The New York Times

PAGE ONE

Special Commemorative Edition Celebrating the 100th Anniversary of the Purchase of The New York Times by Adolph S. Ochs

1896-1996

Galahad Books
New York

First Galahad Books edition published in 1996.

Galahad Books
A division of Budget Book Service, Inc.
386 Park Avenue South
New York, NY 10016

Galahad Books is a registered trademark of Budget Book Service, Inc.

Published by arrangement with The New York Times Company.

Library of Congress Catalog Card Number: 96-77957

ISBN: 0-88365-961-1

Printed in the United States of America.

The New York Times
229 WEST 43 STREET
NEW YORK, N.Y. 10036

ARTHUR O. SULZBERGER, JR.
Publisher

In 1896, a young newspaper publisher from Chattanooga, Tenn., named Adolph S. Ochs gambled his fame and fortune by purchasing an all but bankrupt newspaper called The New York Times.

Mr. Ochs brought with him a commitment to unbiased journalism and a belief that a newspaper could succeed by offering its readers the finest news report available anywhere. He laid down this philosophy in the first edition printed under his leadership: "to give the news impartially, without fear or favor, regardless of any part, sect or interest involved."

As we celebrate the centennial of that purchase, it seems an appropriate time to reissue this book recalling the most famous front pages of The New York Times. It portrays a century of triumph and tragedy, of human greatness and human failures, and above all, it reflects an unparalleled period of progress and change.

Journalism has been called the first rough draft of history. As such it captures events which quickly pass from memory as well as those which continue to deeply affect our lives. Recorded here are some of the most significant moments of the past 100 years, as seen through the eyes of reporters and editors of The New York Times.

It is history at its most intimate—for it only happened yesterday.

PAGE ONE

1896-1996

The New York Times

PAGE ONE

1896-1909

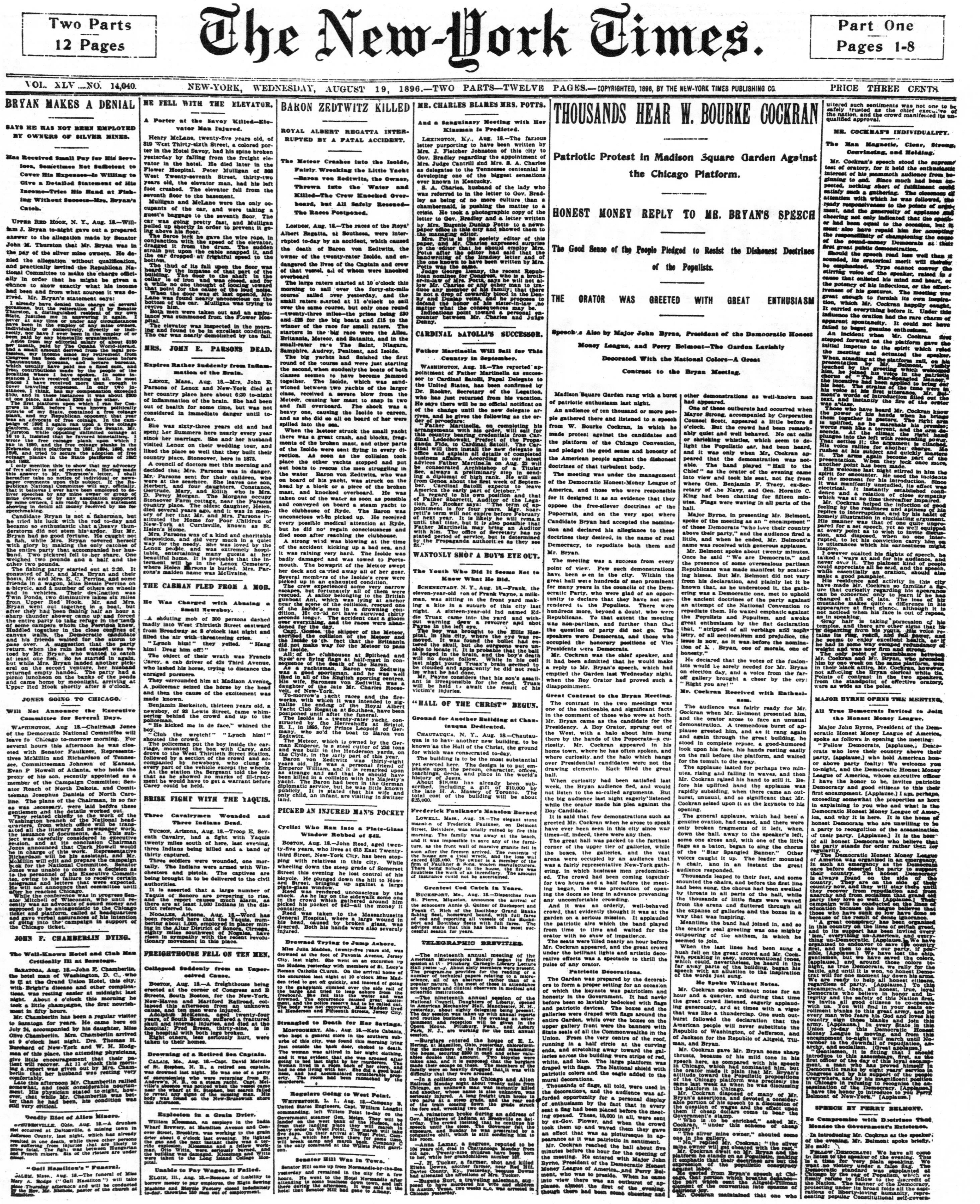

The New-York Times.

VOL. XLV....NO. 14,040. NEW-YORK, WEDNESDAY, AUGUST 19, 1896.—TWO PARTS—TWELVE PAGES.—COPYRIGHTED, 1896, BY THE NEW-YORK TIMES PUBLISHING CO. PRICE THREE CENTS.

BRYAN MAKES A DENIAL

SAYS HE HAS NOT BEEN EMPLOYED BY OWNERS OF SILVER MINES.

Has Received Small Pay for His Services, Sometimes Not Sufficient to Cover His Expenses—Is Willing to Give a Detailed Statement of His Income—Tries His Hand at Fishing Without Success—Mrs. Bryan's Catch.

UPPER RED HOOK, N. Y., Aug. 18.—William J. Bryan to-night gave out a general answer to the allegation made by Senator John M. Thurston that Mr. Bryan was in the pay of the silver mine owners.

HE FELL WITH THE ELEVATOR.

A Porter at the Savoy Killed—Elevator Man Injured.

Henry McLane, twenty-five years old, of 319 West Thirty-sixth Street, a colored porter in the Hotel Savoy, had his spine broken yesterday by falling from the freight elevator in the hotel.

MRS. JOHN E. PARSONS DEAD.

Expires Rather Suddenly from Inflammation of the Brain.

LENOX, Mass., Aug. 18.—Mrs. John E. Parsons of Lenox and New-York died at her country place here about 6:30 to-night of inflammation of the brain.

THE CABMAN FLED FROM A MOB.

He Was Charged with Abusing a Small Newsboy.

BRISK FIGHT WITH THE YAQUIS.

Three Cavalrymen Wounded and Three Indians Dead.

JONES GOING TO CHICAGO.

Will Not Announce the Executive Committee for Several Days.

JOHN F. CHAMBERLIN DYING.

The Well-Known Hotel and Club Man Critically Ill at Saratoga.

FREIGHTHOUSE FELL ON TEN MEN.

Collapsed Suddenly from an Unperceived Cause.

Deadly Riot of Alien Miners.

BARON ZEDTWITZ KILLED

ROYAL ALBERT REGATTA INTERRUPTED BY A FATAL ACCIDENT.

The Meteor Crashes into the Isolde, Fairly Wrecking the Little Yacht—Baron von Zedtwitz, the Owner, Thrown into the Water and Killed—The Crew Knocked Overboard, but All Safely Rescued—The Races Postponed.

LONDON, Aug. 18.—The races of the Royal Albert Regatta, at Southsea, were interrupted to-day by an accident, which caused the death of Baron von Zedtwitz, the owner of the twenty-rater Isolde.

CARDINAL SATOLLI'S SUCCESSOR.

Father Martinelli Will Sail for This Country in September.

WANTONLY SHOT A BOY'S EYE OUT.

The Youth Who Did It Seems Not to Know What He Did.

"HALL OF THE CHRIST" BEGUN.

Ground for Another Building at Chautauqua Dedicated.

PICKED AN INJURED MAN'S POCKET

Cyclist Who Ran into a Plate-Glass Window Robbed of $42.

Greatest Cod Catch in Years.

Frederick Faulkner's Mansion Burned.

TELEGRAPHIC BREVITIES.

MR. CHARLES BLAMES MRS. POTTS.

And a Sanguinary Meeting with Her Kinsman Is Predicted.

LEXINGTON, Ky., Aug. 18.—The famous letter reported to have been written by Mrs. J. Fletcher Johnston of this city to Gov. Bradley regarding the appointment of Mrs. Judge Cantrill and Mrs. S. A. Charles as delegates to the Tennessee centennial is developing one of the biggest sensations ever known in Kentucky.

THOUSANDS HEAR W. BOURKE COCKRAN

Patriotic Protest in Madison Square Garden Against the Chicago Platform.

HONEST MONEY REPLY TO MR. BRYAN'S SPEECH

The Good Sense of the People Pledged to Resist the Dishonest Doctrines of the Populists.

THE ORATOR WAS GREETED WITH GREAT ENTHUSIASM

Speeches Also by Major John Byrne, President of the Democratic Honest Money League, and Perry Belmont—The Garden Lavishly Decorated With the National Colors—A Great Contrast to the Bryan Meeting.

Madison Square Garden rang with a burst of patriotic enthusiasm last night.

An audience of ten thousand or more people gathered there and listened to a speech from W. Bourke Cockran, in which he made protest against the candidates and the platform of the Chicago Convention.

MR. COCKRAN'S INDIVIDUALITY.

The Man Magnetic, Clear, Strong, Convincing, and Holding.

Mr. Cockran's speech stood the supreme test of oratory, for it held the enthusiastic interest of his mammoth audience.

MAJOR BYRNE OPENS THE MEETING.

All True Democrats Invited to Join the honest Money League.

Major John Byrne, President of the Democratic Honest Money League of America, spoke as follows in opening the meeting.

SPEECH BY PERRY BELMONT.

To Compromise with Doctrines That Menace the Government's Existence.

In introducing Mr. Belmont as the next speaker of the evening, Mr. Cockran said.

The first front page after the purchase of The New York Times by Adolph S. Ochs. His letter discussing the purchase appears in the first column on the facing page.

The New-York Times

PUBLISHED EVERY DAY IN THE YEAR.

Offices.

Publication....Printing House Square, New-York
Up-Town..............1,269 Broadway, (32d St.)
All American District Telegraph Offices.
Washington..................513 Fourteenth St.

Subscription Rates—Specimen Copies Free.

	1 Yr.	6 Mos.	3 Mos.	1 Mo.	1 Wk.
Daily, with Sunday..	$10.00	$5.00	$2.50	$ .90	$ .25
Daily, without Sunday..	8.00	4.00	2.00	.75	.20
Sunday edition only..	2.00	1.00	.50	....	.05
Any one day (except Sunday)..	1.50	.75	.40	....	.03
Weekly edition......	1.00	.50	.30	....	.03

Postage prepaid to all points in the United States, Canada, and Mexico, except in New-York City, where the postage is 1 cent per copy; in all other countries, 2 cents per copy per day, payable by the subscriber.

The Times will be sent to any address in Europe, postage included, for $1.80 per month. It is sold in Europe as follows:

London: Low's Exchange, 3 Northumberland Av.
Geneva, Switzerland: Librairie, Georg & Co.; Librairie, A. Cherbuliez, Rue Bovy, Lysberg.
Mainz, Germany: Saarbach's News Agency, agency for Germany and Austria.
Rome, Italy: Loescher & Co.

The address of subscribers will be changed as often as desired. In ordering a change of address both the old and the new address MUST be given.

Cash in advance always. Remittances at the risk of the subscriber, unless made by Registered Letter, Check, Money Order, or Express Order, payable to "The New-York Times Publishing Co."

ADVERTISEMENTS may be left at either of The Times Branch Offices, at any District Messenger Office in New-York City, and at regularly authorized newsdealers' offices, where they will be taken at the same rate as at the Publication Office. Rate cards mailed on application to the publisher. Estimates promptly given.

COMPLAINTS.—Subscribers who fail to receive a single copy of The Times should immediately notify the publisher. Readers who are unable to purchase The Times at any news stand or on any railroad train or steamboat will oblige us by promptly reporting that fact.

TWELVE PAGES.

NEW-YORK, WEDNESDAY, AUG. 19, 1896.

The Times does not undertake to return rejected manuscripts. In all cases where a return of manuscript is desired postage must be inclosed.

To Readers Going Out of Town.

The New-York Times will be mailed, daily and Sunday, for 90 cents per month, and the address changed as often as desired.

BUSINESS ANNOUNCEMENT.

The New-York Times Publishing Company, proprietor of THE NEW-YORK TIMES, has been reorganized. The new organization assumes the ownership today. Mr. ADOLPH S. OCHS of Chattanooga, Tenn., in the interest of the new owners, becomes the publisher and general manager. Mr. CHARLES R. MILLER will continue to be the editor.

NEW-YORK, Aug. 18, 1896.

To undertake the management of THE NEW-YORK TIMES, with its great history for right doing, and to attempt to keep bright the lustre which HENRY J. RAYMOND and GEORGE JONES have given it is an extraordinary task. But if a sincere desire to conduct a high-standard newspaper, clean, dignified, and trustworthy, requires honesty, watchfulness, earnestness, industry, and practical knowledge applied with common sense, I entertain the hope that I can succeed in maintaining the high estimate that thoughtful, pure-minded people have ever had of THE NEW-YORK TIMES.

It will be my earnest aim that THE NEW-YORK TIMES give the news, all the news, in concise and attractive form, in language that is parliamentary in good society, and give it as early, if not earlier, than it can be learned through any other reliable medium; to give the news impartially, without fear or favor, regardless of party, sect, or interests involved; to make of the columns of THE NEW-YORK TIMES a forum for the consideration of all questions of public importance, and to that end to invite intelligent discussion from all shades of opinion.

There will be no radical changes in the personnel of the present efficient staff. Mr. CHARLES R. MILLER, who has so ably for many years presided over the editorial pages, will continue to be the editor; nor will there be a departure from the general tone and character and policies pursued with relation to public questions that have distinguished THE NEW-YORK TIMES as a non-partisan newspaper—unless it be, if possible, to intensify its devotion to the cause of sound money and tariff reform, opposition to wastefulness and peculation in administering public affairs, and in its advocacy of the lowest tax consistent with good government, and no more government than is absolutely necessary to protect society, maintain individual and vested rights, and assure the free exercise of a sound conscience.

ADOLPH S. OCHS.

NEW-YORK, Aug. 18, 1896.

THE PRICE OF SILVER.

Silver touched 68 cents per ounce yesterday for certificates. At this rate the bullion in the dollar that Mr. BRYAN advocates would be worth 51 1-6 cents. This is a fall of about 2 cents since the Populist candidate was put in the field, or a decline of nearly 4 per cent.

There are several inferences to be drawn from this. One is practically forced upon us by Mr. BRYAN himself. It is his professed belief that his election and the policy he sustains would bring the market value of silver to $1.29 an ounce and the value of the silver in a dollar to 100 cents. The fall in price [illegible] that his election is not expected and that the success of his policy is not looked for.

Another inference is that the speculators who bought silver bullion in the belief that the silver craze would at least for a time be general enough to promote a rise in price, have abandoned that belief and are either unloading or threatening to unload.

There are, of course, other causes, purely commercial, which affect the price of silver as that of any other commodity is affected. With these it is not now necessary to concern ourselves. Mr. BRYAN refuses to recognize their existence, and those who understand them are regarding them without reference to politics.

THE NATIONAL DEMOCRATIC ADDRESS.

"For more than a century no man was ever in doubt as to what constituted Democracy." This is the basis of the statement of the Executive Committee of the National Democratic Party just issued from Chicago. The statement founded upon it is admirably simple and complete. Not only every Democrat, but in all essential regards every sensible and patriotic citizen, can accept it. "Every Democrat believed," says the address, "in the rule of law and the rule of an impartial law, in the unhesitating protection not only of the lives of citizens, but of private rights of property, and in the enforcement of obedience to duly constituted authority."

While every Democrat believed this, "he profoundly disbelieved in the ability of Government, through paternal legislation or supervision, to increase the happiness of the Nation." "He believed that it is the function of Government to provide the people with an honest and stable medium of exchange, thus enabling them to transact their business safely and conveniently in every market of the world. He reprobated every attempt to supply to money by means of legislation that value which it can possess only by return of those qualities that render it acceptable to the world when unsupported by legislative fiat."

What can a Democrat with these beliefs and disbeliefs have to do with the Populist policy represented by BRYAN, SEWALL, and WATSON? Every feature of that policy violates some honored Democratic principle. Its chief measure, the free and unlimited coinage of silver at 16 to 1, as proposed, openly defies nearly all those principles. It invades private rights by forcing inferior money on every man to whom a dollar is owing, from the capitalist to the wage earner. It destroys the right of contract. It assumes power in the Government which JEFFERSON would have abhorred. It is class legislation for the direct profit of the mine owners solely. It threatens public credit and private security.

The address declares, and justly, that "all good citizens are bound to repudiate these doctrines and exert every lawful means to insure the defeat of the candidates that represent them." Especially is it the duty of Democrats to "stand steadfast in the defense of our ancient faith. In this crisis there is at stake more than the possibility of temporary victory. The honor and perpetuity of the Democratic Party are at stake."

We are quite ready to concede that even the radical errors of the Populists may sincerely be supported by those who believe in them, but they have no claim on the support of Democrats as such. To these they are simply party treason, and party loyalty joins with patriotism in demanding their utter condemnation and rejection.

THE GREATER NEW-YORK COUNTIES

It seems to us desirable, if it is practicable, to do away entirely with the separate county organizations within the limits of the Greater New-York when a common Municipal Government is established. The mere declaration in the act providing for the consolidation that it was not its intent to affect the boundaries or government of counties is no bar to future action by the Legislature if it is deemed expedient and is within the Constitutional authority of that body.

There is no doubt about the power of the Legislature to set off a part of one county and add it to another, though it cannot in doing so change the boundaries of legislative or judicial districts, which are fixed by the Constitution. This was decided in the case of the last annexation of a part of Westchester County to the City and County of New-York. The only county divided by the proposed consolidation is Queens, and it would be competent for the Legislature to add the portion left out of the enlarged municipality to Suffolk.

But could it then consolidate the four Counties of New-York, Kings, Queens, and Richmond into one? The counties are not created by the Constitution, but their existence is recognized and they are all enumerated in the provisions relating to the apportionment of representation in the two branches of the Legislature. The decision in the Westchester case makes it plain that the Senate, Assembly, and judicial districts must remain as described by county lines when the Constitution was adopted, but it does not follow that the county boundaries must remain for county purposes.

It is desirable to get rid of the county division if possible, because otherwise not only will the Boards of Supervisors of Queens and Richmond have to be retained, but those of New-York and Kings will have to be revived, as neither would any longer have the same boundaries as a city. The counties would also have a separate debt-incurring capacity. So far as other county officers are concerned—Sheriffs, clerks, District Attorneys, and Registers—there seems to be no reason why their offices might not be consolidated as well as those of the municipality, with proper provision for branches and deputies. The county question is a somewhat awkward factor in the consolidation problem, and it is possible that it can [illegible] amendment, but the general lines of the charter for the Greater New-York ought really to be fixed in the Constitution instead of being left liable to continual disturbance by legislative action at Albany. As it is now, the whole charter in its outlines and in its details is a matter of legislation, subject to amendment at any time.

THE BOY ORATOR AND THE MAN ORATOR.

There has very seldom been offered in New-York a more pointed and instructive contrast than was furnished in Madison Square Garden a week ago to-night and last night. The contrast was not only in the speeches, but in the audiences and in the arrangements. Last night the arrangements both on the part of the organizers of the meeting and of the police were immeasurably improved from the previous occasion. Nobody who was furnished with a ticket had any considerable delay or trouble in finding his seat. The queer and picturesque element added to the Bryan meeting by the intense heat was absent last night, the spectacle of a coatless crowd relieving itself by the waving of fans. But the management provided an efficient substitute for it last night by furnishing every seat with a little American flag, which produced an effect equally bizarre and more attractive.

But the main contrast was in the speeches themselves. Nobody who was at both meetings needs to be told that this contrast was so frightfully to the disadvantage of Mr. BRYAN that he will be not only very bold, but very ill advised, if he presumes again during the campaign to confront an audience in this part of the "enemy's country." He was known on his first appearance, apart from his character of the chosen champion of repudiation, as the "Boy Orator of the Platte" and as the man whose sudden eloquence had stampeded into nominating him a body, if not of entirely sane persons, at least of adult males who were at large. To hear the eloquence which had performed such a feat was the motive which assembled the most respectable of his auditors. These connoisseurs of oratory were the most disappointed and the most resentful of all his hearers, except those who had their money on him, so to speak, the men who expected either commercial profit or political preferment in the event of his election, and had made sacrifices of money or of reputation in view of that event. How the connoisseurs in oratory felt, who had gone to hear him in the hope of receiving the sensation that eloquence gives, without regard to the sentiments it adorns, we tried to explain the next morning. The simplest expression is that they felt deceived and imposed upon, and that it would be quite impossible to get any of them to hear BRYAN again.

The most conclusive criticism of him as an orator was the fact that he made two-thirds of his speech to a fleeing audience, and the last third to an audience a third the size of that which had eagerly applauded him before he began to speak.

Of course, everybody in the audience last night, which was about as large as BRYAN's at the beginning and three times as large at the end, knew that Mr. BOURKE COCKRAN knew how to talk. But those who had not heard him before and who had heard BRYAN were scarcely prepared for the full force of the contrast that was impressed upon them. The orator's affluent eloquence flowed on, interrupted only by applause as spontaneous as the applause for BRYAN was perfunctory and managed, and by the hearty laughter which BRYAN did not once elicit, and there must have been many who remembered with dim and remote wonder how they had suffered less than a week before in the place in which they were now delighted, and marveled at the vastness of the difference between an orator and a bore.

The difference is indeed very wide. The old saying about a poet being born and an orator made seems to need revision in view of such a contrast, and to be corrected by the statement that "temperament" counts for as much with an oratorical as with a musical artist. Perhaps that is the difference. The oratorical temperament Mr. COCKRAN evidently has in abundant measure, and Mr. BRYAN, so far as can be judged from his essay in New-York, has it not at all. The meaning of the saying "orator fit" we may take to be that any man may by application arrive at the power of clear expression. That may be conceded to the industrious, or, as they used to say about preachers, the "painful" Mr. BRYAN. For, if he was not clear at all points in his speech, it was partly because there were points in it about which it was not prudent for him to be clear. The trouble with him as an orator is that he is so intensely average, to use the vulgar saying, as common as a yellow dog. This remark applies to his appearance, to his manner, to his gesticulations, so far as his attention to his manuscript allowed him any, to his language, and to his thought. It was all hopelessly humdrum and dog-trot, and utterly without distinction or individuality. Anybody could have written it and anybody could have spoken it.

It seems that a man born so can no more acquire eloquence than he can add a cubit to his stature. And it seems so even more vividly when one has had a chance of hearing the genuine article. Mr. BRYAN appears to have two phases, one of extravagant rhetoric and one of bald monotony of statement or misstatement. Mr. COCKRAN decorates, without effort or parade, a substantial and serious staple of thought. He has every advantage of stature, expressiveness of face and voice, and becoming gesture, which Mr. BRYAN lacks. His voice is remarkably rich and expressive. Mr. BRYAN's name denotes that he is of Irish origin, but nothing in his speeches bewrays him. Mr. COCKRAN's race, on the other hand, is quite unmistakable. The remains of [illegible] still abide with him, insomuch that he leaves it doubtful whether he really regards "BRYAN" as a dissyllable. What is more to the purpose, the Milesian "twinkle" is eminently his, the welling drollery of which the Populist candidate has not a single trace. Moreover, his language, instead of being the bald commercial English of the Nebraskan, is the English of a scholar, full of unexpectedness and allusion. In short, Mr. BOURKE COCKRAN is an orator who would be alluring on the wrong side, and Mr. BRYAN a proser who would be intolerable on the right. If the sound-money Democrats could inveigle the Populist candidate into a joint debate with his critic, of which there is unluckily no hope, what would be the wonder of the hearers of that debate at the reflection that it was on account of his oratorical powers that Mr. BRYAN was a candidate for the Presidency of the United States?

WANTED—POLICEMEN.

It was the simple notion of our old-fashioned forefathers that the office should seek the man. For something like two generations the politics of this country have, in great degree, been run on exactly the opposite principle, often with results that no sane and honest American could look upon without disgust. Even at the highest tide of patriotic feeling that the Republic has ever known Mr. LINCOLN was wont to declare that the office hunters bothered him as much as the insurgents in arms. And only a dozen years ago the men who believed that the sound rule of the fathers was practicable were sneered at as theorists, idealists, and amateur politicians.

Among the men whom these sneers in no way disturbed was THEODORE ROOSEVELT, then a member of Assembly from this city. To his energy, zeal, and skill the State largely owed the civil service law, the chief object of which was to put an end to the use of offices as the spoils of political victory. At that time and until very recently there was no department of the city or State service in which party politics of the worst sort had so much and such mischievous influence. To-day Mr. ROOSEVELT, speaking for the Police Commissioners, gives public notice that in the next four months 800 appointments will be made to the police force, and invites young men who are fit for these places to enter competition for them. "There probably never has been," he says, "such a chance offered in New-York for the employment of young men of good intelligence, of bodily vigor, and of good character. We desire all such to enter our examinations. If they pass them, they will be admitted strictly on their merits and without regard to personal or political influence of any kind."

Every word of this statement is absolutely true. It shows such a change as the most sanguine believers in reform did not dare five years ago to hope for. And the best thing about these changes is that they have been all in one direction and each one has been more decided than those that went before.

THE NEW-YORK SAVINGS BANKS.

The report of the Superintendent of the Banking Department of this State on the condition of the savings banks for the year ending with June 30 comes as a timely argument in favor of sound money. It shows that the number of depositors is considerably larger than the number of voters in the State. Many of them are women and children and other non-voters, but it is not unlikely that they include a majority of the voting citizens. Of the effect upon the value of the savings-bank deposits of degrading our currency to the silver basis by free coinage we have frequently spoken, but this report suggests various considerations for the contemplation of the community.

The total amount of resources, including the surplus held in excess of deposit accounts, is more than $800,000,000. Where is all that capital? Very little of it is lying idle in bank vaults, for it would earn no interest for depositors there. A very large proportion of it has been invested in mortgages on real estate; in other words, has been advanced to purchasers of land and builders. It is part of the invested capital of the community, the value of which and the returns from which depend upon the stability of the currency. Another part is invested in securities paying interest, which would be largely reduced in actual value by a debasement of the money standard.

What does it mean that, notwithstanding the hard times of the last year, the number of depositors has increased and the amount of new deposits was greater than the amount of withdrawals? In part it means that it has been hard to make use of capital in business or in any form of investment that will pay more than the savings-bank rate of 3½ per cent., and there has been a disposition to hoard as well as to save, due to uncertainty about the future. That the sole decrease in the figures is to be found in the aggregate surplus of the banks is significant. It shows that the investments have been less easy to make and less profitable than before, and that in order to keep up the rate of interest it has been necessary to draw upon previous accumulations. This indicates at once the importance of having the surplus and the financial difficulty caused by fear of a currency disturbance. The calamity of any policy that would reduce by nearly one-half the purchasing power of this vast capital, accumulated in investment, but distributed in ownership among more people than there are separate families in the State, can hardly be estimated.

Superintendent KILBURN does well to remind the people of what the well informed in this State knew before—that interest in this vast fund is chiefly that of the depositors. The savings banks are not money-making corporations. They have no stockholders or bondholders, and their Trustees are allowed to have no pecuniary interest in their transactions or investments. No officer is paid anything but for actual services in the management of the banks, and the cost of management, in receiving, safekeeping, investing, and repaying the funds, is only one-third of a cent on the dollar. No savings-bank depositor who understands his own interest can cast a vote in favor of debasing the standard of value and producing financial disturbance.

Mr. BRYAN seems to be no more concerned about the accuracy of his quotations than the originality of his metaphors. In his speech at Barrytown he made bold to say that "SOLOMON said he desired neither riches nor poverty." In fact, the quotation which the Boy Orator was groping at reads "neither poverty nor riches." But waiving that, and waiving also the question raised by modern criticism whether SOLOMON had anything whatever to do with the compilation of proverbs that have his name, it is evident that he had nothing to do with this particular saying. It is expressly credited, in the King James version, at the beginning of the chapter to "AGAR, the son of JAKEH," and it is always known, in and out of the pulpit, as "the prayer of AGAR." That Mr. BRYAN is ignorant of this raises a painful suspicion that he does not know much more about his Bible than he does about bimetallism or the intentions of the American people regarding himself.

"This campaign is characterized by more thinking than we younger men have ever seen," says Mr. BRYAN. This sounds as if Mr. BRYAN were unused to thinking. Men as young as he can recall the campaign of 1876, when the hold of the Republican Party, as the great war party, was broken; the campaign of 1884, when independence became a powerful element in National politics; the campaign of 1892, when for the first time in a generation a definite adverse verdict on extreme protection was given at a Presidential election. No, the quantity of thinking is not so extraordinary as Mr. BRYAN thinks. It is the result of it that puzzles him, and will puzzle him more and more.

Of course the Park Commissioners will not grant special privileges in Central Park to the well-meaning folks who are going to drive all sickness out of America by introducing Father KNEIPP's barefoot cure. If the advocates of KNEIPP are to have favors bestowed upon them, the advocates of all other systems of medicine must be treated with the same indulgence, and presently Central Park will be an open-air sanitarium, with lawns kept continually damp for barefooted invalids to walk over, with mud baths and blood baths and water-cure pavilions innumerable. Generations come and go, creeds change, political parties rise and fall, the world moves on, but the misunderstanding of the design and purpose of our beautiful Park, a place of recreation and flower garden for all, not particularly for poor or rich or moderately well-to-do, is persistent and unchanging.

CAMPAIGN LITERATURE DEMANDED

The Two Congressional Committees Have Their Hands Full of Business.

WASHINGTON, Aug. 18.—Since the opening of the campaign the Republican Congressional Committee has sent out a little more than 13,000,000 of documents. On Saturday alone 337,000 copies of various speeches were started on their way. So great has been the demands for literature that the committee has been compelled to again enlarge its quarters. The speech for which there is the greatest demand is that of Mr. Cleary of Minnesota in reply to Representative Towne, one of the bolting Republicans at the St. Louis Convention.

A very large edition of Secretary Carlisle's Chicago speech to workingmen has been exhausted, and another is on the press. Another popular tract that has been printed by the hundred thousand is written in a conversational vein, and is entitled "Three Evenings with Money."

One of the most popular things issued by this committee is a speech made on the stump in Texas by Judge Aldridge. Singularly enough, this comes to them under the franking privilege through the agency of a Democrat—Senator Caffery of Louisiana, who in a speech in the Senate on the financial question incorporated this Texas speech. The committee has lifted it and made a separate document of it.

Over at Democratic headquarters the committee finds it impossible to keep up with the demand that comes from all sections of the country. The State of Arkansas, the home of Chairman Jones, admitted on all sides to be absolutely certain for the Democratic ticket by a very handsome majority, is clamorous for free-silver literature, and the names of hundreds of Republicans are being sent in with the request that this sort of thing be mailed to them. The Middle Western States are consuming vast quantities of free-silver literature, and the printers having contracts with the committee are forced to operate their works to the limit to come anywhere near getting the work out. In Ohio alone tons of literature have been distributed, and every line of it pertains solely to the financial problem. Thousands and thousands of Republicans whose names are secured by Democratic workers are regularly supplied with this food, and the increasing demands for it in letters written by the recipients themselves is one of the things that leads the committee to believe that the State is to be overturned at the coming election.

The Chairmen of both committees agree that never before was there such a "reading" campaign. The Republican preparation of this literature for distribution will cost hundreds of thousands of dollars. No one is refused, and every letter asking for information at headquarters is referred to some particular individual and an answer written. If it can be replied to with printed matter such is used; if not, a written letter is sent. Thus the committee is kept in touch not only with the political worker, but with the voter himself. The mailing rooms of the two committees are vast beehives, where every employe puts in from eight to ten hours' work a day, and frequently another force is engaged until midnight on the same work.

TO BUY THE WALLACE HOUSE.

It Was Washington's Headquarters at Somerville, N. J.

NEWARK, N. J., Aug. 18.—The Executive Committee of the Revolutionary Society of New-Jersey held a meeting in the office of John Whitehead, Prudential Building, at noon to-day, and contemplated the purchase of the old Wallace House, at Somerville, where Gen. Washington had his headquarters during the Winter and Spring of 1778-9. The Sullivan campaign against the Indians was planned at this place, and near it the Pluckamin fête celebrating the treaty with France was held.

Mr. Whitehead moved that the Executive Committee, at its judgment, be authorized to procure a refusal of the Wallace House until Jan. 1, 1897. The price set upon the house is $6,500. As the Revolutionary Memorial Society is the outgrowth of the Society for the Preservation of Washington's Headquarters at Rocky Hill, and as negotiations for the Herriam house at that place did not culminate, a circular was directed to be sent to all original subscribers, notifying them of the proposed change of location.

A meeting of the historico-patriotic societies of New-Jersey will probably be held at Somerville on Sept. 19, to commemorate the centennial anniversary of Washington's farewell address to the people of the United States. President Stevens of the society is Chairman of the committee, and six others to be named later, are to be associated with him.

SILVER HAS RETARDED PROGRESS.

Responsibility Rests on It for the Panic of 1893.

To the Editor of The New-York Times:

The civil war ended in 1865. Personal liberty was then established throughout this broad land. From that date down to the year 1892 the industrial progress of this country had been continuous, subject to temporary retardations, such as may always occur in the ordinary conduct of business. In 1893 that progress suddenly stopped, enterprise ceased, and from that time to the present day there have been financial chaos, depression, disaster, and compulsory idleness. Although specie payment was suspended from 1865 to 1879, every one had confidence in the ultimate redemption of every promise of the United States in gold coin of the legal standard.

It may be judicious to give the facts proving progress not only in National and personal wealth, but in individual welfare, and to that end the following statement of facts is submitted, covering the period in part from 1865, or an earlier period, to 1890, and in part to 1892.

Relative progress in population and in the principal elements of wealth and welfare compared at various periods:

	Per Cent.
1. Gain in population—1865, 34,748,000; 1892, 65,520,000	88½
2. National expenditures per capita, 1879 to 1882, average $5.16; 1889 to 1892, 5.08. Excess in first period	3
3. National taxation per capita, 1865, $15.73; 1892, $5.43. Excess in 1865	190
4. National debt per capita, 1865, $76.98; 1892, $12.85. Excess in 1865	500
5. The combined imports and exports of the United States were, in 1865, $404,744,893; in 1892, $1,857,680,610. Increase	361
6. The cost of moving a bushel of wheat from Chicago to New-York, by lake and rail, from 1865 to 1868, was 26 6-10 cents; in 1892, 5 61-100 cents. Excess in first period	352
7. The charge for moving merchandise over the New-York Central Railroad in 1865 averaged 3.31 cents per ton per mile; in 1892, average, 0.70 cent per ton. Excess in 1865	370
8. The postal receipts of the United States in 1865, $14,556,159; in 1892, $70,930,475. Increase	387
9. Appropriations for common schools, in 1865, $60,107,612; in 1892, $155,000,000. Increase	158
10. Production of grain, corn, wheat, rye, oats, barley, and buckwheat, in 1865 to 1868, inclusive, an average of 1,312,761,319 bushels; in 1889 to 1892, an average of 3,109,115,463 bushels. Increase	136
11. Production of cotton, the crops of 1865 to 1869, averaged 2,380,000 bales; in 1888 to 1892, averaged 7,982,000 bales. Increase	234
12. Production of pig iron, 1865, 931,582 tons; 1892 10,275,840 tons. Increase	1,100
13. Production of steel, 1865, 13,627 tons; 1892, 4,927,581 tons. Increase	3,606
14. Property insured against loss by fire, assuming that in 1865 the insurance covered only one-half the value of the insured property, and in 1892 three-quarters, the insurance contracts indicate a value in 1865, $3,362,511,218; in 1892, $26,580,728,188. Increase	690
15. Railway mileage, 1865, miles in operation, 35,085; 1892, miles in operation, 175,000. Increase	400
16. New-York Central Railroad, 1865, tons freight, 1,275,290; 1892, tons freight, 20,721,732. Increase	1,535
17. St. Mary's Ship Canal, 1865 to 1869, average tonnage passing, 464,293; 1889 to 1892, average tonnage passing, 8,681,064. Increase	1,770
18. Purchasing power of a dollar; equal quantities of the same kind of food, fuel, and materials for clothing—In 1865 one dollar in paper would buy 1.80 portions; in 1892 one dollar in gold would buy 3.33 portions. Increase	85
19. Workmen in a New-York gasworks—Firemen's wages, 1845 to 1850, inclusive, were $1.20 per day; 1886 to 1890, $2. Increase	150
20. Weavers in a woolen mill—In 1850, Adult men and women worked in a Rhode Island woolen mill fourteen hours a day at 4 3-10 cents an hour, earning 60¼ cents a day. In 1892 weavers worked in the same mill ten hours a day at 13 16-100 cents per hour, earning $1.34½ per day.	
Increase per hour	212
Increase per day	123
21. Mechanics' Earnings—The average earnings of carpenters, machinists, painters, and other mechanics in establishments of continuous occupations were, in paper, in 1865, $2.34; in gold, in 1892, $2.60. The earnings of 1865 would buy equal quantities of the same kinds of food, fuel, and clothing at 55 60-100 cents per portion in 1892 at 30 cents. Purchasing power in 1865, 4.20 portions; in 1892, 8.61 portions. Increased value of a day's wages	106
22. Standard freight locomotive—1865, price in paper, $21,000; 1892, price in gold, $7,350. The engine of 1892, 50 per cent. more effective. Excess of price in 1865	185
23. Steel stubble plows—The price of a low-grade steel plow in 1865 was $24 in paper; a high-grade steel plow in 1892, $12.30. Excess of price in 1865	95
The average earnings of all the workmen in a large plow works in Illinois were, in paper, in 1865, $1.80; in gold, in 1892, $1.16. The purchasing power of the wages in 1892 in equal quantities of the same kinds of food, fuel, and materials for clothing increased	111

Compiled and computed from various authorities, April, 1896.

The proofs of every one of these statements, with the citation of the authorities on which the proofs rest, may be found in the great work upon the "United States of America," edited by Prof. N. S. Shaler, Vol. II., Chapter 1, to which reference may be had.

The foregoing proofs of progress in every department of industry and in every line of National importance were compiled from various authorities in the Spring of 1893. A little later the whole course of events was altered by force of legislation. The subtle poison of the coinage of silver dollars of full legal tender from bullion purchased by means of a forced loan which increased the demand debt of the United States by nearly $500,000,000, culminated in that year in the doubt of the credit of the Nation and in the distrust of the credit of every individual firm or corporation therein.

This crime brought what had been long anticipated by the few—industrial paralysis, financial panic, a stop to constructive enterprise, and a reversal of the progress of the country. No other term will suffice to describe the cause of the financial chaos, the compulsory idleness, and the stop to enterprise since that date. The conspirators who have taken advantage of political power and who secured a force bill for the purpose of forcing bad money upon the people of this country must be held guilty at the bar of public opinion and are about to be condemned.

I use strong words. Let the offer be made to give the advocates of the free coinage of silver at 16 to 1 free coinage, provided they ask nothing else, and they will refuse it. What they want is to be empowered by law to force bad money into circulation, instead of good money, and they delude honest men by trying to make them believe they will get higher prices. The mere threat and danger of their success brought on the panic of 1893. They forced down prices by stopping credit, stopping constructive energy, and to-day, while the grain rots or wastes in the bins of the farmers, and cannot be sold at the cost of production, thousands and thousands of industrious workmen are standing idle throughout the country, in want of this very food. The distress has been brought upon them by men of the mining States, who have taken advantage of their number in the Senate to threaten both political parties. They have been ejected, and, in their effort to discredit the Nation, they are themselves discredited, if not disgraced.

EDWARD ATKINSON.

BOSTON, Aug. 18, 1896.

JEFFERSON CLUB'S ANNUAL OUTING

Prominent East-Side Democrats Spend a Day at Roton Point.

The residents of Avenues A, B, C, and D turned out in large numbers yesterday morning to assist at the departure of the Jefferson Club on its annual clambake and outing. The Jefferson Club is the leading Democratic association of the Eleventh Ward and is a very popular organization. Its guiding spirit is ex-County Clerk Patrick Keenan.

The club went to Roton Point, Conn., for its day's enjoyment. As early as 7:30 o'clock the excursionists began to assemble at the clubhouse, 247 Seventh Street. About 300 members marched to the dock at the foot of Eighth Street and embarked on the steamboat Isabella. At the head of the line marched Mr. Keenan, on either side of him Judges Giegerich and Newburger. In the front rank was Aaron Hanover, who is known on the east side as the "Mayor of Avenue C."

Others who went were Judge Goldfogle, Henry Hirsch, Alderman William Tait, Senator Ahearn, Congressman Sulzer, Assemblyman Benjamin Hoffman, William Hanna, Moses Newhaus, Lawyers Friend and House, Nathan Heller, Abraham Lazarus, Dr. M. Liebman, Thomas J. Doran, Jerold Fitzgibbon, "Tim" Campbell, Morris Blumenthal, Theodore Koch, and George Widder.

NAVY YARD ACCIDENT INQUIRY

Sunken Caisson and Commandant's Barge Raised.

The caisson of Dry Dock No. 2 in the Brooklyn Navy Yard, which was sunk in the recent accident there, by which the Commandant's barge was wrecked and the torpedo boat Ericsson was damaged, was raised yesterday morning, as was also the barge, which was sunk in the dry dock. A careful inspection of the caisson will be made to-day, to ascertain the cause of the accident, if possible.

The official inquiry into the accident was continued yesterday. Assistant Naval Constructor F. W. Hibbs was present at the morning session, with a table of calculations, from which he figured that the weight of the caisson was 96.7 tons. Civil Engineer Menocal had testified that its weight was estimated by its builders at 104 tons. Mr. Hibbs declined to state his opinion as to the cause of the accident.

"Would you," he was asked, "attempt to replace the ballast in the caisson in the manner in which it was being done prior to the accident?"

"Not knowing anything more than I do at present, and having had no experience in removing ballast from caissons, I should say I would not have attempted it," he replied.

He added that had he been engaged in the work, he would have left a considerable margin for safety.

Mr. Hibbs said the dock and caisson were in good condition before the accident.

Naval Constructor Bowles said he did not know the weight of the caisson. He did not think the warm weather was responsible for the accident. He did not recollect having held a conversation with Civil Engineer Menocal about the weight of the caisson. He did not know how much stone ballast was in the caisson.

Assistant Naval Constructor Zam said he told Mr. Menocal it would be safe to remove all the ballast from the caisson, and he was still of that opinion.

The Board of Inquiry will hold another session at 10 o'clock to-day, though no more testimony may be taken.

LORD RUSSELL IN SARATOGA.

He Will Attend the Meeting of the Bar Association To-day.

DOBBS FERRY, N. Y., Aug. 18.—Lord Chief Justice Russell of England and his party left Mr. Willard's residence this morning for Hudson, N. Y. The party embarked on J. Pierpont Morgan's yacht Corsair. The party on arriving at Hudson took a train for Saratoga.

ALBANY, Aug. 18.—Lord Chief Justice Russell of England and party visited the State Capitol building this afternoon. Superintendent Eaton had kept the forces of orderlies at their posts, and had the party shown through the building. A committee of the National Bar Association accompanied the distinguished party, which, after its tour, left for Saratoga at 7:15 to attend the annual meeting of the American Bar Association there. Among the Bar Association committee which accompanied the party were James C. Carter, ex-Minister Edward J. Phelps of Vermont, Charles Claflin Allen, and United States Attorney General Harmon.

SARATOGA, Aug. 18.—The nineteenth annual meeting of the American Bar Association will open here to-morrow. The presence of Lord Russell of England has awakened a widespread interest, and many of the most distinguished men of the country will attend. Senator Gorman of Maryland, Senator Gray of Delaware, Judge I. E. Wales of Wilmington, United States Judge C. P. Shiras of Iowa, Judge L. D. Brewster of Danbury, Conn., and Judge Howe of New-Orleans have arrived, and others are coming in by every train. It is expected that the attendance will be fully three times as large as that of any previous year. Lord Russell and party are at the United States Hotel, where they have engaged cottages.

Much Good It Will Do the Martyrs.

From The London News.

It has been decided, with the approval of the Rev. Stephen Gladstone, the rector, that the Armenian Martyrs Memorial at Hawarden shall take the form of a cross in the churchyard in addition to the stained glass window which is to be placed in the south aisle of the church. The material for the pedestal will be contributed from quarries in England, Ireland, and Wales, and the cross itself will be of Scotch granite. Inscriptions in Armenian by a distinguished Gregorian ecclesiastic, and in English by a member of the committee, will record the circumstances of the Orfa and of the massacres. Cardinal Langenieux, Archbishop of Reims, has been invited to write the Latin inscriptions.

Nansen Reaches Hammerfest.

HAMMERFEST, Norway, Aug. 18.—The members of the Conway expedition, accompanied by Dr. Fridjoh Nansen, whose failure to reach the north pole by drifting in the steamer Fram was lately chronicled, have arrived here.

The Conway expedition, which included Sir William Martin Conway, D. Trevor Battye, Dr. Gregory E. Garwood, and E. E. Conway, went to explore Central Spitzbergen.

YESTERDAY'S TEMPERATURES.

From THE NEW-YORK TIMES's thermometer, on the face of THE TIMES Building, 6 feet above the street level, and from the thermometer of the Weather Bureau, 282 feet above the street level. Both records show the changes of temperature for the 24 hours ended at midnight, and that of the Weather Bureau gives the temperature on the corresponding date last year:

	Weather Bureau. 1895.	Weather Bureau. 1896.	Times. 1896.
3 A. M.	73	[illegible]	66
6 A. M.	71	[illegible]	66
9 A. M.	75	68	68
12 M.	80	70	74
4 P. M.	83	68	73
6 P. M.	82	59	65
9 P. M.	76	61	65
12 P. M.	73	60	63

Average Temperatures Yesterday.

Printing House Square..............67.13
Weather Bureau........................65.00
Weather Bureau corresponding date 1895..............77.00
Weather Bureau corresponding date for last twenty years..............72.00

Probabilities for To-day.

In this city: Fair, Cooler.

Complete "Weather Forecast" Page 12, Column 1.

Index to Classified Advertisements.

See Amusement Advertisements—Page 7.

"All the News That's Fit to Print."

The New York Times.

With SUNDAY MAGAZINE SUPPLEMENT

COPYRIGHTED, 1897, BY THE NEW YORK TIMES COMPANY.

With SUNDAY MAGAZINE SUPPLEMENT

THE WEATHER.

The indications for to-day in this city and neighborhood are fair, warmer, westerly winds, becoming southerly.

VOL. XLVI...NO. 14,247. NEW YORK, SUNDAY, APRIL 18, 1897.—TWENTY-EIGHT PAGES. PRICE FIVE CENTS.

THE NEWS CONDENSED.

Stock market dull.

Wheat, 82⅜c; corn, 29⅝c; cotton, 7⅝c.

LEGISLATURE.—The Senate did not have a quorum for the Saturday session. Tributes of respect to the late Senator Ballantine were paid by Messrs. Grant, Guy, and Stranahan. The Assembly passed several bills, including one for the improvement of a portion of Bronx Park for zoological purposes. The Committee on Rules indorsed a number of measures.—Page 3.

CONGRESS.—The Democrats thrashed over the dissensions of the recent caucus to the relish of the Republicans. An alignment of the factions on a motion to adjourn was prevented by Mr. Dingley's refusal to yield for the consideration of Mr. Bland's resolution of inquiry concerning the policy of the Government in the Union Pacific foreclosure suits.—Page 3.

FOREIGN.—It has been discovered in Honolulu that Japanese soldiers have emigrated to the Sandwich Islands in the disguise of students. The Prince of Wales has discovered that the entire route of the Queen's jubilee procession has been secured by speculating syndicates. The German press is now discouraging any attempt at retaliation on account of the Dingley tariff. The plans of the Anglo-Egyptian Soudan expedition for next Summer are revealed. Prince Hohenlohe, Chancellor of the German Empire, has resigned his position, but Emperor William declines to accept the resignation. The Prince is now in Paris.—Page 22.

Page 1.

Joseph E. Kelly, a jeweler in Somersworth, N. H., has fled to Canada. He is suspected of the murder of Bank Cashier Stickney and detectives are on his trail.

The suit of Miss Hardenbergh of Saugerties, N. Y., against Lawyer Carroll Whitaker, whom she charges with retaining money due her, was referred to a lawyer for hearing.

The Grand Jury of Franklin County, Ky., has indicted Dr. W. Godfrey Hunter and four others for conspiracy to bribe, in connection with the Senatorial contest.

Page 2.

Masked robbers beat and tortured the members of the Blakesley family, near Findlay, Ohio, and carried off $5,000.

Good Government Club C discussed the Citizens' Union movement and its prospect. Exception was taken to its reported indorsement of Seth Low as a reform candidate.

Capt. Gen. Weyler says that he wants no more reinforcements for Cuba, and no more substitutes. Santa Clara and part of Puerto Principe, he says, are pacified, and the insurgents are rapidly disappearing.

Page 3.

Senator Davis says he will try to secure a vote on the arbitration treaty in the Senate next week.

Senator Ford's bill to prohibit the distributing of advertising matter in private mail boxes is signed by Gov. Black.

President McKinley may give Bellamy Storer, who helped him in financial distress, a foreign appointment. Secretary Sherman and the Ohio Senators do not want him placed in Washington.

The Republican Senators have about decided to consider the Dingley bill in caucus before it is submitted to the Democratic members of the Finance Committee, because of the narrow margin of votes they have to pass it.

Page 4.

The troop drill and military games by the First Signal Corps of the National Guard were very successful and well attended.

Interesting and thrilling exhibitions of horsemanship were given at the mounted tournament in Durland's Riding Academy last night.

The Hudson County Civil Engineer has submitted his requested report on an advisable route for the new branch boulevard from the Hudson Boulevard to Arlington.

Page 5.

James C. Reed, Secretary of the Grant Monument Association, is seriously ill.

Edward E. Rice, just returned from Europe, announced that he has secured a number of productions and engaged several people.

Page 8.

The Government will soon begin to construct fortifications near Port Townsend, Washington.

Samples of the sunken piles and hard pan on which the battleship Oregon grounded have been sent to Washington. They were left in the channel, it is believed, by contractors.

Senator Platt was in consultation yesterday with various of his followers about the filling of Federal offices in this city and State, and also about work to be done by the Legislature before adjournment.

Page 9.

Plans for an eighteen-story hotel at Thirty-seventh Street and Fifth Avenue were filed yesterday by the Paran Stevens estate.

Page 10.

A new Exchange has been formed for the avowed purpose of dealing only in real estate securities.

About sixty manufacturing confectioners have organized a Board of Trade and had it incorporated.

Booker T. Washington lectured at the Berkeley Lyceum on the progress of the negro race in the South, and said their growth in wealth and education would solve the political questions involved.

At a meeting held at Sherry's by the New York City Commission to the Tennessee Centennial and International Exhibition, it was announced that the apparent apathy of New Yorkers had caused the withdrawal of the room originally assigned to the metropolis, and its assignment to Chicago.

President Roosevelt of the Police Board sent his resignation to the Mayor yesterday, along with a letter praising Mr. Andrews and condemning the bi-partisan law. No mention was made of Commissioners Grant and Parker and Chief of Police Conlin. The two Commissioners did not attend the special meeting of the board called by Mr. Roosevelt for yesterday morning.

Page 12.

More flowers will be used by the churches this year than last, the hard times then having an effect. Florists all report heavy sales.

It is estimated that there are 100,000 beggars in this city. All earn a livelihood, but many are marked by the Charity Organization Society.

The delegation appointed by several organizations to go to Albany to urge the Governor not to sign the Greater New York charter will leave this city to-morrow morning.

Arthur W. Dennett, ex-Superintendent of the Parkhurst society, is in this city. He says the stories that he intends proceeding against Bloomingdale Asylum or Bellevue Hospital for alleged ill treatment are untrue.

The casket containing the body of Gen. Grant has been removed from the brick tomb in which it has been for twelve years to the new mausoleum. The two sons and the grandson of the soldier witnessed the transfer.

Page 13.

Chief of Police Conlin replied yesterday to Commissioner Andrews's published statement, and said that he meant no impertinence, and took the course he did as a matter of discipline, objecting to the Commissioner giving orders to the men over his head.

Page 17.

The Giants will play only two more exhibition games this week. The championship season opens at Philadelphia on Thursday.

Page 18.

The Columbia University Union is arranging for a grand college championship bicycle tournament at Manhattan Beach Memorial Day.

Page 19.

Entries for the fifth annual Horse Show in Brooklyn have been closed. The list is given.

Chief Marshal Tilly, who will have charge of the Brooklyn Sunday school anniversary parade, has announced his list of division marshals.

Mrs. Theodore Sutro expresses herself as greatly pleased with the success which has attended the law classes for women which she originated.

Henry Beran has revived an old suit against Daniel O'Connell. Both men live in Brooklyn, and were at one time in partnership as contractors.

Springfield, L. I., having no sewers, utilizes a brook for the purpose. A portion of Brooklyn's water supply comes from that stream. The villagers have organized to compel Brooklyn authorities to purchase the property if they want the water purified.

Page 21.

In his cable letter, Harold Frederic reviews the situation in Greece. He shows how the Turks have refused to be forced into appearing as aggressors by the raids on the frontier, and outlines what are thought to be the Grecian plans of the campaign, both by land and sea. Plans for a possible meeting of the three Caesars to further their plans in the Levantine. War in the Transvaal deemed a certainty, to suit the plans of bankers. The "Bill" Chandler of Germany. Gossip of London and Paris.

Page 26.

An employe of the Metropolitan Street Railway Company has invented a new grip, which, it is believed, will eradicate dangers at sharp curves.

An Industrial Colony Association has been formed for the purpose of taking boys off the streets and teaching them the rudiments of a republican form of government, in order to make good citizens of them.

LAWYER SUED BY A CLIENT.

Miss Hardenbergh's Charge Against Carroll Whitaker.

KINGSTON, N. Y., April 17.—At a special term of the Supreme Court, held here to-day, Judge Chase of Catskill presiding, the adjourned case of Hardenbergh against Whitaker came up, and was referred to a lawyer here to take evidence and decide.

The defendant was a well-known lawyer of Saugerties. Some few weeks ago, when the case was heard before Judge Chase, at Special Term here, the charge of retaining money, about $400, from a client of his, Miss Bessie Hardenbergh of Saugerties, was made against Lawyer Carroll Whitaker. The court was asked to compel Whitaker to pay over to Miss Hardenbergh the money.

Miss Hardenbergh is now a resident of New York. In her petition she alleges that in 1891 she had a cause of action against one John W. Tompkins, a merchant of Saugerties, for defamation of character. Whitaker was employed by her to prosecute the claim. He informed her in February last that he had effected a compromise with the merchant, and said he had settled for $100. He retained $16 for his expenses and gave Miss Hardenbergh $84. She avers that she was induced by Whitaker to sign a receipt for the money, and says that he concealed part of the receipt under some loose papers on the desk, so that she could not read it all. Afterward she learned that the merchant had settled for $500, which, she alleges, Whitaker had received.

A NEW CIVIL SERVICE BILL.

Gen. Grosvenor's Measure to Declare the True Intent of the Act.

WASHINGTON, April 17.—Representative Grosvenor of Ohio, who made a vigorous attack on the civil service laws in the last Congress, to-day introduced a bill to declare the true intent and scope of the Civil Service act.

The bill declares that the Civil Service act shall not be contrued to embrace any of the employes in the Government Printing Office or the Bureau of Engraving and Printing, nor any persons employed merely as workmen or laborers, nor construed to allow the appointment to office or promotion in any classes of the civil service covered by the act of any person who has not passed a competitive examination, and all appointments since March 4, 1893, without a competitive examination, unless such appointees are specially exempted, are declared illegal and contrary to the intent and spirit of the act. The bill proposes that all persons who have been employed or appointed in the classified service since March 4, 1893, without examinations shall appear before the Civil Service Commission for examination within ninety days, the examinations not to give them preference over other citizens who are qualified to enter the service. This bill would compel all those now in offices over which President Cleveland extended the shelter of the Civil Service act to pass examinations.

CROUCH ACCUSES ALLEN.

Bloody Handkerchiefs in the Former's Coat at Sackett's Harbor.

WATERTOWN, N. Y., April 17.—Wilbur Crouch, who is under arrest for being implicated in the murder of his divorced wife, Mary Crouch, and her friend, May Daly, at Sackett's Harbor yesterday morning, talked to a reporter at the jail to-day, and accused George Allen, the soldier who was seriously wounded in the tragedy, of being the murderer of the two women. He said:

"There is no question in my mind that Allen murdered my wife and May Daly. I believe he tried to impose on the women. I do not want to make this statement, however, because I desire to accuse no man. As far as a public statement is concerned, I want to say that I am an innocent man, and that my conscience is as clear as that of a new-born babe."

Late last night, Recorder George H. Cobb went to Sackett's Harbor, and searched the house of Wilbur Crouch, and found an overcoat besmeared with mud. In the pockets of the overcoat were found two handkerchiefs covered with blood. This discovery has changed public opinion, that had begun to think Allen committed the act.

Canadian Pacific's Subsidy.

OTTAWA, Ontario, April 17.—A Minister of the Crown is responsible for the statement that the Canadian Pacific Railway has accepted the proposition of the Government to build the Crow's Nest Pass Railway. This proposition is in effect that the Government give the company $10,000, subsidy per mile, and that in return for this subsidy it will give up certain of its special privileges, which it has in its charter, such as the control of rates. Running powers will also be given over this link to other railroads. The subsidy in all will amount to about $3,250,000.

CLUE TO THE BANK MURDER

Jeweler Joseph E. Kelly Traced by Somersworth, N. H., Police in His Flight to Canada.

HAD A LIVERY RIG WAITING.

He Drove to Milton and Boarded a Train—Kelly Knew Cashier Stickney and Used to Put Jewelry in the Bank Windows.

SOMERSWORTH, N. H., April 17.—The police of this city believe they are now on the track of the man they want on suspicion of having been connected with the murder of Cashier Joseph A. Stickney of the Great Falls National Bank, and the robbery of the bank, yesterday. Word was received from Milton during the forenoon that the team which has figured in the bank case was at the Phoenix Stables, where it had been left by a man answering the description of the one who was seen to enter the bank yesterday noon. As soon as possible a description of the team was given, and it was fully identified as that which was hired at Whitten's stable in Berwick yesterday afternoon.

This news caused a complete reversal of the theory which the police had held up to that time, that two men were involved in the affair, because Joseph E. Kelly, a fellow well known about town, hired the team in question from Whitten's stable at 1 o'clock yesterday, and he is believed to be the man who left the team at the Phoenix stables. After leaving the team, the man boarded a train for North Conway, where, it was reported at Milton this morning, he purchased a ticket for Quebec.

Upon receiving this news Officer William H. Rich of Berwick, Deputy Sheriff James H. McDaniel of Somersworth, and Sheriff George W. Parker of Dover, started in pursuit of the fugitive, although it seemed impossible to head him off on his way toward Canada. The Canadian officials were notified to be on the watch. At the same time the local police began to trace Kelly's movements during yesterday. In this they were only partially successful, as about the only fact they could learn was that Kelly hired a team at Whitten's stable at 1 o'clock, saying he was going fishing. On leaving the stable he drove in the opposite direction from that which he had designated in outlining his proposed trip. The only other clue which the police have been able to discover connecting Kelly with the affair is evidence given by E. B. Cheney, a brakeman on the Rollinsford Branch train, who, on his way to the station shortly after 1 o'clock yesterday afternoon, saw Kelly driving the team which he had hired from Whitten. Kelly perceived him at about the same time and suddenly turned the horse and proceeded in the opposite direction. The police consider this important, claiming that Cheney, who at the time was wearing his brakeman's coat with brass buttons, was mistaken for a police officer, whom Kelly desired to avoid.

Knew Cashier Stickney.

The officers now state positively that they believe the man who committed the deed at the bank carried his booty up Prospect Street and deposited it behind Dr. Hayes's orchard wall, then went to Whitten's stable himself, and hired the team, into which he took the plunder and drove away.

Kelly came here from Amesbury, Mass., about three years ago. He went to work at first as a porter in the Great Falls Hotel, which is not far from the bank. Later he acted as clerk in Grant's Hotel in Berwick. Last Summer he went to South Harpswell, Me., where, he claimed, he conducted a hotel. Upon his return here last Fall, he took rooms in the Lothrop Building, directly opposite the bank, in which he opened a jewelry business. His sudden change from hotel life to that of jewelry excited considerable comment at the time, which, however, soon died out.

It now appears, from what evidence the police have been able to get together, that, since Kelly became thus engaged in the jewelry business, he had frequently placed jewelry on exhibition in one of the windows of the bank, and was a frequent caller upon Cashier Stickney. The police searched Kelly's rooms this morning, but nothing was found to throw any light upon his movements or plans, except the fact that from his shaving outfit the razor was missing, and no trace of it could be found about the premises. They consider this an important clue.

Mayor Hanson Has a Theory.

Mayor Hanson does not coincide with the police in their opinion that only one man was concerned in the robbery, and he states that it is by no means certain that Kelly is the man who entered the bank. The Coroner's jury began an inquest at the office of Coroner L. E. Grant to-day. Before the proceedings were opened the Coroner expressed the opinion that they could not be completed to-day. An examination of the head of the dead cashier by the Coroner revealed ten distinct cuts, and the skull was crushed in several places. The Coroner's theory is that Stickney's throat was not cut until after the vault had been robbed. The injury to the skull would not have caused instant death, but would have undoubtedly resulted fatally in time.

A party of twelve men, headed by G. A. Edgerly of Somersworth, went out to Lebanon to-day and traced the team believed to have been used by the robber into the Lebanon woods. There they found a place where the horse had been tied to a tree. This led to the belief that while in the woods the man buried the $600 in silver, which was too heavy for him to carry without detection, but careful search failed to show anything to substantiate this theory.

Charles M. Dorr, a well-known dry goods merchant, and ex-National Bank Examiner of this State, will be chosen cashier of the Great Falls National Bank, as successor of Cashier Stickney, who was murdered yesterday.

PURSUIT OF THE FUGITIVE.

Kelly Has Twelve Hours' Start of the Detectives Who Followed Him.

MILTON, N. H., April 17.—Landlord Chamberlain of the Phoenix Hotel at Milton was awakened from his slumbers early this morning by a party looking for bank robbers. It was learned that Joseph Kelly, who is suspected of the crime, had arrived at Milton about 3:30 yesterday afternoon, placed his horse in the stable connected with the Phoenix, purchased a hat, and then boarded the 4:07 train for Montreal.

Deputy McDaniel was assured that this was the best clue obtainable. With two men they reached Milton soon after midnight, engaged a fresh horse, and drove on to Sanbornville. At that place they obtained a special engine and pressed for North Conway. The deputies in McDaniel's company followed by team. When they got up to North Conway, the locomotive had to return. The searchers found trace of the fugitive, but were unable to run him down. He had seven hours' start of them.

MONTREAL, Quebec, April 17.—Two men, suspected of having committed the murder and bank robbery at Somersworth, N. H., yesterday are said to have boarded a Boston and Maine train at St. Johnsbury, Vt., and jumped the train at a station near this city. The local detectives have been advised of this, and are searching for the men.

KELLY ARRESTED BEFORE.

Sentenced in Amesbury for Housebreaking in 1892.

AMESBURY, Mass., April 17.—Joseph E. Kelly, who is wanted at Somersworth on suspicion of having been connected with the murder of Cashier Stickney and the robbery of the bank, is a native of Amesbury. He is twenty-four years of age. Although his parents are among the most estimable citizens, he was arrested on Sept. 18, 1892, for breaking and entering, on which he was sentenced to the reformatory at Concord. His father keeps a hotel at Salisbury Beach.

Kelly's parents learned for the first time of his being involved in the case, and will probably go to Somersworth to-morrow. The Kelly family consists of his father and mother, and nine brothers and sisters.

WALTHAM SUSPECTS CLEARED.

"Con" Hardigan and John Briggs Prove an Alibi.

WALTHAM, Mass., April 17.—Cornelius Hardigan and John Briggs were arraigned in the District Court to-day before Judge Kennedy, on the charge of murdering Joseph Stickney, cashier of the Great Falls National Bank, at Somersworth, N. H., yesterday. They were both found not guilty and discharged.

George L. Sanderson, baggagemaster of the Fitchburg Railroad, testified to seeing both prisoners alight from the train a few moments before 3 o'clock, showing conclusively that they could not have been in Somersworth at the time of the robbery and murder.

Hardigan was rearrested on two warrants, one charging him with breaking and entering the house of Charles Keele, on Tuesday afternoon, and committing an assault upon him. Hardigan was held in $5,000 bonds for his appearance Wednesday morning.

LIKE THE YONKERS ROBBERY.

Cashier Cobb May Go on to Identify Any Men Arrested.

YONKERS, April 17.—The account of the murder of Treasurer Joseph A. Stickney and the robbery of the Great Falls National Bank, at Somersworth, N. H., on Friday at noon, was closely read in this city this morning, because there were many things in connection with the robbery identical with the theft at the Yonkers Savings Bank here last Monday. The description of the man who murdered the cashier tallies with that of the fellow who held-up Cashier Lyman Cobb of the Yonkers bank.

Then again the time was the same, noon time, when there was no one in the bank besides the cashier. The Yonkers Savings Bank was in charge of Cashier Cobb when the robbery occurred. Cashier Stickney was murdered before he could utter an outcry. Cashier Cobb was compelled to keep quiet at the point of a revolver. Both burglars were desperadoes. Another remarkable incident is that the thieves in Yonkers secured about $4,250, while in New Hampshire they got a very similar amount.

Cashier Cobb says that on account of the meagre description furnished of the New Hampshire burglars, he cannot tell whether they are his visitors. He says that should they be captured and a good description sent on to warrant him going to New Hampshire, he would do so, to see whether he could recognize them.

SHE CAUSED THREE SUICIDES.

Remarkable Confession of a Dying Widow of Middletown.

MIDDLETOWN, N. Y., April 17.—A local paper here prints a strange deathbed confession, alleged to have been made by Mrs. Susan C. Evans, widow of David Evans. She died in New York on Sunday last, but owing to the objections of relatives to her interment in the family plot in this city, her remains were not brought here until Thursday, when they were buried in a new plot.

The article in question states that she was in a repentant mood at the time of her death, and that she confessed that she was the cause of three suicides—those of her husband, another man, and her daughter.

To Serve as President.

ANN ARBOR, Mich., April 17.—Dean A. L. D'Ooge of the Literary Department, and Dean H. B. Hutchins of the Law Department, are most frequently mentioned as liable to be appointed Acting President of the University, to serve while President Angell is away as Minister to Turkey. Both Prof. D'Ooge and Prof. Hutchins are thoroughly familiar with the methods by which the university has been conducted, and either would fill the place most creditably. Regent Levi L. Barbour of Detroit, Prof. S. A. Pattengill, and F. W. Kelsey have also been talked of as possible successors to Dr. Angell. The Regents will meet April 28, when the matter will be acted upon.

Condition of Yale Crews.

NEW HAVEN, Conn., April 17.—The members of the Yale Freshman and 'Varsity crews, who have been here since college closed, took their final practice to-day and left to-night for the usual Easter Sunday recess. All the men are in fine condition. Coach Bob Cook at the beginning of the vacation took two promising freshmen, J. C. Greenway and F. W. Allen, out of the freshman boat and has been keeping them in the 'Varsity shell since then.

Killed by a Train.

PORT CHESTER, N. Y., April 17.—Michael Haduk, a section hand on the New York, New Haven and Hartford Railroad, died to-day in the Port Chester Hospital. He had been struck while at work on the tracks by the Boston express. He was thirty-four years of age. A widow and six children, almost in destitute circumstances, survive him.

Powell Clayton Seriously Ill.

ST. LOUIS, April 17.—Gen. Powell Clayton is confined to bed in his room at the Planters Hotel. He has a very severe cold, bordering closely upon pneumonia. He coughs very hard, and suffers considerable pain.

DR. HUNTER IS INDICTED

A True Bill Returned by the Grand Jury of Franklin County, Ky., Against Political Leaders.

FIVE MEN ARE IMPLICATED.

The Senatorial Candidate Is Not Expected to Withdraw—His Friends Denounce the Action—A Prompt Trial to be Demanded—Hunter's Clash with Hanna.

FRANKFORT, Ky., April 17.—The Franklin County Grand Jury has returned true bills against Dr. W. Godfrey Hunter, the Republican nominee for the United States Senate; ex-Congressman John Henry Wilson of the Eleventh District, the Hon. E. T. Franks of the Second District, Capt. Noel Gaines, and his brother-in-law, Thomas Tanner of Frankfort.

Those named have been indicted for conspiracy to bribe. All are Republicans, with the exception of Gaines and Tanner.

The indictments were all included in one bill, and were filed in court at 10:20 o'clock. The news at once became public, and created the greatest indignation among the Republicans, all of whom denounced it as a conspiracy among Frankfort Democrats to defeat and humiliate Hunter. They claimed that the indictments against Gaines and Tanner, the Democrats, were returned simply as "savers" to prevent the public generally from gaining the impression that the Grand Jury had been made an engine of political persecution, and that they would be dismissed at the first hearing on account of insufficient evidence.

The Specific Charges.

The vital portion of the true bill returned by the Franklin County Grand Jury is as follows:

"The said W. Godfrey Hunter, John H. Wilson, Noel Gaines, E. T. Franks, and T. R. Tanner did unlawfully, corruptly, and wickedly conspire, combine, confederate, and agree together to attempt to bribe them, the said W. G. Gossam, Norge Clarke, and Johns, (members of the Legislature,) and did offer to them the sum of $15,000 each for the vile purpose of securing and influencing them to cast their votes at the time and in manner provided by law for said election for the said W. Godfrey Hunter, and by such unlawful means to secure his election to the said office."

When the indictments had been returned, Judge Cantrill ordered that bench warrants be issued for the arrest of the accused, and made returnable for the next term of the court, which is in September. Bail was fixed at $250 in each case. When asked why he set the cases for next September Judge Cantrill said: "I do not think it proper to try the cases at this term of the court, but if the parties come in and ask for an immediate trail, I will proceed with it at once, otherwise it will go over until September."

Conspiracy to bribe is a common-law offense in Kentucky, the penalty being a fine or imprisonment, or both, at the discretion of the Grand Jury. The friends of Dr. Hunter are greatly rejoiced that no indictment charging perjury was returned, as this is a felony.

Will Ask for Trials at Once.

The accused have engaged the best attorneys in the State to defend them, and, while no consultation has been held and no steps decided on, it is said that immediate trials will be asked for.

Capt. Noel Gaines, one of the indicted parties, and the man who claimed that Hunter and his lieutenants had endeavored to secure his assistance in obtaining votes, gave out an interview this morning, asserting his innocence.

Dr. Hunter was absolutely noncommittal. When asked what effect the indictments would have on his candidacy he asked a legislator to reply for him. "Hunter is the victim of a conspiracy, and will be elected yet," was the answer, and Dr. Hunter smiled grimly. The same reticence is maintained by Wilson and Franks.

Chairman Jones of the Republican caucus said that it was a "diabolical conspiracy" and that the Republicans would disprove and resent it in proper spirit. State Senator Deboe was of the same opinion, and not one of the Republican leaders hesitated to condemn the action of the Grand Jury as partisan and prejudiced.

Hunter Will Not Withdraw.

The session of the General Assembly this morning was uneventful, the bribery indictments overshadowing all else. Many of the members were absent, and those who were not had made pairs. According to previous agreement, a formal ballot was taken, and one vote was cast for each of the candidates, Hunter, Blackburn, Martin, Boyle, and Stone. It is not believed here that the indictments will force Hunter to withdraw. On the contrary, it is believed that it will solidify his forces, and that he will stand against all opposing forces from now on, as the majority of the Republicans are inclined to the opinion that it is nothing more or less than political persecution. The bolting Republicans, however, are gleeful, and are urging a call for another caucus. Hunter men insist that if a new caucus is called they will again win.

Hunter and Hanna Clash.

Dr. Hunter has at last rebelled against Hanna and his agent here, Mr. Samuel Taylor of Ohio, and yesterday afternoon sent a request to Mr. Taylor that he leave Frankfort at once and not return to meddle in the Senatorial muddle.

This was not done, however, until it became known that the Administration had withdrawn its support from Hunter and that it was the desire of Mr. Hanna that Hunter retire in favor of some candidate who could unite the party. Then it was that Dr. Hunter asked Mr. Taylor to leave. Mr. Taylor communicated with Mr. Hanna at once, and was told to use his own discretion. He will remain at least for a time.

Coming to New York to Preach.

PARKERSBURG, West Va., April 17.—The Rev. W. S. Winans, Jr., who has for four years been pastor of the Methodist Episcopal Church, will preach his last sermon as pastor of that large and influential church to-morrow. Mr. Winans will go to the Twenty-seventh Street Methodist Episcopal Church, New York, having agreed to exchange charges with the Rev. C. S. Townsend. Mr. Winans is a tireless minister, an eloquent and interesting preacher, and possesses the graces and courtesies of a scholarly gentleman. During his citizenship in Parkersburg he has made hosts of warm friends among people of all creeds, who will learn with regret his intention of again becoming a New Yorker.

THE BRITISH TAKE GAMASEP.

The Capture Made by the Duke of Edinburgh's Rifles.

CAPE TOWN, April 17.—The stronghold of Gamasep, Bechuanaland, has been captured by the Duke of Edinburgh's Own Volunteer Rifles. Galishowe lost 300 horses, many cattle, and many warriors. The British lost six wounded.

SENATOR MASON'S MAIL.

Only Hanna, He Says, Receives More Letters Than He.

WASHINGTON, April 17.—"The Senate Postmaster tells me," said Senator Mason to-day "that my mail is larger than that of any other Senator, save Hanna. I don't know just how many letters I receive. But this I know, I have had five clerks at work on it ever since I came here, and it cost me just exactly one-half of my salary last month to attend to it.

"I don't know how long other Senators have to work, but I have put in fourteen hours every day. My constituents ask for everything, from a charwoman's job to an Embassy, and I see them all."

FAMILY MADE ILL BY COFFEE.

Verdigris Forms in Copper Kettle in Newark.

NEWARK, April 17.—As a result of drinking coffee made in a vesel with a copper bottom a whole family has suffered from copper poisoning for two days. The victims are William Wegener, his wife, and their children—Frederick, nineteen years old; William, Jr., seventeen; Charles, fifteen; Henry, twelve—and Charles Bonorand, a young man who lives with them, at 22 Brenner Street. The copper had become coated with verdigris.

Charles Bonorand and William Wegener, Jr., came home rather late on Thursday night and took some coffee before going to bed. Each woke Friday morning with a "brassy" taste in his mouth, and had a bad headache.

Mr. Wegener drank the coffee at breakfast, and was taken sick on his way to work. He fell several times, and was taken home by a friend. Henry fell unconscious on Mulberry Street. Dr. Henry Ost administered emetics and milk. All of the victims will recover.

A WOMAN ESCAPES FROM JAIL.

In Taking Her Departure She Writes an Interesting Letter.

MALONE, N. Y., April 17.—Miss Louisa Wiess, a young German, who came to Malone with Dr. Edwin T. Osbaldeston about two years ago as an assistant in his massage treatment, and who, with the doctor, was arrested in Montreal last Fall and extradited, charged with having stolen goods from Fay Brothers of this place, escaped from the Malone Jail this morning and took the early train for Canada. She had been in the habit of assisting in the housework at the jail. Of late, however, she did not leave her cell as early as usual because extra help had been obtained, and when she was missed to-day she had evidently been gone for hours. She left a letter for the Sheriff and another for the District Attorney, which is appended:

To Mr. F. G. Paddock:

Sir: To be in this suspense is too awful for me to stand any longer, and I think that I have already suffered more than my case demands, as I am dying by inches in here. I beg your forgiveness, and please do not chase me as you would a wild deer. I am mad for want of being again with mother. Good-bye, and God bless you. LOUISA.

When the couple were arraigned, about two or three months ago, the doctor was admitted to bail in the sum of $700, and soon after disappeared, and the amount was collected from the bondsmen early this week.

RAILROADS TO CONSOLIDATE.

Agreement Reported of Colorado Midland and Gulf Lines.

DENVER, Col., April 17.—Information has been received here to the effect that the Colorado Midland and Denver, Texas and Gulf Roads will soon enter into a consolidation, and that Receivers Ristine of the former and Trumbull of the Gulf, who are now in New York, have partially concluded all arrangements to this end.

The Midland runs from Colorado Springs to Grand Junction, via Leadville and Aspen, a distance of 384 miles. It recently severed its traffic arrangements with the Santa Fé, and all its trains now enter Denver from Colorado Springs over the tracks of the Denver, Texas and Gulf.

Heavy Loss by Fire in Boston.

BOSTON, April 18.—A fierce fire broke out about 12:30 o'clock this morning in what is known as the "dangerous district" on Summer Street, covering the entire block between Arch and Otis Streets. The block was occupied by three large jewelry firms, whose loss is likely to be over $100,000. J. C. Sawyer, William Fenton, and Smith, Peterson & Co., are the principal sufferers.

THE WEATHER.

A depression is central over the Gulf of St. Lawrence and is moving slowly eastward. A storm of considerable energy is forming to the north of North Dakota. An area of high pressure covers the central valleys and the Gulf States. The barometer has fallen in New England and in all districts west of the Mississippi River; it has risen from the lower lake region southward to the East Gulf States. The temperature is lower in New England and the Atlantic States; it is higher in the Mississippi Valley and throughout the Rocky Mountain districts. Rain has occurred in New England and the lower lake region, but the weather has been fair in all other districts. Occasional showers may occur in northern regions, in the lake regions, and in the Upper Missouri Valleys, but the weather will be fair in all other districts. Slowly rising temperature is indicated for the Atlantic States and the central valleys, and a fall is indicated for the Northern Rocky Mountain plateau.

The record of temperature for the twenty-four hours ended at midnight, taken from THE NEW YORK TIMES's thermometer and from the thermometer of the Weather Bureau, is as follows:

	—Weather Bureau.— 1896.	1897.	Times. 1897.
3 A. M.	68	47	50
6 A. M.	69	45	47
9 A. M.	76	46	48
12 M.	81	53	54
4 P. M.	70	54	53
6 P. M.	64	52	54
9 P. M.	58	48	50
12 P. M.	54	43	46

THE TIMES's thermometer is 6 feet above the street level; that of the Weather Bureau is 285 feet above the street level.

Average temperatures yesterday were as follows:

Printing House Square	50¼
Weather Bureau	48
Corresponding date 1896	69
Corresponding date for last 20 years	49

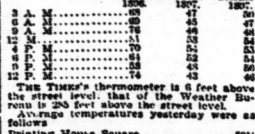

TURKEY ASSUMES WAR

She Says that Hostilities Have Begun and Throws the Blame on Greece.

ORDERS HER TROOPS TO ADVANCE

The Regular Greek Forces Took Part in the Fighting in Thessaly.

THE PORTE ABSOLVES HIMSELF FROM ALL RESPONSIBILITY.

He Offers to Withdraw the Troops from the Frontier if Greece Will Do the Same and Evacuate Crete—War Actually Established.

CONSTANTINOPLE, April 17.—The Council of Ministers, after a session at the palace to-day, declared that war had broken out on the frontier owing to the incursion by the Greeks on Turkish territory, and Edhem Pasha, the Turkish military commander, was ordered to assume the offensive.

This announcement of the actual existence of a state of war on the frontier was at first misunderstood, reports that the Council of Ministers had declared war upon Greece being widely circulated. It was also reported that the Council of Ministers had decided to recall Assim Bey, the Turkish Minister at Athens, and give passports to Prince Maurocordato, the Greek Minister at Constantinople.

The situation is summed up in a detailed circular sent this evening to the Turkish representatives abroad. This circular recalls the week's invasions of Turkish territory, and states that the newest incursion was participated in by Greek troops, thereby establishing war, which has broken out. The circular expresses the hope that the powers, in a spirit of justice, will agree that the entire responsibility for the war falls on Greece. Turkey has no idea of conquest, the circular adds, and as a fresh proof of pacific sentiments, the Sublime Porte offers to retire the Turkish troops on the frontier, if Greece will retire her forces from the frontier and from Crete.

ATHENS, April 17—10 P. M.—Orders were sent this afternoon to the Greek troops to keep strictly on the defensive, but to maintain their positions at all costs.

Turkey's Diplomatic Move.

LONDON, April 18.—The Greco-Turkish situation is understood here to be substantially as follows:

War has not been officially declared between Turkey and Greece, but has been declared officially to have "broken out." The Turkish Cabinet has decided to sever diplomatic relations with Greece, and has ordered Edhem Pasha, the Commander of the Turkish forces, to take the offensive.

It is considered in London that war between Turkey and Greece has actually begun, the Turkish declarations that war has "broken out," being merely for the purpose of diplomatically putting the onus of the war upon the Kingdom of Greece.

ATTACKED IN THE DARKNESS.

An Invasion by the Turkish Commander Expected by Greece.

ATHENS, April 18—1 A. M.—An official dispatch from Larissa, dated at 9 o'clock last night, says that the Turks, under cover of darkness, are assaulting the Greek forces at Mount Analipsis with great fierceness. The Greek resistance so far has been magnificent and spirited. The Greeks still maintain their positions.

The firing began at Gritsovali. The fighting at Gritsovali commenced in an attempt of the Turks to occupy a strategic position in the neutral zone. The Turks continue to abandon their advance posts, a general movement apparently taking place. Firing is reported from Moluna. From Larissa the flashing of guns can be seen. In yesterday's fight at Mount Analipsis the Greeks lost forty wounded and three killed.

ATHENS, April 18—1:30 A. M.—The Cabinet has decided to protest to the powers against the aggressive action of Turkey. An invasion by Edhem Pasha, the Turkish commander, is expected, and the Greek army has taken up positions for the purpose of being in readiness to repel the advance.

THE TURKS FORCED BACK.

The Fight on the Frontier Lasted Until Five o'Clock Yesterday.

ATHENS, April 17—Midnight.—In spite of the fact that official reports indicate that firing on the frontier ceased at midday, a telegram from Larissa at 7 o'clock in the evening says that firing continued past 4 o'clock this afternoon. The line of fire extended from Mount Analipsis Post to Kiephtika Gentekia, a distance equal to ninety minutes' march.

The Turks, falling back, abandoned several stations, which the Greeks promptly occupied. The Greeks cannonaded the Turks from the Greek position at Tsamteja, in the rear. The cannonading caused much excitement at other points. Since noon strong bodies of the Turks have concentrated in the direction of Mount Analipsis. At 5 o'clock the firing slackened. It is expected that the Turks will attempt a night attack upon Analipsis, which was the central point of the battle.

Greek reinforcements have arrived, and there is a general movement of troops toward the frontier. Reinforcements are being hurried toward the frontier from all directions.

Attack on Turks.

HEADQUARTERS OF THE TURKISH ARMY IN MACEDONIA, ELASSONA, April 17, 8 A. M.—News has reached here that a Greek band has attacked the Turkish troops at Karya, northwest of Neseros. A Turkish officer and two men were wounded. As this message is forwarded the fighting

"All the News That's Fit to Print."

The New York Times.

THE WEATHER.
Rain or snow, followed by fair; much colder, with a cold wave.

VOL. XLVII...NO. 15,008. NEW YORK, WEDNESDAY, FEBRUARY 16, 1898.—TWELVE PAGES. PRICE THREE CENTS.

THE NEWS CONDENSED.

Stock market strong.

Cash wheat, No. 2 red, $1.05¾; cash corn, No. 2 mixed, 37⅝c.; cash cotton, 6⅛c.

CONGRESS.—The Senate yesterday adopted a resolution calling on the Attorney General for information as to the coming sale of the Kansas Pacific Railroad. The Attorney General promptly furnished the information called for. The House passed a bill regulating loans to officers of National banks.—Page 3.

FOREIGN.—Lord William Nevill, fourth son of the Marquis of Abergavenny, was sentenced in London to five years' penal servitude for forgery. The Indian frontier war was discussed in the House of Commons. The Russian chargé at Pekin discussed the question of the Southern Manchurian Railway with the Tsung-li-Yamen. The Ambassadors at Constantinople are trying to arrange for the Autonomous Government of Crete without a provisional Governor. S. W. Rudolph of Philadelphia, an artist, expired at sea on the Aller, and was buried at Gibraltar. The British battleship Victorious is still aground at Port Said.—Page 7.

Page 1.

Fire of unknown origin destroyed the West End Hotel and seven cottages at Rockaway Beach.

The Classis of Kingston removed the Rev. Chandler A. Oakes as pastor of the Fair Street Reformed Church.

C. H. Rutherford of New York was arrested on the American Line steamer St. Louis at Newport News for passing a spurious check for $75 drawn on the Chemical Bank of New York.

Handwriting experts at Zola's trial in Paris expressed the opinion that Count Esterhazy was the author of the bordereau for writing which Dreyfus is serving a life sentence on Devil's Island.

It is reported that the Canadian Government has dispatched a note to Washington threatening to exclude Americans from the Klondike in case of hostile legislation by the United States.

A. J. Bowie, a mining engineer in the employ of James R. Keene, draws a dark picture of the outlook at the Klondike. Supplies, skilled miners, and machinery are wanting, he says, for successful work this year.

The proposed law taxing bachelors in New Jersey has brought to light a unique bachelors' club, which has hitherto been unknown to all but the initiated. Its objects are to promote gallantry toward the fair sex and discourage matrimony.

Señor Dupuy de Lome, the ex-Minister to the United States from Spain, with his family, reached the city last night en route for Spain. He declined to talk for publication, and was driven at once to the Hotel St. Marc. Two detectives from the Central Office met him as he landed from the Pennsylvania Railroad's ferryboat and remained on duty at the hotel all night. Señor de Lome and his party will sail to-day on the Britannic.

Page 2.

The Grand Trunk Railway is said to have purchased land near Toledo, which will give it an entrance into that city.

Contracts are said to have been made with the railroads to carry the greater part of Leiter's wheat holdings from Chicago to the seaboard. The Chicago market was strong yesterday.

It was said yesterday that the first of the four vessels being constructed for the American Mail Steamship Company will be ready in August, and that the new line will engage in the fruit trade between Jamaica and other West Indian points and the United States.

Page 3.

Arguments in favor of woman's suffrage were presented to the Senate and House committees in Washington by leading members of the National Woman Suffrage Association.

James B. Angell, United States Minister to Turkey, has announced his intention to resign in time to resume his duties as President of the University of Michigan next Fall.

Pay Director Luther G. Billings, United States Navy, has been convicted by a court-martial of falsehood and scandalous conduct and sentenced to dismissal from the navy.

Addresses to the silver men of the country urging united action in coming elections have been issued by the Democratic and Populist and Silver Republican National Committees.

Proposals were opened in Washington for carrying the mails to Jamaica. The American Mail Steamship Company of New Jersey proposes to furnish four new American twin-screw vessels for 66 2-3 cents per statute mile.

Commissioner Evans admitted the justice of THE NEW YORK TIMES's account of the abuses in the Pension Office. Reform in the selection and employment of clerks as well as a transfer of the bureau to the War Department have been proposed, but are not popular with Congress.

Page 4.

The old steamboat Narragansett, which has been fitted as a houseboat for detained immigrants, arrived at Ellis Island yesterday from Groton, Conn.

It is understood at Albany that the Democratic leaders propose next Fall to separate the State and Congressional campaigns, so that the fight for State officers and the Legislature shall be made on State issues and the fights in the Congressional districts on issues drawn to suit the conditions in each district. On the other hand, it is stated that the Republican leaders propose to make their fight chiefly on the financial issue.

The State Senate yesterday dicussed the proposed Constitutional amendment providing for biennial sessions of the Legislature. There was a hearing before the Senate Cities Committee on the Brush bill relating to the Board of Health. Many bills of local interest were introduced in both houses, and others were reported favorably by committees. The Judiciary Committees of the Senate and Assembly will hold a joint meeting to-day to begin the preparation of a primary election bill.

Page 5.

A waiter's version of the story told by Beck of loaning $10 to Noonan, taking his cuff as security, tended to discredit the testimony given by Beck.

The twelfth annual convention of the American Newspaper Publishers' Association will begin its sessions at the Waldorf-Astoria this morning.

The Executive Committee of the Insurance Tariff Association will meet to-day and frame its recommendation in reference to the maintenance of rates.

Mrs. Clara Baldwin, daughter-in-law of William S. Baldwin, has had him committed for examination as to his sanity. He imagines, she says, that he is Napoleon's son.

George Richards, an old man, was killed at a Newark crossing by a fast train. He had warned the railroad previously that the place was inadequately guarded and dangerous.

Serious trouble was narrowly averted at a game of basket ball between a team of New Rochelle players and Connecticut Guardsmen. A rival local club annoyed the home team.

A girl from Rockland Lake died of rabies in Roosevelt Hospital. She is said last Summer to have fondled a dog afflicted with the disease, the saliva coming in contact with her chapped hands.

There was a large attendance yesterday at the auction sale of trotters and pacers in progress at Madison Square Garden, but the bidding lacked spirit, and a number of well-bred and speedy animals were knocked down at low prices.

The Board of Home Missions of the Presbytery held a special meeting yesterday, at which the Rev. Charles L. Thompson of the Madison Avenue Presbyterian Church was formally accepted as Secretary, to succeed the Rev. William C. Roberts.

John Moje, a Third Avenue saloon keeper, was fleeced of $280 in Philadelphia by three men. He says that he and his manager came up with one of the men and walked him about for six hours before he found a policeman, who arrested the man. Mr. Moje says a cigar he smoked dazed him.

Patrick Vaughan, the policeman who shot and wounded John Lawler, was discharged yesterday in Morrisania Police Court. Lawler pleaded for the officer. He said it was all his own fault, and vowed that he would live a better life in future, whereupon he was also discharged.

Nearly 700 covers, it is expected, will be laid at the banquet of the Merchants' and Manufacturers' Board of Trade of New York, which will be held at the Waldorf-Astoria on Tuesday. The various industries and trades will be grouped at separate tables. Several United States Senators and Representatives will be present. A Reception Committee was appointed last night.

Page 7.

Charles L. Tiffany, who was eighty-six years old yesterday, received the congratulations of many old employes, some of whom have been with him for over forty years.

At a meeting of musical people at the home of Mr. and Mrs. A. W. Drake yesterday afternoon it was decided that the project to establish here a permanent orchestra should be energetically carried out. A committee will be appointed to raise the necessary amount, $1,000,000. There is already $115,000 in hand.

Page 9.

Opposition to the proposed combination of Western tin-plate manufacturers is developing in several quarters. New York dealers regard the scheme as impracticable.

A meeting of committees representing the Rapid Transit Commissioners and the Manhattan Railway Company was held, but a strict silence was maintained as to their proceedings.

Page 12.

Frank Moss denied yesterday the statement that the Society for the Prevention of Crime contemplates legal action against the promotion of William S. Devery to be Deputy Chief of Police.

The model tenement houses on Sixty-eighth and Sixty-ninth Streets, west of Amsterdam Avenue, were opened yesterday for inspection. One is ready for occupancy, and the first tenant will move in to-day.

Chairman Maxwell of the Brooklyn Committee of the Board of Education appeared before the Board of Estimate yesterday and asked for an allowance to pay the teachers for January. They will probably be paid Friday or Monday.

At the third monthly conference held under the auspices of the Charity Organization Society yesterday, the conditions of life of poor children in the city were discussed and the work done and in progress in their behalf was described. The necessity for more small parks in the congested districts was insisted upon, and examples were cited demonstrating the beneficial effects of rural surroundings upon health and morals.

Miss Dellaripha Richardson, daughter of the "Spite House" millionaire, appeared in Surrogate Fitzgerald's court yesterday during the hearing of the contest of her father's will brought by her brother and herself, made mysterious charges of murder and conspiracy, including the Surrogate in her accusations, and then went away. The evidence regarding Mr. Richardson's sanity when he made the will in dispute was conflicting.

At yesterday's meeting of the City Council a resolution was introduced to compel department stores to pay a license of $500 a year for each department; another to investigate the price and quality of gas in various parts of the city, and a third contained a protest against the usurpation of municipal functions by the State Legislature. All were referred to committees. A protest from Queens against the centralization of all municipal power in Manhattan received scant courtesy from the Aldermen at their meeting.

FIRE AT ROCKAWAY BEACH.

The West End Hotel and Seven Cottages Destroyed by Flames of Unknown Origin.

The West End Hotel and seven cottages at Rockaway Beach were destroyed by fire which started shortly after 11 o'clock last night in the hotel. The hotel was a four-story frame structure at the corner of Grove, Hammels, and Ocean Avenues. It contained 200 rooms and was owned by Paul Hauk, who lives in Seventy-fifth Street. He purchased it three years ago, paying $70,000 for it. He has since made extensive repairs and largely refurnished it.

The building was being repainted, and painters were at work in the building during the day. There was no one in the building when the fire started. The flames appeared to have spread through a large portion of the frame building when discovered. The fire was seen simultaneously by two policemen and a life saver.

When the volunteer firemen of Arverne, Hammels, and Rockaway Beach reached the building it was a mass of flame, and they turned their attention to the cottages, some of which were even then burning. Nothing was saved from the hotel. Four of the cottages were partially saved.

KINGSTON PREACHER REMOVED.

The Rev. C. A. Oakes No Longer Pastor of the Fair Street Reformed Church—He Will Appeal.

KINGSTON, Feb. 15.—The Classis of Kingston, after a special session which began yesterday morning and ended this afternoon, decided to dissolve the relations existing between the Rev. Chandler A. Oakes, Ph. D., and the Fair Street Reformed Church. Charges had been brought against Dr. Oakes by the consistory to the effect that the spiritual and financial condition of the church would be bettered by his dismissal. The case was summed up this afternoon for the consistory by the Rev. Dr. Oggel and by Dr. Oakes for himself. The Classis then retired, and after a deliberation of half an hour returned a verdict that the pastoral relations between Dr. Oakes and the church be dissolved on March 1. The vote of the Classis was 15 to 4.

Dr. Oakes is to be allowed to occupy the parsonage until April 1, and will be paid his salary up to June 1. The verdict was received in silence. Dr. Oakes announced his determination to appeal to the Synod, and said that he considered the offer of salary until June 1 as adding insult to injury.

"It is trying to bribe a man for a few hundred dollars, when life, honor, and justice are at stake," he said. This statement was received with applause. Moderator Davis stated that it would take twenty days for an appeal, and until that time the decision of Classis would stand and be in force.

A committee, composed of Dr. Oggel, the Rev. Mr. McNair, Dr. Oakes's counsel, and the Rev. Herman Hageman, was appointed to revise the stenographer's minutes for the appeal. Dr. Oakes says he will preach in the church.

MISS DEANS'S CLAIM ON TRIAL.

Aged Witness Heard in the Suit for a Share of the Stewart Estate.

The actual trial of the suit brought by Miss Euphemia Deans against ex-Judge Henry Hilton to recover a one-sixth interest in the old A. T. Stewart property at Thirty-fourth Street and Madison Avenue, was begun before Justice Scott.

Miss Deans, who is a school teacher, claims that through her mother she is one of the next of kin to the late A. T. Stewart. Her mother, Mary Bailey Deans, she contends, was an aunt of the dead millionaire. Judge Hilton denies the relationship.

The most important witness was James Bailey, eighty-six years old, who said he came to this country from Ireland on May 4, 1838. He said that when he came to this city in 1838 he met Mr. Stewart, to whom he had a letter of introduction from his mother, Mrs. Martin, and that Mr. Stewart spoke of him as the son of "his Aunt Mary." This testimony was intended to show the relationship between the plaintiff and her relatives in Europe. The case will go on.

ESTERHAZY IN THE TOILS

Handwriting Experts at Zola's Trial Affirm that He Was the Author of the Bordereau.

MME. DE BOULANCEY A FACTOR

She Received Letters from Esterhazy Animadverting on France and the Army—His Statements Startle the Court.

PARIS, Feb. 15.—The Zola trial will be concluded this week, according to programme, although it is expected that at least one night session will be necessary to get through on Saturday. So successful have been the efforts of M. Zola and his counsel, M. Laborie, to shatter the position taken by the Ministry on the Dreyfus case that already there are many who feel that Zola's acquittal is certain. When it is taken into consideration that the court was convened for the express purpose of securing a conviction, and that this seemed to be a foregone conclusion at the start, some idea may be obtained of the effect which the trial has had on public opinion in Paris. Even the Court itself, so bitterly hostile at the start, shows every day more and more evidence of being favorably disposed toward Zola. But this, of course, is no assurance that he will not be convicted by the Court.

It was rumored in the lobbies of the court to-day that MM. Laborie and Clemenceau are prolonging the examination of the witnesses in order to extend the trial, in the hope that the question of a revision of the Dreyfus trial will come before the Chamber of Deputies, now that it is generally admitted that Dreyfus was convicted on a secret document, and in the hope that something will happen in their favor.

While the examination of the experts proved rather tiresome, the flimsiness of their methods has turned favor toward Zola, and the mute sulkiness of the Advocate General is a strong indication of how matters are going.

To-day Col. Picquart seemed to come in for the hostility hitherto reserved for M. Zola. Mlle. Comminge's deposition tended to show that Lieut. Col. Paty du Clam wrote the telegrams, signed "Speranza," which were sent to Col. Picquart while he was in Tunis, with the intention to frighten him from following the Esterhazy trial. Prof. Grimand's testimony created a deep impression.

It is said to-night that Commandant Ravary, who compiled the unsatisfactory report for the Esterhazy trial, has had a sudden attack of congestion of the brain.

There were several quarrels outside the court to-day. In one case two barristers had a hand-to-hand fight.

High Prices Paid for Seats.

The visible excitement caused by the trial has greatly abated, but the real interest is absorbing and grows daily. The courtroom is packed, although the price of seats paid to those ready to wait all night to secure places has risen from 5f. to 25f.

Count Esterhazy will be examined to-morrow, so that the interest will be still higher, just as to-day's evidence exceeded yesterday's in exciting qualities.

When the trial is finished the discussion will be moved to the Chamber of Deputies and the Senate, where the Cabinet will be on its trial. There are still thirteen witnesses to be examined, and then will come the addresses of the Advocate General, M. Van Cassel; M. Laborie, and M. Clémenceau. M. Laborie is expected to speak four or five hours. M. Zola will speak very briefly.

The crowd present at the opening of the trial to-day was not so large as yesterday, and Zola's arrival at the court was not marked by any incident.

At the opening of the proceedings the Presiding Judge, M. Delagorgne, disallowed the request of counsel for M. Zola, M. Laborie, that the experts heard at the Esterhazy court-martial should be called to testify.

Gen. Gonse reappeared on the witness stand and protested against the assertion made by M. Jaures, the Socialist Deputy, on Saturday last, that the General Staff had refused to enlighten the Dreyfus affair.

M. Laborie, replying to Gen. Gonse, said that if he desired to throw light upon the case he could ask the War Minister's permission to do so.

To this Gen. Gonse answered that it was not within his province to transmit such a request to the Minister for War.

M. Crepieux Janin, a handwriting expert, was the next witness. He strenuously denied M. Teyssonnières's statement, made by the latter, who is also an expert in handwriting, yesterday, that he had attempted to bribe M. Teyssonnières to modify his reports of the Dreyfus bordereau.

M. Teyssonnières, M. Crepieux Janin added, had declared that it was on his (M. Teyssonnières's) report alone and not on M. Bertillon's that Dreyfus was convicted. This statement created a sensation.

M. Janin added that it was because M. Teyssonnières was angry with the witness for not sharing his opinion in regard to the Dreyfus case that he tried to compromise the matter. The witness further said he was a Frenchman and a Catholic, and exercised the profession of a dentist, and did not exercise the profession of an expert in handwriting.

M. Laborie Overruled by the Court.

Director Meyer of the French Record Office opened his testimony by affirming himself a Catholic. He declared that the published fac similes of the bordereau were as exact as possible, and he thought that Gen. Pellieux's contention that the fac similes looked like forgeries was an exaggeration. The witness added that he only desired an enlightenment of this sad affair, and if he was allowed to compare the fac similes with the original, if mistaken he would loyally say so. Continuing, the witness admitted that he had acted wrongly in intrusting the examination of the bordereau to M. Bertillon, who, the witness asserted, had acted in a manner devoid of all sense.

M. Meyer concluded with saying that the handwriting of Major Esterhazy resembled that of the bordereau.

M. Laborie then asked permission to examine the experts Couard, Belhomme, and Varinard, but the Court refused the request, upon which M. Laborie drew up conclusions, asking the Court to take cognizance of the fact. But the Presiding Judge, before even hearing the question, refused to let it be put, after which the Court retired to deliberate and decided that the Presiding Judge was right in refusing to allow questions "the only effect of which would be uselessly to prolong the proceedings."

Prof. Ernest Molinier of the College of France testified that Major Esterhazy's handwriting absolutely resembled that of the bordereau.

M. Clémenceau, counsel for the Aurore, read letters from Mme. de Boulancey admitting the possession of letters which Major Esterhazy wrote her between 1881 and 1884, and containing serious animadversions on France and the French Army. Major Esterhazy, it appeared, asked that the letters be returned to him; but Mme. de Boulancey refused to do so, in order to be able to prove that she had not committed forgery.

M. Clémenceau urged the Court to appoint a magistrate to ask Mme. de Boulancey if, among the letters, there was not one containing the following expressions:

"First 'Gen. Saussier [then the Commander in Chief of the French Army and Military Governor of Paris] is a clown. In our country the Germans would not show him in a circus.' [Uproar in court.]

"Second 'If the Prussians got as far as Lyons, they might throw away their guns and keep only their riding whips to drive the French in front of them.'" [Prolonged sensation.]

Blackboard for Demonstration.

Three amateur experts in handwriting testified that the fac simile was an exact reproduction of Major Esterhazy's handwriting, statements which caused further sensations in court.

M. Felix Frank, a lawyer of Brussels, testified that in order to demonstrate his evidence it would be necessary to have a blackboard, and that it would require an hour to demonstrate his theory.

Amid an uproar in court the session was suspended while a blackboard was procured and placed on an easel, after which M. Frank traced on the blackboard a fac simile of the bordereau and of Major Esterhazy's handwriting, and commenced his demonstration.

M. Frank made some long technical demonstrations and said:

"The majority of the experts started on the false idea that the writer of the bordereau had disguised his handwriting. The bordereau, however, was written naturally and in a running hand, which is identical with that of Major Esterhazy.

The latter, continued the witness, had recognized the bordereau as being his own handwriting, but had declared it had been traced by a forger. M. Frank proceeded technically to demonstrate the improbability of this explanation, showing how recurring words presented certain divergencies.

The lengthy demonstration of the witness caused impatience among the public in court, culminating in open murmurs, when M. Frank affirmed that the bordereau was written by one person alone, and added that this person was Major Esterhazy.

Annoyed at the murmurs, M. Frank turned and cried:

"I intended to end here, but since I am interrupted I will continue."

The Presiding Judge here remarked:

"I will ask you to use different language than that, which is discourteous."

M. Laborie thereupon intervened, asking the Presiding Judge to order silence in the court, pointing out that the lawyers were following the evidence with the closest attention.

"I am convinced," M. Frank resumed, "that the writer of the bordereau has a German mind."

The witness concluded with predicting that some day it would be recognized that the bordereau was not written by Dreyfus, which remark was greeted with murmurs.

The blackboard was then removed, and Prof. Grimaud of the Polytechnic School deposed that he signed the protests against the conduct of the Dreyfus affair because he was convinced that respect for the law, honor, and the fatherland was involved. The whole procedure struck this witness as being extraordinary. He added:

"In spite of the disguised threats and acts of intimidation of which I have been the victim, I here affirm that a revision of the case is a crying necessity, and I intend to do my utmost to obtain it."

The witness concluded with asserting his rights as a patriot and his love for the army, which brought forth hearty applause.

Prof. Havet of the College of France said he examined, as an expert, the bordereau and the letters of Major Esterhazy and Dreyfus, as well as a letter written by Dreyfus since his condemnation. The latter, the witness continued, was devoid of resemblance to the bordereau, of which he was convinced Major Esterhazy was the author.

Court was then adjourned. The crowd made no demonstration, and the officers, including Major Esterhazy and Gen. Pellieux, left amid silence.

At the Cabinet council to-day the trial of M. Zola and the publisher of Aurora was under discussion.

ARRESTED ON THE ST. LOUIS.

C. H. Rutherford in Custody at Newport News for Passing a Spurious Check on the Chemical Bank.

NEWPORT NEWS, Feb. 15.—A man representing himself to be C. H. Rutherford of New York, was arrested by Chief of Police Harwood on board the American Line steamship St. Louis this afternoon, charged with passing a spurious check for $75. Rutherford has been staying at the Hygeia Hotel, at Old Point, for a week or two. He spent money freely, mingling among the guests of the hotel and the officers at Fort Monroe and soon became well acquainted. Saturday he requested Harry Phoebus, a druggist at Old Point, to cash a check for $75, drawn on the Chemical National Bank of New York. After giving the money to Rutherford Phoebus became suspicious, and telegraphed to the bank for information as to his responsibility.

He received a reply pronouncing the check worthless. Rutherford came to this city, and to-day he went to the shipyard where the St. Louis is tied up for repairs, and requested permission to inspect the vessel. While walking about the big liner he was confronted by the Chief of Police. He attempted to elude the officer, but was soon arrested. Rutherford is now in jail at Hampton. He will be tried as soon as the check is returned from New York. The incident has created a sensation at the hotel, where Rutherford made himself quite popular. It is understood that he swindled several military officers at the fort out of small sums of money.

A UNIQUE JERSEY CLUB.

Its Object Is to Promote Gallantry Toward the Fair Sex and Discourage Matrimony.

TRENTON, N. J., Feb. 15.—The bill introduced by Assemblyman Weller of this city to tax bachelors has brought to light the Bachelors' Club of Trenton. Although the club is one of the oldest in the State, it was not known that such an organization existed until it was forced to announce itself and to formally protest against the passage of the bill now pending. The object of the club as disclosed by its by-laws is rather unique. It is to widen the scope and increase the possibilities of gallantry, and at the same time discourage the seemingly inevitable result of the law of association between persons of opposite sex, namely, matrimony.

Article VII. of the constitution sets forth the principles upon which the club is founded, and is as follows:

"Section 1. No member of the Bachelors' Club shall call upon any one friend among the gentler sex, nor escort her to entertainments or social functions, except in case of formal invitation, oftener than once a month; and it is hereby made mandatory that each member shall call upon, escort to entertainments or social functions, or show some direct gallantry to friends of the gentler sex upon at least three separate and distinct occasions in each month.

"Sec. 2. Violation or disregard of the preceding section shall, after due hearing before the Executive Committee, be deemed sufficient cause for dismissal from membership."

The rigidity of this regulation has had the effect of depleting the membership from time to time, and has, to an extent, discouraged new acquisitions, but, despite this fact, the club has flourished and become popular. John Hartpence of the Supreme Court office has been President of the club since its organization, early in 1891, and J. Harry Woodruff has been Secretary and Treasurer. It is authoritatively stated that Senator Edward C. Stokes of Cumberland will be added shortly to the membership of the club.

MR. HOYT SUED FOR $10,000.

E. G. Bates Asks Damages in Boston as a Result of a Word War.

BOSTON, Feb. 15.—The trial of a suit for $10,000 damages against Charles H. Hoyt, playwright and ex-member of the New Hampshire Legislature, was begun before Judge Sherman and a jury in the Second Session of the Suffolk Superior Court this afternoon.

The suit is brought by Edwin G. Bates, a member of the firm of Bates & Bendix, music publishers, for alleged injuries to character and reputation. Mr. Bates is also musical director of the Castle Square Theatre. Mr. Bates alleges in his bill that in the Park Theatre one night Mr. Hoyt called him a liar and in an uncontrollable fit of passion added a boisterous, loud, and blasphemous tirade of words. He adds that this took place before a large concourse of people and in the presence of ladies, and that Mr. Hoyt after exhausting his vocabulary spit upon him.

It was alleged that Mr. Hoyt continued his talk at the bar of the Hotel Reynolds when Mr. Bates was not present. Mr. Bates says that he has been greatly injured in his feelings and put to great mental suffering, and asks $10,000 damages.

The trouble grew out of a controversy over the song "Sweet Daisy Stokes," which was sung by Otis Harlan in the play "The Black Sheep."

Mr. Hoyt says that any words spoken to the plaintiff were not publicly uttered or published, and were justified and proper, in that they were true.

Mr. Hoyt was in the court room accompanied by Fred Wright, his managed.

DARK TALE FROM KLONDIKE

A. J. Bowie, James R. Keene's Engineer, Says There Are Few Miners There.

EXORBITANT PRICES FOR FOOD

Many Men Drowned in the Ice Floe on the Way—Famine Sure to Kill Many Laborers—Corporations Needed for Good Work.

SAN FRANCISCO, Feb. 15.—A letter has been received from Augustus J. Bowie, a mining engineer sent to the Klondike by James R. Keene in the interests of a New York syndicate, dated at Dawson Jan. 3. After stating that the cold is 20 degrees below zero, with no wind, he says meat is sold at $1.50 per pound wholesale, and flour at $125 for a sack of fifty pounds. Men are paid $1.50 an hour who are not worth that much per diem. "Without exception," he says, "there are fewer mining men than in any other place I was ever in. They have not the slightest conception of mining. The only wonder to me is the fact that the place has been able to exist as long as it has under the terrible prices demanded for everything.

"People in San Francisco and elsewhere cannot conceive the condition of affairs here. Absolutely nothing is to be obtained, and it will be fully two years before the mines can be handled as they should be, on account of the want of ordinary essentials for work, let alone living. Wood sells at $50 per cord. There is plenty of it, but no means for quick or easy transportation. The mines are certainly extraordinarily rich, but the present system of work must be largely or entirely abandoned.

"Corporations must take hold and clean out the crowd of good-for-nothings." A new era will dawn. The Alaska Commercial Company and North American Transportation and Trading Company are the only two business concerns here, where there is ample room for more, if transportation lines were established. Situated as these companies are, they will throw every obstacle in the way of any and every body coming in to compete with them, and thus keep up their sales. They will slowly but surely absorb all the gold output by charging infamous prices for supplies. The Alaska Commercial Company during the present famine has never raised prices on any staple article and has been very just, but when the North American Transportation and Trading Company finds that the Alaska Commercial Company has sold out any article, it raises the price 300 per cent. or more. Coal oil is $40 per gallon, candles fetch $1 each, and are esteemed a luxury. The restaurants are all closed, as are the bakers, and choice bacon is a thing of the past. The poorest whisky, made on the spot, commands $5 a bottle, and you can buy but little at that figure.

"Light just now is the most important thing. One cannot buy candles or oil now for love or money. I have spent only one night in town, as the place is absolutely too disgusting for anything. Gin mills, women, dance houses, and gambling dens are everywhere.

"There is not the slightest doubt that many a poor fellow died en route here, and will never more be heard of. A man who came in the other day by way of Dyea told me that on the way down he saw men's arms sticking up out of the ice. Their bodies were out of sight. They were grasping oars, planks, and pieces of wood, which they had grabbed as they were drowning in the ice floe. The famine hereabouts cannot be pictured in too awful form. Soon the fuel will give out. Men cannot work without food, and there is no food for wood cutters. Some large sales have been made to Eastern parties, $324,000 having been paid for three claims on Bonanza Creek, and $24,000 for two others. Twenty have been bought on Eldorado Creek for $100,000.

"Sulphur and Dominion Creeks now offer the best advantage for the money. The yield of all claims will, I think, be less than last year, as there are no supplies here, labor or materials to work with, and famine is sure to kill off many laborers. If I do not starve to death I shall be very lucky."

CANADA WILL RETALIATE.

Hostile Washington Legislation to be Met by Exclusion of Americans from the Klondike.

MONTREAL, Feb. 15.—A special dispatch from Ottawa says that the Dominion Government this afternoon dispatched a communication to Washington stating the determination of Canada, in the event of the passage by Congress of the bill introduced in the House by Mr. Payne and in the Senate by Senator Frye, to issue a proclamation barring all but British subjects from the right to mine in the Klondike or other Canadian territory in the Yukon region. The contents of the note, it is added, probably will be laid before the American Government by the British Ambassador, Sir Julian Pauncefote.

No official announcement has been made by the Government of the dispatch of such a note, but neither is it denied, and the general belief is that the step has been taken. There has been considerable agitation in favor of a move of this nature by the Canadian Government, and for some days the Government press has been hinting that it might have to come to that.

Sir Wilfrid Laurier and his Cabinet have been much annoyed at the threatened blocking of the "all Canadian Railroad" project by legislation at Washington, and the taunts of the opposition in Parliament probably have determined the Government to carry its plans through at any cost. It is now stated that in view of the disposition shown by the United States in its customs regulations at Fort Wrangell, the Canadian Government may abandon the proposed Stickeen River route and build the railroad from Port Simpson, which will bring it all in Canadian territory.

KLONDIKE RELIEF DELAYED.

SEATTLE, Washington, Feb. 15.—The three-masted ship Lucille, chartered by the Government to convey to Alaska the army pack train of twenty-two officers and men and 110 animals, was libeled for $6,000 to-day by the Alaska Forwarding Company of San Francisco. Five officers of this company boarded the Lucille at San Francisco with 44 animals and 50 tons of freight. A contract was entered into with Havner & Co., owners of the Lucille, to land the expedition at Skaguay, where the company intends to establish a pack train to be used over White Pass.

On the arrival of the Lucille at this port, Havner & Co. contracted to take the Government expedition, which is the advance detachment of the Klondike relief party. One thing after another delayed the departure of the Lucille, culminating to-day, when the San Francisco company libelled the ship because it was found that there was no room for both parties, and that the private expedition was to be left on the dock. A deputy marshal was put in charge of the ship. It is expected that the matter will be settled so that the Lucille can sail some time to-night or in the morning.

LOSS OF THE CLARA NEVADA.

SEATTLE, Washington, Feb. 15.—No further news has been received concerning the reported loss of the steamer Clara Nevada in Alaskan waters. Owing to the many conflicting rumors, hope for her safety has not yet been abandoned. Unless some unexpected steamer arrives, no definite news is expected before next Thursday.

The latest report was brought down by the steamer Excelsior, which arrived to-day. Capt. Donnellson said that just before he left Juneau the steamer Coleman arrived and reported that wreckage and bedding marked "Hassler" had been washed ashore at Seward. He said: "The Clara Nevada was formerly a Government vessel, known as the Hassler, and I have no doubt that she is at the bottom of the sea, at least such part of her as was not burned, for the Seward citizens report having seen a blazing vessel on the water."

The Excelsior arrived at Juneau five hours after the steamer Rosalie, which reported passing the Clara Nevada.

LAKE FISHERMEN LOST.

Carried Off on the Ice into Lake Erie—Between Twenty and Thirty in the Party.

BUFFALO, Feb. 15.—A number of men, estimated at between twenty and thirty, who were fishing through the ice on Lake Erie several miles up the lake, are believed to have lost their lives or to be adrift on the ice on the lake.

A heavy wind blowing from the east caused the ice to break away from the shore, and nothing can now be seen or heard of the men.

A large rescue party is on the way through a blinding snowstorm up the lake shore, but will not return before morning.

TALE OF MURDER MYSTERY.

A Jamaica (L. I.) Contractor Arrested as a Result of a Child's Strange Story.

Robert Brower, a contractor of Jamaica, L. I., was arrested last night by the police of Queens Borough on the strength of a story told by Mrs. Eliza Jackson of 102 Smith Street and her daughter Helen, aged seven years. The daughter says that on the morning of July 11 of last year she saw Brower and a young man employed by him place the body of a colored man in a box and bury it in his back yard.

Brower at first denied to the police that he had a colored man working for him at the time, but later admitted it, and said the man had gone away. Mrs. Jackson said that a son of Brower told her some time after the alleged interment that their colored man, named John, had been kicked by a horse, and had died and was buried in the yard.

RIOTERS KILLED IN HUNGARY.

Village Held Against Troops Sent to Restore Order—The Agrarian Socialist Movement.

VIENNA, Feb. 15.—The Agrarian Socialist movement in Hungary is becoming most serious. At Kistarkany, in the Kaschau District, a thousand peasants are in open revolt. They have murdered the local magistrate, and are holding the village against the troops sent to restore order.

At Agrad, in the same district, in a desperate fight between the gendarmes and the peasants, four were killed and twenty wounded.

At Karasz the Socialists tried to liberate their imprisoned comrades, and the gendarmes were obliged to prevent an onset with leveled bayonets. A woman tried to wrest his rifle from a gendarme, and the latter stabbed her in the breast. She fell dead.

There have been many arrests and much disorder in other districts. At Szathmar a rioter has been killed. The sale of gunpowder has been prohibited in the disturbed localities, and nobody is allowed out of doors after 7 in the evening without a special permit. There is talk of proclaiming a siege.

HANNA BRIBERY CHARGES.

C. C. Shayne Declines to Go to Ohio as a Witness.

C. C. Shayne, who was asked to appear as a witness before the committee of the Ohio Senate, which is investigating the bribery charges in connection with the election of Senator Hanna, has sent the following reply:

New York, Feb. 15, 1898.

Hon. Newman H. Burke, Chairman Senate Committee, Columbus, Ohio:

Engagements until after the London fur sales in March will prevent me from accepting your kind invitation. If, however, you desire a chapter for your Ohio political history, I refer you to my statements already published in the leading journals; or you can send a committee here, to whom every courtesy will be extended.

C. C. SHAYNE.

WEDDING OF MISS HANNA.

The Ohio Senator's Sister Married to a Young Man of Cleveland.

THOMASVILLE, Ga., Feb. 15.—Miss Lillian C. Hanna, the sister of Senator Hanna of Ohio, was married here this evening to S. Prentiss Baldwin of Cleveland.

The ceremony was performed at the country residence of Mrs. J. Wyman Jones, a sister of Miss Hanna, by the Rev. Mr. Whitney, rector of St. Thomas's Church of this city.

In addition to the family, those present were Gov. and Mrs. Merriam of Minnesota, Mr. and Mrs. Arthur Ely and M. J. C. Morse of Chicago, and Mr. and Mrs. Haskell of Cleveland.

Mr. Baldwin is twenty-eight years old; his bride is forty-five.

Glut of Money in Louisville.

LOUISVILLE, Ky., Feb. 15.—Owing to the money plethora the Louisville Clearing House Association has decided to reduce interest paid country correspondents from 2½ to 2 per cent. after March 1. The average balances of Louisville banks held for country correspondents is $10,000,000. Two years ago the banks paid 3 per cent. for country balances.

THE WEATHER.

The local forecast may be found at the top of this page to the right of the title.

The storm of Monday night in Illinois has moved very rapidly to New Jersey, increasing in intensity, a pressure of 29.34 inches being reported from Block Island and a northwest wind of sixty miles an hour from Norfolk. This storm has caused snow or rain from the Middle and Upper Mississippi Valley to the Atlantic Coast, and violent gales in the lower lake region. A second storm of considerable intensity has appeared to the north of Montana. It has grown colder from the interior of the Middle and North Atlantic States to the Rocky Mountains.

The record of temperature for the twenty-four hours ended at midnight, taken from THE NEW YORK TIMES's thermometer and from the thermometer of the Weather Bureau, is as follows:

	—Weather Bureau.— 1897.	1898.	TIMES. 1898.
3 A. M.	38	33	38
6 A. M.	37	33	36
9 A. M.	41	34	41
12 M.	38	36	42
4 P. M.	36	35	42
6 P. M.	35	35	39
9 P. M.	36	36	39
12 P. M.	32	32	39

THE TIMES's thermometer is 6 feet above the street level; that of the Weather Bureau is 285 feet above the street level.

Average temperatures yesterday were as follows:

Printing House Square	39⅝
Weather Bureau	36
Corresponding date 1897	36
Corresponding date for last 20 years	32

The maximum temperature yesterday was 40 degrees at 1 P. M.; the minimum was 32 degrees at 4 A. M. The humidity at 8 A. M. was .73, and at 8 P. M., .83.

THE MAINE BLOWN UP.

Terrible Explosion on Board the United States Battleship in Havana Harbor.

MANY PERSONS KILLED AND WOUNDED.

All the Boats of the Spanish Cruiser Alfonso XII. Assisting in the Work of Relief.

None of the Wounded Men Able to Give Any Explanation of the Cause of the Disaster.

HAVANA, Feb. 15.—At 9:45 o'clock this evening a terrible explosion took place on board the United States battleship Maine in Havana Harbor.

Many persons were killed or wounded. All the boats of the Spanish cruiser Alfonso XII. are assisting.

As yet the cause of the explosion is not apparent. The wounded sailors of the Maine are unable to explain it. It is believed that the battleship is totally destroyed.

The explosion shook the whole city. The windows were broken in nearly all the houses.

The correspondent of the Associated Press says he has conversed with several of the wounded sailors and understands from them that the explosion took place while they were asleep, so that they can give no particulars as to the cause.

WHAT SENOR DE LOME SAYS.

He Declares That No Spaniard Would Be Guilty of Causing Such a Disaster.

Señor de Lome, the departing ex-Minister of Spain to this country, who arrived in this city last night, and went to the Hotel St. Marc, at Fifth Avenue and Thirty-ninth Street, was awakened on the receipt of the news from Havana.

He refused to believe the report at first. When he had been assured of the truth of the story he said that there was no possibility that the Spaniards had anything to do with the destruction of the Maine.

No Spaniard, he said, would be guilty of such an act. If the report was true, he said, the explosion must have been caused by some accident on board the warship.

THE MAINE'S VISIT TO HAVANA.

First American Warship to Visit Cuba Since the Struggle Began.

The Maine was ordered to Havana on Jan. 24 last, and was the first American warship to visit that port since the outbreak of the Cuban rebellion. In explanation of the visit of the American battleship to Cuba Secretary Long issued the following statement:

"So far from there being any foundation for the rumors yesterday of trouble at Havana, matters are now in such condition that our vessels are going to resume their friendly calls at Cuban ports and go in and out just as the vessels of other nations do. The Maine will go in a day or two on just such a visit. The department has issued orders for vessels to attend the public celebrations in Mobile and the Mardi Gras at New Orleans, and for the torpedo flotilla to visit Galveston, Texas."

The Maine was commanded by Capt. Charles D. Sigsbee. Her other officers were Lieut. Commander Richard Wainwright, Lieuts. G. F. Holman, John Hood, and C. W. Yungen, Lieuts. (junior grade) G. W. Blow, J. T. Blandin, F. W. Jenkins, Cadets J. H. Holden, W. T. Cluverius, Amos Bronson, and D. F. Boyd, Jr.; Surgeon L. G. Heneberger, Paymaster C. W. Littlefield, Chief Engineer L. G. Howell, Passed Assistant Engineer E. C. Bowers, Assistant Engineers J. R. Morris and D. R. Merritt, Cadet Engineers Pope, Washington, and Arthur Crenshaw, Chaplain J. P. Chidwick, and Lieutenant of Marines A. W. Catlin.

The commander of the Maine, Capt. Sigsbee, is a favorite in the Navy Department. For four years he was Chief of the Hydrographic Office, and by his energy brought the office up to a high standard.

He justified the department's judgment in the selection by running his ship straight into a dock in New York harbor to avoid sinking a packed excursion boat. This was a display of quick judgment, nerve, and pluck that pleased the department so highly that the Captain was sent a complimentary letter.

ARMAMENT OF THE MAINE.

A Second-Class Battleship Built at the Brooklyn Navy Yard.

The Maine was placed in commission Aug. 17, 1895. She is a twin-screw, armored turret ship, of the belted type, and is known as a second-class battleship. Like the Texas, the Maine was built at a Government navy yard. The Texas was built at Norfolk; the Maine at the New York Navy Yard. Both ships were authorized when Secretary Whitney began the work of rehabilitating a then degenerate navy.

The Maine is of Navy Department designs throughout. The hull was built by navy yard workmen, and the engines were constructed by the Quintard Iron Works. That firm obtained the contract on its bid of $735,000. There were no other bidders.

The vitals of the ship are protected from gun-fire by an armor belt 180 feet in length. This belt has a maximum thickness of 11½ inches. Below the water line the armor tapers to a thickness of 6 inches. To deflect an end-on or a fore-and-aft fire, heavily armored and sharply inclined V-shaped bulkheads are placed forward and aft, the ends joining the armor belt. The bulkheads are 6 inches thick, and well backed.

In her main battery the ship mounts four 10-inch and six 6-inch rifles. A number of guns of smaller calibre are distributed in advantageous places. The 10-inch rifles are mounted in pairs in two steel turrets. One of these is situated aft, the other forward. The turret armor is 10½ inches thick. The protective power of these massive shields is increased by their circular shape, which tends to deflect a missile unless the impact is directly given.

The guns are breech-loading rifles, with bores 10 inches in diameter. The length of each gun is 320 inches. The weight is a little more than 24 tons. From them a full-service charge of 250 pounds of powder throws a 500-pound shell a distance of nine miles, with an initial velocity of 2,000 feet per second.

The 6-inch rifles are of the breech-loading pattern. These weapons measure 188 inches in length and weigh five tons each. The

"All the News That's Fit to Print."

The New York Times.

With FINANCIAL REVIEW and QUOTATION SUPPLEMENT

COPYRIGHTED, 1898, BY THE NEW YORK TIMES COMPANY.

With FINANCIAL REVIEW and QUOTATION SUPPLEMENT

VOL. XLVII...NO. 15,066. NEW YORK, MONDAY, APRIL 25, 1898.—TEN PAGES. PRICE THREE CENTS.

THE WEATHER.

Rain, followed by fair; brisk northerly winds.

THE NEWS CONDENSED.

Cash wheat, No. 2 red, $1.13; cash corn, No. 2 mixed, 38⅝c; cash cotton, 6 7-16c.

FOREIGN—Alarmist reports regarding the condition of Mr. Gladstone are circulating in London. The newspapers say that he is sinking fast and the members of his family have been summoned to Hawarden. A bulletin issued by his physicians at 5 P. M. yesterday says: "Mr. Gladstone's condition is one of increasing weakness, though he is more free from pain."—Page 7.

Page 2.

The men of the Massachusetts Naval Militia arrived and are quartered temporarily at a Brooklyn hotel, the cruiser Prairie not being ready for them. All will offer themselves to-day for enlistment in the regular service.

The work of connecting the life-saving stations and observatories on the Long Island Coast which are to be manned by the Signal Corps is practically completed. The stations at Montauk Point, Southampton, and Fire Island are in readiness.

Page 3.

Gens. Roe, Butt, and Smith went to Albany yesterday and conferred with Adjt. Gen. Tillinghast. The call for volunteers from the President is expected to-day and everything is in readiness for a prompt response.

The first provisional regiment of the State has been formed, according to information given out yesterday. It is composed of nine separate companies of the Fourth Brigade, with headquarters at Rochester. The other separate companies of the State have been attached to regiments or merged into battalions.

A rally of the First New York Volunteer Artillery was held yesterday in the Central Opera House, and more than 1,500 persons showed their patriotism by attending, despite the rain. The new uniform, which is a bluish gray, was exhibited. The recruiting was continued, and more than 300 are said to have enlisted.

Page 4.

Miss Edith Agostini and Eugene J. Beales were secretly married on Feb. 15 in the Transfiguration Church two months before their engagement was announced.

A bolt of lightning struck a house in Bronx, and is said by the inmates to have overturned a bed. Then it ran down a water pipe, ripped a piazza roof off, threw a plank in the air, and entering the house again knocked a woman senseless.

Page 5.

Abraham R. Ratsky is charged with having conducted extensive swindles in the dry good district by means of fraudulent checks.

Peter Wade, colored, of New Durham, N. J., who was accused by Conrad Brill of having stolen a ham, slashed Brill with a knife and nearly killed him late Saturday night.

The Rev. Dr. MacDonald of Brooklyn holds that the war is justifiable, but deplores the seizure of merchantmen and the proposed capture of the Philippines as un-Christianlike.

The Rev. Dr. Lindsay Parker of Brooklyn preached a farewell sermon justifying the war with Spain. He announced that he intended to go to th front with the Twenty-third Regiment, of which he is Chaplain.

The American liner New York arrived from Southampton in water ballast, after a rough voyage. She now becomes the Harvard and in the service of the Government. Most of the old crew reshipped for one year.

The Central Labor Union discussed the city's excess of the debt limit, and saw that it menaced labor by the shutting down of public improvements. The rich tax dodgers were denounced, and an attempt will be made to get workingmen on the Grand Juries.

The Rev. Dr. David H. Gregg preached a patriotic sermon in the Lafayette Avenue Presbyterian Church yesterday, and when he had finished a man in the audience, whose name was not learned, arose and severely denounced the war with Spain. He declared the Maine had been blown up by order of the Cuban Junta. He was loudly hissed, and then Justice Goodrich, who was in the congregation, on the pastor's permission led three hearty cheers for the flag and the Government.

Page 7.

Senator T. C. Platt was at the Fifth Avenue Hotel yesterday and announced that his choice for Chairman of the Republican State Committee is Benjamin B. Odell.

Prof. Felix Adler delivered his last lecture of the season in Carnegie Music Hall yesterday. He spoke on "A New Vocation," and said there was great need for the services of men who can be moral teachers without having theological affiliations.

Page 10.

The Rev. Dr. S. L. Beiler, late of Washington, preached in Calvary Methodist Church at both services yesterday, because the congregation refuses to have its provisional pastor, the Rev. S. F. Jones.

The Roman Catholic Church of St. Michael the Archangel, at West Hoboken, was reconsecrated and rededicated by Bishop Wigger. Mgr. Martinelli and other Church dignitaries were present at the ceremonies.

The Rev. John L. Scudder preached a war sermon entitled "Seventy Million Jingoes." He said, while we are ordinarily not a pugnacious nation, that our boast of patriotism, following the destruction of the Maine, will blow every Spaniard out of the Western Hemisphere.

Arrivals at Hotels and Out-of-Town Buyers.—Page 2.
Marine News and Foreign Mails.—Page 4.
Court Calendars.—Pages 8 and 9.
New Corporations.—Page 8.
Yesterday's Fires.—Page 2.
Real Estate.—Page 9.

THE ASIATIC FLEET MOVING.

Five American Warships Leave Hongkong Under Sealed Orders and Two More to Follow.

HONGKONG, April 24.—Five warships belonging to the United States squadron, accompanied by two storeships, will leave here to-day under sealed orders.

The United States cruisers Olympia and Baltimore will await the arrival of the United States Consul, O. F. Williams, from Manila, and will follow the fleet to-morrow.

WASHINGTON, April 24.—The Asiatic Squadron is under command of Commodore George Dewey, a trusted naval officer, and is made up of seven vessels, excluding the colliers recently purchased by the department. The Olympia, a protected cruiser, with a speed of over 21 knots, is the flagship, while the other ships are the protected cruiser Baltimore, 20 knots; the protected cruiser Raleigh, 19 knots; the protected cruiser Boston, 15½ knots; the gunboat Concord, 17 knots; the gunboat Petrel, 12 knots, and the iron ship Monocacy, 11 knots.

MANILA REASSURES MADRID.

Philippine Loyalists to Resist the American Squadron.

MADRID, April 24.—Advices have been received from Manila, Philippine Islands, to the effect that when news was recived there of the sailing of the American squadron from Hongkong an imposing popular demonstration took place, all classes offering their property and lives in defense of the country. The enthusiasm is described as "tremendous."

Rumors are being circulated that the Philippine filibusters are co-operating with the American squadron, but there is no official confirmation of them.

CRISIS IN PUERTO RICO.

Martial Law Proclaimed and Americans in Danger—A Revolution Threatened.

ST. THOMAS, West Indies, April 24.—Refugees from Puerto Rico who reached here by schooner this evening report that the condition of the island is critical. Martial law har been proclaimed, and Americans there are in danger, as they are without protection.

The agitation there is increasing and food prices are rising fast. The authorities have taken steps to prevent the departure of refugees.

At Mayagues, seventy miles southwest of San Juan, there is talk of a revolution.

SPAIN TO USE PRIVATEERS

An Official Decree Declares that She Is Determined to Reserve This Right.

A STATE OF WAR DECLARED

Regulations of the Declaration of Paris to be Adhered to with the Exception of That Relating to Privateering.

MADRID, April 24.—The following decree was gazetted to-day:

"Diplomatic relations are broken off between Spain and the United States, and, the state of war being begun between the two countries, numerous questions of international law arise, which must be precisely defined, chiefly because the injustice and provocation come from our adversaries, and it is they who, by their detestable conduct, have caused this grave conflict.

"We have observed with the strictest fidelity the principles of international law, and have shown the most scrupulous respect for morality and the right of government. There is an opinion that the fact that we have not adhered to the Declaration of Paris does not exempt us from the duty of respecting the principles therein enunciated. The principle Spain unquestionably refused to admit then was the abolition of privateering. The Government now considers it most indispensable to make absolute reserve on this point, in order to maintain our liberty of action and uncontested right to have recourse to privateering when we consider it expedient, by organizing immediately a force of cruisers, auxiliary to the navy, which will be composed of vessels of our mercantile marine, and with equal distinction in the work of our navy."

The rules which Spain will observe during the war are outlined as follows:

"Clause 1.—The state of war existing between Spain and the United States annuls the treaty of peace and comity of Oct. 27, 1895, and the protocol of Jan. 12, 1877, and all other agreements, treaties, or conventions in force between the two countries.

"Clause 2.—From the publication of these presents, thirty days are granted to all ships of the United States, anchored in our harbors, to take their departure free of hindrance.

"Clause 3.—Notwithstanding that Spain has not adhered to the Declaration of Paris, the Government, respecting the principles of the law of nations, proposes to observe, and hereby orders to be observed, the following regulations of maritime law:

"First.—Neutral flags cover the enemy's merchandise, except contraband of war.

"Second.—Neutral merchandise, except contraband of war, is not seizable under the enemy's flag.

"Third.—A blockade, to be obligatory, must be effective, viz.: It must be maintained with sufficient force to prevent access to the enemy's littoral.

"Fourth.—The Spanish Government, upholding its right to grant letters of marque, will at present confine itself to organizing, with the vessels of the mercantile marine, a force of auxiliary cruisers, which will co-operate with the navy, according to the needs of the campaign, and will be under naval control.

"Fifth.—In order to capture the enemy's ships and confiscate the enemy's merchandise and contraband of war under whatever form, the auxiliary cruisers will exercise the right of search on the high seas, and in the waters under the enemy's jurisdiction, in accordance with international law and the regulations which will be published.

"Sixth.—Defines what is included in contraband of war, naming weapons, ammunition, equipments, engines, and, 'in general, all the appliances used in war.'

"Seventh.—To be regarded and judged as pirates, with all the rigor of the law, are Captains, masters, officers, and two-thirds of the crew of vessels which, not being American, shall commit acts of war against Spain, even if provided with letters of marque issued by the United States."

CONTRABAND OF WAR.

Statement by Solicitor Penfield of the State Department—The Right of Search.

WASHINGTON, April 24.—The Spanish decree published by the Gaceta as to the attitude of that Government regarding privateering, and the question whether or not coal shall be held contraband of war, was discussed by the State Department officials to-day. In response to questions, Judge William L. Penfield, the Solicitor of the department, made the following unofficial statement, which he said was not to be regarded as indicating in any way the action and policy of this Government, but was given for the information of merchants and shippers.

"This Government has not yet officially presented a list of articles which it will treat as contraband of war. If Spain has taken any such action, it is not yet made public. Each Government is competent to prescribe its own list for the guidance of its own authorities. Such list is conclusive upon the Government making it and upon all neutral nations, in the absence of any disregard of treaty engagement and of international law. Any gross disregard of such law or treaty obligation would perhaps provoke the interposition of any neutral state affected.

"Until such a list is prescribed, the question whether articles captured are contraband of war will be governed generally by the law of nations, and specifically by the treaty stipulations between the belligerent captor and the neutral state to whose subject the articles belong.

"International law gives no hard and fast rule for the determination of the question whether articles are contraband, except the general rule that all articles of an essentially warlike character and destined for an enemy's use are contraband. Many articles, such as provisions, coal, &c., are of an equivocal character, and if destined for the enemy's use, are deemed contraband.

"It follows that if such lists should be prepared by the United States and Spain, they may be identical or may be widely divergent, depending on the policy of each Government. The action of each Government will bind only itself and its own prize courts and neutrals. The question whether contraband or not might therefore depend on whether the captor was American or Spanish. And shippers in neutral vessels would not only consider the character of the goods shipped, but whether destined for American or Spanish ports, and whether the goods are included in the list denounced as contraband by the one or the other State.

"This Government has already announced that it will not resort to privateering. In the light of this declaration Spain's announcement that she will treat our privateers as pirates is worthy of Don Quixote. The Spanish Government has published its intention to exercise the right of search. The right to do so is undoubted. But the right can be lawfully exercised only for the purpose of determining the nationality of the ship and its destination, whether its goods are neutral or enemy, whether contraband or not, and whether its conduct is unneutral or neutral.

"If Spain adopts the policy announced by this Government, that the neutral flag protects the goods, if the vessel and its conduct are neutral, only contraband goods in such ships are subject to capture. Of course all merchant ships must respect an effective blockade on the penalty of capture and confiscation."

Educating the Madrid Public.

LONDON, April 25.—The Madrid correspondent of The Daily News says:

"The various false rumors current to-day reminded one of Paris in August, 1870. The Government intends to allow the fullest liberty of publication of news, good and bad, in order to enable the public to form its own education in the habit of self-reliance."

CONCERT OF THE POWERS.

Contemplated Action to Enforce the Observance of Neutrality Law—America Gaining Friends.

WASHINGTON, April 24.—The proposed concerted action for the protection of the flags of neutral powers is believed here to be designed more as a warning to Spain than to have any other significance. The representatives of the powers say the contemplated action is a very likely and natural move, although their home Governments have transmitted to them no notification of the negotiations to that end. It is a measure of precaution sanctioned by the usages of past conflicts, but there is not to be implied in it, as understood here, any disposition to question the sincerity of this Government, as expressed in the formal notification as to the course it will adopt, which has been communicated to all the foreign Governments.

At the Embassies of the powers seeking concerted action, Germany, France, Austria, and Italy, and at several others likely to be interested, no information on the subject has been received. This shows that the powers are carrying on their negotiations independent of conferences with their representatives in the two contending countries, and will await some definite result in the way of a formal understanding and agreement on concerted action before communications are opened with Washington and Madrid. It is possible that no concert of action can be agreed on. On various occasions efforts at concerted action on neutrality enforcement have failed by the refusal of one of the great powers to participate.

LONDON, April 24.—Spain's adherence to the right of privateering, if expedient, has given great satisfaction in that country, where the public press markedly approves the attitude of the Government. Fears are expressed on the Continent that the United States will find it necessary to retaliate, despite the adhesion of the Government to the Declaration of Paris. In any case, Spain's attitude will enhance the importance of the negotiations of the powers, which, it is understood, have been initiated by Italy with a view to making arrangements to protect neutrals on the seas. It is reported from Vienna that England holds aloof from the negotiations, though this is discredited.

The Kolnische Zeitung remarks that "as neither Spain nor the United States occupies anything like a position of supremacy on the seas, neutral Governments will easily be able to insist on the adherence of both to the Declaration of Paris," and "looking to the importance of American markets for German industry and commerce," it expresses doubts "whether the provisions of the existing law of nations are adequate to meet the necessities of the case." This journal thinks it "possible that the war will result in a fresh extension of the principles applicable to the matter."

In fact, it looks as though trade interests will compel a veering of German feeling in the dispute toward the United States. A tendency in this direction is also noticed in France and Italy.

The Berlin correspondent of The Standard says:

"Germany will take no steps prejudicial to the United States, nor, probably, join in any intervention on Spain's behalf. It is evident, therefore, that the meeting yesterday (Saturday) at Dresden between Emperor William and Emperor Francis Joseph signally failed to bring Germany into line with Austria."

GREAT BRITAIN'S NEUTRALITY.

The Proclamation Submitted to the Prince of Wales—Decision on the Coaling Question.

LONDON, April 24.—It is announced that the Prince of Wales held a council yesterday at Marlborough House on behalf of the Queen for the purpose of approving the draft of the neutrality proclamation. It is supposed that the proclamation will be strictly in line of precedents, calling attention to the British Foreign Enlistment act and warning British subjects against blockade breaking or aiding the belligerents in any way.

The Foreign Office will send to the Treasury, the Home, Colonial, War, and India Offices the usual notices prohibiting Spanish and American ships the use of British harbors for warlike purposes.

The coaling question will be met by a provision that belligerents will be supplied at British ports with not more coal than is sufficient to carry them to the nearest port of their own country or some nearer destination, and no more coal will be supplied to the same vessel within three months except by special permission.

Armed ships will be prohibited from carrying prizes into British ports, including those of the colonies.

SPAIN'S PRIVATEERING PLANS.

Frenchmen Apply for Letters of Marque Against America.

LONDON, April 25.—The Madrid correspondent of The Daily Mail says:

"Spain adopts privateering in fact, but not in name. The reservation in the decree issued means very little and what the cancellation of agreements with the United States means can well be appreciated, particularly by Americans remaining behind in Cuba and those who own property there.

"Urgent orders have been issued for the movement of the various Spanish men-of-war and vigorous action is anticipated. Many French ship owners and not a few private Frenchmen have applied for letters of marque against the United States."

NEUTRALITY OF HONGKONG.

British Authorities Proclaim the Foreign Enlistment Act.

WASHINGTON, April 24.—The State Department to-day received information that the Governor of Hongkong had issued a neutrality proclamation as to the United States and Spain. It is similar in terms to those already issued by Jamaica and Newfoundland.

HONGKONG, April 24.—The Foreign Enlistment act has been proclaimed by the British authorities here, thus enforcing the neutrality of British subjects.

Liverpool Shipping Precautions.

LIVERPOOL, April 24.—Many Liverpool steamship owners have instructed their agents to avoid shipping contraband of war, and have ordered their Captains to comply instantly with the commands of any war vessels they may meet and to make no attempt to escape.

ATTITUDE OF THE POPE.

One Report Says He Is Neutral, but It Is Disputed.

LONDON, April 25.—The Rome correspondent of The Daily Mail says:

"Cardinal Rampolla, the Papal Secretary of State, declares that the Vatican will observe the strictest neutrality. The Pope desires prayers only for a speedy conclusion of peace. He considers the singing of the Te Deums for victories an utterly incongruous proceeding."

The Rome correspondent of The Standard says:

"The Queen Regent asked the blessing of the Pope upon Spanish arms. His Holiness replied that he sent it from his heart, and hoped to see a vindication of Spain's rights, which had been trampled upon."

FRENCH COAL STEAMER HELD.

WASHINGTON, April 24.—The New York agents of the French-Atlantic Steamship Company have telegraphed a formal complaint that this Government has refused to clear one of their vessels, the steamer St. Andrew, for St. Thomas, from Philadelphia, on account of suspicion of her coal cargo. The French Embassy, which has been appealed to, to-morrow will make formal representations to the State Department, and insist on its release.

The St. Andrew has 3,300 tons of coal on board, and when she started to leave was refused clearance papers by the Collector of the port. The latter was acting under instructions for the enforcement of the coal embargo law. The action of the Collector doubtless was due to apprehension that the coal taken was destined for the use of the Spanish Government. St. Thomas is neutral ground, and the French company, it is understood, has indicated that it does not contemplate taking the coal to any outside source.

THE PARIS NOT CAUGHT YET.

Spanish Naval Authorities Get Tardy Orders to Capture the American Liner.

MADRID, April 24.—It is said here that, as a result of a meeting of the Cabinet held to-day, instructions were sent to the Spanish naval authorities to effect the capture of the American Line steamship Paris, on her way from Southampton to New York.

LONDON, April 25.—A point of vital interest for Londoners is whether the Paris has escaped the Spanish warships. Up to midnight there was absolutely no news as to the liner at Southampton.

NO SPANISH WARSHIPS SEEN.

Vessels Arriving at British Ports Failed to Sight Any.

SOUTHAMPTON, April 24.—The British steamer Mexican, which sailed from Cape Town on April 6 for this port, via the Island of Madeira, arrived here at noon. Her commander reports that she did not sight a single Spanish war vessel during the voyage.

LONDON, April 24.—Ships arriving at different Channel ports report that they have not sighted any Spanish warships.

EXTENDING THE BLOCKADE.

The Puritan, Cincinnati, and Other Ships to Close Matanzas, Mariel, and Cardenas.

On Board the United States Flagship New York, off Havana, April 23—2 P. M.—The Puritan, Nashville, Marblehead, and Ericsson arrived from Key West this morning.

The Ericsson almost immediately returned to Key West with dispatches. At 10 o'clock this morning the monitor Puritan, the cruiser Cincinnati, the gunboats Machias, Nashville, Castine, and Newport, and the torpedo boats Foote and Winslow left the squadron to blockade Matanzas, Mariel, and Cardenas. They formed separate divisions.

SPAIN'S NAVAL PROGRAMME.

Nothing Disclosed Regarding the Plans of the Admirals—American Ships Threatened.

MADRID, April 24.—It is believed that the Spanish Admirals at their meeting yesterday approved of a plan of campaign against the United States. All information on the subject is refused. Despite statements published in New York to the contrary, it is declared here that the Spanish Navy is fully supplied with coal.

The Government has received no official information of the capture of any American vessels. The Imparcial prints a list of the American ships in the Mediterranean, pointing out that they will be easy prey for the Spanish warships.

Other Madrid papers point out that some excellent prizes are now obtainable in the Mediterranean in the yachts of millionaire Americans.

THE AUDAZ GOES TO SEA.

Spanish Torpedo Boat Destroyer Leaves Queenstown.

QUEENSTOWN, April 25.—The thirty-knot Spanish torpedo boat destroyer Audaz passed Roche's Point at 5:45 A. M. to-day, (Monday,) going seaward, after three weeks in the Queenstown dry dock.

REPORTS FROM SPAIN'S FLEETS.

The Government Informed of Their Movements by Agents Abroad.

WASHINGTON, April 24.—It was said at the Navy Department to-day that no additional information had been received concerning the Spanish fleets at Cadiz and the Cape Verde Islands. Every movement of these fleets is reported promptly to the department by agents abroad.

One officer explained to-day that it was necessary to receive with the greatest caution reports emanating from Madrid of the movements of the Spanish ships, as Spain naturally will try in every way to mislead the United States.

REFUGEES REACH KINGSTON.

Consul at Baracoa Debarks—Americans Mobbed at Guantanamo—Spanish Devastating Cuba.

KINGSTON, Jamaica, April 24.—The United States Consul at Baracoa, Cuba, Mr. Alfredo T. Triay, his wife and two children, two Spanish merchants, and twenty-two Cubans and Cuban-Americans, mostly women and children, from Guantanamo, debarked from the Ely here to-day, after a twenty-four-hour quarantine.

When the steamer left Guantanamo on Friday last a Spanish mob, including many soldiers, filled the public square and adjacent streets, yelling "Death to the Yankees!" Several American flags were soiled, torn, trampled, and treated with other indignities. Some naturalized Americans were compelled to take part in the insulting work on the threat of death if they refused.

Mr. Triay, the Consul at Baracoa, received a letter from a Santiago friend, dated April 15, saying that the American Consul had left a week before and advising him to leave. The coasting steamer San Juan happened to be in port at Baracoa. Mr. Triay, with his wife and children and two handbags, sailed, leaving the Consulate unoccupied and the business unprovided for.

When he reached Santiago he claimed the protection of the British Consul and promptly cabled to Washington, asking why he had not been looked after when all the other Consuls were directed to reach Jamaica at the earliest opportunity. He staid at a hotel in Santiago for a week unmolested, and then the British Consul got him and his family safely to the Ely.

Mr. Triay says he has been treated shamefully. As there is no telegraph at Baracoa he did not know what was happening on the outside. It is assumed, as he is an American, that he will lay the matter before Congress. He does not know who was to blame.

According to his statement, the southern coast garrisons have been weakened to strengthen the defenses at Havana. Last Thursday the San Juan sailed from Santiago with a regiment, and another coastal steamer, pressed into the service by Spain, took troops the same day from Manzanillo for Havana.

It was reported last Thursday at Baracoa that the place would be evacuated by 2,000 Spanish troops.

Orders to the Spanish Army declaring the cessation of hostilities ended were publicly posted at Guantanamo last Friday. Two days previous the troops began concentrating at the principal seacoast cities, abandoning all the interior towns and plantations, in many cases burning them. The passengers by the Ely believe the devastation of that part of the island will be completed before the Americans can invade the ports held by the Spaniards.

Ordinarily there are 2,000 Spanish soldiers at Guantanamo. Now there are 7,000 there. New defenses, earthworks chiefly, are under construction, and the mounting of field pieces is in progress. Two rapid-fire two-pounders, one rapid-fire three-pounder, and four ancient models have been received.

THE CHARLESTON DAMAGED.

Serious Result of the Earthquake at Mare Island.

SAN FRANCISCO, April 24.—The Mare Island Navy Yard officials will not be able to place the cruiser Charleston in commission on Sunday, May 1, as they have all along expected to do.

The Charleston was badly damaged by the earthquake of March 30, as has just been discovered. It was found that nearly every condensing tube was perforated and the diaphragm plate "buckled." The earthquake occurred while the Charleston was in the dry dock.

WAR TO BE DECLARED

Resolution Approved at a White House Sunday Conference to Go to Congress To-day.

NO DELAY EXPECTED IN EITHER HOUSE.

Sampson's Fleet Vigilant and Active Off the Cuban Coast Blockading Ports and Capturing Prizes.

Flying Squadron Still at Fort Monroe—Hongkong Ships Sailing for the Philippines—No News of the Spanish Fleet.

WASHINGTON, April 24.—A resolution formally declaring war against Spain will be introduced in Congress to-morrow. The decision to take this course has been reached after mature deliberation, in order to safeguard the interests of the United States.

All the arguments pro and con were discussed this afternoon at the White House at a conference, in which President McKinley, Attorney General Griggs, Assistant Secretary Day, and Senators Davis and Hale participated, and on its breaking up announcement was made that Congress to-morrow would be asked to declare what it is held already exists.

The President will send a message to Congress to-morrow to be delivered immediately after its convening, setting forth the facts in the case and asking Congress to formally declare war in order that there may be no misunderstanding on the part of other nations.

The most important point in the message from a news point of view will be the announcement that Spain has made formal reply to our ultimatum. This reply has not been given to the public, and it was supposed that none had been received. The document is a formal acknowledgment by Spain and also acceptance by that country of the ultimatum as a virtual declaration of war. Congress therefore will be asked to recognize this condition of affairs and to declare it to the world.

The war resolution has been prepared, and it is understood that the two committees having in charge the foreign affairs of the two houses of Congress will be prepared to repor upon it very speedily—probably immediately after the reading of the message. An effort will then be made to have the resolution taken up and passed forthwith, and it is believed there will be no formidable opposition to this course in either house.

OUTLINES OF THE CAMPAIGN.

Operations Contemplated by the Fleets and Army—The Prospective Invasion of Cuba.

WASHINGTON, April 24.—Washington devoured the Sunday morning papers with avidity, but since morning has been obliged to fret without news. A few brief bulletins upon the boards of newspaper offices, reporting the situation at Havana, have been read and reread. Everywhere there has been speculation as to what shall be done next, and amateur strategists have criticised the plans of the Government, or what are supposed to be the plans of the Government, and have urged immediate activity with the army and the navy, in order that the expectation may be fulfilled of a short, sharp, and decisive campaign.

Persons who are qualified to judge of the merits of the blockading plan insist that it has many advantageous features. The length of coast to be covered by the vessels of the fleet is not great, but it includes all of the island to which the bulk of the commerce usually transacted finds access.

There is agreement of evidence in the War and Navy Departments that the supplies of meat and other food for the Spanish army must be imported or not obtained at all, the cattle in the island having been about used up by the war.

Then, excepting Cienfuegos on the south side, the ports blockaded are so close together that the blockading vessels can communicate speedily, thus affording abundant time in which to notify all vessels if the Spanish fleet should approach with the intention of attacking the blockaders and destroying the vessels of Admiral Sampson's squadron.

The Administration has not overlooked the fact that Spain has been using Portuguese territory as a base of operations. Several days ago reports came from Europe that the Spanish fleet had sailed from the Cape Verde Islands, but the latest report states that the fleet is still there, although hostilities have begun and have existed for three days. The Government has taken the precaution to notify Portugal that it will expect the neutrality laws to be observed by the Government controlling the Cape Verde Islands. If the Government of Portugal heeds this admonition the Spanish fleet at Cape Verde Islands will be required to fall back to the Canary Islands, unless it is part of the Spanish plan of operations to send the fleet across the Atlantic Ocean to meet and give battle to the fleet under Admiral Sampson.

It is stated that the departure of the Asiatic Squadron from Hongkong was made with strict observance of the neutrality laws. The ships of Commodore Dewey's squadron had been assembling there, and they were informed that war had begun. Whether their destination is Manila or some other place the Navy Department does not say. But it is admitted that they left temporarily, and may be expected to return in a few days.

The squadron sails with a collier and a supply ship, and there is a stock of coal owned by the United States at Hongkong. Another shipment of coal is on the way to Hongkong and will reach there soon. As long as the fleet remains near the Philippine Islands the Spanish naval vessels in those waters will not venture to leave their stations, and if they are attacked, the United States fleet is so superior that Spain's resistance would be futile.

It is not considered that there is any necessity for haste in a movement against Manila, but when detailed information is sought as to that matter the officers of the navy become officially reticent.

The international rule providing that a ship may go into a neutral port to obtain provisions and coal sufficient to carry her to the nearest home port affords enough margin of operation and visitation for all the purposes of the navy. If any question should arise about the propriety of frequent visits to Hongkong, Honolulu will be used as a base for coal supplies, and the coal would be sent across the intervening distance from colliers, from which it could be taken at sea if necessary.

Bye and bye it may be possible to establish a supply port at Manila itself.

The army men at the War Department are saying little about the plans of co-operation with the insurgents, but it is ascertained that some expectations are being indulged in on that account. Although the volunteers to be called for to-morrow cannot, it is asserted by competent judges, be ready for field work in less than six weeks or two months, the United States regular forces now accumulated at several Southern points, are to be employed.

It seems altogether probable that when Gen. Gomez has been acquainted with the hopes of the United States he will move up his forces toward Havana from the east and worry the Spanish as much as possible. At the same time the insurgent forces in Pinar Del Rio will be prepared to join the 10,000 or 15,000 United States troops that may be landed at some point to be agreed upon, and to press the Spanish forces from the land side of Havana.

It is believed that this can be done before the wet season is fully established, and without serious impairment of the health of troops.

If it is found that the Spanish resistance is too great and too persistent to be overcome until the volunteer forces are made ready for work on the island, the landing of regulars may be postponed until a later period.

The suggestion of an alternative plan makes it plain that the War Department is not expecting the campaign to be over in a few weeks or months.

Washington to Send Troops.

Washington will have its first camp of citizen soldiers to-morrow. The entire National Guard of the District, amounting to 1,800 men, is to go into camp out on the Soldiers' Home grounds, north of the city, in anticipation of the call to be promulgated by the War Department under the proclamation of the President calling for 125,000 men. The entire Guard cannot enter the service under the call, but 1,000 men will be selected to represent the District.

Gen. Harries, the commanding officer of the Guard, has stimulated the soldier feeling amazingly and promises to give a good account of the District when the opportunity is offered. The Soldiers' Home grounds are admirably situated for a healthful camp, but much must be done to render them comfortable for men who may be compelled to live in camp for six weeks or two months as may be necessary in order to give the mass of volunteers time to organize and obtain sufficient skill to be useful in any movement that may be contemplated.

ERRAND OF THE MANGROVE.

Expected that She Will Cut Off Communication Between Cuba and Spain.

WASHINGTON, April 24.—Important information is expected in a day or two from Key West, when the Mangrove returns to that point. It is believed she will bring the report that she has broken cable communication between Havana and Spain.

She left Key West yesterday morning with a cable outfit on board. A warship convoyed her. Her destination was not announced, but it is believed to be to the sonth of Cuba and to the neibhborhood of Cienfuegos. At that point the cable that connects Havana with Santiago de Cuba takes to the water, and from Santiago crosses to Jamaica, from which point it runs to Bermuda and Halifax. If cut between Havana and Santiago the two routes to Spain, one of which is by way of Haiti to New York, would be cut off.

The officers of the navy are well supplied with charts showing the location of the wires. With appliances for the purpose, the Mangrove can speedily take up the cable, cut out a section and render it next to impossible for the Spanish authorities in Cuba to communicate with the outside world. To effect this isolation of a nervous and anxious people, who soon, under the blockade, will begin to worry about help from the Spanish fleet, will, it is believed, add materially to their discomfort and despair.

The only way by which this expedition could be thwarted would be by dispatching a Spanish force after the Mangrove to keep her off the Cuban coast, but the Spanish vessels that undertake the service would be in danger of capture or destruction by the convoy of the Mangrove.

Spain Says It Is a British Cable.

MADRID, April 24.—Attention is called to the fact that the cable south of Cuba which the United States is credited with intending to cut belongs to a British company.

LONDON, April 25.—The Times this morning protests editorially against the intention attributed to the United States to cut a cable belonging to an English company and expresses the hope that America will not establish so evil a precedent, which might be held by Spain to justify the cutting of any cable landing on American soil.

BUYING COAL IN ST. THOMAS.

1,500 Tons Purchased and 4,000 More Offered—Prices Rising.

ST. THOMAS, West Indies, April 24.—United States Consul Van Horn here has bought 1,500 tons of coal for the United States Government, which will arrive here to-morrow. Four thousand tons now at St. Thomas have been offered to the United States, but owing to cable delays and the complicated character of the transaction the negotiations are still pending.

The Governments of Denmark and the Netherlands are cabling to their West Indian possessions to have coal reserved for naval uses. Only a moderate supply is in store in any of the islands, and prices are rising. At Barbados, St. Lucia, and St. Thomas prices range from 45s. to 50s. a ton.

Greeks Offer to Serve Uncle Sam.

ATHENS, April 24.—Many Greeks are presenting themselves at the United States Consulate here, seeking enlistment in the United States forces for the war against Spain.

Sunday War Extras in London.

LONDON, April 24.—The newspapers here are issuing war extras all day long, but with little new in them beyond the fact that Morro Castle opened fire on the United States fleet.

THE WEATHER.

The local forecast may be found at the top of this page to the right of the title.

The pressure has risen throughout the central valleys, the lake regions and over the Rocky Mountain slope. The storm centre has continued northeastward to the Southern New England Coast. The weather remains cloudy in the North Atlantic States, the lower lake region, and the Ohio Valley, and is nearly clear elsewhere. An abundant rain has fallen in the Atlantic Coast districts, the Upper Ohio Valley, and lower lake region during the last twenty-four hours. The temperature has changed comparatively little. For to-day clearing weather is indicated for New England and New York and generally fair weather for all other districts. It will be somewhat colder in the Middle and South Atlantic States and warmer in the Mississippi Valley.

The record of temperature for the twenty-four hours ended at midnight, taken from THE NEW YORK TIMES's thermometer and from the thermometer of the Weather Bureau, is as follows:

	—Weather Bureau.— 1897.	1898.	TIMES. 1898.
3 A. M.	53	52	56
6 A. M.	51	53	56
9 A. M.	55	56	60
12 M.	65	57	64
4 P. M.	67	61	64
6 P. M.	63	56	58
9 P. M.	61	51	56
12 P. M.	61	50	53

THE TIMES's thermometer is 6 feet above the street level; that of the Weather Bureau is 285 feet above the street level.

Average temperatures yesterday were as follows:

Printing House Square	58⅞
Weather Bureau	54½
Corresponding date 1897	60½
Corresponding date for last 20 years	52

The maximum temperature yesterday was 65° at 2 P. M.; the minimum was 51° at 4 A. M. The humidity at 8 A. M. was 100 and at 8 P. M. 1.00.

TWO PRIZES AT KEY WEST

The Helena Catches the Steamer Miguel Jover and the Detroit Gets the Catalina.

CHASED EIGHT MILES AT SEA

The Catalina Heaves to Only When a Solid Shot Is Fired from the Detroit—Both Vessels Left New Orleans for Barcelona.

KEY WEST, Fla., April 24.—Two Spanish steamers were brought in here to-day, having been captured by vessels of the blockading squadron. The gunboat Helena, Commander W. T. Swinburne, arrived this morning with the Miguel Jover.

Ensign Christy, with a crew of sixteen from the cruiser Detroit and four from the flagship, brought in this afternoon the captured Spanish steamer Catalina, Capt. Fano, which left Cadiz March 7 and was bound from New Orleans for Barcelona, via Havana, for which latter port she was making when taken.

The Helena did not sail with the fleet Friday morning, but remained here until yesterday, when she steamed out to sea. She was cruising about 150 miles in a southwesterly direction when the Jover, steering a southeasterly course, hove in sight early this morning. The Helena fired a blank shot and the Spaniard instantly hove to. The gunboat then put a prize crew of twelve marines, an engineer, and sixteen bluejackets on board the Jover, under the command of Ensign McClellan, who had with him Ensigns Davis and McFarland. The gunboat convoyed the prize into port.

The Jover was bound from New Orleans for Barcelona, via Havana. She has a crew of fifty-two men. She has a cargo of cotton and staves. The prize is estimated to be worth $400,000, her cargo alone being valued at $150,000.

The Catalina was captured about 4 o'clock this (Sunday) morning twelve miles from Havana. She was taken by the cruiser Detroit. When the first shot was fired her Captain made a desperate effort to escape his pursuer and the chase was prolonged for eight miles. Finally a solid shot brought her to. She is carrying a cargo of staves.

According to the Bureau Veritas, the Miguel Jover, Capt. Bil, is a Spanish steamer which sailed from New Orleans on April 22 for Barcelona. She was formerly the Port Denison, is bark rigged, of 2,554 tons net register, and was built at Newcastle, England, in 1877. She is 375 feet 5 inches long, has 42 feet 2 inches beam, and is 20 feet 9 inches deep.

The Bureau Veritas has it that her owners are the Empresa Trasatlantica, (Hijo de Jover y Serra,) of Barcelona.

The Havana agents of the Empresa Trasatlantica of Barcelona, the owners of the Miguel Jover, are Balcelio & Co., 43 Cuba Street. She has a capacity of 5,500 tons, triple expansion engines, and an electric lighting plant. She is classified A1 by Lloyds. She has been used as a passenger rather than as a freight vessel, and has been plying between Havana, Malaga, and Barcelona, stopping at Santa Cruz de Teneriffe, Santa Cruz de la Palma, and Las Palmas, Gran Canaria.

The Catalina was surveyed in the Port of New York in September, 1893. Her agents here are Charles P. Sumner & Co. She was owned before her capture by Pinillos, Izquierdo & Co., and her hailing port was Cadiz. Her Captain is J. Abrusqueta. She is a schooner-rigged screw steel vessel, provided with six bulkheads and two tier of beams, and is 415 feet long, 48 feet beam, and 21.3 feet depth. Her net tonnage is 3,491 and gross 4,706. She was built at Glasgow in 1808 by C. Connell & Co. Her engines are of the cylinder, triple-expansion type.

STEAMER SATURNINA TAKEN.

Revenue Cutter Winona Captures a Spanish Steamer Near Ship Island, Miss.

MOBILE, Ala., April 24.—A special from Biloxi, Miss., says the revenue cutter Winona from Mobile captured the Spanish steamer Saturnina at Ship Island, Miss., at 1 o'clock to-day, but likely will have to remain in quarantine with the prize until the time of quarantine detention is out, to-morrow or next day. The Saturnina is from Sagua to Ship Island. Capt. Zuclaga is in command. She is of 1,876 tons.

Fishing Vessel Caught and Set Free.

On Board Flagship New York, Off Havana, April 23.—The United States cruiser Cincinnati, Capt. C. M. Chester, reported to the flagship at midnight, "I have a prize." This morning it was learned that the Cincinnati's prize was a fishing vessel, and it was allowed to depart in peace.

ITALIAN CRUISER PURSUED.

The Giovanni Bausan Mistaken for a Spanish Vessel—Capture of the Schooner Mathilde.

ON BOARD THE FLAGSHIP NEW YORK, OFF HAVANA, April 23—2 P. M.—After the departure this morning of the Puritan and other boats sent from the fleet to blockade Matanzas, Mariel, and Cardenas, the remainder of the fleet took up a regular formation, having drifted some fifteen miles from Morro Castle. The general advance was made at half speed. Capt. Evans, not quite certain of the position he was entitled to take with the Iowa, came up abreast of the flagship and shouted through the megaphone, "How near may I go?" Rear Admiral Sampson, who was standing on the after bridge, replied, "As near as you can without drawing the fire of the batteries." "All right," Capt. Evans shouted back in tones that expressed the keenest disappointment. The Iowa then went ahead.

About half an hour after the squadron was well under way the cruiser Cincinnati was seen on the eastern horizon, the smoke pouring from her funnels. She had been headed for Matanzas and evidently had turned back to chase some vessel. The object of her pursuit was soon made out, standing well in toward the coast. The flagship, the cruiser Marblehead, and the gunboat Wilmington immediately turned out of course to head the vessel off. The remainder of the squadron proceeded to the westward.

Smoke poured from our ships. The flagship was making eighteen knots, the whole vessel throbbing with the vibrations of her twin screws. The little Wilmington steamed up in splendid shape and the fast cruiser Marblehead kept nearly abreast. The formidable trio bore down upon the warship. Then a shout went up, "She is a Spaniard!" For the next ten minutes the excitement was terrific. The distance which separated the vessels rendered it impossible to make out the warship's identity. She was thought to be the Vizcaya or the Almirante Oquendo heading for Havana.

The New York Prepares to Fight.

The men at the guns shouted with glee. The stokers off duty below cheered vociferously, and begged to be allowed to go on deck to help shoot at the first armed enemy met. The officers crowded on the quarter deck as elated as the men, though under better control. The bugler blew "general quarters." All hands flew to their posts. Down came the shrouds with a rattle. The life lines vanished from the deck. Rear

"All the News That's Fit to Print."

The New York Times.

With FINANCIAL REVIEW and QUOTATION SUPPLEMENT

COPYRIGHTED, 1898, BY THE NEW YORK TIMES COMPANY.

With FINANCIAL REVIEW and QUOTATION SUPPLEMENT

VOL. XLVII...NO. 15,072. NEW YORK, MONDAY, MAY 2, 1898.—TWELVE PAGES. PRICE THREE CENTS.

THE WEATHER.

Probably rain to-night or to-morrow; winds becoming southeasterly.

THE NEWS CONDENSED.

According to official advices received in Madrid from the Governor General of the Philippines, the United States fleet, under Commodore DEWEY, achieved a decisive victory in the harbor of Manila yesterday morning. As all of the news comes from Spanish sources, it is believed in London that the full extent of the disaster to the Spaniards has not been revealed.

From the official reports, it appears that one Spanish warship was blown up, two were burned, and several others were damaged or sunk by their crews to prevent their capture. The loss of life on the Spanish side is reported to be heavy, Capt. CADARSO, commanding the Maria Cristina, being among the killed.

The Spanish reports do not say that any of the American warships were destroyed, but speak vaguely of damage and loss of life sustained by our fleet. It is thought that Manila is still in the hands of the Spaniards, but that it may be taken by the combined action of Commodore DEWEY's warships and the Philippine insurgents on land.

It is reported in Washington that the plan of an immediate invasion of Cuba has been abandoned and that the troops will not leave Tampa Wednesday, as expected.

In explanation of this reported change in programme it is said the President fears that it would be unsafe in this season of the year to send our soldiers to Cuba; it also is said that the President wishes to leave Admiral Sampson's fleet free to fight any Spanish fleet that may come to oppose him.

Still further it is reported the President hopes for a decisive naval victory in Cuban waters, in the event of which it might not be necessary to send any of our soldiers to help the insurgents.

News comes from Madrid that Gen. Blanco has announced the capture off Cienfuegos by American warships of a Spanish merchant steamship having on board a Spanish Colonel and several other Spanish officers.

The Government tug Leyden yesterday took into Key West a small Spanish schooner caught off Havana by the torpedo boat Foote.

Wheat, No. 2 red, $1.20¾. Corn, No. 2 mixed, 40⅝ cents. Oats, No. 2 mixed, 35 cents. Cotton, middling, 6⅝ cents. Butter, Western creamery, 17 cents. Iron No. 1 foundry, $11.75.

Page 2.

Capt. Potter of John R. Drexel's yacht Sultana says her owner will keep her tied up at Marseilles, France, until the war is over, as the Spaniards are on the lookout.

The New Orleans left the Navy Yard yesterday morning and stood out to sea. The Government, it was announced, has purchased F. W. Vanderbilt's yacht, Conqueror, and will fit her as a gunboat.

The new cruiser Topeka arrived in port and anchored off Tompkinsville. Lieut. Knapp saw no Spanish warship on the way over, but did not feel safe, as not a gun is mounted. The Topeka may be ready for service in about ten days.

Page 3.

Everything is in readiness at Camp Voorhees, Sea Girt, for the reception to-day of the New Jersey volunteers.

Nearly 12,000 soldiers will pass through the streets of this city to-day on their way to the camps at Hempstead and Peekskill. The programme of the marches has all been arranged.

Page 5.

At the meeting of the Central Labor Federation yesterday, Chief McCullagh was denounced for prohibiting the Socialist parade that was to have taken place on Saturday evening. Some of the members say they will take the matter to the courts.

The Rev. Dr. A. J. F. Behrends, Chaplain of the Thirteenth Regiment of Brooklyn, which its officers say will not volunteer, preached to the regiment last night. He said he did not intend to volunteer himself, and said: "Remember that somebody must stay at home to plow and weave."

During a fight between a colored butler and a white stewardess at the Union Club, Cranford, the man was nearly killed. A mob of blacks gathered and threatened to lynch the woman and her husband. They were driven to a jail, five miles away, for safe keeping, pursued by a number of men on bicycles. The negroes threaten to burn the clubhouse.

Major A. G. Girard of the army has arrived from Madrid. He says a revolution is imminent, and only needs the knowledge of defeat of Spanish arms in Cuba and the Philippines to break out. The Spanish Navy he believes is inferior and its officers not efficient in sea tactics. He has been told it is the belief of Europe that the fleet will soon appear at Cuba.

Page 7.

The Electrical Exhibition at Madison Square Garden will be opened to-night at 8 o'clock with elaborate exercises.

G. A. Howland of Kleinschmidt & Howland, jewelers, missed a pocketbook containing $6,000 in gems, between Boston and this city, and thinks it was stolen on a Madison Avenue car.

At the fortnightly conference of Christian Workingmen's Clubs, at Amity Hall, last night, Josiah C. Pumpelly lectured upon "Industrial Sovereignty and Privilege," and in the course of his remarks insisted upon the necessity for National ownership and control of railroads.

Page 10.

Mrs. Hannah Bartow of New Brunswick, N. J., celebrated her one hundred and second birthday yesterday. She enjoys excellent health and can sew without glasses.

Page 12.

"What Can Stay-at-Home Patriots Do for Their Country During the War?" was the subject of the sermon delivered last night at the Church of the Divine Paternity by the Rev. Charles H. Eaton.

The Rev. J. Thompson Cole has definitely resigned his position of General Secretary of the American Church Missionary Society, to accept a call as assistant minister to St. Paul's Church, Cheltenham, Penn.

The Rev. Dr. W. S. Rainsford in his sermon yesterday declared that compliance with evil surroundings is worse than war. He thinks it is our manifest duty to intervene in Cuba, but said, "Let us deny and denounce all this talk about 'Remember the Maine.'"

The Rev. Henry Van Dyke yesterday preached a sermon on "The Sacrifice of War and the Cross of Christ," at the Brick Presbyterian Church, Fifth Avenue and Thirty-seventh Street, in which he justified the position taken by the United States in the controversy with Spain.

Marine News and Foreign Mails.—Page 8.
Arrivals at Hotels and Out-of-Town Buyers.—Page 2.
Yesterday's Fires.—Page 3.
Real Estate.—Page 11.
Court Calendars.—Page 9.

POSTSCRIPT

4:30 A. M.

VICTORY AT MANILA

The Governor General of the Philippines Concedes a Spanish Defeat.

SHIPS BLOWN UP, SUNK, AND BURNED.

No Disaster Reported to Vessels of Commodore Dewey's Fleet in the Fierce Engagement.

Spanish Disptaches Admit Heavy Loss of Life on Their Side and Destruction of Their Warships.

MADRID, May 1.—The following is the text of an official dispatch from the Governor General of the Philippines to the Minister of War, Lieut. Gen. Correa, received here at 8 P. M., reporting a naval engagement off Manila to-day:

"Last night, April 30, the batteries at the entrance to the fort announced the arrival of the enemy's squadron, forcing a passage under the obscurity of the night. At daybreak the enemy took up positions, opening with a strong fire against Fort Cavite and the arsenal.

"Our fleet engaged the enemy in a brilliant combat, protected by the Cavite and Manila forts. They obliged the enemy with heavy loss to manoeuvre repeatedly. At 9 o'clock the American squadron took refuge behind the foreign merchant shipping on the west side of the bay.

"Our fleet, considering the enemy's superiority, naturally suffered a severe loss. The Maria Christina is on fire, and another ship, believed to be the Don Juan de Austria, was blown up.

"There was considerable loss of life. Capt. Cadarso, commanding the Maria Christina, is among the killed. I cannot now give further details. The spirit of the army, navy, and volunteers is excellent."

Ships Sunk to Avoid Capture.

An official telegram received at a later hour from the Governor General of the Philippines says:

"Admiral Montejo has transferred his flag to the cruiser Isla de Cuba from the cruiser Reina Maria Christina. The Reina Maria Christina was completely burned, as was also the cruiser Castilla, the other ships having to retire from the combat, and some being sunk to avoid their falling into the hands of the enemy."

The official dispatch does not mention the destruction of any American vessel, although it says that the United States Squadron finally cast anchor in the bay behind the foreign merchantmen.

Another official dispatch from the Governor General of the Philippines says: "The equipping of volunteers continues. We are ready to oppose any debarkation and to defend the integrity of the country."

Report of the Spanish Naval Bureau.

The Naval Bureau at Manila sends the following report of the encounter with the United States squadron, signed "Montejo, Admiral":

"In the middle of the night the American squadron forced the forts, and before daybreak appeared off Cavite. The night was completely dark. At half-past 7 the bow of the Reina Maria Christina took fire, and soon after the poop also was burned. At 8 o'clock, with my staff, I went on board the Isla de Cuba. The Reina Maria Christina and the Castilla were then entirely enveloped in flames.

"The other ships having been damaged retired into Baker Bay. Some had to be sunk to prevent their falling into the hands of the enemy. The losses are numerous, notably Capt. Cadarso, a priest, and nine other persons."

A Manila dispatch to The Liberal says the Spanish land forces are watching the coast to prevent a landing, which, according to the correspondent, would be a difficult operation.

Admiral Montejo's Escape.

El Heraldo de Madrid says that Admiral Montejo changed his flagship during the engagement, or between the two encounters, in order the better to direct the manoeuvres. In this way he escaped the fate of the commander of the Reina Maria Cristina.

The second engagement, according to El Heraldo, was apparently begun by the Americans, after landing their wounded on the west side of the bay. In the latter engagement the Spanish ships Mindanao and Ulloa suffered heavily.

Other unofficial advices from Manila say that the American squadron, under Commodore Dewey, appeared off the Bay of Manila at 5 o'clock this morning and opened a strong cannonade against the Spanish squadron and forts protecting the harbor.

The Spanish second-class cruiser Don Juan de Austria was severely damaged and her commander was killed. Another Spanish vessel was burned. The American squadron retired, having also sustained severe damage.

A second naval engagement followed, in which the American squadron again suffered considerable loss, and the Spanish warships Mindanao and Ulloa were damaged slightly. During this engagement the Cavite forts maintained a steadier and stronger fire upon the American squadron than in the first engagement.

Madrid Calls It a Victory.

Admiral Bermejo, the Minister of Marine, has expressed himself as highly pleased with the heroism of the Spanish marines, and has telegraphed congratulation to Admiral Montejo and the valorous crews of the Spanish squadron under fire of superior warships.

Admiral Bermejo joined the Cabinet Council this evening and informed his colleagues that the Spanish forces had gained a victory in the Philippines. He asserted that he found difficulty in restraining his joyful emotions.

Other Ministers speak of "serious but honorable losses."

Notwithstanding the severe damage the Spanish ships sustained, naval officers here consider that further operations by the American squadron will be conducted under great difficulty, owing to their having no base where they could repair and recoal or obtain fresh supplies of ammunition.

MUTTERING IN MADRID.

Great Excitement Produced by the Serious News Received from the Philippines.

MADRID, May 1—11:30 P. M.—The town is greatly excited by the serious news from the Philippines, and there is an immense gathering in the Calla de Savilla. The Civil Guards on horseback were called out to preserve order, and all precautions have been taken.

There is much muttering, but, up to the present, nothing more serious has occurred.

LONDON, May 2.—Dispatches from Madrid, dated 2:20 A. M., say the city is now tranquil, although the mounted guards are patrolling all the main streets. At the theatres, cafés, and in front of the newspaper offices last evening people loudly lamented the unpreparedness of Manila to resist the American warships, whose attack had long been expected. The Madrid authorities are determined vigorously to suppress all street demonstrations.

THE NEWS IN LONDON.

Dispatches from Spanish Sources Leave Commodore Dewey's Situation in Doubt.

LONDON, May 1.—While it is quite clear that the Spanish squadron has suffered a crushing defeat, the dispatches leave in doubt the intensely interesting question whether the American squadron has suffered material damage.

Neither the Reuter Telegram Company nor The Times nor The Daily Mail, hitherto the only sources of direct information from Manila, has received a word on the subject.

All news thus far comes from Spanish sources, but it seems evident that Commodore Dewey has not captured Manila. Unless he is able to make another attack and capture the town, he will be in an awkward position, having no base upon which to retire and to refit. In such an event the United States squadron would be obliged to make for San Francisco.

As the entrance to Manila Bay was heavily mined with torpedoes, Commodore Dewey displayed great pluck and daring in making for the inner harbor. According to private advices received from Madrid, the United States cruisers Olympia and Raleigh and two other vessels, the names of which are not given, entered the harbor. No dispatches give details as to the vessels actually engaged on either side.

Probabilities point in the direction of the second engagement having occurred through the Spaniards trying to prevent the landing of the American wounded.

Reliable details cannot be had until Commodore Dewey's squadron is able to communicate with Hongkong. There is, however, a suspicious frankness about the Spanish dispatches that savors of a desire to break unpleasant news to the Spaniards. It is not unlikely, therefore, that Commodore Dewey may be able to renew the attack

NEWS CONFIRMED IN LISBON.

Reliable Report of Complete Rout of the Spanish Fleet.

LISBON, May 1—11 P. M.—Reliable news has been received here that the Spanish fleet was completely defeated off Cavite.

MADRID HOPED FOR VICTORY.

MADRID, May 1 (Noon.)—All is quiet here, but the festival being organized for to-morrow promises to be an unusual demonstration, being the anniversary both of the liberation of Spain from France, and of the naval "victory" of Spain at Callao, Peru, in 1866, while interest in the event is heightened by the hope of the Spaniards that the Spanish fleet will be victorious over the United States fleet, commanded by Commodore Dewey, thus giving them a triple celebration.

The Mayor of Madrid has issued a manifesto, inviting all the inhabitants of this city to participate in the celebration. He says:

"Spain is engaged in a struggle to repel the unjustifiable attempts of the Yankees to rob her of her rights in Cuba; but the Yankees will not find it an easy task to conquer a race whose history during twenty centuries has been notable only for warlike exploits."

Philippine Independence Scheme.

LONDON, May 1.—The Evening News publishes a dispatch from Hongkong saying that the insurgent leaders in the Philippines have submitted to Commodore Dewey a scheme for Philippine independence, embracing free trade.

HOW THE NEWS CAME.

The cable map in the office of the Anglo-American Cable Company, at 8 Broad Street, shows the route of the wires which furnish superior advantages to Madrid in the prompt communication the Spanish capital has with Manila.

The cable starts from a point on the coast about forty miles distant from Manila, called Cabo Bolinao, these points being connected by telegraph. The cable is direct from Cabo Bolinao to Hongkong. From Hongkong it stretches to Saigon in Siam, and to Singapore and Madras. From the latter place an overland telegraph leads to Bombay, and here the cable is engaged to Aden, then up the Red Sea to Suez, and finally through the Mediterranean to Lisbon, which is in direct telegraphic connection with Madrid.

THE SITUATION IN MANILA.

HONGKONG, May 1.—Letters to the insurgent Junta here, which were smuggled on board the British steamer Memnon, at Manila, which arrived here yesterday from the capital of the Philippine Islands, assert that the Philippine insurgents are occupying all the hills surrounding Manila, in a radius of ten to twenty miles, awaiting the arrival of the United States fleet, under Commodore Dewey, which was expected off Manila at any moment when the Memnon sailed. The insurgents say that if the United States fleet blockades Manila they can starve the place into submission in about two weeks.

Corroboration has been received of the report that the British residents of Manila expected that the British steamer Esmeralda, which went there to take on board the specie belonging to the Hongkong banks, would have a full cargo of food stuff, as usual, but this was not the case, and much distress is anticipated in consequence, if the insurgent land blockade and the United States sea blockade are enforced.

According to the insurgent leaders, the forces of the Philippine insurgents propose, when the right moment arrives, to make a feint attack upon the City of Manila, to mask a strong and determined attack upon the seaward forts. This plan, however, may be upset by the Spanish authorities, who are well aware of the intention of the insurgents to co-operate with the United States fleet.

The real danger appears to be from internal causes at Manila, where a massacre of the foreign population is apprehended. The British Consul there, E. H. Rawson-Walker, has cabled here asking for the dispatch to Manila immediately of the British first-class cruiser Edgar, to protect British interests there.

It is asserted that the Spanish cruiser Castilla of 3,342 tons displacement and 4,400 indicated horse power, recently grounded near the entrance of Manila Bay, and was afterward scuttled in shallow water. It is added that it is the intention of the Spaniards to use her as a stationary battery, although some of her guns have been landed and mounted on the fortifications at the entrance of the harbor, where other guns have also recently been mounted.

SHANGHAI, May 1.—Famine prices for food are said to prevail in Manila, and it is claimed the Spanish authorities are maintaining order with difficulty. People are burying their valuables, to prevent their seizure by the insurgents or Americans. The military authorities are endeavoring to put a bold front on the situation, but the Manila correspondent of The Shanghai Gazette asserts that it is considered certain that the insurgents will sack the city when the United States fleet appears, not discriminating between Spaniards and other foreigners.

The dispatches received by The Gazette say that Manila is short of food and ammunition and that the conditions prevailing have been made worse by the flocking into Manila of the Spaniards from the provinces. It is added that the natives are already looting and killing in the provinces, Spanish women and children being included in the victims. It is further asserted that the priests are the special objects of the natives' vengeance, about a dozen priests having been killed during the last week.

CHASED BY A SPANISH SHIP.

The Cherokee, Loaded with Sugar and Bound for New York, Reports an Adventure at Sea.

TURKS ISLAND, May 1.—The American steamer Cherokee, Capt. Garvin, of the Clyde Line, arrived here yesterday with 1,800 bags of sugar, and sailed for New York in the evening.

Her Captain reported that on Tuesday night, when she was leaving Macoris for San Domingo, the Cherokee was chased by a Spanish ship.

LOOKING FOR SPAIN'S FLEET.

Naval Authorities Hopeful that the Warships from Cape Verde Are Coming This Way.

WASHINGTON, May 1.—The Naval Strategy Board was in session for a time to-day, but their discussions, as usual, were guarded with much secrecy. It is understood that the course of the Spanish fleet, which left Cape Verde on Friday, is a source of much interest.

If, as reported, the fleet is actually coming this way, it will be hailed with delight by naval authorities here. What they have most feared was that the Spanish ships would hug the other side, compelling our fleets to go in quest of them. If they come to Puerto Rico it will meet the best hopes of the naval authorities here.

TO BOMBARD AN AMERICAN PORT.

PARIS, May 1.—The Eclair says that an Autonomist Deputy from Havana to the Spanish Chamber reports that the Spanish Squadron, which has just left St. Vincent, contemplates the bombardment of an American port.

The Eclair asserts that it is not likely that there will be a fight in Cuban waters, Havana being amply fortified to resist the American fleet.

A New Spanish Ironclad.

MADRID, May 1.—It is reported that a new Spanish ironclad, which is being fitted out at Carthagena, will soon join the Spanish Squadron at Cadiz.

ANOTHER PRIZE TAKEN.

Blanco Informs Madrid that a Spanish Steamer Has Been Caught Off Cienfuegos.

MADRID, May 1—10 P. M.—The Government has received a cablegram from Gen. Blanco saying that the American warships blockading Cienfuegos have captured a Spanish merchant steamer.

A Colonel, a surgeon, six officers, and three non-commissioned officers who were on board the steamer were detained as prisoners of war.

The civilian passengers were released.

LONDON, May 2.—The Madrid correspondent of The Daily Mail, telegraphing Sunday, says:

"The Americans were pillaging the steamer Argonauta, seized off Cienfuegos, and carrying a quantity of arms and ammunition, when three Spanish gunboats went out and compelled them to withdraw."

The Foote Captures a Schooner.

KEY WEST, Fla., May 1.—The Government tug Leyden brought in to-day the small Spanish schooner Mascota, captured near Havana yesterday by the torpedo boat Foote.

She is a small coaster, loaded with fruit. She was bound for Havana. She is not a valuable prize.

THE OREGON AND MARIETTA.

Coming from Rio de Janeiro with the Nichtheroy.

MONTEVIDEO, Uruguay, May 1.—It is announced here to-day in a dispatch from Rio de Janeiro, Brazil, that the United States gunboat Marietta, as well as the United States battleship Oregon, arrived at that port yesterday.

It is added that they will resume their voyage north to-day, accompanied by the United States dynamite cruiser Nichtheroy, recently purchased from Brazil by the Government of the United States.

WASHINGTON, May 1.—The Navy Department to-day received official confirmation of the report of the arrival of the battleship Oregon at Rio de Janeiro. This was the subject of general satisfaction, for it means the very material strengthening of Admiral Sampson's fleet before Havana within the next fortnight.

The Oregon has been making 13 knots an hour, or about 320 miles a day, and it is calculated that she will cover the 3,000 miles between Rio and Cuba in ten days. When she joins the blockading fleet Admiral Sampson's first line will be made up of four superb battleships, of practically the same strength and equipment.

The Temerario Laid Up for Repairs.

BUENOS AYRES, May 1.—The Spanish torpedo gunboat Temerario, which was supposed to be on the watch for the United States battleship Oregon, is at Ensenada, on La Platte, undergoing repairs to a portion of her machinery. It is expected that she will leave within a week.

REJOICING IN WASHINGTON

News of the Victory at Manila Causes Great Excitement at the Capital.

SPANISH REPORTS BELIEVED

It Is Thought, However, that the Full Extent of Commodore Dewey's Success Is Not Yet Revealed—No Official News.

WASHINGTON, May 1.—Coming at the close of the quietest day since the war crisis came on, the news of the victory of the American fleet in the Philippines woke the capital to wild rejoicing.

From early in the evening, when the first bulletin bore the tidings the public had been hungering for since the Maine went down—that there really had been a fight—until midnight, the bulletin boards were surrounded by crowds whose enthusiasm grew with each fresh announcement. Newsboys vended extras with strident cries, in defiance of the local regulations forbidding them to call aloud their wares after 8 o'clock in the evening, and the police did not interfere.

The people in the streets accepted the news as being a part of the truth, if not all, taking it for granted that if the Spaniards had been faking they would have distorted the cable story in their own favor. Much the same view was taken in official circles.

President McKinley received the bulletins as fast as they came in and read them with great interest. Like everybody else, he had been expecting to receive stories of a Spanish victory, since the first news must come from Spanish sources, but he could not imagine any inducement for the Spaniards to misrepresent the facts in our favor.

The News in Official Circles.

At midnight Secretary Porter announced to a group of newspaper correspondents gathered at the White House that there had been no official confirmation of the press dispatches from Manila. "It looks, however, as if the news must be about straight," said Mr. Porter. He added that the President did not expect to receive Commodore Dewey's official report of the engagement for forty-eight hours at least, as it would be necessary for him to send it to Hongkong by one of the vessels of his fleet.

Secretary Long saw the first bulletin and retired without waiting to learn the result of the battle. He would express no opinion concerning the authenticity of the dispatches. Assistant Secretary of the Navy Roosevelt also retired before the receipt of the news of the battle. Secretary of State Day is not in the city.

When Secretary Bliss was shown the first dispatch briefly recounting the victory of the American squadron, he unhesitatingly expressed his gratification at the result, and gave utterance to the hope that Commodore Dewey's fleet had not suffered greatly. Senator Hanna and Chauncey M. Depew of New York, who were with Secretary Bliss at the time, were delighted with the advices and made no concealment of their pleasure.

Army and Navy Rejoice.

Secretary Alger declared that it was a "glorious victory," but, in common with other officials of the Administration, declined to make extended comment upon it.

Navy and army circles, after manifesting throughout the day the greatest eagerness for news from the Philippines, received with intense joy the advices telling of the victory of Commodore Dewey's fleet. At the Army and Navy Club a large company was gathered and read and commented upon the story of the engagements as it was presented in the bulletins. At the club, downtown, at their homes, and wherever seen, the officers were free in giving vent to the pleasure they felt at the news, and declaring the confidence which they had entertained throughout, that the American ships and their officers and men would demonstrate their superiority over the Spanish fleet in Philippine waters.

The absence of any specific statement of injury to the American vessels in the Madrid advices was construed as a convincing indication that they had not suffered appreciable injury, and this was especially pleasing to the naval students of the news. Not only was the preservation of the American ships and men considered in itself a happy outcome, but it was commented upon as clearly indicating that Commodore Dewey and his assistant officers and the men under their command had discharged splendidly their several duties in directing and executing the fight.

In this connection it was pointed out as little less than marvelous that the American squadron escaped without severe injury, because, notwithstanding the disparity in the naval forces, the Spanish fleet, assisted by the shore batteries, should have been able to inflict severe damage on its foe before itself being destroyed. Its failure to do so was explicable only upon the hypothesis of perfect and swift work by the Americans.

Battle May End the War.

An opinion freely expressed to-night by naval officers is that the very decisive victory of Commodore Dewey's fleet will mean probably an early end to the war without further naval battles of importance. The American fleet, it is suggested, is now supreme in the waters of Spain's Pacific possessions, and indications were strongly toward the slipping of the Philippines from her control. It was said that only by quickly yielding to our demands in Cuba could their loss possibly be averted. Spain, it was argued, was confronted with a situation which promised naught save disaster in case she elected to force more fighting.

Judge McComas, Senator-elect from Maryland, after expressing his joy over the result of the conflict, struck a keynote of the expected result of the cannonading at Manila to-day when he said that it was likely to have a tremendous effect, not only on Spain, but throughout Europe. He expressed the belief that it would turn the tide of European sentiment toward the United States.

The idea advanced by Judge McComas was expressed by others to-night. It is regarded by some as likely that the decisive victory gained by Commodore Dewey's squadron may open the eyes of Spain to the seriousness of the conflict upon which she has entered. In official circles it is regarded as almost certain that trouble of a most critical kind will confront the Sagasta Government within Spain's own borders. It is pointed out that the Spanish people have been led to believe that their navy was invincible, and the bitter disappointment that will ensue over the result of the first engagement of the war is likely to precipitate internal dissension, if not a revolution.

Another result of Commodore Dewey's victory, it is thought, may be action on the part of the powers of Europe to induce Spain to abandon what is regarded as a hopeless contest for her. Representations may be made to Spain that she would better relinquish her hold upon Cuba than to risk losing all of her West Indian possessions and the Philippines as well. It is believed to be not unlikely that the representations will indicate that, since Spanish honor has been satisfied by a conflict, Spain can now yield to the inevitable and accept the good offices of the powers to bring about an adjustment.

Joint Attack on Manila Next.

In the dispatches from Madrid, the statement was made that Commodore Dewey effected a landing on the west side of Manila Bay for the men of his fleet who were wounded in the engagements. It was suggested in official circles that this landing had a two-fold purpose. It was not only that the wounded might have better care than they could receive on shipboard, in the face of other probable engagements, but also to carry out what was known to be Commodore Dewey's purpose to effect a junction with the insurgents as soon as possible.

The insurgent forces probably surround Manila on the land sides of the city, and, with the intention of securing control of Manila as soon as possible, Commodore Dewey was to obtain a footing on the island at the earliest practicable moment. As soon as the junction of the American and insurgent forces, the one on sea and the other on land, is effected, a demand is likely to be made for the surrender of the city, and in the event of a refusal a combined attack would be made upon it. The result of such an attack, in the absence of a Spanish fleet and effective shore batteries, seems a foregone conclusion.

In general it may be said that Washington accepts the news received to-night as probably true as far as it goes, with the expectation that when the American version of the affair is received Commodore Dewey's victory will turn out to be more sweeping and signal than the Madrid advices make it.

SPAIN MAY GIVE UP NOW.

A Surrender When Disaster Had Satisfied Honor Advocated in the House of Deputies.

LONDON, May 2.—The Madrid correspondent of The Standard says:

"The sitting of the House of Deputies yesterday (Saturday) was extremely interesting. The Carlists and Republicans had bitterly criticised the action of the Governments of the Regency and the monarchy with persisting during the last twenty-four years in a policy of too systematic neutrality and isolation in Europe, which now, in Spain's hour of trial, has deprived her of anything but platonic sympathies.

"Señor Gullon, the Foreign Minister, in the course of his reply, remarked that this was a positivist epoch in which alliances were founded upon interest alone, and, as Spain could offer but little, other powers could only give her little. Señor Silvela, in a speech which has made a profound impression, and is regarded as marking a turning point in Spanish politics, declared that as the Cuban problem was now reduced to a question of 'honor for the Spanish arms,' it behooved Ministers to assume without hesitation the responsibility of deciding when the point of honor had been sufficiently satisfied. When that time had been reached, he said, it would be time to appeal to the European powers so that they could decide what ought to be done to restore peace and determine the fate of Cuba, because all the powers were interested in Cuba's future.

"Señor Silvela declared that all the idealist foreign policies were things of the past; that nations nowadays were only moved by their interests, and that, therefore, if Spain sought the intervention of the powers she must 'approach them with something practical, for instance, on the basis of the Philippine Islands and with her hands full.'

"Everybody was much struck by Señor Silvela's transparent allusions to future inevitable sacrifices and concessions. His eloquent and powerful speech concluded with the plain declaration that he and his party were ready for office if the Liberal Ministry recoiled from assuming the heavy responsibility of such a policy. The speech will prolong the debates on the address, as the leaders of the Opposition and Señor Sagasta have intimated that they will reply on Tuesday.

"El Imparcial says: 'It behooves the nation, not the Cabinet, to say when honor is satisfied.' This criticism practically confirms Señor Silvela's views."

SPANIARDS FEAR TREACHERY.

Dread in Paris that Some Commander May Espouse Cuba's Cause.

LONDON, May 1.—The Daily Chronicle's correspondent notes among the thoughtful members of the Spanish colony in Paris a lurking dread that some spontaneous act of treachery is looming in the distance. Allusions to Espartero and the Carlist General Maroto, and the convention of Vergara (Aug. 31, 1839,) are made by Spaniards and Cubans who have played their part in politics and who assert that "a commanding officer might be tempted to throw in his lot with the champions of Cuban independence."

The correspondent says this impression is undoubtedly founded upon rumors caused by private letters, in which names are freely mentioned.

CECIL RHODES OUR FRIEND.

He Justifies This Government's Action and Favors a British-American Alliance.

LONDON, May 2.—The Daily Chronicle publishes this morning Cecil Rhodes's view of Anglo-American relations. Mr. Rhodes says:

"In my opinion nothing is so vital to the future of the British and American peoples as a cordial understanding now, and a deeply rooted conviction of mutual good will. From this, if future events render it necessary, a formal alliance may be born.

"It is obvious that if America crushes Spain from the outset there will be an unthinking tendency in England to sympathize with the little boy thrashed by the big boy. But what we must not forget is Spanish atrocity in Cuba. America has done, in view of this atrocity, precisely what Great Britain would have done if it had occurred in an island close to the British coast. In fact, we should not probably have been as patient as America has been. At any rate the two peoples would meet the same circumstances with the same action.

"It is not for us to run after America with offers of alliance. Such a result must of course, be a meeting half way, but it seems to me perfectly obvious that in any division of world interests those of the British Empire and America will be found together. England and America need each other, and this need will grow rapidly in the future."

THE WEATHER.

The local forecast may be found at the top of this page to the right of the title.

The pressure has risen west of the Mississippi and fallen to the eastward. A belt of low pressure extends from the upper lake region southwestward to Texas, with a high pressure in the Northwest and a second high pressure on the South Atlantic Coats. The weather is nearly clear on the Atlantic and Gulf Coasts and cloudy in the lake regions, Central and Upper Mississippi Valley, and the Northwest. Rain has fallen in the Central Rocky Mountain districts, the Missouri and Upper Mississippi Valley, and the lake regions. The temperature has fallen sharply on the middle plateau and slope and has risen in the lake regions and Ohio Valley. Increasing cloudiness is indicated for to-day in the North Atlantic States, followed by showers this afternoon or to-night. Showers are probable in the lake regions, the Ohio, Central Mississippi and Arkansas Valleys. Fair weather will continue in the South Atlantic and Gulf States and the weather will clear in the Northwest. The temperature will be higher on the Atlantic Coast and lower in the Central and Upper Mississippi and Lower Ohio and Missouri Vallies.

The record of temperature for the twenty-four hours ended at midnight, taken from THE NEW YORK TIMES's thermometer and from the thermometer of the Weather Bureau, is as follows:

	—Weather Bureau.— 1897.	1898.	TIMES. 1898.
3 A. M.	54	53	56
6 A. M.	51	50	54
9 A. M.	51	54	61
12 M.	59	62	64
4 P. M.	54	67	67
6 P. M.	52	65	63
9 P. M.	51	59	63
12 P. M.	52	58	61

THE TIMES's thermometer is 6 feet above the street level; that of the Weather Bureau is 285 feet above the street level.

Average temperatures yesterday were as follows:

Printing House Square	61⅝
Weather Bureau	58⅜
Corresponding date 1897	53
Corresponding date for last 20 years	53

The maximum temperature was 69 degrees at 3 P. M., and the minimum, 50 degrees at 6 A. M. The humidity at 8 A. M. was 53 per cent., and at 8 P. M., 41 per cent.

STRENGTH OF THE FLEETS

The American Ships Much Superior in Size and Quality to the Spanish.

DIFFERENCE IN ARMAMENT

Commodore Dewey Had One First, Three Second, and One Third Class Cruiser Against the Spaniards' Less Powerful Ships.

A comparison of the relative strength of the American and Spanish fleets engaged off Manila shows the former to have been considerably superior not only in the size and quality of vessels, but also in the armament, as may be seen from the detailed description of the two fleets which follows:

The American fleet in the Asiatic station consists of the first-class protected cruiser Olympia, which also serves as the flagship; the Baltimore, Boston, and Raleigh, second-class cruisers; the Concord, a third-class cruiser, the gun vessel Petrel, the revenue cutter McCulloch, the collier Nanshan, and the supply vessel Zafru. Their descriptions follow:

The protected cruiser Olympia, of 5,800 tons displacement, is 340 feet long, 53 feet beam, and has a mean draught of 21.6 feet. She was launched in 1892 and has a speed of 21.69 knots. Her battery consists of four eight-inch guns, ten five-inch rapid-fire guns, fourteen six-pounders, six one-pounders, four machine guns, and four torpedo tubes.

The Baltimore is a second-class cruiser of 4,600 tons, with a speed of 20.6 knots. She was launched in 1888, and is armed with 4 eight-inch and 6 six-inch guns, 4 six-pounder rapid-fire guns, 2 one-pounders, and 6 machine guns.

The Boston is also a second-class cruiser. Her displacement is 3,189 tons, and her speed 15 knots. She was launched in 1884, and carries a battery consisting of 2 eight-inch, 6 six-inch, 2 six-pounder rapid-fire, 2 three-pounders, 2 one-pounders, 2.8-inch, 2 1.4-inch, and 2 machine guns.

The Raleigh is a second-class cruiser of 3,183 tons. She was launched in 1892, and has a speed of 19 knots. Her battery includes 1 six-inch and 10 five-inch rapid-fire guns, 8 six-pounders, 4 one-pounders, and two machine guns.

The Concord is a third-class cruiser of 1,700 tons, and her speed is 17 knots. She was launched in 1892, and has a formidable battery of 6 six-inch, 2 six-pounder rapid-fire, 2 three-pounders, 1 one-pounder, and four machine guns.

The Petrel is a gun vessel of 890 tons. She was launched in 1888, has a speed of 13.7 knots, and carries four 6-inch, two -pounder rapid-fire, one 1-pounder, and four machine guns.

Roster of the Squadron.

The roster of the Asiatic Squadron is as follows:

Commodore—George Dewey, Commander in Chief.

Lieutenant—T. M. Brumby, Flag Lieutenant.

Ensign—H. H. Caldwell, Secretary.

On board the flagship Olympia: Capt. Charles V. Gridley, Lieut. Commander S. C. Paine, Lieuts. C. G. Calkins, V. S. Nelson, G. S. Morgan, W. G. Miller, and S. M. Strite; Ensigns M. M. Taylor, F. B. Upham, W. P. Scott, and A. G. Kavanagh; Medical Inspector A. F. Price, Passed Assistant Surgeon J. E. Page, Assistant Surgeon C. P. Kindleberger, Pay Inspector D. A. Smith, Chief Engineer J. Entwistle, Assistant Engineers E. H. De Laney and J. F. Marshall, Jr., Chaplain J. B. Frasier, Captain of Marines W. P. Biddle, Gunner L. J. G. Kuhlwein, Carpenter W. Macdonald, and Acting Boatswain E. J. Norcott.

On board the Raleigh: Capt. J. B. Coghlan, Lieut. Commander F. Singer, Lieuts. W. Winder, B. Tappan, H. Rodman, and C. B. Morgan; Ensigns F. L. Chadwick and P. Babin; Surgeon E. H. Marsteller, Assistant Surgeon D. N. Carpenter, Passed Assistant Paymaster S. R. Heap, Chief Engineer F. H. Bailey, Passed Assistant Engineer A. S. Halstead, Assistant Engineer J. R. Brady, First Lieut. of Marines T. C. Treadwell, Acting Gunner G. D. Johnstone, and Acting Carpenter T. E. Kiley.

On Board the Boston—Capt. F. Wildes, Lieut. Commander J. A. Norris, Lieuts. J. Gibson and W. L. Howard, Ensigns S. S. Robinson, L. H. Everhart, and J. S. Doddridge; Surgeon M. H. Crawford, Assistant Surgeon R. S. Blakeman, Paymaster J. R. Martin, Chief Engineer G. B. Ransom, Assistant Engineer L. J. James, First Lieut. of Marines R. McM. Dutton, Gunner J. C. Evans, and Carpenter O. H. Hilton.

On board the Baltimore—Captain, N. M. Dyer; Lieutenant Commander, G. Blocklinger; Lieutenants, W. Braunersreuther, A. G. Winterhalter, F. W. Kelogg, J. M. Ellicott, C. S. Stanwoorth; Ensigns, G. H. Hayward, M. J. McCormack; naval cadets, D. W. Wurtsbaugh, I. Z. Wettensell, C. M. Tozer, T. A. Karney; Passed Assistant Surgeon, F. A. Hesler; Assistant Surgeon, R. K. Smith; Pay Inspector, E. Bellows; Chief Engineer, A. Kirby; Assistant Engineers, H. B. Price, H. I. Cone; naval cadet, (engineer,) C. P. Burt; Chaplain, T. S. K. Freeman; First Lieutenant of Marines, D. Williams; Acting Boatswain, H. R. Brayton; gunner, L. J. Connelly; carpenter, O. Bath.

On board the Concord—Commander, A. S. Walker; Lieutenant Commander, G. P. Colvocoresses; Lieutenants, T. B. Howard, P. W. Hourigan; Ensigns, L. A. Kaiser, W. C. Davidson, H. V. Butler, Jr., O. S. Knepper; Passed Assistant Surgeon, R. G. Broderick; Passed Assistant Paymaster, E. D. Ryan; Chief Engineer, Richard Inch; Passed Assistant Engineer, H. W. Jones; Assistant Engineer, E. H. Dunn.

On board the Petrel—Commander, E. P. Wood; Lieutenants, E. M. Hughes, B. A. Fiske, A. N. Wood, C. P. Plunkett; Ensigns, G. L. Fermier, W. S. Montgomery; Passed Assistant Surgeon, C. D. Brownell; Assistant Paymaster, G. G. Seibels; Passed Assistant Engineer, R. T. Hall.

On the revenue cutter McCulloch—Capt. D. B. Hodgdon.

The Spanish Fleet.

When the Spanish fleet went into the engagement it consisted of fourteen vessels, including the flagship, five cruisers, five gunboats, and three troop ships, as follows:

The Reina Christina, the flagship and largest vessel of the fleet, a steel cruiser of 3,520 tons, and 3,970 indicated horse-power. Length, 280 feet, 42 feet breadth of beam, and 16 feet deep. Built at Ferrol in 1886, with a battery of six 6.2-inch Hontoria guns, two 2.7-inch guns, three 6-pounder rapid-fire guns, two 4-pounder rapid-fire guns, six 3-pounder rapid-fire guns, two machine guns, and five torpedo tubes. Crew composed of 370 men and officers.

Cruiser Castilla, a wooden vessel of 3,342 tons, 246 feet long, 46 feet beam, and 21 feet draught. Indicated horse power, 4,400. Built at Cadiz in 1881. Battery: four 5.9-inch guns, two 4.7-inch, two 3.4-inch, and two 2.9-inch, four 1-pounder revolving cannon, and two torpedo tubes. Crew, 300.

The Don Antonio de Ulloa and Don Juan de Austria, sister ships, each of 1,152 tons, 210 feet long, speed 14 knots, and equipped with a battery each of four 4.7-inch guns, four 6-pounder rapid-fire guns, one machine gun, and two torpedo tubes. Crew, 173.

The Velasco, a cruiser of 1,139 tons, 210 feet long, speed 14.2 knots, and carrying three 6-inch and two 2.7-inch guns and two machine guns, with a crew of 173 men. She was built in 1881.

The Isla de Luzon and the Isla de Cuba, sister ships, protected cruisers of 1,040 tons and 200 feet long; speed, 14.2 knots, and battery consisting of six 4.7-inch guns, four six-pound rapid-fire guns, two one-inch Nordenfeldts, two 5.3-inch Nordenfeldts, and three torpedo tubes.

The General Lezo and El Cano, gunboats, of 524 tons each, built in 1885, speed 11½ knots. The General Lezo carried two 4.7-inch Hontoria guns, one 3.5-inch, two small rapid-fire, and one machine gun; the El Cano had three 4.7-inch guns, two small rapid-fire, and two machine guns.

The Marques del Duero, an iron gunboat built in 1875, of 500 tons, speed 10 knots, and armament one smooth bore 6.2-inch gun, two 4.7-inch, and one machine gun.

The Argos, a wooden gunboat, built in

"All the News That's Fit to Print."

The New York Times.

With REVIEW OF BOOKS AND ART

COPYRIGHTED, 1898, BY THE NEW YORK TIMES COMPANY.

With REVIEW OF BOOKS AND ART

VOL. XLVII...NO. 15,125. NEW YORK, SATURDAY, JULY 2, 1898.—TWELVE PAGES. PRICE THREE CENTS.

THE WEATHER.

Fair; high temperature; southerly winds.

THE NEWS CONDENSED.

Stock market inactive.

Cash wheat, No. 2 red, 88c.; cash corn, No. 2 mixed, 37⅜c.; cash cotton, 6⅛c.

Page 3.

Col. Francis of the One Hundred and seventy-first Regiment declared yesterday that he would surely close the armory to-night to Capt. Stoddard and his men. He said he had no orders from the Governor to allow the Captain to use the armory.

The auxiliary cruiser St. Paul, Capt. Sigsbee, returned to this port last evening, all well on board. Details of her fight with the torpedo boat destroyer off San Juan de Puerto Rico and of the fighting in Guantanamo Bay were obtained from the vessel's War Budget, which is edited and printed by members of the crew.

Page 4.

New York's baseball team won a game at Chicago. Brooklyn won a ten-inning game at Pittsburg.

In the open tournament of the Seabright Golf Club Walter J. Travis of the Oakland Golf Club won the gold medal, leading a field of nearly seventy competitors.

The suit of Mrs. Anna Corbin Borrowe against the executors of the estate of the late Austin Corbin, her father, has been decided against her by the Appellate Division of the Supreme Court.

Mrs. U. S. Grant, at present in the city, states it as her belief that the relief associations should aid the soldiers at the front, and not the destitute families. Her personal memoirs have been completed.

At the risk of her own life Miss Alice Goodwin, seventeen years of age, rescued Edward Burke, an actor, from drowning at Sea Cliff. He had sustained a concussion of the brain and was sinking for the third time.

Owing to strong winds the boat races between the freshman crews of Cornell, Columbia, and Pennsylvania, and the 'Varsity of these three colleges, and the University of Wisconsin, which were to have been rowed at Saratoga yesterday were postponed until this morning.

Gen. Howard Carroll and Major Theodore L. Poole, appointed by Gov. Black to investigate into the condition of the New York State troops at the big camps, have returned after a three weeks' inspection and pronounce as absolutely false the allegations of suffering and hardship made in certain quarters. Gen. Carroll praises the New York troops very highly.

Page 5.

Debate on the Hawaiian Annexation bill was continued in the Senate yesterday, Mr. Pettus of Alabama making the first formal speech in favor of the resolutions. Mr Mallory of Florida opposed him. No proceedings of consequence were carried on in the House.

Page 7.

Julius Schmidt of 251 Canal Street was stabbed to death in his saloon by William Faue, his chef. There were no witnesses to the murder.

Vincenza Rosano, a young Italian bride of Newark, was shot and killed by a rejected Italian suitor named Marighetti, who after the murder committed suicide by throwing himself from a four-story window.

Page 10.

There was a burst of sympathetic cheering for Jockey Taral when he won the stake race at Sheepshead Bay yesterday.

Caroline Jansen, sixteen years old, of Brooklyn, killed herself by drinking carbolic acid because she had been reprimanded by her father.

The Staten Island Midland Railroad has abolished its system of transfers, and the residents of the island strongly object. It is said the action of the railroad company is unconstitutional, and the matter may be carried to the courts.

Page 12.

The Board of Estimate and Apportionment met yesterday and voted money for various purposes.

Yesterday was the hottest day of the year, and the hottest July 1 since 1872. The mercury registered as high as 93 degrees. Several prostrations were reported.

W. W. Durant, reputed to be worth over $1,000,000, was arrested, charged by his sister with withholding her share of a $1,300,000 estate. He gave bail in $10,000.

Fifteen members of the Brooklyn School Board were appointed yesterday by Mayor Van Wyck, the terms of fifteen having expired. None of the women was reappointed.

All the provisions of the war revenue law which did not take effect on June 14 became operative yesterday. The annoyances incidental to the enforcement of the law were borne with patriotic cheerfulness by the business community generally, but the scarcity of proprietary stamps gave rise to vigorous complaint from manufacturers who for a week past have been vainly clamoring for them at the internal revenue offices, and who declared that their July trade would suffer seriously by the delay in distributing the stamps.

THE WEATHER.

The local forecast may be found at the top of this page to the right of the title.

The pressure is high in the Gulf and Atlantic States and the lower lake regions; also in the Rocky Mountain districts. A depression, central in Nebraska, covers the Rocky Mountain slope. The barometer has fallen in the St. Lawrence Valley and on the middle Rocky Mountain plateau; it has fallen in the Missouri Valley.

The temperature is higher in New England, the Atlantic States, and the Ohio Valley, and lower on the middle Rocky Mountain slope. The following maximum temperatures occurred this afternoon: Montgomery, 100 degrees; Washington City and Philadelphia, 98 degrees; Lynchburg, Charlotte, Raleigh, Atlanta, Knoxville, and Chattanooga, 96 degrees. Showers and thunderstorms have occurred in the lake regions, the Missouri Valley, and on the Rocky Mountain slope.

Fair weather and continued high temperature is indicated for Saturday in New England, the Atlantic States, and the Ohio Valley. Showers and thunderstorms will occur in the Gulf States, the lake regions, the upper Mississippi and Missouri Valleys. The temperature will fall generally in the Missouri Valley and on the middle Rocky Mountain slope.

The record of temperature for the twenty-four hours ended at midnight, taken from THE NEW YORK TIMES's thermometer and from the thermometer of the Weather Bureau, is as follows:

	—Weather Bureau.—		—TIMES.
	1897.	1898.	1898.
3 A. M.	67	71	78
6 A. M.	68	70	78
9 A. M.	73	80	80
12 M.	77	90	86
4 P. M.	[illegible]	93	93
6 P. M.	[illegible]	89	93
9 P. M.	71	[illegible]	88
12 P. M.	70	82	85

THE TIMES's thermometer is 6 feet above the street level; that of the Weather Bureau is 285 feet above the street level.

Average temperatures yesterday were as follows:

Printing House Square....85
Weather Bureau....82
Corresponding date 1897....72
Corresponding date for last twenty years....72

The maximum temperature yesterday was 93 degrees, at 4 o'clock; the minimum was 70 degrees, at 6 A. M. The humidity at 8 A. M. was .68, and at 8 P. M., .46.

BIG BATTLE AROUND SANTIAGO

General Assault Upon Spaniards by Land and Sea.

OUR ARMY IS VICTORIOUS

Captures Enemy's Outer Works and Occupies Them.

THE AMERICAN LOSS HEAVY

Shafter Reports the Casualties as Over 400.

NOT MANY KILLED

Battle to Go On To-day—Our Troops Within Three-quarters of a Mile of the City.

WASHINGTON, July 1.—The War Department has received the following from Gen. Shafter, dated at Siboney:

"Had a very heavy engagement to-day which lasted from 8 A. M. until sundown. We have carried their outworks, and now in possession of them.

"There is now about three-quarters of a mile of open between my lines and the city. By morning troops will be intrenched and considerable augmentation of forces will be there.

"Gen. Lawton's division and Gen. Bates's brigade, which have been engaged all day in carrying El Caney, which was accomplished at 4 P. M., will be in line and in front of Santiago during the night.

"I regret to say that our casualties will be above 400, of these not many killed.

"SHAFTER."

PLAYA DEL ESTE, Province of Santiago de Cuba, July 1.—A general assault on the City of Santiago de Cuba, by land and sea forces of the United States, began at 7 o'clock this morning.

Gen. Lawton advanced and took possession of Cabona, a suburb of Santiago.

Morro Castle and the other forts at the entrance of the harbor were bombarded by our fleet. The Vesuvius used her dynamite guns with good effect.

The Spanish fleet in the harbor fired on the American troops, who were very close to the city.

The fighting continued until dark.

Our forces have carried the enemy's outer works and have occupied them this evening.

The battle will probably be resumed at daybreak.

The American loss is heavy. Some estimates place it at 500 killed and wounded.

SIBONEY, July 1—3:30 P. M.—At 1 o'clock this afternoon, after over five hours' terrific fighting, the Spanish began to leave their intrenchments and retreat into the city. Many Americans were wounded, and are being brought in. One man had had both arms shot off and was wounded in the hip, but was laughing.

COMMENT AT WASHINGTON.

WASHINGTON, July 2.—The suspense which followed the receipt of Gen. Shafter's dispatch early yesterday morning announcing that a battle had been begun near Santiago was relieved at 12:30 this morning when a preliminary report of the day's operations was received by Gen. Corbin from Gen. Shafter.

The President and the war officials are immensely pleased at the information conveyed in Shafter's message. While they learned with sincerest regret that so many of the American troops had fallen in the fight, the ground gained by the day's conflict is regarded as a great victory.

The battle establishes pretty conclusively that the Spaniards are no match for the enthusiastic and aggressive United States troops. The Spaniards were driven from their intrenchments in front back into the city, and the Americans are now occupying the intrenchments and awaiting only the dawn to resume the greater battle which will result, it is confidently believed by the war officials, in the fall of Santiago before Sunday night and perhaps before nightfall to-day.

Adjt. Gen. Corbin put the situation strongly and picturesquely this morning while speaking briefly of the aggressiveness and tenacity of Gen. Shafter:

"The old bulldog," said he, referring thus half-affectionately to the distinguished commander of the Fifth Corps, "is lying right there with his teeth in their neck, only waiting the coming of daylight to finish the work he has so magnificently begun. The engagement yesterday was very heavy for a preliminary fight, but is seems a decided victory for us. I regret to know that Shafter has sustained so heavy a loss, but we may hope that there are not, as he says, many killed.

"It is, however, pretty apt to be true that the loss of an army in an engagement like that of yesterday, where the battle line extended over several miles, will be much heavier than is indicated by the first reports. It is manifestly impossible, in cases where the battle has raged all day and until dark to ascertain with definiteness the loss sustained."

During the early night there was much speculation concerning the reasons for the delay in receiving news from the battle. Capt. Nesmith, who is acting as Chief Signal Officer during the temporary absence of Gen. Greely, feared that cable communication with Cuba might have been interrupted, and none of the other officials would offer a suggestion as to the reason for the delay.

Early in the evening Secretary Alger went to the White House and remained with the President until the dispatch from Gen. Shafter had been received.

SANTIAGO DE CUBA AND ITS ENVIRONS.

(Taken from the Most Recent Maps and Drawings.)

Parallel lines indicate highways and cross lines railways; paths are marked by single lines leading from the highways.

FIRST NEWS OF THE ATTACK.

WASHINGTON, July 1.—The battle has begun. This was the startling news conveyed in the following brief dispatch received from Gen. Shafter at 10 o'clock this morning:

"Secretary of War, Washington, D. C.

"Camp, Near Savilla, Cuba.—Action now going on. The firing only light and desultory. Began on the right near Caney by Lawton's division. He will move on the northeast part of the Town of Santiago. Will keep you continually advised of progress.

SHAFTER,

"Major General."

Brief as it was it told the whole story that the first shots of the long-expected crash of arms, probably the first great land engagement of the war, was under way. It sent a thrill throughout official circles from the highest to the lowest. Secretary Alger was the first to read it. He passed it to Gen. Corbin, Adjutant General of the army, and directed him to take it at once to the White House. Gen. Corbin went to the President, carrying the original dispatch. He was back shortly, and then a bulletin was posted, giving the dispatch verbatim. Until then only the higher officials had known that the decisive hour was at hand. The news spread through the corridor, and a wave of awelike agitation and expectancy took hold of every one. A great crowd of correspondents struggled about the bulletin board; messenger boys dashed off with dispatches; the clerks, men and women, turned from their desks and gathered at the doorways.

Meantime Secretary Alger remained at his desk, while the usual train of callers pushed their way forward. The Secretary preserved his usual outward calm, but those near him said the news from the field had sent the same thrill through the Secretary that prevailed everywhere, and even more, for there was the personal consideration that the Secretary's son, young Capt. Alger, now on the staff of Gen. Duffield, was participating in the engagement now on.

As the Secretary started to the Cabinet meeting he spoke with satisfaction of the fact that sufficient time had elapsed to permit Gen. Shafter to get his army well concentrated at the front, and thrown out into good battle formation. The Secretary felt that our forces were on the aggressive and that the fact that the action was now going on showed that Shafter had bided his time and was ready to strike his blow.

Artillery Well Placed.

Word had come prior to the Shafter dispatch, showing that the artillery, which had been brought to the front, was well placed.

Gen. Miles, commanding the army, received a copy of the dispatch soon after it arrived. He had anticipated it, for only a few hours before a dispatch came to him from Gen. Breckinridge, Inspector General of the army, stating that the spirit of the troops was high, and that they were eager and expectant of action. Gen. Breckinridge's dispatch indicated that results might be expected very soon.

After the first announcement of Shafter was bulletined the time dragged wearily, with nothing from the field to answer the intense anxiety to which every one was wrought. Gen. Shafter's assurance that he would "keep you constantly advised of the progress" gave promise of early details. It had been arranged that they should go first to the White House while the Cabinet was in session, and then should be bulletined so far as warranted. The officials showed every disposition to keep the public completely advised of actual occurrences.

Gen. Lawton's Command.

According to Gen. Shafter's report, the attack on Santiago was begun by the fifth division of the Fifth Army Corps, commanded by Brig. Gen. H. W. Lawton. This division consists of three brigades, made up as follows:

First Brigade, commanded by Col. J. J. Van Horne—Eighth United States Infantry, Twenty-second United States Infantry, and Second Massachusetts Infantry.

Second Brigade, commanding officer unknown, but supposed to be Col. Bates—First United States Infantry, Fourth United States Infantry, and Twenty-fifth United States Infantry.

Third Brigade, commanded by Brig. Gen. A. R. Chaffee—Seventh United States Infantry, Twelfth United States Infantry, and Seventeenth United States Infantry.

It thus appears that the entire division which opened the hostilities of the day is composed entirely of regular troops, seasoned and experienced in battle, with the exception of the Second Massachusetts Volunteer Infantry, which is regarded as one of the best volunteer organizations of the army.

THE PRESIDENT SATISFIED.

Evidences of a Speedy Peace Looked for by Monday—Gen. Corbin Praises Shafter's Army.

WASHINGTON, July 1.—The President is well satisfied with Gen. Shafter's success, and, without having arranged business so as to make the Fourth of July a great day for news, it begins to look at the White House as if by Monday, if not earlier, there will be information that should promise the early termination of the war and the speedy conclusion by Spain that further bloodshed and waste of material is useless.

By Monday, if Gen. Shafter continues to press the enemy as he has since landing, Santiago may be in his possession; by Monday, it is expected, there will be news from Manila of the arrival of the first expedition carrying troops under Gen. Anderson, and by Monday it will be known whether Admiral Camara has really gone toward the Philippines to meet Admiral Dewey or to keep his ships out of the way in order to save them by avoiding war.

At the White House and the War Department, ever since Gen. Shafter landed at Daiquiri and pushed his forces into the Cuban hills, there has been every indication that he was to be heard from soon as having begun operations against the Spanish. Secretary Alger, usually very communicative, told much about what he expected, but he reserved the information which he and Gen. Miles now seem to have had, that Gen. Shafter intended to proceed seriously against the enemy to-day. At all events, when the dispatch came, early this morning, announcing that an advance had begun, and that there was fighting along the entire line, with particular activity at the right, where Gen. Lawton commanded, the news was received at the White House and the War Department as if it had been looked for.

Adjt. Gen. Corbin, who received the early dispatch from Gen. Shafter and took it to the White House at the request of Secretary Alger, is not an enthusiastic man, but he is a confident one. He manifested no surprise at the success indicated in the dispatch of Gen. Shafter.

"There is every reason why we should win," he said. "Our army is the best physically, the best equipped, the best clothed and shod, the best fed, and the most intelligent that ever undertook to defeat a foe."

He made no qualifications. Knowing some of the difficulties that attended getting the army into the field, appreciating all the discomforts complained of by those who are not soldiers, and who do not look at the matter from the soldier's point of view, he insisted that in all matters personal and other qualifications the 15,000, more or less, who are with Shafter to take Santiago are the best men who ever undertook military service.

A Tribute to Shafter's Bravery.

The officials here are confident that they have done everything possible to strengthen Shafter's hands for the great conflict he is waging, and they have an unlimited confidence in his discretion, his bravery, and his energy. The attack to-day, several days before the public mind expected the battle, is a tribute to his energy as well as to his judgment, according to the present lights, for he undoubtedly found it necessary to crush the foe in detail, following Napoleon's favorite maxim, instead of allowing them to consolidate and outnumber him.

As the day wore along without bringing any news the anxiety increased, and the question was in every one's mouth: "Why did he not report?" Adjt. Gen. Corbin's response was brief but pointed: "He is fighting, not writing," and this was accepted as a likely and sound explanation. Just before 4 o'clock came a brief dispatch from Plaza del Este, the cable station near Santiago. But it was from an engineer officer to Gen. Miles, and made no reference to the progress of the battle, merely referring to certain necessary material and live stock. On the whole, this very absence of official news was regarded as rather a favorable indication, the reasoning being that this morning's engagement was but a heavy skirmish, and that our army was feeling the enemy to discover and strike at his weak spot. It was nearly 6 o'clock when the signal officer received the welcome news that the enemy was retreating.

Gen. Miles's Opinion.

Gen. Miles was of the opinion that the action of to-day was in the nature of a heavy skirmish all along the American front, particularly the right, and that its main purpose was to develop the strength of the enemy and, if possible, learn the vulnerable point along the Spanish front. This, however, was based only on the lack of definite information, and Gen. Miles felt that any hour might bring word of a general engagement. Brig. Gen. Stone was inclined to believe that, after maintaining their stand to-day, the Spaniards would retire during the night, leaving the city evacuated.

The military authorities here are fully considering the chances of such a retreat of the Spanish Army from Santiago, and are endeavoring so to shape events that Gen. Shafter's force will not only take Santiago, but the 12,000 Spaniards before they get away north to effect a juncture with Gen. Pando. Full information as to possible lines of retreat has been placed at the disposal of the War Department.

Lines of Spanish Retreat.

One of the most interesting statements is that of General Manager Cox of the Spanish-American Mining Company at Daiquiri, who is thoroughly acquainted with all the country surrounding Santiago. He shows that the two possible lines of retreat are: First, by the road to El Cobre; or, second, by following the line of the Sabanillo and Marato Railroad. The first line will be easy for about the first ten miles or as far as El Cobre, but after that the country is mountainous and barren, and would not afford subsistence, and the pass to reach the central plateau of the island would be difficult.

The more likely line of retreat would be along the line of the above-mentioned railroad, crossing the Sierra Maestra at El Cristo, a pass 600 feet above the sea, ten miles south of Santiago, which is the lowest pass through the Sierra Maestra for many miles. The country back of this is a rolling plateau of rich agricultural land. At Manacas, on the railroad, two miles north of the pass, is a bridge, consisting of a series of thirty-foot spans on iron trestle bents. This point is about two miles beyond the Cristo summit, and just beyond this bridge the railroad divides into two branches. The destruction of this bridge would be the most feasible method of preventing the approach of Gen. Pando's Spanish troops to relieve Santiago.

Possible Base for the Enemy.

It is probable that if the Spaniards retreat by this road they will make a stand on the plateau at El Cristo and hold the pass of El Cristo. The only other pass through the mountains near this point is at Escandel Summit, about six miles in a straight line east of El Cristo Pass. Escandel Summit is 1,200 feet above the sea, and is reached from Santiago via Caney. The road from Santiago to Caney is fairly good, being wide enough for vehicles.

Between Caney and Escandel the road, which is no more than a trail, ascends the mountains, and is very winding and broken. Beyond Escandel, across the range, the country is heavily timbered and broken, and the roads are not good. It is an ideal country for ambush. This is probably the only pass through which the Spanish position could be turned should the Spanish troops occupy the El Cristo plateau and pass.

The railroad has been fortified by a line of blockhouses, protecting the bridges, and certain zones of cultivation inclosed between these forts have been planted during all the time of the war, and would afford a supply for the army for a certain time. In the meanwhile sweet potatoes could be planted, which in three months would ripen. These zones of cultivation exist along the road as far as San Luis, at which point there is considerable country in cultivation. On the other branch (the Sabanilla branch) the zones of cultivation extend as far as Songe.

AT THE CABINET MEETING.

The Battle Discussed—Secretary Long Expects Great Results from the Co-operation of the Fleet.

WASHINGTON, July 1.—The Cabinet was in session for almost two hours to-day, but took no important action. The session was mainly occupied with a discussion of the news from Santiago. Gen. Shafter's dispatch was read aloud before the members of the Cabinet. Other dispatches also were read verbatim to the Cabinet. There was a general feeling of gratification shown at the co-operation rendered by Admiral Sampson's fleet. Careful plans to this end were made in a general way some time ago, though leaving to Sampson the widest discretion.

Besides the Santiago fight, the Cabinet devoted some time to questions connected with the operation of the war revenue law.

After the Cabinet meeting Secretary Long said that the fleet under Sampson was co-operating to the fullest extent with the land forces, and that he expected great results. He suggested that there were two conditions certain in the Santiago situation. "One is," he said, "we will surely win, and the other that it will come about after hard fighting that will tell. Of this we are certain."

Postmaster General Emory Smith remained with the President for some time after the other members went away.

The sentiment in the Cabinet was that there was a strong possibility that the fall of Santiago might be announced at any time now.

ON THE EVE OF THE BATTLE.

Plan of Gen. Lawton's Advance—Caney the Objective Point—How the Land Lies.

GEN. LAWTON'S HEADQUARTERS, RIO GUAMO, June 30.—Daylight to-morrow will see a movement of the Fifth Division, under Gen. Lawton, to a new base north and east of Santiago. All this morning Gen. Garcia's Cubans have been moving from their hill camp, on the east, and have been passing headquarters almost at a jog trot.

Assuming that 4,000 men will be deployed on the northeast, the American advance is one mass of network, which is now drawing closer around the doomed city.

Three miles east of Gen. Lawton's position there rises a narrow ridge in the Santiago Valley. Southward from here the troops can look down on Caney, tiny, picturesque, old, and once a thriving Spanish town, almost at their feet. Three miles west, crowning a low ridge that crosses the Santiago Valley, are seen the Spanish barracks and a large red building, over which floats the Red Cross Society's flag. This is the Reina Mercedes Hospital, where, according to all pacifico accounts, are now Lieut. Hobson and the heroic seven.

The valley, three miles wide, would be a garden spot in time of peace. Now it is filled with a rank tropical growth, covering abandoned plantations. The only sign of a habitation between Santiago and Cavite is Dugure House, once a hospitable country hotel, now used by the Spanish as a barracks, but, like Cavite, abandoned, except for a Corporal's guard of Spaniards.

Opposite, on the northern side of the valley, is a broad plateau, accessible by a good road. This is the key to Santiago. Artillery there could command the city and force the Spaniards to evacuate, or to storm the heights to capture the battery. The latter course the Americans consider extremely unlikely.

Gen. Lawton and his command from the ridge will first take Caney. A slight skirmish is expected, but nothing serious, the captured pacificos all alleging that the Spanish main force, which was here four days ago, has now been withdrawn into Santiago in pursuance of a general plan of concentration.

Linares's Continuous Retreat.

Spies report Gen. Linares's continuous retreat from Daiquiri to Santiago. This plan is said to be much against his own wishes, but to be forced upon him by his superior officer, Gen. Toral, commanding at Santiago. It is evident the Spanish stand is to be made inside the strong entrenchments about the city. With well-armed men, eager for a final clash, this stand might well be desperate. The temper of the Spaniards is hard to ascertain. Owing to the Cubans' biased estimate of Spanish ability, they predict a merely nominal resistance; but the Americans think otherwise. At any rate, the Spanish are eating horses and the civilians are gathering mangroves in a suburban wood, where some twenty have been captured by the American patrol. The Spaniards have, therefore, the spur of hunger. Whether it has broken their fighting spirit a few days may tell.

The capture of Caney and possibly the occupation of the commanding plateau is now thought to be the limit of to-morrow's movement. Gen. Lawton's command carries provision sufficient to last until July 4. With the present supply train service continuing without any accident, he will easily have food enough to last to July 12. By that time, according to one well-informed officer, and perhaps sooner, Santiago will be taken.

This move of the Fifth Division will completely turn the Spanish eastern flank. Gen. Kent's command will be able to move up parallel to its present position, acting as a wall against the horde of Spaniards from three strong lines south and east. Should a serious effort be made to prevent Gen. Lawton's gaining the desired plateau and the Spanish interior force thereby be weakened, Gen. Kent and Gen. Wheeler may be thrown forward and a general engagement be precipitated.

A large detail has been at work all day improving a military road to Caney, with a view of the artillery and the supplies for the other force cutting through the woods parallel to the Old Santiago road. It is also possible that this opening may bring the siege guns that are now working up the coast in the hands of our troops, inland from the railway.

Men in Excellent Condition.

The condition of the American troops is excellent. Despite the hard rains and the hot sun, only eighteen men out of Gen. Lawton's 5,093 were reported ill on to-day's sick call. The other commands are equally well off. The men are full of snap and eager for the big fight.

In preparation for the final assault upon Santiago, sixty tried men in each brigade—non-commissioned officers and privates—have been promoted to be wire clippers, and they will precede the first firing line about 200 or 300 yards for the purpose of cutting the barbed-wire fences that obstruct the way to the city. Their mission is a most hazardous one, as they will be exposed to the fire of our own men as well as that of the enemy.

The pacificos who have been brought into the American camp during the last few days are in a pitiable condition. Men, women, and children are absolutely starving, and they welcome American shelter.

Gen. Shafter has established his headquarters with Gen. Lawton and to-day hoisted the corps flag. To-day the signal corps used an observation balloon, obtaining a perfect view of the Spanish entrenchments, the city, and the harbor.

CUBANS MAKE A DASH.

Advance Within Two Miles of the Arsenal and Prepare for an Early Assault.

CHICAGO, July 1.—A special copyright cable to The Chicago Daily News, dated at Sevilla, Cuba, June 30, says: "Caracas Cubans made a dash west this afternoon and penetrated further into the defenses of Santiago than any troops have yet succeeded in doing. Led by the gray-haired General, they skirted Caney, a cluster of villas two miles from the arsenal, and passed in plain view of the Spanish pickets. To-night they are camped near by preparing for an attack as soon as permission is obtained.

The Cubans have rations for only twenty-four hours, and argue that an early advance is probable from these circumstances. Many of Garcia's men formerly resided in Santiago, being driven thence by the barbarity of Gen. Weyler, and to-day, when they caught a glimpse of their former homes, they gave a tremendous cheer and demanded to be led forward immediately. Gen. Garcia and his officers restrained them with difficulty. Caney is composed of residences of the wealthy classes, and Gen. Garcia expects to occupy it without difficulty, as the Spanish are evidently disposed to abandon the town. From Caney the main road enters Santiago from the northeast, thus making it an important point in the impending operations.

Gen. Garcia hopes to have the honor of leading the grand assault, and has exhorted his men to fight desperately.

A reconnoitring party started to-day to Aguadores by the railroad, but can go no further, a trestle being broken.

The warships are coaling at Guantanamo to their full capacity, and the colliers will be sent North for complete cargoes.

The Texas last night approached within 1,700 yards of Morro Castle, under orders, and used her searchlight, but failed to attract notice. The Spaniards are saving their ammunition. Admiral Sampson can reduce the outer defenses when the army is ready.

Cable communication was established this morning by the Signal Corps, under Allen. The army base is at Siboney, with a naval base at Playa del Este.

Capt. Chanler made a reconnoisance, and discovered the Spaniards busily working on their intrenchments around Santiago.

Red Cross flags were flying on many buildings and church steeples in the city. It has been suggested here that this may be a ruse to prevent cannonading.

An advance reconnoissance was made toward Caney Wednesday. Five hundred Spanish guerrillas were encamped there, intrenched behind a barbed wire fence and a ditch. They had one small gun, and an old church had been turned into a fort.

MANZANILLO BOMBARDED.

(From a Spanish Correspondent.)

HAVANA, July 1—9 P. M.—Advices received at the Palace say that about 4 o'clock yesterday afternoon three American warships bombarded Manzanillo. The Spanish gunboats Cuba Espanola and Guardian and the "pontoon" Maria answered the fire, lying at anchor off the port, while the gunboats Delgarde Parejo, Estrella, and Guantanamo went to meet the American ships and to silence their fire.

The combat lasted forty-five minutes. Over forty shells fell in Manzanillo, but doing slight damage to the houses. The Spanish loss was two sailors wounded and eight "bruised." Among the latter were the Commander of the gunboat Delgardo Parejo and the physician of the "pontoon" Maria.

The American ships retired toward the northwest, by the Manzanillo Keys, towing one ship whose engines were damaged. All the Spanish warships were slightly injured.

Yesterday an American merchant ship fired four shots into Cayo Francis, Cardenas, but no damage was done.

MADRID, July 1.—The Imparcial of this city to-day publishes a dispatch from San-

"All the News That's Fit to Print."

The New York Times.

With REVIEW OF BOOKS AND ART

COPYRIGHTED, 1898, BY THE NEW YORK TIMES COMPANY.

With REVIEW OF BOOKS AND ART

VOL. XLVII...NO. 15,161. NEW YORK, SATURDAY, AUGUST 13, 1898.—TWELVE PAGES. PRICE THREE CENTS.

THE WEATHER.

Rain, clearing in the afternoon; southeasterly winds, becoming southwesterly.

THE NEWS CONDENSED.

Stock market reactionary.

Cash wheat, No. 2 red, 80¼c.; cash corn, No. 2 mixed, 39⅛c.; cash cotton, 6 1-16c.

FOREIGN.—The British Parliament was prorogued until Oct. 20; the speech of the Queen congratulated both houses upon the acts passed, and reviewed the Government's relations with other countries. The Pope was able to receive callers yesterday, having recovered from his recent illness. The Hooley case, involving charges of bribery against certain Lords and Earls, was resumed in English courts. Two American women missionaries were accidentally killed in Yokohama Harbor.

Page 1.

There is continued and increasing indignation in England at the recent agreement between Russia and China and the rebuffs England has been dealt in such negotiations.

Page 2.

Gen. Palma, Delegate of the Cuban Republic, says the leading men of that Government are confident that the United States Government will turn Cuba over to the Cubans.

The transport Seguranca arrived at Quarantine last evening, bringing 331 sick soldiers from Shafter's army at Santiago. One man died at sea. Other transports, bearing Col. Roosevelt and his Rough Riders; Gen. "Joe" Wheeler, and others, are expected to reach port to-day. All are bound for Camp Wikoff, at Montauk Point. The camp site was visited and praised by city and port health authorities. The camp is not in readiness to accommodate more men than the 2,500 now there.

Page 3.

Grace Boone, great-granddaughter of Daniel Boone, was saved from eviction and semi-starvation.

Mrs. J. Polk Deane of Dover, Del., and her sister, Mrs. J. P. Dunning, are dead, as the result of eating poisonous candy which came by mail from an unknown source.

The Campania, which arrived yesterday, sighted the body of a child, probably drowned from La Bourgogne, off Sable Island. The Campania brought many passengers, notably Archbishop Keane.

The President says a soldier's field of duty is prescribed by his Government, and that those who have been kept in camp are as much entitled to the Nation's thanks as those who were engaged in battle.

Page 4.

The convention of the National Buyers' Association adjourned.

Three Englishmen who have just completed a journey of 19,000 miles on a trip around the world, are stopping in town.

Sir William Marriott and W. Morshead arrived from England yesterday to push the complaint of the British stockholders in the Central Pacific against the management of C. P. Huntington.

George Lynch, war correspondent of The London Daily Chronicle, who arrived here from Santiago yesterday on his way back to England, highly praised the courage and endurance of our soldiers, but severely criticised the Commissary, Transportation, and Medical Departments, which, he said, totally lacked organization from the outset and seemed to vie with each other in incompetence. Many soldiers, he declared, were left to die of their wounds.

Page 5.

Lieut.-Col. A. S. Doggett has written to a friend here of the gallant conduct of the Twenty-Fifth Regular Infantry at El Caney.

Gen. "Joe" Wheeler writes to a friend here saying that news from the United States is infrequent and that "we are all begging to go to Puerto Rico."

A crowd of working people at Smith Street and Atlantic Avenue, Brooklyn, raised $20 for a sick man and his evicted family. A truckman volunteered his services and the crowd did the moving and denounced the landlord.

Page 7.

Rear Admiral Kirkland, commandant of the Mare Island Navy Yard, died at Vallejo, Cal., yesterday evening.

Ex-Secretary of State John Sherman arrived in this city Thursday night and left yesterday morning for Washington.

Ex-Senator Hill and Elliot Danforth left for Saratoga. Mr. Hill said he had always favored the holding of the Democratic Convention there.

Lieut. Hobson superintended, at Staten Island, the work of testing air bags to be used in raising the Cristobal Colon. He held an informal reception at the Hotel Majestic in the evening.

Page 9.

American manufacturers of iron and steel, since 1880, have secured control of five-sixths of the foreign trade in America and increased their exports 400 per cent.

The Commissioner of Internal Revenue shows that the receipts for the fiscal year ended June 30 amounted to $170,-900,519. The increase over the previous fiscal year's collections is $24,249,925.

Page 10.

The New Yorks won a victory over the Chicago baseball team at the Polo Grounds yesterday and regained fifth place —the Cincinnatis won a closely contested game in Brooklyn.

Page 11.

Vice Chancellor Emery of New Jersey ruled that the New York and New Jersey Telephone Company may lawfully string its wire across public streets from poles on abutting property without obtaining consent from Summit Township.

Page 12.

A break in a five-foot brick sewer caused a cave-in in West Ninety-eighth Street.

A. J. Heinemann replied to accusations against the Druggists' League for Shorter Hours.

A young man was arrested for stealing bicycles, and implicated a man who he says keeps a fence.

The Board of Classification of the United States General Appraisers handed down decisions on a number of new questions.

As a result of the war revenue tax of 10 cents per pound on tea it is expected that this year's imports will show a decrease of 10,000,000 pounds.

A large clothespole fell in a Hoboken back yard, breaking the skull of Helen Disch, four years old, and injuring several other persons. The child may die.

The estate of A. T. Stewart, the merchant, has again been made the object of legal attack, this time in behalf of Agnes and James Joseph Carroll, minors.

Howard G. Hill, a recent patient of the Kings County Hospital at Flatbush, makes charges of neglect and ill-treatment against the officials of that institution.

A Cleveland and a New York bank which made a joint bid for the last issue of city bonds authorized seek to enjoin the Controller from awarding the bonds to Vermilye & Co. and Kuhn, Loeb & Co.

Nathan H. Wilson and his wife of 497 Sixth Avenue, Brooklyn, started eight days ago on a vacation trip to Vermont, leaving their three small children a scant two days' supply of food. The little ones were found starving and their wants relieved by the Children's Society.

Affidavits submitted in the Supreme Court yesterday in the suit of Calhoun against Pettit assert that the missing real estate operator traded through "dummies" to escape liability on bonds. These affidavits are made by Pettit's business associates. No trace of the missing man has yet been found.

Suicide Epidemic in German Army.

BERLIN, Aug. 12.—There is an epidemic of suicide in the army. The Frankfort Gazette reports four cases in Saxony, and the Ludwigsburg Gazette tells of a fifth, due to an officer's brutality.

ENGLAND IS HUMILIATED

China's Marked Favor to Russia Considered as a Defiant Rebuff Well-nigh Unbearable.

LORD SALISBURY CENSURED

The London Papers Declare that If Such Indignities Continue, "the Guns Will Go Off of Themselves"—Other Comments.

LONDON, Aug. 12.—In the House of Commons to-day the Government leader, Mr. A. J. Balfour, First Lord of the Treasury, declined to pledge the Government to prevent the ratification of the Franco-Belgian Pekin-Han-Kow concessions in China.

But Mr. Balfour promised that in the event of British capitalists purchasing railroad concessions obtained by French or Belgian syndicates in the Yang-tse-Kiang Valley her Majesty's Government will support and assist them, both in London and at Pekin, in this and in all other legitimate British commercial enterprises.

The morning papers express the growing indignation of the country at the position of affairs in China.

The Daily Graphic says: "If this state of things continues, the guns will go off of themselves."

The Shanghai correspondent of The Daily Mail, who professes to divulge the terms of a long existing secret treaty between China and Russia, says: "It is nothing less than an offensive alliance. China undertakes to regard Russia as having a preponderating influence in all questions of commercial and internal politics, while Russia will support China against all 'open door' demands. Russia finances China in internal developments, and China grants Russia preferential rates in certain areas, and railways built in the joint interests of the two countries will be under Russia's practical control.

"Russia will assist China in developing her military and naval forces, and China will co-operate with Russia as an ally. This treaty has been in abeyance since Li Hung Chang visited the Czar. That it has become operative at the present moment in respect to the Pekin-Han-Kow and Niu-Chwang contracts is significant."

If The Daily Mail's version may be trusted it will explain much that had hitherto been inexplicable in the development of the question. The manager of the Hongkong and Shanghai Bank in London in the course of an interview yesterday said:

"I believe the Pekin-Han-Kow Line, owing to natural obstructions and its costliness, will never be built, Russia merely wishing to keep England out."

The French comment gleefully upon the situation, and the newspapers at Berlin and Vienna are at no pains to hide their satisfaction at the discomfiture of England. The Continental press regards the project of an Anglo-American alliance as chimerical. These journals consider that the United States have had enough of war for the present, and will not care to give Great Britain anything more than moral support in China. Therefore, they argue, England is not likely to pick a quarrel with Russia, but will content herself with seeking compensation elsewhere.

A special dispatch from Shanghai says: "The Russian agents are again intriguing to obtain control of the Chinese Maritime Customs Department."

The Peking correspondent of The Times, telegraphing with reference to the Peking-Han-Kow contract, says: "The rebuff is all the more serious because the Tsung-li-Yamen gave assurances that the decree confirming the contract would not be issued until after a further conference with Sir Claude Macdonald, the British Minister."

The Daily Chronicle, in an editorial which reflects the general opinion of the London morning press, comments upon the fact that the Marquis of Salisbury and all the responsible officials are leaving London at such a critical moment. It says: "The curtain is deliberately dropped upon a scene of national humiliation and national indignation."

CITY OF KAZAN IN FLAMES.

Many Buildings Are Already in Ashes and the Fire Raging.

MOSCOW, Aug. 12.—The City of Kazan, capital of the Government of the same name, on the River Kazandka, is threatened with destruction by fire.

The flames are fanned by a strong wind. Several large factories, the arsenal, barracks, and a hundred other buildings are in ashes.

The City of Kazan is the entrepot of the commerce between Siberia, Bokhara, and European Russia, and has an extensive trade on the Volga. It is the see of a Bishop, and has a magnetic observatory, an arsenal, and a powder magazine. It has long been celebrated for its educational establishments. Kazan has several times been nearly ruined by fire.

MORE LEITER LAND MORTGAGED.

Wheat Speculator Gives Real Estate Security for $500,000.

CHICAGO, Aug. 12.—Two more pieces of the Leiter properties were mortgaged to-day by the filing of a deed in the Recorder's office.

As security for a note for $500,000 at 5 per cent. interest, made April 11 last to the Illinois Trust and Savings Bank, Joseph Leiter transferred to John P. Wilson a piece of property 40 by 180 feet on Washington Street, 80 feet east of Dearborn Street, and another, 90 by 180 feet, on Adams Street, 90 feet east of Fifth Avenue.

The deed is made to Mr. Wilson as trustee of the bank in consideration of the loan named. In the transaction Leiter agrees to pay all taxes and assessments, and failing to do so the trustee is to be entitled to 7 per cent. per annum on all sums advanced. The deed recites that the indebtedness secured is a part of the indebtedness of Joseph Leiter to the bank, secured by the quit claim deed given June 13. It is of date Aug. 8, 1898, and is signed by Joseph Leiter of "the Borough of Manhattan."

YELLOW FEVER IN MEXICO.

The Heat is Intense and Sanitary Conditions Very Incomplete.

MEXICO CITY, Aug. 12.—Yellow fever of the worst type prevails at Merida, and has appeared in the interior of the States of Yucatan and Campaso.

The heat is suffocating. The health of the City of Mexico has not been improved since the rains began, and it is proposed to adopt the cremation system here on a large scale.

Yellow Fever Impedes Travel.

HOUSTON, Texas, Aug. 12.—The Southern Pacific has been notified by the State Health Officer to run no more trains from the East till further orders, on account of yellow fever at Franklin, La.

ERMINE FOR SECRETARY DAY?

Report that the President Will Appoint Him to the Bench in the Sixth Circuit.

LOUISVILLE, Ky., Aug. 12.—A special to The Commercial from Chattanooga, Tenn., says:

"Secretary of State Day will be appointed United States Judge for the Sixth Circuit as soon as he resigns from the Cabinet at the close of the war. This was learned from the most reliable authority here to-day.

"It is learned that several months ago Judge Taft of Ohio, the Associate Judge of the Sixth Circuit, went to President McKinley and made a personal request that another Judge for the circuit should be appointed. His reason for this was that the circuit embraces four important States—Ohio, Michigan, Kentucky, and Tennessee—and that only two Judges are allowed, whereas other circuits not so large are given four or more. The work of the circuit, he showed, required an additional Judge.

"The result of the conference with the President was very frankly and unreservedly stated. The President said he intended to appoint Judge Day to the place at the close of the war."

MACIAS REPORTS A REPULSE.

He Informs His Government that Three Were Killed and Nine Wounded at Mayagues.

MADRID, Aug. 12.—An official dispatch has been received here from San Juan de Puerto Rico confirming the report that the American troops have occupied Mayaguez, the important town on the western coast of Puerto Rico. The dispatch adds that the Spanish garrison, consisting of a regiment of infantry and some guerrillas, with two mountain guns, commanded by Col. Toto, made a sortie from the place, and during the engagement which followed the Spaniards had three men killed and nine wounded.

Some gendarmes, it is announced, overtook the Castillo band of insurgents at Cuevas yesterday and exchanged shots with the insurgents, who retired into the mountains.

LEE EXPECTS TO GO TO CUBA.

This Is the Construction Put on His Giving Up His Richmond House.

RICHMOND, Va., Aug. 12.—Gen. Lee telegraphed to-day that he did not want to keep his house here for another year. This is taken to mean that he expects to go to Cuba this Fall and take his family with him.

ALL READY FOR PROSPERITY.

Secretary Long Looks for a Profitable Renewal of Industry.

HINGHAM, Mass., Aug. 12.—Secretary of the Navy Long had this to say of the questions on which, in his judgment, Congressional elections would turn this Fall:

"I think that the old sectional feeling is absolutely and utterly wiped out. The tariff and currency questions are utterly overshadowed by the tremendous rapidity with which recent important events have followed each other. The success of the Administration and its ability to successfully cope with large questions has, I believe, been universally recognized. President McKinley has been confronted with the gravest problems, and it seems as if the destiny of the Republic has been enlarged in scope.

"I don't think it is going to be a good time for contests, as Thomas B. Reed expressed it in his district, and I believe that to be true of other districts throughout the country. There is general feeling in favor of helping the Administration instead of fighting it. Then, too, the war being over, there is an intense readiness for a renewal of prosperous conditions. I look to see the renewal of industry and enterprises that will be of profit to capital and to labor alike."

HUNGARIAN CABINET TO RESIGN

Baron Banffy Visits the Emperor in Upper Austria.

LONDON, Aug. 13.—The Vienna correspondent of The Daily Chronicle says:

"Baron Banffy, the Hungarian Premier, has gone to Ischel, Upper Austria, to see the Emperor-King, and to tender the resignation of the Hungarian Cabinet."

The present Hungarian Cabinet, which was appointed in January, 1895, is composed as follows:

President of the Council—Baron Desiderius Banffy.
Minister of Finance—Dr. Ladislaus de Lukacs.
Minister of National Defense (Honved)—Baron Geza Fejervary.
Minister Near the King's Person (ad latus)—Baron Desiderius Banffy (ad interim.)
Minister of the Interior—Desiderius de Percell.
Minister of Education and of Public Worship—Dr. Julius de Wlassics.
Minister of Justice—Dr. Alexander Erdely.
Minister of Industry and Commerce—Baron Ernest de Daniel.
Minister of Agriculture—Dr. Ignatius de Daranyi.
Minister for Croatia and Slavonia—Emerich de Josipevichid.

Rumors of impending crises in the Austrian and Hungarian Cabinets have been freely circulated of late at Vienna and Budapest, and there has been no little mutual recrimination between the members of the dual monarchy, with a good deal of confusion and uncertainty behind the scenes at both capitals.

The question is as to the renewal of the Ausgleich, the Austro-Hungarian Constitutional compact, which is the basis of the union between the two Governments. A deadlock has been caused by the undertaking of the Hungarian Cabinet not to renew the agreement under Article XIV. of the Austrian Constitution, and the impossibility for the Austrian Ministry, in the present condition of the Reichsrath, to make any other arrangement.

SUTRO WILL TO BE CONTESTED.

Alleged Widow and Recognized Heirs Are Not Satisfied.

SAN FRANCISCO, Aug. 12.—The will of Adolph Sutro will be contested by Mrs. Kluge, the alleged widow, who says she married the deceased millionaire by contract, and also by the recognized legal heirs, who will fight the trust clause in the will. Mrs. Kluge claims there is a will of recent date in existence, in which she and her children are liberally provided for.

The eighteenth clause of the will which has been filed for probate is as follows:

"Unto Miss Hattie Trundle of Washington, heretofore known as Mrs. George Allen, the sum of $50,000 as a reparation, as far as it may be possible, for the injury done her by a scandalous charge, falsely and maliciously, at Virginia City, State of Nevada, in the month of July, 1879, then and there brought against her."

The nature of the "scandalous charge" is set forth in the following dispatch to The Chronicle, published July 9, 1879: "Virginia City, Nev., July 8, 1879.—For some three months a Washington woman, known in the town as 'the $80,000 widow,' has been stopping at the hotel. Her name is Mrs. Allen, and the scandal touches her and Adolph Sutro, of tunnel notoriety. Last Thursday evening Mr. Sutro's family came up to Virginia.

After dinner the inmates of the hotel were startled by screams of women. A general rush was made in the direction of the cries, which led to the room of Mrs. Allen, where Mrs. Sutro was beating her over the head with a champagne bottle and making outcries calling her all sorts of names. Mrs. Sutro declared that she had caught her husband with Mrs Allen. Mrs. Sutro was removed to her room and commenced making things lively for Mr. Sutro. It is stated that E. B. Stonehill has been retained as attorney for Mrs. Sutro in a suit for divorce which will be commenced immediately.

THE FLAG OVER HAWAII.

It Will Be Raised Upon the Arrival of the United States Commissioners—Great Preparations.

HONOLULU, Aug. 4.—The United States ship Philadelphia arrived here yesterday, six days and twenty hours from San Francisco, with Admiral Miller and staff on board. Admiral Miller has orders to confer with Minister Sewall, and until after the conference nothing definite will be decided as to the flag-raising programme. A conference with the Hawaiian Government will be held this afternoon. It is generally understood that the flag will not be raised until the Commissioners arrive, on the 17th inst.

F. M. Hatch has resigned his position as Minister to the United States.

The Ewa plantation, the best-paying sugar estate in Hawaii, has decided to increase its capital stock to $2,000,000. The present capitalization is $1,000,000.

The Japanese imbroglio of 1897 has been settled by the payment of $75,000 to Japan. In making the payment, the Government does not admit the justice of the claim or right of Japan to indemnity. The payment was made at the request of President McKinley.

Queen Liliuokalani returned to Hawaii on the 2d inst., glad, as she said to her friends, to be back in her own country, among her own people. She was given an enthusiastic reception by several hundred of her native friends. She declined to be interviewed. To her friends she said her health was good, but the trip had fatigued her greatly.

The United States transport steamers Rio de Janeiro and Pennsylvania sailed for Manila Aug. 3, and this morning the transports Para and City of Puebla took their departure for the same destination. While the vessels were in port twenty-six measles patients on board the Puebla were cared for at the local hospital, but were removed to their vessel before her departure. On July 27 Isaac Strickland, private of Battery G, Third Artillery, died. He was buried under the auspices of the local Red Cross Society.

FIGHTING CHICAGO GAS TRUST.

E. C. Benedict of This City Defies the Big Corporation.

CHICAGO, Aug. 12.—A battle royal is on between E. C. Benedict, the New York capitalist, and the Gas Trust. Efforts are being made to purchase the Ogden Gas Company, in order that it may be used as a weapon against the Trust. E. C. Benedict, as President of the Gas Trust, contracted with the Indiana Natural Gas Company to supply the syndicate with natural gas. Then Mr. Benedict bought a controlling interest in the Indiana Company. When he resigned, his successor opposed the interests of the outside concern in every way possible. The original contract expires in a few months, and the Trust is unwilling to renew it.

EARTHQUAKES AT MESSINA.

Mount Vesuvius Breaks Forth from a New Crater.

MESSINA, Sicily, Aug. 12.—An earthquake shock was felt here this afternoon and at various points in the island and the southern part of the peninsula. No damage resulted from the disturbance.

NAPLES, Aug. 12.—Mount Vesuvius is now in a state of eruption from a new crater. The eruption is supposed to be connected with the seismic disturbance felt at Messina and in Southern Italy.

Messina is a city and seaport in the northeastern part of Sicily and is the capital of the Province of Messina. It commands the Straits of Messina, which at this point are only four miles wide. It is eight miles northwest of Reggio, Italy, and 130 miles east by north of Palermo, Sicily. It is defended by walls and bastions, a citadel and many forts and is considered as a fortress of the highest importance. Its harbor is one of the finest in the world and vessels of the deepest draught can enter it, which has made Messina a port of considerable commercial standing in the world at large.

The city is built between the sea and the Dinnamare Hills to the westward. It extends in a semi-circle around the harbor, and is one of the most picturesque places along the Mediterranean. It is the northeast terminus of the Sicilian Railway system, which extends to Catania, Palermo, and other important places of the island.

Historically, Messina is of interest. It served in Caesar's time as a station for part of his fleet. Through the Middle Ages it was of importance. Later, in 1743, it was visited by a plague. In 1783 an earthquake almost destroyed the town and killed many of its inhabitants, but it was rebuilt on a much finer scale. Another misfortune befell the town when an inundation came in 1823. Since 1848 it has been the scene of several insurrectionary troubles, which led partly to the building of the strong fortification there.

The city itself is beautiful. Its wide streets are paved with lava and adorned with fountains. It has a cathedral dating from Norman times, a Viceroy's palace, a university, (founded in 1549,) a public library, several private palaces, and many public buildings. Its population in 1891 was estimated at 142,580.

THE WEATHER.

The local forecast may be found at the top of this page to the right of the title.

An extraordinary rainfall of 4.92 inches occurred during the past ten hours at Washington City. This is all the more remarkable because no neighboring stations report heavy rains. Lynchburg and Parkersburg had only a trace of rain in twelve hours, Hatteras, 0.04; Norfolk, 0.24; Philadelphia, 0.34; Atlantic City, 0.12; Cape May, 1.20, and Pittsburg, 0.44. Rain has also occurred in the South Atlantic States.

The temperature has fallen in the lake regions and the Ohio Valley.

Relatively high pressure covers the whole country east of the Rocky Mountains, except in the lower lake region, where there is a slight depression. The pressure continues high off the Atlantic and North Pacific Coasts.

Rain may be expected to-day on the Atlantic Coast and in New England. Generally fair weather is indicated elsewhere.

The record of temperature for the twenty-four hours ended at midnight, taken from THE NEW YORK TIMES's thermometer and from the thermometer of the Weather Bureau, is as follows:

	—Weather Bureau.— 1897.	1898.	—TIMES. 1898.
3 A. M.	67	66	67
6 A. M.	66	65	69
9 A. M.	71	69	74
12 M.	75	72	78
4 P. M.	76	71	78
6 P. M.	78	71	76
9 P. M.	71	71	74
12 P. M.	68	68	71

THE TIMES's thermometer is 6 feet above the street level; that of the Weather Bureau is 295 feet above the street level.

Average temperatures yesterday were as follows:

Printing House Square.....73
Weather Bureau.....70
Corresponding date 1897.....71
Corresponding date for last twenty years..74

The maximum temperature yesterday was 75 degrees at 9 P. M., and the minimum 65 degrees at 4 A. M. The humidity at 8 A. M. was 88 per cent., and at 8 P. M. 93 per cent.

WAR SUSPENDED, PEACE ASSURED

President Proclaims a Cessation of Hostilities.

PROTOCOL IS NOW IN FORCE

Cambon and Day Formally Complete Preliminary Agreement.

CONCESSIONS MADE BY SPAIN

Yields Cuba and Puerto Rico and Occupation of Manila.

WORK ON THE TREATY

Not More Than Five Commissioners on Each Side, to Meet in Paris by Oct. 1.

WASHINGTON, Aug. 12.—The plenipotentiaries of the United States and Spain having this afternoon at 4:23 o'clock signed the protocol defining the terms on which peace negotiations are to be carried on between the two countries, President McKinley has issued the following proclamation:

By the President of the United States of America.

A PROCLAMATION.

Whereas, By a protocol concluded and signed Aug. 12, 1898, by William R. Day, Secretary of State of the United States, and his Excellency Jules Cambon, Ambassador Extraordinary and Plenipotentiary of the Republic of France at Washington, respectively representing, for this purpose, the Government of the United States and the Government of Spain, the Governments of the United States and Spain have formally agreed upon the terms on which negotiations for the establishment of peace between the two countries shall be undertaken; and,

Whereas, It is in said protocol agreed that upon its conclusion and signature hostilities between the two countries shall be suspended, and that notice to that effect shall be given as soon as possible by each Government to the commanders of its military and naval forces:

Now, therefore, I, William McKinley, President of the United States, do, in accordance with the stipulations of the protocol, declare and proclaim on the part of the United States a suspension of hostilities, and do hereby command that orders be immediately given through the proper channels to the commanders of the military and naval forces of the United States to abstain from all acts inconsistent with this proclamation.

In witness whereof I have hereunto set my hand and caused the seal of the United States to be affixed.

Done at the City of Washington, this 12th day of August, in the year of our Lord one thousand eight hundred and ninety-eight, and of the independence of the United States the one hundred and twenty-third.

WILLIAM McKINLEY.

By the President,
WILLIAM R. DAY,
Secretary of State.

A copy of this proclamation has been cabled to our army and navy commanders. Spain will cable her commanders like instructions.

TERMS OF THE PROTOCOL.

WASHINGTON, Aug. 12.—Secretary of State Day, after the peace protocol had been signed by him and by Ambassador Cambon this afternoon, prepared and gave to the press the following official statement of the terms of the document:

1. Spain will relinquish all claim of sovereignty over and title to Cuba.

2. Puerto Rico and other Spanish islands in the West Indies and an island in the Ladrones, to be selected by the United States, shall be ceded to the latter.

3. The United States will occupy and hold the city, bay, and harbor of Manila pending the conclusion of a treaty of peace, which shall determine the control, disposition, and government of the Philippines.

4. Cuba, Puerto Rico, and other Spanish islands in the West Indies shall be immediately evacuated and Commissioners, to be appointed within ten days, shall, within thirty days from the signing of the protocol, meet at Havana and San Juan, respectively, to arrange and execute the details of the evacuation.

5. The United States and Spain will each appoint not more than five Commissioners to negotiate and conclude a treaty of peace. The Commissioners are to meet at Paris not later than the 1st of October.

6. On the signing of the protocol hostilities will be suspended and notice to that effect will be given as soon as possible by each Government to the commanders of its military and naval forces.

SIGNING THE PROTOCOL.

Impressive Scene at the White House—First Event of the Kind in Its History.

WASHINGTON, Aug. 12.—The closing chapter of events that led up to the signing of the protocol and the cessation of hostilities was full of interest. There were rumors early in the morning that over night the French Embassy had received the long-expected final instructions from Madrid, but these, upon inquiry, proved groundless, and it was not until 12:30 that the Madrid note began to come in small installments.

The State Department was soon advised of the fact that the message was under transmission, but as it was evident that it would be long, and that its reception would occupy much time, the Secretary of State left the Department for his luncheon. At 2:45 o'clock Secretary Thiebaut of the French Embassy appeared at the State Department to inform Secretary Day that the Ambassador was in full possession of the note; was fully empowered to sign the protocol for Spain, and only awaited the pleasure of the State Department. He intimated that the Ambassador would be pleased to have the final ceremony conducted in the presence of President McKinley, where the negotiations were begun.

Leaving the Secretary of Embassy in his own office, Secretary Day made a short visit to the White House to learn the President's wishes in the matter. The latter immediately consented to accept the suggestion, and Mr. Thiebaut hastened to inform his principal that the President would receive him at the White House at 4 o'clock.

At the appointed hour, a driving rainstorm prevailed, obliging all the parties to resort to carriages for transportation to the White House. Secretary Day came first, with a large portfolio under his arm, inclosing copies of the protocol, of the proclamation to be issued by the President stopping hostilities, and of some other necessary papers. He was accompanied by Assistant Secretary Moore, Second Assistant Secretary Adee, and Third Assistant Secretary Cridler. They were shown immediately into the Cabinet Room, where the President sat in waiting. He had invited to be present Assistant Secretaries Pruden and Cortelyou and Lieut. Col. Montgomery.

Cambon Reaches the Executive Mansion.

When Ambassador Cambon reached the White House it was just 3:55 o'clock, five minutes in advance of the appointed hour. The rain was still violent, and the Ambassador abandoned his usual custom of alighting at the outer gates of the Executive grounds. He was driven under the carriage porch, passing through a cordon of newspaper men before he and Secretary Thiebaut were ushered inside. They went directly to the library, adjoining the Cabinet Room, on the upper floor. At 4:05 they were announced to the waiting party in the Cabinet Room, and were ushered into its presence.

After an exchange of diplomatic courtesies no unnecessary waste of time occurred, and Assistant Secretary of State Cridler, on the part of the United States, and First Secretary Thiebaut on the part of Spain, retired to a window, where there was a critical examination of the protocol. This inspection had all the outward formalities due a document of this importance. It was prepared in duplicate at the State Department, one copy to be retained by the United States Government and the other to become the property of Spain.

The text is handsomely engrossed in a running old English script. Each copy of the protocol is arranged in double column, French and English standing side by side for easy comparison as to the exactness of translation. The two copies are alike, except that the one held by this Government has the English text in the first column and the signature of Secretary Day ahead of that of M. Cambon, while the copy transmitted to Spain has French in the first column and the signature of M. Cambon ahead of that of Secretary Day.

The protocol sent to Spain was accompanied by the credentials issued by President McKinley, specially empowering the Secretary of State to affix his signature to this document. The authorization was brief and in typewriting, save for the President's characteristic bold signature. Later, the American copy of the protocol will be accompanied by the written credentials of the Spanish Government sent to M. Cambon and bearing the signature of Queen Christina.

The cable dispatch received by him to-day conferred full authority to sign the protocol, and stated that the written authorization would follow, signed by the Queen Regent in the name of the King. Prior to the ceremony of to-day, M. Thiebaut showed the cable dispatch to Secretary Day, and it was accepted as sufficient to enable the Ambassador to sign in behalf of Spain. When the written authorization arrives it will be presented to the State Department to accompany the protocol.

The Signatures Affixed.

The examination of the protocol was satisfactory, and the document was handed to M. Cambon first and then to Secretary Day, who affixed signatures in that order to each side of the two copies. Then the last detail in making the protocol binding was administered by Assistant Secretary Cridler, who attached the seal of the United States.

Throughout the ceremony all but the two signers remained standing. M. Cambon, in signing for Spain, occupied the seat which Secretary of the Navy Long, now on a vacation, usually occupies. The President stood at the left-hand corner, at the head of the great Cabinet table; Secretary Day, M. Thiebaut, and M. Cambon in the order named on the left side of the table. The rest of the party were standing in other parts of the room.

No credentials were produced during the meeting at the White House, the President accepting Secretary Day's assurance that this had been settled to his satisfaction at the State Department. It was 4:23 o'clock when the final signatures were attached to the protocol, and within the knowledge of all the officials present this was the first time that a protocol or treaty had been signed at the White House.

As this ceremony concluded, Acting Secretary Allen of the Navy Department, Secretary Alger, and Adjt. Gen. Corbin appeared, having been summoned to the White House by the President, and they were admitted into the Cabinet room just in season to witness one of the most impressive features of the occasion, when the President requested the hand of the Ambassador and through him returned thanks to the sister Republic of France for the exercise of her good offices in bringing about peace. He also thanked the Ambassador personally for the important part he has played in this matter and the latter replied in suitable terms.

As a further mark of his disposition, President McKinley called for the proclamation which he had caused to be drawn up suspending hostilities and signed it in the presence of M. Cambon, who expressed his appreciation of the action. Without delay Acting Secretary Allen hastened to the telephone and directed that cable messages be immediately sent to all of the naval commanders—Dewey in the Philippines, Sampson at Guantanamo, and the various commandants at navy yards and stations—to cease hostilities immediately. There is a dispatch boat at Hongkong, and it is believed that it can reach Gen. Merritt in forty-eight hours at top speed.

Army Officers Notified.

On the part of the army, while Secretary Alger availed himself of the telegraph, Adjt. Gen. Corbin braved the storm and rushed across to the War Department, where he immediately issued the orders which had been prepared in advance to all of the military commanders to cease their operations. The State Department filled its duty by notifying all diplomatic and Consular agents of the action taken.

All the formalities having been disposed of, the President spent half an hour chatting with those present, and then, at 4:56, the rain still continuing in force, the Ambassador and his secretary entered their carriage and were driven to the embassy. The pen which was used by Secretary Day in signing the protocol was given to Chief Clerk Michael of the State Department, who had bespoken it. M. Thiebaut secured that used by the French Ambassador. Upon emerging from the White House, Secretary Day received the earnest congratulations of the persons present upon the conclusion of the protocol.

While the document signed is properly enough described as a protocol, it is still technically something more than that. So far as it goes, this protocol is absolutely a peace treaty. Thus having provided for the disposition of Cuba, Puerto Rico, and one of the Ladrone Islands there is nothing more for any Peace Commission to do in relation to those subjects; their fate is sealed, and the protocol in that respect is as binding as any definitive treaty of peace.

It was such a protocol as this that was signed by President Thiers and Prince Bismarck to terminate the Franco-Prussian war, and the conditions therein laid down were not even subject to revision at the hands of the Peace Commission that followed.

NOTICE TO CEASE FIGHTING.

Orders to Army and Navy Chiefs—Sampson and Schley Coming Here with Their Ships.

WASHINGTON, Aug. 12.—In accordance with the proclamation issued by the President suspending hostilities, orders were issued this evening to the naval commanders at the several stations in the United States, Cuba, and the Philippines carrying into effect the directions of the proclamation. The Navy Department not only transmitted the President's proclamation in full to the several Commanders in Chief, but also sent directions as to the disposition of their vessels. The following orders are in that sense self-explanatory:

"Navy Department,
"Washington, Aug. 12, 1898.

"Sampson, Santiago: Suspend all hostilities. Blockade of Cuba and Puerto Rico is raised. Howell ordered to assemble vessels at Key West. Proceed with New York, Brooklyn, Indiana, Oregon, Iowa, and Massachusetts to Tompkinsville. Place monitors in safe harbor in Puerto Rico. Watson transfers his flag to Newark, and will remain at Guantanamo. Assemble all cruisers in safe harbors. Order marines north in Resolute.

"ALLEN, Acting Secretary."

"Navy Department,
"Washington, Aug. 12, 1898.

"Remy, Key West: Accordance with the President's proclamation telegraphed you, suspend immediately all hostilities. Commence withdrawal of vessels from blockade. Order blockading vessels in Cuban waters to assemble at Key West.

"ALLEN, Acting Secretary."

The notification to Admiral Dewey was not made public, but Assistant Secretary Allen states that besides being put in possession of the President's proclamation, he was ordered to cease hostilities and raise the blockade of Manila.

In compliance with the orders sent, Admiral Sampson and Commodore Remy will each send a vessel around the coast of Cuba to notify the blockading squadron that the blockade has been raised.

Admiral Schley being on the Brooklyn, and included in the orders to that vessel, will come north with her.

The order sent by the War Department to Gen. Merritt to suspend hostilities was as follows:

"Adjutant General's Office,
"Washington, Aug. 12, 1898.

"Merritt, Manila: The President directs that all military operations against the enemy be suspended. Peace negotiations are nearing completion, a protocol having just been signed by representatives of the two countries. You will inform the commanders of the Spanish forces in the Philippines of these instructions. Further orders will follow. Acknowledge receipt.

"By order of the Secretary of War.

"H. C. CORBIN, Adjutant General."

The orders sent to Gen. Miles and Gen. Shafter were identical with the above, save as to names. As the order states, further instructions will be sent to each General. Gen. Merritt will be directed to confer with the Spanish commandant at Manila to carry out the terms of the protocol and to occupy Manila immediately. Gen. Miles will put himself in communication with the chief authority in Puerto Rico for the purpose of having Spanish forces turn over San Juan and other points to him preparatory to evacuation. Owing to conditions in Cuba the orders to Gen. Shafter, to be sent hereafter, will be very different from those to other Generals.

SHAFTER AND LEE REPLY.

WASHINGTON, Aug. 12.—At 11 o'clock to-night Adjt. Gen. Corbin received from Gen. Shafter an acknowledgment of the receipt by him of the proclamation of the President. Up to midnight no reply had been received from Gen. Miles, it having been impossible to get into communication with him.

All of the Corps Commanders of the army were notified of the suspension of hostilities. In response to the notification sent to Gen. Fitzhugh Lee, the former Consul General at Havana, wired the War Department:

"Thanks. The Seventh Corps has ceased firing. Unofficial."

It is well understood that Gen. Lee's command was being reserved for the attack upon Havana, if the necessity for one should arise. As an official of the War Department expressed it to-night: "It was a bit of the sarcasm of fate that Lee did

"All the News That's Fit to Print."

The New York Times.

WITH ILLUSTRATED WEEKLY MAGAZINE

COPYRIGHTED, 1898, BY THE NEW YORK TIMES COMPANY.

WITH ILLUSTRATED WEEKLY MAGAZINE

VOL. XLVIII...NO. 15,263. NEW YORK, SUNDAY, DECEMBER 11, 1898.—TWENTY-FOUR PAGES. PRICE FIVE CENTS.

THE WEATHER.

Partly cloudy; high westerly winds.

THE NEWS CONDENSED.

CLEMENT SCOTT RESIGNS.

The Well-Known Dramatic Critic Severs His Connection with The Daily Telegraph of London.

Cable Correspondence.

[Copyright, 1898, THE NEW YORK TIMES.]

LONDON, Dec. 10.—Clement Scott has resigned the post of dramatic critic on The Daily Telegraph.

Ever since 1873, Clement William Scott, or "Clemmy," as he is called by the dramatic and journalistic professions, has contributed articles of dramatic criticism to The Daily Telegraph. He has been the only critic in all London for whom a box was always reserved on "first nights." Managers have feelingly declared, when questioned, that they dared not do otherwise. Mr. Scott has so written that he has made many friends. He has also made many enemies.

About a year ago Mr. Scott stirred up a storm of anger and reproach in an interview prepared for a London publication entitled Great Thoughts, in which he was reported as saying that it was nearly impossible for a woman who adopts the stage as a profession to remain pure. He is said to have added that "the freedom of life, speech, and gesture behind the curtain renders it almost impossible for a woman to preserve that simplicity of manner which is her greatest charm."

Continuing, he was quoted with the remarks:

"What is infinitely more to be deplored is that a woman who endeavors to keep her purity is almost of a necessity foredoomed to failure in her career."

The resentment to his words was so great that the proprietors of The Daily Telegraph were asked to dismiss him. They increased his salary. The question was taken up in Paris, where well-known playwrights and managers were invited to contribute their ideas to Le Figaro concerning the correctness of Mr. Scott's dictum. Here in New York also some journals canvassed the actors and actresses then in the city on the subject. Mr. Scott received a [illegible] able amount of abuse from the local theatre people of all ranks and conditions.

In speaking of Mr. Scott's statement the late Harold Frederic said in his cable letter to THE NEW YORK TIMES of Sunday, Jan. 2, 1898:

"The public gets up but a languid interest in the manufactured frenzy of the actor world against Clement Scott. That his wholesale attacks on actresses was both stupid and unjust may all be, but the whole dramatic profession has been crawling on its belly before him for so many years, toadying to him for sugary notices, cringing under his criticism, buying plays from him which were never produced, that there is small wonder that he was emboldened to express his low opinion of it. There are all sorts of talk of physical violence, of the theatres boycotting The Daily Telegraph till he is discharged, and the like, but of actual sport and fear there will be very little. On both sides there is a wealth of rhetoric, and eloquent gestures of aversion and disdain, but not much else."

On April 7 last Mr. Scott made an abject apology in The Daily Telegraph, saying:

"I suggest that the words published, and which have evidently given such offense, were spoken at a moment of great mental strain, when my surroundings were such as to prevent me from clearly appreciating the distress they were likely to cause."

Sir Henry Irving, it is reported, accepted the apology for the profession. Mr. Frederic, in commenting on the affair, said in his letter which succeeded the publication of the apology: "The pity is that the interviewer had not the wit to grasp this view [Mr. Scott's view] of the situation and consign at least one sheet of his interview to the waste-paper basket."

With the exception of a few words of discontent at the alleged inadequacy of the apology from Mr. Willard, Mrs. Kendal, and some others, the matter was allowed to drop.

Mr. Scott is about fifty-seven years of age. At one time he had ambitions as a playwright, but his plays have not succeeded. In late years he has confined his efforts of this nature to prologues and epilogues and to verses which comedians recite at benefits. He has also written some verses for publication. He is the author of "Lays of a Londoner," "Poems for Recitation," and "Lays and Lyrics." He has also written "Round About the Islands," "Poppy Land Papers," and "Blossom Land," all being a collection of holiday articles contributed to The Daily Telegraph and other papers. In 1891 he edited the life and reminiscences of E. L. Blanchard, and in 1892 was part author of "The Fate of Fenella," and four or five years ago, as the result of foreign journeys, he wrote "Cheery Ceylon" and "Pictures of the World."

Previous to his connection with The Daily Telegraph, Mr. Scott was successively clerk in the War Office dramatic critic to The Sunday Times, to The Weekly Dispatch, and to The Observer.

He is considered to be the most widely known and most influential of any London critic. The oft-used phrase that he is the "leading dramatic critic of London" is capable of being interpreted in various ways. What Englishmen, Londoners, say it really means is that he is the critic for the daily paper with the largest circulation, and that his criticisms are consequently more widely read than those of his contemporaries; that he has appealed to the public in several capacities, hence his personality and name are familiar to the crowd. Whether Mr. Scott is the ablest of the London critics, whether his judgment is the best or not, are never-ceasing matters of discussion.

SKATERS NEARLY DROWNED.

WAKEFIELD JUNCTION, Mass., Dec. 10.—As a Boston and Maine train was passing Crystal Lake this forenoon some of the passengers saw two boys struggling in the water, surrounded by broken ice.

No one was near. The conductor stopped the train and five men ran to the lake and rescued the boys, who were almost exhausted. They had broken through while skating.

SLOT MACHINES HIS RUIN.

NEWARK, N. J., Dec. 10.—George Clark, thirteen years old, of 12 Straight Street, was arrested yesterday on a charge of grand larceny, having stolen watches from the offices of W. V. Egbert and Roe & Conover, in Mechanic Street. The first watch disappeared on Dec. 6 and the second two days following.

Young Clark displayed great cunning in disposing of his plunder. He knew that, on account of his youth, he could not pawn the watches without being regarded as suspicious, so he wrote a note and signed his mother's name to it, asking the pawnbroker to receive the watches as a pledge and stating that she wanted the money in order to obtain enough to enable her to make a trip to Ireland. When Clark got the money he gambled it away on the slot machines.

PEACE TREATY SIGNED AT LAST

An Impressive Ceremony at the French Foreign Office.

SPANIARDS WERE VERY GLOOMY

Afterward Made Acrid Remarks About American Bad Taste.

Were Annoyed by the Presence of Our Attaches and Their Eagerness to Secure Pens as Souvenirs.

PARIS, Dec. 10.—The treaty of peace was signed at 8:45 this evening.

The event would have afforded a subject for a great historical painting. The group gathered about the table in the stately chamber of the Foreign Office was impressive in itself; while the fact that the sense of the momentousness of the issues which the act decided was deeply felt by all the participants gave additional solemnity to the scene.

Around the great mahogany table sat the ten arbiters of the destinies of an old and a young nation. Ranged standing behind them were numerous attachés of the American Commission. The jets from the crystal chandeliers above the heads of those present magnified the brilliant green and scarlet of the upholsterings into gaudiness.

There was a theatrical contrast between the black-clothed actors and the scenery. To the Americans it was a happy ending of the epilogue of war; for the Spaniards it was plainly a bitter tragedy, none the less painful because long foreseen. They sat silently as though almost crushed, and none could withhold sympathy from Señor Montero Rios, the President of the Spanish Commission, who, coming from his bed, was bundled in a great overcoat, though logs were burning in the fireplace near by.

The spirits of the two bodies were symbolized by the clothes worn by the members of the commissions, for the Americans were attired in evening dress for the dinner given to them immediately after the meeting by the Duc de Loubat, and the Spaniards wore black frock coats.

Although the commissions met at 3:30 o'clock, expecting to finish their work in a half hour, the engrossing of the treaty on parchment was found to be such a lengthy task that at 5:15 a recess was taken until 7 o'clock. Clerk Martin of the American Commission worked all day without even stopping to eat. When he came into the chamber at 7:30 with the document he found the Commissioners waiting. The Spanish copy had arrived a half hour earlier.

Mr. Arthur Ferguson, the interpreter of the American Commission, then proceeded to read first the English, and after that the Spanish, version of the treaty. This finished, two copies were passed around the table, the Commissioners signing them in the order of their rank—Judge William R. Day, Senator Cushman K. Davis, Senator William P. Frye, Mr. Whitelaw Reid, and Senator George Gray; Señor Montero Rios, Señor Abarzuza, Señor Garnica, Señor Villaurutia, and Gen. Cerero y Saens—each commission signing its opponent's treaty. Both were tied with the Spanish and American colors.

When the seals were prepared to be affixed attendants were sent scurrying for ribbons of the French tricolor with which the documents were sealed, as a compliment to the French hosts of the commissions.

Many officials interestedly watched every detail of the proceedings.

The last seal being impressed, the Commissioners rose and without formality each shook the hands of all his antagonists and exchanged assurances of sincere personal esteem.

There has been a great contest among the families and friends of the American Commissioners for possession of the pens with which the signatures to the treaty were written. Some of the Americans were provided with handsome pens purchased for the purpose. The Spaniards appeared to be unaffected by the souvenir craze and contented themselves with the ordinary quill pens strewn on the table.

Mr. Arthur Ferguson requested Señor Montero Rios to give him his pen, saying:

"Have you any desire to preserve the pen with which you will sign?"

"Not in the slightest," said the Spaniard, with a courtly bow.

The signing was finished at 8:45. At that time the door of the chamber opened, and Señor Villaurutia appeared and exclaimed to a group of correspondents who were waiting in the corridor, "C'est fini." The other members of the Spanish Commission followed Señor Villaurutia, and hurried silently through the vestibule to their waiting carriage. The American Commission strolled out, chatting complacently, and, as they descended the steps, the lights in the chamber were darkened.

The Spaniards subsequently commented acridly upon what they termed the bad taste of the Americans in mustering a crowd of attachés to gloat over the consummation of their downfall and to scramble for relics.

The treaty as signed consists of seventeen articles, it having been found advisable to sub-divide two or three of the articles in the draft agreed upon at the last meeting.

The Commissioners of the two nations wrote their signatures on two copies of the treaty, one copy being for the archives.

The document was prepared by Secretary Moore in behalf of the United States Commission, and by Señor Villaurutia, for Spain, on account of the continued illness of Secretary Ojeda of the Spanish Commission.

Each copy contained the English and Spanish texts of the treaty in parallel columns. The wording had been approved previously by the commissions without a joint meeting, so there was no controversy on this subject.

THE NEWS IN WASHINGTON.

The President Is Congratulated, and in Turn Cables Congratulations to Our Peace Commissioners.

WASHINGTON, Dec. 10.—The official news of the signing of the peace treaty was received in Washington a little later than the press reports. It was in cipher form, as usual, from Judge Day. It was at once transmitted to the President, who was alone at the time, but within a comparatively short time all the members of the Cabinet had either called or sent their congratulations. The President's congratulations were promptly cabled to the commission.

The news of the signing having been so thoroughly discounted in advance, the actual receipt of the official advices created little stir here. There was a general feeling of relief, however, that no unforeseen circumstances intervened at the last moment to blockade the peaceful close of the negotiations.

THE NEXT MINISTER TO SPAIN.

Not Likely that Gen. Woodford Will Return to Madrid.

WASHINGTON, Dec. 10.—The peace treaty having been signed, the Government will be obliged very speedily to take steps looking to the restoration of the diplomatic machinery necessary to friendly relations with Spain. So far the President has not given much consideration to the selection of a United States Minister to Madrid.

The recent visit to the White House of Gen. Woodford, late Minister to that capital, has been erroneously construed to indicate a determination on the part of the President to return the Minister to Madrid. As a matter of fact, this is improbable, as the whole line of diplomatic precedent is in the direction of wiping out all old issues and starting afresh after a war with new Ministers on both sides. The reappointment of Mr. Woodford might mean the return to Washington of Señor Polo y Bernabe, whose residence in Canada during the war rendered him so obnoxious to the American public.

If custom is followed, either the next United States Minister to Madrid or the next Spanish Minister to Washington will be accredited with credentials as a special envoy to exchange the ratifications of the treaty now being negotiated at Paris. Having fulfilled that function he will then present his credentials as Minister Resident and will remain in that capacity.

Just which of the Ministers will be called upon to perform this function depends upon the place selected by the Paris Commissioners for the exchange of final ratifications.

SPAIN'S CABINET TOTTERING.

Its Resignation Is Expected to Follow the Signing of the Treaty of Peace.

LONDON, Dec. 10.—A special dispatch from Madrid says the position of the Cabinet is most critical, and that the resignation of the Ministry is expected as soon as the treaty of peace is signed.

In commercial circles, it is added, the fall of the Cabinet has been discounted, owing to the dull state of business and the heavy taxation.

MADRID, Dec. 10.—The Imparcial to-day says it hopes the Government will unreservedly approve of the energetic conduct of the Spanish Commissioners, and adds:

"Other nations must not think we are thorough cowards and will accept all kinds of humiliations. We congratulate the Spanish Commissioners on rendering a great service to the nation, which owes them deep gratitude."

How Spain Will Get Revenge.

LONDON, Dec. 10.—It is said that Spain has resolved to give permission for the cultivation of tobacco in the Spanish provinces. This will increase the revenue of Spain and she will also revenge herself on the United States, as the Spanish tobacco is expected to seriously compete with the American-grown weed.

COL. BRYAN WILL RESIGN.

Members of the Third Nebraska Understand that Their Commander Is About to Leave the Service.

SAVANNAH, Ga., Dec. 10.—Col. William Jennings Bryan of the Third Nebraska Regiment has either forwarded his resignation to Washington or is about to do so. Of this there seems to be no doubt. To-day he called upon Gen. Lee, commander of the Seventh Corps, and Gen. Keifer, commander of the Second Division of the corps, of which Col. Bryan's regiment is a part, and is understood to have announced his intention of quitting the service. Gen. Lee is to sail for Cuba on the transport to-morrow, and Col. Bryan is believed to have hastened his decision in order that he might acquaint his corps commander with his intention prior to his departure for the island. Neither of the commanding Generals would discuss the matter, and referred to Col. Bryan as the proper source to get any news.

Col. Bryan would neither deny nor confirm the rumor, but he said that when the time came he would prepare a written statement and give it to the press, so that there would be no possibility of any misstatement of his position.

"It is well to have the newspapers to talk through," he said, with a laugh. "They beat your hat all hollow."

Col. Bryan's regiment understands to-day that he will be its commander but a few days longer. Lieut. Col. Vifquain is quoted by other officers of the regiment as having told them that there would soon be promotions in the regiment, as Col. Bryan would resign and he would succeed him as Colonel.

GEN. MERRITT SAILS FOR HOME.

Likely to Resume Control of the Department of the East.

LONDON, Dec. 10.—Major Gen. Wesley Merritt, Mrs. Merritt, and the General's aide de camp, Lieut. Strother, sail from Liverpool for New York to-day on board the steamer Lucania.

WASHINGTON, Dec. 10.—Gen. Wesley Merritt recently notified the War Department that he probably would sail for home to-day. His return will be of special interest at this time, owing to his service in command of the first expedition to the Philippines, and later as Military Governor General of the islands, and also from the fact that he will be the first of those prominently identified with the work of the Peace Commission at Paris to reach here.

No decision has been reached as to Gen. Merritt's future command, but he probably will resume control of the Department of the East, with headquarters at New York, now temporarily held by Gen. Shafter.

TRAINS COLLIDE IN MICHIGAN.

Chicago and Northwestern Engines Crash Together Head On.

MENOMINEE, Mich., Dec. 10.—The southbound and the northbound passenger trains on the Chicago and Northwestern collided head on at 8 o'clock to-day 100 feet from the Menominee iron bridge. The northbound train, which was two hours late, had baggage and mail cars, two day coaches, and a sleeper, and carried seventy-five people.

The engines were badly smashed and the tender of the northbound was covered by the baggage car. A number of passengers were slightly hurt and some women fainted. H. Hanrahan, fireman of the northbound train, was badly injured and had to be cut out of the wreck. Engineer Michael Killian of the southbound train was hurt about the head.

Both trains were running at the same speed and they sustained about equal damage.

DEFENDS HER ACCUSED HUSBAND

New Hampshire Woman Declares She Was Shot by a Stranger.

CONCORD, N. H., Dec. 10.—Daniel Moses, a farmer of North Pembroke, whose wife was mysteriously shot and dangerously injured at her home yesterday morning, has been placed under arrest on suspicion of being his wife's assailant. This morning Moses was lodged in the Merrimac County jail, in this city.

Mr. Moses strongly declares his innocence, and Mrs. Moses, who is barely alive as the result of her wound, says that a stranger entered her home yesterday forenoon during the absence of her husband, and without uttering a word, shot her.

An investigation followed, which disclosed the fact that Mr. Moses possessed a revolver, which was found in a bureau drawer of Mrs. Moses's room, where the shooting took place. One chamber of the revolver was empty, and later both Mr. and Mrs. Moses said that the weapon had not been discharged for months. When told of the empty chamber, Mrs. Moses said she fired one shot at the fence a week ago.

THE MASSACHUSETTS HURT

Battleship Strikes a Sunken Obstruction Off Governors Island.

FIVE COMPARTMENTS LEAKING

Compelled to Return to the Navy Yard, Where She Will Have to Go Into Dry Dock for Repairs.

The United States battleship Massachusetts, while on her way from the Brooklyn Navy Yard to the anchorage off Tompkinsville, S. I., yesterday, struck a sunken obstruction near Diamond Reef off Castle Williams, Governor's Island, and sprung aleak in five of her forward water-tight compartments. The vessel was so badly injured that she was forced to put back to the navy yard, where she will be placed in dry dock for repairs.

There is a diversity of opinion as to the exact cause of the accident. The ship's officers as well as the navy yard officials are reticent about the matter, and it was impossible yesterday to determine the full extent of the injuries the battleship had sustained. That the vessel is seriously damaged, however, is indicated by the hurried preparations being made to dock her.

The Massachusetts left the navy yard yesterday shortly before noon. She was under orders to proceed to the naval anchorage off Tompkinsville, preliminary to sailing for Hampton Roads, where she was to join the North Atlantic Squadron for the annual manœuvres under Commodore Philip. The battleship left the yard under her own steam, with Naval Pilot James A. Bell directing her course.

While rounding Governors Island and off Castle William, the warship struck the obstruction hard enough to make her shiver from stem to stern. There was a momentary commotion aboard the big fighting craft, but the well-disciplined crew quickly regained its composure and calmly stood by awaiting orders. The engines were stopped at a signal from the pilot and the ship lay to.

Then it was discovered that the vessel had struck on the port side, near the bow, and that she was making water fast in five of the water-tight compartments on that side. The leaking compartments were quickly closed and the ship continued on her way to Tompkinsville, that being the nearest anchorage. Before getting under way again, Capt. Nicol Ludlow, commanding the battleship, signaled the fort on Governor's Island to telegraph to the navy yard to send three tugs to assist the Massachusetts, as she was leaking and in danger.

Rear Admiral Bunce, commandant of the navy yard, received a dispatch from Governors Island a few minutes later, and promptly ordered the powerful tug Wompatuck to the assistance of the battleship. The Wompatuck proceeded with all speed to Tompkinsville, where she found the Massachusetts at anchor.

When the tug arrived, Capt. Ludlow deemed it advisable to return to the navy yard without attempting to temporarily stop the leaks. The Massachusetts came back up the bay under her own steam, with the Wompatuck hovering about her, ready to lend assistance if needed. When the battleship entered the East River the tug took her in tow.

The Massachusetts had a slight list to port and was down by the head, just so much so that the red paint below her water line aft showed above the water. This was due to the water she had taken in her forward compartments. When the Wompatuck with her tow reached the mouth of Wallabout Basin she made vain efforts to get her unwieldy charge inside.

The appearance of the battleship down by the head and with a list to one side, coupled with the apparent distress of her convoy, the tug, threw a scare into the navy yard officials. They believed that the Massachusetts was sinking, and the navy yard tugs Nina and Narkeeta were sent out to assist the Wampatuck. The three tugs, after half an hour's hard work, succeeded in getting the battleship into the berth she had vacated, at the foot of Main Street.

As soon as the Massachusetts was moored to the dock Capt. Ludlow went ashore and reported to Admiral Bunce, who in turn reported the matter by wire to Washington. Naval Constructor Hill went aboard the ship to make an examination for the purpose of determining the extent of her injuries.

Capt. Ludlow gave orders to exclude everybody but the navy yard officials from the ship. When Constructor Hill left the vessel he was questioned as to the ship's injuries, but he refused to talk. Capt. Ludlow and Admiral Bunce also declined to make any statement.

From another source, however, it was learned that the ship's plates for a distance of about 15 feet on her port side forward had been either started or ripped open by the blow. As she lay at her dock there was four feet of water in her five leaking compartments, despite the fact that her pumps had been kept working steadily from the time the accident happened.

The officers and crew of the ship who could be induced to talk gave it as their opinion that the vessel had struck a spur of the reef off Governors Island. Pilot Bell, however, expressed an altogether different opinion. He was positive, he said, that the battleship did not strike a reef, but that she grounded in the channel.

The tide at the time the vessels struck, he said, was fully four feet lower than usual, and there was a correspondingly lesser depth of water in the channel off Castle William. Pilot Bell declared that he had taken the battleship Oregon safely through the same channel when she sailed for Manila a short time ago.

The Oregon, he said, drew twenty-seven feet of water, while the Massachusetts' draught was but a small fraction over twenty-six feet. If the Oregon, with her greater draught, could safely navigate the channel, he declared, it was reasonable to assume that the Massachusetts could also, unless, as he had said, the tide was abnormally low. He was certain that if the ship had struck the reef, as claimed, she could not have been kept afloat. On the way back from Tompkinsville, the pilot said, the Massachusetts passed within fifteen feet of the spot where she had struck.

The Massachusetts will be placed in Dry Dock No. 3 as soon as possible. The cruiser Newark is at present in the dock being overhauled. As this dock is the only one at the yard which can accommodate a ship of the size of the Massachusetts, the Newark will have to be floated out before the battleship can be docked.

The Massachusetts is a first-class battleship. She is a sister ship of the Iowa and Indiana, and is one of the finest vessels in the navy. The Massachusetts has been in service about four years. She cost $3,020,000 to build, has a displacement of 10,288 tons, is 348 feet long on the load waterline, has twin-screw vertical triple-expansion engines of 9,000 horse power.

The maximum speed of the ship is sixteen knots. She carries a complement of about 450 officers and men, and her armament consists of 4 thirteen-inch guns, 20 six-pounder rapid-fire guns, 6 one-pounder rapid-fire guns, and 4 Gatling guns. In addition, she is fitted with 6 torpedo tubes. Her commander is Capt. Nicol Ludlow, formerly commanding officer of the monitor Terror. Lieut. Schroeder is executive officer of the ship and Lieut. Potts navigator.

The Massachusetts engaged in the bombardment and blockade of Santiago and in the destruction of Cervera's fleet. At the cessation of hostilities she came North with other ships of Sampson's fleet and after the naval parade in these waters went to the Brooklyn Navy Yard for an overhauling.

THE CLEVELAND BAR SCANDAL.

Burke to be Expelled and Judge Dellenbaugh Investigated.

CLEVELAND, Dec. 10.—State Senator Vernon H. Burke will be expelled from the Cleveland Bar Association. Judge Frank E. Dellenbaugh will be investigated.

This the Bar Association decided to do at its meeting this afternoon. The conclusion was not reached, however, until after three hours of deliberation. Then the vote was taken by calling the roll. The result was largely in favor of adopting the report as submitted by the Trial Committee. This carried with it the expulsion of Burke and the investigation of Dellenbaugh.

James A. Garfield, Chairman of the meeting, announced that the findings of the Investigating Committee would be presented to the Circuit Court for such action as it might consider proper.

BRITISH BOOKS AND AUTHORS.

Gladstonian Documents Pouring in Upon John Morley.

[Copyright, 1898, THE NEW YORK TIMES.]

Cable Correspondence.

LONDON, Dec. 10.—A new edition of "The Open Question", will, by bearing Elizabeth Robins's name on the title page, confirm the news I cabled three weeks ago.

Sir Robert Peel's papers are to be published by Messrs. Murray in January, and will contain important correspondence with the Queen, the Duke of Wellington and with many other statesmen of the period of 1827-41.

Gladstoniana, in response to John Morley's request, has been supplied in such number that the Macmillans have set aside certain rooms in their new building to accommodate and classify them all. The documents at Hawarden are to be dealt with by Mr. Morley on the spot.

NEW PLAYS IN LONDON.

Dialogue for "The Egoist" Written by George Meredith Himself.

[Copyright, 1898, THE NEW YORK TIMES.]

Cable Correspondence.

LONDON, Dec. 10.—Stephen Phillips has finished a play in verse, founded upon the story of Paolo and Francesca, for George Alexander.

George Meredith has himself written all the dialogue in the dramatization of "The Egoist," which Forbes Robertson and Mrs. Patrick Campbell will produce on a date not yet fixed. Meredith feels some anxiety whether the British public will like a play in which the central figure is not a sympathetic character.

George Alexander will produce in January Mrs. Craigie's play, called "A Repentance." The scene is laid in Spain in 1835. The action deals with the Carlist struggle. He has also accepted a three-act play, "The Leaden Casket," by Miss Margaret Young, a new playwright.

A melodrama by Sutton Vane in five acts is to be produced at the Princess Theatre Christmas Eve. It is adapted from "La Jeunesse d'Orgue," by Xavier de Montépin and Jules Dornay.

FRANK HARRIS'S NEW VENTURE.

Reported that the London Editor Will Open a Hotel at Monte Carlo.

[Copyright, 1898, THE NEW YORK TIMES.]

Cable Correspondence.

LONDON, Dec. 10.—It is reported that Frank Harris, late editor of The Saturday Review, is going to Monte Carlo to run a hotel there.

CAUGHT IN BANK OF ENGLAND.

Armed Man Supposed to be Mad or an Anarchist Arrested at Night After Desperate Resistance.

LONDON, Dec. 10.—A wretched, middle-aged, wild-looking man was arrested at the Bank of England at 11 o'clock to-night, after a sharp struggle.

According to one account, the man rang the bell at the main entrance of the bank, and when the janitor opened the door the man rushed in and drew a revolver, which he was prevented from usuing by the military guard, with fixed bayonets, closing around him.

Another version of the affair is that he managed to gain admittance in some unexplained manner, and offered as an excuse for his presence in the bank the statement that he wanted to cash a check.

However this may be, he made a frantic resistance when taken into custody.

In his pockets were found a loaded revolver, a dozen silver and several gold foreign coins, and some jewelry.

The man speaks English with a foreign accent, and it is suspected that he is an Anarchist. When questioned at the police station he gave the name of George Taylor. He was examined by a doctor, who ordered his removal to Bow Infirmary.

The news of the affair spread rapidly through the neighborhood, and a crowd quickly surrounded the entrance to the bank.

THE LONDON EMBASSY.

Report that the Post Had Been Offered to Whitelaw Reid Not Confirmed in Washington.

WASHINGTON, Dec. 10.—Renewed interest was excited to-night in the expected appointment of an Ambassador to Great Britain by the report from London that the President has offered the embassy to Whitelaw Reid, and that he has been urged to accept it.

Indications of this kind have been heard here before this week, and THE NEW YORK TIMES was informed that it was understood that Secretary Hay indicated a preference for Mr. Reid because of the fact that he does not altogether lack diplomatic experience.

The President is averse to talking about this matter, and at the White House the report could not be verified or denied. Secretary Hay was absent from his home this evening, but on all occasions when appointments have been mentioned to him he has declined to say anything about a matter that is strictly the affair of the President.

State Department officers who have read the recent reports about the probable appointment to London regard the chances of Mr. Reid to be quite as good as those of either of the gentlemen who have been named. The reported opposition of Mr. Platt to Mr. Reid will not, they believe, be stubborn.

THE WEATHER.

The local forecast may be found at the top of this page to the right of the title.

The weather conditions have moderated greatly from the Rocky Mountains to the Mississippi River. A rise in temperature of 18 to 20 degrees is reported from Northern Missouri and in Iowa.

The storm in the Gulf of St. Lawrence has increased markedly in intensity, Father Point reporting a pressure of 29.28 inches, a fall of .30 of an inch in the past twenty-four hours. This storm has caused gales in the lake regions and on the Atlantic Coast, Buffalo reporting a west wind of fifty-six miles an hour. Rain has fallen in the Gulf and in the South Atlantic States and light snow in the lower lake region.

Storm signals are displayed on Lake Superior and on the lower lakes from Detroit to Oswego; also on the Atlantic Coast from Delaware Breakwater to Eastport.

The record of temperature for the twenty-four hours ended at midnight, taken from THE NEW YORK TIMES's thermometer and from the thermometer of the Weather Bureau, is as follows:

	—Weather Bureau.— 1897.	1898.	Times. 1898.
3 A. M.	45	26	31
6 A. M.	42	25	30
9 A. M.	44	24	30
12 M.	52	26	34
4 P. M.	55	31	36
6 P. M.	53	31	34
9 P. M.	52	29	32
12 P. M.	50	28	32

THE TIMES's thermometer is 6 feet above the street level; that of the Weather Bureau is 265 feet above the street level.

Average temperatures yesterday were as follows:

Printing House Square	32
Weather Bureau	28
Corresponding date 1897	48
Corresponding date for last twenty years	36

The maximum temperature yesterday was 32 degrees at 3 P. M. and the minimum 28 degrees at 7:30 A. M. The humidity at 8 A. M. and 8 P. M. was 66 per cent.

MILLER WINS CYCLE RACE

Champion Rides 2,007 Miles and Eclipses All Records.

MARRIED IN A RACING SUIT

Ceases Pedaling Long Enough to Wed Miss Hanson—Waller Finishes Second and Pierce Third.

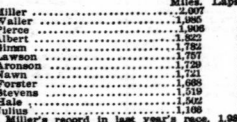

	Miles.	Laps.
Miller	2,007	4
Waller	1,985	2
Pierce	1,906	7
Albert	1,822	6
Gimm	1,782	2
Lawson	1,757	6
Aronson	1,729	5
Nawn	1,721	7
Forster	1,688	8
Stevens	1,519	8
Hale	1,502	2
Julius	1,166	7

Miller's record in last year's race, 1,983 miles 883 yards.

Charles W. Miller of Chicago won the six-day bicycle race, finishing at 10 o'clock last night. He beat the record he made last year by 23 miles and 1,587 yards. He added $2,650 to his bankroll and took to himself a wife.

This is a pretty good record for one man to make in one day, and according to those who went to the Madison Square Garden last night Miller is a good man, and he was cheered and cheered again when he rode around the ring in advance of all the other riders who finished a few minutes before 10 o'clock.

In the last twenty-two hours of the race, or from 12:08 A. M. to the finish, Miller rode 220 miles and 5 laps. He rested frequently, not because of his inability to keep on with the race, but because there was no necessity for him to exert himself to any extent.

He was a long way ahead of Waller, the second man in the race, and all he wanted to do was to stay in front and to reel off enough laps to enable him to beat the record and so win the extra $200 offered for this accomplishment.

With the public the most important of the many happenings of yesterday was the fact that Miller won the race, and the next that he beat the record, but to Miller the most important event of that very eventful day was his marriage to Miss Genevieve Hanson of Chicago.

Miller had been pleading with this young woman ever since the last race, but she had been coy and continually put him off. Before he entered or the race just ended, she made the wedding conditional on his finishing first, and so Miller had an additional stimulus to make him ride.

"Pat" Powers, one of the managers of the race, conceived the idea of having the two married in the Garden as soon as it was certain that Miller had won, and arrangements were made for the wedding, which Mrs. O'Donnell, the mother of the bride, sanctioned.

The time fixed was yesterday afternoon, and all the necessary arrangements were soon completed. A wedding in such a place as Madison Square Garden is a novelty to New Yorkers, and the big building was crowded when the ceremony took place.

The bride had been in the Garden constantly since the race was started, and every one who has visited the race has seen her. She retired to prepare for the wedding early in the afternoon, and Miller quit the track a few minutes after 3 o'clock.

At 4:40 o'clock the band started to play the Wedding March and "They're coming!" was shouted about the arena. The crowd had to wait a little while, though, and after a few minutes the wedding procession was seen walking down the north side of the track from the Madison Avenue end.

"Pat" Powers was in the lead. He had on a new silk hat, which he had just purchased for the occasion. He blushed, so it was said, as he walked down the track, and some thought he was the bridegroom.

Arthur Gardiner, the well-known bicycle rider, wearing a frock coat, silk hat, and gloves, and with a big chrysanthemum in the lapel of his coat, was the next in the procession.

Next came the bride and with her was Mrs. Schineer, the wife of one of the contestants. The bride's costume was a dove-colored broadcloth dress, with a small hat and gloves to match. She carried a bouquet of Bride roses.

Mrs. O'Donnell followed. The crowd cheered itself hoarse and the bride blushed. Mr. Powers led the way to Box 45, which had been specially decorated with floral pieces and bunting for the occasion, and over which Capt. Price kept guard and gracefully handed the bride to a seat.

Then the crowd began to shout for Miller, and he was soon seen emerging from one of the side entrances, clad in an orange-and-white bath robe, and accompanied by his trainer, West. A tremendous cheer greeted the bridegroom, and Miller smiled faintly.

When he reached the box Trainer West lifted him up and stood him by the side of the bride, facing the crowd, which continued to shout and cheer.

Miller threw off his bathrobe and displayed a wonderful costume. He was clad in a new racing suit and the colors were gorgeous. The tights were pink and white, one leg pink and the other white.

His sweater was blue and white, and over this he wore a shirt colored like his tights, only the colors were reversed so that the pink half of the shirt came over the white leg of the tights. Around his waist was a silk American flag, and on the back of the shirt was embroidered an eagle and shield.

Miller was self-possessed and appeared to think nothing more of what was about to take place than he did of the race that he had practically won.

When all was ready Alderman Wentz appeared on the track. He went to the box and arranged every one in it as he thought they should be. He asked the pair a few questions, and then declared them man and wife and blessed them by virtue of Aldermanic dignity.

This was the signal for more cheers, and during the cheering Powers, Gardiner, and others who were around the box kissed the bride and congratulated Miller.

Waller, who was sitting in the front of the box, caused a little fun at this time by rushing up the stairs, grasping Miller by the hand, and then, going up to the bride, he gave her a kiss that could be heard halfway across the Garden. Then the band played "Auld Lang Syne," and Mr. and Mrs. Miller held a brief reception in the box. Presently Miller got on his wheel and rode around the Garden at racing speed for a few minutes, and the crowd cheered again.

At the time the wedding ceremony took place, Miller had ridden 1,970 miles. Announcer Prunty said that he would take a short rest and would then go for the record, which he intended to beat before the race was over. This caused more cheering, and then the crowd began to thin out.

Miller returned to the track shortly before 6 o'clock, and then went to work at the record. Lap after lap he reeled off, and at 6:35 o'clock he equaled the score he made in the race last year—1,983 miles 883 yards. At 7 o'clock he had made 1,990 miles 6 laps, and still he kept on. At 8 o'clock the scoring board showed 2,000 miles, and after riding 6 more miles Miller left the track.

At 9 o'clock every one of the six-day men had gone off the track, and exhibition miles were ridden by some of the crack bicyclists. For a while things were dull, but at 9:45 o'clock all the men who had staid on the track for six days came out again. They went to the old starting place, and were arranged in the order in which they had finished in the race. Then they were started again, with Miller in the front, Waller next, followed by Pierce, Albert, Gimm, Lawson, Aronson, Nawn, Forster, Stevens, Hale, and Julius.

They looked like new men, and it was hard to recognize the men who had been riding in the big race. They all had on clean clothes, had been shaved, and nearly all looked as though they were ready to start in another contest instead of just finishing one. All the cuts and bruises seemed to have disappeared. They rode around for five minutes and then the race ended with the score as at the head of this column.

This did not satisfy the crowd, though, and every one began to shout for Miller, "the champion of the world." Manager Powers, who was master of ceremonies, told Miller to walk around the track with his trainer. Miller started, and West carried a big floral piece on which the word "Miller" was formed of pink roses.

"All the News That's Fit to Print."

The New York Times.

WITH ILLUSTRATED WEEKLY MAGAZINE

WITH ILLUSTRATED WEEKLY MAGAZINE

THE WEATHER.
Fair; high westerly winds diminishing.

VOL. XLVIII..NO. 15,287. NEW YORK, SUNDAY, JANUARY 8, 1899.—TWENTY-FOUR PAGES. PRICE FIVE CENTS.

THE NEWS CONDENSED.

Stock market variable.

CONGRESS. — Representative Grosvenor (Rep., Ohio,) addressed the House yesterday concerning the attitude of the political parties of the country toward the financial question. The House, in Committee of the Whole, resumed consideration of the Legislative, Executive, and Judicial Appropriation bill. Mr. Handy (Dem., Del.,) introduced a bill authorizing American registry for foreign-built ships engaged in the foreign carrying trade when owned by citizens of the United States. The Senate passed the District of Columbia Appropriation bill, and the House bill, authorizing extra pay for volunteers. Mr. Mason (Rep., Ill.,) offered a resolution against the forcible annexation of territory, and will address the Senate upon it Tuesday. Mr. Allen, (Pop., Neb.,) referring to another protest from Southern veterans against the pensioning of Confederates, said he believed Senator Butler, who introduced the suggested amendment, and the President were carried "away by their feelings."—Page 5.

FOREIGN.—At a meeting yesterday evening of the Conservative Club at Madrid, Señor Silvela confirmed the reported agreement between himself and Gen. Polavieja, and made an important announcement of the Conservative policy in Spain, declaring himself as favoring the liberal encouragement of industries and the reorganization of the army and navy. It is believed Premier Sagasta will retire from politics. The recent speech of Viscount Cromer to Soudanese Sheiks, in which he outlined the policy of government in the Soudan, is still receiving approval in England, and, according to advices, provoking much consternation among the French. It is said the case of Cerrutti, involving the peaceful relations of Italy and Colombia, will soon be definitely decided. It is reported from Berlin that the Meat Inspection bill, which is about to become law, will not seriously interfere with the American trade. William Waldorf Astor, who has sued The London Daily Mail for libel for publishing a story that he gave a dinner to forty persons around the trunk of a California tree in order to win a wager, will be heard in court soon. Brazil has abolished two naval and three military arsenals. Count Karolyi, Attaché of the Austria-Hungary Embassy at London, is reported to have committed suicide at London yesterday.—Pages 7 and 19.

Page 1.

Representative Dingley grows constantly weaker and a change for the worse may occur at any time.

There was still no arrest in the Adams poisoning case yesterday. It was learned that men in high places would be subject to disagreeable exposure in case the suspected person was arrested.

A Syrian boy, lost overboard from the Ellis Island ferryboat, was picked up in the bay by a tug yesterday morning, clinging to a cake of ice.

Gov. Roosevelt had a busy day yesterday, rushing about the city to keep various engagements. He had talks with several political leaders.

Within a few hours after Gen. Otis had promulgated his proclamation to the Filipinos, the agents of Aguinaldo billed the town of Manila with a manifesto in which the rebels display resistance to American sway in the Philippines.

Page 2.

"Count" Mariano de Zaremba was held yesterday in the Centre Street Police Court for the larceny of $40.50.

The Business Men's Democratic Association celebrated Jackson Day last night at the Hotel Savoy with a dinner, at which the Democratic Congressmen-elect from this city were the guests of honor.

Admiral Sampson was the guest of honor last night at a dinner given by the Colonial Club. Gov. Roosevelt, Capt. Evans, Capt. Mahan, and Gen. Tracy were among those who made addresses.

The Cercle Français de l'Harmonie held its thirty-third annual dinner, preceding its annual ball, at Sherry's last night. President Maurice F. Holahan of the Board of Public Improvements outlined a number of improvements which, he said, the board had in mind, among them being a system of drainage to cover 17,000 acres of the outlying districts of Brooklyn.

Page 4.

Congressman Sulzer made an address at the Jacksonian Club banquet in Omaha last night.

William Jennings Bryan made a caustic attack upon expansion and the adoption of an imperialist policy by the United States at a Jackson Day banquet in Chicago.

Louis Gimm won the twenty-four-hour bicycle race at the Garden, finishing a few inches ahead of Pierce. Turville was third and Fredericks fourth.

Page 7.

The Spanish Bank of the Island of Cuba has been made the agent of the War Department for the collection of taxes in the island.

Page 9.

The Havana Electric Railway Company, capitalized at $5,000,000, was incorporated in New Jersey yesterday.

Page 11.

Gov. Smith of Vermont has appointed Benjamin F. Fifield of Montpelier as Mr. Morrill's successor in the United States Senate.

A friendly suit has been brought in the Supreme Court for permission to sell the residence at 105 and 107 Fifth Avenue, part of the estate of the late Marshall O. Roberts.

Page 12.

Increased pay for several city employes in the various boroughs was announced yesterday.

Angelo Lamrano, alleged to be a member of a dangerous gang of counterfeiters, was arrested yesterday aboard the Concho, ready to sail for Havana.

J. M. Martin of London yesterday delivered the first of his lectures before the League for Political Education. His subject was "Practical Socialism on the London County Council."

Justice Gaynor, in the Supreme Court, in Brooklyn yesterday adjudged invalid a clause in the will of James M. Waterbury, leaving $50,000 to Eastern District charitable institutions.

Page 13.

The quickness and bravery of Policeman Teever of the East One Hundred and Twenty-sixth Street Station probably saved the life yesterday of little Rosie Dowd of 2,395 First Avenue.

Page 19.

Henry Norman in his weekly cable letter says that the announcement of the coming appointment of Mr. Choate as Ambassador to the Court of St. James's has been received in the warmest possible manner by the London press. The proposed visit of the American fleet to Portsmouth is an event offering the American Ambassador great opportunities, it is said. The English Liberals are getting ready for action on the opening of Parliament. It is expected that the leadership of the Opposition will be offered to Sir Henry Campbell-Bannerman, but that he will refuse it, and that Mr. Herbert H. Asquith will finally accept the position. The Gladstone memorial is not meeting with a popular response. Only £22,000 out of £50,000 has so far been contributed. Rapid-fire field guns are to be provided the English artillery batteries as soon as possible. The weapon is a modification of the Vickers-Maxim gun, which gave such a fine record at some recent gun trials. The police of Leith, in Scotland, the other day published by mistake a royal proclamation calling out the army reserve, militia, and volunteers. The men assembled for duty. This is cited to show that the British Government has all along believed the situation to be very grave. It is still thought in London that a revolution is imminent in Paris. Some notes are given concerning the personality of Prince Victor. The publication of the correspondence between the French and British Governments regarding Madagascar is commented on in the light of recent complications, as is also the coming discussion over the French treaty rights in Newfoundland, and Lord Salisbury's reply to the Czar's note calling for a convention on armaments. The Czar is said to be contemplating some radical reforms in the treatment of prisoners in Siberia.

AGUINALDO IS DEFIANT

Issues a Manifesto at Manila After Gen. Otis's Proclamation.

PROTESTS AGAINST OUR SWAY

Says We Recognized Rebels as Belligerents—Urges His Followers to Stand Firm.

MANILA, Jan. 7.—Within a few hours of the proclamation issued by Gen. Otis, in behalf of President McKinley, the agents of Aguinaldo billed Manila with a manifesto which attracted considerable attention. The revolutionary President protested against Gen. Otis signing himself Military Governor of the Philippine Islands.

Aguinaldo in this manifesto declared he had never agreed, at Singapore, Hongkong, or elsewhere, to recognize the sovereignty of the Americans here, and insisted that he returned to the Philippines on an American warship solely to conquer the Spaniards and win independence. He asserted that both his proclamations of May 24 and June 12 stated this fact officially, and he claimed that Major Gen. Merritt confirmed this by a proclamation days before the Spaniards capitulated, stating clearly and definitely that the American forces came to overthrow the Spanish Government and liberate the Filipinos.

In conclusion, Aguinaldo declared that he had natives and foreigners as witnesses that the American forces recognized not only by acts that the Filipinos were belligerents but by publicly saluting the Filipino flag "as it triumphantly sailed these seas before the eyes of all nations."

Aguinaldo then solemnly protested, in the name of the Deity who empowered him to direct his brethren in the difficult task of regeneration, against the intrusion of the American Government, and reiterated that he can produce proof that he was brought here on the understanding that the Americans promised him their co-operation to attain independence.

The revolutionary leader then called upon all his followers to work together with force, assuring them he is convinced that they will obtain absolute independence, urging them never to return "from the glorious road" on which they have "already so far advanced."

Gen. Otis attaches no importance to the manifesto. He says he feels confident that the opinion of the better classes of the Filipinos is not expressed in it, but as to whether the Filipino masses can be controlled and the Filipino Army kept in check he does not know, although he hopes for a pacific outcome of the trouble.

MADRID, Jan. 7.—Gen. Rios, in command of the Spanish troops in the Philippine Islands, cables that the hostility between the Americans and the Tagalos is increasing.

REINFORCEMENTS FOR MANILA.

Secretary Long Sends the Solace, Princeton, and Yorktown to the Philippines—War Department's Preparations.

WASHINGTON, Jan. 7.—The activity of the Navy and War Departments in preparing for an emergency in the Philippines dictates that there will be no delay in sending adequate naval and military forces to the archipelago.

Secretary Long has ordered the Solace to proceed to Manila as soon as she can be made ready for the voyage. Admiral Dewey has asked for supplies of various kinds, and the Solace will carry a heavy load of these, sufficient to supply the fleet on the Asiatic station for six months at least.

The vessel will be attached to Admiral Dewey's fleet, and in all probability, if this voyage turns out successfully, she will form one of a regular line of transports which will ply between the United States and the Philippines for the special benefit of the navy.

The Solace is a large ship, of about 6,000 tons burden and of comparatively light draught. She was fitted up at the beginning of the war by the Medical Department as a hospital ship, being the first vessel of that type ever put afloat.

The vessel is now at the New York Navy Yard and is expected to sail for Manila via the Mediterranean and Suez in about two weeks. The Navy Department is now making up the detail of her officers.

The department has not yet finally decided upon the increase of naval strength to be allowed Admiral Dewey. Apparently he is in want of small, light-draught gunboats, but it is believed at the department that when the vessels now under way or ordered to Manila reach there, they, with the renovated Spanish gunboats captured by Admiral Dewey, will give him a sufficient force of vessels of this class.

The department has given some consideration to the feasibility of employing in this service some of the larger converted yachts which rendered such effective service on the blockade. The difficulty is that few of them suited for the work from their light draught are large enough to make the long run from Aden across the Gulf of Arabia and the Bay of Bengal to Singapore. Of the few converted yachts that might meet this requirement, the Gloucester, which participated in the battle of July 3 so brilliantly, has been most favorably considered, though the Navy Department has not yet concluded to make use of her.

Besides the Solace, Secretary Long has ordered the gunboats Princeton and Yorktown to the same point. The Princeton is now at New York and will go via Suez. The Yorktown is at San Francisco, and will cross the Pacific.

The War Department issued orders to-day that the three transports now being prepared for the Philippines shall be named as follows: The Mohawk shall hereafter be known as Grant, in honor of the late Gen. U. S. Grant; the Mobile shall be known as Sherman, in honor of the late Gen. William T. Sherman, and the Massachusetts as Sheridan, in honor of the late Gen. P. H. Sheridan. In addition, it has been decided to name two other transports yet to be selected the Thomas and the Logan.

Secretary Alger has decided to send four regiments of infantry to the islands. The Fourth, Twelfth, and Seventeenth have been designated, and, in addition, the Third Infantry, now at Fort Snelling, Minn., will go by the same route—namely, across the Atlantic. The telegraphic orders of the 5th inst., directing that six companies of the Seventeenth Infantry accompany the Fourth Infantry, to sail Jan. 15, have been modified so as to read:

"One battalion of four companies of the Seventeenth, the remaining eight companies to sail later."

THE GERMANS AT ILOILO.

Reported that Gen. Rios Asked Them for Protection and Was Refused.

The New Yorker Staats-Zeitung will publish to-day the following from its Berlin special cable correspondent:

"I am informed, from an unquestionable source, that after the surrender of Iloilo the Spanish General tried to induce the German Consul at Manila and the German Vice Consul at Iloilo to take charge of the protection of the private interests of the Spaniards. The two Consuls wired to Berlin for instructions, and received the following answer:

"'The German Empire, being a neutral power, is not in a position to take charge of functions which could easily be construed as partiality for Spain. All we endeavor to obtain in the Philippines is protection and unrestricted movement of our commerce. Since we see that both are secured under the United States flag we are fully confident that there will never arise a situation which could cause us to deviate from the strictly neutral attitude observed by us up to this day.'

"The Washington Government has been notified of this declaration."

LAWTON ON AN INSPECTION TOUR.

He Says Only Strong Soldiers Will Be Taken to Manila.

PITTSBURG, Penn., Jan. 7.—Major Gen. H. W. Lawton, who commanded a division at Santiago, will go to Chicago in a few days to inspect the troops at Fort Sheridan, who have been ordered to join the first Philippine expedition, leaving New York on the 15th. Some of the troopers who are anticipating a trip to Manila will be disappointed. Asked why he will make the inspection, Gen. Lawton said:

"The Government can't afford to send men on a long trip like this who are physically unfit for such a fatiguing voyage. All the weaklings will be culled out and the very choice of American manhood will compose the rank and file of the army which the Europeans will see for the first time. I will sail on the Mohawk. We expect that official note of our passage will be taken by the foreigners.

"It will be a strange sight to see the boys in blue sailing along on the clear waters of the Mediterranean, and the great powers will not be blind to its significance. They have not seen much of us over there since the days of Decatur, and it will surely have a good effect on the "unspeakable Turk." The ships will sail in small fleets in order to prevent congestion at the coaling stations."

Asked about the outlook for trouble in Cuba, Gen. Lawton said it will come from the professional revolutionists.

SIR WALTER BESANT'S "GUIDE."

The Way Publishers Conduct Their Business Severely Criticised.

(Copyright, 1899.)
Special Cablegram to THE NEW YORK TIMES.

LONDON, Jan. 7.—Sir Walter Besant's guide to literary aspirants, which was announced a fortnight ago, has now been privately published under the title of "The Pen and the Book," and is certain to provoke bitter controversy. Along with much very valuable and experienced advice to young people desirous of entering upon the profession of letters, with instructions how to qualify themselves for its various branches, the book contains elaborate criticisms of the relations between authors and publishers and analyses of the cost of production, intended to show that publishers make excessive profits at the cost of authors.

The following extract shows the direct nature of Sir Walter's attack: "I have no hesitation whatever in alleging as a simple fact that it has been brought home to me by ten or twelve years of investigation into the commercial side of literature, that many publishers, including some of the great houses, have made it their common practice to take secret percentages on the cost of every item, to charge advertisements which they have not paid for, and in this manner to take from the proceeds of the book very much more than they were entitled to by agreement.

"Some have tried to soothe the reproaches of outraged conscience by pretending the custom of the trade. Why, then, is the practice secret? A custom of the trade is a thing known and recognized by both parties to the bargain. This is of course nonsense. They know and they must know that they are thieving."

TWO CANADA SHIPS OVERDUE.

The Damara and Manchester Trader Have Not Arrived at Halifax.

ST. JOHN'S, N. F.—The Furness Line steamer Damara, Capt. Wilson, from Liverpool Dec. 18 for St. John's and Halifax, is still overdue. She is now twenty-one days out, and, as no tidings have been received here, it is feared that she has broken down if not foundered. She has a number of passengers on board, besides a crew of thirty men.

Incoming vessels report tempestuous weather in the Atlantic. Several small coasting vessels have been driven off and may go to the bottom. Many more have sought harbor. All the latter have lost sails, rigging, or spars.

HALIFAX, N. S., Jan. 7.—The Beaver Line steamer Tongariro, which arrived to-day from Liverpool with 300 passengers, reports a succession of heavy head gales. The steamer was fourteen days on the passage, which was one of the roughest voyages in years. High seas accompanied the gales, but only minor damage was sustained. The Tongariro saw nothing of the overdue steamers Damara and Manchester Trader, both running in the Furness Line. It is thought possible one steamer is disabled and in tow of the other. The Manchester Trader is eighteen days overdue.

SPALDING WANTS FREEDOM.

The Former Chicago Banker Asks to be Released from Jail.

CHICAGO, Jan. 7.—Charles Warren Spalding, convict and ex-banker, is an applicant for official clemency before the State Board of Pardons, which will convene at Springfield on Tuesday. The petition filed in his behalf by his attorney, Ross C. Hall, declares that the former head of the Globe Savings Bank has already suffered sufficient punishment for his alleged crimes, and death will soon claim him unless he is again allowed the associations he once enjoyed. It is claimed, however, by some lawyers that should Spalding be released even on parole he could be arrested and prosecuted on one of the twenty-six indictments found against him by the Grand Jury.

In his fight for release from the penitentiary at Joliet Spalding has enlisted the services of twoscore well-known business and professional men.

ACCUSED OF TRAIN ROBBERY.

Arrest of Men Charged with Stopping an Express in Missouri.

MANSFIELD, Mo., Jan. 7.—Deputy United States Marshal Joseph Huffman and four assistants to-day went to the home of Lon Nye, south of Macomb, and arrested Nye and a son, Ben Nye, with William Jennings and Joe Shepherd, who claim to be from Barton County. Later the officers arrested Oscar Nye.

All the prisoners are supposed to be connected with the robbery of a passenger train on the Kansas City, Fort Scott and Memphis Railroad at Macomb, Mo., on the night of Jan. 3. The alleged robbers were brought to Mansfield on a special train. The prisoners were at once taken to the Ozark Hotel, where they are guarded by several officers.

They made no attempt to resist arrest and talked very freely, but the officers say there is very convincing evidence that the prisoners are the guilty persons. Taken away separately, the prisoners were questioned, but denied having had anything to do with the robbery.

SALE OF ALBANY NEWSPAPER.

The Press-Knickerbocker Absorbs The Morning Express.

ALBANY, N. Y., Jan. 7.—The Press-Knickerbocker to-day purchased The Albany Morning Express. The combined paper will be known for the present as the Press-Knickerbocker and Express. The Express was the morning edition of the Evening Journal and was Republican in politics. The Press-Knickerbocker is independent, and the combined newspaper will be conducted upon independent lines.

The Daily Press was started in 1877, and a few years later it absorbed The Daily Knickerbocker. The Express was founded in 1847 by Alfred Stone and Edward Henley. In 1870 Postmaster General Charles Emory Smith, now proprietor of The Philadelphia Press, secured control. William Barnes, Jr., secured control of the property in 1888 and held it until to-day, when it passed to the control of The Press-Knickerbocker.

The controlling interest in The Press Company, proprietors of the combined newspapers, is owned by the family of the late Myron H. Rooker.

LONDON BOOKS AND AUTHORS.

New Volumes Announced from London—Lectures on Copyright—Leon Daudet's New Novel.

(Copyright, 1899.)
Special Cablegram to THE NEW YORK TIMES.

LONDON, Jan. 7.—Augustine Burrell's lectures on the law and history of copyright in books are being published shortly by Cassell.

Lord Ronald Gower's expensive "Life of Sir Thomas Lawrence" will appear next month.

Mr. Constable is publishing next week "French Literature of To-day," by Mlle. Blaze de Bury, who treats the subject in a partly personal and partly critical manner.

M. P. Shiel, the author of "The Yellow Danger," has written another sensational romance dealing with the men and times of Henry VIII.

A novel called "The Vision Splendid" is being published by Hutchinson next month. It purports to be a faithful picture of the inner life of the English stage. Miss Florence Bright, who has collaborated in writing it with Robert Machray, was for several years an actress.

W. B. Yeats's new volume of poems, which Elkin Mathews is publishing at the end of the month, will be called "The Wind Among the Reeds."

Marion H. Spielmann, the editor of The Magazine of Art, has nearly finished her biography of George Frederick Watts. It includes a catalogue of Watts's paintings, comprising 800 items.

T. C. Porter, the Science Master of Eton College, has written a volume of impressions of America, which Pearson is publishing.

Percy Fitzgerald, the well-known authority on Dickens, has written a life of the good Queen Charlotte, wife of George III., which Downey will publish in the Springtime.

According to The Publishers' Circular 6,008 new books were published last year, 236 fewer than in 1897. Novels, including juvenile works, number 1,758, or a decrease of 202.

Léon Daudet's new novel, "Sebastien Gouves," is almost ready. It is the story of a man of genius preyed upon by a band of charlatans. He has also written a pamphlet called "The Dignity of Literature," in which he inveighs against the commercial considerations invading modern literature and denounces the advertising methods upon which so much contemporary literary success is based.

MR. DINGLEY STILL VERY ILL.

WASHINGTON, Jan. 7.—Representative Dingley to-night is resting quietly, and his physicians announce that there has been no recent change in the patient's condition. Mr. Dingley is barely holding his own. He is a little weaker and in a most critical situation, where a change for the worse may occur at any moment. At the same time, there are some favorable signs as to the pneumonia itself, the involved lung clearing steadily.

The illness of Representative Dingley excites deep solicitude at the Capitol, and when word was received that the crisis of yesterday was succeeded by very slight better symptoms to-day there was general satisfaction, although it is known that the patient is still in a critical condition. Speaker Reed and other close associates of Mr. Dingley are kept constantly advised of every material change in the case.

It was noted that while he was delirious and at times unconscious yesterday he had possession of his faculties to-day, recognizing Mrs. Dingley and her daughter, evincing some interest in his breakfast, and in particular showing great interest in what was occurring in the House of Representatives. While these conditions were encouraging, they were offset by the extreme weakness of the patient, which is even greater than yesterday.

The physicians who remained most of the night, reported at midnight:

"Mr. Dingley is certainly no worse, and resting quietly."

Edward N. and A. H. Dingley of Kalamazoo, two of Mr. Dingley's sons, who speeded between Kalamazoo and Fort Wayne on a special switch engine to catch the flier there, arrived here to-night, and A. G. Dingley, another son, will reach here Monday from Mexico. President McKinley called at the hotel to inquire in person this afternoon, and Mrs. McKinley sent the distinguished patient a bunch of flowers.

SCHLEY TO VISIT CHICAGO.

CHICAGO, Jan. 7.—Resplendent in the full uniform of a Knight Templar Admiral Winfield Scott Schley will grace the annual ball of the Knight Templar Commanderies of this city at the Auditorium Monday night. Accompanied by Mrs. Schley and his personal staff, the hero of the Santiago naval battle will arrive Monday afternoon and will be escorted to the Grand Pacific Hotel by a committee of fifteen brother knights. The Admiral and Mrs. Schley will remain in this city some days, and will be the guests of Chicago's Masonic Commanderies.

At a midnight banquet succeeding the ball the guests of honor will be the Admiral and his wife. It is expected that at least 1,000 Knights Templar in full uniform will be seen at the ball and banquet.

From the preparations being made by the dozen local commanderies as well as by individual members of the Masonic fraternity, it seems certain that the "man who smashed Cervera" will be lionized beyond all precedent during his stay in Chicago.

Innumerable hostesses prominent in society are striving for the honor of entertaining him at dinners and receptions in their homes. He is not known to have accepted any invitations from the hero-admiring ones, however, and the committee believes he may decide to put a quietus on all social rivalries by the easy expedient of refusing to be a guest in any private household.

TO SUE CORPORATIONS.

PEORIA, Ill., Jan. 7.—In compliance with an order from the Attorney General of the State, John Dailly, State's Attorney of Peoria County, will file suits against 300 corporations in the county which failed to report to the Secretary of State by Sept. 1 their condition, also whether they were members of any trust, pool, or combine.

The penalty for not making such report is a fine of $50 and a forfeiture of charter. Only a very few of the local corporations have complied with the law.

THE GOVERNOR'S BUSY DAY

Col. Roosevelt Rushes About Rapidly to Keep His Engagements.

TALKS WITH MANY LEADERS

He Meets Senator Platt, Chairman Odell, and Elihu Root, but Says Nothing Was Decided On.

Gov. Roosevelt rushed through a tremendous amount of work yesterday. As he had to attend the celebration of Twelfth Night Friday night there was left only one working day in which to look after the many things he had on hand. Part of that day he had already pledged for the dinner at the Colonial Club, but he accomplished everything he had planned, by rushing with almost feverish haste and eagerness from one point to another, now conferring at his sister's home, 689 Madison Avenue, with political leaders, or applicants for office, now lunching and consulting with other leaders down town, and finally meeting still other leaders at the Fifth Avenue Hotel.

After a late stay at the Century Association clubhouse the night before, the Governor was still able to rise early and receive his callers. To all who asked him about his life in Albany he replied that he was enjoying it, "just as I enjoy everything."

Among his callers yesterday morning were Chairman Odell, John N. Partridge, George Oscar Eaton, John Notman, William R. Stewart, Miss Louisa Lee Schuyler, and Gen. Daniel Butterfield. Mr. Partridge and Mr. Eaton are both considered as candidates for the office of Superintendent of Public Works. Mr. Eaton appeared in the field for the first time yesterday, and the Governor said, when asked who he was, that he was a candidate for this place.

As soon as he had finished with these visitors, Gov. Roosevelt hurried with Chairman Odell to the Lawyers' Club, down town, where they had an engagement to lunch with Senator Platt and Elihu Root. According to Col. Roosevelt, these four were all that were at the luncheon.

In the afternoon the Governor returned up town and called in at the Fifth Avenue Hotel, where conferences had been progressing from early morning. He did not enter any of these conferences, and talked to only a few of his friends while in the hotel. He talked with Lieut. Gov. Woodruff, Frank S. Witherbee of the State Committee, Senator Raines, and a few others.

He said he had only one more man to see—Charles A. Schieren, ex-Mayor of Brooklyn—and that he would then go to the Colonial Club. He then hastened away to meet Mr. Schieren and to attend the dinner to Admiral Sampson.

While at the Fifth Avenue Hotel Gov. Roosevelt said:

"The conference I have just had with Senator Platt, Chairman Odell, and Mr. Root settled nothing. We discussed questions of local legislation and appointments and general policy, but we decided upon nothing. I may add that nothing definite will be determined until I return to Albany next week."

In speaking about the selection of a Superintendent of Public Works, he said it was generally understood that Excise Commissioner Henry H. Lyman would not accept the post. He spoke favorably of J. N. Partridge of Brooklyn, and it was said that the Governor had requested an interview with the latter yesterday. As to Mr. Eaton, he merely said he was an applicant for the place.

The appearance of Mr. Eaton in the race seemed to discomfit some of the politicians yesterday. Few of them knew who he was, and immediately instituted inquiries right and left. The City Directory describes George O. Eaton as an ice dealer, with office at 131 East Twenty-third Street and a home at 20 East One Hundred and First Street. It was said last night that he had some business relation with Chairman Odell, and some politicians were predicting his success upon this connection.

Gov. Roosevelt said that he would return to Albany to-day, probably leaving in the evening.

The politicians swarmed like bees in a hive in the corridors and halls of the Fifth Avenue Hotel all day yesterday. The hotel looked like the lobby of the Capitol at Albany, and for forty-eight hours at least the legislative work of the State has been done there.

Early in the day Senator Thomas F. Grady, Democratic leader, had another conference with Senator Ellsworth, Republican leader, and with Chairman Odell of the Republican State Committee. As an outcome of this conference another conference was held in Senator Platt's rooms between the Senator and Chairman Odell, Senator Ellsworth, and Assemblyman Samuel Frederick Nixon. It dealt with the proposition from Senator Grady that the Democrats be allowed five representatives on all committees in the Senate and Assembly having twelve and thirteen members. Senator Ellsworth had insisted upon allowing them only three on such committees. The conference, however, was more liberal, and consented to allow the Democrats four members on the three principal committees in the two branches of the Legislature, that is, the Committees on Finance, Judiciary, and Cities. On the other committees it was decided the Democrats should retain the proportion of members they were allowed last year.

After this conference Lieut. Gov. Woodruff, together with Michael J. Dady and Walter B. Atterbury, called on Senator Platt to confer about Kings County's part in the legislative committees and concerning appointments and questions of legislation. This ended the series, and the politicians deserted the hotel.

Senator Platt and Mr. Odell will leave for Washington to-night. Lieut. Gov. Woodruff and the members of the Senate and Assembly will return to Albany or to their homes to-day.

Gov. Roosevelt's Staff Complete.

ALBANY, N. Y., Jan. 7.—Major Gen. Roe issued an order this evening designating Harry Hayden Treadwell of New York, a Lieutenant and Battalion Adjutant of the Twenty-second Regiment, as an aide on the staff of Gov. Roosevelt. This completes the staff.

NEW TIN PLATE COMPANY.

Outside of the Trust and to be Established in Wilmington, Ill.

JOLIET, Ill., Jan. 7.—The Wilmington Tin Plate Company, which was licensed as a corporation yesterday by the Secretary of State, is composed of three Joliet men—Dr. William Dougall, D. Trevor Lewis, and T. W. Jenkins. They have secured a tract of eighty acres in Wilmington, this county, and purpose to erect a tin plate plant to cost $150,000.

The plant, it is said, will be in operation by June 1, and will employ between 300 and 400 men, with an annual output of 135,000 boxes. The concern is outside the new tin plate trust. The capital stock is $250,000.

SAVED CHILDREN FROM DEATH.

Mrs. Goodrich Dragged One Boy Unconscious from Blazing Room.

Mrs. Ellen L. Goodrich of 107 South Fifth Street, Brooklyn, was burned about the face and hands last evening while trying to extinguish a fire which started in a Christmas tree, and saving the lives of her four children. The Christmas tree was in a bedroom on the upper floor. While Mrs. Goodrich was lighting it she held her youngest child, one and a half years old, in her arms. The tree caught fire. Mrs. Goodrich tried to put out the blaze, but failed. She then ran with her baby and six-year-old daughter to the basement and left them with the servant. Rushing back to the room, which was then in flames, Mrs. Goodrich found her four-year-old son Clarence crouched in a corner. She succeeded in carrying him from the room. The boy was unconscious and was burned about the face. The eldest child, a boy, eleven years old, escaped from the room uninjured.

While Mrs. Goodrich was saving her children the servant ran to the street and had an alarm turned in. The firemen extinguished the blaze, with a loss of $200. Mrs. Goodrich had considerable of her hair singed off. She and her children were cared for by neighbors.

RUMORED DUEL IN FRANCE.

Count de Castellane, Who Married Miss Anna Gould, Said to Have Wounded M. Deroulede.

PARIS, Jan. 7.—The Liberté to-day says the friends of M. Paul Déroulède, the founder of the Patriotic League, and member of the Chamber of Deputies for the Angoulême Division of Charente, deny that he was wounded in the abdomen in a duel fought two weeks ago with Count de Castellane, Member of the Chamber of Deputies representing the Castellane District of the Lower Alps. The dispute which caused the alleged duel was said to have grown out of a quarrel regarding an actress. The friends of M. Déroulède, in denying the story, say he is suffering from bronchitis.

At a meeting of 4,000 members of the League of Patriots, held in Paris on Dec. 29, it was decided in view of the situation created by the Dreyfus affair to form a new League of Patriots, and M. Paul Déroulède, the founder of the original League of Patriots and personally one of the most active opponents of the revision of the Dreyfus case, was elected President of the new league. He was born in Paris in 1846, was wounded and taken prisoner at Sedan, escaped, and again served against the Prussians. He was a Lieutenant of cavalry when he resigned from the army, and is the author of several patriotic songs.

Count de Castellane is known in the United States, where he married Miss Anna Gould of New York.

NEWS OF LONDON THEATRES.

Mr. Clement Scott's History of the Stage to be Published.

(Copyright, 1899.)
Special Cablegram to THE NEW YORK TIMES.

LONDON, Jan. 7.—Clement Scott's history of the stage will begin with Phelps, at Sadler's Wells, and come down to Irving. The work will appear in the Summer, entitled "The Drama of Yesterday and To-day."

Mrs. James Brown Potter resumes her part in "The Three Musketeers" on Monday evening.

Sir Edward Clarke and Mr. Carson have been briefed to appear for Mr. Augustin Daly in his action against George Edwardes respecting the ejectment of Mr. Daly's representatives from Daly's Theatre.

Miss Fanny Brough produces at the Worcester, Jan. 16, a new four-act comedy by John T. Day.

At the Comedy Theatre on the following day Miss Annie Hughes produces a new play of three acts, "Matches," the central character being a cheery street match seller.

"Grierson's Way Boy," by H. V. Esmond will be the next novelty at the New Century Theatre.

G. P. Bancroft's new play, "What Will the World Say?" will be produced at Terry's on Jan. 26.

At the end of the season Mrs. Patrick Campbell and Forbes Robertson may again be associated in congenial parts.

BANQUET TO NAVAL OFFICERS.

Commanders of the Oregon and Iowa Honored by Minister Dudley.

LIMA, Peru, Jan. 7.—The United States Minister here, Mr. Irving B. Dudley, gave a banquet last night to the commanders of the United States battleships Oregon and Iowa, now at Callao. Among those present were the Peruvian Minister of Foreign Affairs, Señor Porras, and the British Minister here, Mr. W. N. Beauclerk.

There was an excursion to Chosica and a breakfast there to-day in honor of the American officers.

BRITISH STEAMER LOST.

Four of the Wooler's Crew Rescued, the Remainder Missing.

LISBON, Jan. 7.—The British steamer Loch Etive, bound from Newcastle-on-Tyne to Alexandria, Egypt, has passed Penich, on the south side of the peninsula of that name, and signaled that she has rescued four members of the crew of the British steamer Wooler, Capt. Cole, from Barry, on Dec. 30, for Las Palmas, Canary Islands, which vessel sank. The remainder of the crew of the Wooler are missing.

The Wooler was a steel, schooner-rigged steamer, with five bulkheads. She was built at West Hartlepool in 1891, and registered 2,403 tons gross and 1,548 tons net. Her measurements were 290 feet long, 38.1 feet beam, and 20 feet hold. She was owned by Steel, Young & Co., and hailed from London.

Advance in Tin Plate Quotations.

PITTSBURG, Penn., Jan. 7.—An official dispatch was received in this city to-day from headquarters of the tin-plate combine giving notice that the list has been withdrawn and that advanced quotations will rule at once. The advance is 25 cents on each standard 100-pound box. The jobbers have therefore put up prices 30 cents, thus jumping from $3.10 to $3.40 within twenty-four hours. It is believed quotations will advance until $4 is reached.

THE WEATHER.

The local forecast may be found at the top of this page to the right of the title.

The area of high pressure central Friday night in Oklahoma has moved to Northern Georgia, increasing in magnitude, and extends over the whole country from the lake regions to the gulf. The pressure is also high in the plateau regions. The temperature has fallen in the Atlantic States and the lake regions, it has risen from the Mississippi River to the plateau region, and has remained stationary on the Pacific Coast. Snow has fallen in the North Atlantic States and the lake region, rain or snow in the Middle Atlantic States, and rain in the South Atlantic States, and light rain has also fallen on the Middle and Northern Pacific Coast. Increasing cloudiness and snow may be expected in the upper lake region, the Upper Mississippi and Missouri Valleys, and generally fair weather elsewhere. It will grow warmer over the whole country from the Mississippi River to the Atlantic Coast, except in New England, where the temperature will remain stationary. On the Middle and South Atlantic Coast the wind will be light from the west and northwest, with low temperature to-day, and warmer, variable winds to-morrow. Storm signals are displayed on the Atlantic Coast from New Haven to Eastport.

The record of temperature for the twenty-four hours ended at midnight, taken from THE NEW YORK TIMES's thermometer and from the thermometer of the Weather Bureau, is as follows:

	Weather Bureau. 1898.	Weather Bureau. 1899.	TIMES. 1899.
3 A. M.	41	35	40
6 A. M.	38	33	36
9 A. M.	39	26	33
12 M.	41	25	32
4 P. M.	42	28	32
6 P. M.	38	23	30
9 P. M.	35	23	29
12 P. M.	34	25	28

THE TIMES's thermometer is 6 feet above the street level; that of the Weather Bureau is 283 feet above the street level.

Average temperatures yesterday were as follows:

Printing House Square	32¼
Weather Bureau	27¾
Corresponding date 1898	38⅝
Corresponding date for last twenty-five years	32

The maximum temperature yesterday was 35 degrees at 12:30 A. M. and the minimum 25 degrees at 1 P. M. The humidity at 8 A. M. was 68 per cent. and at 8 P. M. 50 per cent.

POISONER STILL SHIELDED

Police Officials Deterred from Moving in the Adams Case.

TRYING TO AVERT A SCANDAL

Men in High Places Threatened with Disagreeable Exposure—What McClusky Is Doing.

There is still no arrest in the Adams poisoning case, and there is now every indication that there will be none until the mysterious influence that is saving the person under suspicion from the clutches of the law is unmasked and the police are forced to show their hands. The ring which has so far prevented an arrest is no stronger than those who have set themselves the task of finding out who compose it, and just as the person suspected has been put in the position of calling on those in high places for protection, so will the members of the ring make an undoubted move that will disclose their identity.

Of course the police officials, from the highest to the lowest, are horror-stricken at the mere thought that they could even be suspected of conniving at such a state of affairs, and they are making strenuous efforts to show that politics has cut no figure in the investigation. As a matter of fact, it is not politics at all, but self-interest which is the moving power. If the person suspected is arrested, there is not a particle of doubt that men occupying high places will be dragged into the unsavory scandal, and it is to protect themselves that they are shielding the suspect. All day yesterday newspaper men were interviewing prominent police officials and getting their denials. And they got just what they expected, for the most guileless of the craft would not admit that he expected to get a confirmation of the rumor from the very men who have prevented the arrest.

Capt. McClusky, as usual, said yesterday that there was nothing new. He is having photographed the wrapper of the package in which the poison came to Cornish, and fac simile copies will be sent out broadcast on the chance that some one will recognize the handwriting thereon. The police cannot stop work entirely, and they must make a reasonable "bluff" to make the public believe that they are still anxious to apprehend the culprit. There is also an indication that the Newark police have been told to cease their too aggressive tactics.

Three days ago Capt. Cosgrove of Newark said that he had come to an arrangement with Capt. McClusky, and that whatever was done in the case would be done in the next twenty-four hours. He also stated that matters had been put in shape, and there was no need for further delay. Thrice twenty-four hours have gone by since then, and yesterday Capt. Cosgrove said that he did not think there would be any developments in the case for the present. When it was pointed out to him that these two statements did not agree, he declined to have anything further to say.

It was stated yesterday that Expert Kinsley had asked for more letters to use in his handwriting investigation, and that three more of a person suspected, and one from a woman to the late Henry C. Barnet had been sent to him. As usual, the signatures had been cut from these, so that if Mr. Kinsley does come to any conclusion that the handwriting of the letters he has in his possession and the writing on the poison package are one, he will still be ignorant of the name of the person suspected, and cannot therefore become a dangerous factor if the case is dropped by the police.

According to Capt. McClusky, his men are still going over the many thousand names furnished by Kutnow Brothers of persons to whom sample packages of their powders have been sent. The poison sent to Barnet came in one of these sample boxes. Capt. McClusky said that the search among the names would not be completed for several days.

Prof. Witthaus yesterday denied that he had ever told any one that he had found Kutnow powder in the bottle of poison sent to Cornish. He said his investigation was not yet complete, and that he did not know the component parts of Kutnow powder.

Bartow S. Weeks, counsel for Roland B. Molineux, said yesterday that his client had been in this city all day in attendance on his wife, who is very ill as a result of the unpleasant notoriety that has been given to her husband's name in connection with the case. Mr. Weeks said, however, that he had no reason to believe that Mrs. Molineux's condition was serious. At 257 West End Avenue, where Mr. and Mrs. Molineux reside, all information about her condition was refused last night.

BEERBOHM TREE'S SCHEME.

A Grand Review of the Century at the Close of 1899.

(Copyright, 1899.)
Special Cablegram to THE NEW YORK TIMES.

LONDON, Jan. 7.—It is announced that Mr. Beerbohm Tree is contemplating a great revue according to the French custom at Her Majesty's Theatre at the end of this year to mark the close of the century. It will be on a magnificent scale and take the form of a series of incidents woven round a central dramatic idea, each culminating in a superb tableau illustrating the forward march of Peace, War, Art, Science, and other fields which the dying century has witnessed.

Literature and poetic charm will, however, be the dominant notes. The best artists will be requisitioned to arrange the tableaus and eminent writers to supply the literary grace. The fashions and customs of the century will be illustrated, full scope being given to the arts of the costumer and the musician.

The project is only in the preliminary stage, but it is practically certain of fulfillment.

AFLOAT IN BAY ON CAKE OF ICE.

Syrian Boy Rescued Midway Between the Battery and Liberty Island.

The tug Edward Annan was midway between Liberty Island and the Battery yesterday morning, when a small boy was seen in the water clinging to a cake of ice. The tug put about and the boy was hauled aboard with a boathook. Though not unconscious, he was unable to give any account of himself. He was landed at the Barge Office, where he was identified as the child of a Syrian woman immigrant who had just been brought from Ellis Island to the Barge Office, and who was wringing her hands because one of her three children was missing. The boy had fallen overboard from the Ellis Island boat without the fact having been discovered.

The boy's mother was Kofa Dyaub, a widow, who arrived here on the steamship La Normandie Christmas Day, and had been detained because she had no money. Bondsmen had been obtained for her Friday, and the family was about to be released when on the trip to the Battery from Ellis Island the boy fell overboard.

WESTERN UNION ENJOINED.

Fight With Cincinnati's Chamber of Commerce Over Stock Tickers.

CINCINNATI, Ohio, Jan. 7.—The Western Union Telegraph Company has been enjoined from removing its stock tickers from the Chamber of Commerce. The Chamber has transferred part of its business to the Postal Telegraph Company, and the Western Union proposes to abandon the Chamber altogether. The Western Union officials began action to-day to have the injunction dissolved.

The Chamber of Commerce has been paying $9,000 a year for the market service, and upon refusal of the Western Union to reduce charges it transferred most of the business to the rival company

"All the News That's Fit to Print."

The New York Times.

ONE CENT — COPYRIGHTED, 1899, BY THE NEW YORK TIMES COMPANY. — ONE CENT

THE WEATHER. Snow early, cold wave, south-westerly gales becoming northwesterly.

VOL. XLVIII..NO. 15,304. NEW YORK, FRIDAY, JANUARY 27, 1899.—TWELVE PAGES. PRICE ONE CENT in Greater New York, Elsewhere, and Jersey City. TWO CENTS.

THE NEWS CONDENSED.

Stock market broad and strong.

Cash wheat, No. 2, red, 80⅝; cash corn, No. 2, mixed, 45⅛; cash cotton, 6⅛.

LEGISLATURE.—The State Assembly passed the resolution providing for an investigation of the official acts of Surrogate Arnold, and a committee composed of five Republicans and two Democrats was appointed to conduct the inquiry. The General Appropriation bill was introduced, carrying an aggregate of $9,396,783.43, which is $812,118.63 less than last year. Among other bills introduced was one to repeal the retaliatory insurance law, which was passed three years ago on account of the hostile attitude of the Prussian Government toward American companies.—Page 3.

CONGRESS.—The debate on the Army Reorganization bill was continued yesterday in the House. Addresses were made by Mr. Grosvenor (Rep., Ohio,) Mr. Marsh (Rep., Ill.,) and others. The Senate had the Pension Appropriation bill under discussion, and Mr. Butler (Dem., N. C.,) offered his amendment providing for pensions to Confederate soldiers, which, however, he afterward withdrew. Mr. Mallory (Dem., Fla.) spoke in support of the Vest anti-colonial resolution.—Page 5.

FOREIGN.—Cable advices from London announce that it is the purpose of the British Government to establish a permanent post as military attaché with its embassy at Washington. The letter of Mr. Balfour concerning the British plan to establish universities in Ireland has been received with general approval in Ireland and England. Sir Matthew White Ridley, Secretary of State for the British Home Department, in a speech before Unionists, said that the increasing friendship between the United States and Great Britain is more desirable than a formal alliance. Earthquakes throughout Jamaica are reported. Bank robbers who stole £47,000 from a London bank returned £40,000 by post. Ambassador White, at Berlin, has had a harmonious conference with von Bülow concerning the Samoan situation.—Pages 1 and 7.

Page 1.

Commissary General Eagan testified before the court-martial at Washington yesterday.

W. M. Cox, a stockholder of the Continental National Bank of Memphis, in his complaint in a legal action, accuses Controller of the Currency Dawes and the cashier of the bank of being in collusion to prevent exposure of the alleged fraudulent management of the institution.

Page 2.

Mr. Quay still lacked 14 votes on yesterday's ballot for United States Senator from Pennsylvania.

The Rev. Dr. Murray, Dean of Princeton University, who underwent an operation on Wednesday, was yesterday reported to be recovering.

Page 3.

Dr. Lyman Abbott in a lecture on "The Duty and Destiny of the Nation" at Barnard College yesterday, advocated present protection of the Philippines and Cuba from aggression and anarchy and giving them the choice of the government they want when they have been educated to free institutions.

Page 4.

The plans for the new home of the New York Yacht Club, to be erected in West Forty-fourth Street, have been placed on exhibition in the clubhouse at 67 Madison Avenue.

Page 5.

Mrs. Esther Herrman has sent $10,000 to the Council of the Scientific Alliance for the building fund.

The rectorship of the Protestant Episcopal Church of St. Mary the Virgin has been offered to the Rev. Dr. George M. Christian of Grace Church, Newark, N. J.

The Grand Jury yesterday found a second indictment against Lawyer P. O'Conner, and also indicted William Rapp and Jacob Bossbardt in connection with the alleged damage suit conspiracy. Bossbardt made a confession implicating Rapp and O'Conner.

Page 7.

Mrs. William Sinsser, Jr., was granted a decree of separation from her husband yesterday, and awarded $2,000 a year alimony.

Page 9.

Charles R. [illegible], President of the Union Institute, has invented a machine that records deposits and disbursements, and it is claimed renders mistakes or falsification of entries by bank employes impossible.

Page 12.

The Committee on Building Department of the Board of Aldermen held a public hearing yesterday on the question of the better protection of high buildings in case of fire.

The Rapid Transit Commissioners yesterday approved the bill which they are preparing for submission to the Legislature. The measure probably will be ready by Tuesday.

At a meeting yesterday authorized representatives of the fire insurance companies doing business in this city unanimously approved a plan for the organization of a fire insurance exchange.

It was learned yesterday that the firm of Von Mohl & Co. of Cincinnati, which sent samples of medicine to an "H. Cornish" at 1,620 Broadway, had been as early as last May in communication with an "H. C. Barnet."

CONTROLLER DAWES ACCUSED.

Charges in a Suit Involving Him and the Cashier of a Memphis Bank.

CHATTANOOGA, Tenn., Jan. 26.—A bill making sensational allegations against Controller of the Currency Charles G. Dawes was filed in the Chancery Court at Memphis on Tuesday, but the fact was suppressed till to-day.

W. M. Cox, a stockholder of the Continental National Bank of Memphis, which has a capital of $500,000, alleges that H. L. Armstrong, cashier of the bank, and Controller Dawes have entered into collusion for the purpose of preventing the complainant from exposing "fraudulent management" of the bank. It is alleged that Armstrong is running the bank in open violation of the law "eventually with the full consent and knowledge of the Controller." Cox alleges that Armstrong has formed a "combine" with influential capitalists for the purpose of depreciating the price of the bank's stock, and by "false statements" frightening non-resident stockholders into selling to a "friendly stock broker, who delivers the goods to Armstrong."

The complainant says he made repeated demands for the lawful right to examine the bank stock books, but the demands were refused. It is charged that false statements of the bank's condition were published, and that Armstrong's personal account was overdrawn $41,000. After making further charges of irregularities by the cashier, the petitioner charges that on June 3, 1898, Bank Examiner J. S. Escott wrote to the Controller: "The cashier is a scheming rascal, totally unfit to hold the position."

Cox appends a letter from Eugene Snowden, former teller of the bank, dated June 23, 1898, in which Snowden made charges of mismanagement. Then follows a letter from George M. Coffin, Deputy and Acting Controller, in which Coffin is quoted as saying: "We would advise you not to follow this matter up, as it might result in serious trouble to all concerned."

In conclusion the petitioner prays that the Controller be required to show cause for not taking proper steps to protect the stockholders of the bank, and also asks for the appointment of a receiver.

Ambassador White Sees von Bülow.

LONDON, Jan. 27.—The Berlin correspondent of The Standard says that Mr. White, the United States Ambassador to Germany, had a long and cordial conversation on Wednesday with Herr von Bülow, Imperial Secretary for Foreign Affairs, regarding the Samoan question, as to which it is evident, the correspondent observes, that no serious differences will arise.

THE PEACE TREATY SAFE

President No Longer Doubtful of Its Ratification.

OPPOSED TO FURTHER DELAY

Visitors at the White House Told of the Desirability of Speedy Action.

WASHINGTON, Jan. 26.—Very promptly following the speech of Representative Johnson in the House in opposition to the Paris treaty and the extension of the rule of the United States over the Philippines came the report to-day that the President's doubts about the ratification of the treaty have been dissipated and that he is confident the Senate will dispose of it favorably on or before Feb. 6.

All sorts of opinions have been expressed about Mr. Johnson's speech, but many of those who admire its lively delivery and the audacity of the Speaker, denounce it as being just the mass of "glittering generalities" which he described the speech of Mr. Dolliver to be. The prevailing opinion on both sides of the House was that the speech was mischievous, and that if it were followed to its logical effect, it would bring about a renewal of the war with Spain, and encourage those agents of Spain who are suspected by the Administration of conniving with Spain to induce the Filipinos to bring on the war so that there may be a chance to rob the United States of the territory ceded to this Government by the Paris treaty.

It is impossible to ascertain what the report is based upon that the Filipinos under Aguinaldo are being assisted by Spain, but the fact was pointed out to-day at the Department of State that the assertion of the Filipinos that the people are averse to the United States is not corroborated by the dispatches and reports of Admiral Dewey and others, who insist that the majority of the islanders would welcome the assertion by the United States of the authority it has acquired by the Paris treaty. Representative Johnson, it is further pointed out, has not obtained information of the attitude of the natives to entitle his word to be preferred to that of such men as Admiral Dewey, Gen. Merritt, and Gen. Greene, all of whom, it is understood at the War Department, still favor the assertion and maintenance of American authority over the islands. They are quoted as saying that the President is well advised as to the attitude of the people of the islands as is Aguinaldo.

The discussion of the situation is not weakening the treaty in the Senate. Every reason that was urged against recognition of the fitness of the Cubans to assume control of Cuba is now urged by the supporters of the treaty as a reason for refusing to admit the readiness of the Filipinos to assume control of all affairs in the Philippines.

Visitors to the White House to-day found the President more inclined than ever to press for ratification of the treaty. He will do almost anything rather than consent to the use of force to overcome the resistance of the Filipinos, but some of the most merciful of his advisers insist that the Filipinos must be suppressed at all hazards. Their chief reason for advising such a course is that they fear that upon the withdrawal of the forces of the United States, in case it should be decided to abandon the islands, the Spaniards left in the Philippines, and all not Spaniards who did not sympathize with or assist the insurgents, would be in danger of massacre. There is no doubt that the Roman Catholic friends of the President, who know the perilous situation of the clericals in the Philippines, have protested strenuously against the surrender of power to the natives, who hate and will revenge themselves upon the priests and all who have been friendly to them.

One of the Commissioners to the Philippines is to be Col. Denby, formerly Minister to China. It is understood that Col. Denby's appointment on the commission to the islands was made upon the strong request of the Chinese Minister, Mr. Wu, and in the interest of the two or three hundred thousand Chinese population of the Philippines. The Minister has given an idea, in a recent interview, of the great interest felt by China in the future of the Philippines and the confidence displayed by the Chinese in Col. Denby, for whom the authorities of that country have great respect, led them to urge his selection as a measure of protection to Chinese who might be exposed to bodily injury and personal loss in case the Filipinos should succeed in driving the Americans out of the islands.

A Senate Democrat said this afternoon, after the executive session, that he believed the treaty could have been ratified yesterday or to-day, and that in his opinion it would be ratified at once. He gave it as his personal opinion that President McKinley would be fully justified in adopting any course to bring about a pacification of the Filipinos as he justified his course in using the $50,000,000 placed in his hands for war purposes. "In my opinion," said he, "nothing can prevent the ratification of the treaty."

PEACE DOCUMENTS WITHHELD.

Complaint that the President Has Not Furnished All the Details.

WASHINGTON, Jan. 26.—To-day's executive session of the Senate was consumed in discussion of the failure of the President so far to send the Senate the documents in his possession and on file in the State Department bearing upon the Paris Conference. Senator Gorman raised the point as soon as the doors were closed that the resolution had been adopted several days since, and addressed the Senate at some length on the failure of the President to respond to the Senate's request for information.

The attack of the Maryland Senator was followed by similar speeches by Senators Vest and Hoar, and they were replied to by Senator Spooner and Frye. The two Senators engaged in a running debate, the opponents of the treaty contending that the Senate was entitled, as part of the treaty-making power, to all the facts bearing upon the case, and the supporters of the document holding that the President could withhold any papers which he did not consider in the interest of the general welfare to give out.

Senator Spooner cited the precedents to show that the President could withhold information of this character at his pleasure, and that such a course frequently had been followed in cases in which the President deemed it unwise to communicate facts bearing upon international negotiations when to do so might prejudice the country's best interests and promote the very evils which it was sought to ameliorate. The point was also made that the President might feel more free to communicate with the Senate if he could be sure of privacy in doing so. No one professed to speak by authority, and all the Senators who were heard in support of the President's course, expressed confidence that the President's action, whatever it might be, would be for the best interests of the public.

Replying to this latter point, Senator Hoar said that he could yield to him in admiration for the personal qualifications of the President or in confidence in his patriotism. At the same time he contended for his original proposition that the Senate was entitled to the President's full confidence in passing upon a question of so much importance as the acquisition of territory thousands of miles from our own shores, and with millions of people totally unlike our own population. He thought there must be some reason for putting the Philippines on a footing so different from the footing on which Cuba had been placed in the treaty.

The opinion is generally expressed that the time allowed for debate of the treaty in executive session will not be by any means consumed, as very few Senators on either side desire to make speeches behind closed doors. The friends of the treaty profess increasing confidence for ratification, but there is yet some talk of adopting a negative resolution to the effect that the treaty does not bind the United States to the adoption of a colonial policy.

SPANISH CABINET MEETS.

Senor Sagasta Says the Cortes Should Meet to Act on the Treaty.

MADRID, Jan. 26.—At the Cabinet meeting to-day the Premier, Señor Sagasta, outlined the Government's intentions relative to the peace treaty. He said that information received by the Minister of Foreign Affairs, Duke Almodovar de Rio, had created the impression that President McKinley feared the treaty would be defeated in the Senate and apprehended "an ultimatum resistance upon the part of the Philippine insurgents against the Americans, who desire to deprive them of independence and debase the Spanish Government, which are sufficient reason for the triumph of the anti-annexationists in the Senate."

Therefore the Premier insisted that the convocation of the Cortes should no longer be delayed.

SPANISH OFFICERS CENSURED.

Gen. Toral, Gen. Jaudenes, and Admiral Cervera to be Tried.

MADRID, Jan. 26.—The Cabinet met this afternoon under the Presidency of the Queen Regent. The absence of Gen. Correa, the Minister of War, was much commented upon and is believed to have been connected with a decision, not yet divulged, reached by the Supreme Military Tribunal relative to Gen. Jaudenes, the Spanish commander who capitulated at Manila, who has been in prison since yesterday, and Gen. Toral, who capitulated at Santiago de Cuba, who is absent from Madrid.

The Cabinet met again this evening, Señor Sagasta presiding. It appears that the evidence before the court-martial showed that Gen. Jaudenes had sufficient ammunition and food to have enabled him to resist longer. The court ordered his arrest, whereupon he surrendered himself, attired in mufti, (civilian dress,) and accompanied by his son and several Ministers of State. Gen. Correa confirmed the arrest.

It is reported that the court-martial will exonerate Gen. Toral on the ground that he acted under superior instructions, but that Admiral Montojo, who was defeated by Admiral Dewey at Cavite, will be tried for the incompetent condition of his fleet.

The newspapers assert also that Admiral Cervera is awaiting his trial, and that therefore he will not be able to take his seat as a Senator or the reassembling of the Cortes.

It is understood that at the Cabinet meeting this evening Señor Capdepon, Minister of the Interior, proposed that the suspension of the constitutional guarantees should now cease.

THE FILIPINOS AGGRESSIVE.

Their Congress Votes Confidence in Aguinaldo and Empowers Him to Declare War.

MANILA, Jan. 23, via Hongkong, Jan. 26.—The Republica, official organ of the Filipino Government, announces that the Congress at Malolos has adopted the Philippine Constitution, passed a vote of confidence in Aguinaldo, and empowered him to declare war on the Americans whenever he deems it advisable.

At a mass meeting of women at Cavite, the paper adds, it was enthusiastically resolved to petition Aguinaldo for permission to take men's places in defense of independence and to bear arms if necessary. Paterno has asked for the privilege of "taking a prominent place in the line of battle against the Americans," and it appears, it has been granted him.

An American sentry recently killed a Captain of Filipino artillery at the Tondo outpost. As a result the Filipinos are intensely excited and denounce it as a "cowardly assassination." On Saturday evening, Jan. 21, five Filipinos, determined to have revenge for their Captain's death, attempted to enter our lines. An American sentry killed one of them, who was armed with a revolver. After an exchange of shots the others were arrested. The incident has intensified the excitement here.

The Mabini Cabinet yesterday insisted upon the liberation of the Spanish civil prisoners in commemoration of the proclamation of the Philippine Republic, and demanded money to the native clergy. A decree to that effect was signed. The Spanish clergy, however, remain prisoners.

An elaborate programme has been arranged for the formal ratification of the Constitution to-day.

Nothing was accomplished at the conference here yesterday, and it is rumored that the Filipinos at their next meeting will give the American eight days in which to accede to their demand for recognition. The rumor is discredited.

Ships on the Way to Manila.

WASHINGTON, Jan. 26.—The cruiser Buffalo is making excellent time on her trip to Manila. According to a cable message received at the Navy Department yesterday she has left Singapore, and will make no more stops until her arrival at Manila. The gunboat Princeton, which also is on her way to the Philippines, arrived at Gibraltar yesterday, and will continue her voyage without delay. The gunboat Marietta, which is likewise destined for service with Admiral Dewey's fleet, has left Cartagena for Savanilla.

Agoncillo to Make Another Move.

WASHINGTON, Jan. 26.—Having failed to receive from the State Department any answer to his latest communication, Senor Agoncillo, the envoy of Aguinaldo, in a few days will take another step to bring the latter's case to the attention of the Government. The envoy here is keeping in touch with the conditions existing in the islands, and, it is said, is using his influence with Aguinaldo to avoid hostilities with the Americans as long as possible.

Satisfactory News from Gen. Otis.

WASHINGTON, Jan. 26.—Gen. Otis cabled the War Department to-day from Manila that the transport Zealandia left yesterday for San Francisco with 124 officers and enlisted men. The soldiers on the Zealandia are said at the War Department to be convalescent. This dispatch, like the last received from Gen. Otis, was regarded as satisfactory, because he made no reference to any change in the conditions at Manila, such as he would be sure to do had there been any insurgent outbreak.

SMALLPOX RAGES IN ARKANSAS.

Four Hundred Cases in Fulton County Within Two Months.

LITTLE ROCK, Ark., Jan. 26.—Dr. H. C. Dunavant, President of the State Board of Health, in speaking of the smallpox situation to-day, told of a terrible state of affairs at Salem, in Fulton County.

Dr. Dunavant has been in that place, where he made a thorough investigation. He says that there have been at least 400 cases of smallpox in the locality within the last two months and that a number of deaths have occurred. He found people walking about the streets of the town, broken out with the disease, pockmarked and pitted, and others falling ill every day.

The local physicians contended that the disease was not smallpox, and little effort had been made to check its ravages. As a result, the disease has become scattered along the line of the Memphis and Fort Scott and Cotton Belt Railroads, and many neighboring towns are now infected.

The disease was first brought to Fulton County about two months ago by a returned soldier.

STRANGE BURIAL AT AMESBURY.

Reuben J. Smith's Body Rests in a Chair in His Sarcophagus.

AMESBURY, Mass., Jan. 26.—The funeral of Reuben J. Smith, whose desire was that his body should be placed in a chair in a sarcophagus the construction of which he personally directed some time ago, was held here to-day.

The arrangements were carried out in accordance with the desire of Mr. Smith. The Rev. Joseph Lambert of the Christian Church conducted a brief service over the body in the room where Mr. Smith formerly lived. The reclining chair which Mr. Smith selected for the repose of his remains had been brought to the apartment, and the body was placed thereon. The room in which the burial service was held was crowded.

Instead of a hearse, the peculiar receptacle necessitated the use of an undertaker's covered wagon. This vehicle, followed by three carriages, proceeded to Mount Prospect Cemetery, where the chair containing the body was placed in its designated position within the tomb. Mr. Smith had expressed the desire that the door of the sarcophagus should be left open, and hundreds were permitted to view the body before the sarcophagus was finally locked and sealed. The key was destroyed after the closing ceremonies.

THE IRISH UNIVERSITIES.

Proposed Plan of Establishing Them at Dublin and Belfast Accepted with Favor in Britain.

[Copyright, 1899.]

Special Cablegram to THE NEW YORK TIMES.

LONDON, Jan. 26.—On the whole, the reception of Mr. Balfour's letter concerning the Irish university scheme has been favorable. The Irish Catholic press receives the proposal warmly. The Times adopts a cautious attitude, and the Liberals are more enthusiastic than the Conservatives. There has been no time yet for opposition, either Nonconformist or Orange, to develop, as the letter took the public by surprise. To-morrow's papers will probably contain a mass of letters on the subject.

THE PROPOSED INSTITUTIONS.

Judge O'Brien Voices Satisfaction at Mr. Balfour's Step.

Henry Norman's cable dispatch to THE TIMES yesterday morning announcing that the Right Hon. A. J. Balfour, First Lord of the Treasury and the Government leader in the House of Commons, had definitely adopted the scheme for establishing two universities for Ireland, was read with much interest by many influential Irish-Americans whose interest in the welfare of their native land has never abated. Justice Morgan J. O'Brien of the Supreme Court, Appellate Division, who is also President of the Society of Friendly Sons of St. Patrick, read the long dispatch carefully and said, after a little deliberation:

"It is a difficult thing for us to understand in this country the conditions in Ireland relating to education. The conditions there are entirely different from our own. The great drawback which existed for many years with reference to primary or elementary education in Ireland was removed by Mr. Gladstone's administration by the establishment of a system which is practically the same as exists in Canada, viz.: the denominational system. This was a very long step in advance of anything that ever had been done by the English Government for Ireland, and my own observations while in that country in 1890, together with expressions that I heard from the Catholic clergy, many of them members of the local boards of education, were favorable to, and commendatory of, the system.

"In the schools in Ireland they have succeeded in solving what in this country has been a vexed question. That is the question of uniting secular education with religious training. Without interfering with the religious convictions of the different denominations, schools have been provided in Ireland where the very best kind of primary education is given. The theory of putting a dome on what is seemingly a good foundation, while it is an advanced and progressive idea, is the natural and logical result of the primary system already established. It was found that with regard to primary education the denominational system worked well, and I do not see why in the higher or university education it should not be equally effective. I have myself heard within a year, from the lecture platform, the statement that the system of primary education in Ireland is the best in the world. This statement was made by a priest who came from Ireland and who was a pronounced home ruler and advocate of more liberal treatment for Ireland. He said that his assertion was borne out by the evidence that in the tests for scholarships and prizes offered by the English and Scottish universities more than 75 per cent. year after year, were won by the Irish students who were educated in the Irish schools.

"My own views would naturally be modified and controlled by the opinions and views of those best able to speak for Ireland with regard to the education of the people of that country. In the absence of such an expression of opinion, however, I may say that I think this latest action of Mr. Balfour is a great step in the right direction. Whether or not something additional to what he proposes is necessary to make the scheme acceptable to the Irish people, it is quite clear that with the principle conceded of according to three-fourths of the people of Ireland the benefits of a higher education, the mere details of administration, or minor differences, can in some way be arranged consistently with the effective advancement and establishment of a great university.

"I therefore personally view with pleasure the evidences given by the English Government, as represented by one of its most advanced statesmen, of according to the Irish people in one direction the rights for which they have contended for centuries."

A BARON AND BARONESS HELD.

A Requisition from London Detains Them in Pensacola.

PENSACOLA, Fla., Jan. 26.—Baron and Baroness de Barra, who were yesterday arrested here, are still held in detention. The officers intended to take them to Jacksonville to-day, but a Deputy Marshal arrived from New York with a requisition for the pair from the English Government, they being charged with having fraudulently obtained £5,000 in England.

President McKinley has been asked to grant the requisition.

INSISTENT PULLER-IN SHOT.

Tried to Convince a Man He Needed New Clothes and Is Wounded.

Charles Marks, the puller-in of Meyer's clothing store, at Park Row and Pearl Street, had a bad scare yesterday afternoon, and, although he escaped with the little finger of his right hand split by a bullet and a few bruises, he will probably be more careful hereafter in his quest for customers. Marks was standing in front of the store at 4:30 o'clock, when Rafello Carolo of 1 Grand Street came along with a friend.

Carolo did not want any new clothes, but this did not deter the puller-in from trying to convince him that he did. The two men were just returning from work, and Carolo was armed with a revolver, while his friend carried a shovel. Angry words were being spoken when Policeman Alexander Smith of the Elizabeth Street Station rode by in a Third Avenue cable car.

Smith saw Carolo draw his revolver and fire two shots at the puller-in, while his friend made a pass with the shovel at Marks's head. Smith jumped off the car, and, running up behind Carolo, seized the weapon and knocked the man down. Carolo's friend ran away, but Marks stood bleeding from a wound in his hand, too frightened to move.

An ambulance was called, and Surgeon Dodge found that only one of the two shots had taken effect, a bullet having split the little finger of Marks's hand. The other missile had bored holes through Marks's clothing. Marks's wound was dressed and Carolo was taken to the police station.

The Art of Making Champagne

MR. PLATT AS AN ORATOR

New York's Junior Senator Gives Notice of a Speech.

WILL TALK ABOUT EXPANSION

His Previous Efforts in Addressing the Senate Confined to a Few Formal Requests.

WASHINGTON, Jan. 26.—In the Senate to-day Mr. Platt of New York gave notice of a speech on Mr. Vest's anti-expansion resolution. Mr. Platt will speak to-morrow after the morning business.

New York Republicans who have heard Mr. Platt speak at State conventions and in Republican meetings know that the Senator can talk when he desires to say something, but he has not been moved to speak since he became a member of the Senate. His remarks since he entered the body at the beginning of the Fifty-fifth Congress would not fill half a column of The Congressional Record. The index to that work shows that he has introduced a few relief bills and many pension measures, and a few public bills, together with many petitions. But for the three years he has enjoyed the opportunity to talk to people in the gallery of the Senate he has been silent, affording opportunity, in the meantime, for such voluminous orators as Peffer and Morgan and Stewart to fill many pages of The Record.

The reports of the utterances of Mr. Platt have been collected for this dispatch in a form which makes it necessary to give a few remarks of others in order to make Mr. Platt's part seem intelligible. Senator Platt's first speech in the Senate was made on March 16, 1898, when he appears as having spoken as follows:

Mr. Platt of New York—I ask unanimous consent for the immediate consideration of the bill (S. R. 101) to correct the naval record of and grant an honorable discharge to Thomas H. Holden of Pawtucket, R. I.

The next remarks reported from Mr. Platt were made April 20, 1898, when he said:

Mr. Platt of New York—I ask unanimous consent for the present consideration of the bill (H. R. 4929) extending the time for the completion of the bridge across St. Lawrence River.

Again, on April 28, he is recorded as having spoken thus:

Mr. Platt of New York—I ask unanimous consent for the present consideration of the joint resolution (S. R. 141) regarding the holding of a Pan-American exposition in the year 1901 upon Cayuga Island, between the cities of Buffalo and Niagara Falls, in the State of New York, to illustrate the development of the Western Hemisphere during the nineteenth century.

On June 14, 1898, this report appears:

Mr. Platt of New York—I ask unanimous consent for the present consideration of the bill (H. R. 6368) to correct the military record of W. Cady Ward, late Major of Second Mounted Rifles, New York Volunteers, and to grant him an honorable discharge.

On June 21, 1898, Mr. Platt occupied the attention of the Senate with these remarks:

Mr. Platt of New York—I ask unanimous consent for the present consideration of the bill (H. R. 10173) to provide for the construction of a bridge across Niagara River.

In the present session also Mr. Platt has been heard. The record of Jan. 5 shows the following:

The President pro tempore—The Chair lays before the Senate a bill from the House of Representatives, and calls the attention of the Senator from New York (Mr. Platt) to it.

The bill (H. R. 1,574) for the relief of the estate of Abel Adams, deceased, was read the first time by its title.

Mr. Platt of New York—I ask unanimous consent that the bill be submitted in lieu of the Senate bill on the same subject, and that it be put upon its passage.

The President pro tempore—The Chair understands that the Senate has passed a similar bill.

Mr. Platt of New York—But it has been passed in a slightly amended form by the House, and I ask unanimous consent for the present consideration of the House bill.

Mr. Cockrell—Let it be read for information.

The bill was read; and by its terms it was provided for the payment to the representative of the estate of Abel Adams of $2,500 for United States coupon bonds that were lost.

The President pro tempore—Is there objection to the present consideration of the bill?

There being no objection, the bill was considered as in committee of the whole.

The bill was reported to the Senate without amendment, ordered to a third reading, read the third time, and passed.

Mr. Platt of New York—I ask that the House bill be referred to the Committee on Finance.

Mr. Platt of New York—I ask that the Senate be requested to return to the Senate the Senate bill upon the same subject, being the bill (S. 4,583) for the relief of the estate of Abel Adams, deceased.

In every instance the Senate granted the requests of Mr. Platt, and passed the bills called up by him.

TO FORM A VAST ICE TRUST.

Standard Oil Company Said to be Behind the Proposed Combination of Corporations.

GARDINER, Me., Jan. 26.—From facts in possession of the men engaged in the ice business on the Kennebec, it appears that the bill to incorporate the American Ice Company, which Representative Manley introduced in the Maine Legislature on Monday, is a measure of greater magnitude than has yet been understood by outsiders.

It is taken here to mean not only a union of the Knickerbocker and Consolidated Ice Companies, but also a consolidation of all the ice companies of any note in the country. The Knickerbocker Company of Philadelphia, the Consolidated Company of New York, the Knickerbocker Company of Chicago, the Independent and Great Falls Companies of Washington, the Richmond Company of Richmond, Va., and subordinate companies, are believed to be in the movement, and while each will come into the combination under its individual name, all will be owned and controlled by the American Ice Company.

A new feature of the deal suggested here, and one which is considered well substantiated by the magnitude of the transaction, which promises to develop a combination almost equal to the great Standard Oil Company, is that the latter is behind the new ice company. It is known that many persons interested in the Standard Oil Company are large stockholders also in the ice companies of this section.

FELTING MAKERS TO COMBINE.

Manufacturers Seek to Stop Competition and Increase Profits.

BOSTON, Jan. 26.—It was learned to-day that the various manufacturers of felting have agreed to combine, it is claimed, for the purpose of correcting abuses which have grown up in the trade, and to call a halt to an unhealthy competition which has reduced the profits of manufacturers very materially.

The parties to the transaction are said to include Tingue, House & Co., who will conduct the New York business; Alfred Dolge & Son whose plant is at Dolgeville, N. Y., is being opened by Jacob Dolge, son of Dr. J. B. Bloodgood, Pilton, N. J.; the City Mills, Franklin, Mass., and the Boston Felting Company of this city. The latter concern will have charge of the Boston business, while a well-known Chicago wholesale house will take care of the Western trade. This comprises practically all the felt plants in active operation in the country.

BIG RUBBER COMBINATION.

New Yorkers in Concern with a Capital of $50,000,000.

The Rubber Goods Manufacturing Company was incorporated yesterday at Trenton, N. J., by the law firm of Ivins, Kidder & Mercer. The company has a capital of $25,000,000 7 per cent. cumulative preferred stock, and $25,000,000 of common stock, and was organized for the purpose of acquiring plants engaged in the manufacture of rubber goods. The incorporators are Charles Stewart Smith of Smith, Hogg & Gardner; Charles H. Dale, Henry Steers, Alvah Trowbridge, Ulysses D. Eddy, George W. Hebard, R. L. Edwards, Percy Chubb, Herbert J. Davis, Alden S. Swan, William A. Towner, Thomas Russell, Ansel L. White, and George S. Dearborn of New York, and Camillus G. Kidder of Orange, N. J. The promoters of the corporation say that it is policy is not to acquire all of the companies engaged in the manufacture of rubber goods, but to acquire properties that have demonstrated their capacity to manufacture goods cheaper than their competitors, and by economies in administration and through the securing of special facilities for obtaining crude rubber, it is expected that the cost of producing rubber goods can be still further reduced.

Among the bankers interested in this enterprise are: J. P. Morgan & Co., Kuhn, Loeb & Co., Kidder, Peabody & Co. of Boston, August Belmont & Co., Speyer & Co., Lee, Higginson & Co. of Boston, Brown Brothers & Co., Blake Brothers & Co., Hollister, Leadbeater & Co., Morton, Bliss & Co., J. & W. Seligman & Co., F. S. Smithers & Co., and Baring, Magoun & Co.

The authorization of the incorporation empowers the company to manufacture and deal in goods of which india rubber, gutta percha, balata, or their substitutes form a component part.

TIN PLATE CORPORATIONS.

Organizing Opposition to the National Enameling and Stamping Co.

TRENTON, N. J., Jan. 26.—Articles of incorporation were filed to-day of three allied concerns, the National Tin Plate Company, the United States Tin Plate Company, and the National Tin Plate and Stamped Ware Company. The two former have an authorized capital stock of $125,000 each and the latter has an authorized capital of $20,000,000. The companies are empowered to manufacture and deal in tin, terne, black plate, and steel plate, and the larger concern is in addition authorized to manufacture steel and iron.

The incorporators of the three companies are the same individuals, viz.: David G. Reid, William B. Leeds, and James B. Dill. The capital stock of the National Tin Plate and Stamped Ware Company is divided into $10,000,000 preferred stock, with 7 per cent. cumulative dividend, and $10,000,000 common stock. The companies are understood to be organized in opposition to the National Enameling and Stamping Company, incorporated on Saturday last with an authorized capital of $30,000,000.

BRITAIN'S MILITARY ATTACHE.

A Permanent Post Will Be Established at Washington—Capt. Arthur H. Lee Will Probably Be Selected.

[Copyright, 1899.]

Special Cablegram to THE NEW YORK TIMES.

LONDON, Jan. 26.—The British Government has decided to create a post permanent as British military attaché to its embassy at Washington.

Of course, the United States Government will previously have been asked whether such a step will be agreeable to it and will have given an affirmative answer. Hitherto the British Government has had military attachés attached to embassies and legations at Berlin, Paris, St. Petersburg, Vienna, Rome, Constantinople, Teheran, Tokio, and Peking.

I am able to add that the first British Military Attaché at Washington will be Capt. Arthur H. Lee, Royal Artillery, who was for nearly five years Professor of Military Topography at the Royal Military College at Kingston, Ontario, and who accompanied the American forces throughout the Cuban and Puerto Rican campaigns as Military Attaché and whose article on American regulars in a recent Scribner's Magazine attracted much attention. He will be raised to the rank of Lieutenant Colonel in his new post.

I feel sure that this appointment will be welcome news to the American Army officers, among whom Capt. Lee made many warm friends while sharing their hardships in the field. It need not be added that the British Government does not make appointments like this unless it is well pleased with an officer's past services.

13TH SKATER MET DEATH.

Train Killed Member of a Party Bound for Crotona Park Lake.

Harry Blundell, eighteen years old, of 848 East One Hundred and Thirty-sixth Street, was killed while on his way to a skating party on the lake in Crotona Park last evening. Eager for the sport, he hurried home from work, ate his supper, and joined the party near the One Hundred and Thirty-eighth Street station of the New York, New Haven and Hartford Railroad. There was just a dozen merry boys and girls there when he reached the rendezvous. One of the lads counted noses.

"You make the thirteenth, Harry," he said when Blundell came up, "and there's trouble ahead for you, old man, to-night."

Blundell laughed at the joke, and they started for the lake, taking a short cut along the tracks of the railroad. They had not gone many yards when a train came along, and to avoid it they crossed over to the north-bound track. Just then a second train, bound in the opposite direction, rounded the curve at full speed. All the members of the party got off the track with the exception of Blundell. He was struck by the train and hurled thirty feet into a ditch. The engineer, Thomas Burke, of New Rochelle, stopped the train and picked the boy up. He had been horribly mangled, and killed instantly. The body was removed to the home of his parents.

Several of the girls in the skating party fainted and had to be taken home.

THE WEATHER.

The local forecast may be found at the top of this page to the right of the title.

The storm central Wednesday night in Wisconsin has moved to Ontario, increasing in intensity, and has caused snow and violent gales in the lake region. Rain has fallen on the West Gulf coast. The storm has been followed by a marked high pressure area which was central last night in North Dakota, and which has caused a sharp fall in temperature from the Middle and Northern Rocky Mountain regions to the Ohio Valley and upper lake regions. St. Paul reports a fall of 38 degrees in twenty-four hours and is 4 degrees below zero, and Davenport and Dubuque a fall of 36 degrees and 34 degrees. The temperature has risen in the Atlantic States and has remained stationary elsewhere, including the Pacific Coast, where the cold weather continues. The cold wave will move eastward and reach the Atlantic Coast to-night, and snow will occur in the lake region, the Ohio Valley, and the Eastern Florida, Southern Florida, where it will be generally fair, and the temperature will rise slowly, with northwesterly gales on the lower lake region, the Ohio Valley, and New England, with much colder in the lower lake region; ... [illegible] ...

The record of temperature for the twenty-four hours ended at midnight taken from the thermometer at THE NEW YORK TIMES building is shown in the annexed table of the Weather Bureau, is as follows:

	1898.	1899.	1898.	1899.
3 A. M.	26	33	26	33
6 A. M.	25	33	25	33
9 A. M.	27	34	27	34
12 M.	30	38	30	38
3 P. M.	32	44	32	44
6 P. M.	30	44	30	44
9 P. M.	29	44	29	44
12 P. M.	28	45	28	45

THE TIMES'S thermometer is 6 feet above the street level; that of the Weather Bureau is 335 feet above the street level.

Average temperature yesterday was as follows:

Printing House Square	41¼
Weather Bureau	40½
Corresponding date 1898	27¾

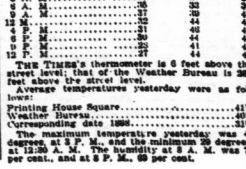

The maximum temperature yesterday was 48 degrees, at 3 P. M., and the minimum 32 degrees, at 12:30 A. M. The humidity at 8 A. M. was 77 per cent., and at 8 P. M., 80 per cent.

GEN. EAGAN ON THE STAND

Justification and Extreme Provocation His Defense.

DESCRIBES HIS MENTAL STATE

Says He Felt Himself Condemned by the Press for Poisoning Soldiers by Wholesale.

WASHINGTON, Jan. 26.—The feature of the proceedings before the Eagan court-martial to-day was the testimony of Commissary General Eagan himself. Not more than fifteen or twenty people outside of the court and a dozen or so newspaper correspondents were admitted to the trial room. Several witnesses preceded the chief figure in the trial. Gen. Eagan listened intently to the testimony of these witnesses, and occasionally held brief whispered consultations with his counsel. He was dressed in full uniform, without sword, and his florid face, white hair and mustache, and soldierly bearing recalled to many the late Gen. Sheridan, to whom he bears a distinct resemblance.

His call to the stand this morning was something of a surprise, as it had been thought that, if he testified at all, it would be later. When his name was called he rose, and standing before the witness chair, raised his right hand, took the oath administered by the Judge Advocate, and at first related his army career. As he proceeded in his testimony it became apparent that the line of defense would be justification and extreme provocation, finally bringing on a serious nervous condition which rendered the witness unfit for business, and made him to a degree irresponsible for his acts. The President's order of immunity, it was also made evident, would be relied on as applicable to Gen. Eagan's testimony before the War Investigating Commission, and that, therefore, the court-martial had no proper jurisdiction in the case.

Gen. Eagan began the story of Gen. Miles's aspersions on him he raised his voice somewhat and spoke with great earnestness, though with perfect enunciation. In speaking of the criticisms of the newspapers, which he said had been called forth by Gen. Miles's testimony, his manner was intensely dramatic and impressive. His eyes filled with tears and his voice trembled and the impression he left with many was decidedly favorable. After the court adjourned several members shook his hand and in a friendly way asked after his health.

GEN. EAGAN'S TESTIMONY.

When the court-martial reassembled today Judge Advocate Davis formally submitted, as an exhibit in the trial, the testimony given by Gen. Miles, which was read yesterday. With this the prosecution rested its case and the defense began the introduction of its evidence. After several witnesses had been heard Gen. Eagan took the stand and was questioned by his counsel. Following is a stenographic report of the more important parts of his testimony:

Q.—Do you remember how long before you appeared before the commission to make your statement in reply to Gen. Miles you had in your possession notice that you could appear? A.—No sir, I do not.

Q.—Was it the day that you then appeared? A.—Yes, Sir.

Q.—Do you remember the date? A.—No, Sir.

Q.—Did you take any steps looking toward having the question which was raised between you and Gen. Miles by his statement adjudicated by a court-martial? A.—Yes, Sir.

Q.—What was it? A.—I had a conversation with the Secretary of War. I do not remember the exact language, but it impressed me as peremptory that Gen. Miles should be tried by court-martial or be charged with the matter. I do not remember exactly the exact language, and it was greatly impressed on me.

Q.—Before you go on, I will ask you what you said to the Secretary. A.—That I desired to continue those grave charges that I was a murderer and a thief, wholesale.

Q.—You took some action, did you not, with relation to an article which appeared in the newspapers. A.—When I saw the alleged interview with Gen. Miles in the New York Journal it drove me nearly crazy, because it emphasized a charge of "embalmed beef" and emphasized a "pretense of experiment." I emphasized to my mind the charge that I was guilty of feeding poisonous food to soldiers for gain. I addressed a letter to the Adjutant General and asked that action be taken, believing at that time that the immunity granted by the President did not extend outside of the court room. I believed that the immunity covered any and everything there, and I believed that it was a very good thing at the time, because the meaning of that so far as it would keep from the papers, was that it was necessary to satisfy the country that the investigation was honest, was complete, and that everybody would be given an opportunity to come forward and testify to everything he knew. I was not astonished that Gen. Miles should be covered by the immunity granted by the President, but I did not believe it extended to his going into newspapers in this alleged interview, and so I sought to ascertain the question by writing to the Adjutant General, and then through him to the Secretary of War, addressing a letter to him through the Adjutant General, asking that the Secretary take up what I considered to be an evasive answer.

Q.—Will you state to the court what impression the testimony of Gen. Miles before the commission made upon you as to the meaning of the statements that he made, and especially by his words "pretense of experiment"? A.—The effect on me, Sir, was that he had taken away that honorable position that I had obtained after all these years of service. He stated that I was unfit for my place as an officer, and that I should go before the country and the world as a man unfit for my court, civil or military, to be thrown out of the army. I had been thrown into the gutter and that I was unfit to associate with people. The whole country has looked upon me as a man from whom physical courage and honor had departed, and that he did not believe I had a particle of it. The trend of the papers, as I have seen them, I was sure to be a good sort of soldier. I had been there, and I could have sought a civil court if I had a wish. It was a mortal insult, and I felt that I am unfit to associate with gentlemen. He took away from me the character of being an honest man and a brave man, and branded me a thief and a murderer. I had a character for honesty and truthfulness, and these things were shown by the papers...

"PRETENSE OF EXPERIMENT."

Q.—I think your answer has covered the question, but I ask you particularly what you understand to be meant by the words "pretense of experiment." A.—That I had furnished such a beef as an experiment; that it was not an experiment, but that it was put up to cover corruption and had fed it to the soldiers; that I had made money by it, and that it was a pretense of experiment; and that I was under a heavy charge of this "pretense of experiment," making it out that I was guilty of corruption in the treatment of the troops, and that I was unfit to hold my place in the army...

Q.—Generally, as perhaps in part accounting for the feeling you had when you came into the court, was it not true that you were for the past few months very much worried and deprived of sleep? A.—Yes, Sir. I do not remember when I have had a night's sleep. I have been under a great mental strain... [illegible]

Q.—You will pardon me for asking the question, but whether or not it is true that you have not entered the office of Commissary General ... any compensation at any time from the ... [illegible]

SUNDAY, THREE CENTS. DAILY, ONE CENT.

"All the News That's Fit to Print."

The New York Times.

THE WEATHER. Generally fair; warmer; fresh southerly winds.

COPYRIGHT, 1900, BY THE NEW YORK TIMES COMPANY.

VOL. XLIX...NO. 15,722. NEW YORK, WEDNESDAY, MAY 30, 1900.—TWELVE PAGES. ONE CENT In Greater New York and Jersey City. Elsewhere, TWO CENTS.

THE NEWS CONDENSED.

Stocks firmer.

Wheat, No. 2 red, 79¾c; corn, No. 2 mixed, 43c; oats, No. 2 mixed, 26½c; cotton, middling, .09⅛c; iron, northern, No. 1 foundry, $21.00; butter, western creamery, 20½c.

CONGRESS.—The House yesterday refused to agree to the Senate amendment to the Naval bill relating to armor plate and an armor plate factory. It adopted an amendment authorizing the Secretary of the Navy to buy armor at such price as he may deem necessary to pay, and sent the bill to conference. The anti-trust measures will be taken up in the House and voted on this week. The Senate considered the Sundry Civil Appropriation bill, adopted several amendments, among them one conditionally appropriating $5,000,000 for the St. Louis Exposition in 1903. The Senate adjourned until Thursday. The Senate Committee reported unfavorably on the Constitutional amendment providing for election of Senators by popular vote.—Page 5.

FOREIGN.—Lord Roberts is now just outside Johannesburg, and reports that he intends to enter the city at noon to-day. He evidently expects no opposition, and says that he has received word that the mines have not been injured. Confirmation of the latter statement comes from other sources. The Orange Free State was formally annexed to the British Empire yesterday. It is to be known in the future as the Orange River State. At a dinner in London last evening Lord Salisbury made a definite statement as to the future of the two Boer republics. He said that no shred of independence would be allowed to them; there would never be a chance of a repetition of the present war. Russian interest in the war continues in a marked degree, and many of the newspapers call on the Czar to intervene. It is declared that the South African Republic is about to open peace negotiations. The Chinese rebellion is assuming larger proportions. It is said the "Boxers" have the support of the Empress and the whole Manchu army. Rioting and massacre at Peking are feared, and the foreign envoys have called for guards. Authority has been sent Minister Conger, on his request, to call on the nearest United States naval vessel. Mrs. Gladstone is growing weaker. Gen. de Galliffet yesterday resigned the War Portfolio of the French Ministry. The leader of the Venezuela rebels is a prisoner. Sir Thomas Lipton entertained Americans at a banquet yesterday.—Pages 1, 2, and 6.

Page 1.

At places on the Lower Rio Grande the ignorant Mexican population were badly frightened by the eclipse. At Iguale they broke into the church for protection.

Page 2.

It is reported in Washington that John D. Long has been selected for the Republican nomination for Vice President.

Page 3.

Willard A. Cobb, President of the State Civil Service Commission, died at Lockport, N. Y.

Republicans from up the State believe that either Senator White or Senator Stranahan will be nominated for Lieutenant Governor.

The American Ice Company yesterday secured an order from Justice Andrews to show cause why proceedings against it should not be stopped.

By the secession of a supporter of Charles A. Hess the partisans of Capt. Goddard obtained a quorum last night, organized the Twelfth Congress Republican District Convention, and elected Bliss and Goddard delegates to the Philadelphia Convention.

Page 6.

The Methodist General Conference at Chicago completed the business before it and adjourned.

Page 7.

Dr. Parkhurst yesterday, on the eve of his departure for Europe, freely expressed his views on Tammany, the Ice Trust, and Gov. Roosevelt.

It became known yesterday that Assemblyman Fallows is entitled to receive a fee for an inheritance tax case in which he took no part, having been appointed to assist in collection of the tax after the check therefor had been received at the Department of Finance.

Page 12.

The final negotiations by which the Consolidated Gas Company will take over the Standard Company have been completed.

Joseph Collins, steward of Fort Hancock, yesterday made further charges against Lieut. Martin, that caused another sensation at the court-martial.

Curator Ditmars and Keeper Snyder of Bronx Zoological Park yesterday, after an exciting experience, bagged two deadly king cobras in a roomful of snakes that had escaped from their cages.

In the contest of the will of Robert Bonner yesterday, Lawyer Van Vorst testified that Mr. Bonner was dissatisfied with the widow of his son, Andrew Allen Bonner, and wanted to prevent her from sharing in the estate.

WILLIAM ROCKEFELLER ILL.

Has Been Successfully Operated Upon for Appendicitis.

William Rockefeller is at his home, 689 Fifth Avenue, recovering from an operation for appendicitis. The following statement was given out last night in connection with the case:

"Mr. William Rockefeller had a slight attack several weeks ago that indicated appendicitis. Under the advice of his physician he had an operation for appendicitis performed after he had recovered from the attack, and he is doing splendidly. The operation was performed by Dr. Robert F. Weir, assisted by Dr. Henry Walker and Dr. Walter B. James.

"The advice of his physicians was that the attack might recur at any time unless the operation was performed, and that it was best to operate while his general health was normal and there was a minimum of risk."

RAILROAD WAR IN CHICAGO.

Surface Lines Prepare to Meet the Five-Cent Elevated Road Fare.

Special to The New York Times.

CHICAGO, May 29.—With the opening of the Northwestern Elevated Road Thursday there will be inaugurated an intramural transportation warfare that promises to bring lower fares within reach of Chicagoans.

The Chicago Union Traction Company, under its new management, has prepared to offset the influence of a five-cent fare from Wilson Avenue and Evanston Avenue to the heart of the down-town district by issuing transfers on its Evanston Avenue line good to the extremities of Edgewater. It costs 10 cents to get to Edgewater at present.

It is a war between the Yerkes interests and the Chicago Union Traction Company, and is attributed to the efforts of Mr. Yerkes to make his elevated roads the trunk lines for suburban traffic.

To Extend Call to Western Pastor.

Special to The New York Times.

GREENWICH, Conn., May 29.—At a meeting of the Second Congregational Church this evening it was voted unanimously to tender a call to the Rev. W. H. Selden of Elgin, Ill. The church has been without a pastor since last August, when the Rev. Dr. Walter M. Barrows died as a result, it is said, of the criticisms which reflected on him after he married Perry Belmont and Mrs. Sloane, a few hours after Mrs. Sloane's divorce.

LAWYERS OPPOSE HAZEL'S APPOINTMENT

Buffalo Deputation Say He Is Unfitted for Judgeship.

CALL ON THE NEW YORK BAR

Meeting of Committee on Judicial Nominations Hurriedly Summoned to Meet Them Late Last Night.

A committee of five members of the bar of Buffalo came to the city last night on the Empire State express and met the Committee on Judicial Nominations of the Association of the Bar of the City of New York at the clubhouse, 42 West Forty-fourth Street. The object of the visit of the lawyers from Buffalo was to convince the New York lawyers that John R. Hazel of Buffalo was not fitted for the position of United States District Judge for the Western District of New York, to which position he has been nominated by President McKinley.

The Committee on Judicial Nominations of the Local Bar Association had already decided on a special meeting of the entire association for to-morrow night to discuss the situation. The call for the meeting had been sent out signed by seven members of the committee and fifteen other members of the association. The meeting of the committee at which this action was decided on was held on Thursday evening last. Robert W. De Forest, Chairman of the committee; Horace Russell and William E. Curtis, members, declined to sign the call.

The meeting called last night by the committee to hear the lawyers from Buffalo was rather unexpected, and it was called in a hurry, after a telegram had been received from the Buffalo committee. It was nearly 11 o'clock when the delegation from Buffalo arrived, and at once they went into secret session with the local committee. The session lasted until nearly 2 o'clock this morning.

Members of the association who were at the clubhouse while the committee was in session were free in the expression of opinion that the fight was strictly a Republican partisan affair, and that it should be left to the Platt and anti-Platt forces to settle. This means that if the same opinion prevails at the meeting to-morrow night there will be an exciting time among the members of the association. Some will be opposed to the association's taking any action at all, while others will be divided upon the question of passing resolutions condemning the nomination.

The call which was sent out yesterday for the meeting to-morrow is signed by twenty-two members of the association, among them being Paul D. Cravath, ex-Justice William N. Cohen, John De Witt Warner, John McLean Nash, John L. Cadwalader, William G. Choate, Theodore Connoly, George F. Butterworth, and Everett P. Wheeler.

The greatest secrecy was maintained as to the names of the members of the Buffalo committee. One of this delegation, asked to tell who he and his companions were, replied:

"We are the guests of the Association of the Bar of the City of New York, and, as the guests of this organization, we do not feel inclined to say anything about our mission to the city or give the names of those in the party. We will remain here until after the meeting to-morrow night, and at that meeting we may present the same arguments that we presented to the committee here to-night."

Col. R. G. Monroe, one of the members of the local committee, said that a subcommittee of the Committee on Judicial Nominations would meet some time to-day and hear further argument from the Buffalo representatives as to the situation, and that the sub-committee would make a report to be presented at the meeting of the association to-morrow night.

Ex-Justice William N. Cohen, another member of the committee, said:

"Nothing will be made public until the meeting of the entire association on Thursday night."

It was understood that as part of the argument against Mr. Hazel's appointment one of the Buffalo delegation presented to the committee copies of letters written by several Judges, some now in the United States District Courts. These letters were addressed to President McKinley and protested against the appointment, on the grounds that Mr. Hazel did not have the necessary experience as a lawyer to qualify him for the position.

Another protest was that from the Lake Carriers' Association of Buffalo, which is a powerful organization, having control of shipping interests on the great lakes. The delegate presenting these documents is understood to have declared that numerous indorsements had been obtained in Buffalo for Mr. Hazel by threats of political destruction on the part of those who had control of the Republican Party in Erie County.

Just what was said by other Buffalo representatives could not be learned from either them or the local committee.

MR. DEPEW STANDS BY HAZEL.

Senator Justifies His Action in Indorsing the Buffalo Man's Application for Judgeship.

Special to The New York Times.

WASHINGTON, May 29.—The storm of protest aroused in Western New York by the appointment of John R. Hazel to a Federal Judgeship has made itself felt here with some rather unlooked for results.

President McKinley shifted the responsibility to the shoulders of Senator Depew by telling Buffalo men who visited him to protest against Hazel's appointment that he would withdraw the nomination if they would get Mr. Depew to withdraw his indorsement. They made this known to Mr. Depew, who was placed in a rather embarrassing position, particularly as the President had not hinted a thing of the sort to him, and also as Senator Platt, not Senator Depew, was the chief mover in applying for the appointment of Hazel. He told the Buffalo people that he could not withdraw his indorsement.

Mr. Depew was asked to-night whether he had any intention of withdrawing his recommendation of Hazel in view of the protests made during the past few days, and replied that he had not. In view of the fact that by the President's action Mr. Depew is now charged with the responsibility of Mr. Hazel's appointment, the Senator was asked for a statement of his position.

"Mr. Hazel," replied Senator Depew, "came first to Mr. Platt, not to me. I am not much of a patronage dispenser. Mr. Platt agreed to support him, and he then came to me. I always like to know something about a man when he asks for my indorsement, and in response to my request Mr. Hazel submitted the most remarkable recommendations I ever have seen.

"He produced letters from every Judge in the Eighth Judicial District, a district whose bench compares favorably with the bench of any district in the State of New York. These eminent Judges did not merely sign their names to a petition, but wrote letters, cordial, emphatic letters. He had the indorsement of every County Judge in the Western District of New York. He had the indorsement of every District Attorney in the district, and he had the indorsement of more than half the bar of Buffalo, including many of the most eminent lawyers there.

"I recognized the names of men whose standing at the bar I knew well, men who had been retained as counsel in past times by the road. The name of Spencer Clinton alone would have been enough to decide me. He occupies a place at the Buffalo bar similar to those occupied by Choate and Root in New York; and he is no politician—doesn't know anything about politics.

"When I saw these recommendations, I said very frankly to Mr. Hazel: 'You have the most extraordinary lot of indorsements I have seen in all my life.' I told him that I should support him with pleasure, and I did so. I heard of no opposition to him then. I knew that there were two or three other candidates for the place—lawyers who wanted to be Judges—but they had no indorsements except their own letters. I did not ask for any further indorsement of Mr. Hazel, and do not see what more it would be possible to ask.

"The Judges who recommended Mr. Hazel so cordially were, some of them, men who had twelve years yet to serve; some who had just been elected; some who were about to retire by reason of the age limit, and, even if I were disposed to hunt for selfish motives in the actions of some of the ablest and most irreproachable Judges in the State of New York, it would be hard to suspect a selfish motive in such cases.

"Then eight or ten very reputable gentlemen from Buffalo came to Washington to protest against Mr. Hazel's appointment. They saw the President, and gathered from him that if I would withdraw my recommendation he would withdraw the nomination. They told me so, and asked me to withdraw my indorsement. I have heard nothing whatever from the White House to this effect. I suppose if a Senator who had recommended a man to office should withdraw the recommendation the President would naturally feel disposed to withdraw the nomination.

"I told them that I had made this recommendation on the recommendations of the Supreme Court Justices, County Judges, District Attorneys, and a majority of the bar, and that I could not withdraw it. To do so, after basing my recommendation on theirs, would be to imply that I now felt a doubt of their veracity and suspected them of falsehood and unworthy motives. It would be a direct insult to every member of the bench of Western New York.

"My recommendation of Mr. Hazel was based entirely on these indorsements. I had no personal knowledge of his standing at the bar, but that is not surprising, since a man who has won such fame in his profession that his professional standing is known throughout the State will not usually be a candidate for a twenty-five-hundred-dollar-a-year Judgeship.

"As to the opposition to Mr. Hazel, I think it originated in politics. A man who has been active in politics, so active as to become the party leader in his county, cannot aspire to office without arousing political opposition."

"But it is said, Senator," it was suggested, "that Mr. Hazel has no experience in Federal practice."

"That was said of Judge Wallace," replied Mr. Depew, "when he was appointed. He had had no experience in admiralty or patent law, and he had served in the army, which, it was urged, was likely to make him still rustier. He was backed by Roscoe Conkling, and precisely the fight that is now being made against Mr. Hazel was made against him. The same arguments were advanced, almost in the same language. Judge Wallace was appointed. It was true that he did not know much about Federal practice, but he was a hard student and an energetic man, like Mr. Hazel; and he has proved to be one of the best Judges on the Federal bench. He is now a Circuit Judge, a promotion for merit.

"Judge Coxe, whose judicial district comprises the new district to which Mr. Hazel has been appointed, was opposed in the same way. He had practiced very little, and in Federal courts not at all. He was a nephew of Roscoe Conkling, and it was claimed that his appointment was due to political influence. But it did not take long for him to make an impression on the bar, and he is held in deservedly high esteem as a Judge. Neither of these Judges had such backing as Mr. Hazel had from Judges and lawyers."

It was suggested to Mr. Depew that the action of the Judges in recommending Mr. Hazel is explained by his opponents on the ground that they were afraid he would become a Supreme Court Judge, and wanted to sidetrack him into the Federal court.

"Well," commented the Senator, "that is an attack on the integrity of the Judges, and a much more serious reflection on their fitness for the positions they hold than any that has been made against Mr. Hazel."

ECLIPSE SCARED MEXICANS.

Frantic Mob Broke Into Church to Secure Protection.

Special to The New York Times.

SAN ANTONIO, Texas, May 29.—Reports from the Lower Rio Grande, which was in the path of the totality of the solar eclipse, tell of serious disturbances in some benighted regions there through the superstitious fears of the ignorant Mexicans. In the little village of Iguala, on the Rio Grande, the Catholic Church Del Carmen suffered severely at the hands of an ignorant mob. During the first contact the people began streaming toward the church, but the doors were locked. At the main entrance complacently stood the padre, a young French priest named Agierre. He waved the crowd back and tried to make them overcome their superstitious fear by bravely awaiting the approaching total eclipse.

For a while he held the crowd in subjection, but at the sight of the heavy black shadow sweeping toward them the mob in affright made a rush for the doorway, trampled down the padre, and broke the heavy doors from their hangings. Many broke in through the low windows, and for a few minutes, in a heap of wrecked benches and amid fragments of statuary from an overturned altar, nearly the entire population of Iguala sat crouched until the bright sunlight reappeared.

News of the affair reached Edinborough, and an expedition, headed by Dr. W. R. Love, started in wagons for Iguala. Some eighteen or twenty people were more or less bruised and injured.

At Brownsville, Edinborough, and Reynosa there was some excitement, but through the foresight of the authorities in warning the people of the coming phenomenon nothing more serious than a general rush for the churches and cathedral was experienced.

On the Mexican side of the river the Government also prepared the people for the coming of the eclipse, and had all the troops in readiness in case of serious alarm or outbreak.

ALABAMA TRADE WITH EUROPE.

Trial Shipments of Steel and Bar Iron from Birmingham.

Special to The New York Times.

BIRMINGHAM, Ala., May 29.—The return of Vice President James Bowron of the Tennessee Coal, Iron and Railroad Company from Europe has been followed by the shipment of several trial orders of Alabama bar iron and steel to the Old World.

Heretofore only raw pig iron has been exported, but it is understood that Mr. Bowron induced European consumers to make a test of finished ore and steel bars from this district, and as a result shipments of 20 tons of steel and 100 tons of bar iron were made to-day, and more will follow in the near future.

Alabama producers believe that a trial of these products is all that is necessary to build up a permanent trade in them abroad.

Commencement at Harvard.

Special to The New York Times.

CAMBRIDGE, Mass., May 29.—The following have been picked by competition from the senior class to deliver the commencement parts at Harvard: Murray Seasongood, Cincinnati; H. L. Seaver, Dorchester, Mass.; R. S. Forbes, Brooklyn, N. Y.; F. G. Bauer, Jamaica Plain, Mass. F. W. C. Hersey of Lincoln, Mass., will represent the Graduate School.

Contractor Dies Suddenly in the Street.

Special to The New York Times.

RAHWAY, N. J., May 29.—Henry Rau, a contractor of Elizabeth, who drove here this afternoon, was taken ... with heart trouble and died in the street before help could reach him.

THE REBELLION IN CHINA

"Boxers" Said to Have Support of the Imperial Troops.

MASSACRE AT PEKING FEARED

Rebels Massed Outside—Foreign Envoys Call for Guards—Nine Methodist Missionaries Killed.

LONDON, May 30.—The Daily Express has the following from Shanghai, dated Tuesday:

"The rebellion continues to grow in intensity, and the gravest fears are entertained of its ultimate extent. The foreign envoys at Peking, fearing a massacre within the capital, have decided to bring up the guards of the legations.

"The rebels are now massing outside of Peking, and their numbers are reported to be constantly augmenting. Fresh contingents of armed malcontents are coming up almost hourly from the north.

"The imperial troops who were sent to disperse the rebels found themselves hopelessly outnumbered. Several hundreds were killed, and two guns and many rifles were captured, after which the greater part of the remaining troops went over to the rebels. They are now marching side by side.

"It is believed that the 'Boxers' have the sympathy of the entire Manchu Army in the anti-foreign crusade; and there is no doubt that they have the countenance of the Empress Dowager and of Prince Ching.

"The Belgian Minister, escorted by a strong body guard, has gone to obtain an audience of the Tsung-li-Yamen, a number of his countrymen, with their families, having been cut off by the rebels at Chang-hsin-tien.

"The position of the missionaries is one of extreme peril, unless aid is speedily forthcoming. It is feared that they will meet with the same fate as their unfortunate converts, whom the 'Boxers' are ruthlessly murdering."

Another dispatch from Shanghai says:

"It is believed that Russia is about to land troops at Taku from Port Arthur, where 20,000 men are in readiness. The Chinese are reported to be sending large masses of troops overland from Hu-nan and Kiang, but the Generalissimo refuses to assume command on the plea of sickness.

"The 'Boxers' assert that they are confident of receiving support from the Dowager Empress, Princes Kang-yi and Ching-Tuan, and the entire Manchu army. Throughout the North the 'Boxers' are enlisting hordes of desperadoes. They are intent upon expelling everything foreign."

The Peking correspondent of The Times, telegraphing Tuesday, says:

"The foreign guards have been summoned by the legations and will arrive immediately. This decision was well taken. The opinion is widespread that the powers should compel China to defray the cost of a measure which the apathy of the Chinese Government necessitates. All the French engineers and their families are reported safe."

The Times, commenting upon the situation in Peking, says:

"We must follow the excellent example set us by the Americans and must lose no time in telling the Tsung-li-Yamen that, unless they re-establish security for the life and property of our fellow-subjects in China without delay we shall take strong measures on our part."

The Times expresses the opinion that Great Britain will have to intervene vigorously for the defense of the elementary rights of British subjects.

SHANGHAI, May 29.—The Russian Minister at Peking has telegraphed asking that all the available gunboats be sent to Taku.

TIEN-TSIN, May 29.—A hundred American marines from the United States cruiser Newark are expected here at 11 o'clock to-night.

An armed rescue party of Frenchmen and Germans started this afternoon to try to relieve the besieged Belgians. The Viceroy, under the pressure of the French Consul, has permitted the rescuers to travel by railroad to Feng-tai, where Chinese protection ends.

A detachment of 200 Chinese soldiers has cleared the railway between here and Peking, and the ordinary service was resumed at noon.

Thirty Japanese have arrived from the gunboat Atagokan. The French flagship and the gunboat Surprise have left Taku.

PEKING, May 29.—The relief party has returned from Chang-hsin-tien, bringing twenty-five persons, including several women and children.

MINISTER CONGER ASKS AID.

Authorization Sent Him to Call on Nearest American Naval Vessel.

WASHINGTON, May 29.—Such advices as have reached here indicate that the situation in China has assumed a very critical phase, and one calculated to tax the entire resources of the Chinese Government. The State Department has been in close communication with Mr. Conger, the Minister at Peking, and the Navy Department is doing its share, having placed the flagship Newark as far up the Pei-ho River as the Taku forts, which is the nearest point to Peking that the ship can reach.

The operations of the "Boxers" are increasing in magnitude. Their demonstrations are no longer local, and they appear to be governed in their movements by some well-settled design. They have murdered nine Methodist missionaries in one province, at the town of Pachow, and have closed in on Peking. Meanwhile the Chinese Army is suspected of disloyalty, this belief being strengthened by wholesale desertions of the soldiers to the "Boxers."

Minister Conger has appealed to the State Department for the protection of a marine guard for his legation. The department has promptly sent him an authorization to call upon the nearest United States naval vessel for assistance. It is not known yet whether he has availed himself of the permission. The ship he would naturally look to would be the Newark, and it is assumed that he has already communicated with Admiral Kempff on board that flagship.

According to reports, the Chinese Government has done everything in its power to meet the demands of the diplomatic body at Peking for the dispersion of the "Boxers," but it appears that the uprising is more serious than was at first apprehended, and even the resident Ministers at Peking are inclined to admit that the task is not an easy one for the Chinese Government.

So far all of the measures taken by the State Department look merely to the protection of the American Legation at Peking, the American Consulates in the vicinity, and the lives of such Americans as may be obliged to take refuge therein in the event of general rioting. The State Department is closely adhering to the practice it has always observed of non-interference in the Chinese disturbances, and it is not contemplated that the American forces shall take any part in the contest between the Chinese Government and the "Boxers," though it is assumed that Rear Admiral Remey, the Commander in Chief of the Asiatic Station, will take immediate steps to supply Rear Admiral Kempff, the senior squadron commander, with such naval force as he may need for safeguarding American interests at the treaty ports.

FRENCH MINISTER RESIGNS

Gen. de Galliffet Surrenders the War Portfolio.

Says He Is Ill, but Public Believes His Action Due to the Premier's Utterances.

PARIS, May 30.—Gen. the Marquis de Galliffet, Minister of War, has resigned. It is officially announced that his successor is Gen. André.

In his letter to M. Waldeck-Rousseau, the Premier, asking him to place the resignation in the hands of the President of the Republic, Gen. de Galliffet pleads ill-health as a reason for his decision. His exact words are:

"I am very ill, and my health prevents me resisting all emotions of the moment."

The Official Journal this morning therefore contains the acceptance of the resignation, embodied in a decree signed by M. Loubet, which also appoints the new Minister of War.

After deciding upon Gen. André as the most suitable successor, the Premier telegraphed to him at Nemours, where he was taking part in the manoeuvres. Gen. André left immediately, arriving in Paris about 11:15 o'clock last evening. The interview at the Ministry of the Interior lasted about three-quarters of an hour. An understanding was rapidly reached regarding all points in the Ministerial programme, and at midnight the Premier was able to send the decree to the Official Journal.

In spite of his plea of ill-health this is not generally considered the sole reason for the resignation of Gen. de Galliffet. Having in view the apologetic statement made by M. Waldeck-Rousseau in the Chamber of Deputies yesterday, there seems little doubt that he was annoyed by the word "felony" applied to an officer of the French Army, although there is little difference between this language of the Premier and that which Gen. de Galliffet himself had used at a previous sitting.

The Ministerial organs continue to give ill-health as the sole reason, the Figaro pointing out that, strictly speaking, Gen. de Galliffet's word "crime" is much harsher than "felony," which "exactly describes Capt. Fritsch's attitude of revolt toward his superior."

For a month his doctor had urged Gen. de Galliffet to resign, and a letter announcing his decision was read at the Cabinet council yesterday.

Whatever the true explanation, there can be no doubt on one point. Gen. de Galliffet's retirement is regarded with considerable regret. His straightforward conduct and his vigorous manner of dealing with opponents were the delight of his friends; and his rugged eloquence at times compelled even the admiration of his enemies.

Under his direction the army has benefited by quite a number of reforms, the most recent of which was his prohibition of the sale of harmful intoxicants. He also forbade that certain newspapers, noted for their attacks upon the army, should be placed at the military clubs.

It is difficult to say yet what effect the resignation will have upon the Cabinet.

Gen. André was appointed a General of Division a year ago and commands the Tenth Division of the Fifth Army Corps. He is sixty-two years old and an excellent type of the well-educated French soldier, distinguished by physical vigor and cool energy, as well as for intellectual quality. While commander of the Polytechnic School from December, 1893, to May, 1899, he showed himself a skillful as well as an energetic administrator. He has strenuously opposed the introduction of politics into the army, and it is therefore certain that he will co-operate with the Cabinet to make France peaceful. He is an officer of the Legion of Honor.

[Gaston Alexandre Auguste, Marquis de Galliffet, who became Minister of War when the Waldeck-Rousseau Ministry was formed, June 22, 1899, was born in Paris, Jan. 30, 1830. He is one of the most highly respected men in France. He has always been considered clever and daring. In the days of the last Empire he was a favorite at Court and was the most popular leader of cotillions in the gay capital. His ancestors were great personages at the Court of Versailles in the days of Queen Marie Antoinette.

The Marquis entered the army at seventeen, as a private in the First Hussars. A year later he killed the fencing master of his corps in a duel, but this did not prevent his advancement, for four years later he became a Lieutenant, after having passed through the non-commissioned grades one after another.

During the Crimean war the Marquis was made a Knight of the Legion of Honor and attained the rank of Major for innumerable feats of courage and gallantry in the same campaign. In Mexico he was severely injured at the battle of Puebla and almost died from exposure and the heat. He was struck in the stomach by a shell and the military surgeon pronounced it a hopeless case. He survived, however, and when the wound had healed a little a silver plate was made to cover it. He was able to resume service in 1868. He was later removed for engaging in a duel, but was reinstated, and in 1870 led the memorable cavalry charge at Sedan.

The troops which put down the Communists in Paris were under command of the Marquis de Galliffet. In 1872 he was in charge of the El Goleah expedition, which presented many difficulties for the transportation of troops. He overcame all obstacles by executing a rapid march through a desert country and subdued the tribes in revolt. For these services he was made a Commander of the Legion of Honor. He was one of the first of the recognized Royalists to rally to the support of the republic and became the personal friend of Gambetta.

In 1875 the Marquis was raised to the rank of a General of Division, retaining it until he retired in 1894, having reached the age limit. He remained in retirement until called to enter the Cabinet as Minister of War.

COMMENT ON GEN. ANDRE.

PARIS, May 30.—The news of the change in the Cabinet became known at too late an hour last evening to allow the morning papers to comment upon it. Most of them merely announced the fact. The anti-Semite and Nationalist papers, however, cannot resist the temptation to indulge in violent language.

The Libre Parole accuses Gen. André of being the "only General in the French Army who has publicly manifested sympathy with Dreyfus."

The Echo De Paris recognized Gen. André's high qualities, but regrets that he consents to associate himself with the "evil work" of the Ministry.

The Gaulois predicts that before three months are over André will "show himself a true French General by abandoning those who now applaud him as they did Chanoine and Galliffet."

The Socialist Aurore considers the departure of Gen. de Galliffet unimportant politically, declaring that "it rather strengthens the Cabinet, because the ex-Minister had lost the sympathy of many Radicals and Socialists."

FRENCH AMNESTY BILL.

PARIS, May 29.—The Senate reassembled to-day and M. Eugène Guérin presented his report on the Amnesty bill, the provisions of which prevent further criminal proceedings arising out of recriminations in the Dreyfus case, and, in accordance with the wishes of the Government, he asked for a discussion of the measure next Friday, to which the Senate agreed.

The report says ex-Capt. Alfred Dreyfus is excluded from the amnesty, owing to the serious double objection that the amnesty, in effacing all trace of the condemnation and crime itself, would have as a consequence the reinstatement of Dreyfus in all his rights, while, on the other hand, it would deprive him of the rights to seek a revision of his case.

The bill, it is further pointed out, will have the effect of removing various suits from the criminal courts to those of civil jurisdiction, and the most complete light may thus be thrown on the Dreyfus affair, but without noise and without scandal.

EXTORTION AT PARIS FAIR?

Special to The New York Times.

WASHINGTON, May 29.—A local newspaper announced this morning that the State Department would be asked to-day to investigate some serious charges which have been sent to this city regarding the conduct of American officials connected with the Paris Exposition. It was asserted that these officials are allotting space to the highest bidders, and are applying the money so received to their own use.

The French Government gives the space free of cost to foreign exhibitors, but it was charged that the American officials in question make the exhibitor pay whatever can be extorted, the minimum being $150, before he is allowed to exhibit. No names were given.

The story was emphatically denied at the State Department. It was said there that no such request had been made, and that the department had no reason to believe than any was in contemplation. A high official declared his belief that the story had no basis whatever. Nevertheless, should any such charge be made at the State Department it will be investigated.

EX-SENATOR'S NARROW ESCAPE

Edward Floyd-Jones Almost Suffocated in His Burning Country Residence.

AMITYVILLE, L. I., May 29.—The residence of ex-Senator Edward Floyd-Jones burned this morning. Its contents, which included an art collection valued at more than $5,000, were also destroyed. The fire broke out at 1:30 o'clock, and before the firemen could get to work the building was beyond saving. Efforts were directed solely to preventing the flames from spreading to adjoining residences. The latter were occupied by E. W. Burdett and C. R. Canfield and were not injured.

Mr. Jones and his servants were asleep in the house, and all had narrow escapes, being aroused by the smoke. They left through the windows, with nothing on but their night clothes. Mr. Jones was almost suffocated. He was removed to a neighbor's house and a physician summoned. The firemen were unable to save anything from the burning building.

Mr. Jones estimates the loss at $15,000, partly covered by insurance. The cause of the fire is unknown.

KILLED BY RUNAWAY HORSE.

Charles Manthey Tries to Stop Animal and His Neck Is Broken.

Charles Manthey, twenty-eight years old, a foreman in Marks & Co.'s wagon factory, 414 East Thirteenth Street, and living at 220 Avenue A, was killed yesterday afternoon in front of 424 East Thirteenth Street by being thrown to the street while trying to stop a runaway horse. His neck was broken. The horse was driven by John Schnieble of 616 East Thirteenth Street, who was arrested. Schnieble is a driver for Rouen, Buehler & Son of 157 Lewis Street.

Manthey saw the horse coming, ran out and seized him by the bridle. He was lifted off his feet. He hung on, however, till he had been dragged about thirty feet, when, in front of No. 424, he was tossed toward the curb, which his head struck. He was picked up, dead. Several men succeeded in stopping the horse a few yards further on. The animal was not hurt and the wagon was not damaged.

Manthey was single. His body was taken care of by the police. Schnieble was later arraigned before Coroner Fitzpatrick and held in $500 bail. The bail was furnished and he was released.

ROBERT GOELET'S CONDITION.

Removed from Hospital in Boston—Injuries May Be Serious.

Special to The New York Times.

BOSTON, May 29.—The family and friends of Robert Goelet are keeping news of his condition and even of his whereabouts from the public.

He was taken from the hospital to-day, and the only thing known further than that is that he is not at his rooms in Cambridge.

The hospital reported this morning that the ultimate result of his injuries was somewhat doubtful.

COFFEE WAGON FOR FIREMEN.

Port Chester Plan to Supply Hot Drink to the Men on Duty.

Special to The New York Times.

PORT CHESTER, May 29.—The Rev. Charles E. Brugler, rector of St. Peter's Church of Port Chester, has induced the members of the junior guild of the church to secure a coffee wagon to attend the fire companies when they go to fires. When wet and cold the firemen have resorted to saloons, and Mr. Brugler hopes to break them of the habit.

The idea is to procure a low wagon, which can be pulled up hills easily and to place huge coffee urns at both ends with fires beneath them. A small supply of bandages and splints will also be carried in case of accidents.

HARVARD STUDENT TO WED.

Dean Sage of New York Will Go on Honeymoon Between Examinations.

Special to The New York Times.

CAMBRIDGE, Mass., May 29.—It has been announced at Harvard that Dean Sage, a prominent Yale man, and a well-known New Yorker, now in the Harvard Law School, will marry Miss Hannah Parker of Albany during his final law examinations.

This announcement has created something like a sensation. To most men the final law examinations are a great terror. Men begin weeks in advance, and put in day and night in reviewing cases. Not so this year with Sage. He will take a couple of examinations, then be married, go on a week's honeymoon, and then take the three remaining examinations. It is an unparalleled feat.

Sage is an honor man in the Law School, having pulled an "A" for two years. In recognition of this unusual honor he has been elected an editor of The Harvard Law Review. He is one of the most popular and brilliant men in the Law School. At Yale he was equally well known, liked and prominent. He was a member of the Psi Upsilon in his junior year, and of the Skull and Bones in his senior year.

Miss Parker is a daughter of Gen. and Mrs. A. Parker of Albany, and a well-known society woman of that city.

A GIFT OF $5,000,000.

Donation by Two St. Louis Men to Washington University.

Special to The New York Times.

ST. LOUIS, May 29.—Samuel Cupples and Robert Brookings have donated $5,000,000 to Washington University. This makes a total endowment of $7,000,000.

The two donors will deed over the immensely valuable tract of city property known as Cupples Station with all its franchises. The income from the $5,000,000 amounts to $400,000 annually.

FIRE ON ELEVATED TRACK.

Something set fire to the ties on the elevated railroad structure at Ninth Avenue and Forty-fourth Street last night. The engineer of a north-bound train saw the fire. He stopped his train and gave the alarm with his whistle to citizens, who called the firemen. In the meantime a down train was also stopped, and engineers and firemen of both engines threw water from their tanks on the fire, keeping it subdued until the firemen came.

The latter used their axes and cut out the burning timbers. The damage won't exceed $10, and the delay to the trains was hardly more than fifteen minutes.

LORD ROBERTS NOW AT JOHANNESBURG

Reports That He Will Enter the City at Noon To-day.

NO OPPOSITION EXPECTED

Confirmatory News as to the Safety of the Mines.

BOERS ARE DESERTING

Transvaal Believed to be About to Open Peace Negotiations—Krueger Wants Promise that He Shall Not Be Exiled.

LONDON, May 30.—Lord Roberts is bivouacking in the suburbs of Johannesburg, and intends to make a victorious entry at noon to-day. Judging from his dispatch he must have private information regarding the disposition of the garrison in the fort, as he does not seem to expect opposition.

Lord Roberts's cavalry have flowed on beyond Johannesburg. A portion is understood to be at Zuurfontein, seven miles north of Johannesburg, and within twenty miles of Pretoria. Lord Roberts, although with a broken bridge at Vereeniging and a wrecked railway behind him, has somehow managed to get forward sufficient supplies for his large force.

As he has been able to do so much, it is considered possible that he will be outside of Pretoria on Friday. The rapidity of his advance is thought an extraordinary achievement, even by grudging Continental critics.

The Boers, who were expected to fight along the line of hills known as Klipriversberg, abandoned the eastern end of the range, near Lord Roberts's advance line, but they stood their ground on the extreme right, near Van Wyck's Rust, where they met Gen. French's turning movement. The fight continued all day, and the result is as yet mere conjecture. Probably the Boer rear guard succeeded in keeping Gen. French off, and is now in the hills northwest of Johannesburg.

Lord Roberts's last dispatch to the War Office, received yesterday evening, was as follows. It was dated "Germiston, May 29, 6:30 P. M."

"We arrived here this afternoon without being seriously opposed. No casualties so far as I am aware in the main column, and not many, I trust, in the cavalry and mounted infantry.

"The enemy did not expect us until to-morrow, and had not, therefore, carried off all their rolling stock. We have possession of the junction connecting Johannesburg with Natal, Pretoria, and Klerksdorp by railroad.

"Johannesburg is reported quiet. No mines, I understand, have been injured.

"I shall summon the Commandant in the morning, and if, as I expect, there is no opposition, I propose to enter the town with all the troops at noon."

Germiston is a suburb to the southeast of the Johannesburg Railway Junction, and Lord Roberts probably mentions it in his message to the War Office because Elandsfontein Station is further eastward.

Additional evidence that the mines are intact comes in a message received by a mining company here to-day from its Johannesburg representative, dated May 28, via Delagoa Bay, and saying "All right."

Prisoners taken at Klip River state that there was no intention of blowing up the mines, declaring that the threat was made simply with the intention of frightening away the burghers.

It was rumored at Cape Town yesterday that Gen. French had cut the Boer communications between Heidelberg and Boksburg, within a few miles of Johannesburg.

The Standard has the following from Pretoria under Monday's date:

"The Transvaal Government has opened, or is about to open peace negotiations. It has cabled a final inquiry to its agents abroad, asking whether any hope exists of aid."

Without doubt the presence of Lord Roberts with 40,000 men at Johannesburg will hasten the Transvaal's decision. Dispatches from Lorenzo Marques yesterday described President Krüger as "wavering, but demanding a guarantee that he shall not be exiled to St. Helena."

The fighting burghers still continue to desert, and the total collapse of the Boer military organization is not far off. Bennet Burleigh, wiring from Lord Roberts's headquarters at Vereeniging on Sunday, says:

"I doubt if President Krüger can muster 15,000 men, as many of the burghers have gone to their homes."

The stancher Boers are sending their families, with wagons and stores, to the Zoutpansberg district.

Whether Pretoria will be defended is uncertain, although a Pretoria message, dated Sunday, pictures the work of preparing the defenses of the capital as going on with "feverish activity." Pretoria is situated in the midst of a wilderness of kopjes and ranges, and is provided with defenses that require at least 20,000 men to man them properly. There may still be one hard nut for the British to crack.

The last message out of Pretoria is the following, dated May 28, and censored by the Boer Government:

"Cranse, acting as special Commandant at Johannesburg, has issued a circular to the officials concerned, warning them of the necessity of controlling the foreign element in the town and directing them to resist all attempts to destroy property or life, meeting force by force."

The Netherlands Railway Company yesterday notified the authorities at Lorenzo Marques that they must decline to accept goods for delivery at Johannesburg. Johannesburg telegrams are still accepted, subject to stoppage at Pretoria.

The following dispatch from Pretoria, dated May 28, was received yesterday:

"The British occupied Zeerust this morning, and a large force is marching on to Lichtenburg.

"An official bulletin states that the British crossed the Vaal River on Saturday. Gen. Lemmer had a severe fight at Klip River. Five of the burghers were wounded and two were captured. The British were 5,000 strong.

"By an order recently issued, the President decreed that May 27 and the two following days be observed by the whole country as days of prayer, humiliation and the confession of sins, and that petitions should be offered for relief from oppression.

"Fighting took place at Vanwyktrust, fifteen miles south of Johannesburg, with a large force of British which broke through from the Klip River."

Newcastle, Natal, telegram of yesterday's date says:

"The British guns at Ingogo have been

SUNDAY, THREE CENTS. DAILY, ONE CENT.

"All the News That's Fit to Print."

The New York Times.

THE WEATHER. Showers; southerly winds.

VOL. XLIX...NO. 15,730. NEW YORK, FRIDAY, JUNE 8, 1900.—FOURTEEN PAGES. ONE CENT In Greater New York and Jersey City. Elsewhere, TWO CENTS.

THE NEWS CONDENSED.

Stocks dull.

Cash wheat, No. 2 red, 82¼c; corn, No. 2 mixed, 45¼c; oats, No. 2 mixed, 26¼c; cotton, middling, 8⅞c; iron, No. 1 foundry, $20; butter, creamery, extra, 19c.

FOREIGN.—A correspondent of The London Daily Express interviewed President Krüger near Machadorp, where his capital is situated, in a railway car fitted up for the emergency. The President and State Secretary Reitz said that the war was not over, and that guerrilla warfare would continue so long as 500 burghers were left to fight. He spoke hopefully of an early return to Pretoria, and said he would not leave the country. There are few telegrams from British sources. The list of casualties in the Thirteenth Yeomanry, captured on May 31, includes Sir John Elliott Cecil Power, Bart., killed, and the Earl of Longford wounded. The breach between Lord Lansdowne and Lord Wolseley has widened, and the latter has appealed to Premier Salisbury. Sir Alfred Milner, British Lord High Commissioner in South Africa, has sent a dispatch to the Colonial Office warning miners not to return to Cape Town from England. The situation in China grows worse. A big battle has been fought with the Boxers, in which 200 dead were left on the field. The British have landed 900 troops, a larger force than that of any other power. A detachment of 180 British marines is about to force a passage from Tien-Tsin to Peking. It is suggested in Berlin that there is a lack of harmony among the powers. The King of Sweden arrived at Paris to visit the exposition. The American Chamber of Commerce in Paris entertained the French Exposition officials. —Pages 1, 3, and 6.

CONGRESS.—The House yielded on the items in dispute on the Naval Appropriation bill and Congress adjourned. Mr. Cannon suffered a complete defeat; his proposed compromise being voted down. The closing scenes in the House were marked by great enthusiasm, roused by the singing of patriotic songs by the members, in which the galleries joined. Several Senators defended Commander Todd against the charges made in the House; after adjournment his suspension was revoked by Secretary Long.—Pages 1 and 2.

Page 1.

The Mayor of Newport threatened to arrest W. K. Vanderbilt, Jr., for fast locomobile driving. The Council will meet to-day to take action in regard to the speed rate.

Amendments to the Rules and Regulations of the Republican Party of the county, among other things providing for an executive committee, were adopted by the County Committee last night.

Page 2.

The American Ice Company has reduced the price of ice from 60 to 40 cents per hundred pounds.

Page 3.

Gov. Roosevelt addressed the boys of St. Paul's School at Concord, N. H.

One of the possibilities of the coming National campaign is a third Presidential ticket to be placed in the field by the National, or gold, Democracy.

The Democratic State Convention of Connecticut elected delegates to the National Convention and instructed them for Bryan and the Chicago platform.

Page 5.

Dr. Edward Everett Hale delivered an address yesterday at the annual commencement of Teachers College.

Page 6.

Capt. Frank F. Crenshaw and Capt. Flint are reported wounded in a dispatch from Manila.

The Secretary of War has directed the Military Governor of the Philippines to appoint a board to revise the tariff schedules.

Page 11.

President Wilson of the Consolidated Exchange replied to Moses Hirshfield's circular, defending his administration, and Gen. Watson and John Stanton joined with him in a statement of the Exchange's finances.

Page 14.

Capt. Frederick Bouchard of the barge Harvest Home late Wednesday night rescued a woman and child from drowning off Ellis Island.

Major Clinton H. Smith of the Seventy-first Regiment, who was dismissed from the National Guard of the State, has sent a letter of protest to Gov. Roosevelt. He declares that the officers of the Seventy-first will uphold him.

Arrivals at Hotels and Out-of-Town Buyers.—Page 3.
Business Troubles.—Page 12.
Court Calendars.—Page 12.
Insurance Notes.—Page 10.
Marine Intelligence and Foreign Mails.—Page 9.
Markets.—Page 9.
New Corporations.—Page 3.
Railroads.—Page 11.
Real Estate.—Page 12.
Society.—Page 7.
United Service.—Page 6.
Weather Report.—Page 3.
Yesterday's Fires.—Page 3.

BIG TORNADO IN THE WEST.

Much Damage in Indian Territory and Kansas—A Train Wrecked.

Special to The New York Times.

VINITA, Indian Territory, June 7.—The Town of Miami, Indian Territory, was struck by a tornado at 12:30 o'clock this morning. Several lives were reported lost, and great damage was done to property. Thomas Skinner, who had camped near the town, was sleeping in his wagon when the wagon was hurled into the Neosho River. Skinner was blown against a tree and instantly killed. Several persons were blown into the Neosho River, but were rescued easily on account of the river being low. The Christian church was completely wrecked, and the large livery barn of Manford Cooler was destroyed.

The loss in the town is estimated to exceed $10,000. Telegraph wires were blown down, heavy losses in hay barns and hay along the storm's path are reported. At Quawpaw, a few miles from Miami, nine large hay barns were destroyed, and all the barns at Oceuma were blown away.

The farmers began cutting their wheat a few days ago and the cyclone has destroyed nearly all the wheat along its path. Farmers were just laying by their corn and it is now blown down.

PARSONS, Kan., June 7.—A severe windstorm swept over this section, doing much damage to buildings, fences, trees, and growing crops. The clock tower of the Missouri, Kansas and Texas station was damaged and the elevator at St. Paul, Kan., twelve miles north of here, was destroyed.

At Emporia, Kan., the Crown Point Milling plant was badly damaged by wind and lightning. Many elevators and smokestacks of crushing mills were blown down.

The west-bound St. Louis and San Francisco passenger train was wrecked this morning two miles west of Oswego by a windstorm. The entire train was twisted loose from the engine and lifted from the track. Two express cars full of fruit were thrown about twenty feet and dropped on one side. Two tramps riding on the trucks were injured. The Pullman chair cars were thrown across the track.

CHETOPA, Kan., June 7.—A windstorm to-day almost destroyed the village of Faulkner, seven miles northeast of here. A schoolhouse, a church, and several dwellings were destroyed. The buildings were scattered over the adjacent country. Several farmhouses in the country were unroofed or blown from their foundations. Much damage was done to crops. No casualties are reported.

Twelve Injured in Wreck.

OMAHA, Neb., June 7.—The Milwaukee passenger train which leaves Council Bluffs at 11 A. M., was wrecked to-day at Persia, Iowa, by spreading rails. The dining car was overturned. Porter White and Conductor Kellogg were seriously injured. J. E. Boyer of Temona, Iowa, had his skull fractured, and will probably die. A Kansas City traveling man was seriously hurt, and eight other passengers were more or less injured.

"BOXERS" ENGAGED IN BIG BATTLE

Reported that 200 Dead Were Left on the Field.

UNITED STATES URGED TO ACT

Only Power Which Can Intervene Without Making Trouble.

British Land 900 Troops, and 180 Marines Start to Force a Passage from Tien-Tsin to Peking.

LONDON, June 8.—A dispatch from Shanghai, dated 7:30 P. M. to-day, says the Dowager Empress has ordered Gen. Neih-Si-Chong, with 3,000 men, to protect the railroad at Peking.

A severe fight, it is added, has occurred with the "Boxers," whose ranks include many soldiers from other Generals' commands. When the battle ended 200 dead were left on the field. The dispatch goes on to say:

"One hundred and eighty British marines, with a machine gun, are about to force a passage from Tien-Tsin to Peking. Altogether about 900 British have been landed from the fleet, a greater number than have landed from the combined vessels of the other powers. This evidence of Great Britain's intention to assert her position strongly gives great satisfaction here."

The Daily Express has the following dispatch from Shanghai, dated June 7:

"Attempts to repair the damage to the railway between Tien-Tsin and Peking have been frustrated by the Boxers, who, thousands strong, hold the line against the engineers, gangs attacking the trains arriving.

"The nearest undamaged point is forty-five miles from Tien-Tsin. All the children and ladies, except Lady Macdonald, have left the legations. There are the gravest fears for missionaries in outlying parts. They number hundreds, and the stations are isolated. Concerted action is impossible.

IMPERIAL EDICT IS EVASIVE.

The Peking correspondent of The Times, telegraphing yesterday, says:

"An imperial decree has been issued, but it is of the same evasive character as the preceding one. Throughout it is apologetic in tone and virtually gives justification to the 'Boxers' for their recent anti-foreign and anti-Christian outbreaks.

"The edict repeats the accusation against native Christians who 'joined the church for their own base ends,' and refers to the 'Boxers' as a 'brotherhood,' and not as rebels.

"It avoids all reference to the murders of missionaries or of native Christians, and implies that the destruction of the railway and mission property is due to lawless characters who have joined the Boxers to profit by the disturbances. It blames the officials, orders that the lawless shall be punished, and condemns the Chi-Li soldiers for assisting the disturbances. Nevertheless its character on the whole is quite unsatisfactory.

"The Tsung-li-Yamen undertakes that railway communication shall be restored by Saturday. They have protested against the arrival of more British guards."

WANT UNITED STATES TO ACT.

The morning papers, in long editorials dealing with the Chinese situation, refer to the possible course of the United States. The Daily Mail, which goes beyond any other in urging America to take the lead in intervention, under the caption "McKinley's Opportunity," says:

"The United States has secured definite pledges as to the maintenance of the open door, and their intervention would not produce friction, danger of which is to be anticipated should either England or Russia act alone. We have no desire to provoke a worldwide conflict. Yet our movements are regarded with so much suspicion by many Russians that serious complications might ensue did we land a strong force near Peking.

"The same applies to Russia, face to face with ourselves, but the United States has traditions of friendship with Russia and a community of interests with England. Their action would therefore assure the hostility of neither power. It need scarcely be said that they would have the moral support of the British people, and our material support also, if only the policy of our Government in the Far East were stronger than it is. They would certainly be assisted by Japan.

"In this way a world conflict, disastrous to the interests of all great States, could best be avoided and at the same time the pledges which the skillful negotiations of Mr. Hay have extracted from the various powers would be vindicated.

"The opportunity for America has come. Will she be equal to it, or will she let it slip from her hands and lose her vast potentialities of trade in Northern China?"

BRITISH INTERESTS IN CHINA.

Great Britain's financial interests in China, interests that can be named on the Stock Exchange, aggregate £40,000,000. These, on an average, have declined 1 per cent. There are also many trading companies and syndicates holding concessions which are capitalized for vast unknown sums. The English money in China is probably close to £500,000,000.

The report that Sir Claude Macdonald is too ill to attend to his duties is declared to be unfounded. He has been in constant communication with the Government.

COMMANDERS' INSTRUCTIONS.

The naval commanders in Chinese waters have received identical instructions as to procedure, the question of an emergency being left to their discretion. No fear is entertained for the safety of the legations at Peking. European residents, however, are escaping from the capital to the coast. Peking is still under control, according to a dispatch to the Morning Post dated yesterday, but in a very excited state. A thousand foreign guards were garrisoning the legation houses.

Six hundred international troops are at Tien-Tsin, with six guns. A dispatch to The Daily Mail from Shanghai, dated June 7, takes a gloomy view of things, which are pictured as going from bad to worse. The correspondent says:

"The authorities are displaying palpably guilty supineness in dealing with the Boxers; and the powers are more and more taking matters into their own hands. The Boxers' revolt is spreading and is rapidly changing its character. The Boxers are getting arms, preparing to meet force with force.

"There has been no communications between Peking and Tien-Tsin since Tuesday, although one miserable, half-hearted attempt has been made by Chinese soldiery to reach the capital. The troops were fired upon, and the train had to come back. Another station has been burned on the line."

BOXERS STILL RAIDING.

A news agency dispatch from Tien-Tsin, dated yesterday, says:

"The 'Boxers' are still raiding and pillaging over a wide area. They have wrecked and burned the stations at Long-Pong and Langoo. It has been definitely ascertained that Mme. Astier and Messrs. Ossent and Cades have been murdered. Gen. Nieh claims to have defeated the 'Boxers,' killing 500."

Telegraphing from Tien-Tsin, under date of June 6, a correspondent says:

"I left Tien-Tsin this morning en route for Peking, accompanied by Gen. Nieh, supposed to be one of the best of the Chinese Generals, with sixty troops. We proceeded to Lofa, a distance of thirty-one miles. We found the plate layers' cabins in flames and telegraph poles cut, and men engaged in destroying others in villages near the railway, where flags were seen bearing the inscription: 'Kill All Foreigners.'

"I saw smoke, evidently from burning houses, in the distance, but Gen. Nieh refused to proceed further, being in mortal fear of the Boxers, though the foreigners endeavored to persuade him to disentrain his troops, who are firmly convinced that it is useless to fight the Boxers, as other Chinese say they have seen Boxers hit with bullets rise and run away.

"There seems to be little prospect of a resumption of traffic to Peking unless the foreign powers assume control of the railway until the Chinese Government proves itself capable of managing communications with its capital."

GREAT BRITAIN'S ATTITUDE.

It is understood here that if the United States expects Great Britain to take independent or initiative action in China, as might be gathered from the special cable dispatches quoting Congressman Hitt, the Chairman of the House Committee on Foreign Affairs, it is depending on a contingency which appears very remote indeed.

A correspondent was informed officially to-day that the British Minister at Peking, Sir Claude M. Macdonald, and his assistants, are still in complete charge of the situation, and are relied upon to meet any circumstances which may arise, armed as they are with authority to requisition from the British-China squadron more troops if they are needed.

Replying to a private letter the other day, which suggested that Great Britain should show her teeth more, Lord Salisbury, it is learned, replied that "unfortunately England's teeth were now in South Africa."

SOUNDING THE POWERS.

In spite of the fact that it is officially stated that Great Britain has neither sounded other powers with the view of securing co-operation in a new and vigorous Chinese policy nor been sounded as to such action by any power, there are many rumors that such steps are under consideration. A member of a foreign Embassy in London says that it is certain the British Foreign Office is contemplating sending instructions to all its Ministers to secure the support of other governments, especially the United States Government, in a plan of action.

Although Russia might be included in this concert it would have for its ulterior object the frustration of any designs Russia may harbor for making capital out of the present troubled state of affairs in China. This statement the British Foreign Office categorically and emphatically denies.

ATTITUDE OF UNITED STATES.

WASHINGTON, June 7.—Perhaps a published rumor to the effect that the United States might join with other powers in prohibiting Russia from landing more troops than those of other powers in China led to the early appearance at the State Department to-day of Mr. De Wollant, the First Secretary of the Russian Embassy. The Ambassador, Count Cassini, is absent on leave from his post, and the First Secretary is acting as Chargé.

If that was the subject of his inquiries, the charge was speedily reassured, for the State Department has made no concealment of its policy respecting the Chinese situation, and has repeatedly intimated that it is concerned solely for the safety of the American Legation and Consulates in China, and for the direct interests of American citizens there.

An indication of the care exercised by the department in confining its officers strictly to these lines is afforded by the instruction to Minister Conger, sent yesterday, to draw upon Admiral Kempf for any force needed to protect his legation and such refugees as might claim the right of asylum there or in the consulates. The Minister was not even charged to send out the United States naval forces and marines to points where American missionaries are reported to be beset and in jeopardy, although much pressure has been brought to bear upon the State Department by the missionary interests to secure an order to this effect.

Mr. Conger's powers are regarded as ample, but he is not expected to take action in the matter of dispatching military expeditions to the interior of China that might be equivalent to a declaration of war. The department hopes to be able to adhere closely to the old-time policy of abstention from interference with internal matters in China, and especially to refrain from entangling movements in connection with the projects of other powers.

The Helena has not yet sailed from Manila to reinforce Admiral Kempf's force at Taku, and it is surmised that at the moment the order was received from the Navy Department, the vessel was either absent from Manila, or was not available for immediate service. The Navy Department was in communication to-day with Admiral Remey, presumably with reference to the speedy movement of the Helena, or some other ship, to Taku.

NO HARMONY AMONG POWERS.

BERLIN, June 7.—The Foreign Office regards the situation in China as no worse than it was last evening. No official reports indicating an unfavorable change have been received. The papers this evening, however, take a different view of the matter. The Vossische Zeitung says:

"Evidences are lacking of harmony among the powers interested in China, and the probability is that if the Boxer movement is allowed to spread and the dangers growing out of it become more serious this result will be owing to the want of harmony."

The National Zeitung, which expresses its views in similar terms, says it hopes that until the present troubles are over Russia, Great Britain, and Japan will bury their differences.

It is understood that Germany has officially declared her readiness to act in concert with the other powers. But, having no interests outside of Shan-Tung Province, she is not disposed to take the leading part in intervention in China.

The German newspapers claim to have discovered that the alleged secret agreement arrived at between Russia and Japan to act together against Great Britain in the Far East is purely fictitious. The National Zeitung avers that Great Britain stands hand in glove with Japan.

The officer commanding the German squadron at Che-Foo has been directed by cable to send a detachment of sailors and marines to Tien-Tsin and, after conferring with the German Minister at Peking, to arrange with the commanders of the other squadrons regarding further measures to be taken for the protection of Europeans.

Orders to Austrian Cruiser.

VIENNA, June 7. The Austrian cruiser Zenta has been instructed to take part in the projected blockade, if finally decided upon.

ASKS MR. HAY'S AID.

Board of Foreign Missions Can Get No Reply from Peking.

The following letter was sent to the Secretary of State at Washington yesterday by the Secretary of the Presbyterian Board of Foreign Missions here:

Sir: Our board has fifty-eight American missionaries in the Shangtung Provinces, China, sixteen in Peking, and ten in Paotingfu, eighty-four altogether, besides, of course, large property interests.

We, as well as many relatives and friends, are intensely anxious about the personal safety of those missionaries, and particularly those at Paotingfu, where, according to the telegraphic dispatches in the daily press, some missionaries have recently been murdered.

A cabled inquiry of our own to Peking has brought no reply. I therefore venture to ask you to inquire by cable, through United States Minister Conger, whether the American missionaries are safe. We shall greatly appreciate your inquiry, and your prompt action will relieve a strain which is now very trying.

ARTHUR J. BROWN, Secretary.

A telegram was also sent to Secretary Hay by Darwin R. James, requesting that prompt attention be given to the above communication.

PLAN OF GOLD DEMOCRATS

May Place a Third National Ticket in the Field.

Executive Committee, After a Secret Meeting, Calls National Committee to Meet in July.

A third Presidential ticket to be placed in the field by the National, or gold, Democratic Party is one of the possibilities of the coming National campaign. This assertion was made yesterday afternoon by George Foster Peabody, Chairman of the National Committee. A meeting of the National Committee will be held in Indianapolis on July 25, at which time the course to be followed in the coming contest by the forces which battled for Palmer and Buckner four years ago will be mapped out.

The Executive Committee held a secret meeting in this city last Friday and after a full discussion of the National situation it was decided to authorize Secretary John P. Frenzel of Indiana to issue a call for a meeting of the National Committee.

Mr. Peabody yesterday explained to a reporter for THE NEW YORK TIMES the conditions which, in his opinion, might make it necessary for the gold Democrats to name their own ticket this year, as they did in 1896. He said:

"At our meeting last Friday we agreed that it would be wise for us to wait until after the Philadelphia and Kansas City Conventions have both been held before announcing what we intend to do this year. We will meet in Indianapolis three weeks after the holding of the Kansas City Convention. By that time the declarations of both conventions will have been made and we will have had time to form an opinion as to what to do. Of course, the question of candidates has been settled and we have some idea of what to expect in the way of platforms from the Philadelphia and Kansas City Conventions, but we will have to wait until we see the actual declarations made in those platforms.

"We want to see what the Republicans have to say on what is called imperialism, and then again the Republican currency plank may not be satisfactory. The same reasons apply to the convention to be held in Kansas City. It may be found that the delegates to that gathering will listen to reason, and that the conservative element is in control. Until we know the exact situation it would not be wise to commit ourselves to any policy.

"It had been hoped that it would not be necessary to reorganize our forces this year, but we decided that in our keeping reposed the old-fashioned Democratic principles, and that it was our duty to guard them well and to take in this coming campaign whatever action may be found necessary to keep those principles before the people."

Mr. Peabody has received many letters from Gold Democrats in all parts of the country asking him to have something definite done, and it was in response to these communications and visits from persons who took part in the fight of four years ago that Mr. Peabody summoned the Executive Committee to meet in this city last week. The committeemen who were here reported that there was much sentiment among those who cannot affiliate with the Republicans and who are opposed to William J. Bryan for the nomination of a third ticket. It is said that if at the meeting of the National Committee it is decided to hold a National convention it will probably be held in Indianapolis, as a compliment to the Indiana Gold Democrats, who were the first to take any action demanding that the anti-silver men in the party place a National ticket in the field. It was in Indianapolis that the Palmer and Buckner ticket was nominated in 1896.

The members of the National Committee are:

George Foster Peabody, New York, Chairman; John P. Frenzel, Indiana, Secretary and Treasurer; J. M. Faulkner, Alabama; P. J. Cole, Arizona; C. B. Moore, Arkansas; E. B. Pond, California; Louis R. Ehrich, Colorado; Joel A. Sperry, Connecticut; John S. Russell, Delaware; D. G. Ambler, Florida; Thomas F. Corrigan, Georgia; Benjamin T. Cable, Illinois; John R. Wilson, Indiana; Edwin Ludlow, Indian Territory; L. M. Martin, Iowa; Eugene Hagan, Kansas; Zack Phelps, Kentucky; M. R. Spellman, Louisiana; C. Vey Holman, Maine; William Pinckney Whyte, Maryland; N. Matthews, Jr., Massachusetts; Thomas A. Wilson, Michigan; F. W. M. Cutcheon, Minnesota; H. M. Street, Mississippi; L. C. Krauthoff, Missouri; A. H. Nelson, Montana; Euclid Martin, Nebraska; G. Woodbury, New Hampshire; William J. Curtis, New Jersey; William B. Childers, New Mexico; Charles Tracey, New York; H. E. Fries, North Carolina; H. L. Whitehed, North Dakota; Talfourd P. Lenn, Ohio; C. E. S. Wood, Oregon; S. T. McCormick, Pennsylvania; C. C. Mumford, Rhode Island; W. R. Davie, South Carolina; John B. Hanton, South Dakota; Michael Savage, Tennessee; M. L. Crawford, Texas; Parley Williams, Utah; W. H. Creamer, Vermont; Joseph Bryan, Virginia; Hugh C. Wallace, Washington; Randolph Stainaker, West Virginia; Ellis B. Usher, Wisconsin.

ELKINS FOR VICE PRESIDENT.

His Name Considered by New Jersey—Views of Senator Stokes.

Special to The New York Times.

TRENTON, N. J., June 7.—A number of the New Jersey delegates to the Republican National Convention have been here this week attending the Supreme Court. When asked as to the attitude of the New Jersey delegation on the Vice Presidency, each one said that the delegation was entirely at sea in the matter, but it was ascertained that the name of Senator Stephen B. Elkins of West Virginia is being considered with favor.

Senator Stokes of Cumberland County, one of the party leaders, when seen at his office in the Mechanics' Bank, of which he is President, was free to say that while he regarded the situation as perplexing and while he had no personal preferences, it seemed clear to him that Senator Elkins was the most desirable candidate from a party point of view.

"He combines," said Senator Stokes, "more elements of availability than any other prominent Republican. Born in Ohio, brought up in Missouri, where he taught school and was admitted to the bar, identified for fourteen years with the development and political life of New Mexico, and now a resident of West Virginia, he is representative of the West and South, and his large business connections make him acceptable to Pennsylvania, New Jersey, and Maryland, while New York would probably regard him with almost as much favor as Cornelius N. Bliss.

"No," said Senator Stokes, "don't ask me to say to what extent Mr. Elkins's name is being considered by our delegation. These are merely my personal views as to his availability territorially and to the business world. Whether the convention accepts the logic of the situation or not remains to be seen."

DARKNESS AT BATH BEACH.

Electric Lights Extinguished, Creating Confusion and Annoyance.

Every electric light at Bath Beach suddenly went out early last night while a big crowd of visitors was moving about among the various concert halls and other places of amusement there. Up to 1 o'clock this morning the defective circuit had not been repaired, and for several hours total darkness prevailed in almost every direction. A dozen or more kerosene lamps furnished all the illumination that existed during that time.

To judge from the noises that rose from the beach for a couple of hours after the dark season began, it was with no slight difficulty that the visitors found their way to the trolley cars. Exactly what happened is still a matter for conjecture, and it is expected that later discoveries will expose many incidents both comic and criminal, as there was abundant opportunity for either.

NEW REPUBLICAN RULES

Adoption of Amendment Providing for Executive Committee.

TEN EYCK MAY BE CHAIRMAN

Not to be Hampered by County Committee's President—Making Way for General Greene.

The Republican County Committee met in special session at the Murray Hill Lyceum last night. In the absence of President Lemuel E. Quigg, who is confined to his home by illness, McDougall Hawkes of the Twenty-fifth Assembly District presided.

Secretary George R. Manchester, in obedience to the action taken at the meeting of the Executive Committee in the afternoon, presented amendments to the rules and regulations of the Republican Party of the County of New York.

These amendments provided, first, that the County Committee elected at the official primary in August, 1900, shall meet for organization on the third Thursday in December, 1900.

This, it will be noticed, is subsequent to the Presidential election.

Next, it was decided to amend Article 4 by striking out the words "and also the Executive Committee," and "these bodies," and substituting therefor "that body," so that the paragraph shall read: "The President shall be the Chairman of the County Committee, and it shall be his duty to preside at all meetings of that body, and he shall be ex-officio a member of all standing and special committees."

Article 5 was amended to add after the "Treasurer" "and the Chairman of the Finance Committee," and, to add to the clause the following:

"The Executive Committee shall meet for the purpose of organization within ten days after its appointment upon the call of the President of the County Committee, and shall forthwith elect its Chairman, who shall be ex officio a member of the Finance Committee and the Committee on Election Officers.

"The Executive Committee shall meet on the call of its Chairman to consider such business as may be brought forward. Meetings of the committee must be called by the Chairman upon the written request of seven members of the committee, stating the object for which a meeting is desired."

This divorces the Chairman of the Executive Committee from the Presidency of the County Committee.

Another amendment provides that delegates to each convention shall be apportioned among the several units of representation according to the primary election law.

Either the County Committee or the Executive Committee may call future conventions, and all delegates must be elected on the official primary day in September of each year, except in Presidential years, when they shall be chosen in August.

All the amendments were adopted on motion of Postmaster Van Cott.

Leader Charles A. Hess of the Twenty-fifth District presented the resignation of Arthur T. Sturges. In his place Gen. Francis Vinton Greene was unanimously chosen.

This prepares the way for the election of Gen. Greene to the Presidency of the committee at the meeting to be held on June 21.

It is generally understood that Aqueduct Commissioner William H. Ten Eyck will be the Chairman of the proposed Executive Committee. Other members will be F. S. Gibbs, Collector of Customs George R. Bidwell, John Sabine Smith, Postmaster Cornelius Van Cott, Gen. Francis Vinton Greene, and Lemuel E. Quigg.

GEN. GREENE TO SEE MR. PLATT.

Conference of Republican Leaders Is Announced for To-day.

Senator Platt and Chairman Odell of the Republican State Committee are in town. The former was very much fatigued on his return from Washington, and retired early. Mr. Odell had no news.

It is admitted, however, that there will be a conference to-day, at which Messrs. Platt, Odell, and Gen. Francis V. Greene, the coming President of the Republican County Committee, will be present.

Chairman Odell had several callers yesterday, including Congressman James S. Sherman of Oneida, who is said to have Gubernatorial aspirations, and Lieut. Gov. T. L. Woodruff, who would like to be Vice President. Mr. Woodruff would not discuss the Vice Presidency.

ELEPHANT PUT TO DEATH.

Hanged on a Mammoth Freight Derrick.

Special to The New York Times.

BALTIMORE, Md., June 7.—Sport, the big elephant of Bostock's Zoo, was put to death by hanging at 6 o'clock this evening. The novel execution took place in the Bolton yards of the Pennsylvania Railroad here. The gallows was the powerful derrick used by the railroad for lifting stone and other heavy freight. The mammoth beast was given large quantities of ether before the execution. Chains were placed about his neck so as to draw upon his windpipe and choke him to death. As the derrick raised the beast, he trumpeted fiercely for a moment, and then was still. Life was extinct in nine minutes. A number of physicians witnessed the hanging and made an examination of the body afterward.

While Sport was being transported in a freight car from Scranton, Penn., in company with an elephant named Jolly, which died of heart disease yesterday, the big beasts became playful. Sport backed with some force against the door, which gave way beneath his weight. The elephant was precipitated from the moving train to the ground. He fell on his back and emitted a terrific scream. The train was stopped and a wrecking crew was telegraphed for. When they arrived Sport was lifted by a derrick into the train. When examined by Baltimore surgeons it was found that while Sport had broken no bones, he had suffered partial paralysis of the spinal column. It required a number of conferences to determine how to kill the big beast.

LAKE BORGNE CANAL BOUGHT.

Alabama Products Will Reach New Orleans by an All-Water Route.

Special to The New York Times.

NEW ORLEANS, June 7.—A company with ample financial backing has just purchased the Lake Borgne Canal property, on which a vast amount of money has been spent, and will push the work to completion. This waterway will connect Lake Borgne and the Mississippi Sound with the Mississippi River seven miles below New Orleans, and will furnish a connecting link between the extensive system of inland waterways made available by the costly work that is being done in improving and opening the Warrior River. The purpose is to establish an unbroken line of slackwater navigation from the Alabama coal and iron fields to New Orleans.

By this route the products of the far interior of Alabama, including coal, iron, turpentine and resin, pitch pine and other timber of value, will find their way down the Warrior and Alabama Rivers to Mississippi Sound, and thence by a sheltered route behind the chain of islands which inclose the sound to Lake Borgne. After crossing Lake Borgne they will reach the canal, and passing through it, be afloat in the Mississippi River, reaching New Orleans by an all-water route without once breaking bulk. This water way will enable the Alabama coal mines to undersell the Pittsburg coal combine in Southern markets, and will also open up a large export business in naval stores for New Orleans.

MAY ARREST MR. VANDERBILT.

He Runs Down a Child—Mayor of Newport Threatens Him for Fast Locomobile Driving.

Special to The New York Times.

NEWPORT, June 7.—Rumors of complaints regarding the speed which William K. Vanderbilt, Jr., has been driving his locomobile through this city have been heard for the past three days, but nothing official has been done by the local authorities until to-day, when Frederick Sheldon, one of the prominent cottagers, called upon Mayor Boyle and lodged a complaint against Mr. Vanderbilt, for the speed with which he passed through the city this morning. According to his complaint, he had a narrow escape from being badly injured. Mr. Sheldon demanded that something should be done to prevent Mr. Vanderbilt from driving his machine at the speed he has been going, and after fully explaining the circumstances, he drove home satisfied.

Later Mr. Vanderbilt chanced to meet the Mayor and his Honor threatened him with arrest if he persisted in racing his locomobile through the streets of Newport.

This afternoon Mr. Vanderbilt came from the Herreshoff works at Bristol, landing at Bristol ferry, where his locomobile was in waiting and, with a party of guests, drove into Newport with his usual speed.

Later as Mr. Vanderbilt was passing along the lower part of Thames Street in a runabout automobile a little girl, who attempted to run across the roadway, was struck by one wheel and was thrown to the ground. Mr. Vanderbilt immediately stopped the automobile and jumping to the roadway quickly picked the child up in his arms and held it until the mother arrived.

The child apparently was not injured, and after handing her over to her mother Mr. Vanderbilt informed the parent that any medical attention or care the child might need, as a result of the accident, would be furnished at his expense.

The farmers in Middletown are considerably worked up over the rapid speed with which W. K. Vanderbilt, Jr., passed through that town a few days ago with his "lightning machine," as it has been named in the rural districts, and the Council will hold a special meeting to regulate the speed of such carriages.

The Ordinance Committee of the City Council of Newport will hold a special meeting to-morrow afternoon to take action in regard to the speed rate and other matters pertaining to the regulation of automobiles in Newport.

BOSTON AND ALBANY LEASE.

Provisions of the Bill to be Reported in Massachusetts Senate.

Special to The New York Times.

BOSTON, June 7.—In the Massachusetts Senate to-morrow Senator Soule, Chairman of the Committee on Railroads, will present the Boston and Albany lease as recommended in the bill voted by the committee after a protracted session last evening. The vote was virtually 12 in favor to 3 against the measure in committee. Senators Joy and Ross and Representative Blood dissent, while Representative Weston reserves his right to dissent, although his name does not appear as against the bill.

By the terms of the bill the Commonwealth does not waive or release any rights or privileges that it may now have, but expressly reserves and retains such rights. These include the right to reduce rates and fares, to compel service, &c. It is stipulated that there shall be no higher rate for freight from any point to Boston than is charged to New York. Nor shall the New York Central diminish or allow to be diminished the facilities for travel and business over the Boston and Albany. It shall expend not less than $250,000 per year, beginning July 1, 1901, until the full sum of $2,500,000 shall have been expended in improving East Boston terminals and double-tracking the Grand Junction Railway.

No change in the lease shall be valid unless it is approved by the Massachusetts Legislature. Whenever the Railroad Commissioners shall deem that the provisions of the act are not complied with they shall transmit a statement to the Attorney General, who shall institute proceedings to obtain compliance. The Supreme Judicial Court of Massachusetts is given full jurisdiction to act on the petition of the Attorney General, and to enforce its decree against the lessee.

The term of the lease is for ninety-nine years, and the act takes effect July 1, 1901. There is no referendum attached

WILLIAM T. PARKER DEAD.

Became Suddenly Insane at the Harvard Law School Examinations.

Special to The New York Times.

CAMBRIDGE, Mass., June 7.—William Thornton Parker, Jr., of the Harvard Law School died this afternoon at 3 o'clock at the Cambridge Hospital of an abscess on the brain caused by overstudy. Thornton was one of the hardest working students in the Law School, and as this was his last year he had been applying himself with unusual vigor.

A few days ago he was taking the examination in Constitutional law when suddenly in the midst of the examination he became insane, and waving his hands wildly, cried out a number of unintelligible sentences. His condition became rapidly worse, and he died this afternoon. He came from Springfield, Mass., and was about twenty-four years of age. He was also a graduate of the Massachusetts Institute of Technology, where he obtained the highest honors.

COLLEGE ATHLETE DROWNED.

S. L. Bahny Loses His Life While Swimming in Mohawk River.

Special to The New York Times.

SCHENECTADY, N. Y., June 7.—The commencement of Union College this year is again overshadowed by the drowning fatality. S. L. Bahny of Olean, a member of the Class of 1902, and a well-known athlete, lost his life this afternoon while swimming in the Mohawk River.

With four companions, Leroy Taylor, George Walrath, E. H. Rider, and W. J. Dickenson, Bahny essayed to swim across the stream. He lost his strength when about half the distance had been accomplished, and cried for help. Taylor, who was about twenty-five yards from Bahny, went to his assistance and tried to tow him ashore. Bahny, however, struggled, and finally succeeded in getting so firm a hold on the would-be rescuer that the two men sank to the bottom. On coming to the surface Taylor freed himself from the grasp of Bahny and made the rest of his way to shore. Walrath then tried to save Bahny, but after a struggle of several minutes he, too, was forced to seek his own safety. Bahny's body was recovered shortly afterward.

ACTOR'S BRAVE RESCUE.

Grasps Two Drowning Women by the Hair and Swims Ashore with Them.

Special to The New York Times.

PORT JERVIS, N. Y., June 7.—Richard Lyle of New York City, in company with Miss Niva Sutterly and Mrs. Beatrice Jensen, was enjoying a boat ride on Culvert Lake, near Branchville, N. J., to-day. The ladies decided to exchange seats during the trip, and as they were passing him, Lyle, who weighs 200 pounds, leaned toward the ladies and the boat capsized. When the three returned to the surface the boat had drifted away, but Lyle, who is an expert swimmer, grasped the ladies by the hair, and holding their heads above the water, swam to shore. The ladies fainted, but restoratives were administered, and they are now none the worse for their experience.

Lyle and the ladies are members of the Lyle theatrical company of New York, which is playing at Branchville, and when Mr. Lyle appeared on the stage last evening he was greeted with tremendous applause by the audience, who had heard of his brave deed

THE HOUSE YIELDS; CONGRESS ADJOURNS

Senate Wins Fight Over Naval Appropriation Bill.

BAD DEFEAT FOR CANNON

His Proposed Compromise Voted Down—Cummings Tells Him He Is "Only a Toy Musket."

Special to The New York Times.

WASHINGTON, June 7.—The fifty-sixth Congress, first session, adjourned this afternoon at 5 o'clock. Joseph G. Cannon, Representative from Illinois, and hitherto the real leader in the House on the Republican side, at midnight the victor over the Senate in the long contest over the Naval Appropriation bill, may have held the opinion, before to-day's session was at an end, that it should have adjourned yesterday, for the sole purpose in holding it together seems to have been to administer to him a complete, conspicuous, and unexpected defeat.

When the two houses dispersed late last night the Senate was smarting under what it considered the insulting treatment accorded to the Naval bill conferrees and the Senate in overturning the conference report on the Appropriation bill and adjourning without attempting to bring about another meeting. Even the form of the new conference was offensive, for the House had taken the matter out of the hands of the Naval Committee and placed it in the care of the Committee on Appropriations. This meant that Mr. Hale and his associates of the Senate were to meet the men who had inspired the opposition that had made possible the prolongation of the session.

A REACTION IN THE HOUSE.

Before the House met to-day a reaction had set in, not altogether an uninspired reaction, for Senators who understood the situation were at work. Fifteen or twenty of them visited the House from time to time to warn their representatives not to join the crusade against the Hydrographic Office of the Navy Department merely to contribute to the political strength of the Coast and Geodetic Survey.

The reaction had been fully established before a vote was reached. Mr. Cannon, still aglow and confident after the rout last night of the Hydrographic office forces, marched up with abundant confidence. The deposed conferrees of the Naval Committee were buoyed up by the assurances and the promises of the visiting Senators. Upon a viva voce vote to recede and concur, which preceded in order the motion of Mr. Cannon to nonconcur, Mr. Dayton (Rep., W. Va.) of the Naval Committee won by a few votes.

Mr. Cannon believed that the rollcall would sustain him and preserve the fruits of the victory achieved last night. The roll-call showed 118 votes to accept the proposition of the Senate, and only 98 for Cannon. Cannon was a beaten leader. He surrendered without conditions, giving over the charge of the bill to Mr. Dayton, one of the men last night discredited and deposed. Everything remaining in dispute went the Senate's way.

For a time it was uncertain whether the President, after his experience of yesterday, would not decline to again wait upon Congress, adopting instead the practice of his predecessor, and ask committees of that body to wait upon him at the White House after the Naval bill had been completed. He was informed, however, when the agreement had been reached, and sent word that he would come to the President's room at the Capitol between 4 and 5. When he reached the Capitol he had little to do, and he was on his way back to the White House a few moments after 5.

HOUSE YIELDS TO SENATE.

WASHINGTON, June 7.—The story of to-day's contest over the Naval Appropriation bill is practically a story of the proceedings in the House with reference to the bill. The Senate simply waited on the House.

Early in the day the conferrees on the bill decided to report a disagreement. Their conference developed the fact that the representatives of both houses were willing to make mutual concessions, and in reality an agreement practically was reached, though it was decided to first report a disagreement to both houses in order to test the feeling.

The tentative agreement eliminated all inland and coast work, confined the survey to the ocean, eliminated all reference to the lakes and to "hydrographic surveys," and reduced the $100,000 appropriated by the Senate amendment to $50,000. The amendment as thus agreed upon was as follows:

Ocean Survey—Including the waters of Cuba and the Philippine archipelago, but not the coast thereof, and for the purchase of nautical books, charts, and sailing directions, and freight and express charges on the same, $50,000.

Mr. Cannon, on behalf of the House conferrees on the Naval Appropriation bill, formally reported the disagreement to the House. The former conferrees, who were superseded last night after a bitter fight, evidently were ready to resume the struggle. Mr. Cannon moved that the House recede and concur in the Senate amendment with an amendment which struck out the word "hydrographic" and provided for ocean, but not coast, surveys.

In his statement Mr. Cannon said the proposed amendment was in harmony with the instructions given by the House a week ago not to agree to any surveys for the coasts of the great lakes, the seaboard, or the islands of our new possessions. The amendment would confine the naval surveys to the deep water of the ocean.

DAYTON MOVES TO RECEDE.

Mr. Dayton, (Rep., West Va.,) one of the superseded conferrees, moved to recede and concur in the Senate amendment in order to bring the question squarely before the House. This motion took precedence over that of Mr. Cannon.

Mr. Moody, (Dem., Mass.,) who last night charged the conferrees with betraying their trust, apologized for his words amid applause.

Mr. Cummings, (Dem., N. Y.,) one of the conferrees, said the apology was "justly due and handsomely done."

He then explained the difficulties under which the old conferrees had labored. He contrasted the result of their work with that of the new conferrees, who, he said, had offered a new proposition which practically violated the House instructions while technically observing them. He somewhat startled the House by referring to a "junketing trip" which Mr. Cannon had taken as the guest of the Coast Survey, and then proceeded to pay his respects to the Chairman of the Appropriations Committee. Mr. Cummings wields a keen blade and the House enjoyed his dextrous thrusts.

CUMMINGS ON CANNON.

He pictured Mr. Cannon, the Chairman of the great Appropriations Committee, as a lion lashing his sides and roaring while the crowd of jackals followed as they smelt fresh meat. Then he described how the House, following blindly the lion's leadership, had done everything it could to degrade its conferrees, despite their appeals that they were powerless.

"I told you," said he, with great vehemence, "that we were up against a stone wall, but you turned us down and turned the controversy over to the Appropriations Committee to settle. And they went up against the same stone wall with the result that they are back here crawling before this House with another proposition. Why, if you were so loyal, did you come crawling back into the House?" he asked, addressing Mr. Cannon. "Why did you not continue your opposition?" Then, with sarcasm and with a contemptuous wave of his hand, he said as took his seat:

"You have been misnamed; you are no Cannon, you are a toy musket." This shot

"All the News That's Fit to Print."

The New York Times.

THE WEATHER. Fair; wind northeasterly, becoming southerly.

COPYRIGHT, 1901, BY THE NEW YORK TIMES COMPANY.

VOL. L...NO. 15,926. NEW YORK, WEDNESDAY, JANUARY 23, 1901.—SIXTEEN PAGES. ONE CENT In Greater New York, Jersey City, and Newark. | Elsewhere, TWO CENTS.

QUEEN VICTORIA DEAD AT OSBORNE

Passed Away Quietly at 6:30 o'Clock Last Evening.

SCENE AT THE BEDSIDE

Family, with Bowed Heads, Listened to Bishop's Prayers.

QUEEN BADE THEM FAREWELL

Said to Have Spoken Words of Great Moment to Prince of Wales.

ALBERT EDWARD NOW KING

Privy Council and Parliament Will Meet in London To-day, and the Proclamation of the New Monarch's Succession Will Follow—Grief Over the Queen's Death and Admiration for Her Character Universal in the United Kingdom, the British Colonies, Europe, and America—Arrangements for the Funeral Not Yet Announced.

COWES, Isle of Wight, Jan. 23.—Queen Victoria is dead. The greatest event in the memory of this generation, almost the most stupendous change in existing conditions in England that could be imagined, has taken place quietly, almost gently, upon the anniversary of the death of Queen Victoria's father, the Duke of Kent.

The end of this splendid career came in a simply furnished room in Osborne House. This most respected of all women, living or dead, lay in a great four-posted bed. Around her were gathered the majority of her descendants. Well within view of her dying eyes there hung a portrait of the Prince Consort. It was he who designed the room and every part of the Castle. In scarcely audible words the white-haired Bishop of Winchester prayed beside her, as he had often before prayed with his sovereign, for he was her Chaplain at Windsor.

With bowed heads the imperious ruler of the German Empire, the man who is now King of England, the woman who has succeeded to the title of Queen, the Princes and Princesses, and those of less than royal designation listened to the Bishop's ceaseless prayer.

Naturally, the family, while recognizing the claim for public information, insist that some details of the events around the deathbed shall be sacred for the present, and have imposed the strictest secrecy on the whole household. The Queen is, however, said to have bidden farewell, in a feeble voice, to her family. She first recognized the Prince of Wales, to whom she spoke a few words of great moment; then Emperor William and the others present filed past and heard a whispered good-bye. All those in the bedroom were in tears.

Six o'clock passed. The Bishop continued his intercession. One of the younger children asked a question in a shrill, childish treble, and was immediately silenced. The women of the royal family sobbed faintly and the men shuffled uneasily.

THE END QUITE PEACEFUL.

At exactly 6:30 Sir James Reid held up a hand, and the people in the room knew that England had lost her Queen. The Bishop pronounced the benediction.

The Queen passed away quite peacefully. She suffered no pain. Those who were now mourners went to their rooms. A few minutes later the inevitable element of materialism stepped into this pathetic chapter of international history, for the Court ladies went busily to work ordering their mourning from London.

The wheels of the world were jarred when the announcement came; but in this palace at Osborne everything pursued the usual course. Down in the kitchen they were cooking a huge dinner for an assemblage the like of which has seldom been known in England, and the dinner preparations proceeded just as if nothing had happened.

An incident characteristic of the Queen's solicitude for others occurred two days ago, when, in one of the intervals of consciousness, she summoned strength to suggest to her dressers, who had been acting as nurses, that they take the opportunity of getting some fresh air.

QUEEN ASKS FOR HER DOG.

On Monday afternoon the Queen asked that her little Pomeranian be brought to her bedside.

It was feared that the Queen was dying at about 9 o'clock yesterday morning, and carriages were sent to Osborne cottage and the rectory to bring all the Princes and Princesses and the Bishop of Winchester to her bedside. It seemed then very near the end; but, when things looked the worst, the Queen, in one of the rallies due to her wonderful constitution, opened her eyes and recognized the Prince of Wales, the Princess, and Emperor William. She asked to see one of her faithful servants, a member of the household. He hastened to the room, but before he got there the Queen had passed into a fitful sleep.

Four o'clock marked the beginning of the end. Again the family were summoned, and this time the relapse was not followed by recovery.

The Prince of Wales was very much affected when the doctors at length informed him that his mother had breathed her last. Emperor William, himself deeply affected, did his best to minister comfort to his sorrow-stricken uncle, whose new dignity he was the first to acknowledge.

OUTSIDE OSBORNE HOUSE GATES.

No member of the royal family left Osborne House yesterday for the customary drives. A changing group of correspondents and townspeople loitered about the gates all day long, but never reached the proportions of the crowd of Monday.

It was a melancholy day. Occasional drizzles obscured the emerald hills beyond the castle. Greater simplicity or a more entire lack of any of that pomp traditionally attached to royalty could not be found in any country house in the kingdom than here, where the best-beloved monarch of centuries was dying and the ruler of another great nation waited by her bedside as grandson rather than as Emperor.

Two stalwart policemen guarding the gates against intruders were the sole reminders of officialdom. They were compelled in the morning to refuse admission to three dusky visitors from India who drove up arrayed in such gorgeous robes that the bystanders instinctively lifted their hats, mistaking them for potentates. The trio announced themselves as lecturers touring England in behalf of a foreign mission, and insisted upon an audience with the Prince of Wales to tender the sympathies of India.

Many of the country gentry and a few titled personages appeared at the lodge and registered their names in the visitors' book, the thrifty flunky who officiated doing a profitable business by selling the original copies of official bulletins to souvenir enthusiasts. Artists and photographers obtained pictures of the gates and grounds and any prominent persons who appeared.

THE LORD CHAMBERLAIN ARRIVES

Everybody feared that the Queen would never waken from the sleep which the noontime bulletin spoke of, and everybody was watching the flag on the castle tower, expecting it to sink to half mast. Lord Clarendon, the new Lord Chamberlain, with Prince Christian of Schleswig-Holstein and the Duke of Argyll, arrived at Osborne in the afternoon. The arrival of the Lord Chamberlain was an ominous sign, as he announces to a new monarch his accession to the throne.

When the 4 o'clock bulletin announced that the Queen was sinking, all the watchers at the gates of Osborne House made up their minds to remain to the end. The cold was intense, and a few favored ones sought shelter in the royal lodge, just inside, where they waited in absolute silence.

NEWS OF THE EVENT ANNOUNCED.

The telephone bell rang at 7:04 P. M., but before a royal servant had time to take the message the Chief of the Queen's Police emerged from the darkness, and, with bared head, said:

"Gentlemen, the Queen passed away at 6:30."

All present reverently uncovered, and then shrill whistles outside and the ringing of the bells of the bicycles in waiting were the signals for messengers to race to Cowes with the news. In a few moments the place was deserted. Simultaneously, mounted messengers, on white horses, dashed from Osborne. What happened within the royal residence is purely surmise.

On their arrival at Cowes the correspondents found the news had been known both at East and West Cowes fifteen minutes before it had been announced to those in waiting at the gates of Osborne House. The streets were already filled with sorrowful crowds discussing her Majesty's death.

Prince and Princess Louis of Battenberg arrived at Osborne just too late to see her Majesty alive.

From all parts of the world there are still pouring into Cowes messages of condolence. They come from crowned heads, millionaires, tradesmen, and paupers, and are variously addressed to the Prince of Wales and the King of England.

RESULT OF ROBERTS'S NEWS?

The record of the last days of the reign of Victoria is not yet fully known. The correspondent of The Associated Press was the only correspondent admitted to Osborne House, and his interview with Sir Arthur John Bigge, private secretary to the late Queen, was the only official statement that was given out.

For several weeks the Queen had been failing. On Monday week she summoned Lord Roberts and asked him some very searching questions regarding the war in South Africa. On Tuesday she went for a drive, but was visibly affected. On Wednesday she suffered a paralytic stroke, accompanied by intense physical weakness. It was her first illness in all her eighty-one years, and she would not admit she was sick. Then her condition grew so serious that, against her wishes, the family were summoned. When they arrived her reason had practically succumbed to paralysis and weakness.

The events of the last few days, described in the bulletins, are too fresh to need repetition.

THE LAST BULLETINS.

OSBORNE HOUSE GATES, Isle of Wight, Jan. 22.—An official bulletin issued at 8 o'clock said:

The Queen this morning shows signs of diminishing strength, and her Majesty's condition again assumes a more serious aspect.

JAMES REID,
R. DOUGLAS POWELL,
THOMAS BARLOW.

The bulletin issued at noon said there had been no change for the worse in the Queen's condition since the morning bulletin.

At 4 P. M. another bulletin was posted. It said the Queen was slowly sinking.

At 6:45 P. M. the end was announced as follows:

Her Majesty the Queen breathed her last at 6:30 P. M., surrounded by her children and grandchildren.

JAMES REID,
R. DOUGLAS POWELL,
THOMAS BARLOW.

THE QUEEN'S FUNERAL.

Will Probably Be at Frogmore—Many Royalties Expected.

COWES, Isle of Wight, Jan. 23.—The body of Queen Victoria is being embalmed to-night, and will probably be taken to Windsor on Saturday.

The coffin arrived last evening from London.

Emperor William's arrangements are not settled, but it is believed that he will not depart until after the funeral, which will probably be a ceremony never before equaled in this country.

LONDON, Jan. 23.—There is little doubt that the funeral of Queen Victoria will take place at Frogmore, Hertfordshire, though nothing in regard to this matter has yet been announced.

Her Majesty was so closely related to the European Courts, big and little, that the gathering of royalties at the obsequies will be unprecedented.

ATHENS, Jan. 22.—King George will start for London to-night.

PARIS, Jan. 23.—The French Government will be represented at the funeral of Queen Victoria by an extraordinary embassy.

The members have not yet been chosen, but the embassy will be headed by Vice Admiral de Lajaille, who on several occasions welcomed Queen Victoria at Cherbourg in the name of France.

TO-DAY'S CEREMONIES.

Privy Council and Parliament to Meet—The Proclamation of the King.

LONDON, Jan. 23.—The Privy Council will meet in London to-day, and the proclamation of the King will take place thereafter at all places required by custom.

The King will come to London to preside over the Council. The Ministers will attend, give up their seals of office, be resworn, receive the proclamation of the King, pass votes of condolence and congratulation, and adjourn.

After giving up their seals the Ministers receive them back from the new ruler. The Privy Councilors will also be sworn afresh.

Shortly before midnight yesterday an official announcement was issued calling Parliament to assemble at 4 o'clock this afternoon to enable members of the House of Lords and House of Commons to take the oath of allegiance to the King. Precedent orders that Parliament shall meet within twenty-four hours of the death of the ruler.

At the offices of the Lord Chamberlain and of the City Remembrancer, at the Guildhall and at the College of Heralds, the officials were busy yesterday preparing for the formalities which for the first time in a generation, are to take place—the proclaiming of a new ruler of the United Kingdom. All the ancient gazettes, Court circulars, and other papers which describe the ceremonial of 1837 were taken from the libraries, that the officials might familiarize themselves with the ancient pageantry whereby a sovereign is proclaimed. The City Remembrancer said yesterday:

"It will depend on the pleasure of the new monarch to decide how far the ancient customs will be modified to suit modern methods; but, in a country where precedents are so firmly adhered to as England, it may be anticipated that we shall follow closely on the acts which prevailed when the Queen ascended the throne. The Privy Council, which is a very large body, will meet at once at St. James's Palace, where the form of proclamation declaring that 'we, etcetera, with one voice and consent of tongue and heart declare and proclaim the high mighty Prince Albert Edward, etcetera, who, by the death of the monarch, has become our only lawful and rightful liege, etcetera.'

"This proclamation will give the new title the King may assume, but this is not yet announced to us. The proclamation will then be sent to Heralds' College, and the following day the Earl Marshal, the Garter King at Arms, the Herald's Pursuivants, and other officials, with the college members and the Household troops, will proceed from the palace, clad in their splendid surcoats, and proceed to Trafalgar Square. There the King at Arms will halt, command silence, and read the proclamation. Proceeding down the Strand to Temple Bar, a halt will again be made, to demand an entrance into the City to proclaim the King. There the Lord Mayor and Sheriffs, in their state carriages, will form a great procession, and when the Earl Marshal's party comes just within the City boundary the proclamation will be read again, and the procession will pass down Ludgate Hill and Cheapside to the Royal Exchange, where similar ceremonies will close the spectacle."

DEEP GLOOM IN LONDON.

Places of Amusement All Closed—How the News Was Received.

LONDON, Jan. 23.—Silence, gloom, and darkness characterize London to-night. From Whitechapel to Mayfair streets usually gay with nightly festivity are dark, deserted, and desolate, and this depression of the public mind is likely to continue for many days to come.

Only a few hours ago the pleasure-seeking populace was hurrying to the theatres and music halls, only to find in every case the doors closed and big, black-bordered bills announcing that the performances had been suspended. The people, thus turned into the streets, gave for a short time an unusually thronged appearance to the West End. Many turned in the direction of Buckingham Palace and Marlborough House, where absolute silence reigned. Small bills, signed "Balfour," were posted outside, announcing the death of the monarch.

Everywhere, in vehicles and on the streets, the one topic of conversation was what would happen under the new reign, rather than the life and death of Victoria. Much interest was evinced in the way in which the enormous fortune of the dead Queen would be distributed, the general notion being that Osborne House would go to Princess Beatrice, and that she and Princess Christian would come into a considerable portion of Queen Victoria's wealth.

The probability that the King will take up a practically permanent residence in Buckingham Palace was much canvassed. This is a question that comes very much home to Londoners. Queen Victoria's preference for Balmoral Castle and Osborne House has been a complaint of long standing in the metropolis, and it is hoped that the new reign will see a change in this respect. The presence of the Court in London would give a brightness and gayety to the city which have long been absent.

Not until Queen Victoria has been laid to rest beside the Prince Consort at Frogmore will the theatres or music halls reopen. Moreover, business will come to a practical standstill. Music in all the hotels and public places ceased last evening. Fashionable resorts were empty, and very few of the nightly habitués were in evidence.

Americans who have passed through great National calamities may recall the crêpe-draped buildings and the National hush; but they can ill-conceive, since the death of Lincoln, any such expression of gloom as has already fallen on the United Kingdom. Marlborough House, so long the home of the new monarch; Buckingham Palace, where Queen Victoria made her last stay in London, and St. James's Palace, the residence of so many former monarchs, are to-night all black and deserted. Sentries in black overcoats keep silent vigil before the closed gates and bolted doors.

Early in the evening from St. Paul's, Westminster Abbey, and other churches bells were solemnly tolling or ringing muffled peals. In some cases the shops were already exhibiting signs of mourning. Beyond these things, however, and the boys crying extra editions in every direction, there was little that would outwardly indicate the passing of the country through an experience novel to almost the whole people.

SORROW IS UNIVERSAL.

Telegrams arriving from all parts of the country and the colonies re-echo the deep feeling of sorrow pervading all classes. These show that everywhere bells have been tolled and public performances and private functions suspended.

In Dublin the expressions of regret were universal. The bells of St. Patrick's Cathedral were tolled. Earl Cadogan, the Lord Lieutenant, was absent from Dublin yesterday, but it is expected that he will return immediately to preside at a meeting of the Irish Privy Council to proclaim the new King.

The news was received with the greatest sorrow at Balmoral, Windsor, and Eton, where Queen Victoria was regarded in an especially personal manner by the inhabitants.

Princess Beatrice telegraphed the tidings to ex-Empress Eugénie at Farnborough.

SCENES YESTERDAY AFTERNOON.

The gloomy faces of the crowds incessantly approaching the bulletin board at the Mansion House indicated yesterday how little the public hoped to receive better news of the condition of the Queen. Men of all ages and conditions, women and even children were content to spend a long time in awaiting their turn to get within reading distance of the board. As the throng moved slowly past the notice board, those who were unable to get there personally sent messenger boys with notebook and pencils to copy the text of everything posted. The grief of all was evident. Never were there so many black ties in the city before the actual arrival of a time of general mourning.

There was a remarkable scene outside the Mansion House early in the afternoon. On receipt of the alarming reports something resembling a groan was uttered by the hundreds of people assembled, and then some one started singing the national anthem. All heads were bared, and in a moment the crowds were singing "God Save the Queen" with a fervor proving how earnestly they wished for her Majesty's recovery. The passengers in passing carriages, cabs, and omnibuses joined in the singing, the drivers reverently doffing their hats.

At 4:35 P. M. the following was posted:

Osborne, 4 P. M.

My painful duty obliges me to inform you that the life of our beloved Queen is in the greatest danger. ALBERT EDWARD.

In reply the Lord Mayor, Frank Green, dispatched the following:

"I have received your Royal Highness's sad intimation with profound grief, which is shared by the citizens of London, who still pray that under Divine Providence the irreparable loss to her Majesty's devoted family and loyal subjects throughout the empire may still be averted. Will your Royal Highness be pleased to accept this heart-felt expression of my deep and sincere sympathy?"

THE FINAL ANNOUNCEMENT.

The latest bulletins previous to the announcement of the Queen's death, especially the message sent by the Prince of Wales, dispelled the last gleam of hope. The crowds silently dispersed from in front of the Mansion House, and only a few groups awaited the appearance of the inevitable announcement. This came at 7 o'clock in the form of a dispatch to the Lord Mayor from the new King as follows:

Osborne, 6:45 P. M.

My beloved mother has just passed away, surrounded by her children and grandchildren. ALBERT EDWARD.

The Lord Mayor immediately sent the following reply:

"Your Royal Highness's telegram announcing the nation's great loss I have received with profound distress and grief, and have communicated this most sad intimation to my fellow-citizens. Her Majesty's name and memory will forever live in the hearts of her people.

"May I respectfully convey to your Royal Highness and to all the members of the royal family the earnest sympathy and condolence of the City of London in your great sorrow?"

The scrap of paper a foot square, posted on the wall of the Mansion House, gave the first notice to London's homeward hurrying thousands of the death of the Queen. Excavations by which the street had been torn up made access to the bulletin difficult, but the bared heads of a silent group under a flickering gas jet told the crowds on the 'bus tops and sidewalks that the Queen was no more.

"BIG BEN" IS TOLLED.

A quarter of an hour later more than a thousand newsboys had invaded the streets with black-ruled newspapers, crying, "Death of the Queen," while through the dark streets boomed the deep-toned notes of "Big Ben," the big bell of St. Paul's Cathedral, the bells of the city re-echoing the news.

The shops closed as soon as the bells began to toll, and the blinds of the Mansion House were drawn down as soon as the message from the Prince of Wales was received by the Lord Mayor.

The bell tolled at St. Paul's Cathedral was the gift of William III., and is used only on occasions of the death of royal personages, Archbishops of Canterbury, Lord Mayors of London, and Bishops of London. The tolling continued for two hours at intervals of a minute and could be heard for miles in the direction of the wind.

Some hundreds of people stood in front of the cathedral around the spot where Queen Victoria prayed on the sixtieth anniversary of her accession to the throne.

LONDON PRESS COMMENTS.

Universal Grief Reflected in Editorials—Labouchere's Warm Eulogy.

LONDON, Jan. 23.—All the morning papers appear in heavy mourning borders, with editorials eulogistic of the dead Queen and recalling the leading events and characteristics of her reign. Very few political references as to the future are made. The Daily Mail says:

"We can but regret that the Queen was not permitted to see the end of the South African struggle. She has been taken from us in a dark hour which, we may hope, is a prelude to the dawn, and when we can ill spare her ripe experience and her vast knowledge of measures and men."

"Let us think of her this morning," says the Daily Chronicle, "by her highest title, not by her crown and sceptre, but by her own magnificent and splendid ideal of womanhood. This it is which touches the heart's core of a proud and imperial race. We have lost mother, wife, and Queen."

The Chronicle remarks that President McKinley was slightly premature in sending a communication to "His Majesty, the King," inasmuch as the Prince of Wales has not yet been proclaimed by the Privy Council.

The Daily Telegraph publishes two editorials under the captions "The Queen" and "The King." In the latter it says:

"Most happily for him, he has, with infinite credit to himself, passed through a period of probation in some ways more difficult and certainly more prolonged than that to which any successor to a throne in modern times has been subjected. He assumes the burden of his imperial task equipped with all the invaluable experience which the most painstaking discharge of great duties could secure him during the lifetime of his august mother. So accustomed have we become to his direct, personal patronage of every charity and every beneficial movement, many of which he initiated himself, that we are apt to forget the exhausting nature of the strain almost daily imposed upon his strength. He has won among the masses of the people a popularity that has been vouchsafed to few of his predecessors."

The Times says:

"The confidence inspired by her personal character enabled Queen Victoria on many occasions to use her intimate knowledge with effect in smoothing the rugged places of international relations or in modifying a policy which, through sheer inadequacy of information, would have led to undesirable friction. We have also to thank the Queen for influence of the most potent kind consistently and vigorously used to enforce high ideals of social and personal virtue, of religious faith and of Christian life."

Referring to the intellectual upheaval and the enormous social and economic progress which characterized the Victorian era, The Times expresses regret that the impetus has to some extent spent itself.

"At the close of Victoria's reign," continues The Times, "we find ourselves somewhat less secure of our position than we could desire, somewhat less abreast of the problems of the age than we ought to be, considering the initial advantages we secured."

"The great English-speaking Republic beyond the Atlantic has not failed to send us officially by the mouth of President McKinley, and unofficially by innumerable newspaper articles and other tokens of popular feeling, proof of how heartily and profoundly it shares in our grief. Need we say for ourselves and our colonies how dear to us in such an hour is the fellowship in woe which our American kinsmen so generously and warmly tender us?"

In another article The Times says:

"If anything can in some measure console the nation for the irreparable loss it has sustained, it is the well-founded conviction that the Queen has left behind her a worthy successor, who may be trusted to walk in her footsteps.

"In the whole range of English social and political life no position is more difficult to fill satisfactorily and without reproach than that of the heir apparent, and it may be justly said that the way this position has been filled has contributed to the remarkable increase in the devotion to the throne and the dynasty which has been one of the most striking characteristics of Victoria's reign.

"As Albert Edward has been a scrupulously constitutional Prince, we may confidently predict that he will be a scrupulously constitutional King. In the fulfillment of this onerous task he will have by his side a Queen who is already enthroned in the hearts of her loving subjects."

Henry Labouchère, M. P., in Truth has a remarkable tribute to Queen Victoria, a tribute all the more remarkable because of his democratic ideas and frank criticisms of royalty.

"Among all her millions of subjects," he says, "there are but few who will not mourn for her loss as for one of their own household. Nor will the mourners be found among her own subjects alone. It is not too much to say that never in the history of the world has a single death caused such universal grief. Alike in happiness and sorrow, she lived a life beyond reproach, without thought of self and unreservedly devoted to the duties of the hour. Although occupying perhaps the proudest position ever filled by a woman, and never wanting in a certain queenly dignity, her tastes, habits, demeanor, and even her dress were marked by the rarest simplicity.

"She has been indeed the mother of her people, and as a mother she will be mourned. In all the affairs of State she manifested the same wisdom that inspired her private life, nor did her own country alone enjoy the fruits of her experience and sagacity. Through her kindred and descendants abroad her influence for many years has been felt in Continental politics, always on the side of peace; and, in at least one crisis, she is known to have rendered service to the whole of Europe.

"Her sudden and lamentable breakdown was due entirely to worry and overwork. She had been greatly distressed by events in South Africa and by domestic griefs."

The Daily News says that Queen Victoria was always a peacemaker. It refers to the incident of her modifying in a pacific sense Lord Russell's dispatch in the Trent case.

The Standard, expressing regret that the Queen was not spared to see peace restored in South Africa, says: "The end for which she strove and prayed has yet to come, and the hope is perhaps visionary that the common grief of Britons and Afrikanders may abate those racial animosities which stand in the way of pacification."

Referring to the conspicuous success of Queen Victoria's reign, The Standard says:

"There was a time when republicanism was a serious phrase on English lips. To-day no whisper of discontent with the monarchical Constitution breaks the mourning of a loyal nation around the bier of the sovereign. It will be said of her in the annals of our land that she strengthened the Throne by loving the people, and that she was a great Queen and the mother of Kings because she was a good, noble, and true-hearted woman."

THE NATIONS' TRIBUTES.

Enmity for Great Britain Hushed and Only Sympathy Expressed.

PARIS, Jan. 23.—The news of the death of Queen Victoria was known in Paris at 8 o'clock last evening through special editions of the evening papers, which newsboys carried throughout the city. Great sympathy was expressed on all sides.

As soon as definite information reached Parliament the Presidents of the chambers announced that the next session would be adjourned as a sign of mourning.

When the news was known at the Ministry of Foreign Affairs, M. Delcassé, the Foreign Minister, went to the British Embassy to express to the Acting Ambassador the condolence of the French Government. President Loubet postponed his visit until the return of Sir Edmund Monson.

Not until then, moreover, will the arrangements relative to mourning be made. The British flag, draped with crape, will be placed over the entrance to the embassy to-day.

Last evening there was a steady stream of callers to inscribe their names in the register at the embassy.

Few and far between, indeed, are the Paris papers this morning which do not sound the note of regret at the passing of Victoria. In addition to long obituaries, special writers publish appreciations, reviewing the Queen's life work, noting in what respects it contributed to the greatness of the British nation, and speculating in some cases upon the reign about to open. Foremost of these special writers is M. Hanotaux, who, in Le Journal, refers to the extent of England's debt to Victoria.

"Her temperament and judgment, thanks to the precious lessons of Lord Melbourne," says M. Hanotaux, "were in complete accord with English Parliamentary institutions. Her success as a sovereign was due to her close attention to the affairs of State, her frequent journeys, her interviews with foreign statesmen, and above all, to the extraordinary position of being allied to several of the reigning sovereigns of Europe."

Le Gaulois says:

"Her action may be summed up in a brief phrase, little authority and much influence. The changes which are about to take place express better than blind and foolish flattery the place she occupied in Europe. That will be her true funeral oration, the final word of which will be that she, the possessor of most ordinary faculties, accomplished more than certain conquerors, and has left a greater gap than Catherine or Elizabeth."

Le Siecle says:

"Doubtless the Prince of Wales will follow the good example of his mother, whose death will mark no change of policy or opinion in Great Britain. He will peaceably enjoy the loyalty of the empire, accorded during the long reign of the Queen."

Le Temps, discussing the outlook, says:

"The sadness, alarm, anxieties, moral sufferings, and pecuniary cares arising out of the Transvaal war have created a new feeling in England. Queen Victoria has been like a mother of a family, a living link with the prosperity of the past, an anchor of security for the British people. With her disappearance will come the unknown, the groping into the dark future."

BERLIN, Jan. 22.—The news of the death of Queen Victoria had been hourly expected in Berlin, and on its arrival special editions of the newspapers sold like wildfire, the announcement being read with silent and respectful sympathy. The fact that Empress Augusta Victoria started to-day for Homburg to be near Dowager Empress Frederick added to the sad circumstances of the occasion.

Immediately after the receipt of the news Count von Eulenburg, the Chief Court Marshal, ordered the flags half masted on all public buildings. Although the hour of the evening was somewhat advanced, a number of the embassies and legations, including the United States Embassy, did the same.

Special mourning orders to the Schloss, the army, the Court, and the public departments were issued this evening. These will be published to-morrow and go immediately into effect.

The German nation fully shares in the feelings of the British people toward the venerable and illustrious sovereign who has just breathed her last.

Semi-official paragraphs in the press this evening rebut the idea, commonly held in Germany, that the new King will be inclined to be hostile toward Germany. On the contrary, they assert that he will act in the interests of Great Britain and the British people alone.

A sense of gratification is felt by all Germans that Emperor William was present at Osborne during the last hours of Queen Victoria's life and that the lofty feelings of filial piety which prompted his action have met with such full and unqualified recognition on the part of the British nation.

THE HAGUE, Jan. 22.—The Dutch press printed the news of the death of Queen Victoria with mourning borders.

The Court will go into mourning; but it is probable that there will be no change in the arrangements for the marriage of Queen Wilhelmina.

ROME, Jan. 22.—A most painful impression was produced by the receipt of the news of Queen Victoria's death.

King Victor Emmanuel, Queen Helena, the Pope, and members of the Government immediately telegraphed condolences.

GRIEF IN CANADA.

Flags at Half Mast Everywhere and Amusement Places Closed.

TORONTO, Ontario, Jan. 22.—To Torontonians no tidings fraught with greater sorrow ever flashed over the wires than those which recorded the death of the Queen. All classes of the community show their heartfelt grief. From early morning till the announcement of her Majesty's death, great crowds gathered and waited around the different newspaper offices, eagerly scanning each bulletin as it was posted up. When at last the dreaded news came, heads were reverently uncovered, and the crowds dispersed silently. For half an hour the bells kept tolling their mournful messages, while national flags, half-masted, swung from every pole.

The children in every school in the city this forenoon sang for the last time "God Save the Queen." The Mayor will proclaim a day of mourning.

MONTREAL, Jan. 22.—The bulletin officially announcing the death of her Majesty turned Montreal into a city of mourning. No sooner was the fact announced than the fire bells began to ring out at minute intervals, and mingled with them came the tolling of the big cathedral bells of both the English and Catholic churches. Flags appeared at half-mast everywhere, and the crowds in the streets and at the bulletin boards of the various papers, their heads in most cases bared, reverently read the announcement.

All entertainments of a social nature have been canceled, and even skating rinks, hockey rinks, and places of public amusement have been closed.

OTTAWA, Jan. 22.—The news of the Queen's death reached Ottawa at 2 P. M. The Secretary of State at once issued a proclamation continuing in office all who held positions under the Crown. This is merely formal.

All public buildings in the Dominion at once placed the union jack at half mast, and it will so remain until sundown on the day of the Queen's funeral.

ST. JOHN'S, N. F., Jan. 22.—The announcement of Queen Victoria's death has called forth expressions of the keenest regret in Newfoundland, the oldest colony of the British Empire. The Colonial Cabinet met this evening and adopted resolutions of condolence, which were cabled to London.

To-morrow will be observed as a day of mourning throughout the colony.

Arrangements are being made for the proclamation of the new sovereign upon receipt of an official intimation of his accession.

HALIFAX, N. S., Jan. 22.—Symbols of mourning for Queen Victoria are everywhere displayed. Flags fly half-mast on ships and from the frowning fortress, and the royal standard, for the first time in many years, is half-mast at the Citadel.

All performances have been canceled, and on the day of the Queen's funeral the tolling of half a hundred bells will mingle with the loud notes of minute guns for the departed sovereign.

A sketch of the life of Queen Victoria will be found on Pages 6 and 7 of this issue.

AMERICAN TRIBUTES TO QUEEN VICTORIA

President McKinley Cables Condolences to the New King.

WASHINGTON FLAGS LOWERED

Such a Mark of Respect Had Never Been Before Paid on the Death of a Monarch—Action by Congress.

WASHINGTON, Jan. 22.—Four days of anxiety, in a large measure, prepared official Washington for the news which was flashed across the cable this afternoon from England. So it happened that all things that could be decently done in anticipation of the death of Queen Victoria had been disposed of, and all was in readiness for the execution of the formalities which are indispensable to such occasions. The President and his advisers were in receipt from time to time of all news which came from Osborne House. When the end came it found appropriate measures of condolence framed, and even orders, ready for execution, looking to the half-masting of the flags over the executive departments and the carrying out of the usual formalities.

The half-masting of the National ensign was an unusual tribute. This has been done once or twice on the occasion of the funeral of some great ruler, but never before in the case of the death of a monarch. The adjournment of the House was also an unusual mark of respect.

THE PRESIDENT'S MESSAGE.

The news announcing the death of Queen Victoria was conveyed to President McKinley simultaneously with its receipt by the newspapers. Soon afterward the President sent the following message of condolence to the new King:

Washington, Jan. 22, 1901.

His Majesty the King, Osborne House, Isle of Wight:

I have received with profound sorrow the lamentable tidings of the death of her Majesty the Queen. Allow me, Sir, to offer my sincere sympathy and that of the American people in your personal bereavement and in the loss Great Britain has suffered in the death of its venerable and illustrious sovereign, whose noble life and beneficent influence have promoted the peace and won the affection of the world.

WILLIAM McKINLEY.

Secretary of State Hay cabled the following message to Ambassador Choate at London:

Department of State, Jan. 22, 1901.

Choate, Ambassador, London:

You will express to Lord Lansdowne the profound sorrow of the Government and people of the United States at the death of the Queen and the deep sympathy we feel with the people of the British Empire in their great affliction. JOHN HAY.

The actual dispatch of the message from the President to the new King of England and from Secretary Hay to Ambassador Choate was delayed only long enough to receive the physicians' statement announcing the demise of the Queen, and then they were sent forward at once and copies were furnished to the press.

The flag on the Executive Mansion was placed at half-mast at 3:30 o'clock.

THE SENATE'S RESOLUTION.

The Senate was in executive session when the news of Queen Victoria's death was announced, but the bulletin announcing her death was passed around by the doorkeepers. Expressions of regret and of admiration for the virtues of the dead sovereign were heard on all hands. Senators Allison and Morgan held a hurried consultation, as the result of which the latter drew up a resolution, which the former presented when the executive session closed. The resolution was as follows:

"That the death of her Royal and Imperial Majesty, Victoria, of noble virtues and great renown, is sincerely deplored by the Senate of the United States of America."

The resolution was adopted unanimously.

Afterward Mr. Allison offered the following resolution:

"That the President pro tem. of the Senate cause to be conveyed to the Prime Minister of Great Britain a suitably engrossed copy of the foregoing resolution."

This was agreed to.

Senator Lodge, evidently voicing the sentiment of most of his colleagues, said later:

"The Queen's death is to the people of the United States a real sorrow. Her reign, the longest in English history, has been a great and memorable one, but it has perhaps nothing greater or more memorable than her own ability and purity of character; her fidelity to her high duties, and her devotion to those ideals of conduct and domestic life which appeal most profoundly to all English-speaking people. The Queen has always been a steadfast friend to the United States, and during her long life has made that friendship traditional in her family. Americans can never forget that England was withheld from active interference in our own civil war largely, if not wholly, by the influence of the Queen and the wise counsels of Prince Albert."

THE HOUSE ADJOURNS.

The House received the news at about 2 o'clock, and for the time being it was the theme of universal discussion among the members. Speaker Henderson had shown deep interest in the Queen's condition, and the first bulletin announcing her death was taken to him in his private office and to Chairman Hitt of the Committee on Foreign Affairs. Mr. Hitt conferred with his colleagues as to the precedents in such cases, and then framed a brief and expressive resolution of sympathy and respect to be introduced in the House later. For a time it was feared that this might give rise to some expressions from Boer sympathizers, but, on the contrary, it was developed that the sentiment of respect for the departed sovereign was shared by all alike.

At the conclusion of the general debate on the District of Columbia Appropriation bill Mr. Hitt offered the resolution, which was as follows:

"Resolved, That the House of Representatives of the United States of America has learned with profound sorrow of the death of her Majesty Queen Victoria and sympathizes with her people in the loss of their beloved sovereign; that the President be requested to communicate this expression of the sentiment of the House to the Government of Great Britain; that, as a further mark of respect to the memory of Queen Victoria, the House do now adjourn."

The reading of the resolution was listened to with impressive silence. Mr. Hitt stated very briefly that this resolution followed the precedents in similar cases. It was, he said, copied almost literally from the resolution adopted upon the occasion of the death of the President of the French Republic, and followed the expression adopted upon the death of the Czar of Russia. He did not, he said, think that the occasion called for any extended remarks, and asked for a vote.

The resolution was unanimously adopted, and the House at 3:05 P. M. stood adjourned until noon to-morrow.

After the adjournment members gathered in knots and discussed the event, the tributes being to the womanly virtues and purity of home life of the Queen, no less than to her national service.

PRAISE FROM CABINET MINISTERS.

Secretary of State Hay, on being informed of the Queen's death, declined to make a statement for publication [illegible] ground that, being under obligation [illegible] ficial message to the British Govern[illegible] on the subject, he did not feel called upon to make a further supplementary private statement.

Attorney General Griggs said:

"Hers has been a noble life. Whether she was greater as a Queen or as a woman is hard to say. Her good influence upon

"All the News That's Fit to Print."

The New York Times.

THE WEATHER.
Fair, with variable winds, mostly east to south.

COPYRIGHT, 1901, BY THE NEW YORK TIMES COMPANY.

VOL. L...NO. 16,121. NEW YORK, SATURDAY, SEPTEMBER 7, 1901.—SIXTEEN PAGES. ONE CENT In Greater New York, Jersey City, and Newark. Elsewhere, TWO CENTS.

PRESIDENT SHOT AT BUFFALO FAIR

Wounded in the Breast and Abdomen.

HE IS RESTING EASILY

One Bullet Extracted, Other Cannot Be Found.

Assassin Is Leon Czolgosz of Cleveland, Who Says He Is an Anarchist and Follower of Emma Goldman.

BUFFALO, Sept. 6.—President McKinley, while holding a reception in the Temple of Music at the Pan-American Exposition at 4 o'clock this afternoon, was shot and twice wounded by Leon Czolgosz, an Anarchist, who lives in Cleveland.

One bullet entered the President's breast, struck the breast bone, glanced and was later easily extracted. The other bullet entered the abdomen, penetrated the stomach, and has not been found, although the wounds have been closed.

The physicians in attendance upon the President at 10:40 o'clock to-night issued the following bulletin:

"The President is rallying satisfactorily and is resting comfortably. 10:15 P. M., temperature, 100.4 degrees; pulse, 124; respiration, 24.

"P. M. RIXEY,
"M. B. MANN,
"R. E. PARKE,
"H. MYNTER,
"EUGENE WASDIN.

"Signed by George B. Cortelyou, Secretary to the President."

This condition was maintained until 1 o'clock A. M., when the physicians issued the following bulletin:

"The President is free from pain and resting well. Temperature, 100.2; pulse, 120; respiration, 24."

The assassin was immediately overpowered and taken to a police station on the Exposition grounds, but not before a number of the throng had tried to lynch him. Later he was taken to Police Headquarters.

The exact nature of the President's injuries is described in the following bulletin issued by Secretary Cortelyou for the physicians who were called:

"The President was shot about 4 o'clock. One bullet struck him on the upper portion of the breast bone, glancing and not penetrating; the second bullet penetrated the abdomen five inches below the left nipple and one and one-half inches to the left of the median line. The abdomen was opened through the line of the bullet wound. It was found that the bullet had penetrated the stomach.

"The opening in the front wall of the stomach was carefully closed with silk sutures; after which a search was made for a hole in the back wall of the stomach. This was found and also closed in the same way. The further course of the bullet could not be discovered, although careful search was made. The abdominal wound was closed without drainage. No injury to the intestines or other abdominal organs was discovered.

"The patient stood the operation well, pulse of good quality, rate of 130, and his condition at the conclusion of operation was gratifying. The result cannot be foretold. His condition at present justifies hope of recovery."

Leon Czolgosz, the assassin, has signed a confession, covering six pages of foolscap, in which he states that he is an Anarchist and that he became an enthusiastic member of that body through the influence of Emma Goldman, whose writings he had read and whose lectures he had listened to. He denies having any confederate, and says he decided on the act three days ago and bought the revolver with which the act was committed in Buffalo.

He has seven brothers and sisters in Cleveland, and the Cleveland Directory has the names of about that number living in Hosmer Street and Ackland Avenue, which adjoin. Some of them are butchers and others are in other trades.

Czolgosz is now detained at Police Headquarters, pending the result of the President's injuries. He does not appear in the least degree uneasy or penitent for his action. He says he was induced by his attention to Emma Goldman's lectures and writings to decide that the present form of government in this country was all wrong, and he thought the best way to end it was by the killing of the President. He shows no sign of insanity, but is very reticent about much of his career.

While acknowledging himself an Anarchist, he does not state to what branch of the organization he belongs.

HOW THE DEED WAS DONE.

Assassin Came with the Crowd to Greet the President and Shot When Two Feet from Him.

BUFFALO, Sept. 6.—Czolgosz's attempt on the life of the President was made at about 4 o'clock in the Temple of Music, where Mr. McKinley had gone to hold a reception at that hour. He had spent the day at Niagara with about 100 invited guests, and arrived at the exposition grounds at 3:30. Mrs. McKinley proceeded to the Mission Building and the President went directly to the Temple of Music.

A vast crowd had assembled long before the arrival of Mr. McKinley. The daily organ recital was nearing its end as the President entered and went to the slightly raised dais at one end of the hall.

The President, though well guarded by United States Secret Service detectives, was fully exposed to such an attack as occurred. He stood at the edge of the raised dais, and throngs of people crowded in at the various entrances to see their Chief Executive, perchance to clasp his hand, and then fight their way out in the good-natured mob that every minute swelled and multiplied at the points of ingress and egress to the building.

The President was in a cheerful mood and was enjoying the hearty evidences of good-will which everywhere met his gaze. Upon his right stood John G. Milburn of Buffalo, President of the Pan-American Exposition, chatting with the President, and introducing to him persons of note who approached. Upon the President's left stood Mr. Cortelyou.

THE ASSASSIN APPEARS.

It was shortly after 4 o'clock when one of the throng which surrounded the Presidential party, a medium-sized man of ordinary appearance and plainly dressed in black, approached as if to greet the President. Both Secretary Cortelyou and President Milburn noticed that the man's hand was swathed in a bandage or handkerchief. Reports of bystanders differ as to which hand. He worked his way with the stream of people up to the edge of the dais, until he was within two feet of the President.

President McKinley smiled, bowed, and extended his hand in that spirit of geniality the American people so well know, when suddenly the man raised his hand and two sharp reports of a revolver rang out loud and clear above the hum of voices and the shuffling of myriad feet. The assassin had fired through the handkerchief which concealed the revolver.

There was an instant of almost complete silence, like the hush that follows a clap of thunder. The President stood stock still, a look of hesitancy, almost of bewilderment, on his face. Then he retreated a step while a pallor began to steal over his features. The multitude seemed only partially aware that something serious had happened.

Then came a commotion. With the leap of a tiger three men threw themselves forward as with one impulse and sprang toward the would-be assassin. Two of them were United States Secret Service men, who were on the lookout and whose duty it was to guard against just such a calamity as had here befallen the President and the Nation. The third was a bystander, a negro, who had only an instant before grasped the hand of the President. In a twinkling the assassin was borne to the ground, his weapon was wrested from his grasp, and strong arms pinioned him down.

Then the vast multitude which thronged the edifice began to come to a realizing sense of the awfulness of the scene of which they had been witnesses. A murmur arose, spread, and swelled to a hum of confusion, then grew to a babel of sounds, and later to a pandemonium of noises.

The crowds that a moment before had stood mute and motionless in bewildered ignorance of the enormity of the deed, now with a single impulse surged forward, while a hoarse cry welled up from a thousand throats, and a thousand men charged forward to lay hands upon the perpetrator of the dastardly crime.

CONFUSION REIGNS.

For a moment the confusion was terrible. The crowd surged forward regardless of consequences. Men shouted and fought, women screamed and children cried. Some of those nearest the doors fled from the edifice in fear of a stampede, while hundreds of others from the outside struggled blindly forward in the effort to enter the crowded building and solve the mystery of excitement and panic which every moment grew and swelled within the congested interior of the palatial edifice.

Inside on the slightly raised dais was enacted within those few feverish moments a tragedy, so dramatic in character, so thrilling in its intensity, that few who looked on will ever be able to give a succinct account of what really did transpire. Even the actors who were playing the principal rôles came out of it with blanched faces, trembling limbs, and beating hearts, while their brains throbbed with a tumult of conflicting emotions which left behind only a chaotic jumble of impressions which could not be clarified into a lucid narrative of the events as they really transpired.

But of the multitude which witnessed or bore a part in the scene there was but one mind which seemed to retain it's equilibrium, one hand which remained steady, one eye which gazed with unflinching calmness, and one voice which retained its even tenor and faltered not at the most critical juncture.

They were the mind and the hand and the eye and the voice of President McKinley.

After the first shock of the assassin's shots, he retreated a step, then, as the detectives leaped upon his assailant, he turned, walked steadily to a chair and seated himself, at the same time removing his hat and bowing his head in his hands.

In an instant Secretary Cortelyou and President Milburn were at his side. His waistcoat was hurriedly opened, the President meanwhile admonishing those about him to remain calm and telling them not to be alarmed.

"But you are wounded," cried his secretary; "let me examine."

"No, I think not," answered the President. "I am not badly hurt, I assure you."

Nevertheless his outer garments were hastily loosened, and when a trickling stream of crimson was seen to wind its way down his breast spreading its stain over the white surface of the linen their worst fears were confirmed.

A force of Exposition guards were on the scene by this time, and an effort was made to clear the building. The crush was terrific. Spectators crowded down the stairways from the galleries, the crowd on the floor surged forward toward the rostrum, while despite the strenuous efforts of police and guards the throng without struggled madly to obtain admission.

IN THE HOSPITAL.

The President's assailant in the meantime had been hustled to the rear of the building by Exposition Guards McCauley and James, where he was held while the building was cleared, and later turned over to Superintendent Bull of the Buffalo Police Department, who took the prisoner to No. 13 Police Station, and later to Police Headquarters.

As soon as the crowd in the Temple of Music had been dispersed sufficiently the President was removed in the automobile ambulance and taken to the Exposition Hospital, where an examination was made.

The best medical skill was summoned and within a brief period several of Buffalo's best-known practitioners were at the patient's side. The President retained the full exercise of his faculties until placed on the operating table and subjected to an anaesthetic.

Upon the first examination it was ascertained that one bullet had taken effect in the right breast just below the nipple, causing a comparatively harmless wound. The other took effect in the abdomen, about five inches below the left nipple, two inches to the left of the navel, and about on a level with it.

Upon arriving at the Exposition Hospital the second bullet was probed for. The walls of the abdomen were opened, but teh ball was not located. The incision was hastily closed and after a hasty consultation it was decided to the remove the patient to the home of President Milburn. This was done, the automobile-ambulance being used for the purpose.

Arrived at the Milburn residence, all persons outside the medical attendants, nurses, and the officials immediately concerned were excluded and the task of probing for the bullet, which had lodged in the abdomen, was begun by Dr. Roswell Park.

When it was decided to remove the President from the Exposition Hospital to the Milburn residence, the news was broken to Mrs. McKinley as gently as might be, by the members of the Milburn family. She bore the shock remarkably well, and displayed the utmost fortitude.

CROWD READY TO LYNCH.

While the wounded President was being borne from the Exposition to the Milburn residence between rows of onlookers with bared heads, a far different spectacle was being witnessed along the route of his assailant's journey from the scene of his crime to Police Headquarters. The trip was made so quickly that the prisoner was safely landed within the wide portals of the police station and the doors closed before any one was aware of his presence.

The news of the attempted assassination had in the meanwhile been spread broadcast by the newspapers. Like wildfire it spread from mouth to mouth. Then bulletins began to appear on the boards along "Newspaper Row," and when the announcement was made that the prisoner had been taken to Police Headquarters, only two blocks distant from the newspaper section, the crowds surged down toward the terrace, eager for a glimpse of the prisoner. At Police Headquarters they were met by a strong cordon of police, drawn up across the pavement on Pearl Street, who denied admittance to any but officials authorized to take part in the examination of the prisoner.

In a few minutes the crowd had grown from tens to hundreds, and these in turn quickly swelled to thousands, until the street was completely blocked by a surging mass of eager humanity. It was at this juncture that some one raised the cry of "Lynch him!" Like a flash the cry was taken up, and the whole crowd re-echoed the cry, "Lynch him!" "Hang him!" Closer the crowd surged forward.

Denser the throng became as new arrivals each moment swelled the swaying multitude. The situation was becoming critical when suddenly the big doors were flung open and a squad of reserves advanced with solid front, drove the crowd back from the curb, then across the street, and gradually succeeded in dispersing them from about the entrance to the station.

By this time there were probably 30,000 people assembled in the vicinity of Pearl, Seneca, Erie Streets, and the Terrace. The crowd was so great that it became necessary to rope off the entire street in front of Police Headquarters, and at a late hour to-night the police were still patrolling in the streets in the neighborhood, in squads of three or four. Inside the station house were assembled District Attorney Penny, Superintendent of Police Bull, Capt. Reagan of the First Precinct, and other officials.

The prisoner at first proved quite communicative, so much so in fact, that little dependence could be placed on what he said. He first gave his name as Fred Nieman, said his home was in Detroit, and that he had been in Buffalo about a week. He said he had been boarding at a place in Broadway. Later this place was located as John Nowak's saloon, a Raines-law hotel, 1,078 Broadway. Here the prisoner occupied Room 8.

THE PRISONER'S STORY.

Nowak, the proprietor, said he knew very little about his guest. He came there, he declared, last Saturday, saying he had come to see the Pan-American, and that his home was in Toledo. He had been alone at all times about Nowak's place, and had had no visitors. In his room was found a small traveling bag of cheap make. It contained an empty cartridge box and a few articles of clothing.

With these facts in hand the police went at the prisoner with renewed vigor in the effort to obtain either a full confession or a straight account of his identity and movements prior to his arrival in Buffalo. He at first admitted that he was an Anarchist in sympathy at least, but denied strenuously that the attempt on the life of the President was a result of a preconcerted plot on the part of any Anarchist society.

At times he was defiant and again indifferent. But at no time did he betray the remotest sign of remorse. He declared the deed was not premeditated, but in the same breath refused to say why he perpetrated it. When charged by District Attorney Penny with being the instrument of an organized band of conspirators, he protested vehemently that he never even thought of perpetrating the crime until this morning.

After long and persistent questioning it was announced at Police Headquarters that the prisoner had made a confession, which he signed.

MRS. McKINLEY COURAGEOUS.

Bears Up Well When She Hears of the Attempt on Mr. McKinley's Life.

BUFFALO, N. Y., Sept. 6.—After the President was cared for at the Exposition grounds, Director General W. I. Buchanan started for the Milburn residence to forestall any information that might reach Mrs. McKinley there by telephone or otherwise. Very luckily, he was first to arrive with the information. The Niagara Falls trip had tired Mrs. McKinley, and on returning to the Milburn residence she went to her room to rest.

Mr. Buchanan broke the news as gently as possible to the nieces of Mr. and Mrs. McKinley, and consulted with them and Mrs. Milburn as to the best course to pursue in breaking the news to Mrs. McKinley. It was finally decided that on her awaking, or shortly thereafter, Mr. Buchanan should break the news to her, if, in the meantime her physician, Dr. Rixey, had not yet arrived.

Mrs. McKinley awoke from her sleep at about 5:30 o'clock. She was feeling splendidly, she said, and at once took up her crocheting, which, as is well known, is one of her favorite diversions.

Immediately on Mr. Buchanan's arrival at the Milburn home he had telephonic communication therewith cut off, for already there had been several calls, and he decided on this as the wisest course to pursue lest Mrs. McKinley, hearing the continued ringing of the bells, might inquire what it meant.

While the light of day remained, Mrs. McKinley continued with her crocheting, keeping to her room. When the day began to wane and the President had not arrived, she began to feel anxious concerning him. "I wonder why he does not come?" she asked one of her nieces. There was no clock in Mrs. McKinley's room, and when it was 7 o'clock she had no idea it was so late, and this is when she began to feel anxious concerning her husband, for he was due to return to Mr. Milburn's house about 6 o'clock.

At 7 o'clock Dr. Rixey arrived at the Milburn residence. He had been driven hurriedly down Delaware Avenue in an open carriage, and at once entered the house. At 7:20 o'clock Dr. Rixey came out of the house accompanied by Col. Webb Hayes, a son of the late ex-President Hayes, who is a friend of President McKinley. They entered a carriage and returned to the Exposition hospital.

After Dr. Rixey had gone, Mr. Buchanan said that the doctor had broken the news in a most gentle way to Mrs. McKinley. He said she stood it bravely, though considerably affected. If it was possible to bring him to her, she wanted it done. Dr. Rixey assured her that the President could be brought with safety from the Exposition grounds, and when he left the Milburn house it was to complete all arrangements for the removal of the President.

A big force of regular patrolmen were assigned to the Milburn residence.

"CAUGHT THE ASSASSIN."

Capt. Wiser of Coast Artillery Says His Men Did So.

WASHINGTON, Sept. 6.—The War Department to-night received the following telegram from Capt. John B. Wiser, commanding the Seventy-third Company of Coast Artillery at Buffalo:

"BUFFALO, N. Y., Sept. 6, 1901.—Adjutant General, U. S. A., Washington: President shot at reception in Temple of Music about 4 P. M. Corporal Bertschey and detail of men of my company caught the assassin at once and held him down till the secret service men overpowered him and took the prisoner out of their hands, my men being unarmed. Condition of President not known. Revolver in my possession.

"WISER, Commanding."

OPINIONS OF SURGEONS.

Injury to Stomach Serious for a Man of the President's Age—Danger of Peritonitis.

According to well-known surgeons, there are in New York four or five persons each year who, through various causes, suffer from injuries similar to those received yesterday by President McKinley at Buffalo. Operations similar to those performed on the President have been successful and the patients have recovered. The prominent surgeons interviewed last evening said that the chances of recovery would be much greater if President McKinley were a younger man.

Dr. John B. Walker of 33 West Thirty-third Street said:

"Any injury to the stomach similar to that which has been inflicted on President McKinley is serious. There have been cases of stomach perforation where the patients have recovered. The diagnosis of any perforated wound of the stomach in an adult is very serious. The trouble is that inflammation following such an injury is more acute to an older person than to one more youthful. The fear is that the contents of the stomach will ooze into the intestines and peritonitis set in."

"Do you recall any recent cases similar to that of President McKinley," was asked.

"Dr. Bull performed an operation on a young man a short time ago. The intestines were perforated and an operation similar to that performed on President McKinley resulted in complete recovery. If President McKinley were a man between thirty-five and forty years of age the chances would be more in his favor. I cannot recall at this time a case of a man of the age of the President recovering from similar wounds. There is one advantage the President had, and that is the prompt assistance of a surgeon. Dr. Roswell Park is one of the most eminent surgeons in the United States."

"What other cases do you recall?"

"The case of the football player in Princeton who was shot by a negro is one of the latest. In that case the young man was of powerful physique. He did not receive the attention of a surgeon for twelve hours, and the result was that peritonitis set in and death occurred in a few days."

MR. ROOSEVELT EN ROUTE.

One Receipt of News the Vice President Leaves for Buffalo.

BURLINGTON, Vt., Sept. 6.—The first news of the attempted assassination of President McKinley reached Vice President Roosevelt at Isle La Motte at 5:30 o'clock this afternoon, when the Vice President was informed over the telephone that there was a rumor that the President had been shot. It was confirmed by another message a moment later.

The Vice President seemed stunned by the news, and put his hands to his head, then exclaimed, "My God!" Those around him were immediately informed of the tragedy, and it was decided to announce it to the company of a thousand persons who had gathered to hear Col. Roosevelt speak at the annual outing of the Vermont Fish and Game League. Senator Proctor made the announcement, and men, women, and children wept.

A later bulletin was received, stating that the President was resting quietly and that the chances were favorable for his recovery. "Good!" exclaimed the Vice President, and his face lighted up. He showed his pleasure by eagerly announcing the good news to the assembly.

The Vice President then left immediately on the yacht Elfrida, owned by W. Seward Webb, and came to this city as quickly as possible, having directed that all messages should be held for him here. The yacht was to have gone to Arrow Point, where a special train was waiting for the Vice President, but the train was sent on to Burlington, and was there when the yacht came into the harbor, at 8:15.

President Clement of the Rutland Railroad placed the train at the disposal of the Vice President, and made arrangements to take him on it to Buffalo. Col. Roosevelt was asked at the wharf for a statement for publication, and said:

"I am so inexpressibly grieved, shocked, and horrified that I can say nothing."

He boarded the train at once and left for Buffalo.

CABINET WILL ASSEMBLE.

Postmaster General Smith and Secretaries Root and Gage Off for Buffalo.

PHILADELPHIA, Sept. 6. — Postmaster General Charles Emory Smith was greatly affected by the news of the shooting of President McKinley, and expressed himself as shocked beyond measure. He immediately telegraphed to Washington and Buffalo, asking for further particulars than the early news dispatches contained. Mr. Smith said he hoped the President's injuries might not prove so serious as was at first intimated.

Mr. Smith left here on a late train to-night for Buffalo. He expects to be at the President's bedside by 9 o'clock to-morrow morning.

NEWBURY, N. H., Sept. 6.—A message containing information from Buffalo was received here early this evening and forwarded by messenger to the home of Secretary Hay. No reply came to it, and up to a late hour Secretary Hay could not be reached.

BUCKFIELD, Me., Sept. 6.—John D. Long, Secretary of the Navy, who has been passing his vacation at the Long homestead, two miles from this place, learned to-night of the shooting of President McKinley. He was deeply affected, and proceeded to his home at once, declaring that he was undecided about future plans. The Secretary positively refused to say anything for publication.

PITTSBURG, Sept. 6.—When informed of the shooting of President McKinley, Attorney General Knox said: "I cannot imagine how any living creature could harbor such a thought as to take the life of the President. I am so shocked at the awful news that I cannot talk further."

Mr. Knox left at 11 P. M. for Buffalo. Just before leaving he said:

"I can only express the common sentiment of horror at the cruelty of the dastardly blow inflicted upon the lovable and beloved man who has stood for all that is best for the people, who have so implicitly trusted him. His bodily wounds, grievous as they are, will cause him less pain than the thought that any human heart could have harbored against him the malice that inspired the deed."

DUBLIN, N. H., Sept. 6.—Secretary of the Interior Hitchcock, who has been at Mount Monadnock, when informed to-night of the tragic incident at Buffalo, said:

"I am too horrified to make any expression whatever." He immediately prepared to leave for Buffalo.

Secretary of War Elihu Root left the Grand Central Station at 11:10 last night for Buffalo in a special train. He was accompanied by a Dr. Dixon, a specialist, with whom he is hastening to the bedside of the President. The train was made up of a single coach and locomotive, and all possible speed will be made to reach Buffalo on record-breaking time.

When Secretary Root was asked to express an opinion of the President's injury, he said:

"What is there to say? I do not know how seriously injured President McKinley is, but I hope his condition is not so serious as reported. I am almost overcome by the terrible news."

Secretary Root came up from Southampton, L. I., in a special train. With Dr. Dixon and a valet, he rode in a cab to the Grand Central Station. The special train had already been made up, and in less than three minutes after their arrival at the station they were speeding on their way to Buffalo.

Special to The New York Times.

CHICAGO, Sept. 6.—Secretary of the Treasury Gage, who was visiting his son, Eli Gage, in Evanston, seemed dazed by the news, and with bowed head walked slowly into the house. Preparations were made at once for the Secretary to go to Buffalo, accompanied by his son. Before he took the train for Buffalo, an hour later, Secretary Gage said:

"I am too shocked to speak. The news of such a happening is simply overwhelming to me. The President was always confident that no harm would ever come to him. He is a man who is honored by all. I received no official message that he had been assassinated. The first tidings were brought me by friends."

WASHINGTON STUNNED BY THE TRAGEDY

No Member of Cabinet Is at the Capital City.

MILITARY GUARD DETAILED

Under the Law Vice President Roosevelt Will Discharge the Purely Routine Duties of the President.

Special to The New York Times.

WASHINGTON, Sept. 6.—For the third time in thirty-seven years Washington has been stunned by the shooting of a President of the United States. Like lightning out of the fair September sky the report from Buffalo arrested attention here about 5 o'clock, and in a few moments anxious crowds were hurrying from all parts of the city to the offices of the newspapers seeking additional information. People stopped in their hurry to ask of every one met whether the President had been killed, and there was the utmost impatience because of the brevity and indefiniteness of the bulletins and the failure of assurance that the wounds inflicted upon Mr. McKinley were not fatal. To-night the street in front of the newspaper offices is crowded with women and men hungering with anxiety and waiting to catch the announcements that come at long intervals through a megaphone operated by a man in an upper window of a newspaper office.

Grief has not checked a torrent of indignation at the crime committed against humanity and a President who has always trusted himself implicity to the protection of his fellows, venturing from day to day to walk the streets without guard. The rage against the assassin was immediate and outspoken with men of all parties, for Mr. McKinley has no personal enemies here or elsewhere.

The disability of the President occurred at a moment when the Administration was entirely unrepresented at Washington by a Cabinet officer. When the information of the shooting reached the White House by a telephone message from Buffalo, Col. Montgomery and a few clerks were the only members of the President's official family present, Col. Pruden getting the news while he was dining at home. From the moment he heard the news, Col. Montgomery began making efforts to reach the members of the Cabinet, except Secretary of Agriculture Wilson, who is in Buffalo. There was a stream of visitors to the White House from the moment the news of the shooting was received until late to-night, but few of the visitors were persons high in official life.

HOW THE NEWS WAS RECEIVED.

The force at the White House since the President's departure has been in constant communication with him, and while he has conducted most of the business of his office at his home, in Canton, Ohio, the majority of the papers with which he has had to deal have been prepared in Washington and forwarded through the White House clerical force. All reports received from him by officials here were cheerful and high-spirited.

The work of the official day was done when the news of the calamity arrived here and the executive departments had generally emptied themselves of their workmen, and very few of the officials were to be found at their desks.

Mr. Adee, the acting head of the State Department, was met at the station as he was leaving for his country home near Laurel, Md., and returned at once to the State Department. He waited for official confirmation of the news, and it was not until he received a copy of the bulletin issued by the physicians through Secretary Cortelyou that he undertook to acquaint officially the Governments of all the nations of the world with the facts of the shooting. He then drew up a message, which will be sent to every United States Embassy, Legation, and Consulate throughout the civilized world directing them to acquaint the Governments to which they are accredited of the facts. With these he embodied a condensation of the physicians' bulletin with Mr. Cortelyou's statement.

In the Navy Department Mr. Hackett, the acting Secretary, who had also quitted the building, was speedily recalled by Capt. Cowles, the acting head of the Navigation Bureau, and he immediately put himself in readiness to take any official action that might be necessary to meet the emergency. At Buffalo in the Exposition grounds the navy had a splendid representation in the shape of the marine battalion under Capt. Leonard, and this force will be immediately available if it is decided by the persons about the President that a guard is necessary near his person.

At the War Department Gen. Gillespie, Chief Engineer of the army, was acting Secretary in the absence of Secretary Root, and Assistant Secretary Sanger, who is away on leave. He also had quitted the building, but he had not been gone half an hour before word reached him and he hastily returned to his desk. He immediately sent messages to the Secretary of war and to Gen. Brooke, commanding the Department of the East, giving such unofficial information as was available.

Gen. Gillespie finally got into communication with Secretary Root and Assistant Secretary Sanger, and as a result of the telephonic talk he proceeded to use some of the forces at his disposal. He telegraphed an order to Fort Foster, N. H., to have an officer, a physician, and a squad of men proceed immediately to the house where the President is lying to act as a guard.

PROVIDING FOR EMERGENCIES.

Steps were next taken to provide for the future of the Executive branch of the Government. It was realized that even under the most favorable conditions the President's injuries are of such a character as to make it almost certain that he cannot undertake for a long time to discharge the duties of Chief Executive, even in the most formal way. Every member of the Cabinet able to travel is expected to at once go to Buffalo, and there a Cabinet council will be held to decide upon the course to be followed by the Executive branch. Vice President Roosevelt is in readiness to do whatever is necessary and to meet the obligations imposed upon the Vice President by the Constitution of the United States. These are contained in Paragraph 6, Section 1, Article II., in the following words:

6. In case of the removal of the President from office, or of his death, resignation, or inability to discharge the powers and duties of the said office, the same shall devolve on the Vice President, &c.

Under the terms of this article, as soon as Mr. Roosevelt is assured by proper authority, probably in this case by the senior member of the Cabinet, Secretary Hay, who will doubtless be in Buffalo by to-morrow evening, he will undertake at once in a provisional way to discharge such duties as may devolve on him. Much will depend upon the report of the physicians on the character of the President's injuries as to the extent to which Mr. Roosevelt will discharge the Presidential duties, if he undertakes them at all, and it is almost certain that in the absence of great emergency in public affairs, even if called to assume these obligations, the Vice President will confine himself in the exercise of his powers to the discharge of the most routine and indispensable functions.

Such public men as were in the city called at the White House during the evening. They included Assistant Secretary Spaulding of the Treasury Department, Assistant Secretary Hackett of the Navy Department, ex-United States Senator H. W. Blair, Controller Dawes, and Register Lyons of the Treasury, and Capt. Towner, Assistant Commissioner of Indian Affairs. There were also calls from representatives of several foreign legations.

No official confirmation of the shooting came to the White House for three hours after its occurrence, when Col. Montgomery, the chief operator at the White House, was informed at 7:20 o'clock by Secretary Cortelyou at Buffalo that a surgical operation upon the President was in progress, and that "so far everything is favorable." Later he gave information of the completion of the operation, and followed that statement with other messages giving private information as to the President's condition and his removal to Mr. Milburn's residence.

STRONG MILITARY GUARD.

During the early evening a conference was held at the War Department of such of the prominent army officers as could be gathered at short notice by Gen. Gillespie. He informed them that he had communicated with Gen. Brooke at Governors Island and that the General had replied that he would start immediately for Buffalo, where he expected in the early morning to take personal charge of all arrangements made for the guarding of the President.

Meanwhile he had directed that the troops which had been placed as a guard around the hospital in the Exposition grounds be transferred to the Milburn home, where the President lies, to serve as a guard and keep back the public and preserve quiet. Gen. Brooke has at Buffalo at his disposal a company of coast artillery, stationed in the Exposition grounds; a company of the Fifteenth Infantry, also stationed at Fort Porter, within the limits of the Exposition preserves, and other troops at Fort Niagara.

The conference decided that there was little more that the War Department could undertake at this time. Surgeon General Van Reypen of the Navy, who came down to the Navy Department, called at Gen. Gillespie's office, and, discussing the case from a medical point of view, took occasion to mention Dr. Nicholas Senn of Chicago as an expert of high grade in such cases of injury, and the suggestion was promptly telegraphed to Buffalo that his services be secured.

Assistant Secretary Alles of the Treasury Department received a message to-night from Secretary Gage at Chicago stating that he was about to leave at once for Buffalo, where he will arrive to-morrow morning.

Admiral Dewey arrived in Washington early in the afternoon. He proceeded at once to his suburban home and was occupied with the details of the approaching Schley court of inquiry when the news reached him by the telephone. He at once sought all the particulars and placed himself in readiness for any service that might be required of him, informing Acting Secretary Hackett of that fact.

The Admiral found himself unable to express his feelings at the news, and all that could be extracted from him was that he was plunged in grief too deep for utterance at this time. He said that he could not now express an opinion as to the effect that the calamity might have on the court of inquiry, or even whether it would result in the postponement of the approaching sitting.

DIPLOMATS' CONDOLENCES.

Owing to the absence of many of the Diplomatic Corps at Buffalo and of many others at the various Summer resorts there were only two representatives of this body of rank in Washington to-day. Minister Wu was one of these, and when seen to-night he was a picture of distress. He said he realized keenly the tremendous indebtedness of China to President McKinley's kindly impulses in her great trials in the past year, and was shocked at the great calamity that had befallen him. He said he could not conceive of any sort of motive for such an inexcusable deed as that of Nieman's, and he was severe in his denunciation of Anarchists. He asked why they were permitted to hatch such plots as this in a Republic where the people could readily change their President if they were in the slightest degree dissatisfied with his official conduct or his private personality. In conclusion, he expressed the hope that the President would shortly recover.

Another diplomatic representative in Washington was Señor Herran, representing the Government of the United States of Colombia. He also was greatly distressed and he affirmed that his whole country would sympathize with the President in this moment of pain. He also could not understand, he said, why such a benevolent character as President McKinley should be thus assaulted by one of the people, and he declared it is time that the Anarchists should be suppressed.

It was somewhat gratifying to the officials here that the very first expression of official sympathy should come from the Island of Cuba, in the shape of the following telegram:

Sept. 6, 1901.
(Received at War Department, 7:45 P. M.
Havana.

Adjutant General, Washington:
Mayor and City Council of Havana have called, expressing sorrow and solicitude for the President, and desire that his family be advised of these expressions.
SCOTT, Adjutant General.

Mr. H. T. Scott of the Union Iron Works at San Francisco, at whose house the President staid while visiting that city, telegraphed the Navy Department as follows:

"So shocked with news, words fail to express our feelings."

Messages of sympathy and of inquiry already have begun to arrive at the State Department.

TO-DAY: SIXTEEN PAGES,

INDEX TO DEPARTMENTS.

"All the News That's Fit to Print."

The New York Times.

THE WEATHER.
Fair; light to fresh north winds.

VOL. LIV....NO. 17,178. NEW YORK, MONDAY, JANUARY 23, 1905.—TWELVE PAGES. ONE CENT In Greater New York, Jersey City and Newark. | Elsewhere, TWO CENTS.

CZAR'S SUBJECTS ARM FOR REVOLT

St. Petersburg Strike Leaders Decide to Fight.

WORKMEN WANT REVENGE

Rumors of Outbreaks in Finland and Elsewhere.

DOWAGER CZARINA FLEES

Joins Czar at Tsarskoe-Selo—Number Shot in Capital Placed as High as 5,000.

ST. PETERSBURG, Monday, Jan. 23.—Leaders of the strikers who came into conflict with the troops yesterday assembled last night and decided to continue the struggle with arms.

The strikers, goaded to desperation by the events yesterday, a day of violence, fury, and bloodshed, are in a state of open insurrection against the Government. It is rumored that 30,000 or 40,000 armed strikers from Kolpino, sixteen miles distant, are marching on St. Petersburg.

The workmen are now arming with every available weapon for a renewal of the struggle. They have few firearms, but are turning the implements of trade into improvised weapons.

There are rumors of trouble in Finland and disaffection on the part of the troops. Strike leaders say they are awaiting news from Moscow and other large cities, where the troops are not believed to be so loyal as the Guards regiments.

The Moscow Regiment yesterday refused to fire on the working people.

No one knows how many men, women, and children were killed and wounded yesterday by the volleys of the troops. Some estimates are as high as 5,000, but 500 is probably nearer the true number.

The Emperor is at Tsarskoe-Selo, whither the Empress Dowager has fled.

PEACEABLE MEN SHOT DOWN.

Petitioners Met by the Troops of Grand Duke Vladimir.

Special Cable to THE NEW YORK TIMES.
Copyright, 1905, THE NEW YORK TIMES.

LONDON, Jan. 22.—St. Petersburg's streets were the theatre to-day of scenes unparalleled in the history of the world. A wholesale massacre of Russian strikers occurred, and the dead and wounded are numbered by thousands.

The strikers undertook to-day to present to the Czar a petition for the redress of their wrongs.

Instead of meeting the Czar they had to deal with Grand Duke Vladimir, and the morgues and hospitals are full of the victims of his cruelty. The correspondent of The Daily Mail, in telegraphing an account of the tragedy, says:

"This morning all was still and strangely quiet. It was bitterly cold, with a piercing wind and driving fine snow. People muffled in furs went to church as usual. A few strolled toward the Palace Square to see what was to be seen, and, finding nothing, started away again.

"There were no troops in front of the palace, and the bridges across the Neva were open to traffic.

"St. Petersburg under the freshly fallen snow was a white, fair city, from which the gilt minarets of the Admiralty, the cathedral, and the St. Peter and St. Paul fortress shot up tongues of flame in the growing sunshine.

"The church bells were calling. Swift sleighs with splendid horses were gliding by. It was impossible then to connect the scene with the pitiful tragedy that was so swiftly to follow.

"At 10 o'clock the troops began to move about, passing in different directions along the radiating suburban thoroughfares. Cavalry, infantry, and Cossacks in small detachments made no great military display, but infantry and some Guards marched away in regiments, their fixed bayonets glittering wickedly.

"The official programme was going to be literally carried out. Evidently no procession from any industrial suburb was to be allowed to approach the centre of the capital.

"An hour later a little tour in a fast sleigh showed that Central St. Petersburg was ringed with a triple cordon of defenses, terrible as those of Liao-Yang, as if to resist an invading army.

"Out on every main road, on the Ekaterinoffsky Prospect on the left bank of the river, at every strategic point where there were cross-roads, detachments of troops were placed on the further side. Every bridge crossing the Neva to Vassili Ostrov was strongly held, while from the inside of the great courtyards of the Winter Palace a mass of troops came out into the Palace Square.

"Most noticeable, as always, were the Preobrajensky Guards in their striking uniform, and the Pavlovsky Guards in high bronze helmets. There were also grenadier guards and the glittering cuirasses and eagle caps of the cuirassiers of guards, the Czarina's regiment, mounted all on black

"The cavalcade was a magnificent sight as it wheeled round in the great square.

"It was plain thus early that there would be no demonstration in front of the Palace. It only remained to see with how much consideration any attempt to hold one would be repressed.

"It was not long to wait before all uncertainty was removed. What followed it is impossible to describe, because it is impossible to know what occurred in many places widely apart.

"The narratives of eye-witnesses are as yet uncollected, but from many different directions people set out upon the projected pilgrimage, only to be shot down in masses by their uniformed brothers almost before their procession had started from the suburbs.

"The Putiloff strikers left their barrack homes about the factory according to their programme, bringing with them their wives and children, even their babies, as had been arranged. Father Gopon marched at their head, bearing a crucifix aloft above the great roll containing the precious petition.

"They marched down the Peterhoff Chaussée, where the works stand, down hill to where, at the Neva gate, the triumphal arch erected after the Turkish war stands at the junction with the main Baltic thoroughfare.

"There the Ismailovsky Guards, a regiment of which the Czar is honorary Colonel, were drawn up in waiting.

"As the head of the procession approached the acting Colonel called upon them to stop. Father Gopon, still holding the crucifix, advanced and demanded that the Colonel receive and forward the petition.

"This request was declined. Then, after a minute's hesitation and discussion, the procession continued to advance. A sharp order was given. The soldiers raised their rifles, and a volley rang out, but they had only used blank cartridges.

"Another order. This time ball cartridge, and men, women, and children fell in heaps.

"Father Gopon, still clutching the crucifix, stood among the dead and dying with the petition.

"Still another volley, and then the crowd no longer. The procession turned and fled, all but 300, who were lying dead, and 500 writhing wounded.

"Some who had revolvers fired as they fled. Others carried icepicks, some had stones, but practically they were unarmed.

"It was all over with the Putiloff strike procession, and at 11:41 o'clock the strikers were still in sight of their works. As they retreated the soldiers followed, and before a quarter of an hour most of them had fled to their homes, and there only remained the dead and wounded, who were removed with the usual Russian skill to be taken to hospital or home.

"What happened to the Putiloff contingent happened at other places. A procession starting its advance found its progress barred almost before it was begun, and as it attempted to continue it was mowed down by volleys.

"Twenty thousand people started from Kolpino, a manufacturing village twenty-five miles away. At the Moscow arch, on the confines of the town, they met with six volleys. A thousand fell dead and 1,500 were wounded.

"From up the river a great crowd marched to the Nevsky gate, where 500 fell dead and 700 were founded

"The Vassili Ostrov workers only lost 200 killed and 700 wounded."

TROOPS FIRE AT LODZ.

Many Demonstrators Shot Down—Rising in Finland Feared.

LONDON TIMES—NEW YORK TIMES Special Cablegram.
Copyright, 1905, THE NEW YORK TIMES.

PARIS, Jan. 22.—A dispatch from St. Petersburg gives an account of a public demonstration at Lodz, a manufacturing town in Russian Poland, in which the crowd carried flags and raised cries of "Long Live Poland!"

Troops stationed in houses along the route of the procession fired upon it through the windows. Some persons were killed and several wounded.

Great excitement prevails.

Another St. Petersburg dispatch says very serious news has been received from Finland, where all the factory hands are on strike and a general rising is feared.

CIVIL WAR THREATENED.

Workmen Have Lost Faith in Czar, and Now Mean to Fight.

ST. PETERSBURG, Monday, Jan. 23.—A condition almost bordering on civil war exists in the terror-stricken Russian capital.

The city is under martial law, with Prince Vasilchikoff as commander of over 50,000 of the Emperor's crack guards. Troops are bivouacked in the streets and at various places on the Nevsky Prospect, the main thoroughfare of the city.

It is rumored that M. Witte will be appointed dictator to-day, but the report is not confirmed.

A member of the Emperor's household is quoted as saying that the conflict of yesterday will end the war with Japan, and that Russia will have a Constitution or Emperor Nicholas will lose his head.

The authorities, while they seem to realize the magnitude of the crisis with which the dynasty and the autocracy are confronted on account of yesterday's events, are apparently paralyzed for the moment.

An official statement was promised at midnight, at which hour it was announced that it had been postponed till to-morrow.

Intense indignation is bound to be aroused all over Russia. The workmen and revolutionists expect news from Moscow and other big centres, where the troops are not of the same class as the Guard regiments of St. Petersburg.

The Warsaw and Baltic Railroad is reported to have been torn up for a mile and a half, but the damage is said to have been repaired.

The blood which crimsoned the snow has fired the brains and passions of the strikers and turned women as well as men into wild beasts, and the cry of the infuriated populace is for vengeance.

The sympathy of the middle classes is with the workmen. Comment on the action of the troops and authorities is very bitter, and sarcastic remarks are made that officers are braver against the defenseless public than against the Japanese, and that "ammunition may be scarce in the Far East, but is too plentiful here."

If Father Gopon, the master mind of the movement, aimed at open revolution, he managed the affair like a genius, for he has done a great deal to break the faith of the people in the "Little Father," who, they were convinced and who Father Gopon had taught them to believe, would right their wrongs and redress their grievances.

Maxim Gorky the Russian novelist, expresses the opinion that yesterday's work will break the faith of the people in the Emperor. He said last evening:

"To-day inaugurated revolution in Russia. The Emperor's prestige will be irrevocably shattered by the shedding of innocent blood. He has alienated himself forever from this people.

"Gopon taught the workmen to believe that an appeal direct to the 'Little Father' would be heeded. They have been undeceived.

"Gopon is now convinced that peaceful means have failed and that the only remedy is force. It is now the people against the oppressors, and the battle will be fought to the bitter end."

At a big meeting last night the following message from M. Gorky was read:

"Beloved Associates: We have no Emperor. Innocent blood lies between him and the people. Now begins the people's struggle for freedom. May it prosper. My blessing upon you all. Would I might be with you to-night; but I have much to do."

A workman who was introduced to speak in Father Gopon's name made a fiery speech. He appealed to the Liberals to furnish arms. The meeting adopted a letter denouncing the officers and regiments that fired on the workmen and another letter extolling the Moscow regiment which refused to fire.

The following is the text of a letter addressed by Father Gopon to Emperor Nicholas on Saturday night:

"Sovereign: I fear your Ministers have not told you the full truth about the situation. The whole people, trusting in you, have resolved to appear at the Winter Palace at 2 P. M. in order to inform you of their needs. If, vacillating, you do not appear before the people, then the moral bonds between you and the people, who trust in you, will disappear, because innocent blood will flow between you and the people.

"Appear to-morrow before your people and receive our address of devotion in a courageous spirit. I and the representatives of labor and my brave workingmen and comrades guarantee the inviolability of your person."

With darkness it was feared that the mob might begin to loot and pillage, and even burn; but beyond the breaking of a few windows in the Nevsky Prospect and the pillaging of fruit shops, little disorder was reported. Some windows of the palace of Grand Duke Alexis were smashed.

Most of the theatres were closed, but at the People's Palace, which was open, two Liberals attempted to harangue the audience, proposing at the close of the performance that the audience testify to their sympathy with their fallen brothers. The orators were promptly arrested, but the audience walked out.

St. Petersburg is sleeping quietly at this hour, 4:45 A. M., worn out by the excitement of a long day. Laborers and spectators have long since left the streets, and the military and police have had little to do for hours beyond driving off occasional riotous bands of irresponsible rogues bent on window-breaking and marauding and dispersing groups of too demonstrative Socialists or Liberals returning from protracted meetings where their minds were filled with incendiary speeches.

Since midnight the Russian capital has been as peaceful as it was the preceding night; but in the Palace Square and in all the principal streets and open places throughout the town bivouac fires are gleaming and infantrymen sleeping near their stacked rifles or marching hither and thither.

Cavalrymen on wearied horses are patrolling the long thoroughfares. No further firing has been heard and no more reports of collisions have been received.

A renewal of rioting is not expected until late in the morning, if at all today, as the strikers, thoroughly wearied by yesterday's events, will be inclined to wait until the military precautions have somewhat relaxed.

Two hundred journalists and professional men met in this city on Saturday evening to discuss means to avoid bloodshed. A committee, consisting of the authors Kharsenieff, Gorky, Annensky, and Gesief, several professors, and the workmen's advocate Kedrim, was appointed to interview Minister of the Interior Sviatopolk-Mirsky.

They arrived at the Ministry of the Interior at 10 o'clock Saturday night, but were received coldly, the officials declaring that it was impossible for them to see the Minister that night. The committeemen announcing their intention to wait till the Minister would see them, they were persuaded to go away by Assistant Minister Rydzefsky, who, being told that their errand was to prevent bloodshed, resolutely refused to call Prince Sviatopolk-Mirsky and ironically told the committeemen they had better persuade the workmen to abandon their plan of a procession to the palace.

Thus rebuffed, the committeemen proceeded to M. Witte's residence. M. Witte received them affably and offered tea to them, which they declined. Having heard them, M. Witte expressed himself with great sympathy, but maintained that all measures had been decided without consulting him, adding: "I am nothing in the administration."

M. Witte then referred them to Minister Sviatopolk-Mirsky, regretting his inability to do anything, and advising them to get the demonstration abandoned. He said the workmen had taken a wrong course, which was incompatible with autocracy. The Emperor could only receive a deputation by application through proper channels.

He then telephoned to Minister Sviatopolk-Mirsky and tried to persuade him to receive the committee. The Minister, however, still declined, and the deputation departed.

Late last night at a conference of editors of St. Petersburg newspapers it was agreed to address to the censorship administration a protest against the censorship of the day's events, and it was also resolved to send a deputation to negotiate with the workmen's union regarding the resumption of work by the printers.

DAY OF TERROR IN CZAR'S CAPITAL

Troops Slay Women and Children with Men.

LED BY PRIEST TO DEATH

Workmen Force Guards to Fire to Stop Them.

BARRICADES IN STREETS

A General Killed and Other Officers Attacked—Crowds Shout "Down With the Czar."

ST. PETERSBURG, Jan. 22.—This has been a day of unspeakable horror in St. Petersburg.

Minister of the Interior Sviatopolk-Mirsky presented to his Majesty last night the invitation of the workmen to appear at the Winter Palace this afternoon and receive their petition, but the Emperor's advisers had already taken the decision to show a firm and resolute front, and the Emperor's answer to the 100,000 workmen trying to force their way to the Palace Square to-day was a solid array of troops who met them with rifle, bayonet, and sabre.

The priest Gopon, the leader and idol of the men, in his golden vestments, holding aloft the cross and marching at the head of thousands of workmen through the Narva Gate, miraculously escaped a volley which laid low half a hundred persons.

The figures of the total number killed or wounded at the Narva Gate, the Moscow Gate, at various bridges and islands, and at the Winter Palace vary. The best estimate is 500, although there are exaggerated figures placing the number as high as 5,000.

Many men were accompanied by their wives and children, and in the confusion, which left no time for discrimination, these shared the fate of the men.

One Regiment Mutinied.

The troops, with the exception of the Moscow Regiment, which is reported to have thrown down its arms, remained loyal and obeyed orders.

The military authorities had a firm grip on every artery in the city. At daybreak guard regiments, cavalry, and infantry held every bridge across the frozen Neva, the network of canals which interlace the city, and the gates leading from the industrial section, while in the Palace Square, as the storm centre, were massed Dragoon regiments, infantry, and Cossacks of the Guards.

Barred from the bridges and gates, men, women, and children crossed the frozen river and canals on the ice by twos and threes, hurrying to the Palace Square, where they were sure the Emperor would be present to hear them.

But the street approaches to the square were cleared by volleys and Cossack charges. Men and women, infuriated to frenzy by the loss of loved ones, cursed the soldiers while they retreated.

Strikers Built Barricades.

Men harangued the crowds, telling them that the Emperor had foiled them and that the time had come to act. Strikers began to build barricades in the Nevsky Prospect and at other points, using any material that came to hand, and even chopping down telegraph poles.

Fighting meantime continued at various places, soldiers firing volleys and charging the mob. The whole city was in a state of panic. Women were running through the streets seeking lost members of their families. Several barricades were carried by the troops.

Toward 8 o'clock in the evening the crowds, exhausted, began to disperse, leaving the military in possession. As they retreated up the Nevsky Prospect the workmen put out all the lights.

The little chapel at the Narva gate was wrecked.

On Kaminostov Island all the lights were extinguished.

Every officer wearing the uniform of the Emperor who was found alone was mobbed. A General was killed on the Nicholas Bridge, and a dozen officers were seized, stripped of their epaulets, and deprived of their swords.

Troops Spared Father Gopon.

There was a very dramatic scene at the Narva Gate when Father Gopon, in golden vestments and bearing aloft an ikon, and flanked by two clergymen carrying religious banners, approached at the head of a procession of 8,000 workmen.

Troops were drawn up across the entrance. Several times an officer called upon the procession to stop, but Father Gopon did not falter. Then an order was given to fire, first with blank cartridges. Two volleys rang out, but the line still did not waver.

Then, with seeming reluctance, an officer gave the command to load with ball, and the next volley was followed by shrieks of the wounded.

As the Cossacks followed up the volley with a charge the workmen fled before them, leaving about 100 dead or wounded.

It was evident that the soldiers deliberately spared Father Gopon. One of the clergymen by his side was wounded, but he escaped untouched and hid behind a wall until the Cossacks passed. He was then spirited away by workmen.

The Scenes in Palace Square.

The most harrowing scenes of the day were around the Palace Square.

This enormous place back of the Winter Palace is surrounded by gardens fronting the Admiralty and by a vast semi-circular building containing the offices of the General Staff, the Ministry of Finance, and the Foreign Office. In the centre of the block is cut an arched gateway surmounted by a bronze quadriga. The gateway serves as an entrance to the Grand Morskaia, one of the most fashionable streets of the city, which crosses the Nevsky Prospect.

Beyond the semi-circular building is a wide space leading to the Moikal Canal, and beyond this stands an enormous square building, the headquarters of the St. Petersburg Military District. From this building the Grand Duke Vladimir had issued orders for the whole military preparations, and from it he directed the day's operations.

In the centre of the square stands a great granite column supporting a statue of Victory, commemorating the defeat of the Napoleonic invasion, at which a veteran guard in the uniform of the period of Alexander I. stands sentinel.

Like a Military Camp.

When The Associated Press correspondent arrived at the Palace Square early this morning he found a considerable crowd of demonstrators already lining the railings of the Admiralty Gardens and the Boulevard. The square itself presented the appearance of a military encampment.

Several companies of the Pavlovsky and Preobrajensky Guards had piled their arms, while the men were sitting around campfires or stamping on the snow to keep warm. Beyond the infantry stood squadrons of the Chevalier Guards and the Horse Guards, without their lances, cuirasses, or the usual gay trappings.

The men carried carbines slung across their shoulders, and their stirrups were covered with felt or straw to keep off the cold. All the soldiers wore bashliks, or hoods, to protect their ears from the keen, searching wind. A field kitchen steamed merrily, disseminating the odor of viands.

Many of the men wrestled or boxed, cracking jokes as one or another rolled on the snow.

A whole row of ambulances drawn up near the palace served as a grim reminder of the stern business on hand.

Meanwhile pickets were stationed at all the entrances of the palace, and cavalry patrols kept promenaders moving along the sidewalk. Sleigh traffic continued uninterrupted till the time came for the cavalry to charge.

The crowd of strikers in and outside the Admiralty Gardens continued to grow hourly, swelled by arrivals from the Nevsky Prospect, which debouches upon the boulevard skirting the Gardens.

Constantly Reproached Troops.

The strikers manned and held a small edifice at the corner of the Gardens and poured out constant objurgations and reproaches at the troops. It was in vain that officers requested them to disperse.

"We have come to present our homage and grievances to the Emperor."

"Let the Emperor come out and hear us; we do not wish to do harm."

"Long live Nicholas II.! If he only listens to our grievances we are sure he will be just and merciful!"

"We cannot longer endure our sufferings. Better die at once and end all!"

Such were the cries repeatedly heard.

Many strikers brought their wives and children. "You soldiers are our brothers; you cannot shoot these little ones," they exclaimed. But as the pickets and patrols continued driving off the people the demonstrators began to give way, and the bitterest insults and oaths, in which the Russian vocabulary is particularly rich, became frequent.

"We are not Japanese; why brutalize us? Will you shame the mother who bore you, who was a Russian like ourselves?" were some of the cries that were heard. Later such expressions as "Scoundrels!" "Mercenaries!" "Dogs!" and worse were heard. A long-haired student among the crowd hurled an insulting epithet at an officer, who sent a couple of men to arrest him.

The crowd tried to rescue the student, but he was dragged and kicked across the sunlit square, his long hair tossing in the wind. The crowd broke out into a storm of hoots and hisses. Then a young workman jeered at a soldier, who applied his rifle butt, and, with the help of comrades, dragged the workman, despite his piteous pleadings, to the lock-up.

Every time the troops moved the crowds hissed them. Strikers also gathered at the entrance of the Grand Morskaia and of the avenue leading to the Moika. The crowd at the latter place swelled to huge proportions, blocking the bridge across the canal.

Ordered to Disperse Crowd.

The order came at 1:30 P. M. to clear off the crowd. The Colonel commanding the Horse Guards uttered a short, sharp command; the troopers drew their swords and advanced at a quick trot, and then broke into a gallop, heading straight for the Moika, where they were lost in a cloud of snow.

Shrieks from the wounded resounded. Then came silence, broken only by the galloping of ambulance horses.

The next twenty minutes passed without incident. Nothing indicated the approach of the horrible butchery which was destined to stain the corner of the Admiralty Gardens with human blood.

The crowd there persisted in refusing to move on, clamoring for the Emperor and continually hurling abuse at the troops, but attempting no violence.

Two companies of the Preobrajensky Guards, of which Emperor Nicholas himself was formerly Colonel, which had been standing at ease in front of the Palace, formed up and marched at double quick toward the fatal corner.

Events followed with awful swiftness.

The commanding officer shouted "Disperse! Disperse! Disperse!"

Many in the crowd turned to flee, but it was too late. A bugle sounded and the men in the front ranks sank to their knees and both companies fired three volleys, the first two with blank cartridges and the last with ball.

A hundred corpses strewed the sidewalk. Many women were pierced through the back as they were trying to escape.

The Associated Press correspondent, standing behind the troops, saw mangled corpses of persons of all ages and both sexes strewing the ground. One boy of thirteen had his skull pierced and rent by bullets. Great splashes and streams of blood stained the snow.

Only a few of the victims remained alive, for the fatal volley was fired at a distance of not more than twenty paces, and so the ambulances had little to do.

Sleighs Carried Off the Dead.

The police recruited a large number of sleighs to carry off the dead.

Heartrending scenes were witnessed as wives, husbands, and mothers came up to claim their dear ones and were carried off with them in the sleighs.

Meanwhile the crowd had drifted up the Nevsky Prospect, yelling, "Murderers! Murderers!" and the square resumed its calm aspect, the troops returning to their stations.

It was now the turn for the crowd stationed at the Morskaia entrance to the square, where the Horse Guards repeated the exploit with which they had cleared the Moika, and drove the people pell mell down the thoroughfare.

From thenceforward the Palace Square ceased to be the centre of interest. The Associated Press correspondent went to the Grand Morskaia, and stood a whole hour near the corner of the Nevsky Prospect. The fashionable hotels on either side of the Grand Morskaia were crowded, but the doors were closed except to well-known visitors. Fashionable jewelers' and other stores were barred, but mostly unshuttered. Quite a number of prominent personages stood on the sidewalks watching the developments.

Secretary Spencer Eddy of the American Embassy chatted with Grand Duke Boris, who had driven up in a stylish sleigh, drawn by a magnificent trotter. M. Bompard, the French Ambassador, drove past with his wife. As a couple of squadrons of red-capped hussars trotted by the officers gave the command, "Use the flats of your swords."

Then the troopers moved off and disappeared down the street, the crowds shrieking "Murderous dogs!" but quickly vanishing before them. A few who were wounded were picked up and conveyed to a drug store on the opposite corner of the Grand Morskaia and the Nevsky Prospect.

An Impromptu Oration.

No troops were visible for as much as half an hour. A crowd quickly formed outside the drug store, and an orator was found for the occasion. Standing on the steps of the drug store, he addressed the impromptu meeting thus:

"Comrades: We came humbly and peacefully to meet the Emperor and lay our grievances before him; but the Emperor refuses to see us, and instead soldiers were sent to shoot us down. Then all I can say is he is no Emperor." "Down with the Emperor!" shouted the crowd. The orator proceeded:

"We have suffered under the sway of the Chinovniks." ("Down with the Chinovniks!" exclaimed the crowd.) "We hoped for redress, but hope is no longer possible; we can win our rights only by fighting." ("Down with the autocracy!" yelled the crowd.)

"Our only chance of redress is from representatives of the people." ("Long live the Constitutional Assembly!") "Then all I have to say is, To arms, comrades, to arms!"

"To arms!" was the thunderous response.

The crowd, now aroused to a state of frenzy, at the sight of the wounded who were being brought out of the drug store and placed in ambulances, saluted them as martyrs. Every head was uncovered as the victims were conveyed away.

The wilder element in the crowd had now obtained the upper hand and pro-

INDEX TO DEPARTMENTS.

"All the News That's Fit to Print."

The New York Times.

THE WEATHER.
Fair to-day and to-morrow; rising southerly winds.

VOL. LV...NO. 17,617. NEW YORK, THURSDAY, APRIL 19, 1906.—TWENTY TWO PAGES. ONE CENT In Greater New York, Jersey City and Newark. | Elsewhere, TWO CENTS.

OVER 500 DEAD, $200,000,000 LOST IN SAN FRANCISCO EARTHQUAKE

Nearly Half the City Is in Ruins and 50,000 Are Homeless.

WATER SUPPLY FAILS AND DYNAMITE IS USED IN VAIN

Great Buildings Consumed Before Helpless Firemen--Federal Troops and Militia Guard the City, With Orders to Shoot Down Thieves—Citizens Roused in Early Morning by Great Convulsion and Hundreds Caught by Falling Walls.

SAN FRANCISCO, April 18.—Earthquake and fire to-day have put nearly half of San Francisco in ruins. About 500 persons have been killed, a thousand injured, and the property loss will exceed $200,000,000.

Fifty thousand people are homeless and destitute, and all day long streams of people have been fleeing from the stricken districts to places of safety.

It was 5:13 this morning when a terrific earthquake shock shook the whole city and surrounding country. One shock apparently lasted two minutes, and there was almost immediate collapse of flimsy structures all over the city.

The water supply was cut off, and when fires started in various sections there was nothing to do but let the buildings burn. Telegraph and telephone communication was cut off for a time.

The Western Union was put completely out of business and the Postal Company was the only one that managed to get a wire out of the city. About 10 o'clock even the Postal was forced to suspend.

Electric power was stopped and street cars did not run, railroads and ferry-boats also ceased operations. The various fires raged all day and the fire department has been powerless to do anything except dynamite buildings threatened. All day long explosions have shaken the city and added to the terror of the inhabitants.

Following the first shock there was another within five minutes, but not nearly so severe. Three hours later there was another slight quake.

First Warning at 5:13 A. M.

Most of the people of San Francisco were asleep at 5:13 o'clock this morning when the terrible earthquake came without warning.

The motion of the disturbance apparently was from east to west. At first the upheaval of the earth was gradual, but in a few seconds it increased in intensity. Chimneys began to fall and buildings to crack, tottering on their foundations.

The people became panic-stricken, and rushed into the streets, most of them in their night attire. They were met by showers of falling bricks, cornices, and walls of buildings.

Many were crushed to death, while others were badly mangled. Those who remained indoors generally escaped with their lives, though scores were hit by detached plaster, pictures, and articles thrown to the floor by the shock. It is believed that more or less loss was sustained by nearly every family in the city.

Steel Frame Buildings Stand.

The tall, steel-frame structures stood the strain better than brick buildings, few of them being badly damaged. The big eleven-story Monadnock office building, in course of construction, adjoining the Palace Hotel, was an exception, however, its rear wall collapsing and many cracks being made across its front.

Some of the docks and freight sheds along the water front slid into the bay. Deep fissures opened in the filled-in ground near the shore, and the Union Ferry Station was badly injured. Its high tower still stands, but will have to be torn down.

A portion of the new City Hall, which cost more than $7,000,000, collapsed, the roof sliding into the courtyard, and the smaller towers tumbling down. The great dome was moved, but did not fall.

The new Post Office, one of the finest in the United States, was badly shattered.

The Valencia Hotel, a four-story wooden building, sank into the basement, a pile of splintered timbers, under which were pinned many dead and dying occupants of the house. The basement was full of water, and some of the helpless victims were drowned.

Fires Start in Many Places.

Scarcely had the earth ceased to shake when fires started simultaneously in many places. The Fire Department promptly responded to the first calls for aid, but it was found that the water mains had been rendered useless by the underground movement.

Fanned by a light breeze, the flames quickly spread, and soon many blocks were seen to be doomed. Then dynamite was resorted to, and the sound of frequent explosions added to the terror of the people. These efforts to stay the progress of the fire, however, proved futile.

The south side of Market Street, from Ninth Street to the bay, was soon ablaze, the fire covering a belt two blocks wide. On this, the main thoroughfare, were many of the finest edifices in the city, including the Grant, Parrott, Flood, Call, Examiner, and Monadnock Buildings, and the Palace and Grand Hotels.

At the same time commercial establishments and banks north of Market Street were burning. The burning district in this section of the city extended from Sansome Street to the water front, and from Market Street to Broadway.

Fires also started in the Mission, and the entire city seemed to be in flames.

Long Detours Around Fires.

The flames, fanned by the rising breeze, swept down the main streets until within a few hundred feet of the ferry station, the high tower of which stood at a dangerous angle.

The big wholesale grocery establishment of Weelman, Peck & Co. was on fire from cellar to roof, and the heat was so oppressive that passengers from the ferry boats were obliged to keep close to the water's edge, in order to get past the burning structure.

It was impossible to reach the centre of the city from the bay without skirting the shore for a long distance so as to get entirely around the burning district.

About 8 o'clock the Southern Pacific officials refused to allow any more passengers from trans-bay points to land, and sent back those already on the boats. The ferry and train service of the Key Route was entirely abandoned owing to damage done to the power house by the earthquake at Emeryville.

Lack of Dynamite Felt.

There was little dynamite available in the city. The Southern Pacific soon brought some in. At 9 o'clock Mayor Schmitz sent a tug to Pinola for several cases of explosives. He sent also a telegram to Mayor Mott of Oakland. At 10:30 he received this reply to his Oakland message:

"Three engines and hose companies leave here immediately. Will forward dynamite as soon as obtainable."

The town of San Rafael, despite its own needs, sent fire fighting apparatus here.

Mayor Schmitz gave orders to use dynamite wherever necessary, and the firemen and United States soldiers, who assisted them, blew down building after building. Their efforts, however, were useless, so far as checking the headway of the flames was concerned.

The shortage of water was due to the breaking of the mains of the Spring Valley Water Company at San Mateo. The water needed so badly in the city ran in a flood over San Mateo.

Burning of the Opera House.

The fire swept down the streets so rapidly that it was practically impossible to save anything in its way. It reached the Grand Opera House on Mission Street, and in a moment had burned through the roof. The Metropolitan Opera Company from New York had just opened its season there, and all the expensive scenery and costumes were soon reduced to ashes.

From the opera house the fire leaped from building to building, leveling them almost to the ground in quick succession.

The Call editorial and mechanical departments, in the handsome building at Third and Market Streets, were totally destroyed in a few minutes, and the flames leaped across Stevenson Street toward the fine fifteen-story stone and iron building of Claus Spreckels, which, with its lofty dome, was the most notable structure in San Francisco. Two small wooden buildings furnished fuel to ignite the splendid pile.

Thousands of people watched the hungry tongues of flames licking the stone walls. At first no impression was made, but suddenly there was a cracking of glass and an entrance was effected. The inner furnishings of the fourth floor were the first to go. Then, as if by magic, smoke issued from the top of the dome.

This was followed by a most spectacular illumination. The round windows of the dome shone like so many full moons; they burst and gave vent to long, waving streamers of flames. The crowd watched the spectacle with bated breath. One woman wrung her hands and burst into a torrent of tears.

"It is so terrible," she said.

The tall and slender structure which had withstood the forces of the earth appeared doomed to fall a prey to fire. After a while, however, the light grew less intense, and the flames, finding nothing to consume, gradually went out, leaving the building standing, but completely gutted.

At California and Sansome Streets stood the Mutual Life Building, a modern structure of architectural beauty, to which the flames were soon communicated. An attempt was made to save it, but the fire was irrepressible. The flames gained, and in a few moments the big building was beyond hope. The Anglo California Bank was swept by the flames and came down in a rush.

Time and again attempts were made with dynamite to clear a space which should prevent the flames from spreading to other buildings, but freely as the explosive was used the fire crept and climbed from one structure to another.

An unusually loud report showed that a gas house at Eighteenth and Market Streets had blown up. The fire caused by the explosion quickly communicated in various directions. As the gas house exploded a feeling of despair overcame the men who were performing the rescue work.

Scare at Palace Hotel.

The Palace Hotel, the rear of which was constantly threatened, was the scene of much excitement, the guests leaving in haste, many with only the clothing they wore. Finding that the hotel was surrounded on all sides by streets, and was likely to remain immune, many returned and made arrangements for the removal of their belongings, though little could be taken away owing to the utter absence of transportation facilities.

The Parrott Building, in which was located the chambers of the State Supreme Court, the lower floors being devoted to an immense department store, was ruined, though its massive walls were not all destroyed.

A little further down Market Street, the Academy of Sciences and the Jennie Flood Building and the History Building kindled and burned like so much tinder. Sparks carried across the wide street, ignited the Phelan Building, and the army headquarters of California, Gen. Funston commanding, were burned.

Still nearing the bay, the waters of which did the firemen good service along the docks, the fire took the Rialto Building, a handsome skyscraper, and converted scores of solid business blocks into smoldering piles of bricks.

Thousands Watch the Flames.

Banks and commercial houses, supposed to be fireproof, though not of modern build, burned quickly, and the roar of the flames could be heard even on the hills, which were out of the danger zone. Here many thousands of people congregated and viewed the awful scene.

Great sheets of flame rose high in the heavens, or rushed down some narrow street, joining midway between the sidewalks, making a horizontal chimney of the former passageway.

The dense smoke that arose from the entire business district spread out like an immense funnel and could have been seen miles out at sea. Occasionally as some drug house or place stored with chemicals was reached, most fantastic effects were produced by the centred flames and smoke which rolled out against the darker background.

One of the first orders issued by Chief of Police Dinan this morning was for the closing of every saloon in the city. This step is taken to prevent drink-crazed men from rioting in the streets.

Mayor Schmitz sent out word to the bakeries and milk stations throughout the city that their food supplies must be harbored for the homeless. Provisions were made to place tents in every park in the city, and those who have lost all will be given food and shelter.

Early in the morning the prisoners confined in the city prison on the fifth floor of the Hall of Justice were transferred in irons to the basement of the structure. Later they were removed to the Broadway Jail, and if necessity arises they will be taken to a branch county jail on the Mission Road.

The Mayor also established a base of rescue, and soon had forces out where they could accomplish most. Many men were sent down to the lodging house district near Market Street. There it was found that many frame buildings, packed with people, had collapsed, burying their occupants in the ruins.

The rescuers jumped into the wrecks and pulled out the dead, the dying, and the injured. Practically every physician in the city immediately volunteered his assistance, and soon there was a well-equipped medical corps organized which began ministering to the injured.

For hours bodies were taken out in the lodging house district, and hundreds of men volunteered to go into the ruins to get more.

The pretentious City Hall, bounded by Larkin and McAllister Streets and City Hall Avenue, was badly shattered by the earthquake, and the ruins later were burned. It took twenty years to build the City Hall, the pride of the coast. When the first shock was felt the building rocked and swayed until it cracked. Part of the interior fell and the ruins caught fire. An alarm was turned in and the firemen responded. Chief Sullivan, awakened by the shock at his quarters in a firehouse, hastened to put on his clothes. As he reached for them the tower of the California Hotel dropped upon his building and crushing through the roof killed him.

The firemen arrived at the City Hall, but were helpless. They hitched their hose to the fire plugs, but there was no water supply.

Every possible precaution has been taken to guard property. Immediately after the destructive shocks the police turned out on guard, and the Governor and Gen. Funston, commanding the Pacific Division of the United States Army, were asked to send troops.

A thousand men from the Presidio, sent by Gen. Funston, arrived downtown at 9 o'clock to patrol the streets. The Thirteenth Infantry, 1,000 strong, arrived from Angel Island a little later and went on patrol duty at once.

The soldiers were ordered to shoot down vandals caught robbing the dead and to guard with their lives the millions of dollars' worth of property placed in the streets to escape the flames.

The First California Artillery, 200 strong, two companies, was detailed to patrol duty on Ellis Street. Two more companies patrolled Broadway in the Italian section. The Ellis Street contingent of guardsmen were under the command of Capt. G. A. Grattan. Capt. William A. Miller commanded the forces on Broadway.

The city is under martial law, and all the downtown streets are patroled by cavalry and infantry. Details of troops are also guarding the banks.

Early this morning Mayor Schmitz, who established his office at Police Headquarters, named the following citizens as a Committee of Safety:

James D. Phelan,	Paul Cowles,
Herbert Law,	M. H. De Young,
Thomas Magee,	Claus Spreckles,
Charles Fee,	Rudolph Spreckles,
W. F. Herrin,	C. W. Fay,
Thornwell Mullalley,	John McNaught,
Garret W. Enerney,	Dent Robert,
W. H. Leahy,	Thomas Garrett,
J. Downey Harvey,	Frank Shea,
Jeremiah Dinan,	James Shea,
John J. Mahoney,	Robert Pisis,
Henry T. Scott,	T. P. Woodward,
I. W. Hellman,	Howard Holmes,
George A. Knight,	George Dillman,
I. Steinhart,	J. B. Rogers,
S. G. Murphy,	David Rich,
Homer King,	H. T. Cresswell,
Frank Anderson,	J. A. Howell,
W. J. Bartnett,	Frank Maestretti,
John Martin,	Clem Tobin,
Allan Pollock,	George Toumey,
Mark Gerstle,	E. D. Pond,
H. V. Ramsdell,	George A. Newhall,
W. G. Harrison,	William Watson.
R. A. Crothers,	

THE BUILDINGS DESTROYED.

A Partial List of the Structures Torn Down or Injured.

SAN FRANCISCO, April 18.—The following is an incomplete list of the buildings destroyed or injured:

Call Building, entirely destroyed.

Claus Spreckels Building, burned out.

Hearst Building, collapsed.

New Chronicle Building, hardly damaged.

The White House, walls badly cracked; all plate glass windows gone; every piece of stock in building removed before 9:30 A. M.

Winchester Hotel, Third Street, totally destroyed by earthquake shock.

Grand Opera House, entirely destroyed.

Claus Spreckels house and stables, Van Ness Avenue, badly damaged and will have to be largely rebuilt.

St. Luke's Episcopal Church, Van Ness Avenue, will have to be pulled down.

Mechanics' Library Building, Post Street, cornices fell to street; building slightly injured.

Crocker Building, Market and Post Streets, slightly damaged, principally around light shaft.

Lick House, walls and roof largely caved in.

Upham Building, Pine and Battery Streets, totally destroyed; loss, $550,000.

Fire house adjoining California Hotel in Bush Street; Chief Sullivan and wife, sleeping in engine house, severely bruised by bricks crashing through roof from hotel.

California Hotel, Bush Street, upper walls collapsed and upper floors wrecked.

The building in course of construction to be occupied by the Hamman baths will have to be rebuilt. It is in Post Street near the Olympic Club. The walls are badly warped and twisted and the roof has fallen in.

San Francisco Gas and Electric Company's Post Street plant, only slightly injured.

St. Francis Hotel, exterior slightly cracked and seamed, but not seriously injured.

Pacific Union Club, Post and Stockton Streets, front injured and fissures in rear wall.

St. Dominic's Church in Pierce Street, total loss. The interior of the church is wrecked and there are fissures in the walls. The structure will have to be pulled down. The parochial house in the same block is nearly a wreck. It is estimated that the loss to the parish is $300,000.

The ornamental top on St. Dunstan's, the apartment house at Sutter Street and Van Ness Avenue, fell into the street.

The Concordia Club building in Van Ness Avenue has several fissures in the side, and rebuilding will be necessary.

The Hotel Grinado, badly damaged; stone coping about roof fell.

EARTHQUAKE'S AUTOGRAPH AS IT WROTE IT 3,000 MILES AWAY.

Tracing Made by the Seismograph Needle in the Office of State Geologist John M. Clarke, State Museum, Albany, Showing How the Earthquake Traveled Across Continent in 19 Minutes.

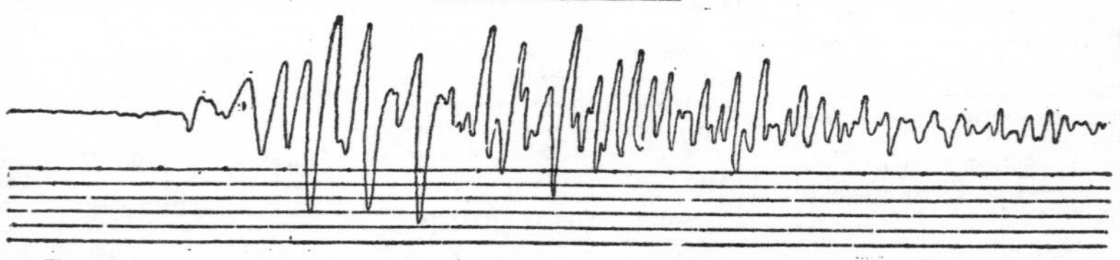

The drawing represents the vibration of the north and south pendulum of the seismograph during the time of the most intense activity, beginning in San Francisco at 5:13 A. M., in Albany at 8:32. In Albany the violent agitation ended at 8:43 A. M. The straight lines at the side of the wavy line indicate the normal condition of the record as the recording drum revolves, and this serves to show the contrast between the ordinary progress of the record and that during a disturbance. The spaces between the dots indicate lapses of one minute each.

The same violent disturbance was noticeable on the seismograph at Washington between 8:32 and 8:35 A. M., thus verifying the time of transit across the continent—19 minutes.

ALL SAN FRANCISCO MAY BURN; CLIFF HOUSE RESORT IN SEA

Flames Carried From the Business Quarter to Residences

PALACE HOTEL AND MINT GO; BIG BUILDINGS BLOWN UP.

Other Shocks Felt During the Afternoon—Insane Asylum Is Wrecked and Hundreds of Former Inmates Are Roaming About the Country—Reports of Heavy Loss of Life at San Jose.

SAN FRANCISCO, Thursday, April 19.—12:15 A. M. (3:15 A. M. New York Time.)—At midnight the fire still roars. Fleeing inhabitants can see from miles around the pillars of fire towering skyward. The crash of falling ruins and the muffled reports of the exploding dynamite reach the ear at regular intervals.

A disaster that staggers comprehension and in point of terror and damage is unprecedented on the coast has not yet reached its culmination.

The Merchants' Exchange Building, one of the handsomest and most substantial edifices in the city, is in flames, as is also the Crocker-Woolworth Building.

The former building is a fourteen-story structure, seven floors of which are occupied by the Southern Pacific Railway Company as offices. The Crocker-Woolworth Building is a twelve-story terra cotta and granite structure and stood directly opposite the Palace Hotel.

The immense D. O. Mills Building is surrounded by fire and probably will burn. The Lick House, the Occidental Hotel, and the Russ House in this immediate vicinity are in immediate danger.

The exact loss of life never will be known. Hundreds have been incinerated. To-night the city resembles one vast shambles with the red glare of the fire throwing shadows across the worn and panic-stricken faces of the homeless.

At the morgue in the Hall of Justice fifty bodies lie. Before the eyes of an Associated Press reporter three thieves were shot dead.

The Japanese quarter has been burned and the people fled in terror, packing on their backs what household effects they could tie together.

At 9 o'clock to-night an Associated Press man who went to a high hill overlooking the city noted that the sky on the east and south sides was illuminated for a distance of four or five miles. The illumination on the southern side was in a duller glow, showing that the flames were not consuming property of such great proportions as was the case on the east side.

In the business district toward the water front the flames were either checked or blocked at about Washington Street, and at the corner of Kearny Street the Hall of Justice could be noted standing, but it was impossible to determine what damage had been done to the interior. From the Hall of Justice to the south the fire cut its way through some of the choicest buildings in the city, the Pacific Mutual and the Italian-American Bank Building being reduced to ashes.

Down Kearny Street on both sides at 10 o'clock the conflagration was still raging with fury, but the direction of the wind prevented its advance up the hills to the west toward the residence quarter.

To the west of Kearny, up to Dupont, most of the buildings were burned as far south as California Street. All around the new fourteen-story Merchants' Exchange Building the fire burned fiercely, licking the sides of the steel giant, but it resisted the influence of the heat.

Then came the destruction of the Western Union Building, at the corner of Pick and Montgomery Streets. In this building were the offices of the Associated Press. Earlier in the day the occupants had been ordered out by the authorities on account of danger, and The Associated Press established a temporary station in The Bulletin editorial rooms. Then the latter place was closed, and this dispatch is written on a doorstep near Chinatown, the illumination of the burning buildings furnishing light for the writer.

It appeared that the great Mills Building would block some of the southward sweep of the blaze, as it had already checked an advance northward earlier in the night. If this proves true the limits of the fire will be determined, but predictions on this point are as unreliable as the strong wind, which every five minutes is changing from one direction to another.

The city to-night in face of its appalling disaster, is fairly quiet and orderly. Liquor cannot be had anywhere and the formidable presence of Federal troops, militia and naval reserves has had its effect on the element that might be disposed to be disorderly.

The Mayor's proclamation authorizing the shooting of looters on sight has been scattered broadcast in circulars and few reports of thieving are received.

It is impossible to give anything like an accurate statement concerning the killed. Unquestionably many people were either killed outright, imprisoned or rendered unconscious in collapsed buildings which were afterward burned.

At 10 o'clock the Occidental Hotel began burning and the great Crocker Building containing the Crocker-Woolworth National Bank was ablaze.

On Geary Street the Albert Pike Memorial Temple of the California bodies of the Scottish Rites Masons, containing scenery that cost $20,000 and costumes valued at $15,000, collapsed. The new Jewish synagogue adjoining was cracked to its foundations.

While five dying men were taken from a collapsed building at Second and Jessie Streets Fathers Hogan, Rogers, and Huber of St. Patrick's Church granted them the last rites of the Catholic Church. This ceremony was performed while a mass of coping overhead threatened to crush the priests to death. Three of the men died.

A shoemaker, Joseph Lindsay, was four hours in a demolished building and when dug out it was found that he had not been hurt.

The entire Larkin Street frontage of the City Hall for a distance of several hundred feet was thrown out into the street, and that thoroughfare for two blocks is piled high with boulders of mortared brick and twisted iron.

Latest reports from Leland Stanford University at Palo Alto indicate that the magnificent stone buildings of that institution have suffered severe damage. Many of the buildings were ruined by cracks that split them from cornice to foundation.

The University of California at Berkeley, across the bay, escaped serious injury. The buildings are intact. Only a few structures collapsed in Berkeley, the shock being slight there.

Artillerymen from the Presidio with their supply wagons and the army commissary wagons are aiding in getting the fleeing inhabitants and their baggage out of the threatened quarters.

270 Dead in an Asylum.

The insane asylum, at Agnews is a total wreck, 270 of the inmates being killed. It is reported that the attachés of the institution who were about at the time of the earthquake were saved. The ruins took fire shortly after the collapse. One hundred and twenty bodies have been removed.

There were about 700 persons in the building. Hundreds of the inmates who escaped death are roaming about the country in a state of panic.

Half San Francisco Gone.

OAKLAND, Cal., April 18, 10 P. M.—It looks now as if the entire City of San Francisco would be burned.

At 10 o'clock to-night the fire

"All the News That's Fit to Print."

The New York Times.

THE WEATHER.
Generally fair to-day and to-morrow; wind variable.

VOL. LV...NO. 17,685 • • • • NEW YORK, TUESDAY, JUNE 26, 1906.—FOURTEEN PAGES. ONE CENT In Greater New York, Elsewhere, Jersey City and Newark. TWO CENTS.

CAPT. WYNNE GUILTY, NAVAL COURT SAYS

Marine Officer May Be Dismissed from the Service.

THE PRESIDENT WILL DECIDE

Will Review the Findings in the Case of the ex-Postmaster General's Son.

If President Roosevelt approves the findings of the court-martial that recently tried Capt. Robert F. Wynne, United States Marine Corps, on charges of insubordination, Capt. Wynne will be dismissed from the service. The record of the court-martial is now in the hands of Secretary Bonaparte, and in a few days will be sent to President Roosevelt for final review.

Although it has not been officially announced, it is generally known in the service that the verdict of the court-martial is entirely against Capt. Wynne, the court finding him guilty on all three charges and fixing his punishment at dismissal. The charges on which the Captain was tried were, first, neglect of duty in not reporting the guard at quarters; second, willful disobedience of orders, and, third, conduct prejudicial to good order and discipline.

It has now been seventeen days since the court-martial, which was held on the armored cruiser Pennsylvania, at the New York Navy Yard, concluded its inquiry into the charges preferred against Capt. Wynne by Lieut. Commander Bryan, who, on the morning of May 21, the date of Capt. Wynne's alleged insubordination, was, in the absence of Capt. Samuel P. Comly, the senior officer on board the Alabama, the flagship of the Second Division of the First Squadron of the Atlantic Fleet.

President Roosevelt, with whom the final decision in the case rests, is a warm personal friend of Capt. Wynne's father, Consul General Wynne, who was Mr. Cortelyou's predecessor as Postmaster General.

Since the court-martial adjourned, Capt. Wynne has received numerous assurances of good will from his friends in and out of the service. There are many persons who have the deepest sympathy for the young officer. His father and mother, who sailed for London on the Atlantic Transport liner Minneapolis last Saturday, were with him on Friday last.

In addition to his court-martial Capt. Wynne also had to face a medical board of inquiry. This inquiry was held a few days after the court-martial adjourned, the board being composed of Medical Inspector Howard E. Ames of the battleship Maine, Surgeon John F. Uria of the armored cruiser Pennsylvania, and Passed Assistant Surgeon Richard B. Williams of the armored cruiser West Virginia. The medical examination was the result of the testimony offered at the [illegible] to the effect that owing to a sunstroke Capt. Wynne suffered in the Boxer troubles in China he was not in a condition to appreciate his obligations to his superiors properly and that he should be retired from the service. Capt. Wynne appeared before the medical board and testified that on Aug. 6, 1900, while on the march to Peking for the relief of the legations, he had suffered a sunstroke near Yang-Tsun. In 1903, while at Guantanamo, Cuba, and again in March of this year, at the same place, he was prostrated in China.

The medical board found Capt. Wynne sane in every way, but it is understood to have recommended that in the future he should not again be assigned to service in the tropics. This report is a part of the record, which will in a few days be forwarded by the Secretary of the Navy to President Roosevelt.

Capt. Wynne was arrested on May 31 on the order of Lieut. Commander Bryan of the Alabama. Capt. Wynne at the time was assigned to duty on a Board of Inquiry, which duty he interpreted to mean that he was exempt from other service. Following this construction, on the morning of May 1 he failed to report when the call to quarters was sounded aboard his ship. Lieut. Commander Bryan noted his absence and sent to Capt. Wynne's quarters to ascertain why he had not appeared. Capt. Wynne sent back word that his assignment on the Board of Inquiry relieved him from any other duty and stayed in his quarters.

Lieut. Commander Bryan then directed an officer and two marines to bring Capt. Wynne on deck. Capt. Wynne refused at first to report, the situation finally becoming so serious that a subordinate officer, a friend of Capt. Wynne's, went to him and persuaded him to report to Lieut. Commander Bryan in order to avoid any further trouble.

PEABODY'S SPECIAL TRAIN.

New Yorker Hires One Rather Than Have His Party Rise at 5:30 A. M.

Special to The New York Times.

ATLANTA, Ga., June 25.—Because he did not desire to have the members of his party awakened in the early morning hours to take the southern train at 5:30 o'clock, George Foster Peabody of New York chartered a special train to make the trip, paying $668 for the cars and engine that were used.

The conductor and others of the crew were rewarded liberally for the special run they made.

INDEX TO DEPARTMENTS.

DOESN'T TAINT ALL TRADE.

London Times Editorially Defends Business Methods in This Country.

Special Cable to THE NEW YORK TIMES.
[Copyright, 1906.]

LONDON, Tuesday, June 26.—The Times this morning publishes a letter from an American correspondent protesting against the alleged readiness of Europe to condemn the whole American people and their business on account of the scandalous disclosures respecting American life insurance methods and the operations of the Chicago meat packers. Commenting on the letter editorially, The Times says:

"It would be a great mistake to suppose that every Englishman believes everything said by every newspaper. No sensible man believes that American business is rotten because some swindles have been exposed, any more than he thinks that all French business is rotten because there was a Panama scandal, or that all our own business is in the same condition because we have scandals from time to time and are aware of much that is wrong, though it may not yet have come in so striking a form before the world.

"Strong language about scandal is not to be taken to show that even those who use it suppose the whole business world in the country where it occurs to be corrupt. It is not their aim or business to offer a careful judicial view of American business as a whole. They are concerned with the scandal alone, and the general perspective must be left for adjustment on some other occasion.

"Americans may dismiss the idea, if they ever entertained it, that the people of this country regard them as all in the same boat with the Beef Trust, Standard Oil Company, dishonest railway managers, and people who control yellow dog funds. There are Pharisees and foolish individuals in all countries. We have some among us, and as they are generally very ready to talk, they probably do some mischief, but the mass of the people understand very well that the mass of American people are very like themselves, and that in America, as here and elsewhere, society is held together only by the saving remnant of which our correspondent speaks—the quiet, inarticulate people who still believe in probity and honor and try to do their duty and fulfill their obligations honestly."

TRUST MEN GO TO JAIL.

Five Ice Men Sentenced for Conspiracy in Ohio.

Special to The New York Times.

TOLEDO, Ohio, June 25.—After a consultation between the five convicted ice men and their attorneys this afternoon it was decided to make an effort to have a modification of the sentence of $5,000 fine and one year's imprisonment made in the morning. Pending the making out of the commitment papers which will send these five men—Joseph A. Miller, R. C. Lemmon, R. A. Beard, H. P. Breining, and P. H. Watters, all prominent in business and social circles—to the Toledo Workhouse, they are prisoners in the county jail, under the supervision of Sheriff Chambers. There is little hope held out to them by their attorneys for escaping all of their Workhouse penalty.

When Judge Kinkade sentenced the men this morning for being guilty of being members of a conspiracy in restraint of trade he told the prisoners and their counsel that when they brought to him papers showing that the money illegally exacted from the public since the 11th of March by the increase of prices had been returned to the public, and when they showed that the trust was broken and that prices would go back to the standard in existence prior to March 11, the date of the formation of the trust, he would listen to a plea of modification. He did not say that he would modify the sentence, or what the modification would be if he did so do.

He further told the prisoners that until he was relieved of a great congestion of criminal work that had piled up while he was hearing the ice trials he would not have time to listen to their statements, giving them to understand in this manner that they must stay at least a short time in the Workhouse.

In spite of this statement the lawyers are trying by every means known to their profession to get the Judge to hear them to-morrow so that their clients may be saved from the Workhouse. Friends of the convicted men have sent them their meals to-day, but on the strict order of the court no one has seen them since they returned from a visit to their counsel this afternoon. While making their trip to the lawyers several of the prisoners were seen. All were in the deepest despair. They had each expected a fine, and were prepared for a heavy one, but the imprisonment was unlooked for.

SHAW AND THE STEEL TRUST.

Leader Williams Asks Inquiry Into Alleged Tariff Favoritism.

Special to The New York Times.

WASHINGTON, June 25.—John Sharp Williams introduced in the House to-day a resolution calling on the Secretary of the Treasury for the correspondence and reports in the matter of certain rulings of the Treasury Department with regard to the levying of an additional 1 cent a pound on certain steel imports.

Mr. Williams is after the motive of the Secretary in insisting on the attempt to collect 2 cents per pound duty on strip steel, after the Board of General Appraisers of New York has repeatedly decided that such importations are subject only to the duty of 1.2 cents per pound provided in paragraph 135 of the Dingley act.

It is charged on information which Mr. Williams has obtained that the basis for the claim for the higher duty was made up, partly at the instigation of a man who had been an examiner at New York, but has now become an employe of the Steel Trust. This man, it is said, when he was examiner made several decisions contrary to what he is now upholding. The material that has been supplied to Mr. Williams charges Secretary Shaw, by inference, with making a ruling in favor of the Steel Trust and against independent manufacturers, and with insisting upon it after the courts have decisively turned him down.

Ohio's New Governor Better.

COLUMBUS, Ohio, June 25.—Gov. Harris returned to the capital from his home at Eaton this evening. He said that he was feeling much better.

MISS FULLER SUDDENLY DECIDES ON A WEDDING

Surprise When Chief Justice's Daughter Quietly Marries.

ENGAGEMENT NOT ANNOUNCED

Ceremony Was Planned for Next Winter, but Dr. Mason's Urgings Upset the Plans.

Special to The New York Times.

WASHINGTON, June 25.—With only a few relatives present and without the knowledge of their friends, Miss Frances Louise Fuller, daughter of Chief Justice Melville W. Fuller, was married at noon to-day to Dr. Robert French Mason of this city.

Their engagement had never been formally announced, and the few who knew of it had been told that the wedding would not take place till next season. Dr. Mason, however, did not wish their engagement to be so long and his urgings suddenly won the day, and no time was taken to prepare for an elaborate ceremony.

The marriage ceremony was performed in the home of the bride's father, in this city, by the Rev. Herbert Scott Smith, rector of St. Margaret's Episcopal Church. The wedding party was a small one, George L. Mason, brother of the bridegroom, acting as best man, and Mrs. White of Chicago, sister of the bride, acting as matron of honor and giving the bride in marriage. The only other guests were Mrs. Hugh Wallace, another sister of the bride; Mr. and Mrs. Benjamin S. Minor, brother-in-law and sister of the bridegroom, and Miss Margaret Mason, his sister. A few of the Fuller servants who remained in town to care for the house while the family were in their Summer home at Sorrento, Me., were also present.

After an informal breakfast following the ceremony the bride and bridegroom left for one of the coast resorts and Mrs. White returned to her home in Chicago. Dr. Mason and his bride will join the Chief Justice next month in Sorrento for a visit, after which they will temporarily live here at the Dupont, where Dr. Mason has lived for some time.

The wedding has thrown what remains of society here into a flutter. Friends of the couple had rested in the assurance that they would be present at the marriage next season.

After the departure of the Chief Justice and his daughter for Chicago, about two weeks ago, however, Dr. Mason became impatient, went on to Chicago, and gained the consent of his fiancée and her father to have the ceremony take place this month. Miss Fuller was unwilling to be married anywhere but in Washington, even though her father was not well enough to make the trip back again to witness the ceremony. Accompanied by her sister, the bride-elect arrived here on Saturday and all arrangements were made hurriedly.

Mrs. Mason has acted as hostess for her father since the death of her mother, two years ago. She was in Europe at that time, studying music, but came immediately home and has been at the head of the judicial household ever since. She discharged the duties of hostess with dignity, grace, and tact, although there have been no formal entertainments, owing to their deep mourning.

Miss Fuller has no own sisters, as the daughters of the Chief Justice who have previously figured so prominently in Washington society, all now married, were the daughters of his first marriage. They include Mrs. Nathaniel Francis and Mrs. Hugh Wallace of this city and Mrs. White of Chicago.

INDEPENDENT PLANTS BAD.

Chicago Inspectors Find Improvement in Some, However.

Special to The New York Times.

CHICAGO, June 25.—Sanitary Inspectors in a report to-day condemn independent packing plants of this city.

Filthy pens, rooms covered with dirt and clotted blood, decayed and neglected vats used daily, and general unsanitary conditions were found in some of the smaller plants. The worst conditions were discovered in the plant of David Levi & Co. at the Union Stock Yards. Chief Sanitary Inspector Perry L. Hedrick cites the details in his report delivered to Health Commissioner Whalen.

In the plants of H. Boore & Co., Boyd, Dunham & Co., and Henry Guth, efforts were being made to improve the conditions, and these places were generally clean. Aside from improper toilet facilities and walls and ceilings that need cleaning, signs of improvement were noticed.

In the Levi plant the Inspectors could find nothing to commend.

COREY TO FIGHT SUIT.

Answers Wife's Divorce Plea and Says He Didn't Desert Her.

RENO, Nev., June 25.—William Ellis Corey, President of the United States Steel Corporation, this afternoon filed an answer to the petition of Mrs. Corey for divorce.

He denies that she is a legal resident of Nevada, and further denies that he ever abandoned her. He asks that her suit be dismissed.

Special to The New York Times.

BRADDOCK, Penn., June 25.—The news that W. Ellis Corey had filed an answer to his wife's suit for divorce and that the answer showed fight in every line evidently came as a blow at the home here of his father, A. A. Corey, to-night. Mrs. Laura Cook Corey, wife of the steel man, is with her father-in-law, but she declined to be seen this evening.

Mrs. Gilman, mother of Mabelle Gilman, the actress, was in Pittsburg today. The rumor is that she and Mrs. Corey met this afternoon in Pittsburg, but that cannot be confirmed.

Curfew Law in Ballston.

BALLSTON, N. Y., June 25.—The Board of Trustees to-night passed a curfew law which forbids children to be on the streets after 9 o'clock at night under penalty of being taken home by the police.

REJECT ROCKEFELLER CASH.

Reformers of the Young Do Not Want His $5,000,000.

Special to The New York Times.

CHICAGO, June 25.—Judge Lindsey of the Denver Juvenile Court has pledged himself to refuse the $5,000,000 promised to him by John D. Rockefeller with which to finance a National Juvenile Improvement Association. His alternative was to take the money with the active condemnation of the leaders of different charities of the country having a like aim. Jane Addams of Hull House, Chicago, negotiated the affair while she and Judge Lindsey were in St. Paul at the biennial meeting of Women's Clubs just closed.

Judge Lindsey asked to have a convention of juvenile workers called in Chicago. Judge Mack issued the call. The convention was to be held in Hull House, Chicago. In the week previous, when both were in St. Paul, Jane Addams told Judge Lindsey that the other workers, herself included, could not federate with any association that was to be financed by John D. Rockefeller. She said she was sure Judge Lindsey would coincide with their views when they were put to him. Otherwise the leaders would refuse to attend the meeting in Chicago. It was an open revolt against Judge Lindsey's connection with Rockefeller's money.

"I do not know where we shall get the money to do the work of organizing and carrying out the plans, but I promise you I will not accept any money whatever from Mr. Rockefeller," was Judge Lindsey's reply.

Miss Addams immediately reported his pledge to her colleagues, and the convention in Chicago was attended with enthusiasm.

TO SPEND $20,000,000.

Pennsylvania Road Plans Big Increase in Equipment.

Special to The New York Times.

PHILADELPHIA, June 25.—More than $20,000,000 is about to be expended by the Pennsylvania Railroad Company for the purpose of equipment and for general construction work. This determination has been reached by President Cassatt, and a construction and equipment list will be submitted to the Board of Directors for its approval at the meeting to be held on Wednesday. The requisition will include the construction of 300 locomotives and not less than 15,000 freight cars.

The decision to spend such a large sum is the outcome of the coal investigation by the Inter-State Commerce Commission, and the belief held by Mr. Cassatt that the outlook for business is bright. The funds to pay for the improvements to be ordered by the Board of Directors will become available through the French loan of $20,000,000 and the $50,000,000 bond issue recently negotiated through Kuhn, Loeb & Co. of New York.

The $20,000,00 to be spent for locomotives, cars, and general construction work does not include the money that will be erquired to take over the 15,000 individual coal cars now being operated on the Pennsylvania system, and which Vice President Thayer announced it is the purpose of the management to buy as soon as plans have been worked out in detail.

JOHN D. CRIMMINS RALLIES.

Not Out of Danger, However, and Improvement Will Be Slow.

Special to The New York Times.

STAMFORD, Conn., June 25.—John D. Crimmins rallied to-day, and his condition to-night was reported as more hopeful. Dr. J. W. Avery, the attending physician, issued this bulletin to-night:

"Mr. Crimmins has had a comfortable day and is resting well this evening. He has made a slight improvement. No further complications have arisen, and the outlook is rather more hopeful, although he is by no means out of danger. His improvement will be slow, as his condition is one from which he cannot recover quickly."

SMOTHERED BY SAND SLIDE.

Two Laborers Dug Out Within Fifteen Minutes, but Life Was Extinct.

Special to The New York Times.

PEEKSKILL, June 25.—An unexpected slide of fine sand in one of James A. De Groat's sand banks at Jones's Point, opposite this village, this morning smothered two men to death. Another was slightly injured.

The other men on the gang escaped unhurt. The bodies were recovered within fifteen minutes after the sand had fallen, but life was extinct.

John Pesti, single, 29 years old, and Louis Suyoke, 24 years old, laborers, were the victims. Both men had been employed by De Groat for several years.

PRATT'S GIFT TO AMHERST.

New Yorker Gave $40,000 for Natatorium Dedicated Yesterday.

AMHERST, Mass., June 25.—The dedication of the new Pratt Natatorium, given to Amherst College by Harold I. Pratt, 1900, of New York, was the feature of today's observances of commencement week.

Mr. Pratt, Mortimer L. Schiff, '96, of New York; Dr. Edward Hitchcock, Athletic Supervisor, and President George Harris made addresses. The Brookline Swimming Club gave an exhibition in the large tank.

The building cost $50,000, of which $40,000 was given by Mr. Pratt for the natatorium, and $10,000 by Mr. Schiff for squash tennis courts on the upper floor of the structure.

TROOPS CONTROL ALLENTOWN

State Constabulary Take Charge in Presence of Car Strikers.

ALLENTOWN, Penn., June 25.—Following the strike of the motormen and conductors of the Lehigh Valley Transit Company, the corporation turned off its power at midnight, but resumed operations this morning, after the arrival of Troop C, State Constabulary, with thirty-four men, under Lieut. Smith.

PURE FOOD BILL CONFERENCE

Senate Objects to House Amendments —The House Insists.

WASHINGTON, June 25.—The House insisted to-day on its amendments to the Pure Food bill, and asked for a conference. The Speaker appointed as conferrees Mr. Mann, (Ill.,) Mr. Hepburn, (Iowa,) and Mr. Ryan, (N. Y.)

The Senate voted not to concur in the amendment of the House, but subsequently agreed to the conference, and Senators Heyburn, McCumber, and Latimer were appointed as conferrees.

THAW MURDERS STANFORD WHITE

Shoots Him on the Madison Square Garden Roof.

ABOUT EVELYN NESBIT

"He Ruined My Wife," Witness Says He Said.

AUDIENCE IN A PANIC

Chairs and Tables Are Overturned in a Wild Scramble for the Exits.

Harry Kendall Thaw of Pittsburg, husband of Florence Evelyn Nesbit, former actress and artist's model, shot and killed Stanford White, the architect, on the roof of Madison Square Garden at 11:05 o'clock last night, just as the first performance of the musical comedy "Mamzelle Champagne" was drawing to a close. Thaw, who is a brother of the Countess of Yarmouth and a member of a well known and wealthy family, left his seat near the stage, passed between a number of tables, and, in full view of the players and of scores of persons, shot White through the head. Mr. White was the designer of the building on the roof of which he was killed. He it was who put Miss Nesbit, now Mrs. Thaw, on the stage.

Thaw, who was in evening clothes, had evidently been waiting for Mr. White's appearance. The latter entered the Garden at 10:55 and took a seat at a table five rows from the stage. He rested his chin in his right hand and seemed lost in contemplation.

Thaw had a pistol concealed under his coat. His face was deathly white. According to A. L. Belstone, who sat near, White must have seen Thaw approaching. But he made no move. Thaw placed the pistol almost against the head of the sitting man and fired three shots in quick succession.

Body Fell to the Floor.

White's elbow slid from the table, the table crashed over, sending a glass clinking along with the heavier sound. The body then tumbled from the chair.

On the stage one of the characters was singing a song entitled "I Could Love a Million Girls." The refrain seemed to freeze upon his lips. There was dead silence for a second, and then Thaw lifted his pistol over his head, the barrel hanging downward, as if to show the audience that he was not going to harm any one else.

With a firm stride Thaw started for the exit, holding his pistol as if anxious to have some one take it from his hand.

Then came the realization on the part of the audience that the farce had closed with a tragedy. A woman jumped to her feet and screamed. Many persons followed her example, and there was wild excitement.

L. Lawrence, the manager of the show, jumped on a table and above the uproar commanded the show to go on.

"Go on playing!" he shouted. "Bring on that chorus!"

Girls Too Terrified to Sing.

The musicians made a feeble effort at gathering their wits and playing the chorus music, but the girls who romped on the stage were paralyzed with horror, and it was impossible to bring the performance to an orderly close.

Then the manager shouted for quiet, and he informed the audience that a serious accident had happened, and begged the people to move out of the place quietly.

In the meanwhile Thaw had reached the entrance to the elevators. On duty there was Fireman Paul Broodin. He took the pistol from Thaw's hand, but did not attempt to arrest him. Policeman Debes of the Tenderloin Station appeared and seized his arm.

"He deserved it," Thaw said to the policeman. "I can prove it. He ruined my life and then deserted the girl." Another witness said the word was "wife" instead of "life."

A Woman Kissed Thaw.

Just as the policeman started into the elevator with Thaw a woman described as dark-haired and short of stature reached up to him and kissed him on the cheek. This woman some witnesses declare was Mrs. Thaw.

The crowd was then scrambling wildly for the elevators and stairs. The employes of the Garden who knew Thaw, and nearly all of them did, as he visited the place often, did not seem greatly surprised at the tragedy. When Thaw entered the Garden in the early part of the show he seemed greatly agitated. He strolled from one part of the place to another, and finally took a seat in a little niche near the stage.

He was half hidden from the audience, but could see any one who might enter. It is believed that he knew just where White would sit, and had picked out this place in order to get at him without interference.

Henry Rogers of 222 Henry Street was seated at the table next to the one at which White was sitting when he was killed. He says that Thaw fired when the muzzle of his pistol was only a few inches from White's temple.

Another witness said that after firing three shots and looking at White as if to be sure that he was stone dead, Thaw uttered a curse and added:

"You'll never go out with that woman again."

A Woman Sat Near White.

At another table adjoining that at which White was killed sat a woman dressed in white. It was believed for a time that she was a companion of White's, and it was reported that she leaned over and kissed the face of the dead man, but this could not be verified, and it is positive that White was alone when he entered the Garden.

Some one in the audience hurried to the fallen man to see if assistance was needed. A great pool of blood had quickly formed on the floor. The tables had been pulled back and in the bright glare of thousands of electric lights it was quickly seen that White was beyond any earthly help.

A number of the actors and actresses left the stage, and away from the calcium and the footlights their painted faces showed strangely in the group of employes and friends of Thaw and the dead man which formed as the last of the audience left.

Thought It a Stage Trick.

Two of them said that the reason the fright of the audience was not worse when the shots rang out was that just before the tragedy a dialogue concerning a burlesque duel had been carried on by two of the characters, and many people thought that the old trick of playing in the audience had been tried again.

As the lights of the Garden were dimmed, the body of White was straightened out, the arms brought to the sides, and the legs placed together. A sheet was obtained in one of the dressing rooms, and this was stretched over it.

While all of this was going on, Policeman Debes and his prisoner had reached the street entrance. Thaw never once lost his composure. His linen and his evening suit showed no signs of ruffling. Only the paleness of his face showed that anything had happened to excite him.

Wanted Mr. Carnegie to Know.

"Here's a bill, officer," he said to the policeman before he started for the station. "Get Carnegie on the telephone and tell him that I'm in trouble."

The policeman and prisoner then walked through the crowd to Fifth Avenue, up the avenue to Thirtieth Street. As they turned the corner at the Holland House a number of cabmen who knew Thaw tipped their hats to him and he recognised their salute in return.

The trip up Thirtieth Street, across Broadway and Sixth Avenue, was without any excitement, and the prisoner reached the station without the usual crowd of curious people following.

Thaw did not seem to be intoxicated, but walked in a sort of daze. He made few comments on the way to the Tenderloin Station. Sergt. McCarthy asked him what his name was, and he answered:

"John Smith, 18 Lafayette Square, Philadelphia."

"What's your business?" he was asked.

"I am a student."

No charge was made on the books against this "John Smith." The detectives were sent out to investigate fully before a charge was made. Sergt. McCarthy asked him:

"Why did you do this?"

"I can't say," he replied apathetically.

Cards found on the prisoner read "Harry Kendall Thaw, Pittsburg." He made no comment when they were pulled out of his pocketbook.

Thaw Sent for Two Friends.

Young Thaw walked dazedly to the back room. He waited a while, and then sent for Frederick W. Lowenfellow and Frederick Delafield. The reporters asked him to make a statement. He refused to do it.

Young Thaw had lighted a cigarette while he stood in front of the Sergeant's desk. In the back room he sat on a long bench that is used by reserves, between two big policemen. He pushed his hat back on his head, stretched out his feet, and lit another cigarette. His eyes had a far-away look.

A number of his friends hurried over to the station to talk with the prisoner, but they were not allowed to see him. William Thaw, a brother of his who is stopping at the Holland House, had not been to see him up to nearly 3 o'clock.

When the detectives put on the case had brought in the witnesses and they had been examined in Capt. Hodgins's room, Thaw was charged with homicide and was locked in a cell.

The following witnesses were detained until the arrival of Coroner Dooley:

Paul Brodin, a fireman, 697 Prospect Avenue, the Bronx; Lionel Lawrence, manager of the company playing at the Madison Square Roof Garden, 325 West Forty-second Street; Harry Silverstein, Marvin Pincher, 84 West Thirteenth Street; Warren Paxsen, 146 East Twentieth Street; Edward Carney, 467 Second Avenue.

Thaw Not Ready to Talk.

Coroner Dooley reached the Tenderloin Station at 1:30 this morning and asked to see the prisoner. Thaw had sent the doorman out to buy him some cigars. He was smoking and seemed calm when the Coroner entered.

"Have you any statement to make to me?" the Coroner asked after he had made himself known.

"I don't care to make any statement now," Thaw replied. "I would appreciate it if you would tell Burr McIntosh or ex-Judge Hornblower or Joseph H. Choate of what has happened."

"Mr. McIntosh is upstairs," he was told. "Do you want to see him?"

"No," he replied, "just tell him to call up Mr. Hornblower or Mr. Choate. Tell him not to call up Mr. Choate until morning. I would not like to get him out of bed."

Mr. Choate is at Stockbridge, Mass.

Mr. McIntosh took the message and left the station.

Coroner Dooley said that he found Thaw in good mental condition. He added that he believed the murder was done through jealousy.

When Thaw was searched in the station $125 in paper money, $2.36 in coin, two silk handkerchiefs, two gold pencils, a gold watch, and a little pocket combination mirror case were found. These were taken by the Sergeant.

Mrs. White at St. James, L. I.

Mrs. Lizzie Hanlon, housekeeper for Mr. White at his residence, 121 East Twenty-first Street, had not heard of the shooting when a reporter from THE TIMES called shortly before midnight. She expressed the utmost horror, and could suggest no explanation.

The house is one of the most magnificently decorated in the city. Standing amid elaborate Italian decorations with carved marble and graceful fountains on every hand, Mrs. Hanlon gave what information she could. She said:

"Mr. White has been alone in the house for some time. Mrs. White has been away in the West for about three weeks or a month, but is now at her country residence at St. James, L. I.

"Lawrence White, Mr. White's son, came down from Harvard the other day. Both he and his father came in and dressed for dinner to-night, but they did not go out together, Mr. White leaving alone a few minutes before his son. I do not know where either of them went."

"Has Mr. Thaw been to the house to see Mr. White recently?" Mrs. Hanlon was asked.

"Mr. Thaw? I never heard of him. As far as I know Mr. White did not have any visitors here to-day."

Young White, with a friend, Leroy King, dined with his father last night at the Café Martin. Mr. White, his son says, was in the best of spirits and said nothing about any trouble.

After the dinner the party entered an electric automobile and went up to the New Amsterdam roof garden. There the two boys asked the elder White to stay and see the performance.

He said: "No, I thank you," adding that he was going elsewhere.

That was the last they saw of him.

Meant to Go to Philadelphia.

Lawrence White says his father was thinking of going to Philadelphia last evening on a matter of business, and intended to up to the last possible moment, and only changed his plans in order to dine with the boys, who had just come down from Harvard.

"If he had only gone!" exclaimed the son in his grief.

Lawrence White said he had never seen Harry Thaw in his life and had never heard his father speak of him, and that he knew of absolutely nothing that could lead to such a tragedy.

He was then informed that his father was dead and that the body was still

"All the News That's Fit to Print."

The New York Times.

THE WEATHER.

Fair, warmer to-day; fair Thursday; fresh south winds.

VOL. LVIII...NO. 18,519. * * * NEW YORK, WEDNESDAY, OCTOBER 7, 1908.—SIXTEEN PAGES. ONE CENT In Greater New York, Jersey City, and Newark { Elsewhere, TWO CENTS.

CAPT. ERB SHOT DEAD BY HIS SISTER-IN-LAW

Philadelphia Political Leader, Who Had Family Troubles, Killed by Mrs. Beisel.

SHE IS IN MEDIA JAIL

Mrs. Erb Says Her Sister Took Pistol from Captain and Fired Six Bullets Into Him.

Special to The New York Times.

PHILADELPHIA, Oct. 6.—Capt. J. Clayton Erb, a wealthy politician and prominent officer of the National Guard, is dead with a bullet wound in his body at his country home, Red Gables, near Glen Riddle, Delaware County. He was found late to-night, and his sister-in-law, Mrs. Beisel, says she shot him by accident.

Mrs. Beisel was arrested by the Coroner and taken to Media Jail. After much questioning she broke down and admitted that she had killed the Captain, but did it to save her own life. She said he had come home and found the sister-in-law and a quarrel ensued. Capt. Erb ordered her to leave the house and she refused. She said he cursed her and went upstairs to his room. He got a heavy army pistol and emerging met her in the hall.

"Now, will you get out or not?" he is reported to have said.

"I will not," replied Mrs. Beisel. She flew at him and grabbed the weapon. A struggle followed and Mrs. Beisel got the weapon.

Mrs. Erb supplied the rest of the facts. She said her sister raised the revolver and cried:

"Take that, you wretch, and that and that," pulling the trigger six times. Every bullet took effect and Erb fell to the floor. Death was instantaneous. The first shot pierced his forehead and the others riddled his breast. Several entered the heart.

Mrs. Beisel is a young and attractive woman. She did not appear excited while being taken in an automobile to the jail.

For the last three months Capt. Erb had been having trouble with his wife. He recently tried to drive her from his house, and was preparing to bring suit for divorce. These troubles came to light when Mrs. Erb caused the arrest of Ernest Poulson, the negro coachman, charging him with having attempted to shoot her.

It developed at the hearing that Mrs. Erb had accused the negro of being a spy in the pay of her husband and that he had been ordered to watch her every movement and report to him. Erb immediately came to the aid of the coachman and secured his release on bail.

The trouble culminated a week ago, when Mrs. Erb had her husband arrested. She said that when she tried to take a carriage from the stables without his consent he had set three of his dogs on her and frightened her so that she fell beneath the wheels of the carriage and was badly hurt.

At various times Mrs. Erb has declared that Erb tried to brain her sister, Mrs. Catherine Beisel, with an ice pitcher, and that he bore a bitter enmity to her.

Poulson's trial was to have come up at Media, the county seat, last week, but was postponed.

Later developments, the police said, tended to show that Erb was shot during a quarrel by Mrs. Erb's sister, Mrs. Catharine Beisel, whom he had bitterly opposed. A physician called to the house at 11:30 said he had found Erb lying in the hallway outside his bedroom door. He had a bullet wound in his head and was dead. No weapon was near. The shot had evidently been fired from some distance.

Mrs. Erb and Mrs. Beisel and the servants were the only persons in the house at the time. Mrs. Erb declared Erb did not commit suicide, but refused to make any other statement.

Mrs. Beisel was a frequent visitor to her sister at Red Gables, although Capt. Erb had forbidden her to be there. Two weeks ago a treaty of peace was arranged between Erb and his wife. Mrs. Erb was about to sign the agreement, which provided that she should have free use of the horses and carriages.

"But your sister shall not use them and she must keep away from the house," remarked Erb.

"Then I will not sign," replied the wife, as she threw down the pen.

The proceedings occurred in the office of Justice Griffith, at Glen Riddle. When the parties failed to agree the matter was taken to Media. All the cases in which Erb and his wife were involved were adjourned to the December term of court for Delaware County. Counsel for Erb denied ten days ago that a divorce had been applied for.

Four weeks ago Capt. Erb became seriously ill, and it was reported at that time that he had been poisoned. Physicians soon relieved him and beyond declaring that he had not attempted suicide, Capt. Erb refused to discuss his illness.

Capt. Erb was known to every Republican politician of Pennsylvania. He was the right-hand man of Israel W. Durham, former boss of Philadelphia, and had done the quiet work in obtaining the election of Matthew Stanley Quay to the Senate in 1901.

Mrs. Erb before her marriage was Mrs. Florence Rothermel. She is an expert horsewoman, and has ridden blue-ribbon winners at many horse shows in this vicinity.

Capt. Erb was an expert in the State Insurance office under Insurance Commissioner Israel W. Durham. He was for many years private secretary to Mr. Durham, and was still connected with his office. He entered political life in the Twenty-ninth Ward under Hamilton Disston, and was later associated with the leadership of James McManes. When Mr. Durham became Insurance Commissioner he made Capt. Erb his expert and actuary. In addition to being active politically Capt. Erb had engaged in the brokerage business, and was for a time in the oil trade.

Three years ago, when the Insurance Department was under investigation by the Legislature, Erb was the chief witness. He testified that the enormous fees, amounting to more than $100,000, which were supposed to have gone to Mr. Durham, were paid to him as actuary. During Durham's incumbency Erb virtually managed the office.

Of late years Capt. Erb has confined his political activity to the Seventh Ward. For many years he has been a leading figure in the military life of the State. At the time of his death he was Captain of the Third Regiment and appeared with his regiment in the Founders' Week military parade Monday. Through Capt. Erb's influence the Third Regiment was aboard ship ready to sail from Tampa for Cuba during the Spanish war. This was accomplished through political influence, but the War Department discovered it before the transport sailed and the regiment was ordered to disembark, and it never saw active duty.

Erb lived until his marriage several years ago in South Thirteenth Street, near Pine. He was more than 50 years old, and is survived by an unmarried sister.

HANGS BY WIRE FROM AIRSHIP

Daring Feat by Knabenshue's Assistant Saves Two from Death.

Special to The New York Times.

PITTSBURG, Penn., Oct. 6.—Roy Knabenshue, the Toledo aviator, had a narrow escape with his mechanic, George Deusler, from being dashed to death on the streets of Pittsburg at noon to-day while making a trip over the city in his dirigible balloon. When about half a mile in the air directly over the high Frick Building, one of the wires of the second cylinder of his machine broke, and the great airship became unmanageable.

About 100,000 people were watching the airship, and they wildly applauded the dippings and twistings of the great winged thing, thinking Knabenshue was giving them a free exhibition. It was not until one of the two men in the basket was seen to creep over the edge of the basket and hang suspended from some invisible wire that the great crowd knew that there was anything wrong.

The human fly who was performing this remarkable feat in the air was Deusler, who made of himself a human ballast hanging to the broken wire to steady the hanging, somersaulting, dipping, runaway airship. Hanging this way Deusler was carried much of the distance back to Schenley Oval, three miles away, where the ship landed safely. Several times Deusler had to clamber back into the basket to rest, but he invariably was called out again to do the human ballast act.

The mechanic saved not only his own life, but that of Knabenshue as well.

APPEAL OF COAL CASE.

Court Grants Government's Plea in Hepburn Rate Bill Suit.

PHILADELPHIA, Oct. 6.—Judges Dallas, Gray, and Buffington of the United States Circuit Court to-day handed down an order allowing the Government to appeal from the decision of the court in the suit of the United States in the matter of the constitutionality of the "commodities clause" of the Hepburn Rate bill.

Counsel for both the Government and the defendant coal roads will petition the Supreme Court of the United States to give this case precedence over all others on account of its great importance.

The assignment of errors upon which the appeal was allowed are about ten in number and were filed by L. Allison Wilmer, special assistant to Attorney General Bonaparte, and by District Attorney J. Whitaker Thompson.

It is contended that the Circuit Court erred in holding that the "clause" is not a valid exercise of the powers of Congress under the Constitution, as to the regulation of commerce, and that the measure would deprive the railroads of their property without due process of law.

It is also contended that the court was wrong in declaring the law discriminative and a prohibition, and not a regulation of inter-State commerce.

BLUMENSTIEL FOR BENCH.

Said to be Slated by Tammany—Against Beckett for Surrogate.

It is not the intention of Tammany Hall to fuse with the Republicans in nominating Charles H. Beckett for Surrogate. Tammany, it was learned last night, intends to have its own candidate, who in all probability will be Senator John P. Cohalan. The nomination for Surrogate as well as the nominations for the vacancy on the Supreme Court bench, the two City Court nominations will be made to-night at 8 o'clock by the County Convention in Tammany Hall.

Emanuel Blumenstiel will, almost certainly, be the Tammany candidate for the Supreme Court Justiceship. He is a member of the law firm of Blumenstiel & Blumenstiel of 27 Pine Street, and has been a member of the Tammany Hall Law Committee for many years. John J. Delany had been prominently mentioned for the place, and so had R. Burnham Moffatt. Both of these men, according to the last unofficial report from the sanctum of Charles F. Murphy, have been turned down in favor of Mr. Blumenstiel.

For the two nominations for Justice of the City Court there are a score of men mentioned. Among those who really figure may be mentioned Maurice B. Blumenthal, Edward B. La Fetra, Abraham Levy, and Robert L. Luce. Mr. Blumenthal's nomination is likely. The other nomination is in doubt.

POLICEMAN SHOOTS ANOTHER.

Patrolman Greenbaum Puts Bullet Into One of Bugher's Men.

Policeman Michael J. McGrath, attached to the personal squad of Deputy Police Commissioner Bugher, was shot in the right arm last night at Forty-second Street and Third Avenue by Patrolman Max Greenbaum of the East Fifty-first Street Station. He was taken to Flower Hospital, where his injury was found to be slight.

Greenbaum was in uniform and on duty when he saw McGrath sitting on a box at a doorway in Third Avenue, near the corner of Forty-second Street. McGrath was in plain clothes. According to Greenbaum, he had a felt hat pulled over his eyes and his coat collar was turned up.

Greenbaum thought McGrath was a suspicious character and asked him what he was doing there.

"None of your business," the patrolman says McGrath answered.

"Move on," said Greenbaum.

Greenbaum says McGrath then pulled a blackjack and struck him in the face. He fell back and started to draw his revolver. He says McGrath reached into his own pocket, and that as he did so he, (Greenbaum,) with an oath, called to him: "Shoot if you're going to!"

Greenbaum said after the shooting that he believed McGrath intended to shoot him, and pulled his own gun as quickly as he could and fired two shots.

McGrath will be held on the charge of resisting an officer as soon as he leaves the hospital.

TOOK BLAME FOR GIRL'S ACT.

Ex-Lawyer Told Court He Was Responsible for Her Thefts.

Margaret Clark of 128 East Twenty-seventh Street, who was arrested on Sept. 20 on a charge of shoplifting, was in Special Sessions before Justices Olmsted, Wyatt, and Deuel yesterday, charged with taking four yards of silk valued at $3.88 from the counter of a Sixth Avenue department store. As Miss Clark stepped up to the bar, a man came forward and said:

"I wish to enter a plea of guilty, your Honor, in behalf of this unfortunate young woman."

"Are you a lawyer?" said the Judge.

"I was at one time," replied the man, "and I now wish to represent this girl both as a counsel and a friend. I brought here here from Pittsburg and I feel responsible for her presence and her actions in this city. It is my fault that she is in this predicament."

Justice Olmsted postponed sentence until to-day, and the young woman was taken back to the Tombs. Immediately afterward Mrs. Axman, the probation officer, and the girl's counsel, who gave his name as Edward Terrall, had a long conference. It is understood that Mrs. Axman will recommend that the girl be released under a suspended sentence.

Miss Clark later in her cell would not talk about her arrest or relations in Pittsburg.

SHELDON CONFERS WITH ROOSEVELT

Reports on Small Campaign Funds—Urges President to Take the Stump.

A NIGHT CONFERENCE HELD

Committeeman Ward and Cabinet Members Discuss the Situation with the President.

Special to The New York Times.

WASHINGTON, Oct. 6.—George R. Sheldon, Treasurer of the Republican National Committee, spent a large part of to-day at the White House. His interview with the President is said to have involved some plain talk on both sides, Mr. Roosevelt criticising Mr. Sheldon for his failure to gather funds for the Republican cause, and Mr. Sheldon expressing his opinion that the funds could be gathered only if Mr. Roosevelt would get out into the open and create enthusiasm among his own following.

Mr. Sheldon called at the executive office in the morning and had a long talk with Secretary Loeb, going afterward to see Secretary Root, who is said to have been the special agent of the President in the recent investigation of Chairman Hitchcock's management of the campaign. Mr. Sheldon returned to the White House at 2 o'clock and lunched with Mr. Roosevelt. Afterward the two entered upon a thorough discussion of the political situation. The National Treasurer returned to New York to-night.

Promised Statement Withheld.

As a result of the conference of the afternoon, Secretary Loeb let it be understood that an official statement from the White House would be forthcoming later in the day. The afternoon wore away, however, without any statement, and late this evening it was announced that the President had changed his mind. No reason was given.

In the last few days Mr. Sheldon has been the object of much criticism because of his inability to collect funds, and there are reasons to believe that he considered the strictures to be inspired by the White House. He insisted, on leaving the Executive office, however, that all was harmonious.

"Chairman Hitchcock has the entire confidence of the Administration in the conduct of the Taft campaign," he said. "Am I to resign? Well, I should say not."

Afterward he gave out this statement:

> The President asked me to come over and lunch or dine with him two or three weeks ago, but the duties of my position have made it impossible for me to come until now. We went completely over the general situation.
>
> On his authority, as well as from my own knowledge, I can say most positively that the relations between him and Mr. Hitchcock are of the closest and most friendly character, that Mr. Hitchcock has his entire confidence, and that the President heartily approves of the manner in which Mr. Hitchcock is managing the campaign, and, I may add, the President is entirely confident of the result.

Criticisms of the President.

While no person at the conference will disclose just what took place, it is understood that Mr. Roosevelt asked for an explanation from Mr. Sheldon as to the plans adopted for the collection of funds. Reports had reached the President's ears that the methods employed had been crude and that many would-be contributors had not even been advised where to send their money. He wanted to know about it.

In other campaigns the Republican Treasurers have carefully looked over the territory, choosing in big commercial or industrial centres men of standing to act as local custodians of campaign cash. In many of the principal cities this has been overlooked entirely in the present campaign, according to reports to the White House. Many thousands of dollars that might easily have been collected have thus been lost because of the absence of official party canvassers.

Mr. Sheldon's explanation of the alleged deficiencies along these lines is not known. It is understood, however, that he did not hesitate to declare that the President must take an active part in the campaign, even to going on the stump, his argument being that enthusiasm was needed to inspire Republicans to contribute, and that the President more than any other man in the party could inspire that enthusiasm.

Denounces Publicity Plan.

The agreement to make public all contributions also has had a serious effect on Mr. Sheldon's campaign for funds. The corporations cannot contribute, and various men of means do not care which party wins, apparently. In spite of all he can do, Mr. Sheldon has found that neither "ginger" nor party pride can be aroused by ordinary methods this year. This lethargy has seized upon the small contributors, and has shut off the only channels through which contributions can come.

Mr. Sheldon condemned the publicity plan for political contributions. He also denounced the press of the country as decadent, on the ground that it had disseminated the letters produced by Hearst, showing the alleged connection of certain men with the Standard Oil Company.

"Hearst acknowledges the letters were stolen," he said, "and the papers in attacking and blackening the characters of many prominent men have aided and abetted a crime. I understand Hearst has one hundred or more letters of the same scurrilous character."

There is much speculation as to the character of the statement that was determined upon to-day and then failed to appear. One story had it that the President practically had decided upon making public the contributions to the Republican campaign fund on or before the 15th of the present month.

Night Conference at White House.

The political situation at large, and practically the prospects for the State and National ticket in New York, was carefully gone over at a prolonged conference at the White House to-night.

Those who talked with the President were William L. Ward, the New York member of the Republican National Committee; Secretary Root, Secretary Cortelyou, Postmaster General Meyer, Secretary Loeb, and Assistant Secretary of State Bacon.

The conference began about 10 o'clock and lasted until midnight. Secretary Loeb later told the newspaper men that there would be no statement relative to it.

One of those who took part said, however, that a review of conditions showed that the general situation was very encouraging to the Republicans, and that especially good reports were coming in as to the chances of the New York State ticket to win.

The campaign for Judge Taft had thrown off the last vestige of lethargy, he said, and was being pushed with all the swing and vigor of previous National contests.

Incidentally the question of campaign finances came up as a result of the visit of Treasurer Sheldon to the White House during the afternoon.

THIEVES TOOK THEIR TIME.

Sat Around and Smoked While Selecting $5,000 Worth of Choice Silks.

Two or more burglars who like to smoke while they work and are not above leaving mementos of their visit broke into the establishment of Kunstler & Heyman, neckwear manufacturers of 60 East Tenth Street, some time between the end of the business day on Saturday and the opening of the building yesterday morning and stole at least $5,000 worth of silk.

The robbery was probably committed Saturday night by thieves who were aware that the firm would observe the Jewish Day of Atonement on Monday, and that the place would be closed until yesterday morning. This gave the burglars ample time to get away. Things were topsy-turvey when the factory was opened yesterday, and bolts of silk were scattered over the floors and tables.

The invaders were evidently thieves of discrimination. They did not take silks of individual or striking designs, but selected the finest fabrics. Some flaming red was taken, but dark or pure white silks were evidently more to the liking of the thieves. The burglars broke into the place at the rear by lifting a window catch with a wire. Once inside candles were used to light the thieves in their work, as several candles burned to the end were left behind.

The visitors evidently selected carefully, and were not in a hurry. Chairs stood grouped about, and a lot of cigarette stumps on the floor bore mute but eloquent evidence that the party had seen no reason to hurry and had enjoyed themselves. They left three whole cigarettes and two masks as another evidence that they bore no hard feelings toward their hosts for not being on hand to receive them.

The police believe the men loaded their plunder on a wagon when they had made their choice of silks, as it would have been impossible for them to have carried off the quantity of goods they did otherwise without attracting attention. There is no promising clue to the identity of the thieves, though the firm kept one of the masks left behind and the police have the other. Unless the owners call at the factory or Police Headquarters for these articles they will be kept as souvenirs.

SIX HURT IN AUTO SMASH.

Chauffeur and His Party Collide with Wagon and Car Turns Over.

Special to The New York Times.

NEW HYDE PARK, L. I., Oct. 6.—A big touring car containing three men and three women turned turtle on the Jericho turnpike at 3:30 o'clock this morning, after colliding with a butcher's wagon belonging to Maurice Loew of Mineola. Both wagon and car were going west when the latter plunged into the butcher's cart and turned over into the ditch. The members of the motor party were all injured. They refused to give their names. The women were picked up by a baker's wagon and driven to Mineola, while the men followed in the first trap they could get. At the office of Dr. Cleghorn it was found that one woman's nose was broken, a cut disfigured the face of another, and one of the men had his collarbone broken. They left on the first train for Brooklyn.

It was learned later that the auto belonged to Ernest Stuts of 126 Bainbridge Street, Brooklyn, and Mrs. Stuts said last night that the accident had occurred while her husband's chauffeur, Arthur Smith, had the car out without their permission.

"Smith has offered to pay all damages," said Mrs. Stutz, "and my husband will keep him in his employ."

It was learned that a friend of Smith's named Harry Grady had received the broken collarbone. The names of Smith's young women companions could not be learned.

HOPE TO CHECK "DRY" WAVE.

Ohio Brewers, Alarmed by Local Option Vote, Meet for Defense.

Special to The New York Times.

CLEVELAND, Ohio, Oct. 6.—With two more counties, Paulding and Wyandotte, voting dry to-day, thirty Ohio counties have driven out saloons in ten days, forcing nearly 900 liquor shops to go out of business. But one county out of thirty-one to hold elections has gone wet. Local option elections will keep right on taking place in Ohio until Jan. 1, by which time the Anti-Saloon League hopes to have made fifty counties dry. There are eighty-eight in the State.

To-day ninety brewers met in Cleveland to devise some plan of checking the anti-saloon wave. Adam Schantz of Dayton, President of the Ohio State Brewers' Association, said to-night:

"The Anti-Saloon League officials have already announced that their next move will be for State-wide prohibition, which would mean a loss to the State in revenue of $10,000,000.

"I believe that as soon as the people fully appreciate the gravity of the situation which confronts them they will cease to be influenced by appeals to their emotional nature and important victories will be won by the liberal elements all over the State."

ANTI-SALOON PARADE.

4,000 Men, Women, and Children Make a Demonstration in Atlantic City.

Special to The New York Times.

ATLANTIC CITY, Oct. 6.—Nearly 4,000 men, women, and children paraded from Chelsea on Atlantic Avenue and thence to the Steel Pier by way of Pennsylvania Avenue to-night, carrying banners, headed by brass bands, shouting that the saloons must go and singing psalms.

There were dozens of wagons, and one was an old sprinkling cart to demonstrate the water-wagon riding contingent, and the old cart was well loaded. Red fire burned freely, and there was more enthusiasm displayed than in any other parade held here during the Presidential campaign.

The parade was an incidental note in the convention of the State W. C. T. U., which is being held here. On the way from the starting point to the pier, dozens of saloons were passed by the paraders, and into the doors of some of these the paraders shouted that the saloons would soon have to close.

Banners and signs were displayed. "Saloons Must Go" seemed to be the favorite inscription, and hundreds of these were in the line.

The paraders attended a mass meeting at the Steel Pier, which was addressed by the President of the Law and Order League of New York City.

$500 to $1,000 on Missouri for Taft.

Special to The New York Times.

ST. LOUIS, Mo., Oct. 6.—St. Louis has begun to speculate on the outcome of the November election. The general odds are 4 to 1 that Taft will defeat Bryan for President. Otto Stifel, the wealthy brewer and a Republican, has bet Abe Slupsky $300 to $1,000 that Taft carries Missouri.

$100,000 IS GAINED BY AIRSHIP FLIGHT

Wilbur Wright Stays Up Over 64 Minutes with a Passenger at Le Mans.

FRENCH RIGHTS ARE SOLD

Latest Test Would Fulfill the Time Requirement Made by the American Signal Corps.

LE MANS, Oct. 6.—Wilbur Wright, who on Saturday established a world's record for an aeroplane flight, while carrying one passenger, made a new record this evening when, under similar conditions, he remained in the air for 1 hour 4 minutes and 26 seconds. His best previous record with a passenger was 55 minutes 37 seconds.

Mr. Wright thus fulfilled the conditions of the contract signed by him and Lazare Weiller, representing a syndicate, whereby Mr. Wright was required to make two flights within a week, with a passenger or equal weight of fifty kilometers each.

The contract calls for the payment to Mr. Wright of $100,000 by the syndicate, in return for which the syndicate obtains the patent rights of the machine in France and the colonies. M. Weiller has already given an order to a French manufacturer for fifty aeroplanes on the Wright model.

The record made by Wilbur Wright, which closes his contract for the sale of the patents of his aeroplane in France for $100,000, also is sufficient to fulfill as to time of flight with a passenger the requirement of the United States Signal Service Corps which his brother Orville has been endeavoring to meet at Fort Myer, Va. The United States War Department wants an aeroplane which can carry two persons for an hour in a still atmosphere at a speed of forty miles an hour. The requirement of the United States service is open to all competitors, and Orville Wright has been endeavoring to meet them on this side, as his brother has been endeavoring to meet the demands of his French contract.

Orville Wright hoped to meet the requirements here on Sept. 17, when he took Lieut. Selfridge in a flight with him. An accident to the propeller sent the machine shooting to the earth and resulted in the death of the army officer and the serious injury of the inventor.

Before the fatal experiment at Fort Myer there had been flights with passengers over the field of Le Mans. On Sept. 14 Wilbur Wright took aloft Major George O. Squier and broke a record with a flight of two passengers. On Oct. 3 he carried a French journalist through the air in a flight of over fifty-five minutes. Prior to this he had flown with a companion for nine minutes on Sept. 25 at Le Mans.

Mr. Farman carried two passengers besides himself during flights in Europe last May, and was able to remain up several minutes.

The $100,000 which will come to the Wrights through the French contract will aid them greatly, for they are men of little means and have been working to get enough funds to develop and finish as far as possible their conquest of the problem of flight by a machine heavier than air.

NAVY ASKS AIRSHIP BIDS.

Washington Officials Hope to Have Aerial Scouts by Next Spring.

Special to The New York Times.

WASHINGTON, Oct. 6.—The Navy Department to-day authorized a call for bids for aeroplanes to be used in the service. The intention of the department is to have the air craft ready for trial next Spring, though the time limit may be extended. Unless some foreign power takes immediate steps to anticipate the action of the Navy Department, this country will be the first to have a fleet of heavier-than-air flying machines as an auxiliary squadron for the navy.

Though the experiments at Fort Myer, in which Orville Wright figured so largely, were under the direct auspices of the Signal Corps of the army, Lieut. Commander Sweet was present at most of the trial flights as official observer for the Navy Department, and had many long conversations with Mr. Wright as to the specifications the department should require.

The plans of the Navy Department at present do not contemplate an aerial auxiliary fleet of fighting units. The most that is hoped for is to have a number of flying planes capable of extended reconnoitring, of making high observations, and possibly of acting as dispatch craft in the face of the enemy. This last duty in the Spanish war was left in great measure to torpedo boats, and the results were far from satisfactory.

The specifications will call for a speed of from forty-five to fifty miles an hour, with a possible endurance of four or five hours. If fulfilled, they will give the aerial auxiliaries a cruising radius of 100 miles, thereby greatly increasing the fleet's protection against surprise and giving it splendid opportunities for watching the movement of a hostile fleet or for reconnoitring over land works with practical impunity.

The trials for the new craft will probably be held in the open stretches of Hampton Roads, though a final decision has not yet been reached. It is expected that only few changes will be made from the type already designated as satisfactory to the army. One change will be that the flying ships will have to be capable of launching from the deck of a war vessel and of alighting on the deck, or, if necessary, both rising from and alighting on the water.

LAWSON TO SELL HIS STABLE.

Soon to Hold Auction of Horses in New York.

BOSTON, Oct. 6.—Arnold Lawson, son of Thomas W. Lawson, announced to-night that it had been decided to sell the Lawson stables at auction in New York this Fall. In all about thirty-five horses will be sold, but Boralma, Dare Devil, and a few other favorites will be retained.

Arnold Lawson, who is a Director of the New England Breeders' Association, owners of the Readville race track, states that the coming foreclosure sale of the association's property and the consequent end of the well-known race course, are the reasons for his decision to quit the turf. With Readville gone, he said, there will be no opportunity to speed the horses.

NORMAN E. MACK ILL.

Democratic National Chairman Suffers a Breakdown in Chicago.

CHICAGO, Oct. 6.—Norman E. Mack, Chairman of the Democratic National Committee, collapsed to-night as a result of fatigue and a severe cold. He is under the care of a physician and a trained nurse.

The illness of Mr. Mack came suddenly, and alarmed fellow-members of the Democratic Committee.

Dr. Hammond of the Auditorium Hotel was summoned, and he said that Mr. Mack was suffering from overwork and nervous exhaustion. He did not believe the illness serious, and intimated that the patient would be able to resume his duties in a few days.

Chairman Mack arrived in Chicago from New York yesterday afternoon.

MILLIONS FOR NEW YORKER.

Theodore B. Shear Will Share in the Estate of John O. Packard.

MARYSVILLE, Cal., Oct. 6.—The will of John O. Packard, who died at Santa Cruz Saturday, was filed for probate in the Superior Court here to-day.

The value of the estate is estimated at $20,000,000. It is to be equally divided between Edward Winslow Packard of Salt Lake City and Theodore B. Shear of New York City, after twelve bequests of $10,000 each to relatives are provided for.

GOVERNMENT'S BEST SELLER.

Agricultural Department to Issue 360,000 Copies of the Year Book.

Special to The New York Times.

WASHINGTON, Oct. 6.—The Department of Agriculture is about to issue a first edition of 360,000 copies of the year book—the volume that is said to have more general readers than any other Government publication. The full issue, as authorized by Congress, is 500,000, and the remaining copies will be printed in subsequent editions if the demand warrants it.

The physical labor involved in getting out the Government's best seller is enormous. The full edition requires 3,100 reams of plate paper and 21,810 of print paper, while the thread used in the bindery reaches the enormous length of 9,600,000 yards—nearly one-fifth of the circumference of the earth. The covers take up 62,000 yards of book cloth, while 8,000 pounds of glue and 30 barrels of flour go to pasting the covers on.

ARLISS SEES THE EAST SIDE.

Actor Goes Slumming and Sees the Essex Market Court.

George Arliss, the actor, went down to look at the east side yesterday through a monocle. He started in at the Essex Market Court, where Magistrate Kernochan invited him to a seat on the bench.

Mr. Arliss heard a man complain about his wife hurling a flat iron into his back in a fit of peevishness; heard a young woman tell about how a young man had agreed to marry her, had accepted $500, and had then disappeared, and heard wrangles of janitors and "white wings" on the subject of garbage.

The actor was personally conducted through Orchard and other push-cart streets. He saw the Bowery, got a glance at Chinatown, and fed a tramp kitten milk out of a wine glass. At the end of it all he remarked:

"My word; such a queer place!"

The east side and the Bowery didn't pay even that much attention to him.

HONOR MRS. LONGWORTH.

Pittsburg Gives Her Much Attention in Republican Campaign Rally.

Special to The New York Times.

PITTSBURG, Penn., Oct. 6.—Congressman Nicholas Longworth of Ohio, Senator Julius Caesar Burrows, and Congressman James Francis Burke opened the active Republican campaign here to-night, and Mrs. Alice Roosevelt Longworth also took part. The President's daughter did not appear in the street parade, but she had an automobile parade of her own from the Duquesne Club to Old City Hall about 8 o'clock. The crowd recognized the President's daughter on her way to the Republican mass meeting and she got a warm reception.

Mrs. Longworth occupied a prominent place on the stage to-night with the wife of Congressman Burke and other friends from Pittsburg. She declined to discuss politics, but on several occasions she led the applause as Burrows or Burke made a hit. She refrained, however, from applauding points in her husband's address.

At the Duquesne Club this afternoon Mrs. Longworth met the wives of many Pittsburg business men.

MESSAGE ON THE FARMERS.

President Roosevelt Will Tell Congress of Their Needs.

Special to The New York Times.

WASHINGTON, Oct. 6.—President Roosevelt is worried over the condition of the poor farmers. In spite of the fact that the ruralists have automobiles and other luxuries unknown to many city folk, the President is planning to send a special message to Congress dealing with the necessity for improving the conditions of life in the country.

In preparation for this message he has directed the Country Life Commission to make a detailed report of its findings before the end of December.

"BEATING" HUGHES.

One Method of Campaigning Arouses Uncomplimentary Comments.

While a Broadway crowd was listening last night to a speech by John S. Crosby comparing W. J. Bryan with Thomas Jefferson on the ground floor hall at No. 1,414, a little, wizened old man, dressed as Father Knickerbocker, with velvet coat, ruffled collar, powdered wig, buckled shoes, and all, sat blinking in a wire cage near the entrance, where all coming in or out could see him. In the old man's hand was a copy of "Pilgrim's Progress."

On the outside of the cage was a placard inscribed in large letters "Hughes's Jail." On the floor at the old man's feet were several croquet mallets and balls, evidently intended as symbols of Gov. Hughes's support of Puritanical tendencies.

The exhibition attracted a great deal of attention, but the general comments on the author of this method of political attack were not complimentary.

AUSTRIA TAKES TWO PROVINCES

Bosnia and Herzegovina Are Annexed and a Liberal Constitution Granted.

SERVIAN ARMY MOBILIZED

Leaders of All Parties Angered by Austria and War Talk Is Popular.

CONFERENCE ON BULGARIA

Britain, France, and Russia Acting Together—Bulgarian Minister Explains the Declaration of Independence.

LONDON, Oct. 6.—The second and culminating step in the Austro-Bulgarian programme for the aggrandisement of themselves at the expense of the status established by the Treaty of Berlin was consummated to-night when Emperor Francis Joseph formally proclaimed the practical annexation of Bosnia and Herzegovina to the dual monarchy, with a pledge of a Constitution guaranteeing civic rights and a representative assembly.

The present situation is as follows: Turkey calls upon the powers to preserve to her what they guaranteed by that treaty. Austria and Bulgaria strongly declare their determination to keep what they have taken. Servia is protesting belligerently against being hemmed in more strongly between two unpopular neighbors and against having the Servians in Bosnia absorbed into the Austro-Hungarian nationality.

The other powers concerned in the Berlin Treaty are discussing the holding of an international conference. Turkey's unexpectedly restrained policy minimizes the possibilities of war, which now is considered out of the question.

A conference of the powers is expected to be held within two or three months if it can be arranged, but no one imagines that it will undo this week's work. Austria declines even to discuss the matter of its annexation of the provinces, and the most that is expected is some arrangement that will save Turkey's pride.

Before the powers agree to enter upon a conference they probably will be obliged to define its scope, which will be a hard task. British statesmen suggest that compensation be made to Turkey, and that guarantees be given against further disturbance of the status quo. Sir Edward Grey, the Foreign Secretary, will address his constituents to-morrow evening, when it is expected he will explain the attitude of the British Government.

The English papers unite in praising Turkey's moderation and in denouncing Austria. The Standard, in a typical utterance, says: "We are sorry for the aged Emperor. We regret that so late in his long and honorable career he has chosen to sully his name with a deed which will go down in history alongside of the partition of Poland."

Several of the London newspapers question whether or not Emperor Francis Joseph is acting against his will.

VIENNA, Oct. 6.—A proclamation will be issued to-morrow by Emperor Francis Joseph declaring that the Austro-Hungarian rights of sovereignty and succession have been extended over Bosnia and Herzegovina. The new imperial provinces will be informed in the same proclamation that they will have a Constitution and a special Diet. The document will say:

> When a generation ago our troops crossed the boundaries of your countries you were assured that they came not as enemies, but as friends, with a firm resolution to put a stop to the ills from which your fatherland for so many years so severely suffered. This promise was given in a solemn moment and was righteously kept. It has been the steadfast endeavor of our Government by peaceful observance of the law and by vigorous efforts to lead the land to a happier future.
>
> To our great pleasure we can say that the seed which was then scattered in the furrow of ploughed soil has come up richly. You yourselves must feel the benefits of a situation whereby order and security have taken the place of force and oppression. Trade and communications are steadily spreading; the civilizing influence of a wider education has made itself felt, and every man may enjoy the fruits of his labors under the protection of a well-ordered Government.
>
> We consider it our most solemn duty to move forward along this path, and with that goal before our eyes we are of the opinion that the time has come to give the inhabitants of both countries fresh proof of our trust in their political maturity.

The Emperor has also addressed a rescript to Baron Von Aehrenthal, the Austro-Hungarian Minister of Foreign Affairs, in which he says:

> Being imbued with the unalterable conviction that the lofty, civilizing, and political objects for which the Austro-Hungarian monarchy undertook the occupation and administration of Bosnia and Herzegovina and the result which that administration has already obtained with costly sacrifices, can be permanently assured only by granting the constitutional institutions corresponding to their needs—institutions for the setting up of which the establishment of a clear and unequivocal legal position for the two provinces forms an indispensable condition—I extend the sovereignty over Bosnia and Herzegovina and, at the same time, bring into force in these provinces the rules of succession applying to my house.
>
> As a demonstration of the peaceful purposes which have led me to this irrevocable decree, I at the same time order the evacuation of the Sanjak of Novipazar by the troops of my army stationed therein.

The rescript is signed by the Emperor and dated at Budapest, Oct. 5, 1908.

A second rescript, addressed to the Gov-

"All the News That's Fit to Print."

The New York Times.

THE WEATHER.
Fair, warmer to-day; clouding to-morrow; light, variable winds.

VOL. LVIII...NO. 18,854. * * * NEW YORK, TUESDAY, SEPTEMBER 7, 1909.—EIGHTEEN PAGES. ONE CENT In Greater New York, Jersey City, and Newark | Elsewhere, TWO CENTS.

GAYNOR, UNPLEDGED, CONSENTS TO RUN

Writes Business Men He Will Accept Support of Any Party, but Make No Promises.

SAYS TAMMANY IS FOR HIM

Assured by Leaders of the Nomination, He Declares—Is for War on Machine Control and "City Spoliation."

Supreme Court Justice William J. Gaynor of Brooklyn has announced his willingness to become a candidate for Mayor in a letter written to a committee of influential Brooklyn citizens who urged him soon after his return from Europe to enter the fight. The long-awaited declaration of his position was made public last night together with the names of the committee of citizens and their letter to the Brooklyn jurist.

Justice Gaynor reviews the entire Mayoralty situation, assails "mere political control," which has resulted in "spoliation of the city treasury." He declares, however, that he has reason to believe that he will receive the Democratic nomination and Republican support, as well as that of the Independence League.

An interesting part of the letter is that in which Justice Gaynor refers to the printed statements that he would not receive the indorsement of the Republican organization unless he made some definite pledge of his position. While declaring that he does not believe that the majority of the organization demand any such condition of him, he emphatically states that he will pledge himself to no organization.

"I shall not take a nomination from any organization to which is annexed any pledge, promise or condition whatsoever other than to be Mayor in fact, and do my duty if elected," says he.

In referring to his expectation of welcoming all voters to his standard, Justice Gaynor says: "When an organization or party vouches for one and nominates him and wants him elected I have always understood that it welcomes help from any and all quarters to elect him."

Promises from Tammany.

He goes on to make the significant declaration that he has received assurance from influential Democrats that the Tammany City Convention will give him an "unconditional nomination" and that "no one can prevent the election of delegates who will nominate me." He states that he is aware that there is opposition to him in the organization, but that he does not believe "an undivided delegation can be brought into the convention opposed to my nomination."

"As to the Independence League," he continues, "inasmuch as it has always stood for the uplifting of city government, I think I may justly expect its support."

Justice Gaynor concludes with a solemn pledge to discharge his trust with fidelity and honesty, ending with the words, "No party or party machine can drag us down if we stand fast together: on the contrary, we may lift city politics up in all parties, and make the spoliation of the city's treasury, through mere machine political control, a thing impossible in the future."

Here is Justice Gaynor's answer:

Justice Gaynor's Letter.

Sept. 4, 1909.

"Messrs. Abraham Abraham, James McMahon, Archibald R. Watson, Judson G. Wall, Michael H. Drummond, James Creelman, Charles M. Higgins, M. M. Belding, Jr., and Frank J. Price.

Dear Sirs—Your letter added to my very great anxiety, already caused by similar letters and requests and public discussion, but has finally helped to enable me to see my way through it. I put myself in your hands, and consent to be a candidate for nomination for Mayor. No doubt you have observed that several bodies of citizens have nominated me already. I specially note your statement, 'We do not care who, or what party convention, joins in nominating and voting for you if you will give us your consent to run,' etc. It requires me to say something of recent occurrences in order that there may be no misunderstanding, and I trust I may say it without a bit of unkindness to any one.

The Republican City Committee has met since your letter was written and apparently give out a statement that the Republican City Convention will not nominate any one who will not pledge himself in advance not to accept a nomination from the Democratic City Convention also. Although published in all of the newspapers, and in no way questioned, I have doubted whether it was in fact authorized. I know that many Republicans will not acquiesce in it. As is well enough known, I have long been of those who look upon such extreme partisanship in city or local elections as most unfortunate. Its main result is to play everything year after year into the hands of party machines.

In years gone by I have worked shoulder to shoulder with Republicans and Democrats alike and together in efforts to prevent official wrongdoing and lift the city Government up and make it intelligent and decent. I so worked successfully with those who prevented the fraudulent purchase of the water company, and other even worse things, still in general remembrance, and with those who moved upon and destroyed John Y. McKane and his corrupt control, results and benefits from which were accepted by leaders and the machines of both parties in turn through series of years.

We never paused then to inquire of one another's politics, or to put any ban or bar on one another because of politics, and we shall not do the like now. Must I now in order to run for Mayor first get up and unjustly offend men who so worked with us then, and thousands of others who gave us their good-will and sympathy in such work, by saying that I shall not suffer the city convention of their party to also nominate me? If I should do so I could not expect their votes.

The great bulk of the voters here who are Democrats in National politics are in favor of intelligent and good local government the same as the corresponding bulk of Republican voters are. How much better it would be for the city if they should work together instead of proscribing and ostracizing each other.

Base Men in the Minority.

Base men are in the minority in all parties and everywhere. There are 75,000 or more voters in this great city who now never allow National politics to influence their votes in city elections. What,

Continued on Page 7.

HARRIMAN SUFFERS RELAPSE.

Diagnosed as Acute Indigestion—His Physician Says, 'We Hope for the Best.'

Special to The New York Times.

TURNER'S, N. Y., Sept. 6.—That E. H. Harriman has had a relapse was admitted this afternoon by Dr. W. M. Gordon Lyle, his physician, at the Harriman home here. Acute indigestion is Dr. Lyle's diagnosis of his patient's trouble.

The attack came on yesterday after Mr. Harriman had appeared to be doing nicely for several days. A telephone message was sent from the Harriman home in the early hours of this morning to Miss Taylor, Superintendent of St. Luke's Hospital nurses' registry, at 214 West 108th Street, Manhattan, asking her to send her best nurse here with all speed. The nurse arrived within three hours.

According to Dr. Lyle, Mr. Harriman is resting easily to-night. He said that it was he who sent for the nurse. There is a report that there are four other nurses here, but this could not be confirmed. Certain it is that Mr. Harriman's state of health is such that both day and night nurses are required.

When Dr. Lyle was seen this afternoon he was much perturbed over the presence here again of newspaper men. It was pointed out to him, however, that they were withdrawn on the understanding that the press was to be apprised of any change in Mr. Harriman's condition through his office at 120 Broadway. He was told that nothing could be learned from that source to-day.

"It is true," said Dr. Lyle, "that Mr. Harriman has had a relapse. Yesterday he had a sharp attack of indigestion, but he is better to-day, and is now resting comfortably. We hope for the best."

Mr. Harriman's entire family is at Tower Hill, while Judge Robert S. Lovett, general counsel to most of the important Harriman interests, was summoned to Arden and arrived last night. It is said that two of the physicians who were called into consultation with Dr. George W. Crile, the Cleveland surgeon, shortly after Mr. Harriman's return from Europe, are again at Arden. They are Dr. Walter B. James of 17 West Fifty-fourth Street and Dr. George E. Brewer of 61 West Forty-eighth Street.

Dr. Lyle gave out this bulletin at 4 P. M.: "Mr. Harriman had an attack of acute indigestion at 11 P. M. last night, having partaken of a dinner a little heartier than his strength would allow. His condition is improved to-day, although there are still slight indications of a bad stomach."

At Dr. Brewer's home last night it was said that the doctor was at Cedar Camp in the Adirondacks, so far as any of his household here knew. He may have gone to Arden from there, however. There was no response to the telephone when a Times reporter tried to reach Dr. James's house over the wire.

DYNAMITE HOUSE AND PLANT.

Official Who Had Discharged Men Kicks Explosive to the Ground.

Special to The New York Times.

TYRONE, Penn., Sept. 6.—The handsome residence of Thomas Calderwood, an official of the American Lime and Stone Company, and all of the buildings of the company at the quarry near here, were completely wrecked and one unidentified fire engineer was killed by explosions of dynamite early to-day.

Calderwood some time ago discharged some foreign employes of his company, and it was the general belief here that the explosions were acts of revenge.

Mr. Calderwood arose at 5 o'clock and smelled something burning. Upon investigation he found a large bundle of dynamite securely bound with wire on his kitchen window. He immediately tore the window open, and kicked it to the ground, and shouted for his wife and daughter to run for their lives. They had barely reached the street before the explosion occurred. Every window in the house was smashed to atoms. The doors and walls were badly damaged. Windows for blocks were broken.

At the quarries a ton of dynamite had been stored. The whole amount was exploded, completely destroying the buildings about the works, and blowing a large steel car 100 feet from the tracks.

The home of Harry Houck, near the quarries, was completely destroyed. The scales used for weighing cars were wrecked, and windows were broken in the houses within a radius of five miles.

HUGHES'S DEPUTIES AT RACES

Make No Secret of Their Mission, but Find No Betting at Sheepshead Bay.

Four investigators of race-track conditions from Albany visited the Sheepshead Bay race course yesterday, as the representatives of Gov. Hughes, after presenting themselves, with credentials which were accepted, to Sheriff Hobley of Kings County

The investigators made no secret of their mission, but made no claim to official standing of any kind, except to say that they came to observe what was going on and ascertain the conditions concerning betting at the race track for a report to the Governor.

The visitors watched the proceedings of the holiday crowd through the afternoon, and agreed that they saw nothing fitting the description of race-track betting published in an afternoon newspaper early last week, which report caused Gov. Hughes to request reports from the New York police officials and the officials of Kings County on the matter of race-track bookmaking.

MISS STEWART A PRINCESS.

Emperor Francis Joseph Confers the Rank in Her Own Right.

VIENNA, Sept. 6.—Emperor Francis Joseph has conferred upon Miss Anita Stewart, whose marriage to Prince Miguel of Braganza will take place Sept. 15, the rank of Princess in her own right.

Miss Anita Stewart is the daughter of Mrs. James Henry Smith by her first husband, William Rhinelander Stewart, whom she divorced in South Dakota to marry Mr. Smith. When Mr. Smith died in Kobe, Japan, he left his stepdaughter an income of $40,000 a year, to which her mother will add another $40,000 a year on her marriage to Prince Miguel next month in London.

In order to get the consent of his father, Dom Miguel, the Prince had to renounce all claim to the throne of Portugal in favor of his younger brother, Prince Francis Joseph.

LONDON APPLAUDS PEARY'S EXPLOIT

Instant Acceptance of His Report a Contrast to Skepticism Toward Dr. Cook.

HAD AWAITED HIS VERDICT

Admiral Nares Thinks It Peculiar That the Announcements Should Come So Close Together.

Special Cable to THE NEW YORK TIMES.

LONDON, Sept. 6.—The news that Commander Robert E. Peary had reached the north pole was made known throughout London by late editions of the evening papers, which displayed the brief announcement under headlines which suggested none of the reservations with which the reports of the discovery by Dr. Cook have been received.

In marked contrast with the skepticism with which Dr. Cook's reports were printed is the immediate and whole-hearted acceptance of Peary's dispatch. Nothing could show this better than a comparison of headlines upon the two announcements.

A Difference in Headlines.

"North pole reached by Peary. Official news that the American flag was hoisted April 6, 1909." That is the way in which Commander Peary's dispatch is presented to its readers by a London paper which headed Dr. Cook's report as follows: "The north pole reported discovered. American explorer's statement."

With the general public a similar readiness to accept Commander Peary's statement is strikingly apparent and bears out the saying frequently heard here recently to the effect that had it been Commander Peary instead of Dr. Cook who had come forward with a bare announcement of the discovery of the pole not a single voice would have been raised in question. It is a testimony to Commander Peary's high reputation as a man and an explorer that the world accepts his word without a shadow of hesitation.

Had Awaited Peary's Testimony

Mr. Peary's announcement is hailed with peculiar satisfaction, because, throughout the controversy that has been raging in the last few days, it has been stated again and again that Mr. Peary's testimony would settle the question definitely. "Peary will know the truth," it was said. Thus, Peary is the witness for whom the whole world is waiting. There was a consensus of opinion among the people with whom I talked to-night that if Commander Peary contests the claims put forward by Dr. Cook, the latter will find it an extremely difficult task to establish his pretensions to be the discoverer of the pole, even should the "proofs" which he is now withholding prove to be as good as he says they are.

Cook Expects Confirmation.

Dr. Cook, on being informed in Copenhagen to-night of the news from Mr. Peary, said:

"I hope it is true, for Peary's reports will confirm all my claims."

An arctic explorer to whom to-night I showed Mr. Peary's message to THE NEW YORK TIMES, saying, "I have the pole," made the comment that Mr. Peary, by implication, denied any other claim to the honor of discovering the pole, and that, consequently, it was to be inferred that the confirmation which Dr. Cook expects from Mr. Peary is hardly likely to be forthcoming.

Peculiar Coincidence, Says Nares.

Sir George Nares, who led the arctic expedition of 1875-6, when interviewed to-night with regard to Commander Peary's message announcing the discovery, said:

"It is difficult to avoid the conclusion that Commander Peary's Eskimos at Etah must have known that Dr. Cook had crossed Smith's Sound and passed Etah last Winter to reach Ellsmere Land. Dr. Cook, then," continued the Admiral, "gets down from his Eskimo headquarters at Annotook to Upernavik by a Greenland route never before traversed, passing all the sea glaciers in Baffin Bay just in time to catch a Danish Government vessel which leaves Upernavik early in the year before the whaling vessels are due.

"My first impression was that Dr. Cook had got hold of Commander Peary's Eskimos in some way or other and ought to have communicated either with Commander Peary or with the Eskimos at Etah.

"The question now arises how it comes about that Cook and Peary announce at practically the same time the discovery of the north pole. Is it not a peculiar fact that this coincidence takes place, in view of the possibility of news having reached Etah of the success of one or the other of the men?"

Capt. Scott of the exploring ship Discovery stated to-night that Commander Peary's message put it beyond doubt that the Stars and Stripes was the first flag to fly at the north pole.

The Proper Witness Arrives.

"Just at the very moment when men were saying that only the evidence of an independent witness who had himself visited the north pole could estab-

Continued on Page 2.

In order not to miss The New York Times of to-morrow, in which will be printed exclusively Lieut. Peary's own story of his discovery of the North Pole, order a copy from your newsdealer early to-day.

COOK GLAD PEARY REACHED THE POLE

Unmoved When, Wreathed with Flowers at Banquet, He Hears the News.

HOPE NOW FOR OTHERS

Believes More Expeditions Will Reach the Pole Within the Next Ten Years.

COPENHAGEN, Sept. 6.—Copenhagen was electrified to-night by the report of Commander Peary's announcement that he had reached the north pole. Dr. Cook was immensely interested and said:

"That is good news. I hope Peary did get to the pole. His observations and reports on that region will confirm mine."

Asked if there was any probability of Peary's having found the tube containing his records, Dr. Cook replied:

"I hope so, but that is doubtful on account of the drift. Commander Peary would have reached the pole this year, probably, while I was there last year. His route was several hundred miles east of mine. We are rivals, of course, but the pole is good enough for two.

"The fact of two men having reached the pole along different paths," continued the explorer, "should furnish large additions to scientific knowledge. Probably other parties will reach it in the next ten years, since every explorer is helped by the experience of his predecessors, just as Sverdrup's observations and reports were of immeasurable help to me.

"I can say nothing more concerning Commander Peary's success without knowing further details, than that I am glad of it."

While Dr. Cook was conversing casually this morning with some friends, a possibility of the dénouement which electrified the world to-day was laughingly suggested. Dr. Cook remarked:

"It is quite possible that Peary will turn up now. He is about due to get back if he carries out his plans."

Those who have had the best opportunities to become acquainted with Dr. Cook here believe that he is not likely to enter into a controversy with Commander Peary.

It is doubtful if history furnishes a more dramatic episode than the breaking of the news to Dr. Cook that Peary had realized the goal of his life's ambition and repeated struggles. Dr. Cook was seated at a dinner, surrounded by explorers and correspondents, in the gilded ballroom of the Tivoli Casino. Around his neck was hung a garland of pink roses, according to the Scandinavian method of honoring heroes, which the explorer wore blushingly and with visible embarrassment. Several speeches, acclaiming him, had been given and repeated toasts to him drunk with clamorous cheers.

Amid this scene a whisper went around that Peary had planted the Stars and Stripes at the pole. Cook was perfectly cool and unmoved. He made a striking speech, in which he paid high tribute to the work of Sverdrup, who sat near, to whose discoveries he largely owed his success; to John R. Bradley, who had financed the expedition; to "the intelligence, endurance, and faithfulness" of the Eskimos who had assisted in the preparations, and those who had accompanied him. The whole story of the expedition, he said, has not come out, and will not come out for some time, nor will it come out in installments, but only when it is completed.

Dr. Cook did not permit the whispers which came to his ear of Peary's success to move him in the least, but when he had finished he was surrounded by correspondents who looked for some sign of emotion, but the explorer said smilingly: "I am glad."

Nothing but arctic exploration has been thought of here for the last few days. The people at first refused to believe that such a report as that telling of Peary's success had been received. They thought it must be a canard or a practical joke. The Danish news agency, which received the telegram from London, feared that it had been imposed upon and cabled to London for confirmation before it would circulate the report.

Minister Egan characterized it as one of the most dramatic events of history. The rumor spread that Peary was returning by way of Denmark, and this made an immense sensation. Some questioned the authority of the Peary telegram on the ground that it was improbable that a scientific man would use such dramatic language.

After the dinner to-night Dr. Cook stood about talking with Sverdrup and the other guests in a most unconcerned manner. Later, with the roses still decorating his shoulders, his hosts led him through the Casino grounds to an automobile. A crowd of several hundred, half of the number being women, surrounded and followed him, cheering, but the people were not able to get near enough to shake hands, because of a cordon of police.

PEARY DISCOVERS THE NORTH POLE AFTER EIGHT TRIALS IN 23 YEARS

Notifies The New York Times That He Reached It on April 6, 1909.

HE WIRES FROM LABRADOR

Returning on the Roosevelt, Which He Reports to Bridgman Is Safe.

IS NEARING NEWFOUNDLAND

Expects to Reach Chateau Bay To-day, When He Will Send Full Particulars.

McMILLAN SENDS WORD

Explorer's Companion Telegraphs Sister: "We Have the Pole on Board."

SEVEN VAIN EXPEDITIONS

Many Years Consumed in Learning the Feasible Route—Picked Men Were His Assistants.

Commander Robert E. Peary, U. S. N., has discovered the north pole. Following the report of Dr F. A. Cook that he had reached the top of the world comes the certain announcement from Mr. Peary, the hero of eight polar expeditions, covering a period of twenty-three years, that at last his ambition has been realized, and from all over the world comes full acknowledgment of Peary's feat and congratulations on his success.

The first announcement of Peary's exploit was received in the following message to THE NEW YORK TIMES:

Indian Harbor, Labrador, via Cape Ray, N. F., Sept. 6.
THE NEW YORK TIMES, New York:
I have the pole, April sixth. Expect arrive Chateau Bay, September seventh. Secure control wire for me there and arrange expedite transmission big story. PEARY.

Following the receipt of Commander Peary's message to THE NEW YORK TIMES several other messages were received in this city from the explorer to the same effect.

Soon afterward The Associated Press received the following:

INDIAN HARBOR, Via Cape Ray, N. F., Sept. 6.—To Associated Press, New York:
Stars and Stripes nailed to the pole. PEARY.

To Herbert L. Bridgman, Secretary of the Peary Arctic Club, he telegraphed as follows:

Herbert L. Bridgman, Brooklyn, N. Y.:
Pole reached. Roosevelt safe. PEARY.

This message was received at the New York Yacht Club in West Forty-fourth Street:

INDIAN HARBOR, Via Cape Ray, N. F., Sept. 6.—George A. Carmack, Secretary New York Yacht Club:
Steam yacht Roosevelt, flying club burgee, has enabled me to add north pole to club's other trophies.
(Signed) PEARY.

Cipher Shows Authenticity.

The telegram to Mr. Bridgman was sent in cipher. The cipher used was a private one and indicated clearly that the dispatch was undoubtedly from Commander Peary.

Commander Peary also sent a message to his wife at South Harpswell, Me., where she has been spending the Summer.

"Have made good at last," said the explorer to his wife. "I have the old pole. Am well. Love. Will wire again from Chateau."

The message was signed simply "Bert," an abbreviation of Robert, Commander Peary's first name. Mrs. Peary sent a wife's characteristic reply, with love and a blessing and a request for him to "hurry home."

By a strange coincidence, Mrs. Frederick A. Cook, too, was in South Harpswell, Me., when she received the first news from her husband.

Peary's Companion Reports.

Two messages were received in this country also from Donald B. McMillan, who accompanied Peary. Mr. McMillan was an instructor in mathematics and physical training at the academy in Worcester, Mass., until the close of school last year, when he obtained a leave of absence of two years to go on the Peary expedition.

In addition to his message to Dr. D. L. Abercrombie, Principal of the academy, Mr. McMillan sent the following to Mrs. W. C. Fogg, his sister, who is Postmistress at Freeport, Me.:

Indian Harbor, Sept. 6, 1909.
Mrs. W. C. Fogg, Freeport, Me.:
Arrived safe. Pole on board. Best year of my life. BEN.

Follows Cook's Report Quickly.

These messages, flashed from the coast of Labrador to New York and thence to the four corners of the globe while Dr. Frederick A. Cook is being acclaimed by the crowned heads of Europe and the world at large as the discoverer of the north pole, added a remarkable chapter to the story of an achievement that has held the civilized world up to the highest pitch of interest since Sept. 1, when Dr. Cook's claim to having reached the "top of the world" was first telegraphed from the Shetland Islands.

The two explorers, Dr. Frederick A. Cook and Commander Robert E. Peary, both Americans, had been in the arctic seeking the goal of centuries, the impossible north pole, whose attainment has at times seemed beyond the reach of man. Both were determined and courageous, and both had started expressing the belief that their efforts would be crowned with success.

Peary the Better Known.

Peary was well known to both scientists and the general public as a persistent striver for the honor of reaching the "farthest north." Dr. Cook, on the other hand, had held the public attention to a lesser degree. He made his departure quietly and his purpose was hardly known except to those keenly interested in polar research.

Then suddenly, and with no word of warning, a steamer touched at Lerwick, in the Shetland Islands, and Dr. Cook's claim to having succeeded where expedition after expedition of the hardiest explorers of the world had failed was made known. Dr. Cook's announcement was that he had reached the pole on April 21, 1908.

Three days later Dr. Cook arrived at Copenhagen and received a welcome such as no explorer had ever received before.

Peary Announces Success.

Five days after the receipt of the Lerwick message, almost to the hour, came the sensational statement from Indian Harbor, Labrador, that Commander Peary also had been successful on his third expedition to the coveted goal, the date being April 6, 1909.

He filed his brief messages and continued on his way to the south, leaving the world to marvel at a dramatic situation such as has seldom been recorded —the double achievement of a purpose that for almost ten centuries had baffled the endeavor of man and had taken many an explorer to his death in the frozen north.

It is almost certain that Commander Peary did not know of Dr. Cook's announcement when he sent his messages from Indian Harbor.

Under ordinary circumstances Commander Peary's announcement would have evoked world-wide interest, but the existing conditions conspired to add many times to the importance of his communication.

According to Dr. Cook's account of his expedition, he buried the American flag at the pole in a metal tube; Peary's words would indicate that the Stars and Stripes were raised by him and left standing.

How the News Came.

The message from Commander Peary to THE NEW YORK TIMES was received in New York at 12:39 yesterday through the Postal Telegraph Company. It was handed in at Indian Harbor, Labrador, and was sent from there by wireless telegraph to Cape Ray, Newfoundland, and from Cape Ray to Port aux Basques by the Newfoundland Government land lines; thence to Canso, Nova Scotia, by cable, and to New York from there over the lines of the Commercial Cable Company.

WASHINGTON CREDITS PEARY.

Believes Cook, Too, but Has Said That He Must Produce Records.

Special to The New York Times.

WASHINGTON, Sept. 6.—There was instant acceptance among the geographers in Washington of the assertion in Commander Peary's laconic cable message that he had discovered the north pole. And there was just as ready rejoicing for Peary is popular with the scientific men in the National capitol, and they are ready to take his word at its face value without examination or delay.

In the manner of their acceptance of this announcement of a second discovery of the point that has baffled discoverers for so many years there is a sharp contrast to the attitude of the same men toward the announcement from Dr. Cook. Most of them, indeed, accept Cook's assertion, and announce their belief that the Brooklyn man actually did reach the north pole in April, 1908. But th

PEARY REPORTS TO THE TIMES

ANNOUNCES HIS DISCOVERY OF THE POLE AND WILL SEND A FULL AND EXCLUSIVE ACCOUNT TO-DAY.

Indian Harbor, Labrador, via Cape Ray, N. F., Sept. 6.

The New York Times, New York:

I have the pole, April sixth. Expect arrive Chateau Bay September seventh. Secure control wire for me there and arrange expedite transmission big story.

PEARY.

PEARY'S MESSAGE TO HIS WIFE.

SOUTH HARPSWELL, Me., Sept. 6.—Commander Robert E. Peary announced his success in discovering the North Pole to his wife, who is summering at Eagle Island here, as follows:

INDIAN HARBOR, via Cape Ray, Sept. 6, 1909.
Mrs. R. E. Peary, South Harpswell, Me.:
Have made good at last. I have the old Pole. Am well. Love. Will wire again from Chateau.
(Signed) BERT.

In replying Mrs. Peary sent the following dispatch:

SOUTH HARPSWELL, Me., Sept. 6, 1909.
To Commander R. E. Peary, Steamer Roosevelt, Chateau Bay:
All well. Best love. God bless you. Hurry home.
(Signed) JO.

CONFIRMED BY FELLOW-VOYAGER.

INDIAN HARBOR, Labrador, Sept. 6, 1909.
Dr. D. W. Abercrombie, Worcester Academy, Worcester, Mass.:
Top of the earth reached at last. Greetings to Faculty and boys.
(Signed) D. B. McMILLAN.

DR. COOK CABLES THE TIMES.

To the Editor of The New York Times:

COPENHAGEN, Sept. 6.
Glad Peary did it. Two records are better than one, and the work over a more easterly route has added value.
COOK.

The New York Times

PAGE ONE

1910-1919

"All the News That's Fit to Print."

The New York Times.

THE WEATHER.
Fair, warmer Sunday; rain probably Monday; moderate south winds.
For full weather report see Page 10, Part 3.

VOL. LX...NO. 19,419. ** NEW YORK, SUNDAY, MARCH 26, 1911.—90 PAGES, In Eight Parts, Including Picture Section and Review of Books. PRICE FIVE CENTS.

141 MEN AND GIRLS DIE IN WAIST FACTORY FIRE; TRAPPED HIGH UP IN WASHINGTON PLACE BUILDING; STREET STREWN WITH BODIES; PILES OF DEAD INSIDE

LIMANTOUR, VICTOR, PROMISES REFORMS

He Remains in Mexican Cabinet and de la Barra Will Displace Creel.

FORCE WILL MEET FORCE

Minister, However, Appeals to Mexicans and Nations to Believe in the Government's Good Faith.

FROM VICE PRESIDENT CORRAL.
Mexico City, March 25.
To the Editor of The New York Times:
The resignation of Gen. Diaz's Cabinet has been well received, because its object is to make it easier for the President to introduce reforms in public administration which it is thought will contribute to re-establish peace.
RAMON CORRAL.

FROM MINISTER OF WAR COSIO.
Mexico City, March 25.
To the Editor of The New York Times:
I am not in a position to answer your question since it is for the public to discuss the effects of the resignation.
G. COSIO.

Señor Limantour seems to have gained full sway in the Mexican Government. He is to remain as Minister of Finance. Ambassador de la Barra, with whom he had long consultations in New York, has been summoned from Washington to be Minister of Foreign Affairs in place of Enrique Creel, Limantour's rival. Four other new names are on the Cabinet slate.

Señor Limantour in an interview appeals to all Mexicans to rally to the Government. He promises needed reforms, but declares force will be met with force.

The Maderos, who were in New York, have gone to Texas to be nearer to Francisco I. Madero, the rebel leader. Insurrectos have appeared at new and widely scattered places. Successful operations are reported in Coahuila and Neuvo Leon in the North and Guerrero and Oaxaca in the South.

APPEAL BY LIMANTOUR.

Assures Mexicans of Reform and Appeals for Their Support.

Special to The New York Times.

MEXICO CITY, March 25.—Señor José Yves Limantour, whose return to this city has been followed by the upsetting of the Diaz cabinet, and who is expected to be a figure of great importance in the new Ministry, in an interview with the correspondent of THE NEW YORK TIMES this afternoon outlined the policy which he believes will be followed by the Government. Señor Limantour, whose resignation went in with those of his colleagues, spoke as an individual.

"I hope and earnestly trust," he said, "that the present difficulties will soon be solved in the best interests of the country and to the satisfaction of all reasonable and patriotic citizens; and I feel that I can say that the administration of Gen. Diaz is prepared to take such measures and implant such reforms as will satisfy the best public opinion of the country; and that, while meeting force with force, it will leave nothing undone in the present circumstances to unite all good Mexicans.

"A united Mexico is our watchword. I ask all patriotic and progressive Mexicans to be patient, and while the Government is working at the problem before it that they practically display the love of the fatherland, which has been and must be the basic principle of Mexico's proud position in the world. The putting aside of all personal resentments is imperatively demanded and a common cause to overcome a national difficulty is a necessity.

"If the citizens and friends of Mexico will continue to prove their devotion to the glorious past and the promising future of this nation in a brief time all complexities can readily be overcome. The Mexican people and the Governments friendly to us must believe—and I say this in all solemnity of verity—that the Government is determined to properly and progressively satisfy all legitimate demands for reformative measures, and that it is doing this in its line of duty as a representative Government, honestly, sincerely, and fearlessly."

The resignation of the Cabinet yesterday is taken as an indication that Señor Limantour's policies are prevailing with President Diaz. Señor Limantour's recognized value in his present office and his unfamiliarity with diplomatic duties is advanced as a strong argument against a change in his office, and he will remain as Finance Minister.

While high officials will not admit that Gen. Bernardo Reyes has been recalled from Europe, it can be stated with practical certainty that the summons has gone to him. To Gen. Reyes, who has long been called the "idol of the Mexican Army," may be intrusted the task of handling the rebellion, as Minister of War and Marine. He will succeed the aged Gen. Cosio, who has been severely criticised for the campaign so far conducted. Gen. Reyes, who has long been abroad on a mission to study the military methods of Europe, was last heard from in Rome, whence he had gone from Paris.

Six Chosen For Ministry.

MEXICO CITY, March 25.—Although no official announcement has been made, it is known that five of the new members of President Diaz's Cabinet have been chosen and it is almost certain that Jose Yves Limantour will remain as Minister of Finance. Other selections besides that of Señor de la Barra as Minister of Foreign Relations, are:

DEMETRO SODI, Judge of the Supreme Court, Minister of Justice, succeeding Justino Fernandez.

NORDBETT DOMINGUEZ, Postmaster General, Department of Communications, succeeding Leander Fernandez.

MANUEL MAROQUIN, well-known civil engineer, Department of Fomento, succeeding Olegario Molina.

JORGE VERA ESTANOL, attorney, Minister of Education, succeeding Justo Sierra.

So far as official announcement of the

Continued on Page 9.

TO-DAY'S SUNDAY TIMES

CONSISTS OF

Part I. Pictorial Section.

WIRELESS NEWS BY KITES.

Got Calls 4,000 and 6,000 Miles Away, Say San Francisco Men.

SAN FRANCISCO, March 25.—Notable achievements in wireless telegraphy are reported by a party that conducted experiments in receiving messages with the aid of high-flying kites on a beach near the Golden Gate last night.

The experimenters say they have distinctly heard calls from San Juan, Porto Rico, Washington, D. C.; Key West, Fla.; Brooklyn Navy Yard, Colon, Guantanamo, Cuba, and the station at Otichishi, Japan, which is 4,900 miles distant. They also detected an indistinct Marconi spark, which they believe was sent from Cornwall, England, a distance of 6,500 miles.

The receiving aerials were strung between two pairs of 16-foot kites, which rose to a height estimated at 1,500 feet.

To-day reports of the experiments are being prepared for transmission to the War Department, together with suggestions for the use of such an appliance for the detection of distant activities of enemies.

SENDS WIRELESS 2,500 MILES.

The White Star Liner Megantic Forwards a Message to England.

HALIFAX, N. S., March 25.—What is said to be an entirely new feat in direct wireless communication, the sending of a message over the Atlantic a distance of 2,500 miles from a ship at sea to England, was reported by the White Star Dominion liner Megantic, which arrived to-day from Liverpool.

While off the coast last night Purser Pomeroy of the Megantic sent a wireless dispatch to Liverpool via Poldhu, Cornwall. The message was received and to-day when the ship docked, a reply by cable was handed to the purser.

Hitherto messages from ships in this part of the Atlantic have gone by way of Cape Race or Glace Bay and a range of 600 miles has been considered as practically the limit.

RAILROAD STRIKE IS OFF.

Queen & Crescent Firemen Return to Work, Both Sides Yielding Points.

Special to The New York Times.

CINCINNATI, Ohio, March 25.—The strike of firemen on the Queen and Crescent road, which caused considerable loss of freight and passenger service, was called off late to-night following a conference of the road's officials and representatives of the Firemen's Union. Both parties found it necessary to concede points of difference.

The company retains the right to employ such firemen as are now in service between Oakdale and Chattanooga, and to give them one-half the passenger and preferred freight runs.

It is understood that the strike, which has lasted sixteen days, has cost the company at least $250,000, besides the cost of operating trains with new firemen.

It is significant that the agreement is not signed by Vice President Powell of the road, who took the matter out of the hands of General Manager Baker. It is signed by Baker for the road and Vice President H. O. Teat, Chairman J. L. Payne, Vice Chairman G. A. Odenwald, and Secretary-Treasurer J. L. Fetterman of the Firemen's Union.

TALK OF CHARGES AGAINST THE MAYOR

Civic Organizations Taking Up Magistrate Corrigan's Attack—Want Police Control Shifted.

MAY GO TO THE GOVERNOR

Former District Attorney Philbin Says the Force Is Demoralized and Gaynor Doesn't Understand It.

An attempt was made yesterday to start an official investigation of police conditions in this city. Various civic organizations communicated with Magistrate Joseph E. Corrigan, who in a letter to the newspapers described the situation as intolerable and put the blame directly upon Mayor Gaynor.

It is the intention of the organizations to find out if things are as bad as has been set forth by Magistrate Corrigan and to have the responsibility placed somewhere.

Magistrate Corrigan has been asked to submit all the information and data relating to the subject he has on hand or can get, and he will comply with the request. This is as far as the Magistrate will go, he said, as he considers that he has done his duty in drawing the attention of the public to the abuses.

"I have nothing to add to what I stated in my letter," said Magistrate Corrigan yesterday, "but I am ready to stand by everything I wrote. My deductions are more than borne out by the letters which I receive by every mail. Most of these are from responsible people and contain specific instances of how the police of New York City are demoralized. These letters I am willing, with the consent of the owners, to turn over to any investigating committee, with any other information which I possess. I hope a full investigation will be made, either by the Grand Jury or some civic body."

Magistrate Butts Takes Notice, Too.

It was reported that the civic organizations will endeavor to have police control taken entirely out of the hands of the Mayor. It was said that they will even go so far as to bring charges before the Governor against the Mayor if he does not remedy defects of his own accord.

City Magistrate Butts substantiated in a measure yesterday the charges of Magistrate Corrigan. On Thursday Magistrate Butts praised Magistrate Corrigan's sincerity and courage, and he was not invited to the meeting of Magistrates on Thursday evening at which thirteen Magistrates disclaimed sympathy with Magistrate Corrigan's attack.

Magistrate Butts's position was defined when two policemen from the West 125th Street Station offered newspaper clippings in the Harlem Court describing proceedings at the Polo Athletic Club as a basis for warrants for the boxers. They said they had been unable to get into the club.

"It is a barefaced confession of the general inefficiency of the Police Department for you to offer me such evidence," said Magistrate Butts. "It reflects small credit on the police affairs of the city. How absurd it is for you men to come here and ask for a warrant or even a summons, when you make no straight charge based upon any real evidence that a crime has been committed.

"Now, understand me. I do not blame you two men or your Lieutenant or your Captain, but it certainly shows inexperience, if not stupidity, in the police administration of the City of New York. The court is powerless to put in motion its processes on such 'evidence' as this. The application for a warrant is denied."

Among those who openly backed up Magistrate Corrigan's charges yesterday were former District Attorney Eugene A. Philbin, who helped to break up the old police "system," convicting a number of Captains for neglect of duty and forcing others to retire from the department.

Force Demoralized, Says Philbin.

"I consider the police force of New York the finest body of men in the world for its size," said Mr. Philbin. "For the most part it is made up of splendid fellows, but they are now working purely under the stimulus of their own innate virtue. The force as a force is demoralized; never in my time has it been in such a state, and I believe that whether his statement was judicious and well timed or not, Magistrate Corrigan was entirely correct in his description of the conditions.

"Men are afraid of their commanding officers, not in the old sense of knowing that they must obey them, but in the sense of having no confidence in them. They are afraid to make an arrest, almost to call their souls their own. Of course, such a condition is intolerable.

"A Captain in the old days was held strictly accountable for what happened in his precinct, and although an honest patrolman, with a grievance or a wrong to report, did not have a chance in the world if he went to Headquarters with it, the discipline was splendid and New York was protected. I did my best to destroy that old system while I was in the District Attorney's office, thinking that thereby I could do a permanent good to the city. It seems, however, that I really did an injury, as so far nothing has been found as a substitute for what was called the police 'business.'

Criticisms of the Mayor.

"I do not believe that Mayor Gaynor is fully informed on police matters, or so thoroughly conversant with them as those who have studied them for years. In my opinion the only solution is to appoint a Police Commissioner for a long tenure of office, say fourteen years, so that he may be free from all influence.

"I am convinced that all the Magistrates who signed the statement condemning the action of Magistrate Corrigan, though they believed it impolitic and, perhaps, tending further to upset the discipline and efficiency of the force, really agreed with him."

James Forbes, Secretary and Director of the National Association for the Prevention of Mendicancy and Charitable Imposture, who is well acquainted with police conditions in New York, also supports Magistrate Corrigan.

"There is no question about it," he said, "the whole police force of the city is utterly demoralized. The police realize that the Mayor dislikes the police, mistrusts them, takes every opportunity to side against them.

"Now, the police force is a peculiar body, with a psychology all its own. They are very closely bound together, so that the slightest influence spreads at once through the entire force, and the Mayor's constraint, which has been carried to the extent of persecution, has simply wiped out their spirit."

Letters to Corrigan.

Letters from all kinds of people praising him for the stand he has taken in regard to the police continue to pour in on Magistrate Corrigan. The following is from a prominent lawyer:

"I congratulate you on having at last brought the public to a realization of present conditions. Whatever the other

Continued on Page 8.

The Flames Spread with Deadly Rapidity Through Flimsy Material Used in the Factory.

600 GIRLS ARE HEMMED IN

When Elevators Stop Many Jump to Certain Death and Others Perish in Fire-Filled Lofts.

STUDENTS RESCUE SOME

Help Them to Roof of New York University Building, Keeping the Panic-Stricken in Check.

ONE MAN TAKEN OUT ALIVE

Plunged to Bottom of Elevator Shaft and Lived There Amid Flames for Four Hours.

ONLY ONE FIRE ESCAPE

Coroner Declares Building Laws Were Not Enforced—Building Modern—Classed Fireproof.

JUST READY TO GO HOME

Victims Would Have Ended Day's Work in a Few Minutes—Pay Envelopes Identify Many.

MOB STORMS THE MORGUE

Seeking to Learn Fate of Relatives Employed by the Triangle Waist Company.

The Burning Building at 23 Washington Place.

Three stories of a ten-floor building at the corner of Greene Street and Washington Place were burned yesterday, and while the fire was going on 141 young men and women—at least 125 of them mere girls—were burned to death or killed by jumping to the pavement below.

The building was fireproof. It shows now hardly any signs of the disaster that overtook it. The walls are as good as ever; so are the floors; nothing is the worse for the fire except the furniture and 141 of the 600 men and girls that were employed in its upper three stories.

Most of the victims were suffocated or burned to death within the building, but some who fought their way to the windows and leaped met death as surely, but perhaps more quickly, on the pavements below.

All Over in Half an Hour.

Nothing like it has been seen in New York since the burning of the General Slocum. The fire was practically all over in half an hour. It was confined to three floors—the eighth, ninth, and tenth of the building. But it was the most murderous fire that New York has seen in many years.

The victims who are now lying at the Morgue waiting for some one to identify them by a tooth or the remains of a burned shoe were mostly girls of from 16 to 23 years of age. They were employed at making shirtwaists by the Triangle Waist Company, the principal owners of which are Isaac Harris and Max Blanck. Most of them could barely speak English. Many of them came from Brooklyn. Almost all were the main support of their hard-working families.

There is just one fire escape in the building. That one is an interior fire escape. In Greene Street, where the terrified unfortunates crowded before they began to make their mad leaps to death, the whole big front of the building is guiltless of one. Nor is there a fire escape in the back.

The building was fireproof and the owners had put their trust in that. In fact, after the flames had done their worst last night, the building hardly showed a sign. Only the stock within it and the girl employes were burned.

A heap of corpses lay on the sidewalk for more than an hour. The firemen were too busy dealing with the fire to pay any attention to people whom they supposed beyond their aid. When the excitement had subsided to such an extent that some of the firemen and policemen could pay attention to this mass of the supposedly dead they found, about half way down in the pack, a girl who was still breathing. She died two minutes after she was found.

The Triangle Waist Company was the only sufferer by the disaster. There are other concerns in the building, but it was Saturday and the other companies had let their people go home. Messrs. Harris and Blanck, however, were busy and their girls—and some men—stayed.

Leaped Out of the Flames.

At 4:40 o'clock, nearly five hours after the employes in the rest of the building had gone home, the fire broke out. The one little fire escape in the interior was never resorted to by any of the doomed victims. Some of them escaped by running down the stairs, but in a moment or two this avenue was cut off by flame. The girls rushed to the windows and looked down at Greene Street, 100 feet below them. Then one poor, little creature jumped. There was a plate glass protection over part of the sidewalk, but she crashed through it, wrecking it and breaking her body into a thousand pieces.

Then they all began to drop. The crowd yelled "Don't jump!" but it was jump or be burned—the proof of which is found in the fact that fifty burned bodies were taken from the ninth floor alone.

They jumped, they crashed through broken glass, they crushed themselves to death on the sidewalk. Of those who stayed behind it is better to say nothing—except what a veteran policeman said as he gazed at a headless and charred trunk on the Greene Street sidewalk hours after the worst cases had been taken out:

"I saw the Slocum disaster, but it was nothing to this."

"Is it a man or a woman?" asked the reporter.

"It's human, that's all you can tell," answered the policeman.

It was just a mass of ashes, with blood congealed on what had probably been the neck.

Messrs. Harris and Blanck were in the building, but they escaped. They carried with them Mr. Blanck's children and a governess, and they fled over the roofs. Their employes did not know the way, because they had been in the habit of using the two freight elevators, and one of these elevators was not in service when the fire broke out.

Found Alive After the Fire.

The first living victim, Hyman Meshel of 332 East Fifteenth Street, was taken from the ruins four hours after the fire was discovered. He was found paralysed with fear and whimpering like a wounded animal in the basement, immersed in water to his neck, crouched on the top of a cable drum, and with his head just below the floor of the elevator.

Meantime the remains of the dead—it is hardly possible to call them bodies, because that word suggests something human, and there was nothing human about most of these—were being taken in a steady stream to the Morgue for identification. First Avenue was lined with the usual curious east side crowd. Twenty-sixth Street was impassable. But in the Morgue they received the charred remnants with no more emotion than they ever display over anything.

Back in Greene Street there was another crowd. At midnight it had not decreased in the least. The police were holding it back to the fire lines, and discussing the tragedy in a tone which those [illegible] seldom use.

"It's the worst thing I ever saw," said one old policeman.

Chief Croker said it was an outrage. He spoke bitterly of the way in which the Manufacturers' Association had called a meeting in Wall Street to take measures against his proposal for enforcing better methods of protection for employes in cases of fire.

No Chance to Save Victims.

Four alarms were rung in fifteen minutes. The first five girls who jumped did so before the first engine could respond. That fact may not convey much of a picture to the mind of an unimaginative man, but anybody who has ever seen a fire can get from it some idea of the terrific rapidity with which the flames spread.

It may convey some idea, too, to say that thirty bodies clogged the elevator shafts. These dead were all girls. They had made their rush their blindly when they discovered that there was no chance to get out by the fire escape. Then they found that the elevator was as hopeless as anything else, and they fell there in their tracks and died.

The Triangle Waist Company employed about 600 women and less than 100 men. One of the saddest features of the thing is the fact that they had almost finished for the day. In five minutes more, if the fire had started then, probably not a life would have been lost.

Last night District Attorney Whitman started an investigation—not of this disaster alone but of the whole condition which makes it possible for a firetrap of such a kind to exist. Mr. Whitman's intention is to find out if the present laws cover such cases, and if they do not to frame laws that will.

GIRLS JUMP TO SURE DEATH.

Fire Nets Prove Useless—Firemen Helpless to Save Life.

The fire, which was first discovered at 4:40 o'clock on the eighth floor of the ten-story building at the corner of Washington Place and Greene Street, leaped through the three upper stories occupied by the Triangle Waist Company with a sudden rush that left the Fire Department helpless.

How the fire started no one knows. On the three upper floors of the building were 600 employes of the waist company, 500 of whom were girls. The victims—mostly Italians, Russians, Hungarians, and Germans—were girls and men who had been employed by the firm of Harris & Blanck, owners of the Triangle Waist Company, after the strike in which the Jewish girls, formerly employed, had become unionised and had demanded better working conditions. The building had experienced four recent fires and had been reported by the Fire Department to the Building Department as unsafe, on account of the insufficiency of its exits.

The building itself was of the most modern construction and classed as fireproof. What burned so quickly and disastrously for the victims were shirtwaists, hanging on lines above tiers of workers, sewing machines placed so closely together that there was hardly aisle room for the girls between them, and shirtwaist trimmings and cuttings which littered the floors above the eighth and ninth stories.

Girls had begun leaping from the eighth story windows before the firemen arrived. The firemen had trouble bringing their apparatus into position because of the bodies which strewed the pavement and sidewalks. While more bodies crashed down among them, they worked with desperation to run their ladders into position and to spread fire-nets.

One fireman, running ahead of a hose wagon, which halted to avoid running over a body, spread a firenet, and two more seized hold of it. A girl's body, coming end over end, struck on the side of it, and there was hope for an instant that she would be the first one of the score who had already jumped to be saved.

Thousands of people, who had crushed in from Broadway and Washington Square and were screaming with horror at what they saw, watched closely the work with the firenet. Three other girls, who had leaped for it a moment after the first one, struck it on top of her, and all four rolled out and lay still upon the pavement.

Five girls who stood together at a window close to the Greene Street corner held their places while a fire ladder was worked toward them, but which stopped at its full length two stories lower down. They leaped together, clinging to each other, with fire streaming back from their hair and dresses. They struck a glass sidewalk cover and crashed through it to the basement. There was no time to aid them. With water pouring in upon them from a dozen hose nozzles the bodies lay for two hours where they struck, as did the many others who leaped to their deaths.

One girl, who waved a handkerchief at the crowd, leaped from a window adjoining the New York University Building on the westward. Her dress caught on a wire, and the crowd watched her hang there till her dress burned free and she came toppling down.

Many jumped whom the firemen believe they could have saved. A girl who saw the glass roof of a sidewalk cover at the first-story level of the New York University Building leaped for it, and her body crashed through to the sidewalk.

On Greene Street, running along the eastern face of the building, more people leaped to the pavement than on Washington Place to the south. Fire nets proved just as useless to catch them and the ladders to reach them. None waited for the firemen to attempt to reach them with the scaling ladders.

All Would Soon Have Been Out.

Strewn about as the firemen worked, the bodies indicated clearly the preponderance of women workers. Here and there was a man, but almost always they were women. One wore furs and a muff, and had a purse hanging from her arm. Nearly all were dressed for the street. The fire had flashed through their workroom just as they were expecting the signal to leave the building. In ten minutes more all would have been out, as many had stopped work in advance of the signal and had started to put on their wraps.

What happened inside there were few who could tell with any definiteness. All that those who escaped seemed to remember was that there was a flash of flames, leaping first among the girls in the southeast corner of the eighth floor, and then suddenly over the entire room, spreading through the linens and cottons with which the girls were working. The girls on the ninth floor caught sight of the flames through the windows, up the stairway, and up the elevator shaft.

On the tenth floor they got them a moment later, but most of those on that floor escaped by rushing to the roof and then on to the roof of the New York University Building, with the assistance of 100 university students who had been dismissed from a tenth story classroom.

There were in the building, according to the estimates of Fire Chief Croker, about 600 girls and 100 men. The bodies of those

"All the News That's Fit to Print."

The New York Times.

THE WEATHER.
Fair to-day and to-morrow; moderate winds.
For full weather report see Page 5.

VOL. LXI...NO. 19,620. * * * NEW YORK, FRIDAY, OCTOBER 13, 1911.—EIGHTEEN PAGES. ONE CENT In Greater New York, Jersey City, and Newark. | Elsewhere, TWO CENTS.

CALIFORNIA FARMERS GIVE VOTE TO WOMEN

Suffrage Has a Lead of 1,500, While Eventual Majority May Be 3,500 or More.

500 PRECINCTS TO REPORT

Liquor Question a Big Factor—Where the Saloon Influence Was Strong the Suffrage Vote Was Weak.

Special to The New York Times.

SAN FRANCISCO, Cal., Oct. 12.—Women of California have won the ballot, and it was the farmers that gave it to them. Overcoming a majority of 16,000 in this city and Oakland against suffrage, an avalanche of votes from Los Angeles and rural counties gave the amendment a majority that may exceed 4,000 when all the votes are counted. On the face of the returns at 9 o'clock to-night suffrage has a clear lead of about 1,500, and there are still some 500 precincts in outside counties to be heard from. At the rate of the gain that has continued all day, these missing precincts will raise the total majority to at least 3,500, and it may go much higher.

When the returns first began to come in the figures were all from populous centres, where the vote against suffrage was very heavy. This is explained by women workers at the polls by the fact that the saloon interests were almost solid against suffrage, because liquor men fear that women if given the ballot would endeavor to make California a dry State. In many of the towns the liquor question is or may soon become an important issue in local politics, and it is asserted that the saloon people felt that women if given the chance would close hundreds of country saloons by local option votes.

For the first twelve hours after the voting was over the tide ran steadily against suffrage except in Southern California. Then the rural votes began to come in. Steadily the big lead of the anti-suffrage forces was cut down, and suffrage leaders, who had given up hope, took new courage. Slowly but steadily the suffrage column grew, and early this morning, when the majority against had been reduced to 500, the farmers were still increasing the vote enfranchising women.

At noon suffrage had gained a lead of 400, and by night it had passed the thousand mark. It is now conceded by all opponents of suffrage that the women have won.

Early in the fight it was thought that the rural vote would be light, as only amendments were submitted. But it was proved that the farmers were keenly interested in the measures presented at the polls, and the vote in the country was heavier than in the cities. Granges and other farmers' organizations had indorsed suffrage.

Los Angeles gave suffrage a majority of a little more than 5,000, but with this exception all gains of suffrage were made in the country. Most of the strictly farming and mining counties voted for suffrage. Where the saloon influence was weak the suffrage vote was large, but where the saloon was powerful suffrage was beaten.

SEES BEGINNING OF THE END.

Other States Bound to Follow California's Example, Says Dr. Anna Shaw.

"We have been expecting word of our victory in California all day, and we are greatly rejoiced," said Dr. Anna Howard Shaw, National President of the Suffrage Party, last night. "First I want to congratulate the party in California on its magnificent fight, and heap on all the praise I possibly can.

"One thing that makes us especially jubilant is that the victory in California gives to the cause as many voters as in the five other States where we had won the fight. I believe that it is the beginning of the end. Kansas, Oregon, Wisconsin, and other Western States are bound to follow the lead at the next elections. The politicians are also sure to realize that the women are winning their long fight, and will climb on the band wagon along with the rest of us.

"The politicians must now come to see that the Woman Suffrage Party is soon to be a great power in the Presidential campaign; in fact, has become so now that California is won. President Taft yesterday made his first speech about woman suffrage and spoke in favor of it. I am quite sure that if Col. Roosevelt was now President he would not be the least timid about speaking of the movement.

"California is the most important State in the West, and that means much to us. The States that were won over first were considered insignificant. And then we won Washington, and then came this splendid victory."

Mrs. Pankhurst, the English suffrage leader who is visiting Mrs. John Winters Brannan of 11 West Twelfth Street, when assured of the victory in California, spoke with great enthusiasm of the effect that it would, in her belief, have on the movement.

"It is very gratifying not only to the party in this country but all over the world," she exclaimed. "In England the news will be heard with the greatest rejoicing. English women will be particularly glad, because it will be a very great help in our campaign. I am so overjoyed that I am going to cable to the headquarters in London in the morning.

"We have been looking forward to this result in the California fight, and we felt sure that there would be a splendid victory. Of course we are all the happier now that our hopes are realized. Every gain for the women here is a gain for us in England and gives a new impetus to the movement. The men must realize that we are going to win."

When informed of the majority for the amendment in California Mrs. Harriet Stanton Blatch of 46 East Twenty-ninth Street, President of the Woman's Political Union, said:

"We are gloriously happy over the victory in California, because we feel that the vote for the amendment in that State will have an influence on the voters in Oregon next year. When we have won Oregon we shall have the Pacific Coast solid.

"The last days of the contest in California have been trying to us. We have received advices, both pessimistic and optimistic, in regard to the probable results of the election, but all the time we have been hopeful.

"The success in California means the heartening up of women over the whole world. It will give a great impetus to our efforts locally to have passed through the next Legislature of this State a bill providing political rights of women."

Mrs. Ida Husted Parker said that she had been sure of the victory all day long, despite the fact that reports of a defeat had come earlier in the day.

"One great effect will be to show that

Continued on Page 3.

AEROPLANE SPEEDS INTO SEA

Curtiss's Hydro-Flier Beats the Fastest Boat at Atlantic City.

Special to The New York Times.

ATLANTIC CITY, N. J., Oct. 12.—C. C. Witmer, one of the Curtiss fliers, gave an exhibition of the possibilities of the new hydro-aeroplane here this afternoon before an applauding crowd of 10,000 persons. There was a thrill in every minute of the flight, which was from the crest of the breakers into the air and then back on the water again. The Sand Burr II., a speed boat, engaged in several spectacular races with the aeroplane, in which the aeroplane was every time the victor. Witmer narrowly missed disaster on two occasions during his first flight, but three attempts within an hour were successful. It was the first time the hydro-aeroplane has been tried on the ocean.

Starting from the beach, Witmer was soon skimming along the water like a speed boat, making forty miles an hour. After getting out as far as the end of the Million Dollar Pier the aviator turned and faced down the beach. Again he put on power, and an instant later soared into the air. At no time did he rise more than fifty feet. After traveling a half mile at an elevation, he effected a good landing on the water, switched his planes, and scooted back over his course.

It was while making this turn that one of the pontoons used as rudders dipped too deep in the waves. The plane careened far over. The canvas became water soaked, and under the extra weight failed to right on an even keel. The Federal life-saving crew rushed to the aviator's assistance, but he refused its aid. By this time the hydro-aeroplane had drifted within easy calling distance of the crowds on the pier. They could see Witmer crawl from his seat, after starting his propeller, and then, steering with his right hand, throw one leg over a support running from the boat which formed the understructure of the craft. In this way he shifted his weight to overcome that of the water-soaked plane, and manoeuvred almost a mile to the beach on the water in safety, while the spectators cheered.

The mechanicians adjusted the plane, and he once more started out. Near the same spot where he encountered trouble before Witmer almost collided with the Princeton, one of the big inlet yachts, carrying fifty passengers. The sailboat cut across his path just as he had put on high speed preparatory to mounting into the air. The water held him down too long, and he barely skimmed by the bow of the boat. A collective gasp went up from the crowd, who expected to witness a smash-up.

Clifford L. Webster, who was granted a pilot's license only last Wednesday, had his aeroplane smashed yesterday on the Hempstead Plains, and he was bruised. Webster was flying about fifty feet above the ground when his engine stopped. His Wright-Burgess biplane started to fall tail first. Webster succeeded, by throwing his weight to the front of the machine, in bringing it on an even keel, where he held it until it struck the ground. He was thrown out, but escaped with a few bruises.

AN HONEST $1,000,000.

Leslie M. Shaw Says It Can Be Made with Courage and Aptitude.

Special to The New York Times.

CHICAGO, Oct. 12.—"A man can make $1,000,000 and make it honestly if he has courage and aptitude." So declared Leslie M. Shaw, ex-Secretary of the Treasury and President of the First Mortgage Guarantee and Trust Company of Philadelphia, addressing to-day the annual convention of the National Convention of Life Underwriters, now in session in this city. Mr. Shaw added that at one time he saw an opportunity to make $1,000,000, but failed because of the lack of qualities he described.

"Those who try to make $1,000,000 dishonestly and fail think that nobody can make it honestly," he said. "There are those you know who have said that it is impossible to do such a thing honestly.

"As far as I have seen in my time, no man has served his country faithfully without receiving adequate reward, and that reward is usually money. Once in a while there is a monument, but not often."

Regarding the necessity of application to one's business, Mr. Shaw said:

"Mark Hanna once told me that he had occasion to call on Phil Armour. He did not say what was the purpose of his call, but it was in 1896. He declared that he found it necessary to make an appointment with Mr. Armour through his stenographer. When he called he found Phil Armour sitting in a chair and being shaved, eating his lunch, and dictating to his stenographer.

"It may not be necessary for you to work as hard as that, but that is the price that Phil Armour paid to have his name written in high places in every nation on the globe, and you can be sure that there are no bargain counters for such goods.

"Baseball is absorbing more interest among the boys of the country than is business," said Mr. Shaw in concluding his speech.

GIRL DREW BOGUS CHECKS.

Cornell Stenographer Admits She Used Them to Get Money for Vacation.

Special to The New York Times.

ITHACA, N. Y., Oct. 12.—In order to get money to continue her vacation, Miss Lorena C. Gibbs, a pretty young stenographer employed in the office of Dean C. A. Martin of the Cornell College of Architecture, drew checks on the First National Bank of this city under the assumed name of Alice M. King and cashed them in business places in Perry, N. Y., where she was spending her vacation last Summer. Miss Gibbs, who was taken into custody here last night, confessed that she had passed checks and this morning was taken back to Perry by Chief Butler of that place, who had been working up the case. As one of the checks was for $25, it is said, a charge of grand larceny will be lodged against her. There are several minor charges on smaller checks.

Miss Gibbs was found at work in her office yesterday afternoon by two officers. She was identified by Chief Butler as tallying with the description he had of her, and after being closely questioned admitted that she had cashed checks under the name of Alice M. King. She declared that she was spending her vacation in Perry and becoming short of funds had to get money some how to live. Chief Butler says that the checks had been coming back to Perry from the First National Bank in Ithaca marked "no funds." The police learned of Miss Gibbs's whereabouts through her letters to a young man in Perry whom she met last Summer.

MR. CARNEGIE SAILS, STILL OPTIMISTIC

Is in the Celtic on His Way Here—Martin Littleton a Fellow Passenger.

TO TESTIFY ON STEEL TRUST

Carnegie Says He'll Tell All He Knows, but That It Is Not Much—Thinks Present Unrest a Good Thing.

Special Cable to The New York Times.

LONDON, Oct. 12.—Mr. and Mrs. Andrew Carnegie and their daughter, accompanied by Mr. and Mrs. George Lauder, are passengers in the Celtic, which sailed for New York to-day.

Mr. Carnegie, who looked in splendid health, had bought a copy of The New York Times, which is now on sale on outgoing boat trains, and gave The New York Times correspondent a ten minutes' chat.

"I am glad to get home," he said, "although I have had a delightful vacation. That is a great speech the President made at Seattle. Mr. Taft is a great statesman."

Asked whether in the course of Mr. Lloyd-George's stay at Skibo Castle his Insurance bill was discussed, Mr. Carnegie replied:

"Yes, we talked about it a great deal. I am very interested in it. Mr. Lloyd-George's scheme stamps him as a great statesman. It is something which in good time our own country must imitate. The distribution of wealth is to be greatly accelerated, and the condition of the masses must be vastly improved. This agitation among the laboring classes is healthful and has only to be judiciously guided to bring us to happier conditions."

When told that Martin Littleton, a member of the committee which is investigating the Steel Trust, was a fellow-passenger in the Celtic, Mr. Carnegie said:

"Then I shall have an opportunity of preaching to him the true gospel."

Asked whether he would testify before the committee, Mr. Carnegie replied:

"Yes, I shall tell them all I know," adding, after a pause, "which isn't much."

The Turkish-Italian war was next spoken of, Mr. Carnegie reiterating his disappointment that "beloved Italia" should have issued her ultimatum, and adding:

"However, I believe it will be peacefully adjusted. You know, I have given a million and a quarter dollars for her hero fund, and don't regret it in the least. Italy has always been beloved of the nations, and I am very glad she accepted the money."

Asked concerning the oath of loyalty to George V. that he took at the presentation to him of the freedom of the City of St. Albans, Mr. Carnegie laughingly admitted it, excusing himself by saying:

"I apprehend no difficulty on that score. King George will have to give me a fair deal. He will have to obey me as well, because, you know, we are all kings in our country."

Finally, Mr. Carnegie spoke of the world's present unrest, saying it was a good thing because "when the world becomes stagnant it wants something to wake it up and keep things marching forward. You will find it will all come right in the end."

Mr. Littleton said he was returning home to attend the Steel Committee meetings, which will begin on Oct. 16. Told that Mr. Carnegie hoped to preach to him the "true gospel," Mr. Littleton laughed, saying, "I've chased him all over Europe, and am now taking him back a prisoner."

While here Mr. Littleton spent some time in studying industrial questions. He is to deliver an address to the Pittsburgh Chamber of Commerce on Oct. 31, on "Industrial Liberty."

WRECKERS DITCH A TRAIN.

Thieves for the Fourth Time in a Month Cause Disaster in Georgia.

Special to The New York Times.

FORT VALLEY, Ga., Oct. 12.—For the fourth time in a month wreckers threw a Central of Georgia train from the rails near here this afternoon. The engine and several coaches left the track, but no one was killed, though the engineer, fireman, and several passengers were injured.

The train was wrecked by spikes being driven between the joints of the rails. When the engine hit the obstruction it left the rails and the coaches followed. Detectives found signs near the track where the wreckers camped.

Three other Central trains have been recently wrecked near here in a similar way, lives being lost in two instances. The repeated attempts to wreck trains has caused the officials of the road to decide to have the track near here patrolled. Detectives think that the wreckers planned to rob the trains after they were derailed, but lost their nerve. Each of the trains wrecked carried large sums of money in the express cars. The Central of Georgia is owned by the Illinois Central.

BEULAH BINFORD PICTURES

On View in a City Theatre Despite the Mayor's Prohibition.

At the Garden Theatre last night motion pictures of Beulah Binford, the girl who became notorious in the trial of Henry Clay Beattie in Virginia recently, were shown for the first time in New York. When Beulah Binford came to New York at the end of the sensational trial, and it was announced that she was posing for a motion-picture concern, orders were issued to the managers of the motion-picture theatres warning them against the exhibition of the films. Revocation of licenses was threatened by the Police Department. There was no interference at the Garden Theatre last night, however. The pictures were put on immediately after Beulah Binford herself had appeared in a short sketch. They purported to tell her life story from childhood up to the trial.

SENATOR CALLS FOR A TRADE YARDSTICK

Jonathan Bourne, Jr., Thinks That Regulation of Corporations Now Demands One.

PROBLEMS NOW TO BE MET

Senate Committee to Attempt a Solution of the Vexatious Ones at Hearings Next Month.

Senator Jonathan Bourne, Jr., of Oregon, President of the National Progressive Republican League, gave out this statement in New York yesterday:

"What is needed is a business yard stick, one that is rigid, never changeable, not fluctuating. What is 'reasonable'? What is 'unreasonable'? Here are two yard sticks provided by the Supreme Court. Are they definite, fixed, ascertained, entirely recognized? Certainly not.

"The Supreme Court has decided that the Standard Oil and Tobacco Companies, as operated in the past, have exceeded in their operations the length or latitude of the legal yard stick.

"How about United States Steel, International Harvester, Smelters, and hundreds of other corporations? They must have the Supreme Court designate their legal yard stick. This means uncertainty, expensive litigation, and long delay. Each corporation must get a clean bill of health from the Supreme Court to know that it is doing a legal business.

"Each yard stick will be different because of the different conditions and methods of each corporation. This is the problem that confronts us. What is the answer? No single brain or single experience can evolve the solution or construct the yard stick. Then what is the desideratum?

"It is to evolve a yard stick that will be applicable to all corporations and business combinations. Is this a judicial, administrative, or legislative function? A legislative Congress, not the Supreme Court, and assuredly not the President or the Attorney General, must solve the problem and must evolve and clearly describe the yard stick.

"How can Congress best accomplish it? At its last extraordinary session the Senate instructed its Committee on Inter-State Commerce by subcommittee, or otherwise, to hold hearings, to summon witnesses. The committee will meet on Nov. 15. Its purpose, presumably, will be ascertainment, not investigation; relief, not persecution; co-operation, not harassment.

"Through this action on the part of the Senate an open forum will be provided where honest and free interchange of ideas based on experience can be assured, where able representatives of both labor and capital, financiers, business magnates, efficiency experts, economic students, producers, and consumers can all be heard. No one person will furnish the solution, evolve the yard stick, but many will furnish experience and ideas having a bearing on the subject.

"Assuming that the hearings will be public, the press, if it has awakened to the realization of the desirability of giving both sides of great questions, should give the American people the benefit of those ideas as expressed by specialists on various lines. Thus great education will be accomplished.

"After the committee has received all these views, opinions based on experience and individual development, it will doubtless arrange, tabulate, analyze, deduce, and conclude as to what exact legal yard stick will best regulate the efforts of centralized wealth so as to serve, first, the general welfare of the Nation, and, second, the co-operative rights of labor and capital, employe, and employer, and the committee's conclusions will be submitted to the Senate, discussed, and undoubtedly legislative action taken. By this process we can get the ideas of the composite citizen, and not the idea of the individual, as represented in the President or in the Attorney General, or the few individuals as represented in the Supreme Court.

"The first question is not the legal form, but the determination based on practical experience and ethics rather than law as to just what is wanted, and just what legislation will supply the want. When that is determined then the lawyers can draw the bill, frame the legislation as to its legal verbiage, Congress enact the legislation, the Supreme Court construe the legal draft rather than the practical purpose, and the Executive, through the administrative machinery, see that its directions are complied with and the individual breaking beyond the legal bars provided in same sent to the penitentiary."

COLUMBUS ABUSED, TOO, MAYOR SAYS

But He Didn't Have to Face a Fresh Edition Every Five Minutes, His Honor Muses.

ALWAYS SO WITH GENIUS

Columbus Day Diners Chuckle as Mr. Gaynor, with an Accusing Eye on Mr. Brisbane, Reviews History.

With an eye on Arthur Brisbane, sitting only a few seats away, Mayor Gaynor at the Columbus Day dinner at the Hotel Astor last night, waxed eloquent over the troubles of Columbus, the subject of libel and slander—"though there wasn't a fresh edition every five minutes." The Mayor's audience chuckled, then laughed, and some rose to their feet and cheered the hit.

Seated beside his Honor at the guest table was William Michael Byrne. Next to Mr. Byrne was George Gordon Battle, and on the right of Mr. Battle was Mr. Brisbane. Mr. Hearst's editor smiled good-naturedly but did not look up.

The Mayor declared that Columbus was one of the greatest men that ever lived, and worthy of every honor this country could bestow on him; that eight States—an interrupter said twenty-nine—had already made Oct. 12 a holiday, and then went on to express the opinion that Europeans should be welcomed to this country, and no steps should be taken to lessen or discourage European immigration, this country being large enough for all.

The Mayor's Speech.

The Mayor said:

"I see one thing that I did which I had no intention of doing in opposing the giving of any money by the city to aid this celebration. I brought about one good result anyway, and that is, a toastmaster that does not talk everybody to death. Heretofore a speaker could not get a word in edgewise.

"Now, that puts me in good accord with you, I hope. I do not really know whether I am or not. I was always afraid to come over, to tell the truth, because I thought some of you might harbor up this matter about the money and give me a very cold reception, if not a cold shoulder.

"But I guess it is all right, Mr. Loft, by the looks of things. In fact, I know it is, because in witnessing the magnificent parade this afternoon, one of the finest ever seen in the City of New York, or on this continent, I believe, I was informed officially that not only had money enough been raised by private subscription, including my own small one, to pay for the parade, but to pay for everything, and have $1,500 left over.

"It was not so much a misfortune that the city treasury did not help you out. It taught you that you can do it yourselves. If there were not public sentiment in this great city of five millions and its environments to pay for a pageant and a celebration here in honor of the discoverer of this continent, then this celebration might well be left undone.

"All's well that ends well, and this thing has ended magnificently. After it is a fixed fact, the wonder is that Columbus Day was not made a legal holiday a hundred years ago in this country. I believe that eight other States have made it a legal holiday. (Voice in the audience, "twenty-nine States all told.") You see how little I know about it. It is well to have somebody to tell me when I make a misstatement.

"I suppose sooner or later the National Government will make it a legal holiday. It was the fortune of this man to achieve a thing so great as to make his name immortal for ever.

Discovery an Accident.

"It is true that by accident, or at all events without design, that Columbus discovered this continent. But his great achievement was not an accident. He had brooded on it for years. It was life study. He patiently toiled at it. I see him to-night off this remote coast patiently and calmly and silently pacing the deck of his flagship and brooding over that one subject that had occupied his mind for many many years.

"He had gone about with that project here and there. It was the same as it is with men of genius now. Nobody entertained him. There were plenty to rebuff him. There were plenty to slander him. There were plenty to libel him, although there was no edition issued every five minutes at that time as there sometimes is now.

"But through it all we see his monumental greatness as exhibited in his patience and his perseverance. No expression is truer in this world than that patience is the possession of great souls, and never was it better illustrated and shown than in the great soul of this man, Christopher Columbus.

"This preparation for his work we seldom get in history. His life is stated and given as though it all occurred in three months. Oh, dear me! Three months!

"You would think it was all done up in a month or two with Caesar. But he was ten long years patiently toiling in Gaul, fighting a battle once or twice a year. You would think from history that he was fighting all the time and doing nothing else. But it was not so. He was patiently toiling, as Columbus toiled. He was getting ready.

"You can do nothing in this world without getting ready. Genius consists in getting ready. To accomplish a result you have to organize the conditions. There is no other way to do it. These are lessons which we have to learn from such events and such men.

"Another reason why it is fitting that Columbus Day should be made a legal holiday is that so many of his countrymen have come to this country. I don't really know how many are in this city, but I suppose there are more Italians here than in any city in Italy. How is that, Judge Freschi? You will have to correct me if I am wrong.

Italians in This City.

"One man told me yesterday there were 250,000 Italians in the City of New York, and a man told me to-day there were 800,000. So I reckon there are about 500,000. I think that is about right. And good citizens they are, too. They have the traits of their nation. They come from a great race. They come from that great Mediterranean basin, where the civilization of the world once clustered—in that Mediterranean basin that gave light and letters to Europe. That has a history, a long history, of the most exalted character in ancient and modern times.

"And they have the traits of their ancestors, and they are good citizens. Some people say, with a tone of disgust, 'Oh, we ought to shut them all out, and not allow them to come into this country!' Oh, dear me!

"How did those people get into this country, I wonder, except in the same way? Some of them, maybe, came over or their ancestors, on ticket-of-leave. They don't seem to remember that very

Continued on Page 3.

OWEN WISTER DYING.

Wife Hurrying to Him in Wyoming in Special Train.

Special to The New York Times.

CLEVELAND, Ohio, Oct. 12.—Speeding westward in a special train, Mrs. Mary Channing Wister, wife of Owen Wister, author of "The Virginian," is hurrying to his bedside in Wyoming, where he is reported as near death.

Mrs. Wister was attending the convention of the Pennsylvania Federation of Women's Clubs at Erie and arrived there Tuesday. She was scheduled to deliver an address and was ready to speak when she received a telegram announcing the fact that her husband was seriously ill. She left the hall immediately, hired a special train, and started for the West.

Mr. Wister is on Struther Burt's ranch in Wyoming, where he got the material for many of his Western stories. Mrs. Wister has been with him all Summer up to the time of her trip to Cleveland. He was in poor health when he went away from his home in Philadelphia and has not been well for three years.

ANOTHER JEFFERSON DAVIS.

A Great-Grandson of the Confederacy's President Is Born.

Special to The New York Times.

DENVER, Col., Oct. 12.—The first great-grandson of the President of the Southern Confederacy, Jefferson Davis, was born to Mr. and Mrs. Jefferson Hayes Davis here to-day. He is named after his great-grandfather.

The baby's father is the son of Winnie Davis Hayes and J. A. Hayes, a banker, of Colorado Springs. He had his name changed to Jefferson Davis in honor of his grandfather on the maternal side. The change in name was legalized by an act of the Colorado Legislature.

Mrs. Davis was formerly Miss Dora De Witt, daughter of Dr. Theodore De Witt of Broadmoore, a fashionable suburb of Colorado Springs. The baby, if he lives, will inherit a million or more.

GAINED $107,000 IN TRANSIT.

But Cargo of Sugar from Java Had to Pay $180,000 Duty.

PHILADELPHIA, Oct. 12.—Unusual interest was manifested in the arrival of the British steamship Kwarra with sugar from Java to-day by reason of the fact that the vessel's cargo increased in value in transit more than $107,000. The Kwarra sailed from Java on Aug. 1, bound for the McCahan refinery here. When the six thousand tons of sugar were put on board the value per 112 pounds was 14s 6d. Yesterday's quotations for Java sugar were 18s 6d. The advance of four shillings in the price will net the owners $107,140 over the original purchase price.

The duty paid on the Kwarra's cargo amounted to $180,000, on a basis of $30 per ton.

LABOR TROUBLE SHOOTING.

Marble Worker Shot and Left Badly Wounded in the Street.

Shot twice as the outcome of labor troubles, as he claimed, Thomas Bernie, a marble polisher, was removed from Thirteenth Street and Avenue A late last night to Bellevue Hospital in a serious condition. He had been wounded in the right shoulder, and there was also a bullet in his chest. The unidentified man, who attempted to kill Bernie, made his escape before the arrival of Policeman Brennan of the Fifth Street Station.

Bernie said that for the past two weeks he had been living with a sister in Thirteenth Street, between Avenues A and B. He said he was employed by the Astoria marble firm of Voska, Goetsch & Siglo, and that he had been working on an uncompleted building for the firm at Forty-eighth Street and Broadway.

There had been trouble, Bernie asserted, between the men employed on the building. He admitted, the police say, that he had taken an active part with one of the factions, and declared he believed that his assailant was one of the workmen on the other side. He could not give an accurate description of his assailant. He is expected to die.

THREE AIRMEN DYING.

MM. Level, Germain, and Horta All Believed to be Mortally Injured.

RHEIMS, Oct. 12.—M. Level, the aviator, was probably mortally injured by a fall to-day. He was sweeping along in his biplane about 250 feet from the earth, in superb weather, when something went wrong with the machinery, and the aeroplane plunged down, striking a telegraph pole in its descent.

M. Level was senseless and barely alive when he was taken from the wreck. It was found that his skull and spine had been fractured.

The condition of Andre Germain, who was injured in a fall with his aeroplane yesterday, is considered hopeless.

CHARLEVILLE, France, Oct. 12.—M. Horta, a student of aviation, while practicing at a height of thirty feet to-day, fell, receiving internal injuries which, it is expected, will cause his death.

His machine capsized.

DENIES CANAL WORK DELAY.

Bensel Answers Republican Club's Attack Regarding the Troy Dam.

SYRACUSE, N. Y., Oct. 12.—John A. Bensel, State Engineer, in an address before the Chamber of Commerce to-day answered the attack made on him a few days ago by the Republican Club of New York in regard to the Troy dam and the delay in the construction of the Barge Canal. Mr. Bensel said:

"This season has seen the largest amount of construction work done on the canal since the work was begun. It has also seen the failure on the part of the canal system to hold water in the vicinity of Rochester, due to poor engineering, and the most rapid repair work on this same section, considering its magnitude, ever accomplished was done under the direction of the present Superintendent of Public Works, who put the canal in a workable condition in four weeks.

"No delay has been occasioned by any action which the State has taken looking toward the building by the State of the dam at the outlet of the canal system in the Hudson River, and thus preserve for the people their rights in the water power developed, and there is no reason in my mind why the United States Government should be requested to take charge of this easterly end of the canal system."

LORD STRATHCONA VERY ILL.

Nonogenarian Canadian Reported to be in a Dangerous Condition.

Special to The New York Times.

CHICAGO, Oct. 12.—A brief cablegram received in this city to-night says that Lord Strathcona, High Commissioner of Canada in London, who is 91 years old, is dangerously ill in London.

Lord Strathcona, the telegram states, was stricken upon his arrival in London yesterday after a journey from England to Canada and back that occupied only fifteen days.

CHINA REVOLT GROWING FAST

Concerted Rising of People Aims at Republic in Place of Manchu Empire.

MANY REBEL SUCCESSES

Hankow and Han-Yang, with Imperial Arsenal, Taken—Capitals of Other Provinces in Revolt.

FOREIGNERS ARE PROTECTED

Rebels Organized and Well Financed—Peking Rushing Army and Navy to Stem Rising Tide.

HANKOW, Oct. 12.—The revolution which has been hanging over China for months past and of which the rising in the province of Sze-Chuen was only a small part has begun in earnest. It is a concerted movement to take the empire and declare a republic. The noted exiled revolutionist, Dr. Sun Yat Sen, leader of the anti-Manchu party, if the plans do not miscarry, is to be elected President. He was the delegate of the revolutionary party to the United States in 1910 and is believed, during that tour, to have made arrangements for the financing of the movement.

Sun Yu, a brother of Dr. Sun Yat Sen, who is now in Hankow, has been elected President of the Provincial Assembly, and Tang Hua Lung, the retiring President of the Assembly and a well-known scholar, has been elected Governor of Hu-Peh.

The whole Assembly has seceded from the imperial Government. The rebels are well organized and financially strong. They have confiscated the local treasuries and banks and are issuing their own paper money, redeeming the Government notes with this, as the foreign banks are refusing the Government notes.

The revolutionaries who two days ago captured Wu-Chang have crossed the Yang-Tse River and occupied the native section—comprising the whole city except the foreign concessions of Hankow and Han-Yang. All are adjoining cities in Hu-Peh Province. Chang-Sha, capital of Hu-Nen, is reported to have risen in revolt, and Nanking, capital of the Province of Kiang-Su, is on the verge of a rising, several public buildings having been destroyed, including the yamens of the Viceroy and the Tartar General.

Thousands of soldiers have joined the mutiny in Hu-Peh.

Twenty miles of the Peking & Hankow Railway has been torn up and the bridges burned.

Many Manchus have been killed and the terrified people are fleeing from the cities into the country, carrying their belongings. The prisons have been opened and the criminals liberated. There has been fighting in the streets, but the most stringent orders have been issued that the lives of foreigners and their property shall be respected.

An American expedition which was dispatched from Hankow to Wu-Chang for the purpose of aiding the missionaries there returned here to-day with all the missionaries, with the exception of Miss R. A. Kemp of the Episcopal Society, the members of the Roman Catholic mission, including the sisters and the London mission, who declined to depart.

There was a brief exchange of shots to-day between the Wu-Chang forts and a loyal Chinese cruiser. The firing ceased after the British and Japanese officials had protested that it endangered the foreign concessions.

When the revolutionists swept across the river they followed their previous policy in Wu-Chang, avoiding any attack on the foreign concessions. The Methodist missionaries in Wu-Chang escaped over the walls and are known to be safe.

A special proclamation issued by the rebel General in charge of the forces in Hu-Peh states that the penalty for any interference with foreigners or with commerce shall be instant death. The proclamation further declares: "This is the army of the people. We will overthrow the tyrant Manchu dynasty and revive the rights of the real Chinese."

The foreigners of Hankow, Wu-Chang, and Han-Yang have been assembled and were entering the foreign concessions this evening. They report that they received every attention and consideration at the hands of the revolutionists.

The capture of Han-Yang, which is a town of perhaps 100,000 just north of Hankow, has delivered into the hands of the revolutionists the arsenal and the important Han-Yang iron works. The revolutionists had no trouble in Han-Yang, overwhelmingly outnumbering the local troops. Gen. Chang Piao escaped by flight, and the members of the local Government were dispersed.

The popularity of the revolutionary movement all along the river and in the interior is indicated by apparently authentic reports that several near-by cities have fallen. Where resistance was offered the rebel forces, the towns appear to have been put to the torch.

The losses in the fighting aggregate several hundred, but practically all the dead are Manchus. The slogan of the movement, which is guided by shrewd and temperate leaders, is evidently "down with the Manchus."

PEKING SENDS TROOPS.

Two Divisions Ordered to Hankow—Navy Also Ordered There.

PEKING, Oct. 12.—The Chinese Government has awakened to the danger of the revolution in Hu-Peh Province. Gen. Yin Tchang, the Minister of War, left hurriedly this evening for Pao-Ting-Fu, 100 miles to the south of Peking, where the Sixth Division of the army is making hasty preparations to leave to-morrow for Hankow. An imperial edict issued to-day ordered the immediate dispatch of

"All the News That's Fit to Print."

The New York Times.

THE WEATHER.
Increasingly cloudy, rain to-night and on Saturday; colder Saturday night; wind variable.
For full weather report see Page 21.

VOL. LXI...NO. 19,767. * * * NEW YORK, FRIDAY, MARCH 8, 1912.—TWENTY-TWO PAGES. ONE CENT In Greater New York, Jersey City, and Newark. | Elsewhere, TWO CENTS.

MRS. W. W. JACOBS IS SENT TO PRISON

Wife of Novelist Sentenced to Month's Hard Labor for Smashing Windows in London.

"DUTY TO HER CHILDREN"

Her Defense and Husband's Plea Fail—More Suffragette Window-Breaking Yesterday.

By Marconi Transatlantic Wireless Telegraph to The New York Times.

LONDON, Friday, March 8.—Undeterred by the hard labor sentences passed by the Magistrates on suffragists earlier in the week, a number of women early yesterday morning waited in the West End for the taking down of the shutters in front of the shops, and as soon as the glass was exposed smashed the expensive windows of some big establishments. Among the windows destroyed were some of the largest in London. Half a dozen of the "militants" were arrested, and doubtless heavy sentences await them.

The latest prominent convict-recruit to the ranks of the militant suffragettes is Mrs. Eleanor Jacobs, wife of W. W. Jacobs, the novelist, who was sentenced to a month's imprisonment at hard labor by Magistrate Fordham at the West London Police Court yesterday for breaking four windows in the Earl's Court Road Post Office on Wednesday afternoon. When asked by the Magistrate what she had to say, she replied:

"I have done this because I think it is my duty as the mother of five children."

"Was it your duty as the mother of children to smash property?" asked the Magistrate.

"Yes, that is the only way we can protest against the action, or rather the inaction of the Government in refusing us justice," responded Mrs. Jacobs.

The Magistrate remarked that her statement was absurd and started to remand her for eight days to have a doctor report on her state of mind.

The defendant smilingly replied:

"My mind is quite sound. I have done my duty to my children for twelve years. I think my daughters, when they grow up, should have equal rights and responsibilities and duties with my sons."

Later in the afternoon Mr. Jacobs appeared before the Magistrate and pleaded for his wife, saying that she had taken this attitude because she conceived it her duty to her children that she should support the movement. He asked the Magistrate to consider that for a long time persons like his wife had been under the influence of two leaders of the movement, Mr. and Mrs. Pethick Lawrence.

He said he could not speak too highly of her as a wife and mother, and hoped the court would extend leniency to her and not inflict on her the hardships which very properly, no doubt, had been inflicted on many of these misguided women. His wife, he said, could not stand hardship, and if called upon to endure it her health would be permanently affected; she did not realize what she was doing.

He wished to say that if the Government had not played with the question, his wife and those other unhappy women would not have been brought into their present position.

The Magistrate, while expressing sympathy with the novelist, said there was no reason why he should deal more leniently with Mrs. Jacobs than with a vagabond who broke a window for a night's lodging, and passed sentence of one month's imprisonment at hard labor.

LONDON, Friday, March 8.—The extent to which the window-smashing raids of the suffragettes has aroused public feeling against them was evidenced by the large force of foot and mounted police necessary to protect them from a great mob, carrying an effigy of Miss Christabel Pankhurst, which gathered outside Oscar Hammerstein's London Opera House, where the militant section of the suffragists held a meeting last night. The speeches at the meeting were tame and there was a noticeable absence of all incitement to violence.

One woman speaker said that, if any woman desired to judge the panic the latest actions of the suffragettes had caused, let her go to the nearest store and try to borrow a hammer.

A large band of medical students created disorderly scenes outside the Opera House.

The excitement into which London has been thrown by the activity of the suffragettes is indicated by the instructions last night that ladies will not be admitted to Buckingham Palace for the Court tonight unless they present their invitation cards, and also by the announcement that both Houses of Parliament will be closed to the public to-day.

The public was practically asked yesterday to help the police catch the window smashers. The Commissioner of Police issued a circular calling attention to the fact that under the common law anybody is empowered to restrain persons attempting to do such damage and to hold them until a policeman arrives, and, similarly, persons detected after the damage is done.

WOULD SMASH IN PHILADELPHIA

Militant Suffragist Threatens Violence Like That in London.

Special to The New York Times.

PHILADELPHIA, March 7.—Miss Lida Stokes Adams, prominent in the National Women's Suffrage Association, declares that unless the women of Pennsylvania get the ballot the suffragette riots of London may be repeated in this city.

Miss Adams is a militant suffragist. She believes that the women of this country are seeking the ballot in too mild a manner and that if they would use a little muscle instead of voice for argument the cause would advance in a more rapid manner.

FOUR DEAD IN TRAIN WRECK.

Thirty Also Hurt in Wabash Crash—Six Coaches Off the Track.

Special to The New York Times.

LAFAYETTE, Ind., March 7.—The Continental Limited No. 1 of the Wabash Railroad, which left Lafayette an hour and a half late, was wrecked at Redwood Curve, a mile and a half west of West Lebanon, Ind., thirty-five miles from here, at 3 o'clock this afternoon, and as the accident tore down all wires, communication with the scene of the wreck was difficult.

Four persons were killed and thirty injured.

The dead are Mrs. U. G. Good, who boarded the train at Fort Wayne, Ind., en route to St. Louis, and died almost instantly, her back being broken; Mrs. Grant, en route from Adrian, Mich., to Kansas City; a Pullman porter, name unknown, and an unknown youth about 18 years old.

The seriously injured are Mrs. Paul Triesce, Danville, internally hurt; May Hudson, Sidney, Ill., cut and bruised; Fred Henschen, St. Louis, traveling auditor Wabash Railroad, hurt about head. Among those less seriously hurt are William P. Howell, Indianapolis; W. C. Thoma, Toledo; Sherman Sayres, Lafayette, Ind.; A. R. Kitsero, Peru, Ind.; Charles Rhodenburg, Dallas, Texas; E. F. Jennings, Buffalo, N. Y.; E. C. Kohl, Crawfordsville, Ind.; L. H. Robinson, Camden, N. J., and F. Barker, Elmira, N. Y.

The entire train of six coaches left the track, but the engine remained on the rails. A wreck train with physicians on board hurried to the scene.

A broken rail is believed to have caused the wreck. The coaches are piled in confusion on the side of a thirty-foot embankment. The tracks are all blocked, and other trains are detouring.

LONE WINDOW SMASHER HERE

Staten Island Girl Takes a Cue from the London Suffragettes.

Miss Annie Glisman, 22 years old, whose home is between Prince's Bay and Pleasant Plains, S. I., has been deeply interested in reading of the exploits of the London suffragettes, and last night she started out on a lone window-smashing crusade.

Miss Glisman first made her way to the home of Alderman Charles Cole, in Prince's Bay, and, after announcing her presence by breaking a window with a stone, rang the doorbell. The Alderman opened the door, and to him the young woman announced that she was a suffragette and had come to demand her rights. She did not explain what she deemed her rights, but declared that if the Alderman did not do something she would stone the house.

Mr. Cole tried to calm her and cautioned her against violence. Then he called his wife to the door to talk to the young woman while he went to the telephone to notify the police. While he was at the telephone the young woman went away, but she was soon heard from in the neighborhood. Stopping in front of several houses, she hurled stones through the windows.

Detectives responded to the call of Alderman Cole, but Miss Glisman eluded them for some time. Finally she was taken to the station, and from there was sent to the City Farm Colony in New Springville, where she will be examined as to her sanity.

OLD MAN-O'-WAR IN CHAIRS.

Daedalus, Sea-Fighter of a Century Ago, Done Into Furniture.

Timbers from the man-o-war Daedalus, which was an aristocrat of the British Navy a century ago when fighting ships were wearing oak armor belts, have been lying for the past month in the wood yard of F. Eckenroth & Son, 921 East Fifth Street.

They were brought over from England several weeks ago in the Mesaba, of the Atlantic Transportation Company's line to be worked up into household furniture for a residence which is being built at 46 East Seventeenth Street for Stephen C. Clark, a real estate dealer at 149 Broadway.

The timbers were square sawed stanchions of oak fourteen and sixteen inches in thickness, which had acted as supports to the main deck of the man-o'-war. It took several weeks to get them ready for the saw by drawing out the spikes and bolts with which every piece was found to be loaded.

The timbers, cut up, were taken yesterday to Sherwin & Co., wood workers, at 287 East 137th Street, where they will be finished into chairs, tables and trimmings for the dining room and library of Mr. Clark's house.

Mr. Clark said last night that seasoned oak had been ordered from England and that it was purely accidental that the wood purchased had been part of a dismantled warship.

JUMPS INTO NIAGARA RAPIDS.

Man on Freight Train Seeks Death in the Whirlpool.

Special to The New York Times.

BUFFALO, N. Y., March 7.—An unidentified man jumped from a Michigan Central freight train to death in the Niagara whirlpool rapids late this evening. The train was on its way from Canada, and it is believed by the Niagara Falls police that the suicide boarded the train at the Canadian end of the bridge.

When the train was about half way across the cantilever bridge and directly over the whirlpool one of the crew saw a man climb to the top of a car, jump over the low rail a few feet away, and disappear.

NEW OIL CAPITAL $30,000,000.

Standard Company of Indiana Arranging for Increase of Stock.

WHITING, Ind., March 7.—The stockholders of the Standard Oil Company of Indiana to-day voted to increase the capital stock of the Indiana corporation from $1,000,000 to $30,000,000.

After the increase has been referred to the Indiana State authorities and a certificate issued by the Secretary of State the Directors of the Standard Oil Company of Indiana will direct the distribution of the stock of the company in accordance with the reorganization plan approved by the United States Court.

HONORS FOR MRS. ROOSEVELT

Costa Rica Government Put Special Train at Her Disposal.

SAN JOSE, Costa Rica, March 7.—Mrs. Theodore Roosevelt and her daughter, Miss Ethel, arrived at Port Limon this morning.

The visit of the wife and daughter of the ex-President of the United States was a surprise to the Government, which took steps immediately to place a special train at their disposal to bring them to San José. Preparations are being made by a women's Reception Committee to entertain the visitors.

TREATIES, SHORN, PASS SENATE, 76 TO 3

Clause Invading Senate's Rights Is Eliminated and Other Restrictions Are Added.

ROOSEVELTIAN VOTES DECIDE

Four Such Senators Defeat Taft's Arbitration Aims—Existing Treaties Suffice, Say Opponents.

Special to The New York Times.

WASHINGTON, March 7.—The Senate brought the debate on the general arbitration treaties with Great Britain and France to an end to-day by unanimous consent, and then proceeded to take from the treaties nearly everything that marked their least advance on the fifteen treaties drafted in 1908 and 1909, when Senator Root was Secretary of State. The single point of advance left in the treaties provides for a Joint High Commission of Inquiry to investigate disputes and their arbitrability, but gives the commission no powers of award. As amended, the treaties were ratified by a vote of 76 to 3.

The turn of affairs adverse to the textual integrity of the treaties came as a surprise to the leaders of the Senate and the supporters of the Administration. It had been known that the ratification of the treaties by the Senate could be obtained only by means of some device like the Lodge resolution of ratification, which, while leaving the treaties unamended internally, so construed them as to deprive the Joint High Commission of its final powers of sending disputes to arbitration and reserved the Senate's full powers of advice and consent. But it had been hoped that the appearance of victory would be saved to the Administration by retaining unimpaired the language in which the treaties were submitted to the Senate.

The defeat of Mr. Taft's plans resulted from the defection of four Roosevelt Senators, who, with two other Republicans, joined the almost solid Democratic vote in insisting upon the elimination bodily from the treaties of the third clause of Article III., which made the decisions of the High Commission final as to the arbitrability of differences.

Col. Roosevelt has sharply assailed the treaties in editorials and speeches. In general, it can be said that the amendments seeking to weaken the treaties had the support of the Democrats, Roosevelt Republicans, and a few unclassified Republicans. But by a strange coincidence the only Senator who voted throughout for every proposal to weaken the treaties was William Lorimer of Illinois, who is Mr. Roosevelt's bitterest enemy in the Senate. At the last it was he who, with Mr. Reed of Missouri, and Mr. Martine of New Jersey—two radical Democrats—voted against ratification.

Bone of Contention Removed.

The test vote came as soon as debate ended. It was on the original amendment reported last Summer from the Committee on Foreign Relations eliminating Clause 3 of Article III., which has always been the bone of contention. The clause was stricken out by a vote of 42 to 40.

The vote for the amendment was made up of thirty-six Democrats and six Republicans. The vote against the amendment was made up of thirty-seven Republicans and three Democrats. The Republicans who voted to strike out the important clause were Mr. Borah of Idaho, Mr. Bourne of Oregon, Mr. Bristow of Kansas, and Mr. Dixon of Montana—all Roosevelt sympathizers—and Mr. Lorimer of Illinois and Mr. Smith of Michigan. The Democrats who voted for the retention of the clause were Mr. Rayner of Maryland, Mr. Thornton of Alabama, and John Sharp Williams of Mississippi.

Then Mr. Culberson of Texas offered an amendment to the body of the treaties exempting from its terms all questions of vital interest, independence, honor, or the interests of third parties. That amendment failed by a vote of 37 to 45, though subsequently the object of the amendment was accomplished in an amendment to the resolution of ratification. Mr. Bacon then unsuccessfully offered to the body of the treaties the amendment, subsequently adopted as part of the resolution of ratification, exempting from the operation of the treaty all questions of immigration, State bonds, Territorial integrity, the Monroe Doctrine, and all issues of American policy. As an amendment to the body of the treaty this motion was lost by a tie vote, 41 to 41.

The second change actually made in the text of the treaties was contained in an amendment offered by Mr. Chamberlain, a Democrat from Oregon. He excepted from the operation of the treaties all questions concerning the admission of aliens to the schools of the several States or their admission into the United States. This amendment, which, of course, has no bearing upon the present treaties, but looks merely to the possible negotiation of similar treaties with Japan and China, was adopted by a vote of 40 to 38.

The question of final ratification then came up, and Mr. Lodge, after explaining that the elimination of Clause 3 of Article III. made his carefully worded resolution of ratification unnecessary, withdrew it and offered instead a simple resolution declaring the treaty with Great Britain ratified. To that Mr. Bacon of Georgia offered his former amendment, and by the change in half a dozen votes it was adopted, 46 to 36. The amended resolution was then adopted, a two-thirds vote being necessary. All votes affecting the British treaty were then voted to apply to the French convention.

Treaties' Purpose Destroyed.

The language of the Bacon amendment shows how completely the significance of the new treaties has been destroyed. It reads:

Resolved further, That the Senate advises and consents to the ratification of the said treaty with the understanding, to be made a part of such ratification, that the treaty does not authorize the submission to arbitration of any question which affects the admission of aliens into the United States, or the admission of aliens to the educational institutions of the several States, or the territorial integrity of the several States or of the United States, or concerning the question of the alleged indebtedness or moneyed obligation of any State of the United States, or any question which depends upon or involves the maintenance of the traditional attitude of the United States concerning American questions, commonly described as the Monroe Doctrine, or other purely Governmental policy.

The debate was significant from the fact that all the opponents of the pending treaties, declared their belief that the treaties already in force as negotiated by Mr. Root as Secretary of State were superior in phraseology and definiteness. Mr. Root himself made a striking address in behalf of the treaties, though, like Mr. Lodge, who also supported them, he favored the Lodge resolution of ratification on striking out the plenary powers of the Joint High Commission.

A SWEDISH GIANT.

Intellectually, August Strindberg is looked up to as a power in literature. One who visited him writes of this big personality in

NEXT SUNDAY'S TIMES.

TRIES TO KILL GIRLS, BLOWS HIMSELF UP

Coachman George Mead Terribly Beats Young Women with Steel Molding, Then Ends His Life.

USED A STICK OF DYNAMITE

Fancied Injury by the Girls' Father, the Rev. Frank Hartfield, Cause of Tragedy Near Brewsters, N. Y.

Special to The New York Times.

BREWSTERS, N. Y., March 7.—In their home, Stonehenge Cottage, in Sodom, twelve miles from here, the Misses Ruby and Amy Hartfield, daughters of the Rev. Frank Hartfield, rector of the Episcopal Church here, and granddaughters of Mrs. Seth B. Howes, widow of a wealthy showman and owner of a large estate known as the Castle, about a mile and a half from this village, are recovering from the attack made on them yesterday by George Mead, their grandmother's coachman and the caretaker of her house, in her absence.

All that remains of Mead was taken to-day from the morgue to the little cottage near the Howes estate, to which he brought his bride less than six months ago. Mead, facing capture at the hands of employes of H. H. Vreeland, former head of the Metropolitan Street Railway Company, blew himself to pieces with a stick of dynamite. His young wife is prostrated.

Miss Ruby Hartfield is 20 years old, and her sister is 18. Mead was 32 years old, having entered the employ of Mr. Howes 16 years ago.

Apparently, Mead intended to kill both the girls and perhaps himself at the same time, to avenge a fancied wrong at the hands of their father. Mead is known to have believed it was by the rector's advice that Mrs. Howes, on leaving for the Winter, four months ago, refused to allow him the use of her automobiles, that he might learn to be a chauffeur, and also reduced his coachman's wages of $45 a month to $30 a month for acting as caretaker. No later than Tuesday Mead threatened to "get square" with the rector.

The attack on the girls was made at about 3 o'clock, when they reached The Castle, after a twelve-mile drive from home, bringing keys to the place, in response to a telephone message from Mead that the wind had blown loose a shutter and he must enter the house to repair this. The girls drove into the stable, from an upper window of which they had seen Mead peering as they ascended the driveway. The man was down the stairs almost before the girls were in the stable, and he bolted the door behind them.

Struck Girls Down.

Both girls were alarmed at his action, but alighted from their pony carriage. Ruby stepped toward Mead to hand him the keys, and he sprang at her, bringing up a steel moulding which he had held behind him, and striking her on the head. As the girl sank, he caught her and struck her again and again.

As Mead dragged Ruby into a washroom, Amy stood, too frightened to scream. Then she rushed toward Mead, crying:

"If you are going to kill her, kill me, too."

Mead dropped the elder sister and sprang at Amy. He struck her once on the head, and the girl fell to her knees. Evidently believing that he had stunned her, Mead jumped back to the other girl. Amy, however, staggered to the stable door, pushed it outward a few inches, and screamed.

Her cries were heard by Dennis Hogan, gardener on the Vreeland estate, who hurried to the stable. Amy faltered an explanation. On the floor of the washroom he found Ruby, her face covered with blood. Mead was not to be seen, but a door into the carriage house showed how he had escaped.

Hogan raised the girl, and carrying her started toward the Vreeland place with Amy clinging to his arm. They had nearly reached the road when they were prostrated by an explosion.

The report reached the ears of A. B. Yates in the Vreeland stable, and he hurried to the scene. With Hogan he got the girls to a safe place, and telephoned to Dr. F. Robert Ritchey, who came with Constable Arthur Brown and Deputy Sheriff H. S. Brown.

The officers found the front of the building almost blown to pieces. Every window was shattered and the south wall bulged outward. Within, the flooring was blown into splinters, but the pony and the cart stood unharmed in the wreckage. The post to which the pony had been tethered was torn from the floor. The two-inch oak partition, which separated the washroom from the main stable, was blown out.

Man Blown to Pieces.

In a corner of the washroom lay Mead's head, neck, part of his left shoulder, and his left arm. His body had been blown to pieces, and his legs and right arm were found in different corners of the room. Most of the damage was confined to the washroom. In the stable two horses, besides the pony, were unhurt, and both of Mrs. Howes's automobiles were not damaged.

On a shelf in the washroom the officers found two sticks of dynamite. One end of the shelf on which they rested was blown away, but the sticks had not exploded. It was with one like these, it is believed, that Mead killed himself. He had the dynamite there to blow up stumps on the place.

Mead's body was taken to the morgue here and afterward claimed by his young wife. Coroner Smith said he would hold an inquest as soon as the Misses Hartfield were well enough to appear before him as witnesses.

Seven stitches were taken in Amy's scalp and thirteen in patching up wounds on the head of Ruby. The girls are still confined to their bed.

PREDICT STOCKING FAMINE.

White Costumes Will Be Incomplete Unless the Retailers Hurry Up.

The increased demand for white dress fabrics for summer is regarded in the New York hosiery market as an infallible indication that white hosiery will be popular.

Many of the stocking mills are preparing to meet the expected demand, which it is believed will exceed that of last year. It is predicted that the failure of retail buyers to appreciate this will cause a shortage in the supply before the season is very far advanced. At the present time buyers are ordering sparingly, and it is said that the rush of orders later on will overwhelm the mills.

AMUNDSEN REACHES THE SOUTH POLE; STAYS FOUR DAYS, DEC. 14 TO 17, 1911; PARTY ALL WELL, HE TELLS THE TIMES

Norwegian Explorer Sends Word of His Success From Tasmania.

NO NEWS FROM CAPT. SCOTT

London Waits Anxiously for Word That He, Too, Has Attained the Goal.

AMUNDSEN'S FULL STORY

Will Be Published Exclusively in The New York Times, Probably To-morrow.

SHACKLETON GIVES PRAISE

Believes Norwegian Was Aided by Good Weather and His Special Equipment.

EXPLORERS MAY HAVE MET

Possible That Their Parties Came Together on the Routes Converging Toward the Goal.

AMUNDSEN ANNOUNCES HIS DISCOVERY

Special Cable to The New York Times.

Christiania, Norway, March 7.

I have received the following message:

HOBART, Tasmania, Thursday, March 7, 1912—Pole attained, fourteenth—seventeenth December, 1911. All well. ROALD AMUNDSEN.

(Signed) LEON AMUNDSEN.

WARNING.

For the protection of Capt. Amundsen, who has risked his life in the attainment of the south pole, and whose chief material reward must be the proceeds of the sale of his narrative, The New York Times, which has purchased the rights thereto for the United States, to be duly protected by copyright, gives notice that it will prosecute any infringement whatsoever of such copyright.

(Photograph, American Press Association.)

Roald Amundsen

He Discovered the Northwest Passage, and To-day His Triumphant Attainment of the South Pole Is Announced.

SHACKLETON ON THE FEAT.

Famous Antarctic Explorer Analyzes the Performance of Amundsen.

By SIR ERNEST SHACKLETON.

Specially Contributed to The New York Times and London Chronicle.

Special Cable to THE NEW YORK TIMES.

LONDON, March 7.—Analyzing the somewhat brief cable to hand, announcing Capt. Amundsen's attainment of the south pole, one, from previous experience, would assume that the journey was done with extreme rapidity and under very favorable conditions as regards the weather.

Capt. Amundsen has attained the geographical south pole, the long-sought-for spot, and that finishes record breaking as far as the ends of the earth are concerned.

Assuming that the latitude of Amundsen's Winter quarters was 74° 44′, that is only 676 geographical miles from the south pole. This place was named Bay of Whales by me on my expedition, and was formerly known as Balloon Bight. If Amundsen did fifteen miles a day and reached the south pole on Dec. 14, he would have started south about the beginning of November, but it is much more likely that he did not travel at that rate, especially for the first hundred or two odd miles, so we may assume that he started for the pole about the beginning of October.

There is no indication in the cable whether Amundsen followed the route of my expedition in reaching the mountains that guard the approach to the pole. It may be possible that he found a new route and an easier one up to the plateau which lies about 9,000 to 11,000 feet above sea level. He may have had good weather.

Took Three Days to be Sure.

The words of the cablegram, "Pole attained, Dec. 14 to 17," evidently mean that on reaching the geographical pole, so that no uncertainty should exist as to his exact position, he waited three days, taking noon observations so as accurately to determine his position.

The advantage of taking three days of continuous observations at the pole are as follows:

Assuming that an explorer took a noon observation of the altitude of the sun and found that he was at the pole, a degree of uncertainty would still exist because of the slow movement of the sun, which completes the circle with hardly any perceptible rise or fall. If an observation is taken for the second day at the same spot, and the difference of declination of the sun in its north or south path corresponds with his observation of the day before, and it does this for the third day, he may safely assume that his position is accurate.

A flying snapshot is not as reliable as a continuous series of observations. If he were using a theodolite, undoubtedly the most accurate instrument, there is no doubt that he could ascertain the position of the pole to one mile.

If Capt. Amundsen left the pole on Dec. 17 he would very likely, with a fair wind behind him, return to Winter quarters in about forty-five days. We left our "furthest south," which was, roughly speaking, 100 miles north of the pole, on Jan. 9, and reached our Winter quarters on Feb. 28. They were 650 geographical miles from the pole, approximately the same length of journey that Amundsen would have covered from the pole to his Winter quarters, as they were ninety miles further south than ours.

We then assume that Capt. Amundsen reached Bay of Whales at the end of January. He would take two or three days loading up and getting under way with the Fram. He would then presumably go north and work to the westward of Cape Adare, and then get into the westerly winds and make Hobart, Tasmania. The Fram, being a slow vessel, doing about five knots, it would take quite a month, unless there were strong winds behind her, to reach Hobart.

Did Scott Reach the Pole?

The question naturally arises in one's mind, did Capt. Scott reach the pole before Dec. 14?

If so, the honor flies with the British flag, but the same endurance, the same skill, and the same meed of endeavor must be granted to Capt. Amundsen as the Norwegian people would grant to Capt.

"All the News That's Fit to Print."

The New York Times.

THE WEATHER.
Unsettled Tuesday; Wednesday, fair, cooler; moderate southerly winds, becoming variable.
For full weather report see Page 23.

VOL. LXI...NO. 19,896. NEW YORK, TUESDAY, APRIL 16, 1912.—TWENTY-FOUR PAGES, ONE CENT In Greater New York, Jersey City, and Newark. | Elsewhere, TWO CENTS.

TITANIC SINKS FOUR HOURS AFTER HITTING ICEBERG; 866 RESCUED BY CARPATHIA, PROBABLY 1250 PERISH; ISMAY SAFE, MRS. ASTOR MAYBE, NOTED NAMES MISSING

Col. Astor and Bride, Isidor Straus and Wife, and Maj. Butt Aboard.

"RULE OF SEA" FOLLOWED

Women and Children Put Over in Lifeboats and Are Supposed to be Safe on Carpathia.

PICKED UP AFTER 8 HOURS

Vincent Astor Calls at White Star Office for News of His Father and Leaves Weeping.

FRANKLIN HOPEFUL ALL DAY

Manager of the Line Insisted Titanic Was Unsinkable Even After She Had Gone Down.

HEAD OF THE LINE ABOARD

J. Bruce Ismay Making First Trip on Gigantic Ship That Was to Surpass All Others.

The admission that the Titanic, the biggest steamship in the world, had been sunk by an iceberg and had gone to the bottom of the Atlantic, probably carrying more than 1,400 of her passengers and crew with her, was made at the White Star Line offices, 9 Broadway, at 8:20 o'clock last night. Then P. A. S. Franklin, Vice President and General Manager of the International Mercantile Marine, conceded that probably only those passengers who were picked up by the Cunarder Carpathia had been saved. Advices received early this morning tended to increase the number of survivers by 200.

The admission followed a day in which the White Star Line officials had been optimistic in the extreme. At no time was the admission made that every one aboard the huge steamer was not safe. The ship itself, it was confidently asserted, was unsinkable, and inquirers were informed that she would reach port, under her own steam probably, but surely with the help of the Allan liner Virginian, which was reported to be towing her.

As the day passed, however, with no new authentic reports from the Titanic or any of the ships which were known to have responded to her wireless call for help, it became apparent that authentic news of the disaster probably could come only from the Titanic's sister ship, the Olympic. The wireless range of the Olympic is 500 miles. That of the Carpathia, the Parisian, and the Virginian is much less, and as they neared the position of the Titanic they drew further and further out of shore range. From the Titanic's position at the time of the disaster it is doubtful if any of the ships except the Olympic could establish communication with shore.

Titanic Sank at 2:20 A. M. Monday.

In the White Star offices the hope was held out all day that the Parisian and the Virginian had taken off some of the Titanic's passengers, and efforts were made to get into communication with these liners. Until such communication was established the White Star officials refused to recognize the possibility that there were none of the Titanic's passengers aboard them.

But by nightfall came the message from Capt. Haddock of the Olympic to Cape Race, Newfoundland, telling of the foundering of the Titanic and of the rescue of 655 of her passengers by the Cunarder Carpathia, which, the wireless message said, reached the position of the Titanic at daybreak. All they found there, however, was lifeboats and wreckage. The biggest ship in the world had sunk at 2:20 o'clock yesterday morning.

Mr. Franklin admitted late last night that the Parisian and the Virginian, though they were among the first to answer the Titanic's calls for help, could not have reached the scene before 10 o'clock yesterday morning, seven and a half hours after the big Titanic buried her nose beneath the waves and pitched downward out of sight. The Carpathia, so the wireless dispatch from Capt. Haddock to Cape Race announced, reached the scene of the Titanic's foundering at daybreak, several hours before the expected arrival of the Virginian and the Parisian.

1,465 Lives Lost First Report.

It is unbelievable, so White Star Line officials were compelled to concede finally, that the Carpathia should have failed to pick up every lifeboat which still floated on the waves. If they failed to pick up more than 655 passengers, it was because the others of the ship's complement had gone with her to the bottom.

But it was not until nearly nightfall that the extent of the disaster was realized. Before that the reassuring nature of the bulletins issued by the White Star line was sufficient to quiet the fears of those who had relatives or friends aboard the unfortunate ship and to prevent widespread belief in a serious disaster.

Capt. Haddock's message from the Olympic, which is printed in another column of THE TIMES, strongly indicated that none but the 655 taken from life boats by the Carpathia had been saved. This message was relayed immediately to the White Star offices, but Mr. Franklin positively declined to make the text of the message public. He offered still the hope that passengers were aboard the Parisian and the Virginian, and even when the admission was wrung from him that there seemed little hope of the saving of any others than the 655 aboard the Carpathia, he clung to the hope that in some unexplained way there were other passengers abroad the two Allan liners.

First Reported Titanic in Tow.

Throughout the day there had been reassurances that the Titanic was being towed to port by the Virginian, and when Capt. Haddock's message proved this to be untrue only the admission was made at the White Star offices that the Titanic had sunk. Mr. Franklin said that Capt. Haddock's message was brief and "neglected to say that all the crew had been saved." But the inference was not that all the passengers had been saved. Rather it was that many of them had died, and presently Mr. Franklin admitted the fear that there had been a terrible loss of life on the Titanic.

This version of Capt. Haddock's wireless had been given at the White Star offices:

Capt. Haddock of the Olympic sends a wireless message to the White Star offices here that the steamer Titanic sank at 2:20 A. M., after all the passengers and crew had been lowered to life boats and transferred to the Virginian. The steamship Carpathia, with several hundred passengers of the Titanic, is now en route to New York.

At 9 o'clock, however, he modified this statement, declaring:

As far as we know the situation, there have been rumors from Halifax that three steamers were at the scene of the Titanic's sinking, namely, the Virginian, the Parisian, and the Carpathia. We have heard from Capt. Haddock of the Olympic, who says the . the Titanic sank at 2:20 o'clock this morning. Haddock also informs us that the Carpathia has 675 survivors on board. It is very difficult to say whether the Virginian and the Parisian have any survivors on board until we can get a report from those vessels.

Fears Serious Loss of Life.

We have asked for that report from Capt. Haddock, and we are expecting a reply at any time. The Carpathia is proceeding to New York direct. We very much fear that there has been serious loss of life, but it is impossible for us to say definitely concerning this and part of the situation until we are able to reassure ourselves whether or not any of the Titanic's passengers are aboard the Allan liners.

We are hopeful that the rumors which have reached us by telegraph from Halifax that there are passengers aboard the Virginian and the Parisian will prove to be true, and that these vessels will turn up with some of the passengers. It is the loss of life that makes this thing so awful. We can replace the money loss, but not the lives of those who went down.

Another version of the message from the Olympic was current last night and included the sentence: "Loss likely total 1,800 souls." This sentence was not in the message received by THE TIMES from Cape Race nor in that sent to the White Star line offices.

Continued on Page 2.

THE PROBABLE LOSS.

Number Aboard.	
First cabin	325
Second cabin	285
Steerage	710
Crew, (estimated)	800
Total	2,120
Saved.	
By the Carpathia	866
Probably drowned	1,254

The Lost Titanic Being Towed Out of Belfast Harbor.

CAPT. E. J. SMITH,
Commander of the Titanic.

PARTIAL LIST OF THE SAVED.

Includes Bruce Ismay, Mrs. Widener, Mrs. H. B. Harris, and an Incomplete name, suggesting Mrs. Astor's.

Special to The New York Times.

CAPE RACE, N. F., Tuesday, April 16.—Following is a partial list of survivors among the first-class passengers of the Titanic, received by the Marconi wireless station this morning from the Carpathia, via the steapship Olympic:

Mrs. JACOB P. —— and maid.
Mr. HARRY ANDERSON.
Mrs. ED. W. APPLETON.
Mrs. ROSE ABBOTT.
Miss G. M. BURNS.
Miss D. D. CASSEBERE.
Mrs. WM. M. CLARKE.
Mrs. B. CHIBINACE.
Miss E. G. CROSSBIE.
Miss H. ROSEBIE.
Miss JEAN HIPACK.
Mrs. HY. B. HARRIS.
Mrs. ALEX. HALVERSON.
Miss MARGARET BAYS.
Mr. BRUCE ISMAY.
Mr. and Mrs. ED. KIMBERLEY.
Mr. F. A. KENNYMAN.
Miss EMILE KENCHEN.
Miss G. F. LONGLEY.
Mrs. A. F. LEADER.
Miss BERTHA LAVORY.
Mrs. ERNEST LIVES.
Miss MARY CLINES.
Mrs. SINGRID LINDSTROM.
Mr. GUSTAVE J. LESNEUR.
Miss GIORGETTA A. MADILL.
Mme. MELICARD.
Mrs. TUCKER and maid.
Mrs. J. B. THAYER.
Mr. J. B. THAYER, Jr.
Mr. HENRY WOOLMER.
Miss ANNA WARD.
Mr. RICHARD M. WILLIAMS.
Mrs. F. M. WARNER.
Miss HELEN A. WILSON.
Miss WILLARD.
Miss MARY WICKS.
Mrs. GEO. D. WIDENER and maid.
Mrs. J. STEWART WHITE.
Miss MARIE YOUNG.
Mrs. THOMAS POTTER, Jr.
Mrs. EDNA S. ROBERTS.
Countess of ROTHES.
Mr. C. ROLMANE.
Mrs. SUSAN P. ROGERSON. (Probably Ryerson).
Miss EMILY B. ROGERSON.
Mrs. ARTHUR ROGERSON.
Master ALLISON and nurse.
Miss K. T. ANDREWS.
Miss NINETTE PANHART.
Miss E. W. ALLEN.
Mr. and Mrs. D. BISHOP.
Mr. H. BLANK.
Miss A. BASSINA.
Mrs. JAMES BAXTER.
Mr. GEORGE A. BAYT—
Miss C. BONNELL.
Mrs. J. M. BROWN.
Miss G. C. BOWEN.
Mr. and Mrs. R. L. BECKW—
Miss RUTH TAUSSIG.
Miss ELLA THOR.
Mr. and Mrs. E. Z. TAYLOR.
GILBERT M. TUCKER.
Mr. J. B. THAYER.
Mr. JOHN B. ROGERSON.
Mrs. M. ROTHSCHILD.
Miss MADELEINE NEWELL.
Mrs. MARJORIE NEWELL.
HELEN W. NEWSOM.
Mr. FIENNAD OMOND.
Mr. E. C. OSTBY.
Miss HELEN R. OSTBY.
Mrs. MAMAM J. RENAGO.
Mlle. OLIVIA.
Mrs. D. W. MERVIN.
Mr. PHILIP EMOCK.
Mr. JAMES GOOGHT.
Miss RUBERTA MAIMY.
Mr. PIERRE MARECHAL.
Mrs. W. E. MINEHAN.
Miss APPIE RANELT.
Major ARTUR PEUCHEN.
Mrs. KARL H. BEHR.
Miss DESSETTE.
Mrs. WILLIAM BUCKNELL.
Mrs. O. H. BARKWORTH.
Mrs. H. B. STEFFASON.
Mrs. ELSIE BOWERMAN.

The Marconi station reports that it missed the word after "Mrs. Jacob P." In a list received by the Associated Press this morning this name appeared well down, but in THE TIMES list it is first, suggesting that the name of Mrs. John Jacob Astor is intended. This supposition is strengthened by the fact that, except for Mrs. H. J. Allison, Mrs. Astor is the only lady in the "A" column of the ship's pasenger list attended by a maid.

NAMES PICKED UP AT BOSTON.

BOSTON, April 15.—Among the names of survivors of the Titanic picked up by wireless from the steamer Carpathia here to-night were the following:

Mr. and Mrs. L. HENRY.
Mrs. W. A. HOOPER.
Mr. MILE.
Mr. J. FLYNN.
Miss ALICE FORTUNE.
Mrs. ROBERT DOUGLAS.
Miss HILDA SLAYTER.
Mrs. P. SMITH.
Mrs. BRAHAM.
Miss LUCILLE CARTER.
Mr. WILLIAM CARTER.
Miss CUMMINGS.
Mrs. FLORENCE MARE.
Miss ALICE PHILLIPS.
Mrs. PAULA MUNGE.
Mrs. JANE ——
Miss PHYLLIS O. ——
HOWARD B. CASE.
Miss MINEHAN.
Miss BERTHA ——

Biggest Liner Plunges to the Bottom at 2:20 A. M.

RESCUERS THERE TOO LATE

Except to Pick Up the Few Hundreds Who Took to the Lifeboats.

WOMEN AND CHILDREN FIRST

Cunarder Carpathia Rushing to New York with the Survivors.

SEA SEARCH FOR OTHERS

The California Stands By on Chance of Picking Up Other Boats or Rafts.

OLYMPIC SENDS THE NEWS

Only Ship to Flash Wireless Messages to Shore After the Disaster.

LATER REPORT SAVES 866.

BOSTON, April 15.—A wireless message picked up late to-night, relayed from the Olympic, says that the Carpathia is on her way to New York with 866 passengers from the steamer Titanic aboard. They are mostly women and children, the message said, and it concluded: "Grave fears are felt for the safety of the balance of the passengers and crew."

Special to The New York Times.

CAPE RACE, N. F., April 15.—The White Star liner Olympic reports by wireless this evening that the Cunarder Carpathia reached, at daybreak this morning, the position from which wireless calls for help were sent out last night by the Titanic after her collision with an iceberg. The Carpathia found only the lifeboats and the wreckage of what had been the biggest steamship afloat.

The Titanic had foundered at about 2:20 A. M., in latitude 41:16 north and longitude 50:14 west. This is about 30 minutes of latitude, or about 34 miles, due south of the position at which she struck the iceberg. All her boats are accounted for and about 655 souls have been saved of the crew and passengers, most of the latter presumably women and children.

There were about 2,100 persons aboard the Titanic.

The Leyland liner California is remaining and searching the position of the disaster, while the Carpathia is returning to New York with the survivors.

It can be positively stated that up to 11 o'clock to-night nothing whatever had been received at or heard by the Marconi station here to the effect that the Parisian, Virginian or any other ships had picked up any survivors, other than those picked up by the Carpathia.

First News of the Disaster.

The first news of the disaster to the Titanic was received by the Marconi wireless station here at 10:25 o'clock last night [as told in yesterday's New York Times.] The Titanic was first heard giving the distress signal "C. Q. D.," which was answered by a number of ships, including the Carpathia,

"All the News That's Fit to Print."

The New York Times.

THE WEATHER. Increasing cloudiness, warmer, probably snow; Wednesday, clearing; brisk southeasterly winds. For full weather report see Page 22.

VOL. LXII...NO. 20,107. NEW YORK, TUESDAY, FEBRUARY 11, 1913.—TWENTY-FOUR PAGES. ONE CENT In Greater New York, Jersey City, and Newark. Elsewhere, TWO CENTS.

SCOTT FINDS SOUTH POLE; THEN PERISHES WITH FOUR MEN IN ANTARCTIC BLIZZARD; BODIES FOUND AFTER EIGHT MONTHS

SCOTT'S LAST MESSAGE TO THE WORLD.

Not Faulty Organization, but Misfortune, Caused the Disaster Which He Foresaw—Asks Aid for Families of the Dead.

Copyright, 1913, by The New York Times Co.

MESSAGE TO THE PUBLIC.

The causes of this disaster are not due to faulty organization, but to misfortune in all the risks which had to be undertaken. One, the loss of pony transport in March, 1911, obliged me to start later than I had intended, and obliged the limits of stuff transported to be narrowed. The weather throughout the outward journey, and especially the long gale in 83 degrees south, stopped us. The soft snow in the lower reaches of the glacier again reduced the pace.

We fought these untoward events with will and conquered, but it ate into our provisions reserve. Every detail of our food supplies, clothing and depots made on the interior ice-sheet and on that long stretch of 700 miles to the pole and back worked out to perfection. The advance party would have returned to the glacier in fine form and with a surplus of food but for the astonishing failure of the man whom we had least expected to fail. Seaman Edgar Evans was thought to be the strongest man of the party, and Beardmore glacier is not difficult in fine weather. But on our return we did not get a single completely fine day. This, with a sick companion, enormously increased our anxieties. I have said elsewhere that we got into frightfully rough ice, and Edgar Evans received a concussion of the brain. He died a natural death, but left us a shaken party, with the season unduly advanced.

But all the facts above enumerated were as nothing to the surprise which awaited us at the Barrier. I maintain that our arrangements for returning were quite adequate, and that no one in the world would have done better in the weather which we encountered at this time of the year. On the summit, in latitude 85 degrees to 86 degrees, we had minus twenty to minus thirty. On the Barrier, in latitude 82 degrees, 10,000 feet lower, we had minus thirty in the day and minus forty-seven at night pretty regularly, with a continuous headwind during our day marches.

These circumstances came on very suddenly, and our wreck is certainly due to this sudden advent of severe weather, which does not seem to have any satisfactory cause.

I do not think human beings ever came through such a month as we have come through, and we should have got through in spite of the weather but for the sickening of a second companion, Capt. Oates, and a shortage of fuel in our depots, for which I cannot account, and, finally, but for the storm which has fallen on us within eleven miles of the depot at which we hoped to secure the final supplies. Surely misfortune could scarcely have exceeded this last blow!

We arrived within eleven miles of our old One Ton camp with fuel for one hot meal and food for two days. For four days we have been unable to leave the tent, the gale blowing about us. We are weak.

Writing is difficult, but for my own sake I do not regret this journey, which has shown that Englishmen can endure hardships, help one another, and meet death with as great a fortitude as ever in the past. We took risks. We knew we took them. Things have come out against us, and therefore we have no cause for complaint, but bow to the will of Providence, determined still to do our best to the last.

But if we have been willing to give our lives to this enterprise, which is for the honor of our country, I appeal to our countrymen to see that those who depend on us are properly cared for. Had we lived, I should have had a tale to tell of the hardihood, endurance, and courage of my companions, which would have stirred the heart of every Englishman.

These rough notes and our dead bodies must tell the tale, but surely, surely, a great, rich country like ours will see that those who are dependent on us are properly provided for.

March 25, 1912. (Signed) R. SCOTT.

Death Wipes Out Brave Party on Return Trip to Winter Quarters

LEAVES MESSAGE TO PUBLIC

Disaster Not Due to Faulty Organization, but to Misfortune, His Last Word.

THREE BODIES IN ONE TENT

There Scott, Wilson, and Bowers Succumbed to Starvation and Exhaustion.

OATES BRAVED DEATH ALONE

Knowing His Fate, He Marched Out Into the Blizzard—"Brave Soul," Wrote Scott.

EVANS KILLED BY A FALL

Storm Wrecked Last Hope of Saving Themselves When Only 11 Miles from a Food Depot.

REACHED POLE JAN. 18, 1912

Found Amundsen's Records There—Perished March 29, 1912, and Bodies Were Found in the Following November.

By Lieut. E.R.G.R. EVANS, R.N.
Second in Command of the Scott Expedition.

Special Cable to THE NEW YORK TIMES.

CHRISTCHURCH, New Zealand, Feb. 10.----Capt. Robert F. Scott's antarctic ship, the Terra Nova, on Jan. 18, this year, arrived at Cape Evans, the base on McMurdo Sound, where it was to meet the explorers on their return from the expedition in search of the south pole and bring them back, if they were ready. It was learned from the shore party found at this base that Capt. Scott and the four men with him had reached the pole on Jan. 18, 1912, but all had perished on the return journey, about the end of March. Their bodies were not found until a searching party discovered them on Nov. 12, nearly eight months after the disaster.

Capt. Scott, Dr. Edward A. Wilson, chief of the scientific staff, and Lieut. H. R. Bowers had made their way back to within 155 miles of Cape Evans, when they were caught in a blizzard and were overcome about March 29. They were then within eleven miles of One Ton Depot, where they would have found shelter and supplies.

Previously Petty Officer Edgar Evans and Capt. L. E. G. Oates of the Inniskillen Dragoons, who had been in charge of the ponies and dogs, had succumbed. Evans was the first to give way, dying from concussion of the brain due to a fall on Feb. 17. Oates died from exposure on March 17.

Found Amundsen's Records.

The records of Capt. Scott were recovered by a relief expedition. They showed that he and his party had reached the south pole on Jan. 18, 1912. There they found the tent and records left by Capt. Roald Amundsen when he quit the pole on Dec. 17, 1911.

Six other men of the Scott expedition who had been through a perilous experience were found to be safe and well. They composed Lieut. V. L. A. Campbell's expedition, which had been sent to make geological investigations to the east of Cape Evans. The Terra Nova had been unable to take the men off the year before on account of ice, and they were left to spend another Winter in the antarctic. In this party were Dr. Levick, Priestly, Abott, Browning, and Dickerson.

Relief Party Had to Return.

Before the Terra Nova sailed for New Zealand last March Surgeon Atkinson, who had been left in charge of the western party until Capt. Scott's return, dispatched Garrard and Demetri with two dog teams to assist the southern party, whose return to Hut Point was expected about March 10, 1912. Atkinson would have accompanied this party, but was kept back in medical charge of Lieut. Evans, the second in command, who, it will be remembered, nearly died from scurvy.

This relief party reached One Ton Depot on March 3, but was compelled to return on March 10, owing primarily to the dog food running short, also to persistent bad weather and the poor condition of the dogs after the strain of a hard season's work. The dog teams returned to Hut Point on March 16, the poor animals being mostly frostbitten and incapable of furthe work.

Garrard collapsed through an overstrained heart. His companion was also sick. It was impossible to communicate with Cape Evans, the ship having sailed on March 4, and the open sea lying between Atkinson and Keohane.

The only two men left sledged out to Corner Camp to render any help that might be wanted by the southern party. They fought their way out to Corner Camp against the unusually severe weather, and, realizing that they could be of no assistance, they were forced to return to Hut Point after depoting one week's provisions.

In April, when communication with Cape Evans was established, a gallant attempt to relieve Lieut. Campbell was made by Atkinson, Wright, Williamson, and Keohane. This party reached Butter Point, when they were stopped by open water. Their return was exciting and nearly ended in disaster, owing to the sea ice breaking up.

Search Party's Journey.

The search party left Cape Evans after the Winter on Oct. 30 last. The party, which was organized by Surgeon Atkinson, consisted of two divisions, Atkinson taking the dog teams with Garrard and Demetri, and Mr. Wright being in charge of a party including Nelson, Gran, Lashley, Crean, Williamson, Keohane, and Hooper, with seven Indian mules. They were provisioned for three months, as they expected an extended search.

One Ton camp was found in order, and all provisioned.

Proceeding along the old southern route, Wright's party sighted Capt. Scott's tent on Nov. 12. Within it were found the bodies of Capt. Scott, Dr. Wilson, and Lieut. Bowers. They had saved their records, hard pressed as they wer .

From these papers the following information was gleaned:

The first death was that of Seaman Edgar Evans, petty officer

Capt. Robert Falcon Scott.

The continuation of the authentic narrative of Capt. Scott's expedition will appear exclusively in The New York Times to-morrow.

ARMED TRUCE IN MEXICO CITY; MADERO RETURNS

Called Upon by Diaz for His Resignation, the President Cries, "I Will Die First!"

REBEL LEADER INSISTENT

He Held Off to Prevent [illegible]aughter, but the Federals Have Not Done the Same.

BATTLE PREDICTED TO-DAY

[illegible]Sides Have Been Strength-[illegible] Their Positions and [illegible]eking Reinforcements.

[illegible]GNERS NOT MOLESTED

Executions Take Place at the Palace—Son of Reyes Kills Himself.

NORTHERN GENERALS WAITING

Washington Hurries Warships to Convenient Ports to Watch Events in Republic.

General Diaz to The Times.

By Cable to the Editor of THE NEW YORK TIMES.

MEXICO CITY, Feb. 10.—The revolt is in progress and in a few hours will have to be decided. All the chances are in our favor. I will pro[illegible]zens and properties.

[illegible] DIAZ.

[illegible] MEXICO CITY, Feb. [illegible] city at 10 o'clock to-night was [illegible].

The Federals and Revolutionists still held their positions. The Government was taking ammunition to the palace under a heavy guard.

Gen. Diaz says he delayed battle in order to avoid slaughter of non-combatants, but as the Government has not refrained from hostile movements he has about lost patience.

Fighting, it is expected, will begin at daybreak.

Special Cable to THE NEW YORK TIMES.

MEXICO CITY, Feb. 10.—An armed truce prevailed between the Federals and the revolutionists all day.

Gen. Diaz still held the arsenal and had practical control of all the heavy artillery. He is equipped with rifles and machine guns and has an unlimited supply of ammunition. According to reports, he is arming and drilling several hundred men in the arsenal.

A conference was held this morning between Gen. Diaz, two of his suporters, and Cabinet Ministers at a café in the centre of the city. What occurred at the conference was not made public, but after it was over a red flag was raised on the arsenal, and war without quarter was declared.

Several cannon were taken from the arsenal last night to the suburbs. They were placed where they would command the Chapultepec Castle. Officers in the castle say they will raze it if necessary to save it.

The movements of President Madero are kept secret. It is reported that he went to Cuernavaca last night and returned to the city at dawn this morning. Gen. Felipe Angeles, commander of Cuernavaca, it is said, is at Contreras, twelve miles south of the capital, with about a thousand Madero troops.

Gen. Angeles, it is said, has some heavy artillery.

The populace is maintaining neutrality.

A small riot in the Colonia del Carmen early this morning was stopped by mounted police.

The number of dead has not beer reported, as it is impossible to pass the lines.

Genoveve de la O and Felipe Neri, rebel leaders from the State of Mexico, occupy a position within ten miles of the capital at Tlalpam and Xicpimilco, awaiting the orders of Gen. Diaz to enter the capital. Tlalpam is five miles beyond the Country Club. Foreigners are leaving that place.

Messengers were sent to Gen. Diaz this morning, protesting loyalty to him and asking permission to enter and join his forces. He sent an officer with instructions to take the positions and wait further orders.

Higinio Aguilar and Gaudencio de la

Continued on Page 8.

EDISON 66 YEARS OLD TO-DAY

Wife Will Make Him Quit Work Long Enough to Dine with Friends.

Special to The New York Times.

WEST ORANGE, N. J., Feb. 10.—Thomas A. Edison, who will be 66 years old to-morrow, will pass the day just as he does the other 364 in the year, with the exception of an occasional Sunday, when he yields to the insistence of Mrs. Edison and goes to church. He will work in the laboratory and offices, but has promised to "knock off" in the evening to be the guest at a family dinner party which Mrs. Edison is arranging.

The employes of the works will observe the day by wearing buttons or pins bearing the numerals "66." The workers at the Edison plant are grateful because since Edison took charge of the commercial branches in December many of the pay envelopes of the humbler employes have been fattened.

The production of the kinetophone, the further perfection of the storage battery, and the development of the disk phonograph record are among the achievements of the inventor during the past year. For his storage battery Edison received the Rathenau medal, donated by Emile Rathenau of Berlin.

"I feel like twenty-five," said Edison this afternoon. "I'm sure I'm going to keep right at it, too, for a good many years more."

POPE DECORATES EDITORS.

Medals to Cardinal for Those Who Compiled Catholic Encyclopedia.

Cardinal Farley received from Pope Pius X. yesterday the "Pro Ecclesia et Pontifice," an important decoration, to be bestowed upon the Board of Editors of the Catholic Encyclopedia. The order was instituted by Pope Leo XIII., July 17, 1888, and the decoration was made a permanent distinction only in October, 1898. It is to reward those, who, in a general way, deserve well of the Pope. The medal is made of gold, silver, and bronze. It is cross shaped, made rectangular in form by fleurs de lis, fixed in the angles of the cross. In the centre of the cross is a small medal with an image of its founder, Pope Leo XIII. The ribbon is purple, with delicate lines of white and yellow on each border. The decoration is worn on the right side of the chest.

The Board of Editors of the Catholic Encyclopedia consists of Charles G. Herbermann, Ph. D., L. L. D., Professor of Latin Language and Literature at the College of the City of New York; Edward A. Pace, Ph. D., D. D., Professor of Philosophy at the Catholic University in Washington; Conde B. Pallen, Ph. D., L. L. D., of New Rochelle; Mgr. Thomas J. Shahan, D. D., rector of the Catholic University, Washington, and the Rev. J. J. Wynnee, S. J.

Dr. Pallen has just returned from Rome, where he presented the Pope with a set of the Vatican edition of the encyclopedia.

LEFT CHANGE FOR $50 BILL.

Clerks Wonder if Their Customer Was Absent-Minded or Crazy.

All day yesterday the clerks at the Broadway and Thirtieth Street store of Hackett Carhart & Co. expected to see a wild-eyed man run in and demand if any one had seen on Saturday a perfectly good $50 bill. No such person turned up, and last night as the employes put out the lights they wondered if there really could be any one in this city who cared so little for money.

On Saturday afternoon a customer asked to be shown some neckties. He seemed perfectly rational and betrayed no more than the proper amount of interest in the adornment of his person. He selected ties worth $4.50 and handed the salesman a $50 bill. This was sent on its way to the cashier for change and the ties were wrapped up. The man took his parcel, put it in his pocket, and quit the store. When the salesman received the change he had gone. The man ran out into Broadway, but the customer had disappeared.

The salesman reported the incident and the cashier decided at once that the note must be a counterfeit. But examination proved that it was genuine.

SOON TO WED, DISAPPEARS.

Rockfellow's Friends Unable to Account for His Sudden Departure.

Special to The New York Times.

PLAINFIELD, N. J., Feb. 10.—Rowland C. Rockfellow, son of the late Mayor George W. Rockfellow, disappeared from his home on Saturday, leaving two notes for his mother, who was prostrated by his absence. His wedding to Miss Rae Warnock, daughter of Mr. and Mrs. W. W. Warnock, was set for Tuesday night, Feb. 18, and one of the letters addressed to his mother said:

"I wil lnot be responsible for any debts unless contracted by myself." The wedding invitations had been issued when the young man disappeared.

Mrs. Rockfellow said to-day that she could not account for her son's action. She exhibited the other note he had left, which read:

Dear Mother: I have been a good boy. I am not dishonest, but I can't help going away. Don't blame me.

W. R. Causbrook, district manager of the Public Service Corporation's local office, where Rockfellow was employed as cashier, said this afternoon that his accounts were correct. His fiancée, Miss Warnock, said she had not had any quarrel with Rockfellow. The first intimation she had had of his absence, she asserted, was on Saturday night when he failed to appear at a dinner party given to them.

WILSON WON'T SEE CASTRO.

Declines Request of ex-President of Venezuela for an Interview.

TRENTON, N. J., Feb. 10.—Representatives of ex-President Castro of Venezuela came to Trenton to-day to obtain an interview for the General with President-elect Wilson. Castro wished to see the Governor, but Mr. Wilson declined to receive him on the ground that he would not mix in any affairs of the Taft Administration before his inauguration as President.

Castro has been building hopes on the possibility of friendly action by Mr. Wilson. He has said that if Mr. Wilson was President instead of Mr. Taft he would have no trouble in obtaining admission to this country. When Mr. Wilson visited Ellis Island some time ago the ex-President expressed much regret that he had been unable to see him. One of Mr. Wilson's companions on that trip, Mrs. J. Borden Harriman, did ask Commissioner Williams to let the Governor's party talk with Castro, but Mr. Williams refused the request curtly. Mr. Wilson seemingly did not know of Mrs. Harriman's request at the time it was made.

INDICT WALSH, NEWELL AND FOYE

True Bills Found Against Police Captain and Lawyer on Bribery Charge.

WHITMAN AFTER HOCHSTIM

Ready Now to Indict One of the Heads of Syndicate Running Disorderly Hotels.

WALDO HUNTING DOWN GRAFT

Big Police Official Reported Called for Examination To-day—Costigan Aids Curran Inquiry.

The Extraordinary Grand Jury returned indictments yesterday against Police Capt. Thomas W. Walsh, Patrolman Charles E. Foye, and Edward J. Newell, the lawyer. Walsh and Newell were charged with bribery and against the lawyer there was a second indictment charging him also with misdemeanor. The first bill found against Newell a fortnight ago was dismissed and the new ones returned. Foye was charged with perjury because of his sworn testimony before the Curran Committee that Chairman Curran had tried to persuade him not to press a charge against a saloonkeeper whom he had arrested.

The witnesses against Walsh and Newell were Thomas J. Dorian and Nathan J. Michaels, the managers of the Hotel Avenel; George A. Sipp, and Patrolman Eugene Fox. All of them were willing witnesses except Michaels. Sipp's story, covering five years of paying graft to Capt. Walsh for protection, was corroborated by Dorian before the Curran Committee, and then Dorian fled the city. District Attorney Whitman made a long and fruitless effort to find him. It was lea[illegible] that he was receiving his weekly pay from the hotel syndicate that employed him, and a search began for evidence to show that these payments were really made to keep Dorian away.

Mr. Whitman threatened to proceed against the syndicate and to indict Dorian. Then Dorian returned and told a story to Mr. Whitman that not only confirmed the confession made by Fox, but gave information that showed that the disorderly hotel syndicate had paid graft to the police for many years in the many districts in which they owned hotels. It was discovered that there were several of these hotels in various sections of the city. Yesterday Mr. Whitman said that he was ready to submit enough evidence before the Grand Jury to indict at least one of the leading spirit of the syndicate.

Whitman After Hochstim.

The man that Mr. Whitman is after is Max Hochstim, who, with Philip Blau, Jacob Spielberg, and a man named Fromberg, composed the Baltic Hotel Company that owns the Hotel Avenel and other hotels of the same character. Mr. Whitman learned yesterday that Mrs. Hochstim owns thirty-nine shares of the Baltic Hotel Company, and that Hochstim owns one share. The sixty other shares are scattered. Some of the information against the syndicate was gathered yesterday in the course of the investigation in connection with police graft bearing upon the cases directly aimed against Walsh and Newell.

The moment the indictment against Newell was returned Justice Goff issued a bench warrant for his arrest. It was served by Detective Flood of Mr. Whitman's office, who found Newell in his office at 42 Broadway. He was brought before Justice Goff and his bail on the bribery charge was fixed at $2,000, while the $1,000 on which he was held on the misdemeanor charge was continued. A surety company furnished the bail, and Newell went about his business. Foye is away on a vacation. He will be taken into custody this morning as soon as he returns and bail will be set. If he fails to furnish it he will be locked up. No action was taken against Capt. Walsh because of his illness. As soon as he is physically able to go abroad he will be arraigned and released on bail.

W. M. K. Olcott, Newell's lawyer, had a talk with Mr. Whitman between the time of Newell's indictment and his arraignment in court. Before Mr. Whitman went home last night it was said that there were prospects that Newell would tell all he knew of his connection with Sipp and Capt. Walsh.

It was explained that if he told all he knew it would be to the effect that a well known lawyer handed him $1,000 to give to Sipp in return for Sipp's promise to remain out of this State until after Jan. 1, 1914; that he held out $300 to pay himself for the services he had rendered Sipp while the latter was a prisoner at Atlantic City on the charge made against him by the police and that the money came originally from Capt. Walsh. But if Newell's story goes beyond this transaction it might reach a point where the system of the police to get legal services from certain influential sources, directly or indirectly, would be uncovered.

Newell Proved Obdurate.

When Newell was indicted first for a misdemeanor, under Section 2,441 of the

Continued on Page 9.

"All the News That's Fit to Print."

The New York Times.

THE WEATHER
Local showers today; Tuesday, fair; fresh, shifting winds, becoming northwest.
For full weather report see Page 17.

VOL. LXIII...NO. 20,610. NEW YORK, MONDAY, JUNE 29, 1914.—EIGHTEEN PAGES. ONE CENT In Greater New York, Jersey City and Newark. { Elsewhere, TWO CENTS.

HEIR TO AUSTRIA'S THRONE IS SLAIN WITH HIS WIFE BY A BOSNIAN YOUTH TO AVENGE SEIZURE OF HIS COUNTRY

CALIFORNIA GOES ON ROCKS IN FOG

Tory Island, Off Northwest Irish Coast, Scene of Mishap to Anchor Liner.

IN NO IMMEDIATE DANGER

Bows Badly Stove In and Ship Taking Water Through Two Holes in Hold.

PASSENGERS STILL ABOARD

Ship Carries 1,000 Persons—Rescue Vessels, Called by Wireless, Standing By Throughout Night.

Special Cable to THE NEW YORK TIMES.

LONDON, June 28.—The Anchor liner California, with more than 1,000 persons aboard, has gone ashore on Tory Island, off the northern coast of Ireland. The destroyer Swift, the fastest and largest vessel of her class in the world, and other vessels have gone to her assistance in response to wireless calls for aid.

The ship is said to be in no immediate danger.

The accident to the California occurred in a thick fog. The latest news received early this morning was that although the position of the liner was serious, no lives had been lost.

In reply to a wireless message, the Captain sent the following details:

California ran ashore Tory Island in fog, about half mile from lighthouse. Did not hear foghorn blowing. Quiet sea. No danger. Three men of war and steamer Cassandra standing by to transfer passengers.

The California went on the rocks with such force that the lower part of her bows were badly stove in, and the two front holds soon filled with water. She is in five fathoms of water forward and seven fathoms aft. There was no panic on board.

News has been received from Londonderry that the landing of the Irish passengers may be expected before noon today.

News of the stranding was caught by the Malin Head wireless station and the entire torpedo boat destroyer flotilla which was for duty off the Ulster voast looking for gun runners, was called up and wireless orders were given to all the destroyers from the cruiser Hecla in Lough Swilly to hurry with all speed to the scene of the accident.

Subsequently orders were received by all the telephone and telegraph stations on the coast from Bangor to Bunbeg, County Donegal, to keep their offices open all night.

By 11 o'clock six destroyers were making for Tory Island.

LONDONDERRY, June 28.—In a thick fog and rain which rendered Tory Island invisible from the mainland, the Anchor Line steamer California, bound from New York for Glasgow, went ashore tonight on the rocks off that island. Wireless calls for help brought speedy assistance from a number of small gunboats and torpedo boats which were patrolling the Northwest Irish Coast for gun runners in connection with the Ulster movement.

The latest news received here is that the California is stuck fast on the rocks, but is in no immediate danger. She struck with such force that the lower part of her bows was badly stove in, and she is making water through two holes in her forehold and second hold.

The steamer, which has on board 121 saloon and more than 300 second cabin passengers, lies in five fathoms of water forward and seven fathoms aft.

The passengers and crew are still on board. There was no panic when she struck the rocks.

Several steamers, including one liner, and the gunboats are standing by, and other vessels are expected to arrive at the scene during the night.

[illegible], June 28.—Capt. Coverley of the [illegible] late tonight sent out this [illegible] dispatch:

[illegible] ashore in fog about half mile [illegible] lighthouse. Did not hear fog-[illegible] quiet. Three men-of-war [illegible] Cassandra standing by to [illegible] passengers."

[illegible]ED 841 PASSENGERS.

[illegible] Where California Struck Ten [illegible] Out of Her Course.

[illegible]fornia sailed from New York [illegible] on Saturday, June 20, for Glasgow [illegible] Moville with 116 first-class, [illegible]d-class, and 375 third-class [illegible]. She signaled Malin Head [illegible] afternoon, and should have [illegible] Moville about 8 o'clock. Tory [illegible] more than ten miles out of [illegible].

[illegible]fornia carried a crew of 240 [illegible] and men, and was commanded by J. A. Coverley, one of the most experienced Captains in the Anchor Line service. This was his second voyage on the California after having been twelve years on the Calabria in the New York-Mediterranean service, and more recently in command of the liner Elysia in the Indian service of the Anchor Line.

The California is the second largest vessel of the Anchor Line in the New York trade, and was built at Glasgow by D. & W. Henderson Bros. in 1907. She is 470 feet long, with a beam of 56 feet 2 inches and a depth of hold of 28 feet 6 inches. She is a twin-screw steamer, with an average speed of 15 [illegible].

[illegible] Captains and other officers of the [illegible] Line are accustomed to fog [illegible] coasts of Scotland and Ire[illegible] [illegible]

STAYS IN AIR 21 HOURS.

Berlin Aviator's Feat Held to be a World's Record.

BERLIN, June 28.—Herr Landmann, an aviator, today concluded a non-stop flight of 21 hours 49 minutes.

It is asserted that this flight constitutes a world record.

Twenty-one hours would be almost enough to carry the seaplane America either to the coast of Ireland, or to the Azores. Plans for the forthcoming trans-Atlantic flight are based on the America's reaching the Azores in twenty hours.

DEWEY IN CANAL PARADE.

Will Be Invited to Make Trip Aboard His Old Flagship Olympia.

Special to The New York Times.

WASHINGTON, June 28.—Admiral George Dewey may take his old flagship, the Olympia, through the Panama Canal next March in the naval parade. Rear Admiral Clark, retired, has been ordered to take command of his old ship, the Oregon, for the occasion, and Secretary Daniels said this afternoon that he had decided to invite Admiral Dewey to take part. If the Admiral does not feel like making the journey via the canal, he may go overland to San Francisco and go aboard the Olympia upon the arrival of the pageant fleet there.

The President and Secretary Daniels will make addresses upon the arrival of the fleet at the exposition city. It is likely that Admiral Dewey and Admiral Clark also will speak. The entire brigade of midshipmen will be taken to San Francisco for the occasion. This will probably take the place of their annual cruise.

The Oregon and the Olympia will be moored at a specially constructed wharf and will be on exhibition throughout the entire exposition. Behind them will be anchored seven typical modern naval ships—a dreadnought of the New York or Oklahoma type, a battleship of the Connecticut or Minnesota type, an armored cruiser of the Tennessee or Montana type, one of the three scout cruisers, a destroyer, a submarine, and a collier, each of the latest build. In addition, the entire Atlantic Fleet will remain throughout nearly the whole of the exposition.

Neither Admiral Dewey nor Rear Admiral Clark has been aboard his ship since relinquishing their commands shortly after the close of the Spanish-American war.

A NEW GAME FOR BROADWAY.

But Auto Owners Hope Trundling Stolen Tires Won't Become Popular.

Harry E. Sullivan with his brother and two women rode up to Shanley's Restaurant, in West Forty-third Street, last evening in a limousine auto with a new white tire strapped like a life preserver to the back. Two men, who had the appearance of chauffeurs came down the street after the owners of the auto entered the restaurant. With businesslike briskness they unbuckled the new white tire and trundled it down the street. The taxicab starter at Shanley's scratched his head. Then he spoke to Patrolman Louis Fick.

"They did it so natural," he explained, "that I didn't think to bother them."

The patrolman jumped into an auto and started in pursuit of the tire. By its tread-prints on the damp pavement he followed it down to Ninth Avenue, up to Forty-fourth Street, around the corner, and there the artful dodgers foiled him by rolling it into the street where its trail was lost in a maze of tire tracks. The tire was worth $75.

"If it's as easy as that," said Mr. Sullivan when he heard of his loss, "rolling rubber hoops in Broadway is apt to become a popular pastime. The first rule of the game is: 'A rolling tire must gather no moss.'"

SCORES BRYAN AND TREATY.

Francis B. Loomis Calls Colombian Agreement "Stupendous Blunder."

Special to The New York Times.

SAN FRANCISCO, June 28.—Bryan's proposed treaty between the United States and Colombia is vicious as to motives and purpose, says Francis B. Loomis, former Assistant Secretary of State. In a statement here tonight Mr. Loomis said:

"Bryan's Colombian treaty is a covert attempt to loot the United States Treasury by lobbyists and political brigands, into whose hands the Secretary of State is playing.

"Bryan and the President are trying to besmirch and discredit the achievement of the previous Administration, which made the canal a reality.

"The treaty is one of the most stupendous blunders made by Bryan, who is running wild with his 'world peace' theories. The United States owes Colombia nothing, either by treaty or otherwise.

"Mr. Bryan's contention that the people of Latin America feel aggrieved because we refuse to permit the Colombian troops to cross the Isthmus for the purpose of engaging in bloody encounters, and closing the lines of transit is not supported by ascertainable facts. The truth is the important Governments of South America such as Argentina, Brazil, and Chile care nothing about Colombia, and they deplore her misdeeds as much as we do."

STATE'S TOLL OF ACCIDENTS

Automobiles Killed Nearly Half as Many as Railroads in April.

Special to The New York Times.

ALBANY, June 28.—There were nearly half as many deaths in New York State from automobile accidents during April as there were from railroad accidents. This is shown in the vital statistics issued by the State Department of Health for April. The deaths resulting from railroad accidents numbered 56, from automobiles 25, from street cars 15, and other vehicles 20. Landslides killed 12 individuals, and 3 others died from injuries inflicted by animals. There were 128 suicides during the month and 35 homicides.

The other external causes of death ran the total up to 735 for the month.

$120,000 FOR SHACKLETON.

Sir James Caird's Gift for His Antarctic Expedition.

Special Cable to THE NEW YORK TIMES.

LONDON, June 28.—Sir James Key Caird, the millionaire jute manufacturer of Dundee, has given $120,000 toward the expenses of the Shackleton antarctic expedition.

Sir James made the gift after Sir Ernest Shackleton had personally explained to him the programme which he hoped to carry out.

Sir Ernest says the gift puts the expedition on a sound basis, and there is now no fear that it will not start well [illegible]

FEDERALS DESERT AGUASCALIENTES

Town South of Zacatecas Evacuated by Huerta's Forces, but Villa Turns Back.

IS CAMPAIGN ABANDONED?

Border Hears His Ammunition Is Exhausted — Row with Carranza Will Not Down.

ENVOYS WAIT ON CARRANZA

Rebel Chief Said He Must Consult Generals—Reply Called Favorable.

ZACETAS, June 27, via El Paso, June 28.—Aguascalientes, capital of the States of the same name, has been evacuated by the Federals, according to information reaching Gen. Villa's headquarters today.

Owing to this, his plan of campaign has been changed, and the troops of the division are returning to Torreon.

Part of the division left last night. The rest will leave for the north today. Gen. Villa will follow his troops during the day. Last Wednesday it was announced that the Villa troops would be taken toward Aguas Calientes overland.

Late reports show that the losses of the Federals here were much greater than at first supposed. The number of prisoners taken by Villa's troops exceed 4,300. The number of killed was close to that figure.

The latest casualty report of the Constitutionalists was over 700 dead and 1,100 wounded, but these figures are not complete.

EL PASO, June 28.—Gen Villa's campaigns are apparently postponed indefinitely.

Lack of ammunition is given as the principal cause, but recent developments, still concealed in the Carranza-Villa estrangement, are believe by partisans of trangement, are believed by partisans of the quiet situation below this point.

The victory of Zacatecas, won by Villa last week, occasioned the expenditure of nearly all his ammunition during the four days of almost continuous fighting.

Since then Villa has not been able to replenish his supply from the United States on account of the strict embargo by United States troops along the frontier. It is said that he has not been assisted in this regard by Gen. Carranza, who could draw on the arsenals at Monterey and Saltillo.

He has only the little ammunition left after the fighting at Zacatecas and an unstated quantity captured from the Federals there.

Gen. Villa returned today to Torreon, according to telegrams from him dated from that place. Some matters connected with his relations with Carranza, it is stated, will be taken up by Villa as well as the obtaining of ammunition for his army.

The statements of Alfredo Breceda, one of Carranza's agents at Washngton, fell here today as oil on the fire.

Carranza and Villa adherents are now outspoken in their views of the recent estrangement, and regard Breceda's statements as an additional indication that discussion of the matter will not subside for some time. Breceda's remarks closely followed in effect those made a few days previously by Roberto Pesqueira, Constitutionalist confidential agent. The Villa men have remained silent.

CARRANZA-HUERTA DEAL?

Report of Peace Negotiations Comes from Mexico City.

VERA CRUZ, June 28.—Secret peace negotiations between Gen. Carranza and President Huerta have been in progress in the capital, according to Antonio Magnon, an American who arrived from Mexico City today. Mr. Magnon said it was positively known that representatives from Carranza had been in the capital for several days in conference with President Huerta, but that the details of the discussions had been kept secret.

It was thought in the capital that a peace agreement between Huerta and Carranza based upon Huerta resignation, was certain to come soon, Carranza having been forced to make some concessions because of his disagreements with Gen. Villa and Gen. Angeles.

It is reported in Mexico City that supporters of Villa and Carranza have been fighting near Monterey.

Mr. Magnon said also that President Huerta's volunteer forces at San Luis Potosi, including all the noted chieftains, such as Gen. Pasquale Orozco and Gen. Antonio Rojas, had refused to cooperate further with the regular army or to withdraw toward the capital, but would fight the Constitutionalists in that region. The volunteer leaders, most of whom are veterans of the three years' border warfare, and all frontiersmen, and, according to Mr. Magnon, say that the Federal recruits are hopeless as soldiers and only hamper the actions of the veteran volunteers.

Gen. Joaquin Maass, Federal commander at San Lois Potosi, went to the capital last Friday to confer with President Huerta, Mr. Magnon said, and was still there when Magnon left Saturday. Mr. Magnon said Gen. Maass, whom he had known for years, confirmed the reported action of the volunteers.

The Federals are fortifying Aguascalientes against a Constitutionalist advance, but it is understood in the capital that Gen. Villa plans to direct his next blow against Queretaro, cutting both the National and Central Railways and compelling the abandonment by the Federal forces of much territory in order to prevent themselves from being cut off from the capital.

Mr. Magnon said that he learned at Soledad that the Federals were gathering railway equipment for the narrow

Continued on Page 5.

Propose Pan-American Memorial to Columbus

A splendid tomb topped by a great light is proposed to be erected in Santo Domingo, in the Caribbean Sea, by subscriptions from peoples of all lands. See

NEXT SUNDAY'S TIMES.

OUR GUNS FIRE ON SANTO DOMINGO

Few Shots from the Machias Stop Bombardment of Puerto Plata by President Bordas.

WARNED BY CAPT. RUSSELL

Told Not to Endanger Foreigners in Attack on Rebels There—Refugees Taken Off by Our Boats.

Special to The New York Times.

WASHINGTON, June 28.—Following general instructions from the Navy Department to protect the lives and property of Americans and foreigners in Santo Domingo, the little American gunboat Machias on Friday afternoon entered the inner harbor of Puerto Plata, and with a few shots from her main battery silenced a battery of President Bordas's forces that was bombarding the town.

The bombardment was in violation of emphatic orders from Capt. Russell, commanding the American squadron, that the attack on the city, which is in the hands of rebels, be conducted in such a way as not to imperil the lives of foreigners.

Capt. Russell is in personal command of the first line battleship South Carolina, that was detached from service at Vera Cruz when conditions in Santo Domingo became threatening. His dispatch to the department, which, like all dispatches from Santo Domingo, took two days to come, makes no mention of casualties. His dispatch follows:

PUERTO PLATA, June 26, 1914.

This afternoon, about 5:30, when the Bordas artillery ashore fired shells into the city of Puerto Plata, the Machias anchored in the inner harbor and with some shots from her main battery stopped the artillery fire into the city, after which there was no further firing. We have the situation well in hand, and no additional vessels, either United States or foreign, will be needed to prevent the bombardment of Puerto Plata. The prompt stopping of the artillery fire into the city this afternoon will have a very reassuring effect upon the Americans and other foreigners in the city, who have recently displayed great anxiety about their protection and safety.

At 8:30 P. M. Friday the revenue cutter Algonquin took on board forty-two persons for passage to San Juan, thirty-three being Porto Ricans and nine Americans, ten men, thirteen women, and nineteen children, and then steamed for San Juan. The Clyde Line steamer Seminole, from Norfolk en route to Santo Domingo City, arrived at 3 P. M. Friday, and after delivering mail took away from Puerto Plata four persons—one French, two Spanish, and one Chinaman. The Clyde Line steamer Algonquin, en route to New York, arrived at 7 P. M. Friday and took away from Puerto Plata twenty-four persons—five Americans, thirteen British, three French, and three Cubans. These passengers were put on board the three vessels named by the South Carolina boats. RUSSELL.

The Navy Department today was emphatic that Capt. Russell's summary enforcement of his orders indicated no change in policy, and that the silencing of President Bordas's battery did not mean that American intervention on a wider scale would be undertaken. The orders had been emphatic, and the attacking forces seemed to think they could be disregarded with impunity. The United States has never indicated its sympathies as to the contending forces, though as under the treaty it was responsible for the Custom House at Puerto Plata, its obligation in this instance was clearly not to encourage attack by the Government's troops.

The Machias is a gunboat of 1,177 tons, 204 feet in length, and with 32 feet beam. Her main battery consists of eight guns of about 4-inch calibre and four smaller guns. She was formerly used by the Naval Militia of Connecticut.

Secretary of the Navy Daniels said the other day that there was no intention to send more ships to the island, and Friday's incident is not thought to have changed his mind on that score.

$500,000 FIRE AT DOVER, N. J.

Incendiaries Destroy Richardson & Boynton Stove Plant.

DOVER, N. J., June 28.—All of the plant of the Richardson & Boynton Company, except the shipping department building, was destroyed by fire today. The firm manufactured stoves and ranges, and its plant, which was Dover's largest industry, covered thirty acres of ground. The loss is $500,000, partly covered by insurance. The works, which ordinarily employ 1,100 men, were shut down three weeks ago for repairs.

Charles Helfer, a night watchman, says he made the rounds of the works at 6:30 A. M. and found everything all right. At 7:30 o'clock he saw smoke coming from the trimming shop. Men who were in the street say they saw flames in three or four different places at the same time.

Dover's two steamers and an auto chemical engine and truck manned by the Volunteer Fire Department responded to the general alarm. All the buildings were frame except the shipping building, which is built of concrete. The water pressure was inadequate, and the flames spread rapidly to the casting and cleaning shop, the mounting, boiler, patent filing, drill and patternmakers' shops, each in a separate building. Three Lackawanna Railroad box cars in the yard near the shipping building were burned. All the finished stock on hand was in the shipping building. The firemen concentrated their efforts to save that building.

For an hour or two there was fear the flames might spread to the town. The firemen successfully defended the nearest buildings.

Incendiarism is suspected. Secretary and Treasurer W. L. R. Lynd, who is also Mayor of Dover, said he couldn't account for the fire. There was no fire in any building of the plant, and the engines had been cold since the shutdown. It is recalled that a threatening letter was sent to Mayor Lynd demanding he should prevent the delivery of the Slattery anti-Catholic lectures. He declined to interfere, and the lectures were delivered on May 15 and 16 last.

The plant will be rebuilt at once. At noon a gang of laborers was put to removing the débris. The company has offices in New York.

Francis Ferdinand Shot During State Visit to Sarajevo.

TWO ATTACKS IN A DAY

Archduke Saves His Life First Time by Knocking Aside a Bomb Hurled at Auto.

SLAIN IN SECOND ATTEMPT

Lad Dashes at Car as the Royal Couple Return from Town Hall and Kills Both of Them.

LAID TO A SERVIAN PLOT

Heir Warned Not to Go to Bosnia, Where Populace Met Him with Servian Flags.

AGED EMPEROR IS STRICKEN

Shock of Tragedy Prostrates Francis Joseph—Young Assassin Proud of His Crime.

Archduke Francis Ferdinand and his Consort the Duchess of Hohenberg

Slain by Assassin's Bullets.

Special Cable to THE NEW YORK TIMES.

SARAJEVO, Bosnia, June 28. (By courtesy of the Vienna Neue Freie Presse.)—Archduke Francis Ferdinand, heir to the throne of Austria-Hungary, and his wife, the Duchess of Hohenberg, were shot and killed by a Bosnian student here today. The fatal shooting was the second attempt upon the lives of the couple during the day, and is believed to have been the result of a political conspiracy.

This morning, as Archduke Francis Ferdinand and the Duchess were driving to a reception at the Town Hall a bomb was thrown at their motor car. The Archduke pushed it off with his arm.

The bomb did not explode until after the Archduke's car had passed on, and the occupants of the next car, Count von Boos-Waldeck and Col. Morizzi, the Archduke's aide de camp, were slightly injured. Among the spectators, six persons were more or less seriously hurt.

The author of the attempt at assassination was a compositor named Gabrinovics, who comes from Trebinje.

After the attempt upon his life the Archduke ordered his car to halt, and after he found out what had happened he drove to the Town Hall, where the Town Councillors, with the Mayor at their head, awaited him. The Mayor was about to begin his address of welcome, when the Archduke interrupted him angrily, saying:

"Herr Burgermeister, it is perfectly outrageous! We have come to Sarajevo on a visit and have had a bomb thrown at us."

The Archduke paused a moment, and then said: "Now you may go on."

Thereupon the Mayor delivered his address and the Archduke made a suitable reply.

The public by this time had heard of the bomb attempt, and burst into the hall with loud cries of "Zivio!" the Slav word for "hurrah."

After going around the Town Hall, which took half an hour, the Archduke started for the Garrison Hospital to visit Col. Morizzi, who had been taken there after the outrage.

As the Archduke reached the corner of Rudolf Street two pistol shots were fired in quick succession by an individual who called himself Gavrio Princip. The first shot struck the Duchess in the abdomen, while the second hit the Archduke in the neck and pierced the jugular vein. The Duchess became unconscious immediately and fell across the knees of her husband. The Archduke also lost consciousness in a few seconds.

The motor car in which they were seated drove straight to the Konak, where an army Surgeon rendered first aid, but in vain. Neither the Archduke nor the Duchess gave any sign of life, and the head of the hospital could only certify they were both dead.

The authors of both attacks upon the Archduke are born Bosnians. Gabrinovics is a compositor, and worked for a few weeks in the Government printing works at Belgrade. He returned to Sarajevo a Servian chauvinist, and made no concealment of his sympathies with the King of Servia. Both he and the actual murderer of the Archduke and the Duchess expressed themselves to the police in the most cynical fashion about their crimes.

ARCHDUKE IGNORED WARNING.

Servian Minister Feared Trouble if Heir Went to Bosnia.

Special Cable to THE NEW YORK TIMES.
[Dispatch to The London Daily Mail.]

VIENNA, June 28.—When the news of the assassination of the Archduke Francis Ferdinand and the Duchess was broken to the aged Emperor Francis Joseph he said: "Horrible, horrible! No sorrow is spared me."

The Emperor, who yesterday left here for Ischl, his favorite Summer resort, amid acclamations of the people, will return to Vienna at once, in spite of the hardships of the journey in the terrible heat.

The Archduke, who was created head of the army, went to Bosnia to represent the Emperor at the grand manoeuvres there. This was the first time the Archduke had paid an official visit to Bosnia. The Emperor visited the provinces immediately after their annexation, in 1908, and the manner in which he mixed freely with the people was much criticised at the time, as those in his party were always afraid lest some Slav or Mohammedan fanatic might attempt the monarch's life. The Emperor's popularity, however, saved him from all danger of this kind.

Before the Archduke went to Bosnia last Wednesday the Servian Minister here expressed doubt as to the wisdom of the journey, saying the country was in a very turbulent condition and the Servian part of the population might organize a demonstration against the Archduke. The Minister said if the Archduke went himself he certainly ought to leave his wife at home, because Bosnia was no place for a woman in its present disturbed state.

The Minister's word proved correct. The people of Sarajevo welcomed the Archduke with a display of Servian flags, and the authorities had some difficulty in removing them before the Archduke made his state entry into the city yesterday, after the conclusion of the manoeuvres. In these manoeuvres were the famous Fifteenth and Sixteenth Army Corps, which were stationed on the frontier throughout the recent Balkan war, and they carried out the evolutions before the Archduke.

Greeted with Cheers.

The details of the tragedy, as received in Vienna, were as follows: The Archduke was driving in a motor car toward the Town Hall in Sarajevo, with the Duchess of Hohenberg by his side. A large crowd assembled to watch them go by. The Archduke, raising his hand to his military cap, acknowledged the cheers, while the Duchess was smiling and bowing, her pretty face framed by her blonde hair.

Suddenly the Archduke's sharp eye caught sight of a bomb hurling through the air. His first thought was for his wife, and he threw up his arm in time to catch the bomb, which thus was turned aside from its course and fell on the pavement and exploded. The Archduke's motor car hastened on its way, its occupants unharmed, but the two Adjutants who were seated in the next motor car were injured by splinters from the bomb. Several persons on the pavement were very seriously hurt by the explosion of the bomb, which was thrown by a young man named Tabrinovitch, (Gabrinovics,) who is a typist from Trebenje, in Herzegovina, and is of Servian nationality. He was arrested some twenty minutes later.

The Archduke and his wife left the Town Hall, intending to visit those who had been injured by the bomb, when a schoolboy 19 years old, named Prinzip, who came from Grahovo, fired a shot at the Archduke's head. The boy fired from the shelter of a projecting house.

Wore Bullet-Proof Coat.

The boy must have been carefully instructed in his part, for it was a well-guarded secret that the Archduke always wore a coat of silk strands which were woven obliquely, so that no weapon or bullet could pierce it. I once saw a strip of this fabric used for a motor-car tire, and it was puncture-proof. This new invention enabled the Archduke to brave attempts on his life, but his head naturally was uncovered.

The Duchess was shot in the body. The boy fired several times, but only two shots took effect. The Archduke and his wife were carried to the Konak, or palace, in a dying condition.

Later details show that the assassin darted forth from his hiding place behind a house and actually got on the motor car in which the Archduke and his wife were sitting. He took close aim first at the Archduke, and then at the Duchess. The fact that no one stopped him, and that he was allowed to perpetrate the dastardly act indicate that the conspiracy was carefully planned and that the Archduke fell a victim to a political plot. The aspiration of the Servian population in Bosnia to join with Servia and form a great Servian kingdom is well known. No doubt today's assassination was regarded as a means of forwarding this plan.

Break News to Children.

The Archduke's children are at Glumex, in Bohemia, and relatives already have left Vienna to break the news to them. The Duke of Cumberland motored to Ischl immediately upon receipt of the news and was received by the Emperor, who will arrive in Vienna at 6 o'clock tomorrow. The bodies of the Archduke and his wife will not be brought to Vienna until tomorrow a week.

The Archduke Charles Francis Joseph, the new heir to the throne, is at Reichenau, near Vienna, with his wife, Princess Zita of Parma, and their little son and daughter. He is expected in Vienna tonight.

When the first news of the assassination became known in Vienna, early this afternoon, crowds collected in solemn silence and discussed the report, which was not credited at first. Every one connected with the press was stormed by crowds asking whether confirmation had been received, and on hearing the truth they said, "How awful!" and then dispersed, to go about their ordinary business or pleasure. The newspapers are getting out extra editions, and the whole city talks of nothing else.

New Heir Popular.

The Archduke Charles Francis Joseph, who is now heir to the throne, always has enjoyed great popularity. He was trained for the throne from the first, although he was kept somewhat in the background, being sent to country garrisons. He was not allowed to undertake to act as the representative of the Duchy of Vienna to as great an extent as the Viennese would have wished. This, however, did not detract from his popularity, while the Princess Zita, his wife, won all hearts before she married the heir to the throne, and the birth of a son two years ago completed her popularity, if indeed, anything was lacking.

General opinion here sympathizes the [illegible] with the Servian faction, and it is feared that it will lead to serious complications with that unruly kingdom, and may have far-reaching results. The future of the empire is a subject of general discussion. It is felt that the Servians have been treated too leniently, and some hard words are being said about the present foreign policy.

All the public buildings are draped in long black streamers and the flags are all at half-mast.

BRAVERY OF ARCHDUKE.

Gave First Aid to Those Wounded by the Bomb.

SARAJEVO, Bosnia, June 28.—Archduke Francis Ferdinand, heir to the Austro-Hungarian throne, and the Duchess of Hohenberg, his morganatic wife, were shot dead in the main street of the Bosnian capital by a student today while they were making an apparently triumphant progress through the city on their annual visit to the annexed provinces of Bosnia and Herzegovina.

The Archduke was hit full in the face and the Duchess was shot through the abdomen and throat. Their wounds proved fatal within a few minutes after they reached the palace, whence they were hurried with all speed.

Those responsible for the assassination took care that it would prove effective, as there were two assailants, the first armed with a bomb and the other with a revolver. The bomb was thrown at the royal automobile as it was proceeding to the Town Hall, where a reception was to be held, but the Archduke saw the deadly missile coming and warded it off with his arm. It fell outside the car and exploded, slightly wounding two aids de camp in a second car, and half a dozen spectators. It was on the return of the procession that the tragedy was added to the long list of those that have darkened the pages of the recent history of the Hapsburgs.

As the royal automobile reached a prominent point in the route to the palace, an eighth grade student, Gavrio Prinzip, sprang out of the crowd and poured a fusillade of bullets from an automatic pistol at the Archduke and the Duchess. Both fell mortally wounded.

Prinzip and a fellow-conspirator, a compositor from Trebinje, Nedeljo Gabrinovics, barely escaped lynching by the infuriated spectators and were finally seized by the police, who afforded them protection. Both men are natives of the annexed province of Herzegovina.

Wards Off the Bomb.

The first attempt against the Archduke occurred just outside the Girls' High School. The Archduke's car had restarted after a brief pause for an inspection of the building, when Gabrinovics hurled the bomb. This was so successfully warded off by the Archduke that it fell directly beneath the following car, the occupants of which, Count von Boos-Waldeck and Col. Merizzo, were struck by splinters of iron.

Archduke Francis Ferdinand stopped his car, and after making inquiries as to the injuries of his aids and lending what aid he could, continued his journey to the Town Hall. There the Mayor began the customary address, but the Archduke sharply interrupted and snapped out, "Herr Burgomeister, we have come here to pay you a visit and bombs have been thrown at us. This is altogether an amazing indignity."

After a pause, the Archduke said: "Now you may speak."

On leaving the hall the Archduke and his wife announced their intention of visiting the wounded members of their suite at the hospital on their way back to the palace. They were actually bound on their mission of mercy when, at the corner of Rudolf Street and Franz Josef Street, Prinzip opened his deadly fusillade.

A bullet struck the Archduke in the face. The Duchess was wounded in the abdomen and another bullet struck her in the throat, severing an artery. She fell unconscious across her husband's knees. At the same moment the Archduke sank to the floor of the car.

Plunges Into River.

After his unsuccessful attempt to blow up the imperial visitors Gabrinovics sprang into the River Miljachka in [illegible] effort to escape, but witnesses [illegible] after him and seized him.

[illegible]

"All the News That's Fit to Print."

The New York Times.

THE WEATHER
Fair today and Thursday; fresh north and northeast winds.
☞For full weather report see Page 18.

VOL. LXIII...NO. 20,640. ... NEW YORK, WEDNESDAY, JULY 29, 1914.—EIGHTEEN PAGES. ONE CENT In Greater New York, Jersey City and Newark. | Elsewhere TWO CENTS.

AUSTRIA FORMALLY DECLARES WAR ON SERVIA; RUSSIA THREATENS, ALREADY MOVING TROOPS; PEACE OF EUROPE NOW IN KAISER'S HANDS

MME. CAILLAUX FREED BY JURY

Wild Tumult in Court After the Verdict—Mobs in Streets Display Anger.

'MURDERESS!' CRIES CROWD

Spectacle of Opposing Counsel Embracing Calms the Uproar for a Moment.

MME. CAILLAUX RECEIVES

Attired in an Evening Gown, is Congratulated by Her Friends—Says Labori Obtained Acquittal.

Special Cable to THE NEW YORK TIMES.

PARIS, July 28.—The jury in the trial of Mme. Henriette Caillaux, wife of the ex-Premier and ex-Minister of Finance, tonight acquitted her of the charge of murdering, on March 16, Gaston Calmette, editor of the Figaro.

The jury had been out for fifty minutes. Although no one expected a severe sentence, the verdict for the moment stunned all in the courtroom except a crowd in the extreme rear, which apparently had a premonition of what was going to happen and was prepared to voice its emotions in loud cheers.

M. Caillaux evidently had a similar vision, for exactly at the moment when the jury left the court room to go through the form of meditating and deliberating its verdict the large Caillaux limousine, stocked with pillows, rugs, and attendants, drew aside at the entrance to the prisoners' exit of the Conciergerie.

By the time the angry crowd left the court room and a mob of several thousand in the street had realized what had happened, the released woman had signed the book at the Conciergerie and had been safely driven away.

A cordon of gendarmes surrounded both the prison and the Palais de Justice adjoining it from early evening, but the crowd broke the ranks and a wild fight ensued.

Mobs Shout "Assassin!"

The boulevards until a late hour were filled with mobs numbering thousands, yelling "Assassin!" and "Down with Caillaux!" The crowds were finally dispersed by dragoons.

There was pandemonium in the courtroom from the time the jury went out until the guards cleared it half an hour after the verdict was returned. It was impossible for anybody to sit, see, or hear. Free fights occurred all over the place, even within the rail marking the space reserved for the court officials. When the jury returned the noise reached the climax, Judges and guards trying to produce order.

It was several minutes before the foreman of the jury could be heard. After the verdict Mme. Caillaux, who had been lying back in her chair, threw her arms about her counsel, Maitre Labori. M. Caillaux was not in court, but was in his car outside.

The demonstrations in the courtroom were chiefly against the verdict, there being "boos" and hisses and cries of "Assassin!" Finally there was a round of cheers for Maitre Labori and another for Maitre Chenu, counsel for The Figaro, who smiled grimly as the verdict was read.

The day's session was devoted to the summing-up speeches of the barristers. There were few incidents, except at the beginning, when the crowd, which was bigger than on any preceding day, became unruly.

At a critical moment of Maitre Chenu's speech—just as he began to describe the scene of the shooting—Mme. Caillaux had another fainting spell, and was carried from the prisoners' inclosure.

There were many arrests of boulevard demonstrators tonight. The trouble would probably have been more serious had not the war situation attracted the greater attention.

Prisoner Falls on Labori's Neck.

PARIS, July 28.—Mme. Caillaux was acquitted after a trial lasting nine days.

The announcement of the jury's verdict was followed by the wildest tumult.

Mme. Caillaux tottered and fell on the neck of her counsel, Fernand Labori, and embraced him. Her hair was undone and fell over her shoulders. Her hat dropped to the floor. The spectators stood up on desks and chairs. "Caillaux!" "Labori!" and cries of "Caillaux! Assassin!" merged into one.

The din was deafening. Several groups of barristers came to blows, and Republican Guards, in an endeavor to separate them, joined in the mêlée. The spectacle of Maitre Labori and Maitre Chêne, the latter counsel for the Calmette family, embracing each other, calmed the tumult for a moment, but it was redoubled when they left the building with Mme. Caillaux.

Failing to make himself heard, the presiding Judge, followed by the other Judges, marched out of the room. The advocates took complete possession of the court, and some of them mounted the Judges' desks and harangued the crowd. The guards then cleared a portion of the court, and, comparative quiet being re-established, Presiding Judge Albanel returned and read the judgment, ordering the release of Mme. Caillaux.

Much shaken with emotion, Mme. Caillaux departed by the witnesses' door, the guards making a lane through the crowd. She covered her face with her hands as if to shield herself from the furious cries of "murderess!" by way of a number of narrow corridors and back staircases, reaching a small side door in the Palace of Justice, where an automobile was waiting, and she drove off unobserved.

M. Caillaux left the building by the main entrance on the arm of his devoted friend, Deputy Pascal Ceccaldi, amid mingled cheers and hoots.

Thus ended the most sensational trial that the Paris courts have had to deal with in years. Each day provided its dramatic thrill, and although the verdict has been pronounced the ultimate outcome cannot be foretold.

The session of the court today was devoted to speeches by counsel. Mme. Caillaux had come into the prisoner's dock pale and worn, and she collapsed in the course of the address of Maitre Chene, who denounced her bitterly.

Prosecutor's Speech Mild.

The speech of the Procurator General, Jules Herbaux, was unusually mild in tone. To the jurors he said: "Your duty, as the defenders of the interests of society, requires you to find a verdict of guilty, but no one expects you to be pitiless."

Maitre Labori, who came last, delivered a masterpiece of passionate eloquence. He concluded amid tempestuous applause:

"My wish is that Mme. Caillaux shall leave here acquitted, and that the press shall be purified. Let us keep our anger for our enemies abroad. Let us leave this court resolute and united to face the perils which threaten us!"

Mme. Caillaux had been becoming visibly weaker as the sitting continued today, and appeared unconscious of what was taking place in court. A hot-water bottle was placed beneath her feet and a cushion at her back soon after she entered the court.

Meanwhile Maitre Elward Seligman, one of the attorneys representing the family of the murdered editor, continued his address. He said:

"The sons of Gaston Calmette asked us to bring them to this court to seek justice. We refused to do so, but do not forget, gentlemen of the jury, with what anguish the orphans await your verdict. You have heard witness after witness speak in praise of the late M. Calmette. There has been only one discordant note, and that came from M. Caillaux. What connection with the case has the fortune of the murdered man? How many millions must a man have in order to permit his being assassinated with complete impunity?"

Following Maitre Seligman came Maitre Chenu, and his cutting analysis of the actions of Mme. Caillaux on the day of the tragedy was too much for the prisoner. She collapsed and fell in a heap on the floor of the prisoners' enclosure.

At the moment Mme. Caillaux swooned Maitre Chenu was saying:

"I will speak of nothing except the assassination of M. Calmette. I will ask the accused whether, when she spoke of her love for her daughter, she thought of the two children of M. Calmette, whose pictures never left him. I shall not attempt to go into the biography of Mme. Caillaux. She is a cool, sensible woman, without emotion or pity. She has tears only for herself. She worked with tenacity to break up her lover's home. You see the result—the mistress triumphed over the lawful spouse. They are bound up in each other—in their happiness, in their hopes, even in their murder plans.

"M. Caillaux is a man of inordinate and limitless ambition, whose power rests on his own audacity and on the fear he inspires.

"M. Caillaux omitted to tell his wife of the assurances given by President Poincaré that Calmette was incapable of printing private letters. They did not fear that. What they feared was the publication of the report by Victor Fabre on the Rochette swindle.

"The husband's violent words at the lunch table decided the wife to substitute herself for him, and she prepared the assassination with as much calm as a society woman fitting in calls between two tea parties."

"Down With Caillaux!"

Demonstrations against the Caillaux verdict occurred in several places tonight. In the Boulevards excited crowds discussing the merits of the case, grew to large proportions, and when the jury's verdict became known there were shouts of derision and cries of "Down with Caillaux!"

In one section the mob became so disorderly that mounted Republican Guards were hastily summoned to assist the police in quelling the disturbances. A large number of police and rioters were injured, and many arrests were made.

Maurice and Jean Rostand, sons of the dramatist, were among those taken into custody.

The Figaro office was also the scene of a demonstration.

After dining at home with her husband and a few friends Mme. Caillaux attired in a handsome evening gown, received a number of intimate acquaintances.

"It is Maitre Labori," she said, "to whom I owe the good fortune to be finally free. He pleaded today with all his fine talent, and I am profoundly grateful to him."

Press Condemns the Verdict.

Special Cable to THE NEW YORK TIMES.

PARIS, Wednesday, July 29.—The acquittal of Mme. Caillaux rouses scanty but hostile comment. The Eclair says: "When the news was published yesterday Paris growled." Echo de Paris says: "The country will attribute the result to the baneful influence of politics."

The Figaro says: "It is the most enormous scandal of our epoch and covers the radical republic with mud and blood. It is an abominable parody of justice. Mme. Caillaux has torn an acquittal from a dazed jury, a terrified Government, and sold Judges."

The Matin gives an account of the incidents following the acquittal and refrains from comment, as does The Journal.

STORY OF THE CRIME.

Shooting Due to Calmette's Newspaper Campaign Against Caillaux.

The Caillaux case, the most celebrated French trial since the Dreyfus case, began on the evening of March 16, when Gaston Calmette, editor of The Figaro, was shot in his office by Mme. Henriette Caillaux, wife of Joseph Caillaux, ex-Premier and Minister of Finance in Premier Doumergues's Cabinet. He died a few hours later. The shooting was the consequence of a vigorous newspaper campaign carried on by Calmette against Caillaux.

Caillaux is an excellent financier and campaign manager. He was Premier in 1911, holding office during the Morocco crisis, and resigning in January, 1912, on account of popular dissatisfaction at the settlement made with Germany at that time.

Calmette's attacks charged, among other things, that Caillaux had used his influence to delay the trial of the swindler, Henri Rochette, in 1908, so as to give him time to escape to Mexico, and that as Minister of Finance he had promised to certain claimants against the Government $1,200,000 on condition that they subscribe 80 per cent. of that sum to the Radical campaign fund. It is said that Calmette had various letters in his possession charging that Caillaux was a tool of Germany in the Morocco crisis, which he had not yet published at the time of his death.

WARBURG IS WON, HITCHCOCK THINKS

Expects Nominee for the Reserve Board to Appear Before Committee.

SECRET CONFERENCE HERE

Banker Is Made to Understand There Is No Discrimination Against Him.

TECHNICAL POINT EXPLAINED

Charles R. Crane Called to White House, Presumably to Get Offer of Jones's Place.

Senator Gilbert M. Hitchcock of Nebraska, who has been acting as Chairman of the Banking and Currency Committee during the absence of Senator Owen in Europe, had an unofficial conference in this city last night with Paul M. Warburg in which he urged on Mr. Warburg that he should appear before the committee, which has under consideration his nomination for membership in the Federal Reserve Board.

Senator Hitchcock was found at the Pennsylvania Station just as he was leaving for Washington at midnight. He seemed greatly pleased with the result of his conversation with Mr. Warburg, and said he saw no reason now why Mr. Warburg should not consent to appear before the committee.

"Did Mr. Warburg say whether or not he would do so?" Senator Hitchcock was asked.

"No," the Senator replied, "but he seemed to understand after our talk just how the committee felt toward him, and that there had been no discrimination against him, and he indicated in every way that he would be willing to appear. I believe Mr. Warburg's attitude has been changed by the explanation I have been able to make to him. I think it has been made clear to him that it is the wish of President Wilson that he should understand that no desire to discriminate against him was intended."

Senator Hitchcock had been down to Southampton, L. I., to visit his family and stopped over in the city a few hours on his way to Washington. He would not say where the interview was held.

No Discrimination Intended.

"I think Mr. Warburg's attitude," he said, "was due to the feeling that there was some discrimination in the committee against him, but generally a committee always has the privilege of inviting before it for investigation men who are nominated to Judgeships and other high offices. This is due only to a desire on the part of the Senate to acquaint itself fully with these men and what they have done.

"Personally I know that Mr. Warburg is an important man in the business and financial world, and has been connected with big things, but he has been in this country only a comparatively short time, and it is to inform itself further of his achievements that the committee has invited him before it. I think the Senate feels the same way toward Mr. Warburg as the committee feels.

"The reason Mr. Warburg felt that he had been discriminated against was probably because three of the five nominees for members of the Federal Reserve Board were readily confirmed. Two of these were officials in Washington, and there was little that could be asked of them that was not already known in official life in Washington. The third man was W. P. G. Harding of Birmingham, Ala. He wrote out for the committee a complete history of his life, and this was sufficient for its purposes."

SUGGEST A. BARTON HEPBURN.

Administration Still Hopeful of Warburg's Confirmation.

Special to The New York Times.

WASHINGTON, July 28.—While the Administration is hopeful that Paul M. Warburg will appear before the Senate Committee on Banking and Currency to testify in regard to his appointment on the Federal Reserve Board, nothing definite has been heard from Mr. Warburg on the subject.

While the impression prevails that Mr. Warburg would be confirmed if he found it consistent with his dignity to accept the committee's invitation to appear, his continued refusal has resulted in the suggestion of others to take his place. A. Barton Hepburn of the Chase National Bank of New York was the most prominently mentioned today, though there is nothing official indicating that serious consideration has been given to any candidate other than Mr. Warburg.

Senators of the Committee on Banking and Currency were mildly shocked today to learn that Chairman Owen favored for the place his lifelong friend, the Rev. Dr. J. M. T. Johnston, a retired minister now in the banking business in Kansas City. At Mr. Owen's request Dr. Johnston appeared before the committee last Summer in support of the Owen-Glass Currency bill. Much of the anecdotal part of his testimony has been stricken from the committee's record. Quickly wearying of the academic topic assigned to him, the Rev. Dr. Johnston branched out into stories of an intimate domesticity that were received in silent astonishment by his mixed audience.

C. R. CRANE CALLED BY WILSON

Chicago Capitalist May Be Offered Jones's Place.

Special to The New York Times.

CHICAGO, July 28.—Charles R. Crane, who is about to retire from the Presidency of the Crane Company, has been invited to Washington by President Wilson.

The action of the President is taken to mean that Mr. Crane will be offered the place on the Federal Reserve Board made vacant by the withdrawal of the nomination of Thomas D. Jones.

According to the intimate friends of Mr. Crane, he is not disposed to undertake the duties of a member of the Federal Reserve Board, since they would tie him to Washington. Should the President persuade him, however, to take the position, it is declared he undoubtedly would be of service in the organization and administration of the new banking and currency systems, as his long business experience would be invaluable in this connection.

President Wilson is to see Mr. Crane at the White House tomorrow.

Notice Sent to the Powers of the Opening of Hostilities.

SERVIAN VESSELS SEIZED

Sharp Fighting Begins Along the River Drina on the Bosnian Frontier.

COUNTER INVASION PLAN

Montenegrin and Serb Armies to Invade Bosnia and Start a Rebellion There.

GREY'S PEACE PLAN FAILS

Kaiser Declines to Join in Conference to Exert Pressure on Austrian Ally.

BUT REPLY IS CONCILIATORY

And London Still Has Faith That His Influence Will Avert General Conflict.

Special Cable to THE NEW YORK TIMES.

LONDON, Wednesday, July 29.—Austria-Hungary declared war on Servia yesterday. The declaration was made at noon to the Servian Government by means of an open telegram. The Austro-Hungarian forces followed up the declaration by seizing two Servian vessels at Orsova, on the Danube, together with a number of boats.

The question whether the Austro-Servian war can be localized and a European Armageddon can be avoided now depends, so far as anything can depend on one man, upon Emperor William.

THE NEW YORK TIMES correspondent referred yesterday to the hopes of the British Foreign Office that the Kaiser's personal influence would be exercised for peace. Now that Germany has refused to accept Sir Edward Grey's suggestion of an ambassadorial conference and Austria has declared war on Servia, the only hope of avoiding that greater conflict, which the whole world apprehends, lies in the conversations that are proceeding directly between Vienna and St. Petersburg, and particularly the turn which can be given them by the German monarch.

The Kaiser's Role.

THE TIMES correspondent is informed on the best authority that great hopes are based on Emperor William's influence in this direction. This information is reflected in The Times editorial this morning, which says:

"There is reason to believe that in the most exalted quarter of Germany the maintenance of European peace is warmly and honestly desired. The pressure from all manner of influential personages and groups is doubtless being exerted to overcome the pacific leanings of the Emperor. It may tax his powers of resistance severely, but in foreign affairs he is the undoubted master and he has often shown that he has a will and judgment of his own. We still hope with some confidence that they will be exerted on the side of that peace which it has often been his honorable boast he helped to keep for six and twenty years.

"Our Paris correspondent repeats that grounds exist for the belief that Germany has already given a better proof of her wish for peace than is known to France."

In London Germany's reply to Sir Edward Grey's proposal is not looked upon as a diplomatic rebuff. The tone of the reply was conciliatory, and Prince Lichnowsky, the German Ambassador here, explained that Germany, while most anxious to co-operate with Great Britain in the attempt to find a settlement, was unable to accept the rôle of a mediator so far as the Austro-Servian dispute was concerned, as she must eschew anything calculated to create the impression that she was not in entire harmony with her Austrian ally. The German Ambassador particularly insisted on the weight which Germany attaches to co-operation with Great Britain with a view to localizing the conflict.

The conversations at St. Petersburg between Count Szapary, the Austrian Ambassador, and Premier Sazonoff, are understood to be proceeding on a tone which gives good hope that it will be found possible to prevent the conflagration spreading beyond the present limits.

Up to a late hour this morning no definite confirmation had been received here of the various reports that Russia had begun a general mobilization.

Statements that the army corps in the west and southwest of Russia were being brought up to their war strength were accepted without hesitation as part of the precautionary measures which every country in Europe, big or small, with the exception of Spain, Portugal, and Switzerland, considered necessary. The news of the issue of orders for a general mobilization of Russian forces would mean that a great European conflict would be precipitated.

May Strike First at France.

Berlin dispatches state that Germany has made it quite clear in St. Petersburg that even "a partial mobilization" will be answered immediately by the mobilization of the German Army, which, according to one dispatch, "nothing could then hold back."

This is in accordance with what is known of the German war policy. The German General Staff does not contemplate simultaneous campaigns on a great scale against both France and Russia. France can mobilize nearly as quickly as herself. Russia takes some weeks to mobilize and more weeks to move her armies from mobilization centres to the frontier.

Germany's safety lies in taking advantage of the slowness of Russian mobilization. She will content herself with a comparatively slight screen of troops along her Eastern frontier to hold back the Russians and will launch all her striking force against the French lines of defense, hoping to pierce them and break the back of the French armies before Russia is ready to act.

The next few hours is likely to show whether Germany thinks the extensive military movements which are taking place along the Russian side of the German-Austrian frontiers constitutes a partial mobilization.

In this connection extreme importance attaches to the statement made in a special dispatch to THE NEW YORK TIMES from St. Petersburg that Russia will declare a general mobilization if Austria occupies Belgrade.

A military expert who is acquainted with the European situation said, when shown the dispatch, that he hoped the correspondent's forecast was incorrect, for such a step would precipitate an Armageddon, as Germany could not afford to throw away the advantage which the slowness of Russian mobilization, the chief weakness of the Dual Alliance, gave her, and would immediately strike at France.

Probable Plans of Opposing Armies.

The Servians are reported to have formed a division in the Sanjak of Novi Bazar and to be concentrating strong forces on the River Lim, which runs through the Sanjak. Montenegrin troops are stated to be in close contact with the Servian forces.

The object of these movements, according to The London Times, is apparently to threaten Herzegovina and Bosnia, where the nature of the ground is favorable for guerrilla operations.

Rumors of fighting on the Drina River that forms the frontier between Bosnia and Servia, were circulated in Vienna and Berlin. Part of the Austro-Hungarian forces is expected to advance across the Drina in the direction of Kraguoyevatz. The Servian forces, on the other hand, are expected to cross into Bosnian territory with the object of raising an insurrection among the Bosnian Serbs.

It is stated on Austrian authority that the object of Austria-Hungary is to crush and disarm Servia and, in particular, capture the Servian artillery and compel Servia to reduce her army in future to inoffensive proportions.

Austria-Hungary also is determined to sieze Mount Lovtchen, a Montenegrin stronghold, which commands the important naval base of Bocche di Cattaro, despite the opposition which Italy is expected to offer to this proceeding.

Three Italian training ships now on a visit to the Clyde have been recalled.

Austrian naval concentration has been ordered at Fiume.

Black Sea Lights Out.

The Russian authorities have ordered all lights along the Russian Black Sea coast extinguished, with the exception of the Chersonese Lighthouse near Sebastopol harbor. Sebastopol itself is open only to Russian warships.

Russia has ordered the mobilization of fourteen army corps in the neighborhood of the Austrian frontier, but these orders are understood to be merely preparatory, not final. In diplomatic circles it is stated that Germany will not reply to this partial mobilization unless a Russian army is mobilized also in the north.

Two French Cabinet councils were held yesterday. No mobilization order has been issued, but considerable military preparations are being made. All officers and men on leave have been recalled to the colors. The French Socialists have issued a manifesto calling upon the Government to use its influence in Russia in favor of peace.

Military preparations are proceeding in Holland and Belgium, with the view of maintaining the neutrality of those countries against an attack by the great powers.

Hungarian Diet Enthusiastic.

Great enthusiasm prevailed in the Hungarian Chamber when Count Tiza, the Prime Minister, announced the outbreak of war and declared the situation demanded a deed of arms, not words. Count Apponyi, leader of the Opposition, supported the Premier. The Parliament was prorogued by royal decree.

Patriotic demonstrations took place in St. Petersburg, the crowds cheering the friendly embassies and legations, including those of Great Britain and Servia.

The Times St. Petersburg correspondent reports the growth of pessimism in official circles. News of the Austro-Hungarian occupation of Belgrade would inflame public feeling. Russian statesmen are convinced that England alone can save the situation, and that Sir Edward Grey's proposals by no means exhaust all his possibilities of persuasion.

Captured Passengers Detained.

BELGRADE, July 28, (by Indirect Route.)—The Servian steamers Deligrad and Morava were seized today at Orsova, on the Danube, by Austrians. The Servian colors were hauled down and the Austrian flag hoisted. The passengers were detained.

Many Servian families have left the capital for the country districts in spite of the advice of the authorities, while there has been a great exodus of Austrians and Hungarians from Belgrade and other parts of Servia.

Perfect order prevails in the capital, the police duties having been undertaken by a corps of volunteers composed of students.

Military preparations are being carried out with feverish activity. The troops have been concentrated in fortified positions. The headquarters of the army has been established at Kragouyevatz, but in the event of necessity will be transferred to Krushevatz, ninety miles southeast of Belgrade.

Two Army Corps at the Border.

BERLIN, July 28.—Reports from the Austrian border today state that the transport of the Eighth and Ninth Austrian Army Corps from Bohemia toward the Servian frontier began yesterday, and that there was no other traffic on the Bohemian railroads except troop trains. The two army corps in Bohemia consist of thirty-two battalions of infantry with a large number of quick-firing machine guns, six regiments of cavalry, two regiments of field artillery, and two regiments of the Army Service Corps.

An unconfirmed dispatch from Gumbinnen, Eastern Prussia, to the Taegliche Rundschau, today says Russia has occupied Wirballen, Russian Poland, with a force of engineers, cavalry, artillery, and two regiments of infantry while Russian guards have been placed along all roads on the frontier. The dispatch adds that a squadron of German Uhlans has advanced to Eydtkuhnen on the Russian frontier.

AUSTRIA MAY PAUSE.

Suggestion in Paris That She May Take Some Territory and Wait.

PARIS, July 28.—According to what is believed to be responsible opinion, there remains the possibility that when Austria has occupied some Servian territory she will in a day or two announce her intention not to proceed further, but to hold what she has taken until Servia gives competent guarantees that she will observe Austria's wishes. Russia would not then be likely to intervene, it is argued, except diplomatically, and negotiations appear to be going on at the present time between Austria and Russia.

On the announcement of war tonight Paris became animated. There were patriotic demonstrations in the capital and many other cities throughout the republic, but there were also demonstrations against the war.

A large number of noted French aviators, led by Roland Garros, in a letter to the Minister of War, have offered their services.

Maurice Barres, member of the Chamber of Deputies and President of the League of Patriots, has issued a call for a big demonstration on the arrival at Paris of President Poincaré to signify affirmation of the Triple Entente and readiness for the service of France.

Text of Austria-Hungary's Declaration of War.

VIENNA, July 28.—Austria-Hungary's declaration of war against Servia was gazetted here late this afternoon. The text is as follows:

"The Royal Government of Servia not having replied in a satisfactory manner to the note remitted to it by the Austro-Hungarian Minister in Belgrade on July 23, 1914, the Imperial and Royal Government finds itself compelled to proceed itself to safeguard its rights and interests and to have recourse for this purpose to force of arms.

"Austria-Hungary considers itself, therefore, from this moment in a state of war with Servia.

(Signed) "COUNT BERCHTOLD,
"Minister of Foreign Affairs of Austria-Hungary."

Russia Announces Its Wish to Remain at Peace Yet Is Determined to Guard Its Interests.

ST. PETERSBURG, July 28.—The Russian Government tonight issued the following official communication:

"Numerous patriotic demonstrations of the last few days in St. Petersburg and other cities prove that the firm pacific policy of Russia finds a sympathetic echo among all classes of the population.

"The Government hopes, nevertheless, that the expression of feeling of the people will not be tinged with enmity against the powers with whom Russia is at peace, and with whom she wishes to remain at peace.

"While the Government gathers strength from this wave of popular feeling and expects its subjects to retain their reticence and tranquillity, it rests confidently on the guardianship of the dignity and the interests of Russia."

CZAR'S FORCES MASS ON EASTERN BORDER

His Capital Expects War and Counts Confidently on England's Aid.

MOBILIZATION ORDER READY

German Official Says Its Issue Would Mean Launching of Kaiser's Army.

Special Cable to THE NEW YORK TIMES.

ST. PETERSBURG, July 28.—With the actual opening of the war the localization of the conflict becomes impossible. Even if Austria-Hungary goes no further than the occupation of Belgrade by the troops thrown across the Save at Semlin, Russia will declare a general mobilization.

Already rapid mobilization is proceeding in the west and southwest, virtually from the German frontier to the Black Sea.

The gravity of the situation is reflected in the diplomatic movements in this capital. The Emperor today gave audience to both the Foreign Minister and the War Minister.

A strong opinion prevails here that in the event of the outbreak of a general European war England would actively support Russia and France, her co-partners in the Triple Entente.

ST. PETERSBURG, July 28.—The fact that Austria had declared war became known here late this evening.

Thousands of persons then gathered, and, cheering wildly, marched through the main streets to the British and French Embassies, where there were scenes of enthusiasm.

Mounted police eventually scattered the crowds, without great disorder.

Says Germany Will Strike Hard.

BERLIN, July 28.—No confirmation had been received up to a late hour this evening by the German Foreign Office or the Russian Embassy of the mobilization of army corps in Russia reported in dispatches to London.

A German official said flatly that any Russian mobilization against Austria, partially or otherwise, meant war. German mobilization orders would then, he said, immediately be issued, and when these once had been sent there would be no possibility of recalling them or of Germany resting on her arms while negotiations continued, as the strategic necessities of war on her two fronts would force Germany to strike immediately and hard.

The opinion was expressed tonight in well-informed Russian circles, however, that partial mobilization of Russian troops along the Austrian frontier was quite probable as an answer to the Austrian declaration of war on Servia.

Servian officials here appeared to think that such a step could be undertaken without evoking a German counter mobilization.

PEACE CONGRESS PROTEST.

Meeting Place to be Changed from Vienna to Berne.

BRUSSELS, Belgium, July 28.—The International Peace Association, at the request of the American delegates now here, has called a meeting for next Friday.

As a protest against the warlike action of Austria the association has decided to change the meeting place of the Universal Peace Congress in September from Vienna to Berne.

Austrian Emperor to Take Command at Vienna Headquarters.

WAR FEVER AT CAPITAL

Crowds Cheer Outbreak of Hostilities and Demonstrate at Friendly Embassies.

OUTBREAK OF FOOD RIOTS

Prices Soar as Hostilities Are Declared and the Government Steps In to Regulate Them.

MANIFESTO FROM EMPEROR

Forced to Grasp the Sword, He Says, to Defend the Honor of His Monarchy.

FRANCE FEARS A GREAT WAR

Army Moves to the Frontier—Belief in Paris That Russia Will Not Desert Servia.

Special Cable to THE NEW YORK TIMES.

VIENNA, July 28.—Upon the issue of the formal declaration of war against Servia today Emperor Franz Josef gave orders for the removal of the Summer Court from Ischl to the capital. His entourage tried to persuade him that Vienna air would not suit him, but the aged Emperor replied:

"I do not want the air of Vienna. I want the atmosphere of headquarters."

The opening of the war has caused the imposition of all kinds of restrictions upon public business. All the railways, of course, are under military control, and the telegraphs are being reserved entirely for the service of the State.

The hope is still entertained here that the war will be confined to Austria-Hungary and Servia. The report that Russia and France have intervened in Vienna is incorrect. In official circles here it is maintained that any action by those powers must be supported by the third party to the Triple Entente, namely, Great Britain. It is known that Great Britain and France do not want a European war. Peace among the great powers or war among the great powers must depend on the action of St. Petersburg.

At the Foreign Office here it is freely stated that now that war has begun Austria-Hungary will be bound to no more conditions such as she propounded prior to the outbreak of hostilities.

Food Prices Up in Vienna.

There was an abnormal rise in the price of provisions today, which caused great indignation on the part of the public, who flocked to the markets to lay in stores in anticipation of a possible scarcity. Vegetables in many cases trebled in price. Feeling ran so high that in many instances stallkeepers in the markets were mobbed or assaulted, and the police had to be called out to restore order. The authorities declare that the sudden increase in the prices of provisions and vegetables is totally unwarranted.

A permanent committee appointed to deal with the question of provisioning the country, sat today to discuss the regulation of prices in order to prevent the public being cheated. A similar meeting with the same object also was held in the Diet.

It was officialy asserted that there was no reason for apprehension with regard to the food suply, and that it was needless for citizens to start the accumulation of stores of provisions. The only effect of such procedure, it was added, would be to still further raise prices.

Official arrangements have been made to take care of families of reservists called to the colors. In the event of a reservist being killed or reported missing an allowance of about 25 cents per day for each adult and 12 1-2 cents a day for children will be continued for six months.

The Declaration of War.

By The Associated Press.

VIENNA, July 28.—It is with a feeling of intense relief that the people in the dual monarchy look forward to the war with Servia, which for several days has seemed to be inevitable, and

"All the News That's Fit to Print."

The New York Times.

THE WEATHER
Generally fair today and Monday; gentle to moderate south winds.
For full weather report see PAGE 3, SPORTS SECTION.

VOL. LXIII...NO. 20,644. .... NEW YORK, SUNDAY, AUGUST 2, 1914.—88 PAGES, In Seven Parts, Including Picture and Rotogravure Section, Real Estate Directory, and Review of Books. PRICE FIVE CENTS.

GERMANY DECLARES WAR ON RUSSIA, FIRST SHOTS ARE FIRED; FRANCE IS MOBILIZING AND MAY BE DRAWN IN TOMORROW; PLANS TO RESCUE THE 100,000 AMERICANS NOW IN EUROPE

Transports for Refugees Being Considered by State Department.

MAY CHARTER VESSELS

Appropriation Will Probably Be Asked from Congress to Rescue Stranded Americans.

MIGHT SEND OVER GOLD

To Relieve Those Unable to Get Cash on Paper or to Obtain Passage.

FEW WARSHIPS NOW THERE

Consuls Being Confronted with Many Urgent Calls for Assistance.

ANXIOUS INQUIRIES POUR IN

Washington Can Only Reply That Our Representatives Are Instructed to Give All Possible Aid.

WASHINGTON, Aug. 1.—The Administration has under consideration the sending of army and navy transports to bring American refugees back from Europe, and a special request to Congress for an appropriation is expected to be made.

The President and Mr. Bryan discussed several plans, but will not make a final decision until tomorrow, when they will confer again and get the opinion of the bankers who usually serve the State Department abroad in normal times.

If necessary the Washington Government is prepared to send American vessels abroad with gold for the relief of Americans. Immediately after the conference with the President Mr. Bryan cabled all consulates, legations and embassies to spare no pains in caring for Americans who remain in the war zones, and to give every facility to those who wished to leave.

State Department officials admitted that a most serious problem was confronting them in the plight of Americans abroad. They estimated that at least 100,000, and possibly as many as 300,000, were scattered throughout Europe. The disorganization of European exchange has made it practically impossible to cash checks or letters of credit. American consulates, legations and embassies are devoid of funds for the emergency which has suddenly confronted them. They are being besieged on all sides with requests for financial assistance.

With the cancellation by several steamship lines of their sailings many Americans find themselves unable to get passage on the overcrowded boats of American register. American warships would be of little use, as they have hardly any capacity for passengers. Naval officers have suggested that the Government could charter immediately some of the big ocean liners of foreign register to bring Americans home.

By special arrangement, officials believe the American Government could obtain the use of foreign ships, securing exemption from seizure if used only for transportation of Americans.

The only American warships in European waters are the little gunboat Scorpion, station ship at Constantinople, and the battleship Maine at Villefranche, with Annapolis midshipmen and the officers and crew of the battleship Idaho taken over at that port by the Greek Government. The Maine will leave Villefranche today for Annapolis.

A special appropriation would be required to charter steamships to bring Americans home. Congress always has acted promptly in such emergencies, and is expected to do so again.

Many applications were received at the State Department from persons in the United States desirous of having American Consuls investigate and report upon the safety of their friends and relatives in Europe. The State Department is returning the uniform answer that under their general instructions the Consuls will look after and report the case of any Americans in distress in their respective districts, and consequently that no special instructions are needed.

ENGLAND HESITATES WHAT COURSE TO TAKE

Grey Wants to Throw the Weight of Great Navy at Once in Favor of Russia and France.

Special Cable to THE NEW YORK TIMES.

LONDON, Sunday, Aug. 2.—Great Britain's rôle in the European war now begun is now a great question. THE TIMES correspondent learns on good authority that the Cabinet is practically divided into equal parts on the question whether to take immediate action or await developments in the hope of remaining outside of the struggle.

Sir Edward Grey, according to this information, heads the party which believes that it is England's duty and interest to throw the weight of her navy at once into the scales on behalf of France and Russia.

Lloyd George leads the other faction, which believes that this country can with honor and advantage hold itself outside and not engage in a European conflict.

One statement, which is given for what it is worth, is that the Chancellor of the Exchequer thinks that England and the United States can together intervene at a propitious moment in such fashion as to reduce to some extent the horrors of a Continental Armageddon. In passing it may be mentioned that the wildest reports have been current on all aspects of the situation for a week past. THE TIMES correspondent refrained from chronicling them because the actual facts of the situation require no sensational embroidery.

Cabinet to Meet Tonight.

A special meeting of the Cabinet has been summoned for the unprecedented hour of 11 o'clock tonight. Most of the Ministers are remaining in town till then, and none is going out of reach. Some hope to get a day's golfing as a respite.

The Cabinet Council sat for two and a half hours yesterday. Sir Edward Grey left in the middle of the proceedings for the Foreign Office.

With reference to the Cabinet's position, The Observer this morning says:

"France and Germany have cast the die on their frontiers. Before nightfall, or even before these lines see the light may be fired in the western and decisive theatre of war the first shots of a tremendous struggle that will decide the destinies of the Old World for generations. The first great actions may decide the final issue, first in the West and then in the Near East.

"If after the lamentable wavering of last week we hesitate one day more we shall be too late to influence an arbitrament which indirectly but surely will decide our own fate no less than that of France. Our hours are numbered. If the Ministry decides today to desert France, then they will strike us out of the list of nations that any power can trust."

Fleet Ready for a Blow.

It is said that the Cabinet is likely to reach a decision tonight. One factor that will probably influence the decision is the total absence of indications of any of that anti-German sentiment which has been a feature of the spurious agitation of recent years. In the event of the Cabinet deciding upon war, speculation is rife as to what the fleet will do first.

The First Home Fleet, which sailed under sealed orders, is believed to be off the coast of Holland or in the neighborhood of Denmark. A high official of the Admiralty said to THE TIMES correspondent tonight:

"It is idle to speculate. Only three men in England know what its orders are."

Thanks to the recent Spithead review by the King, Great Britain's navy is practically ready for war, and a proclamation of mobilization would only really affect the second line. Its ability to strike a sudden, serious blow is not doubted in England, and, as is evident from the orders given to German liners, the blow is apprehended in Germany.

The Admiralty is, of course, in wireless touch with the commanding officers, and to prevent any possibility of interference with the radio communications stringent instructions have been issued that all amateur or private wireless systems must be stopped.

France Orders Mobilization After Germany Asks Her Intentions.

DELCASSE WAR MINISTER

Germany's Old Enemy Heads Army Organization—Once Nearly Caused Conflict.

CLEMENCEAU IN CABINET

President and Cabinet Issue a Manifesto to French Nation.

PLAIN WORDS TO GERMANY

"You Are Mobilizing; We Know It," Says Prime Minister to German Envoy.

ORDERS TO FOREIGNERS

Americans May Stay on Getting Permits—Austrians and Germans Liable to Arrest.

PARIS, Aug. 1.—An official decree orders a general mobilization of the French Army, beginning tomorrow.

The mobilization, according to the official decree, is to be completed at 11:30 o'clock Sunday night.

The wildest enthusiasm was manifested on the Paris boulevards when the news of the order became known. Bodies of men, formed into regular companies in ranks ten deep, paraded the streets, waving the Tricolor and other national emblems and cheering and singing the "Marseillaise" and the "Internationale," at the same time throwing their hats in the air.

Here and there the cry, "On to Berlin!" was raised.

On the sidewalks were many weeping women and children. All the stores and cafés were deserted.

Relations Not Yet Severed.

The decree of mobilization of the French Army, which was followed by a proclamation by the President and the Cabinet to the nation, has, however, not terminated diplomatic relations between France and Germany. Conversations between the powers, notably between Russia and Austria and between France and Germany, continued this evening.

Up to a late hour tonight, it was stated, the German Ambassador was still in Paris.

A rumor in circulation here tonight was to the effect that there were some waverers in the Cabinet yesterday on the question of ordering the mobilization, but that the views of those who asserted that it would be suicidal to allow Germany to put France to further expense with regard to war preparations without actual mobilization prevailed.

The course of diplomatic events since yesterday afternoon can be stated briefly as follows:

Baron von Schön, the German Ambassador to France, called on the French Premier, René Viviani, at 7 o'clock last evening and formally notified him that Germany had addressed an ultimatum to Russia, desiring to know by noon today whether the St. Petersburg Government would discontinue the mobilization of the Russian Army.

Baron von Schön was directed by his Government to ask what were the intentions of France should Russia's reply to Germany be a refusal to demobilize.

The German Government fixed "before 1 P. M. today" as the period within which France must answer. Baron von Schön called at the French Foreign Office at 11:40 A. M. to receive France's reply. Premier Viviani made an earnest appeal to the German Ambassador, asking if Germany could not yet do something to avert war.

The Baron promised to communicate with Berlin and to return to the Foreign Office at 4 P. M., which he did.

"You Are Mobilizing. We Know It."

In the course of their second interview today Premier Viviani said to the German Ambassador:

"You are mobilizing. We know it."

Baron von Schön did not reply, and M. Viviani continued:

"This attitude of your Government has dictated ours. We were compelled to take precautions similar to yours. Our peaceful intentions remain unchanged. We wish peace, and the best proof we can give you of this is that at the present moment the French Parliament has not been convoked. Under our constitution we should be compelled to convoke it if our intentions were not peaceful."

Baron von Schön said: "But frontier incidents are unfortunately to be feared."

Premier Viviani replied:

"How can you suppose such things? Our troops are five miles from the frontier. We are, in fact, exposed to the violation of our frontier, and there is not another power in the world which would have consented to do such a thing."

This refers to the withdrawal of the French troops from the immediate frontier.

The Premier proceeded to point out that the German troops were at the very foot of the frontier posts, and said he concluded from this that if incidents occurred they could only be provoked by the German military forces.

The German reply was submitted to a French Cabinet Council, which, within a few minutes afterward, ordered a general mobilization of the French Army.

The date of the mobilization was set for tomorrow, but it really begins immediately. The men are called out in classes at intervals of days, according to the year in which they entered the army. Precise instructions are always in the possession of every man, so that he may know what to do when a general mobilization is posted.

Reservists Obey Instantly.

The response to the order of mobilization was instant, and the stations of all the railways, particularly those leading to the eastward, were crowded tonight with departing reservists. Many women accompanied the men until close to the stations, where, the women softly crying, farewells were said.

The Russian Ambassador, M. Iswolsky, called on Premier Viviani at 11 o'clock tonight and informed him that Germany had declared war on Russia.

Nothing is known among the general public as to what is going on behind the screen which fell along the German frontier at about 4 o'clock yesterday afternoon.

Arrangements were made last night by Myron T. Herrick, the American Ambassador, acting under instructions from Washington, to take over the affairs of the German Embassy, while Alexander H. Thackara, the American Consul General, is to look after the affairs of the German Consulate.

All foreigners may leave Paris or France before the end of the first day of mobilization by train, but not by automobile. Those deciding to leave France may do so by certain trains, the time tables of which are posted on the walls of Paris tonight, or by sea.

American citizens or British subjects may remain in France, except in the regions on the eastern frontier and near certain fortresses, provided they make declarations to the police and obtain special permits.

No foreigner will be permitted to leave France after the first day of mobilization without a passport signed by a Prefect. Americans, Englishmen, and other foreigners may remain in Paris by obtaining special permits from the police.

Delcasse War Minister.

LONDON, Aug. 1.—A Paris dispatch to the Central News by indirect route reports that Premier Viviani has made changes in the Cabinet.

Théophile Delcassé becomes Minister of War, and Georges Clemenceau, the ex-Premier, joins the Ministry.

M. Delcassé is one of the bitterest enemies of Germany among French statesmen. He nearly caused a war with that country in 1905.

Cabinet Council in Session Till 4 A. M.

PARIS, Sunday, Aug. 2.—The Council of Ministers, which held a late night session to discuss the European situation, adjourned shortly after 4 o'clock this morning. It will continue its discussion of the situation this afternoon. No announcement of the result of the deliberations has been given out.

Poincare Orders Mobilization, Telling France It Is Not War Yet

PARIS, Aug. 1.—President Poincaré and the members of the Cabinet today issued the following joint proclamation to the French nation:

For some days the States of Europe have been considerably aggravated, and, notwithstanding the efforts of diplomacy, the horizon has darkened. At the present hour a greater part of the nations have mobilized their forces. Even the countries protected by neutrality conventions have deemed it their duty to take this measure as a precaution.

The powers whose constitutional or military legislation differs from ours have, without issuing a decree of mobilization, begun and carried on preparations which, in reality, are equivalent to mobilization, and are but the anticipated execution of it.

France, who always has affirmed her desire for peace, who on many a tragic day has given to Europe counsels of moderation and a living example of decorum, and who has multiplied her efforts to maintain the peace of the world, has now prepared herself for all eventualities, and has taken from henceforth her first indispensable dispositions for the safeguarding of her territory.

But our legislation does not permit the completion of these preparations without a decree of mobilization. Conscious of its high responsibility, and feeling that it would fail in its sacred duty if it did not take this measure, the Government has signed the decree.

Mobilization is not war. Under the present circumstances it would appear, on the contrary, to be the best means of assuring peace with honor.

Strong in its ardent desire of arriving at a peaceful solution of this crisis, the Government under cover of these essential precautions will continue its diplomatic efforts, and still hopes to succeed. It counts upon the coolness of the people not to give itself up to unjustified emotion. It counts upon the patriotism of every Frenchman, and it knows that there is not a single one who is not ready to do his duty at this hour.

There are no longer any parties. There is an eternal France—a France peaceful and resolute. There is a fatherland of peace and justice, all united in calm vigilance and dignity.

KAISER SIGNS ORDER MOBILIZING HIS ARMY

"Let Your Hearts Beat for God and Your Fists on the Enemy," Cries Chancellor.

BERLIN, Aug. 1.—Emperor William, at 5:15 o'clock this evening, signed an order mobilizing the German Army.

A semi-official statement says that the threatening danger of war necessitates that military measures be taken for the protection of the German frontier and railway lines. Restrictions, therefore, on the postal, telegraph, and railway services are inevitable, owing to the requirements of the military authorities.

It was officially announced that the time limit of the German ultimatum to Russia expired at noon.

An official communication published in the North German Gazette says the Russian Emperor on July 29 telegraphed to Emperor William urgently requesting him to help in averting the misfortune of a European war and to try to restrain his ally Austria-Hungary from going too far.

Emperor William replied that he would willingly take up the task of mediator, and accordingly diplomatic action was initiated in Vienna.

While this was in progress the news that Russia was mobilizing arrived in Berlin, and Emperor William telegraphed to the Emperor of Russia that his rôle as mediator was by this endangered, if not made impossible.

The communication adds that a decision was to have been taken in Vienna today in regard to the mediation proposals in which Great Britain had joined Germany, but that meanwhile Russia had ordered the full mobilization of her forces. Upon this Emperor William addressed a last telegram to Emperor Nicholas emphatically declaring that his own responsibility for the safety of the German Empire had forced him to take defensive measures.

War Speech by Chancellor.

The German Imperial Chancellor, Dr. von Bethmann-Hollweg, addressed a huge procession of demonstrators today from the window of his official residence, making a stirring speech, in which he said:

"At this serious hour in order to give expression to your feelings for your Fatherland you have come to the house of Bismarck, who with Emperor William the Great and Field Marshal von Moltke welded the German Empire for us.

"We wished to go on living in peace in the empire which we have developed in forty-four years of peaceful labor.

"The whole work of Emperor William has been devoted to the maintenance of peace. To the last hour he has worked for peace in Europe, and he is still working for it. Should all his efforts prove vain and should the sword be forced into our hands we will take the field with a clear conscience in the knowledge that we did not seek war. We shall then wage war for our existence and for the national honor to the last drop of our blood.

"In the gravity of this hour I remind you of the words of Prince Frederick Charles to the men of Brandenburg:

"'Let your hearts beat for God and your fists on the enemy.'"

Enthusiastic cheers and the singing of the national anthem greeted the close of the Imperial Chancellor's speech.

Germany's War Challenge Delivered to Russia at 7:30 Last Evening

EMBASSY THEN DEPARTS

Enrollment of Reservists Begun Throughout the Czar's Vast Empire.

STIRRING SCENES ATTEND IT

Hardly a Family but Loses a Protector, Yet They Take the Call Submissively.

FRANCE HAS TILL MONDAY

Reply to Germany Due Then, but Issue May Be Forced Earlier.

ITALY REMAINS NEUTRAL

Triple Alliance Obligations Not Touched, She Says—Feared a Revolution.

LUXEMBURG INVADED.

Germans Seize a Neutral State Between Them and Paris.

LONDON, Aug. 2.—The Germans have invaded the Duchy of Luxemburg. They seized the Government offices and telephones. The news reached here in a Reuter telephone message from Brussels at 4 A. M. New York time.

Luxemburg is a neutral State southward of Brussels, with its borders on Germany and France. A straight line drawn between Berlin and Paris would pass through the heart of the Duchy of Luxemburg.

Special Cable to THE NEW YORK TIMES.

LONDON, Sunday, Aug. 2.—The news that Germany had declared war against Russia reached London from St. Petersburg late last evening, only half an hour after a Central News dispatch from Paris had raised the hopes of all by the statement that Germany had extended for forty-eight hours, that is, until Monday noon, the period in which Russia and France could reply to the German ultimatums.

The first of these ultimatums was one demanding that Russia cease the mobilization of her army in twelve hours.

The second was a note presented by Baron von Schoen, the German Ambassador in Paris, to Foreign Minister Viviani calling upon France to inform Germany whether in the event of the outbreak of war between Germany and Russia, France would remain neutral.

These notes were regarded as diplomatic skirmishing, designed to cover the hard fact that Germany was bending all her energies to the delivery of the first blow, which might affect the whole course of the war, now officially begun.

In the history of modern warfare an official declaration of war is either accompanied or preceded by an actual stroke of war.

In London this morning it is believed Germany would not officially declare war upon Russia unless her plans for a rapid attack had been entirely completed. Where or how the first blow will be struck is a matter of the widest speculation.

France Next to Be Involved.

France's reply to the German request as to the former's attitude in case Germany engaged in war with Russia is stated to have proved unsatisfactory to Berlin. It was bound to be. Germany could count confidently on it being so. Therefore, according to speculation in London this morning, the eventual news is likely to show that Germany has taken an unsatisfactory reply from France for granted, and while declaring war on Russia has struck or has made her chief preparations to strike at France. This, of course, is pure speculation, and THE NEW YORK TIMES correspondent mentions it for what it is worth.

The established facts, bearing on the crisis in yesterday's developments, are important to note. The first is that the effort made by King George to bring influence to bear on the Czar in favor of peace failed of effect.

The terms of the King's telegram are guarded as the strictest secret. All information THE TIMES correspondent could obtain was that the message was of a highly personal and confidential nature. It followed an interview with Premier Asquith at 2 o'clock yesterday morning.

Italy Feared a Revolution.

The second development was a confirmation of the report that Italy would remain neutral as long as she was assured that her interests were not menaced.

From an official source THE TIMES correspondent learns that the Italian Government was practically forced to this decision by the apprehension that the taking up of arms on behalf of Austria in a quarrel, precipitated by the hereditary enemy of Italy, would have caused an immediate revolution in Italy.

Italy's abstention is a serious blow to the Triple Alliance and may yet prove an important factor in determining, if not the issue of peace or war, at least the duration of the conflict.

One of the ways suggested to prevent the outbreak of war was that Italy and Great Britain should combine and declare themselves on the side of France and Russia. The suggestion utterly disregarded the treaty by which Italy was bound to the Triple Alliance, but it was given some color of vraisemblance by the fact that the British and Italian Ambassadors in various capitals have been working together in a manner which indicated that the Italian Government preferred any peaceable solution of the war to the treaties which bound her to Germany and Austria.

The third important development of the night was the news that the French Government had issued orders for general mobilization.

This came a few hours after the severance of telephonic communications between London and Paris. The French Government informed the British authorities that the telephone was cut for ordinary communication in order to prevent any leakage of news.

Up to 2 o'clock this morning practically no news beyond the announcement of the mobilization had been received here from Paris.

The fullest confirmation of the general mobilization was obtained in London by the issue of a notice to the French Embassy here. This called upon all Frenchmen liable to military service to return to France within twenty-four hours. The news speedily became known in Soho, the French quarter of London, and this morning bands of enthusiastic Frenchmen paraded through Leicester Square.

The almost complete severance of telegraphic and telephonic communication with Paris was shown by the fact that a London paper which had made most elaborate arrangements to obtain a special wire, under a guarantee that nothing in the nature of leakage of military secrets could possibly occur, had not received a word out of Paris up to 3 o'clock this morning.

Telephonic and telegraphic communications with the Continent were generally interrupted.

GERMANY'S DECLARATION

Served by the Retiring Ambassador as Russian Enrollment Begins.

ST. PETERSBURG, Aug. 1.—The German Ambassador, in the name of his Government, sent a declaration of war to the Russian Minister of Foreign Affairs at 7:30 o'clock this evening. Count von Pourtales and the entire staff of the German Embassy then left St. Petersburg.

Martial law has been proclaimed in the capital and its suburbs.

Announcement of the declaration of war was made to the people two hours after it had been received. The city immediately presented a spectacle of extraordinary animation. The Nevsky Prospect and all the leading thoroughfares are filled with war-frenzied people marching in processions, carrying portraits of the Emperor, with flags waving and torches blazing. From time to time there is an outburst of cheering, followed by singing.

Speakers fired with patriotic fervor harangue the crowds. In front of the Kazan Cathedral each procession halts and a sudden hush falls over the processionists, then the strains of the national anthem, sung in perfect harmony by a section of the procession, are heard, and the crowds listen silently with bared heads. On the conclusion of the hymn the procession moves forward and the demonstrations are resumed with greater ardor.

Enrollment of the reservists started at a hundred centres in St. Petersburg at 6 o'clock this morning and was accompanied by stirring scenes. Crowds of women and children accompanied their husbands and fathers to the assembling stations, while priests everywhere blessed the reservists as they marched through the streets singing hymns.

The Municipal Council of Warsaw has voted 1,000,000 roubles (about $500,000) for the Red Cross service of Russia and friendly powers.

The Fateful Red Posters.

Special Cable to THE NEW YORK TIMES.

ST. PETERSBURG, Aug. 1.—All attention is now concentrated on the mobilization of the troops. During the night bills were posted in all parts of the city summoning the whole of the reservists to the colors, and the population awoke to read the startling news on posters printed in red.

Women wept, but the men took it for the most part quietly and seriously, in sad submissiveness.

"I don't care for my life," said one peasant to me, "but I am sorry for the children."

Such expressions are frequent on all hands. Hardly a house, hardly a family

Chronology of Yesterday's Fateful Events

12 Midnight—Germany demands that Russia cease mobilization and gives a twelve-hour limit.

2 A. M.—King George of England, after an audience with Premier Asquith, telegraphs to the Czar, making a strong appeal for peace.

12 Noon—The time limit of Germany's ultimatum to Russia expires.

5:15 P. M.—Emperor William signs an order for the mobilization of the German Army.

7:30 P. M.—The German Ambassador at St. Petersburg delivers to the Russian Government a declaration of war in the name of Germany and leaves St. Petersburg.

First Shots Fired in the Russo-German War.

BERLIN, Aug. 1.—A German patrol near Prostken was fired on this afternoon by a Russian frontier patrol. The Germans returned the fire. There were no losses.

Prostken is a village of 2,300 inhabitants, in East Prussia. It is situated about two and one-half miles west of the international boundary line, on the Konigsberg & Lyck Railroad. The nearest Russian village is Grajevo, about three miles across the international boundary.

Kaiser Forgives Enemies, Prays for Victory.

BERLIN, Aug. 2.—The Emperor again spoke from a window of the Castle tonight to a crowd of 50,000 beneath, who cheered and sang patriotic songs until he appeared. He said:

"I thank you for the love and loyalty shown me. When I enter upon a fight let all party strife cease. We are German brothers and nothing else. All parties have attacked me in times of peace. I forgive them with all my heart. I hope and wish that the good German sword will emerge victorious in the right."

The speech was thrice interrupted by vociferous cheering. At its conclusion the Kaiser bowed in all directions, retiring amid a frenzied demonstration.

The Imperial Chancellor also addressed the assembly, saying:

"All stand as one man for our Emperor, whatever our opinions or our creeds. I am sure that all the young German men are ready to shed their blood for the fame and greatness of Germany. We can only trust in God, Who hitherto has always given us victory."

An imperial decree convokes the Reichstag on Aug. 4.

"All the News That's Fit to Print."

The New York Times.

EXTRA 5:30 A. M.

VOL. LXIV...NO. 20,923. NEW YORK, SATURDAY, MAY 8, 1915.—TWENTY-FOUR PAGES. ONE CENT In Greater New York, Jersey City and Newark. | Elsewhere TWO CENTS.

LUSITANIA SUNK BY A SUBMARINE, PROBABLY 1,260 DEAD; TWICE TORPEDOED OFF IRISH COAST; SINKS IN 15 MINUTES; CAPT. TURNER SAVED, FROHMAN AND VANDERBILT MISSING; WASHINGTON BELIEVES THAT A GRAVE CRISIS IS AT HAND

SHOCKS THE PRESIDENT

Washington Deeply Stirred by the Loss of American Lives.

BULLETINS AT WHITE HOUSE

Wilson Reads Them Closely, but Is Silent on the Nation's Course.

HINTS OF CONGRESS CALL

Loss of Lusitania Recalls Firm Tone of Our First Warning to Germany.

CAPITAL FULL OF RUMORS

Reports That Liner Was to be Sunk Were Heard Before Actual News Came.

Special to The New York Times.

WASHINGTON, May 7.—Never since that April day, three years ago, when word came that the Titanic had gone down, has Washington been so stirred as it is tonight over the sinking of the Lusitania. The early reports told that there had been no loss of life, but the relief that these advices caused gave way to the greatest concern late this evening when it became known that there had been many deaths. Although they are profoundly reticent, officials realize that this tragedy, involving the loss of American citizens, is likely to bring about a crisis in the international relations of the United States.

It is pointed out that the sinking of the Lusitania is the outcome of a series of incidents that have been the cause of concern to this Government in its endeavor to maintain a strictly neutral position in the great European war.

Nation's Course in Doubt.

It is impossible to say tonight what effect the loss of American lives on the Lusitania will have on the Government. Judged from the little that can be learned it is a safe prediction that President Wilson will endeavor to ascertain all the facts, including evidence as to whether a German submarine was responsible for the sinking of the vessel, before proceeding to determine the course to be pursued. The news that many lives had been sacrificed, probably as many as a thousand, was given to him at the White House about 10 o'clock this morning, but no word came from him as to what effect this intelligence had on him.

The State Department tonight sent instructions to the American Embassy in London to send the names of any Americans who might have been killed or injured in the disaster. A bulletin from THE TIMES, saying probably 1,000 lives had been lost, was sent to the White House as soon as received and laid before President Wilson. The news that two torpedoes had been fired into the Lusitania by a submarine and that the Lusitania sank fifteen minutes afterward was also sent to the White House, but reached there after the President had gone to bed. The President retired about 11 o'clock.

On account of the many inquiries it had received from friends and relatives of passengers on the Lusitania and the intense public interest in the tragedy, orders were given tonight to the telegraphers and cipher clerks in charge of the telegraph office in the State Department to remain at their posts all night. They also had instructions to make public any messages bringing official details regarding the Lusitania's passengers. Usually the telegraph office closes at midnight.

Rumors of Congress Session.

There were reports this evening that Congress would be called in extra session, but these were not justified and the most that can be said is that while the Government is greatly concerned over the situation, it has shown no inclination toward excitement or taking hasty action.

Senator W. J. Stone, Chairman of the Committee on Foreign Relations, said tonight:

"I cannot comment on a supposed

Continued on Page 4.

The Lost Cunard Steamship Lusitania

X Where the First Torpedo Struck. XX Where the Second Torpedo Struck.

Cunard Office Here Besieged for News; Fate of 1,918 on Lusitania Long in Doubt

Nothing Heard from the Well-Known Passengers on Board—Story of Disaster Long Unconfirmed While Anxious Crowds Seek Details.

Official news of the sinking of the Lusitania yesterday reached New York in fragmentary reports, and several hours elapsed between the first unverified rumor of the disaster and the cable messages that told at night of the saving of some of the passengers and gave meagre details of the most sensational incident of its kind in the war.

The early accounts that indicated all on board had been saved reassured hundreds of friends and relatives of passengers. Later, it was made known that lives had been lost and probably many persons had been injured.

Among the prominent passengers rescued was George A. Kessler. The list of those of whom no word was received included A. G. Vanderbilt, Charles Frohman, Charles Klein, Justus Miles Forman, and Elbert Hubbard, besides persons widely known in society.

A cablegram sent to Farley Hopkins of The Yale News staff at New Haven, by his father, who was aboard the Lusitania, stated that the vessel was sunk, not beached, that three hundred persons had been already landed, and that the rest in small boats were making for shore. The message reached New York at 8:15 o'clock and was signed "Lee Higginson & Co., London."

Word of the safety of Charles E. Lauriat, Jr., of Boston, Mass., a member of the firm of Charles E. Lauriat & Co., booksellers, who was a first-cabin passenger, reached relatives there in a cablegram early this morning. The message, dated at Queenstown, 2:40 A. M. Read simply:

> Charles E. Lauriat, Jr., safe and well.

For more than half a century it was the boast of the Cunard Line that it never had lost a life. The regon was sunk in collision near Fire Island in 1886, but no lives were lost until five passengers were swept off the Campania's forward deck by a wave on Oct. 5, 1906. The sinking of the Lusitania is the first big disaster the Cunard Line has had.

Message to Cunard Office.

The first word of the sinking of the Lusitania received here reached the local offices of the Cunard Line, 21 State Street, at 11:41 o'clock yesterday morning, but was not made public until late in the afternoon. The message, which was sent from the head office in Liverpool, read:

> The Lusitania, we regret to advise, an unconfirmed report states to have been torpedoed by a submarine at 2 P. M., Friday, ten miles from Kinsale, and sunk at 2.30. There is no news as to the safety of passengers or crew.

Following this dispatch there was a message which had been picked up by the wireless station at Land's End, evidently a distress call from the liner, which said:

> Come at once. Big list. Position ten miles west Kinsale.

A third dispatch from Queenstown stated:

> All available craft in harbor dispatched to assist. Weather here beautifully fine. Wind southeast, light.

By 3 o'clock in the afternoon the news of the sinking of the Lusitania had been spread in the city and the Cunard offices were besieged by relatives and friends of the passengers on board. Owing to the alterations in and additions to the passenger list on sailing day, last Saturday, it took some time to get the correct figures, which were finally given out as 290 first, 601 second, and 362 third class passengers. Of the cabin passengers thirty-six had been transferred fro mthe Cameronia on Saturday morning. This delayed the Lusitania's departure from 10 o'clock to 12:28.

1,918 Persons on Board.

The officers and crew numbered 665 men instead of the usual complement of 950, on account of fewer men being carried in the engineers' and stewards' departments. Thus there were in all 1,918 persons on board.

The Cunard agents told all inquirers that they would give out the messages as fast as they were received and had no intention of keeping back the news from the public. Several bulletins were received from the Liverpool office, but few of them contained any definite statements and they were cancelled, in some instances, within an hour. One received at 4 P. M. read:

> Motor fishing boats towing two boats filled with passengers, probably fifty. Tug Stormcock making Kinsale. Some passengers on board. Many rescue vessels are now apparently making Queenstown.

The first dispatch stating positively that the Lusitania had sunk reached the Cunard office at 5 P. M. It read:

> Old Head Kinsale Station reports about twenty boats, all belonging to Lusitania, are in vicinity where sunk. About fifteen boats are making for the spot to resume.

An unconfirmed report was received late in the afternoon that all the passengers and crew had been saved in small boats and rafts. This information was given out to the people waiting in the Cunard office, and many of them went home. It was estimated that fully 300 inquiries were received by telephone and telegraph in the afternoon from relatives and friends of passengers on board. Long-distance calls were received from St. Louis, Atlanta, Montreal, and Toronto.

The next bulletin made public at the Cunard office was the following:

> Liverpool, May 7.
> 1.31 P. M., (New York Time.)
> Following received by Admiralty, Galley Head, 4.25 P. M. Several boats, apparently survivors, southeast nine miles. Greek steamer proceeding to assist.

The next bulletin was:

> Liverpool, May 7.
> 2.33 P. M. (New York Time.)
> Queenstown wires Old Head: Large steamer just arrived in vicinity, apparently sending assistance. Tugs, patrols, &c.,

Continued on Page 3.

List of Saved Includes Capt. Turner; Vanderbilt and Frohman Reported Lost

LONDON, Saturday, May 8.—5:30 A. M.—The Press Bureau has received from the British Admiralty at Queenstown a report that all the torpedo boats and tugs and armed trawlers, except the Heron which went out from Queenstown to the relief of the Lusitania have returned.

These vessels have landed 595 survivors and forty dead. Fifty-two more survivors are reported aboard a steamer, while eleven others and five bodies have been landed at Kinsale, making the total number of survivors 658, besides forty-five dead. The numbers will be verified later, and it is considered possible Kinsale fishing boats may have rescued a few more.

Among the survivors is the Captain of the Lusitania, William T Turner. Some of the survivors at Queenstown say that Alfred Gwynne Vanderbilt was drowned. Every effort to find Mr. Vanderbilt and Charles Frohman, the theatrical manager, among the survivors has failed.

The Central News says that the number of the Lusitania's passengers who died of injuries while being taken to Queenstown will reach 100.

QUEENSTOWN Saturday, May 8, 4:45 A. M.—The list of the Lusitania's survivors, as far as compiled, follows.

TURNER, Captain.
MATHEWS, A. T., Montreal.
ABRAMOWITZ, S.
LANE, G. B.
MEYERS, W. G. E.
TRIMMINS, J. T.
WITHERBEE, Mrs. A. F.
MACKWORTH, Lady.
ADAMS, Mrs. HENRY, Boston.
RANKIN, ROBERT, New York.
SHARP, SAMUEL.
BYRNE, M. B., New York.
DAVIS, EMILY.
WALKER, ANNIE.
HOUSNELL, E.
CROSS, A. B.
YOUNG, PHILIP, Montreal.
VASSAR, W. A. F., London.
STEELE, GEORGE.
CROSLEY, CYRUS.
PARKER, JAMES.
COLEBROOK, the Rev. R.
MORRIS, H. C. S.
FISH, Mrs., and two children.
MARTIN, Miss R.
GAUTLETT, F. J., New York.
MAYCOCK, Miss MAY.
HENDERSON, VIOLET.
MARDERUD, UNO.
LEVIN, THOMAS D.
THOMAS, D. A., Cardiff, Wales.
EVANS, T. J. M.
CLARKE, A. R.
BURGESS, W. G.
CHARLES, J. H., and daughter, Toronto.
LONEY, Miss, New York.
HERRIS, JOHN.
HOLLAND, Miss.
BRANDELL, Miss JOSEPHINE, New York.
PERRY, F. K. A.
GRAB, O. H.
MOSLEY, G. G., New York.
BROOKS, J. H., New York.
JEFFRY, A. M.
CAIRNS, M.
HAMMOND, O. H., New York.
MANLEY, A.
NEATH, H.
NORTH, Miss.
WINTER, Miss.
WINTER, Miss.
DUGUID, GEORGE.
MOORE, DANIEL.
McCONNELL, JOHN W., Memphis, Tenn.
SHARPE, Miss.
CONNER, Miss.
DALY, H. M.
CLIFFE, PATRICK.
BOHAN, JAMES, Toronto.
CROSLEY, Mrs. CYRUS.
BRETHERTON, Mrs. CYRIL H., and two children, Los Angeles, Cal.
HOPKINS, A. L., New York.
LASSETTER, Mrs. H. B., of Sydney, Australia, wife of General Lassetter.
LASSETTER, Master P.
LAURIAT, CHARLES E., Jr., Boston, Mass.
PAYNTER, Miss IRENE, Liverpool, England.

KINSALE, Ireland, May 8.—Eleven survivors of the Lusitania have been landed here, together with the bodies of five persons who were dead. Among the survivors are:

SMITH, J. RESTON, New York.
BOTTOMLEY, FREDERICK.
BOYLE, N. L.
HOTCHKISS, CHARLES.
HARRIMAN, CORNELIUS.
LIVERMORE, VERNAR.
SULLIVAN, Mrs. F.

Consul's List of Saved.

WASHINGTON, May 8.—Consul Lauriat at Queenstown sends this report:

"Total saved of all nationalities, 700. The following are American survivors of Lusitania; other names will follow:

CRAB, O. S.
PEARL, Major and Mrs., and two children.
SMITH, Mrs. JESSIE TAFT.
HARDWICK, CHARLES C.
EARL, STUART D.
PEARL, AMY.
STANLEY, Mrs.
LINES, L. B.
HILL, C. T.
RANKIN, ROBERT.
LONEY, Miss.
DOHERTY, Mrs. WILLIAM and infant.
PHILLIPS, THOMAS.
McADAMS, WILLIAM.
HOUGHTON, J. H.
SWEENEY, JOHN M.
HAMMOND, OADEN H.
BROOKS, J. H.
JEFFRY, CHARLES T.
LUND, Mrs. C. H.
SHEPPERDSON, ARTHUR.
MOORE, Dr. D. V.
BERNARD, CLINTON.
LIGHT, HERBERT.
LINNSON, J., Jr.
WILLIAMS, EDITH.
LEARY, JAMES J.
SLIDELL, THOMAS.
WOLFENDEN, Mrs. JOHN.
HOLLAND, Mrs. NINA.
MESH, Mrs. THOMAS.
KESSLER, GEORGE A.
McMURRAY, L.
KAY, ROBERT.
LOCKHART, R. P.
CANNON, OWEN.
HARRIS, DURIGHT C.
JUDSON, FRED S.
COLLIS, ED M.
WRIGHT, R. C.
GAUNTLET, F. J.
KNOX, S. N.
O'DONNELL, PATRICK.

Saw the Submarine 100 Yards Off and Watched Torpedo as It Struck Ship

Ernest Cowper, a Toronto Newspaper Man, Describes Attack, Seen from Ship's Rail—Poison Gas Used in Torpedoes, Say Other Passengers.

Queenstown, Saturday, May 8, 3:18 A. M.

A sharp lookout for submarines was kept aboard the Lusitania as she approached the Irish coast, according to Ernest Cowper, a Toronto newspaper man, who was among the survivors landed at Queenstown.

He said that after the ship was torpedoed there was no panic among the crew, but that they went about the work of getting passengers into the boats in a prompt and efficient manner.

"As we neared the coast of Ireland," said Mr. Cowper, "we all joined in the lookout, for a possible attack by a submarine was the sole topic of conversation.

"I was chatting with a friend at the rail about 2 o'clock when suddenly I caught a glimpse of the conning tower of a submarine about a thousand yards distant. I immediately called my friend's attention to it. Immediately we both saw the track of a torpedo followed almost instantly by an explosion. Portions of splintered hull were sent flying into the air, and then another torpedo struck. The ship began to list to starboard.

"The crew at once proceeded to get the passengers into boats in an orderly, prompt, and efficient manner. Miss Helen Smith appealed to me to save her. I placed her in a boat and saw her safely away. I got into one of the last boats to leave.

"Some of the boats could not be launched as the vessel was sinking. There was a large number of women and children in the second cabin. Forty of the children were less than a year old."

Poison Fumes from Torpedoes.

From interviews with passengers it appears that when the torpedoes burst they sent forth suffocating fumes which had their effect on the passengers, causing some of them to lose consciousness.

Two stokers, Byrne and Hussey of Liverpool, gave a few details. They said the submarine gave no notice and fired two torpedoes, one hitting No. 1 stoke hole and the second the engine room. The first torpedo was discharged at 2 o'clock. In twenty-five minutes the great liner disappeared.

Signals have been received at Queenstown that an armed trawler, believed to be the Heron, and two fishing trawlers are bringing in 100 more bodies.

The Cunard Line agent states that the total number of persons aboard the Lusitania was 2,160.

Loss of the Lusitania Fills London With Horror and Utter Amazement

Special Cable to THE NEW YORK TIMES.

LONDON, Saturday, May 8.—Stupefaction is the word which best describes the first impression created by the news of the sinking of the Lusitania. People seemed unable to realize that at such a stage of the world's progress such a [illegible] could be committed as an act of war.

"I have no words for it," said Lord Rosebery, and everywhere one found the same sentiment repeated.

[illegible]

Continued on Page 3.

SOME DEAD TAKEN ASHORE

Several Hundred Survivors at Queenstown and Kinsale.

STEWARD TELLS OF DISASTER

One Torpedo Crashes Into the Doomed Liner's Bow, Another Into the Engine Room.

SHIP LISTS OVER TO PORT

Makes It Impossible to Lower Many Boats, So Hundreds Must Have Gone Down.

ATTACKED IN BROAD DAY

Passengers at Luncheon—Warning Had Been Given by Germans Before the Ship Left New York.

Only 650 Were Saved, Few Cabin Passengers

QUEENSTOWN, Saturday, May 8, 4:28 A. M.—Survivors of the Lusitania who have arrived here estimate that only about 650 of those aboard the steamer were saved, and say only a small proportion of those rescued were saloon passengers.

Official Confirmation

WASHINGTON, May 8.—A dispatch to the State Department early today from American Consul Lauriet at Queenstown stated that the total number of survivors of the Lusitania was about 700.

LONDON, Saturday, May 8.—The Cunard liner Lusitania, which sailed out of New York last Saturday with 1,918 souls aboard, lies at the bottom of the ocean off the Irish coast.

She was sunk by a German submarine, which sent two torpedoes crashing into her side at 2:30 o'clock yesterday afternoon while the passengers, seemingly confident that the great, swift vessel could elude the German underwater craft, were having luncheon.

The great inrush of water caused the liner to list heavily to port, so that she could not launch many of her lifeboats.

About 1,260 of those on board the great ship, including many Americans, apparently went down with her, as a statement issued late this morning by the Admiralty says the total number of survivors is only 658.

There were 1,253 passengers on board the steamship, including 200 who were transferred to her from the steamer Cameronia. The Americans totaled 188. The crew numbered 665.

It is believed that only a few first class passengers were saved as they thought the ship would remain afloat, and made little effort to escape.

There appears to be a large proportion of the ship's crew among the survivors landed at Queenstown. Only a few of.

"All the News That's Fit to Print."

The New York Times.

THE WEATHER
Overcast today and Thursday; moderate, variable winds.
For full weather report see Page 21.

VOL. LXV...NO. 21,277. NEW YORK, WEDNESDAY, APRIL 26, 1916.—TWENTY-TWO PAGES. ONE CENT In Greater New York, Jersey City and Newark. | Elsewhere, TWO CENTS.

CHANCELLOR SEES GERARD; HURRIES BACK TO KAISER

Strong Hint in Berlin That Germany Will Offer Modus Vivendi on U-Boat War.

WISH FOR AN UNDERSTANDING

Bethmann Hollweg Confers with Envoy to See What Terms Will Satisfy Us.

PRESS WANTS SETTLEMENT

Continues to View Situation Gravely—Washington Awaits Word from Gerard.

Exodus of Americans From Germany Begun

GENEVA, Wednesday, April 26, (via Paris.)—An exodus of Americans from Germany has begun. Several of them have already arrived at Basle.

They are convinced that a rupture between Germany and the United States is inevitable.

BERLIN, April 25, 8 P. M., (via London, Wednesday, April 26.)—Prior to his departure for headquarters tonight to consult with Emperor William, the submarine issue and Germany's relations with the United States were again under discussion today by Dr. von Bethmann Hollweg, the Imperial Chancellor, and James W. Gerard, the American Ambassador.

No definite decision in the premises apparently has yet been reached, and one probably will not be arrived at until the Chancellor reaches headquarters tomorrow afternoon.

All the surface indications, however, point more and more to the probability that an arrangement regarding the Sussex and a modus vivendi on the submarine problem will be offered to the United States, and that a sincere endeavor to reach an understanding will be made from this side, putting the decision regarding the future status of relations up to Washington.

The public and the press continue to view the situation gravely, but calmly, and for the greater part with a desire that a way out of the controversy may be found.

The Wolf Bureau today circulates an appeal from the German University League of America to the rector of Berlin University for a dispassionate consideration of the American position.

At the Foreign Office today the correspondents were informed that the Chancellor was devoting the holidays to conferences on the submarine issue with the departments concerned.

The main purpose of the Imperial Chancellor's flying trip to Berlin, which involves twenty hours' travel in each direction, has been, as is evident from his protracted conferences with Ambassador Gerard, the desire to obtain as clear an idea as possible of the attitude and policy of the American Government; what, if anything, lies behind and beyond the American note, and what measures are necessary to satisfy the American demand, before the momentous decision is taken by the Emperor and his advisers at headquarters.

The crisis has come to a head in the midst of the Easter holidays—a season playing a highly important rôle in German life, when public men are widely scattered from Berlin, and their views, which the Emperor would naturally wish to ascertain before reaching a decision, not quickly assembled. Thus the formulation of a reply to the American note, which presumably would spell peace or war, cannot be rushed.

Still Hope for Settlement.

So far as Germany is concerned there is still a possibility of a settlement, and hope has not been abandoned here. But the Germans, as is apparent from many conversations which The Associated Press correspondent has had with prominent men since the beginning of this crisis, wish to know before giving their answer, what sort of answer would satisfy the United States, whether assurances of a properly conducted submarine campaign would be adequate, and whether concessions now would be the prelude to further demands later.

It can be stated positively that Dr. von Bethmann Hollweg and his advisers realize fully the disadvantages of a break with the United States, and that they do not desire it if it can be avoided, but they feel, if a breach must come ultimately, it would be useless to indulge in concessions and compromises now, and that they might as well have the matter settled.

Ambassador Gerard conferred on Monday with the Imperial Chancellor alone, none of the Chancellor's advisers participating in the interview. He was able to give the Chancellor little positive or authoritative information on the limits of the American policy beyond the notes themselves, but the Washington policy so far as it was indicated in the various notes to Germany, it is understood, was discussed at length, and possible solutions to the questions which have given rise to the crisis were considered in this long and confidential interview, concerning which the Ambassador naturally declined to talk to the correspondents.

Gerard Cables to Washington.

Mr. Gerard immediately cabled a long account of the conversation to Secretary Lansing, and the feeling here is that if it were possible to obtain an answer from Washington before the German Council were concluded and a decision adopted it might aid materially in the solution. There is little expectation of that, however.

There has been a distinctly better atmosphere in Berlin of late. On the day of the publication of the American note and for some time afterward an air of gloom prevailed regarding future German-American relations, and many men spoke of a rupture as inevitable. The word now is that a settlement is within the reach of possibility, and although it would be wrong to use the word optimism, at least the spirit of pessimism has notably abated, and everywhere one hears the query: "What does America want? Can we satisfy President Wilson without abandoning the submarine campaign, or does he want to prevent us from winning the war?"

During the crisis there has been an

Continued on Page 2.

Mexican Officials Expect Recall of American Troops

Special to The New York Times.

SALTILLO, Coahuila, Mexico, April 25, (en route with General Obregon.)—General Obregon, Minister of War of the de facto Government, arrived here today on his way to a conference with Major Gen. Scott, American Chief of Staff, and Major Gen. Funston in Juarez or El Paso. Officials here are sure that American troops will be withdrawn from Mexico within two weeks, as they contend that American officials agree with Mexicans that the campaign against Villa has resolved itself into a pursuit of one man, the Villa bands having been broken up. The Mexicans also assert that with the impending surrender of General Canuto Reyes at Torreon and the loyalty to Carranza pledged by the Aerieta brothers in Durango, the Villistas have no hopes of procuring a following, as all the Carranza Generals have demonstrated their fealty.

SCOTT AND OBREGON TO MEET IN EL PASO

General Gavira Takes Steps to Suppress Any Disturbance During Conference.

REASSURES GENERAL BELL

New Plot to Seize Chihuahua City and Kill De Facto Authorities Is Unearthed.

Special to The New York Times.

EL PASO, Texas, April 25.—It was announced officially here tonight that the conference between Major Gen. Hugh L. Scott, Chief of Staff of the United States Army, and General Alvaro Obregon, Minister of War of the de facto Mexican Government, would be held in El Paso, and would start as soon as General Obregon reached the border.

General Carranza, in an official statement, declares he has fully approved the plan for having the meeting at El Paso, and announces that he is especially pleased at the assurances given by General Bell and the announcement that General Scott will call on General Obregon in Juarez first.

While the conference is caused by the American expedition's pursuit of Villa, there is much speculation as to just what will be discussed. Mexicans profess to believe that it is details of the withdrawal of the Americans which will be considered. That is not the view expressed in other quarters. It is generally regarded as more likely that General Scott will urge increased cooperation by Carranza troops in the pursuit of Villa and the stamping out of brigandage along the border—or, at least, increased activity by the de facto Government's forces on their own account to accomplish the same object.

General Gavira, Carranza commander at Juarez, was advised by telegraph this afternoon that General Obregon was leaving San Luis Potosi for Saltillo, and was expected to reach Juarez by Saturday by way of Torreon and Monterey. He will establish his headquarters in Juarez in the fine home which Villa seized from old General Ochoa, and where William Benton, an Englishman, was killed. He will then confer with General Scott through his aids and arrange for the first meeting to be held in the Juarez Custom House, probably Sunday or Monday, if his arrival is not delayed.

Gutierrez May Attend.

Since it became known that General Funston would accompany General Scott, General Gavira has wired to General Obregon advising him to have General Gutierrez, Commander of the Northern Division, accompany him to the border in order that he may have a man on his staff who will be of equal rank with the American General, as both General Scott and General Obregon will be acting as diplomatic representatives of the State Department and Foreign Ministry of Mexico.

A big reception and celebration is being planned for General Obregon in Juarez. This will be patterned after the Taft-Diaz celebration, including the decoration of the streets with flowers and arches and the holding of a public reception in the old Custom House. General Scott will be invited to participate in this reception and will be asked to make his first formal call on General Obregon at that time. Subsequent meetings will be held in the Federal Building in El Paso.

General George Bell, Jr., and General Gavira discussed today the proposed conference with a view toward the closest co-operation to prevent any demonstrations.

"I want you to feel reassured, General Gavira, that if there is any indications of trouble along this part of the border the trouble will be started on your side of the line," General Bell said.

"There will be no trouble," General Gavira replied. "I can assure you of that. My men are too well disciplined and too well trained to attempt such a thing, and we have shown by the rigid use of our authority that we deal hard with enemies of the Constitutional Government who seek to cause trouble between us and our good friend of the North."

Gavira Instructs Officers.

Following out General Bell's suggestion, General Gavira then called all of his officers around him and gave them orders that if there should be any firing across the line of whatever nature there should be no return of the fire until a full investigation had been made in order to avoid friction at a time when a peaceful solution of the troubles of the two countries was so near at hand.

Mexican officials in Juarez may make recommendations to General Carranza asking that the conference between General Scott and General Obregon be held at some other point than Juarez or El Paso. This move, if it is made, will be based on the strong interventionist feeling here and in the fear that influences adverse to the de facto Government might be brought to bear on the conferees. Interventionists have caused friction by circulating rumors of outrages committed on Americans by Mexicans and of the destruction by Mexican mobs of American property. These stories were either grossly exaggerated or purely imaginary, and have caused deep resentment on the part of the Mexican officials in Juarez.

The "Rumorists" have fought sanguinary battles in the last few days at Satevo, San Antonio, Namiquipa, Parral, and points east and west, but every reliable report received here from the interior shows no serious disturbance of any kind.

Another plot against the Chihuahua

Continued on Page 4.

ROOSEVELT LOSES IN THE BAY STATE BY 15,000 VOTES

Massachusetts Elects an Unpledged "Big Four" to Head Chicago Delegation.

TWO DISTRICTS FOR T. R.

This Gives Him Four Delegates—Other Thirty-two from the State Are Unpledged.

COLONEL'S MEN UNDAUNTED

Regard the Result as Not a Fair Indication of Massachusetts Sentiment.

Special to The New York Times.

BOSTON, Mass., April 25.—Unpledged delegates at large to the Republican National Convention were elected at the Presidential primaries today over four candidates pledged to the nomination of Colonel Theodore Roosevelt.

Returns from 1,120 out of the 1,140 districts of the State show that the Roosevelt delegates have been defeated by an average majority of 15,000. Governor S. W. McCall, the highest man on the unpledged delegation, runs nearly 17,000 above the highest man among the Roosevelt candidates, Charles S. Bird.

The indications are that "unpledged," or anti-Roosevelt, delegates will be sent to Chicago from fourteen of the sixteen Congressional districts of the State. That will give Colonel Roosevelt only four of the thirty-six delegates from Massachusetts.

While the "straight goods" Republican leaders, headed by ex-Senator W. Murray Crane, have been confident for some days of victory in the primary fight, the majority rolled up for the unpledged delegation of which ex-Senator Crane himself is a member exceeded their expectations.

While Governor McCall or Senator Weeks and possibly both may receive complimentary votes from the delegation, few here believe they have a chance of being nominated. With favorite sons barred, it is said that the delegation will show an impressive majority for Justice Hughes.

The totals in the 1,120 districts as reported at a late hour are:

Unpledged Candidates.

Governor Samuel W. McCall	62,259
Senator Henry C. Lodge	60,683
W. Murray Crane	58,340
Senator John W. Weeks	56,672

Candidates Pledged to Roosevelt.

Charles Sumner Bird	45,538
Grafton D. Cushing	45,484
Augustus P. Gardner	44,862
R. M. Washburn	42,549

Of the district delegates the indications at midnight were that the following had been elected from the Congressional districts:

Delegates Unpledged.

1. William H. Brooks, Charles R. Hull.
2. George A. Bacon, Alexander McCallum.
3. Herbert E. Cummings, J. Lovell Johnson.
4. W. A. L. Bazeley, Charles G. Washburn.
5. Herbert E. Fletcher, John N. Cole.
6. John L. Saltonstall, Edward R. Hale.
7. Eugene B. Fraser, A. N. Frost.
8. George B. Wason, Wilton B. Fay.
10. E. C. R. Bagley, Abraham C. Ratschesky.
11. Charles H. Innes, Warren F. Freeman.
12. J. Waldo Pond, Walter B. Grant.
13. George H. Doty, Martin Hays.
15. Edward Thurston, Joseph Martin, Jr.
16. Charles L. Gifford, Thomas F. Glennon.

Pledged to Roosevelt.

9. Fred P. Greenwood, Alvah T. Fuller.
14. Henry L. Kincaide, C. Chester Eaton.

The showing made by the unpledged forces in the campaign for district delegates came as a complete surprise to the other side. The defeat of the Roosevelt delegates in the Sixth Congressional District represented by Augustus P. Gardner, one of the Roosevelt delegates at large, came as a stunning blow to the managers of the campaign for the pledged delegation.

Congressman Gardner when asked to comment on the victory of the "straight goods" delegates over those pledged to the Colonel said:

"It was a pity the vote was so light, but I suppose a majority of 15,000 would have been too great to overcome even with a bigger vote. Of course there is this to consider that the candidates on the "unpledged" ticket were the most prominent Republicans in the State, while those pledged to Colonel Roosevelt were not of first prominence. I believe the result would have been very different had we used a ballot by which the voters could have cast their ballots directly for the Presidential nominee of their choice. Under said circumstances I firmly believe Colonel Roosevelt would have defeated any other candidate, not even excluding Justice Hughes, by 15,000."

Commenting on the primary results, Governor McCall said tonight: "I am naturally gratified that the unpledged delegates were elected. The campaign has been conducted without rancor, and I feel sure that it will have no ill effects upon the party."

There was one candidate for district delegate in the field pledged to the nomination of Justice Hughes. He was Charles H. Brown of Medford, running in the Eighth Congressional District. Returns indicate his defeat.

No returns indicating even approximately the vote cast for the Democratic delegates at large were available up to midnight. There was no contest, all the delegates at large being pledged to the renomination of President Wilson. There was little interest and a very light vote in the Democratic primaries.

Apathy in the Campaign.

Despite ideal Spring weather that should have brought the voters out in great numbers the vote throughout the entire State was very light. From the early returns it would appear that less than half the vote of four years ago was cast. The lack of interest was particularly marked in this city, where every district, except those in the Back Bay district, fell far behind the vote of other years.

Generally the light vote is regarded here as reflecting the apathy which has been noticeable throughout the campaign, which was in marked contrast to the interest that was shown in the preferential primaries four years ago, when

Continued on Page 22.

Eight British Airmen Rout Turkish Force Near Suez Canal with a Shower of Bombs

LONDON, April 25.—Eight British aeroplanes bombarded the hostile camp at Quatia in Egypt, near the Suez Canal, it was announced officially today. The camp was destroyed, and the hostile troops, the aviators reported, apparently began to withdraw from that district.

The statement on the recent operations in the vicinity of Quatia says:

"With reference to the fighting in the Quatia district on April 23, the general officer commanding in Egypt reports that it was of a more severe character than at first intimated. The defense of Dueidar was gallantly maintained by one company of Royal Scots. The enemy casualties amounted to seventy killed, and he left behind twenty-eight prisoners taken by us, and war material amounting to 5,000 rounds of small-arm ammunition, four machine-gun belt boxes full, twenty-eight shells, and eighty rifles.

"The pursuing column mentioned in yesterday's report took several more prisoners. Our aeroplanes effected severe casualties with bombs and machine gun fire. One of our mounted brigades was engaged all day with the enemy.

"On April 24 eight aeroplanes took part in an attack on the enemy camp near Quatia, effecting a complete surprise. The hostile camp was destroyed. The enemy suffered severe casualties from bombs dropped and from machine gun fire.

"There was no further fighting on the 24th, and the enemy appeared to be withdrawing from the Quatia district."

In an official statement from London yesterday it was said a hostile column 3,000 strong had attacked the village of Quatia, compelling the withdrawal of the defending small force after a severe engagement. Simultaneously with this battle an action occurred in the neighborhood of Dueidar, which was attacked by 500 men. This force was beaten off after British reinforcements had been brought up. It was said the known casualties of the hostile detachment amounted to forty killed, in addition to which thirty men were made prisoners.

The presence near the Suez Canal of hostile organized forces in such numbers had not been disclosed previously. Quatia is twenty-five miles east of the canal, on a road to El Kantara, where the Turks made their previous unsuccessful attempt to reach the canal. This attack was made in November of 1915, and since that time, so far as has been known, no organized efforts have been made by the Turks to invade Egypt.

MORGENTHAU QUITS AS ENVOY TO TURKEY

Will Take Active Part in President Wilson's Campaign for Re-election.

WILL ORGANIZE LEAGUE

Of Nonpartisan Supporters of Administration—Elkus Expected to be Sent to Turkey.

Special to The New York Times.

WASHINGTON, April 25.—Henry Morgenthau of New York has tendered to President Wilson his resignation as Ambassador to Turkey. No action has been taken on the resignation, but it is assured that the President will accept it. Mr. Morgenthau has been credited with an intention to leave the Diplomatic Service, and, according to gossip here, Abram I. Elkus of New York will be offered the Ambassadorship to Turkey.

The purpose of Mr. Morgenthau in resigning is to enable him to take an active part in the forthcoming political campaign in behalf of President Wilson. When he returned to the United States from Constantinople last February he laid before Secretary McAdoo and other close friends and supporters of the Administration a plan for the formation of a league in the interest of Mr. Wilson's re-election, this league to be composed of business men and others, and to include in its membership independents and persons formerly affiliated with other political parties who were willing to support the Democratic cause this year.

While Mr. Morgenthau was willing to take charge of the formation of the league, he felt that he could not remain in this country engaged in political work while he retained his Ambassadorial office. Men prominent in the Administration urged him not to resign, and expressed the opinion that there would be no impropriety in his remaining in the Diplomatic Service.

At Mr. Morgenthau's home last night it was said that no statement could be made on the subject of his resignation. Reporters were told to call the Ambassador in the morning, that he would see no one until then.

DR. STEIN FALLS DEAD TALKING TO DOCTORS

Brother-in-Law of Henry Morgenthau Stricken on Rostrum at Academy of Medicine.

Dr. Richard Stein, a prominent physician and a brother-in-law of Henry Morgenthau, Ambassador to Turkey, dropped dead last night of apoplexy while reading a paper before the Metropolitan Medical Society at the New York Academy of Medicine, in West Forty-third Street.

Dr. Stein was apparently in the best of health when he ascended the rostrum, shortly after 10 o'clock. He had been reading possibly for fifteen minutes when he suddenly let go his hold on the desk before him and fell backward. The thirty physicians present gathered around him. Several applied artificial respiration and powerful heart stimulants were used, but death had been instantaneous, for all their efforts failed to bring a trace of life.

The body was left on the platform where he had fallen pending the action of Coroner Feinberg, who gave permission at once for its removal. In the meantime Mr. Morgenthau had been notified, and he went first to the Academy building and then to the home of Dr. Stein, at 79 East Seventy-ninth Street, where he broke the news to Mrs. Stein, who is a sister of Mrs. Morgenthau. The body of Dr. Stein was still in the Academy at midnight, where some of his close friends in the profession still remained.

Dr. Stein was born fifty-five years ago in Bohemia. He was a graduate of the College of the City of New York, and his medical degree was from the University of Berlin. He stood high as a general practitioner and gave special attention to diseases of the heart.

Dr. Stein was visiting physician to the German and the Lebanon Hospitals. He was a member of the American Medical Association, the New York Academy of Medicine, the County Medical Society, the Pathological Society, and the Metropolitan Medical Society, the last of which he was addressing at the time of his death.

The society, whose meeting was brought to an abrupt close, was to have been entertained by Drs. J. Teschner and P. Fridenberg. The members of the organization, several of whom were seen last night at the Academy, expressed their deep sorrow over the death of their colleague. They said, however, that, as his life had been so given to the advancement of general medicine, it was in keeping with his devotion to his profession that he should be stricken while reading a paper intended to add to the common fund of medical knowledge.

Mrs. Stein was Miss Sophie Sykes of this city. They had no children.

BERNSTORFF MUST IDENTIFY PAPERS

Lansing Decides Envoy Can Have Only Those That He Declares Official.

PRECEDENT FOR DECISION

Washington Sees Possibility of a Diplomatic Snarl Over the von Igel Documents.

Special to The New York Times.

WASHINGTON, April 25.—Secretary Lansing has decided to give to Count von Bernstorff, the German Ambassador, only those documents which the Ambassador identifies as "official" from among the papers taken from the raided New York office of Wolf von Igel of the German Embassy staff, who was arrested by Department of Justice agents in connection with the plot to destroy the Welland Canal.

It was learned today that the Secretary of State is determined in the stand he has taken not to authorize the return of any of these papers until and unless they are identified by the Ambassador as being "official," which means that they must be claimed as Embassy records. Officials of the Government will not attempt to identify any papers as official. The identification must be made by the Ambassador or someone designated to represent his Embassy. Papers not identified as official will be held by the Government. Should some documents be claimed as official, such identification is expected to prove embarrassing to the Embassy because it would be regarded as linking the Embassy with knowledge of illegal activities covered by these particular documents.

The fact that the Administration is determined to make an issue over the return of the papers is likely to precipitate a stiff diplomatic row unless the German Ambassador should withdraw his demand for the return of all the von Igel papers. There had been intimations during the past few days that this Government might be willing to permit the return of all the von Igel documents. The fact that only such documents as Count von Bernstorff may identify as "official" may be claimed indicates that the Administration has decided to take a firm stand in the matter.

It became evident today that this Government is prepared to resist Count von Bernstorff's claim that all papers belonging to diplomatic agents are immune from seizure.

An interesting precedent that may, and probably will, be invoked during the consideration of the claims made on behalf of the German Embassy for the return of the papers was discovered today. The Prussian Government more than a century ago virtually acquiesced in the abstraction of American diplomatic papers by British diplomats who had been sent to Berlin during the American Revolution. These papers were returned, but copies of them were made by the British Minister in Berlin and sent to London.

Frederick the Great, then King of Prussia, despite the fact that these papers were taken by the diplomatic representative of a nation with which the American colonists were then at war, Prussia having recognized the belligerency of the colonists, did not demand the recall of the British Minister who was charged with having planned and perfected the seizure. The United States Government has never forgotten this rifling of an American diplomatic agent's "red box" in Berlin, and is expected to resort to this, among other precedents, in its treatment of the diplomatic aspect of the von Igel case.

ASK TRUCKMAN ABOUT PLOT.

Grand Jury Hears from Men Dr. Schule Employed.

The Federal Grand Jury, which is continuing the investigation into alleged German bomb manufacturing plots, strikes at munition plants and steamship piers and the expenditure by Franz Rintelen and other German secret agents of money in propaganda work, had before it yesterday afternoon three Hoboken truckmen—E. Hiney, Frederick Rittman, and Frederick Conway. They were interrogated by Assistant United States District Attorney Wood regarding their employment by Dr. Walter T. Scheele, the chemist who operated the factory of the New Jersey Agricultural Chemical Company at Twelfth and Clinton Streets, Hoboken.

Mr. Wood said yesterday that among the papers found in von Igel's office were some which illuminated evidence already in possession of the Government concerning the first Welland Canal plot. These papers indicate, he added, that the plot to destroy the canal did not necessitate an expenditure of more than $1,000, and out of this came the money used to purchase 300 pounds of dynamite, and to pay the expenses of the men sent to Niagara Falls, N. Y.

Von Igel's arraignment is now set for next Monday morning before Judge Harland B. Howe in the United States District Court.

Count von Bernstorff, the German Ambassador, went to Washington yesterday.

TROOPS CRUSH REVOLT IN DUBLIN; TAKE POST OFFICE SEIZED BY RIOTERS; MANY KILLED IN STREET FIGHTING

Sir Roger Casement in London for Trial; He is Detained in Military Custody

LONDON, Wednesday, April 26.—It was announced officially yesterday that Sir Roger Casement had been brought to London for trial. The announcement follows:

Sir Roger Casement, who was arrested in connection with an abortive attempt to land arms in Ireland from a German vessel, was brought to London on Sunday morning. He was met at Euston by officers from Scotland Yard, and is now detained in military custody.

It is understood evidence of his proceedings in Germany since the outbreak of the war will be produced at his trial.

BRITISH HOUSES IN SECRET SESSION

Curzon and Rosebery Resume Their Seats in the Lords for the Momentous Occasion.

GREAT PRECAUTIONS TAKEN

Even Ventilator Sealed to Prevent Eavesdropping—Recruiting Plan to be Made Public.

LONDON, Wednesday, April 26.—The most crowded houses since the war began were drawn to Westminster Palace yesterday by the excitement attending the secret session of Parliament, coupled with the news of various stirring incidents. Earl Curzon made his first appearance in the House of Lords since his illness. The Earl of Rosebery, who had not been seen there since the commencement of the war, also was in his seat. The interest of the public was shown by the large crowd which assembled to watch the arrival of the Ministers and members.

Extraordinary precautions were taken to prevent unauthorized persons overhearing the proceedings. All the doors leading to the House of Commons not only were locked but secured by padlocks which had been specially provided, while the police searched every nook and cranny of the great building, scoured the vaults and underground corridors, and even sealed the grille of the ventilator in the floor of the chamber so that nothing said could by any chance reach the ears of any one below.

Traditional customs were followed in the House of Commons, which was open as usual to attachés, representatives of the press, and spectators until the end of the question period. At that time Premier Asquith observed the ancient practice of taking notice that strangers were present. The question was put that strangers must be ordered to withdraw, which does not permit of debate or amendment. Before the house was adjourned at night it was arranged that the sitting should be resumed today under similar conditions.

In the House of Lords the only procedure was to give notice that no one except members would be permitted in the Chamber.

The Marquis of Crewe, Lord President of the Council, in moving that the sitting be in secret, made a statement on behalf of the Government why this course should be adopted. Although the members of the Cabinet were all set on the achievement of a victory, the Marquis said, they did not agree concerning the number of men or the kind of men who were available for service in the army and navy, nor did they agree as to the proper means for securing those who were available.

The course which the Government proposed to recommend to Parliament might not meet with the full desires of persons of either extreme views, and therefore it was the Government's duty to recommend it as far as possible to the opinion of Parliament as a whole, which necessitated the making of a statement containing confidential information. Hence the Government had decided to hold a secret session, "publishing at an early date a considered description of the proposal which the Government in due course would make to Parliament and the country."

The Marquis of Lincolnshire as Lord Great Chamberlain explained that, in accordance with the hereditary duties of his office, he had taken steps to see that the secrecy would be "most strictly and solemnly observed." He had, he said, caused a search to be made "of the whole House, the lobbies, and the vaults below."

Special Cable to THE NEW YORK TIMES.

LONDON, Wednesday, April 26.—The Daily Chronicle's Parliamentary correspondent says this morning of yesterday's secret session:

"The stringent and comprehensive second paragraph of the new Order in Council, forbidding 'any person or newspaper publishing any report of or purporting to describe or refer to the proceedings at any Cabinet,' pleases nobody but its authors, and the House may have something to say on the subject. To a question by Sir H. Dalziel as to whether the House would have an early opportunity of discussing it, Premier Asquith replied with a request for a notice.

"At 3:12, Asquith, whose rising was a signal for a cordial outburst of applause, addressing the Speaker, said: 'Sir, I beg to call your attention to the fact that strangers are present.' The use of this formula precluded the possibility of debate, the rule being that in these circumstances the Speaker has to put the question forthwith without discussion.

"On Mr. Lowther putting it to the House that strangers be ordered to withdraw, there were many cries of dissent, and it seemed as if the opponents of a secret session would challenge the division. After a lapse of a few moments the Speaker again put the question, and the dissentients were now less vocal, only one solitary voice exclaiming 'No!' Thereupon the motion was adopted by general consent and everybody save the members withdrew from the chamber."

SEA AND AIR RAID ON ENGLISH COAST

German Battle Cruiser Fleet and Two Zeppelins Driven Off After Brief Fight.

SHIPS BOMBARD LOWESTOFT

Four Persons Killed on Shore—Three British Vessels Hit and Aviator Lost.

LONDON, April 25.—German warships and Zeppelins attacked the east coast of England early today, but were driven off after a brief engagement by British warships and aeroplanes. One English air pilot was wounded and another is missing, with his aeroplane.

The German naval fleet—battle cruisers, light cruisers, destroyers, and submarines—appeared off Lowestoft at 4:30 A. M. Local naval forces and British light cruisers, with aircraft, engaged the raiders. The German warships retreated in twenty minutes.

The German warships opened fire on the coast before departing. Two men, one woman, and a child were killed. The material damage done apparently was small.

In the engagement two British light cruisers and a destroyer were hit, but none of them were sunk.

The Official Reports.

The following official announcement was made:

At about 4:30 o'clock this morning the German battle cruiser squadron, accompanied by light cruisers and destroyers, appeared off Lowestoft. The local naval force engaged it and in about twenty minutes it returned to Germany, chased by our light cruisers and destroyers.

On shore two men, one woman, and a child were killed. The material damage seems to have been insignificant, so far as is known at present. Two British light cruisers and a destroyer were hit, but none were sunk.

A later official statement contained this information:

During the operations against the German battle cruiser squadron off the east coast two Zeppelins were pursued by naval and land machines over sixty miles out to sea. Bombs and darts were dropped, but apparently without serious effect.

An aeroplane and a seaplane attacked the German ships off Lowestoft, dropping heavy bombs. Four enemy submarines also were attacked by bombs. One seaplane came under a heavy fire from the hostile fleet, but the pilot, although seriously wounded, succeeded in bringing his machine safely back to land.

It is regretted that one pilot is reported missing. He ascended during the Zeppelin raid earlier in the morning and appears from reports to have attacked a Zeppelin off Lowestoft at about 1:05 A. M. He has not been heard from since.

PREVIOUS NAVAL RAIDS.

Several Since the War Began—In One 130 Persons Were Killed.

Lowestoft, bombarded yesterday by a German fleet, is on the North Sea coast of England, to the northeast of London. It is almost opposite The Hague and is the most easterly town in England. It is a fishing station and a fashionable seashore resort. Its population is about 30,000.

On previous occasions during the war attacks on the English coast have been made by German warships. The most important raid was made on Dec. 16, 1914. The towns of Scarborough, Whitby, and Hartlepool, about 150 miles north of Lowestoft were bombarded and about 130 persons were killed. Aided by fog, the German vessels escaped.

On Jan. 24, 1915, a further attempt of the kind was made, but the German squadron was met off Dogger Bank by the British battle cruiser squadron under Vice Admiral Sir David Beatty. On being sighted the Germans made for home at high speed. Their rear ship, the Bluecher, was sunk, and two other cruisers were set on fire and damaged severely. The British flagship Lion was disabled by a shot in one of her feed tanks and was towed home.

The first German naval raid on the British coast was made on Nov. 3, 1914. Three battle cruisers, the Seydlitz, Moltke, and Von der Tann, the armored cruisers Bluecher and Yorck, and the protected cruisers Kolberg, Graudenz, and Strassburg, left port on the evening of Nov. 2, and at dawn appeared off Yarmouth. They bombarded Yarmouth and Lowestoft for about twenty minutes and then returned. A British submarine—the D-5—attempted to pursue the Germans, but struck a mine and sank. The Yorck also struck a mine, and went down with 300 men.

In the raid on Hartlepool, Scarborough, and Whitby, the German cruisers poured a hail of shells into the towns for an hour and a half, and in addition to the large number killed, 200 or more

Continued on Page 2.

WIRES FROM CITY ARE CUT

But Government Says Trouble Is in Hand and Has Not Spread.

SINN FEIN SOCIETY COUP

Outbreak Is Almost Coincident with Casement's Attempt to Land German Arms.

MILITARY LOSE 12 KILLED

Score of Regulars, Volunteers, and Police Wounded—Losses of Rebels Not Given.

LONDON, Wednesday, April 26.—Almost coincidental with the capture of Sir Roger Casement, leader of the Separatist faction in Ireland, while he was attempting to land arms from Germany on the coast of Ireland, there has occurred in Ireland a revolutionary outbreak of considerable proportions.

So far as has been announced by the British Government only Dublin is affected. Here serious fighting took place Monday between regular troops, volunteers, and policemen against members of the Sinn Fein Society who had captured the Post Office and Stephen's Green and numerous houses in various parts of the city.

Three of the officers of the troops, four or five soldiers, two volunteers, and two policemen were killed, and about a score of others wounded. The losses of the revolutionists have not been made known.

The Government last evening reported that the military authorities had the situation well in hand. The official statement said:

At noon yesterday serious disturbances broke out in Dublin. A large party of men identified with the Sinn Fein Party, mostly armed, occupied Stephens Green, and took possession forcibly of the Post Office, where they cut the telegraphic and telephonic wires. Houses also were occupied in Stephens Green, Sackville Street, Abbey Street, and along the quays.

In the course of the day soldiers arrived from the Curragh and the situation is now well in hand. So far as is known here, three military officers, four or five soldiers, two loyal volunteers and two policemen have been killed and four or five military officers and seven or eight soldiers and six volunteers wounded. No exact information has been received of the casualties on the side of the Sinn Feiners.

Reports received from Cork, Limerick, Ennis, Tralee, and both ridings of Tipperary show that no disturbances of any kind have occurred in these localities.

The first announcement of the trouble was made in the House of Commons yesterday by Augustine Birrell, Chief Secretary for Ireland, who said that the situation was well in hand, but that communication with Dublin was still difficult. There had been several arrests there, but he could not give the names, he said.

While the only details surrounding the situation are the meagre ones contained in the official announcements Government officials expressed the opinion that with Sir Roger Casement and two of his aids in prison in London the troops were in control of the situation.

The arrest of Sir Roger Casement was dealt with by The Pall Mall Gazette yesterday in an editorial which is extremely significant at this moment, but which, for obvious reasons, cannot be dilated upon.

"Before Germany took the trouble to send arms to Ireland," says the newspaper, "she must have been satisfied of the existence of agents in that country who were prepared to receive and use them in her interests. That is to say that there must have been active communication between Irish traitors and their confederates in Berlin despite all existing precautions of censorship and supervision.

"When we find a force devoid of arms undergoing military training in Ireland and a cargo of arms from our enemies seeking a landing place in that country it becomes highly desirable that the connection, if any, between these two striking phenomena should be more fully explained."

LONDON HAD HEARD RUMORS.

Failure to Avert Outbreak May Lead to Official Investigation.

Special Cable to THE NEW YORK TIMES.

LONDON, Wednesday, April 26.—The bulk of informed comment in London in regard to the outbreak in Dublin was expressed in terms of astonishment that, in view of the information which must have been in the possession of the authorities as to the preparations for a rebellion, which was known to be in making, no precautionary measures adequate to crush the movement in its inception were taken.

For some time past rumors of impending trouble have been current in London, and the Irish papers have printed information of an alarming character. Although the London papers generally refrained from or were not allowed to print news of this nature from Dublin, The Times about ten days ago gave a half-column report from its Dublin correspondent of the seditious movement there.

Birrell's replies in Commons to Captain Craig, Edward Carson and Sharman Crawford were described by members of the Commons as surprising.

In the early part of last week THE NEW YORK TIMES correspondent heard reports that an Irish rebellion was timed to break out between Good Friday and Easter Monday. These reports were spread broadcast, and it was naturally

"All the News That's Fit to Print."

The New York Times.

THE WEATHER
Fair Sunday; Monday partly cloudy; light, variable winds.
For full weather report see Page 23.

VOL. LXV...NO. 21,281. NEW YORK, SUNDAY, APRIL 30, 1916.—96 PAGES, In Seven Parts, Including Picture and Rotogravure Section and Review of Books. PRICE FIVE CENTS.

CONFEREES OPEN MEXICAN PARLEY; VIEWS CONFLICT

Obregon Asks for Withdrawal of Our Troops and Scott for Co-operation.

BOTH QUESTIONS DEFERRED

Long Discussion Over the Conditions in Territory Where Pershing's Men Are.

CORDIALITY SHOWN AT END

Impressive Military Display Marks Reception of Obregon and Staff in El Paso.

From a Staff Correspondent.
Special to The New York Times.

EL PASO, Tex., April 29.—The first conference between the representatives of the United States and Mexico began at 5 o'clock this afternoon in the Mexican Customs House in Juarez, and at exactly 7 o'clock, when the four American Army officers and six Mexican representatives left the building, General Scott was seen to pat General Obregon on the shoulder as they went down the steps.

Both the American Chief of Staff and the Mexican Minister of War were smiling, and the conferees of both sides shook hands with one another. Beyond this manifestation of cordiality, they disclosed nothing that had occurred at the discussion of the operations of the American punitive expedition in Mexico, but THE NEW YORK TIMES correspondent is able to state with authority that this is what occurred at the first conference:

General Obregon communicated to General Scott what amounted to a demand that all American troops be withdrawn from Mexico. This was discussed for a few minutes, then it was practically tabled.

Scott's Counter-Proposal.

General Scott presented then the counter-proposal that the Carranza Government co-operate with the American force in Mexico in further pursuit of the Villista bandits. After brief discussion this counter-proposal was tabled to be taken up again at a later conference.

It was agreed between the representatives of the two Governments that these two proposals could not be passed on until there had been discussion regarding the actual conditions prevailing in Mexico in general, and particularly in the State of Chihuahua. Thereupon a prolonged discussion of conditions in the northern State in which the American troops are now situated began. This discussion lasted throughout the remainder of the conference.

General Scott said after the first conference:

"You may say for me that the meeting was very satisfactory. I will notify General Obregon as to the time of our next meeting."

The Mexican representatives have with them the Civil Governor of Chihuahua, Ignacio Enriquez, a clean-cut young Mexican who was educated at the University of Illinois. He is here practically as a "witness in the case."

In presenting their arguments in the discussion of conditions in the North of Mexico, the official representatives will call Enriquez to bear testimony that the State is now under the control of Carranza. And the reports of Mexican secret agents are already here, to be introduced as documentary evidence to the same end.

Mexicans Prepare a "Brief."

The Mexicans have prepared their case like a lawyer's brief. Another "witness" will be Luis Gutierrez, Military Governor of Chihuahua. From sources which THE TIMES correspondent is unable to disclose it was learned authoritatively tonight that General Obregon has complete authority to conduct the conferences without awaiting new instructions of any sort from General Carranza.

General Scott, however, will communicate each day while the conferences are in progress with the Washington Administration and receive new instructions with which to enter the next session.

General Scott is communicating the result of the first conference to Washington this evening, and expects further instructions by tomorrow morning.

The next conference was tentatively set for tomorrow to be held in the same room in the Mexican Custom House. The time is undecided. General Scott will set the hour after hearing from Washington. Those in a position to know estimated tonight that the conferences would last at least four or five days, and probably longer.

The officials who attended the conference this evening were:

Representing the United States, General Hugh L. Scott, Chief of Staff; General Frederick Funston, Lieut. Col. R. E. L. Michie of the General Staff, and Captain Fitzhugh Lee, General Funston's Aid.

Representing Mexico: General Obregon, the Minister of War; General Jacinto Trevino, commander of the Department of the Northeast; General Luis Gutierrez, General Plutarco, and General Elias Calles, Military Governor of Sonora.

The Mexicans also had present as an interpreter Andreas Garcia, their consul at El Paso, and there was an American interpreter with General Scott.

General Calles arrived here this morning. He had not been included in the list of conferees at first, but yesterday telegraphed a request that he be allowed to attend, and was invited by General Funston. The representatives of both countries agreed at this evening's conference that they would make no official statements for publication until all of the conferences were over.

Obregon and Suite Received.

The first official conference, which did not begin until 5 o'clock this afternoon, followed an exchange of formal visits on the part of the representatives of the two Governments. The American officials took the initiative and made the first call last night, motoring across the international bridge and visiting General Obregon and his associates in the Juarez custom house.

The Mexican officials paid a return visit this morning, General Obregon and his large retinue of Generals and minor officers calling on Generals Scott and Funston in their private car parked at the railroad station here. But before they reached the car the Mexicans had an opportunity to learn that despite the fact that about 12,000 American troops are now in Mexico there is still an impressive number of them at a particular point of the border. When the Americans crossed the

Continued on Page 4.

VILLISTAS SMASHED, ARMY OFFICERS THINK

Americans' Hard and Frequent Blows Have Taken Fight Out of Scattered Bandits.

By FRANK B. ELSER.
Special Correspondent of The New York Times.

RANCHO PROVIDENCIA, Chihuahua, Mexico, April 28, (by Carrier to Headquarters of General Pershing, Namiquipa, thence by Wireless to Columbus, N. M., April 29.)—Officers of the Seventh Cavalry arriving at this camp this afternoon from Minaca, Santo Tomas, and other towns in the Guerrero district were of the opinion that Villa forces in the Sierra Madre, in broken up bands, had been hit so hard and so often since the Americans came into the country that all the fight had been taken out of them.

These officers said that to the Americans had been given valuable assistance by the Carranzistas during the thirty-day campaign, which closed with the defeat of the last band of Villistas of considerable size at Temachi on Saturday, April 22.

Carranzistas, with large reinforcements from Torreon and from Zacatecas, San Luis Potosi, and other States in the southern part of the Republic, began to arrive today. As they have nothing in common with the natives of this region, it is now believed that they are in a position to keep Villistas from reassembling in numbers sufficiently large to do damage or levy tribute.

The opinion prevails among men arriving from the west that Villa is dead. This opinion is said to be entertained by natives regardless of political leanings.

CONFEREES DEADLOCK ON ARMY BILL ITEM

Can't Agree on Number of Regulars, on Volunteer Reserve or on Nitrate Plant.

WASHINGTON, April 29.—Conferees of the House and Senate, after three days of deliberation on the Army Reorganization bill, the first of the big preparedness measures, have come to a complete deadlock over several important features. It was strongly intimated tonight that they would report a disagreement and ask their respective branches of Congress for further instructions.

"Hopelessly apart on the size of the regular army, on the proposals for a volunteer reserve army, and on a Government nitrate plant," was the report of one member of the conference tonight, and he declared Congress would be asked in the near future to pass again on these features of the measure.

The Senate conferees are insisting determinedly upon the provision in the Senate bill for a regular army of 250,000 men and Representative Kahn, the Republican House conferee, is standing with them. Representatives Hay and Dent, however, are insistent upon the House provision for 140,000 men.

Representative Kahn pointed out to the conferees today that his amendment for an army of 200,000 had been defeated by only a small majority when the House had the bill under consideration. Since that time, big army men contend, international developments have caused a change of feeling on the part of many representatives. Some Administration leaders think the House might now be brought to accept the 250,000 Senate proposal should the conferees fail to agree.

It was said tonight that should a disagreement be reported the Senate might agree to give up its volunteer army plan and accept instead the National Guard reserve provision of the House bill, and might also abandon the Government nitrate plant provision, which, it is conceded generally, never will be accepted by the House.

900 RECRUITS A WEEK ARMY'S AVERAGE NOW

5,417 Men Enlisted in Last 44 Days—18,413 Applicants Rejected.

WASHINGTON, April 29.—Figures compiled by the War Department based on reports from recruiting stations in all parts of the country show that 5,417 recruits have been obtained for the army in the last forty-four days. This is a fraction over one-fourth of the total of 20,000 men to be added to the regular army under the Hay emergency resolution, which was passed by Congress immediately after the Pershing expedition went into Mexico. At the present rate of enlistment it will take all Summer to obtain 20,000 recruits.

During the forty-four days in which the enlistment has been pushed under high pressure the recruiting officers have received applications from 23,830 young men. Of this number the applications of 18,413 were rejected on account of failure to measure up to the high standard required by the recruiting officers.

Every five days the War Department receives telegraphic reports showing the progress in recruiting, the last of these periods having ended at noon yesterday. These reports show that the recruits are being obtained at the rate of about 900 a week. To date the enlistment record has been as follows, for each of the periods:

Period Ending	Applications.	Acceptances.
March 20	2,453	550
March 25	2,652	[illegible]
March 31	3,963	[illegible]
April 5	2,880	620
April 14	4,966	1,048
April 21	3,513	772
April 28	3,436	718
Total	23,830	5,417

Chicago has been the banner recruiting centre for the country, reporting that during the last forty-four days there have been 2,440 applications and 321 recruits accepted. San Francisco ranks second with 2,762 applicants and 404 recruits accepted, while New York City is third, with 2,122 applicants and 392 recruits accepted. St. Louis stands fourth with 884 applicants and 242 recruits accepted, while Philadelphia has a records of 582 applicants, of whom 221 were accepted.

COMPULSION VOTE GROWS.

Scottish Trades Union Congress Now Stands 66 to 46 Against.

GLASGOW, April 29.—The Scottish Trades Union Congress, by a vote of 66 to 46, today declared its opposition to compulsory military service.

The vote is considered significant, as heretofore the Scottish trades unionists have been virtually unanimous against compulsory service.

8,970 BRITISH AT KUT SURRENDER TO TURKISH FOES

Tigris Force Which Gen. Townshend Led Almost to Bagdad Is Starved Out.

RELIEF FORCE 20 MILES OFF

Hordes of Turks, Strongly Intrenched, Twice Defeated Efforts to Reach Town.

FLOODS ALSO HALT ADVANCE

England Laments Surrender, but Praises Commander for His Brilliant Defense.

LONDON, Sunday, April 30.—The British Tigris army under the command of Major Gen. Charles Townshend, which has been besieged at Kut-el-Amara, has surrendered to the Turkish foes. Exhaustion of supplies compelled the force to yield.

This official announcement was made here yesterday:

After a resistance protracted for 143 days and conducted with a gallantry and fortitude that will be forever memorable, General Townshend has been compelled by the final exhaustion of his supplies to surrender.

Before doing so he destroyed his guns and munitions.

The force under him consists of 2,970 British troops of all ranks and services, and some 6,000 Indian troops and their followers.

The eventual surrender of General Townshend had been expected since the recent failure of the forces under Lieut. Gen. Gorringe and General Keary to break through the Turkish position at Sannayyat, about twenty miles below Kut-el-Amara on the Tigris River, and an unsuccessful attempt to send to the blockaded army provisions by steamers. It had been touch and go with the small British force for many days.

The location of Kut-el-Amara, on a peninsula extending into the Tigris River, made it impossible to send supplies by air as there was no landing place for aeroplanes.

While a supply vessel a few days ago got beyond the main Turkish lines at Es-Sinn, it was a forlorn hope, as the Turks investing the city, advised of her coming, could have easily sunk her from shore, even if she had escaped the artificial barriers in the river.

As for the forces, which attempted to relieve General Townshend, they met with almost continual misfortunes. Several times when it was believed they were on the point of success, rising waters made further progress impossible. After penetrating Turkish positions they were compelled to fall back or remain stationary, owing to the impossibility of attacking the position at Sannayyat, which was surrounded by water. The British troops did actually attack the prepared position there, after wading through mud and water waist deep, but while meeting with some success, failure at other points made their sacrifices futile.

The British public never lost faith in General Townshend, and even now that he has been forced to capitulate after destroying everything at Kut-el-Amara that might be valuable to the Turks, they look back upon his campaign as a brilliant one.

END OF 10 MONTHS' CAMPAIGN.

Surrender Is a Climax of Disasters to British Forces.

The surrender of General Townshend's army to the Turks is one of the few instances of the war in which an entire fighting unit of important numbers has laid down its arms. It is one of the largest body of troops of the Entente Allies which has surrendered at one time and larger than any other captured French or British force.

Signs have not been wanting for a month that the Anglo-Indian force at Kut-el-Amara was in sore straits. Communication had been kept up by aeroplanes, but the official British statement of Friday that a vessel loaded with food had grounded four miles below the city was a strong indication that the force had lacked supplies to a dangerous degree.

A recent Turkish official bulletin said the position of the British at Kut-el-Amara was critical and that they were expecting to receive small supplies of food by aeroplane.

Up to a late day General Townshend had kept alive the hope that he would be relieved. King George sent a message of encouragement to him several weeks ago, and in a message sent out as late as April 7 the General said he expected to be relieved soon.

Less than a score of miles away down the Tigris is a relief army which for months had been attempting to reach the besieged forces. A few weeks ago several successes over the Turks were announced and hope then ran high in England that the mission would succeed.

The Kut-el-Amara disaster is an unfortunate ending of a campaign which for a short time promised to be crowned with remarkable success by the capture of Bagdad.

It was early in June, 1915, that General Townshend, moving northward on his way to Bagdad, captured Kut-el-Amara with the Turkish force of 730 men and the Governor.

Led 40,000 Men Northward.

Townshend had had with him two divisions of Anglo-Indian troops, or a few over 40,000 men. There are no towns deserving the name between Kut-el-Amara and Bagdad, and, receiving fresh supplies the following week, Townshend

Continued on Page 3.

Turks Report That the Kut Garrison Numbered 13,300 And That Surrender Was Made Without Conditions

LONDON, April 29.—A Constantinople dispatch, received by way of Berlin, says that the Vice Chief Commander of the Turkish Army announces that the British garrison at Kut-el-Amara, under General Townshend, which surrendered unconditionally, numbered 13,300 men.

Although the British report puts the size of the surrendered garrison at 8,970 men, it refers to the Indian troops "and their followers." This may account for the additional 4,300 reported from Constantinople and the seeming discrepancy between the British and the Turkish official reports of the surrender.

ROOSEVELT STIRS CHICAGO AUDIENCE

"I'm Proud of You!" He Cries as Diners Cheer His Plea for Preparedness.

WANTS UNIVERSAL SERVICE

Objects to Uncle Sam with a Chinese Pigtail, and Liberty as a Female Huckster.

Special to The New York Times.

CHICAGO, April 29.—Into the Middle West, territory classed by many political leaders as only lukewarm toward his doctrines of preparedness, Colonel Roosevelt today brought from New York his views, conceded to be preliminary to an avowed Presidential candidacy.

If his political chances are to be judged by the warmth of his welcome, his most ardent friends could not have been disappointed. For the reception he got from the time he stepped off the Twentieth Century Limited this morning until he had concluded his address before the Illinois Bar Association tonight was enthusiastic, and bore all the appearance of spontaneity.

He came to Chicago to address the jurists on "National Duty and International Ideals" in a 4,000-word speech, which was interpreted as a straight-out declaration of the issues on which the Roosevelt-for-President campaign shall be based.

A crowd of 1,000 or more greeted the Colonel when he arrived at the La Salle Street Station and thousands cheered him as he passed through the streets in his motor car. On every side the slogan: "We want Teddy! We want Teddy!" adopted by hundreds of delegates to the Republican National Convention of 1912, was chanted. In many ways the scenes enacted were not unlike those witnessed at the time of the 1912 convention upon the arrival of the Colonel, only the situation was more tense then and the crowds greater in size.

If the reception today was a manufactured one, it was well staged and the Roosevelt adherents, far from admitting that it was arranged in advance, assert that little publicity was given to the fact that the Colonel was to arrive here at a certain hour.

The cordiality of the earlier reception was repeated tonight at the Illinois Bar Association dinner at the Hotel La Salle, which was attended by Governor Dunne and hundreds of prominent jurists and attorneys of the State. In all more than 1,300 obtained seats, and the entire nineteenth floor was given over to the affair.

Hundreds of applicants were turned away. It was the biggest dinner ever held in Chicago, according to the management, and this gave an inkling of the interest which the Colonel has aroused in the campaign he has undertaken.

He Assails Wilson's Policies.

The jurists and their guests gave the Colonel a rousing reception and listened with the deepest attention to his carefully prepared address, much of which was in the form of an attack upon the Wilson Administration and the country's policies in handling international problems. If it has accomplished nothing else, the trip has served to place Colonel Roosevelt before the people of the Middle West as openly and uncompromisingly a candidate for the Republican nomination. Where there were a number, and among them several political leaders of prominence, who found it difficult to believe that Colonel Roosevelt actually hoped to capture the Republican Convention after sending the Republican ticket to defeat four years ago there are none now.

"Yes, Teddy's in it for sure," was a remark frequently heard from the lips of those who watched his strenuous entry and heard his address.

Colonel Roosevelt, by his appearance here, has unquestionably created a new atmosphere in connection with national preparedness. He has added, also, a new "punch" to the pre-convention campaign, and where it was lagging a bit has set it ahead at least two weeks in this section. Where many had given little heed before to the fact that the National Convention was only a few weeks off they have been brought to a full realization of the fact that the decision must soon be made, and that if Roosevelt is to be headed off the job must quickly be undertaken.

The greatest demonstration came tonight at the dinner when the jurists, attorneys, and their guests rose and shouted themselves hoarse when the Colonel placed himself on record for universal service founded on a modified form of the Swiss system.

From the moment that he began to speak the Colonel had the crowd with him, and his words were interrupted a score of times by applause. At the final outburst, spontaneous and sustained, with the diners on their feet, waving napkins and shouting, the Colonel gave way to the emotions he felt.

"My heart is thrilled," he exclaimed when his voice could be heard above the din. "I know you are sound. I knew the West meant business—that you would stand for the nation.

"By George, I'm Proud of You!"

The cheering was redoubled and drowned out the Colonel's voice for more than a minute, and he stood there, his face glowing.

"I can't do you the good you have done me," he continued, pounding with his clenched fist to emphasize his feelings. "But I'll go on with my head up and my heart strong to preach preparedness to the people.

"By George, I'm proud of you—it's great! And I can't tell you how glad I am that you showed your feelings in this manner when I spoke of universal service in which all of us would take our man's part in upholding the welfare of this nation.

"I did not know how you'd take it when I said that but I believe it with all my heart, and I didn't care a darn what the effect would be. I'm going to tell you what I thought and felt. I'm proud of you as American citizens. I can't tell you how proud I am."

And the demonstration did not end there. At the conclusion of the

Continued on Page 3.

GERARD APPRISED OF KAISER'S STAND

Berlin Believes the Ambassador Has Been Told What Germany's Reply Will Be.

WASHINGTON GETS NO WORD

Awaits Envoy's Report on Visit to the Emperor—President Will Allow No More Parleying.

BERLIN, April 29.—Ambassador Gerard was received in audience by Emperor William last night and conferred with other leaders of the Empire. No intimation has been given as to when the German reply to the American note will be ready, except a hint contained in a Berlin dispatch to the Cologne Gazette, which said:

"The consultations at Great Headquarters probably are near a conclusion. The visit of the American Ambassador was designed to permit him to consult with persons in authority there over the situation. It is assumed their final decision also will be communicated to him there."

The Tageblatt explains this morning that its statement that the basic features of the answer already have been settled was misunderstood. The paper asserts it meant only to say that a draft of the answer had been made, but that a decision had not yet been reached. The wording of this morning's statement indicates clearly, however, that there was no misunderstanding on the part of the readers, but that the Tageblatt made an error yesterday.

There is virtually no comment in the press upon the situation except that from the pen of Count Ernst von Reventlow, who still appears to believe a breach with the United States is inevitable.

The official organ of the Hansabund, the organization of commercial interests, refers to the gravity of the decision to be reached. It says the representatives of commerce, industry, and trade belonging to the Hansabund are certain the decision will be reached with the dispassionate care which it demands, but are equally certain that Germany's dignity as a nation and its freedom to use all weapons of defense will be fully regarded.

The Hansabund hopes, however, it is declared, that an honorable and peaceful understanding will be reached, but that if such a solution proves impossible all Germans will stand united behind the Emperor.

PRESIDENT WILL NOT PARLEY.

Germany Must Comply or Break Will Follow—Optimism Abating.

Special to The New York Times.

WASHINGTON, April 29.—The feeling of optimism that has prevailed here over the indications that Germany would meet the American demands for the abandonment of present methods of German submarine warfare began to wane today on account of the view that appeared to prevail in Berlin that the issue would be discussed between the two Governments before the German answer was transmitted. This Government wants no discussion. It holds that the time for discussion has passed. There is every reason to believe that President Wilson has determined to break relations with Germany if his demand is not complied with literally.

The supposition in some quarters that Emperor William asked Ambassador Gerard to convey a message to President Wilson which would suggest a modification of the American attitude or permit a discussion of the principle involved, has not tended to increase the hopefulness of those who understand the President's position. Even the Kaiser's personal request along such lines would not influence the President, it is gathered, to consent to further exchanges concerning the merits of the submarine controversy.

Much of the optimism that has prevailed here has been based on information to the German Embassy that the Berlin Government would endeavor to meet the desires of the United States. In German circles this optimism continues, and it is shared to a great extent by officials of the Washington Government. But those officials in a position to know the inside of the situation are not indulging in any high hopes. They know the determination of President Wilson to have a settlement of the submarine issue one way or the other, and realize that he has made up his mind that a severance of diplomatic relations must come if Germany attempts to evade the American demand by suggestions of parley or otherwise.

The President, there is good reason to believe, has decided irrevocably that he will take the course set forth in the note to Germany if a satisfactory answer is not forthcoming, and will not be influenced by opposition in Congress or elsewhere. The pro-German deluge of telegrams to Senators and Representatives has not had the slighest effect on the President. If anything, this phase of the German propaganda has made the President and his advisers even more determined to adhere to the course they have outlined.

Mr. Gerard was expected to have reached Berlin on his return from his visit to the Kaiser some time today. At the State Department just before the closing hour it was said that no message had come from the Ambassador as to his conference with the German Emperor and none was expected today on account of the unusual delays in telegraphic transmission of cipher dispatches. The department has not heard from the Ambassador since he cabled that he had been invited by the Kaiser to visit him, and was leaving Berlin for the front on Thursday.

It was reported today that the Administration was becoming anxious over the failure of the German Government to respond to its demand, which called for a declaration "immediately" that present methods of German submarine warfare had been abandoned and made effective, but nothing to bear out that impression could be obtained from officials. The Administration has no inten-

Continued on Page 3.

DUBLIN REVOLT IS NEAR COLLAPSE; POST OFFICE REBELS SEIZED IS BURNED; WIMBORNE TELLS STORY OF RISING

Redmond Tells Nationalists to Aid the Troops in Suppressing Revolt

LONDON, April 29.—John Redmond, leader of the Irish Nationalists, has placed himself absolutely at the disposal of the authorities and is in constant touch with them. He has instructed Nationalist supporters in all parts of Ireland to hold themselves at the disposal of the military authorities.

In many places besides Dublin the Nationalist voters have already, on their own initiative, mobilized in support of the troops. At Tipperary yesterday volunteers offered their services.

Irish Rebels Proclaimed Republic; Seven Headed It, Wimborne Says

Failure to Cut Wire to Curragh Camp a Fatal Error—Sailors Landed from Fleet to Aid Troops in County Galway.

DUBLIN, April 29.—Baron Wimborne, Lord Lieutenant of Ireland, expressed to The Associated Press at the Viceregal Lodge today the assurance that the seditious movement would be suppressed in the course of a few days.

The Viceroy was full of praise for the loyalty displayed by the great majority of the Irish people, and considered the momentary success gained and the damage done by the rebels as small when viewed in connection with the surprise of the outbreak and the evident preparations made for it.

The country outside of Dublin, except for a few isolated places, has, he declared, remained peaceful.

Requested to give an account of what had happened since the rebels had proclaimed an Irish republic last Monday afternoon, Baron Wimborne said:

"The outbreak began Monday morning about 11:30 o'clock. About that time information was received that Dublin Castle had been attacked, Stephens Green occupied, and the Post Office seized by the rebels. Telephonic communication with the Curragh Camp was immediately obtained by the authorities and the reserve troops there were brought to Dublin that night and the following morning.

"Meanwhile the situation at the Castle, which had never been captured by the rebels, was strengthened. The only casualty there was the shooting of a policeman at the gate. A very few hours after the outbreak large forces had been assembled in the Castle, which, however, was never in real danger.

Failed to Cut Wire to Curragh.

"The rebels had cut telegraphic communications with the country districts and England, but had not succeeded in discovering a telephone wire which connected the Curragh Camp with headquarters. This was one of their great mistakes. They did not cut communication with North Ireland, with which we have at all times been able to converse.

"At one time the rebels had possession of the Broadstone Railway Station, which was not protected.

"On Tuesday morning all the reinforcements we had called from Curragh had reached Dublin, and since that moment the rebels have not attempted anything except sniping from certain localities and houses. It is so easy for them to abandon houses by back doors and to get away to other advantageous positions.

"The military cannot distinguish the rebels from other citizens. Sometimes they leave their houses after hiding their rifles and cartridges and mingle with the ordinary inhabitants. After taking observations of the soldiers' positions they return to commence sniping again. Most of the houses they occupy they have entered by force, and not because the householders sympathise with their movement. As a matter of fact, the general run of people do not sympathise with them.

"Since the number of troops has increased, the position of the rebels has remained the same. When their activities at any point become too lively the troops throw a few shells into the houses they occupy and such explosions have caused fires, while other fires have been started by the rebels themselves.

"They have barricaded Sackville Street and are in possession of all the houses there, but they were shelled out of Liberty Hall by a gunboat on Tuesday, and we occupied their headquarters immediately. They burned Linen Hall barracks, and other small fires have occurred.

"In the early stages of the revolt the Sinn Feiners fired on the members of the fire brigade, but later we cleared the area around the fires, and the firemen were able to extinguish the flames.

"Wednesday the military arrangements were completed by the arrival of further reinforcements, and the rebels were hemmed in in Sackville Street. The work of disposing of the troops to deal with the snipers occupied a lot of time and much care, but eventually this district and other rebel quarters were surrounded. Everything done has been carried out according to plans.

"A big cordon has been drawn all around Dublin and shorter cordons around the inner districts.

Fighting in Galway.

"Regarding the situation in the provinces on the whole, it is very good. We were naturally apprehensive lest there might be some response there to the Dublin movement. Fighting occurred in Galway near Athenry, where the police are now in possession of the town, castle. There has also been fighting in a Galway town which the rebels attacked and compelled us to land men from the fleet to support the military.

"Encounters took place at Enniscorthy, County Wexford, and there were certain rebellious assemblages in Meath and Louth, but on the whole reports are quiet. This applies also to Cork, Limerick, Kerry, Clare, Kilkenny, Mayo, Sligo, Tipperary, Leitrim, Kildare, Roscommon, and all of Ulster."

When asked concerning the origin and connections of the rebel movement with the Germans, the Viceroy said there was an absolute certainty the rebellion was timed to take place with the knowledge of Germany, and was intended to bring about the withdrawal of troops from England to Ireland.

"As to the landing of Sir Roger Casement," said Baron Wimborne, "that was all arranged in Germany with the connivance of the Sinn Feiners. On the night of his arrest a motor car upset into a river and the occupants, who were drowned, both wore Sinn Fein badges. The Germans do not seem to have supplied the rebels with arms, which are of all descriptions, even including fowling pieces.

"A proclamation issued by the rebels announcing the foundation of the Irish Republic was signed by seven persons, including J. T. Clark, Connolly, Pearce, and MacDermott."

Augustine Birrell, the Chief Secretary for Ireland, who was present during the interview with the Viceroy, supplemented his remarks by saying the situation would be dealt with according to martial law, which now is in full operation in Ireland, and deprives the citizens of the right of a civil trial. Mr. Birrell was not overwilling to give information as to occurrences, but he said he was satisfied that the situation was well in hand and that the suppression of the movement was a matter of a short time.

The visit of The Associated Press Correspondent to the Viceregal Lodge followed a long drive in an open motor lorry through the disturbed sections of the city and past barricades, where soldiers knelt or lay down in replying to the rebel snipers. Occasional bullets whistled overhead and the rattle of a machine gun salvo was heard.

No soldier is permitted to walk about without a rifle, as such a proceeding would bring almost certain death. Citizens stood behind curtains and windows as the automobile of the correspondent dashed by. Only a few venture onto the porches, and they fear to go to the stores to obtain provisions.

Boys Shot in Bread Line.

This fear was fully justified, as The Associated Press Correspondent saw two small boys shot while waiting at a bakery for bread during the morning. In other parts of the city, also, many civilian casualties were caused, but the number either of the soldiers or civilians killed or wounded could not be obtained.

The rebels today have been confining their activities to sniping in various parts of the city. The scenes of their operations have been circumscribed to the districts about Sackville Street, the cattle market, and Stephen's Green, where they are surrounded by vigilant troops in complete cordons, while the city itself is cut off from approach by another cordon whose limits are around the circular road which surrounds the city.

Every civilian is regarded with suspicion, and passage through the lines can be obtained only with the best of credentials and passes.

Outside the three areas already mentioned as being in possession of the rebels, numbers of isolated snipers occasionally fire pot shots at passing soldiers. These snipers are difficult to locate. At a hotel on the north wall dozens of shots went through windows and struck walls, while spent bullets dropped everywhere in the streets.

BANK SAVED BY STUDENTS.

Trinity College Opened Heavy Fire on Rebels and Drove Them Off.

LIVERPOOL, April 30.—How Trinity College students saved the Bank of Ireland is told by a resident of Liverpool who has just arrived from Dublin.

"It was the intention of the Sinn Feiners," he said, "to take this institution and its valuable contents, and a body of rebels came along with the express purpose of putting this intention into execution. Opposite the bank stands famous Trinity College, where an officer's training corps of students is stationed, and the young officers had a warm reception in readiness.

"The rebels came along in great style, anticipating no trouble and shooting down the half-dozen soldiers always on guard at the bank. But as they advanced there was a rifle volley, and some of the attacking party dropped to the ground.

"The college had been transformed into a veritable fortress. In the windows were sandbags, loopholed, behind which the officers were waiting to give battle. The insurgents were stupified, and for a moment hesitated as to what they should do. Then several sprang forward, shouting to their comrades, and the rebels pressed on.

"Again came a volley from the windows of Trinity College. More men fell and the rebels broke in disorder and fled."

LEADER CONNOLLY KILLED

Artillery Used Against Dublin Section in Which Rebels Are Corralled

CASUALTIES EXCEED 100

Sackville and Grafton Streets Reported to Have Been Set on Fire.

MANY LADS IN THE REVOLT

Old Men, Too, Joined the Ranks—Little Disorder in Other Parts of Ireland.

LONDON, Sunday, April 30.—Field Marshal Viscount French, commander of the home forces, reports that the General Post Office at Dublin, which has been the principal stronghold of the Sinn Feiners, has been burned down.

James Connolly, one of the leaders of the rebels, is reported to have been killed.

It is said Connolly undertook to issue to persons desiring to leave Dublin passports bearing the words: "Pass bearer. James Connolly, Commandant General of the Irish Republican Army."

Many of the rebels have been made prisoner, and the revolt in Dublin is on the verge of collapse.

In the rest of Ireland the situation is generally satisfactory.

It is reported that the casualties in the street fighting in Dublin exceed 100, and that the troops have been compelled to resort to cannon in one section.

A dispatch received yesterday afternoon said that Sackville and Grafton Streets were in flames, and that artillery was being used on the houses, the inhabitants having been removed.

The recent news that the rebels have been driven out of St. Stephen's Green with bombs, suffering heavy losses in killed, wounded, and prisoners, has not been confirmed officially.

From inquiries made among the military authorities at Dublin, the correspondent of The Evening Star concludes that there probably are not more than 1,500 or 2,000 men and lads actually engaged in the rebellion, so far as the central part of the city is concerned. Among them are quite a number of old men who were closely associated with the Fenian troubles, and some youths of 16 or 17. This is shown, the correspondent says, by the appearance of the prisoners already brought in.

Of the situation outside Dublin little is known beyond the official admission that the disaffection has spread to various localities in the west and south of Ireland. Field Marshal French's statement of Friday night described these disturbances as local in character, and so far as has been revealed by information which has passed the censorship they have not been attended by heavy fighting.

A dispatch from Tralee yesterday said that Austin Stack, commander of the Tralee corps of Sinn Feiners, and Cornelius Collins, an accountant in the General Post Office at Dublin, who are charged with abetting in the importation of arms from the enemy, were taken from the Tralee jail under a strong military and police escort and removed on a train to an unknown destination. There was no demonstration.

SCENES IN EMBATTLED CITY.

Newspaper Men Landed with Birrell in Midst of the Fighting.

DUBLIN, Thursday, April 27, (via London, April 29.)—Fifteen hundred or so armed men of the Sinn Fein had a hold on Ireland's capital today. After four days of fighting their rebel flag still flew from a number of central points.

Since Monday some of the chief positions in the city have been in the hands of the rebels. In defending these strongholds against regular troops and Irish Nationalist Volunteers the rebels are fighting with desperation for their lives, which they know may be forfeited on the charge of treason.

Regulars now command all the rebel positions, the fall of which is merely a question of time.

The streets of Dublin were deserted today, except for sentries and military guards. Business was at a standstill. Civilians peeped anxiously from behind curtained windows. Field guns were barking, machine guns rattling, and rifle fire was pattering, apparently from every quarter at the same time.

Birrell Landed with Newspaper Men.

When The Associated Press correspondent landed early this morning at the quay near the Custom House the pinging of bullets from rifles of snipers in the vicinity was frequent. Augustine Birrell, the Secretary for Ireland, had made the passage from England with the newspaper men. As he stepped ashore he shouted cheerily: "I wish you luck, gentlemen! I don't know what will happen to you, now that you're here."

Soldiers and rebels fired at each other from street corners, wharves, roofs, and

"All the News That's Fit to Print."

The New York Times.

THE WEATHER
Rain Thursday; fair, cold wave by night Friday.
For full weather report see Page 21.

VOL. LXVI...NO. 21,558. NEW YORK, THURSDAY, FEBRUARY 1, 1917.—TWENTY-TWO PAGES. ONE CENT In Greater New York, Jersey City and Newark. | Elsewhere TWO CENTS.

GERMANY BEGINS RUTHLESS SEA WARFARE; DRAWS 'BARRED ZONES' AROUND THE ALLIES; CRISIS CONFRONTS THE UNITED STATES

THIS PORT CLOSED

Collector Malone Stops All Outgoing Ships at Narrows.

GERMAN SHIPS SEARCHED

No Evidence of Unusual Activity on Vessels at Hoboken.

GUARD SET ON THIS SIDE

Police Ordered Out at Midnight to Keep Watch Over Ships Off 130th Street.

ANXIOUS FOR SHIPS AT SEA

Shipping Men in This and Other Ports Fear for Them in Blockade.

[illegible]

Colonel E. M. House left hurriedly for Washington on the Pennsylvania Railroad at 12:30 o'clock this morning. He entered the station through a private stairway and secluded himself in the car before the train was opened to the general traveling public.

The Port of New York was sealed tight last night by order of Dudley Field Malone, Collector of the Port. Vessels of every description, including tugboats, were turned back at Quarantine by the torpedo boat stationed there to maintain the neutrality of the United States.

The purpose of Mr. Malone's order remained a mystery upon which he declined to throw any light. He has full authority to act upon his own initiative in case of emergency, as he is held responsible for enforcing neutrality.

Even naval officers are under orders to take instructions from Mr. Malone in all matters affecting the neutrality of New York.

Rumors that the crews of the German ships interned at Hoboken would attempt to scuttle the vessels and destroy the machinery in the event of war, sprang up everywhere last evening as soon as the German note was made public. Collector Malone called up Chief of Police Patrick Hayes of Hoboken, who was attending the annual patrolmen's ball, and the Chief, with half a dozen plain-clothes men, left the dance and hurried down to the piers to reinforce the eleven men of the Neutrality Squad on guard there. Deputy Collector George F. Lamb was present.

A thorough search made by the neutrality guards under Roundsman Miles disclosed no evidence of any preparations to justify the rumors. The Hamburg-American and North German Lloyd liners have been tied up at the piers for two years and a half, during which time there has been no opportunity to dredge out the slips, so it was said that they were practically lying in the mud, and that scuttling them would be rather pointless.

As to the possibility of an attempt to escape from the harbor, it was said that none of the ships had enough coal to last for more than a single day's steaming, at the end of which period they must inevitably be captured, even if they could pass the destroyers on guard at the Narrows. The Vaterland had more coal than any of the others, but in her case it was said that most of the officers of the interned liners have been living on board of her and that the coal was needed to get up steam for heating and lighting.

Watch Put on German Ships Here.

At midnight Police Inspector Thomas Ryan of the Sixth Inspection District, including the district between 116th Street and Spuyten Duyvil and West of Fifth Avenue, received orders to keep in reserve all men who were about to go off duty at that hour. Twenty

Continued on Page 3.

Text of Germany's Note to the United States

Washington, D. C., Jan. 31, 1917.

Mr. Secretary of State:

Your Excellency was good enough to transmit to the Imperial Government a copy of the message which the President of the United States of America addressed to the Senate on the 22d inst. The Imperial Government has given it the earnest consideration which the President's statements deserve, inspired, as they are, by a deep sentiment of responsibility.

It is highly gratifying to the Imperial Government to ascertain that the main tendencies of this important statement correspond largely to the desires and principles professed by Germany. These principles especially include self-government and equality of rights for all nations. Germany would be sincerely glad if in recognition of this principle countries like Ireland and India, which do not enjoy the benefits of political independence, should now obtain their freedom.

The German people also repudiate all alliances which serve to force the countries into a competition for might and to involve them in a net of selfish intrigues. On the other hand, Germany will gladly co-operate in all efforts to prevent future wars.

The freedom of the seas, being a preliminary condition of the free existence of nations and the peaceful intercourse between them, as well as the open-door for the commerce of all nations, has always formed part of the leading principles of Germany's political program. All the more the Imperial Government regrets that the attitude of her enemies, who are so entirely opposed to peace, makes it impossible for the world at present to bring about the realization of these lofty ideals.

Germany and her allies were ready to enter now into a discussion of peace, and had set down as basis the guarantee of existence, honor, and free development of their peoples. Their aims, as has been expressly stated in the note of Dec. 12, 1916, were not directed toward the destruction or annihilation of their enemies and were, according to their conviction, perfectly compatible with the rights of the other nations. As to Belgium, for which such warm and cordial sympathy is felt in the United States, the Chancellor had declared only a few weeks previously that its annexation had never formed part of Germany's intentions. The peace to be signed with Belgium was to provide for such conditions in that country, with which Germany desires to maintain friendly neighborly relations, that Belgium should not be used again by Germany's enemies for the purpose of instigating continuous hostile intrigues. Such precautionary measures are all the more necessary, as Germany's enemies have repeatedly stated, not only in speeches delivered by their leading men, but also in the statutes of the Economical Conference in Paris, that it is their intention not to treat Germany as an equal, even after peace has been restored, but to continue their hostile attitude, and especially to wage a systematical economic war against her.

The attempt of the four allied powers to bring about peace has failed, owing to the lust of conquest of their enemies, who desired to dictate the conditions of peace. Under the pretense of following the principle of nationality, our enemies have disclosed their real aims in this way, viz.: To dismember and dishonor Germany, Austria-Hungary, Turkey, and Bulgaria. To the wish of reconciliation they oppose the will of destruction. They desire a fight to the bitter end.

A new situation has thus been created which forces Germany to new decisions. Since two years and a half England is using her naval power for a criminal attempt to force Germany into submission by starvation. In brutal contempt of international law, the group of powers led by England does not only curtail the legitimate trade of their opponents, but they also, by ruthless pressure, compel neutral countries either to altogether forego every trade not agreeable to the Entente Powers or to limit it according to their arbitrary decrees.

The American Government knows the steps which have been taken to cause England and her Allies to return to the rules of international law and to respect the freedom of the seas. The English Government, however, insists upon continuing its war of starvation, which does not at all affect the military power of its opponents, but compels women and children, the sick and the aged, to suffer for their country pains and privations which endanger the vitality of the nation. Thus British tyranny mercilessly increases the sufferings of the world, indifferent to the laws of humanity, indifferent to the protests of the neutrals whom they severely harm, indifferent even to the silent longing for peace among England's own allies. Each day of the terrible struggle causes new destruction, new sufferings. Each day shortening the war will, on both sides, preserve the lives of thousands of brave soldiers and be a benefit to mankind.

The Imperial Government could not justify before its own conscience, before the German people and before history the neglect of any means destined to bring about the end of the war. Like the President of the United States, the Imperial Government had hoped to reach this goal by negotiations. After the attempts to come to an understanding with the Entente Powers have been answered by the latter with the announcement of an intensified continuation of the war, the Imperial Government—in order to serve the welfare of mankind in a higher sense and not to wrong its own people—is now compelled to continue the fight for existence, again forced upon it, with the full employment of all the weapons which are at its disposal.

Sincerely trusting that the people and the Government of the United States will understand the motives for this decision and its necessity, the Imperial Government hopes that the United States may view the new situation from the lofty heights of impartiality, and assist, on their part, to prevent further misery and unavoidable sacrifice of human life.

Enclosing two memoranda regarding the details of the contemplated military measures at sea, I remain, etc.,

J. BERNSTORFF.

Text of the Annex to German Note, Outlining Barred Zones and Prescribing Conditions for American Vessels

WASHINGTON, Jan. 31.—Following is the text of the annex to the German note presented to the State Department by Count von Bernstorff:

MEMORANDUM.

"From Feb. 1, 1917, sea traffic will be stopped with every available weapon and without further notice in the following blockade zones [" barred zones," according [illegible]

[The Sayville version says: "In the North Sea, the district around England and France, which is limited by a line twenty nautical miles."]

"The zone is confined by a line at a distance of twenty sea miles along the Dutch coast to Terschelling Fireship; the degree [meridian?] of longitude from Terschelling Fireship to Udsire; a line from there across the point 62 degrees north, 0 degrees longitude, to 62 degrees north, 5 degrees west; further to a point three sea miles south of the southern point of the Faroe Islands; from there across a point 62 degrees north, 10 degrees west, to 61 degrees north, 15 degrees west; then 57 degrees north, 20 degrees west, to 47 degrees north, 20 degrees west; further, to 43 degrees north, 15 degrees west; then along the degree [parallel?] of latitude 43 degrees north to twenty sea miles from Cape Finisterre, and at a distance of twenty sea miles along the north coast of Spain to the French boundary.

"In the South—The Mediterranean: [illegible] and 4 degrees east; also north and west of a zone sixty sea miles wide along the North African Coast, beginning at 2 degrees longitude west. For the connection of this sea-zone with Greece there is provided a zone of a width of twenty sea miles north and east of the following line: 38 degrees north and 6 degrees east to 38 degrees north and 10 degrees west, to 37 degrees north and 11 degrees 30 minutes east, to 34 degrees north and 22 degrees 30 minutes east.

"From there leads a zone twenty sea miles wide, west of 22 degrees 30 minutes eastern longitude, into Greek territorial waters.

"Neutral ships navigating these blockade zones do so at their own risk. Although care has been taken that neutral ships which are on their way toward ports of the blockade zones on Feb. 1, 1917, and have come in the vicinity of the latter, will be spared during a sufficiently long period, it is strongly advised to warn them with all available means in order to cause their return.

"Neutral ships which on Feb. 1 are in ports of the [illegible]

"The instructions given to the Commanders of German submarines provide for a sufficiently long period during which the safety of passengers on unarmed enemy passenger ships is guaranteed.

"Americans en route to the blockade zone on enemy freight steamers are not endangered, as the enemy shipping firms can prevent such ships in time from entering the zone.

"Sailing of regular American passenger steamers may continue undisturbed after Feb. 1, 1917, if

(A) The port of destination is Falmouth.

(B) Sailing to or coming from that port course is taken via the Scilly Islands and a point 50 degrees north, 20 degrees west.

[" Along this route," says the Sayville version, " no German mines will be laid."]

(C) The steamers are marked in the following way, which must not be allowed to other vessels in American ports: On ship's hull and superstructure three vertical stripes one meter wide, each to be painted alternately white and red. Each mast should show a large flag checkered white and red, and the stern the American national flag. Care should be taken that, during dark, national flag and painted marks are easily recognizable from a distance, and that the boats are well lighted throughout.

(D) One steamer a week sails in each direction with arrival at Falmouth on Sunday and departure from Falmouth on Wednesday.

(E) United States Government guarantees that no contraband (according to German contraband list) is carried by those steamers.

[" Two copies of maps on which the barred zones are outlined are added," says the version received via Sayville.]

A SHIP A WEEK FOR US

To and From Falmouth on a Prescribed Route.

BECOMES EFFECTIVE TODAY

Bernstorff Delivers a Note Which Ends Germany's Pledges to Us.

BECAUSE OF PEACE FAILURE

The Kaiser Now Proposes to Employ All Means of Sea Warfare at His Command.

CAPITAL TAKES GRAVE VIEW

President Studies Note Alone—Break Predicted in Some Quarters.

President Amazed by News; Spends Evening Studying Note

WASHINGTON, Jan. 31.—When The Associated Press dispatches telling of the German note began arriving at the White House today President Wilson was in his office talking with a friend. Secretary Tumulty hurried to him with the news. The President could not believe it until he was assured that the information was contained in a formal note already before the State Department.

The President went to bed at 11 o'clock after spending the evening alone in his study with a copy of the German note. This apparently disposed of suggestions that some action might be taken before morning.

The President saw no callers, but is understood to have used the telephone freely.

As far as could be learned, no plans have been laid for him to go before Congress, as he did to announce the sending of the Sussex note threatening to break off diplomatic relations.

Special to The New York Times.

WASHINGTON, Jan. 31.—The United States Government tonight faces its greatest international crisis since the Lusitania was sunk. With full knowledge that her action almost certainly means a break with America, Germany announced to this Government today that she intended to abandon the pledges she gave last year to observe the rules of international law in the conduct of her submarine warfare against merchant shipping. How a break can be avoided, observers here are unable to see. The gravity of the situation cannot be exaggerated.

Beginning at midnight tonight the German U-boats will sink without warning any merchant vessel, neutral as well as enemy, entering a prescribed zone that extends from north of the British Isles around into the Mediterranean to include even the waters of Greece.

That is the sum and substance of Germany's communication to this Government today, delivered to Secretary Lansing in Washington by Count von Bernstorff, the Kaiser's Ambassador, and to Ambassador Gerard, in Berlin, by the Imperial Foreign Office.

Recalls Final Warning.

The United States Government is on record as determined to break diplomatic relations with Germany if pledges concerning submarine warfare are not observed in letter and in spirit. Today's notification of the Imperial Government brings the United States to the point where it must decide whether it intends to make good the following warning to Germany, contained in a note of April 18, 1916:

"Unless the Imperial Government should now immediately declare and effect an abandonment of its present methods of submarine warfare against passenger and freight-carrying vessels the Government of the United States can have no choice but to sever diplomatic relations with the German Empire altogether. This action the Government of the United States contemplates

BRITAIN TO MEET GERMAN MENACE

Fleet of 4,000 Vessels Ready to Chase U-Boats and Protect Merchant Ships.

PORTS WILL BE KEPT OPEN

Liverpool and Bordeaux to be Especially Protected—Fore and Aft Guns for All Vessels.

Great Britain and her allies are prepared to meet Germany's moves in her submarine campaign, it was authoritatively asserted in shipping circles last night. The Entente Powers were convinced weeks ago that ruthless warfare with undersea boats would be decreed sooner or later and have known for ten days that the decision had been reached, it was said.

The ports of Liverpool and Bordeaux will be kept open at all hazards, British steamship representatives asserted, even if it becomes necessary to convoy every merchant ship which crosses the Atlantic. The first step to be taken by the British Admiralty, which virtually controls the merchant fleets of the Allies, will be to arm every ship with guns fore and aft for defensive purposes, it was predicted.

To meet the emergency the British Government has been assembling for months, it was said, a large fleet of small, fast cruisers to be used as "submarine chasers." This type of war craft has proved very effective against undersea boats, well informed shipping men declared. Agents of British lines declared the Admiralty now has a fleet of 4,000 vessels available to keep the sea lanes clear of raiders and submarines and to act as convoys.

There are said to be hundreds of patrol boats and mine sweepers, independent of torpedo boat destroyers, which are on the lookout to convoy liners and freighters when they arrive in the danger zone bound for French or British

Continued on Page 3.

"Barred Zones" and "Safety Lanes" Outlined in Germany's Note.

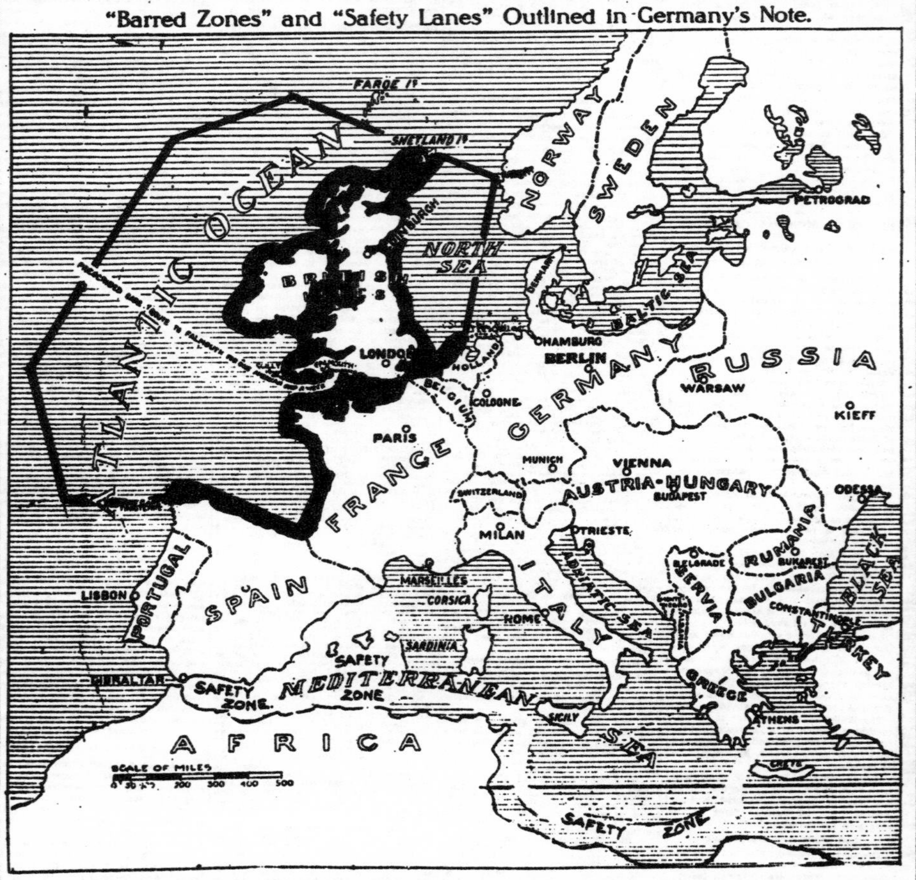

Surrounding the British Isles and bordering the coasts of France, Belgium, and Holland is a "barred zone" (indicated by black areas on the map) twenty nautical miles wide. The boundaries of a secondary "barred zone," shutting off the British Isles and running as far south as Cape Finisterre, on the northwestern coast of Spain, are indicated by a heavy black line. This zone is pierced by the route to Falmouth, as laid down for one American ship a week in the annex to the German note.

In the Mediterranean the safety zone leading to Greek territorial waters is indicated by the white areas shown in the map of that sea. The territorial waters of France, Italy, and the British possessions in the Mediterranean are apparently included in the barred zone.

CHANCELLOR TELLS GERMAN DECISION

He Outlines to Reichstag Committee Measures for Defense by Land and Sea.

AGREED ON AT CONFERENCE

Results of Headquarters Discussion Quickly Told to German Leaders.

BERLIN, Jan. 31, (via London.)—The Imperial Chancellor, Dr. von Bethmann Hollweg, is to make a statement on foreign affairs and the military situation this afternoon to the Ways and Means Committee of the Reichstag. According to the newspapers, the Chancellor will make important declarations regarding "the decisions of the Government," and will explain the grounds upon which these decisions are based.

BERLIN, Jan. 31, (by Wireless to Sayville.)—In its announcement today reporting the result of the recent conference at German Great Headquarters, the Overseas News Agency says:

"Chancellor von Bethmann Hollweg and Foreign Secretary Zimmermann have returned from Great Headquarters, where the planned offensive of the Entente was discussed at the meetings, and a unanimous agreement regarding all measures of defense was formulated. The Central Powers calmly await coming events, conscious of their own power."

LONDON, Jan. 31.—Chancellor von Bethmann Hollweg and Foreign Secretary Zimmermann have returned to Berlin from headquarters at the front, where a complete agreement on measures to be taken by Germany on land and water was reached, according to a Berlin telegram transmitted by Reuter's Amsterdam correspondent.

Kaiser Predicts "Hard Times."

AMSTERDAM, Jan. 31, (via London.)—The Reichsanzeiger publishes an imperial rescript conveying the German Emperor's thanks for birthday congratulations extended to him. It says:

"From these numerous manifestations there ring out with the overwhelming force of unanimity indignation at the contemptuous rejection of our peace

Continued on Page 2.

"All the News That's Fit to Print."

The New York Times.

THE WEATHER
Probably snow or rain today and Friday; wind northeast.
For full weather report see Page 21.

VOL. LXVI...NO. 21,586. NEW YORK, THURSDAY, MARCH 1, 1917.—TWENTY-TWO PAGES. ONE CENT In Greater New York. | TWO CENTS New England and Middle States. | THREE CENTS Elsewhere.

GERMANY SEEKS AN ALLIANCE AGAINST US; ASKS JAPAN AND MEXICO TO JOIN HER; FULL TEXT OF HER PROPOSAL MADE PUBLIC

CONGRESS TO BACK WILSON

Laconia Tragedy Adds Strength to President's Support.

MODIFIED BILL IN HOUSE

Leaders Predict That Senate's Armed Neutrality Measure Will Prevail.

THINK PUBLIC IS AROUSED

Detention of Five Consuls in Germany Increases Crisis—New Demand on Turkey.

President Insists on Passage of Senate Armed Ship Bill

Special to The New York Times.

WASHINGTON, Feb. 28.—The statement was authorized by the White House tonight that President Wilson would insist on the passage of the Senate bill giving him power to arm and protect mechant shipping.

WASHINGTON, Feb. 28.—Opposition in Congress to granting authority to President Wilson to protect American ships and lives at sea began melting and Administration leaders confidently predicted action within another twenty-four hours.

There were indications that many of the Republicans of the Senate who, though favoring the steps proposed, insist that Congress should be called in extra session, would vote for the measure requested by the President when the roll was called. The chief, if not the only, reason for uncertainty was found in the attitude of Senator La Follette, who has given indications of preparing for a single-handed filibuster in the closing hours of the session.

Details of the destruction of the Cunard liner Laconia, published in the morning papers and telling of the suffering and death of an American mother and daughter among the passengers, had its effect during the day. Members of the House and Senate, whose communications had come largely from pacifists, began receiving telegrams from their constituents calling for vigorous action by the Government.

The House Foreign Affairs Committee early in the day reported out the Flood bill, authorizing the President to arm American ships, with amendments eliminating the provision for the use of "other instrumentalities," and adding a prohibition against the insurance of munition ships by the Government War Risk Bureau. A special rule to expedite passage of the measure was introduced by Chairman Flood of the Foreign Affairs Committee, who said he probably would press it tomorrow. It would provide for a vote not later than 4 o'clock P. M.

Hope in Senate Bill.

The Administration plan is to have the Senate substitute for the House measure the bill reported by the Senate Committee and based upon a memorandum prepared by the President. In the form of a conference report the leaders anticipate no difficulty in having the House pass promptly the substitute.

President Wilson probably will pay particular attention to the German crisis in his second inaugural address next Monday. He has not begun work on it yet, and has put off its preparation pending further developments in the foreign situation.

An aggravating incident was added to the German situation today by the receipt of word from Germany that four American Consuls were being held there because a German Consul on his way from the United States to Ecuador had been delayed in Cuba. A statement of the facts, with a request for immediate release of the Americans, was cabled tonight.

Announcement was made at the State Department that instructions had been sent to Ambassador Elkus at Constantinople to report definitely and immediately whether Turkey would guarantee, not only for herself, but for her allies, the safety of the American cruiser Des Moines and the naval collier Caesar in taking relief supplies into Syria and bring out the 1,000 or so marooned Americans there. Ambassador Elkus, having sent a rather ambiguous promise from the Turkish authorities, was told to say that unless definite and specific guarantees were

Continued on Page 4.

No Ships Sunk Yesterday; 456,817 Tons Lost in February

No new sinkings by German submarines were reported yesterday. A record of the tonnage sunk in the German blockade zone during the whole month of February, compiled from British Admiralty figures and reports received from other sources, follows:

NUMBER OF SHIPS SUNK:

American.	Other Neutrals.	British.	Other Belligerents.
2	51	110	20

TOTAL TONNAGE DESTROYED.

American.	Other Neutrals.	British.	Other Belligerents.
3,322	93,019	316,204	44,272

Grand total: (Feb. 1-28.) 456,817 tons.

WILSON GIVES OUT APPEAL FROM HOY

American Whose Mother and Sister Died on the Laconia Asks That They Be Avenged.

OFFERS SERVICES TO NATION

Young, Nephew of Mrs. Hoy, Appeals to Wilson, Lansing, Wadsworth, and Chandler.

WASHINGTON, Feb. 28.—President Wilson has given out for publication the following cablegram which he received from Austin Y. Hoy, whose mother and sister died in a lifeboat after the Laconia was torpedoed by a German submarine:

I am an American citizen, representing the Sullivan Machinery Company of Chicago, living abroad, not as an expatriate, but for the promotion of American trade. I love the flag, believing in its significance. My beloved mother and sister, passengers on the Laconia, have been foully murdered on the high seas.

As an American citizen outraged and as such fully within my rights and as an American son and brother bereaved, I call upon my Government to preserve its citizens' self-respect and save others of my countrymen from such deep grief as I now feel. I am of military age, able to fight. If my country can use me against these brutal assassins, I am at its call.

If it stultifies my manhood and my nation's by remaining passive under outrage, I shall seek a man's chance under another flag.

George A. Young of this city, nephew of Mrs. Mary Elizabeth Hoy, who, with her daughter, lost her life on the Laconia, made public yesterday letters he wrote to President Wilson, Secretary Lansing, Senator Wadsworth of New York and Representative Walter M. Chandler of New York.

To the President, Mr. Young wrote:

I am advised by cable this morning that my aunt, Mrs. Mary Elizabeth Hoy, and my cousin, Miss Elizabeth Hoy, both American born and American citizens, lost their lives as a result of the torpedoing on Sunday of the Cunard liner Laconia.

I am, myself, American born and an American citizen. My father and I are the nearest male relatives in this country of Mrs. and Miss Hoy. Mrs. Hoy, her husband, and her daughter have spent most of their time of late years in London with Mrs. Hoy's only son, Austin Y. Hoy, who is European manager for the Sullivan Machinery Company, an American corporation.

Now, Sir, you will perhaps pardon me if in this moment of distress I speak somewhat strongly. My aunt and cousin are dead, and nothing that can be done by you or the American nation can return them to life. But is it not time, Sir, that you, as leader of this nation, assume your duty of leadership, stop talking, and take some definite action to prevent the recurrence of such a disaster?

With a similar introduction, Mr. Young's letter to Secretary Lansing read:

You will perhaps pardon me if in this moment of distress I ask you if it is not time that the great American Nation, in the government of which you have an important part, should take some definite action other than windy words to prevent the repetition of an occurrence such as that related above? Inevitably, the longer such action is postponed the greater, it seems to me, will be the penalty which must be paid by the American people.

I appreciate fully the responsibility which weighs upon you and the other members of the Administration and the difficulties under which you labor as a result of the apparent differences of opinion among the American people. But this is, it seems to me, a time for leadership to assert itself, and that leadership should be of a much stronger and more definite character than any which has been displayed

Continued on Page 3.

Zimmermann Says Again Neutral Ships Will Be Sunk; Escape of the Orleans Only an Instance of Luck

Special Cable to THE NEW YORK TIMES.

BERLIN, Feb. 28, (via London.)—The report of the safe arrival of the freighter Orleans at Bordeaux did not cause much surprise here, as it was known that there were heavy fogs along the course most likely to be selected by the American vessel, which would naturally render the operations of the U-boats extremely difficult.

The fact that the Orleans, despite her speed, took nearly three weeks for the passage is regarded here as sufficient evidence that her course must have been roundabout and zigzaggy, it being assumed that she was not any too anxious to meet a U-boat.

"One swallow does not make a Summer," is the comment of the newspapers, who say it would be a mistake if the Americans supposed the U-boats had received orders to let American ships pass unmolested. No such orders have been given, according to the Berlin papers, who leave no doubt about it by quoting Foreign Secretary Zimmermann, who in an interview with a Spanish newspaper man recently took occasion to make the following unmistakable statement:

"We make absolutely no distinction in sinking neutrals' ships within the war zone. Our determination is unshakable, since that is the only way to finish the war the coming Summer, in which desire we all share."

This, it is held, can be interpreted in no other way than that American ships, like those of all other neutrals, must comply with the U-boat rulings or take the consequences.

The sinking of the Laconia, a much larger ship than the Orleans, which crossed the danger zone at about the same time, is regarded as proof that even in propitious circumstances, such as foggy weather, it is difficult to escape the U-boats.

"As a casus belli, the Orleans was a failure," says the Zeitung am Mittag, and it would seem as if the people here were rather glad it was.

Says It's Only Luck That No American Ship Has Been Sunk

AMSTERDAM, Feb. 28, (via London.)—Referring to President Wilson's statement to Congress in asking for power to arm American ships that the overt act had not yet occurred, the Cologne Volks-Zeitung says:

"It is only due to a lucky accident that American ships have not been sent to the bottom, and unless American ships avoid the danger zone the overt act is bound to come. There is no doubt that the arming of American merchantmen will mean a fight between submarines and American vessels, which necessarily will produce a state of war."

BERLIN TO REPLACE SEVEN DUTCH SHIPS

Offers Freighters for Vessels Sunk, but Holland Must Buy Them After War.

MOTIVE BEHIND SINKINGS

Hint in Washington That Berlin Ordered Destruction of Ships to Settle Holland's Policy.

THE HAGUE, Feb. 28, (via London.)—The German Government has offered to replace the seven Dutch merchantmen which were torpedoed off the English Coast last week with German freighters until the end of the war, on condition that Holland purchase them afterwards.

LONDON, Feb. 28.—At the Dutch Legation it was said today there was no confirmation of the report published earlier in the week that the Dutch steamship Bandoeng, Eemland, and Zaandijk were still afloat. On the contrary the latest information received by the Dutch officials led to the belief that the vessels had been lost. A search for the steamships proved unavailing.

Special to The New York Times.

WASHINGTON, Feb. 28.—Information received here today has suggested that Germany ordered the destruction of the seven Dutch steamers torpedoed off Falmouth Thursday in order to force the Dutch Government to show its attitude toward the Central Powers. Germany is not blind to the possibilities of danger, contained in the entrance of Holland into the war, with the opportunity it would offer to the Allies to throw an army behind the main German line of defense. Knowing that resentment against her treatment of Dutch shipping was already high, she thought, by her stroke of last week, it is suggested, to force the Netherlands Government to express itself in a way which would commit it definitely to a course of action.

In doing it, it is pointed out, Germany took advantage of certain weaknesses in Holland's immediate military situation. The dykes are frozen and cannot be cut down with the necessary promptness and thoroughness to flood the country. Germany would therefore have an open passage across the country, as the Dutch Army of 500,000 men, while adequately trained and equipped, could not expect to resist successfully the force which Germany could throw into Holland without the dykes as an auxiliary defense.

By attempting to force the Netherlands to show its hand at this time, therefore, the impression has been created in some quarters here that Germany was attempting to force its small neighbor into a subservient attitude when Holland was not in position to assert its rights.

Although the entrance into the war of The Netherlands might result in a second Belgium, and the Dutch Government has made it plain that only wanton aggression would force it into open hostilities, Germany is by no means unaware of the damage which might result from Holland's enmity, whether expressed in actual war or in commercial destruction. Besides the enlargement of the front which she would have to defend, Holland might also harm Germany without entering the war by putting an embargo on commerce between The Netherlands and Germany, thus cutting off one of Germany's principal sources of food supply.

In addition to these considerations, it was pointed out, there are a large number of interned Belgian and British soldiers in Holland, who would be reorganized into fighting units, should Holland break with Germany and decide to resist German attacks and who would be utilized immediately in operations with the Dutch Army.

GERMANY HOLDS FIVE U. S. CONSULS

Held Because a Teuton Was Detained in Cuba—Their Release Now Asked.

RITTER UNDER SUSPICION

Officials Think Swiss Legation Leaked on Detaining of Consuls and Yarrowdale Note.

WASHINGTON, Feb. 28.—Immediate release of five American Consuls being detained in Germany was asked in a note sent the Berlin Government tonight by the United States.

The request was made in a communication replying to a note received from Germany earlier in the day in which it was announced that the American officials would be allowed to travel to new posts in Europe when the Berlin Government had been officially informed that German Consuls in this country ordered to South America and Central America had been permitted to proceed.

The action of Germany was based upon circumstances which, through no fault of this Government, detained Consul Mueller at Havana, Cuba, when he was on his way from Atlanta to his new post at Quito, Ecuador. The United States in its reply made it clear that the departure from this country of German consular officials had not been interfered with and that this Government could not control the movements of German Consuls in Cuba or other foreign territory.

In all, five American consular officers are being held in Germany. Mueller was Acting Consul, representing Germany at Atlanta, when the break in diplomatic relations occurred. After his arrival in Havana he notified Berlin that he had been "detained." It is assumed that the German Government misconstrued his message and concluded that he meant to convey the impression that he was being "held" through some fault of the United States.

"Leak" Displeases Washington.

The facts that five American Consular officers were being held in Germany, pending the satisfaction of the German official mind as to the status of Mueller, and that notes had been delivered to the State Department regarding the Mueller case, were made public here late this afternoon and caused vexation and displeasure at the State Department, where the impression was created that the Swiss Legation in Washington was responsible for the "leak."

Dr. Paul Ritter, the Swiss Minister, is now representing the interests of Germany in Washington. From what could be gathered in official circles today, the State Department would be displeased to learn that Dr. Ritter or any one connected with his legation had been indiscreet enough to disclose for publication the contents of messages passing between the United States and German Governments with the Swiss Government acting as intermediary.

When confirmation of the reported detention of the five Americans was sought at the State Department a high official refused to deny or affirm the story until he could be assured of the source of the information on which the report was based. It was made plain that the State Department had not disclosed anything regarding the case, and the question was even asked in State Department circles whether this story had emanated from the Swiss Legation.

Dr. Ritter's position was described as simply that of a "messenger" be-

Continued on Page 3.

JAPAN CALLS IT MONSTROUS

Embassy Issues Statement Scouting Germany's Proposal.

RELATIONS WITH US CLOSER

Tokio Gratified by Abandonment of Exclusion Bills in Oregon and Idaho.

FLOOD SURE OF CONGRESS

Representative Says Revelation Will Insure Backing of President for Defense Preparation.

Special to The New York Times.

WASHINGTON, Thursday, March 1.—At the Japanese Embassy at an early hour this morning, when THE TIMES correspondent sought information about the German appeal to Mexico and Japan to enter into an alliance with Germany against the United States, the idea that Japan would enter such an alliance was declared to be absolutely impossible and monstrous. One of the highest officials of the embassy, after briefly considering the matter, gave to THE TIMES the following:

STATEMENT BY THE JAPANESE EMBASSY.

"This story is quite unexpected. It is a very monstrous story. It is an impossible story, and an outrageous story. It is the first knowledge that the embassy has had that any such proposal was made. If such a proposal has been made by Germany we have no knowledge that it ever reached the Japanese Government. But if such a proposal were made, it is one that could not be entertained by the Japanese Government, as it is an absolutely impossible proposal. Japan is not only in honor bound to her allies in the Entente, but could not entertain the idea of entering into any such alliance at the expense of the United States."

THE NEW YORK TIMES correspondent feels justified in stating that the United States Government has been for some time in the possession of information concerning the communication of Foreign Minister Zimmermann to the German Minister in Mexico.

Any suggestion that Japan would for a moment entertain a proposition that would mean an abandonment of her conflict with Germany in alliance with Great Britain and the other members of the Entente was scouted as ridiculous in well-informed American quarters this morning.

In this connection it may be of interest to state that THE NEW YORK TIMES correspondent had occasion a few days ago to make inquiry in the proper circles concerning a report that Japan was seeking an arrangement with the United States that would border closely on an alliance.

The information obtained from a source that could be regarded as authoritative was that while it was not true that any such arrangement was in course of consideration there was no doubt that the Japanese Government had a much more cordial regard for the United States on account of several recent occurrences that proved to Japan that the Washington Government was sincerely anxious to live up to its obligations to the Japanese.

An instance of the attitude of the United States that had caused Japan to feel most kindly toward this Government was the action of the Wilson Administration in seeking to have the Legislatures of Oregon and Idaho abandon restrictive legislation aimed at Japanese subjects in those States. There have been other instances here lately indicating that Japan was becoming convinced that her suspicion of American friendship was based on erroneous ideas.

Reports have been in circulation for some time that Japan was seeking an arrangement with the Mexican Government which would give her an advantage in a contemplated war against the United States. These rumors have been persistent. The latest phase of them was that Francisco Villa was preparing to start for Japan, and that when he returned he would bring news that would make every Mexican throw up his hat and cheer. The State Department

Continued on Page 2.

Text of Germany's Proposal to Form an Alliance With Mexico and Japan Against the United States

[Supplied by the Associated Press as an authentic copy of the German Foreign Minister's note to the German Minister in Mexico.]

BERLIN, Jan. 19, 1917.

On the 1st of February we intend to begin submarine warfare unrestricted. In spite of this, it is our intention to endeavor to keep neutral the United States of America.

If this attempt is not successful, we propose an alliance on the following basis with Mexico: That we shall make war together and together make peace. We shall give general financial support, and it is understood that Mexico is to reconquer the lost territory in New Mexico, Texas, and Arizona. The details are left to you for settlement.

You are instructed to inform the President of Mexico of the above in the greatest confidence as soon as it is certain that there will be an outbreak of war with the United States, and suggest that the President of Mexico, on his own initiative, should communicate with Japan suggesting adherence at once to this plan. At the same time, offer to mediate between Germany and Japan.

Please call to the attention of the President of Mexico that the employment of ruthless submarine warfare now promises to compel England to make peace in a few months.

ZIMMERMANN.

FILIBUSTER FOR EXTRA SESSION

Senate Republicans Force Interminable Roll Calls on Amendments to Revenue Bill.

BILL PASSED, 47 TO 33

La Follette Consents to Taking Up Armed Ship Bill Friday, and Senate Recesses.

Special to The New York Times.

WASHINGTON, Thursday, March 1.—Senate Republicans last evening began in earnest a filibuster that seemed the result of a fixed determination to force an extra session. Democratic leaders now practically despair of preventing an extra session, though still bending every effort to beat down the Republican dilatory tactics.

The filibuster began when voting was in order on the Revenue bill. Under the unanimous consent agreement, after 8 o'clock speeches could not be made, but the proceedings were prolonged by formal roll calls on an indefinite number of amendments.

The revenue bill, designed to raise $350,000,000 through special taxes and bond issues was passed by the Senate at 12:10 A. M. by a strict party vote, 47 to 33.

The filibuster was continued until about 1:30 A. M., when the Senate adjourned until 10 A. M.

Immediately after the vote on the Revenue bill Senator Stone, at 12:15 A. M., moved to adjourn until 12:30 A. M. so as to clear the legislative situation for consideration of the Armed Neutrality bill. Senator Penrose countered with a motion to adjourn to 10:30 A. M. That and another by Senator La Follette were beaten.

Then a motion to adjourn until 12:55 A. M. was carried 60 to 6. There were protests in the Republican ranks against the tactics of their leaders, and Senators Borah and Fall told their colleagues they were tired of seeing time wasted and wanted the Senate to get down to business.

Senator La Follette began a single-handed filibuster against the Armed Neutrality bill when the Senate reconvened at 12:55 A. M. after a recess of ten minutes.

Armed Ship Bill Advanced.

Senator Stone, Chairman of the Foreign Relations Committee, sought unanimous consent to dispense with parliamentary formalities in order to get formally before the Senate the armed neutrality measure reported by the committee, which would authorize the President to arm American ships and employ "other instrumentalities" to protect American life and rights on the sea.

Prompt objection came from Senator La Follette, who insisted upon consuming time reading the journal of previous days, over the vigorous objection of Senators Fall and Poindexter, Republicans.

Finally the Wisconsin Senator was induced to withdraw his objection on condition that there should be no attempt to pass the bill before Friday. When Democratic leaders agreed to this the committee presented the bill with a favorable report, and Senator Stone asked that it lay over until Friday.

Then the Senate adjourned until 10 A. M., the majority abandoning plans for taking up the Naval Appropriation bill.

There was no indication as to what would be the attitude of Senator La Follette when the Revenue bill came before the Senate for action. The Democrats are taking it for granted that he will oppose it, but hope he will not undertake to force an extra session by a persistent filibuster.

It was considered significant that during the closing debate on the Revenue bill there were protests from the Republican ranks against the tactics of their leaders. Senators Fall and Borah told their colleagues they were tired of dilatory tactics, that, while they believed there was business requiring an

Continued on Page 3.

PACIFISTS PRESS VIEWS ON WILSON

Bryan, Jane Addams, and Others in Two Groups Confer with the President.

FEAR DECLARATION OF WAR

Approve Executive's Grasp of the Siuation—Bryan Wants Sea Restrictions.

Special to The New York Times.

WASHINGTON, Feb. 28.—William J. Bryan with other pacifists invaded Washington today to bring their influence to bear on the President and Congress to avert war with Germany. Mr. Bryan hurried here from Miami, Fla., last night.

Two groups, the first including Jane Addams, Professor Emily Balch, Joseph Cannon, and William I. Hull, and the second Amos Pinchot, Max Eastman, Paul Kellogg, and Lillian Wald, had conferences with the President this afternoon, both lasting more than an hour. Although none of the eight would discuss their conversations with the President in detail, they said they were impressed with the grasp of the situation the President showed, and that he had assured them he would use his best efforts, as he had in the past, to keep this country out of war if possible.

Mr. Bryan, after conferring in the morning with the leaders of the Emergency Peace Federation, went to the Capitol, where he talked with the members of Congress who are particularly friendly to his peace policies. Although he insisted that he believed the bills now pending before Congress to give the President power to deal with the German crisis should be phrased so as to leave no doubt that Congress was not in any sense declaring war, he would not say that he disapproved of the proposal to give the President added powers in the present emergency.

Asked to commit himself definitely on this point, he said he preferred not to give any one advice on the subject, as his attitude would depend altogether on the phraseology with which the bill was worded when finally approved by Congress.

Mr. Bryan insisted that particular emphasis should be laid on the part of the President's address to Congress in which he said he was not proposing war or measures which must lead to war.

"I am sure that in that the President correctly interpreted the hope of the people," Mr. Bryan said. "The people desire peace, but we have a war element in the country who are doing all in their power to manufacture war sentiment."

He contended that Americans should be prevented from traveling on armed ships, and also that passengers should not be allowed to travel on ships carrying munitions. He called attention in this connection to a dispatch in a New York paper of Feb. 24 saying that the British authorities at Halifax had taken off a number of women and children from a transatlantic steamer under a regulation forbidding them to travel on the ocean during the continuance of the present unrestricted submarine blockade while three American women who were on the same ship were allowed to remain.

"Is it possible," Mr. Bryan said, "that any one will say that our Government is less careful about its people than is the British Government? I believe that American citizens should be restrained from traveling on belligerent ships at a time like this. The Captain of a belligerent ship forfeits every life aboard if he tries to escape when warned to stop.

"Life is more important than merchandise and the first duty of those in charge of a passenger ship is to guard the lives of the passengers. A ship Captain cannot give to his passengers the care and protection to which they are entitled if his thoughts are on a contraband cargo.

"The President in his message said: 'I am not now proposing or contemplating war or any steps that might lead to it.' This statement is so plain that no one ought to suppose for an instant that the President desires Congress to surrender its exclusive right to decide whether the country should go to war and when it should go to war."

WASHINGTON EXPOSES PLOT

Our Government Has Zimmermann's Note of Jan. 19.

BIG PROMISES TO MEXICO

Conquest of Texas, New Mexico, and Arizona Held Out as a Lure to Her.

BERNSTORFF CHIEF AGENT

German Embassy in Washington Head Centre of All Intrigues in This Hemisphere.

[The following dispatch was sent out by The Associated Press last night with the statement that its contents had been fully authenticated.]

WASHINGTON, Feb. 28.—The Associated Press is enabled to reveal that Germany, in planning unrestricted submarine warfare and counting its consequences, proposed an alliance with Mexico and Japan to make war on the United States if this country should not remain neutral.

Japan, through Mexican mediation, was to be urged to abandon her allies and join in the attack on the United States.

Mexico, for her reward, was to receive general financial support from Germany, reconquer Texas, New Mexico, and Arizona—lost provinces—and share in the victorious peace terms Germany contemplated.

Details were left to German Minister von Eckhardt in Mexico City, who by instructions signed by German Foreign Minister Zimmermann at Berlin, Jan. 19, 1917, was directed to propose the alliance with Mexico to General Carranza and suggest that Mexico seek to bring Japan into the plot.

These instructions were transmitted to von Eckhardt through Count von Bernstorff, former German Ambassador here, now on his way home to Germany under a safe conduct obtained from his enemies by the country against which he was plotting war.

Germany pictured to Mexico, by broad intimation, England and the Entente Allies defeated, Germany and her allies trumphant and in world domination by the instrument of unrestricted submarine warfare.

A copy of Foreign Secretary Zimmermann's instructions to von Eckhardt, sent through von Bernstorff, [printed in adjoining columns on this page of THE TIMES] is in the possession of the United States Government.

Document in President's Hands.

This document has been in the hands of the Government since President Wilson broke off diplomatic relations with Germany. It has been kept secret while the President has been asking Congress for full authority to deal with Germany, and while Congress has been hesitating. It was in the President's hands while Chancellor von Bethmann Hollweg was declaring that the United States had placed an interpretation on the submarine declaration "never intended by Germany" and that Germany had promoted and honored friendly relations with the United States "as an heirloom from Frederick the Great."

Of itself, if there were no other, it is considered a sufficient answer to the German Chancellor's plaint that the United States "brusquely" broke off relations without giving "authentic" reasons for its action.

The document supplies the missing link to many separate chains of circumstances which, until now, have seemed to lead to no definite point. It sheds new light upon the frequently reported but indefinable movements of the Mexican Government to couple its situation with the friction between the United States and Japan.

It adds another chapter to the celebrated report of Jules Cambon, French Ambassador in Berlin before the war, of Germany's worldwide plans for stirring strife on every continent where they might aid her in the struggle for world domination which she dreamed was close at hand.

Climax to Bernstorff's Intrigues.

It adds a climax to the operations of Count von Bernstorff and the German

"All the News That's Fit to Print."

The New York Times.

THE WEATHER
Fair today; tomorrow rain or snow; moderate northwesterly winds.
For full weather report see Page 19.

VOL. LXVI...NO. 21,601. NEW YORK, FRIDAY, MARCH 16, 1917.—TWENTY PAGES. ONE CENT In Greater New York. | TWO CENTS New England and Middle States. | THREE CENTS Elsewhere.

REVOLUTION IN RUSSIA; CZAR ABDICATES; MICHAEL MADE REGENT, EMPRESS IN HIDING; PRO-GERMAN MINISTERS REPORTED SLAIN

RAILWAY STRIKE ORDERED TO BEGIN TOMORROW NIGHT

Managers and Heads of Brotherhoods End Final Conference, Both Defiant.

WILSON NOW THE ONLY HOPE

President Seems to Have No Authority, but May Make Appeal to Patriotism.

FIVE DAYS' GRACE FOR MILK

Travelers to Have Time to Get Home—Appeals for the Public's Approval.

The eight-hour fight between the 250 railroads of the United States and the 100,000 trainmen has placed the country again face to face with a nation-wide railway strike.

The National Conference Committee of the Railways yesterday defied the ultimatum of the four brotherhoods that the eight-hour day should be put into effect at once, and the labor chiefs formally served notice that their strike order stood and that a progressive strike program would begin tomorrow night at 7 o'clock. Freight alone will be affected at the start.

As was the case last Fall, when the railroads and the unions broke off diplomatic relations, the only hope of averting a strike lies with President Wilson, and both the managers and the brotherhood leaders remained in New York overnight in the expectation that Mr. Wilson would take a hand in the situation. However, it is a moot question what steps the Government could take to prevent paralysis of transportation facilities and consequent weakening of the nation's resources in the international crisis. The general opinion among officials in Washington last night seemed to be that the President could do little beyond appealing to the patriotism of both sides. A provision to empower him to take over the roads in such an emergency was among the Administration recommendations for railway legislation which failed at the last session of Congress.

Daniel Willard, President of the Baltimore & Ohio, and a member of the National Defense Council, who has been watching the strike developments in New York for the last three days, left late yesterday afternoon for Washington.

Last August after the two sides broke, President Wilson sent the members of the United States Board of Mediation and Conciliation to New York to bring the two sides together. The board failed, and when a strike order was about to be issued, the President sent his Secretary, Joseph P. Tumulty, to New York, with a request that the managers and the labor leaders come to the White House. It was after he kept the two sides in Washington all during the month of August that the Adamson law was passed after a call for a national strike, effective Sept. 4, had been issued. Both sides as represented here now are in readiness to go to Washington.

Monday is decision day for the Supreme Court, and if it should hand down a decision on the Adamson law then it might lead to a renewal of conferences between the two sides regardless of the strike situation. The railroad managers have all along expressed the opinion that the law would be held invalid. The haste of the brotherhoods in forcing the issue has caused the managers to believe that the labor leaders also think the law will be thrown out. While the brotherhood heads say the action of the court one way or the other will not affect their demands, the railroad managers believe that the invalidating of the Adamson law would give them an advantage.

The word of the deadlock here yesterday was flashed to all parts of the country last night, and notices of embargoes and strike preparations were put out by nearly all of the railroads. Appeals to the patriotism of the men were made by many roads. President Wilson was among the first to get notice of the break.

Joseph Hartigan, City Commissioner of Weights and Measures, was quick to appeal to the brotherhoods to permit the movement of food trains into this city. In reply to his plea he received this letter, signed by the chiefs of the four organizations:

"Every indication now seems to warrant the statement that the freight train, engine, and yard employes on certain railways entering this city will peaceably withdraw from service at 7 P. M., Saturday, March 17, and that the employes on other lines will continue in service for several days thereafter, making it possible, in our opinion, to furnish this city food and fuel supplies for several days after the strike becomes effective.

"We regret exceedingly the necessity

Continued on Page [illegible].

Government Heads Hold a Mysterious Conference

Special to The New York Times.

WASHINGTON, March 15.—A conference surrounded with much mystery took place late this afternoon in the office of the Secretary of State. In addition to Secretary Lansing, it was attended by Mr. Baker, the Secretary of War; Mr. Gregory, the Attorney General; Mr. Daniels, the Secretary of the Navy; Mr. Polk, the Counsellor of the State Department, and Mr. Woolsey, personal legal adviser to the Secretary of State.

After the conference it was said by one of those who attended it that no particular subject had been discussed. It had been devoted, he indicated, to many questions that naturally came up for discussion at this critical period in the international relations of the United States. Elsewhere, however, the impression was given that the conference was called to consider matters of rather pressing importance.

FRYATT'S FATE FOR OUR GUNNERS

German Threat to Put to Death Crews of Any Armed American Ships They Capture.

WARNING IN MUNICH PAPER

Assumes That President "Realizes Fate to Which He Is Subjecting His Artillerymen."

BERNE, Switzerland, March 15, (via Paris.)—The crews of armed American merchantmen who venture to fire upon German submarines before a state of war exists between Germany and the United States, must expect to meet the fate of Captain Fryatt, warns the Munich Neueste Nachrichten, a copy of which has reached Berne, in commenting on the announcement of the State Department that American merchantmen will be armed.

"We assume," the newspaper says, "that President Wilson realizes the fate to which he is subjecting his artillerymen. According to the German prize laws it is unneutral support of the enemy if a neutral ship takes part in hostilities. If such a ship opposes the Prize Court then it must be treated as an enemy ship. The prize rules specify as to the crews of such ships. If, without being attached to the forces of the enemy, they take part in hostilities or make forcible resistance, they may be treated according to the usages of war.

"If President Wilson, knowing these provisions of international law, proceeds to arm American merchantmen, he must assume responsibility for the eventuality that American seamen will meet the fate of Captain Fryatt."

The Captain Fryatt referred to in the foregoing dispatch was Captain Charles Fryatt of the Great Eastern Railway steamer Brussels. He was tried before a German naval court-martial in July, 1916, and sentenced to death, on a charge that he had attempted to ram the German submarine U-33. The sentence of the court-martial was executed.

STONE ASKS FOR LIST OF AMERICAN SHIPS

Senate Adopts His Resolution, Which Causes Much Speculation in Washington.

Special to The New York Times.

WASHINGTON, March 15.—Senator Stone of Missouri caused some comment at the Capitol today by introducing a resolution directing the Secretary of Commerce to give the Senate a full list of sea-going vessels applying for American registry between Jan. 1, 1916, and March 15, 1917; the name and character of such vessels before and after registration, the names of the ships' owners, and the precise date of application for registry and date of receiving it. The resolution was read and adopted without discussion, and Secretary Redfield will forward the information tomorrow.

There was a good deal of speculation as to why Mr. Stone, Chairman of the Committee on Foreign Relations, should want this information made public. One suggestion was that he might think that some belligerent nation was permitting its ships to be registered in the United States, so that through the later torpedoing of these ships by German submarines the United States might be drawn into the war. It was suggested that if Mr. Stone wanted the information for his own use, he could have got it by telephoning the Department of Commerce.

Mr. Stone showed no desire to explain his resolution and seemed prepared to rebuff questioners. He said that his resolution spoke for itself. When asked if the changes in the ownership of the Algonquin had prompted his resolution, the Senator said that he would not be interviewed.

LONDON HAILS REVOLUTION

Expected Czar's Overthrow and Sees Brighter Prospects for the Allies.

THINK THE COUP DECISIVE

Well-Informed Observers Believe the Patriotic War Party Has Made Its Control Secure.

FEAR NO SEPARATE PEACE

With Weak Ruler Deposed and Pro-German Advisers Ousted, They Predict New Victories.

Special Cable to THE NEW YORK TIMES.

LONDON, Friday, March 16.—It is the belief in well-informed circles here that the Provisional Government which has been set up in Russia by the military party will be able to keep the upper hand in maintaining a policy that means the uninterruptedly vigorous prosecution of the war to a victorious end.

The overthrow of the Czar was expected, and observers here are confident that the Grand Duke as regent will have the solid support of the war party, while they are equally sure of the elimination of any element with a pro-German taint.

An Anti-German Uprising.

As the situation is explained to THE NEW YORK TIMES correspondent, the revolution simply means that German sympathizers within the Russian Government have been overthrown, and that no chance remains for a separate peace being secretly arranged with Germany. This, it is felt, is the real basis of the revolution that has worked such a sudden change in Russian politics.

This revolution, which has been on the verge of boiling over for months, reached its crisis three days ago, when the military leaders, with the Duma behind them, started outbreaks in Petrograd and Moscow. It is evident from the way in which the uprising was conducted, says THE NEW YORK TIMES correspondent's informant, that it had been carefully planned and skillfully executed.

"After it got under way," he says, "there was no hesitation of movement until the members of the military party were masters of the situation. The details of what occurred in Petrograd and Moscow are lacking, but enough is known to show that they have been in a fever of sanguinary revolution for the last three days.

"Dashes of troops against the headquarters of the pro-German leaders, with the capture of Protopopoff and Stürmer as prisoners of war, were conspicuous features of the revolution. The houses of German sympathizers were burned in both cities, and the occupants either taken captive or forced to flee.

"Now that the military party is in control the situation is said to be settling down, with every prospect that the aim of the Revolutionists will be accomplished."

In fact, the situation was described last night as being "entirely satisfactory."

For months, said the informant of THE NEW YORK TIMES correspondent, Great Britain had been expecting an outcome of the Russian political crisis that would mean the solid intrenchment of the war party and the downfall of those seeking a separate peace with Germany. Now it may be confidently expected that Russia will play her part in the war with even greater vigor than before.

German-Born Czarina Blamed.

The Daily Chronicle in its leading article says:

"From a very early period the German-born Czarina and the clique of pro-German reactionaries whom her influence made powerful with the Czar were bent on ending the war prematurely in the interests of reaction. The Ministers set up under these auspices have for over two years acted in defiance of public opinion. Their policy was not obscure; they hampered the army in respect of munitions, disorganized the country in respect of its distributive services, brought about artificial famine in a land which is one of the world's chief food producers, and themselves, through police agents, tried to stir up abortive revolts in order that they might plead military failure and internal revolution as a reason for withdrawing from the war.

"The people foiled them for long by magnificent and much enduring patriotism. When the Government left the army without munitions the local authorities—the zemstvos and unions of towns—stepped in and organized their

Continued on Page 2.

Duma Appeals to the Army for Unity Against Foe; Gives Pledge of No Weakening or Suspension of War

LONDON, March 15.—The Reuter correspondent at Petrograd telegraphs under date of yesterday:

"The Military Committee of the Duma has asked all the officers not yet employed by the committee to undertake the organization of the soldiers who joined the people, and help guard the capital. The committee issued a statement, pointing out that at the present moment, when facing an enemy who wished to take advantage of the temporary weakness of the country, it was absolutely necessary to make every effort to maintain the power of the army. It added that the blood of the Russians who had died during the two and a half years of war pledged the people to do this.

"The President of the Duma sent telegrams to the commanders of the Baltic and Black Sea fleets, to the chiefs of the armies on the northern, southwestern, western, Rumanian, and Caucasus fronts, and to the Chief of the General Staff, requesting that the army and navy preserve absolute calm, and to be sure that the struggle against the foreign enemy was not suspended or weakened even for a single moment. The telegram sent these commanders added:

> As hitherto, the army and navy must continue firmly and valiantly to defend the country, and while the Provisional Committee is aided by the military element in the capital and with the moral support of the people in restoring calm and regular activity, each officer, soldier, and sailor should fulfill his duty.

"The officers of the Petrograd garrison at a general meeting unanimously agreed to recognize the authority of the Executive Committee of the Duma until the formation of a permanent Government.

"An imperial bodyguard regiment rode into Petrograd today. It is estimated that there are now 60,000 troops in the capital."

People in Revolt Burn and Slay in Streets of Russia's Capital

Fashionable Hotel Riddled by Machine Guns When Pro-German Shoots at Crowd—Count Fredericks's Home Set on Fire and Family Ill-Treated—General de Knorring Shot.

Stuermer and Protopopoff Reported Assassinated

Special Cable to THE NEW YORK TIMES.

LONDON, Friday, March 16.—The Exchange Telegraph's Copenhagen correspondent sends the following:

"A telegram to the Extrabladet reports that the Russian Consul in Haparanda states that the pro-German ex-Prime Minister, Boris Stürmer, and Minister of Home Affairs Protopopoff have been murdered."

Special Cable to THE NEW YORK TIMES.

LONDON, Friday, March 16.—Belated dispatches from Petrograd, giving details of the revolution in Russia, are arriving here. A dispatch to The Morning Post, dated Wednesday, says:

"Every weapon save only heavy artillery has been freely used in Petrograd streets for four days past, and today there is still considerable firing at various points at intervals. Rifles, revolvers, machine guns, and armored motors—all have been used and are still in use.

"The military hotel, formerly the Astoria Hotel, which lodged exclusively officers from the front, their wives and families, with the majority of officers present here as representatives of the Allies, was subjected to a heavy fusillade from machine guns on armored motors, entirely as the result of what was represented as provocation on the part of a pro-German resident, who fired upon the people from the windows.

General's Daughter Wounded.

"The daughter of the Russian General Prince Tumanoff, who is now commanding a cavalry division at the front, was severely wounded in the neck, and her rooms were ruined by the fusillade. A mob of armed men—soldiers, sailors, and civilians—thoroughly searched the Astoria, and disarmed all the Russian officers, but showed marked consideration for the allied officers.

"Similar scenes have been enacted throughout Petrograd, while in the transpontine regions occupied by the factory population, heavy fighting has been in progress for days, until the alleged excessive cruelty of the police caused the Cossacks and soldiery to espouse the side of the people.

"The ease with which the whole of the capital fell into the hands of the revolutionaries very greatly mitigated the bloodshed inevitable in civil tumults, but the butcher's bill is undoubtedly heavy enough."

Supplementing this by a telegram dated Thursday the same correspondent says:

"Precisely one week ago peaceful street demonstrations, at first largely composed of women and children, were made in protest against the inadequate supply of black bread. The police, unable to cope with the movement, which they felt bound to crush by the usual police methods, called in the aid of the Cossacks.

"The workmen, who had held aloof from the overt demonstrations as organized bodies and who were at first represented only by the younger, irresponsible workingmen, were enraged at the rough treatment by the police of their women and children and were encouraged by the obvious reluctance of the Cossacks and soldiery generally to back up the police oppression. Finally the Cossacks turned on the police, who fled before them, and there was a pandemonium of irregular shooting.

"Matters were not improved by the setting at liberty of political prisoners and criminals and the burning of prisons. On the whole, however, the bloodshed, compared with the magnitude of the achievement, has been infinitesimal. Regiment after regiment, brought in from outside the capital, promptly joined their comrades on the side of the people, and when a special body of lifeguards known as the Imperial Convoy also came in it felt that the old régime had fallen indeed.

Rowdy Element Breaks Loose.

"In the meantime the red revolutionary parties were preaching anarchy in all its forms, and the rowdy elements of the population of the great city were busy indulging their professional instincts.

"Happily the worst incentive to violence—alcohol in all its forms—was almost unprocurable, and the disciplined sense of the soldiery, who now formed the majority, was against excesses which disgraced what was now felt to be the great cause of national freedom.

"M. Rodzianko, at the head of the Duma Committee, soon issued commonsense orders for the disarming of civilians and for the checking of red revolutionary manifestations. The soldiers and people themselves put a stop to the looting. Throughout the city a careful search was made for stores of foodstuffs, which were promptly put on sale. The results warrant the belief that unscrupulous profiteering on an incredible scale had long been prevalent.

"At the present moment a careful search is being made for higher military officers and other functionaries, who are being induced to accept the new conditions and carry on their public duties or undergo arrest. The secret police, that scourge of the Russian nation whose service is despised by all, and which has been for a generation past the refuge for defaulters and detected miscreants of all other public services receive no mercy, but the ordinary police are being merely put under arrest.

Police Stations Destroyed.

The Petrograd correspondent of The Daily Chronicle sent the following, bearing Wednesday's date:

"In Moscow, Kiev, and Kharkoff the troops have signified adherence to the new movement, and in Moscow the police have surrendered of their own accord. The Department of Police in Petrograd has been rifled and the building of the secret police, that hotbed of political intrigue, has been burned, and all police stations in town looted and their contents burned or scattered.

"The ordinary and political police, in some cases, were killed. In other cases, they were dragged from their hiding places and lodged in dark cells in the fortress of St. Peter and St. Paul, where so many have suffered martyrdom for Russian freedom. The political prisoners, victims of the old régime, have been freed from the jails, and many are now taking part in the reorganization of the Government."

Count Fredericks's Home Burned.

LONDON, Friday, March 16.—The Times Petrograd correspondent describes the sacking of the residence of Count Fredericks, Minister of the Imperial Court and Aide de Camp to the Emperor, as one of the most deplorable incidents of the revolt.

Count Fredericks's house was set on fire. His aged wife was carried out fainting. His daughter, who is frail, rushed out, carrying her favorite dog. The girl was ill-treated by the drunken mob, and the dog was killed. Both women eventually were taken to a place of safety.

Count Fredericks is now in attendance upon former Emperor Nicholas.

General de Knorring was ordered to report to the Duma, but refused to comply with the summons. On the contrary, he armed himself and the janitor

Continued on Page 2.

ARMY JOINS WITH THE DUMA

Three Days of Conflict Follow Food Riots in Capital.

POPULACE TAKE UP ARMS

But End Comes Suddenly When Troops Guarding Old Ministers Surrender.

CZAR FINDS CAPITAL GONE

Returns from Front After Receiving Warning from Duma and Gives Up His Throne.

Empress Reported Under Guard or Hiding From Angry People

Special Cable to THE NEW YORK TIMES.

PETROGRAD, March 14. (Dispatch to The London Daily Chronicle.)—The Empress of Russia has been placed under guard.

LONDON, March 15.—According to information received here the Russian people have been most distrustful during recent events of the personal influence of Empress Alexandra. She was supposed to exercise the greatest influence over Emperor Nicholas.

It is stated that her whereabouts is not known, but it is believed she is in seclusion, fearing the populace.

The Empress Alexandra before her marriage to the Emperor of Russia in 1894 was the German Princess Alix of Hesse-Darmstadt.

PETROGRAD, March 15.—Emperor Nicholas of Russia has abdicated, and Grand Duke Michael Alexandrovitch, his younger brother, has been named as Regent.

The Russian Ministry, charged with corruption and incompetence, has been swept out of office. One Minister, Alexander Protopopoff, the head of the Interior Department, is reported to have been killed, and the other Ministers, as well as the President of the Imperial Council, are under arrest.

A new national Cabinet is announced, with Prince Lvoff as President of the Council and Premier, and the other offices held by the men who are close to the Russian people.

Petrograd has been the scene of one of the most remarkable risings in history, beginning with minor food riots and labor strikes last week Thursday. The people's cry for food reached the hearts of the soldiers, and one by one the regiments rebelled, until finally those troops which had for a time stood loyal to the Government gathered up their arms and marched into the ranks of the revolutionists.

Duma President Leading Figure.

Michael V. Rodzianko, President of the Duma, was the leading figure among the Deputies, who unanimously decided to oppose the imperial order, issued last week, for a dissolution of the House. They continued their sessions, and M. Rodzianko informed the Emperor, then at the front, that the hour had struck when the will of the people must prevail.

Even the Imperial Council realized the gravity of the situation, and added its appeal to that of the Duma that the Emperor should take steps to give the people a policy and government in accordance with their desires and in order that there should be no interference with carrying on the war to a victorious ending.

The Emperor hastened back to the capital only to find that the revolution had been successful and that a new Government was in control.

The Empress, who, it is alleged, has been influential in the councils opposed to the wishes of the people, is reported to have fled or to be in hiding.

Although considerable fighting took place, it is not believed that the casualties are large. One report says that they do not exceed 200.

A few defenders of the old régime put up a last feeble defense last night from the roofs of the wrecked Astoria Military Hotel and St. Isaac's Cathedral, facing on two sides of the same square.

The city is now quiet and perfect order prevails. So far as is known, no foreigners were injured.

The Imperial Palace at Tsarskoe-Selo is said to have been in a state of siege, but thus far no firing has been reported between the guards defending the palace and the revolutionists and troops.

According to one report the Emperor expected trouble to follow from his decree dissolving the Duma, and so warned the residents of Tsarkoe-Selo to arrange to remain in the suburb for an indefinite period.

Began From Strikes a Week Ago.

The most phenomenal feature of the revolution was the swift and orderly transition whereby the control of the city passed from the régime of the old Government into the hands of its opponents.

The visible signs of revolution began on Thursday, March 8. Strikes were declared in several big munitions factories as a protest against the shortage of bread. Men and women gathered and marched through the streets, most of them in an orderly fashion. A few bread shops were broken into in that section of the city beyond the Neva, and several minor clashes between strikers and police occurred.

Squads of mounted troops appeared, but during Thursday and Friday the utmost friendliness seemed to exist between the troops and the people.

This early period of the uprising bore the character of a mock revolution, staged for an immense audience. Cossacks, charging down the street, did so in a half-hearted fashion, plainly without malice or intent to harm the crowds, which they playfully dispersed. The troops exchanged good-natured raillery with the working men and women, and as they rode were cheered by the populace.

Long lines of soldiers stationed in dramatic attitudes across Nevsky Prospect, with their guns pointed at an imaginary foe, appeared to be taking part in a realistic tableau. Machine guns, firing rounds of blank cartridges, seemed only to add another realistic touch to a tremendous theatric production which was using the whole city as a stage.

On Saturday, however, apparently without provocation, the troops were ordered to fire on people marching in Nevsky Prospect. The troops refused to fire, and the police, replacing them, fired rifles and machine guns.

Then came a clash between troops and police, which continued in desultory fashion throughout Saturday night and Sunday. The Nevsky Prospect was cleared of traffic by the police and notices were posted by the commander of the Petrograd military district warning the people that any attempt to congregate would be met by force.

Until Sunday evening, however, there was no intimation that the affair would grow to the proportions of a revolution. The first serious outbreak came at 4 o'clock, when the men of the Volynsky Regiment shot their officers and refused when they received an order to fire upon striking workingmen in one of the factory districts.

Another regiment detailed against the mutineers also joined the revolt. The news spread rapidly to the other barracks and four more regiments went over. Some of the revolting troops marched to the St. Peter and St. Paul Fortress on the right bank of the Neva, and after a brief skirmish with the garrison took possession of it.

Dissension spread among the troops, who did not understand why they should be compelled to take violent measures against fellow-citizens whose chief offense was that they were hungry and were asking the Government to supply bread. Several regiments deserted. A pitched battle began between the troops who stood with the Government and those who, refusing to obey orders, had mutinied, and even slain their officers.

A long night fight took place between the mutinous regiments and the police at the end of St. Catharine Canal, immediately in front of the historic church built over the spot where Alexander II. was killed by a bomb. The police finally fled to the rooftops all over the city and were seen no more in the streets during the entire term of the fighting.

Turning Point in Revolution.

Still, on Monday morning the Government troops appeared to control all the principal squares of the city. Then came a period when it was impossible to distinguish one side from the other. There was no definite line between the factions. The turning point appeared to come about 3 o'clock in the afternoon. For two hours the opposing regiments passively confronted each other along the wide Liteiny Prospect in almost complete silence.

From time to time emissaries from the revolutionary side rode to the opposing ranks and exhorted them to join the side of the people. For a while the result [illegible] hung in the balance. The troops appeared irresolute, [illegible]

Leading Figures in Russian Revolution.

Czar Nicholas II. who has Abdicated.

Czarevitch Alexis, 12 yrs old, who will succeed to the Throne.

Grand Duke Michael Alexandrovitch, who has been named Regent.

Michael Rodzianko, head of the Revolution and the Temporary Government.

Prince Lvoff Heads Cabinet; Miliukoff Foreign Minister

PETROGRAD, via London, Friday, March 16.—The members of the new National Cabinet are announced as follows:

Premier, President of the Council, and Minister of the Interior—Prince Georges E. Lvoff.

Foreign Minister—Professor Paul N. Miliukoff.

Minister of Public Instruction—Professor Manuiloff of Moscow University.

Minister of War and Navy, ad interim—A. J. Guchkoff, formerly President of the Duma.

Minister of Agriculture—M. Ichingareff, Deputy from Petrograd.

Minister of Finance—M. Terestchenko, Deputy from Kiev.

Minister of Justice—Deputy Kerenski of Saratoff.

Minister of Communications—N. V. Nekrasoff, Vice President of the Duma.

Controller of State—M. Godneff, Deputy from Kazan.

"All the News That's Fit to Print."

The New York Times.

THE WEATHER
Rain by tonight; wind south; Sunday rain, strong northwesterly winds
For full weather report see Page 19.

VOL. LXVI...NO. 21,602. NEW YORK, SATURDAY, MARCH 17, 1917.—TWENTY PAGES. ONE CENT In Greater New York. | TWO CENTS New England and Middle States. | THREE CENTS Elsewhere.

THE ROMANOFF DYNASTY ENDED IN RUSSIA; CZAR'S ABDICATION FOLLOWED BY MICHAEL'S; CONSTITUTIONAL ASSEMBLY TO BE CONVOKED

[illegible]N APPEALS [illegible] PATRIOTISM TO AVERT STRIKE

[illegible]ds Lane, Wilson, Willard, and Gompers of Defense Council Here to Mediate.

NIGHT MEETING FRUITLESS

Committee Asserts Government Has No Plan to Take Over Roads.

EMBARGOES TIGHTENED UP

President Leaves Sickbed to Attend Cabinet Meeting—Gompers Not at First Conference.

The Council of National Defense, at the instance of President Wilson and the Cabinet, last night stepped into the breach between the railroads and the four brotherhoods, and in the name of patriotism appealed to both sides to avert the nation-wide transportation strike called to begin at 7 o'clock tonight. It was the most important action taken by the Council since it was formed recently to mobilize the defense resources of the United States.

President Wilson, after a [illegible] to the brotherhoods: Secretary of the Interior Lane, Secretary of Labor Wilson, Samuel Gompers, President of the American Federation of Labor, and Daniel Willard, President of the Baltimore & Ohio Railroad—all members of the Council or of the advisory council thereof.

Mr. Willard reached New York at 6:30 o'clock to make appointments for peace parleys. Mr. Lane came at 9 o'clock and went at once to the Hotel Biltmore, where he began a conference with the four brotherhood leaders—W. S. Stone of the Engineers, W. S. Carter of the Firemen, L. E. Sheppard, President of the Conductors, and W. G. Lee, President of the Trainmen. Mr. Wilson arrived at 10:30 o'clock, and it was said Mr. Gompers would be here later in the night.

At midnight no intimation had come from the unions that they had receded in any way from their stand, and it seemed probable that the conference would last until dawn. Mr. Gompers had not then arrived, but the other conferrees had no doubt that he would put in an appearance in due course. He was not in Washington when the others left there. Officials of the American Federation of Labor explained that he had been keeping in touch with the brotherhood leaders from a point near New York and could be counted on to attend the proceedings.

Joint Conference Begins.

Shortly after 1 o'clock this morning the railroad managers were called into the conference jointly with the brotherhood representatives. Although no announcement was made, it was assumed that this joint resumption of negotiations seemed to presage possible peace, but this view was altered when, thirty minutes later, the union men walked out. They said they had no statement to make. At 3:45 o'clock this morning the conference adjourned, and Mr. Wilson announced that there was no statement to give out. The conference will be resumed with the brotherhoods at 9:30 o'clock this morning, and with the railroad officials at 11.

It was reported authoritatively that a majority of the managers were considering proposing to the brotherhoods that they accept the terms of the switchmen's award which would give the men nine hours' pay for eight hours' work. The Adamson law provides ten hours' pay for eight hours' work.

The opinion was expressed last night that Mr. Gompers might find himself in an embarrassing situation. The brotherhoods are not affiliated with the American Federation of Labor. They had with the federation a working agreement in the eight-hour fight, but the belief has been exercised that Mr. Gompers does not approve of their pushing the issue at this critical time.

Mr. Lane explained that he had no instructions from the President to threaten that the Federal Government would take over the railroads and operate them in the event the strike started, adding that he "had no club," and had come merely to appeal to the patriotism of the men.

Both the labor leaders and the railroad managers had received late in the afternoon a plea from the White House, in which the President asked them to forget their differences for the time being, and not to call a strike which would further embarrass the Government, already deeply concerned in international complications.

The first thing Secretary Lane did when he met the labor chiefs was to present to them the following letter, signed by Secretary of War Baker, as Chairman of the Council of National Defense:

"At a meeting of the Council of

Continued on Page 4.

President Wilson's Plea for Railway Peace Based on Country's Need and War Danger

Special to The New York Times.

WASHINGTON, March 16.—This is President Wilson's personal appeal to the representatives of the contending factions in the railroad controversy:

"I deem it my duty and right to appeal to you in this time of national peril to open again the questions at issue between the railroads and their operatives with a view to accommodation or settlement.

"With my approval a committee of the Council of National Defense is about to seek a conference with you with that end in view.

"A general interruption of the railway traffic of the country at this time would entail a danger to the nation against which I have the right to enter my most solemn and earnest protest.

"It is now the duty of every patriotic man to bring matters of this sort to immediate accommodation. The safety of the country against manifest perils affecting its own peace and the peace of the whole world makes accommodation absolutely imperative and seems to me to render any other choice or action inconceivable."

The President's message was sent to Elisha Lee, Chairman of the Conference Committee of Railroad Managers; L. E. Sheppard, acting head of the Conductors; W. G. Lee, head of the Trainmen; W. S. Stone, Grand Chief of the Engineers, and W. S. Carter, President of the Firemen and Enginemen.

STRIKE EMBARGOES GROW TIGHTER

New York Central Notifies All Shippers That No Freight Will Be Received.

NEW HAVEN LESS DRASTIC

Pennsylvania Will Haul Food [illegible]

Practically all of the big railroads, including the New York Central, New Haven, and Pennsylvania, with terminal facilities in New York City or New Jersey, which bring the food and other freight vital to the existence of the city's population, issued the expected embargo orders, more or less drastic, yesterday, because of the threatened strike. In most instances the orders became effective last night. The New Haven announced that all sleeping and dining car service would be discontinued, beginning tonight.

The Pennsylvania announced that, for the present, an effort would be made to continue the movement of live stock, food for human and animal consumption, shipments consigned to officers of the United States Government, fuel and supplies for use of the Pennsylvania and affiliated lines, and news print paper, but that these shipments would be accepted only subject to delay, loss, and damage. The New Haven left milk off the restricted list, and added the warning that passenger service might be cut and the limited trains taken off.

The New York Central was the first great Eastern system to take the step, and this order was sent to all agents on its 12,000 miles of line:

> Please notify all shippers that, effective at once, we cannot accept freight from them until further notice.

The New York, New Haven & Hartford followed with an embargo order which read:

> Beginning 6 P. M. Saturday, provided the prospective strike order of the four brotherhoods of train and engine men becomes effective, the passenger and freight service of the New York, New Haven & Hartford Railroad Company will be subject to serious delay and curtailment.
>
> The passenger service is threatened by the calling out of the yard men in Grand Central and other terminals Saturday evening, in connection with the discontinuance of service on other lines. Yard service is an important factor in controlling operation of passenger trains.
>
> All freight and much express are being placed under embargo and the prospects for the continued handling of both are indefinite.
>
> The company will make every endeavor to operate such trains as it can. Patrons are advised of the probable entire suspension of yard and freight train service, curtailment of passenger service, involving a more or less number of trains on such schedules as it may be practicable to establish, and the probable discontinuance of limited trains.

The New York, New Haven & Hartford Railroad Company and the Central New England Railway Company have issued the following freight and express embargoes:

> Effective at 5 P. M. this date these companies will not accept freight of any kind, except milk, for points on or via these lines. This includes freight in transit.
>
> No express will be received through the Grand Central Terminal after 4 P. M., and from or via other points after 10 P. M. Saturday, March 17.

The embargo order of the Pennsylvania Railroad read:

> Effective close of business Friday, March 16, on account of threatened strike, Pennsylvania Railroad, Philadelphia, Baltimore & Washington Railroad, and West Jersey & Seashore Railroad, embargo all freight of all kinds from all points for all destinations, except livestock and foodstuffs for human and animal consumption, (domestic,) shipments consigned to officers of the United States Government, fuel, and supplies for use of Pennsylvania Railroad and affiliated lines, and news print paper.
>
> All freight as above described which may be in transit will not be accepted from the New York, Philadelphia & Norfolk Railroad, the Cumberland Valley Railroad, Cornwall & Lebanon Railroad, the Susquehanna, Bloomsburg & Berwick Railroad, the Pennsylvania Lines West of Pittsburgh, or other connecting lines at any junction point after date and hour above named, regardless of date on which shipment was accepted, as indicated by date on billing.
>
> All bills of lading issued on and after strike March 17, 1917, and until further notice, must bear the following notations:
>
> "This shipment accepted subject to delay, loss, and damage account of threatened strike."

Representatives of the Pennsylvania said the management thought the pre-

Continued on Page 4.

SINISTER HAND SEEN IN STRIKE

Calvin of Union Pacific Fears Brotherhood Heads Don't Speak for Men.

BIG AID TO OUR ENEMIES

Congestion After Walkout Would Block Movement of Troop and [illegible] Trains for Weeks.

OMAHA, Neb., March 16.—E. E. Calvin, President of the Union Pacific Railroad, issued this statement today:

"In connection with the threat of a general railroad strike at this time the question arises, Is some power shrewder and more astute than the brotherhood leaders back of the plan to precipitate a transportation tieup at this time, and establish in this country a condition, which, to the minds of our enemies in Europe, may seem like a revolt against our Government? I am in hearty sympathy with Elisha Lee, Chairman of the National Conference Committee of the Railways, when he calls attention to the fact that the serious international situation should cause every citizen to put every thought of personal right or desire second to his duty to his country.

"In a letter addressed to President Wilson some days ago the brotherhood leaders gave assurance that, in case of war, they would render every possible assistance to the Government. They have overlooked the fact that, in many ways, a railroad strike in this country would be worth more to our enemies than the winning of many battles, for the reason that it would paralyze and stagnate all our resources, and even if the strike be called off, should war be declared, the strike tieup would have resulted in such a congestion of freight in the terminals and on the sidings that weeks, and probably months, would be required to get this congestion cleaned up before the railroads would be in normal running condition again. This would mean that the movement of troops would be seriously interfered with and the movement of commissary supplies and munitions so seriously interrupted as to give our enemies a tremendous advantage.

"A day or two ago an officer of our navy said: 'A tieup of the railroads for even two days would be a serious blow to the national welfare at this critical time. We must keep the fleet fully coaled and equipped with other supplies.'

"Moreover, we are rushing construction work in the navy, and a two days' tieup of transportation of the materials urgently needed might mean a two months' delay in the emergency work we have undertaken. The rank and file of the railroad brotherhoods have waited for ten weeks for the decision of the United States Supreme Court as to the constitutionality of the Adamson law, a decision which may be handed down almost any day.

"In accordance with our agreement, the Union Pacific, in common with the other railroads of the country, kept separate time records since Jan. 1, scrupulously recording the increased pay that would be due to their employes in case the Adamson law was upheld. Further, the strike vote taken by the men was for a specific time and purpose, and in the minds of many of the brotherhood men to make use of the strike vote taken last Summer to call a strike at this time would be illegal.

"When we are on the verge of a decision respecting the legality of the Adamson law, and when we stand face to face with the probability of a war which will tax all our energy, it seems to me that in speaking of the plans of the brotherhood leaders to tie up the transportation industry of the country the people are justified in using a stronger term than ill-advised. To me it seems incredible that the rank and file of brotherhood members would respond to a strike call which must have the universal condemnation of the patriotic citizens of this country.

"It is impossible to believe that the brotherhood leaders, who have heretofore shown real generalship, will lead those who trust in them upon such a fool's errand."

PLEDGE OF REFORM RINGS IN GERMANY; JUNKERS ASSAILED

Bethmann Hollweg's Speech Accepted as Heralding a New Era in the Empire.

PARTY TRUCE IN DANGER

Chancellor Moved to Action by Demands of Socialists in Prussian Diet.

U-BOAT WAR DENOUNCED

London Believes Reform Promises Are the Result of Russian Revolt.

Special Cable to THE NEW YORK TIMES.

BERLIN, March 15, (via London, March 16.)—Chancellor von Bethmann Hollweg's speech before the Prussian Diet yesterday afternoon, which is regarded as the greatest speech that has come from the lips of a German statesman since Bismarck's day, is the subject of comment in every corner of the empire today.

There was every evidence that the Chancellor had not prepared his speech, and that he merely walked into the House, found the subject of [illegible] the moment opportune [illegible] it. In fact, he said he [illegible] thought in the morning [illegible] address the House in the afternoon.

The immediate cause of the eruption which brought about the speech is so insignificant that Americans will have difficulty in understanding how it could ever acquire such importance. But one must remember that for months now the Left, and to some extent Centrists, have lost no opportunity of making it clear to the Right in no unmistakable terms that privileges would have to be curtailed after this war, and that they would insist on thorough reforms, and that only the truce that they swore to keep prevented them from beginning these reforms at once.

The Conservatives listened with ever-increasing wrath and suddenly surprised the Left and Centre with a bill in the lower Prussian House intended to make the inheritance laws of the landocracy still more formidable than they had been. This was regarded as a breach of the truce, and hot words were exchanged over it that should have shown clearly to the Conservatives that the people would not stand for any more privileges.

About a week ago the upper house of the Diet, in the course of its routine work, passed upon and rejected a bill granting to members of the lower house the usual daily allowance and free fare on the railways. The principal Conservative speaker, Yorck von Wartenburg, on this occasion left no doubt that the Conservatives were only using this very unimportant bill as a vehicle to let the other parties know just where the Conservatives stood—namely, exactly in the same spot where they left off the day the great catastrophe broke over the world.

Indignation Even in Prussia.

There was the greatest indignation not only in Prussia, but in the whole of Germany, and the leaders of all parties decided that it must be made clear to the Prussian landocracy that this is the twentieth century.

There was an enormous crowd in the galleries of the House when yesterday's session began. These crowds expected to hear plain speech, and they heard it, first from Dr. Porsch of the Centrist Party, who ridiculed Yorck von Wartenburg as the custodian of antiquity, then from Fredberg, the National Liberal, who not only threw down the gauntlet and said his party would no longer keep the truce but wanted electoral reforms at once.

Dr. Pachnicke of the Progressive Party followed with similar demands, and while he spoke of the Chancellor who had promised them so much and who might afterward be prevented by circumstances from fulfilling his promises, Bethmann Hollweg entered the chamber. He listened quietly to Pachnicke's censure, and when the latter had finished he began his great speech.

"Woe to the statesman who cannot read the signs of the times!" When the Chancellor thundered this variation of the threat by a Conservative orator, it was as though he had cast a spell upon the sentiments of all the parties that only a few minutes before had clashed in violent discord. Everybody present, even the crowds in the galleries, felt as though they had suddenly realized the turning point of a new epoch.

The Chancellor continued:

"Woe to the statesman who believes that after this catastrophe, such as the world has never seen before—a catastrophe whose scope contemporaries and those directly engaged in it cannot possibly measure—woe to him if he believes he can start again from where he left off before the catastrophe. If he should try to put new wine into old bottles—woe to that statesman!"

The Chancellor said he had had no thought in the morning that he would appear at the Chamber. He evidently had not prepared for any speech. Sometimes he stopped to find the right ex-

Continued on Page 3.

WIDE REFORMS PLANNED

Universal Suffrage and Full Political Amnesty Are the Bases.

CROWDS CHEER PROMISE

Duma Committee and Workingmen Busy Planning for a Constituent Assembly.

FOOD PRICES FALL RAPIDLY

Calm Restored in Petrograd, but Partisans of Old Regime Are Still Being Arrested.

LONDON, Saturday, March 17.—Universal suffrage in elections to be held for members of a new constituent Assembly and full political amnesty will be features of the new régime in Russia, according to dispatches from Petrograd. In fact, Deputy Kerenski, the new Minister of Justice, who is a Socialist, accepted the portfolio on the stipulations that there should be absolute freedom of speech and of the press, and full political amnesty, and that the Assembly should be convoked.

Addressing an assemblage of thousands of soldiers and civilians from the gallery of the lobby of the Duma, M. [illegible] office by virtue of an agreement with workingmen's and soldiers' delegates. The council of these delegates approved the agreement by several hundred votes to 15. The first act of the new Government, M. Kerenski stated, was the immediate publication of a decree of full amnesty. Continuing, the Minister said:

"Our comrades of the second and fourth Dumas, who were banished illegally to the tundras of Siberia, will be released forthwith. In my jurisdiction are all the Premiers and Ministers of the old régime. They will answer before the law for all crimes against the people."

"Show them no mercy," many voices in the crowd exclaimed.

"Comrades," M. Kerenski replied, "regenerated Russia will not have recourse to the shameful methods utilized by the old régime. Without trial none will be condemned. All prisoners will be tried in open court.

"Comrades, soldiers, citizens, all measures taken by the new Government will be published. Soldiers, I ask you to co-operate. Free Russia is now born, and none will succeed in wresting liberty from the hands of the people. Do not listen to the promptings of the agents of the old régime. Listen to your officers. Long live free Russia!"

The speech was greeted by a storm of cheering.

The labor leader, Chkueidse, addressing the officers and soldiers, paid a glowing tribute to the soldiers and workingmen who had participated in accomplishing the revolution. He recounted the recent provocative efforts by the secret police in publishing proclamations regarding the murders of officers by soldiers. He exhorted the soldiers to regard their officers as citizens who had helped raise the revolutionary flag and as brothers in the great cause of Russian liberty.

Subsequently officers, soldiers, and workingmen carried M. Chkueidse on their shoulders through a cheering throng of soldiers and civilians.

Apparently the new Provisional Government is proceeding promptly to organize itself on a stable basis, to reconstitute the Governmental departments, and prepare steps for the vigorous carrying on of the war. There is no sign of serious hindrance to the completion of the work of this extraordinarily swift and successful revolution.

Former Premiers Golitzine and Goremykin have been placed in the Fortress of St. Peter and St. Paul, as have Generals Soukhomlinoff and Beliaeff, former Ministers of War; A. B. Protopopoff, former Minister of the Interior; J. G. Chtchegiovitoff and M. Makaroff, former Ministers of Justice, and M. Malakoff and General Kurloff, former Chiefs of Police. Other prominent persons under arrest are being detained temporarily in the Duma Building.

It is announced that there will be no further trials for political offenses, and that the Government has opened the bar to Jewish lawyers, who have been excluded heretofore.

At a conference of the members of the Duma Executive Committee and delegates representing the workmen, which lasted until 5 o'clock this morning, says a dispatch from Petrograd, an agreement was reached concerning the transitional period before the election of a constituent assembly. The executives insisted in the interests of the war on

Continued on Page 2.

New Russian Government Asks People's Support; States Its Policy as Freedom and Suffrage for All

LONDON, March 16.—The Provisional Government in Russia has issued an appeal to the people, according to a Reuter dispatch from Petrograd. The document begins:

"Citizens.—The Executive Committee of the Duma, with the aid and support of the garrison of the capital and its inhabitants, has succeeded in triumphing over the obnoxious forces of the old régime in such a manner that we are able to proceed to a more stable organization of the executive power, with men whose past political activity assures them the country's confidence."

The names of the members of the new Government are then given and the appeal continues:

"The new Cabinet will base its policy on the following principles:

First.—An immediate general amnesty for all political and religious offenses, including terrorist acts and military and agrarian offenses.

Second.—Liberty of speech and of the press; freedom for alliances, unions, and strikes, with the extension of these liberties to military officials within the limits admitted by military requirements.

Third.—Abolition of all social, religious, and national restrictions.

Fourth.—To proceed forthwith to the preparation and convocation of a constitutional Assembly, based on universal suffrage, which will establish a governmental régime.

Fifth.—The substitution of the police by a national militia, with chiefs to be elected and responsible to the Government.

Sixth.—Communal elections to be based on universal suffrage.

Seventh.—The troops which participated in the revolutionary movement will not be disarmed, but will remain in Petrograd.

Eighth.—While maintaining strict military discipline for troops on active service, it is desirable to abrogate for soldiers all restrictions in the enjoyment of social rights accorded other citizens.

"The Provisional Government desires to add that it has no intention to profit by the circumstances of the war to delay the realization of the measures of reform above mentioned."

DUKE NICHOLAS AGAIN HEADS ARMY

The Czar Turns Over Supreme Command to His Uncle, Whom He Deposed.

GENERAL AT THE CAPITAL

With Alexieff, Chief of Staff, He Urged Emperor to Take Only Step to Save Russia.

Golitzin a Suicide?

Special Cable to THE NEW YORK TIMES.

COPENHAGEN, March 17.—A leading Swedish paper, the Social Demokraten, tells that the former Russian Premier, Prince Golitzin, has committed suicide.

LONDON, Saturday, March 17.—A Reuter dispatch from Petrograd says that prior to his abdication the Emperor transferred the supreme command of the Russian armies to the Grand Duke Nicholas, his uncle. The latter has reached Petrograd.

A previous dispatch from Petrograd said that the Grand Duke had telegraphed President Rodzianko of the Duma that, in accord with General Alexieff, Chief of Staff, he had asked the Emperor, in order to save Russia and bring the war to a successful end, to take the only step possible in the present fateful circumstances.

Special Cable to THE NEW YORK TIMES.

COPENHAGEN, March 16.—The Dagens Nyheder states that Russian officials and officers incline to believe that the Grand Duke Nicholas has the confidence of the revolutionists, and that he will get dictatorial authority over the army until conditions are settled.

When the war in Europe began and the Grand Duke Nicholas was appointed Commander in Chief of the Russian armies in the southwest, he came to this distinction partly through inheritance, partly through his intimacy with the Czar, and partly on account of his past service and the affection the mujic soldier had for him. Among the officers he was not popular; he was too hard a worker.

The Grand Duke is 61 years of age and his father, likewise named Nicholas, commanded the Russian forces in the Turkish war of 1877. With his father the young Nicholas, then 21, served with distinction at Plevna, Lovcha, and the Shipka Pass, receiving the decoration of the Cross of St. George.

From 1879 till 1914 the Grand Duke was closely identified with the Russian Army and, at the same time, made himself familiar with most of the other armies of Europe.

At the beginning of the present war he was in command of the Petrograd military district. As Commander in Chief his first invasion of East and West Prussia and Galicia was the carrying out of a plan long before laid. The subsequent retreat, with half-starved soldiers, lacking effective artillery, frequently without rifle ammunition when the rear guard had to use bayonets against machine guns, and over a front of nearly 1,000 miles, and without losing through surrender a single compact army unit, was one of the greatest strategic feats in history.

The retreat began in April, 1915, and six months later the Grand Duke safely brought his armies into prepared works. While military authorities all over the world were praising him, he was suddenly sent to the Caucasus to command the army there, while the Czar had himself proclaimed Commander in Chief of the armies of Russia.

In the Caucasus, with supplies and

Continued on Page 2.

RUSSIANS HERE AID NEW CAUSE

Form a Committee to Take Over Functions of Embassy and Consulates in America.

ASK FIRST FOR AUTHORITY

Overthrow of the Government Causes Wild Joy Among the Jews of the East Side.

Believing that the Russian democracy has come to stay, a number of the leading members of the Russian-American colony in New York held a meeting yesterday and planned to co-operate with the new Government even to the extent of taking over the functions of the embassy, consulates, and heads of various munition departments.

The meeting was held in the office of Professor N. G. Kouznetsoff in the Longacre Building, and an executive committee was formed consisting of Professor Kouznetsoff, who is a member of the Faculty of the Petrograd Military Institution; Ivan Narodny, author and journalist; Ivan Okuntsoff, editor of the Russky Golos, published in this city, and Joseph Dalinda, a correspondent of several Russian newspapers.

According to the announcement made yesterday, this committee, an unofficial and self-appointed body, intends to take over ultimately all the Russian Government offices in the United States and Canada. To accomplish this sweeping change in Russian officialdom on this side of the ocean the committee will get into immediate communication with the members of the provisional Government. Until official sanction has been obtained the committee intends to offer its services to the new régime as an advisory board.

"The Executive Russian Committee of America," reads the official announcement, "is of the opinion that the present newly established form of the Government is merely a stepping stone to the United States of Russia, which is bound to come soon after the end of the war. It makes no difference whether the nominal ruler will be Michael or Grand Duke Nicholas, as the real power will remain in the hands of the Cabinet that will be appointed jointly by the Duma and Council of the Empire. It is even very likely that the Council of the Empire will be abolished. The main question of the new Government is to unite all the nation under the present régime till the end of the war and fight the enemy with all the full vigor.

"This will mean a new era for Russia, new life and new events. The present Russian Cabinet will work hand in hand with England and France. The Czar will remain like the King of England, a decorative figure of the country. The real constitution will be drafted after the war, which may resemble the Constitution of the United States. All the political refugees will get amnesty, all the exiles will be given full freedom.

"The revolution and political change of Russia will not affect the economic and financial life of the country in the least. On the contrary, Russia will be now richer than she ever was, stronger than she ever was, and the world will be surprised by the tremendous reforms that will now take place."

While Russian Liberals and refugees in New York regard the overturning of the Cabinet as the beginning of a new era, the more conservative element is reluctant to concede a complete victory for Russian democracy. Opinions were expressed in several quarters yesterday to the effect that the present upheaval is nothing more than a purely "political coup d'état" without any popular significance whatever. It was pointed out that the best evidence of this fact consists in the retention of the Romanoff family in power. No "revolutionary" program, it was said, could tolerate the continuance of the present dynasty, either through Nicholas II. or any member of his family. The Constitution of the new Cabinet was also believed by several prominent Russians here to be an

Continued on Page 2.

GAVE UP SON'S RIGHTS, TOO

Czar Yielded at Midnight Thursday; Grand Duke Michael Yesterday.

DUMA IS NOW IN CONTROL

Executive Committee Acting with Cabinet It Chose After the Revolution.

NATION BACK OF CHANGE

New Ministers Assume Their Duties and Are Starting Preparations to Push the War.

PETROGRAD, Friday, March 16, 5 P. M., (via London, Saturday, March 17.)—Emperor Nicholas abdicated at midnight last night on behalf of himself and the heir apparent, Grand Duke Alexis, in favor of Grand Duke Michael Alexanderovitch.

At 2:30 o'clock this afternoon Grand Duke Michael himself abdicated, thus bringing the Romanoff dynasty to an end.

The Government, pending a meeting of the Constitutional Assembly, is vested in the Executive Committee of the Duma and the newly-chosen Council of Ministers.

A manifesto to this effect was issued by the Duma Committee today and it will be telegraphed to the General Army Headquarters this evening.

Unless improbable events occur, Russia has today become a republic.

The outcome depends on how the manifesto of the new Government is received by the 6,000,000 soldiers at the front.

Except for the unqualified rejection of the throne by the Czar Nicholas II.'s only brother, the Grand Duke Michael, the Romanoff-Holstein dynasty might be preserved by any number of Czar Nicholas's kinsmen. But the title of Autocrat, since the days of the first Michael Romanoff, in 1613, may only be conferred by a Romanoff. As the Czar chooses no successor after the Grand Duke Michael, and the Grand Duke names no successor at all, the dynasty ends as a reigning house unless a new Government places it upon the throne. Even so, the Romanoffs might decline to recognize the authority of such a Government, as they assert that their right to reign and rule is entirely independent of the will of the people.

The house of Romanoff is descended from Andrei Romanoff, who is said to have gone to Moscow from Prussia in the fourteenth century. Michael Feodorovitch Romanoff was the first of the family to ascend the throne. This was in 1613, when he was 17 years old. He died in 1645. The direct male line of the Romanoffs terminated in 1730 and the female line in 1762, when the Holstein-Gottorp branch came into power and has since ruled.

Miliukoff's Plan That Failed.

Special Cable to THE NEW YORK TIMES.

PETROGRAD, March 16, (Dispatch to The London Daily News.)—Professor Miliukoff announced the list of new Ministers in a speech in Catherine Hall of the Duma, and was finally carried out on the shoulders of the enthusiastic crowd. His speech was often interrupted by questions, and he was repeatedly asked for the program. He said:

"I can already tell you the most important points. [A voice, "the dynasty?"] You ask about the dynasty. I know beforehand that my answer will not please all of you, but I give it. The old despot, who brought Russia to the edge of disaster, will voluntarily abdicate or be deposed. (Applause.)

"The Government will pass to a Regent, the Grand Duke Michael Alexandrovitch [continuous row and applause] and the heir Alexis the Czarevitch [yells—"but that is the old dynasty"].

"Yes, gentlemen, that is the old dynasty, which perhaps you do not like and which perhaps I dislike myself.

"We propose a parliamentary constitutional monarchy. Perhaps others have different views, but if we stop to discuss, instead of instantly deciding, Russia will find herself in a state of civil war and the destroyed régime will be broken."

Order Growing Out of Chaos.

PETROGRAD, March 16, (via London.)—Russia today appeared to be on a fair way toward solving the greatest problem with which any nation, gov-

"All the News That's Fit to Print."

The New York Times.

THE WEATHER
Fair, colder today; tomorrow warmer, probably rain; wind northwest.
For full weather report see Page 21

VOL. LXVI...NO. 21,619. NEW YORK, TUESDAY, APRIL 3, 1917.—TWENTY-FOUR PAGES. ONE CENT In New York City. | TWO CENTS New England and Middle States. | THREE CENTS Elsewhere.

PRESIDENT CALLS FOR WAR DECLARATION, STRONGER NAVY, NEW ARMY OF 500,000 MEN, FULL CO-OPERATION WITH GERMANY'S FOES

ARMED AMERICAN STEAMSHIP SUNK; 11 MEN MISSING

The Aztec Is First Gun-Bearing Vessel Under Our Flag to be Torpedoed.

SURPRISE ATTACK AT NIGHT

12 Navy Men and Their Chief Among 17 Survivors Picked Up by a Patrol.

11 IN A LIFEBOAT THAT SANK

Liner St. Paul, with Cannon, Reaches British Port in Safety—Had 61 Passengers.

PARIS, April 2.—The American steamer Aztec has been sunk by a submarine near an island off Brest. Some of the crew were rescued and are being brought into Brest. A number of the men are missing, and little hope is held that they can be saved, as the steamer was torpedoed at night while a heavy sea was running.

A French patrol picked up nineteen of the crew of the Aztec. Twenty-eight men are reported missing.

William Graves Sharp, the American Ambassador, was informed this afternoon by the French Government of the torpedoing of the Aztec and immediately cabled the State Department at Washington.

Representatives of the American Government will proceed to Brest to take the depositions of survivors of the disaster.

Bluejackets and Officer Saved.

WASHINGTON, April 2.—French Admiralty dispatches to the French Embassy here tonight announcing the sinking without warning of the first armed American merchantman, the freighter Aztec, by a German submarine, said apparently Lieutenant W. F. Gresham and twelve American bluejackets, constituting the armed guard of the vessel, had been saved, but that eleven of the crew were reported missing.

The Admiralty report said the Aztec, bound from New York to Havre, was torpedoed without warning yesterday off Ouessant. The torpedo struck squarely amidships, emitting a powerful gas and putting the wireless out of commission.

The guard with the Captain and three other members of the crew in the second boat to put off apparently were picked up by the French patrol boat Sirrius after three hours. Eleven men are thought to have been drowned when the first boat to put off was smashed.

The third boat, containing the second officer and eighteen men, is not directly accounted for, but the fact that only eleven are reported missing leads to the belief that it must have been picked up.

The Navy Department tonight gave out the names of the navy members on the Aztec as follows:

Officer in charge—Lieutenant William F. Gresham of Tennessee.

Crew—John I. Eopelucci, boatswain's mate; mother, Annie M. Eopelucci, 649 I Street, Southeast, Washington.

Jacob J. Hilfiker, electrician; father, Jake Hilfiker, 2,208 Preston Street, Baltimore, Md.

Thomas E. Dillon, Quartermaster; father, Thomas I. Dillon, 76 Boyd Avenue, Jersey City, N. J.

William H. Douglas, coxswain; mother, Sarah D. Douglas, 1150 South Second Street, Terre Haute, Ind.

Adolph Hendrickson, coxswain; father, Charles Hendrickson, 2,604 Eleventh Avenue, Minneapolis, Minn.

Samuel Earl Israel, seaman; mother, Annie Israel, Kellerman, Ala.

Clarence H. Kelley, Quartermaster; mother, Margaret Kelley, 486 South Broad Street, Trenton, N. J.

Joseph Klewinsky, seaman; father, John Klewinsky, Rural Free Delivery, Route 5, Box 40, Newburg, W. Va.

William F. Rominger, gunner's mate; mother, Dennie Rominger, Elizabethton, Tenn.

Joseph A. Rucker, seaman; guardian, Joseph W. Rucker, Roanoke, Ala.

Clarence W. Whitney, Quartermaster; father, James H. Whitney, Front and Broadway, Cincinnati, Ohio.

All the naval crew were taken from the United States dispatch boat Dolphin at Washington to be placed on the Aztec.

Officials tonight said the disaster would not affect the policy of arming ships, which would be continued in the most efficient manner possible.

First Armed American Ship Sunk.

The American steamship Aztec, the third armed merchant vessel to sail from

Continued on Page 24.

Text of the President's Address

Gentlemen of the Congress:

I have called the Congress into extraordinary session because there are serious, very serious, choices of policy to be made and made immediately, which it was neither right nor constitutionally permissible that I should assume the responsibility of making.

On the 3d of February last I officially laid before you the extraordinary announcement of the Imperial German Government that on and after the first day of February it was its purpose to put aside all restraints of law or of humanity and use its submarines to sink every vessel that sought to approach either the ports of Great Britain and Ireland or the western coasts of Europe or any of the ports controlled by the enemies of Germany within the Mediterranean. That had seemed to be the object of the German submarine warfare earlier in the war, but since April of last year the Imperial Government had somewhat restrained the commanders of its undersea craft, in conformity with its promise, then given to us, that passenger boats should not be sunk and that due warning would be given to all other vessels which its submarines might seek to destroy, when no resistance was offered or escape attempted, and care taken that their crews were given at least a fair chance to save their lives in their open boats. The precautions taken were meagre and haphazard enough, as was proved in distressing instance after instance in the progress of the cruel and unmanly business, but a certain degree of restraint was observed.

The new policy has swept every restriction aside. Vessels of every kind, whatever their flag, their character, their cargo, their destination, their errand, have been ruthlessly sent to the bottom without warning and without thought of help or mercy for those on board, the vessels of friendly neutrals along with those of belligerents. Even hospital ships and ships carrying relief to the sorely bereaved and stricken people of Belgium, though the latter were provided with safe conduct through the proscribed areas by the German Government itself and were distinguished by unmistakable marks of identity, have been sunk with the same reckless lack of compassion or of principle.

I was for a little while unable to believe that such things would in fact be done by any Government that had hitherto subscribed to humane practices of civilised nations. International law had its origin in the attempt to set up some law which would be respected and observed upon the seas, where no nation has right of dominion and where lay the free highways of the world. By painful stage after stage has that law been built up, with meagre enough results, indeed, after all was accomplished that could be accomplished, but always with a clear view, at least, of what the heart and conscience of mankind demanded.

This minimum of right the German Government has swept aside, under the plea of retaliation and necessity and because it had no weapons which it could use at sea except these, which it is impossible to employ, as it is employing them, without throwing to the wind all scruples of humanity or of respect for the understandings that were supposed to underlie the intercourse of the world.

I am not now thinking of the loss of property involved, immense and serious as that is, but only of the wanton and wholesale destruction of the lives of noncombatants, men, women, and children, engaged in pursuits which have always, even in the darkest periods of modern history, been deemed innocent and legitimate. Property can be paid for; the lives of peaceful and innocent people cannot be. The present German submarine warfare against commerce is a warfare against mankind.

It is a war against all nations. American ships have been sunk, American lives taken, in ways which it has stirred us very deeply to learn of, but the ships and people of other neutral and friendly nations have been sunk and overwhelmed in the waters in the same way. There has been no discrimination.

The challenge is to all mankind. Each nation must decide for itself how it will meet it. The choice we make for ourselves must be made with a moderation of counsel and a temperateness of judgment befitting our character and our motives as a nation. We must put excited feeling away. Our motive will not be revenge or the victorious assertion of the physical might of the nation, but only the vindication of right, of human right, of which we are only a single champion.

When I addressed the Congress on the 26th of February last I thought that it would suffice to assert our neutral rights with arms, our right to use the seas against unlawful interference, our right to keep our people safe against unlawful violence. But armed neutrality, it now appears, is impracticable. Because submarines are in effect outlaws, when used as the German submarines have been used against merchant shipping, it is impossible to defend ships against their attacks as the law of nations has assumed that merchantmen would defend themselves against privateers or cruisers, visible craft giving chase upon the open sea. It is common prudence in such circumstances, grim necessity indeed, to endeavor to destroy them before they have shown their own intention. They must be dealt with upon sight, if dealt with at all.

The German Government denies the right of neutrals to use arms at all within the areas of the sea which it has proscribed, even in the defense of rights which no modern publicist has ever before questioned their right to defend. The intimation is conveyed that the armed guards which we have placed on our merchant ships will be treated as beyond the pale of law and subject to be dealt with as pirates would be. Armed neutrality is ineffectual enough at best; in such circumstances and in the face of such pretensions it is worse than ineffectual; it is likely only to produce what it was meant to prevent; it is practically certain to draw us into the war without either the rights or the effectiveness of belligerents. There is one choice we cannot make, we are incapable of making; we will not choose the path of submission and suffer the most sacred rights of our nation and our people to be ignored or violated. The wrongs against which we now array ourselves are no common wrongs; they cut to the very roots of human life.

With a profound sense of the solemn and even tragical character of the step I am taking and of the grave responsibilities which it involves, but in unhesitating obedience to what I deem my constitutional duty, I advise that the Congress declare the recent course of the Imperial German Government to be in fact nothing less than war against the Government and people of the United States; that it formally accept the status of belligerent which has thus been thrust upon it; and that it take immediate steps not only to put the country in a more thorough state of defense, but also to exert all its power and employ all its resources to bring the Government of the German Empire to terms and end the war.

What this will involve is clear. It will involve the utmost practicable co-operation in counsel and action with the Governments now at war with Germany, and, as incident to that, the extension to those Governments of the most liberal financial credits, in order that our resources may so far as possible be added to theirs.

It will involve the organization and mobilization of all the material resources of the country to supply the materials of war and serve the incidental needs of the nation in the most abundant and yet the most economical and efficient way possible.

It will involve the immediate full equipment of the navy in all respects, but particularly in supplying it with the best means of dealing with the enemy's submarines.

It will involve the immediate addition to the armed forces of the United States, already provided for by law in case of war, of at least 500,000 men, who should, in my opinion, be chosen upon the principle of universal liability to service, and also the authorization of subsequent additional increments of equal force so soon as they may be needed and can be handled in training.

It will involve also, of course, the granting of adequate credits to the Government, sustained, I hope, so far as they can equitably be sustained by the present generation, by well conceived taxation.

I say sustained so far as may be equitable by taxation, because it seems to me that it would be most unwise to base the credits, which will now be necessary, entirely on money borrowed. It is our duty, I most respectfully urge, to protect our people, so far as we may, against the very serious hardships and evils which would be likely to arise out of the inflation which would be produced by vast loans.

In carrying out the measures by which these things are to be accomplished we should keep constantly in mind the wisdom of interfering as little as possible in our own preparation and in the equipment of our own military forces with the duty—for it will be a very practical duty—of supplying the nations already at war with Germany with the materials which they can obtain only from us or by our assistance. They are in the field and we should help them, in every way to be effective there.

I shall take the liberty of suggesting, through the several executive departments of the Government, for the consideration of your committees, measures for the accomplishment of the several objects I have mentioned. I hope that it will be your pleasure to deal with them as having been framed after very careful thought by the branch of the Government upon whom the responsibility of conducting the war and safeguarding the nation will most directly fall.

While we do these things, these deeply momentous things, let us be very clear, and make very clear to all the world, what our motives and our objects are. My own thought has not been driven from its habitual and normal course by the unhappy events of the last two months, and I do not believe that the thought of the nation has been altered or clouded by them. I have exactly the same things in mind now that I had in mind when I addressed the Senate on the 22d of January last; the same that I had in mind when I addressed the Congress on the 3d of February and on the 26th of February. Our object now, as then, is to vindicate the principles of peace and justice in the life of the world as against selfish and autocratic power, and to set up among the really free and self-governed peoples of the world such a concert of purpose and of action as will henceforth insure the observance of those principles.

Neutrality is no longer feasible or desirable where the peace of the world is involved and the freedom of its peoples, and the menace to that peace and freedom lies in the existence of autocratic Governments, backed by organized force which is controlled wholly by their will, not by the will of their people. We have seen the last of neutrality in such circumstances. We are at the beginning of an age in which it will be insisted that the same standards of conduct and of responsibility for wrong done shall be observed among nations and their Governments that are observed among the individual citizens of civilized States.

We have no quarrel with the German people. We have no feeling toward them but one of sympathy and friendship. It was not upon their impulse that their Government acted in entering this war. It was not with their previous knowledge or approval. It was a war determined upon as wars used to be determined upon in the old, unhappy days, when peoples were nowhere consulted by their rulers and wars were provoked and waged in the interest of dynasties or of little groups of ambitious men who were accustomed to use their fellow men as pawns and tools.

Self-governed nations do not fill their neighbor States with spies or set the course of intrigue to bring about some critical posture of affairs which will give them an opportunity to strike and make conquest. Such designs can be successfully worked out only under cover and where no one has the right to ask questions. Cunningly contrived plans of deception or aggression, carried, it may be, from generation to generation, can be worked out and kept from the light only within the privacy of courts or behind the carefully guarded confidences of a narrow and privileged class. They are happily impossible where public opinion commands and insists upon full information concerning all the nation's affairs.

A steadfast concert for peace can never be maintained except by a partnership of democratic nations. No autocratic Government could be trusted to keep faith within it or observe its covenants. It must be a league of honor, a partnership of opinion. Intrigue would eat its vitals away; the plottings of inner circles who could plan what they would and render account to no one would be a corruption seated at its very heart. Only free peoples can hold their purpose and their honor steady to a common end and prefer the interests of mankind to any narrow interest of their own.

Does not every American feel that assurance has been added to our hope for the future peace of the world by the wonderful and heartening things that have been happening within the last few weeks in Russia? Russia was known by those who knew her best to have been always in fact democratic at heart in all the vital habits of her thought, in all the intimate relationships of her people that spoke their natural instinct, their habitual attitude toward life. The autocracy that crowned the summit of her political structure, long as it had stood and terrible as was the reality of its power, was not in fact Russian in origin, character, or purpose, and now it has been shaken off and the great, generous Russian people have been added, in all their naive majesty and might, to the forces that are fighting for freedom in the world, for justice, and for peace. Here is a fit partner for a League of Honor.

One of the things that has served to convince us that the Prussian autocracy was not and could never be our friend is that from the very outset of the present war it has filled our unsuspecting communities, and even our offices of government, with spies and set criminal intrigues everywhere afoot against our national unity of counsel, our peace within and without, our industries and our commerce. Indeed, it is now evident that its spies were here even before the war began; and it is unhappily not a matter of conjecture, but a fact proved in our courts of justice, that the intrigues which have more than once come perilously near to disturbing the peace and dislocating the industries of the country, have been carried on at the instigation, with the support, and even under the personal direction of official agents of the Imperial Government, accredited to the Government of the United States.

Even in checking these things and trying to extirpate them we have sought to put the most generous interpretation possible upon them because we knew that their source lay, not in any hostile feeling or purpose of the German people toward us, (who were, no doubt, as ignorant of them as we ourselves were,) but only in the selfish designs of a Government that did what it pleased and told its people nothing. But they have played their part in serving to convince us at last that that Government entertains no real friendship for us, and means to act against our peace and security at its convenience. That it means to stir up enemies against us at our very doors the intercepted note to the German Minister at Mexico City is eloquent evidence.

We are accepting this challenge of hostile purpose because we know that in such a Government, following such methods, we can never have a friend; and that in the presence of its organized power, always lying in wait to accomplish we know not what purpose, can be no assured security for the democratic Governments of the world. We are now about to accept the gauge of battle with this natural foe to liberty and shall, if necessary, spend the whole force of the nation to check and nullify its pretensions and its power. We are glad, now that we see the facts with no veil of false pretense about them, to fight thus for the ultimate peace of the world and for the liberation of its peoples, the German peoples included, for the rights of nations, great and small, and the privilege of men everywhere to choose their way of life and of obedience.

The world must be made safe for democracy. Its peace must be planted upon the tested foundations of political liberty. We have no selfish ends to serve. We desire no conquest, no dominion. We seek no indemnities for ourselves, no material compensation for the sacrifices we shall freely make. We are but one of the champions of the rights of mankind. We shall be satisfied when those rights have been made as secure as the faith and the freedom of nations can make them.

Just because we fight without rancor and without selfish object, seeking nothing for ourselves but what we shall wish to share with all free peoples, we shall, I feel confident, conduct our operations as belligerents without passion and ourselves observe with proud punctilio the principles of right and of fair play we profess to be fighting for.

I have said nothing of the Governments allied with the Imperial Government of Germany because they have not made war upon us or challenged us to defend our right and our honor. The Austro-Hungarian Government has, indeed, avowed its unqualified indorsement and acceptance of the reckless and lawless submarine warfare, adopted now without disguise by the Imperial German Government, and it has therefore not been possible for this Government to receive Count Tarnowski, the Ambassador recently accredited to this Government by the Imperial and Royal Government of Austria-Hungary; but that Government has not actually engaged in warfare against citizens of the United States on the seas, and I take the liberty, for the present at least, of postponing a discussion of our relations with the authorities at Vienna. We enter this war only where we are clearly forced into it because there are no other means of defending our right.

It will be all the easier for us to conduct ourselves as belligerents in a high spirit of right and fairness because we act without animus, not with enmity toward a people or with the desire to bring any injury or disadvantage upon them, but only in armed opposition to an irresponsible Government which has thrown aside all considerations of humanity and of right and is running amuck.

We are, let me say again, the sincere friends of the German people, and shall desire nothing so much as the early re-establishment of intimate relations of mutual advantage between us, however hard it may be for them for the time being to believe that this is spoken from our hearts. We have borne with their present Government through all these bitter months because of that friendship, exercising a patience and forbearance which would otherwise have been impossible.

We shall happily still have an opportunity to prove that friendship in our daily attitude and actions toward the millions of men and women of German birth and native sympathy who live among us and share our life, and we shall be proud to prove it toward all who are in fact loyal to their neighbors and to the Government in the hour of test. They are most of them as true and loyal Americans as if they had never known any other fealty or allegiance. They will be prompt to stand with us in rebuking and restraining the few who may be of a different mind and purpose. If there should be disloyalty, it will be dealt with with a firm hand of stern repression; but, if it lifts its head at all, it will lift it only here and there and without countenance except from a lawless and malignant few.

It is a distressing and oppressive duty, gentlemen of the Congress, which I have performed in thus addressing you. There are, it may be, many months of fiery trial and sacrifice ahead of us. It is a fearful thing to lead this great, peaceful people into war, into the most terrible and disastrous of all wars, civilization itself seeming to be in the balance.

But the right is more precious than peace, and we shall fight for the things which we have always carried nearest our hearts—for democracy, for the right of those who submit to authority to have a voice in their own Governments, for the rights and liberties of small nations, for a universal dominion of right by such a concert of free peoples as shall bring peace and safety to all nations and make the world itself at last free.

To such a task we can dedicate our lives and our fortunes, everything that we are and everything that we have, with the pride of those who know that the day has come when America is privileged to spend her blood and her might for the principles that gave her birth and happiness and the peace which she has treasured.

God helping her, she can do no other.

The War Resolution Now Before Congress

This resolution was introduced in the House of Representatives last night by Representative Flood, Chairman of the Foreign Affairs Committee, immediately after the President's address:

JOINT RESOLUTION, Declaring that a State of War Exists Between the Imperial German Government and the Government and People of the United States and Making Provision to Prosecute the Same.

Whereas, The recent acts of the Imperial German Government are acts of war against the Government and people of the United States:

Resolved, By the Senate and House of Representatives of the United States of America in Congress assembled, that the state of war between the United States and the Imperial German Government which has thus been thrust upon the United States is hereby formally declared; and

That the President be, and he is hereby, authorized and directed to take immediate steps not only to put the country in a thorough state of defense but also to exert all of its power and employ all of its resources to carry on war against the Imperial German Government and to bring the conflict to a successful termination.

MUST EXERT ALL OUR POWER

To Bring a "Government That Is Running Amuck to Terms."

WANTS LIBERAL CREDITS

And Universal Service, for "the World Must Be Made Safe for Democracy."

A TUMULTUOUS GREETING

Congress Adjourns After "State of War" Resolution Is Introduced—Acts Today.

Special to The New York Times.

WASHINGTON, April 2.—At 8:32 o'clock tonight the United States formally made its entrance into the war. At that hour President Wilson appeared before a joint session of the Senate and House and invited it to consider the fact that Germany had been making war upon us and to take action in recognition of that fact in accordance with his recommendations, which included universal military service, the raising of an army of 500,000 men, and co-operation with the Allies in all ways that will help most effectively to defeat Germany.

Resolutions recognizing and declaring the state of war were immediately introduced in the House and Senate by Representative Flood and Senator Martin, both of the President's native State, Virginia, and they are the strongest declarations of war that the United States has ever made in any war in which it has been engaged since it became a nation. They are the Administration resolutions drawn up after conference with the President, and in language approved and probably dictated by him, and they will come before the two Foreign Affairs Committees at meetings which will be held tomorrow morning and will be reported at the earliest practical moment.

Unreservedly With the Allies.

Before an audience that cheered him as he has never been cheered in the Capitol in his life the President cast in the lot of America unreservedly with the Allies and declared for a war that must not end until the issue between autocracy and democracy has been fought out. He recited our injuries at Germany's hands, but he did not rest our cause on these. He went on from that point to range us with the Allies as a factor in an irrepressible conflict between the autocrat and the people. He asserted that peace was impossible for the democracies of the world while this power remained on earth. "The world," he said, "must be made safe for democracy."

We had learned that the German autocracy could never be a friend of this country; she had been our enemy while nominally our friend, and even before the war of 1914 broke out. He called on us to take our stand with the democracies in this irrepressible conflict, with before our eyes "the wonderful and heartening events that have been happening in the last few weeks in Russia." He reaffirmed his hope for peace and for freedom, and looked to the war now forced upon us to bring these about, for, he said, a world covenant for peace can never be maintained except by a concert of the democracies of the world.

The objects for which we fight, he said, are democracy, the right of those who submit to authority to have a voice in their own government, the rights and liberties of small nations, the universal dominion of right, the concert of free peoples to bring peace and safety to all nations, and to make the world free. These have always been our ideals, and to accomplish them we accept the war Germany has made upon us. In fighting it we must not only raise an army and increase the navy, but must aid the Allies in all ways, financial and other, and so order our own preparations as not to interfere with the supply of munitions they are getting from us.

Trouble-making Pacifists Barred.

The President delivered this speech before an audience that had been carefully sifted. All day Washington had been in the hands of belligerent pacifists, truculent in manner, and determined to break into the Capitol. They tried to take possession of the Capitol steps, up which the President must go when he entered, and met the same fate that Coxey's rioters fell in with twenty-three years ago at the hands of the police who dispersed them.

A handful of them fell upon Senator Lodge and assaulted him. Others on

"All the News That's Fit to Print."

The New York Times.

THE WEATHER
Generally fair today and Sunday; moderate west to variable winds.
For full weather report see Page 19.

VOL. LXVI...NO. 21,665. NEW YORK, SATURDAY, MAY 19, 1917.—TWENTY PAGES. ONE CENT In Greater New York. | TWO CENTS Elsewhere N. Y. State, N. J., Conn. | THREE CENTS Other States.

PRESIDENT CALLS THE NATION TO ARMS; DRAFT BILL SIGNED; REGISTRATION ON JUNE 5; REGULARS UNDER PERSHING TO GO TO FRANCE

WILL NOT SEND ROOSEVELT

Wilson Not to Avail Himself of Volunteer Authority at Present.

COMMENDS THE COLONEL

But Declares the Business at Hand Is Scientific and for Trained Men Only.

SAYS RESPONSIBILITY IS HIS

Sending of Pershing Division Believed to be in Direct Response to France's Call.

Special to The New York Times.

WASHINGTON, May 18.—Announcement was made at the War Department tonight by Secretary Baker that an expeditionary force of approximately one division of regular troops, under Major General John J. Pershing had been ordered to proceed to France on as early date as practicable. General Pershing and his staff will precede the troops to the fighting area.

Shortly before this announcement came from Secretary Baker, the White House gave to the press a statement from President Wilson in which he said that he would not avail himself, "at any rate at the present stage of the war," of the authority conferred by the Military Selective Draft act, which he had just approved, to organize volunteer divisions.

While referring in complimentary terms to Colonel Roosevelt's public service and gallantry, the President made it plain that he was entirely out of sympathy with the Roosevelt proposal that volunteers be sent to France without delay.

"Politically, too," said the President, "it would no doubt have a very fine effect and make a profound impression," but he added that "the business now at hand is undramatic, practical, and of scientific directness and precision." The President indicated that he did not regard Colonel Roosevelt as a military expert. He also stressed the point that upon the Executive rested the responsibility for the successful conduct of the war, and that he intended to be influenced by considerations along that line and let everything else wait.

It is apparent from President Wilson's statement that his present state of mind is strongly opposed to sending Colonel Roosevelt or any volunteer force to France.

The official announcement that an expeditionary force of regular troops would be sent to France "at as early date as possible" was handed to newspaper men at the War Department by Major Douglas MacArthur of the General Staff at 9:30 o'clock with the injunctions that it was not to be published through extra editions or otherwise until 10 o'clock. The statement containing this important announcement follows:

"The President has directed an expeditionary force of approximately one division of regular troops under command of Major Gen. John J. Pershing to proceed to France at as early a date as practicable. General Pershing and staff will precede the troops abroad. It is requested that no details or speculations with regard to the mobilization of this command, dates of departure, composition, or other items, be carried by the press, other than the official bulletins given out by the War Department relating thereto."

The President's Statement.

The President's statement regarding Colonel Roosevelt follows:

"I shall not avail myself, at any rate at the present stage of the war, of the authorization conferred by the act to organize volunteer divisions. To do so would seriously interfere with the carrying out of the chief and most immediately important purpose contemplated by this legislation, the prompt creation and early use of an effective army, and would contribute practically nothing to the effective strength of the armies now engaged against Germany.

"I understand that the section of this act which authorizes the creation of volunteer divisions in addition to the draft was added with a view to providing an independent command for Mr. Roosevelt and giving the military authority an opportunity to use his fine vigor and enthusiasm in recruiting forces now at the Western front.

"It would be very agreeable to me to pay Mr. Roosevelt this compliment and the Allies the compliment of sending to their aid one of our most distinguished public men, an ex-President who has

Continued on Page 2.

A Proclamation by the President of the United States

Executive Mansion, Washington, D. C., May 18, 1917.

Whereas, Congress has enacted and the President has on the 18th day of May, one thousand nine hundred and seventeen, approved a law, which contains the following provisions:

SECTION 5.—That all male persons between the ages of 21 and 30, both inclusive, shall be subject to registration in accordance with regulations to be prescribed by the President: And upon proclamation by the President or other public notice given by him or by his direction stating the time and place of such registration, it shall be the duty of all persons of the designated ages, except officers and enlisted men of the regular army, the navy, and the National Guard and Naval Militia while in the service of the United States, to present themselves for and submit to registration under the provisions of this act: And every such person shall be deemed to have notice of the requirements of this act upon the publication of said proclamation or other notice as aforesaid, given by the President or by his direction: And any person who shall willfully fail or refuse to present himself for registration or to submit thereto as herein provided, shall be guilty of a misdemeanor and shall, upon conviction in the District Court of the United States having jurisdiction thereof, be punished by imprisonment for not more than one year, and shall thereupon be duly registered; provided that in the call of the docket precedence shall be given, in courts trying the same, to the trial of criminal proceedings under this act; provided, further, that persons shall be subject to registration as herein provided, who shall have attained their twenty-first birthday and who shall not have attained their thirty-first birthday on or before the day set for the registration; and all persons so registered shall be and remain subject to draft into the forces hereby authorized unless excepted or excused therefrom as in this act provided; provided further, that in the case of temporary absence from actual place of legal residence of any person liable to registration as provided herein, such registration may be made by mail under regulations to be prescribed by the President.

SECTION 6.—That the President is hereby authorized to utilize the service of any or all departments and any or all officers or agents of the United States and of the several States, territories, and the District of Columbia, and subdivisions thereof in the execution of this act, and all officers and agents of the United States and of the several States, territories, and subdivisions thereof, and of the District of Columbia; and all persons designated or appointed under regulations prescribed by the President, whether such appointments are made by the President himself or by the Governor or other officer of any State or territory to perform any duty in the execution of this act, are hereby required to perform such duty as the President shall order or direct, and all such officers and agents and persons so designated or appointed shall hereby have full authority for all acts done by them in the execution of this act by the direction of the President. Correspondence in the execution of this act may be carried in penalty envelopes, bearing the frank of the War Department. Any person charged, as herein provided, with the duty of carrying into effect any of the provisions of this act or the regulations made or directions given thereunder who shall fail or neglect to perform such duty, and any person charged with such duty or having and exercising any authority under said act, regulations, or directions, who shall knowingly make or be a party to the making of any false or incorrect registration, physical examination, exemption, enlistment, enrollment, or muster, and any person who shall make or be a party to the making of any false statement or certificate as to the fitness or liability of himself or any other person for service under the provisions of this act, or regulations made by the President thereunder, or otherwise evades or aids another to evade the requirements of this act or of said regulations, or who, in any manner, shall fail or neglect fully to perform any duty required of him in the execution of this act, shall, if not subject to military law, be guilty of a misdemeanor, and upon conviction in the District Court of the United States, having jurisdiction thereof, be punished by imprisonment for not more than one year, or, if subject to military law, shall be tried by court-martial and suffer such punishment as a court-martial may direct.

Now, Therefore, I, Woodrow Wilson, President of the United States, do call upon the Governor of each of the several States and Territories, the Board of Commissioners of the District of Columbia, and all officers and agents of the several States and Territories, of the District of Columbia, and of the counties and municipalities therein, to perform certain duties in the execution of the foregoing law, which duties will be communicated to them directly in regulations of even date herewith.

And I do further proclaim and give notice to all persons subject to registration in the several States and in the District of Columbia in accordance with the above law, that the time and place of such registration shall be between 7 A. M. and 7 P. M. on the fifth day of June, 1917, at the registration place in the precinct wherein they have their permanent homes. Those who shall have attained their twenty-first birthday and who shall not have attained their thirty-first birthday on or before the day here named are required to register, excepting only officers and enlisted men of the regular army, the navy, the Marine Corps, and the National Guard and Naval Militia, while in the service of the United States, and officers in the Officers' Reserve Corps and enlisted men in the Enlisted Reserve Corps while in active service In the territories of Alaska, Hawaii, and Porto Rico a day for registration will be named in a later proclamation.

And I do charge those who through sickness shall be unable to present themselves for registration that they apply on or before the day of registration to the County Clerk of the County where they may be for instructions as to how they may be registered by agent. Those who expect to be absent on the day named from the counties in which they have their permanent homes may register by mail, but their mailed registration cards must reach the places in which they have their permanent homes by the day named herein. They should apply as soon as practicable to the County Clerk of the county wherein they may be for instructions as to how they may accomplish their registration by mail. In case such persons as, through sickness or absence, may be unable to present themselves personally for registration shall be sojourning in cities of over 30,000 population, they shall apply to the City Clerk of the city wherein they may be sojourning rather than to the Clerk of the County. The Clerks of counties and of cities of over 30,000 population in which numerous applications from the sick and from nonresidents are expected are authorized to establish such agencies and to employ and deputize such clerical force as may be necessary to accommodate these applications.

The Power against which we are arrayed has sought to impose its will upon the world by force. To this end it has increased armament until it has changed the face of war. In the sense in which we have been wont to think of armies, there are no armies in this struggle, there are entire nations armed. Thus, the men who remain to till the soil and man the factories are no less a part of the army that is France than the men beneath the battle flags. It must be so with us. It is not an army that we must shape and train for war; it is a nation.

To this end our people must draw close in one compact front against a common foe. But this cannot be if each man pursues a private purpose. All must pursue one purpose. The nation needs all men; but it needs each man, not in the field that will most pleasure him, but in the endeavor that will best serve the common good. Thus, though a sharpshooter pleases to operate a trip-hammer for the forging of great guns and an expert machinist desires to march with the flag, the nation is being served only when the sharpshooter marches and the machinist remains at his levers.

The whole nation must be a team, in which each man shall play the part for which he is best fitted. To this end, Congress has provided that the nation shall be organized for war by selection; that each man shall be classified for service in the place to which it shall best serve the general good to call him.

The significance of this cannot be overstated. It is a new thing in our history and a landmark in our progress. It is a new manner of accepting and vitalizing our duty to give ourselves with thoughtful devotion to the common purpose of us all. It is in no sense a conscription of the unwilling; it is, rather, selection from a nation which has volunteered in mass. It is no more a choosing of those who shall march with the colors than it is a selection of those who shall serve an equally necessary and devoted purpose in the industries that lie behind the battle line.

The day here named is the time upon which all shall present themselves for assignment to their tasks. It is for that reason destined to be remembered as one of the most conspicuous moments in our history. It is nothing less than the day upon which the manhood of the country shall step forward in one solid rank in defense of the ideals to which this nation is consecrated. It is important to those ideals no less than to the pride of this generation in manifesting its devotion to them, that there be no gaps in the ranks.

It is essential that the day be approached in thoughtful apprehension of its significance, and that we accord to it the honor and the meaning that it deserves. Our industrial need prescribes that it be not made a technical holiday, but the stern sacrifice that is before us urges that it be carried in all our hearts as a great day of patriotic devotion and obligation, when the duty shall lie upon every man, whether he is himself to be registered or not, to see to it that the name of every male person of the designated ages is written on these lists of honor.

In Witness Whereof, I have hereunto set my hand and caused the seal of the United States to be affixed. Done at the City of Washington this 18th day of May in the year of our Lord one thousand nine hundred and seventeen, and of the independence of the United States of America the one hundred and forty-first.

Woodrow Wilson

By the President:
ROBERT LANSING, Secretary of State.

PLANS FOR NATIONAL ARMY

First Draft of 500,000 Men to be Divided Into Sixteen Divisions.

MILITIA SIMILARLY PLACED

Arrangement of Concentration Camps Will Be Near Home Regions of Units.

CALLS OUT NATIONAL GUARD

Entire Force to Mobilize and Recruit to War Strength, Beginning on July 15.

Special to The New York Times.

WASHINGTON, May 18.—President Wilson, tonight at 10 o'clock, issued his proclamation fixing June 5 as the day on which registration is to take place for the national army of 500,000 men to be drafted under authority of the Draft bill, which he signed tonight. On this date all men in the country between the ages of 21 and 30 years, inclusive, will be required to present themselves for registration. Those away from home will register by mail, according to the terms of the proclamation. The registration date for Hawaii, Alaska, and Porto Rico will be announced later.

The President's proclamation sets forth in detail the plans for registration and was telegraphed tonight by the War Department to all parts of the country official posting and publication. It is so as to have the widest publicity by expected that the registration will occupy about five days. After that those entitled to exemption will be excluded from the draft. About 10,000,000 men between 21 and 30, inclusive, are expected to be registered. After the registration and exemptions have been completed, those declared to be eligible for drafting will have their names placed in jury wheels and 500,000 will be drafted for Federal service in the formation of the new national army.

Plans for the formation of the new army have been completed. It will be divided into sixteen divisions, each to consist of 28,000 men. They will be mobilized in sixteen concentration camps, the names of which soon will be announced. The draft army will be officially known as the National Army, in contradistinction to the regular army and the National Guard army. These National Army divisions will be numbered consecutively from one to sixteen.

New York and Pennsylvania will furnish enough men in the draft to form three National Army divisions, exclusive of what they will furnish for the regular army and the National Guard army. New York and Pennsylvania will each furnish about a division and a half for the National Army. The only other State to furnish as much as a division for the National Army will be Illinois. Seven Pacific Coast States, where the population is not so dense, will furnish the sixteenth National Army division.

Distribution of Divisions.

The distribution of the divisions, according to the States that will form them, will be as follows:

First—Massachusetts, Maine, Connecticut, Rhode Island, Vermont, and New Hampshire.
Second—Lower New York State and Long Island.
Third—Upper New York State and Northern Pennsylvania.
Fourth—Southern Pennsylvania.
Fifth—Virginia, Maryland, Delaware, New Jersey, and District of Columbia.
Sixth—Tennessee, North Carolina, and South Carolina.
Seventh—Alabama, Georgia, and Florida.
Eighth—Ohio and West Virginia.
Ninth—Indiana and Kentucky.
Tenth—Wisconsin and Michigan.
Eleventh—Illinois.
Twelfth—Arkansas, Mississippi, and Louisiana.
Thirteenth—North Dakota, South Dakota, Nebraska, Minnesota, and Iowa.
Fourteenth—Colorado, Kansas, and Missouri.
Fifteenth—Arizona, New Mexico, Texas, and Oklahoma.
Sixteenth—Washington, Oregon, Idaho, Montana, California, Nevada, and Utah.

Calls Out the Guard.

President Wilson also issued orders today for the mobilization of the entire National Guard of the country. Instructions were sent to the Adjutant General of the States to the effect that the National Guard not now in Federal service and enlisted men of the National Guard Reserve would be drafted into the Federal service on various dates, ranging from July 15 to Aug. 5. All National Guard coast artillery will be drafted on July 15. The organizations will be held at their rendezvous for about two weeks and will then be sent to concentration camps in the Southern, Southeastern, and Western Departments for training.

There are now 60,000 National Guardsmen in Federal service. There are more than 100,000 not yet in Federal service. These are to be called into Federal service under the orders issued today. New National Guard units will also be formed and all the guard units will be expanded until 400,000 men have been obtained. This will be designated the National Guard Army, and it will comprise

Treasury Plans to Let the Banks Keep Funds Paid for Liberty Bonds

Institutions Subscribing $100,000 Favored—Subscriptions for the Bonds Increase Here — Bank of Commerce Takes $10,000,000 of the Issue.

Special to The New York Times.

WASHINGTON, May 18.—To avoid any disturbance of the money market in placing the Liberty Loan of 1917, the Treasury Department today, in behalf of Secretary McAdoo, who is out of town, issued a circular to banks and trust companies urging that they should buy Treasury certificates in as large amount as practicable, and at least to half their estimated subscriptions, for the new bonds. In the circular, to which his name was signed, Secretary McAdoo also suggested that banks having to make payments for $100,000 or more of bonds, and having qualified as depositaries, will be permitted to cover their payments, in excess of the amount of Treasury certificates taken by them, by placing credit on their books to the account of the Treasurer of the United States.

An indication of the extent to which employers of large forces of men and women are buying Liberty Loan bonds for their employes and permitting payments in small installments was given today when it was learned from one distributing firm in New York that fifty-two corporations either have adopted this plan of aiding their employes or were considering it. Of the fifty-two corporations, thirty-nine reported their number of employes as approximating 163,327. The other thirteen did not report the number of their workers.

California Takes $500,000.

The State of California set an example for other States today by subscribing to $500,000 of the Liberty Loan. Accompanying the application for the bonds was a statement to the effect that the State would take more later.

A subscription for $300,000 of Liberty Loan bonds was made by the Driggs-Seabury Ordnance Company of Utica, N. Y., and Sharon, Penn., makers of the Lewis machine gun, which has large contracts with the Government.

The Treasury circular, issued today, which was signed by Secretary McAdoo, was as follows:

"Banks and trust companies having payments to make on account of subscriptions, and which have qualified as depositaries, may make payment upon such subscriptions on June 28 as to any amounts not paid in Treasury certificates of indebtedness by credit on their books to the account of the Treasurer of the United States, of which credit notice will be given in duplicate to the Treasurer and to the Federal Reserve Bank of the district on or before June 28.

"The amounts so credited will be withdrawn from time to time as required. How long they may be permitted to remain will depend in large measure on the extent to which the privilege of prepayment for the bonds of the Liberty Loan on or before June 28 is availed of. It will be necessary that the early installments paid upon subscriptions to the loan be devoted largely to the payment of the short-term Treasury certificates of indebtedness, which have been and will be placed throughout the country chiefly for making loans to Governments engaged in making war against Germany, and in part to meet unusual war expenditures of our own Government.

Shifting of Credits.

"As practically all the proceeds of the Liberty Loan, whether advanced to foreign Governments or expended directly by departments of the United States, will be spent in this country in payment of indebtedness heretofore or hereafter incurred, the bank resources of the United States as a whole will not be diminished, and the operation involves only a shifting of credits.

"Because of the great amount of work involved in passing upon the qualifications and securities of the banks and trust companies, which will have payments to make, it is deemed necessary until after July 1 to limit to those banks and trust companies having payments to make on subscriptions for $100,000 or more bonds, the provision for making payment by credit, the object in providing for payment by credit being to avoid any disturbance in the money position which might result from large payments being made from June 28 to Monday, July 2, a period when there is customarily a heavy movement of funds due to corporate interest and other payments.

Proceeds to Be Redeposited.

"As soon after July 2 as practicable the qualifications and securities of other banks and trust companies desiring to participate in redeposits will be passed upon, and after provision has been made for the immediate disbursements which the United States will have to make, up to and including July 1, the proceeds of the loan received from time to time, in full or installment payments, will be redeposited with qualified banks and trust companies in a proportion, yet to be determined, based upon the amounts of bonds of the Liberty Loan for which

Continued on Page 11.

Bethmann and Czernin to Confer With the Kaiser

BERLIN, May 18, (via London.)—Chancellor von Bethmann Hollweg and Dr. Zimmermann, the Foreign Minister, left today for German Great Headquarters, where they will meet Count Czernin, the Austro-Hungarian Foreign Secretary. They will continue the conference begun at Vienna recently, when Dr. von Bethmann Hollweg visited there.

The Tageblatt says that it understands that the Polish question and details in connection with the proclamation issued on Nov. 5, 1916, concerning Poland will be discussed.

The Reichstag will reconvene on July 5 for a three days' session, which will comprise the Summer legislative period.

CAMERONIA SUNK; 140 ON BOARD LOST

10,000-Ton Anchor Liner Had Been Used as a Troopship by the British Admiralty.

STAYED AFLOAT 40 MINUTES

Troops Escaped by Jumping to Destroyers—Announcement of Loss Long Delayed.

LONDON, May 17, (Delayed by Censor.)—The British Admiralty announced today that the transport Cameronia has been sunk. The statement follows:

"The British transport Cameronia, with troops, was torpedoed by an enemy submarine in the Eastern Mediterranean on April 15. One hundred and forty men are missing and are presumed to have been drowned."

The survivors of the Cameronia say the vessel was torpedoed in fine, calm weather in the afternoon. The submarine was not seen.

A large number of casualties were due to the explosion of the torpedo, which struck where there happened to be many soldiers. There was some excitement and confusion at the outset after the torpedo had struck, but discipline soon prevailed. The boats were launched, but one of them was smashed, and many lives were lost.

The Cameronia was afloat for forty minutes after she was torpedoed, which enabled several destroyers to run alongside. Soldiers from the Cameronia jumped on these boats in disciplined succession. The destroyers ceased taking on men as soon as they had ob-

Continued on Page 3.

SEA-AND-AIR FIGHT IN THE ADRIATIC

Austrian Light Cruisers Raid Allied Drifter Line and Sink 14 British Minesweepers.

CHASED TO THEIR OWN PORT

Italian Airmen Aiding—British Cruiser Torpedoed and an Italian Destroyer Sunk.

LONDON, May 16.—The British Admiralty announced today that fourteen drifters had been sunk in a raid by Austrian light cruisers in the Adriatic Sea and that the British light cruiser Dartmouth was torpedoed in a subsequent engagement with the Austrian warships, but reached port safely.

The Admiralty said that the British warships Dartmouth and Bristol pursued the Austrian vessels to a point near Cattaro when, battleships coming to their assistance, the British vessels were compelled to withdraw. The text of the statement reads:

"The Admiralty announces that from reports received from the Rear Admiral commanding the Adriatic squadron, supplemented by the Italian official communication, it appears that cruisers, subsequently reinforced by destroyers, raided the allied drifter line and succeeded in sinking fourteen British drifters, from which, according to the Austrian communication, seventy-two prisoners were taken.

"His Majesty's ship Dartmouth, with the Italian Rear Admiral aboard, and H. M. S. Bristol immediately chased the

Continued on Page 3.

Committee Rejects McAdoo's Plan to Levy $445,000,000 More Taxes

Zone Postal Plan May Be Stricken from the Taxation Bill—House Approves Higher Excess Profits and Retroactive Income Imposts.

Special to The New York Times.

WASHINGTON, May 18.—Prior to the convening of the House today the Committee on Ways and Means decided that it would not attempt to raise, at this time, the additional $445,000,000 in indirect taxes requested yesterday in Secretary McAdoo's communication to Chairman Kitchin. Republican members of the committee, as well as some Democrats, rebelled against the proposal to revamp the War Taxation bill and greatly add to its total after the committee had spent weeks in preparing a measure to produce $1,800,000,000.

The House when it met showed a disposition to stand by the bill as presented by the committee. The retroactive income tax section was approved by a vote of 123 to 34, all proposed amendments being rejected. The House likewise approved the excess profits tax carried in the bill, defeating various amendments to reduce and to increase the tax.

That a majority of the members of the Ways and Means Committee have practically reached the conclusion that there should be a change in the second-class mail postage rates recommended in the bill was learned today. Before the bill is put on final passage the committee is to hold another meeting to consider a revision of these rates. The indications are that the "zone system" rates will be stricken from the bill, and the committee will offer an amendment carrying out the suggestion of Chairman Moon of the House Committee on Post Office, reading as follows:

Strike out the section (the zone system section) and insert: Upon all newspapers, magazines and other publications regularly admitted as matter of the second class, when mailed by the publisher and no other, 1 cent per pound. Provided, that parcel post rates shall be charged upon all that portion of such newspapers, magazines or other publications which is devoted to said advertising matter when addressed to any Post Office in the third, fourth, fifth, sixth, seventh, or eighth zones.

Certain members of the committee believe that the Moon amendment will not only produce more revenue, but that it also has a better chance of approval in the House than the original committee proposal, which calls for a flat rate on all second class matter, fixed by zones, ranging from 2 to 6 cents a pound. In the general debate on the Revenue bill the argument was repeatedly made that the Government was carrying advertising matter at a great loss and the levy in postage should be against the advertising rather than the news sections of publications.

If the Moon amendment should be adopted the postal rate legislation will be less burdensome upon newspapers than magazines. Newspapers circulating within a comparatively limited field would not be materially affected. Periodicals and magazines with a country-wide circulation and a surplus of advertising matter would be hard hit by a levy of parcel post rates against the aggregate weight of all the advertising columns.

Excess Profits Tax Approved.

The House made fair progress today in its consideration of the tax measure. It approved the excess profits section and those portions of the bill levying additional taxes on beverages and tobaccos. The House reached but did not dispose of the sections imposing a 5 per cent. tax on various articles, including automobiles and musical instruments.

The Ways and Means Committee has agreed to consider the advisability of modifying the 5 per cent. levy on automobiles. This proposed tax has been strongly opposed by the automobile interests. No assurance has been given by the committee, however, that it will agree to a modification of the tax, but the question will be taken up in committee tomorrow, according to present plans.

Representative Madden of Illinois led an unsuccessful fight against the retroactive tax on incomes. This section provides that there shall be assessed against incomes for the calendar year 1916 an additional tax of one-third of the tax already paid. Under the section each person who has paid a tax on 1916 incomes would have to pay prior to Sept. 15 next, an amount equal to 33 1-3 per cent. of the original levy.

Nevertheless the House adopted the retroactive tax which the Ways and Means Committee estimates will produce $108,000,000.

Wet and Dry Forces Clash.

Wet and dry forces clashed for almost two hours today over an amendment by Representative Howard of Georgia, designed to eliminate the liquor tax increases. Representatives Howard, Cooper of Ohio, Hersey of Maine, and others maintained that the liquor interests were indorsing the proposed increases, hoping thus to strengthen their position against absolute prohibition. The amendment was overwhelmingly defeated. The section as it was approved increases the tax on whisky from $1.10 to $2.20 a gallon and that on beer from $1.25 to $2.50.

Only a perfunctory fight was made on the excess profits tax section. Its opponents will carry their objection to the Senate. Representative Good of Iowa made the chief opposition, offering an amendment patterned somewhat after the English law, but it was decisively beaten.

"All the News That's Fit to Print."

The New York Times.

THE WEATHER
Fair today and tomorrow; moderate northwest to north winds.

VOL. LXVII...NO. 21,839. NEW YORK, FRIDAY, NOVEMBER 9, 1917.—TWENTY-TWO PAGES. ONE CENT In Greater New York. | TWO CENTS Within Commuting Distance. | THREE CENTS Elsewhere.

REVOLUTIONISTS SEIZE PETROGRAD; KERENSKY FLEES; PLEDGE IS GIVEN TO SEEK "AN IMMEDIATE PEACE"; ITALIANS AGAIN DRIVEN BACK; LOSE 17,000 MORE MEN

WOODS MUST GO AS POLICE HEAD, HYLAN DECIDES

Mayor-Elect Will Ask Him to Retire if He Fails to Resign.

SUCCESSOR NOT YET FOUND

Murphy Will Refrain from Interference, Congressman Smith Declares.

HYLAN SHOCKS JOB HUNTERS

Announces Delay in Considering Appointments—Craig Against Pay-as-You-Go Plan.

Mayor-elect John F. Hylan, it was said yesterday, has no intention of retaining Arthur Woods at the head of the Police Department. Friends of the Mayor-elect said that he expected to find a man after his own liking, who measured up to the job, to succeed the Police Commissioner, before Jan. 1, when the Mayor-elect assumes office. Unless Judge Hylan had received the resignation of Commissioner Woods by the time he was ready to appoint his successor, the Police Commissioner, it was said, would be asked to retire.

At the headquarters of Judge Hylan persons who enjoy the confidence of the Mayor-elect said last night that he regarded the administration of the Police Department under Commissioner Woods as having been one of the vital issues in the campaign, even though less attention was paid to it by Judge Hylan in his speeches than to some other branches of the Mitchel Administration.

Expect Woods to Resign.

It is the belief of Judge Hylan's friends that Commissioner Woods will follow the usual practice and submit his resignation when the change of administration occurs, even though a provision in the New York City Charter provides for a five-year term.

Wants Hylan to Feel Free.

Continued on Page 2.

Insists Emperor Charles Will Be Polish Ruler

Special Cable to THE NEW YORK TIMES.

THE HAGUE, Nov. 8.—In spite of recent denials the Lokal-Anzeiger reports that the Austrian Emperor is to be named King of Poland. It says this was decided on at a Crown Council on Monday.

Poland is to be joined to Austria, and Galicia is to belong to the future Kingdom of Poland. Lithuania and Courland will be separate States, such as Prussia, and be represented by Grand Dukes. The paper points out that in Austria even the Germanic parties appear to approve this, but that special emphasis is laid on and guarantees demanded for "the strengthening of Germanic Austria."

The paper seems to question whether German interests have been sufficiently considered in this settlement.

THREAT OF DICTATOR IN GERMAN SNARL

Government Attempts to Force Dropping of Demand for Radical Vice Chancellor.

HERTLING DENIES PROMISES

Opposition to Attack Chancellor as Soon as Reichstag Meets Unless He Yields.

COPENHAGEN, Nov. 8.—The threat that a military dictatorship is inevitable unless insistence upon a radical Vice Chancellor is dropped and the Government of Count von Hertling as it now stands is accepted is held out over the progressive democratic elements in Germany.

Count von Hertling, through a semi-official note in the Norddeutsche Allgemeine Zeitung, announces that no promises whatever were made to give the radicals the two posts they desired.

OTTO H. KAHN TALKS FINANCE WITH WILSON

New Yorker at the White House Discusses Economic Condition of the Country.

WASHINGTON, Nov. 8.—Otto H. Kahn, head of Kahn, Loeb & Co., called today on President Wilson.

Otto H. Kahn has given considerable attention to the question of war taxation, and has advocated methods that would lay as little strain as possible on business.

CADORNA IS OUTFLANKED

A General Among the Troops Cut Off on the Middle Tagliamento.

INVADERS CAPTURE 80 GUNS

Berlin Reckons Total at More Than 2,300; That of Prisoners Over 250,000.

ROME ADMITS WITHDRAWAL

Official Report Shows That Rearguard Actions Are Proceeding West of the Livenza.

BERLIN, Nov. 8, (via London.)—Austro-German forces in Northern Italy have crossed the Livenza River, and in outflanking operations on the middle Tagliamento have captured 17,000 Italian troops, among them a General. Eighty guns have been added to the booty, which now includes more than 2,300 guns. The total number of prisoners taken since the drive began now exceeds 250,000.

These developments of the campaign are announced in the afternoon report from Army Headquarters, the text of which follows:

Our detachments, advancing on the mountain roads, have broken the resistance of the enemy rear guard. By an outflanking movement our attacking columns cut off the retreat of the enemy troops still holding out on the middle Tagliamento between Tolmezzo and Gemona and on the permanent fortified works of Monte San Simeone. Up to the present 17,000 Italians, among them a General, with 80 guns, have had to surrender.

In the plain, fighting has developed along the Livenza River. By a vigorous advance German and Austro-Hungarian divisions, in spite of destroyed bridges, have forced the crossing and have thrown the enemy back westward.

The total number of prisoners captured has now been increased to more than 250,000 and the booty in guns to more than 2,300.

Retreat Continues, Rome Reports.

ROME, Nov. 8.—The withdrawal of the Italian line was continued yesterday, the War Office announced today. The larger units retired unmolested.

Final Stand Beyond the Livenza?

Continued on Page 4.

British Government Denies Lack of Concern for Italy

LONDON, Nov. 8.—The following official announcement was issued tonight:

"A statement from a correspondent of The Associated Press at Italian Headquarters appeared in the British press today. This statement set out to remind the Allies that something more than assurances were needed for getting reinforcements in men and munitions to the threatened Italian lines."

LONDON HAILS OUR WAR MISSION

Comes at Critical Period of the War with New Assurance of Victory.

ENVOYS MAKE BRISK START

Begin Conferences on First Day—Benson Visits Jellicoe—Trip Was Uneventful.

Special Cable to THE NEW YORK TIMES.

LONDON, Nov. 8.—The American mission, headed by Colonel E. M. House, arrived in Europe at a crucial period of the world war. With Russia in the throes of a fresh revolution that may lead to anything, and with Italy engaged in a desperate struggle against both a foreign enemy and internal difficulties the landing of the American mission at a British port is an encouragement to the stalwart and a rebuke to the faint hearted.

Continued on Page 11.

AWAITS LIGHT FROM RUSSIA

Washington Reserves Judgment, Hoping Revolt Is Only Local.

EXPECTS A COUNTER-MOVE

Kerensky, with Conservatives and Perhaps the Army Behind Him, May Save the Country.

DARK DAYS SEEN AHEAD

And Allied War Conference Faces Another Huge Problem—Bigger Burden for Us.

Special to The New York Times.

WASHINGTON, Nov. 8.—Until accurate official reports are received, official and diplomatic Washington are reserving judgment on the new Russian crisis and all that it involves, including possibly civil war, and a still further weakening of Russia's position in the war against Germany.

Expect a New Government.

Continued on Page 2.

Reverses Cited as Showing Greater Need Than Ever For Unified Direction of Allied War Policy

By CHARLES H. GRASTY.

Copyright, 1917, by The New York Times Company.

Special Cable to THE NEW YORK TIMES.

ROME, Nov. 8.—My observations here confirm previous insistence upon the urgent need of centralized methods of managing the war. At bottom this war is the biggest business enterprise ever undertaken, and, while the Kaiser handles his end of it as such, each of the Allies is more or less playing its own separate game. With an infinity of resources, they have discussed and postponed critical decisions until the advantage has been lost.

There has not been a single allied action, with the exception of the battle of the Marne, ranking as a great aggressive stroke.

In a word, after three years, it is time to quit playing amateur against professional.

Plans for the conduct of the war on the basis of a unified western front extending from the North Sea to the Adriatic are now under consideration by Premiers Lloyd George and Painlevé and other high civil and military officials in conference in Rome.

STOCKS TUMBLE ON RUSSIAN NEWS

Flood of Liquidation Hits Exchange, Heightened by Action of Short Sellers.

NEWS CHECKS BROAD RISE

No Action Considered Yet in Regard to Publishing Proportion of Short Sales.

The stock market suffered one of the most drastic declines of the year yesterday, following the receipt of dispatches which told of the Kerensky Government's downfall.

Big Sales of Steel Common.

Russian Bonds Decline.

Continued on Page 3.

HOPE STRONG MAN WILL RULE RUSSIA

Zemstvos' Agent Here and Herman Bernstein Agree That Kerensky Must Go.

GREAT REACTION EXPECTED

Salchnovsky Thinks Revolt May Lead to Constitutional Monarchy.

The elimination of Kerensky from the affairs of the Russian Government was declared to be the most probable as well as the most desirable result of the present Maximalist revolt by persons familiar with Russian affairs and in sympathy with the moderate parties there.

Continued on Page 2.

MINISTERS UNDER ARREST

Winter Palace Is Taken After Fierce Defense by Women Soldiers.

FORT'S GUNS TURNED ON IT

Cruiser and Armored Cars Also Brought Into Battle Waged by Searchlight.

TROTZSKY HEADS REVOLT

Giving Land to the Peasants and Calling of Constituent Assembly Promised.

PETROGRAD, Nov. 8.—With the aid of the capital's garrison complete control of Petrograd has been seized by the Maximalists, or Bolsheviki, headed by Nikolai Lenine, the Radical Socialist leader, and Leon Trotzky, President of the Central Executive Committee of the Petrograd Council of Workmen's and Soldiers' Delegates.

How the Revolt Developed.

Continued on Page 2.

"All the News That's Fit to Print."

The New York Times.

THE WEATHER
Fair today and Thursday; slight temperature change; west winds.
For full weather report see Page 23.

VOL. LXVII...NO. 21,865. NEW YORK, WEDNESDAY, DECEMBER 5, 1917.—TWENTY-FOUR PAGES. ONE CENT In Greater New York. | TWO CENTS Within Commuting Distance. | THREE CENTS Elsewhere.

PRESIDENT CALLS FOR IMMEDIATE WAR ON AUSTRIA; CONGRESS WOULD INCLUDE BULGARIA AND TURKEY; OUR WATCHWORDS ARE: JUSTICE, REPARATION, SECURITY

WILSON FOR VICTORY FIRST

"We Shall Not Slacken or Be Diverted Until It Is Won."

PACIFISTS TOUCH NO HEART

"May Be Left to Strut Their Uneasy Hour and Be Forgotten," Says President.

FIGHTING TO FREE GERMANY

Throng in the House Stands to Cheer Message—La Follette Remains Seated.

Special to The New York Times.

WASHINGTON, Dec. 4.—With dramatic suddenness, yet with no apparent effort at dramatic effect, President Wilson, addressing in person the Senate and the House of Representatives assembled in joint session today, recommended that "the Congress immediately declare the United States in a state of war with Austro-Hungary."

The legislators and the great crowd of spectators who filled floor and galleries were unprepared for the call for a declaration of war. On the contrary, those preceding parts of the President's address had tended to create the impression that the Vienna Government, although allied with Germany, was entitled to special consideration, to charitable treatment, in the realization that it was a mere tool of the military autocracy at Berlin. Then came the call for action against the Dual Monarchy.

The effect was electrical. Not for a moment was the President left in doubt as to the temper of Congress regarding this recommendation. A thrill went through that audience of men and women who had listened with increasing interest to every word that had come with clear-cut distinctness from the lips of the man, who, more than any other, controls the destinies of the nation at this critical time.

War Call Unexpected.

The assemblage had risen before to heights of patriotic enthusiasm over appealing passages of the President's address. But only a minute prior to the stirring declaration his auditors had heard expressions which brought the too ready interpretation that the hour was not at hand when the United States should undertake to deal in a hostile military way with Germany's chief partner in the war. He had named Austria specifically, along with Serbia and Poland, in mentioning the countries he had in mind when, last January, before America entered the great European conflict, he had declared that the nations of the world "were entitled not only to free pathways upon the sea but also to assured and unmolested access to those pathways."

The disappointment of those—and they were many—who had looked for a stirring denunciation of Austro-Hungarian intrigue and international criminality was short-lived. The temporary elation of the few pacifists who were there dropped like a dead weight in a vacuum.

Prior to the remarkable demonstration of patriotic fervor that followed the President's declaration, his auditors had had ample opportunity to find an outlet for their feelings, for the address was filled with statements that appealed in full measure to love of country and determination to see the sanguinary struggle on the battlefields of Europe to a finish.

An important feature of the address was the reiteration and amplification of the war aims of America: Belgium and Northern France must be delivered from Prussian conquest and Prussian menace, but the peoples of Austria-Hungary, the Balkans and Turkey, "alike in Europe and in Asia," must be freed also from Prussian domination; "we do not wish in any way to impair or rearrange the Austro-Hungarian Empire"; "our attitude and purpose with regard to Germany herself are of a like kind"; "we intend no wrong against the German Empire, no interference with her internal affairs."

Assailed Germans' Masters.

If the German people continued after the war to accept the Government of their present masters, the President said, "it might be impossible to admit them to the partnership of nations which must henceforth guarantee the world's peace," and "it might be impossible also to admit Germany to the free economic intercourse which must inevitably spring out of the other partnerships of a real peace"; "the wrongs, the very deep wrongs, committed in this war will have to be righted."

If the Marquis of Lansdowne can find comfort in the analogy between his own statement of war aims and those of President Wilson, he will be disappointed in the President's attitude toward the other proposal of the British statesman—that a reiteration of war aims shall be used as a basis for peace negotiations. President Wilson is not in sympathy with this program. He left no doubt on that score in his address when he declared that "the German power must be crushed," and empha-

Continued on Page 2.

The President's Address to Congress

WASHINGTON, Dec. 4.—Here is the full text of President Wilson's address to Congress today:

Gentlemen of the Congress:

Eight months have elapsed since I last had the honor of addressing you. They have been months crowded with events of immense and grave significance for us. I shall not undertake to detail or even to summarise these events. The practical particulars of the part we have played in them will be laid before you in the reports of the executive departments. I shall discuss only our present outlook upon these vast affairs, our present duties and the immediate means of accomplishing the objects we shall hold always in view.

I shall not go back to debate the causes of the war. The intolerable wrongs done and planned against us by the sinister masters of Germany have long since become too grossly obvious and odious to every true American to need to be rehearsed. But I shall ask you to consider again and with very grave scrutiny our objectives and the measures by which we mean to attain them; for the purpose of discussion here in this place is action and our action must move straight toward definite ends. Our object is, of course, to win the war, and we shall not slacken or suffer ourselves to be diverted until it is won. But it is worth while asking and answering the question, When shall we consider the war won?

From one point of view it is not necessary to broach this fundamental matter. I do not doubt that the American people know what the war is about and what sort of an outcome they will regard as a realization of their purpose in it. As a nation we are united in spirit and intention.

I pay little heed to those who tell me otherwise. I hear the voices of dissent—who does not? I hear the criticism and the clamor of the noisily thoughtless and troublesome. I also see men here and there fling themselves in impotent disloyalty against the calm, indomitable power of the nation. I hear men debate peace who understand neither its nature nor the way in which we may attain it, with uplifted eyes and unbroken spirits. But I know that none of these speaks for the nation. They do not touch the heart of anything. They may safely be left to strut about their uneasy hour and be forgotten.

What the War Is For.

But from another point of view I believe that it is necessary to say plainly what we here at the seat of action consider the war to be for and what part we mean to play in the settlement of its searching issues. We are the spokesmen of the American people and they have a right to know whether their purpose is ours. They desire peace by the overcoming of evil, but the defeat once and for all of the sinister forces that interrupt peace and render it impossible, and they wish to know how closely our thought runs with theirs and what action we propose. They are impatient with those who desire peace by any sort of compromise—deeply and indignantly impatient—but they will be equally impatient with us if we do not make it plain to them what our objectives are and what we are planning for in seeking to make conquest of peace by arms.

I believe that I speak for them when I say two things: First, that this intolerable Thing of which the masters of Germany have shown us the ugly face, this menace of combined intrigue and force, which we now see so clearly as the German power, a Thing without conscience or honor or capacity for covenanted peace, must be crushed, and if it be not utterly brought to an end, at least shut out from the friendly intercourse of the nations; and, second, that when this Thing and its power are indeed defeated and the time comes that we can discuss peace—when the German people have spokesmen whose word we can believe, and when those spokesmen are ready in the name of their people to accept the common judgment of the nations as to what shall henceforth be the bases of law and of covenant for the life of the world—we shall be willing and glad to pay the full price for peace and pay it ungrudgingly. We know what that price will be. It will be full, impartial justice—justice done at every point and to every nation that the final settlement must affect, our enemies as well as our friends.

You catch, with me, the voices of humanity that are in the air. They grow daily more audible, more articulate, more persuasive, and they come from the hearts of men everywhere. They insist that the war shall not end in vindictive action of any kind; that no nation or people shall be robbed or punished because the irresponsible rulers of a single country have themselves done deep and abominable wrong. It is this thought that has been expressed in the formula, "No annexations, no contributions, no punitive indemnities."

Led People of Russia Astray.

Just because this crude formula expresses the instinctive judgment as to the right of plain men everywhere it has been made diligent use of by the masters of German intrigue to lead the people of Russia astray, and the people of every other country their agents could reach, in order that a premature peace might be brought about before autocracy has been taught its final and convincing lesson and the people of the world put in control of their own destinies.

But the fact that a wrong use has been made of a just idea is no reason why a right use should not be made of it. It ought to be brought under the patronage of its real friends. Let it be said again that autocracy must first be shown the utter futility of its claims to power or leadership in the modern world. It is impossible to apply any standard of justice so long as such forces are unchecked and undefeated as the present masters of Germany command. Not until that has been done can right be set up as arbiter and peacemaker among the nations. But when that has been done—as, God willing, it assuredly will be—we shall at last be free to do an unprecedented thing, and this is the time to avow our purpose to do it. We shall be free to base peace on generosity and justice, to the exclusion of all selfish claims to advantage even on the part of the victors.

Let there be no misunderstanding. Our present and immediate task is to win the war, and nothing shall turn us aside from it until it is accomplished. Every power and resource we possess, whether of men, of money, or of materials, is being devoted and will continue to be devoted to that purpose until it is achieved. Those who desire to bring peace about before that purpose is achieved, I counsel to carry their advice elsewhere. We will not entertain it.

Justice and Reparation.

We shall regard the war only as won when the German people say to us, through properly accredited representatives, that they are ready to agree to a settlement based upon justice and the reparation of the wrongs their rulers have done. They have done a wrong to Belgium, which must be repaired. They have established a power over other lands and peoples than their own—over the great empire of Austria-Hungary, over hitherto free Balkan States, over Turkey, and within Asia—which must be relinquished.

Germany's success by skill, by industry, by knowledge, by enterprise we did not grudge or oppose, but admired rather. She had built up for herself a real empire of trade and influence, secured by the peace of the world. We were content to abide the rivalries of manufacture, science, and commerce that were involved for us in her success and stand or fall as we had or did not have the brains and the initiative to surpass her. But at the moment when she had conspicuously won her triumphs of peace she threw them away to establish in their stead what the world will no longer permit to be established, military and political domination by arms, by which to oust where she could not excell the rivals she most feared and hated.

The peace we make must remedy that wrong. It must deliver the once fair lands and happy peoples of Belgium and northern France from the Prussian conquest and the Prussian menace, but it must also deliver the peoples of Austria-Hungary, the peoples of the Balkans, and the peoples of Turkey, alike in Europe and in Asia, from the impudent and alien domination of the Prussian military and commercial autocracy.

We owe it, however, to ourselves to say that we do not wish in any way to impair or to rearrange the Austro-Hungarian empire. It is no affair of ours what they do with their own life, either industrially or politically. We do not purpose nor desire to dictate to them in any way. We only desire to see that their affairs are left in their own hands, in all matters, great or small. We shall hope to secure for the peoples of the Balkan peninsula and for the people of the Turkish empire the right and opportunity to make their own lives safe, their own fortunes secure against oppression or injustice and from the dictation of foreign courts or parties, and our attitude and purpose with regard to Germany herself are of a like kind.

Our Attitude Toward Germany.

We intend no wrong against the German empire, no interference with her internal affairs. We should deem either the one or the other absolutely unjustifiable, absolutely contrary to the principles we have professed to live by and to hold most sacred throughout our life as a nation.

The people of Germany are being told by the men whom they now permit to deceive them and to act as their masters that they are fighting for very life and existence of their empire, a war of desperate self-defense against deliberate aggression. Nothing could be more grossly or wantonly false, and we must seek by the utmost openness and candor as to our real aims to convince them of its falseness. We are in fact fighting for their emancipation from fear, along with our own, from the fear as well as from the fact of unjust attack by neighbors or rivals or schemers after world empire. No one is threatening the existence or the independence or the peaceful enterprise of the German empire.

The worst that can happen to the detriment of the German people is this, that if they should still, after the war is over, continue to be obliged to live under ambitious and intriguing masters interested to disturb the peace of the world, men or classes of men whom the other peoples of the world could not trust, it might be impossible to admit them to the partnership of nations which must henceforth guarantee the world's peace. That partnership must be a partnership of peoples, not a mere partnership of governments.

It might be impossible, also, in such untoward circumstances, to admit Germany to the free economic intercourse which must inevitably spring out of the other partnerships of a real peace. But there would be no aggression in that; and such a situation, inevitable because of distrust, would in the very nature of things sooner or later cure itself, by processes which would assuredly set in.

Rights of Central Powers.

The wrongs, the very deep wrongs, committed in this war will have to be righted. That of course. But they cannot and must not be righted by the commission of similar wrongs against Germany and her allies. The world will not permit the commission of similar wrongs as a means of reparation and settlement. Statesmen must by this time have learned that the opinion of the world is everywhere wide awake and fully comprehends the issues involved. No representative of any self-governed nation will dare disregard it by attempting any such covenants of selfishness and compromise as were entered into at the congress of Vienna.

The thought of the plain people here and everywhere throughout the world, the people who enjoy no privilege and have very simple and unsophisticated standards of right and wrong, is the air all governments must henceforth breathe if they would live. It is in the full disclosing light of that thought that all policies must be conceived and executed in this midday hour of the world's life.

German rulers have been able to upset the peace of the world only because the German people were not suffered under their tutelage to share the comradeship of the other peoples of the world either in thought or in purpose. They were allowed to have no opinion of their own which might be set up as a rule of conduct for those who exercised authority over them. But the congress that concludes this war will feel the full strength of the tides that run now in the hearts and consciences of free men everywhere. Its conclusions will run with those tides.

All these things have been true from the very beginning of this stupendous war; and I cannot help thinking that if they had been made plain at the very outset the sympathy and enthusiasm of the Russian people might have been once for all enlisted on the side of the Allies, suspicion and distrust swept away, and a real and lasting union of purpose effected. Had they believed these things at the very moment of their revolution and had they been confirmed in that belief since, the sad reverses which have recently marked the progress of their affairs toward an ordered and stable government of free men might have been avoided.

Truth as the Antidote.

The Russian people have been poisoned by the very same falsehoods that have kept the German people in the dark, and the poison has been administered by the very same hands. The only possible antidote is the truth. It cannot be uttered too plainly or too often.

From every point of view, therefore, it has seemed to be my duty to speak these declarations of purpose, to add these specific interpretations to what I took the liberty of saying to the Senate in January. Our entrance into the war has not altered our attitude toward the settlement that must come when it is over. When I said in January that the nations of the world were entitled not only to free pathways upon the sea but also to assured and unmolested access to those pathways I was thinking, and I am thinking now, not of the smaller and weaker nations alone, which need our countenance and support, but also of the great and powerful nations, and of our present enemies as well as our present associates in the war. I was thinking, and am thinking now, of Austria herself, among the rest, as well as of Serbia and of Poland. Justice and equality of rights can be had only at a great price. We are seeking permanent, not temporary, foundations for the peace of the world, and must seek them candidly and fearlessly. As always, the right will prove to be the expedient.

What shall we do, then, to push this great war of freedom and justice to its righteous conclusion? We must clear away with a thorough hand all impediments to success, and we must make every adjustment of law that will facilitate the full and free use of our whole capacity and force as a fighting unit.

War Against Austria.

One very embarrassing obstacle that stands in our way is that we are at war with Germany, but not with her allies. I therefore very earnestly recommend that the Congress immediately declare the United States in a state of war with Austria-Hungary. Does it seem strange to you that this should be the conclusion of the argument I have just addressed to you? It is not. It is in fact the inevitable logic of what I have said. Austria-Hungary is for the time being not her own mistress, but simply the vassal of the German Government. We must face the facts as they are and act upon them without sentiment in this stern business.

The Government of Austria-Hungary is not acting upon its own initiative or in response to the wishes and feelings of its own peoples, but as the instrument of another nation. We must meet its force with our own and regard the Central Powers as but one. The war can be successfully conducted in no other way. The same logic would lead also to a declaration of war against Turkey and Bulgaria. They also are the tools of Germany. But they are mere tools and do not yet stand in the direct path of our necessary action. We shall go wherever the necessities of this war carry us, but it seems to me that we should go only where immediate and practical considerations lead us and not heed any others.

Stricter Grip on Enemy Aliens.

The financial and military measures which must be adopted will suggest themselves as the war and its undertakings develop, but I will take the liberty of proposing to you certain other acts of legislation which seem to me to be needed for the support of the war and for the release of our whole force and energy.

It will be necessary to extend in certain particulars the legislation of the last session with regard to alien enemies; and also necessary, I believe, to create a very definite and particular control over the entrance and departure of all persons into and from the United States.

Legislation should be enacted defining as a criminal offense every willful violation of the Presidential proclamations relating to enemy aliens promulgated under Section 4,067 of the Revised Statutes and providing appropriate punishment; and women as well as men should be included under the terms of the acts placing restraints upon alien enemies. It is likely that as time goes on many alien enemies will be willing to be fed and housed at the expense of the Government in the detention camps, and it would be the purpose of the legislation I have suggested to confine offenders among them in penitentiaries and other similar institutions where they could be made to work as other criminals do.

Further Limiting of Prices.

Recent experience has convinced me that the Congress must go further in authorizing the Government to set limits to prices. The law of supply and demand, I am sorry to say, has been replaced by the law of unrestrained selfishness. While we have eliminated profiteering in several branches of industry it still runs impudently rampant in others. The farmers, for example, complain with a great deal of justice that, while the regulation of food prices restricts their incomes, no restraints are placed upon the prices of most of the things they must themselves purchase; and similar inequities obtain on all sides.

It is imperatively necessary that the consideration of the full use of the water power of the country and also the consideration of the systematic and yet economical development of such of the natural resources of the country as are still under the control of the Federal Government should be resumed and affirmatively and constructively dealt with at the earliest possible moment. The pressing need of such legislation is daily becoming more obvious.

The Legislation proposed at the last session with regard to regulated combinations among our exporters, in order to provide for our foreign trade a more effective organization and method of co-operation, ought by all means to be completed at this session.

And I beg that the members of the House of Representatives will permit me to express the opinion that it will be impossible to deal in any way but a very wasteful and extravagant fashion with the enormous appropriations of the public moneys which must continue to be made, if the war is to be properly sustained, unless the House will consent to return to its former practice of initiating and preparing all appropriation bills through a single committee, in order that responsibility may be centred, expenditures standardized and made uniform, and waste and duplication as much as possible avoided.

Additional legislation may also become necessary before the present Congress adjourns in order to effect the most efficient co-ordination and operation of the railway and other transportation systems of the country; but to that I shall, if circumstances should demand, call the attention of Congress upon another occasion.

Task of Winning Foremost.

If I have overlooked anything that ought to be done for the more effective conduct of the war, your own counsels will supply the omission. What I am perfectly clear about is that in the present session of the Congress our whole attention and energy should be concentrated on the vigorous and rapid and successful prosecution of the great task of winning the war.

We can do this with all the greater zeal and enthusiasm because we know that for us this is a war of high principle, debased by no selfish ambition of conquest or spoliation; because we know, and all the world knows, that we have been forced into it to save the very institutions we live under from corruption and destruction. The purposes of the Central Powers strike straight at the very heart of everything we believe in; their methods of warfare outrage every principle of humanity and of knightly honor; their intrigue has corrupted the very thought and spirit of many of our people; their sinister and secret diplomacy has sought to take our very territory away from us and disrupt the union of the States. Our safety would be at an end, our honor forever sullied and brought into contempt were we to permit their triumph. They are striking at the very existence of democracy and liberty.

It is because it is for us a war of high, disinterested purpose, in which all the free people of the world are banded together for the vindication of right, a war for the preservation of our nation and of all that it has held dear of principle and of purpose, that we feel ourselves doubly constrained to propose for its outcome only that which is righteous and of irreproachable intention, for our foes as well as for our friends.

The cause being just and holy, the settlement must be of like motive and quality. For this we can fight, but for nothing less noble or less worthy of our traditions. For this cause we entered the war and for this cause will we battle until the last gun is fired.

I have spoken plainly because this seems to me the time when it is most necessary to speak plainly, in order that all the world may know that even in the heat and ardor of the struggle and when our whole thought is of carrying the war through to its end we have not forgotten any ideal or principle for which the name of America has been held in honor among the nations and for which it has been our glory to contend in the great generations that went before us.

A supreme moment of history has come. The eyes of the people have been opened and they see. The hand of God is laid upon the nations. He will show them favor, I devoutly believe, only if they rise to the clear heights of His own justice and mercy.

WAR DECLARATION READY

Resolution Aligning Austria as Foe Likely to Pass This Week.

MANY WOULD GO FURTHER

Inclined to Declare War on Turkey and Bulgaria Unless Good Reason Is Given.

MESSAGE HIGHLY PRAISED

But Disappointment Keen at Failure to Urge War on All of Germany's Vassals.

Special to The New York Times.

WASHINGTON, Dec. 4.—Immediate action by Congress is to follow President Wilson's demand today for a declaration of war against Austria-Hungary. In both houses the sentiment is unwavering for such a declaration, and it is likely that the country will be arrayed as an enemy of Austria-Hungary by the end of this week.

The House Foreign Affairs Committee will tomorrow draft a resolution, which is likely to be offered before the day is over, declaring war on Austria-Hungary. The Senate Foreign Relations Committee will not meet until Thursday—the Senate having adjourned today until Friday—when a similar resolution will be prepared.

Representative Flood, Chairman of the House Foreign Affairs Committee, has called his committee to meet at 2 o'clock tomorrow afternoon. He is prepared to report a resolution declaring war against Austria-Hungary. There is no opposition to such a course, but action may be delayed by reason of a strong demand to include Turkey and Bulgaria in such a declaration. Indications are that the latter course will be pursued unless the President furnishes the committee with a compelling reason against the inclusion of Turkey and Bulgaria.

As to Austria-Hungary, nothing remains to be done but make the formal declaration, for only scant opposition is expected to spring up. Senators and Representatives who voted against the declaration of war against Germany were not talking today against the President's pronouncement for throwing down the gage of battle to Austria. An almost complete unanimity of sentiment prevailed as to the logic of putting Austria-Hungary in the enemy alignment.

Omission of Turkey and Bulgaria.

The talk at the Capitol after the President's message bore more upon the Executive's advice against a pronouncement against Turkey and Bulgaria than upon the demand for hostilities against Austria-Hungary. Leaders in both houses, Democrats and Republicans alike, expressed not only frank surprise, but regret that the President had not included Turkey and Bulgaria. They felt that Turkey, as one of the arch allies of Germany, ought to be embraced in any declaration of war, and that no obvious reason existed for leaving out Bulgaria.

Members of the Senate Committee on Foreign Relations and the House Committee on Foreign Affairs unhesitatingly expressed the belief that resolutions putting Turkey and Bulgaria along with Austria-Hungary as enemies of the United States would be offered in both houses and passed. For the United States to declare war against Austria-Hungary and not against Turkey, it was suggested by some, smacked of inconsistency. No disposition was manifest to quarrel with the President in having left Turkey and Bulgaria out of it. The opinion was ventured that the President must have had a sufficient reason for naming Austria-Hungary alone, depending, perhaps, upon Congress to take the initiative with the two other countries.

Senator Stone, Chairman of the Senate Committee on Foreign Relations, said that the committee would draft its resolution against Austria-Hungary on Thursday, and that it would be offered to the Senate the following day.

"All along, since the declaration of war against Germany, I have favored putting Austria-Hungary, Turkey, and Bulgaria in the list of America's enemies," said Senator Stone. "Congress will act quickly in declaring war on Austria-Hungary. I hope similar action will just as speedily be taken against Turkey and Bulgaria. If it develops that there is a diplomatic reason why we should not at this time include Turkey and Bulgaria, Congress naturally will withhold action. Such intimation would come, if there were occasion for it, from the White House. I believe I am safe in saying that, unless Congress hears that it would be unwise to act now, declarations will at once be made against Turkey and Bulgaria."

Senator Lodge, another of the Foreign Relations Committee, said he could not understand why the President did not ask for a declaration against Turkey and Bulgaria along with Austria-Hungary.

"I have always favored declaring war against all of Germany's allies," said Senator Lodge. "It seems to me

Assembly May Curb Bolshevist Power But Russia Cannot Continue War

Possible Terms of Peace Forecast—Plea for Friendship and Support of Old Ally to Save Her From Being Thrown Into Germany's Arms.

By HAROLD WILLIAMS.

Special Cable to THE NEW YORK TIMES.

PETROGRAD, Monday, Dec. 3.—Armistice negotiations began last night and will probably continue for several days. We are now faced with an exceedingly complicated situation which needs some unraveling.

First of all there is the internal political position. The Bolshevist movement is by no means simple. It is a curious jumble of conflicting elements ranging from the purest idealism to German intrigue and reactionary monarchism. These elements are temporarily agreed in a peace policy, and derive their authority from the strong pacifist tendencies of the soldiers and Socialists and the pacifist mood of the workmen.

The success or failure of the Bolsheviki depends on fulfillment or non-fulfillment of their promises. They have to deal not only with the fickleness of the mob that now supports them, but with the determined opposition of nearly all the intelligent section of the population and of whole territories, as Ukraine and the Cossack regions and Siberia.

The regular political and social machinery which is interfered with by the Bolsheviki is to a certain extent spoiled by them, but it persists in operating in spite of them. As regards the fickleness of the mob, those reactionaries who now work with the Bolsheviki are preparing to take advantage of a swing round of the popular mood when it does come. Internal rivalries, friction between incongruous and loosely co-ordinated factions, and personal jealousies must also be taken into account in estimating the stability of the Bolshevist power.

Another factor is daily increasing in importance. The elections to the Con-

Continued on Page [illegible].

Dukhonin Slain for Korniloff's Escape When Bolsheviki Take Headquarters

PETROGRAD, Dec. 4.—An official statement was issued today signed by Ensign Krylenko, the Bolshevist Commander in Chief, announcing the killing by infuriated members of the Bolsheviki of General Dukhonin, former Commander in Chief of the Russian Armies, who recently was deposed because of his refusal to request German army officials to enter into an armistice with the Bolsheviki.

General Dukhonin was killed by being thrown from a train after the Bolshevist forces had captured headquarters at Mohilev, where he had remained after his deposition. General Korniloff, also a former Russian Commander in Chief, and who some time ago started an unsuccessful revolt against the Kerensky Government, fled from Mohilev before the arrival of the Bolshevist forces.

The text of the communication of Krylenko follows:

Today I entered into Mohilev at the head of the revolutionary troops. The headquarters was entirely surrounded without fighting. The last obstacle to the cause of peace was fallen.

I cannot be silent on the sad act of lynch law practiced upon the former highest commander in chief, General Dukhonin. Popular hatred surpassed the limits of reason, and in spite of all attempts to save him he was thrown out of a railroad train at the Mohilev Station and killed. The flight of General Korniloff the day before the fall of headquarters was the cause of this excess.

I cannot allow the banner of the revolution to be stained, and it is necessary strongly to condemn such acts. A revolutionary people are fearful in a struggle, but they must be soft after victory.

An unofficial account says that General Dukhonin was dragged from a train in which it was intended to send him to Petrograd, and beaten to death.

A battle between detachments from the Petrograd garrison, commanded by Ensign Krylenko, and Cossacks is reported to be impending at Vitebsk. According to a telegram from Krylenko's Adjutant, the Cossacks have gathered on the flanks and in the rear of Krylenko's forces.

WASHINGTON, Dec. 4.—A cable from Rome today said the Russian Embassy in the Quirinal and the Russian Legation at the Vatican had given notice of their refusal to recognize the Lenine Government in Russia. They have stopped correspondence with the Lenine Ministry of Foreign Affairs.

Allies to Create Joint Naval Board; Framing Army Plan in Full Accord

Paris Council, It Is Announced, Concluded Agreements "Upon the Basis of a Complete Understanding and Close Solidarity" Regarding Economics, Finance, and Fighting Program.

PARIS, Dec. 4.—The Foreign Office officially announced today that at the recent Interallied Conference, in which the United States participated, agreements were concluded "upon the basis of a complete understanding and close solidarity among the Allies for the solution of the questions in which they have a common interest in the war."

It was also announced that the creation of a supreme interallied naval committee had been decided upon.

The Interallied General Staff, it was stated was working upon a definite military program which was placing unity of military action in the way of certain realization.

The announcement regarding the results of the conference was made in the following official statement:

"The Minister of Foreign Affairs reported to the Cabinet today the results of the conference of the Allies. The reading of communications from the Presidents of each section of the Allied Conference, at which were present for the first time representatives of all the countries taking part with us in this war, has given felicitous results from every point of view. They give assurance of practical unity of action, economically, financially, and militarily.

"The agreements have been concluded upon the basis of a complete understanding and close solidarity among the Allies for the solution of the questions in which they have a common interest in the war. The financial needs of each of them, the requirements of their armament, their transport, their food, have been the subject of profound study which guarantees perfect satisfaction.

"The creation of a supreme interallied naval committee has been determined upon. Military unity of action has been placed upon the course of certain realization by the Interallied General Staff, which is at work upon an established program of all military questions.

"From a diplomatic point of view entire accord resulted from the discussions among the representatives of the powers upon all the business, which has been arranged together, to assure the common victory of their countries."

Section 1

"All the [illegible]s That's Fit to Print."

The New York Times.

THE WEATHER
Fair Sunday and Monday; slight temperature change; shifting winds
For full weather report see Page 19.

Section 1

VOL. LXVII...NO. 22,0[illegible]. NEW YORK, SUNDAY, JULY 21, 1918.—92 PAGES, In Nine Parts, including Picture and Magazine Sections in Rotogravure. FIVE CENTS in Greater New York | Elsewhere SEVEN CENTS

ALL GERMANS PUSHED BACK OVER THE MARNE; ALLIES GAIN THREE MILES SOUTH OF SOISSONS; NOW HOLD 20,000 PRISONERS AND 400 GUNS

SAN DIEGO'S LOSS STILL UNEXPLAINED; 1,183 REACH PORT

Captain Christy, in Command, Believes She Was Victim of a U-Boat.

EVIDENCE AGAINST THEORY

Neither Wake of Torpedo Nor Periscope Was Seen—Facts Against Mine, Too.

FEW LIVES LOST WITH SHIP

Men Cheered Captain, Last to Jump from Ship, and Sang National Anthem as She Disappeared.

Special to The New York Times.

WASHINGTON, July 20.—In the opinion of Captain H. H. Christy, commanding the armored cruiser San Diego, formerly the California, which was sunk yesterday ten miles from Fire Island, his ship was torpedoed by a German submarine. He does not make this opinion positive, however, for reasons telegraphed to the Navy Department.

Five or six mines were found in the vicinity of the San Diego's sinking; these may have been sown by a [illegible] but the [illegible] [illegible] seeking to solve. [illegible] is, of course, taking [illegible] measures to ascertain if [illegible] is in or near American coastal [illegible]

All the indications are that [illegible] very little loss of life. The survivors were taken to various places, and it is difficult to get a record of all of them. The process of checking up on the men is complicated also by the fact that only one muster roll of the San Diego is in existence, a duplicate having gone down in the vessel. The sole muster roll at the navy yard at Portsmouth, [illegible] and is now on its way to Washington. Lists of survivors have been coming to the Navy Department by telegraph all day, and as fast as these were received the Bureau of Navigation checked the names from its own records, in order to relieve anxiety sent this to the next of kin of all those reported rescued.

So far the Navy Department has received information that only three members of the crew of the armored cruiser are dead. All of them lost their lives through the explosion which sank the vessel. They are:

DAVIS, THOMAS E., Engineman, [illegible] class; father, Edwin Davis, 215 [illegible] Street, N. W., Canton, Ohio.

THOMAS, FRAZIER O., Machinist's Mate, second class; father, Lockard A. [illegible], Charleston, W. Va.

ROCHET, JAMES F., Engineman, [illegible] class, next of kin, Mrs. C. M. Dean, [illegible] Lake, Cal.

In giving out these names the Navy Department made this statement:

"Others have not been accounted for, and the exact number of the missing cannot be determined until all the survivors are checked up, which is being done as rapidly as possible, but reports indicate that the loss of life was small. The survivors were taken to port on different vessels, and one boatload was landed at a lighthouse on Long Island. The names of the survivors are being telegraphed to the Navy Department, and the next of kin are being notified as fast as the names are received."

Word was received from Canton, Ohio, late tonight that relatives of Thomas E. Davis, given as lost in the Navy Department's list, was safe in Pensacola, Fla.

Captain Christy's Reasons.

The Chief of Staff of the United States Naval Cruiser Force, whose headquarters are in New York, has telegraphed to the Navy Department Captain Christy's reasons for adopting the opinion that the San Diego was sunk by a torpedo. There was no evidence of a U-boat in the vicinity at the time, however, and this and other considerations have caused doubt to be expressed as to Captain Christy's theory. The theory that the vessel struck a mine is also discounted by the fact that the San Diego encountered the explosive abaft the beam. It is contended that if a mine had been the cause it would have been exploded at the very bow or forward of the ship. The report of the Chief of Staff in which Captain Christy's view is given is thus summarized in an official statement of the Navy Department:

The Captain of the San Diego reports that he is inclined to the belief that the ship was sunk by a torpedo. There are no conclusive factors, however, on which to base a definite opinion at present, in view of following circumstances:

1. Torpedo wake was not seen.
2. No convincing evidence that periscope was seen.
3. No submarine appeared, in spite of the fact that three unarmed [illegible]

Continued on Page Seven.

Moscow Now Attacked By Cholera Scourge

LONDON, July 20.—Cholera has spread to Moscow, according to a Russian wireless message received here today. Within the last twenty-four hours, the message says, there have been registered in Moscow 224 known cholera cases, 78 suspected cases, and 26 cases of stomach disease.

The dispatch says that so far as known 120 cases of cholera have occurred in the Province of Petrograd. The message asserts that the Workmen's Commission of Moscow is combating the cholera and has proposed to the Regional Councils that all workrooms be taken over without delay and made freely available to investigation, so that the health of the persons employed in them can be supervised. The commission asks the council to order the compulsory expulsion of the workers from unhealthy rooms and their removal to more sanitary quarters.

ELDEST ROOSEVELT SON IS WOUNDED

News of Theodore's Injury Comes on Heels of Confirmation of Quentin's Death.

THIRD BLOW TO FAMILY

Capt. Archibald Not Yet Recovered from Wounds—President Sends Condolences.

Special to The New York Times.

OYSTER BAY, N. Y., July 20.—Hardly had Colonel Theodore Roosevelt received news today confirming the death of his son, Lieutenant Quentin Roosevelt, than he received a cablegram from his daughter-in-law, Mrs. Theodore Roosevelt, Jr., from Paris which stated that Major Theodore, Jr., had been wounded and was in Paris. The Colonel and his wife bore up bravely under the new trial.

The cable message read:

"Ted wounded. Not seriously. Here with me. Not any danger. No cause for anxiety."

The Colonel explained that Mrs. Theodore Roosevelt, Jr., was connected with the Red Cross hospital in Paris. It is thought that Major Roosevelt had been wounded at the front and removed to the hospital where his wife was.

No further communication has been received by the Roosevelt family and nothing has been heard from the War Department in Washington.

Major Theodore Roosevelt, Jr., went to France with the first American soldiers. About seven weeks ago he was gassed. He refused at that time to go to a hospital. Three weeks ago he was cited for gallantry.

Colonel and Mrs. Roosevelt received the news confirming the death of Quentin during the morning. With them were their two daughters, Mrs. Alice Longworth and Mrs. Richard Derby.

During the afternoon Colonel Roosevelt received the following message from President Wilson:

"The White House,
"Washington, D. C.

"Hon. Theodore Roosevelt:

"Am greatly distressed that the news of your son's death is confirmed. I had hoped for other news. He died serving his country and died with fine gallantry. I am deeply grieved that his service should have come to this tragic end.

WOODROW WILSON."

Colonel Roosevelt replied as follows:

"President Woodrow Wilson, Washington, D. C.:

"I thank you for your courtesy and kindness in telegraphing me, and I deeply appreciate your expression of sympathy and of approval of my son's conduct.

THEODORE ROOSEVELT."

Hundreds of telegrams, cablegrams, and letters of sympathy were received at Sagamore Hill during the day.

Early in the evening the Japanese Red Cross Commission, the members of which are to be the guests of Henry Davison at Locust Valley, L. I., over Sunday, visited Colonel Roosevelt. The Japanese were headed by Prince Tokugawa, and with them were Mr. Davison and his son, Truby.

In addressing the commission the Colonel spoke of the great work the Red Cross was doing. He mentioned the peace at Portsmouth, for which he received the Nobel peace prize. The money, which was turned over to the Government, had been returned to him at his request, he said, and it will be given to war charities, the majority going to the Red Cross. A certain amount, he said, would be given to charities of the allied powers.

"There shall be only one peace," he said, "and that is the peace of right, and the only way to secure it is through a fighting force. No nation has been more efficient in this war than Japan, and no two nations in the world should work together better than Japan and the United States. Any man who works at this time against the interest

Continued on Page Six.

EX-CZAR OF RUSSIA KILLED BY ORDER OF URAL SOVIET

Nicholas Shot on July 16 When It Was Feared That Czechoslovaks Might Seize Him.

WIFE AND HEIR IN SECURITY

Bolshevist Government Approves Act, Alleging Plot for a Counter-Revolution.

PRISONER'S PAPERS SEIZED

Former Emperor's Diary and Letters from Rasputin Soon to be Made Public.

LONDON, July 20.—Nicholas Romanoff, ex-Czar of Russia, was shot July 16, according to a Russian announcement by wireless today.

The former Empress and Alexis Romanoff, the young heir, have been sent to a place of security.

The message announces that a counter-revolutionary conspiracy was discovered, with the object of wresting the ex-Emperor from the authority of the Soviet Council. In view of this fact and the approach of Czechoslovak bands, the President of the Ural Regional Council decided to execute the former ruler, and the decision was carried out [illegible]

The central executive body of the Bolshevist Government announces that it has important documents concerning the former Emperor's affairs, including his own diaries and letters from the monk Rasputin, who was killed shortly before the revolution. These will be published in the near future, the message declares.

The text of the Russian wireless message reads:

"At the first session of the Central Executive Committee, elected by the fifth Congress of the Councils, a message was made public that had been received by direct wire from the Ural Regional Council concerning the shooting of the ex-Czar Nicholas Romanoff.

"Recently Yekaterinburg, the capital of the Red Urals, was seriously threatened by the approach of Czechoslovak bands and a counter-revolutionary conspiracy was discovered which had as its object the wresting of the ex-Czar from the hands of the council's authority. In view of this fact, the President of the Ural Regional Council decided to shoot the ex-Czar, and the decision was carried out on July 16.

"The wife and the son of Nicholas Romanoff have been sent to a place of security.

"Documents concerning the conspiracy which was discovered have been forwarded to Moscow by a special messenger. It had been recently decided to bring the ex-Czar before a tribunal to be tried for his crimes against the people, and only later occurrences led to delay in adopting this course.

"The Presidency of the Central Executive Committee, having discussed the circumstances which compelled the Ural Regional Council to take its decision to shoot Nicholas Romanoff, decided as follows:

"'The Russian Central Executive Committee, in the person of its President, accepts the decision of the Ural Regional Council as being regular.'

"The Central Executive Committee has now at its disposal extremely important documents concerning the affairs of Nicholas Romanoff—his diaries, which he kept almost up to his last days, the diaries of his wife and his children, and his correspondence, among which are the letters of Gregory Rasputin to the Romanoff family. These materials will be examined and published in the near future."

Execution Foreshadowed.

There have been rumors since June 24 that ex-Czar Nicholas of Russia had been assassinated. The first of these stated that he had been killed at Yekaterinburg by Red Guards. This report was denied later, but this denial was closely followed by a Geneva dispatch saying that Nicholas had been executed by the Bolsheviki after a trial at Yekaterinburg. This report seemed to be confirmed by advices to Washington from Stockholm.

The next report was what purported to be an intercepted wireless message from M. Tchitcherin, the Bolshevist Foreign Minister, in which it was stated that Nicholas was dead. Still another report was to the effect that he had been bayonetted by a guard while being taken from Yekaterinburg to Perm. Of all these reports there was no direct confirmation.

There seemingly is no question that

Continued on Page Eight.

Germans Try to Excuse Retreat Over the Marne

AMSTERDAM, July 20.—A semi-official statement received here from Berlin says the German Supreme Army Command had several aims in its attack on the southern bank of the Marne, the crossing of which river, it asserts, was unobserved by the Entente Allies. The statement goes so far as to claim that the German objectives have been fully attained.

The first aims of the Marne crossing, the semi-official statement says, were to broaden the basis of attack for a German blow on both sides of Rheims and to attack and to hold strong enemy forces. Furthermore, the attack on the southern bank of the Marne, which was so menacing for the Entente, the statement adds, finally unloosed the long-expected French counteroffensive.

After urging that the counteroffensive has miscarried because a break through has been prevented, the message naively adds:

"The task of the German troops fighting on the southern bank of the Marne was thereby entirely fulfilled and the further holding of the lines there was unnecessary. The German command could now withdraw the troops to the northern bank for fresh important tasks."

270,000 AMERICANS IN COUNTERBLOW

Also Rainbow Troops and Negro Regiment Are Fighting East of Rheims.

SEVEN DIVISIONS ENGAGED

General March Says 1,200,000 of Our Men Are Now in Europe or on the Atlantic.

Special to The New York Times.

WASHINGTON, July 20.—Seven divisions and one separate regiment of American troops participated, and are participating, in the great counteroffensive between Chateau-Thierry and Soissons and in the resistance to the German onslaught in the Champagne. The 42d, or Rainbow, Division, composed of National Guard troops from twenty-six States and the District of Columbia, including the New York 69th Infantry, now designated as the 165th Infantry, took part in the fighting in the Champagne east of Rheims.

The six other divisions were associated with the French in the counteroffensive between Château-Thierry and Soissons. These divisions are the 1st, 2d, 3d, and 4th of the regular army, the 26th National Guard Division, composed of troops from the six New England States, and the 28th, composed of the Pennsylvania National Guard. Marines are included in this number.

The separate regiment that has been fighting in the Champagne has not been identified at the War Department. It is a negro unit attached to the new 93d Division, which is composed entirely of negro troops. It may be the former 15th New York, now the 369th National Army Regiment, commanded by Colonel William Hayward, formerly Chairman of the New York City Public Service Commission.

1,200,000 Sent Abroad.

The identity of the divisions engaged in the great battle that has been raging west and east of Rheims was disclosed today by General Peyton C. March, Chief of the Army General Staff, in his weekly oral review to newspaper men of military operations in Europe. General March also imparted the information that more than 1,200,000 American troops were in Europe or on their way across the Atlantic. On July 8 President Wilson announced that up to June 30 we had sent overseas 1,019,000 men of all branches of the military service.

General March disclosed in answer to a question that the 77th National Army Division, composed mainly of troops from New York State and which was trained at Camp Upton, Yaphank, L. I., was "in the line near Lunevill and is operating as a division, complete under its own commander." Luneville is in French Lorraine, far down to the southern end of the long battlefront and many miles from the scene of the present conflict around Rheims. The Rainbow Division was employed in this area before its recent transfer to the active sector east of Rheims. Announcement was made last Saturday by General March that the 77th Division was now commanded by Major Gen. George B. Duncan.

The approximate number of American troops engaged in the heavy fighting this week west and east of Rheims is easily ascertainable from an estimate furnished by General March as to the average strength of an American army division. If a division was complete in the current fighting, he said, its

Continued on Page Eight.

FIERCE FIGHTING YESTERDAY

Our Men in a Severe Struggle With the German Reserves.

SUCCESS AS SHOCK TROOPS

Americans, Previously Untried, More Than a Match for the Kaiser's Best.

OVER 6,000 PRISONERS NOW

German Machine Guns Firing Explosive Bullets at Our Men.

By EDWIN L. JAMES.

Copyright, 1918, by The New York Times Company.
Special Cable to THE NEW YORK TIMES.

WITH THE AMERICAN ARMY, July 20.—On the bloody battlefield south of Soissons the American soldiers, along with their comrades of the allied arms, today were matching their strength with the best German warriors.

No one says yet how the battle goes because no one knows yet. We have gained and gained, but the struggle grows in fierceness as both sides threw fresh troops into the maelstrom of death and dust and flying shells out of which may come a result that will have much to do with the end of the war.

The German offensive of July 15 is now turned into a German defensive. Forced back by French and American troops at the start, it was to be expected that when the German high command hurled their shock troops against the French and Americans the progress after the first day would not be so rapid.

Our Men as Shock Troops.

Out of the storm where allied determination, leavened with the new spirit of Americanism, met the famed war machine of the German autocracy has already come one conclusion that augurs well for an allied victory. That is that the backbone of the United States fighting man is a stiff proposition for the Kaiser's warriors.

All the armies class as their best fighters their shock troops. This was a job of shock troops, performed by the Americans, and they have made good.

It was not the brilliant advance of the first day, good as it was, that told the story of the grit of Uncle Sam's fighting lads. It was not the furthest advance that told the real story. That came yesterday, when the new American attacks east of Vierzy and northeast of Chaudon met the German shock troops.

The fighting men were trained for more than a month by Ludendorff to take part in the offensive for Epernay and Châlons. Fresh and in the best of condition and on their tiptoes they were met by our men, who already had been fighting thirty hours.

Then the Germans tried to turn our attack into an advance for themselves. They failed.

Holding Their Gains.

Holding against a murderous machine gun fire, against bombs and bullets from hostile aircraft, against the unquestioned force of the German shock troops, the youthful Americans with their French comrades stood firm, and are so standing as this is written.

The full story of the fast and furious battle cannot yet be told. Word comes one minute that the Germans have a village, and ten minutes later another word comes that the Americans have that village.

Up the roads go trucks of ammunition and down the roads come the ambulances. German shells come groaning over, and in reply one hears a crescendo, oft repeated, which tells that bottled destruction is on its way from the American side.

Down the roads from the front come every now and then a big truckload of slightly wounded Americans, all angry to have been put out of the fight.

The truck halts. A stocky American lad, caked with dust, and with two bullet wounds through the shoulder, asks me for a cigarette, and I ask him what he thinks of it.

"I'll tell you," said he. "I was never in a battle before, and felt kind of squeamish a couple of hours before. I felt squeamish when I went over the top, but as soon as the real fighting started I forgot to be squeamish, and went on until the boche machine gunner got me. Honest to God, I had rather fight than eat now. I hope the 'doc' lets me back soon."

This lad was a coal miner eight months ago.

The Americans started their second attack at 5 o'clock yesterday morning. They had reached their objectives, a varying number of kilometers eastward, and were consolidating their positions when the shock troops struck them about noon.

Then began the battle, which is still going on with the fiercest struggles.

Against one American unit two German shock divisions were hurled. Against another came the famous Prussian Guards.

The Germans had machine guns mounted on wheels, and had rolled them to the edge of the woods. These guns shot explosive bullets, which are the latest piece of barbarity the German has invented.

One story was told by all the wounded whom I talked with, and that was the great number of machine guns the Germans have. This now appears to be the favorite weapon of the Germans against Americans.

Our Huge Bag of Prisoners.

There is one feature of the battle which stands out—the number of prisoners taken by the Americans. The number placed to our credit south of Soissons is now something more than 6,000.

Two regiments have officially booked more than 2,800 German captives, including sixty-six officers.

Coming down the wooded hill I saw a sight that made me think I had run into the German Army, but when I came near I found only a corral of Germans taken by Americans. There were more than 3,000 in a barbed wire cage, and the dirtiest lot of humans I ever saw, with the exception of the Colonel and some of the officers. There they stood, sat, and squatted in the sunlight. The French officer told me they were the most unclean lot of men he had seen during the war.

These prisoners were mostly holding troops, caught in the French-American surprise, and not belonging to the crack German troops. Unshaven and unkempt in every way, they looked like beasts.

The officers captured were entirely different. The Colonel was of the most natty sort, glistening with many decorations. A Captain with whom I talked used to be a business man with an office in Manhattan and a home in New Jersey. He gave it as his opinion that the war would never end in a military victory, but in bankruptcy for one side or the other. He remarked:

"I am thinking of Germany. I am almost sure the Kaiser cannot win a complete military victory, but nothing is left now but to fight on in the hope of a favorable settlement by negotiation, for if we stop now the taxes will be so heavy for Germany that no one can live. We must fight on until the Allies pay us."

I noticed that all the German gas masks on the shock troops were equipped with a new attachment against the new allied gases.

This large number of captives gives reply to the lie that the American troops take no prisoners.

Clark Williams a Worker.

This is the time to pay tribute to an American, Clark Williams, of New York, former Banking Commissioner. In the shade of a noble old château lay a yardful of American wounded, waiting for attention by the surgeons. There were slightly wounded and seriously wounded, happy wounded and discouraged wounded, and hungry wounded. There I found Mr. Williams representing the Red Cross. He had spent the night getting out from Paris five tons of food, and then sent the trucks back for surgical material. He was directing the helpers to feed the half-famished fighting lads, and was himself carrying cans of bouillon around. His pockets were filled with cigarettes and under his arms were packages of prunes. He was truly a working man.

The army surgeon in charge of the hospital asked that public thanks be given to the American Red Cross and Mr. Williams, whose aid had been invaluable.

I spent yesterday back of the fighting line, in territory that had been German the day before. I had seen some scenes of destruction in France, but these scenes were worse. On one road, for three miles, al the trees had been hit by shells and most of them were cut down.

Here is a village with not a building left standing. Here is another with an untouched church steeple, the only whole thing there. Here American and French shells fell when the attack started, and the German shells had hit as well. Caught between the millstones of war, this strip of country was ground to ruin. The shell holes are

Continued on Page Two.

Official Reports of the Day's Operations

French

PARIS, July 20.

Night Report.—We have not had long to wait for the result of our victorious counteroffensive. The Germans, violently attacked on their right flank and south of the Marne, have been compelled to retreat and recross the river.

We hold the whole south bank of the Marne.

Between the Aisne and the Marne Franco-American troops continue to progress and have driven back the enemy, who is resisting stubbornly.

We have reached Ploisy and Parcy-Tigny and have passed beyond St. Remy-Blanzy and Rozet-St. Albin.

Further south we hold the general line of the Priez Plateau, northeast of Courchamps.

The number of prisoners we have taken since July 18 exceeds 20,000. Over 400 guns have been captured.

Between the Marne and Rheims violent combats continue. Franco-British troops, attacking vigorously, encountered large forces. Notwithstanding the enemy's desperate resistance, we gained ground in Courton Wood, the Ardre Valley, and in the direction of St. Euphraise.

Day Report.—Yesterday and last night French and American troops continued their advance over the greater part of the front between the Aisne and the Marne.

Vierzy has been reached and the troops have gone beyond Mauloy Wood, east of Villers-Helon, and conquered Neuilly-St. Front and Licy-Clignon.

South of the Marne our troops have driven back the Germans between Fossoy and Oeuilly and have gained ground toward the Marne.

German

BERLIN, July 20, (via London.)

Day Report.—The activity of the British increased in isolated sectors toward Meteren. They obtained a footing in Meteren, but otherwise their repulse left prisoners in our hands.

Between the Aisne and the Marne the battle continues. Again the enemy started an attack with a view to a breach on the whole front. Tanks penetrated early in the morning into parts of our foremost lines. After a desperate struggle the first enemy thrust had been defeated toward noon on the heights southwest of Soissons, west of Hartennes-St. Neuilly and northwest of Château-Thierry.

Between the Aisne and the Ourcq an attack broke down under our counterthrusts, and to the south of the Ourcq mostly by our fire. North of Hartennes we threw back the enemy beyond the original line. Our troops report the heaviest enemy losses. A large number of tanks were demolished before our front.

South of the Marne there was moderate firing activity during the day. Southeast of Mareuil enemy partial attacks were repulsed.

During the night our troops south of the Marne were withdrawn to the north bank of the river without being noticed by the enemy.

Northwest of Souain French advances were sanguinarily repulsed.

Yesterday again thirty enemy airplanes and seven captive balloons were shot down.

BERLIN ADMITS RETREAT

Says Troops Withdrew Without Being Noticed By the Enemy.

HAD TO RETIRE, SAYS PARIS

Violent Attacks Were Made South of River and Also North—British Aiding Here.

BIG THRUST ON THE OURCQ

French-American Forces Push Ahead Most in Centre—Command Soissons Bridges.

LONDON, July 20.—The German offensive has been broken and the Crown Prince's troops have been thrown back across the Marne River.

The Franco-Americans fighting on the Soissons-Château-Thierry front, up to noon today, had made an average gain of a mile, and an extreme advance, in the centre, of three miles.

The complete collapse of operations south of the Marne, which had previously witnessed a great and decisive defeat of the German invaders early in the war, was announced laconically by a Reuter correspondent at French Headquarters in a dispatch, timed this evening, which said:

"No Germans remain south of the Marne except prisoners and dead."

Official communications from the Paris and Berlin War Offices quickly confirmed the withdrawal, the imminence of which had been indicated by earlier dispatches from correspondents at the front.

These told how the Germans south of the river had suffered a repulse at the hands of the Allies and were retreating toward the river, with French and American troops on their heels. Capture of the Bois de Misy and Port-à-Binsone (one and one-half miles west of Oeuilly) was announced early.

German Version of Retreat.

The day bulletin from the German headquarters, in announcing the retirement, says:

"South of the Marne there was moderate firing activity during the day. Southeast of Mareuil enemy partial attacks were repulsed.

"During the night our troops south of the Marne were withdrawn to the north bank of the river without being noticed by the enemy."

The German communication insists that allied thrusts southwest of Soissons and southward along the Aisne-Marne front were repulsed, with heavy losses.

The French official bulletin says that the enemy was compelled to retire from below the Marne by the violent attacks of the allied forces. Its statement concerning the operations in that area reads:

"We have not had long to wait for the result of our victorious counteroffensive.

"The Germans, violently attacked on their right flank and south of the Marne, have been compelled to retreat and recross the river. We hold the whole south bank of the Marne."

The Paris bulletin also reveals that British troops are in action with the French on the front between the Marne and Rheims. Here vigorous attacks were made by the allied forces in co-operation with the drive south of the river, and important ground was gained in the region along the Ardre.

Continuation of the French and American advance between the Aisne and the Marne is chronicled.

Since and including Thursday the allied troops have captured more

"All the News That's Fit to Print."

The New York Times.

THE WEATHER
Cloudy today; local showers; Tuesday fair; moderate south winds.
For full weather report see Page 15.

VOL. LXVII...NO. 22,150. NEW YORK, MONDAY, SEPTEMBER 16, 1918.—TWENTY PAGES. TWO CENTS Metropolitan District 50 Mile Radius. | THREE CENTS Within 200 Miles. | FOUR CENTS Elsewhere.

AUSTRIA APPEALS FOR A GENERAL PEACE, GERMANY FOLLOWS WITH OFFER TO BELGIUM; AMERICANS ADVANCE ON A 33-MILE FRONT

OUR AVERAGE GAIN 3 MILES

Guns of Metz Forts Now in Action Against Our Line.

PERSHING WINS ON MOSELLE

Captures Villages of Norroy and Vilcey—Total of Guns Taken Is 200.

GERMANS BEGIN DIGGING IN

Apparently Planning to Protect Railroads to Metz, Which Are Under Our Fire.

A "Magnificent Victory," Foch's Word to Pershing

By EDWIN L. JAMES.
Special Cable to THE NEW YORK TIMES.

WITH THE AMERICAN ARMY IN FRANCE, Sept. 15.—General Pershing has received from the allied Generalissimo the following message:

My Dear General:

The 1st American Army, under your command, on this first day won a magnificent victory by a manoeuvre as skillfully prepared as it was gallantly executed.

I extend to you, as well as to the officers and troops under your command, my warmest compliments.

MARSHAL FOCH.

LONDON, Sept. 15. — General Pershing's army is making fine progress. This afternoon it had advanced two to three miles on a thirty-three-mile front since yesterday afternoon, and the fortress guns of Metz have come into action against it.

American patrols are advancing at various points a couple of miles beyond the general advance.

The enemy appears to be withdrawing to some line which will protect the railway communications in the vicinity of Metz, which at present are under the long-range gunfire of the Americans.

The American line at noon today ran through Norroy, on the Moselle, Haumont, Doncourt and to Abaucourt [on the Verdun-Etain road] on the old line.

It has been discovered that there were six German divisions operating in the St. Mihiel salient. That would give a total strength of 60,000 men, or a rifle strength of 36,000. The Germans had broken up for them two more divisions in this action, thus reducing their strength in the west to 191 divisions, plus four Austrian divisions and some dismounted cavalry.

An unofficial report from the American front on the Moselle says that American patrols are approaching Pagny, on the west bank of that river.

German Defense Is Weak.

WITH THE AMERICAN ARMY IN LORRAINE, Sept. 15, (Associated Press.)—The advance of the victorious First Army continued today, but on a restricted front near the Moselle River. There was little opposition on the whole.

In the edge of a wood where the Germans had concentrated some [illegible] machine-gun resistance was [illegible], but a smashing artillery fire [illegible] the enemy. A few additional [illegible] were taken.

The Germans gave further evidence today that they intended to [illegible] on that part of the Hindenburg line running through this section. A detachment was digging in [illegible] about Dommartin [four and a [illegible] miles north of Thiaucourt], while [illegible] La Chaussée [two and a half

Continued on Page Six.

Austria's Statement and Her Note to the Powers

AMSTERDAM, Sept. 15, (by Associated Press.)—The official communication of the Austro-Hungarian Government and the text of its note to belligerent and neutral powers, suggesting a meeting for a preliminary and non-binding discussion of war aims, with a view to the possible calling of a peace conference, are as follows:

The Communication:

An objective and conscientious examination of the situation of all the belligerent States no longer leaves doubt that all peoples, on whatever side they may be fighting, long for a speedy end to the bloody struggle. Despite this natural and comprehensible desire for peace, it has not so far been possible to create those preliminary conditions calculated to bring the peace efforts nearer to realization and bridge the gap which at present still separates the belligerents from one another.

A more effective means must therefore be considered whereby the responsible factors of all the countries can be offered an opportunity to investigate the present possibilities of an understanding.

The first step which Austria-Hungary, in accord with her allies, undertook on Dec. 12, 1916, for the bringing about of peace did not lead to the end hoped for.

The grounds for this lay assuredly in the situation at that time. In order to maintain in their peoples the war spirit, which was steadily declining, the allied Governments had by the most severe means suppressed even any discussion of the peace idea. And so it came about that the ground for a peace understanding was not properly prepared. The natural transition from the wildest war agitation to a condition of conciliation was lacking.

It would, however, be wrong to believe that the peace step we then took was entirely without result. Its fruits consist of something which is not to be overlooked—that the peace question has not since vanished from the order of the day. The discussions which have been carried on before the tribunal of public opinion have disclosed proof of the not slight differences which today still separate the warring powers in their conception of peace conditions.

Nevertheless an atmosphere has been created which no longer excludes the discussion of the peace problem.

Without optimism, it at least assuredly may be deduced from the utterances of responsible statesmen that the desire to reach an understanding and not to decide the war exclusively by force of arms is also gradually beginning to penetrate into allied States save for some exceptions in the case of blinded war agitators, which are certainly not to be estimated lightly.

The Austro-Hungarian Government is aware that after the deep-reaching convulsions which have been caused in the life of the peoples by the devastating effects of the world war it will not be possible to re-establish order in the tottering world at a single stroke. The path that leads to the restoration of peaceful relations between the peoples is cut by hatred and embitterment. It is toilsome and wearisome, yet it is our duty to tread this path—the path of negotiation—and if there are still such responsible factors as desire to overcome the opponent by military means and to force the will to victory upon him, there can, nevertheless, no longer be doubt that this aim, even assuming that it is attainable, would first necessitate a further sanguinary and protracted struggle.

But even a later victorious peace will no longer be able to make good the consequences of such a policy—consequences which will be fatal to all the States and peoples of Europe. The only peace which could righteously adjust the still divergent conceptions of the opponents would be a peace desired by all the peoples. With this consciousness, and in its unswerving endeavor to work in the interests of peace, the Austro-Hungarian Government now again comes forward with a suggestion with the object of bringing about a direct discussion between the enemy powers.

The earnest will to peace of wide classes of the population of all the States who are jointly suffering through the war—the indisputable rapprochement in individual controversial questions—as well as the more conciliatory atmosphere that is general, seem to the Austro-Hungarian Government to give a certain guarantee that a fresh step in the interests of peace, which also takes account of past experiences in this domain, might at the present moment offer the possibility of success.

The Austro-Hungarian Government has therefore resolved to point out to all the belligerents, friend and foe, a path considered practicable by it, and to propose to them jointly to examine in a free exchange of views whether those prerequisites exist which would make the speedy inauguration of peace negotiations appear promising. To this end the Austro-Hungarian Government has today invited the Governments of all the belligerent States to a confidential and unbinding discussion at a neutral meeting place, and has addressed to them a note drawn up in this sense.

This step has been brought to the knowledge of the Holy See in a special note, and an appeal thereby made to the Pope's interest in peace. Furthermore, the Governments of the neutral States have been acquainted with the step taken.

The constant close accord which exists between the four allied powers warrants the assumption that the allies of Austria-Hungary, to whom the proposal is being sent in the same manner, share the views developed in the note.

[The official telegram proceeds to say that the note has been drawn up in French, and runs as follows:]

Text of the Note to the Powers:

The peace offer which the Powers of the Quadruple Alliance addressed to their opponents on Dec. 12, 1916, and the conciliatory basic ideas of which they have never given up, signifies, despite the rejection which it experienced, an important stage in the history of this war. In contrast to the first two and a half war years, the question of peace has from that moment been the centre of European, aye, of world discussion, and dominates it in ever increasing measure.

Almost all the belligerent States have in turn again and again expressed themselves on the question of peace, its prerequisites and conditions. The line of development of this discussion, however, has not been uniform and steady. The basic standpoint changed under the influence of the military and political position, and hitherto, at any rate, it has not led to a tangible general result that could be utilized.

It is true that, independent of all these oscillations, it can be stated that the distance between the conceptions of the two sides has, on the whole, grown somewhat less; that despite the indisputable continuance of decided and hitherto unbridged differences, a partial turning from many of the most extreme concrete war aims is visible and a certain agreement upon the relative general basic principles of a world peace manifests itself. In both camps there is undoubtedly observable in wide classes of the population a growth of the will to peace and understanding. Moreover, a comparison of the reception of the peace proposal of the Powers of the Quadruple Alliance on the part of their opponents with the later utterances of responsible statesmen of the latter, as well as of the non-responsible but, in a political respect, nowise uninfluential personalities, confirms this impression.

While, for example, the reply of the Allies to President Wilson made demands which amounted to the dismemberment of Austria-Hungary, to a diminution and a deep internal transformation of the German Empire, and the destruction of Turkish European ownership, these demands, the realization of which was based on the supposition of an overwhelming victory, were later modified in many declarations from official Entente quarters, or in part were dropped.

Thus, in a declaration made in the British House of Commons a year ago, Secretary Balfour expressly recognized that Austria-Hungary must itself solve its internal problems, and that none could impose a Constitution upon Germany from the outside. Premier Lloyd George declared at the beginning of this year that it was not one of the Allies' war aims to partition Austria-Hungary, to rob the Ottoman Empire of its Turkish provinces, or to reform Germany internally. It may also be considered symptomatic that in December, 1917, Mr. Balfour categorically repudiated the assumption that British policy had ever engaged itself for the creation of an independent State out of the territories on the left bank of the Rhine.

The Central Powers leave it in no doubt that they are only waging a war of defense for the integrity and the security of their territories.

Far more outspoken than in the domain of concrete war aims has the rapprochement of conceptions proceeded regarding those guiding lines upon the basis of which peace shall be concluded and the future order of Europe and the world built up. In this direction President Wilson in his speeches of Feb. 12 and July 4 of this year has formulated principles which have not encountered contradiction on the part of his allies, and the far-reaching application of which is likely to meet with no objection on the part of the Powers of the Quadruple Alliance also, presupposing that this application is general and reconcilable with the vital interests of the States concerned.

It is true it must be remembered that an agreement on general principles is insufficient, but that there remains the further matter of reaching an accord upon their interpretation and their application to individual concrete war and peace questions.

To an unprejudiced observer there can be no doubt that in all the belligerent States, without exception, the desire for a peace of understanding has been enormously strengthened; that the conviction is increasingly spreading that the further continuance of the bloody struggle must transform Europe into ruins and into a state of exhaustion that will mar its development for decades to come, and this without any guarantee of thereby bringing about that decision by arms which has been vainly striven after by both sides in four years filled with enormous sacrifices, sufferings, and exertions.

In what manner, however, can the way be paved for an understanding, and an understanding finally attained? Is there any serious prospect whatever of reaching this aim by continuing the discussion of the peace problem in the way hitherto followed?

We have not the courage to answer the latter question in the affirmative. The discussion from one public tribune to another, as has hitherto taken place between statesmen of the various countries, was really only a series of monologues. It lacked, above everything, directness. Speech and counterspeech did not fit into each other. The speakers spoke over one another's heads.

On the other hand, it was the publicity and the ground of these discussions which robbed them of the possibility of fruitful progress. In all public statements of this nature a form of eloquence is used which reckons with the effect at great distances and on the masses. Consciously or unconsciously, however, one thereby increases the distance of the opponents' conception, produces misunderstandings which take root and are not removed, and makes the frank exchange of ideas more difficult. Every pronouncement of leading statesmen is, directly after its delivery and before the authoritative quarters of the opposite side can reply to it, made the subject of passionate or exaggerated discussion of irresponsible elements.

But anxiety lest they should endanger the interests of their arms by unfavorably influencing feeling at home, and lest they prematurely betray their own ultimate intentions, also causes the responsible statesmen themselves to strike a higher tone and stubbornly to adhere to extreme standpoints.

If, therefore, an attempt is made to see whether the basis exists for an understanding calculated to deliver Europe from the catastrophe of the suicidal continuation of the struggle, then, in any case, another method should be chosen which renders possible a direct, verbal discussion between the representatives of the Governments, and only between them. The opposing conceptions of individual belligerent States would likewise have to form the subject of such a discussion, for mutual enlightenment, as well as the general principles that shall serve as the basis for peace and the future relations of the States to one another, and regarding which, in the first place, an accord can be sought with a prospect of success.

As soon as an agreement were reached on the fundamental principles, an attempt would have to be made in the course of the discussions concretely to apply them to individual peace questions, and thereby bring about their solution.

We venture to hope that there will be no objection on the part of any belligerents to such an exchange of views. The war activities would experience no interruption. The discussions, too, would only go so far as was considered by the participants to offer a prospect of success. No disadvantages would arise therefrom for the States represented. Far from harming, such an exchange of views could only be useful to the cause of peace.

What did not succeed the first time can be repeated, and perhaps it has already at least contributed to the clarification of views. Mountains of old misunderstandings might be removed and many new things perceived. Streams of pent-up human kindness would be released, in the warmth of which everything essential would remain, and, on the other hand, much that is antagonistic, to which excessive importance is still attributed, would disappear.

According to our conviction, all the belligerents jointly owe to humanity to examine whether now, after so many years of a costly but undecided struggle, the entire course of which points to an understanding, it is possible to make an end to the terrible grapple.

The Royal and Imperial Government would like, therefore, to propose to the Governments of all the belligerent States to send delegates to a confidential and unbinding discussion on the basic principles for the conclusion of peace, in a place in a neutral country and at a near date that would yet have to be agreed upon—delegates who were charged to make known to one another the conception of their Governments regarding those principles and to receive analogous communications, as well as to request and give frank and candid explanations on all those points which need to be precisely defined.

The Royal and Imperial Government has the honor to request the Government of ——; through the kind mediation of your Excellency, to bring this communication to the knowledge of the Government of ——.

[The names of the intermediary Government and of that addressed in the particular note dispatched are left blank.]

Teutonic Allies Agreed Austria Should Make a Bid for Peace

Kaiser Karl's Government Forced Germany to Consent at Recent Headquarters Conclave—Appeal to Catch Entente Pacifists and, Through Rejection, to Silence Cry at Home for Peace.

By GEORGE RENWICK.
Copyright, 1918, by The New York Times Company.
Special Cable to THE NEW YORK TIMES.

AMSTERDAM, Sept. 15.—The Austrian proposal for a peace conference, as I have good grounds for knowing, was first seriously considered at the recent imposing meeting at German headquarters. In fact, it is now quite clear that it was the only subject discussed at any length during the gathering.

So insistent was the Austrian demand that such a step should be taken that the German Government had to give rather unwilling consent. In doing so, according to my information, it acted in the hope that such a move might have a certain influence on Entente pacifists, whom the German Government persists in believing to be a very much stronger force than they really are.

It was thought, too, that the proposal might be not without effect in the event of a British general election, but, above all, that the German powers that be consented largely because of the renewed cry of peace. An offer mockingly rejected would be highly valuable at home.

Opposed by Military Men.

It is beyond all doubt that the German military authorities and the German Government do not want any such conference as Austria-Hungary suggests. I say the German Government without reservation because von Payer's speech clearly demonstrates that despite some advances there are no elements in the administration inclined or bold enough to break sufficiently away from Pan Germanism to make negotiations remotely posible for the Entente.

Much which I have recently reported regarding the state of affairs in

Continued on Page Two.

Germany Wants Belgium to Help Her Obtain the Return of Her Colonies

Proposes That Kingdom, Its Economic and Political Independence Restored, Shall Be Neutral—Germany Through Finland Also Offers Not to Invade Karelia if Allies Will Quit Murman Coast.

LONDON, Sept. 15.—Germany has made a definite peace offer to Belgium, according to information received here. The terms of this proposal are as follows:

That Belgium shall remain neutral until the end of the war.

That thereafter the entire economic and political independence of Belgium shall be reconstituted.

That the pre-war commercial treaties between Germany and Belgium shall again be put into operation after the war for an indefinite period.

That Belgium shall use her good offices to secure the return of the German colonies.

That the Flemish question shall be considered and the Flemish minority, which aided the German invaders, shall not be penalized.

The proposal contains no word respecting reparation or indemnities, no admission that Germany wronged Belgium.

It is understood that the Government has received the Austro-Hungarian peace note, and also a proposal that all the powers should withdraw their troops from the Murman territory.

Copyright, 1918, by The New York Times Company.
Special Cable to THE NEW YORK TIMES.

LONDON, Sept. 15.—It is not only toward Belgium that German secret diplomacy has been stretching out its tentacles in the hope of catching and breaking some of the strands of the Entente. Definite information of one other offer which will be made public in due time has reached THE NEW YORK TIMES.

These backstairs efforts, which in the main are chiefly concerned with exchanging "pawns" which Germany holds for colonial possessions whence Kaiserdom can draw raw material after the war, afford some indication of the uses to which Germany would put the confidential conference asked

Continued on Page Two.

London Regards the Proposals as Insincere Manoeuvers by Foe

Austrian Plea Will Be Considered, It Is Thought—If Reply Is Sent, Wilson May Be Spokesman—No Peace Requirements Met, It Is Held.

Copyright, 1918, by The New York Times Company.
Special Cable to THE NEW YORK TIMES.

LONDON, Sept. 15.—It is stated here that Austria's invitation to preliminary unbinding peace discussions will receive the full consideration of the allied Governments. This statement may be taken to mean nothing more than it literally says. Whatever form it may be decided by the allied Governments, who will act as one in accordance with the stipulations of the pact of London, to give to the reply, or whether any reply will be made by the Entente powers, individually or unitedly, cannot, of course, be yet stated, for there has been no time for consultation, but it is suggested that probabilities are that the Entente powers will simply notify the Austrian Government that they have taken notice of the proposals made and leave it at that.

Another suggestion is that President Wilson, whose expression of the Allies' policy has won universal admiration, will again act as spokesman of all the powers arrayed against Austria-Hungary and her confederates. In some quarters it is believed that Lloyd George had foreknowledge of the Austrian move, and that his speech at Manchester, in which he said victory was essential to a sound peace, sounded the note on which allied consideration of the Austrian note will be pitched.

The first impression today was that acceptance of Austria's invitation could have but one of two results, either it would prolong the war or it would lead toward an unsatisfactory peace, in which would be found the germs of future wars.

The Austrian proposals meet none of the requirements which British statesmen have laid down as essential preliminaries to peace discussions. It is also held here that they omit to take into consideration the vital point that President Wilson has laid down certain

Continued on Page Two.

WASHINGTON IS HOSTILE

Feeling There that 'Force Without Stint' Should Answer Foe's Offer.

OFFICIALS AWAIT TEXT

White House Comment Withheld, but It Is Believed Overture Will Be Rejected.

FORMAL REPLY TO BE MADE

President Will Act After Full Consideration and Conference with Allies.

Special to The New York Times.

WASHINGTON, Sept. 15.—The feeling in Washington tonight is that "force without stint" until victory is achieved and a rejection of the overture will be the American Government's response to the Austro-Hungarian Government's invitation to all the belligerent powers to send delegates to some neutral meeting place to enter into nonbinding discussions with a view to peace.

Official comment on the Austrian communication was withheld tonight pending the official receipt of the message, which is probably being forwarded through the courtesy of the Swedish Government. But the unofficial text of the note reached Washington through news channels tonight, and after its contents had become known the most careful canvass of the situation failed to detect any disposition on the part of the Washington Government to accept the invitation to enter at this time such a conference as has been proposed by the Vienna Government.

Secretary Lansing declined to comment on the note, and, in the absence of the official text or of an exchange of views with our allies, no statement, naturally, was forthcoming for publication from the White House.

Note Will Be Answered.

There is no disposition to deal cavalierly with the communication from the Austrian Government. It will receive the same careful consideration that has been accorded by President Wilson and Secretary Lansing to the earlier peace overtures made by the German and Austrian Governments.

The communication is of a character that calls for a response, and there will be a reply. How that answer will be given remains to be determined after the Washington Government has had full opportunity to exchange views with its allies.

The substantially unanimous view of Congressional leaders, regardless of party affiliations, is that this is not the time to enter into peace discussions with the Central Powers. They feel that the tide of battle turned when the Germans were turned back from the Marne at Château-Thierry; that the initiative gained by the allied forces under the masterly leadership of Marshal Foch will be retained, and that the achievements of General Pershing's forces, as well as the victories of the British, French, and Italians, assure a victorious ending of the war on such terms as the Allies are disposed to grant.

The Administration attitude toward the continuation of the war toward a victorious end was voiced by General March in his talk with the Washington newspaper correspondents yesterday, by Secretary Tumulty the day before in his letter to Chairman Hays of the Republican National Committee, and ever since the President's milestone speech at Baltimore last Spring, in which he declared it to be the purpose to fight Germany with "force without stint." The President himself has emphasized and driven home the idea that this war is one of emancipation, and should be continued until it has been conclusively won.

No Inconclusive Peace.

"The President's war aims," said Mr. Tumulty in his letter to Chairman Hays on Sept. 12, a letter read by President Wilson before it was dispatched, "have been made the aims of all the nations fighting against the German Government. These aims have been stated unequivocally by the President upon a number of occasions since the war began. Not merely the American people, but all the world is familiar with these aims,

"All the News That's Fit to Print."

The New York Times.

THE WEATHER
Fair, slightly cooler today; tomorrow, fair; moderate south winds.
For weather report see next to last page.

VOL. LXVIII...NO. 22,193. NEW YORK, TUESDAY, OCTOBER 29, 1918. TWENTY-TWO PAGES. TWO CENTS Metropolitan District 50 Mile Radius | THREE CENTS Within 200 Miles | FOUR CENTS Elsewhere

AUSTRIA 'ACCEPTS' ALL OF WILSON'S CONDITIONS, ASKS FOR IMMEDIATE AND SEPARATE PEACE; LONDON AND PARIS SAY GERMANY IS ISOLATED; ITALIANS AND BRITISH TAKE 9,000 AUSTRIANS

ROOSEVELT BITTER IN BEGINNING WAR ON THE PRESIDENT

Says President Puts Loyalty to Himself Before Loyalty to the Nation.

DENOUNCES WAR'S CONDUCT

"If We Had Prepared," He Declares, It Would Have Been Over in Ninety Days.

SEES NEED OF REPUBLICANS

Carnegie Hall Packed to Hear the Colonel's Speech at Rally for G. O. P. Candidates.

Speaking for more than two hours last night to a crowd that packed Carnegie Hall, Colonel Theodore Roosevelt bitterly assailed President Wilson and his conduct of the war. It was one of the longest speeches the Colonel ever [illegible] rally in support of the Republican State ticket, given under the auspices of the Republican Club and the County Committee of New York, it was in reality a call to the Republicans of the nation to fight to the last ditch to offset the President's appeal and to return an overwhelming Republican Congress at the election. The Colonel referred to the State situation, but merely in passing.

Mr. Roosevelt in his address made this reference to Mr. Wilson:

"He does not ask for loyalty to the Nation. He asks only for support of himself. There is not the slightest suggestion that he disapproves of disloyalty to the Nation. I do not doubt that he feels some disapproval of such disloyalty; but apparently this feeling on his part is so tepid that it slips from his mind when he contemplates what he regards as the far greater sin of failure in adherence to himself."

Altogether the Colonel spoke nearly 20,000 words. He had prepared his speech early last week, and had to add a long insert to deal specifically with the President's last Friday's appeal. There were other speakers, and all dealt largely with the President's appeal, but the Colonel was the main attraction. Besides the 5,000 or so within the hall, several thousand fought for admission and completely overwhelmed the police. Half a dozen speakers filled in the time till the Colonel arrived at 9:15 o'clock. His appearance on the stage was the signal for a great outburst of cheering. Fully one-half of the audience were women, and on the stage sat practically every Republican of prominence in the city and many from up-State.

Colonel Roosevelt's Speech.

After four minutes of cheering, yelling, and handclapping, the Colonel was allowed to start. In his speech he said:

"I come to this meeting as an American, and only as an American. In this crisis I do not consider politics at all whenever doing so conflicts in the slightest degree with the great cause of Americanism or with our immediate purpose of winning the war and of securing the peace of unconditional surrender by Germany. I make my appeal to all good Americans, in the name of Americanism, and I make it just as much to all independents and to all far-sighted, patriotic Democrats who are awake to the real needs of the situation as I do to Republicans.

"This meeting is held under peculiar circumstances. If the President of the United States is right in the appeal he has just made to the voters, then you and I, my hearers, have no right to vote at this election or to discuss public questions while the war lasts. If his appeal is justified, only that faction of the Democratic Party which accepts toward the President the rubber-stamp attitude of complete servility is entitled to control Congress; and no man who is a Republican, and no man whether a Republican or not who puts loyalty to the people ahead of loyalty to the servant of the people, is to have a voice in determining the greatest questions ever brought before this nation.

"In this election appeal which the President has issued to the voters of the country he states that he 'earnestly begs' the voters to return 'a Democratic majority to both the Senate and the House of Representatives,' and that although 'the leaders of the minority in the present Congress have unquestionably been pro-war, they have been anti-Administration,' and that 'the return of a Republican majority to either house of Congress would certainly be interpreted on the other side of the water as a repudiation of my (President Wilson's) leadership.'

"This is an extraordinary document. It is an emphatic repudiation and reversal of the President's announcement of a few months back that "poli-

Continued on Page Seven.

Senate Republicans Refuse to Take Recess at This Time

Special to The New York Times.

WASHINGTON, Oct. 28.—Republican leaders of the Senate today declined to agree to a resolution to adjourn Congress from tomorrow until Nov. 12. This disagreement was made in an informal talk which Senators Martin and Simmons had with Senators Lodge and Penrose. The latter held it was the duty of Congress to remain in session while peace overtures and other important matters were pending.

In expectation of an agreement by the Senate, the House passed a joint resolution, providing for adjournment. After the disagreement, Representative Kitchin asked for its reconsideration by the House and announced that Congress would remain in session unless the Senate should change its attitude Thursday, when the House meets again.

SENATE BATTLE OVER PRESIDENT

Wilson's Denial That His Peace Terms Look to Free Trade Read Into Record.

DEFENDED BY DEMOCRATS

[illegible] **Attack Both His Terms for Peace and Political Appeal.**

Special to The New York Times.

WASHINGTON, Oct. 28.—In a turbulent debate in the Senate today, inspired by President Wilson's call to the country for a return of a Democratic Congress, Republicans and Democrats hurled charges of partisanship at one another. Republican Senators bitterly attacked the President's appeal as an affront to loyal voters of their party.

President Wilson's allusion in his fourteen peace proposals to the "removal, as far as possible, of economic barriers and the establishment of trade conditions among all nations" after the war was attacked by Senators Brandegee of Connecticut and Penrose of Pennsylvania. They argued it would let down the bars to German commerce on an equality with that of the allied nations.

This assertion was denied by Senator Hitchcock of Nebraska, Chairman of the Foreign Relations Committee, who insisted that the President intended that the issue should be put up to the league of nations, so there would be no unjust discrimination against any signatory of the peace treaty.

Senator Hitchcock read into the record a letter he had received from President Wilson and one that Senator Simmons of North Carolina had received in response to letters of theirs in which the President had been informed of criticism by Republican leaders of his "economic barrier" proposal as tending to let down the barriers to Germany after the war.

The Senate debate, which raged for four hours, was precipitated by Senator Knox of Pennsylvania, who took up the President's appeal to the voters to elect a Democratic Congress. Senator Hitchcock replied to Mr. Knox and later Senator Pittman of Nevada vigorously attacked the Republican leaders in Congress, Colonel Roosevelt and Chairman Hays of the Republican National Committee, asserting that they were undermining the war policies of the President. Senator Poindexter of Washington wound up the debate for the Republicans with a vehement reply to Mr. Pittman, in which he insisted that the Republicans had supported the President, but that the President himself had been playing politics.

Prerogatives of Congress.

Mr. Knox insisted that the Senate's prerogative as the treaty-making body must not be usurped by the President.

"The excessive intermingling of the problem of a victorious ending of the war with a great variety of projects of world reconstruction renders our task most difficult," said Mr. Knox. "As a co-ordinate branch of this Government it is our duty, I believe, to make clear the Senate sense of the immediate necessity of clarification and simplification of any program that enters into the ending of the war or the building of the future, and the Senate's sense of the instant necessity of full counsel and accord upon all such programs between the Government of the United States and the Governments of our allies.

"And there is a necessity that underlies these needs. That is classification for the Senate itself of the policies to which it may be later called upon to consider giving its sanction. In this

Continued on Page Six.

NAMES CAILLAUX IN PLOT TO SPLIT ALLIES IN NEW WAR

Count James Minotto Confesses, Revealing Intrigue with Luxburg in Buenos Aires.

HE WAS THE GO-BETWEEN

Swift's Son-in law Says France, Italy, and Spain Were to Join the Teutons.

AGAINST BRITAIN AND RUSSIA

Confession Made Here to Deputy Attorney General Becker as Agent of French Republic.

Count James Minotto, the German nobleman who is a son-in-law of Louis F. Swift, the Chicago packer, and who, according to Secretary of the Navy Josephus Daniels, tried to get a place in the Naval Intelligence Service of this country, has made a startling [illegible] the American authorities [illegible] engaged in by Joseph [illegible] the former French Premier; Count Luxburg, former German Minister to the Argentine, and himself, to disrupt the Entente Alliance and to bring about a new war, in which the Teutonic powers, France, Italy, and Spain would be arrayed against Great Britain and Russia. The full report of the Minotto confession is now on the way to the French authorities in Paris.

Minotto, whose internment as an enemy alien was fought by his wife's family, who maintained that the Count was an Italian and an ally of the United States, was brought to New York last week from the internment prison near Fort Oglethorpe, Ga. He was taken before Deputy Attorney General Alfred L. Becker, who represented the French Government and the Federal authorities. At first, Minotto was not inclined to talk, but he finally told the story in all its details.

The Countess Minotto, mother of Count James, was, before her marriage, the famous German actress Agnes Sorma. Mme. Sorma will be remembered by old theatregoers as the star in Hauptmann's "Sunken Bell," which was played in German at the Irving Place Theatre some twenty years ago. The Countess and her husband are both in the United States at present. They went to Chicago last November to aid their son when he was fighting against the Government's order of internment.

Mr. Becker said last night that for the present he was not in a position to make public the full details of the confession made by Minotto. The story when told in full, he said, would be one of the most remarkable in the history of international intrigue and would show up Caillaux as a plotter compared to whom Bolo Pacha, was a mere novice. Bolo sought to corrupt French public opinion through the publication of a few newspapers. Caillaux on the other hand, sought to betray not only his own but two other nations as well, one of them Italy, an ally of France, and the other Spain, a friend of France. Had the plot succeeded, it was pointed

Continued on Last Page.

'Hold Fast' in This Grave Hour, Hindenburg Tells the Army

WITH THE AMERICAN ARMY NORTHWEST OF VERDUN, Oct. 28, (Associated Press.)—"Hold fast, an armistice has not yet been concluded," is the word sent to the German troops by Field Marshal von Hindenburg, Chief of the General Staff, according to a captured document now in the hands of the Americans. The German commander's appeal reads:

"German soldiers, be vigilant. The word 'armistice' is current in the trenches and camps, but we have not yet reached that point. To some the word represents a certainty, to others it is even a synonym of the peace so long desired. They believe that events no longer depend upon them. Their vigilance is relaxed, their courage and their endurance, as well as their spirit of defiance toward the enemy, are diminished.

"We have not yet reached our aim. The armistice has not been concluded. The war is still on—the same war as ever.

"Now, more than ever, you must be vigilant and hold fast. You are upon the enemy's soil, and on the soil of Alsace-Lorraine, the bulwark of our country. In this grave hour the Fatherland relies on you for its prosperity and for its safety."

FRENCH KEEP UP DRIVE BEYOND OISE

[illegible] **on the Whole Front to the Serre.**

GREATEST GAIN IS 2 MILES

They Have Crossed the Peron River, Capturing Many Villages in a Wide Area.

LONDON, Oct. 28.—While operations on the British front today have been limited to a slight advance of the lines south of Valenciennes, the French, continuing their pressure on the Germans between the Oise and the Serre, have thrown the enemy back about two miles at the apex of their attack, which was in the region of Bois-les-Pargny, east of the little River Peron, and have made substantial gains on either side.

French troops are in fresh contact with the enemy on the whole front between the Oise and Serre, and on the Aisne front, west of Château-Porcien, they have made an advance north of Herpy.

In Eastern Champagne American units in a brilliant local operation gained ground east of Attigny to a depth of about two-thirds of a mile.

French aviators on Sunday, flying over German back areas with 128 machines, effectively bombed enemy transport and troops. They reported many fires in the German-held parts of the Serre Valley and on the right bank of the Aisne.

The French operations of the day

Continued on Page Five.

Americans' Huge Guns Now Turned On Germans' Main Supply Railway

By EDWIN L. JAMES.

Copyright, 1918, by The New York Times Company.
Special Cable to THE NEW YORK TIMES.

WITH THE AMERICAN ARMY NORTHWEST OF VERDUN, Oct. 28.—American guns of large calibre have begun firing on the Longuyon-Sedan-Mezières Railroad, the most important German line of communication, with the object of interrupting traffic and ultimately breaking the line.

Thus the offensive of the American First Army begun Sept. 26 begins to achieve its objective. Our advance of some eighteen kilometers now makes possible the shelling of the German communication line to defend which the German command has made such enormous efforts in past weeks. Of course, the nearer we get to the line the greater is the number of guns which can be used against it. It is not permitted to give details about the big guns, but it may be said that they are among the largest that have been used in the war.

Brisk local fighting continued today on both sides of the Meuse. East of the river there were heavy contacts in the Bois de la Grand Montagne and in the vicinity of Bois Belleu. We took Belleu Wood for the fifth time yesterday afternoon, only to be later driven out again. We have now retaken it again, despite terrific German artillery fire.

Just west of the Meuse our patrols pushing forward found that the Germans had deserted Clery le Grand.

North of Grand Pré the Germans also withdrew from Bellejoyeuse Farm, which has changed hands eleven times in the last ten days. We sent patrols into the farm to have the Germans open heavy machine gun fire from dominating woods. They had evidently set a trap, expecting a large force of Americans to rush into the place.

We have not occupied the farm, which is under constant fire from the hills of Bourgogne Woods. The farm in turn had firing command of the valley to the south, which we hold.

Two new German divisions have been identified north of Verdun.

Due to weather conditions the aerial activities today were slight.

DOOM OF GERMANY SEEN

With Austria Gone, She Cannot Hold Out Long, London Believes.

ALLIES CAN HIT FROM SOUTH

Likely to Harden Terms and Demand Complete Surrender by Deserted Berlin.

PARIS SEES END VERY NEAR

Whole Edifice of Central Alliance Crumbling and Peace Must Come Quickly.

Copyright, 1918, by The New York Times Company.
Special Cable to THE NEW YORK TIMES.

LONDON, Oct. 28.—Suspicion, with which every German move, rightly or wrongly, is regarded here, is absent from the view taken of the Austrian position. While Germany wavers on the brink of surrender, it is said, Austria-Hungary has taken the [illegible]

The British Government has received a communication of Count Andrassy's unconditional acceptance of all the conditions upon which President Wilson made the entry into negotiations regarding armistice and peace dependent. Comparisons to the disadvantage of Germany and to the advantage of Austria-Hungary are made between the plain whole-heartedness of the Austro-Hungarian acceptance and the verbal trickeries which possibly exist in the guarded language of the German notes.

Austria-Hungary has followed Bulgaria in complete surrender, a fact which, it is pointed out, is very important, because it completes the isolation of Germany. Germany's reluctance to tread the same path is comprehensible, but that she will inevitably be forced to walk this Via Dolorosa is beyond doubt.

Although the terms of armistice to Austria-Hungary may not repeat in all respects the terms to Bulgaria, it is assumed that, in one case as in the other, provision will be made for the Allies to use the territory and railways of the surrendering country against any associate who continues the war.

Thus the Germans, if they decide on a war of defense, must be prepared to meet invasion of Germany from the Austrian side. They will find the whole Italian Army free to operate against them, while they themselves will lose the co-operation of the Austrian divisions on the west front. At the same time they will be cut in on from Rumania, and to a large extent from the Ukraine, and their supply problems will become insoluble. It is obvious that, without Austria-Hungary, Germany can only hold out for a strictly limited period, that all possibility of her improving her situation disappears, and that the only effect of further resistance on her part will be to render her still weaker after the war.

The action of Vienna in throwing up the sponge seems therefore the beginning of the end. The inevitable deduction is that Germany's claims to treat a purely military question, like the conditions of an armistice, on the basis of equality merit even less consideration than was the case when the President clearly indicated his view that an armistice must be determined on the basis of allied supremacy.

The news of the Austro-Hungarian surrender can only strengthen the determination of the military and naval chiefs of the Allies to exact adequate guarantees that Germany, if granted an armistice, will be in no position to renew hostilities in case the terms of peace ultimately to be put before her do not meet her views as to what constitutes a peace of justice.

While all the world waits on the decisions to be rendered in Paris, it is expected here that an essential feature of the reply which will be made

Continued on Page Two.

Text of the Austrian Note Replying to President Wilson

BASLE, Oct. 28.—The Austro-Hungarian Foreign Minister instructed the Austro-Hungarian Minister at Stockholm yesterday to ask the Swedish Government to send the following note to the Washington Government:

VIENNA, Oct. 28.

In reply to the note of President Wilson of the 19th of this month, addressed to the Austro-Hungarian Government and giving the decision of the President to speak directly with the Austro-Hungarian Government on the question of an armistice and of peace, the Austro-Hungarian Government has the honor to declare that equally with the preceding proclamations of the President, it adheres also to the same point of view contained in the last note upon the rights of the Austro-Hungarian peoples, especially those of the Czechoslovaks and the Jugoslavs.

Consequently, Austria-Hungary accepting all the conditions the President has laid down for the entry into negotiations for an armistice and peace, no obstacle exists, according to the judgment of the Austro-Hungarian Government, to the beginning of these negotiations.

The Austro-Hungarian Government declares itself ready, in consequence, without awaiting the result of other negotiations, to enter into negotiations upon peace between Austria-Hungary and the States in the opposing group and for an immediate armistice upon all Austro-Hungarian fronts.

It asks President Wilson to be so kind as to begin overtures on this subject. ANDRASSY.

Text of President Wilson's Note to Austria-Hungary

Department of [illegible]
WASHINGTON, Oct. [illegible]

From the Secretary of State to the Minister of Sweden.

SIR: *I have the honor to acknowledge the receipt of your note of the seventh instant in which you transmit a communication of the Imperial and Royal Government of Austria-Hungary to the President. I am now instructed by the President to request you to be good enough through your Government to convey to the Imperial and Royal Government the following reply:*

The President deems it his duty to say to the Austro-Hungarian Government that he cannot entertain the present suggestions of that Government because of certain events of utmost importance, which, occurring since the delivery of his address of the eighth of January last, have necessarily altered the attitude and responsibility of the Government of the United States. Among the fourteen terms of peace which the President formulated at that time, occurred the following:

X.—The peoples of Austria-Hungary, whose place among the nations we wish to see safeguarded and assured, should be accorded the freest opportunity of autonomous development.

Since that sentence was written and uttered to the Congress of the United States, the Government of the United States has recognized that a state of belligerency exists between the Czechoslovaks and the German and Austro-Hungarian Empires and that the Czechoslovak National Council is a de facto belligerent Government clothed with proper authority to direct the military and political affairs of the Czechoslovaks. It has also recognized in the fullest manner the justice of the nationalistic aspirations of the Jugoslavs for freedom.

The President is, therefore, no longer at liberty to accept the mere "autonomy" of these peoples as a basis of peace, but is obliged to insist that they, and not he, shall be the judges of what action on the part of the Austro-Hungarian Government will satisfy their aspirations and their conception of their rights and destiny as members of the family of nations.

Accept, Sir, the renewed assurances of my highest consideration.

(Signed) ROBERT LANSING.

MILITARY REGIME SEES ITS DOOM

Domestic Situation in Germany Serious as Feeling Against Old Regime Rises.

By GEORGE RENWICK.

Copyright, 1918, by The New York Times Company.
Special Cable to THE NEW YORK TIMES.

AMSTERDAM, Oct. 27.—Germany has come to the end of an astounding and historic week and to the beginning probably of a more remarkable one.

The week, which concluded with the resignation of Ludendorff, was characterized throughout by extraordinary outspokenness in the Reichstag. It began with some hints that the reactionaries were in the ascendant. It ended with clear indications that their day is over.

It leaves behind the outstanding impression that Germany is in a parlous political condition. Now that Liebknecht is free, her "insurgent sons" have thrown to the winds all the restraint which autocracy so long imposed on them.

Ludendorff's resignation was a sensation in Berlin, and for it there were several causes. In the first place, his continuous interference in

Continued on Page Two.

9,000 AUSTRIANS, 51 GUNS CAPTURED

Italian and British Forces Advance Four Miles East of the Piave River.

ROME, Oct. 28.—More than 9,000 Austrians were taken prisoner in the operations on the Italian front yesterday, according to the War Office announcement today. Fifty-one guns were also captured. Subjoined is the text of the communication:

Our army, in conjunction with allied contingents, has crossed the Piave River by force of arms, engaging in bitter battles the enemy, who strove desperately to bar the way.

Between the slopes and heights of Valdobbiadene and the mouth of the Soligo Torrent our infantry assault troops passed, during the night, under violent fire to the left bank of the river, broke into the enemy's front lines, and carried them.

Supported by the fire of the artillery on the right bank they gained ground and repulsed enemy counter-attacks throughout the day.

To the south the Tenth Army, taking advantage of the successes of the British at Grave di Papadopoli, compelled the enemy to retire, and repulsed two counterattacks in the direction of Borgo Malanotte and Roncadelle. The prisoners taken yesterday aggregated more than 9,000. Fifty-one guns were captured.

Allied aircraft, with extreme daring,

Continued on Page Six.

VIENNA'S PLEA IS URGENT

Lays Stress on Desire for "Immediate" End of the Conflict.

LOOKS TO WILSON FOR AID

"Adheres to" President's Viewpoint Regarding the Czechoslovaks and Jugoslavs.

BELIEVED TO ECHO [illegible]

Washington Thinks Central Empires Are Seeking Peace in Full Accord.

WASHINGTON, Oct. 28.—While Germany's latest note to President Wilson was being delivered to the State Department today through the Swiss Legation, cable dispatches from Europe brought the information that the Austro-Hungarian Government had caused another communication to be dispatched to the President, asking that immediate negotiations for peace and an armistice be entered into without awaiting the results of exchanges with Germany.

The Vienna Government asserted that it adhered to the same point of view expressed by the President in his last communication upon the rights of the Austro-Hungarian peoples, especially those of the Czechoslovaks and Jugoslavs, and requested that he begin overtures with the allied Governments, with a view to ending immediately the hostilities on all Austro-Hungarian fronts.

The official text of the German note did not differ materially from the unofficial version as received by cable. No official comment was forthcoming, but it is known that no response will be made at present to the communication, which is believed to have been dispatched with the primary purpose of satisfying the German public that their Government was not omitting any opportunity to forward the negotiations for an armistice and peace.

Armistice Question Separate.

Regarding the renewed assurance in the German note that the constitutional structure of the German Government has been and is being changed to democratic lines, it is pointed out that the truth of this statement and the scope of the changes already made or projected, after all, are matters to be dealt with in connection with peace and not in arranging an armistice. A strong indisposition seems evidenced officially to yield to the apparent intent of both the German and Austrian negotiators to combine these two essentially different functions in one phase of the negotiations.

In the case of the Austrian communication, now supposed to be on its way to Washington, through the medium of the Swedish Government, it also was noted that the effort was made to show that Austria had complied with the President's demand for the recognition of the rights of the Czechoslovaks, the Jugoslavs, and other oppressed nationalities in Austria. It does not appear that the complete independence of these people has been guaranteed, and probably sufficient assurance must be had on that point before the Austrian proposal will be transmitted to the Entente Powers for submission to the military experts.

Because of the wide extent of the disaffection in the Dual Empire, developments in that quarter are believed to be fraught with greater possibilities in the way of peace than in Germany. In some official quarters the opinion is freely expressed that Emperor Charles fully realizes that he must submit to any terms which the Entente Powers and America choose to impose, and that at present he is seeking simply to [illegible] onerous and humiliating.

He will be obliged to permit the Hungarians to shift for themselves in the peace settlement if they persist in the separatist movement already in full swing, but there are intimations in official quarters that by no means can the Magyars escape the assumption of full responsibility for their share in the war and [illegible]

Section 1

"All the News That's Fit to Print."

The New York Times.

THE WEATHER
Fair, slightly colder Sunday; Monday fair; fresh west winds.
For full weather report see Page 22.

Section 1

VOL. LXVIII...NO. 22,205. NEW YORK, SUNDAY, NOVEMBER 10, 1918.—84 PAGES, In Seven Parts, Including Picture Section in Rotogravure and Book Section. FIVE CENTS In Greater New York | Elsewhere SEVEN CENTS

KAISER AND CROWN PRINCE ABDICATE; NATION TO CHOOSE NEW GOVERNMENT; MAX IS REGENT; ARMISTICE DELAYED; REVOLT SPREADS ON LAND AND SEA

FRENCH CROSS BELGIAN BORDER; CAPTURE HIRSON

Advance on a 30-Mile Front at Some Points Exceeds Nine Miles.

HAIG WINS ON WHOLE LINE

Germans in Hasty Retreat Before His Armies in Belgium and France.

IN TOURNAI AND MAUBEUGE

British Have Crossed Long Reaches of the Scheldt—Now Approaching Mons.

PARIS, Nov. 9.—French cavalry has crossed the Belgian border north and east of Hirson, the War Office announces tonight. Hirson itself, an important German position, has been occupied as well as several villages in its general neighborhood, and the French line has been carried forward more than nine miles at certain points.

Considerable gains have been made along the whole front of about thirty miles extending from the junction of the French and British armies to the Meuse east of Mezières.

The two water barriers of the Thon and Aure have been forced, and the plateaus to the north occupied.

Mezières has been more closely invested, and the Meuse has been crossed at a point three miles south-east of that town.

The night bulletin reads as follows:

Our troops continued their forward march, advancing fifteen kilometers at certain points during the course of the day.

On the left our cavalry crossed the Belgian frontier, overthrowing the enemy rearguards, taking prisoners, and capturing guns and considerable material, notably several railway trains.

Glageon, Formies, Hirson, Anor, and St. Michel were occupied by us. Our forces continued their pursuit beyond these localities on the general line of Momignies, the northern outskirts of the St. Michel Forest, Maquenoise, and Philippe Forge.

Further east, after having forced a passage of the Thop and Aure Rivers, we occupied the plateaus to the north, despite the enemy's spirited resistance. We took Signy-le-Petit, which was passed for considerable distance, and reached the Mezières-Hirson railway at the village of Wagny and south of Maubert-Fonta .e.

On our right we are along the course of the Sormonne and have reached and surrounded Mezières and Mohon. We crossed the Meuse further east, opposite Lumes.

The text of the day statement follows:

There was artillery and machine-gun activity at several points on the front during the night. This morning the French resumed their march forward along the entire line.

Fires Behind the German Lines.

WITH THE FRENCH ARMIES IN FRANCE, Nov. 9. (Associated Press.)—The French forces today continued their push toward the Belgian frontier, with the Germans persisting in their delaying tactics of the last few days. The Germans used artillery and machine-gun fire at points where they needed more time to break contact with the French.

At other places on the front the progress of the French was maintained with undiminished speed.

HAIG ADVANCES RAPIDLY ON HIS WHOLE FRONT

British Capture Maubeuge and Tournai, Pass the Scheldt Over Wide Area.

LONDON, Nov. 9.—All the armies on the British front are advancing, according to the night bulletin from Field Marshal Haig.

The capture of Tournai has been

Continued on Page Seven.

Province of Poland Rebels and Germans Deport All Males

LONDON, Nov. 7.—The population of the Polish Province of Plock has risen against the Germans, and there have been conflicts in which a number of persons of both sides have been killed, according to a Zurich dispatch to the Exchange Telegraph Company.

The Germans have arrested and shot members of the Polish military organization, and the whole male population is being deported to Germany.

AMERICANS GAIN ALL ALONG FRONT

Clinch Control on Both Sides of Meuse and Take Ground East of River.

HEAR ABDICATION REPORT

Pershing's Men Think the War Virtually Over, but Are Not Eager to Stop.

By EDWIN L. JAMES.

Copyright, 1918, by The New York Times Company. Special Cable to THE NEW YORK TIMES.

WITH THE AMERICAN ARMY IN FRANCE, Nov. 9, (9 P. M.)—The message that the Kaiser has decided to abdicate reached the American front this afternoon, being picked up by wireless and quickly spread among all ranks. This latest development in whirlwind world happenings increased the feeling of our fighters that so far as the Germans were considered, the war was "all over but the squealing." As for themselves, they are getting to like victories and would just as well have the war go on as end. They feel now, as they have always felt, that the war is going to end in but one way.

East of the Meuse Americans are pushing on in the direction of Montmedy. During the day two new crossings of the river were made at Mouzay and Villers-devant-Dun. This work was done under rather heavy shellfire, although the Germans abstained from infantry attacks. We have cleaned out Bois Remoiville.

Just east of Sedan there were the usual artillery and machine-gun duels during the day, while our engineers repaired mined roads and needed supplies and ammunition were got up.

Our aviators report that Montmedy is a scene of great activity, with the Germans moving north. Therefore, we bombed and shelled Montmedy. All the roads in front of the Americans are crowded with boche trains carrying war material out of our reach. Heavy forces still hold the areas in front of us east of the Meuse, below Stenay, while above the enemy has an extra heavy aggregation of artillery and heavy infantry forces.

Unless the war ends our doughboys will be ready soon to tackle this job. News that the German emissaries have until Monday morning to accept or reject the armistice terms is known to soldiers of each side, and needless to say there is the keenest interest in the situation. American lads figure that they can keep the war going if the Germans choose.

Gains All Along the Line.

WITH THE AMERICAN ARMY ON THE SEDAN FRONT, Nov. 9, (Associated Press.)—The American troops fought their way forward today along virtually their entire line, despite the fact that the weather was about as bad as could be.

The resistance encountered was spirited on the whole, though consisting largely of machine-gun activity. The terrain crossed and captured was on par with the most difficult ground the Americans have taken thus far. It

Continued on Page Six.

GERMAN WARSHIPS CLASH

Loyalist Vessels Attack Fleet Seized by Reds—Kiel Is Under Fire.

MEANT TO ATTACK ENGLAND

Naval Officers Were Against Peace, but Men Rebelled Against Their Enterprise.

MANY CITIES JOIN REVOLT

Cologne, Hanover, Oldenburg, and Other Places Reported in Eruption.

Copyright, 1918, by The New York Times Company. Special Cable to THE NEW YORK TIMES.

COPENHAGEN, Nov. 9.—The Politiken states that the reason of the mutiny of the German fleet at Kiel was that the officers would not recognize the Government's peace policy, and had decided to attack England with the fleet.

The sailors then rebelled and forced the officers to leave the warships.

A special to the Koebenhaven from Vamdrup states that several hundred officers were killed at Kiel, and now the fleet, the depots, and the railway station are in the hands of the rioting mariners and soldiers.

Reports from Hamburg state that the railway connections from there are broken and trains to Denmark are starting from Neumunster.

Specials to both the Koebenhaven and the Politiken report the fleet firing at Kiel.

LONDON, Nov. 9.—German warships, manned by crews loyal to the monarchy, and others seized by Reds and now at Flensburg on the Schleswig coast are in battle, according to Copenhagen advices.

It is stated that six battleships anchored outside of Flensburg have directed their guns against the revolutionists. A bombardment was expected. The battleship Koenig, which refused to surrender, was taken after a hard fight.

Reports of growing disaffection and uprisings by the populace continue to pour in from the Continent.

An Associated Press dispatch from Copenhagen says:

"Rebellions have occurred in Hanover, Cologne, Brunswick, and Magdeburg, according to an official announcement at Berlin. These cities, however, are not wholly in the hands of the mutineers, the statement adds. At Magdeburg the garrison resisted."

A previous dispatch from The Associated Press correspondent at Copenhagen reads:

"The uprising in Northwestern Germany, according to the only direct news from Germany early today, is reported to have spread to Hanover, Oldenburg, and other cities. Generally the revolt is not attended by serious disturbances.

"Reports from the Danish border

Continued on Page Two.

Geddes Sure the German Fleet Was Ordered Out, But Men Rebelled Rather Than Fight British

LONDON, Nov. 9.—(British Wireless Service.)—At the banquet following the Lord Mayor's "Victory" show tonight, Sir Eric Geddes, First Lord of the Admiralty, made interesting disclosures. He said that those who were charged with responsibility had waited hourly for the possibility of a naval Armageddon. The whole stage was set for a great sea battle, but something was wrong. The arm that was going to try the last desperate gambling stroke was paralyzed.

"The German Navy, I am as convinced as I am standing here tonight," said the First Lord, "was ordered out, and the men would not come."

Half the German fleet, he declared, was flying the red flag—and the German fleet was flying the red flag because it realized that it was not engaged in a good cause.

BARRAGE DELAYS TRUCE COURIER

Paris Thinks German Government May Wireless Final Reply to Foch.

TERMS READ BY MARSHAL

Enemy Delegates Stunned by Realization of Extent of Nation's Defeat.

LONDON, Nov. 9, (British Wireless Service.) — The British Press Bureau issued the following announcement this afternoon:

"Owing to the heavy German barrage and machine gun fire on the battlefront the passage of the courier from Marshal Foch's headquarters to Spa was so delayed that he is not expected to reach German Headquarters until this afternoon. Consequently it is unlikely that any decision in regard to the armistice will be reached today."

AMSTERDAM, Nov. 9.—The German courier, bearing Marshal Foch's armistice terms, had some difficulty in crossing the German lines.

He was led to believe through the blowing up of an ammunition dump with a series of explosions that the Germans had not ceased firing, but he was informed of the cause of the explosions by wireless and instructed to pass the German lines without delay.

The terms are expected to reach Berlin momentarily.

PARIS, Nov. 9.—Germany's armistice delegates were received by Marshal Foch yesterday morning at 9 o'clock in a railroad car, in which the Commander in Chief of the allied force has his headquarters, according to the Petit Journal.

When the Germans' credentials had been opened and verified, Mathias Erzberger, leader of the enemy delegation, speaking in French, announced that the German Government had been advised by President Wilson that Marshal Foch was qualified to communicate to them the Allies' conditions and had oppointed them plenipotentiaries to take cognizance of the terms and eventually sign an armistice.

Marshal Foch then read the terms

Continued on Page Two.

MAY SIGN TRUCE IN TOWN OF SENLIS

Marshal Foch's Headquarters Scene of Atrocities by Germans Early in War.

PEOPLE AWAIT THE DAY

Remember When the Invaders Wantonly Shot Mayor and Fellow-Townsmen.

By WALTER DURANTY.

Copyright, 1918, by The New York Times Company. Special Cable to THE NEW YORK TIMES.

PARIS, Nov. 9.—The Temps says tonight:

"If the German answer is in the affirmative an armistice will be signed at Senlis, the headquarters of the allied Generalissimo."

It must be a strange experience for the inhabitants of the little French town, the whole main street of which was gutted by boche incendiaries in 1914, to see the French military automobiles containing the travel-worn German envoys flash by on their errand of humiliation. Doubtless they will remember that tragic day of September when their Mayor and fellow-townsmen were wantonly shot and nights far more recent when the earth shook, as I often experienced in that very spot, to the crash of bursting air bombs and the thunder of answering batteries.

With such memories in their hearts the people of Senlis salute the day of retribution.

"There is a striking change in the attitude of the German soldiers during the last few days," said a Lieutenant who arrived in Paris today on leave from Gouraud's army. "Until the beginning of the week the rearguards resisted strongly, but now the boches' chief anxiety seems to be to hurry backward, even if they must leave cannon or machine guns behind. The statement of a Saxon Feldwebel captured two days ago illustrates the general tone.

"'We would have been willing to fight to the end if there was anything to be gained thereby,' he said, 'but the people at home have lost their heads and the country is crumbling to pieces, so why sacrifice ourselves uselessly?'

"The Feldwebel, in charge of twelve men in a machine gun nest, surrendered without firing a shot when a patrol of French cavalry appeared on a hill crest—where they were an easy mark—to the right."

My informant thought the incident typical, adding:

"However one abominates the atrocities the boches committed, it

Continued on Page Two.

Irish Nationalists Appeal to Wilson to Support Demands Made on England

LONDON, Nov. 9.—The Irish Nationalist Party is sending to President Wilson a manifesto appealing for his assistance in settling the Irish question.

The document quotes at length from President Wilson's "great utterances on this war which we hold justify us to enforce the demand we have made for our nation on the British Government."

SOCIALIST AS CHANCELLOR

Prince Max Announces He Will Name Ebert Head of Cabinet.

PLAN NATIONAL ASSEMBLY

This Will Make Provision for the Future Form of German Government.

BRUNSWICK DUKE OUT

Head of House, Who Is Kaiser's Son-in-Law, Abdicates with His Heir.

Copyright, 1918, by The New York Times Company. Special Cable to THE NEW YORK TIMES.

LONDON, Nov. 9, 4:40 P. M.—Emperor William of Germany has abdicated.

PARIS, Nov. 9.—The abdication of Emperor William is officially announced from Berlin, according to a Havas dispatch from Basle.

LONDON, Nov. 9.—A Havas Agency dispatch from Amsterdam says that Prince Max of Baden has been appointed Regent of the Empire, according to the Berlin newspapers.

A Reuter dispatch, however, says he is yet to be named.

According to a German wireless message received here which announces the Kaiser's abdication, Friedrich Ebert, Vice President of the Social Democratic Party, is to be Imperial Chancellor under the regency, and wide reforms are planned, including the calling of a Constitutional German National Assembly to determine the future good of the nation.

The resignations of the German Ministers of the Interior, Instruction, Agriculture, and Finance are reported in a telegram from Berlin.

The Prussian Food Controller again requested to be relieved from office, and the resignation of the Prussian Minister of Public Works has been in the hands of the Cabinet some time.

Emperor William had not at a late hour [before his abdication] accepted the resignation of Prince Max of Baden, the Chancellor, according to a Berlin message to Copenhagen. The Emperor, who was kept thoroughly informed by the Chancellor regarding the general situation, the message adds, asked Prince Max to continue holding the office provisionally until the Emperor's final decision was reached.

The Socialists decided not to carry out at the time set their threat to withdraw from the Government if Emperor William had not abdicated by that hour, according to a Berlin dispatch. Instead they extended the time limit, it is stated, "in consideration of an eventual armistice."

Text of Decree Announcing Kaiser's Abdication and the Plans for Other Changes in Germany

LONDON, Nov. 9.—A German wireless message received in London this afternoon states:

"The German Imperial Chancellor, Prince Max of Baden, has issued the following decree:

The Kaiser and King has decided to renounce the throne.

The Imperial Chancellor will remain in office until the questions connected with the abdication of the Kaiser, the renouncing by the Crown Prince of the throne of the German Empire and of Prussia, and the setting up of a regency have been settled.

For the regency he intends to appoint Deputy Ebert as Imperial Chancellor, and he proposes that a bill shall be brought in for the establishment of a law providing for the immediate promulgation of general suffrage and for a constitutional German National Assembly, which will settle finally the future form of government of the German nation and of those peoples which might be desirous of coming within the empire. THE IMPERIAL CHANCELLOR.

Berlin, Nov. 9, 1918.

Kaiser's Son-in-Law Abdicates.

LONDON, Nov. 9, (British Wireless Service.)—A telegram received at Copenhagen, from Brunswick by way of Berlin, asserts that Emperor William's son-in-law, the Duke of Brunswick, and his successor have abdicated.

The reigning Duke of Brunswick, Ernest Augustus, married the German Kaiser's only daughter, Princess Victoria Louisa, on May 24, 1913. He was then 26 years of age and she was five years younger. The Duke's heir is Prince Ernest Augustus, born on March 12, 1914. Two other sons came during the war—George William, born March 25, 1915, and Frederick, April 18, 1917.

The father of the Duke is the Duke of Cumberland, son of the late King George V. of Hanover and cousin of the late Queen Victoria. The kingdom of Hanover was absorbed by Prussia in 1866.

Chancellor Sees All Hope Gone; Says Germany Is Forced to Yield.

LONDON, Nov. 9, (British Wireless Service.)—Just before Prince Maximilian of Baden offered his resignation as Imperial Chancellor he issued an appeal "To Germans abroad" in which he said:

"In the fifth year, (of hostilities,) abandoned by its allies, the German people could no longer wage war against the increasingly superior forces."

The text of the Chancellor's statement follows:

"In these difficult days the hearts of many among you, my fellow-countrymen, who outside the frontier of the German Fatherland are surrounded by manifestations of malicious joy and hatred, will be heavy. Do not despair of the German people.

"Our soldiers have fought to the last moment as heroically as any army has ever done. The homeland has shown unprecedented strength in suffering and endurance.

"In the fifth year, abandoned by its allies, the German people could no longer wage war against the increasingly superior forces.

"The victory for which many had hoped has not been granted to us. But the German people has won this still greater victory over itself and its belief in the right of might.

"From this victory we shall draw new strength for the hard time which faces us and on which you also can build."

AMSTERDAM, Nov. 7.—Absolute unity is necessary among the German people if they wish to avert unforeseen consequences, says Chancellor Maximillian in an appeal to the German people, which, according to an official dispatch from Berlin, reads as follows:

"For more than four years the German nation, united and calm, has endured the most severe sufferings and sacrifices. If at this decisive hour, when only absolute unity can avert from the entire German people great dangers for its future, internal strength gives way, then the consequences are unforeseeable.

"An indispensable demand in these decisive hours, which must be made by every people's Government, is the maintenance of the hitherto existing calm, under voluntary discipline. May every citizen be conscious of the high responsibility toward his people in the fulfillment of their duty!"

"Issue is Settled," Says Lloyd George, Who Announces Regency in Germany

LONDON, Nov. 9, (British Wireless Service.)—Premier Lloyd George spoke tonight at a banquet which followed the Lord Mayor's "Victory" Show.

"I have no news for you," said the Premier to the banqueters, who were expecting an announcement from him regarding the possible signing of an armistice with Germany.

"Owing to the rapid and triumphant advance of the allied troops and to their relentless pursuit, the German envoys have not been able to get through, and other means have had to be devised to enable them to cross the lines. Owing to these circumstances I have nothing to say to you this evening as to the result of the armistice negotiations. But for all that, it does not matter.

"The issue is settled. In the Spring we were being sorely pressed. The Channel ports were being threatened, and the steel of the enemy was pointed at our hearts.

"It is Autumn. The capital of Turkey is now almost within gunfire of our ships. Austria is shattered and broken. The Kaiser and the Crown Prince have abdicated, [Prince Max's decree said that the Kaiser had decided to abdicate] A

"All the News That's Fit to Print."

The New York Times.

THE WEATHER
Fair today and Tuesday; diminishing northwest winds.
For weather report see next to last page.

VOL. LXVIII...NO. 22,206. NEW YORK, MONDAY, NOVEMBER 11, 1918. TWENTY-FOUR PAGES. TWO CENTS Metropolitan District 50 Mile Radius | THREE CENTS Within 200 Miles | FOUR CENTS Elsewhere

ARMISTICE SIGNED, END OF THE WAR! BERLIN SEIZED BY REVOLUTIONISTS; NEW CHANCELLOR BEGS FOR ORDER; OUSTED KAISER FLEES TO HOLLAND

SON FLEES WITH EX-KAISER

Hindenburg Also Believed to be Among Those in His Party.

ALL ARE HEAVILY ARMED

Automobiles Bristle with Rifles as Fugitives Arrive at Dutch Frontier.

ON THEIR WAY TO DE STEEG

Belgians Yell to Them, "Are You On Your Way to Paris?"

LONDON, Nov. 10.—Both the former German Emperor and his eldest son, Frederick William, crossed the Dutch frontier Sunday morning, according to advices from The Hague. His reported destination is De Steeg, near Utrecht.

The former German Emperor's party, which is believed to include Field Marshal von Hindenburg, arrived at Eysden, [midway between Liége and Maastricht,] on the Dutch frontier, at 7:30 o'clock Sunday morning, according to Daily Mail advices.

Practically the whole German General Staff accompanied the former Emperor, and ten automobiles carried the party. The automobiles were bristling with rifles, and all the fugitives were armed.

The ex-Kaiser was in uniform. He alighted at the Eysden station and paced the platform, smoking a cigarette.

Many photographs were taken by [of?] the members of the Imperial party. On the whole the people were very quiet, but Belgians among them yelled out "En voyage a Paris." (Are you on your way to Paris?)

Chatting with the members of the staff, the former Emperor, the correspondent says, did not look in the least distressed. A few minutes later an imperial train, including restaurant and sleeping cars, ran into the station. Only servants were aboard.

The engine returned to Visé, Belgium, and brought back a second train, in which were a large number of staff officers and others, and also stores of food.

The preparations began for the departure at 10 o'clock this morning, but at 10:40 o'clock the train was still at Eysden. The blinds of the train were all drawn.

The Daily Mail remarks that, if the party arrived in Holland armed, all of them must be interned.

Whiie other dispatches con-

Continued on Page Three.

Kaiser Fought Hindenburg's Call for Abdication; Failed to Get Army's Support in Keeping Throne

By GEORGE RENWICK.

Special Cable to The New York Times.

AMSTERDAM, Nov. 10.—I learn on very good authority that the Kaiser made a determined effort to stave off abdication. He went to headquarters with the deliberate intention of bringing the army around to his side. In this he failed miserably.

His main support consisted of a number of officers, nearly all of Prussian regiments, who formed themselves into two regiments and placed themselves at his Majesty's disposal. To do anything with such support was seen, of course, to be Gilbertian.

During the night the Kaiser called the Crown Prince, Hindenburg, and General Gröner to him, and the consultation lasted a couple of hours. Both officers strongly pressed the Kaiser to bow to the inevitable, and Hindenburg informed him that any more delay in coming to a decision to abdicate would certainly have the most terrible consequences and lead to serious events in the army. For those consequences Hindenburg said he must refuse responsibility.

The Crown Prince, it is said, was the first to give way. General Gröner fully supported Hindenburg's view, but when the conference broke up the Kaiser remained unconvinced of the advisability of abdication. He is said to have come to his final decision an hour or so later, after several communications had reached him from Berlin and after another short and stormy talk with Hindenburg.

Meanwhile, his son-in-law, the Duke of Brunswick, for himself and his heir, had abdicated. "Brunswick's Fated Chieftain". was forced without fighting to abdicate. Reports have it that the republican movement in Brunswick, which long before the war was chafing under autocratic conditions, began to be noticed even before it was set in motion at Kiel.

Kaiser Shivered as He Signed Abdication

LONDON, Nov. 10.—Emperor William signed his letter of abdication on Saturday morning at the German Grand Headquarters in the presence of Crown Prince Frederick William and Field Marshal Hindenburg, according to a dispatch from Amsterdam to the Exchange Telegraph Company.

The Crown Prince signed his renunciation of the throne shortly afterward.

Before placing his signature to the document, an urgent message from Philipp Scheidemann, who was a Socialist member without portfolio in the Imperial Cabinet, was handed to the Emperor. He read it with a shiver. Then he signed the paper, saying:

"It may be for the good of Germany."

The Emperor was deeply moved. He consented to sign the document only when he got the news of the latest events in the empire.

The ex-Kaiser and former Crown Prince were expected to take leave of their troops on Saturday, but nothing had then been settled regarding their future movements.

GERMAN DYNASTIES BEING WIPED OUT

King of Wuerttemberg Abdicates — Sovereign of Saxony to Follow Suit.

PRINCES MAY BE EXILED

Socialists Are Demanding That Every Sovereign in the Empire Shall be Dethroned.

LONDON, Nov. 10.—A Havas dispatch from Basle says:

"Wilhelm II., the reigning King of the monarchy of Württemberg, abdicated on Friday night."

A Wolff Bureau dispatch from Stuttgart, by way of Amsterdam, says that the King has issued a proclamation saying that his person would never serve to hinder the development of the wishes of the people.

According to a report received from Berne, the German Socialists are demanding that every dynasty in Germany be suppressed and all the Princes exiled. It is reported that the Kings of Bavaria and Saxony intend to abdicate soon.

Here is a list of the rules, until several days ago, of the various parts of the German Empire. Those who have abdicated and those reported to be on the point of abdication are marked by an asterisk:

ANHALT—Duke Edward, son of the late Duke Friedrich of Anhalt and of Princess Antoinette of Saxe-Altenberg. Succeeded his brother April 18, 1861.

BADEN—Friedrich II., succeeded to

Continued on Page Two.

MORE WARSHIPS JOIN THE REDS

Four Dreadnoughts in Kiel Harbor Espouse the Revolutionary Cause.

GUARDSHIPS ALSO GO OVER

Those Protecting Mines in the Great Belt and the Baltic Abandon Their Posts.

LONDON, Nov. 10.—The crews of the German dreadnoughts Posen, Ostfriesland, Nassau, and Oldenburg, in Kiel Harbor, have joined the revolution, says a Copenhagen dispatch. Marines occupied the lock gates at Ostmoor and fought down a coast artillery division which offered resistance.

According to the British Wireless Service three German destroyers have anchored outside of Stockholm. All the guardships in the Baltic, it is said, have joined the revolutionary movement.

Six more cruisers flying the red flag arrived at Hamburg last night, says a Wolff News Agency dispatch received in Copenhagen.

An Amsterdam dispatch states that the Berlin Vossische Zeitung and Vorwärts confirm the fact that the inception of the revolution at Kiel was mistaken for the idea that a cruise had been ordered and that it was intended to give battle to the British fleet.

Up to Friday night the number of persons killed at Kiel was twenty-eight, according to information re-

Continued on Page Three.

BERLIN TROOPS JOIN REVOLT

Reds Shell Building in Which Officers Vainly Resist.

THRONGS DEMAND REPUBLIC

Revolutionary Flag on Royal Palace — Crown Prince's Palace Also Seized.

GENERAL STRIKE IS BEGUN

Burgomaster and Police Submit—War Office Now Under Socialist Control.

LONDON, Nov. 10. — The greater part of Berlin is in control of revolutionists, the former Kaiser has fled to Holland, and Friedrich Ebert, the new Socialist Chancellor, has taken command of the situation. The revolt is spreading throughout Germany with great rapidity.

Dispatches received in London today announce these startling developments. The Workmen's and Soldiers' Council is now administering the municipal government of the German capital.

The War Ministry has submitted, and its acts are valid only when countersigned by a Socialist representative. The official Wolff telegraphic agency has been taken over by the Reds.

The red flag has been hoisted over the royal palace and the Brandenburg Gate. The former Crown Prince's palace is also in possession of the revolutionists.

There was severe fighting in Berlin between 8 and 10 o'clock last night and a violent cannonade was heard from the heart of the city.

Burgomaster and Police Join.

A Copenhagen dispatch states that Dr. Liebknecht, the famous Socialist, who spent many months in prison for antagonizing the German Imperial Government and who was recently released, has issued the following announcement in Berlin in behalf of the Workmen's and Soldiers' Council:

"The Presidency of the police, as well as the Chief Command, is in our hands. Our comrades will be released."

A dispatch from Berne states that the Burgomaster of Berlin has placed himself and his staff at the disposal of the new Government.

Some German newspapers describe the movement as Bolshevism. The people are shouting "Long live the Republic!" and singing the "Marseillaise."

Officers Shelled by Reds.

When revolutionary soldiers attempted to enter a building in Berlin in which they supposed that a number of officers were concealed shots were fired from the windows. The Reds then began shelling the building. Many persons were killed and wounded before the officers surrendered.

When the cannonade began the people thought the Reichsbank was being bombarded, and thousands rushed to the square in front of the Crown Prince's palace. It was later determined that other buildings were under fire. Among those killed in the fighting at the "Cockchafer" Barracks was one of the workmen's leaders known as "Comrade" Habersroth.

The Reds, at last reports, were maintaining order.

Berlin was occupied by forces of the Soldiers' and Workmen's Councils on Saturday afternoon, according to a Wolff Bureau report received in Copenhagen. News of Emperor William's abdication was received in the city on that afternoon with general rejoicing, which was tempered by the fear that it had come too late.

Russians Aid in Outbreak.

How far the example of the Russian Bolsheviki influenced the German upheaval is an interesting question. Red flags figured frequently in the various risings and Chancellor Ebert's motor car floets the international emblem.

The shoulder straps were torn from the uniforms of officers in a number of German cities and even the soldiers' insignia were stripped from them. Russian prisoners played a part in the demonstrations in two or three towns.

Delegates of the revolutionary German navy arrived in Berlin on Friday, according to a dispatch from Copenhagen. They conferred for several hours with the Minister of Marine and with members of the Reichstag majority parties.

It is stated that Hugo Haase, a Socialist leader in the Reichstag, has the situation at Hamburg in hand.

It is officially announced from Berlin, according to a Copenhagen dispatch, that the War Ministry has placed itself at the disposal of Chancellor Ebert. This action was for the purpose of assuring the provisioning of the army and assisting in the solution of demobilization problems.

Serious food difficulties are expected in Germany, owing to the stoppage of trains. The Council of the Regency will take the most drastic steps to re-establish order.

In the new German Government there will be only three representatives of the majority parties, namely, Erzberger, Gothein, and Richthofen, says a dispatch from Copenhagen. The other posts will be occupied by Socialists and independents.

Reds Announce Success.

BERLIN, Nov. 9, (German Wireless to London, Nov. 10)—(Associated Press.)—The German People's Government has been instituted in the greater part of Berlin. The garrison has gone over to the Government.

The Workmen's and Soldiers' Council has declared a general strike. Troops and machine guns have been placed at the disposal of the Council. Guards which had been stationed at the public offices and other buildings have been withdrawn.

Friedrich Ebert (Vice President of the Social Democratic Party) is carrying on the Chancellorship.

The text of a statement issued by the People's Government reads:

In the course of the forenoon of Saturday the formation of a new German People's Government was initiated. The greater part of the Berlin garrison, and other troops stationed there temporarily, went over to the new Government.

The leaders of the deputations of the Social Democratic Party declared that they would not shoot against the people. They said they would, in accordance with the People's Government, intercede in favor of the maintenance of order. Thereupon in the offices and public buildings the guards which had been stationed there were withdrawn.

The business of the Imperial Chancellor is being carried on by the Social Democratic Deputy, Herr Ebert.

It is presumed that, apart from the representatives of the recent majority group, three independent Social Democrats will enter the future Government.

Scheidemann Exhorts Calm.

Deputy Scheidemann, (leader of the majority Socialists in the Reichstag,) in a speech today, said:

"The Kaiser and the Crown Prince have abdicated. The dynasty

Continued on Page Four.

Socialist Chancellor Appeals to All Germans To Help Him Save Fatherland from Anarchy

BERNE, Nov. 10, (Associated Press.)—In an address to the people, the new German Chancellor, Friedrich Ebert, says:

Citizens: The ex-Chancellor, Prince Max of Baden, in agreement with all the Secretaries of State, has handed over to me the task of liquidating his affairs as Chancellor. I am on the point of forming a new Government in accord with the various parties, and will keep public opinion freely informed of the course of events.

The new Government will be a Government of the people. It must make every effort to secure in the quickest possible time peace for the German people and consolidate the liberty which they have won.

The new Government has taken charge of the administration, to preserve the German people from civil war and famine and to accomplish their legitimate claim to autonomy. The Government can solve this problem only if all the officials in town and country will help.

I know it will be difficult for some to work with the new men who have taken charge of the empire, but I appeal to their love of the people. Lack of organization would in this heavy time mean anarchy in Germany and the surrender of the country to tremendous misery. Therefore, help your native country with fearless, indefatigable work for the future, every one at his post.

I demand every one's support in the hard task awaiting us. You know how seriously the war has menaced the provisioning of the people, which is the first condition of the people's existence. The political transformation should not trouble the people. The food supply is the first duty of all, whether in town or country, and they should not embarrass, but rather aid, the production of food supplies and their transport to the towns.

Food shortage signifies pillage and robbery, with great misery. The poorest will suffer the most, and the industrial worker will be affected hardest. All who illicitly lay hands on food supplies or other supplies of prime necessity or the means of transport necessary for their distribution will be guilty in the highest degree toward the community.

I ask you immediately to leave the streets and remain orderly and calm.

COPENHAGEN, Nov. 10.—The new Berlin Government, according to a Wolff Bureau dispatch, has issued the following proclamation:

Fellow-Citizens: This day the people's deliverance has been fulfilled. The Social Democratic Party has undertaken to form a Government. It has invited the Independent Socialist Party to enter the Government with equal rights.

WAR ENDS AT 6 O'CLOCK THIS MORNING

The State Department in Washington Made the Announcement at 2:45 o'Clock.

ARMISTICE WAS SIGNED IN FRANCE AT MIDNIGHT

Terms Include Withdrawal from Alsace-Lorraine, Disarming and Demobilization of Army and Navy, and Occupation of Strategic Naval and Military Points.

By The Associated Press.

WASHINGTON, Monday, Nov. 11, 2:48 A. M.—The armistice between Germany, on the one hand, and the allied Governments and the United States, on the other, has been signed.

The State Department announced at 2:45 o'clock this morning that Germany had signed.

The department's announcement simply said: "The armistice has been signed."

The world war will end this morning at 6 o'clock, Washington time, 11 o'clock Paris time.

The armistice was signed by the German representatives at midnight.

This announcement was made by the State Department at 2:50 o'clock this morning.

The announcement was made verbally by an officila of the State Department in this form:

"The armistice has been signed. It was signed at 5 o'clock A. M., Paris time, [midnight, New York time,] and hostilities will cease at 11 o'clock this morning, Paris time, [6 o'clock, New York time.]

The terms of the armistice, it was announced, will not be made public until later. Military men here, however, regard it as certain that they include:

Immediate retirement of the German military forces from France, Belgium, and Alsace-Lorraine.

Disarming and demobilization of the German armies.

Occupation by the allied and American forces of such strategic points in Germany as will make impossible a renewal of hostilities.

Delivery of part of the German High Seas Fleet and a certain number of submarines to the allied and American naval forces.

Disarmament of all other German warships

"All the News That's Fit to Print."

The New York Times.

THE WEATHER
Fair today; Thursday cloudy; mild temperature; wind southeast.
For weather report see next to last page.

VOL. LXVIII...NO. 22,278. • • • NEW YORK, WEDNESDAY, JANUARY 22, 1919. TWENTY-TWO PAGES TWO CENTS Metropolitan District 30 Mile Radius | THREE CENTS Within 200 Miles | FOUR CENTS Elsewhere

NEW YORK TO ASK COURTS TO ANNUL NEW PHONE RATES

Service Board Orders Attorney to Join Other States in Fight on Burleson's Order.

JERSEY AND MICHIGAN SUE

Governor of Massachusetts Declares That State's Rights Should Be Protected.

PLEA FOR PRIVATE CONTROL

National Association of State Commissions Opposed to Present Management.

Special to The New York Times.

ALBANY, Jan. 21.—At its session here today the Public Service Commission of the Second District directed its counsel to begin an action, either by mandamus or injunction, to restrain the New York Telephone Company from putting into operation its new tariff of rates under the order of the Postmaster General. The telephone company, it is stated, is now charging substantially increased rates for services.

The new tariff has not been filed with the commission, and it is the opinion of that body that the telephone company is violating Section 92 of the Public Service Commission law. Attorney Ledyard P. Hale will at once proceed against the telephone company under the commission's authority.

"The commission delayed taking action," said Chairman Hill today, "because it was thought that its position would be stronger by waiting until the Postmaster General had put the order into effect. The new rates were promulgated by the Postmaster General with the statement that they brought about a decrease in charges, but analysis by the commission gives the same results as those made by the commissions in Illinois, Ohio, Nebraska, New Jersey, Indiana, Missouri, and other States; that is, that the increase in rates varies from 20 to 100 per cent.

"The general effect of the order of the Postmaster General is to increase charges for certain telephone service covering the bulk of traffic and making charges for certain services which were heretofore free."

Stands for State's Rights.

BOSTON, Jan. 21.—The action of the New England Telephone and Telegraph Company in putting into effect today the new telephone toll rates determined by the Postmaster General was called to the attention of Attorney General Attwill by the Public Service Commission, with a request that proceedings looking to a suspension of the rates be instituted in the State Supreme Court. The commission alleged that the company had violated the laws of the State in ignoring an order of the commission.

"I see no reason," said Governor Coolidge, "why any of the States should surrender any of their rate-making powers to the Federal Government. In times of war emergencies may arise making it advisable not to stand upon the Constitution, but at the present time I feel that the State's interests should be fully protected. I feel strongly that the Public Service Commission, as in the past, should continue to make rates for Massachusetts patrons."

Michigan Asks an Injunction.

LANSING, Mich., Jan. 21.—First steps to test the right of Postmaster General Burleson to fix long-distance telephone rates in Michigan were taken today by Attorney General Groesbeck in petitions in the Circuit Court for an injunction. Separate petitions were filed for each of the companies involved. They ask in addition to the restraining writ, an order requiring the companies to continue the present rates "until they are legally modified."

Order Obtained in Jersey.

TRENTON, N. J., Jan. 21.—Postmaster General Albert S. Burleson, the New York Telephone Company, the Delaware and Atlantic Telephone and Telegraph Company, and the American Telephone and Telegraph Company were ordered tonight, through an order issued by Judge John Rellstab, in the United States court, to appear and show cause at 10:30 o'clock on Monday morning next, in the Federal court here, why an injunction should not issue to restrain the Postmaster General and the telephone companies from continuing in force the order of the Postmaster General increasing telephone rates in New Jersey. These new rates, effective today, should first be approved by the Public Utility Commission, it is alleged.

Judge Rellstab, however, refused to issue a restraining order which would prohibit the immediate continuance of the new rates until the court had had an opportunity to pass upon the application for an injunction.

The petition was presented by Alfred N. Barber, Secretary of the State Utility Commission, through L. Edward Herrmann, counsel for the commission. Mr. Barber contends that the board is empowered by the State laws to have supervision, regulation, and control over all public utilities in the State. He also asserts the board has power to fix "just and reasonable" rates and may require every public utility concern in the State to file with it complete schedules and classification of rates.

The petition sets forth that the Utility Board issued an order yesterday directing the suspension of the new rates in

Continued on Page Four.

France Had 5,192,372 Men Mobilized on Jan. 1, 1918

LYONS, Jan. 21, (Havas.)—The number of effectives mobilized by France from the outbreak of the war is given as follows in the report of Deputy Benazet on the war budget:

Aug. 15, 1914.—Officers, 92,828; soldiers, 3,780,000.

Feb. 15, 1915.—Officers, 97,753; soldiers, 4,900,000.

Jan. 1, 1916.—Officers, 109,814; soldiers, 5,060,000.

Jan. 1, 1917.—Officers, 113,004; soldiers, 5,026,000.

Jan. 1, 1918.—Officers, 128,372; soldiers, 5,064,000.

On Jan. 1, 1918, the infantry numbered 2,106,773; artillery, 899,645; aviation, 59,285; cavalry, 166,422; engineering corps, 185,110.

TREASON CHARGE AT WIRE INQUIRY

Moon Accuses Reynolds, Postal Official, Because He Fought Burleson's Plans.

AID FOR SMALL SYSTEMS

Mackay Manager Insists Control Is in Interest of Crippled Companies and Western Union.

Special to The New York Times.

WASHINGTON, Jan. 21.—Because Edward Reynolds, Vice President and General Manager of the Postal Telegraph-Cable Company, would not comply with orders issued by Postmaster General Burleson, Chairman Moon of the House Post Office Committee this afternoon charged Mr. Reynolds with "treason" at the committee hearing on the bill Judge Moon has written to extend the period of Federal control over the telegraph and telephone system. Trembling with indignation Mr. Reynolds resented the accusation, while members of the committee protested against Judge Moon's treatment of the witness.

The hearing was marked with bitterness all day. Witnesses representing the Minnesota State Railroad and Warehouse Commission, whom Representative Steenerson of that State presented, were accused by Judge Moon of being actuated by the desire to retain their places, which, he said, would be eliminated by Government regulation. There was distinct line-up in the committee, headed by Judge Moon on one side, and Representatives Steenerson and Madden of Illinois, both Republicans, on the other. Solicitor William H. Lamar of the Post Office Department sat beside Judge Moon and coached the Chairman with questions during the session.

It developed during the testimony that Mr. Reynolds had been dismissed on Dec. 1 because he indorsed a letter written by one of his subordinates urging delay and obstruction to the Federal plan of control.

"You were dismissed, were you?" asked Judge Moon.

"I certainly was," replied Mr. Reynolds.

"Because you were treasonable?"

"I take exception to that," exclaimed Mr. Reynolds, while members at the other end of the table shouted "No, No!" One of them, Mr. Madden, interjected:

"That should certainly be stricken from the record."

"You were disloyal to Mr. Burleson," continued Judge Moon.

"My daughter and son are in France and I won't permit you or any one else to impugn my loyalty," responded Mr. Reynolds.

"I think we should proceed with the hearing as if the witness was a human being," said Mr. Madden. "There's no reason that the power of Government should be used to bulldoze the witness."

Produces Reynolds's Letter.

Judge Moon explained that Mr. Reynolds, in his opinion, had been disloyal to the Postmaster General. The letter in question was of few lines and indorsing one in which a district superintendent said that, "as the war was over" the Postmaster General's plans should be rearded, and added, "Thank God for a Republican House and presumably a Republican Senate." Mr. Reynolds said:

"I sent the letter out to some eight officials. It came into the hands of Mr. Burleson, and he dismissed me."

Mr. Reynolds testified he had started with the Postal Company thirty years ago as a messenger and read a prepared statement, in the course of which he said:

"Mr. Burleson's Operating Committee, consisting of a Western Union man, two Bell Telephone men and one Independent Telephone man, has within the last few days tried to get the Postal Company to agree to increased telegraph rates and the Postal Company has refused.

"I am reliably informed that most of the independent telephone companies were making money at the time the Government took them over, and I am also informed that they wish their properties returned at once, notwithstanding the statements made to this committee to the contrary.

"Public sentiment is opposed to retaining the wires, and no one is willing to admit he wishes the Government to keep the telephone lines in order to bring about Government ownership, except Mr. Burleson, himself, because that purpose is a perversion of the purpose for which Congress authorized the seizure of the lines.

"The whole situation looks to me like a scheme for the raising of telephone rates and the financing of crippled tele-

Continued on Page Four.

LIBERAL GROUPS GAIN IN RETURNS OF GERMAN VOTE

Predicted in Berlin That a Socialist-Democratic Alliance Will Control Convention.

EBERT PARTY FACES FIGHT

May Be in a Minority if the Opposition Combines, Copenhagen Estimates.

RHINELAND FOR CENTRISTS

Weimar Reported to Have Been Selected as Meeting Place of National Assembly.

BERLIN, Jan. 20, (Associated Press.)—Full election returns from all sections of Germany are coming into Berlin slowly because of the work in apportioning the vote among the six leading parties.

Based on incomplete returns available at 8 o'clock tonight, the Majority Socialists had from 43 to 45 per cent. of the total vote. With the Independent Socialists and the German Democrats, the Majority Socialists will constitute the Left of the National Assembly, with 65 per cent. of the seats.

The Democratic Party has made an excellent showing, and may outstrip the Centrists (Christian People's Party) in the final count.

The Independent Socialists made a strong eleventh-hour rally in Berlin, and probably will get four out of the fourteen seats from Greater Berlin. The Majority Socialists will get five seats from Greater Berlin, the Democrats two, and the three parties of the Right one each.

Socialists Outvoted in Württemberg.

The combined bourgeois parties in the Kingdom of Württemberg and the Province of Hohenzollern, Prussia, elected ten delegates to the National Assembly. The Majority Socialists seated seven and the Independent Socialists none. The combined popular vote of the Socialists was 506,000, and of the bourgeois parties 920,000.

In Mecklenburg and Lübeck the combined bourgeois parties elected three delegates and the Socialists three.

The Majority Socialists appear to have made big gains in East Prussia.

In Hanover and Bremen the Socialists had a large majority over the Independents.

The Independent Socialists in Leipsic polled 195,000 votes against 95,000 for the Majority Socialists.

At Frankfort-on-the-Oder the Majority Socialists elected four delegates, the German Democrats two, the National People's Party two, while the Independent Socialists, the German People's Party, and the Centrists failed to get a seat.

In the Magdeburg-Anhalt district the German Democrats got three delegates, the Majority Socialists seven, the National People's Party one, and the Independent Socialists, German People's Party, and Centrists none.

May Get Final Count Today.

The official final count of the national vote probably will not be available before Wednesday. Numerous votes in Berlin are being contested by the Independent Socialists, who charge the Majority Socialists with having used an illegal caption on their party ballot.

It is probable that former Chief of

Continued on Page Three.

Denial That Root or Taft Will Be Wilson's Alternate

By RICHARD V. OULAHAN.

Copyright, 1919, by The New York Times Co.
By Wireless to The New York Times.

PARIS, Jan. 21.—Statements from New York printed in the Paris afternoon newspapers that Elihu Root or William Howard Taft will succeed President Wilson on the American delegation when the President returns to America are said by those close to the President to be unfounded, although no authoritative statement has been issued.

These reports are entirely contrary to the President's announced intentions when he left America. He had arranged then that Secretary Baker should come to France to take his place in the plenipotentiary panel, and there is every reason to believe that there has been no change in his plans. The system for the rotation of plenipotentiaries was adopted, it is understood, partly to fit Mr. Baker's case.

MANUEL READY TO RESUME CROWN

Has Placed Himself Entirely at Disposal of Portugal, His Lord-in-Waiting Says.

ROYALIST CABINET FORMED

Revolt Successful in North, Spanish Government Hears—Lisbon Remains Loyal.

Copyright, 1919, by The New York Times Company.
Special Cable to The New York Times.

LONDON, Jan. 21.—Viscount Asseca, Lord-in-Waiting to former King Manuel of Portugal, received The Daily Chronicle representative tonight at the hotel in London where the ex-King is staying. When the latest message from Vigo was shown to the Viscount he made the following statement:

"At the beginning of the war King Manuel made it distinctly understood that there was to be no movement in his favor in Portugal and that his country was to devote the whole of its energies to prosecution of the war. The assassination of the President in December altered the situation and seemed to threaten the country with chaos.

"In the circumstances a new situation was opened up, the possibility of which before was out of the question. The King's position was this, that he placed himself entirely at the disposal of Portugal. If his country wished him to return he would at once do so without any reference to difficulties or dangers that the course would involve.

"He has been treated with infinite kindness in this country, where he has greatly enjoyed his stay, but he has lived with no other idea than to return to his throne."

MADRID, Jan. 21.—The monarchist movement in Portugal, headed by Paiva Conceiro, has been successful in Northern Portugal, and a Government has been formed at Oporto, according to a report received by the Spanish Government yesterday from the Governor of the Province of Ponte Vedra, in Northwestern Spain, who added that Lisbon was believed to have joined the movement.

The monarchical Government, it was said, was constituted with Paiva Conceiro as President of the Council and Food Minister; M. Saleri, Minister of Home Affairs; Viscount Barro, Minister of Justice and Instruction; Magalhaes Lima, Minister of Foreign Affairs; Silva Ramos, Minister of Communication and Public Works; Count Asevedo, Minister of Labor, and Tamagnini Barbosa, Minister of War.

Advices from another source state that the telegraph and telephone lines between Lisbon and Oporto have been cut, and declare that Manuel has also been proclaimed King in Lisbon.

Direct news from Lisbon, received here in an official message, however, states that the Government controls the

Continued on Page Two.

Latest Returns of the German Election Show Socialist Lead for Assembly Seats

The following table shows the definite elections to seats in the German National Assembly, as shown by the latest cabled returns:

	Maj. Soc.	Ind. Soc.	Democrats.	People's.	Chris. People's.	National.	Comb'd Anti-Soc.
Berlin	5	4	2	1	1	1	..
Saxony	17	3	6	2	..	4	..
Württemberg	7	..	..	..	..	..	10
Mecklenburg and Lübeck	3	..	..	1	1	1	..
Baden	5	..	3	..	5	8	..
Hamburg	7	1	3	..	..	..	..
Magdeburg-Anhalt	7	..	3	1	..	..	..
Frankfort-on-Oder	4	..	2	2	..	..	..
Totals	55	8	19	7	7	14	10

Estimated distribution of seats in the National Assembly, based on incomplete returns: Majority Socialists, 184; Majority and Independent Socialists and German Democrats combined, 268; other parties, 144. Total seats in the Assembly, about 410.

Total popular vote so far announced in detail—5,791,430.

Party Totals—Majority Socialists, 1,593,366; Independent Socialists, 548,795; Democrats, 088,315; Christian People's Party, 707,730; People's Party, 198,373; National Party, 218,635; Bavarian parties, 410,224, in Württemberg only. Combined Socialists, 506,000; Combined Anti-Socialists, 920,000.

A Copenhagen compilation of the vote gives a total of 6,082,311, of which the Majority Socialists are said to have received 2,093,422.

The Majority Socialists are the party of Premier Ebert, from which the radical element split and formed the Independent Socialist Party.

The Democratic Party is a radical combination of the former National Liberals and Progressives.

The People's Party is the Pan-German element.

The Christian People's Party is the old Centrist or Catholic Party, now joined by many Protestants.

The National Party is made up of former Conservatives.

IRISH ASSEMBLY PROCLAIMS THE IRISH REPUBLIC

Declaration of Independence Read to First Sinn Fein Assembly in Dublin.

MEETING AT MANSION HOUSE

Evacuation of Ireland by the Garrison of British Troops Is Demanded.

APPEAL TO FREE NATIONS

Urges Recognition of National Status and "Right to Vindication" at Peace Conference.

DUBLIN, Jan. 21, (Associated Press).—Twenty-five members of the Sinn Fein Society elected to the British House of Commons assembled here this afternoon and formally constituted themselves the "Dail Eireann," which is Irish Gaelic for "Irish Parliament."

They elected Charles Burgess, whose Irish name is Cathal Brugha, Speaker. They also adopted a declaration of independence and an address to the free nations of the world and appointed a committee consisting of Count Plunkett, Arthur Griffiths and Professor Edward De Valeera to present the claims of Ireland to self-determination to the Peace Conference at Paris.

The two last named being in British prisons, only the venerable Count Plunkett can proceed to Paris, and then only provided the British Government consents to give him passports.

Proceedings Were Dull.

The walls of the hall were quaintly embellished with classic statues in plaster and coats of arms. Past Lord Mayors have witnessed many more exciting dramas, notably in recent years the conventions of the Nationalist Party, when there were impassioned speeches and hot party contests. That today's proceedings seemed tame by contrast was due to the fact that they were conducted in the dead language of the Irish tongue. This was a tribute to sentiment, but it was deadening to interest. Few of the 2,000 auditors understood the addresses.

Oratory was killed by the process of reading all the speeches, and even some of the delegates had trouble in following them on their manuscripts. The only concession to popular interest was the translation of the declaration of independence and the address to the free nations in English and French, and this was a wearisome process.

It should not be inferred there was any lack of emotion or want of feeling or responsibility on the part of the delegates. They evidently felt themselves men playing great parts in a solemn sacrament.

A crowd of perhaps a thousand, including many women and children, wearing green, white and yellow ribbons, pressed around the door of the Mansion House, watching the delegates enter. Only two policemen were visible, but the Sinn Fein had its own police—youths wearing white arm bands—to keep order.

Another crowd of different type was on hand—repatriated war prisoners of the Dublin Fusiliers. They had been entertained at luncheon in the Mansion House, and their friends and the public generally were waiting outside to cheer them.

This combination furnished the possibilities of a clash. But none occurred.

A Dingy Meeting Place.

The rotunda of the Mansion House, where the congress met, is a dingy old place, lighted by stained glass windows overhead. The platform and half the floor were fitted with tables for officers and delegates. The remainder of the floor and the circular gallery were reserved for the public, admission being by ticket.

A large proportion of the audience consisted of women. The number of young priests was conspicuous. One of the popular figures arriving first was Father O'Flanagan, who recently was dismissed from his parish by the Bishop on account of his political activity.

There was a brief demonstration when the delegates advanced down the centre aisle, the people standing on their seats and applauding them.

The youthfulness of the Sinn Fein leaders was their most noticeable characteristic. There were hardly a half dozen gray heads in the group. Count Plunkett, Member of Parliament and one of the leaders of the party, introduced in a few terse sentences Charles S. Burgess, a young man who acted as Chairman and who made a short speech which was much applauded. Most of the members of the party crossed themselves frequently during the prayer of the Rev. Father O'Flanagan.

The roll call was made in English. It included all the Members of Parliament elected from Ireland to the British Parliament. Naturally a majority of these men failed to respond, as they are in prison.

Mention of the name of Sir Edward Carson, leader of the Ulsterites, was the cause of much merriment during the session. The most striking feature of the program was the reading of the Declaration of Independence. First in Irish, with the delegates standing, and afterward in English and French, "Ireland's address to the free nations" was read. It began:

"The nation of Ireland, having her national independence, calls through her elected representatives, in Parliament as-

Continued on Page Two.

COUNCIL TO DECIDE ON RUSSIA TODAY; COMPROMISE INQUIRY PLAN EXPECTED; WON'T RECEIVE ANY PARTY SPOKESMAN

See in Reinforcement of Polish Army A Means of Checking Russian Bolshevism

Copyright, 1919, by The New York Times Company.
By Wireless to The New York Times.

LONDON, Jan. 21.—The Daily Chronicle's diplomatic correspondent, discussing the Russian problem now before the Peace Conference, says that the telegrams exchanged between Great Britain and America alone on this portentous subject would fill a volume.

"The opinion obtains here," he says, "that if any intervention is sanctioned it will take the form of reinforcing the Polish Army, which would thus offer a wall to Bolshevism from the east to the west. Polish forces hitherto employed in the west would be strengthened by the addition of two American divisions."

The correspondent proceeds to point out that the weak point in this proposal is the uncertainty as to the disposition of the populace, and whether Bolshevism can be fought by such means. Premier Paderewski's difficulties are considerable, and are as great in the economic as in the political field. The question is how Poland can exist without close economic relations with Russia, since she cannot hope to find a market for her manufactures in the German or Austrian States. The correspondent proceeds:

"The interdependence of Poland, Esthonia, and other constituent parts of the old empire inspire the belief in many quarters that the only real remedy for the present anarchy is federation. Such a solution will probably receive sympathetic consideration from the conference. It is obvious that Russia is too large a territory to be administered from one centre, and its interests also are too diverse. Federation, then, seems to be the most workable system."

DOMINIONS SEEK TO ENTER LEAGUE

British Colonies Want Admission, with Same Status as Other Nations.

EARNED IT, SAYS HUGHES

Nationhood Won by Australia's Efforts in War—Natural Outcome, Says Borden.

PARIS, Jan. 21, (Associated Press.)—Canada, Australia, and the other self-governing Dominions of Great Britain have begun an effort for individual representation in the projected League of Nations. They claim the right to enter the league with the same status as other nations.

The question is now being discussed by the British and Dominion officials, and it will be for the British Government to say whether it shall ask the Peace Conference to accord the Dominions individual membership in the League.

The admission by the Peace Conference of the right of the Dominions to a separate representation at the sessions is held to have been in itself tacit recognition of their nationhood. The new proposal, however, goes further, and it is considered that its acceptance would be a formal acknowledgment by the world of the Dominions existing autonomously within the British Empire and of their equality with other nations. Unofficially it is stated that England will probably approve the plan, although the matter is still the subject of grave discussion.

Premier Hughes of Australia, discussing the claims of the dominions with The Associated Press, said:

"We have earned the right by our sacrifices and efforts in this great war to a place in the family of nations. We expect to come in with the same status as any other nation. So far as I understand it, President Wilson's conception of the League of Nations is that all nations shall come in on a basis of equality, the nations to come in as entities and retain their sovereign rights as nations.

"That being so, of course, once the status of nationhood is established, the Dominions would come in as the other nations and would be accorded whatever right they have."

Sir Robert L. Borden, Premier of Canada, gave to The Associated Press tonight the following statement regarding the claims of the Dominions:

"In the Imperial War Council in 1917 I had the honor of moving in behalf of Canada a resolution which was accepted by the United Kingdom and the other dominions and which declared that the readjustment of the constitutional relations of the component parts of the British Empire should be based on the full recognition of the dominions as autonomous nations of the Imperial Commonwealth.

"The principle thus established has been illustrated and carried into effect by the Peace Conference, in which the several Dominions have distinctive representation as members of the worldwide Britannic commonwealth, which, in open sense, is itself a League of Nations.

"The resolution of 1917, to which I have alluded, declared in emphatic terms the right of each Dominion to an adequate voice in the foreign policy and foreign relations with which the proposed League of Nations is intimately and vitally concerned.

"It is neither necessary nor desirable to forecast the exact method by which this essential purpose shall be fulfilled in framing the constitution of the proposed league."

Canada, Australia, and New Zealand have for several years claimed for themselves absolute independence, so far as the conduct of internal affairs was concerned, but this principle has never been formally admitted by England. The Dominions, it is said, will now ask for formal recognition of it.

The announcement of the aspirations of the Dominions is being discussed with the keenest interest in official circles in Paris. The question is being frequently asked whether this present important step is to be followed later by insistence on the part of the Dominions of a right as nations to have a full share in dictating the foreign policy of the empire as far as it affects the Dominions.

"The British Empire is in one sense a national entity and in another a League of Nations in itself," was the way one high personage summarized the situation tonight.

The Italian Government has nominated Senator Scialoja, former Minister of Justice, as the Italian member of the international committee in Paris to study the question of the League of Nations. Leon Bourgeois and Lord Robert Cecil are the French and British members respectively.

LICHNOWSKY PLEA FOR A JUST PEACE

German Diplomat Expresses His Faith in Wilson and British Statesmen.

ANXIOUS ABOUT FRONTIERS

But Believes Germany's Rights Will Be Respected, "Especially in the East."

BERLIN, Jan. 21, (Associated Press.)—Prince Lichnowsky, former German Ambassador to Great Britain, today gave the following statement to The Associated Press:

"A peace of right and justice, provided it is not merely to be a phrase behind which a peace of violence conceals itself as a Pax Britannica, can only be such a peace as neither enslaves nor mutilates the conquered and which leaves him the possibility of recuperating, of paying his debts and of entering with complete confidence into the peaceful competition of a Society of Nations. A League of Nations which has its roots only in statutes and is not in the hearts of peoples is worthless.

"Just as the conquerors hundreds of years ago treated France forbearingly and left in its possession its old borders, including even German Alsace, which had earlier been taken away from us just as forcibly as we later took it back, so I believe there will be left to us, especially in the East, our borders which are indispensable for us politically and economically.

"Not only ethnography, but also geography, should be taken into consideration in establishing borders. The Poles and Czechs have no more right to our mixed-language territories, which owe their prosperity alone to German organization and to the German market, than we have to all the German territories outside the empire, including the German parts of Alsace-Lorraine.

"Hence a peace of justice would be only such a one as neither boycotts us nor lays upon us intolerable financial burdens which would make us dependents for all time, nor one which creates untenable borders and robs us of lands which we require geographically and economically.

"Mr. Wilson and the British statesmen have announced their war aims to be the abolishing of autocracy and militarism and making good the harm the war has done to Belgium and France. I expect confidently that they will now demonstrate the uprightness of their intentions and that they will not create the impression that a war psychosis now rules them, just as it ruled with us during the war."

STEVENS TO BE HEAD OF TRANS-SIBERIAN

Russian General Horvath to be Co-Director—Allies to Speed Up Work on Road.

VLADIVOSTOK, Jan. 20, (via Montreal.)—The agreement for Allied control of the Trans-Siberian Railway gives the Americans control of the line from Pogranichana to Omsk, a distance of 3,000 miles; the British will have charge of the line from Omsk to the fighting front; the French will control the Khabarovsk line, and the Japanese the line from Blagovieshchensk to Chita.

The administrative positions are to be filled by Russians and Americans in equal numbers. There are to be Russians only on the working staff. John F. Stevens, head of the American Railway Commission to Russia, is to be chief administrator of the railway, with the Russian General Horvath as co-director. Americans are to guard the line.

Cars and engines are being supplied from the United States. Great workshops are being opened in Vladivostok, and every effort is to be made to speed up operations.

AGAINST DEAL WITH SOVIETS

Danish Diplomat Emphasizes the Futility of Treating With Them.

CALL WILSON REACTIONARY

Red Leaders Scoff at the President and Lloyd George, Council Is Told.

OUR LEAGUE PLAN UP SOON

Wilson Expected to Present Memorial at Full Session Late This Week.

PARIS, Jan. 21, (Associated Press.)—The Supreme Council of the Great Powers hopes to formulate a concrete proposal on Russia at tomorrow's meeting. This was the definite official announcement of the communiqué issued tonight after the council had been considering the Russian situation continuously for two days.

It can be added that, while this concrete proposal was not finally decided upon and reduced to writing, its main features were agreed upon in principle. The members came from the session, however, feeling that there was no sovereign remedy insuring a certain cure for the difficult and dangerous situation, and that it would be desirable to embody several lines of action in the proposal.

The first effect of this decision will be that neither Sergius Sazonoff, the Russian Minister of Foreign Affairs before the revolution, nor any Soviet agents will be received in Paris as exponents of Russian affairs, but that some form of inquiry or investigation of political conditions in Russia will be made without considering the presence in Paris of the champions of either side of the dispute. This determination is largely the result of a strong sentiment in some quarters against having any direct dealings with the Bolsheviki.

Early indications were that Premier Lloyd George's proposal to M. Pichon, the French Foreign Minister, would again take form in having Soviet agents come here, and three names of prominent leaders were mentioned as possible emissaries. But this is now said to have been definitely superseded by a plan of inquiry or investigation without involving the presence of Soviet agents.

Dane's Testimony Against Soviets.

The Danish Minister to Russia, Harold Scavenius, who took charge of French interests on the departure of the Ambassador, made a statement before the executive session of the council today on conditions in Russia, which also had a strong influence in determining that Soviet representatives should not come to Paris. He was the last of the Ministers to leave Petrograd, and today he emphasized the futility of trying to conduct any intercourse with the Soviet leaders.

He read an article written by one of the Soviet chiefs declaring that Premier Lloyd George and President Wilson were too conservative and reactionary for the Soviets to deal with.

He also gave exact data on the Bolshevist forces, showing that they did not exceed 90,000 armed men, the remainder being without arms or ammunition, clothing or shoes. He said also that the Red Army was largely recruited from the famished peasants, who took this means to obtain food and the pay the Soviet seemed able to give them.

Polish Question Up Today.

The Polish question will come up at tomorrow's session as well as the matter of Russia. It is understood in this connection that President Wilson has received information concerning the spread of the Bolshevist movement in Poland, where the Russian Red Army is nearing Warsaw. It is expected that proposals will be renewed for the allied armies to help the Polish Army with war material, but this has not yet been decided.

The official communiqué tonight also announces that the question of procedure of the conference was again discussed. The nature of this discussion was in determining the appointment of two committees, the first to deal with reparation for the damages of the war, the second to deal with the subject of the League of Nations.

Another full session of the Peace Conference will probably be held next Friday or Saturday for the purpose of the presentation of a memorial on the League of Nations by President Wilson. The English and French me-

1

"All the News That's Fit to Print."

The New York Times.

THE WEATHER
Cloudy, probably rain Sunday; Monday clearing; southeast winds.
For full weather report see Page 22.

Section 1

VOL. LXVIII...NO. 22,282. NEW YORK, SUNDAY, JANUARY 26, 1919.—96 PAGES, In Eight Parts, Including Picture and Magazine Sections (Rotogravure) and Book Section. FIVE CENTS In Greater New York | Elsewhere SEVEN CENTS

LEAGUE OF NATIONS PLAN IS ADOPTED; PEACE CONFERENCE ACTS ON WILSON PLEA, STRONGLY SUPPORTED BY LLOYD GEORGE

[illegible]OVE TO CANCEL 15 BILLIONS IN WAR EXPENSES

[illegible] Bill Revokes $7,179,-[illegible]944 in Contracts and $8,-221,029,294 in Authorizations.

[illegible]TS ARMY AND NAVY

[illegible] Has Not Yet Found [illegible] to Cut Allotments to Other Departments.

[illegible] SAVING IN THE ARMY

[illegible] in Ordnance Department Alone $9,217,648,304, and Quartermaster $3,756,135,307.

Special to The New York Times.

[illegible]ASHINGTON, Jan. 25.—The cessa[illegible] of war saved the nation billions [illegible] dollars through the cancellation of [illegible]tracts and authorizations. In the [illegible]ficiency bill reported to the House by [illegible] Appropriations Committee, today, [illegible]tracts for $7,179,156,944 are ordered [illegible] and authorizations amounting [illegible]221,029,294 are withdrawn. If the [illegible] had continued another six months [illegible] estimated that the expenditure of [illegible] these amounts, or more than $15,-[illegible] would have been necessary. [illegible] bill carries recommendations for [illegible]propriations of $285,244,259.45 for the [illegible] services of the Government, [illegible]ded as follows: War Department, [illegible]473,782.68; Navy Establishment, $280,-[illegible].225.38; Civil Service, $7,833,750.57; [illegible]vy Department, $154,370.84.

[illegible] largest items for which appro[illegible]ations are recommended follow:

[illegible]ar Department — Temporary em[illegible]ees, $4,000,000; disposition of remains [illegible] officers and men, $2,473,782.68.

[illegible]avy Department: Bureau of Navi[illegible]tion, $1,331,178.64; Bureau of Yards and Docks, $4,100,000; Bureau of Construction, $15,000,000; Bureau of Steam Engineering, $4,330,582.

Representative Swagar Sherley, Chairman, in his report said:

"The repeal of appropriations and withdrawal of authorizations has been confined to the military and naval establishments, not because funds voted to other departments are all required, for such is not the fact, but because the magnitude of the task made impossible at this time a review of the other departments, and it is hoped that in connection with the Sundry Civil and other bills many of these surplus funds may be dealt with. The committee in recommending that various sums shall be covered into the Treasury does not mean to affirm in any sense that the total of the moneys left with the various bureaus is needed or should be expended, or to approve or disapprove various activities set forth in the hearings. There should, and doubless will be, large savings made from these balances.

"What the committee has endeavored to do is to cover into the Treasury such sums that plainly are not needed, but as it is necessarily uncertain just to what extent the Government may be able by cancellation of contracts and discontinuance of projects to reduce its obligations, the committee has deemed it wise to leave funds amply sufficient to meet such obligations. To have undertaken to pass judgment on remaining activities would have been to usurp the prerogatives of many of the committees and would have required a detailed examination that would have taken many additional months.

"The labors of the committee have been greatly added to because of the absence of any uniform system of keeping accounts by the various departments, and it desires to express the [illegible] that Congress may provide soon [illegible] such a system of accounting. While [illegible] work of the committee by some may [illegible] thought unnecessary on the ground [illegible] the departments probably would [illegible] have expended the sums anyway it [illegible] the judgment of the committee that [illegible] was wise directly to provide against [illegible] expenditure, and it cannot be [illegible]ted that the examination of their [illegible]ances and survey of their activities [illegible] needs by the various corps of the [illegible] and navy brought about by the [illegible] of the committee should enable [illegible] departments to make savings of [illegible] millions."

[illegible] following table shows the savings [illegible] cancellation of contracts and authori[illegible]:

ARMY ESTABLISHMENT.

	Appropriations.	Authorizations.
[illegible]derv....	$83,373,290.04	$15,000,000.00
Aeron...	85,000,000.00	....
[illegible]ft prod.	492,000,000.00	....
[illegible] Corps...	3,740,385,307.76	15,750,000.00
[illegible] Dept...	54,145,713.73	65,000,000.00
[illegible] Corps..	792,580,435.76	200,000,000.00
[illegible] Dept...	1,563,309,088.55	7,714,279,294.70
[illegible]m. Warf.	153,932,610.68	150,000,000.00
Total army	$6,844,795,077.70	$8,190,029,274.70

NAVAL ESTABLISHMENT.

[illegible]ation	$58,000,000.00	....
[illegible]igation	4,500,000.00	....
[illegible]ance ...	164,835,843.60	$31,000,000.00
[illegible] Works	2,173,627.00	....
[illegible]p. and Ac.	23,080,000.00	....
[illegible]an Eng..	1,420.33	....
[illegible]e Corps	41,216,975.06	....
Total navy	$334,361,806.98	$31,000,000.00
Grand total army and navy	$7,179,156,944.68	$8,221,029,294.70

Combined appropriation and authorization, $15,400,186,239.38.

Text of the Resolution to Create a World League As Unanimously Adopted by Peace Conference

PARIS, Jan. 25.—Following is the text of the resolution relating to the creation of a League of Nations, which was adopted by the plenary session of the Peace Conference today:

The conference, having considered the proposals for the creation of a League of Nations, resolved that:

It is essential to the maintenance of the world settlement which the associated nations are now met to establish that a League of Nations be created to promote international obligations and to provide safeguards against war.

This league should be created as an integral part of the general treaty of peace and should be open to every civilized nation which can be relied on to promote its objects.

The members of the league should periodically meet in international conference and should have a permanent organization and secretaries to carry on the business of the league in the intervals between the conferences.

The conference therefore appoints a committee, representative of the associated Governments, to work out the details of the constitution and the functions of the league and the draft of resolutions in regard to breaches of the laws of war for presentation to the Peace Conference.

Responsibility.

That a commission, composed of two representatives apiece from the five great powers and five representatives to be elected by the other powers, be appointed to inquire and report upon the following:

First—The responsibility of the authors of the war.

Second—The facts as to breaches of the laws and customs of war committed by the forces of the German Empire and their allies on land, on sea, and in the air during the present war.

Third—The degree of responsibility for these offenses attaching to particular members of the enemy's forces, including members of the General Staffs and other individuals, however highly placed.

Fourth—The constitution and procedure of a tribunal appropriate to the trial of these offenses.

Fifth—Any other matters, cognate or ancillary to the above, which may arise in the course of the inquiry and which the commission finds it useful and relevant to take into consideration.

Reparation.

Following is the draft of a resolution in regard to reparation which the conference adopted:

That a commission be appointed, which shall comprise not more than three representatives apiece from each of the five great powers and not more than two representatives apiece from Belgium, Greece, Poland, Rumania, and Serbia, to examine and report:

First—On the amount of reparation which the enemy countries ought to pay.

Second—On what they are capable of paying, and,

Third—On the method, the form, and time within which payment should be made.

International Legislation.

A resolution in regard to international legislation on industrial and labor questions was passed. It reads:

That a commission, composed of two representatives apiece from the five great powers and five representatives to be elected by the other powers represented at the Peace Conference, be appointed to inquire into the conditions of employment from the international aspect and to consider the international means necessary to secure common action on matters affecting conditions of employment and to recommend the form of a permanent agency to continue such inquiry and consideration, in co-operation with and under the direction of the League of Nations.

This resolution was adopted regarding international control of ports, waterways, and railways:

International Control.

That a commission composed of two representatives apiece from the five great powers and five representatives of the other powers be appointed, to inquire and report upon the international régime for ports, waterways, and railways.

CROMWELL DEATHS NOW CONFIRMED

Bordeaux Police Chief Reports That Young Women Committed Suicide.

PARIS, Jan. 25, (Associated Press.)—The Commissioner of Police at Bordeaux confirms the report of the suicide of the Misses Gladys and Dorothea Cromwell.

The American Red Cross Headquarters here, in answer to inquiries, says it has been informed that the Misses Cromwell sailed on the French steamer La Lorraine. Friends of the twin sisters accompanied them to the pier.

The officer in charge of the Red Cross party on board the ship sent by wireless to the Red Cross a copy of the note found in the stateroom occupied by the sisters in which they said they intended to commit suicide.

The drowning of the Misses Dorothea and Gladys Cromwell from the French liner La Lorraine soon after the vessel sailed from France is still a mystery to members of their family in New York.

Seymour L. Cromwell, the only brother of the young women, discredits the reports and declared last night at his residence, 160 East Seventy-fourth Street, that he believed a mistake had been made, because of the conflicting dispatches and a cheerful letter he had received from his sisters less than a week ago.

Mr. Cromwell said late last night:

"Not only I, but the State Department and of course the Red Cross have sent cables to France endeavoring to find out some definite explanation. As yet I have received no satisfying word, but I was given to understand when the cables were sent that no answer would be forthcoming for thirty-six hours.

"The only thing that can convince me that such a thing could ever have happened would be to receive a wireless from the liner Espagne stating that my sisters were not aboard that vessel. Returning from France on La Lorraine is one of my most intimate friends and also two close friends of my partner in business. Wireless messages have been sent to these friends, but as yet no answer has come."

The Misses Cromwell were 32 years old and not 22 as first reported.

SEEK TO INSTALL STATE SOCIALISM

North Dakota Nonpartisan League, Controlling Legislature, Plans Legislation.

Special to The New York Times.

BISMARCK, N. D., Jan. 25.—Seven million dollars would be invested by North Dakota in the establishment of a State bank and a system of terminal elevators and flour mills under the industrial program introduced in the State Legislature by the Nonpartisan League, which controls both houses.

Complete revision of the State's scheme of taxation, by which the taxation burden would be transferred from personal property to corporations, incomes, and land, also has been proposed, and has the support of the league majorities, which are bound by a caucus pledge to pass all legislation indorsed by such caucus.

The abandonment of the old system of appointive State officials for fixed terms also is due, with the substitution of the Socialist plan, by which officers such as State Tax Commissioners, educational directors, charitable institution directors, &c., may be removed at will.

These, in a general way, are the big problems which confront the Legislature, now twenty days old, and which William Lemke, Vice President of the Nonpartisan League, says will be adjourned by Feb. 10.

This is the first State Legislature completely controlled by the nonpartisans. They have more than two-thirds of the members of the House and Senate, and by using emergency clauses in their administration measures they will come very near to beating referendum of their bills, as 30,000 signatures are required to refer bills to which emergency clauses are attached, and the State has only about 100,000 voters all told.

In carrying out their program for industrial enterprises, the nonpartisans

Continued on Page Five.

REDS WANT PARLEY NEARER

Tchitcherin, Foreign Minister, Says Princes' Islands Are Too Remote.

BUT WILL CONSIDER PLAN

Promises to Do So on Receipt of Confirmation of Council's Reported Decision.

TAKES A SUPERCILIOUS TONE

Invitation Comes, He Says, When Soviets Have Settled Internal Troubles of Russia.

PARIS, Jan. 25.—M. Tchitcherin, the Bolshevist Foreign Minister, has sent a wireless message to the Soviet representative in Sweden asking for confirmation of the decision of the Supreme Council of the Peace Conference to send a mission to confer with representatives of the different factions in Russia on Princes' Islands.

M. Tchitcherin's message says that the islands are too remote for such a meeting. He objects to the isolation of the islands as tending to surround the conference with secrecy, and also objects to leaving to the Entente the choice of participants.

This proposition of the Supreme Council, the message says, is made at a time when the Bolsheviki are victorious over their opponents and the internal situation of Russia has been settled, but the Soviet Government, on receipt of the confirmation requested, will carefully consider the proposal.

More Russians Enter Protests.

The Council of the national and democratic bloc of Russian political organizations abroad has sent a strongly worded protest to Premier Clemenceau against the decision of the Supreme Council to call a conference of the Russian factions.

"We would be men without honor and courage if we accepted for a single moment a truce such as proposed to us while all that are dear are in danger of death—violent death by execution or assassination or slow death through hunger," the protest says.

"The interest of humanity in general and democracy in particular requires the establishment in Russia of a régime based on the sovereignty of the people freely expressed. An improvised meeting at the Princes' Islands cannot be an expression of this sort. Russia has long clamored for the free election of a Constituent Assembly. The attempt was stifled by the Bolsheviki by force of arms, and they are today asked to make the voice of Russia heard."

The Russian Bolshevist Government at Moscow, according to information received by the Socialist newspaper L'Humanité, is surprised that the suggestion made by the allied and associated Powers for a conference between the Russian factions comes at a time when the Bolsheviki are victorious in the field. The Bolsheviki, however, the advices add, do not reject the principle of a conference.

Vladimir Bourtzeff, a well-known Russian revolutionist, in an article in the Matin says that the Russian parties opposed to the Bolsheviki will positively refuse to attend the conference on Princes' Islands, because they look on the Bolsheviki as traitors to the fatherland and as murderers who have dishonored Russia.

Vasili Maklakoff, the latest Russian Ambassador accredited to France, according to the same article, says that all Russians in Paris feel deeply humiliated by the proposal of the allied and associated Powers. The Ambassador adds that a party truce and cessation of hostilities, as requested by the Allies, could have only one result—the hampering of the armies which are about to liberate Northern Russia—without putting an end to the reign of terror. The Ambassador is also quoted as declaring that only the Bolsheviki will profit by such a conference.

Alluding to the decision of the Supreme Council of the Peace Conference to send a delegation to meet representatives of the various Russian factions, which decision has been objected to in some Russian quarters as not in the real interest of the Russian people, M. Maklakoff said yesterday:

"The presence of France and America at the Peace Conference is a guarantee that any unfriendly intention toward Russia, even if there were such, would not be countenanced. It is most strange, however, that France, which on Dec. 29, in alluding to Bolshevism while stating her attitude toward Russia, declared that she would 'never have anything to do with crime,' should now have joined in the proposal to hold a discussion with Bolshevist delegates at the Princes' Islands."

It may be noted in connection with the attitude of Ambassador Maklakoff to-

Continued on Page Three.

Text of Wilson's Speech to Peace Conference Pointing Out Need of a League of Nations

PARIS, Jan. 25.—President Wilson's address before the Peace Conference today was as follows:

Mr. Chairman—I consider it a distinguished privilege to be permitted to open the discussion in this conference on the League of Nations. We have assembled for two purposes, to make the present settlements which have been rendered necessary by this war and also to secure the peace of the world, not only by the present settlements but by the arrangements we shall make at this conference for its maintenance.

The League of Nations seems to me to be necessary for both of these purposes. There are many complicated questions connected with the present settlements, which perhaps cannot be successfully worked out to an ultimate issue by the decisions we shall arrive at here. I can easily conceive that many of these settlements will need subsequent consideration; that many of the decisions we make shall need subsequent alteration in some degree, for if I may judge by my own study of some of these questions they are not susceptible for confident judgments at present.

It is therefore necessary that we should set up some machinery by which the work of this conference should be rendered complete.

We have assembled here for the purpose of doing very much more than making the present settlements that are necessary. We are assembled under very peculiar conditions of world opinion. I may say, without straining the point, that we are not the representatives of Governments, but representatives of the peoples.

It will not suffice to satisfy governmental circles anywhere. It is necessary that we should satisfy the opinion of mankind.

The burdens of this war have fallen in an unusual degree upon the whole population of the countries involved. I do not need to draw for you the picture of how the burden has been thrown back from the front upon the older men, upon the women, upon the children, upon the homes of the civilized world, and how the real strain of the war has come where the eyes of the Government could not reach, but where the heart of humanity beats.

We are bidden by these people to make a peace which will make them secure. We are bidden by these people to see to it that this strain does not come upon them again. And I venture to say that it has been possible for them to bear this strain because they hoped that those who represented them could get together after this war and make such another sacrifice unnecessary.

It is a solemn obligation on our part, therefore, to make permanent arrangements that justice shall be rendered and peace maintained.

This is the central object of our meeting. Settlements may be temporary, but the action of the nations in the interest of peace and justice must be permanent. We can set up permanent processes. We may not be able to set up a permanent decision.

Therefore, it seems to me that we must take as far as we can a picture of the world into our minds. Is it not a startling circumstance, for one thing, that the great discoveries of science, that the quiet studies of men in laboratories, that the thoughtful developments which have taken place in quiet lecture rooms have now been turned to the destruction of civilization? The powers of destruction have not so much multiplied as they have gained facilities.

The enemy, whom we have just overcome, had at his seats of learning some of the principal centres of scientific study and discovery, and he used them in order to make destruction sudden and complete. And only the watchful and continuous co-operation of men can see to it that science, as well as armed men, is kept within the harness of civilization.

In a sense the United States is less interested in this subject than the other nations here assembled. With her great territory and her extensive sea borders, it is less likely that the United States should suffer from the attack of enemies than that other nations should suffer. And the ardor of the United States—for it is a very deep and genuine ardor—for the society of nations is not an ardor springing out of fear or apprehension, but an ardor springing out of the ideals which have come in the consciousness of this war.

In coming into this war the United States never for a moment thought that she was intervening in the politics of Europe, or the politics of Asia, or the politics of any part of the world. Her thought was that all the world had now become conscious that there was a single cause of justice and of liberty for men of every kind and place.

Therefore, the United States should feel that its part in this war should be played in vain if there ensued upon it abortive European settlements. It would feel that it could not take part in guaranteeing those European settlements unless that guarantee involved the continuous superintendence of the peace of the world by the associated nations of the world.

Therefore, it seems to me that we must concern our best judgment in order to make this League of Nations a vital thing—a thin sometimes called into life to meet an exigency—but always functioning in watchful attendance upon the interests of the nations, and that its continuity should be a vital continuity; that its functions are continuing functions that do not permit an intermission of its watchfulness and of its labor; that it should be the eye of the nations, to keep watch upon the common interest—an eye that did not slumber, an eye that was everywhere watchful and attentive.

And if we do not make it vital, what shall we do? We shall disappoint the expectations of the peoples. This is what their thought centres upon.

I have had the very delightful experience of visiting several nations since I came to this side of the water, and every time the voice of the body of the people reached me, through any representative, at the front of the plea stood the hope of the League of Nations.

Gentlemen, the select classes of mankind are no longer the governors of mankind. The fortunes of mankind are now in the hands of the plain people of the whole world. Satisfy them, and you have justified their confidence not only, but have established peace. Fail to satisfy them, and no arrangement that you can make will either set up or steady the peace of the world.

You can imagine, I dare say, the sentiments and the purpose with which the representatives of the United States support this great project for a League of Nations. We regard it as the keynote of the whole, which expressed our purposes and ideals in this war and which the associated nations have accepted as the basis of a settlement.

If we return to the United States without having made every effort in our power to realize this program, we should return to meet the merited scorn of our fellow-citizens. For they are a body that constitute a great democracy. They expect their leaders to speak; their representatives to be their servants.

We have no choice but to obey their mandate. But it is with the greatest enthusiasm and pleasure that we accept that mandate. And because this is the keynote of the whole fabric, we have pledged our every purpose to it, as we have to every item of the fabric. We would not dare abate a single item of the program which constitutes our instructions; we would not dare to compromise upon any matter as the champion of this thing—this peace of the world, this attitude of justice, this principle that we are the masters of no peoples, but are here to see that every people in the world shall choose its own masters and govern its own destinies, not as we wish, but as they wish.

We are here to see, in short, that the very foundations of this war are swept away. Those foundations were the private choice of a small coterie of civil rulers and military staffs. Those foundations were the aggression of great powers upon the small. Those foundations were the holding together of empires of unwilling subjects by the duress of arms. Those foundations were the power of small bodies of men to wield their will and use mankind as pawns in a game. And nothing less than the emancipation of the world from these things will accomplish peace.

You can see that the representatives of the United States are, therefore, never put to the embarrassment of choosing a way of expediency, because they have had laid down before them the unalterable lines of principles. And, thank God, these lines have been accepted as the lines of settlements by all the high-minded men who have had to do with the beginning of this great business.

I hope, Mr. Chairman, when it is known, as I feel confident it will be known, that we have adopted the principle of the League of Nations and mean to work out that principle in effective action, we shall by that single thing have lifted a great part of the load of anxiety from the hearts of men everywhere.

We stand in a peculiar cause. As I go about the streets here I see everywhere the American uniform. Those men came into the war after we had uttered our purpose. They came as crusaders, not merely to win a war, but to win a cause. And I am responsible to them, for it falls to me to formulate the purpose for which I asked them to fight, and I, like them, must be a crusader for these things, whatever it costs and whatever it may be necessary to do in honor to accomplish the object for which they fought.

I have been glad to find from day to day that there is no question of our standing alone in this matter, for there are champions of this cause upon every hand. I am merely avowing this in order that you may understand why, perhaps, it fell to us, who are disengaged from the politics of this great continent and of the Orient, to suggest that this was the keystone of the arch, and why it occurred to the generous mind of your President to call upon me to open this debate. It is not because we alone represent this idea, but because it is our privilege to associate ourselves with you in representing it.

I have only tried in what I have said to give you the fountains of the enthusiasm which is within us for this thing, for those fountains spring, it seems to me, from all the ancient wrongs and sympathies of mankind, and the very pulse of the world seems to beat to the fullest in this enterprise.

CONFERENCE ACTS SWIFTLY

Hears Speeches in Favor of League and Gives Quick Approval

FIRST ADDRESS BY WILSON

Lloyd George Warmly Voices Great Britain's Support of the Proposal.

ORLANDO ALSO BACKS IT

Wilson and House Are American Members of Commission to Draft League Plan.

Delegates of Great Powers on Peace League Commission

PARIS, Jan. 25.—The delegates of the Great Powers on the League of Nations, it was learned tonight, will be:

For the United States—President Wilson and Colonel Edward M. House.

For Great Britain—Lord Robert Cecil and General Jan Christian Smuts.

For France—Leon Bourgeois and Ferdinand Larnaude, Dean of the Faculty of Law of the University of Paris.

For Italy—Premier Orlando and Viterio Scialoia.

For Japan—Viscount Chinda and K. Ochiai.

The delegates of the small nations will be announced later.

PARIS, Jan. 25, (Associated Press.)—The plenary session of the Peace Conference today unanimously adopted the project to establish a League of Nations and name a commission to draft the complete plan.

President Wilson and Colonel House are the two American members of the commission.

The session of the conference began at 3 o'clock in the afternoon in the Salle de la Paix of the Foreign Office with the same imposing setting as the first session, but with little ceremony and a manifest purpose of business.

M. Clemenceau was again in the chair, with President Wilson and the full American delegation at his right, and Premier Lloyd George and the British delegation at his left.

When the session opened it was addressed by President Wilson on the subject of the proposed world league.

The President declared that the conference had solemn obligations to make a permanent settlement.

With great earnestness he asserted that the conference could not complete its work until some further machinery of settlement should be set up.

"We are not here alone," he went on, "as representatives of Governments, but as representatives of peoples, and in the settlements we make we need to satisfy, not the opinions of Governments, but the opinion of mankind."

League Must Have Continuity.

The President contended that a League of Nations must be a vital thing and not casual or occasional. It must have continuity.

"It should be the eye of nations, an eye which never slumbers," he added.

On his travels, the President said, people everywhere had greeted the league as the first thing in their interest.

"Select classes of men no longer direct the affairs of the world," said the President, "but the fortunes of the world are now in the hands of the plain people."

The wish of the people, therefore, must be heard. The war had swept away those old foundations by which small coteries had "used mankind as pawns in a game." Nothing but emancipation from the old system, he contended, would accomplish real peace.

The President said he had seen American soldiers in the street—soldiers who had come, not alone for war, but as "crusaders in a great cause." He added, "And I, like them, must be a crusader, whatever it costs to accomplish that end."

After declaring that the conference was for the purpose of a settlement arising out of the war and to make

1
"All the News That's Fit to Print."

The New York Times.

THE WEATHER
Fair and continued cool Sunday; fair Monday; moderate winds.
For full weather report see Page 23.

Section 1

VOL. LXVIII...NO. 22,436. NEW YORK, SUNDAY, JUNE 29, 1919. 122 PAGES, In Nine Parts, Including Picture and Magazine Sections (Rotogravure) and Book Section. FIVE CENTS In Greater New York | Elsewhere SEVEN CENTS

PEACE SIGNED, ENDS THE GREAT WAR; GERMANS DEPART STILL PROTESTING; PROHIBITION TILL TROOPS DISBAND

WILSON PROMISES TO ACT

Must Wait Until Complete Demobilization, His Word from Paris.

THIS WILL TAKE 7 WEEKS

President Calls Attention of Congress to His Request for Repeal.

LIQUOR MEN UNPREPARED

Had Hoped Until Announcement That Executive Would Intervene at the Eleventh Hour.

Special to The New York Times.

WASHINGTON, June 28.—President Wilson will not lift the ban which provides for war-time prohibition until the demobilization of the army has been terminated.

But when demobilization has been completed, the President will lift the ban. Formal announcement to this effect was made at the White House tonight. The President is in agreement with A. Mitchell Palmer, his Attorney General, that he cannot at this time lift the ban on wartime prohibition. He agrees with the Attorney General that the language of the law is such that he will be free to act on his own initiative, without Congressional action, not immediately after the signing of the treaty of peace, but when the army has been demobilized. As the army has not yet been demobilized, and there are yet a million men in the army, called into service under the emergency of war, the President, in the failure of Congress to vest him with power to call off wartime prohibition, takes the position that he cannot interfere with the putting of wartime prohibition into effect.

The responsibility for putting wartime prohibition into effect is put squarely up to Congress by the President. He takes the position that the law calling for wartime prohibition was an act of Congress, that its terms are clear, and that he had asked Congress to provide for the repeal of the legislation. Congress, having failed to act so far, has left the President's hands tied with legal strings so far as lifting the ban is concerned, and he makes this situation very plain in a cablegram sent to the White House just before he left Paris today.

President Wilson's cablegram was made public at the White House at 8 o'clock tonight by Joseph P. Tumulty, the Private Secretary to the President.

In his message the President said that he could not act until the army had been completely demobilized, and since there were still a million men in the service there was no chance of his taking immediate action. He called attention to the fact that the present difficulty could have been obviated if Congress had heeded his recommendation of several months ago.

The President in his message left no doubt as to what action he will take when demobilization is terminated.

"When demobilization is terminated," says the final sentence of his cablegram, "my power to act without Congressional action will be exercised."

When demobilization has been terminated will be determined by the President upon information to be supplied to him by Secretary Baker and by Attorney General Palmer. The prospects are that six, or perhaps seven, weeks will elapse before demobilization is terminated, which means that the President will probably not be in position, under his construction of the law, to act before the middle or latter part of August in lifting the ban.

It means that wartime prohibition will go into effect on July 1, even though there is no adequate provision legally made for its real enforcement, and that it will remain in effect until the termination of demobilization unless Congress meanwhile adopts the President's request for a repeal of the legislation which provided for the institution of war-time prohibition.

Congress is free at any time to enact the necessary legislation. So far all attempts to bring about repeal have failed on Capitol Hill and there is no present indication that Congress intends to change.

Not only has the President asked Congress to repeal the legislation standing in the way of lifting the ban, but in his cabled statement of today the President declares without equivocation that he will exercise his power to act when demobilization is terminated, and makes it clear he will then lift the ban unless Congress by repealing the act of Nov. 21, 1918, does away with wartime pro-

Continued on Page Eleven.

President Sends A Prohibition Message; Says He Will Act When Demobilization Ends

WASHINGTON, July 28.—The following message from President Wilson, stating his stand on the prohibition question, was made public at the White House tonight by Secretary Tumulty:

I am convinced that the Attorney General is right in advising me that I have no legal power at this time in the matter of the ban on liquor. Under the act of November, 1918, my power to take action is restricted. The act provides that after June 30, 1919, "until the conclusion of the present war and thereafter until the termination of demobilization, the date of which shall be determined and proclaimed by the President, it shall be unlawful, &c." This law does not specify that the ban shall be lifted with the signing of peace, but with the termination of the demobilization of the troops, and I cannot say that this has been accomplished. My information from the War Department is that there are still a million men in the army under the emergency call. It is clear, therefore, that the failure of Congress to act upon the suggestion contained in my message of the twentieth of May, 1919, asking for a repeal of the act of Nov. 21, 1918, so far as it applies to wines and beers, makes it impossible to act in this matter at this time. When demobilization is terminated, my power to act without Congressional action will be exercised.

WOODROW WILSON.

VIOLENCE GROWS IN BERLIN FERMENT

Bomb Hurled at Building in Which Officials Were Conferring on Strike.

SHOTS FIRED AT MINISTERS

Railway Strikers Ignore Orders from Noske and Union Chiefs to Resume Work.

Copyright, 1919, by The New York Times Company.
Special Cable to THE NEW YORK TIMES.

BERLIN, June 28, (via Copenhagen.)—Vorwärts, even Die Freiheit and also Ledebour, in his first speech after his release from prison, earnestly warn the people against riots and political revolt which, in view of the enormous military strength gathered in Berlin, can only lead to awful bloodshed.

Doubtless the big leaders of the Independent Socialists do not wish any outbreaks at present. Nevertheless the air is charged with the spirit of rebellion, and nobody here would be surprised if tomorrow there were a repetition of the events of January and March on a much larger scale.

The minor leaders of the Independents, Communists and Sparticides desire to inflame this unrest, communicating it to ever-growing circles of the workers, and inciting the lawless elements to the most audacious and wholesale crimes. Unknown parties shortly after 2 o'clock this morning threw a bomb against the façade of the building of the Public Works Department. It exploded with a terrific noise, shattering about 200 windows. Nobody was hurt. Later, when the ministers and the railway employes' delegates left the building, after trying vainly all night to reach an agreement, unknown persons fired revolvers at the government members, without hitting any one.

Incite Lawlessness in Berlin.

Though ten or more members of the Executive Committee of the Berlin Soldiers' and Workers' Councils, after being arrested yesterday on suspicion of conniving with the Hamburg revolutionists for the overthrow of the Federal Government, have been released for lack of evidence nobody doubts for one moment that telephone congratulations were exchanged between them and the Hamburg revolutionists, as overheard by officials, but the identity of the man who answered the Hamburg announcement of the successful revolt with "Bravo!" and promised the Executive Committee's aid in starting a revolt against the Government in Berlin could not be established.

Members of that Executive Committee have never made any secret of their intention to overthrow the Government at the first opportunity, and doubtless the weaker heads among them yesterday believed that the time had come. The lawless element believe this, and it cannot be denied that they are quite right, if the absence of any effective policing of the capital is any justification.

Insecurity has reached an incredible degree. Lately men disguised as officers have been ascending street cars and, with pointed revolvers, collecting pocketbooks and jewels from the passengers in true Wild West fashion. This

Continued on Page Three.

DUTCH UNWILLING TO GIVE UP KAISER

Majority of the People Firmly Opposed to Yielding to Allies' Demand.

HOPEFUL AT AMERONGEN

Troelstra Says Chamber Would Surrender Ex-Ruler to Germany Only.

Copyright, 1919, by The New York Times Company.
Special Cable to THE NEW YORK TIMES.

THE HAGUE, June 27.—The question of the delivery of the ex-Kaiser is again on the tapis here. There is no doubt that a majority of Netherlanders are already forgetting Germany's and the ex-monarch's record and violently oppose his surrender.

Appeals such as the recent one from the German Officers League and echoes from the German press only serve to strengthen these feelings. The officers' appeal stated that the German officers would be dishonored forever if Holland delivered the ex-Kaiser to the Allies, and ended with the statement: "It is even yet not certain whether a German can be found to sign the peace treaty."

THE NEW YORK TIMES correspondent questioned Pieter Troelstra, the Socialist leader, the report emanating from Germany that the Dutch Social Democrats opposed the surrender of the ex-Kaiser. Troelstra replied:

"Our party has taken no official attitude. As we have not yet considered the question officially no resolution has been taken and no official correspondence carried on.

"It is true that we are against his surender on principle and would oppose it. I consider that we must wait until we receive the allied demand, so that the matter is not urgent.

"I can certainly say that as Socialists we believe in the right of asylum. English Socialists defend the right of asylum and London has always been a city for political refugees. Switzerland and the Netherlands have been free for centuries and it is a matter of tradition."

When asked if the question were put to a vote in the Dutch Chamber other parties would oppose the delivery of the ex-monarch, Troelstra replied in the affirmative.

"It is impossible," he said, "to deliver a refugee to an enemy. It is against all rights. If Germany should demand the Kaiser it would be another question. We should be in favor of that. I feel nothing but antipathy for his personality, but only his own Government has a right to demand him. I believe that all parties would vote in favor of a demand from the German Government."

Plead Ties with Dutch Queen.

Copyright, 1919, by The New York Times Company.
Special Cable to THE NEW YORK TIMES.

BERLIN, June 28.—The League of Officers of the Former Prussian Army and German Navy has addressed a message to the Dutch Queen pleading that she had refused to extradite the "all highest war lord, our beloved unforgettable King, his Majesty Kaiser Wilhelm, who because of high treason in his own country, and not forced by the enemy's arms,

Continued on Page Three.

LEAGUE OPPONENTS UNITING

Republican Senators Now Seem Agreed on Policy of Reservations.

McCUMBER IS WON OVER

But North Dakota Senator Opposes Any Action Nullifying the Covenant.

SHANTUNG ACTION ASSAILED

Borah Calls It Indefensible—Norris Demands a Reservation Regarding It.

Special to The New York Times.

WASHINGTON, June 28.—With unexpected swiftness the Republican opposition in the Senate to the League of Nations covenant, as embraced in the Treaty of Peace, began to crystallize today, after the cables had brought word that Germany had signed the treaty, and that the President, in his message to the American people, had expressed the hope that the treaty would be "ratified and acted upon in full and sincere execution of its terms."

The President's message, coupled with his statement in interviews at Paris that he hoped the Senate woud ratify the treaty with the League of Nations covenant in it, without amendment, had the effect, it appeared, of bringing closer the elements of opposition among the opponents of the League. Instead of influencing wavering Senators toward an attitude favoring the ratification of the League of Nations covenant, the President's appeal appeared to have exactly the opposite effect.

While the opponents of the covenants, before Germany signed, were admittedly divided as to a policy to pursue in fighting the covenant when the treaty should come before the Senate, they seemed, for the first time since the League fight started, to have come to some general agreement.

Every Republican Senator to whom THE NEW YORK TIMES correspondent talked said decisively that he believed that, if the League covenant was to be accepted by the Senate some character of qualifying resolution would have to be passed, along with the treaty ratification, to express dissent from features objected to.

Even Senator McCumber of North Dakota, the one Republican member of the Foreign Relations Committee who has all along advocated adoption of the covenant, after the President's message had been read in the Senate, said that he believed it would be necessary for that body to adopt "explanatory reservations" in the ratification of the treaty, respecting features involved in the covenant. Mr. McCumber spoke of such reservations being necessary as to the Monroe Doctrine and the right of the United States to determine its purely domestic questions, like immigration, racial equality, and the tariff.

The North Dakota Senator made it clear that he would not favor any resolution of reservation that would have the effect of nullifying the covenant. He wanted the treaty of peace ratified, with the League of Nations included. But he insisted that the Senate should not hesitate to express its dissent from features that affected purely American affairs. If this were not done, he said, there might come some development in the future that might impel the Senate to take action which, in effect, would take America out of the League.

McNary for Interpretation.

Senator McNary, Republican, Oregon, who only a few days ago announced himself as favoring the League of Nations, declared today that he would not oppose a resolution that would enable opponents of the covenant to make clear their dissent from matters to which they objected. This, he said, might be done through a resolution of "interpretation," which was another way of saying one of "qualification."

At the same time Senator McNary agreed with Senator McCumber that no resolution ought to be adopted that would have the effect of rejecting the League of Nations covenant.

Talk of direct amendment of the covenant was not so insistent today among the more radical Senators. They appeared to be willing now to stand behind qualifying resolutions that would amply set forth the features subject to objection. They maintained, however, that Article X., guaranteeing the territorial integrity of members of the League, should come out. On this point

Continued on Page Five.

Wilson Says Treaty Will Furnish the Charter for a New Order of Affairs in the World

WASHINGTON, June 28.—The following address by President Wilson to the American people on the occasion of the signing of the Peace Treaty was given out here today by Secretary Tumulty:

My Fellow Countrymen: The treaty of peace has been signed. If it is ratified and acted upon in full and sincere execution of its terms it will furnish the charter for a new order of affairs in the world. It is a severe treaty in the duties and penalties it imposes upon Germany; but it is severe only because great wrongs done by Germany are to be righted and repaired; it imposes nothing that Germany cannot do; and she can regain her rightful standing in the world by the prompt and honorable fulfillment of its terms.

And it is much more than a treaty of peace with Germany. It liberates great peoples who have never before been able to find the way to liberty. It ends, once for all, an old and intolerable order under which small groups of selfish men could use the peoples of great empires to serve their ambition for power and dominion. It associates the free Governments of the world in a permanent League in which they are pledged to use their united power to maintain peace by maintaining right and justice.

It makes international law a reality supported by imperative sanctions. It does away with the right of conquest and rejects the policy of annexation and substitutes a new order under which backward nations—populations which have not yet come to political consciousness and peoples who are ready for independence but not yet quite prepared to dispense with protection and guidance—shall no more be subjected to the domination and exploitation of a stronger nation, but shall be put under the friendly direction and afforded the helpful assistance of governments which undertake to be responsible to the opinion of mankind in the execution of their task by accepting the direction of the League of Nations.

It recognizes the inalienable rights of nationality, the rights of minorities and the sanctity of religious belief and practice. It lays the basis for conventions which shall free the commercial intercourse of the world from unjust and vexatious restrictions and for every sort of international co-operation that will serve to cleanse the life of the world and facilitate its common action in beneficent service of every kind. It furnishes guarantees such as were never given or even contemplated for the fair treatment of all who labor at the daily tasks of the world.

It is for this reason that I have spoken of it as a great charter for a new order of affairs. There is ground here for deep satisfaction, universal reassurance, and confident hope.

WOODROW WILSON.

DEPORT THIRTY 'RED' AGITATORS

Fifteen Have Been Shipped Away in a Week—18 More Waiting at Ellis Island.

MOST OF THEM ANARCHISTS

Number Includes Some Suspected of Having a Hand in Plot Against Officials.

The deportation of alien agitators and conspirators who have abused their sojourn in America by preaching the overthrow of the United States Government, some of them coming under suspicion of the Secret Service for plots against President Wilson and other high public officials, has begun. Within the last seven days, fifteen of these disturbers, among them the editors of two anarchist newspapers, have been deported from New York, and eighteen others are now on Ellis Island awaiting the sailing of ships that will return them to the lands of their nativity.

The Secret Service agencies of the Government have been quietly, but thoroughly, at work for weeks, and every day or two a new batch of aliens who have urged the destruction of American institutions are rounded up and their records submitted to the proper authorities with a view to immediate deportation.

In the last four weeks thirty anarchist, I. W. W., and Bolshevist agitators have been deported by way of Ellis Island. This number does not include the Seattle and Spokane I. W. W. disturbers and other radicals who were sent East for deportation as a result of Bolshevist strikes in the Pacific Northwest several months ago. Some of those agitators also have been deported, and the cases of several others, recommended for the "homeward voyage," are soon to be decided by the courts.

Most of the deportations have taken place since bombs were set off at the homes of Attorney General Palmer and

Continued on Page Nine.

AMERICA GREETED BY KING GEORGE

"Brothers in Arms Will Continue Forever to be Brothers in Peace."

SENDS MESSAGE TO WILSON

"We Lay Down Our Arms in Proud Consciousness of Valiant Deeds Nobly Done."

LONDON, June 28, (Associated Press.)—King George has sent the following message to President Wilson:

"In this glorious hour when the long struggle of nations for right, justice and freedom is at last crowned by a triumphant peace, I greet you, Mr. President, and the great American people in the name of the British nation.

"At a time when fortune seemed to frown, and the issues of the war trembled in the balance, the American people stretched out the hand of fellowship to those, who on this side of the ocean were battling for a righteous cause. Light and hope at once shone brighter in our hearts, and a new day dawned.

Together we have fought to a happy end; together we lay down our arms in proud consciousness of valiant deeds nobly done.

Mr. President, it is on this day one of our happiest thoughts that the American and British people, brothers in arms, will continue forever to be brothers in peace. United before by language, traditions, kinship, and ideals, there has been set upon our fellowship the sacred seal of common sacrifice.

GEORGE, R. I.

After news of the signing of peace had been received here the following was issued over King George's signature:

The signing of the treaty of peace will be received with deep thankfulness throughout the British Empire. This formal act brings to its concluding stages the terrible war which has

Continued on Page Three.

ENEMY ENVOYS IN TRUCULENT SPIRIT

Say Afterward They Would Not Have Signed Had They Known They Were to Leave First by Different Way.

CHINA REFUSES TO SIGN, SMUTS MAKES PROTEST

These Events Somewhat Cloud the Great Occasion at Versailles—Wilson, Clemenceau, and Lloyd George Receive a Tremendous Ovation.

President Wilson Starts for Home

PARIS, June 28, (Associated Press.)—President Wilson left Paris on his homeward journey tonight. His train started from the Gare des Invalides for Brest at 9:45 P. M.

Mr. Wilson's party was accompanied to Brest by General Leorat and Colonel Lobez, the President's French aids, and also by Stephen Pichon, French Foreign Minister; Georges Leygues, French Minister of Marine, and Captain André Tardieu, a member of the French peace delegation. Ambassador Wallace, General Pershing, Premier Clemenceau, and Colonel House were at the station to say good-bye.

The crowd in the station, numbering upward of a thousand, wildly cheered the departure of the President, who raised his hat to cries of "Vive Wilson." Mrs. Wilson threw kisses to the crowd as the train departed.

The superdreadnought Oklahoma will accompany the George Washington to the United States.

VERSAILLES, June 28, (Associated Press.)—Germany and the allied and associated powers signed the peace terms here today in the same imperial hall where the Germans humbled the French so ignominiously forty-eight years ago.

This formally ended the world war, which lasted just thirty-seven days less than five years. Today, the day of peace, was the fifth anniversary of the murder of Archduke Francis Ferdinand by a Serbian student at Serajevo.

The peace was signed under circumstances which somewhat dimmed the expectations of those who had worked and fought during long years of war and months of negotiations for its achievement.

Absence of the Chinese delegates, who at the last moment were unable to reconcile themselves to the Shantung settlement, struck the first discordant note. A written protest which General Smuts lodged with his signature was another disappointment.

But bulking larger than these was the attitude of Germany and the German plenipotentiaries, which left them, as evident from the expression of M. Clemenceau, still outside of formal reconciliation and made the actual restoration to regular relations and intercourse with the allied nations dependent, not upon the signature of the "preliminaries of peace" today, but upon ratification by the National Assembly.

To M. Clemenceau's warning in his opening remarks that they would be expected, and held, to observe the treaty provisions loyally and completely the German delegates, through Dr. Haniel von Haimhausen, replied after returning to the hotel that had they known that they would be treated on a different status after signing than the allied representatives, as shown by their separate exit before the general body of the conference, they never would have signed.

Under the circumstances the general tone of sentiment in the historic sitting was one rather of relief at the uncontrovertible end of hostilities than of complete satisfaction.

The ceremony had been planned deliberately to be austere, befitting the sufferings of almost five years, and the lack of impressiveness and picturesque color, of which many spectators, who had expected a magnificent State pageant, complained, was a matter of design, not merely omission.

The actual ceremony was far shorter than had been expected, in view of the number of signatures which were to be appended to the treaty and the two accompanying conventions, ending a bare forty-nine minutes after the hour set for the opening.

Premier Clemenceau called the session to order in the Hall of Mirrors at 3:10 P. M.

The signing began when Dr. Hermann Müller and Johannes Bell, the German signatories, affixed their names. Herr Müller signed at 3:12 o'clock and Herr Bell 3:13 o'clock.

President Wilson, the first of the allied delegates, signed a minute later. At 3:49 o'clock the momentous session was over.

The most dramatic moment connected with the signing came unexpectedly and spontaneously at the conclusion of the ceremony, when Premier Clemenceau, President Wilson and Premier Lloyd George descended from the Hall of Mirrors to the terrace at the rear of the palace, where thousands of spectators were massed.

GREAT DEMONSTRATION FOR ALLIED LEADERS.

With the appearance of the three who had dominated the councils of the Allies there began a most remarkable demonstration. With cries of "Vive Clemenceau!" "Vive Wilson!" "Vive Lloyd George!" dense crowds swept forward from all parts of the spacious terrace. In an instant the three were surrounded by struggling, cheering masses of people, fighting among themselves for a chance to get near the statesmen.

It had been planned that all the allied delegates would walk across the terrace after signing, to see the great fountains play, but none of the other plenipotentiaries got further than the door.

President Wilson, M. Clemenceau and Mr. Lloyd George were caught in the living stream which flowed across the great space, and became part of the crowd themselves. Soldiers and bodyguards struggled vainly t-

The New York Times

PAGE ONE

1920-1929

Section 1

"All the News That's Fit to Print."

The New York Times.

THE WEATHER
Partly cloudy and warmer today; Monday, fair.
For full weather report see Page 28.

Section 1

VOL. LXIX...No. 22,632. NEW YORK, SUNDAY, JANUARY 11, 1920. In Eleven Parts, including Picture and Magazine Sections (Rotogravure) and Book Section. FIVE CENTS In Greater New York | Elsewhere TEN CENTS

PEACE SIGNED IN PARIS AND THE TREATY IS NOW IN FORCE; WILSON TO SUMMON FIRST LEAGUE MEETING FOR FRIDAY; LODGE REBUFFS KENDRICK COMPROMISE PROPOSALS

SWEET DEFENDS ASSEMBLY'S ACTION AGAINST SOCIALISTS

Speaker Writes in Reply to Hughes and Condemns Attitude of Socialist Party.

PROMISES A SQUARE DEAL

Republican State Committee Ignores Subject—Major Mills's Protest Sidetracked.

CITY LEADERS ANGERED

Up-State Members Stand with Sweet—Text of the Speaker's Letter.

Speaker Thaddeus C. Sweet of the Assembly last night replied to the letter of Charles E. Hughes condemning the Speaker and the Assembly for suspending the five Socialist Assemblymen-elect at the opening session of the Legislature last Wednesday.

The letter was sent and made public by the Speaker after he had been in protracted conference at the Republican Club and the Murray Hill Hotel with Senator Clayton R. Lusk, who has been investigating seditious activities; Attorney General Charles D. Newton, chief counsel of the Lusk Committee; Archibald E. Stevenson, J. Henry Walters, President Pro Tem. of the Senate, and other Republican leaders.

A meeting of the Republican State Committee had brought Republican leaders from all parts of the State to this city, and that Mr. Hughes's letter had set many of them thinking and had thoroughly angered Speaker Sweet and his friends was quite evident. It was clear that a majority of the up-State leaders sided with Sweet, while with only one notable exception leaders in this city and prominent party men were vexed and disturbed as they pondered the possibility that the Assembly's action might react unfavorably in this Presidential and Gubernatorial year.

No mention was made of the Socialists at the State Committee meeting, which was attended by Sweet and many Assemblymen. Major Ogden L. Mills went to the meeting with a proxy and a prepared speech, ready to vent wrath, which he voiced freely to friends.

A dozen Republican leaders, among them Senator Walters, labored with Major Mills before the meeting began and after it had been called to order. Major Mills was earnestly requested by Walters to join him in the billiard room. In the meantime Chairman Glynn rushed through with the routine committee proceedings and by the time Major Mills and Senator Walters were through talking the meeting had ended.

"The proposition which contemplates the right of a majority to exclude a minority because of political beliefs, is revolutionary and as serious a threat to representative Government as can be found in our entire history," said Major Mills after the meeting. "In fact, I do not think anything like it has been attempted since the British Parliament expelled Wilkes back in the eighteenth century. I recommend to Speaker Sweet a thorough perusal of the Letters of Junius."

Speaker Sweet refused to answer questions of reporters but said he would write a letter in reply to Mr. Hughes. The Speaker's letter follows:

Speaker Sweet's Letter.

"New York, Jan. 10, 1920.

"Hon. Charles E. Hughes.

"My dear Judge Hughes: I notice in today's columns of the press that you communicated to me your views upon the action of the Assembly in the adoption of the resolution suspending the right of the five Socialists to seats in that body pending an investigation of the charges that they are unfit to occupy a seat in the Assembly of the State of New York. It seems from your communication that you have assumed that the action of the Assembly was in the nature of expulsion. If you read carefully and were familiar with the language of the resolution adopted you would see that the resolution provides as follows: 'Therefore, be it resolved, that the said (naming the five Socialist members be denied seats in this Assembly pending the determination of their qualifications and eligibility to their respectvie seats.'

"You should bear clearly in mind that no attack is made upon the views of the Assemblymen-elect in question, however opposed they may be in theory to the institutions of the United States and this State. The question presented squarely is whether the different organizations of which they are members and which they seek to represent in the Legislature advocate methods and employ tactics to bring about the overturn

Continued on Page Twenty-one.

D'Annunzio May Stake Out Rome-Tokio Air Race Course

LONDON, Jan. 10.—A Caproni airplane left Rome yesterday to stake a route to be covered in the Rome to Tokio flight which is being arranged and financed by the Italian Government, according to a Central News dispatch from Rome, under date of Friday. The plane was said to have reached Avlona last night and to have departed immediately for Saloniki.

Three more planes engaged in the same work are scheduled to leave Rome in ten days, and it is reported that Gabriele d'Annunzio, who made an aviation record during the war and now is in command of insurgent forces at Fiume, will be in charge of this contingent.

HOUSE AGAIN DENIES BERGER HIS SEAT

Refuses by Vote of 328 to 6 to Admit Milwaukee Socialist to Membership.

MANN OPPOSES REJECTION

Berger Reiterates Opposition to War—Promptly Renominated at Milwaukee.

Special to The New York Times.

WASHINGTON, Jan. 10.—Victor L. Berger of Milwaukee, re-elected to Congress on the Socialist ticket from the Fifth Wisconsin District, was today, for the second time within two months, refused a seat in the House of Representatives. The vote was 328 to 6, taken after Representative James R. Mann of Illinois, formerly Republican leader of the House, and a supporter of the McLemore resolution, had led a fight in Berger's behalf. Those voting in the negative were Representatives Mann, and Voigt of Wisconsin, the latter the only member of the House who had voted for Berger, when he was first refused a seat, and Harrold of Oklahoma, Republicans, and Sisson of Mississippi, Sherwood of Ohio, and Griffin of New York, Democrats. Representative Sabath of Illinois, Democrat, voted "present."

The issue came before the House upon a resolution offered by Representative Dallinger of Massachusetts, who cited that "Victor L. Berger is hereby declared not entitled to a seat in the Sixty-sixth Congress as a Representative from the Fifth Wisconsin District and the House declines to permit him to take the oath and qualify as a Representative."

Convicted under the Espionage act and sentenced to twenty years' imprisonment, Mr. Berger presented today the credentials of his re-election last month. When the House assembled Mr. Berger walked down the aisle from the cloakroom and seated himself in the second row, immediately under the Speaker's rostrum, on the Republican side. He appeared to be very nervous during the one-hour debate in which he was denounced as a "traitor and a friend of Germany." He chewed his gray mustache and moved uneasily. But when a Wisconsin member said that he had not recanted his disloyal doctrines, but continued preaching them, Mr. Berger was noticed to nod approval.

Berger Says He Will Run Again.

Following the action of the House, Mr. Berger gave out a statement in which he announced that he would again seek re-election, and that "he held the same position that he did during the war"—opposition to war and recruiting, which brought about his conviction under the Espionage act.

Anticipating disorder, special officers were stationed in the galleries, but while there was intense feeling against some of the utterances made in behalf of Mr. Berger, the only disapproval came from the House itself which hissed one or two points and demanded that the vote be taken after half of the one hour apportioned to debate had been consumed.

As the champion of Mr. Berger, the former Republican leader of the House, Mr. Mann, opposed the resolution, which was supported by Mr. Mondell, the present leader of the House, and the other responsible House leaders.

"Mr. Berger," said Mr. Mann, "has been elected anew to the House by a majority of those who vote in his district, and to me the question is whether we shall maintain inviolate the representative form of government where people who desire changes in the fundamental or other laws of the land shall have the right to be represented on the floor of this House, when they control a majority of the votes in a Congressional district.

"Has it come to the point that a man who believes certain things cannot be heard? His people, his constituents, desire him to represent them. It is not our duty to select a representative from

Continued on Page Twenty.

GLASS URGES LOAN OF $150,000,000 TO STARVING EUROPE

Says America Alone Can Avert Anarchy in Austria, Poland and Armenia.

ASKS USE OF WHEAT FUND

Part of $1,000,000,000 Could Be Directed to Establish Credits, He Tells Committee.

AUSTRIA SEES END IN MONTH

Is Ready to Mortgage Her Forests and Customs for Food—300,000 Hungry in Armenia.

Special to The New York Times.

WASHINGTON, Jan. 10.—Secretary Glass, in a letter sent to the Ways and Means Committee today, appealed for an appropriation of $150,000,000 to aid the starving inhabitants of Poland, Armenia and Austria, giving a vivid picture of the distressing situation existing in these countries. Norman Davis, Assistant Secretary of the Treasury, presented additional details of conditions which, he said, must be remedied to prevent actual starvation and the spread of Bolshevism. He read to the committee excerpts from private reports received from American agents which bore out his statements.

Secretary Glass, appreciating the opposition to extending direct financial aid to the war-torn countries, recommended that the assistance go through the grain corporation, which could use its fund of nearly $1,000,000,000 to extend aid through credits or gifts where necessary. This recommendation seemed to meet with the approval of the committee, which will probably authorize the Grain Corporation to expend $150,000,000 of its fund in aid of these countries.

The fund and food would be divided as follows: Armenia, 7,500 tons of flour and other necessities at a cost of $500,000 monthly; Austria, $100,000,000, with a probable reduction to $70,000,000 due to assistance by Great Britain; Poland, 300,000 tons of grain at a cost of $50,000,000; other parts of Europe, $25,000,000.

Norman Davis told the committee that this country must continue to supply food to these three countries until the next harvest. Austria and Poland, he said, could furnish satisfactory security for food furnished them, but in the case of Armenia the aid must be in the nature of charity as that country is without funds or means of establishing credits. Food is also needed in parts of Italy, Hungary and Czechoslovakia, he said.

"The United States has a surplus of food and is the only nation that can prevent the famine," added Mr. Davis. "Great Britain in a formal note to the United States has promised to co-operate to the full extent of its ability, which probably will be mainly in supplying ships to transport the supplies, as Great Britain, France, and Italy already have lent Austria $48,000,000.

Would Mortgage Natural Resources.

"The condition in Austria is so desperate that she is willing to mortgage her forests, the tobacco monopoly, the water power facilities, and even the collection of customs, to obtain food. The Treasury does not believe that customs should be taken because it would cause great delay to economic rehabilitation. Vienna has 2,500,000 people, and it is probable that many of these will have to leave because the surrounding country, since the separation of Hungary, will not support them. Poland deserves help because she is rendering great service to the world fighting the Bolsheviki."

Secretary Glass in his letter summarizes conditions in the respective countries as follows:

"POLAND—According to the best information obtainable, the minimum grain requirement necessary to carry Poland until the next harvest, and which cannot be filled anywhere but in the United States, is 300,000 tons. This deficiency is due to a partial failure of the wheat crop and to a lack of fuel for threshing. Poland is at present living under a hand-to-mouth régime, which can be remedied only by a steady flow of imports from the only available surplus stocks of food, namely, those in the United States.

"The potato crop, which is the staple food of the poorer classes, has been destroyed by frosts to the extent of 50 per cent. in many districts, as it is impossible properly to care for potatoes in transit. Due to delays in transportation, Poland has been unable to procure clothing since the beginning of the war, and the result is that during the past five years practically all clothing has been worn out and has not yet been replaced.

"The food situation in Poland is so serious that the European Children's Re-

Continued on Page Seven.

Reports China and Japan Negotiating on Shantung

SAN FRANCISCO, Jan. 10.—Japan and China have started negotiations on the question of the restoration of Shantung to China, according to a cable dispatch received today from Tokio by the New World, a Japanese newspaper.

SWINDLED CLERGY, WIDOW CONFESSES

Mrs. May J. Bennett, in Tombs, Says "Divine Psychologist" Dominated Her.

WAS A MISSIONARY LEADER

Church, Social and Political Circles of Washington Heights Her Principal Field.

Blaming her downfall upon the influence of a "divine psychologist" who "dominated" her, Mrs. May Jennings Bennett, a handsome, distinguished-looking widow, confessed in the Tombs last night that she had swindled various persons out of large sums of money and that clergymen had been her chief victims.

Mrs. Bennett, one of the Vice-Presidents of the Women's Foreign Missionary Society of the New York Presbytery, and last year its Corresponding Secretary, made her confession to newspaper men in the presence of the Tombs Warden and said that, after fleeing her bail, she had surrendered herself in the hope that the court would show her mercy and that she would be allowed her liberty that she might work to repay her victims.

The scheme she used in church, social, and political circles, particularly in Washington Heights, she said, was to pretend that she had leases on a large number of furnished room houses which she was about to convert into apartment hotels at large profit. How much she got she did not know, but it was "enough to keep me busy a long time paying it back." Of the money with which she induced sympathetic persons to part she invested $10,000 in Mexican oil wells "which aren't paying dividends."

Among those she victimized, she told, was a Paulist Father upon whom she prevailed to write a letter to Assistant District Attorney Alfred J. Talley after she had convinced him she had been badly treated. Once the priest had been won over Mrs. Bennett borrowed $200 from him.

Discussing the influence the "divine psychologist" wielded over her, Mrs. Bennett begged that his cult should not be confused with Christian Science, "which is all right."

She recalled how she was arraigned in the West Side Court last June on a charge of grand larceny, how after she had been indicted she was arraigned in General Sessions, where the case was postponed after it was learned there were three other indictments against her and, despite the urgings of several clergymen, who later proved to have been among her victims, her bail was raised to $3,500. She told of running away and of the bail furnished for her by a surety company being forfeited when she failed to appear when her case was called again last December. Then, reverting to the man upon whom she sought to cast the blame, she said:

"I met a man who advertised a sort of 'new thought.' He told me when I went to him that he could make people prosperous. I told him I wanted to be wealthy. I paid him more than $1,000 at different times and he always told me to go right ahead with my schemes and he was with me, that he would pray for their success. I was under a sort of hypnotic influence; I knew what I was doing was not just right, but had not the power to resist.

"Finally, when I was indicted for grand larceny, I realized that I had been in a terrible dream and that this man, who was or called himself a 'divine psychologist,' had exercised a power for evil and not for good over me. I went to him to help me. He refused to aid me and appeared to be scared to death. I woke up then. I knew I had not been in my right mind."

While she was carrying on her swindles Mrs. Bennett lived luxuriously at Bretton Hall, gave fashionable tea parties and entertained generously. She dressed well, bore herself as a woman of fashion and, in part through her church connections, gained entree to many fashionable homes.

Under the auspices of a church she gave a "charitable affair," ostensibly for the Red Cross, in which she used the names of Collin H. Woodward, a Republican leader in upper Manhattan, and ex-Representative William S. Bennet. The receipts were said to have been large, but nothing remained for the Red Cross when it was over.

The charges thus far brought against Mrs. Bennett, aggregate in the amount of her alleged swindles $7,000, but the sums mentioned in her confession would indicate that she had got more. She admitted last night that her "chain" consisted of a single rooming house.

REPORT OF GERMAN OVERTHROW DENIED; STRIKE SPREADING

Berlin Dispatch Declares Accounts Given by Travelers Are Untrue.

RAILROAD TIEUP IS WORSE

Communists Are Charged with Promoting It for Their Own Political Ends.

CENTRES IN RUHR DISTRICT

Not Even Food Trains Are Moved There—10,000 Berlin Clerks Walk Out of Insurance Offices.

LONDON, Jan. 10.—Reports reached here early today by way of Brussels that the German Government had been overthrown, but these were later denied by an Amsterdam dispatch quoting Berlin advices received this evening. This dispatch reads:

"The report that the German Government has been overthrown is untrue, according to a dispatch received here from Berlin."

Until this dispatch was received there had been no light on the reports, storms having interrupted telegraphic and telephonic communications with Germany since Thursday.

The original Brussels dispatch said that travelers from Germany reaching there had brought unconfirmed reports that the German Government had been overthrown.

It was reported that the Socialists were masters of the situation and that a general strike had been declared throughout the territory not under allied occupation.

Serious Strike Trouble in Germany.

BERLIN, Jan. 9.—The situation created by the railroad strike became worse yesterday, especially in the Ruhr district, where there were additions to the ranks of the strikers.

The committee of Social Democratic railway men here charged the Communists with responsibility for the strike, alleging that while it is ostensibly an economic movement it is in reality a political measure intended to accomplish the introduction of an industrial council system on the Communist plan.

The Independent Socialists and Communists are held to be responsible for further walkouts in the Essen, Elberfeld, and Munster districts. In the Ruhr district it was impossible to move even emergency food trains. At Düsseldorf a gas and electricity shutdown is threatened owing to the lack of coal, and at Dresden the railway men have presented new demands to the Government.

At Dortmund a secret strike vote has resulted overwhelmingly in the affirmative.

Ten thousand Berlin insurance clerks struck yesterday, representing seventy-five companies. The employers claim that the walkout is not complete. The Magdeburg, Frankfort-on-Main, Potsdam, Stuttgart, and Dresden clerks are expected to join in the strike. Labor Ministry mediators are arranging for negotiations with the clerks.

WOULD SEIZE WEALTH ABROAD

Erzberger Proposes Entente Have German Fortunes in Switzerland.

BERLIN, Jan. 9.—Speaking in the Biberach district of Württemberg last night, Mathias Erzberger, Vice Chancellor and Minister of Finance, declared that he proposed to conclude a treaty with Switzerland enabling the recovery of German capital smuggled into that country in 1919. Should the measure fail of its objective, Herr Erzberger asserted he would authorize the Entente to seize such fortunes and credit them to the indemnity to be paid by Germany.

Herr Erzberger has advertised for 3,000 additional rooms to accommodate the staff which he says will be required to administer new tax measures soon to become effective. He has announced that additional taxing measures will be submitted to the Assembly.

KING GEORGE HOPES NEW ERA HAS DAWNED

Prays People of British Empire May Forever Live at Peace with Themselves and with All Men.

LONDON, Jan. 10.—Replying to a loyal message from the citizens of London on the occasion of the ratification of peace, the King has telegraphed the Lord Mayor of London as follows:

"With all my heart I reciprocate their hopes and fervently pray that, please God, this day may be the dawn of a new era, in which the people of the British Empire may forever live at peace with themselves and with all men."

Supreme Council Prompt to Launch the League; Leon Bourgeois to Preside at the First Session

By EDWIN L. JAMES.

Copyright, 1920, by The New York Times Company.
Special Cable to THE NEW YORK TIMES.

PARIS, Jan. 10.—The first meeting of the Council of the League of Nations will be opened in Paris at 10:30 o'clock on the morning of Friday, Jan. 16.

This date was set by Premiers Clemenceau, Lloyd George, and Nitti, sitting with the Supreme Council today, and was at once cabled to President Wilson in order that he might issue immediately the formal call for the historic meeting in accordance with the duty placed upon him by the Versailles Treaty. Premier Clemenceau has notified the powers concerned to have their delegates in Paris on the day set. They will gather at the French Foreign Office, where, it is understood, President Wilson's call will be read and the business of the Council started.

England, France, Italy, Japan, Spain, Belgium, and Brazil will be the nations composing the Supreme Council of the League. Léon Bourgeois, representing France, will preside at the first meeting. There will be two addresses, one by M. Bourgeois and the other by Earl Curzon, representing Great Britain. It was proposed that this gathering be made a big ceremonial event, but the suggestion was vetoed by both Mr. Lloyd George and M. Clemenceau. "No, we won't need any music," added the "Tiger."

It has not been determined whether the Council will meet on the 16th and keep on meeting until it gets its machinery under way. That, however, will be determined before the first meeting takes place. A great deal of quiet preliminary work has been done in outlining the program for the Council prior to the first meeting of the League Assembly, and it is the desire of England to have this work started at once. France, while recognizing the need of haste, rather favors delaying important action until America shall have joined or shown that it will be a long time before she acts.

In other words, if the League is made an issue of the next Presidential election, the League work must go ahead before that time. If there is any chance of early ratification by the Senate, France prefers to wait for the United States.

LODGE SKEPTICAL OF DEMOCRATS' PLAN

Demands Proof of Substantial Party Support Before He Will Discuss It.

COMPROMISE SPIRIT GROWS

Neither Side Anxious to Take Up President's Challenge of Appeal to People.

Special to The New York Times.

WASHINGTON, Jan. 10.—Senator Lodge today furnished the climax to a second day of unusual activity in behalf of a treaty compromise by demanding a showdown from Democratic Senators on reservations proposed as the basis of compromise.

Mr. Lodge sent word to Senators McKellar and Kendrick, coauthors of the recently submitted Democratic reservations, that unless they could present assurances of substantial Democratic support for their proposals further discussion of a compromise upon this basis was useless. Senators with whom Senator Lodge discussed the matter said that the Republican leader had called upon the Democrats to decide whom they would follow—whether President Wilson, insisting upon interpretations as the limit of concession, or Mr. Bryan, counselling ratification upon any basis found practicable, even though that involved Democratic surrender to the Lodge forces.

In spite of Mr. Lodge's position, practically everything that took place in the Senate wing of the Capitol today with reference to the Peace Treaty deadlock indicated that President Wilson's warning that he would call for a "great and solemn referendum" of the American people on the treaty if the League of Nations covenant was modified other than by "interpretations" has had the effect of stimulating rather than retarding efforts at compromise between the opposing groups of Senators. William J. Bryan's appeal for compromise does not figure in the negotiations. His attitude in the situation is looked upon as negligible.

Still Hope for Harmony.

To say that the divergent views of President Wilson and Mr. Bryan have "killed" the treaty and the accompanying covenant is to go beyond the reasonable expectations born of the renewed attempt to harmonize differences between the Senate groups. Friends of the treaty, a good many of whom may also be classed as friends of the President, have by no means given up hope that harmony may result from what earnest Senators on both sides are now undertaking. It is equally clear that neither side, with the exception of the comparatively few irreconcilables, desires to take up the President's challenge to appeal to the people if the pending reservations are attached to the treaty.

That the majority of Senators, Republicans and Democrats, do not sympathize with the President's attitude as outlined in the letter from him read at the Jackson Day dinner in Washington on Thursday night does not mean that there is sympathy with Mr. Bryan's contrary course. That Mr. Bryan advocated the thing that most appeals to the majority of Democratic Senators and apparently to the generality of his party

Continued on Page Two.

BELLS OF LONDON PEAL FOR PEACE

But News of the Treaty Ratification Stirs Little Popular Interest.

CECIL APPEALS FOR LEAGUE

Reiterates His Declaration in Favor of the Early Admission of Former Enemy Powers.

Copyright, 1920, by The New York Times Company.
Special Cable to THE NEW YORK TIMES.

LONDON, Jan. 10.—The London church bells this evening have been pealing in celebration of the conclusion of peace with Germany and the official coming into existence of the League of Nations.

The first report that the treaty had been actually ratified in Paris reached London a little after 6 P. M. But for the bell-ringing, there is no evidence of public interest, and some papers give first place in their news columns to the labor situation at home. For legal purposes in this country the war will be presumed to continue a little longer, and will be terminated by an Order in Council.

People Must Back League, Says Cecil.

LONDON, Jan. 10, (Associated Press).—Whether the League of Nations is to be the real thing or an imposture depends upon the attitude of the peoples, and not least the British people, in the opinion of Lord Robert Cecil, who, as Chairman of the Executive Committee of the League of Nations Union, issued the following statement today:

"The Peace Treaty comes into force today, and with it the *League of Nations*. We, of the League of Nations, welcome its advent, but we must not think that we have yet achieved our ends.

"The League exists, but what is it to be? Is it to be the real thing or an imposture? Are we going to make it an efficient instrument of peace, or is it to become a meaningless addition to the cumberous forms of old-fashioned diplomacy?

"All depends upon the attitude of the peoples, and, not the least, of the British people. Are they going to show themselves worthy of this great opportunity or not? If they are, there is no time to be lost, for there is much to be done. Schemes for the limitation of armaments must be worked out, terms of the mandates must be settled and mandatories appointed, an international court of justice must be established.

"Beyond these and other duties directly imposed upon the League by the covenant and treaty, there are many circumstances at the present time which, in the words of Article XI, 'threaten to disturb international peace or the good understanding between nations upon which peace depends.'

"There is the Russian situation, economic chaos in many European countries and controversies left unsettled by the peace conference, and defects in the Peace Treaty itself and particularly its financial provisions. All these matters are 'within the sphere of action of the league.'

"It will be the duty of the League of Nations Union to formulate a policy on these matters and to urge it upon the Governments, but it would be premature today to lay down that policy in detail.

"Certain points, however, such as the

Continued on Page Two.

PEACE MADE WITHOUT POMP

Simplicity Marks Protocol Signing and Exchange of Ratifications.

LERSNER EXPRESSES JOY

Declares Germany's Determination to "Go to the Limit" in Fulfilling Terms.

GIVES WARNING TO ENTENTE

"Gravest Consequences" Foreseen if War Culprits Are Extradited.

By EDWIN L. JAMES.

Copyright, 1920, by The New York Times Company.
Special Cable to THE NEW YORK TIMES.

PARIS, Jan. 10.—The Allies and Germany are at peace. The world war ended formally this afternoon, when representatives of the Powers which had approved the Versailles Treaty deposited their certificates of ratification and signed the procés-verbal which put the treaty into effect. The United States took no part in the proceedings.

Simplicity marked the ceremony in the Clock Hall of the French Ministry of Foreign Affairs, where the final act of the great struggle was staged. Fourteen allied and associated powers on the one hand and Germany on the other made peace and are again friendly nations.

The allied Premiers and Foreign Ministers gathered around the long green-covered tables, with Baron Kurt von Lersner and Herr von Simson, Germany's representatives, at a separate small table. They arose one by one as they were designated by the master of ceremonies and affixed their signatures to the procès-verbal spread upon a stand in the middle of the long chamber. There was nothing of the dramatic in the actual proceeding; it was dramatic only in its great significance.

Before this ceremony the representatives of England, France, Italy and Japan had met the two German envoys in the office of the French Foreign Minister, and the Germans had signed the protocol binding their nation to pay for the sinking of the German fleet in Scapa Flow and to carry out the unfulfilled terms of the armistice. That done, the Premiers and the Germans were escorted to the Clock Room, where were gathered the diplomats of nearly all the nations of the world; for, besides those signing, other invited statesmen attended the ceremony.

It was two minutes after 4 o'clock when Premier Clemenceau took his seat, closely followed by Premiers Lloyd George and Nitti, with Baron Matsui of Japan not far behind. Scarcely were they seated when Baron von Lersner arose and, walking quickly to the stand, affixed his signature to the document which ended the war. It seemed scarcely two seconds when Mr. Lloyd George was on his feet. He signed quickly and was followed by Mr. Clemenceau, and then by Signor Nitti and Baron Matsui. Then the delegates of the following Nations signed, in the order named: Belgium, Bolivia, Brazil, Guatemala, Panama, Peru, Poland, Siam, Czechoslovackia and Uruguay. America, China, Greece, and Rumania not having ratified the treaty with Germany, did not sign.

It was six minutes after 4 o'clock when Mr. Lloyd George signed. Ten minutes later all had signed.

Then a letter from the Supreme Council promising Germany that the Allies would reduce from 400,000 tons to 275,000 tons their demand for maritime equipment to pay for the Scapa Flow sinking was handed to Baron von Lersner. This done, Mr. Clemenceau arose and said:

Declares That Peace Is Restored.

"The protocol between the allied and associated powers and Germany has been signed. The ratifications of the treaty with Germany have been deposited. From this moment the treaty enters into effect. It will be enforced in all its terms."

That was all. The diplomats filed out and Europe was at peace

The absence of Ambassador Wallace, representing the United States, was a distinct disappointment to the allied statesmen. They had invited all the diplomats and hoped that Mr. Wallace would attend. A formal invitation was received last night by Mr. Wallace from Premier Clemenceau, who had insisted that he attend. The American Ambassador waited until a late hour for instructions from Washington. When none arrived he returned his invitation to M. Clemenceau.

It is announced that tonight the first trains carrying German prisoners will cross the border, thus giving evidence of the good faith of France in promising to give up her prisoners of war as soon as Germany allowed the Peace Treaty to go into effect.

Although the United States did not of course sign the procés-verbal, its name figures in the document which follows:

"Procés-verbal of the ratification of the Treaty of Peace signed at Versailles June 28, 1919.

"Between the United States of America, the British Empire, France, Italy,

"All the News That's Fit to Print."

The New York Times.

THE WEATHER
Fair and colder today; Thursday fair; strong southwest to west winds.
For full weather report see Page 15.

VOL. LXX....No. 22,929. NEW YORK, WEDNESDAY, NOVEMBER 3, 1920. TWO CENTS In Greater New York | THREE CENTS Within 200 Miles | FOUR CENTS Elsewhere

HARDING WINS; MILLION LEAD HERE; BIG REPUBLICAN GAINS IN CONGRESS; MILLER LEADS SMITH FOR GOVERNOR

MILLER BY 57,000

But Democrats Refuse to Concede Governor's Defeat.

SMITH'S SURPRISING RUN

In Some Up-State Strongholds He Surpassed His Former Vote.

WINS EVERY CITY BOROUGH

Strongest in Manhattan, but Could Not Overcome Miller's Up-State Lead.

75,000 VICTORY, GLYNN SAYS

Republicans Here Accuse Tammany of Holding Back City Returns.

WADSWORTH IS ELECTED

Plurality Betters Miller's, but Is Far Behind That on Presidential Ticket.

NEW YORK—Voted for Presidential Electors, United States Senator, Congressmen, Governor and other State officials and on an amendment to the Constitution. Vote in 1916: Democratic, 750,426; Republican, 869,115.
Polls closed at 6 P. M.

After a neck-and-neck race all evening ex-Judge Nathan L. Miller defeated Alfred E. Smith, his Democratic opponent, for the Governorship on the latest returns by about 57,000 plurality. Despite the big Harding landslide, it seemed probable for some time that Governor Smith would be able to pull through, but late returns from rural Republican districts overcame a record vote for him in New York City.

The Democratic managers refused, however, to give up hope, and early this morning still claimed the election of Mr. Smith. The Governor did not put forth any claim himself, asserting that he preferred to wait until remote up-State districts had been heard from. The Democratic leaders based their hopes for final success upon the fact that late returns showed that the Governor had increased his average majority in each election district in the city from 115 to 118 votes. They did not take into account, however, that Mr. Miller had also increased his average in up-State districts from 75 to 83.

If the present ratios are maintained, ex-Judge Miller will have an up-State lead of 379,725, while Governor Smith's plurality in New York City will be 322,494, giving the Republican candidate a plurality in the entire State of 57,231. Republican leaders claimed the election of Mr. Miller by approximately 75,000. Democratic leaders said Smith's plurality would be around 40,000.

Smith Led at First.

Early reports all evening showed the Tammany Governor in the lead, but when reports from rural Republican strongholds came in Mr. Miller's vote picked up considerably and shoved him well into the lead. At the same time Smith's vote in outlying districts in New York City did not keep pace with the huge vote he received in other parts of the city, and the indications were that ex-Judge Miller would be elected by a small plurality.

Some of the members of the Republican County Committee shortly before midnight made the charge that election returns were being held up in some Tammany districts until Mr. Miller's full strength had been reported. The First, Third and Fourth Assembly Districts, in lower Manhattan, where Tammany's strength is greatest, were among those mentioned at Republican county headquarters.

Deputy Attorney General Berger, accompanied by several members of the committee, set out for the polling places in the districts to learn the true state of affairs.

Wadsworth Elected.

United States Senator James W. Wadsworth, Jr., although running behind Senator Harding did not have any difficulty in defeating his Democratic

Continued on Page Four.

State Pluralities.

FOR PRESIDENT.

REPUBLICAN.	
California	500,000
Connecticut	100,000
Colorado	40,000
Delaware	5,000
Idaho	25,000
Illinois	800,000
Indiana	200,000
Iowa	200,000
Kansas	200,000
Maine	75,000
Maryland	20,000
Massachusetts	300,000
Michigan	400,000
Minnesota	100,000
Missouri	40,000
Montana	50,000
Nebraska	100,000
New Hampshire	30,000
Nevada	4,000
New Jersey	200,000
New York	1,000,000
Ohio	400,000
Oregon	5,000
Pennsylvania	750,000
Rhode Island	50,000
South Dakota	80,000
Utah	30,000
Vermont	45,000
Washington	150,000
West Virginia	50,000
Wisconsin	300,000
Wyoming	8,000
DEMOCRATIC.	
Alabama	70,000
Arkansas	100,000
Florida	
Georgia	
Kentucky	20,000
Louisiana	
Mississippi	
New Mexico	
North Carolina	60,000
Oklahoma	7,500
South Carolina	
Tennessee	40,000
Texas	50,000
Virginia	75,000
DOUBTFUL.	
Arizona	
North Dakota	

CITY'S VOTE GOES TO HARDING AND SMITH

For Republican President by 443,000 and Democratic Governor by 325,000.

SEPARATE BALLOTS HELPED

But Some Charges Heard That Tammany Traded Votes—Socialists Make Gains.

New York City, in yesterday's election, gave its vote overwhelmingly to Senator Warren G. Harding, Republican candidate for President; to Calvin Coolidge, Republican candidate for Vice President, and to Alfred E. Smith, Democratic candidate for Governor.

Senator Harding carried every Assembly District in the Greater City with one exception—the First Assembly District, which is Governor Smith's home district. This gave Cox a plurality of about 400 votes.

In the minor contests the Republicans made some gains, although these were nothing like what might have been expected from the overwhelming sweep made by the Presidential ticket.

This result was greatly facilitated by the three ballots instituted by the Board of Elections, one for the Presidency, one for the State ticket (which also included the Congressional candidates), and one for the constitutional amendment and bonus proposal. The separation made ticket splitting easy, and the voters took full advantage of it.

Harding's victory in the city was overwhelming. At 3 A. M. today, on the returns then available, the plurality of the Republican candidate for the Presidency in the city was indicated as about 443,000.

Manhattan gave a Republican Presidential plurality of about 136,000; the Bronx, 62,000; Brooklyn, 177,000; Queens, 61,000, and Richmond, 7,000.

Striking Support of Smith.

But on the State ticket it was quite a different story. The same hour that found Harding victorious by 443,000 in the normally Democratic city of New York, showed Alfred E. Smith, Democrat, leading Judge Nathan Miller, his

Continued on Page Three.

OHIO FOR HARDING; 400,000 PLURALITY IS NOW ESTIMATED

Republicans Ahead in Nearly All the Large Cities of the State.

BIG LEAD IN CINCINNATI

Harding's Margin in Hamilton County Believed to be 20,000.

VICTORY IN CLEVELAND

Cuyahoga County About Two to One—Sweep in Toledo Also.

OHIO—Voted for Presidential Electors, United States Senator, Congressmen, Governor and other State officials. Vote in 1916: Democratic, 604,161; Republican, 516,773.
Polls closed at 5:30 P. M. (6:30 P. M. New York time).

COLUMBUS, Ohio, Nov. 2.—Returns from 2,987 precincts out of a total of 7,145 in the State give Harding 499,355, Cox 336,352.

If this ratio is maintained, the indications are that Senator Harding carried Ohio by more than 400,000 plurality.

Under instructions from State officials county election boards counted Presidential returns first. This made returns on the State ticket and the United States Senatorship unusually slow. Many scratched ballots were voted on the State ticket.

Returns from 128 precincts on the Governorship race show Davis (R.), 15,690; Donahey (D.), 10,833.

Returns from 66 precincts for United States Senator give Willis (R.), 6,341; Julian (D.), 4,794.

Senator Harding has probably carried every large city in the State from which normally the Democrats get their majorities. In some instances his pluralities have been tremendous. He is running even in Columbus, and may have carried it.

Many of the country districts are holding up to normal for Governor Cox. In some instances he is making slight gains there.

Chairman Clark claims the election of the Republican State ticket, including Harry L. Davis for Governor, by 100,000, while Chairman Durbin claims the election of A. V. Donahey (Dem.) for Governor by at least 50,000.

The vote in Cuyahoga County, including Cleveland, is running about two to one for Harding, indicating the sentiment in Northern Ohio. Four years ago Wilson carried the county two to one. Seventy-eight precincts out of 571 in the city of Cleveland gave Harding 13,840, Cox 7,937. In Cuyahoga County, outside of Cleveland, nine precincts out of 133 give Harding 2,926, Cox 830.

Hamilton County, in which Cincinnati is situated, will give 20,000 plurality for Harding.

The first twenty-two precincts to re-

Continued on Page Three.

United States Senators Elected.

REPUBLICANS, 20.	DEMOCRATS, 14.
S. Shortridge, Calif.	O. W. Underwood, Ala.
D. Nicholson, Col.	J. T. Heflin, Ala.
F. B. Brandegee, Conn.	M. A. Smith, Ariz.
F. R. Gooding, Idaho.	T. H. Caraway, Ark.
W. B. McKinley, Ill.	D. U. Fletcher, Fla.
J. E. Watson, Ind.	T. E. Watson, Ga.
A. B. Cummins, Iowa.	J. C. W. Beckham, Ky.
C. Curtis, Kan.	E. S. Broussard, La.
O. E. Weller, Md.	C. S. Henderson, Nev.
S. P. Spencer, Mo.	L. S. Overman, N. C.
G. H. Moses, N. H.	S. Ferris, Okla.
J. W. Wadsworth, Jr., N. Y.	G. E. Chamberlain, Ore.
E. F. Ladd, N. Dakota.	E. D. Smith, S. C.
F. B. Willis, Ohio.	C. Glass, Va.
B. Penrose, Pa.	
P. Norbeck, S. Dakota.	
R. Smoot, Utah.	
W. P. Dillingham, Vt.	
W. L. Jones, Wash.	
I. L. Lenroot, Wis.	

INDIANA IS SWEPT BY REPUBLICANS

Early Returns Indicate That Harding Will Carry State by Upward of 200,000.

WATSON LEADING TAGGART

He Trails Ticket, but on Basis of Returns His Election Is Expected by 185,000 Plurality.

INDIANA—Voted for Presidential Electors, United States Senator, Congressmen, Governor and other State officials. Vote in 1916: Democratic, 334,063; Republican, 341,005.
Polls closed at 6 P. M. (7 P. M. New York time).

Special to The New York Times.

INDIANAPOLIS, Ind., Nov. 2.—Late returns coming in from the rural districts have piled up the Harding plurality in the State with every indication pointing that the Republican landslide will be the largest in the history of Indiana. It was estimated late tonight that Cox will be defeated by at least 200,000 votes. The former Republican plurality record for Indiana in a Presidential race was held by Roosevelt with 93,000.

Of 1,002 precincts out of the 3,384 in the State, Harding has received 330,787 votes and Cox, 239,621.

Warren T. McCray of Kentland, Republican Gubernatorial nominee, has been swept into office by an overwhelming plurality over Dr. Carlton B. McCulloch of Indianapolis, his Democratic opponent. Although James E. Watson ran behind the ticket in several districts in his race for re-election to the Senate against Thomas Taggart, it is estimated that he will trail Harding less than 15,000 votes. Watson ran especially strong in the rural districts, while Taggart made his best showing in the laboring centres.

On the face of incomplete returns it appears that eleven of the thirteen Congressional Districts have piled up a suf-

Continued on Page Three.

ILLINOIS TREBLES REPUBLICAN VOTE

Returns Indicate Harding Has More Than 800,000 Plurality in the State.

McKINLEY CHOSEN SENATOR

Governor, State Officers and Entire Delegation to Congress Probably Republican.

ILLINOIS—Voted for Presidential Electors, United States Senator, Congressmen, Governor and other State officials and on an amendment to the Constitution. Vote in 1916: Democratic, 950,229; Republican, 1,152,549.
Polls closed at 5 P. M. (6 P. M. New York time).

CHICAGO, Nov. 2.—Upon the basis of returns received up to a late hour tonight Harding and Coolidge have carried Illinois by a plurality of more than 800,000. At this hour Harding has an indicated plurality of 331,000 in Chicago. His plurality down State is estimated to be not less than 318,000.

Harding's plurality in Chicago is apparently larger than any ever given a candidate by the city. It exceeds the famous 147,477 which Mayor Thompson got in 1915.

In 966 of 5,730 Illinois precincts, including 475 in Chicago, Harding had 215,913 votes, against 78,906 for Cox.

McKinley, for Senator, had a plurality of 57,621 over Waller, and Small was leading Lewis nearly two to one for Governor.

The Republican sweep apparently is even stronger than in 1904, when Roosevelt carried Cook County by 128,000, the women not voting then. Four years ago Hughes carried the county by 56,000 over Wilson, but Harding's lead over Cox is more than five times greater.

By 1 o'clock it was estimated that 60 per cent. of the 884,000 registered voters had visited the polls. During the afternoon they kept swarming in, and closing time saw many still waiting in line.

Early returns indicate about 825,000 votes were cast in Chicago. The plurality

Continued on Page Three.

CONGRESS HEAVILY REPUBLICAN, GAINS IN BOTH HOUSES

Party Will Have a Majority of 12 in the Senate and 113 in the House.

54 REPUBLICAN SENATORS

House Stands: Republicans 274, Democrats 158, Independents 2, Drys 1

IRRECONCILABLES ELECTED

Brandegee in Connecticut and Moses in New Hampshire Returned.

President Harding will have a Republican Congress to support his policies in the first two years at least of his Administration. Returns received up until the time this edition of THE TIMES goes to press show that the party which was triumphant at the polls yesterday will have increased majorities in both Houses, with that in the House approaching 100.

Returns in the elections for Senators and Representatives are meager from some important States, but the trend of voting in those States in the Presidential and Gubernatorial contests indicates the probable result as far as the Senate is concerned. The returns received indicate that the two houses in the next Congress will stand as follows:

Senate—Republicans, 54 Democrats, 42.

House—Republicans, 274; Democrats, 156; Independents, 2; Prohibitionist, 1.

This gives the Republicans a majority of 12 in the Senate and a majority of 113 in the House. The present Republican majority in the Senate is 2 and in the House 39.

Senator Moses of New Hampshire and Senator Brandegee of Connecticut, both Republicans of the irreconcilable treaty group in the Senate, were strongly opposed on account of their opposition to the League of Nations, but have carried their States by substantial majorities. Senator Brandegee also had the opposition of many women on account of his effort to prevent the ratification of the Nineteenth Amendment.

Phelan Loses California.

Samuel Shortridge, Republican, who supported Senator Hiram Johnson's irreconcilable opposition to the League of Nations, appears to have been elected to the Senate, defeating Senator James D. Phelan, Democrat, a firm friend of the Wilson Administration. Senator James E. Watson, Republican, has been re-elected from Indiana, defeating ex-Senator Thomas Taggart, Democrat. Returns from Iowa are not nearly complete, but they indicate that in spite of the opposition of organizations of farmers and laborers and a great many Re-

Continued on Page Three.

MAP SHOWING HOW THE STATES VOTED

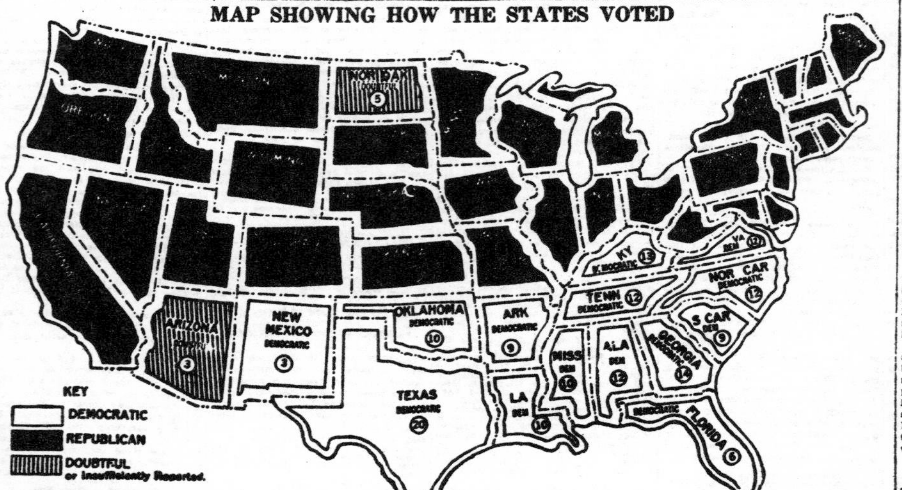

FIGURES IN CIRCLES INDICATE NUMBER OF ELECTORAL VOTES

Electoral Vote.

HARDING.	
California	13
Colorado	6
Connecticut	7
Delaware	3
Illinois	29
Indiana	15
Idaho	4
Iowa	13
Kansas	10
Maine	6
Maryland	8
Massachusetts	18
Michigan	15
Minnesota	12
Missouri	18
Montana	4
Nebraska	8
Nevada	3
New Hampshire	4
New Jersey	14
New York	45
Ohio	24
Oregon	5
Pennsylvania	38
Rhode Island	5
South Dakota	5
Utah	4
Vermont	4
Washington	7
West Virginia	8
Wisconsin	13
Wyoming	3
Total	371
COX.	
Alabama	12
Arkansas	9
Florida	6
Georgia	14
Kentucky	13
Louisiana	10
Mississippi	10
New Mexico	3
North Carolina	12
Oklahoma	10
South Carolina	9
Tennessee	12
Texas	20
Virginia	12
Total	152
Doubtful or Insufficiently Reported	
Arizona	3
North Dakota	5
Total	8

Total number of votes in Electoral College, 531; necessary to a choice, 266.

PRESIDENT HEARD FIRST VOTES ONLY

He Retired at 9 o'Clock, His Physician Leaving the White House Earlier.

NO COMMENT ON RETURNS

Wilson at Afternoon Cabinet Meeting Expressed Confidence in Success of League.

Special to The New York Times.

WASHINGTON, Nov. 2.—Although messages to the White House tonight brought the news that Harding was leading in very nearly all the doubtful localities the attitude seemed to be sit tight and concede nothing until the actual result was ascertained. The experience of the Hughes débâcle four years ago appeared to hold out a lesson in the wisdom of this course for the White House circle.

No public expressions of any kind were made. The atmosphere lacked the gloom usually associated with the news of a reversal. Visitors to the White House found the Secretaries and other members of the staff in perfect good humor.

President Wilson heard bulletins until about 9 o'clock, and this being his usual bed hour, he retired, so it was said. Admiral Cary T. Grayson, his personal physician, left the White House for his home about 8:30 o'clock. This fact seemed to set aside theories that the President would be in a nervous condition if he realized that Senator Harding was far ahead in the Presidential race.

Joseph P. Tumulty, Private Secretary

Continued on Page Four.

GIGANTIC MAJORITIES

Pennsylvania, 750,000; Illinois, 800,000; Ohio, 400,000.

MAY BE 6,000,000 IN ALL

More Than 370 Electoral Votes Won by Harding and Coolidge.

BIG GAINS IN THE WEST

Indiana, Wisconsin, Michigan, Iowa, Kansas, Nebraska and California Won.

NEW JERSEY BY 200,000

Maine, with 75,000, Beats the Plurality She Gave in September.

SOLID SOUTH UNBROKEN

Unless Late Figures Change Tennessee—Cox May Lose All Western States.

By majorities unprecedented in American politics, Warren G. Harding was elected President and Calvin Coolidge Vice President yesterday on Senator Harding's fifty-fifth birthday. Though the addition of women to the electorate might have been expected to make the margins of successful candidates somewhat larger than in past years, it could hardly account for any such unheard of majorities as were rolled up yesterday. From coast to coast records were broken.

Harding's total pluralities in the States he carried may reach 6,500,000 and his net plurality over Cox may be 6,000,000. This surpasses by 3,500,000 the previous record, which was that of Theodore Roosevelt's victory over Alton B. Parker.

The highest State plurality ever previously recorded, Roosevelt's margin of 500,000 over Parker in Pennsylvania in 1904, was surpassed by at least four States yesterday. New York State went for Harding by nearly 1,100,000; Pennsylvania gave him a plurality of 750,000; Illinois gave him 800,000; California, which went for Wilson four years ago by a majority of 2,800, gave Harding a plurality of perhaps 500,000 over James M. Cox. Ohio, the home State of both candidates, went for Harding by 400,000.

At 4 o'clock this morning it seemed that Harding's majority on electoral votes would equal or surpass the record-breaking landslide by which Roosevelt beat Alton B. Parker.

Cox held the solid South, and Kentucky and perhaps Oklahoma among the border States; but West Virginia and Missouri had apparently gone for Harding, as they went for Roosevelt in 1904. Late reports indicate that Cox might possibly lose Tennessee.

The latest reports give Harding 371 electoral votes and Cox 152, with eight votes—those of Arizona and North Dakota—still uncertain. This, however, seems to be due to inadequate reports; the probability is that they are all for Harding.

All over the country the Harding pluralities broke records. Boston, which has been consistently Democratic in recent years, except in 1896, when McKinley carried it over Bryan, showed the effect of the drift of the Irish vote by giving Harding a plurality of more than 20,000.

New York City, however, was even more surprising. The city went for Taft in 1908 by less than 16,000; it seems to have given Harding a plurality of more than 443,000. Buffalo gave Harding a plurality of 46,247.

The effect of the Harding sweep showed everywhere. Though the Southern States stood fast, Harding had carried two wards in Atlanta and two Louisiana parishes. In the Middle West, Indiana and Kansas each gave him more than 200,000 plurality, Iowa about the same; Michigan nearly 400,000; Wisconsin nearly 300,000.

Maine, which surprised observers last September by a Republican plurality of 70,000 in the Gubernatorial election, surpassed this figure by several thousand

"All the News That's Fit to Print."

The New York Times.

THE WEATHER
Generally fair today and Friday; moderate, shifting winds.
For full weather report see Page 18.

VOL. LXX....No. 23,105. NEW YORK, THURSDAY, APRIL 28, 1921. TWO CENTS In Greater New York | THREE CENTS Within 200 Miles | FOUR CENTS Elsewhere

GERMAN OFFER REJECTED, ALLIES PRESENT BILL FOR 132 BILLIONS; FORMALLY HANDED TO GERMAN AGENT IN PARIS LAST NIGHT; HUGHES AWAITS NOTICE OF ALLIED ATTITUDE ON BERLIN NOTE

BONE DRY STATE IN SIXTY DAYS, CHANDLER'S ORDER

Superintendent of State Police Tells His Troopers Two Months Is the Limit.

THEY MAKE FIRST RAIDS

Seize Liquor Worth $30,000 in Saloons in Westchester and Oneida Counties.

MILLER TO AVOID CONFLICT

Governor Opposes Enforcement by State Authorities Where They Conflict With Federal Agents.

Special to The New York Times.

ALBANY, April 27.—Major George F. Chandler, Superintendent of the State Police, began today a drive to make the entire territory in his jurisdiction bone dry within two months. The force with which he expects to do this consists of 232 State troopers, of whom approximately 100 are tied up at the present time by strike duty in this city, Troy and its neighborhood.

The first raids, made early today, netted $30,000 worth of contraband liquor, taken in raids on one saloon on the outskirts of White Plains, Westchester County and two in Oneida County.

Major Chandler said today that every county in the State, outside of counties comprised within the boundaries of New York City and some up-State counties with large cities, which are provided with a police force of sufficient size to cope with the illicit liquor traffic, would be a battleground and under constant surveillance by his men from now on. The State has been divided into zones for the purpose of Major Chandler's enforcement plan, which contemplates making dry some fifty communities every week from now until his purpose has been achieved.

"We are going to wipe out the illicit dives which have been flourishing on the outskirts of small towns up-State," said Major Chandler.

"My men are going about this business in a systematic way which cannot fail but bring the result we are aiming at. We are going to get the illegally possessed liquor. We are going to get the men who sell it and the men who buy and drink it. Each county will be under constant surveillance by my men from the fact that they will pay a business visit to at least one community in each of fifty counties every week from now on. Bootlegging, moonshining, blind tigers and all traffic in liquor in the territory covered by the State police will be entirely wiped out."

Governor Miller was asked this afternoon to comment on the statement of Major Chandler and to say whether he had inspired the constabulary crusade against the illicit traffic in liquor.

"Major Chandler is charged with the duty of enforcing the laws that come within his jurisdiction," said the Governor. "I haven't especially talked with him on this subject. I have entire confidence that he will observe and enforce the law. That is his business."

The Governor made it plain in an interview this afternoon that he would not favor any plan of enforcing the Federal Prohibition Amendment by State officials that would bring them into direct conflict with Federal officers engaged in the same pursuit. The Governor believes that duplication of effort and conflict of authority would be ruinous and bring about the collapse of the campaign now launched by local authorities throughout the State under the Mullan-Gage act against the illicit traffic in liquor.

"As a general proposition," the Governor was asked, "doesn't the enactment of the State Enforcement act place the State as an aid to the Federal Government in suppressing the traffic in liquor rather than the Federal Government as an aid of the State?"

"Of course," the Governor replied, "the very purpose of the State act was to make a law that already existed on the Federal statute books enforcible by local peace officers throughout the State, thus localizing responsibility."

The question was prompted by the fact that Federal enforcement agents had raided some saloons in Albany over the head of the local authorities.

"If a raid is made over the heads of local authorities by Federal agents would you say that this fact laid the local authorities open to censure?" was asked.

"That may or may not be, depending upon the facts," the Governor replied. "The raids are not necessarily made over their heads. The Federal law is the supreme law, and you would have to have more facts than the bare fact that Federal officials had made raids."

"Would you consider raids by Federal agents as evidence that there had been dereliction of duty on the part of local authorities?"

"I would not think it was evidence of

Continued on Page Four.

Proposes a 2½-Cent Coin To Bear Roosevelt's Likeness

WASHINGTON, April 27.—Coinage of a 2½-cent piece, bearing the likeness of Theodore Roosevelt, with the date of his birth and death, is provided for in a bill introduced today by Representative Appleby, Republican, of New Jersey.

The proposed limit of the coin as legal tender would be 40 cents and it would be big enough to distinguish it from the one-cent piece.

HOPE TO ESCAPE TIE-UP OF SHIPS

Both Sides Agree to Make One More Effort Tomorrow to Avert Strike.

SAYS WAGES MUST BE CUT

Benson Tells Conferees Shipping Board Holds Reduction of 15 Per Cent. Is Imperative.

Special to The New York Times.

WASHINGTON, April 27.—While no agreement as to wage reductions and working conditions was reached at the conference of marine workers and ship operators, held here today at the call of Admiral W. S. Benson, Chairman of the United States Shipping Board, hope still is held that a compromise may come which will avert a serious tie-up in New York Harbor on May 1.

This hope is based largely on an announcement made by Andrew Furuseth, President of the International Seamen's Union, that he had a final proposition to make, the details of which he did not wish to discuss at this time. Admiral Benson then called a second conference to be held here on Friday morning.

Admiral Benson laid before the workers and employers at today's conference the policy to which the Government will adhere as an operator of ships. Its basic principles are a decrease in wages of 15 per cent., the elimination of overtime charges and refusal to recognize the "closed shop" as applied to the shipping industry. In calling the second conference, he said, it was for those who wished to attend for a fair and just consideration of the problem. Those who held back, he added, must take the consequences.

The belief here today was that the private ship operators, who had sought a much larger cut in wages, would accept the governmental policy, including the 15 per cent. wage decrease.

As to the workers, it was the belief that all of the labor organizations, with the possible exception of the engineers, finally would accept the Government's proposition. It is possible that the engineers may be brought into line, although their representatives here were in a very warlike frame of mind. It was reported that leaders of some of the organizations of workers believed that the present depression in the shipping industry made this a poor time to strike.

Benson Takes Firm Stand.

The influence of the Government's stand also made itself felt. Admiral Benson, as Chairman of the Shipping Board, and therefore one of the large ship operators, was firm in his attitude. He said he had given the problem the most thoughtful consideration; had heard from both sides in the controversy, and was prepared to stand unalterably behind the conclusions reached.

Entrance of the Government into the controversy through the medium of the Shipping Board gives both workers and private employers an opportunity to come to terms without either side having to admit complete rout. The workers will obtain a very considerable concession in the matter of wage reduction, and also are assured that the Government recognizes their right to demand enforcement of the Seamen's act and other legislation affecting the crews while such laws remain on the statute books. The workers recognize also that if they reject the offer of the Government they will place a weapon in the hands of the private employers with which to fight for the repeal of legislation under which the crews have many privileges.

Early in today's conferences Mr. Furuseth and William S. Brown, the latter representing the Marine Engineers Beneficial Association, asserted that the workers would be unable to accept the wage cut of 15 per cent., placed before them by Admiral Benson as the fixed policy of the Shipping Board. Edward B. Griffin, representing the cooks and stewards, also objected, asserting that the "Shipping Board doesn't know anything about this business."

During the lunch hour the delegation of engineers held a separate conference, and it was announced that resolutions had been adopted refusing to accept the 15 per cent. wage cut. Mr. Brown said that some concessions might be made as to working conditions and minor rules. None of the other organizations went to that extreme, leaving the matter open.

Admiral Benson declared that the 15 per cent. reduction was the best offer

Continued on Page Three.

BIG RING CONTROLS ALL HOUSE FIXTURES; LIKE HETTRICK PLAN

Lockwood Committee Hears of Nine Combinations Doing Hundreds of Millions Yearly.

SECRETARY $50,000 A YEAR

Members Informed Minutely of Prices by System of Colored Charts.

MORE REVELATIONS DUE

Untermyer Says 60 Combinations Grip Everything, "From Boilers to Door-Knobs."

The Lockwood committee yesterday disclosed the existence of nine combinations of national manufacturers of appliances used in buildings doing an annual business of several hundred millions of dollars organized in so-called "open-price" associations, maintaining elaborate systems of price reporting by which competitors were fully informed as to each other's business.

It is the contention of Samuel Untermyer, counsel to the committee, that almost every item that enters into the construction of a house is the centre of a combination of manufacturers who fix and maintain prices by agreement, and before the committee adjourns he expects to show the existence of about sixty such combinations, from boilers to door-knobs.

The inquiry yesterday revealed that the nine open-price associations, organized in a Hettrick-like manner, and known as exchanges, manufacture gas ranges, water meters, pipe fittings, valves, range boilers, sandpaper and sandcloth, steel window sashes, steel lockers, steel shelving, tubular plumbing goods, brass and copper fittings.

The nine combinations of manufacturers operate through a central clearing house at 522 Fifth Avenue, which is in charge of a professional secretary, Albert A. Ainsworth, receiving about $50,000 a year. The manufacturers spend about $200,000 a year in maintaining their organization. This includes the $15,000 salary of Clark McKercher, formerly an Assistant United States Attorney General, who is counsel.

Exchanges Served by Ainsworth.

The exchanges represented by Mr. Ainsworth embrace some of the largest concerns in the country. The combinations are as follows: The American Brass and Copper Statistical Exchange, the Meter Manufacturers' Exchange, the Pipe Fitting and Valve Exchange, the Range Boiler Exchange, the Abrasive Paper and Cloth Manufacturers' Exchange, the Steel Sash Manufacturers' Exchange, the Steel Locker and Shelving Manufacturers' Exchange, the Tubular Plumbing Goods and Tank Filling Exchange and the National Gas Appliance Manufacturers' Exchange.

The information concerning the exchanges was spread on the records during the examination of Frederick H. Loehrs, assistant to Mr. Ainsworth. Ainsworth was asked to "step down" after he refused to waive immunity. Loehrs also refused, but he was permitted to go on. Ainsworth remained in the room at the direction of Mr. Untermyer.

Mr. Untermyer is being assisted in the open-price association phase of the inquiry by former Assemblyman George R. Brennan of Brooklyn.

Loehrs said that Ainsworth was Secretary of thirteen exchanges, but that only nine manufactured articles used in housing. The non-housing exchanges include cotton goods, napthalene and ammonia.

It was brought out that the various firms were known by code numbers, "not for secrecy" but "for brevity," and that keys to the names of the firms in each association were in the hands of the members of the association. The reports sent to the members bore no firm names, only the code numbers.

The reports were sent out on colored charts, which were all colors of the rainbow and a few more, including "canary, salmon and goldenrod."

Counsel Change Minutes.

Loehrs said there were about 150 concerns in the nine combinations. He was questioned concerning the minutes of the meetings of the various associations and said that the proceedings were sent to counsel, but denied that the latter had had certain things expunged from the records. He admitted that counsel suggested changes in the minutes occasionally.

He told of the system whereby some of the members reported day by day the names of customers to whom they sold goods, the date of the sale, character of shipment, price and other details so that by the end of the day a member might know what his competitor's business for the previous day amounted

Continued on Page Seven.

WASHINGTON WANTS LIGHT

Not Even France's Refusal to Accept Berlin Plan Is Yet Received.

OFFICIALS KEEP SILENCE

Great Care Is Taken Not to Give Any Idea of Our Own View of Proposals.

MEANWHILE REPLY WAITS

Capital Feels That Britain Alone Can Prevent Invasion of the Ruhr Now.

French Rejection of Offer Is Announced in Paris

PARIS, April 27 (Associated Press).—Jean Jules Jusserand, French Ambassador to the United States, has been informed by the French Government that the German reparations proposals, as transmitted to the Washington Government, are absolutely unacceptable.

The French point of view is that these proposals, instead of making any advance toward a satisfactory settlement of the reparations question, are rather a step backward.

WASHINGTON, April 27.—An Associated Press dispatch from Paris this evening announced that instructions had gone forward to Ambassador Jusserand to inform the United States that the German propositions were unacceptable to France. It was assumed that M. Jusserand would make this known officially to Mr. Hughes tomorrow.

Special to The New York Times.

WASHINGTON, April 27.—No formal move has been made by the United States Government in connection with the new German proposals on the reparations question, submitted to the Allies through the American Commissioner at Berlin and the State Department. To say that exchanges on the subject are at a standstill would give a wrong impression, but officially this Government has taken no step that would justify any prediction of its ultimate course.

Informally, Secretary Hughes has brought the German note to the attention of the Ambassadors of France, Great Britain, Italy, Belgium and Japan, who would have communicated with their Governments. Whatever advices they have received in return have been communicated to Mr. Hughes in a most informal way. Late this afternoon it was stated in an official quarter that no communication, formal or informal, had come from any allied Government in regard to the Berlin proposals.

The Government knows that the terms of the German proposals are entirely unsatisfactory to France, which is recognized as having superior claims to consideration. But despite press advices from Paris today, stating that the French Government had forwarded instructions to M. Jusserand here, declaring the Berlin suggestions unacceptable and thus confirming the special cable dispatch from Paris, published in THE NEW YORK TIMES this morning, no communication of the sort has been received here. The same is true in respect to other allied Governments.

It is suggested, on the one hand, that the instructions sent to M. Jusserand have been delayed in transmission. Another idea here is that the French Government, while informing M. Jusserand of its position, may have communicated its view to the United States through the medium of an informal conversation with some other person, our Ambassador in Paris, for example.

Official Text Is Withheld.

The State Department is proceeding so cautiously in the present delicate situation that it declines to make public the text of the German communication. Should the proposals be modified by Germany before they reach the allied governments in an official way, the note now under consideration may not be given out officially by this Government. But officials did not hesitate to acknowledge today that the communication as received here, was identical in all respects with the text of the German note cabled to THE NEW YORK TIMES from Paris last night. It was said by some of those who had seen both that even the differences that are usual in translations of the same text done by two different persons were not apparent.

So that portion of Washington outside of the few connected with the Government and the allied Embassies who were privileged to peruse the official text received by Secretary Hughes were dependent upon The TIMES text for their information as to what the Germans had proposed.

It is expected that the allied Governments, in considering the German proposals, will treat as one element in the equation the Hughes note to Germany,

Continued on Page Two.

German Offer Unacceptable, Belgian Official Circles Say

BRUSSELS, April 27.—The German counter-proposals with regard to reparations were declared in political circles here today to be entirely unacceptable.

It was pointed out the new proposals did not differ materially from those submitted by the Germans at the London Conference.

ENGLAND ASKS FOR EXPLANATIONS

German Proposals Found Too Ambiguous to Permit of Definite Judgment.

CONDEMNED BY THE PRESS

Scheme Seen to Involve Allies in Further Interminable Debate—Rejection Foreshadowed.

Special Cable to THE NEW YORK TIMES.

LONDON, Thursday, April 28.—The German note is too ambiguous in the view of official circles here to form a definite opinion about. The Government has taken steps to obtain fuller information as to what the Germans intend to offer, and until that has been received it will maintain the greatest reserve about the matter.

As a matter of fact when the Cabinet met yesterday morning it had heard nothing from Washington and had no official copy of the German proposals before it, but merely a version it had received from Berlin.

Then about the most important point of all, the amount of reparations, there is doubt.

The Germans offer 50,000,000,000 gold marks, or if payment is made by annual instalments, 200,000,000,000, but they do not state over how many years these payments would be distributed or at what rate they are to be discounted. The Paris demand of 226,000,000,000, spread over forty-two years, and discounted at 8, 6 and 5 per cent. might not be so far away from the Berlin offer if the conditions of the latter were much the same, but until these conditions are known it is held here to be utterly useless to institute comparison.

"It is difficult for a layman," said an expert to THE NEW YORK TIMES correspondent, "to appreciate what a tremendous difference, when you are dealing with enormous sums to be paid over a long period of years, the rate of interest charged and the number of instalments required make. The old story of how a sharper cheated a farmer over shoeing his horse by inducing him to pay a penny for the first nail, twopence for the second, and so on, illustrates how conditions may affect payment, and the Germans must define their offer clearly before we can even consider it."

Other Points Obscure.

Then the Government will need full explanation of other points in the German note. What does Berlin mean by an international loan established "on such a basis that it will be possible to reach an extremely high subscription figure"? What does it mean by abolition of the system of sanctions and an agreement that "the present basis of German production is not further reduced"? Does this last mean that Germany is to retain the whole of Silesia in spite of the result of the plebiscite?

Innumerable questions of this sort need answering with regard to the conditions Dr. Simons has tacked on to his offer of cash, and until they are elucidated the British Government considers it useless to enter into a detailed discussion of the proposals.

The ambiguity of the note is, in the view of last night's Evening News, the real reason why it was dispatched to Washington.

"The wording of the offer is so vague," it says, "that it opens up opportunities for interminable discussion. That is just what Germany wants. She is out for delay, for while she talks she does not pay—the paying is done by the Allies. Apparently Germany has yet to learn that it is for the Allies to make conditions. If she persists in that attitude she will have to be undeceived."

The Westminster Gazette considers the German terms are not intended to be more than a good basis for further negotiating. It says:

"Germany makes a gesture of willingness to do the utmost that she conceives to be possible. It is for the Allies to examine the offer and if possible to obtain more. The French Government and the French press vie with one another in declaring the offer totally unacceptable. Of course it is if the test be the destruction which Germany has done, but that by common consent is outside the capacity of any one country to pay. The real test, however, is what Germany can pay provided she has the will to pay. That is a matter for examination and discussion."

The Westminster Gazette considers the new offer is, in essential respects, an

Continued on Page Two.

OFFER DEAD, FRENCH HOLD

Public Opinion Strongly Supports Government's Rejection.

PLEASED WITH OUR PART

Chamber Ready for Action—Payment of Billion Marks by May 1 Might Delay Invasion.

FIND JOKERS IN PROPOSALS

Analyses of the Offer and Conditions Reject Both as Beyond Discussion.

By EDWIN L. JAMES.

By Wireless to THE NEW YORK TIMES.

PARIS, April 27.—Official Paris took it for granted today that the German proposals of April 24 would not be forwarded by Washington to the Allies and that they were dead letters.

The French press strongly backs the Government in its declination to undertake new reparation negotiations with Germany on the basis of Dr. Simons's propositions sent to the United States. As a matter of fact, after reading the newspapers representing all political parties it is very apparent that it would have caused Premier Briand's fall if he had accepted those offers.

All of the afternoon newspapers carry a semiofficial note beginning: "The Government of the United States has not transmitted and will not transmit to the allied Governments the German propositions."

French diplomats are very pleased with the graceful manner in which Secretary Hughes permitted the Paris Government to place a veto on the German proposals and thus halt them. It is understood here that as soon as he got the proposals Mr. Hughes gave M. Jusserand the opportunity to point out that they did not measure up to what France demanded. M. Jusserand cabled to Paris this fact, and last night Paris confirmed his opposition.

No official statement is made as to what France's position may be on any new proposals from Germany, but those proposals will have to go further, much further, than the latest proposals if the French Chamber is to accept them.

The French Chamber is set for action. Probably the only action by Germany now to prevent occupation of the Ruhr the first part of next month is to turn over 1,000,000,000 gold marks cash before May 1.

The Temps tonight publishes a long analysis of the German proposals, and finds the note full of jokers, including a purpose to get all of Silesia and of tearing up the sanctions plan of the Treaty of Versailles. It concludes thus:

"This analysis makes comment useless. Very inferior to the accord of Paris, lacking in precision as to their real value, accompanied by demands which would destroy the treaty and deprive the Allies of all their guarantees, the German propositions cannot form the basis of discussion. They justify fully the firm language M. Briand used yesterday before the Chamber and they only make more intense in all France the will to bring the bosses of Germany to reason."

The Journal des Débats says it is superfluous to consider these proposals, which may be new to Washington, but which are the same brand of foolishness the Allies have been having from Germany for more than a year.

The Journal wants to know how France would be sure collecting ten years from now if she gave up all sanctions. "Either Germany is joking or this offer is a defiance," says the paper, and continues: "Simons poses Germany as a victim in a theatrical manner and cries that if the Allies occupy the Ruhr the German people, reduced to slavery, will wander in the desert like the lost tribes of Israel. That picture will not worry the Allies nor the rest of the world. Unfortunately the only desert is that region devastated by Germany. We don't want to reduce the German people to slavery, but we intend to make them restore that region they reduced to a desert. And we are going to succeed."

The Liberté says Jehovah declared he would have spared Sodom if he could have found ten just men there, and asks where are the just men of Germany.

Estimates of the German Offer.

PARIS, April 27 (Associated Press).—It is pointed out in official circles that the Germans in their proposals are precise in their demands and extremely vague in their offers and that what they propose would yield to France only one-third of the French reparations claims, and that only conditionally.

The Germans, on the other hand, demand, first, release of all pledges held by the Allies in the way of occupation or claims upon German property abroad; second, that Upper Silesia shall remain German territory; third, release from all the cost of the military occu-

Continued on Page Two.

German Blunder Delayed Cabling of Note to Hughes

BERLIN, April 27 (Associated Press).—Clerical blundering in the main telegraph office in Berlin caused a delay of twelve hours in transmission of the German counter-proposals on reparations to Washington. The American mission here filed the last section of the note at 10 o'clock Sunday night, and the cause of the delay was only located when acknowledgment of its receipt came from Washington Tuesday morning, indicating that the note had been an unduly long time in transit.

The night shift at the telegraph office apparently failed to recognize the diplomatic nature of the message and treated it as a routine dispatch.

The English rendering of the original note supplied to the American mission by the Foreign Office not only reveals an imperfect translation, but contains faulty reproduction of the German terms.

HUGHES'S NAME IS MISUSED IN BERLIN

Suggestion for Modification Not His—Did It Come from Unofficial Intruders?

SECRETARY SENT NO WORD

It Is Also Pointed Out That British Inquiries May Have Been Erroneously Attributed to Him.

Special to The New York Times.

WASHINGTON, April 27.—The disclosure today that the United States Government had not communicated with the German Government concerning the latest reparations proposals was intended to apply to the statement from Berlin that American suggestions for a modification of the German terms had been received by the German Government.

This statement is attributed in some quarters to confusion with action taken by the British Government. A press dispatch from London saying that the British Government had requested its representatives in Berlin to enquire informally regarding the German reparations offer for the purpose of clearing ambiguity as to the terms of years in which payments would be made under the offer was confirmed in official advices received here. If this explanation is correct, it was the British Government, therefore, and not the American Government, that communicated with the German Government concerning the German proposals. This action of the British Government may be significant of a willingness of Great Britain to give careful consideration to the German offer, but there is no official sanction for such an inference.

Propagandists Active.

At the same time it is possible that the understanding given currency in Berlin that the United States Government had suggested that it could not transmit the German proposals in their present state indirectly arose from the activities of Americans in Berlin who are endeavoring to have this Government act as mediator between Germany and the Allies. That this group has watchful American connections is not doubted and the free use of cables by the Americans in Berlin in communicating with Senators and others suggests that there may be as free use of cable communication from this side. The length of some of the cablegrams sent from Berlin indicates that money was no consideration.

It was apparent to many people from the moment that they learned what was in the German note that it would not be satisfactory to France, at least. A fair inference was that people in this country who are in close touch with the situation would be able to advise the American group in Berlin that the German proposals were too unsatisfactory to justify the United States in transmitting them.

May Be Federal Inquiry.

The information from Berlin that Secretary Hughes had informed the German Government that the United States could not present the proposals to the Allies was stated without qualification, and it gives rise to the suspicion that somebody has been trying to make the German Government believe that Mr. Hughes took this position. If this somebody has been seeking to make representations to the German Government through the unauthorized use of Mr. Hughes's name or attributing to him views that he never sanctioned, there undoubtedly will be an investigation.

In a broad sense, the German proposals are disappointing. The feeling is general in Washington that they will not meet the situation by affording a basis for further negotiation of the reparations question in their present shape. Whatever may have become of the instructions sent to the French Ambassador in Washington by his Government to inform the United States that the German offer is unacceptable the fact remains that France takes the position and the United States Government,

Continued on Page Two.

GERMANS GET FULL BILL

Reparation Commission Fixes Total Claims of the Allies.

LESS THAN WAS EXPECTED

Commission Finishes Its Work Three Days Ahead of Date Set in the Treaty.

EXCEEDS PARIS DEMAND

But Compares With 50,000,000,000 Marks Offered by Germany in Full Settlement.

By EDWIN L. JAMES.

Special Cable to THE NEW YORK TIMES.

PARIS, April 27.—This evening at 9 o'clock the Reparation Commission summoned to its presence Dr. von Oertzen, head of the German Commission on Reparation, who replaces Herr Bergmann, and officially informed him of the sum which Germany owes in reparation for damage done in the war. The total figure is 132,000,000,000 gold marks.

This figure is considerably below what had been forecast. Details of how it has been arrived at are not yet available, but will be communicated to the German Commission tomorrow in writing.

Even as late as this afternoon the Reparation Commission members were uncertain when they would be able to fix the total, but by night and day work in the last month they have arrived at the end of this part of their labors, three full days before the date of May 1 fixed by the treaty.

After the meeting with Dr. von Oertzen the following communiqué was issued:

"The Reparation Commission, in pursuance of the stipulations of Article 233, Treaty of Versailles, has decided unanimously to fix at 132,000,000,000 gold marks the amount of damages for which reparation is due by Germany in terms of Article 232, second paragraph, and of Annex 1 of Part VIII. of said treaty.

"In fixing this amount the Reparation Commission has effected the necessary deductions from the amount of the damages in order to make allowance for restitutions effected or to be effected in execution of Article 238, and in consequence no credit will be allowed to Germany in respect of such restitutions.

"The commission has not included in the above amount the sum in respect of further obligation incumbent on Germany in virtue of the third paragraph of Article 232 to 'make reimbursement of all sums which Belgium has borrowed from the Allied and Associated Governments up to Nov. 11, 1918, together with interest at the rate of 5 per cent. on such sums.'"

The amount of 132,000,000,000 gold marks as the total damages for which reparation is due from Germany fixed by the Reparation Commission represents what would be demanded of Germany, if she were able to pay in full and liquidate the debt today. It may therefore only be compared with the present cash value of the Allies' proposals made at Paris on Jan. 29, which has been estimated at from 68,000,000,000 to 84,000,000,000 gold marks, if the 226,000,000,000 gold marks demanded, the payment of which was to be completed in forty-two years, were discounted at once; with the cash value of the German counter-proposal made at London, Feb. 28-March 3, estimated at 30,000,000,000 gold marks, and with the present value of Germany's latest offer, 50,000,000,000 gold marks.

Annex 1., of Part VIII., referred to by the commission, defines in ten paragraphs the grounds on which compensation is to be demanded, and the way in which the compensation is to be estimated—damage to persons and property of the Allies, and various costs including the aid given prisoners of war in Germany and the support of their families, &c.

As it was early known that Germany could not possibly meet the total damages to be assessed against her by the Reparation Commission, the Supreme Council approached the subject from another point of view, to determine not what Germany should pay, but what Germany was able to pay.

Thus on Jan. 29, the Supreme Council sent a note to the President of the German delegation in which Articles 1 and 2, fixing the indemnity, or reparations, and describing the manner of payment, read as follows:

For the purpose of satisfying the obligations imposed upon her by Articles 231 and 232 of the Treaty of Versailles, Germany shall, irrespective of the restitutions she is to make under Article 238, and of any other obligation under the Treaty, pay:

(1) Fixed annuities, payable half-yearly in equal parts, as follows:

(a) Two annuities of two milliards of gold marks from May 1, 1921, to May 1, 1923.

(b) Three annuities of three milliards of gold marks from May 1, 1923 to May 1, 1926.

(c) Three annuities of four milliards of gold marks from May 1, 192[illegible] to May 1, 192[illegible].

(d) Three annuities of five milliards

Section 1

"All the News That's Fit to Print."

The New York Times.

THE WEATHER
Generally fair and warmer today; Monday, cloudy, probably thunder showers; southwesterly winds.
For full weather report see Page 19.

Section 1

VOL. LXX....No. 23,171. NEW YORK, SUNDAY, JULY 3, 1921. In Eight Parts, including Rotogravure Picture Sections, Book and Magazine Section. FIVE CENTS In Manhattan, Bronx, and Brooklyn | Elsewhere TEN CENTS

DEMPSEY KNOCKS OUT CARPENTIER IN THE FOURTH ROUND; CHALLENGER BREAKS HIS THUMB AGAINST CHAMPION'S JAW; RECORD CROWD OF 90,000 ORDERLY AND WELL HANDLED

HARDING ENDS WAR; SIGNS PEACE DECREE AT SENATOR'S HOME

Thirty Persons Witness Momentous Act in Frelinghuysen Living Room at Raritan.

DROPS BLOT ON SIGNATURE

Joint Resolution of Congress Made Effective at 4:10 P. M., Daylight Saving Time.

TEXT OF THE RESOLUTION

Steel Pen Used to Be Given to Representative Porter, Author of Historic Document.

Special to The New York Times.

RARITAN, N. J., July 2.—War with Germany ended as it began, by Congressional declaration and Executive signature on American soil.

At 4:10 P. M., local daylight saving time, in the living room of "The Hill," Senator Joseph S. Frelinghuysen's home here, President Harding placed his signature to the Porter joint Congressional resolution declaring peace with Germany and Austria, just two years and four days after the ill-fated Treaty of Versailles was signed.

By a coincidence, a year ago to the day, Warren G. Harding, United States Senator from Ohio and Republican nominee for President, left Washington for his Marion front porch to prepare his speech of acceptance containing the promise of "formal and effective peace so quickly as a Republican Congress can pass its declaration for a Republican Executive to sign."

Scarcely thirty persons in a country home in the hills of Somerset County witnessed the last act that concluded the World War, while a few minutes before, fifty miles away in another part of the State, 90,000 persons saw a wartime riveter in a shipyard knock to the floor of the ring a former French enlisted man and aviation pilot.

Blot on Signature.

"That's all," said President Harding as he held his pen above his signature on a broad vellum typewritten page. The ink dripped from the pen and made a blot the size of a 5-cent piece on the page, almost effacing the "G." of the President's signature.

More ceremony has been connected with making an entry in the family Bible or a débutante's memory book than that accompanying the signature that ended a war that called to the colors 4,800,000 young Americans. And yet the very informality of the occasion heightened its impressiveness. Except for the four cameramen—there were no movies—not one of the witnesses spoke or moved while the President signed the peace resolution. The thirty-odd Government officials and their wives, secret service men, county officers, reporters, butlers, maids, chauffeurs and gardeners that were in Senator Frelinghuysen's living room were busy with their own thoughts, and the modest Frelinghuysen ancestral home will have a place in history long after an international heavyweight championship is forgot.

While President Harding, Senators Frelinghuysen, Hale and Kellogg and Speaker Gillett played golf over the Somerset Hills County Club at Bernardsville this morning, E. W. Smithers, a White House attaché, was on his way from Washington with a leather pouch containing the Porter resolution that the Senate passed yesterday afternoon. "Doc" Smithers reached "The Hill" at 2 o'clock and sat on the Frelinghuysen porch, his pouch between his knees, waiting for the President and his party, who arrived at 3:45.

Receives Papers on Porch.

President Harding, wearing a Palm Beach suit, white shoes, white socks with black clocks, a white shirt, buttoned by removable gold studs, and a green and red bow tie, climbed briskly out of the automobile, and as he sat down in a wicker chair on the porch took a sheaf of papers from the hands of the Washington messenger. Spectators remained a few feet away wondering whether the peace resolution was to be signed there and thereby make another front porch famous.

The President read through the document carefully and then examined some routine papers that had been brought from Washington for his attention. Patsy, a white, wire-haired Irish terrier, sniffed inquiringly at one of the Presidential shoes, while Emily and Joseph Jr., two of the Frelinghuysen children, vainly tried to entice the puppy to their swing seat. For five or ten minutes the President concentrated over official papers and then went indoors.

In the Frelinghuysen living room, an addition to the original house, a small mahogany table, a family heirloom, had been swept bare of its ornaments and was placed in the southwest corner of the room. Two windows, south and west, shed light on the table and to the right was a broad carved wooden mantel of severe lines that would delight a col-

Continued on Page Fifteen.

President Harding Asks, 'Was It a Good Fight?'

RARITAN, N. J., July 2.—President Harding showed little interest when informed late today that Jack Dempsey had defeated Georges Carpentier, French challenger, with a knockout in the fourth round.

"Was it a good fight?" he asked of newspaper men when told the result.

He made no further comment and changed the conversation into other channels.

WIFE AND MOTHER BOTH TAKE POISON

Women Go to Hotel Commodore, Swallow Mercury, and Elder One Phones Physician.

FOUND CLASPING BABY SHOE

Young Woman Was Worried Because Husband Took Child to His Mother—Both May Die.

An attempt is being made to unravel the mystery of why Mrs. Mortimer Weiss, 20 years old, of 46 Fort Washington Avenue, and her mother, Mrs. Frances Weiss, who lived at the Hotel Remington, attempted to commit suicide in the Hotel Commodore by taking bichloride of mercury. They were found there yesterday noon, having taken the poison thirty-six hours before and only let word of their condition get to the outside when their suffering became too great to be borne, and the elder Mrs. Weiss telephoned to a physician.

The only explanation yet given is that the younger Mrs. Weiss had quarreled with her husband, who had taken their baby girl to his mother's home. Clasped in the woman's hand when their room was opened yesterday was a baby's shoe and under her pillow a little rubber dog, such as babies cut their teeth on. She was nearly unconscious and her mother barely able to speak, and neither of them would tell why they tried to die. The daughter is in Bellevue Hospital and the mother in Flower Hospital. Little hope is entertained for the recovery of either, owing to the fact that blood poisoning, also treated immediately, is difficult to check.

Mrs. Frances Weiss is a nurse who has been employed by Dr. Arthur Greenburg, who has offices in the Hotel Remington.

She is about 40 years old. The younger Mrs. Weiss is the wife of Mortimer Weiss, 26 years old, who is associated with his mother, Mrs. Carryl Weiss, in a millinery business at 647 Madison Avenue. They have been married about three years and have a baby a year and a half old. Their married life has not been happy, and on Wednesday Weiss took the baby and went to his mother's home. What the final cause of the break was only the four members of the two Weiss families know, and they would not talk yesterday.

Took Poison From Doctor's Office.

Late Thursday night mother and daughter went to Dr. Greenburg's office in the Hotel Remington. He was out, but the mother opened the office with her key and they remained there for nearly two hours. They apparently took the bichloride tablets from a shelf in his laboratory, for he missed his supply when he went to look for it yesterday, and in the room at the Commodore was found an envelope bearing Dr. Greenburg's name which contained two of the fourteen tablets they had taken.

When they left the Remington they took a cab and drove to the Commodore,

Continued on Page Fifteen.

CROWD EARLY AT GATES

Thousands Wait Through Morning Hours for Opening of Arena

POLICE IN PERFECT CONTROL

Handle Entrance and Exit of Huge Throng Without Difficulty —1,000 Firemen on Guard.

CHEER NOTABLES ON ENTRY

Spectators Eat Lunches in Streets — Bootleggers and Crooks Noticeably Absent.

More than 90,000 men and women, the biggest crowd that ever saw a sporting event in the United States, saw Jack Dempsey knock out Georges Carpentier yesterday.

Such a crowd had never been assembled in this country. It is possible that more persons may have seen some of the championship football matches in England, but there have never been that number seated as spectators of a sporting event. In another way, Tex Rickard, promoter of the fight, achieved a new record. The gate receipts, estimated at approximately $1,600,000 by Mr. Rickard, were far above all previous records.

All day long the crowd had been gathering for the championship battle. From 9 o'clock in the morning, when the gates were opened, until a few minutes before three in the afternoon, when the event of the day was scheduled to begin, a steady stream of men with a noticeable sprinkling of women marched steadily across the muddy fields leading to the saucer-shaped arena, until it seemed as though the latter, large as it was, could hold no more.

This mass of humanity, piled tier on tier in the wooden saucer, was released suddenly by the blow which sent Carpentier to the floor of the ring and retained the championship for Dempsey. Every one started for the exits at once. The pressure increased until the crush became terrific. The policemen and firemen, at least ten of whom were stationed in each section, handled the mass rushing for the exits with the same calm efficiency that they had displayed throughout the day. Regular traffic rules were enforced, the spectators in one aisle being held to let those in another aisle proceed, thus avoiding the cross-currents which usually add to the confusion.

Arena Quickly Emptied.

In one minute after Carpentier had been counted out, streams of men and women were pouring from a hundred exits, though many stayed to see the bout between Miske and Renault, which, though scheduled as a preliminary, was put on after the championship fight.

The last of the huge crowd departed silently and without confusion after the bell and clanged on the Miske-Renault bout. Seven minutes after this had ended the huge arena was empty, except for a few hundred curious ones who clustered around the ringside, watching the newspaper men at work. Policemen quickly had this crowd on the move and the arena was emptied of its non-working spectators at 4:35.

The crowd did not have the expected difficulty in getting out of Jersey City. About one-third of the number went by way of the Hudson Tubes, which carried 60,000 more than the usual number of Saturday passengers and ran its trains on a ninety-second schedule practically all day. Others regained New York by the ferries, which carried 30,000 more back from the fight.

The street cars, taxicabs and motor buses running from Boyd's Thirty Acres were too few to take care of more than a very small percentage of the depart-

Continued on Page Five.

Give Notice of Coming Marriage of Col. Balsan To Consuelo, Duchess of Marlborough

Special Cable to THE NEW YORK TIMES.

LONDON, July 2.—Notice has been given at the Westminster Registry office in Covent Garden of the marriage of Consuelo, Duchess of Marlborough, and Colonel Jacques Balsan.

Louis Jacques Balsan, who himself gave the notice, described himself as a Lieutenant Colonel in the French Army, retired, and gives his age as 52, while the age of the bride-elect is given as 44.

Colonel Balsan is well known in London, where he was a member of the French Aeronautical Mission during the war. He is possessed of considerable wealth, and is a member of a firm which manufactures uniforms and blankets for the French Army.

PARIS, July 2.—The Duchess of Marlborough will be married to J. Balsan at the London Registry office in a few days, it is said by the Continental edition of The Daily Mail. Reports that the Duchess was to marry M. Balsan have been current for several months, but have been frequently denied.

M. Balsan holds a high place in French society. He has been identified with major sports, owning a large racing stable and being an expert pilot of dirigible balloons and airplanes. He distinguished himself in the war, and was promoted to the rank of Lieutenant Colonel just before the armistice was signed.

The Duchess of Marlborough, formerly Consuelo Vanderbilt, was reported last January to be planning her marriage to the French sportsman, Jacques Balsan, when she purchased a magnificent estate at Eze, near Monte Carlo. Rumors of her approaching marriage to Balsan were revived when her divorced husband, the Duke, married Miss Gladys Deacon, formerly of Boston, in Paris, on June 25. The Duchess and Balsan were seen almost daily at tennis in Paris at the same time that the Duke and Miss Deacon were seen continually at dances.

The Duchess of Marlborough is the daughter of the late William K. Vanderbilt and the present Mrs. O. H. P. Belmont. Her marriage to the Duke of Marlborough took place in 1895. They had two children, the Marquis of Blandford, heir to his father's title, and Lord Ivor Churchill. The estrangement of the Duke and Duchess became known in 1907 when they decided to live apart for two years. Temporary reconciliations were effected largely through the intercession of the King in 1919, and the Duke and Duchess took up their residence again at Crowhurst until February, 1920, when they separated for the last time. The following March the Duchess started suit to establish conjugal rights and in May she obtained a final divorce.

Dempsey's First Thought Is Telegram to His Mother

Jack Dempsey's first thought as he came victorious from the ring was of his mother. He took a pencil and wrote her the following telegram:

Mrs. C. Dempsey, 3,572 South State St., Salt Lake City, Utah.
Dear Mother: Won in the fourth round. Received your wire. Will be home soon as possible. Love and kisses. JACK.

REFORMERS DEMAND ARREST OF DEMPSEY

Police Refuse Without Warrant, and They Fail to Get Plea Before Any Judge.

NEW MOVE EXPECTED TODAY

Assault and Battery Charged in Complaint—Not So "Brutal" as They Anticipated.

Herbert Clark Gilson, attorney for the International Reform Bureau, and two other representatives of that organization were among the thousands at the ringside when Dempsey knocked out Carpentier yesterday afternoon. They sat in $50 seats so that they could see everything that went on, but they did not root for either the champion or the challenger, and failed to join in the tumult when the Frenchman was knocked to the floor and counted out.

The reformers were present as witnesses to see whether the law was violated, and they decided that it was. Immediately after the fight Mr. Gilson went to the temporary police station beneath the grand stand and filed a complaint with Lieutenant Michael A. Martin, charging Dempsey with assault and battery and with violating the New Jersey Crimes act, which prohibits prizefighting. He told the police that the knockout was sufficient evidence that the law against prizefighting had been violated.

"Lieutenant," said Mr. Gilson, "I want you to place on the blotter here a complaint against Jack Dempsey, the prizefighter, charging him with assault and battery on Georges Carpentier of France, in this arena a few minutes ago."

Lieutenant Martin made the entry in the blotter, but refused to make an arrest without a warrant. Mr. Gilson wanted quick action and scouted around Jersey City until he found Chief of Police Battersby, who had attended the fight.

The Chief, who had thoroughly enjoyed himself and was busily engaged in discussing the knockout with his friends, could not be found for some time. Then he flatly refused to order Dempsey's arrest without a warrant.

Insist On Prompt Arrest.

"But we want him arrested before he leaves this State and we may not be able to find a Judge to issue a warrant today," said Mr. Gilson.

"That makes no difference," the Chief replied. "I must have a warrant."

"You don't need a warrant," Mr. Gilson argued. "You were at the fight and witnessed the violation of the law yourself. You saw the knockout."

"You must get a warrant first," said the Chief with finality.

Mr. Gilson then attempted to find one of the three County Judges, but was unable to do so last night. He said that he would continue his efforts today and was determined to go through with the reformer's intention of punishing violators of the law.

"Did you see all the fight?" Mr. Gilson was asked.

"Yes," he replied, "I saw it all. Dr. Wilbur F. Crafts, Superintendent of the International Reform Bureau, asked me to attend for the specific purpose of seeing whether the law was violated."

Asked to tell his impressions of the fight, Mr. Gilson said:

"I sat pretty well up front, in one of the $50 seats. A ringside seat? I don't know. There were a number of seats in front of me, but I suppose, as it was a $50 seat, you would call it at the ringside. I could see very well.

"I went in during the next to the last preliminary before the championship bout. This was a brutal affair, but I did not pay so much attention to it or the next fight, in which a man named Tunney clearly outclassed his opponent. Tunney's opponent was groggy long before the fight was stopped by the referee, who should have acted sooner than he did to stop the brutal punishment the loser was receiving.

Called Obvious Prize Fight.

"As to my impressions of the fight between Dempsey and Carpentier, it was obviously a prize fight in violation of the law. There can be no question about it. It was a prize fight, not a boxing exhibition, from the moment the two men entered the ring and put up their hands until the knockout punch was delivered. Both men showed they were out to win by a knockout, not on points or a newspaper decision.

"It was not as brutal as I had expected, however. It was not such a bloody, brutal fight as the fight between Dempsey and Willard at Toledo, for example. I did not see that fight, but I read in the newspapers that Dempsey knocked Willard down seven times

Continued on Page Twelve.

COBB FIGHTS IT OVER AGAIN

Calls Carpentier Soul of the Fray, Dempsey the Body.

ALL WHO'S BALLYHOO THERE

Arts, Science, Drama, Politics, Bar, Bench and Commerce Are Represented.

BOYLE'S 30 ACRES FERTILE

If There Is No New War, He Thinks Jack Will Be Best Fighter for a While.

By IRVIN S. COBB.

It is recorded that, once upon a time, Aaron Burr, being challenged by Alexander Hamilton, bade Hamilton to meet him over in Jersey and there destroyed his enemy. Yesterday afternoon, also New Jersey history, in a way of speaking, repeated itself, which is a habit to which history is addicted. Challenger and challenged met, and again the challenger lost the issue.

Posterity has appraised the loser of that first duel as of more value than the winner who survived. One is moved to wonder whether in the present instance the analogy will continue. Carpentier, an alien, a man who does not speak our language, was the favorite of the crowd before the fight started and while it progressed, and, if I am one to judge, was still its favorite when he came out of it summarily defeated though he was. Dempsey, a native born, will never forget, I am sure, the vast roar of approbation which arose from thirty acres of close-packed humanity about him when for a half-minute it seemed that he was slipping toward defeat. The thing never happened before when an American champion fought before an American audience. But then we never had for a champion a man whose war record—his lack of one rather—was stained with a taint.

Even so, and to the contrary notwithstanding, he showed himself a better man, as a fighter, than the Dempsey who whipped Willard two years ago at Toledo. Carpentier was the soul of the fight, but Dempsey was the body of it. Considering the thing purely in its pugilistic aspects, he won on merit—won because he was bigger and stronger, because he had more endurance than the Frenchman, and because, as it turned out, he was almost as fast upon his feet, when the needs of the moment demanded speed, and almost as clever a boxer as his opponent was. And to top all, he had a short arm blow, using either arm at will to deliver it, the like of which has not been seen on this Continent since Stanley Ketchel passed out.

Loses Like a Gentleman.

It was that drum-fire on his body which wasted Carpentier's substance of resistance, so that when the decisive jolts reached his jaw he had naught left in him with which to weather the blast. He fought fairly, did Carpentier, and like a gentleman he was licked fairly and like a gentleman. As a gentleman and a fighter he bulks tonight as the man the majority of the audience hoped to win and for whom, as a gallant soldier and a brave man, they wish good luck through all his days.

As for Dempsey, unless this country should go to war again, it seems probable that he will continue to be our leading fighter for quite some time to come.

Let us consider the matter chronologically, as it were.

At noon of the day when a championship battle is to be fought two hours later almost anything that happens is news. A prominent music hall performer, entering unostentatiously, accompanied only by his private photographer, his personal press agent and his official announcer—one such just came in as I did—constitutes a thrill. A slew-jawed functionary sowing powdered resin broadcast upon the canvas carpet of the ring amounts to a positive sensation. The sight of a near or Hudson seal society leader eating a proletariat ham sandwich in a box is worth a bulletin. And the mere appearance of a moving picture star is a riot. Such being the case, one begins one's preliminary story thus:

Not since the good old days when the courtesies of the press always were extended to the profession with food and drinks free and no questions asked, have I seen so many distinguished journalists gathered in one spot. We sit, we in whose hands the present destiny of English literature rests, in concentric rows about the fighting platform, like so many drops that have coagulated at the bottom of a huge funnel. Terracing up beyond and behind and on every side of us rise the banked tiers of the biggest ampitheatre this world has seen since the Caesars sat in the Circus Maximus having their Christian martyrs fried on one side. It is the biggest arena ever built of match work and pine planking. Assuredly were the weather as sultry as usually it is in these latitudes it would be the hottest. But the whimsical gods of the weather have been mighty good to us this July day. Under a London-colored sky, as gray and almost as thick as a fog, the centre of population of the United States

Continued on Page Nine.

Dempsey Says He Won Just as He Thought He Would; Carpentier Asserts He Staked His All in the Second

"Carpentier is a good, game fellow, but I think I've got it on him," Jack Dempsey remarked as he entered his dressing room after defending his title. The champion was as happy as a schoolboy and bore no marks to show the effect of the Frenchman's punches.

"I won just as I thought I would," the champion said. "It was a good fight and I think the public was satisfied. They say Carpentier staggered me with a right-hand punch in the second round. I never even remember being hit hard enough to shake me up.

"Perhaps he caught me off balance and it looked as though I was staggering. Perhaps I could have finished him sooner, but I was taking no chances. Carpentier is the heavyweight champion of Europe and I had my own title at stake and wanted to take no unnecessary chance of losing it."

"You've got to hand it to Carpentier; he was surely game," Dempsey said on several occasions.

Georges Carpentier took his defeat gamely and praised Dempsey as a great champion. In his dressing room after the fight Carpentier dictated this statement:

"I staked my all to win in the second round. I hit him hard, but could not drop him. I tried again in the third, but a right to my neck seemed to daze me. I do not know how he got through my guard in the fourth.

"America should be proud of Dempsey. He is a great champion."

CARPENTIER BROKE HIS THUMB IN FIGHT

He Also Sprained His Right Wrist on Dempsey's Jaw in Second Round.

NOT OFFERED AS EXCUSE

Carpentier Cables to Wife That He Is Uninjured and Was Beaten Fairly.

Special to The New York Times.

CARPENTIER'S TRAINING CAMP, MANHASSET, L. I., July 2.—Georges Carpentier returned to his training camp here this afternoon and informed a representative of THE NEW YORK TIMES that he knows no man in the world who is in the same class with Dempsey. He said he put forth every ounce of his strength in the fight and felt that when the American people read their newspapers tomorrow they would believe he had done his best and had not shown the white feather.

On Carpentier's behalf, however, his old friend Thierry Mallet, acting as spokesman, said that an injury to Carpentier's thumb eight days ago, which led to the breaking of the thumb in the second round today, was a contributing cause toward his defeat. Mallet did not attribute the defeat of the Frenchman to this cause, however.

Carpentier's external injuries appeared to be a slight cut under the eye, a slightly swollen nose and a badly swollen right hand, due to the fracture of a bone in the thumb. The injury to the thumb, it was said, was the most serious damage he sustained. In this connection Dr. Joseph B. Connolly, at the training camp here, gave out the following statement:

"This is to certify that I, Dr. Joseph B. Connolly, examined Georges Carpentier after his fight with Jack Dempsey and found him suffering from a fracture of the right metacarpal bone of his thumb, which rendered his right hand useless."

The doctor also said that the wrist was sprained from the blow landed on Dempsey's jaw. The hand has swollen to three times its normal size.

Mallet said that Georges received the injury eight days ago while working Carpentier lost the battle. His trainer, did not care to say anything about it at the time as they felt the announcement might be taken as preparing the groundwork for an excuse in the event Carpentier lost the battle. His manager, Gus Wilson, and the personnel in the camp were anxious to make the point that they did not attribute their man's defeat to the fractured thumb.

Mallet said to THE TIMES representative that Carpentier was a light heavyweight, and was not in the same class as Dempsey, who was a heavyweight. He said:

"On his return Georges said to me, 'You believe that I am a wonder as a light heavyweight. I am. You and I believed Dempsey was not a wonder as a heavyweight. But he is. A very good little man cannot hope to equal a very good big man.'"

"The handicap was too great, that's all," said Mallet. "Carpentier is the best man in the world in his class today, in 170 to 172 pounds weight, the light heavyweight class, but he is not in the same class as Dempsey, who is twenty pounds heavier."

"Georges was further handicapped, in addition to his fractured thumb, by the use of eight-ounce gloves to which he was unaccustomed," added Mallet. "His method is to strike with what may be described as a recoiling blow, but that sort of blow was neutralized by the weight of the glove. He always used four-ounce gloves in previous battles. Georges depended on speed to overcome Dempsey's weight, but in this case speed was overcome by power."

"Who will be your successor as a challenger of Dempsey?" THE TIMES representative asked Carpentier, who appeared cheerful as he walked about under the trees playing with a white rabbit.

"I don't know any man in the world in Dempsey's class," responded the defeated challenger.

"How did Dempsey control himself in the ring?" he was asked.

"His conduct was all that could be

Continued on Page Seven.

BLOW TO THE JAW ENDS THE CONTEST

Story of the Fight by Rounds Shows the Superiority of Dempsey.

ONLY ONCE IN DISTRESS

Carpentier Showed Well in Second Round, but After That Was Beaten Down.

FIRST ROUND.

The gong clanged to start the bout at 3:16 P. M. As the men advanced to the centre of the ring they were both smiling; Dempsey, a sardonic grin which was half sneer; Carpentier, a smile which reflected confidence. There were no preliminaries. Carpentier was the first to lead. He speared the champion with a left jab to the face. A clinch followed in which Carpentier worked his right in an inside uppercut to the champion's chin. Dempsey's head bobbed with the blow. The crowd roared its encouragement of the frail-looking challenger, who wasted no time in his supreme effort. The men were parted and Carpentier again leaped to the attack with characteristic springiness, bounding at the flat-footed champion with a wicked right which curled harmlessly past Dempsey's neck. Carpentier tried again with his right for the jaw, and this time landed on the champion's face with enough force to make Dempsey blink. Dempsey dug a left to the stomach and another clinch followed. Dempsey clubbed his right to the back of Carpentier's head in the clinch. Carpentier hooked a left to the stomach as Dempsey, his left shoulder raised in protection of his jaw and with right poised for immediate use, forced the pace. Carpentier missed a right for the face and in a clinch which followed Dempsey punished his rival severely about the stomach. Dempsey blocked Carpentier's right lead for the stomach and missed with a left hook for the head. Dempsey went in past the challenger's extended, guarding left and jabbed his left to the face. In a clinch the champion battered Carpentier severely about the stomach with rights and lefts. Dempsey missed a right for the jaw and Carpentier grazed the champion's chin with a right. Carpentier led a right which glanced off the champion's hunched left shoulder and landed on Dempsey's guarding left glove. Dempsey, forcing a fast pace, crowded Carpentier continually. In a clinch the champion cuffed Carpentier with rights and lefts and jolted the challenger with a left which shook him. As the men emerged from the clinch Carpentier's nose was bleeding. The skin on the bridge of the nose had been ripped with Dempsey's jolts in close, and the blood trickled down the challenger's face. Carpentier, crouching low, tried a right for the jaw. The blow landed high on Dempsey's temple. Both boxers tried with rights for the jaw. Carpentier missed. Dempsey landed with a glancing blow. A clinch followed in which Dempsey forced Carpentier to the ropes and there pounded the challenger hard about the stomach. Carpentier tried to cover against the blows. He couldn't. Dempsey, the stronger of the two, easily roughed his rival around and landed heavily to the mid-section. As the men were being broken Carpentier was off balance, and with the added weight of a recalcitrant right to the body sprawled over the second strand of the ring, where he hung momentarily doubled up, his glove tips supporting him outside the ropes. Dempsey stepped back as Carpentier quickly came erect without a count. The body punishment plainly hurt Carpentier. Carpentier tried a right and missed before the bell ended the round. Dempsey's round.

SECOND ROUND.

Crouching low, swaying his head from side to side and with his arms drawn protectingly against his jaw, Dempsey forced Carpentier around the ring. Carpentier retreated carefully, slowly, his left extended as he danced back on his toes and his right poised, ready to strike. Suddenly Carpentier leaped in with a left jab and followed with a right high on the head. Dempsey disregarded the blows and shuffled steadily

Continued on Page Two.

DEMPSEY PROVES PROWESS

Forces Carpentier Down With Incessant Rain of Terrific Blows.

TWICE FLOORS OPPONENT

But Frenchman Is Courageous After First Knockdown and Fights Until Knocked Out.

NO "ACCIDENTAL CHAMPION"

Great Throng That Gave Louder Cheer for Georges at Start Acclaims Jack at the End.

Jack Dempsey is still heavyweight champion of the world—it might almost be said that for the first time he is really the champion. Georges Carpentier, in many respects the most serious opponent Dempsey has ever met, stood up against him yesterday afternoon in Tex Rickard's stadium in Jersey City and could not last through the fourth round. And at that, Carpentier fought better than most American critics believed possible.

His end came at a few seconds after 3:30, when the fourth round had been going on one minute and sixteen seconds. Dempsey found the Frenchman's face with his left and followed it up with a hard right just in front of the ear. Carpentier went down, but on the count of nine leaped to his feet and seemed in shape to give the champion more trouble. But he never had the chance.

Dempsey led a light left to the face, and then as Carpentier swayed aside from the blow Dempsey drove a tremendous smash with his right hand into Carpentier's ribs, below the heart. This was quickly followed by a smashing right to the jaw.

The blow to the body was a hard enough blow in itself, because that spot had already been hammered and weakened by a score of fierce short-arm jolts in the desperate in-fighting of the previous rounds, but at the blow to the jaw Carpentier dropped again—dropped on his right side and lay there while Referee Harry Ertle swung his arm above him and counted. At the count of eight Carpentier stirred and made a desperate effort to rise; but he could not move. Nine, ten—and Dempsey's championship was secure.

Witnessed by 90,000 Persons.

So ended the "battle of the century," fought before 90,000 people—a fight which had aroused more interest, in all probability, than any other in all history.

Perhaps this interest had been enhanced by the futile efforts of moral reformers to stop the fight, but there were other elements which made it unique.

When the New World met the Old in the persons of Heenan and Sayers, when Jim Jeffries's gallant effort to come back against Jack Johnson roused the slumbering bitterness of racial feeling, millions of people who had never hitherto paid any attention to prizefighting found themselves roused by a new stimulus and found in the meeting of two boxers an interest such as they would never have supposed could be attached to a mere sporting event.

Yesterday's fight was international, too; it drew a bigger crowd than had ever seen a prizefight. It brought forward for the first time a real heavyweight contender from the Continent of Europe in a sport where heretofore the English-speaking world has had no serious competition.

There was novelty not only in the size of the crowd, but in the composition of it. The throng included thousands of women and a considerable number of public officials such as have rarely been seen in this country at a professional boxing bout. The fight aroused an intensity of interest that would have been impossible but for the still living emotions roused by the war.

No Accidental Champion.

Dempsey was in many ways the most unpopular of white champions. Those who know him best say that this unpopularity is largely undeserved; but the fact remained that millions of people in Dempsey's own country were hoping that the foreign challenger could beat him. The crowd, though it gave the champion a vociferous welcome, seemed to prefer Carpentier by a considerable majority—before the fight. Its speedy end found thousands cheering the winner who, ten minutes before, had been shouting for Carpentier. Dempsey had shown that whatever else might be said about him, he was no accidental champion. He can fight.

He had, to be sure, a big advantage in size. He had a reach longer by an inch than the challenger; he weighed 188 pounds as he stepped into the ring, while Carpentier weighed only 172. To the eye the difference was greater than this. Carpentier seemed fragile, a thing of more nerves and desperate determination against Dempsey's huge bulk.

But Dempsey was no slow-moving leviathan. At long-range Carpentier had the better of him, but from half-way through the first round, when the in-fighting really began, Dempsey had been steadily hammering the [illegible] body, and [illegible] short but [illegible] which broke Carpentier's [illegible] to

Continued on Page Two.

"All the News That's Fit to Print."

The New York Times.

THE WEATHER
Local showers today; Sunday fair; little change in temperature; moderate south and west winds.
For weather report see next to last page

VOL. LXX....No. 23,177.

NEW YORK, SATURDAY, JULY 9, 1921.

TWO CENTS

TRUCE IN IRELAND DECLARED, TO BEGIN ON MONDAY AT NOON; DE VALERA AGREES TO MEET LLOYD GEORGE ON PEACE TERMS; DUBLIN CROWDS CHEER BRITISH COMMANDER AND UNIONISTS

FRANCE CALLS BACK MISSION IN ANGER AT LEIPSIC TRIALS

Holds That German Verdicts on Men Accused of War Crimes Are a Mockery.

THREAT OF ALLIED TRIBUNAL

Paris Is Expected to Demand the Handing Over of Offenders Under the Treaty.

BERLIN JARRED BY MOVE

Professes to Suspect a French Design to Continue the Military Occupation.

Special Cable to THE NEW YORK TIMES.

PARIS, July 8.—On the ground that the German trials of German war criminals are a mockery the French Government has withdrawn its mission to the Leipsic court, thus washing its hands of the procedure, and has notified the allied Governments of its action.

President and Mrs. Harding Observe 30th Anniversary

WASHINGTON, July 8.—President and Mrs. Harding are planning a week-end cruise down the Potomac on the Presidential yacht Mayflower if public affairs will permit Mr. Harding to get away from the capital tomorrow. They do not expect to go ashore.

Today was the thirtieth anniversary of the marriage of President and Mrs. Harding, but they had no formal observance. They were married at the same house in Marion from which the front porch campaign was conducted last year.

At the White House it was stated that nothing was known there of the reported intention of the President to attend the funeral of the World War soldiers in New York Sunday.

HEAT FINDS VICTIMS FROM SEASHORE TO THE ROCKIES

High Humidity Increases Suffering and Many Deaths Are Reported.

DROWNINGS ARE NUMEROUS

One Man Seeking Relief on Roof Rolls Off When Asleep and Is Killed.

TEMPERATURE HERE 89

Thousands Sleep on Sand at the Beaches and on Park Benches—Showers Promised.

Former Kaiser Objects To Paying Dutch Taxes

Copyright, 1921, by The New York Times Company.
Special Cable to THE NEW YORK TIMES.

DOORN, Holland, July 8.—The Municipal Council of Doorn is discussing the vigorous protest lodged by William Hohenzollern against the tax levied by the local authorities. The ex-Kaiser maintains that they have no right whatever to tax him, as he did not come willingly to Holland, and is held practically a prisoner, and is therefore not liable to taxes as if he were a free citizen.

DRAMATIC SCENES IN DUBLIN

General Macready, in Full Uniform, Gets Ovation From Crowds

SALUTES IRISH VOLUNTEERS

People Pray Outside the Mansion House, While De Valera Holds His Council.

WAIT HOURS FOR THE NEWS

When De Valera's Reply to the London Invitation Is Given Out, They Disperse Quietly.

Copyright, 1921, by The New York Times Company.
Special Cable to THE NEW YORK TIMES.

DUBLIN, July 8.—Just at the stroke of 11 today the four Southern Unionists, Midleton, Woods, Jameson and Dockrell, sat down in the Mansion House at Dublin with de Valera and Griffith, President and Vice President of Sinn Fein, to discuss ways and means of an agreement on the Irish problem preparatory to the London conference.

Text of De Valera's Letter to Lloyd George; Official Announcement of Truce on Monday

Special Cable to THE NEW YORK TIMES.

LONDON, July 8.—The text of the letter sent today to Premier Lloyd George by Eamon de Valera follows:

Sir: The desire you expressed on the part of the British Government to end the centuries of conflict between the peoples of these two islands and to establish relations of neighborly harmony is the genuine desire of the people of Ireland.

I have consulted with my colleagues and received the views of the representatives of the minority of our nation in regard to the invitation you have sent me. In reply I desire to say that I am ready to meet and discuss with you on what basis such a conference as that proposed can reasonably hope to achieve the object desired.

EAMON DE VALERA.

The official wording of the statement issued from Downing Street with reference to a truce was as follows:

In accordance with the Prime Minister's offer and Mr. de Valera's reply, arrangements are being made for hostilities to cease from Monday next, July 11, at noon.

DR. BUTLER TO MEET EMPIRE PREMIERS

Is Invited by Mr. Lloyd George to Spend Week-End With Them at Chequers.

DISCUSSES BRITISH POLICY

Convinced Its Guiding Principle Is Close Accord With America—Freedom of Seas Vital.

Copyright, 1921, by The New York Times Company.
Special Cable to THE NEW YORK TIMES.

LONDON, July 8.—Dr. Nicholas Murray Butler of Columbia University and Mrs. and Miss Butler were to have gone to the Continent tomorrow, but THE NEW YORK TIMES correspondent learns from an official source that Prime Minister Lloyd George today sent to Dr. Butler an invitation to pass the week-end with him at Chequers, the country-home donated for the use of British Premiers by Lord Lee.

IRISH HERE PLEASED OVER MONDAY TRUCE

But They Distrust Lloyd George and Expect Little of Conference.

STILL HOPE FOR REPUBLIC

Count on de Valera to Demand Full Autonomy — Some Fear Compromise.

TO MEET PREMIER FIRST

De Valera Asks to Discuss Basis of Proposed Conference

TRUCE COUNTED A BIG GAIN

Suggested by Lloyd George to Lord Midleton, It Is Agreed To by Republicans.

PEACE HOPES NOW BRIGHT

Ulster Expected to Be Called In After British Ministers Have Smoothed the Way.

Copyright, 1921, by The New York Times Company.
Special Cable to THE NEW YORK TIMES.

LONDON, July 8.—Eamon de Valera, replying today to Premier Lloyd George's invitation to a conference of Irish and British representatives in London, agreed to meet Mr. Lloyd George to discuss "on what basis such a conference as that proposed can reasonably hope to achieve the object desired."

BARRICADED MANIAC TAKES LIFE IN FIGHT

Man Crazed With Drink Drove Wife From Home, Then Fought Bloomfield Police.

SHOTS KEPT ATTACKERS OFF

Firemen Failed to Subdue Pole With High-Pressure Stream Turned Into Shack.

Special to The New York Times.

BLOOMFIELD, N. J., July 8.—After turning a little one-story, two-room building on the outskirts of this place into an improvised fort, and defending himself for more than an hour against the attack of policemen and firemen who tried to capture him alive, John Grochacz, a Polish laborer, turned his pistol upon himself and committed suicide this afternoon.

TWO CHILDREN GONE IN THIRD KIDNAPPING

Friendly Neighbors in Cape May Missing With Boy and Girl After Month's Acquaintance.

SAID TO BE FATHER'S AGENTS

No Trace of Men Who Seized Baby at Pompton Lakes or of Mrs. Mayo and Child.

The third kidnapping of children within a week as a result of the separation of parents was reported yesterday in Cape May, N. J., where two children of Mr. Robert Emmett Woodland were taken away by a man and a woman who Mrs. Woodland believes were acting for her husband, from whom she has been separated a year and a half.

Alien Residents, Arriving in First Cabin, Detained Under New Immigration Law

G. F. Burle, representative in New York, at 2 Bridge Street, since 1903, of the grain firm of Sanday & Co., who returned yesterday with his wife and daughter from England on the Royal Mail Steam Packet Oropesa, was in first cabin resident arriving on a first cabin passenger in the port to be held on board under the new interpretation of the immigration restriction law.

London, July 7, 1921.

Dear Lord Midleton: In reference to the conversation I had with you this morning, the Government fully realizes that it would be impossible to conduct negotiations with any hope of achieving satisfactory results if there were bloodshed and violence in Ireland. It would disturb the atmosphere and the settlement...

D. LLOYD GEORGE.

"All the News That's Fit to Print."

The New York Times.

THE WEATHER.
Rain and colder today; Sunday fair; fresh to strong northwest winds.
Temperature Yesterday—Max., 46; Min., 32.
For weather report see next to last page.

VOL. LXXI....No. 23,303. NEW YORK, SATURDAY, NOVEMBER 12, 1921. TWO CENTS In Greater New York | THREE CENTS Within 200 Miles | FOUR CENTS Elsewhere

OUR UNKNOWN WARRIOR BURIED, THE WORLD HONORING HIM; HARDING PLEADS FOR A BAN BY CIVILIZATION ON WAR; DELEGATES ENTER ARMS PARLEY TODAY IN HOPEFUL SPIRIT

ULSTER REJECTS PROPOSED TERMS; DRAFTS NEW ONES

Finds Fundamental Principles Involved Which Are Impossible of Attainment at Present.

WANTS THESE WITHDRAWN

Will "Indicate More Practicable Means" of Obtaining Peace Without Infringing Her Rights.

NEXT MOVE IS UNCERTAIN

British Cabinet Is Expected to Meet Today to Study Reply and to Consider Action.

Special Cable to THE NEW YORK TIMES.

LONDON, Nov. 11.—Ulster replied this afternoon to the British Government's draft suggestions looking to a settlement of the Irish problem with what on its face appears to be a definite rejection of the proposals. There is, however, an intimation that the Ulster Cabinet will indicate other and more practicable means for securing peace without infringing on Ulster's rights."

Sir James Craig and his colleagues take the position that "certain fundamental principles are involved in the suggestions which under existing conditions are impossible of attainment" and that "no useful purpose would be served by holding formal consultation between his Majesty's Government and the Government of Northern Ireland until such suggestions are withdrawn from the subjects to be discussed."

The public is waiting for further developments and elucidations. Ulster's reply today is, of course, a decided setback for the negotiations along the lines laid out by Premier Lloyd George after his conference with the Sinn Fein delegates, and there is said to be grave disappointment in Ministerial circles, but progress along those lines had not been expected with much confidence outside of those circles.

The Ulster Cabinet's main objection to the proposed scheme for settlement is the All-Irish Parliament, and it is an objection that goes to the root of that scheme. It is looked upon as possible that the proposition may be brought back again to discussion of linking the Council of Ireland under the ...

Continued on Page Four.

Boy Scouts to Gather Corn For Armenia in Iowa Fields

DES MOINES, Iowa, Nov. 11.—Thousands of Boy Scouts will sweep Iowa tomorrow to gather corn for famine relief in the Near East. Farmers will co-operate, by permitting the boys to go into the fields and husk limited quantities from standing corn.

Free elevator services, milling and transportation for the corn has been arranged and it will be sent immediately to the famine regions of Armenia.

JOHN M'CORMACK BUYS HALS PAINTING

Singer Pays $150,000 for "Portrait of a Man"—Now on Its Way to America.

SALE IS CONFIRMED HERE

Many Other Pictures Coming—Sir Joseph Duveen Denies "The Blue Boy" Has Been Sold.

John McCormack has paid $150,000 for the "Portrait of a Man" by Frans Hals, and the picture is now on its way to this country, after its removal from the collection of Count Maurice Zamoyski, the Polish Ambassador to France. The report of the purchase was printed in The American Art News and confirmed at the Reinhardt Galleries, who acted for Mr. McCormack in the transaction.

Many other great paintings are on their way to this country, and art dealers predict that the present art season will bring back the pre-war days of large deals in famed pictures. The total of paintings bought abroad this year runs into millions of dollars, and it is predicted that the Winter months will see many more important sales.

Art dealers here were interested yesterday in the report from London that the purchaser of "The Blue Boy," by Gainsborough, was Henry E. Huntington, but Sir Joseph Duveen denied last night that any deal for the picture had been consummated. Sir Joseph repeated that the painting had been bought by Duveen Brothers with no client in mind and that it would not be brought to this country for several months. It is to be exhibited in the National Galleries in London. Another picture bought by the Duveens is "The Tragic Muse," by Sir Joshua Reynolds.

Another important purchase reported this season was that of two Rembrandts for $750,000, for the collection of Joseph Widener. Many other smaller purchases ...

... against the black coat as Hals loved. One hand is gloved, while the other holds the limp glove just taken off."

Special Cable to THE NEW YORK TIMES.

LONDON, Nov. 11.—No confirmation has been received by the Duveens in London of the reported purchase of "The Blue Boy" by H. E. Huntington. The picture is still in the National Gallery, to which it had been lent by Sir Joseph Duveen ... the revelation of the identity of its purchaser.

INJUNCTION STRIPS MILKMEN OF POWER TO HARASS DEALERS

Forbids 12,000 Union Members to Use Violence, Intimidation or Persuasion.

TRIED TO WRECK 4 PLANTS

Tampered With Machines, Threw Away Parts, Left Pasteurizers in Shape to Affect Milk.

SWEEPING COURT ORDER

Prohibits Crowds, Appeals to Consumers or False Reports in Five Boroughs and Westchester.

One of the most sweeping injunctions ever obtained in connection with labor troubles in the metropolitan district has been granted to members of the New York Milk Conference Board. It became effective yesterday, restraining officers and members of the milk wagon drivers' union from violence, interference or intimidation in the five boroughs of New York and Westchester County.

The injunction enjoined the union from the further conduct of the strike by any of the usual methods and practically rendered it powerless to continue the fight of 12,000 wagon drivers and station employes, which has hampered the milk supply of New York for almost two weeks. Although the order, obtained from Supreme Court Justice Charles H. Kelby in Brooklyn, was temporary, counsel for the Milk Board will ask that it be made permanent on Monday, when the union leaders have been summoned to answer the complaint. The unions have obtained counsel and will then begin their fight to prevent the distributors from making the order permanent.

The injunction restrained the strikers from "picketing in any way the depots, places of business or routes of any of the plaintiffs or any point where they or their employes are receiving or distributing milk," ...

... Frank Zollner, Superintendent of the Sheffield pasteurizing plant at 1,380 Fulton Street, Brooklyn, in a sworn statement said that the collection books and records of 161 drivers had been thrown into a sewer by strikers.

Benjamin D. White, a director of the Orange County Milk Association, swore that a union delegate had called him on

Continued on Page Nine.

Gandhi Exhorts Hindus To Remove Lawrence Statue

LAHORE, British India, Nov. 11.—Mohandas K. Gandhi, the Indian Nationalist leader, today urged a large gathering here to remove the statue of Lord Lawrence which stands in the city. Gandhi exhorted his audience to undertake the task "even at the risk of imprisonment or death." Beneath the statue is the inscription, "Will you be governed by the pen or by the sword?"

Lord Lawrence distinguished himself in putting down the Sepoy mutiny in India. He also served as Governor-General from 1863 to 1869.

TROLLEY SMASHED BY WILD FIRE TRUCK

Driver Loses Control and Big Machine Hits Car Head-On—Four Men Hurt.

FIREMAN IS LIKELY TO DIE

Three-Ton Motor Truck Hits Auto on Manhattan Bridge, Injuring Two Persons.

Four men were injured when a fire truck ran wild and crashed head-on into a surface car containing twenty passengers at First Avenue and Eighty-fifth Street about 6:30 o'clock last night. The fright and excitement among the passengers as the heavy truck rammed the front vestibule of the car was intense, but policemen and firemen calmed the people.

One of the injured may die. He is Michael McNamara, fire patrolman, 31 years old, of 2,950 Third Avenue, who was thrown from the truck to the street. Dr. Dunn of Reception Hospital, who responded to an ambulance call, found that McNamara's head was hurt, two ribs were broken and he had other injuries. The fireman was taken to the City Hospital on Blackwell's Island. The others hurt were Edwin Cox, fire patrolman, 29 years old, of 124 East 120th Street, and two passengers of the surface car—Eugene Ortheim, 26 years old, ...

... Fulton Street, Brooklyn, who was sitting beside Walsh, escaped with cuts and bruises. Arthur E. and Walter S. Duane, brothers, of 382 Crescent Street, Brooklyn, who sat in front, were unhurt.

The truck is owned by Joseph McGinness of 172 Duane Street, Manhattan, and was driven by Carl Miller of 690 Summit Avenue, Jersey City. Witnesses said Miller was not to blame. He was not arrested.

Joseph Lacorte, 25 years old, of 224 Sullivan Street, was badly cut about the face and hands when an automobile he was driving east on the Transverse Road in Central Park was struck by an eastbound surface car yesterday. Edgar Wallace of 110 Montague Street, Brooklyn, who was with Lacorte in the machine, also was hurt. John Mulligan, motorman of the surface car, was uninjured. Lacorte and Wallace were taken to Lenox Hill Hospital, but went home after receiving medical attention. Witnesses said Lacorte was trying to cut ahead of the surface car, which hit the auto and threw it in the path of a westbound car, driven by Motorman Edward Nulty, who stopped just in time. The automobile was wrecked.

Thomas Raia, 12 years old, was killed by an automobile truck last night within two blocks of his home, at 328 Leonard Street, Brooklyn. He was roller skating with other boys in Leonard Street, near Jackson, when a truck owned by the American Tobacco Company ran him down and killed him instantly. Charles W. Taylor of 234 Decatur Street, Brooklyn, driver of the truck, was arrested on a charge of manslaughter. Witnesses told the police the truck was moving rapidly.

Seven Hurt on L-6 Are Recovering.

LOS ANGELES, Nov. 11.—Seven men, one an officer, some of whom were overcome by smoke and others burned when fire started in the United States Navy Submarine L-6 yesterday, were reported today to be recovering at the submarine base hospital at Los Angeles Harbor. The blaze started in the forward compartment batteries of the L-6 while she was traveling far below the surface from San Diego to Los Angeles.

LEADERS HAIL CONFERENCE

Briand Sees No Reason to Prevent Results in a Few Weeks.

JAPANESE PREDICT SUCCESS

Millerand and Curzon Send Messages of Encouragement to Washington.

POPE TO GIVE FULL SUPPORT

Delegates Pleased With Harding's Arlington Speech—American Group Confers.

WASHINGTON, Nov. 11 (Associated Press).—With the eyes of all the world fixed hopefully upon them the accredited spokesmen of the powers will meet in Washington tomorrow to try to find a way to ease the heavy burden of armaments.

In the historic quest Great Britain, France, Italy, Japan and the United States, a group which, acting together, can turn the whole tide of civilization into new channels, all have pledged a solemn and determined co-operation.

In addition, China, Belgium, Portugal and the Netherlands, invited because of their vital interests in the pertinent and crucial problems of the Far East, will sit in the conference to complete the circle of those who are to strive for the new day of international relationship.

Expressions from the principal delegations on the eve of the assembly were made as follows:

M. Briand, French Prime Minister—"We enter the conference in an earnest spirit to assist in reaching a common understanding that shall give peace of mind to the world instead of an armed peace. I see no reason why a few weeks hence we should not be separating after having defined how the interests of one have become the interests of all. France wishes to arrive at an accord that will create an atmosphere of peace, in which the nations may work in complete security."

President Harding's Plea for Barring War From the Stage of Righteous Civilization

From President Harding's Speech at Arlington.

The loftiest tribute we can bestow today—the heroically earned tribute—fashioned in deliberate conviction, out of unclouded thought, neither shadowed by remorse nor made vain by fancies, is the commitment of this Republic to an advancement never made before. If American achievement is a cherished pride at home, if our unselfishness among nations is all we wish it to be, and ours is a helpful example in the world, then let us give of our influence and strength, yea, of our aspirations and convictions, to put mankind on a little higher plane, exulting and exalting, with war's distressing and depressing tragedies barred from the stage of righteous civilization.

There have been a thousand defenses justly and patriotically made; a thousand offenses which reason and righteousness ought to have stayed. Let us beseech all men to join us in seeking the rule under which reason and righteousness shall prevail.

Standing today on hallowed ground, conscious that all America has halted to share in the tribute of heart, and mind, and soul to this fellow-American, and knowing that the world is noting this expression of the Republic's mindfulness, it is fitting to say that his sacrifice, and that of the millions dead, shall not be vain. There must be, there shall be, the commanding voice of a conscious civilization against armed warfare.

HOST IN MADISON SQ. HONORS THE DEAD

Fifteen Thousand Guests of the Legion in the Garden, as Many More Outside.

FOLLOW HARDING'S VOICE

The President's Words at Arlington Clearly Heard—50,000 Parade—Thousands Pray.

President Harding's voice rang out in loud and distinct tones to a crowd of 30,000 guests of the American Legion in Madison Square Garden and in Madison Square yesterday, as he delivered his address at Arlington Cemetery in Washington over the grave of the unknown soldier.

Over the amplifying telephone also came the crisp notes of the bugle, the playing of the band, the singing of the quartet and brief words by Admiral Beatty, Marshal Foch, General Diaz and other foreign soldiers, as they laid medals on the casket of the unknown soldier.

OVATION FOR WILSON IN LINE AND AT HOME

Crowds That Watch in Silence as Parade Moves By, Cheer as ex-President Passes.

PILGRIMAGE TO HIS HOUSE

Thousands in Demonstration Lasting an Hour Move Him to Express Thanks.

Special to The New York Times.

WASHINGTON, Nov. 11.—With the last dull boom from the guns which counted off minute after minute of the hours that passed while a reverent and grateful nation paid solemn tribute to its nameless soldier dead through one of their number, and when silence had succeeded eulogy and prayer about the grave at Arlington where his remains had been sealed to the final rest, thousands of the throng which had taken part in those ceremonies turned their thoughts to another "soldier of the World War" who, though among the number of the living, had been grievously ...

SOLEMN JOURNEY OF DEAD

Ceremonial Procession In Which Nation's Leaders Walk Stirs Capital.

HARDING SOUNDS HIGH NOTE

His Appeal Against War Impresses Great Audience at Arlington.

NATIONS DECORATE WARRIOR

And His Body With Wreaths of War Mothers Is Lowered to Last Resting Place.

Special to The New York Times.

WASHINGTON, Nov. 11.—America buried her Unknown Warrior today—placed in the earth the body of that boy whose very namelessness symbolized 50,000 others who had given their lives for America on the field of battle in the World War.

Surrounded by the world's great, with none of them too great to bow in homage, this dead boy's funeral was still no pageant, no spectacular drama, no worldly show. It was more a benediction, a spiritual something whose very realities were less apparent than the thoughts they conjured.

Washington has witnessed many notable ceremonials, but never one like this. Its people saw the bodies of Lincoln and Garfield borne along the broad streets, and under cover of darkness, through a drizzling rain, had watched the solemn progress of that procession which followed the dead McKinley to the White House. There were tears of sorrow then. There were tears today, but most of those who shed them were carried away by the emotion of the symbolism of patriotism which this unknown American embodied.

Taken from that central spot in the Capitol's rotunda where before this only the bodies of Presidents had lain in state, and where it had been designed to place the body of George Washington, this fighting boy whose coffined figure stood for sacrifice to honor and patriotism was followed to his body's final resting place ...

Harvey Sees Tolerance Supplanting Force, He Tells London Armistice Day Diners

LONDON, Nov. 11 (Associated Press).—"Today signalizes the joining of the past with the future," declared Colonel George Harvey, United States Ambassador to Great Britain, in an Armistice Day address here tonight.

The occasion of his commemorative discourse was a dinner to him and Mrs. Harvey given by the English-Speaking Union. It was presided over by Captain Frederick E. Guest, Air Secretary, and attended by a distinguished Anglo-American assemblage.

In his address, Ambassador Harvey alluded to President Harding's proclamation making the day a national holiday, and pointed out the coincidence of the day's falling on the three-hundred and first anniversary of the arrival of the Mayflower.

"On one bank of the Potomac," he said, "in the sacred soil of Arlington Cemetery, the body of our Unknown Soldier was lowered reverently to rest. On the other side of that historic river, in the capital, for the first time in history are gathered the foremost statesmen from the uttermost parts of the earth in a common determination to find for the distracted peoples of the world a way to peace and happiness, which constitutes their priceless heritage from the Maker of the universe. A memorial to our own patriot dead, a harbinger of hope for all the living—such is the true purport of this our holy day."

Ambassador Harvey asked rhetorically if history must be forever mainly a narration of warfare.

"The strength of a country is not measured by armies and navies," he declared. "A schoolhouse at a crossroads is more potent ultimately than a dreadnought on the seas. One little church on a hill is worth a score of regiments. Tolerance has supplanted its antithesis as an actual force. A peculiar responsibility devolves upon our two peoples not only to maintain but to enhance the new, better, higher power among men.

"Mutual respect, confidence and tolerance—these are the essentials of that genius for co-operation which has already won for our Christian President the hearts of our own people, and is destined, I believe, to fetch the English-speaking race into a harmonious relationship so nearly perfect that all mankind will realize in the near future that there is more power and glory in 'Lead, Kindly Light' than in all the fighting anthems of the world."

"All the News That's Fit to Print."

The New York Times.

THE WEATHER. Fair today; Thursday warmer, probably rain; moderate variable winds. Temperature Yesterday—Max. 51, Min. 40. For weather report see next to last page.

VOL. LXXI...No. 23,307. NEW YORK, WEDNESDAY, NOVEMBER 16, 1921. TWO CENTS In Greater New York | THREE CENTS Within 200 Miles | FOUR CENTS Elsewhere

BRITAIN AND JAPAN ACCEPT NAVAL PLAN AMID CHEERS; FAR EAST ISSUE UP TODAY; JAPAN WANTS MANCHURIA OPEN; LODGE MAY NEGOTIATE TO END ANGLO-JAPANESE ALLIANCE

TRACTION HEARINGS BEGIN OVER PROTEST; HYLAN ORDERS FIGHT

Commission Rejects City's Plea for Delay Until Legislature Can Act on Law.

PROCEDURE IS OUTLINED

Evidence Will Show Fares Have Increased and Service Decreased, Says McAneny.

WOULD RESTORE 5c FARE.

Also Keep It Indefinitely—Four Witnesses Examined—Shearn Tells Evaluation Plan.

Denying the plea of Mayor Hylan that hearings on the traction situation be delayed until after the Legislature had reconsidered the transit law of 1921, the Transit Commission yesterday began its examination of witnesses with the declaration that "it hoped not only to restore an actual five-cent fare, but to keep the fare indefinitely at 5 cents."

Mayor Hylan's protest was presented to the commission at the outset of the hearings, but George McAneny, Chairman, said the suggestion for delay could not be taken seriously. Following the commission's decision, the Mayor wrote to John P. O'Brien, the Corporation Counsel, ordering him to "fight these interests every inch of the way and protect the people's rights."

Speaking for Mr. O'Brien and the Mayor, Edgar J. Kohler, an Assistant Corporation Counsel, declared the transit law "was unconstitutional, invalid and void, and that all proceedings conducted by you, all your acts, all your orders, made or to be made, are void and without effect." He said the record plurality for Mayor Hylan in the election was a mandate against the Transit Commission.

Shearn Outlines Procedure.

After Mr. Kohler had finished his statement, Clarence J. Shearn, special counsel for the commission, said "Might we get down to business?" and outlined the evidence as he expected to present it to the commission. Picking up Mr. Shearn's words, which he understood to be "get down to serious business," Mr. Kohler again arose and said he wished to correct any impression that the city administration was not serious.

"The statement of the Corporation Counsel involved not only a protest but also a suggestion to this commission," said Mr. Kohler. "It was a suggestion which the Corporation Counsel makes as his own opinion and the opinion of Mayor Hylan. It was that this commission wait at least until January, until the next Legislature will be in session, before it proceeds further with these hearings."

Snatching the word "serious" out of the quibble over whether the commission's lawyer had used the word, Chairman McAneny smiled at the Assistant Corporation Counsel and replied:

"The commission cannot take your suggestion seriously, Mr. Kohler."

"That puts the commission clearly on the record," said Mr. Kohler as he packed up his papers and started to leave the hearing.

"Mr. Kohler suggests that we wait," said Mr. Shearn. "We have done nothing but wait for the last four or five years. It seems to me that it is time for action, so we will call our first witness—Mr. Monroe!"

Four Experts Are Called.

Mr. Shearn then called four experts of the Transit Commission to prove that service had been reduced on the transit lines, that the margin of safety in operation had been cut on the surface lines of the city, that more than 2,000 free transfer points had been abolished, and that service generally had deteriorated. He brought out facts on the old "welter of franchises" that specified fares varying from 3 to 10 cents, and agreed with Chairman McAneny, who interjected:

"Further disintegration would throw these companies back upon this disordered state of conditions governing rates."

Mr. Shearn in his preliminary statement told how the experts were proceeding with the valuation of the various transit lines, and asserted that the work soon would be finished. He said that the experts were figuring upon the replacement of the lines at pre-war price for materials, less depreciation, and also for the replacement at present prices, less depreciation. Computations of earnings will be also at the prevailing rate of fare and the results placed before the companies and the public "with the utmost frankness and detail."

In the first few hearings the commission will take up its examination of the physical condition of the transit lines and then turn to study the financial conditions. From these premises it will draw its conclusions and formulate a final plan for solution of the transit muddle. It is expected that hearings will continue for several weeks at the rate of three meetings a week—on Tues-

Continued on Page Six.

Reparations Default Report Denied by German Officials

BERLIN, Nov. 15 (Associated Press).—The report that Germany has notified the Allies that she will be unable to meet the next reparation instalment was emphatically denied tonight in official German quarters.

A similar denial was made in Entente diplomatic circles, which are in close touch with the negotiations now proceeding with the Reparations Commission.

MRS. ENRIGHT LOSES $3,000 IN JEWELRY

Police Commissioner's Wife Misses Rings and Gems After Brooklyn Shopping Tour.

REPORT 'NOT FOR THE PRESS'

Slip to Police Stations So Noted—Chamois Bag Was Pinned to Mrs. Enright's Clothing.

Mrs. Richard E. Enright, wife of the Police Commissioner, lost $3,000 worth of jewels, including her wedding ring, while mingling with the shopping crowds in Fulton Street, Brooklyn, on Monday. And last night, although every police agency had been put on the alert by an imperative order from headquarters, the jewels were still missing.

Every effort was made by the detectives assigned to the case to keep the facts from getting into the newspapers. Their attitude was prompted by the order issued from headquarters which advised precinct commanders that the loss by the Commissioner's wife was not for the press.

The desire to keep the matter quiet was further emphasized at the Commissioner's home at 897 St. Mark's Avenue, Brooklyn, last night. Reporters who hurried to the house shortly after the news of the missing $3,000 worth of jewelry had leaked out, found several of the floors brilliantly lighted. But no amount of ringing of the front door bell produced an answer.

Lost Jewels on Monday.

Soon after 1 o'clock on Monday afternoon Mrs. Enright left her home, bound for a tour of the department stores that line Fulton Street. She walked part of the way from her home to Fulton Street and then completed her trip to a well-known store by boarding one of the Fulton Street surface cars. As she entered the store she assured herself that the jewels were still safe, although she had been jostled in forcing her way through the throngs on the sidewalk.

The jewels, it was learned, were put for safekeeping in a small chamois bag which Mrs. Enright securely pinned to her clothing. In the bag were her wedding ring, two wrist watches, three diamond rings, two gem-studded bar-pins, and several other pieces of jewelry.

Mingling with the shoppers in the store, Mrs. Enright visited several departments and then, carrying the parcels, returned to the street and walked for several blocks. It could not be ascertained whether or not she was jostled, a practice of pickpockets, in her short walk, but, at any rate, when she arrived back home she found that the bag had disappeared.

Police Notified at Once.

She notified the store and a hurried search of the departments which she had visited failed to disclose the missing jewels. Mrs. Enright then got in touch with Police Headquarters and Captain John J. McCloskey, in charge of the Brooklyn Detective Bureau, was notified as were most of the other precincts in Brooklyn—with instructions to keep the matter from the newspapers. Subsequently, the stations in the other boroughs were notified and detectives were assigned to visit pawnshops and warn the pawnbrokers to be on the watch for the jewels.

The first detective assigned to the matter of finding the missing gems of the wife of the Police Commissioner was Detective Frank Carberry of the Atlantic Avenue Station. When reporters asked him "what luck," he didn't even move his head. He looked straight ahead and had nothing to say. Finally he referred his questioners to Captain McCloskey, who also had nothing to say.

DRUG RAID IN THEATRE.

Three Alleged Peddlers Arrested in Bowery Film Show.

Special Deputy Commissioner Dr. Carleton Simon, head of the police Narcotic Squad, sent detectives into a Bowery moving picture theatre yesterday afternoon and placed three alleged drug peddlers under arrest in the balcony. So quietly was the raid made that the prisoners were taken without the several hundred men, women and children knowing what was going on.

The prisoners described themselves as Louis Perrotti of 141 Mulberry Street, Michael Arcourt of 62 Eldridge Street and Joseph Guide of 100 Canal Street, [illegible]

BRIAND TO PICTURE DANGER

Will Set Forth to America Why France Cannot Reduce Her Army.

EXCEPT WITH GUARANTEES

He Will Quote German Documents to Prove the Fatherland Still France's Foe.

NAVAL ACCORD WITH ITALY

But Agreement of the Delegations Goes No Further, Declares French Premier.

By EDWIN L. JAMES.

Special to The New York Times.

WASHINGTON, Nov. 15.—Premier Briand of France expects to present at a plenary session of the conference, probably on Friday, the case of his country with regard to the reduction of land armament. He is preparing a strong plea wherein, besides calling attention to the tasks given France as the gendarme of the Versailles Treaty, he will offer documents and statements by German leaders, military and political, to prove that France, with a population of 35,000,000, is still in danger of an attack by Germany, with her 65,000,000, if Germany is left free to nurse a spirit of revenge and continues to train her coming generations in the belief that France is a hereditary enemy.

It is not expected that at his first presentation M. Briand will go at length into political complexities, but will content himself with a statement of the situation that will be understood by those not familiar with the innermost tangles of European relations.

It is probable that he will present the question of guarantees for France only after more concrete proposals have been made for land armament reductions, when he will point out that with assurance from her recent allies France will need fewer soldiers than if she it left to depend largely on her own strength alone.

M. Briand, as well as other members of the French delegation, has been greatly moved by the consistently cordial reception which the delegation has had at Washington. In the very favorable attitude of the galleries at the plenary sessions of the conference the French see a good omen.

Talked Naval Agreement Only.

The French Premier regrets the publication of an agency dispatch yesterday, saying that the French and Italians had formed a working arrangement covering all phases of the conference.

Such a proposition is not in accord with the relations of France and Italy, who by no means march side by side in diplomatic affairs in Europe. Moreover, M. Briand would regard it as altogether impolitic, not to say impolite, to form such a combination at this conference.

What the two chiefs did talk over was the naval disarmament plan as it affected their countries, since they are in a similar position, because the strength of their fleets comes next after that of the three great naval powers. It was seen by M. Briand and Signor Schanzer that application of the proposed ratio of smaller ships to capital ships would work havoc with their navies, and they decided that on this one question it would be well if their experts worked together. I have the assurance of M. Briand that no agreement further than this was reached.

It is understood that the French are working on the calculation that the final settlement will provide for eight capital ships for France. She now has seven, and it is very doubtful if she contemplates building another in the near future. It is reported that under such an arrangement Italy would have an allotment of six capital ships, but both nations would like to have their ratio of auxiliary ships increased largely for the sake of coast defense.

The French were more amused than annoyed at the publication today of a report that M. Briand would undertake to persuade the American Government to recognize the Soviets. Such a suggestion is laughable to any one familiar with the consistent attitude of the French Government toward the Bolsheviki.

May Be No Proposal to Cut Armies.

WASHINGTON, Nov. 15 (Associated Press).—As France is the nation with the largest army, Premier Briand pointed out today, it was appropriate for her to take that question up, but neither at the conference nor in any other quarter is there a suggestion that any such sweeping proposal for the reduction of armies is to be expected at the naval plan put forward by the United States.

So far as the United States is concerned, the army question is largely academic. The American Army, now far below its authorized strength of 150,000 men, is cut to the bone. Further reductions would be opposed by both civil and military chiefs of the War Department. No American plan of army reduction will be presented, and it may

Continued on Page Three.

Cost of Army Supplies Cut $22,516,941 in Last Quarter

WASHINGTON, Nov. 15.—A difference of $22,516,941 is shown in the cost report of the Quartermaster General of the army for supplies, clothing, food and other quartermaster properties bought for the quarter ended Sept. 30, 1921, and the same period of last year. The report was said by army officers today to reflect for the first time in official records the reduced cost of supplying the smaller army of 132,000 men as compared with that of about 200,000 in 1920.

Another difference of $4,301,306 is shown in the net cost of operation of the quartermaster depots for the same periods. For the quarter ended September last the cost was only $3,213,189, against $7,514,496 in 1920.

BRITAIN WOULD END ALL SUBMARINES

Failing That, She Wants Fewer Allowed, More Small Craft, New Replacement Method.

JAPAN SEEKS BIGGER RATIO

A Permanent Tonnage of About 67 Per Cent. of Her Rivals' Total Is Her Idea.

By EDWIN L. JAMES.

Special to The New York Times.

WASHINGTON, Nov. 15.—Considerable light was thrown on today's plenary session of the armament conference upon the modifications which will be sought to the American plan for naval limitation. The talk of members of the various delegations also gives an idea of the changes to be asked.

Because they have been discussed more freely, more is known of the British desires. The main British suggestions are three in number. They relate to submarines, shipbuilding plants and sea police work.

Great Britain stands ready to vote for the suppression of all submarines. Failing that, she wishes their number cut to half the number allowed in the Hughes schedule, and their tonnage limited in a manner to make them capable of only defensive warfare. Thus, large undersea boats fit to make long cruises would be barred.

The British case against the submarines is twofold. In the first place, the British spokesmen proclaim their detestation of submarine warfare as a matter of principle. In the second place, they recognize that the submarine constitutes the greatest war danger to their long lines of communication with their colonies and their food supplies.

Balfour Willing to Ban Submarines.

In his address this morning Mr. Balfour made this indictment of the submarine:

"Our experts are inclined to think too large an amount of tonnage has been permitted for submarines. Submarines are a class of vessel most easily abused in their use and which, in fact, in the late war were most grossly abused. We quite admit the power of the submarine. It is the defensive weapon of the weak and it would be impossible, or, if possible, it might well be thought undesirable to abolish them altogether.

"But the amount of tonnage permitted by the new scheme is far in excess, I believe, of the tonnage possessed by any nation at the presen moment, and I throw it out as a suggestion that it may be well worth considering whether that tonnage might not be further limited and whether in addition to limiting the amount of tonnage it might not be practicable, and if practicable, desirable, to forbid altogether the construction of those vast submarines of great size which are not intended for defense, which are not the weapon of the weaker party, whose whole purpose is attack and whose purpose is probably attack by methods which civilized nations would regard with horror."

Whether the British attitude toward submarines will be wholly approved by the United States with its long coast line and the Panama Canal to defend remains to be seen.

The British view with regard to the replacement of ships, as it affects naval shipbuilding plants, is that the peace of the world would be better preserved by maintaining a small shipbuilding plant, which could build one ship every two years and would be kept constantly at work, than by keeping up large plants that could build four or five ships in two years, but would be kept idle for eight. In case of an emergency, the British argue, these great plants might be put to work at any time and thus upset the whole arrangement.

Want More Small Ships Allowed.

As to sea police, the British believe that the necessity of keeping their lanes of commerce always open might call for an increase in that auxiliary ship tonnage beyond that which might be calculated as necessary for a capital ship fleet in war. They will present a detailed report on this contention.

Another point which the British will urge, as Mr. Balfour indicated, will be a reduction, or at least a fixation, of the fleets of France and Italy, and they would probably like to see the system extended to embrace the fleets of other nations, perhaps those of one or two South American Republics. The French and Italians were disposed to believe that in view of the smallness of their

Continued on Page Three.

LODGE MAY SOUND BALFOUR

British Treaty With Tokio Considered Inimical to Our Interests.

REGARD FOR TOKIO FEELINGS

British Want Arrangement Satisfactory to Japan—Expected to Quit Wei-hai-wei.

TODAY'S SESSION SECRET

Conference to Consider Far East in Committee of Whole—Hughes Proposal Awaited.

By RICHARD V. OULAHAN.

Special to The New York Times.

WASHINGTON, Nov. 15.—Exploding international bombshells is not to be followed by Secretary Hughes as a common practice. There is to be no bombshell exploded by him in the Washington conference in connection with Far Eastern and Pacific questions. Instead, these problems, on account of their extreme delicacy, are to be brought into the conference in a circumspect way, not, however, without a considerable degree of frankness.

The American suggestions for adjustment of the Far Eastern and Pacific questions are to be communicated to the members of the conference sitting as a committee of the whole behind closed doors. Whether Secretary Hughes will present a program of adjustment in complete detail, such as he put before the conference in his "bombshell" speech at the opening session last Saturday, has not been disclosed. The belief prevails that his course will be guided by a full appreciation of and regard for the sensibilities of the governments most intimately interested.

The intention appears to have Far Eastern and Pacific questions developed through suggestion and discussion, rather than through the direct methods applied by Mr. Hughes with respect to the reduction of naval armament. That method would place the United States delegation in the position of saying to the other nations, in proposing a harmonizing of views in connection with Pacific and Far Eastern affairs: "We will do thus and so and so and expect you to do thus and so."

Lodge May Help to End Alliance.

Japan's program for her part in an attempted adjustment of Far Eastern questions may be a long step forward toward harmony, but while it is being said in Japanese quarters that an agreement along the lines proposed by Japan may make the continuance of the Anglo-Japanese alliance is one of the extremely serious problems with which the serious problems with which the conference will have to deal.

It is an open secret that the United States regards the Anglo-Japanese alliance as inimical to its interests and is anxious that it should not be continued. But the subject is one of such great delicacy that it must be approached in a cautious manner by the American delegates in the conference. The fact that this Government is not a party to the alliance makes it essential that the caution shall be of the most advanced order.

There is some reason to believe that the first approach in this delicate situation is to be made by the American delegation to the British delegation. According to the story told, Senator Lodge is likely to be the emissary of the American delegation. He is an old friend of Mr. Balfour, of the British delegation, and it is believed that if this method is adopted, Mr. Lodge will seek the advice of Mr. Balfour in order to ascertain what prospect there is of some arrangement acceptable to Japan which will remove the danger this Government believes to exist in the continuance of the alliance.

The British Government has already furnished ground for overtures by the United States in its public statement last Summer that it desired a conference in Washington preliminary to the current conference with a view to bringing about "some larger arrangement" by the United States, Great Britain and Japan as a substitute for the Anglo-Japanese alliance. Any discussion of the subject between Mr. Balfour and Mr. Lodge would be entirely unofficial and it might be insisted that it was purely personal.

British Defer to Japanese Feelings.

The British attitude toward the alliance is peculiar. Although the Imperial Government and the Governments of the self-governing overseas dominions have admitted through an official statement issued in behalf of the recent imperial conference in London that the alliance had lost its usefulness, the Imperial Government does not desire to end the close relationship with Japan unless it can be accomplished without injuring the sensibilities of that country.

The British point of view, as explained here, is that Great Britain feels under a deep debt of gratitude toward Japan for the part the Japanese Government played in helping Britain during the

Continued on Page Four.

Takahashi Calls Conference Epoch-Making; Says Japan Welcomes Armament Relief

TOKIO, Nov. 15 (Associated Press).—"I am confident that the Washington conference will be epoch-making in the realization of peace and good-will on earth by diminishing, if not removing, causes of distrust and suspicion among nations," said Baron Koretiyo Takahashi, the new Premier, to The Associated Press today.

"The burden of armaments," the Premier continued, "tends to a waste of energy and destruction of purposes and is a curse of the times. Japan's finance feels the pain of the burden of armament as keenly as the other powers. Nothing would be more welcome than relief from this burden through a mutual understanding between the nations based on the principle of equality and fairness.

"The outlay for national defense should be reduced to the minimum necessary for national security. Japan's naval expenditures have been considerably cut down in the budget of 1922-23.

"The success of the Washington conference must be considered to depend on the degree of sincerity on the part of those participating in it, and Japan will be second to none in this respect.

"My fervent prayer is that the meeting in Washington may be successful in insuring lasting peace. This effected, President Harding will be entitled to the gratitude of the world, not only contemporaneous but for generations to come."

Here Is Japan's Far East Program; Shidehara May Present It Today

Integrity of China and Withdrawal From Shantung—Open Door Also but Recognition of Her Special Trade Needs Because Raw Material Supply Is Vital.

Special to The New York Times.

WASHINGTON, Nov. 15.—Japan has a well-defined program for consideration by the Washington conference in connection with the effort to arrive at an international agreement on Pacific and Far Eastern questions.

This program has been worked out in rather elaborate detail, and will soon be disclosed to the conference by Baron Kijuro Shidehara, the Japanese Ambassador to the United States, who will act as Tokio's principal spokesman during the consideration of political questions, just as Admiral Baron Kato is her officially recognized mouthpiece in matters affecting limitation of armaments.

For the present Baron Shidehara is withholding announcement of the Japanese program, but it is understood that in one of the earliest sessions of the Conference Committee on Pacific and Far Eastern Questions, which probably will meet tomorrow morning, Baron Shidehara will unfold the general character of the Japanese Government's views respecting the basis on which an accord in the Far East should be sought.

Points in Japan's Policy.

After a careful canvass of the situation THE NEW YORK TIMES presents what is understood to be a correct outline of the main features of the position the Japanese delegation will assume relative to the Far Eastern problems. They are understood to be as follows:

1. The free and peaceful development of the commerce of Japan, the United States and other nations in the Pacific.

2. Support by all pacific means of the independence and integrity of China and the privilege of equal opportunity and the open door for the commerce and industry of all nations in that country.

3. Withdrawal of Japan's forces from the leased territory of Kiaochow, in the Province of Shantung, on a basis which Japan hopes will be satisfactory to Great Britain and the United States and fair and acceptable to the Chinese.

4. Neither the annexation nor a protectorate over Manchuria, but recognition of the principle that Japan has special interests there, based on considerations of propinquity, vast railway and other investments, and the considerable Japanese population that has penetrated into the region along the railway from Dairen to Changchun, these special interests being regarded by Japan as heightened by the fact that Manchuria stands in the path of possible future Russian aggression against Japan.

5. The open door and equality for other nations in both Manchuria and Siberia.

6. Neither annexation nor protectorial control of Siberia, but recognition of the principle of peaceful penetration of Japanese into that region for purposes of trade and commerce, to obtain raw material, and sell Japanese surplus manufactured products.

7. Withdrawal of Japanese forces from Siberia as soon as there is organized in the Russian Far Eastern Maritime Province and Siberia a government qualified and able to stabilize conditions, and in particular to afford protection to Japanese settlers, fishermen and other subjects of Japan resident there.

8. The hope and expectation of the Japanese that when Japan withdraws from the leased territory of Kiaochow and Tsing-tao, the British will also withdraw from the leased territory of Wei-hai-wei, which is likewise in the Chinese Province of Shantung.

9. The acceptance by China of the new international four-power consortium, in which the present participants are American, British, French and Japanese banking groups, with the object of negotiating and carrying out Chinese foreign loan business and assisting China in the establishment of her great public utilities with the cooperation of Chinese capital, but with consortium control and supervision to insure correct expenditure of foreign loans and to eliminate the possibility of the money being wasted or misap-[illegible]

[illegible] tions in China with a view to closer commercial relations between China and the outside world, China being regarded by Japan as one of the main sources of raw material sorely needed by the Japanese and as a market in which to dispose of Japanese manufactured products, without exclusion of or discrimination against other nations desirous of developing business and commercial relations with the Chinese.

11. The maintenance of the status quo in the Dairen leased territory and of the Japanese leased zone along the South Manchurian Railway.

12. Less concern over the renewal of the Anglo-Japanese alliance, which is not regarded as being so vitally necessary in view of the pronounced tendency of the Washington conference toward an agreement for sweeping reduction of naval armaments of the three leading naval powers.

13. Solution of the Yap question and the problem of trans-Pacific communications on a basis satisfactory to the United States and Japan and with the endorsement of the other Governments interested in Pacific communications.

To Lay Cards on the Table.

Information furnished THE NEW YORK TIMES tonight indicates that this is an accurate outline of the position Japan will take in the discussion and negotiation of the Far Eastern problems. In the submission of these views Baron Kato, Baron Shidehara and Prince Tokugawa hope to be able to convince not only the other delegates in the conference but also the public opinion of the world of the justice of Japan's policies and to dispel whatever suspicion exists against her. If they fail in this they will feel, it is asserted, that their mission to the Washington conference has failed.

In quarters close to the Japanese delegation it is asserted that the Japanese are ready to lay all their cards on the conference table and enter a free and frank interchange of views.

Unless the men in a position to speak for the Japanese delegation are mistaken, that delegation will not seek a solution of Far Eastern problems through secret agreements, but by open diplomacy.

The Japanese representatives in Washington feel there has been too much suspicion and distrust regarding the aims and position of the present Japanese Government. They regard the Washington conference as an opportunity for the complete presentation of Japan's case to the world, and an opportunity that should be welcomed rather than allowed to slip by. It is declared to be the belief of those now in control of the Japanese Government that they have too long delayed a frank presentation of their attitude. They are understood to be fully appreciative of the fact that previous Governments in Japan have made mistakes in international policy, among which might be numbered the twenty-one demands which Tokio made on Peking in 1915. But men close to the Japanese delegation predict that in the Washington conference the world will discover that the Japan of today is not the Japan of the twenty-one demands, and that it stands ready to seek a solution of the Far Eastern question on a basis of justice, friendship and mutual understanding and accommodation.

Want Conditions Improved.

The Japanese delegates are not seeking, according to THE TIMES informants, to have the actual status quo in the Far East retained. What they desire, it is asserted, is an effective improvement of the existing conditions on the basis of the principle of the open door and equality of opportunity. They will assert at the conference table that they are as interested as the Chinese in the rehabilitation of China on sound and stable lines, that China is their nearest and most potentially resourceful neighbor on the mainland of Asia, and that the vital interests and future welfare of Japan are bound up, not in a chaotic China, weakened or embarrassed under the influence of corrupt leaders, but in an economically strong China, friendly to Japan and the other nations of the world.

The Japanese, [illegible]

STIRRING CONFERENCE SCENE

British Willingness to Scrap Half Her Fleet Told by Balfour

BROAD PLAN IS ACCLAIMED

Would Go Further on Submarines Than Hughes—Favors Bringing In Other Powers.

KATO GIVES JAPAN'S ASSENT

Will Suggest Modifications Later—France and Italy Also Agree "in Principle."

By EDWIN L. JAMES.

Special to The New York Times.

WASHINGTON, Nov. 15.—Today a chapter in the history of the world was finished and a new one begun.

A white-haired man, his shoulders bowed as if weighed down by the responsibility he bore, stood with folded arms within the walls which held the armament conference and declared in the name of Great Britain the abandonment of her traditional policy of supremacy on the sea and her willingness to accept a status of naval equality with another nation—the United States of America.

In the cause of the limitation of armaments and better understanding between nations and peoples, Arthur J. Balfour spoke the willingness of his Government to give up half her fleet. And then he read a message, sealing his words—a message from the Prime Minister of Great Britain, written almost within the shadow of Nelson's Monument in Trafalgar Square.

And then a short, spare man, with inky hair, stood up and in the name of Japan pledged his Government to reduce its fleet, disavowing all ambitions to rival the navies of America and England, and pledging his country against aggressiveness on the sea.

Thus the drama was played in the name of many millions of men at the second plenary session of the armament conference in Continental Hall. It was big, almost too big to grasp.

Three short days ago America proposed to a surprised world that a good way to reduce naval armament was to wipe out half the fighting ships of the three big naval powers and she laid down a permanent proportion of five-five-three for the sea strength of England, America and Japan. It was breath-taking. Three short days ago, and today England said "yes" and Japan almost the same thing. Their word was given.

And if one brief week ago it had been openly suggested almost anywhere on earth that the United States was going to propose that England scrap half her mighty fleet, he would probably have been thought an excellent candidate for a padded cell in the nearest lunatic asylum. But what was an impossibility is now a fact.

Big Implications of the Decision.

It is a disarmament conference and today's meeting was a session of a disarmament conference — a conference looking to the general betterment all around of international and national life, a conference calling for general sacrifice for the good of all. Theoretically, every one is concerned, every one benefits and all interests are preserved as much as possible.

Yet, sitting there beneath the spell of mighty events, it seemed as if it was a minor chord which struck home to the heart. The impression swept over one that, after all, it was Great Britain who was giving up the biggest thing—something she might have lost some time, but not just yet—a claim to glory which might have been hers for some time to come.

America was called on to give up something within sight, something she might achieve, but something not yet here. But Great Britain was laying down something which had been hers for a century. The world's encyclopedias for 1916 set down the naval policy of Great Britain as that of having a fleet as great as any other two nations. That is her policy no more. That chapter in the world's history was closed today.

The new chapter which was begun today is America's chapter in history. Who could sit in that hall today and doubt what nation fate had left as the great victor in the World War. Left by events the economic and financial mistress of the world, it is America's prospect today of being the dominating political factor among nations. The success of the present conference can mean no less.

Under the great impulse that the American Government gave the opening of the conference, it seemed almost a matter of fact to attend the second session today; it seemed so natural and businesslike and matter of course that the heavy import of what was going on nearly escaped one. There were the same faces which one saw Saturday; the same figures which took their seats at 11 o'clock this morning. But what a step had been made in the three days!

Promptly on the hour Secretary Hughes, as Chairman of the [illegible]

"All the News That's Fit to Print."

The New York Times.

THE WEATHER
Fair today and Thursday; no change in temperature; north winds.
Temperature yesterday—Max., 40; min., 30.
For full weather report see Page 23.

No. 23,328. NEW YORK, WEDNESDAY, DECEMBER 7, 1921. TWO CENTS In Greater New York | THREE CENTS Within 200 Miles | FOUR CENTS Elsewhere

IRELAND TO BE A FREE STATE WITHIN THE BRITISH EMPIRE; AGREEMENT SIGNED GIVING HER A STATUS LIKE CANADA'S; ULSTER CAN STAY OUT; PARLIAMENT CALLED TO RATIFY

Text of Agreement to Establish the Irish Free State

LONDON, Dec. 6 (Associated Press.)—The text of the agreement signed this morning by the British Government and the Irish representatives follows:

Article I.—Ireland shall have the same constitutional status in the community of nations known as the British Empire as the Dominion of Canada, the Commonwealth of Australia, the Dominion of New Zealand and the Union of South Africa, with a Parliament having powers to make laws for peace and order and good government in Ireland, and an executive responsible to that Parliament, and shall be styled and known as the Irish Free State.

Article II.—Subject to provisions hereinafter set out, the position of the Irish Free State in relation to the Imperial Parliament, the Government and otherwise shall be that of the Dominion of Canada, and the law, practice and constitutional usage governing the relationship of the Crown or representative of the Crown and the Imperial Parliament to the Dominion of Canada shall govern their relationship to the Irish Free State.

Article III.—A representative of the Crown in Ireland shall be appointed in like manner as the Governor General of Canada and in accordance with the practice observed in making such appointments.

Article IV.—The oath to be taken by the members of the Parliament of the Irish Free State shall be in the following form:

"I do solemnly swear true faith and allegiance to the Constitution of the Irish Free State as by law established, and that I will be faithful to his Majesty King George V., and his heirs and successors by law, in virtue of the common citizenship of Ireland with Great Britain and her adherence to and membership of the group of nations forming the British Commonwealth of Nations."

Article V.—The Irish Free State shall assume liability for service of the public debt of the United Kingdom as existing at the date thereof and toward the payment of war pensions as existing on that date in such proportion as may be fair and equitable, having regard for any just claims on the part of Ireland by way of set-off or counter-claim, the amount of such sums being determined, in default of agreement, by the arbitration of one or more independent persons being citizens of the British Empire.

Article VI.—Until an arrangement has been made between the British and Irish Governments whereby the Irish Free State undertakes her own coastal defense, defense by sea of Great Britain and Ireland shall be undertaken by his Majesty's imperial forces, but this shall not prevent the construction or maintenance by the Government of the Irish Free State of such vessels as are necessary for the protection of the revenue or the fisheries. The foregoing provisions of this article shall be reviewed at a conference of representatives of the British and Irish Governments to be held at the expiration of five years from the date hereof with a view to the undertaking by Ireland of a share in her own coastal defense.

Article VII.—The Government of the Irish Free State shall afford to his Majesty's imperial force (a) in time of peace such harbor and other facilities as are indicated in the annex hereto, or such other facilities as may from time to time be agreed between the British Government and the Government of the Irish Free State, and (b) in time of war or of strained relations with a foreign power such harbor and other facilities as the British Government may require for the purposes of such defense, as aforesaid.

Article VIII.—With a view to securing observance of the principle of international limitation of armaments, if the Government of the Irish Free State establishes and maintains a military defense force, the establishment thereof shall not exceed in size such proportion of the military establishments maintained in Great Britain as that which the population of Ireland bears to the population of Great Britain.

Article IX.—The ports of Great Britain and the Irish Free State shall be freely open to the ships of the other country on the payment of the customary port and other dues.

Article X.—The Government of the Irish Free State agrees to pay fair compensation, on terms not less favorable than those accorded by the Act of 1920, to Judges, officials, members of the police forces and other public servants who are discharged by it or who retire in consequence of the change of government effected in pursuance of the hereof paragraph.

Provided that this agreement shall not apply to members of the auxiliary police force or persons recruited in Great Britain for the Royal Irish Constabulary during the two years next preceding the date hereof. The British Government will assume responsibility for such compensation or pensions as may be payable to any of these excepted persons.

Article XI.—Until the expiration of one month from the passing of the Act of Parliament for the ratification of this instrument, the powers of the Parliament and Government of the Irish Free State shall not be exercisable as respects Northern Ireland, and the provisions of the Government of Ireland Act of 1920 shall, so far as they relate to Northern Ireland, remain of full force and effect, and no election shall be held for the return of members to serve in the Parliament of the Irish Free State for the constituencies of Northern Ireland unless a resolution is passed by both houses of Parliament of Northern Ireland in favor of holding such elections before the end of said month.

Article XII.—If before the expiration of said month an address is presented to his Majesty by both houses of Parliament of Northern Ireland to that effect, the powers of the Parliament and Government of the Irish Free State shall no longer extend to Northern Ireland, and the provisions of the Government of Ireland Act of 1920 (including those relating to the Council of Ireland) shall, so far as they relate to Northern Ireland, continue to be of full force and effect, and this instrument shall have effect, subject to the necessary modifications;

Provided, that if such an address is so presented, a commission consisting of three persons, one to be appointed by the Government of the Irish Free State, one to be appointed by the Government of Northern Ireland, and one, who shall be Chairman, to be appointed by the British Government, shall determine in accordance with the wishes of the inhabitants, so far as may be compatible with economic and geographic conditions, the boundaries between Northern Ireland and the rest of Ireland, and for the purposes of the Government of Ireland act of 1920, and of this instrument the boundary of Northern Ireland shall be such as may be determined by such commission.

Article XIII.—For the purpose of the last foregoing article the powers of the Parliament of Southern Ireland under the Government of Ireland Act of 1920, to elect members of the Council of Ireland, shall, after the Parliament of the Irish Free State is constituted, be exercised by that Parliament.

Article XIV.—After the expiration of said month, if no such address as mentioned in Article XII. hereof is presented, the Parliament of the Government of Northern Ireland shall continue to exercise as respects Northern Ireland the powers conferred upon them by the Government of Ireland Act of 1920, but the Parliament of the Government of the Irish Free State shall in Northern Ireland have in relation to matters, in respect of which the Parliament of Northern Ireland has not the power to make laws under that act (including matters which, under said act, are within the jurisdiction of the Council of Ireland), the same powers as in the rest of Ireland, subject to such other provisions as may be agreed to in the manner hereinafter appearing.

Article XV.—At any time after the date hereof the Government of Northern Ireland and the Provisional Government of Southern Ireland, hereinafter constituted, may meet for the purpose of discussing provisions, subject to which the last of the foregoing article is to operate in the event of no such address as is therein mentioned being presented, and those provisions may include: (a) Safeguards with regard to patronage in Northern Ireland; (b) safeguards with regard to the collection of revenue in Northern Ireland; (c) safeguards with regard to import and export duties affecting the trade and industry of Northern Ireland; (d) safeguards for the minorities in Northern Ireland; (e) settlement of financial relations between Northern Ireland and the Irish Free State; (f) establishment and powers of a local militia in Northern Ireland and the relation of the defense forces of the Irish Free State and of Northern Ireland, respectively, and if at any such meeting provisions are agreed to, the same shall have effect as if they were included among the provisions subject to which the powers of Parliament and of the Government of the Irish Free State are to be exercisable in Northern Ireland under Article XIV. hereof.

Article XVI.—Neither the Parliament of the Irish Free State nor the Parliament of Northern Ireland shall make any law so as either directly or indirectly to endow any religion or prohibit or restrict the free exercise thereof or give any preference or impose any disability on the account of religious belief or religious status, or affect prejudicially the right of any child to attend school receiving public money without attending the religious instruction of the school, or make any discrimination as respects State aid between schools under the management of the different religious denominations, or divert from any religious denomination or any educational institution any of its property except for public utility purposes and on the payment of compensation.

Article XVII.—By way of provisional arrangement for the administration of Southern Ireland during the interval which must elapse between the date hereof and the constitution of a Parliament and a Government of the Irish Free State in accordance therewith, steps shall be taken forthwith for summoning a meeting of the Members of Parliament elected for the constituencies in Southern Ireland since the passing of the Government of Ireland act in 1920 and for constituting a Provisional Government. And the British Government shall take steps necessary to transfer to such Provisional Government the powers and machinery requisite for the discharge of its duties, provided that every member of such Provisional Government shall have signified in writing his or her acceptance of this instrument. But this arrangement shall not continue in force beyond the expiration of twelve months from the date hereof.

Article XVIII.—This instrument shall be submitted forthwith by his Majesty's Government for the approval of Parliament and by the Irish signatories to a meeting summoned for the purpose of members elected to sit in the House of Commons of Southern Ireland, and, if approved, it shall be ratified by the necessary legislation.

Signed on behalf of the British delegation:

LLOYD GEORGE.
AUSTEN CHAMBERLAIN.
BIRKENHEAD.
WINSTON CHURCHILL.
WORTHINGTON-EVANS.
GORDON HEWART.
HAMAR GREENWOOD.

On behalf of the Irish delegation:

ART OF GRIOBHTHA (ARTHUR GRIFFITH).
MICHAEL O. O. SILEAIN (MICHAEL COLLINS).
RIOBARD BARTUN (ROBERT C. BARTON).
E. S. DUGAN (EAMON J. DUGGAN).
SEORSA GHABGAIN UI DHUBHTHAIGH (GEORGE GAVAN DUFFY).

Dated the 6th of December, 1921.

ANNEX.

An annex is attached to the treaty. Clause 1 specifies that Admiralty property and rights at the dockyard port of Berehaven are to be retained as at present date and the harbor defenses and facilities for coastal defense by air at Queenstown, Belfast, Lough and Loughswilly to remain under British care, provision also being made for oil, fuel and storage.

Clause 2 provides that a convention shall be made between the two Governments, to give effect to the following conditions: That submarine cables shall not be landed or wireless stations for communication with places outside of Ireland established, except by agreement with the British Government, that existing cable rights and wireless concessions shall not be withdrawn except by agreement with the British Government, and that the British Government shall be entitled to land additional submarine cables or establish additional wireless stations for communication with places outside of Ireland, that lighthouses, buoys, beacons, &c., shall be maintained by the Irish Government and not be removed or added to except by agreement with the British Government, that war signal stations shall be closed down and left in charge of care and maintenance parties, the Government of the Irish Free State being offered the option of taking them over and working them for commercial purposes, subject to Admiralty inspection, and guaranteeing the upkeep of existing telegraphic communication therewith.

Clause 3 provides that a convention shall be made between the two Governments for the regulation of civil communication by air.

HARDING PROPOSES FLEXIBLE TARIFF AND LABOR REGULATION

Asks Congress to Extend the Powers of the Present Tariff Commission.

WOULD FUND FOREIGN DEBT

Will Not Denounce Trade Treaties and Wants Merchant Marine Act Changed.

AGAINST TAX-EXEMPT BONDS

Many Arms Conference Delegates in Throng Which Listens to President's Address to Congress.

Special to The New York Times.

WASHINGTON, Dec. 6.—In an address which President Harding pointed out was not only a message to the Congress but to the people of the entire country he made an appeal today for the united support of his party in the accomplishment of legislation that he considers vital to the peace, prosperity and security not only of the United States but of the world. Senators and Representatives of both parties agreed that it was a very frank expression of the views and hopes of the Chief Executive. In much that he said the President won the outspoken approval of the Democrats as well as the Republicans.

[The full text of the message is published on Page 8.]

Not since the war days has a more representative audience listened to an address by a President on the opening of Congress. Occupying seats of honor directly in front of the rostrum from which the President spoke were statesmen of Europe and the Orient who are representing their respective countries at the Conference for Limitation of Armament. They were an intensely interested body of men who, observing the strictest decorum, did not join in the applause that continually interrupted the delivery of the address.

Behind the diplomats and foreign delegates were grouped the members of the Senate and House, Secretary Hughes and the other members of the Cabinet being in the first row of seats in the House reservation. There were just two uniformed personages on the floor. One was General Pershing and the other his aid, Major Quekemeyer.

Refers Twice to Arms Conference.

Twice in the course of his address, once at the beginning and again as he concluded, the President referred to the Conference fo Limitation of Armament as in session in Washington.

"It is gratifying to report," he said at the start, "that our country is not only free from every impending menace of war, but there are growing assurances of the permanency of the peace which we so deeply cherish."

"Agreeable to your expressed desire," he said, in concluding his address, "and in complete accord with the purposes of the executive branch of the Government, there is in Washington, as you happily know, an international conference now most earnestly at work on plans for the limitation of armament, a naval holiday, and the just settlement of problems which might develop into causes of international disagreement.

"It is easy to believe a world hope is centred on this capital city. A most gratifying world accomplishment is not improbable.

Procedure to Avoid Strikes.

Discussing at considerable length the problem of capital and labor, the President pointed out that the right of labor to organize is as necessary and as fundamental as is the right of capital to organize, and that the right of labor to negotiate through its chosen agents is as essential as is the right of capital to organize to maintain corporations and to limit the liabilities of stockholders. But, he added, just as it is undesirable that a corporation shall not be permitted to impose undue exactions upon the public, it is just as essential that labor shall not be permitted to exact unfair terms of its employers, or subject an innocent public to distress in order to gain its end.

In the same way that nations are seeking procedures to settle their difficulties without resort to war, the President suggested, some procedure should be found whereby labor and capital can reach agreements without resort to those forms of warfare" which are recognized as strikes, lockouts, boycotts and the like.

"Inescapable" World Relationship.

Other outstanding features of the address were the earnestness and the unqualified positiveness with which the President asserted the "inescapable relationship" of the United States to the affairs of the world in finance and in trade. The United States, he declared, would be unworthy of its best traditions, "if we were unmindful of social, moral and political conditions which are not of direct concern to us," but which.

Continued on Page Nine.

B.R.T. DIVIDENDS PAID DAY OF RECEIVERSHIP

Checks for $236,250 Mailed by Operating Company Just Before Garrison Took Charge.

HECTIC HOLIDAY FOR HEDLEY

Got $1,000,000 on New Year's Eve to Stave Off the Failure of Interborough.

Stories of quick shifts of millions between holding companies and subsidiaries, in both the Interborough and Brooklyn Rapid Transit systems on the eve of receiverships were told in the Transit Commission's hearing yesterday by James R. Sheffield, trustee in bankruptcy for the Interborough Consolidated Corporation, and Howard Abel, Controller for the B. R. T.

On Dec. 31, 1918, a few hours before Lindley M. Garrison was appointed receiver for the New York Consolidated Railroad Company, which operates the subway and elevated lines of the B. R. T. system, the companys officers rushed out checks for the last payment of a 1¼ per cent. dividend on $18,900,000 of stock, amounting to about $236,250. The dividends had been declared in the preceding September. As holder of approximately 96 per cent. of the stock of the New York Consolidated, the Brooklyn Rapid Transit Company received the larger part of this payment.

A year later President Frank Hedley and other officers of the Interborough were spending a "hectic New Year's Eve," and finally obtained a loan of $1,000,000 from its bankrupt holding company, the Interborough Consolidated, to aid in averting a receivership for the subway and elevated lines of Manhattan and the Bronx.

A few days before this New Year's Eve loan the Interborough Rapid Transit Company had finished paying back to the Interborough Consolidated $800,000 borrowed from the treasury of the holding company the day before it went into bankruptcy in March, 1919. Mr. Sheffield, trustee in bankruptcy for the Interborough Consolidated, had demanded the return of that $800,000 on the ground that the loan was "illegal."

He also had demanded from the Interborough payment of a note for $300,000, due on April 1, 1919, but which was

Continued on Page Five.

German Explosion Kills 100, Sets Dynamite Works Afire

BERLIN, Dec. 6 (Associated Press).—It is reported that 100 persons lost their lives today as the result of the explosion of an oil tank in the Nobel Dynamite Works at Saarlouis, Rhenish Prussia.

The works are burning.

SAYS UNION ABUSES RAISE BUILDING COST

Witness Tells Lockwood Committee of Expenses Piled Up by Labor Inefficiency.

The Lockwood committee opened a new phase of its housing inquiry late yesterday afternoon by examining witnesses in an endeavor to learn to what extent housing construction was loaded with high costs due to the inefficiency of labor. C. G. Norman, Chairman of the Board of Governors of the Building Trades Employers' Association, detailed a long list of abuses he alleged existed in building trade unions, resulting from severe membership and production restrictions demanded by the organizations.

Patrick J. Crowley, successor of Robert P. Brindell as Chairman of the Building Trades Council, having jurisdiction over 115,000 workers, explained the inefficiency of labor by the phrase "more pay, more pep," and declared he had heard no complaints lately regarding the inefficiency of labor.

Samuel Untermyer, senior counsel to the committee, and Henry Mayer, assistant counsel, again took up the affairs of Inside Electrical Workers' Union 3, which is said to have collected $250,000 a year on "permit" cards which enabled non-union journeymen to work on union jobs if they paid $2.50 a week for journeymen's cards and $1 a week for helpers' cards. Mr. Untermyer examined Joseph Lawlor, Treasurer of the union, concerning the $26,000 of the funds alleged to be missing, but Lawlor became involved in confused statements, saying he believed that William A. Hogan, the financial secretary, had turned the money over to the union, and then that he did not know whether Hogan turned the money over to him or not, finally returning to his original statement.

In introducing the examination of

Continued on Page Six.

America Will Enter No Alliance; Three More Chinese Advisers Out

No Treaty on Far East Likely, but a Less Formal Agreement—Project Shaping Slowly.

By EDWIN L. JAMES.

Special to The New York Times.

WASHINGTON, Dec. 6.—Whatever plans are being worked out for an international treaty, protocol, resolution, agreement, or understanding among three, four, five, six, seven, eight or nine powers to establish a Far Eastern policy do not now form a proper subject for public consideration, according to the official view of the American delegation to the armament conference.

It is stated by spokesman for the delegation that much progress has been made in the working out of a Far Eastern agreement. But just what that "progress" means and just what it is purposed to commit the nation to the American representatives are not yet prepared to say.

While reports originating from other delegations are being published all over the world, emphasizing the idea of an alliance of the United States with other nations, the American delegates think the time is not fit to present the American views on what might be a suitable arrangement.

Efforts made today to induce the American representatives to set correspondents on the right path amid the eddies of conflicting rumors as to what was being done brought only the instructive statement that what had been published about treaties and alliances was not within gunshot of the truth. But just what the truth is—that is not forthcoming.

Observers, and many visiting diplomats, have commented frequently upon the secrecy of the conference since its first days. Not a few of the old-school diplomats who are here and at work feared that the Americans were going to stage the conference doings in the open. It is probable that there was a general expectation that some of the real negotiations would be done at public meetings. It even looked that way just after the first two open sessions.

But the fears of the old school diplomats have proved groundless. For two weeks there has not been a plenary session, and it has become evident that the plenary sessions will be full-dress occasions for announcing decisions previously reached.

While there is no official statement on the subject, there appears no reason to suppose that the American delegation is going to undertake to involve this country in an alliance to take the place of the Anglo-Japanese alliance or to serve any other purpose. Nor will there, in all probability, be any treaty, three-

Continued on Page Four.

Attaches of Delegation Resign in Protest Against 'Negative Results' of Conference.

Special to The New York Times.

WASHINGTON, Dec. 6.—As a protest against "negative results" of the conference concerning China's aspirations, three additional attachés of the Chinese delegation to the Washington conference, two of them superior advisers, today tendered their resignations. This action followed that of Dr. Philip K. C. Tyau, Secretary General of the delegation, yesterday.

Those who resigned today are Yuho M. T. Liang, ex-Minister of Foreign Affairs; Tzu-Chi Chow, ex-Minister of Finance, superior advisers, and Vice Admiral Ting-Kan Tsi, associate director of the revenue council and adviser to the delegation. He was an adviser to the office of the President of China during the incumbency of the late Yuan Shih-Kai. A report that Lieut. Gen. Fu Hwang, adviser to the delegation, also had resigned, was denied.

It was uncertain tonight whether the resignations would be accepted.

China's attitude was criticised by an American official, who said that China had nothing to gain by such a course. He pointed out that the conference was making great progress, and that China found herself in a very strong position, face to face with all the nations interested in the Far East, with their representatives disposed to do everything possible to aid in restoring China's integrity and rehabilitating her finances.

There is divided opinion in the Chinese delegation as to the situation that that country is facing in the conference. One Chinese adviser, deprecating the resignations, said that the action had been premature and would fail of the expected effect. Some of them resigned for the political effect at home, while others, it was said, were absolutely sincere in the course taken.

Another spokesman for China counseled a more determined attitude on the part of China and an insistence that the Shantung Railroad dispute be adjusted first, rather than the minor differences now under consideration in the parley. He said he was in a position to say that the leaders in the conference had decided just how far the Far Eastern matters should be settled and that China would be forced to take what was given her. In his opinion, the conference leaders have agreed not only upon a naval ratio but upon other matters. China, he said, would not be allowed to change her tariff treaties and most of the things in dispute would be left to a commission to study and report upon to another conference.

"We are not too sensitive about the

Continued on Page Four.

Carson Sees for Britain Day of 'Abject Humiliation'

Special Cable to THE NEW YORK TIMES.

LONDON, Dec. 7.—The Morning Post says that after reading the terms of the Irish agreement the comment of Lord Carson, former Ulster leader, was:

"I never thought I should live to see a day of such abject humiliation for Great Britain."

CANADIAN ELECTION LIBERAL LANDSLIDE

Premier Meighen Loses His Seat and His Protection Policy Is Repudiated.

OTTAWA, Dec. 6.—Premier Meighen was defeated in his home constituency, Portage La Prairie, Manitoba, in the Canadian general election today. His opponent was Harry Leader, Progressive.

Returns received tonight indicated the defeat of the Meighen Government and a landslide for the Liberals, led by W. L. Mackenzie King. Seven members of the Cabinet were defeated.

Mr. King, the Liberal leader, was elected in North York, Ontario, a division normally Conservative, by 1,000 majority. T. A. Crerar, leader of the Progressive Party, was elected in Marquette, Manitoba.

In the eastern part of the dominion the Liberals made a clean sweep. Quebec, with sixty-five members in Parliament, will be represented entirely by Liberals. Five of the seven defeated Cabinet members were candidates in Quebec constituencies.

Nova Scotia, with sixteen seats, gave them all to Liberals, two members of the Government going down to defeat in that province. Liberals were reported elected in three out of the four Prince Edward Island divisions, and in six of the eleven constituencies in New Brunswick.

The Cabinet members defeated were F. B. McCurdy, Minister of Public Works, Colchester, N. S.; E. K. Spinney, Minister without portfolio, Yarmouth, N. S.; L. P. Normand, President of the Privy Council, Three Rivers, Quebec; C. C. Ballantyne, Minister of Marine and Fisheries, Montreal, Quebec; A. Fauteux, Solicitor General, Terre Bonne, Quebec; L. G. Belley, Postmaster General, Charlevoix, Quebec; Rudolphe Monty, Secretary of State, Beauharnois, Quebec.

Premier Meighen issued the following

Continued on Page Twelve.

ULSTER RESERVED; DUBLIN REJOICES

Craig Cabinet Begins Sessions to Consider the Terms of the Agreement.

NORTH DISLIKES THE OATH

But Waits to See if Sinn Fein Is Really Friendly—Dail's Acceptance Predicted.

Special Cable to THE NEW YORK TIMES.

BELFAST, Dec. 6.—News that the settlement had been achieved between the British Government and the Sinn Fein delegates caused some surprise in Belfast, particularly in view of De Valera's declaration at Galway in regard to allegiance. The disposition of Ulster people is not to enter upon any hasty criticism or comment, but to wait until the terms are revealed. Should the position of Ulster be safeguarded and southern Ireland accept allegiance and a recognized position within the British Empire there will be a general feeling of satisfaction in the north that the strife in Ireland has been brought to an end.

A specially convened meeting of the Ulster Cabinet was held today. After considering the terms for two and a half hours the Cabinet adjourned further consideration until tomorrow.

Colonel Spender, Secretary to the Northern Cabinet, was asked for the Cabinet's first impression of the terms of settlement. He said they were somewhat puzzled and were anxious to have certain points cleared up. Colonel Spender added that if the proposed changes in area affected any great tract of territory or meant any great disturbance of population they would not be acceptable to Ulster. He understood, however, that they really meant small adjustments along the frontier.

Asked if the form of oath was acceptable, Colonel Spender said that the Ulster people did not like it, but if it were acceptable to the British people they could not object. He regarded with suspicion the fact that the Sinn Feiners were not prepared to take the ordinary form of oath.

Likes the Option for Ulster.

In one form, Colonel Spender remarked, the latest proposals meant an advance, because the former ones provided for forcing Ulster to go in under an all-Ireland Parliament while these gave an option. If the good-will of the Sinn Fein was forthcoming, he added, and there was an intention on their part

Continued on Page Two.

'IRISH FREE STATE' CREATED

All of Ireland Outside of Ulster to Have Dominion Rule.

ULSTER CANNOT STOP IT

Redrawing of Her Frontiers to Follow if She Finally Refuses to Join.

NAVAL RIGHTS RESERVED

Control of Finances, Land Forces and Powers of Council of Ireland Given to New State.

Special Cable to THE NEW YORK TIMES.

LONDON, Dec. 6.—"Ireland shall have the same constitutional status in the community of nations known as the British Empire as the Dominion of Canada, the Commonwealth of Australia, the Dominion of New Zealand and the Union of South Africa, with a Parliament having powers to make laws for the peace and order and good government of Ireland and an Executive responsible to that Parliament, and shall be styled and known as the Irish Free State."

Such is the first article of the "treaty between Great Britain and Ireland" which was signed some minutes after 2 o'clock this morning on behalf of Great Britain by Lloyd George, Austen Chamberlain, Lord Birkenhead, Winston Churchill, Sir L. Worthington-Evans, Sir Hamar Greenwood and Sir Gordon Hewart, and on behalf of Ireland by Arthur Griffith, Michael Collins, Robert Barton, E. J. Duggan and Gavan Duffy.

The signatures were affixed to the document in that historic room of 10 Downing Street on whose walls hang the portraits of the greatest British Premiers of the past and of one American, George Washington, the Father of His Country.

It was that same room, Lord Birkenhead pointed out today, which "witnessed the fateful and melancholy discussions that preceded the final recognition on the part of the statesmen of this country that the American colonies were lost. It was in that room," said the Chancellor of the Exchequer, "in which the anxieties, uncertainties and vicissitudes of the war met with daily reflection, that yesterday was entered upon, in my judgment, a new phase which promises, after all these bitter centuries and generations, that at last an era may dawn which will enable us, of our day and generation, to say that we have not achieved less in settlement here at our own doors of the issue which seems, but is not, domestic than we achieved in the fields of arms when we preserved the security and existence of these islands from the greatest menace that assailed them since the Napoleonic period."

The Cabinet met this morning and approved the agreement reached between the British and Sinn Fein delegates. The Premier was heartily congratulated.

Parliament to Meet Next Week.

Now that the treaty of settlement has been signed the next step will be to submit the terms to the British Parliament for approval. For this purpose both Houses have been summoned to meet on Wednesday next, Dec. 14, by which time it is hoped the agreement as signed by the Sinn Fein delegates will have been ratified by the Dail Eireann.

This meeting of Parliament will be the first of a new session, and this will give added importance to the opening ceremony.

The King will open the session in person and in full state. The greatest emphasis will thus be laid upon it as a great historic occasion, on which the King's speech will no doubt lay due stress. There will be no other business to place before the Houses at this stage, and a day or two would be enough to secure the object in view. Then Parliament would adjourn until the date of assembly previously fixed, Jan. 30, unless there should appear a reason for a meeting a week or two earlier. But the preparation of the necessary bill for giving effect to the Anglo-Irish agreement will require time and its completion before the end of January is unlikely.

The terms of the agreement were carried to Dublin by E. J. Duggan, one of the Sinn Fein plenipotentiaries, and Desmond Fitzgerald, Dail Minister of Publicity.

Meanwhile at the house in Hans Place occupied by the delegates and at the Secretariat in Cadogan Gardens the process of packing up began. There was noticeable slackening in the care with which doors had been guarded ever since the Sinn Feiners came to London, and women secretaries were bustling about packing up big files of documents and getting their own baggage ready. Formal orders had not yet been issued to them, but they expect to leave by the mail train tomorrow night, arriving in Dublin on Thursday morning.

None of the delegates was ready to discuss the settlement, and equal reticence was shown by the rest of the party. They seemed, however, confident that the agreement would be accepted by the Sinn Fein generally, and when it was suggested that De Valera's speeches in the last day or two looked rather ominous, one of the secretaries declared he thought his utterances on Monday quite moderate.

A poster of The Freeman's Journal

"All the News That's Fit to Print."

The New York Times.

THE WEATHER
Unsettled today, probably light snow; Wednesday cloudy.
Temperature yesterday—Max., 45; min., 31.
For full weather report see Page 34.

VOL. LXXI....No. 23,334. NEW YORK, TUESDAY, DECEMBER 13, 1921. TWO CENTS In Greater New York | THREE CENTS Within 200 Miles | FOUR CENTS Elsewhere

YAP AGREEMENT MADE, JAPAN CONCEDES US LEAGUE RIGHTS; NAVY SETTLEMENT NEAR; 4-POWER TREATY TO BE SIGNED TODAY; BORAH ATTACKS IT IN THE SENATE AS AN ARMED ALLIANCE

DE VALERA DENIES HONOR REQUIRES TERMS BE RATIFIED

He Declares Plenipotentiaries Were Sent on Understanding Dail Would Act.

CROWDS FLOCK TO DUBLIN

Many Now Think That the Issue Should Be Submitted to a Plebiscite.

CRAIG REPORTS TO ULSTER

He Declares, It Is Said, That Lloyd George's Attitude Is: "There Is the Treaty, and It Stands."

Special Cable to THE NEW YORK TIMES.

DUBLIN, Dec. 12.—Eamon de Valera issued a further statement today on question of ratification. It reads: "I have been asked whether the honor of Ireland is not involved in the ratification of the agreement arrived at. The honor of Ireland is not involved. The plenipotentiaries were sent on the distinct understanding that any agreement they made was subject to ratification by the Dail Eireann and by the country and could be rejected by the Dail Eireann if it did not commend itself to the country.

"The Parliament of Britain and the people of Britain will on their side similarly consider the agreement solely [illegible]. If the British Parliament [illegible] it can reject it. So can the Irish people. Ratification is then no [illegible] empty formality.

"The United States refused to ratify a treaty signed even by its President. The honor of the nation is not involved, unless and until the treaty is ratified.
EAMON DE VALERA."

This statement is an answer to criticisms that were freely made last week to the effect that the peace delegates were plenipotentiaries representing the Dail Eireann and the Irish nation, and that the nation was therefore in honor bound to uphold their action. Other critics, who have taken an intermediate view, have pointed out that though the Dail is not under obligation to ratify it, the Cabinet is deeply pledged to recommend its acceptance.

De Valera himself does not repudiate this view, but declares that the circumstances are unusual.

Already the members of the Dail are beginning to arrive in Dublin from the various parts of Ireland, and the air is alive with rumor and gossip. Only the members themselves and officials preserve that amazing taciturnity and reserve which have become a second nature with all who have come under the discipline of the last three years. For the rest, speculation still turns nearly around the point how far it is possible that the personal force and idealism of de Valera may turn the current from the direction in which it is setting now.

By what signs, it is asked, do you judge that the peace party will win the day? Will the known feelings of the released internes and the sympathy they have evoked penetrate to the inner councils of the Dail? Can the Bishops who will meet tomorrow speak absolutely for the influence of the Church?

Bishops Meet Today.

The conference of Bishops will meet no doubt in private and will probably issue a statement in favor of the policy of accepting the treaty.

After all, what will carry most weight with the country is not the formal announcement by the higher clergy but the practical enthusiasm and activity of the village priests. In so far as the influence of the Church will affect the decision it will be chiefly exercised through the rank and file, but it is not overlooked that the Dail has never yet been in such a position that it could closely reflect the currents of public opinion. It is more accustomed to direct than to be directed, to be influenced from within than from without. It has never been violently up against clearly expressed public opinion.

It has been intended that the Dail assembly on Wednesday should take place in the small oak room at Mansion House, as the large round room is at present occupied by the Industries of Ireland Fair, but owing to the limited space it has now been decided to hold it at University College, and the press will probably be admitted. The proceedings are likely to be lengthy. It is expected that most of the members will have something to say, so the session may be extended into the second or even the third day.

The actual merits or demerits of the treaty itself have been somewhat obscured by the political differences within the Cabinet, but the supporters of Griffith are now beginning to tell something about the advantages of the treaty. They point out that it will confer on Ireland the same voice as Great Britain in imperial foreign policy, membership in the League of Nations and the right [illegible]. Also, [illegible]

Continued on Page Six.

Legion Head Sees Harding; Predicts Bonus Legislation

Special to The New York Times.

WASHINGTON, Dec. 12.—Hanford MacNider, National Commander of the American Legion, had a fifteen-minute conference with President Harding this morning, and as he left the White House he predicted that the present session of Congress would pass bonus legislation.

Commander MacNider said tonight that Senator McCumber and Representative Joseph W. Fordney had assured him that a Soldiers' Bonus bill would be passed by Congress in the next ninety days.

PRINCE BOYCOTTED IN ALLAHABAD VISIT

Whole Native Population Deserts the Streets at His Arrival in the City.

600 AGITATORS ARRESTED

Chairman of Allahabad Council Gets Jail Sentence—Many Imprisoned in Calcutta.

Special Cable to THE NEW YORK TIMES.

LONDON, Dec. 13.—A dispatch to the Daily Chronicle from Allahabad says:

"The scene in Allahabad this morning on the occasion of the visit of the Prince of Wales was marred by a boycott, which was enforced with the utmost strictness by Gandhi. Practically the whole of the population of the city observed this ordinance, and the roads were therefore bedecked by flags and loyal inscriptions rather than by the gay myriads which attended every movement of the Prince in Rajputana and then in Lucknow.

"It is true that the chief events of the day took place some distance from the densely populated streets, and that the recent arrests are still rankling among those who have the power of intimidating the people in the towns of British India, and it is true, also, that in its determination at all costs to safeguard the person of the Prince of Wales the precautions taken by the Government may well have deterred the easily dismayed Indian crowd from venturing too near the well-guarded avenues through which his Royal Highness drove this morning."

Other dispatches from India show that the situation there daily increases in gravity. It is reported that more than 600 "non-co-operators" are now in prison. In the last few days several agitators were arrested at Allahabad. The Chairman of the Allahabad municipality has been sentenced to eighteen months' imprisonment and a fine of 250 rupees. The editor of The Independent was sentenced to twenty-one months imprisonment and to pay a fine of 2,000 rupees.

Other messages mention arrests at Rangoon, Delhi and Amritsar. Of 155 men arrested for picketing at Calcutta one has been discharged and eight have been sentenced to pay small fines and remanded to six months' imprisonment.

Following up their arrest in Bengal of C. R. Das, President-elect of the All-India Congress, which endorses Gandhi's program of non-co-operation and non-payment of taxes, the authorities have arrested his son, Mrs. C. R. Das and two other women and a large party of volunteers. They declined to give bail or allow bail to be given for them and were remanded in custody in the Presidency Jail at Bengal.

This being the first occasion on which Bengali women had taken such action, the Government released them the same night, warning them that a recurrence of their action would entail grave consequences.

LONDON, Dec. 12 (Associated Press).—Mohandas Karanchand Gandhi, the Nationalist leader, having done "penance" for the Bombay rioting, has written to the Young India Society urging redoubled efforts for the annual All-India Congress at Ahmadabad Christmas week. He says:

"The non-co-operative movement must succeed. While we must not avoid arrest, we must not provoke it by unnecessary offenses. We must hold the Congress at any cost, in spite of the arrest of every leader, unless the Government dissolve the Congress by force."

CALICUT, British India, Dec. 12.—Eighty-one Moplahs have been killed and fifteen made prisoners in a clash with the military near Chervar. The British had only one sepoy wounded.

DELHI, Dec. 12.—A barrister, Asaf Ali, and fifty-three nonco-operationists have been arrested here. They are charged with being members of an unlawful association.

90 DRY AGENTS RAID BROADWAY RESORTS AND A VILLAGE HOTEL

Thomas Healy's, Cafe de Paris, the Little Club and the Hotel Lafayette Visited.

THIRTEEN PRISONERS TAKEN

Raided Premises Searched and Liquors Alleged to Have Been Found in All.

PROTECTION BOAST A CLUE

Raiders, Posing as Western Men Seeking a Good Time, Win Confidence of Proprietors.

Ninety prohibition enforcement agents, some of them disguised as cabaret frequenters and others as longshoremen, shortly before last midnight descended on the Hotel Lafayette, University Place and Ninth Street; Thomas Healy's restaurant at Columbus Avenue and Sixty-sixth Street; the Café de Paris at Broadway and Forty-eighth Street and the Little Club in the Shubert Theatre Building, 212 West Forty-fourth Street, where, after searching each place from cellar to roof, they said that they had found liquors. Summonses were served on ten guests and thirteen employes of the several places were arrested.

The raiders were broken up into four squads of between twenty and twenty-five men each, all under the direction of Roy Q. Merrick, Acting Chief Prohibition Enforcement Agent in this district. The raiders were assembled shortly before 10 o'clock in the headquarters of Supervising Prohibition Enforcement Agent Yellowley, 55 West Twenty-seventh Street, where they were placed under the jurisdiction of three of Chief Yellowley's best men in addition to the Acting Prohibition Enforcement Director.

Merrick led one group down to the Lafayette Hotel shortly after 11 o'clock and he kept his men in Washington Square Park until a few minutes before midnight when he and the leaders of the other groups received simultaneous orders to enter all four suspected places.

"Villagers" Fill Dining Room.

Merrick found the dining rooms in the Hotel Lafayette crowded with frequenters of the Greenwich Village section and men and women on their way to their homes from the theatre, but he cautioned his raiders not to create any excitement among the patrons.

Five of the raiders immediately made their way to the kitchen in the basement of the hotel where they opened an icebox. They said later they found two cases of champagne. In the meantime other groups of Merrick's raiders searched closets, rooms and other parts of the house from the cellar to the roof, but were unsuccessful in finding liquors in any other part of the hotel, except in two small dining rooms, where they said they found several small bottles of wine on the tables.

The seven guests seated about the tables immediately were served with summonses to appear before United States Commissioner Hitchcock in the Federal Building this morning to face charges of violating the Volstead act. Merrick then ordered the arrest of Felix Coumeign, the manager of the hotel, who said he lived at 2 Jane Street, and George Conti, the captain of waiters in the dining room, who gave his address as 319 West Twenty-sixth Street. Then the agents hurried out of the place with their evidence to join other forces which, it had been reported to Merrick, were engaged in a search for liquor in the other suspected places.

Twenty-five agents had all the entrances to Healy's restaurant on the Columbus Avenue and West Sixty-sixth Street sides guarded when Merrick arrived there with his men. Agent Van Tassel, under Merrick's direction, had entered the place with his men while men and women were dancing in the cabaret and the tables in the various dining rooms in the four-story building were crowded with homegoers.

As in the raid on the Hotel Lafayette,

Continued on Page Ten.

British Minority Laborites Ask Harding to Free Debs

LONDON, Dec. 12.—The Independent Labor Party has sent a cablegram to President Harding pleading for the immediate release of Eugene Debs and other political prisoners.

MARKETS IN A WHIRL AS EXCHANGES RISE

Continued Upswing Causes Scramble by Dealers in World's Money Centres.

STERLING TOUCHES $4.24⅛

Variety of Reasons Given for the Extreme Advances—Commodity Markets Unsettled.

An upswing in the exchanges of the principal European countries, which started toward the latter part of last week, continued yesterday and carried sterling up 6⅛ cents, francs 43½ points, lira 20½ points, guilders 35 points, pesetas 81 points and marks .06 points, in a day of intense excitement in all of the money centres of the world, in which occurred repeatedly scrambles by dealers and bankers to execute orders.

A variety of causes for the wild market and the extreme advances in quotations were given, but taken as a whole the impetus back of the market remained a mystery, and Wall Street was puzzled. Ascribed as contributing factors, however, were betterment of the international situation; discounting of the rewriting of the Treaty of Versailles; tremendous developments at the Conference for the Limitation of Armament; probable success of the German-Franco-British conference now under way in London, and a panic of international bears who have sold the exchanges of the world for the decline.

Sterling at Highest in Two Years.

Sterling, at $4.24⅛, is at the highest point since Oct. 4, 1919, when it touched $4.24⅛. The exchanges of Holland and Madrid during the day both touched new maximum figures for the year. An idea of the strength of the upswing may be gained from the following table, which shows yesterday's high and closing quotations of the principal exchanges, together with the quotations of one week ago and one month ago:

	High.	Close.	Week Ago.	Month Ago.
London	4.24⅛	4.20⅝	4.06½	3.98¾
Paris	8.34½	8.28¼	7.45	7.22¾
Rome	4.81½	4.80¼	4.20½	4.09½
Amsterdam	36.40	36.30	35.75	34.87
Berlin	.61¼	.60½	.43¾	.37
Madrid	15.30	15.30	14.12	13.84

Both political and economic factors figure largely in the present movement of exchanges, bankers say. The conference at Washington on the limitation of armaments, hardly considered as a market factor six weeks ago, now is to the fore, and bankers in every financial centre of the world fairly devour the news from Washington from day to day.

Most of the activity in the present exchange market originates from London, Paris and Amsterdam. One banker, recently returned from a study of economic conditions abroad, said that Europe was "literally short to its neck of all exchanges." Speculation in the exchanges is much more popular in Europe than in the United States, he said, and taken as a whole, the people of England, France, Holland, Spain, Italy and Germany have been "bearish" on their own countries for many weeks.

"This day-by-day selling for the decline," he said "has built up a tremendous short interest in the market. The panicky buying of exchanges that we saw Saturday and Monday and that we probably will see again today merely represents the covering of these people."

Discounting of Conditions.

Another banker in close touch with the international situation, described the market as "active and excited," and said that it had broadened to an extent where its upward movement could not possibly be the result of [illegible]ating or manipulating. "It is [illegible]ounting of the improved fi[illegible] [illegible]ositions in all parts of the w[illegible] th[illegible] we are seeing in the foreign [illegible] market today," he said.

The market was so excited during most of the day that bankers and dealers were frequently from one to two cents apart in their quotations. For instance, one dealer last night declared that sterling had sold at $4.24½ during the day, while the highest figure another had received was $4.23⅝. All sorts of rumors were going the rounds of the financial district. One was that the Foreign Relations Committee of the Senate would make an important announcement on Wednesday. Another was that a decision had been reached in England to fund the individual income tax for a term of years.

The advance in sterling particularly had a tendency to unsettle the commodity markets here. Wheat and cotton felt the full effects of the advance. It was pointed out that dealers who purchased cotton last month with the pound at $3.95 now run the further risk of being undersold by competitors who are able to go into the market and purchase cotton with the pound at $4.24. This holds true in every commodity exported.

Dealers in foreign bonds had a wearisome day of it, attempting to find a basis on which to buy and sell. With sterling and the other exchanges jumping erratically, it became almost impossible. The sharp rise in sterling served to carry the price of United Kingdom of Great Britain and Ireland 5½ per cent. bonds to 90⅞, a new high for the year, and an advance of a full point over last week. Bonds of this 1920 external loan are convertible into Great Britain's Internal National War 4s, at the fixed rate of $4.20 to the pound sterling. The advances have pushed the pound up near the point where conversion becomes profitable.

SPIRITED SENATE DEBATE

Reed, Robinson, Stanley and Watson, of Georgia, Support Borah.

POINDEXTER BACKS TREATY

Kellogg Also Defends It—Idaho Member Wants Submarines and Poison Gas Forbidden.

PLEDGE LIKENED TO ART. X.

Long Discussion Now in Prospect, but Ratification Is Still Predicted.

Special to The New York Times.

WASHINGTON, Dec. 12.—The Conference for the Limitation of Armament and the four-power treaty were the subjects of an unexpected and spirited debate in the Senate this afternoon.

Senator Borah of Idaho, a leader in the fight against ratification of the Treaty of Versailles and the League of Nations Covenant, was in command of the assault, which lasted about two hours. Before it ended it was joined in by Senators Poindexter and Kellogg in defense of the new treaty, and by Senators Reed, Robinson, Stanley and Watson from the Democratic side, who supported Mr. Borah. [The full text of the debate is printed on page 4.]

The Idaho Senator argued that this country would be as much bound [illegible]ly to go to the aid of its [illegible] in the event of aggression by some other power under Article II. of the four-power treaty as would have been the case under the provisions of Article X. of the League Covenant.

Before the debate was over those Senators who had been predicting a speedy ratification of the treaty were almost ready to concede that they might have been too optimistic and that instead of easy sailing the treaty might have before it a long and rough road. All the indications, however, are that it will be ratified by much more than the required two-thirds majority when a final vote is reached, some time in 1922.

Senator Poindexter, who was one of the original "irreconcilables" and was the first Senator to speak against the League of Nations, today directed the defense of the four-power treaty, insisting that it was not the "blood-brother" of Article X. of the League, which various Democratic Senators and a few Republican Senators insist is the case.

In opening the debate, Senator Borah paid a tribute to Secretary Hughes for the "masterly" way in which he had presented the American naval reduction program at the first plenary session of the conference. He placed Mr. Hughes among the "great Premiers and Secretaries of State of history."

Holds It Is a Military Alliance.

But the program presented by Secretary Hughes did not go far enough to suit Senator Borah, who made it plain that unless the treaty which will embody the naval reduction program contains a provision that will eliminate from future wars the submarine, poison gas and other "barbarous" instruments for making war, he will oppose ratification.

As the situation now stood, Mr. Borah contended, the four-power treaty was simply a military alliance. He said that under the provisions of Article II. this country could be committed to possible aggressive action in the same way that would have been possible under Article X. of the League covenant.

"When I say 'commit' I do not mean," explained Mr. Borah, "that they could legally bind the Congress of the United States to send an army, but when I say 'commit' I mean precisely what the former President, Mr. Wilson, said with reference to Article X. of the League of Nations, that the moral obligation would be commensurate and more binding than the legal obligation itself."

Senator Borah read several of the provisions of the Anglo-Japanese alliance, which automatically ends with the ratification of the four-power treaty, emphasizing that provision which pledged

Continued on Page Four.

"Brilliant Success," Says Viviani in Farewell; British Delegation Plans to Sail on Dec. 31

WASHINGTON, Dec. 12 (Associated Press).—The Washington conference "is a brilliant success," M. Viviani, head of the French delegation, said tonight in a farewell conference with newspaper correspondents in anticipation of his departure tomorrow for New York, from where he will sail for Paris on Wednesday.

"I am very glad I have had a part in it," he added. "The large questions have either been settled or are about to be. I suppose another conference will be held inside of a year."

M. Viviani plans to sign the four-power Pacific treaty tomorrow, say farewell to President Harding and depart for New York at 4 o'clock with Mme. Viviani and several members of the delegation's staff.

M. Albert Sarraut, the French Minister of Colonies, who is an authority on Far Eastern questions, will succeed him as chief of the French delegation here. Vice Admiral de Bon will assist M. Sarraut and Ambassador Jusserand in naval matters.

All of the British delegates, with the exception of Sir Auckland Geddes, Britain's Ambassador here, have arranged to sail for home Dec. 31 on the steamer Olympic, feeling that the main issues of the conference will have been disposed of by that time.

In making this announcement today a British spokesman said that while there was no positive indication that the work of the conference would be finished by the last day of the year, the British believed that all the big questions will have been decided and the lesser matters may safely be left for the consideration of the Ambassadors who are resident here. Should any questions arise which in the judgment of the Ambassadors appear to require special direction from home offices, they can readily be consulted by cable, it was said.

Beyond the actual work of the conference itself, the British were represented as feeling that the presence of the delegation was not necessary, even in connection with the Shantung matter, which is being dealt with in "direct conversations" between the Chinese and Japanese delegates, assisted by American and British experts. It was suggested from a British source today that a subcommittee might linger after the conference adjourns to deal with the matter. If the conversations are fruitless in bringing about a direct settlement of the Shantung problem, the British delegates say the Chinese delegates have it within their power to bring the matter directly before the conference.

FOUR-POWER TREATY TO BE SIGNED TODAY

Yap Agreement, Which Was a Condition of Our Assent, May Also Be Signed.

CONFERENCE END LOOMS UP

Large Results Counted On by Our Delegates With the Further Agreements Expected.

Special to The New York Times.

WASHINGTON, Dec. 12.—The four-power treaty between the United States, France and Japan and the British Empire, relative to insular possessions and dominions in the region of the Pacific, will be formally signed at 11 A. M. tomorrow in the Diplomatic Room at the State Department.

The official parchment copy of the treaty has been prepared in English and French, and it will be signed by all four American delegates, all four Japanese, seven British, including those from the overseas dominions, and all of the French delegation who are in Washington. M. Viviani, head of the French delegation, will leave the city at 4 o'clock tomorrow afternoon and sail for France on Wednesday on the Paris.

No time will be lost by President Harding in transmitting the treaty to the Senate, where today in anticipation of the coming of the document a memorable debate started over this and other treaties flowing out of the armament conference.

The signing of the four-power treaty by the United States delegation is with the understanding that a convention shall be signed between Japan and the United States with respect to Yap and other mandated islands in the Pacific. It is expected tonight that the agreement between Japan and the United States on Yap will also be signed at the State Department tomorrow by Secretary Hughes and Baron Shidehara.

The success of the conference, according to the Administration point of view, is now complete. Major decisions have been reached, and the rest is regarded as a matter of detail. There is every indication now that all decisions of the conference will be cleared up by Christmas, certainly in time for Mr. Balfour and other British delegates to sail for England on Dec. 31.

The major decisions of the conference will be as follows:

First—The four-power treaty be-

Continued on Page Three.

EXTEND NAVAL RATIO TO FRANCE AND ITALY

Basis of 5-5-3-3-3 Is Studied for Inclusion in Quintuple Limitation Compact.

ORGANIZE NEW COMMITTEE

Heads of Five Delegations and Experts Are Grouped to Expedite Agreement.

Special to The New York Times.

WASHINGTON, Dec. 12.—The program of the Conference for Limitation of Naval Armaments has reached the point where the major problem of ratio has been provisionally decided on—a basis of relative strength of 5-5-3-3-3 for the navies of the United States, the British Empire, Japan, France and Italy.

Under this arrangement the naval ratio of 5-5-3 for the navies of the United States, Britain and Japan, as proposed by Secretary Hughes, will stand, and France and Italy will each, theoretically at least, be brought into the formula on the basis of approximately 300,000 tons each in the matter of capital ships. It is not the expectation that either France or Italy will endeavor to possess a capital ship strength of 300,000 tons, but the tentative understanding reached would authorize that maximum.

It is learned that Great Britain is not opposed to a 3-3 basis for France and Italy as compared with the 5-5-3 ratio for America, Britain and Japan. Early in the conference there were intimations that a basis of 3-3 for France and Italy, on the theory that a combination of the navies of the two nations would make the relative strength between them and Great Britain in the proportion of 6 to 5, might not be satisfactory to Great Britain.

Japan's Assent Assured.

There is no longer any doubt of the acceptance by Japan of the principle of a Japanese capital ship strength of 60 per cent. of that of the American Navy. This was provisionally agreed to by Baron Kato, head of the Japanese delegation, more than a week ago. He has since then received official advices from his Government accepting the 5-5-3 ratio. While this ratio has been provisionally agreed upon and the work of drafting sections of the proposed quintuple naval reduction treaty between the United States, Britain, France, Italy and Japan is under way, final details of the plan remain to be arranged. Japan's approval, it is understood, has been in Baron Kato's hands for several days.

It is understood that in the working out of the details, there may be some readjustment of tonnage by which Japan may save the latest of her capital ships, the Mutsu, and by which the United States may also save the West Virginia and Washington, but without destruction of the fundamental principle of the Hughes naval reduction formula. How this readjustment may be made without disturbing the provisionally agreed upon ratio is now under consideration by Secretary Hughes, Mr. Balfour and Baron Kato.

To facilitate the agreement on details and at the same time bring France and Italy into the projected agreement, the Committee on Naval Armament today agreed to appoint a new committee of fifteen which will deal with the naval limitation question with the utmost expedition. This special committee will consist of the head of each of the five delegations representing the United States, France, England, Japan and Italy. These will each be assisted by a civilian, who, as was explained in a high American quarter today, may or may not be a delegate, and also by a naval expert.

Secretary Hughes, Baron Kato, Mr.

Continued on Page Three.

EQUALITY IN YAP GRANTED

We Recognize Mandate Rights of Japan in Pacific Islands.

COVENANT IS PARALLELED

Accord Reached With Tokio Insures Us Rights Equal to Any League Member.

PLAN WILL BE EXTENDED

Deals With Britain on South Pacific and With Other Mandatories Are Forecast.

By EDWIN L. JAMES.
Special to The New York Times.

WASHINGTON, Dec. 12.—The Administration resurrected today another page of the covenant of the League of Nations to obtain for the United States the rights and privileges of League members in the mandated territories held by Japan in the North Pacific Ocean.

Secretary Hughes announced that Washington and Tokio had reached an accord on Yap and the other islands north of the equator held by Japan under League mandates. That accord is a paraphrase of Article XXII. of the covenant, with specifications as regards Yap. In all the mandated islands held by Japan the United States obtains the benefits of membership in the League of Nations.

An analogous arrangement is to be made with the British Empire for similar rights in mandated territories in the Southern Pacific and later with other mandatories for all mandated territories. As a matter of fact the United States Government, prior to the signing tomorrow of the four-power treaty, establishing the rights of the signatory powers in the Pacific Islands, will send a note to the British delegation, stating that included in those rights are rights the United States would have in the mandated islands were this country a member of the League.

Just as Article II. of the four-power treaty is a paraphrase of Article X. and Article XVII. of the covenant, the treaty between America and Japan with respect to the Northern Pacific islands is a paraphrase of the mandate section of the covenant, Article XXII.

Not only does the United States obtain the benefits of a League member in these mandated territories, but it is also provided that Japan shall submit to the American Government a copy of her annual report on the administration of her mandates, the report which under the covenant Japan must submit to the members of the League Council. It is also stipulated that the United States shall have a say on all modifications of the mandate terms. But, it is made plain that the United States assume no responsibility in the matter. All we ask is to be able to say yes or no to what the League Council may decide. It bears the responsibility; Washington is to be a court of review.

Article XXII. of the covenant, Paragraph 5, says the mandatory "will also secure equal opportunities for the trade and commerce of other members of the League." Article V. of the agreement between America and Japan says that the United States consents to the administration by Japan of the mandated islands in the Pacific Ocean north of the equator subject to the "above conditions" with respect to Yap and the "following conditions":

Then it is set forth that the United States is to have the benefit of the engagements of Japan under the mandate terms, especially Articles III. and IV. This mandate was drafted by the League in accord with Article XXII. of the covenant. Article III. of the mandate prohibits slavery, as the covenant provides in Article XXII., Paragraph 5, Line 5. Article III. of the mandate provides for the regulation of arms traffic, as Article XXII., Paragraph 5, provides.

Article IV. of the mandate prohibits the raising of armies among the natives of mandated territories and forswears fortifications on mandated territories. That guarantee is given by Article XXII. of the covenant to League members. Religious liberty is assured to American missionaries in the agreement, as it is assured to League members by the covenant.

The covenant provides that for Class C mandates, in which category the former German colonies held by Japan falls, shall be administered under the laws of the mandatory, and so the American-Japanese treaty lays down the rule that treaties between America and Japan shall apply to the mandated islands.

Equality in Yap Privileges.

As for Yap, the treaty is most specific. The United States is to have the same opportunities as Japan or any other nation in all that relates to cables and wireless service. America is to have the free operation of the Guam-Yap cable and reserves the right to establish any wireless station she may wish, but it is set down that so long as the Japanese wireless station gives ample and free service this right will not be exercised.

Under Article III. of the treaty it is stipulated that all nationals of America and all property having to do with cables [illegible]

25 Hurt, 1 Missing, in Acid Blast And Fire at Former German Plant

Twenty-five persons were injured, six of them seriously, and one person was missing last night as the result of an explosion and fire yesterday afternoon at the Heyden Chemical Works, Monroe Street and River Road, Garfield, N. J. The explosion, of undetermined origin, occurred on the second floor of a new five-story structure used for the manufacture of salicylic acid. At 9 o'clock last night the fire was said to be under control. The building was destroyed.

Workmen said that immediately after the explosion the fire seemed to be carried to all parts of the building as if by a strong draught. In their panic to leave the flaming structure, workmen from the third and fourth floors slid down cables in the elevator shaft, and others on the lower floors jumped from windows. Spectators say that Martin Jarrak of 215 Monroe Street, Passaic, a foreman, who was the most seriously injured, ran from the building as if crazed by his burns, crying for some one to shoot him.

All the fire apparatus in Garfield was called out, and three companies were sent from Passaic under Chief Bowker. The firemen succeeded in keeping the flames from two tanks near the burning building, one of which contained 30,000 gallons of alcohol and the other chlorosulphonic acid gas.

Until late last night persons who believed that relatives or friends might have lost their lives waited near the plant, although a rollcall of employes revealed that only one person was missing.

The structure destroyed was one of a dozen buildings composing the Heyden Chemical Works, formerly German owned, and bought for $1,500,000 by Allan A. Ryan about two years ago at a sale held by the Alien Property Custodian. The loss was estimated at $250,000.

Two Thousand Women in Leaderless Mob Storm Kansas Mine and Attack Workers

Special to The New York Times.

PITTSBURG, Kan., Dec. 12.—The Howat forces sent their women into the fight in the Kansas mining field today.

Following a secret meeting at Franklin, the "Red" centre, yesterday, the Howat forces organized wives, daughters and other relatives of striking Howat miners into a leaderless mob. This morning the women, 2,000 strong, met at Franklin and went to Mine 17 of the Jackson-Walker Company, a mile from Franklin.

Sheriff Gould and deputies were on the scene this morning before the march of the women began, but they were powerless before the onslaught of the mob. The women stormed the mine as fiercely as any men could have stormed it. Some of them carried red pepper and in one or two instances used it.

The women met an interurban car carrying several miners on their way to the mine. They barred the exit from the car and forced the miners to remain aboard, and the car went on.

Motor cars along the highway were stopped at the mine and the women, nearly all of whom were foreigners, ripped the curtains off the cars. If miners were inside the mob forced them to get out and held them as prisoners. Occupants of cars other than miners also were compelled to wait.

At the mine the women entered the engine house and drove out the engineers and firemen. Then they marched back to Franklin.

Sheriff Gould received reports last night that the women were to be sent to the front this morning in an attempt to get the men out of the mines, and that, failing in that, other methods would be used.

"All the News That's Fit to Print."

The New York Times.

THE WEATHER
Cloudy today; Monday, clear and colder; fresh west winds.
Temperature Yesterday—Max., 36; min., 29.
For full weather report see Page 23.

Section 1

VOL. LXXI....No. 23,374. NEW YORK, SUNDAY, JANUARY 22, 1922. In Nine Parts, including Rotogravure Picture Sections, Book and Magazine Section. FIVE CENTS In Manhattan, Bronx and Brooklyn. | Elsewhere TEN CENTS

POPE BENEDICT XV. PASSES AWAY EARLY THIS MORNING; LINGERS HOURS AFTER WORLD GETS REPORT OF DEATH; TRIBUTES PAID TO THE PONTIFF BY MEN OF ALL RELIGIONS

LLOYD GEORGE ASKS NATIONS TO RESOLVE ON PEACE AT GENOA

Premier Declares International Conferences Alone Can Restore Confidence.

HITS AT POINCARE'S STAND

Those Who Fear Conferences Are Those Unwilling to Face Realities, He Says.

FULL TEXT OF THE SPEECH

Implies Strong Hope for American Co-operation at Genoa—Warns Against Party Strife.

Copyright, 1922, by The New York Times Company.
Special Cable to THE NEW YORK TIMES.

LONDON, Jan. 21.—Prime Minister Lloyd George looks to the Genoa conference to carry the world another stage forward in the paths of peace and recuperation after the war if the United States of America will attend and help to complete the good work done by the Washington conference.

Although he was most guarded in his expression of his views, it was obvious to most of those who listened to the remarkable speech he made at Central Hall, Westminster, today, when he would up the proceedings of the new Liberal Council convention held there, that he counts upon America. He did not say that without America nothing worth while would be accomplished at Genoa, but his whole speech by implication did convey the idea that unless the United States does take a hand there progress at Genoa may be distressingly slow and limited.

He spoke as an optimist struggling hard against adversity. All his emphasis was laid on the necessity of world peace and his conviction that that could be found only through the means of international conferences. His references to the Washington conference, to Mr. Balfour's share in it and to the advantages of an understanding with the United States were made carefully from notes.

The problem which confronted the world, he said, was the restoration of international confidence in every country. Washington had done much to clear away the atmosphere of suspicion. Genoa, he believed, would remove other doubts and fears. Though he did not say it in so many words, he made it clear that his hopes lay in the English-speaking races.

He let his fancy play a little as he spoke of old hatreds, old feuds and old distrusts which complicate European problems and then he almost dramatized his experience of how conferences could solve them as with hands weighing the balance from side to side he pictured the weight of argument.

With arm slowly raised he illustrated the approach to agreement and with a blow of the right fist on the palm of the left hand he exclaimed:

"In the end reason prevails. When you are in conference some one will be there who will bring you face to face with realities, and it is those who never face realities who dislike conferences."

Although the British Premier's speech had to deal with many points of purely domestic politics, Lloyd George obviously regarded them as secondary and subsidiary to his main theme, world reconstruction. Even his appeal for the continuance of the coalition Government in this country was based on the argument that the dominant issue of British domestic politics was need of peace in the world.

"There is one great stable country," he declared with a flash of national pride. "That is Great Britain. Do not deprive the world of the full advantages of the power and prestige of this great land by shattering them upon wretched party feeling."

Lloyd George spoke directly in reply to a resolution congratulating the Government on the Irish settlement.

The full text of the Premier's speech is given below.

FULL TEXT OF LLOYD GEORGE'S SPEECH.

I congratulate the promoters of these meetings upon the finest gathering we have seen, representative of the Liberals who stood in the nation's need for national unity. A resolution has been moved and seconded of congratulation upon a task which if not altogether accomplished is well-nigh accomplished. Congratulations are given to myself and my colleagues on the result of our labors.

The first thing I have to say is that those congratulations have been directed to the wrong address. They ought to have been sent not to those who did it but to those who talked about it [Laughter and cheers] and never did it when they had the chance. It is a fact that we conducted long, difficult and delicate negotiations. It is true that we carried them to a successful issue. It is true we took serious decisions and faced grave responsibilities, some of us graver responsibilities than others, and I notably refer to my Unionist col-

Continued on Page Eighteen.

Freighter Sinking at Sea; Rush to Save Her Crew

BOSTON, Jan. 21.—The new Norwegian steamship Mod, New York for Antwerp, Bremen and Hamburg, is sinking in mid-ocean according to radiograms received here today. The steamer Centennial State reported that all the Mod's lifeboats and her propeller were gone, and that the steamer George Washington was going to her aid. The Mod's position was given as latitude 46:15 north, longitude 41:10 west.

The Mod left New York on Jan. 13. She is a vessel of 2,707 tons and available records indicate that she is a freighter. Her position as given in the wireless messages is about 1,200 miles east of Halifax.

STORM IN FRANCE OVER GEN. PETAIN

Poincare Sharply Criticised for Appointing Him to Post in War Ministry.

CHAMBER TO DISCUSS IT

Nationalists Not Anxious for American Participation at Genoa.

Copyright, 1922, by The New York Times Company.
Special Cable to THE NEW YORK TIMES.

PARIS, Jan. 21.—Premier Poincaré's first governmental act in appointing Marshal Pétain to what is in effect not only the office of Inspector General of the Army but a position in the Ministry of War has been during the last few days one of the subjects of most controversy in all the program of the Government.

The Socialists attacked it at once as an indication of the militaristic intentions of the new Premier. Even in the general opinion it was regarded as an unwise step, however fully qualified for the post the Marshal might be and however little alteration there might be from his former powers.

Then in the Chamber during the debate on Thursday André Lefèvre, himself a former Minister of War, and always one of the hottest advocates of more complete disarmament of Germany, suddenly refused his support to the Government on the ground of this nomination. In a sharp speech he attacked the new arrangement at the Ministry of War as likely to take the army from civilian control and place it in the hands of its military leaders, and by the support he received it became at once apparent that even amid the enthusiasm for the Poincaré administration the Chamber was reserving its right to judge its actions in committing the country to any militarist program.

M. Maginot, the new War Minister, who formerly was Minister of Pensions, at once replied to M. Lefèvre, but his reply was so feeble that Poincaré had to interpose and promise that the matter would be fully debated at the first convenient opportunity.

In the two days that have elapsed opinion has visibly hardened and the first symptoms have appeared of opposition to the Government within the Chamber itself. Two important groups of radicals and radical Socialists, led by M. Klotz, the former Minister, have sent a letter to the Premier informing him that they wish the debate to be fixed as early as possible and in which they characterize Pétain's appointment as "an act contrary to the principle of constitutional responsibility and to republican doctrine."

If the Premier persists in maintaining the appointment in face of the opposition which it has aroused the incident may easily become a vital issue, and though Marshal Pétain's popularity and respect for his modesty and his ability are deep and sincere in the country, there is little doubt that tremendous pressure could easily be aroused on the question.

Premier Poincaré has finished drafting his outline of the preliminary conditions for a Franco-British compact and the terms of the compact itself as he would like to see it. This draft is to be handed to the British Government through the French Ambassador in London, and presumably the reply will be sent by similar channels.

In the new project France is believed to have repeated the request which Briand made that aggression against Poland should form a ground for British intervention, and further to have asked that the treaty be operative for a longer term than ten years.

According to the formula announced in the Premier's ministerial declaration of "a treaty between equals," Poincaré is seeking to have the treaty made reciprocal so as to avoid the suggestion that France is a protected country. Just how he purposes to do this is, however, being kept secret, and even those who are most enthusiastic for "equality" profess their fear that England will not accept easily a guarantee which will appear to carry with it approval of France's military upkeep, and much less will she accept any hard and fast stipulation as to the number of army corps which she must supply in case

Continued on Page Twenty-one.

COLLINS AND CRAIG AGREE ON BOUNDARY AT LONDON MEETING

Terms Give Hope of Peaceable Settlement of Differences of Ulster and South Ireland.

THEY CALL OFF BOYCOTTS

Decide to Devise Better System Than Council of Ireland to Handle Their Relations.

WILL TAKE UP AMNESTY

Ulster Officials Calls News "Best We Have Had, and the Most Cheering."

LONDON, Jan. 21 (Associated Press).—The Irish situation took an unexpected turn today with the announcement that Michael Collins, head of the Irish Provisional Government, and Sir James Craig, Premier of Ulster, had arrived at a mutual agreement, which holds out the promise of a peaceable settlement between the North and the South. It was all the more surprising in view of the fact that Mr. Collins had only left Dublin last night to enter into consultations with Sir James this morning.

In addition to the arrangements made to settle the boundary question, it was decided to cease forthwith mutual boycotts. What is considered of vast importance is the decision to devise a better system than the Council of Ireland, as provided in the 1920 act, to deal with problems affecting the whole of Ireland.

The terms of the agreement are substantially as follows:

1. The boundary commission, as outlined in the Anglo-Irish treaty, is to be altered. The Governments of the Irish Free State and of Northern Island are to appoint one representative each to report to Mr. Collins and Sir James, who will mutually agree on behalf of their respective Governments regarding the future boundaries between the two.

2. Without prejudice to future consideration by his Government of the question of tariffs, Mr. Collins undertakes that the Belfast boycott will be discontinued immediately, and Sir James undertakes to facilitate in every possible way the return of Catholic workmen—without tests—to the shipyards, and whenever trade revival enables the firms concerned to absorb the present unemployed workmen. In the meantime a system of relief on a large scale is being arranged to tide over the period of distress.

3. Representatives of both Governments are to unite in facilitating a settlement of the railway dispute.

4. The Governments are to endeavor to devise a more suitable system than the Council of Ireland for dealing with problems affecting all Ireland.

5. A further meeting will be held at a subsequent date in Ireland between the signatories to this agreement to discuss the question of amnesty for persons who have been imprisoned since the operation of the truce.

Ulster Official Is Hopeful.

BELFAST, Jan. 21 (Associated Press).—John Milne Barbour, who is Sir James Craig's Deputy Finance Minister, described the news of the agreement between Michael Collins and Sir James as "the best we have had yet and the most cheering." He thought it eminently desirable that the north and south combine in the interest of the common country so long as the autonomy of Ulster is reserved.

The general feeling here is that the agreement is an outcome of Mr. Collins's desire to protect the Free State in the coming elections against the menace of a possible combination of Republicans and Communists, as there are many of the latter in the Transport Workers' Union. The Ulster Premier, on his part, is anxious for peace within the six-county borders.

The Ulster Unionists naturally will welcome the raising of the boycott, but are apprehensive of trouble with the shipyard workers on the question of the restoration of Catholic workmen expelled in July, 1920, after the murder of Colonel Smyth in Cork. There has been a heavy increase of unemployment in the shipyards in the last year, and it is considered definitely certain that the Protestant workmen will insist that their coreligionists be given priority in the filling of jobs.

Lord Pirrie holds the same view with regard to the situation as does the Ulster Premier, but believes that it will be a long time before the bitterness engendered by the shootings and bombings on both sides vanishes. Matters, however, he thinks, would be facilitated if the British Government were prepared to finance a large relief scheme, as the Ulster Labor Ministry has been sorely tried by the unemployment problem.

Takes Over Dublin City Hall.

DUBLIN, Jan. 21.—The administration of the Dublin City Hall was handed over today by the British military au-

Continued on Page Fourteen.

Senate Agrees to Take Up Foreign Debt Refunding Monday

WASHINGTON, Jan. 21.—The Senate late today cleared the way for consideration next Monday of the Allied Debt Funding bill. Before adjourning over Sunday, the Senate made the bill its privileged business. A long contest is regarded assured principally over a Democratic amendment to require semi-annual interest payments and to require foreign bonds paying not less than 5 per cent.

The Genoa Economic Conference and many questions relating to the armament conference are expected to be discussed in connection with the measure.

ARREST 'TEX' RICKARD ON A GIRL'S CHARGE

Boxing Promoter Is Accused of Inviting 15-Year-Old Child to 47th Street House.

HE HINTS AT AN ENEMY PLOT

Alleged Victim's 11 and 12 Year Old Companions Give Evidence to Children's Society.

"Tex" Rickard, lessee and manager of Madison Square Garden and the most conspicuous prize-fight promoter in the country, was arrested yesterday on charges involving a 15-year-old girl. This girl, together with two others, aged 11 and 12 years respectively, have told the Society for the Prevention of Cruelty to Children, to the District Attorney's office, and to the police a story of association that began one night last August at Rickard's swimming pool in Madison Square Garden and ended Saturday night when two of the girls, afraid to go home, sought shelter at Bellevue Hospital.

According to the girls' statements, Rickard made their acquaintance when they went to swim in the Garden pool, and invited them to visit his offices in the tower. The girls say that Rickard gave them money and offered them wine. Later, the girls say, they visited him in private houses at 20 and 24 West Forty-seventh Street.

Rickard, who is about 50 years old, denied the accusations and pleaded not guilty when he was arraigned in the West Side Court yesterday morning. He went to court with his wife and lawyers and said he had heard he was wanted. Magistrate George W. Simpson held him in $1,000 bail for examination Wednesday on a charge of criminal assault.

Girls' Charges Against Promoter.

Vincent D. Pisarra, Superintendent of Investigations of the Society for the Prevention of Cruelty to Children, gave reporters a detailed account of the girls' charges against Rickard yesterday afternoon. The girls are Alice Ruck, 15 years old, of 225 East Twenty-fifth Street; Elvira Renzi, 12 years old, of 225 East Twenty-fifth Street, and Anna Hess, 11 years old, of 232 East Twenty-first Street.

"This is the story that the three girls tell," said Mr. Pisarra. "One night last August a boy friend gave the Ruck girl and the Hess girl complimentary tickets to the swimming pool at Madison Square Garden. They went that night and several times in the next few nights. One night they met Rickard, who they say was always at the pool. They just picked up an acquaintance. They were asked if they were sure of his identity, and said that various people came up and called him 'Tex.' They say he gave them $1 each the first night he met them.

"The Renzi girl met Rickard a few nights later. All three girls then began talking to Rickard every night they went to the pool for a swim. He continued to give them money. One night, the Ruck and Hess girls say, Rickard took them upstairs to a room in the tower. They say he offered them wine, but they did not want it. According to the girls, Rickard attempted to attack the Hess girl and did attack the Ruck girl, in a room in the tower.

Met Him by Appointment.

"On a later occasion, the girls say, Rickard gave them a piece of paper on which was written the address, 24 West Forty-seventh Street, and made an appointment to meet them there. The Ruck and Hess girls say they met him on the sidewalk in front of the house and he went in first, after telling them to enter when he made a sign from the window. They say he attacked the Ruck girl again in that house. The Ruck girl says she made three visits to the house at 24 West Forty-seventh Street, accompanied by one of the other two girls on each visit.

"After these visits, the girls say, Rickard directed them to visit another house at 20 West Forty-seventh Street. It is in this house, on Dec. 18, that the complaint alleges specifically that Rickard criminally assaulted the Ruck girl. The Hess girl was in the house at the time."

The story of the girls became known only by accident. About 9 o'clock last Saturday night the Ruck and Hess girls went to Bellevue Hospital and told a story of having been kidnapped by a strange man in a taxicab at 1 o'clock that afternoon. They said the man had

Continued on Page Seventeen.

EX-CONVICT SLAIN; POLICEMAN IS HELD FOR THE KILLING

Victim Shot Down in Dispute Said to Have Grown Out of Boyhood Enmity.

DYING, HE PROTECTS SLAYER

Refuses to Say Who Wounded Him, but Witness Names Patrolman Soden.

OFFICER ARRESTED IN HOME

Pistol Shows Recent Cleaning, but He Is Silent About Tragedy—Prompt Trial Promised.

John R. Soden, a mounted policeman attached to the Glendale Station, Queens, was held yesterday without bail for examination next Friday on suspicion of having shot and mortally wounded John McGuiness, an ex-convict, the night before in a drunken brawl in the saloon at 60 Ninth Avenue. He was arraigned before Magistrate Joseph E. Corrigan in Jefferson Market Court.

Soden is 32 years old and has been a member of the force for eleven years. He was arrested four hours after the shooting in his home, at 8 Bethune Street, a short distance from the saloon, by Captain Thomas Fay, head of the Lower West Side Detective Bureau. He refused to make any statement to Captain Fay or Benedict D. Dineen, Assistant District Attorney, who began an investigation shortly before McGuiness died in St. Vincent's Hospital.

The Assistant District Attorney said four or five men were in the saloon when the shooting occurred, but the police had found only one of them. This witness, Philip Comisky of 411 West Thirtieth Street, told Mr. Dineen the shooting followed an altercation growing out of ill feeling that had existed between Policemen Soden and McGuiness from their boyhood.

Soden, who was in civilian clothes, is six feet one inch tall and weighs 190 pounds. He had struck McGuiness in the face when they were standing at the bar, and the men fought for five minutes, he said. McGuiness, who was two years younger than the policeman, was getting the better of the fight, Comisky said, when onlookers separated the men.

McGuiness Offers Apology.

Comisky told Mr. Dineen that McGuiness then expressed regret that they had fought over the old grudge and, walking up to Soden with his right hand extended, said:

"Well, Jack, let's forget it. We were old schoolmates together."

Soden shook hands with McGuiness, Comisky added, and said:

"Let bygone be bygones."

McGuiness then took a position beside the policeman at the bar, according to Comisky, and Soden suddenly wheeled around on him with his pistol. As McGuiness backed away, the witness said, the policeman shot him in the abdomen, the chest and the right arm.

With the first shot the onlookers fled to the street, Comisky said. Policeman Soden followed.

A policeman, who had been standing a block away, ran into the barroom and found McGuiness dying on the floor. Asked who had shot him, McGuiness refused to reply. He was taken to St. Vincent's Hospital, where Captain Fay and several detectives questioned him. He persisted in his refusal to answer questions, and the only information he gave was his name and his address—328 West Seventeenth Street.

McGuiness was in the hospital about three hours when Detective Sergeant William Quinn again pressed him to tell who shot him. McGuiness, the detective said, impatiently turned his head aside and mumbled the name of a cabaret singer who knew nothing about the shooting.

Witness Tells of Shooting.

In the meantime detectives had arrested Comisky as a material witness. Comisky told Captain Fay that Soden had fired the shots, and the Captain, accompanied by several detectives, went to the policeman's home, where they found him seated with his wife and two children. They asked him if he was in the Ninth Avenue saloon at the time of the shooting, and they told Mr. Dineen he refused to make a statement. Captain Fay then examined the policeman's pistol. It was fully loaded, but had been cleaned recently.

Soden was arrested and taken to the hospital in the hope that McGuiness might be able to identify him, but a few minutes before their arrival McGuiness died. Soden then was taken to the West Thirtieth Street Station, where the policeman said he was scheduled to go on duty at the Glendale Station at midnight—two hours before—but had reported sick to the Lieutenant at the station over the telephone.

A police surgeon was summoned to learn whether Soden was drunk and told Captain Fay the policeman was "fit for duty."

Meanwhile Mr. Dineen had endeavored to get a statement from the prisoner, who refused to speak until he had conferred with his lawyer, James J. Mayer of 119 West Tenth Street.

Soden was locked in a cell at the station until 8 A. M., when he was taken to the Detective Bureau in Police Headquarters and finger printed. The police "line-up" of criminals was going on, but the prisoner was not shown to the assembled detectives.

After Soden was arraigned, Mr. Dineen reported the shooting to District Attorney Banton. He said Michael O'Brien, bartender in the saloon, told him Soden,

Continued on Page Nineteen.

World Is Misled by Premature Report of Death; Berlin Started Rumor, Cardinal's Aid Spread It

LONDON, Jan. 22.—All London went to bed last night in the belief that the Pope had died in the afternoon. The report appears to have been circulated throughout Europe and was accepted by church and civil officials as true. The German Reichstag suspended proceedings, while President Loebe delivered a eulogy on the Pope.

All the London evening papers published extra editions, announcing the death of the Pontiff, and the first editions of the Sunday papers, sent to the Provinces, contained that report.

The report of the Pope's death here emanated from Cardinal Bourne's residence. A member of the Cardinal's staff notified all the English press agencies before 6 P. M. that the Cardinal had received official news of the Pope's death, and confirmed this to all who made special inquiries. Bells were tolled at Westminster and the Southwark Catholic Cathedral, and announcement of the death was made from the pulpit of the latter church, followed by a requiem mass.

Late at night the Cardinal's chief secretary informed the news agencies that the information communicated to them, that the Cardinal had received an official report of the Pope's death, was incorrect. It was impossible to obtain an explanation of the mistake.

The first report of the death of the Pope apparently came from Reuter's News Agency. An Associated Press dispatch from London (not timed there but issued in New York at 12:35 P. M.) said:

"A Berlin dispatch to Reuter's this afternoon says word has been received there that Pope Benedict is dead."

At 1:32 P. M. this Associated Press dispatch from Paris was issued here:

"A Berlin dispatch to the Havas Agency quotes the Wolff Bureau as saying Pope Benedict died at 5:15 o'clock this afternoon, Rome time."

The Cardinal Bourne message to which the above London dispatch refers was timed at London at 6:53 P. M. (1:53 P. M. New York time). It read:

"Cardinal Bourne, Archbishop of Westminster, stated this evening he had been officially notified by telegraph from Rome that Pope Benedict was dead.

At 2:10 P. M. this Reuter's dispatch from Rome was issued by the Associated Press here:

"Pope Benedict died late today."

The time when this message was filed at Rome was not given.

A statement issued last night by the Associated Press said:

"Urgent messages, asking for definite information direct from Rome, brought replies from London that the Italian telegraphic system had been in a state of chaos for more than a year and that undoubtedly the wires were overburdened with hundreds of messages regarding the Pope; that morning messages were coming late in the afternoon, and that doubtless official Vatican messages were given precedence over press dispatches."

ADOPT PLAN TO LIST ALL CHINA TREATIES

Conferees Extensively Amend Hughes Resolution, but Principle Remains.

JAPANESE GAIN A POINT

Agreements Made by Nationals Apart From Government Need Not Be Notified.

By EDWIN L. JAMES.
Special to The New York Times.

WASHINGTON, Jan. 21.—The Far Eastern Committee of the Washington conference today adopted the Hughes resolution providing for the public listing of commitments under which rights in China are claimed. On the motion of the Japanese, the original resolution was altered to place on China the task of publishing agreements with the nationals of the powers with relation to other than public utilities.

The Hughes plan, as adopted, is in four parts. The first lays down that the powers other than China shall file all treaties or other formal documents with relation to China, and that all future treaties shall be notified generally sixty days after their making. Part two says that the powers shall file all commitments between their nationals and the Chinese governmental authorities, so far as possible, where they deal with public utilities. The third part obliges China to notify all treaties or other agreements with any outside Governments, or the nationals of any other Government. Part four provides for inviting other powers to adhere to the arrangement.

Most of the treaties with China have been published; however, it is thought that the operation of the listing arrangement will bring some new ones to light.

The provision for filing future treaties exists already in Article 18 of the Covenant of the League.

The Resolution as Adopted.

Here is the text of the Hughes resolution:

The powers represented in this conference, considering it desirable that there should hereafter be full publicity with respect to all matters affecting the political and other international obligations of China and of the several powers in relation to China, are agreed as follows:

1. The several powers other than China will, at their earliest convenience, file with the Secretariat General of the conference for transmission to the participating powers a list of all treaties, conventions, exchange of notes or other international agreements which they may have with China, or with any other power or powers in relation to China, which they deem to be still in force and upon which they may desire to rely. In each case citations will be given to any official or other publication in which an authoritative text of the documents may be found. In any case in which the document may not have been published, a copy of the text (in its original language or languages) will be filed with the Secretariat General of the conference.

Every treaty or other international agreement of the character described which may be concluded hereafter shall be notified by the Governments concerned within sixty days of its conclusion to the powers who are signatories of or adherents to this agreement.

2. The several powers other than China will file with the Secretariat General of the conference at their earliest convenience for transmission to the participating powers a list, as nearly complete as may be possible, of all those contracts between their nationals, of the one part, and the

Continued on Page Twenty.

MEN OF ALL FAITHS EULOGIZE THE POPE

Protestants Unite With Catholics in Praise of His Great Service to Humanity.

HAYES PAYS HIGH TRIBUTE

"Among the Church's Greatest Pontiffs," Says Archbishop—Bishop Manning's Tribute.

Expressions of sympathy and sorrow on learning of the death of Pope Benedict XV. were given yesterday by officials and prominent citizens as well as church dignitaries throughout the city.

An early report of the Pope's death, which proved to be unfounded, stirred church circles and brought forth many eulogies. When the report of his death was confirmed there were many more such expressions. Orders were given for the draping in purple and black of many church edifices, and announcements of masses for today were made.

Archbishop Patrick J. Hayes made the following statement before the end was announced:

"His death would be a loss not only to the church of which he is the supreme shepherd, but also to the entire world that is longing for peace and stability.

"His services during the war were of the highest order—services which he gave to all mankind, irrespective of race, nation or religion. His thought was to serve humanity, and this he did in a spirit of love and justice and conscientious neutrality.

"His ministry and influence are needed now in the restoration of order and the stabilizing of the terrified social forces and powers that are crying out of the depths of men's sorrowing and distressed souls for a better and a juster world.

"Pope Benedict's name will be placed by history among the Church's greatest Pontiffs and the world's truest benefactors."

Mayor Hylan issued this statement:

"The death of Pope Benedict is a severe loss to religion and one that will be universally lamented. He was an eminent ecclesiastic and a Pontiff who sought to create a real brotherhood of man. I feel a keen and deep, personal sorrow in his death, for his utterances have been a never-ending source of inspiration to me. His memory will ever be cherished not only at the altars of his own Church, but in the heart of every man regardless of his creed."

Tributes by Protestant Clergymen.

The Right Rev. William T. Manning, Episcopal Bishop of New York, said:

"The death of his Holiness Pope Benedict XV. is a matter of concern to the whole Christian world. All Christians will feel deep sympathy with the Bishops, clergy and people of the Roman Catholic Church in their great loss."

The Rev. Caleb R. Stetson, Rector of Trinity Episcopal Church, said:

"The whole Christian world is touched by the death of the Pope, for he is at the head of the largest body of Christian people in the world. Benedict XV. has been known throughout his life as a man devoted to the service of his Church, and one whose interest in latter years as Chief Pastor of the Roman Communion has extended to all parts of the world. His interest in this country was marked, and his expressions of sympathy were warm. My sympathy

Continued on Page Four.

END AT 6 A. M., ROME TIME

Hope Was Given Up Early Yesterday After Two Sinking Spells

BUT HIS STRENGTH REVIVED

Clear-Minded Most of the Time and Full of Affection for Those Around Him.

CROWDS AROUND VATICAN

Messages From the Great of Many Lands Are Received by Gasparri.

ROME, Sunday, Jan. 22 (Associated Press).—Pope Benedict XV. died at 6 o'clock this morning (midnight, New York time).

The end had been expected for several hours. The attending physicians, Cardinal Gasparri and other members of the Pope's household were present at the bedside.

From midnight all hope had been abandoned, and at 2 o'clock Dr. Battistini announced that the Pope could not live longer than four hours at the maximum.

At 3 o'clock this morning Dr. Cherubini, Cardinal Giogri and the Pope's nephew were gathered around the bedside, the end seemingly being near.

The Pope appeared then to be in considerable distress. His extremities were already becoming cold.

At one lucid period late at night the Pope was able to partake of nourishment. He then instructed the major domo to wake him in time for mass, to be celebrated at 5:30 in the morning in his chapel adjoining the bedroom.

Great Power of Resistance.

There had been moments during Saturday when it was feared the end had come, but stimulants revived the Pontiff, and his natural powers of resistance carried him through the turning point temporarily. The Holy Father seemed to cling to life, as did Pope Pius X. in 1914, when the final outcome was in doubt for many hours.

Dr. Battistini, the chief attending physician, visited the patient several times during the night. Each time he said that any minute might see the conclusion of the long hours of suffering through which Benedict XV. had passed in his fight for life.

The last announcement of the evening to the diplomatic representatives, waiting in the antechamber, was made by Cardinal Gasparri, the Papal Secretary of State, who said:

"A catastrophe is imminent. The Holy Father is getting worse and worse. We must be prepared for the inevitable."

The Cardinal's face was downcast and sad. He spoke in quiet tones, with deep emotion, making gestures with his hands.

After the publication of the latest bulletin, Cardinal Giorgi, Mgr. Migone, Father Basil and Dr. Battistini, remained by the bedside. After a time the doctor told his Holiness that they were praying for the peace of the world, to which the Pope replied:

"I would willingly offer my life for the peace of the world." He then turned on his side and lay watching those near him.

Hope Revived, Only to Fade.

Yesterday was a day of great uncertainty and deep anxiety among those who watched and prayed at the Vatican. Virtually all hope of the Pope's recovery was abandoned, even in the early hours of yesterday morning, and as the hours passed the wonder grew at the recuperative powers of the Holy Father, which enabled him to pass from one sinking spell and another to periods of comparative restfulness and strength. It was this changing condition that inspired hope at one moment and gave rise to rumors of death at another.

It was thought that if the Pope passed safely through Friday night he would

"All the News That's Fit to Print."

The New York Times.

THE WEATHER
Rain today, rising temperature; Thursday rain; east to south winds.
Temperature yesterday—Max., 48, min., 34.
For weather report see next to last page.

VOL. LXXI....No. 23,405. NEW YORK, WEDNESDAY, FEBRUARY 22, 1922. TWO CENTS In Greater New York | THREE CENTS Within 200 Miles | FOUR CENTS Elsewhere

GIANT ARMY DIRIGIBLE WRECKED; 34 DEAD, 11 ARE SAVED; VICTIMS PERISH WHEN ROMA BURSTS INTO FLAMES AFTER FALL; COLLAPSE OF RUDDER CAUSES TRAGEDY ON SHORT TRIAL FLIGHT

THE DIRIGIBLE ROMA, 410 FEET LONG, BUILT BY ITALY FOR THE UNITED STATES, BURNED AT NORFOLK YESTERDAY.

FOUR-POWER TREATY WILL BE REPORTED WITH RESERVATION

Brandegee's Modification of the Compact Favored by Senate Committee.

HARDING AND LODGE AGREE

Legal or Moral Obligation to Defend Rights of Other Nations in Pacific Excluded.

MAY BE REPORTED TODAY

Committee Will Choose Between Brandegee's Reservation and a Milder Substitute by Pomerene.

Special to The New York Times.

WASHINGTON, Feb. 21.—The Four-Power Treaty, with a reservation which will stipulate that the United States assumes no "legal or moral" obligation to maintain the rights of other nations signatory to the compact, and that any adjustment or agreement, arrived at under the provisions of Articles I. or II., shall not be binding on this Government unless approved by Congress, will probably be reported out of the Committee on Foreign Relations in the next few days.

It is possible, members of the Committee said tonight, that the treaty may be in the Senate before adjournment tomorrow afternoon.

The reservation, which, it is said, Senator Lodge has accepted, and which the President has agreed to interpose no objections to, if by so doing the situation will be, as one member of the committee expressed it, "eased up," was introduced in committee by Senator Brandegee of Connecticut, one of the original League of Nations "irreconcilables." The reservation has not been approved by the committee, although it is understood that it, or some other reservation along similar lines, will command probably twelve of the sixteen votes in the committee.

The Brandegee resolution, as submitted to the Committee today, reads:

The Senate advises and consents, subject to the following reservation which is to be made a part of the Instrument of Ratification, to wit:

The United States understands that it assumes no obligation, either legal or moral, to maintain the rights, in relation to the insular possessions or insular dominions, of any of the other high contracting parties and that the consent of the Congress of the United States shall be necessary to any adjustment or understanding under Articles I. or II. by which the United States is to be bound in any way and that there is no obligation either legal or moral to give such consent.

Pomerene Substitute Favored.

The Brandegee reservation would probably have been approved today had not Senator Pomerene, one of the Democratic members, offered a substitute which is intended to "soften" the language of the reservation drafted by the Senator from Connecticut. The Pomerene suggestion was favorably received by several of the members, and it is possible that it may be the reservation which the committee will report to the Senate.

The Pomerene reservation, which will be offered in committee tomorrow morning, is very short, and has nothing in it about "legal or moral" obligations, although in the opinion of some Senators it is just as sweeping as the Brandegee draft, in that Congress receives the right to veto any agreement or adjustment that may be reached by the representatives of the signatory nations.

The Pomerene substitute reads:

It is understood, however, that the adjustment provided for under Article I. and the understanding contemplated under Article II. shall be subject to the consent of the Congress of the United States.

According to reliable information emanating from the Committee on Foreign Relations, the following Senators will vote for a reservation along the lines indicated in the Brandegee and Pomerene drafts: Lodge, Borah, Brandegee, Johnson, Moses, McCormick and Wadsworth of the majority, and Hitchcock, Swanson, Pomerene, Pittman and Shields of the minority membership. Senators McCumber, New and Kellogg, Republicans, and Williams, Democrat, are understood to oppose reservations of any kind.

Senator Pomerene agrees with the President's interpretation of the Four-Power Treaty and does not think a reservation necessary, but, realizing that a reservation appears cetain of adoption, is attempting to ender the reservation, if possible, less objectionable.

The Brandegee reservation has been submitted to President Harding. The President is said to have informed the Senators who conferred with him on the matter that while he is of the opinion that the treaty should be ratified without reservation of any kind, he will

Continued on Page Four.

MELLON BACKS UP HARDING ON BONUS

Again Warns Ways and Means Committee That Treasury Cannot Stand the Outlay.

SALES TAX ONLY SOLUTION

Senator Calder Announces in Speech Here He Will Refuse to Vote for Bonus.

Special to The New York Times.

WASHINGTON, Feb. 21.—Secretary Mellon, appearing before the Ways and Means subcommittee considering bonus legislation today, reiterated his opposition to such legislation because of the condition of the Treasury. He agreed with the President, however, that, if bonus legislation were to be passed, the only way to raise the revenue without embarrassing the Government and injuring business was through a sales tax.

Mr. Mellon was asked to appear before the committee to discuss the advantages and disadvantages of different forms of a sales tax. The conference was held in executive session. He said that he was as much opposed to a bill without any provision for revenue as he was against a measure which found the money by the eight-point taxation scheme recently advanced by the committee or by Treasury certificates.

Experts of the Treasury who were with Mr. Mellon said that a final retail tax would be objectionable in that it would be hard to collect and would be obnoxious to the consumer. They urged that if a sales tax were adopted it be placed upon manufactured articles or on the jobber.

2 to 4 Per cent. Tax Favored.

The proposal which seemed to meet with the most favor of the committee was that placing a 2 to 4 per cent. upon specific commodities sold by manufacturers or jobbers. All iron and steel manufactured products would have a fixed tax, and so the tax would be imposed all along the line. In some instances it would be 2 per cent., and the maximum would not exceed 4 per cent.

Under such a plan, taxes would not be imposed on food products and some articles of every-day household consumption. This tax, it is estimated, would raise $500,000,000 annually.

The manufacturers' tax of 1 per cent. advocated by Senator Smoot did not appear to have much support in the committee. This tax, Treasury experts estimated, would yield $250,000,000 annually.

The subcommittee is not seriously considering any form of taxation other than a sales tax. The hearings have not progressed far enough to indicate just what form the sales tax will take, but it can be said upon authority that the committee intends to report a bonus bill carrying a sales tax provision.

Opposition to a sales tax is increasing so rapidly as to make it doubtful whether sufficient votes can be obtained in the Rules Committe for a special rule in

Continued on Page Nine.

Lloyd George Going to Paris For Conference With Poincare

Copyright, 1922, by The New York Times Co.
Special Cable to THE NEW YORK TIMES.

LONDON, Feb. 21.—There is good authority for stating that Premier Lloyd George intends to go to Paris on Saturday to confer with Premier Poincaré on various matters affecting the relations between France and Great Britain in particular the question of the Genoa conference.

SINN FEIN BLOCKS SPLIT OF LEADERS

Insistence of Delegates Forces de Valera and Griffith to Seek a Compromise.

NO VOTE ON THE TREATY

Parish Priests Take the Lead in Demanding Long Delay Before Elections Are Held.

Copyright, 1922, by The New York Times Company.
Special Cable to THE NEW YORK TIMES.

DUBLIN, Feb. 21.—For the first time since their historic duel in the Dail Arthur Griffith and Eamon de Valera met on a public platform in the Mansion House today. In a sense they were there to renew the conflict, but on this occasion the issue was as to which side should capture the organization of Sinn Fein in view of the imminent election on the treaty. Nearly 3,000 delegates from all parts of the country were present to take part in the struggle. It was a remarkable gathering of gray-bearded and young men in the green uniform of the Volunteers and others who limped in on crutches, casualities of the late war, with a sprinkling of parish priests and not a few women, some of them in mourning.

After the dispute had been stated again by de Valera and Griffith, by degrees the feeling to preserve the organization of Sinn Fein against the threatened split became apparent and a parish priest raised a storm of cheers by suggesting that both de Valera's resolution to stand by the Republic and Griffith's amendment, which would recognize the Free State, should be canceled. Another priest urged that the pro-treaty and anti-treaty parties should establish their own electoral machinery and leave the Sinn Fein organization as a weapon to enforce the strict adherence of the British Government to the spirit and letter of the treaty in the framing of the Irish Constitution.

The convention was finally adjourned until tomorrow morning to give the leaders of the opposing forces an opportunity of conferring with a view to evolving a basis whereby the convention could be adjourned for a period without division.

De Valera took the chair nearly half an hour late. Wearing a heavy brown frieze overcoat, he stroke through the nall, which thousands of cigarettes and pipes were already rendering dim and

Continued on Page Three.

Hughes, Mellon, Hoover, Smoot, Burton, Named on Foreign Debt Commission

Special to The New York Times.

WASHINGTON, Feb. 21.—Nominations for the Foreign Debt Funding Commission were sent by President Harding to the Senate today.

In addition to Secretary Mellon, whose appointment was expressly stipulated by the Funding bill signed by the President last week, the nominees are Secretary Hughes, Secretary Hoover, Senator Reed Smoot of Utah and Representative Theodore Burton of Ohio.

Upon this commission will rest the duty of working out satisfactory arrangements for funding foreign debts amounting to more than $11,000,000,000. Initial steps in the negotiations will be taken through diplomatic channels, it was indicated at the White House, and it is expected that Secretary Hughes will undertake these soon after returning from his Bermuda vacation the first of March.

Although there is the possibility that one or more members of the commission may be sent to Europe, it was said by Administration officials today that virtually all of the negotiations will be attempted through diplomatic channels in Washington. It has been stated at the Treasury Department that the funding operations will be taken up with each country in order of the size of their loans from this country. This would place the British negotiations first, followed by the French, Italian and Belgian.

List of the Dead and Survivors In the Wreck of the Big Dirigible

THE DEAD.

Major JOHN G. THORNELL, Air Service; Langley Field.
Major WALTER W. VAUTSMEIER, Coast Artillery Corps; assigned to Air Service; Rockwell Field, Cal.
Captain DALE MABRY, Air Service; Langley Field.
Captain GEORGE D. WATTS, infantry; assigned to Air Service; Ross Field, Cal.
Captain ALLEN P. McFARLAND, Air Service; McCook Field, Ohio.
Captain FREDERICK R. DURRSCHMIDT.
Lieutenant JOHN R. HALL.
Lieutenant WALLACE C. BURNS.
Lieutenant WILLIAM E. RILEY.
Lieutenant CLIFFORD E. SMYTHE.
Lieutenant WALLACE C. CUMMINGS.
Lieutenant AMBROSE V. CLINTON.
Lieutenant HAROLD K. HINE.
Master Sergeant ROGER B. McNALLY.
Master Sergeant MURRAY.
Sergeant LEE M. HARRIS.
Sergeant LEWIS HILLIARD.
Sergeant MYRON G. FIELD.
Sergeant THOMAS YARBOROUGH.
Sergeant BILLY RYAN.
Sergeant VIRGIL C. HOFFMAN.
Sergeant SHUMAKER.
Sergeant HOLMES.
Master Sergeant HOMER GARBY.
Sergeant HEVERON.
Private KINSTON.
Private THOMAS M. BLAKELEY.
Private THOMPSON.
Private MARION HILL.
Civilian STRYKER.
Civilian HANSON.
Civilian O'LAUGHLIN.
Civilian MERRIMAN.
Civilian SCHULENBERGER.

THE SURVIVORS.

Major JOHN D. REARDON, wife, Mrs. Reardon, 300 Elm Street, Washington, D. C.
Captain WALTER J. REED; father, William J. Reed, Scarsdale, N. Y.
Lieutenant CLARENCE H. WELCH; father, W. V. Welch, Papillon, Neb.
Lieutenant BYRON T. BURT Jr.
Sergeant VIRDON T. PEEK; father, Howard Peek, 2,304 Lafayette Avenue, Terre Haute, Ind.
Sergeant HARRY A. CHAPMAN; mother, Mrs. J. H. Ward, 1,626 Frederick Avenue, St. Joseph, Mo.
Sergeant JOSEPH M. BIEDENBACH; father, John Biedenbach, 411 East Market Street, Akron, Ohio.
Corporal ALBERT FLORES.
Civilian WALTER A. McNAIR, Bureau of Standards, Washington, D. C.
Civilian CHARLES DWORACK, McCook Field, Ohio.
Civilian RAY HURLEY, National Advisory Committee on Aeronautics.

STRIKERS SHOT DOWN IN PAWTUCKET RIOT

Police Fire on Mob Fighting to Bar Textile Workers From Mills.

ONE KILLED, SEVEN INJURED

Troops Rushed From Providence Now on Guard—Other Strike Centres Quiet.

PROVIDENCE, R. I., Feb. 21.—A fatal early-morning riot in Pawtucket, the establishment of National Guard units in three troublesome strike centres and a meeting of the State Board of Mediation and Conciliation here were the day's outstanding developments in the textile situation in Rhode Island.

The Pawtucket riot in which one strike sympathizer was killed, two critically wounded and five less seriously hurt by riot gun fire when a crowd came to grips with the police at the Jenckes Spinning Company plant, led to the immediate dispatch of four coast artillery companies to the Blackstone Valley city from Providence. The Woonsocket and East Greenwich companies were under mobilization orders tonight. Their ultimate destination is believed to be Pawtucket.

With the exception of the disturbance at Pawtucket, quiet prevailed throughout the Blackstone and Pawtuxet Valleys today. At Pontiac and Natick, where trouble was experienced yesterday, two troops of cavalry and a coast artillery company were in complete control.

When the troops arrived at Pawtucket they found only guard duty awaiting them, as the strike sympathizers quieted down immediately after their encounter with the police.

Tonight soldiers guarded the Jenckes mills, the plant of the J. & P. Coates Company and the Tamarack mill as a precaution against possible disorders tomorrow. The mills expect to operate on the holiday.

The Board of Mediation and Conciliation, appointed to hear both sides of the strike controversy with a view to arriving at a settlement, declined to make public its progress today. A statement issued after the meeting said:

"In view of the occurrences today in the mill sections of Rhode Island, the board of mediation feels that it should

Continued on Page Ten.

BOTH HOUSES PASS PORT PROJECT BILL

Democrats Fail in Effort to Have Hylan Appoint Two Commissioners.

MILLER WILL APPROVE

Senator Straus Breaks Away From Party, Calling Plan Essential to Cheap Food Supply.

Special to The New York Times.

ALBANY, Feb 21.—Defeating all amendments offered by the opposition, the Senate and Assembly after long debate today, passed Governor Miller's Port Authority bill by very large majorities. The vote in the Senate was 37 to 11 and in the Assembly 97 to 47.

Only one Republican Senator, Smith of Richmond, voted against the bill. One Democratic Senator, Nathan Straus Jr. of New York, and four Democratic Assemblymen voted with the Republicans in support of the measure. The four Democratic Assemblymen were G. T. Cross of Sullivan, Samuel I. Roseman of New York County, Wallace H. Sidney of Schoharie and Frank J Taylor of Kings County.

Both in the Senate and Assembly an effort was made by the leaders of the Democratic minority, Senator Walker and Assemblyman Donohue, to have the bill providing for appointment by the Board of Estimate of two members out of the three on the Port Authority Commission from this State taken from the Finance Committee in the upper house and the Committee on Ways and Means in the lower house for debate and final disposition in the open. In both houses the motion was voted down, in the Senate by a vote of 34 to 14 and in the Assembly by a vote of 89 to 52.

In the upper house Senator Smith of Richmond offered a series of amendments substituting lines leading over Staten Island for the proposed Greenville-Bay Ridge tunnel, which under the Port Authority plan are provided for as the principal connecting link between the New Jersey terminals and the Long Island side of the harbor. These were defeated, also, by a vote of 34 to 14.

The bill now goes to Governor Miller,

Continued on Page Eight.

Survivor Says Roma Often Sailed With a Tilt

NORFOLK, Va., Feb. 21.—One of the survivors of today's disaster said that the Roma often sailed with a slight tilt, and that he paid little attention to the initial lift of the tail of the ship until he heard a man yell that the craft refused to respond to the helm. Then came the crash.

WASHINGTON WAITS FOR A FULL REPORT

General Patrick Flies to Scene to Take Charge of Army Investigation.

AIR MEN NOT DISCOURAGED

Effect of the Disaster on the Future of Military Aviation Is Doubtful.

Special to The New York Times.

WASHINGTON, Feb. 21.—According to information reaching the War Department today from Langley Field, Virginia, the home station of the dirigible Roma, something went wrong with the box-kite elevating planes at the stern of the giant airship, which are used for vertical control, the pilots in charge were unable to keep the nose of the dirigible in the air and it plunged into a high-voltage electric cable, which ignited the hydrogen inside the great gas bag simultaneously with the collapse of the craft.

The capacity of the Roma is 1,100,000 cubic feet and the flames from the ignition of its great cargo of gas not only rendered it impossible for the oficers and other passengers, pinned within the wreckage, to escape, but made it difficult to identify the bodies of those taken later from the wreckage.

The Roma left Langley Field base at 1:30 o'clock this afternoon for its initial test flight with newly installed Liberty motors. The big airship had manoeuvred over Hampton Roads and was approaching the Hampton Roads Naval Base, when something went wrong with the vertical steering planes. It was impossible, according to the stories of survivors, to keep the nose of the Roma in the air. The Roma kept heading downward, its nose struck the charged land cable carrying 2,300 volts of electricity, the craft collapsed and was destroyed by the explosion and fire that followed.

The accident occurred at 2:19 o'clock. There were forty-five passengers on board, according to information given headquarters of the Army Air Service in Washington tonight by officers making verbal report by long distance telephone from headquarters at Langley Field. This preliminary oral report stated that there were eleven survivors, that thirty-four were missing—all regarded as having lost their lives—that the injured had been taken to the hospital of the Public Health Service, near Norfolk, and that all the bodies had not been recovered. This report stated that the only body recovered that had been identified up to 8 o'clock tonight was that of First Lieut. William E. Riley, whose wife, Minnie H. Riley, lives at 526 East Eighty-sixth Street, New York City. Lieutenant Riley died at the hospital to which he was taken. The other bodies recovered were so badly burned that they were unrecognizable.

Officials were informed that the Roma, at the time of the accident, was under command of Captain Dale Mabry of the Army Air Service, who lost his life along with most of the members of his crew.

A phone message to Air Service officers in Washington tonight from an officer at Langley Field stated that Lieutenant Byron T. Burt Jr., Ray Hurley of the National Advisory Committee of Aeronautics, and Sergeant Virden T. Peek of the Air Service, who were fortu-

Continued on Page Two.

INJURED SURVIVORS TELL OF DISASTER

Officers Coolly Remained at Their Posts of Duty Until the Roma Struck.

EXPLOSION FOLLOWED FALL

Flames, Eating Fabric, Opened a Way for Some Imprisoned Men to Escape.

Special to The New York Times.

NORFOLK, Va., Feb. 21.—Lying on cots in the United States Public Health Service Hospital, where they were taken after the Roma disaster, some of the eleven survivors tonight told of their experiences in the collapse and destruction of the giant dirigible.

Several of the survivors appeared more dead than alive. Some were swathed in bandages, some had their faces smeared with cream to relieve them of intense suffering, while others lay asleep or unconscious. Even those who were able to talk were suffering from shock.

Major J. D. Reardon, who was in the control cabin at the time of the accident, said that the work of the officers in charge was admirable.

"Lieutenant Burt and Captain Mabry were at the wheels," the Major said. "The machine gave a duck, and I saw Lieutenant Burt pull with all his might on the elevation lever. He yelled out, 'She won't respond,' and then, 'Cut the motors.' One by one I heard the motors shut off, and then we hit. If the motors had not been shut off we would have hit the ground much harder."

When asked if he had seen any flame, Major Reardon said that he had not.

Corporal Albert Flores was in the observer's pit on top of the bag.

"I felt the ship tilt up from the back," he said, "and start to slide down. I tried to go down inside, but then I decided to come out forward again. By that time we hit the ground and I was thrown out on the ground."

Flores was burned on the hands and is suffering from shock.

Engineer Was Pinned Down.

Joseph N. Biedenbeck, engineer, was burned on the face and hands. In speaking of the accident, he said:

"I did not see any fire. The ship just tilted up and started to nose dive. It took about twenty seconds for us to hit the ground, and an explosion followed. I was pinned down so that I could not get out. The fabric was burning above me and the girders were all around where I was.

"I waited for the fabric to burn through so that I could get out. All the time I was afraid that the big gas bag behind us would explode. As it happened, the fire reached the fabric before the big explosion. If it had been the reverse, I could not have gotten out alive.

"I saw one man try to jump. I don't know who he was or even if he succeeded in making a safe landing. We hit right after that. We were too low for anybody to make a safe jump."

Biedenbeck also spoke of the gallant way in which the officers stood at their posts. Until the instant of the crash the officers were at the wheels.

The survivors showed a peculiar curiosity to know what the wreck looked like. As it was described by others they listened with intense interest, asking questions about the debris.

"What became of the other boys? Did they get out?" one asked.

When one of them was told that the few in the hospital were the only survivors, he gasped, and exclaimed, "Awful."

Vernon Peake, another survivor, said that the Roma was behaving beautifully, until she had trouble with her rudder, but nobody on board thought there was any danger.

"We knew we were dropping," he said, "and we thought a soft spot was being picked out for us to land on. It was not until Lieutenant Burt shouted that the elevation lever would not work,

Continued on Page Two.

HITS HIGH TENSION WIRES

Hydrogen Ignites in Norfolk Flight and Flames Sweep Huge Structure.

FEW SAVED BY LEAPING

One Lieutenant Breaks Neck in Jump—Other Victims Buried in Wreckage.

SAFE HELIUM GAS REMOVED

Rescuers Baffled by Intense Heat—Commander Mabry Stuck to Wheel Till Death Came.

Special to The New York Times.

NORFOLK, Va., Feb. 21.—In the greatest disaster that ever befell American military aeronautics, thirty-four men died this afternoon when the army dirigible airship Roma plunged a thousand feet and crashed to earth in flames near the Hampton Roads army base. Only eleven of the forty-five men aloft with her were saved, and some of them were terribly hurt. Three were slightly injured.

The breaking of the rudder with its vertical controls, affixed in box-kite fashion to the stern, is believed to have been the original cause of the disaster. Its more horrible phase came just as the stricken craft plummeted into the earth. The metal clad nose struck high-tension electric power wires, and with a flash and a roar the dirigible was fired from stem to stern.

Only those whose fortunate positions in the car enabled them to take the desperate hazard of a leap before the flames ran with lightning speed through the gas bag, more than two New York City blocks long, had much chance for their lives. The thirty-three who couldn't jump died. An officer broke his neck in a dive to earth and was dead before he could be got to a hospital.

Captain Dale Mabry, commandant of the Roma and principal pilot, died with his hands on the wheel. He stuck to his post to the last. The clothes were found burned from his body and the flesh from his fingers, but the fingers still grasped the wheel of the aircraft.

Many Officers Among Dead.

The crushed, misshapen mass that thudded onto the field was a funeral pyre of such intense heat that the agonies of those who were not killed in the crash must have been mercifully brief. The bodies were burned beyond recognition and the slow work of listing the victims was carried out partly by a process of elimination and partly through noncombustible objects that the aviators had carried in their pockets. That list when it was completed showed that two Majors, four Captains and seven lieutenants were among the lost.

Horrified watchers, some of them veterans of gallant affairs abroad, rushed toward the blazing wreckage. Blistering heat halted them in their tracks. Some had associates among the ill-fated crew, others were actuated by all the traditional daring of the service—but those walls of heat were beyond human penetration. Not until three fire departments, mobilized at breakneck speed, had exhausted their chemicals and the twisted aluminum metal work was losing its red glow could any one approach. Then there remained only the gruesome job of extricating charred bodies.

The fire burned in the wreckage nearly five hours and it was not until 7 o'clock that it was entirely extinguished and the service men could penetrate far enough to take out all the bodies. The work of examining the débris was completed shortly after 9 o'clock tonight, with the total number of dead officially placed at thirty-four.

Things might have been different had the Roma's gas bag, with its cubical capacity of 1,100,000 feet, not been filled with hydrogen. Non-inflammable helium was the levitating gas used when the Roma, which was bought from the Italian Government, went on her first trial flight here last December. But it had been planned to send the ship—the largest semi-rigid airship in the world—on a Spring cruise over the country to demonstrate her fitness to cross the Atlantic. In her bag had been the whole available supply of helium in the United States. Flying officials wanted that for the Spring journey, so they pumped it into tanks and substituted hydrogen.

Trip to Test Liberty Motors.

The occasion for today's flight that was to prove so tremendous a blow to lighter-than-air flying was a desire to test the Liberty motors which had been installed to replace the Italian motors, which functioned poorly in the cold that marked the brief trial flight last December.

In charge of Captain Dale Mabry, with a full complement of officers and men and a few civilian guests, the huge craft went aloft from Langley Field at 1:30 o'clock in the afternoon. It was just forty-nine minutes later that she lay in ruins, with most of those who had gone up in gay holiday mood dead in the wreckage.

The whole story was compressed into the last minute or so. In that time

"All the News That's Fit to Print."

The New York Times.

THE WEATHER
Rain today; Sunday fair; strong northwest winds.
Temperature yesterday—Max., 43; min., 36.
For weather report see next to last page

VOL. LXXI....No. 23,422. ••• NEW YORK, SATURDAY, MARCH 11, 1922. TWO CENTS In Greater New York | THREE CENTS Within 200 Miles | FOUR CENTS Elsewhere

GANDHI ARRESTED ON CHARGE OF SEDITION; LONDON REPORTS INDIA QUIET THUS FAR; LORD DERBY TO TAKE MONTAGU'S PLACE

WILL DROP ELEVATED OR ACCEPT RECEIVER, INTERBORO DECIDES

New Contract Freeing Subway of $7,600,000 Annual Rent the Alternative.

OWNERS PLAN COURT FIGHT

Interborough Also Wants $30,000,000 for Third Tracks and the New Power Houses.

TO OPPOSE BETTER SERVICE

Ready to Quit if Transit Board Compels Improvements Which Eat Up Present Savings.

The Interborough Rapid Transit Company has refused to make any further payments due on its lease of the elevated lines owned by the Manhattan Railway Company. It has asked the latter company to make a new agreement which would shift from the Interborough payments of $7,600,000 a year, save it from the responsibility of the deficits on the elevated system, and yield in return annual interest payments on betterments aggregating between $1,000,000 and $2,000,000 a year.

In this way the Interborough has answered the question, frequently asked, as to what adjustment could be made in the matter of the lease so far as it concerned the consolidation plan of the Transit Commission.

The Interborough is prepared to consent to the appointment of a receiver for its property if it fails to obtain relief from the payments to the Manhattan Company or if the Transit Commission insists upon enforcing expected orders directing the company to increase its service to the point of absorbing the savings derived from the present restriction of service.

This new development has been known to the commission for some time and it was suggested that this knowledge was responsible for the amendment to the Public Service Commission law introduced in the Legislature at the instance of the commission. The amendment directly bearing on the situation provides that the commission have power to order that the present service of the elevated lines shall not be disturbed in any way, even if separated from the Interborough system.

Rental a Heavy Burden.

Under the terms of the lease between the two companies the Interborough is pledged to pay the Manhattan Company 7 per cent. on a valuation of $60,000,000 for the use of the elevated, at the rate of $1,050,000 every quarter, and to pay in addition taxes and interest on bonds aggregating $3,400,000 a year. These payments, it has been asserted, are responsible for the financial condition of the Interborough and one of the principal reasons why the company has been compelled to pinch service on its subway system, pass interest payments on securities, and delay payments for necessary material.

The new agreement between the Interborough and Manhattan companies, suggested by the former, provides that the Manhattan Company shall pay the Interborough $30,000,000 for the third tracks and power houses built by the Interborough. The plan also requires the Manhattan Company to pay the interest due on this money, to be adjusted on the basis of interest fixed when it was obtained; to relieve the Interborough from all payments of any kind named in the present lease, and to operate the lines independently of any relationship between the two companies save that ordered by State authorities.

Such a plan would leave the Interborough in possession of the new extensions, valued by the company at approximately $17,000,000. These extensions are considered of small moment in the transit system of the city, for the reason that they run in territory where the traffic is not heavy. They were built with an eye to future growth and in the hope that some day they would yield substantial profits.

All of Extensions Short.

One of these extensions is from 155th Street, the original terminal of the Ninth Avenue line, which is owned by the Manhattan Company, to Jerome Avenue, a distance of about three-quarters of a mile. It joins the Jerome Avenue line, which is part of the subway system. Another extension runs from the station of the Third Avenue line at Fordham Road near 190th Street to Gun Hill Road and thence to White Plains Road, about one mile and three-quarters. The third extension is from the Second Avenue line at Fifty-seventh Street, across Queensboro Bridge to Queensboro Plaza, where it joins rapid transit lines to Astoria and Corona, about one mile and a quarter.

It is the opinion of the Interborough that these extensions can be operated without loss, because of the belief that the railroad law of the State would compel the Transit Commission to fix a fare to cover operating expenses. That the commission, under any amendment of the Public Service Commission law, could compel the company to operate these bits of road at a loss is considered unreasonable by the company's lawyers. Such a situation, it was said, would compel the company to carry passengers free because they had paid a fare to the Manhattan Company, or compel the Manhattan Company to carry free passengers who had paid fares to the Interborough. There would have to be a fare for a ride on the lines of the two companies, it was explained, which would reimburse both, under any plan of adjustment.

These extensions, it was said, would not be operated at a loss, and litigation

Continued on Page Three.

University Course to Make Bellhops and Head Waiters

BOSTON, March 10.—Bellhops and head waiters de luxe are to be turned out by Boston University. Seventy-five men have signed for a six weeks' course for college men who work in Summer hotels during their vacation.

The course, which is to start at the university next week, will show the young men how to become any sort of hotel official. It will be given by the vocational department of the College of Business Administration.

RUM RUNNER KILLS BOOTLEGGER IN BOAT

Man Aboard the Imatra Opens Fire on Motor Craft After Dispute.

WOMAN LEADS GUN FIGHT

Wounds Detective in Fusillade Preceding Capture of $10,000 in Whisky.

An alleged bootlegger was killed in a motor boat off a Brooklyn pier last night in a controversy over several cases of liquor which men of the crew of the tramp steamer Imatra had bargained to sell to five young men who came alongside the vessel in a small power craft. A man charged with the shooting was arrested and two men found in the motor boat were taken into custody. The other two are being searched for by the police.

The dead man was George Rauch, 26, of 154 South Fourth Street, Brooklyn, who was one of the five in the motor boat which was to transport the liquor, which had been smuggled into this country. Charged with shooting him, Albert Fosberg, 32, chief engineer of the steamer Imatra, was locked up at the Butler Street Police Station in Brooklyn.

The four men in the motor boat with Rauch, according to the police, were Samuel Kirnsky, 807 Manner Street, Woodhaven, L. I.; Benjamin Raphael, 482 Henry Street, Manhattan, and his two brothers, Lester and Moe Raphael, 135 Henry Street, Manhattan.

Party Comes for Liquor.

According to the story told to the police by Benjamin Raphael and Kirnsky, the party first visited the steamer in the afternoon, making arrangements to purchase several cases of whisky, which were to be taken off last night. In accordance with this arrangement, the party drew alongside the steamer at 7 o'clock in the 30-foot motor boat Harding. The men first said they didn't get the whisky, but later admitted that they got two cases, for which they said they paid $180.

Fosberg, who is charged with homicide in connection with the death of Rauch, tells a different story. He said the men came aboard the steamer and took off two cases, promising to return to the ship and get additional cases and then pay for the whole. Instead of climbing back aboard the vessel, Fosberg said, the men started the boat's motor and drew away.

At sight of the men getting away with the whisky, Fosberg said, he ran back into his room and got a revolver. He said, according to the police, he fired only one shot at the motor boat. That shot took effect in Rauch's chest, causing his death, the police said.

The motor boat continued on to the foot of Montague Street, half a mile away, and the Poplar Street Police Station was notified. Rauch was taken off the boat and was later pronounced dead by Dr. Thompson of the Long Island Hospital.

After leaving the dead man in charge of Benjamin Raphael and Kirnsky, the two other members of the party sped away in the boat. The police said the prisoners admitted later that the boat carried two cases of whisky, and was to land at East Houston Street. The police in Manhattan were notified to look out for the boat.

Benjamin Raphael and Kirnsky are said to have told the police, after admitting that they had actually got whisky, that they paid the third mate, Brynols Garge, $70, and the first mate, whose name they didn't know, $110.

Fifteen Shots Fired in Raid.

A pistol fight between alleged bootleggers and two detectives in which fifteen shots were fired and at least one person, a detective, was wounded, followed a raid yesterday afternoon on a house at 18 Charlton Street. The house is believed by the police to be the terminus in this city of a gang of rum smugglers operating by automobile between this

Continued on Page Fourteen.

FORD'S 'FREEZE-OUT' OF RAIL PARTNERS BLOCKED BY I. C. C.

Small Stockholders of D., T. & I. Defeat Alleged Scheme to Get Rid of Them.

PREVENT LEASE OF ROAD

Commission Sustains Their Contention That It Is Against Public Interest.

WILL KEEP THEIR SHARES

Proposed Lessee Was a Company Owned Entirely by Members of the Ford Family.

Henry Ford, who urged the railroads of the country to "get rid of the unproductive stockholders," has been blocked by the Interstate Commerce Commission in an alleged attempt to "get rid of" the minority stockholders in the Detroit, Toledo & Ironton Railroad Company, Mr. Ford's interesting railroad adventure.

Notice of the decision against Henry Ford was received yesterday in a registered letter from the Interstate Commerce Commission at Washington by Alexander L. Strouse, of Frank, Weil & Strouse, 187 Madison Avenue, counsel for some of the small stockholders.

Leon Tanenbaum and Benjamin M. Strauss of this city and several others, who charged that Mr. Ford was trying to "freeze them out," remain as active associates, though on a small scale, in the automobile manufacturer's railroad enterprise. These men have refused offers of several times the market value of the stock and have represented themselves as determined to remain business colleagues of Mr. Ford, in spite of the latter's well-known aversion to partners of any nationality and in spite of his newspaper campaign against Jews. The holdings of the minority stockholders are less than 2 per cent. of the total.

Stockholders' Contention.

The minority stockholders in their proceedings before the Interstate Commerce Commission alleged that Ford had tried to destroy their rights in the D., T. & I. by leasing the property to a company owned exclusively by the Ford family. They opposed the lease as being against public interest and being purely a device to deprive the small stockholders of any influence or share of profit in the enterprise. The decision of the Interstate Commerce Commission upholding the minority stockholders against Ford and denying permission to make the lease was rendered on Tuesday of last week.

The proceedings had created widespread interest, especially among small holders of stock in different railroads, because of Ford's denunciation of what he called "unproductive stockholders." He had asserted in interviews that the future of the railroads was imperilled by the necessity of paying large dividends to them. Dividends, according to the automobile man, should go only to the "productive stockholders," who were defined by him as employes of the road, persons active in the management and others who continued to contribute actively to its success.

The lease transferring everything of value from the old company to the new would have left the minority stockholders, according to their contention, holding a 2 per cent. interest in the hollow shell of the old company and no interest at all in the new. They alleged that they were victims of an attempt by Ford to translate his railroad theories into practice.

Mr. Ford's Statements.

During the course of the litigation, interviews and statements by Ford, telling what he would do if the Pennsylvania or New York Central were turned over to him, were held to have an interesting bearing on the legal merits of the case, as showing what was going on in Mr. Ford's mind at the time he sought to engineer the alleged "freeze-out" lease. Mr. Strouse made application for permission to cross-examine Ford.

One of the statements of Mr. Ford, ridiculing arguments as to the necessity of protecting the rights of widows and orphans by safeguarding stock from railroad manipulation, was printed by the United States Chamber of Commerce as an authorized interview. In it Mr. Ford urged the policy of "getting

Continued on Page Three.

Plan to Cut Europe's Armies in Half Submitted to League by Commission

By EDWIN L. JAMES.

By Wireless to THE NEW YORK TIMES.

PARIS, March 10.—A temporary mixed commission of the League of Nations Assembly has transmitted to the Governments which are members of the League a draft plan for European armament limitation modeled on the Washington naval reduction treaty. The members have been asked to notify the commission how the allotments of troops compare with their ideas of their needs for national defense. Of course, the plan, which was drafted in accord with instructions of the last League Assembly, held in September, is only in a formative state. The commission will meet again on July 15 and continue work on a scheme to be presented to the third Assembly of the League, which meets in Geneva in September.

The League commission's plan, which was presented at a recent meeting by Lord Esher, representing England, embraces all European countries except the Central Powers, whose armies are limited by the peace treaties, and Russia. The unit taken is 30,000 men. There would be the following allotment of units: Belgium, 2; Czechoslovakia, 3; Denmark, 2; France, 6; Great Britain, 3; Holland, 3; Norway, 2; Poland, 4; Portugal, 1; Rumania, 3; Sweden, 2; Spain, 3; Switzerland, 2.

This would mean forty-six units, or a total of 1,380,000 soldiers for Europe, which would be a reduction of about 50 per cent. under the present armies.

The League Commission also has under consideration another plan to apply the ratios of the Washington naval treaties to the navies of the league members not parties to the Washington agreement.

The weakest point of the League plan is the absence of Russia from the plan. Russia not being a member of the League, the commission naturally could not lay down the size of her army. It is the intention of the League leaders to try to get Russia into limitation negotiations and some statesmen hope to raise the matter at Genoa.

As the plan stands it will meet the opposition of France. France's probable reply to it will be a demand that the League be given some sort of Federal force to enable it to insure observance of the terms of any such limitation agreement.

The plan was tentatively adopted at a meeting of the commission two weeks ago but was kept secret at the time.

Germans to Clear Buildings Of All Monarchical Insignia

BERLIN, March 10 (Associated Press).—All insignia of monarchical Germany must be removed from public buildings, Minister of the Interior Adolf Koester today told the Reichstag. He added that the Government had decided to fix a definite period within which this decision would be carried out.

Exceptions will be made, he said, only where these emblems have been structurally incorporated in buildings where their removal would destroy the architectural value and effect.

All paintings, busts and statues in Government offices must also be removed if their retention is incompatible with the Republican régime. This order will chiefly apply to portraits of former Emperor William, although Herr Koester said exceptions might be made if their removal destroyed the "artistic and historical unity" of the interior decorations.

JURIES OF CITIZENS TO BAR BAD PLAYS

Conference of Actors, Dramatists, Managers and Vice Crusaders Fixes Details.

TO AVOID POLITICAL CENSOR

Theatrical Contracts to Stipulate That They Must Obey Jury's Findings.

The organization of a voluntary jury system, designed to eliminate indecent plays and thereby make unnecessary a political censorship of the stage, was launched late yesterday afternoon at a meeting of dramatists, managers and producers, actors and vice crusaders at the American Dramatists' Society, 148 West Forty-fifth Street.

An important feature of the proposed jury system is the insertion of a clause in all future contracts between dramatists and producers and between actors and producers that they will abide by the decisions of the jury.

Those attending the meeting were informed that Mayor Hylan's approval of the undertaking had been given in an informal manner. Early next week a committee will endeavor to see the Mayor and obtain his formal approval.

Many Interests Represented.

The details of the jury system were worked out at a meeting representing the Authors League of America, through Jesse Lynch Williams, President; Channing Pollock, Vice President, and Le Roy Scott, Chairman of the Executive Committee; its subsidiary, the American Dramatists, represented by Owen Davis, Eugene Buck and George Creel; the Actors' Equity Association, represented by John Emerson, President; Frank Gillmore, Executive Secretary, and John W. Cope of the Equity's council; the Producing Managers' Association, represented by William A. Brady, Charles Coburn and Winthrop Ames; the Better Public Shows Movement, represented by John S. Sumner, head of the Society for the Prevention of Commercialized Vice; Edward J. McGuire and A. G. Boyle of the Y. M. C. A., Mrs. Herbert J. Glover of the Welfare Board of the Protestant Episcopal Church, Mrs. Marian Tucker and Cranston Brenton and Mrs. Coffin of the Drama League.

"These people believe that a political censorship is impossible without destroying all that is finest in what affects," explained Channing Pollock, spokesman for a committee delegated to give out the facts concerning the meeting after its adjournment. "They believe that the theatre is not in a bad way. However, they agree that there are four or five bad plays and that there is a tendency to produce other plays without which the theatre would be better off."

To Draw a Panel of 300.

Their program contemplates the drawing of a panel of 300 citizens. Nominations are to be submitted by the organizations on the joint committee representing the theatrical organizations on the one side, and the Better Public Shows Movement and the City Administration on the other. Each group will be permitted to nominate 150 candidates for the panel, the qualifications for which will be chiefly "good citizenship and common sense," according to Mr. Pollock.

"If a complaint against a given theatrical production is received by the city officials," said Mr. Pollock, "they may call for a jury of twelve to be selected from the panel above described, as representing the theatre on the one side and the public on the other. Each side will have two peremptory challenges. First, they must decide whether any part of the production is objectionable from the point of view of public morals. Second, is the play as a whole objectionable? A vote of 9 to 3 constitutes a verdict. If the jury decides that a manager must readjust his play, he will have one week in which to make the changes. Then the jury will review the play. If the jury decides that the play as a whole is objectionable, all interests, including the dramatists, owners, producers, actors and the public, agree that the play shall be taken off and that there shall be no appeal to the courts. This agreement is to be included in every contract made by the managers with both dramatists and actors.

"We agree with the public," said Mr. Pollock. "The theatre must be a decent place."

AGUINALDO COMING HERE.

Filipino General Accepts Invitation of Spanish War Veterans.

MANILA, P. I., March 10.—General Emelio Aguinaldo has accepted an invitation to be the guest of the Spanish-American War veterans at their annual convention in Los Angeles next Summer. It will be his first visit to the United States.

General Aguinaldo will be the honorary chairman of the Filipino mission, which is expected to sail for the United States late in April to lay before President Harding claims of the Islanders to independence.

SENATOR STANFIELD, THE 'WOOL KING,' ACCUSED OF FRAUD

Idaho National Bank Charges That He Formed a Company to Defraud His Creditors.

HURT BY DROP IN SHEEP

Had Just Bought 400,000—Attempt to Set Aside His Transfer of Real Estate.

THREATENS LIBEL ACTIONS

But Idaho Commissioner Defies Him and Asks Why He Doesn't Pay Farmers What He Owes.

Special to The New York Times.

PORTLAND, Ore., March 10.—Robert Nelson Stanfield, the "wool king" and United States Senator from Oregon, elected in 1920 over former Senator Chamberlain is in difficulties and is rushing home from Washington to save what he can out of property imperiled by the drop in the prices of wool and sheep.

Prayer that a deed of conveyance of real estate made by Stanfield through the R. N. Stanfield Company be set aside is made in an action filed in the Circuit Court today by the First National Bank of Weiser, Idaho, against Stanfield, the R. N. Stanfield Company and the Columbia Basin Wool Warehouse Company.

Claims for about $75,000 against Stanfield on notes for money loaned him during the last year or two are advanced.

The allegation is contained in the complaint that the R. N. Stanfield Company was formed "to hinder, delay and defraud his creditors." When the deed of conveyance was made out, the complaint sets forth, the Wool Warehouse Company assumed the obligation of payment for a mortgage of $200,000. The plaintiff asks that the value of the warehouse liens on real estate be adjudicated and that the plaintiff's rights be determined.

The complaint states that several large judgments against the defendant have been secured in various courts of Oregon and in Boise, Idaho.

Miles Cannon, Idaho Commissioner of Agriculture, announced today that he would welcome suit against him for criminal libel, threatened by Senator Stanfield. The Capitol News this week printed a special dispatch from Washington to the effect that Senator Stanfield had instructed several sheep companies in Idaho and Oregon to start libel suits against Commissioner Cannon because of a published statement by Cannon that these companies had failed to pay for hay and feed furnished in the Spring of 1921 and that many claims have been filed with his department.

Senator Stanfield also advised the managers of his companies to consult attorneys concerning possible action against Cannon on the ground of criminal libel, the dispatch said. When this dispatch was called to the attention of Commissioner Cannon he said:

"I am prepared to make sensational disclosures if this matter is pushed. I made the reports with regard to the Stanfield companies strictly in accordance with the statutes and the evidence submitted to my office. I have not published half the evidence in my possession and I am not particularly worried over this threatened action for alleged criminal libel."

Section 2,059 of the Revised Idaho Statutes, under which Mr. Cannon is acting, reads:

"The Department of Justice is directed to investigate all cases reported to it where a producer of agriculture or products or live stocks have suffered loss in the marketing of his products or has failed to receive a fair and just reasonable compensation by reason of fraud, injustice, extortion, manipulation or profiteering on the part of others."

On Feb. 11 Commissioner Cannon telegraphed to Senator Stanfield at Washington as follows:

"Please wire me immediately whether there are any legal or moral reasons why your sheep companies operating in the State of Idaho should not pay farmers for hay sold and delivered in the Spring of 1921. Quick answer required."

It is known that Mr. Stanfield's losses of wool and sheep have been enormous. In many cases sheep were bought at $16 and when the bottom dropped out of the market they went down to $8.

The Idaho action came to a head when it was published this week that Stanfield had just made a purchase of 400,000 to 500,000 head of sheep. The Idaho Commissioner believes that if Stanfield had money for such a purchase as this, he had money enough to pay the Idaho farmers for hay sold to the Stanfield Companies last year.

United States Senator Stanfield of Oregon is himself authority for the statement that he is America's largest producer of wool and mutton. Here is his autobiography as supplied to the Congressional Directory:

"Robert Nelson Stanfield, Republican, of Portland, Ore., was born at Umatilla, Umatilla County, Ore., July 9, 1877; educated in the public schools and State normal schools of Oregon; engaged in the live stock industry, being America's largest producer of wool and mutton; also engaged in banking, particularly in the financing of livestock producers; served three terms in the Oregon State Legislature; one term as Speaker of the House of Representatives; married to Ines E. Hill in 1897; one daughter, Miss Barbara Stanfield, who is now 17 years of age; nominated as Republican candidate for the United States Senate over one other opponent; elected United States Senator Nov. 2, 1920, defeating the incumbent opponent by 16,500 votes."

Martial Law After Day of Terror in the Rand; Strikers Kill a Manager and Ten of Police

JOHANNESBURG, Union of South Africa, March 10 (Associated Press).—Bold moves by the striking miners, accompanied by fierce fighting between strikers, commandos and police, made the day one of terror in the Rand. Martial law eventually was proclaimed.

Manager Brodigan of the Brakpan mine, the centre of much of the day's fighting, and two special constables were captured and taken out on the veldt and shot. Seven special constables protecting the mine were killed. The strikers also captured twenty-seven policemen at Newlands, west of Johannesburg, where spirited fighting occurred, threatening to shoot them all if other police came to the rescue.

At Fordsburg one man of a commando, or force of burghers, was killed and thirteen members of the commando and four policemen were wounded. The sound of artillery firing at Fordsburg was audible here.

With the proclamation of martial law and the seizure of the strikers' headquarters, where all documents were confiscated, the populace felt a sense of relief. The Ministers of Justice and Defense have issued a statement denying reports of a contemplated native rising in the Rand. They assert there is no disposition on the part of the natives to give trouble. Meanwhile military units are enrolling with remarkable speed and a citizens' protection league is being formed to run public services.

Firing started at Benoni early this morning. Street fighting followed, both sides suffering casualties. Many pedestrians were hit. For two hours the ground between the market square and the workers' hall was a battle area. Then the police formed with the object of surrounding the hall. There was continuous sniping and three persons fell dead, one of them a policeman.

LONDON, March 10.—Premier Smuts of the Union of South Africa today told the legislative Assembly, which is engaged in a discussion of the struggle in the Rand, that the people were face to face with one of the gravest situations that have yet arisen in the country. The Laborite members and Ministerialists are accusing each other of responsibility for the disturbance.

According to the Reuter correspondent at Johannesburg, Premier Smuts declared the behavior of the Rand natives had been beyond reproach, "but the whites had nothing to be proud of." He said the Government had given instructions that very strong measures must be used to suppress lawlessness.

BIG HOUSING BILL NOW SURE TO PASS

Machold Announces Support of Metropolitan $100,000,000 Building Fund Measure.

LOCKWOOD IS ACCUSED

Absence From Hearing Said to Have Endangered Other Bills—He Denies It.

Special to The New York Times.

ALBANY, March 10.—As the result of developments at the Capitol today the passage in both branches of the Legislature of the Lockwood committee's bill which would enable the Metropolitan Life Insurance Company to devote $100,000,000 of its investable funds to housing relief in New York City seems assured. The prospect is also that both Senate and Assembly will act favorably on five other measures already on the calendar of the Senate which are directly concerned with rents and housing.

The financial part of the Lockwood committee's program, however, has been placed in jeopardy through the conduct of Senator Lockwood himself, which has greatly puzzled his colleagues in the Senate. After serving notice that he would move to discharge the Cities Committee from further consideration of those of his committee's bills not already reported, and after filing with Senator Gibbs, Chairman of the Cities Committee, a petition in which seven other members of that committee joined him, demanding that the bills be reported promptly, Senator Lockwood departed for New York City and was not in attendance when the committee met to take action on his bills.

Under the circumstances no action could be taken. At an earlier stage of the session the loss of time would not necessarily prove fatal. But final adjournment is only a week away and bills reported from committees automatically go on what is known as the general orders calendar in the Senate, where they remain until advanced to third reading. General orders is the last order of business in the Senate and is seldom reached during the closing week of a session. In fact, Senator Lusk announced today, while measures on the general orders calendar were under consideration, that the Senate probably would not return to that order of business again before the session ends next Friday. The general orders calendar in the Senate, during the final days, is the morgue to which undesirable measures are consigned if they have not already been left there.

It will probably be necessary when the bills finally are reported by the Senate Cities Committee for Senator Lockwood to ask that they be immediately advanced to final reading when they can be read and acted on. One solitary objection will prevent this, for bills can be advanced in this fashion only by unanimous consent.

The petition sent to Chairman Gibbs of the Cities Committee read as follows:

"We, the undersigned, members of the Cities Committee, respectfully request that you report promptly for the consideration of the Senate, the bills introduced by the Joint Legislative Committee on Housing.

"Very truly yours,
"CHARLES C. LOCKWOOD.
"SEYMOUR LOWMAN.
"HOMER E. DICK.
"WILLIAM W. CAMPBELL.
"PARTON SWIFT.
"C. ERNEST SMITH.
"JAMES J. WALKER.
"PETER J. McGARRY."

Senators Walker and McGarry were the only Democratic signers.

As a result of the petition, Senator Gibbs called a meeting of his committee, which was held immediately after the Senate had adjourned for the day. Only five members appeared, Senator Lockwood not being among them, and three, Campbell, Dick and Smith, had signed the petition. The others were Senator Gibbs and Senator Fearon.

"The five did not constitute a quorum, so we had no right to take action on

Continued on Page Three.

OUR RHINE CLAIM IS NOT ALLOWED

Finance Ministers Continue the Division of German Payments Among Allied Powers.

BOYDEN ASKS $241,000,000

Question Will Go to Governments Upon Whom Washington Is in a Position to Use Pressure.

By EDWIN L. JAMES.

Special Cable to THE NEW YORK TIMES.

PARIS, March 10.—The Washington Government today asked the Finance Ministers of the allied nations engaged in a conference here for dividing up German payments to the Reparation Commission for a settlement of the claim of $241,000,000 of the American Government for the cost of the American Army of Occupation. The allied Ministers did not comply, but by subsequent action presented a direct refusal to grant the American demand.

The American communication was in the form of a statement by Roland W. Boyden, American member of the Reparation Commission, who is sitting in the allied Finance Ministers' meeting. Although the official communiqué makes no mention of the matter, it is understood Mr. Boyden recalled that the Berlin treaty reserved for America the benefits she would enjoy under the Versailles Treaty; that the Versailles Treaty provided that costs of the armies of occupation was a lien on German payments of prior validity to general reparations; that the Allies having practically paid themselves for their occupation costs, the $241,000,000 due America should be paid before any allotment was made for general reparations.

To grant the American demand the allied Ministers, after having allotted sums to meet the French, English and Belgian army occupation costs, would have to assign funds to meet the American claim. What the Finance Ministers did was to complete the division of the 1921 payments and then provide for the allocation of the 1922 payments by Germany, which action included allocation of funds for other purposes than payment of the armies of occupation. No provision was made for meeting the American demand, nor will any be made before the end of the Ministers' conference tomorrow, it was stated tonight officially.

Say We Should Collect Our Own.

The attitude of the Finance Ministers is in accord with that of their Governments, which is that America, having a separate treaty with Germany, should collect direct from Germany. It is always possible the allied Governments may find delicate reasons for changing this attitude, but as the matter stands at present the Allies do not feel that they should collect for America.

The American action is important because for the first time it raises the issue of the validity of the Berlin treaty, that is, it raises the question whether it is a first mortgage, ranking with the Versailles treaty, or a second mortgage ranking after it. It is true the Berlin treaty, in its text, reserves for America the rights she would have had under the Versailles treaty. But that reserving is done by America and Germany, without the consent of the Allies, who under the Versailles treaty, according to the European interpretation, already held a first mortgage on all German resources.

It was the expectation of the allied nations that following the signing of the Berlin treaty Washington would negotiate with them to establish American rights under the Berlin treaty. This was pointed out in the Paris dispatches of THE NEW YORK TIMES last September, which dispatches brought a statement from Washington that no such negotiations were necessary. Because the allied nations owe America immense sums of money and America can bring pressure

Continued on Page Two.

ARREST IS MADE QUIETLY

Leader Taken Into Custody on Order of Government at Delhi.

NEW PLOTS WERE REVEALED

British Opinion Strongly Urged Seizure of Gandhi, First Ordered Last Month.

LORD DERBY TO TAKE OFFICE

Montagu Speaks Today at Cambridge—Resignation of Viceroy Regarded as Inevitable.

BOMBAY, March 10 (Associated Press).—India's non-co-operationist leader, Mohandas K. Gandhi, has been arrested at Ahmedabad, 310 miles north of Bombay. He is charged with sedition.

Special Cable to THE NEW YORK TIMES.

LONDON, March 10.—The announcement by the India Office late tonight that a telegram had been received stating that Gandhi had been arrested and adding there had been no trouble so far follows upon Delhi reports that the Indian Government had decided upon his arrest for today.

London newspapers have been urging that this step should be taken for weeks, and Montagu's statement in the Commons on Feb. 14 that the official order for Gandhi's arrest actually had been issued the week before and then canceled led to charges, as one paper puts it this morning, of "vacillation, hesitation and lack of consistent steadiness" against the Indian and Home Governments.

Montagu on Feb. 14 told the House of Commons that the Government of India had been informed that if in their judgment Gandhi's arrest became necessary they would receive the whole-hearted support of the Imperial Government.

"Last week the official order for his arrest was actually issued," he said, "but since then there has been a dramatic change in the situation, Gandhi and his colleagues having decided not to pursue the policy of civil disobedience, volunteer processions or other illegal activities."

In view of this development the Government of India was holding its hand.

Publication of the Indian Government's demands and the resignation of Montagu have been followed by further sensational disclosures of widespread activities of Indian seditionists and in view of insistent demands of English newspapers it was felt the Indian Government could not longer delay action against Gandhi.

Special Cable to THE NEW YORK TIMES.

LONDON, March 11.—Several political correspondents this morning mention the prediction made in some quarters yesterday that Lord Reading's resignation would shortly be announced.

In that case the Duke of Devonshire is said to be the likely successor.

LAHORE, India, March 10.—Lajpat Rai, a prominent Indian Nationalist, today was sentenced to two years' imprisonment, one year at hard labor was imposed for violation of the Seditious Meeting act, and the other year for violation of the Criminal Law Amendment act. The sentences are to run consecutively.

He was sentenced last December to six months' detention and a fine of 500 rupees, but about a month later he was released and re-arrested immediately on the charge of violating the Criminal Law Amendment act.

DERBY TO TAKE INDIAN OFFICE.

Announcement of His Appointment Is Expected on Tuesday.

Special Cable to THE NEW YORK TIMES.

LONDON, March 10.—It is understood that the Premier has invited Lord Derby to succeed Mr. Montagu as Secretary of State for India.

The opinion in authoritative circles is that Lord Derby will accept and that announcement of his appointment may be expected on next Tuesday.

Reading's Resignation Expected.

LONDON, March 10 (Associated Press).—It was stated authoritatively tonight that an announcement of the name of the successor of Mr. Montagu had been postponed until Monday or Tuesday. It was added that it was virtually certain the new Secretary would not be Andrew Bonar Law. The eventual resignation of the Earl of Reading as Viceroy of India is still regarded as inevitable.

The India incident has intensified the strong feeling between the Liberal and Conservative wings of the Coalition Ministry. The Liberal newspapers without exception lament that Mr. Montagu allowed himself to be drawn into a "false step." But some of them think the result would have been the same in any case, because had he consulted the Cabinet and the Cabinet had refused to permit publication of the India statement the Secretary still would have resigned as a protest.

While awaiting reports from India as to the effect of Mr. Montagu's resignation, the position of Viceroy Reading is the chief subject of the discussions of the press. Official circles which deal with Indian affairs do not concur in the prevailing opinion that the Viceroy necessarily will follow the Secretary of State for India in quitting the Government. It is stated that the Earl of Reading certainly was in his right as

"All the News That's Fit to Print."

The New York Times.

THE WEATHER
Fair and cold today and Sunday; northwest winds.
Temperature yesterday—Max., 28; min., 12.
For weather report see next to last page.

VOL. LXXII....No. 23,765. NEW YORK, SATURDAY, FEBRUARY 17, 1923. TWO CENTS In Greater New York | THREE CENTS Within 200 Miles | FOUR CENTS Elsewhere

TUT-ANKH-AMEN'S INNER TOMB IS OPENED, REVEALING UNDREAMED OF SPLENDORS, STILL UNTOUCHED AFTER 3,400 YEARS

KING TUT-ANKH-AMEN,
wearing the crown and royal vestments, as he appeared to his contemporaries. From a multi-colored decoration on the walls of the tomb of Huy, his Viceroy, discovered some years ago near the tomb of the King.
Courtesy Metropolitan Museum of Art.

KING IN NEST OF SHRINES

Series of Ornate Covers Enclose Pharaoh's Sarcophagus.

WHOLE FILLS LARGE ROOM

Mortuary Chamber Opens Into Another Room, Crowded With Great Treasure.

EXPLORERS ARE DAZZLED

Wealth of Objects of Historic and Artistic Interest Exceeds All Their Wildest Visions.

The Times (London) World Copyright, by Arrangement with the Earl of Carnarvon.
Copyright, 1923, by The New York Times Company.
Special Cable to THE NEW YORK TIMES.

LUXOR, Egypt, Feb. 16.—This has been, perhaps, the most extraordinary day in the whole history of Egyptian excavation. Whatever any one may have guessed or imagined of the secret of Tut-ankh-Amen's tomb, they surely cannot have dreamed the truth as now revealed.

The entrance today was made into the sealed chamber of the tomb of Tut-ankh-Amen, and yet another door opened beyond that. No eyes have yet seen the King, but to practical certainty we know that he lies there close at hand in all his original state, undisturbed.

Moreover, in addition to the great store of treasures which the tomb has already yielded, today has brought to light a new wealth of objects of artistic, historical, and even intrinsic value which is bewildering.

It is such a hoard as the sanguine excavator can hardly have pictured, even in visions in his sleep, and puts Lord Carnarvon's and Mr. Carter's discovery in a class by itself and above all previous finds.

Official Opening Sunday.

Though the official opening of the sealed mortuary chamber of the tomb has been fixed for Sunday, it was obviously impossible to postpone until then the actual work of breaking in the entrance. This was a job involving some hours of work, because it had to be done with the greatest care, so as to keep intact as many of the seals as possible, and also to avoid injury to any of the objects on the other side which might be caused by the falling of material dislodged.

All this could not be done on Sunday while the official guests were kept waiting in the singularly unpleasant atmosphere of the tomb, so an agreement was made with the Egyptian authorities by which the actual breaking through of the wall should be done in their presence today.

Consequently, Howard Carter was very busy inside the tomb all morning with Professor Breasted and Dr. Alan Gardiner, whose assistance has been invaluable from the beginning of the work of examining seals and deciphering and copying inscriptions of all kinds. They had finished by noon, and the tomb was closed till after luncheon, at which Lord Carnarvon, Mr. Carter and Lady Evelyn Herbert entertained all those invited to be present today.

Official Story of Inner Tomb.

It was after 1 o'clock when the official party entered the tomb, and the operation was begun which was to result in such astounding discoveries, of which I am able to give the following authoritative description:

Today between the hours of 1 and 3 in the afternoon the culminating moment in the discovery of Tut-ankh-Amen's tomb took place when Lord Carnarvon and Howard Carter opened the inner sealed doorway in the presence of Lady Evelyn Herbert, Abdel Hamid Suliman Pasha, Under Secretary of Public Works; Pierre Lacau, Director General of the Antiquities Department; Sir William Garstin, Sir Charles Cust, Mr. Lythgoe, the curator of the Metropolitan Museum of Art of New York; Mr. Winlock, Director of the

---

ESSEN IS COWED AFTER WOUNDING OF TWO SOLDIERS

Fight in Beer Hall Causes the French to Turn Out a Stronger Military Display.

CITY NOW WITHOUT POLICE

Chief Arrested, Men Disarmed and Records Seized—Frequent Clashes Elsewhere.

JAIL FOR 2 BURGOMASTERS

Electric Plant Director Is Fined 5,000,000 Marks—Berlin Supplies Funds for Strikers.

Copyright, 1923, by The New York Times Company.
Special Cable to THE NEW YORK TIMES.

DUESSELDORF, Feb. 16.—Every day is adding more and more to the casualty list of the Ruhr occupation.

Last evening in a beer hall at Essen two French soldiers were slightly, and one German policeman gravely, wounded.

At Gunkenrath a French sentinel fired on and killed a German workman who was trespassing on the railroad track.

At several points last evening sentries and posts fired shots as warnings and with every rifle discharged the tension is growing.

The affair at Essen was the most important as affecting the situation in the town. It began, as trouble may at any time begin, trivially enough. Eight French soldiers and two Belgians went into the beer house and called for drinks about 9:30 in the evening. As usual the landlord refused to serve them and the soldiers, as has become their habit, began to draw beer themselves. In protest the landlord called in the German policeman on duty at the door, and, according to all accounts of both the Germans and the French, this policeman entered excitedly with his revolver in his hand crying "Hands up!"

At once the affair which had been a burlesque became serious. The French soldiers instead of obeying such a peremptory order began to draw their revolvers. Then the German fired. Before he could be overpowered he had wounded two men slightly and it was not till he fell with a bullet through his body that he stopped firing.

Attracted by the noise the German police patrol entered at that moment and prevented further fighting.

Police Headquarters Raided.

Today the affair had an aftermath. With armored cars and machine guns a detachment of French troops rode through the town and wheeled sharply into the police barracks before it was known what was intended. They arrested the chief of police, disarmed eighty men in the station and took possession of all records.

Everywhere throughout town patrols have been moving about all day, and as if in warning to the nationalist trouble makers, the French are displaying their strength.

Yesterday the town was silent, depressed and suspicious. Today it is cowed. The French have the whip hand and even the most ardent nationalist must admit it.

All through the province the measures of the French for repressing organized resistance and propaganda are increasing in severity. Over half the newspapers in the Ruhr have now been suspended for one cause or another, police who do not salute, being arrested in batches, and with every new batch the penalty is being increased.

To all this tightening up the Germans are making as yet no new reply. The telephones of Düsseldorf, Essen and several other places are still suspended.

At Bochum the municipal employes today struck for four hours as a protest against the arrests which have been made in the town and against the requisitioning of automobiles. The only return to work was at Duisburg, where the tramway employes have been granted a 110 per cent. increase in wages at a time when the mark is improving by leaps.

Yesterday for the first time the effect of the export prohibition order became patent. As fewer freight trains are leaving the district fewer are coming in, and from 200 the number out and in has fallen to about 40. If that falling off continues a food shortage, which always threatened, may become a reality, and both the French and Germans are doing their utmost to deal with the situation when it arises, each with the hope that their efforts will rally the masses to their support. The Germans are organizing storage and distribution centres as if for a siege, and at the same time the French are accumulating all the food they can in the district. The number of military trains has been largely increased and food is being brought from France far in excess of what is needed by the troops.

To counter all this effort to obtain local support among the workers the Germans have now nearly completed their arrangements for payment of workers forced out of employment by the prohibition of exports. Big firms are prepared themselves to stand a loss, but to small firms the Government, through the Employers' Association and the Reichsbank, is prepared to give all the help that is needed. The total wages roll which it is estimated will have to be met is something like 30,000,000 gold marks a month, and the Government, which in November last asked for a moratorium in reparation payments, seems now prepared to pay this sum to workmen in order to support resistance to the French. So far there has, however, been little or no closing down, and except at the coalpits where little or nothing is being done except for repairs and local consumption work, the Ruhr seems almost normal.

Quick Retaliation by French.

ESSEN, Feb. 16 (Associated Press).—Following the wounding of two French soldiers by German security police in a café brawl last night, Essen was the

Continued on Page Three.

---

89 M. P.'s Ask Harding's Aid; 'One Hope of Saving Europe'

Copyright, 1923, by The New York Times Co.
By Wireless to THE NEW YORK TIMES.

LONDON, Feb. 16.—Signed by eighty-nine Labor and Co-operative members of the British Parliament, the following cablegram was sent to President Harding today:

"America with Britain unwittingly made France's present destructive action possible. We appeal for American co-operation today as the one hope of saving Europe."

Among those who have signed the message are Arthur Henderson, George Lansbury, R. E. Buxton and John Hodge.

$500,000 GEM THEFT SUSPECT ARRESTED

"Marshall" Held as Leader of Gang That Robbed Mrs. Schoellkopf at Drinking Party.

CAUGHT ON MONTREAL TRAIN

Another Arrest Here Said to Have Furnished Clue—Companion Also in Custody.

Inspector John D. Coughlin at Police Headquarters last night announced that the debonair "Marshall," alleged leader of the gang that robbed Mrs. Irene Schoellkopf of $300,000 worth of jewelry in an apartment at 64 West Fifty-second street early on the morning of Jan. 1, had been arrested yesterday on a train between Schenectady and Troy. The arrest was made by Detectives Daly, Horan and Buckley of Inspector Coughlin's staff. They caught "Marshall" when he was attempting to return from Montreal and took him to a house at 73 Lancaster Street, Albany, which he said was his home, to look for the stolen jewels. The detectives reported to Inspector Coughlin by telephone from the Lancaster Street house that they had not found the booty.

The man alleged to be "Marshall" was traveling under the name of M. D. Bidduiph. According to the police, his full name is Matthew Darian Bidduiph. The police say that he is an ex-convict, and that he is known to the police all over the country under the aliases of R. H. Matthews, R. H. Harrison and John F. Derby. According to the police, his photograph is No. 17,553 in the Rogues' Gallery at San Francisco, and he has been arrested many times, and convicted several times.

Inspector Coughlin said the man was wanted in Los Angeles and San Francisco on the charge of passing worthless checks.

Search of the records at Police Headquarters last night showed that "Marshall" had been arrested for passing a worthless check at the Yale Club in New York City in 1917, but had got off with a suspended sentence.

"Marshall," when arrested, said he was 27 years old and gave his occupation as traveling salesman and actor. Under the name of Bidduiph, Inspector Coughlin said, the man had had some success as a moving picture actor, appearing in Universal photoplays. By a coincidence, the last film in which he is known to have appeared was called "Wanted at Headquarters," in which he played a "heavy" part—in other words played a movie villain. This was in 1919.

Companion Also Arrested.

The detectives arrested with "Marshall," a man who identified himself as George F. Daley of 83 Clinton Street, Albany. As far as known, Daley had no connection with the Schoellkopf case, but the police are holding him to investigate why he was traveling with "Marshall." Daley is said to be a New York billposter, with an address in the vicinity of Broadway and 82d Street.

The arrest of "Marshall" and Daley followed a few hours after Horan, one of the detectives who made these arrests, had locked up a man named Charles Curtis in New York. Horan and his partner, Detective Owens, have been detached from all other duty to work exclusively on the Schoellkopf case for several weeks. In the line-up at Police Headquarters yesterday morning, Horan and Owens recognized Curtis, who had been arrested as a suspect in another case, as a man they had been looking for as a friend of one of "Marshall's" alleged confederates in the Schoellkopf robbery.

Curtis was released from the charge on which he was first held, but Horan immediately rearrested him on the charge of suspicion of burglary in another jewel theft—the robbery of Mrs. Lillian Myers of $50,000 worth of jewels in her apartment at 300 West Forty-ninth Street on July 21 last. Curtis is believed to have given the information on which Horan and the other

Continued on Page Six.

ANDERSON ENRICHED BY REALTY TRADING, IS STORY TO PECORA

Prosecutor Quotes Him as Saying $24,700 Came, in Currency, From Deals.

CONTRADICTS HIS AFFIDAVIT

Report to Anti-Saloon Directors in 1919 That Money Came From Loans Is Recalled.

GRAND JURY MOVE HINTED

Inquiry Will Be Pressed "in Some Other Way," Brackett Is Warned in Letter.

In a letter to ex-Senator Edgar T. Brackett, counsel for William H. Anderson, State Superintendent of the Anti-Saloon League, Acting District Attorney Ferdinand Pecora yesterday indicated that unless Mr. Anderson answered questions relating to the source and expenditure of the publicity fund of $24,700, he would take Grand Jury action. Mr. Pecora's letter was in reply to a reiteration by Mr. Brackett that Mr. Anderson should not submit replies to questions pertaining to the fund, details of which Mr. Anderson professes to have withheld from the Board of Directors of the League.

Intimating that he questioned the accuracy of statements made by Mr. Anderson, Mr. Pecora disclosed that Mr. Anderson had asserted he had obtained the money through realty investments negotiated by a friend at a time when he was earning $4,000 a year as an official of the League in Maryland. Mr. Pecora quoted Mr. Anderson as saying that the profits were in excess of $24,700, the sum which he alleged he had loaned the League here for its work when the necessary expenditures exceeded the income. Mr. Pecora pointed out that Mr. Anderson was unable to give the location of any of the realty and declined to divulge the name of his investor friend. Mr. Anderson told the Acting District Attorney that he had received the profits in currency, which he placed in his safe rather than in a bank, according to the letter to Senator Brackett.

Text of Pecora's Letter.

Mr. Pecora's letter follows:

Feb. 16, 1923.

Hon. Edgar T. Brackett, 120 Broadway, New York City.

Dear Senator Brackett:

Much as I regret your adherence to your advice to Mr. Anderson to refuse to answer certain questions which I have asked him as to the sources from which he obtained the sum of $24,700.00, which he claims to have expended on behalf of the Anti-Saloon League during the years 1913 and 1914, and details of such expenditure, I recognize fully your unquestioned right to advise him as his counsel in such manner as you may deem to be in accordance with his own interests.

You express the view that it would seem grotesque to base any prosecution of Mr. Anderson on the facts which have been shown. You also recognize that the ascertainment of the sources from which Mr. Anderson obtained the $24,700, and the methods by which he expended the same, properly comes within the scope of the inquiry which this office is making in so far as light may be shed on the question as to whether the representations which Mr. Anderson made to the Directors of the league in connection therewith are true or false.

In connection with his expenditure of $24,000, Mr. Anderson has declared to me, among other things, that the monies were paid out by him in currency from time to time to certain persons whose identities he will not disclose; that these payments were made for publicity work on behalf of the league; that he has no vouchers or written records of any kind which would show the respective dates and specific amounts of such payments, and that he cannot from memory give such data; that he cannot produce a single copy or piece of printed matter that was used in such publicity work; that all of said monies came from his personal means which he did not keep in any bank or other such depository, but which he kept in a safe in the office of the respective headquarters of the league in the States of Maryland and New York; and that he made such expenditures upon his own initiative and judgment; and without his having consulted the Board of Directors of the league in New York with regard to them.

Tried to Trace Money.

In view of the unusual circumstances under which, according to his own statements, Mr. Anderson made

Continued on Page Four.

Idaho Assembly Bars Japanese From Leasing Any Lands There

BOISE, Idaho, Feb. 16.—The Assembly of the Legislature, by a vote of 54 to 6, today passed a measure to prohibit the leasing of lands in the State to Japanese. The measure, according to its author, Representative Gillis, while aimed primarily at the Japanese, is applicable to all aliens.

Speaking to the Assembly, Representative Gillis said he feared an influx of Japanese and other aliens to Idaho through refusal of the Federal Government to re-lease land now occupied in Washington, and because of other States passing anti-leasing laws.

ENGINEER AMBUSHED AND SLAIN AT DOOR

Earl Remington of Los Angeles, Who Made Planes in War, Is Found Dead in Driveway.

WIFE ASLEEP IN THE HOUSE

Victim, Shot as He Stepped From Automobile, Met Death He Had Feared.

LOS ANGELES, Feb. 16.—Earl Remington, wealthy electrical engineer, found dead from gunshot wounds in the yard of his home here early today, had lived in fear of death for the last week, according to his wife, who was so prostrated with grief that she could not be seen until late today.

Two persons took active parts in the slaying of Remington, according to police conclusions announced late tonight.

Mrs. Remington said her husband had been acting strangely and showed extreme nervousness. Noises outside the house, particularly at night, seemed to distress him, she said. Remington had offered their home, which is in an exclusive residential district, for sale, the widow stated, but had instructed her never to permit any stranger to enter the house.

Although Remington telephoned to his wife yesterday that he was going to their ranch near Chino and would not return until late, it has been established, according to the police, that he did not go to the ranch.

Detectives are attempting to trace his movements yesterday in the hope of finding some clue to the slaying. They stated they had found two friends of the dead man who said they saw him at 5 o'clock yesterday afternoon.

That Remington was slain by some one having a grudge against him is the opinion expressed by the detectives.

Whether an attempted burglary of the office of the safe company of which Remington was the head, on Oct. 15, 1922, had anything to do with the engineer's death also is being investigated. Two of the company's safes were broken into, according to a report, but nothing of value was taken. The police are working on the theory that papers may have been taken at that time which were used later in a blackmailing plot against Remington.

Remington evidently was murdered at about last midnight. A dozen neighbors heard the fatal shot, and his wife lay sleeping within a few feet of him; but the body was not found until 6 o'clock this morning, when Charity Dawson, a negro maid, started downstairs to light the gas heating plant of the house at 1,409 South St. Andrews Street; a fashionable neighborhood.

There was a trail of blood on the driveway and a riddled leather portfolio which Remington had carried. The maid called Mrs. Remington, and the whole neighborhood was soon aroused by their screams.

Remington left his offices early in the afternoon for a trip to his Chino ranch. He was not seen thereafter by either employes or family until his body was found. He rang up his wife at 3:30 P. M. and told her he was going to Chino, according to the maid.

Remington, the police believe, drew up in his Ford coupé at the side of his house, perhaps at the order of his assailant. He stepped around to the back of the car, shifting the leather portfolio now high, now low, in front of his body in an effort to shield himself.

There was a loud report, perhaps two. One charge from the shotgun tore its way to the engineer's heart.

As he staggered away from the machine he fell on his back, arms spread out.

Mrs. Remington, according to the maid, did not hear the report of the gun. As her husband lay dying she was asleep in a bedroom in the northeast corner of the house, directly above the driveway. From her window she could have looked down on the struggle.

Neighbors playing cards heard the shots but thought they were automobile engines backfiring, or tires exploding. If the Remington dog had not been chloroformed for rabies about two weeks ago, the engineer might still be alive, according to the maid. She believes the dog might have awakened the family. Remington had no children.

"The motive may have been robbery, it may have been revenge," said Detective Sergeant Cline after talking with Mrs. Remington.

Remington was Vice President of the International Electric Protective Association, and had a wide reputation as a safe and bank designer.

Aviation was his sporting diversion, and he was adept at stunt flying. During the war he organized and was general manager of an aviation company here.

Charge Hawaiian Coolie Labor Plot.

Special to The New York Times.

WASHINGTON, Feb. 16.—Charges were made today by the Executive Council of the American Federation of Labor that for two years there had been an intensive agitation for the importation of 50,000 Chinese coolies into the Hawaiian Islands, where they would be placed under bond making them "debt slaves" for five years or less if they became rebellious. The council instructed the Federation's legislative representatives to do all in their power to prevent any enactment of laws that would in any degree open the gates to this character of immigration.

SENATE APPROVES BRITISH DEBT BILL; FINAL VOTE, 70-13

46 Republicans, 24 Democrats Favor It—Borah Among the Four Republicans Opposed.

BITTER DEBATE TO FINISH

Many Assail "British Victory," but Glass Wins Applause by Recalling Allies' Sacrifices.

ONLY ONE AMENDMENT

Settlements With Other Allies Must Have Congress Approval—Bill Now Goes to Conference.

Special to The New York Times.

WASHINGTON, Feb. 16.—The Senate passed the British Debt Refunding bill tonight by a vote of 70 to 13, forty-six Republicans and twenty-four Democrats voting to ratify the settlement as agreed to by the Debt Funding Commission, while nine Democrats and four Republicans were recorded in favor of repudiating the settlement.

The final roll-call was ordered at 7:20 o'clock tonight. The Administration victory was much more impressive than had been anticipated, it having been predicted that between fifteen and twenty Senators would oppose the bill when the vote on passage was reached.

The measure passed with only one amendment—that proposed by Senator Robinson of Arkansas, which gives to Congress the right to pass on settlements that may be arrived at in the future with other debtor nations. An amendment to equalize the interest rates and require Great Britain to pay the same interest as the United States itself pays on the loan was defeated, 61 to 21.

It is expected that the House will promptly accept the Robinson amendment and that the bill will be in the hands of the President early next week.

All efforts to amend the bill with regard to interest rates or in other important particulars were signally defeated. An amendment proposed by Senator Harris of Georgia, which authorizes the appointment of three Democrats on the Funding Commission, would undoubtedly have carried, but was withdrawn when the Republican leaders promised to give this matter early consideration when it is presented to the Senate in the form of an independent bill. The Republicans appear as anxious as some of the Democrats to have the minority share the responsibility of adjusting the more than $11,000,000,000 debt now due this country by its former associates in the European war.

Sharp Debate Continued All Day.

Eight lively hours preceded the passage of the bill. At times the debate was spirited to the point of bitterness, but the clean-cut Administration victory was never in doubt. The defeat of the Hitchcock amendment to maintain the British interest charges at a rate as high as rates paid by this Government and a speech by Senator Glass of Virginia broke the back of the opposition. The impassioned plea of the Virginia Senator for favorable action and his fervid defense of Great Britain came near the close of the long day. When Senator Glass concluded it appeared for a minute or two as if the session might have to suspend while Senators, Republicans as well as Democrats, pressed forward to shake his hand and congratulate him.

The leaders of the opposition were La Follette, Reed of Missouri, McKellar, Heflin, Trammell and Norris, while Smoot, Lenroot, Glass and Underwood commanded the defending forces. La Follette made the longest of all the speeches, a carefully prepared utterance in which he denounced Secretary Mellon, ridiculed the President and assailed the majority membership of the Finance Committee for what he charged was its undue and unwarranted haste in rushing the bill to a final vote.

The last day arguments of the opposition were based principally on the claim that the United States, in agreeing to fix the interest Great Britain will pay at 3 per cent. for the first ten and 3½ per cent. for the remaining fifty-two years, had, in fact, canceled what they claimed was approximately $1,000,000,000 of the interest charges.

La Follette Ridicules Harding.

Opening the debate, Senator La Follette recalled the White House dinner of a year ago, which was attended, among others, by J. Pierpont Morgan, Charles H. Sabin and Secretary Mellon, all of them, declared the Wisconsin Senator, of the international banking group.

Continued on Page Five.

GOV. REILY RESIGNS PORTO RICO OFFICE

Tells President Ill Health Forbids Him to Resume Executive Duties.

HAD BEEN LONG UNDER FIRE

Offended by His Inaugural Address, Unionists Made Many Charges Against Him.

WASHINGTON, Feb. 16 (Associated Press).—The resignation of E. Mont Reily as Governor of Porto Rico was received at the White House early this evening, but no announcement was made concerning it, although there was every indication that it would be accepted.

The text of the cablegram of resignation, as made public at the White House, follows:

Hon. Warren G. Harding, President of the United States:

On account of very serious injury while in the States, my trip to Porto Rico prostrated me, and I have been confined to my bed since, not being able to resume my official duties. My physicians inform me it will be several months before I can recover and I must have complete change and rest, free from all care. This being the case, I feel that I should resign and look after my health first.

I would like for my resignation to become effective April 1, believing that by that time I will be able to travel, and if I am not can be taken to a hospital here until I am able to do so.

In offering my resignation, I cannot do so without expressing to you and Secretary Weeks my appreciation of the unfailing loyalty and support you have both continually given to me in my arduous and trying work here.

Your recent statement to me that you were for me 100 per cent. had its echo in the great demonstration tendered me on my return, and shows that the work of your Administration in Porto Rico has not been in vain, but has been appreciated. It was a complete vindication of our American policies instituted in the islands two years ago.

A delegation composed of men of all political parties called on my Secretary yesterday, requesting that I withhold my resignation until you could be communicated with. I have notified them my resignation was irrevocable. Ninety per cent. of the people of the Island are for you and the things you stand for, and are pleading that no backward step be taken in

Continued on Page Five.

GOETHALS DEMANDS COAL FOR UP-STATE

"We Want Action, Not Conferences," He Says in Message to Federal Fuel Distributer.

SEIZURE IS THREATENED

Insists Shipments to Canada Be Diverted—People Will Get Coal, He Asserts.

General George W. Goethals, State Fuel Administrator, serving notice on the Federal Fuel Distributer that "we want action, not conferences" for the relief of suffering localities in Northern New York, suggested in two telegrams yesterday immediate authorization by the Federal officials of drastic relief measures.

Diversion to up-State towns of coal now moving to Canada, priority of New York shipments over shipments to Canada and seizure of cars en route to Canada were some of the measures suggested.

"The people in that part of the State are going to get coal," General Goethals asserted in making public the telegrams. "I am awaiting action from Washington on the telegrams. In case I don't get it, I am not saying what I am going to do."

The seizure of one car of coal consigned to Canada for use of the Saratoga Springs Hospital was authorized yesterday by the shipper, John F. Bermingham, President of the Lackawanna Coal Company. General Goethals called this to the attention of F. R. Wadleigh, Federal Fuel Distributer, in one of his telegrams and asked why the Government could not require the Delaware & Hudson Railroad "to supply our needs."

Reports from Mr. Kilmer to the State Fuel Administration offices yesterday were that people up-State were "on the point of taking coal off the tracks." The people were ready "to take the law in their own hands," he stated and added that "no juries in the afflicted communities would ever vote for conviction."

Predictions of epidemics from influenza and pneumonia unless coal arrived at some of the up-State points today were made by Mr. Kilmer.

General Goethals told reporters that priority must be given both to an emergency shipment of 20,000 tons, which is required immediately, and to future regular allotments.

Schools at many points in the Saratoga district have been closed for lack of fuel, reports to the State Fuel Administration said. Two schools in Corinth have been closed, and unless some coal arrives before Monday, or the school authorities can get some wood, the high school also will close. The school at Schuylerville was ordered closed yesterday for an indefinite period because of the lack of fuel.

Louis Cohen, a landlord of 514 West 182d Street, was sentenced to thirty days in the workhouse in the Court of Special Sessions yesterday for failing to supply sufficient heat and hot water for the house at 522 West 160th Street.

Probation officers reported that the building was badly in need of repairs. Window panes were out and doors were loose, they said, and the temperature recently had been several degrees below the legal minimum.

Mrs. Bertha Becker, who owns a building at 594 West 161st Street, was fined $250 on a similar charge in Special Sessions.

Won't Stop Coal to Canada.

WASHINGTON, Feb. 16.—The proposal for an embargo on anthracite exports, especially to Canada, has been carefully considered and definitely abandoned, it was said today at the White House.

In the view of high Government officials an embargo would have no material effect on the coal shortage which is being experienced in sections of New York and New England.

Doctor and Chauffeur Killed When Train Wrecks Ambulance at Jersey Grade Crossing

A fatal grade crossing accident occurred last evening at Hackensack, N. J., where a train running forty miles an hour, on the New Jersey and New York branch of the Erie Railroad, smashed into an ambulance, crushing a hospital interne and a chauffeur to death. James Reape, 38 years old, of 90 Nassau Street, Brooklyn, the chauffeur, was instantly killed. Dr. Louis Nishawitz, 25, of 830 Kelly Street, the Bronx, an interne at the Hackensack General Hospital, was mortally injured. His skull was fractured and his left leg and right arm were cut off. He died in the hospital half an hour after the accident. The ambulance was wrecked.

Dr. Nishawitz lost his life in the performance of his duty, as he was answering a call to take a sick woman to the hospital from her home on Hudson Street, Hackensack. After the accident a second ambulance was sent for the woman, but the delay had been fatal, and she was dead on its arrival.

The accident occurred about 5:30 P. M. at the Essex Street crossing. The train was a Haverstraw express, carrying commuters from New York.

Owing to a sharp curve south of Essex Street, the engineer could not see the crossing until he was close to it. The crossing gates should have been lowered, but were not. John Burke of Pearl River, N. Y., the gate tender, said the gates were frozen and out of commission. According to Burke, he stood in the middle of the road and swung a red lantern, but the ambulance driver did not heed. Burke was arrested on a technical charge of manslaughter.

Dr. Nishawitz was the son of Max Nishawitz, a shoe merchant in the Bronx. The physician was a graduate of De Witt Clinton High School and the Long Island College Hospital.

Harding Threatens to Cut Shipping Fleet Unless Congress Passes the Subsidy Bill

WASHINGTON, Feb. 16.—The Administration Shipping bill was restored tonight to its former place as the unfinished business of the Senate, after having been laid aside since early in the week to allow consideration of the British debt settlement legislation. This was done on motion of Senator Jones of Washington after advocates of the measure had demonstrated their superior strength by voting down, 38 to 30, a motion by Senator Robinson of Arkansas to adjourn.

The vote on adjournment was not regarded as an accurate test of the strength of the forces supporting and opposing the Shipping bill, as several Senators on both sides were absent.

Opposition of the shipping measure are expected, when the Senate meets tomorrow, to counter with a proposal to lay the bill aside again in favor of the Capper Truth-in-Fabrics bill, and it was considered possible that a test vote on the merchant marine legislation may result.

Although the future of the subsidy bill in the Senate has not been clearly indicated in the face of claims and counter-claims on the possibility of its passage, it was said at the White House today that President Harding would not call a special session of Congress to consider the merchant marine situation if the Shipping bill should fail.

Mr. Harding was said to feel that the necessity for action looking to a solution of the shipping problem had been clearly demonstrated, and to have reached the decision that if the Shipping bill is not enacted the Government will proceed at once to take such steps as will diminish in a very great degree the present losses of the Government's fleet.

Detailed reports on the operation of Shipping Board vessels, showing net losses on individual voyages running as high as $100,000, had been studied by the President and his advisers, it was said, and the consensus of opinion was that the losses would be wiped out under the necessary economics, which would follow the return of the shipping to private ownership.

"All the News That's Fit to Print."

The New York Times.

EXTRA
6 A.M.
THE WEATHER: Fair Today.

VOL. LXXII....No. 23,932. NEW YORK, FRIDAY, AUGUST 3, 1923. TWO CENTS In Greater New York | THREE CENTS Within 200 Miles | FOUR CENTS Elsewhere

PRESIDENT HARDING DIES SUDDENLY; STROKE OF APOPLEXY AT 7:30 P. M.; CALVIN COOLIDGE IS PRESIDENT

COOLIDGE TAKES THE OATH OF OFFICE

His Father, Who Is a Notary Public, Administers It After Form Is Found By Him in His Library.

ANNOUNCES HE WILL FOLLOW THE HARDING POLICIES

Wants All Who Aided Harding to Remain in Office—Roused After Midnight to Be Told the News of the President's Death.

Statement by President Coolidge

Special to The New York Times.

PLYMOUTH, Vt., Aug. 3.—President Calvin Coolidge issued the following statement early this morning:

Reports have reached me, which I fear are correct, that President Harding is gone. The world has lost a great and good man. I mourn his loss. He was my chief and my friend.

It will be my purpose to carry out the policies which he has begun for the service of the American people and for meeting their responsibilities wherever they may arise.

For this purpose I shall seek the co-operation of all those who have been associated with the President during his term of office.

Those who have given their efforts to assist him I wish to remain in office that they may assist me. I have faith that God will direct the destinies of our nation.

It is my intention to remain here until I can secure the correct form for the oath of office, which will be administered to me by my father, who is a notary public, if that will meet the necessary requirement. I expect to leave for Washington during the day.

CALVIN COOLIDGE.

Takes the Oath of Office.

Special to The New York Times.

PLYMOUTH, Vt. (Friday), Aug. 3.—Calvin Coolidge took the oath of office as President of the United States at 2:47, Eastern Standard Time, this morning (3:47 New York time). The oath was administered by his father, John C. Coolidge, who found the text in a book in his library, after having expected to wait until it was received from Washington.

The taking of the oath was a simple and solmn scene. Those who gathered in the living room of the Coolidge rome at Plymouth Notch, besides the President and his father, were Mrs. Coolidge, L. L. Lane, President of the Railway Mail Association of New England; Congressman Porter H. Dale, of Vermont; Joseph H. Fountain, editor of the Springfield Reporter, and Erwin C. Geisser, Mr. Coolidge's Assistant Secretary.

As the elder Mr. Coolidge read the oath Mrs. Coolidge looked on with wet eyes. As the end was reached, President Coolidge, raising his right hand, said in a low, clear voice:

"I do. so help me God."

A moment later the group dissolved, and President and Mrs. Coolidge retired.

Special to The New York Times.

PLYMOUTH, Vt., Friday, Aug. 3.—Calvin Coolidge received the news of the death of President Harding and of his own elevation to the Presidency at ten minutes before 1 o'clock this morning, Daylight Saving Time.

Mr. Coolidge received the first news of President Harding's death from telegrams signed by George C. Christian, the late President's secretary, and from THE NEW YORK TIMES, whose telegram reached him at the same moment.

These telegrams were brought to the Coolidge home at Plymouth Notch by W. A. Perkins of Bridgewater, who owns the telephone line running from Bridgewater to Plymouth. About five minutes later the newspaper men arrived in Ludlow.

The following telegram was sent to Mrs. Harding:

Plymouth, Vt., Aug. 3, 1923.

Mrs. Warren G. Harding,
San Francisco, Cal.

We offer you our deepest sympathy. May God bless you and keep you.

CALVIN COOLIDGE.
GRACE COOLIDGE.

The following telegrams announcing the death of President Harding

Continued on Page Five.

CALVIN COOLIDGE
Thirtieth President of the United States by the Death of President Harding.

WARREN GAMALIEL HARDING
Twenty-ninth President of the United States, Who Died Yesterday in San Francisco.

Public Men Voice Tributes To Harding's Worth and Record

Hughes Says He Was a Brave and Strong Leader—Marshall Calls Him a Great Human American—Honored as Martyr to His Duty—Sympathy Goes Out to Mrs. Harding.

Special to The New York Times.

WASHINGTON, Friday, Aug. 3.—Politics was forgotten in comm[illegible] by public men in Washington when informed of the death of President Harding. On account of the late hour at which the news was received it was difficult to reach officials.

Secretary Hughes, who came to his office in the State Department at an early hour this morning, was shaken by the news.

"No words can express," he said, "the grief into which we are plunged by this calamity. "The nation has suffered an irreparable loss. A quiet, brave, strong leader has fallen, overborne by the burden he was carrying.

"He was not only an able and faithful public servant but one of nature's noblemen. A true hearted, generous spirit, he has left with the people he loved a rare example of gentleness in high office, and of the most conscientious and unselfish devotion to public duty."

Marshall Found Him High Minded.

Thomas R. Marshall, former Vice President of the United States, expressed the deepest sorrow and paid high tribute to the integrity and worth of Mr. Harding.

"The sad intelligence of the President's death has just been communicated to me," said Mr. Marshall. "These are times when all party considerations sink into insignificance. The right kind of a man thinks of the death of his President.

"This has been the death not only of my President but of a man who for many years in the Senate had been my friend of the personal and intimate kind. There is nothing that any man can say, on an occasion like this beyond bearing testimony that aside from political opinions he was a great human American who patriotically and honestly tried to serve his country.

"This is a tribute from a man who did not agree with his political principles, but it is not necessary to agree with his political principles in order to admire the integrity, patriotism and high-mindedness of a man. I think that as the years go by the people will realize that Mr. Harding tried to serve his country well."

Loss to the World, Says New.

Postmaster General New was at his home when the news of President Harding's death was flashed to him from San Francisco.

"I am simply overhelmed," he said. "There are times when a man can not express his grief. This is one of them. The passing of President Harding is a loss to the world, the magnitude of which can not be overestimated."

Joseph P. Tumulty said:

"The new is a dreadful shock to me, as it must be to all who knew President Harding well. While at the White House I had many delightful associations with President Harding, who then was a member of the Senate. Like all men who came in contact with the President I knew him as a kindly gentleman and a true friend."

Says He Had People's Affection.

Senator Walsh of Massachusetts, Chairman of the Democratic Senatorial Campaign Committee, said:

"The President's death is a terrible shock, coming as it does so soon after it was believed that he was on the way to speedy recovery. His death will be mourned in every corner of the land by every class.

"Few Presidents have had a stronger grip upon the affections of our people. His dignity, simplicity, sincerity and graciousness won the hearts of all. His personality, however, did not alone account for his popularity. He has won a place in our history among the most worthy of those who have occupied the Presidency.

"His views were statesmanlike and the honor of our nation was safe and secure in his hands. The nation has lost a noble man, and a sound and safe leader."

Roosevelt Tells of Sacrifice.

Colonel Theodore Roosevelt, Acting Secretary of the Navy in the absence of Secretary Denby, said:

"Words cannot express my grief at the death of my chief, President Harding. It is idle to say that his death is a calamity for the United States, for every one knows it. He gave his life to the service of our country as truly as any one in our history."

Representative Stephen G. Porter of Pennsylvania, Chairman of the House Foreign Affairs Committee, a personal admirer as well as a friend of Mr. Harding said:

"I am simply overwhelmed. I hardly know what to say. He was so gentle, so kind, his every act was in the public interest. It is a terrible shock. I really can't understand it."

Mr. Porter returned recently from Europe, where he represented this country at teh sessions of the commission of the League of Nations on the opium traffic. He was selected for the work by the President.

Senator Curtis of Kansas, Republican whip of the Senate, said:

"The entire world will be shocked at the death of President Harding. His passing at this time was very unfortunate. The extent of his loss cannot be expressed in words. The entire country

Continued on Page Four.

President's Death Shocks Capital, Which Had Expected Recovery

News Telephoned to Executive Clerk From San Francisco—Effort Made to Reach Coolidge in Vermont—Only Two Members of Cabinet in Washington.

Special to The New York Times.

WASHINGTON, Friday, Aug. 3.—News of the death of President Harding not only greatly shocked official and Washington but took the capital com- resident Washington, but took the capital completely by surprise.

It was the sixth time in the history of the nation that the city had been brought face to face with the death of a President, but the shocking word was received under circumstances wholly different from those surrounding the death of any former President.

The only high officials of the Harding Administration in Washington are Secretary of State Hughes and Postmaster General New. All the other members of the Cabinet are out of the city, and two of them, Secretaries Mellon and Davis, are in Europe, while most of the others, with the exception of Secretaries Weeks and Denby, are in the Far West.

Calvin Coolidge, until last night Vice President, and who will immediately be sworn in as the next President of the United Sates, is likewise absent from Washington, but it has occurred several times in American annals that Vice Presidents have been absent from the capital on occasions of deaths of former Presidents.

When last heard from, Mr. Coolidge was at Plymouth, Vt. A message was sent direct from San Francisco notifying him of the death of Mr. Harding. From the Presidential party in San Francisco communications, the White House was advised late tonight, were sent direct to all other members of the Cabinet not now in San Francisco and to personal friends of the President.

Rudolph Forster, Executive Clerk at the White House, was communicated with direct from San Francisco shortly before midnight by long distance telephone. He talked with Mr. Smithers, the ranking member of the White House executive force in San Francisco in the absence of Mr. Christian who had gone to Los Angeles. Mr. Smithers confirmed the death of the President and informed Mr. Forster that messages were being sent to the Vice President and other Cabinet members.

Mr. Hughes is the ranking member of the Administration now in Washington, so that he will take such steps as are necessary in the present situation.

It will also be the duty of the Secretary of State to notify the members of the Diplomatic Corps, who will in turn officially cable their Governments that Mr. Harding is dead.

No plans have or can be made immediately for the swearing in of Mr. Coolidge as President. It is not necessary for him to take the oath from a member of the United States Supreme Court. Another Judge or other officer qualified to administer an oath can act in that capacity. Even a Justice of the Peace back in Vermont, where Mr. Coolidge was last known to be located, can administer the oath.

The first knowledge the White House had of the President's death came from the Rev. Dr. Freeman Anderson, assistant pastor of the Calvary Baptist Church, which President Harding attended. He telephoned to the Executive Mansion and the message was received by E. C. Goss, one of the White House police force, who was one of the few men on duty at that time of the night, as the President had been away since June 20.

In turn Patrolman Goss telephoned to Mr. Forster, who at once summoned the entire White House force. One of the first to arrive was Isaac Hoover for years chief usher at the mansion, and who has known many Presidents intimately, and Joseph Murphy, assistant chief of the Secret Service.

Pedestrians who passed the White House after the news of the President's death noticed that the iron gates on Pennsylvania Avenue were shut and locked, something which has been unknown since the advent of the Harding regime. It was explained, however, that the gates have been shut every night at 8 o'clock since the extensive repairs to the house and grounds have been going on.

Mr. Hoover, who has charge of the renovation of the White House, said at midnight that the mansion could be put in order in two days. In fact, preparations had been made to do this ever since the first news of the President's illness was received in Washington. At any time that notification was sent here that the President was to leave San Francisco the house could have been put in readiness for his reception. Workmen will begin at once this morning arranging the furniture and placing the draperies as usual.

Dancing Stops at the Hotels.

At the big hotels dancing was immediately stopped and a hush and gloom settled over the crowds who slowly began to leave. Extras were on the streets fairly early and residents ran out from their homes to call newsboys, and automobilists stopped their machines to buy the ink-wet sheets. Newsboys were crying extras in Executive Avenue and Pennsylvania Avenue, the two streets bounding the White House on the west and north at midnight, their cries coming clearly into the Executive Offices.

When the news was communicated to William H. Beck, private secretary to the Secretary of State, at midnight, he started by automobile for the State Department and sent word to Mr. Hughes's

Continued on Page Six.

DEATH STROKE CAME WITHOUT WARNING

Mrs. Harding Was Reading to Her Husband When First Sign Appeared —She Ran for Doctor

BUT NOTHING COULD BE DONE TO REVIVE PATIENT

News of Tragic End Shocks Everybody, Coming After Day Said to Have Been the Best Since His Illness Began a Week Ago.

Special to The New York Times.

SAN FRANCISCO, Aug. 2.—President Harding died at 7:30 o'clock tonight [11:30 o'clock New York time] of a stroke of apoplexy.

The end came suddenly while Mrs. Harding was reading to him from the evening newspaper, and after what had been called the best day he had had since the beginning of his illness exactly one week ago.

A shudder ran through the President's frame and he collapsed.

Mrs. Harding and the two nurses in the sick room knew the end had come, and Mrs. Harding rushed out of the room and asked for Dr. Boone and the others to "come quick."

Dr. Boone and Brig. Gen. Sawyer reached the President before he passed away, but were not able to avert the inevitable.

This formal announcement following soon after told the story of the tragic end:

"The President died at 7:30 P. M. Mrs. Harding and the two nurses, Miss Ruth Powderly and Miss Sue Drusser, were in the room at the time. Mrs. Harding was reading to the President, when, utterly without warning, a slight shudder passed through his frame; he collapsed, and all recognized that the end had come. A stroke of apoplexy was the cause of his death.

"Within a few moments all of the President's official party had been summoned."

Shocking in Its Suddenness.

Nothing could have been a more shocking surprise. Shortly before the President's sudden collapse General Sawyer had been telling newspaper men that Mr. Harding had had the best day since he became seriously ill. He said that the President had definitely entered upon the stage of convalescence and that everything went to show that Mr. Harding was on the road to ultimate recovery.

The members of the official party had no warning that the President was in danger. They, like the newspaper men, had been assured that a fatal termination of the President's illness was a thing not likely and with good care he would be able to recover health and strength. Most of the members of the official party were at dinner when the news came. George B. Christian Jr., secretary to the President and his devoted friend, was in Los Angeles with Mrs. Christian. He had gone there at the President's solicitation to read at a gathering of the Knights Templar tonight an address which the President had prepared in the expectation that he would deliver it in person. Mr. Christian had declined to leave San Francisco until he was positively assured by the President's physicians that there was no likelihood of any set-back in the President's condition.

The newspaper men had an engagement with General Sawyer for 8 o'clock. He was to tell them of how the President was progressing toward recovery. In view of what he had said on prior occasions during the day and statements in two official bulletins, the newspaper men had every expectation that they would be able to record that Mr. Harding was one step nearer the goal of recovery.

"There will be a bulletin," said one of the White House messengers gathered in the corridor of the Presidential suite. In a few minutes copies of the bulletin on thin white paper were handed to the waiting reporters. Instead of informing them that the President's condition continued to improve, it gave them the astounding information that he was dead.

Mrs. Harding Is Brave to the End.

First reports that Mrs. Harding had collapsed were denied. The official version indicates that she was calm throughout her husband's last illness. She has been extremely courageous and by her manner and words helped him when he was suffering intensely and was apprehensive of a fatal termination. The official account says:

"Mrs. Harding, who from the beginning of the President's illness had expressed confidence in his recovery, did not break down. On the other hand, she continued, as from the beginning, the bravest member of the group.

"When it was realized that the President had actually passed away, she turned to those in the room, whose concern had turned to her, and said, 'I am not going to break down.'"

Mrs. Harding was seated by the bedside when at 7:10 o'clock the President suddenly collapsed. His breathing, which had been quick ever since the illness overtook him, suddenly became spasmodic. Mrs. Harding, leaving the two nurses to take whatever steps they could in the emergency, ran to the door of the Presidential suite.

"Dr. Boone!" she called, as she ran part way into the almost deserted corridor. A Secret Service operative was seated about twenty feet down the hall. She hurriedly told the Secret Service man that the President had had a sudden and severe relapse and begged the detective to try to locate Dr. Boone or any of the other physicians.

The Secret Service man took up the search for the physicians, while

"All the News That's Fit to Print."

The New York Times.

THE WEATHER
Fair today; unsettled tomorrow; gentle southerly winds.
Temperature yesterday—Max., 84; Min., 69.
For weather report see next to last page.

VOL. LXXII....No. 23,965. NEW YORK, WEDNESDAY, SEPTEMBER 5, 1923. TWO CENTS In Greater New York | THREE CENTS Within 200 Miles | FOUR CENTS Elsewhere

JAPANESE DEATH TOLL MAY REACH 300,000; EARTH STILL ROCKS BUT FIRES ARE WANING; AMERICA IS RAISING MILLIONS FOR RELIEF

GREEKS OFFER PLAN FOR LEAGUE INQUIRY INTO JANINA CRIMES

Want Geneva to Direct Investigation—Will Post 50,000,000 Lire Guarantee.

ASSEMBLY SNUBS ITALIANS

Elections to Committees Result in Their Exclusion From Posts of Honor.

MUSSOLINI RENEWS THREAT

Rome Cabinet Approves Resolution to Quit League if It Intervenes.

Copyright, 1923, by The New York Times Company.
Special Cable to THE NEW YORK TIMES.

GENEVA, Sept. 4.—Nicholas Politis, delegate of the Greek Government, today proposed to the Council of the League of Nations that for the settlement of the dispute between his country and Italy the Council should appoint one or more neutral representatives.

1. To superintend in Greece the judicial inquiry already begun by the Greek authorities and also the trial of those held responsible for the murder of the Italian officers of the Albanian Boundary Commission.

2. To assist in the work of a commission, the appointment of which has been proposed by the Greek Government, through the Council of Ambassadors, to investigate, both in Albania and in Greece, the circumstances which preceded and accompanied the crime.

3. That the Council should instruct a commission composed of three high judicial authorities—one Greek, one Italian and one neutral (for example, the President of the Swiss Federal Tribunal or the President of the Permanent Court of International Justice)—to meet as soon as possible in Geneva to settle the amount of indemnities which it is just that Greece should pay the families of the victims.

4. That the Council should agree that the Greek Government forthwith deposit in a Swiss bank 50,000,000 lire as a guarantee for the immediate payment of whatever indemnities may be decided upon.

Discussion Put Off Till Today.

These proposals were made at a meeting of the Council held this evening at the Secretariat of the League, in the course of which Signor Salandra, head of the Italian delegation, asked for a postponement of the discussion of the Greco-Italian incident until Signor Giurati, his associate, should have returned from Rome with new instructions.

M. Politis was arguing that no sovereign nation could accept dictation as to the nature of the punishment to be inflicted upon its nationals when Signor Salandra interrupted him.

His attitude was most friendly, and it was with a smile that he expostulated that he could not consent to allow the Greek delegate to embark on a controversy in the course of the discussion of a simple question whether the Council should grant a poostponement .

"If M. Politis is allowed to continue, I shall have to reply," he said.

The common sense of this attitude and the politeness of the Italian delegate toward his Greek colleague won general approval, and Lord Robert Cecil suggested that M. Politis should have an opportunity to submit in writing any new proposals he had to make.

M. Politis then retired from the room and at the end of half an hour brought back the suggestions already noted in this dispatch. In the circumstances they could not be immediately taken up by the Council and Lord Robert moved that the discussion of them should be withheld until tomorrow's meeting, when the Council would be in possession of full information as to the Italian attitude.

The attitude of the small nations was strongly shown this morning when Signor Scialoja, who has been President of the Committee on Legal Questions for the last two years and expected to have that honor again conferred upon his country and himself, was defeated, Dr. Motta of Switzerland being elected. The Presidencies of all the committees were given to representatives of small nations.

tA the election of six Vice Presidents of the Assembly at the formal morning session of the body, Lord Robert Cecil and Viscount Ishii headed the ballot with forty-two and forty-one votes, Gabriel Hanotaux of France coming third with thirty-five. The other three Vice Presidents elected were Count Decimeno, Dr. Fortoul of Venezuela and M. Pusta of Esthonia. Italy did not win a single place of honor among the Assembly leaders.

Denies Repudiating League's Authority.

GENEVA, Sept. 4 (Associated Press).—A member of the Italian delegation to the Assembly of the League of Nations today authorized the League Secretariat to deny that Italy had ever officially repudiated the competency of the League to handle the Greco-Italian crisis.

"We are awaiting the return of Major Giuriati from Rome, and then we will

Continued on Page Ten.

Dirigible ZR-1 Makes Perfect Test Flight; 15,000 Cheer Huge Craft Made at Lakehurst

Special to The New York Times.

LAKEHURST, N. J., Sept. 4.—Exceeding the expectations of its builders, the United States Navy dirigible Z R-1 made it maiden flight this afternoon from the Lakehurst air station, where ten months ago construction was started.

Cheered by 15,000 persons, the dirigible, a "made in America" product, rose gracefully, and, after circling the field, took an easterly course to Toms River. Returning to the field at dusk after a flight on an hour, the dirigible made a perfect landing at the station and "went to bed" in its immense hangar.

From the first preparations this morning toward releasing the ZR-1 until after the dirigible had been safely returned to its hangar, the day was replete with interesting events for naval officials. Commander Frank R. McCrary, skipper of the craft, received favorable weather reports from Washington early in the afternoon, and last word instructions to the twenty-two men in the crew were issued by Captain Anton Heinen, German Zeppelin authority, who has been consultant to the navy in the construction of the craft.

A force of 320 marines and enlisted men marched to their posts as guide-rope holders, and 100 civilian employes gathered at the entrance of the hangar to aid in guiding the dirigible to the centre of the field.

When every man was in his place Commander Weyerbacher gave the order, "Start walking," and the small army of men began hauling the ZR-1 from the hangar.

Rear Admiral W. A. Moffett, head of the naval air forces, wished Commander McCrary and his crew "bon voyage." McCrary, Commander Weyerbacher and Captain Heinen then climbed into the pilot gondola, and a moment later the order was shouted, "Let's go."

Propelled by four of the six motors, the dirigible rose to a height of about 1,000 feet, when the pilot started to circle the field. Later the big craft began its real flight, and at a height of 1,200 feet, in full view of the crowds, it soared away in perfect control.

Soon this radio message was received by Admiral Moffett: "In twenty minutes of flying all going well."

Signals in electrically illuminated signboards placed flat on the ground aided in the landing, which was made without a hitch upon an immense stretch of red and white bunting, on which a searchlight was turned.

"The flight was highly satisfactory," said Commander McCrary. "The craft steered exceedingly well, although we did not carry out any tests of severity on the initial trip. We only opened up the motors to half speed, and they functioned entirely to our satisfaction. The ship proceeded smoothly and evenly, as evidenced by the fact that Lieutenant Bauch, one of the passengers, and an enlisted man were able to walk on the roadway on top of the gas bag.

"There are a few minor changes we will have to make before we can take the ZR-1 out again. We plan a series of test flights, the second probably the latter part of next week."

Rear Admiral Moffett was enthusiastic over the results of the trial rip.

One of those who made the flight was Norman O. Walker, the only American who survived the ZR-2 crash in England. He said that the dirigible seemed to him to be a much better craft.

DEMOTTE KILLED IN GUN ACCIDENT

International Art Dealer Shot Dead While on Hunting Expedition in France.

NEWS KEPT SECRET A DAY

Involved in Charges of Extensive Art Frauds, He Was Preparing to Push Suit Here.

Copyright 1923, by The New York Times Company.
Special Cable to THE NEW YORK TIMES.

PARIS, Sept. 4.—George J. Demotte, art dealer of Paris and New York, was killed yesterday while hunting. His companion, Otto Wenger, dropped his gun, causing the discharge of both barrels. Demotte was struck in the shoulder and neck, the jugular vein being severed. Death was almost instantaneous.

The hunting season opened on Saturday, and the art dealer on that day with a party of friends went to the Department of Loir-et-Cher, where he owned property. The accident occurred at the conclusion of the day's hunt, when Wenger was unloading the gun. When he saw his host drop dying to the ground Wenger tried to commit suicide. Other members of the party interfered in time, however, to prevent this.

For unknown reasons the news of the tragic death was kept secret till late this afternoon. Then it became known as a rumor about Paris, and the last evening papers tonight carried a brief notice about it.

Demotte was perhaps the world's greatest dealer in statuary, though he did not confine his business to that branch of art. He had sold numerous pieces to the Louvre in Paris and the Metropolitan Museum in New York and to wealthy collectors, both in France and America.

Recently he had been involved in legal processes over the value of a number of his sales. Recently he accused the famous London, New York and Paris dealer, Sir Joseph Duveen, of conspiring to drive him out of business, and brought suit for half a million dollars against him for his contrary judgment on a piece of alleged Limoges enamel which had been bought by the Dreicer firm, but not paid for, and for remarks alleged to have been made by Duveen about him in connection with this work.

The case was overshadowed, however, by the sudden controversy raised in Paris as to the authenticity of objects sold by Demotte to both the Louvre and the Metropolitan, as well as to a number of private collectors. The charges were made specific by a number of critics, including one who claimed to have heard Demotte's boast as to the restoration of statues for American trade. Jean Vigouroux, former manager of Demotte's New York store, corroborated the charges, specifying some half-dozen "fakes" in the Metropolitan. Vigouroux, however, was under indictment on a charge of retaining illegal commissions on sales, and Demotte made counter-charges that the entire affair was brought up to hurt his character.

Despite this defense persons interested in the Louvre continued to press the charges, and a complaint was lodged with the Prosecutor of the Seine. An investigation followed which tended to confirm allegations that certain Louvre pieces were restored to an extent to make them valueless as specimens of sculpture of the period they represented. This evidence was turned over to the Prosecutor of the Seine only a few weeks ago, and the next step to be taken in the case has not yet been made public.

Two other serious cases arose from the controversy. One was the revelation that a statue sold by Demotte to a

Continued on Page Seven.

COAL PEACE BASIS NOW SEEMS NEAR

Indications Are That $5 Minimum for Day Men Would Satisfy Miners.

MAY DROP OTHER DEMANDS

Lewis Confers With Leaders in Preparation for Conference Today.

Special to The New York Times.

HARRISBURG, Sept. 4.—If the representatives of the anthracite operators agree to grant to day miners a minimum of $5 a day the suspension of work which began Sept. 1 will be lifted and 158,000 miners will return to work. This basis for the settlement of the strike was indicated today on good authority in advance of the meeting tomorrow between Governor Pinchot and the disputants.

Governor Pinchot has asked the operators to give a 10 per cent. wage increase to the contract men. They demanded 20 per cent., but are willing to take half. The day workers, now receiving between $4.20 and $5.60 a day, have signified their unwillingness to take an increase of between 42 and 56 cents a day, as suggested by the Governor. They want a minimum of $5 a day.

A minimum of $5 a day for day men would mean an increase of 80 cents a day. This would give to the day man a daily wage of between $5 and $6. There are 40,000 day workers, and they have declared through their representatives that to grant the comparatively highly paid contract miner as large a percentage increase as they received would further widen the disparity between the wages of the two classes.

Other Demands Offset Each Other.

A minimum of $5 a day for day men, with a 10 per cent. increase for contract workers, would, it was estimated, increase the price of coal $1 a ton at the mines.

With the wage question out of the way there would be two outstanding points left, the check-off and arbitration. The miners have been insistent on the check-off, and the operators just as firmly refused to grant it. The operators demand that the miners agree to a form of permanent arbitration that shall guarantee uninterrupted production during the pendency of wage disputes.

The miners persist in their refusal to arbitrate. Those who have been following the negotiations are of the opinion that these two demands will neutralize each other, thus leaving only the question of the new contract, which probably will be for two years.

A report was received here that a secret agreement had been made between the miners and operators over the week-end and that it would be announced in Washington tomorrow. This report was declared to be utterly without foundation by both sides.

There are still those who insist that the miners will continue the strike unless they obtain the check-off. Sentiment among the rank and file of the miners on the check-off is divided. Some have expressed themselves as favoring it. Others say it is not necessary in the hard coal regions now, but that it should be retained in the soft coal fields.

Officials here who believe the miners will accept Governor Pinchot's suggestions point out that they could not hope to gain more through a long strike than is being offered them without a strike. The Governor is intent on keeping the miners and operators here as long as any hope for a settlement is held out. His friends say that the political asset of a long coal tie-up averted will inspire the Governor to "keep his teeth" in the situation until the end.

It was reported here today that at-

Continued on Page Eight.

RED CROSS ASKS $5,000,000

Sets Its 3,600 American Chapters at Work at Once.

RELIEF SHIPS DUE TODAY

Six Naval Vessels Carrying Supplies Are Nearing Yokohama.

FOOD RUSHED FROM MANILA

Army Transports, Loaded to Capacity, Sail Within 24 Hours.

> ***Prince Regent and Emperor Give $55,000,000 for Relief***
>
> SAN FRANCISCO, Sept. 4 (Associated Press).—Relief work in Japan was furthered today by by several large donations. The Prince Regent gave $50,000,000 for relief; the Emperor gave $5,000,000 from the Privy Exchequer, and the Government donated $4,500,000.
>
> In Kobe $17,500 was raised for the sufferers in ten minutes.
>
> The vessels in Yokohama harbor have given refuge to 5,000 persons.
>
> From Shanghai it was reported that rioting had broken out in the destroyed cities and that the police were arming citizens to aid in maintaining order.

Special to The New York Times.

WASHINGTON, Sept. 4.—The Government of the United States is giving its time and attention almost exclusively to the work of extending in full measure all possible assistance to the stricken people of Japan. This was the official statement that came this afternoon from the White House, where the President is personally directing the relief activities of the Government.

The speed with which the United States is acting to bring succor to the Japanese can be appreciated when it is stated that the army transports Meiggs and Merritt, each carrying a capacity cargo of relief supplies, are expected to sail from Manila within the next twelve hours, or within twenty-four hours after the order directing their dispatch to Japan was cabled to Governor General Wood.

Following a conference between President Coolidge and James L. Fieser, Acting Chairman of the American Red Cross, it was announced that the society immediately will call upon the American people for a fund of at least $5,000,000, of which New York City has been asked to raise $1,000,000. The plans for the relief campaign were worked out in a conference between Mr. Fieser, Secretary of Commerce Hoover, Assistant Secretary of the Treasury Wadsworth, and Masanae Hanihara, the Japanese Ambassador.

Late this afternoon the quotas for the six national Red Cross divisions were announced. They show that while the fund is fixed at $5,000,000 the quotas assigned amount to $5,250,000. The quotas are based on

Continued on Page Two.

> ***Islands of Bonin Group Reported Vanished, Together With Mismia Island and Its Volcano***
>
> Copyright, 1923, by The New York Times Company.
> Special Cable to THE NEW YORK TIMES.
>
> PEKING, Sept 4.—Numerous villages along the coast of the Japanese Peninsula south of Yokohama, where many foreigners were spending the Summer, were washed away by the tidal wave that followed the earthquake.
>
> There is no news from the Bonin Islands and it is feared they have sunk into the sea.
>
> Nothing can be seen of Mismia Island, the volcano on which was reported on Monday to be in violent eruption, and it is believed to have disappeared.
>
> Copyright, 1923, by The New York Times Company.
> Special Cable to THE NEW YORK TIMES.
>
> LONDON, Sept. 4.—The Bonin Islands, called by the Japanese Ogasawarajima, which are reported to have disappeared, were about twenty in number, though only ten were of appreciable size. They lay about 500 miles from the mainland of Japan on a line which would run almost due south from Yokohama or southeast from Nagasaki.
>
> Until 1861 their few inhabitants had somewhat vaguely considered themselves as a British colony, but in that year the British Government recognized Japan's right of possession. Since then the handful of Europeans and Polynesian half-breeds had been outnumbered by Japanese colonists.
>
> Regular steamship communication had been established and a modern system of administration introduced. Exploitation of the islands' resources—valuable timber and agricultural produce—had provided employment for the population, about 5,000.

AMBASSADOR SAFE, U. S. CONSUL DEAD

Woods and Staff Escape When Embassy Is Destroyed—Mr. and Mrs. Kirjassoff Killed.

FOREIGN CASUALTIES HEAVY

State Department Trying to Get News of Americans—All Capitals Anxious.

Special to The New York Times.

WASHINGTON, Sept. 4.—The first direct message from American representatives in Japan to the State Department today brought the news of the safety of Ambassador Cyrus E. Woods and all members of his staff in the embassy at Tokio, and the death of Max D. Kirjassoff, the United States Consul at Yokohama, and his wife.

The American Embassy at Tokio and all other embassies were destroyed, presumably by fire, which it is believed accounts for the safety of those connected with the American Embassy.

Ambassador Woods sent an undated dispatch from Iwaki telling of the safety of himself and staff. It reads:

"Embassy buildings totally destroyed, but no one in embassy injured. Food situation is very acute. Send rations at once from Philippines."

John K. Davis, the American Consul at Shanghai, in a dispatch to the State Department told of the death of Mr. and Mrs. Kirjassoff and reported that there was no information about a number of Americans, among them Representative Ackerman of New Jersey.

Mr. Davis said that his information came by radio from the master of the President Jefferson, of the Admiral Line at Yokohama, to the officials of that line in Shanghai.

His message to the State Department reads:

"Yokohama completely wiped out

Continued on Page Four.

BURSTING OIL TANKS SET YOKOHAMA AFIRE

Explosions Deluged the Doomed City With Flames That Spread Death.

TOKIO BRIDGES COLLAPSE

Thousands of Victims Go Down With Them to Death—Not a House Undamaged.

Copyright, 1923, by The New York Times Company.
Special Cable to THE NEW YORK TIMES.

PEKING, Sept. 4.—The latest news received here by way of the Tomioka wireless station, 150 miles northeast of Tokio, indicates that the catastrophe in Japan equals the worst apprehensions.

In Yokohama the Government oil tanks exploded and the whole city was set on fire. The deaths alone there are still estimated at 100,000.

All bridges across the river in Tokio, which were densely crowded with refugees from the fire, collapsed during the later earthquake shocks and many thousands were drowned or killed by the fall.

All newspaper offices in Tokio have been destroyed except those of the Nichi Nichi, Miyako and Hochi, and in all of these their machines are damaged so that publication of all newspapers is totally suspended.

The University Hospital was destroyed and more than 700 patients perished.

All the hill suburbs of northern Yokohama have been destroyed by earthquakes and fire, and there seems to be no reason to doubt that the foreign quarter on the bluff has suffered a similar fate.

All wards of Tokio have been damaged, but parts of Shiba, Hongo, Kojimachi, Ushicome, Yotsuya and Aoyama wards escaped, though the fire was spreading in Aoyama ward yesterday morning.

Out of about fifty very large buildings in the Marunouchi district only half a dozen are still standing, including the House of Representatives.

Steel-Framed Structures Gone.

The Supreme Court, Imperial Hotel and Central Station, great steel-framed structures recently erected, have been destroyed, either by fire or by the earthquake. This point is of enormous importance to Japan, because, if they were destroyed by the earthquake, buildings of this character will have to be eschewed in the future and this will greatly restrict the country's manufacturing capacity.

The banks burned include the Bank of Japan, Mitsui, Tokai, Yasuda and the Third Bank.

Buildings destroyed in Tokio include the Chinese Legation, French and Italian Embassies, Nicolai and

Continued on Page Three.

Dr. J. Bentley Squier Sails From Kobe To Aid Relief Measures at Yokohama

Copyright, 1923, by The New York Times Company.
Special Cable to THE NEW YORK TIMES.

KYOTO, Japan, Sept. 4.—Dr. J. Bentley Squier of New York has sailed from Kobe on the foreign relief ship West Orowa, bound for Yokohama to engage in relief work there. Dr. Squier's family remain at the Miyako Hotel here.

Dr. Squier and Mrs. Squier and their son and daughter were returning via Japan from a tour in China when the Japanese earthquake occurred. They had intended to sail from Shanghai on the Canadian Pacific liner Empress of Australia for Yokohama, and had they done so the earthquake and fire would probably have caught them in that port, where the Empress had not long before landed her passengers. Instead, they evidently took the overland route and crossed the strait to Japan and were on their way north toward Tokio, but still some 200 miles outside the damage zone, when the shocks occurred which destroyed the capital and the chief port of the island empire.

Dr. Squier is one of the best known surgeons in the United States. He is a former President of the New York County Medical Society.

DEVASTATION COVERS HUNDREDS OF MILES

At Least Five Big Cities Have Been Almost Wiped Out—Millions Are Starving or Dying of Exposure.

THOUSANDS OF MADDENED PEOPLE LEAP INTO RIVER

The Sumida in Tokio Is Clogged With Bodies—Shocks and Explosions Continue—Five Billion Dollars Needed for Reconstruction.

OSAKA, Japan, Sept. 4 (Associated Press).—So vast an area of Japan has been devastated by the greatest earthquake in the history of this country that it will be long before the actual loss of life is known. The most reliable estimates of the dead up to the present are from 200,000 to 320,000.

The newspaper Osaka Asahi estimates the earthquake dead at 320,000, which includes 150,000 dead in Tokio, 100,000 in Yokohama and 60,000 in Yokosuka.

[Other dispatches estimate the casualties as high as 500,000.]

Tokio and Yokohama, with surrounding towns, which formed the centre of the disturbances, are almost completely in ruins. For two days Tokio was swept by flames, and, apart from the loss of life caused directly through the falling of buildings, thousands must have perished in their attempts to make their way through the fire zones and other thousands through exhaustion.

Yokohama, Tokio's busy port, is a city destroyed. Probably more destruction has been wrought there than in the capital itself, for its great docks were torn asunder, its shipping wrecked, its public buildings and homes levelled to the earth.

All advices received here indicate a succession of earth disturbances in that area, extending from many miles inland and to the north, and everywhere the first destructive forces were augmented by explosions, the bursting of water mains, the overflow of rivers and the terrible overpowering rush of tidal waves.

New Islands Arise From the Ocean.

Details of geographical changes are lacking, but it is reported that new islands have been forced up from the bed of the ocean, while whole sections have disappeared. Rivers are said to have changed their courses and volcanoes are erupting in various districts.

The disaster spared none who stood in its path. Many members of noble families have perished, but thus far the only notable foreign resident in the list of killed is the American Consul at Yokohama, Max D. Kirjassoff, who, with his wife, is believed to have been buried in the ruins of the consulate.

The American Ambassador, Cyrus E. Woods, and all the members of the embassy at Tokio are known to be safe, but many of the diplomatic representatives of other nations have not been accounted for, nor has any word been received of their fate.

Word is received that the fires in Tokio burned out on Monday night, but at the same time couriers carry appeals for food supplies and medical supplies and assistance for the hundreds of thousands of homeless refugees who, unless succored speedily, cannot survive.

For the moment all efforts are being directed, first, to ascertaining the extent of Japan's vast losses, both in citizens and foreign residents, and material damage to its cities, and, secondly, to rushing all assistance in every form to the stricken districts.

There has been no time yet for a summing up of the terrible consequences of the earthquake nor for the preparation of a list of the prominent dead Japanese or foreign residents.

The warships of many foreign nations are on the seas already bringing assistance, which fact serves to give encouragement to the Government and the people in their greatest calamity.

Explosion at Hakone Hot Springs.

A great explosion has occurred at Owakidini, in Hakone, one of the hot springs of Japan, located about fifty miles from Tokio.

Earthquake shocks continue at intervals around Kawaguchi, which is on the only railway open out of Tokio.

The shock of yesterday morning, followed by fire, wiped out Kawaguchi.

Reports from eyewitnesses at Hakone say the earthquake left no houses standing at Miyanoshita, the fashionable mountain resort forty-five miles south of Tokio. The Fujiya Hotel was among the buildings destroyed.

In Tokio, the Ichigaya prison was threatened by fire and about 1,500 prisoners were freed. They included Toshihiko Saki, the Communist leader, and other Communists.

Troops of the Fourteenth Division at Utsunomiya and Thirteenth Division at Takata were marching toward Tokio today.

Following the earthquake horrors many of the refugees died from extreme heat and exposure, according to eye-

"All the News That's Fit to Print."

The New York Times.

THE WEATHER
Warmer and cloudy today; tomorrow, fair and colder.
Temperature yesterday—Max., 37; min., 4.
For weather report see Page 19.

VOL. LXXIII....No. 24,105. NEW YORK, WEDNESDAY, JANUARY 23, 1924. TWO CENTS In Greater New York | THREE CENTS Within 200 Miles | FOUR CENTS Elsewhere.

LENIN DIES OF CEREBRAL HEMORRHAGE; MOSCOW THRONGS OVERCOME WITH GRIEF; TROTSKY DEPARTS ILL, RADEK IN DISFAVOR

SOVIET CONGRESS IN TEARS

Mass Hysteria Only Averted by a Leader's Brusque Intervention.

BODY WILL LIE IN STATE

Is to Be Taken to Moscow Today From Village Where Premier Passed Away.

KREMLIN WALL HIS TOMB

Washington Expects No Immediate Change in the Policy of the Russian Government.

By WALTER DURANTY.
Copyright, 1924, by The New York Times Company.
By Wireless to THE NEW YORK TIMES.

MOSCOW, Jan. 22.—Nikolai Lenin died last night at 6:50 o'clock. The immediate cause of death was paralysis of the respiratory centres due to a cerebral hemorrhage.

For some time optimistic reports had been current as the effects of a previous lesion gradually cleared up, but Lenin's nearest frends, realizing the progress of the relentless malady, tried vainly to hope against hope.

At 11:20 o'clock this morning President Kalinin briefly opened the session of the All-Russian Soviet Congress and requested every one to stand. He had not slept all night and tears were streaming down his haggard face. A sudden wave of emotion—not a sound, but a strange stir—passed over the audience, none of whom knew what had happened. The music started to play the Soviet funeral march, but was instantly hushed as Kalinin murmured brokenly:

"I bring you terrible news about our dear comrade, Vladimir Ilyitch." [Nikolai Lenin was his pen name.]

High up in the gallery a woman uttered a low, wailing cry that was followed by a burst of sobs.

Kalinin Breaks the News.

"Yesterday," faltered Kalinin, "yesterday, he suffered a further stroke of paralysis and——" There was a long pause as if the speaker were unable to nerve himself to pronounce the fatal word; then, with an effort which shook his whole body, it came—"died."

The emotional Slav temperament reacted immediately. From all over the huge opera house came sobs and wailing, not loud nor shrill, but pitifully mournful, spreading and increasing. Kalinin could not speak. He tried vainly to motion for silence with his hands and for one appalling moment a dreadful outbreak of mass hysteria seemed certain. A tenth of a second later it could not have been averted, but Yunakidze, Secretary of the Russian Federal Union, thrust forward his powerful frame and with hand and voice demanded calm. Then Kalinin, stumbling, read out the official bulletin.

"'Jan. 21 the condition of Vladimir Ilyitch suddenly underwent sharp aggravation. At 5:30 P. M. his breathing was interrupted and he lost consciousness. At 6:50 Vladimir Ilyitch died from paralysis of the respiratory centres.

"'Dated 3:25 A. M., Jan. 22.

"'Signed:

"'Drs. OHUNK [Lenin's personal physician and chief of the Moscow Health Department, who gave Lenin first treatment when wounded Aug. 30, 1918.]

"'SEMISKO [a close personal friend of Lenin, and Minister of the Health Department],

"'FOERSTER,

"'GTYE,

"'OSIGOF,

"'YEWISTRATOF.'

"We propose," continued Kalinin, "that the twenty-first day of January henceforth be set aside as a day of national mourning." By a tragic coincidence today—Jan. 9, old style, is a similar Bolshevist holiday in memory of Father Gapon's petitioners, massacred by the Czar's troops in the courtyard of the Winter Palace on "Bloody Sunday," 1905.

"Do you agree?" questioned Kalinin.

A confused sound, half sob, half sigh, was the only assent.

Whole Congress Gives Way to Grief.

Kalinin tried to tell the funeral arrangements, but broke down completely.

Kamenief and Zinovief, equally unnerved, and other members of the Presiding Committee had laid their heads on the table and cried like children. Even the daredevil Cossack leader Budyenny was weeping unrestrainedly, while the delegates in the body of the theatre stood motionless, sobbing, with tears coursing down their cheeks.

Finally Lashevitch, a member of the Central Executive Committee of the Communist Party and President of the Siberian Revolutionary Committee, stepped to the speakers' rostrum. His strong, square body in khaki uniform with dull red facings radiated calm as in a firm voice he announced that the members of the Presiding Committee and a group of senior delegates to the Congress would go tomorrow at 6 A. M. by special train to the village of Gorky,

Continued on Page Three.

NIKOLAI LENIN (VLADIMIR ILYITCH ULIANOV),
A sketch made from life for THE NEW YORK TIMES by Oscar Cesare in Moscow, November, 1922, and autographed by Lenin.

EXPERTS PROPOSE GERMAN GOLD BANK

It Would Be Absolutely Independent and Under International Control.

SCHACHT URGES MEASURE

Dawes Committee Will Go to Berlin on Monday to Discuss Proposal There.

Copyright, 1924, by The New York Times Company.
Special Cable to THE NEW YORK TIMES.

PARIS, Jan. 22.—Its first decisive step toward accomplishing the task which has been set it of reorganizing German finance and showing a way of balancing the budget was taken today by the Expert Committee studying the problem under the Chairmanship of General Charles G. Dawes. In a communiqué issued this afternoon the committee announced that it had reached the opinion that an independent gold bank under international control was the first essential to any plan for securing the budget equilibrium and stable currency in Germany.

This opinion, it is emphasized, was a unanimous one, and though the French have been largely instrumental in forwarding the suggestion, they claim no more credit than any other delegates of the five nationalities represented on the committee.

Influenced by Schacht.

To the confirmation of opinion in the minds of the committeemen, Dr. Schacht, President of the Reichsbank, by his replies to the questionnaire submitted to him Saturday and answered yesterday, added considerable influence. As yet the plans for creation of such a bank are not fully elaborated, but the committee, working under high pressure, has given Dr. Schacht a rendezvous in Berlin for Jan. 30, when it promises to discuss with him a definite plan.

The communiqué issued this evening by the committee read as follows:

"The committee of experts appointed by the Reparation Commission to consider stabilization of the currency in Germany and balancing the budget has reached the opinion that an independent gold bank should be established, partly by mobilizing some part of the free reserves of gold and foreign currencies which may exist in the hands of German nationals and which at present discharge no economic function, and partly by co-operation of foreign capital. In their view such a step will form part of the ultimate plan to secure future budget equilibrium and stable currency.

"In this connection the committee think some feature of the plan outlined before them yesterday by Dr. Schacht will prove in due course to be very useful and they were glad to have the advantage of his views as part of the whole field of possible or alternative action to be reviewed.

"The President of the committee has heretofore emphasized the need of allied unification in the program. The committee is convinced that foreign co-operation in the management of such a bank is similarly desirable for its ultimate success.

"The committee, in view of necessary prompt decision and action, has advised Dr. Schaght that it will discuss its definite plan in Berlin on Wednesday, Jan. 30."

As usual the members of the committee today showed the greatest reserve

Continued on Page Six.

BRITAIN ACCEPTS THE LIQUOR TREATY

Document Is Approved by All of the Dominions and Hughes Is Notified.

GEDDES MAY SIGN TODAY

Washington Makes Preliminary Proposals for Similar Compacts to Other Powers.

Copyright, 1924, by The New York Times Company.
Special Cable to THE NEW YORK TIMES.

LONDON, Jan. 22.—The Anglo-American liquor running treaty is ready for the signatures. All the British Dominions have approved it and the British Ambassador at Washington has been asked to notify the United States State Department that Britain is prepared to sign. The treaty, of course, must be ratified by the British and Dominion Parliaments, but with the possible exception of Canada, where the King's Government is in a nominal minority, there is thought to be no likelihood of an upset of the verdicts already given.

British governmental authorities are now satisfied also that the treaty, as revised, will not conflict in any way with the American Constitution. Apprehension had originally existed that the treaty's proposal to allow British ships to carry liquor stores within the three-mile limit might not square with the Eighteenth Amendment, and the British Government was chary of extending the privilege of right of search to an hour's steaming from shore until it was certain that it would receive this quid pro quo.

As stated in official circles, the signing of the treaty will not affect in any way the complaints already filed by the London Government regarding the seizure of British vessels outside the three-mile limit. The Government will continue to seek a decision on the point of law involved in these cases, and to claim compensation for its subjects concerned.

LONDON, Jan. 22 (Associated Press).—Departing from the accepted three-mile limit, which has been the basis of British maritime law, Great Britain and her Dominions have unanimously agreed to grant the United States the right to search British owned vessels carrying contraband liquor within one hour's steaming distance of the American shores. For brevity, it is one of the most remarkable international documents on record.

It consists of less than three short typewritten pages and embraces, first, the decision of the British Government to grant the United States a special extension of the three-mile territorial limit; second, the right of the American authorities to search British vessels for illicit liquor within a boundary described as one-hour's steaming distance from shore; and, third, the right of British passenger liners to bring legitimate alcoholic stores into American waters when such stores are intended for consumption on the homeward voyage.

Marquis Curzon, the Foreign Secretary under Premier Baldwin, had been eager, ever since the Imperial Conference, to have the outgoing Cabinet enjoy credit for completing a treaty which Mr. Baldwin himself cited as one of the most notable achievements of his Administration in fostering Anglo-American relations. The framers of the agreement here are confident that Ramsay Mac-

Continued on Page Eighteen.

Captain of Tacoma and Two Radio Men Lose Their Lives in Vera Cruz Storm

Special to The New York Times.

WASHINGTON, Jan. 22.—Wireless messages from official sources tonight report that Captain Herbert G. Sparrow of the wrecked cruiser Tacoma and two radio operators have lost their lives in a severe hurricane outside Vera Cruz Harbor.

The State Department received this dispatch late tonight from Consul Wood at Vera Cruz by Navy wireless:

Vera Cruz, Jan. 22, 1924.
Secretary of State,
Washington.
I am profoundly distressed to announce the death of Captain of the U. S. S. Tacoma and also of two wireless operators through an accident on board her during a norther, while in the performance of duty. Particulars will follow.
WOOD, American Consul.

The first intimation that the Tacoma had figured in another tragedy reached Washington early in the evening, when Señor Alvarez del Castillo, diplomatic agent of the revolutionary faction, received this radio message from Adolfo de la Huerta:

"By orders of the supreme chief, in the midst of a furious hurricane, our small naval transports steamed out of the port to go to the aid of the Tacoma. Our vessels daringly plunged into the tempest, regardless of danger of their own loss, and succeeded in saving the remainder of the crew of the Tacoma, which is now completely sunk."

Officials have been trying to get word from the Tacoma through the radio of the cruiser Richmond, 180 miles distant at Tampico. The death of Captain Sparrow and the radio operators explains her failure to report.

The news of the tragedy was received in Washington with deep sorrow, for Captain Sparrow was a splendid type of the seasoned naval officer.

The Tacoma was sent to Vera Cruz to re-establish cable communications. She tried to make the breakwater at Vera Cruz at dawn one morning but was caught by a "norther" and thrown on Blanquilla reef.

Most of her men were sent to the beach at Vera Cruz, to be picked up later by the Richmond, on board which they are at Tampico. Captain Sparrow, six officers and forty-eight sailors remained on the Tacoma.

Captain Sparrow, who is an Ohioan, was appointed to the Naval Academy in 1895. He had seen fifteen years of service at sea.

DECLARES ANDERSON FORCED HIM TO SPLIT PART OF HIS 'DRY' PAY

Chief Accuser of Anti-Saloon League Official Then Admits Trying to Sell Exposure.

DENIES HE TRIED BLACKMAIL

Defense Links Witness With Brewers and Wet Organization at Forgery Trial.

Light on the financial arrangements of the Anti-Saloon League of New York State was contributed by O. Bertsall Phillips, former collector for the league, who was the chief witness yesterday at the trial of William H. Anderson, State Superintendent of the league, on a charge of forgery, before Supreme Court Justice Tompkins and a jury. In turn, the defense launched an attack on the personal character of Phillips.

According to Phillips, he entered into a contract with Superintendent Anderson whereby he was to get commissions on all money he collected for the dry propaganda of the league. This contract, according to the witness, stipulated that he was to get 20 per cent. on the first $25,000 he obtained yearly, and 10 per cent. on all money over that figure.

In the course of his direct examination by Chief Assistant District Attorney Pecora, Phillips charged that Anderson had forced him to split "fifty-fifty" on all collection commissions in excess of $10,000. As the witness told it, Anderson declared that his own salary was then only $10,000 a year and that no employe of the league was to get more than he.

Taking over the witness for cross-examination, former Governor Charles S. Whitman, leader of the defense, pounded away unmercifully at Phillips. He asked the witness if he had not "deserted" his wife and six children, and Phillips denying it, was forced to admit that his wife won a "technical" decree of divorce on the grounds of abandonment. He admitted that he had married again and that his wife taught school, but he refused to admit that she worked in order to support herself.

Denies He Tried Blackmail.

Mr. Whitman asked Phillips if he had not tried to "blackmail" the Anti-Saloon League leaders by threats of criminal proceedings, and whether he had not tried to "deliver Anderson and the league" to a Mr. Kaltenbach, an official of the Fleischmann Yeast Company, and, as Mr. Whitman termed it, the "Fleischmann Brewing Company." The former Governor charged that Phillips had approached Kaltenbach, asking $5,000 as the price of the alleged "delivery."

The witness denied this, but admitted that he had visited Kaltenbach several times, and said that he wanted the $5,000 only as a loan to start two suits against Anderson for money which, the witness said, was wrongfully withheld from him. He admitted that the Fleischmann official had advanced $200 or $300. According to the questions of Mr. Whitman, the witness also had sought to interest Colonel Jacob Ruppert, brewer and one of the owners of the New York Yankees, in the alleged "delivery."

Another thing which the cross-examination touched on was Phillips's alleged connection with persons who tried to sell allied munitions secrets, described as having been obtained through the famous "leak" from the office of J. P. Morgan & Co., allied fiscal agents in the early days of the war.

Prior to the advent of Phillips on the witness stand, Miss Mary E. Hill, Assistant Treasurer of the league, and Dr. George Caleb Moor, Secretary of the league and pastor of the Madison Avenue Baptist Church, testified as prosecution witnesses. Miss Hill testified that the alleged false entries in the league's books were unimportant and merely bookkeeping routine which did not alter the actual finances of the organization. Dr. Moor's evidence dealt with the composition of the league's corporate membership, which he estimated to be between forty and fifty persons.

Says Anderson Demanded Split.

Under examination by Mr. Pecora, Phillips testified that he was employed by the league from May 1, 1917, to April 30, 1922. He told of signing the contract for the commissions, said the figures were larger than he expected, and that

Continued on Page Five.

LABOR TAKES OFFICE, FULFILLING ANCIENT BRITISH CEREMONIES

Macdonald Kisses the King's Hand in Accepting Commission to Head Government.

THREE PEERS IN CABINET

New Premier Takes Foreign Office Also and Will Base His Policy on League.

By EDWIN L. JAMES.
Copyright, 1924, by The New York Times Company.
Special Cable to THE NEW YORK TIMES.

LONDON, Jan. 22.—In the historic setting of Buckingham Palace, replete with the symbolism of British monarchy of more than a thousand years, King George today entrusted to a leader of workingmen the chief post in the government of the British Empire.

Events moved swiftly from the moment when Premier Baldwin visited the King this morning and placed the resignation of his Ministry, defeated last night in the House of Commons, in the hands of the King. Mr. Baldwin recommended to the King that he should send for James Ramsay Macdonald, leader of the opposition and head of the Parliamentary Labor Party, as his successor. The King acted on the advice, and before Mr. Baldwin had left the palace Mr. Macdonald had arrived, with J. R. Clynes and J. H. Thomas.

Mr. Macdonald accepted the commission, kissed the King's hand according to custom, and the first Socialist Labor Government in the British Isles came at once into being.

The New Ministry.

The new Ministry was announced as follows:

Prime Minister, First Lord of the Treasury and Secretary of State for Foreign Affairs—JAMES RAMSAY MACDONALD.

Lord Privy Seal and Leader of the House of Commons—JOHN ROBERT CLYNES.

Lord President of the Council—LORD PARMOOR.

Lord Chancellor—THE VISCOUNT HALDANE.

Chancellor of the Exchequer—PHILIP SNOWDEN.

Secretary of State for Home Affairs—ARTHUR HENDERSON.

Secretary of State for the Colonies—J. H. THOMAS.

Secretary of State for War—STEPHEN WALSH.

Secretary of State for India—SIR SIDNEY OLIVIER.

Air Minister—BRIG. GEN. CHRISTOPHER THOMPSON.

First Lord of the Admiralty—THE VISCOUNT CHELMSFORD.

President of the Board of Trade—SIDNEY WEBB.

Minister of Health—JOHN WHEATLEY.

Minister of Agriculture—NOEL BUXTON.

Secretary of State for Scotland—WILLIAM ADAMSON.

President of the Board of Education—C. P. TREVELYAN.

Minister of Labor—THOMAS SHAW.

Postmaster General—VERNON HARTSHORN.

Chancellor for the Duchy of Lancaster—COLONEL JOSIAH WEDGWOOD.

Commissioner of Works—F. W. JOWETT.

Three Laborites Visit the King.

A pacifist, known as an idealist, Mr. Macdonald showed today that he could be practical and swift. With his Cabinet already constituted, it is expected that the old and new Ministers will exchange the seals of office tomorrow at noon, after which Labor will be in power.

Parliament adjourned today until Feb. 12, which leaves the new Prime Minister three weeks to prepare to meet the House of Commons.

After last night's vote, which marked the end of the Baldwin Government, Mr. Baldwin called together his Cabinet at 10 o'clock to receive the resignations of his various Ministers. Then he left No. 10 Downing Street by a back door to walk to Buckingham Palace; but to escape a group of photographers he hailed a passing taxi, which took him to the King's presence. His audience lasted about half an hour.

When Mr. Macdonald met his party leaders at the House of Commons he announced that the King had sent for him, and after conducting his business he left for Buckingham Palace. He wore a frockcoat and high hat, Mr. Thomas had his well known worn derby, while Mr. Clynes had a soft hat pulled over his eyes.

A few moments after they had reached Buckingham Palace Mr. Baldwin came

Continued on Page Four.

COOLIDGE SENDS WATCHER TO OIL HEARING; DAUGHERTY IS ALREADY INVESTIGATING; ASK SINCLAIR TO RETURN, FALL RECALLED

Sinclair Declares Oil Inquiry Is 'Politics'; Denies Paying Fall for Teapot Dome Lease

Copyright, 1924, by The New York Times Company.
Special Cable to THE NEW YORK TIMES.

PLYMOUTH, Eng., Jan. 22.—Harry F. Sinclair was on board the liner Paris, which arrived at Plymouth this afternoon from New York. He was accompanied by Mrs. Sinclair and Mr. Day, Vice President of the Sinclair Oil Company. He did not land at Plymouth, but proceeded to Havre. His name appeared on the supplementary passenger list.

"My trip to Europe," said Mr. Sinclair, "has nothing to do with avoiding being called to give testimony before the committee that has been sitting for the last three or four months. I expect to stay four or five weeks in Europe, and upon my return I shall be perfectly willing to testify again if it is wished. I have already given testimony four or five times, and I was excused.

"There was nothing secret or mysterious about my leaving New York. It was public. Every one knew I was in New York and that I was leaving for Europe. There were forty photographers there when I left.

"I absolutely deny all statements or suggestions that I have brought away documents or papers relating to the case. It is perfectly ridiculous, all these statements that I paid Mr. Fall this money for the lease. I absolutely deny it."

"The entire situation," Mr. Sinclair added, "is a political move and a case of American politics."

WON'T CONFER AGAIN ON ST. MARK'S RITES

Bishop Manning Stands on His Edict Against the New Practices.

RECTOR DEMANDS A JURY

Vestry Backs Up His Request That Services Be Judged by 50 Clergy and Laymen.

The differences between Dr. William Norman Guthrie, rector of St. Mark's-in-the-Bouwerie and Bishop William T. Manning of the Protestant Episcopal Diocese of New York over Dr. Guthrie's eurythmic rituals and "pagan" services reached a climax yesterday.

Dr. Guthrie, his wardens and vestry made it known that the Bishop had refused to meet them again in conference, although on their previous meeting at Synod Hall five weeks ago it had been understood that such a step would be taken.

Dr. Guthrie and the vestry made public two letters which are now in the hands of Bishop Manning. The first is Dr. Guthrie's defense and explanation of his position in view of the Bishop's objection to a further conference. The second sets forth the stand of the wardens and vestry on the same point. Dr. Guthrie says in his letter to the Bishop:

Bishop William T. Manning said last night that he had received both Dr. Guthrie's letter and the communication from the wardens and vestry of St. Mark's, but had not had an opportunity to read them. When a summary of their contents was outlined, including Dr. Guthrie's proposal that the eurythmic rituals and "pagan" services should be judged by fifty representative clergymen and laymen of the Protestant Episcopal Church, the Bishop said that he had no comment to make.

"You officially summoned me on the thirteenth of December, demanding, besides, the presence of all my vestry. You did not open our conference with any inquiry into my work, but greatly surprised us by reading a previously prepared arraignment charging me with disloyalty to the Church of a most serious character, calculated to alienate my vestry from their rector. We respectfully answered you to the effect that your arraignment, and your consequent requests, were not founded on fact but upon newspaper headlines, and on irresponsible, because anonymous, testimony.

Indictment Not Pressed.

"Now this indictment, charging me with disloyalty to the Church, was not pressed by you; but you urged the residual complaint that I had conducted my work in complete disregard of the good name and honor of the Protestant Episcopal Church; and your evidence, was that my work had been of such a nature as to invite objectionable publicity.

"You yourself proposed that we adjourn our conference over the Christmas holidays for thirty days, to consider matters on both sides and discover what common ground there might be between us. We agreed to keep the nature of our conference confidential until the next conference, and especially your requests, though you consented to my consulting my fellow-clergy, with the understanding that they should be warned against any publicity. On my return home, after dinner, I was promptly notified over the telephone by representatives of the press that they were in possession of the tenor of your 'demands.'

"THE NEW YORK TIMES on the 17th of December published, therefore, our formal declaration that such information had not reached the press through us, as must have been amply apparent to you, from the fact that our vestry had resented the at first proposed publication of these requests because of the

Continued on Page Two.

VETO THREATENED ON A HIGH SURTAX

President Stands Inflexibly for Secretary Mellon's 25 Per Cent. Rate.

COMPROMISERS UNMOVED

House Committee Decides to Act on Indirect Taxes First and Surtax Last.

Special to The New York Times.

WASHINGTON, Jan. 22.—In the face of a break in the Republican forces in Congress on the surtax proposals in the Administration tax bill, it was announced today at the White House that President Coolidge had not reversed his position and that he stood inflexibly for the 25 per cent. maximum surtax recommended by Secretary Mellon. He is against any compromise which would fix the rate between this figure and the present 50 per cent.

The Cabinet today discussed the legislative situation, including demands for a compromise on the tax bill so as to expedite its passage. The result of the discussion was that the Administration intends to stand firm against compromises, believing that the Mellon bill is right and based on economic principles, rather than being designed for vote catching purposes.

While the President believes that the bill will not get through Congress without amendments, a White House authority said today that he was more opposed to any fundamental change in it than he was on the day of its introduction. This position is taken by the President in the face of conditions threatening revolt in the conservative faction of his own party, but he believes that he has the support of wide public opinion.

The spokesman represented the President as opposed to any changes in the fundamental rates. He said that Mr. Coolidge would consider as a fundamental change any amendment to the bill which would depart from the surtax rate of 25 per cent.

It was indicated at the White House that the Presidential veto would be stamped on a tax bill which emasculated the Administration proposals. The attaching of a rider for a bonus, it was said, would cause disapproval.

The inflexible stand of the President for the Mellon surtax rates failed to shatter the equanimity of the House leaders, who reiterated that compromises in the Ways and Means Committee were necessary if the bill was to have Republican backing on the floor.

"My job," said Representative Longworth, the party leader, "is to try to get out a bill that will pass the House. The surtax rates will most certainly have to be changed."

Chairman Green repeated his former statement that revenue bills were made at the Capitol. Neither Mr. Green nor Mr. Longworth would comment on the President's view that he would regard a departure from a 25 per cent. surtax maximum as a fundamental change, but it was apparent that they were not influenced by this announcement.

A Democratic view of the Coolidge attitude came from Representative Garner, who said:

"If the President meant that he would accept no rate higher than 25 per cent., then I doubt if there will be any tax bill at all. But I believe that if a bill is sent to him with a surtax between 25 and 50 per cent. he will sign it because the American people want tax reduction."

Objection was voiced by Mr. Garner because Republican members of the committee held sessions of their own today on the program for handling the bill and excluded the Democrats.

At the closed meetings the Republicans practically decided to take up indirect taxes first and the surtaxes last. Outside the committee there was much speculation over this determination, and there must have been considerable discussion inside, for it is known that the action was accomplished only by a narrow vote. The course settled upon cannot please Mr. Longworth, because he believes that surtaxes should be considered at once, as does Mr. Garner.

Representative Longworth, who has been having talks with individual Republicans on the committee, today described the situation as "simmering."

PRESIDENT READY TO ACT

Spokesman Indicates Coolidge Has His Eyes on Developments.

INQUIRY TO BE PRESSED

Senate Committee Wants Fall to Explain Archie Roosevelt's Story.

SINCLAIR'S BOOKS SOUGHT

Mysterious Memorandum Appears of Fall's Ranch Purchase—No Clue to Author.

Special to The New York Times.

WASHINGTON, Jan. 22.—President Coolidge is taking an active personal interest in the developments in the Teapot Dome oil lease hearings before the Senate's special investigating committee. He has ordered the Department of Justice to have an observer at the hearings to watch for any evidence of wrongdoing, and Attorney General Daugherty has been instructed to start action at once if evidence justifying prosecution of any person is presented. Mr. Daugherty declared today that any violation of the law would be prosecuted, "no matter who the person is."

"That's all that can be done now—to observe the evidence brought out at the hearing and [illegible] in accordance with law," [illegible] "If the [illegible] then the Government will take the action required."

In asserting this position it was made clear that the President wanted it understood that the Administration was not making any accusations against any one or expressing any opinion as to the investigation.

The spokesman for the President indicated that Mr. Coolidge did not wish to indicate when and in what way the Government would proceed, on the ground that to do so would embarrass the Department of Justice in its present inquiry.

In addition to the White House announcement that the President had instructed the Department of Justice to follow the testimony before the committee, it was learned in Administration circles that if fraud were committed in the making of the oil leases they would be canceled, and action started civilly and criminally against any persons guilty of wrongdoing in connection with the transfer of the Government properties to oil corporations.

The opinion was expressed by a White House spokesman that all that could be done with dignity and in order had been started by the President when he ordered the Department of Justice to send an observer to the hearing "to see what evidence might disclose as to certain rumors." These rumors dealt with the allegation that a Government official had received money from a corporation interested in the leases.

Sinclair and Fall Summoned.

The Senate Committee today instructed E. T. Stanford, counsel for Harry Sinclair, to notify the latter by cable that it desired his presence without delay, and the production of the books of the Hyva Corporation, which marketed the stock of the company formed to handle the Teapot Dome lease.

Subpoena was also issued for ex-Secretary Fall to appear and answer the testimony of Archie Roosevelt that $[illegible],000 was paid to Fall's ranch foreman by the Sinclair organization. J. W. [illegible]vely, one of the counsel for Sinclair, to whom were loaned 35,000 shares of the Sinclair Corporation's stock, also has been subpoenaed. Senator Lenroot stated that the committee would request E. L. Doheny to testify later. Mr. Doheny is reported on his way [illegible] from New Orleans.

Mr. Fall is expected to appear on [illegible]day, to which day the committee adjourned.

Senator Caraway served notice in writing, as required by the rules of the Senate, that he will move tomorrow to discharge the Committee on Public Lands from further consideration of the resolution he introduced calling for the cancellation of the Teapot Dome lease. This motion, if adopted, would bring the matter before the Senate.

Senator Caraway said tonight that he had the votes to discharge the committee and expected to have a record vote on the resolution itself before the end of the week. Many Republicans are supporting the resolution.

Daugherty Says Department Is W[illegible]

After the announcement from the White House of the attitude of President Coolidge with respect to the Teapot Dome scandal, newspaper men asked Attorney General Daugherty whether he cared to add to the statement [illegible] by the Presidential spokesman or comment on the relation of the Department of Justice to the Senate committee's investigation.

Speaking slowly, Mr. Daugherty dictated this statement:

"You can say that I said that the Department of Justice has been [illegible] this testimony in all these proceedings before the committee and [illegible] [illegible] investigation on its own [illegible]

"During the time that the [illegible] [illegible]

"All the News That's Fit to Print."

The New York Times.

THE WEATHER
Rain today or tonight and tomorrow; no change in temperature.
Temperature yesterday—Max., 46; Min., 34.
For weather report see next to last page.

VOL. LXXIII....No. 24,117. NEW YORK, MONDAY, FEBRUARY 4, 1924. TWO CENTS In Greater New York | THREE CENTS Within 200 Miles | FOUR CENTS Elsewhere

WOODROW WILSON PASSES AWAY IN SLEEP; END COMES AT 11:15 A.M.; NATION SORROWS AND TRIBUTES ARE VOICED IN ALL LANDS

OIL INQUIRY PAUSES IN HONOR OF WILSON; GREGORY RETIRES

Today's Session Is Suspended and Committee May Not Resume Till After Funeral.

SENATE SANCTION AWAITED

Testimony Will Be Postponed Pending Action on Fall's Challenge of Authority.

GREGORY EXPLAINS POSITION

Writes President He Had Been Unaware of Doheny's Share in Paying Fee.

Special to The New York Times.

WASHINGTON, Feb. 3.—The death of former President Wilson may delay for several days the Congressional activities in connection with the Naval Reserve oil lease scandals.

It had been the intention of Senator Lenroot, Chairman of the Public Lands Committee to place before the Senate tomorrow the points made by former Secretary Albert B. Fall on Saturday in refusing to answer questions and to ask for additional power to proceed with the investigation, if that was considered necessary.

But it now develops that the Senate will adjourn immediately tomorrow out of respect to the memory of Mr. Wilson, thus providing no opportunity for consideration of the oil scandals. It is possible that there may be a session of the Senate on Tuesday, at which action will be taken, but the opinion expressed tonight was that all developments might be held back until after the funeral of the former President.

Former Secretary Fall has been subpoenaed to appear before the investigating committee again on Tuesday morning, but this feature of the proceedings probably will also be postponed.

Long Legal Battle in Prospect.

Mr. Fall is remaining in seclusion and his legal advisers are apparently confident that the courts will uphold his right to refuse to testify on the ground that he might incriminate himself. There have been reports that the committee, after obtaining additional power from Congress, would place Fall in custody, if he persisted in defying it, but these are not confirmed. It is probable that a long legal battle will be witnessed, the committee in the meantime going ahead with other phases of the inquiry

During the delay, however, the auditing experts retained by the committee will continue their examination of the books of brokerage firms which have been subpoenaed by the committee in an effort to establish whether any persons prominent in the official life of Washington who may have had advance information profited by the rise in the value of Sinclair Consolidated Securities following the announcement of the leasing of Teapot Dome Reserve to Sinclair.

Thomas Watts Gregory, Attorney General in the Wilson Administration, formally withdrew as special counsel in the oil cases today in a letter sent to President Coolidge which was given out at the White House.

Mr. Gregory made the point that while he had talked on the long distance telephone with the President on Tuesday night, he had not accepted the appointment at that time and had simply agreed to come on to Washington and discuss the proposition. He also stated that he had not recalled at that time that he ever received any money paid out by Doheny.

While the President has made no formal announcement, it was generally accepted tonight that he would appoint former Senator Atlee Pomerene as counsel representing the Democratic Party. It was indicated at the White House that the President desired to talk about it with Senator Walsh, and also would wait until the joint resolution adopted in Congress last week was placed before him.

Silas Strawn, selected as the Republican member of counsel, had a long conference today with Mr. Pomerene about the oil cases, and they said afterward that they had made a good start on the preparation of the case. It is believed that the remote connection of Mr. Strawn's law firm with the Texas Oil Company will not prevent his confirmation by the Senate. In this connection Mr. Strawn said:

"For about ten years, I think, my firm has collected bills for the Texas Company and obtained locations for their filling stations in the Chicago territory. These are matters handled by the young men of our firm and I never have had anything to do with them. My firm never has handled any of the corporate business of the Texas or any other oil

Continued on Page Ten.

Congress to Adjourn Today After Tributes to Wilson

WASHINGTON, Feb. 3.—Congress will pay its tribute tomorrow to Woodrow Wilson.

On convening at noon, both the House and Senate will adjourn out of respect for his memory.

In the House, Representative Longworth, the Republican leader, will give official notification of Mr. Wilson's death, and after a brief eulogy will yield the floor to Representative Garrett, the Democratic leader, who will deliver a eulogy.

In the Senate, Mr. Robinson, the Democratic leader, will deliver an address. Both houses will resume business Tuesday.

EUROPE IS STIRRED BY WILSON'S DEATH

Lloyd George Calls Him Glorious Failure Who Sacrificed His Life for His Ideal.

CECIL PAYS HIM TRIBUTE

France, Italy and Other Allied Capitals Recall His Services in Winning the War.

Special Cable to THE NEW YORK TIMES.

LONDON, Feb. 3.—In common with most of the allied statesmen of Europe and other personalities whom destiny summoned to fill leading rôles in the World War, former Premier Lloyd George sees in Woodrow Wilson an idealist who stood out as perhaps the most remarkable figure of that tremendous cataclysm.

In an interview which THE NEW YORK TIMES correspondent had with him today at his new home at Churt, Surrey, concerning the passing of Mr. Wilson, Mr. Lloyd George said:

"Woodrow Wilson was a very great man, and, like all great men, had his defects, but these will be quickly forgotten in the magnitude of his life work. True he was a failure, but a glorious failure. He failed as Jesus Christ failed, and, like Christ, sacrificed his life in pursuance of his noble ideal.

"He was just as much a victim of the great war as any soldier who died in the trenches. He ruined his health in the endeavor to create a better and happier existence for the people of the whole world, and I am sure that the failure of his altruistic inspirations hastened his tragic end.

"It will perhaps be a generation before the greatness of Woodrow Wilson will be appreciated at its real value by his countrymen and the tragedy which closed his life will bring before the world the unselfishness of his ambitions as nothing else could. Like the tragedy which made for your great martyred Lincoln a permanent place in the hearts of the American people—even of those who disagreed with him, as was made very apparent to me in my recent visit to the Southern States—the sad death of this great Statesman, this great American, will indelibly stamp his name among those at the very top of your history.

Had Violent Likes and Dislikes.

"Like Theodore Roosevelt, Mr. Wilson had violent likes and dislikes, and for this, as always is the penalty of greatness, he was violently criticized. I believe I may say that never have I seen such vicious, cruel vituperation as was heaped upon him at home and in Paris at the time of the Peace Conference. Such abuse never was leveled at any man in like position in history and it hurt him terribly.

"Criticism cut him like a knife. Had he been a lifelong politician he could have overlooked these attacks. Thirty years or so of political life makes one invulnerable. I know. But Wilson's character was such, he was of such fine stuff, that he was immensely sensitive to this public abuse and he suffered more than others would have done. I have no doubt that this helped to bring on his illness.

"Besides, he was a tireless worker. I remember when we were in Paris I would see lights in his room at all hours of the night as he worked at his League idea. The rest of us found time for golf and we took our Sundays off, but Wilson, in his zeal, worked incessantly. Only those who were there and witnessed it can realize the efforts he expended.

His Personality Grew Upon One.

"He was a man whose personality grew upon one. When I first met him here in England I did not understand him, nor did Clemenceau in Paris; but when you spend every day for five months with a man you have opportunity to become well acquainted with him, and when it was over I had learned to appreciate his great gifts and to like him very much personally, and I remember Clemenceau at the time telling me his feelings were similar.

"Yes, Woodrow Wilson was a very good fellow, and I shall mourn his passing. I had the pleasure of spending a

Continued on Page Four.

COOLIDGE ANNOUNCES DEATH

In Formal Proclamation He Calls the Nation to Mourn.

HE LAUDS WILSON'S WORK

With Mrs. Coolidge, He Drives From Church to S Street House and Leaves Cards.

FLAGS ORDERED LOWERED

Will Stay at Half-Staff 30 Days —Government Offices to Close —Receptions Canceled.

Special to The New York Times.

WASHINGTON, Feb. 3.—The death of Woodrow Wilson was formally announced to the people of the nation late this afternoon in a proclamation issued from the White House by President Coolidge, in which he paid high tribute to the war President, and directed that flags on the White House and Government buildings be half-staffed for a period of thirty days.

When the text of the proclamation was made public, the further statement was authorized at the White House that President Coolidge had directed that orders be issued closing all Government departments on the day of Mr. Wilson's funeral. Flags will fly at half-mast on war ships, at military posts and on all American diplomatic and other Government offices abroad.

President Coolidge's proclamation pays high tribute to the life and services of Mr. Wilson, saying that it brings "to many of us" a sense of profound personal bereavement.

Official Social Functions Canceled.

All official social functions—including the brilliant State reception scheduled for the White House on Thursday—have been canceled.

In ordering the flags on Government buildings half-staffed, and arranging for the issuance of orders for closing Government buildings on the day of the funeral, President Coolidge followed the customary procedure. The President feels that the Government, over which Mr. Wilson presided during eight of the most important years in American history, should in every way act in testimony of the respect in which the memory of so great and distinguished a President is held.

President and Mrs. Coolidge were in their pew in the First Congregational Church, at the corner of Tenth and G Streets, when they first heard of the death of the former President. In that church, in common with many others, announcement of the death was made during the services, at the close of which the pastor, the Rev. Jason Noble Pierce, made a special prayer in view of the occasion.

After the close of the service the Coolidges were driven directly to the Wilson home. The big White House car swept into the drive before the Wilson house at 12:25 o'clock, one hour and ten minutes after the death of the ex-President. The door of the car was opened by a Secret Service man, while another stood outside it and between the car and the spectators.

Although a few of the callers at the Wilson home had stayed in their cars and sent in cards by a footman, both the President and Mrs. Coolidge alighted. The President got out first, assisting Mrs. Coolidge. They walked up the flight of three steps to the door. It happened to be open, because two other callers had rung the bell just as the President's car stopped.

Coolidge Hands Cards to the Butler.

Mr. Coolidge himself handed cards to the negro butler, who received them on a silver tray. They re-entered their car, but its long wheelbase was too much for the narrow arc of the Wilson driveway, and the chauffeur was obliged to back and start twice before he could get started for the street.

The President's car started east over the S Street hill and was followed by the car in which the Secret Service men rode.

The President wore a silk hat and a black overcoat with silk lapels. Mrs. Coolidge was dressed in brown, with hat to match. Both were grave, and during their stop at the Wilson house neither was observed to speak a word.

Perhaps half an hour after the Presidential visit C. Bascom Slemp, Secretary to Mr. Coolidge, arrived alone in his car. He entered the house and was inside ten or fifteen minutes. When he emerged, Mr. Slemp said that, in addition to offering his personal condolences as a Virginian and an acquaintance of the family, he had come from the President to tell the members of the Wilson household that the Government was desirous of learning its wishes in respect to funeral arrangements, and that anything they desired would be done.

Mr. Slemp said he had talked to Joseph Wilson, the former President's brother, and John Randolph Bolling, his Secretary. They told him that funeral plans had not been discussed, but it was agreed that as soon as any decision was reached Mr. Slemp would be informed.

WOODROW WILSON

President Coolidge's Proclamation

By the President of the United States of America.

A Proclamation

To the People of the United States:

The death of Woodrow Wilson, President of the United States from March 4, 1913, to March 4. 1921, which occurred at 11:15 o'clock today at his home at Washington, District of Columbia, deprives the country of a most distinguished citizen, and is an event which causes universal and genuine sorrow. To many of us it brings the sense of a profound personal bereavement.

His early profession as a lawyer was abandoned to enter academic life. In this chosen field he attained the highest rank as an educator, and has left his impress upon the intellectual thought of the country.

From the Presidency of Princeton University he was called by his fellow citizens to be the Chief Executive of the State of New Jersey. The duties of this high office he so conducted as to win the confidence of the people of the United States, who twice elected him to the Chief Magistracy of the Republic.

As President of the United States he was moved by an earnest desire to promote the best interests of the country as he conceived them. His acts were prompted by high motives and his sincerity of purpose cannot be questioned. He led the nation through the terrific struggle of the World War with a lofty idealism which never failed him. He gave utterance to the aspiration of humanity with an eloquence which held the attention of all the earth and made America a new and enlarged influence in the destiny of mankind.

In testimony of the respect in which his memory is held by the Government and the people of the United States, I do hereby direct that the flags of the White House and of the several departmental buildings be displayed at half-staff for a period of thirty days, and that suitable military and naval honors, under orders of the Secretary of War and of the Secretary of the Navy, may be rendered on the day of the funeral.

Done at the City of Washington this Third Day of February, in the Year of Our Lord One Thousand Nine Hundred and Twenty-Four, and of the Independence of the United States of America the One Hundred and Forty-Eighth.

By the President, CALVIN COOLIDGE,
CHARLES EVANS HUGHES,
Secretary of State.

GRAYSON DESCRIBES SCENE AT DEATHBED

War President, He Says, Grew Weaker and Weaker Until He Calmly Passed Away.

ONCE CONSCIOUS AT NIGHT

Then He Relapsed Into Virtual Coma, From Which He Did Not Emerge.

Special to The New York Times.

WASHINGTON, Feb. 3.—Woodrow Wilson's death was peaceful, a gradual fading away of life after a long period of unconsciousness, according to Admiral Cary T. Grayson, who was his physician in the days of his strength and vigor at the White House and who was in almost constant attendance upon him since his tragic breakdown more than four years ago.

Mr. Wilson's last spoken word was "Edith," the name of his wife, uttered in a faint whisper late yesterday afternoon, when Mrs. Wilson had left the sick room temporarily. Mrs. Wilson, sent for by Admiral Grayson, returned almost immediately. She remained in the room thereafter until the end, sitting in a chair at the bedside and holding her husband's hand for the greater part of the time.

Mr. Wilson's last completely phrased sentence, so far as Admiral Grayson could recall, was his remark on Friday about the broken machine and the expression of his readiness to go. "I am a broken piece of machinery," he said. "When the machinery is broken—I am ready to go."

The last message to be received by Mr. Wilson from any one outside his immediate family was from Senator Glass of Virginia. Senator Glass, a close friend of Mr. Wilson and a strong supporter of his policies, asked Admiral Grayson to give "the Chief" his love. Admiral Grayson did so early Saturday

Continued on Page Two.

WAR PRESIDENT'S END CAME PEACEFULLY

His Life Ebbed Away While He Slept and His Heart Action Became Fainter Until It Finally Ceased.

WIFE AT THE DYING MAN'S BEDSIDE UNTIL THE END

Her Name Was the Last Word to Pass His Lips and His Last Sentence Was 'I Am Ready,' Spoken Friday.

Special to The New York Times.

WASHINGTON, Feb. 3.—Woodrow Wilson, twenty-eighth President of the United States, a commanding world figure and chief advocate of the League of Nations, is dead. He died at 11:15 o'clock this morning, after being unconscious for nearly twelve hours.

Mrs. Wilson, Miss Margaret Wilson, Joseph Wilson, a brother, and Admiral Grayson, his physician, were at the bedside.

Just before death the war President opened his eyes. His wife and daughter spoke to him, but he did not respond. Ten minutes later he passed quietly away. No word was uttered.

All day yesterday and last night he had been sinking rapidly, his pulse becoming fainter and fainter, until finally it ceased to beat. His "broken machinery" had collapsed.

Washington and the nation were prepared for death. The morning papers had carried the news that he had been "profoundly prostrated." The waiting groups, numbering many hundreds, outside of the Wilson home were silent when Admiral Grayson, five minutes after his patient and friend had expired, opened the door and made the announcement.

Text of the Death Bulletin.

Dr. Grayson read the following bulletin:

11:20 A. M., Feb. 3 ,1924.

Mr. Wilson died at 11:15 o'clock this morning. His heart action became feebler and feebler, and the heart muscle was so fatigued that it refused to act any longer. The end came peacefully. The remote causes of death lie in his ill-health, which began more than four years ago, namely, arteriosclerosis and hemiplegia. The immediate cause of death was exhaustion following a digestive disturbance which began in the early part of last week, but did not reach an acute stage until the early morning hours of Feb. 1. CARY T. GRAYSON.

Arteriosclerosis is a thickening and hardening of the walls of the arteries, and hemiplegia is a paralysis of one side of the body, the limbs on that side losing the power of voluntary motion. Mr. Wilson's left side was so stricken, the outward manifestation being the helpless drop of his left arm and the dragging of the left foot.

Died While Wife Held His Hand.

Mr. Wilson died in a room on the third floor of his home, where for so many months, since his retirement, he sat and looked over Washington, the scene of his greatest achievement. He expired on a large four-poster bed, a replica of the Lincoln bed in the White House.

Mr. Wilson's last word was "Edith," his wife's name. In a faint voice he called for her yesterday afternoon when she had left his bedside for a moment.

His last sentence was spoken on Friday, when he said:

"I am a broken piece of machinery. When the machinery is broken——

"I am ready."

Mrs. Wilson held his right hand as his life slowly ebbed away. Admiral Grayson remained in the death room for a few minutes and then went down stairs leaving Mrs. Wilson and Margaret the only mourners at the bedside.

There had been signs during the morning that the end was a matter of minutes. The first bulletin issued by Dr. Grayson at 8:55 o'clock said:

"Mr. Wilson is unconscious and his pulse is very weak."

His 10:30 o'clock bulletin read:

"After a quiet night Mr. Wilson is very low and the end may be expected any time."

When, therefore, Dr. Grayson appeared on the steps of the house at 11:20 it was realized that he was probably there to announce the end.

Dr. Grayson Deeply Moved.

Dr. Grayson was making a strong effort to keep himself under control. In his hand he held some of the yellow slips on which the bulletins were typewritten. He came toward the newspaper men, who quickly gathered about him near the steps of the house.

"The end came at 11:15," he said in a low tone.

Immediately there was a commotion in the crowd as the newspaper men assigned to flash the news of death which would speed all over the world, broke through their comrades and rushed off.

The crowd across the street, now grown to large proportions, surged forward in an effort to hear Dr. Grayson, but the police lines held and there was nothing for them to do but to listen with strained attention.

Meanwhile Dr. Grayson had begun to read the bulletin. This was the climax of the emotional strain he has been under, and it was only with difficulty that he could force himself to go ahead.

He read slowly. His voice trembled, but did not break. But as he read, very slowly, tears kept rolling down his cheeks and he used his handkerchief.

This action, more than what they could hear, showed the spectators across the street that he was actually announcing Mr. Wilson's death. Here and there in the crowd men began to take off their hats. Soon almost all were uncovered. The women stood with lowered heads, many of them weeping.

Finally, Dr. Grayson finished reading the bulletin. The newspaper men expressed a few words of sympathy and then hurried off to send the detailed news. Dr. Grayson was left standing with only one or two before him.

The physician and friend of the former President, who has been the only link between the sick room and the outside world, was asked whether, now that Mr. Wilson was dead, he would not give a detailed account of his last hours. He demurred, saying he did not believe there was anything more to be added to what had been said.

He was urged to undertake the task as a duty to the memory of his friend and patient. On this ground he assented. He said he would take an automobile ride for the purpose of resting, and that during its course he

"All the News That's Fit to Print."

The New York Times.

EXTRA
5 A. M.
THE WEATHER—Fair today.

VOL. LXXIV....No. 24,392. NEW YORK, WEDNESDAY, NOVEMBER 5, 1924. TWO CENTS In Greater New York | THREE CENTS Within 200 Miles | FOUR CENTS Elsewhere

COOLIDGE WINS, 357 TO DAVIS'S 136; LA FOLLETTE CARRIES WISCONSIN; SMITH BEATS ROOSEVELT BY 140,000

CITY ELECTS SMITH

Big Manhattan and Bronx Vote Wins for Governor.

UP-STATE STRONGLY G. O. P.

Roosevelt Carries Buffalo and Several Large Industrial Centres.

BROOKLYN GOES TO SMITH

Kings County Gives Him 152,000 Plurality, Although Coolidge Carries It by 80,000.

LEGISLATURE REPUBLICAN

Democrats Lose Control of Senate and Their Numbers in Assembly Are Reduced.

SOME OFFICES IN DOUBT

Whole Smith Ticket May Not Be Elected—Vote for the Socialist Nominee, Thomas, Is Small.

Overcoming a Republican Presidential sweep that reached nearly a million plurality, Alfred E. Smith was re-elected Governor of New York in yesterday's election, defeating his Republican opponent, Colonel Theodore Roosevelt, by an estimated plurality of 140,000.

As a vote-getter the Governor surpassed his performance of four years ago when, in the Harding landslide, he went down to defeat, although running more than a million votes ahead of his ticket.

By an enormous city vote the Governor overcame a heavy handicap, for Colonel Roosevelt captured the rock-ribbed Republican counties up-State. The Colonel, reversing the record of Nathan L. Miller, also carried Democratic city strongholds above the Bronx which Governor Smith easily carried two and four years ago.

At 1:30 o'clock this morning Colonel Roosevelt at Oyster Bay issued a statement conceding the election of Governor Smith. He said he congratulated the Governor and also expressed satisfaction over the election of President Coolidge.

While the Governor was taking the measure of his Gubernatorial opponent, President Calvin Coolidge carried the State by 920,000 plurality. His vote up-State not only reached 870,000, but he carried every borough in the City of New York with a plurality over John W. Davis, his Democratic opponent, of 130,000.

La Follette Polls 4[illegible],000.

Senator Robert M. La Follette, running for President on a Third Party ticket, polled 4[illegible],000 votes in the State but ran third.

While Governor Smith was elected by a safe margin there was considerable uncertainty as to the fate of the rest of the State Democratic ticket. Lieutenant Governor George R. Lunn appeared to be safe although he ran fully 100,000 votes behind the Governor in the city. The rest of the ticket was lost in the count of votes for the Governorship.

The Governor's triumph was marred somewhat by the Republican gains in the Legislature. It was admitted by the Democrats that the Republicans elected enough State Senators to take control of that body from the Democrats and had materially increased their majority in the Assembly.

George K. Morris, Republican State Chairman, made the following statement at 1:30 o'clock this morning:

"Indications are that Governor Smith had been re-elected by between [illegible] and 95,000. But we have made substantial gains in the Assembly and have regained control of the State Senate, which will now be 28 to 23 in favor of the Republicans, instead of 26 to 25 in favor of the Democrats. We gained two Senators in Erie County, one in Rensselaer County and one in New York County, with probably an additional gain of one or more in other Senatorial districts. We have [illegible] [illegible] the entire State ticket with the exception of Colonel Roosevelt [illegible]

Continued on Page Two.

GOVERNORS ELECTED.

REPUBLICAN.

Connecticut	Hiram Bingham
Delaware	Robert P. Robinson
Illinois	Len Small*
Idaho	Charles C. Moore*
Indiana	Ed Jackson
Iowa	John Hammill*
Kansas	Ben S. Paulen
Massachusetts	Alvan T. Fuller
Michigan	Alex J. Groesbeck
Nebraska	Adam McMullen
New Hampshire	John G. Winant
Rhode Island	Aram J. Pothier
South Dakota	Carl Gunderson
Vermont	Franklin K. Billings
Washington	Roland H. Hartley
West Virginia	Howard M. Gore
Wisconsin	John J. Blaine*

DEMOCRATIC.

Florida	John W. Martin
Georgia	Clifford Walker*
New York	Alfred E. Smith*
North Carolina	A. W. McLean
South Carolina	T. G. McLeod
Tennessee	Austin Peay*
Texas	Mrs. Miriam A. Ferguson

*Re-elected.

COOLIDGE AND SMITH CARRY THIS CITY

The President's Plurality About 130,000 and the Governor's About 500,000.

LA FOLLETTE VOTE 250,000

Coolidge Wins in Every Borough—Democrats Elect All Local Officers.

New York City gave its vote at yesterday's election to Calvin Coolidge, Republican nominee for President, and Charles G. Dawes, Republican nominee for Vice President, and at the same time rolled up a record plurality for Governor Alfred E. Smith, electing him Chief Executive of New York State for the third time.

As in the Presidential election of 1920, Governor Smith's personal popularity, apparent satisfaction with his administration and possibly some weakness of his opponent, Colonel Theodore Roosevelt, combined to give the Governor a lead never before obtained by any candidate for any office in this city.

President Coolidge obtained a total of approximately 130,000 plurality in New York City and carried every borough, according to fairly complete returns.

The indications were that he would have a plurality of about 9,000 in Manhattan, 4,300 in the Bronx, 73,000 in Brooklyn, 30,000 in Queens and 2,200 in Richmond.

500,000 Plurality for Smith.

Governor Smith, however, carried the city by about 500,000, the "spread" between his vote and that for Davis, the Democratic Presidential candidate, being about 430,000, or nearly equal to the difference between his vote and that for Cox four years ago. Governor Smith carried every Borough heavily.

The indications on incomplete returns were that he had carried Manhattan by more than 196,000, Brooklyn by approximately 130,000, the Bronx by 166,000, Queens by 43,000 and Richmond by 9,000.

Governor Smith apparently carried every Assembly district in the city but one, the Twenty-first District, in Brooklyn. La Follette showed his greatest proportionate strength in the Bronx, where he led in the Third, Fourth and Fifth Assembly Districts and was running close in the Seventh.

The vote in the Nineteenth, Manhattan, Assembly District, which includes a large part of Harlem's "Black belt," showed that the negroes have remained true to the Republican Party's national candidates, but voted for Governor Smith on the Ku Klux Klan issue. With seven districts missing out of forty-four, the [illegible]

Continued on Page Five.

MRS. FERGUSON WINS 2 TO 1 IN TEXAS RACE FOR GOVERNORSHIP

Incomplete Returns Indicate That She Will Have a Majority of 225,000 Over Republican.

RUNS BEHIND IN CITIES

But the Big Majorities in the Rural Districts Carry Her to Victory.

LARGE KLAN VOTE IS CAST

Party Lines Are Ignored as Ku Klux Vote for Republican, While Negroes Vote for Democrat.

Special to The New York Times.

AUSTIN, Texas, Nov. 4.—Returns from the rural districts of Texas coming in late this evening show that Mrs. Miriam A. Ferguson will probably receive a majority of about 225,000 votes over Dr. George C. Butte, Republican, for Governor.

Of a total of about 760,000 votes cast about 218,000 have been counted, giving Mrs. Ferguson a lead of 62,000 votes. According to unofficial returns, the lead which Dr. Butte started with by returns from the larger cities was quickly overcome by the rural returns.

At 10 o'clock the vote for Governor, including returns from 310 towns and cities, stood:

Mrs. Ferguson, 117,345.
Dr. Butte, 68,145.

Interest in the election was intensified by the prominence of the Ku Klux Klan issue in the campaign and it caused an outpouring of people at the polls. It is estimated that nearly 800,000 votes were cast. This is only a few thousand less than the total number polled in the run-off primary. Perfect weather prevailed all over the State, and this was a factor in favor of Mrs. Ferguson, as it meant passable roads for the farmer to travel to the precinct voting boxes.

The early returns show that Mrs. Ferguson's principal strength was in the rural districts. The count in the larger cities is progressing slowly. It shows that Dr. George C. Butte, the Republican candidate for Governor, is running well ahead of Mrs. Ferguson in Dallas, Austin, Houston, Beaumont and other of the larger cities.

Butte is also running ahead of Mrs. Ferguson in a number of the populous counties of North Texas and is making a strong showing in parts of Central Texas. The rural districts, however, are piling up in the early count an almost solid vote for Mrs. Ferguson.

According to these returns, she swept East Texas and the territory south of San Antonio and more than broke even with Butte in other rural districts. It is practically conceded by the Republican leaders that if the estimate that 800,000 votes were polled is correct Mrs. Ferguson's election by the usual big Democratic majority is assured. These leaders contend, however, that the total vote was not more than 600,000 and that this means that Butte has a chance of winning.

The Ku Klux Klan strongholds gave a surprisingly large vote for Butte. It is apparent that he received the bulk of the Klan vote. Party lines were largely lost sight of and thousands of veteran Democrats today cast their first vote for a Republican candidate for office. The election marked the greatest political revolution that ever took place in Texas. Irrespective of the indication that Butte was not elected. Practically all of the German vote, more than 30,000 in number, which is nominally Republican, went to Mrs. Ferguson because of the Klan issue. The same is true of the negro vote which went solid for the woman candidate.

TEMPLE, Texas, Nov. 4.—Mrs. Miriam A. Ferguson of Temple, who on the face of returns in today's general election

Continued on Page Five.

United States Senators Elected

REPUBLICANS—18.

Colorado	*L. C. Phipps
Colorado	†Rice W. Means
Delaware	T. C. du Pont
Idaho	*William E. Borah
Illinois	C. S. Deneen
Kansas	*Arthur Capper
Kentucky	F. M. Sackett
Massachusetts	F. H. Gillett
Michigan	‡James Couzens
Nebraska	*G. W. Norris
New Hampshire	*H. W. Keyes
New Jersey	*W. E. Edge
Oklahoma	W. B. Pine
Oregon	*C. L. McNary
Rhode Island	‡J. H. Metcalf
South Dakota	W. H. McMaster
West Virginia	Guy D. Goff
Wyoming	*F. E. Warren

DEMOCRATS—10.

Alabama	*J. T. Heflin
Arkansas	*J. T. Robinson
Georgia	*W. J. Harris
Louisiana	*J. E. Ransdell
Mississippi	*Pat Harrison
North Carolina	*F. M. Simmons
South Carolina	C. L. Blease
Tennessee	L. D. Tyson
Texas	*M. Sheppard
Virginia	*Carter Glass

Result in Iowa, Minnesota, Montana and New Mexico is in doubt.

*Re-elected.
†Elected for short term to fill vacancy in present Senate.
‡Elected for both short and long terms.

LEGISLATURE AGAIN SOLIDLY REPUBLICAN

Party Recovers Control of the Senate, With a Probable Majority of Four.

STRONGER IN THE ASSEMBLY

J. A. McGinnies of Chautauqua Is Slated for Speaker—One Woman Elected.

Returns from the legislative elections throughout New York State yesterday showed that the Republicans had recaptured control of the State Senate, which during the last two years has been Democratic by the slender majority of one vote. The returns indicated also that the Republicans had increased their lead in the Assembly, which remained Republican during the two years of Governor Smith's present Administration.

Figures, which in some instances have been estimated, give the Republicans a working majority of four in the upper house of the Legislature, with the possibility that this may be increased through changes based on more complete returns.

In the normally Republican Fifteenth Senate District on the upper west side in Manhattan, Senator Nathan Straus won a signal victory, which will return him to the Senate for a third term. He defeated Assemblyman Victor R. Kaufman, whom the Republicans had nominated.

The latest figures received indicate that the Republicans, who have twenty-five members in the present Senate, will have at least twenty-nine in the body elected yesterday.

They gained one Senator in the Seventeenth District, located on the upper west side in Manhattan, where, on partial returns, the election of Courtland Nicoll, the Republican candidate, appeared assured. His Democratic opponent was the present incumbent, Senator Meyer Levy.

In the Eighth Senatorial District in Brooklyn, where early returns indicated re-election of the present incumbent, Dr. W. L. Love, more nearly complete figures pointed to his defeat by R. C. Ellis, his Republican opponent.

Gains by Republicans.

Other gains by the Republicans included the Thirty-first Senate District, which takes in Rensselaer County, where Senator John P. Williams, the Democratic incumbent, was defeated by John R. Williams, a Republican newcomer in the Legislature. In the Forty-ninth, which takes in part of Erie County, Robert C. Lacey, the present Democratic Senator, who enjoyed wide popularity in labor circles and has served two years in the Senate, will be replaced by L. R. Lipowicz, his Republican opponent.

Returns from the Assembly elections showed an increased Republican majority in the lower house of next year's Legislature, where the Republicans this year have a working majority of twelve. In the table a number of the districts within the city were estimated on partial returns from a small number of election districts and the result was subject to change on more complete returns.

Despite the huge pluralities run up by the Republicans for Coolidge and Dawes in New York City, the Democrats retained their hold, with few exceptions, on Senate and Assembly districts in the city which are represented by Democrats in the present Legislature.

The Republican Assembly gains were made up-State for the most part. There they won in Sullivan County, in the First District of Rensselaer, in the First and Third Albany Districts, in the Second Onondaga District and the First District in Schenectady County, all of which sent Democrats to the present Legislature in the election a year ago.

Republican Gain in Kings.

About the only gain made by the Republicans in this city was in the Seventeenth Assembly District in Kings, normally Republican, but for the last two of three years represented by a Demo-

Continued on Page Two.

COOLIDGE AND EDGE WINNERS IN JERSEY

Record Vote Gives President Plurality Which Is Estimated at 350,000.

MRS. NORTON IS ELECTED

First Woman in Congress From the East—Tunnel Bond Issue Adopted.

New Jersey, breaking all previous records in the size of its vote, gave large pluralities to Coolidge and Senator Edge, and increased the Republican majorities in both branches of the State Legislature. The proposed $8,000,000 bond issue for finishing the Hudson vehicular tunnels and the Camden Bridge was receiving large majorities.

The polls were closed at 7 o'clock and the size of the vote was so unprecedented that the first returns were made long after the customary time for reporting them. At 3 o'clock this morning Coolidge had a lead of 167,688 in 1,191 of the 2,559 election districts in New Jersey. On the basis of these figures his estimated plurality reached 350,000 for all the districts.

In the Senatorial contest Edge was leading Donnelly by 27,537 in 324 of the 2,559 districts. Senator Edge declared last night that the Coolidge-Dawes plurality as well as his own would reach 200,000.

The Republicans elected ten members of Congress and the Democrats only two, including Mrs. Mary T. Norton of Jersey City, who won a sweeping victory in the Twelfth District in Hudson County, a Democratic stronghold. Mrs. Norton ran against Douglas D. T. Storey, Republican, and she will be the first woman to go to Congress to represent an Eastern State.

She Thanks the Voters.

When her election was assured Mrs. Norton, in an interview, expressed her gratitude to Mayor Frank Hague of Jersey City for having placed her in nomination in the Twelfth District, which is a Democratic stronghold.

"I congratulate Mayor Hague," she said, "on his foresight and justice in placing New Jersey among the first States of the Union to send a woman to Congress. I thank the organization and I thank the voters. I shall do everything in my power for the people of New Jersey and for the nation."

The success of the Democratic candidate in the Twelfth District of New Jersey was a foregone conclusion. Mrs. Norton was nominated by Mayor Hague with the full approval of other Democratic leaders. Her nomination was hailed at the time as a tribute to her years of work in the interests of the party.

Mrs. Norton cast her ballot in the Twenty-first Election District, in the Eleventh Ward, Jersey City. She was accompanied by her husband when she went to the polling place in a small candy store. Her husband is Robert E. Norton, who is in the cooperage business in Jersey City.

Five election districts in Camden County gave Coolidge 705 votes, Davis 300 and La Follette 80. One election district in Morris County gave Coolidge 118, Davis 25 and La Follette 4. Twenty of the 2,559 election districts in

Continued on Page Seven.

THIRD PARTY POLLS 4,000,000 VOTES IN WHOLE COUNTRY

Showing in Electoral College Far Behind Strength in Popular Support.

CARRIED ONLY WISCONSIN

Mid-West Deserted the Senator but Industrial Districts in Cities Helped Him.

COLLAPSE IN CALIFORNIA

But the Senator Ran Second in That State, the Dakotas, Minnesota, Montana and Nevada.

Returns from the Eastern and Southern States, and a few States in the West, showed that the Progressive Party movement, headed by Senator Robert M. La Follette of Wisconsin, fell far short of the expectations of its leaders. Senator La Follette, apparently, has run a poor third in all States east of the Mississippi River, except his own State of Wisconsin, which he carried and Minnesota, where he is running second. He is running second in Montana, Nevada, California, Iowa and the two Dakotas. Apparently his total vote in the country is about 4,000,000.

La Follette's greatest collapse was in California, where, so far from his carrying the State, as he expected, the Republicans have it by a great majority.

The following table shows the estimated La Follette vote in the various States.

California	330,000
Illinois	350,000
Iowa	275,000
Indiana	80,000
Kansas	90,000
Michigan	125,000
Minnesota	430,000
New York	410,000
Montana	50,000
Nebraska	90,000
North Dakota	100,000
New Jersey	60,000
Ohio	200,000
Pennsylvania	250,000
South Dakota	90,000
Washington	120,000
Wisconsin	375,000

His vote in other States varied from 1,000 or less in Arizona to about 45,000 in Maryland.

The forecasts by the Progressive Party leaders that La Follette and Wheeler would carry Illinois, Ohio and probably a few Eastern States were not made good. In both Illinois and Ohio Senator La Follette was many thousand votes behind John W. Davis, Democratic nominee, and the Wisconsin Senator received only a fraction of the total vote given to President Coolidge.

In New York State, where the backers of La Follette had predicted that the Progressive ticket would carry New York City, La Follette was a bad third. La Follette received fewer than half the votes recorded for Mr. Davis, and President Coolidge beat the Third Party candidate in New York five or six to one. Most of the La Follette strength in New York, as in other Eastern States, was concentrated in a few industrial centres.

In Massachusetts, where President Coolidge beat Mr. Davis six or seven to one, Mr. Davis beat La Follette more than two to one. Even in Boston, a city which La Follette leaders had professed confidence of carrying, Senator La Follette received but a negligible vote.

In Connecticut, another State where the Progressive Party leaders claimed great strength, early returns showed that President Coolidge was getting more than six votes for each given La Follette and that Mr. Davis was leading La Follette about two to one.

Poor Showing in South and West.

The Progressive Party had expected to run first or second in New Hampshire, according to the predictions made, but the returns indicated that President Coolidge would beat Senator La Follette by fifteen to one or better, and that Davis was running ahead of La Follette at the rate of eight votes to one.

Another example of the collapse of the La Follette movement was supplied

Continued on Page Five.

Electoral Vote

COOLIDGE.

California	13
Colorado	6
Connecticut	7
Delaware	3
Idaho	4
Illinois	29
Indiana	15
Iowa	13
Kansas	10
Kentucky	13
Maine	6
Maryland	8
Massachusetts	18
Michigan	15
Missouri	18
Nebraska	8
New Hampshire	4
New Jersey	14
New York	45
North Dakota	5
Ohio	24
Oregon	5
Pennsylvania	38
Rhode Island	5
South Dakota	5
Vermont	4
Utah	4
Washington	7
West Virginia	8
Wyoming	3
Total	357

DAVIS.

Alabama	12
Arkansas	9
Florida	6
Georgia	14
Louisiana	10
Mississippi	10
North Carolina	12
Oklahoma	10
South Carolina	9
Tennessee	12
Texas	20
Virginia	12
Total	136

LA FOLLETTE.

Wisconsin	13
Total	13

DOUBTFUL.

Arizona	3
Minnesota	12
Montana	4
Nevada	3
New Mexico	3
Total	25

Total number of votes in Electoral College, 531; necessary to a choice, 266.

Some of the States in the above list are placed as doubtful only because, due to the difference in time, the returns are inadequate.

REPUBLICANS MAKE GAINS IN CONGRESS

Retain Control of Senate and May Increase House Majority to 50.

BROOKHART LIKELY TO LOSE

Stanley of Kentucky and Walsh of Massachusetts, Democratic Senators, Apparently Beaten.

While the returns on the elections of United States Senators and members of the House of Representatives are incomplete, the indications early this morning were that the Republican Party would retain majorities in both houses of Congress for the two-year period beginning March 4, 1925, the first half of President Coolidge's new administration.

There have been Republican gains in the House sufficiently large to make it apparent that the present majority in that body, which was fifteen when the Congress adjourned in June and has been reduced to ten by resignations and deaths of Republican members, will be considerably exceeded. As for the Senate, Republican candidates have very generally held their own in States from which complete or fairly complete returns have been received.

Figures compiled from the latest returns give the following showing for the next Senate as a result of the elections yesterday:

Republicans, 52; Democrats, 38; Farmer-Labor, 1; four in doubt, with one vacancy not filled yesterday.

The majority the Republicans will have in the House is uncertain but that it will be much larger than the mere nominal majority obtained by the Republicans in the Congressional elections of two years ago is indicated by the following political alignment, based on returns up to an early hour this morning:

Republicans, 2[illegible]; Democrats, 1[illegible]; Socialists, 1; Farmer-Labor, [illegible] [illegible]

NEW YORK BY 900,000

Coolidge's Plurality in This State Little Below Harding's

DAVIS GETS THE SOUTH ONLY

La Follette Apparently Only His Own State, but Large Industrial Vote

CALIFORNIA FOR COOLIDGE

Doubtful States of the Far West Lean to the President as Returns Increase.

DAVIS LOSES WEST VIRGINIA

Refused at Late Hour to Concede Defeat and Hoped for Upset From the West.

BRYAN'S STATE TO COOLIDGE

Plurality of 50,000 in Nebraska for the President Indicated in Latest Dispatches.

Calvin Coolidge has been elected President of the United States in a victory of impressive proportions.

At 5 o'clock this morning the returns indicated that President Coolidge had secured 357 electoral votes, Davis 136 and La Follette 13, and that 25 votes in five Western States were still in doubt. The principal overtures in the late returns were in Kentucky and Missouri. In Kentucky, in 3,431 out of 3,971 precincts, seven-eighths of the State, Coolidge had 337,838, against 331,244 for Davis. It was the opinion of the most competent observers in the State that later returns would not take the State away from the President.

In Missouri Coolidge has 231,502, against Davis's 238,896 in 1,934 out of 4,089 precincts. Correspondents in the State believed that the Republican rural precincts were sure to give the State to the President. The St. Louis Globe-Democrat estimates that Coolidge will carry the State by 59,000.

The five States remaining in doubt are Minnesota, Montana, Nevada, Arizona and New Mexico.

In Montana Coolidge has a slight lead, but the returns are too scant to justify giving the State to him at present. Arizona and New Mexico are close, with indications of going for Davis. In Nevada Coolidge has a lead of 800 votes over La Follette, who is running second, in a little less than one-half the State.

It is not probable that Davis's vote in the Electoral College will exceed 142, which it will be if he carries Arizona and New Mexico. Apparently he has no chance in Minnesota, Montana and Nevada, where he is running third, La Follette being second. On the other hand, it is possible that Coolidge may carry Minnesota, Montana and Nevada, giving him a total of 376, or, with Arizona and New Mexico added, 382 as his utmost limit.

An extreme possibility, but not a very strong one, for La Follette, is the addition of Minnesota, Montana and Nevada, to the one State that he has surely carried, Wisconsin, which would give him a total of 32.

Senator Robert M. La Follette is leading in his home State, Wisconsin, and will undoubtedly win there and get its 13 electoral votes.

Mr. Coolidge is the sixth Vice President to become President through the death of the incumbent and the second to be elected President immediately afterward. The other was Theodore Roosevelt.

Coolidge Victory Overwhelming.

The victory which returns President Coolidge to office and elects Brig. Gen. Charles G. Dawes of Illinois Vice President is overwhelming in the East and Middle West, and early indications are that the Republicans have [illegible] [illegible] in the Far West. Such States as North and South Dakota, which the La Follettites claimed for the Third Party, have gone to President Coolidge. [illegible] Oregon, which [illegible] expected to go to the Third Party [illegible].

[illegible] also has apparently gone for Coolidge by [illegible], according to [illegible]

La Follette Wins Koenig's Home District; Coolidge Captures Davis's and Olvany's

Senator La Follette carried the home election district of Samuel S. Koenig, Manhattan Republican leader, with a vote of 205 to 159 for Coolidge and 160 for Davis. La Follette received 175 of these votes as the Progressive candidate and [illegible] as the Socialist candidate. Four years ago the same district gave Cox 40 and Harding [illegible].

The Rev. Norman Thomas, the Socialist Gubernatorial candidate, ran [illegible] [illegible] in his own home district, [illegible] [illegible] votes as compared with [illegible] for Smith and [illegible] for Roosevelt.

Governor Smith's district on the lower East Side was carried by Davis with a vote of [illegible]. La Follette ran second with [illegible] and Coolidge third with [illegible]. Four years ago the district gave Cox [illegible] and Harding [illegible].

Governor Smith carried his home district by a vote of 494 to 40 for Roosevelt and 2 for Thomas. Two years ago the same district gave Smith 484 and Miller 28.

President Coolidge carried the home district of Tammany Leader George W. Olvany with a vote of 462. Davis had [illegible] and La Follette [illegible]. The President also defeated John W. Davis in the latter's home district at Locust Valley, L. I. The vote was: Coolidge 471 and Davis 176.

Colonel Roosevelt at Oyster Bay received in his own voting district, the [illegible], a smaller vote than President Coolidge, getting [illegible] to Coolidge's [illegible]. In the same district Governor Smith received 120 votes, while John W. Davis polled [illegible].

The home city of Lunn, Governor Lunn was carried by Colonel Roosevelt by a plurality of [illegible].

State Pluralities Rolled Up by Coolidge.

The following table shows President Coolidge's estimated pluralities on the returns so far received from the States carried by him:

California	*800,000	New Jersey	350,000
Colorado	70,000	New York	900,000
Delaware	15,000	North Dakota	*120,000
Illinois	750,000	Ohio	800,000
Indiana	400,000	Pennsylvania	1,100,000
Iowa	*225,000	Rhode Island	35,000
Kansas	250,000	South Dakota	*45,000
Maine	60,000	Utah	4,000
Maryland	13,000	Washington	100,000
Massachusetts	382,000	West Virginia	35,000
Michigan	400,000		
Nebraska	50,000		

*Over La Follette.

"All the News That's Fit to Print."

The New York Times.

THE WEATHER
Fair and cooler today; tomorrow, fair; fresh northwest winds.
Temperature yesterday—Max., 79; min., 54.
For weather report see Page 22.

VOL. LXXIV....No. 24,565. NEW YORK, MONDAY, APRIL 27, 1925. TWO CENTS in Greater New York | THREE CENTS Within 200 Miles | FOUR CENTS Elsewhere in the U. S.

VON HINDENBURG IS ELECTED PRESIDENT OF GERMANY; BEATS MARX, REPUBLICAN LEADER, BY 887,000 VOTES; TWO KILLED AND MANY INJURED IN RIOTING AT POLLS

REAL FIGHT ON HYLAN FOR RENOMINATION EXPECTED THIS WEEK

Smith Will Be in Town and Tammany Conferences May Settle Mayor's Fate.

SOME LEADERS FOR HIM

McCooey's Continued Silence Starts Reports That He May Withhold His Support.

SOMERS IS A POSSIBILITY

President of the Brooklyn Chamber of Commerce Added to List of Candidates.

The fight to prevent the renomination of Mayor Hylan by the Democratic Party of the city is expected to gain added impetus by the visit of Governor Smith here this week. The Governor will probably arrive here Tuesday night or Wednesday noon, and it was said that his visit might bring about a series of conferences in which something definite in the movement to shelve the Mayor might result.

Sentiment among the Assembly district leaders who make up the Tammany Executive Committee was said to be by no means unanimous for denying Mayor Hylan renomination. A minority group of district leaders, some of them holding public office under the Mayor and some because of the fancied sentiment in their districts, was said to be against the plan to pick some other candidate to head the Democratic ticket. It was said that these leaders would have no hesitancy in advising George W. Olvany, leader of Tammany, that it would be a mistake in their opinion to begin a fight.

A few members of this group were said to be willing to go to the extent of supporting Mayor Hylan in the Democratic primaries against a candidate favored by the majority of the Tammany organization and backed by the Governor. So far as could be learned, however, no Tammany district leader has yet said, even privately, that he would support Mayor Hylan as an independent candidate for re-election against the regularly nominated Democratic candidate for Mayor.

The Mayor's Course in Doubt.

Anything like concerted action on the part of the Mayor's supporters in Tammany has been prevented so far by the uncertainty as to whether he would run in the Democratic primaries if opposed by the Tammany leaders, or would run independently. So far there has been no indication as to which course the Mayor would take, although both his friends and his enemies have assumed that he would fight back in some way with the support of William Randolph Hearst.

Tammany leaders, even those inclined to be against a fight on the Mayor, have not taken kindly to the suggestion that Mr. Hearst might take the opportunity of a Democratic primary fight for the Mayoralty nomination to displace some of the present Tammany district leaders to make room for men friendly to him. Such an attempt, it was said, would probably have the result of forcing practically all the present Tammany leaders into the fight against the Mayor. Little fear is felt that Mr. Hearst could succeed in such a plan, as most of the Tammany leaders are rather firmly intrenched in their home districts.

Leaders in the movement to shelve the Mayor were said to have a strong hope that they would be joined by John H. McCooey, the Brooklyn Democratic leader, although they admitted that Mr. McCooey had not committed himself definitely to an anti-Hylan movement. Mr. McCooey is saying nothing for publication just now, and his failure to come out for Mayor Hylan's renomination has been construed as an indication that he was definitely against him. This, it was said, is not necessarily so.

McCooey Is "Listening."

A prominent Tammany man defined Mr. McCooey's attitude as one of "listening." The belief in Tammany is that Mr. McCooey may be induced to desert Mayor Hylan and that his present non-committal policy may be caused by his desire to have a Brooklyn man, perhaps one of the three or four who have already been mentioned, named as the anti-Hylan Democratic candidate for Mayor.

The name of Arthur S. Somers, President of the Brooklyn Chamber of Commerce and a member of the Board of Education, was added yesterday to the list of possible Brooklyn candidates, which previously consisted of General George A. Wingate, former Representative John J. Fitzgerald and County Clerk William E. Kelly. It was suggested that Mr. Somers, who is President of Mr. McCooey's Assembly District Democratic club, was a man whom Mr. McCooey might well back. Mr. Somers has been at frequent odds with Mayor Hylan. He has frequently been mentioned as a possible fusion candidate.

The position of Borough President Maurice E. Connolly of Queens also was said to be undefined. Mr. Connolly would probably like to be renominated for Borough President and will be guided in large part by the exigencies of his local political situation. It was said, that Mr. Connolly, like Mr. McCooey, was "listening," and that if the movement to deny Mayor Hylan renomination assumed the proportions expected he would be likely to join it.

The Bronx Democratic organization, of which Sheriff Edward J. Flynn is the head, is confidently expected to follow the lead of Tammany. A majority of

Continued on Page Seven.

Paris to New York Flight By French Plane Is Planned

Copyright, 1925, by The New York Times Co.
Special Cable to THE NEW YORK TIMES.

PARIS, April 26.—There is being built secretly in Paris a large hydroplane with which it is hoped to fly without stopping 4,000 miles between Paris and New York.

This machine is being constructed on orders of the French navy according to its own plans. It will have a motor of 550 horsepower and will carry 6,000 liters of gasoline. The first trials will take place in June and the flight will be attempted during the Summer.

French aviation headquarters admit the machine is being made, but refuse to reveal any details beyond those given above.

COPPERHEAD BITES GIRL ON SNAKE HUNT

Venom Enters Veins, but First Aid and Serum Apparently Prevent Harm.

INCIDENT AMUSES VICTIM

Officer in Reptile Study Club, Miss Condon Keeps Serpents as Pets in Her Home.

Miss Nellie Louise Condon, Secretary of the Reptile Study Society of America, was bitten on the right index finger by a large copperhead snake yesterday afternoon in the midst of a snake hunt by thirty-five members of the society in Rattlesnake Den, in the Ramapo Mountains, near Suffern, N. Y.

She was treated immediately by the first-aid methods perfected by the society, then rushed to the Good Samaritan Hospital at Suffern, where an anti-venom serum was injected into her side repeatedly. Within an hour she apparently had fully recovered. She was brought last evening to her home at 102 Convent Avenue. To Miss Condon the bite by one of the most venomous of American serpents was only an amusing and interesting episode. She said afterward that she had had no misgivings, but had had perfect confidence in the ability of her associates on the hunt to deal with such an emergency.

The fortuitous circumstance that the snake which bit Miss Condon had been deprived of a large proportion of its poison just before it struck her reduced the dosage of venom that she received, but, as it was, two or three drops were injected into her veins.

The hunt started yesterday morning and was led by Paul W. Snyder of Bloomfield, N. J., one of the most experienced trappers and handlers of reptiles in the society.

Hunters Protected.

The hunters wore their usual field uniform, equipped with leggings, boots and gloves to reduce the danger of snake bites in their scrambling over the rocky ledges which are the favorite sunning places of venomous reptiles. They carried bags in which to bring back their captures and forked sticks with which to catch them and hold them.

Until yesterday no member of the society had ever been bitten by a venomous reptile, but several members of the party carried supplies of the anti-venom serum developed in recent years by the Pasteur Institute.

Early in the hunt yesterday a rattler and a blue-tailed skunk, the latter a variety of lizard, had been caught and studied, and then Miss Condon caught the copperhead. Mr. Snyder took the snake, and while the party gathered around gave a demonstration of how to extract and keep snake venom. He held the angry reptile behind the jaws and let it strike at the edge of a glass phial. The snake deposited about ten drops of his poison, and then was put down on the ground and held with a forked stick.

Miss Condon, intending to transfer him to one of the bags, took charge of him and put a forked stick behind his head. As she stooped to pick up the animal the stick slipped on a loose stone, the snake's head jerked free and he instantly struck her on the hand.

Laughs at Her Wound.

There was no excitement. Miss Condon laughed and said she had been bitten. Within a half minute other members of the party had placed a tourniquet on the finger and another on her arm above the elbow to prevent the poison being carried into her system. Then Frank McLees of Rutherford, N. J., opened the cut with a razor-blade to allow it to bleed freely and Mrs. McLees drew the blood out.

The anti-venom serum was at hand to be applied, but Mr. Snyder thought it better to have it administered by a physician, and so the wound was sterilized with potassium permanganate and bandaged. Then a dose of strichnine to stimulate her heart was administered and Miss Condon was taken in an automobile to the Good Samaritan Hospital in the town nearby, where Dr. C. P. Hussy injected three drams of the serium into her side at intervals during a half hour. The swelling quickly died down and after an hour's rest Miss Condon left with Mr. and Mrs. McLees for Rutherford, and later was brought to New York.

Miss Condon is a strong defender of snakes, most of which she says are harmless and of benefit to man because they destroy insects and other enemies of farmers. She has several harmless ones in her home as pets and finds that though they may not reveal affection, they at least show gratitude when she performs some service for them, such as helping them when they are shedding their old skins.

The society of which she is secretary is headed by Dr. Raymond Lee Ditmars of the New York Zoological Gardens, and has about 100 members, among whom are Dr. Leonard Stejneger of the Smithsonian Institution, Sir Arthur Conan Doyle, Joan Procter, curator of the London Zoo; Dan Beard and Ernest Seton Thompson.

The society boasts that no snake has

Continued on Page Three.

1,909 MURDERS HERE IN LAST 7 YEARS, ARON REPORT SAYS

Republican Publicity Chairman Adds That Only 231 Slayers Have Been Convicted.

INCREASE OF 40 PER CENT.

There Were 333 Homicides Last Year Compared With 240 Reported in 1918.

POLICE ARE CRITICIZED

Statements of Hylan and Enright That Crimes of Violence Are Decreasing Are Denied.

A steady increase in the number of murders during the seven years of Mayor Hylan's Administration and a decline in the efficiency of the police were charged yesterday by Harold G. Aron, Chairman of the Publicity Committee of the Advisory Committee of the New York County Republican Committee.

Mr. Aron asserted that during the seven years ended Dec. 31 last there had been 1,909 murders in the city and only 231 murderers convicted, showing that a murderer in New York City ran only one chance in eight of being caught by the police and convicted. He added that the records showed 333 murders in 1924 as compared with 240 in 1918, an increase of 40 per cent. under Mayor Hylan and Police Commissioner Enright.

Mr. Aron declared that the loose leaf system of records at Police Headquarters made it impossible to get any information and that the only information available to the public came from statements and speeches by the Mayor and the Police Commissioner, in which they said there had been a decrease in "crimes of violence."

More Murders in Hylan's Terms.

Mr. Aron's statement follows:

"Investigation by the Publicity Committee has revealed that during the past seven years there has been a steady increase of murders throughout the city and a decreasing number of murderers brought before juries and convicted. In the seven years ended Dec. 31 last there were 1,909 murders in the city and court records show only 231 murderers convicted by jury.

"In 1924 there were 333 murders, against 240 in 1918. For the seven years of Mayor Hylan and Police Commissioner Enright there has been an increase of 40 per cent. in murders.

"The facts compiled by the committee show that there has been a steady breaking down of efficiency in the Police Department; notwithstanding the public statements by Mayor Hylan and Police Commissioner Enright that police efficiency is the best the city has known.

"No report has been issued by the Police Department since 1922, although the law calls for a yearly report. The only information available to the public has been the repeated statements to the newspapers by the Mayor and the Police Commissioner, and now being spoken nightly by Mr. Enright and his Deputy Police Commissioners around civic associations and other citizen gatherings in all parts of the city.

Police Figures Criticized.

"Mr. Hylan, Mr. Enright and the Deputy Commissioners all are reiterating that there has been a decrease in the seven years of 40 per cent. in what they vaguely term, 'crimes of violence.' In this claim the chief problem of the Police Department is evaded. What Mr. Hylan and Mr. Enright and the Deputy Police Commissioners are not telling the public is that in the seven years there has been a murder increase of 40 per cent. The Mayor, the Police Commissioner, and all under them, are silent on this murder record, which is the worst the city ever has known.

"The following figures sum up the police inefficiency:

	Murders.	Murderers Convicted.
1918	240	28
1919	250	42
1920	253	33
1921	262	34
1922	296	38
1923	275	29
1924	333	27
Totals	1,909	231

"These figures are from the office of the city's Chief Medical Examiner and the court records on murder trials in the five boroughs. The figures exclude shootings by policemen and many other killings which appeared justifiable. Copies of the itemized lists of murders for 1922, 1923 and 1924 are released with this report. The murder lists for 1918, 1919, 1920 and 1921 also were fully compiled by the committee.

"The facts brought to light by the committee show that Mayor Hylan and his Police Commissioner have been misleading the public. Three hundred of the murders of last year remain unsolved. Six murders a week are being added to the list of unsolved crimes.

"No complete record of murders for 1917 is available, because of the legislation in that year abolishing the Cor-

Continued on Page Five.

WASHINGTON UNPERTURBED

General View Is That It Means No Sudden Shift in Berlin Policy.

OFFICIALS ARE SILENT

Question of Effect of Election on American Loans and Dawes Plan Is Discussed.

NO REACTION, SAYS LANSING

Borah Likewise Expresses Optimism—Swanson Is Not So Confident.

Special to The New York Times.

WASHINGTON, April 26.—The election of Field Marshal von Hindenburg as President of Germany was received in Washington with varied emotions, but the general view was that the election of the German Commander-in-Chief did not necessarily represent a reactionary movement, and might not retard Germany's economic recovery or carry the republic toward militarism.

Official Washington declined to say formally what might be the effect of the election upon European affairs or the lending of money by American bankers to Germany. There appeared to be no great surprise in official circles over the election, as late advices from Berlin had indicated that the electorate were rapidly swinging back to the nationalistic spirit which von Hindenburg represented. The hope in official circles was that Germany might be strengthened by the election at home as well as abroad if the new President and his Cabinet should go forward on the plans outlined by the last Government to stabalize German finances and pay reparation.

While those directly interested in foreign affairs did not receive the election results with any great surprise, there were many others here who were astonished. Their offhand comment was that it was the forerunner of a return of the monarchy and the stirring up of more trouble in Europe.

Conflicting reports were received at the German Embassy. The first report had Dr. Marx elected by a good majority, but an hour later the cables told of the turn of the tide in favor of von Hindenburg. No comment was made by the embassy officials, although the impression received there was that they were well satisfied with the results and hoped that the election would aid Germany in her financial efforts.

Little Fear for Dawes Plan.

Pending official word of the election of von Hindenburg, persons who have been closely watching the situation because of the effect it may have on the working out of the Dawes reparations plan and the floating of loans by the German Government and German industry in America would not make public comment.

Informally, however, it is asserted that there is little fear entertained that the operation of the Dawes plan will be threatened at this time. It is pointed out that the Nationalists, who supported von Hinderburg, are also the industrialists of Germany, and that they are deeply concerned in their ability to obtain financial aid in the United States and other foreign countries. For this reason, if for no other, it is contended, this group will see to it that the terms of the Dawes plan are carefully observed.

There are, however, other features of the situation now created by the election of von Hindenburg, in the opinion of an expert who has discussed the possible developments with banking interests. One of them is the reaction among American investors to the turn affairs have taken.

In this connection he said that of all the recent private loans which bankers had floated in the United States that for the Krupps, whose great factories had turned out war material for the German armies during the World War, had been the most unpopular. Investors who had been willing, and even anxious, to subscribe to other loans which they felt would help to build up the new German republic had turned away from the loan bearing the name of the Krupps. Whether the name von Hindenburg would cause the same reaction among investors was a point which has been much discussed.

There has been a great deal more money obtained through private loans in this country for Germany since the war than the sums represented by the part of the German Government loan now in the hands of American investors. Whether the election of the war chief will act as a check upon additional loans

Continued on Page Two.

Fleet Has "Seized" Hawaiian Flying Fields Umpires of the War Manoeuvres Decide

HONOLULU, April 26 (Associated Press).—The umpires in the army-navy manoeuvres here issued a communique at 9 o'clock this morning saying that the attacking "Blue" fleet had "seized" the flying field of the "Black," or defending forces, on the islands of Molokai, Lanai and Maui last night.

The communique said the mine layer Shawmut was "sunk" by seven "Black" planes and a submarine. Enemy destroyers were fired on by shore guns of South Oahu. The "Black" submarine R-20 was "sunk" by the "Blue" submarine S-30 in a running fight. The battleship Wyoming was held to be "disabled" by the submarine T-14 of the main fleet during the close of the general attack on Oahu.

Theoretical loss of life in the engagements was heavy.

The first day of action in the manoeuvres, the purpose of which is to test the defense of the Hawaiian Islands, ended last night with both sides claiming victory. The island of Oahu is the principal objective.

Hindenburg's Statement On Dawes Plan Fulfillment

Field Marshal von Hindenburg, President-elect of Germany, stated his views on the fulfillment of the Dawes program by Germany in an interview with the Associated Press correspondent at Hanover on April 20. Von Hindenburg said:

"Whether the obligations under the Dawes report are capable of fulfillment will become evident only after a certain period of time, since, as you know, the burdens imposed will steadily increase for years.

"We, of course, will not be able to fulfill the conditions unless the foreign powers participating in the pact evince political and economic loyalty."

GERARD SEES DANGER FROM HINDENBURG

Ex-Envoy to Berlin Says Election Means Return to Monarchism and Militarism.

GERMANS HERE HOPEFUL

They Predict Unity and Peace—Blow to Red Influence and Treaty Protest Discerned.

James W. Gerard, former Ambassador to Germany, declared last night that the election of von Hindenburg was a menace to world peace in that it means a return of the German people to militarism and monarchism.

"The election is due partly to the swing toward conservatism which has been in evidence in this country and in England," said Mr. Gerard, "and also to the fact that von Hindenburg is the only person whose reputation survived the war in Germany.

"Nevertheless, it constitutes a menace to the peace of the world, and is a flat declaration by the German people of a return to militarism and monarchism."

Prominent Germans, however, interviewed here last night, expressed hopes for a united, peaceful nation under von Hindenburg's Presidency.

One commentator saw in his victory a strengthening of religious ties against the influence of Soviet Russia, another discovered a protest against the Versailles Treaty, and still another hailed the result as the final defeat of Socialism in Central Europe, and yet declared that the aged General would not take any orders from his former Kaiser.

Prominent Germans here, interviewed last night on von Hindenburg's election, expressed hopes for a united nation under his Presidency.

Views Result as Treaty Protest.

Alphonse G. Koelble, a lawyer, 51 Chambers Street, said:

"The election of von Hindenburg is a protest of the German people against the Versailles treaty, which did not incorporate the fourteen points of President Wilson and did not realize the promises under which the Germans submitted to the armistice.

"In my opinion, it does not mean the restoration of the monarchy. It is not so much a question of the republic or the monarchy as a question of phychology. The German people made a great fight against overwhelming odds and they were led by von Hindenburg, who was a central figure in the conflict.

"Von Hindenburg's election shows a resurgence of the nationalistic spirit in Germany, shows that the German people want to remain Germans, and perhaps is an indication to the world that they will remain German."

The Rev. Dr. William Popcke, pastor of the Evangelical Lutheran Church, 341 East Eighty-fourth Street, said:

"I believe the election of von Hindenburg will result in a united Germany. I believe he will consolidate the various factions, because of his great popularity and because he has the confidence of the German people. Although some persons may be inclined to be fearful, I believe the result of the election will be for peace. Von Hindenburg will not be for war, but for what is for the good of Germany and the promotion of the prosperity of its people."

Discerns Anti-Russian Swing.

F. H. Knubel, President of the United Lutheran Church of America, said:

"From the religious point of view there are considerations in the election of von Hindenburg which can give us genuine satisfaction.

"The best elements of American citizenship have always rejoiced in the definite religiousness of our own President. We cannot but be satisfied, therefore, to see another nation choose as its executive one who likewise is so pronounced in his religious convictions.

"This is above all valuable for the development of the new German republic, since her religious and educational situation is so critical a one at the present time.

"The separation of Church and State has been completed only in part. As this proceeds, the presence of a leader of the State who is sympathetic with the Church is valuable.

"As a final and most important fact it must be realized that the election of a man of von Hindenburg's type means a greater resistance in Germany against Russian influence, with the latter's irreligion. The world, and America especially, must welcome the strengthening of anti-Russian convictions in Germany."

George Sylvester Viereck said:

"The election of von Hindenburg means

Continued on Page Two.

FIELD MARSHAL VON HINDENBURG
First German to Be Elected President by Popular Vote.

HINDENBURG IS IDOL OF GERMAN PEOPLE

Victory Over Russians Raised Him From Obscurity to Place of War Chief.

CALLED WOTAN AND THOR

He Insisted His Candidacy for Presidency Had No Partisan Character.

Field Marshal Paul von Hindenburg became the great idol of the German people in 1914 by his victories over the Russians at Tannenberg and the Masurian Lakes, and has been their idol without interruption ever since. He was the only great war figure who did not fall into disfavor after the war.

Hindenburg kept out of politics and lived the life of a retired soldier, but every time he appeared in public in Germany, he threw everybody else in eclipse. Big popular demonstrations have greeted him on every trip he has made from his home.

In the thousands of accounts that have been printed concerning Hindenburg, two opposing views have been taken of him. One is that he is the incarnation of wisdom, strength and disinterestedness. The other is that he is a stuffed figure who was placed on a pedestal by luck and has been kept there by luck.

It used to be universally thought that Hindenburg was a great automaton and that the engineer inside who worked him was Ludendorff. But since the separation of the two men, Ludendorff's enterprises have all been lamentable failures, while Hindenburg has been all that he ever was, indicating that perhaps Hindenburg was more than a figurehead in the Hindenburg-Ludendorff partnership during the war.

Called a Wotan and a Thor.

In addition to his prestige as a soldier, there are many qualities in Hindenburg which have made their appeal to the German people. In the first place, he looks like one of the old Teutonic gods. The Kaiser called him a modern Wotan. Others have called him a Thor. With the massive, stern and dignified features of a Norse god, he has united the habits and ways of an ordinary German. For birthday presents they sent him from all parts of German warehouses of sausages, sauerkraut and barrels of beer.

He is loyal to the old ways, loyal to the old religion and personally loyal to the House of Hohenzollern, although politically he has declared against a return of a monarchy.

Had he died at the age of 66 years, Hindenburg would have been unknown today. At that age he was just one of many Generals who had been retired on account of age. His career had apparently come to an end in 1907, when he was placed on the retired list with the rank of General and with the nickname of the "Old Man of the Lakes" because he was supposed to be a little cracked on the subject of the Masurian Lakes. He tried to make everybody believe that the war with Russia, when it came, would be fought out amid the marshes of East Prussia, and he spent most of his leisure in the army, and after his retirement working out schemes on paper for trapping the invading Russians.

When the war came, he had been retired seven years and had not been listed for recall. But in September, to save France, Russia threw Rennenkampf and Samsonoff into East Prussia with half-prepared armies. There was a panic throughout Germany. Hindenburg was remembered as the great authority on the terrain where the fight to save Germany must be fought. He was put in command of the Army of the East and Ludendorff was made his Quartermaster.

Between them they tangled up the

Continued on Page Two.

CLASHES REPORTED ALL OVER GERMANY

In Berlin Two Men Are Mortally Injured and Scores Hurt in Fighting Between Gangs.

TWO KILLED IN KARLSRUHE

Silesian Nationalists Besiege Police Headquarters After a Series of Encounters.

Copyright, 1925, by The New York Times Company.
By Wireless to THE NEW YORK TIMES.

BERLIN, April 26.—Two men were mortally injured late this afternoon in a clash in the Moabit section of Berlin largely inhabited by the working classes. Both were members of the Reichsbanner Republican organization. One was removed to a hospital in a dying condition, having been shot through the head by a Nationalist, and the other was so seriously hurt that there is little hope for his recovery.

Throughout the afternoon the neighborhood of the Wilhelma Café, a noted Monarchist stronghold in the fashionable West End district, was the scene of much tumult and brawling despite elaborate police precaution. During the day about thirty persons were injured in this neighborhood as a result of constant fights between Monarchists and Republicans.

Another scene of violence was at Hasenheide, a working-class quarter where Republicans and Communists attacked Nationalist headquarters. In the ensuing fight a Republican youth lost an eye.

In another section of the city a truck full of Communists capsized, burying forty-one occupants under the wheels. Nine were removed to a hospital.

The police took extraordinary precautions in Berlin to prevent trouble. Crowds were kept moving by the police and groups broken up as soon as they looked threatening. Nevertheless, many clashes occurred during the voting hours.

Similar police precautions were taken throughout Germany because of the extreme bitterness prevailing, far surpassing anything before known here. Numerous rows occurred in many cities, towns and country districts.

Two Killed in Karlsruhe.

KARLSRUHE, Germany, April 26 (Associated Press).—In a clash between Republicans and Nationalists at the Presidential elections today two persons were killed and many wounded.

Nationalists Besiege Police.

RATIBOR, Silesia, Germany, April 26 (Associated Press).—An erroneous announcement published here this evening that Dr. Wilhelm Marx was leading von Hindenburg by nearly 2,000,000 votes caused not only consternation, but serious disturbances.

Large bodies of Nationalists began marching through the streets. There were repeated collisions with the security police, and the police used their blackjacks freely. The Nationalists collected reinforcements and besieged the police headquarters in various towns in the area.

The streets in the centre of Ratibor were closed off by the police, who made scores of arrests.

Rival Bands Out for Trouble.

Copyright, 1925, by The Chicago Tribune Co.

BERLIN, April 27.—There is hardly a city in Germany which was not the scene of election violence. Except in Berlin and Karlsruhe the police were able to keep the situation under control.

The demonstrations in Berlin began early. The Nationalists had big motor trucks, filled with boys between the ages

Continued on Page Two.

REPUBLICAN BLOC BEATEN

Marx Gets 13,752,000 Votes to 14,639,000 for Hindenburg.

30,000,000 BALLOTS CAST

Feverish Excitement Prevails as Early Returns Favor One, Then the Other Candidate.

WOMEN SUPPORT MARSHAL

They With Previous Stay-at-Homes Are Believed to Have Swung the Election.

Latest Official Election Totals.

BERLIN, April 27 (Associated Press).—The official provisional figures of the Presidential election follow:

Von Hindenburg	14,639,399
Marx	13,752,660
Thaelmann	1,931,591
Votes declared invalid	21,919
Total	30,345,569

By T. R. YBARRA.

Copyright, 1925, by The New York Times Company.
By Wireless to THE NEW YORK TIMES.

BERLIN, Monday, April 27.—Field Marshal von Hindenburg wins. The German Monarchists have beaten the German Republicans. Germany has turned her eyes back from the new to the old in the election of the Field Marshal, who, though a monarchist at heart, has given his pledge to uphold the Republican Constitution.

After a sensationally exciting election, the returns of which seesawed hour after hour between the Republican and Monarchist candidates, it finally became clear at 1:30 o'clock this morning that the grim old warrior of Hanover, veteran leader of Germany's World War armies, had vanquished ex-Chancellor Marx, on whom the Republicans had pinned all their hopes.

At 1:30 the official election bureau declared Hindenburg elected. At that time 34 out of 35 electoral districts had been heard from. Only Mecklenburg was lacking. The vote then stood:

Hindenburg	14,640,000
Marx	13,740,000
Thaelmann	1,780,000

Thus Hindenburg's plurality was 900,000.

Result Long in Doubt.

From the time the first returns dribbled in, shortly after 8 o'clock, until long after midnight the outcome of the election hung in the balance. Vast crowds, quivering with excitement, surged around the huge bulletin board where results were flashed as soon as received. The same was true of cities throughout Germany, where, as at Berlin, clashes repeatedly occurred between partisans of the rival candidates.

A striking feature of the election was the immense interest manifested by women. The vote was very large, reaching in some sections 85 per cent. of the total registered voters. Whereas at the election on March 29 only 28,000,000 voted, at yesterday's election there were probably more than 31,000,000.

Hindenburg lost his own town of Hanover. The vote there according to figures available at 1 o'clock this morning stood: Marx 130,000, Hindenburg 111,000.

Marx Carries Berlin.

Marx also apparently carried Berlin. At 1 o'clock this morning his lead there was more than 400,000.

Munich went for Hindenburg with a plurality of 80,000.

Stettin and surrounding districts voted as follows: Hindenburg 77,000, Marx 33,000.

In the country district around Stettin, Marx was snowed under, getting only 2,000 votes against Hindenburg's 24,000.

Marx barely nosed out Hindenburg at Nürnberg, the second largest Bavarian city, where he got 110,000 votes against Hindenburg's 95,000.

Stuttgart, metropolis of Württemberg gave Marx 584,000 and Hindenburg 544,000.

Leipsic was carried by Hindenburg with 178,000, whereas Marx got 158,000.

Cassel went for Marx who got 50,000 votes against Hindenburg's 45,000.

Halle voted thus: Hindenburg, 60,000; Marx, 19,000. Thaelmann, the Communist candidate, got 24,000 votes at Halle, known as one of the "Reddest" towns in all Germany.

Heidelberg was carried by Marx with a slight majority and Frankfort by

"All the News That's Fit to Print."

The New York Times.

THE WEATHER
Showers today and tomorrow; fresh south and southwest winds.
Temperature yesterday—Max., 73; min., 69.
For weather report see Page 22.

VOL. LXXIV....No. 24,651. NEW YORK, WEDNESDAY, JULY 22, 1925. TWO CENTS In Greater New York | THREE CENTS Within 200 Miles | FOUR CENTS Elsewhere in the U. S.

SCOPES GUILTY, FINED $100, SCORES LAW; BENEDICTION ENDS TRIAL, APPEAL STARTS; DARROW ANSWERS NINE BRYAN QUESTIONS

LONG STEP TO PEACE IS SEEN BY BRITAIN IN GERMANY'S REPLY

Chamberlain to Consider With Briand Chances of a Parley in August.

WANTS COMPACT PRESSED

Meanwhile the French Think There Are Traps in the Berlin Note.

GERMANS LOOKING TO US

They Want Americans Made Members of the Arbitration Tribunal.

By EDWIN L. JAMES.

Copyright, 1925, by The New York Times Company.
By Wireless to THE NEW YORK TIMES.

LONDON, July 21.—The British Government regards the German security note as a distinct step toward making the Rhine peace compact. While less favorable than London had hoped Dr. Stresemann's communication is seen as opening the way to early negotiations between the Allies and Germany.

Here one finds the belief that some of the most troublesome passages in the German Foreign Minister's note were written for home consumption, especially the section relating to article XVI. of the Covenant of the League. Following the action of the League Council notifying Germany that no special conditions could attend her entry, it is thought here that Dr. Stresemann wrote this part of the note with full knowledge that it was doomed to failure but in the hope of mollifying opposition in the Reich.

As the British see it, the last paragraph of the note is the most important one, in which Berlin says: "On essential points a significant rapprochement of the views of the two sides has already taken place," and in which the German Government hopes for a settlement of outstanding differences and expresses a wish for speedier discussions. That, the British say, really sums up what the Reich's note means, namely, that the matter should be gone ahead with.

Think French Should Be Reassured.

The declaration of the Germans that they have no prime intention of bringing about revisions of the Versailles Treaty is seen here as a passage which should calm French fears, even though the Germans cling to the provision of the League covenant providing for a revision of antiquated treaty provisions.

Likewise, the German statement relative to changing conditions in Rhineland occupation are regarded here as very mild, in view of the report from Berlin that the Reich would demand quick evacuation of the Coblenz and Mayence bridgeheads as part of the compact arrangement.

It was expected that Germany would object to the provisions of M. Briand's note for exceptions and possible Allied crossing of the Rhine peace zone. London does not believe that Germany seriously means the suggestion that the allies should renounce any and all sanctions for possible violations of the Versailles Treaty, especially in regard to reparations, but it is recognized that Berlin has raised a disputable issue in questioning the French claim to the right to guarantee arbitration treaties between Germany and Czechoslovakia.

The only lack of cordial spirit the British see in the German note is the manner in which Berlin refers to Germany's entry into the League. Knowing all along that the allies regarded the Reich's joining the League as an essential part of the bargain, Berlin's condescending agreement to consider the proposal favorably is regarded as slightly in bad taste.

Germany's suggestion for a temporary arrangement of Article XVI until universal disarmament brings other nations' armies down to the level of Germany's is seen as a rather clever move to raise during the coming negotiations the issue of the strength of the French army. The disposition here is not to regard this part of the German note as stating any essential position but rather as intended to seek a bargaining position.

Mr. Chamberlain will at once discuss with M. Briand the conclusions to be drawn from the German note and in particular will consider whether arrangements should be made to invite the Germans to a security conference at Brussels on Aug. 25 or thereabouts. Mr. Chamberlain is anxious to have the security negotiations in shape to be able at Geneva in September to offer the League Assembly something to replace the Geneva protocol work of last year's assembly, which was killed by the unfavorable attitude of the present British Government.

British Press Divided on Note.

The morning papers differ pretty much over the note, according to their political stand. The pro-Government papers find it good and the Opposition press finds it bad.

The Daily Telegraph sees in the friendly tone of the note its chief value. In the arguments raised by the Berlin document this paper perceives an indication of difficult negotiations but fair prospects of success. In the German request for consideration of modifications of the Treaty of Versailles The Telegraph finds the chief stumbling block, but considers the tone of the note indicates a desire for a Rhine compact, and says

Continued on Page Six.

Party Goes South on Yacht To See Dredging by Beebe

The Vanadis, the yacht of Harrison Williams, 60 Broadway, left New York early yesterday morning for Cape Hatteras, where William Beebe and the New York Zoological Society Expedition on the Arcturus are expected Friday afternoon.

A party of friends of Mr. Williams are on board the Vanadis, and George Palmer Putnam, William Beebe's publisher, left New York by rail yesterday morning to join the party at Cape May at the invitation of Mr. Williams.

Beebe, returning from the Sargasso Sea, has notified the New York Zoological Society that he is on his way back to New York and will stop at a designated place off Hatteras to trawl and dredge. This point will be the rendezvous of the Arcturus and the Vanadis.

The Vanadis will also accompany the Arcturus on its return to New York on Saturday. Mr. Williams is chief patron of the zoological society's expedition.

MOB CLUBS DEPUTY, FOE OF THE FASCISTI

Giovanni Amendola, Leader of Aventine Opposition, Is Attacked on Country Road.

BOOED OUT OF MONTECATINI

Assault Follows Siege of Hotel, Peace Truce and Flight From Town of Water Cures.

Copyright, 1925, by The New York Times Company.
By Wireless to THE NEW YORK TIMES.

ROME, July 21.—Deputy Giovanni Amendola, perhaps the most important leader of the Aventine opposition to the Fascist régime, was attacked and clubbed by unidentified persons presumed to have been Fascisti, while fleeing by motor car toward Pistoia from Montecatini, where a Fascist crowd, after besieging him in his hotel for several hours, eventually booed and hissed him out of town.

Deputy Amendola suffered several bruises and superficial wounds on various parts of the body, and will have to remain twenty days in a hospital, it was said at Pistoia, where he went for first aid. He was later brought to Rome by rail accompanied by members of the Fascist railroad police, who guarded him from further attacks.

About half way between Montecatini and Pistoia Signor Amendola's motor car was obliged to halt by two other motor cars drawn up across the road. As soon as Amendola slackened speed fifteen or more individuals who had been hiding behind the hedge sprang up and rushed at the Opposition leader, striking at him with sticks they carried. They then re-entered their motor cars and headed toward Montecatini at a rapid pace.

Amendola, though bleeding from several cuts, was not seriously wounded and ordered the car driven to Pistoia.

Had Gone for Water Cure.

Signor Amendola had gone to Montecatini in order to take a water cure for which the town is famous, but no sooner was his presence known than the hotel was completely surrounded by thousands of Fascist citizens, some even having come from surrounding villages. The crowd booed and hissed lustily.

When that form of amusement began to become monotonous efforts were made to break through the cordons of carabineers which the police officials in order to forestall trouble had placed across each entrance to the hotel.

After several determined rushes had been stopped by the carabineers, the Fascisti succeeded in penetrating into the hotel and chased Deputy Amendola to the fourth floor of the building, where he took refuge in his room, bolting the door. His secretary, who had not been equally fleet of foot, had his eye blackened.

Further hostilities were prevented by the intervention of Fascist Deputies, who prevailed upon the Fascisti to leave the Deputy alone and to enjoin their companions outside the hotel.

The local Fascist leaders and several

Continued on Page Five.

ALL POLICE BELOW 14TH ST. JOIN HUNT FOR A MISSING BOY

Comb East Side Tenements Aided by Forty Detectives for Robert Perles.

ABANDON DROWNING THEORY

Marine Division Fails to Find Clue in River—Lad Seen by Man at 5 P. M. on Sunday.

LITTLE GIRL ALSO SAW HIM

Says She Played With Him but Can Tell No More—Sewers and Intakes to Be Searched Today.

Forty detectives from lower east side precincts and all the uniformed patrolmen between the Battery and Fourteenth Street, on the east side, were brought into the hunt yesterday for Robert Perles, 4 years and 6 months old, who disappeared last Sunday after he had left his home at 272 East Third Street to visit a relative at 95 Ridge Street. Following the abandonment of their first theory that the boy had been drowned in the East River near the recreation pier at the foot of East Third Street, the police decided on an intensive search. Policemen from the Marine Division in launches had dragged the waters in the vicinity of this pier in the forenoon without uncovering any clue that might justify the theory.

A conference of detectives in charge of the quest in the Fifth Street Station at noon led to the issuance of an order to mobolize all detectives from the Old Slip, Beach Street, Oak Street, Mercer Street, Clinton Street and Fifth Street Stations in the block bounded by Delancey, Rivington, Attorney and Ridge Streets, in which lives Mrs. Annie Levine, aunt of the boy, and in which he was last seen playing in front of Public School 4. Mrs. Levine lives in a five-story tenement four blocks from the East River. At 11 A. M. Sunday, she said, she saw her little nephew playing with Daniel Blitz, a companion.

The decision to search every house in this block from cellar to roof was brought about when Lieutenant Detective Louis Dittman recalled that on Oct. 26, 1923, four-year-old Irving Pickelny had disappeared just as mysteriously from in front of his home at 338 Grand Street, and his body had been found in the cellar of the tenement at 71 Suffolk Street a month later.

Detectives Comb Tenements.

The Pickelny home was less than a quarter of a mile from the homes of the parents of the missing Perles boy and his aunt. Detectives were assigned in pairs to comb thoroughly the neighboring tenements as well as the cellar of the public school and tenements in the vicinity of the Perles home in East Third Street, a short distance away.

When they reported after four hours that not a trace of the boy had been found Chief Inspector William J. Lahey then caused an order to be issued from Police Headquarters to all the uniformed men of the section between Fourteenth Street and the Battery to be especially vigilant and arrest any one of subnormal appearance found acting suspiciously.

While the hunt for the boy by the detectives was in full swing hundreds of children and grown-ups were questioned in the hope of obtaining a clue. Samuel Perles, father of the boy, took an active part in this questioning.

As in the hunt for the slain Pickelny boy, the excitement attendant on the police activity aroused the imaginations of many children and much time was lost running down reports of the missing boy's having been seen at various places in the neighborhood, even up to yesterday forenoon.

One witness, however, gave the police information which led them to believe that Robert was alive at 5 P. M. last Sunday. This witness was Max Slissen, who lives on the third floor of 91 Ridge Street, two doors north of the Levine home. Slissen was encountered by Detective Morgan Callahan of the Missing Persons Bureau, who had been assigned

Continued on Page Four.

Buck M'Neil, Saver of 40 Lives, Gets First Honors on Tablet

"Buck" McNeil, the Battery Dock Master, who has saved more than forty persons from drowning off the sea wall at Battery Park, will be the first "Honor Man" to have his name engraved on a tablet to be placed in the office of Dock Commissioner Cosgrove, it was announced yesterday.

The tablet will be a memorial to the late Charles F. Murphy, who served as Dock Commissioner from 1898 to 1902. It will be presented by Charles F. Murphy, a nephew of the Tammany leader. Annually a Dock Department "Honor Man" will have his name engraved on the tablet. McNeil will also be presented with a medal by members of the department. He already has more than three dozen medals for saving life.

COAL STRIKE THREAT IS WIRED TO HOOVER

Miners' Official Warns of General Tie-Up Over West Virginia Wage Fight.

SEEKS ROCKEFELLER AID

Charges Assaults by Armed Guards—Anthracite Conferees Make Little Headway.

Special to The New York Times.

ATLANTIC CITY, N. J., July 21.—While the anthracite operators and miners spent an afternoon in fruitless bickering over a new wage agreement, representatives of the bituminous coal miners here today drew up plans for an intensive campaign against soft coal operators in Northern West Virginia. Van A. Bittner, chief representative of the United Mine Workers in that territory, sent an identical telegram to Secretary of Commerce Hoover and Secretary of Labor Davis denouncing the Bethlehem Mines Corporation, a subsidiary of the Bethlehem Steel Corporation, and the Consolidation Coal Company for their alleged violation of the Jacksonville agreement. He declared that "unless something is done to prevent this abrogation of wage agreements it will be necessary for the miners of the entire State of West Virginia to join with the United Mine Workers of America of the rest of country in a general strike."

At the same time Mr. Bittner, after conferring at the Hotel Ambassador with Thomas C. Townsend, chief counsel for the miners in Northern West Virginia, sent telegrams to John D. Rockefeller Jr. and Samuel Untermyer, alleging that eviction proceedings have been started against hundreds of miners and their families, and that armed guards have assaulted miners. Mr. Untermyer is appealed to because of his large interest in the Bethlehem Steel Corporation, in control of the Bethlehem Mines Corporation. Mr. Rockefeller is supposed to be interested in the Consolidation Company.

Warns of Nation-Wide Strike.

Here is the telegram sent by Mr. Bittner to Secretaries Hoover and Davis:

Several large coal companies in Northern West Virginia, among whom are the Bethlehem Mines Corporation, a subsidiary of the Bethlehem Steel Corporation, and the Consolidation Coal Company, which is controlled by the Rockefeller and Watson interests, have abrogated their wage contracts with the United Mine Workers of America and are attempting to put into effect a wage reduction approximating 50 per cent.

Defenseless miners, their wives and little children are being evicted from their homes by these coal companies because the miners will not agree to violate and abrogate the terms of the wage agreement which is effective until March 31, 1927. Hundreds of armed gunmen are being employed to intimidate, coerce and force our people to accept this reduction in wages.

In the interest of the coal miners and all the people of our country the time has arrived when the Government of the United States should take a definite position against abrogation of wage contracts by the coal operators of Northern West Virginia.

The miners do not propose to have their wage agreements broken down by this method of guerrilla warfare on the part of the Northern West Virginia operators, and unless something is done to prevent this abrogation of wage agreements it will be necessary for the miners of the entire State of West Virginia to join with the United Mine Workers of America of the rest of the country in a general strike.

The United Mine Workers of America are forced to take this position due to the action of the coal operators who have been so unfaithful to our wage agreements solemnly made to insure peace in the coal mining industry.

Ask Rockefeller's Aid.

The following telegram was sent to John D. Rockefeller Jr.:

I wrote you several days ago informing you that the statement made by President Lewis of the United Mine Workers of America that your company in Northern West Virginia, the Consolidation Coal Company, had abrogated its agreement with the United Mine Workers of America was absolutely correct and the Consolidation Coal Company is using every means known to corporate greed to make effective a wage reduction of approxi-

Continued on Page Three.

HYLAN REFUSES BAIT TO GO ON BENCH AND QUIT MAYOR'S RACE

Foes Realize Need for Keeping Him on Ticket to Block Third-Party Plan.

McCOOEY CALLS LEADERS

Brooklyn Chief Confers With Olvany, but Both Refuse to Tell What Was Said.

HEARST EMISSARY ACTIVE

Meeting of Borough Leaders on Mayoralty Situation Is Put Off Until Next Week.

In a final attempt to avert an open break and keep him in line for the ticket, Democrats who do not believe Mayor Hylan could make a winning fight for a third term, yesterday sent friendly emissaries to the Mayor, who now are bringing all their persuasive powers to bear with a view to inducing him to quit the Mayoralty race and accept a nomination for the Supreme Court in the Second Judicial District.

Up to last night these envoys of the anti-Hylan forces had not been able to budge Mayor Hylan from his determination to make a fight for the Mayoralty again. It was stated, however, that the pressure would continue, and that when the Mayor awakened to a realization of his loss of popularity with the voters there was hope that he would yield to their representations.

In the meantime the anti-Hylan forces are sparring for time. It was announced yesterday that the conferences of the five Democratic borough leaders, at which the Democratic city slate is to be decided upon, would be deferred until next week. This announcement was made after John H. McCooey, the Democratic leader in Brooklyn, which is Mayor Hylan's home borough, had met George W. Olvany, the Tammany chieftain, at the Hotel Vanderbilt, where they discussed the tangled Mayoralty situation for an hour or more over luncheon.

Neither Mr. Olvany nor Mr. McCooey would disclose any part of their conversation, except to say that it had been wholly informal and that naturally no decision of any kind had been reached. Prior to meeting Mr. Olvany, the Democratic leader in Brooklyn had talked for almost an hour with James P. Sinnott, one of his district leaders and a high spokesman for Mayor Hylan himself.

Confer in McCooey's Office.

This conference was held in Mr. McCooey's office at the Hall of Records in Brooklyn. What they talked about can only be surmised, for there was no announcement after their meeting. It was presumed, however, that the sole topic was Mayor Hylan's chances to get a renomination for Mayor.

Mr. McCooey is likely to be subjected for the next few days to pressure from sources both friendly and unfriendly to the Mayor and his third term aspirations. An emissary of William R. Hearst arrived in this city yesterday, showing every desire that his presence on the scene of strife should not be bruited about.

The emissary was William A. De Ford, a member of Mayor Hylan's Board of Transportation, and head of the legal department of the Hearst publications in the East. Mr. De Ford had interrupted a vacation to return to the city at a time which may prove crucial to Mayor Hylan's political future. Word had preceded him from Atlantic City, where he has been spending part of his holiday, that he was coming to town for important political conferences. Mr. De Ford when questioned yesterday, declared that he was aware of no such conferences in which he was to be a participant, and that his return at this time was to attend a meeting of the Transportation Board.

Honest Expected Soon.

That the visit of Mr. De Ford was occasioned by reasons purely political, however, was the general opinion among politicians who learned of his presence in the city. Mr. De Ford has been one of Mr. Hearst's political advisers for the last couple of years. He is conversant with all the plans of the editor-politician in relation to the candidacy of Mayor Hylan. Mr. De Ford declined

Continued on Page Fourteen.

Both Sides Speed Procedure for Scopes Appeal; Defense Cost $25,000, With Lawyers Serving Free

Special to The New York Times.

KNOXVILLE, Tenn., July 21.—With the conviction of John Thomas Scopes, attorneys for the defense at Dayton began at once to formulate their plans for the appeal. The case will come before the Supreme Court when that tribunal sits in Knoxville in September. Attorneys for both sides today agreed to expedite the appeal procedure in order to assure a hearing of the issues at that session.

Clarence Darrow, chief of the defense staff, is expected to argue the case before the Supreme Court here. Frank Spurlock, prominent attorney of Chattanooga, assisting the defense, will also plead for Mr. Scopes, being well versed in the peculiarities of Tennessee law. John R. Neal of Knoxville also is expected to take an important part in the appeal proceedings.

For the State, Attorney General Stewart and Ben G. McKenzie doubtless will carry the burden.

The defense's appeal will consist of two main points: First, that the Anti-Evolution law is unconstitutional; second, that even though the law were valid, Mr. Scopes did not violate it, and that the defense was prohibited from proving this at the Dayton trial.

DAYTON, Tenn., July 21 (AP).—A misdemeanor case carrying as a penalty to the guilty offender a fine of $100 and costs of the trial brought an expenditure to the defenders of John Thomas Scopes of about $25,000.

The actual court costs are estimated at well over $800, or more than treble the fine assessed.

The greatest expense of the trial was the cost of bringing expert witnesses, who were not allowed to testify. Defense counsel estimated that cost to be $20,000 to $25,000.

Attorneys on both sides bore their own expenses and served without fees.

In addition several hundred dollars was paid out by the county in preparing the Court House for the trial.

FINAL SCENES DRAMATIC

Defense Suddenly Decides to Make No Plea and Accept Conviction.

BRYAN IS DISAPPOINTED

Loses Chance to Examine Darrow and His Long-Prepared Speech Is Undelivered.

HIS EVIDENCE IS EXPUNGED

Differences Forgotten in the End as All Concerned Exchange Felicitations.

Special to The New York Times.

DAYTON, Tenn., July 21.—The trial of John Thomas Scopes for teaching evolution in Tennessee, which Clarence Darrow characterized today as "the first case of its kind since we stopped trying people for witchcraft," is over. Mr. Scopes was found guilty and fined $100, and his counsel will appeal to the Supreme Court of Tennessee for reversal of the verdict. The scene will then be shifted from Dayton to Knoxville, where the case will probably come up on the first Monday in September.

But the end of the trial did not end the battle on evolution, for not long after its conclusion William Jennings Bryan opened fire on Clarence Darrow with a strong statement and a list of nine questions on the basic principles of the Christian religion. To these Mr. Darrow replied and added a statement explaining Mr. Bryan's "rabies." Dudley Field Malone also contributed a statement predicting ultimate victory for evolution and repeating that Mr. Bryan ran away from the fight.

The end of the trial came as unexpectedly as everything else in this trial, in which nothing has happened according to schedule except the opening of court each morning with prayer. It was reached practically by agreement between counsel in an effort to end the case, which showed signs of going on forever, although all the testimony offered before the jury took only two hours.

Young Scopes, in his shirt sleeves, his collar open at the neck, his carrot-colored hair brushed back, stood up before the bar with a gold epauletted policeman beside him, and Judge Raulston had pronounced sentence before his counsel could suggest that Mr. Scopes might have something to say.

"Oh," exclaimed Judge Raulston. "Have you anything to say, Mr. Scopes, as to why the Court should not impose punishment upon you?"

Scopes Calls Statute Unjust.

Mr. Scopes, who is hardly more than a boy and whose pleasant demeanor and modest bearing have won him many friends since this case started, was nervous. His voice trembled a little as he folded his arms and said:

"Your Honor, I feel that I have been convicted of violating an unjust statute. I will continue in the future, as I have in the past, to oppose the law in any way I can. Any other action would be in violation of my ideal of academic freedom, that is, to teach the truth as guaranteed in our Constitution, of personal and religious freedom. I think the fine is unjust."

No one had expected such a quick ending. Mr. Darrow came into court full of the pleasant anticipation of another "go" at Mr. Bryan, whom he questioned to the delight of hundreds the day before. But the court had no sooner opened than Judge Raulston decided that there would be no further questioning, and then ordered Mr. Bryan's testimony expunged from the record.

Mr. Bryan, who had contented himself with the thought that he would have an opportunity to put Mr. Darrow on the stand and tear into him, was somewhat chagrined at this turn of the case, and announced that he would have to appeal to the fairness of the press to give prominence to the questions which he would have asked Mr. Darrow.

"I had not reached the point where I could give my statement to answer the charges made by the counsel for the defense as to my ignorance and bigotry," he said, bitterly.

Sparrow Poses as Dove of Peace.

But before the day's session was over a dove of peace hovered over the court room in the form of a frightened sparrow, which had strayed in through an open window, and everybody exchanged felicitations except Mr. Bryan and Mr. Darrow. Judge John Raulston declared that the Word of God, "given to man, that man may use it as a waybill to the other world," was an indestructible thing, and prayed God that he had decided right the questions raised in the trial. A minister pronounced a benediction and court adjourned.

The general gratification of the people at the end of a good show was shown by their applause whenever any member of either side, or the visiting spectators, rose to thank Dayton for its hospitality and kindness. And there was a further manifestation of the remarkable change in sentiment which has taken place since this trial began.

The defense faced a [illegible] audience when they started. [illegible]

G. G. HAVEN A SUICIDE, DUE TO ILL HEALTH

Banker and Opera Patron Shoots Himself After Vain Struggle to Recover.

FRIEND DISCOVERS BODY

Dr. E. Eliot Finds Him Dead in His Room While Wife Is Away Shopping.

George Griswold Haven, senior member of the banking firm of Strong, Sturgis & Co. of 11 Wall Street and President of the Metropolitan Opera and Real Estate Company, which controls the Metropolitan Opera House, committed suicide by shooting himself through the head with a revolver at his residence, 6 East Fifty-third Street, yesterday morning.

Mr. Haven, who was 59 years old, had been suffering from a nervous disorder for eighteen months. His mind was clear, but for a year and a half he had been inactive in business and had rested and traveled, seeking to regain his health.

Once or twice recently, according to friends of Mr. Haven, he had expressed himself as despairing of recovery and had shown that he had thoughts of ending his life. He gave no warning of any kind yesterday and left no note or statement explaining his act.

Married Five Months Ago.

Yesterday morning he rose at 8 o'clock and appeared his usual self. He had breakfast with his wife, formerly Miss Dorothy James, daughter of Henry A. James of this city. They were married last February at St. George's Church in this city. The first Mrs. Haven had died two years before.

After breakfast Mrs. Haven went shopping and her husband went to his room on the fourth floor. At 10:30 o'clock yesterday morning Dr. E. Eliot of 34 East Sixty-seventh Street called at the Haven residence. He was an old personal friend of Mr. Haven, but had not been treating him professionally. A servant informed Dr. Eliot that Mr. Haven was in his room.

"I'll go up and see him," said Dr. Eliot. He found Mr. Haven lying dead on his bed. There was a revolver beside him. He had shot himself through the jaw. The bullet had lodged in the brain, killing him instantly. He had been dead about half an hour when Dr. Eliot discovered the body. The revolver was one

Continued on Page Ten.

BONAPARTE GIVES PROPERTY TO WIFE

Great-Grandnephew of the Emperor Signs Away All but $5,000 a Year.

AGREEMENT ENDS HER SUIT

Referee Files Report and Recommends That Leon Jacobs, Lawyer, Get $5,000 Fee.

The details of the settlement of the suit brought by Jerome Napoleon Bonaparte, great-grandnephew of the Emperor, against his wife, Blanche Bonaparte, to set aside an agreement transferring all of his property to her, became known in the Supreme Court yesterday, when a report was filed by Emanuel B. Cohen, appointed referee to determine the amount of the fee to be paid to Leon R. Jacobs, who acted as attorney for Mr. Bonaparte. The referee recommended that the fee be fixed at $5,000, although counsel for Mrs. Bonaparte contended that $250 should be enough.

The report of the referee states that on Dec. 23, 1922, Mr. Bonaparte entered the Craig House, a sanitarium at Beacon, N. Y., "to endeavor to restrain himself of a habit which he had unfortunately contracted." He was discharged as cured on April 21, 1923. Mr. Bonaparte alleged in the suit filed in his behalf by Mr. Jacobs that while he was ill his wife induced him to go to the office of her attorney, William M. K. Olcott, and sign an agreement putting all his property in her hands, and reserving only a small part of the income for himself.

The referee states that Mr. Bonaparte went alone to the office of Attorney Olcott and signed the assignment of his property dictated by Mr. Olcott, whereby he was to get only $5,000 of the income, and the remainder was to go to his wife. The agreement also set forth that he had made a will leaving all of his property inherited from his father and grandparents to his wife.

Value of the Property.

The instrument stated that the property consisted of a half interest in rents from Baltimore property owned by his grandmother, Susane M. Bonaparte, valued at $145,000; an interest in rents from property owned by his great-grandmother, Elizabeth Patterson, valued at $30,000; a half interest in a deed of trust executed by his father, Jerome Napoleon Bonaparte, in 1877, amounting to $11,000; a life interest under the will of his father, from which the income in 1924 was $10,488; a half interest in property owned by his father in Baltimore valued at $3,000, and a claim for a further quarter interest in his father's property, in litigation, which, if successful, would add $30,000 to his income.

The referee states that Mr. Bonaparte, after being released from the sanitarium, made several requests to his wife for the return of his property, but that she refused to return it and also refused to pay his bills at the Craig House. Mr. Bonaparte then consulted Attorney Jacobs as to taking legal action, and in the course of ten weeks saw him twenty times. At these interviews he stated that the value of his property was $300,000. Mr. Jacobs accordingly brought suit to set aside the transfer on the ground that the plaintiff did not realize what he was doing at the time he signed the agreement.

The attorney last saw his client when they called at the Hotel St. Regis to see

Continued on Page Eight.

Girl, Saved by Dog, Shoots Her Assailant; Negro Again Shot by Posse Before Capture

Special to The New York Times.

NEW BRUNSWICK, N. J., July 21.—Shot twice, once by Miss Barbara Long, who lives with her brother Nicholas on a farm near the Lincoln Highway a few miles from here, and a second time by one of a posse which pursued him through the fields after he is alleged to have attacked Miss Long, Jess Williams, a negro, was arrested today on a charge of atrocious assault. After his wounds had been treated at the Middlesex General Hospital he was taken to the New Brunswick Jail.

Miss Long was saved from serious harm by the intervention of a large shepherd dog which made the negro take to his heels through the fields. The negro begged for food, and as Miss Long was preparing it he forced his way into the kitchen of the farmhouse and began to choke her. Miss Long managed to break his grasp on her throat. She screamed and the dog sprang at him. The negro ran from the place and Miss Long fired both barrels of a shotgun at him as he fled. The man was hit, but kept running.

Nicholas Long, the girl's brother, ran to the house when he heard his sister's screams and the shots. He took the gun and followed the negro, being joined by several men working in the fields near by. One man jumped into an automobile and intercepted the negro, who had been wounded a second time by a shot from one of his pursuers.

The negro was later arraigned before Justice of the Peace C. W. Sedam and committed to jail without bail. According to the police, he said he did not intend to harm the girl, but merely tried to rob the place.

Search All London for Wisconsin Professor; He Had $3,000 and Family Suspects Foul Play

Copyright, 1925, by The New York Times Company.
Special Cable to THE NEW YORK TIMES.

LONDON, July 21.—Joseph Victor Collins, Professor of Mathematics at Wisconsin University and candidate in 1910 for the United States Senate, is missing in London and foul play is suspected by his wife and daughter.

Scotland Yard circulated a description and photographs of the missing man, and detectives spent yesterday combing London and hospitals are carrying out a systematic search for him.

Once during the day it was believed he was found and his daughter was called to St. George's Hospital and endured the ordeal of inspecting a suicide's body. It wasn't that of her father.

Professor Collins, when he disappeared, had in his pockets American Express checks and loose change of a value of over $3,000, and the suspicion is that he fell in the hands of sharpers.

With his daughter he boarded an omnibus which passed the corner of a street where his hotel is. The daughter alighted, but the father continued to the railroad station to secure sleeping accommodations for the journey to Edinburgh to the educators' sessions there. That was the last seen of him.

His daughter, in interviews, said she thought he was followed. There were several suspicious-looking men on top of the omnibus, she said. He was the last man in the world, she said, to go off voluntarily, for he had heard all about London gangsters and American visitors.

Mrs. Collins also said she was sure there was foul play behind the disappearance.

EDINBURGH, July 21 (AP).—Professor Collins has not arrived here for the sessions of educators, and no room has been reserved for him in Edinburgh.

Special to The New York Times.

STEVENS POINT, Wis., July 21.—Professor Joseph V. Collins is 66 years old and a member of the Faculty of the Stevens Point State Normal School. He is a widely known mathematician. He was a candidate for State Superintendent of Schools in 1902 and for the United States Senate in 1910.

Members of the Normal School Faculty suggest the disappearance of the professor was due to the fact that he is near-sighted and had wandered into an unknown quarter of London. They think he may have broken his glasses, without which he cannot distinguish a person a few feet away.

Professor Collins had $30,000 in his possession. He has been an instructor at the Normal School since it was organized in 1894.

"All the News That's Fit to Print."

The New York Times.

THE WEATHER
Cloudy and warmer, probably showers, today; tomorrow showers.
Temperature yesterday—Max., 64; min., 42.
For weather report see Page 43.

VOL. LXXV....No. 24,943. NEW YORK, MONDAY, MAY 10, 1926. TWO CENTS in Greater New York | THREE CENTS Within 200 Miles | FOUR CENTS Elsewhere in the U. S.

BYRD FLIES TO NORTH POLE AND BACK; ROUND TRIP FROM KINGS BAY IN 15 HRS. 51 MIN.; CIRCLES TOP OF THE WORLD SEVERAL TIMES

BALDWIN STRATEGY IS WINNING STRIKE FOR GOVERNMENT

Aggressive Action Keeps Vital Services Going as Unions Balk at "Trump Cards."

THOMAS'S TALK SIGNIFICANT

Both Sides Spend a Quiet Sunday, While London Sees Another Food Convoy.

FOOD PRICES KEPT DOWN

Only Rise Allowed Is for Milk—Incoming Cargoes Are Unloaded and Distributed.

By T. R. YBARRA.

Copyright, 1926, by The New York Times Company.
Special Cable to THE NEW YORK TIMES.

LONDON, May 9.—The essence of strategy is robbing the enemy of his freedom of action. If that axiom be transferred from the domain of warfare to that of strikes it must be admitted tonight that so far the British Government, led by Premier Baldwin, has robbed leaders of Britain's great general strike of their freedom of action.

At the close of the sixth day of this gigantic industrial struggle it becomes increasingly apparent that even if the British Government has not won the game yet it has consistently forced the play.

From the very outset of the great strike, at midnight last Monday, most of the aggressiveness recorded has been contributed by those seeking to crush the strike. Each day brings increased railway service. Each day shows a more efficient organization of the Government's emergency food distributing services. Each day has shown a bigger enrollment of volunteers in every branch of strike breaking. Each day has shown hesitation on the part of the strikers to play their trump cards.

They have not tried to smash the great food distribution organization of the Government. They have not called out the "second line of defense" and the "third line of defense." Will they? That is the question, asked in a constantly growing tone of skepticism by those who have lived through these first six days of one of the greatest industrial crises in the entire history of the world.

Thomas Adds to Skepticism.

Tonight this skepticism received decided impetus from J. H. Thomas, the noted labor leader, who has been consistently against extremist measures in the fight to find a panacea for British labor grievances. Speaking at Hammersmith, a London suburb, Mr. Thomas made statements which, as befits a conservative trying to please the moderates without infuriating the extremists, partook largely of the nature of those "weasel words" which so infuriated the late Theodore Roosevelt in the heyday of his acrimonious political combats.

Nevertheless, stripping the speech of all its diplomatic "I don't want to displease anybody" quality, there are in it statements which clearly imply that the general strike is not going exactly as its instigators hoped and that, therefore, Moderates like Mr. Thomas are beginning to hope that the dawn of conciliation is approaching. The most striking statement in Thomas's speech is:

"If the people who talk about a fight to a finish carried it out in that sense the country would not be worth having at the end of it."

"I have never disguised and I do not disguise now that I have never been in favor of the principle of the general strike," said Mr. Thomas. "No one will disagree, however, that the fundamental principle of trade unionism is not only the right for men and women to organize, but the essential part of that legal right is collective bargaining. The workers have no right to say to the employers, 'You must negotiate under the threat of a strike,' but it is equally right and just that the workers should not be asked to carry on negotiations under the threat of a lockout.

"From the start I deliberately went in to get peace. Let there be no mistake about that, and in spite of all that has been said I repeat that it is the duty of both sides to keep the door open.

Extols Workers' Solidarity.

"The response to the appeal of the Trades Union Congress has been the most wonderful, the most marvelous demonstration of solidarity the world has ever seen and has staggered your opponents.

"All attempts to raise the constitutional issue are not only wrong, but

Continued on Page Five.

Strikers Urged 'to Stick to It' If 'Further Steps' Are Needed

LONDON, May 9 (AP).—C. T. Cramp, President of the National Union of Railwaymen, addressing a strikers' meeting in London today, warned that it might be necessary "to take further steps" to gain that for which they were fighting. He said:

"We have entered this fight as railwaymen because we realize that if the miners' standards of living is depressed below the present level, it would not be long before the remainder of the organized workers would find themselves in the same position."

If it were necessary to take further steps to uphold the things which they now required, he asked his hearers to "stick to it," remarking:

"If I am going into a scrap I prefer to scrap with both hands and not with one tied behind my back."

BALFOUR DENOUNCES REVOLUTION INTENT

He Calls Upon Britons to Save "the Civilization of Which They Are the Trustees."

SAYS NATION FACES RUIN

Declares Success of the Revolt Would Put a Minority of Extremists in Power.

Copyright, 1926, by The New York Times Company
By Wireless to THE NEW YORK TIMES.

LONDON, May 9.—The Earl of Balfour declares the general strike to be an attempt at revolution "which would bring ruin, swift, complete and irresistible upon this country," in a statement upon the industrial conflict which appears in tonight's issue of The British Gazette, the official Government organ.

"From such a fate," concludes Lord Balfour, "may the courage and resolution of our countrymen save the civilization of which they are the trustees."

Lord Balfour's Statement.

The text of Lord Balfour's statement is as follows:

"Two hundred and thirty-eight years have passed since a revolution occurred in this country, whose object was to secure the supremacy of parliamentary government and the traditional liberties of our people. Through eight generations it has proved successful.

"But we are now threatened, it seems, with a revolution of a very different kind, and it behooves us seriously to consider what would be its actual results were it, unhappily, to succeed.

"Its methods are being practiced before our eyes; they are to deprive the people of food, transport, employment and a free press. The conveniences of civilized life, which long have been counted among its necessities, are in some cases to be immensely diminished, in others to be brought to an end.

"Personal security is to be threatened; industry is to be seriously hampered, even when it is not wholly stopped. Willing workers are to be kept in idleness; anxious purchasers are to be kept in want; perishable food is to rot in port. All the wheels of social life are to be clogged.

"Such are the methods of the revolutionary movement. What, then, are its objects?

"The nominal object is to maintain unchanged existing conditions of the miners' remuneration as regards hours of work and rates of pay. Now, there is no man who does not heartily share this desire; but neither is there any man who has read the coal mines report who thinks it can be satisfied under existing conditions.

"Were the revolution to succeed tomorrow, the country would suffer, but the miner would not gain.

"No revolution in Great Britain, however triumphant, is going to diminish foreign competition in neutral markets; no revolution is going to hasten the changes recommended by the commission in the methods and organization of the mining industry; no revolution is going to compel the mine owner indefinitely to carry on his industry at a loss. Revolutionary methods would be completely powerless except for evil.

"On the other hand, their power for evil is beyond calculation. All strikes, all lockouts are costly both to employers and employed.

"But neither in fact, nor, I believe, in law, is the course advocated by the trades unions a strike in the proper sense of the term. It is what I have called it—an attempted revolution.

"Were it to succeed, the community would henceforth be ruled not by Parliament, not by the Parliamentary Labor Party, not by the rank and file of the trades unions, not by the moderate members of the Trades Union Council, but by a relatively small body of extremists, who regard

Continued on Page Five.

WETS NOW DEMAND SENATORS SUMMON GARY, ROCKEFELLER

In Brief Filed Today With the Committee They Call for Noted Drys' Testimony.

AIM OF GIFTS CHALLENGED

End of Anti-Trust Prosecution Is Charged When 'Big Business' Allied With Prohibition.

WAYNE WHEELER ATTACKED

Subpoenas Are Urged for Counsel of Anti-Saloon League and the Congress Members in Its Pay.

Special to The New York Times.

WASHINGTON, May 9.—A demand that the Senate Judiciary Committee reopen its prohibition hearings and subpoena Wayne B. Wheeler, John D. Rockefeller Jr., Judge Elbert H. Gary and others and ask them to disclose the sources of the great sums expended by the Anti-Saloon League, is made in a brief which will be filed tomorrow by the wets.

Denouncing Mr. Wheeler for not "keeping his word" to appear as a witness at the recent hearings, the brief declares the anti-prohibitionists wish to question him about the $35,000,000 he has asserted was used by the drys in their fight for the Eighteenth Amendment.

The wets assert that Mr. Wheeler should be forced to tell about contributions by Mr. Rockefeller, Judge Gary and other captains of industry and also "as to the significance of the strange phenomenon that after the alliance of the Anti-Saloon League and big business to keep up a continuous ferment or smoke screen over prohibition, anti-trust prosecutions suddenly ceased."

Members of the House and Senate who have admitted that they are on the League's payroll should also be summoned, as well as Dr. Ernest H. Cherrington of the World League Against Alcohol, who like Mr. Wheeler, escaped cross-examination by Senator Reed, the wets insist.

"Let us have the whole story of prohibition propaganda and prohibition politics as well as the sordid story of prohibition itself," the brief states.

Attack Centred on Reformers.

There is a review of the testimony given at the hearings, but it is upon Mr. Wheeler that the fire is centred.

Declaring that prohibition is costing the United States $500,000,000 annually in direct enforcement and loss of revenue, the wets contend that this is too heavy a price, "even to keep the unctuous Mr. Wheeler—quite voluble enough in the open forum but silent as a clam when it comes to testifying under oath before this committee—in a lifetime job as a parasite upon misguided religious and industrial organizations, and as a super-Government in his own divine right."

Mrs. Ella Boole, President of the Women's Christian Temperance Union is severely criticised for refusing to reply to questions as to whether it would be better to sell mild alcoholic beverages in the open or to allow them to be made at home in the presence of children.

Dr. E. C. Dinwiddie, while described as a man who has earned his living for twenty-seven years as a professional reformer, is complimented as "the highest type of professional dry."

Prohibition has brought in its wake increased drunkenness, secret drinking, deaths from alcoholism, corruption in Government, extensive bootlegging and a widespread use of the still in the home, the wets assert in the brief. Women and children are drinking today, there is an army of rum-runners and moonshiners, denatured alcohol can be easily renatured and prohibition has been an utter failure from a temperance standpoint, the brief adds.

The example of Canada, which sells liquor under Government regulation, is contrasted with conditions in the United States where the public morale has been broken, the modificationists assert.

Reopening of Hearing Unlikely.

In spite of the strenuous nature of the plea for a reopening of the hearings, the request of the wets probably will go unheeded. The Senate subcommittee is 4 to 1 dry, Senator Reed of Missouri, being the only modificationist upon it.

So arid is the committee that there also seems to be no chance that it will favorably report any of the bills which would authorize a modification of the

Continued on Page Twelve.

Only 147 Workless in Paris, Says French Labor Minister

TOURS, France, May 9 (AP).—There are only 147 unemployed persons in Paris, whereas London before the strike there had 800,000 and Berlin 450,000, Minister of Labor Durafour said at a banquet inaugurating the Tours exposition week.

France's birth rate, the Minister asserted, hardly varied from 1913 figures of 192 births for each 10,000 of population, whereas German statistics for the same units of population were 283 in 1913 and 200 in 1926. England, he said, shows 238 in 1913 and 186 in 1926.

"We have done this by organizing against infant mortality," the Minister affairmed, "which, although 13 per cent. before the war, had fallen to 9 per cent. in 1925. Therefore we must not despair. Our percentages of births equal Germany's and surpass England's."

NO TRACE OF WARD; FAMILY IS ALARMED

Brother, Fearing Foul Play, Asks Police to Broadcast Alarm for Missing Man.

SEARCH ON IN THREE STATES

Trenton Police Suspect Ruse in Abandoning His Car—Race Tracks to Be Watched.

The police began a search for Walter S. Ward yesterday at the request of his brother, Ralph D. Ward, who reported his disappearance to the Missing Persons Bureau at Police Headquarters. Mr. Ward said that his brother, who was acquitted three years ago of the murder of Clarence M. Peters, had not been seen or heard from since last Wednesday and that his family feared foul play.

Captain John Ayres, in command of the Missing Persons Bureau, broadcast a confidential alarm for Ward, with his description, among all the police stations in the metropolitan district. Detectives working on the case said last night that they had no clue to Ward's whereabouts, and had no idea whether he had been killed or had disappeared for some reason known only to himself.

No Clue in Abandoned Car.

Ward's automobile was found in Trenton, N. J., last Friday morning, with the windshield broken and a large stone on the front seat. There was neither anything in the car nor any witness to clear up the mysterious circumstances under which the machine had been abandoned.

Ralph Ward told Captain Ayres that at the time his brother disappeared he had been on a business trip to Baltimore on behalf of the Electruck Corporation of 532 West Forty-sixth Street, of which Walter S. Ward is President. Ralph Ward did not know, he said, whether his brother had reached Baltimore and was on his way back or was driving to Baltimore when the car was abandoned.

To reporters who called at his home, 1,010 Fifth Avenue, at Eighty-second Street, Ralph Ward said:

"Walter went to Baltimore early in the week, but came back to New York and was seen here on Wednesday. He went away again in his car and was to have returned home again on Thursday, but we have not seen him since Wednesday."

Thinks It Was Second Trip.

"Was he going to Baltimore on his second trip?"

"I believe so," replied his brother.

"On business?"

"Presumably."

"Have you any clue to what has become of him?"

"Absolutely none," said the brother. "We have no idea what has become of him or where he is."

"Do you think that violence is indicated?"

"Yes, that is the only possible explanation."

Ralph Ward said that the family intended to investigate to see whether Walter might have had an enemy who could have had a motive for attacking him.

At Walter Ward's home, 30 West Seventieth Street, it was said that the missing man's wife was too ill to see reporters. A physician was in attendance on her yesterday morning. Ralph Ward told the police and reporters that his sister-in-law had been "prostrated" by her husband's disappearance.

George S. Ward, former head of a bakery chain company, and father of Walter and Ralph Ward, has been in the South for some time but is expected back soon, it was said at his home.

The Ward family is said to have engaged private detectives to search for

Continued on Page Ten.

PEARY'S OBSERVATIONS ARE CONFIRMED

Flight Is Favored by Sunlight and the Absence of Fog; Sun Compass Functions Perfectly

LEAK DEVELOPS IN PLANE'S OIL SYSTEM NEAR POLE

But Byrd Insists on Going On, Overruling Pilot Bennett—Commander's Nose and Fingers Frozen in Zero Temperature

By WILLIAM BIRD,
The New York Times Correspondent With the Byrd Expedition.
Copyright, 1926, by The New York Times Company and The St. Louis Post-Dispatch.
By Wireless to THE NEW YORK TIMES.

KINGS BAY, Spitzbergen, May 9.—America's claim to the North Pole was cinched tonight when, after a flight of fifteen hours and fifty-one minutes, Commander Richard E. Byrd and Floyd Bennett, his pilot, returned to announce that they had flown to the Pole, circling it several times and verifying Admiral Peary's observations completely.

They were favored by continued sunlight, and there was never the slightest fog, enabling Commander Byrd to use his sun compass and bubble sextant and obtain the most accurate observations possible. There were three magnetic compasses in the plane, but all of them deviated eccentrically after reaching high latitudes. Bennett declared that when he was piloting the magnetic compasses were wholly useless and would swing almost a quarter turn, returning very slowly.

Take Turns in Piloting.

Without the sunlight, navigation would have been almost impossible. Bennett and Commander Byrd alternated in the piloting, Bennett refilling the gasoline containers while the Commander piloted and navigated.

Commander Byrd found that the Bumstead sun compass worked perfectly, even when held in the hand, so when he was in the pilot's seat he held the control stick in one hand while he got his direction from the sun compass held in the other.

When they were within sixty miles of the Pole the oil system of the right-hand motor began leaking badly and it seemed necessary to choose between proceeding with two motors or attempting a landing to make repairs.

Bennett For Landing, Byrd Refuses.

In the neighborhood of the Pole numerous stretches of smooth ice were visible and a landing was favored by Bennett, but Commander Byrd, remembering his difficulties in starting at Kings Bay, vetoed this proposal.

Both agreed, however, to continue the flight to the Pole even if they went on with only two motors. To their surprise, the right-hand motor continued to work effectively, despite the ruptured oil tank, and when the Fokker returned to Kings Bay all three motors were hitting perfectly.

Chantier's Men Embrace Fliers.

The Josephine Ford, after making three circles over Kings Bay, landed at the take-off runway and taxied to her original starting position.

Commander Byrd and Bennett hurried a mile and a half to the shore, where a motor boat rushed them to the Chantier. The crew aboard her went wild with joy, waving flags and their caps. Many of the crew completely broke down with emotion, and with tears streaming from their eyes embraced the fliers.

Commander Byrd's nose and several fingers were frozen while he was taking observations in zero temperature (Fahrenheit) above the North Pole, but treatment here speedily restored circulation, and the Commander is all right now.

At 3 o'clock this morning, Greenwich Time [11 P. M. Sunday, New York Daylight Saving Time], the Norwegian radio station at Stavanger reported that heavy static was interfering with further transmission of The New York Times dispatches from Spitzbergen. These dispatches will be published tomorrow. Commander Byrd's story will be told in New York exclusively in The New York Times.

First News of Byrd's Great Feat As It Reached The New York Times

Whole Population of Kings Bay, Including the Members of the Amundsen-Ellsworth Party, Out to Welcome the Aviator.

From Staff Correspondents of The New York Times.
Copyright, 1926, by The New York Times Co and The St. Louis Post-Dispatch.
By Wireless to THE NEW YORK TIMES.

KINGS BAY, Spitzbergen, Sunday, May 9, 6 P. M. Greenwich Time (2 P. M. New York Time). — Lieut. Commander Richard E. Byrd, U. S. N., leader of the Byrd Polar Expedition, returned from his flight to the North Pole in the airplane Josephine Ford at 4:20 this afternoon, Greenwich Time (12:20 P. M. New York Daylight Time).

The Commander reached the North Pole. He started at 12:50 o'clock this morning, Greenwich Time (8:50 P. M. Saturday, New York Time), which is full daylight at this time of the year in the Arctic, so that his flying time on the dash to the Pole and back was fifteen and a half hours.

[Some error in the wireless transmission of these figures is possible, according to later dispatches to THE TIMES, which state that the commander's total flying time was 15 hours 51 minutes. This is 21 minutes longer than the elapsed time here indicated. It is, however, possible, that the hour 4:20, recorded as marking the commander's return, was the moment at which the returning plane was sighted.]

The Josephine Ford had as its pilot on the trip Floyd G. Bennett, the American pilot of the Byrd Expedition.

The two were welcomed on their return by Captain Roald Amundsen, Lincoln Ellsworth and the entire crew of the airship Norge, now awaiting her chance to fly over the North Pole from Spitzbergen to Alaska, and the entire Summer population of Kings Bay, all of whom had been asleep when the airplane took off fifteen hours previously.

LIEUT. COMMANDER RICHARD E. BYRD, U. S. N.
The American Naval Aviator Who Flew Yesterday to the North Pole and Back.

Coolidge Sends 'Heartiest Congratulations'; Glad That Flight Was Made by an American

Special to The New York Times.

WASHINGTON, May 9.—President Coolidge received the first details of Commander Byrd's successful flight to the Pole from a radio message sent by THE NEW YORK TIMES to the Mayflower, which is cruising tonight in the lower Potomac River.

The message, sent by the Washington Bureau soon after 5 o'clock, furnished the President with all the details known at that time. In reply he radioed:

"Thanks for your message."

Later Mr. Coolidge sent by radio the following comment:

The President sends his heartiest congratulations to Commander Byrd on the report that he has flown to the North Pole. It is a matter of great satisfaction that this record has been made by an American.

The fact that the flight seems to have been accomplished without mishap demonstrates the high development of the art in this country. That it was made by a man trained in the American Navy is a great satisfaction.

CALVIN COOLIDGE.

It is well known that the President was very anxious that the flight should be made, and, although there had been some adverse criticism of the proposal, Mr. Coolidge gave his approval to the plans.

BYRD FAMILY PROUD OF FLIER'S SUCCESS

Governor of Virginia Declares His Brother Never Would Give Up—Mother Rejoices.

Special to The New York Times.

RICHMOND, Va., May 9.—Richmond received its first information of the successful polar flight of Lieut. Commander Richard Evelyn Byrd about 3 o'clock this afternoon, when a message saying the flier had "returned safely" was received by Governor Harry F. Byrd by telephone. The flier's mother, Mrs. Richard Evelyn Byrd, was at the executive mansion when the message was received.

"I am tremendously gratified," Governor Byrd said, "and proud to hear of my brother's success in reaching the Pole."

"Dick has always been so lucky all his life that he believes he will come through, even though ninety-nine of a hundred chances might be plainly against him. I am proud of him. He has always been such an adventurous fellow, we are somewhat relieved, though proud, that he has made the flight. If he had not, and believed there was a ghost of a chance to do so, he would try again as soon as possible."

This one day of the year dedicated to mothers, the message flashed across the frozen miles, brought happiness and comfort to Virginia's "first mother," Mrs. Richard Evelyn Byrd—

"All the News That's Fit to Print."

The New York Times.

THE WEATHER
Fair today; tomorrow fair and warmer; fresh northwest winds.
Temperature yesterday—Max., 58; min., 47.

VOL. LXXV....No. 24,945. NEW YORK, WEDNESDAY, MAY 12, 1926. TWO CENTS in Greater New York | THREE CENTS Within 200 Miles | FOUR CENTS Elsewhere in the U. S.

THE NORGE FLIES OVER NORTH POLE AT 1 A.M.; REPORTS HER FEAT TO TIMES BY WIRELESS; GOING ON OVER ARCTIC WASTES TO ALASKA

EFFORTS FOR PEACE ACTIVE IN LONDON; BOTH SIDES SILENT

Baldwin Waits Until a Late Hour for an Important Message From the Unions.

EXPECTED THIS FORENOON

Strike Leaders in Session Most of Day and Night, With MacDonald Exploring Situation.

MORE MEN ARE CALLED OUT

Meanwhile the Government Reports Still Further Progress in Maintaining Services.

By T. R. YBARRA.

Copyright, 1926, by The New York Times Company
Special Cable to THE NEW YORK TIMES.

LONDON, Wednesday, May 12.—Though the Government and the strikers continued to face each other in full battle formation throughout yesterday, the eighth day of Britain's great general strike, there were signs that the dove of peace was hovering somewhere in the immediate neighborhood. Up to a late hour last night, however, nobody had quite located the bird. Many insisted, nevertheless, that they had distinctly heard the soft whirring of its wings.

They stuck to their assertion despite the declaration in last night's British Worker, the strikers' official organ, that today more workers will join the great strike—the molders and shipyard workers, members of the Amalgamated Engineering Unions and the General Engineering Unions. The strikers' organ also said that instead of "dribbling back to work," according to the Government's statement, the workers are "standing like a rock and more are coming out."

There were also two statements in the official Government communiqué last night which did not partake of the generally rosy hue pervading the bulk of the official statements. One was: "There is as yet little sign of a general collapse of the strike." The other was the admission that the Trades Union Council "is believed to be making efforts to call out certain trades still at work."

Peace Rumors Still Persist.

But these and other similar reports current during the eighth day of the strike could not down the rumors of imminent peace.

The General Council of the Trades Union Congress met last night at strike headquarters to "explore the position with a view to leaving no door shut that could be opened." The meeting was attended by Ramsay MacDonald and J. H. Thomas, who came from Parliament for the purpose. After the meeting had been in session for some hours Mr. MacDonald and Mr. Thomas hastily returned to the Commons, their arrival giving rise to the hope they might have something to announce. They found, however, that the Commons had concluded its sitting.

They went back to the meeting, which lasted until 1:35 o'clock this morning. No announcement was made at its conclusion, but it is understood that there was a spirited discussion between Mr. MacDonald, Mr. Thomas and other members of the Parliamentary Labor Party who are moderate in their views and Ernest Bevin and other leaders of more extreme opinion.

One of those stated to have been active during the day in the interests of conciliation was Ramsay MacDonald. One of the most moderate of the labor chiefs, in addition to visiting the miners' executive and the General Council of the Trades Union Congress today, MacDonald sent the following message to The British Independent, a mimeographed makeshift newspaper run by university students:

"I welcome most heartily your efforts for conciliation. This dispute ought never to have happened, and had the problem in the dispute been handled with ordinary care and common sense there would have been neither a lockout nor a strike.

"On one thing I can give the nation confident assurance. The general strike in support of the miners was never meant as and even now is not a strike against Parliament, the Government or the Constitution. For purely war propaganda purposes the Government says it is.

"Good-will and calm heads will in the end prevail. We are working literally night and day that that may be soon."

It was certainly apparent during the day that something was going on beneath the surface, that it was some-

Continued on Page Five.

'Cop Evangelist' to Retire After 25 Years on Force

Detective Alfred Smith of the Missing Persons Bureau, known as the "cop evangelist," will retire from the force on June 1, after a service of twenty-five years. He will receive an annual pension of $1,250.

In the intervals of his work of seeking missing persons for the last fifteen years Smith had devoted much time to preaching the Gospel in Chinatown, on the Bowery and in the Eighth Avenue Gospel Mission at 290 Eighth Avenue. He will continue at the head of his Bible class under Miss Sarah Gray at the Gospel Mission.

Smith is 55 years old and lives at 62 East Eighty-seventh Street. His son, Robert, is employed in a Wall Street brokerage house and his daughter, Gertrude, is at college.

RAIL LABOR BILL PASSED BY SENATE

By 69 to 13 the Upper Branch Accepts the House Measure Without Amendment.

HARD FIGHT FOR CHANGES

Curtis Fails to Get Commerce Board Power Over Wages—Coolidge's Approval Expected.

Special to The New York Times.

WASHINGTON, May 11.—The bill to abolish the Railroad Labor Board and permit railways and their employes to settle disputes over wages and working conditions by mutual agreement was passed by the Senate by a vote of 69 to 13 late this afternoon. As the Senate approved the bill in identically the same form it passed the House no conference will be necessary and the bill will become law when the President affixes his signature.

Before the Senate passed the bill it was stated at the White House that it was not an Administration measure. The President, it was said, was interested in it to the extent that he believed it would work well because a majority of the railroad managers and employes favored it. But it was also understood that he did not entirely approve the bill as passed, he having suggested that it be amended so as to protect the public interest.

The detailed vote follows:

FOR THE BILL—69.

Republicans—39.

Borah,	Howell,	Robinson (Ind.),
Butler,	Johnson,	Sackett,
Cameron,	Jones (Wash.)	Schall,
Couzens,	LaFollette,	Shortridge,
Cummins,	Lenroot,	Smoot,
Dale,	McMaster,	Stanfield,
Deneen,	McNary,	Wadsworth,
Edge,	Means,	Warren,
Ernst,	Metcalf,	Watson,
Fess,	Norris,	Weller,
Frazier,	Nye,	Willis.
Gillett,	Oddie,	
Gooding,	Pine,	
Harreld,	Reed (Pa.)	

Democrats—29.

Ashurst,	Glass,	Sheppard,
Blease,	Harris,	Simmons,
Bratton,	Heflin,	Steck,
Broussard,	Jones (N. M.),	Stephens,
Bruce,	Kendrick,	Swanson,
Copeland,	McKellar,	Trammell,
Dill,	Mayfield,	Tyson,
Edwards,	Neely,	Walsh,
George,	Overman,	Wheeler.
Gerry,	Pittman,	

Farmer-Laborite—1.

Shipstead.

AGAINST THE BILL—13.

Republicans—9.

Bingham,	Keyes,	Norbeck,
Curtis,	McLean,	Phipps,
Hale,	Moses,	Williams.

Democrats—4.

Bayard,	Robinson (Ark.),	Underwood.
Ransdell,		

Provisions of the Measure.

The bill, which was agreed upon last year by most of the railway executives and heads of the four brotherhoods, and which the President endorsed in principle in his message to Congress, provides:

1. That the railroads and employes shall establish adjustment boards to arrange disputes.

2. That the President shall appoint, with the consent of the Senate, a board of mediation of five persons, none of whom has a pecuniary interest on either side, to intervene when the adjustment boards fail.

3. That boards of arbitration shall be created when both parties consent to arbitration.

4. That when the above methods fail the Board of Mediation shall notify the President, who may appoint an emergency board to investigate and report to him within thirty days. For thirty days after the report has been made there shall be no change in the

Continued on Page Twelve.

FIRST MESSAGE EVER RECEIVED FROM THE NORTH POLE

By FREDRIK RAMM.
New York Times Correspondent Aboard the Norge.
Copyright, 1926, by The New York Times Company and The St. Louis Globe Democrat.
By Wireless to The New York Times.

NORTH POLE, Wednesday, May 12, 1 A. M. (on Board the Dirigible Airship Norge)--We reached the North Pole at 1 A. M. today, and lowered flags for Amundsen, Ellsworth, and Nobile.

LATER, 3.30 A. M.--Lowering the three flags, Norwegian, American and Italian, when the Norge was over the North Pole, was the greatest of all events of this flight. Riiser-Larsen's observations showed that we were over the Pole. The Norge descended and speed was reduced, when the flags were lowered over the wastes whose edges gleamed like gold in the pale sunlight, breaking through the fog which surrounded us.

Roald Amundsen first lowered the Norwegian flag. Then Ellsworth the Stars and Stripes; finally Nobile the Italian flag.

The airship's 1 A. M. time (Norwegian time), was 8 o'clock on Tuesday night, New York daylight time.

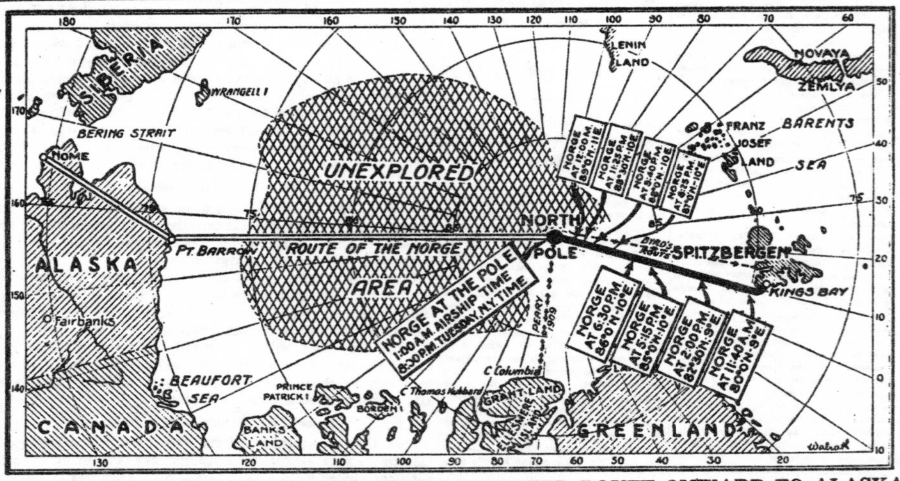

PROGRESS OF THE NORGE AND HER PROJECTED ROUTE ONWARD TO ALASKA

Here is shown the route covered, according to the last wireless reports from the Amundsen-Ellsworth-Nobile airship Norge, which sailed from Kings Bay, Spitzbergen, at 10 o'clock yesterday morning, Norwegian time (5 A. M. New York daylight time) to fly over the North Pole, and her probable course onward toward her ultimate destination, Nome, Alaska.

The hours given in the hollow squares on the map show the position of the Norge at the times stated. The figures are Norwegian time, which is five hours ahead of New York daylight time. The thick black line shows the course the airship has already covered; double line shows her probable future course to Nome. Dotted lines show the routes taken to the Pole by Lieut. Commander Peary in 1909 by dogsled, and by Lieut. Commander Byrd by airplane on Sunday last.

Norge Sails Straight Into the Golden Glow of the Morning Sun, A Silver Creature of the Air, Moving With Grace and Quiet Dignity

Kings Bay Cheers and Weeps as the Giant Dirigible Starts Down the Fjord Accompanied by Commander Byrd and Bennett in Their Polar Airplane, a Striking Contrast in Arctic Exploration—Colonel Nobile Says That the Wind Is His Only Concern—Expedition May Spend Sixty Hours on the Trip to Alaska.

By RUSSELL D. OWEN.
Staff Correspondent of The New York Times.
Copyright, 1926, by The New York Times Company and The St. Louis Globe-Democrat.
By Wireless to THE NEW YORK TIMES.

KINGS BAY, Spitzbergen, May 11.—At 9 o'clock this morning, Greenwich time, or 5 A. M. New York time, the Norge, of the Amundsen-Ellsworth-Nobile expedition, started for Point Barrow, Alaska.

Straight into the morning sun, a tiny speck soon lost in the golden glow of the north, the dirigible disappeared on her journey across the Pole and into the unknown wilderness of the Arctic.

The giant airship, like a silver creature of the air, rose slowly and gracefully from the hands that held her and with her motors humming sailed swiftly down the fjord, following the path Commander Byrd had taken in his spurt to the Pole. She turned over across the bay and rose over Cape Mitre. Then her black silhouette was lost in the sun.

There was rush and swift action to Commander Byrd's departure and the tense hazard of his quick take-off, but the Norge's departure was tremendously impressive because of the ponderous grace and quiet dignity of the great ship, lifting her immense burden from the ground and sailing into the unknown like a liner of the air.. There were power, endurance and swiftness all embodied in her action.

Cheers and Tears at Departure.

Those below the floating fabric raised their hats in the air or flung up their arms in farewell, some cheering and a few moved to tears by the tenseness of the moment which saw their comrades departing on the greatest Arctic feat ever attempted. The air voyagers will spend at least sixty hours in Arctic regions never seen by man and at the end face the greatest hazard, when they may be forced to land the dirigible without assistance from the ground, something never done before.

All the day before Kings Bay was in a fever of preparation, the men of the expedition assembling equipment, packing provisions and small things for comfort, and making sure that nothing was overlooked. Mechanics swarmed over the dirigible, grooming her as though she were a race horse. Every bolt, stay, control wire and girder was gone over carefully. The full tanks were minutely examined, all pipes were overhauled and all instruments tested.

The big motors raced as they received their final turnovers, the immense green curtain near the end of the hangar billowing out in the gale created by the propellers. The new motor was put in splendid condition. Commander Gottwaldt tinkered over the wireless, making sure that the batteries and all the connections were in good condition, for on his direction-finder much depends.

Crew Spurts at Tasks.

There had been uncertainty all day as to the time of departure, but late at night it was announced that the start would

Continued on Page Two.

NORGE SAILS OVER VAST ICE DESERT

Start Made From Kings Bay at 9 A. M. Greenwich Time and Course Is Laid Due North

VOYAGERS SEE POLAR BEARS AND SEALS BELOW

Gentle Wind, Clear Skies and Temperature A Few Degrees Above Zero Accompany Fliers on First Reach to Pole.

By FREDRIK RAMM.
New York Times Correspondent Aboard the Norge.
Copyright, 1926, by The New York Times Company and The St. Louis Globe-Democrat.
By Wireless to THE NEW YORK TIMES.

ON BOARD THE DIRIGIBLE NORGE, KINGS BAY, Spitzbergen, May 11.—The airship Norge, carrying the Amundsen-Ellsworth-Nobile expedition on its flight across the Pole to Nome, Alaska, started today at 10 A. M. Norwegian Time (9 A. M. Greenwich Time, 5 A. M. New York Time).

Make 66 Miles an Hour at Start.

ON BOARD THE DIRIGIBLE NORGE, Flying Poleward, May 11, 11:40 A. M. Norwegian Time (10:40 A. M. Greenwich time, 6:40 New York Time).—We are north of Danes Island, 80 degrees latitude, 9 east longitude. The weather is bright, with the lightest breeze from the south-southeast. The temperature is minus 7 degrees centigrade (19 degrees above zero, Fahrenheit). Our altitude is 425 meters (1,394 feet) and our speed is 107 kilometers (66 miles) an hour. The edge of the ice pack is a few kilometers north of Danes Island. We have sighted seals on the ice. Our motors are running perfectly and we are not feeling cold.

[Later] We are now in latitude 81.12. Our speed is 100 kilometers [62 miles] an hour. The weather is bright with a light easterly breeze. The temperature is minus 10 degrees centigrade (14 degrees above zero, Fahrenheit) and our altitude is 530 meters (1,732 feet).

Espy Polar Bears on Ice.

ON BOARD THE DIRIGIBLE NORGE, Flying Poleward, May 11, 2 P. M., Norwegian Time (1 P. M. Greenwich Time, 9 A. M. New York Time).—We are now in latitude 82.30, longitude 9 east. Our altitude is 560 meters (1,836 feet). The temperature is minus 9 degrees centigrade (15.8 degrees above zero, Fahrenheit). The weather stays clear, with a light southeasterly breeze. The air pressure is 730.

In the sea some lanes are covered with new ice. All the time we have used the left and back motors. Lieutenant Riiser-Larsen has been navigating, assisted by Captain Gottwaldt. Ellsworth has been measuring the atmospheric electricity. Our better speed is due to our new altitude, where the conditions are more favorable.

We have now lost all sight of land and the ice changes the whole aspect. We see several great polar bears and can discern white fish in the small openings in the ice. One meteorological report from the Stavanger radio promises that fine weather will continue far on the other side of the Pole.

All of us are naturally in the highest spirits. We are now eating our first meal and discussing how to celebrate Ellsworth's forty-sixth birthday tomorrow.

View of Ice Desert Most Beautiful.

ON BOARD THE DIRIGIBLE NORGE, Flying Poleward, May 11, 5:15 P. M. Norwegian Time (4:15 Greenwich Time, 12:15 New York Time).—We are now in 85 degrees north latitude 10 east longitude, and heading directly north at a speed of 87 kilometers and a height of 610 meters. A gentle south wind is blowing and the weather is clear. The temperature is minus 12 degrees centigrade (9.8 degrees above zero Fahrenheit) and the barometer stands at 727 millimeters.

We have now flown over the ice a long time. Despite our great height we can clearly see how the ice is cracking and screwing.

The low temperature has as yet had no effect on us. The whole view of this desert of ice is indescribable and most beautiful.

All are well.

Speed North Under Clear Sky.

ON BOARD THE DIRIGIBLE NORGE, Flying Poleward, May 11, 6:30 P. M. Norwegian Time.—We are now in 86 degrees of latitude, 10 degrees east longitude. Our course is due north and our speed is 92 kilometers (57 miles) an hour. We are 570 meters above the ice. A light south-southwest breeze is blowing and the skies are entirely clear. The temperature is minus 12 degrees centigrade [9.8 degrees above zero Fahrenheit] and the barometer stands at 727 millimeters.

Weather reports, which are constantly being received, continue to be favorable. The left engine has been stopped and the right set going. All are well.

The Pole Four Hours Ahead.

ON BOARD THE DIRIGIBLE NORGE, Flying Poleward, May 11, 8:25 P. M. Norwegian Time.—We are now at 87 d

"All the News That's Fit to Print."

The New York Times.

THE WEATHER
Showers today and tonight, followed by clearing and cooler tomorrow.
Temperatures yesterday—Max. 70, min. 62.
For weather report see Page 46.

VOL. LXXVI....No. 25,080. NEW YORK, FRIDAY, SEPTEMBER 24, 1926. TWO CENTS in Greater New York | THREE CENTS Within 200 Miles | FOUR CENTS Elsewhere in the U. S.

TUNNEY WINS CHAMPIONSHIP, BEATS DEMPSEY IN 10 ROUNDS; OUTFIGHTS RIVAL ALL THE WAY, DECISION NEVER IN DOUBT; 135,000 PAY MORE THAN $2,000,000 TO SEE BOUT IN THE RAIN

FLORIDA CONSCRIPTS ALL ITS UNEMPLOYED TO CLEAR WRECKAGE

Police, Militia and Legion Round Up Men in Streets and Set Them to Work.

CALL ISSUED FOR LABORERS

Miami Wants 25,000 Men and Hollywood and Fort Lauderdale 2,000 Each.

LOSS PUT AT $165,000,000

Known Dead Now 365, With 1,100 Injured, 500 Seriously—Fight on Disease Goes On.

By WARREN IRVIN.
Staff Correspondent of The New York Times.

MIAMI, Fla., Sept. 23.—Conscription of all unemployed persons to aid in clearing away wreckage and to speed the work of rehabilitating the Florida storm-swept area was adopted everywhere in that area today. Militiamen and police, aided by several hundred members of the American Legion who have been specially deputized, patrolled all streets and highways, apprehending all persons who could not show that they were employed and putting them immediately to work.

At the same time the city of Miami sent out a call for 25,000 laborers, and officials of Hollywood and Fort Lauderdale announced that they would employ 2,000 laborers in each city.

Mayor E. C. Romfh of Miami predicted this afternoon that within sixty days every trace of the storm's ravages will have been removed from Miami and the city will be as prosperous as ever.

Death Lists Called Inadequate.

Many here believe that the death list lacks scores of names of persons killed. A local newspaper man declared today that he made a check-up of bodies in the city and temporary morgues last Monday, at which time there were 175, but orders were given, he said, to bury the dead as quickly as possible, and many bodies were buried or shipped North for burial without any record being kept of them.

Even now it is almost impossible to get definite information as to the number of dead. The Police Department in Miami keeps no record of dead or injured and persons who inquire there are directed to the newspaper offices for information. Bodies are being taken to half a dozen different undertaking establishments and the only means of keeping a record is by constant checking up at undertaking establishments.

At Miami Beach the situation is still worse. No record was kept there for several days but yesterday the Publicity Director of the Chamber of Commerce was instructed to compile a list of dead and injured.

Hollywood and Fort Lauderdale are the only cities in which accurate records have been kept from the start.

Four new cases of typhoid at Davie, a village of 300 population five miles west of Fort Lauderdale, were reported today and caused health authorities to order the village evacuated. Sanitary conditions at Davie are very bad. The water there is still several feet deep in spots.

Doctor Rows to Patients.

One doctor who was on duty there without rest for seventy-two hours was compelled to row to a house in which a woman and three children were marooned. He said the demand for medicine liquor in the stricken area has caused the warehouse in Miami jail, where seized liquors are kept, to be emptied for the first time since this city became the bootleg distributing point for Florida.

In other sections, such as Hollywood, the police were sent out to raid all speakeasies and bootleg places, with orders to bring in seized liquors for the sick. A storm of protest arose from the church people when word got out that the doctors were using liquor for medicine.

The same doctor at Davie who rowed out to the home of the marooned woman was reported for "drunkenness," because a woman there said she smelled liquor on his breath, and in another case when he prescribed liquor for a woman who had been exposed to the wind and rain for several hours the woman's husband threatened to shoot him if "he dared give my wife a drop of liquor."

A flotilla of destroyers arrived today from the navy base at Charleston, bringing all the anti-typhoid serum available in that district. This amounted to several thousand units.

While City Health Officer Claxton of Miami reported an adequate supply on hand today, health officials at Miami Beach said they needed about 3,000 more units of anti-typhoid serum and about 500 units of anti-tetanus serum. Nearly 10,000 persons have been vaccinated in the Miami area.

One case of tetanus developed yesterday in Miami Beach and two in Hollywood. All available tetanus serums

Continued on Page Eleven.

North Carolinians Weave Homespun Suit for Walker

North Carolina mountaineers, reputed by novelists to be a hard-drinking and generally rough lot, are now sitting peacefully in their hillside homes spinning a new suit for Mayor Walker.

The addition to the Mayor's wardrobe will be made of gray homespun and will be presented to him by citizens of Asheville, who arrive on the "Land of the Sky" special train on Oct. 6 on a boosting tour. The color will be gray—chosen by the Mayor himself.

When the delegation reaches the city it will go directly to the City Hall, where, with appropriate ceremony, the suit will be presented.

GENEVA CONFERENCE ADOPTS COURT PLAN

Right of Powers to Withdraw Approval of American Reservations Is Recommended.

NEW PROTOCOL NEXT STEP

United States Will Be Invited to Help Draft It—President's Action in Doub

By Wireless to THE NEW YORK TIMES.

GENEVA, Sept. 23.—With a single modification, the conference of signatories of the statute of the Permanent Court of International Justice adopted unanimously the conclusions concerning the American reservations which were presented this morning by its committee.

These conclusions were incorporated in "the final act of the conference," which was submitted for signatures.

The single modification concerned the fourth American reservation. The first part of the reservation provided for the withdrawal by the United States of adherence. The committee, to assure equality of treatment to all members, made the provision that the signatory States acting together and by not less than two-thirds majority should have a corresponding right to withdraw consent to the American reservations.

Modified by New Zealander.

On the proposal of Sir Francis Bell of New Zealand this provision was modified so as to extend only to the second paragraph of Reservation 4—by which statute the Court could not be amended without the consent of the United States—and Reservation 5, dealing with advisory opinions. The modification was made after a long debate in which it was agreed that any difficulties which might arise would be confined to the provisions covered by these reservations.

As it stands adopted, a decision by a two-thirds vote against the last points of the American reservations would not in any manner affect America's membership in the Court but only her prerogatives. The United States remains a full member, participating in the election of the Judges, paying her share of Court expenses and possessing the right to withdraw from the Court.

This modification followed a long series of compromises made between national dignity and resentment at the American demands on the one hand and the general desire to extend the influence and jurisdiction of the Permanent Court on the other. The effort made to meet the American demands was stressed by the President tonight in dissolving the conference.

The American reservations, he said quoting Sir George Foster of Canada, comprised a legislative act by a State outside the League and Court and it would be very easy to say "no." But the conference had considered the difficulties were there to be overcome and nothing had been left undone to give satisfaction to the United States and assure her participation in the Permanent Court.

As to the fate of the conference's work nobody could know what this would be. But the spirit and manner in which the work had been done had proved in obvious manner its sincere desire to find a solution. The only thing that remained to be done was for the Governments to hasten their replies to the United States Government.

This spirit mentioned by the President and which had been evident on the part of the great majority of the delegations persisted in the debates today, though Canada and Sweden stood out against giving the United States more than equality.

Sir Francis Bell at the opening of the reading of the committee's conclusions this morning asked that all the provisions for withdrawing consent to American adherence be dropped. This was not the personal demand of a delegate, he said, but a motion by a Government signatory of the statute of the Court. His Government wanted to see the United States come into the Court and stay in it.

Question of Samoa Raised.

Western Samoa, which was now under the flag of New Zealand, was

Continued on Page Sixteen.

CROWD ARRIVES SMOOTHLY

Throngs Ushered Into Philadelphia Stadium Without Confusion.

MANY NOTABLES ATTEND

Governors of Six States and Mayor Walker Among Long List of Officials.

OVER 75,000 FROM HERE

Trains Alone Carry That Number and Others Make the Trip by Automobile.

Special to The New York Times.

PHILADELPHIA, Sept. 23.—One hundred and thirty-five thousand persons, the largest crowd which ever attended a sports event in America, set out a roar when the referee placed the heavyweight crown on the head of Gene Tunney, which must have made the old Liberty Bell at Independence Hall quiver once more.

As the battle began and the heavyweights set to exchanging their jarring blows which rang with a "plop" audible many rows back of the ring, they followed it with a roaring enthusiasm that only the greatest prize-fight crowd in history could produce.

Shortly before the main bout it was announced that the stadium had been completely sold out, breaking both attendance and receipt records. The paid admissions exceeded 130,000 and the gate receipts were over the two-million mark.

In addition to the paid admissions there were unpaid admissions amounting to $30,000 money value. Tex Rickard announced that he had purposely understated the crowd expected in order not to discourage possible last-minute purchasers of seats.

Crowd Is Well Handled.

Old-timers at the ringside who had seen every big fight since Fitzsimmons defeated Corbett said it was the most perfectly handled bout they had ever seen, for the huge concourse was ushered into the stadium without confusion.

The crowd, which had been cheering the preliminary fighters as they mauled each other to while away the spectators' time, broke into their first real frenzy when Gene Tunney appeared in the path alongside the ring and began climbing up to the square. The cheering was continuous from the moment he appeared. It broke into a single great outburst of yells, with shrill whistles from the thousands of lips sharpening it, as he entered the ring and went to his corner, smiling

In the ovation for Tunney there was perhaps a note of sympathy.

Dempsey entered a moment after Tunney, and another great roar went up. Rain began falling but nobody seemed to notice it, least of all the fighters as they squared away and the blows began to fly.

They were yelling madly for Gene as he began swinging into the champion with a force they had not dreamed the young challenger possessed. And when the first round ended with Tunney so unmistakably in the lead there was a minute of sheer delirium.

Women Shout Dismay.

They were at it again, and the voices of the women spectators now and again sounded out over all the clamor as Tunney staggered under the blows of the infuriated champion. There were feminine shouts of dismay as well when Tunney shot a hard one at Dempsey.

As the fight settled down into a give and take and the surprise at Tunney's showing waned, the cries of encouragement and warning became an intermittent hum, punctuated by shouts as the blows landed or missed. The crowd was watching for the fine points now.

As one of the thinly padded fists struck its target of flesh with a whack a concerted groan went through the rows of onlookers.

"The nose, the nose," the crowd yelled as one of Gene's uppercuts brought blood on Dempsey's right cheek. "That fancy nose is a goner. Hit that and he's through."

The fourth round passed and the fifth began. The clamor of the crowd quieted a little, for it gave place to admiration that Tunney had lasted so long. The crowd was yelling for a knockout each time Tunney pushed Dempsey into the ropes.

Dempsey was fighting an unexpectedly good man and the crowd was with his enemy. Then the sixth round began, the round which had been set by the experts as the last one possible for Tunney to fight. The crowd was hushed as Tunney went confidently from his corner.

A sigh of relief swept the stadium as Tunney emerged from it shaken but still strong, and there was a burst of applause as he took his seat. The old-time fight followers wagged their heads. "It's not the same old Dempsey," they said.

"He missed his chance right there," said somebody as Dempsey drove with all his dreadful strength at a point in space which Tunney had just left. "If that had landed we'd been on our way home."

And then a burst of women's cries

Continued on Page Three.

Dempsey's Share $850,000; Tunney to Receive $200,000

Special to The New York Times.

PHILADELPHIA, Sept. 23.—The receipts of the Dempsey-Tunney fight tonight were in excess of $2,000,000. On the basis of $2,000,000, the receipts were divided as follows:

Dempsey	$850,000
Tunney	$200,000
Federal Tax	$200,000
State	$100,000
Sesquicentennial	$200,000
Preliminary fights	$40,000
Tex Rickard, promoter	$410,000

AIRPLANE CARRIES TUNNEY TO SCENE

Challenger Is First to Make Way to Heavyweight Title Bout Through Air.

RISK DEPLORED BY MANY

Tunney, However, Is Calm Throughout—Calls Flying Least Trying on Nerves.

Special to The New York Times.

PHILADELPHIA, Sept. 23.—Not content with the prospect of facing Dempsey and destiny, Gene Tunney had to defy death, too. For the first time in the history of heavyweight championships, the challenger flew forth to the field of battle in an airplane.

From Stroudsburg, Pa., where Tunney trained for the three weeks, to Philadelphia the challenger took the shortest route. He winged above the silvery course of the Delaware River, winding through the Pocono Mountains, and landed at the navy yard in plenty of time to weigh in before the astonished eyes of the Pennsylvania State Boxing Commission.

Gene traveled in a red Curtiss Oriole plan, piloted by the expert hands of Casey Jones, noted for his feats of daring. The only other passenger was Wade Morton, driver of racing cars, who finished fourth in the last five-hundred mile classic at Indianapolis.

Challenger Disdains Danger.

The utter distain Tunney displayed for the battle at hand, with the golden goal for which he has striven seven years in the balance, was unusual in itself. He disregarded entirely the fact that a tremendous gate, the greatest financial success in the history of sports, depended upon his appearance in the ring at the proper time. He laughed at the suggestion of danger which he was tempting. He continued in the same unperturbed, undisturbed, confident mood he had displayed from the start.

When the news spread that the challenger had taken to the air with the chance of his life only a few hours away there was a general outcry of disapproval. But there was no opportunity in which to make the challenger change his course. He had decided on his means of travel a week before and he kept it secret from every one, including his manager, Billy Gibson, and Tex Rickard.

The challenger slept late on his morning of destiny, facing the beckoning call of opportunity with the calmness of a child. He arose at 8 o'clock and relished a special breakfast at the Glen Brook Country Club in Stroudsburg, specially prepared by George Ransberry, his private chef. When he came forth into the misty morning he greeted the small crowd waiting to bid him farewell and godspeed in his quest for the coveted crown with the announcement that he was going to fly to Philadelphia

Cheer Sends Him on Way.

There was gasps of amazement, and after a moment of surprised silence a cheer broke forth from the little knot of well-wishers.

Morton, the race driver, was waiting for the challenger with the motor running in a high-powered Duesenberg. Tunney climbed in beside the driver's seat and was speeded to the Shawnee Country Club at Buckwood Inn, about five miles away. There Jones and his Oriole awaited the coming of the precious passenger.

On arriving at the Buckwood Inn Gene was greeted by Reggie Worthington.

"Where's Casey?" asked the challenger.

"Oh, he's out playing golf," Worthington informed him.

"Say, I might play a couple of holes myself before I leave," Gene suggested in his matter-of-fact way, still calm and unexcited.

However, it was decided that the aerial expedition had better get under way, and Casey Jones was summoned from a bunker. He went over to a near-by shed and in a short time taxied out in a blood red sky chariot. Gene walked over to the third tee on the golf course, accompanied by a few friends and a few strangers who had been playing golf but had deserted their game on hearing that the chal-

Continued on Page Two.

TUNNEY ALWAYS MASTER

Challenger Bewilders His Opponent With His Speed, Accuracy.

AGGRESSIVE IN ALL ROUNDS

Sends Rain of Whiplike Lefts Which Champion Cannot Avoid.

OUTCOME IS A SURPRISE

Dempsey Lacks All Evidence of His Old Aggressiveness—Victor Is Acclaimed.

By JAMES P. DAWSON.
Special to The New York Times.

RINGSIDE, SESQUICENTENNIAL STADIUM, Philadelphia, Sept. 23.—Gene Tunney is the new world's heavyweight champion. The ex-marine fought like a marine here tonight in the Sesquicentennial Stadium, when he carried off the decision over Jack Dempsey, once known as the Manassa Mauler and the ring's man-killer, in a ten-round bout which saw the first passing of a heavyweight championship title on a decision.

Through every round of the ten, Tunney battered and pounded Dempsey. He rained rights on the tottering champion's jaw and he bewildered Dempsey with his speed and the accuracy of a whip-like left hand which Dempsey could not evade. When the decision was announced, the crowd let loose a roar of acclaim for "the man of destiny," who had conquered the man-killer, and the countryside sent the roar echoing back.

Confidence Aids Tunney.

The transfer of the title, the ascension of Tunney to the pinnacle in boxing, surprised the majority of those who witnessed the fight and experienced followers of boxing form. It surprised everybody, almost, but Tunney, whose confidence, more than anything else, perhaps, carried him on to a height which the vast majority thought unattainable for him.

He was complete master, from first bell to last. He out-boxed and he outfought Dempsey at every turn. Where it had been expected that Tunney would break and run before the vicious attack of Dempsey, the tiger man, Tunney, the fighting marine, not only failed to back up, but he went forward all the time with the instinct of the true leatherneck and hammered Dempsey in a driving attack which brooked no restraining effort on the part of the champion.

There was no question of the victor at the finish. There was no question even of the winner of each round as the battle progressed, and Dempsey, instead of flashing the fighting fury which was expected of him, instead of surging forward with the tigerish, vicious rushes he has exhibited in previous and more favorable ring engagements, proved himself instead a floundering, weakened, almost helpless fighting machine from which the spark had gone.

All the evidences of the old Dempsey were merely that; only faint evidences, indications, unexpressive flashes save for their expression of futility of helpless hopelessness, of utter ineffectiveness.

They fought this battle in the rain—a driving, torrential downpour which started when the men entered the ring and which increased in fury as the fight progressed. The ring was flooded, the spectators drenched and the gladiators were drenched, but as the fury of the storm increased so did the fighting of Tunney, and Dempsey had nothing with which to meet this Marine attack.

Knockdown Is Lacking.

It was a disappointing transfer of a heavyweight title in one respect. The battle did not end in a knockout. Indeed, through its ten rounds the struggle held not even a knock down. This was due to the fact that Tunney is a weak hitter in the sense that he is not a finishing or destructive hitter.

He is not of the old Dempsey hitting school. But the New York lad is a punishing hitter, a cruel, tantalizing, tormenting puncher and a cool, unruffled boxer at all times. He did about everything else to Dempsey but knock the defending champion down and out. He battered Dempsey to a pulp, until the beaten champion at the finish was a close resemblance to the giant Jess Willard, whom Dempsey pounded and hammered into a helpless hulk out on the shores of Maumee Bay seven years ago when he won the title.

For the first time in his career

Continued on Page Two.

Times Wide World Photo.

GENE TUNNEY, THE NEW CHAMPION

Champion Tunney Praises the Loser; "I Have No Alibis," Asserts Dempsey

Special to The New York Times.

SESQUICENTENNIAL STADIUM, PHILADELPHIA, Sept. 23—The following statements were made after the bout tonight:

By GENE TUNNEY.

Dempsey fought like the great champion that he was. He has the kick of a mule in his fists and the heart of a lion in his breast. I never fought a harder socker nor do I hope to meet one. Dempsey fought like a gentleman and never took an unfair advantage in the ring. Once or twice he may have hit me a little low, but always it was by accident. He never meant it.

"I'm sorry," he always said following anything close to a foul blow. When the gong rang at the end of the fight he threw his arm over my shoulder and said: "Great fight, Gene; you won." I don't care what they may say about him he is certainly a man in the ring. The hardest blows I felt were two socks on the Adam's apple. That's why I'm so hoarse. I have no plans for the future, but am content to rest a while with the ambition I have nourished for seven years at last realized. The marines, you know, are always first to fight and last to leave. No matter how heavy the going may be you will always find them there in the end.

By JACK DEMPSEY.

I have no alibis to offer. I lost to a good man, an American—a man who speaks the English language. I have no alibis.

Story of the Fight by Rounds

Special to The New York Times.

RINGSIDE, SESQUICENTENNIAL STADIUM, PHILADELPHIA, Sept. 23.—The round by round detail of the Tunney-Dempsey bout fought here tonight follows:

First Round.

Dempsey was attired in blue trunks and Tunney in purple. Dempsey looked rather thin as he stepped forward for a consultation.

As the round started Dempsey, with a scowl on his face, rushed out and drove Tunney to his own corner. Dempsey again rushed. Jack sent a terrific left to the jaw. Dempsey kept rushing in and drove Tunney into his own corner. Dempsey went in and Tunney swung a hard right to Dempsey's chin. Dempsey weaved in again and Tunney was short with a right. They boxed in the centre of the ring for a moment, then Tunney missed a right for the head but ripped two rights to the body. Dempsey jabbed Tunney away, and then Dempsey lunged over the ropes after missing a left swing. Tunney rushed in again and sent a heavy right to the chin. In a terrific exchange Tunney showered left and right swings to Dempsey's jaw and Dempsey was groggy. Gene's only mark in the exchange was a bleeding mouth.

Between rounds Dempsey appeared very tired and his seconds worked hard over him.

Second Round.

Dempsey rushed over to Tunney's corner, trying to get his man. Dempsey swung his right to the jaw, but Tunney got out of the way. They stepped out in the middle of the ring and Tunney swung right and left to the jaw. Dempsey came through with a right to the body and drove Tunney to his corner. Jack drove Gene to a neutral corner and punished him about the head. Tunney sent two lefts to Jack's head. They wrestled across the ring, Dempsey pounding the body. Gene sent short rights and lefts to the jaw. It was now raining heavily. Jack drove Tunney into his own corner with a terrific right to the heart and dazed Tunney. Tunney put over a left and right to the jaw at the bell and the crowd was in an uproar.

Third Round.

Dempsey came out slowly for the third and they met in the middle of the ring. Jack tried a terrific right for the jaw but missed. Gene stood up straight and jabbed lefts and rights to Jack's jaw. Gene put over a heavy right to the head and wrestled Jack back to the ropes. Tunney swung terrific rights and lefts to Jack's jaw. Tunney repeated with a right and had the champion staggering in midring. He graced the champion's jaw and then landed a good right to Jack's jaw. Tunney jumped away and sparred cleverly, but Dempsey kept boring in. Jack came in only to be sent back to the ropes with rights and lefts to the jaw. Tunney sent another left jab to the head, but Jack punished him heavily to the body in return. As Jack came in Tunney ripped lefts and rights to the body at the bell.

Fourth Round.

Dempsey came out with a terrific rush and with a wild right sent Tunney almost over the ropes. Tunney was in bad shape, but he continued to jab Jack away with a left. Jack's eye was cut with one of these lefts. Dempsey went in and sent two lefts to the jaw. Dempsey continued to weave in, trying to land a heavy body blow. Dempsey missed a left to the jaw. Tunney stabbed a left, then swung a heavy right to Jack's jaw. Dempsey's eye was in bad shape and

Continued on Page Three.

VICTORY IS POPULAR ONE

Ex-Marine Gets Ovation as He Enters Ring—Crowd 'Boos' Foe.

BIGGEST IN SPORT HISTORY

Rickard's Luck Turns, However, and Distinguished Gathering Is Thoroughly Drenched.

DEMPSEY'S NOSE SUFFERS

Rebuilt for Movies, It Is Target of Challenger as He Piles Up Points for Victory.

By ELMER DAVIS.
Special to The New York Times.

RINGSIDE, SESQUICENTENNIAL STADIUM, PHILADELPHIA, Sept. 23.—While the rain poured down on the greatest crowd that ever saw a sporting event, Gene Tunney beat Jack Dempsey, and captured the world's heavyweight championship in a ten-round fight here tonight.

The champion, in the phrase of one of the ringside critics, lost his title by a synthetic nose. It was by steady pounding away at the built-in beak which Dempsey acquired a couple of years ago that Tunney piled up a heavy lead on points in the early rounds.

Dempsey rallied toward the middle of the fight, but his effort to come back in a last round finish failed. The ex-marine, against whom the experts were betting three and four to one this afternoon, walked off with the title.

Crowd Is With Tunney.

It was the first time in history that the heavyweight championship of the world has changed hands on points, but there was never the slightest doubt after the start that if there were a decision Tunney would get it. The champion's only chance was to win by a knockout, and here his old power had deserted him. He was in somewhat better shape after three years of idleness than when he fought Tom Gibbons at Shelby, Mont., after a two-year layoff in 1923. The swings and hooks that always missed Gibbons occasionally landed on Tunney. But they never landed hard enough. The young fighter from Greenwich Village could stand up and take it.

Though the experts and the gamblers thought, by a heavy majority, that Dempsey would walk off with the fight, about 90 per cent. of the 130,000 people who saw the encounter were for Tunney. There was an uproarious cheer when the challenger entered the ring. He wore the scarlet trimmed blue dressing gown, with the Marine Corps emblem on the back, which was presented to him by old comrades of the Marine Corps. He climbed through the ropes at 9:30, and stood up to let the crowd see him.

Two minutes later the champion of the world came in. There was a scattering round of applause as he entered the ring, but when Joe Griffo, announcer, introduced him as "the heavyweight champion who has defended his title for the past six years," there was a roar of boos that rocked the whole amphitheatre. If ever a fighting champion, as yet undefeated and favored by all the experts to remain undefeated, had such a reception from a crowd, the episode is buried in the obscurity of the past.

The rain began to fall on the crowd in the Sesquicentennial Stadium just as the big fight started. Hitherto the proverbial Rickard luck had held, even against the weather. Though it rained in Philadelphia early this morning and heaps of dark clouds obscured the sky at nightfall when the crowd began to gather in the stadium, the rain held off.

A dozen fight programs have rained out in New York alone this Summer, but it looked as if Rickard, with the biggest fight of the past three years and the biggest fight crowd and biggest gate of all time, was going to get away untouched.

Five preliminary bouts had gone on and the ring had been cleared for the entrance of the principals to the big event when the rain began at last. The amplifier announcers who relayed Joe Griffo's statements to the farthest edges of the huge stadium had just announced, three or four times, that all persons in the audience were requested to keep their seats.

Crowd Came Prepared.

Suddenly all over the huge U-shaped cup of the permanent amphitheatre and the broad wooden expanse of the temporary seats, people stood up by thousands struggling into rain coats. Then they sat down again, grimly determined to stay to the finish, whatever the weather.

At the end, when the bleeding champion and the eager challenger were exchanging wallops before the bell, the ring was splashed and puddled, the crowd was drowned out, but everybody but Dempsey and his friends was happy.

All the predictions and expectations about this fight were upset. Dempsey had hoped to finish his opponent in one punch and expected to do it within two rounds.

The comparatively few last ditch supporters who expected Tunney to win

"All the News That's Fit to Print."

The New York Times.

THE WEATHER
Mostly cloudy today; tomorrow fair, slightly rising temperature.
Temperature Yesterday—Max. 39; Min. 29.
For weather report see Page 43.

VOL. LXXVI....No. 25,262. NEW YORK, FRIDAY, MARCH 25, 1927. TWO CENTS in Greater New York | THREE CENTS Within 200 Miles | FOUR CENTS Elsewhere in the U. S.

AMERICANS AND BRITISH KILLED IN ATTACKS AT NANKING; WARSHIPS THEN SHELL CITY AND RESCUE SOME FOREIGNERS; ALLIED COMMANDERS SERVE ULTIMATUM; ALL CHINA AFLAME

DEAF TO LAST APPEAL REPUBLICANS KILL SMITH POWER BILLS

He Promises Veto in Special Message Asking That Decision Be Left to People.

BAUMES FENCE BILL DIES

Pistol Measure Is Saved After Defeat—Tammany Members Less Hostile.

CHARGES ROUSE ASSEMBLY

Host of Acts Are Passed as Noon Today Is Set for Final Adjournment.

Special to The New York Times.

ALBANY, March 24.—In a final drive to clear their calendars preparatory to final adjournment tomorrow at noon, the Senate and Assembly labored all day, disposing of approximately 250 bills, of which less than a dozen were defeated.

Among the notable measures that were passed was the constitutional amendment providing for the creation of the Executive budget system in the State, a Smith program proposal adopted in the Senate, and the Friedsam bill providing for State contributions aggregating $16,500,000 for the common schools throughout the State, with a little more than $10,000,000 of the total going to New York City, approved in the Assembly.

The Senate amended the Assembly resolution, which in its original form called for final adjournment on March 18 so as to provide for adjournment sine die at noon tomorrow. The resolution was sent back to the Assembly for approval of the amendment, but up to the time of adjournment this evening the lower house had not concurred. There is no doubt, however, that the curtain will fall over the 1927 session some time tomorrow.

Smith Power Bill Defeated.

Defeat in the Assembly of the Governor's Power Authority bill and his measure providing for a referendum on water power in the election this year and passage of the Republican Water Power bill by a party vote in the lower house, in concurrence with the Senate, which has already approved the bill, were other outstanding features of the day.

The action on the Governor's bill was taken despite an urgent appeal made by the Chief Executive in a special message that the Legislature pass the referendum bill and let the voters determine whether the State or private interests should develop the hydro-electric resources of the State. The Governor will veto the Republican power bill.

Discussion of Baumes anti-crime bills in the Assembly provoked a bitter and prolonged debate, which ended in a second defeat for the so-called "fence" bill, which would legalize testimony by a thief against receivers of goods he had stolen. Considerable progress was made on legislation of this series, however, eight measures being passed. One, the so-called "Pistol bill," was snatched from defeat after it once had been beaten.

Measures Passed by Both Houses.

Measures upon which favorable action was taken today and in which both houses have concurred include:

The executive budget constitutional amendment;

The constitutional amendment providing for an increase to $25,000 in the Governor's salary and increases for Lieutenant Governor and lawmakers;

The tri-State Delaware River compact.

Bills Passed by Senate.

New York City Grade Crossing Elimination bill.

Hickey bill to discourage child marriages.

Westchester Charter.

Bill to license operators at milk-gathering stations.

Lease of Ward Island in part by New York City to be used for establishment of a sewage disposal plant.

Passed by the Assembly.

Friedsam bill appropriating $16,500,000 for additional State aid to public schools.

Republic water power bill providing for a commission to investigate and recommend a State development policy.

Measures Defeated.

Governor Smith's power authority and water power referendum bills.

The Baumes series bill to legalize testimony of thiefs against receivers of stolen goods.

Democratic resolution proposing an amendment to the Constitution which would permit the State to sell or cede the Barge Canal to the Federal Gov-

Continued on Page Four.

14 Big Atlantic Liners Race For Spring Tourist Rush Here

Copyright, 1927, by The New York Times Co.
By Wireless to THE NEW YORK TIMES.

LONDON, March 24.—The pick of the great Atlantic liners are racing to catch the Spring tide of American tourists headed for Europe. Fourteen of the vessels operating between New York and English ports will be on the high seas almost at the same time during the next ten days.

The Majestic and the France sailed westward yesterday. The President Roosevelt and the Antonia will sail tomorrow. The Berengaria, Washington, Ascania, Cedric, Aurania and Minnewaska will sail on Saturday. Closely following will be the Leviathan, Homeric, Lancastria, New York and Mauretania.

SAPIRO CUTS OUT 54 OF ALLEGED LIBELS

Court Tentatively Accepts New Basis of Suit, Refusing Long Recess to Study It.

LAWYERS BATTLE OVER IT

Defense Suggests a Mistrial—Court Bars Questions on Ford Ordering Attacks on Jews.

From a Staff Correspondent of The New York Times.

DETROIT, March 24.—The Sapiro-Ford libel trial produced two cardinal developments today. The first was Aaron Sapiro's elimination of 54 of the 141 libels he had alleged against Henry Ford and the Dearborn Publishing Company. The second was the vain attempt of the plaintiff to show that Mr. Ford motivated an attack on Mr. Sapiro as part of a general onslaught aimed at his race.

The alleged libels which went out of the case were dropped in the amended declaration which William H. Gallagher, counsel for Mr. Sapiro, handed to Federal Judge Fred M. Raymond. The declaration, which sets forth the grounds upon which the suit is based, was criticized by the Court several days ago. In the opinion of Mr. Gallagher, the form submitted today simplified and consolidated his case. Senator James A. Reed and others of the Ford counsel regarded the elimination as a victory.

When the document was tendered Stewart Hanley, who has been most active on the Ford firing line, demanded time in which to study it. He said that the cursory examination he had given it persuaded him that the new declaration altered the whole case. It was possible, he said, although he had no thought of recourse to such a procedure, that the new form might necessitate a mistrial. Mr. Gallagher minimized the importance which the defense attached to the new declaration.

Editorial Is Deleted.

One of the alleged libels which Mr. Sapiro took out voluntarily dealt with an editorial in The Dearborn Independent, published after the series containing the alleged libels, in which the Chicago attorney was accused of unprofessional conduct and pictured as a "cheat" and "fraud" and "grafter" and "faker" and "mountebank." Mr. Gallagher said Mr. Sapiro was not mentioned in the editorial and, further, it was not part of the series which he contends were anti-Jewish. Mr. Hanley countered by saying that the defense had been ready to prove the truth of the editorial, and that the concluding paragraph of the editorial had named Mr. Sapiro.

Mr. Hanley asked that the trial be adjourned to Monday so that he and his associates could readjust their lines of defense, if necessary. Mr. Gallagher opposed that. Judge Raymond, who observed that there had been little "visible progress" in the case, although many issues had been clarified which would result in progress later, settled the matter by adjourning from 10 A. M. to 2 P. M. He then said that he would accept the amended declaration tentatively.

The Court explained that he provisionally accepted the document so that the taking of testimony by William J. Cameron, editor of The Dearborn Independent, could go on. He gave tentative approval to all of the declaration except one clause. He struck that out. This paragraph sought to establish that the periodical, by earlier attacks on Mr. Sapiro's coreligionists, had made the word "Jew" a word of contumely, hate and opprobrium in the minds of The Independent's 600,000 readers.

Amended Basis Taken Up First.

The matter of amended basis of suit was the first order of the session when court convened at 9:30 A. M. Judge Raymond had indicated that he felt the document was insufficient in some of its counts, notably where single phrases, lifted from their context, had been cited as libels. Mr. Gallagher and his associates, Judge Robert F. Marx and Walter F. Lynch, had been revising it since the Judge indicated his opinion. As Mr. Gallagher handed

Continued on Page Twenty-four.

POISONED WHISKY IN SNYDER HOME BARES EARLY PLOT

Scheme That Failed Revealed by Gray and Chemist Finds Bichloride of Mercury.

NO TRACE IN VICTIM'S BODY

Dr. Gettler Says 20 Tablets Must Have Been Used—To Seek Other Drugs Today.

TRIAL IS SET FOR APRIL 11

Newcombe Would Try Both at Once and Will Ask Death Penalty—Woman Protests Her Innocence.

To check up a statement made by Henry Judd Gray that Mrs. Ruth Brown Snyder had tried to poison her husband some time before the murder last Sunday morning, the police took a bottle of whisky from the Snyder cellarette yesterday to Dr. Alexander O. Gettler, city toxicologist, at Bellevue Hospital.

There were several bottles in the cellarette, but the chemist was asked to analyze only the one which had been described by Gray as containing the poison, said to be bichloride of mercury.

As soon as the Snyder whisky bottle was handed to him with this explanation, Dr. Gettler heated up a shining copper wire, dipped it in hydrochloric acid and thrust it in the whisky.

This is the ordinary quick test for bichloride of mercury. If it is present, the mercury deposits on the copper in the presence of hydrochloric acid in minute globules. Usually a microscope has to be used to detect the deposit.

After leaving the copper wire in the whisky for half an hour, Dr. Gettler removed it.

Wire Thickly Coated.

"Great Scott," he exclaimed. The copper wire seemed to be silverplated. There was no need of using the microscope, so thickly was the wire coated with quicksilver (mercury).

"Enough bichloride of mercury was put into that bottle of whisky to kill any man who took one good drink of it," said Dr. Gettler.

Four other copper wires were then heated and dipped into hydrochloric acid. One was inserted into the stomach contents of the murdered man. The others were placed in contact separately with brain, kidney and liver tissue.

After half an hour they were removed. Their appearance was still that of ordinary copper wire. Each wire was examined under the microscope. No globules of quicksilver were found.

"This shows that Snyder had not touched the poisoned whisky recently," said Dr. Gettler. "It has nothing to do with his death. It is possible that he might have tasted the liquor at some time in the past. Mercury, however, remains in the system for some time. We would find traces in the organs probably for two months if he had swallowed any of the whisky with mercury in it."

Dr. Gettler did not have an opportunity yesterday to measure the quicksilver quantitatively, but the evidence of the thickly coated wire made it certain that a large quantity of bichloride of mercury had been used.

"Possibly twenty tablets or more were dissolved in it," said Dr. Gettler. It is probable that the poisoner or poisoners overshot the mark by putting so many mercury tablets in the whisky as to give it a noticeable taste. Whether he was suspicious of the fla-

Continued on Page Nine.

Soviet Warned on Propaganda Hurting Stage as Church Rival

MOSCOW, March 24 (AP).—Mikhail Tomsky, Chairman of the All-Russian Council of Trade Unions, has warned the Soviet authorities that theatres in Russian villages and towns will not keep the public from the churches unless something more than propaganda is offered to entertain audiences.

"Performances in our playhouses must be artistic, esthetic creations, designed to appeal to the taste and pocketbooks of the workers," he declares. "They must be more than propaganda vehicles."

TONGMEN KILL NINE AS WAR FLARES ANEW

Two Chinese Slain in Brooklyn Restaurant While 250 Are Dining There.

KILLINGS OCCUR IN 6 CITIES

27 Bullets Fired Into Man at Newark—Banton Warns He Will Start Deportations.

Chinese tong warfare flared anew yesterday over the eastern part of the United States after a peace of two years between the On Leong Tong and the Hip Sing Tong, and last night nine Chinese had been killed and two wounded in six different cities. The police arrested forty-five.

In Chicago one man was killed early yesterday morning and three were wounded last night. Two of these died later. In Brooklyn two were killed early yesterday morning in a crowded restaurant. In Newark a Chinese from Boston was riddled with bullets in the early morning. Cleveland and Pittsburgh each had one murder during the early hours of the day and in Pittsburgh a second Chinese was wounded.

In New York's Chinatown there was an air of fear and mystery yesterday, and a most unusual number of uniformed patrolmen and detectives. There were more police than Chinese on the three streets of Chinatown. On the "bloody angle" at Doyers and Pell Streets a single uniformed policeman remained alone most of the day.

Tongmen Out of Sight.

The ornate building of the On Leong Tong on Mott Street was deserted and the leaders of that organization congregate elsewhere. The Hip Sings gathered at 15 Pell Street in a room behind a darkened laundry. The once dead-line between Pell and Mott Streets was again drawn, and few if any Chinese turned from one street into the other.

Two years ago, almost to the day, the two tongs signed a peace pact. It was hailed with relief by the police and with rejoicing by the Chinese. It was to last "for all time" it was said, though the skeptical who know the nature of the two tongs and grave doubts. The success of one tong means the decay of the other. Each is jealous, suspicious and watchful of the other.

According to the reports yesterday in Chinatown, the renewal of the warfare was started by the shooting in Chicago of Chin Pock, found shot to death in a gambling house in Chicago's Chinatown. Chin, the story goes, belonged to the On Leong Tong. A few months ago he resigned and joined the Hip Sings. Recently he reversed the process, going back to the On Leongs.

The Hip Sings called him a spy and a traitor. He died in Tom Jack's Chinese gambling house Wednesday night, and by morning Hip Sings had been killed in Brooklyn, Newark and elsewhere, another On Leong man was dead in Pittsburgh and a large part of

Continued on Page Three.

Calls on Gov. Smith to Give His Views On Allegiance to His Church or State

A statement rom Governor Alfred E. Smith setting forth his views regarding the jurisdiction of the Roman Catholic Church, of which he is a member, is asked by Charles C. Marshall, a lawyer of this city, in an open letter to the Governor published in the April number of The Atlantic Monthly. The Governor is asked to state what would be his views in case of possible conflict regarding jurisdiction between the Church and the American Government.

Saying that letters of various Popes made it clear that the Church holds that it has divine ecclesiastical power and that, while it concedes secular power to the State, it remains the judge in its own opinion as to what constitutes secular power, Mr. Marshall contends that the Roman Catholic view is that other churches and ethical associations have no fundamental rights, and asks whether or not Governor Smith concurs in this view.

Mr. Marshall mentions divorce and annulment of marriage, education and the Mexican situation as other matters on which differences of opinion from the Church and American viewpoint are likely, in his opinion, and cites the recent annulment of the Marlborough marriage as a case in point. Mr. Marshall also cites the beatification in 1886 of John Felton, an Englishman, who was convicted of treason in 1570. Felton's offense, three centuries and a half ago, was the posting on the walls of London of the decree of Pope Pius V deposing Queen Elizabeth.

"The honors paid him were rendered 300 years after his treasonable act," Mr. Marshall says, regarding the case of Felton, in his letter to the Governor. "There lies their sinister import. They are no part of the medieval milieu; they belong to the modern world and must have judgment not by medieval but by modern standards.

"Is the record of the Roman Catholic Church in England, sir, in your opinion, consistent with the peace and safety of the State? Nothing will be of greater satisfaction to those of your fellow-citizens who hesitate in their endorsement of your candidacy because of religious issues involved than a disclaimer by you of the convictions here imputed or such an exposition by others of the questions here presented as may justly turn public opinion in your favor."

WASHINGTON ACTS QUICKLY

Orders More Cruisers to China and Gives Admiral Fullest Backing.

GRAVE MESSAGES RECEIVED

Nanking Incident and Unrest Elsewhere Taken Seriously by Officials.

NO LIGHT ON CASUALTIES

Admiral Hough Simply Reports Some Americans Were Slain on Socony Hill.

Special to The New York Times.

WASHINGTON, March 24.—News of the serious incident at Nanking reached Washington early today, when Admiral Charles S. Williams, Commander-in-Chief of the Asiatic Fleet, reported that a "number" of American civilians had been killed and wounded in an attack by Cantonese troops on Socony Hill in that city.

Rear Admiral Harry H. Hough, ranking American naval officer at Nanking, said in his official report, "It is feared that the number of dead is large."

The missions were looted, and 155 Americans, comprising 45 women, 20 children and 90 men, whose fate is uncertain, were left in the city, with firing still going on at 5 o'clock yesterday afternoon, when Admiral Hough reported to Admiral Williams.

Admiral Hough and the British ranking naval officer on the cruiser Emerald then served an ultimatum on the Chinese General, demanding:

First—The immediate protection of all foreigners and foreign property.

Second—The reporting on board of the Cantonese General in command at Nanking before 11 o'clock the night of March 24 (Chinese time) to negotiate respecting the outrages committed.

Third—That all foreigners must be brought to the bund under escort by 10 o'clock the morning of March 25 (Chinese time), which is 9 o'clock New York time tonight.

If the demands of this ultimatum were not complied with, Admiral Hough reported to Admiral Williams, Nanking would be treated as a military area. This meant, according to naval officials today that Nanking could no longer have immunity from extensive attack under the protection of international law, accorded to unfortified cities.

President Coolidge and the Government at Washington, shocked at the sudden turn of events at Nanking, intend to back up Admirals Williams and Hough "100 per cent.," Secretary Wilbur asserted this afternoon.

"Admiral Williams," Mr. Wilbur added, "has full authority to use all the forces under his command at his discretion for the protection of American lives and property. That I have probably said before, but I wish to reiterate it now. He has been given from time to time all the forces he has requested."

At Admiral Williams's request three cruisers were ordered at once from Honolulu to join his forces.

No fresh instructions were sent to the Admiral because he needed none, having, from the beginning, been clothed with the widest authority to act in any emergency threatening the lives of Americans in China.

Late tonight Admiral Williams sent word that the destroyers Peary, Ford and Pillsbury were proceeding to Shanghai from Manila. In addition other destroyers, not yet designated, have been ordered from Manila to Swatow, Amoy and Foochow, one destroyer to each port.

Williams's Report in Summary.

The Navy Department issued this summary of the message from Admiral Williams, which also contains the text of the report from Admiral Hough:

Foreigners on Socony Hill were attacked. British cruiser Emerald and the United States destroyers Noa and Preston shelled the area around the hill to protect the foreigners, opening fire about 3:30 P. M. Landing forces were sent to attempt the rescue of foreigners from the hill.

The commander of the Yangtse patrol force, Rear Admiral H. H. Hough, U. S. N., arrived in the U. S. S. Isabel at 6:30 P. M. and the following dispatch has been received from him through Admiral C. S. Williams, U. S. N., commander-in-chief of the Asiatic Fleet, who has forwarded the entire dispatch to the Navy Department:

"At 5 P. M. the Preston and the Noa ceased heavy gun fire and the British cruiser Emerald sent a landing force to a wall under the Standard Oil house, while the Emerald covered with shrapnel and the Noa and the Preston cleared the bund and far shore of snipers by firing from the ships.

"The landing forces successfully brought off all the foreigners from the Standard Oil house, including the American Consul and his family and all American naval personnel.

Continued on Page Three.

Reports Conflict on Americans Left in Nanking; Shanghai Hears of Negotiations for Release

By The Associated Press

SHANGHAI, Friday, March 25.—Conflicting messages early this morning from the City of Nanking, where a number of foreigners, including Americans, were killed and wounded by Cantonese shelling yesterday, left the fate of a portion of the American community there in doubt.

Prior to yesterday's shelling of Socony Hill, which resulted in counterfire by British and American warships, it was known that 155 Americans, consisting of 90 men, 45 women and 20 children, were ashore. Some of those remained, despite the landing of a rescue party made up of American and British forces, who succeeded in removing most of the stranded.

Other messages from Nanking this morning, however, told of further rescue efforts, which resulted in the rescue and evacuation of all the remaining foreigners, only after further casualties, including some Americans. These messages reported that British and American landing parties approached Socony Hill under renewed fire from the Cantonese, but ultimately rescued all the foreigners.

Nevertheless reports received from Nanking at 5 A. M. said that the fate of 155 Americans was still unknown. There were some Britishers also ashore and the Anglo-American authorities are attempting to negotiate with the Cantonese to effect the rescue of the remaining foreigners without further bloodshed, such as occurred yeserday.

The Americans ashore at Nanking are those who failed to reach the Socony compound. It is believed that they remained at mission centres which are widely separated within Nanking walls. All who reached the Socony compound were believed to have been brought out.

More British Troops at Shanghai And Foreign Defenses There Hold

American Marines, Used Only in Emergency, Chafe for More Active Part—Cantonese Split—Pledges to Restore Order Unfulfilled.

By FREDERICK MOORE.

Copyright, 1927, by The New York Times Company.
Special Cable to THE NEW YORK TIMES.

SHANGHAI, March 24.—Some Americans here are complaining of the inactivities of the American marines and have started a circular letter, to which foreigners other than the British are readily affixing their signatures, thanking the British for protecting their lives and properties.

Ever since their arrival the marines have been anxious to land and participate in the preparations for the defense, but have been restrained aboard their vessels and have not placed a single sandbag or a single reel of barbed wire in position. Finally, when a state of emergency was declared, they came ashore as soon as possible, but six hours after the British and French were in position.

They were then permitted only patrol duty, not even police service. They were not permitted to search for Chinese suspects and not permitted to break up menacing gatherings. Consequently they only paraded the streets in the safer interior sections of the city.

This was commented on as not being adequate defense of American lives and property and neither did they nor civilian Americans profess that it was.

American volunteer soldiers and policemen did not serve under American command. Both of these contingents gladly accepted dangerous orders from the British police chief and commanding officer.

Marines Anxious for Action.

The marines themselves are anxious for more active duty. They themselves point out that had the British not held the lines they would have been required to shoot down many Chinese, civilians as well as soldiers, inside the settlement and that foreigners, including Americans, would have been looted and burned out. They would have been unable to keep the slaughter to a minimum.

Yesterday the marines at the request of the British twice sent detachments, a score of men with two machine guns, into the defenses, immediately withdrawing them in each case after the emergency terminated. In neither case, nor at any other time, have they fired a shot.

I tell this only to contradict exaggerated reports that may have gone to the United States.

Shoot Only in Last Extremity.

The marines have been fully instructed, like the British, not to fire except in the last extremity. I, myself, standing behind a Durham battalion machine gunner in a sandbagged emplacement, witnessed the self-control of the British. An unofficered group, of whom forty were defeated Northerners, with guns and pistols in hand, seemed to charge across the open space. The machine gunner aimed, but held fire till the defeated Northerners were within twenty-five feet. The Shantungese themselves then stopped and none was killed.

American officers tell me they witnessed similar incidents. Yesterday it was arranged and the newspapers announced that Americans would this morning assume a front line position, but the order was rescinded. How and why no outsider knows.

Today 800 men of the Devonshires, namely one battalion, arrived from Hongkong, making the British force total 8,000. Today detachments of the Coldstream Guards and policemen went out into the Chinese city and entered three police stations which were taken over by Communists after the Northerners were defeated and from which snipers with police weapons had been shooting at foreigners. The Coldstream Guards severely beat many, but did not kill any and disarmed and dispersed all.

Cantonese Pledges Unfulfilled.

General Pai Chung-hsi, like the Hankow authorities, is liberal with assurances of restoring order, but is unable or unwilling to fulfill them. The Consuls who visited his headquarters at Lunghua yesterday saw many Nationalist placards, prominent among which was one "Down With Imperialism," which has come to mean "Out with the Foreigners." Marine officers asked me today if I understood the policy of our Government.

Admiral Gen. Pi Shou-chen has left the Astor House Hotel and has gone to a local hospital to recuperate from shattered nerves.

Francis Zia, a youthful Chinese editor, who was saved from beheading by Sun Chuan-fang's Government because of the activities of certain Americans here, has established himself with twelve other radicals, including a woman educated in France, in the Government yamen, styling themselves a new revolutionary government. General Su, who styled himself chief of the Shanghai defense force, has been arrested in the course of the conflict between the contending factions of Nationalists.

With the general strike called off some public utilities are beginning to resume slowly. In the meantime sniping continues in Shanghai, a British armored car being hit. The Italians today returned the fire without apparent slaughter. The warships in the harbor have been hit several times.

Denies Handicapping Marines.

Special to The New York Times.

WASHINGTON, March 24.—Positive denial that American marines at Shanghai are in any way handicapped by orders from Washington was obtained tonight from officials in authority when their attention was called to the reported complaint of

Continued on Page Two.

JOINT FORCES ARE LANDED

Parties From Ships Fight Way to Socony Hill to Reach Nationals.

CHINESE FIRE ON RESCUERS

Cantonese Sympathizers Attack Foreign Consuls, Drive Them Out and Loot Offices.

ANTI-FOREIGN SPIRIT GROWS

Our Consul General Appeals Again to Americans in Interior to Go to Shanghai.

By FREDERICK MOORE.

Copyright, 1927, by The New York Times Company.
Special Cable to THE NEW YORK TIMES.

SHANGHAI, March 24.—In view of the news from Nanking, Hankow, Wuhu and other Yangtse River and neighboring coast ports, all showing that the Nationalists' success at Shanghai has emboldened them to further assaults upon foreigners, American Consul General Clarence E. Gauss is broadcasting tonight prearranged signals summoning all Americans into Shanghai immediately for refuge.

It is evident that Bolshevist propaganda has succeeded in its effort to inflame the Chinese and to embolden them against the foreigners, and, as one success follows another, it is impossible to foresee the conclusion.

Today one of the first acts of the Nationalists entering captured Nanking was to assault the British, American and Japanese Consuls, as well as other foreigners. Only a partial number of these escaped through the courageous dash of a joint British-American naval landing force. There were 45 women, 20 children and 90 men, totaling 155 Americans, left to an unknown fate, besides other foreigners, whose numbers are unobtainable.

No Word of New Attempt.

A series of brief naval wireless messages to the British, American and Japanese warships stationed here told the tale, but said nothing about attempting another effort to relieve the surrounded foreigners tomorrow.

The Nanking news has been daily becoming more serious. Pieced together the story is approximately as follows:

For several days the Northerners, with little fighting, have been falling back upon Nanking, because it is the crossing place to the railway leading back to Shantung. Without the customary warning to civilians, the Southerners, following them, shelled the city.

There were not enough vessels for the Shantungese to recross the river, and they were compelled to fight or surrender to possible decapitation. Consequently the city, inside and outside the walls, became a battleground. The Northerners pillaged at will, but did not attack the foreigners. The incoming Nationalists, however, did not hesitate to attack the consulates today. They killed a Briton, Dr. Smith; wounded the British Consul, Giles, and drove American Consul Davis with his wife and his children from the American Consulate.

A small group of foreigners accompanied by a few American sailors who were protecting the consulate sought safety in the Standard Oil compound immediately inside the city walls, at a point a few miles from the river, but they were unable to escape.

Warships Open Fire.

Evidently the sailors signaled the American destroyers Noa and Preston and the British cruiser Emerald, which created a barrage of shells around the Standard Oil compound, to keep off the assailants, simultaneously landing a joint American and British force, which, it is believed, crossed lowland, creek and moat, finally getting the foreigners down over the city walls and retraversing the route. Altogether it was several miles back and forth to the destroyers.

I reported erroneously yesterday that the American destroyers had left for Shanghai with their 145 American refugee women and chil-

Section 1

"All the News That's Fit to Print."

The New York Times.

THE WEATHER
Generally fair today and tomorrow; moderate to fresh southerly winds.
Temperature yesterday—Max., 66; Min., 52.
For weather report see Page 31.

Section 1

VOL. LXXVI....No. 25,320. NEW YORK, SUNDAY, MAY 22, 1927. FIVE CENTS

LINDBERGH DOES IT! TO PARIS IN 33½ HOURS; FLIES 1,000 MILES THROUGH SNOW AND SLEET; CHEERING FRENCH CARRY HIM OFF FIELD

COULD HAVE GONE 500 MILES FARTHER

Gasoline for at Least That Much More—Flew at Times From 10 Feet to 10,000 Feet Above Water.

ATE ONLY ONE AND A HALF OF HIS FIVE SANDWICHES

Fell Asleep at Times but Quickly Awoke—Glimpses of His Adventure in Brief Interview at the Embassy.

LINDBERGH'S OWN STORY TOMORROW.

Captain Charles A. Lindbergh was too exhausted after his arrival in Paris late last night to do more than indicate, as told below, his experiences during his flight. After he awakes today, he will narrate the full story of his remarkable exploit for readers of Monday's New York Times.

By CARLYLE MACDONALD.

Copyright, 1927, by The New York Times Company.
Special Cable to THE NEW YORK TIMES.

PARIS, Sunday, May 22.—Captain Lindbergh was discovered at the American Embassy at 2:30 o'clock this morning. Attired in a pair of Ambassador Herrick's pajamas, he sat on the edge of a bed and talked of his flight. At the last moment Ambassador Herrick had canceled the plans of the reception committee and, by unanimous consent, took the flier to the embassy in the Place d'Iena.

A staff of American doctors who had arrived at Le Bourget Field early to minister to an "exhausted" aviator found instead a bright-eyed, smiling youth who refused to be examined.

"Oh, don't bother; I am all right," he said.

"I'd like to have a bath and a glass of milk. I would feel better," Lindbergh replied when the Ambassador asked him what he would like to have.

A bath was drawn immediately and in less than five minutes the youth had disrobed in one of the embassy guest rooms, taken his bath and was out again drinking a bottle of milk and eating a roll.

"No Use Worrying," He Tells Envoy.

"There is no use worrying about me, Mr. Ambassador," Lindbergh insisted when Mr. Herrick and members of the embassy staff wanted him to be examined by doctors and then go to bed immediately.

It was apparent that the young man was too full of his experiences to want sleep and he sat on the bed and chatted with the Ambassador, his son and daughter-in-law.

By this time a corps of frantic newspaper men who had been madly chasing the airman, following one false scent after another, had finally tracked him to the embassy. In a body they descended upon the Ambassador, who received them in the salon and informed them that he had just left Lindbergh with strict instructions to go to sleep.

As Mr. Herrick was talking with the reporters his son-in-law came downstairs and said that Lindbergh had rung and announced that he did not care to go to sleep just yet and that he would be glad to see the newspaper men for a few minutes. A cheer went up from the group who dashed by Mr. Herrick and rushed upstairs.

Expected Trouble Over Newfoundland.

In the blue and gold room, with a soft light glowing, sat the conqueror of the Atlantic. He immediately stood up and held out his hands to greet his callers. THE NEW YORK TIMES correspondent being first to greet him.

"Sit down, please," urged every one with one voice, but Lindbergh only smiled again his famous boyish smile and said:

"It's almost as easy to stand up as it is to sit down."

Questions were fired at him from all sides about his trip across the ocean, but Lindbergh seemed to dismiss them all with brief, nonchalant answers.

"I expected trouble over Newfoundland because I had been warned that the situation there was unfavorable. But I got over that hazard with no trouble whatsoever."

Sleet and Snow for 1,000 Miles.

"However, it wasn't easy going. I had sleet and snow for over 1,000 miles. Sometimes it was too high to fly over and sometimes too low to fly under, so I just had to go through it as best I could.

"I flew as low as 10 feet in some places and as high as 10,000 in others. I passed no ships in the daytime, but at night I saw the lights of several ships, the night being bright and clear."

Everyone then wanted to know if the flier had been sleepy on the voyage.

"I didn't really get what you might call downright sleepy," he said, "but I think I sort of nodded several times. In fact, I could have flown half that distance again. I had enough fuel

Continued on Page Two.

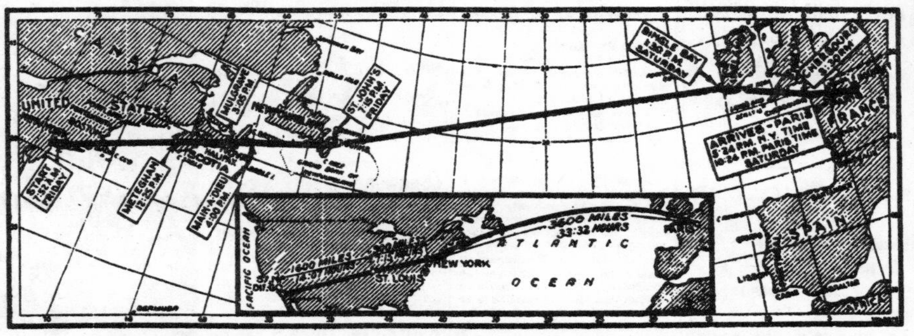

MAP OF LINDBERGH'S TRANSATLANTIC ROUTE, SHOWING THE SPEED OF HIS TRIP.

LEVINE ABANDONS BELLANCA FLIGHT

Venture Given Up as Designer Splits With Him—Plane Narrowly Escapes Burning.

BYRD'S CRAFT IS NAMED

Lindbergh Cheered at Ceremony—Commander, Now Last in Field, Waits on Weather.

Through no fault of his own, Clarence D. Chamberlin, who with Bert Acosta established a world's non-stop flying record a few weeks ago, will not fly the record-breaking monoplane in an attempt to establish a second New York-Paris non-stop flight.

G. M. Bellanca, designer of the plane, and Charles S. Levine of the Columbia Aircraft Company, owner of the ship, came to the parting of the ways last night and the designer finally severed his connection with the promoter. Then Levine issued a statement that the proposed flight, which has been talked of for weeks, was off.

The statement said:

"Due to the crowning blow of Mr. Bellanca's resignation, the plane will be placed in the hangar. Mr. Bellanca's resignation causes us to abandon plans for the New York-Paris flight for the present."

At the very moment that the statement was issued the plane was near the runway at Roosevelt Field with gas tanks filled and oil and equipment aboard ready for the start for Paris.

Plane Threatened by Fire.

A few minutes later, as it was being wheeled off, preparatory to being housed for the night, it narrowly escaped being destroyed by fire. When the word came to the field that the flight was definitely off mechanics were ordered to empty one gasoline tank to lighten the machine. The gasoline spilled on the ground and while the ship was being towed away a careless spectator threw the stub of a lighted cigarette down.

In an instant there was a terrific flare and a dense burst of smoke as the gasoline blazed up.

"The Bellanca's gone," was the cry that rose from thousands of spectators who had gathered at the field.

Word was flashed to the army air station at Mitchel Field that there had been an accident and ambulances and fire-fighting apparatus were sent across the road. An ambulance from the Nassau County Hospital at Mineola was also sent to Roosevelt Field, as well as fire apparatus from Mineola.

The plane, however, was beyond the danger line and was not injured.

It had been announced that the Columbia would take off at 8 o'clock and Chamberlin was in his flying clothes ready to climb into the cockpit with the unnamed pilot who was to have accompanied him on the trip.

With the elimination of the Bellanca monoplane, only Lieut.

Continued on Page Four.

Times Wide World Photo

CAPTAIN CHARLES A. LINDBERGH,
Who Flew Alone Across the Atlantic, New York to Paris, in Thirty-three and One-half Hours.

New York Stages Big Celebration After Hours of Anxious Waiting

Harbor Craft, Factories, Fire Sirens and Radio Carry Message of the Flier's Victory Throughout the City—Theatres Halt While Audiences Cheer.

New York bubbled all day yesterday with excitement and expectancy, first yearning for word of Captain Lindbergh, then half-doubting, gaining confidence as the afternoon progressed and finally acclaiming the victory of the young aviator with street demonstrations where the crowds were thickest, in which the ancient phrase, "I told you so," was often repeated. It was evident during the day that New York had confidence in the lad from the West.

On the streets and elsewhere Lindbergh was the one topic of conversation the whole day long. In the subway, on the elevated, in trains and cars, motion-picture houses, theatres, wherever a few had gathered, or even where one man could find another to talk to, one heard "Lindbergh — Lindbergh — Lindbergh."

And such expressions as this:

"He'll make it, all right."

"Some baby!"

"Well, if he's hit Ireland, he's safe anyway."

"He's away ahead of his time."

"What's the difference in time between here and there, anyway?"

Confused On Difference in Time.

To this latter question there were some amazing answers. One woman who had the aviator's running time mixed with the difference in time between New York and Paris solemnly informed her companion that there was thirty-six hours difference in time between the cities. She said it with an air which signified: "I don't mean maybe." A surprising number of persons insisted that the difference in time was three hours.

Early in the day, even before there was any good reason why there should be definite news, the interest of the people was demonstrated in two ways. At every news stand there were little groups scanning the headlines and buying newspapers. In every newspaper office the switchboards were literally swamped with inquiries. It was not sufficient that the operator said there was no word, or, later, that Lindbergh's plane had been seen over Ireland. The inquirers wanted specific information:

"Well, when will you get the first news?" they asked. And later:

"If he's over Ireland how long will it be before he gets to Paris?"

"Is he all right?"

The questions that were asked, considering that no news could possibly come direct from Captain Lindbergh before he landed, were as surprising as the guesses at the difference in time.

The Times Gets 10,000 Phone Calls.

The telephone inquiries came from all sorts of people and all directions. Not a few rang up THE TIMES office and apologetically explained that they were on golf links or elsewhere at a distance, and hence could not

Continued on Page Three.

LINDBERGH TRIUMPH THRILLS COOLIDGE

President Cables Praise to "Heroic Flier" and Concern for Nungesser and Coli.

CAPITAL THROBS WITH JOY

Kellogg, New, MacNider, Patrick and Many More Join in Paying Tribute to Daring Youth.

Special to The New York Times.

WASHINGTON, May 21.—The triumph of Captain Charles A. Lindbergh in flying from New York to Paris without a stop created a tremendous sensation in the national capital and found immediate response in a host of official messages and statements congratulating the daring aviator upon his achievement.

President Coolidge expressed his admiration in a message transmitted through Ambassador Herrick in Paris for delivery to the young flier in person.

With a single possible exception, this city has never been more thrilled since the armistice, when Woodrow Wilson mingled with noisy thousands in celebrating the end of the war. The exception was when Walter Johnson arose from apparent defeat and won the deciding world series baseball game in 1924.

"The American people," the President said, "rejoice with me at the brilliant termination of your heroic flight. The first non-stop flight of a lone aviator across the Atlantic crowns the record of American aviation, and in bringing the greetings of the American people to France you likewise carry the assurance of our admiration of those intrepid Frenchmen, Nungesser and Coli, whose bold spirits first ventured on your exploit, and likewise a message of our continued anxiety concerning their fate."

Secretary Kellogg, in a message similarly transmitted, said:

"I heartily congratulate you on the success of your great adventure in accomplishing a non-stop flight from New York to Paris. It is a great step in the advancement of aviation. Every one in the United States is proud of your accomplishment."

Knew Lindbergh as a Boy.

In a statement issued here Mr. Kellogg referred to his personal friendship for Lindbergh, whom he has known for years through the young man's late father, a Representative in Congress from the Secretary's home State of Minnesota.

"News has just reached me," Mr. Kellogg said, "of the success of Lindbergh in completing his flight from New York to Paris. It is an achievement of which every American can justly be proud. I have known Lindbergh since he was a boy and rejoice at this culmination of his ambitions, which could only have been gained by scientific knowledge, superb courage and physique and sterling character. Our rejoicing in Lindbergh's success, however, is tempered by our continued ignorance of the fate of Nungesser and Coli, whose courage and valor have now been equaled, but cannot be surpassed."

Hanford MacNider, Acting Secre-

Continued on Page Four.

CROWD ROARS THUNDEROUS WELCOME

Breaks Through Lines of Soldiers and Police and Surging to Plane Lifts Weary Flier from His Cockpit

AVIATORS SAVE HIM FROM FRENZIED MOB OF 100,000

Paris Boulevards Ring With Celebration After Day and Night Watch—American Flag Is Called For and Wildly Acclaimed.

By EDWIN L. JAMES.

Copyright, 1927, by The New York Times Company.
Special Cable to THE NEW YORK TIMES.

PARIS, May 21.—Lindbergh did it. Twenty minutes after 10 o'clock tonight suddenly and softly there slipped out of the darkness a gray-white airplane as 25,000 pairs of eyes strained toward it. At 10:24 the Spirit of St. Louis landed and lines of soldiers, ranks of policemen and stout steel fences went down before a mad rush as irresistible as the tides of the ocean.

"Well, I made it," smiled Lindbergh, as the little white monoplane came to a halt in the middle of the field and the first vanguard reached the plane. Lindbergh made a move to jump out. Twenty hands reached for him and lifted him out as if he were a baby. Several thousands in a minute were around the plane. Thousands more broke the barriers of iron rails round the field, cheering wildly.

Lifted From His Cockpit.

As he was lifted to the ground Lindbergh was pale, and with his hair unkempt, he looked completely worn out. He had strength enough, however, to smile, and waved his hand to the crowd. Soldiers with fixed bayonets were unable to keep back the crowd.

United States Ambassador Herrick was among the first to welcome and congratulate the hero.

A NEW YORK TIMES man was one of the first to reach the machine after its graceful descent to the field. Those first to arrive at the plane had a picture that will live in their minds for the rest of their lives. His cap off, his famous locks falling in disarray around his eyes, "Lucky Lindy" sat peering out over over the rim of the little cockpit of his machine.

Dramatic Scene at the Field.

It was high drama. Picture the scene. Almost if not quite 100,000 people were massed on the east side of Le Bourget air field. Some of them had been there six and seven hours.

Off to the left the giant phare lighthouse of Mount Valerien flashed its guiding light 300 miles into the air. Closer on the left Le Bourget Lighthouse twinkled, and off to the right another giant revolving phare sent its beams high into the heavens.

Big arc lights on all sides with enormous electric glares were flooding the landing field. From time to time rockets rose and burst in varied lights over the field.

Seven thirty, the hour anounced for the arrival, had come and gone. Then 8 o'clock came, and no Lindbergh; at 9 o'clock the sun had set but then came reports that Lindbergh had been seen over Cork. Then he had been seen over Valentia in Ireland and then over Plymouth.

Suddenly a message spread like lightning, the aviator had been seen over Cherbourg. However, remembering the messages telling of Captain Nungesser's flight, the crowd was skeptical.

"One chance in a thousand!" "Oh, he cannot do it without navigating instruments!" "It's a pity, because he was a brave boy." Pessimism had spread over the great throng by 10 o'clock.

The stars came out and a chill wind blew.

Watchers Are Twice Disappointed.

Suddenly the field lights flooded their glares onto the landing ground and there came the roar of an airplane's motor. The crowd was still, then began a cheer, but two minutes later the landing glares went dark for the searchlight had identified the plane and it was not Captain Lindbergh's.

Stamping their feet in the cold, the crowd waited patiently. It seemed quite apparent that nearly every one was willing to wait all night, hoping against hope.

Suddenly—it was 10:16 exactly—another motor roared over the heads of the crowd. In the sky one caught a glimpse of a white gray plane, and for an instant heard the sound of one. Then it dimmed, and the idea spread that it was yet another disappointment.

Again landing lights glared and almost by the time they had flooded the field the gray-white plane had lighted on the far side nearly half a mile from the crowd. It seemed to stop almost as it hit the ground, so gently did it land.

And then occurred a scene which almost passed description. Two companies of soldiers with fixed bayonets and the Le Bourget field police, reinforced by Paris agents, had held the crowd in good order. But as the lights showed the plane

"All the News That's Fit to Print."

The New York Times.

THE WEATHER
Cloudy today, showers tonight or tomorrow; moderate winds.
Temperature yesterday—Max. 78, min. 64.
For weather report see Page 46.

VOL. LXXVI....NO. 25,393. NEW YORK, WEDNESDAY, AUGUST 3, 1927. TWO CENTS In Greater New York | THREE CENTS Within 200 Miles | FOUR CENTS Elsewhere in the U. S.

COOLIDGE DOES NOT CHOOSE TO RUN IN 1928; STARTLES PARTY WITH 12-WORD MESSAGE; SOME DOUBTERS, OTHERS SEE FIELD OPEN

NEW SACCO TRIAL INDICATED AS STEP FULLER WILL TAKE

Governor Is Expected to Call for Reprieve of Men and Action by the Legislature.

POLITICAL ISSUE IS RAISED

Move Would Be 'Expedient,' but Observers Say Executive Feels It Is Right.

PAIR ENTER DEATH HOUSE

Newly Found Vanzetti Alibi Is Presented as Fuller Interviews Last Witnesses.

From a Staff Correspondent of The New York Times.

BOSTON, Aug. 2.—Nicola Sacco and Bartolomeo Vanzetti will not die in the electric chair on the date set. Neither will they be pardoned. Further reprieve pending steps by the Massachusetts Legislature looking to a new trial was indicated at the State House today as the solution of the historic case of the Italian radicals, which Governor Fuller will place before the Executive Council when it meets tomorrow. The Governor will make known the decision tomorrow night.

Commutation to life imprisonment is one alternative that has been discussed, but those who know Governor Fuller are certain that this straddle will not appeal to the State's Chief Executive.

New and overwhelming eleventh-hour evidence is the only factor likely to change the plan for a further reprieve and an appeal to the Legislature for a new trial.

Late tonight, while the Governor and his advisers worked on the report to be laid before the Council tomorrow, the defense was more cheerful than it has been since the Governor's investigation began.

This optimism is not shared by Sacco, whose mind is weakening on the eighteenth day of his hunger strike at Charlestown State Prison. Vanzetti is feeling better and partaking of a little food. He is buoyed up by the news that his sister has sailed from France and is due here on Aug. 10. That is the day set for the execution under the terms of the sentence of the two men.

Every sign today pointed to the fact that Governor Fuller, despite his exhaustive and exhausting inquiry, had not made up his mind on certain phases of the case of the men convicted for the murder of a paymaster and his guard on April 15, 1920.

Interviews Last of Witnesses.

This afternoon Governor Fuller saw the last of the long line of witnesses who have filed into his office for three months, and he then closed the inquiry. He continued his work on the case after lunch away from his office at 5 o'clock. When he returned he gave every indication of being in a comfortable frame of mind.

At 9:10 tonight Sacco and Vanzetti and Celestino Madeiros, facing execution for another murder, whose case is linked with that of the two radicals by his "confession" seeking to exonerate them, were transferred from the Cherry Hill section of the State Prison to the death house, about 100 yards away. The transfer was effected without incident. The removal of the men has no significance, being a routine procedure. Men condemned to die in the electric chair are, according to law, removed to the death house ten days before execution.

Until a few days ago those at the State House who have followed the Governor's inquiry, as well as members of the Sacco-Vanzetti Defense Committee, felt that the result would be clear cut and uncompromising. The defense hoped for an outright pardon. State House sources were of the opinion that the Governor would take no action and permit the death penalty to be imposed.

The tide apparently turned with the latest visit of Superior Court Judge Webster Thayer, who presided at the joint trial as well as at the previous trial of Vanzetti, convicted of an attempted hold-up and sentenced to from twelve to fifteen years. Judge Thayer, who refused the eight applications for a new trial, saw the Governor yesterday, and it was reported afterward that the latter indicated to him the nature of his report.

The stress placed on the meeting of the Council tomorrow is emphasized by the Defense Committee as a certain sign that the Governor could not have made up his mind to send the men to the electric chair. There are eight Councilors from widely separated parts of the State and their bearing on the case is apparent from the following provision in the State Constitution:

"The power of pardoning offenses, except such as persons may be convicted of before the Senate by an impeachment of the House, shall be in the Governor, by and with the advice of the Council."

Since yesterday the idea of a further reprieve and action by the Legis-

Continued on Page Fourteen.

Sept. 19 to Be French Holiday In Honor of American Legion

Special Cable to THE NEW YORK TIMES.

PARIS, Aug. 2.—A law proclaiming Monday, Sept. 19, as a French national holiday this year in honor of the American Legionaires returning to celebrate the tenth anniversary of their entry in the World War was promulgated in the Journal Officiel today.

In this same bill the sum of 3,760,000 francs is allocated to the Minister of Foreign Affairs for expenditures for the entertainment of the American veterans on their visit here.

The announcement declares it to be a joy and an honor for the Government and the French populace to receive the members of the American Legion, who remain an "unshakable base of friendship for France in the United States."

JAPANESE OFFER NEW NAVAL PLAN

Suggestion That May Save Conference Is Wired to Washington and London.

MAINTAINS STATUS QUO

But Gives America and Japan Chance to Catch Up With Britain on Cruisers.

By WYTHE WILLIAMS.

Special Cable to THE NEW YORK TIMES.

GENEVA, Aug. 2.—The plenary session of the tripower naval conference is still set for Thursday, and Ambassador Gibson is expected to attempt the seemingly hopeless task of obtaining a naval limitations treaty acceptable to the United States.

The delegates today were still busy suggesting new compromises, which for the most part are merely old plans re-dressed. They gave it up after lunch and decided they might as well play golf. It is still evident, though, that all the delegations—particularly a portion of the American one—are anxious to avoid adjournment of the conference at almost any cost.

It is not generally clear just what are the newest proposals—at one time labeled Japanese and at another Japano-American—because sometimes the official spokesmen said there were no proposals and at others admitted there were, until interest slackened as the mystery grew. It is evident that they were sized up by Allen Dulles, the legal adviser of the American delegation, who thought they might lead to something being arranged. Thus they assumed a semi-American character.

Mr. Dulles, who recently resigned from the State Department to rejoin a New York law firm, was re-engaged especially for this conference. His most distinguished relative is Robert Lansing, ex-Secretary of State, whom he resembles in his pacific ambition to become a treaty maker rather than a conference breaker.

Meanwhile the unconsulted American navy experts are viewing the civilian members of the delegation askance, fearful that something is being sprung that might have the same effect on the navy as the Treaty of Washington. They are anxiously counting the hours from now until the plenary session. Then if Ambassador Gibson takes the floor and brings the conference to an end they will breathe freely, but not until then.

The only delegates taking the situation placidly and unconcernedly and not indulging in gossip are the British.

Tonight the Japanese delegation gave a full dress dinner in honor of the former Crown Prince of Korea. It was followed by a dance and a midnight supper.

New Plan Submitted by Japanese.

By The Associated Press.

GENEVA, Aug. 2.—The Japanese statesmen today presented to Hugh S. Gibson, chief American representative, a compromise formula on the cruiser problem which has menaced the Tripartite Naval Conference with failure. In handing their formula to the Ambassador, Viscount Ishii and his associates remarked that it was "just an idea."

Despite this new move it was said in responsible quarters tonight that the spectre of failure—failure which, as a prospect, has genuinely alarmed men of many countries—should not yet be deemed definitely avoided. Yet, from the American standpoint at least, the Japanese plan to save the conference is said to appear

Continued on Page Six.

PARTY HERE IS AMAZED

State Organization in Consternation at Coolidge Statement.

IS FINAL, HILLES THINKS

Leaders Expect Effort to Force Renomination by a Popular Demand.

DR. BUTLER LAUDS ACTION

Says President Has Done Wise and Patriotic Act—Ex-Senator Butler Is Silent.

New York State Republicans, with very few exceptions, were thunderstruck yesterday by President Coolidge's announcement regarding his candidacy for another term.

Neither former Senator William M. Butler of Massachusetts, Chairman of the Republican National Committee, who happened to be in the city, nor Charles D. Hilles, the Vice Chairman, had any advance notice of the President's intention. Senator Butler was the President's personal choice for National Chairman and managed his 1924 campaign. Mr. Hilles is considered particularly close to the President and is consulted by him on all matters affecting New York State, and the fact that the President's statement came to them as a surprise indicates the degree of astonishment felt by Republicans here generally.

Hilles Sees Withdrawal.

Mr. Hilles declared that President Coolidge had made his statement without reservation and intended his withdrawal to be final unless some emergency should confront the country in 1928. He said:

"The President's laconic statement was entirely unexpected, and I regret his action. He is a singularly self-reliant man. I believe he took his own counsel until the decision was announced. He is a man of candor and sincerity, and I think he made the statement without reservation. Except that if an emergency should confront the country in 1928, and it should clearly be a duty to run, he will be free to do so. Otherwise I think he intends this to be final.

"He has had the satisfaction of knowing that he would have been renominated by an overwhelming majority.

"I think the President was considerate in announcing his renunciation now. It gives us ten months in which to prepare for the nomination of his successor. I do not agree with those who think he will lose a strategic advantage with the next Congress. He will cease to be a target for partisan attack. Members of his own party who have withheld their support as well as those of the opposition party will now have a kindlier feeling for him and an appreciation of the great service he has rendered."

By the leaders of the State party organization, President Coolidge's renomination and re-election were regarded as virtually certain. With few exceptions, the local Republican leaders accepted the President's statement as final and at its face value, although it was said that a movement would undoubtedly develop to take advantage of the phraseology of his statement that he did "not choose to be a candidate," and seek to bring about his renomination by popular demand.

Think Field Now Wide Open.

The general feeling among those New York Republican leaders who could be found in or near the city, was that the President's statement had left the field wide open for the Republican Presidential nomination in 1928, and that strong movements for former Governor Frank O. Lowden, of Illinois, and Herbert Hoover, Secretary of Commerce, were certain to develop in this State.

The one Republican of prominence who did not feel surprised at the President's announcement was Dr. Nicholas Murray Butler, president of Columbia University, who returned earlier in the day from a trip to Europe. Dr. Butler predicted last February that President Coolidge would not violate the third term tradition by becoming a candidate for renomination, and his attitude of opposition to a third term brought at that time a great deal of criticism from members of the State party organization, who had based all their plans on the probability of President Collidge's renomination.

Dr. Butler's Statement.

Asked to comment on the President's statement, Dr. Butler said:

"As a personal friend and a political supporter of President Coolidge, although without knowledge of his purpose, I have taken it for granted, as I stated in an address to my friends and neighbors of the

Continued on Page Two.

Smith Is Silent on Coolidge, But Democrats See His Gain

President Coolidge's statement that he did "not choose to be a candidate for renomination" was met with silence by leading Democrats here yesterday.

"I have no comment to make," Governor Smith, a leading aspirant for the Democratic Presidential nomination, said at the Hotel Biltmore.

George W. Olvany, leader of Tammany, and Mayor Walker also declined to comment.

The speculation among Democrats was mostly over how the President's statement might affect Governor Smith's chances of nomination for and election to the Presidency. The general offhand opinion was that it would have no material effect on his chance for the nomination, but probably would increase his chance for election.

COOLIDGE'S ACTION PLEASES CORN BELT

Iowa Leaders in Farm Legislation Agitation Think It Will Aid Their Cause.

BOOM IN LOWDEN'S STOCK

His Supporters Think Greatest Obstacle to His Candidacy Has Been Removed.

Special to The New York Times.

DES MOINES, Iowa, Aug. 2.—Iowa's first concern tonight over the announcement of President Coolidge that he does not choose to run for President in 1928 was for the effect of the President's statement on the Middle West's fight for farm relief legislation.

Leaders in the farm agitation were almost unanimous in their belief that the President's action was a victory, or at least a material aid, for the cause of agriculture. Comment also concerned itself largely with the effect of the Coolidge statement on the candidacy of Frank O. Lowden, which has been the chief concern of many of the State's political leaders.

Those who thought first of the bearing of the statement on another term for President Coolidge generally complimented the President on his "courageous act" in taking a stand against breaking the third term tradition.

State Chairman for Lowden.

Perhaps the most significant development in Iowa was the statement of Willis L. Stern, Republican State Chairman, that "this State will doubtless be united for Frank O. Lowden, as all Iowa holds him in high esteem." The statement was interpreted as placing the State party organization back of the Lowden candidacy.

Ex-Governor Lowden's most ardent supporters hailed the Coolidge withdrawal as removing the most serious obstacle to his candidacy, namely the ability of the President to obtain renomination. Organization leaders who have had nothing against Mr. Lowden but who have to stay on the Coolidge reservation may not be disposed to advocate some other candidate against Mr. Lowden, it was pointed out.

Some observers, however, held that the Lowden movement made no gain by the Coolidge statement because the withdrawal of the President had left the Lowden forces without an object against which to direct their attack. This attitude was reflected in the declaration of Frank J. Lund, head of the Iowa Lowden for President League, who predicted that "the East will have another candidate of the same type."

Brookhart Speaks for Norris.

Governor John Hammill, Representative G. C. Dowell, Secretary of State Walter Ramsay and many other party leaders hailed the President's action as a material aid to the Lowden cause which they espouse. Senator Smith W. Brookhart, who has been a confirmed and vigorous opponent of the present Administration, created a mild stir when he came out for Senator George W. Norris of Nebraska. Senator Brookhart's former campaign organization, headed by Mr. Lund, who was his campaign manager, is now in control of the Lowden for President movement in Iowa.

Significant in the Iowa comment was the declaration by some leaders of both parties that Nicholas Longworth "would bear watching." Among those who sounded this note were Secretary of State Ramsay and J. Ray Files, present Democratic State Chairman, who declared that Longworth "speaks the language of the Old Guard." Mr. Files added that "Lowden does not have a Chinaman's chance. The Republican East is in the saddle and the Republican West is in arms."

LEADERS ARE CAUTIOUS

Vice President Dawes Says Public Will Regret the Decision.

LONGWORTH KEEPS SILENT

Ex-Governor Lowden Repeats That No One Can Run Away From the Presidency.

HOOVER TO "THINK IT OVER"

Borah Accepts Announcement as Final—West Did It, Says Brookhart.

President Coolidge's sudden announcement that he did "not choose to be a candidate for renomination in 1928" was manifestly as much a surprise to those who have been mentioned as probable aspirants for the nomination at the next Republican National Convention as to any one else, judging from their expressions as told in the press.

When asked to comment on Mr. Coolidge's declaration Frank O. Lowden would only say that no man could run away from the Presidency.

Vice President Charles G. Dawes at first refused to comment on the President's statement, but later issued a statement of his own, which in effect accepted the President's statement as final on the question of his candidacy for renomination.

Senator Hiram Johnson of California characterized the President's statement as "astonishing."

Speaker Nicholas Longworth of the House of Representatives, who is visiting in San Francisco, declined to comment. Secretary Hoover's views are not available.

Mr. Dawes Voices Regrets.

CHICAGO, Aug. 2 (AP).—Vice President Charles G. Dawes said in a statement here tonight:

"President Coolidge enjoys the confidence and respect of the American people, and his decision will be received with regret by millions of his countrymen."

Ex-Governor Lowden's Comment.

Special to The New York Times.

ALEXANDRIA BAY, N. Y., Aug. 2.—Concerning the announcement made today by President Coolidge on 1928, former Governor Frank O. Lowden of Illinois who, with his family is visiting here, issued the following statement to which he would add nothing: "I have no statement to make beyond the one already made to different delegations calling upon me. That statement was in substance, that I know of no man in all our history who has run away from the Presidency."

Longworth Too Surprised to Talk.

Special to The New York Times.

SAN FRANCISCO, Cal., Aug. 2.—Two of the outstanding possibilities for the Republican nomination for the Presidency were in San Francisco today.

Herbert Hoover, Secretary of Commerce, was at the Bohemian Grove when the message came from the President.

Nicholas Longworth, Speaker of the House of Representatives, received the news from the President's Summer home while attending a luncheon given in his honor at the San Francisco Commercial Club. He declared that he was too surprised to say anything.

"I may have something to say later on," he remarked.

Senator Hiram Johnson admitted that when he first heard of the President's statement he was too astonished to talk. He said:

"If the statement as reported is true, the next Republican Convention will be a grand free-for-all, a regular Donnybrook Fair."

Too Soon to Discuss, Says Hoover.

PALO, ALTO, Cal., Aug. 2 (AP).—Herbert Hoover, Secretary of Commerce, said tonight that he had nothing to say for the present as to President Coolidge's announcement.

"I have no comment to make," the Secretary said. "It is too soon to discuss it. I must think over the President's announcement."

Finality, Borah Thinks.

By Telegraph to the Editor of THE NEW YORK TIMES.

BOISE, Idaho, Aug. 2.—The President could have been renominated by simply remaining silent. His election seemed reasonably certain. His announcement, therefore, that he does not desire to be a candidate in 1928 must be regarded as the result of a profound conviction and as a finality. Naturally, other candidates will be brought out, but it will be a

Continued on Page Five.

A Recent Studio Portrait. Copyright, Harris & Ewing.

CALVIN COOLIDGE.

"I Do Not Choose to Run for President in Nineteen Twenty-eight."

Washington Sees 1928 Field Open; Some Talk of Drafting Coolidge

Hoover, Lowden, Dawes, Longworth, Borah and Norris Are Listed as the Chief of Those Whose Presidential Aspirations Will Now Take Active Form.

By RICHARD V. OULAHAN.
Special to The New York Times.

WASHINGTON, Aug. 2.—It was a real sensation for the infinitesimal segment of political Washington which the hot weather has not driven away, the announcement of President Coolidge at his Summer home in South Dakota that he did not "choose" to run for President in 1928. With it was dovetailed the element of complete surprise.

While some of those concerned or interested in party politics have been expressing the opinion that Mr. Coolidge would decline to be considered as a candidate for another nomination, their number is negligible in comparison with those who were confident that he would be the Republican nominee next year. Besides, nobody expected the President to show his hand at this early date, more than ten months prior to the assembling of the Republican National Convention.

Two Features of Comment.

In the comment which followed the President's terse declaration at Rapid City there were two conspicuous features. One was the speculative slant of whether the President meant it to be understood that in no circumstances would he accept a nomination for another Presidential term. The other was the apparent evidence, cumulative over a period of many months and accentuated by what was learned today, that Mr. Coolidge did not consult close political friends or party leaders with reference to his spectacular statement.

There is reason to believe that he never discussed with any member of his Cabinet the matter of becoming a candidate for President in 1928, with the possible exception of Secretary Hoover, "of whom later," as the compilers of genealogical records say.

Very generally opinion among political observers was that Mr. Coolidge intended his announcement to mean that he had taken himself out of the running. The argument was advanced that a man occupying the high position of President of the United States could not afford, if for no other reason than that of dignity, to make a declaration of such an important character that would be open to the accusation of deception or intentional dubiousness.

A notable exception to this view was the construction placed on the President's announcement by such a conspicuous Republican as Senator Smoot of Utah.

"I construe the statement to mean," said Senator Smoot, "that if the Republican convention nominates him again he will accept the nomination. It does not bar him from running again in such an event."

Want Coolidge, Smoot Thinks.

Senator Smoot, however, would not hazard a guess as to what the party convention would do in the face of the President's declaration. It was too early to make any guesses in that respect, he explained, and then added:

"My opinion is that the American people would like to have Mr. Coolidge for President again, but that is just my personal opinion."

There is no disposition here to dispute Senator Smoot's construction that the President's announcement would not bar Mr. Coolidge from accepting another Presidential nomination if it should be bestowed upon him by the national convention. At the same time, it was contended by most of those who commented on this phase of the subject that Mr. Coolidge has served notice that no effort is to be made to confer the party's highest honor on him again and that this will mean the ascendency of other aspirants for that honor with a division of prominent party workers into various candidatorial camps.

As for the odd wording of the Presidential declaration, it was pointed out by some of those who essayed opinion that the President could not with propriety or with regard for his party come out with a flat declaration that in no circumstances would he accept next year's Presidential nomination. The announcement, according to the generality of opinion here, must be interpreted in the light of all the circumstances. Why should there have been any announcement at all, it was asked, if the President intended to have a string tied to his disclaimer of candidacy?

Discussion of Hoover.

One of Washington's first reactions to the surprise sprung upon the country by Mr. Coolidge was the conviction that Herbert Hoover must be considered as conspicuous in the running for next year's Republican Presidential nomination. Among many political observers the belief prevails that to the country he appears as a national hero. His most recent public service in the administration of relief measures in the flooded areas of the South has given to him a renewed prominence which has served to recall his masterful handling of Belgian and Russian relief and other work for humanity and his direction of the food administration during the World War.

No doubt exists in the minds of those who follow party political tendencies that Mr. Hoover will now be brought forward as a candidate for the Presidential nomination.

A widespread opinion exists in political quarters that his aspirations will have the moral support of President Coolidge. A knowledge of the President's mental processes and habits leads to the conviction that he will not make a declaration in favor of any particular candidate for the nomination, but will find means of having the word passed that Hoover is his favorite against the candidatorial field.

The recent unexplained incident arising from Mr. Coolidge's voluntary assertion that if Mr. Kellogg should retire from the office of Secretary of State Mr. Hoover would not be appointed to succeed him, may be cited as evidence that the President is not particularly cordial toward his Secretary of Commerce, but, in the face of it, the sympathetic good wishes of the President are expected to follow Mr. Hoover's hat as it is cast into the ring.

Will Spur Lowden Boomers.

It goes without saying that the announcement from Rapid City will be followed by increased activities on the part of those who have put Frank O. Lowden forward as their choice for the Republican Presidential nomination.

Mr. Lowden is primarily the favorite of the advanced farm aid advocates and has been regarded as the candidate of these party leaders, chiefly in the Middle West, who resented Mr. Coolidge's attitude toward their Congressional measures for agricultural relief, a resentment translated into open enmity when the President vetoed the McNary-Haugen bill.

As it has been seen by politicians, Mr. Lowden's boom is a protest against what the President's critics term "Coolidgism." In that light it has been construed by the President's friends, and it is not going too

Continued on Page Three.

PRESIDENT ACTED ALONE

His Close Friends Were Unaware of His Stand on Another Term.

CALLS IN NEWSPAPER MEN

President Hands Out Typed Slip in School Room, and Declines to Comment.

DRAMATIC SURPRISE STAGED

Statement Is Issued on the Eve of Coolidge's Fourth Anniversary as President.

From a Staff Correspondent of The New York Times.

RAPID CITY, S. D., Aug. 2.—President Coolidge today dramatically and unexpectedly, and without consultation with friends, issued the following statement to the correspondents here:

"I do not choose to run for President in nineteen twenty-eight."

This brief sentence was written by him on a slip of paper at 9:32 A. M. and later transcribed by stenographers to a slip of paper five inches by two inches. The year was put in words, not figures, and so made a twelve-word statement.

The President had doubled the slips twice and held fifteen of them in his right hand, from which he gave them to the newspaper correspondents, who had been notified to return to his office at noon for a statement. This notice to the correspondents was given at the end of the regular Tuesday morning press conference, in which he had discussed the Geneva Conference and other questions before the public.

The long line of correspondents filed past the President and gasped with surprise as they read the words on the slips of paper. The President was solemn and composed as he gave out the announcement of his desire not to stand for renomination.

"Is there any other comment?" he was asked.

"None," he replied.

The door closed as the correspondents and the secretaries departed from the President's private offices, leaving Mr. Coolidge alone for fifteen minutes to consider the effect of his decision.

Stages Dramatic Surprise.

The startling political statement was made under circumstances simple and dramatic. It came on the eve of the fourth anniversary of the day Mr. Coolidge took the oath of office as President of the United States, by the light of the kerosene lamp in his boyhood home at Plymouth, Vt.

Today's decision in the Black Hills was reached without consultation with friends or advisers, and his associates here say that it effectively takes Mr. Coolidge out of the Presidential race in 1928.

While the word "choose" is subject to popular qualification and reservation, the impression obtained here from the President's associates is that it was selected as properly presenting the President's mind and as expressing completely the President's attitude toward another term.

He avoids saying that he is not a candidate, and what he does say may leave the situation open in the minds of some of his supporters and others, but, according to the views of those close to him here, President Coolidge has closed the doors of the White House to himself after March 4, 1929.

There may be a more definite and final utterance from him, but it is regarded here as doubtful. His announcement today, it is expected here, will be the signal for the entrance of Secretary Hoover, Speaker Longworth, Vice President Dawes and the renewed activity of former Governor Lowden to gain the delegates in the coming Republican primaries.

It is believed here that the President will say nothing more and is not expected to allow his Administration to be used in the promotion of the candidacy of any others who have been mentioned for the nomination.

His now famous announcement takes its place alongside that of his message to Congress, "I do not favor the granting of a bonus." It also follows the line of his announcement in the first step in his political career which ended in his becoming President.

At the close of the legislative ses-

"All the News That's Fit to Print."

The New York Times.

THE WEATHER
Fair and slightly warmer today and tomorrow; moderate winds.
Temperature yesterday—Max. 71, min. 66.
For weather report see Page 42.

VOL. LXXVI....No. 25,394. NEW YORK, THURSDAY, AUGUST 4, 1927. TWO CENTS in Greater New York | THREE CENTS Within 200 Miles | FOUR CENTS Elsewhere in the U. S.

SACCO AND VANZETTI GUILTY, SAYS FULLER, AND MUST DIE; BAY STATE GOVERNOR UPHOLDS JURY, CALLS TRIAL FAIR; HIS BOARD UNANIMOUS, EXECUTION OF PAIR SET FOR AUG. 10

MESSAGES OF REGRET FLOOD COOLIDGE; STRONG DESIRE TO DRAFT HIM SHOWN AS DEBATE OVER STATEMENT GOES ON

PRESIDENT KEEPS SILENT

His Associates Declare He Issued His Statement As a Final Word.

SEEMS IN A HAPPIER MOOD

He Spends an Hour in His Office Reading Telegrams, Then Returns to Lodge.

EXPECT LATER STATEMENT

Politicians at Rapid City See Coolidge Forced by Primaries to Clarify His Stand.

From a Staff Correspondent of The New York Times.

RAPID CITY, S. D., Aug. 3.—President Coolidge, having announced that he does not choose to run for President in 1928, finds himself flooded with telegrams urging him again to lead the Republican Party.

These messages, which have poured in upon him here in the Black Hills, are most complimentary and make clear to him that he has the esteem of a great following. A large proportion of the telegrams seek to prevail upon Mr. Coolidge to accept the nomination if it should come to him after his now famous twelve-word announcement, couched in somewhat indefinite language.

The dispatches not only have come from all parts of this country, but there are scores of cable messages from Americans traveling abroad, insisting that the present situation calls for President Coolidge to permit himself to be renominated by the Republican Party.

Some messages told the President that he had made himself one of the greatest men in recent times by virtually refusing what they declared was certain re-election as President, and going down in history as the man who had longest held that office.

It would be a calamity to the nation, declared some of the messages if Mr. Coolidge should eliminate himself from the race and plunge the country into an uncertain contest for the Presidency, with what was stated as the possibility of radical change in governmental policies that have made the nation strong and prosperous.

Many Talk of Drafting Coolidge.

The nation, judged by these messages that tonight are being digested by the President in his distant lodge in the hills, does not accept as final or conclusive the terse and cryptic statement that the President prepared without consultation and then personally distributed to the press yesterday in his office in the school building.

Apparently a great many people, including many of the dominant Republican leaders, do not believe the statement effectively eliminates President Coolidge from the race. They all construe the announcement as expressing his state of mind and not his actual determination not to accept the nomination if in the face of it the Republican Party should cast aside President Coolidge's apparent personal desires and nominate him next year.

The trend of sentiment reflected in the messages coming here is that the admirers intend to draft Mr. Coolidge and actually show him that there is a real call from the people, a call that rises above his wishes, and disregards the so-called third term talk and the division in the Republican Party in the corn and wheat belt States.

In the opinion of some observers here who have analyzed the messages and read the interviews given in the country, it is necessary for the President to be more definite. It is stated, however, that some move, such as the entrance of a member of his Cabinet in the race, would show that he has fully made up his mind to retire at the end of his term in 1929.

The messages received here indicate that only Mr. Coolidge's refusal to permit his name to be entered in the first primaries in New Hampshire and North Dakota next March will satisfy his supporters and others of the finality of the announcement.

In the last twenty-four hours the Summer White House wires have brought in reports of a great national party readjusting its entire campaign procedure, the fixed opinion of many voters altered and their views as to the strongest candidate the Republican Party can select rendered uncertain. The wires also

Continued on Page Five.

Hoover Declares He Hopes President Will Run Again

PALO ALTO, Cal., Aug. 3 (AP).—Herbert Hoover, Secretary of Commerce, commenting today on President Coolidge's announcement that he did not choose to be a candidate for re-election in 1928, said:

"I regret the suggestion in the President's statement.

"However, I still believe as I stated in Chicago two weeks ago, that President Coolidge should be renominated and re-elected."

BULL MARKET JARRED BY COOLIDGE STAND

Fifty Representative Stocks Decline—Most of Losses Are Regained in Buying Rally.

2,767,170 SHARES SOLD

Trading Next to Heaviest of the Year—Clamor From Exchange Reaches the Street.

Wall Street's "Coolidge bull market" was jarred to its foundations yesterday morning by the President's cryptic announcement that he does not choose to be a candidate for re-election in 1928. There was a pell-mell scramble to sell stocks and opening prices were from 2 to 15½ points lower than the previous day's close. Then banking institutions, individual operators, pool managers and bargain hunters rushed to the market's rescue with such a volume of buying orders that the decline of stocks was turned to a rally within a brief thirty minutes.

The demonstration of the market's inherent strength and its vigorous rallying power was even more impressive than the selling which had taken place, which was mainly of the panic-stricken, save-my-profits sort characteristic of the small trader.

It was the general impression, in banking parlors and brokerage offices, after the close that most stocks had given a good account of themselves. It was a characteristic of the market, and an outstanding one, too, that the trading was most orderly. There were many wide swings, to be sure, and some hurried ones, but the market at all times—even in the hectic fifteen minutes of the first hour when the selling was heaviest—had an outward calm which inspired confidence in it and probably brought in many buying orders.

Market Caught Off Balance.

The sudden injection of an awkward and unsettling political situation into a bull market which has been built on general business prosperity, individual corporate expansion, generally good earnings, easy money conditions and the probability of an upswing in operations in basic industries this Fall was the new element which prompted many stockholders to "sell at the market." The President's announcement had not reached Wall Street until 3:15 P. M. the previous day, too late for any market reaction to it, and nervous groups had gathered in brokerage offices after the close, trying to guess what would happen when trading was resumed in the morning.

The bolt from the Black Hills caught the market off balance. In the first place, the market had behind it a long period of advances, which were mainly perpendicular during July and thus far in August, so far as the leading and pivotal stocks were concerned. This strength had induced wide spread covering of short commitments, leaving many stocks without a comfortable cushion to catch the fall.

A further consideration was the fact that the market has been fairly honeycombed with stop-loss orders placed by those who desired to insure a part, at least, of their profits. Public participation has been on the increase, as was reflected yesterday in the report of an increase of $72,000,000, as of July 1, in Stock Exchange brokers' loans.

Selling Orders Start With Rush.

Selling orders began to come into brokerage offices before the tickers had finished tapping off the President's brief announcement on the previous day. Telephone bells in brokerage offices were jangling before 9 o'clock yesterday morning, registering the impatient calls of customers who were deathly afraid of the uncertainty created and who wanted to save profits which might

Continued on Page Four.

CAPITAL DESIRES LIGHT

Thinks President Should Remove All Doubt as to His Intent.

ACCEPTS HIS WITHDRAWAL

But Fears Accusation of Deception Might Follow Lack of Clearer Explanation.

MUCH TALK OF CANDIDATES

Lowden Held Formidable—Hoover Needs Positive Assurance of Coolidge Withdrawal.

By RICHARD V. OULAHAN.
Special to The New York Times.

WASHINGTON, Aug. 3.—On this, the day following President Coolidge's laconic announcement, "I do not choose to run for President in 1928," Washington's chief reaction is that the President owes to the country a clearer explanation of what his declaration was meant to convey.

This feeling is accentuated by editorial comment throughout the Union, showing there is widespread mystification as to the President's intention with reference to next year's Presidential nomination.

It is easily conceivable that without clarification of his statement the President will lay himself open to the accusation of having made a deceptive utterance. Only a frank explanation from him personally can overcome this accusatory tendency, if a cross-section of Washington opinion is well founded.

Pretty generally the Washington view is that Mr. Coolidge's purpose was to notify the electorate, and especially Republican workers, that he was out of the running. Put in another way, he took the method employed to serve notice that he was not to be considered as a candidate for his party's nomination.

Has High Regard for Dignities.

No man occupying his position, it is held, can afford to practice deception on the nation, and in this connection it may be added that no President has had a higher regard for the dignities which invest the office. Without ostentatious show, he has adhered to the little ceremonials which carry out the idea of dignity. Despite his parading in cowboy regalia, it is the observation of those who have been brought into close contact with him that he looks upon the Presidential office with too much respect to permit him to bring it into even the semblance of the disrepute that might attach to it through any method of deception or questionable practice by its incumbent.

But in the face of all this, the mystification continues. Those who adhere to the belief that Mr. Coolidge intended the country to understand that he would retire from the Presidency at the end of the term he is now serving concede that the element of doubt is still involved. While some of them are willing to insist that the President said all that was necessary in the circumstances, it is apparent that they cannot justify their confidence in that conviction by any positive expression in the brief words which Mr. Coolidge employed in yesterday's statement at Rapid City.

Enough of leading Republican regulars have commented on the President's declaration to indicate that the daze in which it threw them was not sufficiently near unconsciousness to permit them to accept it as meaning definitely that the President in no circumstances would permit his name to be presented to the Republican National Convention next June.

A considerable number of them are resisting the interpretation that Mr. Coolidge has withdrawn from the party contest. There is no mystery about this. The generality of party regulars, and even a large segment of those party men inclined to be spotty in their regularity, have assumed that Mr. Coolidge would be nominated for President next year.

Irregulars Wanted Coolidge.

Certain of the irregulars have been anxious to have Mr. Coolidge run again, their feeling being that of all those in the list of Presidential possibilities he was the most satisfactory. Senator Borah, although he has not hesitated to criticize Administration policies, is believed to be among these.

Another who was credited with satisfaction over the conclusion that Mr. Coolidge would be renominated

Continued on Page Four.

Berlin Talks to Buenos Aires By 7,000-Mile Radio Telephone

Copyright, 1927, by The New York Times Co.
By Wireless to The New York Times.

BERLIN, Aug. 3.—Official tests of a radio telephone service between Berlin and Buenos Aires were carried out tonight, representatives of the various departments of the German Government sending greetings to Argentina. The voices carried over the distance of practically 7,000 miles clearly, a cable from Buenos Aires reported.

Since the South American capital was equipped with only a receiving apparatus, the greetings of the Argentine Government had to be sent via cable.

Experiments with short-wave transmitters have been conducted over a long period. Tonight's success has led to a decision to build a number of sets of this type and it is hoped that regular wireless telephone service can be opened to the public by January.

NAVAL PARLEY FAILS; FINAL MEETING SET FOR THIS AFTERNOON

Cruiser Difficulty, the Crux of Geneva Conference, Brings Break-Down.

JAPAN'S PLAN FRUITLESS

Gibson Says There Would Be No Advantage in Treaty on 'Authorized' British Program.

By The Associated Press.

GENEVA, Aug. 3.—The tripartite naval conference reached a deadlock tonight, it was stated in authoritative American circles, and the last session is planned for tomorrow. This statement was confirmed later by the Japanese spokesman.

It was stated that the delegates had mutually and sorrowfully agreed that no compact could be reached at this time to limit further the naval armaments of Great Britain, the United States and Japan.

This announcement was made after tonight's meeting of the plenipotentiaries to consider the Japanese compromise proposals. The hour of the final session was set for 3 o'clock tomorrow afternoon.

The decision to adjourn the conference tomorrow was brought about by the inability of both Great Britain and the United States to accept clearly the Japanese compromise as a basis of discussion for settling the cruiser question, which was the crux of the whole conference.

British Not Quite Clear on Plan.

When the private meeting of the delegates opened at the villa of Hugh R. Wilson, American Minister to Switzerland, with Ambassador Hugh S. Gibson, chief American delegate, presiding, the Japanese proposal was immediately brought up for discussion.

W. C. Bridgeman, First Lord of the Admiralty and chief British representative, and his colleague, Viscount Cecil of Chelwood (all accounts of the meeting agree here) were not quite clear as to whether the Japanese compromise could be acceptable to them.

This compromise virtually meant a naval holiday for Great Britain until the United States could catch up with her in naval construction. The British delegates, however, indicated that if the compromise were acceptable to both the United States and Japan, more time would be required to look into it.

In the Japanese plan the word "authorized" was employed to emphasize that Great Britain and Japan would finish only their authorized cruiser program.

Gibson-Bridgeman Exchange.

Mr. Gibson asked Mr. Bridgeman what he understood this word to signify, adding:

"Does it mean approved and authorized?"

Viscount Cecil answered that it meant "authorized."

After further dueling, Mr. Gibson asked:

"Does it mean the Birkenhead plan?"

Mr. Bridgeman is understood to have answered "Yes."

"Then that means 498,000 tons for Great Britain by 1931," said Mr. Gibson.

Mr. Gibson added that this was higher than the United States could possibly go and that it would mean that America must build up to that figure.

Mr. Bridgeman's reply was that the British did not wish to speak in terms of total tonnage.

Mr. Gibson insisted that the United States could build only up to 400,000

Continued on Page Three.

NEWS STUNS THE DEFENSE

Decision Is 'Unbelievably Brutal,' Says Statement by the Committee.

WILL CONTINUE THE FIGHT

Asks Millions Throughout the World to Join in Last Desperate Protest.

PATROLS PUT NEAR PRISON

Guard Is Thrown Around the Hotel Where Governor Fuller Spends the Night.

From a Staff Correspondent of The New York Times.

BOSTON, Thursday, Aug. 4.—Gardner Jackson, Chairman of the Sacco-Vanzetti Defense Committee, issued the following statement at 1:15 o'clock this morning.

"The decision of the Governor was delivered at such a late hour that proper answer cannot be prepared to it before morning. The decision is unbelievably brutal in its partisanship, and even more brutal in the omission of facts—not only facts brought out in the course of the case, like the frame-up of expert testimony as shown by the Proctor affidavit, but also facts of the most overwhelming significance established behind closed doors, both before the Advisory Committee and the Governor.

"Inasmuch as the committee and the Governor must justify themselves by reason, and not by partisan fiat, these facts must be disclosed in their entirety. It is a solemn truth that one cannot know the demonstrated facts of the case from the Governor's statement.

"The days separating Sacco and Vanzetti from the electric chair are few, but this defense committee will continue to fight for justice for these two men. Our faith in their innocence is unshaken. We call upon the millions of people throughout the world who have supported them to come forward and join us in this last desperate effort to stay the hand of the judicial hangman."

All through yesterday the defense headquarters of Sacco and Vanzetti housed anxious men and women. A spirit of optimism reigned. Smiles were quick to wreathe the faces of all with the entrance of another visitor. None thought of supper.

As 8 o'clock in the evening drew near, faces appeared drawn and white. What few smiles were seen were ostensibly forced. What little laughs were heard bordered on hysteria. The tension was taut.

With every shrill ring of the telephone all eyes were turned on Mary Donovan, Recording Secretary of the Defense Committee, as she picked up the receiver.

Committee in Despair.

At 9:20 word was telephoned that the Governor had left the State House and that the decision would be announced at 10 o'clock.

"God save the Commonwealth of Massachusetts!" were the first words that greeted the announcement of Governor Fuller's decision by Mary Donovan as she received it over the telephone from the State House.

The words were expressed by Aldino Felicani, at whose instance, seven years ago, the Sacco-Vanzetti Defense Committee was formed, and who has acted as Treasurer since its inception.

A wave of despair swept over the more than forty people assembled there. Some of them had spent each evening of the last few years in the same office, working to free the two men.

No Crowd at Headquarters.

To Miss Donovan fell the lot of going to Mrs. Sacco and breaking the news. Mrs. Sacco received the tidings stoically and would make no comment.

The absence of crowds around defense headquarters was a surprise. In a closely populated Italian section, it was thought that the streets would be filled during the evening and a large squad of plainclothes men was stationed in and about the section. Not more than a handful were at the entrance all during the evening.

After the decision had reached the defense office, a battery of photographers gathered at the entrance flashing pictures of the men and women leaving, their heavy and lagging steps eloquently displaying their frame of mind and spirits.

Thompson Declines Comment.

William G. Thompson, attorney for the condemned men, went to his home in Newton shortly after 6 P. M. planning to return to his office in the Tremont Building to await the news of the Governor's decision. Upon being informed that the decision would not be announced until 9:20 P. M. or later he decided

Continued on Page Three.

Crowds Awaited the Governor's Decision; Fuller's Homes and Other Buildings Guarded

BOSTON, Aug. 3 (AP).—Throngs in the streets in front of the newspaper bulletin boards tonight attested to the wide interest in the Sacco-Vanzetti case. The watchers, who included many women, waited quietly for several hours for the word to come of Governor Fuller's decision. A sprinkling of patrolmen paced the sidewalks where the crowds were the largest.

A detail of patrolmen was assigned to the vicinity of the Phillips house of the Massachusetts General Hospital, where Mrs. Fuller was at the bedside of her son, who is recovering from an operation for appendicitis. Another detail patroled the vicinity of the Ritz-Carlton Hotel in the early part of the evening when the Governor was there.

The Governor's city home in Beacon Street, his Summer home at Rye Beach, N. H.; the State prison, the County Courthouse and jail here and the county jail in Plymouth, Vanzetti's home, also were closely guarded.

Full Text of Gov. Fuller's Decision, Ending Long Fight of Prisoners

He Sketches the Crime of Which Sacco and Vanzetti Were Accused, Reviews the Trial in Detail and Concludes by Declaring the Verdict Right and the Men Guilty as Charged.

From a Staff Correspondent of The New York Times.

STATE HOUSE, Boston, Mass., Aug. 3.—Following is the complete text of the official decision of Governor Fuller in the case of Sacco and Vanzetti:

Decision of Governor Alvan T. Fuller in the matter of the appeal of Bartolomeo Vanzetti and Nicola Sacco from the sentence of death imposed under the laws of the Commonwealth:

On April 15, 1920, a paymaster and his guard were held up, robbed and brutally murdered at Braintree, Mass. On May 15, 1920, Nicola Sacco and Bartolomeo Vanzetti were arrested; they were later tried and found guilty of the murder. The verdict was followed by seven motions for a new trial and two appeals to the Supreme Court of the Commonwealth, all of which were heard and later denied. Prior to the trial of the two men in this case Vanzetti had been arrested, tried and convicted of an attempted hold-up on Dec. 24, 1919, at Bridgewater, Mass., and sentenced to fifteen years' imprisonment.

The appeal to the Governor was presented by counsel for the accused on May 3 of the present year. It was my first official connection with the case.

This appeal, presented to me in accordance with the provision in the Constitution of our Commonwealth, has been considered without intent on my part to sustain the courts if I became convinced that an error had been committed or that the trial had been unfair to the accused.

Saw Doubts in Minds of Many.

I realized at the outset that there were many sober-minded and conscientious men and women who were genuinely troubled about the guilt or innocence of the accused and the fairness of their trial. It seemed to me I ought to attempt to set the minds of such people at rest if it could be done; but I realized that with all I could do personally to find out the truth, some people might well in the end doubt the correctness of any conclusion that I, or in fact any other one man, might reach. I believed that I could best reassure these honest doubters by having a committee conduct an investigation entirely independent of my own, their report to be made to me and to be of help in reaching correct conclusions.

I felt that if, after such a committee had conducted its investigation independently, we were not in substantial agreement, then the course of Massachusetts justice did not flow in as clear a channel as I believed it should. The final decision and responsibility was, of course, mine.

For this committee I desired men who were not only well and favorably known for their achievements in their own lines, but men whose reputation for intelligence, open-mindedness, intellectual honesty and good judgment were above reproach. I asked to serve on that committee, President Abbott Lawrence Lowell of Harvard University, former Judge Robert Grant and President Samuel W. Stratton of Massachusetts Institute of Technology.

No one of them hesitated when asked to serve. They began work as soon as their other affairs could be arranged, labored continuously during much of June and through July, holding their sessions independently, and arrived unanimously at a conclusion which is wholly in accord with mine. The public owes these gentlemen its gratitude for their high-minded, unselfish service on this disagreeable and extremely important problem.

Court Proceedings in Case.

The court proceedings in this case may be divided into two parts: First, the trial before the jury with Judge Thayer presiding; second, the hearings on the successive petitions for a new trial which were addressed to the Judge and passed upon by him. All those proceedings have been attacked by some of the friends of the accused men and their counsel.

The attacks on the jury trial take two forms: First, it is asserted that the men are innocent and that there was not sufficient evidence before the jury to justify a finding of guilty; second, it is asserted that the trial itself was unfair.

The attacks on the proceedings and on the motions for a new trial are in substance that the Judge was biased and unable to give the motions fair and impartial consideration.

The inquiry that I have conducted has had to do with the following questions:

Was the jury trial fair?

Were the accused entitled to a new trial?

Are they guilty or not guilty?

As to the first question, complaint has been made that the defendants were prosecuted and convicted because they were anarchists. As a matter of fact, the issue of anarchy was brought in them as an explanation of their suspicious conduct. Their counsel, against the advice of Judge Thayer, decided to attribute their actions and conduct to the fact that they were anarchists, suggesting that they were armed to protect themselves, that they were about to start out at 10 o'clock at night to collect radical literature and that the reason they lied was to save their friends.

Cites Opinions of Jurors.

I have consulted with every member of the jury now alive, eleven in number. They considered the Judge fair; that he gave them no indication of his own opinion of the case.

Affidavits have been presented claiming that the Judge was prejudiced. I see no evidence of prejudice in his conduct of the trial. That he had an opinion as to the guilt or innocence of the accused after hearing the evidence is natural and inevitable.

The allegation has been made that conditions in the court room were prejudicial to the accused. After careful inquiry of the jury and others, I find no evidence to support this allegation. I find the jurors were thoroughly honest men and that they were reluctant to find these men guilty, but were forced to do so by the evidence.

I can see no warrant for the assertion that the jury trial was unfair.

The charge of the Judge was satisfactory to the counsel for the accused, and no exceptions were taken to it. The Supreme Judicial Court for the Commonwealth has considered such of the more than 250 exceptions taken during the course of the trial as counsel for the accused chose to argue and overruled them all, thus establishing that the proceedings were without legal flaw.

Sees Trial Fairly Conducted.

I have read the record and examined many witnesses and the jurymen to see from a layman's standpoint whether the trial was fairly conducted. I am convinced that it was.

The next question is whether newly discovered evidence was of sufficient merit to warrant a new trial.

After the verdict against these men, their counsel filed and argued before Judge Thayer seven distinct supplementary motions for a new trial, six of them on the ground of newly discovered evidence. All of which were denied.

I have examined all of these motions and read the affidavits in support of them to see whether they presented any valid reason for granting the accused men a new trial. I am convinced that they do not and I am further convinced that the presiding Judge

Continued on Page Two.

DECISION LATE AT NIGHT

State Executive Backs the Original Verdict in Famous Case.

POSITIVE IN CONVICTION

Three Questions Involved in the Case as He Sees It, and He Answers Them Fully.

PRISONERS NOT YET TOLD

Warden Decides It Inadvisable to Inform Them of Doom Until Today.

From a Staff Correspondent of The New York Times.

BOSTON, Aug. 3.—That Nicola Sacco and Bartolomeo Vanzetti were guilty of the payroll murders and robbery at South Braintree on April 15, 1920, for which they have been condemned to die during the week of Aug. 10, was the decision of Governor Alvan T. Fuller, made public at 11:30 o'clock tonight at the State House.

Governor Fuller declared there was no sufficient reason for executive intervention; that there was no justifiable reason for granting a new trial, as the Dedham trial was conducted fairly and without prejudice by Judge Webster Thayer.

The Governor completely exonerate Judge and jury against charges of unfairness; held that there was no valid reason for a new trial on the basis of newly discovered evidence; discarded the confession of Celestino Madeiros, who swore that, while he took part in the South Braintree murders and hold-up, Sacco and Vanzetti were not implicated; and pointed out that the advisory committee designated by him was unanimously of his opinion.

The committee consisted of President A. Lawrence Lowell of Harvard University; President Samuel W. Stratton of the Massachusetts Institute of Technology, and former Judge of Probate Robert Grant.

Warden to Tell Men Today.

Warden Hendry of Charlestown State Prison received the news of Governor Fuller's decision almost as soon as it was given out at the State House. He said he would not convey it to the condemned men until tomorrow, after their second night in the death house.

The decision is expected to speed up world-wide protests on behalf of the two anarchists, whose sympathizers have kept up a continuous agitation for seven years.

The decision made public tonight was perhaps the most carefully guarded secret concerning an appeal in a criminal case that has ever been locked in the bosom of a Chief Executive. Yesterday, an authoritative source in the official family of Governor Fuller stated that the Governor would neither send the men to the electric chair nor would he allow them to go scot free.

The statement was made with emphasis and apparently out of full knowledge of the Governor's decision. There was no equivocation, no "ifs, buts or ands." This gave rise at the eleventh hour to the apparently well-authenticated report that a reprieve under certain conditions would be the solution.

Now that the Governor has decided to allow the law to take its course, it will not be necessary for him to consult with the State Executive Council. That body was to have held a regular meeting at noon today and was requested to hold over until tomorrow. This was interpreted by the defense as a hopeful sign, as consultation with the council meant to them anything but the death sentence.

Governor Defines His Inquiry.

The inquiry of the Governor was concerned, as he explained in his decision, with these questions:

"Was the jury trial fair?"

"Were the accused entitled to a new trial?"

"Are they guilty or not guilty?"

He declared that the eleven living members of the jury were of the opinion that the men had a fair trial.

Discussing the allegations of prejudice against Judge Webster Thayer, Governor Fuller cleared the presiding Judge and said he saw no evidence of prejudice in his conduct of the trial.

The Governor's decision had been awaited by throngs in the Boston streets, a tense situation existing as they waited for hours while copies

"All the News That's Fit to Print."

The New York Times.

THE WEATHER
Cloudy with probable showers today; tomorrow partly cloudy.
Temperature Yesterday—Max. 72; Min. 62.
For weather report see Page 30.

VOL. LXXVI....No. 25,413. NEW YORK, TUESDAY, AUGUST 23, 1927. TWO CENTS in Greater New York | THREE CENTS Within 200 Miles | FOUR CENTS Elsewhere in the U. S.

SACCO AND VANZETTI PUT TO DEATH EARLY THIS MORNING; GOVERNOR FULLER REJECTS LAST-MINUTE PLEAS FOR DELAY AFTER A DAY OF LEGAL MOVES AND DEMONSTRATIONS

COOLIDGE PERCHES GOVERNMENT'S SEAT ON PEAK IN ROCKIES

He Reaches Yellowstone Park and Begins at Once His Sight-Seeing Trips.

VISITS CAMP ROOSEVELT

President Passes First Night in a Cottage Surrounded by Snow-Clad Mountains.

CROWDS EXTEND GREETINGS

Mrs. Coolidge and John Share in Ovations at Stations Where Special Train Halted.

From a Staff Correspondent of The New York Times.

MAMMOTH HOT SPRINGS, Yellowstone Park, Wyo., Aug. 22.—The seat of Government tonight is established on a high peak in the Rockies, the furthermost point west to which it has ever gone, in the majestic scenery of Yellowstone Park. With the arrival of President and Mrs. Coolidge into the national playground through the Gardiner entrance the Presidential flag was unfurled over a gray rambling cottage, the home of H. W. Child, President of the Yellowstone Transportation Company.

Here for [illegible] night the President will remain but in the next four days he will pass each night in a different place as he travels over the park.

The Presidential special train reached Gardiner in a Summer rainstorm. The mountain tops were covered with snow and through the clouds the sun was shining, presenting a rainbow that added to the first view the President and Mrs. Coolidge had of the national playground. A large station crowd followed the President's party through the five miles to the cottage, where hundreds had gathered to greet the visitors.

In less than three quarters of an hour Mr. and Mrs. Coolidge set out on their first expedition, visiting Camp Roosevelt, where they saw the greatest collection of wild game in the United States.

Five-Hour Auto Trip.

As the Presidential party started out on their afternoon auto trip the clouds disappeared, and the President and Mrs. Coolidge had sunshine throughout a five-hour journey through the northern end of the park. Their trip took them over forty-four miles to Camp Roosevelt, along the small canyon road to Tower Falls and to the petrified tree.

H. M. Albright, superintendent of the park, rode in the President's car, in which were the President, Mrs. Coolidge and John. He explained the scenery, delivering a most informative lecture, so the President said later. His recital held the attention of the President, who sat in silence for most of the trip, thrilled by the panoramic scenes unfolded to him at every turn of the road.

The park now is at the height of its beauty, the mountainsides are green, the roads brilliant in early Fall wild flowers and animal life astir as the cold nights approach.

The President not only saw bears at Camp Roosevelt, but antelopes jumping from the crags in Gallatin Range and deer feeding in the pools that indent the lowlands not far from the present Summer White House, opposite the Mammoth Hot Springs Hotel.

On the way to Camp Roosevelt the Forest Rangers had to cut away a tree that the high wind had thrown across the road. All along the roads motors bearing the licenses of distant States and park buses drew aside to give the President right of way, cheering the President as he passed. The drives seemed thronged with travelers. Nearly 10,000 are estimated now to be within the park area.

Camp Roosevelt is a rustic lodge that was built in 1906 to commemorate President Roosevelt's trip to the park in 1903 in company with John Burroughs. There Colonel Roosevelt pitched his camp, fished for many days and studied the wild life so abundant in this region. Today hundreds of tourists' tents, supplied with many modern comforts, surround the lodge.

A mother bear and three cubs ate and frolicked about undisturbed by the visitors. President and Mrs. Coolidge and John stood in the background watching them. This gave the movie men a good setting and the first real picture of the President's day in the park.

Visitors Greeted in Song.

On the porch were assembled a bevy of pretty girls and young men, known as the "Savages," composed of college students who work in the park. They formed a solid mass through which the President and

Continued on Page Fifteen.

Coins Word 'Avigation' For Directing of Aircraft

Special to The New York Times.

WASHINGTON, Aug. 22.—The suggestion that the word "avigation" be used in connection with aeronautics has been made by Lieutenant Lester J. Maitland, who piloted an army plane in the first successful non-stop flight from California to Hawaii. The idea has found favor with officers of the Navy Bureau of Aeronautics

Lieutenant Maitland suggested that "we use the term 'avigation' for the directing or operating of aircraft from one place to another."

The combination of the Latin roots avi (to fly) and agere (to move) is not only etymologically correct, the bureau officers argued, but the word will serve to differentiate navigation and avigation, very different arts. It is not too much to believe, officers of the bureau said, "that in years to come a skilled navigator may be entirely useless in an airplane, while 'avigators' will be in great demand for long-distance commercial flying."

WILBUR PREDICTS STUNT FLIGHT CURB

Naval Secretary Says Federal Law Must Stop Loss of Life as in Pacific Race.

TAKES STAND WITH EBERLE

Navy Extends Search for Dole Fliers by Two Days, but Has No Clues.

By The Associated Press.

SAN FRANCISCO, Cal., Aug. 22.—While navy ships and planes searched under an extended "zero hour," Secretary of the Navy Curtis D. Wilbur, a San Francisco visitor, and officials in Washington agreed today that some Federal move must be made to prevent a recurrence of the disasters that have befallen the Dole air race entrants the seven missing fliers of the Golden Eagle, the Miss Doran and the Dallas Spirit.

Admiral Eberle, Acting Secretary of the Navy, in Washington, predicted the enactment by Congress of a law to prohibit long-distance airplane "stunt flights" except under rigid conditions.

At the same time Admiral Eberle ordered the forty naval vessels searching the Pacific for the missing fliers to continue their efforts until Thursday. The original plans were that the hunt should officially terminate tomorrow night, a week from the date of the start of the Miss Doran and the Golden Eagle.

The extension was made as the result of the disappearance of the Dallas Spirit, piloted by Captain William Erwin of Dallas, Texas, and navigated by A. H. Eichwaldt of Hayward, Cal., which apparently dived into the sea nearly 700 miles west of San Francisco on Friday night after flashing an S O S call on its radio.

Secretary Wilbur was quoted as agreeing that "some step must be taken by the Federal Government to prevent future loss of lives in long-distance stunt flights."

He declined to comment on Admiral Eberle's prediction. He said that the President had some power in this respect, but added he was not sure that this was sufficient to cover the situation.

He declared it was inevitable that some action would be taken "to prevent needless loss of life."

Wide Hunt Lowers Hope for Erwin.

That navy men conducting the hunt for the missing men in the Dallas Spirit held little hope for their rescue was reflected by Lieut. Commander William C. Tooze of the destroyer Hazelwood, who said:

"I do not think there is one chance in a thousand that the Dallas Spirit will ever be found. The Hazelwood, in command of Commander E. H. Connor, covered an area of 3,200 square miles about a point where she gave us her last position and in that space there was not a piece of flotsam—not even an oil spot."

The destroyers Hazelwood, Hull, Kidder, Farenholt and Corry were in San Francisco restocking their larders and refueling, preparatory to proceeding back out to sea to rejoin the airplane carrier Langley, some 500 miles off shore. The Langley has been dispatching observation planes over as wide area for searching purposes.

Reports from Honolulu bore no more hope. The Associated Press correspondent at the island headquarters declared that "another day

Continued on Page Seventeen.

WALKER JOKES WITH BEEFEATER GUIDE IN TOWER OF LONDON

Thinks He Could Find Use for Headsman's Block in New York.

RECEIVES STATE WELCOME

Rides With Mrs. Walker From Station to Hotel in Lord Mayor's Gilded Coach.

TENEMENTS IMPRESS HIM

As Guest of Lord Mayor He Sees Greyhounds Race—Leaves for Berlin Today.

Special Cable to THE NEW YORK TIMES.

LONDON, Aug. 22.—Mayor Walker's last day in London was a busy one. He visited the Tower of London, received a delegation of advertising men, inspected model tenements and after a quiet dinner at his hotel attended the greyhound races at White City tonight as the guest of the Lord Mayor of London.

Mayor and Mrs. Walker plan to leave tomorrow morning at 8:30 for Berlin, where they are due to arrive Wednesday evening at 8 o'clock.

The Mayor on arriving from Dublin on the boat train just after 7 o'clock this morning found, although he had not expected it to meet him, the state coach of the Lord Mayor of London waiting at the railroad station. The coach, an ornate, gilt encrusted affair, with two coachmen on the box and two footmen behind, was drawn by a span of beautifully groomed horses.

At the invitation of the Lord Mayor's representative who met them the Mayor and Mrs. Walker entered it and were driven to their hotel.

Immediately after breakfast the Mayor announced that he wanted to see the Tower of London. Mrs. Walker had planned a shopping tour and could not accompany him. The Mayor's secretary telephoned the Governor of the Tower and made an appointment for 11:30.

Mayor Walker was greeted on his arrival by the Governor, who appointed a stalwart "Beefeater" to conduct him through the Tower. The route led through the Bloody Tower down dark, winding stairs to dungeons, execution rooms of the past, gibbets and all manner of terrifying relics until the Mayor faced the execution block.

The Beefeater pointed to the block and began droning the names of those who perished on it. Mayor Walker stepped forward, the better to examine the block.

"A pretty nifty chin-rest those fellows had," he murmured. "It's nice to inspect close up things you missed. But say," he continued, addressing himself to the Beefeater, "I'd like to see this thing working. Can you arrange it?"

The Beefeater apparently didn't see the humor of the Mayor's remark. He continued explaining that the block was once used as a summary answer to political opponents.

"Then a demonstration's easy," observed the Mayor. "I can provide you material from New York."

He declined to say whom he had in mind, but examined the block closely.

"There are marks which make it look as if the axeman missed and got into the rough," he said.

As the party left the execution chamber the Mayor remarked:

"And no one ever asked for an encore."

Wanted to Meet Gog and Magog.

With the faintest trace of a smile Mayor Walker suggested to the guide that he would like to meet Gog and Magog, the giants whose statues he

Continued on Page Ten.

Society Gets Old Irving Home For Centre of Patriotic Work

The old home of Washington Irving at Seventeenth Street and Irving Place became the property of the National Society of Patriotic Builders of America yesterday when, in the living room, Mrs. William Cumming Story, President of the society, received the title from Algernon S. Bell, the former owner.

The dwelling will be the headquarters of the society. It was selected because it was a type consistent with the aims of the society, which, according to Mrs. Story, are "to preserve historic places, support the Constitution and maintain old American ideals."

Mrs. Story said the society would engage in propaganda for the dissemination of American ideals and culture, asserting that there are "many who come to this country and live and yet remain ignorant of American customs and ideals."

MRS. CHAPLIN WINS DIVORCE AND $825,000

She Gets $625,000 for Herself and $200,000 in Trust for the Two Children.

SUIT BASED ON CRUELTY

Actor Is Not in Los Angeles Court to Hear Her and Friends Tell of Alleged Neglect.

Special to The New York Times.

LOS ANGELES, Aug. 22.—Mrs. Lita Grey Chaplin received an interlocutory decree of divorce from Charles Spencer Chaplin, custody of their two small children and $825,000 in Superior Court today. The film comedian did not appear in court. A year must elapse before a final decree is granted.

When the case was called before Judge Walter Guerin, Edwin T. McMurray, uncle of the plaintiff and chief of her counsel, announced the terms of the property settlement under which Mrs. Chaplin is to receive $625,000, said to be in cash, and $200,000 in trust for the children.

Coming to a sudden and undramatic conclusion, the divorce action, based on charges of cruelty and neglect, was devoid of sensation at its quiet ending, very little different from routine cases. All charges referring to premarital relations of the couple made in the complaint were ruled out by the Judge, who stated that such evidence might be introduced later through testimony, but nothing further was offered.

Chaplin's chief attorney, Gavin McNab, asked the Court to dismiss the comedian's cross-complaint, asserting that his client agreed to the settlement "as an indication of the love of a father for his children, with a desire to keep the taint of scandal from their names."

Only a few sensation-hunters attended the trial, in contrast to the crowds which usually haunt the courts when film colony divorces are on the docket. They heard Mrs. Chaplin testify that her husband had taken her out but twice during the first two months of their married life, and then only for the sake of appearances, and that he never came home before 1 o'clock in the morning. Denying that she interfered with his career, she declared that she hardly ever saw him at all.

The witness described alleged incidents immediately prior to their

Continued on Page Eight.

Dawes Declares He Is Not a Candidate, Declining Young America Union's Support

Special to The New York Times.

CINCINNATI, Aug 22.—Vice President Dawes has informed Douglas T. Atkinson, Judge Advocate of the Young America Union, a secret nonsectarian political organization, that he is not a candidate for the nomination for the Presidency.

Mr. Atkinson received Mr. Dawes's reply at his home here today to a letter sent on behalf of the Young America Union pledging support to Mr. Dawes if he should run. The Vice President wrote as follows:

"I wish you to accept my thanks for your letter and the clipping which you enclosed. Also for your kindly words. They are all much appreciated. I am, however, not a candidate for the nomination."

The Young America Union was founded at Columbus, Ohio, last February. Its chief aim is stated to be to arouse the interest of the younger citizens of the country in civic affairs and to awaken in them a civic pride which it is hoped will be felt in the national issues of the day. The union now has chapters in Cincinnati, Columbus, Youngstown, Cleveland and other large cities in Ohio and is organizing them in other States.

Special to The New York Times.

WASHINGTON, Aug. 22.—The statement by Vice President Dawes in his letter to Mr. Atkinson, that he was not a candidate for the nomination for the Presidency, is viewed by political leaders who are in Washington as merely a reiteration of the position he is said to have taken when approached by others who have sought to sound him out.

The Vice President, it is understood, has not only told friends that he is not seeking the nomination, but that he will not enter the primaries in Illinois or other States. It is not felt, however, that this eliminates him from the race.

The strategy of the leaders who would like to see Mr. Dawes nominated, it is said, is to have him keep out of the primaries in the Middle West and leave the field open for former Governor Lowden of Illinois. Under this arrangement Dawes would fall heir to the Lowden delegates in the event that Mr. Lowden failed to obtain the nomination.

FULLER HEARS PETITIONERS

Governor Is Under Steady Pressure Until the Final Hour.

WOMEN LAST TO APPEAL

Mrs. Sacco and Miss Vanzetti Leave Him and at 11:03 P. M. He Gives Decision.

DEFENSE TRIED EVERY PLEA

Stone, Taft, Holmes and Other Federal as Well as State Judges Refused to Act.

From a Staff Correspondent of The New York Times.

BOSTON, Aug. 22.—Governor Fuller, at the end of a day marked by rapid and continuous action of the defense for Nicola Sacco and Bartolomeo Vanzetti, told Michael A. Musmanno of defense counsel at 11:03 o'clock tonight that he would not interfere in the execution.

The Governor made his decision after a series of extraordinary events. Counsel for the men, augmented by new and distinguished arrivals from New York and Washington, made eight ineffectual attempts to obtain a stay in the Federal courts and in the Superior and Supreme Courts of Massachusetts.

Chief Justice William Howard Taft refused to cross the border from his Summer home in Canada to act on the case. He referred the lawyers to his associates. Subsequently Harlan F. Stone likewise refused. Another effort to get Justice Oliver Wendell Holmes proved futile and other Federal and State Judges likewise declined to take jurisdiction.

A final and dramatic appeal by Mrs. Rose Sacco and Luigia Vanzetti to Governor Fuller at the State House tonight preceded the refusal of the Governor to take any further action to stay the carrying out of the death penalty.

Women Make Family Appeal.

Mrs. Sacco and Miss Vanzetti remained with the Governor for an hour and a half at the State House. In the presence of present and past counsel and State officials, the women begged for a respite. Mrs. Sacco appealed to the Governor as the father of children. She urged her motherhood as an argument that should carry some weight with him.

Miss Vanzetti begged for mercy on behalf of her brother. She urged the Governor to act at once and his name would be blessed. She gave Governor Fuller a message from her brother, saying:

"Some day you will realize my innocence."

To both pleas, Governor Fuller replied:

"I am sorry. My duties are outlined by law."

The women had appeared at the State House at 9:05 P. M. and were at once ushered before the Governor. They left his office at 10:35 P. M. Their eyes were dry. They had wept almost all day and they were bereft of tears at the end.

Effort Is Made to the End.

Among those who pressed into the Governor's office until the last hour before the execution were Francis Fisher Kane, former United States attorney in Philadelphia; State Attorney General Arthur K. Reading, William G. Thompson and Herbert B. Ehrmann, former counsel for the men; Gardner Jackson and Aldini Felicani, members of the Sacco-Vanzetti Defense Committee, and Mr. Musmanno.

The Governor remained at his office until the executions were reported to him before retiring. He had continued to bear the importunities of defense counsel until nearly midnight.

A few minutes before the time for the executions the Governor said good-bye to Mr. Thompson, who had defended Sacco and Vanzetti for many years. When he left Mr. Thompson said:

"Briefly, I outlined to the Governor against the important aspect of the case and did what I considered my duty to my former clients, because, despite the fact that I withdrew from the case, I believe them innocent and they did not have a fair trial."

Fuller Receives Editor's Plea.

Governor Fuller reached his office at the State House at 11:40 A. M. from his Summer residence at Rye Beach, N. H. He greeted newspaper men with "It's a beautiful morning, isn't it." The Governor smiled and seemed in excellent health and spirits.

The Governor was preceded by the first of the day's delegations. Waldo L. Cook, editor of the Springfield Republican; John F. Moors, a Boston banker, and the Rev. Edward Staples Drown of the Episcopal Theological School at Cambridge had called at the Executive offices at 10:15. They left and returned in an hour.

When Mr. Cook and his associates returned they were accompanied by John Lovejoy Elliott of the Hudson Guild, New York City, and Paul U.

Continued on Page Two.

Four Final Legal Pleas Made to the Governor That Failed to Delay Execution of Death Sentence

From a Staff Correspondent of The New York Times.

BOSTON, Aug. 22.—Four final appeals to Governor Fuller for delay in the execution of the death sentences on Sacco and Vanzetti were based on the following grounds:

1. Willingness of the Department of Justice to open its files to the Commonwealth authorities.
2. The official docketing of the appeal for a writ of certiorari in the United States Supreme Court, which could not be acted on by the court until October.
3. A specific request from Arthur D. Hill, chief defense attorney, to allow alienists to examine Sacco and Vanzetti.
4. A request from Mr. Hill, dated last Friday, to delay until the matter of the Supreme Court and the Department of Justice files had been cleared up.

Governor Fuller, after a full day's consideration of these pleas, announced that he would take no further action.

CITY CROWDS SILENT ON NEWS OF DEATHS

Sacco Sympathizers Disperse After Many Protest Meetings Earlier in Night.

POLICE DOUBLY VIGILANT

Force Guards All Vital Points, While Warren and Inspectors Stay on Duty All Night.

The news that the death sentence had been carried out on Sacco and Vanzetti was received in mournful silence by their sympathizers here, who had assembled at various points in the city last night to follow the events in the case to the end. Realizing that their protests had been of no avail, the sympathizers broke up into groups and headed for their homes when the final word came. Some booed as they moved off, but there was no real disorder.

Interest in the fate of the two men was keen throughout the city. Newspaper offices were called by thousands seeking the latest development. Telephone operators of THE NEW YORK TIMES handled 1,755 calls for information from early evening to 1:15 A. M. Crowds gathered in the midtown section for first editions of the newspapers giving the details of the carrying out of the sentence.

Although there had been no reports of disorder up to an early hour this morning, the police guard on transit lines, prominent persons and public and semi-public buildings became doubly vigilant and Police Commissioner Warren announced that he would remain at headquarters throughout the night.

5,000 Wait in Streets.

A crowd of approximately 5,000 persons had stood patiently through the hours leading to the execution outside the offices of The Daily Worker at 30 Union Square East. Brief bulletins told of the approach of the death hour and of demonstrations staged throughout the world. Now and then a cheer would go up at announcement of a foreign protest. A bulletin telling how Sacco's wife and the sister of Vanzetti had arranged to plead with Governor Fuller was received in silence.

As the hour of death grew near the crowd knew that all hope had fled and even the murmur of conversations was stilled. When the final announcement was made to the thousands in the square the murmur of exclamations, blended into one noise, leaped up again, but soon died away. Reinforcements of police had been hurried down to support several hundred patrolmen, under command of Captain William H. Ward, who had patrolled the fringes of the meeting. But the reinforcements were not needed.

Motorcycle Police Ride By.

At 12:25 A. M., a sign was put up in a second floor window of the newspaper building warning the crowd that the end was nearing. Just at that moment fourteen motorcycle policemen, with sirens screeching, rushed down Fourth Avenue, dashed through the square and continued down without a halt. The advance of the motorcycle detachment caused an uneasy stir in the crowd, many apparently thinking that the meeting was about to be dispersed.

A few minutes after the detachment had roared its way by a sign appeared in the window. It read:

"Sacco murdered."

A few moans from women were heard and here and there some one hissed. The crowd, however, was curiously undemonstrative. Another sign came into the window. It said:

"The Workers' Party must not forget its martyrs."

This inscription stared out into the square for a moment and then was replaced by another, which read:

"Vanzetti murdered."

As this went up the police began

Continued on Page Three.

BOSTON BESIEGED; SCORES ARRESTED

Thousands Watch Squad After Squad of Sacco Picketers March Into Police Hands.

CHEERS AND JEERS MINGLE

Advances on State House Last Till Bail Gives Out—Night Move on Bunker Hill Fails

From a Staff Correspondent of The New York Times.

BOSTON, Aug. 22.—Boston, most of whose citizens went calmly about their business twelve days ago when the execution of Nicola Sacco and Bartolomeo Vanzetti was stayed until midnight tonight, lost its indifference today and thousands stood in perspiring masses, blackening the northwest corner of Boston Common, while group after group of picketers, displaying placards and waving banners, were arrested by the police. The number arrested before the State House alone exceeded 150.

A lull came in the picketing at nightfall when bail funds were exhausted, but it started up again at 11 o'clock when two more arrests were made at the State House and two out of sixteen picketers were arrested on Main Street, Charlestown, near the prison.

The first two were Paula Halliday, arrested for the third time in two days, and Frank Shay, actor, author and bookseller, both coming from Provincetown. They staged a small-scale demonstration in the glare of searchlights from the State House roof and were promptly picked up and jailed. Miss Halliday was deprived of her "Is Justice Dead?" slicker.

The two in Charlestown were not identified. The other fourteen who had been marching up and down with banners and placards for twenty minutes mingled with the crowd of curious and escaped.

Police Stop March on Bunker Hill.

Immediately afterward police were dispatched to stop a procession of 300 sympathizers marching from the Defense Committee's headquarters on Salem Street out to the Bunker Hill Monument in Charlestown, a distance of nearly two miles. This was the suggestion of Miss Ruth Hale, who suggested a silent demonstration after a session of prayers had been vetoed on the ground that Sacco and Vanzetti were atheists and would resent being prayed over.

When the marchers reached City Square, Charlestown, the police and their auxiliaries, [illegible] in all, barred the way. Mounted men charged. No one was seriously hurt. Nine were arrested.

Although there had been no outbreak of violence until the Charlestown episode, Beacon Street, Tremont Street, the Common and Rutherford Avenue near the State Prison in Charlestown gave the picture of a town captured and placed under martial law. Police in uniforms and plain clothes, afoot, mounted on horses and motorcycles, and still others packed into automobiles, were everywhere in evidence.

On the streets approaching the prison and the State House every citizen was under suspicion and warned to take himself elsewhere.

Members of the State Constabulary from all parts of Massachusetts arrived in Boston in two and threes throughout the day till 100 of the total force of 156 were concentrated here. In addition to them and the regular police, squads of railroad and other private patrolmen have been drafted, armed and posted about the city. Surrounding the State House alone 239 were on duty and [illegible] others were assigned to the vicinity of the prison in Charlestown.

Police Go Into Action at Noon.

The police were first called into action in connection with Sacco and Vanzetti today at noon when the vanguard of sympathizers arrived before the gates of the State House grounds. There were forty-nine of them, men and women, and some

Continued on Page Four.

WALK TO DEATH CALMLY

Sacco Cries 'Long Live Anarchy'; Vanzetti Insists on His Innocence.

WARDEN CAN ONLY WHISPER

Much Affected as the Long-Delayed Execution Is Carried Out.

MADEIROS FIRST TO DIE

Machine Guns Bristle, Searchlights Glare During Execution—Crowds Kept Far From Prison.

From a Staff Correspondent of The New York Times.

CHARLESTOWN STATE PRISON, Mass., Tuesday, Aug. 23.—Nicola Sacco and Bartolomeo Vanzetti died in the electric chair early this morning, carrying out the sentence imposed on them for the South Braintree murders of April 15, 1920.

Sacco marched to the death chair at 12:11 and was pronounced lifeless at 12:19.

Vanzetti entered the execution room at 12:20 and was declared dead at 12:26.

To the last they protested their innocence, and the efforts of many who believed them guiltless proved futile, although they fought a legal and extra legal battle unprecedented in the history of American jurisprudence.

With them died Celestino F. Madeiros, the young Portuguese, who won seven respites when he "confessed" that he was present at the time of the South Braintree murder and that Sacco and Vanzetti were not with him. He died for the murder of a bank cashier.

Defense Works as They Die.

The six years legal battle on behalf of the condemned men was still on as they were walking to the chair and after the current had been applied, for a lawyer was on the way by airplane to ask Federal Judge George W. Anderson in Williamstown for a writ of habeas corpus.

The men walked to the chair without company of clergy. Father Michael Murphy, prison chaplain, waited until a minute before twelve and then left the prison.

Sacco cried, "Long live anarchy!" as the prison guards strapped him into the chair and applied the electrodes. He added a plea that his family be cared for.

Vanzetti at the last made a short address, declaring his inocence.

Madeiros walked to the chair in a semi-stupor caused by overeating. He shrugged his shoulders and made no farewell statement.

Warden William Hendry was almost overcome by the execution of the men, especially that of Vanzetti, who shook his hand warmly and thanked him for all his kindnesses.

The Warden was barely able to pronounce above a whisper the solemn formula required by law:

"Under the law I now pronounce you dead, the sentence of the court having been legally carried out."

The words were not heard by the official witnesses.

After Governor Fuller had informed counsel for the two condemned radicals that he could take no action, their attorney, Michael A. Musmanno, made a dash to the prison in an automobile and tried to make another call on Sacco and Vanzetti, but Warden Hendry refused, as the legal witnesses were just about to pass into the execution chamber.

The Witnesses Gather.

The witnesses gathered in the Warden's office an hour before midnight. They were instructed as to the part they would take.

W. E. Playfair of The Associated Press was the only reporter permitted to attend the execution, as the State law designated one representative of the press as a witness. The assignment was handed to him six years ago after Sacco and Vanzetti had been convicted in Dedham for the murder of William Parmenter and Alexander Berardelli.

At 11:[illegible] all but the official witnesses were asked to leave the Warden's office. Led by Warden Hendry the official witnesses walked toward the rotunda of the prison. He rapped three times on the inner door. A key turned in the lock. Just then Mr. Musmanno dashed in breathlessly.

"Please, Warden," he said, touching Mr. Hendry on the arm. "A last request."

His voice was faint and broken.

"No, no," the Warden said, sternly, slightly unnerved at the last-minute interruption. Mr. Musmanno turned away, weeping. He had refused to accept as a farewell gift a [illegible]

"All the News That's Fit to Print."

The New York Times.

THE WEATHER
Fair today and tomorrow, not much change in temperature.
Temperature yesterday—Max., 68; min., 53.
For weather report see Page 54.

VOL. LXXVII....No. 25,444. NEW YORK, FRIDAY, SEPTEMBER 23, 1927. TWO CENTS In Greater New York | THREE CENTS Within 200 Miles | FOUR CENTS Elsewhere in the U. S.

GENE TUNNEY KEEPS TITLE BY DECISION AFTER 10 ROUNDS; DEMPSEY INSISTS FOE WAS OUT IN 7TH, AND WILL APPEAL; 150,000 SEE CHICAGO FIGHT, MILLIONS LISTEN ON RADIO

LEGIONAIRES ELECT SPAFFORD AS CHIEF, ENDING CONVENTION

New York Man Is Unanimous Choice for National Commander.

GETS OVATION AT SESSION

Veterans in Paris Approve the Stand of Administration at the Geneva Naval Parley.

PASS MITCHELL'S AIR PLAN

Project for Further Immigration Ban Is Tabled—Bissell of New York Heads '40 and 8.'

Copyright, 1927, by The New York Times Company
Special Cable to THE NEW YORK TIMES.

PARIS, Sept. 22.—The convention in France of the American Legion, so long planned and so long heralded, is now history.

The "greatest ever," as the convention is now known to the Legionaires, came to a close this afternoon in a typical burst of fireworks with the election of the new National Commander and other Legion officials. Edward Elwell Spafford of New York City was the man selected for the Legion's highest honor, and he was chosen unanimously, no other name being even offered to the delegates.

When the choice, which represented the wishes of Legion men from all parts of the country, as he was nominated by the North Carolina delegation and the nomination was seconded by Washington, was announced the convention broke into pandemonium.

Paris had never before witnessed such a scene. The Legionaires started shouting and honking horns, while canes rapped applause like the sputter of machine guns.

Mr. Spafford was escorted to the platform amid the blare of bugles, the shrill of fifes and the thunder of the drums of the band of the Buffalo Post, which went "over the top" into the press box so as to be nearer the centre of activities, scattering the astonished newspaper men.

Nearly Mobbed in Congratulations.

Immediately a seething ocean of Legionaires was trying to shake his hands, thump his back and congratulate him in any way, form and manner as it swirled around him. He climbed into the speaker's box, which was almost the only island of safety, but it was fully ten minutes before the noise was sufficiently quieted to allow him to make a short speech of acceptance and thanks.

It was a fitting way in which to end the spectacular convention, for it was marked by the same combination of seriousness of purpose and uproarious good humor and enthusiasm which so impressed the Paris populace in the big parade of last Monday. America's unmistakable, if occasionally boisterous, sincerity is now a French by-word.

It was also the right spirit in which to close the proceedings, as it wiped out any ill feeling which may have been aroused by the vehement discussions which marked the attempts to map out the Legion's policies in the earlier hours of the session.

As the nominations for the Vice Commanders were made the Legionaires resumed their good-natured gayety. The well-known cry of "Never heard of it!" rang out again and again as the various State delegations were called on. But the greatest opportunity for the now renowned humorous sally of the former soldiers came when, on a point of order, a delegate from the Redwood State said, "California yields to Florida."

"What's that?" was heard from every corner of the enormous room amid general laughter, while the Florida delegate cried, "Louder!" and was greeted with cheers.

Election of Vice Commanders.

The five National Vice Commanders chosen represented all sections of the country. They are John T. Raftis of Washington, Paul R. Younts of North Carolina, Daniel W. Spurlock of Louisiana, J. M. Henry of Minnesota and Ralph T. O'Neill of Kansas.

The Rev. Gill Robb Wilson was elected National Chaplain. He comes from Trenton, N. J., and was formerly an aviator in the Lafayette Escadrille.

The session was called to order at 9 o'clock in the morning and lasted, without recess, until nearly 4 in the afternoon. Almost its first official act was to confer on Count Dejean, head of the American Division in the French Department of Foreign Affairs, the distinguished service cross of the Legion in recognition of his valuable services for Legion, to which he was assigned by Foreign Minister Briand to aid in putting on

Continued on Page Two.

Stinson and Schilling Forced Down and Out Of New York to Spokane Non-Stop Air Derby

From a Staff Correspondent of The New York Times.

FELTS FIELD, SPOKANE, Wash., Sept. 22.—The non-stop race from New York to Spokane came to a definite end today when Eddie Stinson was forced down by engine trouble at Missoula, Mont., and C. A. (Duke) Schiller came down at Billings, Mont.

Stinson would have won the race if he had been flying over country where he could have made a landing at any time. When the intake and exhaust valves on one cylinder of his motor went out, he flew around for several hours, trying to get altitude enough to go on with sufficient gliding distance to make a safe landing.

But he could not get up high enough, and after four or five hours went down at the landing field at Missoula. The field is only 200 miles from Spokane and the time he spent flying in circles would have been sufficient for him to get here. But it was too risky and he wisely quit.

Stinson came in with R. E. Dake in a Waco, the last entry in Class A to arrive. He picked Stinson up as a passenger. Stinson has become a philosopher in his attitude toward long-distance flying. "Sometimes you make it and sometimes you don't," is his motto.

"We had good weather most of the way," he said, "although there was some rain and fog over Michigan. We kept to a great circle course which took us through the centre of Lake Erie and over the other lakes. A good part of the time we were out of sight of land. It got dark while we were over Michigan and dawn found us over North Dakota. I think we kept to our course fairly well all the time until I began circling around after engine trouble developed."

There was much disappointment among the 30,000 people at the field, who had been waiting all day for the non-stop fliers to arrive. The enthusiastic crowd, which cheers every pilot who arrives as if he were a favorite son, gave a rousing reception to Stinson.

INDIANAPOLIS MAYOR QUICKLY CONVICTED

Duvall Faces 30 Days in Jail, $1,000 Fine and 4-Year Bar From Office for Corruption.

TAKES VERDICT IN SILENCE

Bitterness Marks Closing Pleas, Defense Laying Charges to a "Malicious Press."

Special to The New York Times.

INDIANAPOLIS, Sept. 22.—Mayor John L. Duvall was found guilty of violation of the Corrupt Practices act in the Marion County Criminal Court tonight. The penalty is thirty days in the Marion County Jail and a fine of $1,000.

The verdict, reported by the jury at 8 o'clock after three hours' deliberation, makes Mayor Duvall ineligible to hold public office for four years after the date of the crime.

Duvall was pale when the verdict was read and his only comment was: "I have nothing to say."

Under the Corrupt Practices act Duvall was specifically charged with promising William H. Armitage, a politician, the privilege of naming three members of the City Administration in exchange for a cash consideration and support in the 1925 mayoralty campaign. The same Grand Jury which acted upon results of a year's inquiry into alleged political corruption in Indiana also indicted Governor Ed Jackson on a charge of attempting to bribe former Governor Warren T. McCray.

Final Pleas Stir Courtroom.

Ralph Inman, defense counsel, and William H. Remy, Marion County Prosecutor, this afternoon held the packed courtroom spellbound during their pleas which at times became so bitter that the audience gasped.

The crowd got so worked up that once, when work upon a new elevator shaft in the courthouse loosened plaster and showered it through an airduct out into the courtroom, half a hundred spectators sprang to their feet in alarm.

Mr. Remy demanded that the jury send Duvall behind the bars for violating the Corrupt Practices act. Mr. Inman denounced the prosecution of Duvall as the result of acts of a malicious press and demanded that the press be "driven out of town."

With Mr. Remy's argument closing about 4:20 and Special Judge Cassius C. Shirley taking about half an hour for instructions, the case went to the jury at about 5 P. M.

Mr. Inman fired broadsides of ridicule at the State attorneys and the chief State witness, William H. Armitage, and Mr. Remy spent about half of his time in reply.

Answering Mr. Inman's charge that the prosecution of Duvall was a matter of political hatred, Mr. Remy pounded upon the railing of the jury box and declared:

"As long as I am in office this fight against political corruption is going to continue and I pledge myself to the jury and to all the people here that this case will not be the end."

Hurling invectives at the prosecution attorneys and the press, Mr. Inman, who defended D. C. Stephenson, the ex-Klan leader, at Noblesville two years ago and lost, proclaimed Duvall the victim of persecution.

Defense Denounces the Press.

Mr. Inman declared that Duvall was the victim of "a sinister influence in Indianapolis which must be satisfied and should be driven out—a malicious press."

"John Duvall isn't the first Indianapolis man made to stand and defend himself solely because he was unfortunate enough to run and be elected to office," he declared.

In his attack on William H. Freeman and William H. Armitage, the State's chief witnesses, Mr. Inman accused Freeman of "willful, corrupt and deliberate" perjury in part of his testimony.

"It is significant that Armitage never talked before his brother was sentenced to jail," he said. "You could tell by the look in his eyes he would tell any kind of a story to save his brother from going to prison for three months."

DARING FLIER, NUMB, AVOIDS CRASH IN CITY

Steve Lacey, on Western Dash, Dazed by Fumes as Gasoline Swirls About His Feet.

MOTOR SPUTTERED AN HOUR

He Fails to Dump Fuel, Fights Back to Field, Lands Safely and Falls Unconscious.

Special to The New York Times.

ROOSEVELT FIELD, L. I., Sept. 22.—A courageous pilot with a sputtering engine fought for an hour to keep his plane under control over New York City and the surrounding area yesterday afternoon, while gasoline swirled four inches deep around his feet and sent up fumes which numbed his hands and his brain. Battling these obstacles, he brought the plane down on the field here and fell over unconscious.

The pilot was Steve Lacey, who had tried so desperately to take part in the non-stop race to the Pacific against C. S. (Duke) Schiller and Eddie Stinson. With his navigator, Louis A. Yancey, he had worked most of the night repairing his blue and silver biplane Air King, which had lost its tail skid in an unsuccessful effort to take off yesterday.

Today, though the New York-Spokane air derby time limit was past and he could not hope to share in the non-stop prize money, he took off again in an endeavor to make good his promise to fly westward "just for fun." The ill luck which balked him yesterday dogged him today. He and Yancey got away perfectly at 12:52 P. M. and soon disappeared from sight. In a few minutes they reappeared and came down with their heavily laden plane, making a perfect landing at 100 miles an hour. Their engine was not functioning properly. It was tuned again and readjusted and up they soared once more.

Saved City From a Disaster.

Then came the mishap unique in aviation, which almost cost both men their lives and only for their heroism would have sent a plane loaded with hundreds of gallons of gasoline roaring in flames into the streets of New York.

Misfortune threatened them from the start of their last flight. It was 2:21 P. M. The Wright Whirlwind motor apparently was functioning perfectly again as Lacey gave the ship the gun and it rolled along the ground. It was running beautifully at 2,000 feet from the starting point

Continued on Page Three.

TREND TOWARD SMITH PLAIN IN FAR WEST AS LEADERS GATHER

Indications Point to First Raising of His Banner at Ogden (Utah) Conference.

11 STATES REPRESENTED

Iowa Democrats at Own Request, Join Gathering, Which Begins Deliberations Today.

TARIFF IS ON THE AGENDA

Most Available Presidential Candidate and Two-thirds Rule Also Topics.

From a Staff Correspondent of The New York Times.

OGDEN, Utah, Sept. 22.—Democrats in the intermountain States, who went to the Democratic National Convention in 1924 for the most part as enthusiastic supporters of William Gibbs McAdoo, are swinging to Governor Alfred E. Smith of New York. There are indications that at a conference which will begin here tomorrow for the discussion of problems vital to the party they will raise the Smith banner and start the first organized movement in the nation to further the Presidential aspirations of New York's Chief Executive, who, as he did in 1924, will enter next year's Democratic national conclave as the favorite son of his party in the Empire State.

At the Hotel Bigelow, where the conference will be held, fifty rooms have been reserve for prospective conferees, and it is probable that fully that many will attend. Nearly all of those who are expected to answer the roll-call when the meeting is called to order at 10 o'clock tomorrow morning are former adherents of Mr. McAdoo. Almost without exception, too, they are at least politically dry, as are the Democratic organizations in the several States that will be represented at the gathering.

Prominent Conferees.

At least two Democratic National Committeemen who wield considerable influence in party councils have accepted invitations to the conference. They are Isidore B. Dockweiler of California and James H. Moyle of Utah. Today, unexpectedly and to the great delight of those who have taken the initiative in calling the intermountain Democrats together, there was added to the number of prominent participants Delbert M. Draper of Salt Lake City, Chairman of the Central Committee, and, it is said here, a real power in the party organization in this State. Another spokesman for Utah will be J. W. Stringfellow, leader of the organization in Salt Lake County, which supplies approximately one-half of the votes cast in the State. He is openly for Governor Smith for President.

Fred W. Johnson of Rock Springs, Wyo., and former State Senator Joseph Chez of Utah, to whose initiative and earnest labors for many months the Democrats in these Far Western States owe their opportunity for coming together to discuss party problems, said today that it should be clearly understood that no one will be asked at the conference to deliver the delegation from his own State to Governor Smith next year.

Purpose of the Meeting.

It is admitted, in fact, that grave doubt exists whether any of the conferees would be in a position to make

Continued on Page Four.

Pope Pius Sends $100,000 to Flood Sufferers; Bishops in Mississippi Area to Distribute It

Pope Pius XI has contributed $100,000 to the relief of the flood sufferers in the Mississippi Valley. The gift was made public here yesterday by the Right Rev. Dr. Edmond A. Walsh, vice president of Georgetown University and President of the Catholic Near East Welfare Association. Dr. Walsh was Director-General of Papal Relief during the post-war famines in Europe.

The Pope's intention to help victims of the flood was first made known by the Pontiff during a recent visit of Dr. Walsh to the Vatican. Dr. Walsh went to Rome to report on the activities of the new association. Joseph F. Moore, General Secretary of the association, was also present when the Pope first spoke of his intention to make the donation.

Dr. Walsh was designated by the Pontiff to bring the gift to America and present it to the hierarchy of the United States. This he did last week in Washington at the annual meeting of the archbishops and bishops in the Catholic University of America.

Announcement of the contribution was made by Cardinal O'Connell of Boston, Chairman of the meeting. A Committee of Bishops from the flood area was formed immediateley. On the committee are:

The Most Rev. John W. Shaw, Archbishop of New Orleans; the Right Rev. John B. Morris, Bishop of Little Rock, Ark.; the Right Rev. Cornelius Van de Ven, Bishop of Alexandria, Va.; the Right Rev. Jules V. Jeanmard, Bishop of Lafayette, La.; the Right Rev. Richard O. Gerow, Bishop of Natchez, Miss.

The committee is now drawing up recommendations for the most economical and practical disposal of the money.

"As head of the Catholic Church, Pope Pius desired to do something personal in addition to the help already sent to the stricken areas by the various dioceses in the United States," said Dr. Walsh yesterday at his headquarters, 480 Lexington Avenue. "The only regret of his Holiness was that he could not send more."

GREATEST RING SPECTACLE

Crowd Pays $2,800,000 to Watch Contest at Soldier Field.

THRONG IN SEATS EARLY

Largest Boxing Assemblage in History Handled Smoothly by Police and Ushers.

MANY NOTABLES PRESENT

Senators, Governors and Business Leaders Rub Elbows With Obscure Sport Fans.

By JAMES R. HARRISON.
Special to The New York Times.

CHICAGO, Sept. 22.—Out of the welter and turmoil and clamor of the "fight of the ages" one clear fact stands out—that tonight Tex Rickard unveiled the most beautiful picture in the history of sports here or elsewhere.

One hundred and fifty thousand persons watched in the darkness—the greatest of all boxing crowds by about 35,000. It would fill more than two Yankee Stadiums and almost two Yale Bowls; it would pack the Polo Grounds to capacity and leave 100,000 on the outside.

The total receipts were put at $2,800,000.

Governors and Mayors and United States Senators and millionaires lent the right tone to the occasion and millions listened to the story of the fight as it went out "on the air."

Yet the facts and figures do not seem particularly important as compared to the sheer beauty of a picture that only an artist could paint. This may or may not have been "the fight of the ages," but it most certainly was the "sight of the ages."

The veil of darkness over it all; the rippling sea of humanity stretching out as far as the eye could see; the Doric columns of Soldier Field glowing a soft white along the upper battlements of the arena; and finally the ring itself, where two men fought it out with their fists in a pool of white light—these were the high spots of an unforgettable spectacle.

Impressive in Its Vastness.

It was a picture that should have been seen from the air, from the cockpit of an airplane, where the lights and shadows and the blacks and whites of the panorama could have been viewed in their proper perspective.

The ingredients of the picture were striking. A long, low oval stadium of classic lines, filled to its utmost rim. A gently sloping bank of humanity that seemed to stretch to the horizon, and in the centre of the canvas a twenty-foot ring bathed in the fierce light that beats about a throne.

The vastness of the spectacle was its most impressive quality. It filled the eye and staggered the senses. We have seen the Yale Bowl jammed with people, and last November we saw the same Soldier Field at the Army-Navy game, but this was the crowd of crowds and the spectacle of spectacles, lacking only the natural beauty of Poughkeepsie and New London.

Even though he did not sell all of his 163,000 seats, Tex Rickard reached a long cherished goal in his career as an impresario. The 90,000 of Boyle's Thirty Acres and the 115,000 of the Sesquicentennial were left far behind as Chicago and its influx of fight fans poured through the portals of this sports temple.

There they sat, shoulder to shoulder, from the ring up to the top rim where American flags rippled in a brisk western wind. Not that the stadium was full. The cheaper $5 seats, a few city blocks to the north and south, were sparsely settled, proving that you may lead a boxing fan to water but you can't make him drink.

This will probably stand as the record crowd of ring history, because people will sit only so far away from the scene of activities. And tonight Rickard reached the limit in distances. His $5 patrons were 700 or more feet from the ring, which at the Yankee Stadium would locate them somewhere beyond the centre field fence.

Some Bring Radio Sets.

Time was when a fight fan could buy almost any seat and see the proceedings with the naked eye. But no more. As the citizens flocked through the gates half of them were armed with binoculars, opera glasses and telescopes. Here and there one could see some shrewd lads who had brought portable radios with them. They were the $5 boys, who were going to listen even if they did not see.

The weather man was not fooling when he said fair and warmer, for that was a perfect forecast. The fans brought light coats with them, but they were hardly necessary, especially around the ring, where the heat of the bright lights was very noticeable.

The afternoon was gray and overcast and twilight showed a drab, threatening sky and mist which fore-

Continued on Page Twenty.

GENE TUNNEY, STILL THE CHAMPION.

DEMPSEY TO APPEAL DECISION ON FIGHT

He Says Tunney Was Down for 14 or 15 Seconds in the Seventh Round.

TIMEKEEPER CITES RULE

And Boxing Commissioner Says the Point Was Explained Before Bout Started.

Special to The New York Times.

CHICAGO, Sept. 22.—Jack Dempsey and his manager, Leo Flynn, announced tonight that they intend to appeal to the Illinois Boxing Commission to reverse the decision of the referee and two judges allowing Gene Tunney to retain his world's heavyweight title.

"Intentionally or otherwise, I was robbed of the championship," Dempsey said in his dressing room after the bout. "In the seventh round Tunney was down for a count of fourteen or fifteen. Every stop-watch around the ring caught the time as about fifteen seconds, and the inefficiency of the referee or the timekeeper or both deprived me of the fight.

"Everybody knows I am not a whiner. When Tunney beat me last year I admitted that he was the better man that night. I am not an alibi artist, but I know down in my soul that I knocked Tunney out tonight, and, what's more, chased him all around the ring and should have won on points at least."

Tunney Out, Says Flynn.

Flynn paced up and down the dressing room like a caged lion.

"Everything Jack told you goes double for me," said Flynn. "Before the bout the Boxing Commission said they would see that we got a square deal and would step in and reverse an unfair decision. Now I'm going to take them at their word and make a formal appeal tomorrow to have tonight's verdict reversed.

"Tunney was cleanly knocked out for the count of fifteen in the seventh round. Look at that watch here. It has stopped on the figure fifteen. I have not found a watch yet that got the count under ten. I'm not saying the referee was dishonest. I'm saying that he was inefficient, and it amounts to the same thing as far as we are concerned.

"He failed to take up the timekeeper's count at the start—didn't take it up until the timekeeper had got to four or five. This is the biggest injustice I have ever seen in a ring. Leaving aside the knockout in the seventh round, Jack knocked him down again in the ninth and chased him all around the ring. Why didn't Tunney come out and fight like a champion? Dempsey clearly won on points.

"You can say this for me. Dempsey will fight Tunney any time and any place and knock him out."

Dempsey Wants Another Fight.

"Will I fight him again?" echoed Dempsey. "You bet your life. I beat Tunney tonight and I will beat him again any time he wants to get into the same ring with me. I am not ready to retire, by a long shot—not before I've had another crack at Tunney."

There was plenty of high dudgeoning in the Dempsey dressing room

Continued on Page Eighteen.

STORY OF THE FIGHT TOLD BLOW BY BLOW

Detailed Description of Tunney-Dempsey Bout From the Ringside.

BOTH FIGHTERS AGGRESSIVE

Bout Is Marked by Lively Exchanges—Dempsey Hangs On at the End.

Special to The New York Times.

RINGSIDE, SOLDIER FIELD, CHICAGO, Sept. 22.—The detail of the Tunney-Dempsey bout, which was fought here tonight, follows, round by round:

First Round.

Dempsey rushed Tunney, who sidestepped, and Dempsey again swung a left and clinched and Tunney hooked a left. Tunney hit a right to face as they clinched. Referee pulled them apart. Tunney flashed left to Dempsey's face. Dempsey bobbed and weaved and jabbed to Tunney's jaw. Tunney crossed with a right to Dempsey's jaw. Tunney twice jabbed with lefts to the face and they clinched. Tunney followed with a right to Dempsey's jaw and then dodged away from Dempsey's left hook. Gene hooked to Dempsey's body. Gene again got Jack against the ropes and they clinched. Tunney then jabbed a left to the face.

Second Round.

Tunney jabbed a left to face. Dempsey sent one to chest. They clinched and Tunney held Dempsey's arm. Dempsey put a straight left to the body and Tunney a right to the jaw backing Dempsey to the ropes. Tunney missed a right to the jaw as Dempsey ducked and then Tunney drove a right to the head. Dempsey hooked a left to the head and pounded the body when Tunney left himself open. Tunney drove two rights to the head and clinched. Tunney crossed a right to the jaw and another clinch followed. Dempsey put a left to the body and Tunney a left to the face and they clinched. Tunney hooked a left to the face and in a clinch Dempsey sent a left to the body and head. Tunney drove two rights to Dempsey's head. Dempsey put a left to Tunney's face and another to the body.

Third Round.

They danced about at start of the third and Gene led with a right as Dempsey hooked three lefts to the body. Gene started a right hook to Jack's body, but stopped the blow short as they clinched. Tunney rushed Dempsey and landed with short lefts. Jack drove away at Gene's body, the blows being perilously close to the belt line. They got in at close quarters and Dempsey again hit a low and Judge Lytton shouted "Low" to the referee. Dempsey was short with a left and then Tunney missed a short right and Tunney danced away from a short left. Gene missed a left and came in at close quarters to hook at Demp-

Continued on Page Eighteen.

FIGHT FAST AND FURIOUS

On Verge of Knockout in Seventh Round Tunney Comes Back Strong.

FLOORS DEMPSEY IN EIGHTH

Referee and Judges Unanimous in Their Verdict for the Champion.

DISPUTE ON KNOCKDOWN

Challenger Went to Wrong Corner and Thus Delayed Count on Tunney for Few Seconds.

By JAMES P. DAWSON.
Special to The New York Times.

RINGSIDE, SOLDIER FIELD, CHICAGO, Sept. 22.—His refusal to observe the boxing rules of the Illinois State Athletic Commission, or his ignorance of the rules, or both, cost Jack Dempsey the chance to regain the world's heavyweight championship here tonight in the ring at Soldier Field.

By the same token this disregard of rules of ring warfare, or this surprising ignorance, saved the title for Gene Tunney, the fighting ex-marine, who has been king of the ring for just a year.

[illegible] ended with Tunney getting [illegible]decision, and the vast majority in the staggering assemblage of 150,000 people, who paid, it is estimated, $2,800,000 to see this great sport spectacle, approved the verdict.

The decision was given by Referee Dave Barry and Judges George Lytton, wealthy department store owner, and Commodore Sheldon Clark of the Sinclair Oil Company. It was announced as a unanimous decision, but this could not be verified in the excitement attending the finish of the battle. But it should have been unanimous according to all methods of reasoning and boxing scoring, for Tunney won seven of the ten rounds, losing only the third, sixth and seventh, in the last of which, Dempsey made his great mistake. It is known that Judge Lytton voted for Tunney.

Dempsey's Furious Plunge.

In that seventh round Dempsey was being peppered and buffeted about on the end of Tunney's left jabs and hooks and sharp though light right crosses, as he had been in every preceding round, with the exception of the third.

In a masterful exhibition of boxing Tunney was evading the attack of his heavier rival and was countering cleanly, superbly, skillfully, accurately the while for half of the round or so.

Then Dempsey, plunging in recklessly, charging bull-like, furiously and with utter contempt for the blows of the champion, since he had tasted of Tunney's best previously, suddenly lashed a long, wicked left to the jaw with the power of old. This he followed with a right to the jaw, the old "iron mike" as deadly as ever, and quickly drove another left hook to the jaw, under which Tunney toppled like a falling tree, hitting the canvas with a solid thud near Dempsey's corner, his hand reaching blindly for a helping rope which somehow or other refused to be within clutching distance.

Then Dempsey made his mistake, an error which, I believe, cost him the title he values so highly.

Count Begun and Halted.

The knockdown brought the knockdown timekeeper, Paul Beeler, to his feet automatically, watch in hand, eyes glued to the ticking seconds and he bawled "one" before he looked upon the scene in the ring.

There he saw Dempsey in his own corner, directly above the prostrate, brain-numbed Tunney, sitting there looking foolishly serious, his hand finally resting on the middle ring strand. Beeler's count stopped. Referee Barry never started one.

It is the referee's duty to see to it that a boxer scoring a knockdown goes to the corner farthermost from his fallen foe and it is the duty of the knockdown timekeeper

Continued on Page Eighteen.

"All the News That's Fit to Print."

The New York Times.

THE WEATHER
Partly cloudy and continued cold today and tomorrow; west winds.
Temperature yesterday—Max. 33, Min. 24.
☞Per weather report see Page 47.

VOL. LXXVII....No. 25,531. *** NEW YORK, MONDAY, DECEMBER 19, 1927. TWO CENTS in Greater New York | THREE CENTS Within 200 Miles | FOUR CENTS Elsewhere in the U. S.

SIX MEN FOUND ALIVE IN TORPEDO ROOM OF SUNKEN S-4; TAP PATHETIC PLEA 'HOW LONG WILL YOU BE?' TO DIVER; NAVY BATTLES AGAINST TIME TO LIFT SHATTERED CRAFT

AMITY WITH MEXICO IS BROUGHT CLOSER BY LINDBERGH VISIT

Mexico City Hears President Calles Will Go to Havana to Meet Coolidge.

TOTTERING STOCKS RISE

Confidence in Efforts of Ambassador Morrow and the Flier Revives Business.

POPULAR FEELING CHANGING

Parading Workers Cheer Lindbergh and Morrow—Aviator Sees a Bullfight, but Is Silent.

By RUSSELL OWEN.
Staff Correspondent of The New York Times.
Copyright, 1927, by The New York Times Company.
All Rights Reserved.
By Wireless to THE NEW YORK TIMES.

MEXICO CITY, Dec. 18.—The visit of Colonel Charles A. Lindbergh to Mexico already has brought about some remarkable results, political, economic and social. He has acted as a clarifying agent in a slowly developing situation. Not even he nor Ambassador Morrow, who paved the way, probably expected anything so immediately valuable to an accord between the two nations.

Out of the dramatic interest in Colonel Lindbergh, who seems destined to make men of alien race forget their differences in a common admiration of a splendid manhood, has come a definite advance toward a solution of the so-called Mexican problem.

The most significant of the movements in that direction are the reports that President Calles will go to Havana to meet President Coolidge at the Pan-American Congress.

Just what might come of such a meeting in the form of a better economic and social understanding between the two countries men grown old and discouraged in Mexican affairs do not dream of predicting.

Mexico Eager for Amity.

All they know is that with Calles apparently seated firmly in power, with a prospect of comparative internal peace in Mexico and with a wave of sentiment breaking down the barriers between the United States and Mexico, there might come from a meeting of the two Chief Executives an understanding of which the consequences could not be estimated.

Mexico is tired of fighting. Mexico wants peace and a greater degree of prosperity. There are those who believe these lie in a very distant future. But at the same time, under the stir of the emotional reaction of Mexico to Colonel Lindbergh's visit and the honest, common-sense work of Ambassador Morrow, there are many who see a new opportunity for Mexico, both financial and social.

Mexico seems willing to try to win the friendship of the United States, with all that may imply in a country rich in resources and needing only capital and fair dealing to develop them.

Morrow in Leading Rôle.

As a factor in bringing about this situation Ambassador Morrow has played a leading rôle. He has placed diplomacy in Mexico on a new basis, treating those with whom he has dealt as men of their word who wished the best for their country.

If he differed with them, he tried to see their point of view, to find some point of mutual agreement. The result has been remarkable, and it is not stretching the truth to say that Ambassador Morrow is one of the most popular men in Mexico.

Slowly there has penetrated to the minds of the Mexican people a suspicion that the gringo is not the national enemy of Mexico. Ambassador Morrow's unfailing courtesy—his tact, his willingness to go personally to members of the Mexican Government instead of writing notes to them, his refusal to be anything but frank—has brought about the feeling which led today to there being carried in a parade of workmen, the workmen who have been called Bolsheviki, a banner with the inscription, "Morrow is an honest man."

Lindbergh Crystallizes Situation.

This tendency to change the Mexican attitude toward America and its representatives was still inchoate when Colonel Lindbergh crystallized it. When this frank, simple and courageous representative of America dropped over the mountain rim on the wings of his famous plane, Mexico was swept by a wave of pro-Americanism which is difficult to realize, even in the midst of it.

There is something about this young aviator, a magnificent simplic-

Continued on Page Six.

Lindbergh Praises Skill of Riders and Ropers Who Perform for Him

Calls Labor Parade in His Honor Expression of Friendliness for the United States—Not Certain How He Should Wear Gift Cape.

By Colonel CHARLES A. LINDBERGH.

By Mexican War Department Wireless Direct to The New York Times.

MEXICO CITY, Dec. 18.—This has been another of these wonderful Mexican days. There seems to be no end of them. And I have seen two of the sports of Mexico under a perfect sky and brilliant sun.

The exhibition of roping and riding at the Rancho de Charros was one of the finest things of the kind I have ever seen. Then came the review of members of the Mexican Labor Unions at the National Palace, which was a gratifying expression of friendliness toward the United States.

Receives Cape From Matador.

The much debated bull fight came in the afternoon. I received a beautiful cape there, presented by José Ortiz, one of the matadors. The workmanship on it is different from anything of the kind I have ever seen and it is one of the best nationalistic gifts I have had.

I am not quite certain yet how I should wear it, but Señor Ortiz placed it over my shoulders and I suppose that is the way it should be worn.

Last night I had the first opportunity of seeing some of the country around Mexico City from an automobile in which we drove out some way toward Puebla over a wide and smooth road.

The road went up through the mountains, from which there was a splendid view of Mexico City and the valley. I should think this would be a great tourist centre.

Sees Chance for Hotels.

It is one of the most picturesque places on the continent, easy of access and with a delightful climate. If a few hotels were built on these hills, with golf courses laid out near them, so that it would be possible to stay in the country, it should be one of the most attractive places in North America.

This valley has a romantic history and contains the remains of the old Aztec and Toltec civilizations, which were the oldest north of the Isthmus. The Toltecs and Mayas people were cultured peoples whose ruins are among the most interesting in the world. I am looking forward to a visit to the famous pyramids, where I may see what is believed to be the ruins of the Toltec city.

Tourists Would Bring Air Lines.

It is hard to believe now that this whole valley was originally a huge lake, with little islands in it on which the ancient cities were built. It must have been a beautiful spot in those days, even more so than now, although Mexico City is one of the most delightful I have ever visited.

If tourists would come to Mexico in greater numbers it should be possible to build up air lines which would make it much more accessible. The United States is now two days away by railroad, but it would be only a few hours by airplane. Flying in multi-motored planes is as safe as travelling by rail and in the next few years there should be developed a series of airlines to connect all this part of the continent and extend to South America.

BEQUESTS FROM ALL SOUGHT BY COLUMBIA

Dr. Butler in Report Asserts University Merits Mention in Every Citizen's Will.

Columbia University has earned the right to be remembered by some provision in every will that is drawn in New York City because of its service to the community, according to Dr. Nicholas Murray Butler, President of the university, in his 1927 annual report to the Board of Trustees. The report, made public yesterday, again declares that Columbia University "is undercapitalized by some $60,000,000" for the successful discharge of its present obligations.

"The lack of sufficient physical equipment for the present work of the university on Morningside Heights," says President Butler's report, "is glaring and almost impossible to explain satisfactorily to students, to visiting scholars and to the public."

$3,498,380 Gifts in 1927.

The report says that Columbia's total gifts in 1927, including those to Barnard and Teachers Colleges and the College of Pharmacy were $3,498,380.20; that since 1890 gifts to Columbia University have aggregated $71,588,763.64, and that the combined resources of those institutions as of June 30, 1927, were $114,153,749.87, and their budget appropriations were $12,005,670.66. Columbia's teaching staff numbers 2,210, against 2,092 in 1926.

"It is tiresome to repeat the fact, but, as was shown in detail in the last annual report, the university is undercapitalized by some $60,000,000 for the successful and satisfactory discharge of its present public obligations," says the report. "It cannot possibly be put in funds with which to meet those obligations unless the citizens of New York and of the nation, feeling their moral responsibility for the continuance and prosperity of the great institutions that lead and serve the intellectual life and that organize and promote scientific advance, make constant and large benefactions from the fortunes with which they are happily blessed.

"The time should now have come

Continued on Page Nine.

DOUBT ELIGIBILITY OF HOOVER IN 1928

Some Senators Raise Question of His Having Been Resident of Country 14 Years.

Special to The New York Times.

WASHINGTON, Dec. 18.—The question of Secretary Hoover's eligibility to the Presidency under the provision of "fourteen years a resident within the United States" is being seriously raised in Senatorial circles. It is being contended that Mr. Hoover must have been a resident within the United States for fourteen years previous to induction into the Presidency, and the question is being raised as to whether he has been a resident for that length of time.

One of the prominent Republican members of the Senate who is also a constitutional lawyer, but who did not care to be quoted tonight, said:

"The question as to whether Mr. Hoover is eligible under the fourteen-year clause has been seriously raised among some members of the Senate.

"I have no doubt myself that the Constitutional provision means that a man to be eligible for the Presidency must have been a resident within the United States for fourteen years before entering the White House. I do not think it means fourteen years inclusive of early life in the United States."

The Senator in question declined to discuss the matter, he said, because he was not aware of the facts as to the residence of Mr. Hoover here and abroad. The Constitutional provision, found in Paragraph 4, Section 1 of Article II, reads:

"No person except a natural born citizen or a citizen of the United States at the time of the adoption of this Constitution shall be eligible to the office of President; neither shall any person be eligible to that office who shall not have attained to the age of thirty-five years and been fourteen years a resident within the United States."

If Mr. Hoover were nominated and elected in 1928 he would be sworn into office March 4, 1929. Those who argue that "fourteen years a resident within the United States," as used in the Constitution, means fourteen years immediately prior to induction into office contend that Mr. Hoover must show that he has

Continued on Page Thirteen.

YOUTH ARRESTED IN CHILD SLAYING AT LOS ANGELES

Doctor's Son, a University Man, Held as Suspect in Kidnapping of Marion Parker.

ANOTHER TAKEN IN NEVADA

Clues Found in Suitcase, Abandoned Auto and Tailor's Story of Bloody Coat.

$50,000 REWARD POSTED

Volunteers Raise the Fund and Join Full Police Force in Wide Hunt for Murder Gang.

By The Associated Press.

LOS ANGELES, Dec. 18.—The police late today arrested a suspect in the Marian Parker murder case whose name they refused to divulge.

Officers stated, however, that the prisoner was a man of 25 years, the son of a Los Angeles doctor, a military school and university man and known in the past to have committed offenses against young girls.

The police had earlier declared they had fingerprints of the man wanted which would convict him if captured. These prints were taken from the ransom letters and the originals of the filed telegrams.

The police further divulged that the imprisoned suspect was in a position to know intimate details of the Parker family life.

Police Describe Type of Guilty Man.

Police investigators here point out definite qualifications which mark the slayer and which are applied to all suspects taken into custody.

Aside from his physical appearance, which is fairly well known from testimony by several who saw him, and his fingerprints taken from his letters, he is, say the officers, keen-minded, well-educated, egotistic, particularly in believing that he has a master criminal mind.

He has some knowledge of anatomy, as evidenced in the dissection of Marian Parker's body. He has a smattering of education in Greek, but only a smattering, for while he used Greek characters in spelling the word "death" in some of his messages to his little victim's father, he used two of them wrongly.

Also, say the police investigators, he had full information on residents in the neighborhood of the Parker home and was thoroughly acquainted with the district.

They point out as well that his admonition to Parker to seek "aid from God and not from man," combined with the ability to destroy innocence as he destroyed it, places him in the category of the mentally warped and the degenerate.

It may be, investigators declare, that the girl's slayer in penning his letters and telegrams to Parker patterned them after the scholarly style of Leopold and Loeb, Chicago's boy slayers.

Acting on information which they said came from a confidential source a squad of Los Angeles officers tonight descended on Tijuana, across the Mexican border from San Diego, and began combing the dives there for a clue to the killing.

Doubtful on Las Vegas Suspect.

LAS VEGAS, Nev., Dec. 18 (AP).—Lewis D. Wyatt was taken from the Red Feather stage here tonight by Los Angeles detectives seeking the kidnapper and slayer of Marian Parker.

He was held for questioning in the Clark County Jail here. His photographs and fingerprints will be sent to Los Angeles by plane tomorrow.

Wyatt, said the California officers, was too stocky to correctly answer

Continued on Page Four.

P. & A. Photo.

WHERE SIX MEN STILL LIVE IN SUNKEN SUBMARINE.
Diagram Shows the Various Compartments in a Submarine of the Type of the S-4. The Forward One, or Torpedo Room, Is Where the Only Known Survivors Have Answered Signals From the Submerged Craft. The Other Compartments in Order Are: Battery Room, Where the Crew's Quarters Are; Control Room, Directly Under the Conning Tower; Engine Room and Motor or Stern Torpedo Room.

SEWER CHARGES GO TO CONNOLLY TODAY

Scudder Also Expected to Fix Time and Place, Probably Jan. 3 in Queens Court House.

TWO-FOLD DEFENSE LIKELY

Friends Say Borough President Will Attack Motives of His Accusers and Uphold Costs.

Supreme Court Justice Townsend Scudder, who has been designated by Governor Smith to hear the charges of official misconduct against Borough President Maurice E. Connolly of Queens, is expected to have a copy of the charges served upon Mr. Connolly today, together with notification of the time and place of the hearings.

The law provides that the accused shall have at least eight days in which to prepare his answer after the charges are served upon him. As Christmas Day will intervene, Governor Smith has suggested that Justice Scudder give Mr. Connolly ten days to prepare his answer. This would bring the time so close to New Year's Day that it is believed Justice Scudder may not fix the time any earlier than Jan. 3. The Queens County Court House in Long Island City, where Justice Scudder tried the Snyder-Gray murder case, is regarded as the most likely location for the hearings. It is provided by law that the inquiry shall be held within the county where the accused lives.

Justice Scudder, having spent Saturday in Utica to attend a meeting of the trustees of the Masonic Home there—he is a past Grand Master of the Grand Lodge of Masons for New York State—returned to New York yesterday. He went to his home at Glen Head, L. I., in Nassau County, which he left last night for the Hamilton Club, Brooklyn, where he stays while occupying the bench in Brooklyn or Queens. He made no announcement regarding his plans for the inquiry, and, so far as known, has not yet selected a special counsel to assist him.

Steuer Still Undecided.

Max D. Steuer, criminal lawyer, whom Connolly has asked to act as his counsel at the Scudder inquiry, said yesterday that he was still unable to say whether he could accept the retainer. He explained that he had been unable to communicate with three opposing attorneys in law suits in which he is to appear next month, in his effort to persuade them to agree to postponements so that he can accept the Connolly case.

One case, he went on, was in the State courts and had been peremp-

Continued on Page Eight.

Simon Lake Suggests Way To Rescue Men of the S-4

MILFORD, Conn., Dec. 18 (AP).—Simon Lake, inventor of the even keel type of submarine, told The Bridgeport Telegram tonight what he thought was the only possible manner of rescuing members of the crew of S-4 who are alive within its sunken shell.

Mr. Lake said that as long as an air line was pumping air into the submarine the only feasible plan for taking out the men would be for divers to cut a hole through the plate at the bottom of the submerged boat and enter with diving suits or helmets for the survivors.

The water would be kept out of the boat by means of air pressure pumped from above. Pressure of forty-five pounds to the square inch, making an air pressure equal to the water pressure at that depth, would allow the diver to enter with his helmets or suits. Members of the submarine's crew could put on the suits and be pulled to the surface when they came out of the submarine.

HOPE TO SAVE MEN BY TILTING THE S-4

Experts Here Say Craft May Be Up-Ended to Surface by Air Pumped In.

With her hull smashed amidships, her control room a wreck, but with her forward compartments apparently watertight, according to the report of Diver Eadie, naval men here last night saw some hope of saving a part of the crew locked in the sunken submarine S-4 off Provincetown.

With the sweeper Falcon's powerful compressors forcing air into the forward ballast tanks and the Bushnell and the S-8 standing by with more air compressors ready to feed into the manifolds on the Falcon, it is hoped that enough buoyancy can be added to the helpless craft to "upend" her bow first. Then, the engineers say, as was the case in the rescue of the crew of the S-5 in 1920, drills grinding steadily through the thick armor plate might cut the passage for the escape of the entrapped men.

When navy men heard that the control room had been crashed through by the prow of the Coast Guard destroyer Paulding they shook their heads. The diver reported the hole in her as larger than the gash in the S-51; and although later Eadie reported that men were alive in the torpedo compartment, the long, cone shaped room that tapers toward a point and ends, so far as human life is concerned, against the bulkhead housing the torpedo tubes, this news did not greatly cheer them.

The control room is the heart of the submarine. All the main valves for the ballast tanks operate from there, the engine and motor controls, the diving planes and the rising planes. About a dozen men were probably on duty at these controls, and among them several of the officers. Just forward of this compartment is the battery room, where are located the men's sleeping quarters and the ward room for the officers, and ahead of that is the torpedo room, where six men are reported alive.

No one had a chance to escape either forward or aft into the engine room from the control. If men are alive, what happened is this, naval men say: Some one with presence of mind closed the water-tight door between the torpedo room and the battery room and shot home the heavy steel "dogs" that fasten the door. Then the trapped men retreated for-

Continued on Page Two.

City Watches in Vain for Newest Comet; Skjellerup Body Expected by Christmas

The latest visitor from space to make the acquaintance of the solar system, the Skjellerup Comet, which has been making progress in a northerly direction ever since it was discovered by an amateur astronomer of Melbourne, Australia, on Dec. 3, was still invisible to New Yorkers at 5:30 Saturday afternoon. It had been announced in some quarters on Friday that the next day would mark the new comet's appearance over the local horizon.

Dr. Clyde Fisher, curator of astronomy at the American Museum of Natural History, has been looking for it at 5:30 o'clock, just after the sun has set.

"I couldn't pick it up," he said on Saturday. Yesterday he was not at the Museum.

Dr. Harold Jacoby of Columbia University said he thought the comet was "just below the horizon."

"When an object is below the horizon," he said, "you just plain can't see it."

He said that it was barely possible that the comet would be visible tonight at 5:30, or by Christmas, anyway.

The Skjellerup is now so close to the sun that a brilliant sunset would obscure it, even if it were above the horizon. It was discovered by F. J. Skjellerup, and since Dec. 3 it has been seen by persons in Argentina, Chile, Jamaica and other places near the Equator. It is very bright, according to reports from the Southern Hemisphere.

The comet is generally thought to be a new visitor, although there is a bare possibility, according to Dr. Fisher, that it may turn out to be one that was "discovered" many years ago. It will take close observation to be certain on this point, he said.

CAPITAL DUBIOUS ON MANY RESCUES

Crushing of Submarine's Hull Points to Loss of Life in Some Compartments.

SPEED NOW CHIEF FACTOR

Officials Have Full Confidence in Forces Engaged in the Rescue Operations.

Special to The New York Times.

WASHINGTON, Dec. 18.—News that at least six men were still alive in the sunken S-4 was sent to the Navy Department early this evening by Rear Admiral Brumby, who is in charge of the rescue operations off off the tip of Cape Cod. He stated that the information had come from the locked room by means of hammer knocks executed in the Morse code against the side of the submarine. The rescue party in this manner asked questions of and received responses from some of the six who survive. There was no evidence so far, he reported that any one was alive in the submarine other than in the torpedo room.

Rear Admiral Brumby's message read:

> Blowing (air) from the Falcon to the tanks. Air now being hooked up to torpedo compartment.
>
> Following messages sent and received from and to S-4:
>
> First question: "Is gas bad?"
>
> Answer: "No, but the air, how long will you be now?"
>
> Second question: "How many are there?"
>
> Answer: "There are six; please hurry. Will you be long now?"
>
> Answer: "We are doing everything possible."
>
> These messages were by hammer knocks in the Morse code.
>
> No evidence so far that any one is alive anywhere but in the torpedo room.

Admiral Hughes, chief of naval operations, who had been on duty in the Navy Department since 7 o'clock this morning, working on rescue plans, telephoned the message to Secretary Wilbur as soon as it was received.

The Secretary was informed that submarine S-8 was being used in pumping air into the S-4 and that still another submarine, the S-3, has been ordered from Portsmouth, N. H., to the scene.

Previous to this word a dispatch came from Provincetown stating that divers had heard taps from within the submarine in response to their signals.

These sounds came from the torpedo room, which is just forward of the battery room which was shattered by the impact of the collision. Aft of the battery compartment, in the order named, are the control, engine and motor rooms.

Hope is held here that members of the S-4's personnel may be still alive in the engine and motor rooms but none that were caught in the control and battery compartments have survived.

The afternoon dispatch which came from Rear Admiral Brumby read:

> Divers have examined hull and found large hole starboard side 8 feet forward of gun, and in to about centre line. Knocks on torpedo room were answered.
>
> No answers from control room.
>
> No signals possible to engine and motor rooms due to tangled wires on deck.
>
> Divers now securing salvage airline to tanks.

Navy Department officials believe the divers will find a way to establish communication with the men in the engine and motor rooms if any are still living in those compartments. The failure to receive signals from the two central sections of the boat—the control and battery rooms—caused no surprise to those familiar with the submarine's construction, their conjecture being that

Continued on Page Two.

AIR IS BAD, VICTIMS SAY

Faint Sound Once Heard Aft in Vessel, Diver Thought.

BATTERY ROOM CRUSHED

Three to Twelve Men Met Certain Death There, Captain King Declares.

AIR PUMPED INTO TANKS

Rescue Crews Try to Up-End Ill-Fated Craft While Waiting for Pontoons.

From a Staff Correspondent of The New York Times.

PROVINCETOWN, Mass., Dec. 18.—At least six men are alive tonight in the sunken hull of the submarine S-4, which was rammed outside the harbor here yesterday by a Coast Guard boat and went to the bottom with some forty-odd men aboard.

This announcement was made tonight by Rear Admiral Frank Brumby, directing the efforts to bring the disabled craft to the surface and save the lives of the members of the crew. Admiral Brumby based his statement on a report received from a diver who went down 101 feet to the mudbank on which the submarine rests, to converse in code with those inside a forward compartment by hammering on the side of the steel hull.

"How long will you be?" was the pathetic message tapped out by the imprisoned men. The diver answered that everything possible was being done.

"Is the gas bad?" the diver asked.

"No, but the air is," was the reply from inside the hull.

"How many are you?" was slowly tapped out with the diver's hammer.

"Six," was the response. "Please hurry."

Catches Signals From Inside.

It was just about twenty-four hours after the S-4 was rammed and sunk by the Coast Guard destroyer Paulding a mile outside the harbor that the diver, a crack navy expert, working far beneath the surface of a turbulent sea, caught the signals from inside the forward compartment.

The diver reported to Admiral Brumby that the living men who responded to his signals were in the forward part of the submerged vessel. He also brought up an account of heavy damage to the battery room and to the stern of the ship.

This report of the damage to the S-4, which went down after a collision with the Coast Guard boat while running submerged, caused Captain Ernest L. King, submarine rescue specialist, to declare that at least three or four of the crew had been killed in the battery room, which was crushed. There might have been a dozen or more men there, he said.

But with Rear Admiral Brumby affirming that some men were surely alive in the torpedo room forward, Captain King joined him in declaring he would do everything possible with the fleet of rescue ships here to save the lives of all who might be still fighting for existence.

Describes Damage to Craft.

Thomas Eadie, a diver whose rank is that of chief torpedo-man, went down at 3:13 P. M. He did not come up until 4:30, when he made a hurried report to Captain King and Rear Admiral Brumby.

Eadie said he was certain that the men alive were in the forward torpedo room. He told of his hammer signals and of receiving signals in reply.

Heartened by what he heard, he said, he began to explore. As he made his way carefully toward the stern he saw the signs of the severe damage done to the submarine in the crash. The conning tower, he declared, was ripped apart.

Closer examination revealed that a hole had been pierced in the battery chamber. Eadie said that this hole had apparently been opened by the prow of the Paulding. Further toward the stern the damage seemed worse.

The diver told of getting tangled in the wreckage of the superstructure that cluttered the muddy water and of finding it hazardous to proceed. Despite the danger he pushed his way around the craft, resuming his hamering and his listening.

Heard Sound in Rear Room.

Once, Eadie said, he thought he heard a signal from inside a rear compartment. He could not be sure though that what he heard indicated more life in the stern of the boat.

Eadie went back to his examination of the damage. The battery compartment hole was on the starboard side. It was serious.

When Captain King was asked the significance of Eadie's discoveries, he said:

"We are certain that men are alive aboard the submarine and we are going to do our best to get them out safely.

"The damage is apparently serious

"All the News That's Fit to Print."

The New York Times.

THE WEATHER
Showers today, probably tomorrow; not much change in temperature.
Temperature yesterday—Max. [illegible] Min. [illegible]
For weather report see Page [illegible].

VOL. LXXVII....No. 25,714 ••• NEW YORK, TUESDAY, JUNE 19, 1928. TWO CENTS in Greater New York | THREE CENTS Within 200 Miles | FOUR CENTS Elsewhere in the U. S.

AMELIA EARHART FLIES ATLANTIC, FIRST WOMAN TO DO IT; TELLS HER OWN STORY OF PERILOUS 21-HOUR TRIP TO WALES; RADIO QUIT AND THEY FLEW BLIND OVER INVISIBLE OCEAN

RITCHIE WITHDRAWS IN FAVOR OF SMITH, URGING PARTY UNITY

New Yorker's Nomination Will Assure Democratic Victory, He Asserts.

DIRECTS APPEAL TO SOUTH

Smith as President Would Restore Popular Government, Maryland Executive Says.

TURNS OVER HIS DELEGATES

Sees Struggle of 1924 Avoided at Houston—Reed Still in Race, Backer Declares.

Special to The New York Times.

BALTIMORE, June 18.—Governor Albert C. Ritchie tonight withdrew as candidate for the Democratic Presidential nomination, with the announcement that he would instruct the Maryland delegation to cast its sixteen votes at the National Convention at Houston next week for Governor Smith of New York.

In a formal statement, Governor Ritchie urged the Democratic Party to unite behind Governor Smith. The New York Executive, he declared, was "fitted by experience, character and ability to assume the leadership" of the party and had the best chance to win in the November election.

"His record is a guarantee that with him as President, honesty in Government would take the place of corruption in Government," he said of Governor Smith.

Governor Ritchie expressed his gratitude that Maryland had advanced his own name for the Presidential nomination. "The great majority of the Democratic Party in every section of the country" was ready to back Governor Smith, however, he said, and he felt a responsibility to the party so to declare himself.

Makes Especial Plea to South.

Mr. Ritchie directed his plea in behalf of Governor Smith particularly to the South. The national situation demanded, and pointed to, the success of the Democratic Party as the champion of self-government and popular self-rule, principles which the South through the Democratic Party had saved to the nation, he asserted.

He, "as a son of the South," had fought enthusiastically for these principles. As an American and as a Democrat, he now urged a "united and unbroken front" by the party to assure its success next Fall.

"Every Democrat should subordinate himself to this higher call for party unity," he said, to re-establish in national life those principles of which Governor Smith was the "exponent."

Governor Ritchie asserted that, in dropping his candidacy for the Presidential nomination, he also took himself out of the running for second place on the party ticket.

"I have not the slightest thought of the Vice Presidency, nor expectation of it being offered to me, or accepting it if it is," he said. "In taking this action, I do so without any ulterior motive whatsoever. It emanates from a profound sense of duty to the nation and to the Democratic Party, with which the country's well-being is inseparably bound up."

Governor Ritchie's Statement.

The following is Governor Ritchie's statement in full:

I am profoundly convinced that no consideration of self or of personal advancement on any one's part should be allowed to stand for one moment in the way of the success of the Democratic Party, which is the natural champion of self-government and popular self-rule.

These principles are challenging the attention of the country today as they have not done for years. To them I have dedicated such political effort as I am able to exert. Faith in them saved the South during the dark days of reconstruction and made possible a reunited and happy nation; and as a son of the South I have brought to the struggle for these principles the enthusiasm and the loyalty which came to me from ancestors who were ready to die, and some of whom did die, for the cause in which they believed.

As a Democrat I have regarded this struggle as a duty, and as an American I believe that the dictates of patriotism require the re-establishment of these principles in our national life.

That my own State should think me worthy to be the standard-bearer of the Democratic Party is a distinction for which I never can sufficiently express my gratitude, nor can I adequately express it to my friends elsewhere in the coun-

Continued on Page Ten.

President of Porto Rican Senate Stabbed And Badly Hurt by a Maniac Anarchist

Wireless to The New York Times.

SAN JUAN, Porto Rico, June 18.—Antonio Barcelo, President of the Porto Rican Senate, was stabbed with a chisel at the close of a welcoming demonstration at City Hall today and probably owes his life to the fact that he is fat.

The chisel made a four-inch wound, then was deflected by a rib.

Justo Matos, 35 years old and believed to be demented, who attempted the assassination with the unusual instrument, was himself shot through the abdomen by an unidentified bystander after police, they say, actually had him in custody. The condition of Matos is considered critical.

In their efforts to protect Matos police were unable to detect who had shot him.

The assault on Señor Barcelo took place at the close of a noisy welcome while hundreds of persons surged about him with greetings. Señor Barcelo was just returning home from New York where Columbia University gave him an honorary degree of Doctor of Laws and President Butler had referred to him as "captain of his island people."

By The Associated Press.

SAN JUAN, Porto Rico, June 18.—Señor Barcelo tonight was in a hospital undergoing treatment for his wound. Matos was in prison, heavily guarded to protect him from an outraged populace.

A huge crowd met Señor Barcelo at the docks and escorted him to the Plaza, where on a balcony overlooking the promenade he addressed them.

It was while he was speaking that Matos edged through the crowd, pushed his way onto the low balcony and wielded his chisel. The crowd apparently did not comprehend what had happened. There was a shot from somewhere and Matos was seen to fall, writhing in pain, on the street level, where police took charge of him.

At the hospital, where Señor Barcelo was taken, doctors declined to state whether the wound was likely to prove fatal.

The motive for Matos's action is not known. Some in the crowd who noticed him before his deed said he remarked he was ill, and then added that he could kill ten Porto Ricans willingly.

The stabbing itself, perhaps by coincidence, followed the statement in Señor Barcelo's speech that he was not a member of any political party or faction but a Porto Rican, and was proud of the honor accorded him by Columbia University not so much for his own sake as that it went to a citizen of his country.

La Democratica, Señor Barcelo's newspaper, this afternoon said Matos had visited their office and the Barcelo home for a week asking when the legislator would return here. Other afternoon papers refer to him as a "Socialist fanatic," and one calls him a "confessed anarchist."

SMITH SUPPORTERS SEE A QUICK VICTORY

Hope Ritchie's Withdrawal in Favor of Governor Will Be Followed by Others.

AIDES START FOR HOUSTON

Van Namee, Sure of Success, Says "Steam-Roller" Methods Will Not Be Used.

With George R. Van Namee, manager of Governor Smith's preconvention campaign for the Democratic nomination, speeding toward Houston to open headquarters in the Hotel Rice, Smith supporters here were jubilant last night at the announcement by Governor Ritchie of Maryland that he would advise the sixteen delegates from that State to cast their votes for New York's Governor on the first ballot.

Mr. Van Namee predicted, just as he boarded the train at Grand Central Station yesterday noon, that Governor Smith would be nominated on "an early ballot." The more optimistic Smith supporters contended last night that the first ballot would show a strength of 704 votes, or 29 1-3 short of the number required for nomination. The hope was expressed that Governor Ritchie's action might swing other State delegations into line before the voting starts at Houston, in which event Governor Smith might be nominated on the first ballot.

Rules Out "Steam Roller" Plan.

While declining to name the ballot on which he believed Governor Smith would be nominated, Mr. Van Namee declared that with 650 delegates already instructed and many others known to favor the Smith candidacy, his nomination was practically assured. The Smith forces, Mr. Van Namee declared, would not attempt any "steam-roller" methods at Houston and would seek in no way to prevent any candidate from presenting his claims to the nomination. The Smith forces, he added, are concerned with promoting party harmony.

With Mr. Van Namee were Mrs. Van Namee, Howard Cullman of the Port of New York Authority and George C. Norton. Norman E. Mack, Democratic National Com-

Continued on Page Nine.

12 INJURED BY BOMB 'PLANTED' IN DETROIT

County Building Shaken, Windows Shattered and Hundreds Panic-Stricken.

'PURPLE' GANG SUSPECTED

Darrow Attending Court Case Is Jarred—Jokes With Judge About Blast.

Special to The New York Times.

DETROIT, June 18.—A devastating blast which injured twelve county employes, two seriously, shattered dozens of panes of glass and rocked the Wayne County Building to its foundation this afternoon is believed by police to have been another attempt at intimidation of the courts by sympathizers with the "Purple" gang, nine members of which are now on trial on charges of conspiracy to extort.

"The dynamite bomb evidently was intended for the Municipal Courts Building, where the 'Purples' are on trial," Police Inspector John T. Doyle of the First Precinct declared, "but as usual in such cases some stranger was hired to plant the bomb and probably mistook the county building for the City Courts building.

"It is a miracle no one was killed. The bomb was a powerful one. If it had exploded in the confined space of the rest room instead of in the courtway I believe it would have wrecked the building and killed many persons."

The explosion occurred at about 2:50 o'clock. The bomb was left in the men's room on the first floor and was found by Frank Stolpa, a constable, who tossed it into the areaway in the centre of the building and was trying to extinguish it with water when it exploded.

One May Lose an Eye.

Stolpa and Arthur Vercrusse, another constable, who also helped in the efforts to extinguish the bomb, were struck in the face by flying glass and bits of iron from the bomb and taken to Receiving Hospital for treatment. Vercrusse, according to the physicians, may lose the sight of his right eye.

About 100 men and women clerks,

Continued on Page Fourteen.

Keel Laid for Biggest Ship, 1,000 Feet Long; 60,000-Ton 'Oceanic' to Cost $30,000,000

Wireless to The New York Times.

LONDON, June 18.—The biggest ship in the world was begun today at Harland & Wolff's shipyards in Belfast, when the keel was laid for a giant White Star liner to cost $30,000,000. She will be more than 1,000 feet long, with a beam of 100 feet and tonnage of about 60,000.

The ship will not be ready for sailing until 1932, and experts have yet to decide what type of machinery will be installed in her.

When the new ship is added to the White Star fleet she will be called the Oceanic. The six largest steamships in service at the present time, all in the Atlantic trade, are:

The Leviathan of the United States Lines, 59,957 gross tonnage, 907 feet long and 100 feet 3 inches beam.

The Majestic of the White Star Line, claimed by some to be the largest liner afloat, on the basis of the builder and designer's pre-war measurements, which are 56,551 gross tons, 915 feet 5 inches long and 100 feet 1 inch beam.

The Cunarder Berengaria, 52,226 gross tonnage, 883 feet 5 inches long and 98 feet 3 inches beam.

The White Star Olympic, 46,439 gross tonnage, 882 feet 5 inches long, 92 feet 5 inches beam.

The Cunarder Aquitania, 45,647 gross tonnage, 868 feet 7 inches long and 97 feet beam.

The new French liner Ile de France, 43,500 gross tonnage, 757 feet 8 inches long and 91 feet 8 inches beam.

NOBILE VAINLY HAILS FLIERS CIRCLING OVER BUT NOT SEEING HIM

General Radios Base Ship That Rescue Planes Were Over Stranded Men an Hour.

SECOND FLIGHT ALSO FAILS

This Time Italia Castaways Sight One of Planes Piloted by Riiser-Larsen and Holm.

SAVOIA REACHES KINGS BAY

Big Italian Seaplane Ready for Dash North—French and Swedish Craft on Way.

By The Associated Press.

ROME, June 18.—The two Norwegian fliers, Captain Riiser-Larsen and Lieutenant Luetzow Holm, today made a second unsuccessful attempt to find General Umberto Nobile and the party with him north of Spitsbergen. They returned to the icebreaker Braganza without having sighted the marooned men.

Nobile, however, informed the base ship Citta di Milano by wireless that he had seen one of the planes fly within two kilometers of him.

Snow Hides Frantic Signals.

Copyright, 1928, by The Associated Press.

KINGS BAY, Spitsbergen, June 18.—High overhead yesterday General Umberto Nobile saw two seaplanes sent to rescue him and his five comrades from the Arctic ice-floes, but frantic efforts to signal the planes or make known their existence below failed, and, after an hour's reconnaissance above, the craft were seen to disappear in the grim Arctic horizon, flying back toward Spitsbergen.

This news came to the base-ship Citta di Milano today by wireless from the stranded Italia commander, who for days has been awaiting on slowly moving floe ice sight of some one from the outside world who might aid in returning him and his mates on the Italia to civilization and home.

Sunday they thought their days of watching perhaps over. But they failed to count on the trickiness of the snow with visibility, and when help had passed them by their situation was if anything more difficult than before.

Good Visibility of No Avail.

The two seaplanes were those piloted by Captain Riiser-Larsen and Lieutenant Leutzow Holm, the Norwegian fliers. Both set out early Sunday and took a course over Beverly Sound, North Cape and Cape Platen, keeping at a height of from 750 to 900 feet. Both planes carried provisions and clothes for the stranded men.

Visibility was good, but when they returned to Spitsbergen they had not seen a trace of the Italia's commander and the remnant of his crew or of the silk tent he had painted red to aid them. This despite the fact that messages from General Nobile indicated that they had remained above him and in the vicinity for more than an hour.

Today Captain Riiser-Larsen and Lieutenant Holm set out for further reconnaissance, intending, if there were to be variations at all in their course, to keep between their route yesterday and the coast of Northeast Land.

No Chance to Land Amid Ice.

The fliers, on returning yesterday, said that in the area where the fliers are supposed to be they found the ice much too rough for landing. They said that the ice floes were opening considerably, but that the cracks and openings were still too narrow for landing attempts by the seaplanes. They were such, however, as to foster progress by the ice breakers.

In his message to the Citta di Milano conveying the tragic irony of the situation, General Nobile, to aid further searches, gave his present position as 80.33 north and 17.12 east. This would put him about five miles to the east of Foyn Island.

Savoia's Arrival Raises Hopes.

The hydro-airplane Savoia-55, piloted by Major Maddalena, arrived here at 10:45 o'clock tonight. She was the first of the four big seaplanes en route to Spitsbergen to reach the Northern base.

Fine weather was in evidence as the big machine settled in the harbor. Her arrival and the news that at least two others of large cargo and passenger capacity were en route, raised hopes of the watchers here who for weeks have been trying to get into direct touch with General Nobile and the other survivors of the Italia.

It was a bit uncertain as to whether

Continued on Page Six.

Photo copyrighted by G. P. Putnam.

FIRST WOMAN TO FLY THE ATLANTIC.

Amelia Earhart, Co-pilot of the Airplane Friendship, Photographed in Boston, Just Before She Started on Her Great Adventure.

Eager Crowds Imperil Miss Earhart As They Welcome Fliers at Burry Port

Police Aid Weary Trio to Battle Way to Refuge in Zinc Works—Friends Fly From Southampton to Greet Them and Hear Story of Their Adventures.

By ALLEN RAYMOND.

Special Cable to The New York Times.

BURRY PORT, Carmarthenshire, South Wales, June 18.—The first woman to cross the Atlantic successfully by air, Miss Amelia Earhart, Boston settlement worker, alighted in the seaplane Friendship here this morning on the broad expanse of Loughor estuary, after a flight of 20 hours and 40 minutes elapsed time from Trepassey.

Few persons saw the gilt-winged Fokker monoplane descend on the Welsh coast, but this evening, when friends rushing from Southampton brought Miss Earhart ashore, she was the recipient of so enthusiastic a reception by the 2,000 inhabitants of this town that it seemed for a few minutes as if she would not outlive her triumph.

Eager Crowds Imperil Aviatrix.

The arrival of the Friendship was the greatest event this remote district has had since the end of the World War when the town's boys came home. Miss Earhart was nearly crushed by the anxiety of the crowd of men, women and children to touch the hem of her flying suit, get her autograph on a slip of paper, wring her hand and congratulate her upon her triumphant passage over the Atlantic.

The High Sheriff of Carmarthenshire, who had rowed out to greet her; the town's three policemen and a couple of friends had to form a ring with locked arms about the latest popular heroine and literally to fight their way a hundred yards from the shore to the office of the local zinc works, where they found shelter back of locked doors.

"You must remember," the local Police Chief said apologetically, "that our people never saw anything to compare with this. I advise you to remain here until we get extra police."

The Friendship's crew were marooned within the walls of the Frickers Metal Company an hour and a half before police reinforcements arrived and cleared a way to two motor cars to take them to a distant hotel where rest, food and sleep could be obtained after their arduous journey.

Poor Visibility Forced Landing.

Poor visibility forced the plane to come down on the Welsh coast after the first tentative objective—Valentia, Ireland—had been left far behind, but the possible goal of Southampton not yet reached.

Except for the first hour over the Atlantic after leaving the rugged shores of Newfoundland, the fliers never saw sea or land until they had winged their way to the Eastern Irish coast. They flew through fog, rain and snow most of the time, fighting for altitude and clearer weather, but they came fast with the wind behind of twenty to thirty miles per hour speeding them on.

They probably had plenty of gasoline left, when they descended, to reach Southampton—seventy-five gallons—but were struggling in the midst of dense fog and knew they were somewhere off the southern coast of Britain. With their object attained—that of making Miss Earhart the first woman to complete a transatlantic crossing—they decided to take no further risks.

They will go on to Southampton tomorrow.

Stultz and Gordon Elated.

The full story of the flight has yet to be told. The two airmen, Stultz and Gordon, who had the major responsibility and labor of getting the Friendship safely across the ocean, were soon fast asleep after battling their way to the hotel. Both ejaculated their joy at their success and chuckled together over the moments in mid-ocean when they seemed dubious of the outcome.

Miss Earhart, who came through her experience in fine condition and

Continued on Page Two.

FOUGHT RAIN, FOG AND SNOW ALL THE WAY

Miss Earhart Says Motors Spat and Gas Ran Low, But She Had Neither Fear Nor Doubt of Success.

PASSED OVER IRELAND WITHOUT EVEN SEEING IT

Wind Aided Plane—Girl Credits Feat to Stultz and Gordon—She Flew Because It Would Have Been 'Too Inartistic to Refuse.'

By AMELIA EARHART.

Special Cable to The New York Times.

BURRY PORT, Carmarthenshire, South Wales, June 18.—I have arrived and I am happy—naturally.

Why did I do it? When one is offered such a tremendous adventure it would be too inartistic to refuse it. I have been a flier for years. I had planned to spend my vacation flying. I knew the moment this chance came to me that if I turned it down I would never forgive myself.

My trip across the Atlantic aboard the airplane Friendship was all I had imagined it to be as pleasure, and much more, though pretty uncomfortable at times. This is my first trip to England, and it is rather funny dropping in by airplane. Nevertheless I hope to make the trip again some day and make it in the same way by air. What I wanted to demonstrate in this flight was that this type of travel was comparatively safe and ought to be developed.

Gives Great Credit to Companions.

I was a passenger on the journey—just a passenger. Everything that was done to bring us across was done by Wilmer Stultz and "Slim" Gordan. Any praise I can give them they ought to have. You can't pile it on too thick.

Transoceanic flying has to be done by pilots who can fly by instruments alone. I am afraid that some accidents which marred past flights have been caused by pilots not too sure of instrument flying.

Despite the fact that the weather reports promised us fine visibility and fair weather, we had fog, rain and even snow practically all the way across. We only had clear weather for one hour out of the twenty-two we were on the way.

The reason we came down here was because we could not see anything. We had just about enough gasoline left, we reckoned, to make Southampton, but we did not dare attempt it because we were flying blind and we knew we had come across. We will go on there tomorrow.

Calls Waiting the Worst Part.

To go back to the beginning, the hardest strain of all this flight in a way was the waiting at Trepassey. The flight, of course, was a climax piled on top of this worry. That is what made it so tiring. But we had been trying so much to take off at Trepassey that all I can remember thinking of when we took off was that at last we were on the way. I was not really sure till we had flown for half an hour along the coast and headed against the open sea, because I knew that if everything was not all right Bill would go back.

When we started there was such a burst of spray that the outside motors started cutting out. I was afraid we had made another false start, but the motors picked up again, and although they stammered once in a while on the flight when coated with snow, I never had a moment of real trepidation about them and never doubted that we should arrive.

I did not do much. I did not handle the controls once, although I have had more than 500 hours' solo flying and once held the women's altitude record. When Bill Stultz left the controls to work the radio "Slim" would take them.

Thought of Fishing in Newfoundland.

We got two messages from ships on the way, and when I found out what ships they were I did a lot of thinking and jotted down a lot of notes about my feelings, which I hope to expand some day, perhaps.

Leaving the American coast, it was beautiful weather. The jagged coastline beneath us had a grandeur one never forgets, and passing over Newfoundland one could see lots of lakes where they told me there were good trout. I hope to fish there some time.

Beneath us the water was wonderful greens and blues, and everything was serene, though, of course the first thing we did was to start looking for the fog which we knew would meet us off Newfoundland. The first hour over the open sea was the only time we saw it. We did not even see Ireland, though we passed right over it, but when we knew we were over Southern England we could not establish any landmarks and our radio had quit us. We do not know yet how it got out of order, but it was all right when Bill worked it last night and no good when he tried it this morning.

Marvelous Colors in the Clouds.

Last night was gorgeous. The billows of fog shot with pink seemed like a vast sunlit desert, and even when night came there was an interesting color effect. There was the glow of

"All the News That's Fit to Print."

The New York Times.

LATE EDITION
5:30 A.M.
WEATHER—Fair today; cloudy tomorrow.

VOL. LXXVIII....No. 25,855. NEW YORK, WEDNESDAY, NOVEMBER 7, 1928. TWO CENTS in Greater New York | THREE CENTS Within 200 Miles | FOUR CENTS Elsewhere in the U. S.

HOOVER WINS 407 TO 69; DOUBTFUL 55; SMITH LOSES STATE; SOUTH BROKEN; ROOSEVELT IS ELECTED GOVERNOR

HOOVER CARRIES ILLINOIS, SWEEPING IN THE STATE TICKET

Smith Wins in Chicago, but His Republican Rival Gets Big Down-State Vote.

IOWA STRONG FOR HOOVER

Nebraska Puts Republican in Lead and His Victory Seems Certain.

MICHIGAN ALSO REPUBLICAN

Hoover Sweeps Ohio by a Big Majority—Entire State Ticket Elected.

Special to The New York Times.

CHICAGO, Nov. 6.—Illinois went Republican today. Herbert Hoover and the State ticket, headed by Louis L. Emmerson, candidate for Governor, and Otis F. Glenn, nominee for United States Senator, won by such large figures in down-State territory that close battles over some of the places in Cook County were eliminated.

Although he apparently lost Chicago to Governor Smith, incomplete returns indicated that Hoover had carried Cook County, which was counted upon by the Democrats as certain for their entire ticket.

The figures received as this is written forecast a Smith victory in Chicago by about 40,000 and informal reports from the suburbs of the county promised a Republican lead of 73,000.

The vote of 3,208 precincts out of 6,942, including 1,816 from Cook County, gave Hoover 741,167; Smith 604,811. The Republican nominee for President apparently won the State by about 400,000.

Emmerson and his fellow contestants for State executive office apparently fell considerably behind Hoover both in Cook County and down-State, but all apparently were safe on the face of the incomplete figures.

Close Race for Senatorship.

The closest race of all was that for United States Senator which the first reports indicated might be a neck and neck race because of the way that Anton J. Cermak, the "wet" Democrat ran ahead of Governor Smith in Chicago. The first big batch of city precincts to be heard from promised him a Chicago lead of from 250,000 to 275,000.

It was thought that Glenn might not be able to overcome this in the down-State territory because the figures on the Governorship which had been received more fully did not indicate that Emmerson would carry down-State by quite that big a margin. But when the outside counties began to report the returns forecast a margin for Glenn outside Chicago in excess of 350,000.

Cermak was the only Democrat who leaped ahead of his national ticket in Chicago. Floyd E. Thompson, Democratic gubernatorial entry, was allowed by his party to trail Governor Smith and also Thomas J. Courtney, nominee for Attorney General against Oscar E. Carlstrom, the Republican who now holds that office.

The returns on these offices were far ahead of those for the rest of the offices on the State ticket, but Hoover's lead and the leads of Glenn, Emmerson and Carlstrom were taken as proof that all the Republican entries had carried the State.

On incomplete returns Judge William J. Lindsay, Democrat, was leading Judge John A. Swanson, Republican, for State's Attorney, the centre of the battle over Cook County offices.

In the battle over lucrative berths on the Board of Review, Thomas D. Nash, Democrat, is leading Edward R. Litsinger, Republican.

Much Splitting of Votes.

Scattering precinct figures from all the wards, indicate a day of prodigious vote splitting.

The Crowe-Thompsonites whetted their axes for the Dineen Republican candidates, and vice versa. Indications are that if Judge Lindsay maintains his early lead, the entire Democratic ticket may win. Figures on other candidates are slow in arriving but they indicate that the Crowe-Thompson machine was caught in another avalanche, similar to the one that struck it in the popular uprising at the April primaries.

In the fight for drainage trusteeships, where the Crowe-Thompson

Continued on Page Four.

U.S. Senators Elected

REPUBLICAN—18	
California	*H. W. Johnson
Connecticut	‡F. C. Walcott
Delaware	John G. Townsend Jr.
Idaho	§John Thomas
Illinois	§Otis F. Glenn
Indiana	*A. R. Robinson
Maine	‡Frederick Hale
Maryland	‡P. L. Goldsborough
Michigan	†A. H. Vandenberg
Nebraska	*Robert B. Howell
New Jersey	‡Hamilton F. Kean
North Dakota	*Lynn J. Frazier
Ohio	*Simeon D. Fess
Ohio	§T. E. Burton
Pennsylvania	*David A. Reed
Rhode Island	‡Felix Hebert
Vermont	*Frank L. Greene
Wisconsin	*R. M. La Follette Jr.
DEMOCRATS—9	
Arizona	*Henry F. Ashurst
Florida	*Park Trammell
Massachusetts	*David I. Walsh
Mississippi	*H. D. Stephens
New York	*R. S. Copeland
Tennessee	*Kenneth McKellar
Texas	‡Tom Connally
Utah	*William H. King
Virginia	*C. A. Swanson
FARMER-LABORITE—1	
Minnesota	*Henrik Shipstead
IN DOUBT—7	
Missouri	New Mexico
Montana	Washington
Nevada	West Virginia
	Wyoming

*Re-elected for full term ending March 3, 1935.
†Elected for both long and short terms.
‡Elected for full term ending March 3, 1935.
¶Re-elected Sept. 10, 1928, for full term ending March 3, 1935.
§Elected for short term ending March 3, 1929.

BAY STATE IS CLOSE, WITH SMITH AHEAD

Walsh, Democrat, Re-elected to Senate and Cole Is in Front for Governor.

SMITH WINS RHODE ISLAND

But State Ticket Goes Republican—Other New England States for Hoover.

Special to The New York Times.

BOSTON, Mass., Nov. 7.—At 4:30 o'clock this morning, after one of the liveliest election nights ever known in Massachusetts, and when it appeared that the Democrats had swept the State, there was a possibility that Herbert Hoover, though trailing Governor Smith, might receive the eighteen electoral votes of this State.

At the same time there was a probability that the fiani returns would show Frank G. Allen winner of the Gubernatorial contest over his Democratic opponent, General Charles H. Cole, despite the latter's lead.

Senator David D. Walsh, Democrat, running 10,000 votes ahead of Governor Smith, was clearly re-elected over Benjamin Loring Young, Republican.

Smith Carries Textile Cities.

From early in the evening, when Hoover had built up a substantial lead, the returns from Boston and some textile centres pulled him down and pushed Smith out in front.

Then followed a see-sawing back and forth, with Smith slowly forging ahead in the early morning hours, largely as a result of 10,000-vote margins which were given to him in Fall River and Lowell, 4,000 in New Bedford, 5,000 in Salem, 7,000 in Holyoke, and lesser votes in other cities.

For President, 962 precincts out of the 1,605 in the State gave Hoover 405,125, Smith 426,509.

For Governor, 848 precincts, including 300 of the 339 in Boston, gave Allen (R.) 346,495, Cole (D.) 351,091.

For Senator, 848 precincts gave Young (R.) 312,586, Walsh (D.) 321,002.

Unofficial Boston figures for 319 precincts out of 339 gave Hoover

Continued on Page Two.

NEW JERSEY GIVES REPUBLICAN SLATE A HEAVY MAJORITY

Incomplete Figures for State Show Hoover Leads Smith by 116,944.

LARSON AHEAD OF DILL

Victory for Republican by 166,340 Is Indicated in Gubernatorial Race

KEAN BEATING EDWARDS

Strong Republican Showing Is a Damaging Blow to Prestige of Hague as Leader.

Herbert Hoover's indicated plurality in New Jersey was 309,420 early this morning when the tabulation of returns from 1,102 of the 2,920 districts gave Hoover 303,792 and Smith 186,848. In the metropolitan district of New Jersey the Republican and Democratic candidates ran a close race.

In Essex County, which includes Newark, tabulation of the vote in 150 of the 481 districts showed that it stood, Hoover, 39,122; Smith, 31,810.

Hamilton F. Kean was leading Senator Edward I. Edwards, Democrat, by 91,021 in 1,102 districts and his indicated plurality was 239,440.

Larson in the Lead.

In the Gubernatorial contest the returns from 1,102 districts gave Larson 269,391 and Dill 205,692, giving Larson, Republican, a lead of 63,699 and an indicated plurality of 166,340.

In 75 of 506 districts in Hudson County, the stronghold of Mayor Frank Hague, the vote was: Hoover 9,106, Smith, 18,302, Kean 10,204, Edwards 18,896, Larson 10,302, Dill 18,107.

Increasing Republican pluralities reported from the counties of Southern New Jersey were not offset by expected Democratic gains in the metropolitan area.

Republican candidates for Congress were leading their opponents in all counties except Hudson, and Republican candidates for the Assembly were reported generally in the lead in all but counties which are now represented in the Assembly by Democrats.

While the Republicans of Camden County were celebrating the success of their State and national tickets there, State Senator Joseph H. Forsyth was reported to be dying from influenza at his home at Haddonfield. He was stricken several days ago. He was elected in 1926 for three years.

Reports from Trenton were to the effect that a plurality of from 150,000 to 200,000 for Hoover was indicated by the early returns. According to The Associated Press fifty-six districts out of 2,920 in strongly Republican territory gave Hoover a lead of 5,456 over Smith. The vote was Hoover 9,078 and Smith 3,622.

The first 12,000 ballots tabulated in Jersey City gave Smith 7,761 votes, Hoover 4,024, Edwards 7,405, Kean 4,037, Dill 7,276, Larson 4,320.

Forty-five districts reported in the United States Senatorial and Gubernatorial races. These gave Kean, Republican, 7,080; Senator Edwards, Democrat, 3,217. The Governorship figures were William L. Dill, Democrat, 3,580; Morgan F. Larson, Republican, 6,989.

The indicated heavy pluralities of the Republican candidates for United States Senator and Governor were a damaging blow to the prestige of Mayor Hague, Vice Chairman of the Democratic National Committee, whose Democratic stronghold in Hudson has been sufficiently powerful in three Gubernatorial elections to stem the Republican tide in other sections of New Jersey and send Democratic candidates to the Governor's Mansion and to the Senate.

Fight in Hudson County.

The fight of Mayor Frank Hague of Jersey City, Democratic leader in Hudson County, was responsible for the action of election officials in striking the names of apporximately 29,000 voters from the enrollment lists. It was reported that several thousand voters had been disfranchised in Hudson County because of inability of the Commissioner of Registration to deal with the situation resulting from the County Board of Election's ruling at the eleventh hour. Election officials re-

Continued on Page Eighteen.

Gov. Smith's Message to Mr. Hoover

Governor Smith sent the following telegram just after midnight to his successful rival:

Hon. Herbert Hoover,
Palo Alto, Cal.:

I congratulate you heartily on your victory, and extend to you my sincere good wishes for your health and happiness and for the success of your Administration.

ALFRED E. SMITH.

Electoral Vote

HOOVER.			
Arizona	3	Nevada	3
California	13	New Hampshire	4
Colorado	6	New Jersey	14
Connecticut	7	New Mexico	3
Delaware	3	New York	45
Florida	6	Ohio	24
Idaho	4	Oklahoma	10
Illinois	29	Oregon	5
Indiana	15	Pennsylvania	38
Iowa	13	South Dakota	5
Kansas	10	Tennessee	12
Kentucky	13	Utah	4
Maine	6	Vermont	4
Maryland	8	Virginia	12
Michigan	15	Washington	7
Minnesota	12	West Virginia	8
Missouri	18	Wisconsin	13
Montana	4	Wyoming	3
Nebraska	8	Total	407
SMITH.			
Alabama	12	Mississippi	10
Arkansas	9	Rhode Island	5
Georgia	14	South Carolina	9
Louisiana	10	Total	69
DOUBTFUL.			
Massachusetts	18	Texas	20
North Carolina	12	Total	55
North Dakota	5		

Total number of votes in Electoral College, 531; necessary to a choice, 266.

HOOVER BREAKS THE SOLID SOUTH

He Carries Virginia and Probably Florida and North Carolina—Leads in Texas Also.

Special to The New York Times.

RICHMOND, Va., Nov. 6.—Herbert Hoover has carried the Old Dominion and broken the Solid South.

State Democratic headquarters authorized the statement before midnight:

"he unofficial returns indicate that Virginia has gone for Hoover."

At a late hour he had obtained a 21,000 lead over Governor Smith, with two-thirds of the State polled. His plurality had been steadily mounting from the start.

The totals in 1,429 precincts out of 1,665 were: Hoover, 145,641; Smith, 124,520.

Fifteen of forty precincts in Richmond gave Hoover 2,253 and Smith 2,391.

Danville has gone for Hoover. It is a Ku Klux Klan stronghold, but Democrats were as thoroughly organized there as anywhere in the State.

Hoover, as expected, polled heavy votes in the first and second districts while Smith showed great strength in the fourth.

Only in the ninth district did the returns look normal. There were fewer Democratic defections than in other parts of the State, and Hoover and Smith were running neck and neck.

Hoover Leads in Texas.

DALLAS, Texas, Nov. 6 (AP).—The possibility that a Republican Presidential candidate might carry Texas for the first time in history loomed late tonight as Herbert Hoover, for the third time during the tabulation of the vote, went into the lead.

The 11 o'clock tabulation of the Texas Election Bureau showed the Republican ahead by 2,[illegible] votes, with more than half of the ballots counted. It was the largest lead either candidate had gained in the nip and tuck race. Hoover's total, as computed by the bureau, was 208,415, Smith's 205,560. Later a count of 214 counties out of 253, four

Continued on Page Two.

CITY GIVES SMITH 430,000 MAJORITY

Incomplete Count Also Indicates Like Lead for Roosevelt for Governor.

Governor Smith carried New York City by about 430,000 plurality over Mr. Hoover, or about 88,000 less than the plurality he received over Theodore Roosevelt in 1924, which was the largest plurality the city gave him in any of his Gubernatorial campaigns.

With only 28 out of the 3,493 election districts of the city missing, Smith had 1,106,524 against 680,074 for Hoover, a plurality of 426,450. Norman Thomas, Socialist candidate, received less than 50,000 in the city.

Franklin D. Roosevelt, Democratic candidate for Governor, ran behind Smith in the city. With 90 districts missing, Roosevelt had 1,087,418 against 699,441 for his Republican opponent, Attorney General Albert Ottinger, a plurality of 387,977.

Herbert H. Lehman, Democratic candidate for Lieutenant Governor, and United States Senator Royal S. Copeland, Democratic candidate for re-election to the Senate, ran ahead of their ticket in the city.

Lehman Has Big Lead.

With 193 districts missing, Lehman received 1,106,088 votes, against 614,241 for Mr. Lockwood, his Republican opponent, a plurality of 491,847.

With 668 districts missing, Copeland had 958,401 to 498,699 for Alanson B. Houghton, former Ambassador to Germany and Great Britain, the Republican candidate, a plurality of 459,702 for Copeland.

Albert Conway, Democratic candidate for Attorney General, and Maurice S. Tremaine, Democratic candidate for re-election as State Controller, also ran ahead of Smith in the city. With 283 districts missing, Conway had 1,020,920 votes against 564,486 for Hamilton Ward, Republican, a plurality of 456,184. With 285 districts missing, Tremaine had 1,056,027, against 565,780 for

Continued on Page Seven.

ROOSEVELT IS VICTOR BY SLIM PLURALITY; COPELAND ALSO WINS

Democratic Nominee Captures Governorship by Margin Indicated to Be 40,000.

SENATOR IN BY 56,000

Re-elected Over Houghton After Running Up Lead of 523,000 in the City.

LEAVES SMITH FAR BEHIND

Polls 90,000 More Votes Than the Governor—Lehman, Conway and Tremaine Leading.

Franklin D. Roosevelt, Democrat, defeated Attorney General Albert Ottinger, Republican, for the Governorship of New York State, on the basis of returns from 7,718 election districts out of the 8,267 in the State. A plurality of about 40,000 for Mr. Roosevelt was indicated on these figures, and it is possible that this plurality might be cut somewhat by the returns from the missing districts but not enough to give Mr. Ottinger the State.

Senator Royal S. Copeland, candidate for re-election on the Democratic ticket, apparently had won from former Ambassador Alanson B. Houghton by an indicated plurality of about 56,000. Senator Copeland ran surprisingly well in New York City, where his plurality seems likely to reach 523,000, or about 90,000 more than the plurality received by Governor Smith, heretofore regarded as the strongest candidate in the city, personally.

The victories for Mr. Roosevelt and Senator Copeland went some distance toward assuaging the local Democrats for Governor Smith's defeat. Governor Smith's indicated plurality in New York City was about 430,000, and his defeat in the State by about 125,000 was indicated.

Roosevelt Lead 65,565.

Mr. Roosevelt had an actual lead of 68,568, with 549 out of the 8,267 election districts in the State missing, the vote being Roosevelt 2,073,372 and Ottinger 1,954,754.

Outside New York City 4,298 election districts out of 4,774 gave Roosevelt 929,953 and Ottinger 1,257,002, an actual plurality of 327,049 and an indicated up-State plurality for Ottinger of 367,598.

In New York City 3,400 out of 3,393 election districts gave Roosevelt 1,093,369 and Ottinger 697,752, an actual plurality of 395,617 and an indicated plurality of 405,188.

Mr. Roosevelt ran ahead of Governor Smith in virtually every county up-State, while Mr. Ottinger cut into the Democratic vote somewhat in New York City, but not as much as expected.

Senator Copeland's run in New York City was surprising. In 3,144 out of the 3,493 election districts in the city he received 1,033,048 and Houghton 561,539, an actual plurality of 471,509 and an indicated plurality of 523,950.

To offset this tremendous plurality, seemingly the largest ever received in the city by any candidate, Mr. Houghton in 3,645 out of 4,774 Upstate election districts received 1,069,464 to 713,173 for Senator Copeland. This is an actual plurality of 356,291 and an indicated plurality of 467,852 for Mr. Houghton Upstate.

The delay in the returns from about a thousand up-State districts led Mr. Roosevelt to charge early this morning that there were indications which led him to suspect fraud up-State. He announced that Edward S. Dore, Chairman of the Law Committee of the Democratic State Committee, would leave for up-State this morning with a hundred lawyers ready to resist or prevent any fraud which might be attempted.

"Owing to the extreme delay with which about 1,000 districts up-State are sending in election returns, the Democratic State Committee has become convinced that fraud is being committed in an attempt to elect Ottinger as Governor of the State of New York," Mr. Roosevelt said.

"Accordingly, Mr. Dore, John Godfrey Saxe and Maurice Bloch, minority leader of the Assembly, are leaving New York City on the Empire State Express this (Wednesday) morning for up-State cities, together with a staff of 100 lawyers to uncover such frauds as have been com-

Continued on Page Two.

HOOVER CARRIES NEW YORK BY 125,000

Republican Nominee Captures New Jersey, Takes Wisconsin; Breaks Solid South, Winning Virginia, Florida

GAINING IN NORTH CAROLINA AND BAY STATE

Most of Farm Belt in Republican Column in Record-Breaking Vote—Kentucky, Missouri and Tennessee Lost to Democrats.

Voting in unprecedented numbers, a myriad of American citizens yesterday chose Herbert Hoover of California for President of the United States and Charles Curtis of Kansas for Vice President.

How pronounced is the victory of these candidates of the Republican Party over their Democratic competitors, Governor Alfred E. Smith of New York, nominee for President, and Joseph T. Robinson of Arkansas, the Vice Presidential nominee, cannot be determined until the stupendous task of counting 40,000,000 or more votes is completed, but a Republican landslide took place at the polls, and it will be reflected in a heavy Hoover-Curtis majority of the 531 ballots in the Electoral College.

490 Electoral Votes for Hoover

Mr. Hoover is assured of more than 490 electoral votes. It is probable that his majority will increase as further returns are received. He has broken the traditionally Democratic Solid South. He has carried Virginia and returns from Florida indicate that he has won in that State. His tally in the Electoral College may go as high as 444 votes if North Carolina, North Dakota and Texas, which are very close, are added to his strength, or even to the stupendous total of 462, if the count now proceeding in Massachusetts turns in his favor.

Such an outcome would give Mr. Hoover a majority of 397 electoral votes over Governor Smith. It is already apparent that no Presidential candidate of any major party has been beaten as badly as Governor Smith, with the exception of William H. Taft, who got only 8 votes in the Electoral College in his contest for re-election against Woodrow Wilson and Theodore Roosevelt.

According to the latest returns received from Massachusetts, North Carolina, North Dakota and Texas, these States are still in the doubtful column either by reason of inadequate returns or on account of the closeness of contests as the count proceeds, and while Governor Smith may be shown to have carried some of them, his tally of electoral votes may not exceed seventy.

New York Spells Smith's Doom.

Governor Smith's hope of victory began to fade within a few hours after the polls closed in New York State when it was indicated that he had carried New York City, his great stronghold, by less than 450,000, which was much short of the estimate of his managers. As returns began to roll in from up-State it became apparent that the Hoover plurality in that strong Republican area would materially overcome the showing for Governor Smith in New York City, with the prospect that the Republican nominee would carry the State by a lead in the neighborhood of 125,000.

With New York's forty-five electoral votes placed in the Hoover column it became merely a matter of waiting until the full returns determined what the Republican candidates' majority will be in the Electoral College. The tremendous onsweep of the Hoover following was emphasized when State after State in which the Democrats had placed hope of victory went over into the Republican camp.

New Jersey was carried by the Republican national ticket by a heavy majority. Maryland followed suit. Late returns show that Hoover also took Missouri. Of other border States, he captured Kentucky and Oklahoma. Minnesota, which the Smith management was also hopeful of carrying on account of the defection among Republican voters because of Mr. Hoover's attitude on the McNary-Haugen bill, gave him a heavy plurality.

Smith States Only in South.

As for Governor Smith, there is no assurance that he has carried any State outside of the South. With the results in Florida and Texas still in doubt he seems to be certain of having carried only Alabama, Georgia, Louisiana, Mississippi and South Carolina. In the early morning hours late returns had Hoover forging ahead even in North Carolina. Tennessee was conceded to the Republican candidate.

His victories in Alabama and North Carolina are a set back for Senator J. Thomas Heflin and Senator Furnifold M. Simmons, who deserted their party allegiances to oppose him, Simmons on the ground of Governor Smith's anti-prohibition policy and Senator Heflin for the openly stated reason that Governor Smith was a Catholic.

In the early morning hours returns from Wisconsin indicated that the portion of the State outside of Milwaukee had voted so heavily for Hoover that Smith's lead in the metropolis made famous by beer had been overcome and that the State's thirteen electoral votes would be added to the steadily mounting Hoover column.

It was after 4 o'clock this morning before virtually complete returns from Rhode Island showed that Smith had carried Rhode Island, the only State outside the Solid South that can with certainty be placed to his credit. He seems to have carried it by a small majority, probably not exceeding 2,000.

Maine, New Hampshire, Vermont and Connecticut joined the Republican procession. At an early hour this morning the prospect was that where the eighteen electoral votes of Massachusetts would go could not be made certain until late today.

Republican Congress Assured.

The victory for the Republican national ticket is accompanied by the assurance that, as President, Mr. Hoover will have the support of a Congress controlled by those of his own party. While returns are incomplete, the indications are that the Republican majority in the House of Representa-

"All the News That's Fit to Print."

The New York Times.

THE WEATHER
Cloudy, probably rain today and tomorrow; warmer tomorrow.
Temperatures yesterday—Max. [illegible], min. [illegible].
U. S. Weather Forecast—For details see Page [illegible].

VOL. LXXIX....No. 26,212. ****
NEW YORK, WEDNESDAY, OCTOBER 30, 1929.
TWO CENTS In Greater New York | THREE CENTS Within 200 Miles | FOUR CENTS Elsewhere Except 7th and 8th Postal Zones

STOCKS COLLAPSE IN 16,410,030-SHARE DAY, BUT RALLY AT CLOSE CHEERS BROKERS; BANKERS OPTIMISTIC, TO CONTINUE AID

GRUNDY FOR CURBING 'BACKWARD STATES' ON THE TARIFF BILL

Veteran Republican Lobbyist Tells Senate Inquiry the West Needs "Silencing."

PENNSYLVANIA KNOWS BEST

"Unfortunate," He Holds, That the Constitution Gives Equal Voice to States in Senate.

BATTLES INVESTIGATORS

He Assails Borah—Would "Hate to Tell" His Opinion of Wisconsin.

Special to The New York Times.

WASHINGTON, Oct. 29.—Joseph R. Grundy, president of the Pennsylvania Manufacturers' Association, told the Senate Lobby Committee today that certain "backward" States of the West, through their Senators, had been altogether "too vocal" in the consideration of the current tariff bill, and that some method should be found to "silence" them at times when legislation affecting the economic welfare of the United States is under way.

Mr. Grundy declared it "unfortunate" that the framers of the Constitution had seen fit to grant to the States equal rights and representation in the Senate, as the effect of the arrangement was to give sections slow in developing their resources an equal voice in legislation directly involving such great reservoirs of wealth and taxation as Pennsylvania.

Mr. Grundy was recalled today for cross-examination on testimony he gave before the lobby committee on Oct. 24. Last week Mr. Grundy and the Senate investigating committee got along very well, and that session was decorous and orderly in contrast with today, when the witness and his questioners appeared to be antagonistic from the outset.

Criticizes Senator Walsh.

At one stage Mr. Grundy sharply described a series of questions put by Senator Walsh of Montana as "impertinent." There were frequent references to the Vare case, to the party service which Mr. Grundy had performed in the collection of Republican campaign funds, and to the relations of the witness with public men and his activities here as a part of the tariff lobby.

At times the hearing resembled a hot political debate, in which the five members of the committee were arrayed against the witness. Mr. Grundy was once reproved by Senator Blaine of Wisconsin, a member of the committee, for alleged evasion, and Mr. Blaine exclaimed heatedly:

"Look me squarely in the eye and answer my question."

The hearing was marked by frequent spats between Mr. Grundy and Senators Borah, Caraway and Walsh, and in one interchange with the witnesses Mr. Borah denied emphatically a statement that he had opposed the debenture plan at the Kansas City convention.

Chairman Caraway repeatedly indicated that the witness was not frank with the committee and that, while it might be "smart" for him to "sidestep," eventually the investigators would get what they were after.

Hit at "Most Vocal" States.

Mr. Grundy was impelled to enter into a discussion of his belief that "backward Western States" should be silenced on the tariff by questions asked by Senator Walsh. The Senator read from a statement submitted to the committee a week ago, in which Mr. Grundy asserted that if "volume of voice" in the Senate were proportioned to population, productive power or the total contributed toward the national upkeep, some of those States "which are now most vocal would need amplifiers to make their whispers heard."

Mr. Grundy also had declared that "such States as Arizona, South Dakota, Idaho and Mississippi, &c., do not pay enough toward the upkeep of the government to cover the costs of collection." As a result of Mr. Walsh's examination, Mr. Grundy finally included Arkansas and Montana in his list of "backward" States, thus bringing in three of them having representation on the lobby committee.

"You have not mentioned Wisconsin in your list," suggested Senator Walsh. "What do you think about that State?"

"What I think about Wisconsin I'd hate to tell you," replied the witness. This evoked an outburst of laughter in the audience, in which the committee joined.

Favors a Few Concessions.

Mr. Grundy again caused laughter when he said that he would permit the "backward" States, through their Senators, to have their say on questions affecting "Junior Red Cross work and outdoor relief," but that, generally speaking, they should be required to "hold their peace" on

Continued on Page Eighteen.

Von Opel, Rocket Flier, Weds Woman Pilot Who Advised Him

Wireless to The New York Times.

BERLIN, Oct. 29.—Fritz von Opel, the first to fly a rocket plane, and who intends to sail for New York the beginning of November to study and work at General Motors plants, was married on Saturday to Frau Sellnik, née Loewenstein, the former wife of a Wiesbaden actor. For many months she has been von Opel's professional adviser on aviation and she herself is one of Germany's six woman pilots, flying her Handley Page plane with the greatest skill.

Frau von Opel, who is also a daring automobilist, is handsome, slender and blonde. When the airman landed safely from his rocket flight she was the first to congratulate him, shedding tears of joy. She will accompany him to the United States.

COALITION FIGHTING MOVE TO KILL TARIFF

Will Try to Force Through Bill, While Reed Favors Ending Session Nov. 15.

WATSON QUITTING CAPITAL

Departure for Florida Tomorrow for Health Leaves Jones as Republican Senate Leader.

Special to The New York Times.

WASHINGTON, Oct. 29.—Faced by Old Guard Republican willingness to leave the Smoot-Hawley tariff bill to its fate, the Democratic-Progressive coalition was today more determined than ever to drive the bill through the Senate and force the conservatives to accept it in a completely rewritten form.

Coalition strategy was centred upon fixing on the Old Guard leaders any responsibility for abandonment of the remodeled bill with the Simmons-Norris flexible amendment to the farm debenture plan. To those old-line Republicans who are now ready to desert the measure, the coalition applied the unflattering comparison of "rats and a sinking ship."

The administration Republicans refused to be stirred by such criticism. Senator Reed of Pennsylvania reiterated his conviction that the bill would never emerge from conference. Senator Moses announced that he would vote against the bill in the Senate, before it ever went to conference. The Republicans were so dismayed that they even seriously considered a motion to adjourn the Senate about the middle of November until the regular session starts on Dec. 2.

To add to their disorganization it was revealed that Senator Watson, Republican floor leader, would leave for Florida on Thursday to rebuild his shattered health.

McNary to Act as Aide.

Old Guard lieutenants hurriedly announced that Senator Jones of Washington, assistant leader, would take charge in Mr. Watson's absence, aided by Senator McNary of Oregon, who is popular with all Senate factions, has a fine record as a conciliator and more influence than most regular Republicans with the farming public.

When it was first announced that Senator Watson was going to Florida, reports spread that his illness was so serious that he might never return to the Senate as floor leader. His friends, however, denied this. They admitted that he was an ill man and needed a complete rest for a time, but asserted that he would return to assume his duties.

There was some assumption that Mr. McNary would be made temporary leader, because Senator Jones had not sufficiently recovered from the effects of a recent operation, but Mr. Jones assured Old Guard members that he felt capable of taking over the task.

While pessimistic, Senator Watson, who is dropping work by his physician's orders, would not admit that the outlook for passing the tariff bill by the end of the special session was absolutely hopeless. He did not share the view that the session might as well be adjourned, which Senator Reed may propose for about Nov. 15.

Instead, Mr. Watson will work until his departure to bring about "some sort of agreement for some sort of bill," basing this plea on the idea that the coalition must concede increases on industrial as well as agricultural rates.

Says Action Would Aid Business.

"It would have a quieting effect on business to pass the tariff bill," asserted Senator Watson. "Tariff bills are always the occasion of some unrest, though this bill has caused less agitation than usual because a Republican tariff is to be superimposed on a Republican tariff and everybody knows that if this bill fails the country would continue to be prosperous.

"It is true that there ought to be changes in agricultural rates to meet new conditions, but it is equally true

Continued on Page Fifteen.

KAHN REFUSES POST IN SENATE CAMPAIGN; CALLS CHOICE UNWISE

He Writes to Moses to Withhold His Name for Treasurer Due to 'Divided Reception.'

WAS RELUCTANT, HE SAYS

Recalls He Told Senator of His Stand, but Yielded as a Duty to His Party.

HOLDS VIEWS CONFIRMED

Declares He Is a Wall St. Man but a Liberal in Politics—Friends See Him Put in False Light.

Otto H. Kahn in a letter to Senator George H. Moses of New Hampshire, chairman of the Republican Senatorial Campaign Committee, made public yesterday, declined the post of treasurer of that committee because of the "divided reception" which the announcement of his designation as treasurer had met.

Announcement of the selection of Mr. Kahn was made by Senator Moses at the dinner given last Thursday evening at the University Club here by Jeremiah Milbank for Claudius H. Huston, the new chairman of the Republican National Committee. Publication of this announcement, together with the report that speakers at the dinner attacked the members of the Progressive Republican group in the Senate, brought protests from some of these Senators against the selection of Mr. Kahn.

Mr. Kahn in his letter to Senator Moses declared that, while a Wall Street man, he was a liberal in politics. He said some of the interpretations placed on his designation were erroneous, but added that the way it had been received justified his earlier feeling that he was not the right man for the position. No formal action for the appointment of a treasurer of the Senatorial committee has yet been taken, and Mr. Kahn requested Senator Moses not to present his name to the committee.

Mr. Kahn's Letter.

Mr. Kahn's letter follows:

Oct. 28, 1929.

My dear Senator:

When you did me the honor to ask me to act as treasurer of the Republican Senatorial Campaign Committee I told you that I feared your kindly sentiment toward me, springing from a long friendship, was swaying your judgment, that I felt sure that I was not the right man for the position, that, moreover, I was overwhelmed with demands upon my time and energies and that I hoped very much you would not persist in your request.

You argued to the contrary and, among other things, pointed to the fact that, while a Wall Street man, I was known to be, as indeed I am, a liberal in politics. You repeated your invitation when I had the pleasure of seeing you at Mr. Milbank's dinner last Thursday.

I thereupon stated that, though my views were unchanged, I felt that if we want effective party government, such as our political system requires, every citizen should be willing to make good his professions of party allegiance by submitting to being drafted, within the limits of reason and possibility, and that if the leaders of the party to which I belong demanded of me a service which did not conflict with my other duties and responsibilities I was not at liberty to refuse, however reluctant I was to accept.

You regarded this answer as tantamount to an acceptance in principle, as you were perfectly justified in doing, and at what was supposed and intended to be a strictly private dinner, you made informal reference to that acceptance.

Sees His Doubts Confirmed.

But the divided reception with which the report of the appointment of a separate treasurer for your committee and of my designation as such treasurer has met, however erroneous some of the interpretations placed thereon, appears to have confirmed the validity of the doubts which I ventured to express when you offered that position to me, and to justify me in concluding to abstain from occupying it.

I understand that no formal action has been taken as yet by the National Republican Senatorial committee concerning the appointment of a treasurer, and I am making free to write these lines to request that you will please refrain from bringing my name before the committee for appointment to the treasurership.

Believe me, dear Senator,
Very faithfully yours,
OTTO H. KAHN.

Hon. George H. Moses, The Senate, Washington, D. C.

Influential Republicans expressed regret that Mr. Kahn had decided not to take the post of treasurer of the Republican Senatorial committee. It was recalled that he was re-

Continued on Page Fourteen.

Newark Man, 4 Feet 10, Says He Was Smallest in A. E. F.

WASHINGTON, Oct. 29 (AP).—Nicholas Casale of Newark, N. J., wants to be known as the smallest man who went to France with the American Expeditionary Forces.

He has appealed to Representative Hartley of Kearny to establish that fact. Casale recently secured an affidavit from the Veterans' Bureau certifying that he was 4 feet 10 inches tall and weighed 106 pounds when he enlisted. The bureau has refused to declare him the "smallest man," saying it would require months for clerks to scan the record of every man who served with the A. E. F.

It was not explained how Casale secured enlistment when the minimum requirements are 5 feet and 110 pounds.

MISSING AIRLINER BROUGHT IN SAFELY

Pilot Lands Western Express Ship at Albuquerque After Being Forced Down.

WOULD NOT RISK STORM

Passengers Tell of Cold Night in Deserted Ranch House as Snow Swirled Round.

Special to The New York Times.

ALBUQUERQUE, N. M., Oct. 29.—Lost for more than twenty-four hours while marooned on a bleak New Mexico mesa, Western Air Express tri-motored liner 113 escaped today from the snow-swept stretch where it was forced down Monday and landed here with its crew of three and two passengers, chilled but safe.

Caught in a blinding swirl of snow Monday at 10:15 A. M., the plane was forced down near Seechado, seventy-five miles southeast of Gallup, N. M. The crew and passengers found refuge in an abandoned ranch house.

The passengers are Dr. A. W. Ward of San Francisco and W. E. Merz of Mount Vernon, N. Y. The crew includes James E. Doles, chief pilot, of Los Angeles; Allan C. Barrie, co-pilot, of Burbank, Cal., and R. L. Britton, steward, of Los Angeles.

Employes of the airport and pilots of two planes waiting for the weather to clear to resume the search for the 113 stood amazed as the big craft glided along the runway. They rushed out to the plane and as the group of men who had been given up for dead stepped out they danced around them, clapped them on the back and hugged them in delight.

Wild Night of Intense Cold.

Despite their fatigue, Dr. Ward and Mr. Merz were lighthearted and stepped jauntily from the plane. They regretted only the loss of time but joined in praise of Pilot Doles for his skillful manoeuvring to save the ship in the storm when further progress could not be risked.

They told of a harrowing night which followed the forced landing, of tramping through snow to find shelter, of sleeping on an old bed spring covered with seat cushions from the plane and of shivering in intense cold while they took turns in keeping up a fire.

"A half frozen rabbit and a rabbit's foot brought us good luck," Dr. Ward said.

"The half-frozen rabbit had been captured in the bushes by co-pilot Barrie. The rabbit's foot was worn by steward Britten. He had bought it the day the T. A. T. plane City of San Francisco crashed."

Suddenly Enveloped by Storm.

"We left Holbrook, flying east," Doles said, "and were about one hour out when we had to dodge a storm. I nosed her down towards St. John's. Suddenly the storm seemed to break over us all at once, and a landing became a necessity.

"I found a small spot, and it

Continued on Page Seventeen.

LEADERS SEE FEAR WANING

Point to 'Lifting Spells' in Trading as Sign of Buying Activity.

GROUP MEETS TWICE IN DAY

But Resources Are Unable to Stem Selling Tide—Lamont Reassures Investors.

HOPE SEEN IN MARGIN CUTS

Banks Reduce Requirements to 25 Per Cent—Sentiment in Wall St. More Cheerful.

Resources of the banking group which was organized last Thursday to stabilize conditions in the stock market were utilized yesterday to break the force of the terrific flood of selling which accompanied the biggest day, from the point of view of volume, ever experienced on the New York Stock Exchange.

Despite the drastic decline, sentiment in Wall Street last night was more cheerful than it has been on any day since the torrent of selling got under way. Periodic "lifting spells" which developed between intervals of extreme weakness were cited by bankers at the close of the market, as testifying to the presence of investment buying. The public is in some measure regaining its senses and the unreasoning fear which has prompted the sacrifice of securities for any price they would bring is at length subsiding.

While even the tremendous buying power of the banking group was unable to turn the tide of selling in yesterday's market, the group did not relax its concern over the situation on the Exchange. Two meetings were held during the day, one at noon and one at 4:30 P. M., the latter lasting until 6:30 P. M.

Will Continue Support.

After the evening meeting Thomas W. Lamont of J. P. Morgan & Co. spoke to reporters.

"I want to take occasion," Mr. Lamont said, "to explain again, as heretofore, that the banking group was organized to offer certain support in the market and to act as far as possible as somewhat of a stabilizing factor.

"It was not the intention of the group to attempt to maintain prices, but to maintain a free market; in other words, to correct the condition that prevailed last Thursday.

"The group has continued and will continue in a cooperative way to support the market and has not been a seller of stocks."

The statement was issued at the request of reporters to quiet rumors which had been abroad that the banking group had been selling stocks instead of supporting them.

These rumors were, of course, without foundation, for the group is known to have purchased heavily in directions where the force of its buying power would be most effective in stemming demoralization. It was reliably reported that in many instances when no bids could be obtained on the floor for large blocks of stock forced on the market the group had supplied the necessary bids and in other instances had acted as a stabilizing influence upon the list as a whole.

At the noon meeting of the group Owen D. Young, chairman of the General Electric Company, director of the Federal Reserve Bank of New York and head of the Young committee on reparations which recently developed the Young plan, joined the

Continued on Page Three.

Navy Paymaster Leads Way to $47,000 Loot, Dug Up by Night in Washington Chicken Yard

Special to The New York Times.

WASHINGTON, Oct. 29.—Led by Lieutenant Charles Musil, a navy paymaster accused of embezzling $54,600, naval authorities, in a search late at night, recently uncovered $47,000 of the loot buried in a chicken yard in Southeast Washington on the grounds of the Home of the Aged and Infirm.

When Lieutenant Musil voluntarily surrendered himself, on Oct. 14, to the naval authorities at New York, after having disappeared on Sept. 28 from his post as paymaster for Destroyer Division 40 at Charleston, S. C., he is said to have turned over $1,500 to Captain C. T. Owens, commanding the receiving ship Seattle.

This leaves $6,100 unaccounted for and naval officers, in announcing today the discovery in the chicken yard, said they were trying to locate the rest of the money, although they had scant hope of success.

According to the story told to the officers by Lieutenant Musil, he came here directly from Charleston and buried the money in the yard of his former home. He then left for Chicago, where he bought some stock, and went to Detroit and into Canada. From there he proceeded to New York, where he became conscience-stricken and gave himself up.

He was held at the Brooklyn Navy Yard, but when he told his story of the buried money he was brought here to direct the search for it. He is now awaiting general court-martial on specifications covering embezzlement.

Lieutenant Musil was born in Illinois in 1893, enlisted in the navy twenty years ago and was commissioned in 1921. He has a wife and 8-year-old son in New York City.

240 Issues Lose $15,894,818,894 in Month; Slump in Full Exchange List Vastly Larger

The drastic effects of Wall Street's October bear market is shown by valuation tables prepared last night by THE NEW YORK TIMES, which place the decline in the market value of 240 representative issues on the New York Stock Exchange at $15,894,818,894 during the period from Oct. 1 to yesterday's closing. Since there are 1,279 issues listed on the New York Stock Exchange, the total depreciation for the month is estimated at between two and three times the loss for the 240 issues covered by THE TIMES table.

Among the losses of the various groups comprising the 240 stocks in THE TIMES valuation table were the following:

Group.	Number of Stocks.	Decline in Value.
Railroads	25	$1,128,686,488
Public utilities	29	5,135,734,327
Motors	15	1,689,840,902
Oils	22	1,382,617,778
Coppers	13	824,403,820
Chemicals	9	1,621,897,897

The official figures of the New York Stock Exchange showed that the total market value of its listed securities on Oct. 1 was $87,073,630,423. The decline in the 240 representative issues therefore cut more than one-sixth from the total value of the listed securities. Most of this loss was inflicted by the wholesale liquidation of the last week.

U. S. STEEL TO PAY $1 EXTRA DIVIDEND

American Can Votes the Same and Raises Annual Rate From $3 to $4.

BIG GAIN IN STEEL INCOME

Earnings for Nine Months Are $15.82 a Share, Against $8.17 a Year Ago.

Two leading industrial companies yesterday declared extra dividends of $1 a share on the common stock, as a result of their earnings through the Summer months. The companies were the United States Steel Corporation and the American Can Company, whose interests touch every section of the country. Their action caused the Wall Street district to accept the extra dividends as final proof of the prosperity of the country, despite the breaks which have occurred in the stock market.

While the directors of neither of the companies referred to present conditions in the stock market as a reason for taking the extra dividend action at this time, the opinion was expressed that the directors chose this time to declare the extras as reflecting their belief in the fundamental soundness of industry.

Directors of the American Can Company, in addition to declaring the $1 extra disbursement, also increased the regular dividend rate on the common stock from $3 a year to $4 a year, committing themselves to this payment for the future.

The United States Steel directors contented themselves with announcing that earnings for the first nine months of this year were nearly double those of the same period for 1928, namely, $15.82 a share on the common stock outstanding, compared with $8.17 for the nine months of 1928.

Steel Surplus Up $22,909,447.

Earnings of the United States Steel Corporation for the three months ended on Sept. 30 were reported as $72,009,666, equivalent to $5.57 a share on the common stock outstanding, and the extra dividend makes the disbursements for the quarter less than half of the actual earnings. The operation for the three months, after the preferred and common stock dividends, including the extra dividend, increased the surplus of the company by $22,909,447.

September was the lowest for the three months which enter into the quarterly earnings. The amount reported for this month was $21,794,450, which compares with $25,298,059 in August and $24,917,157 for July. The total earnings for the quarter after deducting all expenses incident to operations, including those for ordinary repairs and maintenance of plants, taxes, including the reserve for Federal income taxes, and the interest on bonds of subsidiary companies, amounted to $70,173,713. Allowances for depreciation, depletion and obsolescence took away another $16,819,393, leaving the net income for the three months at $53,354,320. The interest for the quarter on the bonds of the company outstanding amounted to $1,778,970, and the payment of the 1¾ per cent dividends on the preferred stock amounted to another $6,304,919.

Extra Due to Rise in Earnings.

The official statement issued by the company after the meeting of the directors read as follows:

"The United States Steel Corporation's earnings for the first nine

Continued on Page Six.

RESERVE BOARD FINDS ACTION UNNECESSARY

Six-Hour Session Brings No Change in the New York Rediscount Rate.

OFFICIALS ARE OPTIMISTIC

Mellon Also Attends Cabinet Meeting, but Declines to Discuss Developments.

Special to The New York Times.

WASHINGTON, Oct. 29.—The further decline in stock market prices today passed without expressed apprehension on the part of Federal officials. The situation was watched intently by the Federal Reserve Board, which held a continuous session from 10 A. M. until 4 P. M., with Secretary Mellon in attendance.

Secretary Mellon, as ex-officio chairman of the board, attended the early part of the meeting before going to the White House for the Cabinet meeting. It could not be learned whether the market situation was discussed by the President and the Cabinet.

At 2:30 P. M. Mr. Mellon returned to the Reserve Board meeting, and remained until near its close. During the day he had conferred with Under-Secretary Ogden L. Mills and Roy A. Young, Governor of the Reserve Board. After the board adjourned, neither Secretary Mellon nor Mr. Young would even intimate the nature or scope of the discussions.

The Federal Reserve Board was so absorbed in studying the financial problems facing the country as the result of another violent stock fluctuation that most of its members did not leave the board room for luncheon.

Board Reviews Credit Situation.

Members of the board, while admitting that the market situation was under discussion, declared at the end of the day that there was no change which called upon the board for action relative to credits.

There was a report that the board had reviewed the credit situation to determine whether the time had come to lower the rediscount rate to ease credit for business ventures.

The board has hesitated to act on the rediscount rate during the stock market decline, fearing that lowered rates might be employed to bolster up the market. The board's policy is not to aid in speculation, but it feels that the rediscount rate should be lowered to stimulate credits for business when it is apparent that such action would not be accepted as assistance to speculative loans.

Mr. Young said there was no change in financial conditions which the board thought called for its action.

Cut in Discount Rate Expected.

It is thought the question of lowering rediscount rates may come before the Federal Reserve Board shortly. The Boston Federal Reserve Bank directors will meet tomorrow and the New York directors on Thursday. It is possible that one of these banks may suggest a lowering of the rates.

Some observers believe that a reduction in rediscount rates might have a strong psychological effect not only upon business but the market as well. There was no official indication that such a move was imminent, although some observers thought such action might come if suggested by the New York bank directors, since the rate there is 6 per cent as against 5 per cent in other regions. Some thought the New York rediscount rate might be reduced to 5 per cent soon.

Today's session of the board was the longest since the financial flurry

Continued on Page Six.

CLOSING RALLY VIGOROUS

Leading Issues Regain From 4 to 14 Points in 15 Minutes.

INVESTMENT TRUSTS BUY

Large Blocks Thrown on Market at Opening Start Third Break of Week.

BIG TRADERS HARDEST HIT

Bankers Believe Liquidation Now Has Run Its Course and Advise Purchases.

Stock prices virtually collapsed yesterday, swept downward with gigantic losses in the most disastrous trading day in the stock market's history. Billions of dollars in open market values were wiped out as prices crumbled under the pressure of liquidation of securities which had to be sold at any price.

There was an impressive rally just at the close, which brought many leading stocks back from 4 to 14 points from their lowest points of the day.

Trading on the New York Stock Exchange aggregated 16,410,030 shares; on the Curb, 7,096,300 shares were dealt in. Both totals far exceeded any previous day's dealings.

From every point of view, in the extent of losses sustained, in total turnover, in the number of speculators wiped out, the day was the most disastrous in Wall Street's history. Hysteria swept the country and stocks went overboard for just what they would bring at forced sale.

Efforts to estimate yesterday's market losses in dollars are futile because of the vast number of securities quoted over the counter and on out-of-town exchanges on which no calculations are possible. However, it was estimated that 880 issues, on the New York Stock Exchange, lost between $8,000,000,000 and $9,000,000,000 yesterday. Added to that loss is to be reckoned the depreciation on issues on the Curb Market, in the over the counter market and on other exchanges.

Two Extra Dividends Declared.

There were two cheerful notes, however, which sounded through the pall of gloom which overhung the financial centres of the country. One was the brisk rally of stocks at the close, on tremendous buying by those who believe that prices have sunk too low. The other was that the liquidation has been so violent, as well as widespread, that many bankers, brokers and industrial leaders expressed the belief last night that it now has run its course.

A further note of optimism in the soundness of fundamentals was sounded by the directors of the United States Steel Corporation and the American Can Company, each of which declared an extra dividend of $1 a share at their late afternoon meetings.

Banking support, which would have been impressive and successful under ordinary circumstances, was swept violently aside, as block after block of stock, tremendous in proportions, deluged the market. Bid prices placed by bankers, industrial leaders and brokers trying to halt the decline were crashed through violently, their orders were filled, and quotations plunged downward in a day of disorganization, confusion and financial impotence.

Change Is Expected Today.

That there will be a change today seemed likely from statements made last night by financial and business leaders. Organized support will be accorded to the market from the start, it is believed, but those who are staking their all on the country's leading securities are placing a great deal of confidence, too, in the expectation that there will be an overnight change in sentiment; that the counsel of cool heads will prevail and that the mob psychology which has been so largely responsible for the market's debacle will be broken.

The fact that the leading stocks were able to rally in the final fifteen minutes of trading yesterday was considered a good omen, especially as the weakest period of the day had developed just prior to that time and the minimum prices for the day had then been established. It was a quick run-up which followed the announcement that the American Can directors had declared an extra dividend of $1. The advances in leading stocks in this last fifteen minutes represented a measurable snapback from the lows. American Can gained 10; United States Steel common, 7¼; General Electric, 12; New York Central, 14¼; Anaconda Copper, 9¼; Chrysler Motors, 5¼; Montgomery Ward, 4¼, and Johns Man-

"All the News That's Fit to Print."

The New York Times.

THE WEATHER
Fair and continued cold today; tomorrow cloudy and warmer.
Temperatures yesterday—Max. 30, min. 20.
U. S. Weather Forecast—For details See Page [illegible].

VOL. LXXIX....No. 26,243. + * * * * NEW YORK, SATURDAY, NOVEMBER 30, 1929. TWO CENTS In Greater New York | THREE CENTS Within 200 Miles | FOUR CENTS Elsewhere Except 7th and 8th Postal Zones

BYRD SAFELY FLIES TO SOUTH POLE AND BACK, LOOKING OVER 'ALMOST LIMITLESS PLATEAU'; DROPS FOOD, LIGHTENS SHIP ON PERILOUS TRIP

FIRST MESSAGE EVER SENT FROM THE SOUTH POLE

By Commander Richard E. Byrd

WIRELESS TO THE NEW YORK TIMES.

ABOARD AIRPLANE FLOYD BENNETT, in flight, 1:55 P. M. Greenwich mean time [8:55 A. M. New York time], Friday, Nov. 29.—My calculations indicate that we have reached the vicinity of the South Pole, flying high for a survey. The airplane is in good shape, crew all well. Will soon turn north. We can see an almost limitless polar plateau. Our departure from the Pole was at 1:25 P. M.

BYRD

The difference in the times mentioned in this dispatch, that is between 1:55 P. M. in the date line and 1:25 P. M., given by the Commander as that of his departure from the South Pole, is probably accounted for by the lapse between the writing of the dispatch by the Commander and its coding and sending by the wireless operator, Harold I. June. Greenwich time is five hours ahead of New York time and twelve hours ahead of time at Little America.

The Commander's last sentence was evidently added after he began to fly away from the Pole; the first part written before he left there.

CROSSES GLACIER PASS AT 11,500 FEET

Commander Takes Chance and Plane Roars Upward Amid Swirling Drift Out Through Gorge to Tableland

FLYING TIME FOR THE WHOLE CIRCUIT ABOUT 18 HOURS

With Two New Ranges Discovered, the Four Air Argonauts, Guided by Chief, Turn Back to Wild Welcome at Base Camp.

By RUSSELL OWEN.

Wireless to THE NEW YORK TIMES.

LITTLE AMERICA, Antarctica, Nov. 29.—Conqueror of two Poles by air, Commander Richard E. Byrd flew into camp at 10:10 o'clock this morning, having been gone eighteen hours and fifty-nine minutes. An hour of this time was spent at the mountain base refueling.

The first man to fly over the North and South Poles and the only man to fly over the South Pole stepped from his plane and was swept up on the arms of the men in camp who for more than an hour had been anxiously watching the southern horizon for a sight of the plane.

Deaf from the roar of the motors, tired from the continual strain of the flight and the long period of navigation under difficulties, Commander Byrd was still smiling and happy. He had reached the South Pole after as hazardous and as difficult a flight as has ever been made in an airplane, tossed by gusts of wind, climbing desperately up the slopes of glaciers a few hundred feet above the surface.

Radiant Airmen Borne in Triumph.

His companions on the flight tumbled out stiff and weary also, but so happy that they forgot their cramped muscles. They were also tossed aloft, pounded on the back and carried to the entrance of the mess hall.

Bernt Balchen, the calm-eyed pilot who first met Commander Byrd in Spitzbergen and who was with him on the transatlantic flight, came out first. There was a little smudge of soot under the nose, but the infectious smile which has endeared him to those who know him, was radiant.

He was carried away and then came Harold June who, between intervals of helping Balchen and attending to fuel tanks and lines and taking pictures, found time to send the radio bulletins which told of the plane's progress.

And after him Captain Ashley McKinley was lifted from the doorway, beaming like the Cheshire cat because his surveying camera had done its work all the way.

Dumped Food of Forty-five Days, But Not Fuel.

Men crowded about them eager for the story of what they had been through, catching fragments of sentences. It had evidently been a terrific battle to get up through the mountains to the Plateau.

"We had to dump a month and a half of food to do it," said Commander Byrd. "I am glad it wasn't gas. It was nip and tuck all the way."

"Yes," chuckled Balchen. "Do you remember when we were sliding around those knolls picking the wind currents to help us and there wasn't more than 300 feet under us at times? We were just staggering along, with drift and clouds and all sorts of things around us."

When the plane approached the mountains on the way south, Commander Byrd picked out the Livingston Glacier, a large glacier somewhat to the west of the Axel Heiberg Glacier, as the best passageway.

Swooping Upward Through Swirling Drift.

The high mountains shut them in all around as they forced their way upward, Balchen, conserving his fuel to the utmost, coaxing his engines, picking the up-currents of air as best he could to help the plane ride upward.

Clouds swirled about them at times, puff-balls of mist driven down the glacier; drift scurried beneath them; it was a wicked place for an airplane to be, hemmed in by the wall of the towering peaks on either side.

This was the time when they had to lighten ship and Byrd, looking around for what could best be spared, decided to dump some food. There was a dump valve in the fuselage tank, but he had determined to go through and did not know what winds he might face at the top of the glacier. So food was thrown overboard, scattered over the ridged and broken surface of the Livingston Glacier.

"It is an awful looking place," Commander Byrd said.

Over the "Hump" and Vast Panorama Unfolds.

They finally reached the hump at an elevation of 11,500 feet, as indicated by the barograph, although it might have been a little more, because of the difference in pressure inland.

But there was little space under the staggering plane, buffeted by the winds that eddied through the gigantic gorge. Once at the top, Balchen could level off for a time and then gain altitude.

Then there came into view slowly the long sweep of mountains of the Queen Maud Range, stretching to the southeast, and the magnificent panorama of the entire bulwark of mountains along the edge of the Polar Plateau.

Behold Tinted Slopes of Myriad Mountains.

"It was the most magnificent sight I have ever seen," Commander Byrd said. "I never dreamed there were so many mountains in the world. They shone under the sun, wonderfully tinted with color, and in the southeast a bank of clouds hung over the mountains, making a scene that I shall never forget."

Over the plateau the Commander set his course for the pole. They had had a beam wind all the way in to the mountains which

WOMAN HEARD CRASH IN HOTEL AT THE TIME ROTHSTEIN WAS SHOT

Says She Saw Man With Angry or Agonized Look Near McManus's Room.

UNCERTAIN ON HIS IDENTITY

Mrs. M. A. Putnam, "Surprise" Witness for State, Attacked by the Defense.

RAYMOND TELLS OF BIG BET

Testifies He Won $40,000 From Rothstein on One Card—Admits That They Had a Quarrel.

A fragile woman with gray hair, but a schoolgirl complexion, took the stand yesterday in the Criminal Courts Building to aid the State in its effort to convict George A. McManus of the murder of Arnold Rothstein. In clear tones she identified herself as Mrs. Marian A. Putnam of Asheville, N. C., chief of the surprise witnesses for the prosecution.

Loosening the gray squirrel collar of a broadtail fur coat, she said that she had been a guest at the Park Central Hotel on the night of Nov. 4, 1928, when Rothstein received a bullet wound which caused his death two days later. She added that she had registered at the hotel on Oct. 30.

Assistant District Attorney George N. Brothers, urbane in manner and soothing of voice, asked her to tell what she had heard and seen that night. Mrs. Putnam turned her thin face toward the jurymen and folded her hands, asparkle with four diamond rings. Quietly she told how she had heard a "crash" and had seen a man walking down a corridor on the third floor, leading from Room 349, part of a suite hired by McManus.

Saw Agony or Anger in Face.

She had looked at the man's face. It bore the imprint of agony or anger. He had his hands clasped over his abdomen as he followed her down the carpeted passageway. Mrs. Putnam said she locked the door of her room and said nothing about the episode even the following morning when she learned of the shooting.

On through the events of the evening Mr. Brothers led the witness. She told a straightforward story under the prosecutor's questioning and now and then a faint smile curved her tight lips. Mrs. Putnam settled more comfortably in the witness chair and slipped out of the heavy fur coat. As she replied to the questions she smoothed the lace ruffles at the wristbands of her black velvet dress and adjusted the cream-colored lace fichu at her neck.

She completed her story and then James D. C. Murray, attorney for the defense, began his cross-examination. The slow-moving lawyer, his grizzled hair somewhat rumpled, favored the witness with a prolonged stare before he started his questions. Suavely but searchingly he delved into Mrs. Putnam's past. His questions were blunt, but were met with composure by the witness.

Raymond Tells of Winnings.

She made impeaching admissions with a detached calm that almost equaled the perfect poise which had been displayed shortly before by another witness, Nathan (Nigger Nate) Raymond. Raymond, who told how he had won $40,000 from Rothstein when the slain man drew the deuce at high card, admitted that he probably had been guilty of a faux pas—the expression was his own—when he asked Rothstein to give him I. O. U.'s for $200,000 he had won.

During the cross-examination of Raymond the defense developed that he had quarrelled with Rothstein in a taxicab subsequent to the poker game. Raymond said that he had no recollection of any blows having been struck.

When Raymond left the stand the defense sought to have stricken from the record all testimony regarding the poker game. Mr. Murray told the court that the prosecution had failed to carry out its promise to show that the game gave McManus the motive for the murder. Judge Nott refused to grant the motion.

Mrs. Putnam admitted that she had been registered at the Park

Continued on Page Fourteen.

Byrd Lauds Radio Amateurs For Help in Message Relays

LOS ANGELES, Nov. 29 (AP).—A congratulatory message sent by Commander Richard E. Byrd just before the start of his flight over the South Pole, was read today at the convention of the Pacific division of the American Radio Relay League.

The message, received by B. E. Sandham, Los Angeles amateur short wave radio operator, read:

"Greetings from Little America to the radio amateurs of the Pacific division. Am glad for this opportunity to acknowledge the big debt our North and South Pole expeditions owe to the amateur radio operators.

"I wish to thank them for their helpfulness and to express my admiration of the high sense of honor they show in handling messages.

"It is radio that has made this expedition possible.

"Cordial good wishes in which all of Little America join.

"RICHARD BYRD."

WINTER GRIPS NATION; MERCURY AT 20 HERE

Icy Blast Sweeping Out of the Northwest Kills 9, Spreads Damage, Blocks Shipping.

BLIZZARDS RAGE IN WEST

One Frozen to Death in New York and No Let-Up in the Frigid Wave Is Seen.

Winter came howling out of the northwest and the Arctic wastes yesterday, bringing blizzards to the Western States and Canada, hampering shipping on the Great Lakes, and holding the West, the Middle West, the East and many Southern States in the grip of sub-freezing temperatures.

It was the frigid season's first general offensive, and it scattered death, suffering and property damage widely. White River, Ontario, which usually claims the distinction of recording low temperatures, shared with Thief River Falls, Minn., first place on the icy list yesterday, both communities recording 26 below zero. At least eight persons died in the North Central States as a result of the sudden zero snap, according to the Associated Press. New York City added one death to the list. Fears were felt for the safety of hunters caught unprepared for the severe cold in the Minnesota woods. Near the cradle of Winter, where a 30-mile gale was driving a blizzard over the Saskatchewan Lakes, the fate of fifty fishermen, pushing northward on a 30-mile trip, was in doubt. The fishermen had been gone for three days.

Cold to Continue Here Today.

New York had an uncomfortable sample of Winter, and last night the local Weather Bureau gave practically no hope of a let-up today in the cold temperatures.

This city felt its lowest temperature of the season at 10 o'clock last night when the thermometer registered 20 degrees above zero, 12 below freezing. Even the maximum temperature at 9:30 A. M. was only 30 degrees, or 2 below freezing. The average temperature for the day was 26 degrees, compared with a normal Nov. 29 reading of 39. The coldest Nov. 29 on record occurred in 1872 when the thermometer registered 15 degrees.

The cold here was aggravated by a biting northwest wind, blowing at thirty-eight miles an hour. The city's firemen were put to their first severe test of the season in what was a busy "fire" day in Manhattan, the Bronx and Brooklyn. Up to 9 o'clock last night the number of fires for the day totaled thirty in Manhattan, ten in the Bronx and forty-three in Brooklyn.

Fair Weather Forecast.

Although the barometer in the New York Weather Bureau was rising last night, indicating fair weather for today, the cold snap will continue, according to the official forecaster, and the thousands of football spectators who will swarm into the Yankee Stadium for the Army-Notre Dame game this afternoon will have to wear their warmest clothes and wraps.

"Fresh northeast winds and continued cold" was the prediction for today. At the Weather Bureau it was even considered possible that today might be a little colder than yesterday.

A woman on Staten Island was New York's addition to the list of victims of the cold. She was Mrs. Gladys Todd, 53 years old, who was found dead in the back yard of her home, at 4 Schrenkheisen Place, Mar-

Continued on Page Twelve.

CAPITAL DISPLAYS KEENEST INTEREST

President, Waiting News, Is the First in Washington to Hear of Byrd's Success.

OFFICIALS LAUD FLIGHT

Admiral Hughes Says the Commander Is a Worthy Successor to Admiral Wilkes.

Special to The New York Times.

WASHINGTON, Nov. 29.—President Hoover, who had waited anxiously all day for word of the progress of the daring flight to the South Pole, was the first person in Washington, outside of the staff of THE NEW YORK TIMES bureau, to learn of the successful flight of Commander Byrd to the South Pole and back to the base at Little America.

The word was flashed to the White House tonight from the Washington Bureau of THE NEW YORK TIMES. It was transmitted to the President before dinner by Secretary Walter H. Newton.

All day the President had asked for word of the progress of the flight and late in the afternoon had indicated his deep interest. When the news was taken to him, the President expressed his delight over the successful outcome.

Official Washington expressed the most intense relief and the greatest delight at the successful termination of the flight.

Admiral Charles F. Hughes, the Acting Secretary of the Navy, was among the first to be informed.

"We are greatly pleased at the success of Commander Byrd's flight," he said. "He is a worthy successor to Admiral Wilkes, the American naval officer who first discovered the Antarctic Continent."

Earlier in the day Admiral Hughes had said:

"The Navy Department is intensely interested and, knowing Commander Byrd, we are thoroughly confident that he will return successfully."

Davison Congratulates Expedition.

F. Trubee Davison, Assistant Secretary of War for Aeronautics, declared the success of the flight demonstrated again the value of aircraft.

"The flight of Commander Byrd and his brave companions to the South Pole," he said, "is another epic in the annals of the achievements of heavier-than-air craft and proves once again the value of the airplane in exploration of unknown areas where distances can be traveled in hours which under ordinary forms of transportation would require weeks and months. On behalf of the War Department and the Army Air Corps, I wish to congratulate the Byrd Antarctic Expedition. Their achievement will be lauded by Americans the world over."

Major Clarence M. Young, the Assistant Secretary of Commerce for Aeronautics, declared the Byrd flight was simply another demonstration of the "limitless purposes which aviation can serve."

"The flight to the South Pole and back was surely a major accomplish-

Continued on Page Three.

President Sends His Congratulations to Byrd, Saying Spirit of Great Adventure Still Lives

Special to The New York Times.

WASHINGTON, Nov. 29.—After being informed tonight of Commander Byrd's successful flight to the South Pole and back to the base at Little America, President Hoover gave to THE NEW YORK TIMES the following message of congratulations on behalf of himself and the American people, to be transmitted by radio to Commander Byrd:

Commander Richard E. Byrd,
Little America:

I know that I speak for the American people when I express their universal pleasure at your successful flight over the South Pole. We are proud of your courage and your leadership. We are glad of proof that the spirit of great adventure still lives.

Our thoughts of appreciation include also your companions in the flight and your colleagues, whose careful and devoted preparation have contributed to your great success.

HERBERT HOOVER.

BYRD'S FEAT STIRS ENTHUSIASM HERE

Victorious Flight Hailed With Tributes to Commander's Daring and Foresight.

With the reception of news from Little America of the return of Commander Byrd and his companions from their flight over the South Pole, explorers, aviators, aeronautical designers and builders whose names are known throughout the world of aviation and scores of others offered their congratulations to the Commander and expressed their enthusiasm over the success of his efforts. Some of these comments follow:

Anthony H. G. Fokker, designer of the plane in which Commander Byrd crossed the Atlantic—I didn't expect anything but success from Byrd and Balchen. The Commander is an excellent organizer and Balchen is a fine pilot. With all the qualities fliers need for such an expedition, they have proved the unquestioned value and possibility of the airplane.

Mayor Walker—That's marvelous news. I can sum up the way I feel about it in a single sentence. I knew Dick Byrd would do it. He has made another great contribution to scientific advancement and world knowledge. The American flag will certainly look great down there. I know I speak for the people of this city when I say that we rejoice with him and his intrepid companions in this epoch-making exploit. We will await his return to New York with impatience, so that the city can give him the welcome he so richly deserves. New York City has honored Commander Byrd before. It is glad to honor him again, for it feels that in a very real sense he is one of us.

Lieutenant Governor Herbert H. Lehman—It is glorious news. Commander Byrd's successful flight to the South Pole will go down in history as one of the greatest of human exploits. Its success is all the more noteworthy because achieved in the face of great obstacles after the most painstaking preparation. The nation whose flag he has now carried to the uttermost ends of the globe rejoices with him and his gallant crew for the success they have

Continued on Page Four.

BYRD'S FAMILY GETS NEWS OF FLIGHT

Virginia Governor at Capitol Gets News and Mother Hears It at Winchester.

Special to The New York Times.

RICHMOND, Va., Nov. 29.—Although he knew that his brother, Commander Richard Evelyn Byrd, intended to hop to the South Pole "about this time of the year," Governor Harry F. Byrd said in his office tonight that no one in the family or any one else had known exactly what day the plane Floyd Bennett would leave the base.

Commander Byrd's mother, Mrs. Richard E. Byrd Sr., and Thomas Byrd, his brother, received news of the successful flight at their home in Winchester.

Governor Byrd flew to Richmond late today from Norfolk to get news of his brother. He had been at Chapel Hill for the Virginia-Carolina football game on Thanksgiving Day and stopped in the capital to be the guest of Governor O. Max Gardner of North Carolina. Accompanying Governor Byrd in another plane was Colonel Willard D. Newbill of his staff.

From the Executive Mansion the Governor relayed news of the flight to his mother at Winchester.

When Commander Byrd duplicated his top of the world feat by flying over the South Pole at the very bottom of the world his mother, thought it "glorious" and was "thrilled to death," she said tonight.

"I was in Washington when we heard Dick had hopped off," she said. "My son Tom drove up there to get me when I phoned him and we went back to Winchester to wait for news. THE NEW YORK TIMES called me about 6 o'clock but said they would not release the news generally until later.

"Dick had sent me a Thanksgiving radio message a few hours before they hopped off, 'We are off.' We were very uneasy, but I was never so happy in my life as when we heard he had landed safely back at Little America. We really were quite uneasy because this flight seemed more hazardous than anything he ever tried. Nobody knew anything much about Antarctica.

"When Tom heard Dick had gone over safely he said he was 'tremen-

Continued on Page Two.

BRITISH APPLAUD FLIGHT AS TRIUMPH

Thrill Over Byrd's Feat Puts Polar Land Dispute in the Background.

NEWS EAGERLY AWAITED

German Press and People Followed Commander's Course With Keen Interest.

Special Cable to THE NEW YORK TIMES.

LONDON, Saturday, Nov. 30.—Great Britain watched Commander Byrd's progress over the Antarctic wastes to the South Pole and his return as a magnificent adventure, and what claims he may make to any rich coal or mineral deposits over which he has flown or staked with the American flag is an issue that is exciting no comment here.

Even the publication by New York newspapers of a summary of the State Department's answer to the British Government's year-old note concerning sovereignty over the Antarctic lands, which was read here as clearly indicating that the United States does not intend to abandon its claims based on earlier discoveries by American explorers, was not allowed to distract attention from Commander Byrd's performance or to cause a controversy almost on the eve of the five-power naval parley in London.

Hailed as Byrd Triumph.

The Daily Chronicle outstripped its London rivals this morning by alone printing a full account of Commander Byrd's South Pole flight, as transmitted to it by THE NEW YORK TIMES and associated newspapers. The remainder of the London newspapers were able in their final editions to announce only the bare fact of the aviator's epoch-making flight, with full acknowledgment of the source of their information.

The feat, therefore, was hailed here not only as a personal triumph for Commander Byrd and his three companions, Balchen, June and McKinley, but as an outstanding feat in newspaper organization.

Stupendous as is the accomplishment of a flight of 1,580 miles over the frozen wastes to the South Pole and back in 18 hours and 55 minutes in itself, it has been brought home more vividly to the public mind here by the fact that within a few hours of Commander Byrd's return to his base on the Ross ice shelf, at 10:10 o'clock London time last night, the leading newspapers of the world were able to reproduce the story of the exploit.

It has not escaped notice that scientific development, from the short-wave radio to the finer details of aircraft construction, have been pressed into use on this occasion.

Scientists, aviators and public men on every hand are expressing admiration for Commander Byrd's initiative and courage in carrying out successfully a flight which for scientific results may stand alone.

Commander Byrd had been flying over twelve hours before the British

Continued on Page Four.

The New York Times

PAGE ONE

1930-1939

"All the News That's Fit to Print."

The New York Times.

THE WEATHER
Cloudy, with probably occasional rain today; tomorrow fair, colder.
Temperature Yesterday—Max. 50; Min. 44.
U. S. Weather Forecast—For details see Page 46.

Copyright, 1930, by The New York Times Company.

VOL. LXXX....No. 26,583. ***** NEW YORK, WEDNESDAY, NOVEMBER 5, 1930. TWO CENTS In Greater New York | THREE CENTS Within 200 Miles | FOUR CENTS Elsewhere Except 7th and 8th Postal Zones

DEMOCRATIC LANDSLIDE SWEEPS COUNTRY; REPUBLICANS MAY LOSE CONGRESS CONTROL; ROOSEVELT WINNER BY MORE THAN 700,000

WETS GAIN IN HOUSE

Win 32 Seats and Lose None; Hold Senate Places.

AIDED BY ILLINOIS SWEEP

Also Helped by Victory of Bulkley in Ohio—Drys Win in Places.

THREE REFERENDA GO WET

Repeal Proposals Are Carried in Rhode Island, Illinois and Massachusetts.

Forces favoring repeal of the Eighteenth Amendment and liquor laws scored gains in the Congressional elections throughout the country yesterday, adding to these victories substantial majorities in favor of repeal referenda in Illinois, Rhode Island and Massachusetts.

On the basis of returns late last night, the so-called "wet bloc" in the House had picked up thirty new votes to add to the ninety-one which the most optimistic of wets count in the present House.

The Senate wets had picked up several new names, of such imminence as Morrow of New Jersey, Lewis of Illinois and Bulkley of Ohio, but were battling to hold the number of eighteen in the present make-up of the Senate, because of retirements of sitting wet members from States where only dry candidates sought their seats.

Marcus Coolidge of Massachusetts was running well ahead of his dry opponent, William M. Butler, overcoming a substantial lead early in the night.

Results of Referenda.

Wet candidates were carrying with them wet referenda in every State where they were offered. In Illinois the vote went decidedly in favor of repeal of the Eighteenth Amendment. Three proposals, one for repeal of the amendment, another for modification of the Volstead act and the other proposing repeal of the State enforcement act, all carried with good majorities, with the heaviest vote and the heaviest majority recorded on the first question.

Rhode Island registered a vote of more than 2 to 1 in favor of repeal. The vote in Massachusetts was on repeal of the State enforcement act and a majority in favor of the referendum was gaining in size as Marcus Coolidge increased his lead over the dry Butler.

In his landslide in Illinois Mr. Lewis evidently had swept a number of wet Democrats into office, and in Ohio the victory of Mr. Bulkley carried with it an increase in the wet representation of that State in the lower house by at least three. At least two wet gains in the House went with the Morrow victory in New Jersey, and seven apparently had been recorded in Pennsylvania, despite the victories of dry Senate and Gubernatorial candidates.

Many Dry Victories Recorded.

The wets had not actually lost a seat in either house on the face of returns up until early this morning, although dry victories had been scored in a number of States, including three in the South where prohibition figured conspicuously as an issue in the campaign.

The whole delegation in Connecticut, including Representative John Q. Tilson, Hoover spokesman and Republican leader in the House, will be listed among the wets at the next Congress. The only seat in doubt was in the First District, where C. W. Seymour, dry Republican, was pitted with A. Longergan, wet Democrat. Mr. Longergan led on the reports last night.

Four wets evidently had won in Michigan, including S. H. Person, who will occupy the seat held by Grant M. Hudson, former State Superintendent of the Anti-Saloon

Continued on Page Seven.

U. S. SENATORS ELECTED

REPUBLICANS—13.

Delaware	*D. O. Hastings
Idaho	*William E. Borah
Iowa	‡L. J. Dickinson
Kansas	‡Arthur Capper
Maine	¶W. H. White Jr.
Michigan	*James Couzens
Nebraska	*George W. Norris
New Hampshire	*Henry W. Keyes
New Jersey	†Dwight W. Morrow
Oregon	*Charles L. McNary
Pennsylvania	§James J. Davis
Rhode Island	*J. H. Metcalf
Wyoming	†Robert D. Cary

DEMOCRATS—20.

Alabama	‡J. H. Bankhead
Arkansas	*J. T. Robinson
Colorado	‡E. P. Costigan
Georgia	*William J. Harris
Illinois	‡J. H. Lewis
Louisiana	‡Huey P. Long
Massachusetts	‡M. A. Coolidge
Minnesota	‡Einar Hoidale
Mississippi	*Pat Harrison
Montana	*Thomas J. Walsh
New Mexico	*S. G. Bratton
North Carolina	‡Josiah W. Bailey
Ohio	§Robert J. Bulkley
Oklahoma	‡Thomas P. Gore
South Carolina	‡James F. Byrnes
Tennessee	**William E. Brock
Tennessee	‡Cordell Hull
Texas	*Morris Sheppard
Virginia	*Carter Glass
West Virginia	‡M. M. Neely

IN DOUBT—3.

Kansas, South Dakota, Kentucky

*Re-elected for full term ending March 3, 1937. †Elected for both long and short terms. ‡Elected for full term ending March 3, 1937. ¶Elected Sept. 8, 1930 for full term ending March 3, 1937. §Elected for short term ending March 3, 1933. **Elected for short term ending March 3, 1931.

LEWIS, DEMOCRAT, SWEEPS ILLINOIS

Out-and-Out Wet Piles Up 2 to 1 Lead Over Mrs. McCormick, Republican, for Senate.

AHEAD 3 TO 1 IN CHICAGO

Victor Breaks Even or Better in Strong Republican Counties Down-State.

Special to The New York Times.

CHICAGO, Nov. 4.—James Hamilton Lewis, Democrat, and an out-and-out wet, won in a landslide over Representative Ruth Hanna McCormick, Republican and "provisionally wet," in today's election of a Senator from Illinois.

After a campaign in which the Democrats stressed prohibition and prosperity, something of a seismic upheaval struck this rock-ribbed Republican State—the home of Lincoln, the first Republican President—and ex-Senator Lewis's plurality seems likely to approach 700,000. The politicians rate it the greatest blow against national prohibition thus far struck.

Incomplete returns at midnight indicated that the Democrats gained three Congressional seats from Cook County districts, two and possibly three seats down-State, and the two places as members of Congress-at-Large. Correspondingly, the complexion of the Illinois delegation to Washington had been changed by wet gains of eight or nine seats.

Figures from nearly half of the State show Mr. Lewis far in the lead both in Cook County, which includes Chicago, and down-State.

Goes Into Lead Down-State.

In Chicago he was running three to one ahead of Mrs. McCormick, the count indicating that his Chicago plurality will be around 425,000.

Mr. Lewis had 365,982 votes in 1,675 out of 3,009 city precincts; 15,400 in 80 other Cook County precincts, and 256,558 in 1,609 down-State precincts, or a total of 637,940 in 3,394 out of 7,109 precincts in the whole State. His plurality on these returns was 351,676 over Mrs. McCormick, whose vote was 126,724 in Cook County and 286,264 in the 3,394 precincts from all parts of the State. In the same number of districts, Mrs. Lottie Holman O'Neill, Independent Dry, polled 30,448 votes.

Mrs. McCormick seemed likely to

Continued on Page Two.

MORROW WINS EASILY

Majority of 100,000 In Jersey Senate Race Indicated.

PARTY LOSES IN HOUSE

Democrats Leading in Six Districts Nominally Republican.

TWO BOND ISSUES WINNING

Legislature Safely Republican—Anti-Prohibitionists Score Heavily.

Dwight W. Morrow, former Ambassador to Mexico, was leading by a wide margin his two Democratic opponents in his race for both the full and short terms for United States Senator from New Jersey early this morning as the returns were coming in from the 3,321 election districts. Voters in 2,052 districts gave Mr. Morrow 322,014 and Alexander D. Simpson, former State Senator from Hudson County, 227,837.

E. Bertram Mott, chairman of the Republican State Committee, said early this morning a conservative estimate of Mr. Morrow's majority would be 100,000. Republican leaders before the election had predicted a majority of 200,000.

Tabulation of returns from 729 districts showed that Mr. Morrow was leading Miss Thelma Parkinson, Smith College Graduate, in the race for the short term or vacancy caused by the resignation of Walter E. Edge to become Ambassador to France, by a vote of 108,972 to 65,524.

Returns from 1,090 out of 3,321 election districts showed two of the $100,000,000 bond issue proposals winning and one losing as follows: Highways, 83,653 against, 78,740 for; water supply, 78,343 against, 88,442 for, and institutional rehabilitation, 80,105 against and 84,956 for.

Democrats were leading in contests for the House of Representatives in six districts nominally Republican, and that the State Legislature was overwhelmingly Republican.

Mr. Simpson, as candidate for the full term, and Miss Parkinson, as candidate for the short term, polled a surprisingly heavy vote in the early returns although they ran ahead in only three counties, Hudson, Democratic stronghold; Mercer and Middlesex. The Democrats were greatly encouraged by the early returns giving Mr. Simpson and Miss Parkinson leads in half a dozen counties. The leads for the Democratic candidates were accounted for by the fact that they came from industrial centres.

While Mercer, a strongly Republican county, gave Mr. Simpson and Miss Parkinson substantial leads in the early returns, the Republicans expected to see those margins dwindle with the tabulation of returns outside Trenton. The strength of the Democrats in Trenton is said to have been due to the unemployment problem which has been acute there for months.

Representative Mary T. Norton, vice chairman of the Democratic State Committee, conceded the election of Mr. Morrow at 1:25 o'clock this morning.

"Senator Simpson and Miss Thelma Parkinson waged an aggressive and clean battle," said Mrs. Norton. "The opposing forces, wealth and great publicity, supporting fine personality, were hard to overcome and the inevitable resulted. I wish Mr. Morrow every success."

Mrs. Norton Re-elected.

Mrs. Norton was re-elected to the House of Representatives from the Twelfth Congressional District. Fred A. Hartley, Republican, who defeated Paul Moore, Democrat, two years

Continued on Page Five.

Roosevelt Appraises Victory As Expression of Confidence

Governor Franklin D. Roosevelt, speaking over the radio after his re-election had been conceded last night, interpreted the vote he received as one of confidence.

"I want to say a few words to the people of this State tonight," he declared over stations WEAF and WJZ. "I am overwhelmed with gratitude for the vote of confidence you have given to my administration.

"I can only say that in the next two years I will bring all my ability to serve all of the citizens, regardless of party and regardless of locality, in the interest of a program of honest government."

NEW ENGLAND HIT BY DEMOCRATIC WAVE

Massachusetts Elects M. A. Coolidge, Wet, for Senator, and Ely for Governor.

CROSS WINS IN CONNECTICUT

Former Yale Dean Surprises by Victory—Metcalf Rhode Island Winner.

New England Results.

New England Democrats were victorious in two States. Their candidates for United States Senator and Governor, Marcus A. Coolidge and Joseph B. Ely, won in Massachusetts and their nominee for Governor of Connecticut, former Dean Wilbur L. Cross of Yale, was elected. The Republicans carried Rhode Island, New Hampshire and Vermont.

Special to The New York Times.

BOSTON, Nov. 4.—Massachusetts saw a Democratic sweep in today's election which, while not extending throughout the entire State ticket or into the Congressional fight in the sixteen districts, carried a wet Democrat into the United States Senatorship and the Governorship, by decisive margins.

With about two-thirds of the vote counted, it is estimated that former Senator William M. Butler, dry Republican candidate for the Senate, will be defeated by about 75,000 votes by Marcus A. Coolidge, the Democratic candidate. The same returns indicated the defeat of Governor Frank G. Allen, Republican, by 25,000 votes at the hands of Joseph P. Ely, Democrat.

The vote of 1,070 precincts out of the 1,650 in the State gave:

For Governor—Allen, 345,694; Ely, 365,630.

For Senator—Butler, 319,241; Coolidge, 389,432.

State Dry Act Repeal Carried.

At the same time it was indicated that the referendum for repeal of the "baby volstead act," as the State prohibition enforcement law is known, would be carried by more than 200,000.

The vote on the question from 886 precincts, exclusive of Boston, stood: For repeal, 304,951; against repeal, 186,550.

Led by Boston, the cities of the Commonwealth were largely instrumental in piling up the winning Democratic majority. The Boston vote alone, it was estimated, would have

Continued on Page Nine.

TUTTLE IS SWAMPED

Governor's Record Plurality Amazes His Own Party.

CARRIES TICKET WITH HIM

Lehman and Tremaine Re-elected—Bennett Also Victorious.

UP-STATE FOR ROOSEVELT

Sweep Exceeds Smith's Largest Plurality of 385,338—Lieutenant Governor Wins Easily.

Tables of the city and State votes on Pages 10 and 11.

In a Democratic landslide of unprecedented proportions, Governor Franklin D. Roosevelt was re-elected yesterday by a plurality of approximately 730,000 over Charles H. Tuttle, Republican nominee.

In his overwhelming victory, Governor Roosevelt carried with him Lieut. Gov. Herbert H. Lehman, Controller Morris S. Tremaine and John J. Bennett Jr., candidate for Attorney General, who also obtained large pluralities in New York City but ran far behind the Governor up-State.

Professor Robert P. Carroll, Independent dry, running as the candidate of the Law Enforcement party, polled a vote of nearly 170,000, all but about 8,885 of which was outside New York City. Professor Carroll carried Yates County over both Tuttle and Roosevelt and his vote cut heavily into the usual Republican vote in many up-State counties.

556,868 Plurality in City.

New York City gave Governor Roosevelt 556,868 plurality. The vote in the city for Governor was: Roosevelt, 926,665; Tuttle, 369,797; Louis Waldman, Socialist, 88,329, and Carroll, 8,885.

With 168 up-State election districts missing, 4,816 districts out of 4,976 gave Roosevelt, 826,662; Tuttle, 659,163; Carroll, 158,323, an actual plurality for Roosevelt of 167,499 and an indicated up-State plurality of 174,160 and an indicated plurality in the entire State of 730,925. The up-State vote for Roosevelt in these 4,816 districts exceeded the combined vote for Tuttle and Carroll by 10,461.

Carroll's up-State vote was 158,323.

The tremendous vote for Governor Roosevelt was regarded as increasing greatly his chance for the Democratic nomination for President in 1932, for which he is known to be an aspirant. In rolling up his plurality, Governor Roosevelt reached a mark never before attained by any other candidate for State office. His plurality of 556,868 in New York City would have been a record if it had not been exceeded by the city plurality of Lieut. Gov. Lehman, which was 607,087.

The largest plurality ever received in the State by Alfred E. Smith and

Continued on Page Three.

Times Wide World Photo.

OVERWHELMINGLY RE-ELECTED.

Governor Franklin D. Roosevelt, Who, With His Entire Ticket, Is Returned to Office by a Record Plurality.

REPUBLICANS RETAIN CONTROL AT ALBANY

Hold Assembly by a Reduced Margin—Advantage in the Senate Cut to One Seat.

UP-STATE WETS VICTORIOUS

Drys Who Promised to Defeat Them Fail—Hofstadter Elected by 227 Votes.

Despite the landslide which resulted in the re-election of Governor Roosevelt by a towering majority, the Republicans will continue in control of both branches of the Legislature.

Late returns from the legislative elections give the Republicans continued control of both the Senate and Assembly, barring upsets on revised returns in some districts where the vote was close.

Final election returns received early this morning show the Republicans failed to hold their own in the Senate elections. The 1931 Senate, accordingly, will be composed of twenty-six Republicans and twenty-five Democrats.

The Democrats made heavy inroads on the Republicans in the Assembly elections. In the present Assembly the Republicans hold eighty-six seats and the Democrats sixty-four. In the 1931 Assembly the Republicans will have eighty votes and the Democrats seventy, a gain of six votes for the Democrats and a corresponding loss for the Republicans.

The vote necessary to pass a bill in the Senate is twenty-six and in the Assembly seventy-six.

New York City thus will have only one Republican representative in the Senate and only two in the Assembly. In the present Assembly there are four Republican Assemblymen, all from Manhattan. In the 1931 Assembly there will be one from Manhattan, Abbot Lowe Moffat of the Fifteenth, and one from Brooklyn, Robert K. Story Jr. of the Seventeenth Kings District.

Wald Defeated Here.

In the Senate the day was saved to the Republicans through the re-election of Senator Samuel H. Hofstadter of the Seventeenth Senatorial District on the west side of Manhattan. Mr. Hofstadter's victory was won by a slender majority of 227 votes. He defeated Albert Wald, the Democratic nominee, for whom a terrific drive was made by the Democrats in an attempt to gain control of the upper house at Albany

Continued on Page Four.

CITY GIVES GOVERNOR GREATEST PLURALITY

Has Margin of 556,868 as Graft Issue Fails Tuttle—Lehman Leads His Ticket.

MRS. PRATT WINS BY 651

La Guardia Victorious—Miller Elected Judge, Alger Loses—Bond Issue Carries.

Governor Roosevelt carried the city yesterday by the unprecedented plurality of 556,868 votes over his Republican rival, Charles H. Tuttle. His associates on the ticket also piled up huge pluralities over Republican opponents, that of Lieut. Gov. Lehman reaching the mark of 607,087.

The city's vote for Governor was:

Roosevelt	926,665
Tuttle	369,797
Waldman	88,329
Carroll	8,883

Governor Roosevelt's tremendous plurality, although far above the pre-election estimates of John F. Curry and other Democratic leaders, did not arouse the enthusiasm which has greeted the news of large pluralities in the past years. The early estimates were regarded as extremely conservative, the Democratic leaders having somewhat discounted the more optimistic reports which came from the district leaders.

Mrs. Pratt Wins Close Race.

The Democratic landslide carried into office nearly all of the party's local candidates, such strong Republican candidates as Representative Ruth B. Pratt, Representative F. H. La Guardia and State Senator Samuel H. Hofstadter narrowly escaping defeat. The only upset was in Brooklyn where Robert K. Storey Jr., Republican, won against his Democratic rival for an Assembly seat. This was counterbalanced by the victory of D. H. Stephens, Democrat, who was elected to the Assembly in the Nineteenth Manhattan District.

This district, incidentally, is the one in which Martin J. Healy is Democratic leader. Mr. Healy is one of the central figures in the judiciary scandals upon which Mr. Tuttle largely based his fruitless campaign.

The election was one of the quietest in years, there being but few disturbances at the polling places. From the moment that the returns began to come in it was evident that the issue of judicial corruption and alleged bartering of judicial office would have no effect upon the Roosevelt vote. Nor did the driving rain which fell throughout the day keep

Continued on Page Three.

STILL LEAD IN SENATE

But Republican Hold on House Hangs on Belated Returns.

SEE PRESAGE FOR 1932

Democrats Are Victorious in Nearly All the Chief Battles.

PINCHOT BEATS HEMPHILL

Election of Bulkley, a Wet, as Senator in Ohio Seems Indicated.

By RICHARD V. OULAHAN.

A distinct Democratic sweep, suggesting a landslide for that party, extended across the country in yesterday's elections, held in all the forty-eight States except Maine. While the outcome of a number of contests for important public offices is still in doubt, the Democrats were victorious in most of the outstanding battles from which definite returns have been received.

The general trend of these returns up to the time this edition of The New York Times went to press furnished encouraging evidence to Democracy's leaders that the sentiment expressed at the polls throughout a widespread area presaged victory for their Presidential ticket in the elections of 1932.

Democratic Governors were elected in New York, Connecticut, Massacusetts, Rhode Island and Ohio, and in States normally Democratic. In such States as Kansas, Minnesota, Nebraska, Oregan and Wyoming, where the Republicans win more often than not, the result is in doubt on account of the strong trend of Democratic sentiment.

Senate Lead Slender.

Judging by the latest returns, there is a bare chance that the nominal Republican majority in the Senate will be overthrown, although the prospect is that the Republicans may still have a slight excess of members over the Democrats. It is possible, however, that the next Senate will be a tie politically.

Democratic Senators have been elected in place of Republicans in Colorado, Minnesota, Ohio, Oklahoma, West Virginia and Massachusetts, and the chances favor a victory for the Republican Senatorial candidate in South Dakota. Only one Republican Senatorial aspirant has triumphed over a sitting Democratic Senator. This happened in Iowa.

In line with the general Democratic swing, the return showed that candidates of that party have cut heavily into the big Republican majority in the House of Representatives with a fair prospect that the Democrats will get control, though the actual outcome remains in doubt.

Based on the latest returns, the Senate line-up appears to be 45 Democrats, 47 Republicans and 1 Farmer-Laborite, with 3 contests doubtful. This line-up concedes the election of Hoidale, Democrat, over Senator Schall, Republican, in Minnesota. The doubtful contests are in South Dakota, Kansas and Kentucky. Should the Democratic candidates carry all these contests the Senate would stand:

Democrats 48, Republicans 47, Farmer-Laborite 1.

Heavy gains were made by the Democrats in the contest for 431 seats in the House of Representatives, but whether these will be sufficient to wipe out the present Republican majority is uncertain, with returns incomplete from approximately threescore districts.

Results of Latest Figures.

Counting nine vacant seats which had been held by Republicans, the majority of that party in the present House is 103. The latest definite election returns give the Republicans 189 seats, the Democrats 200 and the Farmer-Labor party 1, with 44 in the doubtful column and 1 Independent Republican.

The Democrats have 165 members

Heflin Is Beaten in Alabama by Nearly 2 to 1; Democrats Defeat All Candidates on His Ticket

Special to The New York Times.

BIRMINGHAM, Ala., Nov. 4.—J. Thomas Heflin, senior Senator from Alabama, was defeated by the Democrats of the State today for his defection from the party in the 1928 Presidential election. With three-fourths of the vote counted, John H. Bankhead, his opponent, was leading by 46,007 votes out of a total of 211,627. The vote stood 128,817 for Bankhead and 82,810 for Heflin.

Judge B. M. Miller, for Governor, and Hugh Merrill, for Lieutenant Governor, were holding the same commanding lead over Hugh Locke and Dempsey Powell, "Jeffersonian" candidates running on the same ticket with Senator Heflin.

In a statement to The Montgomery Advertiser tonight Senator Heflin charged "fraud and corruption" in the election and said he would demand an investigation by the Senate Committee on Elections.

"While early returns indicate the vote is going against me, within two hours I will be 100,000 votes ahead."

Boxes which went overwhelmingly for Hoover in the 1928 election went just as strongly for the Democratic nominees today.

No serious political issues were at stake in the election other than whether Alabama would remain in the Democratic column or would become an active two-party State.

"All the News That's Fit to Print."

The New York Times.

Copyright, 1931, by The New York Times Company.

LATE CITY EDITION

THE WEATHER—Fair today and tomorrow; not much change in temperature. Temperatures yesterday—Max. 68, min. 47. U. S. Weather Forecast—For details see Page 54.

VOL. LXXX....No. 26,744. NEW YORK, WEDNESDAY, APRIL 15, 1931. TWO CENTS in Greater New York | THREE CENTS Within 200 Miles | FOUR CENTS Elsewhere Except 7th and 8th Postal Zones

KING ALFONSO QUITS, SPAIN A REPUBLIC; ALCALA ZAMORA IS FIRST PRESIDENT; NATION ORDERLY UNDER MARTIAL LAW

GOVERNOR REQUESTS MINUTES ON CRAIN; QUICK DECISION SEEN

Critics of Prosecutor Predict Early Action—Albany Denies Move Is Significant.

PATHE HEARING ON MONDAY

Seabury Moves to Wind Up the Inquiry May 1—Rothstein Case Is Taken Up.

KLEIN DATA TO PROSECUTOR

Harvey Rebuffed in Plea for Bribe Evidence—Hofstadter Summons Legislative Committee.

Developments yesterday in the investigations into city affairs were:

Governor Roosevelt called upon Samuel Seabury for the minutes of the public hearings on rackets in the removal proceedings against District Attorney Crain.

State Senator Hofstadter called a meeting of the legislative inquiry committee to be held here on Monday.

Controller Berry refused to give Borough President Harvey the transcript of evidence against Irving Klein, borough highway superintendent, to be used at a public hearing today, saying evidence on bribery charge would be sent directly to the Queens District Attorney.

GOVERNOR ACTS ON CRAIN.

Governor Roosevelt wrote to Commissioner Samuel Seabury yesterday requesting a copy of the minutes of the public hearings in the removal proceedings against District Attorney Crain. The Governor took this step twenty-four hours after the elderly prosecutor confessed helplessness against racketeers, who, he said, infest the business structure of the city.

The Governor's letter, made public in Albany before it was received by Mr. Seabury, caused considerable surprise, because it had been understood that the commissioner would make no report until he had concluded his investigation of the City Club's charges against Mr. Crain.

Considerable speculation arose immediately regarding the significance of the Governor's letter. Critics of the District Attorney, pointing out that the Governor has power to remove Mr. Crain at any stage of the proceedings, were inclined to the belief that the Governor was anticipating a request from some civic body for immediate action.

Persons close to the Governor, however, insisted that his action was predicated only upon a desire to keep informed of the progress of the inquiry he set in motion in order to be able to act promptly when Mr. Seabury filed his report. The letter seemed to bear out this belief, for in it the Governor expressed the desire "to keep up with the matter currently."

Text of Governor's Letter.

The letter follows:

April 13, 1931.

My dear Judge Seabury:

If it is not inconsistent with the progress of your work as Commissioner representing the Governor in the matter of the District Attorney in New York, I would appreciate your sending me the copy of the minutes of the public hearings held up to the present time, and also of other public hearings as they occur.

This will enable me to keep up with the matter currently.

Very truly yours,
FRANKLIN D. ROOSEVELT.

Crain Had Attacked Governor.

In closing his defense to the first phase of the charges against him—the allegation that he was lax in prosecuting racketeers in Fulton fish market, Mr. Crain said he would be able to function more effectively if he were not subjected to "attacks from the rear." Part of his helplessness against racketeers, he attributed to Governor Roosevelt's failure to request the Legislature in a special message to grant him the power to issue compulsory subpoenaes and examine witnesses under oath.

Overshadowing all this, however, was Mr. Crain's admission that racketeers were virtually immune from punishment so far as he and the police were concerned, and his declaration that in his opinion the evidence of racketeering in Fulton Market adduced by John Kirkland Clark, counsel to Mr. Seabury, was not sufficient to warrant a resubmission of the case to a new grand jury.

Although the public hearings have been adjourned until next Monday, the private examination of witnesses

Continued on Page Twenty-one.

Crowded Hours of a Busy Day In President Hoover's Life

Special to The New York Times.

WASHINGTON, April 14.—With two addresses, ten innings of an exciting American League game, a Cabinet meeting and a dinner tonight, President Hoover spent one of his busiest days since he entered the White House.

Here is the schedule of the chief events:

8:00 A. M.—Rises.
8:00 A. M.—Medicine ball.
8:00 A. M.—Breakfast.
9:30-10:15 A. M.—Brief conference with callers.
10:30 A. M.—Cabinet meeting.
12:00 M.—Receives delegation of tourists.
12:30 P. M.—Speech at Pan-American Day celebration.
1:00 P. M.—Luncheon.
3:00 P. M.—Attends opening American League baseball game.
5:00 P. M.—Speaks by radio from White House to Tuskegee celebration.
8:00 P. M.—Dines with Secretary of the Navy and Mrs. Adams.
11:00 P. M.—Retires.

The usual noon conference with newspaper men was omitted because of the other demands on the President's time.

BETHLEHEM BONUS GETS 72% OF PROXIES

Management Apparently Wins Approval for System That Paid Grace $1,625,753 in Year.

SCHWAB PARRIES CRITICS

Holds Practice Is an Incentive, and Says Board Voted Him $250,000 in 1930.

The Bethlehem Steel Corporation's bonus plan, under which officers received approximately $36,000,000 in fourteen years and which is being fought in the courts by a minority group, was apparently ratified overwhelmingly yesterday at the annual meeting of the stockholders in Newark.

While a restraining order by Vice Chancellor Backes in Trenton prohibited the stockholders from announcing the result of their vote or recording it pending a determination of the minority stockholders' suit, the management announced that it was voting proxies representing 72 per cent of the outstanding common and preferred stock of the Bethlehem Steel Corporation. So it was assumed that the management had won approval of the bonus system, which in one year added to the $12,000 salary of Eugene G. Grace, president, the sum of $1,625,753.

Schwab Backs System.

Responsibility for the bonus system of the corporation was assumed by Charles M. Schwab, chairman, who maintained that the additional sum to the management was not a "gratuity," which would be an insult, but rather "part payment" by the corporation for services.

With rapier-like swiftness the veteran chairman of Bethlehem parried thrusts so skillfully that even his opponents sometimes joined in the applause that greeted his repartee and his sallies.

His black eyes flashing and a smile of sureness playing around his lips, Mr. Schwab had a ready answer for William H. Gilman, director of the Jefferson County National Bank of Watertown, when he wanted to know why Mr. Grace, with his huge bonus, should have received for his services to the comparatively small body of stockholders of the corporation more than the President of the United States gets for his services to the people of the country.

"I appreciate your sincerity," said Mr. Schwab. "I only object to your comparison of Grace's salary to the President's. The United States Government is not a business enterprise, but I would give five times $75,000 a year to be President of the United States."

At one point of his address Mr. Schwab said that the bonus system as he had originated it for Bethlehem was designed not so much as a reward as an "incentive." He said that he had placed Mr. Grace "upon a pedestal," so that he would have to live up to his high position for the good of the corporation.

He asserted that he had learned the lesson of large rewards to produce large returns from his old employer and mentor, the late Andrew Carnegie, who said that it was necessary to make men feel big and act big to accomplish big things.

Mr. Schwab disclosed that for the first seven years after he organized Bethlehem Steel Corporation he had not only backed the undertaking with his entire fortune, as he later did through many crises, but that he had served as its head without compensation. He was answering the question he said he heard people often ask: "What does C. M. get out of it?"

"I have been the highest paid man in the United States for a good many years," said Mr. Schwab. "Some years my compensation was in

Continued on Page Twenty.

4 AMERICANS KILLED IN SANDINO ADVANCE; WARSHIP LANDS MEN

Three Missing as Nicaraguan Rebels Near Puerto Cabezas After Jungle Skirmishes.

HEAVIER LOSSES FEARED

Fruit Company Hears Eleven Americans and Some British Employes Were Slain.

8 REBELS KILLED BY GUARD

25 Marines Board Gunboat Again When Patrols Return From Clash —300 Americans in Town.

Special to The New York Times.

WASHINGTON, April 14.—According to a report from the gunboat Asheville of the Special Service Squadron, which arrived this morning at Puerto Cabezas on the east coast of Nicaragua, preliminary skirmishes between rebel groups under Augusto Sandino, advancing toward the town, and National Guardsmen have in the past twenty-four hours resulted in four Americans being killed and three missing.

Their names were not given except for that of a Moravian missionary named Briggenzer, who was said to have been killed at Mussias. Other reports said six unnamed foreigners had been killed.

As rebel groups under Sandino, Pedron and Blandon moved through the jungle by way of the Coco River and the Pis-Pis Trail with threats to reach Puerto Cabezas "dead or alive," National Guard reinforcements also moved down the Coco River, the preliminary skirmishes resulting.

Gunboat Lands Men.

The fact that Sandino and his chieftains, who have long operated in the Northwestern Provinces of Nicaragua, were transferring their operations to the east coast, with Puerto Cabezas as their objective, thereby precipitating another serious problem for the government of President Moncada and the American naval forces and marines, was disclosed in reports received by the Navy Department today and made public by the State Department.

Simultaneously it was announced that the Asheville had arrived this morning at Puerto Cabezas from Panama and immediately landed forces which will remain until the Nicaraguan National Guard has arrived in sufficient strength to meet the emergency. Then the bluejackets and marines will be withdrawn and such Americans of the 300 in Puerto Cabezas and vicinity as desire to leave will be evacuated. These Americans are employes of the Standard Fruit and Steamship Company, which owns the Bragman's Bluff Lumber Company.

A disquieting circumstance is that rebels have interposed themselves between the National Guard detachment in the jungle and Puerto Cabezas.

Lieutenant Clyde Roy Darrah of the marines, who is in command of a detachment of the Guard, contrary to unofficial reports yesterday, is alive but at last reports was surrounded by seventy-five rebels under Blandon.

Statement Issued.

The situation was outlined by the State Department today in the following statement:

"The commander of the Asheville, now at Puerto Cabezas, reports that all the Guardia except one officer and a few men have left Puerto Cabezas in operations against the ban-

Continued on Page Fifteen.

Utah Woman Is First Chosen To the Presbyterian Assembly

Special to The New York Times.

PHILADELPHIA, April 14.—Election of Mrs. B. J. Silliman of Green River, Utah, as a commissioner to the Pennsylvania General Assembly was reported today to Presbyterian headquarters here.

Mrs. Silliman, a ruling elder from the Presbytery of Southern Utah, thus becomes the first woman in the United States to be recorded as a commissioner in the highest court of the denomination. Last year's General Assembly made women eligible to the office.

The General Assembly has a total membership of about 950, equally divided between ministers and ruling elders.

PAN-AMERICAN AMITY HAILED BY PRESIDENT

All Major Differences Will Be Settled by Conciliation and Arbitration, He Says.

TIES FOSTER AGREEMENT

Address Opens First Celebration of Pan-American Day Amid Banners of 21 Nations.

Special to The New York Times.

WASHINGTON, April 14.—The time is not far away when every major difference between the American republics will be settled by the orderly processes of conciliation and arbitration, President Hoover declared today at the first celebration of Pan-American Day. Speaking at the auditorium of the Pan American Union, the President was acclaimed by the diplomatic staffs of all the American republics, by official Washington and scores of others.

It was an inspiring sight within and without. Outside the flags of all the American republics stretched to the breeze. Thronging about were hundreds, unable to get into the building, who waited to witness the arrival and departure of the President. Because of the cherry blossoms in Potomac Park, Washington is crowded with visitors from all parts of the country.

At a ceremony in the gardens of the union, the standards of the twenty-one nations of the Pan American Union were presented to schools and colleges located in and near Washington. The presentation was made by the governing board of the union.

Appeals for Understanding.

The President took peace and goodwill among the Americas as the theme of his address. He referred to his visit to many of the Central and South American nations when he was President-elect in 1928. That tour of the sister republics, he declared, had made a deep and lasting impression on him. He was convinced that the twenty-one nations of the union have everything to gain by "keeping in close touch with one another and by developing that spirit of mutual confidence which has its roots in a reciprocal understanding of national aims and aspirations."

"The spirit of mutual helpfulness," the President added, "is the cornerstone of true Pan-Americanism."

It was near the close of his address that President Hoover pictured the bright future of the Americans—one of mediation, conciliation and arbitration, the full significance of which, he said, is not always realized. He pleaded for an unswerving determination to make the union of the American republics, as now expressed in the Pan American Union, an example to all the other nations of the world.

Secretary of State Stimson echoed the words of the President and said that the nations of the Western

Continued on Page Eighteen.

Fire Wrecks the Bluecher Palace in Berlin; Just Bought for $1,800,000 for Our Embassy

Special Cable to THE NEW YORK TIMES.

BERLIN, Wednesday, April 15.—The famous Bluecher Palace on Unter den Linden, which was recently bought by the United States for its embassy, was almost completely destroyed by fire during the night. The fire was under control early this morning.

BERLIN, April 14 (AP).—The right wing of the three-story Bluecher Palace was ablaze when the firemen arrived. Additional alarms emptied the firehouses and almost every piece of apparatus in the city was called out.

Despairing of saving the palace, firemen concentrated on saving nearby buildings.

The offices of the United States Commercial Attaché, which have been located in the palace for several months, were completely destroyed, but there were no known casualties.

The Bluecher Palace, one of the most imposing buildings in the heart of Berlin, was acquired by the American Government on Dec. 10 for about $1,800,000, after negotiations with a Berlin real estate company that began last June, the real estate company acting in the transaction for Prince Bluecher, great-great-grandson of the Bluecher of Waterloo.

The Palace, adjoining the Brandenburger Gate, had about 120 rooms and occupied 65,000 square feet. Built in the eighteenth century, it was one of the historical landmarks in the German capital. The palace was presented to Marshal Bluecher, the "Marshal Vorwärts" of fame, by King Frederick William III in gratitude for his services in the defeat of Napoleon at Waterloo.

The palace figured prominently in the social life of the German capital under the Hohenzollerns, but after the World War it was converted into an office building.

At the time of the sale to the United States it was announced that the leases held by various tenants would not expire until the end of this year and that, with considerable remodeling to be done, the palace would not be ready for occupancy by our embassy until the middle of 1932.

BRITAIN TO WELCOME EXILE

Alfonso Is Regarded as Member of English Royal Family.

HIS WIFE IS KING'S COUSIN

Much of the Huge Fortune of Deposed Monarch Said to Be Safe in London.

REPUBLICANS TO QUIT PARIS

Members of New Cabinet Pack Belongings to Rush to Madrid —They See Huge Task.

By FERDINAND KUHN Jr.
Special Cable to THE NEW YORK TIMES.

LONDON, April 14.—The royal family and the people of Britain are preparing tonight to receive Alfonso of Spain as the latest of royal exiles to find refuge on British soil.

The last of the Bourbons will, however, be an exile with a difference. Unlike Manoel of Portugal and George of Greece—two former kings who are now living in England—Alfonso is a member of the British royal family through his marriage to King George's first cousin. Although the plans are indefinite, there is every reason to believe Alfonso and his English queen will live here with the rank not only of former monarchs but of British royalties as well.

Royal Invitation Likely.

It is expected that King George and Queen Mary will first invite Alfonso to Windsor Castle, where he has been a frequent visitor and where he is enrolled as a voter in the town. Later he is expected to make a home of the imposing Spanish embassy on Belgrave Square where that most royal of all Ambassadors, Marqués de Merry del Val today shut himself in against visitors in his grief at the fall of the throne.

No London house is better fitted to be a king's than the Belgrave Square mansion, only a few doors away from the equally stately home of Prince and Princess Arthur of Connaught. Alfonso and King George have been occasional guests there. As soon as it is decided that ex-King Alfonso is coming to Britain it is expected Marqués de Merry Del Val will offer the house to the fallen monarch, whose most devoted friend he has been for years.

The Ambassador felt the blow keenly today. Until as late as this afternoon he believed everything was quiet and that the throne was in no danger. The King's loss of his throne will be even more heartbreaking to the veteran diplomat than the fact that he is to be succeeded by a Republican as Ambassador. No one, not even Alfonso himself, has been a stauncher Monarchist than Marqués de Merry Del Val, whose brother was Papal Secretary of State for years and who has had an equally notable career as dean of London's diplomatic corps.

British Royalty Concerned.

The British royal family was deeply concerned today by the news from Spain. A few weeks ago, when Alfonso left London, the King and Queen paid him the unusual tribute of going to the railroad station to see him off. Since the war years, when Alfonso alienated the affection of the British royal family by his German sympathies, there has been a complete transformation in the relations between the royal relatives in London and Madrid.

For a few years after the armistice Alfonso seldom visited Buckingham Palace and stayed at Claridge's Hotel. Now, however, his popularity at the palace is greater than ever and the sympathetic help of the British royal family surely will be extended to him in his exile here.

Although Alfonso has lost his throne, he still has a huge fortune. With a prudent eye for eventualities he has been quietly transferring securities and valuables outside of Spain, it is reported here, and much of the private wealth of the royal family has thus been safeguarded. Those who know him intimately say his private fortune is one of the largest in Europe. Much of this wealth, derived largely from investments in Spain, is now believed to be in England.

He has great business and financial ability and is known to have speculated profitably in almost every big

Continued on Page Three.

KING ALFONSO XIII.

Photo by Van Dyck.

WASHINGTON ENVOY OF SPAIN TO RESIGN

Diplomatic Circles Fear Era of Chaos—State Department Awaits Official Report.

BIG CREDIT NOT WITHDRAWN

$60,000,000 Loan to Bank of Spain May Still Be Used, Say New York Financiers.

Special to The New York Times.

WASHINGTON, April 14.—The Spanish Embassy was stunned by the abdication of King Alfonso XIII today. Although, in the absence of any official information from Madrid, it declined to make any statement, there appeared to be no doubt that Señor Don Alejandro Padilla y Bell, who has been Ambassador since Oct. 11, 1926, will resign when he is officially notified of the swift turn of events in Spain.

The Ambassador not only is the personal appointee of King Alfonso XIII, but is personally a monarchist. In the former respect he differs from the other officials of the Embassy, who were appointed by the Foreign Office. Some of them may also tender their resignations, but if they do so it will be because of personal political views and not for official causes.

Ambassador Irwin B. Laughlin cabled from Madrid that King Alfonso had turned the government over to Niceto Alcala Zamora, Republican leader and Provisional President, and that Ministers for the Provisional Government had been named. He said that the King, with the royal family, was expected to leave Spain immediately.

Ambassador Laughlin said considerable excitement in Madrid attended the overturn of the government, but no violence of any consequence.

Although American officials would not discuss possibilities, in diplomatic circles fear was expressed that a period of disorder and even of chaos might result, should the authority of the army and the Church break down. Spaniards, it was asserted, are individualists, but a stable order has been maintained through the centrifugal force of the monarchy, with the army and the Church assisting.

Huge Credit Not Affected.

The status of the $60,000,000 eighteen-month credit extended last month to the Bank of Spain by an international banking group is not affected by the recent political developments in that country in the opinion of bankers who participated in the American portion of the credit. Pending a clearer view of the rapidly moving situation in Spain, no definite statement on the subject could be obtained yesterday from the offices of J. P. Morgan & Co. or the other American banks which sub-

Continued on Page Three.

CATALONIA TO STAY IN SPAIN AS STATE

Separatists Decide on Move After Announcing They Would Be Independent.

ROYALISTS YIELD EASILY

Colonel Macia Takes City Hall Without Resistance and Begins Emptying Jails.

By The Associated Press.

BARCELONA, Wednesday, April 15.—Francisco Macia, Provisional President of the Catalonian Republic, issued a declaration early today that he had "assumed office provisionally under Señor Zamora as head of the Federated Spanish Republic," and that the Catalonian Republic would be an integral State within the Spanish Federation.

Ousted Royalist Mayor.

Special Cable to THE NEW YORK TIMES.

BARCELONA, April 14.—A Catalan Republic has been proclaimed here.

The Municipal Councilors elected on Sunday took possession of the Hotel de Ville today and Colonel Francisco Macia, the Republican leader, took over the government of the province. The Municipal Council and the Provincial Council immediately proclaimed a Catalan Republic.

Colonel Macia is leader of the Catalan separatist movement. In 1927 he proclaimed a Catalan Republic from the Pyrenees and then was arrested by French authorities.

The military authorities of the Fortress Mont Juich have released a number of military prisoners who had been arrested for their Republican leanings. A popular demonstration followed their release, more than 3,000 persons forming a procession and escorting the liberated prisoners to the town hall.

Complete orders reigns thus far, although the carrying of Republican flags through the streets led to one or two minor skirmishes. The military forts of Barcelona have put themselves under the orders of Colonel Macia. All public buildings are flying Republican flags alongside the Catalan colors, and it is generally hoped here that Colonel Macia will succeed in obtaining the chief points of his program—the political liberty of Catalonia, which would become a federal unit of the Spanish Republic.

No Resistance to Coup.

BARCELONA, April 14 (AP).—While thousands cheered for the republic and the end of the monarchy, Colonel Macia took possession of the City Hall today without force of arms and proclaimed the existence of a Spanish republic.

With the plaza packed with a shouting multitude, Colonel Macia, who was elected an Alderman in the Republican victories Sunday, came to the balcony and announced that

Continued on Page Nine.

MONARCH SAILS ON CRUISER

Crown Prince Is With Him —Queen and Others to Go From Madrid Today.

KING BALKED AT ABDICATION

Left to Avert Bloodshed When Revolt Threatened, but Still Claimed Throne.

MOVE REGARDED AS FINAL

New Rulers Plan New Constitution, but Won't Hold Plebiscite on Monarchy.

By FRANK L. KLUCKHOHN.
Special Cable to THE NEW YORK TIMES.

MADRID, April 14.—King Alfonso XIII, the last of the Bourbons, yielded his throne today and Spain became a republic.

The monarchy, which had stood proudly for fifteen centuries with only one brief intermission, was toppled over in a few breathless hours this afternoon without a drop of bloodshed. The Republican Government, headed by Niceto Alcala Zamora as first President, is installed peacefully in Madrid and the Republican flag is flying everywhere in the country.

Through the blackness of this moonless night Alfonso, accompanied only by the Duke of Miranda, his majordomo and two Civil Guards, it is understood, is speeding toward Cartagena, where he will board a ship for Marseilles. The King left the palace by the garden gate and got out of Madrid before any one was aware of it.

An attempt was made to cloak the fact that he had left the palace and his destination is being kept as secret as possible. It was regarded as dangerous to allow him to go by way of Portugal because of the political disturbance there and equally dangerous for him to travel through Northern Spain, which has shown itself so unmistakably hostile.

Monarch Clung to Throne.

With the aid of Melquiades Alvarez, the chief of the Constitutionalist party, Alfonso drew up and signed a proclamation to be issued tomorrow morning. It is neither an abdication nor a renunciation of the throne, as was first announced, but in effect a statement that the King is leaving Spain for the present to avoid bloodshed while the provisional Republican Government holds elections to decide what the country wants. There is no doubt that tonight's demonstrations show the country wants a republic at the moment.

The passing of the most brilliant court left in Europe was typical of Republican simplicity. Miguel Maura walked into the office of the Minister of the Interior and said:

"There is no precedent for what I am going to do, so I shall merely say that I am taking control of this office."

With the other members of the government he immediately went into the Under-Secretary's office and waited while Señor Alcala Zamora signed the amnesty decree.

Government Gives Its Program.

The Provisional Government held a prolonged meeting tonight and started drawing up its program. Afterward it was announced that until a Cortes (Parliament) could be convoked it would proceed by decree.

In the next sentence was the first indication that Spain is not to have any further chance to revise her opinion as to the kind of government she wants. The Cortes, the government' announcement reads, will not discuss the question of monarchy or republic, but will merely draw up a new constitution for Spain.

The government then went on to declare it would begin an inquiry into why the Parliament of 1923 was dissolved to make way for the directorate and of all subsequent happenings. It will open an investigation to determine responsibilities.

The government makes public its decision to support the right of freedom of worship and belief. It will, it promises, do everything to protect personal liberty. It further declares that personal property in the land being guaranteed by law, there can be no expropriation except for public purposes. With regard, however, to the condition of the masses of the

"All the News That's Fit to Print."

The New York Times.

LATE CITY EDITION
THE WEATHER—Generally fair and warmer today, tomorrow partly cloudy; showers.
Temperatures Yesterday—Max., 74; min., 60.
U. S. Weather Forecast—See next to last page

VOL. LXXXI....No. 26,903. **** + NEW YORK, MONDAY, SEPTEMBER 21, 1931. TWO CENTS in New York City | THREE CENTS Within 200 Miles | FOUR CENTS Elsewhere Except 7th and 8th Postal Zones

GREAT BRITAIN SUSPENDS GOLD PAYMENTS TODAY; CLOSES STOCK EXCHANGE, DISCOUNT RATE UP TO 6%; GERMAN BOERSES SHUT, STOCK MARKET HERE OPEN

NANKING WILL INVOKE KELLOGG PEACE PACT; NEW FIGHTING FEARED

Foreign Minister of China Says League Also Will Be Told of Japanese Acts.

MANCHURIANS PLAN BATTLE

Kirin Troops Expected to Attack Japanese Garrison—Harbin Reported Tense.

SOVIET TROOPS AT BORDER

Foreign Observers at Mukden Hold Japanese Military Deliberately Caused Incident.

By HALLETT ABEND.
Wireless to THE NEW YORK TIMES.

NANKING, Sept. 20.—"Appropriate steps are being taken to apprise the League of Nations and the powers signatory to the Kellogg pact of the unwarranted actions of Japanese troops," C. T. Wang, Foreign Minister of the Nanking Government, declared in a statement this morning concerning the lodging of vigorous protests by the Nanking Government with the Japanese Government. Mr. Wang continued:

"The National Government is greatly exercised over the situation caused by the unprovoked attack of Japanese troops on Mukden and other cities in three eastern provinces."

Says Chinese Did Not Resist.

Mr. Wang's statement makes no reference to the Japanese charge that Chinese soldiers tried to damage the South Manchuria Railway north of Mukden, but says Japanese troops fired on Chinese soldiers encamped at Peitaying, that the Chinese withdrew without resisting and that the Japanese disarmed the Chinese and set the buildings afire.

Mr. Wang charges that simultaneously the Japanese bombarded the arsenal and the Peitaying camp, but while the arsenal was not damaged the camp's mortar depot was destroyed. The Nanking Foreign Minister also charges the Japanese fired upon and occupied all Chinese police stations inside and immediately outside Mukden and disarmed the policemen, seized the wireless station, forcibly occupied all government offices and interrupted all electrical communications.

The Japanese Consulate at Nanking announces the transmission last night to Tokyo of the formal protest of the Nanking Foreign Office in regard to the occupation of Mukden by Japanese troops and a formal request that they immediately evacuate the city.

It is officially announced that seventy-one Chinese soldiers were killed in the clash incident to the occupation of Mukden. The number of Chinese wounded is not known. No civilians were killed. The total of the Japanese casualties was one soldier killed and two wounded.

Japanese officially stress the assertion that the magnitude of the incident was due to the extreme nervousness and tension existing in the Mukden area as a result of a long series of minor clashes and growing feeling on both sides of uneasiness and hostility, which resulted in minor Japanese commanders taking the bit in their teeth and quickly extending the zone of operations without the knowledge or approval of the higher command.

More Fighting Expected.

Wireless to THE NEW YORK TIMES.

MUKDEN, Sept. 20.—More fighting was expected tonight between Japanese and Chinese between Dairen and the Mukden area at those points where Chinese soldiers are quartered along the South Manchuria Railway zone. Now everything is peaceful everywhere, with the Japanese in control.

Chinese are looting in the international section of Mukden, which area in ordinary times is under Chinese control. The Japanese are taking steps to protect the area. Foreign opinion here is that the Japanese military were angry because the Nakamura affair was about to be closed diplomatically, so, according to all foreign observers here, the outbreak on Friday night was premeditated. A Japanese statement says:

"We were always prepared for an emergency, but we were surprised on the night of Sept. 18, when Chinese tried to blow up the South Manchuria Railway tracks and to attack a Japanese garrison. The occupation in various cities and towns was necessary to protect everybody. The incident is unfortunate."

This morning Frank Sugden, a British subject, an engineer of the Peiping-Mukden Railway workshop, attempted to go to his office, which

Continued on Page Eight.

Byrd's Old Supply Ship Sails To Load Labrador Lime Shells

By The Canadian Press.

ST. JOHN'S, N. F., Sept. 20.—Carrying out plans of a company, financed largely by Newfoundland capital, to develop the natural resources of Labrador, the steamer Eleanor Bolling sailed yesterday with fifty men and necessary machinery to take marine shell from Hamilton Inlet.

The Eleanor Bolling, which was supply ship of the Byrd Antarctic expedition, is one of several vessels chartered to convey cargoes to St. John's, where equipment for screening the product and preparing it for market has been installed.

The sun-bleached shell deposits, which have lain on the foreshore of Hamilton Inlet for ages, are said to be almost 100 per cent lime, valuable for poultry feeding and horticultural purposes. First shipments are expected early in October.

WALKER BACK TODAY, BUT WANTS NO 'FUSS'

Elaborate Reception Vetoed—He Will Stay Aboard Ship Until It Reaches Pier.

HE PHILOSOPHIZES ON LINER

One 'Must Laugh on the Stage of Politics No Matter What the Sadness Within,' He Remarks.

Having been widely fêted, dined and honored in Europe, Mayor Walker will return to New York today on the North German Lloyd liner Bremen, on which he sailed for a month's "rest cure" in Germany on Aug. 4.

His return, in so far as reception plans and organized welcome are concerned, will be quiet, Charles F. Kerrigan, Assistant Mayor, said yesterday. Mr. Kerrigan, Thomas F. McAndrews, the Mayor's secretary, and Police Commissioner Mulrooney will go down the harbor in a revenue cutter and board the Bremen at Quarantine.

The receiving tug Macom, the city's official craft for the reception of distinguished visitors and homecomers, will not be used. Mayor Walker will remain aboard the Bremen until she docks at Pier 4 at the foot of Fifty-eighth Street, Brooklyn, probably between 8 and 9 P. M.

May Speak Over Radio.

There he will be met by Mrs. Walker and probably by a group of friends and city officials and he will go from the pier to his home at 6 St. Luke's Place. Mr. Kerrigan said there had been some talk of having the Mayor make a short statement over the radio from the pier. While no definite plans have been made, he felt that if the microphone were installed on the pier the Mayor would make a short speech.

In the Mayor's party and returning with him are Dudley Field Malone, former Collector of the Port of New York, and Dr. William Schroeder Jr., chairman of the Department of Sanitation and the Mayor's personal physician.

It was the Mayor's own wish that his homecoming be without "fuss" or noisy reception. Plans had been made for a demonstration, with a parade, a luncheon or dinner and other details, but the Mayor, by long-distance telephone from London, was understood to have vetoed it.

It is understood that his decision was influenced by the many receptions, dinners and celebrations with which he was met in Germany, creating a spirit more festive than restful, which followed him through Europe.

Feted in Many Cities.

After a short stop in Southampton on Aug. 10 the Mayor landed in Bremen the following day and was the guest at a reception in his honor. The next day he proceeded to Berlin, where he spent several days. While there he visited the Baroness von Huenefeld, mother of the late Baron von Huenefeld, who crossed the Atlantic Ocean in the plane Bremen in 1929.

Among the German watering places he visited were Carlsbad and Marienbad. He went to Pilsen, Budapest, Vienna, Cannes, Monaco and Monte Carlo, everywhere seeking rest and finding that his mere presence prevented it. In Paris he was entertained at luncheon by President Doumer of France and was made a Commander of the Legion of Honor. In London he was the luncheon guest of Premier Ramsay MacDonald.

In Berlin he made a tour of the night resorts within a few hours after his arrival. The next day he was the luncheon guest of the Carl Schurz Association, and the next night, over a radio hook-up by which he was heard in Europe and the United States, he made a speech in praise of the spirit of determination to over-

Continued on Page Five.

PRESIDENT DEPARTS TO ADDRESS LEGION AT DETROIT ON BONUS

He Boards Special Train at Martinsburg, W. Va., After Day at Rapidan Camp.

TO WARN OF HEAVY COST

Washington Thinks He May Touch Also on Economic Situation in Europe.

LEGION COMMANDER FIRM

O'Neil Warns Against Cash-Payment Demands and Hints Danger in Prohibition Stand.

From a Staff Correspondent of The New York Times.

MARTINSBURG, W. Va., Sept. 20.—President Hoover left here on a special train at 8:30 o'clock this evening for Detroit where he will deliver an address tomorrow before the national convention of the American Legion.

The President spent the day at his Rapidan camp in Virginia working on his address, which he will deliver at noon tomorrow, but it was not completed when he left here. There were showers throughout the day, and the President remained indoors most of the time.

The President motored from his Rapidan camp to Martinsburg through Sherryville and Winchester. The last twenty-five miles of the trip were made at the slow speed of twenty-two miles an hour so that the President would arrive just before his train was scheduled to leave. As a result, a long line of automobiles which were not permitted by Secret Service men to pass the President's car trailed after it, and there was a wild blowing of horns.

At Martinsburg about 2,000 people were on hand to greet the President and he was called upon for a speech. He waved his hat, but would not make an address.

Accompanying the President are Captain Train and Colonel Hodges, his naval and military aides, and Secretaries Joslin and Richey. Governor Leslie of Indiana and Mrs. Leslie, who were his guests at the camp, will also accompany the President as far as Indianapolis.

Capital Speculates on Speech.

Special to The New York Times.

WASHINGTON, Sept. 20.—With President Hoover on his way to Detroit tonight to address the national convention of the American Legion tomorrow, speculation continues here as to whether there were several compelling motives for the President's sudden decision to attend the convention, after he had made it plain only a few days previously that he would be unable to do so.

There is unanimity of opinion that the President's chief purpose is to set the great power and authority of the influence which comes from his high office against the movements in the ranks of the Legionnaires for the adoption of a resolution calling on Congress to enact legislation permitting World War veterans to borrow from the government up to the full maturity value of their bonus certificates fourteen years before they mature.

As to Conditions Abroad.

Today's speculative comment had to do with whether the President would give attention in his address to matters of pressing public importance other than the bonus, with a rather widespread inclination to surmise that he would take occasion to sketch economic and financial conditions abroad with their effect on the United States.

Those best informed as to the Ad-

Continued on Page Four.

NEW YORK BANKERS CONFER

See No Need for Drastic Action — Investments in London Moderate.

RECENT LOANS PROTECTED

Federal Reserve Can Demand Gold—Morgan Credit Payable in Dollars.

EFFECT ON PRICES FEARED

Britain's Action Also Expected to Have Repercussions on World Credit Situation.

American security markets will not follow the lead of the London Stock Exchange, but will be open for business as usual today. No emergency has developed here to warrant any action similar to that in the foreign countries, it was stated authoritatively last night.

New York bankers held informal conferences here yesterday, at which the new London crisis was discussed, but no concerted action seemed to them to be called for, it was said. The bankers were in communication with British banking authorities by transatlantic telephone.

According to a competent authority, the short-term balances of American banks in London do not exceed $50,000,000, while Great Britain's external obligations in this country, exclusive of the $125,000,000 credit recently granted by the Federal Reserve banks to the Bank of England and the $200,000,000 private banking credit to the British Treasury, do not exceed $500,000,000.

No further supporting measures will be taken to defend the pound sterling at this time, it was stated. The private banking credit which was opened on Aug. 28 last, while not yet actually used up, will be exhausted shortly with the taking up of forward commitments made by the British banking authorities in their recent attempts to bolster the pound.

Banker Sums Up Situation.

The British financial difficulties, as they are understood here, were summed up last night by an important international banker as follows:

The emergency measures taken by the British Government to check the heavy outflow of gold from London will undoubtedly occasion widespread surprise here, although the steps to be taken are by no means unprecedented. During the early days of the Great War, it will be recalled, Great Britain suspended the Bank Act temporarily, and in 1920 sterling went as low as an exchange value of $3.20 as against parity of about $4.86¼. It was not until 1925 that the country returned officially to a gold basis.

The terms of the announcement by the British authorities make it clear that the suspension of gold payments by the Bank of England is a temporary measure and in no way affects the obligation of the British Government to meet in gold such obligations as it may have outstanding in foreign currencies. Undoubtedly the government had a

Continued on Page Two.

The British Government's Statement

Special Cable to THE NEW YORK TIMES.

LONDON, Sept. 20.—This is the statement issued by the government tonight, announcing suspension of the law requiring that the Bank of England sell gold at a fixed price:

His Majesty's Government have decided after consultation with the Bank of England that it has become necessary to suspend for the time being the operation of Subsection 2, Section 1, of the gold standard act of 1925, which requires the Bank to sell gold at a fixed price.

A bill for this purpose will be introduced immediately, and it is the intention of His Majesty's Government to ask Parliament to pass it through all stages Monday, the 21st of September. In the meantime, the Bank of England has been authorized to proceed accordingly in anticipation of the action of Parliament.

The reasons which led to this decision are as follows:

Since the middle of July, funds amounting to more than £200,000,000 (about $1,000,000,00) have been withdrawn from the London market. The withdrawals have been met partly from gold and foreign currency held by the Bank of England, partly from proceeds of a credit of £50,000,000 (about $250,000,000), which shortly matures, secured by the Bank of England from New York and Paris and partly from proceeds of French and American credits amounting to £80,000,000 (about $400,000,000) recently obtained by the government.

During the last few days withdrawals of foreign balances have accelerated so sharply that His Majesty's Government felt that they were bound to take the above decision.

This decision will, of course, not affect the obligations of His Majesty's Government or of the Bank of England which are payable in foreign currencies.

Gold holdings of the Bank of England amount to some £130,000,000 (about $650,000,000) and, having regard to contingencies which may have to be met, it is inadvisable to allow this reserve to be further reduced.

There will be no interruption of ordinary banking business. Banks will be opened as usual for the convenience of their customers, and there is no reason why sterling transactions should be affected in any way.

It has been arranged that the Stock Exchange shall not be opened on Monday, the day on which Parliament is passing the necessary legislation. This will not, however, interfere with the business of current settlement on the Stock Exchange, which will be carried through as usual.

His Majesty's Government have no reason to believe that the present difficulties are due to any substantial extent to the export of capital by British nationals. Undoubtedly the bulk of withdrawals has been for foreign accounts.

They desire, however, to repeat emphatically the warning given by the Chancellor of the Exchequer that any British citizen who increases the strain on exchanges by purchasing foreign securities himself, or is assisting others to do so, is deliberately adding to the country's difficulties.

The banks have undertaken to cooperate in restricting purchases by British citizens of foreign exchange except those required for the actual needs of trade or for meeting contracts, and should further measures prove to be advisable his Majesty's Government will not hesitate to take them.

His Majesty's Government have arrived at their decision with the greatest reluctance. But during the last few days international financial markets have become demoralized and have been liquidating their sterling assets regardless of their intrinsic worth. In the circumstances there was no alternative but to protect the financial position of this country by the only means at our disposal.

His Majesty's Government are securing a balanced budget and the internal position of the country is sound. This position must be maintained. It is one thing to go off the gold standard with an unbalanced budget and uncontrolled inflation. It is quite another thing to take this measure, not because of internal financial difficulties but because of excessive withdrawals of borrowed capital.

The ultimate resources of this country are enormous and there is no doubt that the present exchange difficulties will prove only temporary.

Gold Standard Subsection to Be Suspended.

Subsection 2 of the British Gold Standard act of 1925, which is to be suspended, reads as follows:

The Bank of England shall be bound to sell to any person who makes demand in that behalf at the head office of the Bank during office hours of the Bank, and pay the purchase price in any legal tender, gold bullion at the price of £3 17s 10½d per ounce troy of gold of the standard of fineness prescribed for gold coin by the coinage act of 1870, but only in the form of bars containing approximately 400 ounces troy of fine gold.

EVENTUAL BENEFITS SEEN BY WASHINGTON

British Move Is Held Likely to Affect War Debts—Hoover Informed on Friday.

Special to The New York Times.

WASHINGTON, Sept. 20.—While government officials were unwilling to discuss formally the British financial crisis because of the delicacy of the situation, the announcement by the British government did not come as a surprise, as word had been received here as early as Friday that some drastic step was in contemplation.

While informally some experts referred to the present situation as the most serious since the world war, there was also expressed the opinion that as a long range proposition any move by Great Britain to put her financial house in order would have a salutary effect on world economic affairs.

It was reported here tonight that the White House dinner Friday evening attended by President Hoover and Secretaries Stimson, Mellon and Lamont was arranged after the President first obtained definite information of the step that Britain was contemplating.

Situation Thoroughly Discussed.

It is now understood that there was a thorough discussion at the dinner of the situation as it might affect financial interests of this country and that consideration also was given as to whether this government might be able to do anything to aid the British in facing the financial crisis. None of the officials has made known just what conclusions were reached at the dinner.

Whether the course to be followed by Great Britain would result in the ultimate revaluation of the pound sterling was a matter of considerable conjecture. In some quarters the belief was held that Great Britain would be compelled in the end to go on an "adjusted gold basis" which would in effect mean a stabilization of the pound at a lower level. One official also felt that Great Britain would find it difficult to keep her foreign obligations on a gold basis and handle her domestic financial affairs on another basis.

That any adjustments which Great Britain must make would require a

Continued on Page Two.

Canada "Proposes to Maintain" Gold Standard, Premier Says

By The Associated Press.

OTTAWA, Ont., Sept. 20.—R. B. Bennett, Prime Minister and Acting Minister of Finance, said tonight that Canada proposed to maintain the gold standard.

"What Great Britain may do is for the government of Great Britain to determine," said Mr. Bennett. "As for Canada, we propose to maintain the gold standard."

The Prime Minister auded that he had nothing further to say on the matter.

GERMANY TO CLOSE ALL BOERSES TODAY

To Keep Them Shut Indefinitely if Need Be — Reichsbank Protected by Credit Truce.

By GUIDO ENDERIS.
Special Cable to THE NEW YORK TIMES.

BERLIN, Sept. 20.—The news that the Bank of England had announced the suspension of gold payments, effective tomorrow, struck Berlin banking and Boerse circles as a bolt from the blue and left leading financiers completely nonplussed as to its possible repercussions on the German financial situation.

It was uniformly asserted, however, that the Reichsbank's position was not affected as it was amply protected for the time being through the ratification of the "standstill" agreement on short-term credits.

Pending further developments in London, the German Boerses will remain closed tomorrow and, if necessary, indefinitely thereafter, in keeping with the conclusions reached late today between bank and Boerse leaders and official quarters, as it was commonly feared that the shock resulting from London's procedure would have a devastating reaction upon the German stock markets.

A preponderant number of Berlin bankers incline to the view that the Bank of England's action was an S O S to all capitalistic countries, warning them that the existing currency system was in imminent danger and that the present dislocation

Continued on Page Two.

GENEVA IS SHOCKED BY CRISIS IN LONDON

High French Official There Says Paris and America Must Aid the Pound.

By CLARENCE K. STREIT.
Special Cable to THE NEW YORK TIMES.

GENEVA, Sept. 20.—The news that the Bank of England tomorrow will go off the gold standard and that the London Stock Exchange will not open came as a shock to the few in Geneva who learned of it late tonight.

"If ever there was a time when the United States and France needed to work together it is now," was the incisive comment of a high French official. "Together we can and must support the pound sterling."

Told of reports from Basle that the British development probably meant the loss in value of sterling by a third, Frenchmen here expressed surprise bordering on consternation and obviously felt every effort ought to be made to avoid this.

It was stressed in the French delegation to the League of Nations that Minister of Finance Flandin had gone last night to Paris, where he had been conversing with officers of the Bank of England. The results of the conversations were not known in the delegation, but M. Flandin was expected back here tomorrow. Whether this meant that a move through Geneva was likely none was willing to predict.

In the British delegation the gravity of the situation was indicated by the tone of voices where it was not indicated by the words used. The British stressed that their financial expert, Sir Arthur Salter, did not believe the situation would really turn out as tragically as laymen seemed to fear.

Though admitting that in such unprecedented matters incalculable factors may play a deciding role, the British seemed inclined to think that "in view of the nervousness of foreigners, who are withdrawing their money from London," the trouble had come to a head sooner than it would otherwise and that it was better that it came sooner than later. Hope was somewhat wanly expressed that everything would be all right in a few days if every one kept his head.

The reports that Sir Arthur Salter,

Continued on Page Two.

PARLIAMENT TO BACK MOVE

Cabinet Is Unanimous in Decision to End the Drain on Gold.

KING TO SIGN BILL TONIGHT

London Hopes Drastic Measure Will Not Be Necessary More Than Six Months.

MacDONALD EXPLAINS STEP

Government Says Withdrawals of Funds Since July Forced Its Action.

By CHARLES A. SELDEN.
Special Cable to THE NEW YORK TIMES.

LONDON, Sept. 20.—Great Britain will go off the gold standard tomorrow. Legislation amending the existing financial laws to that effect will be rushed through Parliament in the course of the day and will receive the King's royal assent tomorrow night.

To accomplish this, the new National Government, which is responsible for this drastic step, is assured of the necessary majority in the House of Commons to pass the measure through all its Parliamentary stages in one sitting. The House of Lords, which ordinarily does not sit on Mondays, has been summoned for an emergency session to take the required concurrent action.

Bank of England Approves.

A unanimous decision to abandon the gold standard was reached at an emergency session of Premier MacDonald's Cabinet today after consultation with the Bank of England, which agreed it was the only thing to do.

The Bank of England tomorrow will raise the discount rate to 6 per cent from 4½ per cent.

The London Stock Exchange and all provincial exchanges will be closed for the day.

Although there is no suggestion in the government statement as to how long this state of affairs will continue the official announcement implies it will be only temporary by saying the suspension is "for the time being."

The expectation, or at least the hope, is that it will last only six months if within that period the country manages to balance its international trade as well as its budget.

It was hoped this shock to British government finance would be averted by the change in government a month ago with the subsequent achievement of balancing the budget and cutting down government expenses, but it is evident now that the change was too long delayed.

Blow Was Long Impending.

The present blow has been impending a long time. Now that it has fallen, the situation is explained as due both to international and domestic causes. The foreign factors involved, according to the British appraisal of the situation, have been the hoarding of gold by the United States and France and the recent drain on sterling because of the financial difficulties of other countries.

Diminished foreign confidence in the stability of the pound was another vital factor which had gone too far to be entirely corrected by the recent change in government and by the effect of big loans from New York and Paris. The recent "pay cut mutiny" in the British navy also was one of the various causes of the cumulative effect, which is today's decision to abandon the gold standard.

Also England put a terrific strain on herself six years ago by returning to the gold standard as part of her post-war financial policy and by her whole attitude toward the payment of her war debts. Of all countries on this side of the Atlantic which participated in the war, England is the only one which has not cut the value of its currency. Great Britain alone returned to the pre-war gold parity of its currency while France divided the franc by five.

Plus all this international strain, England has been attempting to carry on at the same time a most expensive experiment in socialism, which, with its enormous cost of unemployment insurance, caused the downfall of the Labor Government just a month ago.

Although the British public dug

Most Severe Quake Since 1924 Rocks Tokyo; Slipping of Strata Alarms Indiana and Ohio

Special Cable to THE NEW YORK TIMES.

TOKYO, Monday, Sept. 21.—The worst earthquake since January, 1924, rocked Tokyo houses violently at 11:53 A. M. today, causing much alarm but apparently little damage. A second and milder shock occurred at 11:58 A. M.

Special to The New York Times.

CINCINNATI, Ohio, Sept. 20.—Earthquake shocks rocked Cincinnati and the surrounding territory shortly after 6 o'clock last night. The shocks were general, reports coming in from every part of Cincinnati—its suburbs. They were felt extensively on the Kentucky side of the river and in a number of up-State, Indiana and Kentucky cities.

No damage was reported here although large buildings were rocked on their foundations, some as much as three inches.

In Mount Adams some residents became alarmed and rushed into their cellars.

The exact time of the tremors was variously reported from 6:05 to 6:10 o'clock. The shocks, half a dozen or more, lasted less than a minute.

CHICAGO, Sept. 20 (AP).—The earth's surface in parts of Indiana and Ohio did a little readjusting of its own today, but beyond momentarily frightening a few residents, damage was slight.

The disturbance, according to Federal geologists here, was caused by the slipping of strata under the earth's surface.

SIDNEY, Ohio, Sept. 20 (AP).—The Methodist and Lutheran churches, the high school and virtually every house in the vilage of Anna, Shelby County, were damaged badly by the earthquake today. Authorities said the total damage would exceed $10,000.

"All the News That's Fit to Print."

The New York Times.

LATE CITY EDITION
POSTSCRIPT
WEATHER—Fair today; tomorrow rain; not much temperature change.
Temperatures Yesterday—Max., 44; Min., 37.

Copyright, 1932, by The New York Times Company.

VOL. LXXXI....No. 27,066. ***** + NEW YORK, WEDNESDAY, MARCH 2, 1932. TWO CENTS In New York City | THREE CENTS Within 200 Miles | FOUR CENTS Elsewhere Except 7th and 8th Postal Zones

JAPANESE ROUTING CHINESE IN FIERCE SHANGHAI BATTLE; DEATH TOLL EXCEEDS 2,000

WHOLE CHINESE LINE FLEES

Pressure From North of Fresh Japanese Troops Forces Quick Move.

PURSUERS LEFT BEHIND

Tachang, Miaoshin and Chapei Fall Before Advance Made Behind Smoke Screen.

TRUCE EXPECTED AT ONCE

Chinese Are Stunned by Sudden Blow—Say Retreat Meets Terms of Japanese.

By HALLETT ABEND.
Wireless to THE NEW YORK TIMES.

SHANGHAI, Wednesday, March 2.—The Chinese were routed this morning by the Japanese in the most sanguinary battle since the World War.

The Japanese killed and wounded before 10 o'clock admittedly exceeded 250. Yesterday's advance in this region totaled two kilometers (more than a mile) and the Japanese losses up to midnight officially were admitted to be slightly in excess of 300 killed and wounded, while the bodies of 1,800 Chinese soldiers were discovered this morning on the ground won yesterday.

Brief reports from General Kenkichi Ueda's headquarters report that the Chinese retreat is degenerating into an utter, panicky rout and the rapid Japanese advance is finding difficulty in maintaining contact with the fast fleeing Chinese soldiers.

The pall of smoke from burning Chinese villages and towns was thickening over Shanghai. Immense exultation was manifested in Japanese circles and the Chinese were stunned by the suddenness and magnitude of the military disaster.

The Japanese captured Tachang at 12:30 today.

Chinese in Pell Mell Retreat.

Early this afternoon the Japanese forces were rapidly approaching from beyond Taching and the Chinese were in pellmell retreat. There was great confusion at Nantao, where Chinese soldiers were attempting to evacuate in railway trains to Hangchow.

The Nineteenth Route Army has voluntarily withdrawn from Chapei, is abandoning other fronts and concentrating at Chenju, according to official oral notification given at 12:30 by the secretary of Mayor Wu Te-chen to United States Consul General Edwin S. Cunningham in his capacity as senior consul.

This withdrawal, the official notification said, also means the evacuation of all Chinese soldiers from Nantao ad Lunghua, but Mr. Cunningham was assured there was danger of disorders at Nantao because 2,000 regular police and 600 picked volunteers already have taken over the maintenance of law and order. It is understood that Chinese will not attempt to police Chapei, declaring "that is dependent upon the Japanese."

Truce Expected Soon.

Presumably the crumpling of the Nineteenth Route Army will be quickly followed by the signing of a truce and by further retirement of the Chinese forces, since Chenju is inside the twenty-kilometer zone which the Japanese insist must be evacuated.

Between 7:30 and 10 o'clock this morning the Japanese had pushed forward to within two kilometres of Tachang. A vast area was being bombed and shelled with unparalleled intensity and the region was dimmed with smoke from huge conflagrations.

The Chinese began the day's hostilities by using two batteries of big guns, firing from Chapei into the Japanese naval headquarters area in Hongkew Park, where many large fires are now burning. For an hour and a half the Chinese batteries kept the city rocking and the roar of their detonations made sleep impossible.

The Japanese had made exceedingly important gains at 10 o'clock toward Tachang, although the terrain is even more difficult than around Kiangwan, with a multitude of vertical banked creeks and sloughs

Continued on Page Twelve.

Settlement Stores Reopen And Shoppers Flock to Them

Special Cable to THE NEW YORK TIMES.

SHANGHAI, March 1.—Acting upon the request of General Tsai Ting-chai three of the largest Chinese-owned department stores on the Nanking Road of the International Settlement reopened today and many smaller stores and shops followed suit. This action contributed largely to a return to approximate normalcy in general business conditions.

SHANGHAI, March 1 (AP).—Stores and offices in the International Settlement reopened today and bargain hunters turned out in droves.

The three big department stores were crowded with shoppers, but the service staff was considerably depleted. Many of the clerks used to live in Chapei and Hongkew and nobody knows where they are now.

JAPAN WILL OFFER NEW TRUCE TERMS

Accepts League Proposal for Armistice at Shanghai With Reservations.

CHINA AFFIRMS AGREEMENT

Plans for Special Assembly at Geneva Tomorrow Await Outcome of Negotiations.

By CLARENCE K. STREIT.
Special Cable to THE NEW YORK TIMES.

GENEVA, March 1.—Naotake Sato this evening gave Joseph Paul-Boncour, President of the League Council, Tokyo's definite acceptance of the latter's so-called "President's plan" for a Shanghai truce and a round-table discussion. Mr. Sato added that the "details"—which is to say, the truce—were to be worked out in Shanghai. Later he confirmed his oral communication in a brief note.

The note merely said Japan was "happy to accept the plan the President has submitted. It mentioned none of the reservations which Mr. Sato gave M. Paul-Boncour orally regarding the details of the truce to be settled on the spot, apparently because Japan thought the terms of the "President's plan" included such reservations.

At any rate, these reservations not merely still stand, but it is understood Mr. Sato explained to M. Paul-Boncour that Japan, instead of accepting Admiral Kelly's armistice terms, was making a counter-proposal.

The United States delegation preferred to reserve comment on Tokyo's reply.

Diplomatic Move Seen.

There is a suspicion in Chinese and Soviet circles that, if Japan does really accept the truce terms, she will then try to win through diplomacy what she failed to win on the battlefield by seeking to have the boundaries of the International Settlement at Shanghai extended to include some districts largely populated by Japanese. There is nothing, certainly, in either the "President's plan" or Mr. Sato's declaration yesterday to prevent such a manoeuvre, for they bar merely any concession or move which exclusively favors the Japanese.

The wording of the second point of the president's plan" and the whole of Mr. Sato's declaration, especially the third point, appear to some to be designed to facilitate such a plan by their references to strengthening the international character of the Settlement.

The Chinese appear to regard the United States as the only one in the group on which they can count not to take advantage of the present situation to try to block China's old fight on the whole question of extraterritoriality.

New Settlement Status Hinted.

There is also some significant, although still vague, talk of the need of improving the status of the Shanghai International Settlement and possibly of putting it under League jurisdiction, like Danzig.

Although the skepticism here is pointed chiefly toward Japan, some are skeptical too of the Chinese Government being able to keep its troops to the terms of the armistice.

Pending definite developments with regard to the armistice and the

Continued on Page Thirteen.

145 in House Force Vote on Dry Law Test; Texan, Last Signer, Rolls Up in Wheelchair

Special to THE NEW YORK TIMES.

WASHINGTON, March 1.—An outright vote on whether the House shall consider a proposal to return liquor control to the States was assured today when the necessary 145 members had signed a petition to cite the Judiciary Committee for discharge from further study of the measure.

The vote probably will be taken on March 14, the first "discharge" day on the calendar.

The wets hailed it as the greatest day since prohibition when the last signature necessary was obtained soon after noon. The 145th member affixing his signature was Representative Mansfield, Texas Democrat. Mr. Mansfield, who is crippled, rolled up to the desk in his wheel chair, while Representative Blanton, Democrat, of Texas, a militant dry, was on his feet chiding the wets for their "failure" to get the required signatures.

The House was set into an uproar when at that moment it was found that Mr. Mansfield, from Mr. Blanton's own State, had made the "wet failure" a literal "howling success." Some observers were quick to remark that March 2 is the Independence Day of Texas, the anniversary of its Declaration of Independence from Mexico.

Representative La Guardia of New York, a wet, was taking Mr. Blanton to task for his remarks when the news was broadcast that Mr. Mansfield had signed.

"Any time that this House has the experience of seeing the distinguished gentleman from Texas (Mr. Blanton) get unduly excited," Mr. La

Continued on Page Two.

SALES TAX ACCEPTED BY ADMINISTRATION, MILLS ANNOUNCES

Secretary Pledges Cooperation on New Bill Despite Changes in Treasury Plan.

$625,000,000 NOW IS GOAL

Basis for Manufacturers' Levy Is Widened as Subcommittee Completes Draft.

Special to THE NEW YORK TIMES.

WASHINGTON, March 1.—Acceptance by the administration of the new tax measure, including a general sales tax applicable to practically every manufacturing industry in the country, was assured today by Secretary Mills.

Mr. Mills told a Ways and Means subcommittee that, even though the original treasury plan had been changed at nearly every major point, the administration would cooperate to the fullest extent in setting in motion and administering the new tax increases.

The subcommittee completed the new tax bill, excepting one or two minor administrative features, this afternoon.

The manufacturers' tax provisions, as agreed on, exempt only a few articles, chiefly commodities for the "poor man's breakfast table" and his daily paper, and the farmer's products, his magazines and periodicals.

The final meeting of the subcommittee resulted in a decision to recommend an even wider base for the manufacturers' levy. Yesterday the subcommittee tentatively agreed to frame the tax so as to produce around $550,000,000 in additional revenue. Today it decided to extend the scope so as to produce $625,000,000.

The additions to the sales tax base were understood to have been made by adding commodities which were being held "in reserve" for special excises.

Members of the subcommittee declined to discuss details, but it was the prevailing idea that gasoline and industrial alcohol had been included in their definition of "manufactured products."

If this is true, gasoline and industrial alcohol would be subject to the 2 per cent general tax instead of the special excises of one cent a gallon as proposed originally.

Agree on Excess Levies.

Final decision on the special excise levies was reached today. Committeemen likewise declined to discuss these, holding that to mention them would be to let loose an "avalanche" of protests on members of Congress.

Other excises most prominently mentioned in discussions of the measure were a 5 to 10 per cent consumers' levy on electric energy and illuminating gas; a tax on oil, with a differential upward on oil imports, and an increase of 3 cents a share on stock transfers.

The bill probably will be presented to the full Ways and Means Committee tomorrow afternoon and may be offered to the House for action by Saturday night, according to Representative Crisp of Georgia, acting chairman.

Actual passage in the House by the end of next week was the confident hope of authors of the measure.

Representative Crisp, fatigued from his strenuous work on the bill, was buoyed in spirit today with the hope that it might even be introduced in the House tomorrow. He will offer the measure as soon as the Ways and Means Committee has agreed to it. It will then be referred back to the committee, which immediately will go through the routine of making a formal report.

Being a revenue bill, it will have priority in the House and, according to Mr. Crisp, will be called up as soon as possible for action.

He mentioned next Tuesday as a

Continued on Page Four.

SENATE BODY ACTS FOR BROAD INQUIRY ON SHORT SELLING

Banking Committee Will Go Beyond Hoover Idea in Stock Exchange Investigation.

EFFECTS ON TRADE SOUGHT

Subcommittee Named to Go Into Long and Short Sales and Interstate Phase.

Special to THE NEW YORK TIMES.

WASHINGTON, March 1.—An investigation of the New York Stock Exchange was recommended today by the Senate Banking and Currency Committee. A subcommittee, headed by Senator Walcott, Republican, of Connecticut, immediately began drafting a resolution requesting authority for such an investigation from the Senate.

The subcommittee was instructed by the full committee to include in the resolution authorizations covering studies of both long and short selling, the effect of speculation on interstate commerce, the use of interstate communications systems by speculators and the value of a proposed stock transfer tax as a check on speculation.

This decision went far beyond the action believed to have been requested by President Hoover Friday when he called Senator Walcott to the White House for a conference on "bear raiding." No intimation of an investigation of trading other than short selling has come from the White House.

The subcommittee was chosen after an executive session, during which the committee members argued the constitutional right of the Senate to investigate the Stock Exchange.

The full committee finally agreed generally that such authority does exist, and the subcommittee, charged with considering this point in more detail, reached the same conclusion late this afternoon.

Regulation Not Contemplated Now.

Leading members of the full committee, including Senator Walcott, indicated that no regulatory measure affecting the Stock Exchange is contemplated at this time. The committee intends to run to the ground rumors about the Stock Exchange and, if questionable practices are found, to suggest means of correcting them, preferably through the action of the governors of the Stock Exchange itself.

"I hope this will not result in Federal legislation," Senator Walcott told newspaper men. "We have no legislative plans. However, the committee feels that if we can by investigation persuade the Stock Exchange to draw such regulations as will abolish bear raids, bull raids and dangerous pool operations, then we will have done the country good service.

"There is not a man on that committee who wants the Stock Exchange abolished. But we want to see what abuses exist. There is so much talk about the Exchange, and we are just as anxious to clear the Stock Exchange of any unwarranted misrepresentations as we are to uncover abuses in security dealings."

The subcommittee was appointed by Senator Norbeck, Republican, of North Dakota, chairman of the full committee, who named Senators Steiwer, Republican, of Oregon, and Bulkley, Democrat, of Ohio, to serve with Senator Walcott.

What sides were taken by committee members on the question of constitutionality was not revealed, but Senator Norbeck said that eventually "almost every member agreed there is authority under some provision or other." The principal point at issue was whether the Stock Exchange could be considered as engaging in interstate commerce or whether its business should be considered as confined to New York.

The committee's executive session

Continued on Page Thirteen.

LINDBERGH BABY KIDNAPPED FROM HOME OF PARENTS ON FARM NEAR PRINCETON; TAKEN FROM HIS CRIB; WIDE SEARCH ON

FOUR STATES JOIN HUNT

Wire Systems Flash Out Alarm on First Word of Kidnapping.

NEW YORK CAR IS SOUGHT

Roads Are Scoured for Pair Said to Have Inquired Way to the Lindbergh Home.

AUTOS STOPPED ON ROAD

Hunt Here Is Led by Mulrooney—Underworld Haunts Visited in Scores of Cities.

The Baby's Description.

HOPEWELL, N. J., March 2 (AP).—A chubby, golden-haired boy closely resembling his famous father—that is the description given Charles Augustus Lindbergh Jr.

He is 20 months old, has blue eyes, curly hair, fair complexion. He is about normal size for a child his age. He has just begun to toddle and is learning to talk.

At 10:40 o'clock last night Colonel Charles A. Lindbergh telephoned the New Jersey State Police Headquarters at Trenton that his son had been kidnapped from the Lindbergh home in Hopewell, N. J. Within ten minutes every communication method of modern science had been utilized to broadcast the alarm and to mobilize the police systems of four States and scores of communities in the search.

Colonel Lindbergh had scarcely poured out his tale when the vast machinery of cooperating police systems began to function. While one man was calling the State police barracks at Lambertville, N. J., ten miles from Hopewell, on the telephone, another was writing out this message to be flashed over the police teletype system:

"Colonel Lindbergh's baby kidnapped from Lindbergh home at Hopewell between 7:30 and 10 P. M. Boy, 19 months, dressed in sleeping suit. Search all cars."

Pair in Stolen Car Hunted.

Shortly before 1 o'clock this morning the Princeton Police Department sent over the network of wires the first message containing anything approaching a definite clue. It read as follows:

"Information received that two men in blue or black sedan bearing New York license plates stopped a man working on highway and asked to be directed to the Lindbergh home in Hopewell."

Relayed to every outpost, this message gave the searchers their first indication of the possible description of the kidnappers' car. It was so vague, however, that they did not permit it to stop them from questioning the occupants of cars of other descriptions.

As the first alarm was being typed out the telephone connection with the Lambertville barracks had been established and Lieutenant Arthur Keaten, in command of that post, had been informed of the situation. With every man who could be spared, he started at once for Hopewell.

Upon their arrival Corporal Joseph Wolf, at Lieutenant Keaten's direction, telephoned back confirmation of the kidnapping, but he was not at that time able to add further details to the few which had been furnished by Colonel Lindbergh.

Meanwhile picked detectives were sent on the rounds of known underworld haunts to see if they could pick up any clues as to the identity of the kidnappers.

Window Found Open.

An open window in the nursery of the Lindbergh home at Hopewell indicated how the kidnappers had gained entrance to the house. A close watch has been kept on the baby since it was born, but apparently no member of the family dreamed of the possibility of a kidnapping and no one remained in the nursery last night after the nurse had placed the child in his crib and made sure he was asleep.

The small force under Lieutenant Keaten at once began a careful search of the woody areas surrounding the Lindbergh home, on the possibility of uncovering some clue to the

Continued on Page Three.

© The Misses Selby.

The Lindbergh baby photographed a year ago. Left to right are Mrs. Dwight W. Morrow, the baby's grandmother; Mrs. Charles Cutter Long, the great-grandmother; Charles Augustus Lindbergh Jr., and Mrs. Charles A. Lindbergh, his mother.

KIDNAPPING OF BABY SPEEDS FEDERAL LAW

Demand in Capital for Statute Providing Death Penalty Expected to Increase.

OFFICIALS HINDERED NOW

Can Act in Almost Any Other Interstate Crime—Patterson Assails "Filthy Act."

Special to THE NEW YORK TIMES.

WASHINGTON, Wednesday, March 2.—Immediate pressure for early passage of the measure making kidnapping a Federal offense is held certain to be the result of the kidnapping of Colonel Lindbergh's son.

Senator Patterson of Missouri recently introduced a bill to this effect. It provides a death penalty. The measure would give authority to the government when the kidnapped person is removed from one State to another. The bill was approved unanimously two weeks ago by the Senate Judiciary Committee and its supporters are confident that it will be adopted by the Senate.

A companion bill introduced by Representative Cochran of Missouri, chairman of the Committee on Expenditures, has been before the Judiciary Committee in that branch for about ten days. The hearings were scheduled for completion soon and the portents, before this morning's news, were for a favorable report.

Patterson Denounces Crime.

"It is a shock to me to hear of this outrage," said Mr. Patterson this morning when informed by THE NEW YORK TIMES. "I hope the child will soon be returned to its parents. This filthy act will aid us in passing the needed legislation, and I am sorry it will not be retroactive, so that the Lindbergh kidnappers can be dealt with by the Federal Government."

On Jan. 23 a telephone message was received by Senator Patterson from Chicago to the effect that there was a plot to kidnap General Charles G. Dawes, who had just been appointed president of the Reconstruction Finance Corporation. Mr. Patterson then said that this information came from a newspaper correspondent. It created excitement in Washington official circles, although the General refused to take it seriously. However, it spurred the efforts of those behind the legislation.

Action Urged in Chicago.

As a result, when the House Judiciary Committee began hearings, Colonel Isham Randolph of Chicago, head of the "Secret Six" of that city, and former Representative Cleveland A. Newton of St. Louis came to Washington to urge early action. Mr. Newton gave the following list of kidnappings which he said had

Continued on Page Three.

FATHER SEARCHES GROUNDS FOR CHILD

Lindbergh and Troopers Hunt With Flashlights for Clues on Big Estate.

NEWS ROUSES COUNTRYSIDE

Hundreds of Autos Rush to the Home in Lonely Woodland, Clogging Narrow Road.

Copyrighted, 1932, by The Associated Press.

HOPEWELL, N. J., Wednesday, March 2.—Charles Augustus Lindbergh Jr., 20-month-old son of the flying Colonel, was kidnapped last night from his nursery in the Lindbergh country home near here. The child, clad in a blue sleeping robe, was put to bed at the usual hour, 7:30 P. M. At about 10 P. M. some-one peered into the nursery. The crib was empty.

Beneath the nursery window, footprints showed in the soft earth. These indicated that the kidnappers, moving with such stealth that the Lindberghs, although in the house, heard no sound, had removed their shoes before climbing a ladder to the window. The trail of the shoeless footprints was followed by The Associated Press reporter to the rutted lane, where police believe a waiting car was parked. Feminine footprints, as well as those of a man, were found.

The first news the Lindberghs had of the crime was when the frightened nurse ran downstairs, screaming that the baby had been kidnapped.

The first newspaper man to reach the home was an Associated Press reporter, who ran a mile over muddy, rut-cut roads to reach a phone to send the first direct news from the residence. This was at 12:40 A. M.

Colonel Lindbergh, bare-headed as usual, was pacing the grounds, while troopers and detectives went over the place with flashlights, seeking clues.

Mrs. Lindbergh, who telephoned the news to her mother, Mrs. Dwight W. Morrow, at the Morrow home in Englewood, N. J., was inside the house. A close friend of Mrs. Lindbergh said she was expecting another child within three months.

The house, glowing with lights from top to bottom, was the only bright spot in the wooded, gloomy district. Wishing to get complete privacy, the Lindberghs picked the site from the air and it is almost inaccessible to the outside world. A winding, muddy lane—their private property—leads to the new house from a country highway, called the Stoutsberg-Worstville Road. The entrance to the Lindbergh road is more than four miles from Hopewell and there are few neighbors near enough to be of any aid in time of

Continued on Page Three.

CHILD STOLEN IN EVENING

At 10 P. M. Nurse Finds Boy, 20 Months Old, Gone, in Nightrobe.

FOOTPRINTS IN THE ROOM

Muddy Trail Leads to Ladder in Wood and Half Mile to Highway, Where Car Waited.

WOMAN BELIEVED INVOLVED

Parents, Distraught, Guarded in Home—Police Deny Report of Ransom Note.

Charles Augustus Lindbergh Jr., 20-month-old son of Colonel and Mrs. Charles A. Lindbergh, was kidnapped between 8:30 and 10 o'clock last night from his crib in the nursery on the second floor of his parents' home at Hopewell, near Princeton, N. J.

Apparently the kidnapping was carried out either while Colonel and Mrs. Lindbergh were at dinner, or soon afterward. The baby's nurse, Miss Betty Gow, visited the nursery about 8:30 o'clock and found everything in order there. When she returned at 10 o'clock, however, the crib was empty.

Muddy footprints that trailed across the floor from the crib to an open window bore mute testimony as to how the baby had disappeared. Miss Gow dashed downstairs. "The baby's been kidnapped!" she shouted. Colonel Lindbergh raced to the nursery, followed closely by his wife. Mrs. Lindbergh recalled that earlier in the day she had tried to fasten a screen on the window that had been opened and had been unable to do so.

Satisfied that there was no mistake and that the baby actually was gone, Colonel Lindbergh telephoned Chief of Police Charles Williamson at Hopewell. Williamson drove to the house accompanied by another officer. Outside the door they met the Colonel. He was bareheaded, and wearing an old black leather jacket such as he frequently wears on his flights.

Footprints Under Window.

Briefly he told Williamson what had occurred. The chief telephoned first to State Police Headquarters at Trenton. Then he, his fellow officer and the Colonel began searching the grounds. Beneath the nursery window were marks where a ladder had stood and the footprints of one person. There were no shoe prints. The kidnapper, apparently, had worn socks or moccasins.

Sixty feet away in rocky ground at the edge of a wood the Colonel and Chief Williamson found a makeshift ladder. Its rungs were caked with mud. Colonel Lindbergh could not say whether it belonged on the premises. He thought it might have been left there by the builders while the house was being constructed during his flight to the Orient last Summer with Mrs. Lindbergh.

The searchers had no difficulty in following the footprints across the muddy ground. A second set of tracks joined them near the edge of the woods. They were much smaller. The two officers thought they might be those of a woman.

The search was interrupted by the arrival of a detachment of State Troopers sent from the barracks at Lambertville and the hunt began anew. The tracks were followed to the main highway, about half a mile from the house, where they disappeared. The kidnappers evidently had entered an automobile at that point.

Lindbergh Aids Search.

Carrying a flashlight, Colonel Lindbergh stayed with the searching party until long after midnight. Once or twice he returned to the house, but he declined to discuss the kidnapping with newspapermen. Instead, he referred them to Major Schoeffel of the State Police, who told the story in detail.

"I hope you boys will oblige me,"

Continued on Page Three.

"All the News That's Fit to Print."

The New York Times.

LATE CITY EDITION

WEATHER—Cloudy, probably rain today; tomorrow fair and warmer.

VOL. LXXXI....No. 27,138. ****+ NEW YORK, FRIDAY, MAY 13, 1932. TWO CENTS In New York City | THREE CENTS Within 200 Miles | FOUR CENTS Elsewhere Except 7th and 8th Postal Zones

WALKER GOT $26,535 BONDS FROM J. A. SISTO AS 'GIFT,' TAXI FINANCIER TESTIFIES

PROFIT IN A STOCK DEAL

Control Board Advocate Bought Shares to Aid Mayor, He Swears.

McKEON WAS INTERMEDIARY

Friend of Walker Says He Took Envelope to City Hall and Handed It Over in Auto.

HASTINGS GOT CAB PROFITS

Terminal Company Hired Him at $18,000 a Year, Seabury Is Told—Unpaid Loans Bared.

J. A. Sisto, who had a hand in financing the Parmelee Transportation Company, gave Mayor Walker bonds worth $26,535.51 before the Municipal Assembly passed the Mayor's bill creating a Board of Taxicab Control, the broker testified yesterday before the Hofstadter committee.

Both Mr. Sisto and John J. McKeon, who delivered the bonds to Mayor Walker in a sealed envelope in the Winter of 1929, demanded that the investigating committee cloak them with immunity before they would say a word about the matter.

Taxi Company Hired Hastings.

Just before Samuel Seabury, chief counsel to the committee, sprang this surprise, B. M. Seymour, vice president and general manager of the Terminal Cab Company, admitted that his company had paid $28,183 in salary to State Senator John A. Hastings, the Mayor's friend.

Colonel George W. Mixter of the firm of Day & Zimmerman testified that it was the Brooklyn Senator who got his company the job of making a traffic survey of New York in 1928. As a result of that survey, the witness said, Mayor Walker appointed a committee, with Frank P. Walsh as chairman, to study the problem of taxicab control.

That committee, of which Colonel Mixter was a member, reported in September, 1930, recommending a board of control, designed eventually to put the city's taxicab industry on a single-franchise basis, which was what the big companies wanted and the independents dreaded. Throughout the entire period of study, Colonel Mixter said, Senator Hastings was in frequent touch with Day & Zimmerman and the taxicab committee. He looked upon the Brooklyn Senator as the "Mayor's messenger or go-between."

More Hastings Loans Bared.

Senator Hastings had been under fire all day as Mr. Seabury sought to show that he had borrowed heavily from companies with which the three backers of the Jamaica Central Railways, an applicant for a Queens bus franchise, were associated, while that company's application was pending in the Board of Estimate.

Park A. Rowley, president of the Manhattan Company, admitted that Hastings had borrowed $7,500 and had not repaid it. William M. Greve, president of New York Investors, was the victim of a $25,000 "touch," which he said he would make good himself. H. P. Williams, chairman of the executive committee of the New York Title and Mortgage Company, admitted that business exigencies had forced him to recommend that Senator Hastings be excused from making good a collateral bond on a $350,000 mortgage because it was cheaper than to resort to litigation.

Throughout the whole proceeding, members of the Democratic minority, especially Assemblyman Louis A. Cuvillier, fought to protect the "dignity of the Senate," as represented in the person of the member from Kings County. Senator Samuel Hofstadter, chairman of the committee, repeatedly overruled their objections to the testimony, and it reached the point where the spectators were laughing every time Assemblyman Cuvillier addressed the chair.

But the court room was gravely sedate and silent, and even the minority dropped their fire of objections, when Mr. Sisto, a slim, gray-haired man, dressed as carefully as the Mayor himself, took the stand and unfolded his story.

He began by refusing to waive im-

Continued on Page Twelve.

Seabury Has a Prior Right To Explanation, Mayor Says

When Mayor Walker was informed at City Hall of the testimony of J. A. Sisto before the Hofstadter committee he broke in and said:

"I received $26,000 in bonds as the profit from that transaction—is that it?"

Informed that his statement was substantially correct, the Mayor parried questions with:

"Well, now, don't you think that Judge Seabury has a prior right to the answer to that question? I have nothing to say about it now, but it will be answered when Judge Seabury asks about it."

METROPOLITAN LISTS NEW AMERICAN OPERA

"Emperor Jones," Gruenberg's Setting of O'Neill Play, to Be Given in Berlin Also.

TIBBETT WILL SING ROLE

14th Native Work Under Gatti Regime Will Be Produced Early in Coming Season.

The Metropolitan Opera Association will present next season a new American opera, "Emperor Jones," based on Eugene O'Neill's play, by the American composer Louis Gruenberg, it became known yesterday.

The libretto has been prepared by Mr. Gruenberg himself. When he sent Mr. O'Neill a copy of his adaptation, the playwright replied that it had been admirably prepared so that the dramatic qualities and flavor of the work were preserved.

Lawrence Tibbett will enact the part of Jones and Tullio Serafin will conduct. No decision has been made by the Metropolitan as to the date of the presentation, but it is believed that it will be early in the season. Erich Kleiber, general music director of the Berlin Staatsoper, one of the largest opera companies in Europe, has already announced that he will produce the opera in Berlin this Fall. It appears, therefore, that Berlin and New York will vie for the right to give the work its world première.

Tom-Tom Used in Score.

Mr. Gruenberg has written the opera in two acts. He has made use, naturally, of the beat of the tom-tom which pursues Jones through the drama. This drum beat, which gradually accelerates in the opera, ceases only in certain brief scenes. These are during the visions and hallucinations which haunt Jones as he flees through the forest.

The work calls for a unique arrangement of the stage. The chorus of pursuing Negroes is grouped out of sight of the audience, below and in front of the stage flooring. At first only crossing hands and arms are seen above it. Then, as the pursuit of Jones draws nearer to its quarry, the bodies of the pursuers gradually emerge as yells of hate and triumph gather in volume.

The hallucinations of Jones—of the murdered crap player, of the sheriff whom Jones has killed, and of the auction block—are shown on small raised stages, to indicate that they are figments of the Negro's imagination.

Finally, Jones is seen, a nearly naked savage, seated on the ground with his fellows, swaying in terror as the medicine man leaps on the stage and indicates him as the tribe's victim. At the end the body of the fugitive, who shoots himself with the silver bullet, is carried by the tribesmen into the forest. Choruses of savage exultation are heard dying away in the distance.

Music Moves Swiftly.

To this drama Gruenberg has written what appears to be swift and pungent music. The principal moment of lyrical expansion is his prayer for the Lord's aid in his plight, which is in the general character, but not in slavish imitation, of a Negro spiritual. The score is also reflective of passing incident and gesture on the stage. Each one of the scenes of hallucination has its special musical counterpart. Toward the end, with an immense crescendo and acceleration, several pairs of drums are employed to intensely stirring effect. The opera takes about one hour to perform.

When Erich Kleiber, who conducted the opening weeks of the recent New

Continued on Page Nine.

Hoover Urges 3-Point Relief Plan Of $1,500,000,000 to Use as Loans

Senate Leaders Are Asked to Put the Proposal Before Colleagues—Finance Corporation Would Help States Handle Jobless and Advance Money for Spurring Business.

By ARTHUR KROCK.

Special to THE NEW YORK TIMES.

WASHINGTON, May 12.—President Hoover today asked Senators Robinson of Arkansas and Watson, the Democratic and Republican leaders of the Senate, to propose to their colleagues a three-point Federal relief program to stimulate private business in reproductive enterprises, to advance money for self-liquidating projects in States and municipalities, to ameliorate agricultural distress and to loan to States—but not municipalities—money for the relief of unemployed citizens.

The President's plan can be achieved simply by extending the powers and financial resources of the Reconstruction Finance Corporation. It involves no new government borrowings; it does not disturb the processes of budget balancing; it contemplates no bond issues for non-reproductive public works, as was proposed by New York financiers. If Congress will pass an amendment to the act establishing the Reconstruction Finance Corporation, the relief measures can be instituted.

The President's plan provides:

1. That the corporation be authorized to issue an additional $1,500,000,000 in debentures, of the proceeds from which $300,000,000 is to be loaned to States for general relief measures; $40,000,000 for export agricultural aid, and the remaining $1,160,000,000 loaned to private business for reproductive enterprises, assured by contracts.

2.—That State bonds and securities which cannot otherwise be floated be purchased by the corporation when the proceeds of these bonds and securities are to be used for unemployment relief.

3.—That the corporation be authorized to loan funds for self-liquidating projects such as toll bridges, tunnels and so forth.

It provides that private business planning reproductive enterprises for which credit cannot be obtained from the banks shall but put on a loaning basis with the corporation, a plan originally proposed by Mr. Hoover when the corporation was created, but rejected by Congress.

Senator Robinson, after a morning conference with the President, called a meeting of Democrats after the Senate adjourned this afternoon and outlined the President's idea. It was favorably received.

Senator Watson talked to a number of Republicans and reported progress with the idea. Speaker Garner and Minority Leader Snell were also consulted, and tonight Republican members of the Senate Committee on Banking and Currency were called to

Continued on Page Eleven.

TAX BILL'S TARIFFS ASSAILED IN REPORT BY MINORITY GROUP

Their Elimination From Senate Measure Is Demanded and 'Log-rolling' Is Condemned.

GAIN IN REVENUE DOUBTED

Imposts on Oil, Lumber, Copper and Coal Will Mean Embargo, Opponents Assert.

Special to THE NEW YORK TIMES.

WASHINGTON, May 12.—Five Democratic members of the Senate Finance Committee opened a fight on the tariff features of the billion-dollar tax bill today in a minority report demanding elimination of the duties on coal, oil, copper and lumber and condemning the "log-rolling" by which, they said, the items were inserted.

Consideration of the measure, expected today, was delayed by further debate on the Glass banking bill. When it appeared that the Glass measure could not be disposed of, even within another day, Republican leaders asked that it be side-tracked to give right of way to the tax bill.

Senator Glass gave rather reluctant consent, explaining that he long since had found it wise "not to go up against a buzz saw."

Senator Smoot will open discussion of the tax bill tomorrow. He had finished preparation tonight of a 4,000-word speech recommending the compromise measure as the prime step toward business recovery through the guarantee of government credit.

Senate leaders at the same time completed plans for a series of night sessions next week, by which it is hoped to complete the revenue measure well before June 10, the date tentatively set for adjournment.

Minority Questions Efficacy.

The minority tax bill report was signed by Senators Harrison, George, Walsh of Massachusetts, Costigan and Hull. Democratic members of the Finance Committee whose names were not attached were Senators Barkley of Kentucky, who voted in committee for the coal tariff; Connally of Texas and Gore of Oklahoma, who favored the duty on oil, and King of Utah, who stood for the copper tariff.

The report questioned whether the duties would result in additional revenues, cited adverse decisions on some of the items by the Tariff Commission and predicted that in many cases the consumer would be a sufferer.

The "log-rolling" methods, it said, would be odious even in a general tariff measure. But to resort to "trades, exchanges of votes and on-again, off-again" practices, the minority charges, such as were used in writing the tariff items into an emergency revenue measure, was held by the Democrats to be "an exhibition that will raise serious questions in the public mind concerning the capacity of representative government to function promptly

Continued on Page Thirteen.

NEW RELIEF GROUP WITH SMITH AT HEAD NAMED BY WALKER

Merged Bureaus on Jobs and Home Aid Have $5,000,000 to Use Until Aug. 1.

UNITY OF EFFORT IS OBJECT

Leading Lawyers, Bankers and Welfare Officials to Begin Tasks on June 1.

Members of the Emergency Work and Relief Administration, formed by a consolidation of the Home Relief Bureau and the Emergency Work Commission, who will assume their tasks on June 1, were notified of their appointments yesterday by Mayor Walker.

The new committee will consist of the following:

ALFRED E. SMITH, Empire State Building, chairman.

FRANK L. POLK, lawyer, former Under Secretary of State, 15 Broad Street.

LAWSON PURDY, executive director, Charity Organization Society, 105 East Twenty-second Street.

GEORGE V. McLAUGHLIN, president, Brooklyn Trust Company, 177 Montague Street, Brooklyn.

JOHN A. STEPHENS, Thompson Starrett Company, 245 East Twenty-third Street.

SOLOMON LOWENSTEIN, executive director, Federation for Support Jewish Philanthropic Societies, 71 West Forty-seventh Street.

FRANK J. TAYLOR, Commissioner of Public Welfare.

MARY L. GIBBONS, Catholic Charities, 10 East Thirty-fourth Street.

WILLIAM EWING, J. P. Morgan & Co., 23 Wall Street.

VICTOR F. RIDDER, president, New York State Board of Social Welfare, 22 North William Street.

WILLIAM J. HODSON, executive director, Welfare Council, 122 East Twenty-second Street.

S. SLOAN COLT, president, Bankers Trust Company, 16 Wall Street.

WILLIAM H. MATTHEWS, Association for Improving the Condition of the Poor; director, work bureau of the Gibson committee, 104 East Twenty-third Street.

JOSEPH J. BAKER, director, Brooklyn Federation of Jewish Charities, 356 First Street.

RALPH WOLF, president, Board of Jewish Social Service, 24 Pine Street.

Coordination of Efforts.

The purpose of the joint committee will be to eliminate the duplication of investigations, obtain a closer cohesion of all public relief under moneys appropriated by the city and to plan for the performance of public work other than by contract. It will also be the task of the committee to select the most beneficial method of assigning those in need to work relief or home relief.

The committee will have $5,000,000 at its disposal from June 1 to Aug. 1.

Mayor Walker announced that he was pleased that so many members of the Emergency Work Commission had agreed to continue with the new organization. Cornelius N. Bliss, chairman of the Emergency Work Commission, whose term began in October, 1931, will relinquish his work on June 1.

Because of the urgent need that still persists among thousands of New York's unemployed for clothing and food the clothing relief and food relief activities of the Emergency Unemployment Relief Committee will continue indefinitely instead of being discontinued as had been planned, it

Continued on Page Eleven.

LINDBERGH BABY FOUND DEAD NEAR HOME; MURDERED SOON AFTER THE KIDNAPPING 72 DAYS AGO AND LEFT LYING IN WOODS

POLICE INTENSIFY HUNT

Curtis, Norfolk Agent, and Condon, Who Paid Ransom, at Hopewell.

TO AID PROSECUTOR TODAY

Schwarzkopf Says Restraints Designed to Safeguard Baby Now Can Be Thrown Off.

A GROUP UNDER SUSPICION

Gov. Moore Pledges Relentless Hunt—Mulrooney Also Promises Full Aid.

Dr. J. F. Condon, the Bronx lecturer who acted as intermediary in the futile payment by Colonel Lindbergh of $50,000 ransom for his son, and John H. Curtis, the Norfolk boat builder, who also has been conducting negotiations, arrived at Hopewell for questioning by the police early this morning. They were scheduled to go to the prosecutor's office in Mercer County later today.

They arrived at the Lindbergh home shortly before 2 o'clock this morning and were at once closeted with the police. A few minutes before their arrival Colonel H. Norman Schwarzkopf, commanding the New Jersey State Police, made this announcement:

"Dr. Condon and Mr. Curtis will be at these headquarters in a few minutes for questioning in connection with this case and they will be turned over by the police authorities at this point to the prosecuting authorities tomorrow morning."

May Have Secret Data.

It is believed that the two intermediaries may have confidential information about the kidnappers which they are now ready to turn over to the authorities.

With this announcement the head of the New Jersey State Police indicated that the hunt for the murderers would be pursued with the aid of State, New York City and Federal authorities, throwing off the restraint that hitherto hampered the police effort. It was disclosed further by the New Jersey authorities that immediate steps are being taken to arrest a group of persons suspected of kidnapping the Lindbergh baby.

The police started their search immediately with a close though apparently unpromising examination of the place where the body was found.

"No footprints were found in the vicinity of where the baby's body was located," said Colonel Schwarzkopf in a statement early this morning. "This whole territory was thoroughly scoured by investigators from this office, even to the extent of scraping the surface of the ground around where the body was found and putting it all in containers and bringing it to these headquarters for the purpose of test and analysis."

Moore Pledges Every Effort.

Governor A. Harry Moore of New Jersey promised that everything possible would be done to "get the murderers" and announced that he expected to confer today with Colonel Schwarzkopf, head of the New Jersey State police. Meanwhile a grand jury investigation of all the Bronx incidents in the case was predicted last night by an aide of the Bronx District Attorney, Charles B. McLaughlin.

President John Grier Hibben of Princeton University called upon the law-enforcement forces of the country to unite in their hunt for the criminals, in a statement issued after he visited the Lindbergh home with Mrs. Hibben last night.

"A national systematic effort must be made right away," he said. "The authorities have been holding off from the beginning in the fear that their actions must cause the death of the child. Now that is over. The forces of law in the country must unite to get the persons who have done this thing."

Schwarzkopf's Statement.

Colonel Schwarzkopf made clear his course in regard to the hunt in an earlier statement, as follows:

"As long as there was a possibility of the baby being alive, the police have been acting with a certain amount of suppressed activity in order not to interfere with any negotiations that might result in the safe return of the baby.

"Now that the body of the baby

Continued on Page Three.

WHERE KIDNAPPERS LEFT SLAIN BABY.

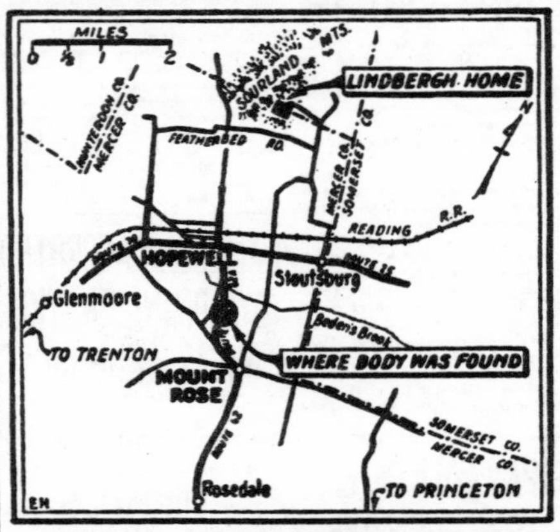

SYMPATHY POURS IN FROM ALL THE WORLD

Grief and Horror Evidenced in Capital Where Hoovers Request Lindbergh News.

ORTIZ RUBIO IS SADDENED

Messages Sent From Mexico City—Inquiries Made From London to Gov. Moore.

Widespread sympathy for the bereaved parents and relatives of Charles A. Lindbergh Jr. and the American people was expressed in messages that poured into the Lindbergh home at Hopewell, N. J., last night from various parts of the world. Officials and civilians who had hastened to join the international search for the kidnappers when the abduction became known sought to assuage the feelings they knew would follow in the wake of the announcement.

The grief and horror with which the nation received the final answer to the question regarding the safety of the child were evidenced at once in Washington, where the report reached the President and Mrs. Hoover among the first. Attachés at the White House, The Associated Press announced, immediately got in touch with the New Jersey authorities to obtain official information.

Deeply moved, Vice President Curtis said, "They have my deepest sympathy, and my most heartfelt condolences go out to the bereaved mother and Colonel Lindbergh and to their families in their sorrow." Mr. Curtis exclaimed with feeling, "It is a most shocking thing."

Unofficial like official Washington was horrified at the news and few persons were able to express their feelings about the tragedy. Captain Emory S. Land, cousin of Colonel Lindbergh, could only declare: "Anything I could say would be futile."

Committee Meeting Halts.

The shocked surprise with which Washington officials, many of them personal friends of the aviator, received the information was exemplified when the meeting of the Democratic steering committee of the Senate broke up on receipt of the barest announcement of the discovery at 6:45 o'clock.

The fifteen Senators present, including Senator Wagner of New York, dropped a momentous question under consideration to express their regrets and seek further details of the development.

"I have never heard more shocking news," Senator Wagner declared.

"It is too awful to talk about," Senator Norris of Nebraska said. Senator Norbeck of South Dakota called the discovery "most tragic," adding "My most heartfelt sympathy goes out to Colonel and Mrs. Lindbergh."

"The world is shocked at the enormity of the crime," Senator Walcott of Connecticut said.

Mrs. Evelyn Walsh McLean, wife of Edward B. McLean, who has put forth great effort and expended upward of $100,000 in an attempt to find the baby, refused to be quoted, but was said by her attorney to be deeply shocked and grieved. He said

Continued on Page Two.

COLONEL BELIEVED ON A YACHT AT SEA

Reported Somewhere Off Block Island on Search for the Kidnappers.

INFORMED OF BABY'S DEATH

Departed May 4 With Norfolk Aides on Mission That Had Seemed Promising.

Colonel Lindbergh was believed to have been on a yacht, somewhere off Block Island, when the body of his son was discovered yesterday. He had been there searching for the kidnappers of his son. There was no question that he had heard of the finding of the body, for Colonel H. Norman Schwarzkopf said that he had been notified, and one of the men with him—telephoning to Norfolk—said that the news had been received.

Colonel Lindbergh set out from Norfolk on May 4, on board the yacht Marcon, owned by Charles H. Consolvo of Baltimore. With him were John H. Curtis, Norfolk boat builder, and one of the trio of negotiators from that city; Edwin A. Bruce of Elmira, N. Y., and Lieutenant George L. Richard, a naval flier. The Marcon cruised up and down the coast near Norfolk until last Saturday, when the men transferred to another boat, which headed out to sea.

Lieutenant Richard Telephones.

The telephone message last night was from Lieutenant Richard to Mrs. Curtis, and was merely "Mr. Curtis is well, and we have heard the news." She could not say from where he had telephoned, nor did he say definitely whether Colonel Lindbergh was still on board. But the Rev. H. Dobson Peacock, one of the other Norfolk negotiators, said that "as far as I know" he was. The second yacht carrying them was generally supposed to have headed directly for Block Island.

When the Marcon sailed from Norfolk it was reported to be going to keep a rendezvous with the kidnappers of Colonel Lindbergh's son, who, according to an unverified rumor at that time, were said be on a foreign ship beyond the twelve-mile limit. Colonel Lindbergh boarded the yacht while in Chesapeake Bay, but bad weather kept the vessel from going out for two days.

The yacht has been running along the Atlantic Coast, it was said, searching for the other ship. Colonel Lindbergh, during the time he was on board, kept watch with the other members of the crew, sleeping in his clothes, always on the lookout for a sign of the second ship. The name of the yacht to which he transferred is not known, nor is its destination. It went straight to sea, however, as soon as he boarded it.

Quest Seemed Promising.

The Norfolk quest had been one of the most promising since the case began. Three prominent citizens of that city were involved, all of them certain that they had been in touch with the kidnappers. They were, besides Mr. Curtis, Rear Admiral Guy H. Burrage, retired, and the Rev. Mr. Peacock. Convinced that they had been in communication with the wanted men, they paid Colonel Lind-

Continued on Page Four.

BODY MILE FROM HOPEWELL

Discovered by Chance Near Centre of Wide Search for Child.

HALF-COVERED BY LEAVES

Skull Fractures Caused Death—Body and Clothing Are Identified by Nurse.

MOTHER IS BRAVE AT NEWS

Neighbors Had Complained That Hunt in Vicinity Had Not Been Thorough.

The baby son of Colonel Charles A. Lindbergh was found dead yesterday afternoon. The child had been murdered.

The body, lying face down in a depression and partly covered with dead leaves and wind-blown débris, was discovered by a Negro truck driver in a patch of woods in the Sourland Mountains less than five miles from the Lindbergh home near Hopewell, N. J.

The discovery was made by accident at 3:15 yesterday afternoon when the driver, walking into the woods from the road, found what he thought was a child's foot sticking out of the ground and notified the police. The identification followed quickly and the official announcement of the Lindbergh baby's fate was made at the Lindbergh home at 6:45 P. M.

The child evidently had been killed soon after he was stolen from his crib in the nursery on the night of March 1. Whether he had been killed with calculating purpose by criminals who found it advantageous to them to get rid of the child, or whether he had been thrown there by kidnappers fleeing in a panic, was not determined last night.

Two Fractures of Skull.

The body showed the marks of two fractures of the skull, one on the left side and the other on the right. The latter was a hole a half-inch in diameter. It was not definitely established whether this was a bullet hole or the result of a blow with a blunt instrument, but since no bullet was found the authorities were inclined to the belief that it was the latter.

The manner in which the baby died was officially stated as follows:

"The diagnosis of the cause of death is a fractured skull due to external violence."

"Unquestionably it was a brutal murder," said Dr. Charles H. Mitchell, County Physician of Mercer County, last night, after he had completed an autopsy.

The condition of the body indicated that the child has been dead at least two months—the kidnapping occurred seventy-two days ago yesterday—and there was a strong possibility that he had been killed on the very night of the kidnapping.

Mother Bearing Up Well.

Mrs. Lindbergh and her mother, Mrs. Dwight W. Morrow, were at home when the body was found, but were in complete seclusion.

Despite the shock of the discovery, Mrs. Lindbergh was bearing up courageously, as she has from the beginning, it was learned last night.

Colonel Lindbergh, who has been away much of the time in recent weeks making fruitless journeys in an attempt to make contact with the kidnappers, was not at home when the discovery was made. Colonel H. Norman Schwarzkopf, commanding the New Jersey State police, said that Colonel Lindbergh had been informed of his baby's death, however, and was on his way home. He did not disclose where the Colonel had been.

Positive identification of the baby's body was furnished last night by Betty Gow, the nursemaid, about whom so much interest in the case

Continued on Page Three.

"All the News That's Fit to Print."

The New York Times.

5 A.M. EDITION

WEATHER—Rain today; tomorrow fair and colder.
Temperatures Yesterday—Max., 56; Min., 50.

Copyright, 1932, by The New York Times Company.

VOL. LXXXII....No. 27,318. Entered as Second-Class Matter, Postoffice, New York, N. Y. NEW YORK, WEDNESDAY, NOVEMBER 9, 1932. TWO CENTS In New York City | THREE CENTS Within 200 Miles | FOUR CENTS Elsewhere Except in 7th and 8th Postal Zones

ROOSEVELT WINNER IN LANDSLIDE! DEMOCRATS CONTROL WET CONGRESS; LEHMAN GOVERNOR, O'BRIEN MAYOR

BIG VOTE FOR M'KEE

O'Brien Is 245,464 Behind Ticket as Protests Rise

BUT FINAL LEAD IS 616,736

Pounds Concedes Defeat Early, Saying 'Day of Miracles Is Past.'

McKEE TOTAL IS 137,538

Thousands of "Write-In" Votes Are Wasted as Backers Fail to Record Choice Properly.

HILLQUIT POLLS 248,425

Gets Greatest Vote in History of City for a Socialist—Runs Far Ahead of Party.

Surrogate John P. O'Brien, Tammany's candidate, was elected Mayor of New York yesterday, but overshadowing his victory, which was a foregone conclusion, was the tremendous "write-in" vote cast for Acting Mayor Joseph V. McKee.

Final returns from the city showed Judge O'Brien to have received a plurality of 616,736 over his nearest opponent, Lewis H. Pounds, Republican. Judge O'Brien's vote was 1,055,768, Mr. Pounds polled 439,032, and Morris Hillquit, Socialist, polled the highest vote ever given a candidate of his party in the city by receiving 248,425 votes.

Vote Listed by Boroughs.

By boroughs, the totals were as follows:

	O'Brien.	Pounds.	Hillquit.
Manhattan	309,256	113,278	39,398
Bronx	181,349	45,284	67,949
Brooklyn	358,605	155,478	112,740
Queens	176,237	105,461	25,821
Richmond	30,321	16,511	2,517
City total	1,055,768	439,032	248,425

The vote for Mr. McKee, put early this morning at 137,538, actually was far more than that, if ballots in which the voters had abbreviated his name, or used initials, or spelled it wrongly, were counted.

The vote was unprecedented, particularly as the use of voting machines made it much more difficult for a name to be writen in than on the old paper ballots.

Judge O'Brien had a clear majority of 215,000 votes over the combined vote of Pounds, Hillquit and McKee, but the McKee ballots cast aside as void would have reduced this, it was pointed out last night.

The vote for Mr. McKee by boroughs was as follows:

Manhattan, 26,336, with ten election districts missing.
Bronx, 24,453, complete.
Brooklyn, 43,328, complete.
Queens, 36,303, complete.
Richmond, 6,790, complete.
City total, 137,538.

The vote for Mr. McKee, made without any campaign on his part, and in the face of his own disavowal of the movement, kept him in the political picture as a candidate to be reckoned with for the full four-year term, to be voted on in 1933.

The term for which Judge O'Brien was elected starts on Jan. 1, 1933, and ends on Jan. 1, 1934.

The vote for Mr. O'Brien indicated he ran 381,263 votes behind Governor Roosevelt in the city, in actual votes cast, though his plurality was only 245,464 smaller than that given to the Presidential candidate.

Mr. Pounds conceded Mr. O'Brien's victory as early as 9:30 in the evening, and he sent the latter a telegram of congratulation.

He said later he could have been elected only by a miracle, and that the days of miracles were past. Mr. McKee, receiving election returns at the Park Lane, also sent a short

Continued on Page Seven.

THE GOVERNOR-ELECT.

© New York Times Studio.
Colonel Herbert H. Lehman.

JUDGES IN 'DEAL' WIN; PROTEST VOTE HEAVY

Steuer and Hofstadter Elected With Lydon and Leary to Supreme Court Bench.

290,000 FOR INDEPENDENTS

Bar Leaders Elated by Big Count for Deutsch and Alger—Call It 'Warning to Bosses.'

City Court Justice Aron Steuer and State Senator Samuel H. Hofstadter were elected yesterday over their independent opponents, Bernard S. Deutsch and George W. Alger, by a vote of about 2 to 1.

The protest vote against the so-called deal by which Senator Hofstadter and Justice Steuer received bipatrisan nominations for two of four vacancies on the Supreme Court bench in the first judicial district exceeded all expectations, but it was not enough to upset the combined strength of the Republican and Democratic organizations.

Justice Richard P. Lydon, who was nominated by both major parties for re-election, and Municipal Court Justice Timothy A. Leary, who had the Democratic nomination for the fourth vacancy on the bench, were elected with comfortable margins. Municipal Court Justice George L. Genung, who had the Republican nomination, trailed far behind the independent candidates.

Since Justice Lydon's re-election was virtually uncontested, his totals were not computed in the early returns. Of the other, Justice Steuer and Judge Leary were running slightly ahead of Senator Hofstadter, whose lead was large enough, however, to preclude the possibility of his being overtaken by Mr. Deutsch, his nearest rival.

The Complete Returns.

The complete returns for the entire first judicial district, comprising the boroughs of Manhattan and the Bronx, follow:

Steuer	565,405
Leary	547,112
Hofstadter	544,032
Deutsch	293,125
Alger	287,167
Genung	205,222

The totals recorded for the judiciary candidates in Manhattan follow:

Steuer	367,295
Hofstadter	357,430
Leary	331,442
Deutsch	147,886
Alger	145,346
Genung	138,304

Final returns from the Bronx, where the independent candidates ran strongest, showed the following totals:

Leary	215,670
Steuer	198,110
Hofstadter	186,602
Deutsch	145,239
Alger	141,821
Genung	66,918

The independent candidates did not

Continued on Page Twelve.

STATE VICTORY SOLID

Lehman Gets Record Party Plurality of 887,000.

WAGNER CLOSE TO HIM

National Ticket Has Margin of 615,000—Full Slate Is Elected.

RELIEF BONDS ARE VOTED

Republicans Have Narrow Edge Up-State—Hill Admits 'Protest' Defeated Them.

By JAMES A. HAGERTY.

Lieut. Gov. Herbert H. Lehman, Democratic nominee for Governor, defeated Colonel William J. Donovan, Republican, yesterday, in the Democratic whirlwind that swept New York State, by a plurality of about 887,000, a record for a Democratic candidate in this State.

Governor Franklin D. Roosevelt and Speaker John N. Garner, the Democratic candidates for President and Vice President, carried the State by a plurality of about 615,000, as against Governor Roosevelt's heretofore record Democratic plurality of 725,000, which he received as candidate for re-election to the Governorship two years ago.

With Governor Roosevelt and Colonel Lehman were swept into office the other Democratic candidates on the State-wide ticket, United States Senator Robert F. Wagner, candidate for re-election; M. William Bray, for Lieutenant Governor; State Controller Morris S. Tremaine, Attorney General John J. Bennett Jr. and the two candidates for Representatives-at-Large, Elmer E. Studley and John Fitzgibbons.

Colonel Lehman led Governor Roosevelt by 88,279 in actual votes cast in New York City and also led the Governor in many cities and counties up-State. His indicated plurality exceeded that of Governor Roosevelt by more than 250,000, but exceeded the indicated plurality for Senator Wagner by only about 35,000.

Returns on the proposition and proposed constitutional amendment were slow in coming in, but a large majority for the proposal to issue $30,000,000 in bonds for unemployment relief was indicated, and scattering returns indicated that the constitutional amendment to throw open the forest reserve to the development of recreational facilities had been beaten.

The vote for President and State-wide candidates follows:

FOR PRESIDENT.

New York City, complete—Roosevelt, Democrat, 1,437,231; Hoover, Republican, 575,031; Thomas, Socialist, 120,486; actual plurality for Roosevelt, 862,200.

Up-State, 431 election districts missing—Roosevelt, 1,022,121; Hoover, 1,254,032; actual plurality for Hoover, 231,911; indicated plurality for Hoover, 247,107; indicated plurality for Roosevelt in the entire State, 615,093.

FOR GOVERNOR.

New York City, complete—Lehman, Democrat, 1,525,510; Donovan, Republican, 542,492; plurality for Lehman, 983,018.

Up-State, 561 election districts missing—Lehman, 1,056,088; Donovan, 1,141,735; actual plurality for Donovan, 85,647; indicated plurality for Donovan, 95,817.

Indicated plurality for Lehman in the entire State, 887,201.

FOR UNITED STATES SENATOR.

New York City, complete—Wagner, Dem., 1,438,343; Medalie, Rep., 517,733; plurality for Wagner, 920,610.

Up-State, 1,301 districts missing—Wagner, 915,699; Medalie, 984,418;

Continued on Page Sixteen.

The President's Message To the President-Elect

From a Staff Correspondent.

PALO ALTO, Cal., Nov. 8.—President Hoover conceded his defeat for re-election at 9:17 o'clock tonight, Pacific Time, and dispatched this telegram of congratulations to Governor Roosevelt:

Palo Alto, Cal., Nov. 8, 1932.

The Hon. Franklin D. Roosevelt,
Biltmore Hotel,
New York, N. Y.

I congratulate you on the opportunity that has come to you to be of service to the country and I wish for you a most successful administration. In the common purpose of all of us I shall dedicate myself to every possible helpful effort.

HERBERT HOOVER.

Governor Roosevelt had not received President Hoover's message when he left for his home shortly before 2 o'clock this morning. Pending its receipt he said he preferred not to make reply or comment on the message.

DEMOCRATS CONTROL STATE SENATE, 26-25

Republican Margin in Assembly of 6 Votes Is Reduced to 2 —Lose by 4 Up-State.

ALSO TWO SENATE SEATS

Moffatt Is Re-elected, While Hastings and Dr. Love Are Defeated in City Race.

The slender working majority of two votes by which the Republicans control the present State Senate was swept away in yesterday's Democratic landslide. The next Senate will be made up of 25 Republicans and 26 Democrats, giving the Democrats a majority of one. The present Senate has 27 Republican and 25 Democratic members. Twenty-six votes are required to pass a bill in that branch of the Legislature.

In the Assembly, where 76 votes are required to control legislation, the Republican majority of six is cut down to two in the 1933 Legislature. The Republicans won 77 seats and the Democrats 73 at yesterday's elections for the Assembly.

The Democrats won four Assembly districts north of the Bronx away from the Republicans; one district in Monroe County, one district in Oneida and two in Sullivan and Schoharie counties. The Republicans, however, reduced the up-State Democratic gains by recapturing from them Schuyler county in the southern tier, where last year they succeeded in electing their candidate for the Lower House.

Post Is Defeated.

The Republicans also managed to strengthen their New York City representation by electing Herbert Brownell Jr. in the Tenth (Manhattan) District. This was the district where Langdon W. Post, Democratic incumbent was turned down by Tammany for supporting legislation to broaden the powers and continue the Hofstadter Committee and ran as an independent, polling 5,053 votes. Mr. Brownell defeated his Tammany opponent by a scant plurality of 307 votes. He received 8,907 votes, Sylva La Chappelle, the Democrat, 8,600.

The Democrats gained two Senate districts up-State, the Thirty-first, made up of Rensselaer County, and the Thirty-sixth, made up of Oneida. In the Thirty-fourth, composed of St. Lawrence and Franklin Counties, Warren T. Thayer, the present Republican incumbent, managed to win again after a hard fight.

The New York City Republicans will have three representatives in the Legislature, Senator-elect George Blumberg, who won by a plurality of approximately 500 over Senator John A. Hastings, Democratic incumbent in the Seventh Senatorial

Continued on Page Five.

OVERTURN IN SENATE

Bingham, Watson, Moses and Smoot Are Defeated.

DEMOCRATIC MAJORITY 12

Party Adds to Control in House—May Rule Both Branches This Winter.

LA GUARDIA LOSES SEAT

Mrs. Pratt Defeated, Wadsworth Wins—Texas Sends Garner Back to the House.

The Democratic wave of victory yesterday gave that party complete control of Congress and in its onrush carried down to defeat the four Republican leaders of the Senate.

Senator Smoot of Utah, Republican dean of the Senate and chairman of the powerful Finance Committee; Senator Watson of Indiana, floor leader; Senator Moses, president pro tempore and Senator Jones of Washington, chairman of the Appropriations Committee, all were relegated to the ranks of "lame ducks." No such upset has occurred in recent history.

While returns early this morning showed the new Senate will be Democratic by a majority of twelve and the House overwhelmingly Democratic, there was a possibility that in the session of the old Congress convening on Dec. 5, the Democrats will achieve a slender control of the whole body.

Changes in Coming Session.

They now have a majority of one in the House, in the old Congress that still is to hold a "lame-duck" session; in the Senate the numbers were evened with the defeat of Senator Barbour of New Jersey for the short term beginning next month, and there was, early this morning, an even chance that Colorado would elect Walter Walker, a Democrat, also for the short term. In that event the Senate in December would be: Democrats 49, Republicans 46, Farmer-Labor 1.

On the basis of incomplete returns, the new Senate stood at Democrats 54, Republicans 34, Farmer-Labor 1, and seven States still in doubt.

The next Congress not only will be Democratic; it will be wet.

New York Republicans fared especially ill in the election, which saw Representative La Guardia, fiery "liberal" Republican who led a bloc that controlled the House temporarily in the last session, defeated by J. J. Lanzetta, Democrat. Representative Ruth Pratt also failed of re-election.

Moses Loses in Close Race.

Of the most prominent Republicans who were unseated, Senator Watson went down first, conceding his defeat by Frederick Van Nuys, Democrat.

Senator Moses ran nip and tuck with Fred H. Brown, Democrat, until after midnight in the poll of ballots, when returns from Manchester, N. H., spelled his certain defeat.

Senator Smoot was defeated by Professor E. D. Thomas and Mr. Jones by Homer T. Bone. Both of the victors were Democrats. Senator Jones, who is better known as the author of the "five-and-ten" law than for his important committee chairmanship, was defeated coincident with adoption of a State referendum in Washington repealing that State's prohibition law.

An important Republican defeat in the House was that of Representative Haugen of Iowa, co-author of the McNary-Haugen bill, who went down before F. Bierman, Democrat.

McAdoo Wins Seat.

William Gibbs McAdoo, former Democratic Secretary of the Treasury, who was credited with switching the Democratic National Convention to Franklin D. Roosevelt through

Continued on Page Six.

THE PRESIDENT-ELECT.

© New York Times Studio.
Franklin D. Roosevelt.

The Electoral Vote

ROOSEVELT 448.

Alabama	11	Nebraska	7
Arizona	3	Nevada	3
Arkansas	9	New Jersey	16
California	22	New Mexico	3
Colorado	6	New York	47
Florida	7	North Carolina	13
Georgia	12	North Dakota	4
Idaho	4	Ohio	26
Illinois	29	Oklahoma	11
Indiana	14	Rhode Island	4
Iowa	11	South Carolina	8
Kansas	9	South Dakota	4
Kentucky	11	Tennessee	11
Louisiana	10	Texas	23
Maryland	8	Utah	4
Massachusetts	17	Virginia	11
Minnesota	11	Washington	8
Mississippi	9	West Virginia	8
Missouri	15	Wisconsin	12
Montana	4	Wyoming	3

HOOVER—59.

Connecticut	8	New Hampshire	4
Delaware	3	Pennsylvania	36
Maine	5	Vermont	3

DOUBTFUL 24.

Michigan	19	Oregon	5

Votes in Electoral College, 531; needed to elect, 266.

Wets in Control in Both Houses, But Short of Two-Thirds in Senate

Modification of Volstead Act Appears Certain, and House Has Easy Majority for Repeal, but Upper Chamber Support Is Uncertain on Basis of Returns.

Complete control of the next Congress by forces opposed to Federal prohibition was one of the results which came with the political upheaval that took place with yesterday's election.

With full returns from the major portion of the country and definite trends established in the remainder, it appeared certain that those demanding a change in the dry laws would hold between fifty and fifty-five seats in the Senate and 300 or more in the House of Representatives.

Up until an early hour this morning, only nineteen outspoken drys had been returned definitely to the House, while twenty-four Senators, most of whom did not come up for re-election this year, remained among the prohibitionists. Around 100 House seats still were in doubt, and several Senators and re-elected Representatives were yet undecided how to align themselves on the question.

The aggregation chosen yesterday represented a veritable checker-board of views on prohibition reform, but the extent of the majorities indicated a good chance for immediate modification of the Volstead act to allow light wines and beer. The gains in both Houses were chiefly among Democrats, whose party has been pledged to that course.

Modification in the next Congress appeared much more probable on the basis of yesterday's election than outright repeal of the Eighteenth Amendment. Sixty-four Senate seats and 290 in the House will be required for the latter, whereas only a bare majority of 49 in the Senate and 218 in the House would be needed to change the national prohibition (Volstead) law.

The House was sure of the necessary two-thirds for repeal, as early this morning the anti-prohibitionists had already captured 282 seats; the

Continued on Page Eight.

SWEEP IS NATIONAL

Democrats Carry 40 States, Electoral Votes 448.

SIX STATES FOR HOOVER

He Loses New York, New Jersey, Bay State, Indiana and Ohio.

DEMOCRATS WIN SENATE

Necessary Majority for Repeal of the Volstead Act in Prospect.

RECORD NATIONAL VOTE

Hoover Felicitates Rival and Promises 'Every Helpful Effort for Common Purpose.'

Roosevelt Statement.

President-elect Roosevelt gave the following statement to THE NEW YORK TIMES early this morning:

"While I am grateful with all my heart for this expression of the confidence of my fellow-Americans, I realize keenly the responsibility I shall assume and I mean to serve with my utmost capacity the interest of the nation.

"The people could not have arrived at this result if they had not been informed properly of my views by an independent press, and I value particularly the high service of THE NEW YORK TIMES in its reporting of my speeches and in its enlightened comment."

By ARTHUR KROCK.

A political cataclysm, unprecedented in the nation's history and produced by three years of depression, thrust President Herbert Hoover and the Republican power from control of the government yesterday, elected Governor Franklin Delano Roosevelt President of the United States, provided the Democrats with a large majority in Congress and gave them administration of the affairs of many States of the Union.

Fifteen minutes after midnight, Eastern Standard Time, The Associated Press flashed from Palo Alto this line: "Hoover concedes defeat."

It was then fifteen minutes after nine in California, and the President had been in his residence on the Leland Stanford campus only a few hours, arriving with expressed confidence of victory.

A few minutes after the flash from Palo Alto the text of Mr. Hoover's message of congratulation to his successful opponent was received by THE NEW YORK TIMES, though it was delayed in direct transmission to the President-elect. After offering his felicitations to Governor Roosevelt on his "opportunity to be of service to the country," and extending wishes for success, the President "dedicated" himself to "every possible helpful effort * * * in the common purpose of us all."

This language strengthened the belief of those who expect that the relations between the victor and the vanquished, in view of the exigent condition of the country, will be more than perfunctory, and that they may soon confer in an effort to arrive at a mutual program of stabilization during the period between now

"All the News That's Fit to Print."

The New York Times.

LATE CITY EDITION
POSTCRIPT
WEATHER—Fair today; tomorrow cloudy, warmer, probably rain
Temperatures Yesterday—Max., 43; Min., 37.

VOL. LXXXII....No. 27,417. Entered as Second-Class Matter. Postoffice, New York, N. Y. NEW YORK, THURSDAY, FEBRUARY 16, 1933. TWO CENTS In New York City. | THREE CENTS Within 200 Miles | FOUR CENTS Elsewhere Except in 7th and 8th Postal Zones

ASSASSIN FIRES INTO ROOSEVELT PARTY AT MIAMI; PRESIDENT-ELECT UNINJURED; MAYOR CERMAK AND 4 OTHERS WOUNDED

REPEAL VOTE TODAY SET IN THE SENATE; FILIBUSTER BROKEN

Wets Win in Test Ballots as Blaine Plan Is Stripped of Protective Clauses.

ROBINSON LEADS FIGHT

Borah Backs Him on Removing the Anti-Saloon Section, Voted Out 33-32.

STATE LIQUOR PLAN OUT

Commission Proposes to Bar the Saloon—Limit on Places to Sell Beer.

Report of the State Liquor Control Commission is on Page 15.

Special to THE NEW YORK TIMES.

WASHINGTON, Feb. 15.—The Senate today stripped the Blaine prohibition resolution to practically "naked" repeal and agreed to vote on the measure at 3 P. M. tomorrow.

Senator Robinson, the Democratic leader, who led the fight to simplify the resolution, predicted that the Senate would furnish the necessary two-thirds majority for adoption on the morrow.

He expressed confidence, too, that the resolution as amended tonight would be acceptable to Speaker Garner and other House leaders, who announced at the outset that the House would be allowed to vote only on the Democratic repeal plan as advocated in the last campaign.

Every prediction was that the vote tomorrow would be extremely close. Senator McNary, assistant Republican leader, described the resolution as "teetering," with the possibility of going one way or the other. He would make no forecast.

Wet leaders, scanning the votes of today, were very hopeful as to the outcome tomorrow. They had succeeded in breaking the filibuster started by the drys to prevent a vote.

Coincidental with the argreement to vote tomorrow, the Senate, by a vote of 33 to 32, struck the so-called anti-saloon provisions from the Blaine resolution and, on a ballot of 45 to 15, decreed that ratification should be by conventions in the several States instead of Legislatures.

Passage in House Predicted.

A deciding vote on the amendment, proposed by Senator Robinson, to strike out the anti-saloon section, was cast by Senator Borah, long a dry stalwart. He held it was impossible for the government properly to exercise any supervision over saloons once the Eighteenth Amendment was repealed.

As the resolution stood tonight, its proposal was only one degree removed from outright repeal. It carried a clause directing Federal protection of dry States which the Garner repeal resolution, submitted at the outset of the session, did not contain but which Senate leaders said tonight was not sufficiently controversial to bring a deadlock between the two branches.

The resolution as it emerged was believed to have a better chance of passage in the House than the proposal submitted by Speaker Garner the first day of Congress. The Speaker's resolution failed by only six votes of obtaining the necessary two-thirds majority, and it was pointed out tonight that the six votes from Senator Robinson's own State, which were cast in the negative at that time, were sufficient to change the tide should repeal be proposed anew to the House.

It was recalled, too, that Senator Robinson was opposed to the Garner resolution, whereas his espousal at this time of the Democratic platform plan was responsible for much of the weight given the revival of the repeal movement.

The dry filibuster against the Blaine resolution broke up in the Senate today when wets announced

Continued on Page Fourteen.

Illinois Senate Passes Bills For Repeal of Prohibition Laws

By The Associated Press.

SPRINGFIELD, Ill., Feb. 15.—The State Senate today passed two prohibition repeal measures and sent them to the House for further action.

The vote on the repeal measures, which had been delayed because of Governor Henry Horner's insistence that regulatory acts should be provided first, was preceded by promises in the debate that they would not be signed until the regulatory bills also had been adopted.

The two bills would remove from the statute books State prohibition and the search and seizure acts.

A measure designed to authorize banking holidays was introduced in the House. Under its terms, the Governor would be empowered to declare a holiday for the State and Mayors authorized to do so for municipalities.

BOY GANG CHIEF, 15, ADMITS KILLING 'FOE'

Says He Stabbed Queens Lad, 12, for "Lying" About Him and Vowed to "Get" Him.

VICTIM MISSING 2 WEEKS

Found Bound in Closet of a Vacant House to Which Killer Had Lured Him by Ruse.

Bound, gagged and stabbed through the heart, the body of 12-year-old William Bender, who disappeared Jan. 31, was found yesterday in a closet in one of a row of partly-built dwellings, less than two blocks from his home at 6 Bergen Landing Road, Richmond Hill Circle, Queens. He had been dead for at least two weeks.

Nine hours after the body was found, Harry Murch, 15-year-old leader of a juvenile gang, confessed he had murdered the Bender boy. Murch and his chum, John Miller, 10, who was with him when the crime was committed, were picked up by the police yesterday afternoon. For more than five hours, despite persistent questioning by officials of the Police Department and the District Attorney's office, they calmly denied all knowledge of the crime. Then finally they broke down.

"I did it," Murch is said to have declared. "Bender lied about me. He told the whole neighborhood that I had hit Mrs. Peterson on the head with a monkey wrench. I said I'd get him and I did."

He is to be arraigned today in children's court, Jamaica, on a charge of homicide.

Tells of Meeting Victim.

Murch said that on the afternoon of Jan. 31 he and Miller had met Bender outside the latter's home.

"I told him," Murch said, "that I was going to stick up a peanut peddler and that if he'd come over to the houses in Mauretania Avenue with me I'd show him how I was going to do it. He came along all right. But he seemed a bit suspicious.

"So I tied up Miller first. Then I untied Miller and tied up Bender. As soon as I had him where I wanted him I took out my knife and stabbed him in the heart."

Miller corroborated Murch's story. Afterward, the boys said, they fled from the house and agreed to say nothing to any one. The knife which Murch used for the crime, they said, was taken from the kitchen of his home.

The clue that broke the case was a small piece of gingham cloth that had been used to gag the dead boy. The fact that Murch had threatened to "get Bender" was well known in the neighborhood and soon after the body was discovered detectives went to the home of Murch's parents, Mr. and Mrs. Charles Murch, in Philbert Avenue, just a short distance from the home of the Bender boy.

In the Murch garage the detectives found other pieces of gingham of exactly the same quality and pattern as that which had been used for the gag. Young Murch and Miller were immediately taken into custody.

The body of the missing boy was

Continued on Page Ten.

TAX RATE OF $2.40 SEEN AS VALUATIONS DROP $1,195,006,742

Sexton Estimates a 19-Point Reduction to the Lowest Basic Levy Since 1920.

REALTY BURDEN EASED

Assessment Totals Cut in All Boroughs—Personalty Less, Franchise Values Rise.

ALDERMEN VOTE BUDGET

Adopt $518,427,972 Document Without Change—Mayor Denies Plea on Sergeants-at-Arms.

Final adoption of the revised 1933 budget at a total of 18 per cent below that of the 1932 budget and announcement of a cut of $1,195,006,742 in assessed valuations of city real estate, personal property and franchises provided yesterday a substantial basis for belief that the basic tax rate this year will be appreciably lower than the 1932 rate of $2.59 per $100 of assessed valuation.

For the first time in the city's history the total of assessed valuations is lower than in a preceding year. Valuations placed upon franchises for tax purposes were increased in every borough this year. Valuations on real estate showed decreases in every borough, while in the Bronx alone the valuations on personal estate showed a rise. The total valuations for all boroughs in 1932 was $19,977,077,315. For 1933 the final valuations aggregate $18,782,070,573.

The Board of Aldermen adopted a final budget of $518,427,972.16, the same total recently approved by the Board of Estimate. This figure shows a decrease of $112,933,325.81 from the total budget for 1932, which was $631,366,297.97. The budget now goes to Mayor O'Brien for his signature. It must be filed with Controller Berry by Feb. 25.

Nineteen-Point Tax Drop Seen.

James J. Sexton, president of the Department of Taxes and Assessments, said that he was certain the basic tax rate would show a decided drop. He expressed the belief that the rate would not exceed $2.40, a drop of nineteen points.

Deputy Controller Frank J. Prial, in the absence of the Controller, said that no accurate estimate of the rate could be made before the amount of the city's general fund for reduction of taxation is known. The general fund, the budget and the final total of assessed valuation, are the three factors used in computing the basic rate. Borough tax rates are added to the basic rate to pay for local improvements.

Mr. Prial said that the amount of the general fund would depend

Continued on Page Nine.

SERIOUSLY WOUNDED.

Times Wide World Photo.

Mayor Anton J. Cermak of Chicago

WOMAN DIVERTED AIM OF ASSASSIN

100-Pound Wife of Miami Doctor Tells How She Forced Up Man's Arm.

HELD ON DURING SHOOTING

Gun Had Been Pointed "Right at Mr. Roosevelt" 15 Feet Away, She Relates.

By Telephone to THE NEW YORK TIMES.

MIAMI, Fla., Feb. 15.—Mrs. Lillian Cross, 48 years old, and weighing only 100 pounds, probably saved the life of the President-elect tonight when she forced the would-be assassin's shooting arm upward and caused the bullets to go high.

"He was aiming right at the President," said Mrs. Cross. "I saw him. That's why I caught his arm and forced the gun up. I said to myself, all in a flash, 'Oh! He's going to kill the President!'"

Mrs. Cross said that she was not frightened when she saw the weapon. Her only thought was for Mr. Roosevelt.

"I didn't begin to get nervous at all until it was all over," she related after she reached her home at 1,069 Northwest Second Street.

"I drove to the park tonight with my husband, Dr. W. F. Cross (he's a physician and surgeon here) and with my friend, Mrs. Willis McCrary of Atlanta, Ga. My husband got a seat somewhere in the back of the crowd, but Mrs. McCrary and I found seats right up front, by the guard rail they'd put up.

"President Roosevelt was only about fifteen feet away from us. He finished his speech and got down from the back of the automobile—an open car it was—and had settled in the back seat. I stood up on the bench on which I'd been sit-

Continued on Page Three.

Cermak in Critical Condition at Hospital; "Glad It Was I, Not You," He Tells Roosevelt

Special to THE NEW YORK TIMES.

MIAMI, Thursday, Feb. 16.—Mayor Cermak was shot in the right side, just below the ribs, and was in a critical condition at Jackson Memorial Hospital. An X-ray showed the bullet lodged in the back of the abdomen.

An emergency operation was considered at 12:30 A. M. and plans were made to undertake it at once. A short time later physicians put off the operation.

When President-elect Roosevelt called to see Mayor Cermak at the hospital the Mayor turned his head and smiled faintly, saying:

"I'm glad it was I, instead of you. I wish you would be very careful. The country needs you badly. You should not take any more such chances as you took tonight."

The President-elect replied:

"The country needs a man like you, too. I can only express my deepest regrets. I have decided not to leave tonight and will return to see you in the morning."

James B. Bowler, Chicago City Councilman, who told of the conversation, said Mr. Roosevelt was expected to call again at the hospital about 8 A. M.

Mr. Bowler was with Mayor Cermak in the emergency room and took from the front of the Mayor's shirt a .32 calibre bullet, which was believed to be a spent shot that had hit one of the other victims.

A bulletin on Mayor Cermak's condition, issued at 2 A. M., said:

"Pulse, 88; temperature, 98.6; respiration, 24. His condition is regarded as dangerous, but not immediately critical. The bullet evidently traversed the diaphragm and margin of the liver and lodged in the body of the eleventh dorsal vertebra. Surgical intervention is deemed unwise unless his condition becomes worse."

The bulletin was signed by Dr. John W. Snyder, Dr. Thomas H. Hutson and Dr. E. S. Nichol. Dr. Snyder is in charge, and at the hospital this morning he said:

"Mrs. Gill and Mayor Cermak have more than a fifty-fifty chance to recover."

WASHINGTON IS STUNNED

Hoover Wires Roosevelt; Rejoicing That He Was Not Wounded.

ASKS NEWS OF CERMAK

Senators Express Gratitude President-Elect Escaped Madman's Shots.

RISK TO PRESIDENT SEEN

Determination Is Voiced That Life of His Successor Be Safeguarded by All Means.

Special to THE NEW YORK TIMES.

WASHINGTON, Feb. 15.—The nation's capital was deeply shocked tonight on hearing of the attempt on the life of President-elect Roosevelt.

From President Hoover to the lowliest citizen the reaction was instant that the country cast every safeguard around the President-elect.

President Hoover himself struck the keynote when he said:

"I am deeply shocked at the news. It is a dastardly act."

Hoover's Message to Roosevelt.

At the same time the President sent a telegram to Mr. Roosevelt which read:

"Together with every citizen I rejoice that you have not been injured. I shall be grateful to you for news of Mayor Cermak's condition."

Official and unofficial Washington was stunned at the first reports of what appeared to be an attempt on the life of the man who within less than three weeks will become Chief Executive. Newspaper extras were on the street almost immediately, and citizens sat close to their radios, receiving the latest news flashes. General relief was expressed that Mr. Roosevelt escaped injury.

Comment of Leaders.

Speaker Garner said:

"I am gratified beyond words that the President-elect is uninjured and that he will assume the administration of the Government of the United States, which is desired by the American people as expressed in the overwhelming result of the November elections."

Secretary Mills said:

"I am thankful that our next President escaped injury and that the act of a misguided or crazy individual will not deprive the American people of their chosen leader."

"Of course, I am overjoyed that the President-elect escaped," said Senator Byrnes, one of Mr. Roosevelt's closest advisers, "but I deplore profoundly that such a thing could happen. It's awful!"

Senator Robinson of Arkansas, Senate minority leader, said:

"Assuming that the shots were fired at Mr. Roosevelt, it should be understood that this is the United States, not Russia. No fanatic, crank or revolutionist, or any number of them will be permitted to prevent the orderly transfer of power in the government of the United States."

Thinks Assailant Deranged.

"How dreadful, and how fortunate he did not hit!" said Senator Lewis of Illinois. "I do not know what to say except that it was a deplorable thing. I do hope it was not attempted out of ill will. It must have been the result of a deranged mind; certainly no one in his right mind would attempt such a thing. If, as appears possible, the shots were actually fired at Mayor Cermak, it undoubtedly was some member of the old lawless element in Chicago with a fancied grievance against the Mayor."

Chief Moran of the Secret Service, ill at his home here, received a report late this evening from Joseph E. Murphy, Assistant Chief, from the hospital in Miami where Mayor Cermak had been taken.

Commenting on the shooting, Senator Shipstead said:

"This unfortunate incident shows the risk the President and the President-elect of the United States are subject to. There are always cranks in the country. Every citi-

Continued on Page Three.

ESCAPES ASSASSIN'S BULLETS.

New York Times Studio Photo.

President-Elect Franklin D. Roosevelt.

GUNMAN LAYS ACT TO BODY 'TORMENT'

Joe Zingara, Hackensack Bricklayer, Says Pain Made Him 'Hate All Presidents.'

DESCRIBED AS ANARCHIST

Man Who Fired at Roosevelt Says He Once Tried in Italy to Kill King Victor Emmanuel.

By Telephone to THE NEW YORK TIMES.

MIAMI, Feb. 15.—Surrounded by detectives and high police officials, the man who shot at President-elect Roosevelt tonight gave his name as Joe Zingara of New York and related, in spasms of words during questioning at Police Headquarters, how "constant torment from a stomach operation" had impelled him to attempt the life of the President-elect.

Zingara, a short, stocky man of about 35, a brick mason who came to Miami two months ago from Hackensack, N. J., betrayed by his manner even in the rational portions of his statement the warped mentality which resulted in his deed tonight.

In an almost boastful tone, he declared that he had attempted the life of King Victor Emmanuel of Italy ten years ago. That failed, he said, for the same reason as his attempt tonight—"there was too big a crowd."

He admitted he had no personal grievance against Mr. Roosevelt. Saying "No, I had none," he swept away questions of that nature.

Nor could the police discover that he had any personal grievance against the King of Italy. But he hated "rich and powerful persons," he said with a hiss, and they were figures, he indicated, for his wrath.

"I Don't Like Presidents."

"I like Roosevelt personally, but I don't like Presidents," he replied when asked if he didn't like the President-elect. He intended to kill him, he said, "and I would be glad if I had killed the President-elect." He did not like Presidents because "rich men send their children to schools."

He said this was because "when I was a young man, rich men's sons went to school while I worked in a brick factory in Italy and burned myself."

Zingara indicated a scar on his stomach which he said was the result of the burn.

He was seized with the idea of trying to kill the President-elect only two days ago, he declared.

"About two days ago I bought a paper for 5 cents and saw that the President-elect was coming to Miami," he related.

"So yesterday I went to a place

Continued on Page Two.

MRS. ROOSEVELT TAKES NEWS CALMLY

She Telephones Immediately to Husband and Is Relieved to Find Him Unhurt.

KEEPS SPEAKING PROGRAM

Assured That "He Is Not Even Excited," She Takes Train Later for Ithaca.

Mrs. Franklin D. Roosevelt returned to her home at 49 East Sixty-fifth Street about 10:30 o'clock last night and found the household upset. The Negro butler's face betrayed his agitation as he admitted her.

"What's it all about?" she demanded.

Stammering, the butler told her that her husband, the President-elect, had been fired upon in Miami. He had only the meager information gleaned from newspapers, which called the house when the first brief reports were received.

Mrs. Roosevelt was met at her home by her daughter, Mrs. Anna Roosevelt Dall, and received the news calmly and without apparent emotion.

"Those things are to be expected," she remarked.

With a calm and steady voice she placed a long distance telephone call which reached the President-elect at the bedside of Mayor Cermak. There followed a few minutes of conversation and then Mrs. Roosevelt turned to the group in the room and said:

"He's all right. He's not the least bit excited."

Leaves for Ithaca.

A few minutes later Mrs. Roosevelt, accompanied only by her maid, was on a railroad train bound for Ithaca, N. Y., to fill a speaking engagement on the program of Cornell University's Home and Farm Week. The train left at 11:35.

Mrs. Roosevelt was speaking at the Warner Club at 321 West Forty-fourth Street when the first of the dramatic incident in Miami was received in New York newspaper offices. She left there without knowledge of what had happened.

In his telephone conversation with Mrs. Roosevelt, members of the household said, the President-elect informed her that it was his belief that the would-be assassin's bullets were aimed at Mayor Cermak, and not at him.

They quoted him as saying that five persons were in the hospital as a result of the shooting, and that he wasn't even scratched. Instead of starting back for New York last night, as he had planned, however,

Continued on Page Two.

ASSASSIN SHOOTS 5 TIMES

Police and Bystanders Leap for Him and Take Him Prisoner.

ACCOMPLICE TAKEN LATER

Cermak and New York Officer Rushed to Hospital—Now in Serious Condition.

ROOSEVELT DELAYS TRIP

Had Been Warmly Welcomed and Intended to Start for North at Once.

By JAMES A. HAGERTY.

Special to THE NEW YORK TIMES.

MIAMI, Feb. 15.—An unsuccessful attempt was made to assassinate President-elect Franklin D. Roosevelt just after he ended a speech in Bay Front Park here at 9:35 o'clock tonight, two hours after his return from an eleven-day fishing cruise on Vincent Astor's yacht Nourmahal.

Although the gunman missed the target at which he was aiming, he probably fatally wounded Mayor Anton Cermak of Chicago and four other persons were hit by five shots from his pistol before a woman destroyed his aim on the last shot by seizing his wrist and a Miami policeman felled him to the ground with a blow of his night stick.

List of the Wounded.

The wounded are:

Mayor Anton Cermak of Chicago, shot through the chest; condition critical.

Miss Margaret Kruis of the Henry Clay Hotel, Miami Beach, a visitor from Newark, N. J., shot through the hand.

Mrs. Joe H. Gill, wife of the president of the Florida Power and Light Company, shot in the abdomen; conditon critical.

William Sinnott, a New York policeman, living at 612 West 178th Street, shot in the head; condition critical.

Russell Caldwell, 22, of Miami, shot in the head.

Roosevelt Was Target.

The would-be assassin, who was arrested immediately and lodged in the city prison on the nineteenth floor of Miami's skyscraper City Hall, is Giuseppe Zingara of Hackensack, N. J.

Although early reports were that he intended to kill Mayor Cermak rather than the President-elect, due to his remark, "Well, I got Cermak," it appeared later that Mr. Roosevelt was his target.

"I'd kill every President," he was reported by the police to have said after his arrest.

"I'd kill them all; I'd kill all the officers," he also is reported to have said, indicating that he may be an Anarchist.

Evidence that the attempted assassination of Roosevelt was premeditated was obtained by the police late tonight and Andrea Valemti, who lived with Zingara, was arrested on suspicion of being an accomplice.

A search of Zingara's clothing disclosed several newspaper clippings, mostly from local newspapers announcing Mr. Roosevelt's intended visit to this city.

Clipping on McKinley.

One clipping, however, contained an account of the assassination of President McKinley by the anarchist Czolgosz. This strengthened the police belief that Zingara might belong to some anarchist group, although no direct evidence has been obtained showing such a connection.

Detectives, deputy sheriffs and policemen were working on several clues, obtained by the questioning of Zingara and Valemti.

Zingara is charged with assault with intent to kill, pending the preferring of the more serious

"All the News That's Fit to Print."

The New York Times.

LATE CITY EDITION
WEATHER—Fair today; tomorrow cloudy, warmer, rain following
Temperatures Yesterday—Max., 40; min., 26.

VOL. LXXXII....No. 27,435. Entered as Second-Class Matter, Postoffice, New York, N. Y. NEW YORK, MONDAY, MARCH 6, 1933. P TWO CENTS In New York City. | THREE CENTS Within 200 Miles | FOUR CENTS Elsewhere Except In 7th and 8th Postal Zones

ROOSEVELT ORDERS 4-DAY BANK HOLIDAY, PUTS EMBARGO ON GOLD, CALLS CONGRESS

HITLER BLOC WINS A REICH MAJORITY; RULES IN PRUSSIA

Stay-at-Homes Turn Out and Give Government 52% of 39,000,000 Record Vote.

NAZIS ROLL UP 17,300,000

Get 44% of Total Poll and Even Wrest the Control of Bavaria From Catholics.

ELECTION IS PEACEFUL

Berlin Is Closely Guarded—The Stahlhelm Holds Parade Under Sunny Skies.

By FREDERICK T. BIRCHALL.
Special Cable to THE NEW YORK TIMES.

BERLIN, Monday, March 6.—With almost mathematical precision the results in yesterday's German elections for the Reichstag and the Prussian Diet bear out the predictions based on the pre-election campaign. Just as two and two make four, so suppression and intimidation have produced a Nazi-Nationalist triumph. The rest of the world may now accept the fact of ultra-Nationalist domination of the Reich and Prussia for a prolonged period with whatever results this may entail.

At 2 o'clock this morning, when 39,000,000 out of the Reich's eligible vote of 44,000,000 counted and with every indication of a probable total vote of 90 per cent, exceeding all precedents Nazi-Nationalist control of the Reichstag was assured. The Nazis will have at least 288 seats and the Nationalists 53 more, giving them together 341 seats, or a clear 52 per cent in a total of 648.

The tabulated vote follows:

	Vote.	Seats.
National Socialists	17,300,000	288
Nationalists	3,100,000	53
Socialists	7,000,000	118
Communists	4,800,000	81
Centrists and Bavarian People's Party	5,500,000	91
People's Party and Allied Groups	1,014,000	12
State (Democratic)	333,000	5
Total	39,047,000	648

The Nazis have increased their vote to 44 per cent of the adult population, or 11 per cent over that of last November and 6½ per cent over their previous high-water total of last July. The Nationalist increase is barely 1 per cent over their vote of last November. This, therefore, is a Nazi rather than a Nationalist triumph.

Nazis Control Bavaria.

Apart from the size of the vote—the 90 per cent of the eligible voters being as nearly unanimous as any election in any large country has ever shown—the sensation of the election is that the Nazis have wrested control of Bavaria from the Catholics. They have wiped out the deficit in their November vote compared with that of July and have beaten the Bavarian People's party by approximately 600,000. This is likely to dispose of any dream of restoring the Wittelsbach monarchy in Bavaria, as it will of the idea of a possible secession of Bavaria from the Reich.

More than this, in the city of Cologne, the Catholic capital of Germany, under the influence of an unexpected 25 per cent increase in the total vote—three-fourths of which has gone into the Nazi column—Herr Hitler's party has come within an ace of seizing control there.

The so-called stay-at-home vote came out with a vengeance and almost the whole of it went to the Nazis; while, in addition, the Hitlerites gained a full 10 per cent from the other parties.

Gain 4,000,000 Votes.

The Nazis have increased their own vote by more than 4,000,000, or almost 30 per cent over the November total. The Centrists and Socialists throughout the country have almost held their own. The Communists lost more than 20 per cent, but their lost votes did not go to the Socialists, as had been expected. While a few may have gone

Continued on Page Eight.

Mob Attacked Stalin's Home In Wide Revolt, Tokyo Hears

Wireless to THE NEW YORK TIMES.

TOKYO, Monday, March 6.—Private information reaching Tokyo states that discontent due to famine conditions is so acute in Soviet Russia that a mob attacked Joseph Stalin's house in Moscow on Jan. 20 and was driven off by troops after 400 persons had been killed. Other reports from Siberia, partly corroborated by information reaching military circles here, indicate the farmers are in widespread revolt. Serious disturbances occurred at Irkutsk, and 80,000 men are said to have joined the revolt, including Communists and Red soldiers.

The Japanese discount a good part of these rumors, but they come from too many sources to be entirely ignored. It is believed these disturbances are much more serious than the Soviet Government has admitted.

CERMAK NEAR END; LAPSES INTO COMA

Death Is Imminent From Shot Aimed by Zangara at Roosevelt.

FAMILY AT HIS BEDSIDE

Third Transfusion Futile in 19-Day Fight to Save Chicago Mayor in Miami Hospital.

By The Associated Press.

MIAMI, Fla., Monday, March 6.—Physicians of Mayor Anton Cermak early this morning relinquished hope for his life.

In a bulletin issued at 12:30 A. M., the physicians said that Mayor Cermak was in a condition of coma and that he probably would live only a few hours. The bulletin said Mr. Cermak was "failing rapidly."

It was issued after a third blood transfusion had been administered yesterday in an attempt to save his life.

The Mayor's right lung, punctured on the night of Feb. 15 by a bullet from the pistol of the assassin, Joseph Zangara, in an attempt to kill Franklin D. Roosevelt, was aspirated yesterday and physicians found a gangrenous condition.

Father Morrison of St. Bartholomew's Church in Chicago entered the sun parlor room at 1:15 A. M. Mayor Cermak's wife was a Roman Catholic and his children are of that faith.

Dr. Frederick Tice of Chicago told newspaper men at 1:25 A. M. that the Mayor probably would live an hour. He said Cermak's breathing was very labored. He called members of the family and said Mr. Cermak's life was "a matter of another hour."

Members of Family Weep.

Members of the family, summoned to the bedside, emerged weeping.

Joseph Cermak, a brother, his wife and Mrs. John Kallal, a sister, came from the sun porch at 12:35 A. M. Mrs. Cermak and Mrs. Kallal took their seats on the lawn before the sun porch door and wept.

Vivian Graham, a granddaughter, emerged soon and joined the group. Daughters of the Mayor had been at his side a short time before.

At midnight newspapermen were allowed to go into the sun porch where the Mayor lies in an oxygen room and see the patient through the glass window of the oxygen apparatus.

The Mayor lay back on his pillow, hands folded over his chest, breathing heavily. Dr. Frank Jirka and Dr. E. S. Nichol were attending him.

Dr. Jirka, who is Mr. Cermak's son-in-law, said the Mayor recognized members of the family. "My wife asked him if he knew her. He told her, 'Yes, kiss me.'"

The greatest air of concern prevailed in the little sun porch, where a heavy guard of police and detectives was maintained.

"Reaction" After Transfusion.

After the blood transfusion yesterday afternoon Mr. Cermak suffered a "slight reaction," causing a weakening of the pulse and irregular respiration, the doctors said.

Reports immediately upon conclusion of the transfusion were that the operation apparently was successful. One pint of blood given by Thomas Pendray Jr. of Miami was

Continued on Page Fourteen.

JAPANESE PUSH ON IN FIERCE FIGHTING; CHINA CLOSES WALL

Jehol Forces Offer Stoutest Resistance of Campaign as They Are Cornered.

BUT LOSE ANOTHER PASS

Chang's Troops at Kupei Bar Retreat Southward to the Peiping Area.

NANKING ADMITS DEFEAT

Asserts 'What Will Happen Next Depends on Military'—Tientsin Fears Clashes.

By The Associated Press.

TOKYO, March 5.—Rengo (Japanese) news agency dispatches from Chengteh (Jehol City) today said the final phase of the Japanese campaign in Jehol Province, a move to seize passes in the Great Wall north and northeast of Peiping, was producing some of the most bitter fighting of the whole drive. Cornered Chinese units were resisting desperately.

The Sixteenth Infantry Brigade of Major Gen. Tadashi Kawahara, en route to Koupei Pass through the wall, fought fiercely with remnants of the troops of Tang Yu-lin, Governor of Jehol Province, ten miles west of the provincial capital, Chengteh. Thereafter the detachment advanced to Changshanku, which is sixteen miles northeast of the pass.

Marshal Chang Hsiao-liang, military commander of North China, was reported to have sealed the pass against Governor Tang and his followers. Governor Tang himself was reported to have fled to Fengning, which is about forty miles northwest of Chengteh.

Pass in Wall Taken.

Fighting in the shadow of the Great Wall preceded the occupation by the Fourteenth Infantry Brigade of Major Gen. Heijiro Hattori of Fanchia Pass, which is one of three important Great Wall passes south of Chengteh. General Hattori faced a large Chinese force south of the wall.

Major Gen. Kaoru Nakamura, commanding the Thirty-third Infantry Brigade, en route from Lingyau to Chiehliing Pass, summoned an air squadron to aid him before he succeeded in routing remnants of Marshal Chang's Sixteenth Brigade.

The Fourth Cavalry Brigade of Major Gen. Kennosuke Mogi, pushing on from Chihfeng, 100 miles northeast of Chengteh, captured Weichang, fifty-five miles to the southwest, the centre of the Jehol opium-producing region, after stiff fighting.

Thousands of Chinese Dead.

Special Cable to THE NEW YORK TIMES.

SHANGHAI, Monday, March 6.—While members of the Nanking Government are expected to discuss a unified policy at Peiping this week, Jehol reports today tell of indescribable confusion among the Chinese forces there, with thousands killed, wounded and missing among the troops in Marshal Chang Hsiao-liang's best brigades, which originally totaled 20,000.

War Minister Ho Yin-ching arrived by airplane at Peiping at noon, and Acting Premier T. V. Soong and others are expected to follow him there for a belated stocktaking of the present situation. The Chinese troops in Jehol appear to be scrambling for the passes out through the Great Wall, with the Japanese bombing Chinese concentrations near Kupei and Haifeng passes and at Dolonnor, in Northern Jehol.

The Japanese artillery is in action at Sanshihchiatze, between Pingchuan and Lingyuan.

The Japanese brigade led by General Hattori is expected to attack the main Chinese force tomorrow at Paishihlatsushan Hill, twenty miles south of Pingchuan and thirty-three miles from Haifeng Pass.

The Charhar Provincial Government is reported to be negotiating with the Japanese for inclusion of that province in Manchukuo, but the Chinese military deny this.

The Nanking Foreign Office yesterday made this terse and incisive statement:

"Jehol is lost. What will happen

Continued on Page Eight.

Relief Wages Will Be Paid Despite Holiday, Gibson Says

Harvey D. Gibson, chairman of the Emergency Unemployment Relief Committee, declared yesterday that the bank holiday would not interfere with the payment of wages to unemployed men and women holding emergency jobs through the committee's work and relief bureau.

"Emergency wages must be paid and some way must be found to pay them," Mr. Gibson said. "I have no doubt that we will find a way to do it. We are not worried about it at all. Arrangements can certainly be made to meet the emergency relief payroll."

The weekly payroll of the committee exceeds $1,000,000.

BEWILDERED CITY STILL PAYS IN CASH

Faces Use of Scrip Calmly and Continues to Patronize the Theatres and Stores.

HOPEFUL MOOD PREVAILS

Merchants and Travel Lines Uncertain on Use of Tender—Many Extending Credit.

Bewildered but still cheerful, the city followed its usual routine yesterday, talked of the possibility of using scrip instead of cash, but still patronized the movie theatres, restaurants and concert halls.

Railroads reported, generally, that there had been no appreciable decrease in week-end travel, that there had been "no embarrassment" and that they were carrying on as usual, on an all-cash basis.

A spokesman for the Pennsylvania Railroad reported that the outward movement yesterday was good and an official of the New York Central reported everything going smoothly with enough cash on hand to meet all the road's needs for the present, including payrolls.

One form of nuisance cropped up at Pennsylvania Station. It started Saturday night, when persons with banknotes of large denominations demanded change. There was a tremendous number of $100 notes, quite a few $500 notes and even a few $1,000 notes were presented for change. One or two of the more timid persons tried to cover up their real purpose by buying Newark tickets.

Railroads Accept Only Cash.

None of the railroads is accepting anything but cash for transportation. This is in accord with general practice, an official pointed out, and up to yesterday no change in that plan had been proposed. Officers of the New York Central Railroad held a special meeting yesterday apparently to arrange for eventualities that might arise from the banking situation, but no decision was reached so far as could be learned.

Airplane lines and steamship lines, on the other hand, were accepting checks from old clients and were following a policy of being "reasonable" about accepting checks from other customers.

"We will maintain a sensible and reasonable attitude during this crisis," said John Gammie, assistant manager of the Cunard Line. "We will try to carry on much as we did in ordinary times. We haven't taken up the matter of scrip, but it is likely that a meeting of steamship line officials may be called to decide on a policy with regard to it."

Rise in Grocery Store Sales.

Increased sales were reported in most of the chain grocery stores in the poorer districts on Saturday, owners reported yesterday. They believed it might have been caused by a desire to stock up before an inflation policy might be decided upon by the government.

The Grand Union Grocery Stores, an official said last night, are planning to issue coupon books redeemable for food at their stores. The books would be sold to industrial and commercial concerns that would use them as part payment to employes. The same official considered it likely that guaranteed Clearing House scrip might be acceptable at the Grand Union stores.

A spokesman for the Great Atlantic and Pacific Tea Company, which maintains chains of grocery stores in several States, said his concern had not yet formulated any

Continued on Page Three.

BANKS HERE ACT AT ONCE

City Scrip to Be Ready Today or Tomorrow to Replace Currency.

EMERGENCY STEP PRAISED

Financiers Look for Little Interruption in Business Under Federal Program.

'TRUST DEPOSITS' TO AID

Cash Now Can Be Placed in New Accounts and Drawn Upon Without Limitation.

Clearing House certificates will be issued in New York, if needed, just as soon as they are printed, possibly today and probably not later than tomorrow, as a result of President Roosevelt's proclamation of last night.

The President's emergency decree not only made the banking holiday national and extended it through Thursday when Congress meets in special session, but it also gave the banks permission to issue scrip in the form of Clearing House certificates to take the place of regular currency.

Thus there will be little or no interruption in the ordinary routine of New York's business affairs, which can be carried on with scrip as a substitute medium of exchange just as well as with other currency. Paychecks, for instance, would be converted into scrip by the banks, which would be open for that purpose and for receiving new deposits.

Leading bankers indicated their approval of the President's proclamation last night and signified their belief that the use of scrip would be just as successful in New York as it was in the 1907 panic.

May Pay in Currency.

There is a possibility, some bankers said, that the New York banks might pay out currency when they reopen in place of, or in addition to, clearing house certificates. Such action would be possible only with the express permission of the Secretary of the Treasury under the President's order. These bankers said that the local banks have large amounts of till money on hand and that they could, if permitted, meet substantial demands from their depositors out of these cash holdings. From the standpoint of the central banking system the paying out of this till money to the public would have no effect upon the position of the national currency, since it is already a part of total money in circulation.

Subject always to the sanction of the Secretary of the Treasury, the banks will be able, under the President's proclamation, to operate along nearly normal lines. Under the provision for creation of special trust accounts, business men, merchants and wage earners will be able to find a safe depository for any cash they receive instead of having to face the dangers of carrying large amounts of currency. Those who withdrew money from the banks just before the shutdown and who have since been worrying about its safety will be able to redeposit the funds in special trust accounts and be assured of getting it back again without limitation.

Lehman Defers State Action.

When informed of the President's proclamation late last night, Governor Lehman withheld comment for the present as to whether he would issue a new decree extending the New York State holiday. Although such an action probably would be regarded as a mere formality, it was thought likely that the Governor would take it. Before President Roosevelt's proclamation was made public, Governor A. Harry Moore of New Jersey issued a decree last night extending the banking holiday in New Jersey indefinitely.

In both New York and New Jersey the banking holiday was proclaimed first for two days—Saturday and today—and was to have ended with the close of business this afternoon. Under the original proclamations by Governors Lehman and Moore the New York and New Jersey banks were to have been reopened tomorrow morning.

All security and commodity exchanges will remain closed, barring unexpected changes in present

Continued on Page Three.

The President's Bank Proclamation

Special to THE NEW YORK TIMES.

WASHINGTON, March 5.—The text of President Roosevelt's proclamation on the banking situation, issued at the White House at 11 o'clock tonight, was as follows:

BY THE PRESIDENT OF THE UNITED STATES OF AMERICA.

A Proclamation

WHEREAS there have been heavy and unwarranted withdrawals of gold and currency from our banking institutions for the purpose of hoarding; and

WHEREAS continuous and increasingly extensive speculative activity abroad in foreign exchange has resulted in severe drains on the nation's stocks of gold; and

WHEREAS these conditions have created a national emergency; and

WHEREAS it is in the best interests of all bank depositors that a period of respite be provided with a view to preventing further hoarding of coin, bullion or currency or speculation in foreign exchange and permitting the application of appropriate measures to protect the interests of our people; and

WHEREAS it is provided in Section 5 (b) of the act of October 6, 1917 (40 stat. L. 411) as amended, "that the President may investigate, regulate or prohibit, under such rules and regulations as he may prescribe, by means of licenses or otherwise, any transactions in foreign exchange and the export, hoarding, melting or earmarkings of gold or silver coin or bullion or currency * * *";

WHEREAS it is provided in Section 16 of the said act "that whoever shall wilfully violate any of the provisions of this act or of any license, rule or regulation issued thereunder, and whoever shall wilfully violate, neglect or refuse to comply with any order of the President issued in compliance with the provisions of this act, shall, upon conviction, be fined not more than $10,000 or, if a natural person, imprisoned for not more than ten years or both * * *";

NOW, THEREFORE, I, FRANKLIN D. ROOSEVELT, PRESIDENT OF THE UNITED STATES OF AMERICA, IN VIEW OF SUCH NATIONAL EMERGENCY AND BY VIRTUE of the authority vested in me by said act and in order to prevent the export, hoarding or earmarking of gold or silver coin or bullion or currency, do hereby proclaim, order, direct and declare that from Monday, the sixth day of March, to Thursday, the ninth day of March, nineteen hundred and thirty-three, both dates inclusive, there shall be maintained and observed by all banking institutions and all branches thereof located in the United States of America, including the Territories and Insular Possessions, a bank holiday, and that during said period all banking transactions shall be suspended.

During such holiday, excepting as hereinafter provided, no such banking institution or branch shall pay out, export, earmark or permit the withdrawal or transfer in any manner or by any device whatsoever of any gold or silver coin or bullion or currency or take any other action which might facilitate the hoarding thereof; nor shall any such banking institution or branch pay out deposits, make loans or discounts, deal in foreign exchange, transfer credits from the United States to any place abroad, or transact any other banking business whatsoever.

During such holiday, the Secretary of the Treasury, with the approval of the President and under such regulations as he may prescribe, is authorized and empowered (a) to permit any or all of such banking institutions to perform any or all of the usual banking functions, (b) to direct, require or permit the issuance of clearing house certificates, or other evidences of claims of assets of banking institutions, and (c) to authorize and direct the creation in such banking institutions of special trust accounts for the receipt of new deposits which shall be subject to withdrawal on demand without any restriction or limitation and shall be kept separately in cash or on deposit in Federal Reserve Banks or invested in obligations of the United States.

As used in this order the term "banking institutions" shall include all Federal Reserve Banks, national banking associations, banks, trust companies, savings banks, building and loan associations, credit unions, or other corporations, partnerships, associations or persons, engaged in the business of receiving deposits, making loans, discounting business paper, or transacting any other form of banking business.

IN WITNESS WHEREOF I have hereunto set my hand and caused the seal of the United States to be affixed.

Done in the City of Washington this 6th day of March, 1 A M., in the year of Our Lord One Thousand Nine Hundred and Thirty-three, and of the Independence of the United States the one hundred and fifty-seventh.

(SEAL) FRANKLIN D. ROOSEVELT.

By the President:
CORDELL HULL,
Secretary of State.

ROOSEVELT MEETS GOVERNORS TODAY

Conference Will Centre on Bank Problem—Confidence in President Apparent.

Special to THE NEW YORK TIMES.

WASHINGTON, March 5.—The Governors conference which President Roosevelt called nearly a month ago to discuss with him interlocking governmental problems will meet with him tomorrow morning in the White House at 11 o'clock. But its discussion will be largely directed toward the more immediate issue of banking moratoriums, with the possibility that what is done may indicate the eventual Federal action to be suggested by President Roosevelt.

The present situation so far overshadows the issues which Mr. Roosevelt stressed in originally calling the conference that they have become entirely secondary. It was his first intention to confine the discussion to a limitation on overlapping Federal and State

Continued on Page Two.

ON GOLD STANDARD, WOODIN DECLARES

Other High Officials Concur in His View of Suspending Payments for Period.

Special to THE NEW YORK TIMES.

WASHINGTON, March 5.—Secretary of the Treasury William H. Woodin declared tonight emphatically that the United States had not gone off the gold standard on account of the proclamation of the President. He was supported in this view by other high officials of the administration, both in the executive and legislative branches, among them Senator Key Pittman, chairman of the Committee on Foreign Relations.

Secretary Woodin said:

"It is ridiculous and misleading to say that we have gone off the gold standard, any more than we have gone off the currency standard.

"We are definitely on the gold standard. Gold merely cannot be obtained for several days. In other

Continued on Page Six.

USE OF SCRIP AUTHORIZED

President Takes Steps Under Sweeping Law of War Time.

PRISON FOR GOLD HOARDER

The Proclamation Provides for Withdrawals From Banks Against New Deposits.

CONGRESS SITS THURSDAY

Day of Conference With the Cabinet and Financial Men Precedes the Decree.

Special to THE NEW YORK TIMES.

WASHINGTON, March 5.—To prevent the export, hoarding or earmarking of gold or silver, coin or bullion or currency, President Roosevelt issued a proclamation at 11 o'clock tonight, in which he ordered a bank holiday from tomorrow through Thursday, March 9. Earlier in the day he had summoned a special session of Congress to meet on Thursday.

This sweeping action was taken after a day of conferences, among officials and bankers, the President taking recourse to war powers granted under the trading-with-the-enemy act.

As a result of the proclamation all banking activities will be suspended during the holiday, except as permitted by regulations of the Secretary of the Treasury, thus taking this country technically off the gold standard until the four-day period expires.

In order that there may not be a complete suspension of all banking and exchange operations, the proclamation authorizes the issuance of Clearing House certificates, which may be used as currency until the banks return to more normal functioning.

Points of the Proclamation.

The main points in the proclamation are:

1. A national banking holiday from March 6 to March 9 inclusive.

An embargo on the withdrawal of gold and silver for export or domestic use during that period, except with permission of the Secretary of the Treasury.

3. The issuance of Clearing House certificates or other evidence of claims against the assets of banking institutions to permit business to carry on.

4. Authorization to banking institutions under regulations of the Secretary of the Treasury to receive new deposits and make them subject to withdrawal on demand without any restrictions or limitations.

Friends of the President said he had a definite three-point program for the solution of the banking problem and that tonight's action included two of them. The first, they said, was a protection of the currency against unreasonable withdrawal. The second was to furnish a temporary currency. The third is permanent reorganization of the whole banking system, which, they predicted would be proposed to the special session of Congress meeting here Thursday.

Officials Act Quickly.

The Federal Reserve Board and Secretary Woodin, with the advice of former Secretary Ogden L. Mills acted immediately after the issuance of the proclamation to make it effective.

The proclamation was issued at 11 o'clock, bringing to an end a series of conferences held by Treasury officials and the new Cabinet throughout the day.

The proclamation affects all Federal Reserve Banks and national banks, trust companies, savings banks, building and loan associations, credit unions or other institutions engaged in any form of banking business.

The proclamation provides for a fine of $10,000 or imprisonment of not more than ten years or both for any violation of its provisions by gold hoarding or otherwise.

The President acted under Section 5 (b) and Section 16 of the trading with the enemy act to place these extraordinary restrictions on the nation's banking structure. The courts have interpreted the act as giving the President authority to bring about a complete suspension of gold and silver payments as well as an embargo on their export.

Section 5 (b) of the trading-with-

"All the News That's Fit to Print."

The New York Times.

LATE CITY EDITION
WEATHER—Fair and warmer today; tomorrow cloudy, showers.
Temperatures Yesterday—Max., 61; Min., 39

Section 1

Copyright, 1933, by The New York Times Company.

VOL. LXXXIII....No. 27,658. Entered as Second-Class Matter, Postoffice, New York, N. Y. NEW YORK, SUNDAY, OCTOBER 15, 1933. F+ Including Rotogravure Picture, Magazine and Book Sections. TEN CENTS | TWELVE CENTS Beyond 200 Miles. Except in 7th and 8th Postal Zones.

GERMANY QUITS LEAGUE AND ARMS PARLEY; HITLER SCORES TREATY, DEMANDS EQUALITY; CALLS ELECTION NOV. 12 TO OBTAIN APPROVAL

REPUBLICANS PLAN FIGHT FOR FUSION TO END DEFECTIONS

Campaign to Begin This Week—Leaders See McKee Defeat as Blow to Roosevelt.

WEIGH NATIONAL RESULTS

Look to Party Victory Here as Step Toward State Triumph in Presidential Drive.

McKEE-LAGUARDIA CLASH

They Exchange Sharp Telegrams as Result of the Seabury Attack on Lehman.

Progress of City Campaign.

City Republicans prepared for aggressive fight for F. H. LaGuardia. National leaders of the party hold defeat of Joseph V. McKee would be a blow to prestige of President Roosevelt.

Mr. McKee demanded to know whether Mr. LaGuardia supported Samuel Seabury's attacks on Governor Lehman. Mr. LaGuardia's reply accused Mr. McKee of attack on Jews eighteen years ago.

Tammany reported that "deserters" were returning to the ranks and said they would be welcomed "if they hustled."

Republicans Plan Fight.

By W. A. WARN.

The Republicans who so far have not taken a very active part in the Fusion campaign are preparing to enter the fight aggressively this week. They are determined to block attempts made by the supporters of Joseph V. McKee to bring about a Republican defection to the Recovery party.

The entry of Mr. McKee into the Mayoralty race, which inevitably will have the effect of dividing the anti-Tammany forces, it was said last night in well-informed Republican quarters, has consolidated Republican sentiment in favor of the candidates on the Fusion ticket.

Announcement is expected within a day or two of a big Republican mass meeting, to be held, probably toward the end of this week, under the auspices of the Republican Mayoralty Committee, of which Charles H. Tuttle is chairman. Plans for the meeting were discussed and perfected at a meeting held behind closed doors at the National Republican Club last week.

Financial Leaders to Meet.

Tomorrow, at a luncheon to be given at the Bankers Club under the auspices of the brokers division, F. H. LaGuardia, the Fusion standard bearer, and some of the other candidates on his ticket will make their appeal to a group of Republicans and Democrats engaged in finance who, although united in their opposition to Tammany, have not been regarded by many as friendly to the candidacy of Mr. LaGuardia.

There will be other gatherings of importance under Republican auspices to signalize the vigorous entry of the local party into the Mayoralty fight in support of the Fusion ticket.

From a purely partisan aspect, the Republicans throughout the country have come to view the Mayoralty fight now in progress in this city as of more than local significance, especially since it is understood that Mr. McKee is making his fight with the support of the Roosevelt administration at Washington.

A defeat for Mr. McKee, as the national Republican strategists look upon it, could not fail to impair the prestige of the President and correspondingly enhance that of their own party.

Republican leaders in this State have sought to impress upon the local leaders and Republicans of prominence who so far have held aloof from the contest that the election of Mr. LaGuardia would give their party a tremendous lift in its attempt to elect a Governor next year, as well as in the Congressional elections, which are of equal importance from a national Republican viewpoint.

A Republican victory in the State next year, as the national leaders view the situation, would almost certainly shift this State from the Democratic to the Republican column in 1936.

Effect on 1936 Is Weighed.

Many prominent Republicans in this city who have not been credited with any personal interest in the election of their fellow Republican, Mr. LaGuardia, are vitally interested in the Presidential campaign three years hence. Ogden L. Mills, former Secretary of the Treasury and strong supporter of Herbert Hoover, has come to be looked upon in party circles as an aspirant

Continued on Page Three.

Major Sports Results

Football—Columbia met unexpectedly strong opposition from Virginia, winning by 15 to 6. N. Y. U. beat Lafayette, 13-12, while Fordham triumphed over West Virginia, 20-0. Yale conquered Washington and Lee, 14-0, and Pittsburgh downed Navy, 34 to 6. Scores of other important games:

Army	52	Delaware	0
Colgate	25	Rutgers	2
Harvard	34	New Hamp.	0
Illinois	21	Wisconsin	0
Lebanon Val.	32	C. C. N. Y.	0
Manhattan	20	Georgetown	20
Michigan	40	Cornell	0
Notre Dame	12	Indiana	2
Princeton	45	Williams	0
Sou. Calif.	14	St. Mary's	7
Stanford	0	Northw'n	0

Racing—Mrs. T. W. Durant's Little Dan won the Long Island Hunt Cup at West Hills, L. I. Sweeping Light took the Continental Handicap at Jamaica, while Dark Secret captured the Laurel Stakes at Laurel.

Full details in Sports Section.

O'BRIEN SIGNS TAX ON UTILITY INCOMES

Levy of 1½% Monthly on Total Revenue of Companies, Effective From Sept. 1.

TO BE USED FOR RELIEF

Mayor Declines to Disclose Whether He Has Vetoed Tax on Savings Banks.

Mayor O'Brien signed yesterday the city bill placing a tax of 1½ per cent on the gross monthly income of public utility companies during the emergency for which the city must provide relief funds.

The Mayor did not disclose whether he had vetoed the city bill taxing savings banks and insurance companies. The veto of this bill was stipulated by the city's bankers as part of their agreement to finance the city and its relief needs over the next four years. The Mayor, it was understood, would defer acting on this measure until the special session of the Legislature convening this week completes its work. The session will enact into law several features of the city's four-year financing agreement.

The bill, which became law yesterday with the Mayor's signature, was passed on Sept. 15 by the Board of Estimate branch of the Municipal Assembly by fifteen affirmative votes. The Board of Aldermen subsequently passed it by a vote of fifty-two to one. The bill places a city tax on the gross income of every corporation, company, association, joint-stock association, copartnership and person operating in the city subject to supervision of the Public Service Commission. The levy is effective from Sept. 1, last, until Feb. 28, 1934, and the proceeds are to go for relief and redemption of relief certificates already outstanding.

Must Be Paid Every Month.

The new city tax must be paid at the end of every month, and is levied in addition to all other license fees and taxes provided by any other section of the law. At first public utilities thought they could obtain a rebate from the city on their special franchise fees, but the bill as explained by the Mayor rules out this possibility.

Returns on the tax must be filed with Controller McAneny on or before the tenth day following the ending of any one month from Oct. 10 to March 10, 1934. The fee must be paid at the time the return is filed.

"In case persons or corporations liable to the payment of the tax fail to make a correct or sufficient return within twenty days after the time required, the Controller is authorized to make an estimate of the gross income of the business and to determine the amount of the tax due," the Mayor said. "The Corporation Counsel, upon request of the Controller, may bring actions to enforce tax payments. A hearing is provided where exception is taken in those cases where the Controller himself makes the estimate of the gross income and fixes the tax.

"The penalty for filing a willfully false return is classed as a misdemeanor. The offense carries a possible sentence of a maximum fine of $1,000 and a maximum imprisonment of one year, or both.

Provision for Refunds.

"Provision is made in the bill," the Mayor said, "that refunds shall be made by the Controller where it has been legally established that a tax was erroneously or illegally collected. The bill expressly states that the revenue obtained from the imposition of this tax must be disposed of as follows:

"1. To defray the cost of granting

Continued on Page Eighteen.

CITY REGISTRATION REACHES 2,322,382, 16,422 UNDER 1932

Turnout of Voters Exceeds Hopes of Leaders of the Fight on Tammany.

TOTAL ALARMS TAMMANY

Five Are Arrested on Charge of Repeating at Booth in Brooklyn.

Registration for the city election reached 2,322,382 last night as the registration period closed. The grand total for the week was only slightly under the record mark of 2,338,804 established in the registration for last year's Presidential election.

The grand total far exceeded the hopes of even the most sanguine of the anti-Tammany leaders and was taken by them as a plain demonstration that the people of the city were aroused in their determination to end the O'Brien administration at City Hall.

Both backers of F. H. LaGuardia, Fusion candidate for Mayor, and Joseph V. McKee, Recovery candidate, contended that the increase over the normal for a Mayoralty election year would go to their candidate. Tammany chieftains made no secret of their alarm at the large turn-out, which usually implies that the so-called independent voter is on the warpath.

Five-Day Record Broken.

When the booths closed Friday night the total registration for five days was 1,611,794, compared with 1,591,019 for 1932, when all previous marks were broken in the registration for the Presidential election. The registration places were open yesterday from 7 A. M. to 10:30 P. M. and far more persons than registered any other day of the week flocked to the polls.

Owing to the increased number of registrants, the final total was not immediately ascertained, but if only approximately the same number of persons registered on the final day this year as registered on the final day of the small registration year of 1929, the last regular Mayoralty election year, the total for this year would be around 2,200,000.

The registration in 1932 was 2,338,804, and there were some indications that this year's total might approach that mark, although for the last few days the daily total of registrants had been gradually decreasing.

The figures for the week showed that many persons registered earlier this year than in the past, and this too was received as evidence that voters were impatient to make themselves eligible to ballot on Nov. 7 against the political group in power in the city.

However, the final all-day listing brought the usual big rush to the registration places, but the exact total was not available some hours after the booths closed.

Five Arrested in Brooklyn.

Five men were arrested in Brooklyn charged with registering twice at a registration place at Public School 133, Fourth Avenue and Butler Street. Mrs. Caroline Maxwell, election inspector, told Lieutenant David McLunn of the Bergen

Continued on Page Two.

Belgians Are Comforted By Work at Border Forts

By The Associated Press.

BRUSSELS, Belgium, Oct. 14.—Belgian political circles declared today that Germany's action in withdrawing from the disarmament conference and the League of Nations had justified last Wednesday's unanimous Cabinet decision to complete the frontier defenses.

An Anglo-French entente presenting a firm front, these circles added, would be the most satisfactory answer to the German withdrawal.

The Belgian reaction appeared to have been summed up in the expression: "Now we know where we all stand."

BERLIN JAILS NAZIS WHO HIT AMERICAN

Velz's Attackers to Be Tried at Once—Troopers Who Beat Briton and Swiss Arrested.

NEURATH GIVES US PLEDGE

Promises Dodd Germany Will Leave Nothing Undone to Render Satisfaction.

Wireless to The New York Times.

BERLIN, Oct. 14.—Following the call made by Ambassador Dodd last night upon Foreign Minister von Neurath, at which the two discussed the state of public feeling aroused in the United States by the failure to inflict punishment upon any Nazis guilty of assault upon Americans for not giving the Hitler salute, two interesting announcements are made by a Berlin news agency tonight.

It is stated that "the persons guilty of assaulting Roland Velz [an American business man] in Duesseldorf have been tracked down" and arrested in Berlin and are "facing prompt sentence by a special court attached to the Berlin Landgericht." The trial, it is said, will probably take place Monday.

"In accord with Commander Ernst of the Berlin Brandenburg division of the storm troops," says the second announcement, "the political police arrested today four storm troopers who had taken part in the outrage on a Swiss citizen, Herr Ruegg, and Mr. Hardy, a member of the staff of the British Embassy. The storm troopers were taken to the Oranienburg concentration camp."

Briton Clerk in Embassy.

Mr. Hardy is a clerk in the British Embassy who was attacked on Unter den Linden some three weeks ago for not saluting a Nazi parade. His assailants ignored his statement that he was a British subject and his offer to produce his passport. The British Embassy has been mak-

Continued on Page Twenty-eight.

Two Stunt Airplanes Crash in Mid-Air; 10 Hurt as One Hits Wilmington House

Special to The New York Times.

WILMINGTON, Del., Oct. 14.—Two "air circus" stunt planes crashed together 2,700 feet above the heart of Wilmington this afternoon and started dropping while several thousand horror-struck spectators looked on.

One of the planes, piloted by Roy (Speed) Hunt of Oklahoma, plunged into the roof of a two-story dwelling, while its motor, torn loose, crashed through the house and buried itself in the ground beneath the first floor. Hunt bailed out at 700 feet and floated to the middle of a street on a parachute which opened only 500 feet above the central section of the city.

The gasoline tank of his plane exploded soon after the crash, burning and injuring three policemen who had climbed to the roof to inspect the damage. Seven other persons suffered minor injuries in two dwellings badly damaged by fire after the explosion.

Lenn Povey of Boston, pilot of the second plane, managed to manoeuvre his ship five miles to Bellanco Airport and land it without injuring either the plane, himself or Harold Newman of Moline, Ill., his co-pilot.

Central Wilmington traffic was demoralized for almost a half hour by hundreds of automobiles and more than 5,000 pedestrians attracted by the collision.

The crashing planes were both units of the American Air Aces, Inc., which had been hired to present an air circus at Bellanca Field, Newcastle, for the Wilmington Junior League in the interest of charity.

The crash occurred just before the show was scheduled to start. Several of the stunt planes were performing high over Wilmington in an effort to arouse further interest in the circus.

Suddenly spectators saw Hunt's plane roll and drop down upon that piloted by Povey. A left wing aileron on the former craft was torn loose and Hunt appeared to go into a tail spin, while Povey's plane also shot downward. Povey righted his ship in a few seconds.

The plunging machine was the one in which Hunt won the transcontinental derby from Los Angeles to Cleveland at the start of the 1932 national air races.

Motorcycle Policeman Louis W. Webb was the most seriously injured. He was held under observation at the Delaware Hospital for a spinal injury. Policemen Hooper Lemmon and Emil Geiger were treated at the hospital for bruises and burns.

Both pilots were able to take part in the air circus.

MOVE DISMAYS GENEVA

Bureau of Arms Parley Called to Meet Today to Study Course.

DELEGATES ARE DIVIDED

Some Favor Session Tomorrow to Prepare Treaty Without German Participation.

4-POWER PACT'S END SEEN

Conference of Leading Powers in Italy With Hitler Suggested to Save Projects.

By CLARENCE K. STREIT.
Wireless to The New York Times.

GENEVA, Oct. 14.—Germany's decision to withdraw from both the League of Nations and the disarmament conference left the delegations here, including many of the Germans, incredulous at first and then dumfounded. There is apparently a unanimous agreement that it is an extremely grave and blundering move, increasing the possibility of the Austrian situation precipitating a further grave development.

The move caused greater surprise not only because of the wholly unexpected withdrawal from the League, but because it came after the Disarmament Bureau meeting this morning, in which the British, United States, French and Italian delegations, though presenting a united program, had taken pains on the request of the German delegation to leave the door open for negotiation. The British and American delegations had just been stressing to their press how the door had been left open when they were nonplussed by the news from Berlin.

Arthur Henderson, president of the disarmament conference, called a special meeting of the bureau for tomorrow morning to consider what to do about the meeting of the general commission scheduled for Monday.

Concessions to Germany.

The German move made a deeper impression since the united program which Sir John Simon explained to the bureau carried with it a considerable increase in Germany's arms in the next four years and promised her, at the end of the four-year period, tanks, war planes and all other weapons forbidden to her at Versailles which the others then retained. That made the break come on Germany's demand for these weapons immediately.

There are many ideas about what to do, but none of the important delegations, including the American, had apparently made up its mind tonight except to study carefully the many possibilities opened, including those of the Locarno Treaty, which is very closely related to Germany's membership in the League.

They are also agreed, as one member of the American delegation put it, that the first essential now is for "every one to keep cool." There is no tendency here to minimize the gravity of the situation.

Five-Power Parley Urged.

One idea, which the British seem to favor, is that Premier Mussolini should invite Prime Minister MacDonald, Premier Daladier, Chancellor Hitler and Norman H. Davis of the United States to a five-power conference in Stresa. This would not be, however, on the basis of the four-power pact which many think the German move has definitely destroyed.

The French appear opposed, the Americans open-minded, Mr. Davis taking the position that he is ready to consider anything that would help peace but that he is not sure yet whether this or any other proposal is wise or possible.

Most of the delegations, including the British and Americans and especially the French, seem favorable to continuing the Disarmament Conference, some partly to bring out more sharply Germany's isolation in the world and the issue on which the break occurred. Others favor this with the view of making a treaty without Germany, on the ground that the rest of the world should meet any menace from Germany by sticking together with arms they have rather than by each nation arming more so as to meet it individually.

Some French circles also suggest

Continued on Page Twenty-eight.

Germany's Note to Parley

By The Associated Press.

GENEVA, Oct. 14.—Germany's withdrawal from the general disarmament conference was announced today in a telegram from Foreign Minister von Neurath to Arthur Henderson, president of the conference, as follows:

BERLIN, Oct. 14, 1933.

On behalf of the German Government I have the honor to make to you the following communication:

In the light of the course which recent discussions of the powers concerned have taken in the matter of disarmament it is now clear that the disarmament conference will not fill what is its sole object, namely, general disarmament.

It is also clear that this failure of the conference is due solely to unwillingness on the part of the highly armed States to carry out their contractual obligations to disarm.

This renders impossible the satisfactory fulfillment of Germany's recognized claim to equality of rights, and the condition on which the German Government agreed at the beginning of this year to take part in the work of the conference thus no longer exists. The German Government accordingly will be compelled to leave the disarmament conference.

BARON VON NEURATH.

HULL HOLDS REICH BALKS ARMS CUTS

Voices Great Disappointment at Germany's Withdrawal From Geneva Parley.

FEARS THE 'ALTERNATIVE'

This Country Is Now Solidly With Former Allies, but No Sanctions Are Considered.

Special to The New York Times.

WASHINGTON, Oct. 14.—The United States Government places squarely upon Germany the blame for slowing down and impeding the movement toward general disarmament, Secretary of State Hull indicated today. He said this government was greatly disappointed and very seriously regretted Germany's move in withdrawing from the disarmament conference.

The news of this step, as well as Germany's notice of withdrawal from the League of Nations, apparently came as a surprise to the State Department. Practically all higher officials were called into conference in Secretary Hull's office, and the scheduled press conference was postponed for two hours.

When Mr. Hull began his conference with newspaper men he was flanked by William Phillips, Under-Secretary; R. Walton Moore, Assistant Secretary; Jefferson Caffery, Assistant Secretary, and Jay Pierrepont Moffat, chief of the Western European Division and disarmament expert of the State Department. It was evident Mr. Hull's remarks were studied, and had been the subject of the conference with his lieutenants.

Teamwork Is Blocked.

The rôle of the United States, Mr. Hull said, has been, throughout the disarmament conference, one of striving wholeheartedly and unremittingly for general disarmament. The action of the Hitler government halted the spirit of teamwork the United States had tried to practice and encourage, he added.

The exact part played by Norman H. Davis on behalf of the United States in precipitating today's crisis was difficult to determine. The State Department had not been informed of any draft resolution, approved by Sir John Simon, British Foreign Secretary; Joseph Paul-Boncour, French Foreign Minister, and Mr. Davis, which Rudolf Nadolny, the German delegate, is said to have taken with him to Berlin, provoking Chancellor Hitler's decision to withdraw from the conference.

Whether or not the United States, Great Britain and France reached the point of agreeing on the wording of a resolution to be introduced at Monday's scheduled preliminary session of the Disarmament Conference, there was no doubt from Mr. Hull's remarks today that the three governments were in accord against any rearming by Germany. Their common meeting ground may have ended there, as the American position has been in favor of carrying out the spirit of the agreement of Dec. 11, 1932, offering equality of rights to Germany within a framework of security.

Reports from Geneva during the past week of jockeying for position by the members of the steering committee have indicated that the United States delegation was seek-

Continued on Page Twenty-nine.

FRENCH ARE CALM; WEIGH NEW CRISIS

German Action Not Wholly Unexpected—Certain Relief Felt Over 'Unmasking.'

BLOW TO PEACE DEPLORED

Le Temps Sees International Efforts Doomed—Return to Versailles Urged.

By P. J. PHILIP.
Wireless to The New York Times.

PARIS, Oct. 14.—France, which becomes easily excited over little matters, learned this morning with astonishing calm of Germany's decision to quit the League of Nations and the disarmament conference. The news came near the end of a Cabinet meeting where financial measures for balancing the budget were discussed. The Cabinet completed its order of the day and then, only informally, talked over this new situation in Europe.

"When an explosion like that occurs," one Cabinet member said, "one must wait until the dust settles down before one can measure the damage and decide what is to be done."

While there is a disposition to take the event calmly, now that it has happened, its extreme gravity is admitted and it is agreed its final consequences cannot be foreseen. It is felt here that Germany has, by her action, challenged the whole Wilsonian principle of international cooperation for insuring peace. Whatever its faults and failures, the League which Germany has rejected was consecrated to that principle.

Skeptics Will Have Their Triumph.

Certainly those who, here as elsewhere, have argued that the League was as powerless to prevent war as laws without police or punishment are to prevent crime, are now going to have their hour of triumph. Those, too, who have, especially during the past few months, been daily urging in the French press that Hitlerism must be destroyed before it gets too strong, are now assured the road has been opened to them, even if they cannot see exactly where it will lead.

For the French people today's decision by the German Government has been indeed grave. The semi-official newspaper Le Temps pleads that the situation "be examined with all calmness," in view of "the questions of paramount importance" it raises for Europe. "It is the end of all attempts at cooperation in organizing peace," declares Le Temps.

In official quarters the German Cabinet's decision is regarded as "grave, extremely important and unexpected at this moment." But it was not an eventuality which had been utterly unforeseen and for which no provision had been made.

Only one conclusion is advanced: "While France has shown herself willing to accept very great sacrifices in order to obtain international control of national armaments, Germany has shown by this action that she is unwilling to accept any control or any limitation whatever."

What is to be done? There are many popular answers to that question, but none is official. At Geneva the disarmament conference continues. There is a good deal of

Continued on Page Twenty-nine.

POST-WAR ERA DENOUNCED

Hitler, Asking Solid Vote, Bars Second-Class Status for Reich.

SEES ARMS PLEDGE BROKEN

Asserting Pacific Aims, He Finds No Possibility of a Franco-German Conflict.

REICHSTAG IS DISSOLVED

State Diets Ended by Decree Wiping Out Old Federal Provinces in Unity Move.

Text of Chancellor Hitler's radio speech is on Page 26.

By FREDERICK T. BIRCHALL.
Wireless to The New York Times.

BERLIN, Oct. 14.—The National Socialist government of Germany announced today the Reich's withdrawal simultaneously from the disarmament conference and from the League of Nations.

At the same time President Paul von Hindenburg by proclamation dissolved the present Reichstag and decreed new elections for Nov. 12. These, however, will not be elections in the normal sense because there exists no organized opposition to the present government. All parties other than the National Socialist have vanished—they have been either self-dissolved or forcibly suppressed.

The new election will be rather in the nature of a plebiscite to range the people behind the present government in any course it may choose to take in foreign affairs. The people are to be enabled, as the Hindenburg proclamation says, "to give expression to their fealty to the Reich Government."

Rebels at Versailles Treaty.

The government itself has issued a statement in which, emphasizing its own and the German people's "coinciding will," it reaffirms its adherence to the completest disarmament, but goes on to say that the German Government and the German people are "determined to accept sufferings, persecution and oppression rather than submit further to a perpetuation of the conditions created by the Versailles Treaty." Therefore it asks the German people to approve its course and thus make that course the expression of the people's will.

The answer can only be unanimous approbation, because no other answer will be possible. Nor can any voice be raised within Germany to ask whither all this is leading.

This notable day has been one of many proclamations. Chancellor Adolf Hitler also has issued one individually as Chancellor and as leader of his party. Germany has suffered bitter disappointment, says the Chancellor, through the action of former governments in putting her into the League of Nations and the disarmament conference. Repeated and studied refusals to accord Germany moral and material equality, he says, have deeply humiliated the German people and their government.

Seeks "Pacification of World."

Since discriminations against her have continued, he proceeds, Germany has no choice but to quit the conference and the League. He proposes, however, that the German people shall have an opportunity to pronounce its solidarity with the government through a popular vote. He is convinced the nation to a man will uphold the determination "to bring about pacification of the world" and to establish equal rights for all.

Thus the stage is set for that unanimous vote that the election cannot fail to produce. But behind all this is something more.

Coincidentally with the calling of this plebiscite under the name of an election there is decreed today the dissolution of all State Diets. They will not be replaced by new bodies. It is even indicated that after the election Chancellor Hitler may withdraw from the States his own personal delegates now there in guise of Statthalters, or Federal Governors.

Thus there will be wiped out the old Federal States. There will be no more Bavaria or Saxony or Württemberg except as geographi-

Continued on Page Twenty-six.

"All the News That's Fit to Print."

The New York Times.

Copyright, 1933, by The New York Times Company.

LATE CITY EDITION
WEATHER—Rain and warmer today; tomorrow fair and colder.
Temperatures Yesterday—Max., 64; min., 34.

VOL. LXXXIII....No. 27,710. Entered as Second-Class Matter, Postoffice, New York, N. Y. NEW YORK, WEDNESDAY, DECEMBER 6, 1933. MP TWO CENTS In New York City | THREE CENTS Within 200 Miles | FOUR CENTS Elsewhere Except in 7th and 8th Postal Zones

PROHIBITION REPEAL IS RATIFIED AT 5:32 P. M.; ROOSEVELT ASKS NATION TO BAR THE SALOON; NEW YORK CELEBRATES WITH QUIET RESTRAINT

LINDBERGHS AT SEA ON BRAZIL FLIGHT; 'O.K.' SHE REPORTS

630 MILES FROM AFRICA

Breeze Starts Fliers After Twenty Attempts in Dead Calm.

MOON LIGHTS THEIR WAY

10,000 Natives See Take-Off as Motor's Roar Stirs Them From Slumber.

RIDE THROUGH SQUALLS

Wife Radios Every Fifteen Minutes of Progress on 1,800-Mile Flight.

Colonel and Mrs. Charles A. Lindbergh were flying across the South Atlantic from Africa to Brazil this morning, reporting their progress by radio every fifteen minutes and their location every half hour.

At 2:20 A. M., New York time, five hours and twenty minutes after taking off from Bathurst, Gambia, in bright moonlight, they were 630 miles on their way across the Southern Ocean.

The first message from the plane was picked up by the Miami, Fla., station of Pan American Airways soon after 9:02 P. M. last night, New York time. It reported that the plane had taken off from Bathurst at that time. At 10 P. M., New York time, another message picked up by the Bahia, Brazil, station of Pan American Airways advised that the plane was flying Course 224 true, and gave its position, which Pan American officials estimated to be about 115 miles southwest of Bathurst. At 10:40 P. M. another message, also picked up by the Bahia station, reported "everything O. K.," and said the plane's position would be given every half hour and a progress O. K. sent out every fifteen minutes. The first progress O. K. was received by the Pan American station at Miami at 11 P. M., New York time.

Made 240 Miles in Two Hours.

At 11 P. M., the Bahia station also picked up a message. It gave for the plane a position approximately 240 miles southwest of Bathurst and right on her course. The operators at Bahia said that in her first message, Mrs. Lindbergh reported considerable static. But her messages, they said, were coming into Bahia strong, fast and clear, as if they were being sent by an experienced wireless operator.

The next message was received by the Pan-American station at Para, Brazil, at 11:50 P. M., New York time. It reported that the plane was flying at an altitude of 2,000 feet and making about 100 knots. There was unlimited visibility, the message said, with the sky about one-tenth overcast, and a quartering ten-knot tail wind.

At 12:30 this morning, the Pan American radio station at Miami and the Chatham, Mass., station of the Radiomarine Corporation each picked up a message from the plane giving a position approximately 446 miles southeast of Bathurst. The message said the plane was flying at an altitude of 1,200 feet, that there was visibility of about ten miles, that the sky was nine-tenths overcast, and that there was a quartering tail wind of 10 knots.

Squalls Met at Daybreak.

A message was received at 1:27 this morning at Pará, Brazil, reporting "skies eight-tenths overcast, scattered squalls, visibility three miles, daybreak; all's well."

At 1:50 A. M. the Bahia station picked up a message, "All's well."

At 2:20 A. M. a message was received at the Pará station reporting the plane's position as 630 miles southwest of Bathurst, flying at 1,000 feet, the skies nine-tenths overcast, frequent squalls, calm seas and no wind. That position indicated the Lindberghs had covered about one-third of the distance to Natal.

Natives Awaken for Start.

Special Cable to THE NEW YORK TIMES.

BATHURST, Gambia, Wednesday, Dec. 6.—With bright moonlight turning the waters around the little island of St. Mary, on which

Continued on Page Twenty-six.

Lindbergh Flight to Fame Twice as Long as New Hop

On the morning of May 20, 1927, six years and six months ago, Captain Charles A. Lindbergh, a mail pilot, left Roosevelt Field for Paris.

He flew alone, and veteran pilots shook their heads when they saw him take off. His silver plane, dripping with rain, lumbered slowly—too slowly—down the muddy runway. It gathered speed, bounced from the ground and settled back again. It barely cleared a tractor at the end of the runway and just climbed over low telephone wires at the end of the field.

Thirty-three and a half hours later the young mail pilot brought his gray plane down at Le Bourget. That famous flight covered 3,610 miles. The present flight, also in a single-engined plane, is about 1,875 miles.

PWA READY TO BAR CITY SUBWAY LOAN

Security for $25,000,000 Advance to Finish System Is Held Inadequate.

BANKERS' PACTS A FACTOR

Officials Here Say Attitude of Washington Is Based on a Misunderstanding.

Special to THE NEW YORK TIMES.

WASHINGTON, Dec. 5.—Inability of New York City to furnish security satisfactory to the Public Works Administration has caused the latter to abandon the allotment of $25,000,000 for completion of the Eighth Avenue subway.

New York officials have not been notified, but it was learned from reliable sources that the application for the loan would be refused.

At his press conference today Secretary Ickes said there was "nothing new" to report on the loan. He added, however, that the matter was held up by the question of security.

Senator Wagner announced virtual assurance of the loan more than two weeks ago. Since then the matter has been before the Special Board of Public Works, while PWA engineers and lawyers were investigating.

Application Signed by Mayor.

The application, for $25,000,000, signed by Mayor O'Brien, was on a loan and grant basis, 30 per cent of the cost of materials and structure to be an outright grant and the rest a loan on security furnished by the city.

The amount of money which completion of the subway would require is indefinite. Public Works Administration officials have scaled the sum down to some $22,500,000 under one estimate.

The money would be applied to equipping, tracking and finishing some eighteen miles of subway already dug, mainly in Brooklyn and Queens, and to the building of stations. Seven thousand men would obtain work through the Winter, it was estimated, and large supplies of capital goods would be purchased.

The allotment was discussed at the recent conference between Secretary Ickes and Mayor-elect La Guardia, but it was not gone into in any detail.

The attitude of the PWA, it was learned, is that the city has tied up the revenues of the subway by its financing agreements with the banks, and would be operating on a margin too slender to enable it to guarantee any return on the investment, even if the PWA funds allowed the subway to open miles of route and thus tap new sources of revenue.

Unification Another Problem.

The PWA feels that the situation is further complicated by the competition of the other New York subway lines. If the other lines were taken over by the city under the unification plan, a campaign promise of the Mayor-elect, the PWA feels that there would be a general scaling down of the demands of creditors and a consequent loss to the government on its investment. The question of the 5-cent fare is not worrying the administration, Secretary Ickes has said.

While Mr. Ickes has already ex-

Continued on Page Twenty-seven.

TAX PLAN OFFERED TO CURB EVASIONS, RAISE $237,000,000

House Subcommittee Urges a Check on Personal Holding Concerns by 35% Levy.

WOULD INCREASE SURTAX

Normal Income Tax of 4% and Revision of Capital Gains Are Also Proposed.

Special to THE NEW YORK TIMES.

WASHINGTON, Dec. 5.—Broad tax reforms designed to increase the Federal revenue $237,000,000 a year and prevent "the avoidance and evasion of the internal revenue laws" were recommended today in a report submitted to the House Ways and Means Committee by a subcommittee.

The full committee immediately began study of the suggestions, and Representative Doughton, the chairman, said a completed bill would probably be ready for presentation soon after Congress meets next month.

Changes sought are aimed principally at persons whose incomes are in the higher brackets, as well as at corporations now legally permitted to take advantage of what committee members said were "unfair but legal" provisions of the revenue laws.

Some discord was apparent within the committee, but no member would publicly express his feelings.

"It isn't law yet, and it is not even past the committee," said one member. "It must go to the House and Senate."

Nine Changes are Urged.

Nine phases of the present law were recommended for modification as follows:

1. Establishment of a normal income tax rate of 4 per cent, instead of the present 4 per cent on the first $4,000 and 8 per cent on the remainder of net income, and revision of the surtax rate on a graduated scale, with the brackets reduced from 53 to 27; estimated to increase revenue $36,000,000 annually.

2. Change for three years in the depreciation and depletion section of the 1932 Revenue Act by reducing allowances by 25 per cent; estimated to add $85,000,000 for each of the three years.

3. Revision of the capital gains and losses section by revising the method of adjustment and prescribing a scale-length of ownership; estimated to add $30,000,000.

4. Amendment of the personal holding companies' section to prevent persons with large incomes from forming companies to evade taxes; estimated to add $25,000,000.

5. Abolition of certain sections of the "exchanges and reorganization" provisions to "close the door to one of the most prevalent methods of tax avoidance"; estimated to add $18,000,000.

6. Imposition of a tax on dividends paid out of corporation earnings accumulated before March 1, 1913; estimated to add $6,000,000.

7. Amendment of the foreign tax credit sections of the 1932 act; estimated to add $10,000,000.

8. Withdrawal of permission for corporations which are affiliated through 95 per cent stock ownership to file consolidated returns; estimated to add $20,000,000.

9. Revision of the partnership losses section of the 1932 Revenue Act; estimated to add $7,000,000.

Eager to expedite the "major problems," the subcommittee passed over a group of minor matters, according to the chairman, Representative Sam B. Hill of Washington. He said the subcommittee would continue study of these problems,

Continued on Page Fourteen.

State House Bootlegger Is Barred in Maryland

Special to THE NEW YORK TIMES.

ANNAPOLIS, Md., Dec. 5.—Wet legislators here will patriotically support legal liquor. The State House bootlegger received formal notice today to discontinue his trade. The notice was served by a policeman on duty at the Capitol.

Throughout this session, the bootlegger has conducted a thriving business; a business which, he says, has been especially arduous because of the sudden demands made on him by legislators and their desire for prompt service.

While his services were cut off eight hours before post-prohibition stuff could be bought, the bootlegger thought the legislators had obtained a sufficient reserve to carry them through until evening and legal liquor.

RATIFYING BY UTAH ENDS PROHIBITION

With Impressive Ceremony, the 36th State Follows Ohio and Pennsylvania in Day.

CONVENTIONS ALL SOLEMN

Moderation Pleas Are Made at Columbus—Hush Greets Vote at Harrisburg.

Special to THE NEW YORK TIMES.

SALT LAKE CITY, Dec. 5—The Eighteenth Amendment to the Constitution of the United States passed out of existence officially at 3:32½ o'clock this afternoon, Mountain standard time (5:32½ New York time) with the ratification of repeal by the convention of Utah, the thirty-sixth required State.

The passing of national prohibition was marked by impressive ceremony in the hall of the House of Representatives in the State Capitol here.

To Delegate S. R. Thurman, a repeal leader of Salt Lake City, whose father was a member of the State's constitutional convention in 1895 before Utah was admitted to the Union, fell the honor of being the last to record his vote, the roll being called in alphabetical order.

His "Yea," placing the Twenty-first Amendment to the Constitution in effect, was greeted by enthusiastic applause from the audience of a few hundred persons.

About ninety seconds later Ray L. Olson of Ogden, president of the convention, who had been manager of the repealists' campaign, brought down his gavel and announced that the repeal amendment had been ratified. Notification was transmitted immediately to the White House by a special wire from the Capitol.

At the same time Delegate A. S. Brown, former president of the Salt Lake Chamber of Commerce, sent out word to President Roosevelt over the Columbia Broadcasting System. He congratulated the President on the successful culmination of the repeal movement.

The whole proceedings were in keeping with the historic aspect of the occasion. Besides high officials

Continued on Page Five.

Italy to Quit League Unless It Is Reformed; Demands Altered Aims and Set-Up at Once

By ARNALDO CORTESI.

Wireless to THE NEW YORK TIMES

ROME, Wednesday, Dec. 6.—At the end of a long sitting lasting far into the night, the Fascist Grand Council, which had been convoked to decide on Italy's relations with the League of Nations, passed a suspended sentence on Geneva.

After having discussed every aspect of the probable effect of Italy's withdrawal, the Grand Council decided "to render Italy's further participation in the League dependent on radical changes in that organization to be brought about within the shortest possible time, which changes must affect the League in its constitution, in its methods and in its objectives."

At the same time the Grand Council reached a temporizing decision also in the matter of payment to the United States of the debt instalment due on Dec. 15. In view of the impossibility of conducting negotiations on the debt problem, the Grand Council decided "to effect on Dec. 15 a token payment of $1,000,000 as renewed proof of Italy's good-will, while awaiting a final settlement of this whole question."

Since the breakdown in the disarmament negotiations Premier Mussolini has been advocating efforts outside Geneva and the League of Nations. He has favored action under the Four-Power Pact initiated by Great Britain, France, Italy and Germany, or at any rate negotiations by the leading powers, including the United States.

As to reforms in the League, the press has suggested that the League be divorced from the Versailles Treaty, and that its constitution be revised to give the larger powers a freer hand in directing its affairs.

CITY TOASTS NEW ERA

Crowds Swamp Licensed Resorts, but the Legal Liquor Is Scarce.

CELEBRATION IN STREETS

Marked by Absence of Undue Hilarity and Only Normal Number of Arrests.

MANY SPEAKEASIES CLOSE

Machine Guns Guard Some Liquor Trucks—Supplies to Be Rushed Out Today.

Slowly gathering momentum from the time when the news began to spread just at nightfall that national prohibition was no more, the public rejoicing at the end of the long dry reign was carried on last night with restraint and absence of undue hilarity.

Throngs of New Yorkers ventured into Times Square and other centres of the metropolis and many of the thousand restaurants, hotels and clubs fortunate enough to have received their licenses for the sale of alcoholic beverages were swamped.

But gay as were their spirits, they were well-behaved. With the city's entire police force of 19,000 men mobilized to guard against overexuberant celebrants, arrests did not exceed the normal number for any day of the last five years. Incidentally, official word that repeal was a fact did not go out to the police until 9:20 P. M., just about four hours after Utah acted.

Stores Fail to Get Stocks.

The thronging to places of public entertainment was enhanced by the fact that only a handful of New Yorkers was able to drink a toast to the occasion with lawful liquor in their own homes. Because Utah did not make repeal effective until 5:32½ P. M., retail liquor stores with only two exceptions were unable to obtain wines and whiskies from the warehouses in the brief time left.

Indeed, the supply of lawful liquor even in the licensed places was woefully scant. Only fifty-four truckloads of bonded liquor were released from the warehouses before they closed last night, and the two largest warehouses shut their doors before the Twenty-first Amendment displaced the Eighteenth.

With 3,000 places licensed to dispense the newly legalized beverages in the metropolitan area and 2,000 more up-State, hardly one in a hundred was able to move in a stock in the few hours available. Some of the others, of course, had had the foresight to lay in supplies under medicinal permits during the dying days of prohibition.

Bootleggers and speakeasies came to the rescue, however, despite a stern warning from Police Commissioner Bolan that his men would not tolerate any such activity. They operated with a little more caution than usual, but nevertheless they took advantage of the occasion to dispose of a large part of their unlawful stocks. The raids threatened by Mr. Bolan proved few and on little known places.

Many Cordial Shops Close.

Cordial shops and other neighborhood dispensaries during the long drought showed fear of police activity last night for the first time in years. Hundreds of them closed their doors, others dealt only with long-known and trusted customers, and only a scattering number, principally in downtown Manhattan, carried on business as usual. Some of them carried signs promising to open as licensed liquor stores in a few days.

There was every indication, however, that New York's long reliance on contraband cheer was near its end. The warehousemen promised deliveries on a large scale would begin today, with 400 trucks licensed to speed legal liquors throughout the city and its suburbs.

A cargo of 6,200 cases of assorted wines and spirits worth about $170,000 arrived on the White Star liner Majestic from France and England late in the afternoon, but the ship was delayed five hours by

Continued on Page Two.

The Repeal Proclamation

Special to THE NEW YORK TIMES.

WASHINGTON, Dec. 5.—The text of the proclamation by William Phillips, Acting Secretary of State, certifying to the adoption of the Twenty-first Amendment repealing prohibition, follows:

WILLIAM PHILLIPS,

Acting Secretary of State of the United States of America.

To all whom these presents shall come, greeting:

KNOW YE, That the Congress of the United States, at the second session, Seventy-second Congress, begun and held at the city of Washington on Monday, the fifth day of December, in the year one thousand nine hundred and thirty-two, passed a joint Resolution in the words and figures as follows:

To wit—

JOINT RESOLUTION.

Proposing an amendment to the Constitution of the United States.

Resolved by the Senate and House of Representatives of the United States of America in Congress assembled (two-thirds of each House concurring therein), That the following article is hereby proposed as an amendment to the Constitution of the United States, which shall be valid to all intents and purposes as part of the Constitution when ratified by conventions in three-fourths of the several States:

ARTICLE.

Section 1. The Eighteenth Article of Amendment to the Constitution of the United States is hereby repealed.

Section 2. The transportation or importation into any State, Territory, or Possession of the United States for delivery or use therein of intoxicating liquors, in violation of the laws thereof, is hereby prohibited.

Section 3. This article shall be inoperative unless it shall have been ratified as an amendment to the Constitution by conventions in the several States, as provided in the Constitution, within seven years from the date of the submission hereof to the States by the Congress.

And, further, that it appears from official notices received at the Department of State that the amendment to the Constitution of the United States proposed as aforesaid has been ratified by conventions in the States of Arizona, Alabama, Arkansas, California, Colorado, Connecticut, Delaware, Florida, Idaho, Illinois, Indiana, Iowa, Kentucky, Maryland, Massachusetts, Michigan, Minnesota, Missouri, Nevada, New Hampshire, New Jersey, New Mexico, New York, Ohio, Oregon, Pennsylvania, Rhode Island, Tennessee, Texas, Utah, Vermont, Virginia, Washington, West Virginia, Wisconsin and Wyoming.

And, further, that the States wherein conventions have so ratified the said proposed amendment constitute the requisite three-fourths of the whole number of States in the United States.

NOW, therefore, be it known that I, William Phillips, Acting Secretary of State of the United States, by virtue and in pursuance of Section 160, Title 5, of the United States Code, do hereby certify that the amendment aforesaid has become valid to all intents and purposes as a part of the Constitution of the United States.

In testimony whereof, I have hereunto set my hand and caused the seal of the Department of State to be affixed.

Done at the city of Washington this fifth day of December in the year of our Lord one thousand nine hundred and thirty-three.

WILLIAM PHILLIPS.

Roosevelt Proclaims Repeal; Urges Temperance in Nation

President's Announcement Is in Accordance With the Instruction of Congress Contained in the Recovery Act—Declares Social Evils of Liquor Shall Not Be Revived.

Special to THE NEW YORK TIMES.

WASHINGTON, Dec. 5.—President Roosevelt's proclamation of the repeal of the Eighteenth Amendment was as follows:

By the President of the United States of America.

A Proclamation.

Whereas the Congress of the United States in the second session of the Seventy-second Congress, begun at Washington on the fifth day of December in the year one thousand nine hundred and thirty-two adopted a resolution in the words and figures following: to wit—

JOINT RESOLUTION.

Proposing an amendment to the Constitution of the United States.

Resolved by the Senate and House of Representatives of the United States of America in Congress assembled (two-thirds of each House concurring therein), That the following article is hereby proposed as an amendment to the Constitution of the United States, which shall be valid to all intents and purposes as part of the Constitution when ratified by conventions in three-fourths of the several States:

ARTICLE.

Section 1. The Eighteenth Article of amendment to the Constitution of the United States is hereby repealed.

Section 2. The transportation or importation into any State, Territory or possession of the United States for delivery or use therein of intoxicating liquors, in violation of the laws thereof, is hereby prohibited.

Section 3. This article shall be inoperative unless it shall have been ratified as an amendment to the Constitution by conventions in the several States, as provided in the Constitution, within seven years from the date of the submission hereof to the States by the Congress.

Declares Amendment Repealed.

Whereas, Section 217 (a) of the Act of Congress entitled "An act to encourage national industrial recovery, to foster competition and to provide for the construction of certain useful public works, and for other purposes," approved June 16, 1933, provides as follows:

Section 217 (a) The President shall proclaim the date of ——

(1) the close of the first fiscal year ending June 30 of any year after the year 1933, during which the total receipts of the

Continued on Page Two.

FINAL ACTION AT CAPITAL

President Proclaims the Nation's New Policy as Utah Ratifies.

PHILLIPS SIGNS DECREE

Orders 21st Amendment in Effect on Receiving Votes of Three Final States.

RECOVERY TAXES TO END

$227,000,000 a Year Automatically Dropped—Canadian Whisky Quota Is Raised.

Special to THE NEW YORK TIMES.

WASHINGTON, Dec. 5.—Legal liquor today was returned to the United States, with President Roosevelt calling on the people to see that "this return of individual freedom shall not be accompanied by the repugnant conditions that obtained prior to the adoption of the Eighteenth Amendment and those that have existed since its adoption."

Prohibition of alcoholic beverages as a national policy ended at 5:32½ P. M., Eastern Standard Time, when Utah, the last of the thirty-six States, furnished by vote of its convention the constitutional majority for ratification of the Twenty-first Amendment. The new amendment repealed the Eighteenth, and with the demise of the latter went the Volstead Act which for more than a decade held legal drinks in America to less than one-half of 1 per cent of alcohol and the enforcement of which cost more than 150 lives and billions in money.

Earlier in the day Pennsylvania had ratified as the thirty-fourth State and Ohio as the thirty-fifth.

Proclamation by President.

President Roosevelt at 6:55 P. M. signed an official proclamation in keeping with terms of the National Industrial Recovery Act, under which prohibition ended and four taxes levied to raise $227,000,000 annually for amortization of the $3,300,000,000 public works fund were repealed.

But the President went further. Accepting certification from Acting Secretary of State Phillips that thirty-six States had ratified the repealing amendment, he improved the occasion to address a plea to the American people to employ their regained liberty first of all for national manliness.

Mr. Roosevelt asked personally for what he and his party had declined to make the subject of Federal mandate—that saloons be barred from the country.

"I ask especially," he said, "that no State shall, by law or otherwise, authorize the return of the saloon, either in its old form or in some modern guise."

Makes Personal Plea.

He enjoined all citizens to cooperate with the government in its endeavor to restore a greater respect for law and order, especially by confining their purchases of liquor to duly licensed agencies. This practice, which he personally requested every individual and every family in the nation to follow, would result, he said, in a better product for consumption, in addition to the "break-up and eventual destruction of the notoriously evil illicit liquor traffic" and in tax benefits to the government.

The President thus announced the policy of his administration—to see that the social and political evils of the preprohibition era shall not be revived or permitted again to exist. Failure of citizens to use their new freedom in helping to advance this policy, he said, would be "a living reproach to us all."

He expressed faith, too, in the "good sense of the American people" in preventing excessive personal use of relegalized liquor. "The objective we seek through a national policy," he said, "is the education of every citizen toward a greater temperance throughout the nation."

As a means of enforcing his policy, the President has the Federal Alcohol Control Administration ready to take control of the liquor traffic and regulate it at the source of supply.

In its first major step today, the

Continued on Page Two.

"All the News That's Fit to Print."

The New York Times.

LATE CITY EDITION
WEATHER—Showers today; tomorrow fair, somewhat cooler.
Temperatures Yesterday—Max., 91, Min., 78

Section 1

VOL. LXXXIII....No. 27,917. Entered as Second-Class Matter, Postoffice, New York, N. Y. NEW YORK, SUNDAY, JULY 1, 1934. Including Rotogravure Picture, Magazine and Book Sections. F TEN CENTS | TWELVE CENTS Beyond 300 Miles. Except in 7th and 8th Postal Zones.

HITLER CRUSHES REVOLT BY NAZI RADICALS; VON SCHLEICHER IS SLAIN, ROEHM A SUICIDE; LOYAL FORCES HOLD BERLIN IN AN IRON GRIP

EXCHANGE, LABOR BOARDS NAMED; FARM BILL SIGNED

KENNEDY IN 'CHANGE POST

The Others Are Mathews, Landis, Healy, Pecora for Varying Terms.

WIRE BOARD IS CHOSEN

Members Are Sykes, Brown, Case, Stuart, Payne, Gary and Walker.

RAIL PENSIONS APPROVED

Clark Howell Heads Air Study —Moffett Made Administrator of the Housing Act.

President Clears His Desk

On the eve of his departure this evening on the cruiser Houston for a month's cruise, President Roosevelt cleared his desk last night.

He named the two commissions to regulate the Stock Exchanges and the operations of telegraph, telephone and radio companies.

He signed the Frazier-Lemke bill setting up new methods for the compromising of agricultural indebtedness.

He signed the railroad employes' pension bill.

He appointed James A. Moffett of New York, prominent oil executive, Administrator of the Housing Act.

He appointed an Aviation Commission, with Clark Howell as chairman.

He created an impartial Labor Relations Board, abolishing the old one and eliminating the NRA from a rôle in settling labor disputes.

Picks Exchange Board

Special to THE NEW YORK TIMES.

WASHINGTON, June 30.—As his last act tonight in cleaning up essential business before sailing from Annapolis for a month's holiday today, President Roosevelt named the personnel of the Securities and Exchange Commission.

He did not designate a chairman, there being some doubt as to his authority to do so, but it was understood in well-informed quarters that responsibility for the commission's work under the sweeping Stock Exchange Control Act would fall upon Joseph P. Kennedy, New York financier, who was designated to serve for five years. Four other commissioners were named for periods varying from one to four years.

The personnel of the commission follows:

JOSEPH P. KENNEDY of New York, five-year term.

GEORGE C. MATHEWS of Wisconsin, four-year term.

JAMES M. LANDIS of Massachusetts, three-year term.

ROBERT E. HEALY of Vermont, two-year term.

FERDINAND PECORA of New York, one-year term.

Messrs. Mathews and Landis are members of the Federal Trade Commission. Mr. Pecora was counsel for the Senate Banking and Currency Committee during the period in which it aired publicly for the first time in twenty years the manifold operations of securities exchanges and investment banking houses. As committee counsel he played a large part in shaping the law under which the commission will operate.

The naming of the Securities and Exchange Commission came after President Roosevelt, in a day of intensive work, had also named the Communications Commission and a commission to plan coordination of aircraft development, and had issued statements announcing the signing of the Frazier-Lemke Farm Mortgage Bill and the Railroad Pensions Bill.

Kennedy Close to Farley.

The membership of the Securities and Exchange Commission had been pretty generally forecast, but even so its composition was full of surprises, particularly the obvious placing in line for the chairmanship of Mr. Kennedy.

This is the first emergence of the New Yorker from what seemed to be political eclipse since the campaign of 1932, when he was distinguished both as a heavy contributor and important raiser of campaign funds, and because of his

Continued on Page Twenty-one.

Major Sports Results

Track—Bill Bonthron of Princeton broke the world's record for the 1,500-meter run in the national A. A. U. championship meet at Milwaukee. Timed in 3:48.8, he beat Glenn Cunningham by two feet. It was the fifth meeting between the stars and the triumph gave Bonthron the edge with three victories.

Tennis—Four Americans advanced at Wimbledon. Frank Shields defeated Christian Boussus of France and George M. Lott Jr. halted Harry Hopman of Australia. Miss Helen Jacobs conquered Mlle. Jacqueline Goldschmidt of France and Miss Sarah Palfrey beat Miss J. Jedrzejowska of Poland.

Baseball—Routing Carl Hubbell, the Dodgers stopped the Giants, 8—4, before 12,000 at the Polo Grounds. At Washington the Yankees were leading the Senators, 4—1, when rain caused the game to be called off in the fifth inning.

(Full details in Sports Section.)

JOHN JACOB ASTOR WEDS ELLEN FRENCH

Notables Fill Newport Church for Ceremony Climaxing Weeks of Social Activity.

ONLOOKERS PACK STREETS

Crowd Delays Both Bride and Bridegroom—Astor's Mother Sits in a Front Pew.

By RUSSELL B. PORTER.

Special to THE NEW YORK TIMES.

NEWPORT, R. I., June 30.—Two of America's oldest families, prominent in both landed wealth and in social position, were united in marriage here today at the wedding of John Jacob Astor 3d and Miss Ellen Tuck French.

The bridegroom is the third of his name in American life. The first John Jacob Astor, fur trader, founded the family in early American days. The second lost his life in the sinking of the Titanic, and the third John Jacob Astor, today's bridegroom, was born .. few months later. He is a half-brother of Vincent Astor, and inherited with the latter the great Astor fortune.

The bride is a granddaughter of Amos Tuck French and is related to the Vanderbilt family.

These young members of old families, the bridegroom only 21 years old and the bride 18, were joined together in a setting replete with symbols of early American traditions.

They were married according to the ancient simple ritual of the Protestant Episcopal Church, whose worshipers came to New England with the first settlers, in old Trinity Church, a long, narrow, weather-beaten white clapboard building with a towering white steeple and gilded spire and weather vane. It was all just as it was when the church was built more than two centuries ago, in 1726, eighty-seven years after the founding of Newport in 1639.

Shading the high steeple was a fine, old elm tree, as tall as or taller than the spire itself, with its great spreading branches almost speaking aloud the story of New England. The tree itself was as old or nearly as old as the church.

Church Recalls Colonial Days.

On the other side of the church, so that the wedding procession walked between it and the old tree to enter the building, was the old burying ground with its plain weather-beaten granite headstones bearing the names of men and women who played leading parts in shaping the history of the colonies and of the first days of the Republic.

All around the church, which is right in the centre of this fine old city, old frame buildings of Colonial architecture, with Grecian columns, steeply slanting roofs and gables, crowding close to the building line of the street, bespoke Newport's history.

The time joined with the place in celebrating the event with appropriate ceremony, for not only was it in the midst of the Summer season, when Newport's social colony is always in full swing, but it was coincident with a visit of a large part of the United States fleet. From time immemorial the navy has been associated with Newport, and

Continued on Page Eighteen.

FORD WILL ACCEPT NRA AND ITS CODE, JOHNSON IS TOLD

General Announces He Awaits Signed Certificate From Auto Maker.

SAYS HE ASKED CHANGES

Recovery Head Asserts His Suggestions Have Been Approved in Detroit.

Special to THE NEW YORK TIMES.

WASHINGTON, June 30.—General Johnson believed tonight that he was nearing such a settlement of his ten months feud with Henry Ford as would let the NRA put another feather in its cap and at the same time allow the automobile maker to re-enter the fertile field of government business.

General Johnson today read a copy of an unsigned letter purporting to be from the Ford Motor Company to a local dealer, setting forth the claims that that firm had been complying and would continue to comply with "pertinent" provisions of the Automobile Code.

The Recovery Administrator s. that if the letter, with certain revisions which he suggested, were returned to him signed by Henry Ford or any other authorized executive of the Ford Motor Company, he would consider it a certificate of compliance, would call off his "crack-down" campaign against the company and recommend to President Roosevelt that it be allowed to resume bidding on government contracts.

A large order of motor trucks for the army, which War Department officials prefer should be Ford products, is said to be the immediate stake in negotiations between the NRA and Mr. Ford. Harry H. Woodring Assistant Secretary of War, has made overtures to General Johnson within the last thirty-six hours to learn what the Ford company would have to do to qualify to bid.

Representative Kvale of Minnesota, active in the House Military Affairs Committee investigating War Department purchases, accompanied the Ford dealer when he called to show the unsigned letter to General Johnson this afternoon.

Talks To Ford Adviser.

General Johnson believed the letter to be entirely authentic and to have originated at the Detroit offices of the Ford Company despite the circumstances under which it was shown to him. This belief was intensified by a telephone conversation which he had with William J. Cameron, editorial adviser to Mr. Ford, regarding the suggested revisions.

The letter, according to General Johnson, was addressed to the Northwest Motor Company of Bethesda, Md., the local dealer that has tried so consistently to keep in contractual relations with the governmental departments regardless of Mr. Ford's refusal to sign a compliance certificate for his code.

In its original form the letter said that although the company had complied and would continue to comply with the provisions of the automobile compact, it reserved its "constitutional rights" as guaranteed by the fundamental law.

This was the section to which General Johnson objected. He told R. P. Sabine, president of the Northwest Motor Company, and Representative Kvale that President Roosevelt would not stand for

Continued on Page Twenty-two.

POLICE FILL THE STREETS

Goering's Forces Keep Curious Throngs on Constant Move.

MACHINE GUNS MOUNTED

Public Buildings on Unter den Linden and Wilhelmstrasse Are Heavily Guarded.

NEWS IS AT A PREMIUM

Rumors Are Rampant as Only a One-Sheet Paper Provides Authentic Information.

Copyright, 1934, by The Associated Press.

BERLIN, June 30.—With the peaceful cool of a Summer evening made strangely tense by squads of armed police and the presence of machine guns, this capital city was facing tonight the possibility of a new unnamed, undefined political event.

Crowds of curious spectators, only partly informed as to events through limited press dispatches, surged up and down Wilhelmstrasse, where public buildings were massed with police ever ready to keep them on the move.

In front of the home of Captain Ernest Roehm, suicide deposed leader of the storm troops, were bristling truckloads of Prussian Premier Hermann Goering's special police. They formed an impressive barricade separate from the thousands who dragged their feet in slow response to demands that streets and sidewalks be kept clear.

Show of Force Excites Crowds.

The presence of police everywhere one turned was a direct stimulant to the excitement of the street and thoroughfare. Never in the history of Berlin, it was pointed out, had so many police appeared in the streets at one time with such obvious readiness for action. In addition to the regular police force, augmented by armed reserves, there was the steel-helmeted, green-clad police of Premier Goering.

The sudden appearance of a police machine gun detachment, with ammunition ready, in historic Potsdammer Platz brought a final touch to the grimness of the situation. The sight of another similar detachment riding up and down Unter den Linden left no doubt in the public mind as to the nature of the emergency.

Men and women rushed like hounds on the scent wherever carriers appeared with copies of one newspaper which had printed one page only for free distribution. This carried a brief account of Captain Roehm's discharge by Chancellor Hitler.

Reactions to the news were various and could be read at will on the faces of newspaper readers. Persons obviously of a conservative mind wreathed their faces in smiles as they read what had happened.

Continued on Page Three.

Dillinger Raids Bank in South Bend, Ind., Reported Shot; Officer Slain, Loot $28,000

By The Associated Press.

SOUTH BEND, Ind., June 30.—A bandit quintet with John Dillinger reported to be in command, stormed the Merchants' National Bank today, scooped up $28,439 and fled in a wild barrage of bullets, leaving a slain policeman and four wounded men in their wake.

The ruthless raiders engaged in gun battles with a detective, two officers and a jeweler as they fled from the bank and made their way to the escape car a half block away. More than fifty shots raked the street in the heart of the city.

Detective Harry Henderson, who identified the bandits' leader as Dillinger, said he believed that he had shot the long-sought gunman as the quintet's car sped away.

Patrolman Harold Wagner encountered the three gangsters who carried out the actual robbery as they were hurrying from the bank. He was fatally wounded before he could reach his pistol.

Those wounded were P. G. Stahley, manager of the Birdsell Manufacturing Company; Jake Soloman, Delos N. Coen, a cashier, and Samuel Toth. At Epworth Hospital it was found that a bullet had struck Soloman in the hip and coursed upward. His condition was described as critical. Toth was wounded in the eye as a bullet smashed the windshield of his automobile.

Leaving an outpost, believed to be John Hamilton, on guard at their automobile, and another bandit closer to the bank, the man identified by a police detective as Dillinger, with two henchmen, one of them believed to be "Baby Face" Nelson, rushed into the bank about noon. Cowing the twenty-five customers with a machine gun, the man identified as Dillinger took up a strategic post and sent a score of slugs into the ceiling while his confederates snatched up $28,439. C. W. Coen, vice president of the institution, who took cover under a desk three feet from the gunner, declared he was positive the leader was the desperado Dillinger.

Bundling their loot, the three commandeered Stahley, Coen and several other patrons and used them as human shields as they marched out the door. Wagner ran toward them from across the crowded street. The machine gunner shot him down, three bullets entering the policeman's body.

THREE OF THE LEADERS WHO DIED IN THE REICH MUTINY.

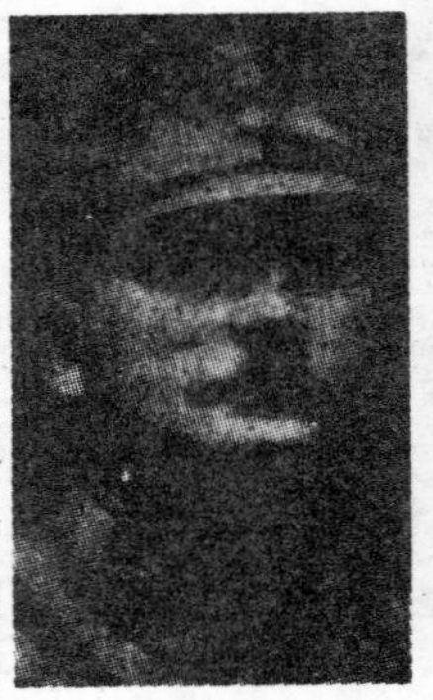

Times Wide World Photo.
Captain Ernst Roehm, ousted Storm Troop head, who committed suicide.

Associated Press Photo.
Karl Ernst, Berlin Storm Troop leader, arrested and later shot.

Times Wide World Photo.
General Kurt von Schleicher, slain by arresting officers.

HITLER COMMANDS NAZI ABSTINENCES

Forbids the Troopers to Spend Money on Banquets and Bans Moral 'Debauches.'

WANTS 'MEN, NOT APES'

Chancellor Asserts All Must Be on Best Behavior or Be Expelled From Ranks.

Wireless to THE NEW YORK TIMES.

BERLIN, June 30.—Chancellor Adolf Hitler issued these eleven commands today to Viktor Lutze, new Chief of Staff of the Storm Troops:

In naming you Chief of Staff of the Storm Troops I expect that you will accept the series of duties that I herewith inform you of.

1—I demand of a Storm Troop leader, just as from a Storm Trooper, blind obedience and unquestioning discipline.

2—I demand that every Storm Troop leader recognize, like every other political leader, that his behavior and reputation must be an example for his organization and for our whole body of followers.

3—I demand that Storm Troop leaders, exactly as in the case of political leaders, be expelled from the Storm Troops without hesitation as soon as their behavior disgraces them in the eyes of the public.

Demands Simplicity.

4—I demand specially from the Storm Troop leader that he be an example of simplicity, not of display. I do not desire Storm Troop leaders to give costly dinners or that they attend such dinners. There was a time when we were not invited to such affairs, and we have nothing to seek there now. Millions of our fellow citizens have not even the necessaries of life. They are not oblivious of those whom fortune has favored, but it is unworthy of a National Socialist to increase the gulf between fortune and misery, which is already great enough.

I prohibit the use of Storm Troop or party funds for festivals and the like. It is shameless to stage debauches with the pennies of our poorest citizens. The luxurious headquarters in Berlin, in which it has now been discovered that some 30,000 marks monthly were spent for banquets, is to be done away with immediately.

State Dinners Excepted.

I prohibit for all party groups banquets and dinners paid for with any variety of public funds. I forbid all party and Storm Troop leaders to partake of such banquets. The only exceptions are functions necessary for reasons of State, notably those for which the Reichspresident and the Reich Foreign Minister are responsible. I forbid all party leaders and Storm Troop leaders to give so-called diplomatic dinners. A Storm Troop leader does not need to engage in representation, but simply to do his duty.

5—I do not desire Storm Troop leaders to undertake business trips in expensive limousines or cabriolets, or to employ public funds for such trips. The same

Continued on Page Two.

Hitler Alone Had Power To Order Shooting of 7

Special Cable to THE NEW YORK TIMES.

BERLIN, June 30.—Over its report of the deaths of seven storm troop leaders who yesterday were in power in German, the Völkischer Beobachter, Chancellor Hitler's own newspaper, carried the headline, "Seven Storm Troop Leaders Shot. End of Convicted Traitors."

The German words used for the verb and adjective taken together in this connection carry a wider meaning than the English equivalent, as is the case with so many German words. They imply that the men were proved guilty and executed.

These men were shot on the spot without trial on the mere allegation of their guilt by order of a higher authority. The only authority which could give an order for their execution unchallenged was Adolf Hitler, who, according to the same article in this newspaper, "is the supreme conscience of the German people."

GOERING POLICE NET CATCHES LEADERS

Suicides and Killings Follow Raids on Homes of Notables in Berlin and Vicinity.

By OTTO D. TOLISCHUS.

Wireless to THE NEW YORK TIMES.

BERLIN, June 30.—General Kurt von Schleicher, former Premier, was killed with his wife while "resisting arrest with a weapon in his hand," according to an official communiqué.

The communiqué was one of a long series issued throughout the day as the criminal police of Premier Hermann Goering of Prussia rushed about Berlin and its vicinity, leaving a heavy wake of arrests, suicides and killings among prominent persons.

General von Schleicher met death at his villa in Neubadelsberg, between Berlin and Potsdam. His wife, Frau Elizabeth von Schleicher, it is stated, fell while trying to shield him with her body during an exchange of shots.

From that point tragedy quickly spread. One squad of General Goering's police rushed to the office of Vice Chancellor Franz von Papen in Vos Strasse, next to the Chancellery, and asked the Vice Chancellor to accompany them to his home. There they kept Colonel von Papen under house arrest, and questioned him regarding his relations with General von Schleicher. The amenities were preserved, and later it was stated Colonel von Papen was "at liberty."

Von Papen Visitors Barred.

Visitors to Colonel von Papen's house, however, were not allowed to see him. His secretary and a Reichswehr officer assured every one that Colonel von Papen was in good spirits, had just finished tea and was smoking his afternoon cigar.

His office meanwhile had been occupied by black uniformed special guards, men with field equipment, rifles and hand grenades. To inquirers they insisted they were merely Colonel von Papen's regular guard, placed there to protect him. Visitors noted, however, that all doors of the building stood open, as if a whirlwind had swept through.

In the face of this action, Colonel

Continued on Page Eight.

NAZI CHIEFS TELL OF ENDING REVOLT

Hitler and Lutze Appeal to the Storm Troops to Be Faithful to Their Movement.

RAID DESCRIBED BY PARTY

Leader of War Veterans Urges Them to Be Calm and to Be Loyal to Government.

Wireless to THE NEW YORK TIMES.

BERLIN, June 30.—A series of statements was issued today by German leaders on their success in crushing the radical Nazi revolt.

NAZI PARTY STATEMENT.

A communiqué from the National Socialist party read:

Munich, June 30.

For many months individual elements have been trying to drive a wedge and produce conflicts between the Storm Troops and the party, as well as between the Storm Troops and the State. Suspicions of this became more and more confirmed, but it was also plain that these endeavors were to be charged to a limited clique of certain leanings.

Chief of Staff Roehm, in whom the leader placed an exceptional amount of confidence, not only did not oppose these endeavors but undoubtedly sponsored them. His well-known unfortunate characteristic gradually led to intolerable burdens which drove the leader of the movement and the Highest Leader of the Storm Troops [Hitler] into most serious conflicts of conscience.

Chief of Staff Roehm established contacts with General von Schleicher without the knowledge of Der Fuehrer [the Leader]. His go-betweens were another Storm Troop leader and an obscure person well known in Berlin, to whom Der Fuehrer had always strongly objected.

Since these negotiations also led —of course without the knowledge of Der Fuehrer—finally to contacts with a foreign power, or rather to its representative, it was not possible to avoid intervention both from the standpoint of the party and the State.

Provocative incidents brought about according to the plan caused Der Fuehrer to fly from Bonn to Munich at 2 o'clock this morning, after visiting labor camps in Westphalia, in order to remove and arrest the most seriously compromised group of leaders. Der Fuehrer himself went with only a few companions to Wiessee in order to still any attempts at resistance.

The execution of the arrests revealed such immorality that any trace of pity was impossible. Some of these Storm Troop leaders had taken male prostitutes along with them. One of them was even disturbed in a most ugly situation and was arrested.

Der Fuehrer gave orders for this plague to be done away with ruthlessly. In the future he will not permit millions of decent people to be compromised by a few of such sick men. Der Fuehrer instructed Premier Goering of Prussia to take similar action in Berlin and especially to arrest the reactionary accomplices of this political plot.

At noon today Der Fuehrer

Continued on Page Four.

STORM TROOP CHIEFS DIE

Killed or Take Own Lives as Chancellor and Goering Strike.

REACTIONARIES ALSO HIT

Wife Shot With Schleicher as He Resists Police—Head of Catholic Action Slain.

HITLER FLIES TO MUNICH

Tears Off Rebels' Insignia and Arrests and Ousts Roehm —Papen Held but Freed.

By FREDERICK T. BIRCHALL.

Wireless to THE NEW YORK TIMES.

BERLIN, June 30.—On the eve of a self-proclaimed month of peace Germany has passed today through the throes of a violent purging that must profoundly affect her future. It is neither a revolution nor a coup d'état nor a counter-revolution but authoritative action intended to head off any of the three.

Chancellor Hitler in Munich, backed by General Hermann Wilhelm Goering, Premier of Prussia, in Berlin, has struck simultaneously at the rebel elements in his own Storm Troops and at certain reactionary elements temporarily allied with them or suspected of being so allied for their own ends in an attempt to upset the present régime in Germany.

When the day was over many Storm Troop leaders had been shot to death or had committed suicide.

In addition, General Kurt von Schleicher, Herr Hitler's predecessor as Chancellor, had been slain while resisting police who attempted to seize him as one of the plotters.

[Captain Ernst Roehm, chief of staff of the Storm Troops, committed suicide after having been ousted by Chancellor Hitler, according to The Associated Press, while Heinrich Klausener, chief of the Catholic Action, was shot to death by a Nazi special guard.]

The Official Version.

The official version is that the attempt was a joint effort "to bring pressure" on the government with a threat of violent action behind it. There is mention of a "foreign power" as being involved. The discerning interpret this reference as being to Russia and the ultimate aim of the rebels as a new national bolshevism.

Whatever the cause, Chancellor Hitler has acted swiftly and decisively. Flying to Munich in the early hours of this morning from Bonn, where he had been ostensibly inspecting work camps, he assembled his trusted special guards in that city and proceeded to gather in the suspected leaders, who had already proceeded to preliminary action.

Captain Roehm, the leader of the conspiracy, was arrested in his bedroom in his country house outside Munich by Herr Hitler himself and then and there deposed from all his offices. His fellow-conspirators were gathered in by the dozen in Munich and around it.

The official story told to foreign correspondents by General Goering this afternoon says that some of them, both in Munich and in Berlin, committed suicide and others were shot while resisting.

Goering Acts Swiftly.

Almost simultaneously in Berlin General Goering, by arrangement with Chancellor Hitler, was taking similar action. It came swiftly and unexpectedly just before noon. But here the members of the reactionary group believed to be acting with the rebel Storm Troop leaders were equally the objects of the assault.

Karl Ernst, group leader of the Berlin Storm Troops, was traced to a house near Bremen and surrounded there. He is dead and the official version is that he was shot while resisting arrest. The unofficial version is that he was brought by airplane to Berlin and executed on his arrival.

Police and special guards at the very outset sought to put General von Schleicher under arrest at his villa outside Potsdam. It is said that he attempted to draw a pistol. A volley of shots brought him down and his wife died with him.

Vice Chancellor Franz von Papen, who seems to have been under sus-

Continued on Page Two.

"All the News That's Fit to Print."

The New York Times.

LATE CITY EDITION
POSTSCRIPT
Fair, slightly cooler today; tomorrow fair.
Temperature Yesterday—Max., 89; min., 72.

VOL. LXXXIII....No. 27,939. Entered as Second-Class Matter, Postoffice, New York, N. Y. NEW YORK, MONDAY, JULY 23, 1934. TWO CENTS In New York City. | THREE CENTS Within 200 Miles | FOUR CENTS Elsewhere Except in 7th and 8th Postal Zones

15 KILLED, 18 HURT AS BUS FALLS 35 FEET AND BURNS ON AN OUTING AT OSSINING

MANY TRAPPED IN FLAMES

Machine Out of Control Plunges Off Ramp Into Lumber Yard.

GASOLINE TANK EXPLODES

Injured Struggle in Vain to Open Jammed Doors of Old-Fashioned Coach.

4, AFIRE, LEAP INTO RIVER

Members of Young Democrats' Club of Brooklyn Bound for Sing Sing Ball Game.

Fifteen persons were killed and eighteen injured, yesterday, when a bus containing about forty men, women and children plunged thirty-five feet from a ramp near the Ossining railroad station and burst into flames.

The bus was one of seven that had been chartered by the Young Men's Democratic League of the Twentieth Assembly District in Brooklyn to take members of the league and their friends to a baseball game in Sing Sing.

Speeding, out of control, down the tortuous Secor Road hill, it mounted the ramp that crosses the New York Central tracks near the Ossining station, crashed through the fragile iron railing on one side of the ramp and landed on its four wheels in a lumber yard.

Gasoline Tank Explodes.

The driver, apparently, failed to turn off the ignition; and as the bus struck the ground the gasoline tank exploded with a deafening roar. Sheets of flame shot out in all directions, and while passengers inside scrambled for the exits, fire enveloped the vehicle and the adjacent lumber piles.

The bus, one of the old-fashioned type with no centre aisle, had eight seats running crosswise and doors on either side of each seat. A few of the doors were opened without difficulty, enabling those inside to escape. But many of the doors, thrown out of alignment by the crash, refused to open.

The occupants of these seats were penned inside, and with the flames mounting around them began screaming for help. Those who had escaped tugged vainly at the closed doors. With the aid of witnesses to the crash they succeeded in opening several doors and releasing some of those inside.

Four Leap Into the Hudson.

Four men, who escaped from the bus with their clothing in flames, rushed to the near-by Hudson River and threw themselves in. Two others raced down along the New York Central Railroad tracks. Those in the river were rescued by Frank McLaughlin, former Fire Chief of Ossining. What became of the two who ran along the tracks could not be definitely ascertained last night, but it is believed that they were taken in charge by near-by residents and rushed to a hospital.

Thomas McGuire Jr. of 828 Halsey Street, Brooklyn, who had escaped from the bus with a broken arm and secondary burns, rushed back to rescue his father, who had been critically burned. Others who had escaped from the bus made every effort to save those still inside. So did witnesses to the accident. George Adcock, an Ossining fireman, got credit for seven rescues. But the old wooden framework of the bus and the sun-dried lumber piled near by burned like tinder and the rescue work had to be abandoned.

All ambulances in Ossining were brought to the scene of the crash and the injured removed to the Ossining, Grasslands and Tarrytown Hospitals. Father John Kelly of Briarcliff, who chanced to be passing in an automobile, had arrived in time to assist in the rescue work. He also administered the last rites of the church to some of the more seriously injured. Afterward, he went to the Ossining Hospital, where he administered the last rites to others.

The regular staff at the Ossining hospital was swamped with work and was reinforced by numerous volunteers. These included Drs. Robert Bloom, James Kearney, John Schofmeister, Edward Huntington of Ossining, Edward Hunt-Miller of Croton.

Many prominent women in the vi-

Continued on Page Three.

Victims of Bus Accident

A partial list of the dead and injured in the bus accident at Ossining, as compiled last night, follows:

THE DEAD.

GALLER, ABRAHAM, 666 Hancock Street, Brooklyn.

HAYES, Mrs. WILLIAM, 27 Cornelia St., Brooklyn.

INCARNATO, FRANK, 28 years old, driver of the bus, 662 Ninety-second St., Brooklyn.

McNICHOLAS, JOHN, Jr., 26, 412 Irving Av., Brooklyn.

An unidentified person.

MISSING (BELIEVED DEAD).

GALLER, Mrs. ABRAHAM, 666 Hancock Street, Brooklyn.

LUFF, ARTHUR, 9 Woodbine St., Brooklyn.

His sister, whose name was not determined.

MEMEY, JOSEPH, 27 Cornelia St., Brooklyn.

McDONALD, Mr. and Mrs. JOSEPH, 100 Gates Av., Brooklyn.

McDONALD, BERNADETTE, 12 years old, their daughter.

MURRAY, Mr. and Mrs. JAMES, 15 Cornelia St., Brooklyn.

THOMPSON, Mrs. ROSE, 9 Woodbine St., Brooklyn.

THE INJURED.

Ossining Hospital.

CONNORS, FRANK, 542 Bainbridge Av., Brooklyn, critical.

CORCORAN, JOSEPH, 666 Putnam Avenue, Brooklyn, not serious.

ELLERY, JAMES, 712 Knickerbocker Av., Brooklyn, left hospital after treatment.

HAYES, WILLIAM, 27 Cornelia St., Brooklyn, not serious.

HAYES, JAMES, 12, his son, critical.

HUPF, FRANK, 831 Monroe St., Brooklyn, not serious.

McCANN, DANIEL, 378 Central Av., Brooklyn, critical.

McGUIRE, THOMAS, 828 Halsey St., Brooklyn, critical.

MERKEL, Mrs. TERESA, 280 Highland Blvd., Brooklyn, left hospital after treatment.

REITMEYER, JOHN, 1,218 Gates Av., Brooklyn, critical.

SCHWARTZ, Mrs. ARCHIBALD, 116 Liberty St., Brooklyn, not serious.

Grasslands Hospital.

KNAUER, FRANK, of 75-07 Sixty-fourth St., Glendale, Queens.

LALOF, MARY, 9 Woodbine Street, Brooklyn; not serious.

McGUIRE, THOMAS, Jr., 828 Halsey Street, Brooklyn; not serious.

SCHNEIDER, EDWIN, 105-11 196th Street, Hollis, Queens; not serious.

SCHWARTZ, ARCHIBALD, 116 Liberty Street, Brooklyn; not serious.

Tarrytown Hospital.

HICKEY, GEORGE, 17 Woodbine Street, Brooklyn; not serious.

MURRAY, WILLIAM, 15 Cornelia Street, Brooklyn; not serious.

BUS BRAKES WEAK, SURVIVORS ASSERT

'We'll Take a Chance,' Driver Said—Stopped Twice for Makeshift Repairs.

MAN SAW WIFE PERISH

Tried to Pull Her From Wreck, but Flames Drove Him Back, He Testifies at Inquest.

Special to THE NEW YORK TIMES.

OSSINING, N. Y., July 22.—Walter Thompson of 9 Woodbine Street, Brooklyn, a survivor of the bus accident that cost fifteen lives here today, testified tonight at the official inquest that the bus driver knew his brakes were bad.

Thompson was the first witness called by Dr. Amos O. Squire, Medical Examiner for Westchester County. His story of the bad brakes and the driver's makeshift repairs was corroborated by other witnesses and in unofficial accounts obtained by newspaper men from other survivors here and in Brooklyn.

"Several times on the way up," Thompson told Dr. Squire, "the driver had trouble with his brakes. I noticed that finally he got up and turned the foot brake around as if he were screwing it on the shaft. After each time the brake held better, and then it seemed to loosen up. At one point the emergency brake held all right, but on the hill in Ossining it was no good.

"In the neighborhood of Tarrytown, where they were fixing the road, the cars ahead stopped for traffic and the driver had to drive off the road because the brakes wouldn't hold.

"We'll Take a Chance."

"I said to him, 'Your brakes are bad.' I told him he'd better be careful and that he ought to stop and fix them.

"The driver said: 'The hell with it. We'll take a chance. I guess we'll get through.' He was completely sober. I thought that he was a good chauffeur—that's what I told the man in the seat with me.

"When we got on the hill on Main Street here and were coming down from the top at a pretty good pace, we got to where he should have taken a turn at Hunter Street [a right-angle turn off Main Street which would have led to the prison] and there were two automobiles parked on the street which partly blocked the turn.

"The driver turned out, swung away over and cleared the automobiles and went on down the hill, swinging from curb to curb almost all the way down the hill. He couldn't get control again.

Yelled to All to Jump.

"Just before the bus crashed through the railing the driver yelled, 'Everybody jump!' We went right through the railing, and the bus fell front first when the hind wheel hit the foundation for the railing, raising up the rear of the bus. The bus struck on the front.

"The motor backed up and drove the steering wheel into the chauf-

Continued on Page Three.

TREASURY OFFERS MORTGAGE BONDS

$100,000,000 in 3% 14-Year Farm Corporation Securities to Go to Highest Bidders.

SALE USHERS NEW POLICY

Marks First Time Treasury Has Acted as Fiscal Agent—Ready Market Expected.

Special to THE NEW YORK TIMES.

WASHINGTON, July 22.—The Treasury Department today announced an offering to the public of $100,000,000 of Federal Farm Mortgage Corporation 3 per cent bonds, thus inaugurating a new policy under which the department acted as the agent of one of the emergency recovery set-ups in floating securities which the corporation is authorized by law to sell to obtain funds.

In the past the Treasury, except in the case of short-term Treasury bills which are sold on a discount basis, has judged the market, determined upon the interest at which a security should be offered and then has sought subscriptions at par or at a small stated premium. Such offerings have been for the purpose of covering the Treasury's own requirements.

In the present offering, however, which the Treasury is making on behalf of the emergency corporations, the department did not have discretion in fixing the interest rate the securities shall carry. It has, therefore, offered the mortgage corporation's bonds to the highest bidders, but in no case at less than par and accrued interest. The bonds will be dated May 15, 1934, mature on May 15, 1949, and may be redeemed on May 15, 1944, or on any subsequent interest payment date which comes semi-annually on May 15 and Nov. 15 of each year.

At present Treasury 3s are selling in the market at slightly over 102, and outstanding bonds of the mortgage corporation are quoted at just over 101. The latter are guaranteed as to principal and interest by law.

Substantial Premium Expected.

In connection with the present offering the Treasury Department expects to market the $100,000,000 issue readily and at a substantial premium. The bonds are exempt both as to principal and interest from Federal, State, municipal and local taxation, except surtaxes, estate, inheritance and gift taxes. They will be issued in denominations of from $100 to $10,000.

The decision to have the Treasury market the bonds and thus further centralize the handling of government-backed security offerings in the public market was reached after conferences between Treasury officials and officials of the Farm Credit Corporation, under the supervision of which the Federal Farm Mortgage Corporation activities are brought.

To a certain extent it is in line with the policy adopted some time ago to suspend the direct sale of debentures by the RFC to banks

Continued on Page Two.

2,320 Planes for Army Asked in Baker Report

Board Declares Congress Should Provide Funds—Separate Unit Plan Rejected —Mail Flying Praised.

Special to THE NEW YORK TIMES.

WASHINGTON, July 22.—Holding that the strengthening of the air forces was essential to adequate national defense, the War Department's special aviation committee recommended today an increase in the aviation strength of the army to 2,320 planes and a corresponding increase in the flying personnel. The present authorized strength of the army air corps is 1,800 planes, which the committee reported to be more than 300 short.

The committee, headed by Newton D. Baker, former Secretary of War, and composed of eleven civilians and generals, declared against consolidation of the army and navy aviation services into a single unit. Its report praised the spirit and manner in which the army carried the mail under difficulties during the period of the cancellation of the air mail contracts. With this was mingled criticism of the actual performance, coupled as it was with fatalities, and whatever there was of failure was attributed to lack of proper equipment and to insufficient training.

While expressing the opinion that the United States was comparatively free from the threat of serious overseas air invasion because of the failure so far to develop an airplane capable of crossing the Atlantic or Pacific with an effective military load, attacking vital areas successfully and returning to its base, the committee held that the army's air corps must be ready at all times for war service.

"The next great war is likely to begin with engagements between opposing aircraft, either sea-based or land-based," the report read, "and early aerial supremacy is quite likely to be an important fac-

Continued on Page Six.

The recommendations of the Baker committee are on page 6.

FALL BUSINESS RISE PREDICTED BY NRA; SUMMER DROP CUT

Upward Trend Held Definite by Leon Henderson, Citing Homely Indicators.

LESS FAMILY DOUBLING-UP

This Despite Increase in Marriages—Small Loans Are Being Rapidly Repaid.

WASHINGTON, July 22.—The NRA has been informed by its experts to "gamble" on a substantial Fall rise in business and a less than usual slump during the remainder of the Summer.

Leon Henderson, chief of the Blue Eagle's research and planning division, held this conclusion today on the basis of a mass of statistical and other data. His advice to NRA is based upon an expectation of an upswing.

Mr. Henderson's searchers have reported to him that the decline thus far this Summer has been less than normal, and that there are now numerous signs of an upward trend in business generally.

There is no expectation, however, of a boom development. Mr. Henderson employs most careful language in his estimate of the future. He himself referred today to his attitude as a "gamble" on the basis of the best facts available.

The research chief is paying especial attention to what he describes as his "homely indicators." For instance, there has been a gain in the sale of living room rugs, one of the first things which housewives like to replace when funds are available.

There also has been a decline in the number of bachelors, he points out. In one city the number of bachelors before the depression was 10,000. This increased to 29,000 at the height of the depression and is now about 22,000, the expert conclusion being that men with funds are less fearful of marriage.

Families Again Spread Out.

For another thing, Mr. Henderson's "doubling up" indicator in reference to housing shows that families which have been crowded now are spreading out and filling vacant apartments and houses.

Small personal loans, his figures show, are being paid up in full at an increasing rate. The index shows the rate of repaying at a record high for the depression, and higher even than in the month when soldiers' cash bonus payments were largest. Similarly, the rate of repayment of building and loan obligations is up and the amount of unrented property held by building and loan associations is down. Repayments to the Home Owners Loan Corporation and Farm Credit Administration are also holding up well.

Mr. Henderson said he was paying increasing attention to this type of statistical indicator because, first, it shows the status of the ordinary person better than the customary type of business statistics, and second, because it tends to get at the beginning of the buying process rather than at the end.

Of particular significance, Mr. Henderson said, are the indicators showing a reduction in personal debt. He holds this to be one of

Continued on Page Two.

FRENCH FACTIONS WARNED BY LEBRUN TO RESTORE TRUCE

President Says Public Will Be Severe With Those Blocking Doumergue's Work.

PREMIER TO SEEK ACCORD

Tardieu Is Said to Be Ready to Make Peace With Herriot to Prevent Cabinet Shifts.

By The Associated Press.

AURILLAC, France, July 22.—President Lebrun took a hand in the bitter Cabinet clash today by warning that there must be no interference with the government of Premier Doumergue.

France will not tolerate anything which blocks M. Doumergue's work of restoration, M. Lebrun said as he unveiled a monument at the birthplace of the assassinated President, Paul Doumer.

M. Lebrun made no direct reference to the Cabinet dissension in which Edouard Herriot and André Tardieu, both Ministers without portfolio and both former Premiers, are the chief figures. But he said pointedly that party fights must be forgotten.

The President expressed pride in M. Doumergue's "wisdom and prudence" and asserted his work must go on.

"Public opinion will not accept a situation that stops his beneficial work," M. Lebrun said. "It will be severe toward those who do not do everything to assure for the future what the wisdom of the efforts of today already is permitting us to hope is being achieved."

Critical Week for France.

Wireless to THE NEW YORK TIMES.

PARIS, July 22.—This coming week seems likely to be as critical for France as was that following the rioting of Feb. 6. There is only this difference in the situation, that this time there is even greater confusion.

It is believed the country as a whole at this vacation time wants a real truce to politics. It has put its trust in Premier Doumergue, and among persons of all classes of opinion one hears expressions of resentment because his Ministers could not keep the truce while his back was turned. Whatever he does will have the approval of most persons, but it also is true that whatever he does is almost certain to arouse resentment in one camp or the other.

In the two camps feeling is running high. André Tardieu's friends on newspapers are reiterating that the Radical Socialists are responsible for breaking the truce and are seeking to thrust them out of the Cabinet because they spoke the truth about Camille Chautemps.

To that the reply of the Radical Socialist press is to describe M. Tardieu as "the man who brought down French bonds."

Newspapers like the Petit Parisien, which more nearly represent average opinion, are being careful to remain outside the quarrel. They are too well aware of its dangers for France, because this quarrel strikes deeper than any political division since the days of the Dreyfus affair. There is no concealment of the fact that below the truce, which is possible only in the person and authority of Premier Doumergue, there is an atmosphere

Continued on Page Four.

DILLINGER SLAIN IN CHICAGO; SHOT DEAD BY FEDERAL MEN IN FRONT OF MOVIE THEATRE

Cummings Says Slaying of Dillinger Is 'Gratifying as Well as Reassuring'

By The Associated Press.

WASHINGTON, July 22.—Smiling in elation, Attorney General Cummings tonight termed the slaying of John Dillinger by Federal agents "gratifying as well as reassuring."

The Attorney General was notified just before he boarded the train for the West, the first leg of a journey to Hawaii. At Union Station he dictated the following statement:

"The search for Dillinger has never been relaxed for a moment.

"He has escaped capture on several occasions by the narrowest of margins.

"The news of tonight is exceedingly gratifying as well as reassuring."

Mr. Cummings said the end of the Indiana bandit reflected great credit on the Chicago office of the division of investigation.

J. Edgar Hoover, chief of the Bureau of Investigation, rushed to his office at word that the desperado had been shot down. He told news men:

"This does not mean the end of the Dillinger case.

"Any one who ever gave any of the Dillinger mob any aid, comfort or assistance will be vigorously prosecuted."

He referred directly to George (Baby Face) Nelson, Homer Van Meter and another gangster. Nelson, named by the department as the killer of Special Agent W. Carter Baum in the Dillinger outbreak in the Wisconsin woods last April, was described by Mr. Hoover as a "rat."

REACHED FOR HIS GUN

Outlaw's Move Met by Four Shots, All Finding Their Mark.

HAD LIFTED HIS FACE

Desperado Had Also Treated Finger Tips With Acid to Defeat Prints.

TWO WOMEN WOUNDED

Agents, Tipped Fugitive Was Going to Theatre, Waited While He Saw Show.

Special to THE NEW YORK TIMES.

CHICAGO, July 22.—John Dillinger, America's Public Enemy No. 1 and the most notorious criminal of recent times, was shot and killed at 10:40 o'clock tonight by Federal agents a few seconds after he had left the Biograph Theatre at 2,433 Lincoln Avenue, on Chicago's North Side.

One bullet penetrated the head and another the chest of the desperate outlaw. He died as he was being taken to the Alexian Brothers Hospital. The body was later removed to the county morgue, where the identification of Dillinger was made positive.

According to Melvin H. Purvis, chief of the investigating forces of the Department of Justice in Chicago, and leader of the band of sixteen men who had waited for more than two hours while the desperado viewed his last picture show, Dillinger attempted to put up a fight.

"He saw me give a signal to my men to close in," Chief Purvis said. "He became alarmed and reached into a belt and was drawing the .38-calibre pistol he carried concealed when two of the agents let him have it. Dillinger was lying prone before he was able to get the gun out and I took it from him."

Surgical Disguise Fails.

Dillinger had taken great precautions to prevent his being recognized. His face had been lifted by a surgical process since his last picture was taken and he had dyed his hair a darker shade than its natural light reddish brown.

"It was a good job the surgeons did," Chief Purvis said, "but I knew him the minute I saw him. You couldn't miss if you had studied that face as much as I have."

Two women, passers-by who had no connection with the outlaw, were wounded by stray bullets fired by the Federal agents. They are Mrs. Etta Natalsky, 45 years old, of 2,433 Lincoln Avenue, and Miss Theresa Paulus. Each was struck in the left leg. Their injuries, it was said, were not serious.

Patron of Gangster Film.

Chief Purvis and twelve of his own men, accompanied by Captain Timothy O'Neill and three members of the East Chicago police force, went to the vicinity of the small theatre at about 8:30 P. M.

They had received information during the afternoon that Dillinger would attend the performance of "Manhattan Melodrama," a gang and gun movie featuring Clark Gable and William Powell, in the evening.

The sixteen men were posted strategically, some at all possible exits of the theatre, with groups to the north and south, and one detail on the opposite side of busy Lincoln Avenue. Chief Purvis, seating himself in his automobile a few feet south of the show house, watched.

It was about 8:30 P. M. when Dillinger walked up to the entrance and bought a ticket, or tickets. A Chicago policeman who happened to be at the scene said he was accompanied by two women, one dressed in red, but Chief Purvis said he saw none. Passing into the theatre, Dillinger took a seat.

While he was inside, the agents completed their preparations for his emergence. There were so many of them, and their actions seemed, to the theatre manager and to observers in the neighborhood, to be so suspicious that the police were notified.

Policemen Frank Slattery, Edward Meisterheimer and Michael Garrity, who investigated, were shown Federal badges by the watchers and interfered not at all, al-

Continued on Page Nine.

HOT WAVE ABATES; SEVEN DROWN HERE

Highest Temperature Is 89 at 4:30 P. M. After Cool Morning—One Heat Death.

DROUGHT SPREADS IN WEST

Total Dead in Nation From Weather 272—Cattle and Crops Loss Mounts.

After three days of oppressive heat and high humidity, the weather here moderated somewhat yesterday.

The day's maximum temperature was 89 degrees at 4:30 P. M.; but the humidity remained comparatively low throughout the day, and a brisk northerly breeze tempered the heat of the sun.

The combination here of the warm sun and cool breeze made perfect weather for the seashore, and all the near-by beaches again were thronged with large Sunday crowds. For the fourth time this season the crowd at Coney Island was estimated at more than 1,000,000. At the Rockaways, it was estimated, there were more than 450,000; at Long Beach, more than 300,000, and at Jones Beach, more than 150,000.

The crowd at Jones Beach was one of the largest of the year. The causeway there was lined throughout the day with automobiles, and both bathhouses did a near-capacity business.

One heat death and one prostration were reported during the day. An unidentified man about 55 years old was stricken with a heart attack induced by the heat at Sheriff and Delancey Streets and died.

Seven Persons Drowned.

Seven drownings were reported:

JOSEPH CERILLA, 16 years old, of 101 Bergen Street, Brooklyn, drowned while bathing off West Twenty-fifth Street, Coney Island.

JAMES CUNNINGHAM, 24, employed at the Overlook Hospital in Summit, N. J.; drowned off Beach 104th Street, Rockaway Beach.

ALLAN SNYDER, 22, of 533 Wingon Street, West Philadelphia, drowned in Mirror Lake at Browns Mills, N. J.

FRANK SELLTENRICH, 15, of 309 Seventh Street, Jersey City; drowned in New York Bay off Linden Avenue, Jersey City.

CATHERINE LeCONTE, 5, of 948 East Third Street, Brooklyn; drowned in Lake Ronkonkoma, L. I.

WILLIAM MAGUIRE, 72; drowned in Salem Creek at Salem, N. J.

MILTON WEYLANDT, 18, of 282 Watchogue Road, Port Richmond, S. I.; seized with heart attack and drowned in Lake Hopatcong, N. J.

It was said last night at the Weather Bureau that today probably would be fair and slightly cooler.

272 Dead in Nation.

Deaths in the protracted heat wave covering most of the country passed 256 yesterday, The Associated Press reported.

Hundreds of prostrations were recorded.

The Southwest and Midwest were hardest hit. Only slight relief for scattered areas was in immediate prospect.

In the grain belt crops wilted and

Continued on Page Eleven.

THREE DOOMED MEN FLEE TEXAS PRISON

Another Convict Killed Climbing Wall, Two Others Shot in Death House Break.

GUARD ALSO IS WOUNDED

Trio of Killers, One of Them an Aide of Clyde Barrow, Escape in Waiting Car.

By The Associated Press.

HUNTSVILLE, Texas, July 22.—Three of the most desperate killers in the Southwest—Raymond Hamilton, Blackie Thompson and Joe Palmer—escaped from the death house of the State penitentiary here today in a daring break in which one convict was killed, two others wounded and a guard shot.

The three convicts who were shot, all bank bandits and life-termers, were mowed down by the gunfire of guards as Hamilton, Thompson and Palmer scampered over the wall to two waiting automobiles.

Whitey Walker was killed by the shots of guards whom the convicts engaged in battle. Charlie Frazier, the man who engineered the break, was shot from the ladder with which he was scaling the wall and was believed to be fatally wounded. Roy Johnson, the third bank robber, was shot and less seriously hurt.

H. E. George, the guard, was momentarily stunned as a bullet creased his scalp. He was not seriously hurt.

The break occurred while the prison yard was almost deserted. All officials and guards not actually on duty and practically all convicts were attending a ball game between the prison team and a Conroe team at the athletic field beside the walls.

The escape was the first ever made from the death house, which is located in the centre of the prison. In daring and cool execution, the break has no parallel in the annals of the penitentiary.

Guard Forced to Unlock Cells.

At 4:30 P. M. Inside Guard Lee Braswell approached the death house to feed the five inmates. Inside guards are not permitted to carry weapons, as they come closely into contact with the convicts, and it would be possible for the latter on occasions to overpower and disarm them.

As Braswell approached the door, Frazier, crouched against the wall, stepped forward and thrust the muzzle of a .45-calibre revolver against his ribs. In his other hand the convict held another .45.

Frazier marched Braswell into the death house, and compelled him to unlock the cells in which Hamilton, Palmer and Thompson were incarcerated. These convicted murderers came out, and Frazier handed Hamilton his extra gun. Braswell was locked in Hamilton's cell.

The quartet of desperadoes sped from the death house and were joined at the door by Walker and Johnson. A few feet from the death house they encountered W. T. Mc-

Continued on Page Eleven.

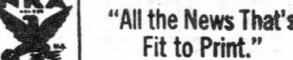

"All the News That's Fit to Print."

The New York Times.

LATE CITY EDITION
WEATHER—Showers, cooler today; fair, cooler tomorrow.
Temperatures Yesterday—Max., 89; min., 68.

VOL. LXXXIII....No. 27,942. Entered as Second-Class Matter, Postoffice, New York, N. Y. NEW YORK, THURSDAY, JULY 26, 1934. P TWO CENTS In New York City | THREE CENTS Within 200 Miles | FOUR CENTS Elsewhere Except in 7th and 8th Postal Zones

AUSTRIAN NAZIS KILL DOLLFUSS, REVOLT FAILS; 147 PLOTTERS HELD; MARTIAL LAW IN EFFECT; ITALIAN ARMY, NAVY, PLANES READY TO ACT

DEATHS FROM HEAT INCREASE TO 1,213 IN THE COUNTRY

Temperatures Continue to Stay Above 100 Degrees in Western Cities.

MISSOURI SUFFERS MOST

Records Show 312 Deaths in State—Intense Drought Suffering in Huge Area.

WALLACE IS PESSIMISTIC

He Says Situation Will Be Very Serious Unless Relief Comes in Two Weeks.

The Daily Heat Record

Following are the maximum heat records set yesterday in Western cities, with deaths for the day and the forecast:

City.	High Mark.	Deaths in Day.	Forecast.
Chicago	96	70	Cooler.
Cincinnati	106	37	Slightly cooler.
Des Moines	104	21	Showers, cooler.
Omaha	100	5	Possible showers.
St. Louis	108	76	Showers, cooler.
Kansas City	106	12	Showers, cooler.

By The Associated Press.

Wind and rain combined forces to afford some slight relief to people on the Atlantic, Pacific and Gulf coasts yesterday, but there was no relief for the parched fields, panting beasts and the perspiring populace of the Middle West where the toll of death and damage continued to mount.

Fatalities listed as "heat deaths" reached 1,213 persons. Thousands of head of livestock have been destroyed and the market value of many additional thousands seriously reduced during the past sixteen days, when most of the nation has suffered under temperatures around the century mark. Irreparable damage has resulted to crops in all great producing areas.

On forecasts from the Weather Bureau of continued drought, Dr. Elwood Mead, Reclamation Commissioner, said that tens of thousands of persons in the Dakotas and eastern slopes of the Rockies "must be evacuated."

The Atlantic Coast was favored with lower temperatures and showers in many places. Several baseball games were postponed. The Pacific Coast also continued to enjoy comfortable weather.

Water shortage is serious in many communities. Two down-State Illinois counties reported the situation "was becoming desperate." Some Iowa cities have been hauling water in tank cars. Hundreds of new wells have been sunk throughout the Middle West.

Grasshoppers, chinch bugs and other insect pests daily add their ravages to the farmers' worries.

Deaths Sweep States.

Missouri with 312 victims continued to lead the list of States. Illinois was second with 300 and Ohio had 127. Among the others were Indiana 54, Nebraska 61, Iowa 62, Minnesota 32, Kansas 29, Kentucky 43, Texas 28, Michigan 19, Pennsylvania 18, Wisconsin 15, Oklahoma 10, South Dakota 7, West Virginia 12, Tennessee 5, New York 4, Massachusetts 3, Maryland 3, Connecticut 4, District of Columbia 2, Arkansas 2, Alabama 1.

Chicago, where a new all-time high record of 104.8 degrees, officially 105, was recorded Tuesday, dropped to a maximum of 93 yesterday, although the humidity continued excessive. St. Louis and Kansas City, with highs of 110 for the previous day, turned in marks of 108 and 106 respectively.

Cincinnati equaled its 106-degree mark for the second successive day, but some hope of relief was held out for Thursday, after a slight drop came in the early afternoon. Cleveland, swept by a lake breeze, enjoyed a 78 at 2 P. M. (Eastern standard time).

The Pacific Coast had little change in temperature and no heat fatalities. Seattle and Los Angeles had 80, Portland 84 and San Francisco 68 degrees.

Oklahoma City dropped from 104 Tuesday to 96 at noon Wednesday. Michigan cities in the midnineties showed a 10 degree drop. Baltimore had a 98, Indianapolis 105, Lincoln 97, Huntington (W. Va.) 100, Pittsburgh 96, Philadelphia 86, St. Paul 76, Milwaukee 84, Cumberland (Md.) 105, Ottumwa (Iowa) 104, Duluth 74, Omaha 101, Springfield (Ill.) 101, Carbondale (Ill.) 112, Louisville 100, Lawrence (Kan.) 111, Columbia (Mo.) 111, Newkirk (Okla.) 105, Topeka (Kan.) 109, Emporia 115.

Oklahoma's parched surface faced a new menace—forest fires, eighteen of which were reported licking up the valuable pasturage—and the State relief administration asked $500,000 immediately to fight conditions, "the worst on record."

Although its cattle purchase ma-

Continued on Page Eleven.

Will Not Tell of 'Hanging,' Reporters Go Back to Jail

By The Associated Press.

DANVILLE, Ky., July 25.—Jack Durham and Wesley Carty, newspaper men who have refused to tell the police court about their advance information on a hanging in effigy, went back to jail late today to serve another six hours. Judge J. W. Harlan ordered them to appear in court again tomorrow.

At the close of today's hearing, after Durham and Carty repeated their refusal to disclose their information on the ground that it was given them in confidence, Judge Harlan said:

"Well, boys, if this is going to be an endurance contest, I can stand it. You understand that this is a challenge to the court."

Yesterday Durham and Carty served a jail sentence of three hours. Monday they were fined $10.

BUS CRASH WITNESS RECEIVES A THREAT

Another Tells Court 'the Boss' Ordered Him to Say Falsely He Overhauled Coach.

3 ARE HELD AS WITNESSES

De Marco, of Rialto Company, Before Grand Jury—New Jersey Pushes New Laws.

Three men were held as material witnesses and Westchester County authorities were told of a threat to one witness and an order to another to commit perjury as the grand jury opened at White Plains yesterday its investigation of the Ossining bus disaster.

Indictments for manslaughter, predicted by the District Attorney's office the day before, did not materialize, and the grand jury heard only one witness before adjourning until next Wednesday. But District Attorney Frank H. Coyne and his aides received evidence, they said, that caused them to characterize many of the companies identified with the Rialto Bus Corporation as "phony, paper corporations with dummy directors."

Jersey Prepares Laws.

Before the end of the day the effects of the investigation had spread far beyond the county in which the accident that cost the lives of nineteen persons occurred.

Aroused by the tragedy and the resultant indications of faulty brakes, inadequate equipment, and lack of legislation to authorize inspection and supervision of sightseeing and chartered buses, New Jersey authorities followed the lead of New York State and prepared to provide remedial laws.

At Albany a resolution authorizing legislative investigation of the bus accident was introduced, and in New York and neighboring States local authorities of various towns and cities were taking the responsibility for inspection and supervision into their own hands.

There were suggestions that bus transportation systems be investigated with a view to more adequate control, and that the Federal Government investigate the tax returns of some companies.

Bus Official Testifies.

The single witness before the White Plains grand jury yesterday was Nicola De Marco, ostensible manager of the Rialto garage at 434 East 105th Street, where the buses that took the Young Men's Democratic League of the Twentieth Assembly District, Brooklyn, on the fatal trip to Ossining were stored. De Marco, who appeared jaunty, had been described by Max E. Greenberg, attorney for the Rialto concerns, as one of those

Continued on Page Twelve.

KENNEDY PLEDGES SECURITIES ACT AID TO BUILD BUSINESS

Chairman Says Commission Will Encourage Legitimate Stock Market Operations.

PROMISES NEW STANDARDS

Speaking at Luncheon, He Assures Capital and Investors Alike of Proper Profit.

The text of Chairman Kennedy's speech is on Page 13.

Special to The New York Times.

WASHINGTON, July 25.—Joseph P. Kennedy spoke words of reassurance today to both capital and investors in connection with the new Securities Act. As chairman of the Securities and Exchange Commission he delivered his first speech since assuming office when he appeared at a luncheon of the National Press Club.

He told business generally that there would be no vindictiveness in the enforcement of the stock market law, but rather an effort to develop the financial market.

If business does the "right thing" it will be protected and have a chance to live and prosper, Mr. Kennedy said in assuring governmental protection of all interests.

The commission's job, although essentially a technical one, would be done, said Mr. Kennedy, "in a businesslike way without political publicity of any sort." Public scrutiny of the commission's activities would never be discouraged or avoided, he declared.

"In our hands has been placed the responsibility of giving all the aid of which government is capable to the better organization of the mechanism through which the savings of the people find their way into securities," Mr. Kennedy said.

Some Old Practices Past.

"Everybody says that what business needs is confidence. I agree. Confidence that if business does the right thing it will be protected and given a chance to live, make profits and grow, helping itself and helping the country. But the old things business did, the old practices it followed, are, some of them, no longer the right ones."

The commission did not view business with suspicion, nor was there any intention by any member of it that business must be "harassed and annoyed and pushed around," he said.

"Domestic tranquillity is as essential to business as it is to our political system, and it was stated as one of the primary objects to be achieved through the Constitution," Mr. Kennedy went on. "We of the Securities and Exchange Commission do not regard ourselves as coroners sitting on the corpse of financial enterprise. On the contrary, we think of ourselves as the means of bringing new life into the body of the security business.

"We are not working on the theory that all the men and all the women connected with finance, either as workers or investors, are to be regarded as guilty of some undefined crime. On the contrary, we hold that business based on good-will should be encouraged so that it may be helpful."

It would be an "idle thing" to deny that business confidence was lacking in the United States, Mr. Kennedy said, and this was especially true in the case of securities. In times of change capital was notoriously timid, but there was nothing unusual in this; it was caution born of experience.

Mr. Kennedy made plain that the commission was not proceeding as a prosecutor hopeful of bringing

Continued on Page Thirteen.

French Forest Fires Menace Thousands; Whole Mediterranean Fleet Standing By

By The Associated Press.

TOULON, France, July 25.—The entire French fleet in the Mediterranean was ordered to be prepared to speed to Toulon today to evacuate thousands of persons menaced by forest fires in the region of Bormes and Lavadou.

Several thousand persons were reported to have been trapped by a serious fire, and high winds were whipping up the flames.

Orders for the fleet to stand by were radioed by Admiral DuBois after the commandant of the marines fighting the flames had reported that roads were blocked and that the fire was surrounding villages, cutting off escape.

The village of Bormes, to which inhabitants returned after having left it last night, was again evacuated.

Officials said that about 25,000 acres of pine trees have been destroyed.

ATHENS, July 25 (AP).—Six persons died of heat here today as the temperature rose as high as 115 degrees. Many forest fires were burning throughout Greece.

WARSAW, July 25 (AP).—The area around Sandomierz, where the surging Vistula River has spread itself into an enormous lake, was the outstanding danger spot today in Poland's flood-devastated scene.

Ten thousand persons already have been evacuated from the section, and as many more are expected to be ordered to move by military patrols. The evacuation everywhere was orderly.

Although it rained persistently last night, there were reassuring reports from the central section of the Vistula today.

Germany Recalls Envoy For Actions in Vienna

Special Cable to The New York Times.

BERLIN, Thursday, July 26.—The German Government at 2 o'clock this morning announced the recall of Dr. Kurt Rieth, German Minister to Austria, and Germany's intention of arresting the assassins of Chancellor Dollfuss, on behalf of whom Dr. Rieth intervened, should they reach German territory. The announcement reads:

"At the request of Austrian governmental authorities and Austrian rebels, respectively, German Minister to Vienna Rieth consented, without asking the German Government itself, to an agreement concluded between the two relative to the safe passage of the rebels to Germany. He was thereupon immediately recalled from his post."

The second official announcement said that the agreement reached between the Austrian rebels and the Austrian Government for safe passage of the rebels did not concern the German Reich and implied no legal obligations for the German Government.

BERLIN DECLARES HANDS-OFF POLICY

Asserts Austrian Revolt Is a Purely Internal Affair and No Concern of Reich.

PARIS AND LONDON GRAVE

Insist Vienna's Independence Must Be Preserved—British Fear Crisis Like 1914.

By FREDERICK T. BIRCHALL.

Wireless to The New York Times.

BERLIN, July 25.—Throughout the day there has been the keenest interest as to what was happening in Vienna. And information to the public has been correspondingly meager and inaccurate and dictated by the National Socialist interest.

Telephone communications during this afternoon were fragmentary and liable to interruption, both from the Austrian and from the German end. Tonight, when this was being written, it is cut off altogether. Since Paris, Rome and London report a similar condition, the interruption probably is from the Austrian end.

The last reliable communication between Berlin and Vienna was between two Americans at about 5 o'clock. The Vienna informant was then able to assure his Berlin questioner that the Dollfuss party had regained full control and that the Chancellor "had withdrawn several promises extorted from him under duress."

Version Reaching Berlin.

At the Austrian Legation it was stated that some 300 Nazis had seized the official radio station earlier in the day, had announced that the Chancellor had resigned and had issued other falsehoods; that the police had since captured them and that the Austrian Minister of Justice had issued an explanation.

At 6 o'clock communication had ceased, and the legation professed not to know whether any Nazis had entered the Chancellery. It was stated, however, that a military cordon had been established around it and that the revolt had failed.

However, every time the press attaché at the legation told an inquirer over the telephone that it was Austrian Nazis that had invaded the radio station, the connection with the legation was immediately broken. Eventually he abandoned all attempt at plain speech and simply said that the disturbers "belonged to the party that one would expect."

Safe Conduct Demanded.

It was understood here tonight that the assassins of Chancellor Dollfuss, wherever they came from, demanded safe conduct to Germany after their crime and further demanded and obtained intervention by the German Ambassador to insure it.

The official German reaction is that this is purely an Austrian internal situation with which Germany has nothing to do and off which she is keeping her hands. It is said that she has kept the Austrian emigrés scattered; that she has moved or called the Aus-

Continued on Page Three.

INTERVENTION IS HINTED

Rome Reports Appeal to Powers by Austria to Guard Independence.

75,000 TROOPS AT BORDER

Italian Forces Whip Equipment Into Order and War Fleet Is Steaming Northward.

VIENNA CONFERENCE TODAY

Representative of Italy, France, Britain and the Little Entente Expected to Act.

By The Associated Press.

ROME, July 25.—A statement emanating from official sources tonight said the Austrian Government had requested intervention by European powers to guarantee Austria's integrity.

The statement, which was given to the government-controlled press, was published soon after it was announced that Premier Mussolini had issued wartime military orders to army, navy and air forces to the north of Padua.

The inspired press reported that the diplomatic representatives of Italy, France, Britain and the Little Entente countries would hold an urgent conference at Vienna tomorrow to determine what action should be taken. The conference also will decide which of the powers should intervene in case armed assistance is determined upon.

Italian troops are prepared to march into Austria on short notice.

Fulvio Suvich, Under-Secretary of Foreign Affairs, was remaining at the Foreign Office throughout the night to keep in touch with the Austrian situation and to confer with Premier Mussolini by telephone. The Premier at the same time was keeping a vigil at Riccione.

No effort was made to disguise the fact that the Austrian question is viewed here in a very grave light.

Responsibility of Italy.

"Italy is in the first line of defense for the peace of Europe," said an authoritative editorial in the newspaper Il Popolo di Roma. "It is difficult, if not impossible, to deny that Germany has had grave responsibility in that which has occurred in Austria.

"For months the radio at Munich has issued insult and calumny against Dollfuss and his government. All the efforts of the powers to obtain an end to this campaign, which is against all the principles of international politics, were wrecked by the ill will of German leaders."

The army and air force at Padua was commanded by the Premier to be in instant readiness to move across the Austrian frontier. Leaves were canceled, and each unit was told to keep itself in full strength with all of its mechanical war devices in order. The order applied to 75,000 men from Padua north.

At the same time, an official communiqué was issued stating that the First Naval Squadron had left Fort Ancona.

The communiqué did not give the destination of the squadron, but naval circles said that it is moving into the Northern Adriatic, particularly Port Trieste, to keep in touch with Austrian developments.

Situation Is Held Grave.

By ARNALDO CORTESI.

Wireless to The New York Times.

ROME, July 25.—The Austrian Nazi outburst caused profound consternation in Italy today, but no particular surprise, as it had been felt for several days that things were rapidly approaching a crisis there as a result of the government's energetic repressive measures.

The impression tonight is that Italy probably is ready to go to any lengths, including military occupation, to prevent Nazi control of Austria. If the development of events justifies such a course, Italy will propose the occupation of Austria by international forces until such time as it is considered safe to leave her to work out her own salvation. If other powers, however, are unwilling to act, Italy is ready to go ahead on her own initiative.

There is reason to believe that preparations for such an eventuality have already been made. In-

Continued on Page Two.

KILLED IN VIENNA REVOLT.

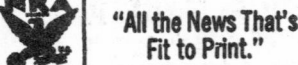

Times Wide World Photo.

Chancellor Engelbert Dollfuss.

Eight Nazis Hold Off 1,000 Men For Hours at Vienna Radio Plant

Correspondent of The New York Times Witnesses Battle From Restaurant Table—Machine Guns and Bombs of Police and Heimwehr Force Their Surrender.

By G. E. R. GEDYE.

Wireless to The New York Times.

BRATISLAVA, Czechoslovakia, July 25.—I had to cross the Austrian frontier, because the Austrian authorities severed all telegraphic and telephonic communication and are severely censoring telegrams. I can tell the astounding story of how fewer than 200 Nazis held the Austrian Cabinet prisoners all day long in the Chancellor's office.

Chancellor Dollfuss was shot dead by the Nazi revolutionaries because he drew a revolver on being arrested by the Nazis.

Life in Vienna went on normally all day, except for the desperate battle, at which I was present.

The battle raged at the offices of Ravag, the Austrian radio broadcasting company. I left this battle in its earlier stages at 1:30 P. M. to follow an armored car which drove to the Chancellor's offices, where trucks were lining up with machine guns.

No more than any one else could I suspect that what seemed to be merely a precautionary measure was in reality an attempt to rescue members of the Austrian Government who were being held prisoners, facing the rifle and pistol muzzles of the desperadoes within the Chancellery.

Until late in the afternoon no one had an inkling that the Chancellor and nearly all his Cabinet, together with the huge staff of civil servants, were being held prisoners. Most of the civil servants were driven into the courtyard and kept there under guard.

Dollfuss Shot in Head.

After their release I spoke tonight with Dr. Schmitt, one of the officials of the Chancellor's Department. He seemed on the point of collapse.

"I was held prisoner all day," he said, "and, like the others, know nothing. Chancellor Dollfuss is dead. I saw wounds on his neck and on his head. He died at 5 P. M. We believe that he was shot shortly after 12 o'clock when the Nazis broke into his room. It was a terrible blow."

At 9 P. M. the Chancellor's office was finally evacuated by the rebels under a guarantee of safe conduct to the German frontier. The telephone service began to function normally again.

I learned that ten men in military uniforms confronted the Chancellor at 12:30, and when he drew a revolver they shot him down.

The first intimation I had that there was anything unusual in Vienna was when I was passing through Johannesgasse shortly before 1 o'clock, when four or five revolver shots were fired. Several policemen took cover at the side of a house and occasionally fired shots at the Ravag building. They did not seem to know what was really afoot. Within a few minutes motor trucks filled with policemen with rifles, with fixed bayonets and with steel helmets began to pour into one end of Johannesgasse. In a few minutes the cracking of rifle fire was added to the popping of revolvers. The astounded passersby had no idea of what was in progress.

Woman Tells of Raid.

A woman, white and trembling, was allowed to come through the police cordon into the street where the firing was now general.

"I saw everything that happened from our house opposite Ravag," she told me. "A group of eight young men tried to enter Ravag about half an hour ago. When the policeman at the door challenged them they shot him dead.

"Inside the building they were resisted by one of the directors, a man named Holt. They shot him dead, also, and on entering the studio they placed their revolvers at the head of the announcer and forced him to broadcast a statement that the Dollfuss Cabinet had fallen. Dr. Rintelen, they stated, had become Chancellor and was forming a new Cabinet.

"Then a police alarm was given and the shooting started."

I was informed by the police that it was correct that only eight Nazi youths had carried out this coup and subsequently had repelled for nearly three hours the biggest force the Vienna police could bring to bear on them in the narrow street. With their revolvers they defended themselves against a heavy attack with machine guns.

As I watched the fighting, truck after truck loaded with police and Heimwehr men rolled up until there must have been 1,000 men taking part in the attack, which was pressed with tremendous vigor.

The police were in an ugly temper. One of them marched up to the Terrace Restaurant, where I had ordered a meal as an excuse to remain on the scene after the street had been cleared, and drove me with his clubbed rifle into the restaurant.

Machine guns were now taken

Continued on Page Two.

ALL OF REBELS PRISONERS

Passage to Germany, Arranged by German Minister, Revoked.

MOB TRIES TO LYNCH THEM

Their 'Chancellor' Is Also Held, While Kurt Schuschnigg Succeeds Dollfuss.

VIENNA IS QUIET AGAIN

But Armed Guards Patrol the Streets—Reports of Fighting in Styria, Nazi Stronghold.

Wireless to The New York Times.

VIENNA, Thursday, July 26.—Calm and quiet settled over Vienna this morning. There was no external evidence of the sensational attack on the Federal Chancellery yesterday by 147 Austrian Nazis who killed Chancellor Engelbert Dollfuss and seized members of the Austrian Cabinet as hostages.

The fate of the rebels seemed to be decided. Though they obtained a pledge of safe conduct into Germany before they released the Cabinet members the Austrian Government early this morning issued a communique saying this had been revoked.

The safe conduct, it was pointed out, had been granted with the consent of President Miklas, after a consultation with representatives of great powers in Vienna, on condition that nobody was killed in the building, but as Chancellor Dollfuss had died following the rebel attack the Nazis will be tried according to Austrian law.

Rebels Under Strong Guard.

The rebels are prisoners in Marokkaner Barracks in Vienna, strongly guarded. Their leader is a man named Holsweber, a former army sergeant. In addition to the barracks guard, policemen, armed with rifles, still patroled the streets and trucks rumbled along the boulevards bringing in more troops.

[A dispatch from Vienna in a late edition of The London Mail said that Heimwehr troops and civilians had sought during the night to lynch the assassins of Chancellor Dollfuss, The Associated Press reported. The dispatch said police, heavily armed, had repulsed all attempts to get at the prisoners by threatening to fire into the approaching crowd.]

Dr. Anton Rintelen, the rebels' candidate for the Chancellorship, has been arrested and is now in military custody in the Building of the Ministry of War.

Reports of alleged Italian military movements along the Austrian border are believed here to be greatly exaggerated. Only those measures were taken which had been prepared automatically in the event of Austrian internal disorder. It is understood that Italian Army airplanes are held ready for flight over Austria in case of emergency.

It was believed in political circles here today that Ministers of the Great Powers will call on Acting Chancellor Kurt Schuschnigg to ask his plans and that he will accept the office of Chancellor.

Cabinet Holds Rebels.

Copyright, 1934, By The Associated Press.

VIENNA, July 25.—A group of Austrian Nazis today seized the federal Chancellery, killed their bitter enemy, Chancellor Engelbert Dollfuss, and held the government building until they received a guarantee of safe conduct to Germany, a guarantee which was revoked when it was discovered that Dr. Dollfuss was dead.

The Nazis were placed in Marokkaner Barracks, stripped of their uniforms and were ordered held after a Cabinet meeting under the leadership of the new Chancellor, Dr. Kurt Schuschnigg, Minister of Education.

An official communiqué stated that the fact that Dr. Dollfuss was killed canceled the promise of safe conduct, in return for which the

Continued on Page Two.

NRA WE DO OUR PART

"All the News That's Fit to Print."

The New York Times.

Copyright, 1934, by The New York Times Company.

5:30 A. M. EXTRA

WEATHER—Cloudy, warmer today; local showers tomorrow.
Temperatures Yesterday—Max., 81; Min., 67

VOL. LXXXIII....No. 27,949. Entered as Second-Class Matter, Postoffice, New York, N. Y. NEW YORK, THURSDAY, AUGUST 2, 1934. P TWO CENTS In New York City. | THREE CENTS Within 200 Miles | FOUR CENTS Elsewhere Except in 7th and 8th Postal Zones

VON HINDENBURG DIES AT 86 AFTER A DAY UNCONSCIOUS; HITLER TAKES PRESIDENCY

Times Wide World Photos.

PRESIDENT PAUL von HINDENBURG

END COMES AT 9 A. M.

Reich President Dies at His Home in East Prussia.

MADE A VALIANT FIGHT

Disappearance of House Flag at Neudeck Announces News to World.

THERE HAD BEEN NO HOPE

He Lapsed Into Coma After Hitler Reached Bedside for Last Meeting.

By The Associated Press.

NEUDECK, Germany, Thursday, Aug. 2.—President von Hindenburg died at 9 A. M. today.

The President's death was indicated to correspondents by the disappearance of the house flag from the flagstaff.

Death came to the 86-year-old leader of the German people and former war marshal after a valiant fight against a complication of ailments.

Chancellor Hitler has assumed the Presidency.

Unconscious For Hours.

By GUIDO ENDERIS.

Wireless to THE NEW YORK TIMES.

BERLIN, Thursday, Aug. 2.—A physician's bulletin at 6 o'clock this morning stated that President Paul von Hindenburg remained in the state of unconsciousness into which he lapsed last evening. His death was believed to be a matter only of hours.

The President had consistently lost strength since early morning. All hope that his once rugged constitution would carry him along for a time was definitely dissipated by bedside bulletins that reached Berlin from Neudeck during the day.

At midnight the Propaganda Ministry announced that no further bulletin would be forthcoming during the night. This secretiveness served only to heighten the mystery surrounding Chancellor Hitler's convocation of his Cabinet.

Neither foreign correspondents in Berlin nor those besieging the President's estate at Neudeck had been able to break the news embargo which hedged the Field Marshal's deathbed. Only what seeped through official quarters was placed at the disposal of the German and foreign press.

Hitler Advances Time of Visit.

Chancellor Hitler advanced the time of his flight to Neudeck by more than an hour yesterday morning because of an urgent summons from Professor Ferdinand Sauerbruck, the President's chief physician. It was reported Dr. Sauerbruck notified Herr Hitler that the patient was rapidly sinking.

The last meeting between the President and the man whom he elevated to the Chancellorship after rebuffs which have now become historic, received only brief mention in the day's official bulletins. Herr Hitler found the President momentarily conscious and assured him of the prayerful thoughts of the saddened nation. The President shook the Chancellor's hand and thanked him cordially for his visit; then he dropped into a fresh sleep.

Herr Hitler flew back to Berlin late in the afternoon. Among those who accompanied him to Neudeck was Ernst F. S. Hanfstaengl, chief of his Anglo-American publicity department, but only Herr Hitler was admitted to the sick chamber.

Hope that the President would linger on vanished early last evening when Dr. Sauerbruck, on behalf of the attending physicians, announced that the patient was lapsing into unconsciousness and that his heart action was fast failing. A bulletin issued at 2:30 P. M. stated that the President was then steadily losing ground, despite a restful night. He was conscious most of the forenoon and was able to converse with those around him during part of the afternoon.

Up to two months ago President von Hindenburg's rugged frame and his soldierly bearing gave no evidence of physical decline. The collapse began to set in a month ago when it was discovered the atrophied prostate gland precluded recourse to a major operation be-

Continued on Page B [Preceding Page 4].

HITLER CONSULTS CABINET IN SECRET

Ministry Meets Two Hours in Emergency Session—Von Papen in Attendance.

NEW ELECTION POSSIBLE

Friend Says Chancellor Intends to Occupy the Presidency—Army an Unknown Factor.

Wireless to THE NEW YORK TIMES.

BERLIN, Aug. 1.—Chancellor Hitler convoked the German Cabinet for an emergency session at 9:30 o'clock tonight.

The Ministers, among them Vice Chancellor Franz von Papen, had been hastily summoned. They remained with the Chancellor about two hours.

Beyond a more-than-laconic bulletin announcing that the Cabinet had been called, nothing was divulged. There was no indication as to the purpose of the session, and this quickly gave rise to rumors that President von Hindenburg had already died, but that the announcement was being withheld until tomorrow.

The reading public has received only official communiqués concerning the Reich President. The controlled press appears to have been instructed to abstain from any speculative comment on the implications involved in a vacancy in the Presidency.

Hitler Is Seen Taking Power.

Copyright, 1934, by The Associated Press.

BERLIN, Aug. 1.—Adolf Hitler intends to be both President and Chancellor of Germany, one of his close friends told The Associated Press today.

This would give to Herr Hitler a dictatorship as absolute as any in the world.

Despair gripped many Conservatives who had looked upon President von Hindenburg as an anchor against extreme Nazism.

Herr Hitler's plan, The Associated Press informant said, is to call the Cabinet together to read a brief law assigning the dual power to himself.

"The whole thing will take but a few minutes," he said, "for the Cabinet will, of course, endorse the proposal. It will simplify the Führer's [Hitler's] whole work immensely if he need not first ask somebody whether he may do this or that."

An indication of the reliability of this source is that Sunday he revealed the President's turn for the worse and was the first to tip off the fact that Herr Hitler was going to Venice to meet Premier Mussolini.

Under the German Constitution Dr. Erwin Bumke, President of the Supreme Court, would become Act-

Continued on Page Two.

SOCIALIST SUPPORT SOUGHT BY AUSTRIA

Neutrality of the Party in Fight With Nazis to Be Rewarded by Release of Leaders.

FOE HANGED IN INNSBRUCK

Minor Rebels to Be Held and Put at Hard Labor—Officials Linked to Putsch.

By G. E. R. GEDYE.

Wireless to THE NEW YORK TIMES.

VIENNA, Aug. 1.—There are signs that the Austrian Government is preparing for radical changes in policy and is contemplating steps calculated to obtain from the Social Democrats assurance of at least neutrality toward the government's fight to the finish with the Nazis.

For eighteen months the Nazis have carried on terroristic activities in Austria, involving a considerable loss of life and enormous property damage. But until yesterday the death penalty had been reserved exclusively for Socialists.

Even the stern ordinance directed against Nazi terrorists, which Chancellor Dollfuss introduced fourteen days before he was slain, proclaiming death as the only admissible penalty for those possessing explosives, had a Socialist for its first victim. He was hanged the night before Dr. Dollfuss was assassinated.

Three Nazis Now Hanged.

Yesterday, however, two Nazis at last were hanged. Today another Nazi was hanged in Innsbruck, Friedrich Wurnig who shot and killed Police Commandant Franz Hickel of Innsbruck on the day of the Dollfuss slaying.

Still more important from the viewpoint of the government, having been committed to a final struggle, is the fact that it has arrested men like Dr. Anton Apold, director of the Alpine Mining Company, and General Karl Bardolf, former adjutant to Archduke Franz Ferdinand, who were always behind the scenes in negotiations between Germany and Austria. Governor Kernmaier of Carinthia, another prominent protector of Nazis, also has been arrested.

The first move to conciliate the Socialists will be the release of prominent leaders who have been imprisoned without trial since February. It is likely they will be free in a day or so. The leaders to be released are Burgomaster Karl Seitz, head of the party, and Herr Danneberg, Herr Helmer, Frau Proft and Frau Postranetzky, members of the central executive committee of the party, and more officers of the Republican Defense Corps, General Koerner, Major Eiffler and Captain Loew.

Whether such release will have

Continued on Page Three.

TWO REFORM BILLS ARE SIDETRACKED; LEHMAN FIGHTS ON

Quorum Lacking for Report on County Plans as Republicans Walk Out of Committee.

BATTLE ON FLOOR IS DUE

Governor, Assailing 'Despicable' Action, Is Expected to Spur Democrats in Assembly.

SMITH TARGET IN SESSION

Republicans Deny Entering Agreement—Say He Is Trying to 'Bedevil' Situation.

By W. A. WARN.

Special to THE NEW YORK TIMES.

ALBANY, Aug. 1.—The Assembly Judiciary Committee met this afternoon and voted to report eleven minor bills, but failed to take any action on the proposed constitutional amendments, sponsored by Senator Dunnigan and Senator Mastick, to prepare the way for county government reforms.

The Republican majority in the Assembly contrived to block these yesterday after their adoption in the Senate, sending them back to committee.

Governor Lehman pronounced as "despicable" the failure of the committee to act on the measures, the adoption of which he and ex-Governor Smith, as head of the New York City Charter Revision Commission, have so much at heart.

The Governor said he was firmly backing the position taken by Mr. Smith in a telegram transmitted on behalf of the entire Charter Commission to Speaker McGinnies yesterday protesting against the action of the Republican majority in "repudiating" its agreement to pass the County Reform Bills.

Governor Is Silent on Plans.

Governor Lehman has not indicated what further steps he may be contemplating to force favorable action on the two side-tracked measures.

They have both been adopted by the Senate, together with another proposed amendment to the Constitution, in which both the Mastick and Dunnigan proposals are joined and which the Assembly yesterday concurred in by unanimous vote.

While the Judiciary Committee, like the Assembly itself, has a Republican majority, it has become apparent through developments of the last few days that the Democrats in the Legislature are no more eager to pass these constitutional amendments than are a majority of the Republicans.

While engaging on the floor of the Assembly today in an apparent effort to make political capital out of the Republican blockade established yesterday against the Dunnigan and Mastick measures, the Democrats did not bestir themselves to rescue the amendments.

Chance for Steingut to Act.

Assemblyman Steingut, minority leader, has not filed the necessary three days' notice of a motion to take the two resolutions from the Judiciary Committee, possibly on the assumption that the committee had not had an opportunity to act when the Assembly met today.

Now that the committee has met and failed to act the way is open for Mr. Steingut to proceed, but unless action is taken by the Assembly before the end of the week the adoption of the two resolutions would be to no purpose.

Under the Election Law, Monday is the deadline for publication of notice that the amendments are to be submitted to the 1935 Legislature for concurrent action.

Governor Lehman was aroused when he learned of developments at the committee meeting.

"The action in refusing to report or act on the bills is despicable," he said. "I am back of the position taken by Governor Smith 100 per cent.

"Until I learned of the action of the Judiciary Committee in refusing to report the bills, I was convinced that in accordance with the agreement reported by former Governor Smith, the bills would be reported out and passed.

"There is still time to pass these bills, and they should be passed. I am amazed that any condition like this could exist."

Lehman Action Is Expected.

Hence, with the Governor so stirred by the situation, observers at the capital believe he will move to compel more vigorous intervention by the Assembly Democrats to save the measures.

Most of the Democrats, and Republicans also, have already quit their legislative labors for the week and returned to their homes or gone to the Saratoga races or elsewhere. In order to get anything

Continued on Page Four.

Giant Seaplane Tops All Records; Lindbergh Hails Test of Clipper

Sikorsky Machine, Under Transport Conditions With a Full Load, Averages 157.5 Miles an Hour Over a 1,242-Mile Course —Range Would Cover Ocean Trade Routes.

By REGINALD M. CLEVELAND.

Special to THE NEW YORK TIMES.

BRIDGEPORT, Conn., Aug. 1.—All existing world's records for transport seaplane flight (previously held abroad) were toppled like ninepins here today as the giant Sikorsky S-42, the Brazilian Clipper, carrying a full transport load and with Colonel Lindbergh in charge for Pan American Airways, flew 1,242.8 miles at an average speed of 157.5 miles an hour. Eight long-standing and recent world marks were shattered by impressive margins. The two other official ones had already been won by the plane in previous test flights.

As Edwin C. Musick, chief pilot of the airlines, sent the four-engined flying boat four times over a course of 311 miles which included Manhattan's river front, Long Island Sound and the Atlantic Ocean, it was evident that history was being written for American aviation.

Starting at the Stratford Lighthouse, the course ran through five control points, George Washington Bridge, Staten Island Lighthouse, Fire Island Lighthouse, Block Island, Point Judith Lighthouse and back to the place of beginning.

The elapsed time for the flight was 7 hours, 53 minutes, 58 seconds, for a distance equal to that from Newfoundland to the Azores. Yet Pilot Musick used only 69 per cent of the 3,000 horsepower of the four Pratt & Whitney Hornet engines streamlined into the wide silver wing. He had fuel enough for another lap when he landed. The margin of range, with a mail load, for any of the ocean trade routes, Atlantic or Pacific, by way of the islands, had been amply proved.

Cruising speed only was used and less than full horsepower because the flight was an acceptance test for the airline of this craft, which will cut two days' time from the run between Miami and Buenos Aires and put that South American capital within five and one-half days of New York.

Strictly transport conditions prevailed during the flight.

When the plane crossed the starting line against the blue of a morning sky at 9:24:38, Eastern daylight time, she had only six persons aboard. They were Colonel Lindbergh, as official representative of Pan American Airways' technical

Continued on Page Seven.

SMITH ACTS TO QUIT IN CHARTER DISPUTE

Reported Ready to Resign if Board Does Not Agree to Reconsider City Rule Vote.

LETTER ALREADY DRAFTED

Seabury Said to Be Weighing Similar Action—Crucial Meeting Tonight.

Alfred E. Smith will resign from the New York City Charter Revision Commission unless the commission at tonight's meeting changes its decision to retain the city legislature in substantially its present form, according to reports last night in Albany from a source close to the former Governor.

Mr. Smith was said to have long been disgusted with the opposition to thoroughgoing reform of the city charter among members of the commission. According to the report from Albany, Mr. Smith was quoted as saying in private conversation that he was "sick and tired of the bickering and opposition in the commission" and that he "would like a vacation."

The fact that the former Governor has for some time been considering resignation or taking some other drastic action to bring sharply to public attention the failure of the commission to make real progress was confirmed by persons in the city close to Mr. Smith.

Letter Already Drafted.

It was felt that Mr. Smith might be led to resign at tonight's meeting if the commission voted to restore to the Borough Presidents their administrative and patronage powers, as some members of the commission fear will be done. According to a report by The Associated Press, Mr. Smith has already drafted his letter of resignation.

Samuel Seabury, vice chairman of the commission, declined last night to deny or to comment on a report that he also intended to resign. Earlier in the day Mr. Seabury had stated that he would make no comment until after the outcome of tonight's meeting on what he plans to do in case the opposition on the commission succeeds in restoring borough government.

These reports came as fear was expressed by members of the commission and civic organizations favoring drastic charter revision that a successful drive would be made at tonight's meeting to restore to the Borough Presidents their present administrative and patronage powers. Such a result, it was said, would largely nullify all the progress made by the commission. Both Mr. Smith and Mr. Seabury have fought for stripping Borough Presidents of their powers and for a single chamber legislature.

Confusion existed yesterday among members of the commission, as well as among civic organizations, over the effect of the action taken Tuesday night by the commission to retain the Board of Estimate and to revamp the Board of Aldermen into a smaller but much stronger Council.

Many condemned it as merely retaining the present form of city legislature, while others saw in it

Continued on Page Four.

BUSINESS TAX YIELD IS UNDER $3,000,000

$2,092,681 Total, With Mail Returns Still Due, Far Short of $8,000,000 Expected.

BUDGET NOW UNBALANCED

Mayor Denies City Plans to Restore Half of Pay Cut—Chides Levy on Figures.

The city's hope of realizing $8,000,000 from its new business tax received a severe blow last night when Controller Joseph D. McGoldrick announced that the total collected up to 6 P. M. on the final day for payment was only $2,092,681.47.

It was pointed out, however, that a last-minute ruling permitting payment of taxes by mail without penalty, provided the letters containing tax checks or money orders were postmarked before midnight, would probably bring in additional payments today.

Nevertheless it was predicted that the total return, even with the last-minute checks, could not possibly come to much more than $3,000,000—only three-eighths of the sum the city had hoped to garner from the new tax.

McGoldrick Withholds Comment.

Mr. McGoldrick withheld comment on the tax payments pending the final compilation today. It was indicated, however, that he was convinced that the total returns would be materially less than the sum expected when the tax was imposed.

Failure of the revenues from the business tax to come up to expectations will have the effect of unbalancing the city budget, it was said. The budget was balanced after the passage of the City Economy Bill by salary reductions and furloughs and by imposition of new taxes, of which the business tax was one.

A total of $1,094,800.27 was received yesterday in payment of the tax in the City Collector's office in the five boroughs. During the day 16,748 returns were filed.

Several times recently administration spokesmen have expressed the fear that the business tax revenue would be materially below the original estimates. None, however, believed that the revenue would be as small as last night's figures indicated it would be.

In view of the fact that failure to pay the tax on time brings with it a 10 per cent penalty plus payment of 5 per cent interest a month on the whole tax sum due, it was felt in the Finance Department that few concerns would withhold their payments. It was not disclosed how many payments were made under protest and threat of court action to test the constitutionality of the tax measure.

Cut in Reserve Is Hailed.

The revision of the bankers' agreement to provide reduction in the tax delinquency reserve fund in the budgets of 1935, 1936 and 1937 from the original $50,000,000 to $25,000,000 was praised yesterday by Peter Grimm, chairman of the Citizens Budget Commission. Mr. Grimm telegraphed Controller McGoldrick and Governor Lehman, who were mainly responsible for

Continued on Page Nine.

NEW ORLEANS TENSE AS POLICE AWAIT A MOVE BY TROOPS

300 More Patrolmen Sworn In as the Militia Removes Machine Guns From View.

GUARD FORCE IS REDUCED

Gov. Allen Orders Guardsmen to Investigate Alleged Gambling and Vice Graft.

Special to THE NEW YORK TIMES.

NEW ORLEANS, Aug. 1.—New Orleans anxiously watched the growing tension tonight as armed State and city forces faced each other in a political crisis precipitated by the tactics of Senator Huey Long.

George Reyer, Superintendent of Police, completed tonight the swearing in of 500 supernumerary policemen for emergency use. The machine guns manned by National Guardsmen, which have been protruding from the windows of the registration office, were removed.

The 500 emergency policemen, called for service by order of Mayor Walmsley, were armed with automatic shotguns and pistols. They were divided into two platoons, 300 on the day shift and 200 on night duty.

Of the former, 200 will be held at police headquarters, and 100 stationed at the City Hall and the First Precinct station. All of the men on night duty are stationed at police headquarters, with police automobiles and patrol wagons held in readiness to transport them wherever they might be needed.

Policemen now ready for duty number 1,300. All regular members of the department have been instructed to be ready for duty at all times, day or night.

Explains Machine Guns.

The appearance of machine guns in the registration office was explained by Adjt. Gen. Fleming at a conference with Mayor Walmsley this afternoon.

"The members of the artillery unit guarding the registration office," Adjutant General Fleming said, "were relieved Tuesday night by members of the machine gun unit. The machine gun unit always carries its machine guns along wherever it is sent."

He denied the machine guns were intended for intimidation.

Mayor Walmsley and the Finance Commissioner, A. Miles Pratt, in statements issued today, denied there was any intention on the part of the city government to seize any records in the registration office.

The presidents of the chief organizations of business men met today and debated the situation. They adopted a resolution which censured no one and asked the world to understand that "the business of this city is being conducted along the usual, efficient lines with no interruptions whatsoever."

Three members of the new police commission created by the Long-controlled Legislature to take supervision of the police force out of the hands of the Mayor and Council filed their credentials. No attempt was made to call a meeting of the board.

Prosecution of the 500 odd men charged with miscounting ballots in the last election, being regarded as impossible under a law taking effect today, District Attorney Stanley nolle prossed the cases. The charges were brought after a

Continued on Page Fourteen.

Overnight Air Service To West Coast Starts

Starting overnight service between the nation's coasts on the "Lindbergh Line," a fourteen-passenger Douglas plane of the Transcontinental & Western Air Line took off from Newark Airport yesterday afternoon at 5:25 Eastern daylight time. It is due in Los Angeles at 7 this morning.

Elliott Roosevelt, second son of the President; Lieut. Commander Frank M. Hawks, noted speed pilot; two paying passengers, newspapermen and airline officials were aboard as passengers.

The plane also carried two copies of THE NEW YORK TIMES addressed respectively to Frank L. Shaw, Mayor of Los Angeles, and Harry Chandler, publisher of The Los Angeles Times.

20% CUT IN NAVIES URGED BY SWANSON

But Secretary, in Rejoinder to Tokyo Premier, Says 5-5-3 Ratio Should Continue.

OUR PLANE PROGRAM CUT

Navy Now Thinks Equipping of All Ships Will Require 274 Fewer Than 1st Estimate.

Special to THE NEW YORK TIMES.

WASHINGTON, Aug. 1.—A general reduction of 20 per cent in naval armaments by all the powers signatory to the London Naval Treaty was advocated today by Secretary Claude A. Swanson, but he insisted that the 5-5-3 ratio of naval strength fixed by the Washington Treaty of 1922 should stand intact. If agreed to by the powers, the 20 per cent reduction should be a real and not a "blue print" one, he declared.

Meanwhile, Admiral William H. Standley, chief of naval operations, made known that the navy had revised its estimates, but had reached no final decision on the number of planes necessary under the Vinson Naval Building Bill to outfit old and new ships in the next five years. High navy officials now figure that only 910 new planes would be needed, or 274 fewer than previously had been estimated. The navy now has 1,000 planes.

No comprehensive reason was given by naval officials for this reduced estimate, but it was partly explained by the fact that when the earlier estimates were made no decision had been reached to abandon the building of flying-deck cruisers.

Secretary Swanson's statement came as a rejoinder to yesterday's declaration by Premier Keisuke Okada that, while Japan did not expect to attain parity with the United States and Britain at the 1935 naval conference, she could not favor continuation of the present ratio system, which "hurts the self-respect of nations."

Asked to comment on the Japanese Premier's speech, Mr. Swanson said:

"I adhere to the same position I always have. The naval powers met in London and distributed to the naval powers the naval strength they thought was just and right. Naval strength is relative. Both naval and military armaments are relative.

"I represented the navy at the Geneva conference and we offered there the proposition to have any reductions up to 33 1-3 per cent in the different categories of ships,

Continued on Page Three.

Wagner and Prall Hurt in Auto Plunge; Senator Drives Into Brook to Avoid Crash

Special to THE NEW YORK TIMES.

WESTPORT, N. Y., Aug. 1.—Trapped on a curve of a narrow Adirondack highway, Senator Robert F. Wagner drove his automobile over a twenty-foot embankment into a mountain brook rather than have a collision with an oncoming car near here this morning. Senator Wagner and Representative Anning S. Prall, his only companion, were both seriously but not critically injured.

Senator Wagner suffered two fractured ribs on the right side, severe lacerations of the face and knees and numerous body bruises. He may also have concussion of the brain.

Representative Prall suffered a compound fracture of both bones of his lower right leg and lacerations of the hands and forehead.

Witnesses of the crash carried the injured men three miles to the offices of Dr. Harold J. Harris here, where both remained tonight. Dr. Harris said that both were resting comfortably and in no great pain, but that because of the severe shock he did not consider it advisable to move them to a hospital.

Dr. Harris said that he thought it might be best for Senator Wagner to remain in the recovery room in his offices for several days, but that Mr. Prall might be taken to a New York City hospital tomorrow. He said there was "no evidence of skull fractures or concussions, but we never are sure until after twenty-four hours."

The legislators were on their way north on a fishing expedition when the accident occurred. They were bound for the Seigneur Club at Lucerne, Que. Senator Wagner had only recently returned from Portland, Ore., where he attempted to adjust the marine workers' strike and was fired on by mistake.

The highway through the mountains between Wadhams and this village, which is on Lake Champlain, is narrow and winding. Senator Wagner attempted to pass a truck on a curve, only to find another truck approaching from the opposite direction.

Rather than hit either truck he turned his machine off the road. It tumbled down the embankment into the brook but did not overturn. Both occupants were thrown against the windshield and dashboard, but were conscious when they were extricated from the wreckage, and remained so while they were being brought to the office of Dr. Harris here.

"All the News That's Fit to Print."

The New York Times.

LATE CITY EDITION
WEATHER—Cloudy, rain or snow today; tomorrow rain.
Temperature Yesterday—Max., 49; Min., 36
Detailed Weather Report Page 42.

VOL. LXXXIV....No. 28,145. Entered as Second-Class Matter, Postoffice, New York, N. Y. NEW YORK, THURSDAY, FEBRUARY 14, 1935. P TWO CENTS | In New York City. | THREE CENTS Within 200 Miles | FOUR CENTS Elsewhere Except in 7th and 8th Postal Zones.

HAUPTMANN GUILTY, SENTENCED TO DEATH FOR THE MURDER OF THE LINDBERGH BABY

MACON'S MEN LAND, SAVED FROM DEATH IN SKY AND ON SEA

Calm Heroism and Unbroken Navy Discipline Revealed as Survivors Reach Port.

ADMIRAL TELLS OF HORROR

Saw Gasoline Flames Spread Over Water to Airship's Crew as the Cruisers Came Up.

WILEY DESCRIBES PLUNGE

Naval Court Is Ordered for Today as Field Inquiry Into the Cause Is Started.

Special to THE NEW YORK TIMES.

SAN FRANCISCO, Feb. 13.—Eighty-one officers and men of the eighty-three who set out on the dirigible Macon to join the fleet off the California Coast came home today to tell how the giant airship was destroyed yesterday evening and death which snatched at them from sky and sea was beaten back.

They stood huddled on three rescue cruisers in San Francisco Bay, laughing, asking for cigarettes, and between puffs relating this latest epic of man's defeat amid his conquests of space.

But though they could describe the first alarm and the fall, of flying minutes after the Macon struck, and dragging anxiety as the navy swept the misty seas in search of them, they were mute on the cause of the disaster.

Some fabric tore away on her fins and along her backbone; gas cells burst, the great structure shuddered and soared and descended and hit, and suddenly they were tumbled out pell mell into the water, fighting for their lives. Flaming gasoline was ignited about them by calcium flares of mercy.

This was the story in brief, different for every man, yet somehow merging into one clear picture of the whole.

Three Warships Reach Port.

The warships Richmond, Cincinnati and Concord brought in the survivors. Lieut. Commander Herbert V. Wiley, the Macon's skipper, was aboard the Concord. When he described what happened it was in terms of telephone calls, buoyancy and lack of it, jettisoned gasoline and crumbling gas cells and frames. He was in the control car, a city block from the source of trouble.

The story of men is another narrative. The Macon was humming along not far at sea south of Monterey Bay. The weather was dark gray and filled with drizzle, but the world's greatest dirigible had seen many such days. She had met the fleet plowing northward toward San Francisco; she was accompanying it, and soon she would go to her home in Sunnyvale.

The time was a little later than 5 o'clock in the afternoon, and daylight was already failing. There was a slight jar. It jerked at the wheel in the helmsman's hands. Some said they did not feel the jar, but immediately noticed the inclination of the ship, nose upward.

However, there were subsequent "jars." Lieutenant C. S. Rounds described them as a "shudder."

"But it was squally outside," he said. "I doubt if many of us in the first sixty seconds anticipated serious trouble. Even when the 'stand by' orders came, I thought it was a minor crisis of navigation."

Gas Cells Begin to Go.

But those jars were the rupturing of gas units; first No. 1, then No. 2, away aft. Lieutenant Rounds was forward and inside the ship. There was no excitement for the first four or five minutes, excepting among those aft who were whipping telephone calls into the control car. The airship was riding rapidly.

Then No. 9 cell burst. About that time it dawned on all that this was no minor crisis.

They stuck by their posts. They slipped gasoline tanks aft and devalved the forward cells to level her out, but it was no good.

Having soared into the mist in a last living effort, the Macon lost buoyancy and began to fall. It was then that Commander Wiley sent out the message that they were falling and first mentioned abandoning ship.

The man who sent that electric

Continued on Page Two.

Opera Threatened Again As Board Balks at Deficit

Metropolitan Directors Cast Doubt on Next Season Unless Production Costs Are Cut and Popular Subscription Enlarged.

There may be no opera at the Metropolitan next season. The board of directors of the Metropolitan Opera Association has decided that opera cannot be continued on the basis of the enormous losses incurred in the last five seasons.

After a meeting of the executive committee yesterday in the office of Paul D. Cravath, chairman of the board, Mr. Cravath issued the following statement:

"The directors of the Metropolitan Opera Association have decided that it is not feasible to give opera at the Metropolitan Opera House next season on the basis of continuing to incur the large deficits of the last five seasons.

"They have requested the preparation of a plan for reducing the cost of producing opera, and increasing the support of the public through subscriptions for seats, that will render the continuation of opera financially possible."

The members of the committee would not elaborate on this statement last night. One member intimated that the announcement had a twofold purpose; to quiet the rumors that have been at large in the last few weeks and to gauge the public reaction as to its willingness to participate in assuring the Metropolitan's future.

It was emphasized that neither the full board nor the executive committee had abandoned the Metropolitan to whatever fate might befall it, and that, despite the immediate doubts, there was every intention to continue consideration of the opera's future.

Besides Mr. Cravath, the members of the executive committee who attended the meeting were Mrs. August Belmont, Cornelius N. Bliss, Frederic Potts Moore, David Sarnoff and Allen Wardwell. Robert S. Brewster, the new president of the Metropolitan Opera and Real Estate Company, and Myron C. Taylor were the only members absent.

The executive committee has been holding frequent meetings since Fall to determine ways and means of continuing opera at the Metropolitan. The first question before it was the establishment of a policy and financial program. The second, depending on the first, was the naming of a general manager to succeed Giulio Gatti-Casazza, whose resignation takes effect next April.

Many plans for the continuation of Metropolitan Opera were proposed and discussed at these meet-

Continued on Page Twenty-five.

HOPE GAINS IN ROME FOR PEACE IN AFRICA

But Italy Is Reported Ready to Spend $850,000,000 in the Event of War.

REPLY TO DEMANDS ASKED

Plan for Solution Reported in Addis Ababa—Fascist Grand Council to Meet.

By ARNALDO CORTESI.

Wireless to THE NEW YORK TIMES.

ROME, Feb. 13.—The optimistic forecasts made yesterday as to a peaceful solution of the Italo-Abyssinian crisis became more positive today following a meeting between Negradas Yesus, Abyssinian Chargé d'Affaires, and Fulvio Suvich, Italian Foreign Under-Secretary. Although it is stated semi-officially that no actual solution has been reached, the impression is that good progress has been made.

Special emphasis is laid on the fact that Signor Suvich began by assuring the Abyssinian envoy that Italy was animated by the most peaceful intentions, to which the envoy replied that his Emperor also wished to avoid war. Signor Suvich then complained that the demands submitted to Emperor Haile Selassie by the Italian Minister at Addis Ababa remained unanswered.

Then the Italian Under-Secretary went on to discuss possible solutions of the crisis. These include the establishment of a neutral zone on the Abyssinian side of the frontier, but it is positively stated that no indication that this condition will be accepted by the Emperor has yet been received by Italy.

The Abyssinian envoy sent a long report of his conversations with Signor Suvich to Addis Ababa, and it is hoped by Italian officials that a reply will be forthcoming in the next few days.

There has been no let-up in the feverish activities to prepare a strong Italian expeditionary force for dispatch to Africa. In view, however, of today's favorable development hope is beginning to be entertained that it may never be necessary for the force to leave Italy.

Mussolini Studies Note.

By The Associated Press.

ROME, Feb. 13.—Premier Mussolini gave deep study tonight to an Abyssinian note calling Italians the aggressors in recent border conflicts. This note, Italian officials said earlier today, made the situation "very serious."

Nevertheless, there appeared this evening to be less concern in government circles over the prospect of hostilities in Africa, although an authoritative source said Italy was prepared to spend about $850,000,000

Continued on Page Sixteen.

LEHMAN TAX BILLS VOTED BY SENATE

Four-Cent Gasoline Levy and Budget Are Among the 11 Measures Approved.

FEARON ATTACKS FIGURES

He Predicts a $100,000,000 Deficit at Fiscal Year End—Five Proposals Held Up.

By W. A. WARN.

Special to THE NEW YORK TIMES.

ALBANY, Feb. 13.—Eleven of the measures included in Governor Lehman's fiscal program were passed in the Senate today. Action on five was deferred, not because the Democrats did not have the votes to pass them, but because legislative leaders doubted whether passage of them would be within the requirements of the Constitution, until after the main budget bills, already passed in the Senate, had been passed in the Assembly also.

Every Democrat in the Senate voted for the Governor's bills. The Republican vote was split in many instances. Senator Fearon, leader of the Republican minority, voted for the main budget bill, but not until he had first denounced it as a measure which did not comply with the Constitutional provision for a balanced budget and had accused Governor Lehman of financial juggling in drafting his measures.

The Senator cited figures intended to show that Mr. Lehman had constantly blundered in estimating revenues. He declared that these futile processes had been repeated by the Chief Executive in making up his new budget, with the probable result that the Governor would be confronted with a $100,000,000 deficit when the next fiscal year ends instead of the $3,000,000 surplus of the Governor's own estimate, cited in his budget message to the Legislature.

Sees 700 New Jobs.

Senator Fearon accused the Democrats of putting more than 700 new jobs into the budget bill without telling anybody anything about it. He said they had refused the taxpayers a public hearing on the budget bill at a time when the Governor himself was demanding public hearings in towns and counties on local budgets.

Senator Dunnigan, Democratic leader, came to the defense of the Governor and the debate was shot through and through with partisan charges. At times it became quite heated, with Senators Fearon and Dunnigan striding up and down the centre aisle.

Senator Fearon gave Senator Twomey, fiscal leader of the Senate, some moments of embarrass-

Continued on Page Six.

SENATE COMMITTEE ADOPTS WORK BILL; TRUCE OVER WAGES

Drive for Pay Under 'Prevailing' Rates Is Beaten and the 'Dole' Also Is Rejected.

ROOSEVELT RETAINS POWER

But His Scale Must Not Cut Private Wages—Floor Fight Due as Labor Protests.

Special to THE NEW YORK TIMES.

WASHINGTON, Feb. 13.—After hours of struggle today, the administration leadership, supported by Senator Glass, regained control of the Senate Appropriations Committee and finished a redraft of the $4,880,000,000 relief bill deemed acceptable to President Roosevelt.

Mr. Glass expects to report the revised measure formally to the Senate tomorrow or next day. Leaders hope it may be acted upon finally before the diminishing funds in the present relief coffers are depleted entirely.

Today's action in the Appropriations Committee was considered both by the administration and organized labor as a victory for the Roosevelt supporters. Instead of yielding to the demand of the American Federation of Labor for an irrevocable "prevailing wage" provision, the committee adopted an amendment giving the President control over pay rates, but with the added prescription that he must pay the "prevailing" scale if he finds the new works program is depressing, or is likely to depress, private wage structures in any locality.

William Green, president of the A. F. of L., said tonight that the substitute was "unacceptable and unsatisfactory to labor," adding that the federation would make its appeal directly to the Senate membership.

"Dole" Amendment Is Beaten.

The committee also withstood a drive from another group and again voted down, by 12 to 11, the so-called "dole" amendment which would have provided a cut in the appropriation to $2,880,000,000 and thereby, according to its supporters, force the President to rely more on direct relief than upon the more expensive new public works.

Thus, after three weeks of varying degrees of fright, administration leaders apparently had taken hold again. They proposed to move at once to break the log-jam of legislation which has backed up behind the relief program, and expressed confidence in predicting that this measure would be well on its way through the Senate before another week had gone.

Through all of its vicissitudes in the committee, the bill emerged today without any change which leaders regarded as a serious violation of the principles laid down by the President in his annual message. He called then for a lump-sum appropriation and for adequate discretionary authority to spend it in a self-diminishing, largely self-liquidating works program, designed to return 3,500,000 able-bodied persons now on relief to employment at lower than prevailing wages.

All of the trouble on the measure,

Continued on Page Eight.

ELEVATORS TIED UP IN 200 BUILDINGS IN STRIKE FLARE-UP

Union Disclaims Action After New Delay in Decision, but Admits Patience Is Gone.

UPTOWN APARTMENTS HIT

Madison Square Offices Also Are Affected—Spread of the Walkout a Possibility.

A general strike of building service employes in office and apartment house buildings loomed last night after sporadic walkouts affecting more than 200 buildings and 2,500 employes were staged in various parts of the city yesterday.

The strikes were called by a so-called "rank and file committee" of members of the Building Service Employes Union, claiming a membership of 140,000, as the arbitration committee headed by Major Henry H. Curran, appointed last December by Mayor La Guardia to settle the differences between the union and realty interests, was struggling to complete its labors and present an award.

The committee was to have made known its award yesterday. It failed to do so, however, and last night Major Curran announced that the award would not be made public until today. The committee remained in session all evening at Major Curran's office, 280 Madison Avenue.

"Ill Advised," Says Mayor.

Mayor La Guardia on being informed of the walkouts, which occurred in the Harlem, Washington Heights and Madison Square sections, termed the strikes as "ill advised."

At the office of the union, 1,450 Broadway, responsibility for the strikes was disclaimed. The walkouts were characterized as "unauthorized," but the statement was added, "We cannot hold them back any longer—our men have lost patience waiting for the award."

Detectives of the West 123d Street Precinct, cruising in a radio car, arrested sixteen men shortly before 1 o'clock this morning, charging them with disorderly conduct for alleged intimidation of building-service employes in three Harlem apartment houses. According to the officers, the sixteen men, nine of whom were Negroes, had entered the apartment houses and compelled attendants on duty to quit their jobs.

Six of the prisoners were picked up at 50 West 112th Street, three at 56 West 112th Street, and seven at 1,980 Seventh Avenue. They will be arraigned in the Fifth District Court today.

Promised to Work for Peace.

A fortnight ago James J. Bambrick, after a meeting of the union's executive committee and the presidents of its fifteen locals in the city, had promised Major Curran that every effort would be made to prevent any strikes, pending the outcome of the arbitration proceedings.

This was in response to a plea from Major Curran to keep the men from striking lest such action jeopardize the arbitration award.

Continued on Page Eight.

Girl Dies in Leap Off Empire State Tower; Impact Smashes Heavy Marquee in 33d St.

Disconsolate because of a quarrel with her fiancé, a 20-year-old girl jumped from the observation landing of the Empire State Building just before 8:30 o'clock last night, her body crashing into a glass and metal marquee nearly a quarter of a mile below.

The impact of the fall, which shattered frosted glass, light bulbs and the sheet-iron covering of the canopy, was at first mistaken for an explosion by passers-by and shop employes in the vicinity. Witnesses in buildings on the opposite side of Thirty-third Street said the young woman's body had struck a sixth-floor set-back of the building before hurtling onto the marquee.

From the contents of her handbag, which was clutched tightly in her fingers, the girl was identified as Irma P. Eberhardt of the Laura Spelman Hall Branch of the Y. W. C. A., 607 Hudson Street. Except for a Y. W. C. A. membership card the black bag contained only 83 cents in change and a compact of lipstick and rouge.

At the moment Miss Eberhardt jumped from the Empire State terrace, according to the police, Raymond Rebecchi of 5,716 136th Street, Flushing, was at the Charles Street station reporting her disappearance to Detective Frank Campbell. Before he had finished, word of her death was received from the police of the West Thirtieth Street precinct.

Rebecchi is said to have told Detective Campbell that he and Miss Eberhardt had quarreled on Tuesday, but that he had called at the Y. W. C. A. last night in the hope of effecting a reconciliation. He asked her to go to dinner, he said, and while he went to a lavatory to wash his hands the young woman vanished.

Rebecchi is said to have told the police he waited about half an hour in the foyer when he received a telephone call from Miss Eberhardt. "I'm going to kill myself," she said and hung up the receiver. Alarmed, the young man hurried to the police station.

Times Wide World Photo.

BRUNO RICHARD HAUPTMANN

Being taken to his cell after hearing death sentence last night.

HAUPTMANN IN CELL FALLS IN COLLAPSE

After Hearing Verdict Without a Sign, He Breaks Down in Fit of Weeping.

WIFE SOBS AFTER HE GOES

Both Prepared for Worst by Warning of Fisher Against Outburst in Court.

By CRAIG THOMPSON.

Special to THE NEW YORK TIMES.

FLEMINGTON, N. J., Feb. 13.—For the first time since his arrest Bruno Richard Hauptmann was reported tonight to be in a state of collapse.

When he marched out of the court room, manacled to Constable Hovey Low on his left and State Trooper Hugh Stockberger on his right, he was pale but erect and his step seemed firm.

He went through the back rooms to his cell tier, which has been occupied by him alone. The minute the door was slammed shut behind him, according to the reports, he slumped, his face striking the floor.

There was a hush in the court room when Hauptmann came in at 10:30 o'clock tonight. For the first time since the trial started he was in irons, manacled to two of his nine guards. The bell in the belfry had already announced that the jury had reached a verdict, and the shouting of the throng outside was an overtone to the inside hush.

Wife Comes to His Side.

Hauptmann walked across the room from the rear door and took his seat. He sat down stiffly, a little awkwardly, as if the manacles impeded his motions.

At almost the same moment his wife, her normally red face growing pale, edged up the outside aisle and around the seats inside the rail to a place close to her husband. She twisted her lips into a wry smile, but her husband, after one glance, looked away.

In the two minutes that passed before the jurors began to file in there was a vivid little picture. C. Lloyd Fisher, the one member of Hauptmann's counsel who has been closest to him, visiting him in the jail daily and taking his life story before the trial, leaned over and put his arm around the prisoner's shoulder.

He whispered: "This is only the beginning. Don't show a sign, because, if you do, it will count against you."

Then the attorney leaned over and placed his arm around Mrs.

Continued on Page Twelve.

JURY COURAGEOUS, WILENTZ DECLARES

Nation Indebted to Them, He Says—Thanks Aides, Foley and New York Police.

'ENDS OF JUSTICE SERVED'

Peacock Says Verdict Is Reply to 'Mothers' Prayer'—Law Points Raised by Defense.

From a Staff Correspondent.

FLEMINGTON, N. J., Feb. 13.—Attorney General David T. Wilentz, commenting tonight upon the Hauptmann verdict, thanked all those associated with the prosecution, and paid special tribute to the jury.

"The tremendous responsibility imposed upon the Hunterdon County jury was shouldered without flinching," he said. "The nation is indebted to these courageous men and women.

"The proper presentation of the case was due in the main to the work of the New Jersey State police. District Attorney Samuel J. Foley of the Bronx and his assistants labored unceasingly and to them I extend my deep thanks, as well as to Inspectors Henry Bruckman, John J. Lyons, the members of the New York police and the agents of the Federal Government."

Mr. Wilentz added that it had been his unwelcome duty to prosecute the case and said that he hoped society would be served by his efforts and those of his associates.

Former Judge George K. Large of Flemington, special counsel to the State, said, "The verdict was fully justified by the evidence."

"Truth Will Prevail."

Assistant Attorney General Robert Peacock said:

"The verdict proves again that truth will prevail. All during the time I was preparing the case at the request of the Attorney General I felt that the simple truth presented in terms the jury could understand would adequately serve the ends of justice.

"The verdict is the answer to the prayers of the mothers of this nation that those who harm their children shall be punished and that men of the accomplishments of Colonel Lindbergh shall be able to maintain homes in the quiet assurance that their families in the hour of their absence shall be protected by the arm of the law."

Colonel H. Norman Schwarzkopf said:

"I feel that the verdict is in accordance with the evidence and that the ends of justice have been served.

Continued on Page Eleven.

JURY OUT FOR 11 HOURS

One of 2 Women Who Held Out for Mercy Near Tears at End.

DEFENDANT PALE, SILENT

Fails to Glance at Wife as He Is Led Back to Cell—She Is Calm.

DEFENSE PLANS TO APPEAL

Execution Set for the Week of March 18—Court's Charge Attacked as Biased.

Judge's charge to the jury and exceptions granted, Pages 10, 11.

By RUSSELL B. PORTER.

Special to THE NEW YORK TIMES.

FLEMINGTON, N. J., Feb. 13.—Bruno Richard Hauptmann was convicted of murder in the first degree at 10:45 o'clock tonight for the killing of Charles A. Lindbergh Jr. at Hopewell on the night of March 1, 1932.

He was sentenced to die in the electric chair at the State prison in Trenton some time during the week of March 18.

The jury of eight men and four women returned its verdict after having been out for eleven hours and twenty-four minutes since it retired from the court room at 11:21 o'clock this morning to deliberate in the jury room.

Handcuffed to two guards, Hauptmann stood between them silent and motionless, his face ashen white and terror in his deep-set eyes, while he heard the jury state its verdict and the judge pronounce sentence.

A few minutes later he was led away to his cell in the county jail. He did not even cast a glance of recognition toward his wife, who sat a few feet away. She looked at him with red-rimmed eyes, but did not weep.

Colonel Charles A. Lindbergh, who attended every session of the thirty-two court days of the trial from its beginning on Jan. 2, six weeks ago, and who heard Supreme Court Justice Thomas W. Trenchard deliver his charge to the jury this morning, was not in court when the verdict was returned. He had returned to his home in Englewood in the afternoon.

Woman Juror Near Tears.

Mrs. Verna Snyder, juror No. 3, was biting her lips to keep from crying and her eyes were wet with tears as she left the jury box. According to well-founded report, she and Mrs. Rosie Pill, juror No. 2, had held out to the last ballot for a verdict of guilty with a recommendation providing imprisonment at hard labor for life.

All the rest of the jurors were grave but appeared serene, as if they were satisfied that they had done their duty.

At 10:28 Sheriff Curtiss came out of the judge's chambers and gave an order to a deputy sheriff. The latter left the room and mounted the stairs to the cupola on the roof of the white court house. In a moment the 125-year-old bell, older than the court house itself, began to toll. By an old custom, revived a few years ago, the bell is rung to notify the town that a jury has reached a verdict and is about to return to the court room.

"There's the bell!" the whisper spread through the court room.

"Quiet! Quiet!" cried the guards as the reporters murmured among themselves, but both the murmurs and the shouts were drowned out by the noise of the crowd in the street, which at this moment rose to a roar.

Prisoner Is Brought In.

Mr. Fisher of defense counsel came in and indicated that Hauptmann was already on the way from his cell. At 10:31 the prisoner was brought in. The Sheriff and five State troopers led the way.

Hauptmann's gait was unusual as he appeared in the doorway. In a moment the reason was clear. For the first time since the trial began, he was brought into court man-

Continued on Page Twelve.

"All the News That's Fit to Print."

The New York Times.

LATE CITY EDITION
WEATHER—Fair, continued warm today; tomorrow cloudy, showers.
Temperatures Yesterday—Max., 85; Min., 73

VOL. LXXXIV....No. 28,329. Entered as Second-Class Matter, Postoffice, New York, N. Y. NEW YORK, SATURDAY, AUGUST 17, 1935. P TWO CENTS In New York City. | THREE CENTS Within 200 Miles | FOUR CENTS Elsewhere Except in 7th and 8th Postal Zones.

WILL ROGERS, WILEY POST DIE IN AIRPLANE CRASH IN ALASKA; NATION SHOCKED BY TRAGEDY

Sergeant Morgan's Report of the Death Of Rogers and Post as Seen by Natives

Special to THE NEW YORK TIMES.

SEATTLE, Wash., Aug. 16.—The radio message sent by relays from Point Barrow, Alaska, to Seattle, in which Staff Sergeant Stanley R. Morgan informed the world of the tragic death of Will Rogers and Wiley Post, read as follows:

"Ten P. M. native runner reported plane crashed fifteen miles south of Barrow.

"Immediately hired fast launch, proceeded to scene.

"Found plane complete wreck, partly submerged, two feet water.

"Recovered body Rogers, then necessary tear plane apart extract body of Post from water.

"Brought bodies Barrow. Turned over Dr. Greist.

"Also salvaged personal effects, which am holding. Advise relatives and instruct this station fully as to procedure.

"Natives camping small river fifteen miles south here claim Post, Rogers landed and asked way to Barrow.

"Taking off, engine misfired on right bank while only fifty feet off water.

"Plane, out of control, crashed nose on, tearing right wing off and nosing over, forcing engine back through body of plane.

"Both apparently killed instantly.

"Both bodies bruised.

"Post's wrist watch broken, stopped 8:18 P. M."

The message was received by Colonel George E. Kumpe, in charge of the army signal corps headquarters here. It had been relayed through two radio stations and took about two hours to reach Seattle.

Sergeant Morgan won fame last Spring when he stayed at his post through a severe influenza epidemic while others, including his wife and 2-year-old son, Barrow, lay seriously ill. Sergeant Morgan and Dr. Henry W. Greist, the Presbyterian medical missionary, waged a bitter fight against the epidemic. While Dr. Greist ministered to the sick, Sergeant Morgan radioed for the aid which finally defeated the epidemic.

10-MINUTE HOP THEIR LAST

Engine Fails on a Take-Off for Final 15 Miles to Point Barrow.

LANDED TO GET BEARINGS

Startled Eskimos See Huge Bird Plunge to River Bank From 50 Feet Above Water.

ONE RUNS 3 HOURS TO TELL

Humorist Revealed as Financing a Trip Around the World With Famous Pilot.

(Copyright, 1935, by The Associated Press.)

POINT BARROW, Alaska, Aug. 16.—Will Rogers, beloved humorist, and Wiley Post, master aviator, were crushed to death last night when a shiny, new airplane motor faltered and became an engine of tragedy near this outpost of civilization.

Both were killed when their red Arctic sky cruiser slipped and fell fifty feet head-on into a river bank. The 550-horse-power motor, driven back into the fuselage, snuffed out the lives of the two men instantly.

A native runner raced to Point Barrow with word of a plane crash. Sergeant Stanley R. Morgan of the Army Signal Corps dashed to the scene to learn the full significance of the tragedy.

First he took the body of Rogers from the cabin. Then he was forced to tear the plane apart to recover that of the flier who twice had flown around the globe—once alone.

Bodies Are Taken to Barrow.

The bodies were brought here and given to the care of Dr. Henry W. Greist, a Presbyterian medical missionary.

It was a trifling ten-minute flight that ended the careers of two famous figures long accustomed to flying. Although Rogers—gentle master of the "wise crack"—never became a pilot, he was perhaps the world's foremost airplane passenger.

Resuming a happy-go-lucky aerial tour of Alaska, a prelude to a flight to Siberia and on to Moscow, the noted travelers left Fairbanks late yesterday for a 500-mile hop to Point Barrow, northernmost white settlement in America.

Fifty miles out they encountered fog. Post "sat down" on Harding Lake for a while, but resumed the journey soon.

Apparently uncertain of his bearings, he again brought his pontooned plane to the surface of a shallow river fifteen miles southwest of here to ask natives the way to Point Barrow.

Rogers chatted with the Eskimos. Post tinkered with the plane during the brief stop. Soon after 5 P. M. (11 P. M. Eastern daylight time) they took off for the last little hop.

Motor Misfires on Take-Off.

The natives told the story to Sergeant Morgan. They said the motor of Post's new specially built plane misfired soon after it rose. The pilot quickly banked to the right; then the ship plummeted nose first, out of control. It dived into the edge of the stream, where the water was only two feet deep.

When Sergeant Morgan arrived at the scene by launch, he said today, he found the monoplane a complete wreck, partly submerged. The right wing was broken off.

The soldier said Post's watch had stopped at 8:18 P. M., apparently the time of the accident. [The difference in time indicated by the aviator's watch and that reported by the natives probably is accounted for by the time zones through which he had flown.]

The runner arrived here at 10 P. M. with word of the tragedy. Recovering the flier's personal effects, Sergeant Morgan turned them over to Dr. Greist, awaiting instructions from Mrs. Rogers and Mrs. Post and from Morgan's superior, Colonel George E. Kumpe at Seattle.

The unrelenting Arctic, grave of other such noted fliers as Carl Ben Eielson and Frank Dorbandt, played a leading part in this new tragedy.

Rogers and Post had left Fairbanks in the face of poor flying conditions. The stop at Harding Lake enabled them to await the

Continued on Page Four.

CAPITAL SADDENED BY ROGERS DEATH

Both House and Senate Halt Business for Tribute to the Humorist and to Post.

GARNER DEEPLY AFFECTED

Robinson Hails 'Best Loved Citizen'—Deaths 'Real Loss,' Speaker Byrns Says.

Special to THE NEW YORK TIMES.

WASHINGTON, Aug. 16.—The death of Will Rogers and Wiley Post shocked and saddened the capital, which knew Rogers as a frequent visitor and liked him as an amiable "josher" of politicians.

Legislative machinery stopped briefly in tribute. The Senate dropped other business to honor the humorist, a friend of Presidents, diplomats and political leaders. The House also listened to a speech of eulogy, while from all quarters came expressions of sorrow over his death.

As soon as the Senate convened, Senator Robinson, the Democratic leader, took the floor and said:

"Probably the most widely known private citizen in the United States and certainly the best beloved met his death some hours ago in a lonely, far-away place.

"We pause for a moment in the midst of our duties to pay brief tribute to his memory and to that of his gallant companion, Wiley Post.

"I do not think of Will Rogers as dead. I shall remember him always as a sensible, courageous, loyal friend, possessed of unusual and notable talents.

"He made fun for all mankind. In nothing that he ever said was there an intentional sting. He was kind, generous, patriotic.

"His companion was a courageous representative of a gallant group who, on wings of adventure, sought remote places and conquered long distances."

News Saddens McNary.

Senator McNary, the Republican leader, said:

"Mr. Rogers has brought happiness, joy and good feeling to the hearts of millions of Americans. In common with all his fellow-citizens, I regret his tragic end and that of his doughty and valiant companion."

Vice President Garner, a friend of long standing, who shared the humorist's dislike of ceremonial attire, could only say, when informed of his death:

"Awful bad! Awful bad!"

Mr. Rogers had boomed Mr. Garner for the Presidency three years ago, and the two had a gay time together Jan. 17 when the Vice President entertained for President Roosevelt.

Speaker Byrns, addressing the House, mentioned Mr. Rogers's in-

Continued on Page Four.

ROOSEVELT CALLS CHIEFS TO ARRANGE CONGRESS WIND-UP

Conference Tomorrow Is Expected to Set Program for Adjournment Thursday.

FIVE MAJOR BILLS FAVORED

Wealth Tax, Banking, Coal, Alcohol Control and Gold Ban Measures Slated to Pass.

UTILITY DEADLOCK HOLDS

Holding Company Curb and Other Major Bills Likely to Wait Till Next Session.

By The Associated Press.

WASHINGTON, Aug. 16.—A semifinal conference of Democratic leaders to make arrangements for a prompt adjournment of Congress was called tonight by President Roosevelt for Sunday night.

The expectation of some of the party chiefs was that at that meeting the President would disclose which measures he was willing for Congress to drop and which he wanted enacted before adjournment.

Among those invited to the conference, beginning at 8:30, were: Vice President Garner, Speaker Byrns, Senator Robinson of Arkansas, the Democratic leader; Chairman O'Connor of the House Rules Committee, Chairman Harrison of the Senate Finance Committee and Chairman Doughton of the House Ways and Means Committee.

It was indicated by one of the conferees that any agreement reached Sunday night, however, would be subject to possible modification if particular pressure developed for the enactment of any measure.

Conjecture on Program.

From what they already had heard directly and indirectly from the President, some of the conferees, talking privately, said the meeting made more clear the possibilities of an end to the present session by the end of next week at the latest.

Some were talking about an adjournment Tuesday, or Thursday. Most agreed that it probably would be the latter part of next week before everything could be wound up to their satisfaction or to that of the President.

The expectation of some of the conferees was that the President would renew his insistence upon enactment of:

1. The Guffey Coal Stabilization Bill, which proponents and some opponents say will pass the House Monday and be approved by the Senate early next week:
2. The Federal alcohol control plan.
3. The $250,000,000 Tax Bill.
4. The Omnibus Banking Bill, on which conferees reached an agreement late today.
5. The measure forbidding suits for gold payments on government contracts.

Six Bills May Be Shelved.

Their belief was that unless action was hastened the following would be left behind when this session ended, with their present status remaining the same until the next session:

1. The Utilities Bill;
2. The rivers and harbors legislation;
3. The measure expanding Federal control over food and drugs;
4. Railroad reorganization;
5. General oil regulation;
6. The Ship Subsidy Bill.

Leaders said the Utilities Bill probably would be left behind, not because the President did not want the legislation, but because the conference deadlock could not be broken.

A possibility was seen by some that the Rivers and Harbors Bill might be insisted upon because it would legalize the millions already spent by the Federal Government on a number of projects, such as the Parker Dam. And they added that they had but scant doubt that before Congress had adjourned it would ratify the oil compacts entered into in Dallas last February.

House Tax Conferees Named.

Special to THE NEW YORK TIMES.

WASHINGTON, Aug. 16.—A determined drive to adjourn Congress by Tuesday night, with Thursday as the latest alternate date, was started today following formal commitment of the Wealth-Tax Bill to conference and a conference agreement on the Eccles Banking Bill.

The promise of Tuesday adjournment was held out by Senator Robinson as the Senate voted to take a recess until Monday. Early in the day he had informed the Senate of his desire to quit at that time and in so doing issued a warning

Continued on Page Fourteen.

Davey Sets Ohio Vote for 1936, Defying Opponents of New Deal

Governor, Here, Denies Delaying Test on Advice of Roosevelt Forces, Gives Economy as Reason—He and President Are Accused of 'Conspiracy' by Republican Leader.

Governor Martin L. Davey of Ohio moved formally yesterday to defy Republican demands for a special State-wide election this year for Representative at Large to test New Deal sentiment in the State.

The Governor was visiting New York City during the day and telephoned his office in Columbus to frame an order in legal form setting the election for next year. All that remains to put the order into effect is the signature of the Governor, which he said he would affix when he reached Ohio tomorrow.

With the Republican national leaders, heartened by a victory in the Rhode Island Congressional elections, demanding that Ohio vote this November to fill the vacancy caused by the death of Representative Charles V. Truax, the Governor insisted that the election should be held next year to avoid imposition of from $500,000 to $600,000 special election costs on hard-pressed taxpayers of the State.

He ridiculed the charge made by his political adversaries that the election was being postponed until next year, apparently under advice from the Roosevelt forces at Washington, to prevent an early test of the New Deal in such a key State as Ohio.

"There is no moral justification of loading that extra cost for a special election on the units of the State," Governor Davey said at the Hotel Biltmore. "The good and ample reason for this order is that a recent referendum reducing the tax limit from 15 mills to 10 mills on the dollar has, with the aid of the depression, depleted the treasuries of the counties and the cities so badly that they could not well stand the expense of a special election.

"Now I want to point out that no district in Ohio will be without representation meanwhile, since this post is that of a Representative at Large. I have an excellent precedent for this action, since the same course was followed in my

Continued on Page Seven.

ROOSEVELT RESTS AT HYDE PARK HOME

Joins Family on Two-Day Visit to Celebrate 21st Birthday of Franklin Jr.

AVOIDS ISSUE ON HOOVER

President Intercedes for Man Caught at Baltimore While Stealing Ride on His Train.

From a Staff Correspondent.

HYDE PARK, N. Y., Aug. 16.—President Roosevelt returned to Hyde Park House today for a brief period of quiet contemplation before undertaking the direction of strategy designed to bring the current session of Congress to a satisfactory conclusion from the administration standpoint.

He came here overnight aboard a special train which arrived at 8:30 o'clock this morning for the announced purpose of attending a family party tomorrow in celebration of the twenty-first birthday anniversary of Franklin D. Roosevelt Jr., his third son.

However, an impromptu "press conference" held by Mr. Roosevelt while he sat in an automobile for the ride from the train to his mother's estate overlooking the Hudson River gave ample indication of the many problems awaiting a directing hand, if not a definite solution, by the President.

These problems he plans to tackle actively on Sunday, when he will return to the White House for a long series of conferences with the individuals and groups representing the administration leadership on Capitol Hill.

A cheery confidence was radiated by Mr. Roosevelt today as he was subjected to a barrage of questions by reporters who clustered around his automobile in the bright morning sunlight.

Questioned on Utility Bill.

The questions dealt principally with the Utility Holding Company Bill, which has been deadlocked in conference between the House and Senate for some time, and the Tax Bill which was sent to conference yesterday after the Senate had approved a measure considerably different than the House bill.

Asked if he expected enactment of the Utility Bill this session, Mr. Roosevelt replied smilingly that he hoped so, with an inflection in his voice which some reporters interpreted as indicating that he intended to have this done.

Would he be willing, he then was asked, to accept the House bill, which differs from the Senate bill and administration recommendations in its omission of the celebrated "death sentence" section? At this question, Mr. Roosevelt smiled and closed the topic with the assertion that he could not comment on details.

A request for comment on the action of the Senate in passing the Tax Bill in changed form brought the rejoinder from the President that the Tax Bill had not been finally passed by Congress yet; that it was still an open question.

Renewed efforts by correspondents to get specific comment from the President on the recent statement by former President Hoover requesting Mr. Roosevelt to set forth definitely his plans regarding possible changes in the Constitution, elicited from the President only the reply that he had read Mr. Hoover's statement very hurriedly and therefore was in no position to comment.

Aside from the conferences Mr.

Continued on Page Fourteen.

CONFEREES AGREE ON BANK MEASURE

Glass and His Senators Win on Nearly All Points, Ending Long Battle on Bill.

ONE VICTORY FOR HOUSE

Effort to Force State Banks Into Reserve Is Put Off—Swift Finish Planned.

Special to THE NEW YORK TIMES.

WASHINGTON, Aug. 16.—Unanimous agreement on every feature of the hotly contested bill to change the nation's banking laws was reached by Senate and House conferees late today and arrangements were made to hurry this highly important measure through both branches of Congress early next week.

Senator Glass and his conservative colleagues of the Senate conferees won a smashing victory over Representatives Steagall and Goldsborough of the House conferees in almost every particular, but the two House liberals succeeded in postponing efforts to force State banks into the Federal Reserve System.

Senator Glass was delighted by the outcome. He and the other members of the conference asserted that the bill would go through both branches with ease.

Action will be taken on the conference report in the House Monday. The conferees arranged to file formal reports to both branches tomorrow.

The end of the conference marks a long and bitter fight over the policies of Marriner S. Eccles, governor of the Federal Reserve Board, as expressed in the bill passed by the House, and the views of the Glass group as set forth in the Senate bill.

Opinion tonight was that Mr. Glass, veteran banking legislator, had once more come out the victor.

Reserve Board Is Increased.

He and the other Senate conferees succeeded in carrying out their views on the open market committee, particularly in the aspect that government securities must be purchased on the open market and not direct from the Treasury.

Likewise, Senate conferees prevailed in their insistence that the Federal Reserve Board must be increased from the present six to seven members, with the Secretary of the Treasury and the Controller of the Currency eliminated as members ex officio.

The suggested permission of the Senate bill for banks of deposit to underwrite securities was stricken out at the request of President Roosevelt, Senator Glass stated.

The provision of the Senate bill that bankers may serve on not more than two bank boards simultaneously was retained but made subject to the discretion of the Reserve Board, however.

A big feature of the bill is the arrangement for the open market committee, which would be composed of seven Reserve Board members and five representatives of the twelve regional Reserve Banks. This committee would have power to influence the flow of credit by purchase and sale of government bonds by the Reserve Banks.

Policy Is Mandatory.

The policy laid down by the committee would be mandatory upon the Reserve Banks.

Following the view of Mr. Eccles, the House gave complete voting control of open market operations entirely to the Reserve Board, with

Continued on Page Fourteen.

HOPSON ADMITS TRYING TO CONTROL PRESS WITH ADS

He Also Tells Senators He Urged Move to Kill Utility Bill in Conference.

ATTACK ON TIMES RENEWED

House Committee Told That His 1934 Income Was Between $300,000 and $500,000.

Special to THE NEW YORK TIMES.

WASHINGTON, Aug. 16.—Howard C. Hopson, who now admits that he was the guiding influence of the $900,000 lobby that the Associated Gas and Electric Company waged against the Wheeler-Rayburn bill, was forced to state before the Senate lobby inquiry committee today that the company had not hesitated to use the advertising columns of newspapers as a club to minimize unfavorable publicity.

He also said he had suggested to another high utility holding company official that a campaign be waged to kill the administration's utility program in conference of the two branches of Congress. As matters stand tonight every indication is that the Wheeler-Rayburn bill will die in conference, where for more than a month the conferees of the Senate and House have been deadlocked. All hope had not been given up by the measure's advocates, however.

Earlier in the day, before the House investigating committee, Mr. Hopson for the first time gave figures on his income last year. He said he had received "some three or four or five hundred thousand dollars" from his private companies.

Admits Borrowing Millions.

He also said that the A. G. E. had borrowed several million dollars since the first of the year, and that had it not been for the Wheeler-Rayburn bill the borrowings might have been a million dollars less.

He was directed to supply the names of the banks from which the money was borrowed, and said he would do so.

Before the Senate committee Mr. Hopson again made charges involving THE NEW YORK TIMES. He asserted that the newspaper was under "the strong influence" of the Morgan and Carlisle interests, and that because of this alleged influence the A. G. E. should expect at "more or less frequent intervals" more "unpleasant attacks from that quarter."

The charges were made in a telegram to the H. C. Hopson Company, New York, which was signed by Duncan Robertson, Mr. Hopson's private secretary.

The telegram was in fact his own, said Mr. Hopson, explaining that it was his custom to have Mr. Robertson sign practically all of his messages to his New York office.

Messages to Hearst Admitted.

William Randolph Hearst was pictured before the committee as the writer of an editorial printed in the Hearst newspapers Sunday, June 2, which Senator Black asserted was strikingly along lines suggested by Mr. Hopson in a telegram to Mr. Hearst dated May 31.

Mr. Hopson admitted sending frequent messages to Mr. Hearst, who was dubbed by Senator Minton "the sage of San Simeon," but insisted that he had no reason to believe his messages inspired editorials or news articles in the Hearst papers.

Arthur Brisbane, Hearst writer, was pilloried, however, and documents placed in evidence showed

Continued on Page Twenty-six.

COAL BILL SPLITS HOUSE DEMOCRATS; PASSAGE HELD SURE

Widest Party Schism Since 'Death Sentence' Marks 'Must' Measure Debate.

VICTORY BY 30 CLAIMED

Administration Leaders Are Confident Despite Attacks as Unconstitutional.

Special to THE NEW YORK TIMES.

WASHINGTON, Aug. 16.—In the face of the most serious party schism which has yet confronted any of President Roosevelt's projects for industrial reform, the Guffey-Snyder Coal Bill was manoeuvred by House leaders tonight into a position for final action on Monday.

With general debate on the measure concluded, they planned to carry it through the amending stage tomorrow and adjourn before the vote on passage.

Not since the vote on the President's demand for the "death sentence" for utility holding companies has the rank and file of the Democratic majority been so thoroughly split as on the merits of the Guffey-Snyder measure, and leaders were working overtime to make good their prediction that the bill would pass by about thirty votes.

Although they conceded that the final count would be close, all said enough votes had been obtained to assure passage of the administration "must" measure. Their estimate of thirty votes was verified by Republican leaders.

"Stalwarts" Oppose Measure.

Shouts of "unconstitutional," "communism," and "regimentation" from some of those who have been among the stanchest supporters of the administration on some other reform programs marked consideration of the bill on the floor today.

The opposition among Democrats was so strong that Republicans either sat back to watch them denounce the measure or left the floor entirely.

Emphasizing the broad difference of opinion on the constitutionality of the measure was the performance of such Ways and Means Committee "stalwarts" as Representatives McCormack of Massachusetts, Cooper of Tennessee and Fuller of Arkansas, all of whom took the floor to oppose it, and sometimes on Republican time. The bill had been reported favorably by the committee by a vote of 12 to 11.

The special rule for consideration of the bill was adopted 241 to 94, after a perfunctory debate. Representative McCormack, one of the two Democrats on the Ways and Means Committee who abstained from voting on reporting out the measure, said that he would vote for the rule but against the bill.

He told other members that there would be no inconsistency in such a position, and that he thought the bill should have a chance for consideration on the floor.

Representative Fuller of Arkansas called Speaker Byrns's attention to the distribution by pages in the hall of copies of the bill bearing typewritten slips which said:

"Bituminous Coal Bill as amended and reprinted. Controversial propaganda largely eliminated. Two-thirds of tonnage output operators favored bill and more than 95 per cent of labor."

Representative Snyder of Pennsylvania, co-author of the bill, said that he had pasted the slips on the measure and had instructed the

Continued on Page Seven.

Lawyer Charges Judge Downs Beat Him; Sues for $50,000 in Contempt Case Row

County Judge Thomas Downs of Queens was sued in the New York Supreme Court yesterday by Lorenzo C. Carlino, a lawyer, for $50,000 damages. The lawyer charged that Judge Downs, after finding him guilty of contempt of court in a trial, and fining him $250, had knocked him down and kicked him at the St. Albans Golf Club in Queens.

Mr. Carlino alleges that his appeal from the contempt order was based on the ground that it was a violation of the section of the Judiciary Act which requires that a contempt order cite the specific facts upon which it is based. The lawyer further asserts that he got an order from the Appellate Division restraining Judge Downs from making any change in the order pending the appeal.

Mr. Carlino served the order on Judge Downs at the golf club on May 7 last, he alleges, when the jurist was about to step into his car. He says that as soon as he showed a signature of Presiding Justice Lazansky on an injunction order, "the defendant, Thomas Downs, struck the plaintiff, knocked him down, then kicked him while on the ground and trampled upon the order which was served upon him. Defendant called plaintiff vile, filthy names and otherwise used vile and filthy language."

In addition to the suit against Judge Downs the lawyer asks $25,000 damages from Sheriff Peter J. McGarry of Queens for brutal treatment when he was arrested on the contempt order, which was later set aside by the Appellate Division.

Judge Downs denied last night he had assaulted Mr. Carlino.

"I was getting into my automobile parked in front of the clubhouse about 10 o'clock one night more than three months ago," the judge explained, "when a man I did not recognize in the darkness rushed out at me from some shrubbery. I was all alone and had received only a few days before an anonymous threat against my life. I hit the man at once. He fell down and a paper dropped to the ground. The man picked up the paper and ran away."

ETHIOPIANS OFFER ITALY GUARANTEES

Bar Military Occupation, but Propose Mine, Rail, Trade and Settlement Rights.

ASK ROME TO STATE CASE

Britain and France Hold That Frank Presentation of Demands Is Essential.

By FREDERICK T. BIRCHALL.

Wireless to THE NEW YORK TIMES.

PARIS, Aug. 16.—Throughout the day and until late this evening, with only an interval for luncheon, Premier Pierre Laval, Anthony Eden of Great Britain and Baron Pompeo Aloisi of Italy have been in conference at the Quai d'Orsay over the Italo-Ethiopian problem in an effort to avert a war, with its resultant repercussions in Europe.

The first day's deliberations closed tonight with one definite, positive step taken toward results. The British and French have made a joint formal request to the Italians to state fully and frankly their complaints against Ethiopia and their consequent claims upon her.

From a British source it is learned that the Ethiopian Government, which is not represented at this conference, has shown a disposition to concede several points that may go far toward satisfying the Italian claims when these are made.

Offers Security Guarantees.

The Addis Ababa government, for instance, has expressed willingness to provide the most complete guarantees of security from Ethiopian aggression for the present Italian colonies and such economic concessions as may be agreed upon, provided the guarantees expected fall short of military occupation.

Emperor Haile Selassie is willing to grant reasonable rights for developing mineral and commercial possibilities within the Ethiopian territory, specific concessions to Italy being made in both fields.

He is further willing to consider granting some rights to Europeans to settle in Ethiopian territory and develop it while maintaining their original nationality. This last point would go a long way toward compliance with the Italian wishes.

Finally, he is willing to renew and even extend by making further concessions the old understanding with Italy, giving her permission to undertake a certain amount of commercial road and railroad construction in this country. This again anticipates an obvious Italian demand.

No answer to the Franco-British query was forthcoming from Rome tonight. Indeed, an immediate response was not expected. Baron Aloisi agreed to submit the request to Rome and to report the result as soon as possible. He received assurance from the others that if Italy would comply with this re-

Continued on Page Three.

"All the News That's Fit to Print."

The New York Times.

LATE CITY EDITION
Cloudy, slowly rising temperature today. Tomorrow cloudy, probably followed by rain or snow.
Temperatures Yesterday—Max., 31; min., 18.

Copyright, 1936, by The New York Times Company.

VOL. LXXXV.....No. 28,486. Entered as Second-Class Matter, Postoffice, New York, N. Y. NEW YORK, TUESDAY, JANUARY 21, 1936. P TWO CENTS In New York City. | THREE CENTS Within 200 Miles | FOUR CENTS Elsewhere Except in 7th and 8th Postal Zones.

KING GEORGE V DIES PEACEFULLY IN SLEEP; PRINCE OF WALES BECOMES EDWARD VIII

BONUS BILL PASSES IN SENATE, 74 TO 16; HOUSE TO CONCUR

BOND PLAN IS TRIUMPHANT

All but 2 Minor Changes Are Beaten in 3-Hour Final Session.

INFLATIONISTS FIGHT HARD

But Neely Move to Pay With Currency and 'Protect' the Taxpayer Loses, 65-23.

14 'ANTIS' SWING OVER

Cost Put at $2,491,000,000 to $2,664,000,000 or More—House Acts Tomorrow.

Special to THE NEW YORK TIMES.

WASHINGTON, Jan. 20.—By a vote of 74 to 16 the Senate today passed after about three hours' further consideration the "baby bond" Soldiers' Bonus Bill, whose total cost in outlays soon and eventually is estimated at from $2,491,000,000 to $2,664,000,000.

The measure now goes to the House, where concurrence, in a vote set for Wednesday, is regarded as certain. The vote there is being deferred, Speaker Byrns said, to allow absent members to return in time to go on record on final passage.

The overwhelming Senate support of nearly 5 to 1 for prepayment of the adjusted compensation certificates, due in 1945, was furnished by fifty-six Democrats, fifteen Republicans, two Farmer-Laborites and one Progressive.

Only nine Democrats and seven Republicans were recorded against. Thirteen names had been called without a dissenting vote before Senator Brown answered "no."

Senator Bulkley voted against, as did Senators Burke and Byrd. Ten more names were called before the next opposing vote, that of Senator Couzens, the first Republican to vote "no."

The following, who voted for the baby bond bill today, had stood against the Patman currency bonus bill May 7:

Ashurst, Bailey, Barkley, Dieterich, Guffey, Harrison, Lonergan, Radcliffe, Robinson and Walsh, Democrats; Austin, Barbour, McNary and White, Republicans.

The following Senators who did not vote on passage of the Patman bill last May voted affirmatively today: Gore, O'Mahoney and Reynolds, Democrats, and Norbeck and Nye, Republicans.

Many Veterans in Gallery.

Veterans packed the galleries today and even the diplomatic section was well filled. Some of the veterans wore overcoats issued to them years ago or bought at salvage stores since. Some had apparently not shaved for several days. They had but one concern: this vote. They listened intently to the debate, to the voting—and departed jubilant.

High up in one of the public galleries Ray Murphy, National Commander of the American Legion, and James E. Van Zandt, National Commander of the Veterans of Foreign Wars, took their seats soon after the session began.

On the final roll-call they kept pace with the vote on their own tally sheets.

"I am pleased, that is all, and I have nothing more to say," Mr. Murphy said afterward as he was being congratulated on all sides.

The Senate had met at noon and at 3:14 P. M. the vote was over and adjournment was quickly taken. Most observers agreed that practically every member who voted for the bill today would vote to override a veto, should President Roosevelt return the bill after the expected concurrence of the House. That would more than suffice to override.

Instead of paying the cost of the certificates in cash, as provided in

Continued on Page Fourteen.

House Votes Bill to Bar Foreign Mail Divorces

Special to THE NEW YORK TIMES.

WASHINGTON, Jan. 20.—A bill designed to restrict "mail order" divorces from Mexico, by closing the mails to all correspondence about them, passed the House and went to the Senate today.

Introduced by Representative Healey of Massachusetts, the bill provides that every sort of communication designed to give information or to solicit divorce business in a foreign country is not mailable. The bill provides a fine of $5,000 and a maximum prison sentence of five years or both.

There has been much agitation for such a bill owing to the issuance of many fraudulent Mexican divorces.

DR. ROBINSON UNFIT, ALUMNI UNIT FINDS

City College Committee Holds President Lacks Qualities Vital to Leadership.

MINORITY DEFENDS RULE

12-to-4 Report on Long Study of Campus Disorders Is Sent to Graduates.

Dr. Frederick B. Robinson, president of City College, lacks "the human qualities necessary to achieve the widespread confidence of his faculty and his student body and to provide genuinely inspired, resourceful and socially imaginative leadership," in the opinion of a special committee of the Associate Alumni of the college. The committee for more than a year has been studying the factors responsible for the frequency of undergraduate demonstrations at the institution.

Twelve members of the committee signed the report, which was mailed last night to 1,500 members of the association. Four others signed a minority draft, warmly defending the record of the Robinson administration. One committeeman did not vote because of his inability to attend meetings.

The committee was appointed on Dec. 17, 1934, by Dr. Stephen P. Duggan, director of the Institute of International Education and then president of the alumni organization. His action followed adoption at the association's annual meeting of a resolution directing him to appoint a committee to "seek all significant facts concerning present conditions in the City College and the nature of the present relations between the administration and the student body and the staff."

The group was to have reported its findings at a special meeting of the alumni a month later, but the mass of testimony gathered by it in "tapping every disclosed source of authentic information" soon made it apparent that the committee's deliberations must be extended.

Alumni Meeting Called.

A special meeting of the Associate Alumni has been called for next Monday night at the college's Twenty-third Street building by Federal Judge Clarence G. Galston, president of the association. Both the majority and the minority reports will be discussed.

Signers of the majority draft were Dr. Henry Moskowitz, '99, chairman of the committee and executive adviser of the League of New York Theatres; Dr. Paul Abelson, impartial chairman in the arbitration of labor disputes; Dr. Louis I. Dublin, '01, third vice president of the Metropolitan Life Insurance Company; Waldemar Kaempffert, '97, science editor of THE NEW YORK TIMES; Professor Charles V. Morrill, '03, of the medical faculty of Cornell University; Dr. Henry Neumann, '00, leader of the Brooklyn Society for Ethical Culture; Louis Salant, '98, attorney; Jonas J. Shapiro, '18, attorney; Professor Herbert Wechsler, '28, of Columbia

Continued on Page Two.

QUICK AAA REFUND SHARPLY ORDERED BY SUPREME COURT

Mandate Is Swiftly Issued as Government Fights for 200 Millions Held in Escrow.

CONTRARY RULING CITED

President Calls Conference of Congress Leaders and Aides to Seek Way Out.

Special to THE NEW YORK TIMES.

WASHINGTON, Jan. 20.—With sudden swiftness breaking a precedent of years, the Supreme Court today issued mandates making immediately effective its recent decisions declaring the Agricultural Adjustment Act unconstitutional and ordering $200,000,000 of impounded AAA taxes returned to processors.

The impact of the action was immediately felt in administration circles. President Roosevelt summoned a group of Congressional and farm leaders to meet at the White House tomorrow to discuss the situation created by the release of the $200,000,000, and the farm situation in general.

Announcement of the court's mandates came two and a half hours after the justices had left the bench and entered upon a two-week recess to catch up with their work. Court attachés said they could not remember when the justices had acted so quickly except in urgent matters such as murder cases. Usually all orders are handed down from the bench while the court is in session, and it was assumed that this would be the procedure today.

One of the orders tersely refused a government request made earlier in the day for reopening of the Louisiana rice millers' case through which the $200,000,000 was ordered turned back to the processors. It also granted the mandate sought by the rice millers and directed that their own impounded $200,000 taxes be released. The other order directed immediate issuance of a mandate releasing $80,000 in the receivership proceedings of the Hoosac Mills, victors in the AAA case decided on Jan. 6.

President Is Urged to Act.

Court action came even while government officials were studying plans to prevent the sequestered $200,000,000 from being recovered by processors without stern legal fights. In the face of the justices' swift moves, the President's advisers urged him to call tomorrow's conference as the present tentative strategy might have to be materially altered.

At the White House, it is understood, will be Senators Bankhead and Smith, and Representative Jones of Texas, Congressional farm leaders and possibly Senator Robinson, Democratic floor leader and and Speaker Byrns. Secretary Wallace and Chester C. Davis of the AAA, M. G. White, solicitor for the Agricultural Department and representatives of the Treasury and Department of Justice are also expected to participate.

Government legal officers said it would be necessary for all processors with taxes impounded as part of the $200,000,000 to make applications in the Federal courts before their money could be released. The money, it was stated, would not be automatically given back without

Continued on Page Fifteen.

NEW KING 41 YEARS OLD

Adopts Name Edward in Signing Notice to London's Mayor.

FACES AN ARDUOUS LIFE

An Ardent Rider and Flier, He Must Settle Down to More Prosaic Tasks.

CORONATION A YEAR AWAY

Period of Court Mourning Will Precede It—Heir to Throne Flew to Sandringham.

By FREDERICK T. BIRCHALL.
Special Cable to THE NEW YORK TIMES.

LONDON, Tuesday, Jan. 21.—Edward VIII, who at the age of 41 became King at the moment of his father's death just before midnight, will be publicly proclaimed as sovereign today.

According to ancient custom, a crier will call out from the steps of the Royal Exchange, "The King is dead, long live the King!" Ceremonial announcements of the same description will be made in every city, town and village in the country.

The new King himself, who is still at Sandringham, may be expected to remain there in such seclusion as can be permitted to him. His great loss came to him last night after a day more strenuous than most of those he has experienced in a life already inured to ceremonial hardships and quick movement.

Visited London Sunday.

King Edward, then the Prince of Wales, was in London Sunday night, having come here in the afternoon to see Prime Minister Stanley Baldwin and to arrange for a special meeting of the Privy Council at Sandringham which, in King George's presence, would appoint a Council of State, now useless and obsolete, to act should the late monarch's illness have continued over a long period.

Edward, with his brother, the Duke of York, flew back to Sandringham yesterday morning and was present when the Privy Council ppointed this intended Council of Regency. Thereafter he was close by his father's death chamber until the end came.

His first task was to console his weeping mother, to whom he is deeply attached and whose favorite son he is. But his duties as King brooked no delay. Already they pressed upon him, and within less than an hour of his father's death and his own accession to the throne he had undertaken his first official act as King by sending the following telegram:

> Sandringham, 12:28 A. M.
> Lord Mayor, London.
> I am deeply grieved to inform you that my beloved father, the King, passed away peacefully at 11:55 P. M. tonight.
> EDWARD.

In the next few days, until the funeral is over, he will have a foretaste of the strenuous life of duty awaiting him. He will be consulted upon a thousand matters of procedure. He must preside over

Continued on Page Nine.

Lieut. Giovannoli Named for Cheney Award; Faced Death in Rescues From Burning Plane

Special to THE NEW YORK TIMES

WASHINGTON, Jan. 20.—Lieutenant Robert K. Giovannoli of Lexington, Ky., on duty with the Army Air Corps at Dayton, was selected today to receive the Cheney Award for 1935, in recognition of his "extreme bravery" in the rescue of two men from a burning plane at Dayton on Oct. 30.

Lieutenant Giovannoli was born in 1904 in the District of Columbia, is a graduate of the University of Kentucky, and was commissioned in 1930.

"Probably not in the entire history of the Air Corps has a more heroic action been recorded," the War Department said of Lieutenant Giovannoli's act. An experimental bombing airplane crashed at Wright Field, the citation said in part, the wreckage catching fire. Three of the crew were rescued, but Major Ployer P. Hill, pilot, and Leslie Tower, civilian test pilot, were trapped in the all-metal cockpit.

Lieutenant Giovannoli extricated Tower through a window of the cabin. He returned, entered the compartment through the window, and began the task of releasing Major Hill. He worked with "seemingly superhuman energy" four or five minutes and cut loose with a pocket knife the pilot's shoe which had become wedged in the wreckage. He then raised the pilot and passed him through the window to waiting hands.

"His own escape from a perilous position in which he suffered serious and painful burns was considered miraculous," the citation said.

Major Hill died several hours later and Mr. Tower several days later.

THE DEAD KING.

THE NEW KING.

MONARCH'S DEATH STIRS WASHINGTON

Roosevelt Cables Condolences—He Is Expected to Appoint Special Envoy for Funeral.

GRIEF IN WORLD CAPITALS

Bitterness Abates in Rome—New Ruler Wins Praise in Berlin—Paris Is Moved.

Special to THE NEW YORK TIMES.

WASHINGTON, Jan. 20.—The death of King George caused deep sorrow and brought many expressions of grief here tonight. Official messages of condolence were sent to London by President Roosevelt and Secretary of State Cordell Hull.

Sir Ronald Lindsay, the British Ambassador, and the Ministers of Legations maintained here by British Dominions were deeply grieved. They refrained, however, from making any statements until they had been officially notified of the death by their governments.

Official periods of mourning will be declared by these missions by authority of royal decree. In addition to the British Embassy, there are maintained here legations of Canada, the Irish Free State and the Union of South Africa.

It is likely that President Roosevelt will designate a Special Ambassador to represent him at the funeral. A decision on this question, however, is being delayed until official information on the funeral arrangements has been received from the United States Embassy in London.

Messages by the President.

The following message was sent by the President to the new King:

> It is with deep sorrow that I learn of the death of His Majesty your father. I send to you my profound sympathy and that of the people of the United States, in whose respect and affection he occupied a high and unique place. I had the privilege of knowing His Majesty during the war days and his passing brings to me personally a special sorrow.

To Dowager Queen Mary the President sent this message:

> Mrs. Roosevelt and I extend to Your Majesty and to the members of your family our heartfelt sympathy and join you in mourning the loss of one whose high qualities of kindness and wisdom have been so powerful an influence for universal peace and justice.

Mr. Roosevelt also sent condolences to the governmental heads of the British Dominions—Australia, Canada, the Irish Free State, New Zealand and the Union of South Africa. The message to Lord Tweedsmuir, Governor General of Canada, was typical. It follows:

> Upon the sad occasion of the death of His Majesty King George, I offer to Your Excel-

Continued on Page Five.

Death Bulletin Posted At Sandringham House

By The Associated Press.

SANDRINGHAM, England, Tuesday, Jan. 21.—The last bulletin posted at "Jubilee Gate" of Sandringham House was done with rural simplicity.

Down the darkened drive a bareheaded youth rode a bicycle with a dim oil lamp flickering in front of him.

In an old brown leather case, which he carried in one hand while the other gripped a handlebar, he brought the announcement of the death of the Sovereign of the world's largest empire.

The chimes of the Sandringham church clock, striking half an hour after midnight, had just died away. Only the moaning of the wind through the elms bordering the drive broke the silence.

The youth, without dismounting, delivered the case at the lodge gate to one of the King's servants. The bulletin was taken out of the case and slowly, in the light of two great lanterns of the lodge, the gatekeeper walked across the drive and posted it.

DEATH IS MOURNED BY WHOLE EMPIRE

Aga Khan Honors the King's Memory in Bombay—Salute Is Fired in Singapore.

Special Cable to THE NEW YORK TIMES.

LONDON, Tuesday, Jan. 21.—Within a few minutes of the King's death almost every corner of the earth had heard the news.

In Bombay, India, the Aga Khan declared that the "King Emperor was not only a great ruler but also a great man." He added:

"I am sure that the new King Emperor will, with his knowledge of the world and the whole empire, be a worthy successor."

Mahatma Gandhi announced from his Bombay sick bed that he had sent "respectful condolences" to the royal family through the Viceroy, the Earl of Willingdon.

In Cape Town most persons were asleep when the news of the King's death was received, but at the Government House high officials waited near telephones.

In Singapore a Royal Air Force airplane flying a long black streamer gave the first general indication that the King was dead. Later a battery fired a salute of seventy guns. Mohammedans, Hindus, Buddhists, Chinese and Jews, as well as Christians of all denominations, plan memorial services. The news of the death caused a suspension of Chinese New Year festivities and all markets were closed.

When Melbourne, Australia, received the news in the middle of the morning public offices were closed. All sports were canceled. Sir Isaacs, performing his last duty as Governor General of the Commonwealth, sent a message of sympathy to the royal family.

Hushed crowds in Wellington,

Continued on Page Five.

LONDON SADDENED BY NEWS OF DEATH

Hushed Crowd at Buckingham Palace Receives Word From Mourning Servant.

END SEEMED ANTICIPATED

Quietness in Piccadilly Circus Long Before Midnight Showed Stress of Nation.

By FERDINAND KUHN Jr.
Special Cable to THE NEW YORK TIMES

LONDON, Tuesday, Jan. 21.—The hand of death lay upon London last night. It was a stunned and silent crowd of several hundreds that stood outside Buckingham Palace just after midnight when the notice announcing that the King had died was posted on the railing.

Few in the crowd could read what it said, but all knew what it meant. Heads were bared as if by a common signal, and all conversation was hushed to whispers.

One light glowed in a window high up in a corner of the palace, but nothing else broke the gloom except the incessant popping of photographers' flashlights and the glare of headlights from automobiles that drew slowly up to the palace gates and then passed on.

Sentry Continues March.

The front of the palace loomed up dimly in the darkness across the great courtyard. A sentry in gray tramped back and forth along the sidewalk as though nothing had happened.

The crowd stayed long after midnight, apparently unwilling to believe or unable to realize the King had died. Some attraction had drawn those hundreds to the palace, although the King was lying at Sandringham far away. After all, it was his home in his capital and it was to this building that thousands had come to acclaim him on Armistice Day and hundreds of thousands on the sunlit morning of his Jubilee.

Slowly the crowd melted away. By this time newsboys were shouting through the empty streets near by and their black-bordered placards announced that a great reign had ended.

But the palace sentry still marched up and down as he had done all evening. One King had died but another was on the throne and Great Britain had not changed at all.

Even before the sad news came the King's capital seemed to anticipate it. The electric signs of Piccadilly Circus flashed their messages as brightly as ever, but all the gayety had gone out of the life of the great city.

The theatres were half empty and the streets were strangely deserted as millions sat at their radios listening for news from Sandringham.

Early in the evening a vaudeville program from a broadcasting studio

Continued on Page Ten.

FAMILY WITH KING AT END

Queen Breaks Down as Long Vigil Closes at Sandringham.

HOPE HAD RISEN A LITTLE

Ruler, 70, Had Signed Paper Naming Council of State to Act in Illness.

PARLIAMENT MEETS TODAY

Theatres and Stock Exchange to Be Closed and Ships at Sea Will Lower Flags.

Outline of the life and reign of King George V, Pages 5 to 10.

By CHARLES A. SELDEN.
Special Cable to THE NEW YORK TIMES.

LONDON, Tuesday, Jan. 21.—George V, King and Emperor, passed peacefully last night in the twenty-sixth year of his reign and the seventy-first year of his life out of a world in which he had faced manfully much tribulation. His eldest son, as Edward VIII, now reigns in his stead over Great Britain, Ireland and the great British Empire overseas.

The King died five minutes before midnight in his own house of Sandringham in Norfolkshire, where he had spent the happiest hours of his life. His Queen and his children, all except one—Henry, Duke of Gloucester, who is himself ill in London—were at the bedside as the King's life ebbed away.

He suffered no pain, the doctors say. Throughout the last twelve hours his strength slowly failed until he fell asleep.

Canterbury Blesses Him.

Just before the end came the Archbishop of Canterbury, the King's lifelong friend, who had shared this last vigil with the royal family, bent over the dying monarch and gave him a last blessing.

A few moments later life was extinct and the news was being telephoned to Prime Minister Stanley Baldwin by Sir John Simon, Secretary of State for Home Affairs, who in virtue of his office had also remained at Sandringham near the King's chamber, and the news was being flashed also to the whole world.

The official bulletin of the death was as follows:

> Death came peacefully to the King at 11:55 o'clock tonight in the presence of Her Majesty the Queen, the Prince of Wales, the Duke of York, the Princess Royal and the Duke and Duchess of Kent.
> FREDERIC WILLANS,
> STANLEY HEWETT,
> DAWSON OF PENN.

From the death chamber there are already coming affecting stories of the last solemn scene. The Queen, who had maintained a constant watch both day and night in the room adjoining the King's bedroom, had at last been persuaded to take some food. Then she joined the others at the bedside. When the end came the iron self-control she had kept through the long, anxious days broke down at last. She turned to her son, the new King, and they exchanged an affectionate embrace. Each looked lovingly at the dead monarch, then with slow steps they turned away and went to another room, where they did their best to console each other.

Ships to Lower Flags.

Immediately on hearing the news from Sandringham the Admiralty Office in London flashed it to all British warships on the seven seas. Today all their flags will fly at halfmast.

Parliament will convene today as by law it must without summons whenever a sovereign dies. Mr. Baldwin has fixed the hour for the session at 6 o'clock in the evening.

In the House of Commons the Speaker will take the chair wearing white bands on the sleeves of his black gown and black shoe-

Continued on Page Five.

"All the News That's Fit to Print."

The New York Times.

LATE CITY EDITION
Fair and somewhat warmer today. Tomorrow rain and warmer.
Temperatures Yesterday—Max., 39; min., 17.

Section 1

VOL. LXXXV....No. 28,533. Entered as Second-Class Matter, Postoffice, New York, N. Y. NEW YORK, SUNDAY, MARCH 8, 1936. P Including Rotogravure Picture, Magazine and Book Review. TEN CENTS | TWELVE CENTS Beyond 200 Miles Except in 7th and 8th Postal Zones.

HITLER SENDS GERMAN TROOPS INTO RHINELAND; OFFERS PARIS 25-YEAR NON-AGGRESSION PACT; FRANCE MANS HER FORTS, BRITAIN STUDIES MOVE

STRIKE PEACE HOPE REVIVED AS MAYOR OFFERS A NEW PLAN

OWNERS ARE RECEPTIVE

Realty Board Acts Today on Move to Submit to Arbitration.

UNION ASSENT IS HINTED

Resumption of Negotiations Is Held Likely After La Guardia and Strikers Confer.

300 AT TUDOR CITY QUIT

More Park Av. Buildings Also Affected—Closed-Shop Issue No Longer a Factor.

Hope for settlement of the strike of elevator operators and other building service employes was revived last night after another appeal to both sides by Mayor La Guardia to submit the dispute to arbitration.

The Mayor made his proposal in identical telegrams addressed to the Building Service Employes Union, the strike organization, and the Realty Advisory Board, which has played the rôle of spokesman for large realty interests in the strike. Accompanying the Mayor's proposal was a detailed plan of settlement minus the closed shop.

The fact that the Mayor dispatched his peace plan after he had conferred at City Hall with strike leaders was taken as a clear indication that it was acceptable to the union, which had previously indicated its readiness to abandon the closed-shop demand.

William D. Rawlins, executive secretary of the Realty Advisory Board, declared after receipt of the Mayor's telegram that the peace plan might be looked upon with favor in the form in which it was submitted.

He announced that the directors of the Realty Advisory Board would consider the Mayor's proposal at a meeting this afternoon at the board's offices, 12 East Forty-first Street. The proposal will be analyzed by Walter Gordon Merritt, counsel for the board, after which a reply to the Mayor will be drafted.

New Negotiations Hoped For.

It was hoped last night that today's meeting of the Realty Advisory Board's directors would lead to a resumption of negotiations at City Hall tomorrow morning and to a settlement of the strike.

The Mayor's appeal for peace came after another day in which there were no important strike developments.

Although the union called out some 300 employes in Tudor City, preliminary to extending the walkout in the Grand Central area tomorrow, and appeared to be holding its lines in other parts of the city, there was no marked extension of the strike during the day.

Upon the intervention of the Mayor the union called off the strike in some 170 buildings controlled by the New York State Mortgage Commission after the commission had agreed to abide by any settlement ultimately reached with the realty interests of the city. The commission controls about 140 buildings in Manhattan and thirty in the Bronx.

In making known the dispatch of telegrams to the contending groups, pleading with them to bring the strike to a termination, Mayor La Guardia said:

"I am convinced that the strike can be settled if both sides are willing to do so. Resistance on one side and provocation on the other will get nowhere. Misrepresentations from either side are not helpful. The real issue now is wages and working conditions, and surely arbitration should be accepted by both sides.

"The Mayor will maintain law and order, protect life and property, and that goes for both sides. He will continue his efforts to end this controversy regardless of abuse from either side."

Closed-Shop Demand Eased.

The Mayor's plea was made public after he had conferred again with James J. Bambrick, strike leader, and other union spokesmen. His statement that "the real issue now is wages and working conditions" was taken as another indication that the union was will-

Continued on Page Thirty-seven.

Butler and Shaw Swap Retorts Not 'Courteous'

By The Associated Press.

SAN PEDRO, Calif., March 7.—Nicholas Murray Butler and George Bernard Shaw let go with both barrels of caustic sarcasm today at each other through the medium of interviews.

Said Dr. Butler, president of Columbia University, with regard to the gibes of G. B. S. at the American Constitution and the President:

"Anything George Bernard Shaw may say about politics is too ludicrous to comment upon. This won't surprise Mr. Shaw because it represents an opinion I have had about him for a long time. And he knows it."

Said G. B. S.:

"I suppose if Dr. Butler had an automobile that had been running for thirty years and was still running he would insist that it shouldn't be exchanged for a new motor car. That is the way with your Constitution. Dr. Butler's antiquated automobile wouldn't bring much of a 'trade-in.'

"Anyway I'm 'G. B. S.' and Dr. Butler isn't 'N. M. B.'"

LEHMAN CRIME PLEA POLITICS, SAYS IVES

Speaker Ascribes Attack on Assembly Members to Quest for Re-election Issue.

DEFENDS ALL COLLEAGUES

He Calls on the Governor for 'Appropriate Action' on Dodge and Geoghan.

The text of Mr. Ives's address is printed on Page 38.

Special to THE NEW YORK TIMES.

ALBANY, March 7.—Governor Lehman is making a "political football" of his crime program and picking a fight with the Legislature merely to develop an issue on which to run for re-election, Speaker Irving M. Ives of the Assembly asserted tonight in a State-wide radio broadcast.

The Speaker went on the air over WOKO and a chain of stations to reply to the radio attack of two weeks ago in which the Governor charged that "powerful groups of lawyer legislators" were banding together to hamstring his program in the Assembly.

Mr. Ives offered a detailed statement of his position on the crime bills, saying that his attitude was that of many Democrats and Republicans, and demanded that Governor Lehman "take appropriate action" in the cases of District Attorney William C. Dodge of New York and District Attorney William F. X. Geoghan of Kings. He said:

"Two glaring examples of the failure of law enforcement are to be found in New York City. The first is the case of District Attorney William F. X. Geoghan of Brooklyn, who, unable to secure convictions in the notorious Drukman case, was superseded by Special Prosecutor Hiram C. Todd, who obtained these convictions with admirable promptness.

Demands Governor Act.

"The second example is that pertaining to District Attorney William C. Dodge of New York County, who, after having shown himself unable to break up racketeering gangs which for years have been preying upon the public of New York, was finally superseded in this assignment by Attorney Thomas Dewey as special prosecutor. Where Mr. Dodge failed, Mr. Dewey has not failed and instead has obtained a number of convictions.

"Obviously, there must be some laxity of law enforcement somewhere in these cases, and I recommend that the Governor, in view of the facts, take appropriate action."

The Speaker enumerated "certain basic truths that have emerged from the confusion and misunderstanding which this anti-crime controversy has provoked."

He declared that "the intemperate charges directed at the Assembly by the Governor are utterly false and ridiculous."

He asserted that "the Governor has sought to claim credit for inaugurating all anti-crime programs offered in this State since the 1935 session of the Legislature, to the

Continued on Page Thirty-eight.

HOOVER DECLARES FREEDOM IN PERIL, LIFE 'MORTGAGED'

He Tells Colorado Republicans We Face Enslaving Taxes, Repudiation or Inflation.

'COMMON MAN' MUST PAY

Future 'Fireside Talks' Will Be With Collector, He Says—Hits 'Planned Economy.'

The text of Mr. Hoover's speech is printed on Page 36.

Special to THE NEW YORK TIMES.

COLORADO SPRINGS, March 7.—Crushing taxes, repudiation of debts or inflation are certain sequels to the New Deal, Herbert Hoover declared tonight before the Young Republican League of Colorado in a speech which was broadcast nationally.

The administration's spending and what he regarded as its steps toward dictatorship have failed to solve the problems of the depression or end unemployment, he said.

The former President asserted that the youth of the nation faced a choice between the old American system, with its political liberty and equality of economic opportunity, and a "planned economy" involving regimentation and bureaucracy.

The freedom and opportunities of youth "are being mortgaged," Mr. Hooover asserted, adding that "taxation enslaves as well as dictatorship."

More Taxes "Inevitable."

He warned that the nation's "future fireside talks" would be with the tax collector, and some believed that present taxes on wealth, designed to complete the cycle of "shirtsleeves to shirtsleeves in three generations," take the shirt also.

"Do not mistake," he went on. "The new taxes of today are but part of them. More of them are as inevitable as the first of the month. The only alternatives are repudiation or inflation. No matter what nonsense you are told about corporations and the rich paying the bill, there will be two-thirds of it for the common man to pay after the corporations and the rich are sucked dry."

He said, further:

"And where do we get to after all this attempt to supplant the American system? At the time of the election in 1932 the American Federation of Labor reported 11,600,000 unemployed. Today, after three years of the New Deal, they report 11,600,000 unemployed.

"To get these people back to their jobs was the outstanding job of our government. It was the excuse given for all these doings. But the grim fact remains that it has failed in its primary purpose. And $15,000,000,000 will be added to the national debt before the New Deal is over."

The Record on Platform Pledges.

Mr. Hoover contrasted the administration's actions and party platform promises of 1932, and said that when he was President all but two of the thirty-seven Republican platform promises were carried out, despite depression difficulties. Two secondary promises, he said, "broke against the obstinacy of a Democratic Congress."

The trend of events in this country since 1932, he said, followed the pattern of European nations that succumbed to dictatorship, and he added that the New Deal had "imitated the intellectual and vocal technique of typical European revolution."

The great contributions to civili-

Continued on Page Thirty-six.

Rumania's War Council Called to Special Session

By The Associated Press.

BUCHAREST, March 7.—The Rumanian Defense Council tonight was called to a special session Monday, to devise means for improving and rapidly increasing the nation's armaments. The council consists of King Carol, former Premiers and the general staff of the army.

The semi-official newspaper, Dimineata, predicted that the League of Nations would apply economic sanctions against Germany as a result of remilitarizing the Rhineland.

Commenting on Chancellor Adolf Hitler's speech before the Reichstag, the newspaper said, "Germany is laughing today, but France and England will be laughing tomorrow."

MUSSOLINI ACCEPTS PEACE PARLEY BID

League Invitation Satisfactory in Principle as Basis for Talks, He Tells Cabinet.

ITALY WILL NOT AID PARIS

Imposition of Sanctions Said to Have Freed Nation of Locarno Obligations.

By ARNALDO CORTESI.
Wireless to THE NEW YORK TIMES.

ROME, March 7.—At almost the minute when Chancellor Adolf Hitler, in Berlin, was announcing the reoccupation of the Rhineland, Premier Benito Mussolini, in Rome, was informing the Italian Cabinet Council that he had decided to accept "in principle" the invitation of the League of Nations to negotiate peace with Ethiopia.

These two facts, though seemingly unrelated, are likely to have some important repercussions on each other. The turmoil created in Europe by Hitler's move, which has directed attention from East Africa and pushed sanctions into the background, is expected to help Mussolini to drive a hard bargain with the Negus and to settle the Italo-Ethiopian conflict with all possible speed.

Italy, as soon as her best energies are no longer fettered in Africa, will be able to make her weight felt in the European balance of power and participate in the process of readjustment in the next few years.

The text of Mussolini's reply to the League's peace appeal is not yet known and will not be made public until it has arrived at Geneva. Therefore, it is still uncertain whether he has agreed unreservedly to negotiate or whether he has pledged his acceptance with important reservations.

Newspapers, usually regarded as the government's mouthpieces, are at variance on this point. The Giornale d'Italia thinks, as the invitation of the League contained no limitations, there are no conditions in Mussolini's reply. The Tribuna on the contrary says that Mussolini's acceptance does not tie him down to anything and implies the widest reservations. It also

Continued on Page Thirty-nine.

Brief Attack of Cold Is Repelled by Sun; Rising Temperatures Forecast for Today

Winter tried to take possession of the city again yesterday, just two weeks before the official arrival of Spring. But a bright sun in a clear sky turned Winter back with a jump of 7 degrees in temperature within little more than an hour in the afternoon.

A forecast for continuing rising temperatures and fair skies is expected to bring a moderate day of above-freezing weather today and warmer weather and rain tomorrow.

From midnight Friday until 3 o'clock yesterday afternoon the mercury remained below freezing and brought a renewed touch of Winter to the city. At 8 A. M. the temperature dropped to a low of 17—the coldest since the days of snow and ice on Fifth Avenue and Broadway.

Within the next hour the mercury rose ten degrees and then dropped back for several hours before renewing an upward course at noon. At 3 P. M., when the mercury stood at 32, a shift in light winds from the north to the southwest sent it up quickly to a high of 39 at 4:15, after which it fell slightly.

The average temperature for the day was 28, which is seven degrees below the normal. The coldest March 7 in the records of the Weather Bureau was in 1890, when the mercury dropped to 6, and the warmest was in 1921, when it rose to 69.

Since Jan. 1, when the day was 9 hours and 17 minutes long, the length of the day has increased gradually and will be 11 hours and 32 minutes long today. On March 18 the vernal equinox will begin with the day and night each 12 hours long. Two days later, on March 20, at 1:58 P. M., Spring will begin.

PARIS APPEALS TO LEAGUE

Rejects Reich Proposal of a Substitute for Locarno Treaty.

ALLIES SUPPORT PROGRAM

Russia and Czechoslovakia to Aid to 'Limit' in Effort to Clear Rhineland.

BELGIUM ACTS AT BORDER

French Officials Say Military Moves to Drive Back Germans Await Geneva Decisions.

By P. J. PHILIP.
Wireless to THE NEW YORK TIMES.

PARIS, March 7.—France has laid Germany's latest treaty violation before the Council of the League of Nations. That is the procedure called for in the situation.

At the same time the French Government today made it quite clear that there could be no negotiation with Germany of any substitute for the Treaty of Locarno or anything else as long as a single German soldier remained in the Rhineland in contravention of Germany's signed undertakings.

While no public mention of French troop movements is being made here, it is obvious that the necessary precautions will be taken, probably on the same scale as last March, when the Reich government denounced the military clauses of the Treaty of Versailles and reorganized her army.

[France ordered all northeastern border fortifications garrisoned at full strength, The Associated Press reports, and Belgium canceled leaves for troops garrisoning her eastern frontier.]

Withdrawal Held Essential.

What is essential, in the French view, is that the German Government must be compelled, by diplomatic pressure first and by stronger pressure if need be, to withdraw from the Rhineland. For what is found most intolerable in all today's happenings is this renewed appearance of the mailed fist in diplomacy—not, in French opinion, in the service of common peace and order, but as a menace and provocation.

Everything that can be done to avoid war will be done. But there should be no mistaking this fact in Germany or elsewhere: that rather than submit to this last crashing piece of Teutonism, France will fight.

Meanwhile, as always, the French have presented their case. The Cabinet met twice today, once in reduced numbers at the Elysée Palace with President Albert Lebrun and later at the Quai d'Orsay. Between the two meetings Foreign Minister Pierre-Etienne Flandin called in the Ambassadors of all signatory powers of the Locarno agreements for consultation and to acquaint them with his government's views.

General Marie Gustave Gamelin, chief of the General Staff, took part in the Elysée Palace meeting.

The Cabinet has been summoned for tomorrow morning to be kept fully apprised of the situation and to learn the attitude of other governments whose opinions have been sought by French diplomatic representatives.

After the second Cabinet meeting, Mr. Flandin, in the famous clock room at the Quai d'Orsay, read to the biggest assembly of newspaper men there had been there since the days of the Versailles treaty a long declaration setting forth his government's views and decisions. It was a direct indictment of German veracity and an exposure of all treaty infractions involved in today's actions.

Invokes Mediation Clause.

One of his most damning declarations was the invocation of that section of the Locarno Pact by which France and Germany agreed that if any difference should arise between them which could not be dealt with by ordinary diplomatic means, they would submit it to conciliation and arbitration.

That procedure, it is argued here,

Continued on Page Thirty.

GERMAN ARMY AGAIN ON THE RHINE.

The shaded portion of the map shows the district demilitarized under the Treaty of Versailles. It included all German territory on the west of the Rhine and a zone fifty kilometers wide along the east bank. The stars show where the principal garrisons were established.

GERMANY'S ACTION ASSAILED BY EDEN

He Uses Severe Tone Toward Reich Envoy, but Attitude of Cabinet Is Deemed Milder.

By AUGUR.
Special Cable to THE NEW YORK TIMES.

LONDON, March 7.—Foreign Secretary Anthony Eden used strong words to condemn the German Government's action when Ambassador Leopold von Hoesch of Germany presented to him this morning Chancellor Adolf Hitler's memorandum concerning the Rhineland.

Mr. Eden said the British Government must consider the entry of German regular troops into the forbidden zone to be in defiance of treaty obligations and a flagrant breach of a territorial frontier. The terms of the Treaty of Locarno impose definite duties on the British Government. The implications of the situation now created will therefore be carefully gone into.

But to Charles Corbin, the French Ambassador, Mr. Eden said that the government, while determined to comply with treaty obligations, was equally desirous of avoiding hasty action and it advised the French Government to study the points of the German offer, for they appear to be not without value.

Action Had Been Expected.

The fact is that at the bottom of their hearts Cabinet Ministers here are not so displeased with Hitler's proposals as it officially must be said they are. For sometime past the demilitarized zone has been written off as lost. A chance to obtain a solid counter-value for a hopeless item on the balance sheet appears attractive for practical politicians in London.

The real question awaiting reply is whether Hitler offers advantages that upon closer inspection may be found ephemeral once the fact of the illegal military occupation of the Rhineland is accepted without demur.

Officials in Berlin, it is known here, were alarmed when Foreign Minister Pierre-Etienne Flandin of France put a direct question to Mr. Eden concerning British aid in case of an infraction by Ger-

Continued on Page Thirty-three.

ARMY MARCHES IN AS HITLER SPEAKS

In Full War Equipment It Goes to Rhineland, Ending Its Advance Near Frontier.

By OTTO D. TOLISCHUS.
Wireless to THE NEW YORK TIMES.

BERLIN, March 7.—Germany today resumed her "watch on the Rhine" when, with an astonishing bravado that dared challenge Europe to war or to peace and left the world breathless for the moment, the new German Army crossed the military frontier, which hitherto has separated it from France, and occupied the demilitarized Rhineland zone created by the Versailles treaty and reaffirmed at Locarno.

The move was carried through with that German efficiency which drew from foreign military experts tribute to the German Army command and amid manifestations of both popular enthusiasm and grave apprehension. It brought back echoes of the last German westward march nearly twenty-two years ago, but also it was made to look like a dress rehearsal for more serious business.

Even while Chancellor Adolf Hitler was serving notice of the contemplated move to diplomats of the Locarno powers assembled in the chancellery at 11 A. M. field-gray masses of the troops of occupation were already on the march.

Planes Circle Cologne.

A few minutes before Hitler began to announce this move to the world in his speech before the Reichstag the first military flying squadrons already were circling Cologne's cathedral spires. As he began to talk infantry, artillery, motorized cavalry, tanks, machine-gun units, anti-aircraft artillery and all other paraphernalia of modern warfare already were closing the Rhine bridges, and two hours after he had finished, his advance guards already had reached Saarbruecken, their westernmost point for the present, only three kilometers from the French frontier.

According to an official announcement, troop movements will continue all day tomorrow. Occupation of the zone, which comprises

Continued on Page Thirty-one.

VERSAILLES CURB BROKEN

Hitler Smashes Locarno Citing Franco-Soviet Treaty as Reason.

READY TO REJOIN LEAGUE

Battle for Equality Ended, He Tells Joyous Reichstag—Sets Vote for March 29.

URGES AIR PACT IN WEST

Bilateral Neutralization of Rhine Proposed—Hand Is Extended to Lithuania.

Hitler's Reichstag speech and other texts on Pages 31, 32, 33.

By GUIDO ENDERIS.
Wireless to THE NEW YORK TIMES.

BERLIN, March 7.—Germany today cast off the last shackles fastened upon her by the Treaty of Versailles when Adolf Hitler, as commander-in-chief of the Reich defense forces, sent his new battalions into the Rhineland demilitarized zone.

The Chancellor's marching orders were timed to synchronize with Germany's notification to the powers concerned and to a listening Reich that she no longer considered herself bound by the Locarno terms because the fundamental basis and inherent purpose of that pact had been destroyed through the conclusion of the mutual assistance treaty between France and the Soviet Union.

Hitler related to the Reichstag all he had done. After he had proposed a daring peace program he was greeted with a burst of enthusiasm when he announced that with complete sovereignty over all German territory restored, the Reich was prepared not only to return to the League of Nations, but also to cooperate in any system of collective security that gave promise of success.

Sees Struggle Closed.

"After three years of ceaseless battle," Hitler concluded, "I look upon this day as marking the close of the struggle for German equality status and with that re-won equality the path is now also clear for Germany's return to European collective cooperation."

To give the German people an opportunity to pass judgment on his leadership, Hitler said, he decided to dissolve the Reichstag and order a plebiscite on Sunday, March 29, in which German voters will be able to record their confidence or lack of it in the government's home and foreign policies.

The announcement of Germany's denunciation of the Locarno pact, which she voluntarily negotiated with France and Belgium in 1925 and for which Great Britain and Italy stood sponsors, provoked less jubilation in the Reichstag than did the news that German troops at that very hour were again marching to their peace garrisons in the Rhineland. That news unloosed a cyclone of rejoicing as the 660 Deputies rose to greet it.

But the Chancellor's speech as a whole must be counted an outstanding political pronouncement and oratorical achievement with respect to both its contents and forceful delivery and also the intense sincerity that marked the recital of the reasons that had determined him to abrogate Locarno.

Offers Non-Aggression Pacts.

The speech was easily Hitler's boldest utterance on German foreign policy. While it was not free from recriminations and indictment of France's refusal to grasp Germany's outstretched hand, that hand was once more revealed as offering France and Belgium a twenty-five-year non-aggression pact at the very moment when the roll of German regimental drums was being heard along the Rhine for the first time since 1919.

The proposed non-aggression pact, which Hitler said was open also to the Netherlands, constituted the only part of his seven-point peace scheme that he offered as a substitute for the discarded Locarno accord.

Germany is also prepared, he continued, to negotiate immediately for the creation of a demilitarized

Continued on Page Thirty.

"All the News That's Fit to Print."

The New York Times.

FINAL EXTRA
Rain and much colder today. To-morrow fair, with little change in temperature.
Temperatures Yesterday—Max., 73; Min., 63

VOL. LXXXVI.....No. 28,774. Entered as Second-Class Matter, Postoffice, New York, N. Y. NEW YORK, WEDNESDAY, NOVEMBER 4, 1936. TWO CENTS In New York City. | THREE CENTS Within 200 Miles. | FOUR CENTS Elsewhere Except in 7th and 8th Postal Zones.

ROOSEVELT SWEEPS THE NATION; HIS ELECTORAL VOTE EXCEEDS 500; LEHMAN WINS; CHARTER ADOPTED

FEW HOUSE SHIFTS

Democrats May Add to Vast Majorities in Both Chambers

THREE SENATORS TRAIL

Barbour, Hastings and Metcalf Appear to Have Lost Seats.

90 HOUSE RACES IN DOUBT

Democrats Elect 254, While Republicans Obtain 84, and Progressives 6.

By TURNER CATLEDGE

Republican hopes of making heavy inroads upon the huge Democratic majorities in Congress were apparently smothered under the pro-Roosevelt landslide in yesterday's election.

As the size of the New Deal avalanche continued to grow into the early morning hours the Democrats gave promise of actually increasing their lop-sided majority in the Senate and were offsetting Republican gains of new House seats by capturing places now held by anti-New Dealers. If the trend of the count persists in the tardy tabulations today the Democrats may hold their own or actually add to their majorities in both branches of Congress.

In the wreckage left by the Democratic sweep also appeared the Senatorial careers of three outstanding Republican Senators—Barbour of New Jersey, Hastings of Delaware and Metcalf of Rhode Island. As the count from their respective States stood early today, these three incumbents appeared defeated.

Moreover, the Democrats threatened to pick up still another Republican Senate seat, that formerly occupied by the late Senator Couzens, and they were pressing hard upon Senator Lester J. Dickinson of Iowa, whose opposition to the administration's farm relief program won for him the enmity of many farmers in his State.

Lodge Leading Curley

The only present Democratic Senate seat which appeared definitely lost to the Democrats was that held by Senator Marcus Coolidge of Massachusetts. Henry Cabot Lodge 2d, Republican, was well ahead of Governor James M. Curley for this post, despite the State's substantial majority for the remainder of the Democratic national and State ticket.

Still another Democratic berth was threatened. Senator W. J. Bulow, Democrat, was trailing Chandler Gurney, Republican, by a slight margin in South Dakota.

The veteran Senator Norris, who left the Republican fold to stand for re-election as an Independent in Nebraska, was increasing his lead over former Representative Robert G. Simmons, Republican, and Terry Carpenter, "regular" Democrat.

Representative Ernest Lundeen, Farmer-Labor candidate, was piling up a commanding lead over former Governor Theodore Christianson, Republican, in Minnesota.

Senator Borah, Republican dean of the Senate, was doing the same to his opponent, Governor C. Ben Ross, Democrat.

As the Senate count stood early today, the Democrats appeared to have elected twenty of the thirty-six Senators who were up for election this year and the Republicans six, while ten were still in doubt. On this showing the Democrats would have a membership of at least sixty-seven Democrats in the new Congress, the Republicans seventeen, Farmer-Laborites one, and Progressives one. The Democrats stood a good chance to pick up still others out of the ten in

Continued on Page Three

Landon Congratulates President, Who Replies

Special to THE NEW YORK TIMES.

TOPEKA, Wednesday, Nov. 4.—Governor Landon conceded his defeat in a message of congratulation to President Roosevelt at 1:30 o'clock this morning, Eastern standard time.

His message read as follows:

"The nation has spoken. Every American will accept the verdict and work for the common cause of the good of our country. That is the spirit of democracy. You have my sincere congratulations."

"ALF M. LANDON."

Governor Landon decided to send the message after he had retired for the night at the Executive Mansion, with the word that no statement would be issued during the night.

Special to THE NEW YORK TIMES.

HYDE PARK, N. Y., Wednesday, Nov. 4.—Half an hour after receiving Governor Landon's message President Roosevelt sent the following reply:

"I am grateful to you for your generous telegram and I am confident that all of us Americans will now pull together for the common good. I send you every good wish."

UNION PARTY VOTE FAR BELOW BOASTS

Coughlin Group Appears to Have Exercised Little Influence on the Electorate.

SUPPORT OF LEMKE WEAK

Even in Ohio and South Dakota His Showing in the Early Returns Is Poor.

By F. RAYMOND DANIELL

Representative William Lemke, the Presidential candidate of the so-called "lunatic fringe," made scarcely a dent in the great totals the nation piled up for President Roosevelt and Alfred M. Landon in yesterday's voting.

Showing his greatest strength in Illinois, Pennsylvania and Massachusetts, the North Dakota Representative, who had the backing of the Rev. Charles E. Coughlin, Dr. Francis E. Townsend and the Rev. Gerald L. K. Smith, still remained a negligible factor in the outcome of the election.

Despite confident predictions by the Union party's backers last August that Mr. Lemke would take enough votes from Mr. Roosevelt to deprive him of a majority in the Electoral College, thus throwing the election into the House of Representatives, nowhere did he poll a substantial enough vote to hurt either major party candidate.

In his home State of North Dakota the co-author of the Frazier-Lemke bill was trailing far behind the President and his Republican opponent. The first seventy-eight precincts reporting gave Mr. Lemke only 1,280 to Mr. Roosevelt's 11,644 and Mr. Landon's 5,333.

Here in New York, Father Coughlin's candidate for the House of Representatives in the Sixteenth Assembly District was snowed under. He was former State Senator John A. Hastings, an intimate friend of former Mayor James J. Walker. His opponent was Representative John J. O'Connor, who incurred Father Coughlin's wrath by threatening to kick the priest of Royal Oak from the Capitol to the White House. Mr. O'Connor seemed an easy winner in the Sixteenth.

Two reasons were advanced to explain the failure of Mr. Lemke to make a better showing. The first was that Father Coughlin, the Rev. Mr. Smith and Dr. Townsend all were inflationists when it came to estimating the size of their following, which each placed in the neighborhood of 6,000,000 voters. The second was that the men and women who cheered so loudly at the Cleveland conventions of the National Union for Social Justice and Old Age Revolving Pensions Ltd., became Republicans and Democrats again after returning home.

The early vote for Representative William Lemke, even in States where Father Coughlin's National Union for Social Justice boasts a

Continued on Page Five

BIG CHARTER VOTE

8-Hour System for Firemen Also Wins Easily

VOTING CHANGE APPROVED

Brunner Is Victor Over Morris by Large Plurality.

ROOSEVELT SWEEP HERE

President's Vote and Margin, Which Reached 1,356,458, Set Highest City Record.

By RUSSELL B. PORTER

President Roosevelt piled up the largest vote and plurality ever accorded to a candidate for any office in the history of New York City at yesterday's election.

With all the city's 3,799 election districts in, the President had the extraordinary plurality of 1,356,458, which was considerably larger even that his campaign managers had estimated.

This was about 50 per cent larger than his 1932 plurality and about three times former Governor Alfred E. Smith's city plurality when he ran against Herbert Hoover for the Presidency in 1928.

The total Presidential vote was 2,747,240, or over 500,000 more than the total vote cast in the 1932 Presidential election and the 1933 Mayoralty election, the previous records.

Governor Lehman ran behind the President, but had a plurality of 921,938 with no election districts missing. He ran about 2 to 1 ahead of William F. Bleakley, his Republican opponent, while President Roosevelt's ratio was 3 to 1 over Governor Landon. Governor Lehman's plurality was not as large as in 1932, when it was 989,844, but was larger than two years ago, when it was 803,956.

Brunner an Easy Winner

In the day's only election for city office, William F. Brunner, Democrat, had a final plurality of 891,880 over Newbold Morris, Republican, in the contest for president of the Board of Aldermen, with no election districts missing.

The voters approved all three local questions on which referenda were taken. They accepted the new city charter by 927,396 to 583,044, an affirmative majority of 344,354, with 689 election districts missing.

With 78 election districts missing, they voted 898,389 for and 551,914

Continued on Page Four

Smith Plans Comment On the Election Today

Alfred E. Smith, former Democratic candidate for President who espoused the cause of Alfred M. Landon in this campaign said last night that he probably would issue a statement today setting forth his views on President Roosevelt's sweeping victory.

Earlier in the evening he had called THE NEW YORK TIMES to ask how the election was going. He was informed that President Roosevelt was leading in all but a handful of States. He made no comment but when he was asked if he were going to a party of Jeffersonian Democrats in the apartment of Raoul Desvernine, Liberty League lawyer, to which he had been invited, he replied:

"No, I'm going to bed."

P. S.—The former Governor did not retire at once. He called up an hour later to get the latest returns.

DEMOCRATS RETAIN STATE SENATE LEAD

They Are Assured of 30 Seats of the 51, One More Than Their Previous Number.

FAIL TO WIN ASSEMBLY

Republicans Are Beaten for Five Places, but Still Hold a Bare Working Majority.

By W. A. WARN

The Democrats will control the State Senate by a subsantial majority and the Republicans will have a bare working majority in the Assembly, according to complete returns from the legislative elections.

The latest returns give the Democrats thirty seats out of fifty-one in the Senate, a net gain of one over their present quota. The Republicans suffered a loss of five seats in the Assembly, but still retain seventy-six seats, which gives them the constitutional majority necessary to pass bills and prevail on important parliamentary motions.

The result in not a few of the districts, however, on the face of the latest returns was so close that in some instances a demand may be made by the losers for recount proceedings.

This city will lose its only Republican Senator through the defeat of Senator Joseph C. Baldwin 3d in the Seventeenth Senatorial District, situated in Manhattan. Leon A. Fischel, Democrat, carried the district by a plurality somewhat below 5,000.

The Democratic solidarity of Albany County in its legislative representatives surprisingly was broken. A Republican candidate for Assembly, John McBain, nominated in

Continued on Page Five

Roosevelt, Speaking to Victory Procession At Hyde Park, Predicted Record Sweep

By CHARLES W. HURD

Special to THE NEW YORK TIMES.

HYDE PARK, Nov. 3.—With wire returns indicating a landslide for President Roosevelt far in excess of the majority necessary to re-elect him, President Roosevelt said tonight that he thought the "sweep" might carry every section of the United States.

Speaking to several hundred loyal followers who staged a victory procession through rain from Hyde Park to Mr. Roosevelt's home, Hyde Park House, at 10:30 P. M., he said:

"The returns are not all in yet, so I can't say anything official or final, but it looks as though we are going to have one of the largest sweeps ever heard of in the United States."

"As a matter of fact, from the returns now, it looks as though this sweep has carried every single section of the country," he exclaimed.

The President, laughing and happy, spoke while standing on the open porch of his house, looking out over a crowd whose faces were illuminated by red-fire torches and the calcium flares used for light for motion pictures.

He waved aside sound microphones, saying: "This is just a home party."

The crowd cheered the President, Mrs. Roosevelt, and his mother, Mrs. Sara Delano Roosevelt.

The assemblage cheered loudly when Mr. Roosevelt said one of his happiest moments came with the word that he had carried the village of Hyde Park, although he lost the township.

The crowd remained for half an hour, with some enthusiastic persons shouting "How about 1940?"

Mr. Roosevelt leaned on the arm of his son, Franklin Jr. Beside him were his wife and mother. Grouped behind him was a small party including his daughter, Mrs. Anna Boettiger, and Mr. Boettiger, Mrs. James Roosevelt, his daughter-in-law, and other relatives.

Others in the party included Secretary and Mrs. Morgenthau, Judge and Mrs. Sam Rosenman, Frederick A. Delano and members of the White House staff and newspaper correspondents.

LEHMAN VOTE CUT

Bleakley Gets a Surprising Total in the City

SWEEP HELPS GOVERNOR

Roosevelt Strong in Industrial Cities—Gets Big Up-State Poll.

OTHER DEMOCRATS SAFE

Bray, Tremaine, Bennett and Others of State Ticket Regarded Certain of Victory.

By JAMES A. HAGERTY

Governor Herbert H. Lehman was re-elected Governor of New York yesterday for a third term. The indicated plurality for the Governor over former Supreme Court Justice William F. Bleakley, his Republican opponent, was about 600,000.

Governor Lehman, who was urged to become a candidate for re-election to help President Roosevelt, ran far behind the President in New York City. With all the election districts reported, his plurality in New York City was 921,938 as compared with the city plurality of 1,356,458, or more than the million and a quarter predicted by Postmaster General Farley, for President Roosevelt. President Roosevelt's plurality in the State was indicated at about 1,150,000.

The tremendous vote for President Roosevelt in New York City and the failure of Governor Landon to carry up-State by much more than 200,000 indicated that the defection of former Governor Alfred E. Smith and other Jeffersonian Democrats had little effect on the Presidential vote, although there apparently were influences within the Democratic party working against Governor Lehman in New York City.

With New York City complete and 480 election districts missing out of 5,151 up-State, the vote for President was:

	Roosevelt.	Landon.
Up-State	1,197,201	1,370,516
New York City	2,016,204	659,746
Totals	3,213,405	2,030,262

Actual plurality for Roosevelt, 1,183,143.

With New York City complete and 892 election districts missing up-State, the vote for Governor was:

	Lehman.	Bleakley.
Up-State	1,060,564	1,338,892
New York City	1,795,124	873,186
Totals	2,855,688	2,212,078

Actual plurality for Lehman, 643,610.

The tremendous vote for President Roosevelt swept to victory the other State-wide Democratic candidates for re-election, Lieut. Gov. M. William Bray, Controller Morris S. Tremaine, Attorney General John J. Bennett Jr., and Mrs. Caroline O'Day and Matthew J. Merritt, Representatives at Large.

Incomplete returns also indicated the election of Harlan W. Rippey, Democratic candidate for Associate Judge of the Court of Appeals over Supreme Court Justice James P. Hill, Republican candidate.

City Margin Is Unprecedented

President Roosevelt carried New York City by the unprecedented plurality of 1,356,458, the total vote being 2,016,204 for the President and 659,746 for Governor Landon. This was more than 50,000 in excess of the results forecast in the surveys made by the five Democratic county leaders, which they believed should be scaled down 10 per cent to give the probable results.

Governor Lehman's New York City plurality increased with the late returns, and he did not run as far behind the President as the early returns had indicated he would do.

With all election districts reported, the vote for Governor in New

Continued on Page Five

©New York Times Studio Photo.

FRANKLIN D. ROOSEVELT

DEMOCRATS SWEEP ALL PENNSYLVANIA

President Wins by More Than 550,000 in First National Party Victory in 70 Years.

PHILADELPHIA IS CARRIED

Whole State Government and the Legislature Go to Democratic Control.

Special to THE NEW YORK TIMES.

PHILADELPHIA, Wednesday, Nov. 4.—Pennsylvania, the Keystone State of Republicanism, was swept yesterday by the Democrats for the first time in a Presidential election since the Civil War era.

With unprecedented Democratic pluralities in Philadelphia and Allegheny Counties, with greatly diminished Republican pluralities in the commuting counties about Philadelphia, and with even the rural districts only half heartedly Republican, President Roosevelt carried the State by a margin which exceeded 550,000 votes.

Returns from 6,733 of the State's 8,010 divisions gave:

Roosevelt, 2,010,343.
Landon, 1,469,679.
Lemke, 44,253.

Complete returns from the 1,291 divisions in this city gave:

Roosevelt 521,941.
Landon, 322,229.

This city plurality of 199,712 exceeds that for Herbert Hoover in 1932 for the whole State by 40,000.

The Democratic victory, the size of which amazed even the leaders of that party, not only gave to President Roosevelt this State's thirty-six electoral votes, but put the State government wholly in the hands of the Democrats.

Democrats Get Legislature

George H. Earle in 1934 seized the Governorship for the Democrats for the first time in forty-four years. Since assuming office he has been at odds constantly with a Republican-controlled State Senate, which has succeeded in balking many of his plans for putting a "little New Deal" in effect in Pennsylvania.

As a result of yesterday's election

Continued on Page Three

JERSEY'S 16 VOTES SAFE FOR NEW DEAL

Upsets in Republican Areas Add to Huge Pluralities in Democratic Counties.

SMATHERS SEEMS WINNER

Senate Aspirant Runs Behind Roosevelt but Has Lead Over Barbour, Incumbent.

New Jersey's sixteen electoral votes seemed at 5 o'clock this morning in possession of President Roosevelt. Reports from 1,719 of the State's 3,551 election districts gave him 493,071 votes to 295,794 for Governor Landon.

Hudson County, the great Democratic stronghold run by the State leader, Mayor Frank Hague of Jersey City, was responsible for this tremendous lead in what had been a doubtful State until the count began. It seemed quite likely that, although Mr. Landon made gains in other areas, he never could overcome the Hudson County handicap, particularly since several normally powerful Republican communities deserted Landon for Roosevelt.

Keeping pace with President Roosevelt in the Democratic territories, but dropping behind him in many Republican sections which the President dominated, State Senator William H. Smathers, Democrat, had in 1,656 districts a total of 404,546 for United States Senator.

His Republican opponent, W. Warren Barbour, the incumbent, was gathering many hundreds here and there, outside Hudson County, having a total in the same districts of 297,000. Though this seemed a difficult lead to overcome, Mr. Barbour was quite confident that the great number of unreported districts would offset the Smathers advantage and pull him through for another stay in Washington.

Even Mayor Hague's prediction of 125,000 plurality in Hudson County for Roosevelt was so far surpassed as to give him a happy surprise. In 545 districts out of 584 in that county, the President received 284,-

Continued on Page Eleven

POLL SETS RECORD

Roosevelt Electoral Vote of 519 Seen as a Minimum

NO SWING TO THE BOLTERS

'JeffersonianDemocrats' Fail to Cause Rift as Expected.

NEIGHBORS HAIL PRESIDENT.

Landon Concedes Defeat and Sends His Congratulations to Victorious Rival.

By ARTHUR KROCK

Accepting the President as the issue, nearly eight million more voters than ever before had gone to the polls in the United States—about 45,000,000 persons—yesterday gave to Franklin Delano Roosevelt the most overwhelming testimonial of approval ever received by a national candidate in the history of the nation.

Except for the small corner of New England occupied by Maine, Vermont and New Hampshire—which was oscillating between Republican and Democratic in the early morning hours of Wednesday—the President was the choice of a vast preponderance of the voters in all parts of the country, and with him were re-elected as Vice President John N. Garner of Texas and an almost untouched Democratic majority in the House of Representatives. The Democratic national ticket will have a minimum of 519 electoral votes and a possible popular majority of ten millions.

The Republican candidates for President and Vice President, Governor Alfred M. Landon of Kansas and Colonel Frank Knox of Illinois, are the worst-beaten aspirants for these offices in the political annals of the United States, with the exception of William H. Taft in 1912, when Colonel Theodore Roosevelt led a formidable revolt in the Republican party and Mr. Taft carried only Vermont and Utah. Yesterday Utah was also in the President's campaign bag. He had carried forty-five States as contrasted with the forty-two he won from Herbert Hoover in 1932. And to assure his reputation as the greatest vote-getter in the annals of the United States he—a Democrat—had overwhelmingly swept Pennsylvania, unfailingly Republican for generations in national elections.

The following table contains a list of the States carried by the President, with a total of 519 electoral votes, to which the four of New Hampshire may yet be added:

Alabama	11	Nebraska	7
Arizona	3	Nevada	3
Arkansas	9	New Jersey	16
California	22	New Mexico	3
Colorado	6	New York	47
Connecticut	8	North Carolina	13
Delaware	3	North Dakota	4
Florida	7	Ohio	26
Georgia	12	Oklahoma	11
Idaho	4	Oregon	5
Illinois	29	Pennsylvania	36
Indiana	14	Rhode Island	4
Iowa	11	South Carolina	8
Kansas	9	South Dakota	4
Kentucky	11	Tennessee	11
Louisiana	10	Texas	23
Maryland	8	Utah	4
Massachusetts	17	Virginia	11
Michigan	19	Washington	8
Minnesota	11	West Virginia	8
Mississippi	9	Wisconsin	12
Missouri	15	Wyoming	3
Montana	4		

Landon Sends Congratulations

After hours of hopeful waiting on rural districts in the Northeast States, Mr. Landon and the Republican national chairman, John D. M. Hamilton, announced their intentions of letting the night pass before agreeing to the fact of the stupendous party defeat. But about 1 A. M. in Topeka, Mr. Landon sent the customary message of congratulation to the President at Hyde Park, and at 1:45 A. M., at headquarters in Chicago, Mr. Hamilton followed suit. All the important newspapers supporting the Republican ticket (about 90 per cent of the metropolitan and country

Continued on Page Three

"All the News That's Fit to Print."

The New York Times.

LATE CITY EDITION
Cloudy, mild, with occasional rain today; clearing, colder tonight. Tomorrow colder.
Temperature Yesterday—Max., 51; Min., 38

VOL. LXXXVI.....No. 28,811. Entered as Second-Class Matter, Postoffice, New York, N. Y. NEW YORK, FRIDAY, DECEMBER 11, 1936. P TWO CENTS In New York City. | THREE CENTS Within 200 Miles. | FOUR CENTS Elsewhere Except in 7th and 8th Postal Zones.

EDWARD VIII RENOUNCES BRITISH CROWN; YORK WILL SUCCEED HIM AS GEORGE VI; PARLIAMENT IS SPEEDING ABDICATION ACT

CODE FOR INDUSTRY VOTED HERE TO BACK AIMS OF NEW DEAL

Association of Manufacturers Pledges Cooperation for 'Era of Good Feeling.'

ASKS FOR CENSUS OF IDLE

Moley Urges Business Join in Federal Planning—McCarl for Industrial Board.

LABOR GIVES 30-HOUR PLAN

Industrial Progress Council in Washington Hears Program for a Shorter Week.

Industry and New Deal

The National Manufacturers Association meeting here adopted a code for industry pledging "era of good feeling" and cooperation with social aims of New Deal. The text of the code is on Page 30.

The Council for Industrial Progress in Washington heard labor's plan to promote employment by a thirty-hour week and Federal regulation of working conditions. Employers did not oppose new labor laws, but spokesmen insisted that they should conform to the Constitution. Page 33.

Code Is Adopted Here

A declaration of principles for American industry, calling for an era of good feeling both at home and abroad, pledging cooperation with the government in the national interest and embracing, at least in principle, some of the most important social reforms of the New Deal, was adopted yesterday afternoon at the final session of the forty-first annual convention of the National Association of Manufacturers, held in the Waldorf-Astoria Hotel.

The declaration was in harmony with the keynote speech delivered at Wednesday's session by Colby M. Chester, chairman of the General Foods Corporation and president of the association, and in striking contrast to the bitter criticisms of the New Deal uttered by industrialists at previous meetings.

In closing the convention Mr. Chester asserted his belief that it had "written a new, sound and progressive note in the industrial life of this nation in its declaration of principles," and predicted that it would have the support of "a united industry" within the year.

Census of Idle Is Urged

Resolutions were adopted urging a government census of unemployed and opposing governmental ownership of the railroads or any transportation system.

Addresses were made by Raymond Moley, editor of the magazine Today; John R. McCarl, former Controller General; George H. Mead, president of the Mead Corporation and chairman of the business advisory council to the Department of Commerce, and James A. Emery, general counsel of the association.

Mr. Moley urged joint economic planning by the government and business. He warned industry that it must recognize the meaning of the election returns—that the people voted for security of wages and living standards—and offer them a rational plan to attain these ends if it does not wish to be compelled to submit to impractical and drastic legislation.

A balanced budget through the reduction of relief expenditures and other government spending was advocated by Mr. McCarl. He urged industry to accept the responsibility for reducing the need for relief by giving more jobs. He also suggested that business organize a National Industrial Board to cooperate with the government in the "collective" solution of social and economic problems.

According to Mr. Mead, business wants "constructive regulation," contrary to a general public impression, although it is opposed to "government ownership or control." Business also believes in economic security, he said, adding that a "practical" economic security and

Continued on Page Thirty-one

4,336,000,000 Francs Set As French Budget Deficit

Wireless to THE NEW YORK TIMES.

PARIS, Dec. 10.—There will be a deficit of 4,336,000,000 francs in the French budget during the coming year, according to figures put before the Chamber of Deputies this morning by the finance commission.

The ordinary expenditure under the budget is estimated at slightly more than 48,000,000,000 francs and the income at 43,685,000,000 francs. With these figures before them, the Deputies began to vote in rapid succession for most of the 140 articles in the law having to do with the collection of revenue despite the protest of one Right Deputy who argued that to vote revenues before expenditures was contrary to all good sense and logic.

JAPAN WITHDRAWS DEMANDS ON CHINA

Indicates Dropping of Moves for Anti-Red Cooperation and Autonomy of North China.

ARMY IS UNDER CRITICISM

Foreign Office Wants Public to Know the Military Interfere With Major Policies.

By HUGH BYAS
Wireless to THE NEW YORK TIMES.

TOKYO, Dec. 10.—Withdrawal of all the Japanese demands regarding North China autonomy and of that for cooperation against communism was implied in a statement issued to the press today by Eiji Amau, Foreign Office spokesman.

Japan asks Nanking to fulfill the agreements already reached on lesser points, but the request is not accompanied by a threat or warning except that if Japanese lives or property are endangered or Japanese rights violated the government will take "adequate measures."

Ambassador Shigeru Kawagoe's failure to obtain satisfaction from China, even in minor matters, is explained as due to Chinese indignation over the invasion of Suiyuan Province by Mongols and Manchukuoans.

Mr. Amau said nothing to connect the Japanese Kwantung Army with these events, but the public was already aware that Manchukuo's Premier had proclaimed sympathy with the Mongolian rising and knew he would not have taken such a step without being prompted.

Mr. Amau's statement, read in conjunction with Foreign Minister Hachiro Arita's answer to the Privy Council yesterday, suggested that the Foreign Office wants the public to know how the Kwantung army interferes with major policies on which all branches of the Tokyo government have agreed.

The statement claims that a definite agreement was reached with China regarding suppression of anti-Japanese movements—including revision of the control of the press and of Kuomintang (Nationalist party) branches—engagement of Japanese advisers, control of Korean exiles and reduction of tariffs.

Consulate Involved

China further agreed to reopening of the Chengtu Japanese Consulate and accepted most of Japan's demands for settlement of recent incidents.

A hitch occurred over air services. No agreement was reached regarding joint defense against communism though both sides concurred on several items.

Economic cooperation in North China was agreed on in principle. This stage having been reached, the Chinese, "taking advantage of the Suiyuan affair," broke off negotiations, threatened to repudiate all the concessions already made and evaded Ambassador Kawagoe's repeated requests for a further interview with Foreign Minister Chang Chun. Mr. Kawagoe was said to have handed Mr. Chang a note embodying the agreed points, requesting that they be put into effect.

"Japan is now watchfully waiting for China's response and is prepared to take adequate measures if China fails to control anti-Japanese movements or if Japanese life and property interests are jeopardized," said the statement.

It is pertinent to recall that Mr.

Continued on Page Twelve

CROWDS IN LONDON CALM

News Is Received With British Reserve as Thousands Gather.

QUEEN MARY IS CHEERED

Many Break Through Police Lines When She Calls at Home of Duke of York.

TENSION OF WEEK ENDED

People Sad at Losing Edward but Relieved the Suspense at Last Is Over.

Wireless to THE NEW YORK TIMES.

LONDON, Dec. 10.—As the news of King Edward's abdication sped to the far corners of the empire this afternoon Britain received confirmation of her worst fear with mixed emotions, sadness at losing so popular and beloved a sovereign and relief that the gnawing suspense of the last week at last had drawn to an end.

Massed thousands stood silently outside the towering iron gates of Parliament while the terse, restrained statement of the first monarch in England's history ever to renounce the throne voluntarily was read to the House of Commons. Presently, as the twilight shadows of Westminster Abbey lengthened over Parliament Square, word sped from mouth to mouth that the reign of Edward was coming to an end.

Although the atmosphere a few minutes before had been highly charged with tension and anxiety the news was received calmly and with typical British reserve. There was no demonstration and no show of feeling save for the serious, strained faces in the crowd and the flutter of women's handkerchiefs here and there.

Crowds Gather Throughout Day

Throughout the day, from dawn until after midnight, crowds of varying proportions gathered outside all the buildings associated with the historic happenings of the day. People clustered about No. 10 Downing Street, the Houses of Parliament and all the royal residences, standing stolidly and silently when allowed or moving along without protest if required. If any emotion was perceptible that could be described as a corporate reaction, it was one of bewilderment and incredulity that such a thing ever could actually happen.

A throng composed mostly of women, which at times reached 10,000 or more, stood on the pavement before Buckingham Palace forming

Continued on Page Twenty

Edward Plans Radio Talk To British Empire Tonight

Special Cable to THE NEW YORK TIMES.

LONDON, Dec. 10.—King Edward will broadcast to the empire tomorrow night at 10 o'clock, immediately after he has signed the Abdication Act and ceased to be King, in the character of a private person. It is expected Parliament will have disposed of its business by then.

[American networks will broadcast the message at 5 P. M., Eastern Standard Time.]

The British Broadcasting Corporation has arranged for a worldwide hook-up.

Many persons feel the King's decision to broadcast is not wise. He has already sent a message to Parliament with a penciled note to the Prime Minister, commending the Duke of York to the support of the whole empire. These will be broadcast four times tonight and printed in every British newspaper.

MRS. SIMPSON CRIES LISTENING AT RADIO

Shaken and Exhausted by the Climax in Career of King Who Forsook Throne for Her.

WILL REMAIN AT CANNES

Edward Will Not Visit Her Now—Britons in France Question Her Course.

Wireless to THE NEW YORK TIMES.

CANNES, France, Dec. 10.—With tears streaming down her face, Mrs. Wallis Warfield Simpson, for whose sake Edward VIII has abdicated as King and Emperor of the greatest empire the world has ever known, listened today as did all the rest of the world to the news over the radio from the scene in the British Parliament.

She heard the words announcing that the King Emperor of whom so much had been expected had laid down his scepter and crown so as to be free to marry her some months hence and live the life of an ordinary mortal.

Says King Won't Go to Riviera

At 1 o'clock this afternoon the following statement was made by Herman L. Rogers, at whose villa Mrs. Simpson is staying:

"There is definitely no change so far as Mrs. Simpson's plans are concerned. She will stay here until after Christmas. She is now at the villa and in the best of health. There has been no change in the household.

"It cannot be stated if she has

Continued on Page Twenty

Soviet Orders Militia Punished for Arrests Without Warrants in Spite of New Charter

Special Cable to THE NEW YORK TIMES.

MOSCOW, Dec. 10.—The first charges of violating the new Constitution were brought at Kazan today in connection with the arrests of eleven persons there by the militia on its own initiative.

According to the new Constitution, "no one may be subjected to arrest except upon the decision of a court or with the sanction of the prosecutor." Apparently no such authorization was obtained, and Moscow authorities have called the Kazan militia's action an "outrageous violation" of the Constitution and ordered that the guilty be suitably punished.

According to an investigation in Kazan, a doorman at a restaurant was arrested this week purely on suspicion. When he failed to arrive home his father made inquiries, and on finding his son in jail complained to the public prosecutor. The latter showed little interest. A correspondent of the Moscow newspaper Izvestia then took up the matter and spurred the prosecutor to visit the jail, where he found eleven persons arrested without warrants.

Today also the first Soviet death sentence for the infringement of private ownership and personal property and the murder of a private individual was imposed in a Moscow court.

Two employes of a State antique shop had been selling valuable old books to two highly paid ballet dancers. Thus the employes had learned their clients had money and valuables. They invaded the young dancers' home in their absence, killed their mother and cook with a brass pestle and looted the apartment. The criminals were traced, arrested, convicted and tonight they will be shot.

Hitherto the death penalty has been imposed in murder cases only where the safety or welfare of the State was involved, the normal penalty for an ordinary murder being not more than ten years.

Nikolai V. Krylenko has assumed his duties as head of the All-Union Commissariat for Justice, newly created under the Constitution. Today he began reorganizing the whole legal profession of the country into voluntary associations, which will give legal aid to any accused persons demanding their services. Any accused person is entitled to free legal counsel if he desires. Legal aid offices are also being established by trade unions.

Because of the new legal guarantees many more lawyers than hitherto will be needed. Accordingly steps are being taken to enroll thousands more students in the law schools already established, and plans are being formed for the creation of many more schools in the various republics.

BALDWIN TELLS OF EVENTS

Relates to the Commons How He Warned King Against Marriage.

DENIES ANY BITTERNESS

Says Ruler, Far From Feeling Resentment, Had Become a Firmer Friend to Him.

LEGAL ISSUE IS REFUTED

Churchill Declares It Is Now Clear That There Was Never a Constitutional Crisis.

By CHARLES A. SELDEN
Special Cable to THE NEW YORK TIMES.

LONDON, Dec. 10.—The momentous session of Parliament that received today King Edward's message of abdication was best described by Prime Minister Stanley Baldwin himself when he said near the close of his narrative of the crisis:

"This House of Commons today is a theatre which is being watched by the whole world."

Never since the first British Parliament was called by Simon de Montfort 672 years ago had it been the theatre for such an impressive tragedy as that enacted today.

There have been greater political issues, perhaps, and more fateful struggles between Crown and Commons. There have been long Parliaments, short Parliaments and rump Parliaments. But there has been no precedent for today's enactment of the tragedy in which a monarch signed away his sovereignty over an empire of 500,000,000 people for his love of a woman.

And while the play was on, the wars of one hemisphere and the efforts in the other hemisphere to end wars were merely side shows.

Extra Police on Hand

Standing room only was the situation in the legislative chamber itself, while there was not even standing room left in the acres of lobbies and for many blocks outside on the streets that lead to the Houses of Parliament.

So many extra companies of police were assigned to duty around the buildings that it was feared serious disorder was anticipated by the authorities, but nothing could have been further from the fact. There was as much decorum in witnessing this self-effacement of Edward VIII as there was last January when the multitudes gathered to mourn for his father and to proclaim him.

Needless to say, the House itself was filled as it had not been since the session at which war was declared in 1914. In the diplomatic gallery, every seat was taken by Ambassadors and Ministers from nearly all nations.

What little daylight sometimes seeps into the Commons chamber on a Winter afternoon was completely shut out by a dense fog, so there was nothing but mellow illumination from the lights above the stained glass ceiling.

House Is Ill at Ease

The House was ill at ease during the hour's interval prior to the great moment when Prime Minister Baldwin entered with the King's message of abdication. The familiar cry, "Prayers are over," after the customary, brief devotional exercise with which every session opens, was followed by many involuntary, at least unusual, "Amens," suggestive of a devout wish that for this once they might be answered quickly.

There were no "King's men" in this House. But it was equally true there were no anti-King men.

The King's own message was received with sorrow and sympathy. When Mr. Baldwin made his long statement of the events that preceded the decision to abandon the throne, there vanished the last trace of the bitterness that had developed in the last week from fear that the Crown might try to override the Commons.

"We are not judges," said Mr. Baldwin, and it was one of his utterances to which members gave their warmest assent.

"While there is not a soul among us who will not regret this from the bottom of his heart," said the

Continued on Page Sixteen

Associated Press Photo.

SUCCESSOR TO THE BRITISH THRONE
The Duke of York

YORK GETS OVATION AT HOME IN LONDON

Cheering and Singing Theatre Crowds Surge About His Car While Auto Horns Salute.

HE DOFFS HAT TO THRONG

New Monarch Expected to Use Name 'George' as Symbol of Strength and Steadiness.

Special Cable to THE NEW YORK TIMES.

LONDON, Dec. 10.—Thousands of Londoners shouted a welcome tonight to a shy and awkward young man who was ready to step into the dazzling light of the greatest throne on earth.

With the abdication of King Edward VIII, the 41-year-old Duke of York was about to take his place on the world wide stage as the latest in the long line of English sovereigns. And tonight, in front of his town house at 145 Piccadilly, the crowds had their first chance to show him that they were glad.

A surging throng of theatre-goers on the way home surrounded his car as he returned after having dinner with Edward at Fort Belvedere. Cheering and waving hats, they filled the wide roadway in front of the house and blocked traffic so completely police were powerless to keep it moving.

Before the Duke entered the house he turned to the crowd and raised his hat several times. That was the signal for a great demonstration. Hundreds of motorists set up a deafening salute with their horns, while the crowd began singing the national anthem and "For He's a Jolly Good Fellow."

Popular Reign Indicated

It was a demonstration of some importance in the story of the British throne, for it showed that the Duke may be a popular King even without any of the brilliant qualities of his elder brother.

Tomorrow night he will become King, and Saturday morning his accession will be proclaimed with the stately pageantry that has come down unchanged from medieval times. For individual kings may come and go, but the British monarchy that has survived many shocks before this will keep its place as the keystone of the vast and loosely jointed empire.

Heralds in uniforms of gold will

Continued on Page Eighteen

EDWARD CHEERFUL AFTER TAKING STEP

Reported Like Man Who Has Had Crushing Load of Worry Lifted From Shoulders.

PACKS FOR HIS DEPARTURE

Knowledge That He Will Not Be Barred From Returning to England Relieves Him.

By FERDINAND KUHN Jr.
Wireless to THE NEW YORK TIMES.

LONDON, Dec. 10.—The blue and white flag of the Duchy of Cornwall fluttered slowly to the foot of its mast at 10 o'clock this morning on the high turret over Fort Belvedere.

It was a signal that made history, for at that moment King Edward was renouncing the greatest throne on earth so that he could marry the woman he loved. With his three brothers as his only witnesses, he signed the instrument of abdication as his "final and irrevocable decision" to retire into private life.

He will remain King until tomorrow afternoon, when the Abdication Bill is expected to reach him from Parliament. As soon as he signs it, however, his unhappy days as King will come to an end after the shortest reign in 453 years. The Duke of York will come to the throne as George VI and Edward will leave England as the first man in all the 1,000 years of the British monarchy to have left the throne of his own accord.

Edward Again Cheerful

Although he has not shown himself to the public for almost a week, it was reported on good authority tonight that he was like a man who had had a crushing load of worry lifted from his shoulders.

The depression and jumpiness of the last few days had vanished and the King was said to be cheerful and purposeful, superintending the packing of his belongings, dealing with State papers, which arrived incessantly from London, and looking forward to more happiness than he has known in a long time.

Workmen and tractors were busy all day on Edward's private flying field at Smith's Lawn in Windsor Great Park, apparently preparing it for the take-off of an important airplane. Four police cars were on duty and a cordon of police and

Continued on Page Sixteen

KING MAKES HIS DECISION

Chooses Woman Over Throne After 'Long and Anxious' Thought.

FINALE LIKELY TOMORROW

New Reign, Expected to Bring Back Calm of George V's, Is to Be Proclaimed Then.

CROWNING PLAN MAY HOLD

Edward Can Use Either of Two Titles, Earl of Rothesay or Baron of Renfrew.

Edward's letter, the Abdication Bill, Baldwin's speech, Page 17.

By FREDERICK T. BIRCHALL
Special Cable to THE NEW YORK TIMES.

LONDON, Dec. 10.—Some time Saturday morning, perhaps even as soon as tomorrow night, Edward VIII will cease to be a King and Emperor. He has made his choice between a woman and a throne and the woman has won.

Today at Fort Belvedere, his country home near Windsor Castle, and in the presence of his three brothers, the Dukes of York, Gloucester and Kent, the King signed a message to his Ministers announcing his determination "after long and anxious consideration" to renounce the throne to which he had succeeded on the death of his father. This, said the message, is "my final and irrevocable decision."

The message was carried by Prime Minister Stanley Baldwin this afternoon to a crowded session of the House of Commons and there read, not without emotion, by the Speaker.

Bill Introduced in House

There is no question of whether the House should accept it. Under the British Constitution there can be none, for it was an expression of the King's will and the King rules, though he does not govern, Britain and the empire. But immediately afterward, as soon as the Prime Minister in a speech that will be memorable for the restrained feeling it expressed and the leaders of the Opposition each after his fashion had voiced their regret, a bill was introduced that will implement the monarch's decision.

Tomorrow this formal bill of abdication will be rushed through all its stages in both houses, Commons and Lords. It will then be carried to the King for his royal assent. The moment he signs it he ceases to be King and his brother, the Duke of York, who is nearest to him, will reign in his stead.

The new King will take the throne, according to the best information available tonight, as George VI and for that choice there is a reason. It is desired, now that this storm is over and the skies are clearing, to get back to the ordered peace and quiet stability of the monarchy under the last King George, to leave behind this brief era of conflict between will and duty and to concentrate anew on the empire and its common destiny.

Proclamation Likely Tomorrow

Another era will begin probably at noon on Saturday when the accession of the new King is proclaimed from the balcony of St. James's Palace, again at old gray Charing Cross and finally from the steps of the Royal Exchange in the City of London, each time with all the pomp and ceremony that the monarchy has upheld here throughout a thousand years Kings may change but the old order remaineth; that is to be Britain's watchword still.

And thus, in circumstances that will arouse wonder and pity as long as history continues to be written, ends the brief reign of King Edward VIII. It has lasted ten months and twenty-two days before this strange storm that love of woman created has brought it to a close, and the empire still endures. Even a newcomer can

Continued on Page Sixteen

"All the News That's Fit to Print."

The New York Times.

LATE CITY EDITION
Fair today, little change in temperature. Tomorrow cloudy and warmer, followed by rain.
Temperatures Yesterday—Max., 37; Min., 27

VOL. LXXXVI.....No. 28,868. Entered as Second-Class Matter, Postoffice, New York, N. Y. NEW YORK, SATURDAY, FEBRUARY 6, 1937. P TWO CENTS In New York City. | THREE CENTS Within 200 Miles. | FOUR CENTS Elsewhere Except in 7th and 8th Postal Zones.

PROGRESS IS MADE IN MOTORS PARLEY; EVICTION DEFERRED

WORKING ON TERMS

Subcommittee Begins Study of Specific Issues in Strike

WILL REPORT THIS MORNING

Pressure From Roosevelt Is Credited With Averting Complete Collapse

MURPHY BLOCKS OUSTERS

Halts Arrest of Union Men After Court Issues Eviction Writs at Flint

Developments in Auto Strike

DETROIT — President Roosevelt's pleas avert a new deadlock in the auto strike conferences. After all-day sessions a subcommittee is named and begins a study of specific issues pending a new joint meeting today.—Page 1.

FLINT—Judge Gadola signs writs for arrest of union leaders and sit-down strikers, but Sheriff, after asking aid of troops, delays action.—Page 2.

NEW YORK—Federal Council of Churches of Christ in America condemns sit-down strikers as a "dangerous weapon." It also assails General Motors for its speed-up program.—Page. 2.

Negotiations Go On

By LOUIS STARK

Special to THE NEW YORK TIMES.

DETROIT, Feb. 5.—John L. Lewis, chairman of the Committee for Industrial Organization, and William S. Knudsen, vice president of General Motors Corporation, comprising a subcommittee designated at today's joint conference of spokesmen for both sides in the automobile strike dispute, sat down tonight with Governor Frank Murphy to formulate a report to go before the full committee tomorrow.

The subcommittee was named today after President Roosevelt's repeated telephonic intervention had saved the deadlocked automobile conference from collapsing. When the second session of the conference closed at 8 o'clock this evening Governor Murphy announced that progress had been made.

While the Governor divulged no details of the conference session today, it was learned that Mr. Lewis had made an important concession toward meeting General Motors spokesmen part way. He agreed to drop his demand that the union be the sole bargaining agency in all the sixty-nine plants of the corporation and to limit this demand to twenty plants where union men are on strike.

Company Reported Wavering

The corporation committee, it was reported, appeared tentatively to be willing to grant sole bargaining rights to the union in six plants on certain conditions, but made no definite commitment that could be regarded by the union as unqualified acceptance of its position in these six plants. Actual and positive agreement on this point awaited further clarification at the hands of the subcommittee tonight.

In announcing progress tonight Governor Murphy, flushed and beaming, warned against over optimism. He indicated that as yet there was no absolute assurance that whatever progress had been made would broaden out until a complete settlement had been written.

Nevertheless, Mr. Murphy's announcement that a sub-committee had been appointed to meet tonight to explore the various subjects in dispute, presumably collective bargaining, wages, hours and creation of machinery for the settlement of disputes, gave rise to hope in many quarters that a settlement might be in sight.

The full joint conference of three on each side will convene again at 10 o'clock tomorrow morning to hear the reports being prepared tonight by the sub-committees.

Presses Roosevelt Plea

Governor Murphy pressed home to both sides today the admonition of President Roosevelt that the nation looked to them to settle their dispute in a manner betokening public-spirited citizens in a civilized community, and without the indus-

Continued on Page Two

Great-Grandmother, 72, Joins Picket Line in Flint

By The Associated Press.

FLINT, Mich., Feb. 5.—A 72-year-old great-grandmother joined union pickets today in front of Fisher Body Plant No. 1, held by sit-down strikers.

She was Mrs. Rebecca Goddard of Clio, Mich., who said she had nine or ten relatives, including a son, inside the plant.

"I just came down from Clio to show some of my neighbors," she said. "There are a lot of sit-down grouches up there. You don't know what sit-down grouches are? Why, they're people who don't believe in the union."

She was asked if it was true she was a great-grandmother.

"Certainly," she replied. "I have six children, twenty grandchildren and about ten great-grandchildren. My youngest son, Robert, is in that plant right now."

She said she also had some grandchildren and nephews in the plant.

FRIARS FACE TRIAL AS SPANISH REBELS

'People's Court' Will Assemble Monday for Case Against 60 Escorial Guardians

1,500 OTHERS ARE INDICTED

Speedy Hearings Are Planned for Prisoners Who Fill the Jails in Madrid

By The Associated Press.

MADRID, Feb. 5.—A special "people's court" will sit in judgment on the Augustinian friars who dwelt in the Escorial monastery built by King Philip II nearly 400 years ago, the government announced today.

The monks are charged with holding "anti-government tendencies" in the civil war. So far the government has kept possession of Escorial, northwest of Madrid, despite encirclement and siege by insurgent armies.

There are perhaps 60 of the friars, and there are nearly 1,500 more persons who are similarly indicted by the Leftist régime in Spain.

Trials Begin Monday

The friars will be tried by a court made up of a judge and two "representatives of the people." The court's session will begin Monday, and it has been instructed to conclude the trial within twenty days.

Simultaneously, Wenceslao Carrillo, Director General of Public Safety, announced he would immediately begin to examine the cases of all prisoners in Madrid's teeming jails with a view to liberating those against whom there is insufficient evidence of Rebel activity. The others will be rushed to trial.

The Augustinian friars were custodians of the edifice which housed the tombs of Spanish Kings since Philip II had it built to commemorate a victory over the French in 1557. He intended it as a retreat from Madrid's court gayety.

When the military uprising plunged Spain into civil war the large Escorial monastery was converted into a temporary prison for 500 Summer residents of the town. On their release a wing of the vast, rectangular structure was converted into barracks. The treasures the monks had guarded were stored in other parts of the building.

Constant improvements on the building, even in modern times, gave Spaniards a figure of speech. They have come to say "This is work on Escorial" when they wish to describe some task never finished.

State Monument Planned

Since the advent of the Spanish Republic it had been planned to remove the friars to allow conversion of the monastery into a national monument along with royal palaces and other properties. But the war gave a different aspect to their evacuation.

The mausoleum has but one vacant sepulcher, that reserved for former King Alfonso XIII, now an exile with slight chance of lying with his predecessors.

One of the friars' most-prized possessions was a rich library of Arabic, Hebrew and Spanish manuscripts. They had a school of higher education bearing the name of Alfonso's father, Alfonso XII, and a university, similarly named, devoted to the education of the sons of the Spanish nobility.

$100,000 CAFE SHUT BY RACKET BOMBS, OWNER TESTIFIES

Stench Missiles Used for Ten Months After He Refused to Pay $3,000, He Says

FOUR OTHERS TELL ILLS

Restaurant Manager Describes Threats to His Children and $2,000 Demand

A $100,000 example was given to the Supreme Court jury hearing evidence in the restaurant racket trial yesterday by Hyman Gross, who had been one of the owners of the Gerard Cafeteria, on Broadway at Times Square, which was closed by a stench bombardment ten months after it opened.

The experience of Mr. Gross, who had refused to pay Louis Beitcher, the racket's collector, $3,000, was one of five cases, three of attempted extortion and two of extortion placed in the record before Justice Philip J. McCook during the day.

In another, John A. Miller, manager of the Anne Miller restaurant, then at 43 West Eighth Street and a place patronized by Juror No. 5, Franklin H. Middleton, told of kidnap threats against his children and a demand for $2,000. Harry A. Vogelstein, one of the defendants, Miller said, told that "only saps" picketed.

Tells of $1,750 Payment

Isidoris Coviris, one of three owners of the Broadway Cafeteria at 2,230 Broadway, testified that he paid Beitcher $1,750 to purchase protection from the "rights of the union," and Richard M. Decker, owner of a night club called the Congress Restaurant at 1,657 Broadway, told of a sudden strike called by Local 16 of the Waiters Union to force him to join the Metropolitan Restaurant and Cafeteria Association, an employers' association, which he did at a cost of $285.

Two of Mr. Decker's waiters had worked for Jules Martin, the man who organized the racket for Arthur (Dutch Schultz) Flegenheimer, when he operated a restaurant in West Forty-eighth Street.

The flow of witnesses was speeded up by the fact that attorneys for the eight defendants, including three officials of Local 16 of the Waiters Union, two of Local 302 of the Cafeteria Workers Union, and three others, two of them lawyers, connected with the Metropolitan Association, shortened their cross-examination.

Run Short of Witnesses

Toward the end of the day the prosecution, conducted by William B. Herlands and Milton C. Schilback, two of Special Prosecutor Thomas E. Dewey's chief assistants, ran short of witnesses and a half-hour wait followed while more were produced after telephone calls.

Mr. Gross was examined by Mr. Schilback. He said his regular business was real estate, but in July, 1933, after he and associates "had spent $100,000 to build the place," the Gerard was opened at 1,508 Broadway. He had personally put up $40,000, he said.

Before they opened, Max Pincus, then in Local 302 but now dead,

Continued on Page Thirty-six

ROOSEVELT ASKS POWER TO REFORM COURTS, INCREASING THE SUPREME BENCH TO 15 JUSTICES; CONGRESS STARTLED, BUT EXPECTED TO APPROVE

Supreme Court Keeps Up With Its Work, Say Aides

By The Associated Press.

WASHINGTON, Feb. 5.—Supreme Court attachés said today that the tribunal was up to date in handling its business.

They explained it had been so since soon after William Howard Taft became Chief Justice in 1921.

When he went on the bench, fulfilling a lifelong ambition, the tribunal was from two to three years behind in its work. He speeded up disposition of the litigation so that soon afterward it was abreast of the docket.

SIX ON HIGH BENCH ELIGIBLE TO RETIRE

They and Six Justices of the Circuit Courts Could Come Under Roosevelt Plan

13 OTHER JURISTS LISTED

These Members of the Lower Courts Also Have Reached 70, With 10 Years of Service

Special to THE NEW YORK TIMES.

WASHINGTON, Feb. 5.—Not only six of the nine justices of the Supreme Court but half a dozen of the judges of the Federal Circuit Courts and an undisclosed number of the judges of the District Courts would be eligible for retirement as having reached the age of 70 after ten years of service on the bench, as urged by President Roosevelt.

There are forty-three judgeships in the Circuit Courts and 163 in the District tribunals, but in some instances there are still vacancies in appointments.

Preferring not to single out individuals, the Department of Justice refused to reveal the details today, but it was established from other sources that about six of the Circuit justices could retire on these qualifications.

As President Roosevelt stated that twenty-five out of a total judiciary of 237 could thus leave the bench, and as it is known that six Supreme Court and six Circuit justices were so classed, the thirteen others must be members of the district benches and special Federal courts.

Chief Justice Hughes is, of course, among those who will be in the 70-year-old, ten-year service class this year. In fact, he will be 75 years old April 11, and Justice Van Devanter will be 78 just six days later.

Justice McReynolds's seventy-fifth birthday fell on last Wednesday. Justice Brandeis, oldest member of the court, reached the age of 80 Nov. 13 last. Justice Sutherland will be 75 on March 25 and Justice Butler 71 on March 17.

Justice Stone will be 65 Oct. 11,

Continued on Page Ten

BILL IS INTRODUCED

Robinson and Bankhead Act for Passage by Senate and House

MAJORITY FOR PROPOSAL

But Most Conservative Democrats Are Silent and Republicans Are Hostile

SPECULATION ON JUSTICES

Those Mentioned for New Places Include J. M. Landis, Richberg and Frankfurter

By TURNER CATLEDGE

Special to THE NEW YORK TIMES.

WASHINGTON, Feb. 5.—President Roosevelt's proposals for a comprehensive reform of the Federal judiciary fell today like a bombshell upon a Congress which thought it already had experienced the ultimate in surprises when it heard his recent messages on reorganization of the executive branch.

Not even the closest of the President's Congressional advisers knew of the plan until they were called to the White House this morning and told to prepare for the shock at noon.

Regardless of the far-reaching nature of the proposals, the balance of Congressional reaction was decidedly in their favor. Judging from the content of the comment, this was due to three main factors—the resentment in Congress at recent decisions of the Supreme Court holding its acts invalid, the continuing faith of the so-called "liberal" element in Mr. Roosevelt and his works, and the unquestioning loyalty of the leadership in both houses to him and his program.

Republican Protest Vehement

On the other side of the scales were the spontaneous objections of the Republicans, characterized by a vehemence akin to that of the last Presidential campaign, and the disapproving attitude of a number of conservative Democrats.

Most of the conservative Democrats declined to comment.

Although the President's plan for a non-amendment approach to the issues raised by the court's interpretations ran counter to the plans of several outstanding legislators, notably Senator Robinson and Senator Ashurst, the leadership started laying general plans for its enactment. Senator Robinson predicted that the recommendations would receive "favorable consideration" in the Senate, and Speaker Bankhead promised quick action in the House on what he considered a "sound principle" of judicial reform.

The details of the plan, particularly the effective proposal for appointment of six new justices to the Supreme Court, brought forth limitless speculation as to the possible appointees. High on practically every list of possibilities were Senator Robinson, James M. Landis, who will shortly resign as chairman of the Securities and Exchange Commission to become dean of the Harvard Law School; Felix Frankfurter, Professor of Law at Harvard; Donald R. Richberg, former general counsel of the National Recovery Administration; Senators Wagner and Ashurst and Chairman Summers of the House Judiciary Committee.

The reform proposals were submitted in accordance with the best approved New Deal practices. They were worked out in every essential detail by the President with his administrative advisers, then the Congressional leaders were called in and informed of the schema. Later a message, with supporting data and the draft of a bill, was sent to Congress.

The only difference today from the practice followed with most of the other measures of major importance was that the three documents—message, supporting data and bill draft—were appended together in a single sheaf of papers, and representatives of the press were called in to be informed in advance of their specifications. The latter was not exactly an innovation, as the President follows this practice regularly on involved budget matters and recently used it in presenting and explaining his plan on executive reorganization.

The President's attitude in explaining the proposal today was in

Continued on Page Nine

President's Message

Special to THE NEW YORK TIMES.

WASHINGTON, Feb. 5.—Following are the text of the President's message to Congress on the judiciary, the draft of his proposed bill and the text of the letter of Attorney General Cummings to the President:

I have recently called the attention of the Congress to the clear need for a comprehensive program to reorganize the administrative machinery of the executive branch of our government. I now make a similar recommendation to the Congress in regard to the judicial branch of the government, in order that it also may function in accord with modern necessities.

The Constitution provides that the President "shall from time to time give to the Congress information of the state of the Union, and recommend to their consideration such measures as he shall judge necessary and expedient." No one else is given a similar mandate. It is therefore the duty of the President to advise the Congress in regard to the judiciary whenever he deems such information or recommendation necessary.

I address you for the further reason that the Constitution vests in the Congress direct responsibility in the creation of courts and judicial offices and in the formulation of rules of practice and procedure. It is, therefore, one of the definite duties of the Congress constantly to maintain the effective functioning of the Federal judiciary.

The judiciary has often found itself handicapped by insufficient personnel with which to meet a growing and more complex business. It is true that the physical facilities of conducting the business of the courts have been greatly improved, in recent years, through the erection of suitable quarters, the provision of adequate libraries and the addition of subordinate court officers. But in many ways these are merely the trappings of judicial office. They play a minor part in the processes of justice.

Since the earliest days of the republic, the problem of the personnel of the courts has needed the attention of the Congress. For example, from the beginning, over repeated protests to President Washington, the justices of the Supreme Court were required to "ride circuit" and, as circuit justices, to hold trials throughout the length and breadth of the land—a practice which endured over a century.

In almost every decade since 1789, changes have been made by the Congress whereby the numbers of judges and the duties of judges in Federal Courts have been altered in one way or an-

Continued on Page Eight

STOCKS DROP FAST ON COURT MESSAGE

Sweeping Declines Stop a Rise, Making Market the Year's Second Largest

BRIEF RALLIES ARE FUTILE

List Closes Only Slightly Above Day's Lows—Some Bankers Say Effect Will Be Mitigated

President Roosevelt's proposals for changes in the Federal judiciary came as a stunning surprise to the financial community yesterday. They evoked uncertainty and alarm among bankers and business men which found expression in a sweeping decline of stock prices.

Prices of representative issues on the New York Stock Exchange, which had been advancing during the morning, broke swiftly as the President's message was being read. The volume of dealings increased, the stock ticker fell five minutes behind the pace of trading and earlier gains were quickly turned to losses of one to three or four points.

Brief rallies in the afternoon gave way repeatedly to renewed selling and closing prices were only slightly above the lowest levels of the day.

From the standpoint of number of shares dealt in, the market was the second largest of the year, the total of transactions being 3,321,000. On the basis of number of issues to appear on the tape, 975, it was the broadest market since Nov. 12.

Course Unexpected by Bankers

A sample of the net declines among important issues showed: United States Steel down 2⅝ points at 96⅝; Bethlehem Steel, off 2⅜ at 81¾; Allied Chemical, 5 points lower at 235; Allis Chalmers, off 2⅛ at 75⅛; Anaconda Copper, down 1⅛ at 54⅜; Chrysler, off 2 at 126⅛, and Standard Oil of New Jersey, off 1⅝ at 70⅝.

Domestic corporation bonds were irregularly weaker, while the market for government securities showed declines fairly evenly matched by advances.

The response of financiers to the news was based upon concern and uncertainty over its implications rather than upon disagreement with the President's objectives. In spite of rumors which have been heard from time to time that Mr. Roosevelt might seek to enlarge the Supreme Court, it had been felt by most bankers that such a course was unlikely.

Consequently, as the chief executive of one big bank expressed it, the financial community was "flabbergasted" at the suddenness of the announcement, the drastic character of the changes proposed and the implications of criticism of

Continued on Page Ten

AIM TO PACK COURT, DECLARES HOOVER

Roosevelt Move Transcends Any Partisanship Question, Ex-President Holds

WIDELY CRITICIZED HERE

'Shameful Day' in Our History, Colby Asserts—Justice Black Hails 'Greatest Advance'

President Roosevelt's message to Congress asking for authority to appoint Federal judges in addition to those more than 70 years old was characterized last night by Herbert Hoover, his predecessor in the White House, as a proposal for "packing" the Supreme Court to get through New Deal measures.

Mr. Hoover declared that the President's proposal went far beyond any question of partisanship, and advised that Congress delay action on it until the people had time to formulate their views. His comment, made public at his suite in the Waldorf-Astoria, was as follows:

"Stripped of subsidiary matters, some of which are admirable, the President's action amounts to this:

"The Supreme Court has proved many of the New Deal proposals as unconstitutional. Instead of the ample alternatives of the Constitution by which these proposals could be submitted to the people through constitutional amendment, it is now proposed to make changes by 'packing' the Supreme Court. It has the implication of subordination of the court to the personal power of the Executive. Because all this reaches to the very depth of our form of government, it far transcends any question of partisanship.

"The Congress should delay action until the people have had ample time to formulate their views on it. In the long sweep of the Republic a few months are not too much to consider a vital change in the repeated judgment of the American people over 150 years. That judgment has always been that their liberties have depended greatly on the independence of the court and that they themselves should determine changes in the Constitution."

Reaction to the President's proposal among New York City lawyers was generally strongly unfavorable. Former Justice Clarence J. Shearn, president of the Bar Association of the City of New York, asserted that it was plainly an attempt to pack the Supreme Court for cases in which the Federal administration would have a political interest and called on all opposed to "mobocracy" or dictatorship to fight it.

Bainbridge Colby, Secretary of State during the Wilson administration, declared it was an attempt to

Continued on Page Nine

SURPRISE MESSAGE

Asks Authority to Name New Justices if Old Do Not Quit at 70

SEES NEED OF 'NEW BLOOD'

Constitutional Amendment and Statutory Judiciary Curb Would Be Side-Stepped

LOWER COURTS AFFECTED

Bench Would Be Expanded, Appeals Speeded and Defense Assured in Injunctions

By ARTHUR KROCK

Special to THE NEW YORK TIMES.

WASHINGTON, Feb. 5.—The President suddenly, at noon today, cut through the tangle of proposals made by his Congressional leaders to "bring legislative and judicial action into closer harmony" with a broadaxe message to Congress recommending the passage of statutes to effect drastic Federal court reforms.

The message—prepared in a small group and with deepest secrecy—was accompanied by a letter from the Attorney General and by a bill, drawn at the Department of Justice, which would permit an increase in the membership of the Supreme Court from nine to a maximum of fifteen if judges reaching the age of 70 declined to retire; add a total of not more than fifty judges to all classes of the Federal courts; send appeals from lower-court decisions on constitutional questions direct to the Supreme Court, and require that government attorneys be heard before any lower-court injunction issue against the enforcement of any act of Congress.

Avoiding both the devices of constitutional amendment and statutory limitation of Supreme Court powers, which were favored by his usual spokesmen in Congress, the President endorsed an ingenious plan which will on passage give him the power to name six new justices of the Supreme Court.

Power Left to the President

Under the provisions of the bill drawn by the Department of Justice for Congress, if the six now sitting justices who are more than 70 years of age do not resign, the President is empowered to name a new member for each justice in that category. These are the Chief Justice and Justices Brandeis, Van Devanter, Butler, McReynolds and Sutherland. Thus, after the passage of the bill, which is generally expected, the court will number anywhere from nine to fifteen justices.

Although the message—an unusually long one for the President—was a general criticism of the effects upon government and private litigants of overburdened courts and superannuated judges, and stressed a general plea to Congress to make provision for "a constant and systematic addition of younger blood" to "vitalize the courts," Congress instantly recognized its outstanding feature and purpose.

Although the message outlined basic defects in the administration of justice in the United States, and contained many reforms to which no exception will be taken, Congress quickly sensed that the President had hurdled the present majority of the Supreme Court on his way to the goal he outlined in his opening message of the session. This, as he stated it, is to find "means to adapt our legal forms and our judicial interpretation to the actual present needs of the largest progressive democracy in the modern world."

Variety of Emotions Aroused

That passage was the one which had brought the most cheers from the floors of Congress when the President uttered it. To achieve its aim was the object of all the proposed amendments and statutes which have heaped high in the Congressional hoppers since the opening of the session. When members of the Senate and the House became aware of the ingenious but effective manner in which the President planned to attain his objective without touching the Constitution or the powers of the court, they were torn by a variety of emotions.

Senator Robinson, the majority leader in his branch, said the mes-

Continued on Page Eight

West Virginian Saved After 8 Days in Mine; Had No Food, Forced to Drink Sulphur Water

By The Associated Press.

FLEMINGTON, W. Va., Feb. 5.—Eight foodless days of utter darkness while lost in the débris-choked passageways of an abandoned mine ended today for Robert Johnson, 36-year-old rural mail carrier.

"I sure thought I was a goner," he said.

Johnson told from his cot in a hospital of praying through the long hours in the damp mine, of giving up all hope, then of seeing a dim glow of lamps carried by rescue workers.

"Thank God, my prayers were answered," he sobbed fervently before a sleeping potion administered by physicians put him to sleep.

Doctors had broken his long fast—he had only sulphur water to drink in the mine—with plenty of black coffee, then with bowls of strained soup.

Rescue crews found Johnson nearly two miles from the mine entrance early today. He was huddled behind a heap of jagged chunks of slate in the mine which he operated to dig coal in his spare time for sale to neighbors.

The crews had expected difficulty in removing the slate, but had little actual trouble in reaching the imprisoned man.

Three of the scores of volunteers who had searched the mine day and night since Johnson disappeared on Jan. 27 heard his feeble cries for help while exploring a narrow tunnel.

His first words were to assure himself he hadn't merely imagined a light had cut through the dark.

C. P. Pride, assistant safety director for the State Department of Mines quoted him:

"I told myself, 'Bob, please don't lose that light.'" He didn't.

As the rescue party came closer he called to Mike Stanko Jr., Edward Whitehair and William Westfall, all his friends and neighbors:

"Take your time, I'll guide you by your light."

They cautiously approached the heap of slate, reached through a hole and gripped Johnson's hand—assurance he was safe.

Then word went to the surface, sped through this little community of about 400 population in Northeastern West Virginia. Pride and eight others gathered stretchers and blankets. They hurried into the mine, waded and swam through a deep pool of water covering nearly an acre where originally, many believed, Johnson had drowned while trying to open clogged drains.

After Johnson was taken out on the mountainside, he was carried a quarter of a mile down a snow-covered path to a waiting ambulance. There he was joined by his wife—among his first questions was "How's my wife?"—and hurried to a hospital fifteen miles away in Clarksburg, the nearest large city.

"All the News That's Fit to Print."

The New York Times.

LATE CITY EDITION
Fair today, temperature unchanged. Tomorrow fair, little change in temperature.
Temperatures Yesterday—Max., 71; Min., 56

VOL. LXXXVI....No. 28,958. Entered as Second-Class Matter, Postoffice, New York, N. Y. NEW YORK, FRIDAY, MAY 7, 1937. P TWO CENTS In New York City. | THREE CENTS Within 200 Miles. | FOUR CENTS Elsewhere Except in 7th and 8th Postal Zones.

HINDENBURG BURNS IN LAKEHURST CRASH; 21 KNOWN DEAD, 12 MISSING; 64 ESCAPE

ANARCHISTS RENEW BARCELONA STRIFE; 5,000 LEAVE BILBAO

Revolters, Regaining Part of Catalan Capital, Demand Shock Troop Dissolution

SOCIALIST MINISTER SLAIN

Insurgents Reported Gaining Unresisted in Aragon as Foes Withdraw 12,000

EVACUATION IN NORTH SPED

British Warships Protect Craft Taking Women and Children From Bilbao to France

The Spanish Situation

PERPIGNAN—Anarchists were reported to have regained positions in Barcelona and to have demanded the dissolution of the government's shock troops. Withdrawal of 12,000 men from the Aragon front, to deal with the situation, was also reported, leading to an advance by the Rebel armies. Page 1.

ROME—A heavy concentration of Rebels, including Italians, to rescue the Italians cut off at Bermeo, was under way on the Bilbao front. Page 10.

BILBAO—Five thousand women and children were taken from the city, and vessels carrying them to France were guarded by British warships. More refugees were preparing to leave. (Follows the above.) Page 10.

LONDON—Foreign Secretary Eden revealed that the British Government had evidence that Guernica was destroyed by airplanes. He favored a neutral inquiry. Page 10.

Anarchists Give Ultimatum

Special Cable to THE NEW YORK TIMES.

PERPIGNAN, France, May 6.—The Anarchists are reported to have regained control in parts of Barcelona this afternoon after the Catalan Generalidad believed it had dominated the situation.

The Anarchists issued an ultimatum to the government demanding the dissolution of the shock troops patroling the city, the government's chief support, within twenty-four hours and declaring that otherwise they would take matters into their own hands and use every means in their power to suppress the shock troops.

The Anarchists also have obtained the upper hand at Junquera in addition to Figueras, according to news received here, and threaten, it is alleged, to use asphyxiating gas unless their ultimatum is obeyed.

Anarchist broadcasts have been picked up here stating that the casualties in the disorders in Barcelona since the Anarchist rebellion Tuesday amounted to 400 dead and 2,000 wounded. Declaring that "enough blood has flowed," the broadcasts continue to appeal for calm every ten minutes, and it is therefore believed that trouble still persists in Barcelona.

French Consulate Menaced

The French Consulate was threatened by Anarchists, who asserted that Rightist sympathizers had taken refuge there. The consul appealed to French warships in the harbor and 200 armed sailors reinforced the consulate guard.

Telephonic communication with Barcelona is still cut off tonight, and telegraphic and telephonic communication with the interior of Catalonia, which was re-established yesterday, was again interrupted this morning.

The Spanish Consul at Perpignan has recommended that Frenchmen and others should not go further than Figueras, and trains do not proceed beyond Gerona.

Francisco Ascasso, leader of the Anarchists in the Aragon Government, is reported to have been murdered.

Rebels Gain on Aragon Front

By The Associated Press.

PERPIGNAN, France, May 6.—Reports of an unresisted Insurgent advance along the whole Aragon front of Northeastern Spain and of the withdrawal of 12,000 government troops from it to keep the peace in troubled Barcelona, put a new and serious face on the Catalan Anarchist insurrection tonight. The reports emanated from Insurgent

Continued on Page Ten

Judge Sentences Himself By Signing Papers Unread

Wireless to THE NEW YORK TIMES.

MOSCOW, May 6.—A judge on one of the most important benches of the Moscow District Court who has the bad habit of signing unread any document placed before him has just sentenced himself to jail.

The court clerks, deciding he needed a lesson in "Bolshevik vigilance," presented to him a sheaf of papers including one reading "To the chief of Butyrky prison: Under Magistrate Abramson is sent to you for further detention." Judge Abramson signed all the papers and picked up his newspaper again.

The clerks, of course, extracted the sentence and were passing it around laughingly when the judge found out about it. He destroyed it in a rage, declaring such jokes tended to undermine Soviet justice.

The government learned about it, however, and today Izvestia delivered to Judge Abramson a stinging rebuke for perfunctoriness, reminding him that he dealt not in inanimate goods but in human fate.

HUGHES SEES CHOICE IN LAW OR TYRANNY

Courts Must Be Maintained, He Tells Law Institute, or We Replace Reason by Force

TEST OF BAR TO ROOSEVELT

Stewardship Is Questioned by Laymen, He Writes in Warning of 'Critical Audience'

Text of Chief Justice Hughes's address is on Page 17.

Special to THE NEW YORK TIMES.

WASHINGTON, May 6.—Chief Justice Hughes made what his hearers construed as a reference to the Supreme Court when he told the American Law Institute today that if society is to choose the processes of reason as opposed to the tyranny of force, "it must maintain the institutions which embody those processes." It was the second time that the Chief Justice of the United States has broken his silence since the controversy over reorganization of the Supreme Court started three months ago.

Vigorous applause, lasting more than a minute, followed the Chief Justice's words, with which he concluded a speech in which he avoided any direct reference to the court issue.

President Roosevelt in a message to the institute likewise refrained from any positive statement about the Supreme Court, but remarked that "law interpreters," among other legal experts, are facing a sometimes critical audience.

President on Lawyers' Position

"I am happy to greet you members of the bench, the bar and the law school faculties who have assembled for the fifteenth annual meeting of the American Law Institute," the President stated.

"I have followed with interest your accomplishments within recent years in the restatement of the law and your proposals for improvement in the administration of criminal justice.

"Today our stewardship as lawyers is being questioned. The laymen of America are not, perhaps, quite so disposed to make a complete delegation of law matters to law men. At least the layman asserts his right to evaluate us.

"Law scholars, law practitioners, lawmakers, law administrators and law interpreters have the stage today. But more significant, they must play their rôles before an intense and sometimes critical audience.

"But this is well. The virtue of the common law was its adaptability to growth and improvement. In generations present and future the lawyer likewise will be measured by the same test.

"It is encouraging today that so many outstanding leaders of the profession assemble to give service in the important and worth-while task to which the American Law Institute is dedicated. I extend again my warm and cordial greetings to your membership and my best wishes for continued success."

Only at one other time since President Roosevelt made his recommendations to Congress on Feb. 5 has the Chief Justice made any

Continued on Page Seventeen

NOTABLES ABOARD

Merchants, Students and Professional Men on the Dirigible

LEHMANN IS A SURVIVOR

Veteran Zeppelin Commander, Acting as Adviser on Trip, Is Seriously Burned

CAPT. PRUSS IS ALSO SAFE

C. L. Osbun, Sales Manager, Who Survived a Plane Crash, Escapes Second Time

Notables from many walks of life were among the passengers on the ill-fated Hindenburg. They included merchants, students and business and professional men and women.

Many of the survivors owed their lives to the fact that they were apparently near windows in the dirigible when the accident happened and were able to leap through them to the ground in safety.

Among the survivors listed were Captain Ernst Lehmann, veteran Zeppelin commander; Captain Max Pruss, the new Hindenburg commander; Herbert O'Laughlin of Chicago, employed by the Consumers Company of Elgin, Ill.; Clifford L. Osbun, export sales manager of the Oliver Farm Equipment Company of Chicago, and Ferdinand Lammot Belin Jr. of Washington, D. C.

Lehmann's Condition Grave

Early this morning Dr. E. G. Herbener, staff surgeon at the Paul Kimball Hospital in Lakewood, said that Captain Lehmann was on the doubtful list. Captain Lehmann is suffering from shock and second and third degree burns of the face and body. Captain Pruss is suffering from second and third degree burns of the face, forehead and arms and will probably recover, Dr. Herbener said.

Among the passengers who were still unaccounted for were John Pannes, passenger traffic manager of the Hamburg-American Line and North German Lloyd at New York, and his wife; Ernst Rudolf Anders, partner of the firm of Seelig & Hille, tea merchants of Dresden, Germany, and his son, R. Herbert Anders, and Hermann Doehner of Mexico, D. F.

Captain Lehmann and Captain Pruss were in the control gondola when the crash occurred. Both officers, together with several other members of the crew, leaped through the gondola windows to safety

Lehmann an Adviser

Captain Lehmann, who was serving as adviser aboard the Hindenburg, had been commander of the ship until this year. He has had long experience with the lighter-than-air craft, and has been associated with Hugo Eckener, world-famous authority on Zeppelins, since 1931.

He was born March 12, 1886, at Ludwigshafen, on the Rhine, the son of a chemist. He became a naval cadet in 1905 and later entered the Polytechnic Institute at Charlottenburg, a borough of Berlin.

During the World War Captain Lehmann received the German Iron Cross award. After the war, as second in command to Eckener, he brought the dirigible Los Angeles to Lakehurst in 1924. When the Hindenburg was completed in 1936 Captain Lehmann was placed in command, a position he held until recently, when Captain Pruss was elevated as commander of the ship.

Mr. Osbun's escape from the disaster marked the second time that he had narrowly missed death as the result of a flying accident. Last year he was aboard a transport plane when it was forced down en route from Puerto Rico to Buenos Aires. Soon after he was transferred to a motorboat with other passengers and the motorboat blew up. Mr. Osbun escaped injury, but two other passengers were seriously burned.

Mr. Osbun declared that he was talking to fellow passengers in the dining salon, looking down through the observation window watching the ship being moored, when the disaster occurred. He was apparently blown through the window and thrown to the ground, suffering injuries. He was taken to the Paul Kimball Hospital in Lakewood, where his condition was said to be not serious.

Mr. Osbun is 37 years old, the fa-

Continued on Page Nineteen

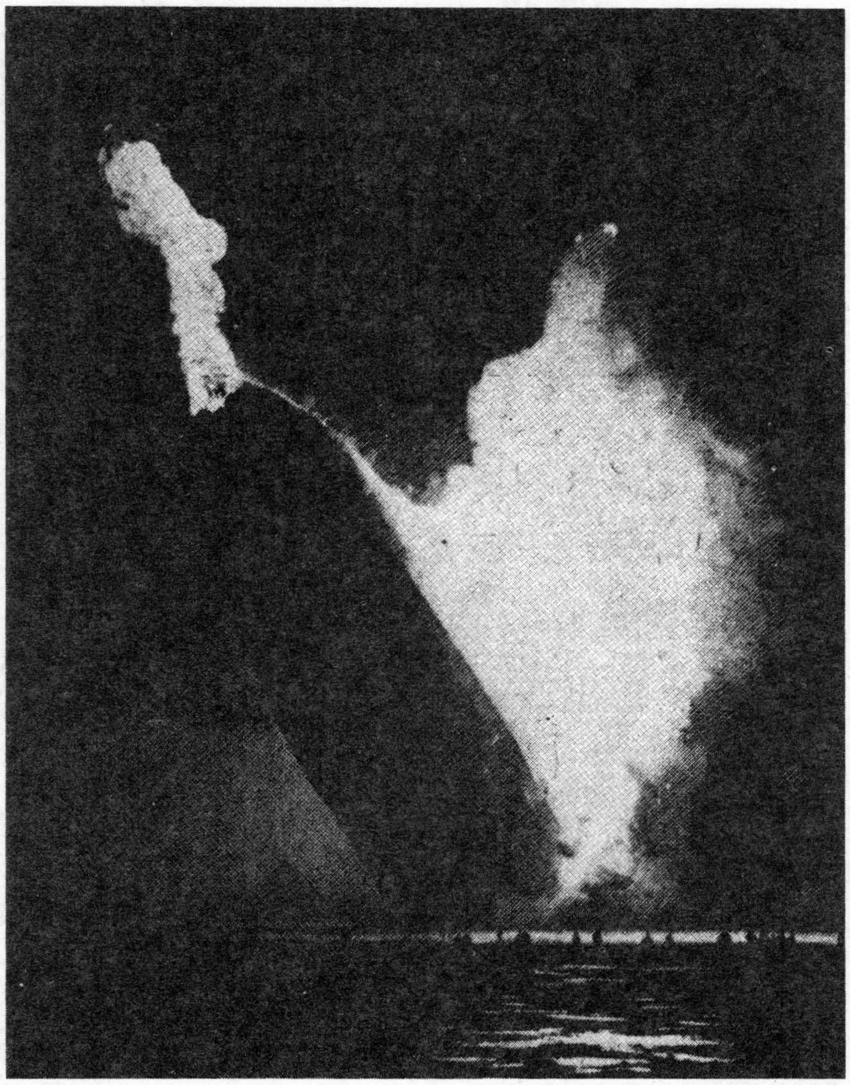

Associated Press Photo.

THE HINDENBURG IN FLAMES ON THE FIELD AT LAKEHURST

The giant airliner as she settled to the ground near her mooring mast at 7:23 o'clock last night

SHIP FALLS ABLAZE

Great Dirigible Bursts Into Flames as It Is About to Land

VICTIMS BURN TO DEATH

Some Passengers Are Thrown From the Blazing Wreckage, Others Crawl to Safety

GROUND CREW AIDS RESCUE

Sparks From Engines or Static Believed to Have Ignited Hydrogen Gas

A page of photographs of the disaster and survivors Page 20.

By RUSSELL B. PORTER

Special to THE NEW YORK TIMES.

NAVAL AIR STATION, LAKEHURST, N. J., May 6.—The zeppelin Hindenburg was destroyed by fire and explosions here at 7:23 o'clock tonight with a loss of thirty-three known dead and unaccounted for out of its ninety-seven passengers and crew.

Three hours after the disaster twenty-one bodies had been recovered, and twelve were still missing. The sixty-four known to be alive included twenty passengers and forty-four of the crew. Many of the survivors were burned or injured or both, and were taken to hospitals here and in near-by towns.

The accident happened just as the great German dirigible was about to tie up to its mooring mast four hours after flying over New York City on the last leg of its first transatlantic voyage of the year. Until today the Hindenburg had never lost a passenger throughout the ten round trips it made across the Atlantic with 1,002 passengers in 1936.

Two Theories of Cause

F. W. von Meister, vice president of the American Zeppelin Company, gave two possible theories to explain the crash. One was that a fire was caused by an electrical circuit "induced by static conditions" as the ship valved hydrogen gas preparatory to landing. Another was that sparks set off when the engines were throttled down while the gas was being valved caused a fire or explosion.

Captain Ernst Lehmann, who commanded the Hindenburg on most of its flights last year and was one of tonight's survivors, gasped, "I couldn't understand it," as he staggered out of the burning control car. Captain Max Pruss, commanding officer of the airship, and Captain Albert Stampf were also among the survivors.

Captain Lehmann was critically burned and injured; the other officers were also burned, but less seriously.

Experts in lighter-than-air operations who saw the accident said tonight that when the two landing lines were dropped by the dirigible at 7:20, they were immediately made fast to the mooring cars on the circular track about the mooring mast. The crew began to make the lines taut, but the ship had gathered too much momentum, according to these observers, and drifted several hundred yards past the mast. The starboard line pulled hard as the nose of the ship passed over the mooring mast at the top.

Order Not Heard

Captain Pruss, making his first trip in command of the dirigible, signaled and shouted, "Pay out!"

This order was heard by the operator on one mooring car, but not by the other, as the shout went against the wind and could not be heard. Consequently, one mooring car paid out and the other did not. The result was that the ship was thrown off its balance and lost the perfect equilibrium it had previously had.

Its nose dipped, forward ballast was dropped and the elevators were set to raise the ship. Instead the ship was held tight by one yaw line. The nose was pulled over and the elevators had an effect opposite to that which they were intended to have, according to this version. The tail dropped sharply and the bottom rudder hit the

Continued on Page Nineteen

DISASTER ASCRIBED TO GAS BY EXPERTS

Washington Sees Dangerous Combination of Hydrogen and Blue Gas as Cause

Special to THE NEW YORK TIMES.

WASHINGTON, May 6.—Washington airship experts and Congressional leaders received the news of the Hindenburg disaster with amazement and expressions of sorrow. But in every instance those who commented pointed out that the three disasters of the United States Navy were structural, while that of the German craft was due to the use of a combination of hydrogen and blue gas, the most dangerous of all gases for inflation of airships.

Dr. Hans Luther, the German Ambassador, said the disaster must not cause the world to lose faith in dirigibles and that it could not have been caused by technical defects.

"It is terrible," the Ambassador said. "I was horrified by the news, but it could not have been a technical matter. It must not cause us to lose faith in dirigibles because the Graf Zeppelin has operated safely and efficiently for eight years on the run from Europe to South America and elsewhere."

Secretary Hull sent the following message tonight to Konstantin von Neurath, the German Minister of Foreign Affairs:

"I extend to you and to the people of Germany my profound sympathy at the tragic accident to the dirigible Hindenburg and the resultant loss of life to passengers and crew."

"It is too terrible to believe," Admiral A. B. Cook, Chief of Naval Aeronautics, said. "From what I

Continued on Page Twenty-one

Airship Like a Giant Torch On Darkening Jersey Field

Routine Landing Converted Into Hysterical Scene in Moment's Time—Witnesses Tell of 'Blinding Flash' From Zeppelin

By CRAIG THOMPSON

Special to THE NEW YORK TIMES.

LAKEHURST, N. J., May 6.—The Hindenburg, giant silver liner of the air, suddenly became a torch above the naval air station here tonight. What began as a routine landing of the transatlantic airship ended in a holocaust.

The ground crew, officials of the naval air base, spectators, reporters and press photographers were going about their customary business of aiding or watching the ship nose into the mooring mast.

Two ground lines had been dropped from the nose. These, attached to the cars running on a circular track around the mast, were holding the ship nose down at a thirty-degree angle, and helping it jockey into a position favorable with the wind for a mooring.

A thunderstorm had passed over the field a short time before and a drizzly rain was still falling. Twilight was beginning, although the visibility was still good.

So suddenly that it left spectators on the verge of hysteria for some time afterward, the ship burst into flame. Some one in the ground crew yelled "Run for your lives!" and the crew did. The stern of the ship settled and the photographers, squinting through the view finders of their cameras, ran toward the ship.

The occurrence sounded, witnesses said, like two explosions, one following the other about thirty seconds apart. Some said they saw one burst of flame, others two, but the noises they described as explosions gave way to the sounds of human screams.

In the "heavier-than-air" hangar, the pilot of an American Air Lines plane, waiting to ferry passengers from the airship into Newark, watched from a window.

"It seemed to happen so fast that I didn't think anybody could escape," he said afterward.

He was wrong, for about at that moment a man ran into the hangar.

"His face was black, but he seemed to be all right otherwise. He wanted to telephone his mother in Chicago."

The passenger was Herbert James O'Laughlin of Chicago.

On the field was an army detachment from Philadelphia, detailed there for just such an emergency. This detail promptly went to work, trucks scurrying over the field seeking the injured, while in the hangar telephone calls were being put through to all points in New Jersey and New York City calling for ambulances, doctors, nurses, medicine.

All this occurred while the flames spread toward the uptilted nose of the ship, while the stern sank to the ground to be followed shortly by the entire length, girder and strut, the bared ribs of the ship from which the skin had disappeared.

Robert Seelig, Murray Becker and Larry Kennedy, all newspaper camera men, related what they had seen.

"There was a noise that sounded like bullets coming out of the gondolas," Seelig said. "I saw nobody

Continued on Page Twenty-one

GERMANY SHOCKED BY THE TRAGEDY

At First Disbelieving, Line's Officials Tell of Receiving Message of Landing

Special Cable to THE NEW YORK TIMES.

BERLIN, Friday, May 7.—It was a few minutes after 1 o'clock this morning when the first news of the disaster to the Hindenburg reached Berlin by telephone from The New York Times Bureau in London. The bureau forwarded the brief bulletin to the effect that the airship had been destroyed while making its landing. No details were given.

At that hour the German newspapers were without news. Several first editions, in fact, had reported the Hindenburg's supposedly safe arrival on the strength of an erroneous telegram received by the company in Frankfort on the Main. It was almost two hours later before the news of the disaster with some few details reached the newspapers through the medium of the German official news agency.

Facts Difficult to Get

In the meantime such facts about the airship and its passengers proved difficult to obtain. The Frankfort and Berlin offices of the Zeppelin company were closed and no complete list of the passengers or crew was available. A list of twenty-one names comprising foreign passengers out of a total list of thirty-nine was obtained by telephone from Frankfort, where this correspondent had retained it since the sailing day.

Dr. Hugo Eckener, veteran chief of the Zeppelin service, was in Austria, where he had lectured last night in Vienna. The Vienna bureau of THE NEW YORK TIMES traced him to Graz and obtained his ad-

Continued on Page Nineteen

"All the News That's Fit to Print."

The New York Times.

LATE CITY EDITION
Showers and cooler today. Tomorrow generally fair and continued cool.
Temperatures Yesterday—Max., 73; Min., 56

VOL. LXXXVI.....No. 28,964. Entered as Second-Class Matter, Postoffice, New York, N. Y. NEW YORK, THURSDAY, MAY 13, 1937. PP TWO CENTS in New York City. | THREE CENTS Within 200 Miles. | FOUR CENTS Elsewhere Except in 7th and 8th Postal Zones.

GEORGE VI AND ELIZABETH CROWNED IN ABBEY; MILLIONS OF THEIR SUBJECTS ACCLAIM THEM; KING, ON AIR, PLEDGES SERVICE TO THE EMPIRE

Times Wide World Radiophoto.

THE ROYAL FAMILY ACKNOWLEDGES GREETINGS OF CORONATION CROWDS

King George VI, Queen Elizabeth and the Princesses Elizabeth and Margaret Rose on the balcony of Buckingham Palace after the ceremony at Westminster Abbey. Behind the Queen, on the left, is Lady Ursula Manners, daughter of the Duke of Rutland, and on the right Lady Diana Legge, daughter of the Earl of Dartmouth, both train bearers for the Queen. Behind King George are two members of the Palace staff.

C. I. O. STEEL STRIKE SHUTS TWO PLANTS OF JONES-LAUGHLIN

27,000 MEN ARE IDLE

Corporation Puts Blame on Murray, Says It Will Sign Pact

DRIVE AT INDEPENDENTS

Picketing Begins at Pittsburgh and Aliquippa Mills, Backing Recognition for Union

REPUBLIC BARS CONTRACT

Cleveland Letter Tells 55,000 Workers Company Will Not Agree to a Closed Shop

By The Associated Press.

PITTSBURGH, May 12.—Thousands of union steel workers picketed the giant plants of the Jones & Laughlin Steel Corporation tonight in the first major steel strike since John L. Lewis began his drive to organize the nation's millmen into one big union.

The strike began at 11 P. M. as the first move in the campaign of the Steel Workers Organizing Committee to obtain written collective bargaining contracts with the independent steel producers of the country, employing about 202,000 men.

Cheers from the picket lines greeted union members on the early night shifts who walked from the mills in Pittsburgh and Aliquippa, in answer to the strike order of Philip Murray, chairman of the S. W. O. C.

Walkout on Murray's Order

Mr. Murray ordered the walkout after a two-hour conference with H. E. Lewis, chairman of the board of Jones & Laughlin had failed to effect an agreement on the union's demand.

The corporation, in a formal announcement, stated that it had offered to sign a contract provided an identical contract could be granted to non-union workers among its 27,000 employes.

The company also announced that it had offered to grant a sole collective bargaining contract to the group obtaining a majority vote at an employes' election, supervised by the National Labor Relations Board.

A company representative said no attempt would be made to operate the plants "for the time being."

Mr. Murray declined to state what effect the Jones & Laughlin strike would have on union activities at other independent companies, and he would not comment on the company's statement.

The Steel Workers Organizing Committee, as an affiliate of the Committee for Industrial Organization, received a rebuff from Republic Steel Corporation at Cleveland during the day.

The Republic corporation, with 55,000 employes, made public a letter to its workers, refusing to sign a C. I. O. contract. It said, "Republic does not believe in the closed-shop principle."

Biggest Steel Strike Since 1919

The Jones & Laughlin walkout is the biggest strike blow aimed at the steel industry since 1919. The 1919 strike cut production 40 per cent.

Mr. Murray said the Jones & Laughlin mills would be shut "tight," except for maintenance crews, which were ordered to keep up the blast furnaces.

A further conference would be held with the company tomorrow, Mr. Murray said.

Flames from the blast furnaces shot high into the air, intermittently lighting up the faces of the crowds of men, women and children who packed the streets in front of mill gates more than an hour before the strike call went into effect.

Two score municipal police mingled with the crowd, but made no attempt to break the picket lines.

Without disorder, the union men prevented non-union workers from entering the mill gates.

They held two American flags across the main entrance at the Aliquippa works.

Night Shift Men Parade

The throng was increased by the night shift members who fell into line, clasped arms with one another, and paraded in front of the gates.

A light rain before midnight sent many of the women and children of the strikers' families to their

Continued on Page Four

Home Relief Families Get $1,200,000 WPA Clothes

Distribution to home relief families of 2,056,989 articles of clothing made by seamstresses on WPA sewing projects was reported yesterday by Miss Charlotte E. Carr, executive director of the Emergency Relief Bureau. The clothing, which had an estimated retail value of $1,200,000, was distributed between April 13, 1936, and April 23, 1937.

In addition to these WPA products, home relief families received $2,562,410 in cash for the purchase of apparel.

The cash sum to be distributed by the ERB as a clothing allowance for the quarter ending June 30 has been raised to $1,500,000, Miss Carr announced. Of this amount $750,000 was disbursed last month.

REBELS BEAT BACK ATTACK ON TOLEDO

Report Loyalists Have Lost 3,000 There—Government Claims 7-Mile Gain

BILBAO SUBURBS BOMBED

More Than 100 Missiles Were Dropped—Madrid Shelled, Toll Rising to 217

By The Associated Press.

TOLEDO, Spain, May 12.—Heavy government attacks against Insurgent-held Toledo developed today into a mass offensive in which, Insurgents said, the attackers suffered "unprecedented slaughter."

Government prisoners estimated their dead in the campaign at more than 3,000, with total casualties not calculated, Insurgent reports said.

Waves of government infantry charged Insurgent positions south of the Tagus River as a climax to four days of fighting.

Insurgents braced their lines tonight along a six-mile front south of the Tagus. Estimates of government troops in the offensive ranged from 18,000 to 22,000 men.

No-man's land was covered with dead and wounded after a terrific battle yesterday. Squads from both armies roamed the area in the night looking for wounded.

The brilliant defense of Insurgent militiamen in one sector, it is stated, won for them the collective award of the Laureada, the highest honor for bravery in the Spanish Army.

Prisoners taken by the Insurgents were quoted as saying the government army in the Toledo sector included two brigades of the Lister Division and two other international outfits, the Campesina Brigade and the Dimitroff Battalion, in addition to the units already on the front. Apparently they were sent to reinforce government troops trying to recapture the city won by Insurgents last October, when they freed comrades besieged in the Alcazar.

[The government asserted its troops had advanced about seven miles on the Toledo front.]

100 Bombs Dropped Near Bilbao

BILBAO, Spain, May 12 (AP).—Insurgent airplanes dumped more than 100 bombs into the suburbs of Bilbao today but did not fulfill General Emilio Mola's threat to blast the Basque capital to bits.

Terror-stricken inhabitants, mindful of the Insurgent Northern commander's warning he would bombard the city "without mercy" if it did not surrender by today, ducked for cover three times as nine bombing planes and seven pursuit planes roared over Bilbao. Several gasoline tanks were set afire and nearby buildings were destroyed. Clouds of dark smoke billowed over the city.

Basque officials asserted they were informed General Mola had chosen today for the expiration of his ultimatum because the eyes of the world would be turned away from the Spanish civil war toward the London coronation. The indignation that would follow a violent attack on the civilians in the city thus would be lessened, they said.

One person was killed and several wounded in the air bombing of the town of Sorroza. Planes also bombed Larrauri and Mangula, north of Bilbao.

Bilbao's food situation was grave again. Bread supplies were almost exhausted. Only enough re-

Continued on Page Thirteen

142 PLAYGROUNDS, CLOSED BY MOSES, SEIZED BY POLICE

Patrolmen Force Locks to Reopen Them as Park Head Defies Mayor on Control

STAFF FURNISHED BY WPA

Somervell, in Control Again, Provides Labor That Moses Lost in Personnel Cuts

One hundred and forty-two playgrounds in the city became the battlefield yesterday for confused conflict between Mayor La Guardia, Lieut. Col. Brehon B. Somervell, WPA Administrator, and Police Commissioner Lewis J. Valentine on the one side, and Park Commissioner Robert Moses on the other. By nightfall, however, "New York's finest" were in full control.

With the Mayor heading by train for California but keeping in touch with the situation by long-distance telephone, the police late in the afternoon picked or broke the padlocks on the playgrounds which had been closed by Mr. Moses because WPA play directors had been withdrawn, and replaced them with police padlocks.

Facilities Normal Today

Today the playgrounds will be reopened to the children, with WPA directors working for the Police Department under direct WPA jurisdiction, aided by 135 men and women from the police juvenile aid bureau. The children can play in safety, the police promised.

The police advanced on the locked gates of the playgrounds only after Mr. Moses had announced to the press there would be "no armed conflict between his park guardsmen and the police" and after he had refused the request of Commissioner Valentine for keys to the padlocks.

The Park Commissioner, asserting that no one was more interested in keeping the playgrounds open for the children than he, stood off the Police Commissioner on legal grounds. The Mayor's order to have the police take over any closed playgrounds, in effect transferring jurisdiction to the police, was a "clear violation of the charter and absolutely illegal," he declared.

Keep Up Other Play Areas

Playgrounds that had been locked "because of the outrageous way in which the WPA has done this" will stay locked, Mr. Moses said, but he added that "if the police want to take the locks off, it will be all right." The 215 playgrounds which were manned by Park Department employes will continue to be run by the department, he said.

The Mayor, anticipating a playground crisis because of the long feud between Mr. Moses and the WPA administrator, had issued his order to the police Tuesday night when he left for California. The order was made public at City Hall by his secretary, Lester Stone, after Mr. Moses had announced the closing of the playgrounds.

With the playgrounds still locked at 3 o'clock, Mr. Stone put in a telephone call for the Mayor at Toledo, and when the Mayor's train arrived informed him of the general situation. He then announced that the Mayor issued the following statement:

"I confirm my order to keep all the playgrounds open. The children of the city, for whom the playgrounds were built, cannot be made to suffer, and I expect the Police Department to reopen the play-

Continued on Page Two

YOUNGER PRINCESS IS BORED BY AFFAIR

Margaret Rose, 6, Even Goes to the Extent of Yawning at Archbishop of Canterbury

OLDER SISTER NUDGES HER

Elizabeth, for the First Time, Takes Precedence Over Other Ladies of Royal Family

By The Associated Press.

LONDON, May 12.—Two little Princesses saw their father crowned King today, but their reactions were very different.

Eleven-year-old Princess Elizabeth sat primly in her seat in the royal box, her attention fastened on the dramatic spectacle before her. One day she may play the leading rôle in such a ceremony, for she is heir presumptive to the throne.

Beside her, Princess Margaret Rose, 6½, tried her best to act as a princess should at a coronation. But she couldn't keep from squirming and lounging in her seat as the proceedings went on, and once she yawned right at the venerable Archbishop of Canterbury, head of the Anglican Church.

The little girls had risen at 7:30 for the great day. They peeped out of the nursery windows of Buckingham Palace to see thousands

Continued on Page Sixteen

Housewives Entitled to Fixed Salaries, Like Any Worker, Mrs. Roosevelt Holds

The suggestion that wives who stay at home to look after the household should receive a definite salary for their work was advanced last night by Mrs. Franklin D. Roosevelt, wife of the President.

Remarking that a housewife earns the right to a salary, "without any question," Mrs. Roosevelt added that "any girl who is needed at home has a job just as surely as the girl who operates a machine in a factory; if she is not needed at home, she loses out by not working."

Mrs. Roosevelt expressed her views in a discussion of "The Home vs. Work for Women," with Miss Rose Schneiderman, president of the Women's Trade Union League and secretary of the New York State Department of Labor. The discussion was broadcast over a radio network.

Asked for her opinion of the most vital question facing working women, Miss Schneiderman said it was "getting over their economic inferiority complex." Women often carry a feeling of inferiority into business and industry and are willing to work for much less pay, she said.

Mrs. Roosevelt remarked that there was no question that "a woman who works to give her children the necessities and some of the advantages of life should have her work day limited to eight hours."

Miss Schneiderman said that when the working conditions of women were bettered "those of men automatically rise too."

"When women work long hours and for next to nothing," she continued, "they are not only competing against each other, but are pulling down the wages of their men folks."

Asked by Mrs. Roosevelt if she thought men resented women in industry, Miss Schneiderman replied that emotionally they did, "sometimes."

"But can you imagine," she continued, "what would happen if the 11,000,000 working women in the United States suddenly quit their jobs and just waited for the men to support them?"

Vast Throngs Cheer Royalty In Procession and at Palace

Rain Fails to Lessen Enthusiasm of More Than 1,000,000 on London Route—Queen, Queen Mother, Baldwin Get Ovations

By CHARLES W. HURD
Wireless to THE NEW YORK TIMES.

LONDON, May 12.—The most representative military spectacle the British Empire could muster escorted King George today through six miles of London streets to signalize his coronation, while more than 1,000,000 Londoners and visitors from all countries looked on and cheered even in the last hour, when a cloudburst fell from the skies.

The procession was at once a display of most impressive pageantry and a graphic demonstration of British feeling that the monarchy is an integral part of the empire's soul.

There were plenty of cheers for the troops and the famous personages in line, but most were reserved for four persons—the King and Queen, who got the greatest ovation; Queen Mary, whose popularity is undimmed, and Prime Minister Stanley Baldwin, who steered the throne through its greatest modern crisis last December.

Following their triumphal ride the royal family had another great ovation from the crowds at Buckingham Palace when, in response to cheers, the King appeared on the balcony wearing his robe and crown. The crowd roared, "God save the King!" and then sang "For He's a Jolly Good Fellow."

More prolonged cheers were given Princess Elizabeth and Princess Margaret Rose when they joined their parents. There was an ovation for Queen Mary when she appeared to stand between the King and Queen.

The King and Queen, although tired by the day's responsibilities, made four more appearances later in the evening. Responding to the cheers of the crowds, they walked out on the balcony at 9 o'clock. Immediately after the loud-speakers were employed to announce that they would appear no more tonight. However, they made bows from the balcony three more times, the last at 11:50.

Heavy Rain in Afternoon

By seven o'clock this morning most of the stands along the parade route were filled by ticketholders who had tucked their lunches and mackintoshes under their chairs and hoped they would not have to use the coats despite the lowering skies. Hope for good weather became large when, almost coincident with the King's departure from Buckingham Palace, the sun peeked momentarily through the clouds, but it was its first and last appearance. Thenceforward the clouds yielded intermittent showers, followed by a heavy downpour starting at 3 o'clock.

With the coming of the heavy rain those who had yet to see the procession pulled on their coats, raised their umbrellas and waited. The newspapers they brought to read while waiting were used to wrap legs and feet and to cover women's hats.

Those who left their umbrellas up after the parade appeared were pelted with balls of wet paper until they gave up the struggle to keep dry either in the open seats or among the standing crowds. It was notable that few yielded their places until they had seen the King and Queen at the close of the procession.

Britons saw their King in his full story-book rôle attired in royal raiment—the symbol of all honor and protection—riding with the Queen in a golden coach surrounded by the panoply of greatness which every Briton loves as the symbol of spiritual possessions that all share alike.

Affection for King Displayed

George, looking through the glass windows of his coach, obviously sincere but modest to the point of shyness, saw manifestations of affection and regard which promise at some future day to raise him to a status approximating that of his father, George V, as the average Briton's ideal of a modest gentleman.

Some enthusiastic reports placed the size of the crowd greeting the King at 3,000,000 to 5,000,000, but a conservative estimate would reduce this—possibly to less than the number that turned out for George V's funeral early last year, but an extraordinary number considering the threatening weather and the bus strike which paralyzed this highly important transportation system.

Moreover, with the exception of the estimated 250,000 persons who bought reserved seats, most of the spectators had stood eight to fifteen hours by the time they saw the procession. They paid a heavy price, fainting by thousands, requiring attention by a large corps of doctors, nurses and ambulances. During the wait for the Westminster Abbey ceremonies the writer saw hundreds of them in one limited area drop down to rest or sleep on the soaked ground.

Show Love of Triumphs

This picture of the sleepers on the wet ground encompassed the whole story, the love of government, King and pageantry by average Britons and their dogged determination to participate in the nation's triumphs even though many

Continued on Page Eighteen

GEORGE VI THANKS PEOPLE OF EMPIRE

His Broadcast Is Received as Promise of a Reign Like That of His Father

HE GREETS THE DOMINIONS

Recalls That Kingship Arises From 'Will of Free Peoples' Associated in Amity

By FERDINAND KUHN Jr.
Wireless to THE NEW YORK TIMES.

LONDON, May 12.—With the cheers of London crowds still ringing in his ears, King George gave his personal thanks tonight to his peoples throughout the empire and promised to serve them faithfully in the years ahead.

He chose the evening of his coronation day to speak into the microphone from his study in Buckingham Palace as his father had after his silver jubilee two years ago. He talked not only as a king who had just had a crown placed on his head but as a simple young man without great brilliance who had been called to great responsibilities and was determined to live up to them.

Voices Thanks for Loyalty

It was an unassuming little speech, and there was more than a hint of George V in the new King's voice when he said:

"I cannot find words with which to thank you for your love and loyalty to the Queen and myself. Your good will in the streets today and your countless messages from overseas and from every quarter of these islands have filled our hearts to overflowing. I will only say this: that if in the coming years I can show my gratitude in service to you that is the way above all others that I should choose."

All this, so sincerely meant and so modestly spoken, might have come from the lips of George V if there had been a broadcast on the day of his coronation. It was evident in every sentence that in his coronation George V had set the pattern for this reign of the son who resembles him so closely in his temperament and in his attitude toward his royal job.

Later in his speech King George recalled that he had assumed his crown not only by the grace of God, but "by the will of the free peoples of the British Commonwealth," a reminder that he, like his father, realizes the source whence his kingship comes.

He talked, too, of today's ceremonial as a solemn "dedication" of himself and his Queen, and in one moving passage he reminded unnumbered millions of listeners that "the highest of distinctions is service to others."

Finally there was a reference to

Continued on Page Seventeen

RITE IS MEDIEVAL

Westminster Relives Past Age as Ruler Comes Into His Kingdom

KING A FRAIL, GRAVE FIGURE

Anointed and Robed in Regal Garb, He Receives Crown and Is Cheered by Peers

GIVES VOW WITH EMOTION

Queen, Serious and Nervous, Takes Place on Throne—Historic Service Drags

By FREDERICK T. BIRCHALL
Wireless to THE NEW YORK TIMES.

LONDON, May 12.—In a setting of medieval splendor such as seemed scarcely to belong to this day and age George VI was crowned King and Emperor in Westminster Abbey today.

He rode there with his Queen in their golden coach drawn by eight gray horses through streets lined with troops brought from all parts of the empire, and millions of his subjects acclaimed him as he passed.

In the Abbey he went through the ceremony of being accepted by his people. He took a vow to care for their welfare, to maintain and obey the laws passed by their Parliament, to be just and to temper justice with mercy.

Anointed With Holy Oil

He was disrobed of the outer garments he had worn on entering and anointed on his hands, breast and forehead with holy oil and thus dedicated to the kingship. Then he was freshly robed in cloth of gold and royal purple. The Sword of State was girt to his side and his heels were touched with the Spurs of Power.

They put the Ring on his finger. Two scepters—emblems of power and justice, equity and mercy—were placed in his hands. Then St. Edward's ancient crown of pure gold and costly jewels was pressed upon his bowed head with a prayer to God to crown him with all princely virtues.

Trumpets sounded, drums rolled and the Abbey sprang into full illumination at his crowning, while outside the church bells rang for joy and guns thundered a royal salute. The peers of his realm surrounding him put on their own coronets and the great edifice rang with the shout, "God save the King!" Archbishops, Bishops, the King's royal brothers and the nobles of his realm knelt in turn before him and swore fealty.

Then Queen Is Crowned

Then the Queen was anointed and crowned in like manner and took her place on her lower throne beside him. They went together to the high altar, knelt in prayer and partook of the communion. Finally, in a new splendid procession, they passed down the great nave and out among the plain people, who are the mainstay of their kingdom, yet had had little share in all this ceremony. And throughout the long drive they were again acclaimed in a thunder of cheers echoing through all London—"God save the King!"

The pageant within the Abbey followed the lines that already have been so fully described in advance. The King and Queen entered the Abbey at 11:20 A. M. from the temporary annex, to which the street procession had carried them. They left it at 2:40 P. M. The historic service had dragged a little.

Most of those within the edifice had arrived before 7 o'clock. Few were able to depart before 3:30. The last did not get away before 8. That was due to bad management and it made a long day for many persons no longer young.

So the sixth George and the second Elizabeth, his consort, came at last into their kingdom. Into more than a kingdom; into an empire of kindred and equal great States that overspreads the world. To keep these firmly linked and insure justice to their countless millions is no easy task in these troublous times. But that is of tomorrow.

Scene One of Splendor

The splendor of the scene in which this pageant was enacted is not easy to convey.

Picture the great gray Abbey, shrine and temple of the English race throughout a thousand years,

Continued on Page Sixteen

"All the News That's Fit to Print."

The New York Times.

Copyright, 1937, by The New York Times Company.

LATE CITY EDITION
Partly cloudy and cooler today. Tomorrow fair with little change in temperature.
Temperatures Yesterday—Max., 75; Min., 64

VOL. LXXXVII....No. 29,111. Entered as Second-Class Matter, Postoffice, New York, N. Y. NEW YORK, THURSDAY, OCTOBER 7, 1937. PPP TWO CENTS In New York City. | THREE CENTS Within 200 Miles. | FOUR CENTS Elsewhere Except in 7th and 8th Postal Zones.

U. S. CONDEMNS JAPAN AS INVADER OF CHINA; DROPS NEUTRALITY POLICY TO BACK LEAGUE; GENEVA CALLS MEETING OF 9-POWER NATIONS

61,000 SEE YANKS CRUSH GIANTS, 8-1, IN SERIES OPENER

Hubbell Routed in Sixth as Victors Stage Seven-Run Uprising at Stadium

GOMEZ PITCHES SUPERBLY

Holds Rivals to Six Hits and Yields Only Tally in Fifth—Lazzeri Gets Homer

DIMAGGIO STAR IN RALLY

Singles With Bases Full to Start the Onslaught—Gate Receipts Are $234,256

By JOHN DREBINGER

Bursting out of the misty haze like an enveloping flame such as a man might encounter on locating that leak in a gas pipe with the aid of a match, the Yankee juggernaut exploded only once at the Stadium yesterday, but that once sufficed to blow the opening clash of the 1937 world series virtually into atoms.

It came with cyclonic effect in the sixth inning, toppled Carl Hubbell like a reed in a high gale, tossed Colonel Bill Terry and his Giants into such confusion that they even nominated a relief pitcher who was sitting awed and spellbound in the dugout, and went on to hurtle seven runs across the plate.

Two rounds later the venerable Anthony Lazzeri wafted a towering home run into the stands and the sum total of all this was a smashing victory for Marse Joe McCarthy's amazing American League champions behind their own left-hander, Vernon Gomez. The final score, 8 to 1, left a crowd of 61,000 almost as stunned and bewildered by it all as were the crestfallen National Leaguers.

Clings Tenaciously to Lead

For five innings, Hubbell, ace pitcher of his circuit, strove heroically to repeat his notable triumph in the series opener of 1936. In four of these rounds, in fact, the work of the famous screwball maestro was absolutely flawless as he clung tenaciously to a one-run margin he had gained over his left-handed adversary.

But in this, perhaps, he made a mistake, for it is a matter of scientific knowledge that at times it is extremely dangerous to keep a highly volatile explosive too tightly bottled up. Something simply had to give and in the sixth it was ol' Hub himself.

Confronted by the inviting set-up of the bases full and nobody out but a few less hardy Giant rooters who doubtless already felt what was coming, Joe DiMaggio, he whom they call the wonder player of his time, crashed a single to center field to start the avalanche of Yankee runs pouring across the plate.

More Shells Are Fired

Presently the bases again filled. In fact, those Yankees seemed to keep the bases filled for an almost interminable period while Bill Dickey and George Selkirk fired more shells into the gaunt frame of ol' Hub, who was unmistakably going down with all his comrades on board.

Finally, with the seven big tallies tucked away, the Yankee storm subsided, leaving only Gomez to move serenely on to his fourth victory in world series warfare.

The singular Castillian, who once made the classic remark that he would rather be lucky than good, now reveled in the picture of combining both of these rare qualities so vital to success in any venture.

For not only had fortune smiled on him to the extent of having runs poured in for him in a carload lot, but he was undeniably superb as well. He pitched smoothly and easily, held the straining National League standard bearers to six blows, only two of which did any damage at all, and all in all was a far cry from the Gomez who stumbled badly to two victories last Fall behind a similar withering barrage.

Open Gaps in Stands

As had been half feared, the capacity crowd which was expected to total 70,000 did not materialize. There were a few open gaps in the lower end of the reserved sections and, what was even more surprising, the unreserved upper tier revealed vacant spaces as well.

The paid attendance totaled 60,573, more than 6,000 short of the all-time record set last year, and the receipts were $234,256.

Following a night of heavy rains which for a time threatened to postpone the whole program a day, a clear but intensely humid morning greeted the early arrivals. It assured a ball game, even if the sun remained behind a haze that hung over the arena like a smoke screen throughout the sultry afternoon.

The bulk of the crowd, in fact,

Continued on Page Thirty-two

Only Three Days Remain For Registration Here

Registration throughout the city continued yesterday to lag behind both last year's figures and those of 1933, the year of the last Mayoralty campaign. The total registration in the city for the first three days of this year was 960,403, which compared with 962,072 in 1933, and 1,152,272 last year, when the all-time record was set.

Yesterday's registration did, however, show an upturn in most boroughs, and in Manhattan and the Bronx exceeded the 1933 total for the same period, although it lagged far behind the 1936 figures.

Residents of New York who desire to cast a vote in the municipal election on Nov. 2 must qualify by registering this week. There are only three days left. Registration places will be open from 5 P. M. to 10:30 P. M. today and tomorrow, and from 7 A. M. to 10:30 P. M. on Saturday.

MAYOR AND TAYLOR BREAK OVER BUDGET

La Guardia Quits Meeting in Rage, Charging Political Plot by Colleagues

WON'T CUT PAY, HE SAYS

Insists Controller Must Make Up Shortage Due to Cut in Water Rates

Enraged to the point of tears by the attempts of Democratic members of the Board of Estimate to make him responsible for finding the additional $12,000,000 for next year's budget, Mayor La Guardia slammed out of an executive session of the board yesterday after the bitterest battle he has ever had with Controller Frank J. Taylor.

Controller Taylor suggested in the course of the executive session that the Mayor order the Budget Director to reduce salaries next year to make up the $12,000,000 taken off the city's revenues when the Aldermen cut city water rates last Monday. Through the closed doors of the committee room in City Hall the Mayor's sledge-hammer blows on the table were plainly heard.

"Damn it," he shouted, "you're not going to put me on the spot. I'm a candidate too. Your Democratic Aldermen overrode my veto on the water rates, and now you want me to take the rap. I'll be damned if I will.

Tells Colleagues to Do Cutting

"Mahoney and the rest of you are going around town taking credit for getting the water rate cut through, and now you want me and my Budget Director to take the rap by trying to make us cut salaries in the budget next year.

"You cut the revenue," the Mayor stormed at his colleagues. "Now go ahead and cut the budget. I warned you that you either would have to cut relief or cut salaries, if you cut the water rate. Now, damn it, you go ahead and do it. I won't."

With a mighty tug, the door of the chamber flew open and the Mayor charged out, his face a choleric red and tears of rage starting from his eyes. He tore by every one in the hall, clattered down the stairs and dashed into his office, and every door in his path got a resounding slam as he went.

The board formally adopted the Mayor's executive budget of $589,222,376 yesterday, and it became the tentative budget through that action. The open meeting at which the vote was taken was marked by sharp exchanges among the Mayor, Mr. Taylor and Borough President James J. Lyons of the Bronx.

"The Controller is the financial officer of the city—let him find the $12,000,000 to make up the water rate cut," the Mayor remarked.

"I won't take that responsibility," retorted Mr. Taylor. "It's your budget."

"Well, I can't print the money," the Mayor shot back.

Lyons in Clash

Mr. Lyons tried to introduce a motion stating that the Mayor was equally responsible with other members of the Board for local legislation which increases the budget by $22,905,038. In his budget message last Saturday the Mayor said these were items over which he had neither power nor control.

"The Borough President of the Bronx doesn't know what he's talking about and apparently can't read English," the Mayor lashed out. "He is one of those who is trying to force the tax rate up, or salaries down, through the cut in water rates."

"We're not going to tamper with

Continued on Page Eleven

LONDON AND PARIS SAID TO GIVE ITALY 24 HOURS TO REPLY

Patience Is Exhausted in Issue of Withdrawal of Italians From War in Spain

SHOW OF FORCE EXPECTED

Opening of French Frontier to Arm Madrid Is Held to Be Sufficient

Twenty-four hours in which to reply to the invitation to a three-power meeting on withdrawal of "volunteers" from Spain was understood to have been given to Italy yesterday by Great Britain and France. An Anglo-French display of force was indicated if a prompt reply from Italy was not forthcoming. In Rome it was said the answer was not yet ready. [Page 1.]

Rain and fog continued to hold up the Insurgent drive near Gijon on the north coast of Spain. In the southwest around Huelva the Rebels were harassed by guerrilla warfare. [Page 20.]

In London a group of British Protestants, having issued an appeal for a united Christian front to combat anti-church activities in connection with the civil war, was collecting funds to help this work. [Page 20.]

Firm Stand Toward Italy

By The Associated Press.

LONDON, Oct. 6.—France and Great Britain tonight gave Premier Benito Mussolini twenty-four hours' grace to respond to their joint bid for a three-power discussion of the withdrawal of "volunteers" from Spain.

The two governments, alarmed by the new Italian aid to the Spanish Insurgents, strongly indicated their patience with Mussolini was not unlimited after Foreign Secretary Anthony Eden conferred lengthily with Prime Minister Neville Chamberlain and Ambassador Charles Corbin of France.

"The two Governments have agreed on the desirability of receiving an early reply from Italy," said a statement issued following the conferences.

Show of Force Suggested

The feeling grew in authoritative quarters that a stern show of Anglo-French force might be the only way to get Italian Black Shirt legions out of Spain, a problem that worries Britain as much as the Far Eastern crisis does.

"We may have to take quick, very decisive action to strangle at its source the prolonged Italian intervention in behalf of the Insurgents," said one informed source, though just what direct action the British Cabinet might take remained a secret.

The opinion was expressed that Italy's obvious attempts to impress Britain and France of her strength—by sending new, powerful planes and troops to Spain—actually were

Continued on Page Twenty

Rome Held Ready to Aid Any U. S. Peace Parley

By The Associated Press.

ROME, Oct. 6.—Diplomatic circles here were stirred by the potentialities of President Roosevelt's comments on world affairs.

There was considerable speculation in Fascist circles over whether the President, in announcing more active American cooperation in the cause of world peace, was planning an international conference to halt "international anarchy and instability" and if his strength was great enough to obtain a positive peace agreement.

Informed sources said Italy would be willing to take part in such a parley if sufficient preliminary work preceded the actual conference.

American condemnation of Japan as a treaty violator in China today fell sharply athwart an Italian tendency to justify Japanese activity. For example, the Popolo d'Italia of Milan said yesterday, "We fully understand and justify" Japanese efforts at expansion.

Reliable sources reported that weeks ago the Fascist press was instructed to play up the Japanese side of the Sino-Japanese conflict.

JAPANESE CONFER ON CENSURE BY U.S.

Emergency Conference Called by Foreign Office as Extras Appear With Condemnation

ROOSEVELT IS CRITICIZED

But Press Is Convinced That We Will Shun Entanglement in Other People's Quarrels

By The Associated Press.

TOKYO, Thursday, Oct. 7.—The Japanese Foreign Office called an emergency conference today following United States action condemning Japan as a treaty violator.

Simultaneously, newspaper extras began appearing with the bare text of the pronouncement issued by the State Department in Washington. No comment was published immediately. Excitement spread through the streets as crowds clustered around the newsboys.

Government officials earlier had reserved comment on the action by the United States and by the League of Nations Assembly also condemning Japan for her role in the undeclared war with China.

They said they were awaiting

Continued on Page Thirteen

Hepburn Government Wins in Ontario; He Hails Victory as Endorsing Fight on CIO

Special to THE NEW YORK TIMES.

TORONTO, Oct. 6.—After three stormy years in office, Premier Mitchell Hepburn of Ontario was re-elected tonight by a majority almost as sweeping as that which first swept him into power in 1934.

The Conservatives lost their leader, Earl Rowe, who was defeated by Mr. Hepburn's Minister of Education, Dr. L. J. Simpson. All the other Liberal Ministers were reelected, with the exception of Duncan Marshall, who held the portfolio of agriculture.

Mr. Hepburn's Liberal party won 63 and the Conservatives 23 out of the Legislature's ninety seats.

Two Liberal Progressives, one independent Liberal and one United Farmer were returned. Labor, Social Credit and Communist candidates were left at the post. The Cooperative Commonwealth party (Fabian Socialist) lost the one seat it held in the last Legislature.

The result was interpreted by Mr. Hepburn chiefly as an endorsement of his determined stand last Spring against the incursion of C. I. O. organizers from the United States. "The people of Ontario," he declared, "may rest assured they will have another five years of industrial peace. Ontario has given endorsement to the first jurisdiction that had enough courage openly to defy and resist the threatened C. I. O. invasion."

Ontario farmers, to whom Mr. Hepburn made his chief appeal, gave him solid support. In Oshawa, where the General Motors strike last Spring provoked his intervention and caused the resignation of two Ministers from his Cabinet, a Liberal candidate, Gordon Conant, was returned. Northern Ontario, whose miners were said to have been recruited by the C. I. O., gave the Government almost as large a vote as in 1934.

Against this, however, was the fact that in Windsor and Toronto, David A. Croll and Arthur W. Roebuck, two former Hepburn Ministers, who lost their Cabinet portfolios as the result of an open break with the Premier over the C. I. O. issue, were re-elected with handsome majorities.

Credit for his victory is given both by the government's friends and foes to Mr. Hepburn himself. For eight weeks he waged what was virtually a one-man campaign, principally on his opposition to the C. I. O. and communism which, he contended, was following hot on its heels.

TORONTO, Oct. 6 (Canadian Press).—The Conservatives gained nine seats from the Liberals in the Ontario election: Dufferin-Simcoe, Fort William, Hastings West, Leeds, Peel, Prince Edward-Lennox, Simcoe East, Toronto Riverdale, Victoria. The Liberals gained three from the Conservatives: Peterborough, Toronto Bracondale, Toronto St. David, and one from the Cooperative Commonwealth party, Hamilton East.

LEAGUE UNANIMOUS

Fifty Countries Endorse Move for a Parley to Seek Settlement

19 NATIONS ARE INVITED

Germany and Russia Also Are Expected to Be Asked—Roosevelt Speech Hailed

Wireless to THE NEW YORK TIMES.

GENEVA, Oct. 6.—With the tacit approval of fifty countries and the remaining two, Poland and Siam, abstaining, the League of Nations Assembly adopted tonight the resolution of its Far Eastern Advisory Committee. This resolution authorizes League members who are parties to the Nine-Power treaty to invite the United States and other interested powers to initiate the consultation provided for in this treaty with a view to ending the Sino-Japanese conflict by agreement.

Then, instead of closing the session, the Assembly followed the precedents set during the Manchurian and Ethiopian crises and recessed. By this action its President, the Aga Khan, was left free to call another session whenever he considers it necessary.

Tonight's meeting was brief, lasting slightly more than a half hour. There were only two speakers, Carl J. Hambro of Norway and Stefanus F. Gie of South Africa. Both supported the resolution.

Declares Move Adopted

When they had finished and no further speakers expressed a wish to be heard the President announced that unless a vote were requested he would take it that the Assembly did not want one. There being no objection he declared the resolution adopted.

Immediately thereafter, in accordance with the Assembly's decision, he signed letters to seventeen League members who are signatories of the Nine-Power treaty, inviting them to initiate the consultation provided for under the pact's Article VII at the earliest possible moment. The seventeen League signatories are Australia, Belgium, Bolivia, Canada, China, Denmark, France, India, Italy, Mexico, the Netherlands, New Zealand, Norway, Portugal, Sweden, the United Kingdom and the Union of South Africa.

[Article VII of the Nine-Power treaty, signed at Washington Feb. 6, 1922, reads: "The Contracting Powers agree that whenever a situation arises which in the opinion of any one of them involves the application of the stipulations of the present treaty and renders desirable discussion of such application, there shall be full and frank communication between the Contracting Powers concerned.]

League circles hinted that an invitation from Washington to hold the consultation in the capital of the United States would be particularly acceptable, as under those circumstances the Japanese might be disposed to accept. The British are especially known to hold this view.

Besides Japan, the United States and the seventeen other countries mentioned above, Germany and Soviet Russia are almost certain to be invited, though it is regarded as unlikely that Germany will accept.

Since the Advisory Committee meets again within a month it is hoped here that consultation will be called within a fortnight. The results could then be transmitted to the Advisory Committee when it meets and, if the circumstances require it, the Assembly might be reconvened.

Other Measures Threatened

GENEVA, Oct. 6 (AP).—The League of Nations put pressure on Japan tonight to end her undeclared war on China. The League Assembly threw its "moral support" to China, called on the Nine-Power treaty group to act and told Japan there might be other measures if she did not quit her war.

The Nine-Power signatories also were expected to assemble quickly. Representatives of League members involved said the conference might be held in London within two weeks. Some suggested that the conferees might meet in Washington, where the treaty was created. Arrangements probably will be made through triangular conversations among London, Paris and

Continued on Page Twelve

U. S. Statement on Japan

Special to THE NEW YORK TIMES.

WASHINGTON, Oct. 6.—Following is the text of the State Department statement issued today condemning Japan's action in China:

The Department of State has been informed by the American Minister to Switzerland of the text of the report adopted by the advisory committee of the League of Nations setting forth the advisory committee's examination of the facts of the present situation in China and the treaty obligations of Japan. The Minister has further informed the department that this report was adopted and aproved by the Assembly of the League of Nations today, Oct. 6.

Since the beginning of the present controversy in the Far East the Government of the United States has urged upon both the Chinese and the Japanese Governments that they refrain from hostilities and has offered to be of assistance in an effort to find some means, acceptable to both parties to the conflict, of composing by pacific methods the situation in the Far East.

The Secretary of State in statements made public on July 16 and Aug. 23 made clear the position of the Government of the United States in regard to international problems and international relationships throughout the world and as applied specifically to the hostilities which are at present unfortunately going on between China and Japan. Among the principles which in the opinion of the Government of the United States should govern international relationships, if peace is to be maintained, are abstinence by all nations from use of force in the pursuit of policy and from interference in the internal affairs of other nations; adjustment of problems in international relations by process of peaceful negotiation and agreement; respect by all nations for the rights of others and observance by all nations of established obligations; and the upholding of the principle of the sanctity of treaties.

On Oct. 5 at Chicago the President elaborated these principles, emphasizing their importance, and in a discussion of the world situation pointed out that there can be no stability or peace either within nations or between nations except under laws and moral standards adhered to by all; that international anarchy de-

Continued on Page Twelve

STIMSON FAVORS ACTION ON JAPAN

Urges Joint Move by U. S. and Britain to Stop Supplying War Goods to Tokyo

HE PRAISES ROOSEVELT

Terms Chicago Speech 'an Act of Leadership'—Supports Our Backing of League

The text of Mr. Stimson's letter is on page 12.

An appeal that the United States lend support to the League of Nations "by a statement of its concurrence" in efforts to stop Japan's war upon China was made yesterday by former Secretary of State Henry L. Stimson in a letter to THE NEW YORK TIMES discussing the Sino-Japanese situation.

Mr. Stimson, whose letter had been completed before President Roosevelt made his Chicago address, added a paragraph in which he hailed the talk, which called for "concerted action" for peace and assailed war makers. He referred to it as "an act of leadership" which, he hoped, "will result in a new birth of American courage in facing and carrying through our responsibilities in this crisis."

"In this grave crisis in the Far East we not only must not fear to face issues of right and wrong but we must not fear to cooperate with other nations who are similarly attempting to face those issues," Mr. Stimson declared.

Failure to act, he warned, will not keep this country out of war, but will endanger our own peace,

Assails Neutrality Laws

Assailing the recent neutrality legislation of the United States as "a policy of amoral drift" which, if continued, will make our entanglement in war more certain, Mr. Stimson suggested as one measure of practical action that the United States and Great Britain stop supplying Japan with commodities essential to the pursuit of her military and naval operations.

The United States and the British Empire, he pointed out, now furnish Japan with the bulk of these commodities.

"China's principal need is not that something should be done by outside nations to help her, but that outside nations should cease helping her enemy," Mr. Stimson declared after an exhaustive analysis of the situation, in which he branded Japan as a militarist aggressor acting in violation of international obligations under the Nine Power treaty.

While rejecting the idea of armed intervention in the Sino-Japanese conflict, Mr. Stimson emphasized that "that is very far from saying that the only alternative is inaction or a passive and shameful

Continued on Page Twelve

OSTRACIZE JAPAN, PITTMAN DEMANDS

Senator Asserts an 'Economic Quarantine' Would End Conflict in 30 Days

HOLDS WORLD SHOULD ACT

Calls on 'Civilized' Nations, Especially Britain, to Join U. S. in Strong Move

Special to THE NEW YORK TIMES.

RENO, Nev., Oct. 6.—Senator Key Pittman, chairman of the Senate Foreign Relations Committee, recommended an economic quarantine of Japan in a statement issued here tonight.

He declared that President Roosevelt has been "very patient and has made every effort to persuade the military government of Japan to abandon its unlawful, immoral and brutal conduct in China," and that "the continued conduct of the military government of Japan" has conclusively proved to the world that Japan's "excuse" that she has been only protecting her subjects in China is false.

"The Government of the United States, while not a member of the League of Nations," said Senator Pittman, "is a signatory to the Nine-Power pact guaranteeing the territorial integrity of China and bears all of the obligations that fall upon Japan, Great Britain, France, Belgium, Poland and other great signatories. Our government can no longer refrain from asserting the facts and publicly condemning Japan.

Action Under Nine-Power Pact

"The action of our Government is taken under the Nine-Power pact and not under the covenant of the League of Nations. Japan has offered the excuse of a hold-up—that is, the hold-up man needs money and the victim has it.

"Great Britain is more directly affected by Japan's aggression than is the United States or any other country. Great Britain backed down in 1932 and left our Government out on a limb. Our Government has gone as far as it can until the other Governments that are responsible come out of the brush and assume their part of the responsibilities.

"The President has suggested the method of compelling Japan to desist from its barbarous warfare of destruction. He holds that Japan is disseminating war disease which may involve the world and that Japan should be quarantined as every civilized community quarantines against contagious disease.

"The Neutrality Act was never intended to meet such contagion. It was intended solely to eliminate certain causes that might lead us into foreign war. What is required now is a quarantine to prevent spread of the war disease and to stamp it out.

Continued on Page Nineteen

TWO PACTS CITED

State Department Says Tokyo Breaks 9-Power and Kellogg Treaties

EMBARKS ON NEW COURSE

Acceptance by Washington of Bid to Conference Asked by League Is Foreseen

By BERTRAM D. HULEN
Special to THE NEW YORK TIMES.

WASHINGTON, Oct. 6.—Japan was condemned by the United States for her action in China and accused of having violated the Nine-Power treaty for safeguarding China and the Kellogg-Briand antiwar pact in a formal statement issued late today by the State Department.

The declaration aligned this country with the League of Nations in the condemnation of Japan as an aggressor. It is to be followed, from all indications, by American acceptance of an invitation, which has not yet been received, to participate in a conference called under the Nine-Power treaty to consider what the interested nations should do to meet the emergency.

The statement, which was issued in response to official notification of the analysis of and the conclusions on the Sino-Japanese controversy by the League of Nations, marked a radical shift in American policy and represented the first step in implementing the views President Roosevelt enunciated in his Chicago speech yesterday.

New Course for U. S. Seen

Together the two moves mean, in diplomatic and political opinion, that President Roosevelt has made a dead letter of American neutrality policy and is embarked on a new course of dealing actively with aggressor nations.

The State Department statement reviewed the efforts Secretary Hull has made heretofore to encourage peace between Japan and China, recalled the pertinent points of President Roosevelt's Chicago speech, and concluded by saying:

"In the light of the unfolding developments in the Far East the Government of the United States has been forced to the conclusion that the action of Japan in China is inconsistent with the principles which should govern the relationships between nations and is contrary to the provisions of the Nine-Power treaty of Feb. 6, 1922, regarding principles and policies to be followed in matters concerning China, and to those of the Kellogg-Briand pact of Aug. 27, 1928. Thus the conclusions of this Government with respect to the foregoing are in general accord with those of the Assembly of the League of Nations."

The condemnation of Japan marks the first time the United States has declared a nation an aggressor or a violator of treaties.

First Move of the Kind

Similarly, the call for a conference under the Nine-Power treaty constitutes the first time that that pact has been invoked. Secretary of State Henry L. Stimson planned to invoke it in 1932 at the time of Japan's invasion of Manchuria, but was dissuaded when Great Britain displayed no enthusiasm for the plan. Instead, Mr. Stimson invoked American rights under the treaty and implemented the Kellogg-Briand pact by announcing the United States would not recognize gains won contrary to its terms.

[This is the second instance within eight days in which the United States has supported action taken by the League of Nations. Secretary Hull issued a statement on Sept. 28 condemning Japanese bombings of open cities in China after the League had adopted a resolution taking a similar stand.]

Officials in issuing the statement were thoroughly aware of the significance of the step and of its implications in relation to association of the United States with the League of Nations and in the renewed force it gives the Kellogg-Briand pact.

They appreciated, although perhaps only in broad outline, that it might well lead to similar steps in future emergencies and that it might also produce adverse reactions from isolationist elements in this country. Even today peace organizations attacked President

Continued on Page Twelve

"All the News That's Fit to Print."

The New York Times.

LATE CITY EDITION
Partly cloudy, continued cold to-day. Tomorrow cloudy, probably snow, temperature unchanged.
Temperatures Yesterday—Max., 32; Min., 19

VOL. LXXXVII....No. 29,178. | Entered as Second-Class Matter, Postoffice, New York, N. Y. | NEW YORK, MONDAY, DECEMBER 13, 1937. | PPP | TWO CENTS In New York City. | THREE CENTS Within 200 Miles. | FOUR CENTS Elsewhere Except in 7th and 8th Postal Zones.

U. S. GUNBOAT SUNK BY JAPANESE BOMBS; 1 DEAD AND 15 HURT; 54 SAVED, 18 MISSING; BRITISH WARSHIP HIT, SEAMAN DEAD

DIES CLAIMS VOTES TO BEAT WAGE BILL BY RECOMMITTAL

But Despite His Poll House Leaders Hope to Pass Measure This Week

HARD FIGHT IN PROSPECT

Some Expect Norton Change in Administration to Be Turned Down

CROP PLAN TEST IS NEAR

Senate Action This Week Seen—Harrison Predicts Tax Revision by Feb. 1

Special to THE NEW YORK TIMES.

WASHINGTON, Dec. 12.—Congressional leaders plan to make a determined effort to send to conference this week two of the four measures for which the special session was called, the Farm Bill voted by the House last week and the Wages and Hours measure, which has long been tied up in the House Rules Committee.

The latter bill faces perhaps the bitterest fight of the session. When the House convenes tomorrow noon Representative Mary Norton, chairman of the Labor Committee, will call up the measure, changed in many respects from the Black-Connery bill passed by the Senate at the last regular session.

By means of a discharge petition to which 218 signatures were obtained ten days ago to force it out of the Rules Committee, the bill comes before the House, where its enemies threaten the strongest kind of opposition.

Representative Dies of Texas, a member of the Rules Committee, disclosed tonight that with other opponents he had been quietly taking a poll of the House and felt that they had enough backing to force recommittal of the bill.

Count 202 for Recommittal

"Our poll shows that 202 House members will vote for recommittal," he said. "It indicated that two-thirds of the Republicans in the House favor recommittal."

He added that at least thirty-five of the members who signed the discharge petition would vote for the motion to recommit and that Southern foes of the measure could count on enough additional votes from the Middle West and rural towns in the East to give them a majority when the test came.

"If the bill passed, taking the most optimistic figures, it would affect not more than 500,000 workers after you deduct those who are exempt and those who are engaged in intrastate employment," said Mr. Dies.

"This bill can only help a handful but at the same time its passage would increase the cost of living and thus affect the whole nation. Its real effect would be to lower wage scales and lengthen hours."

Representative Cox of Georgia, likewise a member of the Rules Committee, also expressed hostility to the measure.

"The passage of this measure is the worst thing that could take place at this time," he said. "It would throw a million out of work."

The House leadership expresses equal confidence that a wages and hours measure in some form will be passed by the end of Wednesday's session.

Boland Predicts Passage

Representative Boland, the Democratic whip, canvassed the situation over the week-end, and predicted that a bill resembling in essentials the Senate measure, which provides for a five-man administrative board with differentials as to minimum wages and maximum hours for various parts of the country, would be approved.

The leaders will fight the motion to recommit and say they regard a victory in that fight as virtually certain. Mr. Boland said a handful of those who signed the discharge petition might vote to recommit, but that there were enough votes to compensate for such a defection.

Besides having to thwart efforts of Southern members who seek recommittal, the leadership faces what may develop into a major struggle over the content of the legislation to be passed. Representative Dockweiler of California seeks to substitute for the bill a measure, strongly backed by the American Federation of Labor, which provides for a flat forty-hour maximum work week and a forty-cent minimum pay per hour and for administration by existing agencies, with Federal courts and the

Continued on Page Twelve

Convicts Kill Captive Guard As Governor Begs Mercy

South Carolina Executive Pleads 2 Hours for Hostage Held in Prison Office, Then Troops Rout 6 Men With Gas

By The Associated Press.

COLUMBIA, S. C., Dec. 12.—A machine-gun company of National Guardsmen fired tear-gas shells today to subdue six convicts who stabbed a prison guard captain to death and barricaded themselves in the captain's office in a desperate attempt to escape from the State penitentiary.

The victim, Captain Olin Sanders, was stabbed five times after the felons had defied a dramatic two-hour plea by Governor Olin Johnston to give themselves up.

The youthful Governor shouted to them through the door of their barricaded refuge, urging them to submit to avoid bloodshed and obviate the necessity of calling out the National Guard.

"Get us a car. Open the gates. Otherwise it'll be too bad for Sanders," one of the felons retorted.

In vain the Governor begged them to release their captaive. Two hours later the khaki-clad troopers arrived. Another plea was made by Adjt. Gen. James C. Dozier, commanding the guardsmen. Again the convicts bluntly refused, announcing they would stay there "until hell freezes over."

Governor Johnston made one final effort to persuade them.

"If you boys will walk out of there and let Captain Sanders walk out first, I'll see that nothing goes against your record," he promised.

A hoarse rumble of defiance replied, and Governor Johnston signaled the guardsmen.

"Go ahead, boys—let them have it."

A barrage of tear gas brought quick surrender. Gasping and choking, with tears streaming down their cheeks, the desperadoes emerged, one by one, with their hands up.

On the floor, bleeding profusely from stab wounds, lay Sanders. He died in a hospital a few minutes later.

The victim apparently was stabbed immediately after the guardsmen opened their tear-gas attack.

Prison officials said that Sanders was unarmed at the time of the attack because strict prison rules forbade carrying a gun into the prison yard.

Guards said he had "checked"

Continued on Page Four

SLOAN BACKS FUND BY $10,000,000 GIFT

General Motors Head Endows Foundation He Established for Economic Research

ASKS THAT STOCK BE HELD

Transfer of Holdings in His Own Concern Explained—Gains in Education Sought

Alfred P. Sloan Jr. announced plans yesterday for endowing the Alfred P. Sloan Foundation for economic research with securities worth about $10,000,000. A little more than one-third of the proposed endowment, his statement said, consists of common stock of General Motors Corporation, of which Mr. Sloan is chairman.

Lest the public misapprehend the situation, Mr. Sloan included in his statement announcing the gift a promise to recommend to the trustees of the fund that they retain the General Motors stock in their portfolio. Under SEC rules the transfer of ownership of the stock is a matter of public record.

The trust Mr. Sloan purposes to endow was established by him on July 6, 1936, as a non-profit corporation under the laws of Delaware. Harold S. Sloan, his brother, a former Associate Professor of Economics at State Teachers College, Montclair, N. J., was named executive director of the fund.

The organization of the trust was not announced until Feb. 27, 1937. At the time it was explained that the founder had been too busy with labor troubles to determine details of the fund's operation or the size of the endowment needed for its work. In the meantime, Harold Sloan established an office at 30 Rockefeller Plaza.

Sloan Explains His Gift

Mr. Sloan's statement, announcing his intention of transferring $10,000,000 of securities to the fund, follows:

"I take this means of announcing that I am in the process of donating as an endowment to the Alfred P. Sloan Foundation, which I have been developing for some years past, securities of an estimated worth of approximately $10,000,000. The specific purpose of this statement is twofold: first, to avoid any misconception as to the aims involved, and, second, to establish the objectives that I have in mind.

"I particularly wish to emphasize the fact, even if it appears self-evident, that this transaction has nothing whatsoever to do with General Motors Corporation or my official relationship with same. It is entirely a personal matter. However, among the securities involved are over 100,000 shares of the common stock of General Motors.

"Due to government regulations, changes in my General Motors holdings are a matter of public record on account of my official relationship with that organization; hence it is important, especially in the period of uncertainty now existing, that no prejudice should develop as to the reasons for the action that I am taking. I shall recommend to the trustees of the foundation that they continue to hold these securities as part of its portfolio.

"As to the objectives: The Alfred P. Sloan Foundation has as its general purposes, in common with all

Continued on Page Ten

PRINCETON SENIOR IS KILLED IN FIRE

Lawrence H. Clark, 21, Found Slumped in Dormitory After Flames Sweep His Room

VICTIM OF DENSE SMOKE

Fellow-Student Arouses Seven Other Sleepers, but Fails to Locate His Friend

Special to THE NEW YORK TIMES.

PRINCETON, N. J., Dec. 12.—Lawrence H. Clark, a 21-year-old senior at the university here, was killed this morning by smoke from a fire which apparently originated in an upholstered chair in his dormitory room at 44 Mitchell Hall. He died in the room of another student across the hall from his own, his body partly draped in bedclothing which he had sought before running out into the cold.

At about 3:45 o'clock Richard B. Duane Jr., a sophomore, of Locust, N. J., and the occupant of the room in which Clark's body was found, was awakened by the noisy entrance of Clark from the hall. He saw Clark drop on one knee, seemingly having tripped over the door sill. Duane's room was instantly filled with smoke, and, clad only in pajamas and a pair of hastily snatched shoes, he ran out of the building and to the university police office on the campus, where he turned in a fire alarm. He said he believed Clark had followed him out.

Awakens Other Students

After turning in the alarm, Duane ran back to the dormitory and awakened the other students by shouting through the building. Five students were asleep in two double rooms on the ground floor and four more in single rooms on the second floor. Only when they were all out, shivering in heavy coats over pajamas, did Duane realize that Clark was not among them.

He went back into the building, climbing the stairs to the second floor, and finding that the flames, mounting through the ceiling in Clark's room, had cut off the electric current, he struck a match. By the imperfect light he looked over his own room, but could not enter Clark's because of the smoke, and concluded that Clark had somehow got out.

Back downstairs again, he once more became alarmed at the absence of Clark and once again went into the building. This time the smoke was so thick he could not even reach the second floor.

All the fire apparatus of Princeton had arrived meanwhile. The clangor had resulted in the assembly of a large number of students, police and others. The firemen, on ladders, attacked the fire through the windows of Clark's room.

In a few moments it had been subdued sufficiently to permit a more thorough search. In Duane's room Clark's body was found, wedged between a chest of drawers and the wall, at the foot of Duane's bed. Apparently he had sought to find clothing in Duane's room, became blinded by the smoke and dropped unconscious. The bedclothing from Duane's bed was partly draped around his body.

Clark was taken to the university hospital immediately and, although apparently dead, Dr. C. Douglas

Continued on Page Eight

RUSSIA'S MILLIONS VOTE STALIN TICKET AMID HOLIDAY AIR

Bands Play as Most of Nation's 90,000,000 Electors Join in First Secret, Direct Poll

SUPREME SOVIET CHOSEN

Heads of Air and Tank Corps, Removed From Ballot, Are Believed in Trouble

By HAROLD DENNY

Wireless to THE NEW YORK TIMES.

MOSCOW, Dec. 12.—The Soviet Union elected its first Supreme Soviet under its new constitution today in a beautifully conducted vote that was carried out with all the precision, order and colorful decor of a May Day parade or a Bolshoi Theatre spectacle.

The authorities succeeded fully as well as they could have expected in bringing out the total electorate numbering probably 90,000,000 to vote for the only ticket in the field—the ticket headed by Joseph Stalin himself and including virtually every high government and Communist party official.

Thus the present Soviet regime can now show the world the most complete endorsement in terms of number of votes cast ever given to any government in the world's history.

Huge Turn-Out at Polls

As there was no semblance of opposition in today's election the only question was how many votes would be cast. It seemed tonight on the basis of this correspondent's visits to typical polling places in Moscow and several surrounding villages and of radio reports from all parts of the Soviet Union that virtually every one, male and female, above the age of 18 who was able to get to the polls afoot, on skis or in automobiles, trucks or sleighs had voted, and naturally for the one ticket.

Agitators went through dwellings hunting for non-voters. Where they found sick persons who were able to leave their beds cars were summoned to transport them to the polls. In one election district in Moscow a number of ill persons reported they were unable to leave their beds and requested that ballots be sent them so they could vote.

It could not be determined what was done in most such cases, but in one at least an absentee vote by a bedridden elector was allowed. This case was that of Constantin Stanislavsky, famous director of the Moscow Art Theatre, who is now 75 years old and ill of pneumonia. A ballot was sent to him and he sealed it himself and dispatched it by a member of his family, who deposited it in a box in Mr. Stanislavky's election district here.

Results Are Broadcast

All afternoon and evening election results were broadcast as in the United States. As there was no contest, however, the bulletins were devoted to what percentage of the eligible vote had been cast.

So expeditiously were the voters handled that most polling places had little to do after midday. Bulletins late tonight showed that very nearly 100 per cent of the total possible vote had been cast in Moscow and other big centers.

As far as Moscow was concerned

Continued on Page Sixteen

NANKING INVESTED

Japanese Expect Its Fall Soon Because Troops Are Rushing In

VITAL GATE IS CAPTURED

Naval Force Is Expected to Arrive Today to Join Land and Air Assault

By HALLETT ABEND

Special Cable to THE NEW YORK TIMES.

SHANGHAI, Monday, Dec. 13.—Japanese troops, preceded by tanks, have been pouring into Nanking since 4 A. M., when they captured Chungshan gate. The city's capitulation is imminent, according to Japanese army headquarters.

The Nanking fighting continued unabated throughout last night under clear skies and a half moon. The Japanese took yesterday the shores of Lotus Lake, which borders Nanking's north wall. Colonel and Mrs. Charles A. Lindbergh landed on this lake after their flight to China in September, 1931.

Japanese flags flew along all of the south wall before sunset yesterday. The Japanese first held Kwanghwa gate and the corner west of the gate and Chunghwa gate and another corner near it.

The Japanese Army contingent that crossed to the north bank of the Yangtze to Wukiang Sunday has captured Pukow, the southern terminus of the Tientsin-Pukow railway, directly opposite Nanking. They thus cut off the last chance of escape for the Chinese forces in the Nanking and near-by areas.

Chinese Show Bravery

Once more the rank and file of Chinese soldiery demonstrated at Nanking their extraordinary ability to take terrible punishment and hold fast under conditions which ordinarily would dishearten any fighting men.

Mostly unpaid and underfed, without any provisions for their wounded, the Chinese forced the Japanese to pay a terrific price for every foot gained around the gates.

As in 1900, when Chinese forces held Tientsin's walls until a hill of corpses exceeded 7,000 and conspicuously again at Tsinan in Shantung in 1928, when they fought with similar valor, the Chinese contested every foot of the Japanese advance.

From many vantage points on the wall at Kwanghwa gate, from Purple Mountain and from other dominant heights surrounding the city the Japanese for nearly fifty hours poured shells of all sizes and machine-gun fire into the area inside Nanking's wall. There were almost hourly aerial bombings, but the Chinese continued their suicidal battle.

With the city surrounded on all land fronts the Japanese crossed the Yangtze River yesterday at Taiping, between Nanking and

Continued on Page Fifteen

Old Treaty Permits U. S. Patrol; Ships Not on Aggressive Mission

Nationals Are Protected on Yangtze Through Agreement—Silver Island Blockade by Chinese Not Responsible for Difficulties

Special to THE NEW YORK TIMES.

WASHINGTON, Dec. 12.—The United States gunboat Panay, sunk today by bombs in the Nanking battle area, was one of six or seven such patrol boats maintained in the Yangtze River by the United States under the Sino-American treaty of 1858. Other nations also maintain patrols in the river.

This treaty was conceded by China following the joint attack on that country by Britain and France in 1857-58, when they captured Canton and reduced the Taku forts guarding Tientsin. The United States and Russia did not join in the war but they insisted on sharing the rights gained by the others.

Among these was permission for foreigners to travel in the interior of China and the entrance of Christian missionaries into this field. Four ports were opened on the Yangtze and extraterritorial rights were granted to the nations concerned so they could protect their nationals. In order to protect these foreigners and their trade and religious activities the patrol of the river was established.

Commander L. P. Lovette, naval press relations officer, who formerly commanded such craft said tonight that these vessels comprised a sort of civil "police force" for the United States and China.

Naval orders say that these boats are on duty for the special purposes of protecting United States nationals from violence, to protect them in times of emergency, to maintain uninterrupted communications, and to protect United States diplomatic and consular establishments.

He said the ships acted as police not only for the United States but for China, offering protection to China's citizens as well as to our own in times of violence or emergency. Sometimes, he said, it became necessary for the United

Continued on Page Fourteen

TROTSKY CLEARED BY DEWEY BOARD

International Group Finds He and Son Were 'Not Guilty' of Plot Against Soviet

A 'FRAME-UP' IS CHARGED

New Evidence Contradicts the Moscow Verdicts on 21 Counts, Report Says

An international commission of inquiry headed by Dr. John Dewey declared last night that Leon Trotsky was "not guilty" of the charges against him in the Moscow trials of August, 1936, and January, 1937, and that the trials were a "frame-up."

The commission's verdict of "not guilty" applied also to Leon Sedov, Mr. Trotsky's son now residing in Paris and condemned in absentia with his father in the two trials.

Dr. Dewey reported the commission's findings at a mass meeting in the Hotel Center, 108 West Forty-third Street, attended by more than 2,000 persons, including many prominent liberals and representatives of various schools of political thought specially invited to hear a summary of the commission's report.

The report, a document of 80,000 words, will be published in book form, continuing the series of publications begun with the record of the preliminary hearings held by the commission last April in Mexico City and at which Mr. Trotsky testified at great length and was subjected to exhaustive interrogation.

Contradicts the Verdicts

The commission's conclusions, as reported by Dr. Dewey at last night's meeting, flatly contradicted the verdicts of the Moscow court on twenty-one separate counts. On the basis of "much new documentary evidence" assembled over a period of nine months in Mexico, the United States, Canada and European countries, and study of the official Soviet trial records, the commission reached the conclusion that Mr. Trotsky and Mr. Sedov were the victims of a conspiracy to discredit them, and that "independent of extrinsic evidence" the conduct of the Moscow trials "was such as to convince any unprejudiced person that no effort was made to ascertain the truth."

The commission found also that the confessions of the accused in the Moscow trials "contain such inherent improbabilities as to convince the commission that they do not represent the truth, irrespective of any means used to obtain them."

At the same time, the commission expressed the belief that the confessions were obtained by duress.

The Chief Findings

Supporting itself upon a "mass of new documentary evidence and affidavits," the commission affirmed

Continued on Page Sixteen

3 DRIVES STARTED BY SPANISH REBELS

Collapse of Loyalists Is Said to Have Resulted at Toledo, Brunete and Teruel

MADRID IS AGAIN SHELLED

Insurgents Claim 270 Planes Took Part in Friday Battle, With Victory for Them

By The Associated Press.

HENDAYE, France, at the Franco-Spanish Frontier, Dec. 12.—The Spanish Insurgent armies launched today their long-awaited general offensive, Insurgent authorities announced at Irun. They struck simultaneously on the Toledo, Brunete and Teruel fronts.

An Insurgent communiqué announced the government lines had collapsed under the offensive, which hit "like a bolt of lightning."

"The Reds [Government] were unable to resist the attacks," the Insurgents declared.

The offensives at Brunete and Toledo were directed at Madrid, Spain's long besieged capital, while the drive on the Teruel front is faced toward Valencia.

270 Planes in Battle

Insurgent dispatches today gave further details of Friday's aerial battle near Saragossa. They said massed air fleets totaling 270 warplanes had clashed. Twenty-five Government planes were shot down and only one Insurgent plane was lost, it was said.

The great air battle coincided with the holiday of Notre Dame de Lorette, the patron saint of aviation. Under her auspices, Insurgent dispatches said, twenty Insurgent planes from Saragossa flew over Government lines to lure enemy pilots.

When 100 Government planes encircled the supposed raiders, 150 Insurgent warplanes suddenly swooped, putting the Government fleet to flight with a quarter of its strength lost in a few minutes.

Insurgent planes made a number of fresh incursions in Government zones Saturday, meeting renewed resistance. One Insurgent squadron invaded the Aragon front, east of Saragossa, bombing the outskirts of Castejon del Puetente. A Government communiqué said the raid was checked with a minimum of damage.

Madrid Heavily Shelled

By HERBERT L. MATTHEWS

Wireless to THE NEW YORK TIMES.

MADRID, Dec. 12.—Many dinners were spoiled in Madrid tonight when the Rebels chose from 7:40 to 8:50 to bombard the center of the city with considerable intensity. They may not have been good dinners, for the Madrileños are not indulging in feasts this Winter.

We had a perfectly good dish of succotash partly ruined in our hotel by one of three shells which hit

Continued on Page Thirteen

JAPAN TAKES ONUS

Officers Admit Attack on Panay With Regrets—Craft Sought Safety

BRITISH VESSELS TARGETS

Two Fire at Planes as Bombs Are Aimed at Them—Two Standard Oil Ships Sunk

By The Associated Press.

SHANGHAI, Monday, Dec. 13.—Japanese bombs sank the United States gunboat Panay in the Yangtze River twenty-five miles above Nanking yesterday.

One American sailor died of his wounds. His name was not given. Eighteen other persons were unaccounted for.

There were fifty-four known survivors, some of them wounded. Among the wounded were Lieut. Comdr. James J. Hughes, commander of the Panay, and Lieutenant Arthur F. Anders, executive officer.

[Ambassador Nelson T. Johnson reported to the State Department at Washington that fifteen of the survivors had been wounded, some of them seriously, according to The Associated Press. One of the injured was an Italian subject, he said.]

The gunboat's normal complement was fifty-five officers and men. In addition, the "mercy ship" carried at least nine American refugees, including four embassy officials.

Two Standard Oil Company ships were also sunk at the same time. No word was received of the fate of those aboard these vessels.

The Japanese Navy quickly accepted responsibility for the grave incident. A Japanese communique pledged immediate steps to place the blame on the military units responsible, and it regretted the bombing "most deeply."

British Gunboat Shelled

Earlier British naval reports said that Colonel Hashimoto, senior Japanese officer, had declared he had orders to "fire on every ship on the river." His statement was made in reply to a British protest against shelling of the British gunboat Ladybird at Wuhu. A British seaman was killed and two other Britons were wounded there.

Officers of the United States flagship Augusta said they believed seventy-two persons had been aboard the Panay. Those missing apparently were killed by the Japanese bombs or were drowned when the vessel sank. However, some might have reached a place without communication facilities.

Most of the survivors were put ashore by rescue vessels at Hohsien, Anhwei Province.

Rear Admiral Harry E. Yarnell, commander of the United States Asiatic Fleet, canceled his departure for Manila, scheduled for tomorrow, in face of the serious incident.

Other Ships Rush to Aid

The U. S. gunboat Oahu and the British gunboat Bee steamed under forced draught for the scene of the sinking.

The Bee was expected to reach the scene of the sinking some time tonight, but because of the distance the Oahu was not expected until Tuesday.

The 450-ton Panay, especially made for river service in China, had stood by to save Americans during the Japanese siege of Nanking. Anchored in the Yangtze, the Panay was a haven for Embassy officials and other refugees until the Japanese shells crashing dangerously near caused her to seek safety up the river.

It was while steaming away from the battle zone that the vessel was sent to the bottom by Japanese bombs.

Among those aboard the Panay were George Atcheson Jr., second secretary in charge of the United States Embassy at Nanking; J. Hall Paxton, second secretary; Captain Frank Roberts, assistant military attaché, and Emile Gassie, embassy clerk.

The United States Consulate here said that other civilians believed to have been aboard were: Norman Alley, Fox Movietone cameraman; Weldon James, United Press correspondent; Norman Soong, a correspondent of THE NEW YORK TIMES; Roy Squires, American born in China; James Marshall, Collier's Magazine writer; T. J. Broderick, Standard Oil Company representa-

Continued on Page Fourteen

Doctor Arrested in Park Ave. Hit-Run Death; Traced by Car Part Found Near the Victim

Dr. John E. Toole, 41 years old, Yale graduate and urologist, was awakened by detectives at his home, 120 East Eighty-fifth Street, shortly after 7 o'clock yesterday morning and arrested on a technical charge of homicide. The arrest followed an all-night investigation of the death of Miss Mary McCormack, 60, of 22 East 119th Street, who was hit and dragged more than 100 feet by an automobile at 10 o'clock Saturday night as she was crossing Fifty-eighth Street at Park Avenue. The motorist failed to stop.

Detectives Charles L. McGowan and Hugh Fox took Dr. Toole to the East Fifty-first Street station, where he denied responsibility for the death of the woman, whose body was not identified at the morgue until yesterday afternoon. The identification was made by her sister, Anna McCormick, a housemaid in the home of Dr. Nicholas Murray Butler, president of Columbia University.

Although Dr. Toole insisted his automobile did not hit any pedestrian, the detectives quoted him as saying he felt a jar when the car was passing Fifty-eighth Street on Park Avenue. The doctor explained he thought he had passed over a depression in the street and kept on toward his home.

When the body of Miss McCormack was picked up, near by was found part of a broken automobile radiator grill and the emblem of a Dodge car. A search of all garages in the city was started for an automobile with broken grillwork and a missing emblem. It was not until early yesterday morning that such a car, with the front blood spattered, was found in a garage at 150 East Eighty-fourth Street. The detectives said the piece of broken radiator fitted perfectly into the frame. The automobile was listed as the property of Dr. Toole. When the detectives called at his home, Dr. Toole was asleep. He was said to have admitted he drove the automobile Saturday night, but insisted that beyond the slight jar at the scene of the accident he did not notice anything out of the ordinary. Miss McCormack was crossing Park Avenue from west to east when she was struck by a northbound automobile traveling at considerable speed.

Dr. Toole was taken from the East Fifty-first Street police station to police headquarters, where he was booked and remained pending arraignment this morning in Homicide Court.

Dr. Toole, who is single, is a graduate of the Yale class of 1920. He practices here and in Hempstead, L. I., specializing in urology and radiology.

"All the News That's Fit to Print."

The New York Times.

LATE CITY EDITION
Fair and moderately cold today. Tomorrow fair, with slowly rising temperature.
Temperatures Yesterday—Max., 38; Min., 29

Copyright, 1938, by The New York Times Company.

VOL. LXXXVII....No. 29,248. Entered as Second-Class Matter, Postoffice, New York, N. Y. NEW YORK, MONDAY, FEBRUARY 21, 1938. PP TWO CENTS In New York City. | THREE CENTS Within 200 Miles. | FOUR CENTS Elsewhere Except in 7th and 8th Postal Zones.

HITLER DEMANDS RIGHT OF SELF-DETERMINATION FOR GERMANS IN AUSTRIA AND CZECHOSLOVAKIA; EDEN RESIGNS IN CRISIS OVER BRITAIN'S POLICY

FEDERAL AGENCIES CONSIDER FORCING RAILROAD MERGERS

Groups Shaping Rehabilitation Plans Believe Plight Inclines Congress to Idea

FAVOR THREE YEARS' GRACE

Would Allow Time for Voluntary Consolidations, With Federal Action Afterward

FOR TEMPORARY POOLING

Some Officials Hold This a Need Until a Long-Range Plan Becomes Effective

By JOHN H. CRIDER
Special to THE NEW YORK TIMES.

WASHINGTON, Feb. 20.—Legislation for forced consolidations of railroads is being considered seriously in at least three of the government offices now preparing plans to be laid before President Roosevelt at his rail conference scheduled for the coming week.

It was learned that some officials are advancing a plan which would apply the "death sentence" technique of the Holding Company Act to railroad consolidations. Under this procedure the railroads would have a certain period of years in which to submit voluntary unification plans, after which a government agency would prepare a plan for them.

'Like most remedies for the nation's rail problems, the idea of forced or compulsory consolidation has been considered for years, with little favorable response from Congress, even for milder remedies than the one now gaining ground. Rail reformers are hopeful that this time Congress will relent in view of the unusually sad plight of the railroads.

"Wasteful" Competition a Factor

President Roosevelt, Senator Burton K. Wheeler, in charge of the Senate investigation of railroad finances, and the Interstate Commerce Commission in its annual report have stated that "wasteful" competition is one of the fundamental railroad ills.

The I. C. C. went so far in its annual report as to state that "no competitive industry can work out its salvation through a price-increasing policy alone." The best expert opinion in official Washington seems to be that a rate increase, such as the $517,000,000 rate rise which the I. C. C. is expected to grant to the railroads can be at most only a temporary remedy.

It is felt that compulsory consolidations cannot solve the immediate economic emergency faced by the railroads and that rate increases and perhaps some form of pooling may have to be employed until a long-range plan can be effected. Pooling is condemned by some as an incentive to inefficiency since the weak railroads are carried along by the strong.

Senator Wheeler's investigating committee, the I. C. C., the Securities and Exchange Commission, and the Reconstruction Finance Corporation are among the government agencies now formulating plans to be considered at the White House conference.

Financial Position Weak

The current efforts in official circles to work out a permanent solution to the railroad problem arises from the unusually weak financial position of the country's railroads, due partly to increased operating costs, the decline in general business activity, and competition from other forms of transportation, but the real work was started when the President discussed the problem at a press conference on Dec. 10. He questioned the necessity for maintaining parallel lines of railroad with inadequate traffic.

He also referred to the reports of Commissioner Joseph B. Eastman of the Interstate Commerce Commission as Federal Coordinator of Transportation in 1933 and 1934 which discussed the problems of consolidation at some length. As a consequence there has been a considerable demand for these reports, particularly for the first one, which contained in the appendix a report by Leslie Craven, counsel to the coord'nator, upholding the constitutionality of compulsory consolidations and recommending a modification of the method employed in England.

Some of those now preparing plans to lay before the President feel with Mr. Craven that under "any consolidation program which is non-compulsory and not fully comprehensive, it is almost certain that uneconomic and inefficient groupings will result due to the inevitable 'nclination of the carriers which initiate consolidations to grab favorable lines in the effort

Continued on Page Eight

Swiss Make Romansh Fourth Official Tongue

By The Associated Press.

BERNE, Switzerland, Feb. 20.—Swiss voted by an overwhelming majority today to establish Romansh as the fourth official language of Switzerland.

The vote was considered by some observers as a slap at Italy, where Fascisti say Romansh, an obscure language that is spoken only in part of Grisons canton, is an Italian dialect.

German is spoken by about 71 per cent of the Swiss, French by 22 per cent, Italian by 6 per cent and Romansh by 1 per cent.

A resolution giving the Federal Council power to prevent arms shipments to warring nations and providing for partial control of armament industries also was approved.

TENEMENT BLAZE KILLS 3, INJURES 9

Families Routed in 165th St. Fire, Third in Building Unit in Less Than Two Years

DARING RESCUES CUT TOLL

Cripple Is Carried to Safety—Man Leaps to Death, Wife Is Killed Shielding Baby

The third fire since June, 1936, in adjoining three-story buildings at 761-63 East 165th Street, between Forest and Tinton Avenues, the Bronx, killed three persons early yesterday morning and caused injuries to nine others, including an infant orphaned by the blaze.

Hampered by the collapse of a stairway under which the flames were believed to have started, firemen of seven engine companies and two hook-and-ladder units made a series of dangerous rescues from the second and third floors of No. 763, virtually all of which was destroyed except its yellow-brick front.

One of the firemen, exhausted by the struggle in the building, which had no fire escape, was among those treated later by Dr. Harry M. Archer, honorary departmental surgeon.

Fire Not Incendiary

At first it was believed that the fire was incendiary, but after an all-day investigation Assistant District Attorney George Pilzer and Assistant Fire Marshal Martin Scott announced at 9:30 o'clock last night that the fire was not of suspicious origin. They had spent hours questioning tenants of the building and others living near by.

One of those hurt was a passerby who aided in the rescue work. Another volunteer, boosted on the shoulders of friends before the apparatus arrived, cut his hand in smashing a second-floor window to warn tenants. The two were Thomas Smith, 38, of 1,009 Union Avenue, who suffered a sprained knee and cut thumb, and Joseph Barrett, 27, of 486 East 165th Street, whose left hand was injured.

Francis Dunn, 38, of 857 Fox Street, who was later cut on the head by falling glass, turned in the alarm at 3:04. He was on his way home when he noticed curling flames in the building. By the time the first fire apparatus arrived, Smith, Dunn and others had awakened all the tenants in No. 761 and the building had been cleared.

Flames Burst Through Roof

The blaze centered, however, beneath the stairway of No. 763 and spread rapidly to the top, where it divided and ate its way into the top floor of both units of the building. One witness said it suddenly burst through the roof like a great torch.

Smoke in the hallway thickened, but members of Engine Company 50 tried to get up the stairs anyway. Fireman Terence A. Nugent, who subsequently needed medical aid, was one of those nearly trapped when the stairs crumbled.

While his colleagues swung their ladders toward the building, a man appeared at the third floor window over the entrance, clambered to the sill and stared down, terrified.

A confusion of shouts rose from the street. Some cried "Jump!" and others yelled "Back! Back!" The man jumped. But while would-be rescuers extended their arms, his body struck the broad, jutting cornice between the second and ground floors. The deflection catapulted him beyond them to the street, and he was fatally injured. He was William Theofanna, 42, whose wife, Armione, 41, was burned in the bedroom while shielding their baby, 5-month-old Betsy.

With the fire-fighting crew augmented by men summoned by a second alarm, rescues by ladder were accomplished with comparatively little difficulty. But in the case of William Sculla, 65-year-old paralytic, Firemen John Mullen and Vincent Howard risked their lives to fight their way to his bed,

Continued on Page Twenty

ORTIZ INAUGURATED AMID WIDE ACCLAIM BY THE ARGENTINES

Nation Greets Six American Airplanes as a Major Part of Colorful Ceremony

PRESIDENT IS A CIVILIAN

Public Reaffirms Its Faith in Free Rule, Regarding U. S. as Example and Friend

By JOHN W. WHITE
Special Cable to THE NEW YORK TIMES.

BUENOS AIRES, Argentina, Feb. 20.—Dr. Roberto M. Ortiz was inaugurated the twenty-first constitutional President of the Argentine Republic this afternoon in a colorful ceremony amid widespread popular acclaim. In Argentina lawyers have the title of Doctor and this puts the Presidency again under a civilian title; the last two Presidents were generals.

The presence of six giant U. S. Army bombers of the type known as "flying fortresses" associated the United States with Argentina on this occasion in a manner in which no foreign country has participated at any inauguration in recent years. The planes arrived on Friday after a record-smashing flight from Miami, bearing a letter from President Roosevelt to President Ortiz, expressing the best wishes of the American Government and the American people for his forthcoming government.

Nothing that the United States has done in Latin America, with the possible exception of President Roosevelt's visit a year ago, has ever aroused such an enthusiastic response on the part of the Argentine people. The newspapers have published the most laudatory editorials extending a hearty welcome to the American fliers and expressing their appreciation of the good-will of the government that sent them.

Faith in Democracy

People here have seized upon the visit of the United States fliers as an opportunity to reaffirm their faith in democracy and express their disapproval of totalitarian regimes. South America, including Argentina, has been subjected to such intense propaganda from European totalitarian countries, especially Italy, during the last year that this propaganda has now reached the state expressed in the Spanish words "contra producente"—working to defeat its own aims.

The people have become resentful of this high-pressure propaganda. They have enthusiastically greeted the big American fighting planes as messengers of peace and good-will from the country to which the South Americans have always looked as their model democracy.

Public opinion in Argentina was very cold to the intimation that the Italian planes that recently visited Brazil might come to Buenos Aires for the inauguration. The Italians changed their minds and did not come. No foreign mission has ever been more enthusiastically received than the American aviators whose flight was not announced until two days before they started.

Italian newspapers both here and in Italy have not mentioned the American flight. German papers here gave it a paragraph hidden away on an inside page. Both devoted pages to two recent Italian flights.

This was an ideally beautiful Summer day with the bright blue sky and blazing sun that are featured in the Argentine flag. The Argentine Army and Navy Flying

Continued on Page Seven

Roosevelt Silent on Hitler, But May Give Views Soon

Special to THE NEW YORK TIMES.

HYDE PARK, N. Y., Feb. 20.—The temporary White House was completely silent today on President Roosevelt's reaction to the address of Chancellor Hitler to the German Reichstag. But there were suggestions that he might soon make known in an informal way the views of his Administration toward the political situation abroad.

Marvin H. McIntyre, the President's secretary, insisted that Mr. Roosevelt passed the day resting from the cares of his office, and that he had talked only with members of his immediate family and the vestrymen of St. James Episcopal Church here.

Despite the official reticence, however, there was no doubt that the President was in close touch with the State Department.

EDEN'S RESIGNATION DISTRESSES FRANCE

Belief Prevails That British 'Capitulation' Must Reduce Leadership of Paris

SMALL ALLIES FEARED FOR

Chautemps and Delbos Confer With Ambassador Phipps, Calling Him Urgently

By P. J. PHILIP
Wireless to THE NEW YORK TIMES.

PARIS, Feb. 20.—The resignation of British Foreign Secretary Anthony Eden has caused much more concern in France than anything that Chancellor Adolf Hitler said today. Immediately after the announcement was made, Ambassador Sir Eric Phipps hurried over to see Premier Camille Chautemps and Foreign Minister Yvon Delbos, presumably to assure them that British friendship for France and Anglo-French cooperation would remain as close as ever.

But such assurances are not likely to alter the conclusion that what is called here the Germanophile clique in Great Britain has won, and that henceforth France will be reduced to a very different role in European affairs from that which she has been accustomed to play.

It is a poor consolation to be told by Hitler that she has nothing to fear from Germany "if she minds her own business." And it will be meat for much criticism of M. Delbos and his aids that this abandonment should be the reward of their steady support of British policy during the past two years, or rather, as it will be called, their constant subservient agreement.

Bitter Clash Forthcoming

It is too early to forecast what the effects will be here. What is clear, however, is that there will be a bitter fight between those who clamor for complete abandonment of the non-intervention policy in Spain and a frank espousal of the republican cause, and those who will counsel prudence and that France

Continued on Page Three

King Issues Fascist Charter for Rumania; Constitution Sets Up a Corporative State

Wireless to THE NEW YORK TIMES.

VIENNA, Feb. 20.—A dictatorial Constitution was given to Rumania tonight by a proclamation signed by King Carol. It was not countersigned by any of his Ministers.

The democratic parliamentary system is abolished and replaced by a Fascist corporative Chamber and Senate, where various trades and occupations will be represented. The distribution of land under the land reform scheme stands, but increased compensation will be given for mineral rights taken over by the State. Special measures will be taken against corruption. Trial by jury is abolished.

In the proclamation Carol says: "I have been moved by one idea only—the love of my people and the need to rescue the fatherland."

The Constitution promises to peoples that have lived for centuries on the soil of present-day Rumania the same treatment as the "Rumanian race" will receive, but it indicates that State jobs will go mostly to ethnical Rumanians.

There are rumors that on Thursday Rumania will go through the form of taking a plebiscite of the people's views on this dictated Constitution.

King Carol assumed direct control of the Rumanian Government early this month, when he forced the pro-Fascist Premier Octavian Goga out of office to make way for a national Cabinet headed by Dr. Miron Cristea, Patriarch of the Rumanian Orthodox Church.

The King suspended the Constitution, promising to replace it as soon as the situation created by M. Goga's leanings toward Germany and Italy and his anti-Semitism had calmed.

The new Constitution had been generally expected to provide for a dual administration: a Crown Council, composed of distinguished Rumanians, that would lay down general principles of policy, and a Cabinet to frame legislation that would be submitted to the King and the Crown Council.

Under a corporative State, such a dual system would resemble that of Italy, with her Fascist Grand Council and Cabinet.

BRITAIN IS SHOCKED

Foreign Secretary Quits Over Issue of Seeking Deals With Dictators

CRANBORNE GOES OUT, TOO

Two Other Ministers Waver—Outburst Is Expected in Commons Today

By FERDINAND KUHN Jr.
Special Cable to THE NEW YORK TIMES.

LONDON, Feb. 20.—Foreign Secretary Anthony Eden resigned from the British Cabinet tonight, no longer willing to approve or support the methods of Prime Minister Neville Chamberlain and a majority of his colleagues in seeking settlements with Italy and Germany.

He took with him into retirement Viscount Cranborne, Under-Secretary for Foreign Affairs. At least two other Ministers—Walter E. Elliot, Secretary of State for Scotland, and William S. Morrison, Minister of Agriculture—had contemplated resigning with Mr. Eden, but late tonight they had not carried their intentions to the point of action.

Viscount Halifax, Lord President of the Council, will direct the Foreign Office temporarily, with Mr. Chamberlain himself probably taking charge of foreign affairs for a time in the House of Commons.

Eden Is Determined

The Cabinet had tried for more than three hours in the afternoon to persuade Mr. Eden to change his mind, but this time nothing could shake his determination.

As a last resort the Ministers begged Mr. Eden to accept some other office or to say he was resigning on grounds of ill health. But he refused all such suggestions. A break had come on a question of policy and he saw no reason why he should conceal it.

Tonight, pale and haggard, Mr. Eden walked dejectedly across Downing Street, where a crowd was waiting to cheer him, and called at No. 10. Inside the historic Prime Minister's house Mr. Chamberlain was in anxious consultation with his Ministers.

But Mr. Eden stayed only long enough to hand in a formal letter of resignation. After four minutes he strode back to the Foreign Office in the darkness with his two years and two months of incessant responsibilities at an end.

The Foreign Secretary's letter and Mr. Chamberlain's reply threw light on what had been known abroad and at home but persistently denied in official quarters and in pro-Government newspapers here. They showed that the resignation had been precipitated by the interview with the Italian Ambassador, Count Dino Grandi, on Friday, but also that disagreements between Mr. Eden and Mr. Chamberlain had been going on for months.

Refers to 'Difference'

"The events of the last few days," wrote Mr. Eden, "have made plain a difference between us on a decision of great importance in itself and far-reaching in its consequences. I cannot recommend to Parliament a policy with which I am not in agreement."

Mr. Eden went on to admit a "difference of outlook between us in respect to international problems of the day and also as to the methods whereby we should seek to resolve them." He reminded Mr. Chamberlain that it was not in the interests of the nation that Ministers should work "in uneasy partnership," especially the Foreign Secretary and the Prime Minister.

The letter ended with a note of thanks for "help and counsel" and a polite and doubtless sincere assurance that "our differences, whatever they may be, cannot efface that memory or influence our friendship."

The stilted wording of Mr. Chamberlain's reply showed what a shock to him and his Cabinet this resignation had been. The Prime Minister wrote of his "most profound regret" and of the "distinction" with which Mr. Eden had administered the Foreign Office. His regret was all the greater, said Mr. Chamberlain, "because such differences as have arisen between us in no way concern the ultimate aims or fundamentals of our policy."

"The decision you find yourself unable to accept," wrote the Prime Minister, "is whether the present

Continued on Page Two

Eden-Chamberlain Letters

By The Associated Press.

LONDON, Feb. 20.—The texts of Foreign Secretary Anthony Eden's letter of resignation to Prime Minister Neville Chamberlain and the Prime Minister's reply follow:

My Dear Prime Minister:

The events of the last few days have made plain a difference between us on a decision of great importance in itself and far-reaching in its consequences.

I cannot recommend to Parliament a policy with which I am not in agreement.

Apart from this, I have become increasingly conscious, as I know you have also, of the difference in outlook between us in respect to the international problems of the day and also as to the methods whereby we should seek to resolve them.

It cannot be in the country's interest that those who are called upon to direct its affairs should work in uneasy partnership, fully conscious of differences in outlook yet hoping they will not recur.

This applies with special force to the relationship between the Prime Minister and the Foreign Secretary.

It is for these reasons that with very deep regret I have decided I must leave you and your colleagues with whom I have been associated during years of great difficulty and stress.

May I end on a personal note?

I can never forget the help and counsel you have always so readily given me, both before and since you became Prime Minister.

Our differences, whatever they may be, cannot efface that memory nor influence our friendship.

Yours ever,
ANTHONY EDEN.

Mr. Chamberlain's Reply

My Dear Anthony:

It is with the most profound regret, shared by all our colleagues, that I have received your intimation of your decision

Continued on Page Three

ITALY IS JUBILANT AS EDEN QUITS POST

Sees Relations With Britain Improved With Change in the Foreign Office

HITLER SPEECH IS HAILED

But Strain on Friendship Is Seen if Reich Interferes Actively in Austria

By ARNALDO CORTESI
Wireless to THE NEW YORK TIMES.

ROME, Feb. 20.—The news of the resignation of Anthony Eden, British Foreign Secretary, reached Rome late this evening and quickly spread throughout the city, causing great satisfaction everywhere, as was to be expected. In the Foreign Office Mr. Eden's resignation is believed to remove one of the great obstacles to the conclusion of an Italian-British understanding and, as this is still one of the main objectives of the present foreign policy, it is thought that official negotiations soon will be opened with better chances of success than in the past.

Italians have, whether rightly or wrongly, been convinced that for a long time there has been a conflict of opinion in the British Cabinet between one school of thought, headed by Prime Minister Neville Chamberlain, that was in favor of an agreement with Italy, and another, headed by Mr. Eden, that made an agreement dependent on conditions, such as the withdrawal of Italians from Spain, that Italy could not accept or was not willing to accept.

Mr. Eden's resignation is regarded as a victory for Mr. Chamberlain's faction and, therefore, likely to bring an Italian-British understanding nearer by insuring that Italy's desire to make friends with Britain is met by an equal desire on Britain's part to make friends with Italy.

Claim Personal Defeat

It is thought in Italy that Mr. Eden is more or less smarting under the failure of his scheme to upset Premier Benito Mussolini's plans in Ethiopia by means of sanctions which it is believed were actuated by personal animosity against Italy.

Mr. Eden has, therefore, always been the target of strong attacks by the Italian press which, sometimes openly and sometimes by innuendo, accused him of allowing his private grudges to play too large a part in his handling of his country's foreign affairs. Italians feel, in other words, that Mr. Eden's fall has caused a personal enemy to disappear as head of the British Foreign Office.

It cannot be doubted that Italy will take advantage of the new sit-

Continued on Page Five

NAZIS CELEBRATE IN AUSTRIAN FETES

Great Strength Is Shown in the Provinces, but Numbers Are Small in Vienna

HITLER THREAT IS FEARED

Patriots Are Bitter, Hearing No Pledge of Independence in Chancellor's Talk

By G. E. R. GEDYE
Wireless to THE NEW YORK TIMES.

VIENNA, Feb. 20. — Throughout Chancellor Adolf Hitler's speech Vienna's streets were like those of a dead city. Patriots and Nazis alike were indoors, patiently listening, the former hoping to hear the promises made at the Berchtesgaden meeting with the Austrian Chancellor fulfilled, the latter to learn whether there would be flaming words with which to light the torch of a Nazi uprising.

Instructions had come from Munich for small but peaceful Nazi demonstrations today. A Nazi journalist told me today, however, that three or four days hence there would be large-scale demonstrations. He would not give the date. Presumably it is Thursday, when Chancellor Kurt Schuschnigg speaks.

It has become fairly common knowledge here that Hitler solemnly promised Dr. Schuschnigg that if he accepted the terms dictated under the threat of invasion Germany would today recognize Austria's independence, the political monopoly of the Fatherland Front and guarantee suspension of the support of the Austrian Nazis with money and propaganda material from Germany.

Newspapers had promised the Austrian population that Hitler's speech would carry out his side of the bargain and repay Austria for the heavy sacrifices she made to avoid invasion.

Threat to Austria Seen

When the speech ended without the least effort by Hitler to fulfill his part of the bargain, there was great indignation. But more serious than this was the bitterness caused by Hitler's silence on the question of Austrian independence, which was taken as equivalent to a threat that will soon be put into execution.

During the broadcast Vienna Nazis listened quietly in their favorite cafes. Immediately afterward street demonstrations began, but not on any serious scale. Three hundred Nazis marched past the German Legation singing the "Horst Wessel Song" and shouting "Heil Hitler." The police allowed the demonstrators to parade but did not allow them to stand outside the legation.

Soon afterward similar small

Continued on Page Three

NAZI POWER CITED

Status Quo Repudiated by Fuehrer—Restates Colonial Demands

TONE OF TALK ANTI-BRITISH

Resignation of Eden Is Hailed as Greatest Victory of German Diplomacy

Chancellor Hitler in a militant speech to the Reichstag yesterday made a strong point of the right of "self-determination" for the 10,000,000 Germans in Austria and Czechoslovakia. He indicated force must be used in the end to break the status quo. He promised to go ahead with plans to enlarge the army. He assailed British policy, making a direct attack on Mr. Eden, and demanded colonies.

Disputes in the British Cabinet over proposed negotiations for a settlement with Italy and Germany led to the resignation of Foreign Secretary Eden. Viscount Halifax took temporary control of the Foreign Office, but Prime Minister Chamberlain will direct its policies.

France was fearful of losing her position as leader on the European Continent as a result of Mr. Eden's retirement. Italians, on the other hand, were jubilant over the passing of the Secretary, long regarded as a foe of their country.

Nazis held large demonstrations in Austrian provinces, but made a poor showing in Vienna.
[All stories on Page 1.]

Main Points of Hitler's Speech to the Reichstag on Page 4.

Hitler Shows Militancy

By OTTO D. TOLISCHUS
Wireless to THE NEW YORK TIMES.

BERLIN, Feb. 20.—In the most militant speech of his career, which is already hailed here as the final cause for the overthrow of British Foreign Secretary Anthony Eden, Chancellor Hitler outlined today before the Reichstag those principles and conditions through which National Socialist Germany proposes to retain her place in the sun and which, in her view, are alone able to preserve peace.

In some respects this most anxiously awaited speech was sufficiently vague to allay some of the worst fears in certain capitals, already primed for sensational extras. In respect to the two events which have most alarmed the world recently, namely the reorganization of the government and the army command and Austria's "cold Anschluss" with the Third Reich, it was even disappointing in its paucity of new revelations.

In both of these cases Hitler has stuck entirely to the understatements of the official communiqués previously published.

Right of Self-Determination

The speech's real keynote was the proposition that by virtue of their efficiency and accomplishments the German people, organized in and represented by the National Socialist Third Reich, constituted a great power therefore entitled to equal rights with all other great powers, including the right of self-determination. This right of self-determination, according to Wilson's fourteen points, was specifically proclaimed by Hitler for the "10,000,000 Germans" living in the two states adjacent to German borders.

These States are Austria, with nearly 7,000,000 inhabitants, and Czechoslovakia, with a German minority of more than 3,000,000.

Despite its occasional vagueness there was no possibility of mistaking the final implications of this speech, with which the world will have to reckon henceforth. It was a frank repudiation of the status quo and any mere legalistic conception of world politics and an equally frank avowal of power politics based on the vital, if egotistic, interests of nations—a dedication to the proposition that might creates new right.

League Policies Repudiated

It is in this sense that the whole speech was also an outspoken repudiation of the legalistic League of Nations policy of Mr. Eden. It was further underlined by the open if ironic attacks on Mr. Eden per-

Continued on Page Three

"All the News That's Fit to Print."

The New York Times.

LATE CITY EDITION
Generally fair and warmer today. Tomorrow mostly cloudy, mild temperatures, colder at night.
Temperatures Yesterday—Max., 46; Min., 31

Copyright, 1938, by The New York Times Company.

VOL. LXXXVII.. .No. 29,267. Entered as Second-Class Matter, Postoffice, New York, N. Y. NEW YORK, SATURDAY, MARCH 12, 1938. PP TWO CENTS In New York City. | THREE CENTS Within 200 Miles. | FOUR CENTS Elsewhere Except in 7th and 8th Postal Zones.

NAZIS SEIZE AUSTRIA AFTER HITLER ULTIMATUM; GERMAN TROOPS INVITED TO MAINTAIN ORDER; SEYSS-INQUART CHANCELLOR; POWERS PROTEST

A. E. MORGAN DEFIES PRESIDENT'S AIRING OF TVA BOARD ROW

Again and Again He Declines at Hearing in Roosevelt's Office to Give 'Facts'

SAYS IT IS UP TO CONGRESS

He Is Told He Should Resign if Not Willing to Support Accusations He Made

TWO COLLEAGUES HEARD

Lilienthal and H. A. Morgan Put Before Chief Executive Data Defending Their Course

A summary of Mr. Roosevelt's inquiry in TVA on Page 8.

By TURNER CATLEDGE
Special to THE NEW YORK TIMES.

WASHINGTON, March 11.—President Roosevelt met open defiance today in his efforts to investigate dissension in the Tennessee Valley Authority when Arthur E. Morgan, chairman of the board, refused to submit evidence in support of his charges against his fellow-directors and reiterated, instead, his demand for a Congressional investigation.

Chairman Morgan sat with the other board members, Dr. Harcourt A. Morgan and David E. Lilienthal, for six hours in the President's office, the most unusual meeting of its kind ever held in Washington.

Time and time again the TVA chairman heard the President repeat demands for him to bring forth evidence to back his charges. He heard the other directors spread before the President the grounds on which they had countercharged that the chairman was undermining the TVA and that they could work with him no longer.

Dr. Morgan even heard the suggestion from the President's lips that he should resign if he were unwilling to support with facts his accusations that "fairness" and "decency" were impossible in the TVA administration with the other two members on the board.

Says He Is an "Observer"

Except for rare intervals when he defended himself with a sentence or two against the charges of his associate directors, Chairman Morgan remained openly defiant of the proceedings. Throughout, he maintained the position he had stated shortly after 11 A. M. when he marched into the President's office behind the others:

"I am an observer and not a participant in this alleged process of fact finding."

As the conference temporarily ended early tonight, President Roosevelt told the three TVA board members that it was their duty to the country not to continue their "personal" row any longer. He told them that if they could not reach a settlement among themselves, it was the duty of those who could not see their way to do so, to resign. He gave them until 11 A. M. next Friday to submit any other statements or evidence to prove their charges, and, furthermore, to determine whether they would be able to compose their differences without a resignation.

This statement from the President was widely interpreted in Washington as an ultimatum to Chairman Morgan either to drop or substantiate his statement by next Friday or quit.

Expect Morgan to Resist

Simultaneously the Presidential statements aroused wide speculation as to whether Mr. Roosevelt had the power to remove Chairman Morgan or any of the other two TVA directors. From Dr. Morgan's attitude, observers concluded that he would resist any effort at ouster until his case was heard before a Congressional committee.

Various data concerning the dispute were brought into the open at the Presidential hearing and the two groups made it plainer than ever that they are separated by a chasm of professional and personal feeling which will require little short of a political miracle if it is to be patched up.

Opening the meeting with a statement of the necessity, in the public interest, of disclosing the facts upon which Chairman Morgan had based his charges against the other directors, the President turned to Dr. Morgan for a reply, but received, instead, a refusal to answer.

The President read the accusations made in recent statements by Chairman Morgan and at the end of each asked for specifications. As often as Mr. Roosevelt demanded "facts," Dr. Morgan stood on his previous statement, in which he had said in effect that he would have nothing to do with the President's personal inquiry.

The questioning revealed that Dr.

Continued on Page Nine

Flower Peddler Freed By Defiant Magistrate

In defiance of a letter from Chief Magistrate Jacob Gould Schurman urging city magistrates to impose heavier fines on flower vendors, Magistrate Sabbatino suspended sentence yesterday on a peddler in Coney Island Court, declaring that "nobody can tell me what to do except my Creator, through my conscience."

After releasing Thomas Hyden, 23-year-old peddler, of 257 Eighty-seventh Street, Brooklyn, Judge Sabbatino made public the letter from his chief. Terming the instructions "insulting," he said:

"In the letter I received, I was told that I should sentence floral peddlers to pay fines of $5 or to serve two-day jail terms, and should be even stricter with second offenders. The people of this city should heed the many robberies that are committed instead of worrying about floral peddlers."

WHITNEY ARRESTED ON SECOND CHARGE

Accused by the State of Using $109,384 Yacht Club Fund to Get a Loan

BAIL PLACED AT $25,000

Prompt Indictment Will Be Sought—Bennett-Dewey Feud Is Revealed

For the second time in two days Richard Whitney, senior partner of the brokerage film which bears his name and former president of the New York Stock Exchange, was arrested, fingerprinted, photographed, haled into court and held in bail yesterday on a charge of grand larceny in the first degree.

This time he was accused of the theft of bonds with a face value of $153,200 and present market value of $109,384 belonging to the New York Yacht Club, of which he had custody as treasurer of the club, and their use as collateral for a personal loan of $450,000 from the Public National Bank and Trust Company of New York without the permission or knowledge of the club. He was released in $25,000 bail on this charge after arraignment in the Felony Court before City Magistrate Thomas A. Aurelio, who held him for the grand jury.

The penalty fixed by law for conviction on the charge of grand larceny in the first degree is from five to ten years in State's prison for each offense.

Total Bail $35,000

Mr. Whitney now has his liberty on $35,000 bail, as he was freed in $10,000 on Thursday by Judge William Allen in the Court of General Sessions on the charge of stealing $105,000 in securities from the estate of his father-in-law, George R. Sheldon, of which he was an executor and trustee, and of which his wife, his sister-in-law, the widow of Judge Daniel F. Murphy of the Court of Special Sessions; Harvard University and St. Paul's School at Concord, N. H., were the beneficiaries.

Ambrose V. McCall, Assistant State Attorney General, who has been conducting daily hearings on behalf of Attorney General John J. Bennett Jr. since the Whitney firm was suspended by the Stock Exchange on Tuesday, informed Magistrate Aurelio that his investigation had already shown shortages of nearly $1,000,000 in the Whitney accounts. He said that in view of this and other circumstances Attorney General Bennett regarded the $10,000 bail asked by District Attorney Thomas E. Dewey of New York County in the Sheldon estate case as entirely insufficient.

Feud Is Revealed

Mr. McCall's statements brought into the open a feud that has been developing behind the scenes since District Attorney Dewey called a witness from the Attorney General's inquiry before the grand jury and obtained the indictment in the Sheldon case by a surprise move.

Hurrying here from Albany yesterday morning, Attorney General Bennett made no secret of his resentment at Mr. Dewey's action. He said that a district attorney had never before stepped into a case while it was under investigation by the Attorney General, and that he saw no necessity of Mr. Dewey acting as he had done. In the ordinary course of events, Mr. Bennett explained, his office would have presented the Sheldon case to the grand jury and prosecuted it just as it intends to do with the yacht club case, under Article 23-A of the General Business Law. He said his office has concurrent jurisdiction with the county prosecutor.

In view of the indictment obtained by Mr. Dewey, the Attorney General said he did not intend to accept Mr. Whitney's offer to testify at the State investigation. If it had not been for Thursday's indictment, he added, the broker would have

Continued on Page Eighteen

TAX BILL IS PASSED BY HOUSE, 294 TO 97; SENATE TO SPEED IT

Three Hours of Continuous Voting on Amendments Precede House Action

'THIRD BASKET' IS OUT

Liquor, Pork Import Levies Replace It—Profits, Gains Imposts Are Retained

By CHARLES W. HURD
Special to THE NEW YORK TIMES.

WASHINGTON, March 11.—The House passed the new Tax Bill today after three hours of continuous voting, in which a roll-call confirmed its former informal action eliminating a special levy of 20 per cent on the income of large closely held corporations. Adopted in place of the "third basket" surtax were new taxes on liquor and imported pork products. Final passage was voted 294 to 97.

The bill, which is expected to yield between $5,000,000,000 and $5,300,000,000 annually was ordered sent to the Senate immediately. There the Finance Committee will begin studies of it on Monday in expectation of a quick report.

Final House action on the bill occurred in the presence of almost all members on the floor, that being in itself a rare occurrence.

These members, permitted by the leadership only to vote and not to debate, carried on loud conversation among themselves, laughed and occasionally applauded as some member shouted "Aye" or "Nay" in response to his name through the dreary succession of roll-calls, one teller count and one standing division.

New Corporation Clause Voted

The most important change in the bill, as compared with current tax laws, consists of readjusted rates and schedules for corporation taxes, reported in detail previously, which are expected to make their burden more equitable.

However, the House refused again today, by an overwhelming vote on a roll-call, to reconsider its action continuing in effect the much criticized undistributed profits tax and the capital gains tax.

The results of the roll-calls, in the order in which they were taken, follow:

The House adopted, 233 to 153, the McCormack Amendment which eliminated the "third basket" contained in Section 1B.

It adopted, 201 to 182, an amendment by Representative Thompson of Illinois placing a new excise of six cents a pound on imported pork and three cents a pound on imported pork.

It approved, 290 to 96, an additional tax of 25 cents a gallon on spirits, proposed by Representative Robertson, to be added to the $2 rate now in effect.

It defeated, 292 to 94, a motion by Representative Treadway of Massachusetts, to recommit the bill to the Ways and Means Committee with instructions to eliminate the undistributed profits tax and to modify the corporate gains.

The final roll-call was on adoption of the bill.

A teller vote resulted in approval, by 135 to 96, of an amendment by Representative Boileau to include Engleman spruce among woods ex-

Continued on Page Nine

Netherlands Likens Crisis To Invasion of Belgium

Wireless to THE NEW YORK TIMES.

THE HAGUE, The Netherlands, March 11.—The news of the dramatic events in Austria has seriously impressed The Netherlands, where it is considered the most alarming intelligence for smaller European countries since August, 1914, when German troops invaded Belgium.

Although German relations with The Netherlands are quite different from those with Austria, it is felt that some pretext or other might serve the Reich some day to intervene in The Netherlands' internal affairs as well.

The attitude of the British Government in the face of the new situation is impatiently awaited. In any case the lesson of Austria will not be lost on The Netherlands.

ROME CHECKS PARIS ON AID FOR VIENNA

Refuses to Cooperate With France and Britain for the Support of Austria

FAILURE FOR BLUM IS SEEN

Premier Designate Is Unable to Form Union Government From All the Parties

By P. J. PHILIP
Wireless to THE NEW YORK TIMES.

PARIS, March 11.—It was learned here tonight that yesterday the French and British Governments jointly sounded out Italy as to whether cooperation could be expected in maintaining Austrian independence and that they received a firm negative reply.

However, Nazi Germany's annexation of Austria this evening has profoundly affected the French political situation and, in the opinion of every political party, made the immediate constitution of a government essential. That being so, Premier-designate Léon Blum tonight, after a day of continuous negotiation and argument with one party and another, informed the press that toward noon tomorrow he will announce his decision and intentions.

It is believed that he hopes to be able to announce the formation of a national government including most, if not all, of the parties. Before then, however, he will meet the National Council of the Socialist party, which last January ran counter to his wishes and by a small majority opposed every Socialist Minister in the Chautemps Cabinet.

What course events will take depends on M. Blum's ability to persuade his own party that the time has come for them to take the lead in the formation of a government which will represent France and not

Continued on Page Two

Mechanic on New Army Planes Held as Spy; Trapped by Counter-Espionage in Plant

Following several days of intensified counter-espionage activities around Long Island air fields, Federal authorities yesterday arraigned Otto Hermann Voss, a naturalized German mechanic employed in the Seversky aircraft plant, for espionage. Waiving examination, Voss was held in $10,000 bail.

The government invoked the same severe World War statute under which two renegade soldiers and a German woman were held as German spies on Feb. 26. Voss was charged with delivering and inducing others to deliver "to agents of a foreign power certain documents, writings, code books, signal books, photographs, instruments and information relating to the defense of the United States." The maximum punishment for conviction is imprisonment for twenty years.

The Seversky Aircraft Corporation at Farmingdale, L. I., is now building pursuit planes for the army that have broken several world records at speeds over 300 miles an hour and are recognized as one of the best types of fighting ships.

The background of the case was not revealed beyond what appeared in the complaint and the few words spoken by Lester C. Dunigan, assistant United States attorney, at the arraignment before United States Commissioner Isaac Platt. Mr. Dunigan said that after a conference with John F. Dailey, Acting United States Attorney, it had been decided that any statement at this time "would be out of order."

It was reported, however, that four men who were poor mechanics worked near Voss for three weeks until two Department of Justice agents arrested him Wednesday. Then they disappeared. Voss worked in the "day-dreaming" or experimental, section of the plant's assembly division, where Major de Seversky tests new ideas and materials.

Voss, it was learned, visited Germany for about a month last Summer. His wife at their home at 225 Jericho Turnpike, Floral Park, was on the verge of collapse after two long sessions of questioning by Federal agents. They were at her home on Wednesday and Thursday. Mrs. Voss asserted her husband was innocent and believed he came under suspicion when his name was found in a paper on the person of a friend arrested as a spy suspect recently.

The defendant, 30 years old, was silent at his arraignment. He is 6 feet tall with old scars on both cheeks. Mr. Dunigan said Voss worked at the plant at intervals for several years. His alleged illegal activities were dated from Jan. 2, 1936.

ITALY GETS SHOCK

Visit of Hitler Probably Will Be Canceled as Result of the Coup

ROME-BERLIN AXIS SHAKEN

Parleys With Britain Likely to Be Speeded and Accord Is Now Thought Probable

By ARNALDO CORTESI
Wireless to THE NEW YORK TIMES.

ROME, March 11.—The news from Austria struck Italy with the impact of an exploding bomb and left the official world here aghast. An official spokesman told an unusually large audience of newspaper men this evening that the Italian Government considered the situation so grave that it did not feel it could make any statement at present.

The general impression is, however, that whatever Italy may decide to do she will not make any attempt to intervene in Austria militarily and will not concentrate divisions at the Brenner Pass as in July, 1934, after the assassination of Chancellor Engelbert Dollfuss. Certainly no troop movements have been reported.

The greatest uncertainty and confusion reigned in Italian quarters, where the day's developments apparently were entirely unexpected. But it seems clear that Chancellor Hitler's action in forcing Chancellor Kurt Schuschnigg to resign has shaken the Rome-Berlin axis to its very foundations. Whether the axis will be able to survive depends on the turn of events in the next few days and the explanations Berlin furnishes in reply to Rome's inquiries. Worth recording in any case are the widespread rumors that Hitler's visit to Italy in May will be canceled. Such a cancellation would be an unmistakable symptom that the axis was doomed.

No Hint to Rome

The very surprise and shock caused by Dr. Schuschnigg's resignation prove that Hitler acted without giving the Rome end of the axis the slightest inkling of his intentions. As late as last night Italian circles close to the government were still saying that the Austrian plebiscite would lead to a clarification, which Rome heartily favored. Now the latest developments have brought the Italo-German situation to a climax.

It is declared here that Hitler could not have chosen a better moment for a coup in Austria. The Anglo-Italian negotiations are not yet properly under way and therefore Italy cannot definitely count on British support in any action she might meditate in Central Europe. France is in the throes of a Cabinet crisis, while Russia also is going through a far from happy period internally.

The events in Austria are also likely to have deep repercussions on the Anglo-Italian negotiations. Italy obviously will now enter them in a much weaker position, since her principal strength in relation to Britain hitherto was that in the field of foreign politics she and Germany acted as a unit. The wabbling of the axis cannot but increase for Italy the necessity of reaching an understanding with Britain and thus deprive her of a considerable part of her bargaining points.

Agreement Facilitated

On the other hand, the events in Austria cannot but make both Italy and Britain more determined to reach an agreement as soon as possible.

Even if the Rome-Berlin axis survives this blow, it is doubtful whether it will ever again regain the strength it had hitherto. Public opinion is convinced Germany has betrayed Italy: therefore it is difficult to imagine that the atmosphere of perfect cordiality and mutual confidence existing hitherto can ever be restored. Perhaps an open break will be avoided so as to gloss over the fact that a pillar that has upheld the whole of Italian foreign policy in the last two years has fallen to the ground, but it seems that the process of a breaking up of the axis has begun.

No course appears open to Italy but to save what she can of her position in Central Europe by diplomacy. Germany today is very different in a military sense from the Germany of 1934, so the use of force can in all probability be ruled out.

Perhaps Germany still counts

Continued on Page Two

The Austrian Situation

Following an ultimatum from Berlin, the Schuschnigg government in Austria retired yesterday evening and was succeeded by one headed by the Nazi leader, Arthur Seyss-Inquart, as Chancellor. He immediately asked Germany to send troops to help in preserving order. Some 50,000 highly armed and mechanized forces marched to the border. Both Munich and Vienna report some crossed into Austria. Berlin denies this. Nazi mobs took possession of Vienna and raided the Jewish quarter. The swastika was flown over public buildings, and Fatherland Front forces were disarmed. There were similar demonstrations in other cities.

Europe was aghast at the coup of Hitler. His action struck Italy with the force of an exploding bomb. The impression was that Italy would not retort with force, but it was believed the Rome-Berlin axis had been shaken and that Hitler's visit to Rome might be canceled. No advance notice of Germany's intention is believed to have been given to Mussolini.

Britain delivered a sharp protest to Berlin, saying Germany's action was bound to produce "the gravest reactions, of which it is impossible to foretell the issue." Other warnings were delivered earlier, but Foreign Minister von Ribbentrop retorted that Germany saw no reasons to confer with Britain until her purposes had been achieved elsewhere.

In Paris it was understood Italy had been asked if she would join in a united effort to save Austria, but had refused. France, however, took action similar to that of Britain in protesting the Reich's action. The parties tried to get together to form a new Cabinet to deal with the situation, but they were still too deeply divided to make that accomplishment possible. It was believed Léon Blum would not be able to gain sufficient support to head a government. [All the above dispatches on Page 1.]

Premier Negrin of Spain announced that Italy and Germany had made unofficial proposals for some agreement with the Loyalists, but they were determined not to enter on negotiations. [Page 2.]

BRITISH APPALLED BY REICH METHODS

Government Sends to Berlin a Sharp Rebuke Assailing the Tactics Employed

LONDON NOT TO INTERVENE

German Troops Start Across Border While Ribbentrop Is Guest of Chamberlain

By FERDINAND KUHN Jr.
Special Cable to THE NEW YORK TIMES.

LONDON, March 11.—At the very moment when German troops were crossing the Austrian frontier the British Government tonight delivered to Berlin one of the sharpest protests it has yet made in its post-war relations with Germany.

[France also protested to Germany along the same lines as the British rebuke, it was reported in Paris.]

The strength of the protest showed how strongly the British Government felt over the day's events and particularly over the methods by which Germany had finally attained her ends in Austria.

Referring especially to the second German ultimatum that had preceded the actual invasion, the British described it as the "coercion, backed by force, of an independent State in order to create a situation incompatible with its national independence."

Such action, it was pointed out, was bound to produce the "gravest reactions of which it is impossible to foretell the issue."

The protest was delivered at the Wilhelmstrasse by Sir Nevile Henderson, the British Ambassador.

British Warning Disregarded

In invading Austria tonight Germany flatly disregarded the warnings of the British Government earlier in the day that threat or use of force would damage the prospects of the Anglo-German talks and threaten future chances for reconciliation in Europe.

The warning was delivered personally to Joachim von Ribbentrop, German Foreign Minister, by Prime Minister Neville Chamberlain and Foreign Minister Viscount Halifax after luncheon at 10 Downing Street.

But the British Minister's words produced no effect upon Herr von Ribbentrop or upon his master in Berlin. Herr von Ribbentrop is said to have told Mr. Chamberlain, indeed, that the Fuehrer saw no reason for starting negotiations for reconciliation with Britain until German purposes "elsewhere" had been achieved.

While these words were being spoken the German Army was rolling along the express highways leading to the Austrian border and Berlin was preparing the ultimatums that forced the Austrian Government from power.

Britain will, of course, do nothing in the way of intervention. At this late stage in the absorption of Austria there is little left for Britain

Continued on Page Two

REICH ARMY MOVES; 50,000 AT FRONTIER

Force of Infantry, Artillery and Engineers Said to Have Entered Austria With Planes

BUT BERLIN MAKES DENIAL

Bavarian Roads Choked, Cars Taken Over—Border Towns Fired by Excitement

Wireless to THE NEW YORK TIMES.

MUNICH, Germany, Saturday, March 12.—With a dramatic suddenness that stunned the world the German Army embarked yesterday on its first campaign beyond the Reich's borders and without firing a shot achieved a victory that laid Austria prostrate at its feet, transformed the European equilibrium and set the borders fixed by the peace treaties into motion for a readjustment, of which the end is not yet in sight.

All day yesterday German forces, some 50,000 strong, made up of infantry, cavalry, artillery, motorized divisions, air force units and engineers with bridge building materials were moving to the Austrian frontier. Their mission was to avenge what is termed in Germany "the betrayal of Berchtesgaden'—Chancellor Kurt Schuschnigg's recent proclamation of a plebiscite on Austrian independence.

Last night, following Dr. Schuschnigg's overthrow and a telegram from the new Chancellor, Dr. Arthur Seyss-Inquart, to Chancellor Hitler requesting German military aid in preventing bloodshed, German troops were reported to have marched into Austria in close formation at three points—Salzburg, Kufstein and Mittenwalde.

[According to an Associated Press dispatch from Vienna, German troops crossed also at Passau, on the way to Linz, Austria, and a contingent of Reich troops, numbering about 1,000 men in trucks, was expected to reach Vienna at 6 A. M., New York time.]

Orders No Resistance

Information given out at the Munich army headquarters said the troops had begun to cross the border shortly after 10 o'clock, although their coming had been heralded by Dr. Seyss-Inquart in semihourly broadcasts beginning soon after 7 o'clock. The broadcasts included instructions to the Austrian military and civil authorities and the population not to resist the troops.

Whether the statements of the Munich army headquarters are correct or whether insistent denials in Berlin of a German march into Austria are the real truth does not much matter, for, even if the troops did halt at the border without crossing it, theirs is still the victory. It was their march that turned the tide in Austria and, after a bloodless Sadowa, enabled the Austrian

Continued on Page Three

SCHUSCHNIGG GOES

Resigns After Threat of Invasion as Powers Fail to Back Him

PLEBISCITE IS CALLED OFF

Goering and Hess Expected in Vienna Today—Nazis Rule Streets, Rout Foes

Censorship Imposed

By The Associated Press.

VIENNA, March 11.—Censorship has started.

An order posted in the correspondents' room in the Central Telegraph Office tonight said all telephone conversations from the room must be in German.

Correspondents for the International News Service, an American organization, were detained against their will, without charges, at the office.

By G. E. R. GEDYE
Wireless to THE NEW YORK TIMES.

VIENNA, Saturday, March 12.—Under threats of force from Berlin, Chancellor Kurt Schuschnigg of Austria yielded last evening and resigned in dramatic circumstances. The Nazis, with Dr. Arthur Seyss-Inquart, Interior Minister in the Schuschnigg Cabinet, as Chancellor, are in power.

To an unprepared public listening over the radio to a typical program of pleasant Viennese melodies the voice of the man who may have been the last Chancellor of an independent Austria announced at 7:45 P. M. that, in his own words, he had "yielded only to force" to avoid bloodshed and that under the threat of a German invasion that was to start at the very moment he spoke, he had resigned his office.

Plebiscite Is Postponed

Apart from the statement in a broadcast at 6 o'clock that "the Chancellor and Fatherland Front Leader, in consultation with President Miklas, has decided to postpone the plebiscite," there was no warning for the public when the program was interrupted for the announcer to say, "An important declaration is just coming." Then, without even mention of Dr. Schuschnigg's name, his voice was heard at the microphone.

When Dr. Schuschnigg had finished, thousands of Nazis began swarming into Vienna's streets to take over control unopposed. An hour afterward Dr. Seyss-Inquart also addressed the nation over the radio, calling on every one to maintain order and declaring that there was no question of resistance if the German Army should march in.

Dr. Seyss-Inquart's first official act as Chancellor appears to have been a message to Chancellor Hitler requesting the speedy dispatch of German troops to his support. The message read:

"Following the retirement of the Schuschnigg government, the Provisional Government of Austria regards the restoration and maintenance of law and order in Austria as its first duty.

"To this end it urgently requests the German Government to support it in this undertaking and assist it in the prevention of bloodshed. I therefore appeal to the German Government for the earliest possible dispatch of troops."

Up to noon Dr. Schuschnigg had remained firm in the face of all threats. Then came the first ultimatum from Germany, conveyed by Dr. Edmund Glaise-Horstenau, Minister Without Portfolio in the Schuschnigg Cabinet, on his return from Berlin. Austria was to postpone the plebiscite or she would be invaded.

Final Ultimatum Delivered

At 4 P. M. an airplane landed in Vienna. It brought Dr. Schuschnigg a final and, this time, an official ultimatum. The man who delivered it was believed to have been Josef Buerckl, Nazi leader in the Saar.

At first it was rumored that Field Marshal Hermann Goering and Rudolf Hess, deputy leader of the German Nazi party, had arrived with the ultimatum and were going to speak to the crowds in the Karlsplatz at 10 P. M., but this proved untrue. It was stated later, however, that Marshal Goering and Herr Hess would arrive today.

In any event, this ultimatum was quite different from that Dr. Glaise-Horstenau had delivered. It was an

Continued on Page Three

"All the News That's Fit to Print."

The New York Times.

LATE CITY EDITION
POSTSCRIPT
Showers today, cooler tonight. Tomorrow fair.
Temperatures Yesterday—Max., 75; Min., 63.

Copyright, 1938, by The New York Times Company.

VOL. LXXXVII....No. 29,454. Entered as Second-Class Matter, Postoffice, New York, N. Y. NEW YORK, THURSDAY, SEPTEMBER 15, 1938. P THREE CENTS NEW YORK CITY and Vicinity | FOUR CENTS Elsewhere Except in 7th and 8th Postal Zones.

CHAMBERLAIN OFF BY PLANE TO SEE HITLER; WILL MAKE A PERSONAL PLEA TO AVERT WAR; PRAGUE FIRM AS SUDETENS BATTLE THE POLICE

GEORGE IS WINNING IN GEORGIA POLL; CAMP RUNS THIRD

TALMADGE SECOND

Choice of President in 'Purge' Primary Admits His Defeat

TALMADGE CLAIMS VICTORY

Former Governor Lost Lead Won in the Early Returns in Rural District Counts

Senator George went into the lead on the late count from the Georgia Senatorial primary after a nip-and-tuck race in the returns with Former Governor Eugene Talmadge, an even more direct critic of the New Deal than the Senator whom President Roosevelt marked for elimination in the party "purge" campaign. Lawrence Camp, the choice of the President, trailed throughout the count and conceded defeat. [Page 1.]

Democrats of Connecticut, in State convention, renominated Senator Lonergan and Governor Cross. Attorney General Cummings advocated letting "the dead past bury its dead." [Page 14.]

Former Governor Frank D. Fitzgerald of Michigan won over two opponents and will oppose Frank Murphy for the Governorship. [Page 16.]

Senator Tydings's lead in Maryland's popular vote rose to 56,000 on late returns. [Page 18.]

'Purge' Again Defeated

By TURNER CATLEDGE
Special to THE NEW YORK TIMES.

ATLANTA, Thursday, Sept. 15.—President Roosevelt's drive to "purge" less than 100 per cent followers from the Senate was rounded out here early today in an apparently disastrous finale.

Senator Walter F. George, whom the President personally requested Georgia voters to oust from the seat which he has held in the Senate for 16 years, forged ahead in the returns from yesterday's Democratic Senatorial primary. The Senator was leading both in popular and county unit votes at midnight.

The runner-up was former Governor Eugene Talmadge, a more consistent and certainly more bitter critic of the President and the New Deal than Senator George. After running ahead in the early returns, Mr. Talmadge dropped behind the Senator, but at the same time went on the radio and claimed the nomination, saying that if he lost, it would be stolen from him.

Federal District Attorney Lawrence Camp, over whom the President waved the once-magic New Deal wand in his celebrated speech at Barnesville five weeks ago today, ran a poor third and formally conceded defeat at 11:30 P. M.

70 of 159 Counties Complete

At midnight 70 of the State's 159 counties had reported complete returns, accounting for 170 of the total 410 county unit votes, a majority of which a candidate must receive to be nominated. Out of the number Senator George had collected a total of 110 county unit votes in forty-two counties; Mr. Talmadge 54 unit votes in twenty-six counties, and Mr. Camp six in two counties.

Senator George had amassed 100,093 popular votes; Mr. Talmadge 75,881 and Mr. Camp 55,265. Senator George was leading in counties having a total of 192 unit votes; Mr. Talmadge in counties having a total of 194 and Mr. Camp in counties with a total of 7. However, a trend toward Mr. George had set in late in the evening and was still running.

In a radio broadcast at 11:30 P. M., Mr. Camp said:

"I am deeply grateful to all the people who have supported me in this fight. I regret the fight was not successful at this time, but I believe that the fight for liberalism will be successful in the end and that the people will demand liberal representation. I bow to the will of the electorate and offer my congratulations to the successful candidate."

On many of the first returns Mr. Talmadge would be leading in one county after another, with only one to three boxes in each to be heard from. But in most of these, when the county tabulation was complet-

Continued on Page Eighteen

Corcoran 'Deaf and Dumb' When Queried on Tydings

Thomas G. Corcoran, one of President Roosevelt's closest advisers in the current "purge" campaign, visited the local WPA offices yesterday to renew an old friendship with Lieut. Col. Brehon B. Somervell, Works Progress Administrator. He smilingly denied that there was any political significance to his visit.

Asked whether he had anything to say about Senator Millard Tydings's renomination in Maryland, Mr. Corcoran replied:

"I never have anything to say. Professionally I am deaf, dumb and blind."

TRANSIT EXPANSION TO COST $827,102,344

Delaney Submits Long-Range Program to Planning Board —Many Items Must Wait

A long-range program for expansion of the city's rapid transit facilities, at an estimated total cost of $827,102,344, was submitted to the City Planning Commission yesterday by the Board of Transportation.

In submitting the program, John H. Delaney, chairman of the board, explained that it was not to be regarded as inflexible, but as subject to changes in the city's financial condition, the volume of rapid transit traffic, the fate of pending transit unification proposals and other factors.

"This board," Mr. Delaney wrote, "is aware that the present financial resources of the city are not sufficient to permit the adoption at this time of any considerable part of this future program, but is of the opinion that the City Planning Commission should have before it a comprehensive outline of what this board deems to be the most useful development of transit facilities during the coming years."

Early Unification Assumed

Explaining that the list of projects was arranged generally in the order of priority desired, Mr. Delaney declared that it was drawn on the assumption that "rapid transit unification will be effected in the near future."

The list is a comprehensive summary of the many rapid transit projects put forward by the Board of Transportation since it began to function in 1924. It includes the proposed additional system based upon a trunk line subway under Second Avenue, the proposed acquisition of parts of the Long Island Railroad right of way in Queens, the recapture of the Hudson & Manhattan Railway tubes in Manhattan and the building of a rapid transit tunnel between Brooklyn and Staten Island.

The list, which will come before the City Planning Commission for consideration this afternoon, includes the proposed demolition of the Sixth Avenue elevated line at an estimated cost of $225,000, less possible salvage. Proceedings are now pending under which the city hopes to acquire the line itself at a cost of $12,500,000.

Projects as Submitted

Following is the complete list of projects submitted by the Board of Transportation:

Transportation building...$3,000,000

Rockaway Line, Acquisition and Reconstruction, Queens—Four and two tracks; subway, embankment and elevated.....$40,568,544

Fulton Street Line Extension:

Via Pitkin Avenue and Linden Boulevard, Grant Avenue to 108th Street, with provision for a connection to the Rockaway line, Brooklyn and Queens; four tracks, subway $21,300,000

Connection from Rockaway line to Fulton Street extension, Queens; two tracks, subway and open cut $2,220,000

Hillside Avenue Extension—178th Street to 212th Street, Queens; four tracks, subway..........$22,750,000

Flushing Line—I. R. T. Extension:

Via Roosevelt Avenue, public streets and private property parallel and adjacent to L. I. R. R.; Main Street, Flushing, to Bell Boulevard, Bayside, Queens; four tracks to 149th Street, thence two tracks to Bell Boulevard; subway, embankment and open cut....$5,380,000

Via 149th Street and 111th Avenue, from Roosevelt Avenue to 122d Street, College Point, Queens; two tracks, elevated throughout $7,580,000

Continued on Page Fourteen

RED HOOK HOUSING TO COST $12,000,000, A $4,600,000 SAVING

Total Per Room of $1,125 Is About Half That for Harlem and Williamsburg Projects

BIDS FAR BELOW BUDGET

Rheinstein Wires Mayor That Queensbridge Should Now Provide for 9,000 More

The total cost of the Red Hook low-rental housing development, including land, will be about $12,000,000, or approximately $4,600,000 less than the $16,592,766 provided in the budget allowed by the United States Housing Authority, it was announced yesterday by Alfred Rheinstein, chairman of the New York City Housing Authority.

Mr. Rheinstein, who is also Commissioner of Housing and Buildings, telegraphed Mayor La Guardia at Prescott, Ariz., that the bids for the Red Hook superstructures, which were opened Tuesday, showed that the project could be completed at a cost per room, including land, carrying charges and overheard, of $1,125.

Cost of Other Projects

The cost per room of Williamsburg Houses, built by the housing division of the Public Works Administration, was $2,284, while Harlem River Houses cost $2,150 a room, Mr. Rheinstein said, adding that the lower cost for Red Hook was due to "an accurate definition of the problem, careful planning, unusual cooperation of the building industry and a favorable market."

Mr. Rheinstein expressed confidence that similar economies would be revealed when bids for the $16,500,000 Queensbridge development were opened some time next month. He advised Mayor La Guardia that as a result it would be possible to provide housing in the Queensbridge development for 31,000 persons, or 9,000 more than the plans approved by the Federal authorities contemplated.

"This saving undoubtedly will permit slum clearance which, in the past, was a doubtful prospect because of the high cost of land in New York City," Mr. Rheinstein said in discussing the reduction in cost.

"This is the first fruit of intensive effort by an organization which has labored with great skill and faithfulness. Credit is due Alfred Easton Poor, the chief architect, and his associates; to the engineers and to our own technical staff, which is headed by Allan S. Harrison."

Rheinstein Praises Builders

Mr. Rheinstein paid tribute to the cooperative attitude of the building industry, which he said had been a factor in the saving. He said the building industry and the Housing Authority had worked in close harmony and "on a practical basis" for many months.

The text of Mr. Rheinstein's telegram to the Mayor follows:

"Bids on the superstructures for Red Hook opened last night. Total cost, including land, carrying

Continued on Page Thirteen

Ultimatum of Henlein Disavowed in Germany

Wireless to THE NEW YORK TIMES.

BERLIN, Sept. 14.—The ultimatum sent to the Czech Government by the Sudeten party yesterday is declared here to have been drawn up without Chancellor Adolf Hitler's approval.

It was stated here today that Konrad Henlein could not communicate with Berchtesgaden yesterday because of alleged intervention by Prague in telephonic communication with Germany. Herr Henlein is thereupon said to have dispatched his belligerent statement to the Czech Government on his own responsibility.

Apparently he was not sharply reproved for doing so, and his subsequent decision to break off negotiations with Prague had Hitler's complete approval.

The German Foreign Office stated today that it was unable to get in touch with the German Legation in Prague yesterday between 8 P. M. and midnight.

PRESIDENT SPEEDS BACK TO CAPITAL

Tells Rochester, Minn., Crowd That the European Crisis Changed His Plans

By HENRY N. DORRIS
Special to THE NEW YORK TIMES.

ON BOARD THE PRESIDENTIAL TRAIN EN ROUTE TO WASHINGTON, Sept. 14.—President Roosevelt sped toward Washington tonight to be at the seat of government during the present crisis in Europe.

Concerned over what he described in extemporaneous remarks at Rochester, Minn., as the "extremely serious" situation in Europe, Mr. Roosevelt cut short his visit to his son, James, who was reported to be progressing well after his operation Sunday for a gastric ulcer.

Standing on the rear platform of his special train after he had paid his son a morning visit, the President said to several hundred Rochester citizens gathered to bid him farewell:

"I am going back now, not to my house on the Hudson River, but straight through to Washington, because, as you know, having read the newspapers, the condition of affairs in other parts of the world is extremely serious. That is why, as President, I have to go back to the national capital."

Until this morning the President was undecided as to going to Hyde Park or Washington, but after a long conversation with Secretary Hull, Mr. Roosevelt ordered that the train go direct to the capital.

After he reaches Washington tomorrow night he is expected to go

Continued on Page Twelve

Americans Informally Told to Return Home; Many Ship Bookings to Europe Canceled

By The Associated Press.

BERLIN, Sept. 14.—American travelers have been advised "unofficially and informally" by the United States Consulate here to return home "if they could conveniently alter their European travel plans," officials said today.

Members of the consulate staff disclosed that numerous United States citizens had inquired what they ought to do in view of the critical situation in Central Europe.

The officials said, however, that American residents in Berlin have not been advised to leave Germany.

Consulates of other countries have given their nationals similar advice.

Special to THE NEW YORK TIMES.

WASHINGTON, Sept. 14.—Asked about a press report that the American consulate in London was advising Americans to book early passages for home, Secretary of State Cordell Hull today said he had received nothing officially on that subject.

He pointed out that some years ago a survey was taken of possible eventualities in various parts of the world and general instructions were then issued to consulates for their guidance in such matters in a threatening war situation. These instructions, he said, had not been supplemented by special instructions in the present crisis.

Special Cable to THE NEW YORK TIMES.

LONDON, Sept. 14.—The United States cruiser Nashville anchored in the Thames off Gravesend today after a hurried trip from Portland—a move made ostensibly to "let the men see another port" but in reality, London suspected, to care for American residents in case of danger.

WASHINGTON, Sept. 14 (AP).—It was announced today that a bombproof cement and steel shelter was being built under a wing of the American Legation in Prague, Czechoslovakia.

It was authorized by the State Department after the Czech Government had given its approval.

The American Embassy in Berlin is also about to undergo extensive repairs, and it is reported another bombproof shelter may be built there.

Shipping executives said last night that European developments of the last few days had affected shipping in both passenger and freight fields.

Tramp ships of foreign registry, which are generally available for service to any part of the world depending upon the nature of the freight, were said yesterday to have been withdrawn from the market.

In the passenger field cancellations of bookings have already been reported. Nine cancellations were reported last night on a ship scheduled to sail during the next few days.

The ship lines also have notified their booking clerks to restrict their promises of accommodations on ships in westbound sailings during the next few weeks.

There have been no cancellations of sailings from Europe as yet. The Europa will dock here today and the New York of the Hamburg Line tomorrow.

FIGHTING IS BITTER

Dead Mount to 23 as Six Are Killed in a Struggle in Eger

GERMAN ARMS ARE SEIZED

Troops Victorious After Long Struggle in Schwaderbach —Martial Law Extended

By G. E. R. GEDYE
Wireless to THE NEW YORK TIMES.

PRAGUE, Czechoslovakia, Thursday, Sept. 15.—After perfect order had apparently been restored in most of the Sudeten German areas yesterday, further serious firing on the police occurred in Eger last night that developed into a pitched battle, with six killed.

A government communiqué last night said that investigations into events in various parts of the frontier areas had established that the shooting of individual police and attacks on various gendarmerie stations and State buildings that set in immediately after Chancellor Adolf Hitler's speech at Nuremberg Monday night were part of an attempted revolt.

Despite the restoration of order, it asserted, danger still remained that irresponsible elements would continue their "cruel and ruthless attempts at violence against fellow citizens of a different race and different political opinions."

"Altogether," the communiqué declared, "there have been twenty-three deaths—thirteen Czechs, of whom ten belonged to the forces of public order. Of the German assailants ten were killed. Of the seventy-five wounded fourteen are Germans; thirty-seven of the others are police and gendarmes."

Moderate Measures Stressed

"These figures clearly show with what reserve and moderation the necessary measures have been taken. Firearms have been employed only on absolutely unavoidable occasions; the attackers have had machine guns and even hand grenades among their arms.

"The government has had every right to suppress this revolt and to do it energetically in the interests of the State and for the sake of European peace."

The writer had left Eger absolutely normal in the afternoon, save for many drawn shutters concealing the wreckage of Monday night's wave of violence following Hitler's speech. An occasional double police patrol with rifles and bayonets indicated that martial law was in force.

Late in the evening it was reported that a police patrol had been fired on from the headquarters of the Henlein party in the Hotel Victoria in the town.

The fighting began, according to the official account, when, acting on information that there was a secret munitions depot in the party headquarters, two police detachments in armored cars were sent to carry out a search. They found the doors of the hotel closed and were received with fire from the windows.

Armored Cars Return Fire

The armored cars returned the fire and with the help of hand grenades the doors were finally burst open. Inside a considerable armory of German revolvers and automatic pistols and a radio transmitting station were found. Those inside who had not already escaped were arrested.

During these operations the police were constantly fired on from the cellars of the neighboring Hotel Wenzel. The shooting continued until late in the evening, when that hotel was taken by storm and every one found inside was placed under arrest.

The six persons killed included one policeman, one Czech railwayman and one Henleinist. Three bodies of persons apparently killed by stray bullets were lying in the market square. One was a woman. Their identity has not yet been established.

By 9:30 P. M. order was stated to have been fully restored in Eger. The ringleaders were arrested and will be tried summarily by a military court.

The only other place in the republic where the Henleinist revolutionaries were still causing trouble last night was the village of Schwaderbach, near Graslitz. Schwaderbach is really a suburb of the German township of Sachsenberg. There the Henleinists had been armed, allegedly by Germany, not

Continued on Page Four

Chamberlain Visit Stuns Reich; Hitler Looks to British Fair Play

Czech-Sudeten Crisis Seen as Drawing Further Away From Brink of War as Result—Berlin to Delay Action

By GUIDO ENDERIS
Wireless to THE NEW YORK TIMES.

BERLIN, Sept. 14.—The Czech-Sudeten German crisis drew further away from the brink of war tonight with the announcement that Prime Minister Neville Chamberlain and Chancellor Hitler would meet in Berchtesgaden tomorrow afternoon for a man-to-man talk.

Following a day of nervous apprehensions over the intensification of the situation in Sudetenland and the breakdown of negotiations between the Czech Government and Konrad Henlein the news that the British Prime Minister had sought an appointment with Hitler stunned the unsuspecting radio public tonight. Mr. Chamberlain's visit was announced in a communiqué containing the Prime Minister's messages and Hitler's reply, which was remarkable alike for its informally personal formulation and its dramatic contents.

Mr. Chamberlain, it is expected, will reach Hitler's mountain chalet early tomorrow afternoon. He will land at Munich and will immediately motor to Berchtesgaden, which once again is to become a cynosure of world-wide curiosity. The announcement of the British Prime Minister's visit came long after official quarters had closed down for the day, and it was no less a surprise to Berlin officialdom than to the public generally. As a demonstration of British desire to assuage the crisis it is assured a cordial reception here.

It is also received as a vindication of Hitler's faith in British fair play. If that faith has experienced passing shocks they were never sufficiently violent to modify Hitler's conviction that he could see eye to eye with British statesmen in critical moments.

The conference between Hitler and the British Prime Minister will follow the breakdown in negotiations between the Sudeten party and the Czech Government. Their complete collapse in an atmosphere of mutual recrimination suggested to German diplomacy, as it undoubtedly did to Britain's, that the Czech crisis has now become the exclusive concern of European statesmen.

This was the German position

Continued on Page Two

TOKYO CZECH STAND ALARMS SHANGHAI

Pledge to Back Reich and Italy by Arms, if Necessary, Seen as Threat to Foreigners

By HALLETT ABEND
Special Cable to THE NEW YORK TIMES.

SHANGHAI, Sept. 14.—Consternation over the European crisis spread and deepened here and in other centers of foreign residence in China upon receipt from Tokyo of a declaration by a Foreign Office spokesman to the effect that Japan is prepared to join forces with Germany and Italy in accordance with the anti-Comintern agreement.

This statement apparently implies an immediate spread of a European conflict to the Far East and places enormous interests in jeopardy.

An immediate question arises concerning the British and French concessions in Tientsin, where there are stationed only a handful of troops of each nation. There, presumably, Japan and Italy would act in unison since Italy has her own Tientsin concession, a considerable Tientsin garrison and a river gunboat.

Limited Forces

At Shanghai there are only two regiments of British troops, about 4,500 French forces and Annamites and 1,200 United States Marines. Anchored in the Whangpoo River are three French warships, one British cruiser, two Italian light cruisers, the U. S. S. Asheville, ocean-going gunboat, and the U. S. S. Oahu, river gunboat, while for miles downstream are many Japanese warships of all sizes. Other fighting craft, however, are within striking distance. The British have a force at Hong Kong while the United States Asiatic Fleet bases at Manila and spends its Summers on the China coast.

British interests in the International Settlement and also the French Concession at Shanghai are utterly indefensible and the entire surrounding countryside is in the hands of the Japanese Army.

At Canton there are only two foreign concessions, the British and French, both on the Island of Shameen. There is nothing larger than the river gunboats, but the larger craft would be dispatched from Hong Kong, which is well-garrisoned and stoutly defensible from land and sea.

Inexplicable to Americans

Special Cable to THE NEW YORK TIMES.

TOKYO, Sept. 14.—A statement by a Foreign Office spokesman early today that the Comintern is primarily responsible for the Sudeten trouble is considered inexplicable in American and other foreign circles in Tokyo.

The afternoon edition of the newspaper Miyako editorially supports this statement but other papers at present are silent.

The Miyako especially praises Chancellor Adolf Hitler's Nuremberg speech, saying that it will have

Continued on Page Seven

FRENCH HOPES RISE ON BRITAIN'S MOVE

Daladier Not Only Endorses the Chamberlain Plan, but Claims Initiative in It

By P. J. PHILIP
Wireless to THE NEW YORK TIMES.

PARIS, Sept. 14.—With special trains ready outside Paris to take the civilian population away and with the president of the American Chamber of Commerce here asking that provision for gas masks be made for American citizens, all seemed set tonight for a tragic finale to the tension of past days and weeks, when the news of Prime Minister Neville Chamberlain's proposal to visit Chancellor Adolf Hitler caused such surprise and relief as had not been experienced since the news broke in November, 1918, that the Germans were seeking an armistice.

Of course, there are all kinds of different opinions about the British Prime Minister's action. There is, first, the official one. In a communiqué issued late this evening Premier Eduoard Daladier in some ways claims credit for the suggestion, for he always has been a partisan of a get-together policy with Germany, and late last evening, he says, he suggested by telephone to Mr. Chamberlain that something should be done for having something like a three-power conversation to consider the situation.

Tells of Taking Initiative

In his statement this evening M. Daladier said:

"At the end of yesterday afternoon, in the presence of a rapid sequence of events in Czechoslovakia, which made local negotiations difficult, I took the initiative in establishing direct personal contact with the British Prime Minister with a view to examining with him the possibility of attempting exceptional procedure that would permit an examination with Germany of the most effective means of assuring a friendly solution of the differences that separate the Sudetens and the Prague government and, in consequence, of maintaining peace in Europe.

"I am, therefore, extremely happy at the agreement in the ideas of the two governments."

The British Prime Minister's action has, therefore, official French sanction and approval. At the same time the French, because of the fact that the British are acting alone, are relieved of certain grave embarrassments. They are bound by their treaties with Czechoslovakia to go to that country's aid if her territorial integrity is threatened.

But the French are also on record as defenders of minorities, and the behavior of the Sudeten Nazis during these last few weeks has left no doubt in any French mind that, whatever they may want, they do not want to continue under the old regime or anything like it. From a purely French viewpoint, therefore, the whole basis on which war might

Continued on Page Ten

LONDON HAILS PLAN

Prime Minister Hopeful of a Temporary Accord at Berchtesgaden

KING HASTENS TO CAPITAL

In Case of a Rebuff Britain Will Have Stressed to World Her Efforts for Peace

Prime Minister Chamberlain, in a dramatic move to avert Europe's threatened war, is flying to Germany to meet Chancellor Hitler face to face. [Page 1.] The step, which was approved by the full British Cabinet yesterday, was understood to have been suggested by Premier Daladier of France. [Page 1.] It electrified Germany, where Hitler conferred all day with his diplomatic advisers. [Page 1.]

This development came after a day of continued violence in the Sudeten areas of Czechoslovakia. In the border town of Schwaderbach Henleinists seized the police station and for hours held the Czech forces at bay. Prague charged that they were helped by arms from abroad. In Eger six were killed in a police attack on Henleinist headquarters. [Page 1.]

Meanwhile Konrad Henlein said events had left his original demands far behind and he balked at further negotiations. [Page 10.]

As a solution to the Sudeten German problem a letter published in Italy, attributed to Premier Mussolini, called on Viscount Runciman, British mediator, to sponsor a plebiscite. [Page 5.]

At Geneva preparations were made to convene the League Council immediately after any German invasion of Czechoslovakia. [Page 6.]

A Tokyo statement that Japan would support her anti-Communist allies, Germany and Italy, with arms if necessary caused alarm in foreign circles in China because of the peril to huge foreign interests there. [Page 1.]

While Washington took hope from the Chamberlain development [Page 2], American tourists in Germany were advised as a precautionary measure to leave the country. [Page 1.]

Locally, the stock market again was hit by a wave of selling [Page 2], and underwriters suspended rates on marine insurance, with higher ones likely to be fixed today. [Page 3].

Chamberlain Flying to Reich

By FERDINAND KUHN Jr.
Special Cable to THE NEW YORK TIMES.

LONDON, Thursday, Sept. 15.—Prime Minister Neville Chamberlain flew today from the Heston Airdrome for Berchtesgaden, Germany, to keep an appointment with Chancellor Adolf Hitler in a last attempt to save Europe from war.

At 8:36 A. M. the wheels of the big silver Lockheed monoplane lifted from the runway into a cloudless sky. Its first stop will be Munich, 600 miles away, whence Mr. Chamberlain will go to Hitler's mountain chalet by automobile.

He made a statement for the newsreels as follows:

"I am going to meet the German Chancellor because the situation seems to me to be one in which discussions between me and him would be fruitful. My policy has always been to seek peace. The Fuehrer's ready acceptance of my invitation leads me to hope my visit will not be without result."

Only about 100 newspapermen, photographers and officials were allowed near the airplane. They cheered and shouted, "Good luck! God speed you!"

A moment later Mr. Chamberlain turned and bowed his head to enter the plane. But photographers called him back and then the Prime Minister found time to joke. He struck a stiff attitude, his hands on his hips, like an old-fashioned daguerreotype.

The crowd gasped and then gave three cheers, waving hats. The individual cries redoubled and Mr. Chamberlain's face broke into a surprised smile and he waved his own hat. Within five minutes after the engines had been warmed up

Continued on Page Three

"All the News That's Fit to Print."

The New York Times.

LATE CITY EDITION
Cloudy, little change in temperatures today; showers tonight. Tomorrow fair, cooler.
Temperatures Yesterday—Max., 71; Min., 55

VOL. LXXXVIII...No. 29,466. Entered as Second-Class Matter, Postoffice, New York, N. Y. NEW YORK, TUESDAY, SEPTEMBER 27, 1938. PPPP THREE CENTS NEW YORK CITY and Vicinity | FOUR CENTS Elsewhere Except in 7th and 8th Postal Zones.

BRITAIN PLEDGES AID IF CZECHS ARE ATTACKED; ALSO GUARANTEES SURRENDER OF SUDETEN AREA AS HITLER IN SPEECH KEEPS PEACE DOOR OPEN

TRUCK FIRMS HALT THE MAYOR'S PLAN; DRIVERS ACCEPT IT

Operators Reject Peace Terms as 'Unfair' After All-Day Conference Fails

CITY HAS A FLEET READY

1,000 Sanitation Vehicles Are Mobilized for Emergency—15,000 Quit in Jersey

Convinced that further negotiations between union and operator representatives would produce no settlement of the truck drivers' strike that has paralyzed shipping in New York City for more than a week, Mayor La Guardia submitted a compromise proposal to the negotiators whom he locked in City Hall last night and demanded an end of the strike by noon today.

Michael J. Cashal, vice president of the International Brotherhood of Teamsters, submitted the Mayor's proposal to the strikers' committee and within a few minutes announced their acceptance.

The Mayor's proposal was unanimously rejected by the truck operators early this morning at a meeting at the Capitol Hotel, Eighth Avenue and Fifty-first Street, attended by more than 300 members of the Merchant Truckmen's Bureau and the Highway Transport Association.

The vote was taken at about 1:40 A. M. at the end of a two-hour meeting at which members of the operators' negotiating committee reported on the Mayor's proposal and asked for instructions.

The operators also voted to set up a committee to enlist support among shippers and to seek to persuade operators not to sign separate agreements.

Although the committee made no formal recommendation for acceptance or rejection of the Mayor's proposal, members of the committee assailed it as "unfair" and requiring the operators to concede everything while the union gave nothing in return.

Rise in Costs Seen

D. L. Sutherland, president of the Highway Transport Association, estimated that the proposal, if accepted, would raise costs between 7 and 9 per cent. He termed the proposal "not a compromise but a piece of political skulduggery." Operators at the meeting applauded declarations from the floor that it was time to make a stand and fight it out.

The operators met late in the afternoon, and recessed until evening to hear reports on the City Hall negotiations. The committee arrived from City Hall at about 11:30 P. M. and discussion of the Mayor's plan began a few minutes later. The operators will meet again at the Capitol Hotel at 3 P. M. today.

The operators' committee is to report its answer at City Hall at 9 o'clock this morning, in accordance with the Mayor's request. Arthur G. McKeever, managing director of the Merchant Truckmen's Bureau, told the Mayor at the conclusion of the City Hall conference last night that some points would require clearing up and would have to be submitted to the operators' organizations.

In the meantime, the Mayor ordered mobilization of the Department of Sanitation's emergency fleet of 1,000 trucks, which began arriving at City Hall Plaza shortly after 12 o'clock. The fleet was being mobilized to handle any essential food stuffs or other material held up by the strike.

2-Year Contract Urged

Mayor La Guardia's proposal was for an agreement to run for two years. Where the union had demanded a forty-hour week at the forty-four-hour rate of pay, the Mayor proposed a forty-four-hour week at forty-seven hours' pay, an eight-hour day, beginning at 8 A. M., with four hours on Saturday, no man to be permitted to work more than forty-four hours weekly.

The Mayor submitted his compromise plan at a joint meeting of driver and operator committees of eleven members each at City Hall. He expressed a determination to end today the strike which he pointed out had caused not only losses to the business community but hardship to citizens, particularly those in the storm-stricken areas.

The plight of the hurricane-swept communities of New England, which need building supplies and materials, was described by Governors Robert E. Quinn of Rhode Island and Wilbur L. Cross of Connecticut in telegrams to the Mayor to start storm relief supplies moving again.

Meanwhile, the strike of 15,000 drivers in New York City had spread to 15,000 drivers in North New Jersey, while a strike of bus drivers, not involved in the dispute, had halted the transportation of

Continued on Page Six

Southampton Declines WPA Storm Clean-Up Aid

Special to THE NEW YORK TIMES.

SOUTHAMPTON, L. I., Sept. 26.—The Village Board of Southampton voted today to decline an offer of WPA aid in cleaning up after Wednesday's hurricane. Many trees were blown over and considerable damage was done to the waterfront of this exclusive Summer resort.

After the Village Board meeting Mayor Albert P. Loening said:

"The Village Board has declined WPA aid in cleaning up the highways and for other rehabilitation work in the village. In Southampton we have always been able to handle our own affairs in the 300 years of our existence. The Village Board appreciates WPA offers of help, but the members feel that the sister communities of Southampton, which sustained greater damage, should receive whatsoever assistance would have gone to us."

LABOR LAW CHANGE DEMANDED BY FREY

Its Administration 'Disrupting' Factor in Industry, He Tells Metal Trades Group

By The Associated Press.

HOUSTON, Texas, Sept. 26.—John P. Frey, chief of the A. F. of L. Metal Trades Department, attacked Federal regulation of wages and industrial relations today in his annual report to the metal trades conference, and called for greater cooperation between labor and industry.

Mr. Frey said that the trade union movement was founded on "self-government in industry instead of government by bureaus and administrators."

Congress, he declared, would do much to prevent recurring depressions by establishing "the proper and adequate rules under which business is to be conducted."

"Business and organized labor, through the conference room and collective bargaining, must then work out the problem of stable production and the economically sound division of the wealth being created," he said.

Mr. Frey's report criticized both the Wage-Hour Law and the National Labor Relations Act. The administration of the latter, he said, was a "disrupting" factor in American industry.

"Both the law and the personnel must be changed before the board under the Wagner act can constructively and sanely apply its authority to protect the right of wage-earners to be represented by organizations of their own choosing," he said.

The Wage-Hour Law, he continued, conferred "extraordinary authority" on the administrator amounting to "bureaucratic or commissar control."

Communist Activity Assailed

The metal trades chief also criticized the activity of Communists in the labor movement, the political ventures of the rival C. I. O. and its contributions to political campaigns.

In less specific terms, he struck at centralization of government authority, "college professors and theorists in administrative posts," and at a "super-intelligent, highly educated minority" he said was preaching that workers should trade their independence for security.

"Should the day come," he continued, "when American workmen, instead of depending upon themselves, depend upon outsiders for leadership and guidance, then American wage-earners will have lost their independence and their capacity for self-government."

Recalling some of the political activities of the C. I. O., Frey said:

"The definite entry of the C. I. O. into the political fields creates an issue which we cannot escape. The political activities of the C. I. O. have led many representatives in State Legislatures and in Congress to give more consideration to the probabilities of C. I. O. strength than the merits of the legislative measures coming to their attention.

"The nonpartisan political policy of the American Federation of Labor serves to indicate the most effective method of meeting this problem." (The federation's policy has been to reward its friends and punish its enemies regardless of party.)

The political expenditures of the C. I. O.'s United Mine Workers in the 1936 Democratic Presidential campaign and later in the 1938 Pennsylvania Democratic primary, Mr. Frey declared, "eclipsed all political records."

"Enormous Expenditures"

"These enormous campaign expenditures," he added, "are an evidence of what labor may expect if it is to indulge in partisan politics, a larger expenditure for political purposes than for all other trade union activities combined."

Reiterating some of his anti-communism testimony before the Dies House committee investigating un-American activities, Mr. Frey

Continued on Page Five

PREPARE TO FIGHT 'OLD GUARD' SLATE ON DEWEY TICKET

Republican Liberals Fear Move to Give All Other Places to Conservatives

SPRAGUE BOOM IS HINTED

Young Element in Party Hears He Is Talked for Long-Term Senate Nomination

By JAMES A. HAGERTY

Special to THE NEW YORK TIMES.

SARATOGA SPRINGS, Sept. 26.—Reports of a possible clash between the liberal and Old Guard elements in the Republican party over the nomination of candidates other than for Governor reached here tonight as the first of the delegates arrived for the opening of the State convention Wednesday.

There was no difference of opinion over the desirability of nominating District Attorney Thomas E. Dewey of New York County for Governor, but fear was expressed by some of the liberal faction that the conservative party leaders might try to name conservatives for the rest of the ticket.

This feeling is likely to be reflected at meetings of the board of governors of the State Association of Young Republican Clubs tomorrow afternoon and of the executive committee of the association tomorrow evening. The board of governors will confine itself to making suggestions for the platform while the executive committee will make recommendations concerning candidates.

The Young Republicans favor the nomination of Edward Corsi of Manhattan for the short Senatorial term. They are not wholly satisfied with all of those suggested for nomination for the full Senatorial term of six years.

Mentioned for Long Term

The word here is that J. Russell Sprague of Nassau County and Representative Bruce Barton of Manhattan are under consideration for this nomination in addition to Edward H. Butler, publisher of The Buffalo Evening News, and Jerome D. Barnum, publisher of The Syracuse Post-Standard.

District Attorney Alfred L. Simon of Saratoga County, president of the Association of Young Republican Clubs, has the support of this section for nomination for Attorney General. State Senator Benjamin F. Feinberg of Clinton County also has strong support for this nomination.

The boom for Assemblyman Jeremiah J. Wadsworth of Livingston County arrived tonight in the custody of Mark Welch, his campaign manager. State Senator Frederic H. Bontecou of Dutchess County also is a candidate for this nomination. Delegates from Western New York brought a boom for E. E. Holmquist, Jamestown furniture manufacturer, for the nomination for Controller.

Miss Katherine Kennedy, acting secretary of the Republican State Committee, was overwhelmed with requests for tickets of admission to the convention on her arrival.

There will be 1,936 delegates and the same number of alternates, in excess of 1,600 more than at any previous convention of the party, and the convention hall seats only

Continued on Page Four

Reich Is Accelerating Inflation of Currency

Wireless to THE NEW YORK TIMES.

BERLIN, Sept. 26.—Inflation of German currency is being accelerated alarmingly by military preparations. Contrary to the general rule for the third week in September the Reichsbank return for Sept. 23 shows a large increase in loans and a substantial rise in banknote and total circulation.

In consequence the Sept. 30 return will show a very serious inflation in the total.

On Sept. 23 the bills portfolio was 1,785,000,000 marks higher than in the same period in 1937. The note circulation was 2,078,000,000 marks higher, which means a 40 per cent rise in one year.

The total note circulation is 8,786,000,000 marks, against 6,565,000,000 marks for the same period in 1937. Reichsbank gold and exchange reserves show virtually no change.

3 NATIONS IN REPLY PRAISE ROOSEVELT

Germany Is Silent, but Czechs, British and French Send Notes—U. S. Cabinet Called

Replies by Benes, Chamberlain and Daladier are on Page 10.

Special to THE NEW YORK TIMES.

WASHINGTON, Sept. 26.—A Presidential call for a special meeting of the Cabinet tomorrow afternoon, "because of the existing situation," coupled with feverish activity at the State Department on behalf of Americans stranded in European danger zones, combined today to make official Washington keenly aware of the fast-developing war crisis in the wake of Chancellor Adolf Hitler's Berlin address.

At the White House and at the State Department, particularly, there was an obvious effort to present an appearance of calm in the face of an admittedly serious situation in Europe. President Roosevelt remained in his blue-paneled study in the White House, from which in the early hours this morning he authorized his appeal for peace to the European powers directly concerned.

Replies were received from the British, French and Czechoslovak Governments expressing gratification at President Roosevelt's eleventh-hour peace plea and they were relayed to the White House as quickly as they were received at the State Department. At the close of business for the day no reply had been received from the German Government, and officials did not know when to expect one.

[Advices from Berlin showed that no mention was made of Mr. Roosevelt's message in the German press and Herr Hitler did not mention it in his speech.]

Mr. Roosevelt conferred with

Continued on Page Ten

Geoghan, Angered by Rumors, Subpoenas Officials to Inquiry Into 'Corruption'

For the second time within two months, District Attorney William F. X. Geoghan of Brooklyn proceeded yesterday to conduct a personal investigation into rumors of "official corruption" involving a member of his office and this time centering about a fur swindle in which five policemen and four other persons have been indicted.

Making one of his rare appearances before a grand jury, Mr. Geoghan spent several hours in the afternoon interrogating three witnesses, including Police Inspector Michael F. McDermott. Afterward, he announced that he had issued grand jury subpoenas for the appearance today and tomorrow of William B. Herlands, Commissioner of Investigation, Chief City Magistrate Jacob Gould Schurman Jr., Magistrate Matthew J. Troy, S. Harvey Posner of the Citizens Committee for Crime Control, and "others reported to know something about this matter."

"Aspersions have been cast upon my office and I now propose to have a show-down," Mr. Geoghan, angered, declared. "With the aid of this grand jury, I am going to probe these charges of reported, or rumored, official corruption in connection with this case.

"I will subpoena every single person connected in any way with this matter. If anyone has anything to say, let him say it before this grand jury. I want it all on the record in black and white. I'm the prosecutor of this county and if there is anything to this I'll prosecute it to the limit."

Later in the day Mr. Geoghan announced that the investigation concerned Isidore Jaffe, 48 years old, of 332 East Fourteenth Street, Brooklyn, a suspect in the fur swindle, against whom grand larceny charges twice have been dismissed because of insufficient evidence, and who is alleged to have said that he was freed "because I paid plenty." Mr. Geoghan said that Jaffe had been an informer in the case and that he had made a statement recently denying the payment of money and explaining that he "was only trying to throw the others off the trail."

It was just two months ago that Mr. Geoghan, acting on the basis of rumors and unofficial charges, initiated a personal investigation into reports that one of his staff assistants had accepted a bribe of $100 to "fix" a perjury case. As a result William F. McGuinness, suspended assistant district attorney of Brooklyn, and George F. Murphy, city-employed elevator operator, recently were indicted for conspiracy to obstruct justice and are awaiting trial.

BENES IS ASSAILED

Hitler Says Czech State Was Conceived as Lie by 'Mad' Statesmen

SUDETENLAND ONLY CLAIM

Address Seen as Facade Behind Which Anything Can Happen —Oct. 1 Still Deadline

Text of Chancellor Hitler's speech is on Page 17.

By FREDERICK T. BIRCHALL

Wireless to THE NEW YORK TIMES.

BERLIN, Sept. 26.—For an hour tonight, facing directly an audience of 15,000 in the Sportspalast, Chancellor Hitler addressed the German people listening in by order at loudspeakers over all the land and his speech was far from being the expected defiance of British and French public opinion steadily rising against his Czechoslovak ultimatum.

Uncompromising in the matter of his demands for the evacuation of Sudeten German areas, he stressed equally his having agreed to a plebiscite in the disputed territories after German forces came into possession of them.

It was notable that Herr Hitler had really harsh words only for President Eduard Benes and the present Czechoslovak State, which he characterized as "conceived as a lie and conducted as a swindle for twenty years." The Czech people escaped vituperation and Herr Hitler addressed soothing phrases to the Poles, Ukrainians, Slovaks, French, British and even Hungarians, all of whom he reminded of his manifested desire to seek no quarrel with them.

It was almost as though, knowing himself about to take an action that would be universally reprehended, he sought in advance to create a friendlier atmosphere.

Last Territorial Demand

Twice he asserted that if the Sudeten territories were ceded this would be the last territorial demand Germany would make in Europe. There was no special emphasis on the last two words, but there might have been. Not once did Herr Hitler demand the alienation of the Czechoslovak State entirely.

While utterly uncompromising in his insistence that the Sudeten areas should be surrendered by Saturday he stressed the sweet reasonableness of this demand rather than the desire to acquire them forcibly. The Czech Government, he argued, had already consented to surrender the territories; he only wanted it to keep its word. The British and French had agreed to it and they should stand by their agreement.

The fact that his memorandum handed to Prime Minister Neville Chamberlain had extended beyond the original limits of the areas to be surrendered and that the conditions for evacuation were harsh and humiliating beyond any expectation, Herr Hitler ignored. He glossed over the demand for German military occupation of the disputed areas also pending and during the plebiscite stressing instead that he had granted Mr. Chamberlain's request to have an international commission manage the plebiscite.

Way Left Open for Hitler

The speech, in fact, while fervent and impassioned in the Hitler manner, left the impression on account of its very reticences that it was a facade behind which anything can happen without in the least controverting its contents. Herr Hitler can negotiate through France and Britain for a peaceful surrender or he can wait the prescribed period and then march in dealing as harshly as he chooses with the Czech resistance. Either way he will be consistent and he can claim and will probably receive the initial applause of his people.

It is common knowledge that Sir Horace Wilson of the British Foreign Office arrived by air from London bringing a message from Mr. Chamberlain that had the endorsement of the French ministers who had gone to London as well as the French Cabinet, and that Sir Horace was closeted with Herr Hitler for more than a half hour before his speech. The message, it is understood, was a final appeal not to close the door to negotiation

Continued on Page Twelve

Two British Declarations

By The Associated Press.

LONDON, Tuesday, Sept. 27.—Following are the texts of the authoritative statement issued yesterday on Britain's decision to join in defending Czechoslovakia in case of attack and of Prime Minister Chamberlain's statement early this morning replying to Chancellor Hitler's speech:

Statement of Policy

It is stated in official quarters that during the last week Prime Minister Chamberlain has tried with the German Chancellor to find a way of settling peacefully the Czechoslovak question.

It is still possible to do so by negotiation.

Germany's claim to transfer of the Sudeten areas has already been conceded by the French, British and Czechoslovak Governments.

But if, in spite of all efforts made by the British Prime Minister, a German attack is made upon Czechoslovakia, the immediate result must be that France will be bound to come to her assistance and Great Britain and Russia will stand by France.

It is still not too late to stop this great tragedy and for the peoples of all nations to insist on settlement by free negotiation.

Chamberlain Declaration

I have read the speech of Chancellor Hitler and I appreciate his reference to the efforts I have made to save peace.

I cannot abandon those efforts since it seems to me incredible that the peoples of Europe who do not want war with one another should be plunged into a bloody struggle over a question on which agreement has already been largely obtained.

It is evident that the Chancellor has no faith that the promises made will be carried out. These promises were made not to the German Government direct but to the British and French Governments in the first instance.

Speaking for the British Government, we regard ourselves as morally responsible for seeing that the promises are carried out fairly and fully and we are prepared to undertake that they shall be so carried out with all reasonable promptitude, provided that the German Government will agree to settlement of terms and conditions to the transfer by discussions and not by force.

I trust that the Chancellor will not reject this proposal, which is made in the same spirit of friendliness as that in which I was received in Germany and which if it is accepted will satisfy the German desire for union of the Sudeten Germans with the Reich without the shedding of blood in any part of Europe.

CZECHS RESIGNED AFTER HITLER TALK

No Hope Taken by the People From Speech—Officials Are Urged to Stand Fast

By G. E. R. GEDYE

Wireless to THE NEW YORK TIMES.

PRAGUE, Czechoslovakia, Sept. 26.—Knowledge that Chancellor Adolf Hitler would speak tonight hung like a thundercloud over the political atmosphere of this capital all day. Czechoslovakia had already rejected the Godesberg memorandum as furnishing no basis whatever for discussion, and it was felt quite possible that Herr Hitler's speech would contain an announcement that German troops would be ordered to attack Czechoslovakia.

People hurried from shops and offices with unusual speed for the comparative safety and security of their homes and far more than the usual number of gas masks were carried by civilians in the streets during the afternoon and evening.

The fact that Dr. Joseph Goebbels, German Propaganda Minister, with his well-known desire for war, introduced Herr Hitler tonight seemed at once an ominous sign. When the speech of the German Chancellor closed without a declaration of hostilities there was a slight relaxation of tension here. The relaxation, however, did not go very far because it is universally felt that the speech of Herr Hitler now makes war inevitable by Saturday.

Czechoslovakia Is Silent

It is not likely that there will be any official Czechoslovak reply to the speech, which, it is felt here, did nothing but repeat the Godesberg memorandum, with no important variations. That memorandum had already been rejected, and Czechoslovakia has nothing more to say.

There is full confidence that when the blow falls both of Czechoslovakia's allies, France and Russia, will fulfill their treaty obligations to the letter, as will her allies of the Little Entente, Rumania and Yugoslavia, should their intervention be necessary by reason of Hungary's participation in an attempt to wreck this country.

As for Britain, the news received here concerning last night's Cabinet sitting awakened a strong hope that she also would join her friends.

Meantime, until dusk falls with its uncannily darkened streets and pitch black windows, daily life continues almost normal in Prague. The virtually complete absence of taxicabs—perhaps six are plying in the entire city, but nobody sees them—makes it necessary to fight for a place in street cars, where Russian conditions prevail. The cars are packed from morning to night with passengers clinging to every inch of space, even on the steps.

For those who have no automobiles of their own, the street cars are now the only means of trans-

Continued on Page Fourteen

FRANCE SEES ISSUE DRAWN FOR HITLER

Ministers Say Chancellor Must Choose Now Between War and Peace

By P. J. PHILIP

Wireless to THE NEW YORK TIMES.

PARIS, Sept. 26.—From their London conference Premier Edouard Daladier and Foreign Minister Georges Bonnet returned this afternoon by air to find there was no necessity even for calling a Cabinet meeting before tomorrow morning. Events had spoken for themselves. There was no need to explain.

M. Daladier's reply to President Roosevelt, Prime Minister Neville Chamberlain's final appeal to Chancellor Adolf Hitler, the decision of Foreign Minister Georges Bonnet to summon at once the Council of the League of Nations if Czechoslovakia should be attacked, interviews that General Marie Gustave Gamelin, Chief of Staff of the French Army, had had, London warnings, preparations against air attack that are being made in Paris and finally Chancellor Hitler's speech all contributed to make the situation clear to every one. If Herr Hitler insists on having his way, he will have war. There is no other issue.

Opens Way for Russia

By deciding to summon at once the League Council, M. Bonnet is opening the way for Russian intervention with the consent of Rumania. The only uncertain element in today's doings, as far as the French public was concerned, was exactly what was contained in Mr. Chamberlain's appeal to Herr Hitler, which had been sent with M. Daladier's full approval. Everything else that had been done and said seemed to point to war.

London reports late today of a proposal to Herr Hitler to negotiate with the Czechoslovaks and a warning that if he does not reach a satisfactory settlement and tries force, Great Britain and Russia will automatically join France in protection of Czechoslovak independence, swiftly changed the outlook. Even Chancellor Hitler's speech was found, in the light of these new reports, to read somewhat differently than it had sounded. There were significant omissions. It will not be until his reply, which Sir Horace Wilson is taking to London tomorrow, is made public, that any one can be quite sure, if even then.

Fears of the general public who heard or read Herr Hitler's speech concurred that it looked like war. In inner circles of those engaged in this immense diplomatic game it is still hoped, even believed, that inch by inch the German leader can be forced from his position.

No one here has any quarrel with the German people. It is the Nazi system, personified in Hitler, Goering and Goebbels that is the enemy of what France believes in. If some check can be interposed to that system without war, then so much the

Continued on Page Fourteen

ENTENTE REVIVING

London Warns It Will Share Defense With Paris and Moscow

APPEALS TO HITLER ANEW

Offers to Enforce the Cession Pledge of Czechs—Meeting of Parliament Tomorrow

Britain announced last night that she and Russia "will certainly stand by France" if that nation should go to the defense of Czechoslovakia. This information was not delivered to Herr Hitler before his speech but a personal note from Prime Minister Chamberlain was given to him urging further negotiations. Mr. Chamberlain announced he would see that Sudeten territory was transferred to Germany fairly if she did not go to war.

Herr Hitler refrained from defiance in his speech to the German people. He was uncompromising in his demands for annexation of Sudeten territory and threatened to take it if surrender was denied but was believed to have left the door open to negotiations.

Czechoslovakia gave no indication that she would make a reply to Herr Hitler's speech, and the people resigned themselves to the worst. It was felt in Prague that the speech made war inevitable by Saturday.

The French Premier and Foreign Minister, on their return from London, declared the issue had boiled down simply to whether Hitler wanted war. If Germany should attack, the League Council is to be convened to give Russia a chance to intervene with Rumania's consent.

President Roosevelt called a special session of the Cabinet for today "because of the existing situation" and the State Department rushed activities in getting Americans out of Europe. [All the above dispatches on Page 1.]

Premier Mussolini appealed to Britain and France to abandon Czechoslovakia before it was too late. [Page 16.]

Germans and French strung barbed wire along the Rhine and challenging signs were erected on both sides. [Page 14.]

Britain Is Pledged to Fight

By FERDINAND KUHN Jr.

Special Cable to THE NEW YORK TIMES.

LONDON, Tuesday, Sept. 27.—The British Government took its most momentous decision in twenty years yesterday by accepting a clear-cut military commitment in case of German aggression against the Czechoslovak Republic.

An authoritative statement came from Downing Street last night that if a German attack was made against Czechoslovakia "the immediate result must be that France will be bound to come to her assistance and Great Britain and Russia will certainly stand by France."

So at the eleventh hour and as a last resort the hesitations of the past months and years have been wiped away. Prime Minister Neville Chamberlain's carefully qualified warning to Germany on March 24 and that of Sir John Simon, Chancellor of the Exchequer, last month have been swept into the forgotten past by the rush of tremendous events.

Triple Entente Revived

From now on France knows she can count definitely, without quibbles and evasions, upon British help if she springs to the defense of Czechoslovakia. Britain has had to swallow her dislike of Continental commitments and by an odd twist of history Conservative Britain and Bolshevist Russia will find themselves, if war now begins, allied once more in spite of all their mutual antipathies of the past twenty years.

In other words, if Chancellor Hitler fulfills last night's threat to "go" and liberate our Germans" in Czechoslovakia he will find himself confronting a revival of the old Triple Entente.

There is one big "if" in the decision taken by the united British Cabinet early yesterday morning and approved by the heads of the British and French Governments later in the day. The new alignment of Britain, France and Russia

Continued on Page Sixteen

"All the News That's Fit to Print."

The New York Times.

LATE CITY EDITION
Generally fair, cooler today. Tomorrow cloudy, probably followed by rain; temperature unchanged.
Temperatures Yesterday—Max., 73; Min., 54

Copyright, 1938, by The New York Times Company.

VOL. LXXXVIII...No. 29,468. Entered as Second-Class Matter, Postoffice, New York, N. Y. NEW YORK, THURSDAY, SEPTEMBER 29, 1938. PPP THREE CENTS NEW YORK CITY and Vicinity | FOUR CENTS Elsewhere Except in 7th and 8th Postal Zones.

HITLER HALTS WAR MOVES, CALLS 4-POWER CONFERENCE; MEETS MUSSOLINI, CHAMBERLAIN AND DALADIER TODAY; MUNICH TALK MAY COVER WHOLE EUROPEAN SITUATION

DEWEY SLATE HITS CONVENTION SNAG; KEY POSTS IN DOUBT

Barton and Heck, at Opening Session, Score New Deal on 'Vote Buying' and 'Waste'

LEHMAN UNDER PRESSURE

Farley Says He Will Be Drafted —Hoover in West Backs Roosevelt Peace Plan

The Republican State Convention opened with a snag developing over completing the Dewey slate. Bruce Barton and Oswald D. Heck condemned the New Deal on "vote buying" and as failing to solve the unemployment problem. [Page 1.]

At Rochester, on the eve of the Democratic State convention, the leaders were exerting all their pressure to induce Governor Lehman to run again and Chairman Farley expressed the opinion that the convention would draft him. [Page 21].

Herbert Hoover in a speech in Kansas City backed President Roosevelt's peace efforts, but attacked his home policies. [Page 22.]

Senator Vandenberg told the Michigan League of Women voters that the "yes-but-man" was the essential factor in a system of "nonpartisan politics" that he asserted would be a strengthening element in the development of the two major parties. [Page 23.]

Speeches at the Republican Convention, Pages 18, 19; Hoover's Kansas City speech, Page 22.

State Republicans Meet

By JAMES A. HAGERTY

Special to THE NEW YORK TIMES.

SARATOGA SPRINGS, Sept. 28.—With complete agreement on District Attorney Dewey as the candidate for Governor, the slate makers at the Republican State Convention struck a snag today when Mayor Rolland B. Marvin of Syracuse refused to be drafted for the nomination for the long Senatorial term.

Concurrently, a difference of opinion developed between Kenneth F. Simpson, New York County chairman and national committeeman, and Edwin F. Jaeckle, Erie County leader, and there was a revolt of a minority of the Brooklyn delegation, who expressed opposition to the candidates for the nomination for Controller suggested by John R. Crews, Brooklyn leader.

Agreement seemed to have been reached on the nomination of Edward Corsi of Manhattan for the short Senatorial term, to fill the vacancy caused by the death of Senator Royal S. Copeland, and on the nomination of Richard B. Scandrett Jr. of Orange County and Mrs. Helen Rogers of Buffalo for Representatives at Large. The selection of candidates for the long Senatorial term, Lieutenant Governor, Attorney General and Controller awaited the results of further conferences to be held after the night session of the convention.

The name of Jerome D. Barnum, publisher of The Syracuse Post-Standard, was the only one mentioned for the long Senatorial term nomination after it became known that Mayor Marvin had repeatedly refused efforts to draft him.

Marvin Favors Present Posts

Mr. Marvin is under commitment to serve the three remaining years of his Mayoralty term. He also is the head of the Onondaga Republican organization, and is reported to be reluctant to leave these two positions.

The nomination of Mr. Barnum, understood to be opposed to any possible alliance with the American Labor party, would not be satisfactory to sponsors of Mr. Dewey's candidacy, it was said.

Mayor Marvin this evening called members of the Onondaga County delegation together for a conference. He said at midnight that his position was unchanged and that he would not take the nomination for Senator. Reluctant to lose him, those back of Mr. Dewey's candidacy will make a further effort tomorrow to get him to run. In case of failure, the indications tonight were that the nomination would go to Mr. Barnum.

No meeting of the executive committee of the State committee was held tonight and the conferences which went on were confined to a small number of the party leaders. Resentment among the delegates and leaders of the less populous counties increased as no apparent progress was made in agreeing on a ticket, and a meeting of the county chairmen of rural counties was called for tomorrow morning in the Grand Union Hotel at which it is expected that protests will be

Continued on Page Eighteen

Gain of 369,000 Jobs Shown in August Survey

The National Industrial Conference Board reported yesterday that 10,590,000 workers were unemployed in August, a drop of 369,000 from the July total. This estimate included as unemployed 3,475,000 workers in the WPA, Civilian Conservation Corps and other government works agencies.

The hiring of 338,000 additional workers in manufacturing helped increase total national employment to 43,453,000, or 422,000 above the July figure. Construction employment rose by 126,000, transportation 12,000, forestry and fishing 5,000 and agriculture 3,000, according to the report.

Declines of 41,000 in employment in the service industries and of 32,000 in trade, distribution and finance were recorded.

TRUCK PEACE NEAR; MANY OWNERS SIGN

Only the Out-of-Town Haulers Still Oppose Mayor's Plan—Shipments Move Again

An end of the two weeks' strike of 15,000 truck drivers today was expected last night when the Merchant Truckmen's Bureau, representing local operators, voted to accept the compromise terms of Mayor La Guardia. The Highway Transport Association, representing long-distance haulers, voted to reject the terms, but decided later to defer action until today.

The Highway Transport Association adopted a five-point resolution to send a committee to see Mayor La Guardia this morning, to defer action meanwhile on the Mayor's compromise, to register a vote of confidence in its wage scale committee, to draw up as soon as possible a new contract to be submitted to the Mayor and to meet again this evening at 8 o'clock. At the second meeting the long-distance haulers rescinded their rejection of the Mayor's plan.

The operators, who earlier in the day had declared they would stand pat "until hell freezes over," quickly came to terms after Mayor La Guardia had appeared at a joint meeting of the two groups at the Hotel Capitol, Eighth Avenue and Fifty-first Street.

The Mayor appealed to the operators to end the dispute, told them that disaffections in their ranks had resulted in separate agreements releasing 2,500 trucks during the day and, incidentally, admitted that he had no desire to continue "in the trucking business," referring to his emergency mobilization of 800 obsolete trucks of the Department of Sanitation.

Offers to Name Committee

The Mayor's appearance before the operators apparently turned the tide in favor of a settlement. He offered to appoint a fact-finding committee to study economic and other factors in the trucking industry and to make recommendations on wages and working conditions. Furthermore, the Mayor was able to cite the widespread response of truck operators to sign separate agreements following the appeal he made to the operators when their organizations rejected his compromise offer.

As a result of these disaffections the movement of commerce had resumed to such an extent that merchants reported increasing shipments and Port Authority executives noted a rise in truck traffic through the Holland Tunnel.

The compromise plan which the Mayor submitted late Monday night provides among other things for a forty-four-hour week at the rate of forty-seven hours' pay. The strikers originally demanded a forty-hour week at forty-seven hours' pay.

Decide to Vote Separately

The Merchant Truckmen's Bureau and the Highway Transport Association, which had met jointly 500 strong to consider every proposal up to last night, finally decided to vote separately on the Mayor's compromise terms. At the time of the division their number had dwindled to about 300 and of that number only half cast ballots. The ballot of the Merchant Truckmen's Bureau totaled about eighty.

The bureau's members accepted the Mayor's terms, it was learned, after their joint wage scale committee of nineteen had been reduced to four members by disaffections. The four members of the "old guard" who stood pat were P. J. Murphy, president; Arthur G. McKeever, managing director; Ted Ficke, past president, and Hugh E. Sheridan, chairman of the joint wage scale committee.

The end of the strike was assured when the United States Trucking Corporation and other important operators announced soon after Mayor La Guardia's address that they would follow the lead of Daniels & Kennedy and hundreds of other operators who already had signed separate agreements with the International Brotherhood of

Continued on Page Twenty-six

BERLIN IS RELIEVED

Hopes Talks on Czechs May Lead to Wider European Accord

ROOSEVELT PLEA A FACTOR

Hitler Described as Desirous of Removing Parley From 'Benes Atmosphere'

By GUIDO ENDERIS

Wireless to THE NEW YORK TIMES.

BERLIN, Sept. 28.—Announcement today of the four-power conference in Munich tomorrow followed a day of high-pressure diplomatic exchanges and long-distance telephone calls between Berlin, London, Paris and Rome. It burst in upon the stagnant political atmosphere like a freshening breeze.

The circumstances under which the four Premiers will meet is not unlike that existing when Neville Chamberlain, the British Prime Minister, undertook his dramatic flight to Berchtesgaden.

With the German ultimatum nearing its deadline it was recognized that the statesmen concerned with the Czech crisis were largely talking past each other and that only a frank, intimate exchange across a conference table gave promise of breaking the deadlock.

Chancellor Adolf Hitler was reported determined not only to react to Mr. Chamberlain's appeal but to expand the British Prime Minister's suggestion by making further conversations a four-power affair.

Roosevelt's Plea a Factor

There were other factors, too, that pressed for early inter-governmental action. One of decisive weight, it was admitted here, was President Roosevelt's second appeal to Chancellor Hitler, which reached Berlin early this morning.

In view of the atmosphere of recrimination engendered by foreign and German press controversies over the German memorandum, the proposal that the four statesmen meet provoked no surprise in Berlin diplomatic quarters. It was realized that important time had been lost through the fruitless Hitler-Chamberlain negotiations at Berchtesgaden and Godesberg.

The outcome of those negotiations, it now seems, contributed to making the Czech crisis even more complicated and acrimonious. Charges that Czech mobilization was undertaken at British instigation also provoked irritation here.

Meanwhile Herr Hitler watched developments with a calm born of unconcern, convinced that the German case was securely grounded and that Great Britain would not abandon her peace initiative merely because of conflicting interpretations of the German memorandum,

Continued on Page Six

Chamberlain Off to Reich; Cites 'Try, Try, Try Again'

By The Associated Press.

HESTON AIRPORT, London, Thursday, Sept. 29.—Prime Minister Neville Chamberlain took off for the Munich four-power conference at 8:35 o'clock this morning (2:35 A. M. in New York).

Most of the Cabinet and a large crowd cheered him. Like admiring schoolboys, the Ministers had brought a gift of fruit for him to eat en route on this third journey to Chancellor Adolf Hitler in the cause of peace.

Standing outside his plane, the Prime Minister said:

"When I was a little boy, I used to repeat: 'If at first you don't succeed, try, try, try again.' That's what I'm doing."

BRENNER PASS, Thursday, Sept. 29 (AP).—Premier Benito Mussolini and his Foreign Minister, Count Galeazzo Ciano, arrived here today by special train at 6:08 A. M. (12:08 A. M. in New York) on their way to Munich. They were greeted by Rudolf Hess, Chancellor Hitler's deputy in party affairs. An hour later the train continued toward Munich.

PARIS, Thursday, Sept. 29 (AP).—Premier Edouard Daladier, accompanied by his staff, left Le Bourget Field by airplane today at 8:45 A. M. (2:45 A. M. in New York) for Munich.

CZECHS SUSPICIOUS OF MUNICH PARLEY

Fear Four-Power Accord at Their Expense—Hope Hitler Simply Aims to Save Face

By G. E. R. GEDYE

Wireless to THE NEW YORK TIMES.

PRAGUE, Czechoslovakia, Sept. 28.—Prime Minister Neville Chamberlain's speech tonight and the forthcoming conference in Munich had a mixed reception here. In official circles a reserved attitude was maintained.

For years what Europe's small nations that have remained outside the German orbit have most dreaded is a four-power pact in which the so-called Western democracies would in the end find themselves led by the nose by the two Fascist powers. This four-power conference looks to Czechoslovak eyes alarmingly like that.

An early release of the Czechoslovak News Agency tonight labeled it the "Fuehrer Conference," an innocent misprint, which was corrected subsequently to the "Vierer Conference," or Conference of Four.

There is another interpretation that seems not without foundation—that Chancellor Adolf Hitler and the Nazi party find themselves losing the war within their own

Continued on Page Seventeen

Italy Reported Forsaking General Franco; Angry at His Neutrality in Czech Quarrel

Wireless to THE NEW YORK TIMES.

ROME, Sept. 28.—In connection with the other problems now confronting Europe, a report circulated in Rome today that, although still lacking confirmation and indeed officially denied, nevertheless is worth noticing.

It was stated that the Italian Government, incensed at Generalissimo Francisco Franco's declaration of absolute neutrality in the present European crisis, had decided to withdraw all Italian troops from Spain immediately. Some reports even went as far as to say the first contingents were already on their way back.

It is obviously useless, say many indignant Italians, to continue spending Italian money and shedding Italian blood in Spain if Italy cannot count on General Franco in an hour of need.

All such reports must be accepted with the greatest prudence, since Italy is heavily committed in Spain and can scarcely afford to see General Franco lose. Nevertheless, Italian enthusiasm for the Spanish venture has waned noticeably of late. Hence it is not to be excluded that some compromise solution may be broached at the conference in Munich, Germany, tomorrow.

The offer of the Spanish Premier, Dr. Juan Negrin, to withdraw all foreign volunteers on the Loyalist side seems to offer a possible starting point for negotiations aiming at the institution of a constitutional monarchy in Spain with definite safeguards for the two warring parties.

Elimination of the Spanish question would have the immediate advantage for Italy of permitting application of the Anglo-Italian agreement and facilitating the resumption of Italo-French negotiations. It is deemed significant, in any case, that the Italian Foreign Minister, Count Galeazzo Ciano, before his departure for Munich, had a long conversation with the Spanish Ambassador here.

Wireless to THE NEW YORK TIMES.

GENEVA, Sept. 28.—In the League of Nations Assembly's political committee tonight the request of the Spanish Premier, Dr. Juan Negrin, for a League Commission to verify the withdrawal of non-Spanish combatants from the Loyalist army hit a snag.

The British and French agreed to it on the condition, which Spain accepted, that this should not prevent the London Non-Intervention Committee later from sending its committee to both sides for the same purpose if Generalissimo Francisco Franco ever accepted its plan. Portugal, Albania and Poland, however, opposed even this and insisted that only the Non-Intervention Committee should act in this respect.

DUCE SWAYS HITLER

Persuades Him by Phone to Delay Mobilizing and Join Parley

HEEDS CHAMBERLAIN PLEA

Appeal by Roosevelt Is Also Delivered to Mussolini—Italian Hopes Soar

By ARNALDO CORTESI

Wireless to THE NEW YORK TIMES.

ROME, Sept. 28.—The war clouds hanging over Europe were torn asunder in dramatic fashion this morning and admitted a pale ray of sunshine when Premier Benito Mussolini had a long personal telephone conversation with Chancellor Adolf Hitler of Germany and prevailed upon him to postpone German mobilization and give his adherence to a conference in Munich at noon tomorrow among Prime Minister Neville Chamberlain of Britain, Premier Edouard Daladier of France, Herr Hitler and Signor Mussolini himself.

Premier Mussolini telephoned the German Chancellor after the first of two calls by the Earl of Perth, the British Ambassador to Rome, on Count Galeazzo Ciano, the Italian Foreign Minister. On his first visit Lord Perth delivered the following message to Signor Mussolini from Mr. Chamberlain:

> I have today addressed an appeal to Chancellor Hitler to abstain from the use of force to solve the Sudeten problem, which I feel sure could be solved by means of a brief discussion while giving him essential territory, population and the protection of both Sudetens and Czechs during the transference.
>
> I offered to go myself to Berlin to discuss a compromise with the German and Czech representatives and, if the Chancellor so desires, also with the representatives of Italy and France.
>
> I trust that Your Excellency will inform the German Chancellor that you are willing to be represented and will exhort him to adhere to my suggestions. I have guaranteed that the Czech promises will be carried out and I am confident that complete agreement could be reached within a week.

Roosevelt Appeal Received

William Phillips, the United States Ambassador, was received by Premier Mussolini at 4 o'clock this afternoon and delivered a personal message from President Roosevelt. It is understood that Signor Mussolini expressed his appreciation of the President's efforts on behalf of peace and declared himself happy to be able to announce that a solution in accordance with Mr. Roosevelt's suggestion had already been adopted with the decision to hold the Anglo-French-Italian-German conference in Munich tomorrow.

[A summary issued by Stefani, official Italian news agency, said, according to The Associated Press, that the President in his message, "after having recalled efforts exerted by him to assure a peaceful solution of the German-Czechoslovak conflict and after having emphasized the tragic consequences that a European war would have for every one, asked Il Duce to lend his aid to settle the controversy by negotiation or other peaceful means and without recourse to force."]

Lord Perth first called on Count Ciano at 10 A. M. and then at noon. As Signor Mussolini's telephone conversation with Herr Hitler occurred between the two visits, Count Ciano was able to inform the British Ambassador on the second that Signor Mussolini had induced Herr Hitler to agree to a conference.

Signor Mussolini assured Herr Hitler personally, as well as through an official step through the Italian Ambassador to Berlin, that Italy was ready to stand by her pledges to Germany but begged him not to disregard the opportunity Mr. Chamberlain offered for getting what he wanted without using violence.

The Italian Premier left for Munich by special train at 6 o'clock this evening accompanied by Count Ciano.

The wave of hopefulness that swept over Italy when this news became known is heightened by reports that Signor Mussolini succeeded in inducing Herr Hitler not only to meet Mr. Chamberlain and

Continued on Page Nine

German Liners Are Called Home; Thousands of Tourists Stranded

Other Lines Take as Many as Possible—2,000 on the Washington—Freighter Slips From Puerto Rico and Eludes a Cutter

Germany withdrew the far-flung tentacles of her mercantile marine yesterday in a drastic move that threw shipping on the Atlantic into unprecedented confusion, turned liners around at sea and sent two vessels out from New York Harbor empty, before all their prospective passengers could be warned.

With other steamship companies altering schedules on a moment's notice in efforts to accommodate stranded passengers and shipping on extra cots, lifebelts and other equipment required by international safety laws, the entire industry was in a state of disruption unknown here since the World War.

There was no explanation of the recall either abroad or here. Local shipping officials, long accustomed to soldierly discharge of orders from the Reich Government, said they knew only that the order had been issued and had been complied with as quickly as circumstances permitted. It was construed here as an attempt to get the fleet into safe German harbors to avoid possible repetition of the elimination of the German merchant marine in the World War.

All the way across the Atlantic, from the North Sea to America, ships are either plowing along on their usual courses devoid of passengers and carrying only such cargoes as could be shipped at the last moment or are retracing their courses and omitting ports that in more peaceful times are regularly on their schedules.

The first ship affected was the 50,000-ton express liner Europa, which turned around in the English Channel before reaching Cherbourg and Southampton and hurried back toward Bremerhaven, leaving hundreds of passengers waiting on piers in the French and English ports.

Her sister ship, the Bremen, had sailed from New York at 12:25 A. M. yesterday, on schedule. At the end of the day, however, the recall order had been extended to the entire fleet of the German lines with a few exceptions in which execution of the order was impossible.

Early yesterday morning, after a few hours of hurried preparation, the Hamburg-American liner Hansa steamed out of New York, leaving

Continued on Page Twelve

WASHINGTON'S HOPE FOR PEACE MOUNTS

Roosevelt Made Final Plea to Hitler on Hearing Reich Might March Yesterday

Special to THE NEW YORK TIMES.

WASHINGTON, Sept. 28.—Upon receiving official confirmation through diplomatic channels of the summoning of the four-power conference at Munich tomorrow, the White House, through Stephen T. Early, secretary to the President, said today that the meeting "offers great hope and encouragement."

This was the one definite Administration comment on the development, but the relief here was evidenced in a relaxation of the tension that had gripped the government. For the first time in several days it was really believed that the grave danger of war could be averted.

Mr. Early revealed that President Roosevelt had decided upon his final plea to Chancellor Hitler for peace last night after having received press and radio reports that Germany might march into the Sudeten area of Czechoslovakia today. There was no official confirmation, but Mr. Roosevelt felt that he should make his last effort then or never. If the troops marched today it would be too late.

Stresses No Involvements

It was also disclosed by Mr. Early that the President's suggestion for a conference to decide the detailed questions at issue would enlarge the negotiations to include Poland, Russia and Hungary. At the same time Mr. Early stressed that the United States has no involvements in Europe.

According to Mr. Early the President decided to send his plea early last night during a two-hour conference on the day's developments with Secretary of State Cordell Hull and Sumner Welles, Under-Secretary of State.

Previously, at his late afternoon press conference, the President had rather indicated that there would be no developments during the night, but the unofficial reports of possible German military movements this morning decided his course. When he reached his decision he dictated the telegram instead of writing it in longhand, as he did his earlier peace appeal that was dispatched early Monday morning.

This illustrates, Mr. Early said, how closely the President has watched the situation by reading press dispatches and listening to the radio when he was confined to the Executive Mansion by a head cold.

"It is a great advantage," Mr. Early said, "to have the President sitting in the White House Mansion in a rather detached way, and his cold, therefore, has been a blessing."

There was no attempt here today to forecast what the result of the Munich conversations would be.

Continued on Page Eight

FRENCH NOW WANT SOLID PEACE BASIS

Nation Firmer Toward Hitler —Mussolini Moves Watched —Many Abandon Paris

By P. J. PHILIP

Wireless to THE NEW YORK TIMES.

PARIS, Thursday, Sept. 29.—How will they line up, two and two or three and one? Is Premier Eduard Daladier of France strong enough to carry this immense argument? In which camp will Premier Benito Mussolini of Italy be? Will Chancellor Adolf Hitler scream, as he did at Berchtesgaden? Will it bring real peace?

All these and a thousand other questions poured out in an unceasing stream yesterday as bit by bit the news leaked out in France that this ever-towering crisis, which has seemed each day certain to crash in a great welter of blood and ruin, had shot up to a new pinnacle with hope perched higher than ever.

And now what? After these successive days crowded with events, with their alternating hopes and fears, even peace will seem an anticlimax. To satisfy France in her present grim mood it must at least be a real peace, such a peace of confidence as there is between Britain and France or between France and the United States. Is that possible with Adolf Hitler and Benito Mussolini in power in their respective countries with Nazi and Fascist systems?

Daladier Must Be Wary

M. Daladier will have to go warily. His people are not trustful by nature—and, perhaps, with cause. And yet it is realized that the French Premier cannot go to this conference with nothing to offer. There must be something for Signor Mussolini, whose ways have seemed devious, but to whom in the end and for whatever cause a debt of gratitude seems due for yesterday's action.

There must be something for Herr Hitler, if only a Roman triumph in a Mercedes car through the winding streets of Karlsbad, Czechoslovakia. M. Daladier is big enough to do it, but he will need Prime Minister Neville Chamberlain's protecting shadow if he is to bring back honor with peace in a manner sufficient to satisfy even some of his immediate colleagues.

What comes first, of course, is a settlement of the Sudeten issue. There the line-up seems almost certain to be three to one, for Signor Mussolini knows that anything more than the first Anglo-French settlement proposal will mean the Czechs will fight, and the chances that such a war might be localized are very small. He has other reasons, some of which go back to the annexation of Austria and others that look forward to the future and the necessity of doing a service for those who have something to give.

Can Herr Hitler, who has never gone back from what he said he would, do so now? That is the great question of tomorrow. Signor

Continued on Page Thirteen

COMMONS JUBILANT

Chamberlain's News of a Delay by Hitler on Czechs Stirs Bedlam

FINAL PLEAS SUCCESSFUL

Mussolini and Roosevelt Are Credited—Germany Warned She Would Attack Today

As Prime Minister Chamberlain was delivering a grave speech to the House of Commons yesterday two slips of paper were handed to him that bore tidings which instantly dispelled the war clouds hanging over Europe. The slips related that Chancellor Hitler had agreed to meet Mr. Chamberlain, Premier Daladier and Premier Mussolini at Munich today for a peace conference, and meanwhile had deferred his war measures.

This development resulted from a Chamberlain appeal to Herr Hitler, a second Roosevelt appeal to the Chancellor and especially from an appeal by Mr. Chamberlain to Signor Mussolini. The Italian Premier promptly got in touch with the Chancellor and begged him not to disregard the opportunity for peace.

There was talk in Rome that the Munich conference would range over the entire European situation, including Spain, and also that Signor Mussolini might forsake the cause of the Spanish Insurgents.

Washington was hopeful. It was revealed in the capital that President Roosevelt had sent a personal message to Premier Mussolini asking his intervention.

Berlin was relieved by the new turn, as was Paris, but the French are insistent that a real settlement must develop out of the four-power talks. Prague was suspicious, fearing that a settlement would be at its expense.

Meanwhile, as a result of German action in recalling merchant ships, many of which sailed swiftly without passengers, the Atlantic tourist trade was thrown into confusion.

[All the above dispatches on Page 1.]

The stock market here reacted to the good news in Europe with gains of 1 to 4 points. [Page 7.]

Mr. Chamberlain's speech is printed on Page 14; British White Paper, Pages 16-17.

Hitler Agrees to Parley

By FERDINAND KUHN Jr.

Special Cable to THE NEW YORK TIMES.

LONDON, Thursday, Sept. 29.—Prime Minister Neville Chamberlain won the greatest and sweetest triumph of his life yesterday when he suddenly announced to a wildly cheering House of Commons that Chancellor Adolf Hitler had summoned a four-power meeting for today at Munich, Germany, to find a peaceful way out of the Czech crisis.

A "last last" appeal from Mr. Chamberlain to Herr Hitler and another to Premier Benito Mussolini, together with the second message from President Roosevelt, had produced the desired result in Berlin when all hope of averting war appeared lost. It came only twenty-four hours after Herr Hitler had sent word to London that Germany would mobilize yesterday and march across the Czech frontier today unless his demands upon Czechoslovakia were fulfilled.

Instead Mr. Chamberlain is flying to Munich this morning and hopes to meet Herr Hitler, Signor Mussolini and Premier Edouard Daladier of France about midday. The same advisers who went to Godesberg are accompanying Mr. Chamberlain, with the addition of Frank Ashton-Gwatkin, the expert who served with Viscount Runciman's mediatory mission in Prague.

Whether the meeting at Munich succeeds or not, there was a strong belief throughout Britain today that Europe might soon awaken from its nightmare. Relief and thankfulness without parallel since the Armistice swept the country at the

Continued on Page Fifteen

"All the News That's Fit to Print."

The New York Times.

LATE CITY EDITION
Mostly cloudy, not quite so cool today. Tomorrow probably fair with moderate temperatures.
Temperatures Yesterday—Max., 48; Min., 44

VOL. LXXXVIII...No. 29,680. Entered as Second-Class Matter, Postoffice, New York, N. Y. NEW YORK, SATURDAY, APRIL 29, 1939. P THREE CENTS

HITLER SAYS NO TO ROOSEVELT, INSISTS ON DANZIG; SCRAPS POLISH, BRITISH NAVAL AND MUNICH PACTS; WARSAW DEFIANT; ITALY MAY END LONDON TREATY

MOSCOW AVIATORS DOWN IN CANADA; RELIEF IS RUSHED

One Flier Hurt and Plane Is Badly Damaged in Landing on New Brunswick Marsh

ON DASH TO NEW YORK

Mishap in Northern Wilds Comes After 23 Hours and 40 Minutes in the Air

By Telephone to THE NEW YORK TIMES.

MISCOU PLAIN, N. B., April 28.—Forced down on their flight over the Arctic Circle route from Moscow to New York, Colonel Vladimir Kokkinaki and his co-pilot, Major Mikhail Gordienko, Soviet airmen, wrecked their twin-motored monoplane in landing in a marsh five miles from this village on Miscou Island, northeasternmost point of the Province of New Brunswick.

Clearing the ice covering Chaleur Bay on the west and the Gulf of St. Lawrence on the east, the airmen found a landing spot on the snow-covered marsh to bring their flight to a halt, but in making the landing both right and left wings were smashed, the two propellers shattered and one of the two engines was torn from the fuselage.

One of the fliers was injured in landing, but it was believed that he was not badly hurt. He made light of his injury, indicating that it was only a broken rib and, with the aid of his comrade, made himself comfortable in an improvised bed beside the wrecked plane, sheltered from the frozen marshland by a single blanket. It was cold, but not severely so.

The fliers had made their presence known to the residents of this hamlet and others of the 1,200 on Miscou Island by circling before landing. Their motors sputtered as if they were having engine trouble or were running short of fuel. It was thought at first, because they were flying so low, that they might land here, but they continued on.

Inhabitant Finds Plane

When the big red plane swung down toward the marsh and it was apparent the fliers were going to land, Lawrence Vibert of this village set out to find them. He discovered them on the marsh, five miles from the village, resting beside their plane. Vibert was unable to speak to them, however, for the fliers spoke only Russian.

For several minutes Vibert tried to make himself understood in English and French and the Russians attempted to talk with him in their native tongue. Gesticulating, the uninjured airman at last hauled out a map and showed Vibert that the plane had flown from Moscow along a course set out on the paper and that it was due in New York at 8 P. M. The plane had been 23 hours 40 minutes in the air.

Vibert, by gestures, attempted to get the fliers to leave their wrecked plane in the desolate marsh and come to his house for shelter. Both pilots gestured that they would remain on guard beside their plane, and the injured man, lying on the frozen ground in his improvised bed, indicated that he was comfortable so long as he did not attempt to move.

Returning to the village, Vibert telephoned to Miss Jeannette Newton, telephone operator at Shippigan, a railroad trunk station on the mainland twenty-five miles from here, and reported his discovery. Loading up with food and fuel and blankets at his house, he started trudging back to the plane, intending to stay through the night with the airmen.

Vibert said as far as he could discover the men had a single blanket and no tent or other material to afford shelter from the cold.

Stay to Guard Plane

It was believed the men were remaining by their plane to guard it, as the injured flier did not indicate that he felt he was hurt too badly to be moved by villagers, who were ready to send out a stretcher for him. However, no medical aid could be sent to the men as Dr. A. Robichaud of Shippigan (the nearest physician) would have to cross two dangerous ice-covered strips of water and two islands to reach them.

A rescue party headed by Constable Marcel Therriault of the Royal Canadian Mounted Police, stationed at Shippigan, will escort Dr. Robichaud to the scene at dawn. Once the party takes the men off the island, they will be able to go from Shippigan to the railroad terminal at Bathurst and thence down to Moncton and St. Johns.

The end of the flight in this section of the Canadian wilds was caused by lack of knowledge of the terrain, the same cause which prevented several Moscow-New York airmen, flying the Pacific route, from reaching their destination non-stop. Colonel Kokkinaki and

Continued on Page Two

Daylight-Saving Time Starts At 2 Tomorrow Morning

Daylight-saving time will go into effect at 2 A. M., Eastern standard time, tomorrow. Before retiring many New Yorkers will turn their clocks and watches forward one hour.

More than 30,000,000 persons in the United States are affected by the time change, of whom about 10,000,000 are in New York. Daylight saving will continue in effect until the last Sunday in September, when the lost hour of sleep will be regained.

As has been the custom in past years, most railroad time-tables will continue to show Eastern standard time, while nearly all the trains will be changed an hour to conform to the new daylight time. The Long Island Railroad, however, will operate all its trains on the new time.

THRONGS ARRIVING FOR START OF FAIR

Incoming Travel Rises, Hotels Filling Up With Visitors for Opening Fete

The advance guard of World's Fair visitors began to trickle through New York's railroad terminals, bridges and tunnels yesterday, with indications that many thousands would arrive today, tonight and tomorrow morning for Sunday's official opening.

With the Weather Bureau predicting "probably fair" for tomorrow, with more than thirty vessels of the Atlantic fleet nearing port, and with the Bronx-Whitestone Bridge to be dedicated today. Fair officials were confident that their estimate of an attendance of 1,000,000 for the opening day would be realized.

Although the Fair will not be 100 per cent ready, by any means, when the gates open, the management was satisfied that it would be as nearly ready as any other World's Fair has been, or more so. They felt that this one will be so much bigger than previous fairs that even in its incompleted stage it will have so much more to see than any one can possibly cover in a day that no one will be disappointed at the failure of some of the exhibits to be ready.

Most of Features Ready

Bad weather in the last few weeks, labor troubles and the foreign situation were given as factors that have delayed construction and the receipt of exhibits in some cases. It was emphasized, however, that the buildings that will not open, or will open in a seriously incomplete condition, will be in a distinct minority.

Even in the amusement zone, which is the most retarded part of the Fair from a construction standpoint, it was said that fifty-five or more attractions would be ready for business when the first-day crowds arrive. The management promised that the streets in the amusement zone would be satisfactorily paved by tomorrow.

Grover A. Whalen, president, and Bayard F. Pope, treasurer of the Fair Corporation, made a tour of the grounds last night and expressed themselves afterward as satisfied with the conditions they found. They saw thousands of painters, carpenters, landscape gardeners and other artisans working through the night to get things ready both outside and inside the exposition buildings.

Both at the Fair Grounds and throughout the rest of the city New York was getting ready to entertain the throngs of visitors expected. All over the city the Fair's orange and blue colors and its trylon and perisphere symbols were displayed on public and private buildings, including City Hall.

40,000 Work at High Speed

Despite the damp, misty rain that prevailed most of the day, about 40,000 men were working at high speed inside the Fair Grounds, putting up many-colored flags, pennants and banners, taking down scaffolding and doing other last-minute jobs. Trucks and automobiles, which will be barred from the grounds after today, continued to dash about, and the wheel-chairs and buses in which visitors will be able to go from place to place throughout the 1,216-acre tract began to appear in large numbers.

Hotels, restaurants and bars, as well as railroad stations, throughout the city also were filling up with people from out-of-town who exhibited an eager friendliness and talkativeness unusual to New Yorkers, and told utter strangers their personal histories and their views on the foreign situation, as well as their plans for visiting the Fair.

The police, especially the traffic policemen, began to have their hands full with visitors unaccustomed to the ways and regulations of the metropolis. Just outside Pennsylvania Station yesterday afternoon an elderly woman, evidently from out-of-town, put a traffic policeman to the test, and he came through with flying colors under

Continued on Page Three

LEGISLATURE VOTES REPUBLICAN BUDGET, SLASHING LEHMAN'S

Both Houses, on Party Lines, Pass $388,000,000 Bill, a $31,000,000 Reduction

GOVERNOR PLEADS IN VAIN

Warns of Harm to Public Service—Majority Holds Cut Vital—Court Test Ahead

By WARREN MOSCOW
Special to THE NEW YORK TIMES.

ALBANY, April 28.—Both houses of the Legislature, by practically a straight party vote, adopted the Republican budget late today. The Assembly balloted 82 to 64 for the measure and the Senate approved it, 27 to 24.

The total of the budget, as revised by the Republican majority, is $388,000,000, as contrasted with the $419,000,000 budget submitted by Governor Lehman, a reduction on paper of $31,000,000. The Governor submitted a budget of $415,000,000, but by transferring special fund revenues and appropriations to the general fund the totals of the Governor's budget and that of the Republican majority were raised by about $4,000,000 of bookkeeping transactions.

The vote in the Assembly came late in the afternoon after an all-day debate wherein the Democrats charged the Republicans with crippling State services, and the repudiation of platform pledges, and the Republicans retorted that a check in spending was necessary.

Senate Session Is Short

The Senate, worn out by the Assembly debate, to which most of the Senators listened as visitors, cut its discussion to less than an hour. The only deviation from party affiliation in either house came in the Assembly, where Joseph Boccia, Republican of New York City, elected with the support of the American Labor Party, voted with the Democrats against the revised budget.

Both houses acted after they had received another special message from Governor Lehman, in which the Governor accused the Republicans of hampering State services, and pursuing an unconstitutional course of action.

The budget will now go to the Governor, who has the power to veto any addition to estimates and also any of the special acts necessary to carry out the Republican program. These special acts have not yet been passed. He has no power to veto cuts in the budget. Both sides have served notice that the question of the constitutionality of the "lump sum" budget prepared by the Republicans will be carried to the Court of Appeals, but it is not now known whether the Governor will attempt to veto the budget on the grounds that it is unconstitutional or sign it for the purpose of expediting a test case.

Nor is it certain how the test case will be brought. The most probable sponsor is the State Association of Civil Service Employes, which has announced that it would bring an action if the Republicans carried out their announced plans. This they did today.

On the floor of the Assembly the

Continued on Page Four

Riot in Saar Reported Over New 60-Hour Week

Special Cable to THE NEW YORK TIMES.

PARIS, April 28.—A French news agency reports that twenty Saar workers have been jailed for rioting against the new sixty-hour week.

At Forbach on the French frontier gendarmes reported that all was quiet on the eastern front. Metz and Strasbourg also reported apparent quiet across the frontier.

Wireless to THE NEW YORK TIMES.

VIENNA, April 28.—Twelve men, most of them former officers of the Austrian Army, were arrested today in a wine cellar in the center of Vienna. They are suspected of a monarchist conspiracy. All are known to have monarchist sympathies.

ROME-LONDON PACT MAY BE NEXT TO GO

Following of Hitler's Lead Is Rumored in Italy—Public Fears Step Toward War

By HERBERT L. MATTHEWS
Wireless to THE NEW YORK TIMES.

ROME, April 28.—Amid a general fear of an approaching war, which Chancellor Adolf Hitler's address intensified here today, came rumors that Italy might in her turn denounce the Anglo-Italian Pact of April 16, 1938. These reports, however must be taken cautiously and they cannot be confirmed in official quarters.

These reports are, perhaps, more symptomatic of the rising tension in Italy since the announcement of British conscription than a true foreshadowing of events to come. But something is expected.

Herr Hitler's reply to President Roosevelt was very different from Premier Benito Mussolini's mild protestation of peace, and there well may be some move from this end of the Axis to bring Italy's policies into line with Germany's.

Alarm Felt by Public

Herr Hitler's speech has been interpreted by the ordinary Italian as another step toward war and from that viewpoint it has brought regret and disappointment. Such feelings, of course, are not expressed in official circles or in the first reactions that are to be found in the press.

Herr Hitler's reaffirmation of the strength of the Axis echoes what is constantly being said here and because of that the official attitude on everything that Herr Hitler states is praise as a matter of policy. The newspapers reflect the same attitude and outwardly one gets the impression of complete harmony.

Yet, when there is a controlled press, the commentator has to distinguish between spontaneous natural feelings, as far as they are

Continued on Page Five

$325 Car Set to Go 50 Miles Per Fuel Gallon; Crosley Puts Its Speed at 50 Miles an Hour

Special to THE NEW YORK TIMES.

INDIANAPOLIS, April 28.—A new low-cost, two-cylinder automobile, designed for a top speed of fifty miles an hour and a gasoline mileage of fifty to the gallon, was introduced to distributors and newspaper men today at the Indianapolis Motor Speedway here by Powel Crosley Jr., Cincinnati manufacturer and owner of the Cincinnati Baseball Club.

Radical in design, the car will sell f. o. b. for $325 for the two-passenger convertible coupe and $350 for the four-passenger convertible sedan, the only models in which it is to be manufactured, at Richmond, Ind. The car will be manufactured in Cincinnati as well, but Richmond will be the final shipping point.

It is said that the car will accommodate persons taller than six feet, although the automobile itself is only ten feet long from bumper to bumper, mounted on a wheelbase of eighty inches. It has three speeds forward and reverse, four-wheel mechanical brakes and is equipped with safety glass.

The two-cylinder engine is of a light aviation four-cycle type. An aviation-type suction blower, an integral part of the flywheel, provides air cooling. The drive shaft runs straight to the rear axle without going through universal joints as in the conventional car.

The Crosley automobile weighs only 925 pounds and has a gasoline tank of four-gallon capacity which is estimated to be at least a 200-mile fuel supply. The crankcase holds only two quarts of oil.

The gear shift and steering arrangements are not essentially different from those of other makes.

The cars shown at the introductory display today were in the standard colors of gray, yellow and blue. They had red wheels with chrome hub caps and black tops. The car can be used as a light commercial vehicle by the removal of one of the seats in the convertible coupe for added transportation space, offering a quarter-ton carrying capacity, Mr. Crosley said.

"I always have wanted to build a practical car that would not only operate at a low cost, but also would sell at a low price," Mr. Crosley stated. "I have been dreaming of this car for twenty-eight years."

The car was christened by Lewis L'Hommedieu Crosley, grandson of the manufacturer, who broke a bottle containing a sample of all standard brands of gasoline.

Crosley officials announced that the new cars would be manufactured at the rate of about 200 a day.

POLAND PREPARED

Return of Danzig to the Reich Opposed as Well as a Corridor Road

ARMS PLAN TO BE RUSHED

Attempts to Exert Pressure Will Be Met by Poles—End of Pact Seen as Warning

By JERZY SZAPIRO
Wireless to THE NEW YORK TIMES.

WARSAW, April 28.—The memorandum from the Reich government outlining its views in the present state of Polish-German relations was delivered to the Foreign Office here today by the German Chargé d'Affaires at the very moment Chancellor Hitler began his speech.

No information is obtainable here as to the contents of the memorandum but official circles declare that it will be examined carefully and attentively. There is a tendency to regard the document as a preliminary step to the opening of new negotiations between Poland and Germany with a view to concluding a new agreement replacing the 1934 non-aggression pact that Herr Hitler denounced today.

The Poles, it is understood, are prepared to negotiate a new understanding and to discuss the Danzig problem but under normal conditions without pressure or intimidation.

[Poland intensified her military precautions at the Polish-German frontier where many of Poland's 1,300,000 men now under arms are stationed and military activity especially was noticeable near Danzig, The Associated Press reported.]

The memorandum, it is believed, repeats in more diplomatic form the views Herr Hitler expressed in his speech and declares that the non-aggression pact must be considered non-existent because it was violated by the Poles when they entered an agreement with Britain.

Official circles explained that so far as Danzig is concerned the Germans, during the last five years, have always maintained that the fate of this provincial city was of minor importance to them but that the Danzig problem should not adversely affect Polish-German relations and undermine the non-aggression agreement.

As far as German communications through the so-called Corridor, they have always been treated favorably by the Polish Government although Germany violated certain conventions in connection with traffic such as, for instance, the prompt payment for railroad transit.

Road Held Out of Question

The extra-territorial road through the Corridor is out of the question, it was added. Such a demand, it was said, had already served the Germans as a pretext to disrupt a neighboring country; such methods could not be applied to Poland.

The Polish-German non-aggression pact, it was further said, was a bilateral arrangement and a unilateral denunciation of the agreement was sure to provoke a strong reaction. Germany never received the right to decide what was best for Poland's interests, it was added, and the 1934 pact could never be interpreted as preventing Poland's cooperation with the western powers.

The question of whether the Polish-British agreement was contrary to the non-aggression pact should be left for diplomatic exchanges, it was said. In this case such exchanges were rendered impossible by the fact that since April 6—the date of Prime Minister Neville Chamberlain's pronouncement of the Polish-British guarantee—diplomatic contacts with the Reich government have been cut off because Foreign Minister Joachim von Ribbentrop would not see the Polish Ambassador, Josef Lipski, and the German Ambassador here, Hans Adolf von Moltke, never returned from his Easter vacation.

Statement Surprises Warsaw

Warsaw was surprised by Herr Hitler's revelation that he had offered the extension of the Polish-German non-aggression pact for twenty-five years and a common Polish-Hungarian-German guarantee of Slovakia's independence in return for Danzig's incorporation in the Reich and a motor road through the Corridor. It was indicated in official circles that up to

Continued on Page Seven

President Tells Norwegian Guest Hitler Leaves Door Open 'an Inch'

Remark to Crown Princess at Poughkeepsie Roosevelt's Only Comment on Speech—He Slept Through the Broadcast

By FELIX BELAIR Jr.
Special to THE NEW YORK TIMES.

POUGHKEEPSIE, N. Y., April 28.—"It left the door about an inch open," President Roosevelt commented on Chancellor Adolf Hitler's reply to his proposal that the Rome-Berlin Axis pledge a ten to twenty year guarantee of the territorial integrity of thirty-one European States, in which the Nazi chief called for specific proposals on the basis of absolute reciprocity.

The Chief Executive's off-hand judgment, presumably directed at the opportunities for an amicably negotiated settlement of Germany's demands within the limits of Chancellor Hitler's statement of his attitude, was offered in response to a direct question from Crown Princess Martha of Norway as to what he thought of the speech.

Fewer than fifty persons were within earshot of the exchange that followed, and some of it was missed entirely amid the hub-bub that followed the handshaking and picture taking of the President and Mrs. Roosevelt with the Princess Martha and Crown Prince Olav and their entourage as they debarked at a lumber yard dock at Poughkeepsie.

Without waiting for a formal introduction to the royal couple by George Summerlin, chief of protocol of the State Department, the President extended his hand in greeting first to the Princess and then to the Prince, just behind her. Camera men manoeuvred for position while keen-eyed Secret Service operatives and local and State police kept back the crowds.

"What did you think of Hitler's speech, Mr. President?" inquired the Crown Princess.

"Six o'clock in the morning is rather early, don't you think?" Mr. Roosevelt parried first, referring to the hour the broadcast of the speech started here.

Newspaper photographers and newsreel cameramen began jostling each other, and for a moment or two the President's conversation was blanked out. Then he was heard by those closest to remark:

"How can any one have a reaction to a speech that lasts more than two hours?"

The remark about the door's being left open about an inch followed a few seconds later.

Exactly to what part of the Hitler address the President directed this remark was left to the imagination of those who heard it. From as much of the context as was heard

Continued on Page Eight

FRENCH SEE PERIL IN BOND TO POLES

Fear Call to War for Danzig Which They Do Not Regard as a Good Issue

By P. J. PHILIP
Wireless to THE NEW YORK TIMES.

PARIS, April 28.—Both in official circles and among the general public Chancellor Hitler's speech today has been judged as unlikely to increase, although it does not diminish, the present state of tension.

In manner it sounded aggressive. In matter it is described as being a very astute lawyer's presentation of the German case, carefully compiled, well argued and marked by a tendency toward caution.

This tendency is shown in the inclination to appeal to juries—the British, French and American peoples—by insinuating that their governments are hostile judges. It is shown also, it is considered here, in the manner in which, while the Chancellor denounces the Anglo-German naval agreement and the German-Polish accord he still seems to leave the doors open for future arrangements.

Where he was least at ease was in defense of his action regarding Bohemia. He devoted twenty typewritten pages, nearly a fifth of the whole speech, to that question as if it needed all that space to convince himself as well as his listeners that he had not departed from his doctrine and policy. He seemed, French experts judged, uncomfortable, as if he knew instinctively that he had acted in contradiction to himself.

Uneasiness Over Danzig

By far the greatest importance is attached to his denunciation of the pact with Poland and his account of the rejection by Warsaw of the offer he had made concerning Danzig and operation through the Polish Corridor. While the Chancellor based his denunciation of the pact with Poland on the fact that that country had joined the ranks of the western nations in an agreement that he considers hostile to Germany there seems little doubt that his major reason was the rejection of the Danzig agreement by Warsaw, for the Franco-Polish treaty existed when the Germano-Polish pact was made.

There is uneasiness here because Warsaw was solely responsible for rejection of the German proposal. Paris was not informed until afterward and even then not fully of all its terms. That Germany had proposed that Poland and Hungary should participate in a guarantee of the independence of the Slovak State was news to the French Foreign Office.

In rejecting the Chancellor's proposals Warsaw was not, therefore,

Continued on Page Six

BRITAIN UNSOLACED BY HITLER'S SPEECH

Finds Situation Full of Danger—Home Fleet Concentrates—Russian Plan Speeded

By FERDINAND KUHN Jr.
Wireless to THE NEW YORK TIMES.

LONDON, April 28.—The British Government pushed ahead today with its conscription plans and its defensive alliances in spite of the comparatively mild and almost apologetic tone of certain passages in Chancellor Adolf Hitler's speech.

Prime Minister Neville Chamberlain met his leading Cabinet colleagues to discuss the draft of the conscription bill that will be published Monday night and debated in the House of Commons Thursday. At the same time British diplomacy showed no signs of slackening in its efforts to bring Russia and Turkey into the anti-aggression front of Europe.

Soviet Ambassador Ivan M. Maisky returned here today from his consultations in Moscow and found a message saying that Viscount Halifax, Foreign Secretary, would be delighted to see him at the Foreign Office at his earliest opportunity. So the two men arranged to compare notes tomorrow morning on the progress of the Anglo-Russian talks, which aim to create an Eastern front against Germany in case of war.

British Fleet Assembles

By coincidence or design, warships of the British Home Fleet, led by the giant battleship, Nelson, assembled at Portland today after their Easter leave. The ships concentrated while Herr Hitler was speaking, just as last September they arrived at their battle stations in Scotland on the day of the Nuremberg speech that helped to precipitate the Czech crisis.

Such friendly references as Herr Hitler made to Britain today may, no doubt, be reciprocated publicly by Mr. Chamberlain in the House of Commons next week. Taking a leaf from Herr Hitler's book, the Prime Minister can say with perfect sincerity that he admired Germany's past achievements and would regard war between Britain and Germany as a needless tragedy for mankind, but the British found nothing in the speech to justify even the slightest abandonment of their new policy, which has led them in six short weeks to assume military responsibilities to three countries in Eastern Europe and to impose compulsory military training at home.

In fact, the more Herr Hitler's speech was studied here today the less reason was seen for the optimism that shot prices upward on the Stock Exchange this afternoon. The speech, as viewed in high quarters

Continued on Page Six

BID TO POLES BARED

Chancellor Reports 25-Year Pact Offer for Free City's Return

SPEECH A BLISTERING ONE

Nazi Leader Willing to Give Non-Aggression Pledges to Nations Asking for Them

Chancellor Hitler, in a scornful speech before the Reichstag yesterday, denounced three treaties, replied in critical tones to President Roosevelt's truce proposal and defended his actions in Europe. One pact he abrogated was the non-aggression treaty with Poland [text of note to Warsaw, Page 7], and at the same time he emphasized he wished the return of Danzig and cession of a right-of-way across Pomorze. Another accord he canceled was the Anglo-German naval treaty [text of note to London, Page 6], and the third was the Munich consultative agreement with Britain. To Mr. Roosevelt, the Chancellor declared he was ready to pledge non-aggression to the thirty-one nations named by the President provided such pledges were reciprocal and the other nations took the initiative. [Page 1; text of the speech, Pages 9, 10 and 11.]

Poland's reaction was one of firm refusal to cede any territory and of renewed military precautions. [Page 1.]

Rumors circulated in Rome that Premier Mussolini might follow his partner's lead by denouncing the Anglo-Italian agreement. [Page 1.]

In the opinion of President Roosevelt the Chancellor "left the door about an inch open" [Page 1], and the State Department seemed to agree. [Page 8.]

London found the speech had done nothing to relieve the tension [Page 1], Paris was somewhat encouraged yet was apprehensive over the danger spot at Danzig [Page 1], while Moscow took solace in the thought that the Chancellor had divided Europe into two camps and thus removed the long-standing Bolshevist bogey. [Page 5.]

Chancellor Hitler Speaks

By GUIDO ENDERIS
Wireless to THE NEW YORK TIMES.

BERLIN, April 28.—An American President's political philosophy underwent searching scrutiny by Chancellor Adolf Hitler before the National Socialist Reichstag today and he found it wanting.

But President Roosevelt's peace appeal of April 15 to Herr Hitler was not the only document to crumble in the white heat created by one of the most blistering speeches that the Chancellor has delivered before the Reichstag.

Today that body literally worked itself into a frenzy of approval as Herr Hitler announced the abrogation of the German-Polish non-aggression pact of 1934, the Anglo-German naval agreement of 1935 and the Anglo-German consultative pact concluded between Herr Hitler and Prime Minister Neville Chamberlain in Munich last September.

If the political equilibrium in an already restless Europe is not placed further in jeopardy by the German Government's decisions announced today it will be because of calmer judgments in Chancelleries elsewhere, which probably have discounted today's speech on the ground that it was motivated by internal considerations.

Diplomats Gasp at Decisions

The tension in the chamber of the Kroll Opera House mounted as Herr Hitler announced the decisions, which made neutral spectators and the occupants of the diplomatic gallery gasp at the manner in which he defied Britain and fretted the nerves of Polish statesmen.

His caustic rejection of President Roosevelt's message concluded a two-hour speech already packed with thrills. Its climactic effect was attributable to the shrivelling sarcasm bestowed upon the President's proposals.

Herr Hitler dealt with them as twenty-one points, each of which gave him a succulent opportunity

Continued on Page Eight

"All the News That's Fit to Print."

The New York Times.

LATE CITY EDITION
Generally fair and continued cool today. Tomorrow fair, slowly rising temperatures.
Temperatures Yesterday—Max., 60; Min., 45.

Copyright, 1939, by The New York Times Company.

VOL. LXXXVIII...No. 29,682. Entered as Second-Class Matter, Postoffice, New York, N. Y. NEW YORK, MONDAY, MAY 1, 1939. PP THREE CENTS NEW YORK CITY and Vicinity | FOUR CENTS Elsewhere Except in 7th and 8th Postal Zones.

PRESIDENT OPENS FAIR AS A SYMBOL OF PEACE; VAST SPECTACLE OF COLOR AND WORLD PROGRESS THRILLS ENTHUSIASTIC CROWDS ON THE FIRST DAY

POLES CONSIDERING COUNTER DEMANDS IN REPLY TO HITLER

Military Circles Say Claim on Danzig Should Be Dropped Before Further Parleys

BALTIC OUTLET STRESSED

Reich Specification of Width of Right of Way in Corridor Said to Be 15.5 Miles

In Warsaw there were indications yesterday that the Polish reply to Germany might call for a dropping of the Nazi demands regarding Danzig and the replacing of the League of Nations link to the Free City by a new Polish one. It was also reported that Chancellor Hitler in a detailed demand had asked a fifteen-and-a-half-mile motor road right-of-way across Pomorze. [Page 1.]

Both Paris and London seemed to be hopeful that a Polish-German compromise on Danzig could be reached. Reports from the two capitals indicated a disinclination to be forced to fight on this issue. [Page 12.]

The question of peace or war, however, was considered by Nazi spokesmen to have been put up to the democracies and their partners. [Page 13.]

With the arrival of the German Army commander in Rome it was believed new pressure was being put on Italy by Germany for a full-fledged military alliance. But it was significant that according to all reports the Brenner Pass between the two countries was being fortified on both sides. [Page 11.]

Poles to Use Hitler Tactics

By JERZY SZAPIRO
Wireless to THE NEW YORK TIMES.

WARSAW, Poland, April 30.—The German memorandum delivered to the Polish Foreign Office on Friday while Chancellor Adolf Hitler was attacking Poland will be answered in the same manner. A Polish memorandum, repudiating the German accusation and rejecting Danzig's incorporation into Germany and a highway across Pomorze [the Polish Corridor], but leaving the door open for further negotiations, will be delivered at the Berlin Foreign Office while Foreign Minister Josef Beck and Premier Felicjan Slawoj-Skladkowski are addressing the Sejm [Parliament], probably on Friday.

[It was reported in Poland that Chancellor Hitler had demanded a German motor road right of way across Pomorze 15.5 miles wide, The Associated Press stated.]

Certain influential military circles hold that Warsaw should not enter into new negotiations with the Nazis unless the Germans withdraw their demands regarding Danzig. This view is expressed in the military journal, Polska Zbrojna, which published one of the strongest criticisms of Herr Hitler's speech and of German policy generally.

"Danzig is at the mouth of a great Polish river," it says, "and we cannot give it up. The Polonization of Danzig is notable; wherefore, why should the Germans show so much interest in what to them is but one of their provincial towns?"

Poland to Make Demands

The Gazeta Polska, official organ of the Polish Government, tomorrow will publish a noteworthy statement concerning the position of Danzig.

"Germany," it will say, "has shown her regard for international engagements by her recent occupation of Memel, by her denunciation of solemn treaties. She has demonstrated quite clearly that German policy aims at separating Poland from her outlet on the Baltic Sea, the importance of which to Poland needs no emphasis.

"The policy of Berlin thus creates a situation that forces Poland to go further in her demands concerning the status of Danzig than she did formerly when concluding with Germany the pact of 1934."

Although it is not explicitly stated, there is reason to believe that Poland's demands will include the transference of the functions of the League Commissioner to the Polish Government.

Will Close Exchanges

The Polish official answer to the German memorandum, it is believed, will close German-Polish exchanges for the time being. The Poles expect to delay the negotiations until there is a general clarification of the European situation.

No chances are being taken, however. All the military precautions ordered last month are still in force and the army is strengthened by

Continued on Page Twelve

Rider Will Ask Pensions For Congress Members

By The Associated Press.

WASHINGTON, April 30.—A quiet campaign to give pensions to members of Congress has materialized into a legislative proposal.

Chairman Ramspeck of the House Civil Service Committee said today that he intended to add provisions for the pensions to a bill making amendments to the Civil Service Law which has just been passed by the Senate.

Under the proposal, the government and the members would bear about equal shares of the cost. Five per cent of the salary of each member would be deducted monthly and would go toward the purchase of an annuity to be added to the amount to be paid by the government.

Civil service workers receive pensions which increase with length of service. They contribute 3½ per cent of their salaries.

Mr. Ramspeck reported that almost every member he had talked to favored the pension idea.

"They're getting security-minded," he added, laughing.

PARI-MUTUEL VOTE AGAIN UP IN STATE

Republicans Plan Assembly Test on Betting System—Democratic Split Reported

Special to THE NEW YORK TIMES.

ALBANY, April 30.—The question of pari-mutuel betting on horse-racing is returning to plague the 1939 session of the Legislature.

Pressure from pari-mutuel advocates has resulted in a decision on the part of Republican leaders to put the matter to a vote on the Assembly floor. If the proposed constitutional amendment should be passed by both Houses this year, it would be submitted to the people for approval in the Fall, as the 1938 Legislature approved the system.

Despite considerable support on the Republican side, there is no guarantee that the pari-mutuel proposal will pass in either House. The Democrats, who have blown hot and cold on the measure for years, are again reported to be divided on the subject.

In one recent year the proposed amendment was passed by the Senate, and when it came up a second time as is required by the Constitution, its original sponsor voted against it. Last year John J. Dunnigan, the Democratic leader of the Senate, pushed the proposal through the Upper House, and it gained approval in the Republican controlled Assembly as well.

Senate Sponsor Now Lacking

With the intervening elections, the Republicans gained control of the Senate as well and Senator Dunnigan has made no move to introduce the proposal in the Senate. In fact, it has yet to have an official sponsor there. However, John D. Bennett and Norman F. Penny, Nassau County Republican Assemblymen, have introduced in the Assembly resolutions identical with the Dunnigan resolution of the year before, and passage this year by both Houses would constitute the required second action by the Legislature, even if the sponsors are not the same.

In the Assembly the practice of the Republican leadership, under Speaker Heck, is to refuse to throttle in committee any bill of the type of the pari-mutuel proposal, because of rumors always circulated about bookmakers' lobbies. Putting the bill out for a vote leaves it up to the individual membership. The Republicans will seek passage of the measure in the Assembly, but its final fate would appear to rest on the number of Democratic votes it can command.

Whether the matter will be brought to a vote this week, or the following week, was not disclosed today.

Sales Tax Vote Awaited

Tomorrow night the Legislature is expected to adopt the rest of the budget bills, and either then, or the next day, adopt the tax program which will be used to finance the Republican budget. The new taxes on this program are the increase in the liquor tax, effective on May 1, and the two-cent-per-package cigarette tax, effective on July 1.

Later in the week the sales tax probably will come up for a vote, with its eventual fate still depending on the support the Republicans can muster for it in the Senate, where they control by a margin of only two votes. The political aspects of the battle over the budget itself appear to make it unlikely that the Republican sales tax idea can gain any Democratic votes on the Senate side.

Local bills have been cleaned up to a large extent in both houses, and after the enactment of the tax bills, the settling of the sales tax problem, the revision of the unemployment insurance law, and the enactment of a housing measure, the Legislature will be in a position to quit and go home, to await a possible special-session call.

CONGRESS FACING SEVEN BIG ISSUES AS TIME SHORTENS

None Is on Week's Calendars, But All Except Taxes Are in Legislative Process

WAY CLEARED FOR ACTION

Routine Money Bills Passed, Reporting of Vital Measures to Floor Is Expected

By LUTHER A. HUSTON
Special to THE NEW YORK TIMES.

WASHINGTON, April 30.—Congress has been in session nearly four months and has disposed of only two of the major controversial items on its calendar. At least seven important issues remain to be settled in the two months that remain of the session if present plans are followed and a late Summer sitting is avoided by adjournment around July 1.

None of the major measures is on the calendar of either chamber for this week. The most progress that can be expected is that one or more of these measures may come from committees to the floor of the House or Senate.

The two issues that have been settled are the limited authorization for the President to reorganize executive agencies and the expansion of national defense, for which necessary appropriation bills have been passed. The decks also have been cleared of considerable of the routine, most of the important departmental appropriation bills having been disposed of.

Major Questions Outstanding

The following matters remain to be dealt with:

Amendments to the Social Security Act, the National Labor Relations Act and the Wages and Hours Law.

Revision or extension of existing neutrality laws.

The amount of the appropriation and the method of disbursement for relief during the 1940 fiscal year.

A farm program including the highly controversial question of export and domestic subsidies on farm products.

Legislation to repeal, modify or continue in effect certain provisions of the tax laws that are estimated to yield an annual revenue of around $2,000,000,000 even if general tax revision is not attempted.

Except for tax proposals, all of these measures are in the legislative mill. On some of them committee hearings are in progress; on others committee action has ended.

There is a possibility that proposed amendments to the Wages and Hours Law may come up in the House tomorrow. Representative Mary Norton, chairman of the Labor Committee, has indicated that she will try to bring up under suspension of the rules the proposals which her committee has approved. If this is not done, the proposals must lie over at least a week.

To Hear Green on C. I. O. Charges

On Capitol Hill tomorrow, however, interest probably will center in the hearing by the Senate Education and Labor Committee on proposed amendments to the National Labor Relations Act, where William Green, president of the American Federation of Labor, will be the witness.

Mr. Green is expected to reply to

Continued on Page Twenty-four

Times Sq. May Be Closed To Autos During Fair

Times Square may be turned over as a playground for World's Fair visitors if their numbers become great enough to warrant special police arrangements in the theatrical area.

Police Commissioner Valentine said yesterday that the Fair crowds may approximate the number of American Legion members who came to New York for their national convention in September, 1937. If that should develop, Mr. Valentine said, it would be advisable to turn over Times Square to the city's guests.

Automobile traffic would be routed north and south on either side of the Square, as it was during the Legion convention. For the last two weeks heavy police details have handled the crowds in Times Square, directing pedestrians to the right to obtain the maximum amount of order.

RUSSIAN AVIATORS, RESCUED, ARRIVE

Two Who Crashed in Canada Here in American Plane—One Fainted During Flight

Brig. Gen. Vladimir Kokkinaki and Major Mikhail Gordienko, the two Soviet airmen who crashed Friday night in a swamp off the coast of New Brunswick were landed in a rescue plane last night at Floyd Bennett Field at 10:31 o'clock.

The two men were brought to New York in the plane of Commodore Harold Vanderbilt, which was chartered by Soviet and American officials for the rescue work, which took more than thirty hours.

They and the rescue party, which left here Friday night after word of the crash of the Moscow-New York non-stop flight came through from Miscou Point, N. B., were "ferried" to the end of the scheduled flight in an American airplane.

Their own craft, in which they sped toward New York from Moscow in 23 hours and 40 minutes, still lay in the frozen morass where Major Gordienko squashed it in an emergency landing. He landed it, because General Kokkinaki had fainted at an altitude of more than 27,000 feet, it was learned yesterday when the party first brought the two men as far south as Moncton, N. B.

In recounting last night the events which led up to the forced landing at the field General Kokkinaki said the main difficulty of flying in the substratosphere was at 27,000 feet, where his compass liquids froze and his radio reception was so poor that he could not tune in the directional beams. He offered this explanation as a reason why the ship apparently lost its course, having been reported in the same area for nearly four and a half hours prior to its final landing.

In the plane were the two Russian aces; Russell Thaw, pilot, and his co-pilot, John Revely; V. P. Butosov, Dr. Louis S. Spector and Peter Baranov, all of the Amtorg

Continued on Page Twenty-four

Hague Ignores Own Plea for Patriotic Rally; Skips Americanization Fete for Ball Game

Special to THE NEW YORK TIMES.

JERSEY CITY, N. J., April 30.—Mayor Frank Hague, who issued a proclamation yesterday calling on residents of Jersey City to "show your Americanism" by attending the city's tenth annual celebration today of Americanization Day, did not appear at that event this afternoon. Instead he attended the double-header baseball game between the Jersey City and Toronto teams of the International League at Roosevelt Stadium.

"As Mayor of Jersey City, I earnestly and respectfully invite all the people of our city to participate actively in the Americanization Day exercises, Sunday, April 30, 2 P. M., at Pershing Field," declared the Mayor's signed proclamation, published yesterday in newspaper advertisements.

"Show your Americanism by parading or being present Sunday afternoon. It is my request that the American flag be displayed on all homes and buildings Sunday. Every citizen should remove his hat as the colors pass by."

The proclamation listed Mayor Frank Hague among the speakers at Pershing Field, from which representative Jerry O'Connell, Montana Democrat and foe of the Jersey City Mayor, was whisked away by police several months ago when he attempted to speak there.

A crowd estimated at 4,000 persons assembled in the field today and 10,000 others marched there. During the parade and speechmaking, however, the Mayor was one of 29,362 baseball fans who did not take part in the Americanization celebration. He occupied a box at the baseball stadium with his nephew and private secretary, former Judge Frank Hague Eggers.

The Jersey City team won both games.

Commissioner Arthur Potterton, who spoke at Pershing Field, declared that "Jersey City takes the lead to show the world that nothing un-American will creep into our lives in this part of the State." Referring to other parts of the State and the nation, he said that "we have given them the courage they did not possess."

Representative Edward J. Hart, Democrat, was another speaker. Governor A. Harry Moore was present, but did not speak.

The Americanization Day celebration is sponsored by Captain Clinton Fisk Post, Veterans of Foreign Wars.

ROOSEVELT SPEAKS

He Sees Nations of This Hemisphere United in Desire for Peace

U. S. DEMOCRACY STRONG

Exposition Here and in West Born of Singleness of the American Ideal, He Says

By FELIX BELAIR JR.

In his first public utterance since Chancellor Hitler's virtual rejection of his plan to assure the peace of Europe for another ten years, President Roosevelt served notice on the world yesterday that the nations of the Western Hemisphere were "united in a desire to encourage peace and good-will among all nations" and voiced their hope that time would break down the barriers to tranquillity on the Continent.

In a brief address dedicating the New York's World's Fair to the cause of international amity and declaring it "open to all mankind," the President said that the American wagon was hitched to the star of peace, and asked that the months ahead "may carry us forward in the rays of that hope."

Avoids Any Direct Reference

For those who had expected a more direct reference by President Roosevelt to the state of affairs in Europe or something that might be interpreted as a reply to the German Chancellor's all but complete throwdown of his peace guarantee proposal there was disappointment, for his attitude regarding that had to be inferred from what he said of the traditional aspirations of the American republics.

Of recent years American historians would write that "sectionalism and regional jealousies diminished and that the people of every part of your land acquired a national solidarity of economic and social thought such as had never been seen before," the President said.

He added that "wise tolerance" almost as much as the American form of government had made possible this unity of sentiment in a nation made up of so many different creeds and national derivations. The President recalled that democratic government had endured unchanged in this country longer than in any other country on the globe at any period of history, a circumstance he attributed to the wisdom of the framers of the Constitution.

He Sees Aim Accomplished

"That this has been accomplished," the President added a little later, "has been due first to our own form of government itself and, secondly, to a spirit of wise tolerance which, with few exceptions, has been the rule.

"We in the United States, and, indeed, in all the Americas, remember that our population stems from many races and kindreds and tongues. Often, I think, we Americans offer up the silent prayer that on the continent of Europe, from which the American hemisphere was principally colonized, the years to come will break down many barriers to intercourse between nations—barriers which may be historic, but which so greatly, through the centuries, have led to strife and hindered friendship and normal intercourse."

From the distant reaches of the Court of Peace, at the head of which he spoke in front of the Federal Building, the President's voice came echoing back. The spectators sat motionless on folding chairs down the long concourse ending with the Trylon and Perisphere as Mr. Roosevelt slowly spoke the principal address of the day.

Not until the completion of his remarks, which carried for at least half a mile through the amplifiers arranged for the occasion, was there a suggestion of applause. The President deliberately had phrased his speech so as not to play upon the emotions and he received none of the clapping that punctuated a preceding address by Mayor La Guardia until he finished what he had to say.

The throng that came to hear him was apparently too much absorbed in his remarks to give any outward demonstration of approval until he was done. But cheering and applause was as spontaneous as it was general when Mr. Roosevelt stepped from the microphone after his concluding pronunciation:

"I hereby dedicate the New York

Continued on Page Four

Crowds Awed by Fair's Vastness And Medley of Sound and Color

Opening Day Has Everything, Including All Kinds of Weather—Spirit of Gayety Wanes When Pelting Rain Menaces Finery

The Fair had everything for its opening yesterday, including all kinds of weather. Early trains rolled to the Flushing Meadows under skies clear and blue, flooded with rich sunlight, carrying thousands come to look upon the miracle wrought by Grover Whalen's armies in the last three years.

Silk-hatted dignitaries, sailors on shore leave, men and women of all ages, dressed for fair weather and a great holiday. They came in hordes down the railroad and subway ramps, forty and fifty abreast, to gaze upon the wonders, to buy guide books from the shouting peddlers and to scramble for the observation cars.

Wealthier fairgoers climbed into motor-driven and man-powered chairs for their first tour of the grounds. Hundreds of thousands preferred to make it on foot, all a little bewildered and puzzled by the tremendous sweep of grounds, by the dazzling color, almost blinding in the bright sun. Guides, ushers, policemen and policewomen were breathless the first hour trying to keep up with the flood of questions.

Men and women, rank amateurs at reading maps, assembled in the walks or took over the benches, to puzzle out the direction of the various exhibits. Thousands were misled by the dazzling sun into thinking that the destinations they had marked off were close at hand. In most cases they learned that this was an illusion. The strong light had something of the effect of a mirage.

Above the grounds, despite notice that aircraft were to be kept from the Fair zone until the President's address, silver ships careened and darted, like gilded gnats. Two lazy blimps, reflecting the sun from their sides, came over the reviewing stand and crossed to the outer border of the Fair. The crowds craned their necks to watch their antics in the sky, and drivers of observation cars kept sounding their musical horns to warn them to safer spots.

Everywhere, far as the eye could see, men in blue, gray, green and yellow uniforms assembled in military formations and headed toward the parade ground in the Court of Peace. Bugle notes, brassy and thin, sounded and echoed from all corners of the field. Drums rolled and fifes piped sharp marching tunes. The non-military visitors were in a dither, racing from one group to another.

Groups representing the foreign nations caught the eye as they

Continued on Page Two

CITY AND THE FLEET TAKE TURN AS HOST

1,000 Officers and Men Under Admiral Johnson Help Open Fair—Ships Draw Crowds

By HANSON W. BALDWIN

The city played host to the navy yesterday and the navy played host to the city.

It was—all things considered—an even exchange. Some 1,000 officers and men of the thirty-five visiting men-of-war, led by Rear Admiral Alfred W. Johnson, commanding the Atlantic Squadron, took part in the opening ceremonies for the World's Fair, and thousands of others rolled along Broadway and throughout the five boroughs with that walk peculiar to sailors home from the sea.

But the boats that brought the parties ashore took crowds of visitors back to the ships, while other thousands climbed the gangways of ships berthed at piers and stared with absorbing interest at turrets, the burnished muzzles of guns, the ranks of planes aboard the aircraft carrier Ranger, the ominous black hulls of the submarines and the torpedo tubes of the destroyers.

It was the visiting squadron's second day—and first Sunday—in port, and the public took full advantage of it. The men-of-war were a rival attraction, and a stellar one, to the World's Fair, and the crush of visitors was more than the navy could handle.

Estimates of Throng Vary

The crowd estimates varied widely. The police said 23,000 got aboard, while the navy thought 56,000 had crowded onto the battleships, cruisers, destroyers, submarines and auxiliaries in the five hours of the afternoon that the ships received the public. Perhaps 10,000 to 15,000 others were turned away—some of them after several hours in line—when ships' officers and the beach guard said the men-of-war were unable to accommodate any more visitors.

The visiting hours were supposed to have been from 1 to 5 P. M., but at the Ninety-sixth Street landing no more visitors were permitted to leave shore after 3:25 P. M. Naval officials explained that it took some time to clear the ships of visitors, especially when the vessels were lying out in the stream and all visitors had to be transported by small boats.

They explained that it was necessary at times to allow no visitors to leave the shore landing places later than 4 P. M. There was, however, despite the navy's announcement that all ships would be open daily from 1 to 5 P. M., considerable variation on individual ships.

The Ranger, aircraft carrier berthed alongside a pier at Canal

Continued on Page Ten

LIGHT AUTO TRAFFIC 'SURPRISE' TO POLICE

Elaborate System to Cope With Expected Snarls on Roads Goes Unused

Although Police Department traffic experts were ready for the worst, streams of automobiles flowed evenly along principal Queens highways yesterday and not a single accident involving a serious injury was reported.

An elaborate system for emergency communications, worked out to cope with expected road snarls, went unused as 3,300 patrolmen, 523 of the traffic division, and 300 detectives—a total of 4,123—worked overtime to assure a safe and orderly opening to the World's Fair.

By 11 P. M. most of the motorists had either gone home or were on their ways there and reports to police centers indicated there was no more congestion than there had been on the way out.

The only mishap on the record—spoiling what otherwise would have been a virtually incredible perfect mark—occurred at 1:10 P. M. just outside the Fair Grounds, at Lawrence and Sanford Avenues.

Louis Hoffman, 70 years old, of 1,266 Spofford Avenue, the Bronx, suffered lacerations of the left leg when struck by a car that the police said was driven by Louis Anzelone of 27-41 108th Street, Corona. Mr. Hoffman went home after treatment by an interne from Flushing Hospital. The driver was not held.

Policeman Is Injured

A patrolman was hurt inside the grounds a little later, when a crush developed outside the French Building. There were seven children lost, a man had an epileptic fit, and fifty peddlers were arrested for operating on the ramp leading from the combined I. R. T.-B. M. T. subway terminal, but otherwise, the first day was as safe as a lawn party.

A false fire alarm was turned in at the box in the R. C. A. building shortly before the opening parade, while the walks near the Fire Chief Thomas F. Dougherty said it was "malicious."

Patrolman Bartholomew Nicastro, 35 years old, of 113-02 178th Street, St. Albans, was the man injured. The accident occurred at about 5 P. M. when the resurgent crowd he was trying to keep back threw him against a wooden "horse," which had been used in construction work. He was treated for a cut right leg by one of the Fair surgeons under Dr. Joseph Peter Hoguet, and remained on duty. In general, the Fair's six first aid stations had a dull day.

A checkup by the Fair police at 10 P. M. indicated that the stations,

Continued on Page Four

NATIONS IN PARADE

Mayor and the Governor Voice Welcome to the 'World of Tomorrow'

WEATHER REDUCES THRONG

Attendance Reported Above 600,000—Centers of Religion and Freedom Dedicated

By RUSSELL B. PORTER

The biggest international exposition in history was officially opened at 3:12 o'clock yesterday afternoon when President Roosevelt formally dedicated the New York World's Fair 1939 in an address before a gathering of 60,000 persons in the open-air Court of Peace.

Governor Lehman, Mayor La Guardia, Sir Louis Beale, British Commissioner General to the Fair and spokesman for the nearly sixty foreign nations that have exhibits, and Grover A. Whalen, president of the Fair Corporation, also made speeches at the opening ceremonies. They joined the President in emphasizing the message of peaceful progress that the Fair brings to mankind in an era when the whole world is troubled by war and threats of war.

When the President officially declared the Fair open he brought to a climax ceremonies that included a parade of 20,000 uniformed soldiers, sailors and marines, foreign groups in picturesque native costumes from nearly all the countries of Europe, Asia and the Americas, and the workmen who built the Fair, in their overalls and white caps.

Starting at the Trylon and Perisphere, the Theme Center of the Fair, the parade passed down Constitution Mall to the Court of Peace with flags waving, bands playing and spectators applauding until it ended with a colorful pageant in the Court of Peace.

Spectacle Impresses Visitors

Although the official exercises were the important part of the day from a formal viewpoint, actually the Fair itself made the greatest impression upon the visitors, judging from their comments as they strolled through the 1,216-acre Fair Grounds and as they journeyed homeward last night.

What they saw was a spectacle of surprising beauty and magnificence, especially last night when the whole Fair and the heavens above it were bathed in soft, glowing colors with the most modern lighting effects, and when fireworks combined with flame, water and color displays on the Lagoon of Nations, the pools in Constitution Mall and the surface of Fountain Lake.

In the daytime also the Fair is a beautiful sight, with the whole scene dominated by the 700-foot Trylon and the 200-foot Perisphere, from which radiates a rainbow of many-colored buildings of modernistic, functional architecture, some bizarre in shape and hue, others strikingly handsome and impressive in their suggestion of strength and use.

Green trees, shrubbery and lawns, playing fountains, shady benches and restful spots on all sides make a garden spot of this artificial city within a city which has been constructed within the past three and one-half years on what was formerly the ash dumps of the Flushing Meadows, and will be a great city park after the Fair is over.

See "World of Tomorrow"

In the huge crystal ball of the Perisphere, visitors peered to see what "the World of Tomorrow" would be like, finding it to be a conception of more and more progress in democracy and in the advance of science, industry, commerce, transportation, communication, the arts and the professions to bring peace and happiness to mankind. They found the same ideas expressed in the streamlined, futuristic dimensions of the buildings, statues, murals, dioramas, landscapes and exhibits of the Fair as a whole.

Like the worlds of yesterday and today, and also like the City of New York, which has the reputation of never being finished but of always changing, the "World of Tomorrow" has a great deal of unfinished business before it. The heart of the Fair, the half-mile stretch between the Theme Center and the Court of Peace where the official ceremonies were held, was virtually complete yesterday, but many other sections,

Continued on Page Three

"All the News That's Fit to Print."

The New York Times.

LATE CITY EDITION
Partly cloudy and warm with scattered showers today and tomorrow.
Temperatures Yesterday—Max., 88; Min., 70

Copyright, 1939, by The New York Times Company.

VOL. LXXXVIII...No. 29,797. Entered as Second-Class Matter. Postoffice, New York, N. Y. NEW YORK, THURSDAY, AUGUST 24, 1939. PP THREE CENTS NEW YORK CITY and Vicinity | FOUR CENTS Elsewhere Except in 7th and 8th Postal Zones.

GERMANY AND RUSSIA SIGN 10-YEAR NON-AGGRESSION PACT; BIND EACH OTHER NOT TO AID OPPONENTS IN WAR ACTS; HITLER REBUFFS LONDON; BRITAIN AND FRANCE MOBILIZE

U.S. AND ARGENTINA PLAN TRADE PACT, WELLES DISCLOSES

Our Commerce Will Get Full Equality With That of All Foreigners, He Asserts

BEEF NOT TO BE INCLUDED

Long Preliminary Talks Ease Difficulties, With Offset Seen to Our Recent Losses

Special to THE NEW YORK TIMES.

WASHINGTON, Aug. 23.—The United States intends to negotiate a reciprocal trade treaty with Argentina as a move to put American commerce with that republic on a footing of equality with that of European competitors, Sumner Welles, Acting Secretary of State, stated today. There have been more than four years of preliminary discussion.

The State Department, making public a list of products upon which this country would make tariff concessions, set Oct. 4 as the closing date for submission of briefs by interested Americans and Oct. 16 for the opening of public hearings.

It was emphasized that fresh, chilled or frozen Argentine meats, the entry of which into this country is banned by the Tariff Act of 1930, and fine wools would not be a subject of discussion in the negotiations. This was expected by officials to remove the most serious objections which might have been advanced to conclusion of a reciprocal agreement. Barring of the entry of Argentine fresh beef here has long been a subject of some friction between the two countries in their commercial relations.

"It may be noted that during the fifteen-year period 1924-38 our exports to Argentina have exceeded our imports from that country by $486,900,000," Mr. Welles said in a statement.

Trade Cut by Foreign Pacts

"Our trade with Argentina has suffered in recent years for lack of a trade agreement. The trade of certain European countries with Argentina has been developing at our expense under the influence of their commercial agreements with Argentina. The placing of American commerce in Argentina on a footing of full equality with that of our European competitors was a subject which was gone into fully in preliminary discussions leading up to the present announcement.

"The agreement will enable us to maintain our competitive position in a market of great present and prospective importance.

"On our side we must, of course, offer reciprocal benefits. The products of interest to Argentina with respect to which consideration will be given in the course of the negotiations, with a view to seeing what concessions could be granted, are listed in connection with the announcement of the proposed negotiations. The concessions, which will in due course be formulated, should, of course, permit an increase in Argentina's exports to this country, but will not have injurious effect upon American production.

"The types of wool included in the list are the coarser types, of which there is only a very small production in this country."

Barter Agreement With Germany

It was presumed that in referring to European competitors Mr. Welles was speaking principally of Germany, which concluded a barter agreement with Argentina after the Pan-American Conference in Lima last December. England has long been a large trader with Argentina, however, and is a heavy buyer of Argentine beef.

Among the products upon which the United States will consider lowering duties in favor of Argentina are:

Tallow, oleo oil and oleo stearin, extract of meat, including fluid, pickled or cured beef packed or not packed in air-tight containers; dead turkeys, dead birds, chicken eggs, corn or maize, including cracked corn; asparagus in its natural state, and some wools.

With the possible exception of that made with Brazil, a reciprocal trade treaty with the Argentine would be the most important yet consummated with a Latin-American country, officials indicated. Be-

Continued on Page Thirty-five

BRITAIN ACTS FAST

Air Force Is Ready for Hostilities—Warships Mass in Skagerrak

EXPORT EMBARGO IS FIXED

Parliament Meets Today in an Emergency Session—King to Convene Privy Council

By FERDINAND KUHN Jr.

Special Cable to THE NEW YORK TIMES.

LONDON, Aug. 23.—The British Government prepared for action today with every indication that it was ready to go to war with Germany whenever a call for help from Poland should come.

Warning notices went out to reservists in all departments of the armed and civilian services; the King was returning to London to hold a meeting of the Privy Council tomorrow; Londoners were ordered to darken their windows until further notice; the air force was poised for instant action, and a concentration of an undisclosed number of British warships was reported in the Skagerrak, between the Norwegian and Danish coasts, as if to remind Germany of the blockade that she had to endure during the World War.

The emergency was underlined by a Board of Trade announcement placing an immediate embargo on unlicensed exports of essential war materials "in order to conserve the stocks in this country." The list included copper, nickel and rubber, which the Germans have been buying in large quantities in the past week or two, and also aluminum, lead, iron and steel scrap and raw cotton.

Parliament Session Today

Tomorrow both houses of Parliament will meet in emergency sesison to give the government sweeping powers of a sort unknown in democratic England since World War days. The new law will be something like the old Defense of the Realm Act, enabling the government to issue Orders in Council, without prior or subsequent Parliamentary sanction, for any purpose that the national interest may require.

Trade-union leaders were invited to examine the bill today and they came away satisfied that all possible safeguards of individual liberty would be included.

The real business of the Parliamentary session, however, will be to hear a complete review of the international situation by Prime Minister Chamberlain in the House of Commons and by Viscount Halifax, the Foreign Secretary, in the House of Lords. All indications are that the Prime Minister's words and the subsequent debate will be more sombre in tone than anything heard in the Commons chamber since Aug. 3, 1914, when Sir Edward Grey made his famous speech on the eve of the World War.

Everywhere it was agreed that a crisis of the utmost gravity now confronts Britain, a crisis far more serious than that of last Autumn, when this country was not committed as it is now. The British determination to carry out all the pledges to Poland was reaffirmed in the government message handed to Chancellor Hitler today by Sir

Continued on Page Five

The Developments in Europe

The signing of the Russo-German non-aggression pact, which many world capitals feared might be Chancellor Hitler's "go-ahead signal," took place in Moscow early this morning, half a day after German Foreign Minister von Ribbentrop had arrived in the Russian capital. The pact, which runs for ten years, in addition to prohibiting attack by either party against the other, forbids either to join any association of powers aimed at the other. Moreover, it provides that if one party is an "object of warlike acts" the other will not support such acts. [Page 1; text of the treaty, also Page 1.]

Signature of the pact followed a day that seemed to bring Europe closer to the brink. When the British Ambassador to Germany conveyed to Chancellor Hitler a warning that Britain would fight for Poland he was bluntly rebuffed. In Berlin word freely circulated that the German Army would march at 6 P. M. today (noon in New York). [Page 1.]

In the face of Herr Hitler's rebuff Britain went ahead with war preparations, including the sending of notices to reservists, poising of the air force and concentration of warships in the Skagerrak, north of Denmark. Parliament prepared to meet today to grant the government sweeping emergency powers. [Page 1.] Reinforcements were reported being sent to the Mediterranean, where the bases at Gibraltar and Malta were on the alert. [Page 3.] The dominions, led by Canada and Australia, were beginning to swing into line behind Britain. [Page 6.]

France, convinced that Germany intends to invade Poland within a few days, called up further reservists after a meeting of the Permanent Committee on National Defense. [Page 1.]

Poland remained outwardly calm, still doubting that Herr Hitler would risk precipitating a general war. [Page 2.]

In Turkey allegiance to the coalition powers was affirmed, although German Ambassador von Papen was flying to Angora from Germany, presumably to try to break that allegiance. [Page 1.] But in Rumania, another State guaranteed by France and Britain, informed circles said that country would strive to remain neutral [Page 7.]

Only in Rome were signs of war lacking. Although the press continued to attack Poland, no unusual defense preparations were evident. [Page 1.]

In an attempt to head off disaster King Leopold of the Belgians, speaking for the seven Oslo powers, appealed for peace. [With the text of the appeal, Page 5.]

President Roosevelt, disturbed by the outlook, was speeding back to Washington [Page 1], where officials were clearing the decks for action if it became necessary to safeguard United States neutrality and help Americans to escape from danger zones. [Page 3.] The State Department advised citizens not to go to Europe [Page 3] and those who were trying to return home found ships still running normally from foreign ports. [Page 3.]

In the Far East the army and navy leaders in Japan were understood to have shaped a policy to be followed in view of the new situation arising from the Russo-German treaty. [Page 4.] In China some observers believed the treaty would mean increased Soviet aid in resisting Japan. [Page 4.]

FRANCE MOBILIZES; NOW EXPECTS WAR

People Confident of Strength to Meet Aggressor as Hopes of Peace Diminish

By P. J. PHILIP

Wireless to THE NEW YORK TIMES.

PARIS, Thursday, Aug. 24.—Convinced by a report from French Ambassador Robert Coulondre at Berlin and by a reply that Chancellor Adolf Hitler gave yesterday to Prime Minister Neville Chamberlain's message through British Ambassador Sir Nevile Henderson at Berchtesgaden that an invasion of Poland is intended by the German Government within the next few days, the French Government last night decided to call up a further contingent of reservists today.

This decision was communicated to the press in an official statement from Premier Edouard Daladier's office as follows:

"On account of the international situation the French Government has decided to complete military measures already taken by calling up an additional contingent of reserve soldiers."

During last night notices were

Continued on Page Two

TURKEY REAFFIRMS PLEDGES TO ALLIES

Will Honor Pact With France and Britain—German Envoy Flies to Woo Her

Special Cable to THE NEW YORK TIMES.

ISTANBUL, Turkey, Aug. 23.—No official pronouncement has yet been made about the Russo-German non-aggression pact. In official quarters the position of Turkey is said to be unchanged; she has made agreements for mutual assistance against aggression with France and Britain and stands by them.

The Turkish people are still bewildered over yesterday's news, but less alarm about its possibilities is noticeable since last night's official British communiqué was published.

Until the Turkish Government has authentic information about the terms of the pact Turkish newspapers will be reticent. Cumhuriet, only Turkish newspaper with an editorial on the subject today, assumed the Soviet Union would stipulate that if Germany was guilty of aggression against any of her Western neighbors, the pact would become null and void.

In this case, the newspaper said, it should act as a deterrent against war in Europe, for the newspaper could not believe the Soviet Government will remain indifferent to the fate of its neighbors on the Baltic and Black Seas simply because it signed a pact of non-aggression with Germany.

Cumhuriet added that although a pact of non-aggreison was not an alliance, it implied friendly feelings, and it believed, therefore, that the anti-Comintern pact was political, not ideological, and that the Russo-German pact may be regarded as a truce.

Von Papen Flies to Turkey

BUDAPEST, Hungary, Aug. 23 (AP).—Franz von Papen, Germany's Ambassador to Turkey, passed by plane through Budapest today, en route from Salzburg to Angora.

Diplomatic circles conjectured his mission now was to renew attempts to draw Turkey out of the British-French bloc. They recalled German and Italian claims that Turkey's alliance with Britain and France was dependent upon Russia's not joining the opposition camp.

Wireless to THE NEW YORK TIMES.

BUDAPEST, Hungary, Aug. 23.—The international situation was dis-

Continued on Page Five

Sidney Howard Killed by Tractor on Estate; Playwright Is Crushed in Berkshire Garage

Special to THE NEW YORK TIMES.

TYRINGHAM, Mass., Aug. 23.—Sidney Coe Howard, playwright, was crushed to death today by a two and a half ton tractor in his garage on his 700-acre estate here.

Mr. Howard had put in a morning of hard work on a new play based on Carl Van Doren's "Benjamin Franklin" and, as was his custom, was going to seek relaxation in physical work on his estate, which included one of the most modern dairy farms in this part of the State. The chore he had set for himself was harrowing a twenty-eight-acre field which he had recently bought to extend his property.

Driving alone to the garage a quarter of a mile from his studio in the fields, Mr. Howard entered, turned on the ignition switch of the tractor and cranked it. The machine lurched forward, pinning the playwright against the wall of the structure. The tractor, put in the garage the night before by an employe, was believed to have been left in high gear.

Fred L. Fairbanks, superintendent of the estate, discovered Mr. Howard while on an inspection trip. The garage, a former Shaker schoolroom, is set off by itself on the estate and is seldom visited by any one except by those on business.

Mr. Fairbanks found his employer in, an upright position, his head bent over his chest. He was pinned at the chest by the hood of the tractor, which had stalled after crushing him against the wall.

After starting the tractor and moving Mr. Howard's body, Mr. Fairbanks ran to the nearest telephone on the estate to notify Mrs. Howard and summon aid. Mrs. Howard was shopping in Lee, five miles away. When she returned

Continued on Page Nineteen

QUICK ACTION SEEN

Berlin Talks of 6 P. M. Deadline for Move Against Poland

DICTATOR WARNS BRITISH

Henderson So Wrought Up on Leaving Parley With Hitler That He Is Speechless

By OTTO D. TOLISCHUS

Wireless to THE NEW YORK TIMES.

BERLIN, Thursday, Aug. 24.—While Foreign Minister Joachim von Ribbentrop was in Moscow discussing, in the view of some German quarters, not so much a new non-aggression pact as "Poland's fourth and final partition," Chancellor Hitler yesterday received Sir Nevile Henderson, the British Ambassador, for a fifteen-minute conference.

According to reliable information, the conference ended on a rather blunt note that is interpreted in diplomatic quarters as possibly Herr Hitler's last word. The communiqué, issued last night, reads:

"Complying with the wish of the British Government, the Fuehrer received Sir Nevile Henderson at the Berghof today. The Ambassador delivered a letter from the British Prime Minister addressed to the Fuehrer, which was drawn up in the same sense as yesterday's British communication regarding the Cabinet session.

"The Fuehrer left no doubt in the mind of the British Ambassador that the obligations assumed by the British Government could not induce Germany to renounce the defense of her vital national interest."

Hitler's Tone Reported Blunt

Actually Herr Hitler's tone to Sir Nevile was reported to have been even more blunt than the communiqué indicates. In effect, Herr Hitler told the Ambassador that Britain had no business in Eastern Europe and that her guarantee of Poland merely encouraged Polish resistance to German demands, therefore it was up to Britain to persuade the Poles to yield or face the consequences.

Sir Nevile left the conference so wrought up he was speechless. Not trusting his memory to repeat the exact shadings of Herr Hitler's answer, he asked that it be put in writing and he returned for it a half hour later. He got it couched in the same strong terms that Herr Hitler used to him before.

At the same time there are also well-authenticated reports that, in addition to Prime Minister Chamberlain's letter, Sir Nevile also delivered to Herr Hitler an oral message that if Herr Hitler would give the Poles time Britain would try to induce Poland to come forth with new proposals. In that connection some circles launched—perhaps not unintentionally—the suggestion that Foreign Minister Josef Beck of Poland might after all ask to see Herr von Ribbentrop and even Herr Hitler. A preliminary meeting with the former might be arranged at Riga, Latvia, on Herr von Ribbentrop's return from Moscow. But Polish circles declare the suggestion was "extremely unlikely" because it spelled surrender.

As during the last few days the word in Berlin is that the zero hour, which will set the German Army on the march, will come today, and these rumors are supplemented with the additional detail that the exact hour is 6 P. M. [noon, New York time], which might mean "contact with the enemy" some time tomorrow. Furthermore, orders to postpone action, issued after Herr von Ribbentrop's departure for Moscow, have been canceled again.

Germans Elated by News

How much all that is merely a part of the "war of nerves" and how much is bitter reality remains to be seen. In fact the tension developing in Germany, at least in an atmosphere of fantastic unreality, is made no more real by the delayed Summer heat that lures the populace to the woods and beaches, and, together with the elation over the Russian pact and renewed confidence in Herr Hitler's diplomatic superiority over the democratic statesmen, helps to hide the war clouds.

However, the rebuff to Britain yesterday, which in some quarters is compared with the rebuff administered to the French Ambassador by King William of Prussia just preceding the Franco-Prussian War

Continued on Page Two

Text of the Berlin-Moscow Treaty

By The Associated Press.

MOSCOW, Thursday, Aug. 24.—The text of the German-Russian non-aggression pact announced here today follows:

The German Reich Government and the Union of Soviet Socialist Republics, moved by a desire to strengthen the state of peace between Germany and the U.S.S.R. and in the spirit of the provisions of the neutrality treaty of April, 1926, between Germany and the U.S.S.R., decided the following:

Article I

The two contracting parties obligate themselves to refrain from every act of force, every aggressive action and every attack against one another, including any single action or that taken in conjunction with other powers.

Article II

In case one of the parties of this treaty should become the object of warlike acts by a third power, the other party will in no way support this third power.

Article III

The governments of the two contracting parties in the future will constantly remain in consultation with one another in order to inform each other regarding questions of common interest.

Article IV

Neither of the high contracting parties will associate itself with any other grouping of powers which directly or indirectly is aimed at the other party.

Article V

In the event of a conflict between the contracting parties concerning any question, the two parties will adjust this difference or conflict exclusively by friendly exchange of opinions or, if necessary, by an arbitration commission.

Article VI

The present treaty will extend for a period of ten years with the condition that if neither of the contracting parties announces its abrogation within one year of expiration of this period, it will continue in force automatically for another period of five years.

Article VII

The present treaty shall be ratified within the shortest possible time. The exchange of ratification documents shall take place in Berlin. The treaty becomes effective immediately upon signature.

Drawn up in two languages, German and Russian.
Moscow, 23d *of August*, 1939.

For the German Government:
RIBBENTROP.

In the name of the Government of the U.S.S.R.:
MOLOTOFF.

NO MILITARY MOVES APPARENT IN ITALY

Country Remains Tranquil as Regime Fails to Whip Up Any War Fervor Among People

By HERBERT L. MATTHEWS

Wireless to THE NEW YORK TIMES.

ROME, Aug. 23.—The Italian ship of state sailed tranquilly on the edge of the European tornado today. There have been no conferences, communiqués, evacuation orders, special mobilization or troop movements.

There have been only some diplomatic visits to Count Ciano, the Foreign Minister, including those of the British and French Ambassadors. This is the fourth time since last Thursday that Sir Percy Loraine saw Count Ciano, which shows the degree of pressure the British are bringing to bear as well as their anxiety to make the Italian leaders realize Britain's determination to support Poland. Presumably, Sir Percy delivered a copy of the same note that was presented to Chancellor Hitler, although that has not been admitted.

André François-Poncet's visit was his first since returning to Rome last Friday. He has tried steadily to see the Foreign Minister but hitherto without success. It is believed he also impressed on Count Ciano France's intention to abide by her pledges.

The Hungarian Minister, Baron Frederick Villani, also saw Count Ciano today, reviving reports about Germany's demands on Budapest.

Italian People Are Calm

The Italian people are not being whipped up to the fervor that would be required to enter a war in the next few days. Nowhere do you see air shelters being hastily dug or gas masks being distributed.

Only in the newspapers do the commentators warn their readers that a conflict seems near, while relatively full accounts of the developments in various capitals are given. The British Cabinet's statement last night is published fully in all newspapers here, whereas the German press ignored it. If readers trusted their Italian newspapers this evening they would have a biased but reasonably correct appreciation of the dangers of the present situation.

On the other hand, so far as they know their country is making no last-minute efforts to meet the

Continued on Page Four

PRESIDENT SPEEDS TO ACT ON CRISIS

Disturbed by War Threat, He Will End Cruise Today and Board Train at Red Bank

By FELIX BELAIR Jr.

Special to THE NEW YORK TIMES.

RED BANK, N. J., Aug. 23.—Admittedly disturbed by the European war crisis, President Roosevelt is hurrying here aboard the navy cruiser Tuscaloosa after scrapping plans for a more ceremonious landing at Annapolis in order to be back at the White House in the event of an outbreak of hostilities.

A small White House secretarial staff is awaiting the arrival of the President off Sandy Hook early tomorrow to give him a bundle of official diplomatic reports on the latest developments abroad. Mr. Roosevelt plans to study the reports aboard his special train en route to Washington.

After debarking from the Tuscaloosa about 8 A. M. tomorrow the President will motor here with Brig. Gen. Edwin M. Watson, his secretary, and Rear Admiral Ross T. McIntire, White House physician. He is expected to stop long enough before entraining for the capital to telephone Secretary of State Cordell Hull, as well as to the embassies in London and Paris about overnight developments.

To Get War Supplies Report

Back at the White House in the early afternoon the President will have before him a report of the War Industries Committee on the status of the nation's munitions and other heavy industries. The committee has been canvassing the aviation and other industries in the past few days with a view to American preparedness.

Prior to the departure of the White House staff late today it was understood the War Industries Committee had drafted a report informing the President that the aviation and several other industries were prepared for any emergency that might arise and that aircraft manufacturers were ahead of schedule on orders of military planes from France and Great Britain.

Among Presidential intimates as well as the capital's political observers interest centered during the day on the question of whether Mr. Roosevelt considered the situation abroad sufficiently grave to call a

Continued on Page Three

BARS HOSTILE UNION

Treaty Forbids Either to Join Any Group Aimed at Other

ESCAPE CLAUSE OMITTED

Von Ribbentrop's Car, Flying Swastika, Passes Beneath Red Flag at Kremlin

By The Associated Press.

MOSCOW, Thursday, Aug. 24.—Germany and Soviet Russia early today signed a non-aggression pact binding each of them for ten years not to "associate itself with any other grouping of powers which directly or indirectly is aimed at the other party."

By the pact they also agreed to "constantly remain in consultation with one another" on their common interests and to adjust differences by arbitration.

The non-aggression clauses bound each power to refrain from any act of force against the other and if either party is "the object of warlike acts by a third power" to refrain from supporting that third power.

The pact did not include the usual escape clause providing for its denunciation in case one of the contracting parties attacked a third power. This provision has been written into most non-aggression agreements signed in the past by Moscow.

Arrives by Plane

By G. E. R. GEDYE

Special Cable to THE NEW YORK TIMES.

MOSCOW, Thursday, Aug. 24.—With the meticulous punctuality of a perfectly staged arrival, two huge Focke-Wulf Condor planes conveying Joachim von Ribbentrop, the German Foreign Minister, and his thirty-two assistants, landed at the Moscow airdrome on the stroke of 1 P. M. yesterday.

Adequate but not excessive police precautions were taken at the airdrome. For the first time the Soviet authorities displayed the swastika banner, five of which flew from the front of the airdrome building, but were placed so as not to be visible from the outside.

Vyacheslaff M. Molotoff was not present to welcome Herr von Ribbentrop, probably because he is not only Commissar of Foreign Affairs but also Premier, and therefore higher in rank than Herr von Ribbentrop. Instead the visitor was received by Vladimir P. Potemkin, Vice Commissar of Foreign Affairs; Mr. Barkoff, protocol chief; Mr. Merkuloff, Vice Commissar of Internal Affairs, under whom falls the NKVD, formerly the GPU; Mr. Alexandroff, chief of the Central European Department of the Foreign Office, and General Suvoroff, commander of the Moscow garrison.

Almost the entire staff of the huge German Embassy, headed by the Ambassador, Count Friedrich Werner von der Schulenburg, with the military, naval and air attachés in uniform, was present. The German civilians mostly wore top hats and cutaway coats.

The Italian Ambassador, Augusto Russo, with his military attaché in uniform, also was present. The feature of the reception most commented upon was the absence of any Japanese representative.

The German Embassy staff stood lined up like troops on parade. As each was presented to Herr von Ribbentrop he sprang to attention, clicked his heels, gave the Hitler salute and shook hands, again saluting and heel-clicking.

In Old Austrian Embassy

From the airdrome the party drove to the city through streets where police in their white Summer jackets stood every ten paces. For Herr von Ribbentrop the Soviet Government provided a large American car from the Kremlin car park, flying the swastika flag.

The party drove directly to the former Austrian Embassy, where they are being housed. Subsequently Herr von Ribbentrop and leading members of his mission had luncheon at the embassy with Count von der Schulenburg.

At about 3:30 P. M. Herr von Ribbentrop, accompanied by Count von der Schulenburg and an expert translator whom the Germans brought from Berlin, drove through the gates of the Kremlin with its

Continued on Page Six

"All the News That's Fit to Print."

The New York Times.

EXTRA

Partly cloudy and somewhat warmer today. Tomorrow generally fair with moderate temperatures.

Temperatures Yesterday—Max., 67; Min., 61

VOL. LXXXVIII...No. 29,805. Entered as Second-Class Matter, Postoffice, New York, N. Y. NEW YORK, FRIDAY, SEPTEMBER 1, 1939. THREE CENTS NEW YORK CITY and Vicinity | FOUR CENTS Elsewhere Except in 7th and 8th Postal Zones.

GERMAN ARMY ATTACKS POLAND; CITIES BOMBED, PORT BLOCKADED; DANZIG IS ACCEPTED INTO REICH

BRITISH MOBILIZING

Navy Raised to Its Full Strength, Army and Air Reserves Called Up

PARLIAMENT IS CONVOKED

Midnight Meeting Is Held by Ministers—Negotiations Admitted Failure

By The Associated Press.

LONDON, Friday, Sept. 1.—The British Parliament was summoned to meet today at 5 P. M. [12 noon in New York].

British Call Up Forces

By FERDINAND KUHN Jr.

Special Cable to THE NEW YORK TIMES.

LONDON, Friday, Sept. 1.—All attempts to bring about direct negotiations between Germany and Poland appeared to have broken down tonight as Great Britain mobilized her fleet to full strength, stretched her other defensive preparations close to the limit and began moving 3,000,000 school children and invalids from the crowded cities into the safety of the countryside.

Censorship was established over cables after London had been cut off for hours from communication with the Continent.

It was the peak of the crisis, but a day of rumors had not shifted the fundamental issue nor given a conclusive answer to the question of peace or war.

At midnight the British Government was not yet convinced that Germany really intended to attack Poland and provoke a world war.

Terms Called Smoke Screen

All that had happened during yesterday, including the sudden broadcasting of Chancellor Hitler's sixteen-point demands, was interpreted here as a smoke screen rather than as the flash of guns.

After hearing Herr Hitler's "terms" officials here quietly announced tonight that "the government primarily interested in the proposals is, of course, the Polish Government."

Until the Polish Government has had time to consider them, it was said in Whitehall that "it would be highly undesirable for any comment to be made."

It was fully expected that Poland would reject them later today; indeed, Polish circles here were describing them tonight as "utterly unacceptable," for they would involve dismemberment of Poland and loss of Poland's capacity to defend her independence. In any event, there was no sign of any intention here to put pressure on Warsaw to accept.

Much might have been said about the German "proposals" here tonight if the government had not been so anxious to leave the first decision to Warsaw without any prompting. That the British regarded them as artful went without saying, since they conveyed a first impression of reasonableness that was not borne out by the terms themselves.

Until the announcement on the German wireless tonight, the British Government had not been told about them officially, and the Polish Government was not informed until Josef Lipski, Polish Ambassador to Berlin, visited Foreign Minister Joachim von Ribbentrop a few minutes before the broadcast took place.

Shortly after midnight last night, Sir Nevile Henderson, the British Ambassador in Berlin, had heard the "points" read to him by Herr von Ribbentrop, but the reading was so fast that the Ambassador could not even take notes of them in detail. In any event, he was told Herr Hitler's "points" were not being given to him or his government officially, on the ground that it was already too late.

Time Limit Expired

On Tuesday Herr Hitler had asked that a Polish negotiator should arrive in Berlin within twenty-four hours; and as nobody had arrived from Warsaw when the time limit expired, Sir Nevile was told that the "points" could not be communicated officially to [illegible]

[illegible] German time table with the

Continued on Page Four

Bulletins on Europe's Conflict

London Hears of Warsaw Bombing

LONDON, Friday, Sept. 1 (AP).—Reuters British news agency said it had learned from Polish sources in Paris that Warsaw was bombed today.

French Confirm Beginning of War

PARIS, Friday, Sept. 1 (AP).—The Havas news agency said today that official French dispatches from Germany indicated that "the Reich began hostilities on Poland this morning."

The agency also reported that the Polish Embassy here had announced that "Germany violated the Polish frontier at four points."

"German reports of pretended violation of German territory by Poland are pure invention, as is the fable of 'attack' by Polish insurgents on Gleiwitz," the embassy announcement said.

Attack on Entire Front Reported

LONDON, Friday, Sept. 1 (AP).—A Reuters dispatch from Paris said:

"The following is given with all reserve: According to unconfirmed reports received here, the Germans have begun an offensive with extreme violence on the whole Polish front."

First Wounded Brought Into Gleiwitz

GLEIWITZ, Germany, Friday, Sept. 1 (AP).—An army ambulance carrying wounded soldiers arrived at the emergency hospital here today at 9:10 A. M.

The men, carried in a wagon, were on stretchers. One had on a first-aid field bandage. It could not be ascertained where the ambulance came from.

At about 9:30 a half-mile long truck train manned by the engineering corps drove through the heart of the city with pontoon bridge building material. In the train were caterpillar tread, twenty-passenger motor vans.

Obviously the train had been on the road for a considerable time. All equipment was thickly covered with gray mud.

A scouting plane of the air force was patrolling an area over Gleiwitz.

Early today Gleiwitz residents reported that artillery fire

Continued on Page Four

DALADIER SUMMONS CABINET TO CONFER

News of Attack on Poland Spurs Prompt Action—Military Move Thought Likely

By The Associated Press.

PARIS, Friday, Sept. 1.—Edouard Daladier, Premier and War Minister of France, informed that German troops crossed the Polish frontier today, summoned an urgent meeting of his Cabinet for 10:30 A. M.

It was probable that Parliament would be called tomorrow.

Reports of the German invasion came from Berlin and from the Polish Embassy here. The Ministers were called to the Elysee Palace to meet with President Albert Lebrun.

Upon receipt of word of the German operations M. Daladier rushed to the War Ministry and called General Marie Gustave Gamelin, supreme commander of land, sea and air forces, into consultation.

A little later Daladier summoned Foreign Minister Georges Bonnet.

The Polish Embassy said that Germans violated the Polish frontier at four points and at the same time it characterized German charges that Poles had crossed into Germany as "pure invention."

Havas, Frnch news agency, announced that "a German declaration of war against Poland probably will lead France and Great Britain to take new military measures."

Britain and France are committed to aid Poland in any fight to save her independence.

Ministers Stand Firm

By P. J. PHILIP

Wireless to THE NEW YORK TIMES.

PARIS, Aug. 31.—The Cabinet met with President Albert Lebrun for more than two hours this evening at the Elysée Palace. At the close of the meeting Minister of the Interior Albert Sarraut handed the press the following communiqué:

"MM. Edouard Daladier, President of the Council, and Georges Bonnet, Minister of Foreign Affairs, laid before the Cabinet a detailed account of the international situation as a whole.

"The Cabinet was unanimous in formally maintaining the engagements taken by France."

Later M. Daladier had further conversations with M. Bonnet, Fi-

Continued on Page Four

BRITISH CHILDREN TAKEN FROM CITIES

3,000,000 Persons Are in First Evacuation Group, Which Is to Be Moved Today

By FREDERICK T. BIRCHALL

Special Cable to THE NEW YORK TIMES.

LONDON, Friday, Sept. 1.—The greatest mass movement of population at short notice in the history of Great Britain is under way. It is an evacuation, under government order, of little children, invalids, women and old men from congested areas.

From London, Birmingham, Manchester, Liverpool, Edinburgh, Glasgow and twenty-three other cities the great exodus is going on as this dispatch is being written. The numbers are stupendous. More than 3,000,000 of these helpless human beings are being taken out of danger of German bombs.

Nothing like it has ever been attempted anywhere; yet it is going on without mishap—so far, indeed, without serious confusion.

Scenes everywhere were much the same whether in the aristocratic West End or the proletarian East Side, but one that this correspon-

Continued on Page Three

HOSTILITIES BEGUN

Warsaw Reports German Offensive Moving on Three Objectives

ROOSEVELT WARNS NAVY

Also Notifies Army Leaders of Warfare—Envoys Tell of Bombing of 4 Cities

By JERZY SZAPIRO

Wireless to THE NEW YORK TIMES.

WARSAW, Poland, Friday, Sept. 1.—War began at 5 o'clock this morning with German planes attacking Gdynia, Cracow and Katowice.

At Gdynia three bombs exploded in the sea.

The regular German Army started an offensive in the direction of Dzialdowka—in Upper Silesia and Czestochowa. The German plan apparently is to cut off Western Poland along the line of Dzialdowka-Lodz-Czestochowa.

The offensive is developing, from East Prussia, toward Silesia and northwards from Slovakia.

At 9 o'clock an attempt was made to bombard Warsaw. The planes, however, did not reach even the suburbs.

A military attack on the garrison at Westerplatte in the Danzig area was repulsed.

The Foreign Office at 8:45 A. M. issued a communiqué saying that military action had begun in Westerplatte in the Danzig area as well as in Buschkowa near Gdynia, and in Dzialowka, Chojnice and Lowa.

Hostilities have begun and Poland has been attacked, said the communiqué.

Three cities in Upper Silesia suffered artillery bombardment, particulars of which are lacking, it was said.

While this dispatch was being telephoned, the air-raid sirens sounded in Warsaw.

Danzig Fighting Reported

WARSAW, Poland, Friday, Sept. 1 (AP).—It was reported today that Tczew and Czestochowa were bombed by German airplanes early this morning.

There was no official confirmation of the bombing.

Fighting was reported at Danzig. It was reported officially that German troops had attacked Polish defenses near Mlawa, bordering the southern part of East Prussia. There was no announcement of the damage resulting from the bombing.

Mist and clouds were overhanging the city. A light drizzle apparently afforded momentary protection against air raids. Warsaw went to work as usual.

Roosevelt Warns Navy

WASHINGTON, Friday, Sept. 1 (AP).—President Roosevelt directed today that all naval ships and army commands be notified at once by radio of German-Polish hostilities.

The White House issued the following announcement:

"The President received word at 2:50 A. M. Eastern standard time

Continued on Page Five

FREE CITY IS SEIZED

Forster Notifies Hitler of Order Putting Danzig Into the Reich

ACCEPTED BY CHANCELLOR

Poles Ready, Made Their Preparations After Hostilities Appeared Inevitable

Special Cable to THE NEW YORK TIMES.

DANZIG, Friday, Sept. 1.—By a decree issued early this morning Albert Forster, Nazi Chief of State, proclaimed the annexation of the Free City to the Reich, thus settling by a fell stroke the original point of contention in the international crisis.

In a telegram to Chancellor Hitler Herr Forster explained his action as necessary to remove "the pressing necessity of our people and State." Herr Forster also issued a proclamation to the people of Danzig saying the hour awaited for twenty years had arrived because "our Fuehrer, Adolf Hitler, has freed us."

[A NEW YORK TIMES dispatch from Berlin this morning said Herr Hitler telegraphed Herr Forster today thanking him and all Danzigers, and stating:

"The law for reannexation is in effect immediately."

The Chancellor stated, furthermore, that Herr Forster was appointed head of the civil administration of the Danzig area.]

In a four-article decree Herr Forster declared the Constitution of Danzig no longer valid. He declared himself sole administrator of the Danzig part of the German Reich, and he declared that until the Reich's legal system had been introduced by command of Herr Hitler all laws except the Constitution remained in effect. Then Herr Forster immediately wired Herr Hitler of his action, begged the Chancellor to give his approval of the move and through Reich law complete the annexation.

The German flag is now flying everywhere over Danzig, Herr Forster said, and all church bells resound to the event. "We thank God," he declared, "that He gave the Fuehrer the strength and the possibility to free also us from the evil Versailles treaty."

Hitler Accepts Danzig

By The Associated Press.

BERLIN, Friday, Sept. 1.—The German official news agency, D. N. B., announced today that Albert Forster, Nazi Chief of State in Danzig, had proclaimed the reunion of the Free City with the Reich.

Herr Hitler today accepted the Free City of Danzig into the Reich.

"I acknowledge your proclamation of the return of the Free City of Danzig to the Reich," Herr Hitler's telegram said. "I thank you, Gauleiter Forster, and all Danzig men and women, for your loyalty which you have displayed for so many years.

"Greater Germany welcomes you with joy in her heart.

"The law of reunion will be enacted forthwith. I appoint you, Herr Forster, chief of the civil administration in the Danzig territory."

Forster's telegram to Herr Hitler read:

My Fuehrer.

I have just signed and then put into effect the following basic law, concerning the reunion of Danzig with the German Reich.

The basic State law of the Free State of Danzig and the reunion of Danzig with the German Reich is effective Sept. 1, 1939.

To lift the immediate distress of the people and State of the Free City of Danzig, I decree the following basic State law:

ARTICLE I

The Constitution of the Free City of Danzig has been suspended effective immediately.

ARTICLE II

All legal and administrative power will be executed exclusively by the head of State.

ARTICLE III

The Free City of Danzig with its territory and its peoples forms

Continued on Page Five

Soviet Ratifies Reich Non-Aggression Pact; Gibes at British and French Amuse Deputies

By G. E. R. GEDYE

Special Cable to THE NEW YORK TIMES.

MOSCOW, Aug. 31.—With Premier and Foreign Commissar Vyacheslaff M. Molotoff, working under high pressure—so suddenly applied without any previous indication and contrasting so sharply with earlier delaying tactics this week as to suggest German insistence that the matter be finally settled—the Supreme Soviet [Parliament] tonight unanimously ratified the Russo-German non-aggression pact.

Ratification, which was first foreshadowed at midday, was preceded by a speech by Mr. Molotoff so precise in its definition of Soviet obligations to refrain from participating on the side of Great Britain and France in any war against Germany, so voluble in its defense against charges of inconsistency against Communist Russia for embracing Fascist Germany, and so insistent on the inevitability of friendship between "not merely the governments but also the peoples" of Germany and Russia as to extinguish the last faint hopes of the western democracies that Moscow might yet find loopholes or excuses for joining them at some subsequent date in resisting German aggression against Poland.

Mr. Molotoff's speech contained nothing to justify constantly repeated suspicions of the existence of a secret German-Soviet pact entitling the latter to participate in a partition of Poland.

The Premier's speech contained much trenchant and seemingly irrefutable evidence of blunders by the British and French Governments in handling the question of Soviet cooperation. It was not diffi-

Continued on Page Eight

Hitler Acts Against Poland

The port of Gdynia, north of Danzig (toward top of map), was blockaded this morning. At Gleiwitz (shown by cross) artillery fire was heard after a Polish-German skirmish had been reported there. Cracow, to the east, was among Polish cities said to have been bombed.

Hitler Tells the Reichstag 'Bomb Will Be Met by Bomb'

Chancellor Vows 'Fight Until Resolution' Against Poland—Gives Order of Succession As Goering, Hess, Then Senate to Choose

Chancellor Adolf Hitler of Germany, in a world broadcast this morning, opened "a fight until the resolution of the situation" against Poland, announcing that "from now on bomb will be met by bomb."

At the same time he announced, to face any eventuality, that if anything "happened" to him, Field Marshal Hermann Goering was to be in charge; if to Marshal Goering, Rudolph Hess; if to Herr Hess, the Senate, which he proposes to appoint, will select a successor.

The Chancellor, after attempting to narrow the conflict with Poland by assuring the Western powers that he had no designs on their frontiers, by assuring the neutrality of the sideline powers and by acknowledging the friendliness of Italy and the new relations with Russia, issued a defy to Poland's allies.

Says He Will Carry on

"I shall carry on this fight regardless of against whom I may come," he declared.

At the same time he held the door open for Poland to capitulate to his demands, declaring that he did not intend to make war against women and children. He said that if a solution did not come from the present Polish Government, it would come from a future Polish Government.

The Chancellor expressed confidence, toward the close of his address, that his decision, which was being broadcast over amplifiers hastily erected by electricians at the last moment in the streets of Berlin and the provincial capitals, would be accepted by the German people.

The scene enacted in the Kroll Opera House in Berlin was carried over sound waves to most of the nations of the world. From Berlin hook-ups had been arranged with the three major networks of the United States, and, according to the announcer for the German broadcasting system, over the Italian, Hungarian, Spanish, Norwegian, Swedish, Danish, Yugoslav, British and French national networks.

The summons to the Reichstag, ordered by Herr Hitler himself, had been sent out only a few hours before the meeting. Most of the members had been awaiting the signal, and when the opera house opened shortly before 10 o'clock [5 o'clock, New York time] this morning, they were dressed in the uniforms of their military formations.

After Herr Hitler finished speaking the deputies enacted a law incorporating Danzig into the Reich, declaring Danzig citizens were now Germans, voiding the Constitution of the Free City and extending to its territory the jurisdiction of German law.

At 5:10 A. M., Marshal Goering opened the meeting and turned the floor over to the Chancellor.

In the early part of his address, Herr Hitler electrified his audience with this declaration:

"We have all been suffering under the tortures that the Versailles treaty has been inflicting upon us."

Then, speaking with measured deliberateness of Germany's claims to the pre-war German areas, he announced, as he had on a previous occasion:

"The Treaty of Versailles is, for us Germans, and has been, for us Germans, not a law."

Anticipating what the announcement's reiteration would lead to, the Deputies roared applause. Then Herr Hitler, his indignation rising as he proceeded, set about building up the German case, asserting that his proposals for a peaceful solution of the problem of Danzig and the Polish Corridor had been rejected, and charging that the Poles had visited atrocities on Germans, especially women and children, "killing many of them."

SUMMARY OF SPEECH

A summary of Herr Hitler's speech was translated as follows:

"For months we have been suffering under the burdens of the Treaty of Versailles. Danzig was and is a German city. All these regions have only Germany to thank for their cultural development.

"Minorities in the Polish Corridor have been shamefully mistreated. Here, as in other respects, I have tried to solve the problems by peaceful means. In the fifteen years of National Socialism we have been

Continued on Page Three

HITLER GIVES WORD

In a Proclamation He Accuses Warsaw of Appeal to Arms

FOREIGNERS ARE WARNED

They Remain in Poland at Own Risk—Nazis to Shoot at Any Planes Flying Over Reich

By OTTO D. TOLISCHUS

Special Cable to THE NEW YORK TIMES.

BERLIN, Friday, Sept. 1.—Charging that Germany had been attacked, Chancellor Hitler at 5:11 o'clock this morning issued a proclamation to the army declaring that from now on force will be met with force and calling on the armed forces "to fulfill their duty to the end."

The text of the proclamation reads:

To the defense forces:

The Polish nation refused my efforts for a peaceful regulation of neighborly relations; instead it has appealed to weapons.

Germans in Poland are persecuted with a bloody terror and are driven from their homes. The series of border violations, which are unbearable to a great power, prove that the Poles no longer are willing to respect the German frontier. In order to put an end to this frantic activity no other means is left to me now than to meet force with force.

"Battle for Honor"

German defense forces will carry on the battle for the honor of the living rights of the reawakened German people with firm determination.

I expect every German soldier, in view of the great tradition of eternal German soldiery, to do his duty until the end.

Remember always in all situations you are the representatives of National Socialist Greater Germany!

Long live our people and our Reich!

Berlin, Sept. 1, 1939.

ADOLF HITLER.

The commander-in-chief of the air force issued a decree effective immediately prohibiting the passage of any airplanes over German territory excepting those of the Reich air force or the government.

This morning the naval authorities ordered all German mercantile ships in the Baltic Sea not to run to Danzig or Polish ports.

Anti-air raid defenses were mobilized throughout the country early this morning.

A formal declaration of war against Poland had not yet been declared up to 8 o'clock [3 A. M. New York time] this morning and the question of whether the two countries are in a state of active belligerency is still open.

Reichstag Will Meet Today

Foreign correspondents at an official conference at the Reich Press Ministry at 8:30 o'clock [3:30 A. M. New York time] were told that they would receive every opportunity to facilitate the transmission of dispatches. Wireless stations have been instructed to speed up communications and the Ministry is installing additional batteries of telephones.

The Reichstag has been summoned to meet at 10 o'clock [5 A. M. New York time] to receive a more formal declaration from Herr Hitler.

The Hitler army order is interpreted as providing, for the time being, armed defense of the German frontiers against aggression. The action is also suspected of forcing international diplomatic action.

The Germans announced that foreigners remain in Polish territory at their own risk.

Flying over Polish territory as well as the maritime areas is forbidden by the German authorities and any violators will be shot down.

When Herr Hitler made his an-

Continued on Page Three

CHAMBERLAIN ANNOUNCES BRITAIN IS AT WAR WITH GERMANY

"All the News That's Fit to Print."

The New York Times.

EXTRA

Generally fair, little change in temperature today. Tomorrow cloudy, showers in afternoon or night.
Temperatures Yesterday—Max., 80; Min., 64

Section 1

NEWS INDEX, PAGE 21, THIS SECTION

Copyright, 1939, by The New York Times Company.

VOL. LXXXVIII....No. 29,807

Entered as Second-Class Matter, Postoffice, New York, N. Y.

NEW YORK, SUNDAY, SEPTEMBER 3, 1939.

P

Including Rotogravure Picture, Magazine and Book Review. TEN CENTS | TWELVE CENTS Beyond 200 Miles Except in 7th and 8th Postal Zones.

BRITAIN AND FRANCE IN WAR AT 6 A. M.; HITLER WON'T HALT ATTACK ON POLES; CHAMBERLAIN CALLS EMPIRE TO FIGHT

SOVIET IN WARNING

British-French Action to Bring Western Border Revision, Berlin Hears

NAZIS GREET MISSION

Hitler to Receive New Russian Ambassador and General Today

By OTTO D. TOLISCHUS

Wireless to THE NEW YORK TIMES.

BERLIN, Sunday, Sept. 3.—According to well-informed quarters here Moscow is already supposed to have notified Paris and London that if France and Britain join in the present Reich-Polish conflict Russia will find herself compelled to revise her Western borders.

This is tantamount to the threat that any British and French help to Poland will merely hasten the partition of Poland between Germany and Russia. There are hints that Russia might also seek other "compensation" in regions even less convenient to Britain.

As an impressive demonstration of this new cooperation there arrived today by air from Stockholm a new Russian Ambassador and a new embassy secretary, both of whom were said to be very close to Premier Vyacheslaff Molotoff, and a Russian military mission headed by a commanding general.

Officials Greet the Mission

The new Ambassador is Alexander Shkhartzeff, who, it is pointed out here, collaborated with Mr. Molotoff in the Commissariat of Foreign Affairs in Moscow. The new embassy secretary is Vladimir Perloff, up to now Mr. Molotoff's secretary and interpreter.

The military mission consists of General Maxim Purjakoff, designated as the Military Plenipotentiary of the U. S. S. R., and his staff; Brig. Gen. Michael Beljakoff, Colonel Nikolai Skornjakoff, Major Basanoff and Captain Alexander Seditch.

To show the importance of the occasion the members were met at Tempelhof Airfield by Dr. Ernst Woermann, Under-Secretary of State in the Foreign Office; Baron Alexander von Doernberg, Chief of Protocol, and other Foreign Office officials. Lieut. Gen. Seifert, commander of Berlin, headed the list of army officers greeting the Russians. A guard of honor presented arms.

The Russians received an ovation as their automobiles, flying the hammer-and-sickle flag of the Soviet Union, passed the Reich Chancellery. Those assembled along the street gave the Nazi salute.

Hitler to Receive Envoy

Adding importance to all this is the fact that it was announced at midnight that Herr Hitler would receive the new Ambassador, together with the Military Plenipotentiary, for the submission of credentials later today, which sets a precedent for diplomatic speed.

That such a formidable military mission was sent here to work out close collaboration with the German Army is taken for granted here. But German quarters still hold that the consultative clauses of the German-Russian pact are sufficient to cover all the collaboration necessary and a formal military alliance may be signed only as the last trump card to impress London and Paris.

Ambassador Joseph Lipski and his whole embassy staff left Berlin this morning under safe conduct en route to Sweden, which has also taken over the representation of Polish interests. The German Embassy staff was supposed to have left Warsaw at the same time. German interests in Poland are being represented by the Netherlands. Official quarters hold, however, that this merely represents a "cessation of direct diplomatic relations," not a formal break of relations, just as there is no declared state of war.

Meanwhile, since the German-Polish conflict is now being arbitrated by the roar of cannon the re-

Continued on Page Sixteen

Announcement of Final Ultimatum

By The Associated Press.

LONDON, Sunday, Sept. 3.—Following is the text of today's communique revealing the final ultimatum to Germany:

On Sept. 2 His Majesty's Ambassador in Berlin was instructed to inform the German Government that unless they were prepared to give His Majesty's Government in the United Kingdom satisfactory assurances that the German Government had suspended all aggressive action against Poland and were prepared promptly to withdraw their forces from Polish territory, His Majesty's Government in the United Kingdom would without hesitation fulfill their obligations to Poland.

At 9 A. M. this morning His Majesty's Ambassador in Berlin informed the German Government that unless not later than 11 A. M., British Summer time, today, Sept. 3, satisfactory assurances to the above effect had been given by the German Government and had reached His Majesty's Government in London a state of war would exist between the two countries as from that hour.

His Majesty's Government are now awaiting the receipt of any reply that may be made by the German Government.

The Prime Minister will broadcast to the nation at 11:15 A. M.

21 CIVILIANS KILLED IN RAID ON WARSAW

Women, Children Die as Bomb Hits Workers' Apartment—State of War Decreed

By The Associated Press.

WARSAW, Poland, Sept. 2.—Twenty-one dead and more than thirty wounded were counted tonight after German bombs had struck an apartment house in a Warsaw workingmen's quarter.

The bombs tore off the side of the apartment house as if it had been made of paper. Rescue workers still were clearing away the resultant pile of debris in a search for further casualties when this correspondent inspected it.

One of the bombs had dug a crater fully twenty feet in diameter, and the open ground was piled high with furniture and belongings.

In the center of a large park in the southern section of Warsaw, this writer also saw where a bomb had struck a simple wooden dwelling, killing two persons and wounding one. In an open field near the Vistula River, where ten light bombs apparently had been released simultaneously, they had dug craters in a 100-yard circle.

With the writer on this tour of inspection of damage done by the German air bombings were C. Burke Elbrick, secretary of the American Embassy; Clifford Norton, chargé d'affaires of the British Embassy, and officials of the Polish Foreign Office.

During the tour the party twice was forced to take refuge because of air-raid alarms, five of which in all sounded through the city today. Once the party took cover in a shallow dugout filled with working men, their wives and their crying children.

The worst scene of damage was at Kolo, the workingmen's quarter, where, in addition to wrecking one apartment building, the bombs had smashed windows in several others.

An old man gulped back tears as he said his wife and two children were dead. A woman, still staring blankly into space, said: "My husband is gone."

An official news service communiqué stated that yesterday German raiders dropped 120 bombs on Warsaw and its vicinity, killing ten and wounding twenty-five in Warsaw proper, with the number of casualties in the suburbs still undetermined.

President Ignaz Moscicki declared that Poland was under a "state of war" today as official reports said that Polish forces were resisting German invasion on three fronts.

The "state of war" supersedes the

Continued on Page Fourteen

News dispatches from Europe are now virtually all subject to censorship

PARIS AUTHORIZED WAR DECLARATION

Chamber Voted Credits After Hearing Daladier—New Ultimatum Being Drawn

By The Associated Press.

PARIS, Sept. 2.—Premier Edouard Daladier today received implied authority from the Chamber of Deputies to declare war on Germany.

With that to support them, he and his Cabinet met at the War Ministry at 7:30 tonight to frame a demand that Chancellor Hitler reply to the British-French "last warning" of yesterday.

The power to declare war was vested in a war budget bill of 69,000,000,000 francs, which the sober Deputies, many wearing army uniforms, adopted unanimously by a show of hands after hearing M. Daladier say the government was still willing to negotiate if Germany would cease hostilities in Poland.

Whether the Premier uses the authority vested in him by adoption of the budget depends upon the possibility—frankly viewed as slight—that Herr Hitler would avail himself of a last-minute loophole for peace.

The Premier told the finance committee that he planned to call the Chamber to approve an actual declaration of war if that became necessary, but he may simply ask for approval after, rather than before, the action is taken.

"The government will take the same chance as Parisians," M. Daladier told a Deputy who asked whether the government planned to leave Paris immediately.

The session was held in a tense atmosphere from 3 to 3:55 P. M.

Continued on Page Seventeen

ROME ASKED PEACE

Pressed Its Proposal for a 5-Power Parley on Britain and France

WAR MEASURES CUT

Press Expressed the Hope Germany Would Win in Poland

By The Associated Press.

ROME, Sept. 2.—Premier Mussolini tonight sought to prevent Polish-German hostilities from spreading into a general European war by arranging a negotiated settlement.

Conferences that the British and French Ambassadors had with Foreign Minister Count Ciano were believed to be connected directly with an Italian proposal of a five-power conference discussed in London by Prime Minister Neville Chamberlain and Foreign Secretary Viscount Halifax.

The possibility of halting the German-Polish conflict and arranging a peaceable settlement was believed to have been discussed at the diplomatic conferences, but no official information was forthcoming.

Some foreign observers believed, however, that Signor Mussolini had been asked to use his influence on Adolf Hitler to halt fighting in Poland, call his army back and negotiate a settlement of his demands on the Poles.

For Wide Settlement

Here it was regarded as certain that any five-power conference proposed by Premier Mussolini would not be merely for settling the German-Polish conflict but would be aimed at complete revision of the Treaty of Versailles.

Under such a revision Italy and Germany would seek the political and economic concessions that they consider necessary to end European tension once and for all. This has long been Signor Mussolini's idea and Italian newspapers recently have been stressing it as the only real solution. [Italy has been demanding from France concessions concerning Tunisia, the Suez Canal and Jibuti, French Somaliland port.]

While the Ambassadors of France and Britain conferred with Foreign Minister Ciano Italy continued her policy of watchful waiting and avoidance of any military "initiative".

The important commentator, Virginio Gayda, in the Giornale d'Italia noted uneasily that French and British war preparations made it seem that only a miracle could prevent a "more general explosion." Italy, he said, rested on her arms, confident she had done everything possible to avoid war. He said she was following events

Continued on Page Fifteen

NAZIS REPORT GAINS

Hitler's Aims in Corridor Already Won, They Say, Telling of Big 'Trap'

RESISTANCE IS NOTED

But Armies Drive On and Navy Is in Command of Baltic, Germans Hold

Special Cable to THE NEW YORK TIMES.

BERLIN, Sunday, Sept. 3.—Defying the British and French ultimatums, the German armies reported continued advances into Poland yesterday.

By nightfall, it was asserted, not only had they attained the German war aims in the Polish Corridor as outlined in Chancellor Hitler's "sixteen points" but they were pushing forward in a concentric drive toward Warsaw. According to one report, the German forces stood less than fifty miles north of the Polish capital, and a big battle was believed developing along the Narew River.

According to the latest communiqués of the army command, which apparently have already been overtaken by developments, the German armies operating out of East Prussia and Pomerania had virtually cut the Corridor along the Netze and Vistula Rivers, so that all Polish troops remaining in the bottleneck north of it were hopelessly trapped.

Claim Capture of Teschen

In the South the Germans were reported to have taken the heavily fortified Jablunka Pass, the main strategic highway from Slovakia into Poland; to have captured Teschen and Pless [Pszczyna] and to be breaking through the Polish bunker line approaching Biala. The army group apparently has the task of capturing the Upper Silesian industrial section and the Teschen coal mines, taken by Poland from Czecho-Slovakia, and then of advancing along the Vistula toward Sandomierz, the new Polish armament and industrial center.

At the same time two other German Army groups, operating from the north out of East Prussia and from the southwest out of Silesia, apparently were conducting a pincers movement on Warsaw. The southwestern group was declared to have taken Wielun and to be advancing toward Radomsk and Sieradz.

The Northern army group, according to a communiqué, was advancing on Przasnysz, but, according to private reports, is already beyond that town and approaching a larger Polish army that is supposed to have taken a stand on the Narew, where the first real battle of the undeclared war may take place.

Reich Claims "Air" Domination

The communiqué asserted also that the German air force, after many bombing expeditions against air fields, railroads, military transports, retreating marching columns and other military objectives, in which many planes and the munition factory at Skarzysko-Kamienna were destroyed, now has "unchallenged air domination over the entire Polish territory and so is now free for other tasks in protection of the Reich."

In addition, the Germany Navy, which said it had bombed the fortifications and port of Hela and also Gdynia, reported the sinking of a Polish torpedo boat off Hela. It was said to command the Baltic so completely that the fishing embargo was lifted last night.

A communiqué issued by the high command early today, according to the official German News Bureau, declared:

"The German air force yesterday again proved its absolute superiority. The whole air area over the battle zone and the hinterland is completely controlled by the German air force. Attacks were confined exclusively to military objectives.

"After units of German armored cars had reached the Vistula, approximately at noon, the German

Continued on Page Twelve

Fuller Breaks Own Bendix Race Records; Crosses Continent in 8 Hours 58 Minutes

Frank Fuller, San Francisco sportsman pilot, broke his own record in the Bendix Trophy Race from Burbank, Calif., to Cleveland yesterday and then kept on to Bendix, N. J., to break his own record for a transcontinental crossing in the event, opening feature of the National Air Races and the country's outstanding air derby.

Flying a stripped-down Seversky military plane equipped with the same twin Wasp engine he had in the 1937 race, when his earlier records were set, Fuller flew the 2,450 miles from Burbank to Bendix in an elapsed time of 8 hours 58 minutes 8.46 seconds. His average speed was 273.14 miles an hour. His elapsed time in 1937 was 9 hours 25 minutes.

The record for a transcontinental flight is 7 hours 28 minutes, established by Howard Hughes in a specially built plane about two years ago.

In crossing the finishing line at Bendix, Fuller, a wealthy paint manufacturer, won three prizes totaling $12,500. For being the first to reach Cleveland he received a prize of $9,000. As the first to fly over the line at Bendix he won another $1,000, and for breaking his 1937 record he won $2,500.

Fuller reached Bendix at 4:24:53 P. M., Eastern daylight time, and proceeded, without landing, to Floyd Bennett Field, where he brought his plane to earth at 4:35 P. M.

Max Constant of Burbank was the second racer to fly over Bendix, reaching there at 6:13:29 P. M. Arthur C. Bussy of Roversford, Pa., appeared at 7:06:15 P. M.

Although Constant arrived at Bendix ahead of Bussy, he took off from Burbank before him and Bussy was declared the second prize winner and received $5,000 for the flight to Cleveland and an additional $800 for continuing to Bendix and Floyd Bennett Field.

Mrs. Arline Davis of Cleveland landed at Newark Airport at 8 P. M., believing that she had crossed the official marker at Bendix and thereby won the $2,500 prize for the first woman to finish

Continued on Page Three

Text of Chamberlain Address

The following is the text of the address by Prime Minister Chamberlain from 10 Downing Street this morning:

I am speaking to you from the Cabinet Room from 10 Downing Street. This morning the British Ambassador in Berlin handed the German Government the final note stating unless we heard from them by 11 o'clock [6 o'clock New York time] that they were prepared at once to withdraw their troops from Poland a state of war would exist between us. I have to tell you now that no such undertaking has been received and consequently this country is at war with Germany.

You can imagine what a bitter blow it is to me that all my long struggle to win peace has failed. Up to the very last it should have been quite possible to arrange a peaceful settlement between Germany and Poland.

Hitler has evidently made up his mind to attack Poland whatever may happen. Hitler claims that his proposals were shown to Poland and to us. That is not a true statement. The proposals never were shown to the Poles or to us.

The German Government prepared the proposals in German and the same night the German troops crossed the Polish frontier. Germany will never give up force and can only be stopped by force.

We are prepared to uphold our treaty with Poland and to protect them from the wicked and unprovoked attacks on the Polish people. France is joining Britain in fulfillment of her pledges. We have a clear conscience and the situation has become intolerable. Now that we have determined to finish it I know that you will all play your part.

When I have finished speaking several detailed announcements will be made on behalf of the government giving you plans under which it will be possible to carry on the work of the nation in these days of stress which may be ahead, but these plans need your help. You may be taking part in one of the fighting services or one of the other branches.

It is of vital importance that you carry on with your jobs. May God bless you all and may He defend the right for it is the evil things we shall be fighting against—brute force, broken promises, bad faith. But I am certain that right shall prevail.

Bulletins on European Conflict

Air Raid Warning in London

LONDON, Sept. 3 (Sunday).—Air raid sirens sounded an alarm in London today at 11:32 A. M. (5:32 A. M., E.S.T.).

The whole city was sent to shelters by the wail of the alarm but all clear signals were sounded seventeen minutes later.

Ribbentrop Gives Reply to British Envoy

BERLIN, Sunday, Sept. 3 (AP).—German Foreign Minister Joachim von Ribbentrop received British Ambassador Sir Nevile Henderson at 9 A. M. [4 A. M. in New York] today to hand him Germany's answer to the "final warnings" of Britain and France. Herr von Ribbentrop was expected to see the French Ambassador, Robert Coulondre, shortly before noon.

American Diplomats' Families Leave Reich

BERLIN, Sunday, Sept. 3 (AP).—About fifty women and children of the United States Embassy and consular staffs, as well as several other American families, left Berlin today at 8:50 A. M. [3:50 A. M. in New York] for Copenhagen in compartments reserved for them in a regular train.

They were due in Copenhagen at 5:35 P. M. [12:35 A. M. in New York].

War Announced in France

PARIS, Sunday, Sept. 3 (AP).—The radio announced to the French nation today that British Prime Minister Chamberlain had proclaimed Great Britain at war with Germany.

"No News" at the German Embassy

LONDON, Sunday, Sept. 3 (AP).—At the German Embassy in London at 9:30 A. M. today [5:30 A. M., New York], a half hour before the expiration of the British ultimatum, it was said, "There is no news." A spokesman said, "We are in constant communication with Berlin."

Denies Poles Got Five-Power Parley Offer

LONDON, Sunday, Sept. 3 (AP).—Exchange Telegraph Agency, British news agency, said today that Count Edward Raczynski, Polish Ambassador in London, informed it that "the Italian Government did not approach Poland" concerning a reported five-power conference to settle German-Polish issues.

"Apart from the declarations made yesterday in the British Parliament and apart from contradictory reports in the press," the agency quoted him, "the Polish Government has not knowledge of such a scheme."

Exchange Telegraph said the Ambassador declared that "any talk of such a conference" would be "ludicrous and fantastic" as long as "a single enemy soldier stands on Polish soil."

1,000 Americans Sail on French Liner

PARIS, Sunday, Sept. 3 (AP).—The French Line said today that the Ile de France had sailed from Havre with more than 1,000 Americans on board, bound for home.

Heavy Fighting Is Reported in Silesia

WARSAW, Sept. 2 (AP).—Although official information was lacking, it was reported tonight that severe fighting be-

Continued on Page Twelve

TO END OPPRESSION

Premier Calls It 'Bitter Blow' That Efforts for Peace Have Failed

WARNING UNHEEDED

Demand on Reich to Withdraw Army From Poland Ignored

Prime Minister Neville Chamberlain announced to the world at 6:10 o'clock this morning that Great Britain and France were at war with Germany. He made the announcement over the radio, with short waves carrying the measured tones of his voice throughout all continents, from 10 Downing Street in London.

Mr. Chamberlain disclosed that Great Britain and France had taken concurrent action, announcing that "we and France are, today, in fulfillment of our obligations, going to the aid of Poland."

France, however, had not made any announcement beyond stating that the French Ambassador to Berlin would make a final call upon Foreign Minister Joachim von Ribbentrop at 6 o'clock this morning, and it was assumed the French had proclaimed the existence of the state of war.

Speaks With Solemnity

With the greatest solemnity Mr. Chamberlain began his declaration by reporting that the British Ambassador to Berlin had handed in Great Britain's final ultimatum and that it had not been accepted. Without hesitation he announced Britain's decision and, after touching briefly on the background of the crisis, he expressed the highest confidence that "injustice, oppression and persecution" would be vanquished and that his cause would triumph.

Mr. Chamberlain appealed to his people, schooled during the last year as the crisis deepened in measures of defense and offense, to carry on with their jobs and begged a blessing upon them, warning that "we shall be fighting against brute force."

The declaration came after Great Britain had given Chancellor Adolf Hitler of Germany extended time in which to answer the British Government's final ultimatum of Friday. In the final ultimatum Herr Hitler had been told that unless German aggression in Poland ceased, Britain was prepared to fulfill her obligations to Poland.

Warning Was Sharp

Britain's last warning at 4 o'clock this morning, New York time, left no doubt of her stand, for the phrase, "fulfillment of Britain's obligations to Poland," was replaced by a flat statement that a state of war would exist between the two countries as of the hour of the deadline.

After Mr. Chamberlain had finished his statement, which had been introduced as "an announcement of national importance," the announcer warned the British people not to gather together, broadcast an order that all meeting places for entertainment be closed, and gave precautions to prepare the people against air bombings and poison gas attacks.

Mr. Chamberlain began his

Continued on Page Fifteen

"All the News That's Fit to Print."

The New York Times.

LATE CITY EDITION
POSTSCRIPT
Generally fair with showers tonight, continued warm.
Temperatures Yesterday—Max., 79; Min., 64

VOL. LXXXVIII...No. 29,808. Entered as Second-Class Matter, Postoffice, New York, N. Y. NEW YORK, MONDAY, SEPTEMBER 4, 1939. P THREE CENTS NEW YORK CITY and Vicinity | FOUR CENTS Elsewhere Except in 7th and 8th Postal Zones.

BRITISH LINER ATHENIA TORPEDOED, SUNK; 1,400 PASSENGERS ABOARD, 292 AMERICANS; ALL EXCEPT A FEW ARE REPORTED SAVED

ROOSEVELT IN PLEA

President, on Air, Asks the Nation to Observe True Neutrality

CALLS ALL TO UNITY

Draws Ring Around Americas—'Even a Neutral' May Judge, He Says

By TURNER CATLEDGE
Special to THE NEW YORK TIMES.

WASHINGTON, Sept. 3.—In an extraordinary message broadcast by radio to "the whole of America," President Roosevelt tonight called for an adjournment of all partisanship and selfishness and substitution of complete national unity in the United States to the end that the newest world war may be kept from the Western Hemisphere.

He declared that, as long as it remained within his power to prevent, "there will be no blackout of peace in the United States."

Linking the present European conflagration to the "invasion of Poland by Germany," the President announced that a proclamation of American neutrality was being prepared for issuance under the present Neutrality Act.

"I trust that in the days to come our neutrality can be made a true neutrality," he added.

Would Seek a "Final Peace"

But it seemed clear to him, he said, "even at the outbreak of this great war," that the influence of America should be consistent "in seeking for humanity a final peace which will eliminate, as far as it is possible to do so, the continued use of force between nations."

In his flat declaration that "this nation will remain a neutral nation," the President said he could not ask that every American remain neutral in thought as well. "Even a neutral has a right to take account of facts," he said. "Even a neutral cannot be asked to close his mind or his conscience."

The President gave no inkling of his intentions about calling Congress into special session to revise the stringent Neutrality Law which places certain mandatory obligations upon him. The universal opinion among observers at the capital was that he would issue a call soon, and that it might come upon the heels of the obligatory neutrality proclamation, placing an embargo on arms and munitions of war to Germany, Poland, France and England. White House sources said the neutrality proclamation could be expected within the next forty-eight hours.

Gives Ideas of Safety

Under the law, the neutrality proclamation, which carries with it the proclamation of an arms embargo, is required as soon as the President makes a finding that a state of war exists between two or more countries. Officials were standing today on the technicality that this government had not been officially notified of Britain's and France's declarations. They conceded, however, that this was a mere technicality.

In the course of his message, the President drew a ring around the Western Hemisphere, saying in substance that this was the area which the United States must and would seek to protect and keep neutral.

This country, he said, had certain ideas and ideals of national safety "and we must act to preserve that safety today and to preserve the safety of our children in future years."

That safety, he continued, is and will be bound up with the safety of the Western Hemisphere "and the seas adjacent thereto."

"We seek to keep war from our firesides by keeping war from coming to the Americas," he said.

Recalls Efforts for Peace

He claimed historic precedent, going back to the days of George Washington, for this country's assuming the responsibility of protecting the whole of the Americas. It is serious enough and tragic enough to every American family in every State in the Union to live in a world torn by wars on other continents, he said. Therefore he considered it our national duty to use

Continued on Page Six

Poles Charge Aerial Gas Attacks on Cities As Germany Agrees to 'Humanize' the War

LONDON, Sept. 3 (AP).—The Polish Ambassador to London, Count Edward Raczynski, tonight declared that new German air attacks in all parts of Poland had disclosed that the civilian population was suffering with the Germans using gas in their raids.

WARSAW, Sept. 3 (Polish Telegraphic Agency).—German bombers threw gas bombs on the unfortified village of Grudisk in the county of Ciechanow.

Wireless to THE NEW YORK TIMES.

BERLIN, Sept. 3.—It was announced today that Germany and the Western Powers had agreed to "humanize" the war by not employing poison gas, not bombing open cities from the air, even when in the zone of war operations, and not taking military measures against civilians as long as both sides observed the agreement.

The reported dropping of gas bombs on Polish towns represents the first use of gas from planes in European warfare.

The inauguration of this form of attack recalls that in 1915 the Germans began the use of poison gas on the battlefields and the Allies followed suit.

In 1917 the German General Staff gave consideration to the use of gas from planes in attacking cities, but after a long debate it was decided not to do so. The reason was that the British and French air forces combined were superior to the air force of the Germans, and the fear of what might happen to German cities deterred the Germans from using gas in air attacks at that time.

ITALY FAILS TO ACT AS HER ALLY FIGHTS

Rome Plans to Stay Neutral Unless Attacked—Fascist Moves Kept Secret

By HERBERT L. MATTHEWS
Special Cable to THE NEW YORK TIMES.

ROME, Monday, Sept. 4.—Although Great Britain and France are at war with Germany, Italy has taken no step to join her Axis partner. She remains friendly to Germany but neutral, and she will make no move against the French and British unless attacked. This was made clear in Premier Mussolini's newspaper, the Popolo d'Italia, this morning, which reaffirmed the declaration of neutrality contained in the Council of Ministers' communiqué Friday.

Whether there is any possibility of Italy going beyond that attitude toward one side or the other cannot be stated yet, for the Italians continue to be completely secret. Since history always repeats itself, one may well suppose that the French and British are doing everything they can to win Italian benevolence, if not aid. That is the normal and natural thing for them to do whether they have hopes for success or not. After all, diplomatic relations between Rome and Paris and London continue on a friendly basis, and none need be surprised if André François-Poncet and Sir Percy Loraine, the French and British Ambassadors, who see Count Ciano, the Foreign Minister, so often these days, should be exerting their greatest efforts to win Italy away from Germany. It is their business to do so.

Attitude Is Not Changing

None can say yet what success, if any, they are having. So far as today is concerned there is that Popolo d'Italia article to go upon, which indicates clearly enough that Italy is not changing her attitude because Britain and France have entered the conflict. Although it was printed before those countries acted it was written at a time when there could be no doubt of what was going to happen.

The editorial begins by saying that the Council of Ministers' communiqué should be "re-read and meditated." Its words were "sculpted in stone," says the editorial, meaning that it was meant to last.

From Premier Mussolini's efforts for "peace with justice," two things are to be deduced it continues:

First, that notwithstanding certain foreign interpretations which are too hasty or ingenuous nothing is changed on the plane of Italo-German friendship.

Second, that Signor Mussolini has worked not only for the solution of the German-Polish problem but for all other problems which like this one now being solved by arms, have their origin in the Versailles Treaty.

"It is therefore natural," the article goes on, "that whatever happens, whether the German-Polish conflict remains localized or spreads to a catastrophe, the Duce's work—that is to say the work that

Continued on Page Seven

HITLER WITH ARMY ON EASTERN FRONT

Leaves Berlin After Placing Blame for War on Britain—Allied Envoys Depart

By OTTO D. TOLISCHUS
Wireless to THE NEW YORK TIMES.

BERLIN, Sept. 3.—At 9 o'clock tonight Chancellor Hitler left Berlin, presumably for the Eastern Front. He had previously sent a message to the Eastern Army stating that he was joining them.

He left the city in a heavily guarded special train that mounted anti-aircraft artillery. He was accompanied by his Foreign Minister, Joachim von Ribbentrop, and by Field Marshal Hermann Goering. It was supposed that their destination was Stolp, Pomerania, where the headquarters of the Eastern Army is believed to be located.

The departure of the Chancellor ended a day of proclamations from the chancellery. There was an appeal to the German people, a proclamation to the Nazi party, a message to the soldiers of the East Army and another to the troops manning the Westwall. There was also given out the text of a German memorandum answering the British ultimatum.

Perhaps the most significant feature of all these proclamations and of the memorandum is that they do not mention France, sidetrack

Continued on Page Two

POLES REPORT GAIN

Tell of Fighting on Foe's Soil After Horsemen Retake 2 Towns

SHELL GERMAN AREA

But Invaders Announce Wide Advances—They Capture Rail Center

By The Associated Press.

LONDON, Monday, Sept. 4.—An Exchange Telegraph dispatch from Warsaw reported early today that Polish troops had crossed the German frontier north of Breslau and were fighting on German soil.

Quoting a Polish short-wave radio broadcast, the news agency said the troops had crossed between Rawicz and Leszno. These towns are on the border about twenty-five miles apart and approximately forty-five miles north of Breslau. The report said Polish cavalry was in the action.

[The Polish Telegraphic Agency reported earlier that Polish cavalry had driven German forces from Rawicz and Leszno, which they had captured in surprise attacks on Friday.]

The agency quoted the following communiqué issued last night by the Polish supreme command:

"During the day the German air force carried out raids on numerous unfortified towns, including Warsaw, Deblin, Radom and Cracow. Near Radom and Cracow twenty-six enemy aircraft were brought down. The total number brought down today was sixty-four. The Polish losses amounted to eleven machines. German raiders did not spare the peasant population working in the fields near their villages.

"Considerable enemy forces launched a strong attack in the direction of Silesia and the region of Podhale. Under the pressure of the enemy, Polish forces were compelled to abandon Czestochowa on the Silesian frontier.

"Our lines were slightly pressed in the Silesia sector. In the north Polish troops recaptured Puck and Orlowo."

In an air encounter over Poznan late yesterday, Exchange Telegraph said, six German bombers were shot down near Wolbrom after they had dropped a number of gas bombs.

The agency said that the German radio had announced that a German Army had crossed the Warta [Warthe] River yesterday east of Wielun in Western Poland.

An attempt by Polish troops cut

Continued on Page Nine

The Developments in Europe

Britain and France plunged into war yesterday morning and soon events began to gather momentum.

The most sensational was the torpedoing and sinking of the British liner Athenia off the Hebrides this morning. She was carrying 1,400 passengers, including 292 Americans, from Liverpool to Montreal. The news shocked the White House. [Page 1].

On top of this came charges by Poles that the Germans had dropped gas bombs on towns. [Page 1.]

Britain, following her tactics of the last war, quickly blockaded Germany and closed the entrances to the Mediterranean Sea as well. The British public was calm and grimly determined after it had heard Prime Minister Chamberlain gravely announce on the radio that "this country is at war with Germany." [Page 1.] He made the same announcement in the House of Commons, where he immediately received the support of such former opponents as Winston Churchill and David Lloyd George. In a new War Cabinet Mr. Churchill resumed the post of First Lord of the Admiralty, which he had held in the last war; Lord Hankey, another veteran statesman of that conflict, became Minister Without Portfolio, and Anthony Eden became Secretary for the Dominions. [Page 8; texts of Mr. Chamberlain's addresses and of addresses in the Commons, Page 8.]

In France Premier Daladier, declaring that the responsibility for bloodshed was Chancellor Hitler's, said that France's cause was the cause of justice. [Page 1; text of Daladier's radio speech, Page 8.]

Herr Hitler in a series of statements during the day put the blame for the strife on the British whom he accused of seeking to encircle Germany. He left for the Polish front. [Page 1; texts of these statements, Page 2.]

On that front the Poles were reported to have carried the fighting to German soil in one sector, but were declared to be giving ground in Silesia and at points in Pomorze [Page 1].

Italy still took no step to join her Axis partner in the conflict and it seemed obvious that the British and the French were doing what they could to win her to their side. [Page 1.]

Russia likewise kept a middle-of-the-road position [Page 6.]

President Roosevelt, in an extraordinary message radioed to "the whole of America," called for national unity as a measure for keeping the Western Hemisphere from becoming embroiled. [Page 1; text of the message, Page 6.]

BRITISH NAVY ACTS

It Cuts Off Entrances to the Baltic, North and Mediterranean Seas

LONDON IS UNSHAKEN

Declaration of War Is Met With Resolve—Air Alarm Orderly

Special to THE NEW YORK TIMES.

WASHINGTON, Sept. 3.—The British Government has ordered a naval blockade of Germany, according to information reaching officials here tonight. This government has not been informed officially by the British Government of this fact, however.

It was understood here that the naval blockade went into effect immediately upon the declaration of war and that British naval vessels were blocking the entrance to the Baltic Sea near Skagerrak and were stretched across the North Sea near the Scandinavian peninsula. It was also understood here that the entrances to the Mediterranean at Gibraltar and Suez were being carefully controlled.

Both Britain and France were cloaking their naval and military moves with greatest secrecy and neither the Navy nor the War Department had specific information about them up to 8 o'clock, Eastern standard time, tonight.

Britain Is Determined

By FREDERICK T. BIRCHALL
Special Cable to THE NEW YORK TIMES.

LONDON, Monday, Sept. 4.—At last midnight Great Britain had been at war with Germany for thirteen hours. France had been at war for seven hours—since 5 o'clock.

A darkened London, in which only hooded red and green crosses at the traffic halts, invisible from above, indicate that there are streets, houses and human life below a clear starry sky, awaits calmly the air attacks that it confidently expects despite Chancellor Hitler's professed desire to avoid bombing open cities. Even these tiny indications will be extinguished the moment that sirens hoot their warnings of approaching raiders.

There are few people in the streets because the authorities have broadcast warnings to every one to stay at home and to go out no more than is necessary. Cinemas, theatres and every other form of entertainment likely to draw a crowd have been shut down by order for the time being, at least. Only the churches have held their customary services.

People Grimly Determined

Thus war has come to Britain, to a people grimly determined to meet it and to see it through. The predominating sentiment, if any, is one of relief that the long period of suspense is over. Throughout the land the watchword now is: "Let's get on with it."

War became a reality yesterday morning just after the church bells had ceased ringing. It came in the shape of a sudden interruption of the regular radio program by an announcer:

"The Prime Minister will broadcast an important announcement to the nation."

Then came Mr. Chamberlain's well-known voice, quiet and sad but clear and firm:

"I am speaking to you from the Cabinet room at 10 Downing Street."

Then followed his terse narration of the course of events. That morning (it was actually at 9 o'clock, two hours earlier) the British Ambassador at Berlin had handed Foreign Minister Joachim von Ribbentrop a final note stating that unless the Germans had agreed by 11 o'clock to withdraw their troops from Poland, a "state of war would exist between us."

"I have to tell you now," continued Mr. Chamberlain in the same level tones, "that no such

Continued on Page Four

FIRST SHIP SUNK IN THE WAR
The Athenia, with 1,400 aboard, torpedoed off the Hebrides
Wired Photo—Times Wide World

List of the American Passengers Aboard the Torpedoed Athenia

Special to THE NEW YORK TIMES.

WASHINGTON, Monday, Sept. 4.—The list of American citizens who embarked on the liner Athenia in Liverpool follows; no addresses were given in the cable received at the State Department from Ambassador Joseph P. Kennedy:

Ralph Ruffieau
Katheryn McGuire
Hasel Casserly
Charles Grant
Florence Malik
Edith Bridge
Harry Bridge
Robert Harris
Gustaf Petersen
Margaret Buchan
Laura Cattle
Mrs. Thomas Kerr
Kate Hinds
Herbert Spierelberg
Mrs. Davis
Margaret McGuire
Elizabeth Wise
William Buchanan
Master Charles Grant
Bernice Jansen
Constance Bridge
Sarah Warenreich
John Hughes
Gertrude Reed
George Cattle
Thomas Kerr
Rhoda Thomas
William Hinds
J. Davis
William Peers
Lillian Peers
Charles Prince
Harold Etherington
Ellen Harrington
Jessie Forle
Francis Cooley
Charles Prince (two Charles Princes)
Geoffrey Etherington
R. Casey
George Keliher
Harry Trehearne
Ella Trehearne
Annie Word
Duncan Wood (Two Duncan Woods)
Ernest Ratcliffe
Faith Ratcliffe
Irene de Munn
Edward O'Connell
Aileen Philipsen
Mary Steinberg
Ralph Child
Peter Birchall
Duncan Wood
Ellin Ratcliffe
Donald Gifford
Jozef Karnowski
Dorris O'Connel
John Youngquist
Donald Edwards
John Lawrence
Tryphene Humphrey
Louise Horte
Mary, Dick and Edward Belton
Elsa Philipsen
Adolph Sadowski
John Harju
Charles Stork
Harold Ruggs
Adolph Leocha
Florence Dery
Wiktor Ponjola
Ethel Russell
William Bohn
Ada Bohn
Montgomery Evans
Franklin Dexter
Cathleen Schurr
Agnes Stappel
Lillian Eilstrap
Rose Churchill
Ellen Howland
Miarine Dexter
Maud Shearer
Alexander Sheshunoff
Cosby Eilstrap
Sarah Burdett
Yvette Pepin
Ena Logan
Herbert Bonn
Thomas Quine
Lulu Sweigard
Romona Allen
Gus Anderson
Eleanor Crowley
Harriet Tolley
Janet Elsen
Annie Quine
Carol Allen
Susan Allen

The following Americans boarded the Athenia at Glasgow, the American Consulate there reports:

James Boyle
Cathryn Brennan
Margaret Campbell
Elva Campbell
Agnes Craig
William Diller
Margaret Diller
Louis Diven
Mary Diven
Mary Dowie
Thomas Fielder
John Bernard
Margaret Ford
Cora Gilroy
Don Gilroy
Helen Hannah
Jan Hannah
Florence Hargreave
Selena Isaacs
Jeanette Jordan
Margaret Little
Harriet McFadzean
Mary McKellar
Alexander Nichol
Edith Nichol
Marion Nichol
Alice Tocklington
John Pringle
Lottie Tringle
Katherine Scott
Essie Mallery
William Mallery
Helen Stewart
Edgar Wilkes
Margaret Wilkes
Donald Wilkes
William Wilkes
Myrtle Barber
Barbara Bradfield
Joan Outhwaite
Alberta Wood
Lucile Lucas
Elizabeth Martin
Gertrude Martin
Ila Vincent
Michael Flynn
Alice Robinson
Robert Townsend
Bainbridge Hayden
Dirus Ekaube
Doris Elaine Kent
William Ralph Singleton
Margaret Moore
Sarah Bloom
Olive Bloom
Fred Tinney
Madeline Tinney
Charles Cotterman
Bunson Price
Elizabeth Alton (two listed)
Louis Burns
Mary Burns
Harriette Jones
Joan Moffett
Elsie Moffett
Joseph MacDonald
Elmetta MacDonald
Harriet Roney
Wendell Sherk
Nicola Lubitsch
Henry Smith
Ellen Smith
Jeannette Smith
Caroline Stuart
Frieda Windmann
Matthew Brown
Mary Brown
Elizabeth Brown
James Curran
Isobel Bruce
Betsy Brown
Dorothy Fox
W. E. MacBain
Marjorie MacBain
Gus Anderson
Caroline Rice
William Bown
Ada Bown
Elizabeth Lewis
May Lewis
Donald Lewis
William Aitken
Anne Baker
Alma Bloom
Dorothy Feder
Martha Bonnet
William Brown
George Calder (Two listed)
Margaret Calder
Alice Chalmers
William Chalmers
Margaret Doggett
Eileen Duncombe

The names of the Americans who boarded the Athenia at Belfast could not be obtained up to 5 o'clock this morning.

News dispatches from Europe and the Far East are now virtually all subject to censorship.

HIT OFF HEBRIDES

Ship Bound for Canada Carried Some Children Among Americans

CAPITAL IS SHOCKED

President's Aide Notes Liner Had Refugees, Not Munitions

By The Associated Press.

BELFAST, Northern Ireland, Monday, Sept. 4.—All persons aboard the sunken British liner Athenia, except some killed by a German torpedo, were reported saved today.

An agent of the ship's owners here issued the report. He said all survivors had been picked up by other vessels.

By The Associated Press.

LONDON, Monday, Sept. 4.—The British Liner Athenia, with 246 United States citizens among her 1,400 passengers, was torpedoed and sunk 200 miles west of the Hebrides, the British Ministry of Information announced early today. [Washington reports said 292 Americans were aboard the Athenia.]

The United States Embassy, checking on the departures of Americans hurrying home in flight from the European war, said 101 boarded the ship at Liverpool and 145 at Glasgow. [Forty-six more Americans boarded the vessel at Belfast, Washington was informed.]

The Athenia sailed Saturday from Liverpool.

The British Ministry of Information said the 13,581-ton ship reported to the Admiralty she had been torpedoed 200 miles off the Hebrides, west of Northern Scotland.

The Ministry of Information said the last official information received by the Admiralty from the ship was that she was sinking "rapidly." Since there were no further advices, it was then assumed she had gone down.

[Stephen Early, secretary to President Roosevelt, said in Washington that official reports indicated the Athenia was carrying "mostly Canadians and some Americans."

["I'd like to point out," he said, according to The Associated Press, "that, according to official information, the ship had gone from Glasgow to Liverpool and was bound for Canada, bringing refugees.

["I point this out to show that there was no possibility, according to official information, that the ship was carrying any munitions or anything of that kind."]

292 Americans Were Aboard

WASHINGTON, Monday, Sept. 4 (AP).—Dispatches to the State Department indicated today that at least 246 [later news brought the figure to 292] Americans were aboard the liner Athenia, torpedoed in the North Atlantic.

White House Is Informed

Special to THE NEW YORK TIMES.

WASHINGTON, Monday, Sept. 4.—Information received here last night that the Cunard White Star liner Athenia had been torpedoed off the coast of Ireland while en route to the United States brought a prompt statement from the White House acknowledging receipt of the news and information from the State Department that it had received eighteen long-distance calls within a few minutes of a radio broadcast of the news. The calls appealed for information about relatives aboard.

The White House said that the vessel was bound from Glasgow and Liverpool to Montreal with a large group of Canadian passengers and with an undetermined number of Americans among them.

At 6 A. M., British Summer Time [1 A. M. in New York] Ambassador Joseph P. Kennedy cabled the State Department as follows:

"Admiralty unable as yet to indicate whether Athenia has sunk or rescue arrangements; 101 American citizens embarked on her at

Continued on Page Five

"All the News That's Fit to Print."

The New York Times.

LATE CITY EDITION
Generally fair and cooler today and tonight. Tomorrow fair with moderate temperature.
Temperatures Yesterday—Max., 84; Min., 64

Section 1

NEWS INDEX, PAGE 51, THIS SECTION

VOL. LXXXVIII....No. 29,821 — Entered as Second-Class Matter, Postoffice, New York, N. Y. — NEW YORK, SUNDAY, SEPTEMBER 17, 1939. — PPP — Including Rotogravure Picture, Magazine and Book Review. TEN CENTS | TWELVE CENTS Beyond 200 Miles Except in 7th and 8th Postal Zones.

SOVIET TROOPS MARCHED INTO POLAND AT 11 P. M.; NAZIS DEMAND WARSAW GIVE UP OR BE SHELLED; FIERCE BATTLE IS RAGING ON WESTERN FRONT

2 SENATORS BLAST EMBARGO REPEAL AS LEADING TO WAR

Clark, Disavowing Filibuster, Asks Prolonging of Session to Curb Rule by Decree

DEFENDS 'INSULATIONISTS'

Vandenberg Calls Favoring Any Belligerent 'Unneutral' and Urges 'Middle Ground'

By TURNER CATLEDGE
Special to THE NEW YORK TIMES.

WASHINGTON, Sept. 16—The fight over lifting the embargo against export of arms was intensified further today as Senators Clark of Missouri and Vandenberg of Michigan aimed new blasts at the Administration's program to alter the Neutrality Act at the special session of Congress.

Following upon the radio address last night of Colonel Lindbergh, the Senators, a Democrat and a Republican, took up Senator Borah's thesis—that the issue was more of intervention or non-intervention in the affairs of Europe than of mere methods of neutrality.

Senator Clark's remarks were contained in a statement telegraphed from his home in St. Louis for release at the capital.

Senator Vandenberg made his plea to his own constituents at a Republican rally at Grand Rapids, telling them not to allow their minds to be taken off domestic problems by the agitation over the conflict abroad.

In his address, Senator Vandenberg declared that the arms embargo should not be repealed by a revision of the present neutrality laws.

"In my view," he said, "it is not 'neutrality' for us to change that code today to make it fit some favored belligerent, no matter what our sympathies. In my view, that is unneutrality. It is trying to be half in this war and yet to safely stay out. I do not believe there can be any such middle ground."

Clark for Check on Executive

"I welcome the President's call for an extraordinary session of the Congress," Senator Clark said in his statement.

"Since the President has by proclamation declared the existence of a national emergency, it is the duty of the Congress to remain in session and share fully in the responsibilities of government during the duration of the national emergency. This is and should remain a government by law and not by decree.

"So far as the Neutrality Act is concerned there has been no suggestion of a 'filibuster' on the part of any of the Senators who oppose the emasculation and perversion of the whole neutrality policy heretofore adopted by the Congress and approved by the President by the repeal of the provision for a mandatory arms embargo.

"The suggestions of a 'filibuster' have been put out in inspired articles from Washington and Hyde Park designed to promote gag rule and stifle free and fair discussion of perhaps the most important question of public policy which has confronted the Congress of the United States since that tragic day in 1917 when the decision was made to throw the United States into the World War.

Sees Decision on "Taking Sides"

"We are now to determine whether or not we have learned anything from that awful experience by deciding whether by repealing the arms embargo we shall again deliberately set our feet on the path which inevitably leads to war.

"Those of us who oppose the abandonment of a bona fide neutrality policy stand precisely where President Roosevelt stood in his eloquent Chautauqua speech in 1936 when he was a candidate for reelection when he said in defending the law containing a mandatory arms embargo:

"'We are not isolationists except in so far as we seek to isolate ourselves completely from war.'

"My friend, Senator Elbert Thomas of Utah, one of the leading revisionists, let the cat out of the bag the other night as to the real posi-

Continued on Page Thirty-seven

White House Gate Closed To Keep Out Trysting Cars

Special to THE NEW YORK TIMES.

WASHINGTON, Sept. 16—Neither wars nor rumors of wars, but the popularity among motorists of the White House grounds on Summer nights is the reason one of the iron gates on Pennsylvania Avenue is now closed after dark and a guard stands at the other, day and night, to tell all comers that only those having appointments may park their cars inside.

People have been driving in, especially at night, and parking there, Mrs. Roosevelt revealed at a press conference today. And though it is a pleasant place to sit, under the trees, the White House driveway is really not a good trysting place, she said. Too many motorists were attracted by it.

As the number of parking parties increased, so did the problem of keeping the driveway open and free of obstruction. Now an extra all-night guard is on duty, from dark to dawn, to keep it so.

LATIN TRIP FOR FAIR PLEDGED BY MAYOR

'If They Want Me to Go, I Am Going,' He Says—Crowds Set New Record for Saturday

By SIDNEY M. SHALETT

Clarifying his position as the possible World's Fair ambassador of good-will to South America, Mayor La Guardia, in two statements yesterday, agreed that he would go "if necessary," but hinted that the trip might not take place for at least several months.

There was even a third statement issued by Stanley Howe, the Mayor's executive secretary, to settle the "incident" created Friday night when Grover A. Whalen, Fair president, announced in the Mayor's absence that Mr. La Guardia would fly "at an early date" to sell the United States' neighbors to the South on the idea of participating in the 1940 exposition.

As Mr. Howe viewed it, the Mayor would like, with permission of the State Department, to make a trip both to sell South American nations on the 1940 Fair and to "unsell" them on any totalitarian ideas that may have crept in.

These matters yesterday were exceedingly important to the administrators who run the Fair, but despite all the flurry about South American envoys and European participation the Fair itself was entertaining the biggest Saturday crowd in its history. From early morning on thousands of visitors streamed past the turnstiles, and early in the evening it became evident that a new record for a Saturday would be set.

The Mayor issued his first statement shortly after noon, after a hurried dash from the World's Fair City Hall to Hoboken to see Mr. Whalen off on the Statendam. The Fair president, who had made the announcement Friday in which the Mayor did not fully concur, was sailing for Europe as salesman for the 1940 Fair.

Boat Held Up for Mayor

Arriving at the dock only four minutes before sailing time, Mayor La Guardia induced the captain to hold up the boat until he could hurry aboard, have a word with Mr. Whalen and pose with him for a farewell picture. It was such an eleventh-hour affair that the last gangplank was partly dismantled and had to be made secure again before the Mayor and his retinue could leave the ship.

Then, on the pier, the Mayor gave out the following statement concerning his South American plans:

"There are a great many preliminaries. If it can do the Fair any good, and if these necessary preliminaries can be made, and if there is a real need, I'll go. But there is nothing definite yet."

Then he whisked off in his car. His next appearance, late in the afternoon, was at a ceremony of the United Spanish War Veterans in the Court of Peace at the Fair. There he was asked again if he would fly south, and this time he made it a little stronger.

"I'll do anything that is helpful and necessary for the World's Fair," the Mayor said. "If they want me to go, I am going. Of course, that requires a good deal of preliminary preparation and is al-

Continued on Page Forty-eight

6 U. S. SHIPS KEPT IN PORT AS SEAMEN HOLD OUT FOR PAY

Stalemate Results Over War Risk Insurance Demands—No Solution Seen Near

FRIED CALLS 12 SAILORS

Plans Inquiry on Tie-Up of American Trader—Owners Say Capital Must Act

American merchant shipping was badly hampered in New York harbor yesterday when the crews of six vessels refused to sail their ships, insisting on concrete concessions to their demands for extra compensation for entering European waters affected by the war.

With Federal agencies already overburdened by the unusual duties laid on them as a result of the war, confusion reigned on the waterfront, and at a late hour there appeared to be little chance of solution or compromise.

Two of the ships, one with passengers, were to have sailed Friday afternoon but their crews staged a sit-down strike after signing the ship's articles. In other cases, the men declined to sign the articles, leaving vessels with no manning force.

Fried Sends Out Summonses

On the United States liner American Trader, which was at the Chelsea piers of the company with passengers and cargo, twelve union men received summonses from the office of Captain George Fried, supervising inspector of the Bureau of Marine Inspection and Navigation.

The summons in each case was returnable immediately at 45 Broadway, but a representative of the National Maritime Union appeared in the men's stead and received an adjournment until 10 A. M. tomorrow, allowing the union time to obtain counsel for them.

Captain Fried had boarded the American Trader on Friday night and had been at the piers yesterday, but he declined to reveal the nature of the charges to be filed against the men, saying that the public would be admitted to the hearing.

He also declined to explain why only twelve of the seventy seamen had been called, or to say how they had been selected.

Will Set Up Special Board

He planned to constitute a "C" board to preside at the inquiry, headed by himself and including Captain Karl Nielsen and Howard C. Bridges, inspectors of the district. The "C" board would sit in the same manner as a grand jury, to determine if charges should be filed against the men.

The National Maritime Union, which has disclaimed responsibility for the strike on Friday, issued a

Continued on Page Forty-six

Blast Shakes Offices Of Reich Air Ministry

By The Associated Press.

BERLIN, Sunday, Sept. 17—An explosion occurred in the Air Ministry headquarters on the Leipzigerstrasse early today. Firemen and police closed off an extensive area around the building.

The Propaganda Ministry acknowledged that there had been an explosion, but no immediate explanation was forthcoming. It was reported that no one had been injured. There was shattered glass in the street, but the extent of the damage was not immediately apparent.

The Propaganda Ministry refused to speculate whether the blast might have been caused by a bomb. It said merely that an investigation was under way.

"The persons responsible are being sought energetically," a Propaganda Ministry spokesman declared.

The blast came during the regular nightly blackout and the streets were deserted.

TOKYO MINIMIZES SOVIET AGREEMENT

Denies Non-Aggression Pact Is to Follow Truce—Policy on Russia Is Held Unchanged

By HUGH BYAS
Wireless to THE NEW YORK TIMES.

TOKYO, Sept. 16—Japanese officials emphatically deny and characterize as "absolute nonsense" reports that a non-aggression pact with Russia is under negotiation or is contemplated. They also deny that Germany had a hand in arranging the armistice on the Manchukuoan-Mongolian border or that German influence could induce Japan to change her policy toward the Soviet.

The Japanese Government regards the armistice as a means of terminating the border fighting. It is part of the new Cabinet's policy for a speedy settlement of the China "incident." Not only does it assure peace on the Mongolian frontier, it is asserted, but it shows Generalissimo Chiang Kai-shek that he cannot expect further diversions in the north, and it helps demonstrate that the Soviet has lost faith in the possibility of a Chinese victory.

According to Domei, the Japanese news agency, the armistice is a definite help toward a settlement in China by enabling Japan to devote her entire energy to the impending peace moves. When asked what Russia receives, the Japanese answer is that she wins a cessation of potentially serious disputes with Japan and possibly certain territorial concessions during the frontier adjustment.

On the broader question whether the armistice is a first step toward a revolutionary realignment of world forces, officials suggest that the move is adequately explained

Continued on Page Thirty-two

Major Sports Yesterday

BASEBALL

The Yankees clinched their fourth consecutive American League pennant under Manager Joe McCarthy and equaled the record set by John McGraw's Giants of 1921 to 1924. It was the eleventh flag victory for the New Yorkers, who beat the Tigers at the Stadium, 8—5. The second-place Red Sox lost. In Cincinnati the Reds halted the Giants, 6—1, and maintained their lead of three and a half games over the victorious Cards.

GOLF

Marvin (Bud) Ward of Spokane defeated Ray Billows of Poughkeepsie, N. Y., 7 and 5, to win the national amateur championship on the North Shore Country Club links, Glenview, Ill. Ward is the first Pacific Coast golfer to take the title.

TENNIS

Welby Van Horn upset John Bromwich, 2—6, 4—6, 6—2, 6—4, 8—6, to gain the final of the national singles championship with Robert L. Riggs, who eliminated Joe Hunt, 6—1, 6—2, 4—6, 6—1. Miss Alice Marble and Miss Helen Jacobs entered the women's final.

HORSE RACING

Hash won the Edgemere Handicap at Aqueduct, where Merry Knight annexed the Junior Champion Stakes. At Chicago, Challedon captured the Hawthorne Gold Cup. Farndale took the Foxcatcher National Cup Steeplechase at Fair Hill, Md.

POLO

The Bostwick Field four beat Westbury, 9—8, in the first match of the national open tournament.

(Complete Details of These and Other Sports Events in Section 5.)

GERMANS SET BACK

Heavy Counter-Attacks Repulsed by the French Drive

NAZIS BLAST TOWNS

Gamelin Hits at Three Points in Saar Area, Hardest on Moselle

By G. H. ARCHAMBAULT
Wireless to THE NEW YORK TIMES.

PARIS, Sept. 16—The Germans are bringing up more and more troops on the western front, where the fighting grows fiercer daily. That is the salient point in the French headquarters communiqués today. This morning's bulletin, Communiqué 25, said:

"There was a restless night on numerous parts of the front. Enemy artillery was very active in the region south of Saarbruecken.

"Our troops made some progress east of the Moselle.

"A strong enemy counter-attack, following artillery preparation, was driven back in the region near the lower valley of the Nied River."

This evening Communiqué 26 announced:

"There was great activity on both sides on the part of artillery and of first-line troops on the entire front.

"The enemy is constantly reinforcing before us.

"At several points the enemy abandoned and destroyed several of his villages from which he retreated."

Battle West of Saarbruecken

The heaviest fighting at present is on that portion of the front running some twenty miles west of Saarbruecken. The object is the possession of observation points dominating not only the Saar Valley but also certain parts of the Westwall.

The specific purpose of the German attack near the River Nied, which is a tributary of the Saar, was to regain a number of observation points along the plateau from which the town of Saarlautern can be brought under the fire of French guns.

After artillery preparation the German infantry left its cover for a swift attack. The duration of this preparation, however, had sufficiently indicated its purpose. The French guns came into action as soon as the infantry got on the move and the attack was soon stopped. It is reported that the Germans employed a relatively large force for this attempt.

There is also heavy fighting for the establishment of the Saar bridgeheads. The possession of the banks of the river at divers points is important for the bringing up of heavy tanks.

That the Germans should be bringing up reinforcements continuously, as reported in the evening communiqué, may imply the intention of attempting stronger counter-attacks than any hitherto. It may even suggest an endeavor to wrest the initiative from the French. It is manifest that important developments may be expected soon.

Three Main Sectors

As the second week of the war ends, the operations on the west front are clearly divided into three main sectors. These are, reading the map from the east to the west:

1. From the Rhine, in the vicinity of Lauterbourg to the highway from Zweibruecken to Bitche.

2. From this highway to a point on the Saar north of Forbach, taking in Saarbruecken, the industrial heart of the Saarland.

3. From this point west of Saarbruecken to the Moselle River in the vicinity of the village of Perl.

In each of these three sectors French troops are operating on German soil.

At the beginning of the hostilities the eastern sector was the most active, with the French occupation of the forest called Bienwald, in order to gain ground at the point where the Maginot Line and the Westwall describe a right angle before following the Rhine Valley southward. In that valley itself scarcely a shot has been fired as yet; the garrisons of the respective fortified lines are merely sentries.

Continued on Page Forty-two

The International Situation

A Poland already tottering under the blows of the German military machine was subjected to another invasion last night, this time by Soviet forces, according to an official announcement in Berlin.

It was declared that the Russian Government had informed the Polish Ambassador it was marching in "to protect its own interests and to protect the White Russian and Ukrainian minorities."

Nevertheless, Moscow said, Soviet neutrality is being maintained. Berlin said the action had German sanction. [Page 1.]

The German sweep in Poland was unabated. Kutno, Bialystok and Przemysl fell. But at Warsaw the invaders were still encountering furious resistance. As a result they issued an ultimatum to the Poles to quit Warsaw within twelve hours on pain of bombardment of the entire city. [Page 1.] The effects of previous bombardments and air raids on the Polish countryside were described by a correspondent, who found towns in flames, inhabitants wailing over ruins of homes and chaos everywhere. [Page 28.] In general, military experts found that Poland's despair was undermining her resistance. [Page 40.]

Meanwhile, the "Battle of the Saar," snowballing daily into a major engagement, was being fiercely fought. The French reported that after a heavy artillery exchange the Germans had destroyed and abandoned several villages and had retreated. [Page 1.]

In the face of continued harrying of commerce by German submarines, which yesterday sank two more British ships, the Admiralty set up convoy service for merchant vessels. [Page 1.] Three South American countries, Argentina, Brazil and Uruguay, fearing violations of their neutrality by belligerent warships, were negotiating to pool their naval strength for protection of the entire coast of South America. [Page 31.]

The full significance of the Russo-Japanese truce on the Mongolian border was still unclear, as was Germany's role, if any, in its conclusion. Japanese officials emphatically denied reports that a non-aggression pact with Russia would follow, insisting that Japan remained an anti-Comintern power. [Page 1.] But one result of the new truce emerged in the form of reports that the Japanese, freed of fears for the Manchukuoan border, had launched a general offensive in Central China. [Page 30.] In London news of the truce was received with equanimity; statesmen there had become accustomed to surprises from Moscow. [Page 34.]

In this country Senators Clark and Vandenberg rallied to Senator Borah's fight against alteration of the Neutrality Act. [Page 1.]

MERCHANT CONVOYS SET UP BY BRITAIN

Guard Pressed After Her Loss of 21 Ships—Three More Vessels Are Victims

By The Associated Press.

LONDON, Sept. 16—The British Admiralty pressed into service tonight convoys for merchant shipping after it was disclosed authoritatively that enemy craft had sunk twenty-one British ships, involving a tonnage of 122,843, during the first two weeks of the war.

The use of convoys was not instituted by the British in the last war until 1917.

While slim cruisers and racing destroyers roved and struck on the shipping lanes, planes of the Royal Aircraft patrolled the skies around the United Kingdom in redoubled efforts to halt the persistent shipping losses to U-boats or mines.

Despite the casualties, naval quarters expressed optimism about the situation at sea.

Understatement in Reports

Increasing patrol activity and the Admiralty's cautious announcement that "a number of U-boats have been destroyed," was taken by naval authorities to tell a story of far greater successes than the guarded statement indicated.

Britain placed responsibility on Germany for the sinking last night of the 8,000-ton Belgian motorship Alex Van Opstal in the Channel off Weymouth, asserting she was sunk by mine or torpedo in violation of international law.

[In Brussels, Belgian authorities refrained from lodging a protest, pending a report from the master of the vessel as to whether she was sunk by torpedo or mine.]

A British communiqué said there were no British mines in the neighborhood, that Germany had sent no notification of German mines there and that attack without warning was in violation of the submarine protocol to which Germany subscribed.

[The Alex Van Opstal left New York on Sept. 6 for Antwerp with eight passengers and 3,400 tons of grain.]

The latest ship to be added to the list of British losses was the tanker Cheyenne of the Anglo-American Oil Con., any, which was announced officially to have been attacked and sunk by a submarine off the southwest coast of Ireland.

[The Anglo-American Oil Company, according to Poor's Man-

Continued on Page Forty-six

Dispatches from Europe and the Far East are now subject to censorship.

ORDER GIVES POLES 12 HOURS TO LEAVE

Nazis Say Citizens Will Have to Take 'Consequences' Today Since Army Is Defiant

Wireless to THE NEW YORK TIMES.

BERLIN, Sept. 16—The German Army High Command has given Warsaw until 3:10 o'clock tomorrow morning to decide whether or not to surrender. In the event the Polish capital does not give in to the German troops now surrounding it on all sides, the city will "take the full consequences of being regarded as a military sector."

[The German High Command reported at 4:30 o'clock this morning, an hour and twenty minutes after expiration of the ultimatum, that its army in the field had had no word from the Polish authorities, The Associated Press reported.]

The notice was served in the form of a double ultimatum: First, a military ultimatum expiring at 3:10 o'clock tomorrow morning, and the second ultimatum to the civilian population to leave the city by 3:10 o'clock in the afternoon [10:10 A. M. New York time].

A German officer entered Warsaw with a white flag at 8 o'clock this morning to demand the surrender of the city. According to the report of the official German News Agency the commandant of the city refused to see him or accept a written demand for the surrender of the city.

The officer, it is stated, thereupon returned to the German lines and this afternoon a squadron of the German air force distributed the pamphlets.

Nazis Cite Law Violation

Warsaw already has been subjected to a partial bombardment by the German air force and artillery but, according to German report, only objects of a military nature have been fired upon. Preparations for defense by the civilian population, however, are regarded by the German High Command as being a "violation of international law depriving the city of its character as an open city." German shells and German bombs will crash into the city tomorrow afternoon unless it is "surrendered without resistance" by dawn tomorrow.

"The patience of the German Army is now exhausted," states the official news agency. "The German Army is no longer willing to observe inactively these conditions which are a slap in the face of all international law, but is determined to put an end to these activities of the Warsaw power holders which, though of no importance whatever in a military sense, constitute a

Continued on Page Forty

FRONTIER CROSSED

Reich Ministry States That Invasion Has German Sanction

ENVOY IS NOTIFIED

Soviet Pleads Need to Aid Minorities, but Claims Neutrality

By The United Press.

BERLIN, Sunday, Sept. 17—A spokesman for the Propaganda Ministry announced that Russian troops had marched into Poland today at 4 A. M. Moscow time [11 P. M. Saturday in New York].

The Soviet troops entered Poland with the full knowledge and approval of the German Government, he said.

The spokesman made his statement after D. N. B., the official German news agency, had reported from Moscow that the Soviet Government had informed the Polish Ambassador, Dr. Waclaw Grzybowski, Saturday night that Soviet troops were about to cross the frontier.

The agency said that the note handed to the Ambassador informed the Poles that the troops would cross the frontier along its entire length from Polosk in the north to Kamenets-Podolski in the south "in order to protect our own interests and to protect the White Russian and Ukrainian minorities."

The Soviet Government, the agency said, told the Poles that it maintained its neutrality despite its military action, but added that its treaties with the Polish State could be regarded as canceled because the Polish State could no longer be regarded as existing.

To Occupy Two Districts

MOSCOW, Sunday, Sept. 17 (P).—Soviet Russia has decided to send her army across the Polish frontier today and to occupy the Polish Ukraine and White Russia.

The government was understood unofficially to have sent a note last night to the Polish Ambassador here saying that the Red Army would enter the Polish Ukraine and White Russia today from Polosk to Kamanets-Podolski.

Copies of this note were said also to have been sent simultaneously to all diplomatic representatives here saying the action was taken because Poland no longer exists. It was said to have declared there no longer is a Polish Government because its whereabouts are unknown.

The note was said to have declared that "the Soviet Union will retain neutrality, but feels it necessary to protect White Russian and Ukrainian minorities in Poland and will do everything to keep peace and order."

[Poland not only has a non-aggression pact with Russia but in mutual assistance treaties by which the British and French are pledged to aid Poland in defense of her independence against any aggression. Polish invocation of this treaty brought Great Britain and France into war against Germany on Sept. 3, two days after a German army invaded Western Poland.]

Covers Entire Frontier

The scene of the Russian action would extend across the whole of Russia's Polish frontier.

It would increase considerably Russia's frontier with Rumania. Rumania holds Bessarabia, wrested from Russia after the World War, and the Soviet Government never has relinquished its claims on this territory.

Russia's decision to act came after she had sent a vast number of men to her western frontier in semi-mobilization and had followed with her "peace" with Japan.

It was believed here that the Polish Embassy in Moscow would leave and that, possibly, the British also would leave, since they are allies of Poland.

Man Power Is Threat

If necessary, Soviet Russia could throw nearly 2,000,000 trained soldiers against the struggling Poles.

The official Communist party newspaper Pravda this Spring estimated Russia's peacetime army at 1,800,000. This estimate did not include the millions of semi-trained

Continued on Page Thirty-six

"All the News That's Fit to Print"

The New York Times.

LATE CITY EDITION
POSTSCRIPT
Mostly cloudy, mild temperatures today, followed by light rain.
Temperatures Yesterday—Max.,51; Min.,39

Copyright, 1939, by The New York Times Company.

VOL. LXXXIX...No. 29,895. Entered as Second-Class Matter, Postoffice, New York, N. Y. NEW YORK, THURSDAY, NOVEMBER 30, 1939. P THREE CENTS NEW YORK CITY and Vicinity | FOUR CENTS Elsewhere Except in 7th and 8th Postal Zones.

RUSSIANS START THEIR INVASION OF FINLAND; PLANES DROP BOMBS ON AIRFIELD AT HELSINKI; WAR STARTS AS U. S. MOVE FOR PEACE IS MADE

KUHN FOUND GUILTY ON ALL FIVE COUNTS; HE FACES 30 YEARS

Leader of the Bund Here Will Be Sentenced Tuesday as Thief and Forger

JURY OUT FOR 8½ HOURS

Defense Counsel Rebuked by the Court as Clashes Mark Final Day of Trial

Fritz Kuhn, the leader of the German-American Bund, was convicted shortly after 10 o'clock last night of grand larceny and forgery in General Sessions Court.

He stood up, with only his forefinger on his left hand waving along the side seam of his trousers, and heard without a blink the verdict of a jury that had deliberated eight and a half hours. The maximum sentence he can receive is thirty years, and the day on which he will hear his fate was set by Judge James G. Wallace as Tuesday.

Pending the sentence Judge Wallace told Peter L. F. Sabbatino, the counsel who had defended Kuhn during his trial in General Sessions Court, that action on a promised contempt of court would be suspended until then. He gave Mr. Sabbatino leave to make any motions he desired in the intervening time.

Kuhn marched off to the Tombs with the stoical attitude of a good German soldier, which he says he once was. There was no tremor on his face, and the three courtroom bailiffs who surrounded him when Morris C. Bullock, the foreman of the jury, pronounced him guilty, had only to tug at his sleeve to lead him away to prison. There was not even an interchange of glances between him and Mr. Sabbatino or Wilbur V. Keegan, associate counsel.

What the Verdict Meant

The verdict was that he was guilty of grand larceny in the first and second degree in the theft of $717 from the bund to pay for the transportation of the furniture of Mrs. Florence Camp across the country, and of second degree larceny and two counts of forgery in the "Murray transaction."

The Murray transaction was a $500 item which Kuhn listed on the bund books of record and told the bund members that he had paid to James D. C. Murray for legal services. These two items, totaling $1,217, were all that the jury had to pass on of an indictment which originally charged thefts amounting to more than $14,000.

One pair of counts, dealing with more than $8,000 charged against Kuhn as a theft had been eliminated before the trial began and Judge Wallace knocked out another pair charging that he had stolen $4,424 of the bund funds because, the judge ruled, the prosecution had not proved this beyond a reasonable doubt.

During a long afternoon and early evening while the jury was out, Kuhn sat in the court room talking to his counsel. He had sandwiches brought in to him and munched on them while Assistant District Attorney Herman J. McCarthy, who prosecuted him, walked the corridors of the Criminal Courts Building.

Part of Charge Is Re-read

After seven and a half hours the jury came in shortly before 9 P. M. to ask Judge Wallace for a re-reading of a part of his charge dealing with the Camp transactions.

When the verdict finally did come in a half-hour later he stood up again. But this time the bailiff who was behind him asked him to step outside the rail enclosing the space for the attorneys, and as he stood there two other bailiffs came up behind him.

The precaution of three men surrounding the man who says his war record covered service as a machine gunner in Alpine service during the World War was not necessary. He made no move and there was no sign of emotion on his face.

The index finger of his left hand wiggled spasmodically. But he did not even move his hand.

Then, in a voice that was not even audible a few feet away, he gave his "pedigree" to a bailiff. He said that he was born in Germany forty-two years ago and revealed

Continued on Page Twelve

Must Stay Day in Mexico Or Pay San Diego Duties

Special to THE NEW YORK TIMES.

WASHINGTON, Nov. 29—The twenty-four hour limit goes into effect Friday on the Mexican border in the San Diego Customs District and persons wishing to avail themselves of the $100 customs exemption on goods brought into this country must stay in Mexico at least twenty-four hours.

Collectors have been instructed that in their discretion they may permit tourists staying a shorter time to bring in goods with an aggregate value of not more than $5 without paying duty.

The unusual situation in the San Diego district is created by the proximity of the Free Port of Tijuana, into which European merchandise may enter duty-free. Large retail establishments there maintain billboards along the roads to Tijuana advertising bargains on selected European imports.

CITY WILL SET UP A 'BOOSTER' BUREAU

Mayor Reveals Plans for New Department to Attract More Business Here

Reviewing the accomplishments of his administration before a gathering of merchants and property owners yesterday, Mayor La Guardia disclosed plans for still another project for the betterment of the city—a Department of Commerce—to bring more business and industry here.

He told the Central Mercantile Association at its Fall luncheon in the Hotel Pennsylvania that he had often boosted New York on his frequent flights out of town and that now he would have a municipal organization for this purpose, "and I am going to out-small-town the smallest town in the country."

The Mayor had reviewed the difficulties of city finance, education costs, the new pension plan for policemen and firemen, the Sixth Avenue improvement, transit unification, plans for Ninth and Second Avenues, the North Beach Airport and the new information bureau under the Park Avenue ramp in Pershing Square, not mentioning other accomplishments.

Will Combat Adverse Reports

"We have been confronted with a lot of small-town stuff about business in New York being more costly than elsewhere," he then went on. "I am going to out-small-town the smallest town in the country. I am going to establish a Department of Commerce which will have the function of providing information and advice to business men interested in coming to New York."

The Mayor's bureau will add no cost to the city government, he said, because he will "pick up employes from various city departments to do the work." He also will invite business and labor here to cooperate, he said, adding that "labor will have to assume its responsibility and I expect it to do its part."

The first step in the functioning of such a new program, the Mayor said, has already been taken in his invitation to the film industry to return to New York. He said there was no reason why this industry should be centered in one city "but we should have our share." He reported that, "notwithstanding ridicule and opposition, we are making progress."

Ryan Seen as Likely Head

A report that a municipal department of commerce would be established was published last Sunday but had not been publicly acknowledged by the Mayor until yesterday. The report said that Clendenin J. Ryan, Deputy Commissioner of Sanitation, would head the new department and would be sworn in as its first Commissioner this week.

In his address, which lasted for more than an hour, the Mayor dwelt particularly on his new pension plan for policemen and firemen. The establishment of the plan was prompted by the fact that any pension plan in existence July 1, 1940, will, under constitutional amendment, become a contractual obligation of the city.

The Mayor noted that the Legislature had failed to put the policemen and firemen pension system on

Continued on Page Twelve

DIES AT RALLY HERE WARNS U. S. TO STOP ITS 'APING' OF EUROPE

10,000 Cheer His Plea for National Unity and a Fight on All Alien Forces

HE PLEADS FOR TOLERANCE

Calls on Administration to Provide Funds to Continue Work of His Committee

Speaking last night in Madison Square Garden before an enthusiastic throng estimated at 10,000 to 12,000 persons, representing many patriotic and religious organizations, Representative Martin Dies of Texas denounced communism, fascism and nazism as alien forces tearing at American unity. He made a strong plea also for racial and religious tolerance.

Asserting that there was an organized campaign to discredit the work of the Congressional Committee Investigating un-American Activities which he heads, Mr. Dies made a demand for public funds with which to continue hearings on subversive groups next year. He also called on the Administration, which he implied was opposed to the committee, to come out openly and say whether or not it favored the drive against foreign "isms."

On this question Mr. Dies got strong support from the audience and from the other speakers, who urged those present to demand from Congress an appropriation that would preserve the committee as it is.

The husky, 6-foot Representative who has achieved national prominence since he was named chairman of the committee in 1938 was escorted to the platform by a guard of American Legionnaires while the drums of the Seventh Regiment band announced him with a fanfare.

Mr. Dies's fellow-speakers were Colonel George U. Harvey, Borough President of Queens; Joseph P. Ryan, president of the International Longshoremen's Association; Jeremiah Cross, past State commander of the American Legion; Laurens Hamilton, president of the New York State chapter, Sons of the American Revolution, and Jean Mathias, New York State commander, Jewish War Veterans of the United States.

As chairman of the meeting, Merwin K. Hart, president of the New York State Economic Council, opened the meeting at 8:30 P. M. Frederick Jagel of the Metropolitan Opera sang the "Star-Spangled Banner," although he advocates the adoption of a new anthem for the United States.

Among those who attended, it was reported but not confirmed, were

Continued on Page Thirteen

Intelligence Chief Quits; Dutch Blame Venloo Case

Wireless to THE NEW YORK TIMES.

AMSTERDAM, the Netherlands, Nov. 29—Major Gen. J. W. van Oorschot, 64-year-old head of the Netherlands intelligence service, resigned today. He had headed the department since 1919.

Observers are inclined to link his resignation with the Venloo frontier incident.

THE HAGUE, the Netherlands, Nov. 29 (UP)—The Venloo incident involved the shooting of a Netherlands intelligence officer, Lieutenant Klop, and the kidnapping of two British intelligence agents and a chauffeur by German Gestapo [secret police] agents. General J. W. van Oorschot, who resigned today, was responsible for sending Lieutenant Klop to Venloo.

The British version of the incident was that two British intelligence officers, Sigismund Payne Best and Captain Richard Henry Stevens, went to Venloo to investigate presumably legitimate German peace talk on Nov. 9.

REICH OIL SITUATION VIEWED AS CRITICAL

Germany Isolated From Great Sources of Supply—Imports From U. S. Virtually Ended

Special to THE NEW YORK TIMES.

WASHINGTON, Nov. 29—The oil situation in Germany, especially the Reich's reserve of fuel oils, is the most serious problem facing the Hitler government today, in the opinion of American naval and military experts. Export data in the Department of Commerce appear to substantiate this opinion.

Germany is one of the few great nations without oil resources and since the war started she has received virtually no crude, lubricating or gasoline supplies from the United States, the one market that under normal conditions would be in a position to make up at least part of the deficit.

Official statistics, plus reports considered reliable, all indicate that Germany is completely isolated from the great oil markets of the world. So grave is the situation that Germany is making frantic efforts to develop synthetic gasoline plants, which, it is hoped, may be in partial operation by the middle of 1940. Even the Germans do not expect the plants to be operating to capacity before the end of 1941.

Any hopes the Germans might have of getting appreciable quantities of oil from the Russian fields are dispelled, according to official information, by the fact that Russia is having a hard time producing enough for her own needs. This is

Continued on Page Seven

Unofficial Thanks to Be Given Here Today By Irreconcilables Clinging to 'Old Style'

It will be just another day on New York's official calendar today, but half the nation, led by New England, will observe Thanksgiving with a determination to make the celebration of the traditional date outshine the "new Thanksgiving" fixed by President Roosevelt and marked by the other half of the country a week ago.

They will be joined here in unofficial joy by those New York irreconcilables who refuse to eat turkey on any but the last Thursday of November, by those who have children coming home from school or college in "old-style" States, and by those who feel that any holiday is worth celebrating again even if it did occur only seven days before. These double celebrators will be following the example of Colorado, Mississippi and Texas, which are observing a second holiday in addition to the one last week.

Including these three, twenty-six States have proclaimed today as Thanksgiving Day. Americans in Sao Paulo, Brazil, dissenting from their fellows in Rio de Janeiro, and most other Americans abroad also will observe the day—which has been termed the "Republican Thanksgiving" in contrast to the "New Deal Thanksgiving" of Nov. 23.

In New York many theatres are giving special matinees, and numerous restaurants will have turkey dinners for those who wish to partake. Private clubs are in some cases holding special events which were scheduled for today before the President changed the date. The Volunteer Rescue Army, which fed turkey to 2,018 unemployed last week, will give the same menu today for 3,000 at its chapel at 379 First Avenue.

Magistrate Henry H. Curran, sitting in Felony Court yesterday, declared he would observe the holiday today to "give thanks for the twenty-three States that didn't fall for this tyrannical novelty which came out of Washington." But he will eat chicken because "it's not fair to make the turkeys suffer on two days."

In Highland Park, N. J., a suburb of New Brunswick, school pupils will be dismissed at 1 P. M. as a "gesture toward those who believe the day is still the oldtime Thanksgiving."

Rutgers University, in New Brunswick, will observe its second Thanksgiving today to permit students to go to Providence, R. I., to the Brown-Rutgers football game. Mayor C. D. White of Atlantic City has also proclaimed today as a second Thanksgiving.

The nation's principal observance

Continued on Page Fifteen

HULL ACTS QUICKLY

Offer of Good Offices in Ending Dispute Sent to Finland and Russia

HELSINKI LIKELY TO AGREE

But Moscow's Reaction Is Held to Be Highly Problematical —Pittman Assails Soviet

U. S. Offer Received

By The United Press.

MOSCOW, Thursday, Nov. 30—The United States' offer to mediate in the Soviet-Finnish dispute was received at the American Embassy here at 10:30 A. M. (3:30 A. M. Eastern Standard Time).

The offer will be presented or delivered to the Soviet Foreign Office some time this morning by Walter Thurston, Chargé d'Affaires.

By BERTRAM D. HULEN

Special to THE NEW YORK TIMES.

WASHINGTON, Nov. 29—The increasingly serious developments in relations between Russia and Finland led the United States today to proclaim her readiness to extend good offices for a pacific adjustment of the points at issue, if that should be agreeable to both parties.

The move was made in an effort to leave no stone unturned that would prevent a spread of European hostilities. It was in the form of a statement issued by Secretary of State Cordell Hull after several telephone conversations with President Roosevelt. In particular, it represented their views of a way in which the American Government could throw its weight into the scales for peace after consideration had been given in the State Department to possible courses of action.

The text of the statement follows:

This government is following with serious concern the intensification of the Finnish-Soviet dispute. It would view with extreme regret any extension of the present area of war and the consequent further deterioration of international relations.

Without in any way becoming involved in the merits of the dispute, and limiting its interest to the solution of the dispute by peaceful processes only, this government would, if agreeable to both parties, gladly extend its good offices.

Text Is Cabled to Envoys

The force of a diplomatic appeal was given the statement when Secretary Hull late today cabled the text to the United States Legation in Finland and the United States Embassy in Russia with instructions that it be delivered to the Foreign Offices.

The statement was issued at 3:05 P. M., one hour before word was received of Russia's severance of diplomatic relations with Finland, and an hour and a half before the press carried reports of the speech of Vyacheslaff M. Molotoff, Soviet Premier and Foreign Commissar.

In comment on the statement the State Department said it did not constitute intervention, nor did it necessarily mean mediation. It simply meant, it was stated, that this government is using what efforts it can to help Russia and Finland settle the dispute themselves.

Although Secretary Hull merely expressed a readiness to extend good offices if Russia and Finland are agreeable, his action threw open the possibility of an adjustment that might be worked out along any one of several lines. An offer of good offices, mediation and arbitration are the three recognized methods for pacific adjustment of disputes under The Hague convention of 1907 and have been utilized by the United States on many occasions, particularly in Latin America.

In the case of an offer of good offices the country making the tender sets no limitations upon the form that will be used in seeking to facilitate an adjustment. It could be by diplomatic conversations, mediation, arbitration, reference to a commission of inquiry or any other method. The country making the tender, moreover, usually does not figure in the ad-

Continued on Page Six

The International Situation

Soviet Russia severed diplomatic relations with Finland last night and this morning the Red Army crossed the border while Soviet planes bombed the airfield at Helsinki. Explaining the break over the radio, Premier Molotoff said that Finnish hostility had become "unbearable," and virtually demanded that a different government be set up in Helsinki. He also indicated rejection to a tender of good offices by the United States. [Page 1.] This offer had been made by Secretary Hull after he had been in touch with President Roosevelt. [Page 1.]

Finland, meanwhile, revealed that the Russian action had been taken before she had delivered a note to the Kremlin offering to withdraw forces from the border and suggesting conciliation. [Page 1.]

London evinced friendliness for the Finns and welcomed the news of the American offer. [Page 6.] Likewise Italy, fearing that near-by Rumania might next claim Russia's attention, expressed through her press sympathy for the Finns. [Page 7.] Germany, on the other hand, supported Russia, although she indicated that her attitude if a conflict began would be one of "benevolent neutrality." [Page 4.]

The Reich's most serious problem of the moment, according to Washington experts, is its critical oil situation. Germany was revealed as completely isolated from the world's oil markets. [Page 1.]

There was little actual war activity during the day. The British reported having driven off two German air raid attempts. [Page 2.] The French said one of their patrols had penetrated deep into German territory in the Vosges sector and had brought back valuable information. [Page 8.] And at sea two more British ships were sunk. [Page 3.]

Japan, a possible sufferer from the hostilities at sea, studied measures of reprisal against the Anglo-French blockade of German exports. It was reported that such measures might include seizure of Allied cargoes in the Orient. [Page 1.]

In the Balkans the Rumanian Foreign Minister turned down Hungary's revisionist demands, but at the same time invited her to help improve relations between the two countries. [Page 10.]

Today Premier Daladier will go before the French Parliament and ask, with every expectation of success, that his emergency powers be continued. [Page 9.]

JAPAN MAY SEIZE CARGOES OF ALLIES

Studies Plan for Reprisals if Anglo-French Ban on Reich Exports Continues

By HUGH BYAS

Wireless to THE NEW YORK TIMES.

TOKYO, Thursday, Nov. 30—The Japanese Government is considering retaliatory measures against Great Britain's two-way blockade of Germany. These may include seizure of Anglo-French ship cargoes in Far Eastern waters.

This threat appears in the newspaper Nichi Nichi this morning as part of its report of a conference held at the Foreign Office yesterday to discuss the British reply to Ambassador Mamoru Shigemitsu's protest against the Order in Council for seizure of German exports on neutral ships.

Reports from other sources indicate that interference with Anglo-French shipping in the Far East still is a somewhat distant possibility, depending on the British response to Japan's demand for special consideration of her German imports. Asahi says that Mr. Shigemitsu has been instructed to press the British Government to give assurances that Japanese trade will receive special consideration in enforcement of the blockade.

The Foreign Office conference in which Foreign Minister Kichisaburo Nomura, Vice Foreign Minister Masayuki Tani and several bureau chiefs participated, found the British order had been formulated in flexible terms so that its effect could not be ascertained until it has been enforced. It was decided to await the text and to continue the policy of pressing Britain to give consideration to Japan's "imported" imports from Germany.

If the Japanese representations to Britain are disregarded, a further measure will be considered in the terms of Japan's original protest, which threatened appropriate counter-measures.

Norway Adds Her Protest

OSLO, Norway, Nov. 29 (UP)—Foreign Minister Halvdan Koht announced today that the Norwegian Government has made representations to the Allied Governments regarding their decision to seize German exports.

The Norwegian Government, Mr. Koht said, "fails to see how such a move can be in accord with international law." He added that Norway claimed the right to demand compensation for any losses involved, and urged Great Britain to reconsider her decision. Norway is

Continued on Page Three

Dispatches from Europe and the Far East are subject to censorship.

FINLAND IS BLOCKED IN MEDIATION PLEA

Note Delivered After Rupture Offers to Recall Troops—Soviet Move Awaited

The text of the last Finnish note appears on Page 5.

By The Associated Press.

HELSINKI, Finland, Thursday, Nov. 30—Profoundly disturbed by Moscow's action rupturing diplomatic relations, but still determined to stand fast, Finns uneasily awaited developments today, fearing the beginning of hostilities at any time. But early this morning officials said there had been no troop movements across the borders so far as they could learn.

It was all the more shocking to the Finns because the Moscow action came before they could deliver a note to the Kremlin offering to withdraw Finnish defense forces from the frontier as a gesture toward settling their quarrel.

The offer was made by Foreign Minister Eljas Erkko in his reply to Russia's denunciation of the 1932 Finnish-Soviet non-aggression treaty.

"My government is ready to settle with the Soviet Government the question of the removal of Finnish defense forces on the Karelian Isthmus, with the exception of frontier customs guard forces, to such a distance from Leningrad that it could not even be alleged that they threaten its security," Mr. Erkko's note said.

Making a Sincere Effort

He prefaced this statement with the explanation that Finland was motivated by a desire "to prove emphatically that there is a sincere effort to reach an accord with the Soviet Government and refute the Soviet Government's allegations that Finland has adopted a hostile attitude toward the U.S.S.R. and is desirous of threatening the security of Leningrad."

Despite the breaking off of diplomatic relations, and despite the midnight broadcast of Soviet Premier Vyacheslaff M. Molotoff, who announced the action, Finland's note answering Moscow's denunciation of their non-aggression pact was delivered to the Kremlin at 1:10 A. M., Moscow time.

This was almost three hours after the Vice Commissar of Foreign Affairs, Vladimir Potemkin, had notified the Finnish Minister that relations were broken.

The Finnish answer said the Helsinki Government thought Russia unjustified in denouncing the non-aggression pact and suggested that a conciliation commission be named to examine the controversy.

The news from Moscow spread rapidly through Helsinki. Grim Finns gathered in clusters to discuss the situation. Government of-

Continued on Page Five

BORDER IS CROSSED

Soviet Artillery Opens Fire as Troops March in Karelian Sector

AIR RAID WARNING SOUNDED

People Run to Shelters as the Capital Sees Russian Planes —Five Bombs Are Dropped

Special Cable to THE NEW YORK TIMES.

COPENHAGEN, Denmark, Thursday, Nov. 30—At 9:15 A. M. today the first Russian troops crossed the Karelian frontier into Finland. At 9:20 o'clock an air raid warning was sounded in Helsinki, causing panic in the streets.

At 9:25 o'clock Russian bombers flew over the Finnish capital.

Five Bombs Dropped

HELSINKI, Finland, Nov. 30 (UP)—Five bombs were dropped on the city's airfield today. A report from the border station at Terijoki said Russian troops had opened artillery fire against the Finns early this morning.

Terijoki is on the Karelian Isthmus, twenty-two miles from Leningrad.

The bombing of Helsinki occurred a few minutes after a Russian two-motored airplane flew over the city, driving people to shelter.

Earlier, a squadron of six Russian airplanes had been sighted over the Gulf of Finland, approaching the city.

Finnish anti-aircraft guns fired on the squadron as well as on the single plane over the capital.

Finnish anti-aircraft batteries fired on the plane here and coastal batteries attacked the Russian squadron in the gulf.

Molotoff Proclaims Split

By G. E. R. GEDYE

Wireless to THE NEW YORK TIMES.

MOSCOW, Thursday, Nov. 30—Premier Vyacheslaff M. Molotoff announced in a thirteen-minute radio speech last midnight the breaking off of diplomatic relations with Finland by the Soviet Union through the recall of all Soviet diplomatic, consular and economic representatives in Finland. At the same time he warned all units of the Red Army and Red Navy to stand ready for every emergency.

In contrast to the last Soviet note to Finland and in glaring contrast to the abusive violence of the inspired press and radio campaign, Mr. Molotoff's speech, except for one important particular, conformed entirely to international usage.

Although it accepted, of course, without any effort to substantiate their accuracy, all the Soviet charges concerning the alleged extraordinary violations of the frontier by the Finns in the last few days, the language was restrained and contained indications that the Soviet was prepared to grant concessions to reach a settlement—with the "Finnish people." In that, however, lay the important exception to conformity with international usage.

Appeals to "Finnish People"

Despite the sentences asserting no desire to interfere in internal Finnish affairs and that the Finnish regime's relations with other States was exclusively the affair of Finland, the speech directly appealed over the heads of the present Finnish Government "to the Finnish people." Thus it confirmed the belief expressed more than once that the Soviet Union intended to try to force the surrender of the bases demanded from Finland through a change in the Finnish Government rather than through involving the Soviet Union in an invasion of Finnish territory.

By these passages of his speech Mr. Molotoff would seem to have confronted the Finnish Government with the alternatives of immediately recalling its diplomatic mission from Moscow at the peril of a still further increase in Soviet military pressure, if not of invasion, or of resignation. If the latter alternative were chosen, it would open the

Continued on Page Four

"All the News That's Fit to Print."

The New York Times.

LATE CITY EDITION
Cloudy and colder today. Tomorrow partly cloudy with slowly rising temperatures.
Temperatures Yesterday—Max., 43; Min., 31

VOL. LXXXIX...No. 29,909. Entered as Second-Class Matter, Postoffice, New York, N. Y. NEW YORK, THURSDAY, DECEMBER 14, 1939. PP THREE CENTS NEW YORK CITY and Vicinity | FOUR CENTS Elsewhere Except in 7th and 8th Postal Zones.

BRITISH DEFEAT NAZI RAIDER IN ALL-DAY FIGHT; SHE RUNS TO MONTEVIDEO WITH 36 DEAD, 60 HURT; U-BOAT SUNK, REICH CRUISER HIT IN NORTH SEA

A.F.L. LEADER SAYS NLRB 'PLAN' SAVED LEWIS' COAL UNION

Area Jurisdiction Ruling Led Thousands to Quit the Rival P.M.W., Ozanic Tells Inquiry

'SHOOTING' ORDER CHARGED

NLRB Report Said U. M. W. Officer Urged This Treatment for Progressive Miners

By The Associated Press.

WASHINGTON, Dec. 13—Joe Ozanic, young leader of the Progressive Mine Workers (A. F. L.), charged before a House investigating committee today that the National Labor Relations Board had followed a "plan" to give the United Mine Workers (C. I. O.) "a way out" in the desperate rivalry between the two unions.

The "plan," as he described it, was embodied in a controlling decision, which certified the C. I. O. union as the bargaining agent for all the coal mines in a specified geographic area. This was done, he said, despite provable majorities for the Progressives in individual mines affected.

As a result, he asserted, the United Mine Workers and employers in the field had forced thousands of Progressive members to switch to the C. I. O. union, and pay its dues, regardless of their own desires in the matter.

In one instance which he cited, that of the Acme Semi-Anthracite Coal Company of Williams, Okla., members of the Progressive union were unemployed, he said, because their jobs had been taken by miners imported by the United Mine Workers.

Bitterness of Feud Evidenced

All the accumulated bitterness of the fierce battle between the C. I. O. and the American Federation of Labor was epitomized for the committee in the day's testimony. Mr. Ozanic spoke repeatedly of "Dictator John L. Lewis." and of alleged "coercion" by C. I. O. members against his own followers.

At one point Edmund M. Toland, the committee's counsel, introduced a memorandum from Philip G. Phillips, the West Virginia regional director of the Labor Board, which quoted "Van Bitner" as having advised United Mine Workers' organizers to shoot Progressive organizers "faster than they would shoot a rabbit."

"Who is Van Bitner?" Chairman Smith, Democrat of Virginia, inquired.

"Van Bitner," Mr. Ozanic replied, "why, he's the provisional district president for District 17 of the United Mine Workers. He was appointed by Dictator John L. Lewis and never in his life elected by the United Mine Workers. That, gentlemen, is Mr. Bitner."

Later Van A. Bittner, who spells his name with two "t's" and is president of District No. 17, and also a member of the U. M. W. International Board, denied that he had ever made the shooting statement.

Denial by U. M. W. Official

"That statement of Phillips is absolutely untrue and made out of whole cloth," he told reporters. The memorandum mentioned that "Bitner" spoke at a Labor Day meeting in Charleston, W. Va., but the U. M. W. official said that the union held no Labor Day meeting in Charleston in 1938.

When Mr. Ozanic took the stand he told the committee that he started work as a coal miner at the age of 15 and was a member of the United Mine Workers of America.

After twenty-two years in that union, he said that he and fellow-miners in the Illinois fields "seceded" because of the U. M. W.'s dictatorial policies" and formed the Progressive Mine Workers of Illinois in 1932.

The new union soon recruited 35,000 of the State's 42,000 miners, he said, and, he added, still had them. After the Progressives received an international charter from the A. F. L. in 1938, Mr. Ozanic said, it recruited an additional 80,000 workers in coal fields outside Illinois. To the latter, however, rec-

Continued on Page Eighteen

Revolutionary Landmark In Queens Being Razed

The old frame building in Elmhurst, Queens, used during the Battle of Long Island as the headquarters of the British Army, was being razed by its present owner yesterday despite efforts of Borough President George U. Harvey to have the property purchased by the city and restored as a historic landmark.

The building, which stands at what is now Fifty-seventh Avenue and Queens Boulevard, was erected in 1762. On Sept. 3, 1776, General William Howe, commanding the British forces, wrote his official report to the King on what happened during the Battle of Long Island six days before, while using the house as his headquarters.

The present owner, Dr. Hevia, Cuban tobacco planter, who has a home in Richmond Hill, decided to raze the building when it became in need of repair. He has no plans for future use of the land.

RALLY HERE SCORES REICH AND SOVIET

Hoover, Landon, La Guardia and Green Are Heard by 20,000 in Garden

Before a mass meeting of more than 20,000 persons who filled every seat in Madison Square Garden last night, former President Herbert Hoover, former Governor Alf M. Landon of Kansas, Mayor La Guardia and William Green, president of the American Federation of Labor, headed prominent Christian and Jewish speakers who joined in protest against the persecution of Jews by Nazi Germany and in an appeal for the mobilization of the moral forces of the world against Hitlerism and Stalinism.

The meeting, held under the auspices of the American Jewish Congress and the Jewish Labor Committee, unanimously adopted by rising vote a resolution asking President Roosevelt to convey American condemnation of the persecution of the Jews in Nazi Poland to the German Government and to use every possible means to succor the victims of the oppression. It was decided to appoint a committee representing the two organizations to take the resolution to Washington.

Hitler and Stalin Booed

Cheering every reference to President Roosevelt's neutrality program, the audience booed equally every mention of Hitler and Stalin. They laughed loudly when speakers ridiculed Nazi and Communist propaganda that Hitler and Stalin are working for peace against the imperialistic war aims of England and France.

They also applauded statements that the real issue was the defense of democracy against totalitarianism, whether its label was Nazi, Fascist or Communist, and that anti-Semitism was only the first step toward the destruction of all religions, labor unions and civil liberties. Many in the audience came in delegations from New York labor unions in which Jewish membership predominates.

The speakers and the audience made it clear that their protests were aimed at the Russian invasion of Finland as well as German aggression in Poland, and that their appeals for help were directed in behalf of the Finns as well as the Jews in Poland, Austria Czecho-Slovakia and Germany.

It was announced that part of a collection taken up at the meeting to defray its expenses and to help Jewish victims of Hitlerism would be turned over to former President Hoover's Finnish relief fund if the collection was large enough. The total was not announced, as the contributions were not to be counted until today.

About seventy policemen were stationed outside the Garden in case of disturbances, but there was no trouble.

Several hundred persons were turned away when the gates of the Garden were closed by Fire Department order at 8:35 P. M., half an hour after the meeting opened. About 200 clustered outside the police lines, despite the rain.

Mayor La Guardia received the biggest ovation of all the speakers when he arrived on the platform after flying in from Chicago on a night plane. He expressed his "horror" at what is taking place in Europe and said he hoped that what

Continued on Page Eight

RUSSIA CONDEMNED

League Certain to Expel Her as Committee of 13 Calls Her Aggressor

PLANS AID TO FINNS

U. S. Will Be Invited to Help—Victim One of Invader's Judges

Text of League report on Russia is on Page 6.

By P. J. PHILIP

Wireless to THE NEW YORK TIMES.

GENEVA, Dec. 13—Soviet Russia, it is now considered certain, will be thrust forth from the company of the League of Nations, having, in the opinion of her fellow-members, by her own acts placed herself outside the Covenant.

A report by thirteen of them—the committee appointed by the Assembly to consider Finland's appeal—held today that Russia has been the aggressor and called on member States to lend all possible aid to the victim. It also offered the facilities of the League to coordinate such help and suggested that non-members be invited to cooperate.

The report was drafted by a subcommittee composed of the representatives of Great Britain, France, Sweden, Bolivia and Portugal.

In the public meeting of the Assembly during the morning Argentina demanded the expulsion, declaring that she would no longer remain a member of the League if the Soviet Union continued to enjoy that title.

Russia Not Represented

The Russian Government was not there to defend itself and no one cared to assume its defense. Jacob Suritz, Soviet Ambassador to France, anticipating events, had left Geneva on the morning train.

Alternative suggestions to that of expulsion proposed by Argentina were invited. It was stipulated that they should be heard in private committee so as to avoid embarrassment to those who feel that their geographic position as Russia's neighbors affects their judgment of both the legal and moral aspects of the question.

Cuba wanted to speak after Argentina in the Assembly, but was overruled as Mexico and India already had agreed to submit their proposals in private.

The Assembly then prepared one more step on the way to expulsion by electing the Union of South Africa and Finland to the council in the place of New Zealand and Sweden, re-electing Bolivia and shelving until after the council shall have taken its decision on the Russian issue the re-election of

Continued on Page Six

Liner Columbus Cleared For Transatlantic Dash

By The Associated Press.

VERACRUZ, Mexico, Dec. 13—Port authorities disclosed tonight that the 32,581-ton German liner Columbus had obtained clearance papers for a transatlantic voyage and was prepared to sail without further notice.

All crew members on shore leave have been ordered to report aboard to prepare for a "long voyage."

The ship's representatives said her destination was Oslo, Norway.

It was believed that the Columbus would slip from port shortly, but in view of persistent rumors of British warships in the Gulf of Mexico and Caribbean she was expected to sail as secretly as possible, probably at night without lights.

The same agency also arranged for the departure of the German freighter Arauca, also here since the start of the war. The crew was busy this afternoon painting the vessel black.

VALPARAISO, Chile, Dec. 13—The 4,930-ton German steamer Dusseldorf sailed from this Pacific Ocean harbor today, the fourth to sail of five German ships here at the outbreak of war. The only remaining one is the school ship Velero Priwall.

FINNS REPORT GAIN IN COUNTER-THRUST

Say Russians Are Hurled Back as Major Battle Impends—Soviet Is 'Invaded'

By The United Press.

COPENHAGEN, Denmark, Thursday, Dec. 14—Heavily reinforced Finnish troops early today were reported to be laying siege to the strategic town of Salla, just above the Arctic Circle, where the Russians were said to have lost 7,000 men.

The Finns, concentrating large forces in an effort to prevent the Red Army from reaching the Gulf of Bothnia and cutting Finland in two, hoped to recapture Salla today, frontier dispatches said.

Salla is about 125 miles northeast of the top of the Gulf of Bothnia at the Swedish-Finnish border and slightly northeast of the town of Kemijaervi, where fierce fighting was reported.

Thrust Into Russia Reported

[Finnish forces had carried the war to Russian soil in a strong drive north of Lake Ladoga, according to unofficial reports in Helsinki. This followed closely the reported bombing of the Soviet's Leningrad-Murmansk railway, which was said to have halted an attempt to transport submarines to the Arctic.]

Against the Russians' reported losses of 7,000 men in the new Finnish counter-offensive, the Finns claim to have lost only 250 men.

Continued on Page Nine

Davies Will Resign as Envoy to Belgium To Become an Adviser on Europe to Hull

By FELIX BELAIR Jr.

Special to THE NEW YORK TIMES.

WASHINGTON, Dec. 13—Joseph E. Davies is soon to give up his post as Ambassador to Belgium and take a place in the special division of the State Department dealing with war emergencies.

The Ambassador's resignation is lying on the President's desk. Whether it was offered when Mr. Davies called on the President today or was sent ahead of his return to the United States was not ascertained. The resignation was technical, in any event. Arrangements for the transfer were completed several weeks ago.

The duties to be assigned to Mr. Davies will be similar to those now being performed by Hugh R. Wilson, who recently resigned as Ambassador to Germany, and Breckenridge Long, former Ambassador to Italy. President Roosevelt is said to be desirous of putting the details of the emergency situations abroad in the hands of diplomats who have had experience in the field.

Mr. Davies entered the diplomatic service as Ambassador to Russia and later was transferred to Brussels. He has been credited at various times with an ambition to represent this country in London. He returned to this country yesterday, ostensibly to participate in negotiations over revision of the reciprocal trade agreement with Belgium.

As he left the Executive Office today after conferring with the President, Mr. Davies said that he wanted to be on record as having stated that he was not a candidate for the Secretaryship of the Navy, a post with which his name had been connected in recent rumors.

Mr. Davies will probably go back to Brussels to wind up the affairs of his ambassadorship and also to participate in official activities incident to the start of operation of the trade agreement.

After it became known that information regarding Mr. Davies's resignation had been obtained by THE NEW YORK TIMES, a spokesman of the State Department said that Mr. Davies had been instructed to return here and that he reported today to the President, Secretary Hull and Under-Secretary Welles. The spokesman issued this statement:

"No decision has been reached as to what his future duties will be either in Washington or in the event that he returns to Belgium.

Continued on Page Sixteen

NORTH SEA SUCCESS

British Submarine That Spared Bremen Said to Have Scored Twice

NEW TACTICS IN AIR

Planes Patrol Nazi Base to Prevent Laying of Mines at Night

Special Cable to THE NEW YORK TIMES.

LONDON, Dec. 13—The British Admiralty announced tonight that the British submarine that sighted and spared the German liner Bremen a few days ago had sunk a German U-boat and torpedoed a German cruiser in the North Sea.

The announcement marked the first time that any British submarine had been in action against enemy seacraft. Details of the British submarine's exploit were not given and officials would not make any comment on the identity of the German cruiser involved.

When asked whether the cruiser had sunk after the torpedoing the officials pointed out that the communiqué specified sinking in the case of the U-boat but used the word "torpedoed" in the case of the cruiser. This was taken to mean the cruiser had been damaged. When the action took place was not revealed.

New Air Patrol Fixed

The Air Ministry issued today a statement hinting at new tactics in the evolving strategy of war in the air and on the sea. British planes, it was said, had maintained an all-night watch over the German seaplane bases at Sylt, Borkum and Norderney in Helgoland bight.

The official announcement indicated that a new arm of defense against air attack had been formed and that it was its duty to squelch attacks from the air on enemy territory instead of awaiting the arrival of Nazi air armadas.

Hindsight is sometimes helpful in interpreting the mysterious diplomatic manoeuvring in these uncertain times, but yesterday's announcement that a British submarine failed to sink the Bremen and the latest announcement that British planes roared harmlessly over German naval bases last night do not help much in understanding the way this strange war is developing.

Presumably, the British Admiralty thinks more was gained diplomatically by the strict observance of international law than could have been gained by the sinking of the queen of Germany's merchant navy. Likewise, it may be presumed the British feel there is more to be gained by sending planes to hover over the nests of Germany's mine-laying flying boats than by bombing their bases and that it is better to hold the threat of attack above the Nazi fliers' heads than to try to drive them from British coasts with all the advantage that falls to the fighter who rises fresh to the fray.

Nazis Scoff at Statement

The Germans, of course, scoff at the British statement that they could have sunk the Bremen but did not think it sporting or legal. The truth is, the Germans say, that the British are just trying to put the best face possible on their naval impotence.

The official announcement of the new patrols over the German bases in Helgoland Bight said they were "continuously maintained." Their purpose, it was said, was "to interrupt the activities of mine-laying aircraft operating from these bases." Despite anti-aircraft opposition "the operations were successfully carried out."

Today's Air Ministry statement indicated that Britain's method of meeting the new magnetic mine menace included not only some method of sweeping up the destructive eggs laid by planes and submarines in coastal shipping channels but also contemplated measures to prevent their being laid at all. Aviation experts said there was much about the establishment of what already have been dubbed "security patrols" that is mysterious.

It was pointed out, for instance, that the official statement rather indicated that bombing planes were used, that they circled more or less

Continued on Page Three

The International Situation

Britain's far-flung sea power caught up with a raiding German pocket battleship yesterday in the Western Hemisphere.

A running battle was fought during the day and last night off the Uruguayan coast between the Nazi craft, identified as the Admiral Graf Spee, and two small British cruisers, the Ajax and the Achilles. The cruiser Exeter had also been in the battle, but was damaged and forced to drop out. The pursuit continued with hits scored on both sides until the pocket battleship raced into neutral Montevideo harbor badly damaged and with thirty dead aboard. The Ajax and the Achilles followed and lay outside the harbor. Page 1.]

Under international law Uruguay must now determine the minimum repairs needed to make the German ship seaworthy, and when these repairs have been made the vessel must either put to sea or be interned for the duration of the war. [Page 4.]

London claimed another naval success, reporting that the British submarine that had sighted the liner Bremen on her dash to Germany had sunk a U-boat and torpedoed a German cruiser. At the same time the Air Ministry indicated a new policy of an all-night air patrol over German seaplane bases to frustrate aerial mine-laying. [Page 1.]

Following his adventurous voyage homeward, the Bremen's commander declared at a reception that he believed the liner had been held up in New York last August to help the British. [Page 3.]

While the Finns reported having thrown the Russians back in counter-offensives and were unofficially said to have carried the war to Russian soil [Page 1], a League of Nations committee condemned Russia as an aggressor, called for all possible aid to the Finns by members and non-members alike and suggested expulsion of the Soviet, a development that now seems certain. [Page 1.]

What the League was doing was still kept from the Soviet people. [Page 8.] But a hint that Moscow was not insensitive to criticism was seen in the hasty summoning home of the new Russian Ambassador to Rome, who had not yet had time to present his credentials. [Page 1.]

While the British House of Commons in its first secret session since the World War debated Opposition charges of government bungling on supplies [Page 11], peace talk in the House of Lords by a few members caused Foreign Secretary Halifax to characterize the debate as "unfortunate." [Page 1.]

SOVIET CALLS HOME NEW ROME ENVOY

Italians Believe He Will Be Asked How Seriously They Mean Balkan Warning

By HERBERT L. MATTHEWS

By Telephone to THE NEW YORK TIMES.

ROME, Dec. 13—Nikolai Gorelchin, the new Russian Ambassador, who has not yet had time to present his credentials, was hastily summoned back to Moscow by telegram and left Rome on Monday, it was learned today. The Russian Embassy claims it is a mere informative visit without particular significance and that Mr. Gorelchin, who saw Count Ciano, the Foreign Minister, last week, will return to Rome shortly.

However, it is at least a coincidence that his sudden recall should come at a time when there are almost daily hostile demonstrations against Russia and when the Fascist Grand Council, to say nothing of the entire Italian press, has been issuing warnings to Moscow to keep out of the Balkans. One is entitled to suppose that Joseph Stalin wants to know just what the Italians mean and how serious they are with their threats.

Italy's Earnestness Clear

If that is what his visit is about, Mr. Gorelchin will doubtless inform his government that Italy means business, for genuinely strong measures are being taken to parry the expected Russian thrust, should it try to go beyond Bessarabia. On the other hand, the Soviet Government may have become sensitive about criticism and hostility and may not intend to send Mr. Gorelchin back here.

In connection with the press criticism, Roberto Farinacci's newspaper, the Regime Fascista, offers a novel explanation for the Russo-German alliance. After saying that Finnish resistance has proved Russian weakness, the writer concludes:

"So when England, France and the Osservatore Romano [the Vatican City newspaper] speak of the Russian peril, it is in bad faith. Russia preferred the German alliance because she thought that if she had to fight Germany she would be beaten."

Premier Georges Kiosseivanoff of Bulgaria, in an interview with the Giornale d'Italia's correspondent today, says that while Bulgaria has not renounced "the realization of

Continued on Page Seven

Dispatches from Europe and the Far East are subject to censorship.

BRITISH PEERS URGE NEW PEACE MOVES

Mediation Call Hurts Nation, Halifax Replies—Commons Holds Secret Session

Special Cable to THE NEW YORK TIMES.

LONDON, Dec. 13—The question of making peace now and without military victory arose in the House of Lords today in a debate described by Foreign Secretary Viscount Halifax as "unfortunate because it would create a wrong impression abroad that Britain was not united in her determination to fulfill her war aims."

The debate centered around the problem of whether a lasting peace could be obtained at this time and whether a long war would not mean that the country paid a terrible price in vain.

[Meanwhile the House of Commons in its first secret session since the last war debated for seven hours and a half Opposition charges that the government is bungling the production of vital war supplies.]

The debate was precipitated by a suggestion from the Earl of Darnley that Britain take up the Belgian and Netherland proposal for mediation, which, he said, still is open. Supported by Lord Arnold and the Bishop of Chichester, he said Britain had not done enough after the Versailles treaty to conciliate Germany and warned against a "revenge-producing victory."

Three Peers Reply

Lord Balfour, Viscount Samuel and Lord Snell opposed the Earl amid cheers. Lord Balfour declared there was a reign of violence and terror in Germany, "and as long as that persisted any idea that there was a change of heart or that a freely negotiated peace was possible was illusory."

Lord Darnley maintained that Chancellor Hitler's actions were aimed partly to make Germany free and prosperous but chiefly to make her free from any danger in the future, and every threat made against him made him think aggression more necessary.

Lord Arnold said it was unfortunate the Earl's proposal could not be discussed at a secret session. He contended that laying down peace conditions in advance did not help negotiations, but hindered them. He added:

"If a satisfactory peace could be secured in other respects, this country would not wish to continue the war on account of Austria."

Lord Arnold believed that if the war continued until Herr Hitler was overthrown by revolution, Germany would become Communist and enter into an alliance with Russia. He feared that communism might spread over Eastern Europe and "not only would any peace at the end of a long war be

Continued on Page Twelve

PREY OF 3 CRUISERS

Pocket Battleship Puts In South America Port After 18-Hour Fight

EXETER FORCED OUT

Foe Badly Damaged 1 Ship, but Two Others Continue Chase

By JOHN W. WHITE

Special Cable to THE NEW YORK TIMES.

BUENOS AIRES, Argentina, Thursday, Dec. 14—The German pocket battleship Admiral Graf Spee struggled into Montevideo harbor shortly before last midnight with thirty-six of her crew dead, sixty wounded and the ship badly damaged as the result of an eighteen-hour running battle with the British cruisers Exeter, Ajax and Achilles.

Shortly after the Graf Spee's arrival two British cruisers, the Ajax and the Achilles, arrived in the outer roads off Montevideo, but at an early hour this morning had not reported to the authorities ashore regarding their casualties.

[Returning from a visit aboard the Admiral Graf Spee, the German Minister to Uruguay, Otto Langman, said that the dead included a lieutenant and the wounded the commander of the ship, The Associated Press reported. His statement that the ship was the Spee and not the Admiral Scheer as reported at first was the first indication that the Graf Spee had been operating in the Atlantic.

[The spokesman for the German Legation at Montevideo said that "there are thirty-six dead and sixty wounded aboard the Graf Spee, mostly because the British used mustard gas shells," The United Press reported. The spokesman said that the damage to the battleship was insignificant.

[Captains of six British ships captured by the Graf Spee off the South American and South African coasts will be landed at Montevideo, the spokesman added.]

Open Fire on the Spee

The British squadron was under the command of Commodore H. H. Harwood.

Contact with the Graf Spee was established six times during the morning when the pocket battleship attacked the Ajax while the latter was convoying the French passenger liner Formosa from Rio de Janeiro to Montevideo. The Ajax called for help and the Exeter and Achilles arrived at full speed and opened fire on the battleship.

The four warships fought an intense artillery duel from 6 o'clock until 10. Despite the Admiral Spee's speed and heavier armament she was repeatedly hit by shells from the British cruisers, especially the Exeter. The Spee, accordingly, directed her main efforts to putting the Exeter out of commission. By this time all four warships were running southward, the Formosa having dropped back for safety.

The Exeter, finally disabled, was forced to drop out of the battle but by this time the Spee was so badly damaged that the commander began running at full speed for the River Plate, closely followed by the Ajax and Achilles.

The battle apparently lasted on and off all day, as the firing was renewed twice after the warships were within sight of the Uruguayan shore. Just after the warships passed Punta del Este, which projects far out to sea, the two British cruisers turned westward toward the shore to take advantage of the setting sun by getting the Graf Spee silhouetted against the reflected light in the eastern sky while they were protected by the shadow of the land.

Spee Changes Her Course

This forced the Spee to change her course disadvantageously to the southeast. Then the British warships renewed their heavy firing, which continued until well after dark. Under cover of night the Graf Spee changed her course and finally reached the refuge of Montevideo,

Continued on Page Four

The New York Times

PAGE ONE

1940-1949

"All the News That's Fit to Print."

The New York Times.

LATE CITY EDITION
POSTSCRIPT
Cloudy, preceded by rain today, slightly colder tonight.
Temperatures Yesterday—Max., 51; Min., 44

VOL. LXXXIX...No. 30,026. Entered as Second-Class Matter, Postoffice, New York, N. Y. NEW YORK, TUESDAY, APRIL 9, 1940. P THREE CENTS NEW YORK CITY and Vicinity | FOUR CENTS Elsewhere Except in 7th and 8th Postal Zones.

GERMANS OCCUPY DENMARK, ATTACK OSLO; NORWAY THEN JOINS WAR AGAINST HITLER; CAPITAL IS REPORTED BOMBED FROM AIR

HOUSE TO CONSIDER WAGE ACT CHANGES EARLY NEXT WEEK

Leaders in Surprise Moves Also Slate Bill for Court Review of Agency Rulings

LABOR LAW ACTION LIKELY

Proponents of Amendments Expect Drive to Dispose of All Labor Legislation

House consideration next week was slated for the bill to amend the Wages and Hours Act and for the Logan-Walter bill to provide for a court review of decisions by governmental agencies. [Page 1.]

A refusal by the Supreme Court to review the Labor Board's order in the Republic Steel case sustained the reinstatement of 5,000 C. I. O. strikers with $5,000,000 back pay. [Page 20.]

The Socialist party convention, at Washington, stated in a resolution that "the interests of American working men and women will best be served by the making of an immediate peace between the C. I. O. and A. F. L." [Page 1.]

Colonel Harrington, WPA Administrator, will be questioned Thursday by the House Appropriations Subcommittee on evidence gathered by its investigators bearing on the 1941 relief outlay. [Page 20.]

The NLRB refused to relieve Mrs. Elinore M. Herrick of further responsibility in connection with the election of employes of the Consolidated Edison Company of New York after a charge of collusion with the company. [Page 20.]

Two Revision Bills Slated

By HENRY N. DORRIS

Special to THE NEW YORK TIMES.

WASHINGTON, April 8—House leaders decided today on consideration early next week of the Barden bill to amend the Wages and Hours Act, a decision which occasioned surprise in labor quarters since it had been assumed this measure would follow the Smith or Norton amendments to the National Labor Relations Act.

But this was not the only surprise, because the tentative calendar for next week also contained a place for the Logan-Walter bill providing court review of any decision of a governmental agency which has the force of law.

When these two measures are out of the way, proponents of amendments to the Wagner Act expect to win consideration of their measures. Just how they will manage this was not revealed, but it was said by one member that the procedure was for a "Bang! Bang! Bang!" program that would wipe the House calendar clean of labor legislation that has "plagued" it for more than a year.

The Barden bill has been pending since last August, when a rule was granted for its consideration. It was never considered, however, because of the "compromise" by which the lending-spending and United States Housing Authority bills—desired by the Administration—were taken up. Both of these failed to obtain consideration, but they served to crowd out the Barden bill, which primarily aims at a redefinition of the "area of production" provision of the Wages and Hours Act.

Would Remove "Ambiguities"

The amendment proposed by Representative Barden of North Carolina, a member of the House Labor Committee, proposes to remove the "ambiguities" of the "area of production" clause and the ruling subsequently made on it by the former Wages and Hours Administrator, Elmer F. Andrews.

Under that ruling processing plants located within ten miles of the area where agricultural products are grown or harvested are exempt from the provisions which require them to pay a minimum wage of thirty cents an hour or work their employes not to exceed forty-two hours per week without overtime pay of time and a half. The Barden amendment proposes

Continued on Page Twenty

The International Situation

War caught up two more countries in its clutches today as the Germans invaded Denmark and attacked Norway.

In the early morning Nazi troops crossed the southern border of Denmark, landed on Danish soil from warships and occupied the Danish capital, Copenhagen—all apparently without resistance. [Page 1.]

Almost at the same time a diplomatic dispatch to Washington announced that Norway was at war with Germany. [Page 1.] This development followed an attempt by German warships—more than 100 of which had been sighted last night moving northward in the Kattegat—to force an entry, with aerial support, into Oslo Fjord. At latest reports German troops were debarking on the Norwegian coast and had entered Navik, Bergen and Trondheim, while the Norwegians were said to have moved their capital, which was reported bombed.

Berlin explained it was taking Denmark and Norway under its "protection" to prevent any hostile attack upon them. [Page 4.]

There had been at least one suggestion yesterday of German troop movements in Scandinavia. A Nazi transport had been torpedoed off Southern Norway with a loss of 150 out of some 300 uniformed men aboard. In the same neighborhood a large German tanker was sent to the bottom. [Page 1.]

The mining of Norwegian waters had taken Norway completely by surprise and eight German freighters were apparently in the same predicament, as they were trapped in those waters and unable to get home. With British warships patrolling the mine fields the ore traffic at Narvik was halted and it seemed likely that Swedish iron shipments would be halved. [Page 3.] Norway protested to both Britain and France against the mining, terming it "an open breach of international law" and demanding that the mines be removed. [Page 1.] London had expected the protest and discounted it. But the British were believed to be ready to go to Norway's aid against the Germans. [Page 2.]

With a loophole in the blockade apparently plugged in Scandinavia the British gave some of their attention to the Balkans; their envoys to the countries of that region began their conferences. [Page 9.] At the same time Southeastern Europe was startled by Rumania's detention of a fleet of British barges carrying dynamite, which, according to the Germans, was to have been used for blocking the Danube. British quarters insisted the explosives were to have been used only for destroying river craft in the event of a German invasion of Rumania. [Page 1.]

ROOSEVELT EFFIGY 'FRONT' GUN TARGET

Healy Also Swears Cassidy Wanted 12 in Congress Shot in Capital as Gesture

Denis A. Healy, star prosecution witness in the trial of seventeen men indicted for conspiring to overthrow the United States Government, testified yesterday in the Brooklyn Federal Court that some of the defendants had used a likeness of President Roosevelt's head as a target during rifle practice.

He swore that John F. Cassidy, a defendant who was prominent in the Christian Front, had favored "going to Washington and shooting twelve Congressmen to show that the Christian Front means business," and he testified that William Gerald Bishop, another defendant, wanted to place Major General Van Horn Mosely, U. S. A. retired, at the head of a dictatorship after overthrowing the present government.

Telling of how members of the group practiced making crude bombs out of empty beer cans, Healy said that they had discussed committing acts of sabotage here if the United States entered the war. He declared that Bishop had boasted to him of knowing who was responsible for an explosion he said had occurred on an oil tanker in the lower bay a few days earlier.

Cross-Examination Begun

Healy finished his direct testimony at 2:30 P. M. yesterday after having been on the witness stand for five hours, beginning Friday afternoon. He began at once a hammering cross-examination at the hands of defense counsel, which they estimated would last for at least two full court days in their effort to discredit his story of having posed as one of the plotters, meanwhile keeping the Federal Bureau of Investigation informed of every development.

He was forced to admit that he had lied on numerous occasions, that he had pretended to be anti-Semitic in order to "carry out my role"; that he had once approached Bishop for aid in smuggling a relative into this country from Canada, and that he had once been convicted of street fighting, for which he received a suspended sentence.

Conceding that he had testified for the government in a previous case, Healy denied that he was a "professional witness," as was charged by former Magistrate Leo J. Healy, counsel for eleven of the defendants. He said the government had arranged a leave of absence for him from the New York Central Railroad, and was paying him the same salary while he was

Continued on Page Sixteen

BRITISH EXPLOSIVES HELD BY RUMANIANS

Fleet of Barges Detained at Danube Port—Nazis Charge Plot to Block River

By The Associated Press.

BUCHAREST, Rumania, April 8—Detention of a fleet of dynamite-laden British barges, said by Germans to be designed to blow up a narrow Danube gateway and block a German supply line, today electrified Southeastern Europe with the fear war soon might spread to this quarter of the world.

Rumanian police, acting on a tip said to have been supplied by the pro-Nazi Iron Guard, halted the fleet near Giurgiu, Danube River port whence Germany ships much-needed Rumanian oil supplies. Aboard were tons of dynamite.

Germans alleged the British planned to blockade the spot in the Danube known as the Iron Gate by sinking the barges and wrecking the narrow channel where the river cuts through the Carpathian barrier between high cliffs. The Iron Gate is 280 miles up river from Giurgiu.

Official British quarters, acknowledging the barges were loaded with explosives, insisted they were to be used only for destroying Allied river craft in case of a German invasion of Rumania.

The only official British statement on the matter was a communiqué saying merely that Rumanian authorities had seized two cases of firearms which a British barge captain had neglected to declare in passing customs.

Troops Guard Gateway

The British aim was reported in Germany to be the blocking of the Iron Gate with sunken barges and blasting of the narrow artificial channel through which all river shipping must pass.

Two hundred Rumanian and Yugoslav soldiers armed with machine guns tonight were guarding the gateway where the Danube forms the boundary between Rumania and Yugoslavia. Giurgiu was turned into a military zone by the Rumanian Army, which banned all entries without special permits.

The German version of the seizure, said to have taken place Saturday, reported more than 100 British Army, Navy and Air Force men, who were to have participated in the coup, had been arrested.

Both the Rumanian Foreign Office and British quarters, however, insisted there was no basis to the German reports that Britons had been seized aboard the barges, and official London sources declined to

Continued on Page Eight

REICH SHIP IS SUNK

150 Lost Off Transport Torpedoed by British Off South Norway

ALL MEN IN UNIFORM

Large Nazi Tanker Also Sunk by Allies, but Crew Is Rescued

Special Cable to THE NEW YORK TIMES.

OSLO, Norway, April 8—A British submarine torpedoed and sank the German troop ship Rio de Janeiro today off Lillesand, on the south coast of Norway. At least 150 German soldiers are believed to have perished.

It is reported here that the German transport, formerly a freighter on the South American run, had at least 300 men aboard and that fewer than 150 are accounted for. The ship, of 5,261 tons, was out of Hamburg and was classified here as a transport because all the men aboard were in uniform.

Another large German vessel, the tanker Posidonia, was also reported torpedoed today off the south Norwegian coast, but without loss of life.

[Lloyd's Register of Shipping does not list a German tanker Posidonia. The Associated Press, in recording the report of still a third sinking, that of the German tanker Kreta, indicated that there might be some confusion over the Posidonia's case, since the Kreta, apparently to conceal her identity, had sent out the call letters of the Posidonia. Other reports said that the Posidonia used the Kreta's signals.]

The report of the torpedoing of the Rio de Janiero received here states that the British submarine intercepted the transport off the Norwegian coast, hailed her and fired a warning shot across her bows. This was disregarded and the troopship altered her course, speeding toward land or territorial waters. The submarine then fired a torpedo.

Some Jump Overboard

With the explosion some of the Germans immediately jumped overboard. A Norwegian fishing vessel was near by and went to the rescue, taking these men out of the water.

As the transport appeared to be settling, the submarine fired a second torpedo, with terrific result. An iron bar from the ship was hurled 150 feet and struck the rescuing fishing vessel, killing three of the Germans who had been taken aboard.

The fishing vessel continued its work of rescue and was aided by other fishing craft that hurried out when an alarm was sounded along the coast. These ships took a total

Continued on Page Five

NAZIS IN NORWAY

Troops Debark at Ports —Government Leaves Oslo for Hamar

NARVIK IS OCCUPIED

Air Attacks on Capital Reported—Civilians Are to Be Evacuated

Sweden Is Mobilizing

By The United Press.

STOCKHOLM, Sweden, April 9—The Swedish radio announced today that the government had ordered general mobilization.

Wireless to THE NEW YORK TIMES.

LONDON, Tuesday, April 9—The Paris correspondent of Reuters, British news agency, reported this morning that the Oslo radio had announced that German troops had debarked in Norwegian ports at 3 A. M.

[Mrs. J. Borden Harriman, United States Minister to Norway, notified the State Department early this morning that she had been informed by the Foreign Minister that Norway considered herself at war with Germany.

[Mrs. Harriman also reported that at 5:30 A. M. Norwegian shore batteries were still engaged in battle with four invading German warships that were trying to force entry into Oslo Fjord.]

It was also announced that the Norwegian Government had left Oslo for Hamar, in Central Norway.

Reuters further reported that the Germans had occupied the cities of Bergen and Trondheim.

[The Oslo radio announced this morning that the Norwegian Government had ordered general mobilization after an all night session of the Cabinet, The Associated Press reported.]

Reuters also reported from Paris that the Oslo radio announced this morning that the Germans had occupied Narvik.

The Norwegian legation here issued the following communiqué this morning:

"The German Minister in Oslo saw the Norwegian Foreign Secretary at 4:30 o'clock this morning and demanded that Norway should be handed over to the German administration. If this was not done all resistance would be defeated. This demand was refused and hostilities have started."

LONDON, Tuesday, April 9 (UP)—A Reuters, British news agency,

Continued on Page Two

Canadian Premier to See Roosevelt Soon, Stopping Off En Route South for a Vacation

By FREDERICK T. BIRCHALL

By Telephone to THE NEW YORK TIMES.

OTTAWA, April 8—Prime Minister W. L. Mackenzie King will leave Ottawa in a few days for a short holiday in the South of the United States. On his way through Washington he will pay a visit to President Roosevelt at the White House.

This will be Mr. Mackenzie King's first visit to Washington since war was declared. There are several questions he would like to take up with Mr. Roosevelt. There are doubtless also matters the President will be glad to discuss with the Canadian Prime Minister.

While there is no information here as to the precise subjects that may figure in the conversation, some of those ripe for discussion are well known. Among these are the progress of the St. Lawrence Waterway project, continuance of the trade agreements renewed last year and the extent to which the United States can aid Canada's war effort.

As to the St. Lawrence project, it is known that both administrations are anxious to have the treaty signed with as little delay as possible so that it may be submitted to Congress in time for consideration before adjournment. Since the project again came up opposition to it has developed in both countries. It will not have easy sailing.

Among matters even more pressing are the exemption of Americans resident in Canada from the conditions affecting the ownership of foreign currency and securities and the status of American fliers who desire to come here and enlist under the Air Training Plan and for overseas service.

It has been strongly urged that Canada modify for these the oath of allegiance now required from all who join her forces, which does not automatically give them Canadian citizenship, while causing them to lose their own.

Another point of interest is Canada's desire to obtain from the United States more airplanes for use in the initial stages of the commonwealth air training plan. The present prospect is that there will be a shortage of planes until Canadian plants, now in receipt of about $40,000,000 worth of orders, can reach the stage of advanced production.

Any or all of these topics may be profitably discussed between the

Continued on Page Five

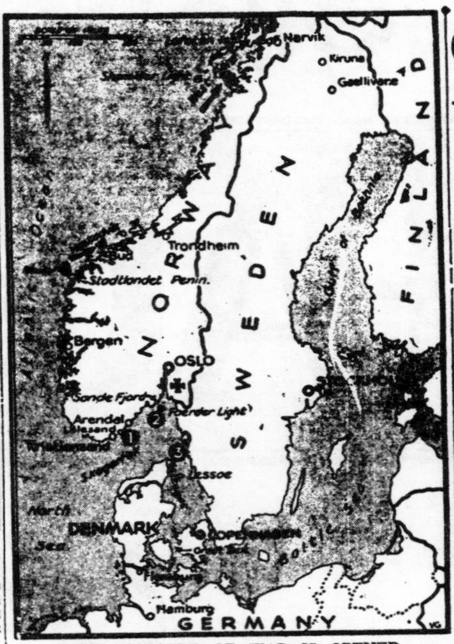

NEW THEATRE OF WAR IS OPENED

German troops invaded Denmark at 5 A. M. today. A few hours previously German warships attempted to force an entry into Oslo Fjord (cross). This action, which brought Norway into the war against the Reich, followed the sighting last night of a German armada steaming northward off Lessoe (3). Near Lillesand (1) a German troop transport was torpedoed by a British submarine and a U-boat was rumored to have been sunk. Off Faerder Light (2) one and perhaps two German tankers were sent down. The Allied mine fields off Norway are indicated by arrows.

NORWAY DECLARES WAR ON GERMANY

Washington Notified of Action by U. S. Minister at Oslo—Warships Sent There

Special to THE NEW YORK TIMES.

WASHINGTON, Tuesday, April 9—Norway is at war with Germany. This was the word received soon after 1 o'clock this morning by the State Department from Mrs. J. Borden Harriman, the American Minister at Oslo.

The startling information was received less than two hours after equally disturbing intelligence had been received of the German occupation of Denmark.

[President Roosevelt, at Hyde Park, kept in close touch with the State Department and his special train was held ready for a quick return to Washington, The United Press reported.]

The State Department announced the state of war in the following communique:

"The American Minister at Oslo, Mrs. J. Borden Harriman, telegraphed the Department tonight that the Foreign Minister had informed her that the Norwegians had fired on four German warships coming up Oslo Fjord and that Norway was at war with Germany. In response to a request by the British Minister to Norway the American Legation at Oslo has been authorized to take over British interests in Norway in case he is forced to leave."

Envoy's Request Explained

State Department officials, in answer to queries regarding the apparently ambiguous last paragraph of Mrs. Harriman's cable, said that there could be no doubt that Norway was at war against Germany. They pointed out that the Norwegians were firing on German warships and the British envoy was considering the possibility that he might have to evacuate, although he was not certain he would have to do so.

[The United Press said Mrs. Harriman reported that she had taken charge of the British and French Legations.]

It was reported on usually good authority that American warships in European waters had been ordered to proceed northward so they could take part in the evacuation of American citizens in Denmark,

Continued on Page Four

ALLIED MINES BRING A PROTEST BY OSLO

Breach of International Law Charged by Koht—Sweden Takes Defense Measures

By The Associated Press.

OSLO, Norway, April 8—Foreign Minister Halvdan Koht told Parliament today that Norway had protested to Paris and London against the mining of her waters at dawn, a sudden move by which the Allies hope to cut off Germany's Swedish ore shipments through Norway's western coastal waters.

In a public statement Mr. Koht charged the Allies with an "open breach of international law" and demanded that the mines "be removed at once and that the guard by foreign warships cease." Britain was patrolling Norway's waters near the new mine fields, stating such action would be for forty-eight hours to warn away neutral vessels.

In all Scandinavia statesmen, in realization that the dreaded day had arrived bringing the European war to the north, gathered to discuss the cloudy future and await a feared retaliation from Germany.

Leaders of the Norwegian Parliament, which was called into special session, said they were behind the government's action in the crisis. A Cabinet meeting was held in Oslo, which military and naval leaders attended.

Political Leaders Meet

Leaders of all of Denmark's political parties met in Copenhagen, and in Stockholm Swedish leaders watched gravely. The Swedish Foreign Office announced there had been no violation of Swedish waters, but officials admittedly were worried.

The Oslo newspaper Arbejdarbladet, a government organ, said that "the situation is particularly grave for our country, but in such times we must keep our heads cool."

"Any tendency toward nervousness or panic would only make it worse," the paper said. "Norway naturally will protest in a most emphatic way against any closing of her waters and demand respect for international laws. But it is a ques-

Continued on Page Four

Dispatches from Europe and the Far East are subject to censorship at the source.

COPENHAGEN TAKEN

Troops Cross Border as Ships Debark Others in Sudden Nazi Blow

DANES FALLING BACK

Germans Say They Act to Forestall Foe and Protect Neighbor

By SVEND CARSTENSEN

Wireless to THE NEW YORK TIMES.

COPENHAGEN, Denmark, Tuesday, April 9—German troops crossed the Danish frontier at 5 o'clock this morning.

Three German cruisers arrived at that same hour at Middelfart and troops immediately occupied streets of the town.

Copenhagen was also occupied by German troops this morning.

The invasion came without warning. For some hours before the crossing of the border reports had circulated here that the Germans of South Jutland were expecting German troop trains carrying 45,000 men to arrive at the town of Flensburg during the night. That German town on the border was characterized as a convenient port for shipping troops northward, and although Danish border guards had been put in the highest state of preparedness it was not thought that there would be any threat to Denmark.

This belief had been bolstered by the fact that the fleet of more than a hundred German warships that passed through the Great Belt into the Kattegat and Skagerrak yesterday and early today included troopships—and it was presumed that this fleet was on the way to Norway to retaliate against the British Navy.

More Centers Seized

Mr. Carstensen left Copenhagen after the entry of German forces and went to Kolding, where he filed the following dispatch:

Special Cable to THE NEW YORK TIMES.

KOLDING, Denmark, Tuesday, April 9—The German occupation continues here. It is reported that two ferry points on the Great Belt—Nyborg and Korsoer—have been occupied.

Troops have landed at Middelfart on a large scale. A Little Belt bridge has been reported seized and the city of Aalborg in North Jutland has been occupied.

Although there were no reports of clashes between Danish troops and the invaders today, military resistance was expected at Haderslében, about thirty miles north of the German border. The placing of guns and erection of barricades were reported from that town.

After leaving Copenhagen I observed from my automobile swarms of fast German planes flying over towns dropping badly printed leaflets that laid responsibility for Germany's invading Denmark and Norway to what was termed a British intention to make Scandinavia a theatre of war.

The leaflets termed Winston Churchill, Britain's First Lord of the Admiralty, "the century's greatest warmonger," who planned to police Norwegian and Danish waters against the wills of the two countries.

The statement said that, since Norway and Denmark were unable to resist effectively, Germany had resolved to act in advance of a British attack and by her own forces take over "protection" of Danish and Norwegian neutrality and "guard" the countries during the war. It was asserted that Germany did not intend to obtain bases for her fight against Britain but solely aimed at preventing Scandinavia from being a battlefield for "British expansion of the war."

According to the statement, negotiations were going on between the German and Danish Governments to make Denmark "secure" and assure that her army and navy were maintained and the Danish people's freedom respected. The country's independence, it was said, is fully secured. The resin-

Continued on Page Two

"All the News That's Fit to Print."

The New York Times.

LATE CITY EDITION
POSTSCRIPT
Fair, not much change in temperature today. Tomorrow cloudy.
Temperatures Yesterday—Max. [illegible]

VOL. LXXXIX...No. 30,057. Entered as Second-Class Matter, Postoffice, New York, N. Y. NEW YORK, FRIDAY, MAY 10, 1940. THREE CENTS NEW YORK CITY and Vicinity | FOUR CENTS Elsewhere Except in 7th and 8th Postal Zones.

NAZIS INVADE HOLLAND, BELGIUM, LUXEMBOURG BY LAND AND AIR; DIKES OPENED; ALLIES RUSH AID

U.S. FREEZES CREDIT

President Acts to Guard Funds Here of Three Invaded Nations

SHIP RULING TODAY

Envoy Reports to Hull on Germany's Attacks by Air and Land

Special to THE NEW YORK TIMES.

WASHINGTON, Friday, May 10—President Roosevelt early today ordered the freezing of all credits held by Belgium, the Netherlands and Luxembourg in this country.

He called a conference for 10:30 A. M. of heads of the State, War and Navy Departments to consider pressing problems of neutrality.

The President acted swiftly after news of Germany's invasion of the three European neutral countries reached Washington and galvanized high officials into action. His order with regard to the freezing of all the invaded countries' credits and cash balances here was a counterpart of the action taken after Germany invaded Norway and Denmark.

Congress this week completed action on legislation that specifically authorizes the President by decree to freeze all such cash and credits of any belligerent. The object is to prevent these resources from falling into the hands of the invading power.

Ships to Be Considered

The President's order directed Secretary of the Treasury Henry Morgenthau Jr. to freeze all Belgian, French and Luxembourg credits before the markets open this morning.

It was announced also that the conference to be held at 10:30 will consider the question of Belgian and Netherland ships that may be in United States ports. Attorney General Robert H. Jackson also will attend this conference.

The White House, meanwhile, indicated some skepticism of the official explanation of the invasion given by German Propaganda Minister Joseph Goebbels, who was reported to have said that the Germans moved because of information that Great Britain and France intended to invade the countries involved.

"Nevertheless," said Stephen T. Early, Presidential secretary, after he had quoted the Goebbels statement, "it remains to be seen who invaded who."

It was announced that the President would remain awake throughout the night, if necessary, to receive reports and consult with officials. Sumner Welles, Under-Secretary of State, at 1:45 A. M. joined the group of State Department officials who remained on duty at the department.

Report From Ambassador

A general invasion of the three neutrals by heavy German land and air forces was reported to the State Department and Mr. Roosevelt early today by Ambassador John J. Cudahy at Brussels.

After trying vainly to re-establish telephone connection with Secretary of State Cordell Hull, over which he had relayed a "blow-by-blow" description of developments several hours earlier, the Ambassador got through the following terse message:

"German planes continue to cross the border and are bombing the airport near Brussels. It seems to be a general attack on all three countries."

A State Department press liaison officer who was relaying latest diplomatic bulletins to reporters as they came in by transatlantic telephone, dropped the cryptic remark:

"As the American Ambassador spoke from Brussels, an embassy military attaché stood at his elbow."

After relaying the information to the President that the Belgian Government had ordered all hands to stand by, Ambassador Cudahy again called Secretary Hull between 10 and 11 o'clock and said he had been informed by officials in Brussels that one German and

Continued on Page Two

The International Situation

In the midst of Britain's Cabinet crisis Germany struck another powerful blow early this morning by invading the Netherlands, Belgium and Luxembourg.

After swarms of planes had engaged in air fights over Amsterdam, parachute troops, some of them clad in Netherland uniforms, descended at strategic points while planes bombed air fields. The Netherlands resisted the incursion and promptly opened the dikes that are part of her water defense system. [Page 1.]

Parachute troops likewise made surprise landings in Belgium and bombs from 100 planes blasted the Brussels airport. [Page 1.]

Appeals for help were dispatched to the Allies by the invaded countries and it was understood that machinery of assistance was being set in motion. Queen Wilhelmina in a proclamation issued at The Hague declared, "I and my government will do our duty." [Page 1.]

As in the case of Norway, Berlin explained that the German action had been taken to forestall the Allies; an announcement said that an attack on Germany had been planned through the territory of the Low Countries. What the Reich was doing, it was declared, was safeguarding the neutrality of those countries. [Page 1.]

President Roosevelt lost no time in acting on the new situation. After night conferences he ordered the freezing of credits of the three invaded countries. Further measures are to be taken today. [Page 1.]

London, meanwhile, announced that British troops had occupied Iceland to prevent a possible German seizure of that former Danish possession. [Page 1.]

Before all these happenings Neville Chamberlain had appeared to be on his way out as Prime Minister, but today it was expected the new developments might save him.

Following upon his relatively narrow escape in the House of Commons vote on Wednesday night, Mr. Chamberlain set about yesterday to see what could be done to satisfy his critics. He offered Cabinet posts to two leaders of the Labor Opposition, but they refused to serve under him. As to whether they would serve under another Conservative, they delayed their reply. If Mr. Chamberlain steps out of office, it is thought probable his place will be taken by the present Foreign Secretary, Viscount Halifax, with Winston Churchill acting as government spokesman in the Commons, from the floor of which the peer would by tradition be barred. [Page 1.]

A new offset to the Norwegian reverses was a London announcement that British submarines had attacked three German convoys and scored eleven torpedo hits, in addition to destroying two ships sailing home. [Page 6.]

Moreover, the Allies' Narvik campaign seemed to be making progress. From that far northern area it was reported that two Allied columns closing in on the railway to the port were within ten miles of each other near the Swedish border; their intention apparently was to join and drive westward along the railroad to Narvik itself, which is held by the Nazis. The Germans, in their effort to thwart the besiegers, were said to be landing parachute troops and supplying them by air. [Page 4.]

In the aftermath of the campaign in the south of the country Foreign Minister Koht disclosed that four of Norway's six divisions had been lost—killed, wounded or captured by the Nazis or interned by Sweden. [Page 6.]

Bombs Drop on Swiss Soil

By The United Press.

BERNE, Switzerland, Friday, May 10—The army staff announced today that foreign airplanes had dropped bombs in the Berne Jura Alpine district between Delemont, near the frontier, and Mount Terr, damaging a railroad.

Traffic continued over the road, the army staff said. It added that other foreign planes were flying over Swiss territory near Basle but that no details had been received.

MUSSOLINI TO LET 'ONLY FACTS' SPEAK

Press Assures Yugoslavia, but Reminds Her of Fate of Poland and Norway

By HERBERT L. MATTHEWS

By Telephone to THE NEW YORK TIMES.

ROME, May 9—The fourth anniversary of the founding of the new Italian Empire was celebrated today in an atmosphere of warlike preparation. The army was honored, Italian armed strength was glorified and the country was told by its leading commentators that the empire would soon earn that "freedom of the seas" which to Italians means domination of the Mediterranean.

Rome, like every other city in the empire, resounded today to martial music while thousands of soldiers paraded through streets from whose buildings hung innumerable flags. The great ceremony was at the Piazza Venezia this morning. Premier Mussolini awarded gold and silver medals to the kin of soldiers fallen in Fascismo's three wars in Ethiopia, Spain and Albania. Later, responding to the insistent appeal of the thousands of men massed below his balcony, he spoke very briefly, only to say that he was resuming his cloak of silence.

"May 9, 1936, was a great day in the history of the country, a day of solar victory," he said. "After my speeches, you must accustom yourself to my silence. Only facts will break it."

Small groups in the crowd thereupon began yelling "Tunisia!" and "Malta!" but the cries were not general.

At the same time this morning

Continued on Page Seven

ICELAND OCCUPIED BY BRITISH FORCE

Secret Expedition Is Justified as Thwarting Action There by Germany

By JAMES MacDONALD

Special Cable to THE NEW YORK TIMES.

LONDON, Friday, May 10—Forestalling a possible German swoop on the strategically valuable former Danish dominion of Iceland, the British have landed an expeditionary force there, it was announced this morning by the Foreign Office here.

Neither the size of the British contingent, which was sent out in the deepest secrecy, nor its place of landing was revealed in the official communiqué.

The landing of the expeditionary force was still going at an early hour this morning. Observers guessed that the landing place must be Reykjavik.

TEXT OF COMMUNIQUE

The official announcement read as follows:

Since the German seizure of Denmark it has become necessary to reckon with the possibility of a sudden German descent on Iceland.

It is clear that in the face of an attack on Iceland, even on a very small scale, the Icelandic Government would be unable to prevent their country from falling completely into German hands.

His Majesty's Government have accordingly decided to preclude this possibility which would de-

Continued on Page Three

ALLIED HELP SPED

Netherland and Belgian Appeals Answered by British and French

TACTICS ARE WATCHED

London Thinks Move an Effort to Get Bases to Attack Britain

Italians Reported Massing

By The United Press.

BUENOS AIRES, Argentina, Friday, May 10—The Madrid radio was heard broadcasting today that the British had closed the Strait of Gibraltar and that Italy was massing troops on the French frontier.

Special Cable to THE NEW YORK TIMES.

LONDON, Friday, May 10—The British Government received appeals for help early today from both the Netherlands and Belgium.

The British and French reply to the Netherland-Belgian appeals was prompt. Representatives of the respective governments here were told by 8:30 A. M. (3:30 A. M. New York time) they could expect all the help Britain could give them.

The Netherland Legation here received assurance that its country and Belgium were now regarded as Allies of Britain and France.

Within a few minutes after receipt of official news of the invasion of the Low Countries, the British Cabinet was called to 10 Downing Street and was in session with Prime Minister Neville Chamberlain.

According to information here, the Belgian Cabinet was in Brussels and Premier Hubert Pierlot conferred with King Leopold.

The German invasion of the Low Countries had been expected in London, and it must be presumed the Allies were ready for it to some extent.

Allies Visible to Planes

The biggest handicap to the British and French was in the timing of the German thrust at dawn. This prevented the Allies moving troops under cover of darkness, and since hundreds of German planes already had flown over practically all of Netherland and Belgian territory for some hours, the disposition of Allied troops and their every movement must have been known to the German High Command.

While the Netherlanders and Belgians had taken every precaution

Continued on Page Four

BRUSSELS IS RAIDED

400 Reported Killed—Troops Cross Border at Four Points

PARACHUTE INVASION

Mobilization Is Ordered and Allied Aid Asked—Luxembourg Attacked

Wireless to THE NEW YORK TIMES.

BRUSSELS, Belgium, Friday, May 10—The invasion Belgium had feared since the outbreak of the European war came before dawn this morning. About a hundred German planes flew over this city and bombed the airport.

The airfield at Antwerp also was bombed. Parachute troops were landed at Hasselt in Eastern Belgium. Artillery fire was reported heard along the German and Luxembourg frontiers.

Anti-aircraft guns at the airport commenced firing with the appearance of the first invaders and kept up a steady barrage. Those in the center of the city went into action at 5:30 A. M.

Above the drone of airplane engines could be heard the staccato of machine guns. Bombs wrecked many houses in the vicinity of the airport and caused some loss of life. [Exchange Telegraph (British news agency) said 400 persons had been killed in the first raid.]

Reports from Antwerp and other parts of the country said German planes had flown constantly over since 4:30 A. M., keeping anti-aircraft batteries steadily in action.

Premier Hubert Pierlot and Foreign Minister Paul-Henri Spaak conferred with King Leopold and then called an emergency meeting of the Cabinet. The radio broadcast repeated summonses to all soldiers to join their units at once. A "state of alarm" was decreed throughout the country with the appearance of the first planes.

The Belgian radio also stated German parachute troops had fluttered down at Nivelles, less than twenty miles south of Brussels, and at Saint Trond, about thirty-five miles east of the capital.

The broadcast stated that Germany had made no demarche in Brussels before the invasion.

Wireless to THE NEW YORK TIMES.

LONDON, Friday, May 10—The Germans crossed the Belgian frontier at four points this morning, according to an announcement over

Continued on Page Two

Chamberlain Saved by Nazi Blow In Low Countries, London Thinks

By RAYMOND DANIELL

Special Cable to THE NEW YORK TIMES.

LONDON, Friday, May 10—The first effect of the German attack on the Low Countries is expected to be that Prime Minister Chamberlain will be saved just when it looked as if he was sure to fall.

It was believed that the Labor party, which so far has refused to serve under him in a truly national government, and only yesterday rejected a formal offer to do so, will now close ranks, forget political difficulties and take any Cabinet job offered to its leaders. Furthermore, the Labor party conference, which was supposed to start at Bournemouth on Monday, now will probably be called off.

There is just a possibility that Mr. Chamberlain may quit immediately and turn his seals of office over to First Lord of the Admiralty Winston Churchill. This was a strong but unconfirmed rumor as a Cabinet meeting held this morning came to an end.

In addition, it was said that under Mr. Churchill, Alfred Duff Cooper would receive the Admiralty post, Anthony Eden the War Office and that Viscount Halifax would remain at the Foreign Office.

Until the invasion of the Low Countries was known, the consensus of political observers here had been that the end of the Chamberlain Government could not be long delayed.

The two questions uppermost were how soon it would take place and who would succeed him at No. 10 Downing Street. The betting had been that it would be sooner rather than later and that Foreign Secretary Viscount Halifax would be the next Prime Minister, with Mr. Churchill serving as his spokesman in the House of Commons, from whose floor the present Foreign Secretary, as a peer, is barred by tradition.

The troubles of the 71-year-old Prime Minister, who struggled vainly to maintain Europe's peace by appeasement and who was accused in the House of Commons of bungling the business of war-making, increased rather than diminished during the day. However, the House, despite the gravity of the internal crisis and perils abroad, decided to take its usual twelve-day Whitsuntide holiday, subject to recall in the event of major developments, which followed promptly.

Mr. Chamberlain's efforts to broaden the base of his Cabinet by

Continued on Page Five

NAZIS SWOOP ON THE LOW COUNTRIES

By land and air German troops descended this morning upon the Netherlands, Belgium and Luxembourg. The principal land incursion into the Netherlands was at Roermond.

Ribbentrop Charges Allies Plotted With the Lowlands

By GEORGE AXELSSON

Wireless to THE NEW YORK TIMES.

BERLIN, Friday, May 10—Foreign Minister Joachim von Ribbentrop at 9 o'clock this morning announced that Reich forces had launched military operations against Holland, Belgium and Luxembourg to "protect their neutrality."

Earlier it was reported that German troops had occupied Maastricht, the Netherlands, and had "landed" contingents in Brussels, probably meaning parachute troops.

Herr von Ribbentrop said that Germany had received unimpeachable proof that the Allies were engineering an imminent attack through the Lowlands into the German Ruhr district wherefore the Germans felt compelled to take corresponding measures. He said the time had come for settling the final account with the "Franco-British leaders."

And thus the war to a decisive finish has at last started in the West. This was the assumption when Herr von Ribbentrop informed the world through newspaper men that the German action meant that she had decided to settle all accounts with the Allies.

"France and Britain dropped their mask," said Herr von Ribbentrop. "The alarm in the Mediterranean was a feint behind which the Allies were preparing an onslaught on German territory which the Reich could not tolerate."

The notes—handed to The Hague and Brussels simultaneously with a shorter note to the Grand Duchy of Luxembourg just prior to their invasion by Germany—accused the Lowlands with having been overwhelmingly partial toward the Allies, adding that the attitude of the press was objectionable to the Reich.

A memorandum similar in tone to that handed to Denmark and Norway last month stated:

"In the life-and-death struggle thrust upon the German people, the government does not intend to await an attack by Britain and France inactively allowing the war to be carried through Belgium and Holland onto German soil. The government, therefore, has issued orders to safeguard the neutrality of the two countries with all the military means of the Reich."

Ribbentrop Reads Statement

In eight points the memorandum outlines the German argument that Belgium and Holland had not observed the strictest neutrality upon which German respect for their territories was founded. The document accuses them with having even supported Germany's enemies in their hostile intentions. Belgium fortified exclusively her Eastern frontier against Germany, leaving the French frontier unfortified, one argument reads.

Berlin slept peacefully unaware

Continued on Page Four

HOLLAND'S QUEEN PROTESTS INVASION

Wilhelmina Vows She and the Government Will Do Duty—Bars Negotiation With Foe

By The United Press.

THE HAGUE, the Netherlands, Friday, May 10—Queen Wilhelmina said today in a statement on the German invasion of the country that "I and my government will do our duty."

The Queen, in a proclamation addressed to "my people," said:

"After our country, with scrupulous conscientiousness, had observed strict neutrality during all these months, and while Holland had no other plan than to maintain strictly this attitude, Germany last night made a sudden attack on our territory without any warning.

"This was done notwithstanding a solemn promise that the neutrality of our country would be respected so long as we ourselves maintained that neutrality.

"I herewith direct a flaming protest against this unprecedented violation of good faith and violation of all that is decent in relations between cultured States.

"I and my government now will do our duty.

"Do your duty everywhere and under all circumstances. And let every one go to the post to which he has been appointed and, with the utmost vigilance and with that inner calm and serenity which comes from a clear conscience, do his work."

The Netherland general military headquarters in a communiqué said:

"Never will the High Command or government enter into negotiations with the enemy."

Dispatches from Europe and the Far East are subject to censorship at the source.

AIR FIELDS BOMBED

Nazi Parachute Troops Land at Key Centers as Flooding Starts

RIVER MAAS CROSSED

Defenders Battle Foe in Sky, Claim 6 Planes as War Is Proclaimed

First Bombing in France

Special Cable to THE NEW YORK TIMES.

PARIS, Friday, May 10—The Bron airdrome, a big airport near Lyon, was bombed by German planes today. One German aircraft was shot down. The alarm was first given at 4:25 A. M. The all-clear signal was given at 6:45 A. M.

WASHINGTON, Friday, May 10 (AP)—United States Ambassador William C. Bullitt telephoned the State Department from Paris at 4 A. M. today that the Germans had bombed a number of fortified towns in France, "such as Dunkerque and Calais."

By The United Press.

AMSTERDAM, The Netherlands, Friday, May 10—Germany invaded the Netherlands early today, land troops being preceded by widespread air attacks on airdromes and by the landing of parachute troops.

The Netherlands resisted and announced she was at war with Germany. Anti-aircraft batteries and fighter planes engaged swarms of German aircraft when they appeared simultaneously over a score of Netherland cities.

An official proclamation said:

"Since 3 A. M. German troops have crossed the Netherland frontier and German planes have tried to attack airports. Inundations are effective according to plans. The army anti-aircraft batteries were found prepared. So far as is known six German planes have been shot down."

[French, Belgian and British planes were sighted over the Netherlands this morning, a Reuters (British news agency) dispatch said in quoting the Netherland radio station at Hilversum, near Amsterdam.

German troops were first reported crossing the Netherland frontier near Roermond, eight miles north of the Belgian frontier. German planes landed troops by parachute at strategic points near Rotterdam, The Hague, Amsterdam and other large cities.

A large number of the German troops landed by parachute were said to be dressed in Netherland military uniforms.

Other Germans crossed the Maas River in rubber boats to Netherland territory. They were said to be reaching the Netherland side in "considerable numbers."

A fierce air battle raged over Amsterdam as Netherland fighter planes dived repeatedly on German bombers and troop transport planes with chattering machine guns.

Schiphol Airdrome outside Amsterdam, the nation's largest, was heavily bombed. Military authorities immediately threw a heavy guard around the airdrome in an effort to defend it against German parachute troops.

Planes identified as German Heinkels bombed Schiphol Airdrome repeatedly, loosing some thirty heavy caliber bombs on the landing field between 5:15 and 5:30 A. M.

Reports poured in of planes in great numbers over a score of Netherland cities. Netherland authorities, hurriedly organizing defense, flashed orders to the whole country to be on the alert against parachute troops.

Fifty planes were over Nijmegen, sixty miles southeast of Amsterdam on the German border.

A number of parachute troops reportedly landed at Sliedrecht, Delft and several other points. Delft is twelve and a half miles from The Hague. About 100 parachute troops

Continued on Page Three

"All the News That's Fit to Print."

The New York Times.

LATE CITY EDITION
Fair, continued cool today. Tomorrow increasing cloudiness, slightly warmer.

Copyright, 1940, by The New York Times Company.

VOL. LXXXIX...No. 30,065. Entered as Second-Class Matter, Postoffice, New York, N. Y. NEW YORK, SATURDAY, MAY 18, 1940. PPPP THREE CENTS

NAZIS PIERCE FRENCH LINES ON 62-MILE FRONT; TAKE BRUSSELS, LOUVAIN, MALINES AND NAMUR; WASHINGTON SPEEDS ITS BIG DEFENSE PROGRAM

ROOSEVELT IS BUSY

Calls Parley on Great Air Force, Considers Bigger Sea Patrol

UNITY IN CONGRESS

Partisanship Shelved in Drive—Midwest May Get Arms Plants

By FELIX BELAIR Jr.
Special to THE NEW YORK TIMES.

WASHINGTON, May 17—National defense preparations were begun by government agencies today on a scale unapproached since the World War.

In response to President Roosevelt's preparedness message calling for an impregnable America, first steps were taken toward proposed far-reaching undertakings, such as construction of airplane and munitions factories in the Middle West, out of reach of possible quick bombing raids.

The President followed his request to Congress for a goal of 50,000 first-line fighting planes by calling a conference of aviation industry leaders with army, navy and Treasury officials to be held in the office of Secretary Morgenthau Monday morning. Earlier in the day he disclosed plans to recommission thirty-five more World War destroyers for emergency patrol duty at a cost of $6,000,000.

Developments of the Day

As the executive and legislative branches gave evidence of the "partnership" for which the President appealed in his $1,182,000,000 national defense message yesterday, the preparedness campaign brought the following developments:

1. The House Military Affairs Committee began hearings on the President's defense program envisaging an army nucleus of 750,000 regulars and 250,000 reserves, fully equipped for active service by June 30, 1941.

2. Military authorities shaped plans calling for a $300,000,000 outlay to bring actual aircraft production up to 30,000 planes a year as quickly as possible under a program specifying a number of factories between the Allegheny and Rocky Mountains capable of producing a hundred planes a month, the government to build the plants and rent them on a "fixed-fee basis."

3. House leaders organized a drive for modification of the Walsh-Healey Act to permit the President to waive forty-hour week limitations governing shipbuilding to speed up the present expansion program.

4. Mr. Roosevelt made known plans to call to Washington soon several recognized industrialists to speed industrial mobilization required to carry out his unprecedented peacetime defense program.

5. The White House placed its stamp of approval on plans of Colonel Frank Knox, Chicago publisher, to sponsor the creation of a chain of aviation training camps throughout the country to supplement the military and naval training facilities.

6. The Navy Department considered proclaiming all industrial navy yards, air bases and fields as restricted areas and sought ways and means of increasing the number of its skilled mechanics from 75,000 to 150,000 or 200,000 men. The President's defense plan included the placing of the navy's expansion program on a twenty-four-hour basis instead of eight hours as at present.

Leaders Discard Partisanship

Political leaders, meanwhile, declared a moratorium on partisanship to expedite early enactment of legislation carrying out the President's plan to make our defenses invulnerable. The statement of former President Hoover endorsing Mr. Roosevelt's message to Congress was received by the White House as "an indication of national unity which we welcome and that political differences are being cast aside in the emergency."

The President, apparently convinced of Republican good will for his program, invited Alfred M. Landon to a White House luncheon conference next Wednesday.

In announcing the President's endorsement of the aviation training plan suggested by Colonel Knox, Stephen T. Early, White House

Continued on Page Six

The International Situation

The War in the West

German arms struck yesterday along the whole Western Front from the Netherland border to the northern anchor of the Maginot Line at the Luxembourg corner. As night fell the situation was as follows:

The Nazis claimed that on the northern wing against the British and Belgians they had penetrated to the outlying forts of Antwerp and occupied Malines and Louvain and that advance units were in Brussels, the Belgian capital. On the southern wing, against the French, the German High Command said it had broken through the fortifications along the Belgian-French border for a distance of 100 kilometers (62 miles) from just south of Maubeuge to Carignan, south of Sedan, and had penetrated into France as far as Le Cateau, La Capelle and to a point north of Rethel. The communiqué admitted, however, that the lines were changing hourly. The Germans claimed 12,000 French prisoners, including two generals. On the central Belgian front advances were reported at Namur and Wavre. [Page 1.]

The Allies did not deny that the situation was critical. General Gamelin, supreme commander of the Allied forces, issued a general order to all troops stating that the "fate of our country, of our Allies, the destiny of the world depend on the battle now being fought." The command was, "Conquer or die." The order recalled Marshal Joffre's famous message to the French Armies before the 1914 First Battle of the Marne, where the "taxicab army" from Paris stopped the Kaiser's legions, and saved Paris. A communiqué said that the Germans had penetrated as far as Avesnes and Vervins, about fifteen miles into France along the Belgian border. It estimated the Germans had engaged the "greatest part" of their heavy tank divisions in the attack. Attacks south of Sedan in the vicinity of Montmedy and Sedan were said to have been repulsed. Allied bomber and fighter squadrons were reported carrying out their missions of harassing enemy troop concentrations and rear lines of communication. [Page 1.]

While London admitted a withdrawal of its forces to a new defense line behind Brussels, advices from field headquarters in Belgium indicated the retreat had been orderly and that British air forces were more than holding their own in harassing the enemy and protecting their own rear from German bombing and machine-gunning attacks on communication lines. [Page 1.]

The Air Ministry at London said the German advance was not being made without cost. It estimated German plane losses in the last seven days at 1,000. However, it said, large reserves (estimated at 23,000 planes) made it probable the German air effort could be sustained for some time. [Page 4.]

Tragic victims of the horror were uncounted numbers of refugees who choked all roads in Belgium not already filled with troops and guns moving up to the fighting lines, homeless, unfed, many wounded, seeking a sanctuary which appeared not to exist. [Included in the above.]

King Leopold of the Belgians, his capital lost, moved his government to Ostend. [Page 1.]

Repercussions Elsewhere

Scenes in government departments reminiscent of World War days were seen in Washington as the Federal agencies involved moved to put into effect the needed defense measures outlined by President Roosevelt in his speech to Congress Thursday. The President called a conference of Army, Navy and Treasury officials and aviation leaders to discuss his program to build up the United States air force to 50,000 planes. [Page 1.]

War fever mounted in Rome. Premier Mussolini's newspaper, Popolo d'Italia, thundered: "The Italian people must now or never achieve their Mediterranean destiny." The Senate, in an atmosphere of war hysteria, heard a budget report with a record deficit and warning of more taxes; the stock market suffered another "Black Friday" recession. [Page 1.]

On the Balkan diplomatic front Russia was reported bringing pressure on all interested countries to retain the status quo there under threat of forming an alliance with Yugoslavia and Bulgaria and reviving the idea of a union of all the Slavs in Europe. [Page 5.]

COL. KNOX TO FORM AIR 'PLATTSBURGS'

Roosevelt Authorizes Civilian Groups to Promote Training of Students as Pilots

Special to THE NEW YORK TIMES.

CHICAGO, May 17—With the authorization of President Roosevelt, Colonel Frank Knox, publisher of The Chicago Daily News and Republican Vice Presidential nominee in 1936, stated here today that a civilian group would be formed to cooperate with the government in training 10,000 pilots at volunteer camps this Summer in the nine army corps areas. Colonel Knox discussed the project in a White House conference yesterday with the President.

The training camps will be opened about July 1, Colonel Knox said, and will be designed primarily to accommodate 10,000 college students who have been receiving preliminary training through the Civil Aeronautics Authority.

"What we are undertaking," Colonel Knox said, "is not to replace any of the present activities, but to extend and increase them. We can turn out airplanes rapidly, but not top pilots, and we need at least two pilots for each plane."

World War Comparison

Colonel Knox described the new organization as a parallel to the army training camps of the last World War, such as Plattsburg, N. Y.

The cost of promoting the volunteer enlistments in the camps will be financed privately, he continued. The army has agreed for its part to provide tents, reserve officers for training, cooks and camp sites.

"Most of all," Colonel Knox said,

Continued on Page Seven

WAR BASIS EVIDENT IN ITALIAN BUDGET

With Record Deficit Figures, Senators Cheer Belligerent Speeches of Leaders

By HERBERT L. MATTHEWS
By Telephone to THE NEW YORK TIMES.

ROME, May 17—While nothing startling happened in Italy today, there have been a number of minor developments to drive home further the feeling that Italian intervention in the European war is not very far off.

The Senate held a session in the morning full of genuine war fervor. The Minister of Finance, Count Paolo Thaon di Revel, presented what amounts to a war budget and admitted a deficit for this year of more than 26,000,000,000 lire. Premier Mussolini's own newspaper, in a highly significant editorial, as good as told the nation that it was about to enter the conflict. The Stock Exchanges had a singularly black day; the great successes claimed by Germany on the French front provided a temptation of the first magnitude for the Fascist leaders.

The temperature in the Senate session was feverish. Every time the name of King Victor Emmanuel or of Premier Mussolini was mentioned there was a remarkably emotional reaction. Count Suardo, the President of the Senate, spoke words like these:

"The Italian people press around you, Duce, to form an iron block of energy and will, ready for your orders wherever you wish to guide them, because they know that the road you will take at their head to preserve our vital rights has just one goal—the grandeur and power of Italy."

At the end of Count Suardo's

Continued on Page Five

GAMELIN IN APPEAL

Says Fate of Nation and World's Destiny Hang on Present Conflict

FIGHTING IS AT PEAK

Full Air Forces Battle—Attacks at Sedan and Montmedy Repulsed

By G. H. ARCHAMBAULT
Wireless to THE NEW YORK TIMES.

PARIS, May 17—"The fate of our country and that of our allies and the destiny of the world depend on the battle now being fought."

Thus begins a general order to all troops issued this evening by General Maurice Gustave Gamelin, supreme Allied commander.

Taken in conjunction with the communiqué issued from General Headquarters tonight, it reveals the situation as tragic.

"Today the German attack developed on a massive scale," the communiqué stated, "not only in Belgium but in the region of Avesnes and Vervins. On those fronts the enemy engaged the greater part of his heavy tank divisions. The battle took the form of a veritable melee."

Avesnes and Vervins are in the North of France, the latter some fifteen miles from the Belgian border.

[Cannonading was heard today on the outskirts of Paris, according to The Associated Press. It was not learned whether this was anti-aircraft or other fire.]

All United in Battle

General Gamelin's order adds that British, Belgian and Polish soldiers are fighting by the side of the French, together with foreign volunteers. The British Air Force, he added, like the French, is fighting to the last man.

Every troop that cannot advance, the general asserted, must die where it stands rather than abandon the portion of national soil entrusted to it. Concluding, he said:

"As always in the critical hours of our history, the watchword is 'Conquer or die.' We must conquer."

This general order so reminiscent of that issued by Marshal Joffre in 1914 on the first day of the Battle of the Marne tells the story. There are no details. A terrific struggle is being fought for the future of mankind. All else is of no moment.

That the Allied General Headquarters has not departed from its calm is indicated in the remainder of the communiqué, which proceeds to refer to minor incidents as follows:

"Further to the east the enemy attacked in the region of Sedan and Montmedy without success.

Aviation Continues Activity

"In close collaboration with the Royal Air Force our aviation continued its energetic and efficacious action against ground troops, crossroads and railways. While assuring the protection of our troops our fighters engaged in numerous encounters. Many enemy planes were brought down. In the present conditions of open warfare it is not possible to know the exact number."

Nor is it of moment to refer to this morning's news relating to the actions on the Meuse. They all pale into insignificance with the day's developments. Since the outline of the pocket formed by the Germans was indicated by a spokesman for the general staff that pocket has been burst.

Any appreciation of the situation, any comment would be mere guesswork utterly out of place in the circumstances.

Decisive Victory Sought

PARIS, May 17 (AP)—The French armies, under orders from General Maurice Gustave Gamelin to "die on the spot rather than give further ground," battled a massive German tank drive into Northern France tonight in a clash described by the high command as "a veritable melee."

Adolf Hitler's fighters carried their week-old offensive on the Western Front to a peak during the day with violent blasts both in Belgium and France in a desperate effort to drive home a decisive victory.

The German thrust through Bel-

Continued on Page Three

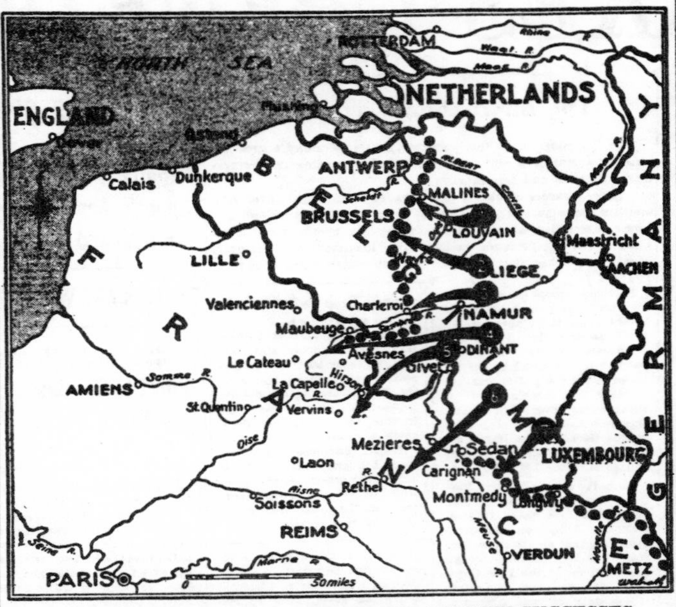

GERMANY'S SWIFT COLUMNS SWEEP TO NEW SUCCESSES

Nazi forces, breaking through the extension of the Maginot Line in Northern France across the Belgian border, have reached the vicinity of Avesnes (4) and Vervins (5) and are reported north of Rethel (6) in a thrust toward Laon. The Allies claim to have halted a further attempt to widen the gap south of Sedan (7). In Belgium the Germans occupied Louvain and Malines (1) and claim to have reached the outer fortifications of Antwerp; they also crashed through the Dyle River defenses and marched into Brussels (2) as British forces withdrew to the west, and reported the capture of Namur (3). The dotted line indicates approximate Allied fixed positions.

Gamelin, 1940; Joffre, 1914

Gamelin Order

By The United Press.

PARIS, May 17—Following is the text of General Maurice Gustave Gamelin's order of the day to the French armies:

"The fate of our country and that of our Allies and the destiny of the world depend on the battle now being fought.

"English, Belgian and Polish soldiers and foreign volunteers fight at our side.

"The British Air Force is engaged up to the hilt like ours.

"Every unit that is unable to advance must accept death rather than abandon that part of the national territory entrusted to it.

"As always in the critical hours of our history the watchword today is 'Conquer or die.' We must conquer."

Joffre Order

Following is the text of the order addressed by Marshal Joffre to all army headquarters and to troops on Sept. 6, 1914:

"We are about to engage a battle on which the fate of our country depends and it is important to remind all ranks that the moment has passed for looking to the rear; all our efforts must be directed to attacking and driving back the enemy.

"Troops that can advance no further must, at any price, hold on to the ground they have conquered and die on the spot rather than give way. Under the circumstances which face us, no act of weakness can be tolerated."

BELGIANS REMOVE CAPITAL TO OSTEND

Vacating of Brussels Laid to 'Obvious Necessity'—U. S. Envoy Remains at Post

Wireless to THE NEW YORK TIMES.

PARIS, May 17—The removal of the Belgian capital from Brussels to another point in Belgian territory was announced today in a broadcast from Brussels by M. Vanderpoorten, Minister of the Interior, speaking for Premier Hubert Pierlot.

[The Belgian Government is now established at Ostend, on Belgium's North Sea coast, The Associated Press reported in a dispatch from Ostend.]

"This painful decision," he said, "has been forced upon us by obvious necessity. The Allied troops are defending themselves step by step, but the rapidity of movement that armies have today causes events to transpire with greater rapidity than ever. After a few days of war we find ourselves in a situation which, without being so grave, recalls in certain respects what it was after the first weeks of war in 1914. We shall soon witness, we firmly believe, the same recovery which took place then."

The Minister praised the courage of the Belgian Armies and people, and added:

"The Premier yesterday after-

Continued on Page Four

FRANCE PAYS PRICE FOR SHIFTING UNITS

Penetration by Nazi Armored Forces Laid to Fact Aid Had to Be Rushed to Neutrals

Wireless to THE NEW YORK TIMES.

PARIS, May 17—Outside military circles, the public mind not only here but seemingly all over the world is much exercised over the swift advance of German armored columns into French territory. The briefest explanation is that the Allies have paid that price for moving immediately to the aid of Belgium and the Netherlands despite the fact that both countries steadfastly refused to consider any joint plan of campaign in the event of invasion.

Apparently what seems most inexplicable to the layman is that the line of defenses along the French frontier should have been penetrated. The answer is twofold:

First, these defenses were not the Maginot Line of solid permanent concrete works that extends only from Montmedy eastward to the Rhine, but field fortifications—trenches, ditches, pits and the like—reinforced since the war by pill boxes and blockhouses.

Second, that the value of field works is determined by the forces behind them.

Since the Allied High Command decided early in the campaign to

Continued on Page Four

BRITISH FALL BACK BEHIND BRUSSELS

'Adjustment' West of City Is Announced—Troops Steady Against Nazi Blows

Special Cable to THE NEW YORK TIMES.

LONDON, May 17—The War Office announced tonight that the British Army in Belgium had retired the night before to positions west of Brussels, "certain adjustments at the front having become necessary."

"This readjustment," the communiqué said, "was carried out without interference. There is no question of any collapse or break through in this sector as suggested by the German communiqué."

By HAROLD DENNY
Wireless to THE NEW YORK TIMES.

WITH THE BRITISH ARMY IN BELGIUM, May 17—The Germans renewed today their assaults on the British positions, hurling tanks supported by airplanes with especial severity on the right side of the British line.

The British are withstanding these terrific mechanized assaults with great steadiness and can be counted upon to continue doing so. The British Expeditionary Force is fighting under the French High Command, and its employment is governed by the working out of the grand battle plan. The British are playing the role assigned to them no matter what their local situation. Should the French be hard pressed in the Sedan area—enough, that is, to threaten the splitting of the Allied general line—a realignment of the British forces might be necessary.

British Staff Pleased

British staff officers are pleased with the fine qualities their troops are exhibiting against attacks such as soldiers never had encountered before this war. They are equally confident of the ability of the French High Command to meet any situation presented by the German drive. The French must have foreseen every emergency which could develop and devised effective counter-measures. The French seem to have the gift of choosing the exact moment to strike most effectively.

The British now are fighting side by side with the Belgians, who made contact with them in the vicinity of Malines.

British resistance to the German

Continued on Page Three

Dispatches from Europe and the Far East are subject to censorship at the source.

NAZIS REPORT ROUT

Allies 'in Full Retreat' Westward Into France, Germans Declare

AIR VICTORIES NOTED

Sedan Prisoners Said to Total 12,000, Among Them 2 Generals

By GEORGE AXELSSON
Wireless to THE NEW YORK TIMES.

BERLIN, May 17—Brussels, Malines and Louvain have fallen to the relentlessly advancing Germans, who also claim to have broken into France across the defenses of the Maginot Line extension on a wide front, standing not more than ninety miles from Paris at the nearest point.

The German High Command today broke a three days' silence on its Western Front operations to announce two major successes. First was the driving of a sixty-two-mile wedge into the French lines from south of Maubeuge to Carignan, southeast of Sedan. Second was a break through the Belgian Dyle line positions south of Wavre, along with the capture of Namur.

The spearhead of the German advance into France—where, a General Headquarters communiqué significantly says, "Our infantry units and air force are pursuing the enemy in full retreat westward"—is tonight said to be in the vicinity of La Capelle and Le Cateau, halfway between Maubeuge and St. Quentin.

In the sector southeast of Sedan the Germans, according to their communiqué, have taken 12,000 prisoners, including two generals, and also captured abundant war material.

British Throw in Tank Units

In Belgium, the Germans early this morning already had advanced their lines to Malines, the vicinity of Louvain and south of Brussels in the Waterloo area, making the military situation of the capital seem hopeless for the defenders.

Here, it is admitted, the British had thrown in particularly powerful tank units in a desperate attempt to stem the German advance to the coast. The lines were swaying back and forth along this entire sector, with tank meeting tank and infantry against infantry in vicious hand-to-hand encounters of a ceaseless attack and counter-attack.

The Germans evidently were following the Polish campaign method of launching giant tanks in wild forward lunges fanwise, as though along the fingers of an outspread hand, and trusting to skill and chance to hold the spearheads and eventually close the gaps between.

With Paris and the English Channel coast directly threatened, the military plight of the Allies appears most grave, as seen from Berlin. The British, it is said, must now devote every ounce of their resources to saving the coast, while the French must be equally occupied with the defense of their capital, rendering mutual aid difficult if not impossible.

French Attacks Said to Fail

The Germans admit violent French attacks on their south flank, presumably in the Longwy sector, but say these attempts to relieve the main fronts met with no success. Instead, it is claimed, the Germans gained further ground in their counter-attacks.

That the struggles in Belgium and France have changed their aspect in the last forty-eight hours is asserted by military observers here. Only Wednesday the two battle zones, that in front of Brussels and that to the south in France, formed one connected front from Antwerp by Charleville to Sedan.

The German break through between Namur and Givet and into the Maginot Line across the Meuse was thrust at the point where the south flank of the Belgian battle zone joined the northern flank of the French. Widening of the breach between Namur and Givet and the rapid German push westward in the Maubeuge sector are said to have separated the two battle lines and doubled over the flanks.

The Belgian front is now reported turned back on the Sambre River westward where, according to the Germans, the Allied forces now are threatened with a flanking move-

Continued on Page Two

"All the News That's Fit to Print."

The New York Times.

LATE CITY EDITION
Cloudy, little change in temperature today. Tomorrow rain, not much change in temperature.
Temperatures Yesterday—Max., 70; Min., 58

Copyright, 1940, by The New York Times Company.

VOL. LXXXIX No. 30,069. Entered as Second-Class Matter, Postoffice, New York, N. Y. NEW YORK, WEDNESDAY, MAY 22, 1940. THREE CENTS NEW YORK CITY and Vicinity | FOUR CENTS Elsewhere Except in 7th and 8th Postal Zones.

NAZIS AT CHANNEL, TRAP ALLIES IN BELGIUM; CROSS AISNE RIVER 60 MILES FROM PARIS; FRANCE CAN'T DIE, REYNAUD TELLS PEOPLE

PRESIDENT SPEEDS DEFENSE PROGRAM; APPEALS FOR UNITY

At Press Talk He Condemns Nazis as Machine-Gunning Fleeing French Civilians

MOVES ON 'FIFTH COLUMN'

New Reorganization Order Will Put Immigration Bureau in Justice Department

The International Situation

On the Battle Fronts

Eleven days after the start of their offensive on the Western Front, the Germans yesterday drove a spearhead to the English Channel, cutting off the Allied troops in Belgium and the northwest tip of France from the main body of the French Army. The German command estimated that half a million to a million men had thus been trapped between a steadily pressing mass of German attackers and the North Sea. [Page 1.]

The German thrust, described by Berlin as "the greatest attack of all time," swept sixty miles along the Valley of the Somme, reaching Abbeville, on the estuary of that river. Amiens and Arras fell. The Germans claimed that their air force, aided by submarines and torpedo-carrying mosquito boats, was in command of the Channel. However that may be, French and Belgian ports, from which the British must embark if all effort to hold the northern line is abandoned, were being unmercifully bombed last night. Despite all this activity in the west, the Germans did not let up in the southern part of their huge salient. The push toward Paris continued, with semi-official sources in Berlin saying the invaders had crossed the Aisne at Soissons, sixty miles from the capital. [Included in foregoing.]

Paris contended that only motorcycle troops had reached Abbeville. Despite the breakthrough, French authorities said, there still was furious fighting in the neighborhood of Cambrai, far to the German rear, where the invaders had not yet succeeded in consolidating their positions. But there was as yet no sign of large-scale counter-attack. [Page 1.]

The French admitted that the Somme Valley above St. Quentin was in chaos. Parachutists set hundreds of fires around Arras and Amiens; in the triangle between the Belgian border, Amiens and the Channel, not one railway station stood intact. [Page 1.]

The Germans apparently had succeeded in capturing the commander of the French Ninth Army, General Henri Honoré Giraud. A Berlin dispatch said the capture had been "half-tragic, half-comic"—that the general had walked into his headquarters and found German officers there. Paris admitted there had been no communication with the general for forty-eight hours. [Page 1.]

Early this morning waves of Allied fliers bombed Aachen (Aix-la-Chapelle), on the west border of Germany. Bombs showered on the city and on Westwall fortifications. This raid was outstanding among many aimed at the German rear. The British Air Ministry announced that during the night German planes had dropped bombs on two districts in Southeastern England; no damage or casualties were reported. [Page 1.]

Alfred Duff Cooper, British Minister of Information, warned his countrymen by radio that they might expect invasion at any time. Volunteer "parashoots" were rushed to positions guarding points vulnerable to attack by German soldiers floating down from the skies. [Page 3.]

Premier Reynaud, addressing the French Senate, said the inefficient training and handling of General André Georges Corap's army was responsible for France's plight. "Unbelievable faults" would be punished, he declared. The Premier said the classic French conception of war had been demolished by armored divisions, fighting planes and disorganization of the rear by parachutists. He emphasized his faith in France to surmount her period of trial, and asserted: "Abroad they are beginning to understand * * * that what is happening affects them and their children. Let them not come to this understanding too late." [Page 1.]

Repercussions Elsewhere

Italy, which is expected shortly to join the German side, closed the border between Italian-owned Albania and Yugoslavia, where Allied sentiment has been strong. There were reports in Yugoslavia that munitions were being rushed in below the border and that barrack and other military construction work was being pressed in twenty-four-hour shifts. [Page 5.]

President Roosevelt, at a press conference in Washington, appealed for national unity in preparedness. He set forth three points to govern policy in building up our defenses: (1) No war millionaires will be created; (2) labor must not take advantage of its collective power to foment strikes interfering with the defense program; (3) there must be no weakening of social legislation of the last seven years, notably laws affecting labor standards. [Page 1.]

As President Roosevelt outlined yesterday at his press conference further details of plans for the nation's defense [Page 1] various departments of the government took action to speed up preparedness. The navy submitted to Congress a program calling for 10,000 planes and 16,000 pilots. It also ordered a forty-eight-hour work week in navy yards and the hiring of 15,000 more civilian employes. [Page 13.]

Senator Pepper offered a resolution authorizing the President to sell to any invaded country any of the army's or navy's airplanes. The Senate sped action on the War Department Appropriation Bill, now increased to almost $1,500,000,000 in cash grants and close to $325,000,000 in contract authorizations. [Page 10.]

The President asked the House to lift its $50,000 limit on WPA grants, because such a restriction would hamper projects for defense. [Page 8.] He also vetoed a $109,985,450 Rivers and Harbors bill in order to give preference to military projects. [Page 11.]

States 3-Point Plan

By FELIX BELAIR Jr.

Special to THE NEW YORK TIMES.

WASHINGTON, May 21—President Roosevelt today coupled an appeal for national unity behind his preparedness drive with the grimmest picture of German military tactics yet painted in any official American quarter—a picture of the deliberate machine-gunning of millions of fleeing French women, children and old men by Nazi war planes. He said Americans well understood the implications of such ruthless methods and would be guided accordingly.

Then the President, employing the gravest tone he has used in referring to the war in Europe, outlined the following three-point policy which he said would govern the nation's defense preparations:

Not a single war millionaire will be created in this country as a result of the war disaster.

Labor will not attempt to take advantage of its collective power to foment strikes and interfere with the national defense program to squeeze higher wages from employers in the so-called war industries.

Under no circumstances will the Administration sanction a weakening of the social legislative gains attained during the last seven years. Labor standards prescribed in the Walsh-Healey act and the Wage-Hour Law must not be relaxed in the name of the national defense.

Plans Attack on "Fifth Column"

As the President gave further impetus to the preparedness drive there were the following developments in his national defense program:

1. Mr. Roosevelt sought to strengthen the country against "fifth column" activities by providing for an early transfer of the Bureau of Immigration and Naturalization from the Labor Department to the Department of Justice. He said he would send to Congress tomorrow another reorganization plan giving effect to the transfer proposal.

2. With full Administration backing, chairmen of the Senate and House Naval Affairs Committees introduced companion bills to spend an additional $124,000,000 for a naval air armada of 10,000 planes and 16,000 pilots. Introduced by Senator Walsh and Representative Vinson after a White House conference, the proposed legislation would increase the navy's authorized aerial fleet by 7,000 units, of

Continued on Page Ten

HENDRICKSON LEADS IN JERSEY PRIMARY

Willkie Gets Surprise Write-In Vote Against Dewey in Presidential Contest

A write-in vote for Wendell L. Willkie in the New Jersey primaries yesterday disclosed surprising strength for the utilities executive as a candidate for President. State Senator Robert C. Hendrickson of Gloucester County was leading former Governor Harold G. Hoffman for the Republican nomination for Governor.

A total of 2,395 election districts out of 3,631 in the State gave 165,650 votes to Mr. Hendrickson and 144,290 to Mr. Hoffman, a commanding lead of 21,360 for Mr. Hendrickson.

Contrary to pre-election predictions, Hendrickson carried Bergen and Union Counties on the basis of incomplete returns. His margin in both counties was small, however. His plurality in Essex County was larger than had been expected.

State Senator Winant Van Winkle, a Hendrickson supporter, was defeated for renomination in Bergen County by a Hoffman candidate, Lloyd L. Schroeder. Complete returns gave Schroeder 27,385 votes to 26,251 for Van Winkle.

District Attorney Thomas E. Dewey entered the Republican primary as a preferential candidate

Continued on Page Sixteen

ALLIES FIGHT BACK AT FURIOUS DRIVES

Admit Penetration of Nazis to Abbeville, but Look for Re-forming of Lines

By The Associated Press.

PARIS, May 21—The Allies, with their backs to the English Channel, tonight fought against a new German advance that spread a path of fire across Northern France and threatened to isolate England.

The French High Command's night communiqué admitted the Germans had driven their advance guard to Amiens and Arras, on the edge of the coastal plain leading to the English Channel.

A War Ministry spokesman added that German motorcycle troops had pushed on to penetrate the outskirts of the Abbeville region. The city of Abbeville is on the Somme estuary, twelve miles from the Channel's open waters, and about twenty-five miles west of Arras and Amiens. The War Ministry spokesman said he believed the French still held Abbeville itself, but that he could "give no official confirmation."

German motorcycle units thrust along roads to the west of Arras and Amiens behind advance bombardments and machine gunning from Nazi planes. Other roads radiating from the French towns, filled with refugees, were reported strafed by the Germans from the

Continued on Page Four

PREMIER IS CANDID

'Unbelievable Faults' in Allied Defense to Be Punished, He Says

'DISASTER' ADMITTED

But France Is Told Hope and Savage Energy Can Still Bring Victory

The text of Premier Reynaud's address is on Page 6.

By P. J. PHILIP

Wireless to THE NEW YORK TIMES.

PARIS, May 21—Announcing quietly, amid a chilly silence, that since 8 o'clock this morning the advancing German forces had occupied Amiens and Arras, Premier Paul Reynaud in the Senate this afternoon called on the people of France, soldiers and civilians alike, to be worthy of the "grandeur of the hour in which we are living" and to "rise to the height of the misfortunes of our country."

Succinctly, sparing no one, he told the tragic story of the mistakes that had been made in the Belgian campaign, of the lack of preparation, of the miscalculations, of the terrible exactness of the German calculations and their consequences.

The Germans had broken the hinge on which the whole left wing of the Allied armies swung, the Premier explained. They had pounded through the breach and driven forward with their armored divisions and airplanes far behind the French northern defense line. The French classic conception of war had been utterly routed by this new conception which disorganized the country behind the lines while it piled hammer blow on hammer blow at strategic points.

Cites "Unbelievable Faults"

There had been, he went on, "unbelievable faults which will be punished." Bridges over the Meuse that should have been destroyed had not been destroyed. Describing what happened to General André Corap's army, he called it a "disaster" and "total disorganization."

M. Reynaud seems not to have given up hope. He demanded that that hope should be backed by confidence and savage energy on the part of all who are fighting and working for the salvation of the country.

This new method of war must be met by new methods of defense, he held. France had in the past repeatedly overcome such initial mistakes and miscalculations; she had risen from the pit of defeat to victory under Marshal Henri Philippe Petain and Marshal Foch's lieutenant, General Maxime Weygand, in the past and could do so again.

There was an indirect word directed toward America and all the peoples far removed from the struggle. They were beginning to understand and to see that their future also was involved, M. Reynaud de-

Continued on Page Six

NAZIS SPRINT TO COAST AND PUSH NEARER TO PARIS

Allied forces have been put in peril by a German spearhead driven between French and Belgian troops at Valenciennes (2) and by the westward push of the German right wing in Belgium, where the Belgians were engaged east of Ghent (1). Even more serious, however, was the advance to Abbeville (4) near the shore of the English Channel. As fighting raged north of Cambrai (3) motorized units swept south of that town and then, while some of them moved northwest to Arras, the rest raced along the Somme valley, took Amiens and continued on to the coast. Nor was the threat to Paris lessened. At Amiens the Nazis claimed to have a bridgehead across the Somme, while to the east the German advance beyond Laon (5) was semi-officially declared to have resulted in the capture of Soissons, within sixty miles of Paris, and threats to both Noyon and Compiegne. At Rethel (6), however, the French said they were clinging to the south bank of the Aisne. The approximate limit of the German advance is shown by the broken line, which is based on dispatches received from both Berlin and Paris.

'Chutists and Cyclists Set Fires Behind Allied Lines

By The United Press.

PARIS, May 21—Germany unleashed the full fury of "total war" on Northern France today, dropping parachutists with torches to set fire to wide areas around Arras, Amiens and other cities in the Nazi drive to the English Channel.

Hundreds of German planes rained incendiary bombs on every city, village and community in the Picardy and Flanders lowlands, military dispatches said.

At the same time giant air transports unloaded aerial incendiaries who were instructed to race through the countryside and set fire to or dynamite factories, railway stations, munitions and fuel dumps and other such objectives in scores of cities between Cambrai and the sea.

In the triangle between the Belgian frontier, the Channel and Amiens, not one railway station stood intact tonight, military spokesmen said.

Property losses were tremendous. Spokesmen said they could be figured in tens of billions of francs along a corridor of destruction thirty-five miles wide in which not a building stood undamaged and

Continued on Page Two

Women, Children Begin Evacuation of Gibraltar

Wireless to THE NEW YORK TIMES.

GIBRALTAR, May 21—Women and children are being evacuated from Gibraltar. The first batches left today for French Morocco. Others will follow tomorrow and subsequent days.

The action follows an official announcement today that the Governor of Gibraltar, Lieut. Gen. Sir Clive Liddell, had received instructions from the War Cabinet that owing to the international situation the evacuation of women and children from Gibraltar would be compulsory immediately.

AACHEN IS BOMBED HEAVILY BY ALLIES

Troop Concentrations There—German Bombs Dropped in Southeast England

By The United Press.

AACHEN, Germany, Wednesday, May 22—Waves of Allied bombing planes early today attacked this German city along the German Westwall fortifications, bombing and battling Nazi Messerschmitt fighters.

The first air raid alarm was sounded at 12:45 A. M., when the first enemy bombers appeared over the city and began dropping bombs. The attack was met by anti-aircraft fire for fifteen minutes, and Messerschmitt fighters went into the sky to battle the raiders. From then on the Allied planes came in waves and were still sweeping upon the city at 1:05 A. M.

[Aachen, also known as Aix-la-Chapelle, lies at the point of the German, Netherland and Belgian borders and was the "jumping off" place for the German in-

Continued on Page Four

Dispatches from Europe and the Far East are subject to censorship at the source.

Nazis Report Capture of Giraud; Say General Walked Into a Trap

Wireless to THE NEW YORK TIMES.

BERLIN, May 21—The Germans told an astounding story today of how General Henri Giraud, commander of the French Ninth Army, was captured. In a lightning advance in the Cambrai sector, Nazi forces occupied the château headquarters of the French Ninth Army. Here they learned that the commanding general had left, having been relieved by order of the new Commander in Chief, General Maxime Weygand, by General Giraud, who had been head of the Seventh Army.

According to accounts here, the Germans set their trap by merely remaining and taking General Giraud and his staff into custody as they arrived to take charge, ignorant of the situation. The story of the capture leaked out in Berlin yesterday, but the High Command did not want it spread, hoping that dispatch riders and others attached to the Ninth Army headquarters, uninformed of the change, would fall into the net.

BERLIN, May 21 (UP)—General Henri Honore Giraud, commander of the French Ninth Army, which had struggled to stem the German tide for eleven days, was said to have been taken prisoner in a "half-tragic, half-comic manner" when he walked into his headquarters and found German officers there.

General Giraud, 61 years old and one of France's most famous strategists, had been placed in command of the main Allied defense along the German "bulge" front in Northern France and Southern Belgium only on Saturday, it was said by German officials.

As a captain in the World War, he was captured by the Germans two weeks after the outbreak of the conflict and finally escaped through Belgium and the Netherlands to

Continued on Page Five

BRITISH FIGHT HARD TO AVOID DISASTER

Their Whole Force in Belgium Is Trapped in Untenable Position, Allies Admit

By The United Press.

LONDON, May 21—The lightning German thrust to the English Channel has separated the main French and British armies and trapped the entire British expeditionary force in an untenable position, the Allied High Command recognized tonight.

The writer left one of the Channel ports today when the German drive was reaching its peak. It was directly menaced by advancing German mechanized units.

The British have their choice of attempting evacuation under a rain of German bombs over the entire Channel area or facing the enemy in a last-ditch effort to hold the only avenue of escape left to them—the Channel ports of Calais, Boulogne, Ostend and Blankenberge.

In either event, the B. E. F. is fighting desperately to escape annihilation.

[In Berlin it was said that the British had received orders to embark for England and that "our planes are bombing embarkation centers."]

Le Touquet Threatened

The Germans are completing encircling tactics in their drive on the coast between Abbeville and Le Touquet, which they are due to reach at any hour.

[Le Touquet is about twenty miles north of Abbeville, from which a double-trunk railroad line runs to the French resort.]

German mechanized divisions were rumbling along roads leading to the principal ports. Allied forces were rushing to oppose them, but the Nazis were flushed with victory and no obstacle seemed capable of checking them.

The roads were crowded with refugees from Northern France, Belgium and the Netherlands. They blocked the roads and made Allied military manoeuvres more difficult.

The B. E. F. at present is awaiting the order of the Commander in Chief to make a terrific last stand in which it would throw all it possesses of gun power, tanks, infantry divisions and aircraft.

The French, on the other (southwestern) flank of the German columns, have been assembling for

Continued on Page Four

500,000 'ISOLATED'

Swift Thrust to Coast Cuts Off Huge Force, Berlin Claims

SOISSONS 'TAKEN,' TOO

Invaders Stab at Paris as Threat to Britain Progresses

By GEORGE AXELSSON

Wireless to THE NEW YORK TIMES.

BERLIN, May 21—In a crowning series of staggering blows dealt to the Allies in the last few days, the Germans claim tonight to have reached Abbeville on the Picardy coast, fifteen miles from Le Treport on the English Channel. Thus they have now virtually achieved their aim to isolate the combined Allied armies in the western corner of Belgium and the northwestern tip of France. Unless they can fight their way out, this should seal the fate of the Belgian Army and numerous divisions of the French, altogether totaling perhaps between 500,000 and 1,000,000 men, including whatever British forces are left in this area.

[The German thrust toward Paris has reached the region of Reims, it was said in official German circles early today, according to an Associated Press dispatch from Berlin.]

In an apparently masterful enveloping movement rapidly closing in, the Germans claim to have definitely broken up the entire French Ninth Army, taking prisoner its commander, General Henri Giraud, with his complete staff. The mission of the Ninth Army was to insure liaison between the strong Allied units in Belgium and the Maginot Line south of Sedan.

En route to Abbeville, the Germans say, they occupied Amiens and Arras. The River Somme up to the estuary that the Germans tried in vain to reach in their "risk it all" drive in March, 1918, should thus be in their hands after brisk fighting that apparently lasted fewer hours than it did months during the World War.

Soissons Reported Taken

At the same time they are pushing toward Paris, and it is semi-officially said here tonight that they have taken the city of Soissons, a bare sixty miles by air from the French capital. Noyon and Compiègne, in this same area, appear to be seriously endangered and likely to be occupied at one moment or another.

With perhaps 1,000,000 Allied troops hopelessly cut off and squeezed by powerful German armies between the mouths of the Rivers Scheldt and Somme, the question arises here in the minds of neutral military observers: How could the Allied Army leaders have permitted a situation threatening such a major disaster?

One explanation is that it is perhaps the outcome of a desperate French attempt at a counter-offensive aimed at the flank of the German right wing without having sufficiently insured the rear lines of communication. It is suggested that German tanks of the mastodon type may have charged the French laterally, cutting off their supply lines and forcing the bulk of the attackers clear through the fronts into the jaws of German tongs as flocks of Nazi dive-bombers efficiently supported the deadly ground work of the tank divisions.

French Effort Criticized

In this connection, it is asked here: What has happened to the French artillery? It is a matter of record that the French have the most efficient artillery, from light field pieces including the famous 75's up to railway and other heavy long-range guns.

None of these, any more than French supertanks reputedly weighing in the neighborhood of fifty tons, have figured in reports of the fighting available here. The superiority of the German tank and of the German plane seems definitely established, in the eyes of observers here.

With the Channel ports from Ostend to Boulogne strongly compromised, a powerful German bid for final victory seemingly enters a decisive stage. As seen from here, the Allied position is not altogether

Continued on Page Two

"All the News That's Fit to Print."

The New York Times.

LATE CITY EDITION
Partly cloudy today, showers tonight, little change in temperature. Tomorrow showers.
Temperature Yesterday—Max., 64; Min., 53

Copyright, 1940, by The New York Times Company.

VOL. LXXXIX...No. 30,077. Entered as Second-Class Matter, Postoffice, New York, N. Y. NEW YORK, THURSDAY, MAY 30, 1940. THREE CENTS NEW YORK CITY and Vicinity | FOUR CENTS Elsewhere Except in 7th and 8th Postal Zones.

ALLIES ABANDONING FLANDERS, FLOOD YSER AREA; A RESCUE FLEET AT DUNKERQUE; FOE POUNDS PORT; ONE FORCE CUT OFF FROM THE SEA AS LILLE FALLS

PRESIDENT TO ASK $750,000,000 MORE FOR ARMY PROGRAM

Nazi Blitzkrieg Held to Show the $3,300,000,000 Allotted Fails to Meet Needs

FOR TANKS, GUNS, PLANES

Tax Bill to Be Offered in House Today—D. M. Nelson Named Procurement Director

By FELIX BELAIR Jr.
Special to THE NEW YORK TIMES.

WASHINGTON, May 29—On the eve of his first meeting with the reconstituted Council of National Defense, President Roosevelt was putting finishing touches today on a new request for $750,000,000 as a supplemental appropriation for further expansion and mechanization of the military establishment to take account of European war developments since he sent his preparedness message to Congress two weeks ago.

The projected increase in funds for the Army, over and above the omnibus $3,300,000,000 defense program already pending, was mapped by the President in a White House conference with Treasury and War Department officials.

It was the President's plan to send up the supplemental request in a few days. Subject to additions, the new program contemplates placing orders immediately for the following:

About 3,000 new pursuit and bombing planes.

Between 1,500 and 2,000 tanks.

About 500 heavy howitzers.

A supply of aerial bombs of various sizes, to cost between $20,000,000 and $30,000,000.

Other modern weapons of war which have been developed in Army laboratories, but not yet put into actual production.

German Drive Appraised

There was no official announcement on the results of the meeting, and Secretary Woodring, who acted as spokesman for the group, said only that they had reviewed "the whole military situation."

From others present, however, it was learned that the nation's military establishment had been reappraised in the light of Germany's advances in Western Europe since the President's preparedness message was first submitted to Congress.

Other developments in the national defense program were:

1. The Senate Naval Affairs Committee brought out a measure increasing the air force limit of the Navy to 10,000 planes and 16,000 pilots, with a report warning that the "country at this time is facing the possibility that the Allies may be defeated and that we may have to defend ourselves in both oceans at the same time."

2. Senate leaders were planning to take up tomorrow the $1,500,000,000 bill providing an 11 per cent increase in under-age surface tonnage, with indications that the measure would be disposed of without delay.

Procurement Officer Named

3. Secretary Morgenthau named Donald M. Nelson, executive vice president of Sears, Roebuck & Co., as director of the Treasury's Procurement Division, thereby adding another business executive to the list of those on whom the administration is relying for the success of the defense program.

4. Administration - Congressional plans for placing emergency rearmament financing on a "pay-as-you-go" basis gathered momentum, with an announcement by Representative Doughton, chairman of the House Ways and Means Committee, that he would introduce tomorrow a measure raising the statutory debt limit by $3,000,000,000 and imposing upward of $656,000,000 in new defense taxes.

5. Secretary Hull modified aviation restrictions under the Neutrality Act to permit the delivery of American planes by American pilots to Halifax, N. S., thereby removing the ban on through deliveries over the Maritime Provinces.

6. White House sources explained that there would be the closest possible relations between Presi-

Continued on Page Eight

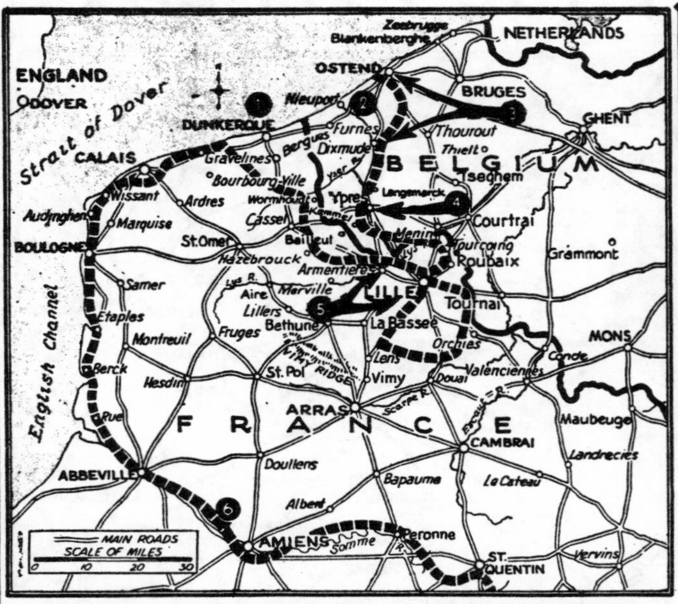

ALLIES STRIKE FOR COAST IN EVER-TIGHTENING POCKET

To keep the exit at Dunkerque (1) open French and British sea, land and air forces were waging a furious struggle yesterday; to retard the German advance the Allies were understood to have opened sluice gates on the Yser to flood the region below Nieuport (2). In the sector that had been held by the Belgians the Nazis pushed to Ostend and Dixmude (3). Farther south they were reported to have taken Ypres (4). Their most important operation of the day, however, was the bisecting of the pocket by the capture of Lille and Armentieres (5), thus cutting off from the sea the Allied forces in the lower section. Along the Somme the French eliminated a German bridgehead west of Amiens (6). The broken lines show the approximate battlefronts.

HULL ORDER SPEEDS PLANES TO ALLIES

Allows Our Pilots to Fly Craft Over Three Canadian Maritime Provinces

Special to THE NEW YORK TIMES.

WASHINGTON, May 29—The way was opened today for expediting deliveries of American airplanes to the Allied fighting lines when Secretary Hull modified regulations of the Neutrality Act to permit the delivery of such aircraft by American pilots to ports in the three eastern Canadian Provinces.

The step was designed to facilitate deliveries to the Allies because of the urgency of their military situation. It was taken at the request of the French Government.

Mr. Hull ruled that "American nationals may travel in belligerent aircraft over the Canadian Provinces of New Brunswick, Nova Scotia and Prince Edward Island." This means that pilots from the United States may fly new planes to Halifax, whence they will be flown across the Atlantic by pilots of the Allies or sent across by ship.

American pilots have been delivering planes in Ottawa and other Canadian cities. As before, they must still conform under the new order to regulations by pushing planes over the Canadian border from the United States.

Previously, while American pilots could fly planes over Canadian territory, once they were pushed over the border the fliers could not enter the three eastern maritime Provinces because American ships are barred from them and aircraft regulations conform to shipping rules. Newfoundland was excluded from the modification today because there was no actual need for including it.

The Department of Commerce announced that April shipments of aircraft and equipment to the Allies included 195 planes and 285 engines.

Of the planes, France received seventy completely powered craft and ninety-eight in a knock-down condition. The United Kingdom obtained twenty-three assembled and powered and Canada four.

Of the engines, 230 went to France, forty-three to Canada and twelve to the United Kingdom. The French plane acquisitions were valued at $9,176,538, those of the United Kingdom at $2,139,000 and those of Canada at $288,296.

With a variety of other equipment included, French purchases for the month totaled $14,443,071; those of the United Kingdom $2,908,621 and those of Canada $728,929.

The Department of Commerce announced that total exports of aero-

Continued on Page Ten

Berlin Exchange Slumps As Optimism Is Decried

Wireless to THE NEW YORK TIMES.

BERLIN, May 29—In what was apparently a strong reaction to warnings against over-optimism, which have been circulated generally among the population following the German victories in the West, the Berlin Boerse today took a sudden nose dive.

Most issues dropped between 1 and 4 per cent. In shipping, Hapag dropped 5 per cent and North German Lloyd dropped 3 per cent. Fixed interest securities were quiet and generally unchanged. The close was irregular, with call money at 1⅞-2⅛.

Utilities, motor works and other heavy industries led the recession, while metal works in the Rhineland were among those that showed the maximum decline.

URUGUAY ON GUARD FOR FIFTH COLUMN

Check on Assembly, Increase in Army Urged—Nazis Take Bold Tone in Ecuador

Special Cable to THE NEW YORK TIMES.

MONTEVIDEO, Uruguay, May 29—The Uruguayan Government is frankly alarmed over Nazi fifth column activities.

After several Cabinet meetings at which the problem was closely studied, President Alfredo Baldomir has sent to Congress, with a request for urgent action, two bills. One provides for general rearmament and the other modifies Article 38 of the Constitution, which guarantees the right of assembly.

It has been rumored in well-informed diplomatic circles in more than one South American capital yesterday and today that Uruguay fears an invasion of Nazi fifth columnists from Southern Brazil. Official circles tonight emphatically denied any such fear and also denied that Uruguay had requested assistance from any other government.

The President's office earlier in the day, however, had published the details of the plans for rearmament and for modifying the constitutional guarantees.

Article 38 of the Constitution says that "all persons have a right to form themselves into associations," whatever may be the object sought, except they do not constitute an association declared by law to be illicit.

Since the law doesn't define what constitutes an illicit association, the bill that President Baldomir sent to Congress yesterday defines such il-

Continued on Page Six

ITALY BARS IMPORTS EXCEPT BY BARTER

Cancels Permits to Bring In Goods or to Buy Exchange for Payments Abroad

By HERBERT L. MATTHEWS
By Telephone to THE NEW YORK TIMES.

ROME, May 29—The Ministry of Foreign Exchange issued an order today to all banks and industrial firms canceling permits for importation and permission to acquire foreign currency to pay for imports. Thus Italy cuts herself off commercially from the world, except for barter agreements, and even there Italian ships coming in are not departing to bring back further imports.

This is the most serious indication yet given of the expectation of war, certainly as serious as the postponement of the sailing of Italian vessels announced last Friday.

The Conte di Savoia is due back from New York Sunday. No one expects her to depart, even on June 23, when she is scheduled to go. That will leave only the Conte Grande out of the Mediterranean among the large Italian ships. She sailed for South America a week ago.

[The steamship Roma arrived yesterday at Naples, according to The Associated Press, and is now expected to remain there instead of proceeding to Genoa, as scheduled. The Roma was to have left Genoa for New York June 29.]

Trade with the United States will suffer most heavily by the decision taken today. It has been possible for importers to acquire dollars at

Continued on Page Four

NAZIS TIGHTEN TRAP

They Drive a Line Across Pocket, Encircling Foes in South

SAY YPRES IS TAKEN

Zeebrugge and Ostend Fall—Large Stores Are Reported Seized

By GEORGE AXELSSON
Wireless to THE NEW YORK TIMES.

BERLIN, May 29—Remnants of the Allied Armies cut off in Flanders came a step nearer to being wiped out today when the Germans, simultaneously pressing from east and west toward the middle, managed to drive a wedge right across the pocket, thus separating the French and British divisions north of Lille from those in the south, who now are surrounded on all sides, no longer having access to the sea.

The Germans tonight claim to be in the city of Lille, in Ypres and Armentières and to have burned Dunkerque under heavy artillery bombardment. The Belgian capitulation permitted the Germans to take Bruges, Zeebrugge, Ostend and Thourout without a struggle.

Piercing the Allied lines at Lille, where, however, fortifications still seem to hold out, permitted the Germans to make two pockets out of the big one. The smaller of these, south of Lille, is square with the sides between nine and twelve miles long, and inside this narrow space are compressed the French divisions that only a few days ago tried to break the strong German hold at Valenciènnes, as well as British contingents that figured in desperate resistance in the sector between Arras and Cambrai.

Refugees Also in Trap

Hemmed in with these troops is an incalculable number of refugees and other civilians, who are exposed to bombs and shell fire on the same terms as the soldiers fighting one another in this area.

The larger northern pocket reaches from Lille to the sea, and although it is some thirty miles wide the situation of the troops enclosed in it appears to be hardly more enviable than that of their comrades surrounded to the south. They are being hard pressed on three sides by withering German fire as well as from the air.

Their only chance of retreat, should they choose this way out, seems to be the narrow strip of coast between Dunkerque and Nieuport, but the Germans are said to be continuously shelling and bombing this district, making an exit, even if protected by Allied warships, seem most difficult.

Crowded together in an area bounded by Dixmude, Ypres—which the Germans claim to have taken by storm tonight—Armentières, Bailleul and Bergues, remnants of the British Expeditionary Force and whatever French and Belgians remain thereabout appear to have a choice only between death or surrender.

The situation up there, according to latest reports received in Berlin, indicates that the Allies have chosen to fight to the last. The Germans stand before Dixmude, where the British are holding them, and a similarly bitter struggle is raging at

Continued on Page Four

11,000 Times Speedier Way Found To Obtain Atomic Power Element

By WILLIAM L. LAURENCE

Development of a process that speeds up by 11,000 times the extraction of U-235, the element recently discovered to possess 5,000,000 times the power output of coal, promising to make it possible to utilize atomic energy as a new source of enormous power for all purposes, and to place in the hands of the nations at war, especially Germany, the most powerful fuel ever to be discovered, is to be announced in the forthcoming issue of Nature, leading British scientific weekly, advance proofs of which have reached THE NEW YORK TIMES. Germany, more than any other European nation, has been concentrating on developing this power. If the tests succeed the Allied blockade could be materially offset.

The new process for extracting U-235 that promises to revolutionize methods of power production and to usher in a new civilization based on the utilization of atomic power, was developed by Professor Wilhelm Krasny-Ergen of the Wenner-Grens Institute, Stockholm, Sweden, one of the leading scientific research institutions in Europe.

On May 5 it was announced that a tiny amount of U-235, a relative of uranium, had been isolated at the University of Minnesota and at the General Electric Company, and that pioneer experiments at the physics laboratories at Columbia University, under the direction of Professor

Continued on Page Eighteen

The International Situation

On the Battle Fronts

The Battle of Flanders became yesterday a wholly rear-guard action, with the Allies trying to evacuate as many as possible of the troops caught in the German pocket. The trapped men fought on "desperately but not despairingly," Paris reported. [Page 1.]

The port of Dunkerque was still in Allied hands (although the Germans reported its embarkation area in ruins), as was Nieuport, just above the Belgian border. Ships were said to be waiting at the coast to take off the men who could get to them, although how they stayed afloat in the torrent of German bombing seemed a mystery. The British and French fleets were furiously bombarding German forces on the Channel, hoping to cover the withdrawal. The task of evacuation was made doubly difficult by a German force that, Paris reported, had straddled the Franco-Belgian border near Cassel and Mount Kemmel. The French said that defense floodgates had been opened, inundating part of the area west of the Yser. On other fronts the French asserted that they had eliminated a German bridgehead on the Somme west of Amiens, and had repulsed a German thrust near Rethel, on the left flank of the invaders. [Included in the foregoing.]

The desperate situation of the Allied army of the north was made evident by Berlin dispatches telling of the success of the German effort to cut the opposing forces in two. The invaders drove a wedge between the two Allied wings to the north of Lille. Thus there are now two pockets; the forces south of Lille are completely surrounded, in a square-shaped area whose sides measure only nine to twelve miles. The pocket above Lille was greatly reduced by German advances pressing down from the north and up from the south. [Page 1.]

Early this morning shattered remnants of the British Expeditionary Force began arriving at British ports. Most of them were wounded. To the survivors still in Flanders King George sent a message saying they had displayed "gallantry that has never been surpassed in the annals of the British Army." [Page 1.]

The Allies recorded a victory in Norway. They took Narvik, and the Germans admitted its loss. The British said their warships had sunk seven German troop transports in the Narvik area in the last three days. [Page 1.]

Repercussions Elsewhere

Britain took drastic measures to guard against possible fifth column activities on the part of aliens. Beginning June 3, all aliens must be in their "ordinary place of residence" from 10:30 P. M. to 6 A. M.; they are forbidden to own bicycles, boats or aircraft without special permission. [Page 3.]

Italy, by decreeing an end to import and foreign currency permits, cut herself off from the world commercially, except for her barter arrangements. And even they have ceased to mean anything, as Italian vessels no longer are being sent abroad for cargoes. The new regulations gave the strongest indication yet of Italy's intention to join Germany in the field soon. [Page 1.]

Because Russia had refused to accept Sir Stafford Cripps, Left-Wing Labor member of the British Parliament, as a "special trade envoy," London conferred Ambassadorial status on him. Sir Stafford is in Athens, en route to Moscow. With offers of improved trade with Britain, he will seek to woo Russia away from Germany. [Page 4.]

The Nazi fifth-column technique stirred fears in South America. Uruguay's Congress received from President Baldomir two bills, one of which would provide for rearmament, the other modifying the Constitution to deny the right of assembly to anti-democratic organizations with foreign connections. [Page 1.]

What has happened in Flanders impelled a reappraisal in Washington of American defense plans, with the result that President Roosevelt decided to ask Congress for $750,000,000 (in addition to the $3,300,000,000 already projected) to be used to buy 3,000 pursuit and bombing planes, 1,500 tanks, 500 heavy howitzers and at least $20,000,000 in aerial bombs. [Page 1.] The Senate Naval Affairs Committee, recommending House-adopted bills to speed air and naval preparedness, said the country's defense plans must be based on the possibility of defeat for the Allies. [Page 9.]

ALLIES GET NARVIK IN LAND-SEA FIGHT

Warships Support Troops in Final Thrust From Beis and Rombaks Fjords

By JAMES MacDONALD
Special Cable to THE NEW YORK TIMES.

LONDON, May 29—Narvik, Norway's important iron ore port, the prize of an unrelenting struggle ever since Germany invaded Norway on April 9, has been captured by Allied forces, the War Office and Admiralty announced in a joint communiqué today. The communiqué also announced the capture of Fagernaes, on the shore of Narvik Harbor, and Forsneset, five miles east of Narvik on the railway line over which Swedish iron ore reaches Narvik for shipment to Germany.

Fierce fighting by Norwegian, French, British and Polish forces continues in the district. An unofficial report received here today said British naval forces had sunk seven German troop transports in Narvik waters since Sunday.

British warships are reported high up in Rombaks Fjord, shelling German positions on the Ofoten railway. In a narrow part of the fjord the Germans have sunk four ships in an attempt to block off the British naval vessels.

Other reports reaching London today said German planes had raided Bodoe, at the entrance to Vest Fjord, about ninety miles south of Narvik, last evening, dropping 200 bombs and machine-gunning the town. Of the population of 6,000, it is said at least 5,000 are now

Continued on Page Five

HARRIED B. E. F. MEN ARRIVING IN BRITAIN

Many of Wounded Had to Wade Out to Boats Under Constant Fire of German Forces

By The United Press.

LONDON, Thursday, May 30—Shattered remnants of the British Expeditionary Force—blood-stained, muddy and walking like men asleep—began arriving in British ports early today.

Most of the first arrivals were wounded. They described a constant, pitiless German bombing and strafing bombardment of the French ports from which Viscount Gort is attempting to save his trapped divisions.

They said the shattered British forces were "sliding off a stretch of coast thirty miles long."

German bombs rained down continually, even on hospital ships, they said. Quays and harbor works of the French ports were under terrific German air attack, which went on all through last night.

Allied warships and the Royal Air Force worked and fought like beavers to aid the rescue of the battered armies of Flanders whose fate was teetered on the Channel's brink. Under a screen of intense curtain fire from long-range naval guns, the B. E. F. was backing out through the Dunkerque area,

Continued on Page Five

Dispatches from Europe and the Far East are subject to censorship at the source.

COAST FIGHT RAGES

Communications Lines and Bases Bombarded Constantly by Nazis

DUNKERQUE SHELLED

Allies Inflicting Heavy Losses as They Battle in Rear-Guard Actions

By G. H. ARCHAMBAULT
Wireless to THE NEW YORK TIMES.

PARIS, May 29—The full import of the Belgian defection during the course of the battle in Flanders may be gathered from the indication given tonight by a spokesman for the General Staff that King Leopold's army represented about half the Allied forces engaged on that front.

French and British in that area continue to fight desperately, though not despairingly yet, with the knowledge that at present at least little help can be given them. Their valor is described as very comforting in the circumstances, and it is added that whatever happens their honor will be safe.

Breaking the anonymity rule that has prevailed hitherto, it is announced this evening that, under General Georges Maurice Jean Blanchard's direction, General René-Jacques-Adolf Prioux is striving to fight his way to the coast in the general direction of Dunkerque, where Vice Admiral Jean Marie Abrial of the French Navy is cooperating and is holding that base, where he has organized a service of supplies with vessels of all kinds of tonnage.

Prioux a Cavalry Man

General Prioux was a corps commander at the beginning of the war; he is sixty-one years of age and comes from the cavalry arm.

No one has yet come from that inferno in Flanders to describe the scene; doubtless it baffles the imagination. For the battle is being waged on land, in the air, on the sea and under the sea. Every engine of death yet devised by man is in action and the fight never ceases day or night. Nor is it confined to the actual battlefield. All bases, all lines of communication are bombed continually on both sides, with the Germans concentrating a great effort on Dunkerque.

The communiqué issued from French General Headquarters this morning said that "information from accurate sources warrants the affirmation that the losses suffered by the Germans in the engagements yesterday and last night were particularly high."

The French and British are fighting mostly rear-guard actions against very superior numbers, but whenever any unit finds itself in approximately equal strength it counter-attacks "to progress over the enemy dead."

Position Very Critical

Nevertheless despite heroic deeds it cannot be gainsaid that the position of the Allied division is very critical.

The exact position of General Blanchard's forces is not known; his front in any case must be very fluid. Doubtless he has shortened his lines in order to constitute a sort of mobile fortress moving toward the sea and fighting every inch of the way. The tragic aspect of his situation lies in the fact that the prime task of Leopold's army was to cover the coast.

It is revealed today in this connection that it was at the Belgian King's repeated insistence that the Allies took up positions on the Scheldt to protect Antwerp and also that the order to retreat was deferred until May 15, although the Allied High Command had urged withdrawal on the eleventh or twelfth.

There is confirmation today of the indication given yesterday in these dispatches that before the capitulation there were French detachments between the Belgians and the sea. It is hoped that though relatively small they may have acted effectively along the coast. It is believed, moreover, that it has been possible to flood part of the country west of the Yser River. Water lines of this sort proved of great value in the last war in this very region.

On the coast the Allies have lost Ostend. They hold Nieuport and

Continued on Page Two

"All the News That's Fit to Print."

The New York Times.

LATE CITY EDITION
Cloudy with showers and little change in temperature today and tomorrow.
Temperature Yesterday—Max., 65; Min., 57

VOL. LXXXIX..No. 30,089. Entered as Second-Class Matter, Postoffice, New York, N. Y. NEW YORK, TUESDAY, JUNE 11, 1940. THREE CENTS NEW YORK CITY and Vicinity | FOUR CENTS Elsewhere Except in 7th and 8th Postal Zones.

ITALY AT WAR, READY TO ATTACK; STAB IN BACK, SAYS ROOSEVELT; GOVERNMENT HAS LEFT PARIS

NAZIS NEAR PARIS

Units Reported to Have Broken Through Lines to West of Capital

SEINE RIVER CROSSED

3 Columns Branch Out From Soissons—Enemy Held, French State

By The Associated Press.

PARIS, June 10—Marauding German tanks were reported tonight to have reached the Paris region itself as the government left the capital.

While some German armored advance guards were said to have penetrated to the environs of Paris in isolated raids through the French lines, the main front was about thirty-five miles west and northeast of the capital. Although steadily approaching, the battle's roar still could not be heard here.

[The German High Command has no knowledge that Nazi tank units have reached the Paris region, The United Press reported.]

The battle, which had been waged heretofore on familiar World War territory for the most part, swung into virgin soil as the Germans advanced west of Paris.

In the triangle bounded by Amiens on the Somme, Rouen, seventy miles west of Paris on the Seine, and Vernon, forty miles west on the Seine, the Germans redoubled their attacks, crossing the river at several points. An armored column, which crossed the Bresle last week, led the assault.

The French took their main stand west of Paris all along the Seine in an effort to prevent the Germans from effecting further passages and taking the capital from the rear.

In the central sector of the Oise Valley, directly north of Paris where the Germans had suffered tremendous losses, they held back their infantry and sent out dive bombers in an effort to break down French resistance.

They broadened their salient, however, farther east, where they had crossed the Aisne. Three columns fanned out from Soissons through La Ferte Milon and Fere en Tardenois and toward Fismes.

Hold Firm on East Flank

They were just north of Chateau-Thierry and the Marne, where they were stopped in their 1918 thrust by Americans fighting with the French.

On the east flank, where the French have been holding firm, fresh German infantry, tanks and planes battered the French lines, but with small gains.

But France, besieged on two sides by Germans driving on Paris from the north and the Italians entering the war on the south, proclaimed her grim determination to carry on the fight.

The main combats were centered in the Seine Valley to the west of Paris, with the High Command declaring that some German elements had crossed the Seine River at certain points, and in the Ourcq River Valley to the northeast of the capital.

The communiqué, however, said the "enemy is held everywhere by vigorous counter-attacks."

The French communiqué was filed from Paris, but was issued "Somewhere in France." The regular press conference of the War Office was not held this morning, as only a few attachés were in the office.

The High Command reported that the German break-through to the Seine resulted from increased pressure applied by the Nazis between the route from Amiens to Rouen and from Amiens to Vernon as far as the lower Seine.

In the other principal area of combat, east of the Oise River, German columns coming down from the region of Soissons have resumed their attack toward the Ourcq River.

The German offensive in the

Continued on Page Two

The International Situation

On the Battle Fronts

Italian guns will speak today in Europe. Italy's declaration of war against France and Britain became effective at 12:01 A. M., Rome time. Before 100,000 men and women, packed in the Piazza Venezia and near-by streets, Premier Mussolini yesterday announced his decision. It was war against "the plutocratic and reactionary democracies of the West." For the present that does not include the United States, but Rome reports that few Italians, from Signor Mussolini down, believe they will see the end of this war without having America against them.

The Italian Premier specifically excluded Turkey, Switzerland, Yugoslavia, Greece and Egypt from his military designs. Rome hoped Turkey would fail to keep her agreement to support the Allies in a Mediterranean war.

Demonstrators in Rome carried placards naming Italian objectives in the war—Tunisia, Jibuti, Corsica, Suez, Malta, Cyprus. There were reports that action against some of these places already had started. But Rome was convinced that nothing big would get under way until today. [All the foregoing, Page 1, Column 3.]

The sixth day of the Battle of France brought the German invaders still closer to Paris; at one point—south of Beauvais—they were said to be within twenty-five or thirty miles of their goal. On the French left wing the Germans crossed the Seine at several points in a dangerous advance that threatened to envelop the capital. In the center, they pushed through to the Ourcq Valley, a movement that similarly threatened to flank Reims. On the French right wing the German pressure was furiously increased; but the French said no great gains had resulted. Information from the French side was less complete than usual because the government press bureau was evacuated from Paris and had not yet established a stable headquarters. [Page 1, Column 1.]

The French Government moved, apparently to the neighborhood of Tours. An exodus of civilians from Paris got under way. [Page 1, Column 2.]

Berlin analyzed the front thus: A semicircle had been thrown around Paris, from which three wedges were being driven into the defense lines. The first, in the lower Seine Valley, succeeded in cutting off the extreme left of the French Army, which can now be pushed to the coast. The second was progressing toward the Marne from the Aisne below Soissons. The third, on the French right, had pierced the Aisne and was headed toward Reims. [Page 1, Column 5.]

London admitted the loss of the airplane carrier Glorious, two destroyers, a transport and an oil tanker—totaling 50,706 tons—in an engagement in the North Sea. King Haakon of Norway arrived in Britain with his government. Some Norwegian troops also were carried off and will continue the war on the Western Front. [Page 16, Column 3.]

Repercussions Elsewhere

President Roosevelt, in a broadcast speech, termed Italy's entry into the war a threat to the American way of life. "The hand that held the dagger has struck it into the back of its neighbor," he said. Declaring it an "obvious delusion that we of the United States can safely permit the United States to become a lone island in a world dominated by the philosophy of force," he advocated all possible material aid to the Allies. [Page 1, Column 4.]

The Canadian Parliament declared war against Italy; Prime Minister Mackenzie King denounced Premier Mussolini as "a carrion bird waiting for brave men to die." [Page 4, Column 5.]

Premier Reynaud, broadcasting to the French people after Italy's announcement, said France had won out over greater difficulties in the past. He asserted France always had been willing to negotiate Italian demands peaceably. [Page 12, Column 1.]

Berlin, jubilant over the entry of the Italians, expressed the belief that Premier Mussolini's military effort would be concentrated in the Mediterranean. It was said that no immediate Italian land attack on France was expected. [Page 5, Column 1.]

Switzerland reported much military activity, but no rumble of guns, in mountain passes between France and Italy. The Swiss were concerned about rumors that there were new German troop concentrations on the country's northern frontier. [Page 5, Column 5.]

Turkey stood ready to fulfill her engagements to the Allies under the mutual-assistance pact of last October. It was believed that the first step, once Italy made that pact operative by an aggressive move in the Mediterranean, would be the placing of Turkish ports and air fields at the disposal of the Allies. [Page 1, Column 7.]

Belgrade heard reports that the Italians had landed troops and much mechanized equipment at the Italian-owned port of Zara, which is on the Yugoslav coast, and on the Italian-owned island of Lagosta, near by. [Page 1, Column 6.]

FRENCH MINISTRIES MOVED SOUTHWARD

Tours Is Believed New Capital, but Reynaud Goes to Army —No Civilian Panio

By The Associated Press.

PARIS, June 10—The French Government left Paris tonight.

"Paul Reynaud, Premier, has gone with the armies," said a communiqué, which also declared:

"The High Command asked the Ministers to effect their withdrawal to the provinces in conformity with established dispositions. This withdrawal has been effected."

The announcement of the departure of the Ministers was made only after they were safely installed "somewhere in France" in the southern provinces.

The government transfer at General Maxime Weygand's request was approved last night at a Cabinet meeting.

Under cover of darkness the Ministers drove to their new offices

Continued on Page Ten

BRITISH NAVY GUNS HAMMER AT NAZIS

Shelling From Sea, Rushing of Troops and Planes Mark London's Share in Battle

By HAROLD DENNY
Special Cable to THE NEW YORK TIMES.

LONDON, June 10—Britain was rushing all available forces today into the battle in France, which was officially called here the "Battle of Paris and London" because of the Nazi threat to England. This reinforcement across the English Channel will continue, it was stated, "despite the imminent danger of German invasion of the United Kingdom."

The guns of British warships pounded the Germans to support Allied troops near the coast.

"Important contingents" of new troops have already gone to France, it was announced.

Even closer cooperation of the

Continued on Page Twelve

OUR HELP PLEDGED

President Offers Our Full Material Aid to Allies' Cause

AMERICA IN DANGER

Fate Hangs on Training and Arms, He Says at Charlottesville

The text of the President's speech will be found on Page 6.

By FELIX BELAIR Jr.
Special to THE NEW YORK TIMES.

CHARLOTTESVILLE, Va., June 10—"On this 10th day of June, 1940, the hand that held the dagger has struck it into the back of its neighbor." In these words tonight President Roosevelt condemned the decision of Premier Mussolini which took Italy into the war on the side of Germany.

The remark was interpolated by the President in an address at the graduation exercises of the University of Virginia here. There could be no missing the depth of his feeling, since he put into the words all the emphasis at his command.

Italy's intervention was denounced furthermore as a definite threat to the way of life and the trade and commerce of the Americas. This government, he said, would give all material aid to France and Great Britain as "opponents of force."

The Chief Executive of the United States spoke to the nation and to the world only a few hours after Premier Mussolini announced his decision to join hands with Chancellor Hitler and unleashed his fascist legions against France and Great Britain. More details were revealed by Mr. Roosevelt of his correspondence with the Italian dictator in an effort to keep Italy at peace and to prevent the spread of war to the Mediterranean basin.

"To the Regret of Humanity"

"Unfortunately—unfortunately, to the regret of all of us and to the regret of humanity—the chief of the Italian Government was unwilling to accept the procedure suggested, and he has made no counter proposal," the President said.

And a moment later:

"The Government of Italy has now chosen to preserve what it terms its freedom of action and to fulfill what it states are its promises to Germany. In so doing it has manifested disregard for the rights and security of other nations, disregard for the lives of the peoples of those nations which are directly threatened by the spread of this war, and has evidenced its unwillingness to find the means, through pacific negotiation, for the satisfaction of what it believes are its legitimate aspirations."

The President bespoke the prayers and hopes of this nation for those peoples beyond the seas who were battling for their freedom.

"In our American unity," he

Continued on Page Six

Nazi Tide Laps at Paris as Italy Joins War

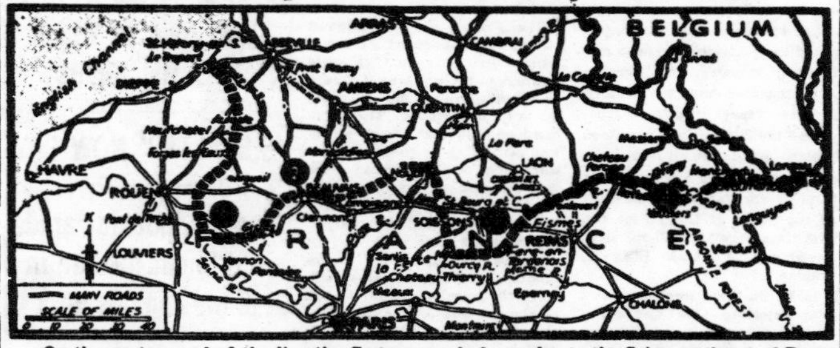

On the western end of the line the Germans pushed a wedge to the Seine southeast of Rouen (1) and struck mighty blows in the region of Beauvais (2). In the center they reached the Ourcq River below Soissons (3). To the east they crossed the Aisne at two points near Vouziers (4).

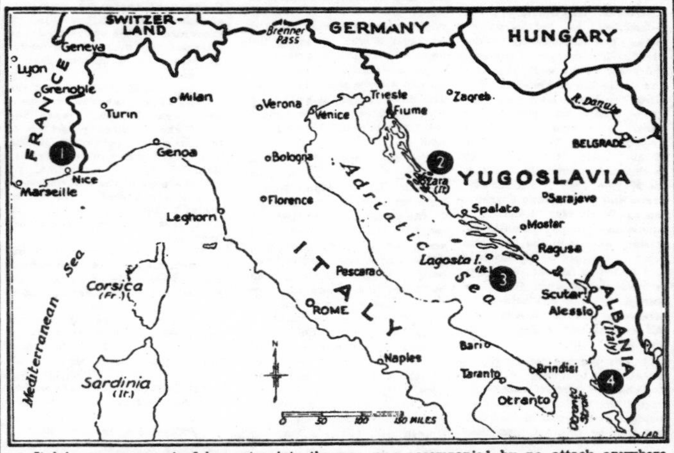

Italy's announcement of her entry into the war was accompanied by no attack anywhere. One report had Italian troops invading the French Riviera (1), but this was unsupported. Rome's troops landed at two Italian-owned points on the Yugoslav coast: Zara (2) and Lagosta (3). In Albania (4) Italian military preparations were accelerated.

NAZIS CLAIM BREAK IN SUPPLY ARTERY

Paris Cut Off From Havre by Thrust to Seine East of Rouen, Berlin Says

By C. BROOKS PETERS
Wireless to THE NEW YORK TIMES.

BERLIN, June 10—German forces in Northern France were fighting tonight to shorten the radius of a semicircle they are drawing about Paris, according to reports received here. Apparently they are attempting to drive three wedges into the remaining French territory north of the capital.

The first is on the Germans' extreme right wing, which is reported to have reached the lower Seine east of Rouen and therewith cuts off Paris from Havre. Mass tank formations, assisted by light motorized units, are claimed here to have made more than a sixty-mile ad-

Continued on Page Eleven

Three Italian Freighters Are Scuttled by Crews

By The Associated Press.

LA LINEA, Spain, Tuesday, June 11—Two Italian merchant ships, the 10,000-ton Chelina and the 2,000-ton Numbolia, were scuttled by their crews in Gibraltar waters late yesterday [Monday] when their crews heard the radio news that Italy had gone to war.

RIMOUSKI, Que., June 10 (UP)—The 3,921-ton Italian freighter Capo Noli was set afire by her crew tonight as she proceeded down the St. Lawrence, but the scuttling attempt failed.

The Marine Department said the Canadian pilot grounded the freighter near the Father Point pilot station. A naval control boat extinguished the flames.

The government salvage boat Lord Strathcona left Quebec tonight for the site with a large derrick in tow. The Capo Noli will be taken over by the Canadian Government and her crew probably will be interned.

ITALIANS REPORTED ON YUGOSLAV COAST

Said to Have Landed at Two Places Controlled by Rome—Mass on Greek Border

By The United Press.

BELGRADE, Yugoslavia, Tuesday, June 11—Large numbers of Italian troops were reported early today to have been landed along the Yugoslav coast at two Italian points as the Yugoslav Government prepared to fight in defense of its territory if necessary.

[It was reported from Berlin yesterday that Italian forces had invaded France through the Riviera, but this was denied in Rome, and German military quarters said later that they had no knowledge of any such movement.]

Reports from Split on the Adriatic coast said that large forces of Italian troops had been landed at

Continued on Page Four

La Guardia Warns of Strict Neutrality Here; Consuls Told to 'Adhere to Consular Duties'

Mayor La Guardia went on the air over WNYC, the city broadcasting station, yesterday afternoon with a strong plea to the million persons of Italian blood in this city to preserve strict neutrality in the face of Italy's declaration of war.

Moving with characteristic rapidity, the Mayor telephoned the city broadcasting studio in the New York City Building at the World's Fair and said he would be on the air ten minutes later. He thought over the message he wanted to deliver while driving over from the World's Fair City Hall, and was prepared to speak immediately upon his arrival. Meantime, Morris S. Novik, director of the station, had made arrangements to rebroadcast the Mayor's talk over five commercial stations at intervals later in the day.

Speaking slowly and impressively, the Mayor stated his policy that the European war must be fought on the battlefields of Europe and not on the sidewalks of New York.

Recalling his war service as an ally of the Italian forces in Italy, the Mayor said he fully realized that the Italian entry into the war on the opposite side must be as painful to others of Italian blood as it was to him. Nevertheless, he insisted that the national policy of neutrality must be observed in the city. While he pledged full protection to consular officers of various European governments in the city, the Mayor made clear that these officials must stay within the bounds of their consular duties.

The Mayor's speech follows:

This is F. H. La Guardia, Mayor of the City of New York, talking.

On Sept. 2, 1939, when the Nazi

Continued on Page Eight

TURKEY PREPARES UNDER ALLIED PACT

Partial Mobilization Expected Today—Troops Are on Move —Precautions in Balkans

By J. W. KERNICK
Special Cable to THE NEW YORK TIMES.

ISTANBUL, Turkey, June 10—Turkey, speeding her military preparations as a result of Italy's entry into the war, stood ready tonight to fulfill her obligations under her mutual-assistance agreement with Britain and France.

That accord, concluded last October, stipulates that Turkey will lend the Allies every assistance in her power in the event of hostilities in the Mediterranean as a result of aggressive action by a European power. Hence Turkish aid can be invoked as soon as the first shot is fired.

The Italian action has already resulted in the calling of several classes to the colors by the Turkish Government. It is believed that the next move will be to place ports and airfields at the disposal of the Allies.

[The Turkish Cabinet met last night to consider the question of war or peace, The Associated Press reported, but it was believed that Turkey's entrance into the war would be by gradual steps, not immediately.]

Italy's declaration of war caused neither surprise nor excitement in Turkey. The Turks had suspected for some time and lately became certain that Premier Mussolini could not forever remain an onlooker while Chancellor Hitler marched.

Premier Mussolini's assurances that he did not intend to attack Yugoslavia, Turkey, Greece, Switz-

Continued on Page Two

Dispatches from Europe and the Far East are subject to censorship at the source.

DUCE GIVES SIGNAL

Announces War on the 'Plutocratic' Nations of the West

ASSURES 5 NEUTRALS

Bid Is Made to Russia, But Rome Has No Pledge of Aid

'Hostilities' Are Reported

"Hostilities were started four hours ago, Central European time," Radio Roma, the official Italian short-wave radio, said last night at 11 o'clock Eastern daylight time in a broadcast recorded by Columbia Broadcasting System's short-wave listening station.

"The first Italian war bulletin is expected to be issued within a few hours."

At 2:18 A. M. today, however, the official British wireless said that "there have been no reports as yet of any engagements growing out of Italy's entrance into the war," Columbia's listening station reported.

By HERBERT L. MATTHEWS
By Telephone to THE NEW YORK TIMES.

ROME, Tuesday, June 11—Italy declared war on Great Britain and France yesterday afternoon, to take effect at one minute past midnight. The land, air and sea forces of the Italian Empire were already in motion.

It is a war, as Premier Benito Mussolini announced to the people from his balcony at the Palazzo Venezia at 6 in the evening, against the "plutocratic and reactionary democracies of the West." For the moment that does not include the United States, but few Italians believe that they will see the war to a finish without having the Americans against them.

Signor Mussolini expressly excluded Turkey, Switzerland, Yugoslavia, Greece and Egypt as enemies unless they attacked Italy or the Italian possessions.

Turkey provides the burning question of the day. Italians are absolutely convinced that the Turks will not move against them and will not honor their agreement with the Allies. It is hoped to confine Italian activity to France, Great Britain and the Mediterranean and to keep the Balkans tranquil. If that can be done, Italians think, the Turks will remain quiet.

Soviet Action Discounted

Russia has washed her hands of the struggle. The Italians know that any disturbance in the Balkans will immediately bring her in; but as long as the struggle is confined to the west and south the Soviet will do nothing either to hinder or help. This was told to your correspondent a few hours ago by a very authoritative source.

It was emphasized there were no agreements about furnishing material or anything else, nor any threats or promises.

The Italian Ambassador, Augusto Rosso, left in the morning for Moscow and Ivan Gorelkin, Soviet Ambassador, is coming back to Rome, thus ending a long period without such representation. The Italians were anxious to restore full diplomatic relations in this critical period, according to this writer's informant, and the Russians agreed, but without compromising themselves.

It thus appears that Premier Mussolini has embarked on this dangerous venture without really knowing what Soviet Russia will do in the long run.

President Roosevelt's speech clearly has come too late. There was nothing that the United States could do to halt this conflict, the Italians say. Whatever brake Mr. Roosevelt may have exercised was overcome by the momentum of the whole Fascist policy. Once it was set in motion, nothing could stop it.

The Italians do not believe that the United States can affect the issue, whatever it does. They are

Continued on Page Four

"All the News That's Fit to Print."

The New York Times.

LATE CITY EDITION
Partly cloudy, warmer today, followed by showers tonight. Tomorrow fair, temperature unchanged.
Temperatures Yesterday—Max., 78; Min., 65

VOL. LXXXIX...No. 30,093. Entered as Second-Class Matter, Postoffice, New York, N. Y. NEW YORK, SATURDAY, JUNE 15, 1940. THREE CENTS NEW YORK CITY and Vicinity | FOUR CENTS Elsewhere Except in 7th and 8th Postal Zones.

GERMANS OCCUPY PARIS, PRESS ON SOUTH; CAPTURE HAVRE, ASSAULT MAGINOT LINE; FRENCH ARMY INTACT; SPAIN SEIZES TANGIER

HITLER IS DOUBTED

Roosevelt Skeptical of Pledge He Will Not Cross Atlantic

HAS RECOLLECTIONS

U. S. Doing All It Can for Allies, He Asserts of French Appeal

By FELIX BELAIR Jr.
Special to THE NEW YORK TIMES.

WASHINGTON, June 14—President Roosevelt replied today to Adolf Hitler's reported denial of territorial aspirations in the Western Hemisphere with a reference to the German Chancellor's record of broken pledges to respect the integrity of European nations over a considerable period of time.

As a part of the same answer the President said the United States was doing and would continue to do everything in its power to give aid to the Allies. He said, in effect, that Chancellor Hitler's statement in an interview that he would confine his activities to Europe was to be taken with considerable quantities of salt.

The President followed up this with an announcement of plans to mobilize American scientific genius in the interest of national defense.

"That brings recollections," the President said when asked at his press conference for his reaction to statements credited to the German Chancellor in an interview published in Hearst newspapers today. Reporters were not permitted to quote directly the rest of the President's statement, in which he said his observation might be enlarged upon with dates and nations going back over quite a period of years.

Many Rumors in Washington

Mr. Roosevelt's press conference remark was the high point of a day in which Washington was thick with rumors of the formation of a new French Cabinet without Premier Reynaud, that France would soon seek a separate peace with the Germans and that the President had been asked by France or Great Britain to propose a declaration of war against the Nazi government.

Both the White House and State Department denied that any proposal had been received from the Allied governments that the United States declare war.

Secretary Hull was asked in connection with the French situation whether the question of a declaration of war by the United States had been projected or raised in any way. He replied that so far as he knew nothing was involved beyond the sale of supplies, under terms and conditions that every one knew.

The question was asked of the Secretary of State at his press conference, which was held at 1 o'clock. Mr. Hull said the appeal Premier Reynaud made to President Roosevelt was then being decoded, that he had not seen it, but he understood it was the same that the French Premier gave by radio last night. Later the French Ambassador, Count de Saint-Quentin, said he assumed it was that or its equivalent.

Day's Other Developments

These other developments in the legislative and executive branches during the day stood out:

1. The President let it be known, by inference, that no accumulation of circumstances in the European war would alter this country's determination to arm to the teeth.

2. The House passed and sent to the Senate a bill authorizing the Reconstruction Finance Corporation to organize and lend money to corporations for plant expansion and acquisition of strategic materials for nationl defense.

3. State Department officials made no secret of their belief that France would soon undertake negotiations with Germany looking to a separate peace and that reorganization of the French Government probably would be attempted with this in mind.

4. Administration sources said legislation would be introduced next week to embargo exports of scrap iron as a measure of national defense.

5. Attorney General Jackson

Continued on Page Ten

The International Situation

On the Battle Fronts

Paris was taken over yesterday by the German war machine.

Led by dust-stained tanks, followed by motorized divisions and then by infantry, the German Army marched down the Champs Elysées. Tense, grim-faced Parisians—the few who had remained behind—stood silently on the curbs as a hostile force marched through the famous boulevards of the "City of Light" for the first time since 1871. Shops were closed and shuttered. [Page 1, Column 7.]

In Berlin there were scenes of wild rejoicing. On Chancellor Hitler's orders church bells were rung for a quarter of an hour and the Nazi flag was ordered displayed for three days. [Page 2, Column 2.]

Berlin said that the fall of Paris—described as "catastrophic" morally and economically for the French—had completed the second phase of the war. The first was the Battle of Flanders. The third, the High Command communiqué said, was pursuit and "final destruction" of all the French forces. The chief drive of this "final" phase appeared to be directed against the flank of the Maginot Line through Champagne and the Argonne Forest—famous World War battlefield of American troops. Montmédy, western anchor of the line, was reported conquered. Spearheads had driven as far east as Vitry-le François, between Paris and Nancy. Verdun was said to be threatened. On the coast Havre's fall was claimed. [Page 1, Column 8.]

Hitler's personal press representative in the field with him said that the German leader considered the fall of Paris only an incident on his road of conquest and that he was not interested in peace now. [Page 2, Column 8.]

The French High Command said it had abandoned Paris because there was no "valuable strategical reason" why it should be defended and it did not want the city devastated. The communiqué said the French Army was retreating in good order. A slackening of the German drive was reported at several points, but the heavy push in Champagne, threatening the rear of the Maginot Line, was still in progress. The armament of the line is useless against an attack from the rear. A frontal attack on the line west of the Saar was reported repulsed. [Page 1, Column 5.]

High sources in London said that Britain had agreed to accept any military or political decision the French Government might make but would fight on whatever it was. [Page 1, Column 6.] If the war is to be waged successfully, however, informed sources said, every available piece of war material in the United States must be sent to the Allies at once. [Page 1, Column 4.]

The war appeared to be developing for Italy. First reports of action on her Alpine frontier were reported in a communiqué. It was divulged for the first time, too, that the Italian fleet was at sea in force. [Page 1, Column 3.] Attacks in Africa were reported, both by the Italian air arm and by Allied troops against Libya, Eritrea and Ethiopia. Successes were claimed by the Italians in all actions. [Page 4, Column 1.]

The French Government abandoned Tours as its provisional capital and started southward, apparently for the port of Bordeaux. It was the seat of the French Government for a short time in 1914. [Page 1, Column 6.]

Repercussions Elsewhere

Spanish troops yesterday took over control of Tangier, the small internationally-policed territory in Northern Africa fronting on the Straits of Gibraltar. Madrid said the action had been taken to "guarantee its neutrality" and had been done with the full consent of the other three guarantors—Britain, France and Italy. Berlin said the consent of the Allies was given after the act. Return of Tangier has been one of the most frequently expressed territorial demands of Franco-Spain. That of British-held Gibraltar is the other. [Page 1, Column 4.] In Washington Secretary Hull said the United States would insist on its extraterritorial rights in Tangier under the treaty of 1906. [Follows the foregoing.]

"That brings up recollections," President Roosevelt said at his press conference when a purported interview with Chancellor Hitler was shown to him quoting the German leader as saying he had no aspirations in this hemisphere. The President's reference was to similar statements made about European countries. Driving ahead with the American defense program, the President announced the appointment of a scientific research commission to work with the defense advisory commission. [Page 1, Column 1.]

COLONNA PROTESTS ON ITALIAN CHARGES

Envoy Sees Hull—Inquiry Here Widened—German Agent to U. S. Warns of Reprisals

Special to THE NEW YORK TIMES.

WASHINGTON, June 14—The Italian Ambassador, Don Ascanio dei Principi Colonna, protested to Secretary of State Cordell Hull today what he considered to be an unjustified effort to foment anti-Italian feeling in the United States.

The protest was directed specifically to the charges made in New York yesterday that the Italian Consulate General there, under orders of Premier Benito Mussolini, was seeking to promote fascism in this country by ideological propaganda. He also implied there were similar activities against Italy in other American cities.

His concern was especially manifested over publication of these charges by newspapers. The fact that the New York charges were issued through Police Commissioner Valentine apparently was not mentioned. No reference was made directly to President Roosevelt's Charlottesville address denouncing Italy.

In making the protest, Prince Colonna declared that Italian consuls in this country restrict their activities to their legal functions and that Italian nationals in the United States are careful to avoid

Continued on Page Nine

ITALIANS IN CLASH ON FRENCH BORDER

Report Attack Repulsed—Fleet Action Revealed—Coast Is Shelled

By HERBERT L. MATTHEWS
By Telephone to THE NEW YORK TIMES.

ROME, June 14—The war began to develop for Italy on land, sea and air, according to this morning's communiqué, with the first activity on the Italo-French frontier and an indication that the Italian Fleet was on its way on some great mission.

The taking of Tangier by the Spaniards is considered a first-rate victory for the Axis, but, of course, the fall of Paris dominates everything else.

Among Fascisti here there is rejoicing over the fate of Paris. The newspaper Lavoro Fascista cheers in an eight-column box whose sentiments are typical.

"C'est Paris," it says. "Capitalists, Jews, Masons and snobs all over the world are in mourning. The spiritual capital of all the old civilization has fallen. Paris has fallen. Paris itself 'la ville lumière—Paris tout entier.' "

As the war shapes up, even this early, the Mediterranean seems more than ever certain to become Italy's main theatre of operations. To be sure, there was some activity for the first time yesterday on the French frontier. There were clashes by patrols and "enemy, al-

Continued on Page Four

MOROCCANS MOVE IN

Spanish Troops Take Over Zone in Which U. S. Has Rights

'GIBRALTAR' NOW CRY

Madrid Students Parade and Shout for Return of the Famous Rock

By T. J. HAMILTON
Special Cable to THE NEW YORK TIMES.

MADRID, June 14—The Spanish Government announced early this afternoon that with the object of guaranteeing "the neutrality of the international zone" in Morocco, Moroccan troops entered Tangier this morning.

It was stated officially that the action had been taken in agreement with Great Britain, France and Italy, who are other guarantors of the zone under a convention of 1903. The United States, which is also a signatory to the convention, received a copy of the announcement in a note delivered to the United States Embassy here at 11 A. M.

The text of the communiqué follows:

"With the object of guaranteeing the neutrality of the international zone and the city of Tangier, the Spanish Government has decided to take charge provisionally of the surveillance, police and public safety services of the international zone; forces of Moroccan troops entered this morning with this object.

"All existing services are assured and they continue functioning normally."

Coveted by the Spanish

Next to Gibraltar, Tangier occupies the front rank in Spanish territorial aims. In the last few days newspapers have devoted special attention to it among African territories that the French, assertedly with the connivance of the British, took away from Spain.

Although the first extra newspapers did not appear on the streets until 4 P. M., word that Tangier had been occupied spread quickly. By noon flags were appearing on houses throughout Madrid and members of the Falange youth movement were marching in uniform through the streets.

The news helped to bring an extra welcome for General Franco when he arrived late in the afternoon to open an exposition showing accomplishments of the government in rebuilding devastated regions. The press confined itself to printing the text of the government communiqué and relating the history of the international zone.

However, there were four demonstrations during the day, in which university student Falangistas predominated, all shouting, "Tangier is ours!" Some of these demonstrations passed the French and British Embassies.

British circles emphasized tonight that the occupation of Tangier had taken place with the complete agreement of Britain and France, who along with Italy and Spain were guarantors of the interna-

Continued on Page Six

FRENCH NOTE LULL

Battle Continues Along Front—At Some Points Its Violence Abates

ATTACK IS REPULSED

Nazi Losses Are Heavy in Maginot Assault—Loire Next Barrier

By G. H. ARCHAMBAULT
Wireless to THE NEW YORK TIMES.

TOURS, France, June 14—Is there any significance in the fact that although the battle continued to be waged today all along the front from the coast to the Argonne, it was notable that at certain points its violence was abating?

That question is in every mind tonight, for it may contain confirmation of the belief that the Germans have now engaged the maximum of their available forces.

The communiqué issued tonight gives little information on the day's operations, but it implies that all the retreating French forces continue to fight rear-guard actions and that at several parts of the front they have, in addition, counter-attacked the advancing Germans.

The only reference to Paris is as follows: "The prescribed withdrawal has been effected in conformity with our plans."

But if there has been a relative lull on the main line of battle the Germans were very active in front of the Maginot Line, especially west of the Saar River. Early in the morning they launched a violent attack with the now customary accompaniment of tanks and dive-bombing planes. The French claim to have thrown back the attacking force, on which they inflicted heavy losses.

Present Front Uncertain

Manifestly this attack must be considered in correlation with the fighting in the Argonne, farther to the west.

It is impossible tonight to indicate the present front even approximately. It is really one long line of pockets and salients, a situation calling for great qualities of generalship in order to preserve cohesion of the French forces.

Meanwhile, with the withdrawal of the French troops charged with the defense of Paris the first phase of the Battle of France was ended in defeat. It may be called the Battle of the Seine. The next phase may be the Battle of the Loire.

The issue was clear from the moment it was decided to declare Paris an open city and the news of withdrawal cannot have surprised many. A communiqué issued this morning from French General Headquarters explained that there were insufficient strategic reasons for defending the capital to justify risking destruction of France's very heart.

From the military point of view it is clear now that a battle for Paris would merely have immobilized troops, added to the loss of life and brought about no com-

Continued on Page Three

British Call on U. S. for Munitions at Once; French Order 120 Bombers Here for 1941

By RAYMOND DANIELL
Special Cable to THE NEW YORK TIMES

LONDON, June 14—In circles close to the government it was said today that every gun, every ounce of war materials that the United States can spare was needed urgently and needed quickly if the cause for which the Allies were fighting was not to be lost on the battlefields of France. It is not a matter of months but of weeks, even days, it was added by those in a position to know the facts, of which the ordinary people in this country only now are becoming dimly aware.

Withdrawal of the battered French armies behind their abandoned capital and contemplation of the possibility that the Government of France may be forced to withdraw from Europe to Africa, led to expressions that made increasingly apparent the extent to which the

After the Anglo-French Purchasing Commission yesterday had announced that French purchases of war material in the United States were being stepped up, the French signed a contract at 7 P. M. for 120 "flying fortresses" to be delivered in the second and third quarters of 1941. The planes are to be built by the Consolidated Aircraft Corporation.

In an interview earlier in the day a spokesman for the Anglo-French commission said that contracts for "many millions of dollars" had been placed during the day.

Instead of curtailing purchases following the capture of Paris by the Germans, France is sending more purchasing experts, this spokesman said. In response to a question relative to the ability to pay cash for purchases, he added:

"There is no immediate end of our

Continued on Page Four

Will Fight On, British Insist, Even if the French Capitulate

London Letting Ally Make Decision on the Immediate Course as Help Is Speeded—New Nazi Peace Offensive Expected

By The United Press.

LONDON, June 14—Britain has agreed to accept any decision France may make regarding military and political policy, but if France is lost as an ally the British will fight on alone against Chancellor Hitler's war machine, it was understood tonight.

The British Government was understood to have agreed this week to any choice the French Government might make in regard to these military and political matters, which weigh more heavily with each hour of Germany's increased drive, provided the choice had the approval of Generalissimo Maxime Weygand.

Foreign observers in London today regarded the German assault against the Maginot Line, particularly the strong flanking attack south of Montmedy around Vitry-le-François, as of far greater strategic importance than yesterday's German occupation of undefended Paris. Nevertheless, the psychological importance of the fall of Paris and the effect on French morale are not underestimated.

The impression prevails in foreign embassies in London that Herr Hitler would respond affirmatively to any possible French peace overture, but would impose harsh conditions as his price for ending the war in France. These conditions, it was felt, might range from dismantling the $500,000,000 Maginot Line to the return to Germany of Alsace-Lorraine and other territorial and economic and financial concessions.

There are strong indications, however, that Herr Hitler would refuse to negotiate with Britain, since he is intent on smashing Britain's financial and industrial power.

How far Germany would be prepared to bid for a completely Nazi-dictated peace presumably would depend upon the extent of the German losses suffered in the war.

If Britain should be compelled to fight on alone without France as an ally she would be able, it is felt in British quarters, to carry on until Autumn with United States aid. The British Navy is relatively intact despite Germany's claims to the contrary. Then, it is asserted, starvation might seriously menace Germany and Italy during the Winter, impairing their military strength and the security of their home fronts.

British morale appears to be firm,

Continued on Page Five

TOURS ABANDONED AS FRENCH CAPITAL

Government Is Expected to Make Seat at Bordeaux—U. S. Move Is Awaited

By P. J. PHILIP
Wireless to THE NEW YORK TIMES.

TOURS, France, June 14—Tours has ceased to be the substitute capital of France after a brief three-day career. Premier Paul Reynaud's speech last night and other symptoms showed clearly before we went to bed that that would be so.

There were already signs of packing up again in different administrations. Sleep seemed, however, more urgent than flight, especially as we ourselves had just obtained a bed—the first we had slept in since Sunday. In that we were luckier than most, although it does seem expensive to have had only one night's sleep in a two-room apartment rented for a month. However, it permitted a proper wash and a change of linen.

And now we and everybody else are on our way again. We don't know what is happening because the information service installed here with so much trouble on Monday has opened its wings and fled with a part of the censorship service. Press Wireless is functioning for a few hours and then good-bye to Tours.

Avalanche Advancing

The morning communiqué told the story of why this should be so—in part at least. The avalanche is advancing from all sides, closing around Paris and pushing forward in Champagne. The problem is where to go to escape it.

During the day, while we are on the road, things are likely to happen that will change the whole situation. It is too much now to hope that they will change it in any way that can be counted as satisfactory.

Along the roads through here the stream of civilian and military cars has recommenced. The embassies and legations have already pulled out. Wherever we go is going to be so congested that the remnants of that camping outfit with which we started are going to be invaluable.

Only 5,000 American bombers and fighters flying across the Atlantic in response to Premier Reynaud's desperate appeal could restore to the French people their belief that they are not alone in this terrible fight. Words and promises and the complicated explanation of political circumstances will not suffice. They will serve only to break further the dying hope there is today in every French heart.

For the British all the French feeling is as if they were of the

Continued on Page Three

REICH TANKS CLANK IN CHAMPS-ELYSEES

Berlin Recounts Parade Into Paris—Third of Citizens Reported Remaining

By The United Press.

BERLIN, June 14—German tanks today clanked across the Seine bridges, past the Arc de Triomphe and down the tree-lined Champs Elysées into the heart of Paris at the head of the first cavalcade of invaders to enter the French capital in nearly seventy years.

Flanked by armored cars, the dust-stained tanks swung triumphantly into Paris from the northwest at the head of Nazi units occupying the "City of Light," German accounts of the event said.

It was the ninth recorded invasion of Paris and the first since Bismarck's legions trod the broad boulevards in 1871. The jubilant German press proclaimed the fall of Paris to be the "symbol of decision" in Chancellor Adolf Hitler's Western offensive.

[Berlin Nazis expected Adolf Hitler to visit Paris June 21, the twenty-first anniversary of Germany's acceptance of the Treaty of Versailles, an Associated Press dispatch said.]

Entry From Northwest

The advance into Paris, through the suburbs of Argenteuil and Neuilly and into the aristocratic western part of the city began early in the morning, the Germans said. It was exactly five weeks after the massive western offensive began with the German drive into the Netherlands and Belgium.

The tanks rumbled between thin lines of tense and silent Parisians, the Germans said. Reports from the French capital estimated that probably a third of the city's normal population of 2,800,000 had remained in Paris.

Behind the tanks rolled anti-tank units, still dusty and laden with evidence of the furious fighting in which they had taken part to the north.

As the long shadows of the early morning retreated, more and more Nazi contingents streamed into the capital, evacuated by French Armies hoping to save their beloved Paris from the fate of Warsaw.

Motorized infantry, riding in steel-shielded trucks mounting machine guns to command the broad streets, converged from the Seine bridges to the Place de l'Etoile.

In that hub from which radiate eleven streets stands the Arc de Triomphe and its tomb of the Unknown World War Soldier, where flickers the Eternal Flame.

German reports indicated that the parade through Paris swung around

Continued on Page Two

2 FORCES TAKE CITY

Berlin Says Industrial Losses May Be Worst Feature for French

MONTMEDY CAPTURED

Anchor of Maginot Line Lost—Nazis Report Foe Is Routed

By C. BROOKS PETERS
Wireless to THE NEW YORK TIMES.

BERLIN, June 14—Today, for the third time within the last century and a quarter, victorious German troops marched into Paris. This time, however, the legions, the clatter of whose hobnailed boots resounds throughout Paris and the entire world, are more than just German soldiers. They are the bearers of a proposed new order for Europe and perhaps the world, a major tenet of which is to destroy the old one.

With the capitulation of Paris, the Germans claim that the destruction of the remaining French forces is but a matter of "the shortest time." Well-informed quarters in Berlin put that time at two weeks at most.

For the German High Command announced today that the second phase of the western campaign has been completed successfully, the resistance of the French northern fronts has been broken and the enemy is "in full retreat along the entire front from Paris to the Maginot Line near Sedan."

Retreat Called Rout

If the statements of German military officials in Berlin are correct, this "full retreat" is really a rout. For the French, forced from their positions, have had no time to construct new ones but are being constantly harassed by German tanks, other motorized units and planes as they move southward, it is reported.

Early this morning, the Germans declare, they unleashed a frontal attack on the Maginot Line along the entire Saar front. Farther east, the fall of Montmedy, "anchor" of the Maginot Line, was claimed as well.

The extreme right wing of the German forces was not idle either. For yesterday it captured Havre, Berlin heard, and thus added approximately another hundred miles to the stretch of French coast that already is in German hands.

Advance on Cherbourg

The lower Seine, moreover, according to the High Command, was crossed on a wide front. The extreme right wing, it is believed, now is advancing on Cherbourg further to cut France off from Great Britain and provide the Germans with still another base for a future raid on the British Isles.

The front is now about 300 miles long as the crow flies, Germans declare, from Havre to the Rhine.

Although no information has been officially released here relative to the progress of the attack on the Maginot Line, it was said in usually accurately informed quarters tonight that the force of the German drive in this sector already has borne fruit and that Reich troops have broken through in several places.

Escape Held Impossible

Forces of the German left wing are reported pushing forward in a southeasterly direction in what now appears to be a plan to storm the triangle of the Maginot fortifications from several sides, while an advance west of the fortifications to Belfort—southern tip of the Maginot Line—would cut off the avenue of escape for the French troops manning the line.

This German left wing yesterday was said to have captured Vitry-le Francois and crossed the Marne-Rhine Canal, which connects that town with Strasbourg. Still farther west another tentacle of the German left wing last evening was reported to have stormed the famous Hill 304 (Dead Man's Hill) northwest of Verdun, in which sector in 1916, Germans say, they lost 80,000 men.

The southern tip of the Argonne Forest also has been reached, Germans declare.

The Meuse defenses and Verdun

Continued on Page Two

"All the News That's Fit to Print."

NEWS INDEX, PAGE 33, THIS SECTION

The New York Times.

LATE CITY EDITION
Cloudy today with little change in temperature. Tomorrow cloudy and slightly warmer.
Temperatures Yesterday—Max., 72; Min., 52

Section 1

VOL. LXXXIX..No. 30,101.

Entered as Second-Class Matter, Postoffice, New York, N. Y.

NEW YORK, SUNDAY, JUNE 23, 1940.

Including Rotogravure Picture, Magazine and Book Review. TEN CENTS | TWELVE CENTS Beyond 200 Miles, Except West of Pa.—South of Md.—North of Mass.

FRENCH SIGN REICH TRUCE, ROME PACT NEXT; BRITISH BOMB KRUPP WORKS AND BREMEN; HOUSE QUICKLY PASSES 2-OCEAN NAVY BILL

REPUBLICAN FIGHT LOOMS ON WAR ISSUE AT THE CONVENTION

Dewey, Taft and Willkie Reach Philadelphia to Appeal to the Delegates

NO GROUP HAS CONTROL

Rival Candidates Make Ballot Claims—Willkie Stronger—Hoover Possibility Seen

A battle between divergent views on the war and peace issue loomed yesterday among delegates to the Republican National Convention, opening tomorrow. Messrs. Dewey, Taft and Willkie, rival candidates for the Presidential nomination, reached Philadelphia to press their campaigns. No leader or group of leaders was in a position to dominate the proceedings or the committee on resolutions. The effect of a speech by Mr. Hoover to the convention Tuesday night is expected to decide what, if any part, he will play as a Presidential nominee. [All the foregoing Page 1, Column 1.]

In press conferences Mr. Dewey declared for aid to the Allies without violating international or domestic law or entering the war; Mr. Willkie for aid to the Allies without going to war, and for reciprocal trade treaties. [Page 2, Column 1.]

The national committee approved a change in the rules under which districts which fail to show a poll of 1,000 Republicans would be deprived of representation at future conventions. Other rules changes approved would ease penalties on States which do not give a majority for the national ticket. [Page 2, Column 4.]

Drafters of the platform, split over aid to the Allies, hinted that a stand on the foreign policy plank might be left largely to the decision of the Presidential nominee. [Page 3, Column 1.]

Convention Unbossed

By JAMES A. HAGERTY

Special to THE NEW YORK TIMES.

PHILADELPHIA, June 22—The Republican National Convention, which will convene here Monday in the Municipal Auditorium, will open without a boss or even under the control of any particular group of minor bosses.

This was the indication, today, when District Attorney Thomas E. Dewey of New York, Senator Robert A. Taft of Ohio and Wendell L. Willkie, president of the Commonwealth and Southern Corporation, just now regarded as the three leading candidates for the Presidential nomination, arrived in the convention city to make direct appeals to the delegates.

With no leader or group of leaders in a position to dominate either the convention or the committee on resolutions, the delegates face the prospect of a hotly contested fight for the nomination for President, and an equally bitter floor contest on the resolution on foreign relations.

Little difficulty is expected in putting through the rest of the platform which is expected to follow the recommendations of the program committee of the National Committee, headed by Dr. Glenn Frank.

Alfred M. Landon, nominee for President in 1936, who is chairman of the subcommittee on foreign relations of the committee on resolutions, continued today his efforts to get a plank that would be satisfactory both to the isolationists and those favoring a declaration of aid to the Allies, but the formula, so far as could be learned, had not been found tonight.

Candidates Give Views

Mr. Dewey, Mr. Willkie and Senator Taft each had a press conference. Mr. Dewey declared for aid for the Allies without violating international or domestic law or getting into the war. Mr. Willkie, who was nearly mobbed by supporters in the Bellevue-Stratford Hotel, also declared for aid to the Allies without going to war and

Continued on Page Two

Major Sports Results

BASEBALL

New York's major league teams all met defeat yesterday. The Reds downed the Giants, 3—1, on Ernie Lombardi's homer with one man on base, the Pirates beat the Dodgers, 7—2, and the Tigers won from the Yankees, 3—2. Despite the setback, the Dodgers stayed in first place in the National League.

RACING

Your Chance won the $13,350 Dwyer Stakes at Aqueduct after Snow Ridge, first past the finish line, was disqualified for bumping in the stretch. Gen'l Manager was placed second and Andy K. third. The crowd of 20,520 bet $1,076,417 on the seven races, this being Aqueduct's first million-dollar day.

TRACK AND FIELD

The University of Southern California won its sixth successive National Collegiate A. A. championship in the meet at Minneapolis. The New York A. C. easily retained the metropolitan A. A. U. senior title.

(Complete Details in Section 5.)

CITY WPA TO PURGE 1,000 NAZIS, REDS

Signing of Affidavits to Be Started Tomorrow—FBI to Aid in Investigations

Without waiting for President Roosevelt to sign the new Relief Appropriations Act, Colonel F. C. Harrington, National Work Projects Commissioner, set in motion yesterday the machinery for purging the WPA rolls of Communists and Nazis by July 1.

The purge in this city will begin tomorrow, and the local administrator, Lieut. Col. Brehon B. Somervell, estimated that at least 1,000 WPA workers would lose their jobs before it was completed. All of the 101,000 persons on the rolls here, and 1,700,000 in other parts of the country, will be required to sign affidavits disavowing Communist or Nazi affiliations. The maximum penalty for false statement will be $2,000 fine and two years' imprisonment.

Colonel Somervell made clear that his office would not rely on affidavits alone in carrying out the mandate of the new law. The registration lists of the Board of Elections will be compared with the WPA payroll to turn up the names of Communists. The full facilities of the Federal Bureau of Investigation, the Police Department and the WPA's own Bureau of Investigation will be invoked as a further means of identification.

Dies Records to Be Used

Still another source of data, Colonel Somervell revealed, will be the reports and testimony gathered by the Dies committee and the record compiled in the recent trial of Fritz Kuhn, leader of the German-American Bund.

Because of "the well-known practice of Communists to deny membership in the party and to use false names in enrollment with the WPA," the administrator called upon all "responsible citizens" to make available any information they had on subversive activities among Federal relief employes. He said he expected at least 50,000 letters, and he promised that "grudge letters would be carefully sifted out from those submitting authentic information."

Although Congress did not complete action on the new Relief Act until yesterday morning, WPA officials in this city have been collecting material on Communists and Nazis on their rolls for several weeks. More than 1,000 names of persons tentatively identified as members of un-American groups are now under scrutiny, it was learned.

Under the wording of the law, Colonel Somervell said, a person does not have to be a member of the Communist party to be ineligible for WPA employment. He said he regarded Trotskyists as Communists within the meaning of the law, and indicated that other "splinter groups" would be subject to a similar interpretation. The administrator said he would function as the court of last resort in determining whether a person entertained subversive views.

The WPA purge creates a problem for municipal relief authorities.

Continued on Page Thirteen

FOR 200 NEW SHIPS

70% Increase in Fleet Authorized as Congress Recesses Till July 1

TO COST 4 BILLIONS

Chambers Enact Tax, Defense and Relief Fund Measures

Special to THE NEW YORK TIMES.

WASHINGTON, June 22—Congress took a recess at 9:10 o'clock tonight, adopting a resolution to reassemble on July 1 after the Republican National Convention at Philadelphia, and to take a similar week's recess during the Democratic National Convention at Chicago.

As a night session began to clear the decks for the recess, the House gave a dramatic flourish to a day devoted to pressing legislation by passing and sending to the Senate the "two-ocean" navy bill. No dissent was heard in the voice vote.

Within less than two hours, the House thus gave its approval to the construction of the world's mightiest navy, designed for defense of the United States and the Western Hemisphere. The Senate did not have time to act.

The "two-ocean" navy bill would authorize about 200 warships, a 70 per cent increase in the nation's fleet, or an expansion of 1,325,000 tons of combatant and auxiliary vessels to be built in the next six years at an estimated cost of $4,000,000,000.

Naval Air Force Augmented

Besides the increase in ship tonnage, the two-ocean navy measure also would increase the naval air force authorized strength from 10,000 to 15,000 planes.

It provides for $25,000,000 for "mosquito" torpedo boats, and authorizes an appropriation of $150,000,000 to expand shipbuilding facilities at government and private yards.

It provides also for the expenditure of $20,000,000 for expansion of facilities for armor plate manufacture and $50,000,000 for added facilities for construction of guns.

In calling for enactment of the bill, as recommended by Admiral Harold R. Stark, Chief of Naval Operations, Chairman Vinson of the House Naval Affairs Committee said that when the bill became law the Administration would ask for $175,000,000 for an immediate start on the program.

Mr. Vinson and Representative Maas of Minnesota, ranking minority member on the committee, led the brief debate by asserting that the United States should not depend upon the Navy of any other power for its defense.

"The time has come to realize that if the United States is to remain free and independent it must depend upon itself," Mr. Maas said. "It is foolish to risk our defense on the thin thread of a (the Panama) canal."

The Navy now has 307 ships in

Continued on Page Fourteen

$5,377,552,058 Voted For Defense This Year

By The Associated Press.

WASHINGTON, June 22—Here are the defense appropriation totals, including contract authorizations, which Congress has approved thus far this session:

*Regular Army bill	$1,[illegible]23,254,624
*Regular Navy bill..	1,492,542,750
Supplemental defense	1,768,913,908
Urgent deficiency.....	28,000,000
Emergency deficiency	252,340,776
Strategic materials (in Treasury appropriation)	12,500,000
Total	$5,377,552,058

*To which supplemental sums were added by the Senate.

There are also items intended for defense in the Civil Aeronautics Authority, Civilian Conservation Corps, WPA and the Army Civil Functions Supply Bills.

COMMITTEE LEANS TO KNOX REJECTION

But Senate Naval Group Votes to Hear Him July 1—Stimson Will Testify Next Day

By HAROLD B. HINTON

Special to THE NEW YORK TIMES.

WASHINGTON, June 22—Confirmation of Colonel Frank Knox as Secretary of the Navy probably will be opposed by the Senate Naval Affairs Committee, according to some members questioned after a stormy executive session today. If members maintain the opposition shown today, an adverse report will be made to the Senate, it was said.

The Naval and the Military Affairs committees, to which the nominations of Colonel Knox and of Henry L. Stimson as Secretary of War have been referred, will hear the nominees in person during the week of July 1, when Congress reassembles after its recess for the Republican National Convention.

There is no indication that the Military Affairs Committee will recommend rejection of Colonel Stimson, although he will probably be closely questioned by such isolationists members as Senators Reynolds and Lundeen.

The Naval Affairs Committee will give Colonel Knox a more searching examination, it was believed. Some members, it was reported, favored rejecting the nomination today, but counsel prevailed that no nominee should be disapproved without having a chance to be heard.

Senator Walsh, its chairman, announced after the meeting that Colonel Knox would be invited to appear on July 1. In other quarters it was said that eleven members attended today's meeting and that most of those who spoke were opposed to the nomination. Only Senators Hale and Barbour took no part in the discussions.

The most outspoken opponents, according to these reports, included Senators Walsh, Tydings, Smith of South Carolina, Byrd, Holt and Gillette, all Democrats. Senator Johnson of California, a Republican, also indicated his opposition. Others attending the meeting were

Continued on Page Fifteen

British Torpedo and Bomb the Scharnhorst; Submarine, Planes Waylay Nazi Battleship

By HAROLD DENNY

Special Cable to THE NEW YORK TIMES.

LONDON, June 22—The Germans' 26,000-ton battle cruiser Scharnhorst has been seriously damaged by a British submarine and airplanes off the Norwegian coast, according to reports given out tonight by the Admiralty and the Air Ministry.

The Scharnhorst was believed to be lying at bay with German destroyers and war planes clustering about her protectively, awaiting further attack by British naval units summoned by the Royal Air Force bombers.

The battle with the Scharnhorst and her escorting forces was the most important of three attacks on German and Italian naval craft reported in London.

The other incidents were the almost unbelievable exploit of the capture of an Italian submarine by a British trawler in the Gulf of Aden opposite British Somaliland and the sinking by an airplane of a German supply ship in the North Sea.

The Scharnhorst, with her sister ship the Gneisenau, the most powerful of German war vessels, had previously taken severe punishment. She was heavily pummeled in April by the British battleship Renown off Narvik, Prime Minister Winston Churchill then reported.

On June 13 she was reported here to have been badly bombed, with one—perhaps two—British bombs making direct hits on the center of the ship when she was in Trondheim Fjord.

"One of our submarines sighted the Scharnhorst soon after she left Trondheim Fjord," the day's reports said. "The battle cruiser was clearly on passage to a safe port where she could repair damage sustained when hit by at least one heavy bomb during an attack by the aircraft of the fleet arm on June 13."

This latest encounter with the Scharnhorst touched off an excep-

Continued on Page Twenty-one

ARMS PLANT IS HIT

R.A.F. Raiders Continue Assault Upon Nazis' Bases of Supply

SCORE NEAR BERLIN

Plane Factory Is Target—Germans Retaliate Along English Coast

By JAMES MacDONALD

Special Cable to THE NEW YORK TIMES.

LONDON, June 22—Royal Air Force bombers pounded the big Krupp arms works at Essen and important aircraft factories and military stores at Bremen, Kassel, Rothenburg and Goettingen and a big naval depot at Willemsoord in German-occupied Netherlands in a heavy series of air raids last night, according to the Air Ministry's communiqué today.

As against their boast of heavy damage done to the Nazis, British officials insisted that Nazi airmen had accomplished little in their retaliatory raids in this country this morning and last night.

Three persons were killed in a Suffolk town and three wounded elsewhere, it was announced. It was declared that bombs burst sporadically in "several counties on the east coast," but that most of them fell in open country, causing small damage. The German raids, it was said, were less intense than those of Tuesday and Wednesday nights. The Ministry did not state whether or not any Nazi planes were shot down, or if any defending fighter machines were lost.

All Appears Quiet

Meanwhile all appeared quiet on the British home air front tonight. There were no unwelcome noises of purring enemy motors that were picked up by the sensitive sound-detecting devices on the ground.

[Alexandria, Egypt, fought off three Italian air raids yesterday, the first of the war. British fliers attacked Tobruk, Libya, and reported hitting a large warship. Rome said bombers had destroyed a British naval base in Egypt and raided Marseille and Bizerte, Tunisia.]

Many sections of British planes are reported to have taken part in widespread raids on German objectives last night, but only one was shot down and only two are reported missing.

The plane that was shot down was one of several that subjected Willemsoord to a terrific aerial bombardment.

Almost five tons of high explosive and incendiary bombs were dropped in less than a minute. During that lightning stroke oil tanks were set afire, naval storehouses blown to rubble, two unidentified ships sunk, another badly damaged, "and German machine-gunners received a dose of their own medicine," the Air Ministry said. American built Lockheed-Hudson planes were used in that sortie.

Two Planes Missing

Many planes were engaged in the big raids over Germany. They returned with only two missing.

British raiders over Bremen directed their attack against the large Focke-Wulf airplane factory. They made direct hits with incendiary and explosive bombs in the middle of the factory buildings. Two violent explosions were seen by the British fliers after their bombs burst.

The airfield adjoining the factory was also bombed and one hangar was badly damaged, according to assertions made here.

Another section of the raiders reported that they had hit several buildings of the Krupp plant at Essen as well as railroad sidings near by. The exact extent of the damage done there, however, was not disclosed in London.

The objective at Kassel was the Fieseler aircraft factory and it was said that several bombs were seen exploding directly on the target.

Airplane hangars were damaged at Rothenberg, where also military buildings and the air field were hit. Another attacking force dropped bombs on the aircraft storage depot

Continued on Page Twenty-six

The International Situation

In Europe and Africa

An armistice between Germany and France was signed in the Forest of Compiegne yesterday at 6:50 P. M. German time (12:50 P. M. New York time). Immediately after the signing the French representatives left by a German plane, German-piloted, for Rome, where they will sign a companion document with Italy. Six hours after the signatures have been appended to the Italian armistice the order to cease fire will become effective. The terms of the armistice are still withheld; in Bordeaux they were described as "hard but honorable." London reported, without confirmation, that these were the principal provisions: (1) Occupation of France by Germany and Italy for the duration of the war with Britain; (2) surrender of all war stores; (3) surrender of all gold and foreign currency reserves; (4) delivery of coal and other raw material supplies to Germany for a fixed period. [Page 1, Column 8.]

Prime Minister Churchill said he had heard "with grief and amazement" of the French acceptance of terms that, to his mind, would mean that France and her empire would be entirely at the mercy of the dictators. He called on the French people to continue resistance. This call was reiterated by General Charles de Gaulle, former French Under-Secretary of War, who broadcast from London, calling on all French people not under Axis guns to mobilize to carry on the war. [Page 1, Column 6.]

The French negotiators arrived in Rome by plane from Compiègne. [Page 27, Column 1.]

Berlin announced that 500,000 French soldiers, encircled in Alsace-Lorraine, had surrendered, among them three army commanders. Only isolated resistance was left in that part of France. The Germans took the port of Lorient, on the southern coast of Brittany. According to Swiss reports, the French repulsed a German attack on L'Ecluse Fort, which dominates the Rhone at the Swiss border. [Page 22, Column 1.]

British bombers struck at the famous Krupp armaments works at Essen and at aircraft factories at several other points in Germany. In a raid on Willemsoord, German-held base in the Netherlands, the British said they had sunk two ships, set one afire and destroyed naval storehouses. Berlin reported that nearly 100 planes took part in Friday night's bombing of Britain. The Germans said that in recent actions they had sunk two British transports, one of 11,000 tons, the other of 32,000, the latter carrying about 5,000 men who were lost. British bombers reached the Berlin area Friday night, the Germans admitted, injuring seven persons and damaging buildings. [Page 1, Column 5.]

The British reported that the German battleship Scharnhorst, 26,000 tons, had been both torpedoed and bombed, with "considerable damage" resulting. The action took place off the Norwegian coast. A destroyer was torpedoed in the same fight, London said. The British trawler Moonstone informed the Admiralty that it had captured a large Italian submarine in the Gulf of Aden. Depth charges forced the submarine to the surface, where guns were brought into play. The Italian commander and several officers were reported killed; three officers and thirty-seven men were captured. [Page 1, Column 3.]

Three groups of Italian bombers attacked the Allied naval base at Alexandria, Egypt, early yesterday. They were driven off, the British reported, by the combined fire of both French and British naval units, and no warships were hit. Rome claimed to have sunk three enemy ships in the Mediterranean. [Page 1, Column 7.]

By the emphatic means of an official government statement, Russia denied that troops were being concentrated on the German frontier. [Page 22, Column 7.]

Developments Elsewhere

Within less than two hours, the House of Representatives adopted the "two-ocean" navy bill, which will give the United States the most powerful navy in the world—a navy 70 per cent greater than the present one. [Page 1, Column 3.]

After a stormy session of the Senate Naval Affairs Committee, it appeared in Washington that Colonel Frank Knox, Republican, would not be approved by the committee for Secretary of the Navy. Colonel Henry L. Stimson, Republican, nominated for Secretary of War, also faces hard going before the Military Affairs Committee. But confirmation of both appointments is expected when the issue gets to the floor. [Page 1, Column 4.]

In Hyde Park, where he was spending the week-end, President Roosevelt contemplated the possibility that the United States might have to shift the fleet to the Atlantic to face a superior sea power of the totalitarian nations. [Page 16, Column 1.]

GENERAL SUMMONS FRENCH TO RESIST

De Gaulle Offers to Organize Fight Abroad—Churchill Supports His Stand

By RAYMOND DANIELL

Special Cable to THE NEW YORK TIMES.

LONDON, Sunday, June 23—A broadcast to the French people by one of their own military leaders calling on them to continue the fight against Germany by every means in their power was made from here last night.

General Charles de Gaulle, assistant and adviser to Paul Reynaud when the former Premier was also War Minister, told his countrymen the proposed armistice would be not only capitulation but "submission and slavery."

[The general undertook to organize such French resistance as was possible himself and urged French fighting men and technicians everywhere to join him in the task, according to The United Press.]

General de Gaulle's arguments were reinforced early this morning by Prime Minister Winston Churchill in a statement expressing "grief and amazement" at the terms. He indicated they would transform France into an active enemy, and he too urged French-

Continued on Page Twenty-seven

ALEXANDRIA FIGHTS FIRST ITALIAN RAIDS

20 Bombs Fall in 3 Attacks—Warship Reported Fired by R. A. F. at Tobruk

By JOSEPH M. LEVY

Wireless to THE NEW YORK TIMES.

CAIRO, Egypt, June 22—Alexandria experienced its first bombing this morning when twenty bombs were dropped in three Italian air raids. Two persons were killed; twenty-three were injured.

The dead were a native woman, who was killed when bombs hit among palm trees growing in a village close to the city, and a man who was killed by a bomb that demolished four Alexandria houses. Here nineteen persons were injured.

[Another air raid warning sounded in Alexandria early today, but no planes appeared, The Associated Press reported, and the all-clear signal was given in fifteen minutes.]

Bombs were reported dropped indiscriminately on the city, harbor and native villages, the bombers flying high and dodging in their attempt to avoid anti-aircraft fire. Two Italian planes were reported badly damaged. It is not certain whether either was shot down.

Only a few bombs fell in the city.

Continued on Page Twenty-three

NAZI TERMS SIGNED

But Hostilities Persist as French Fly to Get Italy's Demands

SEVERITY PROTESTED

Huntziger Voices View at Close of 27-Hour Compiegne Parley

By GUIDO ENDERIS

Wireless to THE NEW YORK TIMES.

BERLIN, June 22—The armistice treaty between Germany and France was signed today in the forest of Compiègne at 6:50 P. M. German Summer time [12:50 P. M. New York time]. Col. Gen. Wilhelm Keitel, Chancellor Hitler's plenipotentiary, signed for Germany and General Charles Huntziger for France.

Its contents will not be made public for the present, but it is announced that the agreement does not provide for immediate cessation of hostilities. The fighting is to end six hours after the Italian Government has notified the German High Command of the signing of an armistice treaty between Italy and France.

As the latter is now believed to be a mere formality, already agreed upon by the leaders of the Axis Powers in their discussion in Munich last Tuesday, its conclusion is expected within the next forty-eight hours. The French delegation that conferred at Compiègne also will negotiate with Italy. Such procedure, it is predicted, will end the war on the Continent early in the coming week.

Scene in Car Dramatic

The French delegation returned to Compiègne from Paris at 10 A. M. and continued its deliberations throughout the day, during which it was in constant communication with the Bordeaux government. To expedite contacts, German military authorities installed a direct telephone wire connecting the armistice car with Bordeaux.

The German radio broadcast announcing the signing of the treaty closed with the words, "We thank our Fuehrer." There was a dramatic scene in the armistice car at Compiègne before the formalities were completed. General Huntziger, in a choked voice, announced that his government had ordered him to sign.

"Before carrying out my government's order," he said, "the French delegation deems it necessary to declare that in a moment when France is compelled by fate of arms to give up the fight, she has a right to expect that the coming negotiations will be dominated by a spirit that will give two great neighboring nations a chance to live and work once more. As a soldier you will well understand the onerous moment that has now come for me to sign."

After the signatures were affixed, General Keitel requested all present to rise from their seats, and then said:

"It is honorable for the victor to do honor to the vanquished. We have risen in commemoration of those who gave their blood to their countries."

Talks With Italy Speeded

The French delegation left Compiegne for Paris tonight and is expected to take up negotiations with Italy without further delay to bring the hostilities to a quick close.

With an Italian-French armistice in imminent prospect, military activities are now expected to give way to diplomatic negotiations and it is not improbable that Germany, Italy, France and possibly also Belgium will meet in conference soon in some German city to discuss steps for an approach to honorable peace.

Meanwhile there is no indication in German official or press utterances to suggest that Germany is not grimly determined to prosecute her war on Britain with all possible speed, and this determination has received fresh impetus through uninterrupted attacks by British bombers on German objectives.

With French Channel ports now available as German air bases, raids on English coastal points also have increased in recent days and with the final liquidation of the war in

Continued on Page Twenty-eight

"All the News That's Fit to Print."

The New York Times.

LATE CITY EDITION
Fair, with little change in temperature today and tomorrow.
Temperatures Yesterday—Max., 80; Min., 68

Copyright, 1940, by The New York Times Company.

VOL. LXXXIX..No. 30,174. Entered as Second-Class Matter, Postoffice, New York, N. Y. NEW YORK, WEDNESDAY, SEPTEMBER 4, 1940. THREE CENTS NEW YORK CITY and Vicinity | FOUR CENTS Elsewhere Except in 7th and 8th Postal Zones.

ROOSEVELT TRADES DESTROYERS FOR SEA BASES; TELLS CONGRESS HE ACTED ON OWN AUTHORITY; BRITAIN PLEDGES NEVER TO YIELD OR SINK FLEET

R. A. F. REPELS RAIDS

Fliers Turn Back Three Drives on London—Reich Perfecting Technique

PLANES REACH BERLIN

2½-Hour Alarm in City—British Hit Hard at French Coast

By JAMES B. RESTON
Special Cable to THE NEW YORK TIMES.

LONDON, Wednesday, Sept. 4—German bombers started ringing that big London doorbell early yesterday morning. They rang it again in the afternoon while Prime Minister Winston Churchill and his Ministers were commemorating the first anniversary of the war, and they kept ringing it right up till last midnight, when the third "all clear" of the day was sounded over the capital.

It was a day of fierce air battles, fought at great height in blue and silver sky all over Southeast England, and at the end, though Reich Marshal Hermann Goering's night shift was still operating all over the island, the British Air Ministry announced that twenty-five Nazi planes had been shot down to fifteen of Britain's planes. Eight British pilots were said to be safe, though it is not known whether they are in condition to fly.

[British bombing planes flew high over Berlin shortly after last midnight. Berlin spokesmen were quoted as saying that most of the Royal Air Force planes were turned back by severe anti-aircraft fire between Wittenberg and Magdeburg, but several planes escaped through the anti-aircraft barrage and reached Berlin, where they were again met with anti-aircraft fire.]

These German bombers, which have already overwhelmed five countries in the past twelve months, have now perfected a technique in attacking this vast, sprawling city, and they tried to work it again yesterday morning in the first raid.

Two Formations Meet

Just at 10 o'clock, timed to perfection, one wave of bombers approached the Thames Estuary from their bases in Belgium. Simultaneously, another formation, flying high through a light haze, came up from bases in France and met them over the Kentish coast. Altogether they were about 250 of them, and defying anti-aircraft batteries at first they started along the banks of the Thames toward London.

As they came inland, however, they met first one, then a second squadron of British fighters, who dived through Nazi fighter patrols into the bombers, broke up the formation and then attacked them singly and drove them back over the coast.

Some German bombers dropped their dynamite in Kent and Essex, but all that is said about the effect of these bombs is that they caused few casualties and little damage.

What can be said is that, if these bombers were trying to get into the heart of London to attack objectives here, they certainly failed, for while sirens were sounded everywhere in Greater London nobody in the heart of the city saw any fighting.

There was an interesting sidelight to the second mass raid of the day. At 2:45 P. M. Mr. Churchill, who somehow contrives to look more confident every day, walked into Westminster Abbey to attend the special service in commemoration of the day a year ago when Britain declared war on Germany. Alongside him walked tall, gaunt Viscount Halifax, Foreign Secretary; dapper Arthur Greenwood, Minister without portfolio; Sir Kingsley Wood, Chancellor of the Exchequer; Anthony Eden, War Secretary, and Joseph P. Kennedy, United States Ambassador to Great Britain.

They took their places in the cool church beside a great audience. At 2:50 P. M., as they were sitting there waiting for the service to start, air-raid sirens started echoing through the great cathedral.

Mr. Churchill got up, walked over to the cloisters and had a long talk with the Dean. In a few minutes he returned and took his place beside his Ministers in the chancel. It was announced that the service would proceed.

Around the city the British fight-

Continued on Page Three

The International Situation

Destroyer-War Base Deal

Completion of a deal by which the United States will transfer to Britain fifty over-age destroyers and obtain ninety-nine-year leases on eight shore and island bases stretching from Newfoundland to British Guiana was announced by President Roosevelt yesterday in a message to Congress. Coincidentally, the British Government pledged not to scuttle or surrender its fleet under any conditions. [Page 1, Column 8.]

The objective of the arrangement with Britain is to build a 4,500-mile iron fence in the Atlantic to assure this country's safety for a century, an authoritative State Department source said. To attain this, any interpretations of international law and parts of treaties in conflict must be subordinated, he said. Since this country's purpose is its defense, no well-intentioned nation can call the move a hostile act, he declared. [Page 1, Column 7.]

President Roosevelt, en route to Washington, disclosed that he looked upon the agreement as a means of keeping an enemy from the country's front door. Listing it as in some ways more important for defense than Jefferson's Louisiana purchase, he hinted there might be other similar arrangements. [Page 1, Column 6.]

The President had acted on an opinion from Attorney General Jackson, who held that the Executive had the right to negotiate the transfer without Senate consent and the constitutional power to dispose of the vessels. [Page 1, Column 5.]

Wendell L. Willkie, Republican Presidential nominee, said the country would undoubtedly approve the arrangement, but criticized Mr. Roosevelt's failure to obtain Congress's approval. [Page 1, Column 3.]

London rejoiced. A Foreign Office spokesman described the agreement as a practical method for each nation to contribute to the other's defense requirements. [Page 1, Column 4.]

Axis spokesmen did not challenge the deal's legality under neutrality laws. In Berlin it was belittled as unlikely to affect the war's outcome. It was said to be a bargain for the United States and evidence that Britain was "cracking up." In Rome it was expected the Italians would be embittered. [Page 15, Column 1.]

Developments in Congress

The House opened debate on the Selective Service Training Bill, the discussion following the lines of the Senate's deliberation. Indications were that the bill would pass by a good margin, the principal controversy centering on the question of industrial conscription. Leaders planned for final action Friday. [Page 17, Column 1.]

The Senate Finance Committee opened hearings on the excess profits tax and defense expansion amortization bill. The probability of changes in the measure increased as witnesses hit at its effects on business. [Page 10, Column 1.]

The War in Europe, Asia and Africa

German bombers hammered at Britain's airfields, harbors and naval bases, engaging the Royal Air Force in battles all over Southern England. Three raids on London were repelled. [Page 1, Column 1.]

Several R. A. F. bombers reached Berlin early today to provoke violent anti-aircraft fire after the British had loosed a powerful aerial counter-offensive in which their planes had bombed German industrial centers, the French coast and Italian power stations. [Page 3, Column 1.]

In the central Mediterranean, new type Italian bombers scored a victory, damaging a British battleship, an aircraft carrier, a cruiser and a destroyer, the Rome High Command announced. The R. A. F. again pounded Assab, port in Italian Eritrea. [Page 4, Column 6.]

Led by Tahiti, France's most important colony in Oceania, the French-protected Society Islands have voted to throw in their lot with Britain, repudiating Vichy, it was reported. [Page 6, Column 1.]

A virtual Japanese ultimatum demanding a military base and passage for troops was reported to have been rejected by French Indo-China and conflict there was believed inevitable. [Page 6, Column 3.]

In an attempted Iron Guard coup three gunmen broke through King Carol's palace guard and fired several shots into the air. Others equally vainly besieged a radio station, fought with troops. [Page 1, Column 2.]

A clash between Hungarian and Rumanian troops over the occupation of Transylvania was reported at Bucharest. [Page 4, Column 1.]

BUCHAREST CHECKS IRON GUARDS' COUP

Shots Fired in Front of Royal Palace—Handbills Call On Carol to Abdicate

By EUGEN KOVACS
Wireless to THE NEW YORK TIMES.

BUCHAREST, Rumania, Sept. 3—A group of the Iron Guards, dissatisfied with the conduct and policy of other Iron Guards who are Ministers and who participated in the Crown Council, organized and carried out several attempts tonight against different public buildings in Bucharest. All these attacks failed.

A small group consisting of three persons appeared in an automobile this evening at 8:30 before the Royal Palace and one of them fired two shots in the air. A policeman on duty in front of the gates of the palace fired at the car but failed. The man who fired the shots tried to escape, however, but was arrested, while the car disappeared.

The regular news bulletin broadcast at 10 o'clock was canceled.

A second group, consisting of young men wearing military uniforms and disguised as Iron Guards, attacked the Bucharest radio station. The guard fired and succeeded in repelling the attacking group.

At the cabin of transmission of the Central Telephone Exchange a man was found who cut off some lines so that the telephone connection with abroad was cut off for a while. At the State Railway repair works in the suburb of Grivitza an-

Continued on Page Four

WILLKIE FOR PACT, BUT HITS SECRECY

Regrets President Did Not Put Deal With Britain Before Congress and People

By JAMES A. HAGERTY
Special to THE NEW YORK TIMES.

RUSHVILLE, Ind., Sept. 3—Asked today to comment on President Roosevelt's announcement of the agreement to turn over to Great Britain fifty over-age destroyers in return for air and naval bases in British Western Hemisphere areas, Wendell L. Willkie, Republican nominee for President, declared that the country undoubtedly would approve the program, but criticized the President's failure to obtain prior approval of Congress as smacking of totalitarianism.

In a statement prepared with care and with realization that it might have important foreign repercussions, Mr. Willkie said:

"The country will undoubtedly approve of the program to add to our naval and air bases and assistance given to Great Britain. It is regrettable, however, that the President did not deem it necessary in connection with this proposal to secure the approval of Congress or permit public discussion prior to adoption.

"The people have a right to know of such important commitments prior to and not after being made. We must be extremely careful in these times when the struggle in the world is between democracy and to-

Continued on Page Fourteen

BRITISH JUBILANT

Destroyers Strengthen Their Fleet at Point of Greatest Strain

MORAL EFFECT GREAT

But Press Warns People Gesture Does Not Mean U. S. Will Enter War

By RAYMOND DANIELL
Special Cable to THE NEW YORK TIMES.

LONDON, Sept. 3—It would be impossible to overstate the jubilation in official and unofficial circles caused today by President Roosevelt's announcement that fifty United States destroyers were coming to help Great Britain in her hour of peril. They will be manned by British crews and will fly the white ensign of the Royal Navy, it is true, but they are coming, nevertheless.

It was tangible proof that American talk of giving "all aid short of war" was more than idle chatter and that this country's friends across the Atlantic, despite German propaganda and the heavy bombardment of British cities and towns, had decided there was still lots of fight left in the British lion and that it was not too late to help turn the tide against totalitarian domination of Europe.

Destroyer Losses Offset

Under the arrangement, it was pointed out by authoritative sources, the United States gained security against future aggression, while the British fleet at one stroke acquired fifty 1,200-ton destroyers as an offset to the thirty lost since the beginning of hostilities.

These destroyers are badly needed at this stage of the war with British seapower engaged in a death grapple with the German Empire. Since the French were knocked out as an ally, the whole job of protecting convoys and maintaining the lifelines of the Empire against the new enemy in the Mediterranean has fallen upon the British fleet, while the air force has concentrated chiefly on destroying the enemy's supplies and defending the homes of the people of this island, which is under repeated bombardment from the air throughout its length and breadth.

Added to this multiplication of the navy's duties has been the necessity of blockading the whole Continent of Europe while standing by to resist the very real threat of a German invasion which, as War Secretary Anthony Eden warned today, still hangs over this country.

As great as was Britain's need the material gain by today's transaction was matched in British minds by the intangible implications of most open indication yet of Anglo-American cooperation for defense against the Nazi threats.

The Times, London, will point out editorially tomorrow that such cooperation between a belligerent and a neutral is "a new departure" but one that is dictated by the necessities of modern war. The editorial goes on to say:

"The tragic fate of some of the smaller peoples of Europe might have been averted if they had not been restrained from planning for

Continued on Page Fifteen

Writer on British Destroyer Sees U-Boats in Raids and One Sunk

By BRYDON TAVES

ABOARD A BRITISH DESTROYER, in the North Atlantic, Sept. 3 (UP)—Germany is shooting the works to make good the threat of total blockade of the British Isles, but after eight days aboard a little British flotilla leader I can say that hundreds of ships are entering and leaving British ports each week.

German submarine and air attacks marked my voyage. Not one day passed without action. The British crew was either manning gun and depth-charge stations to fight off a U-boat or manning anti-aircraft stations to fight attacking planes.

I saw one British merchantman take a long-range torpedo squarely amidships and sink within a half hour. The next day our destroyer evened the score.

A "tin fish," meant for us, missed by a scant thirty feet as we whipped around. Then we rocked from the concussion of our own depth charges and I saw an oil patch spread slowly over the surface, marking that U-boat's end.

The destroyer was engaged in a typical convoy job, and its duties were something between those of a conscientious sheep dog and a sister of charity leading a bunch of orphans across Times Square.

We were one destroyer and one smaller warship escorting a thirty-ship convoy spread over fifteen square miles of ocean. Watching the line of hulls stretching out behind us, I remembered what a naval officer in a convoy control room in a West coast port told me just before I sailed.

"Give me fifty over-age American destroyers," he said, "and I will

Continued on Page Four

RULING BY JACKSON

Opinion Holds Transfer by President Needs No Senate Action

AN 'EXECUTIVE' DEAL

Opponents in Congress Seek to Find Means of Obstructing It

Attorney General Jackson's opinion is printed on Page 16.

By LEWIS WOOD
Special to THE NEW YORK TIMES.

WASHINGTON, Sept. 3—President Roosevelt has unqualified power to exchange fifty over-age destroyers for British naval and air bases in the Western Hemisphere without Senate consent, in the opinion of Attorney General Jackson, made public today, but, while Mr. Jackson asserted the Executive's right to dispose of naval vessels, he again refused to sanction the legality of delivery of "mosquito boats" now under construction.

Under a World War law the Attorney General ruled that it would be entirely proper to transfer the destroyers, since these were not built "with the intent that they should enter the service of a belligerent," but turning over the uncompleted mosquito boats, he argued, would be impossible, as this would legally mean that they were intended for a belligerent.

Opponents of the British-American deal sought tonight to find means of obstruction and delay, but this seemed to hinge upon the extent to which the direct interest of a taxpayer could be proved and the general opinion here was that the adversaries were blocked from court action and could depend only upon sufficient massing of public opinion. Apparently the Administration felt legally secure.

Writing his opinion to President Roosevelt last Tuesday, Mr. Jackson went into detail as to constitutional power and especially stressed the responsibility of the Executive to use every authority for national defense at a time when "present world conditions forbid him to risk" any constitutionally avoidable delay.

"No Future Commitments"

The Attorney General conceded that the wide Presidential power over foreign relations was not unlimited, but in this case, Mr. Jackson contended, there were no promises or future commitments by the United States which would require Senate consent or, indeed, any Congressional action. The agreement provided an opportunity to establish naval and air bases for coastline defense, he maintained, but needed no appropriation of money. Thus it was unnecessary for the Senate to ratify "an opportunity that entails no obligation," he declared.

Alluding to precedents, Mr. Jackson remarked that the "proposition falls far short" of the acquisition of the Louisiana Territory by President Jefferson from a belligerent during a European war. Outside of constitutional power, he went on,

Continued on Page Sixteen

UNITED STATES ACQUIRES DEFENSE BASTIONS

Bases at the places indicated by circled dots are being leased by Great Britain to this country for ninety-nine years. The leases for those in Newfoundland and Bermuda are in effect outright gifts; the leases for the others are in exchange for fifty over-age United States destroyers. The bases in the Caribbean area will supplement present American defense centers (black diamonds) in guarding approaches to the Panama Canal.

ROOSEVELT HAILS GAIN OF NEW BASES

Exchange of Over-Age Ships for British Leases Offers Outer Defense Line, He Says

By CHARLES HURD
Special to THE NEW YORK TIMES.

ON BOARD ROOSEVELT TRAIN, Sept. 3—President Roosevelt indicated that the chief value of the trade with Great Britain of fifty over-age destroyers for naval and air base sites in British crown colonies in the Western Hemisphere lay in the fact that this outer line of defenses would keep any enemy away from this country's front door.

For that reason, he said, his agreement with the British Government was more important for the defense of this country than anything since the Louisiana Purchase in 1803, which assured American military control over the Mississippi River.

There may be other similar negotiations, he added, but he cautioned newspaper reporters not to try to guess where they would be, listing the odds at 10 to 1 that such guesses would be wrong.

The President did not deny a suggestion made by a reporter that perhaps Greenland might be the site for another base. He merely renewed his caution against speculation.

The President's view of the agreement, which has been known to be in progress for several weeks, was given at a special press conference on his private train at the same hour that his offices in Washington sent to Congress a message that the exchange was accomplished.

A dozen newspaper reporters heard Mr. Roosevelt read the text of the message to Congress, which he completed during a trip from Hyde Park, N. Y., to Tennessee, North Carolina and West Virginia. He read the message, after laughingly telling them that there was no story. While the document, with supporting papers, was being made public in Washington at noon, he began his press conference at 11:50 A. M. Eastern time.

Mr. Roosevelt called the press conference to meet in the tiny vestibule of his private car forty-five minutes after he departed from South Charleston, W. Va., where he inspected work being done to restore to high productivity a long abandoned Navy ordnance plant built in 1917-18 to construct armor plate and shells.

Among the statements he made

Continued on Page Ten

SHIP TRADE IS HELD NOT HOSTILE ACTION

State Department Stresses Defense Phase of Exchange of Vessels for Bases

Special to THE NEW YORK TIMES.

WASHINGTON, Sept. 3—No country could consider the transfer of fifty United States destroyers to Great Britain and the obtaining by this country of naval and air bases in British New World territory as a hostile act, an informed State Department source said today.

Only a nation seeking world conquest could use this as a pretext for belligerent action, the source asserted.

The intention of this government in completing the agreement was merely to strengthen its own defenses and no other considerations were entertained, State Department officials said, in insisting that the United States had the opportunity to obtain a 4,000 or 5,0000 mile ring of steel around the eastern part of the hemisphere on terms unequaled since the Louisiana Purchase. They added that the protection would last for 100 years.

It was made clear that it was no time to consider any technical provisions which might be sought in international law by opponents of the agreement but that in these dangerous days, when the world is almost literally on fire, defense considerations must come first.

This view was expressed in answer to questions of correspondents about the Second Hague Convention of 1907, of which the United States and Germany are signatories, but Great Britain is not.

Hague 1907 Convention Is Quoted

Article VI of this convention asserts:

"The support in any manner, directly or indirectly, by a neutral power of a belligerent power, by warships, ammunition or war materials of any kind whatever, is forbidden."

Article VIII says:

"A neutral government is also bound to display the same vigilance to prevent the departure from its jurisdiction of any vessel intended to cruise, or menace in hostile operations, which had been adapted entirely or partly within the said jurisdiction for use in war."

Article XXVIII, however, states: "The provisions of this present convention do not apply except to the contracting powers and then only if all the belligerents are parties to the convention."

One could accurately visualize a

Continued on Page Sixteen

LINE OF 4,500 MILES

Two Defense Outposts Are Gifts, Congress Is Told—No Rent on Rest

FOR 50 OLD VESSELS

President Holds Move Solely Protective, 'No Threat to Any Nation'

Texts of messages on leasing of naval bases, Page 10.

By FRANK L. KLUCKHOHN
Special to THE NEW YORK TIMES.

WASHINGTON, Sept. 3—President Roosevelt informed Congress today that he had completed an arrangement by which the United States will transfer to Great Britain fifty over-age destroyers and obtain from Britain ninety-nine-year leases for sea and air bases at eight strategic continental and island points in the Western Hemisphere.

The new American defense line thus established will stretch 4,500 miles from Newfoundland to British Guiana and include other bases on the islands of Bermuda, the Bahamas, Jamaica, St. Lucia, Trinidad and Antigua.

It is intended to make difficult, if not impossible, naval and air attacks upon the United States and much of the New World. The exact sites of the bases will be determined later by the two governments.

A solemn pledge by the British Government to the United States not to scuttle or surrender the British fleet under any conditions was revealed coincidentally by the State Department's publication of correspondence between Secretary Hull and the British Ambassador, the Marquess of Lothian.

Secretary Hull was informed that it represented the "settled policy" of His Majesty's Government not to "surrender or sink" the British fleet.

Reshaping of Naval Defense

The deal, carrying with it far-flung international as well as domestic defense implications, was hailed by President Roosevelt as the most important since the Jefferson Administration completed the Louisiana Purchase in 1803.

Informed official circles contended that it assured the British Fleet as an Atlantic sea-screen for the United States and made it possible for the American Fleet to remain in the Pacific.

Some thought it might lead to an informal defensive alliance between this country and Australia similar to the arrangement recently completed administratively with Canada, although others disagreed on this point.

President Roosevelt informed Congress that the British Government had given the right to bases in Newfoundland and Bermuda as an outright gift, "generously given and gladly received," but that "the other bases mentioned have been acquired in exchange for fifty of our over-age destroyers."

Previously, the President had insisted that the destroyer and base deals were separate.

Legal Basis for Procedure

Mr. Roosevelt explained in his message that he had acted upon a legal opinion by Attorney General Jackson which held that the Chief Executive had the right to dispose of the destroyers and complete the deal without consultation with the Senate and without its approval.

The President made clear that he would not seek the Senate's endorsement by remarking that he sent his statement merely "for the information of Congress."

Chairman Walsh of the Senate Naval Affairs Committee and several other Senators publicly condemned the proposed deal as illegal under domestic and international law when it was reported in the press some weeks ago that President Roosevelt had agreed to give Britain fifty destroyers after pleas from Prime Minister Winston Churchill.

In view of Senator Walsh's stand, some Senators privately expressed the opinion that there might be an attempt to have the Naval Affairs Committee open an investigation of the whole transaction.

After the President's message was

Continued on Page Twelve

"All the News That's Fit to Print."

The New York Times.

LATE CITY EDITION
Fair and cooler today. Tomorrow fair and continued cool.
Temperatures Yesterday—Max., 72; Min., 64

Copyright, 1940, by The New York Times Company.

VOL. LXXXIX..No. 30,181. Entered as Second-Class Matter, Postoffice, New York, N. Y. NEW YORK, WEDNESDAY, SEPTEMBER 11, 1940 THREE CENTS NEW YORK CITY and Vicinity | FOUR CENTS Elsewhere Except in 7th and 8th Postal Zones.

BRITISH BOMB BERLIN, HIT REICHSTAG BUILDING AND OTHER LANDMARKS IN CENTER OF THE CITY; GERMANS POUND AT LONDON IN 8-HOUR ATTACK

ROOSEVELT TO TALK 'POLITICS' TONIGHT BEFORE TEAMSTERS

First Avowed Campaign Talk Will Be a Paid Broadcast Over Two Networks

'HISTORY' WILL BE A TOPIC

President Professes Not to Know if 8-Year Survey Would Be Political or Historical

By CHARLES HURD
Special to THE NEW YORK TIMES.

HYDE PARK, N. Y., Sept. 10—President Roosevelt dropped tonight the nonpolitical attitude which he has heretofore adopted. He will deliver tomorrow night a major speech in Washington before the annual convention of the Brotherhood of Teamsters, Chauffeurs, Stablemen and Helpers, A. F. of L.

He will speak over two nation-wide radio networks on broadcast time to be paid for by the Democratic National Committee, instead of getting facilities free from all four networks available.

The decision was announced by Stephen T. Early, White House secretary, who told news correspondents:

"I expect that President Roosevelt in all probability will deliver the labor speech of the campaign."

The decision that this speech would be Mr. Roosevelt's first bid for re-election apparently was made at the last minute. The President at a press conference earlier indicated that he did not consider the speech to be political.

Mr. Early, who acted as Presidential spokesman later, said that the decision was dictated to some extent by a desire not to burden the radio circuits by carrying the talk as an unpaid news service by all the radio companies and thereby making them liable for granting equal facilities and time to Wendell L. Willkie.

New Phase of the Campaign

The White House announcement, made only a few hours before the President left on his train for the capital, opened a new phase of his activities as they concern this election year. Heretofore he has insisted that his inspection trips and his talks were made as duties of the President.

He will speak nonpolitically in Philadelphia on Sept. 20, when he receives a degree from the University of Pennsylvania, and here on Oct. 5, when he dedicates in one ceremony a new high school and two grade schools.

This attitude also will characterize other similar trips and talks in the future, but White House sources recalled that Mr. Roosevelt made for himself a loophole in the noncampaign rule in his radio address to the Democratic National Convention at Chicago, on July 19.

In that speech he said:

"Since last Summer I have been compelled to abandon proposed journeys to inspect many of our great national projects from the Alleghanies to the Pacific Coast. Events move so fast in other parts of the world that it has become my duty to remain either in the White House itself or at some near-by point where I can reach Washington and even Europe and Asia by direct telephone.

"I do expect, of course, during the coming months, to make my usual periodic reports to the country through the medium of press conferences and radio talks. I shall not have the time or the inclination to engage in purely political debate, but I shall never be loath to call the attention of the nation to deliberate or unwitting falsifications of fact which are sometimes made by political candidates."

Early Recalls President's Stand

On returning from a work session with the President at the Hyde Park house in late afternoon, Mr. Early gathered reporters in his office and recalled that statement by Mr. Roosevelt, laying emphasis on the President's earlier stipulation that he would use the press conferences and radio speeches to reply to political attacks.

"The address tomorrow night will be on radio time to be paid for by the Democratic National Committee," Mr. Early said, and he added, "That is all."

This announcement served to lift the proposed speech, which Mr.

Continued on Page Fifteen

La Guardia to Reveal Choice for President

Special to THE NEW YORK TIMES.

WASHINGTON, Sept. 10—Mayor La Guardia will announce his choice for President in a nation-wide radio broadcast Thursday evening over the NBC Red Network, he announced here today.

The Mayor, here as chairman of the United States section of the United States-Canadian Joint Defense Commission, issued a typewritten announcement to this effect. It has been reported that the Mayor would work for President Roosevelt's re-election, but he refused to go beyond his formal announcement.

The Democratic National Committee will pay the bill for Mayor La Guardia's broadcast tomorrow evening, Edward J. Flynn, chairman of the committee, said yesterday. The speech will be delivered from 7:15 to 7:30 P. M. and will be repeated later from 11:15 to 11:30 P. M. for Pacific Coast listeners.

Mr. Flynn said that the Mayor had suggested the broadcast to him several days ago.

LEHMAN DEPLORES STATE TAX CURBS

Asserts Attempts at 'Economic Isolation' Are a Threat to Democratic Way of Life

Charging that several States have deliberately attempted a policy of "economic isolation" in recent years, Governor Lehman warned last night that their efforts to "stifle the flow of trade across State lines" might eventually threaten our democratic way of life.

Governor Lehman, Governor A. Harry Moore of New Jersey and Governor Raymond E. Baldwin of Connecticut spoke at the annual dinner of the National Tax Association, which is holding its thirty-third annual conference at the Hotel Pennsylvania. Their addresses followed a day of discussion of current tax problems by many governmental and university specialists in the field.

Governor Moore pointed out that at present three-quarters of the cost of government in New Jersey is defrayed by taxes on real property, and he contended that this is too narrow a tax base. In working out replacement taxes, however, he said, care must be taken not to impose taxes that would harm the State's industries in their competitive position with other States.

Governor Baldwin, pointing out that Connecticut has a balanced budget without a sales tax or a State income tax, said that in his State an indicated deficit of $1,500,000 when he took office in January, 1939, has been changed to a surplus of $1,000,000 by a policy of government "friendly" to business, labor and agriculture, with resultant increased production.

Sees Struggle by States for Gain

In his assault on State tax policies that are creating interstate trade barriers, Governor Lehman said that over a period of years there has arisen "a shameless struggle for gain at the expense of sister States." He said that these policies were of "questionable material benefit" to the States that employ them.

"Laws have employed the power of government not for purposes of revenue but rather to stifle the flow of trade across State lines in behalf of domestic interests and enterprises," Governor Lehman said. "The net result has been to limit open competition, raise prices, lower standards of quality and, finally, to affect adversely the national income."

Turning to the "political and social implications" of this trend, Governor Lehman said that "while our democratic way of life is being challenged more fiercely than at any recent stage of our national history, we quibble among ourselves over questionable material benefit."

"If the time ever arrives when boundary lines of the forty-eight States assume greater significance than as mere geographic borders, our democracy is doomed," Governor Lehman continued. "National strength and solidarity in times of crisis are strongly dependent upon singleness of purpose, absolute

Continued on Page Twenty-nine

WILLKIE OPPOSES DELAYING OF DRAFT DESPITE PRESSURE

Hopes the Senate and House Conferees Will Eliminate the Fish Amendment

HE REBUFFS ISOLATIONISTS

Takes Stand in Face of 140 House Republicans Who Voted to Wait

By JAMES A. HAGERTY
Special to THE NEW YORK TIMES.

RUSHVILLE, Ind., Sept. 10—Disregarding strong pressure from members of the Republican organization, Wendell L. Willkie came out today against the House amendment to the Burke-Wadsworth selective service bill, which, if accepted by the Senate, would delay the draft until after the November election.

"I hope that, as a result of the conference between House and Senate conferees on the selective service bill, the Fish amendment is eliminated," Mr. Willkie said in a formal statement.

In opposing any delay in the draft, or selective service for national defense as Mr. Willkie prefers to phrase it, the Presidential nominee ran counter to 140 Republicans in the House who voted for the amendment, including Representative Joseph W. Martin Jr., chairman of the national committee. Only twenty-two Republicans voted against the amendment.

Resists Isolationist Pressure

Mr. Willkie's declaration confirmed the assertion he made in his speech Saturday night that never during his campaign would he take any position in which he did not believe. He is known to regard the international situation as so serious that there should be no avoidable delay in any of the preparations for national defense. He declared for "selective service" in his acceptance speech and explained afterward that he meant selective service now, not later.

Since that time he has resisted pressure from leading members of his party to modify his position and take more of an isolationist stand. He has been frank at all times regarding his views on foreign policy.

He has said frequently that he favored aid to Great Britain, short of war, adding that when he said "short of war" he meant "short of war." In criticizing President Roosevelt's exchange of over-age destroyers for defense bases in British possessions, he favored the trade but attacked the method used by the President as dictatorial.

Research Aides Arrive

Members of the research staff which will accompany Mr. Willkie on his trip to the Pacific Coast arrived here today. Among them were Russell W. Davenport, who resigned as managing editor of Fortune to join the movement to nominate Mr. Willkie; Raymond Leslie Buell, former director of The Foreign Policy Association, and Elliott

Continued on Page Seventeen

Ford's Party Leaves $46 As Tip After Luncheon

By The Associated Press.

DETROIT, Sept. 10—Ethel Gaff, 19-year-old Fort Wayne (Ind.) hotel waitress, need not worry about the $46 left on the table after Henry Ford and his party ate a $4 luncheon. It was the change from a $50 bill which paid for the luncheon.

Miss Gaff was reported in doubt as to whether the money was a tip or whether the automobile manufacturer had forgotten it in his hurry to resume his motor trip.

"I paid the check, and I left the money purposely as a tip for the young lady," Harry Bennett, personnel director of the Ford Motor Company, said today. "She did a very good job in taking care of us, and particularly in keeping curiosity seekers away from Mr. Ford."

PLANE PRODUCTION HAILED BY KNUDSEN

He Says in Buffalo Interview We Will Have 11,000 Combat Craft by April, 1942

By The Associated Press.

BUFFALO, Sept. 10—In nineteen months the Army and Navy will have about 11,000 combat airplanes, fighters and bombers, William S. Knudsen of the National Defense Commission said today as he approached the end of a nation-wide tour of aircraft plants with Major Gen. H. H. Arnold, chief of the Army Air Corps.

"We know the United States is making the best airplanes," he said, and added:

"I believe that presently we can say we are making the most airplanes."

The figure of 11,000 was based on a total production by April 1, 1942, of 33,000 planes, 14,000 destined for Great Britain and 19,000 for the armed services of the United States. General Arnold said that of those to be delivered to the Army and Navy, about 60 per cent would be so-called combat types.

Mr. Knudsen said the current American airplane production of 900 a month, including both military and large commercial types, would be doubled in twelve months. Seated in the office of Burdette S. Wright, president of the Curtiss Aeroplane Division of the Curtiss-Wright Corporation, he fixed at three a day the delivery of new Curtiss P-40 fighter planes to the Air Corps.

General Arnold added that 524 P-40's, one of the newest types of American fighters, were on order for the Air Corps, and that 140 had been delivered.

The visitors saw two of these fighter planes, the American counterpart of British and German pursuit craft, streak at 330 miles an hour across Buffalo's Municipal Airport in a rare public demonstration of the progress of the nation's air rearmament drive.

Delivery of P-40's to both the Air Corps and to Great Britain's Royal Air Force has been slowed down by the limited manufacture of engines by the Allison Engineering Corporation, a General Motors subsidiary at Indianapolis, but Mr.

Continued on Page Fourteen

Italians Jail Prince Doria as Anti-Fascist; Prince Torlonia Also Reported Arrested

By CAMILLE CIANFARRA
Wireless to THE NEW YORK TIMES.

ROME, Sept. 10—Prince Filippo Andrea Doria-Pamaphili-Landi, 54-year-old head of an Italian princely family, has been put in a concentration camp, it is learned.

It is also reported, but without confirmation, that 23-year-old Prince Alessandro Torlonia, whose mother was Elsie Moore of New York and who married a daughter of the King of Spain, also has been arrested.

Circles close to the government emphatically denied this evening that the "alleged" arrests of two Roman princes were part of a round-up of anti-Fascisti.

"No such round-up has taken place," they stated, "and all reports to the contrary are completely unfounded."

Prince Doria's arrest is stated to have been caused by remarks unfriendly to the Fascist regime, which he made publicly less than a fortnight ago. At present, according to friends of the family, he is doing manual labor. Since it is feared he is affected by heart trouble and rheumatism, there is considerable apprehension for his life among his friends.

Prince Doria, after the death of his first wife, married his English nurse, Gesina Mary Dyckes, who is generally credited with having kept him alive with her constant care.

His anti-Fascist feelings are well known in Rome. He heartily disapproved the Ethiopian campaign.

On Dec. 18, 1935, the "day of the faith," when, following the adoption of sanctions against Italy by the League of Nations, Italian women were asked to donate their wedding rings to increase Italy's gold reserves, Prince Doria refused to display the Italian flag on the balcony of his beautiful eighteenth century palace in the Corso Umberto, Rome's main street.

This gesture did not escape a

Continued on Page Six

LONDON IS HARRIED

Night Invaders Resume Bombing After 4 Raids by Day Are Repelled

BRITONS CARRYING ON

People Now Sleep in the Shelters—Water and Gas Impaired

By RAYMOND DANIELL
Special Cable to THE NEW YORK TIMES.

LONDON, Wednesday, Sept. 11—As darkness fell last night a waxing moon rose above the smoldering embers of the previous night's great fires, which threatened for a time to destroy the beautiful St. Paul's Cathedral and St. Mary-le-Bow Church, whose sweet-toned chimes for generations have lulled the Cockney children to sleep. The German Air Force then returned in force to London to continue the attack that has made life in this capital a nightmare since Saturday.

The all clear was sounded at 4:39 this morning, after the raid had been in progress for eight hours and twenty-four minutes.

[Nazi bombers smashed at London with increasing violence early today, The Associated Press reported. Until early this morning, it was stated, the attack was much less ferocious than the previous three. Then the pace stepped up until four separate squadrons were wheeling about the capital at the same time at opposite points of the compass.]

The screams of their bombs, the earth-shaking crashes, the blazes that lit the sky, the clangor of fire engines and ambulances, the bark of anti-aircraft guns and nerve-racking hum of engines droning like a mosquito that does not bite, brought another sleepless and hideous night to 7,000,000 harried persons who are trying to carry on in the face of an attack that spares neither humble workmen's homes nor the homes of the nobility.

Bombing Is at Random

For nine hours last night explosive-laden planes roared overhead, dropping high explosive and incendiary bombs apparently whenever the spirit moved the man in charge of the bomb racks to press the button. They released death and destruction upon helpless civilians who shuddered each time the ground shook beneath them.

Two hospitals, one filled with ailing children and the other a maternity hospital, suffered heavy damage. It is not accurately known at present, while the raid is still going on, how many homes were wrecked or persons killed, for the rescue workers are still digging among the ruins.

It was estimated, however, that Sunday night's raid caused at least 286 deaths and sent 1,400 persons, including the lame, halt and blind, into hospitals, seriously injured.

Question of Morale

But it is not the dead or the injured, or even the extensive property damage that really counts in this battle for London, which is a mere prelude to the Battle for Britain. It is what is happening to the city's life and the nerves of its people that matters the most.

They are standing up to the punishment that is being rained on them from the skies with a courage that makes the eyes of a neutral observer smart at times. There is no doubt about their bravery, but one cannot help but wonder how long any people's nerves can stand up under this kind of bombardment, in which every one knows that each breath may be the last one, and in which the suspense is awful.

That does not mean that a defeatist attitude is growing. Far from it. These people are getting madder by the minute.

Many homes are without gas and tea. Citizens are forced to undergo tremendous inconveniences in getting to and from the places where they earn their livelihood, and their ingrained politeness to one another is becoming a little strained.

There is hardly any one who has not a friend who has been bombed out of his home or has had a narrow escape from death or injury.

Monday night bombs dropped on every section of London. Slum hovels, wealthy homes, warehouses and luxury apartments, all felt the

Continued on Page Two

The International Situation

The War in Europe and Africa

Berlin last night suffered the most intense raid yet inflicted by Royal Air Force planes. Earlier British craft had ranged over Northwestern Germany, Belgium, the Netherlands, France and the Norwegian coast, raiding twenty-five places. Relays of planes blasted Hamburg wharves, a Berlin power plant, docks, factories, barges and supplies at Continental ports. Four bombers failed to return, the Air Ministry reported. [Page 1, Column 8.]

With fires from Monday's attack still smoldering, Nazi bombers swooped down upon London again last night to give the harassed city its fourth sleepless night. The crash of descending bombs started at dusk, when the air-raid sirens sounded the fifth warning of the day. Previous raids had been limited apparently to reconnaissance flights and the planes had been driven off by British fighters. The early alarms were so timed that they drove workers to air-raid shelters at lunch time, at tea time, and again at the height of the evening rush hour with people jammed around crippled transit facilities. Though harassed at their daily tasks after a sleepless and strained night Londoners' morale was unbroken and they were getting "madder by the minute." [Page 1, Column 5.]

Women and children, many dazed from shell shock, jammed the railroads, begged rides from motorists and pleaded with the authorities to find havens for them in an exodus from battered London. The menfolk were carrying on. The Minister of Transport asked that every one refrain from unnecessary travel; the Minister of Health broadcast a plea for aid to the homeless and warned of increasing destitution as a result of bombing. [Page 3, Column 1.]

Announcing more raids against the British capital, Berlin official sources said that new waves would strike London until the British people bring to power a government willing to accept German terms. The present havoc being wrought in London, German papers said, is not the Battle of Britain but merely the Battle of London, and they promised that the Battle of Britain would follow when London, as the nerve-center of the British Isles and an important military objective, had been destroyed. [Page 1, Column 7.].

London and Berlin reports told of a new secret British weapon, a "self-igniting leaf" of cardboard and phosphorus, that had started fires in Germany. [Page 1, Column 6.]

In what was reported to have been the worst raid in the Middle East, Italian fliers bombed Tel Aviv, Palestine, killing 150 civilians. British claimed there were no military objectives there. Rome reported bombing of the Jaffa harbor, the Alexandria-Matruh Railroad and Port Sudan. [Page 6, Column 3.]

Prince Filippo Andrea Doria-Pamphili-Landi, 54-year-old head of an Italian princely family, is now doing manual labor in a concentration camp for remarks unfriendly to the Fascist regime, it was learned in Rome. Reports that Prince Alessandro Torlonia, whose mother was Elsie Moore of New York and who married a daughter of the King of Spain, had also been arrested were unconfirmed. The government denied that there had been a round-up of anti-Fascisti. [Page 1, Column 3.]

American Developments

The American Red Cross sped plans to provide relief for victims of German air raids in London and other British cities. The Washington office of the Red Cross ordered 500,000 garments shipped from its New York warehouses, made preparations to send additional medical supplies, and cabled funds for purchase in London of twelve mobile canteen units of eight vehicles each for feeding homeless civilians. [Page 14, Column 4.]

House and Senate conferees on the conscription bill spent the day tabulating the differences between the two adopted versions of the measure without conclusive result. Washington opinion is that the final version will accept the House age limits of 21 to 45 and that the Fish amendment to delay the draft sixty days will be dropped. [Page 12, Column 3.]

The Senate agreed to limit debate on the Export-Import Bank Bill to ten minutes today after spending yesterday in fruitless debate. Senator Taft has offered the only amendment, restriction of loans to help Latin-American production of strategic, critical or non-competitive products. [Page11, Column 1.]

INCENDIARY 'CARDS' A BRITISH WEAPON

Damp Discs, Dropped by R.A.F. by Thousands, Dry and Ignite—Nazis Incensed

By The Associated Press.

LONDON, Sept. 10—Britain disclosed tonight a new "secret weapon" in the form of innocent-looking bits of chemically treated cardboard dropped by the millions on Germany as delayed fire-bombs that burst into flame in unexpected quarters.

Germany, in first making public the new British tactics, acknowledged that the fire-secreting "calling cards" carried something more than a mere nuisance threat.

British authorities, in subsequently admitting use of the new weapon, described it only as a "self-igniting leaf," and declined to furnish details.

But the authentic German description, given after chemical analysis, sounded like a sequence from some fertile adventure cartoon or a passage from a detective thriller.

The cards, composed of guncotton and phosphorus, are carried in a moist state, the Germans said. Scattered over the countryside in lots of a quarter-million from a single plane, they dry out naturally and spring suddenly into flames about eight inches high when warmed by natural processes to a moderate temperature.

Implying that the cards may bear a printed message, the Germans said they were particularly dangerous because people had been pick-

Continued on Page Twelve

NAZIS SEE BATTLE AS FIGHT TO FINISH

Air Attacks on London Will Be Pressed Till British Yield, It Is Said in Berlin

By The United Press.

BERLIN, Sept. 10—Nazis, angered by British bombing of Berlin and other cities, reported tonight that the German Air Fleet was roaring against London again in an offensive that would be pressed relentlessly until the British capitulate.

New waves of German bombers flying against London will carry out remorseless and incessant warfare, Nazis said, until "the smoking ruins of industrial and military objectives, decimation of the British Air Force and shattered morale of the British people bring into power a government that will accept German terms."

The German terms were regarded here as unconditional capitulation.

Official German quarters were silent regarding any peace terms, but there were many unofficial suggestions that the collapse of Britain is "only a matter of weeks."

The Nazi press said that "now it is an eye-for-an-eye and a tooth-for-a-tooth" battle and said that "the sword of the German air force strikes pitilessly."

"What effects the heavy caliber bombs have were clearly revealed by Warsaw and Rotterdam," one newspaper said. "If London wishes to taste a similar fate to the full extent, then let Herr Churchill and his criminal clique continue to send pirates at night to Germany."

The Propaganda Ministry said

Continued on Page Four

RAID NAZI CAPITAL

Miss U. S. Embassy, Hit Brandenburg Gate, Germans Say

AIM HELD DELIBERATE

R. A. F. Hammers 25 Vital Points to Weaken Foe's Offensive

By PERCIVAL KNAUTH
Wireless to THE NEW YORK TIMES.

BERLIN, Wednesday, Sept. 11—The Royal Air Force this morning attacked the heart of Berlin's governmental center, dropping explosive and incendiary bombs in the immediate vicinity of the Wilhelmstrasse and the Reich's Chancellory. Appearing over the capital a few minutes after midnight with the moon nearly at full to guide them, the British fliers steered their course straight down "Via Triumphalis" bisecting Berlin from east to west and dropped a veritable hail of incendiary bombs on the famous Unter den Linden and Brandenburg Gate.

Two houses away from the American Embassy incendiary bombs set a small fire. Three hundred yards up the "East-West Axis" a bomb estimated at between 500 and 1,000 pounds in weight smashed into the broad asphalt speedway, rocking buildings in a half-mile radius. Incendiary bombs splattered on the rooftops, on the Brandenburg Gate, the Academy of German Art, the House of German Engineers and the old Reichstag building, setting small fires, which, however, were said to have been quickly extinguished.

In THE NEW YORK TIMES office near the Wilhelmplatz detonations of half a dozen explosive bombs in the vicinity of the cellar were heard in the underground air-raid shelter. Incendiary bombs were said to have set small fires in a Jewish hospital, close to the university buildings, and the Charite Hospital.

The Catholic Saint Hedwig's Hospital, second largest in Berlin, likewise was said to have been struck by incendiary bombs which started several fires.

Two Injured by Bombs

In the Invalidenstrasse, close to the central business section, explosive bombs injured two persons and blasted the front of an apartment house as well as part of another house. In Dorotheenstrasse, which runs parallel to Under den Linden, a dud bomb buried itself many feet deep in the street, while another ripped a wide hole in the office building.

An American news agency, with offices on the top floor of a building on this street, had a narrow escape when a bomb struck a house next door.

The British apparently attacked in four waves coming from the west. German military observers estimated the altitude of the first wave at about 18,000 feet, with each successive wave flying at a lower height, the last dropping its bombs from an altitude of about 6,000 feet. They flew straight into the city and when over the governmental district dropped numerous flares, which were followed by both explosive and incendiary bombs.

Some planes were reported to have flown low and machine-gunned anti-aircraft, artillery and searchlight batteries. The ground defenses followed the planes with a steady barrage, which was louder over the center of the capital than ever heard before.

Official German quarters asserted the attack on the governmental district were obviously premeditated and designed to destroy government buildings. R. A. F. fliers, it is asserted, had every opportunity of sighting their objectives both in the light of the great number of flares and the bright moon. It is concluded here, therefore, that the order had been given in London to attack the governmental district, for it is claimed that "all military objectives whatever were strictly avoided."

What form the German retaliation for this attack will take cannot as yet be said. However, German quarters always have been very clear in stating that retaliation will follow a hundred thousandfold in the same manner as the British attack. Never before have governmental districts in Berlin

Continued on Page Four

"All the News That's Fit to Print."

The New York Times.

LATE CITY EDITION
Cloudy, much colder today. Tomorrow partly cloudy and rather cold
Temperatures Yesterday—Max., 68; Min., 52

Copyright, 1940, by The New York Times Company.

VOL. XC..No. 30,237. Entered as Second-Class Matter, Postoffice, New York, N. Y. NEW YORK, WEDNESDAY, NOVEMBER 6, 1940. THREE CENTS NEW YORK CITY and Vicinity | FOUR CENTS Elsewhere Except in 7th and 8th Postal Zones.

ROOSEVELT ELECTED PRESIDENT; CERTAIN OF 429 ELECTORAL VOTES; DEMOCRATS KEEP HOUSE CONTROL

RETAIN HOUSE GRIP

Democrats, Holding 225 Seats, Gain at Least Ten From Rivals

65 ARE NOW IN DOUBT

Latest Figures Indicate Republican Gain of 1 to 3 Senators

By TURNER CATLEDGE

Unless further complete returns today show more Republican winners in yesterday's election, the Democrats not only will have met successfully the challenge of their opponents to control the house but may actually repair some of the damage to their huge majority in the 1938 Congressional election.

The Republicans, on the other hand, may have added from one to three to their roster in the Senate, but this remains to be determined by complete reports.

Returns received up to 4 o'clock this morning indicated that the President's party had dropped only four seats to the opposition, while they had picked up at least ten now held by Republicans. This made the count 225 Democrats, 143 Republicans, one Independent Democrat and one American Labor, with sixty-five seats still in doubt.

The present House is composed of 259 Democrats, 167 Republicans, one Farmer-Laborite, two Progressives and one American Labor member, with five vacancies due to deaths and resignations.

The status of the Senatorial tabulation at that hour, with thirty-six States in contest—thirty-three for full and three for unexpired terms—showed Democrats, 18; Republicans, 7, and 11 still in doubt. This made sure that the new Senate would have at least 62 Democrats, 22 Republicans, 1 Independent, leaving the 11 in doubt. The present ratio of the Senate is 69 Democrats, 24 Republicans, 1 Progressive, 1 Independent and 1 Farmer-Laborite (Senator Shipstead of Minnesota, who ran this year as a Republican).

The Senate's lone Progressive, Senator Robert M. La Follette, trailed Fred H. Clausen, his Republican opponent, in the earlier returns from Wisconsin, but along in the morning hours he forged ahead and word from the Badger State indicated that he might pull through in the toughest fight of his career.

The four seats dropped by Democrats to Republicans were in the Eighth Oklahoma, Sixteenth New York, Fourth California and the Sixth Missouri districts. More than offsetting these were the ten picked up by the Democrats, including the First, Second and Fourth Connecticut districts and the Congressman at Large of that State; the First and Second Rhode Island districts, the Fift and Twenty-second Pennsylvania districts and the Forty-first New York and the Sixteenth Ohio districts. The Democrats made a clean sweep of the delegations in Connecticut and Rhode Island, annexing six seats held in these two States. Perhaps the greatest upsets in the House were the defeats of Representative Phil Ferguson, Democrat, of Oklahoma by Ross Rizley, Republican, and of the Democratic Representative James Fay of the Sixteenth New York by William E. Pheiffer, Republican.

Incumbent Democrats Sticking

Incumbent Democrats were holding tenaciously to leads in most of the other contests in which they were involved and New Deal nominees were threatening sitting Republican Congressman in a number of districts, particularly in States where the Roosevelt victory was assuming landslide proportions in the popular vote.

The Republicans had entertained no hope from the start of capturing the leadership of the Senate, but they claimed chances of picking up from five to ten new seats to add to the twenty-four they now have.

Continued on Page Two

THE VOTE FOR PRESIDENT

State.	Districts Total.	Districts Reported.	Roosevelt, Democrat.	Willkie, Republican.	Thomas, Socialist.	Electoral Vote Roosevelt.	Electoral Vote Willkie.
Alabama	2,300	1,107	140,984	21,224	....	11	..
Arizona	430	270	40,287	21,603	....	3	..
Arkansas	2,169	642	37,285	8,586	....	9	..
California	13,692	9,394	1,043,200	743,522	....	22	..
Colorado	1,610	387	43,150	54,301	....	..	..
Connecticut	169	168	412,648	358,159	....	8	..
Delaware	249	200	50,890	40,312	....	3	..
Florida	1,451	896	246,183	82,581	....	7	—
Georgia	1,730	896	196,687	39,046	....	12	..
Idaho	792	300	36,113	30,155	....	..	..
Illinois	8,378	6,017	1,514,763	1,376,092	....	29	—
Indiana	3,896	2,188	576,754	576,872	....	..	..
Iowa	2,453	1,806	386,657	376,889	....	—	..
Kansas	2,734	1,377	147,821	216,802	....	..	9
Kentucky	4,341	2,240	307,223	193,622	....	11	..
Louisiana	1,712	481	137,518	22,987	....	10	..
Maine	629	633	154,732	163,782	....	..	5
Maryland	1,331	1,194	351,234	241,447	....	8	..
Massachusetts	1,810	1,151	636,856	575,950	....	17	..
Michigan	3,630	1,349	287,245	367,738	....	..	19
Minnesota	3,696	910	258,715	216,433	....	11	..
Mississippi	1,668	635	87,190	4,179	....	9	..
Missouri	4,479	2,914	526,667	480,110	....	..	..
Montana	1,195	262	43,057	26,829	....	4	..
Nebraska	2,043	1,227	124,825	169,063	....	..	7
Nevada	260	177	15,845	11,212	....	3	..
New Hampshire.	294	287	115,932	103,671	....	4	..
New Jersey	3,630	2,038	529,922	564,294*	....	..	16
New Mexico	914	413	60,990	39,300	....	3	..
New York	9,319	9,297	3,231,032	3,021,536	....	47	..
North Carolina	1,926	686	560,558	175,507	....	13	..
North Dakota	2,262	631	72,669	73,330	....	..	..
Ohio	8,675	7,722	1,485,514	1,385,759	....	26	..
Oklahoma	3,613	2,805	355,765	249,117	....	11	..
Oregon	1,693	923	89,971	89,639	....	..	..
Pennsylvania	8,113	7,132	1,912,401	1,670,032	....	36	..
Rhode Island	259	259	181,881	138,432	....	4	..
South Carolina	1,277	958	81,967	4,144	....	8	..
South Dakota	1,936	1,034	61,211	88,369	....	..	4
Tennessee	2,300	1,891	267,724	119,836	....	11	..
Texas	254	244	504,433	118,198	....	23	..
Utah	831	345	63,298	39,941	....	4	..
Vermont	246	246	64,344	78,255	....	..	3
Virginia	1,714	1,622	233,386	103,030	....	11	..
Washington	3,018	1,068	184,800	102,082	....	8	..
West Virginia	2,300	1,016	217,064	155,899	....	8	—
Wisconsin	3,038	1,782	408,665	377,717	....	12	..
Wyoming	696	490	22,399	21,765	....	..	..
						429	51

*Hudson County returns incomplete.

ROOSEVELT WINNER IN MASSACHUSETTS

Indicated Margin Is Below That of 1936—Saltonstall Ahead in a Close Race

Special to THE NEW YORK TIMES.

BOSTON, Nov. 5—President Roosevelt carried Massachusetts over Wendell Willkie in today's election. Indications tonight were that his margin would be smaller than the 174,000 by which he captured the State's 17 electoral votes four years ago.

The Democratic surge was great enough to re-elect Senator Walsh over Henry Parkman Jr. by a substantial margin and to endanger Governor Leverett Saltonstall's re-election in his contest with Attorney General Paul A. Dever.

Lieut. Gov. Cahill, State Secretary Cook, State Treasurer Hurley and State Auditor Cook apparently were re-elected, while Robert T. Bushnell seemed to have won his contest for Attorney General on the basis of returns which had been counted late tonight.

President Roosevelt was Strongest in the industrial cities outside Boston. He carried Lynn by almost 6,000 votes and New Bedford by a ratio of nearly 2 to 1. It was estimated that Roosevelt's margin in Boston would approach 100,000. He carried Somerville by 4,100 votes.

Governor Saltonstall fared much

Continued on Page Four

The War

Leading developments yesterday in the war, accounts of which appear on Page 25—the first page of the second section, —were as follows:

1. A German pocket battleship appeared in mid-Atlantic and shelled a British convoy.

2. Prime Minister Churchill emphasized before the Commons the growing U-boat threat and said bases in Ireland were needed by Britain.

3. In the Greek-Italian hostilities Rome reported an advance in the Yanina sector, the Greeks were said to be closing in on Koritza and a Yugoslav town was bombed by Italian-type planes.

The summary headed "International Situation" also appears on Page 25.

NEW JERSEY VOTE GOES TO PRESIDENT

Willkie Margin Cut in Normal Republican Areas—Edison and Barbour Win

By RUSSELL B. PORTER

On the basis of incomplete returns at 4 o'clock this morning, President Roosevelt appeared to have carried New Jersey with its sixteen electoral votes by a safe plurality—over Wendell Willkie—drastically reduced from 384,000 margin in 1936, and closer to his 31,000 edge in 1932.

The same returns indicated the election of Charles Edison, former Secretary of the Navy and son of the late Thomas A. Edison, the inventor, over his Republican opponent, State Senator Robert C. Hendrickson. Mr. Edison appeared to have polled more votes than the President.

United States Senator W. Warren Barbour, Republican candidate for re-election, ran far ahead of his ticket, and decisively defeated James H. R. Cromwell, former Minister to Canada and husband of Doris Duke, the tobacco heiress.

Eight hours after the polls closed at 8 P. M. there was still uncertainty over State-wide totals. Only one-half of the State's 3,631 election districts had reported their results by that time, and only a few comparatively of these were from the strong Democratic counties—Hudson, where Mayor Frank Hague of Jersey City, vice chairman of the Democratic National Committee, piled up a big Roosevelt vote, and Camden and Middlesex, where big industries with strong Roosevelt labor strength are located.

Big Vote Adds to Delay

The delay in recording the vote from these counties was caused partly by the record-breaking vote, brought out by perfect weather and unprecedentedly heavy registration, partly by the fact that voting machines are not used in these counties, and partly by the traditional withholding of the Hudson County vote until after the Republican counties have reported.

Surrogate John H. Gavin of Hudson County, spokesman for Mayor Hague, estimated early this morning, with the vote still incomplete, that Hudson would give the President and Mr. Edison a plurality of 110,000, including 80,000 in Jersey City. Mr. Cromwell was running far behind.

Four years ago Mr. Roosevelt re-

Continued on Page Twelve

CITY MARGIN WIDE

Lead Totals 727,254—Queens, Richmond Won by Willkie

P. R. SYSTEM UPHELD

Abolition Move Defeated by About 206,550—Simpson Is Elected

By LEO EGAN

Franklin D. Roosevelt piled up a plurality of 727,254 in New York City yesterday as voters in record-breaking numbers went to the polls under clear skies to record their choice for President. This was far short of the 1,375,396 plurality given to him in 1936, when he was a candidate for a second term.

The President carried the three most populous counties in the city but lost Queens and Richmond. Queens gave Wendell Willkie a plurality of 36,875.

Senator James M. Mead, seeking re-election on the Democratic ticket, ran slightly ahead of the President. He carried the city by 845,063, carrying all five counties.

The President's pluralities of 350,610 in Kings, 219,086 in the Bronx and 195,017 in Manhattan were much less than his supporters had counted on except in Manhattan, but they were enough to please them. The Manhattan plurality was larger than expected.

Results in Other Contests

Other features of yesterday's voting in the city were the defeat by an indicated plurality of 206,550 of the proposal to repeal the proportional representation method of selecting members of the City Council, the apparent defeat of Representative James H. Fay in the Sixteenth District, the election of Kenneth F. Simpson, New York County Republican leader, for the Congressional seat now held by Representative Bruce Barton; the election of John Cashmore and Samuel S. Leibowitz, the Democratic candidates for Borough President and County Judge, respectively, in Brooklyn, and the re-election of Representative Vito Marcantonio, outstanding Congressional foe of conscription and the Roosevelt defense program, in the Twentieth Congressional District on Manhattan's upper East Side.

The President carried all but two Assembly districts in Manhattan, losing the Fifteenth and Tenth, and all but three in King's, losing the Ninth, Tenth and Twentieth. He swept all eight districts in the Bronx and lost three out of six in Queens.

In all but one borough the friends of proportional representation were able to beat down the proposal to repeal it. If the proposal had been carried the voters would have elected Councilmen next year on the basis of State Senate districts with

Continued on Page Four

WINNERS OF PRESIDENCY AND VICE PRESIDENCY
Franklin Delano Roosevelt Henry Agard Wallace

DEMOCRATS CARRY STATE BY 230,000

Mead, O'Day, Merritt and Desmond Join President in New York Victory Column

By JAMES A. HAGERTY

For the third time President Franklin D. Roosevelt carried his home State of New York with its forty-seven electoral votes in yesterday's election, this time by a plurality of about 230,000, over Wendell L. Willkie, his Republican opponent.

The vote in New York City with 40 election districts missing out of 4,051 gave Willkie 1,241,501 and Roosevelt 1,937,017, an actual plurality for Roosevelt of 695,516 and an indicated plurality of 700,823.

Outside New York City in 5,004 out of 5,268 election districts, the vote was Willkie 1,685,043, Roosevelt 1,219,817, an actual plurality of 465,276 for Willkie and an indicated plurality of 489,924. This gave the President an actual plurality of 230,240 on these returnst and an indicated plurality of 215,000, which may be slightly higher because of the small number of votes in the unreported districts.

Bruce Barton, Republican candi-

Continued on Page Ten

Bonfires of All Buttons Urged to Heal Bitterness

Public bonfires of all the Democratic and Republican campaign literature and buttons was suggested yesterday by William Allen White, national chairman of the Committee to Defend America by Aiding the Allies, as a means of "healing partisan bitterness and for launching a nation-wide campaign to safeguard American democracy."

Mr. White, in a statement issued last night, urged "unity mass meetings" as soon as possible after election, in a message to the representatives of the group's 717 local chapters in the forty-eight States.

The meetings should be held, he said, "not in the spirit of exaltation on the part of the victorious party but with the idea that we destroy the symbols of partisan bitterness and unite now on a national program of safeguarding American democracy."

PRESIDENT TAKES KEYSTONE STATE

Republican Chairman Concedes Pennsylvania—Guffey Ahead in Senate Race

Special to THE NEW YORK TIMES.

PHILADELPHIA, Wednesday, Nov. 6—Aided by impressive strength in the industrial areas, President Roosevelt apparently duplicated his feat of 1936 and won the thirty-six electoral votes of traditionally Republican Pennsylvania in yesterday's election.

The trend in the senatorial contest between Senator Joseph F. Guffey, Democrat, and Jay Cooke, chairman of the Philadelphia Republican Committee, was in the direction of the re-election of Mr. Guffey, who campaigned on his record of "100 per cent Roosevelt support."

The Democrats, it seemed likely, would gain an undetermined number of seats in the State's Congressional delegation, which had been Republican by nineteen to fifteen, and they appeared to have an even chance of wresting control of the State House of Representatives from the Republicans, who took it over with the election of Governor James two years ago. The Republicans were hopeful of salvaging their majority in the State Senate.

James F. Torrance, Republican State Chairman, conceded Pennsyl-

Continued on Page Four

ROOSEVELT LOOKS TO 'DIFFICULT DAYS'

But Tells Celebrators That He Will Carry On for the Country 'Just the Same'

By CHARLES HURD

Special to THE NEW YORK TIMES.

HYDE PARK, Wednesday, Nov. 6—Standing on the portico of his mother's home here, Franklin D. Roosevelt early today acknowledged his re-election with a promise to continue to be "the same Franklin Roosevelt you have known."

He made this statement to several hundred residents of Hyde Park and vicinity who formed a torchlight procession that carried out a tradition marking Democratic political victories with rallies at the old house, a parade formed by Democrats as soon as returns indicated the victory.

"We are facing difficult days in this country," Mr. Roosevelt told the throng, "but I think you will find me in the future just the same Franklin Roosevelt you have known a great many years."

The President beamed on the crowd as he leaned on the arm of his third son, Franklin Jr., in the bright light of flares set in place by motion-picture camera men.

He smiled and waved while hundreds of persons trooped through the grounds from cars parked first in the driveways and afterward on the Albany Post Road, some of them a quarter of a mile away.

President Faces His Neighbors

Behind the President were grouped about forty guests who had been entertained by Mrs. Roosevelt at supper at her cottage at Val-Kill. But the President faced a crowd in which there were no prominent politicians, no industrial leaders.

These were exclusively his neighbors, who bear to him the same relationship as the villagers bore to his father when he was a minor Democratic leader and a friend of President Cleveland.

President Roosevelt walked on to the front porch of Hyde Park house just before midnight, when he finally broke a vigil over tables on which he marked election returns behind locked doors in the dining room of his home.

The first glare of red flares was seen far off down the driveway. Ten minutes later, exactly at midnight, a town band marched into the car park in front of the house.

The President, with Franklin Jr., stood at the right side of the porch.

Continued on Page Two

BIG ELECTORAL VOTE

Large Pivotal States Swing to Democrats in East and West

POPULAR VOTE CUT

First Time in History That Third Term Is Granted President

By ARTHUR KROCK

Over an apparently huge popular minority, which under the electoral college system was not able to register its proportion of the total vote in terms of electors, President Roosevelt was chosen yesterday for a third term, the first American in history to break the tradition which began with the Republic. He carried to victory with him Henry A. Wallace to be Vice President, and continued control of the House of Representatives by the Democrats was also indicated in the returns.

But in many of the larger States so many precincts were still missing early this morning, and the contest in these States was so close, that Wendell L. Willkie, the Republican opponent, whose name Mr. Roosevelt never mentioned throughout the campaign, refused to concede defeat. He said it was a "horse race," and that the result would not be known until today. He went to bed in that frame of mind.

As the returns mounted there seemed little, however, to sustain Mr. Willkie's hope. New York, Massachusetts, Connecticut, Rhode Island, Pennsylvania, Ohio and Illinois, of the greater States, all appeared to have been carried safely by the President. The Solid South had resisted all appeals to revolt against Mr. Roosevelt's quest for a third term. The Pacific and Mountain States were following the national trend.

States for Mr. Roosevelt

States sure or probable for the President are:

Alabama, Arizona, Arkansas, California, Connecticut, Delaware, Florida, Georgia, Illinois, Kentucky, Louisiana, Maryland, Massachusetts, Missouri, Minnesota, Mississippi, Montana, Nevada, New Hampshire, New Jersey, New Mexico, New York, North Carolina, Ohio, Oklahoma, Pennsylvania, Rhode Island, South Carolina, Tennessee, Texas, Utah, Virginia, West Virginia and Wisconsin—electoral votes, 429.

States sure or probable for Mr. Willkie:

Kansas, Maine, Michigan, Nebraska, North Dakota, South Dakota, Vermont—electoral votes 51.

States doubtful or insufficiently reported:

Colorado, Idaho, Indiana, Iowa, Oregon, Washington and Wyoming—electoral votes, 51.

The Electoral Vote

Listing as doubtful nine States, including several like California, Ohio and Indiana, which seem certain to join the Democratic column, there were at 3 A. M. only 51 electoral votes in possible dispute. The President had an apparently certain total of 429, while with more or less security in Mr. Willkie's column were only 51 votes.

No shift or series of shifts could affect the electoral result and the indications were that the President's total would reach from 420 to 470.

Either figure would be much less than the nearly clean sweeps he had in 1932, when he carried forty-two States, and in 1936, when only Maine and Vermont went Republican. And unless the Far West and the Mountain States shall be shown to have given incredible majorities and late returns from the Eastern States pile up the President's votes higher than indications seem to make possible, Mr. Roosevelt's popular majority will be far less than he had against Herbert Hoover and Alf M. Landon.

It appeared early this morning that a maximum of 5,000,000 and a minimum of 2,000,000 would represent the final difference between the popular votes cast for the two major Presidential candidates. The Associated Press tabulation at 1:30 A. M. was 14,879,930 for Mr. Roose-

Continued on Page Two

Willkie Retires Refusing to Give Up; He Declines Any Statement Before Today

Grimly clinging to his avowed determination not to give up the fight, Wendell L. Willkie said at 1:30 this morning that he intended to go to bed in his suite at the Hotel Commodore, and that he would have no statement to make concerning the election until some time after he wakes up this morning.

This information, relayed from his fourteenth-floor suite to the waiting crowd of reporters in the press headquarters downstairs, was the only word that came from Mr. Willkie after he had briefly appeared before a crowd of cheering campaign workers at 12:20 A. M., to say that he was neither afraid nor disheartened, and repudiate indignantly suggestions that he should concede his defeat.

When he appeared at that time before about 1,500 faithful supporters in the Grand Ball Room of the Commodore Hotel, Mr. Willkie pleaded with them not to quit and expressed his confidence that the fight they had jointly waged would eventually be won.

His appearance before his campaign workers came after hours of seclusion in his private suite, where he repeatedly characterized the election as "a horse race" and predicted that the result would not be known definitely until some time today. Mr. Willkie appeared before the crowd of campaign workers at 12:19 A. M.

Holding up both hands to ask for silence while they gave him an ear-splitting ovation, Mr. Willkie said:

"Fellow workers: I first want to say to you that I never felt better in my life. I congratulate you in being a part of the greatest crusade of this century. And that the principles for which we have fought will prevail is as sure as that the truth will always prevail.

"And I hope that none of you are either afraid or disheartened because I am not in the slightest.

"I just wanted to come down and thank you so much for being my fellow fighters in this struggle—to

Continued on Page Five

"All the News That's Fit to Print."

NEWS INDEX, PAGE 51, THIS SECTION

The New York Times.

LATE CITY EDITION
Occasional rain, little change in temperature today. Tomorrow partly cloudy, continued cool.
Temperatures Yesterday—Max., 67; Min., 49

Section 1

VOL. XC No. 30,388. Entered as Second-Class Matter, Postoffice, New York, N. Y. NEW YORK, SUNDAY, APRIL 6, 1941. Including Rotogravure Picture, Magazine and Book Review. TEN CENTS New York City and Vicinity

GERMANS INVADE YUGOSLAVIA AND GREECE; HITLER ORDERS WAR, BLAMING THE BRITISH; MOSCOW SIGNS AMITY PACT WITH BELGRADE

U. S. STEEL STRIKE IS CALLED BY C. I. O., EFFECTIVE TUESDAY

Murray Says Wage Talks Failed and Plans Picketing in Tie-Up Involving 261,000 Men

ROOSEVELT MAY STEP IN

President Is Reported to Have Summoned C. I. O. Chief in Move to Bar Walkout

By The Associated Press.

PITTSBURGH, April 5 — The C. I. O. Steel Workers Organizing Committee tonight ordered its members in all steel mills of the giant United States Steel Corporation, employing about 261,000 wage-earners, to stop work at midnight next Tuesday.

The union said that negotiations for a wage increase and other benefits had collapsed.

Philip Murray, C. I. O. president and chairman of the Steel Workers Organizing Committee, telegraphed instructions to local union units of the corporation to establish continuous picket lines at all plant gates.

[The United Press reported from Pittsburgh last night it had learned authoritatively that President Roosevelt, concerned over the threatened stoppage, had invited Mr. Murray to a White House conference tomorrow or Tuesday.]

The company produces more than one-third of America's steel, an amount exceeding all of that made in England. It hold millions of dollars in defense contracts.

Mr. Murray termed the cessation of work a "lockout" rather than a strike, asserting that the company had rejected his suggestion to continue negotiations, which began March 20, another week, with any agreement to be retroactive to April 1. The company was said to be willing to make the agreement retroactive only to April 8.

The sudden development, threatening to spread the nation's strike area to the vital steel industry, came during an interim of wage negotiations, which still are scheduled to be resumed Monday at 10 A. M.

Mr. Murray called in 100 local union leaders today for conference. It was the third such meeting since the union made known its nine-point demands, which included a wage increase of 10 cents an hour, a closed shop, check-off of union dues by the company, liberalized vacations and establishment of seniority rights.

The company's minimum pay, established in 1937, is 62½ cents an hour, with the average pay of wage-earners about 87 cents an hour. This contract expired April 1 and was extended to April 8.

The company's original counter-offer of a 2½ cents an hour wage rise was rejected by Mr. Murray. Tonight it was learned this offer had been raised to five cents an hour but again was refused by the union. The company contended it made but $60,000,000 of its $102,000,000 profit last year in its steel plants. The other profits came from coal, cement shipping and other subsidiaries. The company has insisted it cannot increase wages without increasing the price of steel. The Government has firmly refused to sanction any such price advance.

In his instructions to local unions, Mr. Murray said:

"The Carnegie-Illinois Steel Company has either rejected entirely or submitted unsatisfactory counter proposals with respect to each of the points offered by the S. W. O. C. in its program.

"The S. W. O. C. will attempt to arrive at an agreement with the companies involved to provide for the continuance at work of the necessary maintenance men during the suspension of operations. Further instructions regarding this situation will be forwarded to you by wire.

"Peaceful picket lines shall be established at all plant gates and maintained at all times during the cessation of work. There should be no violence or other unlawful acts on the part of members or representatives of the S. W. O. C."

No comment was forthcoming from the company on the development.

Continued on Page Forty-one

The International Situation

SUNDAY, APRIL 6, 1941

Germany's armies this morning launched a vast attack upon Yugoslavia and Greece. The move was announced over the Berlin radio in an order of the day from Reichsfuehrer Hitler, read by Propoganda Minister Goebbels; it denounced "the Belgrade government of intrigue" and said German troops would not lay down their arms until "this band of ruffians" and every last Briton had been eliminated from Southeastern Europe. [Page 1, Column 8.]

As Belgrade's first air raid was reported, it was believed the principal Nazi attacks had been launched from Bulgaria, one across Southern Yugoslavia and another southward toward Salonika. Bulgaria's army was said to have an active role, but Hungary's was believed inactive for the present. The Yugoslavs were expected to fight a rear-guard delaying action until they reached their strong natural defense positions. The Belgrade Government had planned to evacuate the capital, going to some southern point. The United States Minister was reported remaining in Belgrade. [Page 1, Column 5.]

With dramatic suddenness Yugoslavia and Soviet Russia signed a five-year non-aggression and friendship pact providing that if either signatory became the victim of aggression by a third State the other would maintain a policy of "strictest friendship." The pact will take effect immediately and the articles of ratification will be exchanged in Belgrade "at the earliest possible moment." [Page 1, Column 4.]

On the African front, British Headquarters in Cairo reported that an Axis advance east of Bengazi, Libya, "has been successfully held and the situation is well in hand." Empire forces in Ethiopia crossed the Awash River, to a point only eighty miles from Addis Ababa, while other units driving down on the capital from Eritrea captured Adowa and Adigrat. [Page 1, Column 6; Map, Page 7.]

The British Air Ministry augmented early brief accounts of the R. A. F attack on Brest Friday night and early Saturday by stating that the 26,000-ton German battleships Gneisenau and Scharnhorst had been "very, very lucky" if they had escaped serious damage from new and powerful British bombs. R. A. F. aircraft, it was said, had dived to 1,000 feet to unleash their missiles on the Nazi raiders and had fired oil stores and warehouses near by, while other British planes dropped bombs on Rotterdam and the Ruhr. [Page 9, Column 1.]

The sharp British blow at the two German raiders coincided with a Berlin claim that 718,000 tons of British and Allied shipping had been sunk during March by German surface craft, U-boats, mines and airplanes. A German auxiliary cruiser operating "overseas" was said to have sunk the British auxiliary cruiser Voltaire of 13,255 tons. Moreover, Berlin said, U-boats in two days had sunk eighteen ships, totaling 106,000 tons, in a British convoy. [Page 13, Column 1.]

President Roosevelt's hint that he might soon lift combat-zone restrictions on the Red Sea to permit passage of American ships with war supplies for Britain aroused considerable interest in Washington. Senator George, chairman of the Senate Foreign Relations Committee, was said to feel that such action would necessitate Congressional amendment of the Neutrality Act; other members of Congress were believed to hold the President already had power to do this through provisions of the Lease-Lend Law. [Page 21, Column 1.]

Uruguay formally seized two Italian and two Danish ships in her harbors and placed the crews, comprising 119 men, under the direction of the Italian and Danish consuls, respectively. Many of the Danish seamen were reported to have expressed pleasure over the seizures and to have exhibited pro-British emblems. [Page 19, Column 1.]

COAL TIE-UP ENDED IN 65% OF THE MINES

Southern Operators Hold Out but Contract for Rest Will Be Signed Tomorrow

Yielding to pressure from the Federal Government, representatives of 65 per cent of the nation's soft-coal producers agreed yesterday to sign a new contract with the United Mine Workers tomorrow. At least 300,000 miners are expected to return to work Tuesday or Wednesday, ending a week's stoppage that threatened to cut off vital fuel supplies for defense industries.

Dr. John R. Steelman, director of the United States Conciliation Service, who succeeded in breaking the four-week deadlock between the C. I. O. union and the operators, predicted that virtually all the mines would be open within a week. Other government officials said they believed the settlement in the soft-coal fields would provide a key to peaceful adjustment of employer-union differences in steel and anthracite, thus removing two additional threats of delay in the defense program and insuring uninterrupted work for 1,000,000 men.

Thirteen associations of Southern bituminous operators were the sole holdouts against the tentative accord effected by Dr. Steelman, and there were indications that their ranks were beginning to crumble. Union officials said scattered companies in the Southern States had indicated their intention of signing with the John L. Lewis organization, whether or not their associations went along. The union relied on the pressure of competition to bring the others into line in a few days.

Under the terms of the proposed contract the United Mine Workers will win its full demand for a basic wage of $7 a day. This represents an increase of $1 over the rate previously in effect in the North and $1.40 over the Southern rate. The union's insistence on abolition of

Continued on Page Thirty-three

KNUDSEN ASSAILS RADICALS IN LABOR

Charges They Hamper Output for Defense—Cooperation by All Vital, He Warns

Text of Mr. Knudsen's address appears on Page 40.

Asserting that the most serious thing about the strike in the Allis-Chalmers plant in Milwaukee was not the time lost in the production of defense materials but the fact that it showed that "radical" labor leaders could tell the State and Federal Governments "where to get off," William S. Knudsen last night proposed a program for dealing with labor difficulties that he said would eliminate 90 per cent of the strikes.

The director-general of the Office of Production Management, who spoke at the Army Day dinner of the Military Order of the World War at the Hotel Waldorf-Astoria, said that the labor situation during the last month had grown worse and warned that the epidemic of strikes must be stopped or the effort for defense and aid to Great Britain, Greece and Yugoslavia would fail.

Interrupted by applause when he started to discuss the labor situation, Mr. Knudsen declared that time was the all-important element in America's defense program and declared that if the nation could put on a "little steam" in production during the eighty-nine days remaining before the Fourth of July "we might save a lot of blood later on."

"I do not believe that legislation against strikes is necessary or enforceable," Mr. Knudsen said, "but I do believe that during the emergency period a definite procedure should be followed in order that strikes may be held to a minimum.

"For instance, I believe that strike votes should be taken under the supervision of the Labor Department. I believe a certain mini-

Continued on Page Forty

TREATY NOW VALID

Moscow Discloses That Pledge of Friendship Was Made Yesterday

PEACE IS TERMED AIM

Strictest Neutrality Is Provided—Accord Is Hailed in London

By The Associated Press.

MOSCOW, Sunday, April 6—Soviet Russia and Yugoslavia have signed a treaty of friendship and non-aggression after several days of negotiation, Tass, Soviet official news agency, announced early today.

The agency said the pact had been signed yesterday by the Russian Premier and Foreign Commissar, Vyacheslaff M. Molotoff, and Milan Gavrilovitch, former Yugoslav Cabinet Minister and Yugoslavia's representative in Moscow.

The treaty declared that Russia and Yugoslavia were "inspired by the friendship existing between the countries and convinced that the preservation of peace forms their common interest" and hence had decided to conclude the pact.

The treaty was for five years.

Its first article provided neither country would attack the other and that each would respect the sovereign rights and territorial integrity of the other.

It provided that, in case of aggression against one of the countries by a third power, the other would observe a policy of friendly relations with the country attacked.

TEXT OF THE TREATY

MOSCOW, Sunday, April 6 (UP)—Tass News Agency gave out today the text of the treaty between the Soviets and Yugoslavia, as follows:

A treaty on friendship and non-aggression between the Union of Soviet Socialist Republics and the Kingdom of Yugoslavia.

The Presidium of the Supreme Soviet U. S. S. R. and His Majesty the King of Yugoslavia, inspired by friendship existing between the two countries and convinced that preservation of peace forms their common interest, decided to conclude a treaty on friendship and non-aggression and appointed for this purpose their representatives:

Presidium of the Supreme Soviet U. S. S. R.—Vyacheslaff M. Molotoff, chairman of the Council of Peoples Commissars and Peoples Commissar of Foreign Affairs; His Majesty the King of Yugoslavia — Milan Gavrilovitch, Envoy Extraordinary and Minister Plenipotentiary of Yugoslavia, Bozhin Simich and Colonel Dragutin Savich, which representatives, after exchanging their credentials found in proper form and due order, agreed on the following:

ARTICLE I

The two contracting parties mutually undertake to desist from

Continued on Page Twenty-five

YUGOSLAVIA FIGHTS

Belgrade Has Air Raid as Armies Resist, Berne Hears

DRIVE FROM BULGARIA

Greeks Announce Nazi Attack—Stukas Clear Path, Germans Say

By RAY BROCK

Wireless to THE NEW YORK TIMES.

BELGRADE, Yugoslavia, Sunday, April 6—At 3:25 o'clock this morning the air-raid sirens in Belgrade sounded an alarm. For the Yugoslavs it was the first indication that the nation was at war.

An hour later, at 4:32, two Yugoslav fighter planes appeared over the city, flying in an easterly direction. They came from the Zemun airdrome. Two more fighter planes appeared a short time later.

[At this point wireless connections with Belgrade were cut.]

Greeks Announce Attack

The Greek High Command announced in a communiqué broadcast from Athens that since 5:15 A. M., Athens time, the German troops had been attacking Greek troops on the Bulgarian border, the Columbia Broadcasting System announced this morning. No further details were in the communiqué as it was received here.

The German Propaganda Ministry announced in a broadcast from Berlin, according to CBS, that swarms of German planes, including Stuka dive bombers, were "pouncing like hornets" on Greek and Yugoslav airdromes and railways in an effort to cripple the resistance to the invading German armies. The Nazi Propaganda Ministry also asserted that the planes were clearing a path for tanks and infantry, and that parachute troops were landing at strategic points within the Greek-Yugoslav defenses. There was no confirmation of these claims, however.

Belgrade Has Second Alarm

By Telephone to THE NEW YORK TIMES.

BERNE, Switzerland, Sunday, April 6—The Belgrade correspondent of THE NEW YORK TIMES reported at 5:30 o'clock this morning that naturally he had heard of the situation, but that "you wouldn't know the difference." Aside from two air-raid alarms in the capital early this morning, no incident had yet occurred. Reports as to the exact location of the fighting were very scant.

On the Greek frontier the invasion doubtlessly came from Bulgaria through the Struma Valley with a secondary attack down the Vardar Valley. This latter attack, however, would entail driving across the southeastern border of Yugoslavia—the Third Army region based on Skoplje under General Ilija Brasitch.

For some time before the Yugoslav crisis began to take on even faintly menacing tones, the Yugoslav High Command had been re-

Continued on Page Twenty-four

New Army Marches in Rain Here; Nation Joins in Military Tribute

By HANSON W. BALDWIN

The new Army of the United States paraded down the Fifth Avenues of many cities yesterday as the nation opened an unprecedented week-end celebration of Army Day.

Veterans of past wars marched with youngsters who may become veterans of a future war, as the muffled beats of drumheads dampened by the rain epitomized the somber attitude with which thousands of spectators in many cities viewed their marching men. Not since 1917 and another war has the nation so taken the Army—now truly a national army—to itself with quiet, restrained pride.

For the music of the bands was but a faint echo in people's minds of the growing thunder of Europe's guns, and the serious attitude of the onlookers was matched in New York, Washington and other Eastern cities by the weather. The skies were a sullen gray and the peaks of New York's skyscrapers were veiled in mist as the Army marched and drumheads burst and slickers poured off torrents of the rain.

The New York parade along upper Fifth Avenue, which had been expected to be the greatest Army Day event in the city's history, lost considerably in volume but gained in solemnity because of the weather. Not many more than half of the expected 30,000 marchers participated, and the sparse, umbrellaed crowd that watched could not have numbered at its peak more than 30,000 to 40,000. The crowd dwindled at times during the two-hour parade to less than half that number. The weather, too, turned the march-past into a real test of soldiering, particularly for 4,500 men of the Forty-fourth Division from Fort Dix, N. J., who had negotiated seventy-eight miles of roads slick with rain in motor convoys to participate in the parade.

Mayor La Guardia, huddled be-

Continued on Page Forty-two

Hitler's Order of the Day

Adolf Hitler's declaration that Germany was at war with Yugoslavia was read over the Berlin radio early today by Propaganda Minister Joseph Goebbels. As heard by the National Broadcasting Company's station in New York and translated from the German, it read:

In the name of the Fuehrer, Adolf Hitler, I am reading the following order of the day to the German Army of the East:

Berlin, April 6, 1941.

Soldiers of the Southeast Front:

Since early this morning the German people are at war with the Belgrade government of intrigue. We shall only lay down arms when this band of ruffians has been definitely and most emphatically eliminated, and the last Briton has left this part of the European Continent, and that these misled people realize that they must thank Britain for this situation, they must thank England, the greatest warmonger of all time.

The German people can enter into this new struggle with the inner satisfaction that its leaders have done everything to bring about a peaceful settlement.

We pray to God that He may lead our soldiers on the path and bless them as hitherto.

In accordance with the policy of letting others fight for her, as she did in the case of Poland, Britain again tried to involve Germany in the struggle in which Britain hoped that she would finish off the German people once and for all, to win the war, and if possible to destroy the entire German Army.

In a few weeks long ago the German soldiers on the Eastern Front, Poland, swept aside this instrument of British policy. On April 9, 1940, Britain again attempted to reach its goal by a thrust on the German north flank, the thrust at Norway.

In an unforgettable struggle the German soldiers in Norway eliminated the British within a period of a few weeks.

What the world did not deem possible the German people have achieved. Again, only a few weeks later, Churchill thought the moment right to make a renewed thrust through the British Allies, France and Belgium, into the German region of the Ruhr. The victorious hour of our soldiers on the West Front began.

It is already war history how the German Armies defeated the legions of capitalism and plutocracy. After forty-five days this campaign in the West was equally and emphatically terminated.

Then Churchill concentrated the strength of his Empire

Continued on Page Twenty-six

BRITISH HALT DRIVE IN LIBYA, GET ADOWA

Axis Checked East of Bengazi —South Africans Within 80 Miles of Addis Ababa

Wireless to THE NEW YORK TIMES.

CAIRO, Egypt, April 5—The British announced today that their forces in Libya had halted the advance of German and Italian armored units somewhere east of Bengazi. The situation here after the recapture of that port by the Axis was said to be "well in hand."

At the same time the swift progress of the British Imperial forces in East Africa resulted in the capture of Adowa [and of near-by Adigrat, according to The Associated Press] while South African troops in Ethiopia crossed the Awash River and struck to within eighty miles of Addis Ababa.

[Massawa, the Red Sea port toward which the British armies of East Africa are racing, was reported to have defied a British demand for surrender, according to an Associated Press dispatch from Khartum.]

South African Advance

After the British in the last two days took the two most easily defendable areas in East Africa, Italian resistance appeared to be crumbling fast. The South African troops, who have marched all the way from Italian Somaliland now are moving westward along the Jibuti railway. After a brisk but brief battle at the crossing of the Awash, this column is pushing through the African hill country toward the higher rolling grassland plateau around Addis Ababa.

It is said the South Africans averaged a twenty-five-mile advance every day in the last two months.

North of the capital, combined British and Indian forces are pursuing the fleeing Italians toward Dessye through difficult mountainous terrain. Between Asmara and Adowa they advanced with only slight skirmishing at many points that might have become other Cherens had Italian morale been good.

The occupation of Adowa again frees the battle site where in 1896 Ethiopia's Emperor Menelik routed the Italians, killing 6,000 and capturing 4,000, thus preserving his nation's independence until 1935. The town itself has a population of 6,000.

Despite the lightness of the fighting in this area, advancing British forces surprised and captured a battalion of Italian infantry. Italians are running southward, apparently almost wholly disorganized, throwing away their arms and surrendering on the slightest excuse,

Continued on Page Seven

NAZI UNITS CROWD YUGOSLAV BORDERS

Some Are Reported in Albania, Many in Southern Hungary— German Plane Downed

By C. L. SULZBERGER

By Telephone to THE NEW YORK TIMES.

BELGRADE, Yugoslavia, April 5 —The German military encirclement of Yugoslavia was nearing completion tonight as eight new divisions reportedly jammed the Hungarian roads, a powerful armored unit concentrated at Bela Crkva, on the Rumanian frontier one and a half hours' drive from Belgrade, and the first Nazi troops entered Albania.

British information sources reported from Bucharest and Budapest that the invasion of Southeastern Yugoslavia by the German Army of the Struma was ready to begin at any moment.

It is only worth noting that most of the more pessimistic predictions emanate from German-controlled countries, such as Hungary, Rumania and Bulgaria, or from the Croat capital of Zagreb, which is the center of the small but active German-inspired Fascist movement.

The facts of the situation are clear. Once more the normal peasant life of Hungary has been thrown into turmoil by the huge disruption caused by the passage of German Armies, and eight separate divisions were said to have been sighted. The motorized units on three points of the Hungarian southern frontier—Mohacs, Szeged and Nagy Kanizsa —were increased, as were the concentration in the Rumanian Banat.

An absolutely reliable source said German soldiers were known to have arrived in Albania—the debarkation point coming as somewhat of a surprise and indicating the probability that airplane transport was employed. Four Tyrolean mountain divisions have entered Italy in the last four days.

The government ordered the closing of all frontiers this morning. Outerbridge Horsey, secretary of the United States Legation in Budapest, who is coming here by train for emergency work, was stopped at the Hungarian frontier and the legation here is trying to facilitate his transport now by automobile.

All Danube traffic on the Yugoslav stretch of the river has now been halted. A German Messerschmitt plane was shot down yesterday while cruising over Maribor and it crashed at Ptuj.

Circulation through the country save with special military permit has been halted. All cars are being stopped by the police and are being requisitioned unless they have special passes. A new War Press Bureau has been established. At the same time Yugoslav technical con-

Continued on Page Twenty-five

NAZI TROOPS MARCH

Goebbels Reads Order to Germans to Rid Europe of All Britons

QUICK BLOW PLEDGED

Greece Told She Invited It—U. S. Is Said to Share Blame

By DANIEL T. BRIGHAM

By Telephone to THE NEW YORK TIMES.

BERNE, Switzerland, Sunday, April 6—At 5 o'clock this morning German forces attacked Yugoslavia and Greece in the long-awaited culmination of the Balkan war of nerves.

The news broke on the world with startling suddenness when a German radio station announcer with a triumphant blast this morning introduced Dr. Joseph Goebbels, Minister of Propaganda, who then read Reichsfuehrer Hitler's order of the day to "my forces in Southeast Europe."

"Since dawn this morning," said Dr. Goebbels, "the German Reich has been at war with Yugoslavia and Greece."

It was indicated that the friendship pact signed between Yugoslavia and Russia yesterday was one of the factors of which Germany complained. This was another version of the Nazi charges of "aggressive encirclement of Germany," which have been used since Herr Hitler's advent to power.

Yugoslav Arming Held Cause

Another source of grievance, it would seem, was Belgrade's mobilization, a point that Herr Hitler mentioned in his order of the day as one of the chief reasons for the attack.

Immediately after Dr. Goebbels's broadcast, telephone communications to the eastward from this city —and south to Rome—were cut off.

[United States and British encouragement to the Yugoslavs in their resistance to German demands was also cited as grounds for Germany's attack, according to The Associated Press. Alleged American offers of material aid were also quoted.]

The German Army was told it would not lay down its arms until the "ruffians" and "plotters" in Belgrade had been deposed and the last Briton driven out of this territory.

Friendship for Greeks

German soldiers have been fighting in Greece since dawn today, the proclamation stated. It was indicated that the battle in Greece was not directed against the population but only against the "world enemy," Great Britain, who had dispatched troops there for an attack against the interests of the Reich.

Germany, Herr Hitler was quoted as saying, does not consider herself at war with Greece and will not molest any Greek who does not take up arms against the German Army, but any who lends his support to the British will be crushed.

"Soldiers of the Southeast Front," the Reichfuehrer proclaimed, "your hour has now come."

He then told these troops that they must emulate their comrades in Poland, Scandinavia, the Lowlands and France. He added that the general mobilization in Yugoslavia was considered by the Reich as final proof that Britain had mixed into the internal affairs of Yugoslavia and would lead that country into hostile acts against Germany.

Yugoslav Provocation Charged

BERLIN, Sunday, April 6 (UP)—The German radio, in broadcasting Reichsfuehrer Hitler's order to the German Army, quoted him as saying Germany was unable longer to endure the Yugoslav attitude. The Reich was said to be reacting to the mistreatment, "attacks and murdering" of Germans in the Serb Kingdom.

The order said the greatest patience had been exercised by Germany respecting Yugoslavia and Greece, but that now the moment for action had arrived.

It was said that Herr Hitler had frequently called attention to the dangers in the Southeast.

Now, it was said, Germany was

Continued on Page Twenty-six

"All the News That's Fit to Print."

The New York Times.

LATE CITY EDITION
Fair and continued cool today and tomorrow.
Temperatures Yesterday—Max., 62; Min., 40

VOL. XC..No. 30,425. Entered as Second-Class matter, Postoffice, New York, N. Y. NEW YORK, TUESDAY, MAY 13, 1941. THREE CENTS NEW YORK CITY and Vicinity

HESS, DESERTING HITLER, FLIES TO SCOTLAND; BERLIN REPORTED HIM MISSING AND INSANE; DARLAN MEETS HITLER; R. A. F. POUNDS PORTS

COAST SHIPYARDS SHUT BY PICKETS; RETURN REJECTED

Navy and Maritime Work Stops as Other Crafts Refuse to Pass Heavy Lines

POLICE STAY IN RESERVE

Union Leaders Declare Fight to Finish as Meeting Votes Against Lapsing Strike

By FOSTER HAILEY
Special to THE NEW YORK TIMES.

SAN FRANCISCO, May 12—A request from the Office of Production Management that striking machinists in eleven shipbuilding yards in the San Francisco Bay area return to work pending an attempt to settle their wage and hour demands in conference was unanimously rejected today by a mass meeting of those of the strikers affiliated with the American Federation of Labor.

Picket lines around the eleven plants, established by the 1 200 A. F. of L. machinists and the 700 who belong to the Congress of Industrial Organizations, brought a complete halt to operations as 15,000 to 18,000 other workers who are not on strike refused to pass through the machinists' picket lines.

The strike was called Friday midnight by Local 68 of the A. F. of L. and Lodge 1304 of the C. I. O. The latter is affiliated with the Steel Workers Organizing Committee, headed by Philip Murray, president of the C. I. O. The walkout is in protest against hourly wage and overtime provisions of a master contract for the whole coast signed April 23 in Seattle by representatives of labor, the OPM and the shipbuilders.

Reason for Refusal to Return

The request to go back to work pending a conference came from Joseph Keenan, A. F. of L. representative of the OPM. It was presented to a mass meeting of about 1,000 members of Local 68 by its business agents, E. F. Dillon and Harry Hook, who later said:

"Our members took the position, and passed a resolution to the effect, that inasmuch as we've never been able to get an agreement out of Bethlehem in the past twenty-two years, we don't feel any good purpose would be served by sending the men back to work before an agreement is reached now.

"We feel it would only prolong the controversy and probably result in a repetition of what we are going through now."

Although Bethlehem Shipbuilding, a division of Bethlehem Steel, is only one of the eleven plants involved in the strike, it is by far the largest, employing about 900 of the 1,200 A. F. of L. machinists who are on strike, and it is considered the bellwether of the group.

Out to Compel Settlement

"We intend to tell Mr. Keenan, if he telephones us from Chicago, the attitude of the strikers," Mr. Dillon said. "When he made the request yesterday he said he would call back today. (He had not called up to late tonight.)

"We would be glad to have a representative of the OPM on the ground here to go into a thorough analysis of the situation.

"As things stand now, the strike will continue in effect until we are able to make some agreement with Bethlehem and the rest."

No formal action was taken by the C. I. O. machinists, since the request was not directed to them, but pickets handed out leaflets signed by J. P. Smith, business agent of Lodge 1304, asserting that "hard-won conditions must be preserved and employers, under a smoke screen of national defense, are not going to destroy them." The C. I. O. was not represented in the negotiations for the master contract.

In a joint statement, Mr. Dillon and Mr. Hook said that the machinists, because of the "friendly attitude and fine spirit of the other metal trades organizations," intend to see to it "that all such metal trades men that respected our picket lines will be returned to their jobs without discrimination" and on a basis satisfactory to them.

Apprised of the strikers' position, Frank H. Fox, chairman of the Bay Area Shipbuilders Negotiating Committee and authorized spokesmen

Continued on Page Sixteen

'Peace' Pickets Routed At White House Gates

Special to THE NEW YORK TIMES.

WASHINGTON, May 12—One soldier and one Marine tonight broke up a line of eight pickets marching in front of the White House who represented the American Peace Mobilization. This organization has been charged with being a Communist Front group.

At the hour all Washington theatres were letting out, police emergency cars and motorcyclists roared through downtown Washington to the White House. The two assaulters were arrested and one picketeer was removed to Emergency Hospital where he was reported slightly injured. The picketing continued.

Tonight's fracas followed one at 3 A. M. when a larger group of soldiers and Marines attacked the pickets, tore up their placards and warned them they would be back if the picketing continued. In an earlier assault the policemen did not interfere. Tonight the assailants were seized and one was charged with simple assault. The police then closed and manned the White House gates for the night.

ROOSEVELT TO TALK TO NATION MAY 27

'Fireside Chat' Two Weeks From Today Is Substituted for Address Tomorrow

By FRANK L. KLUCKHOHN
Special to THE NEW YORK TIMES.

WASHINGTON, May 12—President Roosevelt will make a "fireside chat" to the nation May 27, but will not make his scheduled speech before the Pan American Union Wednesday night, it was announced at the White House today.

This change in plans was interpreted generally to mean that the President has in mind no important announcement on American foreign policy for two weeks and that, at least for this period, he does not contemplate any new type of aid for Britain.

The Executive seldom makes fireside chats except upon important matters, however, and his talk on the 27th is generally expected to present an outline of the current position of the United States as he sees it and the future steps that should be taken.

Mr. Roosevelt completed his seventh day in bed because of illness today, and his widely publicized speech was canceled to give him time to recover fully, according to official statements.

Stephen T. Early, White House Secretary, emphasized, however, that the President had never intended his talk before the Pan American Union to be of "world-shaking" importance.

Pressure on President

In informed circles it was understood that the Executive did not intend to be pushed into any important steps and that he considered the present time poor for any announcement of vital importance.

Speaking of the canceled Wednesday address, Mr. Early said:

"So, despite reports from abroad, there will be no world-shaking pronouncement from President Roosevelt Wednesday night, as this office has stated right along."

Three Cabinet officers, Secretaries Henry L. Stimson, Frank Knox and Claude Wickard, have urged use of the American Navy to protect shipment of war supplies to Great Britain, their speeches generally being interpreted as an appeal for escort of convoys by the American Navy. Other individuals or groups publicly have urged the Executive to go so far as ask for a declaration of war. Pressure has come from all sides on these controversial questions and others.

The decision to cancel Wednesday night's speech was revealed through White House announcement of a resolution adopted by the Board of Governors of the Pan American Union.

Diplomats Ask Postponement

"The Ambassadors, Ministers and chargés d'affaires of the republics of Latin America," the resolution said, "realizing that President Roosevelt has recently been indisposed and in view of the fact that the reception to be tendered him would involve strain upon him, take the liberty of suggesting that the reception be postponed until such time as President Roosevelt may

Continued on Page Eight

HAMBURG HIT HARD

Miles of Docks Fired in British Bombing a Second Night

BREMEN LIKE TARGET

U-Boat Yards and War Plants of Reich Bases Kept Under Attack

By DAVID ANDERSON
Special Cable to THE NEW YORK TIMES.

LONDON, Tuesday, May 13—Nine miles of docks along the River Elbe at Hamburg were laced with heavy British bombs and thousands of incendiaries over Sunday night when the Royal Air Force followed up its attack of the previous night with another vigorous raid on German war ports.

The Hamburg docks were "threaded and crossed with fire, continuing the destruction and disorganization of vital parts of this great seaport," the British Air Ministry reported.

Bremen, the Reich's second port in the size of its war activities, was attacked also with what R. A. F. officials moderately termed a "heavyweight of high-explosive and incendiary bombs."

Shipbuilding yards and especially the plants of the two ports where Germany has built most of her U-boat fleet were blasted.

Previous Havoc Extended

Explosives hammered down on industrial works in both cities, the Air Ministry stated, and vast fires were started to continue the havoc of previous attacks.

Last night "objectives" at the great German industrial center of Mannheim, also a frequent target for the British, were attacked by R. A. F. bombers, a brief official report early today said.

Sunday night attacks were made by the R. A. F. on a number of other targets in the Reich, including Emden again, and the docks of Rotterdam were also bombed.

Four aircraft of the Bomber Command were missing from all these operations, British officials said.

The Coastal Command carried out Sunday night attacks on docks at the Netherland port of Ijmuiden, and on the Nazi seaplane base on the island of Texel without loss.

The attacks seemed to mark a definite stepping-up of the R. A. F. offensive, as officials of the Bomber Command, in giving some detail of the operations, said the objective was to strike Hamburg again before that city could "recover from the impact of the attacks made Saturday night."

Weather Right for Bomb-Aimers

Fine weather and the brilliant moonlight enabled the British pilots to pick their spot with relative ease over "the vast expanse of docks which was the particular focus" of this raid, it was stated.

An R. A. F. flier's account of the Bremen attack said:

"It was not so cold as when we visited Bremen three nights before, but there was the same bright sky. All the way over there were patches of cloud which looked like stepping

Continued on Page Six

Russians See Advantage In R. A. F. Planes' Big Load

By The Canadian Press.

LONDON, May 12—Increased bomb loads carried by Royal Air Force bombers "partly offset" the German advantage of having air bases close to Britain, Red Star, organ of the Soviet Army, said in an article quoted today by the British Broadcasting Corporation.

The article commented on "the tremendous load of bombs that now can be carried by a single British machine."

In a review of war developments, the newspaper observed that "the hardest blows delivered by the German Air Force in recent weeks have been aimed at British ports and centers of shipbuilding" and also that "the experience of the last war proved that British and United States industry made up for sinkings by U-boats."

PAPEN SEES HITLER, RETURNS TO TURKEY

Envoy Is Expected to Reveal Nazi Plans for Near East—Soviet Move Studied

The following dispatch was received by direct voice broadcast through the Ankara wireless station last night. C. L. Sulzberger prefaced the broadcast in this way:

"The following direct broadcast from Ankara to THE NEW YORK TIMES, *New York City, contains news dispatches for* THE TIMES. *These are exclusive property of the New York Times Company. Dispatches follow."*

By C. L. SULZBERGER
Special Broadcast to THE NEW YORK TIMES.

ANKARA, Turkey, May 12—Franz von Papen, the German Ambassador to Ankara, came back to his post today aboard a large camouflaged Junkers troop transport plane, following a series of last-minute conferences with Reichsfuehrer Hitler at the latter's Obersalzburg retreat.

The Ambassador, who was accompanied by his wife and daughter, was met at the Ankara Airport by the diplomatic representatives of the countries that have signed the tripartite accord. He appeared in excellent spirits and conferred for several minutes with the Italian Ambassador.

Herr von Papen has been expected back almost daily for the better part of the last fortnight and the fact that he continually delayed his return and then at the last minute had a long personal conversation with Herr Hitler is regarded as significant.

Events are shaping up rapidly in the Middle East, and the only hand that now remains to be disclosed fully is that of Germany. Russia has abandoned her disinterest in this area by according full diplomatic recognition to the bellicose Rashid Ali Beg Gailani government of Iraq.

Britain, already engaged in extensive military operations in Iraq, has

Continued on Page Two

Bodies of Brewster and Wife Found In Plane Wreckage in Alleghenies

The bodies of Benjamin Brewster, New York investment broker, and his wife, the former Leonie de Bary Lyon, who disappeared Friday on a projected flight from Roosevelt Field to Warren, Ohio, were found last night in the charred wreckage of their plane on a rugged mountain top forty miles north of Harrisburg.

The discovery was made after several pilots reported they had seen the badly damaged wreck nestled in tree branches on Shade Mountain near Beavertown.

The report that the bodies had been found was telephoned to Private Charles Hicklin of the Pennsylvania Motor Police by Private John Zeigler, one of a party sent out from the barracks at Selinsgrove.

The bodies were taken in charge by Dr. Charles W. Strand, coroner of Snyder County, who will remove them to Middleburg as soon as permission is received from members of the Brewster family.

Late last night positive identification was made by Whitney Stone, vice president of the Stone & Webster Company, a brother-in-law of Mr. Brewster. In a telephone conversation with his sister, Mrs. Edward C. Brewster, Mr. Stone said the plane crashed against the side of a 1,500-foot mountain and then exploded. A reward of $1,000 had been offered by Mr. Stone to the person locating the plane.

The Brewsters' plane was a radio-equipped black and green Beechcraft with a Wright motor. Mr. Brewster was a prominent sportsman pilot and had more than 1,000 flying hours to his credit.

The tangled, charred wreckage was sighted at about 5 P. M. (daylight saving time) by two private pilots from Philadelphia, who were among more than seventy who searched the mountain area by air. They reported having circled the scene and sighted a twisted wing lying near by. The wing, they said, apparently had escaped the flames, and its black and green striping could be seen clearly. These fliers,

Continued on Page Nineteen

ADMIRAL HAS TALK

Berlin Says Ribbentrop Was Present—Place Is Not Disclosed

VICHY PRESS TENSE

U. S. Attitude Is Cause of Worry—Leahy May Protest Attacks

By The Associated Press.

BERLIN, Tuesday, May 13—Reichsfuehrer Hitler has received the French Vice Premier, Admiral François Darlan, in the presence of German Foreign Minister Joachim von Ribbentrop, it was officially announced early today.

The communiqué announcing the meeting did not say where or when it took place.

The announcement said:

"The Fuehrer, in the presence of the Reichsminister of Foreign Affairs, received the vice president of the French Ministerial Council, Admiral Darlan.

Hitler-Stalin Talk Forecast

VICHY, France, May 12 (AP)—Separate meetings of Reichsfuehrer Hitler with Premier Joseph Stalin and Premier Mussolini were considered in diplomatic circles here tonight as likely to result from the current political moves over Europe.

The object of the meetings, these circles said, probably would be complete economic if not military organization of the Axis-dominated Continent.

Observers listed the current shake-up of Spain's civil and military organization and Vice Premier Admiral François Darlan's negotiations with the Germans as indicators of forthcoming conferences of Herr Hitler and Mr. Stalin and Signor Mussolini.

U. S. Gives Press Concern

By G. H. ARCHAMBAULT
Wireless to THE NEW YORK TIMES.

VICHY, France, May 12—For the time being it is not possible to separate the two hemispheres in any discussion here of the world situation. That the situation is tense and is likely to remain so, at least until President Roosevelt has spoken, is admitted.

In every newspaper as well as in every conversation the United States and what it may or may not do is a recurrent topic.

There are some here who surmise that it may have been mentioned in Paris during the visit there of Vice Premier Admiral François Darlan, who is expected back in Vichy tomorrow to report to Marshal Henri Philippe Pétain, who himself returned this morning after a few days' rest in his Riviera estate.

A semi-official commentary declared today that the Marshal has expressed his satisfaction to the Admiral with the progress of his negotiations hitherto.

It is understood that another Admiral—William D. Leahy, the United States Ambassador—may also see Marshal Pétain in the near future for one of their periodical conversations on food supplies and cognate subjects.

To Stick to Collaboration

While there is complete official silence regarding the negotiations with Germany, as also regarding the United States, the Inter-France News Service, now situated in Vichy, which circulates editorials "for free reproduction by any newspaper," advanced the following arguments:

"Should war occur between the United States and Germany and should it be prolonged, the political reasons which led France to follow the road of collaboration would be reinforced by even more decisive practical reasons. For war between the United States and the Axis would immediately create a European solidarity that would be stronger than any sentimental factor.

"An American blockade, which would necessarily be extended to all our coasts, will develop the notion of a common interest among the peoples of old Europe, since from Brest to Koenigsberg and from Narvik [Norway] to Cadiz [Spain] we should be compelled to do without meat from Argentina and coffee from Brazil, to dispense with cotton from the United States and oil from Mexico. The French

Continued on Page Five

Nazis Allege 'Hallucinations'; Silent on Glasgow Arrival

Arrest of Hess's Aides Ordered Since Hitler Forbade Him to Fly—Letter He Left Said to Show Disordered Mind

By Telephone to THE NEW YORK TIMES.

BERLIN, May 12—Authoritative quarters in Berlin refused to comment late tonight on a British statement that Rudolf Hess, 47-year-old deputy leader of the National Socialist party and Reichsfuehrer Hitler's personal representative, had bailed out of a Messerschmitt plane near Glasgow, Scotland, and was in the hands of the British authorities. Earlier in the evening the Germans had officially reported Herr Hess to be missing.

The man who, on Sept. 1, 1939, was designated by Herr Hitler as his second choice, next to Reich Marshal Hermann Goering, in the line of succession for leadership of the German State, was last heard of in Augsburg, in Bavaria, on Saturday. He was reported to have taken an airplane there for an unknown destination in violation of Herr Hitler's orders prohibiting him from flying because of physical disability.

THE GERMAN STATEMENT

The news of the mysterious disappearance of Herr Hess was released, forty-eight hours after he had been reported missing, in the following communiqué:

Rudolf Hess has met with an accident.

Party Comrade Hess, who because of a disease that for a year has progressively worsened has been categorically forbidden by the Fuehrer to continue his flying activities, recently found means in violation of this command to come into possession of an airplane.

On Saturday, May 10, about 6 P. M., Party Comrade Hess took off from Augsburg for a flight from which until today he has not yet returned. A letter that he left behind unfortunately indicated, by its incoherence, symptoms of a mental derangement that permits the inference that Comrade Hess became the victim of hallucinations.

The Fuehrer immediately ordered the arrest of the adjutants of Party Comrade Hess, who alone knew of these flights and, knowing of their prohibition by the Fuehrer, did not prevent or immediately report them.

Under the circumstances, the National Socialist movement must regretfully assume that Comrade Hess has crashed or met with an accident somewhere on his flight.

Herr Hess last spoke in public in an official capacity on May 1 as the representative of Herr Hitler at the Labor Day demonstration of the party in Augsburg, where he addressed the congress of the Reich Labor Chamber.

Herr Hess, who also was a member of the German Cabinet as Minister Without Portfolio, was born in Alexandria, Egypt, on April 26, 1894. He became identified with the party in 1921, and in recognition of his services Herr Hitler appointed him as private secretary, a post that he held from 1925 until 1932, when he received more responsible positions in the party organization.

Despite his position as deputy

Continued on Page Four

The International Situation

TUESDAY, MAY 13, 1941

A laconic announcement from 10 Downing Street gave to an astounded world last night the news that Rudolf Hess, deputy leader of the Nazi party in Germany and the third most powerful figure in the Reich, had landed by parachute in Scotland and was in safe custody in a Glasgow hospital suffering from a broken ankle. The official statement gave no direct explanation for the dramatic development, but it was presumed that the man who was named at the outset of the war by Adolf Hitler as his second in succession had deliberately fled Germany.

Herr Hess flew to Scotland in a Messerschmitt 110, a plane incapable of carrying sufficient fuel for his return to Germany. The plane crashed Saturday night on the Duke of Hamilton's estate. The flier established his identity in the hospital, and the Foreign Office dispatched an attaché to interview him there. [All the foregoing, Page 1, Column 8.]

Berlin issued a communiqué earlier in the day stating that Herr Hess, apparently suffering from "hallucinations" induced by a long-standing ailment, had taken off by plane from Augsburg Saturday evening against the express orders of Herr Hitler and was "missing" and presumably had "met with an accident." It was announced that Herr Hess's adjutants had been ordered arrested. [Page 1, Column 6.]

Hundreds of German bombers flew over South England and the Midlands Sunday night, attacking airdromes and other objectives, and causing destruction over widespread areas. Nine Nazi planes were shot down. A Berlin statement that forty-five British airfields were attacked was contradicted by the British, who said the military damage was "not considerable." Few raiders were reported over Britain last night. [Page 6, Column 1.]

Over Sunday night the R. A. F. was sending wave after wave of bombers against German ports, particularly Hamburg and Bremen. Nine miles of docks and shipyards on the River Elbe were laced with fires from British incendiaries, and attacks were made on Emden, Rotterdam and Ijmuiden. Last night British planes again bombed Mannheim. [Page 1, Column 3.]

The return to Ankara of German Ambassador von Papen from an extended visit to Berlin gave rise to a belief that Germany would propose a far-reaching economic treaty to all but isolated Turkey. Ankara also looked for an early meeting between the Ambassador and the Iraqi Defense Minister, who has been visiting Ankara. [Page 1, Column 4.]

The situation in Iraq was described by the British as now "stabilized." R. A. F. planes harried remnants of Iraqi forces, and British mechanized forces completed the occupation of Rutbah, a vital point on the oil pipe line and site of an airplane base. [Page 2, Column 6.]

The British forces in Ethiopia tightened their pincer around Alagi, the last Italian stronghold on the Asmara-Dessye road. The Italian garrison at Gondar was said to be virtually isolated. In North Africa, the Admiralty announced, British warships bombarded Bengazi Saturday night, but Rome asserted the British vessels had been routed after having suffered direct hits. [Page 3, Column 4.]

Reichsfuehrer Hitler received Admiral Darlan, the French Vice Premier, in the presence of German Foreign Minister von Ribbentrop at an undisclosed place, it was announced in Berlin. The role that the United States might play in world events was believed in Vichy to loom large in any discussion of European affairs that might be going on. "Collaborationist" sources predicted a "European solidarity" in the event the United States engaged in war with Germany. [Page 1, Column 5.]

In Washington the ship-seizure bill sponsored by the Administration passed its first test in the Senate when the Commerce Committee reported it favorably by a vote of eleven to four, thus making it possible to bring the measure to the floor later this week. The committee defeated an attempt to prevent transfer to a belligerent of any of the ships that might be seized. [Page 7, Column 1.]

President Roosevelt's scheduled speech before the Pan-American Union tomorrow night has been canceled, but he will make a fireside chat to the nation on May 27, in which it is expected that he will deal with the position of the nation in the international situation and the future steps that should be taken. [Page 1, Column 2.]

BRITISH ASTOUNDED

Hitler's Deputy Is in Hospital After Bailing Out of War Plane

HAS A BROKEN ANKLE

London Believes Hess's Flight May Portend a New Purge in Reich

By ROBERT P. POST
Special Cable to THE NEW YORK TIMES.

LONDON, Tuesday, May 13—Rudolf Hess, deputy leader of the German Nazi party and the third-ranking personage in the German State, parachuted to earth in Scotland on Saturday night and is now a prisoner of war.

That may sound like something from a mystery thriller by Oppenheim. But in sober truth, 10 Downing Street issued a communiqué last night that is probably the strangest and most dramatic document ever to come from the official home of a British Prime Minister.

THE BRITISH STATEMENT

This statement said:

Rudolf Hess, the Deputy Fuehrer of Germany and party leader of the National Socialist party, has landed in Scotland in the following circumstances:

On the night of Saturday, the tenth, a Messerschmitt 110 was reported by our patrols to have crossed the coast of Scotland and to be flying in the direction of Glasgow. Since a Messerschmitt 110 would not have fuel to return to Germany, this report was at first disbelieved.

Later on a Messerschmitt 110 crashed near Glasgow with its guns unloaded. Shortly afterward a German officer who had bailed out was found with his parachute in the neighborhood, suffering from a broken ankle.

He was taken to a hospital in Glasgow, where he at first gave his name as Horn, but later on he declared that he was Rudolf Hess.

He brought with him various photographs of himself at different ages, apparently in order to establish his identity.

These photographs were deemed to be photographs of Hess by several people who knew him personally. Accordingly, an officer of the Foreign Office closely acquainted with Hess before the war has been sent up by airplane to see him in the hospital.

Identified by Official

Ivone A. Kirkpatrick, who used to be first secretary in the British Embassy in Berlin, was the official sent to Scotland, and the Ministry of Information announced early this morning that Herr Hess's identification had been definitely established.

Earlier the Germans had announced that Herr Hess, who was outranked only by Reichsfuehrer Hitler and Reich Marshal Hermann Goering in the Nazi hierarchy, had been suffering from hallucinations and had violated Herr Hitler's orders in taking the plane.

It was just before nightfall Saturday that Herr Hess was found by a Scottish farm worker; he was groaning in agony, with his parachute wrapped around him. He was taken first to a little two-roomed cottage and then was turned over to the military authorities. This morning he was in a military hospital somewhere near Glasgow.

That is the bare outline of the facts as they are known so far. What do they mean? The Germans have already announced that Herr Hess's "adjutants" have been arrested. The British are inclined to believe that there may be another purge in Germany—a purge similar to the one following the arrest of Captain Ernst Roehm, who was also one of Herr Hitler's closest collaborators, on June 30, 1934.

But from this distance it is almost impossible to say what this development means as far as Germany is concerned. One can record only what the British believe it means. One Briton told the writer that "this is the first 'break' we have had since the war started."

Alfred Duff Cooper, the Minister of Information, himself acted as messenger boy to take the British

Continued on Page Four

"All the News That's Fit to Print."

NEWS INDEX, PAGE 38, THIS SECTION

The New York Times.

LATE CITY EDITION
Partly cloudy and continued warm today and tomorrow.
Temperatures Yesterday—Max.,91; Min.,73

Section 1

VOL. XC..No. 30,465.
Entered as Second-Class Matter, Postoffice, New York, N. Y.
Copyright, 1941, by The New York Times Company.
NEW YORK, SUNDAY, JUNE 22, 1941.
Including Rotogravure Picture, Magazine and Book Sections
TEN CENTS New York City and Vicinity

HITLER BEGINS WAR ON RUSSIA, WITH ARMIES ON MARCH FROM ARCTIC TO THE BLACK SEA; DAMASCUS FALLS; U.S. OUSTS ROME CONSULS

MUST GO BY JULY 15

Ban on Italians Like Order to German Representatives

U. S. DENIES SPYING

Envoys Told to Protest Axis Charges—Nazis Get 'Moor' Text

By BERTRAM D. HULEN
Special to THE NEW YORK TIMES.

WASHINGTON, June 21—The Italian Embassy was directed by the State Department in a note published today to close all its consular offices and other agencies in this country having connections with the Italian Government by July 15. This was the reply to the Italian demand for the closing of all American Consulates in Italy.

At the same time Sumner Welles, Under-Secretary of State, announced that he had sent to Dr. Hans Thomsen, the German Chargé d'Affaires, the text of President Roosevelt's message to Congress yesterday denouncing the sinking of the American freighter Robin Moor in the South Atlantic on May 21.

This message, which accused Germany of being an international outlaw, engaging in piracy and attempting to intimidate the United States by the sinking and to drive American commerce from the seas, contained notice that this country would not yield before such measures and stated that compensation would be sought for the sinking.

It was transmitted "for the information" of the German Government, but constituted in effect a note of protest. A further communication will be sent asking damages when a final determination has been reached of the extent of damages that should be sought.

Will Deny Improper Acts

In addition, the State Department instructed the American Embassies in Berlin and Rome to inform the respective governments that the United States objects to all allegations of improper acts by American consular officials in those countries and to complete arrangements for the withdrawal of the consular officials and their staffs by July 15, the limit set by the German and Italian Governments.

The Axis governments had charged that the American Consuls had spied for the British. No reply has been made by the State Department to the German protests against the order closing Nazi consulates in this country, but the protest will be rejected. The United States alleged subversive activities as the reason for the demand for them to be closed by July 10.

The notes to the German and Italian Embassies were sent by messenger last night. However, no direct charge of improper activities was made against the Italian consuls in the note Mr. Welles sent to Don Ascanio dei principi Colonna, the Italian Ambassador. He merely stated that the continued functioning of Italian consular establishments within United States territory "would serve no desirable purpose."

In addition, the closing of Italian agencies having connections with the Rome government was requested. The Italian Embassy, as in the earlier case of the German Embassy, was exempted, but the closing of the office of the Italian Commercial Counselor in New York was demanded, along with the consulates.

Welles Note to Colonna

The note from Mr. Welles to Prince Colonna follows:

June 20, 1941

His Excellency
Don Ascanio dei principi Colonna
Royal Italian Ambassador
Excellency:

I have the honor to inform Your Excellency that the President has directed me to request that the Italian Government promptly close all Italian consular establishments within United States territory and remove therefrom all Italian consular of-

Continued on Page Two

Hope Dims for Submarine; Diver Balked at 370 Feet

Knox Believes All 33 Are Dead on the O-9 and Expects Rites at Scene for Navy 'Heroes'—Pressure Halts Descent

By RUSSELL PORTER
Special to THE NEW YORK TIMES.

PORTSMOUTH, N. H., June 21—As hope faded rapidly for the crew of the Submarine O-9, which failed to rise after submerging yesterday morning twenty-four miles east of this city, it became known tonight that the Navy might be unable to complete its salvage operations, and might be compelled to leave the bodies entombed where they lie—440 feet below the surface of the Atlantic.

This theory was based upon the assumption that the two officers and thirty-one men must already be given up as lost, but that assumption has become stronger with every new development since the submarine was reported missing.

Last night cork insulation from the interior of the hull was picked up, showing that at least part of the submarine had collapsed, and early today, after fourteen hours of dragging, grapnels located an object believed to be the sunken craft. Since then no signals from the O-9 have been received on the sensitive sound-detection devices on the salvage ships in response to their repeated messages.

The view that the O-9's fate was sealed was strengthened this afternoon when reporters and photographers, visiting the scene in a Navy press boat, saw one of the Navy's most experienced divers fail in an attempt to reach the O-9 after descending 370 feet, or within seventy feet of where the Navy believes it has located the submarine with grapnel lines.

The diver, George Crocker, 30 years old, of Seattle, asked to be hauled up when he became convinced that he was not getting enough air pressure from his life lines of helium-oxygen mixture to overcome the increasing sea pressure as he went lower and lower.

A message from the Falcon said: "Diver descended 370 feet. Had difficulty in breathing. Brought to surface. Will continue attempts by varying diving techniques."

On the salvage ship the dive was called "the most dangerous in submarine history." It was pointed out that no one had ever made a successful "working" dive at 440 feet and that any diver who went down so far, where he would have to grope his way in complete darkness under terrific sea pressure, 195.8 pounds to the square inch, could do so only at extreme risk to his life.

Colonel Frank Knox, Secretary of the Navy, returning tonight on

Continued on Page Thirty

ARMY ASKS GUARD BE KEPT IN SERVICE

Recommends Congress Act to Hold State Troops, Reserve Officers Indefinitely

By HALLETT ABEND
Special to THE NEW YORK TIMES.

WASHINGTON, June 21—Members of the National Guard and Reserve Officers Corps will be kept in active service beyond the single year planned when they were called, if a recommendation made today by the War Department is approved by President Roosevelt and Congress.

Instead of a return to civilian life, starting Sept. 15, their terms of service in uniform may be extended indefinitely, or at least until the Army selectees have been sufficiently trained in ample numbers to permit the Guardsmen to be demobilized. The recommendation to the President does not specify any limit to the proposed extension of service.

At present there are 289,800 National Guardsmen, including their 21,800 officers, on active duty with the Federal Army. They were inducted into service in increments beginning Sept. 15 of last year. Some went into uniform as late as March of this year. Their terms of service, at time of induction, were limited to twelve months, which may not be extended except by act of Congress.

341,300 Would Be Affected

In addition to the National Guardsmen, who comprise eighteen divisions and one cavalry brigade now on active service, the government has called up 51,500 Reserve officers under the same terms, making collectively 341,300 officers and men who would be affected.

Today's War Department recommendation to the President that steps be taken to retain in the service these Guardsmen and Reserve officers was taken, according to the official announcement, because "the War Department has been flooded with queries from the field" as to whether or not the specified one-year limit of service would hold good or be changed.

"These queries are to be expected," continues the announcement, "because whatever the decision, there are many adjustments which the citizen-soldier must make in his affairs."

As yet no decision has been reached in the War Department whether or not to seek authority to retain selectees in the Army beyond the one-year training period specified in the Selective Service Act, but presumably such a step

Continued on Page Nineteen

NAVY MAY REPLACE SHIPYARD STRIKERS

Weighs Putting Own Machinists to Work to End Long Tie-Up in San Francisco

By The Associated Press.

SAN FRANCISCO, June 21—Striking A. F. L. machinists in a $300,000,000 defense program have come to a showdown with the United States Navy and their own international officers.

Reliable reports, not officially denied, indicated that the Navy might install its own machinists in the huge Bethlehem shipyards Monday if the local union did not heed the order of its international president to call off the strike by that time.

The same reports indicated that the Army also might be on hand

Continued on Page Twenty-eight

R. A. F. BLASTS FOE

Bags 26 Nazi Planes in Record Day Raids on Invasion Coast

GERMANY IS BOMBED

British on 11th Straight Night Offensive Into Western Reich

Special Cable to THE NEW YORK TIMES.

LONDON, Sunday, June 22—Twenty-six Nazi fighter planes were destroyed in daylight yesterday by Royal Air Force fliers on their fifth straight day of raiding the Germans' invasion coast and air bases in Northern France.

Twice before dark, waves of R. A. F. warcraft—reportedly numbering at least 150 planes each—swept over the Channel in offensive operations.

Bombers attacked the Nazi's airdromes on each occasion while strong forces of fighters blasted the way for the big planes through formations of German defense fighters. While the major raids were going on, other strong R. A. F. units patrolled over the French coast and battled Messerschmitts.

Attack Goes On; Big Bombs Used

Last night and early this morning the R. A. F. was still attacking the invasion coast, using some of the latest type of high-powered bombs.

Explosions rolled across the Channel like peals of thunder, shaking the ground and rocking buildings for miles along the Kentish coast, observers there reported.

A night curtain of fog hung over the Strait of Dover and little could be seen of the raids. The latest British attacks were apparently being made in the Boulogne area, where some of the heaviest daylight bombing was carried out.

Meanwhile R. A. F. bomber forces were again attacking Western Germany, officials here said briefly early today. The attacks marked the eleventh consecutive night in which the British have bombed industrial centers and war bases in the Reich.

Two Nazi bombers were shot down during the night in small scattered enemy raids on the east and southeast coasts of England. A few German bombs were reported dropped there; there were no accounts of casualties or damage.

The R. A. F. coastal patrol squadrons reported destroying at least two enemy planes and one Nazi

Continued on Page Eighteen

The International Situation

SUNDAY, JUNE 22, 1941

At 5:30 o'clock this morning, Berlin time, two statements were read over the German radio that constituted a declaration of war upon the Soviet Union by Germany. A proclamation of Adolf Hitler, read by Propaganda Minister Goebbels, said that Russia, with Britain and the United States, had sought to "throttle" Germany and that he had therefore decided to put the fate of the German people in the hands of the army. A statement by Foreign Minister von Ribbentrop contained the actual declaration of war. The Finns and the Rumanians were mentioned as allies. Berlin reported subsequently that troops were on the march in East Prussia. [Page 1, Column 8; with map.]

Yesterday was a good day for British arms.

In the Syrian campaign Damascus was occupied. The British announced its capture and Vichy reported its evacuation to avoid street fighting and destruction of the city. Another British force was pushing nearer Beirut, supported by the fleet and the air arm, while a third column was moving toward Tadmur. [Page 1, Column 5; Map on Page 12.]

No less encouraging to the British was a victory much closer to home in the largest British daylight air attack of the war. In a sweep two waves of 150 planes each pounded the French Channel coast, going particularly for airdromes, and engaged German air defenses. The British reported downing twenty-six Nazi planes in these attacks for a loss of five of their own. Late last night the British were continuing their attacks across the Channel. [Page 1, Column 4; Map, Page 18.]

The Libyan theatre was quiet, but British pressure in East Africa was indicated by a protest from Vichy against what was declared to be a virtual ultimatum from General Wavell to French Somaliland to join the Free French or suffer an intensified blockade. London confirmed the representations of General Wavell. [Page 14, Column 1.]

Washington continued the accelerated pace of its anti-Axis diplomatic offensive. The Italian Embassy was instructed to close the forty-nine Italian consulates and seven agencies in this country before July 15. President Roosevelt's message to Congress on the Robin Moor was handed to the German Embassy while the State Department instructed the United States embassies in Berlin and Rome to inform those governments that the United States objected categorically to any allegations of improper acts by United States consuls. [Page 1, Column 1.]

Italian consular circles here were silent concerning the Washington order, but Italian anti-Fascist quarters expressed jubilation. [Page 3, Column 1.]

SYRIAN CITY TAKEN

French Withdraw After a Hard Fight—British Closer to Beirut

TADMUR PUSH IS ON

Allied Planes Harassing Vichy Troops, Whose Defense Falters

By C. L. SULZBERGER
By Telephone to THE NEW YORK TIMES.

ANKARA, Turkey, June 21—French troops evacuated the city of Damascus today after a persistent bombardment by British artillery and withdrew to new positions outside the Syrian capital, according to official advices from Beirut. Early in the afternoon it was learned that the Allied vanguard was already beginning to enter the city. This evening the British reported complete occupation.

The Damascus airport at Mezze has been taken by Indian detachments of the Allied forces and one of the key points east of Damascus has been surrounded by Druz tribesmen fighting on the side of the British.

The Beirut radio announced tonight that a British motorized column pushing westward from Iraq was now heading toward Tadmur. The British column, it was said, has been bombed constantly by the French Air Force, which has just been reorganized and reinforced by French squadrons coming from North Africa. Some German planes also were said to have arrived in Syria.

Advance in High Gear

It is clear that the Allied advance is beginning to move into high gear. Unconfirmed reports that the British forces have reached Beirut indicate that it may also fall soon. Beirut's fate depends largely on whether the British will call in their superior naval forces to shell the city proper. So far this has been avoided in order to keep damage and casualties at a minimum.

[A dispatch from Cairo said that Australian forces had been progressing toward Beirut for two days and had passed Ras Damour.]

The Allies, convinced of the seriousness of the French resistance, evidently have begun to fight this undeclared war in earnest and intend to get it over with fast at any cost. The main center of French resistance in the east has been Damascus, and the capture of the city is of great importance.

The Allied counter-move to the French attack in the south, which developed earlier in the week, is now proceeding with dispatch in the Merdjayoun district. The fortress of Merdjayoun is in Allied hands and it is obvious that the region is being rapidly cleared, since the coastal advance is dependent to a large degree on a corollary advance in the center.

Considerable concentrations of French artillery had been brought up around Damascus. The French dug in and placed batteries in many of the villas and gardens in the outer sections of the city. These batteries were slowly picked off by British gunners with Royal Air Force support, but the principal British effort was artillery shelling. The British sought to avoid excess damage by aerial bombardment, which is less accurate than artillery fire.

Tadmur Believed in Peril

The French admission that a British column is pressing toward Tadmur would seem to indicate that perhaps the town is endangered. Several days ago reliable sources here reported the existence of the column, but this was steadfastly denied by Beirut.

While there have been new reports that the trouble for the British in Iraq is far from over, the fact that they are able to spare considerable forces from there would indicate that everything is under control. It is known that British forces also are working westward along the North Syrian frontier toward Aleppo, but the exact strength of these units is not known here.

British military circles admit that the Syrian adventure can no longer

Continued on Page Twelve

WHERE GERMAN ARMIES MARCH ON RUSSIA

Shown on the map is the western frontier of the Soviet Union, a battle line of more than 2,000 miles. Berlin indicated an attack from Norway to Rumania.

The Hitler Proclamation

The text of Adolf Hitler's proclamation, as recorded here by Columbia Broadcasting System, follows:

It was a difficult step for me to send my Minister to Moscow in order to attend to work against the policy of encirclement of Britain.

I hoped that at last it would be possible to put away tension.

Germany never intended to occupy Lithuania. The defeat of Poland induced me to again address a peace offer to the Allies. This was declined because Britain was still hoping to bring about European coalition.

That is why Cripps [Sir Stafford Cripps, British Ambassador] was sent to Moscow. He was commissioned under all circumstances to come to an agreement with Moscow. Russia always put out the lying statement that she was protecting these countries [evidently Lithuania, Estonia and Latvia, the Baltic States].

The penetration of Russia into Rumania and the Greek liaison with England threatened to place new, large areas into the war. Rumania, however, believed she was able to accede to Russia only if she received guarantees from Germany and Italy for the remainder of the country. With a heavy heart, I did this, for if Germany gives guarantees, she will fulfill them. We are neither Englishmen nor Jews.

I asked Molotoff [Soviet Foreign Commissar V. M. Molotoff] to come to Berlin, and he asked for a clarification of the situation. He asked, "Is the guarantee for Rumania directed also against Russia?"

I replied, "Against every one."

And Russia never informed us that she had even more far-reaching intentions against Rumania.

Molotoff asked further, "Is Germany prepared not to assist Finland, who was again threatening Russia?"

My reply was that Germany has no political interests in Finland, but another attack on Finland could not be tolerated, especially as we do not believe that Finland is threatening Russia.

Molotoff's third question was, "Is Germany agreeable that Russia give guarantees to Bulgaria?"

My reply was that Bulgaria is a sovereign State and I did not know that Bulgaria needed guarantees. Molotoff said Russia needed a passage through the Dardanelles and demanded bases in the Bosporus.

A few days later she [Russia] concluded the well known friendship agreement which was to incite the Serbs against Germany. Moscow demanded the mobilization of the Serbian Army.

When I still was silent, the men in the Kremlin went one step further. Russia offered to deliver war material against Germany. This was at the same time that I advised Matsuoka [Japanese Foreign Minister Yosuke Matsuoka] to bring about a lessening of the tension with Russia.

Serbian officers flew to Russia, where they were received as allies. Victory of the Axis in the Balkans at first foiled the plan to involve Germany in a long war and then, together with England and with the hope of American supplies, to throttle Germany.

Now the moment has come when I can no longer look at this development. Waiting would be a crime against Germany.

For weeks the Russians have been committing frontier violations. Russian planes have been crossing the frontier again and again to prove that they are the masters. On the night of June 17 and again on June 18 there was large patrol activity.

The march of the German Armies has no precedent. Together with the Finns we stand from Narvik to the Carpathians. At the Danube and on the shores of the Black Sea under Antonescu [Rumanian Dictator Ion Antonescu], German and Rumanian soldiers are united.

The task is to safeguard Europe and thus save all.

I have therefore today decided to give the fate of the German people and the Reich and of Europe again into the hands of our soldiers.

BAD FAITH CHARGED

Goebbels Reads Attack on Soviet—Ribbentrop Announces War

BALTIC MADE ISSUE

Finns and Rumanians Are Called Allies in Pian of Assault

Statement by von Ribbentrop is printed on Page 6.

By C. BROOKS PETERS
By Telephone to THE NEW YORK TIMES.

BERLIN, Sunday, June 22—As dawn broke over Europe today the legions of National Socialist Germany began their long-rumored invasion of Communist Soviet Russia. The non-aggression and amity pact between the two countries, signed in August, 1939, forgotten, the German attack began along a tremendous front, extending from the Arctic regions to the Black Sea. Marching with the forces of Germany are also the troops of Finland and Rumania.

Adolf Hitler, in a proclamation to the German people read over a national hook-up by Propaganda Minister Dr. Joseph Goebbels at 5:30 this morning, termed the military action begun this morning the largest in the history of the world. It was necessary, he added, because in spite of his unceasing efforts to preserve peace in this area it had definitely been proved that Russia was in a coalition with England to ruin Germany by prolonging the war.

Saw Stalemate in West

Herr Hitler, in his proclamation as reported here, made one vitally interesting statement, namely, that the supreme German military command did not feel itself able to force a decisive victory in the West—apparently on the British Isles—when large Russian troop concentrations were on the Reich's borders in the East.

The Russian troop concentrations in the East began in August, 1940, Herr Hitler asserted. "Thus, there occurred the effect intended by the Soviet-British cooperation," he added, "namely, the binding of such powerful German forces in the East that a radical conclusion of the war in the West, particularly as regards aircraft, could no longer be vouched for by the German High Command.

[The German radio announced early today that documentary proof would shortly be given of a secret British-Russian alliance, made behind Germany's back.]

Designed "to Save Reich"

The German action, Herr Hitler explained to his fellow-National Socialists, is designed to save the Reich and with it all Europe from the machinations of the Jewish-Anglo-Saxon warmongers.

The German Foreign Minister, Joachim von Ribbentrop, followed Dr. Goebbels on the air with a declaration of the Reich Government read before the foreign correspondents in the Foreign Office. Herr von Ribbentrop said he received V. G. Dekanosoff, the Russian Ambassador, this morning and informed him that in spite of the Russian-German non-aggression pact of Aug. 23, 1939, and an amity pact of Sept. 28, 1939, Russia had betrayed the trust that the Reich had placed in her.

"Contrary to all engagements which they had undertaken and in absolute contradition to their solemn declarations, the Soviet Union had turned against Germany," the Reich note asserted. "They have first not only continued, but even since the outbreak of war intensified their subversive activities against Germany in Europe. They have second, in a continually increasing measure, developed their foreign policy in a tendency hostile to Germany, and they have third massed their entire forces on the German frontier ready for action."

The Soviet Government, it was charged, had violated its treaties

Continued on Page Seven

"All the News That's Fit to Print."

The New York Times.

LATE CITY EDITION
Increasing cloudiness with rising temperature today. Tomorrow cloudy, somewhat colder.
Temperatures Yesterday—Max., 34; Min., 25

VOL. XCI No. 30,634. Entered as Second-Class Matter, Postoffice, New York, N. Y. NEW YORK, MONDAY, DECEMBER 8, 1941. THREE CENTS NEW YORK CITY and Vicinity

JAPAN WARS ON U. S. AND BRITAIN; MAKES SUDDEN ATTACK ON HAWAII; HEAVY FIGHTING AT SEA REPORTED

CONGRESS DECIDED

Roosevelt Will Address It Today and Find It Ready to Vote War

CONFERENCE IS HELD

Legislative Leaders and Cabinet in Sober White House Talk

By C. P. TRUSSELL
Special to THE NEW YORK TIMES.

WASHINGTON, Dec. 7—President Roosevelt will address a joint session of Congress tomorrow and will find the membership in a mood to vote any steps he asks in connection with the developments in the Pacific.

The President will appear personally at 12:30 P. M. Whether he would call for a flat declaration of war again Japan was left unannounced tonight. But leaders of Congress, shocked and angered by the Japanese attacks, were talking of a declaration of war on not only Japan but on the entire Axis.

The plans for action tomorrow were made tonight in a White House conference at which the President, surrounded by his Cabinet and by Congressional leaders of both parties, went through reports, some official, some unconfirmed, of the continued assaults of the Japanese upon American Pacific outposts.

Meet Far Into Night

The conference lasted until after 11 o'clock and at its close an official statement was issued. This said that the President had reviewed for his conferees the latest advices from the Pacific and declared:

"It should be emphasized that the message to Congress has not yet been written and its tenor will, of course, depend on further information received between 11 o'clock tonight and noon tomorrow. Further news is coming in all the time."

Congressional leaders asserted as they left the White House that they did not know what the President would say tomorrow.

"Will the President ask for a declaration of war?" Speaker Rayburn was asked.

"He didn't say," answered the Speaker.

Asked whether Congress would support a declaration of war, Mr. Rayburn observed:

"I think that is one thing on which there would be unity."

Politics Declared Dropped

"There is no politics here," said Representative Joseph W. Martin Jr., Minority House Leader. "There is only one party when it comes to the integrity and honor of the country."

"The Republicans," said Senator Charles L. McNary of Oregon, the Senate minority leader, "will all go along, in my opinion, with whatever is done."

Unless international developments and plans changed overnight, it was indicated, the Presidential recommendations would be directed for the present, at least, at Japan only. This was asserted authoritatively in the face of widespread expectation that any

Continued on Page Six

NEWS BULLETINS

are broadcast by The New York Times every hour on the hour over Station WMCA—570 on the dial.

WEEKDAYS
8 a. m. through 11 p. m.
SUNDAYS
9 a.m., 1 p.m., 5 p.m., 11 p.m.

TOKYO ACTS FIRST

Declaration Follows Air and Sea Attacks on U. S. and Britain

TOGO CALLS ENVOYS

After Fighting Is On, Grew Gets Japan's Reply to Hull Note of Nov. 26

By The Associated Press.

TOKYO, Monday, Dec. 8—Japan went to war against the United States and Britain today with air and sea attacks against Hawaii, followed by a formal declaration of hostilities.

Japanese Imperial headquarters announced at 6 A. M. [4 P. M. Sunday, Eastern standard time] that a state of war existed among these nations in the Western Pacific, as of dawn.

Soon afterward, Domei, the Japanese official news agency, announced that "naval operations are progressing off Hawaii, with at least one Japanese aircraft carrier in action against Pearl Harbor," the American naval base in the islands.

Japanese bombers were declared to have raided Honolulu at 7:35 A. M., Hawaii time [1;05 Sunday, Eastern standard time].

Premier-War Minister General Hideki Tojo held a twenty-minute Cabinet session at his official residence at 7 A. M.

Soon afterward it was announced that both the United States Ambassador, Joseph C. Grew, and the British Ambassador, Sir Robert Leslie Craigie, had been summoned by Foreign Minister Shigenori Togo.

The Foreign Minister, Domei said, handed to Mr. Grew the Japanese Government's formal reply to the note sent to Japan by United States Secretary of State Cordell Hull on Nov. 26.

[In the course of the diplomatic negotiations leading up to yesterday's events, the Domei agency had stated that Japan could not accept the premises of Mr. Hull's note.]

Sir Robert was summoned by

Continued on Page Five

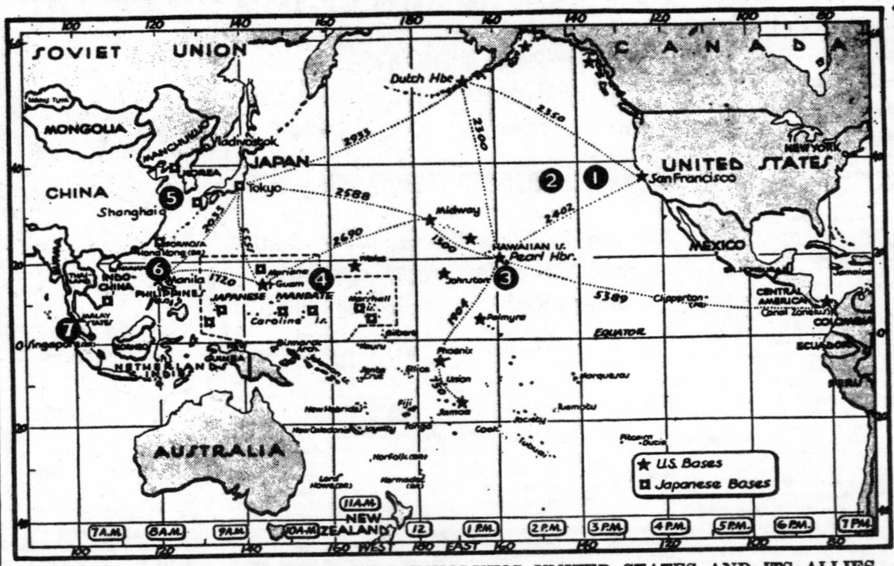

PACIFIC OCEAN: THEATRE OF WAR INVOLVING UNITED STATES AND ITS ALLIES

Shortly after the outbreak of hostilities an American ship sent a distress call from (1) and a United States Army transport carrying lumber was torpedoed at (2). The most important action was at Hawaii (3), where Japanese planes bombed the great Pearl Harbor base. Also attacked was Guam (4). From Manila (6) United States bombers roared northward, while some parts of the Philippines were raided, as was Hong Kong, to the northwest. At Shanghai (5) a British gunboat was sunk and an American gunboat seized. To the south, in the Malaya area (7), the British bombed Japanese ships, Tokyo forces attempted landings on British territory and Singapore underwent an air raid. Distances between key Pacific points are shown on the map in statute miles.

JAPANESE FORCE LANDS IN MALAYA

First Attempt Is Repulsed—Singapore Is Bombed and Thailand Invaded

By The Associated Press.

SINGAPORE, Monday, Dec. 8—The Japanese landed in Northern Malaya, 300 miles north of Singapore, today and bombed this great British naval stronghold, causing small loss of life among civilians and property damage.

About 300 Japanese troops landed on the east coast of Malaya and began filtering through jungle-fringed swamps and rice fields toward Kota Bahru airdrome, which is ten miles from the northern terminus of a railroad leading to Singapore.

An official report from the

Continued on Page Two

The International Situation

MONDAY, DEC. 8, 1941

Yesterday morning Japan attacked the United States at several points in the Pacific. President Roosevelt ordered United States forces into action and a declaration of war is expected this morning. [Page 1, Columns 7 and 8.] Tokyo made its declaration as of this morning against both the United States and Britain. [Page 1, Column 2.] The first Japanese assault was directed at Pearl Harbor Naval base in Hawaii. Many casualties and severe damage resulted. [Page 1, Columns 4 and 5; Map, Page 13.] United States Army aircraft took off from the Philippines this morning and some points in the Archipelago were bombed. [Page 8, Column 2.] Singapore and Hong Kong were bombed and a Japanese landing in Northern Malaya and a move on Thailand were reported. [Page 1, Column 3.] In Shanghai, Japanese marines occupied the waterfront; a British gunboat was sunk, a United States gunboat seized. [Page 9, Column 1.]

Factional lines dissolved as an angered Congress prepared to meet this morning. [Page 1, Column 1.] Secretary of State Hull accused Japan of having made a "treacherous and utterly unprovoked attack" after having been "infamously false and fraudulent." [Page 1, Column 6.] He released the text of diplomatic exchanges with Japan [Page 10], while the President gave out the text of his fruitless appeal to the Japanese Emperor. [Page 12.] The White House was the hub of Washington activity and news bulletins were released there. [Page 12, Column 3.]

The Federal Bureau of Investigation was ordered to begin a round-up of some Japanese in this country. [Page 6, Column 8.] As New York City went on a war footing and public precautions were taken, the FBI began the detention of Japanese nationals. [Page 1, Column 4.]

The unification of the country under the impact of the attack was swift. [Page 6, Column 6.] Formerly conspicuous isolationists indicated full support for the war effort. [Page 6, Column 4.]

Prime Minister Churchill notified Tokyo that a state of war existed. [Page 4, Column 1.] Declarations were made last night or early today by Australia, Canada [Page 14 Column 1], the Netherlands Indies [Page 7, Column 2] and Costa Rica. [Page 15, Column 1.]

Libya was the scene of a renewed tank battle and the Tobruk corridor was reported again clear of Axis forces. [Page 20, Column 2, with map.] On the Moscow front the German line was broken at two places, said Soviet sources. [Page 37, Column 2.]

Tokyo Bombers Strike Hard At Our Main Bases on Oahu

By The United Press.

HONOLULU, Dec. 7—War broke with lightning suddenness in the Pacific today when waves of Japanese bombers attacked Hawaii this morning and the United States Fleet struck back with a thunder of big naval rifles. Japanese bombers, including four-engined dive bombers and torpedo-carrying planes, blasted at Pearl Harbor, the great United States naval base, the city of Honolulu and several outlying American military bases on the Island of Oahu. There were casualties of unstated number.

[The United States battleship Oklahoma was set afire by the Japanese attackers, according to a National Broadcasting Company observer, who also reported in a broadcast yesterday that two other ships in Pearl Harbor were attacked.

[The Japanese news agency, Domei, reported that the battleship Oklahoma had been sunk at Pearl Harbor, according to a United Press dispatch from Shanghai.

[Governor Joseph B. Poindexter of Hawaii talked with President Roosevelt late yesterday afternoon, saying that a second wave of Japanese bombers was just coming over, and the Gov-

Continued on Page Thirteen

ENTIRE CITY PUT ON WAR FOOTING

Japanese Rounded Up by FBI, Sent to Ellis Island—Vital Services Are Guarded

The metropolitan district reacted swiftly yesterday to the Japanese attack in the Pacific. All large communities in the area, including New York City, Newark, Jersey City, Bayonne and Paterson, went on immediate war footing.

One of the first steps taken here last night was a round-up of Japanese nationals by special agents of the Federal Bureau of Investigation, reinforced by squads of city detectives acting under FBI supervision. More than 100 FBI men, fully armed, were assigned to the detail.

The prisoners were sent to Ellis Island, where they will be held pending action at Washington. It was indicated hundreds would be detained.

Earlier Mayor La Guardia had convened his Emergency Board and directed that Japanese nationals be confined to their homes pending decision as to their status and had their clubs and other meeting places closed and put under police guard.

A police sergeant and five policemen immediately went to the Japanese Consulate at 630 Fifth Avenue in Rockefeller Center where the Consul General, Morito Morishima, and his staff were preparing to leave, and posted a guard there. The Consul General and his staff were escorted to their homes when they left. They were not to move about the city without police in attendance.

Rear Admiral Adolphus Andrews, commander of the North Atlantic Squadron, told reporters at a conference in the Federal

Continued on Page Three

HULL DENOUNCES TOKYO 'INFAMY'

Brands Japan 'Fraudulent' in Preparing Attack While Carrying On Parleys

Texts of Secretary Hull's note and Japan's reply, Page 10.

By BERTRAM D. HULEN
Special to THE NEW YORK TIMES.

WASHINGTON, Dec. 7—Japan was accused by Secretary of State Cordell Hull today of making a "treacherous and utterly unprovoked attack" upon the United States and of having been "infamously false and fraudulent" by preparing for the attack while conducting diplomatic negotiations with the professed desire of maintaining peace.

But even before he knew of the attack, Mr. Hull had vehemently brought the diplomatic negotiations to a virtual end with an outburst against Admiral Kichisaburo Nomura, the Japanese Ambassador, and Saburo Kurusu, special envoy, because of the insulting character of the reply they deliv-

Continued on Page Eleven

Lewis Wins Captive Mine Fight; Arbitrators Grant Union Shop

The three-man arbitration board appointed by President Roosevelt to arbitrate the union shop dispute in the captive coal mines last night reversed the decision of the National Defense Mediation Board and ruled that all workers in the captive mines should be required to join John L. Lewis's United Mine Workers as a condition of employment.

The decision was made by a two to one vote, with Benjamin F. Fairless, president of the United States Steel Corporation, dissenting. Dr. John R. Steelman, who took a leave of absence from his post as director of the United States Conciliation Service to serve as chairman of the arbitration panel, and Mr. Lewis voted in favor of extension to the captive mines of the union shop provision of the standard Appalachian agreement.

Despite his dissent, Mr. Fairless promised that the coal mining subsidiaries of United States Steel would put the ruling into effect. All eight steel companies operating captive mines had given formal assurances before the decision was reached that they would accept it as binding.

The arbitration award ended a dispute in which Mr. Lewis had repeatedly defied the President by calling strikes that menaced the production of steel and that had had its repercussions in the enactment by the House of the Smith anti-strike bill.

In explaining his vote for the union shop, Dr. Steelman pointed out that 95 per cent of the 53,000 captive miners had voluntarily assumed membership in Mr. Lewis's C. I. O. union and that 99.5 per cent of all the miners in the nation were now members of the union.

Since the bulk of the industry, including many owners of captive mines, was already operating under the union shop, it could not be argued that the United Mine Workers was endeavoring to take

Continued on Page Forty-three

GUAM BOMBED; ARMY SHIP IS SUNK

U. S. Fliers Head North From Manila—Battleship Oklahoma Set Afire by Torpedo Planes at Honolulu

104 SOLDIERS KILLED AT FIELD IN HAWAII

President Fears 'Very Heavy Losses' on Oahu—Churchill Notifies Japan That a State of War Exists

By FRANK L. KLUCKHOHN
Special to THE NEW YORK TIMES.

WASHINGTON, Monday, Dec. 8—Sudden and unexpected attacks on Pearl Harbor, Honolulu, and other United States possessions in the Pacific early yesterday by the Japanese air force and navy plunged the United States and Japan into active war.

The initial attack in Hawaii, apparently launched by torpedo-carrying bombers and submarines, caused widespread damage and death. It was quickly followed by others. There were unconfirmed reports that German raiders participated in the attacks.

Guam also was assaulted from the air, as were Davao, on the island of Mindanao, and Camp John Hay, in Northern Luzon, both in the Philippines. Lieut. Gen. Douglas MacArthur, commanding the United States Army of the Far East, reported there was little damage, however.

[Japanese parachute troops had been landed in the Philippines and native Japanese had seized some communities, Royal Arch Gunnison said in a broadcast from Manila today to WOR-Mutual. He reported without detail that "in the naval war the ABCD fleets under American command appeared to be successful" against Japanese invasions.]

Japanese submarines, ranging out over the Pacific, sank an American transport carrying lumber 1,300 miles from San Francisco, and distress signals were heard from a freighter 700 miles from that city.

The War Department reported that 104 soldiers died and 300 were wounded as a result of the attack on Hickam Field, Hawaii. The National Broadcasting Company reported from Honolulu that the battleship Oklahoma was afire. [Domei, Japanese news agency, reported the Oklahoma sunk.]

Nation Placed on Full War Basis

The news of these surprise attacks fell like a bombshell on Washington. President Roosevelt immediately ordered the country and the Army and Navy onto a full war footing. He arranged at a White House conference last night to address a joint session of Congress at noon today, presumably to ask for declaration of a formal state of war.

This was disclosed after a long special Cabinet meeting, which was joined later by Congressional leaders. These leaders predicted "action" within a day.

After leaving the White House conference Attorney General Francis Biddle said that "a resolution" would be introduced in Congress tomorrow. He would not amplify or affirm that it would be for a declaration of war.

Congress probably will "act" within the day, and he will call the Senate Foreign Relations Committee for this purpose, Chairman Tom Connally announced.

[A United Press dispatch from London this morning said that Prime Minister Churchill had notified Japan that a state of war existed.]

As the reports of heavy fighting flashed into the White House, London reported semi-officially that the British Empire would carry out Prime Minister Winston Churchill's pledge to give the United States full support in case of hostilities with Japan. The President and Mr. Churchill talked by transatlantic telephone.

This was followed by a statement in London from the Netherland Government in Exile that it considered a state of war to exist between the Netherlands and Japan. Canada, Australia and Costa Rica took similar action.

Landing Made in Malaya

A Singapore communiqué disclosed that Japanese troops had landed in Northern Malaya and that Singapore had been bombed.

The President told those at last night's White House meeting that "doubtless very heavy losses" were sustained by the Navy and also by the Army on the island of Oahu [Honolulu]. It was impossible to obtain confirmation or denial of reports that the battleships Oklahoma and West Virginia had been damaged or sunk at Pearl Harbor, together with six or seven destroyers, and that 350 United States airplanes had been caught on the ground.

The White House took over control of the bulletins, and the Navy Department, therefore, said it could not discuss the matter or answer any questions how the Japanese were able to penetrate the Hawaiian defenses or appear without previous knowledge of their presence in those waters.

Administration circles forecast that the United States soon might be involved in a world-wide war, with Germany supporting Japan, an Axis partner. The German official radio tonight attacked the United States and supported Japan.

Axis diplomats here expressed complete surprise that the Japanese had attacked. But the impression gained from their attitude was that they believed it represented a victory for the Nazi attempt to divert lease-lend aid from Britain, which has been

Continued on Page Four

"All the News That's Fit to Print."

The New York Times.

LATE CITY EDITION
Cloudy followed by clearing and colder today. Tomorrow fair and moderately cold.
Temperatures Yesterday—Max., 44; Min., 25.

VOL. XCI. No. 30,635. Entered as Second-Class Matter, Postoffice, New York, N. Y. NEW YORK, TUESDAY, DECEMBER 9, 1941. THREE CENTS NEW YORK CITY and Vicinity

U. S. DECLARES WAR, PACIFIC BATTLE WIDENS; MANILA AREA BOMBED; 1,500 DEAD IN HAWAII; HOSTILE PLANES SIGHTED AT SAN FRANCISCO

TURN BACK TO SEA

Two Formations Neared City on Radio Beams, Then Went Astray

ALARM IS WIDESPREAD

Whole Coast Has a Nervous Night—Many Cities Blacked Out

By LAWRENCE E. DAVIES
Special to THE NEW YORK TIMES.

SAN FRANCISCO, Dec. 8—Two formations of "many planes," described as undoubtedly enemy aircraft, flew over the San Francisco Bay area tonight, it was announced officially by Brig. Gen. William O. Ryan, commander of the Fourth Interceptor Command, after a progressive blackout had blotted out naval and military establishments and whole cities along the Pacific Coast.

Conflicting reports spread, contributing to the "war of nerves," as the sirens wailed and broadcasting were silenced.

After another spokesman, through an error, had declared the blackout to be an air raid test, General Ryan said at the Presidio that it was no test but "the real thing."

The ships were detected first about 100 miles at sea, he said. In two formations they headed for the Monterey Peninsula, about eighty miles south of this city, and for San Francisco Bay itself.

Radio detectors plotted their course, bringing one formation in just north of the Golden Gate and the other to a point near Fort Barry, at the south end of the Golden Gate Bridge.

Planes Turn Back to Sea

After flying northward for some distance the planes turned south to a point thirty-five or forty miles down the peninsula section below San Francisco. Apparently trying to orient themselves, they flew about a while longer and then headed southwest to sea, General Ryan said.

The commanding officer, whose station is at Riverside and who said he just "happened" to be at the Presidio tonight, declared that the planes followed radio beams to these shores. When radio stations on the West Coast were silenced as part of the blackout the enemy craft apparently were not sure of their position.

No American planes were sent to the attack, he said, because "you don't send planes up unless you know what the enemy is doing and where he is going and you don't send planes up in the dark unless you know what you are doing."

Although there was no official explanation for the absence of anti-aircraft fire, it was indicated that the planes were hardly close enough for effective use of the guns.

Plane Carriers Rumored

Although General Ryan had no information, he said, as to the presence of enemy aircraft carriers hovering off the Pacific Coast, rumors of their presence had been broadcast during the day and this, it was acknowledged, would be the logical explanation for the appearance of the planes.

Lieut. Gen. John L. Dewitt,

Continued on Page Twenty-eight

NEWS BULLETINS

Please do not telephone The New York Times for war news. Every hour on the hour news bulletins are broadcast over Station WMCA—570 on the dial.

WEEKDAYS
8 a.m. through 11 p.m.
SUNDAYS
9 a.m., 1 p.m., 5 p.m., 11 p.m.

Philippines Pounded All Day As Raiders Strike at Troops

Air Base Near Capital Among Targets Hit by Japanese—Landing on Lubang With Aid of Fifth Columnists Reported

By H. FORD WILKINS
Wireless to THE NEW YORK TIMES.

MANILA, Tuesday, Dec. 9—After a day of widespread aerial attacks throughout the Philippines, Japanese bombers swept in over Manila Bay early this morning and attacked Nichols Field, the United States Army air base on the outskirts of this capital, and simultaneously reports were received of a Japanese landing on Lubang Island, off the northwestern tip of Mindoro.

This morning's attack, which began shortly after 3 o'clock, was the first in the Manila area. The damage was believed to have been slight, but some casualties were reported. [A National Broadcasting Company correspondent reported that an official statement issued in Manila after the raid said: "In the raid on Nichols Field, which was conducted by approximately ten Japanese bombers, one hangar was damaged and one officers' quarters was burned. The casualty list consists of one soldier killed and twelve wounded—all Americans."]

The reported landing on Lubang, sixty miles southwest of Manila, was not officially confirmed, but the reports received credence here. [Other unconfirmed reports, relayed by the Columbia Broadcasting System, told of landings in the Davao region, on the southern island of Mindanao.]

The Manila area's first experience with bombs was a climax to a day and night of tension and activity. The explosions could be

Continued on Page Nine

PLANES GUARD CITY FROM AIR ATTACKS

Army Interceptors Join the Navy Patrols—Anti-Aircraft Apparatus Set Up Here

While long lines of men of fighting age waited impatiently outside of every Army, Navy and Marine Corps retruiting office in the city yesterday, representatives of the city, State and Federal Governments went ahead with the grim business of making New York City ready for war.

Beginning at dawn yesterday Army fighting planes took off at regular intervals from Mitchel Field to maintain, in conjunction with a Navy patrol, a constant fighting force in the air, so there could be no repetition here of the surprise in Hawaii. At the same time the First Interceptor Command called to active duty 40,000 volunteer civilian aircraft spotters at 1,300 posts scattered through thirteen eastern coastal States and the District of Columbia.

Anti-Aircraft Guns Set Up

The Sixty-second Coast Artillery of Fort Totten, Bayside, Queens, set up anti-aircraft apparatus at vantage points around the city. One base was in Prospect Park, Brooklyn.

Air raid wardens went on duty at midnight in every part of the city, as a result of a series of conferences among Police and Fire Department officers and representatives of the Board of Education and the Department of Housing, at which it was agreed that air raid warnings would be broadcast by the blowing of the sirens of all police radio cars and emergency trucks and all Fire Department apparatus.

Alternating long and short blasts of the sirens will be sounded from the moment the Army notifies the Police and Fire Departments of the approach of an enemy and will be continued throughout the duration of the raid. The all-clear signal will be given by a series of short blasts from the sirens, it was agreed.

Teachers to Be Warned

The Police and Fire Departments, with their network of communications reaching into every neighborhood in the city, also undertook to advise the 800 public schools of an impending raid when the alarm is sounded, so the teachers can shepherd their pupils to their homes in accordance with plans already made.

Precautions against sabotage of bridges, tunnels, railroads, reservoirs, dams, power plants and other points of key importance throughout the city also were discussed at conferences of high police officials with Commissioner

Continued on Page Twenty-six

MALAYA THWARTS PUSH BY JAPANESE

Thailand Capitulates and Is Seen Virtually in Axis—Two Raids on Singapore

By F. TILLMAN DURDIN
Wireless to THE NEW YORK TIMES.

SINGAPORE, Dec. 8—The Japanese in the first eighteen hours of their attack on the Malaya peninsula have forced Thailand to capitulate, but do not now appear to have achieved any appreciable success in an invasion of British Malaya.

There was an air raid on Singapore this morning. Prai, on the mainland opposite Georgetown, more commonly known as Penang from the name of the island on which it is located, was also bombed, but damage was said to be slight.

[Bombs again started dropping on Singapore at 4 A. M. today, The Associated Press re-

Continued on Page Ten

1 BATTLESHIP LOST

Capsized in Pearl Harbor, Destroyer Is Blown Up, Other Ships Hurt

FLEET NOW IS FIGHTING

Aid Rushed to Hawaii—Some Congressmen Sharply Critical

By CHARLES HURD
Special to THE NEW YORK TIMES.

WASHINGTON, Dec. 8—The Battle of the Pacific spread tonight over a 5,000-mile "front" from Hawaii to the Philippines while a badly battered United States Fleet fought back at Japanese sea and air forces that launched severe attacks yesterday afternoon.

Tonight the Japanese were reported to be launching their main attack at the Philippines, particularly at Palawan, the greatest natural harbor in the archipelago. That attack was preceded today, according to reports from Manila, by an onslaught against the United States military air fields there, which put these out of commission for the time being and set fire to storage tanks containing vital gasoline for air operations.

The Japanese Sunday attack on Hawaii was reported in informed quarters to have been launched from the mandated islands, rather than from Japan proper, and aircraft carriers apparently approached undetected within 250 or 300 miles of Pearl Harbor.

3,000 Casualties on Oahu

The White House announced officially that the attack on the Island of Oahu, site of Honolulu and the Pearl Harbor naval base, probably has cost about 1,500 lives and resulted in an equal number of wounded persons.

To the toll of lives announced for this region, and undisclosed casualties in the Philippines and at other points, was added official word that one "old battleship" had capsized in Pearl Harbor, a destroyer had exploded and that several other

Continued on Page Four

The International Situation

TUESDAY, DECEMBER 9, 1941

The United States yesterday made a formal declaration of war on Japan after President Roosevelt had addressed a joint session of Congress. [Page 1, Column 8.] The Senate approved by unanimous vote [Page 6, Column 1] while one woman in the House of Representatives dissented. [Page 6, Column 4.]

In the national effort the Supply, Priorities and Allocations Board mapped expanding production [Page 36, Column 1], leaders of organized labor pledged support [Page 36, Column 4], and Mayor La Guardia issued a proclamation giving air raid defense instructions [Page 34, Column 1.]

In San Francisco two formations of enemy aircraft were sighted over the city, which was blacked out. [Page 1, Column 1.]

White House announcements indicated that the battle of the Pacific was raging with the United States still on the defensive. [Page 1, Column 4; Map, Page 4.] There were extensive air attacks in the Philippines [Page 1, Columns 2 and 3; Map, Page 9], raids on Hong Kong [Page 11, Column 1] and a Tokyo report that both Guam and Wake had been put under the Japanese flag. [Page 12, Column 1; with map.] The British were mopping up on a Japanese landing party in Malaya, but Thailand had yielded. [Page 1, Column 3; Map, Page 10.]

The small detachment of United States Marines at Tientsin and Peiping was disarmed and detained by the Japanese and they closed the United States Consulate in Shanghai [Page 3, Column 1.] Imperial Headquarters in Tokyo made sweeping claims of victory in the battle of the Pacific, listing great damage to the United States forces. [Page 1, Column 5.]

In London, Prime Minister Churchill announced Britain's declaration of war to Parliament and made a stirring address to the world. [Page 14, Column 1.]

The American nations began to line up behind the United States. A conference will be held, but seven countries have already declared war on Japan, two have broken diplomatic relations and several others are preparing to act. [Page 22, Column 3.] China decided to declare war not merely on Japan but on Germany and Italy as well. [Page 9, Column 4.] The various European governments in exile also supported the United States. [Page 18, Column 1.] Russia's position is obscure. [Page 2, Column 2.]

The United States accused Germany of having egged Japan on; said lease-lend aid would continue. [Page 1, Column 6.] Berlin gave out word that Winter had stopped the Germans short of Moscow and that the capture of the Russian capital had been put off until Spring. [Page 1, Column 7.]

In Libya, the Axis armored forces were attacked from three directions by the British and what was expected to be a major engagement was eventually merely a rearguard action. [Page 24, Column 3.]

The President signs the declaration of war
Associated Press Wirephoto

LARGE U. S. LOSSES CLAIMED BY JAPAN

Tokyo Lists 2 Battleships, 1 Mine-Sweeper Sunk, 4 Capital Ships, 4 Cruisers Damaged

TOKYO, Tuesday, Dec. 9 (From Official Broadcasts, Distributed by The Associated Press)—Japanese Imperial Headquarters announced last night the sinking of two United States battleships and a mine-sweeper, severe damage to four other American capital ships and four cruisers and the destruction of about 100 American planes in Japan's surprise blows at Hawaii, the Philippines and Guam.

The official news agency, Domei, quickly interpreted "these magnificent early gains" as giving Japan naval mastery over the United States in the Pacific, and said that any force that the United States could muster now "would be regarded as utterly inadequate to accomplish any successful outcome in an encounter with the thus-far intact Japanese fleet."

In addition, "many enemy merchant ships were captured" in the Pacific, it was announced, and the communiqué listed an unconfirmed report that a Japanese submarine had sunk an American aircraft carrier off Honolulu.

"No Japanese ships were lost during the fighting," it added.

Domei said today it was "understood that Japanese forces had destroyed more than 300 American planes, including 200 in dogfights and on the ground in Hawaii. The others, it said, were "believed" destroyed in the Philippines. Of the total, the news agency said, thirty were Fortress planes and thirty long-range bombers.

Japanese newspapers identified the two American battleships declared sunk Sunday at Pearl Harbor, Hawaii, as the 31,800-ton West Virginia, and the 29,000-ton Oklahoma. [An Italian broadcast, however, quoted Domei as listing the Oklahoma and the 33,100-ton Pennsylvania as lost. In Berlin, D. N. B. said in a Tokyo dispatch that an American transport ship carrying 350 men had been sunk off Manila.]

Japanese planes were reported to have again attacked the Philippines and British Hong Kong yesterday, inflicting "heavy damage" in a follow-up of the raids launched Sunday. "Twelve out of fourteen enemy planes on the ground were

Continued on Page Thirteen

The President's Message

Following is the text of President Roosevelt's war message to Congress, as recorded by THE NEW YORK TIMES *from a broadcast:*

Mr. Vice President, Mr. Speaker, members of the Senate and the House of Representatives:

Yesterday, Dec. 7, 1941—a date which will live in infamy—the United States of America was suddenly and deliberately attacked by naval and air forces of the empire of Japan.

The United States was at peace with that nation, and, at the solicitation of Japan, was still in conversation with its government and its Emperor looking toward the maintenance of peace in the Pacific.

Indeed, one hour after Japanese air squadrons had commenced bombing in the American island of Oahu the Japanese Ambassador to the United States and his colleague delivered to our Secretary of State a formal reply to a recent American message. And, while this reply stated that it seemed useless to continue the existing diplomatic negotiations, it contained no threat or hint of war or of armed attack.

Attack Deliberately Planned

It will be recorded that the distance of Hawaii from Japan makes it obvious that the attack was deliberately planned many days or even weeks ago. During the intervening time the Japanese Government has deliberately sought to deceive the United States by false statements and expressions of hope for continued peace.

The attack yesterday on the Hawaiian Islands has caused severe damage to American naval and military forces. I regret to tell you that very many American lives have been lost. In

Continued on Page Six

U. S. TO CONTINUE AID TO BRITAIN

White House Charges Nazis Sought Pacific War, but Will Fail to Gain Ends

Special to THE NEW YORK TIMES.

WASHINGTON, Dec. 8—A statement accusing Germany of having done everything in her power "to push Japan into the war" was issued this evening at the White House.

The statement declared that Germany's objective was "to put an end to the lease-lend program," which has aided the European enemies of Germany, including Britain and Russia and their allies and Turkey. It added that this program would continue "in full operation" and that the German attempt to end lease-lend shipments was "100 per cent" mistaken.

This statement took full cognizance of the belief in diplomatic circles here that Germany would carry out its pledges to Japan, its Axis ally, by declaring war on the United States and that Italy would

Continued on Page Seventeen

NAZIS GIVE UP IDEA OF MOSCOW IN 1941

Winter Forces Abandonment of Big Drives in North Till Spring, Berlin Says

By The Associated Press.

BERLIN, Dec. 8—Winter has stopped the Germans short of Moscow and the capture of the Soviet capital is not expected this year, a military spokesman declared tonight.

[A surprise Russian attack on Eastern Crimea from the Caucasus was revealed in a Moscow broadcast. A counter-attack from Sevastopol also was reported. The Soviet claimed important gains around Taganrog and on Moscow's defense lines.]

It seemed likely from the spokesman's statement that until Spring there could be no further major German offensive except along the extreme southern front. This word reduced the Russian campaign to secondary interest for the Germans for the first time, and attention focused instead on Ja-

Continued on Page Twenty-five

UNITY IN CONGRESS

Only One Negative Vote as President Calls to War and Victory

ROUNDS OF CHEERS

Miss Rankin's Is Sole 'No' as Both Houses Act in Quick Time

By FRANK L. KLUCKHOHN
Special to THE NEW YORK TIMES.

WASHINGTON, Dec. 8—The United States today formally declared war on Japan. Congress, with only one dissenting vote, approved the resolution in the record time of 33 minutes after President Roosevelt denounced Japanese aggression in ringing tones. He personally delivered his message to a joint session of the Senate and House. At 4:10 P. M. he affixed his signature to the resolution.

There was no debate like that between April 2, 1917, when President Wilson requested war against Germany, and April 6, when a declaration of war was approved by Congress.

President Roosevelt spoke only 6 minutes and 30 seconds today compared with Woodrow Wilson's 29 minutes and 34 seconds.

The vote today against Japan was 82 to 0 in the Senate and 388 to 1 in the House. The lone vote against the resolution in the House was that of Miss Jeanette Rankin, Republican, of Montana. Her "No" was greeted with boos and hisses. In 1917 she voted against the resolution for war against Germany.

The President did not mention either Germany or Italy in his request. Early this evening a statement was issued at the White House, however, accusing Germany of doing everything possible to push Japan into the war. The objective, the official statement proclaimed, was to cut off American lend-lease aid to Germany's European enemies, and a pledge was made that this aid would continue "100 per cent."

A Sudden and Deliberate Attack

President Roosevelt's brief and decisive words were addressed to the assembled representatives of the basic organizations of American democracy—the Senate, the House, the Cabinet and the Supreme Court.

"America was suddenly and deliberately attacked by naval and air forces of the Empire of Japan," he said. "We will gain the inevitable triumph, so help us God."

Thunderous cheers greeted the Chief Executive and Commander in Chief throughout the address. This was particularly pronounced when he declared that Americans "will remember the character of the onslaught against us," a day, he remarked, which will live in infamy. "This form of treachery shall never endanger us again," he declared amid cheers. "The American people in their righteous might will win through to absolute victory."

Then, to the accompaniment of a

Continued on Page Five

President to Talk On Radio Tonight

By The Associated Press.

WASHINGTON, Dec. 8—President Roosevelt will make a radio address to the nation tomorrow night at 10 P. M., Eastern standard time, at which time the White House said he would make "a more complete documentation" of the Japanese attack than has yet been possible.

Stephen Early, Presidential secretary, announced that the Chief Executive would speak for half an hour and that the address would be carried by all networks.

Mr. Roosevelt began dictating the speech tonight in his White House study.

"All the News That's Fit to Print."

The New York Times.

LATE CITY EDITION
Fair, slowly rising temperature today. Tomorrow cloudy, moderately cold, occasional snow.
Temperatures Yesterday—Max., 34; Min., 24

VOL. XCI. No. 30,638. Entered as Second-Class Matter, Postoffice, New York, N. Y. NEW YORK, FRIDAY, DECEMBER 12, 1941. THREE CENTS NEW YORK CITY and Vicinity

U.S. NOW AT WAR WITH GERMANY AND ITALY; JAPANESE CHECKED IN ALL LAND FIGHTING; 3 OF THEIR SHIPS SUNK, 2D BATTLESHIP HIT

BLOCKED IN LUZON

But Japanese Put Small Force Ashore in South of Philippine Island

SABOTEURS ARE HELD

Some in Manila Seized for Spreading Rumor About City Water

By H. FORD WILKINS
Wireless to THE NEW YORK TIMES.

MANILA, Friday, Dec. 12—The United States Army Far East headquarters announced today that a small Japanese invasion force was reported to have pushed ashore at Legaspi, Southern Luzon, and "the enemy has improved his strength in Northern Luzon," where, however, the situation remains unchanged materially. The announcement added that the report of the Legaspi landing was still unconfirmed and there were no details.

[Small forces of Japanese apparently have been landed at Legaspi, it was said officially three hours after the morning communiqué had said merely that the Legaspi development had not yet been confirmed, a United Press dispatch from Manila said.]

There was no further indication of the progress of the sea war. The office of Admiral Thomas C. Hart, commander in chief of the United States Asiatic Fleet, remained silent.

One Japanese plane was shot down by an American fighter near Bancayan, in the mountain mining district.

2,000 Families Are Moved

Manila took further emergency measures to evacuate portions of the old walled city. The Red Cross supervised the removal of 2,000 families, loading them into buses and trucks and taking them to safety zones considerably removed from the city. Identification cards were issued and checked as the evacuees lined up for removal.

With Lieut. Gen. Douglas MacArthur's United States Far Eastern forces fully in control of the North Luzon invasion threat and his air force sufficiently active to disperse Japanese raiders headed for Manila, his intelligence service turned yesterday to mopping up fifth columnists.

Their latest trick was to circulate rumors that the city water supply had been poisoned. Army, city and government officials quickly scotched the rumors with assurances and proof that nothing whatever was wrong with the water supply. Several persons were arrested, including air-raid wardens, on a city-wide house-to-house campaign warning the people against "impure water."

Several persons entered hospitals asserting that they had been poisoned, but examination disclosed that nothing was wrong with them but upset stomachs and fear. Elaborate analysis proved that the water they drank was not contaminated.

The official communiqué asserting that mopping-up operations were progressing heightened the morale of the nation, suddenly plunged into total war and its first taste of conflict in forty years.

The sinking of a United States Army transport in Manila Bay, as announced by Tokyo, was denied officially here yesterday.

Interned Japanese, numbering around 2,000, were revealed to be extremely uncomfortable under the threat of bombs from Japanese planes, recognizing that bombs do not distinguish nationalities.

Legaspi Move Discounted

MANILA, Friday, Dec. 12 (U.P.)—The small Japanese landings at Legaspi, a port of about 36,000

Continued on Page Eight

Line-Up of World War II

THE ALLIES

Australia	Haiti
†Belgium	*Honduras
Canada	Netherlands Indies
China	New Zealand
Costa Rica	Nicaragua
Cuba	†Norway
†Czecho-Slovakia	*Panama
Dominican Republic	†Poland
*El Salvador	South Africa
Free France	†Soviet Union
Great Britain	United States
†Greece	†Yugoslavia
Guatemala	

THE AXIS

Finland	Japan
Germany	Manchukuo
Hungary	Rumania
Italy	Slovakia

*Have declared war on Japan only.

†At war only with Germany, Italy and their European allies.

CITY CALM AND GRIM AS THE WAR WIDENS

Loyalty and a Determination to Win Are Evident in Every Class and National Group

The people of New York City received the news that we are at war with Germany and Italy as well as Japan with profound calm and a quiet, stern determination to see it through, no matter how long it takes. Patriotism and loyalty were the spontaneous order of the day in every household, every business office, every factory, every school and every institution. The whole city rallied in support of the war.

All over the city the Stars and Stripes flew proudly from public and private buildings, and those in charge of Army, Navy, Coast Guard and civilian defense organizations swung promptly and forcefully into action to protect the city

Continued on Page Twenty-one

U. S. FLIERS SCORE

Bombs Send Battleship, Cruiser and Destroyer to the Bottom

MARINES KEEP WAKE

Small Force Fights Off Foe Despite Loss of Some of Planes

By CHARLES HURD
Special to THE NEW YORK TIMES.

WASHINGTON, Dec. 11—A Japanese battleship, a cruiser and a destroyer have been sunk in the Pacific and a second battleship badly damaged by bomb hits, the United States forces announced in communiqués today recording their first major victories in the warfare that began last Sunday with surprise Japanese attacks.

Damage to the second battleship was revealed tonight in a Navy communiqué, which said a man-of-war of the Kongo class had been hit by Navy patrol planes off the coast of Luzon. This was "the second battleship to be bombed effectively by United States forces," the communiqué asserted.

The battleship sunk, also of the Kongo class, was believed to have been the 29,330-ton Haruna. She went down after having been set afire by aerial bombardment north of Luzon. She had been supporting an attack in which the Japanese effected a landing at Aparri, a remote village on the northern Philippine coast, separated from Manila by mountains and forests.

The cruiser, unidentified except that it was of the light class, and the destroyer were sunk also by fliers who took off from Wake

Continued on Page Six

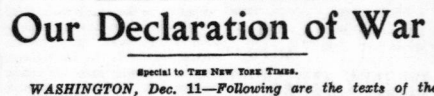

The International Situation

FRIDAY, DECEMBER 12, 1941

The United States declared war yesterday on Germany and Italy. Congress acted swiftly without a dissenting vote. [Page 1, Column 8.] Then, without debate, it passed a bill to permit the use of all United States land forces anywhere in the world. [Page 1, Column 7.]

This action coincided with good news from the Pacific. Washington announced the sinking of a Japanese battleship, a cruiser and a destroyer and reported severe damage to a second battleship by bomb hits. [Page 1, Column 3, Map, Page 6.]

The American declaration came within a few hours after Germany and Italy had declared war on the United States. The Reich's declaration was made in a diplomatic note and in a Reichstag address by Adolf Hitler. [Page 4, Column 1.] Benito Mussolini proclaimed Italy's declaration. [Page 4, Column 5.]

In London, where news of America's full entry into the world war brought predictions of an Allied grand strategy [Page 13, Column 5], Prime Minister Churchill declared that the Allies would win ultimately at any cost. [Page 1, Column 4.] Mexico broke off relations with Germany and Italy, while ten other Latin-American nations declared war on those countries or prepared to take that step. [Page 9, Column 1.]

The Soviet radio asserted that any Axis hopes for a separate peace with Russia were in vain. The radio declared that Russia was determined to fight alongside the United States and Britain until the Allies won. [Page 19, Column 1.]

In all of yesterday's land fighting, Japan was checked. In the Philippines, attempts to win a firm foothold on Luzon appeared smashed, except for a landing of parachutists at an airport 180 miles northeast of Manila and another small landing on the southeastern coast of the island. [Page 1, Column 1; Map, Page 2.] The British reported a slow-down of Japanese attacks in Malaya. [Page 13, Column 1.] While British forces fought off new assaults on Hong Kong, a two-day Chinese offensive to relieve pressure there was reported to have inflicted 15,000 casualties. [Page 11, Column 1, with map.]

Tokyo claimed the destruction of an American destroyer, a submarine and eighty-one planes, in addition to the capture of 350 Americans on Guam. [Page 8, Column 5.] With the commander of Britain's Far Eastern Fleet among 595 men still missing in the sinking of the Prince of Wales and the Repulse, the British named a new commander. [Page 14, Column 3.]

Amid debate in Washington over a proposed investigation of what happened at Pearl Harbor Sunday [Page 10, Column 1], Secretary of the Navy Knox arrived in Honolulu, presumably to seek first-hand information on that attack. [Page 1, Columns 5 and 6.]

President Roosevelt called upon industrial and labor representatives to meet next week and reach a voluntary agreement to end labor disputes for the duration. [Page 29, Column 2.] It was revealed also that the Administration was considering the registration of all men between the ages of 18 and 65 for military and civilian service. [Page 34, Column 1.]

On the European fighting front the Russians reported further gains against German forces. [Page 18, Column 3.] The Berlin radio revealed that the Nazis had replaced their commander on the Moscow front. [Page 19, Column 3.] In Libya, the main Axis forces were still withdrawing westward, Cairo announced. [Page 17, Column 1.]

Left: The President set his signature to the act against Germany. Center: He checked the time with Senator Tom Connally. Right: After that he placed the United States officially at war with Italy.

Associated Press Wirephotos

AXIS TO GET LESSON, CHURCHILL WARNS

He Announces Replacement of Libyan General—Upholds Phillips's Judgment

Text of Mr. Churchill's speech will be found on Page 16.

By CRAIG THOMPSON
Special Cable to THE NEW YORK TIMES.

LONDON, Dec. 11—Prime Minister Winston Churchill delivered a review of the war in the Pacific, North Africa, Russia and the Atlantic today that contained a compound of gloom and of optimism, but he ended with this ringing declaration:

"Just handfuls and cliques of wicked men and their military or party organizations have been able to bring these hideous evils upon mankind. It would indeed bring shame upon our generation if we did not teach them a lesson which will not be forgotten in the records of a thousand years."

Precedes Declarations

He spoke to the House of Commons before the Axis war declarations and the United States' reply.

Mr. Churchill gave hitherto unpublished details about the sinkings of the Prince of Wales and the Repulse, which made plain that the British lost the use of airdromes on the Malay Peninsula and that the ships had had to rely solely on their anti-aircraft guns for protection against the attacking planes. In so doing he stoutly defended the judgment whereby Vice Admiral Sir Tom S. V. Phillips, who appeared tonight to have been lost, undertook an attack on Japanese transports that resulted in the sinkings of the warships.

Mr. Churchill announced that Lieut. Gen. Sir Alan Gordon Cunningham had been replaced in Libya by Major Gen. Neil Methuen Ritchie, adding that General Cunningham "has been reported by medical authorities to be suffering from serious overstrain and was granted sick leave."

General Ritchie, the new commander of the Eighth Army, is 44 years old. His was one of three "young-men" appointments to the General Staff that were made last June. In the last war he was commissioned a second lieutenant in the Black Watch at the age of seventeen and was a captain when he was twenty. He fought in France, Mesopotamia and Palestine, and received the Distinguished Service Order and the Military Cross.

Mr. Churchill gave an indication of the size of British and Allied losses in merchantmen in the Battle of the Atlantic for November that would, from his statement, appear to have been no greater than 100,000 tons. This would be a

Continued on Page Seventeen

Our Declaration of War

Special to THE NEW YORK TIMES.

WASHINGTON, Dec. 11—Following are the texts of the documents wherein the President asked a war declaration against Germany and Italy, and Congress acted:

The President's Message

To the Congress of the United States:

On the morning of Dec. 11 the Government of Germany, pursuing its course of world conquest, declared war against the United States.

The long-known and the long-expected has thus taken place. The forces endeavoring to enslave the entire world now are moving toward this hemisphere.

Never before has there been a greater challenge to life, liberty and civilization.

Delay invites great danger. Rapid and united effort by all of the peoples of the world who are determined to remain free will insure a world victory of the forces of justice and of righteousness over the forces of savagery and of barbarism.

Italy also has declared war against the United States.

I therefore request the Congress to recognize a state of war between the United States and Germany, and between the United States and Italy.

FRANKLIN D. ROOSEVELT.

The War Resolution

Declaring that a state of war exists between the Government of Germany and the government and the people of the United States and making provision to prosecute the same.

Whereas the Government of Germany has formally declared war against the government and the people of the United States of America:

Therefore, be it

Resolved by the Senate and House of Representatives of the United States of America in Congress assembled, that the state of war between the United States and the Government of Germany which has thus been thrust upon the United States is hereby formally declared; and the President is hereby authorized and directed to employ the entire naval and military forces of the United States and the resources of the government to carry on war against the Government of Germany; and, to bring the conflict to a successful termination, all of the resources of the country are hereby pledged by the Congress of the United States.

(An identic resolution regarding Italy was adopted)

Secretary Knox Visits Honolulu; Bases There Were Raided 5 Times

Special to THE NEW YORK TIMES.

WASHINGTON, Dec. 11—The Navy Department announced tonight that Secretary Frank Knox had arrived in Honolulu this afternoon.

There was no previous announcement that he had left for Hawaii, nor was there any intimation of the specific purpose of his visit.

WASHINGTON, Dec. 11 (U.P.)—Delegate Samuel W. King of Hawaii disclosed tonight after a telephone conversation with Governor Joseph B. Poindexter that twenty Japanese planes were shot down during the Sunday raid on Pearl Harbor.

Mr. King said the information was authorized for release in Hawaii by Lieut. Gen. Walter C. Short and that Mr. Poindexter was permitted to make the disclosure by transpacific radio-telephone.

Mr. Poindexter told Mr. King that "civilian morale is 100 per cent throughout the territory.

"Civilian defense measures are working without a hitch," he added.

HONOLULU, Dec. 11 (U.P.)—In addition to two deadly attacks on the United States naval base at Pearl Harbor last Sunday, Japanese bombers followed with a third attack later that day and with a fourth Monday morning, it is possible to disclose today for the first time.

Censorship permits a cautious description of the attack. A few seconds after the first bombers came over, with the rising sun insignia of Japan on their wings, defending anti-aircraft batteries sent up a heavy barrage.

Within a few minutes heavy clouds of black smoke began rolling up from Pearl Harbor, fourteen miles from Honolulu.

Planes roared in over the harbor, dropping bombs on navy centers and ships. Torpedo planes splashed

Continued on Page Eleven

CONGRESS KILLS BAN ON AN A. E. F.

Swift Action Without Debate—Service Terms Are Extended to Six Months After War

Special to THE NEW YORK TIMES.

WASHINGTON, Dec. 11—Congress swiftly eliminated prohibitions against American expeditionary forces today and continued terms of enlistment or induction to a date six months after hostilities end. Acting without debate, the two houses dropped the A. E. F. ban by removing restrictions in the Selective Service Act on the use of troops outside the Western Hemisphere.

The Senate Appropriations Committee, meanwhile, added an undetermined sum to the $8,246,000,000 third supplemental national defense appropriation bill as passed by the House. This change was said to have raised the bill's total above $10,500,000,000.

A ranking member of the committee was unable to say tonight what the exact amount of the bill was, but he said he was "satisfied it is above $10,500,000,000." He added that the amendments approved by the committee were mostly for new items, regarded as emergency ones by the Army and the Navy and Coast Guard. If approved, the measure would set a record for the size of a single appropriation bill.

Fund for Army Pay Specified

Among the amendments approved by the committee was one setting at $314,000,000 the supplemental item for pay of the Army, but immediately following it was a proviso that this amount should not be taken to mean the limit if the Army inducted or enlisted thousands of new personnel. If this took place, under the amendment practical authority would be granted for pay of the personnel under Congressional promise to pass deficiency bills to whatever extent was necessary.

Some $390,000,000 was added to the bill for military air construction. The Signal Corps also received a sizable increase for construction and equipment, while to the Navy were granted increases of many millions for landing fields, yards and docks. The Coast Guard received $4,750,000 for extraordinary expenses and $8,743,000 for new equipment.

The Army Chief of Staff received $125,000,000 as an emergency fund, to be accounted for to Congress every three months, and various sums were voted for additions to forts and posts within the United States.

The measure changing the Selective Service Act regarding the tenure of service and the extent of service came on the heels of action by both houses in declaring war on Germany and Italy, follow-

Continued on Page Thirty-four

WAR OPENED ON US

Congress Acts Quickly as President Meets Hitler Challenge

A GRIM UNANIMITY

Message Warns Nation Foes Aim to Enslave This Hemisphere

By FRANK L. KLUCKHOHN
Special to THE NEW YORK TIMES.

WASHINGTON, Dec. 11—The United States declared war today on Germany and Italy, Japan's Axis partners. This nation acted swiftly after Germany formally declared war on us and Italy followed the German lead. Thus, President Roosevelt told Congress in his message, the long-known and the long-expected has taken place.

"The forces endeavoring to enslave the entire world now are moving toward this hemisphere," he said.

"Never before has there been a greater challenge to life, liberty and civilization."

Delay, the President said, invites great danger. But he added:

"Rapid and united effort by all of the peoples of the world who are determined to remain free will insure a world victory of the forces of justice and righteousness over the forces of savagery and barbarism."

For the first time in its history the United States finds itself at war against powers in both the Atlantic and the Pacific.

Quick and Unanimous Answer

Congress acted not only rapidly but without a dissenting vote to meet the Axis challenge. Within two and three-quarters hours after the reading of Mr. Roosevelt's message was started in the Senate and House at 12:26 P. M., the President had signed the declarations against Germany and Italy. Seventy-two hours previously the Japanese attack on Hawaii had brought about the declaration of war against the other Axis partner.

Congress also quickly completed legislation to allow selectees and National Guardsmen to serve outside the Western Hemisphere and set the term of service in the nation's forces until six months after the termination of the war.

In the Senate the vote was 88 to 0 for war against Germany and 90 to 0 for war against Italy. The vote in the House was 393 to 0 for war against Germany and 399 to 0 for war against Italy. The larger Congressional vote against Italy was attributable to the fact that some members reached the floor too late to vote on the declaration against Germany.

In the House, Miss Jeannette Rankin, Republican, of Montana, who cast the lone dissenting vote on Monday against declaring war on Japan, today voted a non-committal "present" with regard to Germany and Italy.

Ignoring Hitler's declarations before the Reichstag today regarding American policy, and Mussolini's to a crowd before the Palazzo di Venezia in Rome, Congress adopted identical resolutions against Germany and Italy. It merely noted that their governments had thrust war upon the United States.

Grim Mood in Congress

Congress acted in a grim mood, but without excitement. Not only on the floors of the Senate and House, but in the galleries the grim mood prevailed. President Roosevelt, busy at the White House directing the battle and production effort as Commander in Chief, did not appear to read his message, as he did when war was declared upon Japan.

There was a deeply solemn undernote as the members assembled at noon. Senator Walsh, chairman of the Senate Naval Affairs Committee, had announced that the

Continued on Page Five

"All the News That's Fit to Print."

The New York Times.

LATE CITY EDITION
Partly cloudy, slightly warmer today. Tomorrow mostly cloudy, moderate temperature.

VOL. XCI..No. 30,642. Entered as Second-Class Matter, Postoffice, New York, N. Y. NEW YORK, TUESDAY, DECEMBER 16, 1941. THREE CENTS NEW YORK CITY and Vicinity

KNOX REPORTS ONE BATTLESHIP SUNK AT HAWAII, 5 OTHER CRAFT LOST, BUT MAIN FLEET IS AT SEA; PRESIDENT LAYS PERFIDY TO JAPAN'S EMPEROR

AIR WARDEN ORDERS WILL BE BACKED UP BY $500 PENALTIES

Alternate Jail Sentences Are Provided in Bill Council Will Act Upon Today

5 NEW SIRENS DELIVERED

Devices May Be Heard One to Two Miles—Tests Tomorrow—School Rules Unchanged

Failure to obey civil defense regulations or refusal to comply with the orders of air raid wardens would be made punishable by a jail term of not more than six months or a fine of not more than $500 by a local law to be introduced at this afternoon's meeting of the City Council by majority leader Joseph T. Sharkey of Brooklyn.

The measure, which was requested yesterday by Mayor La Guardia, also provides that during an air raid all except duly authorized persons must immediately leave streets, parks and open spaces and proceed to the nearest cover, and that vehicles must be parked immediately and their passengers take to the nearest shelter.

After the air-raid alarms last Tuesday and Wednesday many air-raid wardens complained that crowds thronged into the streets to see what was going on and ignored their directions to seek shelter. The legislation sought by the Mayor is intended to correct this condition and to give the wardens legal authority to disperse crowds which might be subject to heavy casualties in an actual raid.

Warden Cards Printed

The Police Department has completed the printing of 200,000 identification cards for air-raid wardens, it was learned last night at the office of the Coordinator of Civilian Defense at Police Headquarters, and is about to begin issuing them to qualified wardens. Zone wardens will receive white cards, sector wardens yellow cards and post wardens salmon-colored cards.

Each warden must affix a photograph of himself, chauffeur size, to his card and return it to the police through his local precinct. A Police Department seal will then be placed over his picture and signature to guarantee the validity of the card, and then it will be returned to the holder. The cards will be two by three inches in size.

Five big "siro-drones," the first of seventy to be delivered this week, arrived yesterday at the office of Thomas W. Rochester, chief engineer of the Police Department. The five included two different types, one of which is supposed to be audible within a radius of two miles and the other with a range of one mile.

Can Be Heard Mile

Both sirens are about three feet high, with horns twenty inches in diameter, and are electrically operated. The type with a radius of one mile is operated by a two-horsepower motor and the louder horn by a five-horsepower motor. They are ordinarily used as factory whistles and fire alarms in small towns and are manufactured by the H-O-B Company, Inc., of Stapleton, S. I.

Mayor La Guardia, Police Commissioner Valentine, and other local officials and civilian defense leaders will attend tests of both types of the new "siro-drones" tomorrow afternoon. The Mayor's party is to arrive at Spring and Lafayette Street, near Police Headquarters, at 4:30 P. M. to try out the sirens after they have been placed on a Police Department tower truck.

Earlier tomorrow afternoon, at 4 o'clock the Mayor and his entourage will visit the building of the New York Edison Company at Fortieth Street and the East River for a trial of the big whistle, operated by steam and electricity, that is mounted on the structure.

Continued on Page Twenty-four

'Keep Flag Flying,' MacArthur's Order

Wireless to THE NEW YORK TIMES.

MANILA, Dec. 15—Morale at headquarters of the United States Army's Far Eastern Forces is above par.

An officer on the staff of General Douglas MacArthur, Commander in Chief, suggested to him that the American flag atop the bastion that marks the headquarters might serve as a target for Japanese planes. General MacArthur laughed and said:

"Take every other normal precaution for the protection of the headquarters, but let's keep the flag flying."

18-64 AGE LISTING FOR DRAFT RUSHED

House Committee for Military Service at 21, Senate Group for Minimum of 19

By HENRY N. DORRIS

Special to THE NEW YORK TIMES.

WASHINGTON, Dec. 15—Congressional committees speeded legislation today to give full wartime powers to the President and extend the registration requirements of the Selective Service Act to all men from 18 to 64, inclusive.

The House Military Affairs Committee gave final approval to a bill carrying the Selective Service changes. The Senate Military Affairs Committee gave tentative approval to a bill, withholding full approval pending testimony in executive session tomorrow by Brig. Gen. Lewis B. Hershey, Selective Service Administrator.

The bills as they stood tonight differed on the ages subject to military service. The Senate bill contains tentatively the War Department recommendation for the age brackets 19 to 44, inclusive. The House committee approved the bracket 21 to 44, inclusive.

About 41,000,000 men would be affected by the overall registration requirement, which is planned not only to provide an army of 2,800,000 to 7,500,000 but to ascertain

Continued on Page Thirty-one

RUSSIANS TAKE KLIN

Vital Rail Point in Center Seized as Push Gains on Every Front

NAZIS FLEE IN NORTH

Lose 3 Towns in Tula Area—Soviet Claims Crimean Advance

By DANIEL T. BRIGHAM

By Telephone to THE NEW YORK TIMES.

BERNE, Switzerland, Tuesday, Dec. 16—Smashing through ever-weakening German lines of defense, Soviet troops continued their brilliant operations in the fighting yesterday, recapturing Klin, important rail point on the Moscow-Leningrad line, and three communications centers south of Moscow.

The Red Army also advanced in the Volkhov area, southeast of Leningrad, and in Crimea the Germans were pushed back to the outskirts of Balaclava by Russian troops from Sevastopol, a Russian military spokesman announced on the Moscow radio this morning.

In operations intended to disengage the entire Leningrad-Moscow rail line, the Russians carried out encircling movements north of the Valdai Heights that enabled them to smash the German Thirty-ninth Army Corps. According to the spokesman, 20,000 Germans were killed or wounded in this action.

The remainder of the German force was reported to be fleeing in a southwesterly direction in an attempt to rejoin a "fairly large German force" with its back to Lake Ilmen. However, a Russian column threatens the Germans' southern wing on that sector.

On the Leningrad end of the front Red Army troops began a wide-scale operation southwestward from Tosna. It is understood that the main objective is to straighten out a deep salient that the Germans have held for more

Continued on Page Fifteen

U. S. 'WHITE PAPER'

President in Message Reveals How Tokyo Hid Treacherous Aims

AS HITLER DID LATER

Tyrants Will Fall in End to the Free Peoples, He Says on Radio

The President's message to Congress is on Page 6.

Special to THE NEW YORK TIMES.

WASHINGTON, Dec. 15—Emperor Hirohito was accused today by President Roosevelt, in effect, of personal complicity in Japan's course of carrying on peace negotiations with the United States while putting into operation the plan for a treacherous attack upon this country.

The Emperor is regarded by most Japanese as a divinity whose personal honor must be above reproach, and diplomatic circles here expressed the opinion today that the revelation of perfidy might have serious repercussions within Japan later.

The President revealed in a message transmitted to Congress the details of the reply from the Emperor to his personal appeal to peace on Dec. 6. The message, which was looked upon as the equivalent of an American White Paper, outlined the whole course of American-Japanese relations and of step-by-step execution of the joint German-Japanese-Italian plan for world conquest.

[The issue of the war is whether a revival of barbarism is to be forced on the self-respecting peoples of the world by tyrants, President Roosevelt declared last night in his radio address on the 150th anniversary of the ratification of the Bill of Rights. Whereas Hitler's idea is that the individual has no rights whatsoever under an absolute master, the state, the President pledged that this nation will not lay down arms until "liberty is once again secure in the world we live in."]

Talked Peace After War Started

The President emphasized that Hirohito's reply to his peace appeal was delivered orally to Ambassador Joseph C. Grew in Tokyo three hours and forty minutes after Japanese planes and submarines had started the war by a surprise attack on Pearl Harbor.

The full text of the Emperor's reply was not made public, but he was quoted as saying, in part, after Japan had begun the war:

"Establishment of peace in the Pacific, and consequently of the world, has been the cherished desire of His Majesty, for the realization of which he has hitherto made his government to continue its earnest endeavors."

Japan's real reply, the President stressed, had been given earlier by the long-prepared attack without warning on American bases in the Pacific. "There," he said, "is the record, for all history to read in amazement, in sorrow, in horror and disgust."

After outlining the attempt by the United States to maintain friendly relations with the Japanese from the time Commodore Perry opened Japan to the outside world in 1853, and telling of continued American efforts to maintain a peace based on justice and fair-dealing in the Orient, the President stated that Japan openly entered a league of fascism against the free world under the pretext of signing the anti-Comintern Pact in 1936.

Tells of Axis Accord Against Us

He offered evidence to show that Japan, Germany and Italy arranged together to time their blows against free nations in the best manner to effect joint plans for world dominance, and mentioned how the three finally and openly concluded last year "a treaty of

Continued on Page Six

The International Situation

TUESDAY, DECEMBER 16, 1941

Secretary of the Navy Knox yesterday reported losses to the United States Fleet in the Pearl Harbor attack as one battleship, a target ship, a minelayer and three destroyers. Casualties, as he gave them out, were heavier than had been previously reported. He said that defense forces were "not on the alert" and that the Japanese had been aided by a great "fifth column." An investigation is going forward. [Page 1, Column 8.]

The situation in the Philippines appeared to be stabilized, with an air raid on the naval station at Olongapo the only major operation. Midway, as well as Wake, was said in reports from Washington to be still holding out. [Page 1, Column 5; Map, Page 2.] British troops, resisting a Japanese attack in force on the Malay Peninsula, were declared to have dug in on a stronger defense line in southern Kedah and to have abandoned the southern tip of Burma. [Page 14, Column 3.] British and Netherland air units fought off strong Japanese forces. [Page 1, Column 5 and 6.] At Hong Kong the British had retired from the mainland and were strongly defending the island. The Chinese thrust in relief was gaining momentum. [Page 10, Column 2.]

Tokyo's Premier pictured his foes in collapse, but warned of a long war. [Page 1, Columns 6 and 7.]

President Roosevelt, in a message to Congress outlining the events leading up to the war, laid stress on the Japanese bad faith, in which, he implied, the Emperor himself was involved. [Page 1, Column 4.] In a broadcast to the nation on the anniversary of the ratification of the Bill of Rights, he made Adolf Hitler the chief object of his attack and pledged our victory for the sake of liberty. [Page 30, Column 2.]

The President also made his quarterly report to Congress on lease-lend aid and emphasized that our entrance into the war increased its necessity. [Page 4, Column 1.] Military Affairs Committees of the Senate and House approved bills to register all males between 18 and 65 years, but differed slightly on the age for military service. [Page 1, Column 2.]

Moscow reported the recapture of the city of Klin and said the drive around Tula was successful; indeed, there were continued victories of the Russian offensive on all fronts. [Page 1, Column 3; Map, Page 15.]

The Axis also continued to give ground in Libya and the Nazis were reported to be throwing their last tank and infantry strength into a desperate delaying action. [Page 16, Column 1.] Their supply lines were said to have been further impaired with the sinking in the Mediterranean of a large supply ship and the sinking or damaging of half a dozen smaller vessels. [Page 17, Column 1.]

Vichy heard of fresh attacks on Nazis in Paris, including the bombing of a restaurant. There were reports that Marshal Pétain had refused the Germans the use of the French fleet and bases in Tunisia. [Page 18, Column 3.] Secretary of State Hull expressed friendly and encouraging sentiments toward the French people at his press conference. [Page 19, Column 1.]

As the American republics took further actions in support of the United States, Argentina contemplated instituting a state of siege to curb Axis activities. [Page 9, Column 3.]

ENEMY MAKES SOME GAINS IN MALAYA AND SOUTH BURMA

British defenders of Victoria Point (1) were reported to have withdrawn as a Japanese force pushed westward across the Kra Isthmus. An announcement of fighting in Southern Kedah (2) indicated that the Japanese had made progress in that area. "Some activities" were reported in Kelantan (3). Ipoh (4) had an air-raid alarm. Frame on inset shows the area covered by large map.

Allied Fliers Match Japan's In North Malaya Fighting

By F. TILLMAN DURDIN

Special Cable to THE NEW YORK TIMES.

SUNGEI PATANI, North Malaya, Dec. 14 (Delayed)—Against Japanese based on airdromes in Thailand that apparently had been prepared for them long before the attack on Malaya began, British, Australian and Netherland air units in this region are putting up courageous and effective opposition. One Royal Air Force source told me that the Japanese were operating from five different airfields in Southern Thailand within forty-eight hours after the war broke out.

[Japanese forces pushed into the southern part of the State of Kedah, Northern Malaya, and took Victoria Point, the tip of Southern Burma, the British announced. The Japanese, however, moved at a heavy cost in lives, it was said. The defenders were entrenched on the eastern side of the peninsula south of Kota Bharu. Penang was not raided yesterday, but Japanese bombers attacked Ipoh, tin mining center.]

The Japanese at present are using planes chiefly for bombing Malayan airdromes. The city on Penang Island, off the west coast of Malaya, is the only civilian center

Continued on Page Fourteen

FILIPINOS BEAT OFF 154 ENEMY BOATS

Lingayen Guns Blast Japanese for 3 Days—Invading Planes Bomb Olongapo Naval Base

By The United Press.

MANILA, Tuesday, Dec. 16—First details reached here today of an engagement at Lingayen Beach, 110 miles northwest of Manila, where a Filipino Army division, lining the shore with artillery, blasted 154 motorboat loads of invading Japanese soldiers without letting one of them reach land alive.

The fighting lasted three days. It began last Wednesday night and at last report the Filipinos were holding the beach. The colonel in command sent word to Manila that his force would stand their ground "to the last man."

Details were brought here by a correspondent of The Philippines Herald. He quoted the colonel, whom he did not identify, as having said:

"We eagerly awaited the Japanese attempt to land. The enemy showed up Wednesday night. I counted 154 motorboats in all. We held our fire until they were near.

"Then our artillery roared into action. Most of the boats were destroyed. A few managed to escape to warships which must have been anchored far beyond the horizon. Since then the enemy has attempted to land, but each time he has been frustrated."

The correspondent reported that when the colonel promised to fight to the last man "he was merely voicing the sentiments of men of all ranks whom I interviewed." The colonel was said to be con-

Continued on Page Six

Tokyo Premier Claims Triumph, Then Warns of War to Be Fought

By The Associated Press.

TOKYO, Tuesday, Dec. 16 (From Japanese Broadcast) — Premier Hideki Tojo, addressing an extraordinary session of the Japanese Diet, today reiterated his assertions that Japan had declared war on the United States only after trying all means of peaceful settlement. He declared:

"Our fighting services have speedily broken through the enemy key positions within less than ten days. The bulk of the American Fleet which had been at Hawaii is destroyed; the main body of the British Far Eastern Fleet is crushed; the encircling front against Japan, the strength of which the enemy has exaggerated and given wide publicity in an attempt to intimidate Japan, is shattered at various places.

"The anti-Japanese encircling front already is on a fair way to collapse."

He nevertheless cautioned the Japanese that "a war remains waiting to be fought."

Japanese Imperial Headquarters reported that Japanese expeditionary forces had landed on British Borneo at dawn today despite a heavy gale.

The headquarters also reported that Japanese Army and Navy forces completed occupation of the island of Guam last Friday.

A joint communiqué of the army and navy sections of Imperial Headquarters warned Japanese yesterday "against the lurking danger of enemy submarines" off Japan's island coasts and urged them to

Continued on Page Eighteen

Knox Statement on Hawaii

By The Associated Press.

WASHINGTON, Dec. 15—The text of Secretary Knox's statement detailing losses in the Japanese attack on Pearl Harbor follows:

My inspection trip to the island enables me to present the general facts covering the attack which hitherto have been unavailable.

1. The essential fact is that the Japanese purpose was to knock out the United States before the war began. This was made apparent by the deception practiced, by the preparations which had gone on for many weeks before the attack, and the attacks themselves, which were made simultaneously throughout the Pacific. In this purpose the Japanese failed.

2. The United States services were not on the alert against the surprise air attack on Hawaii. This fact calls for a formal investigation, which will be initiated immediately by the President. Further action is, of course, dependent on the facts and recommendations made by this investigating board. We are all entitled to know it if (a) there was any error of judgment which contributed to the surprise, (b) if there was any dereliction of duty prior to the attack.

3. My investigation made clear that after the attack the defense by both services was conducted skillfully and bravely. The Navy lost:

(a) The battleship Arizona, which was destroyed by the explosion of, first, its boiler and then its forward magazine due to a bomb which was said to have literally passed down through the smokestack;

(b) The old target ship Utah, which has not been used as a combatant ship for many years, and which was in service as a training ship for anti-aircraft gunnery and experimental purposes;

(c) Three destroyers, the Cassin, the Downes and the Shaw;

(d) Minelayer Oglala. This was a converted merchantman, formerly a passenger ship on the Fall River Line and converted into a minelayer during the World War.

The Navy sustained damage to other vessels. This damage varies from ships which have been already repaired and are ready for sea, or which have gone to sea, to a few ships which will take from a week to several months to

Continued on Page Seven

HEROIC ACTS CITED

2,897 Defenders Killed in Gallant Battle—Base Not 'on Alert'

FIFTH COLUMN ACTIVE

2-Man Submarine Used—Roosevelt to Name Inquiry Board

By CHARLES HURD

Special to THE NEW YORK TIMES.

WASHINGTON, Dec. 15—Japan did not administer a knockout blow or destroy the effectiveness of American naval forces in the Pacific when she attacked at Pearl Harbor, Hawaii, at dawn on Dec. 7, and thus failed to achieve her objective, Secretary of the Navy Frank Knox reported today on his return from a flight to Hawaii to investigate the attack.

High Japanese officials had asserted that the blow struck at Pearl Harbor destroyed American naval supremacy in the Pacific. Mr. Knox evidenced a different view when he said:

"The Japanese failed to knock out the United States before the war began."

Fleet Now Hunts Enemy

The Secretary said the United States Army and Navy forces in Hawaii "were not on the alert against the surprise attack" of the Japanese and in consequence losses had been heavy. After the action started, however, he said, our soldiers and sailors fought bravely, and he added that all remaining effective units of the Pacific Fleet "are at sea seeking contact with the enemy."

He listed the destroyed vessels as the battleship Arizona, the destroyers Cassin, Downes and Shaw; the minelayer Oglala and the target and training ship Utah. In addition, he said that the battleship Oklahoma had capsized and that an unannounced number of vessels had been damaged.

The Navy casualties in this action were given by Mr. Knox as 91 officers and 2,638 men killed and 20 officers and 636 men wounded. Late this evening the Army announced that its losses in this engagement totaled 168 officers and men, bringing the aggregate service losses to 2,897.

Attack's Objective Failed

Mr. Knox gave his report at a special press conference a few hours after his return from Honolulu. He supplemented a prepared statement by replies to questions that emphasized the fact that the Japanese, launching their attack with carrier-borne planes and submarines, eluded the naval patrols at sea, caught the Army Air Force on the ground and destroyed the great majority of planes there, and showed a detailed knowledge of objectives.

Against these adverse reports, Mr. Knox reported that the sailors and soldiers fought bravely and well after the action started, and he told reporters that the Japanese failed in their objective, which was to knock out the Pacific fleet before the war started.

Responsibility for the errors committed, he said, will be investigated immediately by a Presidential commission. He declined to anticipate the results of such an investigation. After calling on President Roosevelt this evening, Mr. Knox said the President would name the inquiry board tomorrow.

The Japanese losses for this engagement were listed by the Secretary as three submarines, including one large and one small one destroyed and a small one captured, and forty-one planes.

One reason for the success of the Japanese, he asserted, was cooperation from the Hawaiian Islands themselves.

"The most effective fifth-column work in this war was done in Hawaii, with the exception of Norway," Mr. Knox said.

He declined to elaborate on steps

Continued on Page Seven

"All the News That's Fit to Print."

The New York Times.

LATE CITY EDITION
Rain today and not much change in temperature.
Temperatures Yesterday—Max.,53; Min.,35

VOL. XCI. No. 30,757. Entered as Second-Class Matter, Postoffice, New York, N. Y. NEW YORK, FRIDAY, APRIL 10, 1942. THREE CENTS NEW YORK CITY and Vicinity

JAPANESE CAPTURE BATAAN AND 36,000 TROOPS; SINK TWO BRITISH CRUISERS; ITALIANS LOSE ONE; INDIA REPORTED AGREEING ON NATIVE COUNCIL

SENATOR AND JONES CLASH OVER ATTACK ON WAR PLANT DEAL

Bunker Charges DPC Condones 'Unconscionable Profits' for Nevada Magnesium Plant

UNTRUE, SAYS SECRETARY

Fees Paid to 9 Contractors, He Adds, Will Be Less Than 2% of Cost of 70 Millions

Special to THE NEW YORK TIMES.

WASHINGTON, April 9—Senator Bunker, Democrat, of Nevada, today attacked the Defense Plant Corporation, an RFC subsidiary, charging that the terms of its contract with Basic Magnesium, Inc., for a plant at Las Vegas, Nev., meant "unconscionable profits." Secretary Jones, as head of the RFC, immediately replied that the charges were misleading and untrue, and, in effect, challenged Senator Bunker to press them without benefit of Senatorial immunity.

The Secretary of Commerce replied to Senator Bunker in a statement.

"Senator Bunker's statements accusing RFC officials of wrongdoing," he said, "are unworthy of a United States Senator and cannot go unchallenged. The Senator must know these statements are untrue.

"The magnesium plant that is being built by the government near Las Vegas, Nev., will cost approximately $70,000,000 and have an estimated annual capacity of 112,000,000 pounds of metallic magnesium.

Says Fees Total Less Than 2%

"Nine separate contractors are participating in the construction. The fees to be paid the nine contracting and engineering firms, together with the fee to Basic Magnesium, Inc., for its engineering plans, supervision and 'know-how,' will aggregate less than 2 per cent of the total cost of the plant.

"The operating or management fee of the plant is to be half cent per pound of magnesium produced, which is approximately 2 per cent of the estimated cost.

"The royalty for the ores will not exceed ¼ cent per pound of magnesium metal produced.

"No irregularities have been discovered in the construction of the plant that would warrant the irresponsible statements made by Senator Bunker. The plant is wholly owned by the government and will be operated for its account. All expenditures in connection with the construction of the plant as well as its operation are carefully audited as the work progresses.

"Defense Plant Corporation contracted with Basic Magnesium, Inc., for the construction of this plant at the request of OPM and the War Department, and the government's interest is fully protected.

"Senator Bunker's speech contains many false and misleading statements, which it takes no courage to make under his cloak of immunity."

"Sinister," Bunker Contends

In his speech in the Senate the Nevada Senator said:

"Those individuals who have participated in unconscionable profits in America and who have slowed down our war production are worthy of the disgust and contempt of every American."

He contended that the data he presented were sufficient "to warrant the conclusion that the Defense Plant Corporation has entered into an agreement that is so sinister as to indicate that some officials in our government are guilty of malfeasance in the performance of their duties."

"If the agreement between the Defense Plant Corporation and Basic Magnesium, Inc., represents a cross-section of conduct on the part of the Defense Plant Corpora-

Continued on Page Eighteen

Cripps Said to Have Accord On National Regime in India

Plan Is Reported to Envisage Rule by a Council With Briton Directing Army and Native in Defense Ministry

By The United Press.

NEW DELHI, India, April 9—Great Britain and India are in general agreement on a self-government plan that will establish the first all-Indian national government in two centuries and provide for an executive council of fifteen members, all but one of them to come from the various political parties, it was learned tonight.

The plan was reported to be acceptable, with the exception of a few minor adjustments, to the two major political groups—the All-India Congress party and the Moslem League.

Under the plan a native government Minister will handle all Indian defense matters except war strategy and tactics, which a British military chief will control.

With only final details to be smoothed out, formal announcement of the settlement was predicted for late tomorrow or Saturday.

Inquiries late tonight revealed that under the agreement reached between the Congress party and Sir Stafford Cripps, British negotiator, the new national government would be directed not by a Cabinet but by the Executive Council of the Viceroy of India, the Marquess of Linlithgow.

The importance of that point in the agreement, it was said, was the fact that a Prime Minister would not be appointed and asked to form a Cabinet—the usual constitutional procedure—but that the Viceroy would appoint members to the council, after receiving the names of nominees by the various Indian parties.

Under the new government, the country will be mobilized to resist the Japanese, who are pressing closer.

It was learned that an executive

Continued on Page Six

2 Police Officials Suspended On Amen's Charges of Graft

In an unexpected move that may present a test case of far-reaching effect in the Police Department, Special Prosecutor John Harlan Amen's two extraordinary grand juries returned supplemental presentments yesterday against two high-ranking police officers who had sought retirement while under investigation in connection with alleged police protection of a $100,000,000 city-wide gambling racket.

The two, Inspector Camille C. Pierne of the Tenth Division in Brooklyn and Lieutenant Terence J. Harvey of the Brooklyn Borough headquarters squad, were named in Wednesday's presentments that bared the existence of police graft estimated at more than $1,000,000 a year, but no specific charges were lodged against them on the theory that a mere application for retirement was sufficient to preclude the prosecution of departmental charges against them.

However, Police Commissioner Valentine, after conferring behind closed doors with his aides and later in the afternoon with Mayor La Guardia, issued a statement Wednesday night asserting that he had notified Mr. Amen that inasmuch as the retirement applications of several police officers had not been acted upon by the Police Pension Fund he regarded them as members of the uniformed force and would like to be advised if the grand jury had made any charges against them so that he could be "guided accordingly."

Mr. Amen's reply yesterday was to send a letter to Commissioner Valentine asserting that it was because of his understanding of Mr. Valentine's earlier advice that he had not filed charges against men

Continued on Page Thirty-eight

GASOLINE SUPPLIES CUT AGAIN BY WPB

Deliveries to East and 2 States in Northwest Will Be Reduced From 80 to 66⅔ Per Cent

Special to THE NEW YORK TIMES.

WASHINGTON, April 9—The War Production Board issued today an order further curtailing gasoline deliveries to filling stations and bulk consumers in seventeen Eastern States, the District of Columbia and Oregon and Washington.

Effective April 16, deliveries of gasoline to filling stations and bulk consumers in curtailment areas will be cut to 66 2-3 per cent of average deliveries in December, January and February, adjusted for seasonal variations. Deliveries have been reduced 20 per cent since March 19.

Secretary Ickes, Petroleum Coordinator, discussing the WPB order, said at his press conference:

"If this curtailment proves satisfactory, we may go to Leon Henderson and tell him we see no need for rationing."

Mr. Ickes added that the matter

Continued on Page Twenty-six

Jesse Jones Shakes Eugene Meyer; Eye-Glasses Broken in Encounter

Special to THE NEW YORK TIMES.

WASHINGTON, April 9—Jesse Jones, Secretary of Commerce, and Eugene Meyer, editor and publisher of The Washington Post, were participants in a fistic encounter at the annual dinner of the Alfalfa Club at the Hotel Willard tonight.

A sharp verbal exchange arising from resentment by the Secretary of an editorial in which his testimony before the Senate's Truman committee investigating the rubber situation was criticized preceded the encounter, club members said.

As told by eyewitnesses, Secretary Jones was approached by Mr. Meyer, a long-time critic of the banker, as Mr. Jones entered the small ballroom of the hotel. Accounts of witnesses vary as to the words which immediately preceded the encounter, but most members agreed that Secretary Jones grasped Mr. Meyer by the coat and started to shake him. As Mr. Meyer wrenched himself free his eyeglasses fell to the floor and were smashed.

Mr. Meyer, the accounts continue, swung at the Secretary but friends, including John J. O'Connor, former New York Representative, pushed them apart. Secretary Jones left immediately after the fight, while Mr. Meyer stayed for a time chatting with friends.

The men have been frequent adversaries since the Hoover Administration, when both served with the Reconstruction Finance Corporation, of which Mr. Meyer was then chairman. Mr. Jones is also a publisher, owning The Houston Chronicle.

Today's editorial asserted that Mr. Jones had shielded himself behind the President, the British and the Netherlanders in defending his handling of the rubber situation.

PLANES GET SHIPS

Japanese Sink Big Naval Units in Bay of Bengal, Blast Base in Ceylon

BRITISH RAID CARRIER

Score Near-Misses, Get 4 Aircraft—2 Fleets Massing for Battle

By RAYMOND DANIELL
Wireless to THE NEW YORK TIMES.

LONDON, April 9—The Japanese have struck a heavy blow against the British Navy in the struggle for mastery of the Bay of Bengal, which is the key to the Indian Ocean, in sinking by air attack the heavy cruisers Dorsetshire and Cornwall. In return, near-misses were scored by bombers in an attack on a Japanese aircraft carrier in the Bay of Bengal.

Full enemy control of the Bay of Bengal, the eastern half of which the Japanese command already, would lay the eastern coast of India open to invasion. Renewed aerial attacks today on Trincomalee, the main British naval base on the island of Ceylon, off the south coast of India, made it more apparent than ever that the Japanese were seeking to extend their domination westward.

1,100 Are Rescued

News of the sinking of the 10,000-ton Cornwall and 9,975-ton Dorsetshire was given in an Admiralty communiqué, which placed the encounter with the Japanese planes in the Indian Ocean. The announcement said 1,100 survivors,—including the commanders, Captain A. W. S. Agar of the Dorsetshire and Captain P. O. W. Mainwaring of the Cornwall—had been picked up. The Dorsetshire was the ship whose torpedoes administered the coup de grace to the German battleship Bismarck in the Atlantic last year.

The attack on the Japanese aircraft carrier was announced in a communiqué received tonight from Colombo, Ceylon. In the action, which followed today's attack on Trincomalee, four Japanese planes were shot down. Some of the attacking planes did not return, but their number was not disclosed. While Trincomalee was being raided a couple of Japanese planes appeared over Colombo, but dropped no bombs.

[The Colombo communiqué also revealed that in the attack on Trincomalee the Japanese damaged harbor and airdrome facilities and caused a few casualties among dockyard personnel, The Associated Press reported. Six of the Japanese planes were shot down, six others were probably destroyed and two were listed as damaged. The Japanese, who attacked with "a large force of bombers and fighters," caused no damage in the town of Trincomalee.]

Allied Cargo Ships Sunk

The loss of the Cornwall and the Dorsetshire, coupled with an official statement from New Delhi, India, that several merchantmen have been sunk in recent enemy air and naval attacks in the Bay of Bengal, represents a serious blow not only at British naval strength in that area but against United Nations lines of communication.

The number of merchant vessels lost was not announced, but the total of survivors from them—between 400 and 500, who have landed on the coast of Orissa in India—indicates a considerable number. Tokyo said today that the number of ships sunk was twenty-one, with twenty-three others so severely damaged that they must be regarded as lost.

The Japanese naval force in the Bay of Bengal area is operating hundreds of miles from its presumed base in the Andaman Islands. The distance from the Andamans to Ceylon is more than 1,000 miles. Before the occupation of

Continued on Page Six

IN THE FOX HOLES OF BATAAN

U. S. Troops in action on the Philippine peninsula, the fall of which was announced yesterday
Associated Press Wirephoto (U. S. Army Signal Corps)

ITALIAN CRUISER SUNK BY BRITISH

10,000-Ton Vessel Destroyed by Submarine—Foes Spar in Libyan Fighting

By ROBERT P. POST
Wireless to THE NEW YORK TIMES.

LONDON, April 9—A 10,000-ton eight-inch-gun Italian cruiser has been sunk in the Central Mediterranean by torpedoes from a British submarine, the Admiralty announced today.

The cruiser, which may have been convoying reinforcements for Marshal Erwin Rommel in Libya, was accompanied by destroyers and aircraft when Lieut. Comdr. E. P. Tomkinson, who received the Distinguished Service Order with bar in December for his work on submarine patrol, ordered the attack. Eight minutes after his torpedoes struck home, the commander risked attack by the cruiser's escort to show his periscope. The cruiser was heard to break up and sink while the destroyers picked up survivors.

Lieut. Commander Tomkinson's earlier exploits were carried out with the Urge, one of the smallest British submarines. Last April he sank a heavily laden oil tanker of more than 10,000 tons. For this he

Continued on Page Eight

Sacred Saffron of Priests Aids Foe's Burma Advance

By HARRISON FORMAN
Wireless to THE NEW YORK TIMES.

CHUNGKING, China, April 9—Clad in the sacred saffron robes of the Poongee—literally meaning "great glory"—the fifth column in Burma is taking advantage of the historic sanctuary provided by Burmese Buddhism. In the past the Poongees have included, besides the genuinely devout, many thieves, bandits and general malcontents, and they have always been a major problem for British administration.

Unlike most other priesthoods, the Poongees require no special training or lifelong vows. Any man may in practice become a Poongee for any period desired, days or years, by the simple procedure of shaving his head, donning a saffron robe, formally renouncing all things worldly before a temple and thereafter living solely by begging, which is not permitted for more than daily needs.

In practical example, a business man may welch on a contract or a debt by simply becoming a Poongee, and he thereby is cleansed of all worldly obligations and responsibilities. The Poongees are arrogant and sacrosanct in so far as the police are concerned. The Poongees are publicly regarded as holy men who can do no wrong, and the British military confess they are practically helpless in the face of such fanaticism.

An eyewitness on the Burma front reports that at a certain supposedly secret airport there ap-

Continued on Page Five

AMERICANS BAG TEN IN BURMA AIR FIGHT

A. V. G. Routs Twenty of Foe Without One Loss—Lull in Land Fighting Continues

By The United Press.

CHUNGKING, China, April 9—Reinforced American Volunteer Group fliers have roared back into the Battle of Burma, destroying ten planes and damaging two others in a mass dogfight with twenty Japanese Zero fighters in which one American plane was lost but its pilot saved, an A. V. G. communiqué announced tonight.

The battle was fought over the Burmese town of Loi-Win, the communiqué said. [An Associated Press dispatch from Chungking, based on the same official source, said the encounter took place Wednesday over Leiyun in the south of China's Yunnan Province. Neither Loi-Win nor Leiyun appears on available maps.]

Week of Inaction Ended

This was the first challenge to Japanese air superiority over Burma battlegrounds since the invaders launched their all-out offensive against cities and airports in that theatre early last week. The strength of the A. V. G. force—American-made and American-flown planes fighting under the Chinese banner—was not disclosed.

Official Chinese dispatches disclosed that German officers were mapping the Japanese drive against Chinese lines north of Toungoo in Central Burma. One German officer was reported captured by the defenders and reconnaissance revealed that the Japanese were massing troops in Thailand to the east for a possible envelopment move against the Chinese on the Nazi model.

Chinese spokesmen said the Japanese concentrations in the Chiengmai area across the Thailand border not only menaced the Chinese positions around Toungoo but enabled the invaders to threaten a diversion drive into China's Kwangsi and Yunnan Provinces.

The Toungoo front—one-third of the way to bombed-out Mandalay from captured Rangoon—has been fairly static for a week. A belated Chinese communiqué reported the Japanese attacked south of Yedashe, eighteen miles north of Toungoo, on Monday and that fighting continued after dark that night. Subsequent communiqués

Continued on Page Five

War News Summarized

FRIDAY, APRIL 10, 1942

Rocky Bataan Peninsula, the finger of land that still defied the Japanese after they had conquered most of the Southwest Pacific, finally succumbed yesterday. Its 36,853 remaining American and Filipino defenders—drained by hunger, exhaustion and disease—could no longer rally to beat off an enveloping movement that broke their lines on the east flank. For three months they had fought against ever-growing odds. Although Corregidor Island and the other forts in Manila Bay stayed in American hands, it was questionable how long they could hold out. [1-8; map, P. 2.]

The United Nations suffered a probably greater strategic setback in the Bay of Bengal. Japanese planes sank two British 10,000-ton cruisers, the Dorsetshire and the Cornwall, and a great naval battle loomed with the coast of India at stake. Allied bombers attacked a Japanese naval squadron and scored near-misses on an aircraft carrier. In this Allied attack and in a raid on the Ceylon naval base of Trincomalee, the Japanese lost at least ten planes. [1:4; map, P. 6.]

Allied aerial successes were reported from Burma and Australia. Reinforced American volunteer pilots in the Burma theatre shot down ten enemy fighters and damaged two others without a loss of their own. [1:7.] United Nations bombers blasted planes and military targets in a surprise raid on Rabaul, New Britain. [3:1.]

With the threat to India growing daily, the drawn-out negotiations in New Delhi appeared nearing a successful compromise—the establishment of an Indian national government in which the defense minister would share responsibility with General Wavell. [1:2-3.]

The naval defeat in the Indian Ocean was offset somewhat by the sinking of a 10,000-ton Italian cruiser by a British submarine in the Mediterranean. In Libya, the British were jockeying for position against strong Axis forces, whose movements no longer seemed to indicate a large-scale offensive. [1:5.]

Germany flung large units of tanks and planes into the Russian front to feel out the Red Army's strength in virtually every sector, Moscow reports said, but the reinforced Soviet forces broke up their attacks and clung to the initiative. [11:1, with map.]

In occupied Europe, the embittered Norwegian people observed the second anniversary of the German invasion with a "strike" of silence as Quislingists and German troops marched in the streets. [9:1.]

DEFENSE CRUSHED

Stimson Reveals Defeat Followed Failure to Get in More Food

CORREGIDOR IS HELD

Wainwright on the Isle Free to Set Course, Roosevelt Tells Him

What Tokyo Reports

By The Associated Press.

TOKYO, Friday, April 10 (From Japanese broadcasts recorded in New York)—The Domei news agency said today that "60,000 Filipino and American troops resisting the Japanese on Bataan Peninsula have begged for a halt in hostilities after six days of fierce Japanese assault."

"Details of the conditions of surrender are not yet disclosed," said the Domei dispatch, "nor is it known yet whether the Japanese forces have decided to accept the terms."

Corregidor was raided twice yesterday by Japanese bombers and tons of explosives were unleashed on military installations, Domei reported.

By CHARLES HURD
Special to THE NEW YORK TIMES.

WASHINGTON, April 9—An overwhelming Japanese Army, aided by the allies of hunger, fatigue and disease, today crushed the small mixed force that had held Bataan Peninsula since December.

Japanese forces, heretofore estimated at 200,000 men, including fresh assault troops, and supported by tanks, artillery, bombers and attack planes in profusion, enveloped an exhausted defending army of 36,853 men, as counted officially yesterday afternoon.

The defeat of the American and Filipino forces was officially announced as a "probability" in a War Department communiqué issued as of 5:15 A. M. today. A few hours later Secretary of War Henry L. Stimson announced the defeat at his regularly scheduled weekly press conference. He already had carried the word to President Roosevelt.

Reveals Supplies Were Sent In

When Secretary Stimson met reporters in his conference room he paid the highest praise to the spirit of the defenders in a fight recognized as hopeless from the beginning had pledged that the Philippines would be reconquered. In the same talk he described extraordinary efforts made to provision the garrison, saying that "several shiploads of supplies" were sent into the Philippines, "but for every ship that arrived safely we lost nearly two."

As far as was known here today the rocky fortress of Corregidor Island still held its own astride the entrance to Manila Bay and other troops held adjacent fortified islands. The decision as to whether they should continue fighting was laid squarely on Lieut. Gen. Jonathan M. Wainwright, to whom President Roosevelt dispatched yesterday a message giving him absolute authority to continue the fight or make terms, as he might see fit.

Army Records Position

This responsibility is a heavy one for General Wainwright, for it is assumed here that he lacks transport to take more than a handful of the Bataan forces across the four miles of water that separates Bataan Peninsula from Corregidor. Even so his food is desperately short, Secretary Stimson having said this morning that every man in Bataan had been on short rations since Jan. 11. This was a primary reason for the collapse of the defense after five days of savage hand-to-hand fighting.

The long-expected defeat, which by its deferment wrote an epic in American military history, was officially indicated in War Depart-

Continued on Page Two

"All the News That's Fit to Print."

The New York Times.

LATE CITY EDITION
Mild today.
Temperatures Yesterday—Max., 74; Min., 53

Copyright, 1942, by The New York Times Company.

VOL. XCI..No. 30,783. Entered as Second-Class Matter, Postoffice, New York, N. Y. NEW YORK, WEDNESDAY, MAY 6, 1942. THREE CENTS NEW YORK CITY and Vicinity

CORREGIDOR SURRENDERS UNDER LAND ATTACK AFTER WITHSTANDING 300 RAIDS FROM THE AIR; BRITISH HIT MADAGASCAR BASE; VICHY RESISTS

CHARGE ACCOUNTS ARE DUE IN 40 DAYS AS INFLATION CURB

Reserve Board's Regulation, in Effect Today, Is First Check on Such Retail Customers

Bringing retail charge accounts under control for the first time and ruling that installment purchases must be liquidated in twelve months the Federal Reserve Board promulgated yesterday amendment No. 4 to its consumer credit regulation W, carrying into effect the seventh point in President Roosevelt's anti-inflation program.

Under the amendment, which is effective today, charge account customers of retail stores will be required to speed up their payments to complete them within forty days after the end of the month in which purchase is made. If this is not done the account will be transferred to an installment basis requiring liquidation within six months and no further charge account purchases will be permissible until the items in default are paid for.

The amendment also tightened substantially the earlier restrictions on installment sales and broadened the scope of the merchandise covered to forty-six listed classifications, including almost every item used in the American home, and clothing and jewelry as well. The down payment was generally raised to 33 1/3 per cent and the payment period to twelve months.

Explains Aim of Rules

Allan Sproul, president of the Federal Reserve Bank of New York, in announcing the amendment here, said:

"As amended, the regulation is extended to cover a comprehensive list of durable and semi-durable goods for civilian consumption and contemplates that the volume of outstanding consumer credit, already substantially diminished, will be further contracted in keeping with the government's purpose to prevent the rapid bidding up of prices.

"The purpose of this revision is to help make effective the last point in the seven-point program which the President set forth in his special message to Congress of April 27, 1942, as follows: 'To keep the cost of living from spiraling upward, we must discourage credit and installment buying, and encourage the paying off of debts, mortgages and other obligations; for this promotes savings, retards excessive buying and adds to the amount available to the creditors for the purchase of war bonds.'"

With respect to charge accounts, the regulation, in effect and depending upon the date of the purchase, provides for a forty to a seventy day payment period, similar to that in effect in Canada. The average period for payment of

Continued on Page Fourteen

Nazis' War Industry Spurs Plane Output

By Telephone to THE NEW YORK TIMES.

BERNE, Switzerland, May 5—German war industry has been ordered to devote all its attention henceforth to turning out airplanes, even to the detriment of tanks and other matériel. This news from Berlin tonight confirms indications reaching foreign circles here that mastery of the air is the paramount consideration for the moment.

Figures declared to be trustworthy indicate that the peak of plane production in the Reich was reached in June, 1941, when 3,300 were turned out. Now it has fallen to between 2,700 and 2,800. Italy's contribution does not exceed 700 machines a month.

It is understood the Germans' estimate of their opponents' production is: United States, 3,300 planes a month; Britain, 2,400; Russia, 2,600 to 2,900. But the Nazis can draw upon considerable reserves.

WPB CUTS GASOLINE 50 PER CENT IN EAST

Non-Essential Users May Be Down to 5 Gallons a Week After May 16 Order

By The Associated Press.

WASHINGTON, May 5—Gasoline consumption in the East will be slashed 50 per cent below normal starting May 16, the War Production Board said tonight. This means that many of the area's 10,000,000 motorists probably will have to get along with as little as five or six gallons a week.

The reduction will become effective the day the seaboard area begins using ration cards.

[In New York motorists will register for gasoline rationing next Tuesday, Wednesday and Thursday. Rationing will begin on May 15.]

While the overall curtailment will be one-half, informed sources explained that it would amount to about a 60 per cent cut for non-essential users of automobiles, since necessary vehicles will continue to receive their full requirements of fuel.

Action Recommended by Ickes

The WPB action, taken on recommendation of Harold L. Ickes, petroleum coordinator, came shortly after Joseph B. Eastman, defense transportation director, declared "every owner of a motor vehicle in public or private service should realize that he holds this vehicle in trust for the national war effort and that it should be used only for purposes of necessity."

This statement of Mr. Eastman's applied to the whole country, not merely to the East.

Simultaneously with the gasoline order, WPB directed that de-

Continued on Page Thirteen

BRONX GRAND JURY CLEARS EVERYONE IN THE FLYNN CASE

County Is 'Singularly Free of Fraud and Corruption,' Presentment Says

The Bronx County grand jury that has been hearing evidence on the paving with city materials and labor of a courtyard on the Lake Mahopac estate of Edward J. Flynn, chairman of the Democratic National Committee, as well as other irregularities in the Bronx, handed up a seventeen-page presentment yesterday, finding that Bronx County is "singularly free of fraud and corruption," but that many irregularities are prevalent.

The grand jury declared that after hearing all the evidence submitted, it did not find that the facts warranted the indictment of any one.

Work on Flynn Estate Reviewed

In discussing the work done on the Flynn estate on Nov. 14, 15, 17 and 18 of last year, the presentment said city employes had been transported to the estate from the city by city-owned station wagons and that the work had consisted of laying 8,000 second-hand granite blocks.

The city employes, the presentment said, were paid in full for their services; 8,000 blocks were returned to the city and the gasoline and oil issued to the city station wagons for the Mahopac trip were returned in full. The cost of trucking the blocks by private concerns was paid by Mr. Flynn. The courtyard was only part of a general alteration on the estate, with the total job to cost more than $30,000.

The evidence adduced, it continued, showed that Mr. Flynn had never expressed any desire that the work be done under city auspices or by city employes and without expense to him, but that the job would be done by a private contractor and paid for by Mr. Flynn. The work done by city employes was under the supervision of Robert L. Moran, Bronx Commissioner of Public Works.

Paul J. Kern, deposed president of the Civil Service Commission, who conducted an investigation in the paving job while still in office, was severely rebuked by the grand jury for hampering the investigation conducted by William B. Herlands, Commissioner of Investigation.

No Conspiracy Found

"In respect to the second phase of the investigation," the presentment said, "the alleged conspiracy between Mayor La Guardia, Mr. Flynn and Commissioner Herlands to suppress the Kern investigation, the charge was entirely without foundation and we feel that it never would have been made but for the fact that Mr. Kern is greatly influenced by what he terms 'his intuition.'"

Mr. Kern had charged that Mayor La Guardia was trying to suppress his investigation in Mr. Flynn's behalf, and that in return Mr. Flynn was to obtain for the Mayor the Democratic nomination for United States Senator.

The grand jurors found that the records of the Department of Highways and Sewers under Commissioner Moran were in a "deplorable condition." They said they believed Borough President James J. Lyons when he testified that he was ignorant of the Mahopac paving job, and "we strongly condemn this ignorance." Commissioner Moran, they said, was Mr. Lyons's appointee and the Borough President could not avoid responsibility for the manner in which any subordinate conducted a department.

The Grand Jury's Presentment

In its presentment the grand jury said:

"The subject matter of our investigation resolved itself, naturally, into three phases; 1, the Maho-

Continued on Page Twenty-eight

Direct Hit on Tirpitz By British Reported

By Telephone to THE NEW YORK TIMES.

STOCKHOLM, Sweden, May 5—British Royal Air Force bombs scored a direct hit on the battleship Tirpitz when she was in Kiel harbor prior to her transfer to her present anchorage at Trondheim, Norway, according to an eyewitness account by a Swedish seaman published in Ny Dag. The observer also reported a great change of morale among German civilians.

"Although the British attacks on Kiel were usually made from a great height, sometimes from 20,000 feet," he is quoted as saying, "the bombs hit their targets with astonishing precision. Thus in every bombing the biggest wharf in Kiel was regularly set ablaze, and on one occasion a British bomber scored a direct hit on the Tirpitz."

FOE ENTERS CHINA ACROSS BURMA LINE

Advance Units Over Border While Main Columns Wait—Planes Aid British Retreat

By DAVID ANDERSON
Wireless to THE NEW YORK TIMES.

LONDON, May 5—The Japanese have entered Yunnan Province in China via the Burma Road, it was announced today. Their vanguards reached the suburbs of Wangting, which is on a small river dividing Burma and China, and Chungking said the Japanese were being engaged by Chinese troops in the hills. The main enemy column was waiting within Burma at Chukok, near by.

The invading force must have made a detour around the Chinese fighting at Kutkai because the battle there was reported still going on. Other Chinese units were believed holding out north of Mandalay on the banks of the Irrawaddy River. British soldiers were continuing their slow retreat west of Mandalay.

"At times their [the Japanese]

Continued on Page Four

BRITISH ADVANCING

Landing Force Reported Within Four Miles of Madagascar Base

'CHUTISTS ARE USED

Warships and Aircraft Make Frontal Assault to Help Troops

By RAYMOND DANIELL
Wireless to THE NEW YORK TIMES.

LONDON, May 5—Small units of British Commandos and regular troops won a bridgehead at Courier Bay in the action against Madagascar and were reported tonight to be fighting their way across a ten-mile-wide isthmus toward the important naval base of Diego Suarez.

[A London dispatch of The Associated Press quoted Vichy reports that waves of British parachutists had been landed at the outset of a double attack in which warships and squadrons of aircraft made a frontal thrust from the sea timed to coincide with the overland assault on the rear of the base by British light armored units landed at Courier Bay.

[The Associated Press said that, according to advices released by Vichy sources, the British occupying forces had reached Andrakaka, four miles from Diego Suarez. The French estimated that the attacking forces numbered 20,000 and the French and native defenders about 7,000.]

There were only sketchy accounts of the battle for the big French island, which lies athwart vital United Nations supply routes. However, a joint Admiralty-War Office communiqué issued this afternoon clearly indicated that opposition had been offered by the Vichy French garrison. The capture of a defending battery was reported.

A communiqué issued late to-

Continued on Page Two

JAPANESE FINALLY TAKE CORREGIDOR

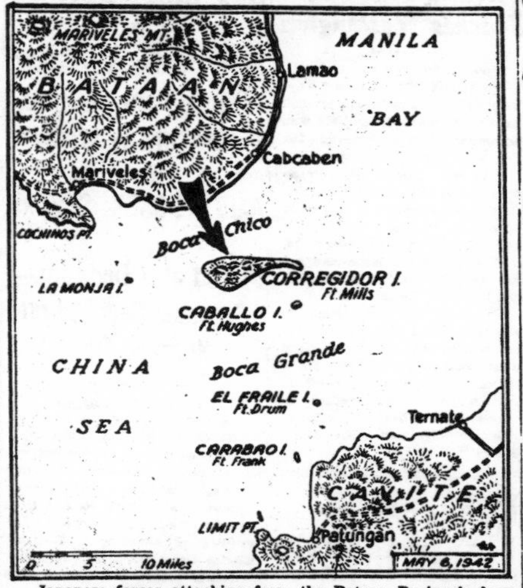

Japanese forces attacking from the Bataan Peninsula have forced the surrender of Corregidor and other United States island fortresses at the entrance to Manila Bay.

Laval Protests 'Aggression' But Won't Seek U. S. Break

By LANSING WARREN
By Telephone to THE NEW YORK TIMES.

VICHY, France, May 5—Replying to the American note expressing approbation of the British occupation of Madagascar, Pierre Laval as Chief of the French Government and Foreign Minister, tonight protested the move as an aggression. He rejected as inadmissible the "pretension of the Government of the United States to forbid France to defend her territory when attacked," and declared that he leaves "to President Roosevelt the share of responsibility that may fall to him in consequence of this aggression."

[In Washington, Secretary Hull made it clear that there would be no deviation from the approval of the British action at Madagascar. After a White House session, Pacific War Council members praised the move.]

M. Laval, in handing his note to the American Chargé d'Affaires, S. Pinckney Tuck, recalled the long record of friendship between France and the United States and added:

"You were present at my recent interview with your Ambassador, Admiral Leahy, and I wish again to repeat to you what I said to him, that no definitive gesture leading to a break will be initiated by France."

Indicates Grave Situation

M. Laval read his reply to the assembled French and foreign press in a salon of the Hotel du Parc, and completed it with comments that indicated the full seriousness for French-American relations because the United States for the first time was directly involved in diplomatic controversy with France.

Following is the text of the note as read to the correspondents by M. Laval:

In replying to the note handed in today by the Chargé d'Affaires of the United States of America, the French Government raises the most energetic protest against the aggression of which Madagascar has just been the object on the part of British forces.

It notes the assurance given that Madagascar will be returned to France some day.

It rejects as inadmissible the pretension of the Government of the United States to forbid France to defend her territory when attacked.

The French Government is the sole judge of the obligations imposed by its honor. In that manner, the defenders of Madagascar have understood correctly their duties. They have not hesitated, despite their numerical inferiority, to carry out their duties according to the most noble tradition of the French Army.

England so often since the Armistice has manifested hostility to France and the aggression

Continued on Page Two

RED ARMY ATTACKS KEY GERMAN BASES

Timoshenko Smashes at Kursk, Kharkov and Taganrog to Forestall Nazi Drive

By The Associated Press.

MOSCOW, May 5—Stealing the jump on Reichsfuehrer Hitler, hundreds of thousands of Russian soldiers, tanks and planes smashed head-on today at three key German bases from which it was believed the Nazi leader was planning his Spring or Summer drive.

Under command of Marshal Semyon Timoshenko, the first Russian general to turn back the German military machine with the recapture of Rostov last November, the Red Army struck at Kharkov, Kursk and Taganrog in the strongest Nazi-held section of the long battle line.

Action was also stepped-up in the northern sectors, particularly the hard-fought Kalinin area northwest of Moscow. The army newspaper Red Star said the Germans were

Continued on Page Ten

OTHER FORTS FALL

American Soldiers Had Held Out in Spite of Supply Shortage

COURAGE IS PRAISED

Roosevelt Views Their Example as Guarantee of Final Victory

By The Associated Press.

AT UNITED NATIONS HEADQUARTERS, Australia, Wednesday, May 6—The American fortress of Corregidor and the other fortified islands in the entrance to Manila Bay surrendered today, it was officially announced here.

Besides the rock that is Corregidor, the United States forts that had held out were Fort Hughes, Fort Drum and Fort Frank.

The end came in the second day of the final Japanese assault, launched at midnight Tuesday, Manila time, with landings from Bataan Peninsula after Corregidor had been pounded again and again by Japanese big guns and aerial bombs. Corregidor alone had had 300 air raids since Dec. 29, when thirty-five Japanese bombers attacked for three hours.

A spokesman for General Douglas MacArthur, who led the brilliant defense of Bataan and the forts at the mouth of Manila Bay until ordered to Australia, made this announcement:

"General Wainwright has surrendered Corregidor and the other fortified islands in Manila Harbor."

There were believed to be about 7,000 men and women altogether on Corregidor and the other fortified islands. Besides the original garrisons, there was a naval detachment consisting originally of some 3,500 Marines and bluejackets who were removed to Corregidor when fighting ceased April 9 on Bataan Peninsula. A group of Army nurses also reached Corregidor.

Troops Half-Starved

By CHARLES HURD
Special to THE NEW YORK TIMES.

WASHINGTON, May 5—The fortified island of Corregidor in Manila Bay, last bastion of the American defenders of the Philippine Island, Luzon, was fighting a landing attack by Japanese troops today.

The issue of the fighting was not known in Washington at 8 P. M., when the War Department issued a communiqué, but two factors indicated grave concern over the outcome of a contest in which the defenders are outnumbered,

Continued on Page Five

War News Summarized

WEDNESDAY, MAY 6, 1942

Corregidor, the island fortress at the entrance to Manila Bay, was surrendered to the Japanese after a furious assault. The British were engaged in breaking French resistance to their landing in Madagascar. Japanese forces reached and crossed the Burma-China frontier. Other war fronts were largely unchanged.

The surrender of Corregidor and other island bases was announced by United Nations Headquarters in Australia, following an earlier Washington communiqué stating that the Japanese had started landing operations. The defenders were reported to be short of both food and ammunition. [1:8.]

British landing forces on Madagascar were reported to be within four miles of the Diego Suarez naval base at the northern extremity of the island. The French garrison was resisting, but Vichy reported that some 20,000 British had landed or were preparing to land. London said the Commandos had encountered little resistance. [1:5; map, P. 2.]

The Vichy regime ordered the garrison at Madagascar to resist. Pierre Laval in a note to the United States Government rejected Washington's warning against French belligerent action, but he insisted his government would not be the first to take measures to break relations with the United States. Admiral Darlan, chief of the Vichy military forces, expressed extreme bitterness toward Britain. [1:6-7.]

Secretary of State Hull indicated clearly at his press conference that the United States would adhere to a policy of full support of British occupation of Madagascar. [3:1.]

Meanwhile, Japanese forces in Burma had reached the Chinese frontier in the Burma Road sector and had penetrated a slight distance into China. A battle was raging on the frontier, and the Japanese had been halted, according to Chungking. United States bombers from India attacked successfully Mingaladon airport north of Rangoon. The Japanese said their planes had set on fire the Chinese city of Yungchang, 120 miles inside China in Yunnan Province. [1:4, map, P. 4.]

Chungking said that Chinese guerrillas in Eastern China had raided fifteen Japanese-occupied cities during the past two weeks and destroyed power plants and communications. [6:3, with map.]

The United Nations Australian Headquarters announced successful air attacks on Lae, New Guinea, and Rabaul, New Britain. A Japanese air attack on Port Moresby was repulsed. [4:4.]

On the other side of the world, London announced Royal Air Force attacks on the Skoda munitions plant in Czechoslovakia and factories at Stuttgart in Southwestern Germany. The Germans raided points on the British south coast. [10:2.]

The story was heard in London that a group of German generals had informed Adolf Hitler that if the campaign in Russia this year should fail, they would seek to abolish the National Socialist system. [8:4-5.]

Moscow reported an offensive in the south against German-held Kharkov, Kursk and Taganrog. [1:7.]

Washington disclosed the sinking of three more merchant vessels off the United States east coast. [5:1.]

Mrs. Rosenberg in 2 Federal Jobs While Making $22,500 on the Side

By LOUIS STARK
Special to THE NEW YORK TIMES.

WASHINGTON, May 5 — Some members of the House Appropriations Committee asserted today that they were determined to write into all future supply bills a provision prohibiting Federal administrative officials from accepting employment outside the government. This came following the disclosure at a closed meeting of an appropriations subcommittee today that Mrs. Anna M. Rosenberg of New York, regional director of the Social Security Board, receives a large income from private industry and also draws pay from another agency.

Mrs. Rosenberg's Social Security Board post pays $7,500 on a full time basis. Besides this Federal position she revealed to the subcommittee today that she received $20,000 a year for part time work as public and labor relations consultant to the Macy-Bamberger stores in New York and Newark, and $2,500 a year for similar services performed for I. Miller, New York shoe dealer.

In addition, Mrs. Rosenberg is a consultant on the staff of Nelson Rockefeller, coordinator of American Affairs. For this service she receives $6,000 a year. Her total earnings therefore are $36,000 a year, $13,500 paid by two government agencies and $22,500 by industry.

Arthur J. Altmeyer, chairman of the Social Security Board, who accompanied Mrs. Rosenberg to the committee meeting today, revealed that when the regional directorship was offered to her six years ago Mrs. Rosenberg made it a condition that she be permitted to continue her work as labor consultant for private concerns. Correspond-

Continued on Page Twenty-eight

G. M. Defies WLB on Double Pay; Hearing Will Take Up Issue Today

Special to THE NEW YORK TIMES.

DETROIT, Mich., May 5—On the eve of the start of negotiations before a panel of the National War Labor Board between the General Motors Corporation and the United Automobile Workers, C. I. O., C. E. Wilson, president of the corporation, revealed today that it had defied the board on the issue of double-time pay for Sunday and holiday work.

The disclosure came in the release by Mr. Wilson of the texts of exchanges of correspondence among the corporation, the board and the union. The correspondence dated from April 27. It included a copy of the order by the board to Mr. Wilson May 1 that double-time pay for Sunday work be continued by the company to May 18.

In reply to the order, the release by Mr. Wilson showed, H. W. Anderson, vice president of General Motors, sent the board on May 2 a telegram which said that "we protest and do not agree to comply with your directive order."

The hearings before the NWLB panel are scheduled to open in Washington tomorrow morning. They aim at a renewal of the union contract which expired April 28. The contract has been continued in effect except for a stipulation by General Motors April 27 that "pending a final adjustment," double time "will not be paid for Sunday and holiday work." It has been agreed that when a new agreement is reached all its terms will be retroactive to April 28.

Walter P. Reuther, director of the General Motors division of the union, has made known that the union wished to have the Washington hearing open to the public, including the press. Mr. Wilson, in a telegram to the board today,

Continued on Page Fourteen

"All the News That's Fit to Print."

The New York Times.

LATE CITY EDITION
Little change in temperature today.
Temperatures Yesterday—Max., 85; Min., 69

Copyright, 1942, by The New York Times Company.

VOL. XCI..No. 30,830. Entered as Second-Class Matter, Postoffice, New York, N. Y. NEW YORK, MONDAY, JUNE 22, 1942. THREE CENTS NEW YORK CITY and Vicinity

TOBRUK FALLS, AXIS CLAIMS 25,000 PRISONERS; GERMANS DRIVE WEDGE INTO SEVASTOPOL LINES; JAPANESE ASHORE ON KISKA IN THE ALEUTIANS

'GAS' DROUGHT CUTS HOLIDAY PLEASURE AS CITY SWELTERS

New Yorkers Stay at Home or Drive Only to Suburbs—Many Avoid Main Roads

CROWDS AT SOME RESORTS

Others Are Hard Hit as Travel Is Spotty—Humidity Soars and Mercury Reaches 84°

New Yorkers, afflicted with the first sweltering Sunday of the season under the gasoline shortage, stayed at home yesterday, sitting on the sidewalks or in penthouse or roof gardens, or went to near-by parks and beaches. Pleasure driving was only half of normal, by and large, and the resorts, particularly the distant ones, bore the brunt of the decline. Relatives and friends in the suburbs apparently had many visitors.

The heat was not record-breaking. Temperatures rose from a low of 69 degrees at 8:45 A. M. to a high of 84 degrees at 5:30 P. M. The humidity, however, remained at 75 per cent, which the Weather Bureau said was extremely high for such high temperatures. In the morning two-tenths of an inch of rain fell and skies were overcast long after, accounting for many of the stay-at-homes in the city.

Brooklyn's first heat prostration of the season was reported last night when John Chambers, 45 years old, of 244 West End Avenue, Coney Island, collapsed as he was walking in Flatbush Avenue near East Twenty-sixth Street, Brooklyn. He was removed to Coney Island Hospital, where his condition was described as fair.

Motoring Is Spotty

The drop in pleasure driving, although marked as far as resorts were concerned, and severe if parkway use was an accurate indication, did not fully reflect the gasoline supply situation. With many stations dry, traffic on the George Washington Bridge was reported normal for a Sunday, through the Holland Tunnel a third off, and over other bridge and tunnel exits the reduction was not significant.

Yet on the Westchester parkways motor traffic was 30 per cent of normal and on the Long Island parkways about 60 per cent of normal. Police traffic experts believed that this reflected the spotty character of the gasoline shortage, which was acute in Westchester and near-by Long Island and some sections of New Jersey, but not serious in others.

Those who had gasoline in their tanks apparently went pleasure driving in spite of the appeals to save gasoline, but avoided the parkways and resorts, where they would be conspicuous. Many, the traffic experts thought, must have gone to visit friends and relatives

Continued on Page Nine

If in Doubt, Put It Out

Carelessness remains the greatest enemy of the Army's dimout regulations, it was said yesterday by civilian lighting experts who have been working with the Army on ways of cutting down the nightly illumination over the city that is used by enemy submarines in spotting shipping off our coast.

Windows and doors thoughtlessly opened for relief from the heat continue to loose light rays that help build up the sky glow over the metropolitan area, these experts said. They urged that whenever a window or door is opened for this purpose, it should be properly shaded or screened to prevent direct rays of light from emerging. These and other precautions should be placed in effect by one hour after sundown, which is at 8:31 P. M. tonight.

Meanwhile, the Army adjures all citizens: "If in doubt, put it out."

Peter of Yugoslavia Reaches Washington

Special to THE NEW YORK TIMES.

WASHINGTON, June 21—King Peter of Yugoslavia arrived here by airplane today. He was accompanied by M. Nincitch, the Yugoslav Foreign Minister.

They will discuss with President Roosevelt and other officials their country's continued opposition to the Axis. One of their objectives, it is understood, will be to obtain lease-lend aid for the guerrilla forces resisting the Nazis in Yugoslavia.

The King and his entourage will spend tonight at Blair House and will leave tomorrow to spend a few days in the country. He is traveling incognito until Wednesday, when he will return to Washington to begin the official program of his visit to the United States.

DIMOUT 'FAILURE' IS LAID TO MAYOR

Defense Council Members Say He Has Not Ordered Police to Enforce Army Rules

Charges that Mayor La Guardia has failed to give the Police Department orders to enforce the Army's dimout regulations, but has endeavored unsuccessfully to get the Army to modify its specifications, were advanced yesterday by two members of the executive board of the Lower West Side Defense Council, acting as a special committee in behalf of the council.

Howard Mulligan, a lawyer, of 103 Waverly Place, and J. B. C. Woods of 38 Perry Street, made public copies of a letter they had sent to the Mayor charging that conditions in their area were "deplorable." Mr. Mulligan explained that he and Mr. Woods had been authorized to take this action at a meeting at the council's headquarters, 27 Barrow Street, last Tuesday evening.

"Nightly, men are dying and ships are being sunk by the enemy off our coast because you, sir, prefer not to carry out the Army's orders," the letter charged.

In his weekly radio broadcast on June 7 Mayor La Guardia an-

Continued on Page Thirteen

RED ARMY RETIRES

Paris Radio Says Nazi Troops Have Reached Town of Sevastopol

AXIS LOSSES SEVERE

Placed at 7 Divisions—Germans Repelled on Kharkov Front

By RALPH PARKER

Wireless to THE NEW YORK TIMES.

MOSCOW, Monday, June 22—The Russian High Command acknowledges in its communiqué this morning that the Germans have succeeded, at a high cost in lives lost, in driving a wedge into the defenses of Sevastopol. But the bulletin also reports the repulse of numerous severe German assaults on the Sevastopol front.

[The German-controlled Paris radio said today that German troops had reached the town of Sevastopol after breaking through the Russian inner defense lines, The United Press reported from London. German sappers smashed their way through the final defense line outside the town with flame throwers, the Paris broadcast claimed.]

[The Germans reported the Red Army forces on the Kharkov front, where fighting on any considerable scale appears to be confined to one narrow sector, are said to have achieved an important success. After two enemy regiments had crossed a river barrier and advanced on the eastern bank, the Russians struck back, driving the Germans into and across the river. The Russians themselves then crossed the river and captured points on the western bank.

Press reports yesterday indicated that the Germans were continuing to pour troops into the Sevastopol fighting and that the situation there was grave. These reports said that waves of German and Rumanian infantry, attacking Russian lines in the southern sector of the Crimean base's defenses while planes dive-bombed Soviet artillery positions, had

Continued on Page Five

NEW LANDING MADE

Japanese Cruiser Is Hit in Army Air Blow at Kiska's Harbor

TRANSPORT IS SUNK

U. S. Fliers See Enemy's Temporary Buildings on Aleutian Isle

By C. BROOKS PETERS

Special to THE NEW YORK TIMES.

WASHINGTON, June 21—The Japanese forces that have been operating in the western Aleutian Islands since June 3 have succeeded in occupying Kiska, 650 miles west of Dutch Harbor, strategic American operations base, the Navy Department announced today.

Enemy occupation of Attu, westernmost island of the American chain and some 275 miles northwest of Kiska, was acknowledged in a Navy announcement on June 12.

Flying conditions in the Aleutian region—in which "foul weather and fog" are the general rule, the Navy reported recently—were sufficiently satisfactory in the last few days to permit "some restricted air operations against Kiska," today's Navy communiqué asserted.

Long-range Army aircraft attacked a small force of Japanese ships in Kiska's harbor and reported hits on a cruiser, the Navy announced. An enemy transport was sunk.

Tents of Japanese Seen

The American planes that finally were able to penetrate to the remote island of Kiska, where until the Japanese occupation the United States Navy maintained a weather station, observed that the enemy had set up tents and "minor temporary structures on land."

The communiqué added that operations in that area continued to be restricted "by considerations of weather and great distances."

Last Monday the Navy Department reported that Army and Navy planes were continuing air assaults "against the Japanese forces which recently were reported to have landed on western islands of the Aleutian group." At that time the Navy asserted that at least three Japanese cruisers, one destroyer, one gunboat and one transport had been damaged, "some of them severely," by air attacks.

Since the announcement on June 12 of the occupation of Attu naval circles in Washington have minimized the seriousness of Japanese landings in the western Aleutians, characterizing them as having been inspired primarily by a desire "to save face" after the defeat administered by American Army and Navy forces in the Coral Sea and off Midway Island.

Supply Problem Difficult

Military experts here have stated that supply would be a major problem for any enemy forces that endeavored to establish themselves in the Aleutians. The distance from bases in Japanese territory to the Aleutian Islands is so great, these circles have contended, that aerial transport is not feasible, particularly in view of the uncertain weather conditions. Therefore, supplies must be transported by surface craft, which are constantly exposed to attack by American submarines.

There is, however, a possibility that in the Rat Island group, of which Kiska is one island, the Japanese could conceal submarine mother ships and perhaps even small aircraft carriers, the experts here said. Submarines from such bases might prove effective should Japan attack Russia, they added.

But for the most part, according to the opinion conveyed to reporters in Washington by military circles, the enemy will have to be

Continued on Page Four

War News Summarized

MONDAY, JUNE 22, 1942

Tobruk fell yesterday, and the resultant threat to Egypt and the British position in the Eastern Mediterranean changed the war picture drastically, while the Russians acknowledged a significant German advance at Sevastopol, though at the cost of heavy enemy losses.

Tobruk fell to a smashing blow delivered by waves of German tanks according to London reports. The Germans claimed that 25,000 prisoners had been taken. In London the opinion prevailed that there had not been time to lay minefields around Tobruk before the Axis attack. [1:8.]

Military observers in London referred to the fall of Tobruk as an "incontestable disaster." The Germans were believed to have obtained a large quantity of stores. General Rommel was expected to drive on Suez. [2:2.]

British bombers attacked Emden, German submarine base, for the second successive night, airfields in the Netherlands and enemy shipping off the Netherland coast. Heavy air attacks were also made on the French and Belgian coasts. [1:5.]

Moscow granted that the defenders of Sevastopol had been forced to fall back as the enemy forced a wedge in their lines, but declared that the action had crippled five German and two Rumanian divisions. Sharp activity was reported in the Kharkov and Leningrad sectors. [1:2.]

President Kalinin of the Soviet Union, in a review of a year of war, stated that the Germans no longer were capable of a general offensive. [5:5; map, P. 5.]

Lord Beaverbrook, addressing a "Salute to Russia" meeting in Britain, again urged the United Nations to open a second front. He asserted that the British Army was now sufficiently prepared. [3:1.]

Chungking reported that the Japanese had been halted in Kiangsi and had lost 1,300 troops in Honan. The Minister of War asserted that the Japanese soon would be so bogged down in China that they would not be able to attack Russia with full strength. [4:1.]

The United States Navy announced that Japanese forces in the Aleutians had succeeded in occupying the island of Kiska, 650 miles west of Dutch Harbor. Bomb hits were made on a Japanese cruiser and a Japanese transport was sunk. [1:4; map, P. 4.]

Colonel J. L. Ralston, Canadian Defense Minister, disclosed that a government telegraph station at Estevan Point, Vancouver Island, had been shelled by a submarine Saturday night, but no damage was done. [1:5-6.]

As President Roosevelt and Prime Minister Churchill continued their conversations yesterday Washington reported that the fall of Tobruk and Russian withdrawals at Sevastopol had checked "second front speculation." Concern was being shown over the necessity for holding the present front in Egypt. [1:7.]

ROMMEL'S FORCES TAKE IMPORTANT PORT IN LIBYA

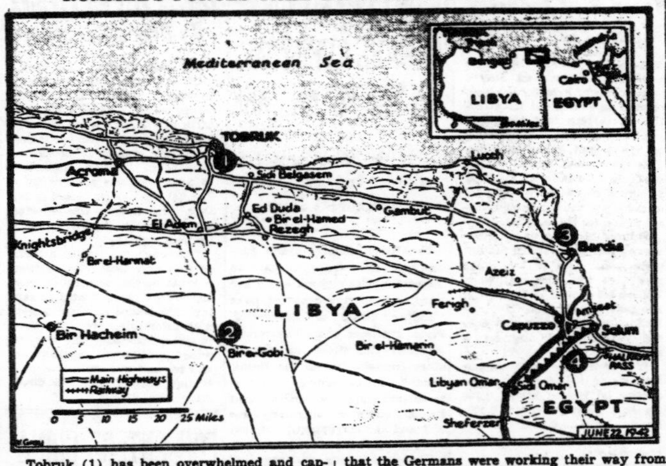

Tobruk (1) has been overwhelmed and captured with its garrison by the Axis, which also claimed the capture of Bir el-Gobi (2) and the minor port of Bardia (3). There were indications that the Germans were working their way from Bardia southward to Capuzzo for an assault across the border into Egypt. Here they will find defenses between Solum and Sidi Omar (4).

Vancouver Island Shelled; Northwest Coast Dims Out

By P. J. PHILIP

Special to THE NEW YORK TIMES.

OTTAWA, June 21—Estevan Point on Vancouver Island was shelled by an enemy submarine at 10:35 o'clock, Pacific time, last night (1:35 A. M., Sunday, Eastern war time), Colonel J. L. Ralston, the Defense Minister, announced here today. The submarine was presumed to be Japanese.

The enemy's objective was the government wireless and telegraph station there. No damage was done, said a report from Lieut. Gen. Kenneth Stuart, Canadian Chief of Staff and acting Commander in Chief of the West Corps defenses.

[Coastal dimouts in the States of Washington and Oregon were put into effect last night, following the shelling of Estevan Point, which is about 125 miles north of the United States border.]

There is an airfield near Estevan Point, but no report has come through as to whether action was taken against the attacking submarine.

The attack was the first against Canadian soil in the history of Canada as a Dominion. Last month two ships were torpedoed and sunk in the Gulf of St. Lawrence.

The Defense Minister's announcement said:

"The Commander in Chief, West Coast defenses, reported that the Dominion Government telegraph station at Estevan Point, Vancouver Island, was shelled by a submarine at 10:35 P. M. (Pacific time) on Saturday night. No damage resulted."

Estevan Point lies halfway along the western shore of Vancouver Island, about 150 miles northwest of Victoria. Its only importance seems to be the estab-

Continued on Page Four

R. A. F. PAYS EMDEN 2D VISIT IN 2 NIGHTS

Also Hammers Other Targets in Northwest Reich—Hits Ship Off Dutch Coast

By JAMES MacDONALD

Wireless to THE NEW YORK TIMES.

LONDON, June 21—A large number of British bombers hammered Emden, Germany, last night for the second night in succession and also other objectives in Northwest Germany and air bases in the Netherlands.

At the same time American-built Hudson planes of the Coastal Command, ever on the lookout for enemy shipping, searched waters off the Netherland coast, where a Canadian flying crew dropped two bombs on a medium-sized cargo vessel.

The communiqué announcing these operations did not divulge the number of planes engaged, but said the raids cost the Royal Air Force six bombers and one Coastal Command plane. The R. A. F. losses were increased today when one fighter plane failed to return home from a daylight attack on Dunkerque.

[The Berlin radio went off the air at 1:50 A. M. today, a possible sign that British bombers were again over Germany, The United Press reported from London.

[German planes dropped bombs early today in a sharp attack on the south coast of England, The Associated Press reported. Two of the raiders were shot down and two more Nazi planes destroyed over Europe.]

As in the case of the R. A. F. raids on Emden late Friday night and early yesterday morning, the Air Ministry did not go into details about the targets for the night or indicate the extent of damage.

While patrolling along the Netherland coast during the night Coastal Command fliers caught up with an enemy convoy of three ships. The rear gunner on a Canadian-manned plane said on his return to his base that he saw two bombs hit one vessel amidship, hurling debris high in the air in the resulting explosions. Whether the vessel sank was not determined. What became of her two companion ships was not learned here.

Although the sky was clear, there was less daylight activity to-

Continued on Page Five

'Never a Dull Moment' at Midway, Reporter Watching Battle Found

The following account of the Battle of Midway is by a correspondent of THE NEW YORK TIMES *who was aboard one of the United States warships.*

By FOSTER HAILEY

Special to THE NEW YORK TIMES.

WITH THE PACIFIC FLEET, at Sea, June 4 (Delayed)—Today is the day. Mark it on your calendar in red ink, Thursday, June 4. It may be the one on which the tide definitely turned in the battle of the Pacific.

This morning at dawn the Japanese launched planes from a strong striking force northwest of Midway. We are in a position to strike them on the flank. If our planes can only get to their carriers before the Japanese planes attacking Midway car return, the result may be a naval disaster for the Japanese.

White water is curling away from the clipper bows of the cruisers and the big carriers, whose escort we are, as we drive on at high speed with the destroyers ahead and on the flanks. It is a relief for the nerves when the first alarm is sounded. It turns out to be false, but the activity has eased the tension.

There is another spurt of activity as another air contact is reported, but it turns out to be a big patrol plane from Midway that joins the force to act as an anti-submarine guard.

"Midway was attacked at 6:48 A. M.," our Admiral and Chief of Staff says crisply when an inquiry on the situation is made.

"We should be in launching distance soon."

The dawn was a gloomy one, but now the clouds are breaking up.

Continued on Page Four

NEWS PUTS DAMPER ON CHURCHILL VISIT

But Washington Sees Mid-East Crisis as Incidental in His Planning With Roosevelt

By JAMES B. RESTON

Special to THE NEW YORK TIMES.

WASHINGTON, June 21—Washington was in a sober and realistic mood tonight. The fall of Tobruk and the situation of the Russians at Sevastopol have put a damper on the unrestrained second-front speculation that has surrounded the Roosevelt-Churchill talks. The chief immediate concern was viewed as the holding of the second front the United Nations now have in Egypt, rather than opening up new fronts on the European Continent.

The President and Mr. Churchill continued their talks during the day, and the chiefs of staff of the United States and Britain, General George C. Marshall and General Sir Alan Brooke, who came to the United States with Mr. Churchill, continued their exchange of information and their planning for the future.

The plain and simple truth about these important discussions is that only a few persons know what has gone on since Mr. Churchill arrived, and they are not telling what they know.

The purpose of the conversations is much less complicated, dramatic and urgent than one would tend to deduce from the secrecy with which they have been surrounded.

It is undoubtedly true, as Stephen Early, White House secretary, has said, that they are dealing with the future plans of the

Continued on Page Eight

NAZIS NEAR EGYPT

British Are on Border as Rommel Presses On After Victory

PORT'S LOSS SERIOUS

Plan for a Second Front Seen Upset by Need to Hold New Line

By DAVID ANDERSON

Special Cable to THE NEW YORK TIMES.

LONDON, June 21—A smashing blow delivered yesterday by waves of German tanks, heavily supported from the air, crushed the defenses of Tobruk in Libya. The War Office tonight confirmed the loss of the town, already claimed by the enemy, who said 25,000 prisoners, including "several generals" had been captured.

The story of what happened, as given by both German and Italian sources, appears to cover the battle fairly fully, but the accuracy of these reports cannot be checked at present. Briefly, it can be said Field Marshal Erwin Rommel's armored units that had passed Tobruk in pursuit of the British Eighth Army did so to make certain whether the British showed any signs of preparing a counter-attack.

When the German Marshal was satisfied this was not the case he reversed his forces, bringing back tanks against Tobruk from the south, driving from the vicinity of Ed Duda, and did this fiercely with every ounce of power at his command. At the same time the Luftwaffe began intensive bombing of Tobruk's defenses. Within a matter of hours the battle was over.

Tobruk Long in Battle

Tobruk must have been softer in its last moments than during the many other attacks it beat off during the last seventeen months since it was captured from the Italians on Jan 22, 1941. It has been on the fringe of the Libyan battlefield for some weeks with inevitable strain as strategy wavered between one of concentration of strength there and one of evacuation.

Despite the presence of a large garrison when Tobruk fell it is believed there was not time to lay minefields on its perimeter or otherwise strengthen its defenses to face an immediate storming.

A Cairo communiqué, released here at noon today, paved the way for the worst. It read:

"Yesterday the enemy attacked the perimeter of Tobruk in great strength. In spite of most determined resistance by our forces the enemy succeeded in penetrating the defenses and in occupying a considerable area inside them."

Twelve strong points in the defenses were taken by the first wave of enemy tanks, according to Berlin. This made a wedge two and a half miles wide, and German sources state the British defenders then realized that further resistance was useless.

Bombers Blast Defenses

But they had other reasons for weighing most seriously the advantages of carrying on the fight. The Germans said today that "numerous bombers' ceaseless attack wrought great destruction in the fortifications and other military works of the port and town."

It was not long after noon yesterday when large formations of German bombers swooped down on a group of four anti-aircraft batteries, all of which were silenced, it was reported by Berlin. Still more of the Luftwaffe's heavy aircraft, laden with high explosives, cruised over a column of twenty tanks, setting many of them ablaze.

Finally, the German radio said, "About 2 P. M. another great attack was made on Tobruk, which lasted three hours without interruption and caused numerous fires.

Continued on Page Two

"All the News That's Fit to Print."

NEWS INDEX, PAGE 55, THIS SECTION

The New York Times.

LATE CITY EDITION
Continued cool today with light winds.
Temperatures Yesterday—Max., 57; Min., 45
Sunrise, 7:34 A. M.; Sunset, 5:46 P. M.

Section 1

Copyright, 1942, by The New York Times Company.

VOL. XCII—No. 30,969. Entered as Second-Class Matter, Postoffice, New York, N. Y. NEW YORK, SUNDAY, NOVEMBER 8, 1942. Including Magazine and Book Sections. TEN CENTS New York City and Vicinity

AMERICAN FORCES LAND IN FRENCH AFRICA; BRITISH NAVAL, AIR UNITS ASSISTING THEM; EFFECTIVE SECOND FRONT, ROOSEVELT SAYS

U.S. DRIVES ON BUNA

American Troops Flown to Area Closing In on Big Japanese Base

PAPUA IS OVERRUN

All Except Beachhead of Buna-Gona Seized in New Guinea Push

By The Associated Press.

AT UNITED NATIONS HEADQUARTERS, Australia, Sunday, Nov. 8—American combat troops are in action near Buna, vital Japanese base on the north New Guinea coast, General Douglas MacArthur disclosed today.

Simultaneously, General MacArthur disclosed that the Allies have occupied Goodenough Island to the northeast of New Guinea, off Collingwood Bay, in an obvious flanking movement.

[American Army troops on Guadalcanal advanced on Friday (Solomons time) in the area to the west of Henderson airfield, the Navy reported yesterday. They crossed the Malimbui River a few miles south of Koli Point, where the Japanese recently landed reinforcements, but met little opposition.]

It was from Buna, in midsummer, that the Japanese began a drive across tortuous trails of the Owen Stanley Mountains which carried to within thirty-two miles of Port Moresby, Allied base on the south coast, before it was stalled. Late in September the Allies began encircling and infiltration movements which rolled the Japanese back and yesterday's communiqué had mentioned bitter fighting at Oivi, which is fifty-five miles south of Buna.

Japanese Resist at Oisi

"American ground troops in force, transported by air from Australia during the last month, have penetrated Central and Northern Papua to the vicinity of Buna," a communiqué stated.

"The Allied forces now control all of Papua except the beach head in the Buna-Gona area."

The surprising development came as a thrust around the eastern end of New Guinea from Milne Bay where Japanese troops landed in July only to be pinned against the sea and slain or forced to their ships.

"Units from Milne Bay," the communiqué said, "have now completed clearing remnants of hostile forces from the islands to the north and have occupied adjacent strategic points."

While this disclosure was being made, Australian ground forces still were meeting fierce resistance at Oivi where the retreating Japanese are making a stand. Today's communiqué said the Australians maintained constant pressure and were resorting to their hitherto successful tactics of local encircling movements in efforts to dislodge the defenders.

The Allied air force continued to support the overland drive with strafing attacks on the Japanese troops.

Island Attacked Oct. 22

AT UNITED NATIONS HEADQUARTERS, Australia, Sunday, Nov. 8 (U.P.)—The announcement of sweeping Allied gains in New Guinea came as a surprise to observers here, although an Australian offensive through mountainous central New Guinea had been making steady progress toward the north coast for the past five weeks.

[Delayed dispatches from Harold Guard, United Press staff correspondent in New Guinea, revealed that the Americans had

Continued on Page Forty-five

LEADS IN AFRICA

Lieut. Gen. Dwight Eisenhower
Associated Press

R. A. F. ROCKS GENOA; U. S. RAID ON BREST

Bombers From Britain Pound North Italy 2 Nights in Row —Hit Nazis on Coast

Special Cable to THE NEW YORK TIMES.

LONDON, Sunday, Nov. 8—Bombers from Britain struck a heavy blow at Northern Italy over Friday night, blasting the port of Genoa again in support of the Eighth Army's battling of the Nazis and Italians in the African desert.

Again last night the Royal Air Force sent its big bombers over Northern Italy, British officials reported briefly early today. The announcement meant that the R. A. F. from here was seeing to it that the Axis forces in Africa got no help from home.

American heavy bombers, both Flying Fortresses and Liberators, escorted by Allied fighters, carried out a smashing attack on the docks and U-boat pens at Brest in occupied France yesterday afternoon, United States Army headquarters here announced.

Bombs were seen to strike the targets at Brest. The communiqué stressed that sharp Nazi anti-aircraft fire and enemy fighter opposition were encountered over the coast of Brittany.

The Brest raiders shot down four Nazi fighters. All the United States bombers returned, but one Allied fighter was lost.

The R. A. F.'s fighter squadrons

Continued on Page Twenty-one

NAZIS NEAR LIBYA

British Drive Out to Bar New Stand by Enemy or Reinforcements

FOE BOMBED ALL NIGHT

Pursuers Reported to Be Within 40 Miles of Halfaya Pass

By The United Press.

CAIRO, Egypt, Nov. 7—The British Eighth Army under Lieut. Gen. Bernard L. Montgomery hurled armored forces, motorized infantry and swarms of planes tonight at the remnants of German General Field Marshal Erwin Rommel's once-proud Afrika Korps—possibly only 25,000 out of an original 140,000—now trying to brace for a stand at Halfaya [Hellfire] Pass on the Libyan frontier, 240 miles west of the Alamein battleground.

The main body of the British forces was reported to be well west of Matruh, 110 miles west of El Alamein, and advance striking forces were believed to be as far as 200 miles west of El Alamein, or close to the Egyptian-Libyan frontier, 240 miles west of El Alamein.

How many men Marshal Rommel had left in the Halfaya area could not be established. Already 20,000 prisoners have been counted in British hands. Marshal Rommel's desert casualties were estimated at approximately 20,000 more. In addition, 75,000 Italian troops had been left far behind the swirling battleground, ready to surrender when the British could find time and men to round them up.

Marshal Rommel entered the battle with a maximum of 140,000 troops in the forward area. It was doubted whether he had more than one or two divisions left to attempt another stand at Halfaya unless he had been able to rush large reinforcements from the rear.

It appeared possible tonight that the Axis forces might not even attempt to stand at Halfaya, but would, instead, continue their headlong flight as deeply as possible into Libya in an effort to open a gap between themselves and the Eighth Army.

Such a manoeuvre, however, may already be doomed to failure. General Montgomery has ordered that every attempt be made to cut off Marshal Rommel's retreat. It was believed that he might have sent a hard-hitting, fast-moving

Continued on Page Four

SHOCK TROOPS LEAD

Simultaneous Landings Made Before Dawn at Numerous Points

PLANES GUARD SKIES

An Armada Pours Men on the Beaches—Early Actions Satisfactory

By WES GALLAGHER
Associated Press Correspondent

ALLIED HEADQUARTERS IN NORTH AFRICA, Sunday, Nov. 8—American soldiers, marines and sailors from one of the greatest armadas ever put into a single military operation swarmed ashore today on the Vichy-controlled North Africa shore before dawn, striking to break Hitler's hold on the Mediterranean.

[Reports reaching Allied headquarters in North Africa today disclosed that successful landings had been made by American assault parties on beaches of North Africa near two main objectives outlined in operational plans, an Associated Press dispatch stated.

[British forces reported attemping a landing at Algiers after a bombardment were said by the Vichy radio to have been "beaten off."]

Tall, decisive Lieut. Gen. Dwight D. (Ike) Eisenhower, supreme commander of the huge forces involved in the operation, worked throughout the night directing the first great American blow at the Axis.

Included in the forces were crack combat troops, Rangers (airborne units) and the cream of America's airmen.

British naval and air force units supported the American landing forces, who were preceded by a snowstorm of leaflets and a radio barrage promising the French that the United States had no intention of seizing French possessions and only sought to prevent Axis infiltration.

It undoubtedly was the longest over-water military operation ever attempted, with hundreds of ships in great convoys coming thousands of miles under the protection of British and American sea and air might.

I came on one of these big convoys.

Fighting-fit American soldiers

Continued on Page Five

WHERE THE UNITED STATES PREPARES FOR NEW FRONT

As the survivors of Marshal Rommel's beaten German legions fled westward toward the Libyan border (1), powerful American land, sea and air forces landed behind them at various places in Vichy France's colonies along the Mediterranean (2) and on the shores of the Atlantic, apparently in Morocco (3). British naval and aerial units are assisting them. There was no indication of military action against Vichy's possessions on the western bulge of the Atlantic (4). A large and comprehensive map of the African and Mediterranean theatre of war will be found on Page 1 of Section 4 of this issue of THE TIMES. However, Section 4 had gone to press before the announcement last night of the landing of American troops.

U.S. MEETS 'THREAT'

Big Expeditions Invade North and West Africa to Forestall Axis

EISENHOWER AT HEAD

President Urges French to Help, Calls Move Aid to Russia

Roosevelt's appeal to French people and Eisenhower's message to North Africans, Pg. 8.

By C. P. TRUSSELL
Special to THE NEW YORK TIMES.

WASHINGTON, Nov. 7—Powerful American forces, supported by British naval and air forces, landed simultaneously tonight at numerous points on the Mediterranean and Atlantic coasts of French North Africa, forestalling an anticipated invasion of Africa by Germany and Italy and launching effective second-front assistance to Russia, President Roosevelt announced tonight.

Lieut. Gen. Dwight D. Eisenhower is in command.

The President made the announcement even as the American forces, equipped with adequate weapons of modern warfare, he emphasized, were making the landings.

President Speaks to France

Soon he was speaking direct to the French Government and the French people by short-wave radio and in their own tongue, giving assurances that the Allies seek no territory and have no intention of interfering with friendly French, official or civilian. He called upon them to cooperate in repelling "the German and Italian international criminals."

By doing so, he said, they could help liberate France and the French Empire.

[United States and British planes dropped leaflets in France and French Africa containing messages to the people from President Roosevelt and General Eisenhower, London reported.]

General Eisenhower himself, the White House let it be known, also spoke by radio to the French people, explaining the purposes of the invasions.

His proclamation, delivered while the American troops were making their landings, gave specific directions to French land, sea and air forces in North Africa as to how they could avoid misunderstanding and prevent action against them by a system of signals. This is a military operation, General Eisen-

Continued on Page Three

LANDING PLAN KEPT SECRET BY WRITERS

Americans Selected for Duty, Bureaus Sworn to Silence—Eisenhower Slipt Away

By RAYMOND DANIELL
Special Cable to THE NEW YORK TIMES.

LONDON, Sunday, Nov. 8—For weeks American newspaper men have been the custodians of one of war's biggest secrets. It was not an easy secret to keep because through all that time they had to improvise excuses for the absence of a large number of the members of their London staffs to conceal the fact that they had gone with the expeditionary forces.

Most London offices of Amer-

Continued on Page Fourteen

President's Statement

Special to THE NEW YORK TIMES.

WASHINGTON, Nov. 7—President Roosevelt's statement announcing the opening of a second front in French North and West Africa follows:

In order to forestall an invasion of Africa by Germany and Italy, which, if successful, would constitute a direct threat to America across the comparatively narrow sea from Western Africa, a powerful American force equipped with adequate weapons of modern warfare and under American command is today landing on the Mediterranean and Atlantic coasts of the French colonies in Africa.

The landing of this American Army is being assisted by the British Navy and air forces, and it will, in the immediate future, be reinforced by a considerable number of divisions of the British Army.

This combined Allied force, under American command, in conjunction with the British campaign in Egypt is designed to prevent an occupation by the Axis armies of any part of Northern or Western Africa and to deny to the aggressor nations a starting point from which to launch an attack against the Atlantic coast of the Americas.

In addition, it provides an effective second-front assistance to our heroic allies in Russia.

The French Government and the French people have been informed of the purpose of this expedition and have been assured that the Allies seek no territory and have no intention of interfering with friendly French authorities in Africa.

The government of France and the people of France and the French possessions have been requested to cooperate with and assist the American expedition in its effort to repel the German and Italian international criminals, and by so doing to liberate France and the French Empire from the Axis yoke.

This expedition will develop into a major effort by the Allied Nations and there is every expectation that it will be successful in repelling the planned German and Italian invasion of Africa and prove the first historic step to the liberation and restoration of France.

Major Sports Yesterday

FOOTBALL

Making both touchdowns in the second half, Notre Dame defeated Army before 75,142 spectators at the Yankee Stadium. With a scoring pass in the first period and several goal-line stands, Navy thrilled 74,000 fans at Philadelphia by upsetting Penn. Both Fordham and Columbia lost free-scoring contests here and the Big Three—Princeton, Yale and Harvard—all went down to defeat. Iowa toppled hitherto unbeaten Wisconsin. Scores of leading games:

Alabama	29	So. Carolina	0	Miss. State	7	Tulane	0
Amherst	35	Trinity	6	Missouri	26	Nebraska	6
Boston Coll.	28	Temple	0	Moravian	32	C. C. N. Y.	0
Brown	20	Holy Cross	14	Navy	7	Penn.	0
Colgate	35	Columbia	26	Notre Dame	13	Army	0
Cornell	13	Yale	7	Ohio State	59	Pittsburgh	19
Dartmouth	19	Princeton	7	Oklahoma	76	Kan. State	0
Duke	42	Maryland	0	Oregon	14	U. C. L. A.	7
Duquesne	7	St. Mary's	7	Penn State	18	Syracuse	13
Georgia	75	Florida	0	Rice	40	Arkansas	9
Ga. Pre-Fl.	41	Auburn	14	So. Calif.	21	California	7
Ga. Tech	47	Kentucky	7	Stanford	20	Washington	7
Great Lakes	42	Purdue	0	Texas	20	Baylor	0
Illinois	14	Northwestern	7	Tex. A. & M.	27	S. M. U.	20
Indiana	7	Minnesota	0	Texas Tech	13	T. C. U.	6
Iowa	6	Wisconsin	0	Vanderbilt	19	Mississippi	0
La. State	26	Fordham	13	Wash. State	25	Mich. State	13
Michigan	35	Harvard	7	Williams	31	Wesleyan	6

HORSE RACING

Good Morning won the Florence Nightingale Purse by half a length from Too Timely on the war-relief program before 22,099 racegoers who bet $1,550,089 at Belmont Park. Aonbarr defeated Riverland by a neck in the Grayson Handicap at Pimlico.

HOCKEY

The New York Rangers downed the Montreal Canadiens, 4—3, in the overtime opening game at Madison Square Garden.

(Complete Details of These and Other Sports Events in Section 5.)

War News Summarized

SUNDAY, NOVEMBER 8, 1942

The White House announced last night that powerful American forces were landing on the Atlantic and Mediterranean coasts of French North Africa to forestall a German invasion. The announcement stated that the landing was to prevent the creation of an Axis threat to the Atlantic coast of the Americas across the narrow sea in Western Africa. France has been assured that the Allies seek no territory. [1:8.]

American correspondents with the African expeditionary force told of simultaneous landings by the United States troops at many points hundreds of miles apart. [1:4.]

Britain's Eighth Army continued its pursuit in North Africa of Marshal Rommel's shattered army. Twenty thousand prisoners had been taken, according to Cairo. British columns were said to be 200 miles west of El Alamein, close to the Libyan border. [1:3; map, P. 4.]

London announced that British heavy bombers had launched a "concentrated and effective" attack on Genoa Friday night and again raided Northern Italy last night. United States bombers attacked the U-boat base at Brest, France, and other planes from Britain pounded Nazi targets from the Netherlands to the Bay of Biscay. [1:2; map, P. 21.]

Moscow reported that the Soviet armies held on all fronts and killed some 1,800 of the enemy on the Stalingrad and Caucasus fronts. The German advances in the Nalchik region had apparently been halted. [38:4-5.]

General Douglas MacArthur's headquarters announced that American troops in force had been transported by air to New Guinea and had penetrated to the vicinity of Buna, Japanese base on the north coast. [1:1; map, P. 45.]

The United States Navy announced that Army forces on Guadalcanal Island in the Solomons had attacked Japanese troops to the east of the airfield Nov. 6 and had encountered little opposition. Announcement was also made that at least 5,188 Japanese had been killed in land fighting on Tulagi and Guadalcanal since the United States occupation Aug. 7. [46:1 with map.]

United States bombers attacked successfully the docks at Rangoon, Burma, and returned to their bases in India. [46:8.]

Blow to Knock Italy Out of the War Called Goal of American Invasion

Special Cable to THE NEW YORK TIMES.

LONDON, Sunday, Nov. 8—Allied Army, Navy and air forces commanded by Lieut. Gen. Dwight D. Eisenhower, commander of all American forces in the European theatre, have struck a powerful blow to free the Mediterranean from Axis control and knock Italy out of the war. That, in the opinion of military observers here, is the meaning of the movement of United States forces that now become part of the gigantic pincers with which it is expected that the last vestiges of the German and Italian forces in North Africa will be annihilated.

The movement now under way called for the finest timing. It was essential that, before that huge armada of whose presence at Gibraltar the Nazis were aware got under way, Britain's Eighth Army in Egypt should break through Marshal Erwin Rommel's defenses and start the westward push that is fast becoming a rout. Now United States soldiers swarming ashore at many points in French North Africa are closing Marshal Rommel's back door.

The first stage of the battle just beginning will be a struggle for the control of roads, railways and airfields in Algeria and the neighboring colony of Tunisia. Once the control of these has been won, Allied reinforcements and supplies will be able to dispense with the long journey around the Cape of Good Hope that has been one of

Continued on Page Thirteen

Petain Says Vichy Will 'Defend' Lands

By The Associated Press.

LONDON, Sunday, Nov. 8—The Vichy radio said today that Marshal Henri Philippe Pétain had sent President Roosevelt a message expressing his "astonishment and sadness" at learning of "the aggression of your troops against North Africa."

Marshal Pétain said that the reasons given by the President for the landings failed to justify them and added:

"France and its honor are involved. We are attacked and we will defend ourselves."

The Vichy government issued a communiqué opening with an "appeal to Frenchmen not to allow yourselves to be swayed by foreign broadcasts."

"All the News That's Fit to Print."

The New York Times.

LATE CITY EDITION
Continued cool with moderate winds today.
Temperatures Yesterday—Max., 68; Min., 60
Sunrise, 5:27 A. M.; Sunset, 8:31 P. M.

VOL. XCII—No. 31,204. Entered as Second-Class Matter, Postoffice, New York, N. Y. NEW YORK, THURSDAY, JULY 1, 1943. THREE CENTS IN NEW YORK CITY

M'ARTHUR STARTS ALLIED OFFENSIVE IN PACIFIC; NEW GUINEA ISLES WON, LANDINGS IN SOLOMONS; CHURCHILL PROMISES BLOWS IN EUROPE BY FALL

MAYOR FACES FIGHT WITH OPA ON PLAN FOR HANDLING MEAT

Gives Approval for Sales by Slaughterers to Retailers on Consignment Basis

FEDERAL ACTION LOOMS

Price Agency Director Here Promises Move Should Violation Be Found

A direct conflict between Mayor Fiorello H. La Guardia and the Office of Price Administration appeared inevitable last night, after the Mayor had announced that he had approved, on his own responsibility, a plan for independent slaughterers to sell meat to the public at consumer ceiling prices through consignments to retailers, despite the OPA's objections to the plan.

"If they go ahead with a plan that is in violation of the regulations, OPA will be forced to take action," Frank C. Russell, district OPA director, retorted when informed of the Mayor's decision. "Apparently, the Mayor has given his permission for something which the OPA legal department has turned down."

Former Municipal Court Justice Nathan Sweedler of 225 Broadway, who, as counsel for the Eastern States Independent Meat Packers and Slaughterers, proposed the plan approved by the Mayor after the OPA had turned it down, announced that his organization hoped to have meat on sale in some retail shops today and expected to have a large quantity available by Saturday.

Sees Quick Meat Supply

Mr. Sweedler has estimated that his group could provide 25,000 pounds of beef within twenty-four hours after the Mayor gave his approval to the plan and eventually could gear its output to 1,000,000 pounds a week, but the Mayor was even more optimistic. He said that the plan might provide the city with 1,000,000 pounds a week "and it may be 5,000,000 pounds."

Under the plan the meat would be sold on consignment, the retailer keeping 21 per cent of the selling price. According to Mr. Sweedler, the remaining 79 per cent would pay for the cost of livestock, freight and slaughtering. He contends that under his plan meat could be sold at the consumer ceiling prices, and any butcher violating the ceiling would be deprived of meat through a voluntary policing system.

The Mayor announced his approval of the plan to reporters at City Hall and then released a letter to Commissioner of Markets Daniel P. Woolley in which he argued that the plan did not conflict with any existing regulations and that it should be accepted as a temporary measure.

Holds Plan Feasible

"I have carefully studied the report you submitted to me with plan for direct consignment of food from the original processor to retailer direct, and selling by such retailer to consumer at ceiling prices or lower," the Mayor said in his letter. "I do not see how any such plan could conflict with any existing rules or regulations of any Federal agency, provided the producer, farmer or livestock man is paid the market price and the retailer sells at ceiling prices or lower.

"The whole purpose of food control is to make food available and fix ceiling prices. There is nothing in the rules that prevents anyone from selling below ceiling prices. Surely, in the protection of the consumer, we could not or would not prosecute a retailer for selling below ceiling prices provided his food is wholesome and complies with all health requirements and government inspection.

"In fact, if an original processor or retailer wanted to give food

Continued on Page Seventeen

OWI Closes Twelve Regional Branches

By The Associated Press.

WASHINGTON, June 30—Twelve regional and thirty-six branch offices of the Office of War Information throughout the country began closing at midnight tonight as the fiscal year ended.

The OWI said an official would remain in each of the twelve regional offices for a few days to liquidate the affairs of both the regional and branch offices.

The shutdown was made necessary, the OWI said, because the Senate voted to appropriate only $3,000,000 for the domestic branch of the organization and earmarked the amount, allowing none for maintaining the regional and branch offices. The House had voted to abolish the domestic service entirely.

"It isn't likely that the Congressional conference committee, which has yet to act finally, would go above the Senate's $3,000,000, so we are closing down the offices," an agency spokesman said.

CONGRESS CRUSHES SUBSIDY PROGRAM

Ban on Payments to Cut Prices Stays in CCC Bill Passed by Overwhelming Majorities

By The Associated Press.

WASHINGTON, June 30—Congress, handing the Roosevelt Administration another legislative setback, today forbade use of subsidies to push down retail food prices and ordered the meat-butter price "roll back" ended by Aug. 1.

The ban was incorporated in legislation extending the life of the Commodity Credit Corporation for two more years from midnight tonight and adding $750,000,000 to its present $2,650,000,000 lending powers. Both Senate and House approved the measure by far more than the two-thirds majority which would be necessary to override a veto. The House vote was 160 to 32, and the Senate vote, 62 to 13.

Less restrictive than the original House measure, the bill permits continued use of subsidies, up to $150,000,000 to meet increased transportation costs such as are now being paid on the movement of oil to the East Coast and on coffee imports, and to promote production of critical metals and war-essential foods. It also allows incentive payments on canning and specialty crops, price support for domestic vegetable oils and fats, and payments for sale of wheat for feeding purposes. However, no subsidies could be paid simply to reduce prices.

Before final passage, a provision prohibiting Government agencies from deducting farm benefit payments in calculating agricultural price ceilings was stricken out.

Just before final Congressional action, Lou R. Maxon, deputy administrator of the Office of Price

Continued on Page Seventeen

WALLACE AND JONES RENEW THEIR ROW AFTER 2-HOUR TALK

Conference Called by Byrnes Fails 'to Resolve and Determine' Controversy

SHARP STATEMENTS ISSUED

Secretary Says Charge of Delay by RFC in War Effort Is 'Dastardly' and 'Untrue'

By JOHN H. CRIDER
Special to THE NEW YORK TIMES.

WASHINGTON, June 30—An attempt by the War Mobilization Director, James F. Byrnes, to harmonize the differences between Vice President Henry A. Wallace and Secretary of Commerce Jesse H. Jones, failed today after he had summoned them to his office for a two-hour discussion this afternoon.

Tonight the Vice President issued a statement which somewhat tempered his bitter accusations against Mr. Jones made yesterday but said the fundamental differences remained.

To this the Secretary replied:

"Mr. Wallace in his statement tonight repeats that delays of the RFC have retarded the war effort. This dastardly charge is as untrue as when he first made it. As for the rest of his statement, Mr. Wallace was not authorized to speak for me. I will continue to speak for myself, and as previously stated, I shall insist upon a Congressional investigation."

The Vice President's statement made it clear that the basic differences between himself and Mr. Jones had been altered only to the extent that "Mr. Jones did not object" to Mr. Wallace's plan to ask Congress after its recess for funds for foreign procurement which would make it independent of the Reconstruction Finance Corporation, headed by the Secretary of Commerce.

There was no mention of Mr. Byrnes in the Vice President's statement, although it was the fruit of the War Mobilization Director's efforts to play the role of peacemaker for the Federal Bureaucracy cast for him by President Roosevelt's Executive Order of May 28 calling upon him to "resolve and determine controversies between such agencies or departments."

Meanwhile, the Senate, showing little indication at this point of being in a mood to grant the broad authority over foreign procurement expenditures sought by Mr. Wallace, inserted in the War Agencies Appropriation Bill an amendment by Senator Kenneth McKellar, Democrat, of Tennessee, providing that BEW could not use for foreign purchases any of the $36,000,000 appropriated without approval of a majority of the

Continued on Page Eleven

UNITED NATIONS FORCES MOVE FORWARD IN THE SOUTHWEST PACIFIC

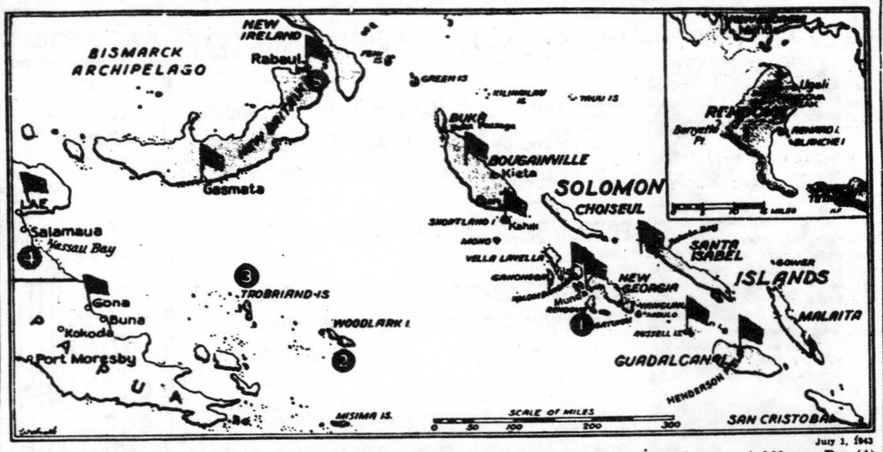

American troops landed on Rendova and New Georgia Islands (1), in the vicinity of the enemy air base at Munda, and engaged the Japanese. The inset shows this area in detail. To the west the Allies occupied Woodlark Island (2) and the Trobriand Islands (3) without opposition. In New Guinea they occupied Nassau Bay (4), just below Salamaua; the landing craft encountered only slight resistance. Apparently these widespread operations have as their ultimate goal the reduction of Rabaul (5), which was bombed.

76 BILLIONS SPENT IN U. S. FISCAL YEAR

71 of the Total Were for War—Public Debt Up to 140 Billions, Deficit to 55

Special to THE NEW YORK TIMES.

WASHINGTON, June 30—The United States ended its fiscal year tonight with a record of expenditures of more than $76,000,000,000, receipts of more than $21,000,000,000, a gross public debt of more that $140,000,000,000 and a deficit of more than $55,000,000,000.

The latest figures available at the Treasury were for June 26, four days before the actual end of the fiscal year. On that date total war expenditures for the year were $71,014,000,000, as against $25,515,000,000 on the same date in 1942.

Spending for civilian purposes was $5,375,000,000, as compared with $5,800,000,000 on the same day a year earlier. The War Department spent $41,690,000,000 and the Navy $20,513,000,000. War expenditures of the Agriculture Department totaled $2,005,000,000. The Maritime Commission spent $2,733,000,000.

In one year the public debt increased from $76,560,000,000 to $140,028,000,000 and the deficit advanced from $19,152,000,000 to $55,242,000,000.

Receipts of $21,625,000,000 up to

Continued on Page Twelve

Prime Minister Warns Axis Allied Attacks Are Imminent

By RAYMOND DANIELL
By Cable to THE NEW YORK TIMES.

LONDON, June 30—Prime Minister Churchill warned the Axis today that the Allies were preparing heavier blows on land and sea and by air from east, south and west to bring about the unconditional surrender that he and President Roosevelt declared at Casablanca was the price of peace.

The text of Mr. Churchill's address is printed on Page 4.

In the Mediterranean and "elsewhere," he said, heavy fighting probably would develop "before the leaves of autumn fall," but he added that large-scale amphibious operations take months to prepare.

Significantly, he dwelt at length and in considerable detail upon the growing scale and intensity of the British-American air offensive against Germany from this island, and indicated that Russian air power, long tied down to the battle lines, would soon be able to join in the attack on Nazi industry from the east.

A Major Victory at Sea

Reviewing the Battle of the Atlantic, he said a victory had been won at sea against the submarines two months ago comparable with the Allied conquest of Africa with the capture of 350,000 German and Italian prisoners and vast quantities of war material. He likened the victory in Tunisia to the Russian triumph at Stalingrad.

The Prime Minister was speaking in the ancient Guildhall, where he received freedom of the City of London, that square mile of the British capital that still bears the

Continued on Page Four

BERLIN EVACUATION REPORTED PLANNED

Swedes Hear Exodus Is to Start in Fall—Wuppertal Held Beyond Rebuilding

By GEORGE AXELSSON
By Telephone to THE NEW YORK TIMES.

STOCKHOLM, Sweden, June 30—Berlin will evacuate in the Fall women and children not engaged in the war industries, according to reliable information received here today through private channels.

Fear of heavier and more frequent Allied air raids with the coming of longer nights has prompted this decision, and authorities have already begun the preliminary arrangements, it is stated.

The extent to which the Ruhr has been hit by the RAF raids is indicated by a statement by Adolf Hitler's chief city planning consultant, Armaments Minister Albert Speer, just back from a tour of inspection of the devastated area.

He said it was not worth while to try to rebuild Wuppertal.

Continued on Page Three

MARTINIQUE YIELDS, ASKS TERMS OF U. S.

Robert, 'to Avoid Bloodshed,' Ready to Accept Change of French Authority

The Martinique radio broadcast a statement last night by Admiral Georges Robert, Vichy's High Commissioner on the island, asserting that he had asked the United States Government to dispatch a "plenipotentiary to fix the terms for a change of French authority."

The broadcast said that Admiral Robert had taken the action "to avoid bloodshed." It was recorded by Federal Communications Commission monitors, The United Press said.

The admiral has, since the fall of France, stood firm in his determination to hold Martinique and nearby French islands in the Caribbean under his own rule, loyal to Marshal Henri-Philippe Pétain, French Chief of State.

The reception of the broadcast was marred by technical difficulties, but those portions of the broadcast that could be heard said:

"Communiqué to the population:

"In order to avoid bloodshed between the French and * * * I have asked the Government of the United States, under the double condition of its renewing the guarantee to maintain French sovereignty in these islands and of the nonintervention of American forces, to send a plenipotentiary to fix the terms for a change of French authority.

"* * * my duty to the people and the Marshal * * *

"Admiral Robert."

Recently there have been unconfirmed reports of clashes between the Admiral's troops and elements favoring the rule of the islands by

Continued on Page Eight

War News Summarized

THURSDAY, JULY 1, 1943

The Allied Southwest Pacific and South Pacific Commands have started a broad offensive against Japanese positions. The first results of the combined naval, air and land operations are:

Landings on Rendova and New Georgia Islands in the Central Solomons, where fighting is going on.

Occupation, without opposition, of the Trobriand Islands and Woodlark Island off the southeastern tip of New Guinea at the north end of the Coral Sea.

A landing at Nassau Bay, ten miles south of Salamaua in New Guinea.

Heavy aerial bombardment of the big Japanese base at Rabaul, New Britain.

Gen. Douglas MacArthur is in general command of the combined operations, with Admiral William F. Halsey Jr. directing the offensive of the South Pacific forces. The battle area extends 300 miles north of Guadalcanal to Rabaul and 750 miles northwest to Salamaua [All the foregoing, 1:8.]

In London, Prime Minister Churchill pledged that after Hitler's defeat "every man, every ship and every airplane in the King's service that can be moved to the Pacific will be sent and there maintained in action * * * for as many years as are needed to make the Japanese, in their turn, submit or bite the dust."

Mr. Churchill then announced that "very probably there will be heavy fighting in the Mediterranean and elsewhere before the leaves of autumn fall." He characterized Tunisia and the campaign against the U-boat as the two greatest Allied victories of the war, and promised that every corner of Germany would be bombed as thoroughly as the Ruhr had been. [All the foregoing, 1:5-6.]

On the other war fronts, Flying Fortresses raided Le Mans in France and the RAF hit targets in western Europe [5:2-3], Reggio Calabria and Messina were bombed in the Mediterranean [6:2], and Russian troops captured a strong position on the Velikiye Luki front. [7:1.]

Admiral Robert, Vichy's High Commissioner in Martinique, asked the United States for terms under which the West Indies islands could be transferred to other French authority. [1:7.]

Cattle Grower Says 'Policymakers' Are to Blame in Meat Shortage

By JAY G. HAYDEN
North American Newspaper Alliance.

WASHINGTON, June 30—Joseph G. Montague, general counsel for the Texas and Southwestern Cattle Raisers Association, put the blame for the meat shortage today on "the unofficial policy-makers close to the President," thereby bringing into the open a charge which figured behind the scenes in the Congressional rejection of food subsidies and the retirement of Chester C. Davis as Food Administrator.

Speaking before the Senate Agricultural Committee, Mr. Montague said:

"Surrounding the President are a group of people who have no responsibility, yet determine policy and cause confusion in the meat situation. They are entrenched in power and determined to change the economic and social order."

Mr. Davis is believed to have had substantially this same thought in mind when he gave as his first reason for resignation that "I find I have assumed a public responsibility while the authority, not only over broad food policy, but day-to-day actions, is being exercised elsewhere."

Mr. Davis, according to his close friends, became convinced that the real policy-makers were the same old New Deal inner cabinet, including particularly Harry L. Hopkins, Associate Justice Felix Frankfurter and Judge Samuel Rosenman, which has functioned prominently throughout the Roosevelt Administration. Whether he was speaking of his own knowledge or merely

Continued on Page Seventeen

Laundry Workers Held Essential But the WMC Restricts Services

Special to THE NEW YORK TIMES.

WASHINGTON, June 30—The War Manpower Commission extended to the country's laundries today the same preferential treatment in the allocation of manpower as is given to essential war industries.

Laundries classified as "locally needed" by regional directors of the WMC will be supplied with workers by the United States Employment Service, will be protected from labor piracy and will have their existing labor force stabilized, except that there will be no occupational deferment under the Selective Service Act. They will receive this aid only if they discontinue luxury services to their patrons.

To be classified as "locally needed" they must meet standards agreed upon by the War Labor Board's Office of Civilian Requirements and the WMC. These standards are designed to enable the laundries to give adequate essential service to more people than they are now doing with their available labor force and to put maintenance services on a "rock-bottom, first-things-first basis."

Under the new ruling hand ironing, the retouching of all flat work and the retouching of wearing apparel by hand after pressing, except for a bare minimum required to make it presentable; fancy packaging and unnecessary folding are eliminated, and customers will be limited to one grade of starching of their shirts and other wearing apparel.

Laundries are expected to cooperate in inducing hotels, boarding houses and tourist homes to change bed linen only once a week for any one patron; limit each patron to one face towel and one bath towel

Continued on Page Ten

2-PRONGED DRIVE

Americans Battle Enemy on New Georgia and Rendova Islands

SALAMAUA IN PERIL

Allies Seize Trobriand and Woodlark Isles—Rabaul Pounded

By SIDNEY SHALETT
Special to THE NEW YORK TIMES.

WASHINGTON, Thursday, July 1—Combined Army and Navy forces under General Douglas MacArthur have opened the long expected offensive against the Japanese in the south and southwest Pacific.

Fighting was in progress on Rendova and New Georgia islands, which were hit by ground, naval and air forces in "closest synchronization," a communiqué from General MacArthur's headquarters in Australia reported today. Nassau Bay, ten miles south of the big Japanese base of Salamaua in New Guinea, fell to the Allies after a slight skirmish, and the Tobriand and Woodlark island groups, 300 to 400 miles west of the New Georgia group, were occupied without opposition.

The Allied push—aimed, observers here believe, at the major Japanese base of Rabaul, on New Britain Island—got under way yesterday, Solomons time, which was Tuesday here.

Nutcracker Move Seen

It was believed here, on the basis of early reports, that the fighting and occupations reported so far were preliminary to major actions to come. If bases in the New Georgias are consolidated, a two-way push against Rabaul might be developing, with one arm advancing northwestward from the Central Solomons and the other swinging across eastward from new bases in New Guinea.

United States heavy bombers carried out an attack on Rabaul during the night, dropping nearly twenty-three tons of high-explosive, fragmentation and incendiary bombs throughout the dispersal areas at the Vunakanau and Lakunai airdromes, the communiqué from Australian headquarters reported. "Several explosions" and "numerous fires" were observed, one of which was visible for 100 miles, the announcement said.

The big bombers, which have punished Rabaul extensively in recent weeks, ran into heavy Japanese anti-aircraft fire and interference from some enemy night fighters. One American bomber was missing after the raid.

The Tobriand and Woodlark islands will be valuable as steppingstones in a chain of fighter-plane bases from the Allied stronghold of Milne Bay, on the tip of New Guinea. Japanese-held Gasmata and Rabaul may be raided with comparative ease with the aid of these bays.

Navy Gives First News

The first report of landing actions came early yesterday when the Navy announced here in a communiqué that combined United States forces had landed June 30 (Solomons time) on Rendova Island, in the New Georgia group, which is only five miles from the important Japanese air base of Munda, on New Georgia Island, but that communiqué said, "No details have been received."

A hint that the fighting had extended came later from Secretary of the Navy Frank Knox in Los Angeles, where he is inspecting Pacific Coast installations. The Secretary declared that the Rendova attack was the beginning of "an offensive against the Japanese base at Munda and surrounding bases." Navy officials in Washington yesterday declined, however, to con-

Continued on Page Three

"All the News That's Fit to Print."

The New York Times.

LATE CITY EDITION
Moderately cool with gentle winds today.
Temperatures Yesterday—Max., 80; Min., 73
Sunrise, 6:23 A. M.; Sunset, 7:27 P. M.

Copyright, 1943, by The New York Times Company.

VOL. XCII..No. 31,268. Entered as Second-Class Matter, Postoffice, New York, N. Y. NEW YORK, FRIDAY, SEPTEMBER 3, 1943. THREE CENTS IN NEW YORK CITY

ALLIES LAND IN ITALY OPPOSITE MESSINA; 8TH ARMY LEADS, WITH AIR-NAVAL COVER; RUSSIANS DRIVE AHEAD, CAPTURING SUMY

HULL TO TAKE REINS OVER ALL AGENCIES IN ECONOMIC FIELD

Coordination of OEW, OFRRO and Lend-Lease Under State Department Is Due Soon

NOT ALL FRICTION ENDED

WFA and OEW at Odds—Capital Speculates on What Course Lehman Will Pursue

By JOHN MacCORMAC
Special to THE NEW YORK TIMES.

WASHINGTON, Sept. 2—The coordination of the Office of Economic Warfare, the Office of Lend-Lease Administration and the Office of Foreign Relief and Rehabilitation Operations by the State Department in a way which will give the department complete control over their activities and leave them as instruments executing its policies has been planned and will shortly be put in effect, it was learned today.

Part of the plan is the formulation of a definite and coordinated policy with regard to the international economic activities of the Government. Hitherto there has been a general understanding in theory, but in practice some of the agencies which were supposed to execute economic policy have worked at cross-purposes.

The conflict between the foreign activities of some of the Reconstruction Finance Corporation subsidiaries and those of the Board of Economic Warfare exploded recently in the row between Vice President Wallace and Secretary Jones, which led to the coordination of these activities by the OEW under Leo T. Crowley as its new head.

Some Friction Still Exists

But there is still uncertainty regarding the representative spheres of OEW, Lend-Lease and OFRRO and, for that matter, friction between OEW and the War Food Administration as regards foreign food purchases. The plan, therefore, is to have the State Department effect a final coordination of their efforts, and there is a possibility that some or all of them might be absorbed in the process.

This is not only believed to be the policy of the President and Secretary Hull, but it is understood to be approved by Mr. Crowley and Edward Stettinius Jr., lend-lease administrator. There is some doubt, however, whether ex-Gov. Herbert H. Lehman is willing to subordinate OFRRO to the State Department to the extent desired.

From a spokesman for Mr. Crowley it was learned that close collaboration with the State Department has from the first been one of his objectives. Mr. Crowley has indicated that as soon as the coordination is made and the administrative facilities have been set up, the time will have arrived for a substantial simplification of the Government's foreign economic set-up.

OEW Changes Held Temporary

It was because of these views that the reorganization of OEW announced Tuesday was regarded as of a transitory rather than permanent character.

For instance, James L. McCamy, who was appointed assistant to the director, will soon leave again to join the Bureau of the Budget. Hugh B. Cox, who will act as general counsel, will work only part time with OEW, and the rest of the time as assistant attorney general of the United States. No executive director was named, and Lauchlin Currie, who will act as executive officer, is on "loan" from the President's office.

Before OEW and lend-lease are placed under the State Department, however, the details of foreign economic policy will have been worked out and men of the requisite business ability will have been added

Continued on Page Seven

Meat Ration Points Are Cut But Butter Will Need More

Thirty-five Meat Items Are Reduced 1 to 2 Points on Report of Larger Supplies—Changes Take Effect Sunday

Special to THE NEW YORK TIMES.

WASHINGTON, Sept. 2—Point values of most meats were lowered today by the Office of Price Administration, effective Sunday through September. An exception to the increased purchasing power of red stamps was creamery butter. It will call for twelve instead of ten points a pound. The buying power of blue stamps was reduced by an increase in the point values of many processed fruits and vegetables.

The changes in red stamp values were based on the belief that more meat would be available to civilians for the rest of this month. The ration costs of most lamb and bacon cuts were reduced one to two points a pound. Lower values were fixed for sirloin steak, roasts of beef and several variety meats.

The increase in the point value of creamery butter is not likely to be noticed in most urban areas, where dealers, because of acute shortages, have been restricting customers to a quarter pound at a time and getting three points for the quarter pound, or twelve points a pound.

Farm or country butter was listed separately for the first time in the new point value schedules. To it a point value of six points a pound was assigned. Previously country butter had the same point value as creamery butter. The reduction was intended to spur the movement of farm-churned butter to urban markets to relieve the shortage of creamery butter.

"The further increase in the point value of creamery butter is necessary because purchases near butter-producing areas have been so large at a ten-point value that shortages developed in other parts of the country," the OPA said. "In addition butter production during

Continued on Page Eight

CONGRESS TAX MOVE IRKS MORGENTHAU

Joint Committee Plans to Subpoena Data Direct From Internal Revenue Body

Special to THE NEW YORK TIMES.

WASHINGTON, Sept. 2—A conflict has arisen between the joint committee of Congress on internal revenue taxation and the Treasury over the committee's power to obtain tax data direct from officials of any Government department or agency and this may lead to a test in the courts of the committee's authority.

The 1942 revenue act empowered the committee to obtain such data from officials of the Bureau of Internal Revenue or any other department without sending its requests through departmental heads.

The committee, jointly set up by the Senate Finance and House Ways and Means Committees, has seldom agreed with the Treasury on tax matters in recent years. Of late it has been paying less and less attention to the Treasury's views and insisting on writing its own tax bills.

It was to give Colin F. Stam, the committee's chief of tax experts, opportunity to make use of the fiscal and economic experience to be found in Government departments and particularly in the Internal Revenue Bureau that Congress was asked to authorize it to go over the head of Secretary Morgenthau to his subordinates and to deal similarly with other divisions.

Although neither the Treasury nor Mr. Stam would comment on

Continued on Page Ten

1,330 JAPANESE SAIL ON EXCHANGE LINER

Gripsholm Leaves on Second Trip—Teia Maru to Bring Americans Back Home

The exchange liner Gripsholm, painted white and carrying in huge letters on her side the word "Diplomat," sailed from her anchorage in New York Harbor early yesterday on her second mission to exchange Japanese civilians for Americans who have been interned in the Orient since December, 1941.

Gaily painted like the cruise ship she was before the United States Government chartered her in the spring of 1942 from the Swedish-American Line, the big vessel carried the gold and blue marks of Sweden, painted flags and brilliant lighting arrangements to identify her through submarine-infested waters.

In her cabins there were, according to announcements of the War and State Departments in Washington, 1,330 Japanese civilians who will be exchanged for Americans and nationals of other Western Hemisphere nations in the port of Mormugao, Portuguese India, on or about Oct. 15.

The Americans and their fellow internees—1,500 of them, including 1,250 citizens of the United States—are to travel from the Orient on the Japanese-flag liner Teia Maru.

The Washington announcements said that the Teia Maru was scheduled to leave Japan on Sept. 15, touching at ports in China, the Philippines and Indo-China to take on additional passengers, and calling at Singapore for fuel and wa-

Continued on Page Five

Browder Charges 'Bad Faith' Delays Opening a Second Front

Earl Browder, general secretary of the Communist party of the United States, asserted at a party meeting last night in Manhattan Center, 311 West Thirty-fourth Street, that Anglo-American relations with Soviet Russia would "deteriorate sharply" unless a second front in Western Europe was opened before the end of summer.

The meeting was a special one called to hear Mr. Browder discuss the present situation. About 3,000 persons were in the hall.

Mr. Browder argued that we should not wait until next spring in the hope that victory can then be "bought much more cheaply," but should land in full force now in an effort to win a quick victory and take some of the burden of land fighting off the Red Army. He held that military occupation by "fighting armies" was the only way nazism could be ended.

Mr. Browder, who is not a military expert, vigorously expressed the opinion that our troops were overwhelmingly able to open a second front whenever their leaders gave the word. But the British and American general staffs, he charged, have acted in the role of "politicians subject to reactionary influence," and have overruled themselves as military leaders, in which capacity, he said, they realize the need for a second front. Counting out "weakness" as a reason for not opening a second front, he said the only alternative was "bad faith."

Mr. Browder charged that "dark and sinister forces" in this country were accusing the Soviet Union of

Continued on Page Four

AIR BLOWS PRESSED

French Fields Pounded as Fortresses Join British in Sweeps

POWER PLANT IS HIT

Canal Locks Smashed on Key Dutch Route Serving Antwerp

New, Heavy Air Raids As Allies Land in Italy

By The United Press.

LONDON, Friday, Sept. 3—Powerful forces of Allied bombers ranged over the northern flank of the European continent early today, almost simultaneously with the invasion of Italy.

A long procession of bombers streamed out over the British coast, flying so high they could not be seen from the ground, although the roar of their motors was audible.

By The United Press.

LONDON, Friday, Sept. 3—American Flying Fortresses, culminating an evening of widespread activity that saw Royal Air Force Fighter Command planes in their biggest operation of the year, blasted enemy airfields at Mardyck and Denain in northern France late yesterday, a joint British-American communiqué reported today.

Squadrons of British Spitfires and Typhoons escorted medium B-26 Marauder bombers of the Eighth United States Air Force and RAF Boston, Mitchell and Ventura bombers in attacks on targets in Pas de Calais Department.

Fast and deadly P-49 Thunderbolts covered the Fortresses in their hard-hitting foray against the northern French airfields. "Good bombing results were observed on all targets," the joint communiqué said, adding that four enemy aircraft were destroyed—one by the Fortresses and three by Spitfires. One medium and one light bomber and two fighters were lost in the heavy operation.

The B-26 Marauder medium bombers of the Eighth United States Air Force attacked the power station at Mazingarbe, near Bethune, France, "with good results," the fighter pilots reported.

Continued on Page Six

RED ARMY ROLLING

Storms Ukraine Citadel and Seizes Towns on Kiev Rail Line

DONBAS KEYS TAKEN

Nazis Retreat Toward Dnieper—550 Places Fall in Two Days

By The Associated Press.

LONDON, Friday, Sept. 3—Moscow announced early today that five Red armies plunging westward had cut the Bryansk-Kiev railway 150 miles from Kiev, smashed German reinforcements in a six-mile gain on Smolensk and rolled up Axis lines in a new forty-five-mile-wide spurt in the Donets Basin.

Premier Joseph Stalin, in an order of the day, announced late yesterday that the Ukraine citadel of Sumy, ninety miles northwest of Kharkov, had fallen to Gen. Nikolai Vatutin's army, and a communiqué announced the capture of Krolevets and Yampol, two points on the vital Bryansk-Kiev railway linking the enemy's central and southern fronts.

Lisichansk, Voroshilovsk, Slavyanoserbsk and other cities were seized in the Donets Basin, while Budennovka, twenty miles from Mariupol, was taken in the push along the rim of the Sea of Azov, said the communiqué, recorded by the Soviet monitor.

250 More Places Overrun

The swiftness of the Russian advances and the tone of the communiqué indicated that the Germans were engaged in a large-scale retreat toward the Dnieper River, particularly in the huge Donets Basin. The bulletin, however, emphasized that the Germans were fighting stubbornly all along the 600-mile front.

More than 9,000 Germans were killed yesterday as the Red Armies overran nearly 250 cities and villages, many of them strategic prizes, for a two-day bag of nearly 550 localities.

Germany's 1941 invasion lines now have been cracked by the Russians in a 1943 offensive that has carried the Red Army more than half way along the comeback trail

Continued on Page Four

War News Summarized

FRIDAY, SEPTEMBER 3, 1943

Allied forces crossed the Strait of Messina from Sicily and landed in southern Italy early this morning to start the long-awaited invasion of Europe, according to a communiqué issued by the Allied Headquarters in North Africa. The landing was the culmination of a series of devastating air blows. [1:8, maps pages 1, 2 and 3.]

The Russian war machine rolled relentlessly on yesterday. The important Ukrainian town of Sumy was captured, the Bryansk-Kiev railway was severed and a wide advance was made in the Donets Basin, with every indication that a German retreat to the Dnieper River was in full swing. [1:5, map P. 4.]

Continuing the softening-up process on the Continent, Allied fighters and bombers hit airfields in Northern France shortly after RAF fighters had returned from the Netherlands, where they struck at some of the most vital water communications controlled by the Germans. The bomb racks were unloaded on the strategic Hansweert Canal, where three locks were hit. The RAF reported that 107,520 American tons of bombs had been dropped on Germany in the first eight months of 1943. [1:4, map p. 6.]

The Navy Department in Washington still withheld details of Tuesday's raid on the Marcus Islands, but some of the mystery was dispelled by the Japanese, who acknowledged damage to the strategic air and observation base and estimated the American task force at 160 fighter and bomber planes from two carriers. Military observers at Pearl Harbor believe that the Marcus raid was just a feint and that a major blow against Japan's outer defenses is near. [5:1.]

Allied bombers dropped a record of 206 tons of bombs on the Japanese bases at Madang, New Guinea, General MacArthur reported. Ground troops also were strafed at Salamaua. [5:5, with map.]

The Pacific phase of the war is believed to be one of the principal subjects being discussed by Prime Minister Churchill and President Roosevelt in Washington. They have been holding day and night sessions. The Prime Minister also has conferred with high military and supply mission heads. [4:4.]

Another indication of the stepped-up pace to launch a second or a third front was the report from Washington of an August output of 7,700 planes as against 7,373 for July and indications that the figure might top 8,000 in September. [1:7.]

ACROSS NARROW WATERS TO EUROPE

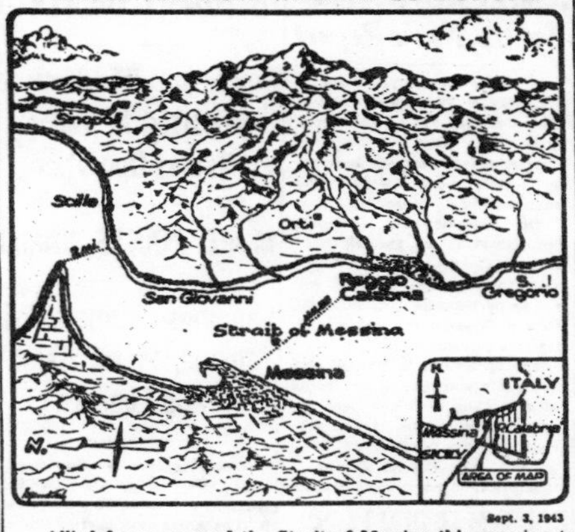

Sept. 3, 1943

Allied forces spanned the Strait of Messina this morning to land on the toe of Italy. This map, a perspective view looking eastward, gives an idea how the mainland appeared to the invaders.

Other Invasions This Year Anticipated in Washington

By ROBERT F. WHITNEY
Special to THE NEW YORK TIMES.

WASHINGTON, Friday, Sept. 3—While Washington slept, its somnolent thousands secure in the knowledge that plans laid at Quebec last week would be efficiently carried out, the word was flashed to the capital that the invasion of the Italian mainland had begun. It was the first penetration by the Allies of Fortress Europe and thus a historic event which defied the pledge of Adolf Hitler that his Reich, by its aggressions, would secure its future for a "thousand years."

Unlike the invasion of North Africa by American troops nearly a year ago and the opening of the Sicilian campaign about two months ago, the invasion was not announced in Washington. The first news to the public came in flashes from North Africa.

The announcement, as received here, told of Allied troops swarming across the Strait of Messina. Only on Tuesday Prime Minister Churchill, in his Canadian speech, had stated that the Germans had augmented their forces in Italy and intended to make a battleground of that country.

The Allied invasion was seen here as an answer both to that challenge by the Germans and to the demands that a second front be opened in Europe this year.

When the news came, it is probable that the President and Mr. Churchill, the pair who are directing the strategy of the two English-speaking nations of the United Nations, were awaiting the news of a successful landing together in the White House study, as it is known that when they meet neither one retires early.

It was hoped here in semi-official quarters that the invasion of Italy would answer the prayers of Russia that her Allies in the west would lift some of the load off her shoulders by an attack on the European Continent.

While it was confidently expected that the invasion of Italy

Continued on Page Three

PLANE OUTPUT 7,700 FOR AUGUST, A JUMP

Production This Month May Reach 8,000, WPB Says—Rise Despite New Designs

Special to THE NEW YORK TIMES.

WASHINGTON, Sept. 2—Aircraft production last month totaled 7,700 planes, compared with 7,373 in July, the WPB reported today in tones of elation.

On the basis of the August figure, airplane production in September will top 8,000, it was said.

The rise in output last month as compared with July was at the rate called for in the production schedule. Both July and August production were below the original schedule, WPB officials said. But they maintain that the schedules are "unrealistic" in that they do not take into consideration the shifts in production occasioned by design changes and by many other factors.

Schedules have been adjusted three times so far this year, one official said, and are likely to be changed again. He added that "I'd rather make 6,500 planes of the type we needed than to meet the schedules which include many of the types we don't need and would rather not have."

He contended that "we got the planes we wanted. Those we didn't want we didn't get."

The discrepancy between the

Continued on Page Seven

Portugal Weighs Idea of Fighting; Premier Tells People to Prepare

Neutral diplomatic quarters in London reported yesterday that Portugal was contemplating a declaration of war against Japan and might follow it with declarations against other Axis powers, according to The United Press.

The Portuguese action is said to arise from the fact that the Japanese established military control over Macao, in China near Hong Kong, as well as from Japanese occupation of Timor, in the southwest Pacific north of Australia.

Portuguese naval reservists have been called up during the past ten days. It was understood reliably that 10,000 reservists were being called to the Army. It was suggested that Portugal was now prepared to send expeditionary forces to free Macao and Timor.

The Government of Portugal on Wednesday night issued a formal statement "following fantastic rumors" and this statement gave the impression Portugal was on the eve of some important action.

LISBON, Sept. 2 (AP)—Premier Antonio de Oliveira Salazar stated today that Portugal's stepped-up military preparations were defensive but "in the unfortunate times in which we are living may have to be used against foreign enemies as much as against internal elements of national disintegration."

Clamping a tight censorship on speculation regarding the military preparations, Dr. Salazar cautioned against expecting any change in the country's foreign policy.

[The London Evening Standard interpreted the "mobiliza-

Continued on Page Five

DAWN IS ZERO HOUR

British and Canadians Storm Over Narrow Strait of Messina

ROME SAYS NOTHING

Allies Invade on Fourth Anniversary of Their War Declaration

By MILTON BRACKER
By Wireless to THE NEW YORK TIMES

ALLIED HEADQUARTERS IN NORTH AFRICA, Friday, Sept. 3—The Allies have breached the "Fortress of Europe." On the fourth anniversary of the British and French declaration of war against Germany, Allied troops are striving to establish a bridgehead on the Italian side of the Strait of Messina.

Under the thunderous support of Allied sea and air power, British and Canadian forces of the British Eighth Army crossed the narrow strip of water to bring the war at long last to the mainland of the Continent that Germany has enslaved.

Preceded by a pounding artillery barrage across the strait and by a number of reconnaissance landings, the main party set foot on the tip of the Calabrian Peninsula, opposite Messina, at 4:30 A. M. today [10:30 P. M. Thursday, Eastern War Time].

No details were available on either this morning's historic assault or the previous reconnaissance missions. The latter were, plainly, those referred to in German broadcasts as landing attempts beginning on Aug. 29, which the Germans said had been repulsed with heavy losses.

[A Mutual Broadcasting System commentator, speaking from Algiers, quoted an official Allied spokesman today as saying that the Allies were "apparently engaged in heavy fighting." The Associated Press reported from London.]

A special communiqué issued here at 7:20 A. M. said merely: "Allied forces under General Eisenhower continued their advance. British and Canadian troops of the Eighth Army, supported by Allied sea and air power, attacked across the Strait of Messina early today and landed on the mainland of Italy."

Field Guns Pave Way

ALLIED HEAQUARTERS IN NORTH AFRICA, Sept. 3 (U.P.)—British, Canadian and other troops of the British Eighth Army spearheaded the invasion armies, swarming across the Strait of Messina from Sicily under cover of Allied aircraft and the big guns of British and American warships. The Eighth Army's field guns helped to pave the way for the invasion troops with a thunderous barrage that silenced several of the

Continued on Page Two

Arnold in Britain To Meet Air Chiefs

By The Associated Press.

LONDON, Sept. 2—Lieut. Gen. Henry H. Arnold, chief of the United States Army Air Forces, and Maj. Gen. William C. Lee, commander of an air-borne division, who is known as the father of American parachute troops, arrived in Britain today from the United States. They plunged immediately into a study of the military set-up and recent operations by the Eighth United States Air Force.

General Arnold is here for conferences with Air Chief Marshal Sir Charles Portal, Lieut. Gen. Jacob L. Devers, commanding all United States forces in the European theatre; Maj. Gen. Ira C. Eaker, commander of the Eighth Air Force, and other British and American officers.

"All the News That's Fit to Print."

The New York Times.

LATE CITY EDITION
Continued moderately cool today; moderate winds.
Temperatures Yesterday—Max., 74; Min., 67
Sunrise, 6:30 A. M.; Sunset, 7:27 P. M.

VOL. XCII..No. 31,274. Entered as Second-Class Matter, Postoffice, New York, N. Y. NEW YORK, THURSDAY, SEPTEMBER 9, 1943. THREE CENTS IN NEW YORK CITY

ITALY SURRENDERS, WILL RESIST GERMANS; ALLIED FORCES LAND IN THE NAPLES AREA; RUSSIANS IN STALINO, CLEAR DONETS BASIN

SOVIET TIDE RISES

Swift Red Army Blows Capture Key City, Free Rich Region

DRIVE NEARS DNIEPER

More Rail Hubs Fall—Thrust Toward Kiev Also Extended

By The United Press.

LONDON, Thursday, Sept. 9—The Red Army recaptured Stalino, Russia's twelfth city, yesterday and freed the Donets Basin, which before the war produced more steel than Japan and Italy combined, in a great surge that took it to Grishino, ninety miles east of Dniepropetrovsk on the lower Dnieper River.

While the armies of Gen. Rodion Y. Malinovsky and Gen. Fedor Tolbukhin drove the enemy from the rich Donets Basin, crowded with coal mines and factories, the army of Gen. Konstantin Rokossovsky drove to a point ninety-six miles northeast of Kiev by capturing Borzna, twenty-three miles west of Bakhmach.

Bakhmach and Romni, forty-two miles to the southeast, were surrounded on three sides, a Moscow radio bulletin reported, and thus the Bakhmach-Kremenchug railroad was cut. The roads leading from Bakhmach to Kursk and Gomel had been cut previously and only the lines to Kiev and Odessa remained open.

Picked Troops Take Stalino

Red Army shock troops, picked from the sixteen infantry divisions that had driven the Germans through city after city in six days of tireless fighting, took Stalino by storm.

The Russian communiqué said the Red Army troops drove in on Stalino throughout Tuesday night and yesterday morning. They fought through the suburbs and then stormed the city from north and south, routing the enemy in a street-by-street fight and capturing a great store of spoils.

Twenty-five miles northwest of Stalino the Russians took Krasnoarmeiskoye, a big railroad junction controlling two of four rail roads leading west from the basin.

In all the Russians took, in addition to Stalino, a city of 462,000 persons, more than 150 towns in the Donbas alone, twenty of them important, in gains of up to twelve and a half miles. During their Donbas offensive the Russians took twelve towns of more than 50,000 persons each.

The Germans at Krasnoarmeiskoye were so swiftly beaten that the Russians took nineteen planes and several loaded railroad trains.

March on Kiev Gains

On the Kiev front, the Russians took more than sixty towns in advances of up to twelve and a half miles. Their capture of Borzna in that area meant that the battle for the Dnieper River line had started. An advance of twenty-three miles to Nezhin would cut the only remaining German supply line east of the river. The Russians had already advanced 101 miles in nine days from Rylsk, half the distance to Kiev.

More than 1,000 Germans were killed at Borzna, and 1,000 were killed in another sector.

South of Bryansk the Russians advanced up to six miles to take several villages. They were reported only twenty miles south of Bryansk. The Soviet communiqué, recorded from the Moscow radio, reported that the Russians were advancing west of the Navlya railroad junction in this area, driving the Germans through dense forests.

West and southwest of Kharkov nearly four miles were gained in some sectors and about 1,200 Germans were killed.

The Germans were first to ad-

Continued on Page Twenty-two

New Fascist Regime Set Up, Nazis Report

By Cable to The New York Times.

LONDON, Thursday, Sept. 9—The German radio announced early today that a "National Fascist government has been set up in Italy and functions in the name of Benito Mussolini."

The announcement, called a "proclamation by the National Fascist Government of Italy," said "this Badoglio betrayal will not be perpetrated. The National Fascist Government will punish traitors pitilessly."

The broadcast, in Italian, said nothing about the whereabouts of Mussolini, who has been reported under arrest. It was preceded by the playing of "Giovinezza," the Fascist anthem.

FOE'S MARCUS LOSS 80%, NIMITZ SAYS

U. S. Carrier Planes Alone Hit at Japanese Isle—Hell Cat Fighter Excels in Test

By ROBERT TRUMBULL
By Telephone to The New York Times.

PEARL HARBOR, Sept. 8—Admiral Chester W. Nimitz, Commander in Chief of the Pacific Fleet, issued today a communiqué that gave the first details of the raid on Marcus Island Sept. 1. Coincidentally three naval air officers who participated in the action gave an interview covering all phases of the raid, which they said destroyed a surprisingly well-fortified Japanese air base.

Action Consisted of Bombing

Admiral Nimitz's communiqué said that a United States Pacific Fleet task force under command of Rear Admiral Charles A. Pownall attacked the little island, 1,185 miles southeast of Tokyo, at dawn Sept. 1. The air officers revealed that the action consisted entirely of bombing and strafing by carrier-borne aircraft.

They said that the new Grumman F6F Hellcat fighter was employed in combat for the first time in the

Continued on Page Twenty-two

IN HEART OF ITALY

American 7th Army Is Reported in Van of Naples Operation

MORE POINTS NAMED

Landings Rumored at Genoa, Pizzo, Gaeta and Leghorn

By Wireless to The New York Times.

ALLIED HEADQUARTERS IN NORTH AFRICA, Thursday, Sept. 9—The Allies have carried the land campaign against the Nazis in Italy to the vicinity of Naples in new operations announced within twelve hours of the disclosure by Gen. Dwight D. Eisenhower that the Italian armed forces had unconditionally surrendered.

The news was announced here a few minutes past 6:30 A. M. in the following thirteen words:

"Further operations have started on the Italian mainland in the vicinity of Naples."

In the absence of the slightest expansion of the communiqué, no details are available as to the forces participating. The single fact remained that the attack had been pressed near Italy's southern metropolis and port, second only to Genoa, in what obviously was a major amphibious thrust.

Naples is a city of more than 700,000 population—nearer 1,000,000 if the suburbs are included. The assault was launched eighty-three years and two days after Garibaldi entered the city alone in a dramatic liberation gesture, which culminated in the unification of the country ten years later.

Although there is no indication just how near the city itself the landing or landings were carried out, it is plain that Naples is the objective of the sea-borne invaders.

[This dispatch did not indicate the make-up of the landing parties. A Tunis radio broadcast

Continued on Page Four

War News Summarized

THURSDAY, SEPTEMBER 9, 1943

Italy has surrendered unconditionally, and all hostilities between that country and the United Nations ceased yesterday. An armistice was signed last Friday, the same day that Italy was invaded, but the victors reserved the right to withhold announcement until the most favorable moment for the Allies. The armistice terms had been approved by the United States, Britain and Russia.

General Eisenhower, announcing the surrender, promised support to all Italians who helped fight the Germans. Marshal Badoglio issued a proclamation ordering all fighting against the "Anglo-American forces" to cease and commanding resistance to "attacks from any other quarter."

Allied radios and planes carried messages urging the Italians to take vengeance on their "German oppressors" and to prevent trains, ships and trucks from carrying German troops or supplies. [All the foregoing, 1:8; map, P.3.]

Landings in the Naples area followed only a few hours after the surrender announcement and it was believed the Allies were attempting to cut off German troops in southern Italy. The American Seventh Army was reported among the invading forces. [1:3; map, P. 4.] Earlier, the Italian Navy and merchant marine had been urged to take their ships to designated points and to scuttle the vessels as a last resort to keep them from the Germans. [7:4.]

Wild demonstrations of joy were reported from all over Italy, but in the north they gave way to sober realization of continued danger when the Germans occupied Milan and other cities and imposed martial law. [3:1.] No official comment came from Berlin, but the German radio, after withholding the news for hours, was furious at the "treachery." [1:5-6.]

Germany's Balkan satellites were so shaken by the Italian surrender that Bulgaria, Rumania and Hungary were reported ready to follow Italy out of the war. [10:3.]

President Roosevelt, in a radio address last night, termed the surrender a great victory for the Italian people as well as for the United Nations. But he warned: "The time for celebration is not yet. Our ultimate objectives in this war continue to be Berlin and Tokyo." [1:5-6.]

The actual fighting in Italy was of a minor nature. Land forces advanced on both coasts. [3:6.] Airfields were hit by Allied bombers and the Rome radio reported heavy raids on suburbs of the city. [4:1.]

With one Axis partner out of the war, the two others continued to be hit hard. The Red Army captured Stalino and cleared the Germans out of the Donets Basin. [1:1; map, P. 22.] Allied bombers from Britain struck enemy airfields in France and Belgium [23:2], while down in New Guinea Japanese troops were providing weak opposition as the Allies closed in on Lae. [22:1.]

The naval task force that raided Marcus Island Sept. 1 destroyed 80 per cent of the Japanese military installations. We lost three planes. [1:2.]

U. S. SOLDIERS IN LONDON CHEER THE NEWS

Americans in front of the Red Cross Washington Club in the British capital when the news of Italy's surrender was announced.

Associated Press Radiophoto, passed yesterday by censor

Announcements of the Surrender

By Broadcast to The New York Times.

ALLIED HEADQUARTERS IN NORTH AFRICA, Sept. 8 — The texts of the proclamations by Gen. Dwight D. Eisenhower and Premier Pietro Badoglio follow:

By GENERAL EISENHOWER

This is Gen. Dwight D. Eisenhower, Commander in Chief of the Allied Forces.

The Italian Government has surrendered its armed forces unconditionally. As Allied Commander in Chief, I have granted a military armistice, the terms of which have been approved by the Governments of the United Kingdom, the United States and the Union of Soviet Socialist Republics. Thus I am acting in the interest of the United Nations.

The Italian Government has bound itself to abide by these terms without reservation. The armistice was signed by my representative and the representative of Marshal Badoglio and it becomes effective this instant.

Hostilities between the armed forces of the United Nations and those of Italy terminate at once. All Italians who now act to help eject the German aggressor from Italian soil will have the assistance and the support of the United Nations.

By PREMIER BADOGLIO

The Italian Government, recognizing the impossibility of continuing the unequal struggle against the overwhelming power of the enemy, with the object of avoiding further and more grievous harm to the nation, has requested an armistice from General Eisenhower, Commander in Chief of the Anglo-American Allied forces. This request has been granted. The Italian forces will therefore cease all acts of hostility against the Anglo-American forces wherever they may be met. They will, however, oppose attack from any other quarter.

CITY 'JUMPS GUN' IN WAR BOND DRIVE

Rallies, Sales Begin on Vast Scale—State Savings Banks Will Invest $600,000,000

As President Roosevelt and Secretary of the Treasury Henry J. Morgenthau Jr. opened the Third War Loan Drive for $15,000,000,000 last night over the radio, it was announced here that in the campaign to raise the State's quota of $4,709,000,000 the mutual savings banks in the State would buy $600,000,000 in Government bonds. The United States Steel Corporation and its subsidiaries will buy $100,000,000 in Government securities, with parts of the total allocated to districts where the corporation operates.

Restive to get its drive under way, New York City held preliminary rallies yesterday as Army convoys took into the five boroughs Navy gunners who had been rescued at sea. The largest meetings were held in Times Square and on the steps of the Sub-Treasury Building at Wall and Broad Streets.

Burgess Hails Italy's Surrender

The thousands assembled in the streets for these two gatherings cheered wildly as speakers announced the capitulation of Italy. Ticker tape, confetti and torn paper were thrown from the windows of buildings where workers in the financial community were listening to the rally.

The unconditional surrender of Italy is "bullish news" and will be a great help in the bond drive, W. Randolph Burgess, chairman of the War Finance Committee for New York State, said later in the

Continued on Page Sixteen

President Hails Victory But Warns of Real Foes

By JOHN H. CRIDER
Special to The New York Times.

WASHINGTON, Sept. 8—President Roosevelt hailed the surrender of Italy tonight as "a great victory for the United Nations" and also "a great victory for the Italian people" against "their real enemies, the Nazis," but cautioned against over-optimism. Addressing the nation on the opening of the Third War Bond drive, the President said "the time for celebration is not yet" and added that "our ultimate objectives in this war continue to be Berlin and Tokyo."

Toward the middle of his speech the President interpolated three words which gave basis to reports that Allied armies already were on the move again in the Mediterranean when he spoke of troops in landing barges moving up to enemy coasts "at this moment."

"This war does not and must not stop for one single instant," he declared. "Your fighting men know that. Those of them who are moving forward through jungles against lurking Japs—those who are landing at this moment in barges moving through the dawn up the strange enemy coasts—those who are diving their bombs down on the target at roof-top level at this moment—every one of these men knows that this war is a full-time job and that it will

Continued on Page Seventeen

Germans Charge Betrayal by Italy In Plot With Russian Government

By GEORGE AXELSSON
By Wireless to The New York Times.

STOCKHOLM, Sweden, Sept. 8—Berlin's newspapers branded Italy's capitulation as cowardly treachery last night. The German press abounds in scatching denunciation of Premier Pietro Badoglio and King Victor Emmanuel, as well as the Italian people.

"Mussolini was too great a person for a nation like that," a German official said. This is the second time that Victor Emmanuel has broken his word, the newspapers say, because the King "left Germany in the lurch" in 1915 when he joined the Allies.

Forgetting its praise of the Italians during the heyday of their pact, Berlin now condemns the Italians as third-rate individuals. "The cowardly perfidy of Badoglio caps the crime," one paper said, "by being committed in collusion with the Soviet Government, which is treason not only against Italy and Germany but also against all Europe."

Berlin added that the Germans had no intention of giving up their entrenchments in Italy, where they hoped to offer efficient resistance. Italy, since last night, is German-occupied territory to the extent that the Germans have been able to gain a firm footing there. In the Italian provinces occupied by the Germans, Berlin boasts fascism will be revived even if "we leave it to the Italians in those provinces to organize themselves along fascist lines.

Official circles are reviving accusations of broken words of honor

Continued on Page Nine

GEN. EISENHOWER ANNOUNCES ARMISTICE

Capitulation Acceptable to U. S., Britain and Russia Is Confirmed in Speech by Badoglio

TERMS SIGNED ON DAY OF INVASION

Disclosure Withheld by Both Sides Until Moment Most Favorable for the Allies—Italians Exhorted to Aid United Nations

By MILTON BRACKER
By Wireless to The New York Times.

ALLIED HEADQUARTERS IN NORTH AFRICA, Sept. 8—Italy has surrendered her armed forces unconditionally and all hostilities between the soldiers of the United Nations and those of the weakest of the three Axis partners ceased as of 16:30 Greenwich Mean Time today [12:30 P. M., Eastern War Time].

At that time, Gen. Dwight D. Eisenhower announced here over the United Nations radio that a secret military armistice had been signed in Sicily on the afternoon of Friday, Sept. 3, by his representative and one sent by Premier Pietro Badoglio. That was the day when, at 4:50 A. M., British and Canadian troops crossed the Strait of Messina and landed on the Italian mainland to open a campaign in which, up to yesterday, they had occupied about sixty miles of the Calabrian coast from the Petrace River in the north to Bova Marina in the south.

The complete collapse of Italian military resistance in no way suggested that the Germans would not defend Italy with all the strength at their command. But the capitulation, in undisclosed terms that were acceptable to the United States, the United Kingdom and the Union of Soviet Socialist Republics, came exactly forty days after the downfall of Benito Mussolini, the dictator who, by playing jackal to Adolf Hitler, led his country to the catastrophic mistake of declaring war on France three years and three months ago this Friday.

Negotiations Begun Several Weeks Ago

The negotiations leading to the armistice were opened by the war-weary and bomb-battered nation a few weeks ago, it was revealed today, and a preliminary meeting was arranged and held in an unnamed neutral country.

The Italians who had approached the British and American authorities were bluntly told that the terms remained what they had been: unconditional surrender. They agreed, and the document was signed five days ago. But it was agreed to hold back the announcement and its effective date until the moment most favorable to the Allies.

That moment came today, when the Allied Commander in Chief, in a historic broadcast, announced the armistice. He concluded with the reminder that all Italians who aided in the ejection of the Germans from Italy would have the support and assistance of the United Nations.

One hour and fifteen minutes after the General's voice had gone out over the air, Marshal Badoglio faced a microphone in Rome and confirmed the armistice. He concluded with the promise that the Italian forces would oppose attacks "from any other quarter," although they were laying down the arms that they had taken up against the Anglo-American armies.

Military Aspect Emphasized

Although it was emphasized that the armistice was a strictly military instrument, "signed by soldiers," it was disclosed that it contained a clause binding Italy to comply with political, economic and financial conditions to be imposed at the Allies' discretion.

[It was believed that the armistice conditions were substantially the same as those imposed on France in 1940, which allowed the Germans to use all strategic French ports and military bases to wage war against Britain, The United Press reported.]

Immediately after the announcement of the armistice, the Allies made two appeals—one to the Italian people and one to the Italian Fleet—urging them to rally to a cause that was, in effect, the liberation of their own country. The appeal to the people was disseminated by radio and air-borne leaflet, while that to the Navy was broadcast by Admiral Sir Andrew Browne Cunningham, the Allies' Mediterranean naval commander.

The Italian people, particularly transport, railroad and dock workers, were asked not to give the slightest aid to the Germans. The men who man Italian ships received specific instructions how to bring their vessels into the protection of the United Nations.

Although the fear was proved unjustified by Marshal Badoglio's broadcast, the Allies had taken no chances of a German move to forestall his giving the news to the people. As a safeguard, they had obtained from the Italians an agreement to leave one senior military representative behind when the others returned to Rome. This man is now in Sicily and presumably, had Marshal Badoglio not gone on the air, his representative would have broadcast the decision to the Italian public.

As a further earnest of good faith, Marshal Badoglio had arranged to send the text of the proclamation that he made this evening to Allied Headquarters here. He kept his word.

1,181 Days at War and Losses

Italy quit the war after 1,181 days, during which she steadily lost territory and prestige. Last May 7, with the fall of Tunis and Bizerte, the last Italian soldier in North Africa was doomed. Since then, Sicily, part of Metropolitan Italy, was occupied in thirty-eight days.

The Italians endured two raids on military targets in Rome

Continued on Page Three

"All the News That's Fit to Print."

The New York Times.

LATE CITY EDITION
Cloudy and warmer today; fresh winds.
Temperatures Yesterday—Max., 30; Min., 9
Sunrise, 8:18 A. M.; Sunset, 5:34 P. M.

VOL. XCIII. No. 31,381. Entered as Second-Class Matter, Postoffice, New York, N. Y. NEW YORK, SATURDAY, DECEMBER 25, 1943. THREE CENTS IN NEW YORK CITY

EISENHOWER NAMED COMMANDER FOR INVASION; 3,000 PLANES SMASH FRENCH COAST; BERLIN HIT; ROOSEVELT PROMISES NATION A DURABLE PEACE

STRIKE CALLED OFF BY 230,000 IN TRAIN AND ENGINE UNIONS

But Non-Operating Men Meet Carriers and Reject Offer Made for Overtime Pay

GIVE BYRNES NO ANSWER

He Says Agreement Must Meet Requirements Set Forth in the Stabilization Program

By LOUIS STARK
Special to THE NEW YORK TIMES.

WASHINGTON, Dec. 24—The Brotherhood of Locomotive Engineers and the Brotherhood of Railroad Trainmen today canceled notices for a strike of their 230,000 members on Dec. 30 in view of President Roosevelt's offer and their acceptance of arbitration by the Chief Executive.

The conductors, firemen and switchmen's unions, also members of the "Big Five" operating and transportation brotherhoods, representing more than 120,000 employes, have rejected arbitration by the President and have not called off the strike of their members set for Dec. 30.

The other major development today in the railroad wage situation was a three-hour conference in the office of James F. Byrnes, chief of the Office of War Mobilization, participated in by committees of the railroads and of spokesmen for the fifteen non-operating unions, whose 1,100,000 members are scheduled to strike on Dec. 30.

At this meeting it was reported that the non-operating unions asked for a wage increase of 6 cents an hour as compensation for overtime after forty hours. These employes receive overtime after forty-eight hours of service. The carriers are reported to have offered 4 cents an hour for overtime, but it is understood that this was rejected by the unions.

Insists on Negotiations

B. M. Jewell, chief negotiator for the unions, is said to have been pressed by Mr. Byrnes for a reply to the President's demand that the non-operating employes permit him to act as sole and final arbiter in their dispute with the carriers.

The union leader is said to have replied with some asperity that the President last night gave the unions until Monday to reply to the arbitration proposal, and that in the meantime they had obtained from the President authority to proceed and seek an agreement with the carriers, whose committees were headed by Jacob Aronson, vice president of the New York Central Railroad.

The offer of 4 cents an hour for overtime was understood to be above the 4 to 10 cents an hour sliding scale wage increase recommended in the non-operating unions' case by an emergency board, convened after Frank M. Vinson, the Economic Stabilization Director, had rejected the 8 cents an hour proposal of a previous emergency board.

Byrnes' Statement

The conference in Mr. Byrnes' office, which was attended for a short time by Mr. Vinson, ended at 5:30 P. M. and the following statement was issued on Mr. Byrnes' behalf:

"The representatives of the carriers and the non-operating brotherhoods met in the conference room of the Office of War Mobilization.

"The representatives of the carriers were not present at the conference the President held with the representatives of the brotherhoods yesterday afternoon. Justice Byrnes advised the carriers' representatives that the President desired to know whether they would object to his arbitrating the differences between the carriers and the non-operating brotherhoods.

"The representatives of the carriers stated that they were entirely willing to agree that the President should arbitrate the differences just as they had agreed in

Continued on Page Twenty-six

17 Perish as Fire Sweeps 42d Street Lodging House

Scores Hurt in 'Bowery-Type' Building Disaster, Worst of Its Kind Here in Years—Many Trapped Asleep

Sixteen bodies had been removed last night from a five-story brick structure at 437-439 West Forty-second Street, between Ninth and Tenth Avenues, the four upper floors of which were occupied by a "Bowery-type" lodging house, after one of the city's worst fires in years virtually had consumed the entire interior.

A seventeenth victim died at 7:15 P. M. in Roosevelt Hospital, to which most of the score of injured were removed.

The actual loss of life probably never will be known. With most of the victims burned beyond recognition and in many cases nothing remaining but bones, the task of counting the dead and identifying them was proving almost impossible. Authorities, after checking for hours, could not even determine how many persons were in the building at the time of the fire. They were faced with the fact that the lodging house had beds in three-foot by six cubicles, separated by flimsy plywood partitions, and in hall-like dormitories "accommodating" 248 persons. It was said the beds were well filled with restaurant and other night workers.

The fire, believed to have smoldered for three hours, started at 2 P. M. as if set by a hundred torches. Trapped in their sleep many were burned to death in their "cells," rooms so tiny that a lodger had literally to crawl into bed through a special door on a central vertical hinge that folded to permit entry.

The victims groped through con-

Continued on Page Twenty-six

WLB PEACE OFFER WIRED STEEL UNION

Davis Tells Murray Retroactivity Can Be Reconsidered Within Wage Formula

Special to THE NEW YORK TIMES.

WASHINGTON, Dec. 24—William H. Davis, chairman of the War Labor Board, telegraphed today to Philip Murray, president of the CIO United Steel Workers, that if labor members of the board desired to reconsider their vote on the retroactive pay issue "the public members will favor such reconsideration."

But, while he indicated that a retroactive basis might be approved within the framework of the present ("Little Steel") wage stabilization formula, Mr. Davis stated in his message that the public members could not now determine "any question of retroactivity that might come up in any future change in the wage stabilization policy."

Presuming that any such future change would be applied to "all wage-earners," he wrote that retroactivity in general or in particular ought to be decided when and if the change is made.

[A production stoppage was reported early this morning by The Associated Press with the expiration of contracts at midnight covering 35,000 employes at the Republic Steel Corporation and Youngstown Sheet and Tube Company. At these plants in Youngstown and in Cleveland picketing began.]

"Misunderstanding" Deplored

Mr. Davis' telegram said:

"You are quoted as saying that the proposal of the public members of the War Labor Board as to retroactivity in the steel negotiations violates principles enunciated by the board in the recent cases affecting hundreds of thousands of workers, that the proposal of the

Continued on Page Twenty-six

CITY AN OPEN HOUSE FOR WARTIME YULE

Heart-Warming Parties for Service Men and Women Are Chief Among Festivities

New York was far from a big, cold, gray city as it ushered in its third wartime Christmas last night with heart-warming church services, gay parties, gifts for the ill and unfortunate, and messages of good-will that brought cheer to its teeming millions and to the men and women visitors in the services.

It will not be a white Christmas, according to the weather man, but it will be cold.

Tens of thousands of visitors, many of them members of the families of service men, were in the city for the week-end. Railroads, doing a peak business, were handicapped by the bitter cold in the surrounding country. Virtually every train to and from the city was loaded to capacity, with standees in the aisles. Because of the cold, many trains were late.

Grand Central Terminal and the Pennsylvania Station were packed. Policemen kept the crowds moving. Buses and bus terminals throughout the city did a land-office business, too.

Stores Experience Let-Up

Only in the stores did Christmas Eve bring a let-up. While business was brisk, the real crush had subsided and only last-minute shoppers were on hand.

The churches of all faiths welcomed the Holy Day with midnight services, offering prayers for a victorious peace. There were many men in uniform at masses, carol services and communion.

Virtually every Roman Catholic church celebrated a midnight mass by permission of Archbishop Francis J. Spellman. Episcopal churches celebrated communion, while many churches of other faiths held can-

Continued on Page Nine

Biggest of War Plants Will Make Army Bomber Engines at Chicago

By The United Press.

CHICAGO, Dec. 24—The country's largest war plant, a series of structures sprawling over 500 acres of land, was ready today to turn out an unending stream of engines for Army bombing planes.

The giant inland plant on Chicago's South Side was built by the Dodge division of the Chrysler Corporation. Willow Run could be set down in the main building with enough room left to lay out twenty baseball diamonds.

There are nineteen buildings in the plant, all ready for production. The main building, the machining-assembly unit, covers eighty-two acres.

The plant has fourteen cafeterias and kitchens, butcher shops and bakeries to feed employes.

A parking lot a mile and a quarter long will accommodate 14,000 automobiles. The interplant communication system has 500 miles of telephone lines. Utility services are sufficient for a city of 75,000 population.

Officials revealed that the machine shops had been turning out parts for 2,200-horsepower, eighteen-cylinder Wright engines.

The plant, already called "Hitler's headache," will employ more than 25,000 persons when it enters mass production.

Prior to the completion of the Chicago plant, the bomber factory owned by the Government and operated by Henry Ford at Willow Run, twenty-five miles from Detroit, was called the largest war production unit in the world. It covers two square miles.

RECORD AIR BLOW

'Forts,' Liberators and Medium Bombers Rock 'Special' Targets

ALL CRAFT RETURN

RAF Pounds the German Capital With 1,120 Tons Before Dawn

By DAVID ANDERSON
By Cable to THE NEW YORK TIMES.

LONDON, Dec. 24—The greatest number of American heavy bombers ever to take off from Britain attacked "special military installations" of the Germans along the coast of northern France today as part of record operations of probably 3,000 Allied warplanes across the Channel.

Before dawn hundreds of the most powerful bombers of the Royal Air Force struck Berlin again with more than 1,120 tons of high explosives and fire missiles.

Several features of this two-fisted battering by the Allied air forces on the eve of Christmas made the day a memorable one for the enemy, even taking into account the Anglo-American achievements of recent weeks.

Headquarters of the United States Eighth Air Force announced that 1,300 planes handled by American crews took part in the daylight missions.

An even greater number of RAF, Dominion and Allied planes were out. Every one of the bombers and fighters of the joint forces returned to its base, according to a communiqué issued by headquarters of the United States Army here and the British Air Ministry.

Included in the American force were the largest formations of Flying Fortresses and Liberators ever sent into the air. Since an estimated 750 United States "heavies" at one time have attacked targets in western Germany within the past month, the day's operations entailed the use of close to, if not exceeding, 800 four-motored bombers.

The most concentrated attacks were carried out in the Pas-de-Ca-

Continued on Page Three

TO KEEP IT BY ARMS

President Says 4 Nations Agree on This for as Long as Necessary

'COST MAY BE HIGH'

German Might Must End, He Says on Air, Warning 'Japs' of Bad News

The text of the President's address appears on Page 8.

By JOHN H. CRIDER
Special to THE NEW YORK TIMES.

HYDE PARK, N. Y., Dec. 24—President Roosevelt promised the country and the world this Christmas Eve that they could look for insured peace with "certainty," even though "the cost may be high and the time long," and said that the United States, Great Britain, Soviet Russia and China were agreed to use force to maintain that peace "for as long as it may be necessary."

Speaking from the study in the Franklin D. Roosevelt Library, one of his favorite rendezvous, with his family gathered informally around him, the President gave his first comprehensive report on his recent conferences in the Middle East over the most extensive broadcast facilities ever set up in this country.

For the first time the President tempered his "unconditional surrender" ultimatum of Casablanca by stating that the United Nations did not want to enslave the German people but wanted them to have "a normal chance to develop in peace as useful and respectable members of the European family."

Here appeared to be one of the great achievements of the conference at Teheran—a united view by the Allies in Europe on what kind of a post-war Germany they would look for, which closes the gulf which appeared to exist between the Anglo-American "unconditional surrender" demand, and the more hopeful outlook for the future which the Russians have been

Continued on Page Eight

War News Summarized

SATURDAY, DECEMBER 25, 1943

President Roosevelt proudly announced to the world yesterday the appointment of General Dwight D. Eisenhower as supreme commander of the Anglo-American invasion forces—a selection, he said, that was made at the Teheran conference, where every point concerning the impending east-west-south attack on Germany had been decided.

It was announced from London that General Wilson would succeed General Eisenhower as commander of the Allied forces in the Mediterranean theatre; that General Montgomery would be chief of British Army units under General Eisenhower; that General Alexander would head the Allied forces in Italy, and that General Spaatz would be American Air Force commander against Germany. [All the foregoing, 1:8.]

Peace is certain, but the cost of bringing it about will be high and the realization may be distant, President Roosevelt declared during the Christmas Eve broadcast from his Hyde Park home. He said the United Nations had no desire to enslave the German people but wanted them to develop as respectable members of the European family. As for Japan, he said that empire is being enveloped in a band of steel and there is plenty of bad news for the Japanese in the offing. [1:5.]

Speaking from the German-surrounded Vatican, Pope Pius XII made a plea for a just peace and declared that a normal measure of power and the employment of force were needed to achieve it, but he decried any harsh imposition supported by arms alone. [1:6-7.]

An estimated 3,000 American and British planes of virtually all types—the greatest concentration in air history—bombed the Pas-de-Calais area of France, where, it is believed, the Germans have implanted rocket guns. In this, the fifth straight assault on these targets, the American Eighth Air Force sent 1,300 planes, a record number for any single operation. All Allied planes returned. The attack followed a Royal Air Force blow at Berlin, reportedly hitting the southeast industrial area near Tempelhof. [1:4, map P. 3.]

The fortified town of Gorodok, seventeen miles from Vitebsk and on the Vitebsk-Nevel railroad, was successfully stormed by the Russian Army, which drove ahead to capture sixty other places. Southwest of Zhlobin, in southern White Russia, large German tank and infantry attacks were beaten back. [1:7, map, P. 5.]

The British Eighth Army captured Vezzani, three miles southwest of the Adriatic port of Ortona, where fighting continued in the streets. There was little activity except for patrol thrusts on the Fifth Army front, because of deep mud. Medium Allied bombers struck at the Riviera coast, hitting bridges, railroads and viaducts. [1:6-7.]

Cape Gloucester, which seems to be shaping up as another possible invasion point on New Britain Island, was hit by 300 more tons of Allied aerial bombs, bringing the total tonnage dropped since Dec. 1 to 2,500. [6:1.]

The Navy announced that the United States submarine Grayling was presumably lost with her complement of sixty-five men. [6:2.]

NEW INVASION COMMANDER IN CHIEF

Gen. Dwight D. Eisenhower

The New York Times, 1943

Pope Prays for Just Peace Kept by Wise Use of Force

By The Associated Press.

LONDON, Dec. 24—Praying that this may be the last war Christmas and that a truly Christian peace may be celebrated in the coming year, Pope Pius XII today called for the world's responsible leaders to check the instincts of hate and vengeance and give rise to "the resplendent dawn of a new spirit of world union."

The text of the Pope's address appears on Page 10.

Raising his voice to a vibrant ring in outlining "the principles for a peace program," the Pontiff called for a "normal measure of power," sanctions and "the employment of force" to achieve and maintain peace, but warned that true peace "can never be a harsh imposition supported by arms" alone.

"An hour like the present—so full of possibilities for vast beneficent progress no less than for fatal defects and blunders—has perhaps never been seen in the history of mankind," said the Holy Father, who spoke on Christmas Eve from the bayonet-circled Vatican, where he has been isolated except by radio since the Germans occupied Rome in September.

The 35-minute address was delivered on the radio in Italian, but an official English language translation later was made available.

Juridical Basis for Peace

"A true peace is not the mathematical result of a proportion of forces, but in its last and deepest meaning is a moral and juridical process," said the Pope, speaking from what he called the "abysmal ruins of this terrible war."

"It (peace) is not, in fact, achieved without the employment of force, and its very existence

Continued on Page Ten

RED ARMY TAKES KEY TO VITEBSK

Gorodok, 17 Miles From Goal, Falls After Russian Feint Outwits Nazi Defense

By The Associated Press.

LONDON, Saturday, Dec. 25—The Russian Baltic Army cracked a model German defense-in-depth line and captured the heavily fortified lake town of Gorodok, seventeen miles north of Vitebsk yesterday, sweeping on over 2,000 German dead in a continuing offensive to take sixty more towns and hamlets, Moscow announced early today.

Resuming their drive after a two-day slow-down, the Russians swept to within fifteen miles of the Vitebsk-Polotsk rail line, an important east-west supply artery for the Germans, as they advanced southward along the Nevel-Vitebsk railroad.

In another fighting area to the south—southwest of Zhlobin—the

Continued on Page Five

8th Army Wins Town Near Ortona; Americans Take a Hill, Lose One

By MILTON BRACKER
By Wireless to THE NEW YORK TIMES.

ALGIERS, Dec. 24—The Allied armies in Italy kept up pressure all along the line yesterday despite the imminence of Christmas, but were unable quite to complete the capture of Ortona or accomplish substantial gains on the Tyrrhenian half of the front.

Although Canadian units of Gen. Sir Bernard L. Montgomery's Eighth Army had driven back the last German defenders of Ortona to the northwest corner of the shell-blasted and tank-razed town, the defenders kept returning fire and apparently intended to deprive the Allies of the full use of the most important port immediately below Pescara as long as possible.

Evidence of the toll the Germans have been paying for their desperate defense of the area was the discovery of a new cemetery at the crossroads just southwest of Ortona with at least 100 German graves.

The Eighth Army did manage to wrest from the enemy another village three miles southwest of Ortona and a mile beyond the Ortona-Orsogna road. It was Vezzani, which is three and a half miles from the coast and, like Ortona, just about twelve from Pescara. Other units of General Montgomery's veteran army have also penetrated to the outskirts of Villa Grande, a mile northeast of Vezzani on a secondary road paralleling the coast.

On the Fifth Army front the

Continued on Page Three

GENERAL IS SHIFTED

Choice of 'Big 3' Parley, He Has Montgomery as British Field Leader

WILSON IS SUCCESSOR

Mid-East Head Honored—Spaatz to Direct U. S. Air Strategy

Special to THE NEW YORK TIMES.

HYDE PARK, N. Y., Dec. 24—President Roosevelt announced today the appointment of Gen. Dwight D. Eisenhower to lead the invasion of Europe from the north and west, and from London came word that Gen. Sir Bernard L. Montgomery of North African fame would head the British troops under General Eisenhower to form a proved and hard-hitting team to lead the assault on Adolf Hitler's "Fortress Europe."

The President's announcement of General Eisenhower's selection at the recent Teheran conference to lead the main attack against Germany also set to rest the old rumors regarding the probable appointment of Gen. George C. Marshall, Army Chief of Staff, to that post.

The President, in his radio report today on the recent conferences at Teheran and Cairo, also named Lieut. Gen. Carl A. Spaatz as commander of "the entire American strategic bombing force operating against Germany."

This was taken to mean that while General Eisenhower will confine his command to the mass attack on Europe from the north and west, General Spaatz' command over all American strategic bombardment of Germany extends to operations against Germany from all neighboring bases.

Quashes Marshall Rumors

The President gave a vivid picture in his radio report of complete agreement between Prime Minister Churchill, Premier Stalin and himself regarding a detailed program for the annihilation of Germany by land and air from all directions.

He also paid high tribute to General Marshall, presumably to set old rumors at rest. Some persons have argued that the position to be occupied by General Eisenhower is of greatest importance, but the official decision now revealed seems to give credence to the opinion that the most important position in the Army is that of Chief of Staff, just as Washington is the only place from which the whole global operation can be commanded.

"To the members of our armed forces, to their wives, mothers and fathers, I want to affirm the great faith and confidence that we have in General Marshall and Admiral King (Chief of Naval Operations), who direct all of our armed might throughout the world," the President declared.

Their Military Genius Stressed

"Upon them," he said, "falls the responsibility of planning the strategy; of determining where and when to fight. Both of these men have already gained high places in American history; places which will record in that history many evidences of their military genius that cannot be published today."

The announcement from London told, not only of General Montgomery's appointment to head the British invasion forces under General Eisenhower but also of Gen. Sir Henry Maitland Wilson's appointment to replace General Eisenhower as commander of the Mediterranean Theatre and Gen. Sir Harold R. L. G. Alexander's appointment to command all Allied forces in Italy.

The Teheran military decision announced by the President proved as much as anything else that the American handling of the invasion of North Africa and of Italy had deeply impressed the United States allies. Those invasions may now be regarded as the testing phase of the main European invasion, since the American officers identi-

Continued on Page Two

"All the News That's Fit to Print"

The New York Times.

LATE CITY EDITION

Partly cloudy, slightly warmer today; gentle to moderate winds.

Temperatures Yesterday—Max., 63; Min., 55

Sunrise, 5:26 A. M.; Sunset, 8:23 P. M.

VOL. XCIII . No. 31,544. Entered as Second-Class Matter, Postoffice, New York, N. Y. NEW YORK, MONDAY, JUNE 5, 1944. THREE CENTS NEW YORK CITY

ROME CAPTURED INTACT BY THE 5TH ARMY AFTER FIERCE BATTLE THROUGH SUBURBS; NAZIS MOVE NORTHWEST; AIR WAR RAGES ON

TRANSIT MEN BALK AT MAYOR'S INQUIRY INTO OUTSIDE JOBS

Demand for Sworn Statements Covering Family Earnings Evokes Union Protest

RESENTMENT WIDESPREAD

Many Department Heads Cold Toward Policy and Some Authorize Dual Work

By PAUL CROWELL

Widespread resentment among city employes against Mayor La Guardia's crusade to keep them from holding outside jobs on their own time was intensified yesterday. It became known that Investigation Commissioner Edgar Bromberger, by direction of the Mayor, had asked the 35,000 employes of the unified transit system to make sworn answers to forty questions concerning their own employment and that of all working members of their families.

The Transport Workers Union and other organizations representing city transit workers already have registered informal protests and are considering formal action. It was reported that the TWU was prepared to ask its members receiving such questionnaires from Commissioner Bromberger's office to turn them over to the union.

The questionnaire, of a type said to have been sent to employes of other city agencies, asks the transit worker to give full details about his own job, any job he may have outside, any job his wife may hold, any jobs his children may be filling Full details concerning pay rates on all such jobs are demanded. The workers are asked also how they obtained outside jobs, whether they paid anyone to get them and whether they are making payments to anyone in connection with outside jobs.

Board Members Dislike Policy

The regulations of the Board of Transportation do not forbid the holding of outside jobs and individual members of the board were known to feel that so long as employes were punctual and efficient in their tasks their outside activities were their own affair. Despite this feeling, however, the board is prepared to carry out the policy laid down by the Mayor. An informal survey of other city agencies conducted last week indicated that most of their heads held about the same attitude, but felt that the Mayor's policy must be carried out if he insisted upon it.

The Mayor's insistence that city employes, regardless of departmental rules forego such activities, led him recently to demand that charges be brought against an electrical engineer employed by the Board of Transportation who was teaching one night a week at City College, receiving $12 for each night's work. An exchange of views between the Mayor and the Board of Transportation resulted in a decision to let the employe continue teaching until the end of the current term, with the understanding that he would not resume teaching in the fall.

The electrical engineer, who is a graduate of one of the country's leading technical schools, was certified by the Board of Transportation, after investigation, to be efficient, painstaking and punctual, and the Mayor was told that his outside work made him a better city servant, while the small additional income was a welcome addition to his modest salary. It was also pointed out to the Mayor that there was nothing in the board's rules or the law to bar the outside work The Mayor is reported to have replied that the man must keep one job or the other, but could not hold both.

Outside work by employes is a live issue in the Board of Transportation, where it is estimated that at least 10 per cent of the 35,000 transit workers have extra work to increase family income.

Resentment against the Mayor's

Continued on Page 11

Laval Tries to Shift Funds to Argentina

Pierre Laval, chief of the Vichy government, recently tried to transfer $50,000 from Spain to Argentina, the Brazzaville radio said yesterday in a broadcast recorded at the Columbia Broadcasting System's short-wave listening station.

"A Madrid bank revealed to the Spanish authorities that a deposit of $50,000 had been made with them for transfer to an Argentinian bank," the French radio said. "An inquiry was opened, and the person behind the depositor was discovered: He is Pierre Laval."

The same broadcast reported:

"Germans in France have been buying gold at very high prices. Among the German agents arrested by French police for illegal traffic in gold was one who identified himself in order to be freed. He told the police commissioner that he was the director of a bank in a small German town. Because of his age, he had not been drafted into active military service, but his competence in financial matters made possible his being used in this work, in which he had been engaged since 1940."

JOHNSTON IN RUSSIA SCOFFS AT U. S. REDS

Business Leader Also Praises Soviet 'Capitalism'—Calls Ideologies Bridgeable

By The United Press.

MOSCOW, June 4—With straight-from-the-shoulder frankness, Eric Johnston, president of the United States Chamber of Commerce, told 100 Soviet trade leaders yesterday that a gulf separated the economies of the United States and Russia, but that bridges of practical cooperation could be thrown across that gulf.

Mr. Johnston advocated extensive post-war trade and visits between American business and "Soviet capitalists" as one bridge, but said that "each of our countries should be allowed to pursue its own unique economic experiment unimpeded by the other."

Bluntly, he told the Russians that Americans "were most private-minded and most individual-minded and, make no mistake, we are determined to remain so and even become more so."

Mr. Johnston, who arrived in Russia last week, was luncheon guest of A. I. Mikoyan, Soviet Foreign Trade Commissar, at Spiridonovka House. At the table sat Soviet trade experts, members of the Soviet Foreign Office, United States Ambassador W. Averell Harriman and Soviet military men.

At first the Russians appeared nonplussed by Mr. Johnston's bluntness, but later they burst into gales of mirth at his sallies at American Communists and Marxians.

"I shall try to show you my admiration for your heroic deeds and

Continued on Page 6

FOE 'EXPLAINS' STEP

Hitler Ordered Troops Out to Save Rome, Germans Assert

ENEMY PLEA BARED

Kesselring Made Last-Minute Renewal of Open-City Offer

By The Associated Press.

LONDON, June 4—The Germans announced tonight in a special communiqué—broadcast after the Allies had liberated Rome—the withdrawal of German troops to the northwest of the city and said that the Allies had received a plan whereby Rome would have been regarded as an "open city."

The open-city proposals were said to have been advanced at 11 P. M. on Saturday, less than twenty-four hours before Rome changed hands. The first word from Adolf Hitler's headquarters in several days asserted that the fight in Italy would continue and that measures were being taken "to force final victory for Germany and her allies." The communiqué said:

"As the front line, in the course of the present fighting in Italy, was gradually approaching nearer and nearer to the city of Rome, there was danger that Rome, one of the oldest cultural centers of the world, would be directly involved in the present fighting. Hitler has ordered the withdrawal of German troops to the northwest of Rome to prevent the destruction of Rome.

"The struggle in Italy will be continued with unshakable determination to break the enemy attacks and to force final victory for Germany and her allies. The necessary measures for an eventual German victory are being taken in close collaboration with fascist Italy and other allied powers.

"The year of invasion will bring Germany's enemies an annihilating defeat at the most decisive moment."

Kesselring's Proposals Listed

Field Marshal Gen. Albert Kesselring, the German commander in Italy, sent the Allies proposals that Rome be regarded as an open city, a special announcement from Hitler's headquarters said. The statement was broadcast by the German radio and was received only after a dispatch filed from Rome had announced the crushing of the last German resistance units within the city. The broadcast said:

"The German High Command announced that the supreme commander of German troops in Italy, Field Marshal Kesselring, had submitted proposals to the Vatican with the request that they should be conveyed to the Anglo-American High Command. The proposals confirmed the recognition of Rome

Continued on Page 4

Enraged Bull Kills 2 Brothers, Gores Neighbor on Long Island

Special to THE NEW YORK TIMES.

BABYLON, L. I., June 4 — Two dairy farmers, brothers, were found this morning gored and trampled to death on the Ames Farm in North Babylon, victims of their Guernsey bull, which had run wild and scattered their herd of thirty cows over near-by roads. A neighbor, trying to round up the scattered herd, was gored in the groin by the infuriated animal.

State troopers were forced to shoot and kill the belligerent bull.

The victims were George W. Ames, 41 years old, and his brother, James Hawley Ames, 35, who operated the Ames Farm on Phelps Lane, North Babylon. So far as is known no one saw the unequal encounter that cost them their lives. Their bodies were discovered, lying about 100 feet apart, several hundred yards from the cow barn.

The first intimation that anything was amiss came with complaints to the State Police in North Babylon that the Ames cows were wandering off the pasture and on the near-by Phelps Lane and Belmont Road. Two State troopers were sent to the farm and succeeded in getting most of the cows back into the pasture along with the bull. They put in a call for two additional troopers to round up the remainder of the herd.

Their suspicions aroused by the fact that the milk delivery truck, fully loaded, was standing in its place although it usually left on its rural route at 8 A. M., the troopers made their way to the farmhouse. There they found Mrs. Kathleen Ames, mother of the two men, and her daughter, Jane L. Ames, a school teacher.

A search of the farm was begun and Trooper Anthony Cherry came

Continued on Page 20

THE FIRST OF EUROPE'S WAR CAPITALS TO FALL TO THE ALLIES

The sign tells the troops they have entered Rome. The New York Times (U. S. Signal Corps Radiotelephoto)

U. S. 'HEAVIES' BOMB IN FRANCE ALL DAY

Attack Boulogne Area Twice, Rip Rail, Air Targets Near Paris—Genoa Blasted

By JAMES MacDONALD

By Cable to THE NEW YORK TIMES.

LONDON, Monday, June 5—Continuing to pave the way for the Allied invasion of the Continent hundreds of Allied bombers and fighters from Britain scorched a 200-mile stretch of the French coast yesterday and penetrated inland.

Three separate missions were carried out by the Flying Fortresses and Liberators of the United States Eighth Air Force with fighter escort over northwestern France. They met little Luftwaffe opposition; the enemy flak ranged from moderate to heavy.

In the morning and again in the afternoon strong formations of the

Continued on Page 5

Road to Rome Hard Fought, Yet Crowded With Civilians

By MILTON BRACKER

By Wireless to THE NEW YORK TIMES.

IN THE OUTSKIRTS OF ROME, June 4—The Fifth Army's entry into the suburbs of Rome was made along Highway 6—the Via Casilina—which runs into Rome at Centocelle, a suburb test known for its airport. But the advance did not mean a simple triumphal procession into the heart of Rome. It meant going in in careful infantry columns along the sides of the road. Most of the men had their bayonets fixed and they wore deadly earnest expressions because two wrecked Sherman tanks along the approaches told what had happened to other Americans earlier today.

Just before 4 P. M., a huge column of smoke billowed up from the southwest corner of the city, indicating a demolition. At the same time, a mine went off with a terrible burst beyond the farthest of the two tanks, and it tore an Italian woman to pieces. As the afternoon wore on, the sniping

Continued on Page 4

CONQUERORS' GOAL REACHED BY ALLIES

Fifth and Eighth Armies Drive Up From South on Rome in a Historic Campaign

By HERBERT L. MATTHEWS

By Wireless to THE NEW YORK TIMES.

ROME, June 4—The Allies' troops fought their way into Rome this morning and at nightfall they were still fighting on the outer edges, which the Germans were defending despite all their protestations about considering Rome an open city. Other large German units faced entrapment south of Highway 6 unless they could be pulled back across the Tiber or through Rome.

But Rome has been reached—the goal of conquerors throughout the ages, though none was ever before able to make the almost impossible south-north campaign. What Hannibal did not dare to do, the Allies' generals accomplished, but at such a cost in blood, matériel and time that it will probably never again be attempted.

All roads from all over the world led to Rome today as a United

Continued on Page 3

CITY'S FALL FOCUSES POLITICAL CHANGES

Victor Emmanuel's Promise to Retire Recalled — Badoglio Cabinet May Step Down

Special to THE NEW YORK TIMES.

WASHINGTON, June 4 — Pending receipt of final details of the fall of Rome, most Government leaders tonight refrained from direct comment. It was felt that the first official reaction to the Allied victory would come from President Roosevelt in the radio address that the White House announced he would make tomorrow night.

Interest in the news of the capture of the Italian capital centered not so much in the military victory as in the probable political consequences, particularly those stemming from King Victor Emmanuel's recent statement that he planned to retire as Italy's ruler as soon as Rome fell to the Allies.

The King announced April 12 that he intended to turn Italy's affairs over to Crown Prince Humbert, and said the transfer of power would take place "on the day on which the Allied troops entered Rome."

Even more important than this move are the effects the change may have on the future of the Italian Government now headed by Marshal Pietro Badoglio. Developments, it was said, will be watched closely not only as to other high appointments to be made after Prince Humbert takes over control but also as to any alterations in the structure of the Italian Government.

While the diplomatic and politi-

Continued on Page 4

War News Summarized

MONDAY, JUNE 5, 1944

Rome was liberated from the Nazi-Fascist aggressors last night. The first European capital to be wrested from the enemy came under full Allied control when a force that had fought its way up from the old Anzio beachhead knocked out a German scout car in the center of the city. There was fierce fighting with enemy rear-guard detachments at the outskirts of Rome before the city was liberated.

Fifth Army units and the vanguard of the Eighth Army, which entered the Eternal City later, were sent in hot pursuit of the fleeing Germans. Rome was found to be 95 per cent intact, with destruction centered in the railroad yards. [All the foregoing 1:8; maps P. 2.]

German artillery and snipers held off the Allied advance between the airport at Centocello and the city limits. Civilians, obviously happy over the departure of the Nazis, remained calm as United Nations troops moved in. [1:5-6.]

Hitler's headquarters announced after the Fifth Army had entered the city that the Germans had withdrawn to new lines northwest of Rome. Shortly before the city fell they dispatched a proposal that Rome be declared an open city. [1:3.]

Capture of Rome, according to military observers in London, made it much more likely that the main objective of the offensive—destruction of the German Tenth and Fourteenth armies—would be accomplished, with possible enemy losses reaching up to 100,000. [3:1.]

The AMG, following closely upon the victorious Allied forces, was fully prepared to undertake the gigantic task of feeding some 2,000,000 civilians. Vast stocks of food have been accumulated for distribution. [1:6-7.]

Washington withheld official comment until President Roosevelt's radio address tonight, but the capital was interested in how soon King Victor Emmanuel would fulfill his promise to retire when Rome had fallen to the Allies. [1:7.]

American heavy bombers from Britain smashed three times at enemy installations in France yesterday as the air invasion continued unabated against little enemy opposition. Italian-based aircraft struck rail lines on the French-Italian border. [1:4.]

United States troops resumed the offensive against the three airfields on Biak Island, off New Guinea. Thirty Japanese planes were shot down in widespread fights from Biak to Truk. [8:2.] Continued improvement in Allied positions was reported from Burma [8:3] although in China the Japanese made some gains toward Changsha while losing ground in other sectors. [8:4-5.]

Eric Johnston, president of the United States Chamber of Commerce, told 100 Soviet trade leaders at a Moscow luncheon that the way to bridge the economic gulf separating American and Russian economies lay in closer knowledge and greater mutual respect. [1:2.]

AMG Will Rush Food for Rome, Teeming With 750,000 Refugees

By HAROLD CALLENDER

By Wireless to THE NEW YORK TIMES.

ALGIERS, June 4—The fall of Rome will add about 2,000,000 persons to those whom the Allies have assumed responsibility of feeding, Allied authorities estimated today. But the Allied Military Government, now operating under the Allied Control Commission, has long prepared for the task and is believed to be ready.

The normal population of the Italian capital is estimated to have been swollen by 750,000 refugees from Naples and other places.

Allied authorities have stocks of wheat, canned milk and dehydrated vegetables ready to send to Rome quickly with the cooperation of the Fifth and Eighth Armies regarding transport by trucks.

At Anzio landing facilities have been built since the establishment of the bridgehead, and ships can be unloaded at Gaeta.

In the plans already made Rome has been divided into regions for the distribution of foodstuffs by Italian and Allied personnel under the authority of the commission. An emergency system has been prepared to provide strict control over the black market, which otherwise might absorb the local produce destined to go into the Allied pool for distribution on a ration basis to the masses who cannot afford the black market.

Capt. Matthias F. Correa, former United States Attorney for the Southern District of New York, has a staff of investigators, including 150 Guardia di Finanza, ready to combat the black market

Continued on Page 4

AMERICANS IN FIRST

U. S. Armor Spearheads Thrust Through Last Defenses of Rome

FINAL BATTLE BITTER

Fifth and Eighth Armies Rush On Beyond City in Pursuit of Foe

By The United Press.

NAPLES, June 4—The Fifth Army captured Rome tonight, liberating for the first time a German-enslaved European capital. German rear guards were fleeing in disorganized retreat to the northwest.

Except for the railway yards, smashed by the Allies' bombs, the city is 95 per cent intact United Press correspondents reported, after their arrival in the city.

Late tonight, the British Eighth Army, rushing into Rome from the southeast along the Via Casilina, was reported to be joining the Fifth Army in close pursuit of the hard-pressed enemy remnants, under orders to destroy them to a man if possible. Only enough troops to maintain order and ferret out any German snipers or suicide nests were to be left in Rome as the Allies' main armies pounded on without pausing to celebrate their greatest triumph, coming 270 days after the start of the Italian campaign.

[The Allies battled German rear guards to the edge of the ancient Forum, The Associated Press reported. A force from the old Anzio beachhead completed the mopping up of German forces at 9:15 P. M. by knocking out an enemy scout car in front of the Bank of Italy, almost within the shadow of Trajan's Column.]

Final Stand at Rome's Gates

At the very gates of Rome, the Germans had made a final stand but Lieut. Gen. Mark W. Clark, after having waited three hours for the enemy troops to withdraw in accordance with their own declaration of Rome as an open city, ordered a violent anti-tank barrage. Then masses of Fifth Army men and weapons crashed into the city and began mopping up enemy snipers and a few tanks and mobile guns trying to cover the retreat.

More of the enemy survivors of the Allies' whirlwind offensive were streaming in congested retreat to the northwest at the mercy of the Allies' planes, which, during the day, destroyed or damaged 600 enemy trucks and other vehicles. The Germans' jammed traffic columns stretched fifty-five miles to Lake Bolsena.

Direct radio contact with American correspondents in Rome was established tonight. A United Press reporter said that the main entry into the city had been made along the Via Casilina, which passes through the Porta Maggiore at the southeastern edge of the city. Other Allied troops were reported to have fought their way through the Ostiense freight yards, just south of St. Paul Gate, the main entrance to the city from due south and only one and one-quarter miles from the Venice Palace.

The entry into Rome came with dramatic suddenness after the Al-

Continued on Page 3

President to Talk On Rome Tonight

By The United Press.

WASHINGTON, June 4—A fifteen-minute radio address will be made by President Roosevelt to the nation tomorrow night on the liberation of Rome, the White House announced tonight.

Mr. Roosevelt will speak from 8:30 to 8:45 P. M.

The President's message will be broadcast over all major networks.

"All the News That's Fit to Print"

The New York Times.

Copyright, 1944, by The New York Times Company.

6 A. M. EXTRA

Partly cloudy and warmer today; moderate to fresh winds.

Temperatures Yesterday—Max., 67; Min., 51

Sunrise, 5:35 A. M.; Sunset, 8:26 P. M.

VOL. XCIII. No. 31,545. Entered as Second-Class Matter, Postoffice, New York, N. Y. NEW YORK, TUESDAY, JUNE 6, 1944. THREE CENTS IN NEW YORK CITY

ALLIED ARMIES LAND IN FRANCE IN THE HAVRE-CHERBOURG AREA; GREAT INVASION IS UNDER WAY

ROOSEVELT SPEAKS

Says Rome's Fall Marks 'One Up and Two to Go' Among Axis Capitals

WARNS WAY IS HARD

Asks World to Give the Italians a Chance for Recovery

The text of President Roosevelt's address is on Page 5.

By CHARLES HURD

Special to THE NEW YORK TIMES.

WASHINGTON, June 5—President Roosevelt hailed tonight the capture of Rome, first of the three major Axis capitals to fall, as a great achievement on the road toward total conquest of the Axis. Rome, he said, marked "one up and two to go."

The President spoke for a quarter-hour on the radio, as had been announced yesterday, but his speech was notable for its lack of heroics. It was in no sense a speech of triumph, but rather a tribute to the United Nations forces and leadership that drove the Germans from Rome.

With this tribute he combined a solemn warning that much greater fighting lies ahead before the Axis is defeated, as well as high tributes to the Italian people, whom he again welcomed as a people into the family of nations opposed to the Axis.

"Italy should go on," Mr. Roosevelt said, "as a great mother nation, contributing to the culture and the progress and the good-will of mankind, developing her special talents in the arts, crafts, and sciences, and preserving her historic and cultural heritage for the benefit of all peoples.

"We want and expect the help of the future Italy toward lasting peace. All the other nations opposed to fascism and nazism ought to help to give Italy a chance."

Shrines Should Live, He Says

President Roosevelt saw considerable significance in the fact that Rome should be the first Axis capital to fall. He remarked its shrines, "visible symbols of the faith and determination of the early saints and martyrs that Christianity should live and become universal," and added that "it will be a source of deep satisfaction that the freedom of the Pope and of Vatican City is assured by the armies of the United Nations."

There is significance, too, he added, in the fact that Rome was liberated by a composite force of soldiers from many nations.

Reviewing the military picture, the President pointed out that "it would be unwise to inflate in our own minds the military importance of the capture of Rome." He cautioned his auditors that while the Germans have retreated "thousands of miles" across Africa and back through Italy "they have suffered heavy losses, but not great enough yet to cause collapse."

"Therefore," he added, "the victory still lies some distance ahead. That distance will be covered in due time—have no fear of that. But it will be tough and it will be costly."

Turning to the relief problem in the newly liberated portion of Italy, Mr. Roosevelt noted that some persons thought of the financial cost, but he maintained that the work would pay dividends "by eliminating fascism" and any future desire by Italians to "start another war of aggression." Relief has been planned, he added, but transport demands are so great that "improvement must be gradual."

He warned Italy that it "cannot grow in stature by seeking to build up a great militaristic empire,"

Continued on Page 5

Conferees Accept Cabaret Tax Cut

By The Associated Press.

WASHINGTON, June 5—A House-Senate conference committee agreed today to cut back the cabaret tax from 30 to 20 per cent, but eliminated a provision exempting service men and women from the levy.

The group decided to put the national debt limit at $260,000,000,000 as originally requested by the Administration.

The action is subject to House and Senate votes. The conferees met informally today, but members said that the decisions probably would stand as their final recommendation.

The House, at the insistence of a group of Republicans, passed a bill raising the debt ceiling only from $210,000,000,000 to $240,000,000,000. The Senate then put the figure at $260,000,000,000 and attached a rider reducing the cabaret tax from 30 to 20 per cent and exempting men and women in uniform from paying the tax on their checks.

Some tax experts argued that this exemption would make administration of the excise on night clubs impossible.

FEDERAL LAW HELD RULING INSURANCE

Supreme Court, 4-3, Decides Business Is Interstate and Subject to Trust Act

Special to THE NEW YORK TIMES.

WASHINGTON, June 5—The Supreme Court, by a four-to-three decision today, held that the insurance companies of the country, with assets of $37,000,000,000 and annual premium collections in excess of $6,000,000,000, are in interstate commerce and thus subject to the Sherman Anti-Trust Law.

The decision upset precedents which began with a contrary decision by the court more than seventy-five years ago and have been reaffirmed repeatedly since the adoption of the anti-trust law in 1890.

The majority decision, written

Continued on Page 13

War News Summarized

TUESDAY, JUNE 6, 1944

The invasion of western Europe began this morning.

General Eisenhower, in his first communiqué from Supreme Headquarters, Allied Expeditionary Force, issued at 3:30 A. M., said that "Allied naval forces supported by strong air forces began landing Allied armies this morning on the northern coast of France."

The assault was made by British, American and Canadian troops who, under command of Gen. Sir Bernard L. Montgomery, landed in Normandy. London gave no further details but earlier Berlin had broadcast that parachute troops had landed on the Normandy Peninsula near Cherbourg and that invasion forces were pouring from landing craft under cover of warships near Havre. Dunkerque and Calais were being heavily bombed, the Germans said.

Later announcements from Berlin said that there was fighting between Caen and Trouville and that shock troops had swung into action to halt the invasion. [All the foregoing, 1:8.]

General Eisenhower, in an order of the day to each member of the "great crusade," told his men the enemy would fight savagely and added: "We will accept nothing less than full victory. Good luck." In a broadcast to the "Peoples of Western Europe," he said the day would come when he would need their full help. A special word to France added that Frenchmen would rule the country. [1:6-7.] Almost simultaneously it was announced that General de Gaulle had arrived in London. [6:2.]

The liberation of Rome in no way slowed the Allied pursuit of the tired and disorganized German armies in Italy yesterday. Armored and motorized units sped across the Tiber River to press hard upon the retreating enemy's heels. Five hundred heavy bombers joined with lighter aircraft to smash rail and road routes leading to northern Italy and to add to the foe's demoralization. The Eighth Army, despite heavy opposition, especially northeast of Valmontone, captured a number of strategic towns. [1:3; map P. 2.]

General Clark said that parts of the two German armies had been smashed. He doubted the ability of the German Fourteenth to put up effective opposition and declared that the Tenth had taken a bad beating. [3:1.]

King Victor Emmanuel fulfilled his promise and turned over all authority to his son, Crown Prince Humbert. [1:5-6.]

President Roosevelt warned the people of the United States in a radio talk last night not to over-emphasize the military significance of the liberation of Rome. "Germany has not yet been driven to surrender," he said. "Victory still lies some distance ahead. * * * It will be tough and it will be costly." The President appealed to the world to give Italy a chance to contribute her share to a lasting peace. [1:1.]

In the Pacific theatre Americans were converging on the Biak airfields. Allied planes sank one and damaged two Japanese destroyers and shot down at least eighteen aircraft. [8:1.]

PURSUIT ON IN ITALY

Allies Pass Rome, Cross Tiber as Foe Quits Bank Below City

PLANES JOIN IN CHASE

1,200 Vehicles Wrecked —Eighth Army Battles Into More Towns

By The Associated Press.

ROME, June 5—The Allies' armor and motorized infantry roared through Rome today without pausing, crossed the Tiber River and proceeded with the grim task of destroying two battered German armies fleeing to the north.

Fighter-bombers spearheaded the pursuit, jamming the escape highways with burning enemy transport and littering the fields with dead and wounded Germans. The enemy was tired, disorganized and bewildered by the slashing assault, which in twenty-five days had inflicted a major catastrophe on the Germans and liberated Rome almost without damage.

Railway Yards Bombed

Five hundred American heavy bombers blasted railway yards at five points in northern Italy between Venice and Rimini along which the Germas might attempt to move reinforcements and equipment to bolster their beaten armies. Hour after hour, the Allies' planes swept down on highways leading northward and tore the fleeing enemy apart. Twelve hundred combat vehicles were destroyed from dawn to dark yesterday, and hundreds more today. Farther north, medium bombers smashed bridges and rail facilities.

[The Germans have abandoned the entire left bank of the Tiber from Ostia, at its mouth, to Rome, according to a Vichy broadcast quoted by The Associated Press.

[The Germans are already entrenched in mountain positions

Continued on Page 2

FIRST ALLIED LANDING MADE ON SHORES OF WESTERN EUROPE

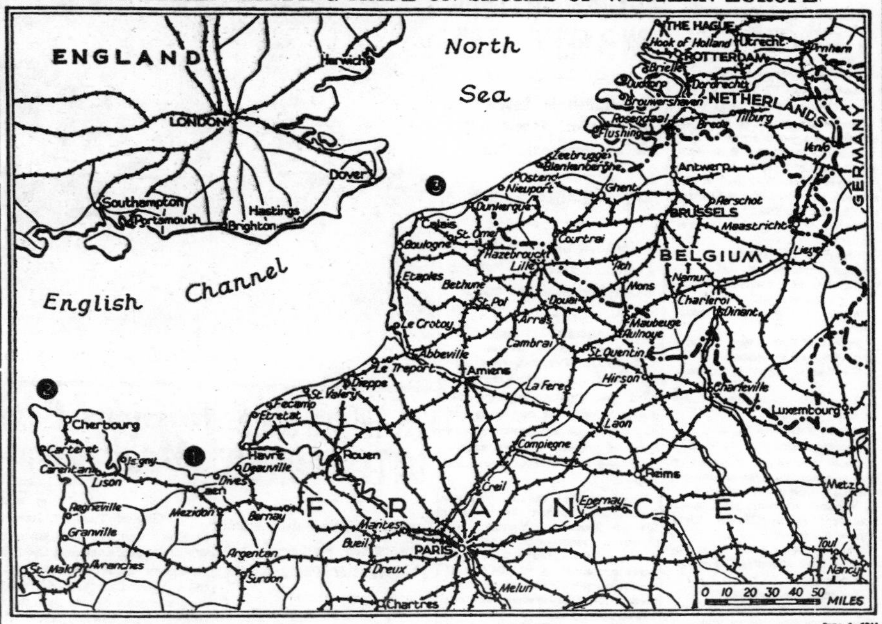

June 6, 1944

General Eisenhower's armies invaded northern France this morning. While the landing points were not specified, the Germans said that troops had gone ashore near Havre and that fighting raged at Caen (1). The enemy also said that parachutists had descended at the northern tip of the Normandy Peninsula (2) and heavy bombing had been visited on Calais and Dunkerque (3).

POPE GIVES THANKS ROME WAS SPARED

Voices Appreciation to Both Belligerents in Message to Throng at St. Peter's

By Wireless to THE NEW YORK TIMES.

VATICAN CITY, June 5—Pope Pius XII appeared on the balcony of St. Peter's at 6 P. M. today to thank God that Rome had been spared from the ravages of war while before him in the densely packed square of St. Peter's and the new broad Via Della Conciliazione tens of thousands of Romans cheered themselves hoarse.

It was the third time today that the Pontiff had showed himself to cheering crowds, as he had appeared twice at a window of his office this morning. But this was a solemn, sacred occasion and no one knowing anything about Pius XII can doubt the fervor of his thankfulness that Rome had been saved.

The Pontiff seemed strong and well and his voice carried far, though it was difficult to hear every word he said because of the crowd.

"We must give thanks to God for the favors we have received," said the Pope. "Rome has been spared. This day will go down in the annals of Rome."

He went on to say he hoped that Italians would be worthy of the grace shown them and put aside hatred and all personal vendettas. He then thanked both belligerents—the Allies and Germany—for having left Rome intact.

After a prayer of thankfulness to the Blessed Virgin and Saints Peter and Paul, guardians of Rome, the Pontiff gave his blessing, "urbe et orbis," as the immense crowd knelt before him.

[The Associated Press estimated the crowd was between 250,000 and 500,000.]

The world has changed for Rome but the Vatican goes on imperturbably as it has through so many other conquests in centuries gone by. It is neutral in fact and spirit. The Pope and all high officials went about their daily routine today as in the past. Except for the tanks and armored cars running along the street in front of St. Peter's one could never know what had happened today.

Continued on Page 5

Italy's Monarch Yields Rule To Son, but Retains Throne

By The Associated Press.

NAPLES, June 5—Victor Emmanuel III stepped aside as King of Italy today, as he previously had said he would do upon the liberation of Rome, and handed to his 39-year-old son, Crown Prince Humbert, all "royal prerogatives." Italian political pressure had been brought to bear against him since the occupation of Naples.

In a decree signed by himself and countersigned by Premier Pietro Badoglio, head of the Italian Liberation Government, the King named his son Lieutenant General of the Realm. The monarch, however, retained his title as head of the House of Savoy and remains as King without power.

[The first act of the Council of Ministers after the transfer of royal powers was a formal denunciation of the 1940 armistice treaty inflicted on France, The United Press said.]

Victor Emmanuel, who became King July 29, 1900, had announced last April 12 his "irrevocable' decision to withdraw from public life "on the day on which Allied troops enter Rome."

Little more than a figurehead since Benito Mussolini assumed the dictatorship of Italy, Victor Emmanuel had won a reputation in the first years of his reign as a sympathetic monarch, interested in his people and their problems.

Prince Humbert, tall and erect, opposed fascism in Italy at the start, but later made a truce with Mussolini. In effect, Humbert becomes the King's regent.

TEXT OF ROYAL DECREE

The King's withdrawal decree:

I, Victor Emmanuel III, by the grace of God and by the will of the nation King of Italy, in collaboration with the President of the Council of Ministers and with the agreement of the Council, have ordered and order as follows:

My beloved son, Humbert of Savoy, Prince of Piedmont, is nominated our Lieutenant General. In collaboration with responsible Ministers he will in our name superintend all matters of administration and exercise all royal prerogatives without exception, signing royal decrees which will be countersigned and authenticated in the usual way.

We order all concerned to observe this decree and to see that it is observed as the law of the State.

Given at Ravello June 5, 1944.
VICTOR EMMANUEL.
(Countersigned) PIETRO BADOGLIO.

The withdrawal was presented to

Continued on Page 6

ALLIED WARNING FLASHED TO COAST

People Told to Clear Area 22 Miles Inland as Soon as Instructions Are Given

By Cable to THE NEW YORK TIMES.

LONDON, Tuesday, June 6—The British Broadcasting Corporation began its 8 A. M. news bulletin this morning with quotations from a Supreme Headquarters' "urgent warning" to inhabitants of the enemy-occupied countries living near the coast.

Gen. Dwight D. Eisenhower has directed that whenever possible in France a warning shall be given to towns in which certain targets will be intensively bombed.

This warning, the broadcast said,

Continued on Page B

PARADE OF PLANES CARRIES INVADERS

Witness Says First 'Chutists Met Only Light Fire When They Landed in France

The first eyewitness account of the Allies' invasion of Europe was given in a pool broadcast from London this morning by Wright Bryan of the National Broadcasting Company, who accompanied the airborne troops in their landings.

His account said the first spearhead of Allied forces landed by parachute in northern France in the first hour of D-day.

"In the navigator's dome in the flight deck of a C-47, I rode across the English Channel with the first group of planes from the United States Ninth Air Force Troop Carrier Command to take our fighting men into Europe," Mr. Bryan said.

He added that just before he left French soil for the return trip he saw seventeen American paratroopers, led by a lieutenant colonel, jump with their arms, ammunition and equipment into German-occupied France."

He declared that his group at the head of the leading wing was met with "only scattering small

Continued on Page B

Eisenhower Instructs Europeans; Gives Battle Order to His Armies

Following are the texts of a statement by Gen. Dwight D. Eisenhower broadcast to the people of western Europe and his Order of the Day to the Allied Expeditionary Force as recorded by The New York Times and the Columbia Broadcasting System:

People of western Europe! A landing was made this morning on the coast of France by troops of the Allied Expeditionary Force. This landing is part of the concerted United Nations plan for the liberation of Europe made in conjunction with our great Russian Allies. I have this message for all of you. Although the initial assault may not have been made in your own country, the hour of your liberation is approaching.

All patriots, men and women, young and old, have a part to play in the achievement of final victory. To members of resistance movements, whether led by national or outside leaders, I say: "Follow the instructions you have received." To patriots who are not members of organized resistance groups I say, "continue your passive resistance, but do not needlessly endanger your lives until I give you the signal to rise and strike the enemy. The day will come when I shall need your united strength. Until that day, I call on you for the hard task of discipline and restraint."

Citizens of France! I am proud to have again under my command the gallant forces of France. Fighting beside their Allies, they will play a worthy part in the liberation of their

Continued on Page 3

EISENHOWER ACTS

U. S., British, Canadian Troops Backed by Sea, Air Forces

MONTGOMERY LEADS

Nazis Say Their Shock Units Are Battling Our Parachutists

Communique No. 1 On Allied Invasion

By Broadcast to THE NEW YORK TIMES.

LONDON, Tuesday, June 6—The Supreme Headquarters of the Allied Expeditionary Force issued this communiqué this morning:

"Under the command of General Eisenhower, Allied naval forces, supported by strong air forces, began landing Allied armies this morning on the northern coast of France."

By RAYMOND DANIELL

By Cable to THE NEW YORK TIMES.

SUPREME HEADQUARTERS ALLIED EXPEDITIONARY FORCES, Tuesday, June 6—The invasion of Europe from the west has begun.

In the gray light of a summer dawn Gen. Dwight D. Eisenhower threw his great Anglo-American force into action today for the liberation of the Continent. The spearhead of attack was an Army group commanded by Gen. Sir Bernard L. Montgomery and comprising troops of the United States, Britain and Canada.

General Eisenhower's first communiqué was terse and calculated to give little information to the enemy. It said merely that "Allied naval forces supported by strong air forces began landing Allied armies this morning on the northern coast of France."

After the first communiqué was released it was announced that the Allied landing was in Normandy.

Caen Battle Reported

German broadcasts, beginning at 6:30 A. M., London time, [12:30 A. M. Eastern war time] gave first word of the assault. [The Associated Press said General Eisenhower, for the sake of surprise, deliberately let the Germans have the "first word."]

The German DNB agency said the Allied invasion operations began with the landing of airborne troops in the area of the mouth of the Seine River.

[Berlin said the "center of gravity" of the fierce fighting was at Caen, thirty miles southwest of Havre and sixty-five miles southeast of Cherbourg, The Associated Press reported. Caen is ten miles inland from the sea, at the base of the seventy-five-mile-wide Normandy Peninsula, and fighting there might indicate the Allies' seizing of a beachhead.

[DNB said in a broadcast just before 10 A. M. (4 A. M. Eastern war time) that the Anglo-American troops had been reinforced at dawn at the mouth of the Seine River in the Havre area.]

[An Allied correspondent broadcasting from Supreme Headquarters, according to the Columbia Broadcasting System, said this morning that "German tanks are moving up

Continued on Page A Following Page 3

"All the News That's Fit to Print"

The New York Times.

LATE CITY EDITION
POSTSCRIPT
Partly cloudy and warm today
Temperatures Yesterday—Max., 84; Min., 64
Sunrise, 5:26 A. M.; Sunset, 8:32 P. M.

VOL. XCIII. No. 31,566. Entered as Second-Class Matter, Postoffice, New York, N. Y. NEW YORK, TUESDAY, JUNE 27, 1944. THREE CENTS IN NEW YORK CITY

CHERBOURG FALLS TO AMERICAN TROOPS; ENEMY LEADERS AMONG 30,000 PRISONERS; RUSSIANS CAPTURE VITEBSK AND ZHLOBIN

REPUBLICANS MAKE QUICK END TO WAR THEIR BATTLE CRY

Warren, Keynoter, Says Party Will Bring Victorious Boys Home With All Speed

DISPUTES OVER PLATFORM

Dewey Avalanche Piles Up, With Californian Unchallenged as His Running Mate

Governor Warren's keynote address is printed on Page 10.

By TURNER CATLEDGE
Special to THE NEW YORK TIMES.

CHICAGO, Tuesday, June 27—A triple pledge to bring the boys back home quickly and "victorious," to reopen the doors of opportunity to "all Americans," and to guard the peace in the future, was sounded yesterday as the Republican battle-cry at the opening of the party's twenty-third national convention.

While it was being uttered by Gov. Earl Warren of California, temporary chairman, in his keynote address to a cheering throng in the Chicago Stadium, THE NEW YORK TIMES gained access to a plank which policy writers had evolved Saturday, pledging the party to a post-war cooperative organization "among sovereign nations," to prevent military aggression and attain permanent peace in the future.

Word had come meanwhile from Wendell L. Willkie, the nominee of 1940, that he considered the foreign policy plank, as he understood it, ambiguous, and therefore was disappointed in it.

Willkie's Backers Upset

This note of controversy came as a distinct shock to a group of former backers of Mr. Willkie who have been attempting these last few days to bring him in line with the platform, and with a ticket of Thomas E. Dewey of New York for President and Governor Warren for Vice President, which is considered certain of nomination by tomorrow night.

Meanwhile, another complication appeared in the hitherto placid convention picture when the seventeen Governors who are delegates demanded opportunity to examine and possibly suggest changes in the platform before it is submitted to the convention, probably tonight, for ratification.

The Governors did not protest any particular item in the platform as it was agreed to in principle last night. They did protest the fact, however, that, as one of them put it, an "oligarchy" of Senators, members of the House and other party leaders, had assumed the prerogative of speaking for the party.

The Governors feel, as Governor Warren reflected in his keynote address, that they have been the spearhead, more than members of Congress, for the resurgence of Republicanism during the last three years. What happened here when the Governors demanded and obtained permission to appear before the resolutions committee was another chapter in a protest which first came to light at the Mackinac Island conference in September.

Led by New Englanders

The action was led, as was the move at Mackinac, largely by a New England group, in which Gov. Raymond E. Baldwin of Connecticut and Gov. Sumner Sewall of Maine were active.

These new possibilities of trouble ahead did not divert the main line of appeal upon which the party was centering—an appeal to the soldier vote, to those Americans who are weary of the New Deal, and, above all, to those wanting to avoid the tragedy of war in the future.

It was the note on which Gov. Dwight Green of Illinois opened the meeting with a welcoming ad-

Continued on Page 9

Convention Events Listed for Today

Special to THE NEW YORK TIMES.

CHICAGO, June 26—The official program for tomorrow's sessions of the Republican National Convention is as follows:

Tuesday, June 27, 10:15 A. M.
(Central War Time)

Convention called to order by the temporary chairman.

National Anthem: Miss Mildred Maule of East St. Louis, Ill.

Prayer: The Rev. Joseph Simonson, pastor of Christ Lutheran Church, St. Paul.

Report of Committee on Credentials.

Report of Committee on Permanent Organization.

Election of permanent chairman and permanent officers.

Address by permanent chairman.

Report of Committee on Rules and Order of Business.

Election of National Committee.

Report of Resolutions Committee.

Recess until 8:15 P. M.

Tuesday, June 27, 8:15 P. M.

Convention called to order by the permanent chairman, Representative Joseph W. Martin Jr.

National Anthem: Miss Mona Bradford of the Chicago Civic Opera Company.

Prayer: Rabbi Abba Hillel Silver of The Temple, Cleveland.

Music.

Address: Herbert Hoover.

Address: Representative Clare Boothe Luce of Connecticut.

Adjourn until Wednesday.

WILLKIE CONDEMNS PEACE-POLICY PLAN

Republican Draft on Foreign Relations Could Be Used to Balk Cooperation, He Says

A few hours after Wendell Willkie had received the text of the proposed Republican foreign-policy plank, the 1940 Presidential candidate issued a statement denouncing the plan as ambiguous, subject to opposing interpretations and capable of being used to throttle effective collaboration by the United States with other countries to maintain peace.

Mr. Willkie's views on the platform committee's suggestions were presented to reporters who had been invited to visit his offices at 15 Broad Street. He explained that he chose this form of making them public because he was not a delegate to the convention.

Likening the language proposed for this year's platform to that employed in 1920, Mr. Willkie recalled that thirty-one leading Republicans had assured the country that the 1920 formula "was the surest road to an effective international organization," but that President Harding, immediately after the election, "announced that the League of Nations was dead."

"A Republican President elected under the proposed platform of

Continued on Page 13

ACCORD OF NATIONS FAVORED IN PLANK ON FOREIGN POLICY

'Participation in Cooperative Organization' Provided 'to Attain Permanent Peace'

TAFT PREDICTS ADOPTION

Declaration Calls for Seeking 'Economic Stability,' Pledges Constitutional Procedure

By JAMES B. RESTON
Special to THE NEW YORK TIMES.

CHICAGO, Tuesday, June 27—The Republican party platform will favor "participation by the United States in post-war cooperative organization among sovereign nations to prevent military aggression and to attain permanent peace."

The party's Foreign Affairs Committee, headed by Senator Warren Austin of Vermont, has approved unanimously a plank which calls on the future world peace organization to "develop effective cooperative means to direct peace forces to prevent or repel military aggression."

Pending the formation of this world peace organization, the plank recommends that the United States should "pledge continuing collaboration with the United Nations."

Senator Robert A. Taft, chairman of the party's Resolutions Committee, to which the platform will be submitted later this morning, said he was certain that the foreign affairs plank as recommended by Senator Austin's committee would be adopted.

Objectives of Peace Treaties

After stating that the party favored "prosecution of the war to total victory against all our enemies in full cooperation with the United Nations and the speedy return of our armed forces," the plank emphasized that justice in the writing of the peace was the essence of realism.

"We believe that peace and security do not depend upon the sanction of force alone, but should prevail by virtue of reciprocal interests and spiritual values recognized in these security agreements," the Foreign Affairs Committee said.

"The treaties of peace should be just; the nations which are the victims of Axis aggression should be restored to sovereignty and self-government, and the organized cooperation of the nations should concern itself with basic causes of world disorder."

Elaborating on "cooperation," the committee continued:

"We shall seek, in our relations with other nations, conditions calculated to promote world-wide economic stability, not only for the sake of the world, but also the end that our own people may enjoy a high level of employment in an increasingly prosperous world. We

Continued on Page 14

ALLIED WARSHIPS SHELLING GERMAN POSITIONS IN CHERBOURG

The U. S. S. Quincy (left) and H. M. S. Glasgow bombarding the port
The New York Times (British Admiralty via U. S. Signal Corps Radiotelephoto)

U. S. TROOPS SCALE LOFTY SAIPAN PEAK

Tapotchau, Dominating Island, Is Reported Won — Carrier Planes Batter Guam and Rota

By GEORGE F. HORNE
By Telephone to THE NEW YORK TIMES.

PACIFIC FLEET HEADQUARTERS, Pearl Harbor, June 26—Mount Tapotchau on Saipan Island has been scaled by United States Marines who are now established in positions near the summit. Marines and Army troops have made substantial gains on both the eastern and western shores of the island.

[A front dispatch said that Tapotchau which dominated the island and has been the goal of our men ever since they landed on Saipan, had been captured by troops who held it against a before-dawn Japanese counter-attack Sunday.]

Admiral Chester W. Nimitz stated that the Kagman Peninsula, forming the upper arm of Magicienne Bay, was now entirely in our hands and that troops had

Continued on Page 7

Russians Begin Encircling Mogilev and Orsha Citadels

By The United Press.

LONDON, Tuesday, June 27—The Red Army, tearing out the northern and southern anchors of the German defense line in White Russia, captured the fortress cities of Vitebsk and Zhlobin yesterday and seized more than 1,700 towns and settlements, while the vanguard of their victorious forces advanced more than twenty-two miles toward Minsk for a great pincer assault on that city.

Striking with unprecedented power and speed, four Soviet armies sprinting along a 285-mile front raced to within eighty-four miles of Minsk, approached to within thirty-five miles of the Polish border, outflanked Orsha and drove to within six miles of Mogilev.

Vitebsk, the most powerful Nazi stronghold on the route to East Prussia, and Zhlobin, 157 miles to the south, fell on the fourth day of the Red Army's summer offensive—four days in which Russian troops advanced as much as fifty-six miles, seized 3,040 towns and settlements and killed more than 31,500 Germans.

More than 6,000 of the German garrison of five infantry divisions

Continued on Page 6

VIENNA WAR PLANTS GET HEAVY BOMBING

Italy-Based Planes Pound Oil, Aircraft Works—Weather Cuts Invasion Support

By The Associated Press.

SUPREME HEADQUARTERS, Allied Expeditionary Force, Tuesday, June 27—United States Flying Fortresses and Liberators 500 to 750 strong roared from Italian bases to the Vienna area yesterday through the heaviest Luftwaffe opposition in recent weeks and attacked oil refineries, rail yards and a Nazi aircraft plant.

Poor weather over western Europe halted for the day the pounding from Allied air bases in Britain and Normandy of German supply and communication lines behind the French front.

Indications of renewed Allied aerial activity came last night as the German radio interrupted programs to say an alert had been sounded in all parts of southwestern Germany. In Hungary, where British bombers of the Mediterranean Allied Air Forces attacked oil works Sunday night, the Budapest radio went off the air again at 10 P. M.

The Flying Fortresses and Liberators and their escorting Mustangs, Lightnings and Thunderbolts of the United States Fifteenth Air Force shot down large numbers of enemy planes on the route to the Vienna area, headquarters announced.

They struck refineries at Schwechat, ten miles southeast of

Continued on Page 5

14 WARSHIPS SHELL CHERBOURG AT ONCE

British Newsman Describes Destruction of Batteries Defending Harbor

By DESMOND TIGHE
Reuter Correspondent

ABOARD H.M.S. GLASGOW, off Cherbourg Harbor, June 25 (Delayed)—American battleships and heavy cruisers, supported by two British cruisers and seven destroyers, are firing broadside after broadside into German shore batteries at vital key points on the fringes of Cherbourg harbor in support of the Army.

The bombardment started at exactly eleven minutes past 12 this morning and has lasted for more than three hours with German long-range 450-mm. shore batteries returning the fire vigorously.

As I watched this bombardment from the bridge of H.M.S. Glasgow, victor of the recent Bay of Biscay battle, we are steaming steadily some 15,000 yards off the breakwater of Cherbourg harbor.

Air Resounds With Crashes

Our six-inch guns are blazing away as shells scream into a German fort. The air resounds with the crash of broadsides from the battleships, cruisers and destroyers. The Channel sea is whipped with wicked looking grey-black splashes as we are straddled time and time by German shore batteries.

The German gunnery is good and although we are plastering their concrete gun emplacements with tons of high explosives some of them keep on firing.

The United States bombardment task force is commanded by Rear Admiral Morton L. Deyo, United States Navy. Admiral Deyo is flying his flag in the heavy cruiser Tuscaloosa. Among the warships in his battle squadron are the battleships Texas, Nevada, Arkansas; the American cruiser Quincy, and the two British cruisers, Glasgow and Enterprise. We are escorted by a

Continued on Page 4

VICTORY IN FRANCE

Capture of Port Seals First Phase of Allied Liberation of Europe

FIGHT SHARP TO END

British Reported Near Main Enemy Highway at Base of Peninsula

5 A. M. Communique

By The Associated Press.

SUPREME HEADQUARTERS, Allied Expeditionary Force, Tuesday, June 27—The capture of Lieut. Gen. Carl Wilhelm von Schleiben, commander of the Cherbourg garrison, and Rear Admiral Hennecke, Nazi sea defense commander of Normandy, was announced today in Allied communiqué No. 43 confirming the fall of Cherbourg.

"Cherbourg's liberation came after a final day of fierce fighting in the northwestern part of the city," the communiqué said.

"In the battle the enemy has lost the greater part of four infantry divisions, numerous naval and marine units and line of communication troops."

Of the British gains on the east side of the beachhead, it said:

"A strong attack toward the Villers-Bocage-Caen main road has secured Cheux and Fontenay, and has advanced several miles in the face of heavy German armor and infantry. Progress continues."

By DREW MIDDLETON
By Cable to THE NEW YORK TIMES.

SUPREME HEADQUARTERS, Allied Expeditionary Force, Tuesday, June 27—Cherbourg, France's third greatest port, has fallen to the American troops in the first outstanding victory of the Allied campaign to liberate France.

The fall of Cherbourg, after a siege that lasted a week from the moment the first shells from American field guns began to pound its defenses, was officially announced here this morning just after 7 o'clock double British summer time [1 A. M. in New York.]

With the taking of the city the first phase of the campaign in which the Allies were forced to build up their armies without the use of a large port came to an end. It was estimated here recently that supplies for two divisions could be moved through Cherbourg within forty-eight hours after its fall.

Captives May Total 30,000

Last night American patrols mopped up the remaining German resistance in the vicinity of the naval base and arsenal and cleaned out snipers from buildings along the waterfront, where individual Germans held out until the last.

Although there has been no official estimate of the number of prisoners yet, it is probable the city's fall will bring more than 30,000 German soldiers and sailors into the Allied cages.

Cherbourg was the second French port and naval base to fall to Lieut. Gen. Omar N. Bradley. Bizerte in Tunisia was taken by the United States Second Army Corps under his command on May 7, 1943.

The struggle for Cherbourg drew to its victorious close yesterday when in the rain and chill wind doughboys mopped up the port. By nightfall more than one-third of the port had been occupied and by midnight two-thirds of the city was in Allied hands.

At dawn Monday 3,400 German prisoners had been taken and it is probable that twice that number was captured in the mopping up operations yesterday.

The Germans were driven from five remaining strongholds during the early evening by grenade, bay-

Continued on Page 3

War News Summarized

TUESDAY, JUNE 27, 1944

Cherbourg fell to the Americans this morning after General Bradley's troops had fought the desperate German defenders from dock to dock along the ruined waterfront. The enemy held out in four or five strong points, principally around the naval base, until each fortified nucleus had been overrun. Lieut. Gen. von Schleiben, Cherbourg garrison commander, and Admiral Hennecke, head of the German sea force off Normandy, were captured. The total of prisoners may reach 30,000.

At the eastern end of the Normandy line the British opened a new drive from Tilly-sur-Seulles and gained as much as four miles, threatening to cut the Caen-Avranches highway at the base of the Cotentin Peninsula. Since the initial landings three weeks ago the Allies have liberated more than 1,000 square miles of France, have taken more than 50,000 prisoners and have destroyed four German divisions. [All the foregoing 1:8; map, P. 2.]

Three United States battleships headed a force of fourteen Allied vessels that pounded Cherbourg's main fortifications into rubble shortly after noon Sunday. The massed naval rifles poured shells into the targets for more than three hours, clearing the way for the troops. [1:7.]

A British naval intelligence officer said in this city that the Germans had been so skillfully outmaneuvered that they massed their air defenses to counter a feint invasion aimed at Calais and Boulogne, leaving Normandy without protection. [5:1.]

Dense fog halted air operations from Britain, but a heavy force of American bombers from Italy smashed oil refineries, rail yards and an airplane plant in the Vienna area. The Luftwaffe offered the heaviest opposition in weeks. [1:6.]

Another vaunted German line crumbled when the Red Army captured Vitebsk and Zhlobin, anchors of the "Fatherland Line." More than 45,000 enemy troops were trapped at Vitebsk, and at one point the Russians were thirty-four miles from the old Polish frontier. A record number of 1,700 places was liberated in the general advance. Gains were also reported from the Karelian Isthmus on the Finnish front. [1:5-6; map P. 6]

The Fifth Army in Italy entered the port of Piombino without a fight and, inland, advanced to within fifteen miles of Siena and forty-five of Florence. The Eighth Army crossed the Chienti River northeast of Foligno in hard fighting. [6:1.]

Marines on Saipan, in the Marianas, have scaled Mount Tapotchau and dug in at the summit. The southern part of Garapan, on the west, was in American hands, and the Japanese have been cleared from Kagman Peninsula on the east. Carrier planes did widespread damage to shipping, installations and grounded enemy aircraft at enemy bases on Guam and Rota. [1:4; maps P. 7.]

Allied forces have captured Mogaung in Burma and gained on all fronts from the Indian border to China, where Hsiangta was recaptured. [7:5.] The Japanese, after seizing Hengshan and Yuhsien, were unable to push closer to Hengyang in China's Hunan Province. [7:4.]

3-Cornered Baseball Game Yields $56,500,000 in Fifth Bond Drive

A crowd of 50,000 baseball fans, all of whom paid their way into the park by buying war bonds, turned out last night at the Polo Grounds to witness a bizarre contest in which the Yankees, Giants and Dodgers participated in a nine-inning contest. The Brooklyn nine won the game, tallying five runs; the Yankees scored one and the Giants nothing.

The program, as arranged by the Fifth War Loan Sports Committee, helped to swell New York's quota in the current bond drive by $56,500,000. Fifty million dollars of this sum came, according to announcement by Mayor La Guardia, from the coffers of the City of New York. The remainder was contributed by the crowd as "admission fee," plus a one-million-dollar bond purchase of an autographed score card by the Bond Clothing Stores.

During the day the drive moved into high gear with the announcement of many large subscriptions here totalling around $1,000,000,000 and the disclosure that purchases throughout the nation had reached $4,591,000,000, or 29 per cent of the quota for the campaign.

Devised and conceived by Stanley Oshan of the War Finance Committee, the baseball game was followed closely by the huge throng that was seeing three major league teams tangle with each other on the same field for the first time. While Mr. Oshan was the originator of the idea it required a Columbia University professor of mathematics, Paul A. Smith, to produce a method of scoring it.

Professor Smith's assistance proved helpful, indeed, for the

Continued on Page 20

Pockets of Nazis Kept on Sniping As Americans Overran Cherbourg

By HAROLD DENNY
By Wireless to THE NEW YORK TIMES.

WITH THE AMERICAN FORCES at Cherbourg, June 26—The Germans fought a last-ditch defense in Cherbourg this evening, though the outcome was inescapable. Substantial elements of the American forces got into the city from the south only after a piece-by-piece conquest of succeeding strong points and the Germans were still firing on them in the city and from two pillboxes remaining on Fort du Roule with 88-mm. fieldpieces and machine guns. The city has been considerably damaged but less than one would have thought. As a whole it is intact, though many individual buildings have been smashed.

Dominating all was the arsenal, where the last important holdout group was still firing rifles while large portions of the structure were burning with a red glow and towering black smoke.

Holding out about equally with the arsenal was one last desperate little group of cannoniers at Fort du Roule.

It stands like Gibraltar and should have been impregnable. Its fortifications of reinforced concrete, several stories deep and tunneled into solid rock, remind one of the Maginot Line fortresses, which I visited the first winter of this war. They include an electric light plant, underground barracks, an underground hospital and abundant stores of everything conceiv-

Continued on Page 4

"All the News That's Fit to Print"

The New York Times.

LATE CITY EDITION
Fair today and tomorrow with mild afternoons and cool nights.
Temperatures Yesterday—Max., 75; Min., 56
Sunrise, 6:16 A. M.; Sunset, 7:39 P. M.

VOL. XCIII..No. 31,626. Entered as Second-Class Matter, Postoffice, New York, N. Y. NEW YORK, SATURDAY, AUGUST 26, 1944. THREE CENTS IN NEW YORK CITY

ALLIES SWEEP TO TROYES, NAZI ROUT GROWS; GERMAN COMMANDER SURRENDERS IN PARIS; RUMANIA DECLARES WAR, BULGARIA TO QUIT

NELSON UNDER FIRE OF BRADLEY DEWEY; WPB POST IN DOUBT

Former Head of Rubber Agency Defends Program, Accuses Nelson of 'Sniping'

ISSUE PUT TO PRESIDENT

Question of Production Chief's Future Is 'Iffy,' He Says —Krug Takes Firm Hold

By CHARLES E. EGAN
Special to THE NEW YORK TIMES.

WASHINGTON, Aug. 25—The question whether Donald M. Nelson will resume his chairmanship of the War Production Board on his return from a special mission to China for President Roosevelt was raised today when the President told his press conference that he did not know whether Mr. Nelson would resume his duties at that time.

The President's statement came soon after Mr. Nelson departed on the first leg of his China journey and the day after the chairman had apparently won a fight with his executive vice chairman, Charles E. Wilson, who resigned yesterday after charging that his usefulness was being impaired by attacks from Mr. Nelson's staff. It supplied another surprising development in the explosive situation which had developed in the WPB over reconversion.

While official Washington speculated whether the President had a more important job than WPB head in prospect for Mr. Nelson or whether the war agency chairman was to be "let out" along with his first assistant, Mr. Nelson came under fire from another quarter when Col. Bradley Dewey, retiring rubber director, accused him of engaging "in typical Washington sniping" at the rubber director's office.

Dewey Takes Issue on Rubber

Colonel Dewey referred to the testimony given by Mr. Nelson before a closed session of the Senate's committee investigating national defense as the type "that has made many good Americans unwilling to give services that otherwise would be of value to the country and to the conduct of the war."

Mr. Nelson had testified that the rubber program was completed, "all but getting the tires." Questioned about Colonel Dewey's then-recent resignation, Mr. Nelson said that to call the rubber program completed would be "like the Army saying they are completed except for the shooting."

Colonel Dewey told reporters that he had never said the task of providing tires was completed, but rather that the synthetic rubber plants were turning out rubber in surplus.

The problem of providing manpower and tire cords no longer required the special powers which were reposed in the Office of Defense Rubber, Colonel Dewey added.

Krug Demands End of Sniping

"These powers are of no value to the problem of manning the plants and providing the much-needed tires," he concluded. "By Presidential directive these were and are the responsibilities of the WPB and of the War Manpower Commission."

J. A. Krug, who was named yesterday by President Roosevelt as acting chairman of the WPB in the absence of Mr. Nelson, took over the reins today. He called the vice chairmen of the agency into conference this afternoon, and, according to reports, told them that he received a clear grant of authority to run the WPB and "get it back on the track."

He warned the officials that he intended that fights within WPB should end and that he would "fire" anyone who engaged in the future in internal disputes.

Mr. Krug told reporters later

Continued on Page 24

Must Post Ceilings For Diners Monday

The Regional Office of Price Administration reminded restaurant managements yesterday that they have until Monday to file a list of forty food items and the ceiling prices they are required to post on their premises. The list in triplicate must be filed with local war price and rationing boards.

The new OPA national restaurant regulations require the posting of the forty food items and the ceiling prices. Restaurants violating the provisions of the regulation face enforcement action, OPA attachés pointed out. Each list filed by a restaurant will be compared with menus of May, 1943, and, upon approval, a copy of the list, bearing an official stamp to show approval, will be returned to the restaurant owner.

OWN MEN AT FRONT APPEAL TO LABOR

AFL and CIO Leaders in France Link War Supply Shortages to 'Our Quarrels at Home'

By SIDNEY SHALETT
Special to THE NEW YORK TIMES.

WASHINGTON, Aug. 25—"We cannot let the men whose lives depend on this equipment pay the price for our quarrels at home," six American labor leaders who are visiting the French battlefields under War Department sponsorship have declared in a message sent back here to their unions.

The message was transmitted through the War Department to William Green, president of the American Federation of Labor, and Philip Murray, head of the Congress of Industrial Organizations.

"Conscious of the partnership that exists between the fighting fronts and the factory," it read, "the War Department has made it possible for us to travel through the battle areas and see at first hand how our soldiers are using the weapons and equipment made by American labor.

Need of Supplies to Save Lives

"As we travel along roads lined with the wreckage of American and German equipment and pass through shattered French cities and, above all, as we pause at military cemeteries and hospitals that are all too plentiful here, we are struck more forcibly than ever before with the horrible destructiveness of modern war and the importance of superior supplies in cutting down the toll of our dead and wounded.

"We are filled with pride for our Army. Its combat efficiency and morale are high. It is well-staffed and well-manned—an Army representative in the highest sense of our great American democracy.

"Everybody knows his job—from generals to privates—and we are determined to get ourselves to the job of finishing this war with the same single-minded determination as the men at the front.

"We do not know whether the war will last a short time or a long

Continued on Page 24

RED ARMY RACES ON

Russians Attack Galati Gap and Encircle 12 German Divisions

REACH DANUBE DELTA

205,000 Enemy Troops Killed or Taken in Six Days—Tartu Seized

By The Associated Press.

LONDON, Saturday, Aug. 26—Two Russian armies racing toward the heart of Rumania at a better than a mile-an-hour clip yesterday reached the Galati Gap defenses at Tecuci and also drove a spearhead down to the Danube River delta at Kiliya in a six-day whirlwind offensive that Moscow announced had cost the enemy nearly 205,000 in killed or captured.

In perhaps the greatest defeat yet inflicted on the Axis in a comparable period, the Russians also announced they had encircled twelve German divisions of upward of 60,000 men southwest of fallen Kishinev, provincial capital of Bessarabia. Thirteen thousand Germans already have surrenderd in two days, and the remainder are being annihilated, said the Moscow broadcast bulletin.

Thousands of Rumanians were abandoning the struggle against the Russians and turning to fight the Germans, dispatches said, as the Second and Third Ukrainian Armies under General Rodion Y. Malinovsky and Feodor I. Tolbukhin linked up for a quick drive on Bucharest, within 113 miles of Soviet columns that seized Tecuci on the Barlad River.

Danube Delta Reached

A total of 550 towns and villages were swept up by the two armies, and the capture of Tecuci found the Russians within ninety miles northeast of the Ploesti oil wells. General Malinovsky's troops now were at the Galati Gap, a forty-five-mile stretch of defenses prepared along the Putna, Siret and Barlad Rivers just above where those streams empty into the Danube.

To the southeast, a Soviet communiqué said, the Russians had captured Kiliya on the Danube, fifteen miles west of the Black Sea port of Vilkov at the mouth of the delta, and twenty-two miles east of the port of Ismail. General Tolbukhin's Third Army seized that point. To the northwest his troops reached the Prut River on a seventy-mile front between captured Leusheny and Kagul, the latter being thirty miles northeast of the river's confluence and rail junction of Galati. The capture of Gasanbatyr put the Russians thirty miles from the port of Ismail on the northeast.

Soviet aircraft added to the slaughter by attacking Axis military trains at Galati, the supplementary communiqué said.

In six days the Russians have captured nearly all of lower Bessa-

Continued on Page 6

ALLY FIGHTS REICH

Nazis' Bombers Attack Bucharest—City Held Cleared of Germans

FIGHTING CONTINUES

Bulgaria Called Willing to Surrender to Allies Unconditionally

By SIDNEY GRUSON
By Cable to THE NEW YORK TIMES.

LONDON, Aug. 25—The new Rumanian Government, after having denounced German perfidy tonight, openly declared war on the Reich, thereby fulfilling a Russian prerequisite for acceptance of the Rumanian offer to change to the Allied side.

The United States and Great Britain, moreover, have received word from Bulgaria that she is ready to accept unconditional surrender terms. The western allies, it was learned tonight, are now filling in details of the terms. The Rumanian declaration of war came after the Nazis, according to a proclamation broadcast by the Bucharest radio, had bombed the capital heavily and German units had attacked Rumanian forces and machine-gunned civilians of Bucharest and of other places.

Nazis' Plight Called Hopeless

"By these acts of aggression, which occurred simultaneously in various parts of the country, Germany has placed herself in a state of war with Rumania," the proclamation declared. "The Government therefore orders the Rumanian Army to begin the struggle against all German military forces on Rumanian territory for the liberation of the country from German usurpation."

The Germans themselves have acknowledged their position in Rumania as being hopeless. The Nazi-controlled Scandinavian News Service said that encircled German units were trying to break through the Russian lines toward the Carpathians and Transylvania to fight their way to Hungary.

The German "Danube" radio station appealed to the Rumanian Army tonight to "refuse to fight against your former allies." But the appeal was falling on deaf ears, for the Bucharest radio shortly before had declared that the capital had been completely

Continued on Page 3

PARISIANS CELEBRATE ARRIVAL OF ALLIES

Patriots crowding around a jeep after its arrival in the French capital yesterday. This picture, one of the first to be taken inside the city, was sent from the new transmitting station set up in Cherbourg.

The New York Times (U. S. Signal Corps Radiotelephoto)

THIRD NEAR MARNE

Berlin Says Americans Have Driven to Reims, 80 Miles Above Paris

SEINE FOE CRUSHED

River Becomes a Scene of Carnage as Bombs Rain on Germans

By DREW MIDDLETON
By Cable to THE NEW YORK TIMES.

SUPREME HEADQUARTERS, Allied Expeditionary Force, Saturday, Aug. 26—Three resounding victories were won along the 200-mile-long front in northern France yesterday.

Armored patrols of the United States Third Army rumbled into Troyes, a great road and railroad center 130 miles from the German frontier as the thrust eastward on the extreme right flank of the Allies' line broke through German offensive positions in front of Troyes, thirty-seven miles from the Marne River.

Bridgeheads across the Seine south of Paris were widened, and the enemy was driven from Montereau, ten miles east of Fontainebleau, and was retreating hurriedly from the area northeast of Montargis, taken by other American forces late Thursday.

Report Reims Reached

An unconfirmed report, published in The London Chronicle, said the Germans declared that American troops had reached Reims, eighty miles northeast of Paris.

French and American troops penetrated into the center of Paris yesterday.

Aside from its tremendous effect on French morale, the Allies' occupation of Paris, the most important communications center in France, is a military triumph of first magnitude.

Finally, far to the west, British, American and Canadian forces were driving the remnants of the German Seventh Army pell-mell into the Seine. The Elbeuf pocket replaced Falaise as a graveyard. Enemy forces are now contained in an area less than 300 miles square, with the Seine to the east and north and the Risle to the west and the steadily advancing Allied line to the south.

Planes Batter Fleeing Foe

While field guns and tanks searched the forests for fleeing Germans, hundreds of medium and light fighter bombers scourged the Germans seeking to escape across the Seine.

The battle has become a race for Seine crossings, with Allied forces confident they will have killed, wounded or captured at least 40,000 of the Germans before they reach the Seine.

As ground forces drove the Germans to the Seine, American and British light naval craft, attacking German ships leaving Le Havre, blew up an escort vessel, an armed trawler and a German E-boat and damaged at least five other craft.

Between 3 and 4 o'clock yester-

Continued on Page 4

JAPANESE CRUISER FIRED BY U.S. FLIERS

Mast-Head Strike at Manado Also Smashes 7 Freighters —40 Barges Riddled

By FRANK L. KLUCKHOHN
By Cable to THE NEW YORK TIMES.

ALLIED HEADQUARTERS IN AUSTRALIA, Aug. 25—A Japanese cruiser and seven Japanese freighters were sunk or severely damaged and forty barges and luggers were shot up as a force of fewer than twenty-five of Gen. Douglas MacArthur's Liberators made a surprise low-level attack yesterday on Manado, in Netherland Celebes, which is the enemy supply point for Halmahera.

The Mitchells braved heavy ack-

Continued on Page 6

Allied Forces Help French To Rid Capital of Nazis

By The Associated Press.

SUPREME HEADQUARTERS, Allied Expeditionary Force, Aug. 25—The Paris radio announced late tonight that the French capital had been liberated and that the German commander had signed a document ordering his troops to cease fire immediately.

The announcement followed entry of American and French troops into the capital during the day. There was no immediate confirmation here.

The latest word at headquarters was that American and French troops had joined Fighting French patriots on the Ile de la Cité in the heart of the capital after bitter fighting with Germans and French collaborationist militiamen.

Gen. Charles de Gaulle, President of the French Committee of National Liberation, said in a speech broadcast from Paris:

"France will take her place among the great nations which will organize the peace. We will not rest until we march, as we must, into enemy territory as conquerors."

The commander of the Paris region for the French Forces of the Interior, Colonel Raoul, issued this proclamation to his forces, the radio said:

"FFI of the Ile de France (the Paris region), you have unleashed a rising that has liberated Paris. You have improvised your tactics, animated by the strong desire to win, and you have won."

In another broadcast the Paris radio said that the German com-

Continued on Page 5

AMERICANS SEIZE CANNES, PUSH EAST

Drive to 20 Miles From Italy, Spear Along Rhone—Lyon Is Reported in Patriots' Hands

By The Associated Press.

ROME, Aug. 25—American troops lunging suddenly eastward from their Riviera beachhead, in southern France, have captured the famous resort towns of Cannes and Antibes and tonight were fighting forward less than twenty miles from the Italian frontier.

Nice, within short artillery range of the advancing Americans, was expected to fall at any hour.

Other swift Allied columns drove methodically toward the heart of France and a junction with Gen. Dwight D. Eisenhower's armies in the north. Tonight's communiqué said forces probing into the delta of the Rhône valley were close to

Continued on Page 3

War News Summarized

SATURDAY, AUGUST 26, 1944

American forces in northern France entered Troyes, 130 miles from the German frontier, as Allied armies continued yesterday to move forward along a 200-mile front. Our bridgeheads across the Seine south of Paris were widened. The enemy was driven from Montereau, ten miles east of Fontainebleau and was in hurried retreat from the area northeast of Montargis. Far to the northwest, the remnants of the German Seventh Army, trapped with their backs to the Seine, were being driven into the river. [1:8; map P. 4.]

As the famous spire of the Eiffel Tower pierced an early morning fog, French and American forces smashed through to the heart of Paris amid a tumultuous welcome. The Free Paris radio reported that the German commander of the city had surrendered. [1:6-7; map P. 5.]

In southern France, Allied troops captured Cannes and Antibes and stood less than twenty miles from the Italian frontier. Other Allied columns were reported closing in on Lyon, Rhône Valley industrial center 170 miles inland from the Mediterranean, and French patriots were said to be in control of the city. [1:7; map P. 2.]

General de Gaulle—who is in Paris—and his committee will have a greater part in the administration of civil affairs in France by new agreements. [5:1.]

More than 3,000 planes from Britain and Italy ranged over Czechoslovakia and Germany, pounding aircraft plants, airfields and experimental and research centers for Hitler's flying bombs and other new weapons of destruction. [4:6.]

The Red Army has reached the Galati Gap, a forty-five-mile path between the Danube delta and the mountains to the west, and seized Tecuci, a railway junction within that gateway to the Balkan plains. Twelve enemy divisions have been encircled southwest of Kishinev. Moscow also reported the capture of the key city of Tartu on the Riga-Tallinn railroad in Estonia in the Russian drive to wipe out two German Baltic armies. [1:3; map, P. 6.]

Chaos mounted in the Balkans. After German planes had bombed the Rumanian capital, the Bucharest radio went on the air to proclaim that King Michael's new pro-Ally Government was at war with Germany. Rumanians were battling Hungarians as well as Germans. [1:4.] The Russian sweep led Bulgaria to send word to the Allies that she was ready for unconditional surrender. [6:1.]

Allied planes set a Japanese cruiser ablaze and sank or damaged seven enemy freighters near Celebes, an important Japanese supply center for Halmahera Island. [1:5.]

Army Rules Roosevelt Address Was Political, Then Denies It

Special to THE NEW YORK TIMES.

WASHINGTON, Aug. 25—The War Department changed its mind today on whether President Roosevelt's speech at Bremerton, Wash., on Aug. 12 was "political," holding first that it was and several hours later reversing itself to hold that it was "not political."

The issue was raised by the Socialist party, which applied to the War Department for equal radio time to address fighting men overseas on the grounds that the President's Bremerton speech, in which he mainly reviewed his trip to Hawaii and the Aleutians, was "political."

Under Title 5 of the Service Men's Voting Law, the Socialists contended, they were entitled to equal time on the air. Earlier this week the War Department had announced that, under an interpretation of the statute, the Democratic, Republican, Socialist and Prohibition parties would have equal recognition for any political radio time.

Under the first ruling by the War Department today the Socialist party was granted equal time to that of the President to address the men overseas.

"The War Department," said a memorandum issued in reply to press inquiries, "has indicated to the Socialist party that, under the statute, it will accede to this request. The other major political parties have asked for and have been furnished copies of the correspondence between the War De-

Continued on Page 9

Dulles Indicates Republican Idea Is to Cooperate, Yet Criticize

By JAMES B. RESTON
Special to THE NEW YORK TIMES.

WASHINGTON, Aug. 25—Apparently the Republican party will try to lift the specific question of American participation in a world security organization out of party politics in the Presidential campaign, but there will be no moratorium on discussion of the Administration's conduct of foreign policy as a whole.

This seemed clear today at the close of the first phase of the discussion between Secretary Hull and John Foster Dulles, Governor Dewey's representative on foreign affairs, who issued a joint statement which indicated that they had not reached complete agreement on the subject of how to discuss foreign policy during the campaign nor complete agreement on the American security plan now before the Dumbarton Oaks Security Conference.

Mr. Dulles told reporters that he hoped the two major parties could reach an agreement on the American security plan now being discussed at the Dumbarton Oaks conversations and he added that he would see Mr. Hull again to that end, but he indicated that no complete agreement had been reached as yet and emphasized that the Republicans would retain their right to criticize freely the Administration's past conduct of foreign relations.

The joint statement by Secre-

Continued on Page 24

Von Kluge Killed, Stockholm Hears

By The Associated Press.

STOCKHOLM, Saturday, Aug. 26—Field Marshal Gen. Guenther von Kluge has been killed, the newspaper Dagens Nyheter said today on the basis of information received from Germany.

Circumstances of his reported death were not known here and the newspaper had no additional details.

[There was no immediate confirmation of this report in either Axis or Allied official quarters.]

Von Kluge, 61 years old, had held command of the German armies on the western front since July 6, when he succeeded Field Marshal Gen. Karl von Rundstedt.

"All the News That's Fit to Print"

The New York Times.

LATE CITY EDITION
Sunny, cool and windy; fair and becoming cooler tonight.
Temperatures Yesterday—Max., 60; Min., 51
Sunrise, 7:20 A. M.; Sunset, 6:01 P. M.

VOL. XCIV..No. 31,687. Entered as Second-Class Matter, Postoffice, New York, N. Y. NEW YORK, THURSDAY, OCTOBER 26, 1944. THREE CENTS NEW YORK CITY

U. S. DEFEATS JAPANESE NAVY; ALL FOE'S SHIPS IN ONE FLEET HIT; MANY SUNK; BATTLE CONTINUES

SPECIAL PRIVILEGE SOLD BY NEW DEAL, DEWEY CHARGES

Says Roosevelt Backs Plan for 1,000 to Put '$1,000 on the Line' to Aid Campaign

PARTY LETTER IS QUOTED

Governor Declares in Chicago Administration Lacks 'Honesty' to Solve Post-War Problems

The text of Mr. Dewey's speech will be found on Page 13.

By ALEXANDER FEINBERG
Special to The New York Times.

CHICAGO, Oct. 25—Governor Dewey declared tonight that "for $1,000 laid on the line to finance the fourth-term drive, this Administration boldly offers for sale 'special privilege.'" which includes the "assisting in the formulation of Administration policies."

Attacking the "rudimentary honesty" of the New Deal, Mr. Dewey, in a major campaign address preceding the appearance of President Roosevelt here Saturday, charged that the Chief Executive himself was the sponsor of the fund raising idea.

The Chicago Stadium, which accommodates 25,000 persons, was packed to capacity, with several thousand others clamoring to obtain admittance. Gov. Dwight H. Green of Illinois presented Mr. Dewey, who was received with tumultuous acclaim. He kept pointing to the microphone to still the demonstration, but it was just short of five minutes before he could begin his speech.

Governor Dewey said that the fund raising plan was disclosed in a letter signed by H. L. McAlister and Sam J. Watkins, State finance chairman, and written on the letterhead of the National Democratic Campaign Headquarters, Little Rock, Ark.

Dewey Quotes Letter

Mr. Dewey quoted the letter as follows:

"This is an invitation to you to join the One Thousand Club.

"The idea of such a club originated at a recent conference at the White House between the President, Robert E. Hannegan, chairman of the Democratic National Committee, and Edwin W. Pauley, treasurer of the committee. At this meeting the President commented:

"'I think it would be a good idea to have a list of one thousand persons banded together from all over the United States to act as a liaison to see that facts relating to the public interest are presented factually to the President and members of Congress.'

"Members of this organization undoubtedly will be granted special privilege by party leaders. These members will be called into conference from time to time to discuss matters of national importance and to assist in the formulation of Administration policies.

"To be eligible for membership in the One Thousand Club will require a contribution of $1,000 to the National Democratic campaign fund."

Mr. Dewey declared that "there in crude, unblushing words is the ultimate expression of New Deal policies," adding:

"And the sponsor of this idea is frankly stated in that letter to be the President himself. The man who holds the highest office within the gift of the American people at a conference in the White House sponsors an idea to sell 'special privilege' and a voice 'in the formulation of Administration policies' for one thousand dollars on the barrelhead."

The Governor said that New

Continued on Page 12, Column 1

No Extra Gasoline For Trip to Polls

By The Associated Press.

WASHINGTON, Oct. 25—Chester Bowles, OPA head, in a letter to Senator Davis, Republican, of Pennsylvania today stated that the OPA could not allow extra gasoline rations for private automobiles to take voters to the polls if other means of transportation are available.

Pennsylvania has no absentee voting law and Senator Davis contended that many persons from his State working elsewhere would be unable to return to cast their ballots unless they received extra gas rations.

"A special ration may be granted to carry persons to and from the polls for the purpose of voting in public elections (including primary elections), provided reasonably adequate alternative means of transportation are not available," Mr. Bowles wrote.

Where no other form of transportation is available those wishing to use cars for voting may apply to their local ration boards on special forms which the boards have available.

WAGNER ACCLAIMS PARTY FARM POLICY

He Says That Dewey Is Vague on Agriculture—Calls His Platform 'Double Talk'

By CLAYTON P. KNOWLES
Special to The New York Times.

SYRACUSE, N. Y., Oct. 25—The farm plank in the Republican platform offers nothing but "double talk" and Governor Dewey, rather than clarifying the issue, puts forward proposals "as vague and airy as a wisp of smoke," Senator Robert F. Wagner declared tonight as he carried his campaign for re-election into this city in the heart of the farm area.

"Mr. Dewey ridicules the so-called aphabetical agencies," he declared. "But how could low-interest loans have been provided without the Farm Mortgage Corporation? How could farm prices have been supported without the Agricultural Adjustment Administration? How could the number of farms with central electric service have been multiplied three times without the Rural Electrification Administration?

"These programs are not perfect. They need to be improved, but they are solid, they can be seen, they can be felt. When Mr. Dewey talks about the farmer, what he proposes is as vague and airy as a wisp of smoke."

His address, broadcast over a State-wide hook-up by the Columbia Broadcasting System, said that Governor Dewey's Commissioner of Agriculture last spring set minimum milk prices "far above

Continued on Page 12, Column 4

PRESIDENT ELATED

Gives News From Halsey That Foe Is 'Defeated, Damaged, Routed'

TEST IS ON, KING SAYS

Practically All Japanese Fleet in the Battle, Admiral Believes

By LEWIS WOOD
Special to The New York Times.

WASHINGTON, Oct. 25—President Roosevelt exultantly announced late today the receipt of a report from Admiral William F. Halsey saying that the Japanese Navy in the Philippine area had been "defeated, seriously damaged and routed" by our forces.

Two hours earlier Admiral Ernest J. King, Commander in Chief of the United States Fleet and Chief of Naval Operations, had disclosed that virtually all of the long elusive Japanese Fleet had been engaged at last in the furious sea battle of the Philippines.

These two startling revelations, exciting Washington as nothing has done since the European invasions, were taken here to mean that the vaunted Japanese naval power had been seriously crippled and the road to Tokyo made much easier. At last, it was presumed, the principal part of Japanese naval strength had been nettled out of hiding and then decisively beaten.

Announcement Is Dramatic

The circumstances of the President's statement were thrilling. When only a half dozen newsmen remained in the White House press room at 5:20 P. M., Press Secretary Stephen T. Early appeared at the door.

"Come quick," he cried, slapping his palms together for emphasis.

Rushing to the President's oval-shaped office, the reporters found him seated at his desk, smiling broadly. Obviously he had been interrupted in his late afternoon dictation. Before him lay scattered papers, but directly in front of him was a single sheet of paper, inscribed apparently with his own handwriting.

He had, said the President beamingly, a "real flash," just telephoned to him by Admiral William D. Leahy, Chief of Staff to the President as Commander in Chief of the Army and Navy. Picking up the paper, Mr. Roosevelt slowly and distinctly read:

"The President received today a report from Admiral Halsey that the Japanese Navy in the Philippine area has been defeated, seriously damaged and routed by the United States Navy in that area."

For a moment there was a pause. No one said a word. Then

Continued on Page 3, Column 3

U. S. and Britain Recognize Italy; Action Is First With an Ex-Enemy

By BERTRAM D. HULEN
Special to The New York Times.

WASHINGTON, Oct. 25—Diplomatic relations with Italy were resumed by the Allies tonight.

Recognition is being accorded by the United States, the other American republics in the United Nations and Britain. The Soviet Union had previously extended recognition to the Government of Premier Ivanoe Bonomi.

Our action was announced by Edward R. Stettinius Jr., acting Secretary of State, who said that Alexander C. Kirk, who has been serving as our diplomatic representative in Rome with the personal rank of Ambassador, would now be accredited to the Italian Government with the rank of Ambassador.

It is expected that Italy will now send an Ambassador here. The appointment of Count Carlos Sforza, long a friend of the United States, to the post, has been forecast since it became evident that recognition would not long be delayed.

Announcement of the recognition has been made at London and is expected at the Latin-American capitals, except for Buenos Aires. Argentina never severed relations with Italy, although she did with Germany and Japan.

The announcement by Mr. Stettinius follows:

"After consultation with the other American republics, as provided in the Resolutions of Rio de

Continued on Page 10, Column 5

SEA POWER OF LAND OF THE RISING SUN SHATTERED IN BATTLE

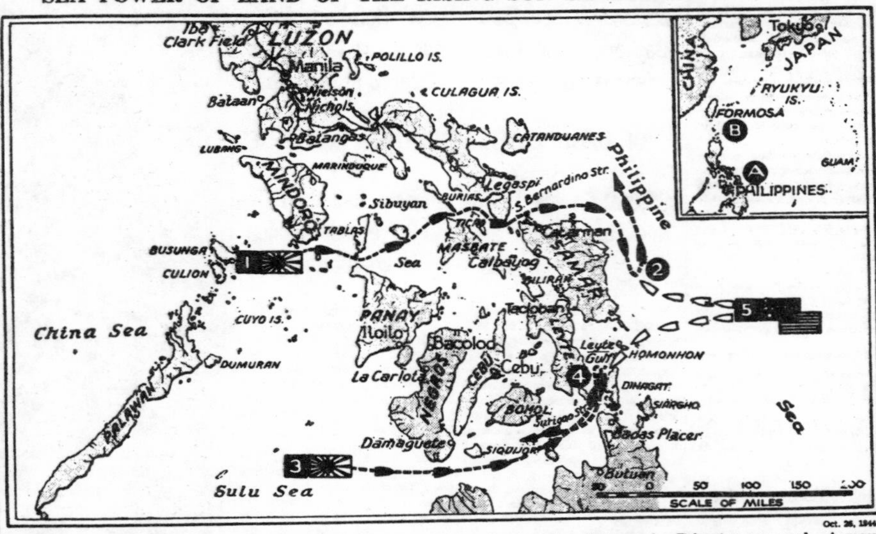

Piecing together the statements of Admiral Nimitz and General MacArthur gives this picture of the battle around the Philippines: One Japanese force, including four battleships, ten cruisers and thirteen destroyers, first sighted south of Mindoro (1) steamed east, across the Sibuyan Sea, through San Bernardino Strait and down the coast of Samar (2), where Admiral Kinkaid's combined force (5) attacked it and forced it to retire northward with perhaps ten ships damaged. It was apparently in this action that the American light carrier Princeton was sunk. A second enemy force, first sighted southwest of Negros (3), included two battleships, one or two cruisers and four destroyers. It moved east across the Sulu Sea and through Surigao Strait (4). Admiral Kinkaid attacked this group and it lost one battleship and several cruisers and destroyers; the rest of the force retreated west through the strait. This whole battle scene is at (A) on the inset. A third Japanese force was engaged southeast of Formosa (B).

ALLIES CUT UP FOE IN WEST HOLLAND

British Hammer Germans in One Area of 's Hertogenbosch—Canadians Tighten Traps

By CLIFTON DANIEL
By Wireless to The New York Times.

SUPREME HEADQUARTERS, Allied Expeditionary Force, Oct. 25—The Germans were rapidly losing their grip tonight on their strongholds between the North Sea and the British Second Army's salient in the Netherlands.

British forces converging from three sides drove them out of all

Continued on Page 7, Column 2

'17 Hours of Hell' Raised In Sea Battle Off Leyte

By RALPH TEATSORTH
United Press Correspondent

ABOARD ADMIRAL KINKAID'S FLAGSHIP, off the Philippines, Thursday, Oct. 26—The Tokyo Express rammed into the American Navy Limited today. The pride of Japan was wrecked so badly it may never make another long run. It was the day our Navy had dreamed about for considerably more than a year.

It was seventeen hours of concentrated hell and the most amazing thing about the battle was that our Pacific Flight Carrier Force—which nobody thought could deliver such a terrific punch—held off the bulk of the Japanese fleet all day and had it on the run all afternoon.

When evening came and most of

Continued on Page 4, Column 7

War News Summarized

THURSDAY, OCTOBER 26, 1944

The Japanese Navy came out to fight in the waters off the Philippines and was severely mauled. One force of four battleships, ten cruisers and thirteen destroyers moved up south of Mindoro into the Sibuyan Sea. Every battleship and at least one cruiser was hit. This flotilla rounded Samar and fled north. We lost an escort carrier.

A second force of two battleships, two cruisers and four destroyers came into the Sulu Sea from southwest of Negros Island. After all the ships had been hit it turned tail and retreated.

A third force, this one with carriers, came down from home waters and the battle was still going on. Most of the engagements were fought from the air and the enemy suffered heavily in plane losses. Our light carrier Princeton was hit and its magazine subsequently exploded. Most of the crew were saved. The Third Pacific Fleet took on the enemy carrier force and the Seventh turned back the two others. [All the foregoing 1:3.]

President Roosevelt, in an impromptu press conference, said that Admiral Halsey, commanding the Third Fleet, had just reported that the Japanese Navy had been "defeated, seriously damaged and routed." Earlier Admiral King had said that almost the entire enemy naval strength was involved in the Philippines battle. Fighting covered an area 600 miles north and south and 250 east and west. Navy officials were elated and felt the whole course of the war might be speeded. [1:3.]

On Leyte American troops had pushed twenty miles north of Tacloban and nine miles inland from Dulag. Additional landings on the northern part of Leyte and the southern part of Samar won control of San Juanico Strait, which separates them. [1:7; map P. 2.]

Superfortresses delivered a smashing assault on Japan's key aircraft plant at Omura on the island of Kyushu. One B-29 was missing. [1:6.]

German positions in the Belgium-Netherland pocket were becoming increasingly untenable as Canadian and British troops drew closer and menaced the enemy retreat line. [1:4; map P. 7.] More than 2,200 American and British bombers lashed rail and oil targets in the Reich. Six bombers and one of a great fighter escort were missing. [9:1.]

Russian forces captured the German port and U-boat base of Kirkenes in Norway and thirty other Norwegian villages. [1:6-7; map P. 11.] To the south the Red Army renewed its drive on Warsaw, gained more ground in East Prussia and liberated all of Transylvania by capturing Satu-Mare and Carei. [12:1, with map.]

Mount Belmonte, guarding the southern approaches to Bologna, was captured by Americans of the Fifth Army in Italy. The British Eighth Army gained three miles in the Adriatic sector. A German withdrawal was indicated. [10:7.]

The United Nations have resumed diplomatic relations with Italy, the first former enemy state to receive recognition. [1:2-3.]

AIR PLANT IN JAPAN SMASHED BY B-29'S

Omura Target Is 'Perfectly Patterned,' Pilots Say—Foe Lists 100 Planes in Attack

Special to The New York Times.

WASHINGTON, Oct. 25—While the remnants of the demoralized Japanese Fleet were fleeing from Admiral William F. Halsey's forces in Philippine waters, United States Army Superfortresses today were carrying the war another step closer to the heart of Japan by carrying out a successful mission against the key aircraft assembly plant at Omura on the island of Kyushu.

Twentieth Air Force Headquarters here announced that a medium-sized task force of the mammoth bombers, operating from Twen-

Continued on Page 4, Column 4

AMERICANS MAKE BIG LEYTE JUMPS

Troops Push Westward on Isle—Southern Coast of Samar to the North Now Held

By The United Press.

ADVANCED HEADQUARTERS ON LEYTE, Thursday, Oct. 26—American dismounted cavalry troops have invaded Samar, third largest of the Philippines and last island barrier on the road to Luzon and Manila, while forces fighting on Leyte have punched nine miles inland to seize the key road junction of Burauen.

Gen. Douglas MacArthur also announced in a special communiqué that Field Marshal Count Juichi Terauchi's Japanese defenders of the northern Leyte front were "disintegrating" under the American hammer blows.

The three-mile American advance that occupied Burauen, southern terminus of an inland highway, split the Japanese lines in northern Leyte and threw the enemy back toward the hills, where Filipino guerrillas were reported in action.

The new American triumphs pushed our lines nine miles inland and raised to thirty-one the number of towns and villages captured. Six airfields also have been seized.

The invasion of Samar, with an

Continued on Page 4, Column 5

Russians Invade North Norway; Take Kirkenes in Wide Advance

By W. H. LAWRENCE
By Wireless to The New York Times.

MOSCOW, Oct. 25—Entering their ninth country in less than seven months, Red Army forces smashed across the Norwegian frontier today and liberated the Barents Sea port of Kirkenes and thirty other Norwegian villages just fifty-four months and twenty-one days after the beginning of Adolf Hitler's treacherous invasion of the Scandinavian country.

This new expedition of Russian troops outside the Soviet Union was announced by Premier Joseph Stalin in a special order of the day and was saluted by Moscow's massed guns and highlighted in tonight's communiqué.

The Soviet Union's Norwegian campaign brings Allied armies back on the soil of that restless country for the first time since June 15, 1941, when the British had to withdraw their poorly equipped forces in the face of numerically superior German forces.

[On its European front the Red Army reopened the battle for Warsaw by outflanking the Polish capital on the north, drove farther into East Prussia against desperate resistance and completed the liberation of Transylvania.]

It would be wrong to assume from this dash across the Norwegian frontier at its northernmost point that the liberation of

Continued on Page 11, Column 6

BATTLESHIP IS SUNK

Seventh Fleet Smashes Two Japanese Forces Converging on Leyte

REMNANTS IN FLIGHT

They Are Hotly Pursued—Third Enemy Force Is Hit Off Formosa

The Imperial Japanese Fleet has been brought to battle. It is suffering a crushing defeat. Two of its divisions have been routed. One has been almost destroyed. Contact has been made with the main force southeast of Formosa by Admiral William F. Halsey's Third Fleet. That engagement is continuing, said the last communiqué.

Two strong Japanese naval forces converged on Leyte Gulf through the San Bernardino Strait in the Philippines to the north and the Surigao Strait to the south. Vice Admiral Thomas C. Kinkaid's Seventh Fleet smashed these two forces and put the remnants to flight after sinking or heavily damaging every ship in the southern enemy force.

One big Japanese carrier has been sunk. Two more have been heavily damaged and undoubtedly are out of action. One Japanese battleship of the Yamasiro class has been sunk. At least four others have been heavily damaged. Several enemy cruisers and destroyers have been sunk. Many others have been hit, both by bombs and torpedoes.

Enemy Defeated and Routed

The only announced American loss is the converted cruiser-carrier Princeton sunk. Other escort carriers were damaged by fire from one of the enemy battleship forces.

Gen. Douglas MacArthur reported triumphantly that "the Japanese Navy has suffered its most crushing defeat of the war." Admiral Ernest J. King, in Washington, said that "practically all" of the Japanese fleet was engaged and that he was confident of the outcome. President Roosevelt called a special press conference to announce receipt of a message from Admiral William F. Halsey reporting that the enemy has been "defeated, seriously damaged and routed."

Pending official word from Pearl Harbor, it appeared the greatest surface and naval air action in the history of naval warfare was being fought and won by the Pacific Fleet, the greatest naval force that ever went down to the sea.

Fate of Leyte Decided

SEVENTH FLEET HEADQUARTERS, Philippines, Thursday, Oct. 26 (AP)—Japan lost the first, and possibly the decisive, round in an all-out battle to halt on the Philippines line the American advance toward her home islands.

This occurred early yesterday morning when Admiral Kinkaid's outnumbered fleet battered and put to rout Japanese battle forces converging on Leyte Gulf.

Complete results are lacking as the action is continuing, with planes from Admiral Kinkaid's hurt but still fighting carrier force hitting the surviving enemy warships as they are retiring. [General MacArthur said the Japanese force that came through Surigao Strait fled back through it to the west and the other was in flight in a northerly direction.]

[Gordon Walker in a Mutual broadcast from the Philippines said "a Navy spokesman here claimed that practically every

Continued on Page 3, Column 2

"All the News That's Fit to Print"

The New York Times.

LATE CITY EDITION
POSTSCRIPT
Considerable cloudiness and milder today; moderate winds.
Temperatures Yesterday—Max., 51; Min., 37
Sunrise, 7:33 A. M.; Sunset, 5:05 P. M.

VOL. XCIV No. 31,700. Entered as Second-Class Matter, Postoffice, New York, N. Y. NEW YORK, WEDNESDAY, NOVEMBER 8, 1944. THREE CENTS IN NEW YORK CITY

ROOSEVELT WINS FOURTH TERM; RECORD POPULAR VOTE IS CLOSE; DEMOCRATS GAIN IN THE HOUSE

2-DAY LUZON BLOWS SMASH 440 PLANES, 30 JAPANESE SHIPS

Halsey's Fliers Destroy 249 Aircraft, Sink Four Vessels in Sunday Sweep

MANILA FIELDS RAVAGED

Ports and Installations Hit Hard—Enemy Lines to Leyte Defenders Are Strained

By GEORGE HORNE
By Telephone to The New York Times.

PEARL HARBOR, Nov. 7—Admiral William F. Halsey's Third Fleet carriers spread death and damage over southern Luzon Island in the Philippines for the second successive day on Sunday, sinking another five ships and destroying 249 additional enemy aircraft.

It was a major air strike, apparently an all-out effort to annihilate the Japanese air forces supporting enemy counter-attacks on Leyte, where American military leaders have reported the campaign nearing its final stages.

Over the two days, according to Admiral Chester W. Nimitz's communiqué today, the enemy has lost 440 aircraft, 327 of which were caught on the ground and 113 shot down in the air. The principal plane concentrations were found on seven fields in the Manila network. They were Nichols, Clark, Nielson, Lipa, Tarlac, Bambam and Mabalacat.

[The two-day toll of enemy ships sunk or damaged was about thirty.]

Unable to Rise in Strength

As the widespread attacks continue, the enemy air opposition is becoming steadily weaker, as is evidenced by the fact that on the second day all but a few of the lost enemy aircraft were caught on the ground, unable to get into the air.

Terrific damage is being inflicted on port facilities and ground installations in and around Manila harbor. In addition to ships sunk and planes destroyed, many air and surface craft were listed as damaged. Reports on the action were still of a preliminary nature and there was no count of our own losses.

Admiral Nimitz said three oil storage areas were left blazing at the northern section of Clark Field and at the northeast of the field a tremendous explosion was observed, followed by fire. North of Malvar a railroad engine and five tank cars were blown up.

Five Ships Sunk at Manila

In the harbor of Manila the fighters, torpedo planes and dive-bombers sank three cargo ships and an oil tanker, probably sank a destroyer and damaged two destroyers, two destroyer escorts, a trawler and several cargo ships. Fourteen cargo ships were damaged during the two-day attack, in which wave after wave of American planes swept in from the sea to wipe out available enemy strength that might be used to bolster the hard-pressed Japanese forces on Leyte.

Meanwhile the steady attacks on the Bonins and Kuriles are continuing. On Sunday a Liberator of the Eleventh Army Air Force, flying hundreds of miles from our Aleutian bases, hit three small transports off Onnekotan Island in the Kuriles and other Liberators flying with it concentrated on land targets of the island base.

Seven enemy fighters fought the big bombers in a running battle, and guns from three Liberators brought down one and probably destroyed another. Two Liberators were damaged.

Otomari and Tori Island, also in the Kuriles, were attacked. Seventh Air Force Liberators

Continued on Page 19, Column 2

War News Summarized

WEDNESDAY, NOVEMBER 8, 1944

Japanese Lose 440 Planes

Japanese air power in the Philippines received a staggering blow on Saturday and Sunday when Third Fleet carrier planes destroyed 440 enemy aircraft in the Manila and southern Luzon areas. Nearly thirty ships, including a number of warcraft, were also destroyed or damaged. Our fliers reaped their greatest harvest at seven airfields where they wiped out 327 planes on the ground. Port and ground installations suffered terrific damage. Reports were still incomplete and our own losses were not known. [1:1.]

Luzon fields pounded from air

Battle Joined on Leyte

American troops on Leyte were battling elements of four Japanese divisions in the hills north of Ormoc and repulsed three heavy attacks, inflicting great loss on the enemy. The area of Valencia, north of Ormoc, was under American artillery fire. [19:1, with map.]

Tokyo Sees B-29's

The jittery Japanese reported more Superfortresses on reconnaissance flights over Tokyo and surrounding territory. They also said that the Bonins and Volcanos had been bombed. [19:2.] In China the enemy scored by driving to within twenty miles of Liuchow, but in Burma the British captured Kennedy Peak and threatened Fort White and Paletwa. [21:1.]

Grim Fight Below Aachen

The United States First Army fought its way back into the streets of Vossenack in some of the bitterest fighting of the war. Three German counter-attacks from Schmidt were repulsed. The Sixth Army Group made important advances in the Vosges Mountains and in the Netherlands Allied troops were mopping up the liberated areas. [19:8, with map.]

Soviet Drive Forecast

Behind the lull on Russia's fighting fronts the Red Army was reported to be preparing for a great new offensive. [19:4.] The Athens radio announced that the Greek Government had ordered dissolution of the guerrilla bands Edes and Elas. [19:5.]

Robot Blows at U. S. 'Possible'

A joint Army-Navy statement said that it was "entirely possible" for flying bombs to reach the United States from Europe, but gave no indication such an attack was expected. [19:6-7.]

FISH IS DEFEATED; CLARE LUCE WINS

Congress Veteran Concedes Bennet's Victory—Close Finish in Connecticut

Special to The New York Times.

NEWBURGH, N. Y., Wednesday, Nov. 8—Representative Hamilton Fish, for twelve terms a Republican member of the House and a leading isolationist and critic of President Roosevelt's foreign policy, conceded his defeat by Augustus W. Bennet just before 1 o'clock this morning.

"From reports I have received to date, it looks like I have lost the district by a 5,000 vote majority," he said.

"It looks as if the Republicans have lost the House, and if that is so, as much as I regret it, I have no great desire to continue to serve as a minority member, which I have for the last fourteen years in an uphill fight."

Mr. Bennet, in a victory statement, paid tribute to those who had supported him from all parties, "including the much-abused Political Action Committee." He hailed his election as the result of the citizens' determination "to eliminate Ham Fish from Congress."

Factors in the Result

Heavy Republican defections to Mr. Bennet in Orange County and strong support for Mr. Fish's opponent in the parts of the district in Rockland, Sullivan and Delaware counties sent the Republican nominee down to defeat in the bitterest Congressional election in this part of the State in years.

Complete returns from Orange County gave Fish 35,126 votes to 27,371 for Bennet, a majority for Fish of 7,755. This indicated that Mr. Bennet's majority for the whole Twenty-ninth Congressional District would be about 5,600.

Complete returns from Rockland County gave Bennet 19,706 votes to 12,323 for Fish, a majority of 7,383.

In Sullivan County, with twenty-four election districts missing, including those where Mr. Bennet was expected to run strongest, the vote was Fish 3,877, Bennet 3,776,

Continued on Page 2, Column 7

ROOSEVELT VICTORY CLAIMED IN JERSEY

Hague Spokesmen Also Say Wene Will Win—Constitution Revision Is Rejected

Despite greatly reduced pluralities in Hudson County, Democratic stronghold of New Jersey, lieutenants of Mayor Frank Hague of Jersey City, Democratic boss of the State, predicted shortly before 4 A. M. today that the State's sixteen electoral votes would be delivered to President Roosevelt, largely by virtue of an estimated plurality of 75,000 votes in Hudson. In 1940 Mr. Roosevelt carried the county by a plurality of 100,877.

Mayor Hague's spokesman also predicted victory for the party nominee for the United States Senate, Representative Elmer H. Wene, although by a close vote, and rejection of the proposed revised State Constitution by a substantial margin.

Mr. Hague himself left headquarters in Jersey City early today without making any statement.

The Jersey City predictions were made despite the fact that eight of the twelve wards in the city had not reported returns up to that hour, but the estimates on the fate of charter revision appeared to be borne out by State-wide returns. At 4 A. M., with 1,311 of the State's 3,657 election districts missing, the vote for rejection was 480,503 to 381,686 for approval.

At the same hour Mr. Dewey was leading Roosevelt by a vote of 481,677 to 456,275, with 1,819 districts missing, and H. Alexander Smith, Mr. Wene's Republican opponent, was leading the Democratic nominee by a vote of 562,261 to 503,763, on the basis of returns from 2,226 districts.

Five Hudson Communities Bolt

The apparent failure of the Hague machine earlier to deliver the expected large Democratic plurality in the county had caused some political observers to place the State in the doubtful class.

Continued on Page 9, Column 4

GET 11 TO 20 SEATS

Victories Blast Hopes of Rivals to Control the House

SENATE UNCHANGED

Democrats Have 180 in House, Republicans 155, 98 in Doubt

By TURNER CATLEDGE

Democratic gains of from eleven to twenty seats in the House and a possible new place or two in the already one-sided Senate, appeared on returns received up to 5 A. M. today to have followed in the wake of yesterday's fourth-term landslide for President Roosevelt.

Republican hopes of controlling the House appeared to have been blasted beyond any possibility of realization and what in the earlier count seemed to portend a G. O. P. gain in the Senate began to fade with the later returns.

These same reports showed the defeat of Representative Hamilton Fish, Republican, of New York, one of the most controversial figures in the lower house; the possible defeat of Senator John A. Danaher, Republican, of Connecticut; a victory for Mrs. Clare Luce, Republican, in a close race in the Fourth Connecticut Congressional District; a trend in the early count against Senator Gerald P. Nye, Republican "isolationist" of North Dakota, and a neck-and-neck contest in which Senator James J. Davis, Republican, of Pennsylvania, was trailing his Democratic opponent, Representative Francis J. Myers, by a slight margin.

Leading Senators Re-elected

These returns also revealed the re-election of Senator Alben W. Barkley, Democratic Majority Leader, in Kentucky; of Senator Scott Lucas, Democrat, in Illinois; of Senator Robert A. Taft, Republican, in Ohio; of Senator Millard Tydings, Democrat, in Maryland, and numerous other sitting Senators, both Democratic and Republican.

With 98 House seats still in doubt, the Democrats had clinched 180 seats in the House of Representatives of the Seventy-ninth Congress; the Republicans were certain of at least 155; the American Labor party of 1 an dthe Progressives of 1.

Seventeen Senate places were still awaiting the decision of the final count, but the Democrats were certain of 49, or an actual majority. The Republicans appeared certain of thirty-one and the Progressives of one.

With the latest returns received the Democrats had garnered a net

Continued on Page 2, Column 5

ELECTED TO PRESIDENCY AND VICE PRESIDENCY

Franklin D. Roosevelt © Pirokle — Harry S. Truman Chase-Statler

ROOSEVELT STRONG IN WAR VOTE TALLY

Partial Count of Ballots of Armed Forces Increases President's Majority

By CHARLES GRUTZNER Jr.

The majority given to President Roosevelt by civilian voters who went to the polls throughout the nation yesterday was increased by the count of war ballots marked, some of them as long as two months ago, by members of the armed forces in camps here and in far-flung theatres of operations.

The decisiveness of the President's victory over Governor Dewey removed the possibility that the outcome of the election might hinge on the soldier vote in some of the eleven States that delayed counting their war ballots, but partial returns from States that counted their war ballots yesterday made it clear that the support of the men and women in the armed forces would be a strong factor in building up the final majority of their Commander in Chief.

A breakdown of the vote into civilian and war ballots was slow in coming in from nearly all of the thirty-seven States that counted their soldier vote yesterday, because election officials were concerned chiefly with transmitting

Continued on Page 4, Column 2

New York for Roosevelt; Wagner Re-elected Senator

By JAMES A. HAGERTY

For the sixth consecutive time, four times as a candidate for President and twice as a candidate for Governor, President Roosevelt carried his home State of New York in yesterday's election and won its forty-seven electoral votes. With 3,609 of the 3,700 election districts in New York City and with 4,978 of the 5,421 election districts outside New York City reporting, President Roosevelt had an actual lead over Governor Dewey, his Republican opponent, of 300,831 and a plurality of about 283,000 for the President in the State was indicated.

Returns from 3,609 election districts out of 3,700 in New York City gave Dewey 1,240,216, Roosevelt 1,966,539. This is an actual plurality of 726,273 and an indicated plurality of 743,700 for Roosevelt.

Returns from 4,978 election districts out of 5,421 outside New York City gave Dewey 1,585,771, Roosevelt 1,160,329. This is an actual plurality of 425,442 and an indicated plurality of 460,785 for Dewey.

Re-elected in the sweep for the President was United States Senator Robert F. Wagner, who defeated Secretary of State Thomas J. Curran by a plurality probably greater than that for Mr. Roosevelt. Also elected was Associate Judge of the Court of Appeals, Marvin R. Dye, who defeated John Van Voorhis, Republican. The President, Senator Harry S. Truman, candidate for Vice President, Senator Wagner and Mr. Dye, all Democrats, also were nominees of the American Labor and Liberal parties.

Returns from 3,566 election districts of the 3,700 in New York City gave Curran 1,183,020, Wagner 1,957,026. This is an actual plurality of 774,006, and an indicated plurality of 802,900 for Wagner.

Returns from 4,797 of 5,421 election districts outside of New York City gave Curran 1,468,985, Wagner 1,086,736. This is an actual plurality of 382,249, and an indicated plurality of 433,680 for Curran.

Both Houses of the State Legislature remain Republican. Among the greatest upsets in the State was the defeat of former Mayor Rolland B. Marvin of Syracuse, Republican candidate for State Senator in the Forty-third Senatorial District, by Richard P. Byrne, Democratic and American Labor party nominee. On incomplete returns, Senator John J. Dunnigan, Democratic leader of the

Continued on Page 6, Column 4

DEWEY STATEMENT ADMITS HIS DEFEAT

Candidate Concedes Loss of Election at 3:12 A. M. and Congratulates Victor

Gov. Thomas E. Dewey, Republican candidate for President, conceded defeat at 3:12 o'clock this morning.

His statement was made at Republican National Headquarters in the Hotel Roosevelt, where both he and Herbert Brownell Jr., chairman of the National Committee, earlier had refused comment on the growing indication of a lopsided electrical college vote for his Democratic opponent, President Franklin D. Roosevelt.

Mr. Dewey said:

It is clear that Mr. Roosevelt has been re-elected for a fourth term, and every good American will whole-heartedly accept the will of the people.

I extend to President Roosevelt my hearty congratulations and my earnest hope that his next term will see speedy victory in the war, the establishment of lasting peace and the restoration of tranquillity among our peoples.

I am deeply grateful for the confidence expressed by so many million Americans for their labors in the campaign.

The Republican party emerges from the election revitalized and a great force for the good of the country and for the preservation of free government in America.

I am confident that all Americans will join me in a devout hope that in the years ahead Divine Providence will guide and protect the President of the United States.

President Roosevelt, from his Hyde Park home, acknowledged, at 3:28 o'clock this morning Gov-

Continued on Page 3, Column 2

Roosevelt Leads as Davis Trails, In Mounting Pennsylvania Count

Special to The New York Times.

PHILADELPHIA, Wednesday, Nov. 8—On the basis of partial returns from all but three of the sixty-seven counties in Pennsylvania, it appeared early that President Roosevelt for the third successive time had captured the State's electoral votes.

Swept on the Roosevelt wave, it appeared, was Representative Francis J. Myers in his race to unseat James J. Davis, 71-year-old Republican Senator who was elected first in 1932 and re-elected six years ago.

Whether the Roosevelt impetus would be sufficient to sweep into office the Democratic candidates for the five State offices remained in doubt. Reports in these instances, lagging far behind the count on the two top contests, were inconclusive.

With 6,012 of 8,202 precincts reporting. President Roosevelt was leading Governor Dewey, 1,282,392, to 1,238,986. Among the returns were all the 1,338 precincts in this city where the President gained a lead of 117,000.

The returns showed that once again the soft coal miners in western Pennsylvania and the anthracite miners in the East repudiated John L. Lewis, president of the United Mine Workers of America, by turning in thumping pluralities for Mr. Roosevelt.

On the other hand, with less than half the precincts reporting and Governor Dewey reducing the President's lead, Republican leaders were hoping that late returns and a fair share of the soldier vote, to be counted on Nov. 22, would mean victory for the party in the State.

Although the President seemed

Continued on Page 5, Column 4

DEWEY CONCEDES

His Action Comes as Roosevelt Leads in 33 States

BIG ELECTORAL VOTE

Late Returns in Seesaw Battles May Push Total Beyond 400

By ARTHUR KROCK

Franklin Delano Roosevelt, who broke more than a century-old tradition in 1940 when he was elected to a third term as President, made another political record yesterday when he was chosen for a fourth term by a heavy electoral but much narrower popular majority over Thomas E. Dewey, Governor of New York.

At 3:15 A. M. Governor Dewey conceded Mr. Roosevelt's re-election, sending his best wishes by radio, to which the President quickly responded with an appreciative telegram.

Early this morning Mr. Roosevelt was leading in mounting returns in thirty-three States with a total of 391 electoral votes and in half a dozen more a trend was developing that could increase this figure to more than 400. Governor Dewey was ahead in fifteen States with 140 electoral votes, but some were see-sawing away from him and back again. Typical of these were Wisconsin, where he overtook the President's lead about 2 A. M.; Nevada, where Mr. Roosevelt passed him at about the same time, and Missouri.

In the contests for seats in Congress, the Democrats had shown gains of 11 to 20 in the House of Representatives, assuring that party's continued control of this branch. In the Senate the net of losses and gains appeared to be an addition of one Republican to the Senate, which would give that party twenty-eight members—far short of the forty-nine necessary to a majority. A surprise was the indicated defeat of the veteran Pennsylvania Republican, Senator James J. Davis.

Mrs. Luce's Opponent Concedes

The Congressional races were featured by a mass Democratic attempt, in which the President and Vice President Henry A. Wallace personally participated, to unseat Representative Clare Boothe Luce of Connecticut. But shortly after 3 A. M., following a night in which the lead had swung back and forth, her election was conceded by her opponent, Miss Margaret Connors. Some hours before, to his neighbors at Hyde Park, the President had expressed rejoicing over Mrs. Luce's "defeat." Her success is the vitriol in the Democratic honey.

Despite the great general victories by the Democratic party, the popular vote will evidently show a huge minority protest against a fourth term for the President. Tabulations by the press associations indicated that the disparity between the ballots cast for the two candidates will be so small that a change of several hundred thousand votes in the key States, distributed in a certain way, would have reversed the electoral majority. At 4:40 A. M. The Associated Press reported 16,387,999 for Mr. Roosevelt and 14,235,051 for Mr. Dewey from more than one-third of the country's election districts. This ratio, if carried through, would leave only about 3,000,000 votes between the candidates.

One of the most interesting struggles for the Presidency was that in Wisconsin, where Mr. Dewey took an early lead, lost it and regained it again. Wisconsin is the State where the late Wendell L. Willkie made his bid for renomination, posing the issue of

Continued on Page 2, Column 3

"All the News That's Fit to Print"

The New York Times.

LATE CITY EDITION

Fair and cold today. Cloudy and slightly warmer tomorrow.

Temperatures Yesterday—Max., 33; Min., 19

Sunrise, 6:17 A. M.; Sunset, 4:56 P. M.

VOL. XCIV...No. 31,771. Entered as Second-Class Matter, Postoffice, New York, N. Y. NEW YORK, THURSDAY, JANUARY 18, 1945. THREE CENTS NEW YORK CITY

RUSSIANS TAKE WARSAW, REPORTED IN CRACOW; WIN A CITY 14 MILES FROM REICH IN 24-MILE GAIN; BRITISH ADVANCE, AMERICANS CLOSE ON ST. VITH

ROOSEVELT URGES WORK-OR-FIGHT BILL TO BACK OFFENSIVES

Letter to May Calls for Prompt Action on 18-to-45 Measure—King, Marshall Tell of Needs

RECENT LOSSES ARE HEAVY

House Group Abruptly Ends Hearings—Approval of Legislation Expected by Tonight

Appeals by the President, Gen. Marshall, Adm. King, Page 13.

By C. P. TRUSSELL

Special to The New York Times.

WASHINGTON, Jan. 17—President Roosevelt called on Congress today for prompt action on a work-or-fight bill for men between 18 and 45, since it was vital that the Allied "total offense should not slacken because of any less than total utilization of our manpower on the home front."

In support of his appeal, which was addressed to Chairman Andrew J. May of the House Military Affairs Committee, the President attached a copy of a joint letter sent to him by General Marshall and Admiral King.

Replacements Needed

As "the agents directly responsible" for the conduct of military operations, they also urged "immediate action" on the home front to meet requirements for young and vigorous replacements in battle zones and to provide the necessary manpower to multiply production of critical munitions, build new ships and repair those damaged in combat.

Mr. Roosevelt said that the need for statutory controls to channel 4-F's into essential war work was more urgent now than it was eleven days ago when he asked for it at a stop gap, pending enactment of a national service law, and urged action "without delay" on the May-Bailey bill providing for "limited national service" and covering all 18 to 45 deferred registrants.

Hearings on the May-Bailey bill were ended abruptly, and Mr. May called an executive session of the committee tomorrow. He predicted that the measure, in some form, would be approved by nightfall.

"Time to Act," May Says

"We've discussed this matter long enough," Mr. May said. "It's now time to act."

Committeemen joined their chairman in expected approval of the bill, but they predicted that changes would be made, warned that much care must be exercised in revising the measure, and looked for a "tough" fight when it reached the House floor.

Earlier, the National Association of Manufacturers joined organized labor in opposing the bill, as well as national service generally, before the committee.

Frederick C. Crawford, chairman of the NAM executive committee, testified that if legislation were to be written, it should only put teeth into the controls of existing machinery and programs. He said that intensified cooperation between Government, management and labor could supply the manpower demands for the armed service and war production replacements now and in the next six months, when an estimated 1,600,000 men will be required. Recent employment gains were cited.

The President in his letter to Mr. May said that it was true that there had been a trend toward increased placement of manpower in the last fortnight, but, he added that there was danger that this trend, accelerated by belief that Congress was about to act on work-or-fight measures, would be reversed by indications that such action was likely to be delayed.

Although the May-Bailey bill is not a complete national service measure, Mr. Roosevelt said, it would "go far" to effect essential

Continued on Page 13, Column 2

Russian Super-Tank Reported by Nazis

By The Associated Press.

LONDON, Jan. 17—A German reporter, speaking on the Berlin radio from the Kielce sector of Poland tonight, paid high tribute to the power of a new Red Army heavy tank, called the Joseph Stalin.

"The Russians are using their new Joseph Stalin super-tank on an ever-increasing scale," the Nazi reporter, Heinz Megerlein, said. "This most powerfully gunned and armored vehicle in the world is more than a match for our best tank, the Royal Tiger."

The German broadcaster said the Russian super-tank carried a 122-mm. [4.8-inch] gun.

The German Royal Tiger tank has been reported to mount a new version of the famous 88-mm. gun.

U.S. POLICY ON ROWS IS FIRM, GREW SAYS

Position, Stated Vigorously, Is Not to Allow Differences to Mar Unity, He Asserts

Joseph C. Grew, Under Secretary of State, declared last night that our State Department has vigorously stated, and would continue to state to its allies, the American position on issues in dispute, but that it was the policy of this Government not to allow these differences to interfere with the unity of action essential to winning the war, or to disrupt that unity after the war.

He made this reply to recent critics of our foreign policy at a meeting in The New York Times Hall, 240 West Forty-fourth Street, at which Senator Warren R. Austin of Vermont called for the earliest practicable meeting to establish the Dumbarton Oaks Organization, and Senator J. William Fulbright of Arkansas assailed our handling of foreign affairs as hesitant, timid, and lacking in forthrightness.

Nicholas Roosevelt was moderator of the meeting, which was arranged by The New York Times on the topic, "America's Place in World Affairs." The prepared addresses of the three speakers were broadcast over radio stations WQXR and WQXQ. Senators Austin and Fulbright then took part in a discussion and question-and-answer period that followed, for which Mr. Grew was unable to remain.

Fulbright Assails Delay

Senator Fulbright said that our failure to take part in formulating decisions in such pressing matters as the situations in Greece, Italy and Poland was forcing Great Britain and Russia to make their own decisions. He declared that our failure to assume a share of the responsibility for the decisions in the case of Greece had had the effect of making "one of our Allies, Great Britain, "the undeserved goat" and had stirred up feeling

Continued on Page 12, Column 3

FOE STIFF IN WEST

Fog and Tanks Help the Germans Slow British and U.S. at Front

OUR AIR ARM BARRED

Montgomery Push Gains Town—Americans Lift Threat to Strasbourg

By CLIFTON DANIEL

By Wireless to The New York Times.

SUPREME HEADQUARTERS, Allied Expeditionary Force, Jan. 17—While the drive to beat back the German salient continued despite thick, freezing weather and repeated German counter-attacks, which cost the Germans at least twenty-four tanks today, British forces northeast of Aachen also made painful progress into the flank of the Maeseyck bulge.

Beating their way with a flail of tanks through mine fields, dense fog and stinging sleet, they advanced 2,000-odd yards in the first twenty-four hours. Their progress was marked on the map by two river crossings and a village captured—Dieteren. The attack seemed less ambitious than originally appeared, but it still held symbolic value as representing a resumption of the Allied initiative.

The American threat to St. Vith, the last important road junction on the Germans' retreat route from the Ardennes, grew serious today as the battle-wise Old Hickory Division pressed down on the devastated town through knee-deep snow, thick woods and treacherous hills, reaching within five miles of St. Vith's outskirts. A forest belt of two and a half miles and a maze of knobby hills still stand between the town and the attacking Americans, however.

Americans Gain in Alsace

In Alsace American forces attacking the perimeter of the German bridgehead over the Rhine north of Strasbourg not only redressed the setback inflicted by the Germans last night but pushed their way into the western stronghold of the German pocket at Herrlisheim. This advance, though local and limited, will be regarded with satisfaction, particularly by the French, who have been viewing the bridgehead and its threat to Strasbourg with apprehension for many days.

Militarily, Strasbourg does not seem more important than any other city, but politically it is a far greater prize for either the Germans or the French. As the capital of the lost and regained province of Alsace and the "second city of France," it is a major symbol for France, and its loss might have a painful effect on French morale, already at a low ebb because of the unduly severe winter.

However, French forces holding the city are regarded as sufficient at the moment to counter any

Continued on Page 9, Column 1

RED ARMY TEARS GERMANS' DEFENSES IN POLAND ASUNDER

Jan. 18, 1945

Breaking from their Narew River positions, the Russians punched out a salient between Ciechanow and Pomiechowek (1). In an encircling operation they finally toppled Warsaw and some units sped westward to Leszno (2). South of the Polish capital the Warsaw-Lodz railroad was cut with the capture of Zyrardow (3). The rail junction of Skarzysko-Kamienna was being encircled as Soviet forces moved into Szydlowiec and Konskie (4). The Red Army's closest approach to Germany was at the important Polish city of Czestochowa, fourteen miles from the Silesian border (5). Although the Lublin radio reported the fall of Cracow, Moscow merely said that Sadowie (6), eight miles away, had been taken, but the city's capture was obviously at least imminent.

U. S. MEN USE TNT TO SLIT ICY GROUND

Fight Polar Weather in Hills of Ardennes as Well as Atrocity-Bent Germans

By Wireless to The New York Times.

SUPREME HEADQUARTERS, Allied Expeditionary Force, Jan. 17—Up in the Ardennes hills, where the United States First Army is attacking toward St. Vith, the ground is so hard that the troops have to use dynamite and mortar shells to dig slit trenches.

The hills are so steep and slippery with snow that tanks sometimes slide down them like sleds. When pinned down by enemy fire or while waiting to attack Ameri-

Continued on Page 5, Column 2

MacArthur Protects Flank By 17-Mile Dash Along Gulf

By LINDESAY PARROTT

By Wireless to The New York Times.

ALLIED HEADQUARTERS, on Leyte, Thursday, Jan. 18—The pace of the American advance on Luzon in the Philippines has been fastest in the extreme northwest where Gen. Douglas MacArthur's infantrymen have been feeling their way into Bolinao Peninsula, which forms the western shore of Lingayen Gulf. Here, in a sprint of seventeen miles from captured Alaminos, Sixth Army men reached Bolinao, a town on the extreme point of the peninsula.

Other detachments are moving southwestward toward Dasol Bay and the highway that leads west of the Zambales Mountains toward Bataan, a communiqué announced today.

[The capture of Bolinao sealed

Continued on Page 3, Column 3

War News Summarized

THURSDAY, JANUARY 18, 1945

Warsaw, the first European capital to fall to Hitler's blitzkrieg five years and four months ago, was liberated by Russian and Polish troops yesterday. The First White Russian Army captured the city after a wide encircling dash that swept up more than 800 other places.

The Red Army steamroller, which at its closest point was 260 miles from Berlin, moved north of the Polish capital when the Second White Russian Army, from its two bridgeheads across the Narew River, advanced twenty-four miles on a sixty-two-mile front, freeing Makow, Pultusk, Ciechanow and 500 other communities.

At the southern end of the long surging line the First Ukrainian Army liberated Czestochowa, Radomsko and 700 more inhabited places, and Lublin reported that Cracow had also fallen. This Russian army was only fourteen miles from the Reich. [All the foregoing 1:8.]

Gloom hung heavy over Germany. The enemy press and radio prepared the people for retreat on the Eastern front as the "final onslaught against Germany planned at Teheran" got under way. [6:1.]

The Warsaw victory brought to a climax the diplomatic impasse over recognition of a single Polish Government by all the Allies. The Polish Government in London indicated it would seek an early return to Warsaw and the Moscow-fostered Lublin regime was expected to move into the capital immediately. [1:7.]

Reverses in the east did not prevent the Germans from stiffening against the new British Second Army drive north of Aachen. The British advanced 2,000 yards, crossed the Roode River in two places and captured two villages, one of which was Dieteren. To the south, Americans took Vielsam and were five miles from St. Vith. The Third Army trapped a German force in the woods southeast of Tettingen. Inconclusive small battles were fought in the Alsace area. [1:3; map, P. 9.]

Some 700 American heavy bombers and 350 fighters carried the air war to oil and submarine plants in the Hamburg-Harburg area and rail targets in northwest Germany. [8:3-4.]

Americans on Luzon speared seventeen miles from Alaminos on the extreme right of the line to capture Bolinao, at the southwest tip of Lingayen Gulf. They also cut across the peninsula toward Dasol Bay, on the China Sea. At the other end of the line patrols entered Pozorrubio while main forces were half a mile from Rosario. Allied planes, in their best day, destroyed sixty-two enemy aircraft, all but one of which were caught on the ground. [1:5-6; map P. 2.]

Tokyo said that Pacific Fleet carrier planes had hit China for the fourth day, 300 of the Navy's aircraft striking Hong Kong, Canton and Hainan Island. A sizable force of B-29's—Tokyo said eighty—hit air installations at Shinchiku, on Formosa's northwest coast, with good effect, and General MacArthur's fliers again struck Okayama, on the southwest coast. [1:6.]

OUR CHINA STRIKE IN 4TH DAY, FOE SAYS

Tokyo Cites 300-Plane Blow at Coast Ports—B-29's Join in Attack on Formosa Base

By The United Press.

PEARL HARBOR, Jan. 17—Tokyo reported today that more than 300 American carrier planes hit the China coast for the fourth successive day, battering Hong Kong, Canton and Hainan Island.

B-29 Superfortresses joined the mounting two-way offensive with new blows against Formosa.

[A new attack on Formosa Wednesday night was reported by General Douglas MacArthur's headquarters on Luzon. The report stated that long-range patrol planes harassed the Okayama airdrome.]

There was no immediate confirmation that Admiral William F. Halsey's Third Fleet planes had

Continued on Page 3, Column 5

ACCORD ON POLAND AT ONCE HELD VITAL

Red Armies' Sweep to West Seen Spurring Need for 'Big 3' Agreement

By RAYMOND DANIELL

By Cable to The New York Times.

LONDON, Jan. 17—The fall of Warsaw and the swift advance of the Red Armies across western Poland toward the old frontiers of Germany have made it imperative that President Roosevelt and Prime Minister Churchill reach a final agreement with Premier Stalin on Poland's territorial and political future at their next meeting, it is believed here.

There are signs that the exiled Polish Government under Premier Tomasz Arciszewski is approaching the problems of its relations with Russia with a new sense of urgency but without much outward evidence to support an optimistic view of the outcome.

Mr. Arciszewski, in a statement on the liberation of Warsaw, cited the words of Lieut. Gen. Tadeusz Komorowski [General Bor], just before he and his underground army defending Warsaw yielded to the Germans after a heroic sixty-three-day struggle: "We are fighting for freedom, we are fighting for the right to be free!" Mr. Arciszewski commented: "At this moment these words embody, as

Continued on Page 6, Column 2

McGuire, Pacific Air Ace, Killed; He Downed 38 Japanese Planes

By The Associated Press.

SAN ANTONIO, Tex., Jan. 17—Major Thomas B. McGuire Jr. of San Antonio and Ridgewood, N. J., the leading American active ace with thirty-eight Japanese planes to his credit, was shot down and killed in the Philippines Jan. 7, Lieut. Gen. George C. Kenney, commanding the Allied Air Forces in the Pacific, informed Mrs. McGuire in a letter dated Jan. 8.

Mrs. McGuire received General Kenney's letter today. The Allied air chief said that the word Major McGuire had been shot down brought him the worst of a number of bad moments he had had to face since the war began.

"I felt that he would make a name for command as well as for leadership and for great personal courage," the letter stated.

"The accident, which left him vulnerable on Jan. 7 and in which he met his death, was sheer chance as Major McGuire was one of the most capable fighter pilots I have ever known."

"Your husband was one of the best. We at the Air Forces can never forget. We will find it more difficult to carry on without him," General Kenney added.

The letter indicated that Major McGuire's plane was in some way disabled in the air, making him an easy prey to defending enemy fighters. Mrs. McGuire said she had received no official notification of her husband's death from the War Department.

Major McGuire became the leading ace when Maj. Richard I. Bong of Poplar, Wis., returned to the United States on leave. Major

Continued on Page 5, Column 3

Douds Receives Formal Charges Aimed at Removal From NLRB

Formal charges aimed at forcing his resignation as regional director of the National Labor Relations Board were received yesterday by Charles T. Douds. The document was signed by Lester A. Asher, associate administrative examiner of the board in Washington.

Filing of the charges was announced in a statement on Tuesday by Harry A. Millis, chairman of the board, who said that Mr. Douds' removal was being sought "to promote the efficiency of the service" and on grounds of a "lack of fitness and capacity to supervise and direct the work of the staff" of the New York office. In making known that removal proceedings had been instituted against Mr. Douds, Dr. Millis voiced an implied reprimand to Mr. Douds for carrying the controversy between himself and the board into the press.

Mr. Douds, who had refused to comply with the board's previous request that he resign, demanding that formal charges be filed against him so that he might answer them in accordance with prescribed procedure, confirmed receipt of the charges yesterday but declined to discuss them. He made the following statement:

"This afternoon I received formal charges from the board. I first learned of the transmission of these charges from the papers this morning. I will answer these charges to the board and not through the newspapers.

"Dr. Millis implied in his statement this morning that the information already made public on this matter emanated directly or indirectly

Continued on Page 34, Column 3

RIPS LINE IN POLAND

Red Army Races West After Storming Into Vistula Citadel

KONEFF NEAR SILESIA

Capture of Czestochowa Threatens Heart of Reich's Industries

By The United Press.

LONDON, Thursday, Jan. 18—Russian and Polish troops yesterday captured devastated Warsaw to free its last survivors of five years of Nazi tyranny as the Red Army's greatest offensive surged twenty-four miles across western Poland, taking Czestochowa and reaching within fourteen miles of the German border.

At the same time the Red Army launched another offensive north of Warsaw that carried within 130 miles of Danzig and twenty-two miles south of the East Prussian border. Cracow, the fourth city of Poland, also was reported to have been liberated, but Moscow said only that Russian armored spearheads were eight miles northeast of the city at Sadowie.

Shoulder to shoulder, three crack Soviet armies were driving westward across Poland along a twisting 450-mile front. They were headed straight for Germany and were 260 to 288 miles from Berlin.

Racing Toward Lodz

With Warsaw, the first European capital to be overrun by Adolf Hitler's victory-flushed troops, behind them, the Russians were racing westward toward Lodz, second city of Poland, and Russian spearheads already were at Babsk, thirty-six miles east of Lodz on the main Warsaw-Berlin highway.

German troops were retreating hastily toward the borders of the Reich and Berlin reports indicated that the Nazis might be pulling out of Poland entirely, writing off their 1939 conquest of the country. German newspapers reaching Stockholm said the German High Command had moved the puppet Government General of Poland from Cracow to Central Germany.

The Russians were striking with blitzkrieg speed that paled Germany's lightning marches through Poland in 1939 and France in 1940, and though Berlin protested that its troops were fighting far behind advance Soviet lines, the German Army appeared to be in full rout.

More than 2,000,000 Soviet soldiers were committed to the huge offensive and Moscow dispatches said savagery unparalleled in four winters of war raged on the Eastern Front as the Russians tore gaps in the German lines and split and resplit enemy groups falling back toward the Oder River—the Rhine of the east.

Silesia Center Outflanked

Thousands of German troops were killed yesterday as Soviet troops, advancing at a mile-an-hour clip, outflanked the rich coal and steel region of upper Silesia and split its defenders from the main German armies in the Lodz area. Capturing Slawniow, the Russians were only twenty-four miles northeast of Dabrowa, easternmost industrial center of Silesia.

Premier Joseph Stalin announced the capture of Warsaw, "the capital of our ally, Poland," just five years, three months and twenty days after Hitler's troops marched into the bombed city, and the free Warsaw radio broadcast to the world: "The city is razed, but we live on."

Marshal Stalin announced the victory in an order of the day. In Moscow victory guns fired without interruption for three hours to mark it and two subsequent orders of the day from the Red Army's Commander in Chief.

The second told of the new offensive north of Warsaw by the Second White Russian Army under the command of Marshal Konstantin K. Rokossovsky, which had ad-

Continued on Page 6, Column 3

"All the News That's Fit to Print"

The New York Times.

LATE CITY EDITION
Fair and warm today. Cloudy and warm tomorrow.
Temperatures Yesterday—Max., 50; Min., 34
Sunrise today, 6:34 A. M.; Sunset, 7:12 P. M.

VOL. XCIV..No. 31,836. Entered as Second-Class Matter, Postoffice, New York, N. Y. NEW YORK, SATURDAY, MARCH 24, 1945. THREE CENTS IN NEW YORK CITY

PATTON CROSSES RHINE IN A DARING DRIVE WITHOUT BARRAGE, EXPANDS BRIDGEHEAD; NAZIS SAY RUSSIANS ARE MOVING ON BERLIN

SENATE, BY 52 TO 36, REJECTS WILLIAMS AS DIRECTOR OF REA

Nineteen Democrats Join With 33 Republicans to Defeat the Former Chief of NYA

HE DENOUNCES HIS FOES

And Declares With Patton of Farmers Union That Issue Is Whether People Shall Rule

By WILLIAM S. WHITE
Special to THE NEW YORK TIMES.

WASHINGTON, March 23—The Senate rejected today, 52 to 36, President Roosevelt's nomination of Aubrey Williams to be Rural Electrification Administrator. The adverse vote came through a coalition of Republicans and Conservative Democrats. Most of the latter came from the South, and some of them had been termed "Tories" by the nominee.

Nineteen Democrats joined thirty-three Republicans in voting to deny confirmation to Mr. Williams, the first such denial of an important executive appointment since 1939. Thirty-one Democrats, four Republicans and the Senate's single member of the Progressive party, LaFollette of Wisconsin, voted for the nomination.

Immediately after the Senate vote, the National Farmers Union, of which Mr. Williams has been national director of organization, vowed political vengeance on his opponents, and said that Mrs. Franklin D. Roosevelt would address a "Victory Dinner" for Mr. Williams Wednesday night that would begin "a total war of issues."

The Southern Democrats who opposed Mr. Williams were principally those whose views on economics are radically opposed to the New Dealism of Mr. Williams.

Barkley Upholds Nominee

A last minute speaker for Mr. Williams was Senator Barkley of Kentucky, the majority leader.

"The record shows," he said, "that Williams was not connected with communism, but that he combated communism."

Mr. Williams asserted that he had been rejected by "those who stand for control by the few, fearing an economy in which everybody would share."

Then, in a joint press conference at the headquarters of the Farmers Union, both he and James G. Patton, president of the National Farmers Union, indicated that the Senate's action would be used as the starting point of an intensive national organizing and political campaign by the union to be concentrated in the Deep South.

"We'll be seeing some of those Senators out where the people live," Mr. Patton declared. Remarking that the forthcoming "Victory Dinner" had been so named because the vote in the Senate "showed us how we stand," he added:

"This is the first battle in a total war of issues in this country to decide whether the country is to be conducted for the people or for the vested interests. The Farmers Union people will become much more intense in their feelings because of Mr. Williams' rejection. We are going to take whatever steps are necessary to begin to implement our feelings more drastically."

Denies Competence an Issue

Mr. Patton and Mr. Williams have been associated, as individuals, with the CIO's Political Action Committee, although the Farmers Union as an official entity has not been so connected. What the union's precise mechanism would be in its new campaign had not been determined, Mr. Patton said, although he indicated that no consideration had been given to the question of setting up a separate political organization.

Mr. Williams declared that "such Senators" as Bushfield, Republican of South Dakota; Willis, Republican, of Indiana; McKellar, Democrat, of Tennessee; Taft, Republi-

Continued on Page 15, Column 7

Women's Jury Bill Goes to Governor

Special to THE NEW YORK TIMES.

ALBANY, March 23—With unanimous adoption by the Senate, Governor Dewey received today Assemblyman Philip Schuyler's bill making jury service for women mandatory instead of optional. The only exceptions permitted under the bill are those where a woman has children under 16 years of age or is caring for a sick or invalid person.

Enactment of the measure after several years of experience under permissive jury service follows a considerable demand from women's groups, notable among which is the League of Women Voters.

A year ago former Assemblywoman Jane H. Todd sponsored a similar bill, which passed the Assembly, but died in committee in the upper house. There has been no indication as to what Governor Dewey's views are with regard to the proposal.

RISE OF $14,000,000 IN SCHOOL AID VOTED

Legislature Moves to Adjourn Today—Assembly Passes Merit Rating Truce

By LEO EGAN
Special to THE NEW YORK TIMES.

ALBANY, March 23—By unanimous vote in both houses, the Legislature passed and sent to Governor Dewey today a bill revising the apportionment of State aid for education to increase the total by about $14,000,000 over that provided by existing law and $18,000,000 over that required by the old formula.

The Assembly rejected, 66 to 78, the Young-Demo merit rating bill after a debate lasting almost five hours and then passed unanimously the "harmonizing" merit rating proposal, which had the endorsement of Governor Dewey, the Ives Committee on Labor and Industrial Conditions, the AFL and the CIO.

A majority of the Assembly Republicans favored the Young-Demo bill and threatened for a time to revolt against their leaders, who, along with Governor Dewey, opposed it.

Bowing to Labor Charged

In private conversation and, according to some reports, at a closed party conference, the Young-Demo backers accused the leadership of bowing to organized labor. There was a great deal of private bitterness over the action of Irving M. Ives, the majority leader, and Oswald D. Heck, the Speaker, in persuading a number of Republicans favoring the Young-Demo plan to switch to the "harmonizing" bill.

The "harmonizing" bill, which in most essentials is identical with the last of the Falk-Gugino bills, will be taken up in the Senate tomorrow, with passage, in view of the Assembly action, regarded as certain.

By disposing of the education-aid and merit rating measures, which rank among the most impor-

Continued on Page 15, Column 2

HOUSE UNANIMOUS IN VOTE TO EXTEND DRAFT ACT A YEAR

Senate Leaders Seek Rapid Action on Measure Free of Civilian Job Issue

NO BREAK IN DEADLOCK

New Compromise to 'Freeze' Workers Is Considered by Conferees—Vote Set Today

By C. P. TRUSSELL
Special to THE NEW YORK TIMES.

WASHINGTON, March 23—The House quickly passed by unanimous vote and sent to the Senate today a bill to extend the Selective Service Act for one year beyond May 15.

On the Senate side leaders assumed that chamber also would act promptly on the bill, without the attachment of riders which would link the drafting of men for the armed services to the mobilization of manpower on the home front.

The question of a "labor draft" remained deadlocked, with Senate and House conferees seeking to find a compromise in the conflicting civilian manpower bills which the two branches have passed.

A new compromise, or trade, was proposed today and was scheduled for a vote tomorrow. It was suggested that if the House would abandon its "limited national service," or draft, provisions, the Senate would agree to impose penalties on workers as well as employers for violations of employment ceilings and other War Manpower Commission controls.

Workers Would Be "Frozen"

Under the proposed compromise there would be a "freezing" of essential war workers into their present jobs as long as they were needed.

An expected move to prohibit the sending of draftees into combat zones within five months after their induction into the Army failed to develop in the House.

The Military Affairs Committee, which reported the extension bill yesterday, was told by Maj. Gen. Idwal Edwards, Assistant Chief of Staff in charge of training, that such a restriction would be "very definitely harmful" to an orderly system of providing men for the fighting fronts.

While the House was acting with unanimity, conferees on the manpower bills spent hours this afternoon studying the compromise offered by Senator Austin, Republican, of Vermont, and the amendments to it which have been presented by Representative May, Democrat, of Kentucky.

As a recess was taken, the conferees had before them a proposal for the newer compromise. Concededly, it was not certain that the Senate conferees would be willing to apply penalties to employes when WMC regulations were violated, even though the House conferees should agree to abandon all "labor draft" concepts.

Among Senate conferees there

Continued on Page 14, Column 3

THE RHINE IS BRIDGED AND OUR MATERIEL ROLLS ACROSS

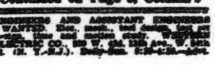

A strong span is stretched on pontoons, over which heavy trucks are carrying supplies to our forces on the east bank
The New York Times (U. S. Signal Corps)

ODER BRIDGEHEADS REPORTED MERGED

Foe Puts Red Army 6 Miles Past Kuestrin—Danzig and Gdynia Split—Push in South Gains

By The Associated Press.

LONDON, Saturday, March 24—Berlin said last night that the Red Army had reopened a blazing battle for the imperiled German capital, while Moscow announced that Russian forces had split the defenders of the prize Baltic ports of Danzig and Gdynia.

Waves of Russian infantry and tanks were reported by the enemy to have broken through defenses along Berlin's Oder River line and to have swept six miles beyond captured Kuestrin to within thirty-one miles east of the capital. [German reports cited by The United Press said that two Oder bridgeheads had been linked.

Continued on Page 7, Column 2

New Rhine Bridgehead Won Without Loss of Single Man

By EDWARD D. BALL
Associated Press Correspondent.

WITH THE UNITED STATES THIRD ARMY east of the Rhine, March 23—The United States Third Army stormed across the Rhine at 10:25 o'clock last night without loss of a man and without drawing a single shot from the Germans until a good twenty minutes after the crossing was made good.

By dawn today a solid bridgehead had been driven into Hitler's inner fortress against opposition that still was spotty and erratic despite some artillery and mortar fire.

Most of the enemy weapons were soon silenced.

By dawn many infantry units had gone across, and by that time the first waves of doughboys had pushed inland.

There was a minimum of noise and confusion at the bridgehead, where droves of assault boats were speeding back and forth with men and supplies.

Within eight hours Lieut. Gen.

Continued on Page 4, Column 4

U. S. CARRIER LOST IN BATTLE OFF IWO

Bismarck Sea, Escort Craft, Is Victim of Air Blow — Fleet Strike in Ryukyus Reported

By The Associated Press.

GUAM, Saturday, March 24—Loss of the U. S. S. Bismarck Sea, an escort aircraft carrier, to enemy aerial attack off Iwo Island on Feb. 21 was announced by Admiral Chester W. Nimitz today. Most of the Bismarck Sea's company was rescued, he stated. The normal complement of an escort carrier is about 1,500 officers and men.

[Delayed dispatches from the fleet off Iwo said there were more than 300 casualties among the crew of the Bismarck Sea, including 100 who, struggling in the water, were strafed and killed by Japanese fliers.

[The Tokyo radio said early Saturday that American carrier aircraft, which earlier in the week ravaged Japanese air and naval strength in the home islands, made attacks Friday and Saturday (today) on Okinawa Island, Japanese air and naval base in the Ryukyu group, mid-

Continued on Page 10, Column 2

AIR FLEETS FLATTEN NAZIS AROUND RUHR

U. S. 'Heavies' Strike at 12 Rail Yards, RAF Hits Bridges and Enemy Troops

By SYDNEY GRUSON
By Wireless to THE NEW YORK TIMES.

LONDON, Saturday, March 24—Allied airmen poured more thousands of tons of bombs on the Germans east of the Rhine, especially in the Ruhr area, yesterday, in the third successive day of record operations to flatten everything in the path of the American and British Armies massing for a crossing of the Rhine on the northern sector of the Western Front.

Last night, as the Ruhr's industrial towns and the great plain leading to north Germany blazed from countless fires set by thousands of heavy, medium and light bombers, more blows were struck in the aerial softening-up.

[A powerful fleet of British heavy bombers battered German troops and positions on the east bank of the Rhine during the night, London officials announced early Saturday, The Associated Press said. British planes also bombed Berlin for the thirty-second straight night.]

More than 1,250 Flying Fortresses and Liberators of the United States Eighth Air Force and three fleets of Lancasters and Halifaxes of the Royal Air Force, all of them escorted by fighters, flew by daylight through towering clouds of smoke rising from the ashes of dead cities.

In weather so clear the heavy bombers' targets could be picked up by naked eye from five miles up, the American and British crews pounded rail yards and

Continued on Page 5, Column 2

War News Summarized

SATURDAY, MARCH 24, 1945

The American Third Army has stormed across the Rhine in large force and established a firm bridgehead, the second one now held by our troops. The new crossing was made at 10:25 P. M. Thursday and the bridgehead has been expanded since then. Its site was not officially disclosed, but the Germans said it was near Frankenthal, four and a half miles north of Ludwigshafen.

The mighty German armies once deployed west of the Rhine have been either destroyed or driven to the east bank almost in their entirety. American tanks crashed into Speyer, one of the last enemy strongholds west of the Rhine, while the enemy bridgehead in the Palatinate was compressed further to an area about fifteen miles from east to west with a base of less than twenty miles along the river. Tremendous aerial blows on German communications north of the Ruhr may be part of preparations for a new offensive by Marshal Montgomery. [All the foregoing 1:8; map, P. 2.]

Thousands of Allied bombers again struck in support of the ground forces, seeking to pulverize enemy installations east of the Rhine and soften the foe's power and will to resist. Countless fires were started in the industrial areas of the Ruhr as our flying artillery pounded marshaling yards. [1:7]

The Red Army has renewed its drive on Berlin after breaking through German defenses along the Oder River line, the enemy reported. The Nazis also said the Russians had smashed six miles beyond Kuestrin to within thirty-one miles of the capital, reaching Golzow on the main Kuestrin-Berlin railroad. Soviet troops on the Baltic split the enemy before Danzig and Gdynia by knifing to the Bay of Danzig midway between the two ports. [1:4; map P. 7.]

An American escort carrier, the Bismarck Sea, was lost to enemy action off Iwo Feb. 21, the Navy announced. Another naval bulletin revealed that our carrier planes had caused extensive damage at seven Japanese ports and bases on Kyushu Island during the attack by Fifth Fleet forces early this week. Further details also put at 731 the number of enemy planes destroyed or damaged. [1:6; map P. 10.] The B-29 attack on Tokyo March 9 knocked out 20 per cent of the city's productive facilities for at least three months and the punishment given the Japanese in the five recent aerial assaults against their industrial cities probably was the most severe suffered by any people in a similar period, it was emphasized by General Norstad. [9:4.]

In the Philippines American forces took Naguilian and its airfield, twelve miles northwest of Baguio, on Luzon. [10:6.]

The Japanese opened a new offensive northwest of Hankow in central China with 60,000 troops. The drive apparently had the twin aims of capturing several Allied airfields in its path and seizing the wheat crop. [9:2; with map.] The British, striking out south of Mandalay in Burma, continued to cut up the foe. [9:5.]

Moses Threatens to Resign in Row Over 'Talk Out of Mayor's Office'

Park Commissioner Robert Moses, for years one of Mayor La Guardia's stanchest political and administrative supporters, told the Board of Estimate yesterday that he keenly resented "talk right out of the Mayor's office" insinuating that he favored a tree-removal appropriation of $145,000 because he "had to take care of favored contractors."

Commissioner Moses appeared at an adjourned meeting of the Board of Estimate to speak in support of a recommendation by Borough President James A. Burke of Queens that $145,000 be appropriated to make possible the removal, by a private contractor, of the 5,330 trees blown down by the hurricane last September and still cluttering city streets in Queens and Brooklyn. The hurricane left 16,730 trees to be removed from the streets. Of these 7,933 have been removed by contract and 3,467 by departmental forces of the Park Department, cooperating with employes of the Department of Sanitation and the offices of the borough presidents.

Discussion of the Burke proposal provoked a heated argument between Commissioner Moses and Deputy Mayor Rufus E. McGahen, who insisted that the proposal be referred to Budget Director Thomas J. Patterson for a report in accordance with routine procedure. Before the argument ended Commissioner Moses, pale with anger, indicated his willingness to

Continued on Page 15, Column 5

Germans Speed Arms to Mountains As Allies Map Their Destruction

By Wireless to THE NEW YORK TIMES.

PARIS, March 23—The Germans are speeding work on a great national redoubt, a defensive position based on the mountains of the southern Reich, where SS divisions, some regular soldiers and Nazi party officials hope to continue the war after the German field armies have been destroyed.

A reliable source who recently returned from Switzerland said the work on the redoubt had been rushed since the last Russian offensive and the Anglo-American victories west of the Rhine and that, according to neutrals who lately had been in the Reich, the Germans also were constructing another redoubt on the Kiel Canal in the north.

The Swiss, he said, are extremely worried, since the preparation of the redoubt in the south foreshadows heavy fighting near their borders by Russian as well as American and British armies.

According to this source a nobleman, who must remain unidentified, recently drove from his domain to Vienna and back. Both trips were exceedingly difficult because the Germans had closed many of the roads leading into the redoubt and he had to detour around the position. He reported that the Germans were pouring many hundreds of tons of supplies of all kinds into the redoubt.

The exact limits of the position where the Germans hope to retire

Continued on Page 3, Column 1

3D WINS FIRM HOLD

Spans the River at Night Above Ludwigshafen, Catches Foe Asleep

1ST SPEEDS UP PUSH

Palatinate Escape Gap Cut Again—Thousands More Captured

By DREW MIDDLETON
By Wireless to THE NEW YORK TIMES.

PARIS, March 23—Troops of Lieut. Gen. George S. Patton's United States Third Army have established a bridgehead over the Rhine in a bold, skillful assault.

The river was crossed at 10:25 o'clock Thursday night. The bridgehead established at that time has been steadily expanded since. [Press services said the crossing was virtually unopposed for two hours.]

The Twelfth Army Group, whose announcement was released here tonight, did not locate the bridgehead, but the German radio said that it was east of Frankenthal, four and a half miles north of the northern outskirts of Ludwigshafen.

[Earlier German broadcasts said that Third Army troops had crossed the Rhine at Oppenheim, ten miles south of Mainz, and that other American troops had attempted crossings at Duesseldorf and six miles south of Cologne, The Associated Press reported. The Germans said the crossings at Duesseldorf and in the Cologne area had been repulsed.]

Crossing Is Bold Stroke

At his headquarters, Lieut. Gen. Omar N. Bradley, Twelfth Army Group Commander, said that the Allies were in a position to cross the Rhine virtually "anywhere at any time."

The Third Army's crossing of the Rhine was an operation as daring as the character of its commander. General Patton hurled his troops across the river without preparation by artillery or air force in a surprise move that evidently caught the enemy asleep.

Since that time his troops have been striking out from the bridgehead and expanding it.

A great east-west highway runs through Frankenthal. There was a bridge under construction there in May, 1944. No recent information concerning the bridge is available here.

Frankenthal, where the Germans said the crossing was made, is six miles northwest of Mannheim on the east bank of the Rhine opposite Ludwigshafen. If the crossing was made in this area, as the enemy claimed, then General Patton has placed his troops in a fine position to attack Mannheim from the north or east. Frankenthal also is twenty-five miles southwest of the industrial city of Darmstadt.

Germans Nearly Wiped Out

Meanwhile Gen. Dwight D. Eisenhower's order to destroy the German Armies west of the Rhine is almost fulfilled.

Tanks of General Patton's Third Army rumbled into Speyer, one of the last German strongholds west of the Rhine, today, while a series of savage blows by armored and infantry divisions of the Third Army and Lieut. Gen. Alexander M. Patch's Seventh Army hammered down the enemy bridgehead in the Palatinate to a rough triangle fifteen miles from east to west with a base of less than twenty miles along the west bank of the Rhine.

The tremendous aerial assault on the German Army's defense depots and communications in the area north of the Ruhr and west of the Rhine opposite the front of Field Marshal Sir Bernard L. Montgomery's Twenty-first Army group was maintained from early morning today.

Nothing more than routine pa-

Continued on Page 3, Column 3

"All the News That's Fit to Print"

The New York Times.

LATE CITY EDITION
Clearing and warm today.
Fair, continued warm tomorrow.
Temperatures Yesterday—Max., 74; Min., 54
Sunrise today, 6:21 A. M.; Sunset, 7:36 P. M.

VOL. XCIV...No. 31,856. Entered as Second-Class Matter, Postoffice, New York, N. Y. NEW YORK, FRIDAY, APRIL 13, 1945. THREE CENTS IN NEW YORK CITY

PRESIDENT ROOSEVELT IS DEAD; TRUMAN TO CONTINUE POLICIES; 9TH CROSSES ELBE, NEARS BERLIN

U. S. AND RED ARMIES DRIVE TO MEET

Americans Across the Elbe in Strength Race Toward Russians Who Have Opened Offensive From Oder

WEIMAR TAKEN, RUHR POCKET SLASHED

Third Army Reported 19 Miles From Czechoslovak Border—British Drive Deeper in the North, Seizing Celle—Canadians Freeing Holland

By DREW MIDDLETON
By Wireless to THE NEW YORK TIMES.

PARIS, April 12—Thousands of tanks and a half million doughboys of the United States First, Third and Ninth Armies are racing through the heart of the Reich on a front of 150 miles, threatening Berlin, Leipzig and the last citadels of the Nazi power.

The Second Armored Division of the Ninth Army has crossed the Elbe River in force and is striking eastward toward Berlin, whose outskirts lie less than sixty miles to the east, according to reports from the front. [A report quoted by The United Press placed the Americans less than fifty miles from the capital.] Beyond Berlin the First White Russian Army has crossed the Oder on a wide front and a junction between the western and eastern Allies is not far off.

[The Moscow radio reported that heavy battles were raging west of the Oder before Berlin, indicating that Marshal Gregory K. Zhukoff had launched his drive toward the Reich's capital. The Soviet communiqué announced further progress by the Red Army forces in and around Vienna.]

Paris is wild with excitement tonight. A special edition of the newspaper France-Soir carries a report by the radio station "Voice of America" that places American forces fifteen and five-eighths miles from Berlin after an airborne landing that had linked up with Lieut. Gen. William H. Simpson's forces advancing eastward from the Elbe. This would put American forces only seventy-five miles from the Red Army vanguard.

No Confirmation at Headquarters

There was no confirmation of this report at Allied Supreme Headquarters, which by its own admission was thirty-six hours behind developments on some sectors of the front.

Resistance was continuing only on the northern and southern flanks. The center had burst wide open. Weimar fell to Lieut. Gen. George S. Patton's infantry, and reports from the front said Erfurt also had been cleared. Schweinfurt and Heilbronn, two German bastions on the south, had fallen to United States Seventh Army forces, who were driving on Bamberg, while farther north Third Army forces were about thirty-five miles from the Czechoslovak frontier in the area east of Coburg.

[The German radio reported American Third Army forces at Lichtenberg, nineteen miles from the Czechoslovak border, The United Press said.]

The offensives to liberate the Netherlands and reduce the Ruhr

Continued on Page 12, Column 2

OUR OKINAWA GUNS DOWN 118 PLANES

Japanese Fliers Start 'Suicide' Attacks on Fleet, Sink a Destroyer, Hit Other Ships

By W. H. LAWRENCE
By Wireless to THE NEW YORK TIMES.

GUAM, Friday, April 13—Japanese attempting to halt the American march to Tokyo, have started "desperate, suicidal" aerial attacks upon our ships and men in the Okinawa area, losing 118 planes on Thursday alone, Fleet Admiral Chester W. Nimitz announced today.

The Japanese succeeded in sinking a destroyer and damaging several other surface units, the communiqué said. All of the damaged vessels remained in action.

It was the first time that the Navy had revealed the suicidal nature of the Japanese air missions against our ships and men. The Japanese radio has been saying that this type of assault was being carried on by a "special attack corps" known in Japanese as "kamakazi," which, translated literally, means "divine wind."

Attack at Low Levels

The Japanese fliers launched their attacks upon our ships and men at a high speed and from low levels, diving directly into a ship or troop concentration to explode their bombs as they crashed.

There was no official estimate of the total number of enemy aircraft engaged in the Okinawa area attack other than the report of the 118 enemy planes destroyed.

Admiral Nimitz reported that the attacks began early on April 12 (Eastern Longitude time) with seven enemy planes shot down during the morning in the vicinity of the Hagushi beaches.

The tempo of the attack was stepped up in the afternoon as the Japanese bore in on our ships in wave after wave. Admiral Nimitz said that ships' guns, carrier aircraft and shore-based anti-aircraft shot down 111 of the attackers.

The revelation of the suicidal Japanese air attacks was the highlight of Admiral Nimitz' regular morning communiqué, which also disclosed the identity of two Marine and two Army divisions that have gone into action on Okinawa. These included the Twenty-seventh Army Division, formed from New York National Guard units, which are seeing action for the first time since the Saipan campaign and previously had engaged in the Gilbert Islands assault. It is com-

Continued on Page 18, Column 2

Army Leaders See Reich End at Hand

By The Associated Press.

WASHINGTON, April 12—High Army officials told Senators today that the end of organized fighting in Germany probably would come within a few days.

Describing the pell-mell dash of American Armies across Germany, General Staff officers expressed the opinion to members of the Senate Military Committee that a collapse of German arms was imminent.

Those who attended said the army chiefs declared that they were so sure of the results that orders had been drawn for a drastic reduction in shipments of durable equipment to Europe.

© Perskie

Franklin Delano Roosevelt
1882-1945

SECURITY PARLEY WON'T BE DELAYED

State Department Urges That World Be Shown We Plan No Changes in Policy

By JAMES B. RESTON
Special to THE NEW YORK TIMES.

WASHINGTON, April 12—The United Nations Security Conference will open in San Francisco on April 25, despite the death of President Roosevelt, Secretary of State Edward R. Stettinius Jr. announced tonight.

Mr. Stettinius said that he had been authorized by President Harry Truman to make this announcement after a meeting of the Cabinet at the White House.

Most of the overseas delegations to the San Francisco conference have either arrived in this country or are now on their way, but while this was said to have been a factor in the decision to proceed with the conference, State Department officials urged that every attempt be made to give immediate evidence to the world that President Roosevelt's foreign policy would be sustained by the new Administration.

President Roosevelt had planned to address the San Francisco conference. His interest in an international organization of nations to maintain peace and security had gone back to his service in the Wilson Administration, when he sat in the gallery of the Senate and listened to the debate that resulted in the rejection of the League of Nations Covenant. He had expressed to friends his desire to participate in the San Francisco conference and to see the United States enter the new league during his term in office.

The sudden elevation of Presi-

Continued on Page 2, Column 1

War News Summarized

FRIDAY, APRIL 13, 1945

President Roosevelt died yesterday afternoon, suddenly and unexpectedly. He was stricken with a massive cerebral hemorrhage at Warm Springs, Ga., on the eve of his greatest military and diplomatic successes—the impending fall of Berlin and the opening of the San Francisco Conference to set up a World Security Organization that would make the world free from martial and economic strife [1:7-8.]

Mr. Roosevelt had been sitting in front of the fireplace of his Little White House, having gone to Warm Springs on March 30 for a three-week rest. About 2:15 Eastern war time he said, "I have a terrific headache," lost consciousness in a few moments and died at 4:35. He was 63 years old. [1:6.]

The tragic word spread quickly around the world. Expressions of sorrow poured in from all sections. [4:5.] American soldiers and sailors refused to believe the reports until there was no longer doubt that their Commander in Chief had gone. [4:2-3.]

Harry S. Truman was sworn in as President at 7:09 o'clock last night, and a few minutes later Mrs. Roosevelt left for Warm Springs. [1:7.] The new President immediately called a Cabinet meeting and declared that Mr. Roosevelt's policies would be continued, that the war would be carried on until Germany and Japan surrendered unconditionally and that the San Francisco Conference would open April 25 as scheduled. [1:3.]

Some 500,000 American soldiers of the Third and Ninth Armies, and thousands of tanks, sped along a 150-mile front toward Berlin and Leipzig. The Ninth, surging across the Elbe, according to delayed reports was less than fifty miles from the German capital and 115 from the Russians along the Oder. The Third Army captured Weimar, home of the late German Republic, and was twenty-three miles below Leipzig, with the First closing a pincers from the north. [1:1-2; map P. 2.]

The Moscow radio reported that the Red Army was waging fierce battles east of Berlin, indicating resumption of the drive on that city. Elsewhere Russian troops scored wide gains and cut the last escape railroad from Vienna. [13:1.]

Open cities were ruled out and every German was ordered by Himmler to fight to the death, although Goebbels said "the war cannot last much longer." [12:6-7.]

The Ninth Air Force destroyed at least 117 more German planes yesterday. [11:8.]

In Italy the Eighth Army advanced along a thirty-mile front toward Bologna and the Po Valley; the Fifth Army also made good gains and was eleven miles from La Spezia. [13:8, with map.]

Japanese planes resumed their suicide attacks on American ships off Okinawa, sinking a destroyer and damaging several other vessels. One hundred and eighteen enemy planes were shot down. [1:2.] The Americal Division invaded Bohol, last of the enemy-held central Philippines. [18:6.] The B-29 attack on Koriyama, 110 miles north of Tokyo, set a new Superfortress distance record. [18:2.]

Secretary of State Stettinius and Secretary of War Stimson, denouncing Germany's "steadily increasing" mistreatment of American prisoners, said those responsible would be brought to justice. [13:6-7.]

Clashes between Right and Left wing elements in Iran were reported from Moscow. [13:2.]

LAST WORDS: 'I HAVE TERRIFIC HEADACHE'

Roosevelt Was Posing for Artist When Hemorrhage Struck —He Died in Bedroom

By The Associated Press.

WARM SPRINGS, Ga., April 12—President Franklin D. Roosevelt's last words were:

"I have a terrific headache."

He spoke them to Comdr. Howard G. Bruenn, naval physician.

Mr. Roosevelt was sitting in front of a fireplace in the Little White House here atop Pine Mountain when what was described as a massive cerebral hemorrhage struck him.

The President's Negro valet, Arthur Prettyman, and a Filipino messboy carried him to his bedroom. He was unconscious at the end. It came without pain.

Dr. Bruenn said that he saw the President this morning and he was in excellent spirits at 9:30 A. M.

"At 1 o'clock," Dr. Bruenn added, "he was sitting in a chair while sketches were being made of him by an artist. He suddenly complained of a very severe occipital headache (back of the head).

"Within a very few minutes he lost consciousness. He was seen by me at 1:30 P. M., fifteen minutes after the episode had started.

"He did not regain consciousness, and he died at 3:35 P. M. (Georgia time)."

The artist sketching Mr. Roosevelt was N. Robbins of 520 West 139th Street, New York.

Only others present in the cottage were Comdr. George Fox, White House pharmacist and long an attendant on the President; William D. Hassett, Presidential secretary; Miss Grace Tully, con-

Continued on Page 4, Column 3

END COMES SUDDENLY AT WARM SPRINGS

Even His Family Unaware of Condition as Cerebral Stroke Brings Death to Nation's Leader at 63

ALL CABINET MEMBERS TO KEEP POSTS

Funeral to Be at White House Tomorrow, With Burial at Hyde Park Home—Impact of News Tremendous

By ARTHUR KROCK
Special to THE NEW YORK TIMES.

WASHINGTON, April 12—Franklin Delano Roosevelt, War President of the United States and the only Chief Executive in history who was chosen for more than two terms, died suddenly and unexpectedly at 4:35 P. M. today at Warm Springs, Ga., and the White House announced his death at 5:48 o'clock. He was 63.

The President, stricken by a cerebral hemorrhage, passed from unconsciousness to death on the eighty-third day of his fourth term and in an hour of high triumph. The armies and fleets under his direction as Commander in Chief were at the gates of Berlin and the shores of Japan's home islands as Mr. Roosevelt died, and the cause he represented and led was nearing the conclusive phase of success.

Less than two hours after the official announcement, Harry S. Truman of Missouri, the Vice President, took the oath as the thirty-second President. The oath was administered by the Chief Justice of the United States, Harlan F. Stone, in a one-minute ceremony at the White House. Mr. Truman immediately let it be known that Mr. Roosevelt's Cabinet is remaining in office at his request, and that he had authorized Secretary of State Edward R. Stettinius Jr. to proceed with plans for the United Nations Conference on international organization at San Francisco, scheduled to begin April 25. A report was circulated that he leans somewhat to the idea of a coalition Cabinet, but this is unsubstantiated.

Funeral Tomorrow Afternoon

It was disclosed by the White House that funeral services for Mr. Roosevelt would take place at 4 P. M. (E. W. T.) Saturday in the East Room of the Executive Mansion. The Rev. Angus Dun, Episcopal Bishop of Washington; the Rev. Howard S. Wilkinson of St. Thomas's Church in Washington and the Rev. John G. McGee of St. John's in Washington will conduct the services.

The body will be interred at Hyde Park, N. Y., Sunday, with the Rev. George W. Anthony of St. James Church officiating. The time has not yet been fixed.

Jonathan Daniels, White House secretary, said Mr. Roosevelt's body would not lie in state. He added that, in view of the limited size of the East Room, which holds only about 200 persons, the list of those attending the funeral services would be limited to high Government officials, representatives of the membership of both

Continued on Page 3, Column 2

TRUMAN IS SWORN IN THE WHITE HOUSE

Members of Cabinet on Hand as Chief Justice Stone Administers the Oath

By C. P. TRUSSELL
Special to THE NEW YORK TIMES.

WASHINGTON, April 12—Vice President Harry S. Truman of Missouri, standing erect, with his sharp features taut and looking straight ahead through his large, round glasses, became the thirty-second President of the United States in a ceremony lasting not more than a minute in the Cabinet Room of the White House at 7:09 o'clock tonight.

The oath was administered by Chief Justice Harlan F. Stone two hours and thirty-four minutes after the sudden death of President Roosevelt at Warm Springs. Mr. Truman had picked up a Bible from the end of the big Cabinet conference table, held it with his left hand and placed his right hand upon the upper cover. After repeating the oath, he bowed his head, lifted the Bible to his lips and kissed it.

Even before he had taken the oath Mr. Truman had asked President Roosevelt's Cabinet to continue in service. He also authorized Edward R. Stettinius Jr., Secretary of State, to announce that the United Nations Conference for International Organization would go on as scheduled.

To the newsmen at the White House he sent this word, through Stephen Early, press secretary:

"For the time being I prefer not to hold a press conference. It will be my effort to carry on as I believe the President would have done, and to that end I have asked the Cabinet to stay on with me."

Soon after he became President, Mr. Truman left the White House for the five-room Connecticut Avenue apartment where he has resided with Mrs. Truman and their 20-year-old daughter, Mary Margaret, for four years. He said he was "going home, to bed."

It was shortly after he had finished presiding over the Senate debate on the United States-Mexican Water Treaty late this afternoon that Mr. Truman received word from the White House of President Roosevelt's death. This was at about 5:15 P. M., a half hour before the news was made public. Reaching for his hat, he dashed out of the office, calling back to his staff that he was going to the White House.

Arriving at the White House, the

Continued on Page 3, Column 6

Byrnes May Take Post With Truman

Special to THE NEW YORK TIMES.

WASHINGTON, April 12—James F. Byrnes, recently resigned as Director of War Mobilization and Reconversion, known to be one of President Truman's warmest friends in official Washington, is expected to be called to the White House for consultation, and possibly to take an important post in the Cabinet, in the immediate future.

President Truman's admiration of former Justice Byrnes is well known here. He undoubtedly would have been Mr. Truman's choice as a successor to Cordell Hull as Secretary of State.

"All the News That's Fit to Print"

The New York Times.

LATE CITY EDITION
Clearing and warmer today. Cloudy with moderate winds tomorrow.
Temperatures Yesterday—Max., 51; Min., 44
Sunrise today, 5:54 A. M.; Sunset, 7:56 P. M.

VOL. XCIV. No. 31,875. Entered as Second-Class Matter, Postoffice, New York, N. Y. NEW YORK, WEDNESDAY, MAY 2, 1945. THREE CENTS IN NEW YORK CITY

HITLER DEAD IN CHANCELLERY, NAZIS SAY; DOENITZ, SUCCESSOR, ORDERS WAR TO GO ON; BERLIN ALMOST WON; U. S. ARMIES ADVANCE

MOLOTOFF EASES PARLEY TENSION; NEW MOVES BEGUN

Russian Says Country Will Cooperate in World Plan Despite Argentine Issue

4 COMMISSIONS SET UP

They Will Deal With Council, Assembly, Court and Some General Problems

By JAMES B. RESTON
Special to The New York Times.

SAN FRANCISCO, May 1—The United Nations Conference on International Organization has survived its first basic crisis and after six days of political maneuvering on secondary issues, it began to move at rapid tempo today toward its primary task—the creation of a world organization which would stop what Field Marshal Jan Christiaan Smuts called "this pilgrimage of death."

The test came last night. Rebuffed by the conference on his attempts to keep Argentina out of the conference and bring the Warsaw Poles in, Soviet Foreign Commissar Vyacheslaff M. Molotoff went late last night to Secretary Stettinius' penthouse at the Fairmont Hotel. He immediately made his position clear.

He still disapproved the conference actions on the Poles and the Argentine, but he wanted the conference to succeed; he would cooperate in its labors, and while he was under urgent pressure by the events in Europe to return to Moscow, he would remain at least for a few days until the major issues on the charter were thrashed out among the four sponsor powers. Then, he said, he would have to leave, probably at the week-end or early next week.

"Friendly Meeting" Is Held

Immediately, in what the Foreign Ministers of the United States, Great Britain and China described to their colleagues as "the most friendly meeting of the conference," the big four approved the formation of the working commissions and committees of the conference, and other committees began discussing, not the personalities or procedures of the conference, but the basic questions of creating an organization which would win the support, with the power, of the great nations without violating the rights and principles of all nations.

The three main developments of the day were as follows:

First, the conference approved four commissions to deal with the security council of the proposed organization, the general assembly, the judicial agency and general problems, and established twelve committees to study specific problems under these four commissions.

The heads of the four commissions were: Trygve Lie of Norway, Security Council; Field Marshal Smuts, General Assembly; Carraciolo Parra Res of Venezuela, judicial organization; and Paul Henri Spaak of Belgium, general provisions.

Second, Field Marshal Smuts called on the four major powers to accept the special responsibilities which flow from the special authority given them under the Dumbarton Oaks proposals and urged all the nations here to pay more attention to the spiritual and economic aspects of the new charter than they had in the past.

Third, the Russians began studying in some detail the sixteen amendments to the Dumbarton Oaks proposals which were submitted by the United States. The other delegations started circulating amendments and exchanging views on proposals already circulated.

The facts on the crisis among the Big Three over Poland, Argentina, White Russia and the Ukraine can now be put down with assur-

Continued on Page 13, Column 6

Allies Invade North Borneo; Fighting Fierce, Tokyo Says

Australia Informed of Landing by Treasury Minister—MacArthur Reports Only Air Attacks and New Gains on Luzon

By The United Press.

MANILA, Wednesday, May 2—An official Australian announcement said yesterday that Allied troops had invaded Borneo, the world's third largest island, but Gen. Douglas MacArthur's communiqué early today reported only that heavy bombers were neutralizing enemy bases and airdromes on the oil-rich island.

Tokyo also reported the landings and said they had been made on the ten-square-mile island of Tarakan on the northeast coast, a region rich in oil wells, which the Netherlanders destroyed before the Japanese captured them in 1942. The enemy broadcast said "fierce fighting" was in progress.

[A later Japanese broadcast, picked up in San Francisco, reported that Allied units had landed on Tarakan Island at 6:30 A. M., Tuesday, Tokyo time. The broadcast said "the enemy had been bombarding the island since April 27, and on Monday morning began approaching the island in their landing attempts." It reported the landing force consisted of "about 5,000 soldiers" and said Japanese forces on the island "are holding secure their positions, obstructing the enemy's advance."]

General MacArthur announced that heavy bombers in attacks on Borneo had struck Kuching, Macassar and Kendari, while medium units and fighters had attacked Japanese gun positions on Tarakan.

General MacArthur announced that on Mindano Island the Twenty-fourth Division, in another swift drive, had advanced eleven miles

Continued on Page 16, Column 2

NEW CIGARETTES FACE PRICE INQUIRY

OPA Calls on Manufacturers of 21-Cent Brands to Prove Quality Merits Charge

By JAMES E. POWERS

Manufacturers of hitherto unheard of brands of cigarettes that have appeared on the market in recent weeks and are being retailed at four or more cents a package higher than ceiling prices for scarce popular brands will be called upon by the Office of Price Administration to show that the new products are of a quality rating the prices charged, it became known yesterday.

Daniel P. Woolley, regional OPA administrator, said an investigation was in progress as a result of complaints by smokers who said they had paid 21 cents a package for cigarettes "they had previously never heard of."

The United Wholesale Tobacco and Cigarette Distributors Association, a sub-jobbers' group, in a telegram to Senator William Langer of North Dakota, who recently introduced a resolution to set up a committee to look into the "black market" in cigarettes, demanded an immediate investigation of the entire cigarette shortage.

Mr. Woolley declared that as a result of OPA prosecution of violators of price ceilings, the black-market condition largely had been corrected here. He said he was centering on the pricing of the new cigarette brands.

Mr. Woolley added that studies were being made to determine

Continued on Page 40, Column 4

HARD COAL 'HOLIDAY' BRINGS WLB BAN

New Order by Board Asserts Output Is Urgent—Seizure Action Is Postponed

By JOSEPH A. LOFTUS
Special to The New York Times.

WASHINGTON, May 1—The War Labor Board issued a new order tonight to the United Mine Workers and the operators to resume the production of hard coal. To give the UMW leaders an opportunity to act on the order it decided to defer for twenty-four to forty-eight hours a recommendation to President Truman for Government seizure of the mines.

The miners went on a holiday today after expiration of their contract at midnight.

Dr. George W. Taylor, WLB chairman, in a telegram to both parties took cognizance of the miners' traditional "no contract, no work" policy.

"The board's order provides for a continuing contract," he said. "It is urgent that production should be immediately resumed."

As in acting on the soft coal dispute a month ago, the WLB provided in the new order that any legal wage adjustment agreed upon or finally ordered be retroactive to the expiration date of the old contract.

Union spokesmen told the WLB at a brief hearing that the Tri-District Scale Committee had voted to advise the miners to return to work when the operators accepted the settlement proposal made by Secretary of Labor Perkins.

Dr. Taylor, in questioning John Owens of the UMW, noted that

Continued on Page 40, Column 3

Eisenhower Halted Forces at Elbe; Ninth Had Hoped to Storm Berlin

By The Associated Press.

WITH THE UNITED STATES NINTH ARMY, in Germany, April 26 (Delayed by Censorship)—A direct order from Supreme Allied Headquarters halted the United States Ninth Army's drive to Berlin at the Elbe River at a time when the most pessimistic officers were predicting that Lieut. Gen. William H. Simpson's forces could reduce the German capital in ten days, "even if the Germans fought hard."

General Eisenhower's order said the Ninth would halt on the Elbe and await the arrival of Russian forces from the east, thereby leaving the capture of the capital to the Red Army. It also was understood that the American First and Third and British and Canadian armies received similar orders to halt at the Elbe.

It was not clear whether General Eisenhower's order was dictated by political policy agreed upon by the Great Powers or in a belief that it was a military necessity.

It was felt by high staff offficers in the field, however, that the Ninth and other American forces could push on to the capital without great difficulty. While the order disappointed some staff officers, it was not altogether unexpected. It was known that the Ninth Army had pushed past the eventual British-American occupation area when it crossed the Weser River.

While the staff officers were disappointed, the American doughboys and tankmen who had to do the fighting and dying to get to Berlin expressed no regret. Almost to a man, they felt they could do with-

Continued on Page 4, Column 4

REDOUBTS ASSAILED

U. S. 3d, 7th and French 1st Armies Charging Into Alpine Hideout

NEAR BRENNER PASS

British in North Close About Hamburg—Poles Gain in Emden Area

Von Rundstedt Caught

By The Associated Press.

WITH UNITED STATES SEVENTH ARMY, Wednesday, May 2—Field Marshal Karl von Rundstedt has been captured by United States Seventh Army troops.

The Seventh Army caught the former German commander in the west in its drive into the Nazis' southeastern redoubt area.

By DREW MIDDLETON
By Wireless to The New York Times.

PARIS, May 1—The last defenses of the Third Reich were crumbling as Allied tanks and infantry swept almost unopposed into the northern and southern redoubts.

Gen. George S. Patton's United States Third Army has resumed its offensive into Austria, crashing to within twenty miles of Linz, and is only fifty-four miles from Amstetten, where Marshal Fedor I. Tolbukhin's Third Ukrainian Army was last reported. According to reports from the front, radio contact has been established between tanks of the United States Eleventh Armored Division and the vanguard of the Soviet armies.

Other armored columns of the

Continued on Page 14, Column 1

NAZI CORE STORMED

Russians Drive Toward Chancellery Fortress, Narrowing Noose

BRANDENBURG TAKEN

Stralsund Port Swept Up in New Baltic Gains—Vah Valley Cleared

By C. L. SULZBERGER
By Wireless to The New York Times.

MOSCOW, Wednesday, May 2—Street battles within smoldering Berlin today entered their twelfth day since the Russians first broke into the city, with Nazi die-hards still holding grimly to the central part of the town, whittled down by yesterday's fighting, in which Marshal Gregory K. Zhukoff's First White Russian Army group completely occupied Charlottenburg and Schoeneberg and more than 100 blocks in the capital's central region.

Some 14,000 prisoners were taken within the city on Monday, the Russians announced. At the same time, the remnants of a hold-out group south of Berlin, part of which had been annihilated at Wendisch Buchholtz, was split in two and the survivors are being ground to death by Marshal Zhukoff's men.

Curiously enough, the midnight communiqué does not mention Marshal Ivan S. Koneff's First Ukrainian Army group, which has been working from the southwestern sector of the city toward the desperately defended Tiergarten.

Marshal Zhukoff's forward spearheads meanwhile struck deep into Brandenburg Province, capturing the city of Brandenburg, halfway to Magdeburg from Berlin.

While Gen. Andrei I. Yeremenko proceeded apace in his lightning

Continued on Page 3, Column 2

War News Summarized

WEDNESDAY, MAY 2, 1945

Hitler is dead, according to the Hamburg radio, and on Monday, the day before he allegedly fell at his command post in the Chancellery in Berlin, he appointed Admiral Karl Doenitz to be the new Fuehrer. The head of the German Navy, who had made his mark directing the enemy's U-boats campaign, pledged continuance of the war. [1:8.]

Washington received the news, as did London, with some skepticism and a desire to see the body. Selection of Admiral Doenitz was considered logical in view of his strong Nazi feelings. [1:7.]

The new development was interpreted in London as a move to counteract Himmler's reported peace bids, but Prime Minister Churchill broadly intimated in the Commons that he might have "information of exceptional importance" to impart before Saturday. Peace will probably come before all enemy forces have surrendered, he said. [1:6-7.] Germany was reported to have begun evacuation of Denmark and to be ready to leave Norway. Count Bernadotte said in Sweden he had no new Himmler proposals, and the Nazis' Scandinavian withdrawals were related there to a prospective general capitulation. [11:1]

Meanwhile, general Allied progress on the battlefields against slight resistance continued. The United States Third Army, on the day Hitler was declared to have died, captured Braunau, his birthplace. The drive into Austria was resumed and had reached to within twenty miles of Linz and fifty-four of the last known Russian position. The Seventh Army smashed through the Tyrol on a broad front and cleared Munich. The British Second Army, by-passing Hamburg, raced to within eighteen miles of the Baltic port of Luebeck. [1:4; map P. 14.]

General Eisenhower, it was revealed, personally ordered the halt of the Allied drive on Berlin from the west to permit the Russians to take the capital. [1:2-3.]

The Russians greatly cut down the German holding in Berlin, capturing the districts of Charlottenburg and Schoeneberg. West of the city they occupied Brandenburg and along the Baltic they seized Stralsund. [1:5; maps Pages 2 and 14.]

New Zealand troops in Italy made contact with Yugoslav Partisans at Monfalcone near Trieste and the British entered Udine. While the Eighth Army was closing a trap along the Swiss border, the Fifth neared France. [1:6-7; map P. 14.]

Mussolini and his mistress were buried in unmarked paupers' graves in Milan. [13:1.] Admiral Horthy, former Regent of Hungary, was captured. [4:3.]

Invasion of Borneo was officially disclosed in Australia, although no word of the break into the Japanese-held Netherlands East Indies had come from General MacArthur. On Mindanao in the Philippines, Americans were within six miles of the city of Davao. [1:2-3; map P. 16.]

Seventh Division troops on Okinawa resumed their southward advance, entering the village of Kuhazu. [15:1.] More than 400 starved, naked Allied prisoners of war were liberated by the British as they drove on Rangoon in Burma. [15:3.]

Good progress was made at the San Francisco Conference. Foreign Commissar Molotoff, after assuring Secretary of State Stettinius of his desire that the conference succeed, announced that pressure of events would compel his return to Moscow within a few days. [1:1.]

ADOLF HITLER — The New York Times, 1939

Clark's Troops Meet Tito's In General Advance in Italy

By VIRGINIA LEE WARREN
By Wireless to The New York Times.

AT ADVANCED ALLIED HEADQUARTERS, in Italy, May 1—After advancing fifty-five miles in less than a day along the coastal road rimming the Gulf of Venice, units of one division of the Fifteenth Army Group made contact this afternoon with Marshal Tito's forces at Monfalcone while other troops under Gen. Mark W. Clark continued to sweep German remnants from the valleys of north Italy and to seal off the few remaining escape routes through the Alps.

No details of the meeting at the small seaport northwest of Trieste between Marshal Tito's men, who had driven fourteen miles from Trieste, and leading elements of the Eighth Army's Second New Zealand Division were given in tonight's communiqué.

On the other side of Italy another historic meeting was imminent as Fifth Army troops, continuing their drive along the Gulf of Genoa, advanced on the Aurelian Way to within sixty miles of the French border, which has already been crossed by French troops headed this way.

General Clark announced yesterday that the military power of Germany had virtually collapsed, but there still are drives for his two armies to make and engagements still to be won. The Germans, trying to regroup for their flight across the Alps, were deprived of two key road junctions leading to mountain passes west of Brenner when Belluno and Udine were occupied this afternoon by units of the Eighth Army.

Udine, which was taken by the British Sixth Armored Division, is twenty-eight miles southwest of Caporetto, the scene of the Italian disaster in World War I. The forces that entered Belluno went on five miles to Ponte nell 'Alpi, guardian of the approach to Italy's

Continued on Page 13, Column 5

DOENITZ' ACCESSION VIEWED AS A BLIND

Capital Lays His Designation to General Ignorance of His Allegiance to Party

By The Associated Press.

WASHINGTON, May 1—If Adolf Hitler really designated Grand Admiral Karl Doenitz his successor, military men here believe, he did so for the following reasons:

1. Doenitz is a Nazi supporter who could be counted on to keep German resistance going if possible.

2. But he is not associated in the Allies' minds with German atrocities and the extreme policies of the Nazi party. Therefore, Hitler probably figured that he might be able to get better treatment from the Allies when the hour of surrender came.

3. He is immensely popular with the German people.

There was a disposition here tonight to look for continued organized resistance whose core would now be centered in the Baltic and North Sea port areas. Those places are the homes of the German Navy and especially of the U-boat fleet that Doenitz commanded from 1936 until he succeeded Grand Admiral Erich

Continued on Page 5, Column 1

Churchill Hints Peace This Week; 2-Day Celebration Is Authorized

By CLIFTON DANIEL
By Wireless to The New York Times.

LONDON, May 1—The general belief that peace with Germany will be announced this week persisted in Britain today, encouraged by Prime Minister Churchill himself and by Grand Admiral Karl Doenitz's announcement of the death of Adolf Hitler.

The War Cabinet again held a session tonight but so far as was known did not have any concrete proposal to consider. The chances that Heinrich Himmler ultimately will deliver an acceptable peace are now held in some official quarters to be only "fifty-fifty."

Nevertheless the buoyant Prime Minister told the House of Commons today that he might have "information of importance" to announce before Saturday.

The public's hopes were raised still further by a long Home Office circular giving the Government's views on how Britain should observe V-E Day, which the British, it appears, will be expected to celebrate strictly according to form.

[Stockholm reported, with the return there of Count Bernadotte, the "imminent liberation" of Denmark and Norway—already taking effect locally in Denmark—as a phase of a prospective general German capitulation that must be acceptable to the Allies' military commands.]

The hurrahing will begin with the announcement of the cessation of hostilities by Mr. Churchill over a nation-wide radio network. The King will speak at 9 o'clock that evening. And throughout that day

Continued on Page 10, Column 4

ADMIRAL IN CHARGE

Proclaims Designation to Rule—Appeals to People and Army

RAISES 'RED MENACE'

Britain to Insist Germans Show Hitler's Body When War Ends

By SYDNEY GRUSON
By Cable to The New York Times.

LONDON, May 1—Adolf Hitler died this afternoon, the Hamburg radio announced tonight, and Grand Admiral Karl Doenitz, proclaiming himself the new Fuehrer by Hitler's appointment, said that the war would continue.

Crowning days of rumors about Hitler's health and whereabouts, the Hamburg radio said that he had fallen in the battle of Berlin at his command post in the Chancellery just three days after Benito Mussolini, the first of the dictators, had been killed by Italian Partisans. Doenitz, a 53-year-old U-boat specialist, broadcast an address to the German people and the surviving armed forces immediately after the announcer had given the news of Hitler's death.

[The British Foreign Office said that it would demand the production of Hitler's body after the end of hostilities, The Associated Press reported.]

First addressing the German people, Doenitz said that they would continue to fight only to save themselves from the Russians but that they would oppose the western Allies as long as they helped the Russians. In an order of the day to the German forces he repeated his thinly veiled attempt to split the Allies.

Radio Prepares Germans

Early this evening the Germans were told that an important announcement would be broadcast tonight. There was no hint of what was coming. The stand-by announcement was repeated at 9:40 P. M., followed by the playing of excerpts from Wagner's "Goetterdaemmerung."

A few minutes later the announcer said: "Achtung! Achtung! In a few moments you will hear a

Continued on Page 5, Column 4

Copenhagen Writer Again Phones Story

By Cable to The New York Times.

STOCKHOLM, Sweden, May 1—For the first time in more than five years THE NEW YORK TIMES correspondent in Copenhagen, Svend Carstensen, tonight telephoned a story from the Danish capital. The Nazi-imposed censorship there has been lifted. Mr. Carstensen said:

"The Danes are overjoyed at their imminent liberation, but it is not noticeable on the Copenhagen streets.

"Anxious to avoid trouble on May Day, Copenhageners have been staying indoors. The black-out is still enforced and it is pitch dark in Copenhagen tonight. All Copenhageners are glued to radios listening to broadcasts on Hitler's death.

"We expect King Christian will resume his functions and name a new Cabinet any day now. In the meantime the strictest discipline is being observed so as not to give the Germans any excuses for starting more trouble."

On April 9, 1940, Mr. Carstensen was the first to give the world the news of the German invasion of Denmark in a wireless dispatch to THE NEW YORK TIMES. His dispatch was cleared less than an hour before the Nazis seized the radio station and was the last to be sent.

"All the News That's Fit to Print"

The New York Times.

LATE CITY EDITION
Cloudy with showers today. Partly cloudy and cooler tomorrow.
Temperatures Yesterday—Max., 64; Min., 47
Sunrise today, 5:46 A. M.; Sunset, 7:59 P. M.

Copyright, 1945, by The New York Times Company.

VOL. XCIV..No. 31,881. Entered as Second-Class Matter, Postoffice, New York, N. Y. NEW YORK, TUESDAY, MAY 8, 1945. THREE CENTS IN NEW YORK CITY

THE WAR IN EUROPE IS ENDED! SURRENDER IS UNCONDITIONAL; V-E WILL BE PROCLAIMED TODAY; OUR TROOPS ON OKINAWA GAIN

ISLAND-WIDE DRIVE

Marines Reach Village a Mile From Naha and Army Lines Advance

7 MORE SHIPS SUNK

Search Planes Again Hit Japan's Life Line—Kyushu Bombed

By WARREN MOSCOW

By Wireless to THE NEW YORK TIMES

GUAM, Tuesday, May 8—In an island-wide American advance on Okinawa yesterday the First Marine Division drove south to the edge of Dakeshi Village, about a mile from Naha, the capital, straightening out the line on our right flank. In the center the Seventy-seventh Army Division used flame-throwing tanks for considerable advances, while the Seventh Army Division moved forward on the left flank.

[Airfields on Kyushu, southern Japan, were bombed Monday and Tuesday by Superfortresses, two of which were lost in heavy air opposition.

[Allied fliers started operating from the Tarakan airfield although fighting continued on that island off Borneo, and in the Philippines American troops made advances on Mindanao and Luzon.]

Japanese Dead at 36,535

As the United States forces on Okinawa resumed their drive, Fleet Admiral Chester W. Nimitz revealed that Japanese killed on the island had mounted to 36,535 on Monday, showing that the Americans were maintaining their rate of 1,000 a day.

The Americans have not yet taken the main Japanese artillery emplacements on Okinawa, which were the principal targets of the fleet off the island. The fleet's guns continued yesterday, along with carrier aircraft, to support the ground movements.

Meanwhile search bombers of Fleet Air Wing 1 continued to give an impressive demonstration of what the tightening air blockade of Japan will mean. Attacking at mast-head height with bombs and machine guns, these long-range aircraft, based in the Okinawa area, sank four more ships in waters off Korea and damaged five others.

The ships sunk were a large cargo ship, a medium cargo ship, a medium oiler and a large fleet tanker. Two small freighters were

Continued on Page 12, Column 2

Leopold Rescued By 7th Army Troops

By The Associated Press.

WITH THE UNITED STATES SEVENTH ARMY, Tuesday, May 8—Léopold III, King of Belgium, and his wife, Princess Rethy, have been liberated by the Seventh Army, it was announced today.

They were found near Strobl, eight miles east of Salzburg. The Americans had been told of their whereabouts by civilians.

With the King and his wife were eighteen members of their staff and four children. All were in good health.

Elements of the American 106th Cavalry Group had to overpower German Elite Guards to make the rescue. Seventh Army troops are now closely guarding the royal party.

The Pulitzer Awards For 1944 Announced

The Pulitzer Prize awards announced yesterday by the trustees of Columbia University included: For a distinguished novel, to "A Bell for Adano," by John Hersey; for an original American play of the current season, to "Harvey," by Mary Chase.

Among the newspaper awards were those to Hal Boyle, Associated Press war reporter, for distinguished correspondence; to James B. Reston of THE NEW YORK TIMES for his reporting of the Dumbarton Oaks Security Conference; to Joe Rosenthal, Associated Press photographer, for his photograph of marines raising the American flag at Iwo and to The Detroit Free Press for "distinguished and meritorious public service" in its investigation of legislative corruption at Lansing, Mich.

Further details of the awards will be found on Page 16.

MOLOTOFF HAILS BASIC 'UNANIMITY'

He Stresses Five Points in World Charter, but His View on One Is Questioned

By JAMES B. RESTON

Special to THE NEW YORK TIMES.

SAN FRANCISCO, May 7—The major allies who forced Germany's unconditional surrender have reached "unanimity" on the kind of world security organization which should be created at the United Nations conference to protect their newly won victory, Vyacheslaff M. Molotoff, Russian Foreign Commissar, said today.

While the delegates at the conference celebrated the end of the European war, and three Foreign Ministers, T. V. Soong of China, Paul Henri Spaak of Belgium and Trygve Lie of Norway left the conference to deal with urgent official business elsewhere, Mr. Molotoff told the press that the Soviet Union attached the "greatest importance" to five agreements reached by the heads of the Big Four delegations.

First, he said, these leaders agreed to support the principles of justice, international law, human rights and fundamental freedom for all.

Second, he added, the Big Four agreed not to make provision in the security charter for the revision of treaties.

His statement on this point was ambiguous and led to some speculation as to the unanimity of all four on the question.

Revision Power Called Danger

A reference in the United Nations charter to the necessity of revising treaties, Mr. Molotoff stated, "would play into the hands of enemy countries, which would certainly like to undermine and emasculate these treaties." Furthermore, he declared, to give the new League of Nations authority to consider revision of treaties would be a violation of national sovereign rights, which are guaranteed in the Dumbarton Oaks Charter.

For these reasons, he concluded, "the idea of revising treaties was rejected as untenable."

Third, Mr. Molotoff said, it was agreed among the Big Four that treaties directed against Germany, such as Russia's twenty-year alliances with Britain, France, Czechoslovakia, Yugoslavia and the Warsaw Poles, "should remain in force until such time as the Government concerned felt that the international security organization was really in a position to undertake the accomplishment of the tasks of

Continued on Page 15, Column 2

GERMANY SURRENDERS: NEW YORKERS MASSED UNDER SYMBOL OF LIBERTY

Thousands filling Times Square in spontaneous celebration yesterday — The New York Times

PRAGUE SAYS FOES ACCEPT SURRENDER

Czechoslovak Radio Reports All Fighting in Bohemia Will Be Ended Today

By The Associated Press.

LONDON, Tuesday, May 8 — The Czechoslovak-controlled Prague radio announced today that the Germans in Prague and throughout Bohemia, a last major holdout pocket of German resistance, had accepted unconditional surrender.

The announcement came as the United States Third Army was reported to have advanced to the outskirts of the Czechoslovak capital, and three Russian armies hammered toward the same goal from the east and north.

"The German military plenipotentiary is negotiating with the Czechoslovak National Council on the modalities of unconditional surrender," said the broadcast, detailing what purported to be the

Continued on Page 11, Column 2

Wild Crowds Greet News In City While Others Pray

By FRANK S. ADAMS

New York City's millions reacted in two sharply contrasting ways yesterday to the news of the unconditional surrender of the German armies. A large and noisy minority greeted it with the turbulent enthusiasm of New Year's Eve and Election Night rolled into one. However, the great bulk of the city's population responded with quiet thanksgiving that the war in Europe was won, tempered by the realization that a grim and bitter struggle still was ahead in the Pacific and the fact that the nation is still in mourning for its fallen President and Commander in Chief.

Times Square, the financial section and the garment district were thronged from mid-morning on with wildly jubilant celebrators who tooted horns, staged impromptu parades and filled the canyons between the skyscrapers with fluttering scraps of paper. Elsewhere in the metropolitan area, however, war plants continued to hum, schools, offices and factories carried on their normal activities, and residential areas were calmly joyful.

One factor that helped to dampen the celebration was the bewilderment of large segments of the population at the absence of an official proclamation to back up the news contained in flaring headlines and radio bulletins. With the premature rumor of ten days ago fresh in everyone's mind, and millions still mindful of the false armistice of 1918, there was widespread skepticism over the authenticity of the news.

By mid-afternoon loudspeakers were blaring into the ears of the exulting thousands in the amusement district the news that President Truman's proclamation was being held up by the necessity of coordinating it with the announcements from London and Moscow, and that the formal celebration of the long-awaited V-E Day would be delayed until today.

This sobering note gradually

Continued on Page 7, Column 6

SHAEF BAN ON AP LIFTED IN 6 HOURS

Action Comes After Protests From Newspapers and Public—Writer Still Barred

Suspension of filing facilities of The Associated Press in the European theatre was clamped on by Supreme Headquarters, Allied Expeditionary Forces (SHAEF), yesterday in an unprecedented action and was lifted six hours and twenty minutes later.

The ban was continued, however, on all copy submitted for clearance by Edward Kennedy, chief of the press association's staff on the Western Front, who sent the momentous story announcing Germany's final surrender in a dispatch from Reims, France, which was received in New York over the AP wires at 9:35 A. M. (EWT).

It was not until seven hours and fifty-five minutes had elapsed aft-

Continued on Page 4, Column 2

Summary of News of the War and German Surrender

TUESDAY, MAY 8, 1945

The war ended in Europe yesterday after five years, eight months and six days of the bloodiest conflict in history. Grand Admiral Karl Doenitz surrendered unconditonally to the Allies in a little red schoolhouse at Reims, France. At 8:41 P. M. Sunday, New York time, Col. Gen. Gustav Jodl signed for the enemy and Lieut. Gen. Walter Bedell Smith, General Eisenhower's Chief of Staff, for the Allies. In the absence of any official announcement there was some confusion as to the compliance with the surrender. Fighting had been going on in Czechoslovakia and nothing had been heard from German pockets along the French coast. [1:7-8.]

President Truman planned a broadcast from the White House at 9 o'clock this morning. Washington, gratified that the war in Europe was over, was confused by lack of confirmation. [2:2.]

Prime Minister Churchill will also broadcast at 9 A. M. from London and Premier Stalin is expected to make a simultaneous announcement in Moscow. King George will talk over the radio six hours later. [2:8.] London will celebrate V-E Day today, but, unable to restrain its joy, staged many impromptu celebrations yesterday. [2:7.]

Most New Yorkers took the news calmly and thankfully, sobered by realization that the war in the Pacific was far from over. There were, however, noisy outbursts in such centers as Times Square and Wall Street. Scrap paper showers fluttered from roofs and windows. [1:4-5.]

German Foreign Minister Lutz Schwerin von Krosigk broke the news to his people. The future will be difficult, he warned, and then added: "We must make right the basis of our nation. In our nation justice shall be the supreme law and the guiding principle. We must also recognize law as the basis of all relations between the nations." This sudden, complete reversal in German policy was received with skepticism by the Allies. [3:1.]

Perhaps one reason for this was the announcement from Moscow that 4,000,000 men, women and children had been done to death by gas, shooting, famine, poisoning and torture in the German extermination camp at Oswiecim, Poland. [12:5.]

The actual situation in Czechoslovakia was obscure. Late last night a Patriot broadcast said the Germans were negotiating with the Czechoslovak National Council details of surrender in Prague and Bohemia. Fighting had continued throughout yesterday and German planes had bombed public buildings and hospitals. [1:3; map P. 11.].

The United States Third Army continued its general advance into Czechoslovakia and the Fifth and Seventh Armies joined again in the Alps. The British Second Army moved to Denmark and Poles entered the shattered port of Wilhelmshaven. [11:1.] Breslau fell to the Red Army after an eighty-four-day siege; 40,000 Germans were captured. [11:5.]

Japan accepted the surrender of her Axis partner with a statement that she never had expected German aid and would go on to victory without the Reich. [13:1.]

Infantry and marines on Okinawa scored another general advance after naval bombardment had pulverized Japanese strong points. Pacific Fleet planes sank or damaged thirteen more ships off Korea and Japan. [1:1; map, P. 12.] B-29's maintained their assault on Kyushu airfields. Two of the big planes were shot down. [14:3-4.]

On Tarakan Allied troops were within a mile and a half of the eastern shore. Americans gained on Mindanao and Luzon in the Philippines. [12:3-4.]

Foreign Commissar Molotoff said in San Francisco that unanimity on amendments to Dumbarton Oaks assured success of the conference. He declared that the Big Four consultations had ended. [1:2.]

GERMANS CAPITULATE ON ALL FRONTS

American, Russian and French Generals Accept Surrender in Eisenhower Headquarters, a Reims School

REICH CHIEF OF STAFF ASKS FOR MERCY

Doenitz Orders All Military Forces of Germany To Drop Arms—Troops in Norway Give Up—Churchill and Truman on Radio Today

By EDWARD KENNEDY

Associated Press Correspondent

REIMS, France, May 7—Germany surrendered unconditionally to the Western Allies and the Soviet Union at 2:41 A. M. French time today. [This was at 8:41 P. M., Eastern Wartime Sunday.]

The surrender took place at a little red schoolhouse that is the headquarters of Gen. Dwight D. Eisenhower.

The surrender, which brought the war in Europe to a formal end after five years, eight months and six days of bloodshed and destruction, was signed for Germany by Col. Gen. Gustav Jodl. General Jodl is the new Chief of Staff of the German Army.

The surrender was signed for the Supreme Allied Command by Lieut. Gen. Walter Bedell Smith, Chief of Staff for General Eisenhower.

It was also signed by Gen. Ivan Susloparoff for the Soviet Union and by Gen. Francois Sevez for France.

[The official Allied announcement will be made at 9 o'clock Tuesday morning when President Truman will broadcast a statement and Prime Minister Churchill will issue a V-E Day proclamation. Gen. Charles de Gaulle also will address the French at the same time.]

General Eisenhower was not present at the signing, but immediately afterward General Jodl and his fellow delegate, Gen. Admiral Hans Georg Friedeburg, were received by the Supreme Commander.

Germans Say They Understand Terms

They were asked sternly if they understood the surrender terms imposed upon Germany and if they would be carried out by Germany.

They answered Yes.

Germany, which began the war with a ruthless attack upon Poland, followed by successive aggressions and brutality in internment camps, surrendered with an appeal to the victors for mercy toward the German people and armed forces.

After having signed the full surrender, General Jodl said he wanted to speak and received leave to do so.

"With this signature," he said in soft-spoken German, "the German people and armed forces are for better or worse delivered into the victors' hands.

"In this war, which has lasted more than five years, both have achieved and suffered more than perhaps any other people in the world."

LONDON, May 7 (AP)—Complete victory in

Continued on Page 3, Columns 2 and 3

"All the News That's Fit to Print"

The New York Times.

LATE CITY EDITION
Showers, thunder showers; warm and humid today and tomorrow.
Temperatures Yesterday—Max., 70; Min., 67
Sunrise today, 5:49 A. M.; Sunset, 8:15 P. M.

Section 1

NEWS INDEX, PAGE 41, THIS SECTION

VOL. XCIV..No. 31,963. Entered as Second-Class Matter, Postoffice, New York, N. Y. NEW YORK, SUNDAY, JULY 29, 1945. Including Magazine and Book Review. TEN CENTS New York City and Suburban Areas (15c Elsewhere)

SENATE RATIFIES CHARTER OF UNITED NATIONS 89 TO 2; TRUMAN HAILS AID TO PEACE

FOES ARE CRUSHED

With Hiram Johnson Ill, Only Shipstead and Langer Vote 'No'

WORLD OBLIGATION CITED

Leaders Say Today's Ratification Is 'Master Plan,' With Military Pacts Secondary

By JAMES B. RESTON

Special to THE NEW YORK TIMES.

WASHINGTON, July 28—The United States Senate paid a first installment on an old debt today. It ratified, 89 to 2, the United Nations Security Charter, successor to the League of Nations Covenant which it rejected twenty-six years ago, and thereby fulfilled Woodrow Wilson's prophecy that one day the upper chamber would reverse its decision.

The vote came 107 days after the death of Franklin D. Roosevelt, who helped guide the Charter past the pitfalls that defeated Wilson's Covenant, and at a moment when American statesmen were settling the fate of a defeated Germany and American warships were closing in on the heart of Japan.

The two Senators who voted against ratification were William Langer of North Dakota and Henrik Shipstead of Minnesota, both Republicans. Mr. Langer, who worked actively for Hiram Johnson and Robert M. La Follette when those two "irreconcilables" were candidates for President, said he was voting against the Charter because it would mean "perpetual war" and the "enslavement" of millions of poor people from Poland to India.

Hiram Johnson Sends Word

Senator Hiram Johnson, Republican, of California, sent word from the Naval Medical Center outside Washington that if he had been well enough to be present he would have joined Mr. Langer and Mr. Shipstead in opposition, but the four other members of the Senate who were with Mr. Johnson in the upper chamber during the League of Nations debate—Arthur Capper, Republican, of Kansas, and Peter G. Gerry of Rhode Island, Kenneth McKellar of Tennessee, and David I. Walsh of Massachusetts, Democrats, all voted for ratification.

As soon as the results were made known, President Truman and Cordell Hull, former Secretary of State, who started work on the Charter in the State Department in 1942, issued statements praising the Senate's action.

"It is deeply gratifying that the Senate has ratified the United Nations' Charter by a virtually unanimous vote," the President's message from Potsdam said. "The action of the Senate substantially advances the cause of world peace."

It was a grim-appearing Senate that rolled off the "ayes" on the final count this evening. Despite the long parliamentary debate in the chamber on the subject, and despite its overwhelming approval at the end, there was no sense of a job finished but merely of a difficult job just beginning.

Since a league to enforce peace had first been mentioned to members of this chamber by Woodrow Wilson in 1914, some 40,000,000 human beings, armed and unarmed, had been killed in two great wars. In the first German war total military casualties were estimated at 37,000,000 men; in the European phase of the second German war some 14,000,000 more had been killed, and our own casualties in this war, still unfinished, were over the million mark.

Chaplain Tells Senate's Hopes

Throughout the debate, the Senate seemed to realize this and to approach the problem more in hope than anything else.

"Under the old order of strife," the Senate's chaplain said in his prayer opening today's session, "we learned how to destroy ourselves. Under a new charter of mutual aid and tolerance of diversity, may we learn at last how to save ourselves."

Today's vote does not put the

Continued on Page 33, Column 4

Truman Deeply Gratified, He Says in Cable Message

President Promptly Recognizes Senate's Action as Advancing 'the Cause of World Peace'—Grew and Hull Applaud

Special to THE NEW YORK TIMES.

WASHINGTON, July 28—President Truman was swift to applaud the passage of the World Security Charter. In a message from Potsdam he said:

"It is deeply gratifying that the Senate has ratified the United Nations Charter by a virtually unanimous vote.

"The action of the Senate substantially advances the cause of world peace."

Joseph C. Grew, Acting Secretary of State, and Cordell Hull, former Secretary of State, also commended the Senate for its approval of the Charter.

Mr. Grew said:

"The passage of the United Nations Charter by the Senate today is a memorable event in the history of the United States and the world. By their action, the members of the Senate have taken a most important step toward establishing security and peace throughout the world.

"Millions of men, women and children have died because nations took to the naked sword instead of the conference table to settle their differences.

"The United Nations Charter, approved by such an overwhelming majority, represents the labor of citizens of fifty nations, united in their desire for a peaceful world. The Charter itself is the foundation and cornerstone on which the international organization to keep the peace will be built. This organization can survive only through the faith and labor of the citizens of all these nations.

"I congratulate the members of the Senate for their work today.

Continued on Page 33, Column 1

Poles, at Big 3 Meeting, Ask Stettin, Oder-Neisse Border

By RAYMOND DANIELL

By Wireless to THE NEW YORK TIMES.

BERLIN, July 28—A delegation of the Polish Government, including Vice Premier Stanislaw Mikolajczyk and, it is believed, Labor Minister Jan Stancczyk, has been here this last week to ask for a final delimitation of their country's western frontier to include Stettin and run from there southward along the east bank of the Oder-Neisse River line.

It was officially announced that Britain's new Prime Minister, Clement R. Attlee, and his Foreign Minister, Ernest Bevin, after formal calls on President Truman, Secretary of State James F. Byrnes, Premier Stalin and Foreign Commissar Vyacheslaff M. Molotoff, had participated today in a plenary session of the tripartite conference.

It is now believed, although there has been no inkling of their plans from official sources, that neither Winston Churchill nor former Foreign Secretary Anthony Eden will return. The new Prime Minister and his Foreign Secretary, who as Labor Minister in Mr. Churchill's coalition Government had access to all secrets of the War Cabinet, are the only new members of the British delegation. Inasmuch as Mr. Attlee sat in at all sessions of the Big Three before his election and saw all the official documents at the conference, it can hardly be said that he is a newcomer to the council table.

Parley Continuity Maintained

The downfall of the Churchill Government has caused little break in the continuity of the conference. Little more than forty-eight hours elapsed between Mr. Churchill's departure from Berlin and Mr. Attlee's return today.

In the absence of the head of the British delegation experts worked steadily to clear the decks

Continued on Page 5, Column 4

WOOLLEY DISMISSES ROSS IN OPA DISPUTE

Refuses to Grant the Public Hearing Demanded by Aide He Suspended June 22

Paul L. Ross, regional enforcement executive of the Office of Price Administration, who was suspended June 22 on charges of maladministration, was discharged yesterday by Daniel P. Woolley, regional OPA administrator, who refused to grant Mr. Ross the public hearing for which he had pleaded.

The discharge, effective at once, was contained in a registered letter mailed to Mr. Ross at noon, and followed by less than forty-eight hours the filing of Mr. Ross' reply to the administrator's charges.

In a brief statement, Mr. Woolley declared "utterly untrue and unfounded" serious counter-charges against him preferred by Mr. Ross in his answer. The enforcement officer had accused Mr. Woolley of hampering the enforcement of OPA regulations, interfering in behalf of certain alleged violators and obstructing the Federal enforcement policies.

Upon learning of his discharge,

Continued on Page 37, Column 5

Kweilin and Three Airfields Seized; Chinese Also Gain in Other Areas

By The Associated Press.

CHUNGKING, China, July 28—Chinese troops recaptured the airbase city of Kweilin yesterday and seized its three former American airfields from the Japanese, the Chinese High Command said tonight. The victory ended a six-week battle.

Kweilin, walled capital of Kwangsi Province, once was the biggest United States airbase in South-Central China. It had been occupied by the Japanese since last November. Its recapture was the most significant victory in the recent comeback of the Chinese armies.

Generalissimo Chiang Kai-shek's veterans smashed into the rubbled streets of Kweilin, 360 miles southeast of Chungking, at 4 P. M. yesterday after mowing down the defenders of the city's south and west gates. Most of the Japanese garrison had fled and enemy rearguard remnants swiftly were routed from machine-gun nests in cellars and on roofs, a communiqué said.

The Japanese, headquarters added, withdrew to the northwest to escape annihilation. Their escape route northeastward to Hengyang was severed several days ago. The Chinese said: "Our troops are in hot pursuit."

Kweilin, abandoned by the United States Fourteenth Air Force eight months ago, was the third former American airbase recovered in three days by the Chinese, whose current drive is rapidly strengthening American air power on the Asiatic mainland. It was

Continued on Page 3, Column 5

CRIPPLED WARSHIPS OF JAPANESE NAVY SMASHED BY FLIERS

2 Battleships and 3 Cruisers Set Afire in Saturday Strike by the Third Fleet

HYUGA IS FOUND SUNK

Returning U. S. Pilots Report Waters Off Kure Strewn With Burning Vessels

By Wireless to THE NEW YORK TIMES.

GUAM, Sunday, July 29—Two Japanese battleships, the Haruna and Ise, and three cruisers were set afire and a third battleship, the Hyuga, which was heavily damaged on Tuesday, was found to be resting on the bottom at her anchorage as United States Third Fleet carrier planes struck heavily Saturday at crippled remnants of the Japanese Navy in the Inland Sea.

An aircraft carrier also was further damaged.

Fleet Admiral Chester W. Nimitz today announced the results of the strike, which were incomplete. No reports had yet been received from British carrier pilots, who also participated.

Enemy Air Opposition Sporadic

The enemy's air opposition was sporadic, with American fighters shooting down one Japanese plane near Task Force 38, another eighteen near the target areas and destroying seventy-five on the ground. Fifty-six other parked enemy aircraft were damaged.

[Pilots returning from the Saturday strike reported waters off the Kure naval base littered with burning ships, and fleet dispatches said every major Japanese warship was believed to have been put out of action for the duration of the war, The United Press stated.]

The Third Fleet assault was directed at Japanese shipping between the once great ports of Kobe and Kure.

Pilots reported that the Hyuga, a modernized battleship with carrier type runway aft permitting it to handle aircraft, was on the bottom, water lapping over her main deck amidships.

It was disclosed also that Saturday's aerial assault, resulted in the sinking of three submarines, presumably in dry dock, and damage to four destroyers, two destroyer escorts, two medium-size freighter transports, three small cargo ships and an unidentified vessel.

Five Warships Left Burning

Whether these ships were among those damaged in the Tuesday attack, which battered twenty-three warships, was not revealed. However, it is definite that yesterday's attack further damaged six warships hit on Tuesday, the battleships Haruna and Ise, the cruisers Tone, Aoba and Oyodo and the escort carrier Kaiyo. All of these ships except the carrier were left burning in the latest assault.

Thus it seems that Admiral Halsey is well along toward his objective—the neutralization of Japan's remaining naval warships in order to provide a thoroughly clear field for future amphibious

Continued on Page 3, Column 2

War News Summarized

SUNDAY, JULY 29, 1945

The United States Senate ratified, 89 to 2, the United Nations Security Charter. The two Senators who voted against ratification were William Langer of North Dakota and Henrik Shipstead of Minnesota, both Republicans. [1:1.]

Two battleships and three cruisers, all previously damaged, were hit again in the latest Third Fleet attack on the Inland Sea area, Admiral Nimitz disclosed, and it was found another battleship had been sunk. Returning pilots reported that the Japanese Navy probably was out of action for the rest of the war. [1:4.]

Between 550 and 600 Superfortresses set fire to six of the eleven Japanese cities warned previously of their coming destruction. [1:5; map P. 2.]

General Minami, chief of Tokyo's would-be totalitarian party, said Japan would be ready to discuss peace when East Asia was free from British-American "colonial exploitation." [9:1.]

Captain Zacharias, United States naval spokesman, broadcast to Japan a declaration that peace with Japan had now been made possible by the Potsdam proclamation. [4:5.]

Chinese forces took Kweilin and three former United States airfields. Other Chinese pressed toward Kukong, 120 miles north of Canton, gaining thirty miles in two days. [1:2-3; map P. 3.]

The British in Burma reported that the Japanese Twenty-eighth Army had been annihilated with more than 5,500 killed and the remnant fleeing toward Thailand. [3:1.]

Prime Minister Attlee and six new Ministers took the oath of office in London. [5-1.]

A Polish Government delegation was in Potsdam pleading for a western frontier running along the Oder and Niesse Rivers. Meanwhile, the conference was resumed with Mr. Attlee and Foreign Secretary Bevin in the places of Winston Churchill and Anthony Eden. [1:2-3; map P. 5.]

Michel Clemenceau accused Marshal Pétain at the latter's treason trial of having been indirectly responsible for handing over Georges Mandel, former Minister of Colonies, to the Germans who killed him. [12:1.]

BOMBER HITS EMPIRE STATE BUILDING, SETTING IT AFIRE AT THE 79TH FLOOR; 13 DEAD, 26 HURT; WIDE AREA ROCKED

WHERE BOMBER CRASHED INTO EMPIRE STATE BUILDING

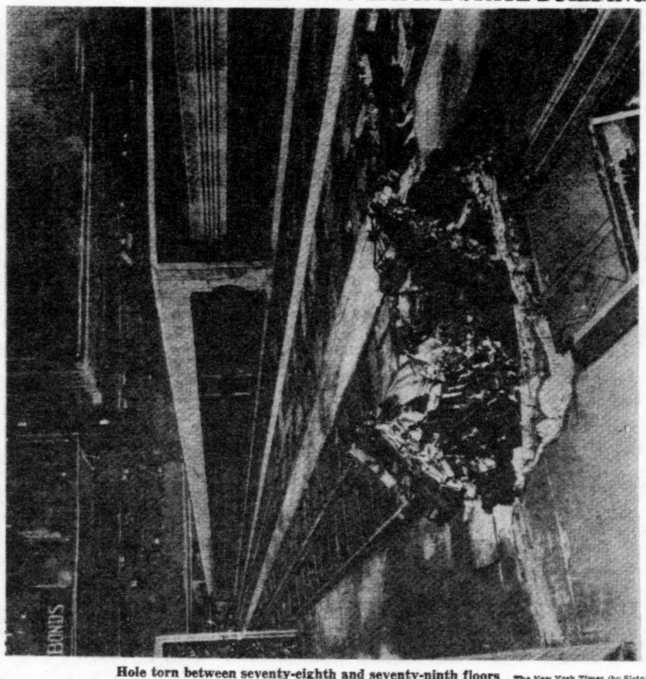

Hole torn between seventy-eighth and seventy-ninth floors The New York Times (by Sisto)

B-25 CRASHES IN FOG

Hole 18 by 20 Feet Torn Through North Wall by Terrific Impact

BLAZING 'GAS' SCATTERED

Flames Put Out in 40-Minute Fight—2 Women Survive Fall in Elevator

By FRANK ADAMS

A twin-engined B-25 Army bomber, lost in a blinding fog, crashed into the Empire State Building at a point 915 feet above the street level at 9:49 A. M. yesterday. Thirteen persons, including the three occupants of the plane and ten persons at work within the building, were killed in the catastrophe, and twenty-six were injured.

Although the crash and the fire that followed wrecked most of the seventy-eighth and seventy-ninth floors of the structure, causing damage estimated at $500,000, Lieut. Gen. Hugh A. Drum, president of the Empire State, Inc., Corporation, said last night that an inspection by the city's building department and by other engineers and architects showed that the structural soundness of the building had not been impaired.

Landing Advice Disregarded

The plane, en route from Bedford, Mass., to Newark on a cross-country mission, had flown over La Guardia Field a few minutes before the crash, and its pilot, Lieut. Col. William F. Smith Jr., deputy commander of the 457th Bomber Group and recently decorated for his service overseas, was advised by the control tower to land. Instead he asked for the weather at Newark Airport and headed in that direction.

Horror-stricken occupants of the building, alarmed by the roar of engines, ran to the windows just in time to see the plane loom out of the gray mists that swathed the upper floors of the world's tallest office building. The plane was banked at an angle of about fifteen degrees as Colonel Smith swung it in a curve out of the northeast.

It crashed with a terrifying impact midway along the north or Thirty-fourth Street wall of the building. Its wings were sheared off by the impact, but the motors and fuselage ripped a hole eighteen feet wide and twenty feet high in the outer wall of the seventy-eighth and seventy-ninth floors of the structure.

Brilliant orange flames shot as high as the observatory on the eighty-sixth floor of the building, 1,050 feet above Fifth Avenue, as the gasoline tanks of the plane exploded. For a moment watchers in the street below saw the tower clearly illumined by the glare. Then it disappeared again in gray murk and the smoke of the burning plane.

Motor Hits Another Building

One of the plane's two motors hurtled clear across the seventy-eighth floor, tore a hole in the south wall of the building, and plummeted to the roof of the twelve-story office building at 10 West Thirty-third Street, where it started a fire that demolished the penthouse of Henry Hering, noted sculptor, with resulting damage estimated at $75,000.

A propeller was imbedded in the wall of the Empire State Building; the other motor and part of the landing gear crashed into an elevator shaft, where they fell to the sub-cellar 1,000 feet below, and other sections of the fuselage were blown as high as the eighty-sixth floor observatory. The steel girder at the seventy-ninth floor level was bent inward eighteen inches by the shock.

Cascading torrents of flaming gasoline poured through the seventy-eighth and seventy-ninth floors, setting fire to everything that was combustible. The burning fuel ran down stair wells into hallways as far as the seventy-fifth floor, while choking fumes

Continued on Page 25, Column 1

B-29'S FIRE 6 CITIES IN PROMISED BLOWS

Oil Refinery Target on Honshu Added to List LeMay Gave Japanese in Advance

By Wireless to THE NEW YORK TIMES.

GUAM, Sunday, July 29—The Twentieth Air Force early today bombed six out of eleven Japanese cities that hardly twenty-four hours previously had been told that they were on a list of enemy communities marked for aerial destruction by Superfortresses.

Seven task forces of the B-29 bombers, totaling 550 to 600 planes, dropped more than 3,500 tons of incendiaries on the six industrial centers situated from Shikoku in the south to northern Honshu and demolition bombs on an oil refinery near Osaka.

[Gen. Douglas MacArthur reported Okinawa-based Army planes had sunk enemy shipping in Japan's Inland Sea area. He disclosed that our new B-32 super-bomber has been in action since May against the foe on Formosa and along the China coast.]

One of the B-29 task forces, sent

Continued on Page 4, Column 1

Catholic War Relief Office Is Chief Victim of Tragedy

By LARRY RESNER

An agency that has been in the vanguard of supplying aid and comfort to thousands of homeless and destitute persons in the war zones became yesterday, through one of those curious quirks of fate, the victim of the worst local tragedy of the war. The point of greatest impact of the low-flying bomber that crashed into the Empire State Building was at the seventy-ninth floor, where the principal tenant was the War Relief Services of the National Catholic Welfare Conference.

Throughout the war years, this agency has sent many field representatives into the lands laid waste by war to work with other relief and welfare agencies in helping war victims.

And only yesterday, as the bomber struck and destroyed their office, the reduced Saturday staff of workers was busily engaged in arranging the final details of a trip to Europe on Tuesday of two of their principal functionaries.

Only five of an estimated working staff of fifteen to twenty persons in the office, including men and women, were known to have escaped the flames that swept the skyscraper floor as the gasoline of the crashing plane exploded.

W. Paul Dearing, correspondent here for The Buffalo Courier-Express and publicity director of the War Relief Services for the last year, either jumped or was blown from his seventy-ninth-floor office to his death on a ledge on the sev-

Continued on Page 32, Column 8

SURVIVOR LIKENS CRASH TO A QUAKE

Building Moved Twice, Then Settled, Says Occupant Who Felt Shocks in China

By ALEXANDER FEINBERG

The towering Empire State Building that is a city of 102 stories, reaching 1,250 feet high, "moved" twice yesterday when struck by the bomber and then it "settled." That was a dread moment for one who had felt that double movement and the settling many times before.

Recently returned from China after twenty-seven years, the man who told of his sensations when the B-25 struck said the impact was precisely that of an earthquake, to which he is no stranger. Preferring not to give his name, he said he was in an office on the sixty-eighth floor of the building when he felt the double "move-

Continued on Page 28, Column 1

Red Cross and Hospital Groups Speed to Aid of Victims, Rescuers

The last fireman barely had leaped from his truck to the raging four-alarm blaze caused by the bomber crash in the Empire State Building when hospital disaster units and two Red Cross Service canteen wagons were on the scene to aid the victims and rescuers of the catastrophe.

While fifteen Red Cross aides set up shop and dispensed hot coffee and doughnuts to the toiling fire fighters and others helping them, two disaster units from Bellevue Hospital, replete with the latest equipment, were making their way into the upper reaches of the building to assist in the rescue work.

Only twelve minutes elapsed between the sounding of the first alarm at 9:49 A. M. and the fourth alarm and from the moment the Telegraph Bureau at Police Headquarters received the first report the city's fire-fighting equipment, a small army of police and squads of Army and Navy units, mostly military police and shore patrols, moved with clock-like precision through the fog-shrouded streets.

The fire sirens screeched constantly as apparatus sped to the scene. The second alarm hit at 9:57 A. M., the third at 10 A. M. and the last at 10:01 A. M. After that there were other calls but only for specialized equipment.

The four alarms brought to the scene forty-one pieces of fire-fighting apparatus, including "walkie-talkie" radio units. All were under the immediate command of Fire Commissioner Patrick Walsh. Almost simultaneously the Police Department's ranking officers dispatched more than 400 policemen,

Continued on Page 32, Column 6

"All the News That's Fit to Print"

The New York Times.

LATE CITY EDITION
Partly cloudy, less humid today.
Cloudy and warm tomorrow.
Temperatures Yesterday—Max., 72; Min., 66
Sunrise today, 5:37 A. M.; Sunset, 8:06 P. M.

VOL. XCIV..No. 31,972. Entered as Second-Class Matter, Postoffice, New York, N. Y. NEW YORK, TUESDAY, AUGUST 7, 1945. THREE CENTS IN NEW YORK CITY

FIRST ATOMIC BOMB DROPPED ON JAPAN; MISSILE IS EQUAL TO 20,000 TONS OF TNT; TRUMAN WARNS FOE OF A 'RAIN OF RUIN'

HIRAM W. JOHNSON, REPUBLICAN DEAN IN THE SENATE, DIES

Isolationist Helped Prevent U. S. Entry Into League—Opposed World Charter

CALIFORNIA EX-GOVERNOR

Ran for Vice President With Theodore Roosevelt in '12 —In Washington Since '17

Special to THE NEW YORK TIMES.

WASHINGTON, Aug. 6—Senator Hiram Warren Johnson of California lifelong isolationist who helped prevent this country's entry into the League of Nations and fought all "foreign entanglements" through a second World War, died in his sleep this morning at Bethesda Naval Hospital, nine days after, ill but consistent, he had paired his vote against ratification of the United Nations Charter. Death was caused by a thrombosis of a cerebral artery. Mrs. Johnson was with him when the end came.

When word reached the Capitol of the passing of the oldest member of the Senate in point of service, save Senator Kenneth McKellar, the President pro tempore, the mourning was deep. With great personal affection colleagues paid humble tribute to his integrity of character, his liberalism and his steadfastness to his ideals and convictions. They joined in declaring that the country had lost a great statesman.

Senator Johnson, who was serving the fourth year of his fifth term in the Senate, would have been 79 years old on Sept. 2. Although his health had been failing during the last two years and though the thundering voice which had conveyed his eloquence through innumerable stirring debates had become little more than a whisper, friends believed he planned to seek a sixth term in 1947.

He went to the hospital July 18. Five days before that he had cast the lone vote in the Foreign Relations Committee, of which he was the ranking minority member, against reporting the new World Charter to the Senate without change. He did not participate in the floor debate on this document, which won Senate approval by a vote of 82—2. However, he clashed spiritedly with colleagues while the hearings were in progress.

Funeral arrangements awaited the arrival of the Senator's son, Lieut. Col. Hiram W. Johnson Jr., who was flying here from California.

Capper Becomes the Dean

The death of Senator Johnson made Senator Arthur Capper of Kansas, who last month marked his eightieth birthday, the Republican dean of the Senate. It also elevated him to the ranking minority membership on the Foreign Relations Committee, with which Senator Johnson had been so conspicuously identified through the many years of his unshaken position on foreign policy. Mr. Capper, too, with Senators McKellar, Carter Glass of Virginia, David I. Walsh of Massachusetts and Peter G. Gerry, was in the League fight of 1919 and 1920. He supported it, with reservations.

The career of Senator Johnson, from his entrance into the Senate from the Governorship of California in March of 1917, was one distinctly lacking in compromise or reservation. In 1912 he had bolted his party with Theodore Roosevelt and had become his running mate on the Bull Moose ticket. In 1932 he again bolted to support Franklin D. Roosevelt for the Presidency but broke bitterly with the President when he ran for his third term.

In 1919 Mr. Johnson joined with Senators Lodge, Borah, Reed,

Continued on Page 23, Column 4

Jet Plane Explosion Kills Major Bong, Top U. S. Ace

Flier Who Downed 40 Japanese Craft, Sent Home to Be 'Safe,' Was Flying New 'Shooting Star' as a Test Pilot

By The United Press.

BURBANK, Calif., Aug. 6—Maj. Richard Bong, America's greatest air ace, died today in the flaming wreckage of a jet propelled fighter plane which crashed while he was testing it.

Only 24 years old, he wore twenty-six decorations including the nation's highest award, the Congressional Medal of Honor. He had survived countless air battles and shot down forty Japanese planes without a scratch.

The knowledge he gained in those battles was too valuable to risk, so he was brought home to "safe" duty. He was on that "safe" duty today when his P-80, the Shooting Star, hurtled over a clump of trees and burst like a bomb in a field.

Witnesses did not agree on the cause of the crash. One Army flier said that Major Bong overshot the Lockheed airport. Another witness, John McKinney of North Hollywood reported that he saw something fall out of the plane's tail.

"The plane started to wobble up and down, then went into a left bank and hit the ground," he stated. "It exploded and burned and scattered wreckage over about a block square."

Major Bong was trying to get out of the ship when it crashed. He had released the escape hatch and was partly clear. He had pulled the ripcord to his parachute, and the silken folds lay about the body as the flames swept over it.

With a roaring sigh, the plane, like a giant blowtorch, shot over the airport just before 3 P. M. and then lurched over the trees and nosed down into the field, a mile away.

Smoke and flame surged up and crowds rushed from the airport. By the time anyone could reach the scene the ship had been almost consumed.

The crash scene was near the intersection of Cahuenga and Oxnard Boulevards and barely out-

Continued on page 15, Column 2

MORRIS IS ACCUSED OF 'TAKING A WALK'

Fusion Official 'Sad to Part Company'—McGoldrick Sees Only Tammany Aided

The No Deal ticket, headed by Council President Newbold Morris, "can only serve the interests of Tammany Hall," Controller Joseph D. McGoldrick, candidate for re-election on the Republican-Liberal-Fusion party slate, declared yesterday in a fresh attack on the third-party ticket injected over the week-end into the city Mayoralty campaign.

A short while later Gabriel A. Wechsler, general secretary of the City Fusion party, which supported Mayor La Guardia and Mr. Morris in previous city campaigns, accused Mr. Morris of "taking a walk away from the good government forces."

To both charges Mr. Morris declared he would stand on his statement of Sunday that he was not interested in "just taking votes" away from Judge Jonah J. Goldstein, Republican-Liberal-Fusion candidate for Mayor, or from William O'Dwyer, his Democratic-American Labor party opponent.

"I have no comment," he said, "since I stand on my statement of Sunday. We are waging an affirmative campaign."

Informed that Hyman Blumberg,

Continued on Page 19, Column 6

CHINESE WIN MORE OF 'INVASION COAST'

Smash Into Port 121 Miles Southwest of Canton—Big Area Open for Landing

By The Associated Press.

CHUNGKING, China, Aug. 6—Chinese troops have broken into the South China port of Yeungkong and cleared a fifty-mile stretch of the Chinese "invasion coast" west of Hong Kong, Generalissimo Chiang Kai-shek's headquarters said today.

Swaying block-by-block street fighting is raging in the strategic coastal highway town, 121 miles southwest of Canton, a communiqué said.

By breaking into Yeungkong Chinese forces won control of a fifty-mile coastal stretch leading west to Tinpak, which lies east of Luichow Peninsula on the South China Sea. The coastal area now is open to a virtually unopposed landing should American forces choose it for a staging point for supplies to the armies of South China.

West of Luichow Peninsula another 145-mile coastal stretch extending to the Indo-China frontier is under Chinese control and observers believe the Chinese soon may launch a concerted drive from the west and east that would seal off the Japanese on the Luichow

Continued on Page 2, Column 7

Turks Talk War if Russia Presses; Prefer Vain Battle to Surrender

By SAM POPE BREWER
By Wireless to THE NEW YORK TIMES.

ANKARA, Turkey, Aug. 6—Russo-Turkish relations weigh heavy on Turkish minds these days. All leading editors commented today on various aspects of the Russian claims against Turkey.

The Potsdam conference leaves the situation virtually unchanged so far as the Turks can see, but they seem to agree that they would go to war, however hopeless such a war might be, rather than yield before the threat of force. Suggestions from London and Washington that the Russians have been asked to moderate their demands give little reassurance here.

The Potsdam communiqué created more confusion than confidence and the Turks are still trying to decide whether the fact that the conference did not deal with certain specific questions means that it was a failure.

Many point out that all the really thorny questions still are unsettled. The Turks probably do not see a relative importance among world problems of Russian demands on Turkey, but point out that the important question of principle is involved. The general and apparently official argument is that the status of the Straits cannot he modified by a bilateral agreement but must be discussed at a conference of the signatories of the Montreux Convention, with America replacing Japan. The signatories were Great Britain, France, Russia, Japan, Turkey, Greece, Rumania, Yugoslavia and Bulgaria.

The grounds for the Russian claims to Kars and Ardahan are not clear, but throughout the Near and Mideast in recent months

Continued on Page 13, Column 1

KYUSHU CITY RAZED

Kenney's Planes Blast Tarumizu in Record Blow From Okinawa

ROCKET SITE IS SEEN

125 B-29's Hit Japan's Toyokawa Naval Arsenal in Demolition Strike

By FRANK L. KLUCKHOHN
By Wireless to THE NEW YORK TIMES.

MANILA, Tuesday, Aug. 7—More than 400 fighters and bombers, speeding at chimney-top level for two hours Sunday over Tarumizu in southern Kyushu in the largest single attack launched by Gen. George C. Kenney's Far East Air Forces to date, leveled that city's munitions factories and aircraft and munitions storage depots and waterfront installations.

Rockets and demolition bombs were poured by waves of B-26 Invaders, B-25 Mitchells and Mustangs and Thunderbolts of the Fifth and Seventh Air Forces from Okinawa, supported by a few B-24 Liberators carrying big bombs.

[Tarumizu, about 350 miles from Okinawa, appeared to be a site at which the Japanese might be preparing a rocket campaign against the American base, said a United Press dispatch. FEAF pilots reported seeing in the area, which has extensive cave construction, what seemed to be Japanese robot planes and also a huge catapult-like machine, extending over the water, that might be a rocket launcher.

[About 125 B-29's hit the Toyokawa naval arsenal of Japan in a demolition bombing Tuesday noon, Strategic Air Forces headquarters at Guam reported.]

The planes over Tarumizu met scant resistance, as our fliers took their time to assure the highest

Continued on Page 11, Column 2

REPORT BY BRITAIN

'By God's Mercy' We Beat Nazis to Bomb, Churchill Says

ROOSEVELT AID CITED

Raiders Wrecked Norse Laboratory in Race for Key to Victory

The text of Mr. Churchill's statement is on Page 8.

By CLIFTON DANIEL
By Wireless to THE NEW YORK TIMES.

LONDON, Aug. 6—The hitherto secret details of the grisly race between Germany and the Allies to find a weapon so destructive that it would insure absolute victory—a race not only between scientists but also between under-cover agents—were recounted in London tonight after it had been disclosed that the first atomic bomb had been dropped on Japan.

"By God's mercy British and American science outpaced all German efforts," said a statement by former Prime Minister Churchill written before he left office and issued from 10 Downing Street by his successor, Clement R. Attlee.

"The possession of these powers by the Germans at any time might have altered the result of the war," Mr. Churchill said, "and profound anxiety was felt by those who were informed."

The British Isles, which endured the terrors of flying bombs and rockets, did hear repeated rumors that Adolf Hitler's V-3 weapon was to be an atomic bomb, but they never knew until tonight how close they came to being the first victims of its destructive power. Much less did they suspect what

Continued on Page 9, Column 1

War News Summarized

TUESDAY, AUGUST 7, 1945

One bomb hit Japan on Sunday night, but it struck with the force of 20,000 tons of TNT. Where it landed had been the city of Hiroshima; what is there now has not yet been learned.

The attack, dramatically announced by President Truman sixteen hours after the missile had struck, was with an atomic bomb, a "harnessing of the basic power of the universe," he said. "The force from which the sun draws its power has been loosed against those who brought war to the Far East. And the end is not yet."

Details of the missile are closely guarded, but the 125,000 workers who saw materials pour into their factories never saw anything go out. The bomb is the result of pooling British-American scientific knowledge begun in 1940. "We have spent two billion dollars on the greatest scientific gamble in history—and won," Mr. Truman said, and warned:

"We are now prepared to obliterate more rapidly and completely every productive enterprise the Japanese have above ground in any city. It was to spare the Japanese public from utter destruction that the ultimatum of July 26 was issued at Potsdam. If they do not now accept our terms they may expect a rain of ruin from the air."

Secretary of War Stimson detailed the story of research and production and forecast improvements to increase the effectiveness of the "atomic bomb" several times. Congress will be asked to establish a committee to control peacetime use.

Hiroshima was a major military target, a city of 318,000 persons thickly settled around a quartermaster's depot, an embarkation port, armament and airplane parts plants. [All the foregoing 1:8.]

All production was in the United States at two plants at Oak Ridge, near Knoxville, Tenn., and one at Richland, Wash. A scientific laboratory was maintained in Sante Fe, N. M. [1:6.]

Former Prime Minister Churchill told of Britain's part, including costly attacks on German "heavy water" plants and the race to outstrip the Nazis. He praised American scientific achievement and gave full credit to President Roosevelt and his advisers. [1:5.]

Tokyo made no mention of what had happened to Hiroshima but rail service in that area was canceled. [1:7.]

Okinawa sent out 400 planes that left Tarumizu, on Kyushu's Kagoshima Bay, in flaming wreckage. About 125 "Superforts" bombed Toyokawa naval arsenal by daylight. [1:4; map p. 11.]

Chinese troops have broken into the port of Yeungkong and have cleared a large stretch of the south China coast west of Hong Kong and east of the Luichow Peninsula. [1:3; map P. 2.]

Moscow, moving to implement Potsdam decisions, has resumed diplomatic relations with Finland and Rumania. [11:4.]

The Germans received an opportunity to develop democratic talents when the United States and Great Britain authorized local trade unions and political parties in their zones of occupation. [12:2.]

France is expected to ratify the United Nations Charter and then the Bretton Woods monetary plan in the near future. [13:6.] Marshal Pétain was accused of having asked Hitler for help in regaining France's colonies. [13:1.]

Argentina has lifted the state of siege in effect since Pearl Harbor. [14:6.]

Steel Tower 'Vaporized' In Trial of Mighty Bomb

Scientists Awe-Struck as Blinding Flash Lighted New Mexico Desert and Great Cloud Bore 40,000 Feet Into Sky

By LEWIS WOOD
Special to THE NEW YORK TIMES.

WASHINGTON, Aug. 6—A blinding flash many times as brilliant as the midday sun and a massive, multi-colored cloud boiling up 40,000 feet into the air accompanied the first test firing of an atomic bomb on July 16, three weeks ago today. Set in the remote desertlands of New Mexico, the experiment was seen against a wild background where rain poured in torrents, and lightning pierced the sky up to the zero hour of the explosion at 5:30 A. M.

A steel tower from which the atomic weapon hung was vaporized. In its place was only a huge, sloping crater. At the moment of the explosion a mountain range three miles distant stood out sharply in brilliant light.

"Then," said the War Department in a description, "came a tremendous, sustained roar and a heavy pressure wave which knocked down two men outside the control tower (10,000 yards, or more than five miles, away.)"

Before the detonation scientists waited in tense expectancy. Minutes lengthened seemingly to hours. Lying face downward, with their feet toward the steel tower, the watchers waited, nearly breathless. They were "reaching into the unknown" and did not know what would happen.

On the instant that all was over these men leaped to their feet. The terrible tension ended, they shook hands, embraced each other and shouted in glee. Behind their triumph was sober consciousness of possessing the means to "insure the speedy conclusion of the war and save thousands of American lives."

The scene of the great drama was the Alamogordo Air Base, 120 miles southeast of Albuquerque. Here the scientists strove to unlock the secret upon which $2,000,000,000 had been spent.

Graphic word pictures of the

Continued on Page 5, Column 1

ATOM BOMBS MADE IN 3 HIDDEN 'CITIES'

Secrecy on Weapon So Great That Not Even Workers Knew of Their Product

By JAY WALZ
Special to THE NEW YORK TIMES.

WASHINGTON, Aug. 6—The War Department revealed today how three "hidden cities" with a total population of 100,000 inhabitants sprang into being as a result of the $2,000,000,000 atomic bomb project, how they did their work without knowing what it was all about, and how they kept the biggest secret of the war.

One of these, Oak Ridge, situated where only oak and pine trees had dotted small farms before, is today the fifth largest city in Tennessee. Its population of 75,000 persons has thirteen supermarkets, nine drug stores and seven theatres.

A second town of 7,000 was built for reasons of isolation and security on a New Mexico mesa. The third, named Richland Village, houses 17,000 men, women and children on remote banks of the Columbia River in the State of Washington.

None of the people, who came to these developments from homes all the way from Maine to California, had the slightest idea of what they were making in the gigantic Gov-

Continued on Page 3, Column 2

TRAINS CANCELED IN STRICKEN AREA

Traffic Around Hiroshima Is Disrupted — Japanese Still Sift Havoc by Split Atoms

By The United Press.

WASHINGTON, Aug. 6—The Osaka radio, without referring to the atomic bomb dropped on Hiroshima, hinted tonight at the terrific damage it must have caused by announcing that train service in the Hiroshima and other areas had been canceled.

First mention of the bomb came in a Japanese Domei agency dispatch announcing that President Truman and Prime Minister Attlee had disclosed that the new missile had been dropped on Hiroshima.

The Office of War Information began telling the Japanese today what hit them. OWI branch transmitters in San Francisco, Hawaii and Saipan beamed President Truman's statement on the atomic bomb to Japan.

Edward Barrett, director of the OWI's overseas branch, said that the President's announcement and related information on the atomic bomb will dominate the OWI's normal Japanese transmissions for the next several days.

LONDON, Tuesday, Aug. 7 (U.P.)—The Japanese Domei news agency, in a dispatch recorded by the British radio, said today that

Continued on Page 7, Column 3

Reich Exile Emerges as Heroine In Denial to Nazis of Atom's Secret

Special to THE NEW YORK TIMES.

WASHINGTON, Aug. 6—How Germany twice narrowly missed the secret of harnessing atomic energy by splitting uranium atoms and releasing the most powerful destructive force on earth was recalled today in War Department reports on the atomic bomb.

Development of the bomb after more than ten years of experimentation and research marks the first time that Prof. Albert Einstein's theory of relativity has been put to practical use outside the laboratory: the equation by which he showed the existence of a definite relationship of matter, energy and the velocity of light.

That the new bomb may be far from its maximum devastating potential was indicated by the War Department's statement that said:

"The energy we are now able to utilize in the atomic bombs, at 100 per cent efficiency, constitutes only one-tenth of 1 per cent of the total energy present in the material. But even one-hundredth of 1 per cent is still the most destructive force by far on this earth."

The principal character in the dramatic story of the long search for a method of releasing atomic energy is Dr. Lise Meitner, a woman physicist whom the Nazis expelled from Germany as a "non-Aryan." With her associates, Dr. Otto Hahn and Dr. F. Strassmann, both chemists, she had been working in the Kaiser Wilhelm Institute in Berlin, bombarding uranium atoms with neutrons and then submitting the uranium to chemical analysis.

As the War Department tells the story:

To their amazement, they found the element barium in the debris of the smashed uranium atoms.

Continued on Page 7, Column 1

NEW AGE USHERED

Day of Atomic Energy Hailed by President, Revealing Weapon

HIROSHIMA IS TARGET

'Impenetrable' Cloud of Dust Hides City After Single Bomb Strikes

Truman, Stimson statements on atomic bomb, Page 4.

By SIDNEY SHALETT
Special to THE NEW YORK TIMES.

WASHINGTON, Aug. 6—The White House and War Department announced today that an atomic bomb, possessing more power than 20,000 tons of TNT, a destructive force equal to the load of 2,000 B-29's and more than 2,000 times the blast power of what previously was the world's most devastating bomb, had been dropped on Japan.

The announcement, first given to the world in utmost solemnity by President Truman, made it plain that one of the scientific landmarks of the century had been passed, and that the "age of atomic energy," which can be a tremendous force for the advancement of civilization as well as for destruction, was at hand.

At 10:45 o'clock this morning, a statement by the President was issued at the White House that sixteen hours earlier—about the time that citizens on the Eastern seaboard were sitting down to their Sunday suppers—an American plane had dropped the single atomic bomb on the Japanese city of Hiroshima, an important army center.

Japanese Solemnly Warned

What happened at Hiroshima is not yet known. The War Department said it "as yet was unable to make an accurate report" because "an impenetrable cloud of dust and smoke" masked the target area from reconnaissance planes. The Secretary of War will release the story "as soon as accurate details of the results of the bombing become available."

But in a statement vividly describing the results of the first test of the atomic bomb in New Mexico, the War Department told how an immense steel tower had been "vaporized" by the tremendous explosion, how a 40,000-foot cloud rushed into the sky, and two observers were knocked down at a point 10,000 yards away. And President Truman solemnly warned:

"It was to spare the Japanese people from utter destruction that the ultimatum of July 26 was issued at Postdam. Their leaders promptly rejected that ultimatum. If they do not now accept our terms, they may expect a rain of ruin from the air the like of which has never been seen on this earth."

Most Closely Guarded Secret

The President referred to the joint statement issued by the heads of the American, British and Chinese Governments, in which terms of surrender were outlined to the Japanese and warning given that rejection would mean complete destruction of Japan's power to make war.

[The atomic bomb weighs about 400 pounds and is capable of utterly destroying a town, a representative of the British Ministry of Aircraft Production said in London, the United Press reported.]

What is this terrible new weapon, which the War Department also calls the "Cosmic Bomb"? It is the harnessing of the energy of the atom, which is the basic power of the universe. As President Truman said, "The force from which the sun draws its power has been loosed against those who brought war to the Far East."

"Atomic fission"—in other

Continued on Page 2, Column 2

"All the News That's Fit to Print"

The New York Times.

LATE CITY EDITION
Sunny with low humidity today.
Partly cloudy, warmer tomorrow.
Temperatures Yesterday—Max., 77; Min., 65
Sunrise today, [illegible] A. M.; Sunset, [illegible] P. M.

VOL. XCIV..No. 31,974. Entered as Second-Class Matter, Postoffice, New York, N. Y. NEW YORK, THURSDAY, AUGUST 9, 1945. THREE CENTS IN NEW YORK CITY

SOVIET DECLARES WAR ON JAPAN; ATTACKS MANCHURIA, TOKYO SAYS; ATOM BOMB LOOSED ON NAGASAKI

TRUMAN TO REPORT TO PEOPLE TONIGHT ON BIG 3 AND WAR

Half-Hour Speech by Radio to Cover a Wide Range of Problems Facing the World

HE SIGNS PEACE CHARTER

And Thus Makes This Country the First to Complete All Ratification Requirements

By The Associated Press.

WASHINGTON, Aug. 8—President Truman will report to the country on the Potsdam conference over all radio networks at 10 P. M., Eastern war time, tomorrow in a thirty-minute speech.

The Presidential secretary, Charles G. Ross, said today that the speech, which probably would also be short-waved abroad, would go into greater detail than the communiqué issued by the Big Three at the close of the meeting July 26.

Mr. Truman worked on the speech today as well as on a mass of other paper work which accumulated during his month-long absence, and signed into full ratification the United Nations Charter.

He held his calling list to a minimum, including brief conferences with Senators Hatch of New Mexico and Kilgore of West Virginia, and Henry L. Stimson, Secretary of War.

The Stimson conference was devoted to further discussion of the atomic bomb.

Associates of the President indicated that his report on the Potsdam conference would probably mention the new and revolutionary bomb used for the first time against Japan.

Full Appraisal May Be Given

A full appraisal of revised conditions, including Russia's declaration of war against Japan, may come in Mr. Truman's broadcast.

Originally the speech was expected to be primarily a report on the Soviet-British-American agreements announced at the end of the Potsdam conference. These dealt mainly with Europe, keeping Germany under strict surveillance, and the writing of peace treaties.

It became known today that Mr. Truman had four or five names under consideration for the vacancy on the Supreme Court, and the decision appeared imminent.

One of the names is that of Senator Austin, Republican, of Vermont, who has been endorsed by his Democratic colleague, Senator Hatch. It was to renew his suggestion that Mr. Austin be appointed to succeed Justice Owen Roberts, who retired, that brought Mr. Hatch to the White House today.

"Of course the President made no commitments," Mr. Hatch told reporters later, "but he definitely is considering both the appointment of a Republican and Senator Austin. Of course that is only a possibility."

Justice Roberts, appointed by President Hoover in 1930, was one of two Republicans in the present makeup of the high court. Chief Justice Harlan F. Stone is the remaining member of that party.

Charter Goes to Archives

Special to The New York Times.

WASHINGTON, Aug. 8—When President Truman signed today the document by which he ratified the Charter of the United Nations, the United States thereby became the first country to complete its action for bringing the Charter into force.

Several other countries have ratified or taken action with a view to ratification, but no instrument of ratification has yet been received from any of them by the State Department, which is the

Continued on Page 3, Column 5

Foreigners Asked To Stay at Home

Special to The New York Times.

WASHINGTON, Aug. 8—Discouragement of unessential travel by foreigners to the United States was ordered by the Government today through the State Department.

"The Department of State has always traditionally done everything in its power to promote the travel of citizens of other countries of the Western Hemisphere to the United States," said the announcement. "However, the United States Government is now engaged in a gigantic military operation in deploying forces and supplies from the European theatre to the Pacific area. This tremendous task places an unprecedented burden on the transportation system."

The citizens of other countries should realize the situation, the statement said, and postpone trips to the United States unless they were directly connected with the war.

TAMMANY OUSTS LAST OF REBELS

County Committee Ratifies Executive Group's Action—Meeting Picketed

Without the slightest opposition, the New York County Democratic Committee, popularly known as Tammany, last night ratified the selection of an executive committee on which there remained no opposition to the leadership of Edward V. Loughlin or to the influence in the organization repeatedly exercised by Bert Stand, secretary, and Clarence H. Neal Jr., chairman of its elections committee.

In Brooklyn the Kings County Democratic Committee nominated United States Attorney Miles F. McDonald for District Attorney of Kings County to run for the vacancy caused by the resignation of William O'Dwyer, Democratic and American Labor party candidate for Mayor. Mr. McDonald, a graduate of Holy Cross College and Fordham Law School, in accepting the nomination, told the members of the committee that he would resign as United States Attorney.

Nearly 2,000 members, the largest number in recent years, attended the Tammany meeting in the Central Commercial High School, 214 East Forty-second Street. All resolutions presented were adopted unanimously by voice vote.

The committee ratified action taken by the executive committee in seating Robert B. Blaikie as leader of the Seventh Assembly District in place of Joseph H. Broderick and Assemblyman Patrick H. Sullivan, in spite of the claim of Mr. Broderick that he had elected a majority of county com-

Continued on Page 17, Column 2

2D BIG AERIAL BLOW

Japanese Port Is Target in Devastating New Midday Assault

RESULT CALLED GOOD

Foe Asserts Hiroshima Toll Is 'Uncountable' —Assails 'Atrocity'

By W. H. LAWRENCE

By Wireless to The New York Times.

GUAM, Thursday, Aug. 9—Gen. Carl A. Spaatz announced today that a second atomic bomb had been dropped, this time on the city of Nagasaki, and that crew members reported "good results."

The second use of the new and terrifying secret weapon which wiped out more than 60 per cent of the city of Hiroshima and, according to the Japanese radio, killed nearly every resident of that town, occurred at noon today, Japanese time. The target today was an important industrial and shipping area with a population of about 253,000.

The great bomb, which harnesses the power of the universe to destroy the enemy by concussion, blast and fire, was dropped on the second enemy city about seven hours after the Japanese had received a political "roundhouse punch" in the form of a declaration of war by the Soviet Union.

Vital Transshipment Point

GUAM, Thursday, Aug. 9 (AP)—Nagasaki is vitally important as a port for transshipment of military supplies and the embarkation of troops in support of Japan's operations in China, Formosa, Southeast Asia and the Southwest Pacific. It was highly important as a major shipbuilding and repair center for both naval and merchantmen.

The city also included industrial surburbs of Inase and Akunoura on the western side of the harbor, and Urakami. The combined area is nearly double Hiroshima's.

Nagasaki, although only two-thirds as large as Hiroshima in population, is considered more important industrially. With a population now estimated at 253,000, its twelve square miles are jam-packed with the eave-to-eave buildings that won it the name of "sea of roofs."

General Spaatz' communiqué reporting the bombing did not say whether one or more than one "mighty atom" was dropped.

Hiroshima a 'City of Dead'

The Tokyo radio yesterday described Hiroshima as a city of ruins and dead "too numerous to be counted," and put forth the claim that the use of the atomic

Continued on Page 6, Column 3

RED ARMY STRIKES

Foe Reports First Blow by Soviet Forces on Asian Frontier

KEY POINTS BOMBED

Action Believed Aimed to Free Vladivostok Area of Threat

By The United Press.

SAN FRANCISCO, Aug. 8—Russia's mighty Far Eastern Army began hostilities against Japan at 12:10 A. M. Thursday [Russian time], launching a sudden attack along the eastern Soviet-Manchuria border only nine minutes after Moscow's declaration of war became effective, the enemy reported today.

A Kwantung Army headquarters communiqué issued at Changchun [Hsinking] and recorded here reported the attack and also announced that the Red Air Force already was bombing strategic points in Manchurian territory behind Japanese lines.

No details of the attack were given, but presumably the Russians would drive west from the Vladivostok area into Japanese-held territory north of the tip of Korea. Vladivostok is only about twenty miles east of the border, separated from the Japanese by fortified positions along the rugged, mountainous terrain.

The communiqué made it clear that ground forces had opened the attack—part of the Soviet Union's Far Eastern Army of more than 1,000,000 well-equipped troops, who never were called into action against Germany, but remained along the border, a constant threat to Japan.

Although the communiqué did not locate the fighting, it was believed the Russians would strike out as quickly as possible from the Vladivostok region, which is highly

Continued on Page 4, Column 6

Allies Cut Austria Into Four Zones With Vienna Under Joint Control

By LANSING WARREN

Special to The New York Times.

WASHINGTON, Aug. 8—A four-power control machinery, including France with the Big Three, has been established in Austria in accordance with an agreement between the Soviet Union, the United States, the United Kingdom and France, it was announced today.

The system resembles the military control arrangement for Germany. It divides Austria into four zones of occupation and provides that Vienna, the capital city, shall also be occupied by the forces of the four controlling powers. It creates an Allied Council, consisting of the four military commissioners, who will govern Austria as a whole. The commissioners will make the decisions for all Austria and will insure a uniformity of action in the different zones.

[The text of the statement on Austria is on Page 11.]

Under the direction of this combined Allied council each military commander will have full authority in his zone. The council will act through the commanders and through an executive committee, which will advise the council and carry out its decisions.

By this means the agreement seeks to prevent a situation that would separate too rigidly the

Continued on Page 11, Column 5

CIRCLE OF SPEARHEADS AROUND JAPAN IS COMPLETED

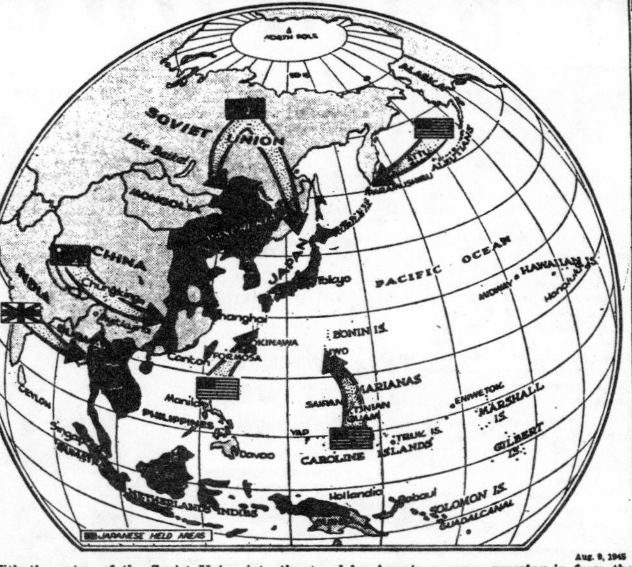

Aug. 9, 1945

With the entry of the Soviet Union into the war against Japan, the enemy is confronted with armed might from new directions—the north and northeast. Japan was already being battered by American power pressing in from the northeast and the south and by Chinese and British power from the west and southwest. The Russians are reported attacking Manchuria.

385 B-29'S SMASH 4 TARGETS IN JAPAN

Tokyo Arsenal and Aircraft Plant Are Seared—Fukuyama and Yawata Cities Ripped

By Wireless to The New York Times.

GUAM, Thursday, Aug. 9—Gen. Carl A. Spaatz, armed with the confirmed knowledge that his Strategic Air Force possesses in the atomic bomb the most powerful destructive agent devised by man since gunpowder was discovered, sent four separate forces

Continued on Page 2, Column 1

U. S. Third Fleet Attacking Targets in Northern Honshu

By ROBERT TRUMBULL

By Wireless to The New York Times.

GUAM, Thursday, Aug. 9—Admiral William F. Halsey's mighty Third Fleet, including British carriers, is now throwing strong air attacks at northern Honshu in the Japanese home islands, where the enemy has twenty to twenty-five airfields, Fleet Admiral Chester W. Nimitz announced this morning.

Although no specific targets were designated, the communiqué said shipping, air installations and "other military targets" were hit by strong air attacks beginning at dawn.

Today's communiqué broke nine days of silence by the Third Fleet after strikes in the Tokyo area July 30. It is possible that persistent fogs, caused by the warm Japanese Current at this time of year, forced Admiral Halsey to desist during that time from the sea-borne attacks carried out in conjunction with land-based air activity over the empire.

Northern Honshu, an area of 30,669 square miles, a little smaller than Maine and populated by 9,500,000 persons, has twenty to twenty-five airfields that are considered operational although some are small, poorly developed bases and probably are used only for the dispersal of the Japanese air force hiding out in that area.

While the northern Honshu district as geographically defined is outside the main military and industrial area of the island there is

Continued on Page 2, Column 8

TRUMAN REVEALS MOVE OF MOSCOW

Announces War Declaration Soon After Russian Action —Capital Is Startled

By FELIX BELAIR JR.

Special to The New York Times.

WASHINGTON, Aug. 8—President Truman announced a few minutes after 3 P. M. today that Russia had just declared war on Japan. The dramatic statement, issued with all the casualness of a routine proclamation, came during the shortest White House press conference on record.

Flanked by Secretary of State James M. Byrnes and Admiral William D. Leahy, his Chief of Staff, the President stood before hastily summoned reporters and in steady, matter-of-fact tones declared: "I have only a simple an-

Continued on Page 3, Column 1

War News Summarized

THURSDAY, AUGUST 9, 1945

Russia has declared war against Japan because that country is the only great power standing in the way of peace. Foreign Commissar Molotoff so informed Ambassador Sato in Moscow yesterday. He said it was in the interests of shortening the war and bringing peace to the world that Moscow acceded to the Allied request to join the war in the Far East and subscribed to the Potsdam ultimatum of July 26. Mr. Molotoff revealed that Japan had asked the Soviet Union to mediate for peace, but that proposal "lost all foundation" when Tokyo rejected the Potsdam demands. [1:8.]

Hostilities were begun nine minutes after the war declaration went into effect at 12:01 this morning, according to Tokyo, when Soviet troops struck along Manchuria's eastern frontier with Siberia. Air attacks, it was said, quickly followed. [1:4.]

President Truman broke the news when he told a hastily called press conference: "Russia has declared war against Japan —that is all." [1:7.] Secretary of State Byrnes declared there was "still time—but little time—for the Japanese to save themselves from the destruction which threatens them." Mr. Byrnes said the President had convinced Premier Stalin that Russia must enter the war if she was to be responsible for peace. [4:2.]

Congress, jubilant and confident that Russia's aid and the atomic bomb would shorten the war materially, expected to be called back soon. [4:1.]

Japan received another blow when the second atomic bomb to fall struck Nagasaki on Kyushu. Crew members reported good results. "Practically all living things" in Hiroshima were destroyed beyond recognition by heat and pressure from the first atomic bomb, Tokyo reported. [1:3.] Fires leaped seven rivers. [6:3, with map.]

The Third Fleet, after nine days of silence, sent its carrier planes in a strong attack, still continuing at last reports, against northern Honshu and its score of airfields. [1:6-7.] B-29's hit four Japanese cities in twenty-four hours and mined home waters. [1:5; map P. 2.]

Wuhu Island, at the mouth of the Min River east of Foochow, was captured by the Chinese. [8:2, with map.]

Russia, Britain, France and the United States have signed an agreement for the occupation and administration of Austria similar to that in effect in Germany. Complete separation from Germany, restoration of the 1937 frontiers and return of democratic government were set as Allied goals. [1:2-3; maps P. 11.]

A new code of international law was adopted by the Big Four listing wars of aggression as a crime against peace. [1:6-7.]

General de Gaulle and his Cabinet, contrary to the wishes of the Consultative Assembly, will submit the questions of a new constitution and government responsibility to a referendum on Oct. 21. [13:5.]

President Truman signed the United Nations Charter yesterday. He will discuss the Potsdam Conference and the military situation in a broadcast at 10 o'clock tonight. [1:1.]

4 Powers Call Aggression Crime In Accord Covering War Trials

By CHARLES E. EGAN

By Wireless to The New York Times.

LONDON, Aug. 8—A new code of international law, defining aggressive warfare as a crime against the world and providing punishment for those who provoke such wars, was announced here today.

By agreement among representatives of the United States, Great Britain, the Soviet Union and France, the legal framework necessary for the trial of the key German and Italian leaders held by the Allies was promulgated this afternoon. The document sets precedents in international law and, in the words of United States Supreme Court Justice Robert H. Jackson, the American representative, "ought to make clear to the world that those who lead their nations into aggressive war face individual accountability for such acts."

"If we can cultivate in the world the idea that aggressive war making is the way to a prisoners' dock rather than the way to honors," he said "we will have accomplished something toward making peace more secure."

[The texts of the War Crimes Committee report and Mr. Jackson's statement are on Page 10.]

The agreement, upon which the international committee has been laboring since June 26, represents

Continued on Page 11, Column 6

RUSSIA AIDS ALLIES

Joins Pacific Struggle After Spurning Foe's Mediation Plea

SEEKS EARLY PEACE

Molotoff Reveals Move Three Months After Victory in Europe

By BROOKS ATKINSON

By Wireless to The New York Times.

MOSCOW, Aug. 8—Russia declared war on Japan tonight. In a dramatic press conference held at 8:30 P. M., Foreign Commissar Vyacheslaff M. Molotoff read the declaration, which was announced to the public at 10 P. M., Moscow time [3 P. M. New York time].

In view of Japan's refusal of the Allies' demand for unconditional surrender, Mr. Molotoff said, the Allies proposed that the Soviet Union "join the war against Japanese aggression and thus shorten the duration of the war, reduce the number of victims and facilitate the speedy restoration of universal peace.

"Loyal to its Allied duty," the Foreign Commissar continued, "the Soviet Government has accepted the proposal of the Allies and has joined in the declaration of the Allied Powers of July 26. The Soviet Government considers that this policy is the only means able to bring peace nearer, free the people from further sacrifice and suffering and give the Japanese people the possibility of avoiding the dangers and destruction suffered by Germany after her refusal to capitulate unconditionally."

Closing his concise statement, Mr. Molotoff declared:

"In view of the above, the Soviet Government declares that from tomorrow, that is Aug. 9, the Soviet Union will consider itself to be at war with Japan."

The Soviet Government's declaration comes three months after the victory over Germany, supporting rumors that some months ago the Soviet Government intimated it would join in the war against Japan three months after victory was won in Europe.

For the first time Mr. Molotoff revealed that the Japanese Government had asked the Soviet Union to mediate for a cessation of hostilities about the middle of June. Japanese Ambassador Naotaka Sato delivered the message, and also a special message from

Continued on Page 3, Column 3

Tokyo 'Flashes' News 3 Hours After Event

By The Associated Press.

SAN FRANCISCO, Aug. 8—Japan's first recorded wireless reaction to Russia's war declaration was a brief factual announcement of that action by the Domei agency in an English-language transmission to Europe.

The Domei account, broadcast five hours and fifty-five minutes after the Moscow announcement, reported:

"Flash! Flash! Tokyo, Aug. 9 —Tass News Agency announced late last night that Foreign Commissar Vyacheslaff M. Molotoff communicated to Naotake Sato, Japanese Ambassador to Russia, that the Soviet Union will consider itself in a state of war with Japan from Thursday, Aug. 9, according to the Moscow radio recorded here this morning."

By the time the "flash" was read, the state of war already had existed for several hours.

"All the News That's Fit to Print"

The New York Times.

LATE CITY EDITION
Thunderstorms, warm, humid; clear and cooler tonight. Fair tomorrow.
Temperatures Yesterday—Max., 84; Min., 71
Sunrise today, 6:06 A. M.; Sunset, 7:55 P. M.

VOL. XCIV..No. 31,980. Entered as Second-Class Matter, Postoffice, New York, N. Y. NEW YORK, WEDNESDAY, AUGUST 15, 1945. THREE CENTS NEW YORK CITY

JAPAN SURRENDERS, END OF WAR! EMPEROR ACCEPTS ALLIED RULE; M'ARTHUR SUPREME COMMANDER; OUR MANPOWER CURBS VOIDED

HIRING MADE LOCAL

Communities, Labor and Management Will Unite Efforts

6,000,000 AFFECTED

Draft Quotas Cut, Services to Drop 5,500,000 in 18 Months

By LEWIS WOOD
Special to THE NEW YORK TIMES.

WASHINGTON, Aug. 14—All manpower controls over employers and workers were abolished tonight, the War Manpower Commission announced, enabling employers to hire men where and when they pleased.

The end of the war threw on the Government the difficult task of trying to readjust perhaps 6,000,000 war workers into new employment. Nevertheless, the WMC said, all its facilities would be used to help workers find new places, with preference going to veterans, displaced migratory war workers and other preferentials.

At the same time President Truman announced that monthly inductions into the Army would be immediately slashed from 80,000 to 50,000, and said 5,000,00 to 5,500,000 men probably would be released from the service within the next year or eighteen months.

The induction rate of 50,000 monthly, the President said, would be sufficient to maintain the occupation forces and allow men of long service overseas to return to their homes.

Under the WMC program, the manpower controls are to be lifted at once and voluntary community action to hurry reconversion will be substituted. In every community, the number of displaced workers and returning veterans will be ascertained in cooperation with local management-labor groups. Full facilities of the United States Employment Service offices will be made available to all employers. Service for veterans will be enlarged.

The WMC program embraced these seven points:

1. All manpower controls are to be lifted at once and in their place voluntary community action to

Continued on Page 12, Column 3

Hirohito on Radio; Minister Ends Life

The Japanese Domei agency said at 11 o'clock last night that Emperor Hirohito had been "graciously pleased to personally read an imperial rescript accepting the Potsdam declaration."

The Domei English-language wireless dispatch, directed to the United States and recorded by the Federal Communications Commission, said that the Emperor had read the rescript over a nation-wide broadcast at noon Wednesday, Tokyo time.

Previously Domei had reported that weeping people had gathered before the Imperial Palace and "bowed to the very ground" in shame.

Japanese War Minister Korechika Anami committed suicide, Domei reported this morning. The wireless dispatch, directed to the American zone, said Anami had taken his life at his "official residence" to "atone for his failure in accomplishing his duties as His Majesty's Minister."

A complete story appears on Page 3.

Third Fleet Fells 5 Planes Since End

By The Associated Press.

GUAM, Wednesday, Aug. 15—Japanese aircraft are approaching the Pacific Fleet off Tokyo and are being shot down, Admiral Chester W. Nimitz announced today.

Five enemy planes have been destroyed since noon today, Japanese time, or 11 P. M. EWT.

Gen. Douglas MacArthur has been requested to tell the Japanese that American defense measures require the Third Fleet to destroy any Japanese planes approaching United States warships.

GUAM, Wednesday, Aug. 15 (UP)—When Admiral Halsey received word of Japan's capitulation today, he sent this message to his fliers:

"It looks like the war is over, but if any enemy planes appear shoot them down in friendly fashion."

SECRETS OF RADAR GIVEN TO WORLD

Its Role in War and Uses for Peacetime Revealed in Washington and London

By WILLIAM S. WHITE
Special to THE NEW YORK TIMES.

WASHINGTON, Aug. 14—The great drama of radar, the war's most powerful "secret weapon" until the atomic bomb was devised, was displayed before a world audience today.

The Joint Board on Scientific Information Policy permitted the Office of Scientific Research and Development, the War Department and the Navy Department to tell the story of a device of which millions had known vaguely for two years, a device which at least three times stood between survival or defeat by the Axis powers for the United States and Great Britain.

It was radar, short for "radio detection and range," that helped the small surviving British air squadrons to beat the German blitz of 1940, thus not only saving the home islands but preserving them as the essential Anglo-American base from which the continental invasion went forward on June 6, 1944.

It was radar, which "sees through the heaviest fog and the blackest night," that more than any other factor broke in 1942 the German submarine attack in the Atlantic which was threatening to starve and strangle the British homeland.

And it was radar that permitted the remnants of the blasted United States Pacific Fleet to stay alive

Continued on Page 14, Column 3

ALL CITY 'LETS GO'

Hundreds of Thousands Roar Joy After Victory Flash Is Received

TIMES SQ. IS JAMMED

Police Estimate Crowd in Area at 2,000,000—Din Overwhelming

By ALEXANDER FEINBERG

Five days of waiting, of rumor, intimation, fact, distortion—five agonizing days following the first indication of a Japanese surrender, days of alternately rising hopes and fears—came to an end for New York, as for the nation and the world, a moment or two after seven o'clock last night. And the metropolis exploded its emotions, harnessed for the most part during the day, with atomic force.

"Official—Truman announces Japanese surrender."

These were the magic words, flashed on the moving electric sign of the Times Tower, at 7:03 P. M. that touched off an unparalleled demonstration in Times Square, packed with half a million persons.

The victory roar that greeted the announcement beat upon the eardrums until it numbed the senses. For twenty minutes wave after wave of that joyous roar surged forth.

Restraint was thrown to the winds. Those in the crowds in the streets tossed hats, boxes and flags into the air. From those leaning perilously out of the windows of office buildings and hotels came a shower of paper, confetti, streamers. Men and women embraced—there were no strangers in New York yesterday. Some were hilarious, others cried softly.

By 7:30 P. M. the crowd in the Square had risen to 750,000 persons; by 8:45 it had swelled to 800,000 and the number continued to rise. People were packed solidly between Forty-third Street and Forty-fifth Street. Individual movement was virtually impossible; one moved not in the crowd but with it.

At 10 P. M. Chief Inspector John J. O'Connell estimated that 2,000,000 persons were in the Times Square area from Fortieth to Fifty-second Street, between Sixth and Eighth Avenues. This constitutes an all-time record, police officials said. At that hour people were still pouring into the Square from subways, buses and on foot.

Those at the north end of the

Continued on Page 5, Column 1

Two-Day Holiday Is Proclaimed; Stores, Banks Close Here Today

By The Associated Press.

WASHINGTON, Aug. 14—Tomorrow and Thursday are days off for Government workers and holidays for pay purposes for workers in general.

And V-J Day, when it comes, will be a premium pay day, too.

President Truman announced both rulings tonight.

He directed agency heads throughout the Government to cut their forces down to a bare skeleton staff Aug. 15 and 16 and not to charge the two days against the employes' annual leave. He said it was in "inadequate" recognition of the four-year efforts on "one of the hardest working groups of war workers."

For other workers under wage control, Wednesday and Thursday count like Christmas and the few other accepted holidays for purposes of overtime pay and in figuring the number of days worked in a week. Many employers already have obtained approval for regular time pay to workers who take the day off.

Postal service for the next two days will "approximate holiday service," the Postoffice Department said.

Local postmasters will have wide discretion in carrying out the President's wishes, it was indicated, and those postal employes required to work tomorrow and next day will have compensating time off at a later date.

It was presumed, but not specifically stated, that Government workers generally will be off on V-J Day, too.

The White House said that the next two days are to be regarded as legal holidays.

Preston Delano, Controller of the

Continued on Page 6, Column 7

PRESIDENT ANNOUNCING SURRENDER OF JAPAN

Mr. Truman reading the message in the White House. Seated are Admiral William D. Leahy, Secretary of State James F. Byrnes and former Secretary of State Cordell Hull. Standing (left to right) are Maj. Gen. Philip Fleming, head of the Federal Works Administration; William H. Davis, Economic Stabilizer; John W. Snyder, Reconversion Director; James Forrestal, Secretary of the Navy; Fred Vinson, Secretary of the Treasury; Tom Clark, Attorney General, and Lewis Schwellenbach, Secretary of Labor. Associated Press Wirephoto

PETAIN CONVICTED, SENTENCED TO DIE

Jurors Recommend Clemency Because of His Age—Long Indictment Upheld

By G. H. ARCHAMBAULT
By Wireless to THE NEW YORK TIMES.

PARIS, Wednesday, Aug. 15—Marshal Henri-Philippe Pétain was convicted at 4:15 A. M. today of intelligence with the enemy and sentenced to death. Because of his age—the former head of the Vichy regime is 89—the jury expressed the hope that the death sentence might not be carried out.

Guards had to arouse Pétain in

Continued on Page 15, Column 5

Terms Will Reduce Japan To Kingdom Perry Visited

By JAMES B. RESTON
Special to THE NEW YORK TIMES.

WASHINGTON, Aug. 14—The Allied terms of surrender will not only demobilize and demilitarize Japan but also deprive her of 80 per cent of the territory and nearly one-third of the population she held when she attacked Pearl Harbor. Thus these terms, already approved by President Truman and our major Allies, will not only destroy the vast empire she conquered in the first eighteen months of this war but also reduce her to little more than the territory she occupied when Commodore Perry introduced her to the western world in 1853.

The main terms of surrender, as

Continued on Page 11, Column 2

World News Summarized

WEDNESDAY, AUGUST 15, 1945

World War II became a page in history last night.

President Truman announced at 7 P. M. that he had received the Japanese reply to the Allied note of last Saturday and that he deemed it full acceptance of the Potsdam declaration of July 26. The Chief Executive said that the Japanese surrender would be made to Gen. Douglas MacArthur in his capacity as Supreme Allied Commander in Chief. Allied military commanders were ordered to stop fighting, but the proclamation of V-J Day will await the signing of the peace treaties. [1:7-8.]

Simultaneously with the President's announcement, Admiral Nimitz flashed "cease fire" orders to all units under his command. [8:3-4.]

The official announcement that the Japanese sneak attack on Pearl Harbor had resulted three years and 250 days later in the inglorious end of the Japanese Empire touched off unrestrained celebrations throughout the Allied world. Here in New York the flash on the moving electric sign on the Times Tower, "Official—Truman announces Japanese surrender," signaled a wild demonstration. [1:3.]

Emperor Hirohito announced the Japanese surrender to his people in his first broadcast to the nation. Weeping Japanese gathered outside the Emperor's palace to bow to the ground in their shame because their "efforts were not enough." [3:2.]

The fury of Allied military might continued to strike the Japanese up to the very last. Even as the Tokyo radio announced that the Japanese reply to the Allied note of Saturday was on its way, our Superfortresses were winging from the Marianas to the Japanese homeland. More than 1,000 planes struck Honshu with 6,000 tons of bombs in a fourteen-hour assault ending early yesterday. [8:1.]

In the midst of rejoicing it was disclosed that the heavy cruiser Indianapolis had been sunk, presumably by an enemy submarine, shortly after she had delivered an atomic bomb cargo to Guam. All men aboard were casualties. [1:6-7.]

The Red Army unleashed fierce new attacks. Russian armored forces raced ninety-three miles unchecked across western Manchuria toward Harbin and other Soviet columns scored new gains all along the 2,300-mile front. [6:6; Pacific area map P. 8.]

The Soviet Union signed "a treaty of friendship and alliance" with China after an agreement had been reached between the two nations on all questions of common interest. [1:6.]

Chinese Communists informed the Generalissimo that they refused to accept his command to remain at their posts. [6:1.]

A French jury sentenced Marshal Pétain to death. [1:4.]

TREATY WITH CHINA SIGNED IN MOSCOW

Complete Agreement Reached With Chungking on All Points at Issue, Russians Say

By Cable to THE NEW YORK TIMES.

LONDON, Aug. 14—The Soviet Union and China have signed a treaty of friendship and alliance, the Moscow radio announced tonight, and have reached "full agreement on all other questions of common interest."

The broadcast said the treaty and "other agreements" would be published shortly after they had been ratified by the two countries.

These are the first fruits of the talks that have been proceeding in

Continued on Page 6, Column 3

Cruiser Sunk, 1,196 Casualties; Took Atom Bomb Cargo to Guam

Special to THE NEW YORK TIMES.

WASHINGTON, Aug. 14—The American heavy cruiser Indianapolis was sunk by enemy action in the Philippine Sea with 1,196 casualties, every man aboard, the Navy announced today.

The 9,950-ton ship left San Francisco on July 16 on a special, high-speed run to deliver essential atomic bomb materials to Guam. The cargo was delivered. The cruiser was lost after having left Guam.

The sinking, which took one of the Navy's heaviest tolls of lives since Pearl Harbor, was disclosed a few minutes before President Truman announced Japan's surrender.

Casualties included five Navy dead, including one officer; 845 Navy missing, including sixty-three officers; 307 Navy wounded, including fifteen officers; thirty Marine missing, including two officers, and nine enlisted Marine wounded. Next of kin have been notified.

The skipper, Capt. Charles B. McVay 3d, 47, of Washington, was wounded.

The Navy Department also reported for the first time that in a previous action on March 31 the Indianapolis, flagship of the Fifth Fleet, was damaged by a suicide plane off Okinawa. She had been at the Mare Island, Calif., Navy

Continued on Page 10, Column 6

YIELDING UNQUALIFIED, TRUMAN SAYS

Japan Is Told to Order End of Hostilities, Notify Allied Supreme Commander and Send Emissaries to Him

MACARTHUR TO RECEIVE SURRENDER

Formal Proclamation of V-J Day Awaits Signing of Those Articles—Cease-Fire Order Given to the Allied Forces

By ARTHUR KROCK
Special to THE NEW YORK TIMES.

WASHINGTON, Aug. 14—Japan today unconditionally surrendered the hemispheric empire taken by force and held almost intact for more than two years against the rising power of the United States and its Allies in the Pacific war.

The bloody dream of the Japanese military caste vanished in the text of a note to the Four Powers accepting the terms of the Potsdam Declaration of July 26, 1945, which amplified the Cairo Declaration of 1943.

Like the previous items in the surrender correspondence, today's Japanese document was forwarded through the Swiss Foreign Office at Berne and the Swiss Legation in Washington. The note of total capitulation was delivered to the State Department by the Legation Charge d'Affaires at 6:10 P. M., after the third and most anxious day of waiting on Tokyo, the anxiety intensified by several premature or false reports of the finale of World War II.

Orders Given to the Japanese

The Department responded with a note to Tokyo through the same channel, ordering the immediate end of hostilities by the Japanese, requiring that the Supreme Allied Commander—who, the President announced, will be Gen. Douglas MacArthur—be notified of the date and hour of the order, and instructing that emissaries of Japan be sent to him at once—at the time and place selected by him—"with full information of the disposition of the Japanese forces and commanders."

President Truman summoned a special press conference in the Executive offices at 7 P. M. He handed to the reporters three texts.

The first—the only one he read aloud—was that he had received the Japanese note and deemed it full acceptance of the Potsdam Declaration, containing no qualification whatsoever; that arrangements for the formal signing of the peace would be made for the "earliest possible moment;" that the Japanese surrender would be made to General MacArthur in his capacity as Supreme Allied Commander in Chief; that Allied military commanders had been instructed to cease hostilities, but that the formal proclamation of V-J Day must await the formal signing.

The text ended with the Japanese note, in which the Four Powers (the United States, Great Britain, China and Russia) were officially informed that the Emperor of Japan had issued an imperial rescript of surrender, was prepared to guarantee the necessary signatures to the terms as prescribed by the Allies, and had instructed all his commanders to cease active operations, to surrender all

Continued on Page 2, Column 3

MacArthur Begins Orders to Hirohito

By Wireless to THE NEW YORK TIMES.

MANILA, Wednesday, Aug. 15—Gen. Douglas MacArthur in his first action as Allied Supreme Commander today directed Emperor Hirohito and the Japanese Government to furnish a radio station in the Tokyo area for "continuous use in handling radio communications between this headquarters and your headquarters." The message, sent in the clear, called for "the earliest practicable" arrangements to end hostilities.

"All the News That's Fit to Print"

NEWS INDEX, PAGE 23, THIS SECTION

The New York Times.

LATE CITY EDITION
Clearing early today; cooler.
Clear and cool tomorrow.
Temperatures Yesterday—Max., 88; Min., 72
Sunrise today, 6:19 A. M.; Sunset, 7:29 P. M.

Section 1

VOL. XCIV..No. 31,998. Entered as Second-Class Matter, Postoffice, New York, N. Y. NEW YORK, SUNDAY, SEPTEMBER 2, 1945. Including Magazine and Book Review. TEN CENTS New York City and Suburban Areas (12c Elsewhere)

JAPAN SURRENDERS TO ALLIES, SIGNS RIGID TERMS ON WARSHIP; TRUMAN SETS TODAY AS V-J DAY

HOLIDAY TRAFFIC NEAR 1941 LEVEL; 'GAS' IS PLENTIFUL

Exodus From City Is Greatest Since Pre-War Days but Congestion Is Avoided

GOOD WEATHER PROMISED

Near-by Resorts Do Capacity Business—3 Persons Die in Queens Accidents

America's millions, deprived since 1941 of the chance to cruise the highways of their nation, hit the road in traditional Labor Day week-end style yesterday.

There was a plentiful supply of gasoline, the sun shone warm out of blue skies, and everyone felt free from war worries. This combined to roll up traffic that continued heavy all day.

New York City's heat-ridden population took to car, train, bus and plane. The exodus to near-by mountain and seashore resorts was the greatest since that of 1941.

The weather formed a perfect lure. Not even the thunder showers predicted by the Weather Bureau for late afternoon took place. Today's prediction is for clearing weather early, followed by cooler, with the highest temperature around 80 degrees, and with fresh to strong northwest winds. A clear and cool Monday is forecast by the bureau. The temperature yesterday reached 88 degrees at 3:30 P. M. with the humidity at 52 per cent. The all-time high for the date was set in 1924 with 92.5 degrees and the low in 1872 with 51.

Many Cars Come Into City

Travel in the city was two-way. As cars streamed out of the city over bridges, on ferries and through tunnels, out-of-towners poured in. The main idea for Labor Day seemed to be change of scenery.

Thousands of automobiles, many of them looking as though they had just been taken off the jacks for the first time in years, formed a continuous procession along the main highways leading up-State, out on Long Island and to the South Jersey shore.

The Port of New York Authority reported that 69,400 automobiles had crossed the George Washington Bridge into New Jersey. Forty-five thousand cars passed through the Holland Tunnel during the sixteen hours preceding 6 o'clock last night. Lincoln Tunnel police said traffic was heavier than usual.

Few serious accidents were reported. "Maybe it's because the cars just don't have the pep," remarked a Westchester County parkway policeman.

Sights along the parkways bore out his contention. Many cars became pathetically silent as their drivers resignedly hauled them over to the side of the road to patch up tires or to fume over engine repairs.

Gasoline Supplies Abundant

Assured of as much gasoline as they wanted, motorists traveled leisurely and did not cause congestion. Filling station pumps received their heaviest workout in years. Station operators estimated that demands for gasoline ranged from 10 to 30 per cent over last week-end, but they reported there was no difficulty in obtaining supplies.

The Cities Service Oil Company said it was having difficulty in meeting orders for premium gasoline, ordinarily accounting for 25 per cent of sales, as the supply was limited, but no company reported shortages of non-premium gasoline. No motorist was forced to stay in town because of lack of fuel.

Trains, buses and airlines were crowded, as they have been all through the war. The airlines re-

Continued on Page 30, Column 2

Times Sq. Takes V-J News Quietly

Times Square throngs, which had greeted Japanese capitulation explosively last month, took the formal signing of terms in much calmer fashion last night.

Two hundred policemen, including twenty-five mounted patrolmen, who had been assigned to the area in case of another outburst of feeling, reported that the street crowds took the flashing of the bulletin from Times Tower at 10:04 P. M. with a few cheers and good-natured remarks, and did not attempt to start a celebration.

In numbers the crowd was no larger than an average Saturday night, and of the persons present perhaps half or more were out-of-town visitors here for the Labor Day week-end, the police estimated. Other parts of the city were similarly quiet.

Mayor La Guardia had said earlier that the people "have had their big time and are satisfied." He decided not to hold a celebration in Central Park today as had been planned.

PRESIDENT STRESSES LABOR DAY OF PEACE

But He Warns That After Six Holidays of Hostilities Great New Problems Lie Ahead

Special to THE NEW YORK TIMES.

WASHINGTON, Sept. 1—President Truman hailed the first Labor Day of peace in six years today and declared a grateful world would always remember the workers of all free nations for their contribution to victory.

Secretary Forrestal and J. A. Krug, chairman of the War Production Board, also lauded the men and women of labor, and Philip Murray, chairman of the Congress of Industrial Organizations, told a radio audience that America's vast war plant must be put to work on peacetime products which would give prosperity unlimited to this country.

Mr. Truman's statement said that six years ago today the workers of the United States, and of the world, awoke to a Labor Day in a world at war, and added:

"We in the United States had two years of grace, but the issue was squarely joined at that hour, as we now know. There was to be no peace until tyranny had been outlawed.

"Today we stand on the threshold of a new world. We must do our part in making this world what it should be, a world in which the bigotries of race and class and creed shall not be permitted to warp the souls of men.

"We enter upon an era of great problems, but to live is to face problems. Our men and women did not falter in the task of saving freedom. They will not falter now in the task of making freedom

Continued on Page 24, Column 3

HAILS ERA OF PEACE

President Calls On U.S. to Stride On Toward a World of Good-Will

SALUTES HEROIC DEAD

Cautions Jubilant Nation Hard Jobs Ahead Need Same Zeal as War

Text of the President's address proclaiming V-J Day, P. 4.

By WILLIAM S. WHITE
Special to THE NEW YORK TIMES.

WASHINGTON, Sept. 1—President Truman, in remembrance of all who have fallen and in an appeal to all Americans to go forward now in hope and fraternity toward "a new and better world of peace and international good-will," tonight solemnly proclaimed tomorrow to be V-J Day.

The moment that he began to speak was, in the official and historical sense, the first moment of peace this country had known since a December day nearly four years ago, when, at a sudden, a harsh and an incredible blow the whole of the Pacific world went into flames.

Into the human calendar of great American holidays, like the Fourth of July and the Eleventh of November, the President thus entered another date, the Second of September, although it does not technically signify the end of the "duration" and will have no basis as a legal end of the war. The termination of hostilities, for purposes of computing military service, for setting the limit to war agencies and for all other like formalities, will be set only by final decision of Congress.

Japanese Surrender Signaled

But Mr. Truman's speech was a speech to the heart of a country that had had the skill to make the atomic bomb and could now "use the same skill and energy and determination to overcome all the difficulties ahead," rather than to the keepers of its books of law.

It was notice from the White House, so long awaited, that nearly four years of war, a struggle of sacrificial grandeur such as the United States had never known, had at last come to an end, and that the terrible ledger opened at Pearl Harbor had now been balanced and closed.

The President spoke in this mood, a mood of valedictory and of dedication, as he proclaimed "this . . . victory of more than arms alone . . . this . . . victory of liberty over tyranny." He had just received the signal from across the world that the Japanese had signed, aboard the great battleship Missouri, the last, humiliat-

Continued on Page 4, Column 1

Public Gets Big Army Food Stocks; Whipping Cream Is Freed of Bans

Special to THE NEW YORK TIMES.

WASHINGTON, Sept. 1—The national food situation continued its steady improvement today as the Department of Agriculture, with four orders, increased the supplies of butter, canned salmon and ice cream and signalled the return of whipping cream.

This action was a direct consequence of the sharp reduction of military requirements of these foods. With the discontinuance of butter purchases by the armed forces, the Department explained, it is now possible to revoke the limitations on the sale of heavy cream and the use of butter fat in the production of all frozen desserts. Both these rulings will make whipping cream and ice cream of a higher butter fat content readily available.

In a simultaneous direction, the agency ordered released for civilian use all butter currently held by creameries and receivers for the armed forces and other Government buyers. Although as much as 20,000,000 pounds of butter may be returned to civilian consumers under this ruling, ration values will not be changed, it was indicated.

"At the time ration point values were established for September, the Office of Price Administration recognized the possibility of these

Continued on Page 33, Column 1

JAPANESE FOREIGN MINISTER SIGNING SURRENDER ARTICLES

Mamoru Shigemitsu (right, seated), on behalf of Emperor Hirohito, affixes his signature to document as Gen. Douglas MacArthur (left) and Lieut. Gen. Richard K. Sutherland (center) look on during ceremony aboard the Missouri in Tokyo Bay.

Associated Press Wirephoto (via Navy Radio from U. S. S. Iowa)

BYRNES FORESEES A PEACEFUL JAPAN

Says People Are Expected to Force Development—World Amity Vital, Hull Warns

Special to THE NEW YORK TIMES.

WASHINGTON, Sept. 1—Secretary of State James F. Byrnes declared tonight that with Japan's surrender we have entered the second phase of our war—"what might be called the spiritual disarmament of that nation, to make them want peace instead of wanting war."

The intention of this Govern-

Continued on Page 5, Column 1

Japan's Surrender Ordered Over Militarist Opposition

By FRANK L. KLUCKHOHN
By Wireless to THE NEW YORK TIMES.

TOKYO, Sept. 1—In the rubble of this once-proud imperial capital the story of how the Japanese Army opposed the surrender and how the Emperor made the final decision to capitulate after having heard the opinions of all his advisers, and how War Minister Korechika Anami had committed suicide was unfolded today by one of a handful of those in a position to know without bias what occurred.

It was also learned how the Japanese reacted step by step to wartime developments and how propaganda that Japan could win had been continued to the last moment, thus leaving the industrious long-

Continued on Page 7, Column 1

U. S. CHIEFS DIVIDED ON ITALY'S COLONIES

State Department Split Over Russia and Influence Zones Is Projected by Issue

By JAMES B. RESTON
Special to THE NEW YORK TIMES.

WASHINGTON, Sept. 1—A fundamental issue has developed in the Department of State over the future of the Italian colonies, particularly Eritrea, Libya and Italian Somaliland.

The issue is whether these colonies should go back to Italy as part of her sovereign territory, be taken from her and administered by the United States, Britain, France and the Soviet Union under the United Nations Organization or be administered by a neutral international commission under the United Nations.

The major powers that defeated Germany are soon to start draft-

Continued on Page 15, Column 1

World News Summarized

SUNDAY, SEPTEMBER 2, 1945

The rulers of Japan, who set the Pacific ablaze nearly four years ago with their surprise attack on Pearl Harbor and hoped to culminate that assault with a peace dictated in the White House, formally signed their unconditional surrender to the Allied powers in Tokyo Bay. Foreign Minister Shigemitsu signed the historic document for his country in the shadow of the sixteen-inch gun muzzles of the battleship Missouri. General MacArthur, who signed in behalf of the Allies, said mankind hoped a better world would result from the solemn occasion. [1:8; map P. 12.]

President Truman proclaimed today as V-J Day. He urged the nation to observe the day of victory over Japan in a spirit of dedication and as a symbol of "victory of liberty over tyranny." He also asked his countrymen to remember "our departed gallant leader, Franklin D. Roosevelt." [1:3.]

Japan's decision to surrender was dictated by Emperor Hirohito after he had overruled a strong faction within the Cabinet and the army that wanted to keep on with the war in the belief that the Japanese could defeat an invasion of the homeland, according to well-informed observers in Tokyo. [1:5-6.]

Medical "experiments" recalling medieval sadism were carried out on dying American prisoners of war by young Japanese Army doctors, two American physicians interned with their compatriots said aboard a United States hospital ship. [1:6-7.]

With the Foreign Ministers' Council scheduled to meet in London next week to begin consideration of peace terms, it was learned that a serious division of opinion over the disposition of the Italian colonies had developed in the State Department. [1:6.]

Former Secretary of State Stettinius said in London that the development of the atomic bomb emphasized the need for "the speedy creation of the United Nations Organization to keep the peace of the world" and predicted that as soon as the organization began functioning it would appoint a military staff to deal with the use of atomic bombs, as well as all other types of force, in preserving peace. [15:2.]

"ALL THE NEWS THAT'S FIT TO PRINT"

In the first eight months of this year, The Times published 6,092 more columns of news than any other newspaper. With World Peace still to be won, and reconversion a topic of daily import, The New York Times continues to print the complete news.

TOKYO AIDES WEEP AS GENERAL SIGNS

Imperial Staff Chief Hastily Scrawls His Signature—Shigemitsu Is Anxious

By The Associated Press.

ABOARD U. S. S. MISSOURI in Tokyo Bay, Sunday, Sept. 2—The solemn surrender ceremony, on this battleship today, marking the first defeat in Japan's 2,600-year-old semi-legendary history, required only a few minutes as twelve signatures were affixed to the articles.

Surrounded by the might of the United States Navy and Army, and under the eyes of the American and British commanders they so ruthlessly defeated in the Philippines and Malaya, the Japanese representatives quietly made the marks on paper that ended the bloody Pacific conflict.

The Japanese delegation came aboard at 8:55 A. M., 7:55 P. M. Saturday, E. W. T., as scheduled. They reached the Missouri in personnel speed boats flying the American flag.

Foreign Minister Mamoru Shigemitsu led the delegation. He climbed stiffly up the ladder and limped forward on his right leg, which is artificial. He was wounded by a bomb tossed by a Korean terrorist in Shanghai many years ago.

On behalf of Emperor Hirohito, Mr. Shigemitsu signed first for

Continued on Page 3, Column 1

Enemy Tortured Dying Americans With Sadist Medical 'Experiments'

By ROBERT TRUMBULL
By Wireless to THE NEW YORK TIMES.

ABOARD THE HOSPITAL SHIP BENEVOLENCE, in Tokyo Bay, Sept. 1 — Seriously ailing American prisoners at Shinagawa, the only hospital serving 8,000 prisoners of war held in the Tokyo area, were guinea pigs for fantastic experiments recalling the sorcery and sadism of the middle ages, Drs. Mack L. Gottlieb and Harold W. Keschner, both of New York, told this correspondent today.

Both doctors are recuperating aboard this ship after their rescue from Shinagawa on Wednesday by a special Navy evacuation mission headed by Comdr. Harold A. Stassen, former Governor of Minnesota and now Assistant Chief of Staff and Flag Secretary to Admiral William F. Halsey, commander of the Third Fleet.

[In an interview in Tokyo the Japanese Army doctor to whom some of these practices were charged confirmed the cruel treatment of American prisoners.]

Dr. Gottlieb, who had his home and office at 307 East Forty-fourth Street, was a Naval officer captured at Guam. Dr. Keschner, of 451 West End Avenue, was taken with an Army force in the Philippines. Both are in good physical

Continued on Page 14, Column 1

WAR COMES TO END

Articles of Capitulation Endorsed by Countries in Pacific Conflict

M'ARTHUR SEES PEACE

Emperor Orders Subjects to Obey All Commands Issued by General

The texts of the surrender documents and statements, P. 3.

By The Associated Press.

ABOARD THE U. S. S. MISSOURI in Tokyo Bay, Sunday, Sept. 2—Japan surrendered formally and unconditionally to the Allies today in a twenty-minute ceremony which ended just as the sun burst through low-hanging clouds as a shining symbol to a ravaged world now done with war.

[A United Press dispatch said the leading Japanese delegate signed the articles at 9:03 A. M. Sunday, Tokyo time, and that General MacArthur signed them at 9:07 A. M.]

Twelve signatures, requiring only a few minutes to inscribe on the articles of surrender, ended the bloody Pacific conflict.

On behalf of Emperor Hirohito, Foreign Minister Mamoru Shigemitsu signed for the Government and Gen. Yoshijiro Umezu for the Imperial General Staff.

MacArthur Voices Peace Hope

Gen. Douglas MacArthur then accepted in behalf of the United Nations, declaring:

"It is my earnest hope and indeed the hope of all mankind that from this solemn occasion a better world shall emerge out of the blood and carnage of the past."

One by one the Allied representatives stepped forward and signed the document that blighted Japan's dream of empire built on bloodshed and tyranny.

First was Admiral Chester W. Nimitz for the United States, then the representatives of China, the United Kingdom, the Soviet, Australia, Canada, France, the Netherlands and New Zealand.

The flags of the United States, Britain, the Soviet and China fluttered from the veranda deck of the famed superdreadnaught, polished and scrubbed as never before. More than 100 high-ranking military and naval officers watched.

Pledges Justice and Tolerance

"As Supreme Commander for the Allied powers," General MacArthur told the Japanese, "I announce it my firm purpose, in the tradition of the countries I represent, to proceed in the discharge of my responsibilities with justice and tolerance, while taking all necessary dispositions to insure that the terms of surrender are fully, promptly and faithfully complied with."

All through this dramatic half hour, only those aboard the battleship knew of what was taking place, because the Missouri has no broadcasting facilities.

But recordings were rushed to the near-by communications ship Ancon, and the solemn words of General MacArthur beginning the ceremony—"We are gathered here, representatives of the major warring powers"—were flashed around the world.

The Japanese representatives were present at the command of Emperor Hirohito contained in a proclamation issued by order of the Supreme Allied Commander.

The Emperor further commanded his officials "to issue general orders to the military and naval forces in accordance with the direction of the Supreme Commander

Continued on Page 2, Column 3

"All the News That's Fit to Print"

The New York Times.

LATE CITY EDITION
Cloudy with showers today. Considerable cloudiness tomorrow.
Temperatures Yesterday—Max., 75; Min., 65
Sunrise today, 6:26 A. M.; Sunset, 7:05 P. M.

VOL. XCIV. No. 32,011. Entered as Second-Class Matter, Postoffice, New York, N. Y. NEW YORK, SATURDAY, SEPTEMBER 15, 1945. THREE CENTS IN NEW YORK CITY

M'ARTHUR PLEDGES IRON RULE, REBUKES CRITICS ON POLICY; CURBS DOMEI NEWS AGENCY

FIRM GRIP MAPPED

General Says All Terms of Surrender Will Be Imposed on Japan

HOMMA READY TO GIVE UP

Japanese Premier Asks U. S. to 'Forget Pearl Harbor' in Interests of Peace

By GEORGE E. JONES
By Wireless to THE NEW YORK TIMES.

YOKOHAMA, Japan, Saturday, Sept. 15—Gen. Douglas MacArthur took cognizance yesterday of criticism of his so-called "soft policy" toward Japan. In an extraordinary statement defining his problems and policies, he emphasized that the surrender terms imposed on the beaten empire would be carried out in a stern, uncompromising fashion.

At the same time the Supreme Commander for the Allied Powers admitted that it was difficult for him to "exercise that degree of patience which is unquestionably demanded if the long-time policies which have been decreed are to be successfully accomplished without repercussions which would be detrimental to the well being of the world."

This was General MacArthur's rebuttal to the criticism, particularly that of the American press, of his policy of working to the fullest possible extent through the existing Japanese Government.

Domei Curbed, Put Under Censor

General MacArthur's patience evidently had worn thin as he ordered the suspension of Domei, the Japanese news agency, which had been foremost in propagating stories of American "brutalities" toward Japanese civilians.

Today Supreme Headquarters rescinded the suspension and permitted Domei to reopen at noon after a shutdown of nearly eighteen hours.

Henceforth, however, Domei must use for its foreign news only what it receives from the United States Office of War Information broadcasts and its local news will be subjected to strict American censorship. Presumably the censorship will be applied also to local news matter gathered by the Japanese newspapers.

This backdown from General MacArthur's original order ended a news drought for Tokyo's large papers that sent them scurrying to American press associations and syndicates seeking to arrange for reception of foreign news from American sources.

The shutdown order was rescinded after conversations between headquarters and Domei representatives in which the Japanese agency was reminded sharply that Japan was a defeated nation and that Domei would take its orders from the occupation authorities without "ifs" and "buts." General MacArthur has been displeased at the tendency of the Japanese press, particularly Domei, to assume that Japan enjoyed equal status with other nations and as such possessed prerogatives of sovereignty in dealings with the American occupation forces.

Still in First Phase of Action

In effect General MacArthur stated that we were still in the first phase, which is primarily one of military considerations—that of deploying sufficient American troops onto Japanese soil and demobilizing Japanese forces. He promised that when this phase had been completed "no one need have any doubt about the prompt, complete, entire fulfillment of the terms of the surrender."

He added that Japan was in a state of utter collapse industrially and militarily and said that her existing structure was controlled completely by the American occupation forces. This amounts in effect to an explanation of his present policy in terms of promises for a stern policy in the future when military conditions permit.

[Lieut. Gen. Masaharu Homma, held responsible by General MacArthur for the Bataan death march, arrived in Tokyo and said he was preparing to surrender himself, The Associated Press reported.

[Earlier Premier Prince Naru-

Continued on Page 4, Column 3

Big 5 Invite Other Powers To Present Views on Italy

Evatt Is Credited With Winning Voice for Smaller Allies on Peace Treaty—Parley Picks Up Speed, Forms Secretariat

By HERBERT L. MATTHEWS
By Cable to THE NEW YORK TIMES.

LONDON, Sept. 14—The Council of Foreign Ministers of the five great powers, pushed by internal and external pressure, suddenly came to its majority today as a full-fledged organization to settle the peace problems of the world.

The Foreign Ministers began their detailed discussions of a treaty with Italy and found surprisingly easy going. The Council called in a number of other powers for discussions, established a joint secretariat to carry on through the coming months and in general adopted methods of procedure that show that this body, which began as a council of five powers, is really a world organization.

If any one man deserves the credit for forcing this issue so quickly it is the fiery Australian Minister for External Affairs, Dr. Herbert V. Evatt, who came to London last week brimming with a determination that the smaller powers would have their say, and today's development was his triumph. The essential points were set forth in two communiqués, one from the Council and the other from Dr. Evatt himself.

The first communiqué begins by saying that there were two meetings today, one presided over by Foreign Minister Wang Shih-chieh of China and the other by Secretary of State James F. Byrnes of the United States, in accordance with the rotation decided upon on the first day. Encouraged by their progress today, the Foreign Ministers decided to forget about the traditional British week-end and to work tomorrow and perhaps Sunday.

"The Council began its discussion of terms for the peace settlement with Italy," says the communiqué. "It was agreed all the United Nations at war with Italy would be invited to submit, if they wished, their views in writing on this subject. It was also decided that the president of the session,

Continued on Page 7, Column 4

POLAND DENOUNCES VATICAN CONCORDAT

Asserts Holy See Violated It—Arrests and Deportations of Clerics Reported

By Wireless to THE NEW YORK TIMES.

LONDON, Sept. 14—The Warsaw Government has denounced the concordat that has governed relations between Poland and the Holy See since 1925, it became known here today. The decision was taken on Sept. 4, with fifteen Cabinet Ministers voting in favor of the denouncement to four against.

It also was reported in Catholic circles here that two Polish priests were arrested this week on charges that are not known. They are Dr. Albert Sztajer, who was attached to Cardinal Hlond's cathedral in Poznan, and Father Kuhn, a German priest of the Danzig diocese. Dr. Sztajer will be put on trial shortly. Father Kuhn already has been sentenced to death.

These arrests followed alleged deportations to Russia of the Bishop of Luck and to Central Poland of the Archbishop of Vilna and the arrest of the Bishop of Danzig, all of which were reported by Polish circles in London opposed to Warsaw.

In an article on religious conditions in Poland, the Catholic weekly Tablet will say tomorrow that these events "confirm the view already forced upon us that the present limited freedom enjoyed by Polish Catholics is only temporary and will end when it is decided that no more Poles abroad can be inveigled back."

Father Piotr Kruszynski, Vicar General of the diocese of Lublin,

Continued on Page 9, Column 2

ARGENTINE REPLY FOUND MISLEADING

Many Errors Shown in Answer to U. S. Charges of Failure to Live Up to Obligations

By ARNALDO CORTESI
By Wireless to THE NEW YORK TIMES.

BUENOS AIRES, Sept. 14—On Tuesday the Foreign Ministry published a 10,000-word document to prove that the Argentine Government had complied faithfully with the commitments it assumed when it signed the final Act of Chapultepec. A careful study of this document shows that it contains so many hiatuses and makes so many erroneous or misleading statements that it can confidently be described as a very poor attempt to justify the Government's far from brilliant position.

Far from proving that Argentina carried out her commitments, it convicts the Government of the most astonishing laxness in almost all matters of fundamental importance. Since the Argentine document was provoked by former Assistant Secretary of State Nelson Rockefeller's charges that Argentina had not taken the measures necessary to eliminate Axis firms, it perhaps would be best to start from this point.

The Argentine Government substantially confirms Mr. Rockefeller's figures. To date the Government has eliminated only two small subsidiaries of the Thyssen Lamental Company and two German banks, while six German insurance companies are in the process of liquidation. Bids also have been requested for the sale of merchandise belonging to about a

Continued on Page 10, Column 1

Chinese Communists Claim Gains Ranging From Yangtze to Peiping

By TILLMAN DURDIN
By Wireless to THE NEW YORK TIMES.

CHUNGKING, China, Sept. 14—Sweeping territorial gains from the Yangtze Valley to areas north and west of Peiping are claimed for the Communist armies in a communiqué issued today from Communist headquarters in Chungking. The communiqué summarized Communist army activities of the last week.

The Communists claim to have "fairly complete control of everything but points on the railways" in an area stretching from Kalgan to the mouth of the Yangtze River and from the Shantung Peninsula to east of Shansi and including northern and northwest Shansi. The communiqué said "puppet armies" in the big cities were strong enough to resist attacks.

At a meeting with the press in Chungking today Mao Tze-tung, chairman of the Central Executive Committee of the Communist party, said the Communists were still fighting because "the Japanese and the puppets are fighting us, and since they are fighting us we are still fighting them."

He claimed the important Hopei port of Chinwangtao north of Tientsin, had been taken by the Communists in addition to Shanhaikwan, where the Great Wall meets the sea, and the capital of Jehol Province.

Gen. Chou En-lai, Communist military leader, who also attended the press conference, stated that Japanese had attacked the Communists in Chahar Province and, after recovering two important towns, and turned them over to

Continued on Page 5, Column 3

Storm Races to Florida; 2 Subways Flooded Here

6th and 8th Ave. Lines Tied Up 3 Hours as Half Inch of Rain Falls in 10 Minutes—Boy Drowned on Newark Street

A torrential rainstorm that began at the start of the rush hour last evening halted service on the Sixth and Eighth Avenue subways through midtown Manhattan for three hours last night, flooded thousands of cellars and delayed millions on their way home. In New Jersey it was responsible for two deaths, one by electrocution, the other by drowning, in addition to uprooting trees and tearing the roof from a home in Elizabeth.

Half an inch of rain fell in Manhattan in the ten minutes between 5 and 5:10 P. M., according to Weather Bureau measurements. This was not a record fall. Last year .76 inches fell in ten minutes on Aug. 16 and .85 inches in ten minutes on Sept. 13, the eve of last year's hurricane.

There was no connection between yesterday's storm and the hurricane moving toward Miami out of the Carribean, according to the Weather Bureau. The local storm, it was explained, was part

Continued on Page 30, Column 4

Exposed Areas Are Prepared as Hurricane With 150-Mile Winds Moves Toward Coast—Bahamas Await Big Blow

By The Associated Press.

MIAMI, Fla., Sept. 14—A tropical hurricane which is reported to have created great havoc in Turks Island with 150-mile winds swirled toward the Florida Keys tonight, and at 11 o'clock was about 310 miles southeast of Miami.

Thousands of persons began to move from exposed areas under Coast Guard, Red Cross and Weather Bureau urgings. Schools, police stations and other public buildings were thrown open to refugees throughout south Florida.

The Federal storm warning service estimated that squalls would be felt in this area tomorrow morning, building up to gales and then howling hurricane winds as the center passed, probably over the Florida Keys, tomorrow afternoon.

The red and black flags of the hurricane warning signal were up from Fort Lauderdale to Key West and Dry Tortugas.

Army, Navy and commercial airplanes sped out of the danger

Continued on Page 30, Column 2

TROLLEY CARS HERE ON WAY TO OBLIVION BY NEXT YEAR'S END

700 New Buses to Assume Travel Burden on Lines in Manhattan and Bronx

The antiquated, clangorous and slow trolley car is to disappear from the streets of Manhattan and most of the Bronx by the end of next year, according to an announcement yesterday by the Third Avenue Transit Corporation.

As replacements for 450 trolleys that are to be scrapped, 700 new buses will travel the seventy-five miles of surface lines scheduled for abandonment in Manhattan and the Bronx, and thirty miles in Yonkers, New Rochelle and Mount Vernon. Most of the buses already have been ordered from General Motors Corporation.

Announcement of the company's program, involving $11,000,000 of financing, was made by its president, Victor McQuistion. The buses, he said, would cost an average of $15,000 each.

In Manhattan the street car lines hat will mark the passing of an .ra are those running up Broad-

Continued on Page 11, Column 5

VALENTINE RETIRES; LA GUARDIA DELAYS NAMING SUCCESSOR

Mayor Tells Police at Promotion Ceremonies New Head Will Come From Ranks

The Police Department is operating today without a commissioner, as the resignation of Lewis J. Valentine, its chief for almost eleven years, became effective at midnight without the appointment of a successor by Mayor La Guardia.

As the time drew near for Mr. Valentine to perform his last official act by presiding at departmental promotion ceremonies at noon yesterday, Centre Street gossip predicted confidently that the climax of the proceedings would be the naming of a new commissioner. The 500 members of the force present in the line-up room sat up expectantly as the Mayor walked to the rostrum, waited eagerly for him to broach the subject and then relaxed as he made it clear that he would take his legal time about swearing in a new commissioner.

With Mr. Valentine out of the department after forty-two years

Continued on Page 11, Column 1

World News Summarized

SATURDAY, SEPTEMBER 15, 1945

General MacArthur pledged that Japan would be made to carry out her terms of unconditional surrender in a stern, uncompromising manner. Taking note of criticism of the occupation as indicating "a soft policy," he said this was an "erroneous concept." He emphasized that the occupation was still in its first phase and that when this phase was completed "no one need have any doubt about prompt, complete, entire fulfillment of the terms of surrender." The Allied commander also curbed the Domei agency, foremost Japanese news outlet. [1:1.]

Premier Higashi-Kuni asked Americans to "forget Pearl Harbor" and declared a new Japan would emerge after reconstruction that would be shorn of militarism and would be "as peace-loving as the United States." [4:1.]

General Homma, Japanese commander in the Philippines during the Bataan "death march," arrived in Tokyo to surrender as a war criminal. [4:6.]

A Communist communiqué issued from Chungking reported large-scale territorial gains and said the Chinese Communists had "fairly complete" control between Kalgan and the mouth of the Yangtze River and from the Shantung Peninsula to east of Shansi. [1:2-3.]

Japanese forces surrendering on Nauru Island were said to have resorted to cannibalism. [5:2.]

On the eve of Viceroy Wavell's return the All-India Congress party working committee voted to contest all elections in India and to continue its program of negotiation and cooperation in seeking independence. [6:2.]

The Foreign Ministers' Council in London began detailed discussions of the treaty with Italy and made encouraging progress. All nations that were at war with Italy will be asked to submit their views. The council also set up a joint secretariat consisting of the secretaries of the five delegations to speed its work. [1:2-3.]

Exchange of operational information between the Red Army and the American-British forces during the war was called "wholly satisfactory" by General Deane, head of the American military mission in Moscow. [9:4.]

Poland denounced its concordat with the Vatican. [1:2.]

A study of a 10,000-word document issued by the Argentine Foreign Ministry led to the conclusion that it was a poor attempt to justify the Argentine Government's position and tended to convict that Government of laxity in carrying out its commitments under the Act of Chapultepec. [1:3.]

The tempo of reconversion suffered a serious setback as the Ford Motor Company shut down after hitting out at "unauthorized" strikes that were interfering with its supplies. [1:8.]

The British Trades Union Congress adopted a resolution urging a general forty-hour week in industry and a government housing program. [9:2.]

The Pearl Harbor disaster will be investigated by a joint Senate-House committee of six Democrats and four Republicans. Senate Majority Leader Barkley is expected to act as chairman of the inquiry. [1:4-5.]

FORD ENDS ALL PRODUCTION, BLAMES CRIPPLING STRIKES; ALL AUTO INDUSTRY MENACED

Labor Rows Worry Capital; Detroit Situation 'Ominous'

Officials Fear Crisis Before Peace Parley of Unions and Management, and Want Early Meeting—Congress Ponders Steps

By LOUIS STARK
Special to THE NEW YORK TIMES.

WASHINGTON, Sept. 14—A national labor-industry crisis, which might even precede President Truman's scheduled "industrial peace" meeting, was regarded as a possibility today by labor officials, who felt that Detroit labor developments were "ominous."

Secretary Schwellenbach called for reports from the Conciliation Service, which has had a commissioner in close touch with the Detroit labor situation.

Other officials felt that the piling up of wage demands by unions and the comparative slowness in settling problems of reconversion pay may touch off a series of strikes and disputes that will keep the Labor Department and the War Labor Board as busy as at some periods during the war.

The difficulty facing the board, however, is that neither labor nor industry fears any possible "sanctions." To labor the no-strike agreement is no longer binding. While high international union officials have in some cases sought to minimize strikes, they have not always succeeded in checking the walkouts that threatened to get out of hand.

Decision by the shop craft unions to ask the railroads for reduction of the forty-eight-hour week to thirty-six hours without loss of pay will go through the procedure provided under the Railway Labor Act, beginning with direct conferences, mediation, proposal for voluntary arbitration and then, if a crisis develops, for investigation by a Presidential fact-finding board.

This slow, step-by-step procedure, with "cooling off" periods during each step, was contrasted by officials today with strikes now under way on short notice or none at all and with threats by the CIO United Automobile Workers Union to "blockade" plants of General Motors Corporation.

Members of Congress, who are

Continued on Page 2, Column 6

50,000 ARE LAID OFF

Company Head Charges Irresponsible Groups Balk Reconversion

UNION PLANS CAMPAIGN

UAW-CIO Leaders Insist on 30% Auto Pay Rise Under Sweeping Strike Plan

The Ford Motor Company halted all production at its plants throughout the country and laid off 50,000 workers, blaming "irresponsible labor groups" for strikes against its supplies [1:8.]

Meanwhile at Flint the Automobile Workers Union's executive board moved to demand a 30 per cent nation-wide pay rise under threat of strikes, and a labor-management showdown loomed. [2:5.]

Washington feared a labor crisis before the labor-management conference, with Detroit situation called ominous. [1:6-7.]

A CIO Electrical Workers Union began an enrollment drive among 12,000 striking "white-collar" workers of Westinghouse Electric. [2:1.]

AFL railway unions will demand a thirty-six hour week with no pay cut. [2:7.]

Benjamin Fairless, president of the United States Steel Corporation, said a union demand for $2 a day wage increase cannot be granted without a sharp rise in steel prices. [2:8.]

Company in Blunt Attack

By JAMES B. RESTON
Special to THE NEW YORK TIMES.

DETROIT, Sept. 14—The Ford Motor Company halted virtually all production in its plants throughout the country today and laid off 50,000 workers, basing its action upon "crippling and unauthorized strikes" against companies supplying it with parts.

The company's action, set forth in a statement signed by Henry Ford 2d, executive vice president, applied to all plants except its Lincoln and Rouge steel factories. The statement said that "continued outbreaks by irresponsible labor groups are impeding the regular progress of reconversion."

The development came as the entire automotive industry appeared heading for a labor-management showdown after the International Executive Board of the CIO United Automobile Workers Union had demanded earlier today a 30 per cent wage increase throughout the industry under a threat of strikes to enforce the demand.

Period of Tension Starts

A period of tension in the automotive capital began this morning when the 22-man Executive Committee of the UAW, largest CIO union in the country with a membership of about 1,250,000, announced at a union meeting in Flint that the UAW would either get its 30 per cent raise or call a series of concentrated strikes, first against one of the Big Three auto companies and its suppliers and then against another, but on a basis of one at a time so that the full force of the international union could be thrown against each individual of the Big Three.

In outlining this "divide and conquer" policy, R. J. Thomas, international president; Walter Reuther, vice president, and George F. Addes, secretary-treasurer, stated that their new drive would be carried out under the law, and that the union would "crack down" on wildcat strikes.

The Ford company statement, coming soon afterward, was blunt. It read as follows:

"After several weeks operations in the face of crippling and unauthorized strikes against many of our suppliers, the Ford Motor Company is being forced to halt virtually all of its production operations late today.

"We have considered all angles of the situation. We wanted to keep men at work. We had hoped that by this time we would be hiring more men. Instead we are telling 50,000 of our employes to stay off their jobs indefinitely.

"In two and one-half months we

Continued on Page 3, Column 3

COLLEGES CHART 2 BILLION OUTLAY

Survey Discloses a Building Program Marking Greatest Expansion in Their History

By BENJAMIN FINE

Colleges and universities in all parts of the United States face the greatest period of expansion in their history, involving a post-war building program of possibly more than $2,000,000,000, a survey conducted by THE NEW YORK TIMES has disclosed.

After four years of war-enforced delay, the colleges report that new dormitories, laboratories, classrooms, gymnasiums and other necessary buildings will be constructed just as soon as help and priorities can be obtained. Almost every one of them needs repair and reconstruction work.

A sampling of forty representative institutions of higher learning showed that blueprints have been prepared for buildings and development of campus facilities which will cost $250,000,000. This sampling, which is less than 10 per cent of the 600 recognized liberal arts institutions and State universities, did not cover the professional schools or junior colleges, where an even greater expansion is planned.

Plainly, the college heads are preparing for a substantial rise in enrollment. Many institutions predict that their students will increase by 50 to 100 per cent. As a result, building must start at once.

Since Pearl Harbor little, if any, work has been done on the campuses. Almost every college and university reported that buildings

Continued on Page 16, Column 2

BRADLEY REVAMPS VETERANS' SERVICE

Sweeping Decentralization to Give 13 Districts Controls—Hospital Changes Planned

By CHARLES HURD
Special to THE NEW YORK TIMES.

WASHINGTON, Sept. 14—The modernized Veterans Administration ordered by President Truman took shape today when Gen. Omar N. Bradley, new administrator, announced a decentralization program for the organization together with innovations in medical service designed to meet criticisms.

General Bradley made public his reorganization program less than twenty-four hours after it was reduced to tabular form, cautioning reporters that for the most part it existed as yet only on paper. But he said he hoped to be able to show accomplishment soon.

"Don't get the idea," he said at a news conference, "that we think this plan will perform a miracle, or get things done right now. But we hope it will show definite improvement in the work of the Veterans Administration."

General Bradley plans to:

1. Decentralize supervision and control over veterans' facilities into thirteen branch offices that will have absolute control over the facilities and offices in their areas.

2. Raise the medical establishment to rank equal to other departments, add a planning section and break insurance away from general finance.

3. Separate vocational training from other activities and make it a specialized project equal in importance to medical care.

4. Reform veterans' hospitals to

Continued on Page 3, Column 5

Ten Lawyers in Congress Named To Conduct Pearl Harbor Inquiry

By WILLIAM S. WHITE
Special to THE NEW YORK TIMES.

WASHINGTON, Sept. 14—A joint Congressional committee of ten members, all lawyers, was appointed today to investigate the Pearl Harbor disaster.

For the Senate, Senator McKellar of Tennessee, the presiding officer, chose Senators Barkley of Kentucky, the majority leader; George of Georgia and Lucas of Illinois, Democrats, and Brewster of Maine, and Ferguson of Michigan, Republicans. Senator George withheld a final acceptance, pointing out that a great amount of work was pending before his own finance committee but promising to make a decision by early next week.

On the part of the House, Speaker Rayburn chose Representatives Cooper of Tennessee, Clark of North Carolina, and Murphy of Pennsylvania, Democrats, and Gearhart of California, and Keefe of Wisconsin, Republicans.

The selection of some of the most widely known and veteran members of the Senate caused some comment that the investigating group would be "a Senate committee."

Speaker Rayburn said he had followed no precise criterion in appointing the House members of the committee. He disclosed that he had acted upon the recommendations of Representative Martin of Massachusetts, the House Republican leader, in selecting the minority members.

The Speaker, who has made it plain that he regretted Congressional insistence on an inquiry and

Continued on Page 5, Column 7

"All the News That's Fit to Print"

The New York Times.

LATE CITY EDITION
Sunny, warm today. Sunny, with increasing cloudiness tomorrow
Temperatures Yesterday—Max., 70; Min., 49
Sunrise today, 5:46 A. M.; Sunset, 6:15 P. M.
Full U. S. Weather Bureau Report, Page 51

VOL. XCV..No. 32,205. Entered as Second-Class Matter. Postoffice, New York, N. Y. NEW YORK, THURSDAY, MARCH 28, 1946. THREE CENTS IN NEW YORK CITY

RUSSIAN, DEFEATED ON IRAN, WALKS OUT OF UNO; TEHERAN'S ENVOY PUTS PLEA BEFORE COUNCIL; SAYS SOVIET ASKED OCCUPATION AND OIL RIGHTS

REUTHER ELECTED PRESIDENT OF UAW BY NARROW MARGIN

8-Year Reign of Thomas Is Ended in Balloting Marked by Fist Fights, Near-Riots

VICTOR MAKES UNITY PLEA

Plans Campaign Among Farm Equipment Makers, Pledges Assistance to Murray

By WALTER W. RUCH
Special to THE NEW YORK TIMES.

ATLANTIC CITY, N. J., March 27—The United Automobile Workers, CIO, crowned ten years of trade unionism for Walter P. Reuther today by electing the 38-year-old red-head to the union presidency that had been held for eight years by R. J. Thomas.

In an election in the Municipal Auditorium that was as close as it was bitter, the delegates at the tenth convention of the huge union elevated the fiery leader from his post of vice president to one of the most powerful positions in the labor movement by a majority of only 124.4 votes.

The final tabulation, under a system of fractional voting, gave Reuther 4,444.8 and Thomas 4,320.4.

Mr. Reuther's first gesture was one of friendliness toward the Left Wing element that had battled furiously to keep him from office. and his first promise was one that he would exercise every power at his command to bring unity into an organization that has, admittedly, been disintegrating at the top level.

Plans Membership Drive

As for the "common enemy," he immediately outlined plans to expand the membership through drives to organize the farm machinery workers, the white collar workers and the engineers and technicians of the automotive industry as part of the UAW.

In his first address as president, Mr. Reuther sought to scotch, once and for all, rumors of dissension between him and Philip Murray, president of the Congress of Industrial Organizations, by extending full cooperation and expressing an anxious desire to walk at Mr. Murray's side to help bear "his heavy burden."

In a word, Mr. Reuther stepped into the presidency with a plea for unity that he might bind up the factionalism that abounds in a union harboring virtually every breed of political faith in the nation.

The man he had defeated, who had lost in a seventh attempt at re-election, was on the verge of tears as he gave up the office he held since Homer Martin, the first president, was ousted in 1938. He accepted a hearty handshake from the winner, who was heard to say: "Well, Tommy, now we can work together for a better union."

Mr. Thomas was understood reliably to be slated for appointment by Mr. Murray to serve as representative of the CIO on the newly formed World Federation of Trade Unions.

A movement was under way late tonight, however, to draft Mr. Thomas as a candidate for one of the two vice-presidential posts, which will be filled tomorrow. Among those urging such action were a number of Reuther delegates, who called at the Thomas headquarters to express their personal good-will toward the defeated candidate. Mr. Thomas promised an answer in the morning.

Fights Enliven Voting

Fist fights and near-riots enlivened the voting session, which began with nominations at noon and ended at 4:30 P. M., with the most tumultuous demonstration of the convention. So near exhaustion were the frenzied partisans as a result of the narrow margin separating the candidates throughout the day that an overnight recess was taken before proceeding with the election of a secretary-treasurer and two vice presidents.

His red locks flecked with red,

Continued on Page 31, Column 5

U. S. Tutor Sought For Hirohito's Son

By Wireless to THE NEW YORK TIMES.

TOKYO, March 27—Emperor Hirohito has asked the members of the American education mission at present here under the chairmanship of Dr. George D. Stoddard, New York State Commissioner of Education, to recommend an American tutor for the 12-year-old Crown Prince Akihito, it was learned in palace circles today.

The report came as members of the mission were received in audience this afternoon, later attended a tea party and witnessed court dances in the presence of the Emperor and his younger brother, Prince Nobushito Takamatsu.

Prince Akihito now is enrolled in the Peers School, of which his father also is a graduate. He also has the tutorial services of R. H. Blythe, an Englishman long resident in Japan, who is teaching him English. It is understood that an American tutor is being sought to supplement Mr. Blythe's teachings.

DRASTIC PROGRAM ON FOOD ADOPTED

UNRRA Resolution Outlines Steps, Including Rationing, to Meet Famine Crisis

UNRRA resolution outlining world food policy, Page 14.

By BESS FURMAN
Special to THE NEW YORK TIMES.

ATLANTIC CITY, N. J., March 27—The eleven-nation special food committee, which has been hard at work here since Friday on ways of meeting the famine crisis, recommended today rigorous food-saving measures. It also called for a recess in this United Nations Relief and Rehabilitation Administration Council to permit assessing the scarce supply situation, with provision to reconvene in Washington as soon as the director general can report.

With a few slight word changes, the resolution of the food committee was adopted unanimously at a session of the committee of the whole on policy held tonight to close the two weeks debate here on world food.

The expectation here was that the Council would reconvene in Washington in two or three weeks. In the interim the UNRRA director general would be requested under the resolution of the food committee "to consult immediately and continuously with representatives of the supplying Governments and with the combined food board to consider the effectiveness of steps being taken and to report thereon to the Central Committee and the Council." This duty no doubt will devolve on Fiorello H. La Guardia, slated to succeed Director General Herbert H. Lehman, although Mr. Lehman earlier had agreed to serve through the Council, not anticipating a recess.

Dallas W. Dort, second alternate of the American delegation, who served as chairman of the eleven-

Continued on Page 14, Column 2

IRAN'S STORY TOLD

Ambassador Ala Says He Does Not Know of Any Agreement in Force

DISCLOSES DEMANDS

Byrnes Asks That Case Be Confined to Purely Procedural Issue

Iranian Ambassador's statement of his country's case, P. 9.

By WILL LISSNER

In relief at becoming a participant in the deliberations of the United Nations Security Council on Iran's case, Ambassador Hussein Ala of Iran took a place at the Council table at 5:50 o'clock yesterday afternoon and disclosed demands made by the Soviet Union upon his country in secret Moscow negotiations between Feb. 19 and March 3 of this year.

The Iranian Ambassador plunged almost at once to one of the most vigorously discussed points, the question of whether or not there was a Soviet-Iranian agreement, as both Marshal Stalin and the Soviet delegate had indicated, when he stated:

"May I say once and for all that I know of no agreement or understanding, secret or otherwise, having been entered into between my Government and the Soviet Union with respect to any of the matters involved in the dispute now referred to this Council."

Mr. Ala, a short, spare man of quiet dignity, moved on the invitation of the chairman, Dr. Quo Tai-chi, from the seat in the front row of the Council chamber, where for two days he had been a mute witness of the Council's proceedings, to a seat on the extreme right of the table next to Dr. Oskar Lange, Polish representative, after the Council had voted to hear him.

"It was a relief," he said at the close of the session. "Imagine being obliged to watch all this discussion and not being able to begin making a statement."

Keen Interest Shown

While the members of the Council listened with keen interest, Mr. Ala began his presentation of Iran's reasons for opposing delay in consideration of her case.

"The issue between Iran and the Soviet Union was that the latter was interfering in the internal affairs of Iran through the medium of Soviet officials and armed forces," he asserted.

When Prime Minister Ahmad Ghavam of Iran went to Moscow on Feb. 19 to negotiate, as directed by the Security Council in its resolution of last Jan. 30, Mr. Ala continued, the Soviet officials "would not agree to withdraw their troops from Iran or to refrain from interfering in the internal affairs of Iran."

Instead, he said, the Soviet officials made a series of proposals. Soviet troops were to continue to stay in some parts of Iran indefi-

Continued on Page 11, Column 2

SOVIET DELEGATE WALKS OUT OF UNO—IRAN'S ENVOY TAKES A SEAT

Ambassador Andrei Gromyko is flanked by newspaper men as he leaves the chamber after the delegates refused to postpone discussion of the Iranian dispute until April 10. The New York Times

Ambassador Hussein Ala addressing the delegates. At the left is an assistant to Dr. Oskar Lange, Poland's representative, and at the right is Akbar Daftari of the Iranian Embassy. Associated Press

IRAN AGAIN DENIES NEW SOVIET PACT

Premier Reiterates No Written or Oral Accord Was Reached in Talks in Moscow

By GENE CURRIVAN
By Wireless to THE NEW YORK TIMES.

TEHERAN, Iran, March 27—Official sources here reiterated today that there was no new agreement with the Soviet Union despite all the clamoring for details from other parts of the world. Premier Ahmad Ghavam has not altered his position one degree since he returned from his conference in Moscow.

He said then that he had failed

Continued on Page 11, Column 5

Gromyko Is Stern and Silent As He Leaves UNO Chamber

By W. H. LAWRENCE

With grim, stony-faced determination, young Andrei A. Gromyko took a fateful walk out of the United Nations Security Council at 5:19 P. M., yesterday. He went because the Kremlin had told him that under no circumstances would the Soviet Union present to the Council before April 10 a defense of its actions in Iran. The Council had just rejected, 9 to 2, his motion to postpone the case for two weeks.

He did not wait for his opponent to begin to speak. He did not wait even until the Council had decided the issue affirmatively by inviting his opponent, Hussein Ala, Iranian Ambassador to the United States, to join the Council table.

But Mr. Gromyko will be back.

Continued on Page 3, Column 5

World News Summarized

THURSDAY, MARCH 28, 1946

The Soviet Union walked out of the UNO Security Council session late yesterday afternoon after the Russian proposal to defer consideration of the Iranian question until April 10 had been defeated, 9 to 2. Only Russia and Poland voted for it. When it became evident that Iranian Ambassador Ala would be invited to the table to present his case, Ambassador Gromyko announced he was unable to participate further in the discussions or remain present, picked up his papers and departed. [1:8.]

Mr. Gromyko's withdrawal was in conformity with strict instructions from Moscow and he is expected to attend any sessions before April 10 at which the merits of the Iranian question are not discussed. [1:5-6.] Oskar Lange, Poland's delegate, defended Mr. Gromyko's action and declared that Poland would continue in attendance. [2:2.]

Russia, at the Moscow conferences with Premier Ghavam, instead of agreeing to withdraw from Iran, made counter-proposals that were unacceptable, Mr. Ala disclosed to the Council. The Russians wanted Soviet troops to remain in some parts of Iran "for an indefinite period"; they demanded recognition of Azerbaijan's autonomy and proposed a joint Soviet-Iranian oil company in which Russia would hold 51 per cent of the stock. There have been no further discussions or agreements, he said, and he had not been authorized to agree to a delay. The session adjourned before Mr. Ala finished. [1:3.]

Official sources in Teheran confirmed the lack of any agreement. [1:4.]

The day of debate was marked by frequent sharp exchanges. The Council will meet in executive session this afternoon. [4:2.]

The Military Staff Committee began work on the international police force to maintain world security and peace through the UNO. [10:2.]

Russian Naval Lieutenant Redin was held in $25,000 bail in Portland, Ore., on espionage charges that Soviet officials called a "frame-up" to damage Russian prestige. He was accused of having induced some unnamed person to obtain data about the destroyer-tender Yellowstone, described as a "floating shipyard." [6:3.]

The British Labor party attacked Communists and dissident left-wingers in a manifesto rejecting a proposal to affiliate with the Communist party, which was accused of harboring fifth columnists. [10:3-4.]

In this country, observers saw a rebuke to leftists in the labor movement [31:2] in the defeat of R. J. Thomas by Walter P. Reuther for president of the United Auto Workers Union, CIO. [1:1.]

All nations were urged to their greatest efforts to cut food consumption and increase production to meet the world famine crisis in an UNRRA resolution. [1:2.]

Yugoslavia was warned in a sharp Allied communiqué that American and British occupation troops would oppose any sudden attempt by Marshal Tito's men to seize part of the Venezia Giulia area. [1:7; map P. 15.] Russia presented new draft peace treaties for Bulgaria and Hungary designed to meet Anglo-American objections. [15:2.]

León Blum told American negotiators that France would have to spend at least $17,000,000,000 in five years to re-establish her economic position and to permit her to play her full part in collective security. [1:6.]

BLUM PUTS NO TOP ON SIZE OF U. S. LOAN

Emissary Says France Needs $5,000,000,000 of Our Goods to Modernize Industry

By JOHN H. CRIDER
Special to THE NEW YORK TIMES.

WASHINGTON, March 27—Léon Blum, special French emissary to the United States, opened the current financial negotiations by painting a pitiable picture of France as "a nation twice ruined in thirty years," but citing the post-war accomplishments of her people as evidence of their courage and determination to recover.

The release today by the French Embassy of excerpts from M. Blum's lengthy presentation at the opening session on Monday was the first of a series of official releases under the rule of liberal public information adopted yesterday by the negotiators.

M. Blum opened on a note of "great solemnity" to stress the unity of all French political parties in supporting the "principles of democracy" and the "unconditional and unqualified" acceptance by France and all her constituent parties of the "principles of collec-

Continued on Page 17, Column 2

ALLIES WARN TITO ON VENEZIA GIULIA

Issue Blunt Statement Against Any Yugoslav Move to Invade Disputed Zone at Trieste

By SAM POPE BREWER
By Wireless to THE NEW YORK TIMES.

ROME, March 27—The Allied Governments issued a firm warning tonight to the Yugoslavs against any effort to stage a sudden invasion of the disputed Zone A of Venezia Giulia, now occupied by Anglo-American forces.

In the most blunt statement made on the subject in many months, Lieut. Gen. William D. Morgan, Supreme Allied Commander in the Mediterranean theatre, from his headquarters in Caserta, speaking in the names of the American and British Governments, said: "Public order will be enforced with justice, and in our zone we shall tolerate no attempt to prejudge in any way the final disposition of the territory.

"To this end, the American and British Governments have authorized me to declare that it is their firm intention to maintain their present position in Venezia Giulia until an agreed settlement of the territorial dispute has been reached and put into effect."

Allied Forces Reduced

This is the first time since the agreement was signed with Marshal Tito last June for the present division of Venezia Giulia into Zones A and B that such action has been necessary by the British and Americans.

[Zone A constitutes about a quarter of the area on the western side of the peninsula against the Italian frontier, and includes

Continued on Page 15. Column 2

Braden Bars a Break With Peron; Says Europe Needs Argentine Aid

Spruille Braden, Assistant Secretary of State and leading exponent of a firm policy in dealing with Argentina, indicated yesterday that there was nothing we could do at the moment about the Perón regime, recently victorious in the election held there.

In a frank discussion here, Mr. Braden ruled out the breaking of diplomatic relations as "silly," and any attempt to impose sanctions as futile, because neither France nor Britain would back us, nor would we, in this country, want to assume the resposibility of depriving the starving of Europe of the food Argentina could supply.

Mr. Braden was the principal speaker at a seminar for women's clubs, arranged by THE NEW YORK TIMES in cooperation with the General Federation of Women's Clubs, held at Times Hall, 240 West Forty-fourth Street.

Other speakers on the program, the first of three scheduled, included Turner Catledge, assistant managing editor; Foster Hailey, editorial writer; James B. Reston, national correspondent; Anne O'Hare McCormick, editorial correspondent, all of THE TIMES; John J. McCloy, former Assistant Secretary of War, Mrs. William Dick Sporborg of the General Federation of Women's Clubs and Mrs. Arthur Hays Sulzberger, who welcomed the guests.

Mr. Braden's exposition of our present attitude toward Argentina came during the question and answer period. The question to which he addressed himself was:

"If the United States applies

Continued on Page 19, Column 1

10c Fare Resolution Withdrawn; Defeat by Board Was Indicated

By PAUL CROWELL

Cornelius A. Hall, Borough President of Richmond, withdrew yesterday, "pending further conferences with Mayor O'Dwyer," the ten-cent subway fare resolution submitted by him to the Board of Estimate on March 14.

Mr. Hall's announcement came soon after the committee of the whole of the Board of Estimate ended a three-hour executive meeting at City Hall. Mayor O'Dwyer and the other Democratic members of the board declined to discuss Mr. Hall's announcement, but it was reliably reported that he decided to withdraw the higher-fare resolution after his colleagues had indicated that they would vote it down today and would not agree to lay it over for consideration at some future meeting.

The resolution called for a ten-cent fare on all transit lines owned and operated by the city, with free transfers for any single continuous trip. It also provided for a ten-cent fare on the Staten Island ferries, with free transfers to subways and certain bus lines. Another provision called for retention of a five-cent fare for school children traveling to and from school.

Mr. Hall declined to discuss details of the proceedings at the executive meeting, but did say that "it was a lengthy discussion."

"I am withdrawing my resolution pending further conferences with Mayor O'Dwyer," he declared.

Mayor O'Dwyer recently indi-

Continued on Page 20, Column 5

COUNCIL PROCEEDS

Soviet Departure Fails to Swerve Body in Hearing of Issue

SOVIET COURSE HAZY

She Will Be Present at a Meeting Today—Poland Backs Her

Transcript of UNO proceedings on Iran question, Page 8.

By JAMES B. RESTON

The Soviet Union took a walk at the United Nations Security Council meeting yesterday, but it will be represented at the Council's Committee of Experts today, and it will come back to the Council when it feels like it, which will probably be on April 10.

This action, which broke, temporarily, the rule of Big Five unanimity, which the Russians have supported from the start, was not a break with the UNO. It was not to be compared, as some observers have been comparing it, with the German, Italian and Japanese departures from the League of Nations; nor was it an indication that the coalition that produced victory had been dissolved.

It is a decision by the Soviet Government, carried out by its Ambassador to Washington, Andrei A. Gromyko, to leave the Council for two weeks while the question of Red Army troops in Iran is being discussed. It is a parliamentary maneuver. It is an expression of protest against the Council. It is, admittedly, a psychological blow to the new organization and an illustration of the Soviet thesis that the great powers should direct, and even dictate, procedure as well as issues of substance in the Council.

Not a Break With Council

But it is not a break with the Council. In fact, not only do the Soviet representatives say they will be in the meeting of the Committee of Experts today, but in addition it is reported that if today's closed session of the Council deals only with the procedural aspects of the Iranian question, they may even attend that, though this is not at all certain.

At 5:04 yesterday afternoon, at the end of what began to look strangely like a filibuster by the Soviet Union, the Council defeated the Soviet Union's motion to postpone discussion of the Iranian case until April 10. Only the U.S.S.R. and Poland voted for it.

At 5:19, before the Council had voted to invite the Iranian Ambassador to sit at the Council table and tell why he thought the case of the Soviet troops in Iran was urgent, the youthful, pokerfaced Soviet delegate, Ambassador Gromyko, raised his hand and addressed the chair.

Soviet Statement on Withdrawal

As he was recognized, the spotlights in the chamber room went on slowly. The chamber was crowded. The delegates, weary of endless argument on legal points, frustrated by the lack of any rules of procedure and frankly out of patience with the Soviet Ambassador's repetitive argument, turned indulgently toward him and settled down for what looked like another long speech. But he was brief and to the point.

"For reasons which I explained clearly enough in our meeting of yesterday and in today's meeting, Mr. Chairman," he said in Russian, "I, as representative of the Soviet Union, am not able to participate further in the discussions of the Security Council because my proposal has not been accepted by the Council, nor am I able to be present at the meeting of the Council, and I therefore leave the meeting."

For a few minutes the audience did not understand the meaning of this, for when he finished speaking he waited expressionless in his chair until the translators had finished. The first indication the

Continued on Page 3, Column 1

"All the News That's Fit to Print"

The New York Times.

LATE CITY EDITION
Partly cloudy and mild today.
Occasional showers tomorrow.
Temperatures Yesterday—Max., [illegible]; Min., [illegible]
[illegible]

VOL. XCV..No. 32,239. Entered as Second-Class Matter. Postoffice, New York, N. Y. NEW YORK, WEDNESDAY, MAY 1, 1946. THREE CENTS IN NEW YORK CITY

JOINT PALESTINE BODY BARS A JEWISH STATE, BUT URGES ENTRY OF 100,000 REFUGEES

WARSHIP BLOWS UP AT MUNITIONS PIER IN PORT, KILLING 5

60 on Escort Vessel Injured—Blasts Shake New Jersey Towns Near Big Depot

BOMBS ASHORE SET OFF

Sailor Is Only Slightly Hurt as Depth Charge Explodes as He Is Carrying It

By MEYER BERGER

Special to THE NEW YORK TIMES.

LEONARDO, N. J., April 30—One officer and four sailors of the destroyer escort Solar's complement of fourteen officers and 136 enlisted men vanished utterly before noon today in an ammunition explosion that tore away one-third of the 306-foot ship's forward structure.

About sixty of the ship's crew were injured, but only thirty-five were hospitalized, and of them only a handful remained tonight for further treatment. The Navy withheld the names of the five missing men and the names of the injured because not all their families had been officially notified.

The explosion happened as the Solar's crew was unloading her ammunition supply in preparation for an overhaul. Normally she carries about fifteen tons of assorted ammunition, including depth bombs and smaller charges, torpedoes and shells for her cannon. Only one-third of this amount was still aboard when the blast occurred.

Tons of Explosives Near By

Near by, when the detonation shook the New Jersey coast in and around the Raritan Bay district, were a number of other vessels preparing to unload ammunition. It was unofficially estimated here that these vessels held, all told, about 25,000 tons of explosives. Tugs dragged these craft out of the danger zone.

Burning fragments from the Solar, hurled at tremendous force against freight cars on the pier, started other explosions. One car in a freight string, filled chiefly with depth charges, blew up and all but vanished in dust and smoke, scattering its parts in all directions. Three strings of cars were hauled shoreward by their locomotive crews, at great risk.

No one seemed certain tonight what had caused the explosion, but what seemed like a possible explanation came from Jack Horne, fireman second class, of Charlotte, N. C. He thought a piece of ammunition carried by Joseph Stuchinski, seaman, of Baltimore, might have done it.

"Ski," the fireman said, "was carrying a 'hedgehog' from the forward magazine. While he was holding it, it just went off. He must have bumped it against something, because those things go off when anything touches them."

Seaman Stuchinski, oddly enough, was not seriously injured. He was deafened, a few minor scratches showed on his chest when he got to the first-aid station and his dungarees were split.

"It went off. The thing just went off," he said.

The "hedgehog" Stuchinski carried was an anti-submarine depth charge. Metal-cased, weighing about sixty pounds, it is generally cylindrical, about thirty inches long and between four and five inches in diameter.

Bow Like Elephant's Trunk

The Solar lay at the northern, or bay end, of the easternmost of the three great piers that jut out from the Navy's Earle Ammunition Depot, when she blew up. She was approximately one and one-half miles from the beach end of the depot. The blast curled her bow in much the same shape as an elephant's back-bent trunk.

The concussion was felt twenty to thirty miles around. The detonation rushed across Raritan Bay to shake homes in Tottenville, Richmond Valley, Pleasant Plains, Princess Bay, Great Kills, Oakwood and New Dorp, all on Staten Island, and shattered panes in some of those communities.

Ground tremors were felt to the west and to the southwest. There were some freakish effects. Residents in Middletown Township, including Rumson, Fair Haven, Red Bank and Little Silver, for example, seemed certain the explosion was local. Several frightened housewives called the police to say, "The boiler just blew up in my cellar."

Dogs raced away from the beach

Continued on Page 2, Column 3

AFTER EXPLOSIONS RIPPED DESTROYER ESCORT

The wrecked U. S. S. Solar at the Navy Ammunition Depot in Earle, N. J., yesterday

The New York Times (U. S. Navy)

BAN BY MUSICIANS BLOW TO TELEVISION

Petrillo Plans to Prolong the Refusal of Union Men to the Industry Indefinitely

By JACK GOULD

The American Federation of Musicians, headed by James C. Petrillo, plans to forbid its members to work in television until some indefinite date in the future when the union can determine the effects of video's advent on present-day radio, it was learned yesterday.

Television broadcasters were agreed that Mr. Petrillo's stand would retard the immediate development of video programs, since it could be a matter of months if not years before anyone could determine to what extent television would supplant or complement sound broadcasting.

Use of "live" musicians was first denied the television industry in February, 1945, by the international executive board of the federation, but yesterday was the first time that Mr. Petrillo explained the action and indicated that the ban would be of prolonged duration.

Musical Films Already Banned

Last week Mr. Petrillo's union and the Hollywood motion picture producers entered into an agreement not to permit films containing music to be used in television, a move leaving the telecasters with only records as a possible source of music. Beginning July 1, under a rule of the Federal Communications Commission, the television stations are scheduled to offer twenty-eight hours of programs a week, but under Mr. Petrillo's edicts they will be forced to rely primarily on talks, sporting events and other non-musical fare.

Coincidentally with stating the union's position on television, Mr. Petrillo also reiterated his stand against permitting standard radio programs containing music to be presented simultaneously on frequency modulation outlets. The union is insisting on double crews of musicians in the event of such duplication.

The re-statement of the union's views on FM were regarded with

Continued on Page 28, Column 2

Stalin Warns of War Plot By 'International Reaction'

By The Associated Press.

LONDON, April 30—Generalissimo Stalin promised tonight that the Soviet Union would be true to a policy of peace and security but charged that what he described as "international reaction" was "hatching plans of a new war." In an order of the day broadcast by the Moscow radio the Russian leader also declared that it was necessary to be constantly vigilant, "to protect as the apple of one's eye the armed forces and defensive power of our country."

TEXT OF STALIN ORDER

His broadcast order, issued in connection with the Soviet Union's May Day celebration, was heard in London by the Soviet monitor, who issued the following text:

Comrades, Red Army and Red Navy men, sergeants and petty officers, comrade officers, generals and admirals, working people of the Soviet Union:

Today, for the first time since the victorious termination of the Great Patriotic War we celebrate May 1—the international holiday of working people—in conditions of peaceful life, won in a hard struggle against the enemies at the cost of heavy sacrifices and privations.

One year ago the Red Army hoisted the banner of victory over Berlin and completed the defeat of fascist Germany. Within four months after the victorious termination of the war against Germany, imperialist Japan downed her arms. The Second World War, prepared by the forces of international reaction and unleashed by the chief fascist states, ended in a full victory of the freedom-loving nations. The smashup and liquidation of the main hotbeds of fascism and world aggression resulted in changes in the political life of the nations of the world, in a wide growth of the democratic movement of the nations.

Taught by the experience of war, the popular masses realized that the destinies of states cannot be entrusted to reactionary leaders, who pursue the narrow caste and selfish anti-popular aims. It is for this reason that nations, which no longer wish to live in the old way, take destinies of their states into their own hands, establish democratic order and actively fight against the forces of reaction, against instigators of a new war. The nations of the

Continued on Page 5, Column 4

INQUIRY FINDS 'PERIL' TO SECRETS OF WAR

Senators Hear Radar Makers on Russian Buying and Urge Law Tightening

By C. P. TRUSSELL

Special to THE NEW YORK TIMES.

WASHINGTON, April 30—Need for a tightening of the laws to provide protection for wartime secrets in the electronics and other fields was declared by Senate investigators today to be "very definite." The statement came after a closed-session inquiry into negotiations for sales of radar and similar equipment to Russia.

Members of a special Senate Judiciary subcommittee, conducting the investigation, said that there was no evidence that "classified,"

Continued on Page 3, Column 4

Sharp Restrictions in Distilling Ordered in Food Conservation

By CHARLES E. EGAN

Special to THE NEW YORK TIMES.

WASHINGTON, April 30—World famine is more than a short term problem, and plans to meet its reappearance next winter should be drafted immediately, Chester C. Davis, chairman of the President's Special Famine Emergency Committee, asserted today.

Mr. Davis, who conferred with President Truman, later said that emergency measures, taken to insure larger relief shipment of grains and other foods to famine-stricken areas in the next few weeks, could not be considered as final, but were merely "the first sprint" in a continuing race to avert death for millions who otherwise would starve.

Meanwhile, Secretary Anderson issued an order restricting distilleries who operated for five days at full mashing capacity in April to three capacity days in May.

The order also limited the use of grain by the entire distilling industry to 2,500,000 bushels a month; banned use of wheat in the manufacture of spirits and restricted distillers to the use of corn which is unsuitable for human consumption.

In January, distillers were permitted ten capacity mashing days, but were cut to seven and one-half in February and to five days in March and April.

Brewers, operating on a 30 per cent reduction of grain, were not included in today's order.

"Every report coming before us makes it plain that the present famine is not a short run emergency that ends on July 1," Mr. Davis' statement said, adding:

"The present food shortages have been seriously aggravated by drought in many parts of the world, but even with good weather the wartime destruction of agricultural facilities will be felt for a long time.

"Farm animals and farm machinery have been destroyed. The strength of farm workers has

Continued on Page 28, Column 3

BIG FOUR RULE OUT AUSTRIA'S DEMAND FOR SOUTH TYROL

Paris Conference Rejects Any Major Frontier Revision in That Region of Italy

NO PROGRESS ON TRIESTE

Rome and Belgrade Are Asked to Send Delegates—Report of Experts Confusing

By C. L. SULZBERGER

By Cable to THE NEW YORK TIMES.

PARIS, April 30—Italy's retention of most of the Province of Bolzano [South Tyrol], which is claimed by Austria, was virtually assured tonight after the Council of Foreign Ministers had agreed that no requests for a major frontier change would be accepted in that area so valuable in hydro-electric power.

At the same time, after examining a verbose and confused report on Trieste and Venezia Giulia, submitted at long last by the special commission sent by the Foreign Ministers' deputies to investigate the Italian-Yugoslav border area, the Ministers agreed to invite the Yugoslav and Italian Governments to send delegates here on Friday to present once again their views on this hotly disputed and vitally important region.

The report showed a complete divergence in opinion between the Soviet investigator and the three other participants on the value of a census taken in 1945 by a Yugoslav, Professor Rodlich. The Soviet member of the commission said the census was fine and the three others said it was just the opposite. Since this census is of vital importance in deciding the ethnic basis for a decision, that leaves everything up in the air.

Suggested by Molotov

The move to widen the scope of the Foreign Ministers' meeting by inviting in the Italians and Yugoslavs was suggested by Vyacheslav M. Molotov. The Soviet Foreign Minister recalled that the Potsdam decisions, the "bible" under which the peace treaties are being drafted, provided that the interested parties should be included when necessary. Thus, the doors have been opened to permit entry of those delegations—Greek, Italian, Yugoslav, Hungarian and Bulgarian—now clamoring for a

Continued on Page 4, Column 2

World News Summarized

WEDNESDAY, MAY 1, 1946

Palestine should become neither a Jewish state nor an Arab state, the Anglo-American Committee of Inquiry declared in its report made public simultaneously last night in Washington and London. Admission of 100,000 Jews this year and virtual abrogation of the 1939 British White Paper with its restrictions on land holdings were recommended. Other suggestions included continuation of the present mandate until establishment of a United Nations trusteeship and resolute suppression of violence and terrorism by Jews or Arabs. [1:8.]

Although President Truman expressed pleasure over certain parts of the report, it was felt in Washington that neither the Jews nor Arabs would be satisfied. [13.1.] In fact, Arab leaders threatened to combat any additional Jewish immigration [13:3] and Zionists expressed their opposition. Bartley C. Crum, a member of the committee, predicted that a directive authorizing the entry of 100,000 Jews into Palestine would "issue forthwith." [1:6-7.]

British reaction counted heavily upon American support in whatever was done, but regretted the absence of any long-term solution. [1:6-7.]

Italy will be permitted to retain most of southern Tyrol despite Austrian claims, the Foreign Ministers tentatively agreed at their conference in Paris, but they were as wide apart as ever on what to do about Trieste and the Venezia Giulia area. It was decided to invite Yugoslavia and Italy to present their cases anew. [1:5.]

Britain tried to meet French desires by suggesting internationalization of either the Ruhr or both the Ruhr and the left bank of the Rhine for fifty years. [3:1.] Secretary Byrnes' proposed four-power treaty to keep Germany disarmed was favorably received in the Senate Foreign Affairs Committee. [3:2.]

The United Nations Security Council subcommittee opens its investigation into Franco Spain this afternoon. [1:7.] Europe's ruined industries should be restored before attempts to eradicate world unemployment, the Economic and Employment Commission heard [8:5], while the Transport and Communications Commission debated the relative merits of free enterprise and government control of shipping. [7:1.] The Commission on Human Rights may seek a new international bill of rights and ask authority to supervise its implementation. [8:2]

Tabriz, capital of Azerbaijan, has been formally evacuated by Russian troops, the Tabriz radio reported. [3:6.] Premier Stalin declared that, while the world must remain vigilant against reaction, it had "no reason to doubt" that Russia would remain steadfast in her devotion to international peace and security. [1:3-4.]

Japan was shocked at the plot to assassinate General MacArthur and the Government offered its apologies. No arrests have been announced. [1:6-7.]

Ammunition being unloaded from the destroyer-escort Solar in Raritan Bay exploded, killing an officer and four sailors. [1:1.]

John L. Lewis served notice that anthracite miners intended to strike on May 31 unless they obtained the same demands that led to the soft-coal strike. Negotiations will start in New York on May 10. No progress was made toward settling the bituminous dispute. [29:1.]

Further restrictions were placed on the use of grain by distillers in order to make more food available for world famine relief. [1:2-3.]

General Motors was authorized by the OPA to raise prices on its cars from $16 to $60 to cover wage increases. [27:6-7.] House members returned to Washington still opposed to extending price control without heavy restrictions. [30:5.]

Arabs 'Outraged' by Report; Jews Are Far From Satisfied

Rival Agencies Reiterate Their Arguments—U. S., British Talks Are Forecast on Easing Burden Too Big for London

By HERBERT L. MATTHEWS

By Wireless to THE NEW YORK TIMES.

LONDON, April 30—Now that the report of the Anglo-American Committee of Inquiry on Palestine has been published, one can safely predict tonight that the next step will be for the British to consult the United States Government about it. The British have reached the point at which they consider that Palestine is far too great a burden for them to be forced to handle alone.

No Government spokesman would say anything about the report tonight because the Cabinet and other officials have not had time to study it. One must keep in mind that the members of the committee had a mandate only to make recommendations, which do not in any sense involve Governmental responsibility.

The Arab Office in London has lost no time in issuing a scorching statement condemning the report lock, stock and barrel. The Jewish Agency for Palestine gave the report a mixed reception. It was happy about the proposal to allow 100,000 Jewish refugees to enter Palestine but asserted that without the formation of a Jewish state there could be no solution to the problem of homeless Jews.

On all sides one hears dubious comment about the fact that the committee's report makes no suggestion in terms of any sort of finality nor does it even offer any kind of long-term solution to the Palestinian problem. It is feared that even moderate elements among the Arabs will be more disturbed about that feature of the report than any other.

In their present mood of shocked disgust over the murder of seven British soldiers in Tel Aviv last Thursday the British are inclined to place the most prominence on that part of the report dealing with security and with making it clear that violence and terrorism will be resolutely repressed. The state-

Continued on Page 14, Column 5

Truman Said to Plan Start Of Jewish Entry 'Forthwith'

By LAWRENCE RESNER

Bartley C. Crum, one of the six United States members of the Joint Anglo-American Committee of Inquiry on Palestine, predicted here yesterday, on the basis of a discussion he had with President Truman at the White House on Monday, that the directives authorizing the admission of 100,000 European Jews into Palestine would "issue forthwith."

Mr. Crum, a San Francisco lawyer, also expressed the belief that most Jewish groups would endorse the affirmative aspects of the report, although reserving their right to continue a fight for the achievement of their ideological tenets, principally a Jewish state.

An immediate endorsement of the recommendation to obtain the admission of the 100,000 European Jews came from Joseph M. Proskauer, president of the American Jewish Committee, who said the provisions for immediate action were "obviously based on the highest considerations of statesmanship and humanity."

The World Zionist Emergency Council, which speaks for some of the largest and most active Zionist groups in the United States, said a statement outlining its position probably would be issued today, after the report had been studied.

The initial negative response by a Jewish group came from the Political Action Committee for Palestine, whose executive vice chairman, Dr. Baruch Korff, said that despite "the report's few fine points, the commission had proved

Continued on Page 13, Column 4

U.N.'S SPAIN INQUIRY COMMENCES TODAY

5-Man Subcommittee to Meet Here In Secret—No Outside Witnesses at First Session

By W. H. LAWRENCE

The Franco regime in Spain goes on trial today on charges that it is a cause of international friction and a threat to world peace.

Meeting privately at 3 P. M., representatives of Australia, China, France, Poland and Brazil will set in motion the first formal investigation by the United Nations, authorized Monday by a 10-to-0 vote of the Security Council, in which Russia did not participate but refrained from exercising an asserted right to veto the inquiry.

How, where and when the Council subcommittee will function presumably will be decided in the early part of today's meeting, and the members then will turn to analyzing the evidence now before them, listing the specific charges

Continued on Page 7, Column 5

MacArthur Plot Alarms Japanese; They See Possible Repercussions

By The Associated Press.

TOKYO, April 30—News of a frustrated assassination plot against General Douglas MacArthur tonight shocked the Japanese.

Their first reaction was twofold: A feeling that their country had lost face; fears that repercussions might be felt in every household.

The Government officially apologized. Katsuo Okazaki, representing Foreign Minister Shigeru Yoshida, visited General MacArthur's office two hours after Allied Headquarters had announced discovery of the plot. He did not see the general personally, but delivered a verbal message to aides.

Mr. Okazaki expressed "deep regret and concern" and said his Government was "greatly embarrassed." He asked if there was anything his Government could do.

Earlier, Premier Kijuro Shidehara, Mr. Yoshida and Home Minister Chuzo Mitsuchi conferred. Japanese reporters speculated that they discussed tighter precautions than previously were planned for the May Day demonstrations.

Many Japanese immediately asked, "Will this create more anti-Japanese feeling in America?" They linked this with fear that adverse American reaction might complicate efforts to obtain food and might mean a longer, harsher occupation.

They also expressed regret that the incident might mar the occupation and change the attitude of General MacArthur, whom the Japanese generally respect.

Allied headquarters had previously given some details of the plot. One conspirator was seized and a nation-wide hunt was launched for a die-hard Japanese militarist named as the arch plotter.

The accused and hunted plot leader was Hideo Tokayama, former member of the dread Kempeitai or "thought police." In the

Continued on Page 12, Column 6

TRUMAN FOR ACTION

Inquiry Upholds His Visa Proposal, Urges End of White Paper

WOULD GUARD ARAB RIGHTS

Report for Change in Holy Land Property Curbs—Demands a Firm Stand on Violence

The text of the report of the Anglo-American Committee of Inquiry on Palestine, Pages 15 to 21, inclusive.

FELIX BELAIR JR.

Special to THE NEW YORK TIMES.

WASHINGTON, April 30—The Anglo-American Committee of Inquiry on problems of Jews in Europe and Palestine, reporting to the two Governments today on its four-month investigation, urged the admission of 100,000 European Jews into the Holy Land as soon as possible, but flatly rejected the idea of a Jewish state, together with Arab claims for dominance. It asserted Christendom's own interest in the area.

Released simultaneously for publication in Washington and London, the report drew from President Truman an expression of satisfaction that his proposal for the admission of 100,000 Jews into Palestine had been recommended. He added that "the transference of these unfortunate people should now be accomplished with the greatest dispatch."

The President declared it significant that the report aimed at guarantees for Arab civil and religious rights and urged measures to improve Arab cultural, educational and economic position.

Land Changes Asked

"I am also pleased," he said, "that the committee recommends, in effect, the abrogation of the White Paper of 1939."

The report repudiated the 1939 White Paper principles, which made further Jewish immigration dependent on Arab consent and banned Jewish land purchases in a major part of Palestine.

Dependent for its final effect on adoption by both Governments, the report covered a wide range of controversial subjects on which President Truman gave no hint of his attitude except to say that he was taking them under advisement.

However, Mr. Truman seemed to have embraced the major policy statement rejecting "once and for all the exclusive claims of Jews and Arabs to Palestine," which the committee enunciated as follows:

"(I, That Jew shall not dominate Arab and Arab shall not dominate Jew in Palestine. (II) That Palestine shall be neither a Jewish state nor an Arab state. (III) That the form of government ultimately to be established shall, under international guarantees, fully protect and preserve the interests in the Holy Land of Christendom and of the Moslem and Jewish faiths."

Stress on Unique Status

With deliberate emphasis, the Committee of Inquiry declared that "Palestine is a Holy Land, sacred to Christian, to Jew and to Moslem alike; and because it is a holy land, Palestine is not, and can never become, a land which any race or religion can justly claim as its very own."

With equal emphasis, the committee said the same considerations set Palestine apart from other lands, and dedicated it to the precepts and practices of the brotherhood of man rather than to those of narrow nationalism.

The 42,000-word report was signed in Lausanne, Switzerland, by Judge Joseph C. Hutcheson, United States chairman, Sir John E. Singleton, British chairman, Frank Aydelotte, Frank W. Buxton, Bartley C. Crum, James G. McDonald and William Phillips, American members, and W. F. Crick, R. H. S. Crossman, Frederick Leggett, R. E. Manningham-Buller and M. Morrison for Britain.

For the immediate future the

Continued on Page 14, Column 3

"All the News That's Fit to Print"

The New York Times.

LATE CITY EDITION
Mostly sunny today. Fair and warmer tomorrow.
Temperatures Yesterday—Max., 54; Min., 4[illegible]
Sunrise today, [illegible] A. M.; Sunset, [illegible] P. M.
Full U. S. Weather Bureau Report, Page [illegible]

VOL. XCVI...No. 32,393. Entered as Second-Class Matter, Postoffice, New York, N. Y. NEW YORK, WEDNESDAY, OCTOBER 2, 1946. THREE CENTS in NEW YORK CITY

12 NAZI WAR LEADERS SENTENCED TO BE HANGED; GOERING HEADS LIST OF THOSE TO DIE BY OCT. 16; HESS GETS LIFE, SIX OTHERS ORDERED TO PRISON

SHIP OFFICERS QUIT, PARALYZING PORT 2D TIME IN MONTH

Never Before Have Masters Been Called From Bridges—Engineers Also Strike

WASHINGTON PLEAS FAIL

But Efforts to Settle Dispute Over Wages and Working Conditions Are Continued

By GEORGE HORNE

The cogs of the nation's merchant marine slowed to a standstill yesterday for the second time in a month as the unprecedented strike of licensed officers got under way.

It was unprecedented because never before in the country's shipping history have shipmasters—captains earning as much as $500 and $600 a month—been called from their bridges in a union action to enforce wage and working demands. But they were leaving their ships on order, along with brother engineer officers of the Marine Engineers Beneficial Association.

Reaction among the captains was mixed, and the situation affecting them at a late hour last night was obscure, after a welter of messages to and from the negotiating headquarters in Washington, where Government authorities were still trying to effect a settlement before the walkout could settle down to a long-term affair.

Many Captains Not in Union

Many captains are not members of the National Organization of Masters, Mates and Pilots (AFL), even on such ships as have MMP contracts. Shipping operators said the captains, who are the owners' supreme representatives aboard, and as such considered beyond the call of strike action, were "being threatened."

They declared that Capt. Harry Martin, East Coast president of the MMP, had agreed in Washington yesterday to leave security watches aboard all ships, including a captain and a day and night mate for stand-by duty. But they said the pledge was not being honored.

At a special meeting of the AFL Maritime Trades Department at the office of the International Longshoremen's Association last night it was announced that "the status quo" remains. That meant that captains were being called off, whether they agreed or not. The AFL spokesman said the response among all MMP officers was excellent.

Ship operators took the position that the masters were "in the middle" and "behind the eight-ball," and they agreed that many would have to leave their ships at the union's call.

The MMP leaders have stood by their original conception of the walkout as being no strike. It was, the union leaders said, simply a case of the men not working in

Continued on Page 4, Column 3

Cards Beat Dodgers In First Game, 4-2

Despite a muscle ailment, Howie Pollet pitched the Cardinals to a 4-2 victory over the Dodgers at St. Louis yesterday in the first of a three-game play-off series for the National League pennant. The Cards meanwhile routed Ralph Branca, first of five Brooklyn pitchers, with three runs in as many innings.

Howie Schultz momentarily tied the score for the Dodgers with his homer in the third and also batted in their second run with a single in the seventh.

The play-offs, first such in the history of major league baseball, will be resumed tomorrow at Ebbets Field, and the third contest, if necessary, will be played there Friday.

(Complete details on Page 35.)

12 Inches of Snow Blanket Several Up-State Areas

Flurries Are Reported as Far South as the Pennsylvania Line—Temperature Here Is Near Record Low for Date

By The Associated Press.

ALBANY, Oct. 1—Canadian-border areas of upper New York dug out tonight from more than a foot of snow as high winds churned the tail-end of the season's first storm into near-blizzard fury.

It was still snowing early tonight, but a United States weather forecaster described the pre-winter blast as a one-day storm. He predicted low temperatures for another 48 hours.

The storm, whipping across the Adirondack area from Canada, forced some schools to close, blocked secondary highways and disrupted power and communications lines in northern New York.

Although the brunt of the storm was felt in the upper Adirondacks, its effect was State-wide. Temperatures plummeted toward the freezing mark and snow flurries were reported in western and southern New York, along the Pennsylvania line.

Syracuse, reporting its earliest snow in forty-four years of official records, had a half-inch.

New York City's 45-degree temperature early this morning was within three degrees of the 1916 record low for the date.

Some up-State areas without snow had steady rain. Saratoga Springs reported a twenty-four-hour fall of 1.5 inches and Schenectady had 2.08 inches in the thirty-six hours ending at 8 A. M.

The villages of Malone in Franklin County and Potsdam in St. Lawrence apparently were hardest hit, with traffic crippled and heavy damage caused by falling trees and branches. Malone had 13 inches of snow and Potsdam a foot. Both were without electric power.

Malone's gas service was cut partly when a falling tree damaged a main. The Alice Hyde Memorial Hospital was without electricity all morning and gas most of the day. Power was re-

Continued on Page 27, Column 2

LEHMAN 'STRADDLE' CHARGED BY IVES

Says Rival Evades Wallace Foreign Policy Issue With Aim to Placate Left

Special to THE NEW YORK TIMES.

ALBANY, Oct. 1—Irving M. Ives, Republican candidate for United States Senator, charged tonight that former Governor Herbert H. Lehman, his Democratic opponent, had issued a "shadow doctrine" on foreign policy designed to placate both old-line Democrats and left-wing groups.

Mr. Lehman, he declared, straddled the issue and took a "vague and insecure" stand which had something to please "each of the political organizations and splinter parties he represents in this campaign."

In a State-wide radio broadcast he challenged Mr. Lehman to tell the people whether he agreed with Secretary of State James F. Byrnes or with former Secretary of Commerce Henry A. Wallace. He declared it impossible to side with both.

Challenge on "Enslavement"

"Mr. Wallace believes in drawing an iron curtain across eastern Europe," he said, adding:

"We have seen that wars arise when people are enslaved and the truth kept from them. Does my opponent favor a policy which would permit this condition to ex-

Continued on Page 8, Column 3

HULL, 75, STRICKEN AFTER PEACE PLEA

United Nations' 'Father' Calls on Powers to Renew Zeal—His Condition Serious

Text of Mr. Hull's statement appears on page 18.

By BERTRAM D. HULEN

Special to THE NEW YORK TIMES.

WASHINGTON, Oct. 1—Cordell Hull, former Secretary of State, suffered a stroke in the United States Naval Hospital at Bethesda, Md., last night, a few hours after he had completed a statement appealing to the Great Powers to compose their differences for the sake of world peace.

The stroke was officially described at first as "light," but the hospital announced later that Mr. Hull's condition had become "more serious during the day." Friends meanwhile had described him as extremely weak and had expressed grave concern. They considered his condition to be critical.

A hospital bulletin issued at 10 o'clock tonight said Mr. Hull remained in serious condition. "No improvement has been noted in his condition since the last bulletin," it said. "No change" was reported at midnight.

Nevertheless, the former Secretary's statement for world peace was issued on his behalf tonight, carrying out his instructions. It

Continued on Page 18, Column 3

City's Search for Meat Supplies Fails to Uncover Any Hoarding

A meat search by three city departments was three-quarters finished yesterday and disclosed holdings in local slaughterhouses, storage plants and railroad cars of 13,312,880 pounds—not much compared to New York's normal consumption of 3,800,000 pounds a day.

With fewer than fifty of the city's 400 major repositories of meat still to be visited by the task force of 225 policemen and inspectors of the Health and Market departments, Mayor O'Dwyer said he saw nothing in the findings so far to warrant municipal action.

Meat supplies in retail stores, meanwhile, continued to shrink, and the Office of Price Administration reported that the black market was shrinking even faster than the supply of available meat. This did not seem any great victory to housewives, since the race was in the direction of a zero supply.

OPA enforcement agents, continuing their daily check on prices and, incidentally, supply, found only one out of ten butcher shops with meat to sell. Many were shut and many others sold only poultry. There was more sausage meat than any other kind. Last week the district OPA had reported one shop out of five selling meat.

Yesterday's report by the district enforcement staff was to the effect that only 5 per cent of the meat being offered for sale was at black market prices, whereas the same office had estimated last week that 20 to 35 per cent of the local sales were at over-ceiling prices.

The City Council, in a majority resolution sent to its rules committee, called upon the Federal Government to seize all cattle and meat in the country and blamed the meat industry for "open defiance to the American people by the creation of a meat famine." The resolution, which also urged that the Government make available to the public as an emergency health measure the meat so

Continued on Page 38, Column 3

11,236-MILE RECORD SET AS NAVY PLANE LANDS IN COLUMBUS

Truculent Turtle Smashes Old Mark by 3,300 Miles in Non-Stop Flight From Australia

UP 55 HOURS 15 MINUTES

Four-Man Crew, Fresh Despite Rough Hop, Is Disappointed at Not Finishing in Washington

By FREDERICK GRAHAM

Special to THE NEW YORK TIMES.

COLUMBUS, Ohio, Oct. 1—A non-stop flight distance record that surpassed the previous mark by more than 3,300 miles was set today when the Truculent Turtle, the Navy's new twin-engine, land-based patrol bomber, landed here to complete an 11,236-mile flight that started Sunday morning in Perth, Australia.

The plane touched down here at 12:25 P. M., Eastern standard time.

The time for the flight, which started in the warm spring weather of Australia and ended in chilly winds here, was 55 hours 15 minutes. Despite a heavy load of fuel and constant headwinds that averaged 11.5 miles an hour for the entire trip, the average speed of the plane was 203.4 miles an hour.

The old distance record, set by the four-motored Dreamboat, a Superfortress, in a flight from Guam to Washington, was 7,916 miles.

Like "Long Patrol Mission"

"You might say it was no tougher than a good, long patrol mission," Comdr. Thomas D. Davies, chief of the four-man crew that manned the flat-sided Lockheed plane, said when he dropped from the exit hatch in the belly of the fuselage and greeted Navy officers at the municipal field.

"We had turbulent air, headwinds and some instrument weather," Commander Davies con-

Continued on Page 12, Column 3

World News Summarized

WEDNESDAY, OCTOBER 2, 1946

Twelve high Nazi conspirators were sentenced by the International Military Tribunal in Nuremberg yesterday to death by hanging for the supreme crime of aggressive war; three received life sentences in prison, four received lesser terms and three were acquitted.

The men who will be executed not later than Oct. 16 are Goering, von Ribbentrop, Kaltenbrunner, Rosenberg, Frank, Frick, Streicher, Sauckel, Seyss-Inquart, Keitel and Jodl. Bormann was sentenced to death in absentia. Hess, Funk and Grand Admiral Raeder received life sentences, von Schirach and Speer twenty years, von Neurath fifteen years and Grand Admiral Doenitz ten years. Schacht, von Papen and Fritzsche were acquitted. [All the foregoing 1:8.]

The verdicts on Hess, von Papen and Schacht and the exoneration of the General Staff, Cabinet and Storm Troops as organizations brought a strong dissent from the Russian Justice, Maj. Gen. Nikitchenko. The chief American prosecutor, Justice Jackson, said he was "disappointed" in the liberation of von Papen and Schacht because it would adversely affect further prosecution of industrialists and militarists. [1:6-7.]

Russia accused the United States at a commission meeting of the Conference of Paris of attempting to change agreements reached by the Foreign Ministers Council on Trieste, and the Slav bloc succeeded in delaying a vote. [1:7.]

Former Secretary of State Hull, who is 75 years old today, was stricken in Bethesda Naval Hospital shortly after completing a statement urging the Great Powers to compose their differences for the sake of peace. His condition is serious. "Incalculable disaster" would follow any irreconcilable division in this "most perilous juncture in history," Mr. Hull said. [1:3.]

A House committee, it was disclosed, has been quietly laying the basis to ask Congressional approval for this country's first integrated, permanent world-wide espionage and counter-espionage service. [13:1]

Iran, rejecting Britain's disavowals, has asked for the recall of a British Embassy secretary accused of conspiring to bring about a revolt of southern tribesmen. [11:1.]

Dmitri Shostakovich's new Ninth Symphony has been condemned in the Soviet press for ideological weakness and failing to reflect the true spirit of the Russian people. [31:3-4.]

Bernard M. Baruch characterized as "either misinformation or complete distortion" charges at a political rally by supporters of former Secretary Wallace that the United States expected other nations to give up their atomic energy secrets while this country withheld all information. [1:6-7.]

The American Merchant Marine was almost completely tied up by the strike of engineers and dock officers that began at midnight yesterday. Federal conciliation efforts continued without result. [1:1.]

No progress was made toward ending the Pittsburgh power walkout that has halted production on vital materials [2:2], and a strike of CIO warehouse and office workers threatens to paralyze the dress manufacturing industry in New York. [2:4.] Thirty-seven persons were injured in a picketing riot at Hollywood studios. [3:1.]

The Navy bomber Truculent Turtle landed at Columbus, Ohio, establishing a new world distance record of 11,236 miles in its non-stop flight from Perth, Australia. [1:4; map P. 12.]

RECEIVING THEIR FREEDOM FROM NUREMBERG COURT

Col. Burton C. Andrus, who headed the prison where the defendants were confined during their trial, handing out letters certifying their liberty to Hans Fritzsche (left), Franz von Papen (second from right) and Hjalmar Schacht (right).

Associated Press Radiophoto

GERMANY NOT FREE, SCHACHT COMPLAINS

Von Papen Says He Has Given Up Politics—Austria Seeks Extradition for Trial

By DANA ADAMS SCHMIDT

Special to THE NEW YORK TIMES.

NUREMBERG, Germany, Oct. 1—Franz von Papen said that his political career was "absolutely ended," Hans Fritzsche asked to be tried again by a German court and Hjalmar Schacht asked for chocolate for his two children today when the three men acquitted by the International Military Tribunal appeared before 200 representatives of the world press.

Schacht got his candy bars and all reaped a harvest of cigarettes

Continued on Page 20, Column 3

Russian and Jackson Object; Schacht Called a Swindler

By The Associated Press.

NUREMBERG, Germany, Oct. 1—Soviet Justice J. I. Nikitchenko tonight assailed the acquittal of three high Nazis by the International Military Tribunal, asserting that the opinion freeing Hjalmar Schacht, banker, was in "obvious contradiction to the evidence." [Justice Nikitchenko also declared Schacht a "swindler," according to a Reuters dispatch.]

The Russian Major General also dissented from the acquittal for the German General Staff, the Reich Cabinet and the decision imprisoning Rudolf Hess for life instead of giving him the death penalty.

Justice Robert Jackson of the United States, speaking for what he called the prosecutors of all nations, declared the decisions on individuals were of secondary importance compared to the fact that the principle was established making aggressive war a crime punishable by death. However, Justice Jackson also assailed the Schacht verdict.

Justice Nikitchenko said Fritzsche, as a radio propagandist, "had a most basic relation to the preparation and conduct of aggressive warfare." The most detailed dissent was in the case of the German General Staff and High Command, of which Justice Nikitchenko said:

"Without their advice and active cooperation, Hitler could not have solved [his] problems. In the majority of cases their opinion was decisive. * * * The General Staff issued most brutal decrees and orders for relentless measures against unarmed, peaceful population and prisoners of war."

Justice Nikitchenko said bluntly

Continued on Page 24, Column 6

SLAV BLOC STALLS VOTING ON TRIESTE

Connally Disputes Vishinsky's Charge That U. S. Seeks to Violate Big Four Accord

By LANSING WARREN

Special to THE NEW YORK TIMES.

PARIS, Oct. 1—Making use of procedural entanglements in an atmosphere of raw nerves, the Slav States succeeded tonight in blocking a vote on the United States proposal to implement the Italian draft treaty's general clauses on a statute for Trieste.

During a tense discussion in the peace conference's Italian Political and Territorial Commission, Senator Tom Connally of the United States and Andrei Y. Vishinsky, Soviet Vice Foreign Minister, exchanged accusations and retorts. Other leading delegates made contradictory suggestions on procedure, and finally the lateness of the hour forced adjournment.

Mr. Vishinsky charged that the United States proposal was an adroit and deliberate effort to evade an agreement by the Big Four's Council of Foreign Min-

Continued on Page 17, Column 2

Baruch Rebukes Wallace Groups For Distorting U. S. Atom Plan

By A. M. ROSENTHAL

Special to THE NEW YORK TIMES.

LAKE SUCCESS, N. Y., Oct. 1—In a sharp reply to followers of former Secretary of Commerce Henry A. Wallace, Bernard M. Baruch, American representative on the United Nations Atomic Energy Commission, categorically denied tonight that this country was asking the rest of the world to stop nuclear research and reveal its uranium resources while the United States retained complete freedom of action.

Mr. Baruch's strongly worded denial was the result of statements made in Chicago on Saturday at a conference of the National Citizens Political Action Committee, Independent Citizens Committee of the Arts, Sciences and Professions, and the Congress of Industrial Organizations' Political Action Committee. It was sent as a telegram addressed to Henry Morgenthau, Harold Ickes and Philip Murray, president of the CIO, who were speakers at the conference.

After noting tht the conference had gone on record as saying that the United States was trying to have other nations accept "binding agreements" while keeping its technical knowledge to itself as long as it saw fit, Mr. Baruch declared:

"I say without reservation that this is either misinformation or complete distortion. Nowhere does any such statement occur in the American proposal."

Mr. Baruch followed his denial with a pointed request for a correction.

"I am sending this to you," he said in the telegrams, "in order that you may see that this is corrected immediately."

The Baruch statement was issued by the American delegation at 7 P. M., on the eve of a meeting tomorrow morning of the Atomic Energy Commission's Committee 2, which will discuss the

Continued on Page 16, Column 3

50-MINUTE SESSION

Tribunal Dooms Keitel, Ribbentrop, Streicher, Rosenberg, Jodl

SIX SAID TO APPEAL

Allied Council in Berlin Last Resort—Doenitz Gets Lightest Term

Verdicts in the Nuremberg trials are on pages 22, 23, 24.

By KATHLEEN McLAUGHLIN

Special to THE NEW YORK TIMES.

NUREMBERG, Germany, Oct. 1—Death by hanging was decreed this afternoon for twelve of the original twenty-four defendants indicted in the Nuremberg war crimes trials. Three others—Dr. Hjalmar Schacht, Franz von Papen and Dr. Hans Fritzsche—were acquitted by the International Military Tribunal over the dissent of the Soviet member of the court, Maj. Gen. Iola T. Nikitchenko.

Those who will die by the noose within fifteen days, unless reprieved through an appeal within four days to the Allied Control Council in Berlin, are Hermann Goering, Joachim von Ribbentrop, Field Marshal Gen. Wilhelm Keitel, Ernst Kaltenbrunner, Dr. Alfred Rosenberg, Hans Frank, Wilhelm Frick, Julius Streicher, Fritz Sauckel, Col. Gen. Alfred Jodl and Arthur Seyss-Inquart.

Martin Bormann, who succeeded Rudolf Hess as Deputy Fuehrer and who was tried in absentia, owing to the lack of conclusive evidence that he is dead, also was sentenced to death by hanging if and when he ever is apprehended.

Mitigation in von Neurath Case

Life imprisonment was meted out to Hess, Walther Funk and Grand Admiral Erich Raeder. General Nikitchenko dissented likewise from his colleagues' judgment on Hess, expressing the opinion that he had merited death by hanging.

Baldur von Schirach, formerly supreme leader of the Hitler Jugend, and Albert Speer, Reich Minister for Armament and Munitions and chief of the Todt Organization, received twenty-year terms.

Possibly in consideration of his advanced years, Baron Constantin von Neurath, former Foreign Minister, although adjudged guilty on all four counts, received the comparatively mild sentence of fifteen years' imprisonment. He is 73. The Tribunal said in mitigation that he had been dismissed by Adolf Hitler for having been too lenient in his administration as Protector for Bohemia and Moravia and that he had intervened to obtain the release of many Czechoslovaks who had been arrested.

The mildest punishment of all fell to Grand Admiral Karl Doenitz, once Commander in Chief of the German Navy and, during the last days of the war, successor to Hitler as head of the German Government. He must serve ten years in prison.

[Six of those convicted—von Ribbentrop, Frank, Seyss-Inquart, von Schirach, Speer and Doenitz—have appealed their sentences, the British Broadcasting Company said, quoting official sources. The BBC broadcast was recorded by the National Broadcasting Company.]

Pattern Is Similar

In the courtroom, which over the last ten months has echoed unceasingly to the testimony of the unprecedented horrors precipitated upon the world through the Nazi hierarchy, the profound drama of the concluding phase of the trial lasted only fifty minutes. Lord Justice Sir Geoffrey Lawrence, as presiding jurist, announced all the sentences to the eighteen convicted men as they were summoned singly before the tribunal. An atmosphere of utter solemnity prevailed throughout this grim interval.

Beginning with Goering, former

Continued on Page 21, Column 3

"All the News That's Fit to Print"

The New York Times.

LATE CITY EDITION
Fair and continued cold today and tomorrow.
Temperature Range Today—Max.,36; Min.,28
Temperatures Yesterday—Max.,45; Min.,30
U.S. Weather Bureau Report, Page 10; Sect. 1

Section 1

NEWS INDEX, PAGE 79, THIS SECTION

VOL. XCVII..No. 32,817. Entered as Second-Class Matter, Postoffice, New York, N.Y. NEW YORK, SUNDAY, NOVEMBER 30, 1947. Including Magazine and Book Review. FIFTEEN CENTS

ASSEMBLY VOTES PALESTINE PARTITION; MARGIN IS 33 TO 13; ARABS WALK OUT; ARANHA HAILS WORK AS SESSION ENDS

SCHUMAN BARS DISCUSSION OF FRENCH LABOR OVERTURE; COMMUNIST PAPERS SEIZED

PREMIER ADAMANT

Strikers Must Go Back on Regime's Terms—Labor Curbs Urged

ASSEMBLY SPLIT ON CODE

324 Saboteurs Are Arrested—Paris to Expel Aliens Who Help Ruin Economy

By HAROLD CALLENDER
Special to The New York Times.

PARIS, Sunday, Nov. 30—Premier Robert Schuman refused early today to meet the leaders of the Confederation of Labor to discuss a strike settlement different from that offered by the French Government.

Meanwhile, the Premier pressed hard for immediate passage by the Assembly of a law to strengthen the Government's hand by enlarging its police force and enabling it to imprison those who sought to force men to strike or who committed or urged sabotage.

As intense activity continued throughout the night inside and outside the Assembly, it became clear that the labor leaders who had encouraged the strikes had at last taken the initiative in seeking to end them, and that the Cabinet was divided regarding the policy the Government should adopt.

Early last evening Paris police surrounded the plants of the two Communist newspapers, l'Humanité and Ce Soir, entered the buildings and seized the plates of special editions whose publication had been forbidden. No papers were allowed to leave the plants. Later the police vacated the premises.

The special edition of l'Humanite, in large headlines printed in red ink, proclaimed: "They wish to assassinate the Republic!"

Minister Begins Parley

Shortly after M. Schuman had placed his proposed law before the Assembly early yesterday, Pierre Lebrun, a Communist secretary of the labor confederation, issued a statement urging renewed negotiations and mentioning that the striking workers would have a hard time when the Dec. 1 pay day came on Monday without pay envelopes.

At the same time, Daniel Mayer, Socialist Minister of Labor, who is understood to have opposed the law that M. Schuman sought, opened negotiations with the executive committee of the confederation, which sat most of the night in his office while the Cabinet met in the Palais Bourbon. Through M. Mayer the committee asked to see M. Schuman, but the Premier refused its request and denied that the Government was negotiating with the strike leaders.

A sharp divergence of view be-

Continued on Page 46, Column 3

Major Sports Results

FOOTBALL

With Rip Rowan passing for the first touchdown and dashing ninety-two yards for the second, Army beat Navy yesterday for the fourth straight year. N.Y.U. rallied to tie Fordham. Scores of leading games:

Alabama	21	Miami, Fla.	6
Army	21	Navy	0
Florida	25	Kansas State	7
Fordham	12	N.Y.U.	12
Ga. Tech	7	Georgia	0
Holy Cross	20	Boston Coll.	6
Maryland	0	N.C. State	0
Mich. State	58	Hawaii	19
Mississippi	33	Miss. State	14
N. Carolina	40	Virginia	7
Oklahoma	21	Okla. A.&M.	13
Oregon Sta.	27	Nebraska	6
Rice	34	Baylor	7
S.M.U.	19	T.C.U.	19
Tennessee	12	Vanderbilt	7
Texas Tech	14	Hardin-Sim.	6
West Va.	17	Pittsburgh	2

CROSS COUNTRY

Curtis Stone of Philadelphia won the National A.A.U. championship at Van Cortlandt Park, but the New York A.C. took the team title for the third successive time.

HORSE RACING

Incline outran Gallorette to capture the Bryan and O'Hara Memorial Handicap at Bowie on the last day of the major Eastern season.

(Full details in Section 5.)

U.S. Troops to Stay in Italy Beyond Dec. 3 Sailing Date

Change in Plans Is Linked to Disturbances Led by Communists—Milan Is Calm Following Compromise on Prefect

By ARNALDO CORTESI
Special to The New York Times.

ROME, Nov. 29—The United States Army Department today ordered Maj. Gen. Lawrence Jaynes, commanding the Mediterranean Theatre of Operations, and his entire staff to postpone their departure from Italy. With them will remain about 2,500 officers and men who are leading specialists of the United States Army in Italy.

The order is believed to reflect the anxiety with which the Government in Washington views the Communist-fomented disturbances in Italy.

General Jaynes and his officers and men had planned to leave from Leghorn on Dec. 3 aboard the Admiral Sims. Washington ordered a postponement of departure until Dec. 14, the deadline set by the Italian peace treaty. No explanation was given for the change of plans and this strengthened the impression that it was dictated by preoccupation over Italy's political outlook.

The officers and men with General Jaynes form the skeleton organization for a large army. They include highly trained specialists, familiar with conditions in Italy. They belong to the Engineer, Signal, Ordnance, Secretariat, Quartermaster, Medical and Military Police Corps and other auxiliary services.

Washington's change of plans came after General Jaynes had said farewell to Pope Pius and President Enrico de Nicola. Ambassador James C. Dunn called on Premier Alcide de Gasperi two days ago, and it is presumed that he informed the Italian Government then of the postponement of the American troops' departure.

Though the American troops should, under present plans, leave

Continued on Page 45, Column 1

No-Parking Area Is Created From City Hall to Canal St.

After a two-hour conference with Mayor O'Dwyer at Police Headquarters, Police Commissioner Arthur W. Wallander announced yesterday two further moves in the department's efforts to ease traffic congestion in the city.

Commissioner Wallander added the section of Manhattan north of City Hall as far as Canal Street and west to but not including West Street to the restricted parking areas already established in a large part of the borough below Fifty-ninth Street.

He also said that a survey was being made throughout the city in an effort to discover additional sites for municipal parking lots like the one established at the old World's Fair parking lot in Flushing, Queens. The lot set up experimentally there "looks promising," he said, reporting that 766 motorists had used it on Friday.

Mayor Explains Needs

The Commissioner announced the moves at a press conference at the end of his talk with the Mayor. Mr. O'Dwyer sat in on the press conference and added some comments of his own after his aide had made the announcement.

About forty traffic policemen will be needed to enforce the parking restrictions in the new area, the Mayor said. Commissioner Wallander has asked for 2,000 additional men for the Police Department to take care of this and other needs, which would add $6,000,000 to the department's budget, he continued.

Together with $4,000,000 for the men added to the force last July, this would amount to a total of $10,000,000 that would have to be appropriated for the Police Department next year in addition to

Continued on Page 78, Column 5

WAR PAY 'RACKET' HUNTED BY TRUMAN

Gen. Vaughan Says President Wants Army, Navy, Air House-Cleaning on Disability Cases

Special to The New York Times.

WASHINGTON, Nov. 29—The armed services are preparing to turn over to President Truman at his request the records of 28,000 wartime Army officers who have been retired for disability on tax-free pay normally amounting to three-fourths of their active service remuneration.

This became known as an aftermath of the case against Maj. Gen. Bennett E. Meyers and was confirmed today by Maj. Gen. Harry H. Vaughan, the President's military aide, who said at Philadelphia that Mr. Truman was determined to "wipe out any possible racket" in tax-free disability retirement pay.

The President has already spoken about the matter to James Forrestal, Secretary of Defense, and it is expected that a formal directive will be received soon.

Presumably the order will apply also to naval officers retired for disability so that once the President has the records in hand he

Continued on Page 27, Column 1

Congress Action Lags on Aid Bill Despite Warnings Need Is Urgent

By JOHN D. MORRIS
Special to The New York Times.

WASHINGTON, Nov. 29—Congress set aside the troublesome problems of European aid and domestic inflation today and attended the Army-Navy game practically en masse, while pressures for accelerated action on the legislative problems awaited members' return to work Monday.

Despite repeated representations of urgency in both fields, the Congressional machinery faced a slowdown in production of the authorization for winter relief to France, Italy and Austria.

Formulation of anti-inflation legislation still had hardly begun, and completion of the task was far out of sight.

The Senate was prepared to resume consideration Monday of the foreign relief bill, but earlier expectations of passage on that day had been diminished by failure yesterday to dispose of four amendments proposed by Senator James P. Kem, Republican, of Missouri.

While some of them are acceptable to the bill's managers, at least one is expected to cause considerable discussion and possible delay of a vote on the bill itself until Tuesday.

This would require detailed, written acknowledgement by every recipient of relief supplies that the goods were gifts of the United States.

Senator Kem successfully opposed action on the amendments yesterday, asserting that he wanted Thanksgiving holiday absentees to be present when the votes were taken. He thus disrupted leaders' plans for clearing the slate of all proposed amendments so that the bill itself could be disposed of Monday.

Hope for a final vote Monday

Continued on Page 26, Column 1

VAST GI HOUSING TO RISE NEAR SITE OF WORLD'S FAIR

21 14-Story Apartment Units to Form Nation's Largest Veterans' Cooperative

COST PUT AT $58,000,000

Occupancy on Tenant-Owner Basis—Work Will Start Before End of Year

By LEE E. COOPER

On a fifty-five-acre tract overlooking the site of the World's Fair of 1939, the country's largest veterans' cooperative apartment community soon will begin to take form, it became known last night.

After nearly a year of negotiations, and with the official blessing of the city and of the Veterans Administration, plans for the $58,000,000 project were revealed by Frederick Briggs, chairman of the board of the Communities Redevelopment Corporation, which is sponsoring the enterprise.

The new Queens housing center, which will occupy a large portion of the former Arrowbrook Golf Club grounds, will be for occupancy exclusively by veterans of World War II and their families on a tenant-ownership basis.

Plans call for the erection of twenty-one fourteen-story apartment houses of the fireproof type, to accommodate 5,699 families. Each building will have its own garage facilities, to be rented separately, for tenants' automobiles.

Shopping Centers Will Rise

In furtherance of the plan to create a self-contained community, the builders will erect shopping centers at the edges of the property, which is bounded by Main Street, Jewel Avenue and Park Drive East, within the boundaries of Forest Hills. A promenade, with stores beneath it, will be constructed on the hillside overlooking Flushing Meadow Park. The residential buildings will be set amid winding tree-lined walks and landscaped park spaces.

The Board of Estimate gave its unanimous sanction to the over-all plan for the project at a special closed session last Wednesday, after receiving a favorable report on it from Robert Moses, City Construction Coordinator who had been in consultation with the sponsors.

The city's cooperation will be limited to street changes and zoning aids permitting stores and the erection of fourteen-story houses on the site. No municipal financial

Continued on Page 12, Column 3

PEACE GAINS NOTED

Brazilian Says Contacts Inspired No Forecast of Imminent War

CITES ROLE OF MINORITY

Lie Regrets That Economic Issues Were Sidetracked—Others Hail Aranha

By MARSHALL E. NEWTON

It is the mission of the United Nations to achieve world peace and the General Assembly made a memorable contribution in that direction, Dr. Oswaldo Aranha of Brazil, president of the Assembly, told the delegates of the fifty-seven member nations yesterday in his speech closing the second regular session in Flushing Meadows.

When he finished his address the delegates rose and applauded Dr. Aranha, whose talents and statesmanlike handling of the difficult task of presiding at the international assembly had been lauded by several preceding speakers.

Dr. Aranha pointed out that the present post-war period had not been marked by the armed conflicts that had followed the Peace of Versailles and he said that we lived today in a different era, in which our minds must turn to the future and not the past.

Calls for Foresight

"But close contact with international political life leads to no forecast of world war in the near future," he said. "The world seeks, however, new forms of political, economic and social integration in which the contest of ideas will supersede the clash of arms. The status quo is no longer possible. A new reality is rising in our days, to which we must impart the spirit of the United Nations, the only conception capable of insuring peace, solidarity, dignity and equality for all peoples.

"Our action should not be post factum. Our task is one of foresight and of organized prevention to eliminate the elements and factors capable of disturbing world

Continued on Page 67, Column 3

Arabs See U.N. 'Murdered,' Disavow Any Partition Role

Angry Delegates Stalk From Assembly Hall Before Formal Closing—Silver Voices Gratification, Offers Friendship

By A. M. ROSENTHAL

Bitter Arab delegates walked out of the General Assembly hall at Flushing Meadow last night after the vote for the partition of Palestine and solemnly announced that in their eyes the United Nations had died.

"No, not died," said Faris el-Khouri of Syria. "Murdered."

The representatives of the Arab states swept out of the building without waiting for the formal end of the Assembly and the farewell speeches. But before they entered their limousines they announced that they would have absolutely nothing to do with the United Nations Commission for Palestine, nothing to do with the transitional period after the end of the mandate and nothing to do with partition.

There was an open thread of warning running through all the Arab delegates' comments on the Assembly's action. They spoke of bloodshed to come and said the responsibility would not be theirs, but would be on the shoulders of the countries that had pressed for partition.

On the other side of the quarter-century Arab-Zionist dispute there was jubilance and hope for the future. Dr. Abba Hillel Silver, chairman of the American section of the Jewish Agency for Palestine, expressed his gratitude to the Assembly and especially to the United States and the Soviet Union.

Dr. Silver's statement follows:

"We are deeply gratified with the action of the General Assembly of the United Nations. It marks a turning point in Jewish history. It is an impressive reaffirmation of the just claim of the Jewish people to rebuild its national life in its ancestral home.

"This noble decision to re-establish the Jewish state and restore

Continued on Page 60, Column 1

U.N. REJECTS DELAY

Proposal Driven Through by U.S. and Soviet Will Set Up Two States

COMMISSION IS APPOINTED

Britain Holds Out Hand to It—Arabs Fail in Last-Minute Resort to Federal Plan

By THOMAS J. HAMILTON

The United Nations General Assembly approved yesterday a proposal to partition Palestine into two states, one Arab and the other Jewish, that are to become fully independent by Oct. 1.

The vote was 33 to 13 with ten abstentions and one delegation, the Siamese, absent.

The decision was primarily a result of the fact that the delegations of the United States and the Soviet Union, which were at loggerheads on every other important issue before the Assembly, stood together on partition. Andrei A. Gromyko and Herschel V. Johnson both urged the Assembly yesterday not to agree to further delay but to vote for partition at once.

The Assembly disregarded last-minute Arab efforts to effect a compromise. Although the votes of a dozen or more delegations seesawed to the last, supporters of partition had two votes more than the required two-thirds majority, or a margin of three.

How Members Voted

The roll-call vote was as follows:

For (33)—Australia, Belgium, Bolivia, Brazil, Canada, Costa Rica, Czechoslovakia, Denmark, Dominican Republic, Ecuador, France, Guatemala, Haiti, Iceland, Liberia, Luxembourg, the Netherlands, New Zealand, Nicaragua, Norway, Panama, Paraguay, Peru, Philippines, Poland, Sweden, the Ukraine, South Africa, Uruguay, the Soviet Union, the United States, Venezuela, White Russia.

Against (13)—Afghanistan, Cuba, Egypt, Greece, India, Iran, Iraq, Lebanon, Pakistan, Saudi Arabia, Syria, Turkey, Yemen.

Abstentions (10) — Argentina, Chile, China, Colombia, El Salvador, Ethiopia, Honduras, Mexico, United Kingdom, Yugoslavia.

Absent (1)—Siam.

All other questions before the Assembly were disposed of a week ago, and it ended the second regular session at 6:57 P.M. after farewell speeches by Dr. Oswaldo Aranha, its President, and Trygve Lie, the Secretary General. The Assembly's third regular session is to open in a European capital on Sept. 21.

The vote on partition was taken at 5:35 P.M. Representatives of Iraq, Saudi Arabia, Syria and Yemen, four of the six Arab member states, announced that they would not be bound by the Assembly's decision and walked determinedly out of the Assembly Hall at Flushing Meadow. The Egyptian and Lebanese delegates were silent but walked out, too.

Briton Seeks Contact

Sir Alexander Cadogan, representative of Britain, which is to terminate the League of Nations mandate over Palestine and withdraw all British troops by Aug. 1, made a brief statement after the vote. He requested the United Nations Palestine Commission to establish contact with the British Government about the date of its arrival in Palestine and the coordination of its plans with the withdrawal of British troops.

The United Nations commission, which will be responsible to the Security Council in the event that the Arabs carry out their threats to fight rather than agree to partition, will be composed of representatives of Bolivia, Czechoslovakia, Denmark, Panama and the Philippines.

This slate, which is understood to have the backing of the United States, was proposed by Dr. Aranha and approved without opposition after the Arab delegates had walked out.

The commission, as proposed by the partition subcommittee of the

Continued on Page 66, Column 2

Molotov Insists on Regime Before Treaty on Germany

By DREW MIDDLETON
Special to The New York Times.

LONDON, Nov. 29—Soviet Foreign Minister Molotov urged with new fervor in the Council of Foreign Ministers today the early establishment of a central German government as a precondition of the peace treaty.

Mr. Molotov's argument was based on the futility of completing a German peace treaty with no German government to sign it or assist in its preparation. But it was obvious that the Soviet delegate was moved by fears that the Western Allies, if this Council meeting failed, would make their own arrangements for a German government and treaty.

With a stridency that disrupted an otherwise decorous meeting, Mr. Molotov declared the Soviet Union would never recognize a peace signed by Western Germany and the Western powers. No government set up in Frankfort on the Main in the United States zone and in the "ersatz government for Bizonia" will be an adequate substitute for the Soviet proposal, he asserted.

Secretary of State Marshall and French Foreign Minister Bidault both flatly opposed any tendency to make the establishment of a German government a precondition of signing the German peace treaty.

A compromise proposal presented by British Foreign Secretary Bevin was as abruptly turned down by Mr. Molotov, who said it did not go far enough. Then he proceeded to add a clause that made the British proposal an echo of the Soviet suggestion.

This brisk exchange of German participation in the peace making followed an encouraging agreement by the Big Four on the ad-

Continued on Page 54, Column 3

ZIONIST AUDIENCE JOYFUL AFTER VOTE

Tears, Excited Laughter Mark Tension—Aranha Commends Public's Good Behavior

By WALTER S. SULLIVAN

The attention of the entire Arab and Jewish worlds focused on Flushing Meadow yesterday to hear the verdict of the United Nations General Assembly on the future of Palestine.

The reaction in the packed hall to the decision for partition typified that of listeners far and near. While members of the Arab delegations walked out, Zionists in the audience rejoiced.

It was a rejoicing that started with silence and grew as the meeting neared its end. In the public lobby there were kisses and tears and excited laughter. In the delegates' lounge a rabbi cried, "This is the day the Lord hath made! Let us rejoice in it and be glad!"

The initial silence resulted from a call to order by the Assembly's president, Dr. Oswaldo Aranha. A burst of applause had greeted the surprise vote of France in favor of partition, and it was this that had

Continued on Page 67, Column 2

World News Summarized

SUNDAY, NOVEMBER 30, 1947

The General Assembly of the United Nations yesterday approved the plan for the partition of Palestine by a vote of 33 to 13 with ten abstentions and one absence. After the vote there were repeated statements of bitterness and disillusion from the Arab representatives. One after another they asserted that the Charter had been violated and that their nations would not be bound by the action and would reserve "freedom of action." The Arabs then walked out of the Assembly. [1:8.]

The Arabs subsequently pronounced the United Nations "dead," and disavowed any intention of playing a part under the partition plan. They went on to say, however, that this did not mean their retirement from the United Nations. Zionist leaders were jubilant over the outcome. [1:6-7.]

Zionists attending the Assembly expressed their joy with tears and excited laughter. Dr. Oswaldo Aranha praised the public for its good behavior. [1:7.]

The Palestine debate concluded the business of the current session of the General Assembly, and Dr. Aranha of Brazil gave his closing address. He declared that the second meeting had made a notable contribution to world peace, and after the delegates had risen to applaud him the session adjourned. [1:5.]

In London, Soviet Foreign Minister Molotov demanded the early establishment of a German government to accept the peace treaty. The other Ministers, seeing this as a move to commit them against any possible partition of Germany, opposed him. [1:6-7.] Secretary Marshall plans to ask the Council of Foreign Ministers next week to achieve the economic unification of Germany through the removal of all zonal barriers in what is expected to be the most important United States proposal at the conference. [50:3.]

In the deputies' meeting the Soviet delegation continued to study the French proposals on Austria and refused to agree on principle at any point. Action was delayed, but it was felt the Russians might accept. [51:1.]

In Paris, Premier Schuman declined to discuss with leaders of the Confederation of Labor any strike settlement on terms other than the Government's. He asked for police powers to suppress Communist agitators and moved against Communist papers. They had charged that a "revolutionary coup" was planned for midnight and that "assassination of the Republic" was its objective. The editions were suppressed. [1:1.]

In Italy, the United States commander and 2,500 American troops were ordered by Washington to postpone departure, presumably because of the troubled situation. The general strike in Milan, however, was ended. [1:2-3.]

The Ronne Expedition in the Antarctic reported the exploration and mapping of a total of about 100,000 square miles of territory in the name of the United States. [56:3.]

A scientific advance that may be of importance in insect pest control was announced by the United States Army. Ultrasonic waves have been developed that are lethal to mice and small insects. [14:1.]

Defense Secretary Forrestal has been instructed by President Truman to turn over the records of 28,000 wartime Army officers who have been retired for disability on tax-free pay, in the determination to wipe out any possible "racket." [1:2.]

Company Asks Rise in Gas Rate From $1.15 to $2 Sliding Scale

The Consolidated Edison Company of New York, Inc., announced yesterday it had applied to the State Public Service Commission for permission to increase the maximum charge for gas from $1.15 a thousand cubic feet to $2 with declining rates after the first thousand.

The petition said that neither Consolidated Edison nor any of its predecessor companies had increased its rates since Oct. 1, 1922, and that existing rates were confiscatory of the company's property. It was estimated that the company would lose $1,498,500 in 1947 through its gas operations.

According to the company, 57 per cent of the gas it supplies is sold at the maximum rate of $1.15 a thousand cubic feet. The company's service area includes 1,100,000 customers in Manhattan, the Bronx and the first and third wards of Queens—Astoria, Long Island City, Flushing, College Point, Whitestone, Douglaston, Bayside, Little Neck and Bellerose.

The company proposed an immediate schedule of temporary rates, which it estimated would increase its annual revenues approximately $8,239,700 on the basis of estimated gas sales for 1947.

If this increase had been in effect through 1947, the company said, it would have provided the company with a net return after taxes of $4,300,000 in connection with its gas operations.

If approved by the Public Service Commission, the new classifications would provide a minimum charge of $2 for the first thousand cubic feet or less of gas consumed in any bi-monthly billing period.

For the first 4,000 cubic feet consumed bi-monthly after the initial 1,000-foot block, residential customers would be charged 12 cents a hundred; 10 cents a hun-

Continued on Page 18, Column 1

"All the News That's Fit to Print"

The New York Times.

LATE CITY EDITION
Increasing cloudiness, cold today.
Snow, not so cold tomorrow.
Temperature Range Today—Max., 18; Min., 9
Temperatures Yesterday—Max., 24; Min., 5.5
Full U. S. Weather Bureau Report, Page 31

VOL. XCVII No. 32,879. Entered as Second-Class Matter, Postoffice, New York, N. Y. NEW YORK, SATURDAY, JANUARY 31, 1948. THREE CENTS IN NEW YORK CITY

MANY HOMES WITHOUT HEAT AS ZERO COLD IS DUE HERE; U. S. CUTS OIL EXPORTS 18½%

FUEL CRISIS GROWS

Hundreds of Families Reported Suffering in City Area

BAY STATE SEIZES PLANT

Bradford Acts When Walkout Threatens Boston Gas—Oil Diversion Denied Here

By WILL LISSNER

Hundreds of families in the city were reported by their landlords to be in cold homes for lack of fuel oil last night as temperatures dropped toward zero in Manhattan and toward subzero levels in the suburbs.

At 3 A. M. today the temperature dropped to 2.2 degrees, establishing a new low record for the season. The previous record was 5 degrees, registered last Saturday.

The winter's coldest weather gripped not only New York but the whole Northwest. The Midwest and South, however, got some relief yesterday from the protracted cold spell. The fuel situation was reported acute in many cities throughout the East.

Temperatures, after falling to points between zero and 5 degrees above in Manhattan and zero and 10 degrees below in the suburbs, are expected to rise today to 20 degrees. The cold is due to continue, according to the United States Weather Bureau, but whereas yesterday was sunny, increasing cloudiness was expected today. More snow is threatened tomorrow. The lowest temperature yesterday was 5.5 degrees at 9:50 A. M.

Yesterday's hourly temperatures were:

1 A. M.	23	2 P. M.	12
2 A. M.	23	3 P. M.	15
3 A. M.	22	4 P. M.	14
4 A. M.	18	5 P. M.	12
5 A. M.	13	6 P. M.	12
6 A. M.	9	7 P. M.	11
7 A. M.	8	8 P. M.	9
8 A. M.	7	9 P. M.	8
9 A. M.	6	10 P. M.	7
9:50 A. M.	5.5	11 P. M.	7
10 A. M.	6	12 M.	6
11 A. M.	7	1 A. M.	5
Noon	9	2 A. M.	4
1 P. M.	10	3 A. M.	2.2

Petroleum Exports Cut

As the fuel shortage produced critical conditions for many apartment and home owners in this and other cities, officials took steps to relieve the situation.

The Commerce Department announced in Washington that it had ordered exports of petroleum products cut 18½ per cent from 11,850,000 to 9,650,000 barrels during the first quarter of the year. Oil exports to Japan and the Ryukyus were cut from 1,600,000 barrels to 100,000. Exports will be allowed only from areas where fuel can be spared best, the department said.

In Massachusetts Gov. Robert F. Bradford ordered the seizure of a gas plant in Everett where a walkout of 900 workers was threatened that would have affected service to sixty-four hospitals and 1,500,000 residents of Greater Boston. After seizure and issuance of a temporary injunction, union leaders ordered their followers to remain at work.

In Tennessee, Governor James McCord proclaimed a state of emergency and announced a voluntary fuel conservation program.

In Rochester, Sheriff's deputies and city policemen were organized to make emergency deliveries of fuel oil in extreme cases.

In Endicott, Mayor E. Raymond Lee declared an emergency due to the gas shortage and urged residents to conserve fuel. Many homes there and in Binghamton and Johnson City were without heat and residents sought emergency shelter.

Philadelphians Warned

Residents of Philadelphia were warned of a gas shortage caused by the oil shortage and were urged to restrict use of gas to the absolute minimum.

Police Commissioner Arthur W. Wallander of this city, regional fuel coordinator, sent telegrams asking eighty-six terminal dealers here to remain open today and tomorrow, because of the expected severe cold, to supply fuel oil to hardship cases.

Mayor O'Dwyer declared during the afternoon that it was not necessary at this time to proclaim a state of emergency and to divert

Continued on Page 12, Column 5

Petroleum Shipment Abroad Is Curbed to Ease Shortage

Department of Commerce Orders Quotas Reduced From 11,850,000 to 9,650,000 Barrels for Quarter—Slashes Japan

Special to The New York Times.

WASHINGTON, Jan. 30—The Department of Commerce announced today that "in view of the serious shortage of fuel oils," in this country it had ordered an 18½ per cent cut in exports of petroleum products during the first quarter of this year. Its action will reduce from 11,850,000 to 9,650,000 the barrels of petroleum designated for overseas.

The Department also announced that it would limit licenses for export of petroleum products to shipments for those areas of the United States where the fuel can best be spared during the emergency.

In addition, it was disclosed that a separate quota of gas oil and distillate fuel oil had been established for the first quarter for shipments to Japan and the Ryukyus, drastically cutting their supply from 1,600,000 barrels to 100,000. The Department said that the difference would be met from oil producing areas outside the United States.

Proposals had been made in Congress to stop all shipments abroad except those going to American military forces. Bills designed to accomplish this end have been introduced in the House and the Senate.

Walter S. Hallanan, chairman of the National Petroleum Council, said today that the petroleum industry had taken "prompt and forthright action to alleviate the shortages of some petroleum products which have been rendered acute in certain sections by the severe cold weather." The industry "takes pride in the fact that it was the first to develop a voluntary agreement under the recent authorization of Congress," he added.

Canada Is Not Affected

WASHINGTON, Jan. 30 (AP)—The action today of the Depart-

Continued on Page 11, Column 4

Hope Wanes in Sea Search For 28 Aboard Lost Airliner

By FREDERICK GRAHAM

The Atlantic area northeast of Bermuda was being searched last night for survivors of a British South American Airways plane that disappeared in the area early yesterday morning with a crew of six and at least twenty-two passengers, but hope had almost been abandoned.

The thirty-two-passenger plane, which listed among those aboard Air Marshal Sir Arthur Coningham, Royal Air Force, who commanded the Second Tactical Air Force of the Allies at the invasion of Normandy, was out of London and on the Azores-to-Bermuda leg of the flight when last heard from about 1 A. M. (EST) yesterday.

At least fifteen United States Air Force, Navy and Coast Guard planes plus three Coast Guard cutters, two commercial steamers and a British South American Airways plane worked over a large area about 400 miles northeast of Bermuda without success. More aircraft are scheduled to continue the search today.

The plane, a converted Lancaster bomber of the type used by the RAF for saturation bombing of Germany, had stopped in Santa Maria in the Azores to refuel. An Associated Press dispatch from Bermuda said the plane, believed to have been commanded by Capt. David Colby, radioed to Bermuda that it would arrive there at midnight Thursday, an hour and a half late. One hour later it reported to Bermuda again, saying it was 440 miles northeast of Bermuda, that there was a moderate sea swell and that it was bucking strong headwinds. Nothing more has been heard from the plane.

The only other report that might

Continued on Page 10, Column 2

ORVILLE WRIGHT, 76, IS DEAD IN DAYTON

Co-Inventor With His Brother, Wilbur, of the Airplane Was Pilot in First Flight

Special to The New York Times

DAYTON, Ohio, Jan. 30—Orville Wright, who with his brother, the late Wilbur Wright, invented the airplane, died here tonight at 10:40 in Miami Valley Hospital. He was 76 years old.

Mr. Wright, who had been confined to a hospital in October, collapsed in his office on Tuesday. He was suffering from lung congestion and coronary arteriosclerosis.

At the bedside when Mr. Wright died were Horace A. Wright, a nephew; Mrs. H. S. Miller, a niece, and Delyle Myers, a nurse.

The announcement of his death was made by Dr. A. B. Brower, family physician.

Engrossing Amusement

In the early fall of 1900 fishermen and Coast Guardsmen dwelling on that lonely and desolated spot of sand dividing Albemarle Sound from the Atlantic Ocean on the coast of North Carolina called

Continued on Page 12, Column 2

Arms Get Atomic Energy Priority In Policy Set by Congress Group

By WILLIAM S. WHITE

Special to The New York Times.

WASHINGTON, Jan. 30—The Joint Committee on Atomic Energy laid down today a firm policy that the production of atomic weapons, rather than work on peacetime applications of atomic energy, must be the "vital business" of the United States for the foreseeable future.

It declared also that "uninterrupted operation" of the "critical," or military, facilities of the Atomic Energy Commission was so essential to national security that an investigation was in motion to find a formula to assure "continuity of work" under all labor eventualities.

In its first report to Congress, the committee indicated some dissatisfaction "in a number of cases" with certain aspects of the handling of internal security within the personnel of the Atomic Energy Commission.

"In certain of these cases," the report went on, "the committee has requested that the commission outline in detail its security policy as applied to these specific instances."

"In the majority of these cases," it was added, the men in question had been employed while atomic energy still was under Army control.

As to the essential policy to be followed in atomic development, the committee declared:

"Until such time as an effective, enforceable and reliable program for the international control of atomic energy is in successful operation, the most vital business of the Atomic Energy Commission must be the meeting of the atomic requirements of national defense.

"The joint committee has been assured that those charged with these responsibilities are keenly aware thereof. This phase of the atomic energy program is of para-

Continued on Page 4, Column 5

Record 799-Million Budget Is Asked by Dewey for State

He Estimates Actual Outlay at 753 Millions for Next Fiscal Year, but Says No Rise in Taxes Is Needed—Warns on Inflation

By LEO EGAN

Special to The New York Times.

ALBANY, Jan. 30—Governor Dewey submitted another record-breaking budget to the Legislature tonight, calling for appropriations of $799,600,000, including deficiencies for the current year, but estimating expenditures in the new budget year at a figure of $753,500,000. The Governor regards the lower figure as his "budget" total.

Appropriations recommended are $128,200,000 higher than those carried in last year's budget message but, because of supplemental grants for teacher pay, veterans' housing, college housing, central schools and rent control, only $53,400,000 higher than actual appropriations, which were $746,200,000.

The expenditures of $753,500,000 contemplated in Mr. Dewey's message compare with an actual total of $707,500,000 in the current year, according to revised estimates. The revised figure reflects increased relief contributions and higher food prices for inmates of state institutions which are being provided for in deficiency appropriations.

Allowing for continuance of the reductions made in 1946, which he recommended, the Governor estimated that existing regular taxes would produce $758,600,000 in the new budget year, enough to balance expenditures and leave a $5,000,000 surplus.

The regular tax structure does not include the additional one-cent-a-package levy on cigarettes or the 20 per cent increase in existing income tax rates which were voted to finance the $400,000,000 veterans' bonus. If the present return from these special levies continued, Mr. Dewey said, the bonus bonds might be retired in eight or

Continued on Page 9, Column 1

Text of Gov. Dewey's budget message will be found on pages 8 and 9.

REALTY VALUATIONS RISE $745,775,468 IN CITY FOR 1948-49

Higher Accrued Value Is Chief Factor in $17,684,240,921 Total, Biggest Since '33

By LEE E. COOPER

New York's land and buildings, regarded as the richest segment of real estate in the world, have risen in value to $17,684,240,921 on the city's tax books for the coming fiscal year.

Municipal assessors have chalked up a tentative increase of $745,775,468 over current figures on taxable properties for the year beginning July 1, 1948, to carry the aggregate valuations to the highest level since 1933.

A report submitted to Mayor O'Dwyer yesterday by Harry B. Chambers, president of the Tax Commission, showed an average rise of about 4½ per cent for the five boroughs, accounted for largely by an upswing in "accrued value" rather than by addition of new construction to the assessment rolls.

The report set the following ten-

Continued on Page 11, Column 3

GOP GROUP SHAPES SHARP ERP REVISION WITH FUND REDUCED

A Proposal to Sell U. S. Goods to Latin America for Food for Europe Wins Favor

By FELIX BELAIR Jr.

Special to The New York Times.

WASHINGTON, Jan. 30—A fighting nucleus of eighteen Senate Republicans agreed late tonight to press for important changes in the Administration's European Recovery Program as the party's legislative leaders brushed aside President Truman's demand for approval of the full $6,800,000,000 asked for the first fifteen months of operations.

The group of eighteen Senators, in which Westerners predominated, called for a complete shift in emphasis of the Marshall Plan "from the underwriting of trade deficits to the support of specific production programs" in which financial aid would be contingent on increased output of food, coal, steel and transportation facilities.

Senator Joseph H. Ball of Minnesota said the principles agreed

Continued on Page 6, Column 2

World News Summarized

SATURDAY, JANUARY 31, 1948

Mohandas K. Gandhi, 78-year-old spiritual leader of hundreds of millions of Indians, was shot in New Delhi yesterday as he walked toward a pergola to lead 1,000 of his followers in evening prayer. He died twenty-five minutes later. His assassin, a Hindu, was seized after he had fired three quick shots into the frail leader, who only recently had ended a hunger strike in protest against communal strife. [1:8.]

News of the tragedy shocked the world. In Bombay, it ignited a new outburst of rioting. [2:3.] United Nations officials at Lake Success feared this might be the beginning of a new wave of violence throughout India. [2:4-5.] President Truman said the whole world would mourn and expressed hope that the assassination would "not retard the peace of India and the world." [2:1.] Similar expressions of regret were voiced in London, where the King and the Queen and Prime Minister Attlee were among the many leaders to pay tribute to Mr. Gandhi. [1:6-7.]

The French National Assembly approved, 308 to 242, the Government's program to establish a free gold market and to allow Frenchmen to repatriate foreign assets by paying a tax. The Socialists reversed their previous stand and voted for the program. [1:6-7.]

Two recent Russian notes protesting the reopening for American use of an airfield in Tripolitania and the presence of American naval craft in Italian ports will be rejected by the State Department. [6:5.] The Navy announced that another 1,000 marines would go to the Mediterranean soon to replace an equal number now serving in that area. [6:4-5.]

The United States consulate in Jerusalem declared American citizens participating in the fighting would lose their passports and right to protection. [1:7.] Britain announced at Lake Success before the Palestine Commission that she could not allow the formation of any armed militia in Palestine before her mandate ends. [4:3.]

In Washington a group of eighteen Senate Republicans urged a change in the European Recovery Program to support specific production goals and brushed aside the Administration's request for approval of the full initial fund of $6,800,000,000. [1:5.]

An 18½ per cent reduction in exports of petroleum products was ordered by the Commerce Department "in view of the serious shortage" of oil in this country. [1:2-3.]

Also in Washington, the Joint Committee on Atomic Energy declared this nation must concentrate for the foreseeable future on the "uninterrupted" production of atomic weapons in preference to the peaceful utilization of atomic energy. [1:2-3.]

Governor Dewey asked the Legislature to appropriate $799,600,000 as he submitted another record-breaking budget. Appropriations last year totaled $746,200,000. [1:4-5.]

Winter's coldest weather hit the metropolitan area, with the thermometer hovering near zero in the city. In the suburbs the temperature was expected to fall to sub-zero levels during the night. Some homes suffered from a shortage of fuel oil. [1:1.]

A thirty-two passenger British plane was feared lost on its way to Bermuda. [1:2-3.]

Orville Wright, air pioneer, died in Dayton, Ohio, at 76. [1:2.]

GANDHI IS KILLED BY A HINDU; INDIA SHAKEN, WORLD MOURNS; 15 DIE IN RIOTING IN BOMBAY

MOHANDAS K. GANDHI

The New York Times

THREE SHOTS FIRED

Slayer Is Seized, Beaten After Felling Victim on Way to Prayer

DOMINION IS BEWILDERED

Nehru Appeals to the Nation to Keep Peace—U. S. Consul Assisted in Capture

By ROBERT TRUMBULL

Special to The New York Times.

NEW DELHI, India, Jan. 30—Mohandas K. Gandhi was killed by an assassin's bullet today. The assassin was a Hindu who fired three shots from a pistol at a range of three feet.

The 78-year-old Gandhi, who was the one person who held discordant elements together and kept some sort of unity in this turbulent land, was shot down at 5:15 P. M. as he was proceeding through the Birla House gardens to the pergola from which he was to deliver his daily prayer meeting message.

The assassin was immediately seized.

He later identified himself as Nathuran Vinayak Godse, 36, a Hindu of the Mahratta tribes in Poona. This has been a center of resistance to Gandhi's ideology.

Mr. Gandhi died twenty-five minutes later. His death left all India stunned and bewildered as to the direction that this newly independent nation would take without its "Mahatma" (Great Teacher).

The loss of Mr. Gandhi brings this country of 300,000,000 abruptly to a crossroads. Mingled with the sadness in this capital tonight was an undercurrent of fear and uncertainty, for now the strongest influence for peace in India that this generation has known is gone.

[Communal riots quickly swept Bombay when news of Mr. Gandhi's death was received. The Associated Press reported that fifteen persons were killed and more than fifty injured before an uneasy peace was established.]

Appeal Made By Nehru

Prime Minister Pandit Jawaharlal Nehru, in a voice choked with emotion, appealed in a radio address tonight for a sane approach to the future. He asked that India's path be turned away from violence in memory of the great peacemaker who had departed.

Mr. Gandhi's body will be cremated in the orthodox Hindu fashion according to his often expressed wishes. His body will be carried from his New Delhi residence on a simple wooden cot covered with a sheet at 11:30 tomorrow morning. The funeral procession will wind through every principal street of the two cities of New and Old Delhi and reach the burning ghats on the bank of the sacred Jumna River at about 4 P. M. There the remains of the greatest Indian since Gautama Buddha will be wrapped in a sheet, laid on a pyre of wood and burned. His ashes will be scattered on the Jumna's waters, eventually to mingle with the Ganges where the two holy rivers meet at the temple city of Allahabad.

These simple ceremonies were announced tonight by Pandit Nehru in respect to Mr. Gandhi's wishes, although many of the leaders desired that his body be embalmed and exhibited in state. India will see the last of Mr. Gandhi as it saw him when he lived—a humble and unassuming Hindu.

News Spreads Quickly

News of the assassination of Mr. Gandhi—only a few days after he had finished a five-day fast to bring about communal friendship—spread quickly through New Delhi. Immediately there was spontaneous movement of thousands to Birla House, home of G. D. Birla, the millionaire industrialist, where Mr. Gandhi and his six secretaries had been guests since he came to New Delhi in the midst of the disturbances in India's capital.

While walking through the gardens to this evening's prayer meeting Mr. Gandhi had just reached the top of a short flight of brick steps, his slender brown arms

Continued on Page 3, Column 6

All Britain Honors Gandhi; Truman Deplores Tragedy

By HERBERT L. MATTHEWS

Special to The New York Times.

LONDON, Jan. 30—Mohandas K. Gandhi, in death, has won the unanimous tribute of Britons—something he never hoped for or expected during his life. Nowhere outside of India has the shock of his assassination contained the feelings and emotions evident here today because Britain and Mr. Gandhi have been linked for good or evil over the last forty years.

In a special broadcast to the British people tonight the Prime Minister said:

"The voice which pleaded for peace and brotherhood has been silenced, but I am certain that his spirit will continue to animate his fellow countrymen and will plead for peace and concord."

[President Truman and Secretary Marshall expressed their grief and condolences in messages to India. Members of Congress were apprehensive. Leaders of many other lands joined in paying tribute and in deploring the manner of Mr. Gandhi's death.]

The sincerity of today's expressions of regret, which came from the King and Queen, the Prime Minister, the political parties—even the Communist—and from many humble Londoners who filed silently into India House this afternoon to pay tribute, cannot be doubted.

Those many quarrels when Mr. Gandhi fought with his passive resistance against the imperial power of Britain are truly things of the past. Mr. Gandhi himself paid high tribute to Britain for her policy of freeing India and of trying to help to keep the two dominions at peace with each other.

The British, on their side, have

Continued on Page 2, Column 2

U. S. WARNS CITIZENS IN PALESTINE FIGHT

Consulate General Says They Face Loss of Passports and All Protective Rights

By SAM POPE BREWER

Special to The New York Times

JERUSALEM, Jan. 30—United States citizens fighting in the armed services of the Jews or the Arabs will lose their passports and their right to protection, the United States Consulate General warned Americans in Palestine tonight. Furthermore, naturalized citizens, it was said, would lose their American nationality if they fought for a foreign power.

[Zionist hopes for getting United Nations help in arming a Jewish militia in Palestine were dimmed by the statement of Sir Alexander Cadogan, chief British representative, that the British Government would not allow formation of such forces before the end of the mandate.]

The consular warning is being twisted by Arab sources into a promise that those fighting for the Jews may have their passports back when the fighting ends. The relevant passage reads: "American passports valid only for direct

Continued on Page 4, Column 4

France Votes Free Gold Market, Legalizes Hidden Assets by a Tax

By HAROLD CALLENDER

Special to The New York Times.

PARIS, Jan. 30—Parliamentary sanction was given today for the Government's devaluation of the franc and its accompanying monetary policy.

By a vote of 308 to 242, the National Assembly passed the Government's bill to create a free gold market and to legalize the hitherto illegal possession of foreign securities held by Frenchmen, if those assets were repatriated and the owners paid a special tax of 25 per cent of the assets' value.

As a comparatively free market in dollars had already been established by decree—although its opening was delayed by the freezing of bank notes of 5,000 francs—today's vote by the Assembly completed the series of measures framed by the Government to derive maximum benefit from devaluation by getting possession of privately owned foreign securities and hoarded gold.

Estimates of the total of these illegal securities have been in the neighborhood of $300,000,000 in the United States alone, while official guesses have placed the value of the hidden gold in France at $2,000,000,000.

Apparently placated by the freezing of the bank notes, the Socialists once again switched their position and voted today for the gold market bill, which they had opposed bitterly Wednesday, although their Ministers had apparently accepted it in the Cabinet meeting last Saturday. They were not reluctant to switch, for they did not desire to upset the Government and wreck the "Third Force," hostile though they were to the Government's departure from a planned economy.

The freezing measure, taken when the Socialists had precipitated a Cabinet crisis by balking at the gold market, was considered mainly a political move. But René Mayer, Finance Minister, told the

Continued on Page 5, Column 2

"All the News That's Fit to Print"

The New York Times.

LATE CITY EDITION
Fair and warmer today and tomorrow.

Copyright, 1948, by The New York Times Company.

VOL. XCVII..No. 32,984. NEW YORK, SATURDAY, MAY 15, 1948. THREE CENTS

ZIONISTS PROCLAIM NEW STATE OF ISRAEL; TRUMAN RECOGNIZES IT AND HOPES FOR PEACE; TEL AVIV IS BOMBED, EGYPT ORDERS INVASION

NAVY PUSHES PLAN FOR CONSTRUCTION OF MISSILE VESSELS

Sullivan Asks House Committee to Approve Halting Work on Battleship, Destroyer Types

WANTS 65,000-TON CARRIER

Floating 'Submarine Killers' Are Also Stressed in Plea for Diverting $300,000,000 Fund

By C. P. TRUSSELL
Special to The New York Times.

WASHINGTON, May 14—The Navy asked Congress today for authority to shift sharply its construction of fighting craft from battleship, cruiser and destroyer types to guided missile vessels, a 65,000-ton carrier able to base, far at sea, planes with an operating radius of 1,700 miles, better submarines and floating "enemy submarine killers."

Such new ships, John L. Sullivan, Secretary of the Navy, told the House Armed Services Committee, must have a higher priority "because of the more immediate need for them in the event of an emergency." The immediate reaction of the committee appeared to favor prompt action.

For such a shift in construction, Secretary Sullivan brought out, the Navy wanted to halt the building of thirteen naval vessels, including the battleship Kentucky, the large cruiser Hawaii, seven destroyers, two destroyer escorts and two submarines. To date about $197,000,000 has been spent on them.

However, this money was not to be abandoned, Mr. Sullivan emphasized. These craft could be converted now to the new program, be explained, or be put aside for a fitting-out later as new weapons were developed.

New Aims for $300,000,000 Fund

What the Navy wanted, Secretary Sullivan asserted, was Congressional permission to divert some $300,000,000 remaining in the present ship construction account to these purposes:

Starting the 65,000-ton aircraft carrier (the biggest ones now are the two of the Midway class, at 45,000 tons), which might cost around $124,000,000.

Building, for reproduction later, of a "submarine killer." (Hearings on the defense program have indicated that Russia has made great progress in the submarine field.) A "killer" machine, it is indicated, is developing in new work on the cruiser type of sea-craft.

The construction of four submarines of types advanced beyond those now building.

In addition, there was under plan a conversion in an unidentified way of a carrier and two submarines.

Secretary Sullivan told the committee that the Kentucky and the Hawaii would not have to stand by for the development of new weapons. It is planned, he disclosed, that they be converted into guided missile ships. Apparently to allay fears in Congress that larger aircraft carriers make easier targets for enemy bombers, Mr. Sullivan drew upon experience in the second World War and the results of atom-bomb tests at Bikini.

Speed Held Bomb Defense

"The experiments at Bikini," Mr. Sullivan said, "have proved that a fast-moving fleet is an unprofitable target for an atomic bomb."

Members of the committee interpreted this as a Navy Department conclusion that even though a potential enemy might acquire the atomic bomb, the revised construction program proposed today promised a maximum of safety. Mr. Sullivan recalled that the Navy lost three large and two light carriers in the Pacific, but none was sunk by aircraft land-based. He indicated that mobility of a fleet, equipped to latest model, would discourage the spending of atomic bombs, even if an enemy had some.

Today, the Senate Republican

Continued on Page 7, Column 4

Heaviest Trading in 8 Years Marks Stock Market Spurt

3,840,000 Shares Change Hands as Wave of Bullish Enthusiasm Increases Securities 1 to 7 Points

The hectic days of the Nineteen Twenties were re-enacted yesterday on the floor of the New York Stock Exchange when the most turbulent session in recent years produced increases of 1 to 7 points in the share list. Accompanied by a burst of bullish enthusiasm not witnessed in almost a decade, the deluge of buying orders so taxed the facilities of the Exchange that the reporting ticker tape lagged behind floor transactions by five minutes.

The cracking of the 1947 high level at the approach of mid-day served as the signal for a buying rush. Public participation suddenly enlarged and buying orders pressed floor traders to the utmost. This condition existed for forty-five minutes in the final hour when 1,350,000 shares were traded.

Accompanied by the broadest market on record with a total of 1,151 issues dealt in, volume on the Stock Exchange spiraled to 3,840,000 shares, the largest since May 21, 1940, in contrast to the Thursday turnover of 2,030,000 shares.

Brokers termed it the "wildest" bull market in twenty years on the premise that at no time in the interval had the industrials and rails advanced with such a unity of force.

While the ground had been well laid for a movement of such scope earlier this week, it was the piercing of the 1947 resistance point that confirmed the presence of a bull market to those who act by the charts, or averages. Early in the day, telegrams were sent by several advisory services to their clients urging the purchase of securities. The response to this advice showed primarily in the late

Continued on Page 23, Column 4

Truman Sees His Election; Calls GOP 'Obstructionist'

By ANTHONY LEVIERO
Special to The New York Times.

WASHINGTON, May 14—President Truman asserted tonight that there would be a Democrat in the White House during the next four years and that he would be the man. He made the statement to a cheering audience of 1,000 young Democrats at their meeting here.

The President's speech was a fighting one in the new Truman manner. He spoke extemporaneously, resorting to whimsy and irony and using forceful gestures of his arms to underscore his points.

Mr. Truman accused the Republican party of stealing Democratic platform planks. "You know," he said, "it has been their habit since 1936 of taking a few planks out of the old Democratic platforms and building a platform and then saying, 'Me, too.'"

[*The text of President Truman's speech is on Page 7.*]

"What have the Republicans done in the last fifteen and a half years?" Mr. Truman asked, then said:

"They have been obstructionists. They spent most of their time while I was in the Senate—and I was there for ten years—in obstructing progressive legislation that was for the welfare of the common man, and throwing bricks and mud at the greatest President that ever sat in the White House."

Mr. Truman was interrupted by applause at this obvious allusion to President Roosevelt.

"That has been their record," he continued, "and they haven't changed a bit. They were against Social Security. They were against TVA. They were against wages

Continued on Page 7, Column 2

MINNESOTA'S GUARD OUT IN MEAT STRIKE

Governor Acts After 200 Raid Cudahy Newport Plant, Attack 60 Workers and Abduct 25

Special to The New York Times.

ST. PAUL, Minn., May 14—National Guard troops were ordered to South St. Paul and Newport, towns on opposite banks of the Mississippi River near here, by Governor Luther Youngdahl today following violent disorders at strike-bound packing plants in the area and the statement of the local sheriffs that their forces could not maintain law and order.

The Governor did not proclaim martial law but said the troops would take their orders from the civil authorities.

The Governor's action followed a serious outbreak at the Cudahy packing plant in Newport shortly before last midnight in which a group of about 200 men raided the plant with clubs, knives and hammers. In South St. Paul on Thursday strikers forced back police who tried to open a way through picket lines at the Swift & Co. plant in

Continued on Page 16, Column 3

Princess Elizabeth, in Paris Talk, Asks Common Effort of 2 Nations

By LANSING WARREN
Special to The New York Times.

PARIS, May 14—Speaking in faultless French with just the touch of a British accent to delight French ears, Princess Elizabeth today asked France and Britain to make a common effort to lead Europe to moral and intellectual as well as economic reconstruction.

Her well-worded and discerning speech was cheered, but she went straight to the hearts of the Parisian throng when, with disarming frankness, she avowed her joy that her first foreign trip since her marriage had brought her here to Paris.

"For a long time," she said, "I have wanted to come to France. More fortunate than I, my husband already knew your admirable capital and he is all the happier to return. This trip is all the more important and agreeable for the warmth of your welcome which has touched us both."

From the time they stepped down from the train at the Gare du Nord early today, Princess Elizabeth and Prince Philip, Duke of Edinburgh, were the center of admiring attention from the throngs that lined the streets and from all the French officials who received them throughout the day.

President Vincent Auriol voiced the general feeling when in a statement issued tonight he said:

"I have been personally struck by her grace, her charm, her modesty and her nobility. I feel sure that the sentiments that she has expressed went straight to the hearts of all the French."

Elizabeth's address, broadcast to the French nation, was delivered from the top of the monumental entry to the Galliera Museum, where she came to open the British Government's exhibition of relics and souvenirs of famous Brit-

Continued on Page 6, Column 3

AIR ATTACK OPENS

Planes Cause Fires at Port—Defense Fliers Go Into Action

BORDER IS BREACHED

Cairo Vanguard Takes Colony—Trans-Jordan Reports a Movement

By The Associated Press.

TEL AVIV, Palestine, Saturday, May 15—Air raiders bombed this all-Jewish city at about dawn today.

First reports said there were "some casualties" near the power and light station.

[Cairo reported that Egyptian armed forces had been ordered to enter Palestine. Arab armies moved from Trans-Jordan at 12:01 A. M. Saturday to "liberate the Holy Land from Zionism," said a Trans-Jordan communiqué reported by The United Press from Amman.]

Tel Aviv was under complete blackout all night but no sirens were sounded during the raid. Civil guards were alerted and fifteen to twenty ships in the port area moved out to sea.

The planes swooped over Tel Aviv little more than twelve hours after Jewish leaders proclaimed the existence of a new Hebrew state of Israel.

Some bombs fell in the vicinity of the power station along the Yarkum River near Tel Aviv.

Persons at the scene said there was one hit on or near the power station, causing "some casualties."

TEL AVIV, Saturday, May 15 (UP)—Some ten bombs were dropped on Tel Aviv by two aircraft described as bombers and accompanied by two small fighters. One Jew was killed and three were hospitalized. Jewish Army aircraft took to the skies a few minutes after the enemy planes whizzed over rooftops at an estimated altitude of 300 feet.

Several fires could be seen north

Continued on Page 2, Column 3

U. S. MOVES QUICKLY

President Acknowledges de Facto Authority of Israel Immediately

TRUCE AIM STRESSED

Soviet Gesture to New Nation Anticipated—Others Due to Act

By BERTRAM D. HULEN
Special to The New York Times.

WASHINGTON, May 14—President Truman announced early tonight recognition by the United States of the new Jewish State of Israel. The President acted instantly upon being informed that the new nation had been proclaimed.

"This Government," he announced, "has been informed that a Jewish state has been proclaimed in Palestine and recognition has been requested by the provisional government thereof.

"The United States recognizes the provisional government as the de facto authority of the new State of Israel."

These two paragraphs constituted the text of the President's statement.

Coupled with the announcement was an expression of hope for peace in Palestine. This was made known through a separate White House statement issued by Charles G. Ross, Presidential press secretary.

"The desire of the United States to obtain a truce in Palestine," this said, "will in no way be lessened by the proclamation of a Jewish state.

"We hope that the new Jewish state will join with the Security Council Truce Commission in redoubled efforts to bring an end to the fighting—which has been throughout the United Nations' consideration of Palestine a principal objective of this Government."

[Pending stabilization of the Palestine situation and indications that the State of Israel

Continued on Page 3, Column 2

World News Summarized

SATURDAY, MAY 15, 1948

Several hours after the state of Israel, the first Hebrew nation in 2,000 years, had been proclaimed in a Zionist declaration of independence in Tel Aviv, [1:8.]. President Truman announced that the United States recognized the "provisional government" of Israel as "the de facto authority of the new state." A second White House statement expressed the hope that the new regime would cooperate with United Nations efforts to bring about peace in Palestine. [1:5.] The British High Commissioner departed from Palestine and boarded a cruiser at Haifa as Britain's rule over the Holy Land formally ended. [1:7.]

The special session of the United Nations General Assembly ended last night after it had agreed to send a mediator to Palestine to try to arrange a truce. [1:6-7.] The trusteeship plan for Jerusalem sponsored by the United States was rejected by the Assembly, with the Arab states and the Soviet opposed to the measure. [1:6-7.]

Tel Aviv was bombed at dawn. Egypt ordered her troops to invade Palestine. Trans-Jordan reported her army on the move also. [1:4.] Haganah claimed that its forces captured Acre in the north. [2:8.]

In Moscow the newspaper Pravda, in the first editorial comment on the recent exchange between Washington and Moscow, accused the United States of double-dealing. [4:8.]

Paris crowds gave an enthusiastic welcome to Princess Elizabeth and the Duke of Edinburgh when they arrived for a visit. [1:2-3.]

Congress received a request from the Navy for authority to shift the emphasis in its construction of fighting craft to guided-missile vessels. [1:1.]

President Truman predicted that he would be re-elected next November. [1:2-3.]

Minnesota National Guard troops were rushed to South St. Paul and Newport after 200 persons had raided the Cudahy meat packing plant at Newport, where a strike is in progress, attacking about sixty workers and abducting twenty-five of them. [1:2.]

The New York Stock Exchange enjoyed one of its biggest days in recent years as an avalanche of buying orders sent stocks up from 1 to 7 points. Trading reached a total of 3,840,000 shares, the largest since May 21, 1940. [1:2-3.]

Winston Churchill's War Memoirs

See Page 17 for today's installment, in which Mr. Churchill describes the invasion of Norway and the clash of the British and German fleets.

AT HELM OF THE JEWISH STATE

David Ben-Gurion, *Premier* — Moshe Shertok, *Foreign Minister*
The New York Times

U. N. Votes for a Mediator; Special Assembly Is Ended

By THOMAS J. HAMILTON

After hearing both the Soviet Union and the Arab delegates denounce the United States for its sudden recognition of the new Jewish state in Palestine, the United Nations General Assembly decided last night to send a Mediator to the Holy Land to do what he could to arrange a truce and carry on public services.

The vote was 31 to 7, with sixteen abstentions and four delegates absent, and the General Assembly, which was called into special session at Flushing Meadow on April 16 at the request of the United States, adjourned for good at 8:32 P. M.

The failure of the General Assembly either to repeal the partition resolution of last November or to provide military force to keep the peace means that the fate of Palestine will be decided by the impending war between Jews and Arabs, not by any United Nations action.

The mediation resolution conformed substantially with a United States proposal announced last Wednesday, after it had become obvious that the General Assembly would not accept the original United States plan for a temporary trusteeship.

However, the General Assembly refused to accept a United States plan for a temporary trusteeship over Jerusalem, which was rejected earlier in the evening by a vote of 20 to 15, less than the necessary two-thirds majority.

Two other proposals regarding Jerusalem were rejected, but presumably the provisions of the partition resolution on Jerusalem, which was to have been established as an international enclave under the administration of the Trusteeship Council, still stand.

In addition, the Assembly de-

Continued on Page 4, Column 4

CUNNINGHAM GOES AS MANDATE ENDS

British Commissioner Boards Cruiser Off Haifa—Jews Take Down Union Jack

By The Associated Press.

HAIFA, Palestine, Saturday, May 15—Britain ended her mandate over the Holy Land last midnight. Lieut. Gen. Sir Alan Cunningham, the last British High Commissioner, sailed from Haifa port, finishing British mandate guidance.

Sir Alan's departure from Palestine's richest port caused little excitement among the Jews, who control most of the city.

The British fired a few rockets and searchlights spotlighted the cruiser as it steamed from the harbor.

Wearing the uniform of a British Army general, Sir Alan walked down a few steps of dock into a launch that took him to the cruiser Euryalus.

Upon getting into the launch, he turned and looked soberly up across the docks. There stood an honor guard of the King's Company of Grenadier Guards and Royal Marine commandos.

The launch pulled away amid the

Continued on Page 2, Column 7

U. N. Bars Jerusalem Trusteeship; Vote Follows Mandate Deadline

By MALLORY BROWNE

The United Nations General Assembly rejected yesterday the United States plan for a temporary trusteeship regime in Jerusalem.

Solidly opposed by the Arab States and the Russian bloc, the plan to set up a United Nations Commissioner authorized to protect the Holy City and its holy places failed to obtain the necessary two-thirds majority at the closing session at Flushing Meadow.

The vote, which came just after the bombshell of the United States recognition of the new Jewish State had burst in the Assembly, was 20 in favor, 15 against and 19 abstentions. The balance was turned by the hostility of Britain and most of the Dominions.

The United States fought hard all day, first in the Political and Security Committee of the Assembly, sitting at Lake Success, and then in the evening session of the Assembly, to get the trusteeship plan adopted before the end of the mandate at 6:01 P. M., New York time.

An Arab filibuster, aided by the Soviet bloc, defeated this effort. It was well past the zero hour when a roll-call vote showed that the Assembly preferred to leave Harold Evans, newly appointed Jerusalem municipal Commissioner, in sole charge of the Holy City and its treasures.

As one Arab after another filed up to the tribune and took up the maximum five-minute period allowed in repeating the arguments against a trusteeship plan, 6:01 o'clock went by.

At once Awni Khalidy of Iraq, who had led the Arab fight against the trusteeship plan, rushed up to the tribune and exultantly proclaimed that the time had passed; that the mandate was at an end, and that, since, as Francis B. Sayre of the United States had said, the measure must

Continued on Page 3, Column 5

THE JEWS REJOICE

Some Weep as Quest for Statehood Ends—White Paper Dies

HELP OF U. N. ASKED

New Regime Holds Out Hand to Arabs—U. S. Gesture Acclaimed

Text of declaration setting up new Jewish state, Page 2.

By GENE CURRIVAN
Special to The New York Times.

TEL AVIV, Palestine, Saturday, May 15—The Jewish state, the world's newest sovereignty, to be known as the State of Israel, came into being in Palestine at midnight upon termination of the British mandate.

Recognition of the state by the United States, which had opposed its establishment at this time, came as a complete surprise to the people, who were tense and ready for the threatened invasion by Arab forces and appealed for help by the United Nations.

In one of the most hopeful periods of their troubled history the Jewish people here gave a sigh of relief and took a new hold on life when they learned that the greatest national power had accepted them into the international fraternity.

Ceremony Simple and Solemn

The declaration of the new state by David Ben-Gurion, chairman of the National Council and the first Premier of reborn Israel, was delivered during a simple and solemn ceremony at 4 P. M., and new life was instilled into his people, but from without there was the rumbling of guns, a flashback to other declarations of independence that had not been easily achieved.

The first action of the new Government was to revoke the Palestine White Paper of 1939, which restricted Jewish immigration and land purchase.

In the proclamation of the new state the Government appealed to the United Nations "to assist the Jewish people in the building of its state and to admit Israel into the family of nations."

The proclamation added:

"We offer peace and amity to all neighboring states and their peoples, and invite them to cooperate with the independent Jewish nation for the common good of all. The State of Israel is ready to contribute its full share to the peaceful progress and reconstitution of the Middle East."

World Jews Asked to Aid

The statement appealed to Jews throughout the world to assist in the task of immigration and development and in the "struggle for the fulfillment of the dream of generations—the redemption of Israel."

Plans for the ceremony had been laid with great secrecy. None but the hundred or more invited guests and journalists was aware of the meeting until it started, and even the guests learned of the site only ten minutes before. It was held in the Tel Aviv Museum of Art, a white, modern-design two-story building. Above it flew the Star of David, which is the state's flag, and below, on the sidewalk, was a guard of honor of the Haganah, the army of the Jewish Agency for Palestine.

As photographers' bulbs flashed and movie cameras ground out reels of the scene, great crowds gathered and cheered the Ministers and other members of the Government as they entered the building. The security arrangements were perfect. Sten guns were brandished in every direction and even the roofs were manned.

The setting for the reading of the proclamation was a dropped gallery whose hall held paintings by prominent Jewish artists. Many of them depicted the sufferings and joys of the people of the Diaspora, the dispersal of the Jews.

The thirteen Ministers of the

Continued on Page 2, Column 6

"All the News That's Fit to Print"

The New York Times.

Copyright, 1948, by The New York Times Company.

7 A.M. EDITION
Partly cloudy today with occasional rain tonight and tomorrow.
Temperature Range Today—Max.,54; Min.,43
Temperature Yesterday—Max.,54; Min.,46
Full U. S. Weather Bureau Report, Page 55

VOL. XCVIII No. 33,156. Entered as Second-Class Matter, Postoffice, New York, N. Y. NEW YORK, WEDNESDAY, NOVEMBER 3, 1948. Times Square, New York 18, N. Y. Telephone LAckawanna 4-1000 THREE CENTS IN NEW YORK CITY

TRUMAN LEADS DEWEY IN LATE RETURNS; THURMOND GETS 40 VOTES; WALLACE TRAILS; DEMOCRATS GAIN IN HOUSE AND SENATE

SHIFT IN CONGRESS

Democrats Win Control of Senate by Wresting Six Seats From GOP

LEADING FOR 3 MORE

Republicans' House Rule Endangered as Rivals Surge in East, West

By C. P. TRUSSELL

Democratic control of both the Senate and House of the Eighty-first Congress was probable if not a certainty on the basis of returns at 6 A. M. today from yesterday's dramatic and surprise-laden election.

From the Senate returns it had been made certain that Democrats had wrested Republican seats from Illinois, Iowa, Oklahoma, West Virginia, Minnesota and Wyoming. It requires a net gain of only four for the Democrats to acquire a majority from the present division of 51 to 45 in favor of the Republicans.

The Democratic sweep, however, had not ended there. They were siding to indicated victory over Republicans in three other states, Kentucky, Delaware and Idaho.

This, it appeared, was a virtual promise to the Democrats that they would have a bare majority, plus four and thus remove, or at least lessen, doubts that they could reorganize the Senate.

Republican Holds Broken

The Republicans also were in desperate danger, despite a need by Democrats of thirty-one Republican-held seats to conquer, of having the House also torn from their grasp. Republicans already had lost many seats in the industrial East, and the Democratic sweep was pressing westward.

In the Senate race the Democrats, while breaking into Republican territory, appeared to be holding solidly in those areas and preserving their present seats. In addition they were causing not only surprises but shocks at many points.

There remained a situation, however, which injected concern into the jubilation that reigned in Democratic camps. How even a "safe" majority in the upper House would make for Democratic harmony was a question left for future developments to answer. The Democratic party split had carried forty Southern electoral votes for the States' Rights party headed by Gov. J. Strom Thurmond of South Carolina—possibly sufficient to throw the whole Presidential and Vice-Presidential election into the hands of the Congress itself.

It was believed by experienced observers that Democratic voting in the Senate on many occasions would distinctly not follow the party line. Whether or to what extent the proved bitterness might delay or block a reorganization of the Senate, if it should be in order in the light of indicated returns, also remained to be seen.

Meanwhile, the completed returns and trends of others appeared to be taking persistent courses.

One of the most spectacular surprises of the Senate returns was in

Continued on Page 3, Column 2

Marshall Will Quit Jan. 20, Paris Says

By The Associated Press.

PARIS, Wednesday, Nov. 3—Secretary of State Marshall will resign next Jan. 20 regardless of the outcome of the Presidential election, an informed source in the American United Nations delegation said today.

The source said that there had been many recent reports that Secretary Marshall might resign.

Secretary Marshall, the source said, planned to retire to his farm.

Senators Elected

Democrats—19

Alabama	*John J. Sparkman
Arkansas	*John L. McClellan
Colorado	*Edwin C. Johnson
Georgia	*Richard B. Russell
Illinois	†Paul H. Douglas
Iowa	†Guy M. Gillette
Louisiana	*Allen J. Ellender Sr.
Louisiana	‡Russell B. Long
Minnesota	†Hubert H. Humphrey
Mississippi	*James O. Eastland
North Carolina	¶J. Melville Broughton
Oklahoma	†Robert S. Kerr
Rhode Island	*Theodore F. Green
South Carolina	*Burnet R. Maybank
Tennessee	†Estes Kefauver
Texas	†Lyndon B. Johnson
Virginia	*A. Willis Robertson
West Virginia	†Matthew M. Neely
Wyoming	†Lester C. Hunt

Republicans—8

Kansas	†Andrew F. Schoeppel
Maine	§Margaret Chase Smith
Massachusetts	*Leverett Saltonstall
Nebraska	*Kenneth S. Wherry
New Hampshire	*Styles Bridges
New Jersey	†Robert C. Hendrickson
Oregon	*Guy Cordon
South Dakota	†Karl E. Mundt

In Doubt—6

Delaware	Michigan
Idaho	Montana
Kentucky	New Mexico

*Re-elected Tuesday for full term ending Jan. 3, 1955.

†Elected Tuesday for full term ending Jan. 3, 1955.

‡Elected Tuesday for unexpired term ending Jan. 3, 1951.

¶Elected Tuesday for unexpired term ending Jan. 3, 1949, and for full term ending Jan. 3, 1955.

§Elected Sept. 13, 1948.

MARCANTONIO WINS BY NARROW MARGIN

His Vote of 35,937 Beats Ellis, Morrissey—Isacson and Pressman Defeated

By WARREN MOSCOW

Representative Vito Marcantonio last night squeaked through to a narrow victory for re-election to Congress over John P. Morrissey, Tammany Democrat, and John Ellis, Republican, in his first contest as a candidate on the American Labor party line alone.

Facing a divided opposition and with the loyal support of thousands who live in the slums of East Harlem to overcome a more conservative vote lower down in Yorkville, the peppery Representative, who has been denounced consistently for being a close adherent of the Communist party line, won by a thin margin. His victory was a minor political miracle on the surface, yet somewhat expected by those familiar with the political conditions in the area.

He was the only leftist to win in the metropolitan area, however, and middle-of-the-road Democrats had a field day as rightist Republicans, elected in the 1946 GOP landslide, also went down in a consistent pattern of Congressional defeat.

Final figures in the contest, with no election districts missing, gave Mr. Marcantonio 35,937, Mr. Morrissey 31,184, and Mr. Ellis, 31,482. Mr. Ellis polled 26,518 Republican votes, and 4,964 on the Liberal Party line.

In one of the closest contests, attracting almost as much interest as the Marcantonio one, Representative Jacob K. Javits, Liberal and Republican nominee in the Twenty-first District, Washington Heights, overcame the normal Democratic voting tendencies in the area for the second time to win re-election. He defeated Paul O'Dwyer, brother of the Mayor, and candidate of the Democratic and American Labor parties, by a vote of 66,455 to 64,297.

When the returns showed him the winner, Mr. Javits issued the following statement:

"The victory in our district is a victory for the people of the district, and I have had the honor of carrying the fight for them in beating down an unprincipled political deal. In carrying out my functions in the Congress, I will continue to be the people's Congressman."

On the debit side for the leftists was the defeat of the incumbent Leo Isacson, ALP member from the Bronx, who won a surprising victory in a by-election last spring. Yesterday, the Democratic candi-

Continued on Page 3, Column 5

DEWEY WINS STATE

Piles Up 525,042 Lead Outside City, Loses by 489,047 Here

LABOR IS BIG FACTOR

Wallace Total 503,404 —Liberals Poll 222,217 for the President

By JAMES A. HAGERTY

Governor Dewey, Republican nominee for President, carried his home state of New York in yesterday's election by a plurality of about 37,000 over President Truman, his Democratic opponent, and won New York's important forty-seven electoral votes.

With fifteen election districts missing out of 5,592 outside New York City, and with the city complete, the vote on the two major-party candidates was:

	Dewey	Truman
New York City	1,108,054	1,597,101
Rest of State	1,720,223	1,195,181
Totals	2,828,277	2,792,281

This gave Governor Dewey an actual plurality in the state of 35,996, which probably will be increased by about 1,500 by returns from the missing up-state districts, probably all Republican. Mr. Dewey carried the state outside New York City by 525,042 on the tabulated returns. Mr. Truman's New York City plurality was 489,047.

Henry A. Wallace, Progressive candidate for President, received a larger vote in the state than had been generally expected. With fifteen up-state election districts missing, he polled 503,404 votes, of which 423,424 were in New York City and 79,980 elsewhere in the state.

The Liberal party polled 222,219 votes for President Truman, of which 194,449 were cast in New York City and 27,770 in the rest of the state.

President Truman's strong showing, which held the plurality for his Republican opponent to several hundred thousand less than most pre-election estimates, was due to strong support from members of

Continued on Page 11, Column 2

THE TRUMANS AND THE DEWEYS VOTING IN YESTERDAY'S ELECTION

The President placing his ballot in the box at the polling place in his home town of Independence, Mo. Waiting their turn to vote are Mrs. Truman and their daughter, Margaret.

Associated Press Wirephoto

Governor Dewey signing the register at the polling place in public school at 121 East Fifty-first Street. Mrs. Dewey is standing beside her husband, and the registrar is Mrs. R. V. Hough.

The New York Times

JERSEY FOR DEWEY BY 70,000 MARGIN

Governor Overtakes Truman —Hendrickson Wins, Party Loses 3 House Seats

By RUSSELL PORTER

With only 101 out of 3,707 election districts unreported at 6 o'clock this morning, New Jersey's sixteen electoral votes went to Governor Dewey by an indicated plurality of about 70,000.

This was a surprisingly small margin over President Truman, in view of claims by Republican managers as late as last night that the Dewey margin would be 234,000.

State Treasurer Robert C. Hendrickson, Republican, of Woodbury defeated Archibald S. Alexander, Democrat, of Bernardsville by

Continued on Page 6, Column 2

World News Summarized

WEDNESDAY, NOVEMBER 3, 1948

President Truman at 7 o'clock this morning, was within sight of an electoral majority that would keep him in the White House for four years more. Maintaining an early lead in the popular vote he gradually won more and more states in a close race with Governor Dewey [1:8.] Governor Thurmond carried four Southern states on the States' Rights ticket [1:5], but the vote for Henry A. Wallace was only a fraction of what his supporters had expected. [1:5-6.]

It was Mr. Wallace's half-million votes in New York State that enabled Mr. Dewey to win by a narrow margin. [1:3.] The New York Governor also carried New Jersey by a close vote. [1:4.] Mr. Dewey won in Connecticut, but Chester Bowles, Democrat, was elected Governor. [1:7.]

Control of Congress passed from the Republicans to the Democrats, unofficial and incomplete returns indicated. The Democrats easily won enough seats to take over the Senate [1:1] and apparently defeated more than enough Republicans to control the House. [9:3.]

In this city Representative Marcantonio was re-elected, but Representative Isacson and other American Labor party candidates were defeated. [1:2.] For the first time since 1938 the Democrats made gains in the State Legislature. [18:3.]

The coveted post of Surrogate in New York County was won by George Frankenthaler, Republican, who had a plurality of 644 over Judge John A. Mullen, Democrat. [7:1.]

Chairman Spaak of the United Nations General Assembly's Political Committee admonished Soviet Deputy Foreign Minister Vishinsky during debate on the Balkan question to stop "insulting other delegates." [21:3-4.] Poland asked in the Economic Committee that action be taken against the United States for alleged economic sanctions under the Marshall Plan. [21:2.]

The Benelux countries have been asked for more detailed information on their four-year recovery plans. The Belgians fear pressure to impose a planned economy. [30:4-5.]

Plans to ban collective disobedience of taxation laws and other Communist moves will be considered by the French Cabinet today. Numerous casualties resulted from clashes between miners and Government forces seizing strike-bound mines. [24:2.]

Although it was denied that peace talks between Israel and Trans-Jordan had begun, it was reported authoritatively that King Abdullah had decided that such talks should be held. [23:4.]

Chinese planes continued to bomb Mukden, occupied by the Communists. [24:3-4.]

Washington took two steps affecting national defense. The inactive National Guard was re-established [54:2] and Selective Service recommended that qualified medical and dental students receive draft deferment until graduation. [54:5.]

Wallace Vote Is Far Short Of His Party's Expectations

By WILL LISSNER

No signs of the 10,000,000 vote that the Progressive party leaders were counting upon for their Presidential candidate, Henry A. Wallace, appeared in returns early today from roughly half the country's projected popular vote in yesterday's election.

As the returns rolled in, it became clear that Mr. Wallace would not get even half the vote his campaign managers expected, and probably not even a quarter of it. Of 25,431,641 votes counted, Mr. Wallace polled 618,705, or about 3 per cent. Undoubtedly this figure was influenced by the failure to count minority party polls in some states in the early counting.

In New York, however, Mr. Wallace's vote was decisive, and in several other states, such as California, it made serious inroads on the Democratic showing for President Truman.

In forty of the forty-five states in which the Progressive party was on the ballot, Mr. Wallace was running better than 1 per cent of the vote in seventeen and at fractions of 1 per cent, some of them infinitesimal, in twenty-three.

The states that were giving Mr. Wallace better than 1 per cent were California, Connecticut, Florida, Idaho, Iowa, Maryland, Massachusetts, Minnesota, Montana, Nevada, New Jersey, New York, North Dakota, Oregon, Pennsylvania, South Dakota and Wisconsin.

The states that were giving him less than 1 per cent of the vote

Continued on Page 15, Column 2

40 ELECTORAL VOTES TO STATES RIGHTERS

Alabama, Mississippi, South Carolina, Louisiana Won, but Popular Vote Is Short

By CLAYTON KNOWLES

The States Rights Democratic ticket, headed by Gov. J. Strom Thurmond of South Carolina, was romping off this morning with forty electoral votes in five Southern states, an electoral total that had been as good as conceded to it even before the balloting began.

With about half the projected national vote recorded, the Thurmond-Wright ticket had polled 552,417 popular votes. It was on the ballot in only thirteen states.

Not beyond the realm of possibility was the prospect that neither President Truman nor Governor Dewey would win a clear majority of the electoral vote. States Righters hoped for such an eventuality in launching their party last July. In such a situation, the election is thrown into the House of Representatives, where each state delegation casts one vote.

The forty States Rights electoral votes were made up of Alabama's eleven, South Carolina's eight, Mississippi's nine, Louisiana's ten and two of Tennessee's twelve.

Two electoral candidates, pledged to the Thurmond-Wright ticket, were running on the Democratic slate which was leading in latest tabulations in Tennessee. They also were running on the States' Rights slate which was showing up a poor third in latest reports.

The forty-vote indication fell far below the predictions of Governor Thurmond and other States' Rights leaders, who forecast that the ticket would win more than 100 electoral votes.

This, the fourth party in the national election, while living up to advance estimates in point of electoral votes, was not polling the great popular vote in the South that had been expected. It did not appear to be making large enough inroads in a number of key Southern states to throw these states to the Republican ticket as some persons had expected.

States that had been placed in this category were North Carolina

Continued on Page 7, Column 3

BOWLES IS ELECTED IN GOVERNOR RACE

He Wins Connecticut by 1,400 Votes, While Dewey Carries State for GOP by 15,000

Special to THE NEW YORK TIMES.

NEW HAVEN, Conn., Nov. 2—With only one town unreported, Chester A. Bowles, Democrat, leading by 1,322 votes, is certain of election as Governor of Connecticut over the incumbent, James C. Shannon.

Governor Dewey, the first Republican to carry the state since Herbert Hoover won it in 1932, has carried the state over President Truman by about 15,000 votes.

The Democrats also disrupted the Republican domination in Congress, which included all six Representatives in the last House. Abraham A. Ribicoff, a lawyer of Hartford, and John A. McGuire, both Democrats, upset the Republican incumbents in the First and Third Districts.

Representatives John Davis Lodge and James T. Patterson of the Fourth and Fifth Districts, respectively, are the only Republicans assured of re-election. Both candidates of the party trail in close contests for the Second District seat and Congressman-at-Large.

In the large cities of New Haven, Hartford and Waterbury, Mr. Bowles piled up a majority of 40,-

Continued on Page 2, Column 6

12,000 See Start of Horse Show; Mexican and French Officers Win

By JOHN RENDEL

New York's wealth and fashion and a large number of plain citizens divided their interest between the election returns and the annual visitations of the horse as a medium for sport and the exchange of social amenities last night. The occasion was the formal opening of the Sixtieth National Horse Show, launched again on an election afternoon for a run of eight days of matinee and evening performances in Madison Square Garden.

In some ways it was the biggest national held since the war stopped. There were more horses, the number exceeding 500 from this country, Canada, Mexico and France. The Royal Canadian Mounted Police, in scarlet and blue, were back with their eye-catching ride to music for the first time since 1936.

France was represented by a military jumping team, also for the first time since 1936. Mexico and Canada were in the same international jumping competition, as they had been a year ago.

Horse and man combined for exciting hunter and jumper contests. There were slick saddle horses, flashy harness rigs to remind the metropolis that a lot of countryside still existed where the horse had a place.

The void in the refulgent panoply was in the absence of a United States Army team, disbanded soon after last summer's Olympic Games because the horse isn't what he was in war any more. America's military riders, always hitherto present as far as memory served, were missed by the 12,000 on hand in the seats around the arena floor to honor the horse and participate, vicariously or otherwise, in the spectacle of society on parade.

There was another parade, too, that was a lot more stirring. It was the traditional one of the in-

Continued on Page 38, Column 1

FORECASTS UPSET

President Surprises by Taking Early Popular Vote Lead, Holds It

AHEAD ON ELECTORS

Truman Has Indicated 227, Governor 176— 88 Are Doubtful

By ARTHUR KROCK

At 6 A. M. today, after a night in which his political fortunes waxed and waned with every passing hour, President Harry S. Truman took an impressive lead over his Republican opponent, Gov. Thomas E. Dewey of New York, in both the popular and electoral vote of the nation which went to the polls yesterday in the forty-eight states of the Union to choose a President, a Vice President, the Eighty-first Congress and thirty-two Governors.

Ahead in the popular vote at all times during the counting, the President gained the electoral lead when Illinois was conceded to him at 5 A. M. and his chance of gaining Ohio steadily improved. At 6 A. M. the division of electoral votes between him and Governor Dewey that appeared to be established was as follows:

Truman, 227; Dewey, 176; doubtful, 88.

The remaining 40 of the total of 531 electoral votes apparently had been won by the Presidential candidate of the Democratic States' Rights party, Gov. J. Strom Thurmond of South Carolina.

Truman Needs 39 More

Only thirty-nine electoral votes were needed by the President to attain the majority of 266 that would give him a full term in the White House in his own right. And fifty-three were in sight—in the doubtful states of Iowa, Montana, Nevada, Washington, Iowa and California. However, in the last named, with a block of twenty-five, Governor Dewey was holding the lead.

If California ends with a Dewey victory, Ohio, with twenty-five electors, can overcome that loss, and Ohio went definitely into the doubtful column in the early hours of today. Therefore the possibility that the election would end without a decision, and the choice of a President would devolve on the House of Representatives in the Eighty-first Congress, remained within the area of strong possibility, with the Senate empowered to choose the next Vice President. But Governor Dewey's chances to win the election were fading fast at dawn today.

The possibility of an election by the House is the consequence of the capture of forty electors in the South by the States' Rights Democratic party, whose nominees were Govs. J. Strom Thurmond of South Carolina and Fielding Wright of Mississippi. And, if this is the eventual outcome, the President will have been defeated by the revolt of Southern Democrats against his "civil rights" program of Federal laws to enforce anti-segregation and a "fair employment practices" act in the states.

The returns at 6 A. M. however, further upset the earlier indication that the Progressive party candidacy of Henry A. Wallace had not proved as costly to the President, or more so, than the Southern Democratic insurrection. For if Mr. Dewey's pluralities in New York and in Ohio are as narrow as was indicated early today, Mr. Truman can attribute his failure to carry them both to the Wallace vote that was subtracted from the normal Democratic following.

The Congressional returns were more definite. Democratic candidates for the Senate appear certain to win the four crucial contests that will give the two wings of the party a numerical Senate majority over the Republicans in

Continued on Page 3, Column 3

"All the News That's Fit to Print"

The New York Times.

LATE CITY EDITION
Partly cloudy and mild today; fair tonight and tomorrow.
Temperature Range Today—Max., 65; Min., 47
Temperatures Yesterday—Max., 60; Min., 48
Full U. S. Weather Bureau Report, Page 35

Copyright, 1949, by The New York Times Company.

VOL. XCVIII..No. 33,346. Entered as Second-Class Matter, Postoffice, New York, N. Y. NEW YORK, THURSDAY, MAY 12, 1949. Times Square, New York 18, N. Y. Telephone Lackawanna 4-1000 THREE CENTS IN NEW YORK CITY

BERLIN LAND BLOCKADE IS LIFTED; FIRST TRAIN, AUTOS REACH CITY; ZONE TROOP RETIREMENT STUDIED

ISRAEL WINS A SEAT IN U.N. BY 37-12 VOTE

ARABS INDIGNANT

Quit the Assembly Hall After Poll—9 Nations Abstain in Ballot

59TH COUNTRY IN BODY

Israel's Foreign Chief Sharett Pledges Peace Effort—Debate Brings Polish Attack

By THOMAS J. HAMILTON

The General Assembly admitted Israel to membership in the United Nations at 7:28 last night by a vote of 37 to 12, with nine abstentions.

The delegations of the six Arab states—Egypt, Iraq, Lebanon, Saudi Arabia, Syria and Yemen—walked out of the Assembly Hall at Flushing Meadow in protest before the applause over the election of Israel as the fifty-ninth member of the United Nations had died away. They indignantly refused to make any statement to correspondents regarding their intentions, but drove away to New York.

The Arab delegates, who also walked out when the General Assembly adopted the resolution recommending the partition of Palestine on Nov. 29, 1947 gave no hint of their impending action in their speeches in the General Assembly in the afternoon.

Charge Israeli Violation

They protested bitterly, however, that Israel had refused to comply with the provisions of a General Assembly resolution adopted on Dec. 11, 1948, calling for an international regime in Jerusalem and the repatriation of Arab refugees. Also, they challenged the validity of a Security Council recommendation for the admission of Israel, since Britain, a permanent member of the Council, had abstained.

The Charter requires the concurring votes of the Big Five on all except procedural questions, and the Arab delegates insisted that the Assembly should first get a ruling from the International Court of Justice. This procedure was contained in a resolution presented by Iraq yesterday afternoon, but Dr. Evatt ruled it out of order on the ground that the General Assembly could not examine the decision of another United Nations body.

The Yemen delegation returned shortly after 10 o'clock for the night session of the Assembly, and an Egyptian delegate came back a few minutes later, but the other desks remained vacant.

Immediately after the vote Dr. Evatt summoned to the platform Moshe Sharett, Israeli Foreign Minister, who had arrived by plane from Tel Aviv early yesterday to hear the final speeches.

"We enter this Assembly, which represents the collective statesmanship of the world, in a spirit of humility, anxious for guidance and enlightenment," said Mr. Sharett, who re-stated the Israeli policy of "loyalty to the fundamental principles of the United Nations' Charter and friendship with all peace-loving states, especially with the United States of America and the Union of Soviet Socialist Republics."

Now a Working Member

Mr. Sharett took his seat at the desk that had previously been prepared for the Israeli delegation in the back of the Assembly hall, between the Iraqi and Lebanese delegations. United Nations officials said no additional formalities were required, and that Israel would have the right to participate in all further proceedings of the General Assembly on the same basis as the fifty-eight other members.

The vote came too late to permit the Israeli flag to be raised in the area in front of the main delegates' entrance. A flag pole, however, had been prepared in advance, and there will be a ceremony at Lake Success at 10:30 A. M. today.

The General Assembly took up the application at its afternoon session and the debate concluded at 7:30 as a result of the fact that the protests of the Arab delegates,

Continued on Page 13, Column 1

Protesters in Tripoli Tear U.S. Flag to Bits

By The United Press.

TRIPOLI, LIBYA, May 11—Demonstrators tore to shreds a United States flag in front of the United States Consulate in Tripoli today and set fire to a number of Italian establishments.

The demonstrators, demanding full independence for this former Italian colony, shouted "Long live Russia! Down with America and the United Nations!"

Special to The New York Times.

LAKE SUCCESS, May 11—A United Kingdom proposal that Eritrea, except for the western province, be incorporated into Ethiopia was approved in a subcommittee of the Political Committee this morning by a vote of ten to three with two abstentions.

A second United Kingdom proposal that the western province be incorporated in the adjacent Sudan also was approved by a vote of seven to two with six abstentions.

WAR PENSION BILL IS SHARPLY LIMITED

House Group Confines Benefit to Unemployable and Reports Measure as Rankin Protests

By JOHN D. MORRIS
Special to The New York Times.

WASHINGTON, May 11 — The new veterans pension bill was further watered down in committee today—to such an extent that its author, Representative John E. Rankin, Democrat, of Mississippi, voted, though in vain, against reporting it to the House.

The action was taken by the House Veterans Affairs Committee at a closed meeting that had been scheduled merely to formalize its action yesterday in approving pensions on a more liberal basis.

The committee voted, 14 to 8, to confine the $72-a-month payments to unemployable veterans. By a voice vote, it then cleared the measure formally to the House.

Approval of the limitation was prompted by Veterans Administration cost estimates, drawn up overnight, that without it the bill would cost $65,000,000,000 in the cost of veterans' benefits over the next fifty years. Yesterday's action had been based on a $12,000,000,000 estimate.

As finally approved, the measure's fifty-year cost was estimated at $8,693,000,000 by Guy H. Birdsall, assistant veterans administrator.

Mr. Rankin was joined by Representative A. Leonard Allen, Democrat, of Louisiana, in voting against reporting the bill. Shortly afterward the Mississippi legislator arose in the House to protest the action of the committee, of which he is chairman.

The employability clause, he asserted, would bar pensions from

Continued on Page 32, Column 4

KENNY TO ASK COURT FOR ORDER TO SEIZE JERSEY CITY BOOKS

Mayor-Elect Seeks to Prevent Any Alterations of Records to Shield Old Regime

FULL INQUIRY IS PLANNED

'It's All Right With Me,' Says Hague of Defeat—Fight for State Rule Likely

By LEO EGAN

The political coalition that dethroned Frank Hague as boss of Jersey City has decided to seek a court order barring the outgoing city administration from destroying or altering official records before it leaves office next Tuesday.

John V. Kenny, who headed the coalition and who will become Mayor in the new administration, said a formal application for an order impounding city books and records would be submitted tomorrow to Judge William Brennan in Hudson County Superior Court.

One of the first acts of the new regime, Mr. Kenny added, will be to order a full-scale audit of the records and accounts of the outgoing administration, headed by Mayor Frank Hague Eggers, nephew of the 73-year-old former Mayor, who was one of the last of the old-time bosses in the United States to yield up his political power.

Drive to End State Rule Seen

While the new regime was making its plans for sifting city records for evidence of illegal acts and misuse of public funds on behalf of the Hague machine, Democrats in other parts of New Jersey were contemplating a drive to strip Mr. Hague of his control of the Democratic party in the state.

Many Democrats fear that unless Mr. Hague's connections with the state organizations are severed the fall elections will result in an overwhelming victory for the Republican State ticket, headed by Gov. Alfred E. Driscoll.

In any reorganization of the Democratic State Committee, Mr. Kenny, who was leader of the Second Ward in Jersey City for the Hague organization for many years, is expected to play a leading role. So are former Mayor Meyer C. Ellenstein of Newark, who topped all candidates for City Commissioner there in Tuesday's elections, and Mayor George Brunner of Camden.

David Wilentz, who prosecuted Bruno Richard Hauptmann for the Lindbergh kidnapping, and Mayor Michael De Vito of Paterson are also expected to play important parts in any reorganization movement.

In the interview yesterday afternoon in which he told of his plans for investigating the outgoing Administration, Mr. Kenny announced also that he would support State Senator Elmer Wene for Governor on the Democratic ticket this fall. Senator Wene won the Democratic nomination with the backing of Mr. Hague in a recent primary.

The interview was sandwiched in between posing for newsreels and making an appearance on a television program. Although he looked tired and his voice was hoarse, the Mayor-elect said he felt "fine."

With respect to his plans on taking over, Mr. Kenny said that

Continued on Page 25, Column 2

Johnson Approves Air Force Plan To Distribute Negroes Among Units

Special to The New York Times.

WASHINGTON, May 11—Latest proposals by the Air Force to conform to armed service policy on racial equality were approved today by Louis Johnson, Secretary of Defense.

W. Stuart Symington, Secretary of the Air Force, wrote to Secretary Johnson on April 30 and assured the defense chief that his directive of April 6 asking equality of treatment and opportunity "without regard to race, color, religion, or national origin" would be put into effect.

One of the principal moves in this direction is an Air Force order disbanding the all-Negro 332nd Fighter Wing at Lockbourne Air Force base at Columbus, Ohio. Its 2,000 officers and men will be distributed throughout the service in non-segregated units, it was stated.

Another assurance given to Mr. Johnson, it was learned, was that "key" positions would be open to Negroes who are individually qualified to hold them.

Letters from Kenneth C. Royall, Secretary of the Army at that time, and Dan A. Kimball, Assistant Secretary of the Navy, answering the same April 6 directive, were in effect rejected by Mr. Johnson on the ground that they were too general. The Secretary of Defense asked the two officials to "clarify" the information contained in their responses. Both letters, it was learned, told Mr. Johnson that his policy was already in effect, and did not indicate that additional changes would be made.

In his reply to the Army and Navy, Mr. Johnson fixed a deadline of May 25 by which the two services are to provide more details of their plans to conform to the equality policy. The services were instructed to make their replies through Thomas R. Reid, chairman of the National Military Establishment's Personnel Policy Board.

Mr. Johnson made his April 6 directive to the armed service secretaries public on April 20, at which time he stated that he in-

Continued on Page 54, Column 1

U. S. PLAN WEIGHED

Big 3 Would Withdraw to Ports in the North Under Proposal

FRENCH WOULD GO HOME

Presentation of Suggestion Will Depend on Soviet Stand in Paris Talks

By JAMES RESTON
Special to The New York Times.

WASHINGTON, May 11—The United States was reported today to have under consideration a plan under which all occupation troops in Germany would be withdrawn into restricted areas at the North German ports.

Under this plan, which is being discussed with Britain and France, Soviet troops would be situated on the West Bank of the Oder in Stettin, British troops would be restricted to the area of Hamburg, and United States troops would be concentrated in Bremen.

[Stettin was included in the Soviet zone in the Potsdam pact, but under a separate agreement reached Sept. 20, 1947, the Russians turned over control of the former German port to Poland. Bremen is a United States enclave in the British zone.]

These troops, it is understood, would be obliged, under this plan, to use only sea communications, and France, which has a common frontier with Germany, would withdraw her occupation troops into her own territory.

An understanding apparently already has been reached among the Western powers to reject any Soviet proposal at the forthcoming meeting of the Council of Foreign Ministers in Paris for the complete evacuation of all occupation troops from all of Germany.

It is felt here that total withdrawal of these troops would be detrimental to the economic recovery and sense of security of Western Europe.

However, if Soviet Foreign Minister Andrei Y. Vishinsky should demonstrate in Paris that his Government was now prepared to establish a central government in Germany along the lines laid down by the Western powers for the

Continued on Page 3, Column 2

IT'S A REAL HOLIDAY FOR THESE BERLIN YOUNGSTERS

Joyous children hold their lunch boxes over their heads as they get news that there will be no school in celebration of the end of the blockade. The sign reads "blockade free."

Associated Press Radiophoto

ACHESON STILL BARS FRANCO AS FASCIST

Says Spanish Regime Denies Basic Rights in the Pattern of Hitler and Mussolini

Secretary Acheson's remarks on Spanish regime, Page 10.

By BERTRAM D. HULEN
Special to The New York Times.

WASHINGTON, May 11—Secretary of State Dean Acheson declared today that the question of restoring full diplomatic relations with Spain turned primarily upon the attitude of Western European countries that were still opposed to bringing her back into their international family for military and economic cooperation.

This attitude, the Secretary told his weekly news conference, was conditioned by the absence of fundamental freedoms under the Franco regime which, he said, originally and still was patterned on Nazi Germany and Fascist Italy. At an-

Continued on Page 10, Column 1

Eisler Reported Stowaway; Seizure in Britain Is Asked

By WILL LISSNER

A man who has identified himself as Gerhart Eisler, native of Germany, is fleeing from the United States aboard the Gdynia-America liner Batory, it became known yesterday. The fugitive is believed to be the former Comintern agent named by the House Un-American Activities Committee as America's No. 1 Communist, jumping $23,500 bail to escape serving a year in jail and other penalties, but his identity has not yet been definitely established.

The Federal Bureau of Investigation and the Immigration and Naturalization Service of the Department of Justice moved yesterday to fix the identity of the fugitive. If the man aboard the Batory is the German-born Communist leader Eisler, he will be placed in custody for eventual return.

The fugitive is bound for Gdynia, but the ship, which sailed last Saturday, will put into Southampton Saturday. To make sure that Polish Communists aboard the ship do not balk a return, the State Department, at the request of the Department of Justice, notified Scotland Yard of the incident and asked that top investigators meet the ship on her arrival in the English port. Scotland Yard was asked to hold the suspect.

If Eisler, the convicted Communist agent, has fled the jurisdiction of the Federal District Court, his bail would be forfeited even though the English authorities return him, it was said at the Federal Building.

The forfeiture of the $23,500 bail would be a blow to the Civil Rights Congress and the American Committee for the Protection of the Foreign Born. For a good part of

Continued on Page 4, Column 3

FIRST BERLIN TRAIN FROM WEST SEALED

Officials Lock Doors and Draw Shades to Keep Russians Out and Reporters In

By The United Press.

BERLIN, Thursday, May 12—The first western passenger train since last year arrived in Berlin at 5:11 A. M. today (11:11 P. M. Wednesday, Eastern Daylight Time)—hauled by a Soviet zone locomotive.

A combined British-American train of twelve cars, it carried approximately 140 Western nationals, including seventy-three British troops and at least a score of reporters.

Anglo-American officials ordered the doors locked and the shades drawn soon after the train left Helmstedt at 1:23 A. M., the first train to make the West-East run on the Helmstedt-Berlin road since last year.

The train officials said that the "sealing" of the cars was necessary "to keep the Russians out and to keep you newsmen in." The reporters peeked anyway but saw only a moonlit empty landscape during the eventless three hours

Continued on Page 2, Column 2

World News Summarized

THURSDAY, MAY 12, 1949

The 328-day Soviet blockade of Berlin ended on schedule at 12:01 o'clock this morning, Berlin time, and approximately an hour and one-half later the first vehicles from the Western zones of Germany entered the city followed by the first train. [1:8; maps P. 2.]

The first Western passenger train to Berlin was sealed; a jeep led the road convoy [1:7.] Russian guards at Berlin ignored automobiles going to Helmstedt; people watched on the Autobahn. [3:1.]

Secretary of State Acheson warned that the end of the blockade did not, in itself, solve the German problem. He said Russia's willingness at the forthcoming Big Four meeting in Paris to consider proposals that would not erase the progress made in Germany by the Western powers would determine the outcome. He praised the draft constitution for a West German state. [4:2.] The United States was said to be considering a plan for withdrawal of all occupation troops to North German ports, except for French forces, which would return to France. [1:4.]

Guarded optimism was expressed by Moscow's New Times in an editorial on the Big Four meeting. The editorial said the talks could be a "turning point" in East-West relations. [4:6.]

Communists, urging at a Senate hearing in Washington that ratification of the North Atlantic treaty be deferred until after the Paris meeting, likened the pact to "Hitler's Axis." [1:6-7.]

The United States will abstain from a United Nations vote to lift the curbs on full diplomatic relations with Spain, Secretary Acheson said, because of the opposition in Western Europe to any change. Explaining this country's position, he denounced the Franco regime as still functioning along Nazi and Fascist lines. [1:5.]

Israel became the fifty-ninth member of the United Nations when the General Assembly voted, 37 to 12, to admit her. The six Arab states left the hall in protest. [1:1.] Foreign Minister Sharett, the first Israeli delegate to the United Nations, pledged his country to work for peace with its Arab neighbors and to remain friendly with both the United States and Russia. [12:3.]

Japan is not what she was ten years ago, Premier Yoshida said in appealing for proper understanding by the world. He asked access to materials and markets to enable Japan to become self-supporting. [19:1.]

Representative Rankin disowned his veterans' pension bill when a "watered-down" version was reported by a House committee. [1:2.]

Labor leaders and President Truman were said to have agreed on pressing passage of the Administration's labor bill with some amendments. [24:2.]

A man who identified himself as Gerhart Eisler, called this country's No. 1 Communist, sailed secretly on a Polish liner now at sea. [1:6-7.]

Victorious anti-Hague forces in Jersey City will seek a court order impounding all public records until an audit can be made. [1:3.]

Index to other news appears on Page 32.

U.S. Reds Liken Pact to Hitler Axis; Norman Thomas Urges Ratification

By WILLIAM S. WHITE
Special to The New York Times.

WASHINGTON, May 11 — The Communist party of the United States, through a statement filed by its general secretary, Eugene Dennis, likened the North Atlantic treaty today to "Hitler's Axis," and demanded that the Senate withhold any action toward its ratification until after the Big Four Foreign Ministers' conference.

However, Norman Thomas, Socialist leader, supported ratification of the treaty before the Senate Foreign Relations Committee, but stressed that he did so with much anxiety because of the "dangers" that might lie in it.

He expressed belief that the pact should not be ratified unless the Senate made it "absolutely plain" that Spain would not be included in it, and equally plain that proposed American military aid should not be used against colonial peoples.

Senator Tom Connally, Democrat, of Texas, committee chairman, said that Spain's inclusion was "highly improbable" since it could be done only by unanimous consent of the twelve countries that signed the treaty.

Above all, Mr. Thomas recommended that before ratification this country issue "a mighty appeal for an end of the armament race under effective international controls which would make the pact unnecessary."

The Communist party proposal that the pact be held back, first advanced last week by Henry A. Wallace, was offered also by representatives of the National Council of American-Soviet Friendship and the National Council of the Arts, Sciences and Professions.

Witnesses for the three organizations appeared before the committee and further urged Soviet-United States conferences looking toward resolving differences between the two countries.

Their recommendations for de-

Continued on Page 7, Column 3

SIEGE ON 328 DAYS

Leading Car Speeds 102 Miles From the British Zone in 1½ Hours

AIRLIFT PLANES CONTINUE

West Concerned as Russians Turn Back Some Trucks—City's Lights Turned On

By DREW MIDDLETON
Special to The New York Times.

BERLIN, Thursday, May 12—Just as the morning sun rose over the jagged skyline of this broken but defiant city a Soviet zone locomotive chugged wearily into the Charlottenburg Station in the British sector hauling the first train to reach Berlin from the West in 328 days.

Arrival of the train completed the relief of the city from the iron vise of the Soviet blockade.

At one minute after midnight [6:01 P. M. Wednesday, Eastern daylight time] two jeeps and a convoy of cars, buses and trucks roared out of the city for the Western zones. An hour and three quarters later the first cars of a flotilla that simultaneously had left Helmstedt, in the British zone at the border of the Soviet zone, swept into Berlin to re-establish the land link with the West broken since the Soviet Military administration established a complete blockade of the city last June.

By morning it was evident that the Russians had observed the letter if not the spirit of the East-West agreement reached in New York. Traffic was flowing freely along the Autobahn.

Although there had been some difficulty over locomotives, the Russians had promised to send sixteen freight trains and one passenger train into Berlin each day. Pending settlement of the dispute the trains will be pulled by Soviet zone locomotives.

Western Officials Disturbed

To Berliners who awoke in the night to find lights burning in the streets and in their homes and intersector barriers dismantled, the blockade for the moment seemed over. Americans and British in Military Government offices, however, were distinctly disturbed by the turning back at Soviet checkpoints of trucks bound for the Western zones with Western sector exports.

This refusal to permit trucks to pass stems from a Soviet order of January, 1948. Hence it is not affected by the New York agreement on ending the blockade. But the Western Powers felt that the action indicated that the Russians would not give an inch more than called for by that agreement.

The first railroad train since June of 1948 passed through the checkpoint at Helmstedt, in the British zone at the border of the Soviet zone, at 1:23 A. M., bound for Berlin.

The first car from Helmstedt, driven by Walter G. Rundle, United Press manager for Germany, arrived at the American checkpoint outside Berlin at 1:44. Mr. Rundle had driven the distance, which the British declare is 102 miles, in an hour and thirty-seven minutes. He said that the bridge across the Elbe at Magdeburg was in good condition.

Aide's Wife Enters City

The first woman to enter Berlin after lifting of the blockade was Adelaide de Neufville, wife of Lawrence de Neufville, consultant to the civil affairs division of the United States Military Government.

The first two railroad trains to start across the Soviet zone for Berlin since June 17, 1948, left the Russian control point at Marienborn early this morning. The first of these was a passenger train carrying correspondents. It moved into the moonlit landscape of the Russian zone at 1:55 after an eleven-minute wait at the checkpoint.

Eight minutes later a freight train of forty-two cars carrying coal from the Ruhr for Berlin passed through the checkpoint en route to Berlin, symbolizing the end not only of the Russian block-

Continued on Page 2, Column 3

"All the News That's Fit to Print"

The New York Times.

LATE CITY EDITION

Fair and quite cool today and tomorrow.

Temperature Range Today—Max.,62; Min.,49
Temperatures Yesterday—Max.,66; Min.,50
Full U. S. Weather Bureau Report, Page 27

Copyright, 1949, by The New York Times Company.

VOL. XCIX..No. 33,481. Entered as Second-Class Matter, Postoffice, New York, N. Y. NEW YORK, SATURDAY, SEPTEMBER 24, 1949. Times Square, New York 18, N. Y. Telephone Lackawanna 4-1000 THREE CENTS IN NEW YORK CITY

ATOM BLAST IN RUSSIA DISCLOSED; TRUMAN AGAIN ASKS U.N. CONTROL; VISHINSKY PROPOSES A PEACE PACT

SMALL STEEL MILL SETS PENSION PLAN, A POSSIBLE PATTERN

Proposal by Employer of 1,200, With Workers Sharing Costs, Is Held Poser for Union

LIMITS CAUSE FOR STRIKE

Murray Is Firm for 'Package' Urged by Panel — Wildcat Walkout Hits Another Plant

By A. H. RASKIN

Special to THE NEW YORK TIMES.

PITTSBURGH, Sept. 23—The first hint at the strategy the steel industry may employ to head off a threatened strike of 500,000 steel workers Oct. 1 came today from one of the smallest companies in the industry.

While the United States Steel Corporation and other big companies marked time on the first day of their renewed negotiations with the United Steel Workers of America, CIO, the Follansbee Steel Corporation made a proposal to the union that was widely regarded here as the forerunner of similar offers to be made by the rest of the industry.

The company, which has 1,200 employes at plants in Follansbee, W. Va., and Toronto, Ohio, informed the union that it was prepared to commit itself to pay 6 cents an hour for pensions, provided its workers put up an additional 3 cents an hour.

Employes Pay for Insurance

The company already has a contributory program of social insurance, to which it gives about 4 cents an hour and the workers 2 cents.

The proposal would bring the company's outlay for pensions and welfare into line with the 10-cent "package" recommended by President Truman's fact-finding board. At the same time it would make an end run around the union's insistence that employers pay the whole cost of industrial social security.

The Truman panel endorsed the idea that employers should meet the bill for pensions and social insurance, but opened the door for supplementary payments by workers to increase the amount of protection that could be provided. The board said such arrangements could be effected through collective bargaining.

If other steel companies subscribe to the 6-cent figure for pensions and 4 cents for health, hospital and other forms of social insurance, on condition that their workers also contribute, the union would be maneuvered into the position of having to decide whether or not to strike solely for establishment of the non-contributory principle.

Philip Murray, president of the union, has stressed the union's belief that the most important element in the Truman board's report was its recommendation that care for the "human machine" should be as much a charge on industry as care of plant equipment. The union has barred any compromise on that issue.

Murray Again Threatening Strike

At a two-hour conference with representatives of United States Steel this afternoon, Mr. Murray reiterated the union's determination to strike unless the company agreed to shoulder the full cost of pensions and welfare on the 6-cent and 4-cent basis suggested by the fact-finders.

The company made no immediate reply. Subcommittees were set up by both sides to continue negotiations Monday, five days before the strike deadline.

There was nothing to indicate that "Big Steel" had abandoned the opposition it expressed in public statements last week to exemption of workers from any direct share of financial responsibility for their own pensions and insurance.

The company has committed itself to give 4 cents an hour for welfare, provided workers made an additional payment on their own, but it has declined to set any specific figure for pensions until a joint study of retirement benefits is completed next March 31.

Negotiations between the union and other large steel companies took place today in a dozen cities, but none of the companies gave any new indication of its position. In virtually all cases the talks were recessed until Monday without any sign of a break in the deadlock that has existed since the first negotiations got under way in June.

Union negotiators warned that the patience of the men in the steel mills was wearing thin at the lack of progress toward employer-

Continued on Page 23, Column 1

Cancer Patient Slain; Daughter Detained

Special to THE NEW YORK TIMES.

STAMFORD, Conn., Sept. 23—Carol Paight, 20 years old, was placed under police guard in Stamford Hospital tonight pending investigation of whether she shot her police-sergeant father in pity after learning that he had an inoperable cancer.

The father, Carl Paight, 52, died seven hours after he was shot with his own service pistol at 5:45 P. M. He had been in the hospital since Sept. 15, suffering from the effects of an operation that showed he had cancer.

The daughter, who had been alone with him, became hysterical. Sedatives were administered before she could be questioned by the police and a psychiatrist.

Father and daughter had been deeply attached, friends said. Police who knew both because of Sergeant Paight's twenty-eight years of service here, said that she had declared upon being told of the cancer that she did not want her father to suffer.

RED DEFENSE RESTS; REBUTTAL WAIVED

Jury in 9-Month Trial Excused Till Summaries Begin Oct. 4, May Get Case Week Later

By RUSSELL PORTER

The defense rested in the nine-month Communist trial yesterday, and the Government waived its right of rebuttal. Federal Judge Harold R. Medina gave counsel until 2 o'clock Tuesday afternoon to submit requests for instructions to be included in his charge to the jury and announced that arguments on closing motions would be heard at 10:30 o'clock Wednesday morning.

Judge Medina excused the jury until Tuesday morning, Oct. 4, when, if he denies the usual defense motions to throw out the case, summaries will begin. In the absence of unexpected developments, the case should go to the jury by the week beginning Monday, Oct. 10.

Eleven members of the Communist party's American Politburo or national board have been on trial since January 17, for criminal conspiracy to teach and advocate overthrow of the Government and destruction of American democracy by force and violence. Government witnesses have testified that the defendants reorganized the party for this purpose in 1945 on orders from Moscow.

The defense took roughly six months to present its case, including a two-month preliminary challenge to the Federal jury system. The Government introduced its evidence in two months.

The defense called thirty-five witnesses and the Government fifteen. The defense offered 429 exhibits, the Government 332.

Of the 158 trial days, the defense used 109—eighty-two in the trial proper and twenty-seven in the jury challenge. The Government spent thirty-seven days in the presentation of evidence. Ten days were devoted to picking the jury and two days to opening statements by opposing counsel.

The Government called its first witness on March 23 and rested on May 19. The defense began to present evidence on May 23, four months ago yesterday.

Nearly 20,000 pages of testimony

Continued on Page 7, Column 2

CIO SEES LEFTISTS QUITTING TO FORM OWN ORGANIZATION

High Officers Say Such Action Is Called for by New Line of Communist Party

FIGHT AT CONVENTION DUE

National Body Plans to Set Up Rival Right-Wing Unions if Pro-Red Groups Depart

By LOUIS STARK

Special to THE NEW YORK TIMES.

WASHINGTON, Sept. 23—High officers of the Congress of Industrial Organizations expressed the view today that the new Communist party line was to split all pro-Communist unions from the CIO and to form a new labor federation. This belief is supported by the following developments:

1. A factional struggle within the CIO Teachers Union in New York, in which the pro-Communists are demanding that the union leave the CIO, though their opponents proclaim loyalty to the parent body.
2. The decision of pro-Communist unions to carry the fight on autonomy and wage policies to the right wing, led by Philip Murray, president of the CIO.
3. The "impossible" demands decided on several days ago by the convention of the United Electrical Radio and Machine Workers that will be served on Mr. Murray.
4. Refusal of the Farm Equipment Workers Union to obey the CIO mandate to merge with the United Automobile Workers.

The Murray forces are prepared for a possible split. If it occurs, they will charter right-wing groups to form the nucleus of new organizations supplanting the dissidents.

Eleven Affiliates Involved

Eleven CIO affiliates may be affected by the possible schism. While they have been generally credited with a membership of 1,000,000 members, informed officials say that their total is more nearly 600,000.

The largest of the dissidents is the UE, which says it bargains for 600,000 members. This union, however, is reported by right-wing officers to be paying to the CIO on about 350,000 members. Some of the leftist-led unions have been in arrears in payments to the national organization for some months.

The largest nut that the CIO has to crack is the UE, its third largest affiliate. This union, well entrenched in General Electric, Westinghouse and other large radio and electrical manufacturing companies, is a strong, well-disciplined organization.

Despite its strength, CIO officials indicated that they would meet any challenge of the UE's re-elected officers. If the union should decide to leave the CIO, the latter's officers feel confident of winning adherence of the workers in the big General Electric and Westinghouse plants as the nucleus of a new electrical union.

Mr. Murray's associates are impatient for the battle because daily evidences of leftist dissidence convinces them that the latter have made up their minds to split the CIO and to put the blame on the right wing.

The latest aspect of the leftist attack on the CIO leadership is

Continued on Page 28, Column 7

Auto Crash Kills Publisher's Wife As He Reaches for Spilling Cup

Special to THE NEW YORK TIMES.

HARRISON, N. Y., Sept. 23—Marvin Pierce, president of the McCall Corporation, magazine and fashion publishers, at 230 Park Avenue, New York, was driving to the Rye railroad station this morning when he tried to prevent a cup of coffee from spilling on his wife's clothes. In an accident that followed, his wife, Mrs. Pauline Robinson Pierce, 53 years old, was killed and Mr. Pierce was injured.

The couple left their Purchase Street home, adjoining the Westchester Country Club, soon after 8 A. M. Mr. Pierce, who is 56, was at the wheel and his wife was beside him, ready to drive home from the station after her husband had boarded a commuters' train for New York.

Mrs. Pierce held in her hands a cup of coffee that she had carried from the breakfast table. After sipping the fluid, she placed the cup for a moment on the seat between her husband and herself. From a corner of his eye Mr. Pierce saw the cup tipping toward his wife.

As Mr. Pierce reached for the cup, the auto swerved to the left side of the road, hit a soft shoulder, plunged 100 feet down a moderate embankment, slid between a pole and a tree and crashed into a tree and a stone wall. Striking the windshield, Mrs. Pierce died of a fractured skull. The accident occurred on Highland Road near Purchase Street.

Taken to the United Hospital in Port Chester, Mr. Pierce told his story to the police. Detectives found the coffee cup, bone China of English manufacture, unbroken in the wreckage of the car and took it to police headquarters. Physicians listed Mr. Pierce's injuries as a cerebral concussion, fractured nose, four broken ribs and several bruises. His condition tonight was improving.

Besides her husband, Mrs. Pierce leaves two sons, James R. and Scott Pierce of Rye, and two daughters, Mrs. Walter G. Rafferty of West Hartford, Conn., and Mrs. G. H. W. Bush of Bakersfield, Calif.

ADDRESSING U. N.

Andrei Y. Vishinsky
The New York Times

VISHINSKY SAYS U.S. PLOTS ATOMIC WAR

Calls for Great Power Treaty to Strengthen World Peace in Assembly Speech

Text of Vishinsky address to U. N. Assembly is on Page 4.

By THOMAS J. HAMILTON

Andrei Y. Vishinsky, the Soviet Foreign Minister, accused the United States and Britain yesterday of planning an atomic war, and introduced a resolution at Flushing Meadow proposing that the United Nations General Assembly request the five Great Powers to conclude "a pact for the strengthening of peace."

The resolution also would call on all nations to settle their disputes without resorting to the use or threat of force, and would take note "of the unbending will and determination of peoples to ward

Continued on Page 4, Column 1

CAPITOL FOR ACCORD

Lucas Says 'Future of Civilization' May Rest on Atom Control

AIRING OF VIEWS URGED

McMahon Holds U. S. Should 'Demand Right' to Put Case Before Russians Via Radio

By WILLIAM S. WHITE

Special to THE NEW YORK TIMES.

WASHINGTON, Sept. 23—In a great anxiety that passed soon into a positive response—demands for fresh tries at international control of the atomic bomb—Congress heard today the news that an atomic explosion had occurred in the Soviet Union.

The atmosphere at the Capitol almost everywhere was consciously quiet and restrained. Some of the most responsible members of Congress issued statements saying that the American people could have confidence, in any possible crisis, in the military leadership and the military power of this country.

Beyond this, Administration Congressional spokesmen said in substance that the implications of the President's disclosure of what had happened in Russia were beyond the scope of any Congressional action. They looked toward the United Nations as the forum for this matter.

Senator Scott W. Lucas of Illinois, the Democratic leader of the Senate, and Senator Brien McMahon, Democrat, of Connecticut, the principal Congressional authority on atomic energy, came out almost at once for another attempt at bringing the bomb under the world's seal.

"I believe," said Senator Lucas, "that nothing could give the world greater confidence in survival than for the delegates at the United Nations to reconsider the question of atomic energy control, and arrive at an agreement acceptable to all.

"The world knows that our rep-

Continued on Page 3, Column 5

World News Summarized

SATURDAY, SEPTEMBER 24, 1949

President Truman issued yesterday a terse statement containing this dramatic disclosure: "We have evidence that within recent weeks an atomic explosion occurred in the U. S. S. R."

His announcement, indicating that United States monopoly in atomic weapons had ended, added that "ever since atomic energy was first released by man, the eventual development of this new force by other nations was to be expected." He said this "probability" had always been "taken into account" by this nation, and he renewed his plea "for that truly effective and enforceable international control of atomic energy which the Government and the large majority of the members of the United Nations support." [1:8.]

Secretary of State Acheson said he assumed that it was an atomic weapon that had been exploded in the Soviet Union. He said the news would not lead to any shift in the United States position on international atomic control. [1:7.]

New efforts to achieve an acceptable plan for international control of atomic weapons were urged in Congress, where Mr. Truman's announcement was received with restrained anxiety. [1:5.] Reassuring statements were made by General Eisenhower and Maj. Gen. Leslie R. Groves, wartime chief of the atomic bomb project. General Eisenhower said he saw no reason why "a development that was anticipated years ago should cause any revolutionary change in our thinking or in our actions." [2:2.] One result expected by Washington observers was a spur to the North Atlantic defense program. Closer cooperation among the United States, Britain and Canada in atomic development was also seen. [2:3-4.]

Scientists who had generally predicted that the Russians would eventually succeed in discovering the secret of setting off an atomic explosion saw the Russian development as having come at least three years earlier than had been expected. [1:6-7.]

Soviet Foreign Minister Vishinsky said nothing about Russian possession of an atomic bomb in his eagerly awaited address to the United Nations General Assembly. He accused the United States and Britain of planning an atomic war. Mr. Vishinsky introduced a resolution calling for "the unconditional prohibition of atomic weapons" and another asking the five major powers to make "a pact for the strengthening of peace." [1:4.]

Renewed negotiations by the Big Four Foreign Ministers' deputies on an Austrian state treaty got off to a bad start. Russian refusal to reconsider the controversial issues forced an indefinite adjournment. [6:2.]

The British Labor Government will ask for a vote of confidence after Parliament convenes next week to debate the Government's devaluation of the pound. [6:3.]

In China the battle for the important seaport of Amoy reached new intensity. [5:1; with map.]

In a move that might set the pattern for the big companies in the steel industry to stave off a threatened strike by 500,000 steelworkers, the Follansbee Steel Corporation offered a pension plan under which the company would pay 6 cents an hour and its employes an additional 3 cents an hour. [1:1.]

High CIO officials were reported to believe that the new Communist party line was to try to split all pro-Communist unions from the CIO to organize a new labor federation. [1:3.]

Index to other news appears on Page 14.

Truman Statement on Atom

By The United Press.

WASHINGTON, Sept. 23—The text of President Truman's statement today announcing a recent atomic explosion in the Soviet Union:

I believe the American people to the fullest extent consistent with the national security are entitled to be informed of all developments in the field of atomic energy. That is my reason for making public the following information.

We have evidence that within recent weeks an atomic explosion occurred in the U.S.S.R.

Ever since atomic energy was first released by man, the eventual development of this new force by other nations was to be expected. This probability has always been taken into account by us.

Nearly four years ago I pointed out that "scientific opinion appears to be practically unanimous that the essential theoretical knowledge upon which the discovery is based is already widely known. There is also substantial agreement that foreign research can come abreast of our present theoretical knowledge in time." And, in the three-nation declaration of the President of the United States and the Prime Ministers of the United Kingdom and of Canada, dated Nov. 15, 1945, it was emphasized that no single nation could, in fact, have a monopoly of atomic weapons.

This recent development emphasizes once again, if indeed such emphasis were needed, the necessity for that truly effective and enforceable international control of atomic energy which this Government and the large majority of the members of the United Nations support.

Soviet Achievement Ahead Of Predictions by 3 Years

By WILLIAM L. LAURENCE

President Truman's announcement that we have evidence of the occurrence of an "atomic explosion" in the Soviet Union within recent weeks ranks only next to his original announcement of the explosion of the first atomic bomb over Hiroshima on Aug. 6, 1945. It marks the end of the first period of the atomic age and the beginning of the second.

The momentous event is bound to have profound repercussions the world over. Though the scientists have predicted its coming, it came at least three years sooner than was expected. This was largely the result of an erroneous assumption that Russian scientists did nothing about developing an atomic bomb until after we informed them about it following Hiroshima. The fact of the matter is that scientists everywhere recognized the tremendous potentialities of atomic energy for war and peace as soon as the discovery of uranium fission was announced to the world in January, 1939.

While it is likely that Soviet scientists tested the first and only bomb they had, it would be dangerous to assume that they are four years behind us and that it would take them that long to catch up with us. It would be much more reasonable to assume that they have geared their plants to produce at the rate of one bomb a week, so that they will have a stockpile of at least fifty bombs a year from now, enough to destroy fifty of our cities with 40,000,000 of our population.

On the other hand, it is also likely that the latest event will make possible a better understanding between us and Russia, leading toward an agreement for the international control of atomic energy. Bargaining between equals is more likely to produce desirable results than bargaining between two principals, one of which holds

Continued on Page 2, Column 6

ACHESON RULES OUT SHIFT IN U. S. PLANS

Western Diplomats and Atomic Experts at U. N. Agree to Uphold Control Program

Text of Secretary Acheson's statement is printed on Page 2.

By A. M. ROSENTHAL

Secretary of State Dean Acheson said yesterday that he assumed the explosion in Russia reported by President Truman had been caused by an actual atomic weapon. He insisted, however, that the news had come as no shock and would not change the United States-sponsored plan for international control of atomic energy.

Other Western diplomats and atomic control specialists at the United Nations Assembly at Flushing Meadow took the same line. Unanimously, they said that the majority of the members of the United Nations would stick to the plan that had been fought by the Soviet Union for more than three years.

United Nations officials took it for granted that the President's announcement had pushed the world organization back into the center of the atomic picture despite the long deadlock on control negotiations. Secretary General Trygve Lie summed up the Secretariat attitude by saying that the

Continued on Page 2, Column 5

Couple Held in Quebec Air Crash; Woman Said to Have Planted Bomb

By The Associated Press.

QUEBEC, Sept. 23—Police reported tonight that a drug-dazed woman confessed to carrying a package, believed to have contained dynamite, which was placed aboard an ill-fated Quebec Airways plane that blew up Sept. 9, killing all twenty-three persons aboard.

Police said the woman, identified as Mrs. Arthur Pitre, admitted taking the package to the Quebec Airport where it was placed aboard the plane, but she insisted that she did not know the contents of the package.

Royal Canadian Mounted Police said the woman was recovering from sleeping pills she took at the suggestion of her lover, whose wife was aboard the plane.

Provincial police detained as a material witness J. A. Guay, a young Quebec jeweler, whose 28-year-old wife was one of the passengers who lost their lives when the plane was ripped open by a blast in its luggage compartment. The plane smashed into a mountain near Sault au Cochon, forty miles northeast of Quebec.

Mrs. Pitre was also being held as a material witness.

Police also are reported to have questioned a third person in connection with the case.

Police described the third person as a 26-year-old "pretty waitress." They said she was a close acquaintance of Guay.

The crash took the lives of three New York executives of the Kennecott Copper Corporation. They were President E. T. Stannard, President-designate Arthur D. Storke and Vice President R. J. Parker.

Quebec Provincial police detained Mrs. Pitre at her home in Quebec. Persons living near by saw police enter the woman's Gauvreau Street home, an apartment. Crowds gathered outside and police were called to keep the curious on the move.

Police Inspector René Belec told newsmen:

"We have definite proof that explosives were aboard the plane to

Continued on Page 23, Column 3

U. S. REACTION FIRM

President Does Not Say Soviet Union Has an Atomic Bomb

PICKS WORDS CAREFULLY

But He Implies Our Absolute Dominance in New Weapons Has Virtually Ended

By ANTHONY LEVIERO

Special to THE NEW YORK TIMES.

WASHINGTON, Sept. 23—President Truman announced this morning that an atomic explosion had occurred in Russia within recent weeks. This statement implied that the absolute dominance of the United States in atomic weapons had virtually ended.

"We have evidence that within recent weeks an atomic explosion occurred in the U.S.S.R.," President Truman said.

These words stood out in red-letter vividness in a brief undramatic statement in which the Chief Executive said that the United States always had taken into account the probability that other nations would develop "this new force."

He pleaded once again for adoption of the system of international control of atomic energy promulgated by the United States and supported by the large majority of countries now assembled in the United Nations General Assembly at Flushing Meadow.

McMahon Reveals News

Mr. Truman announced the discovery to the Cabinet, assembled in the White House at 11 A. M. for the usual Friday meeting. Simultaneously on Capitol Hill Senator Brien McMahon, Democrat, of Connecticut, stood before the members of the Joint Congressional Atomic Energy Committee and gave them the news, which Mr. Truman had passed on to him at 3:15 P. M. yesterday.

White House correspondents had their usual conference with Charles G. Ross, the President's secretary, at 10:30 A. M. It was routine, but as they filed out his secretary, Miss Myrtle Bergheim, advised them not to go away. A moment before 11 A. M. Miss Bergheim entered the press room and said: "Press!"

The news men filed into Mr. Ross' office. He said he wished the door closed, and a secret service man took his post there. Then Mr. Ross said that he would pass out an announcement and that nobody was to leave the room until everyone present had a copy. Then he began passing around the President's mimeographed statement.

Tass Correspondent Attends

One of the first reporters to scan his copy exclaimed, "Russia has the atomic bomb!" There was a wild rush through the door and to the telephones in the near-by press room. One of the news men who sprinted out was the correspondent of Tass, the official Soviet news agency.

"The President has just given it to the Cabinet," said Mr. Ross as they went.

Thus the President did not personally appear, and there was no opportunity then or later to put questions to him.

Secretary of Defense Louis Johnson came out of the Cabinet meeting soon afterward. He began shaking his head as the questions came. Reporters literally clutched his arms as he headed for his limousine.

"Have we made any change in the disposition of our forces since this happened?" This question was asked twice.

"No," Mr. Johnson finally said.

"Does the Cabinet know any more about this than is contained in the President's statement?"

"The Cabinet knows all about it," Mr. Johnson replied to this. "It was fully informed."

"Do you have reason to believe this was the first atomic explosion in Russia?" asked another reporter.

This time Mr. Johnson smilingly shook his head, negatively.

"Don't overplay it," remarked Mr. Johnson, departing. In the cir-

Continued on Page 2, Column 8

"All the News That's Fit to Print"

The New York Times.

LATE CITY EDITION
Sunny and mild today, cool tonight. Fair tomorrow.
Temperature Range Today—Max.,72; Min.,51
Temperature Yesterday—Max.,69; Min.,54
Full U. S. Weather Bureau Report, Page 39

VOL. XCIX...No. 33,488. Entered as Second-Class Matter. Postoffice, New York, N. Y. NEW YORK, SATURDAY, OCTOBER 1, 1949. Times Square, New York 18, N. Y. Telephone Lackawanna 4-1000 THREE CENTS IN NEW YORK CITY

STEEL STRIKE STARTS AS 500,000 QUIT; TRUMAN PLANS NO NEW INTERVENTION; LEWIS RECALLS 102,000 MINERS TO PITS

SOVIET IN U. N. ASKS INDEPENDENT LIBYA, BRITISH EVACUATION

Proposes Military Withdrawal Within Three Months as Colonies Debate Opens

DELEGATES ARE SURPRISED

U. S. Suggests Independence Within 3 to 4 Years, Britain Would Set Like Limit

By THOMAS J. HAMILTON
Special to The New York Times.

LAKE SUCCESS, Sept. 30—In a surprise move the Soviet Union proposed today that the United Nations General Assembly grant Libya immediate independence, and that "within three months all foreign troops and all military personnel shall be withdrawn from Libyan territory."

The proposal was aimed directly at the Western powers, since Britain maintains air bases in Cyrenaica, which, it is generally understood, would be available to the United States in the event of war.

The Soviet proposal, made public just as the Assembly's Political and Security Committee began its debate on disposition of the former Italian colonies in Africa, was timed to anticipate the speeches later in the afternoon announcing United States and British support of independence for Libya.

Dr. Philip C. Jessup, United States Ambassador at Large, said the United States would favor independence for Libya within three to four years.

McNeil Seeks 3-Year Limit

Hector McNeil, British Minister of State, suggested a time limit of three to five years, but he confined his statement to Cyrenaica and Tripolitania, which are being administered by Britain pending a decision by the Assembly. Mr. McNeil said he would leave it to France to say what should be done with the Fezzan, which is under French administration. It is understood that France will propose that she continue to administer the area.

The Soviet resolution was introduced by Georgi N. Zarubin, after Mr. McNeil had spoken, with the comment that the Soviet delegation would explain at a later meeting of the committee the r asons that motivated its proposal.

Mr. McNeil, who was the first speaker, had been shown a copy of the Soviet resolution while he was speaking. He said it looked "distressingly familiar" and that he hoped no attempt would be made to make "propaganda warfare" of the situation.

Until a year ago, the Soviet Union had been trying to persuade the other members of the Big Four that Libya, together with the two other former Italian colonies, Italian Somaliland and Eritrea, should be administered by Italy under a United Nations trusteeship.

Soviet Switches Stand

In Paris, however, before the Big Four handed the question to the General Assembly, the Soviet Union proposed a collective or direct United Nations trusteeship, and it fought unsuccessfully for this solution at the continuation of the General Assembly session here last spring.

The new Soviet proposal still provides for a direct United Nations trusteeship over Eritrea and Italian Somaliland. At the end of five years they would become independent.

In each case, the Trusteeship Council (of which the five great powers are permanent members) would appoint an administrator, who would be assisted by an advisory council consisting of the Big Five, Italy, Ethiopia, and one European and two native residents, to be appointed by the other members. The resolution also provides that at an unspecified time a part of Eritrea needed to give Ethiopia "access to the sea through the port of Assab" would be ceded to Ethiopia.

U. S. Stand Unchanged

Dr. Jessup and Mr. McNeil advocated the same solutions for the two other colonies that they supported at the Assembly's spring session: Italian administration of Italian Somaliland, cession of the western province of Eritrea to the Anglo-Egyptian Sudan, and cession of the remainder to Ethiopia.

The only other speaker today was Abte-Wold Aklilou, the Ethiopian representative, who insisted that Eritrea was an integral part of Ethiopia, and urged the Assembly to allot all of Eritrea, except the western provinces, to Ethiopia. He made no recommendation regarding the western prov-

Continued on Page 4, Column 8

Mao Heads Peiping Regime; Program Supports Moscow

Red Government Launched—Chou's Name Is Linked to Office of Premier

By WALTER SULLIVAN
Special to The New York Times.

SHANGHAI, Sept. 30—Mao Tze-tung, chairman of the Central Committee of the Chinese Communist party, was elected chairman of the new Central Government of the People's Republic of China today as the Chinese People's Political Consultative Council completed its job of launching the new government of Communist China.

Three other leading Communists and three non-Communists were named vice chairmen. The Communists are Gen. Chu Teh, Commander in Chief; Liu Shao-chi, a member of the Political Bureau and usually rated the highest ranking member of the party under Mr. Mao, and Kao Kang, chairman of the Northeast People's Government.

Mao Tze-tung
The New York Times

The three non-Communist vice chairmen are Mme. Sun Yat-sen, widow of the founder of the Chinese Republic; Chang Lan, aged chairman of the Democratic League, and Li Chi-shen, chairman of the Kuomintang Revolutionary Committee.

The organ headed by Mr. Mao

Continued on Page 4, Column 3

Yanks Lose, Trail Red Sox By One Game; Cards Beaten

As the major league pennant races enter upon their final two strides to the wire, Brooklyn's dauntless Dodgers today seemed to be sitting right handsomely in the National League scramble with a full game lead over the second place Cardinals and only two more encounters to play before the curtain rings down on the struggle tomorrow night. Though idle yesterday, they gained their advantage when the St. Louis Redbirds lost to the Cubs in Chicago, 6 to 5.

But not so the Yankees. The battered Bombers, season-long pace-setters in the American League until last Monday, fell out of their brief first place tie with the Red Sox yesterday by losing to the Athletics at the Stadium, 4 to 1, while Boston's Bosox downed the tail-end Senators, 11 to 9.

Thus, as the Yanks and Red Sox move into their final two games at the Stadium today and tomorrow, Joe McCarthy's Bosox, again leading by a full game, need only one victory to clinch the pennant. They could end the struggle by winning today. The Yanks, on the other hand, must win both games to capture the flag, with no chance left for even finishing the race in a deadlock, unless some circumstance, such as weather interference, should prevent one of the games from going to a decision.

At the moment the standing of the two American League contenders reads:

	Won	Lost	P.C.	G.B.	To Play
Boston	96	56	.632	..	2
New York	95	57	.625	1	2

Therefore, should the Red Sox win today, it would settle the race, for even were the Yankees to win the final game of the season tomorrow, the final standing would be:

	Won	Lost	P.C.
Boston	97	57	.630
New York	96	58	.623

Oddly, and perhaps for the first time in major league history, the National League goes into its final two days with the same figures prevailing as in the rival circuit.

However, there is a slight difference. For though the Dodgers lead the Cards by a full game and each club has two more games to play, they do not meet each other.

Continued on Page 17, Column 6

PAY RISE TO 1,355,000 CLEARED BY SENATE

Civil Service and Postal Bills Total $211,000,000—Fourth Spending Authority Ends

By C. P. TRUSSELL
Special to The New York Times.

WASHINGTON, Sept. 30 — The Senate today approved in rapid succession two bills to authorize an estimated $211,000,000 in annual pay increases for 1,355,000 classified and postal employes of the Government. About half a million of those slated for rises are in the Post Office Department.

This action raised the total of prospective increases voted by the Senate this week to more than $500,000,000 and affects 3,000,000 on the civilian and military payrolls. The House, in measures previously adopted, had approved rises of at least $120,000,000 more than the Senate's total.

The average increase for classified Civil Service workers is $124 a year. The increase for the post-office employes is $100. The House bill provides $150.

After the adjustment of differences in conference, appropriations must be authorized to cover the increases.

The pay rises are contained in four measures, these applying to the classified, or Civil Service, employes; to postmasters and postal workers; to top officials in the Executive Branch of the Government, and to military personnel in almost every rank or grade.

As the Senate acted today on the last of the major pay bills, Congress, as a whole, found itself under obligation to authorize, for a fifth time, the continued spending of funds by Federal establishments, even though formal appro-

Continued on Page 23, Column 4

Mrs. Patenotre Pays $2,000,000 In Tax Case; Fine, Term Suspended

By PAUL P. KENNEDY

Mrs. Eleanor Louise Patenotre, 80-year-old former owner of The Philadelphia Inquirer and widow of Jules Patenotre, one-time French Ambassador to the United States, pleaded guilty in Federal court yesterday to a charge of tax evasion and handed over a check for $2,000,000 in civil liability settlement.

The maximum penalty of $10,000 fine and a five-year jail sentence was suspended by Federal Judge Alfred C. Coxe, who placed the defendant on a one-day probation.

The Government has a lien on about $3,400,000 of the defendant's cash and securities in J. P. Morgan & Co., Inc., to satisfy additional tax claims amounting to about $3,000,000, it was announced after yesterday's hearing.

The Government's suit arose over the sale in 1930 of Mrs. Patenotre's 51 per cent interest in The Inquirer to the Curtis-Martin interests for $10,500,000. A few days before the sale, according to Thomas F. Murphy, assistant United States attorney, the stock had been transferred to her son, Raymond, a French citizen living in Montreal, where the sale was consummated.

The Government immediately began an inquiry with a view to recovering taxes, at that time slightly less than $200,000 and which this year amounted to about $2,184,000. When it was learned, however, that the sale had been made by a French citizen outside the United States, the investigation was dropped.

In 1945, however, through a treaty with Canada, some bank

Continued on Page 25, Column 7

POLAND, HUNGARY RENOUNCE PACTS WITH YUGOSLAVIA

Two Countries Move Day After Similar Action by Russia—Warsaw Expels Diplomats

TITO HITS BACK AT SOVIET

Moscow Considers Agreements 'Scraps of Paper,' States Belgrade News Agency

By EDWARD A. MORROW
Special to The New York Times.

WARSAW, Sept. 30—Poland joined Hungary today in formally denouncing a treaty of mutual aid and friendship with Marshal Tito's Yugoslavia. The two countries acted a day after the Soviet Union had similarly voided its treaty of friendship with Yugoslavia.

Following Hungary's lead of last week, Poland also ordered the expulsion of eight Yugoslav diplomats because of alleged spying and diversionary activities.

The friendship treaty was denounced on the ground that Yugoslav agents were sowing confusion in Poland.

[Hungary declared that she had denounced the treaty because Yugoslavia had "defamed" it by plotting to overthrow her Government. Tanyug, official Yugoslav news agency, said that the Soviet Union, in renouncing its treaty with Yugoslavia, had shown that it considered its solemn agreements as "scraps of paper."]

In a note delivered to the Yugoslav Ambassador today, the Polish Government underlined in the strongest possible terms the position it had taken earlier this month when on Sept. 8 it intimated that the friendship treaty was null and void.

Reminding Marshal Tito of that note, the Polish Government said "incontrovertible facts" had proved that the embassy had been engaged in spying and abetting a political diversion within this country. Such activities, the note continued, link Yugoslavia with the "Fascist underground and testify to its complete annexation with the imperialist camp."

Consequently, the note said, the immediate departure of eight Yugoslav officials was ordered. These included Ante Rukavina, counselor (who was mentioned in the recent Budapest spy trials as a diversionist planted in Poland); Lieut. Col. Janko Susnjar, the military attaché; Major Bogic Vlahovitch, his

Continued on Page 6, Column 3

COAL TIE-UP BREAKS

80,000 Anthracite Men and 22,000 Workers in West Return Monday

MAJOR WALKOUT PERSISTS

Big Shafts East of Mississippi Are Not Affected—UMW Calls Order Aid to Homes

Special to The New York Times.

PITTSBURGH, Sept. 30—Orders for the 80,000 miners in the anthracite fields and for 22,000 in bituminous fields west of the Mississippi River to return to work Monday were issued by officials of the United Mine Workers today, but there was no indication of a break in the deadlocked negotiations with the major soft-coal producers of the country.

The UMW orders, which will return 102,000 of the union's estimated 480,000 members, or almost one-fifth of them, to the pits, were designed primarily to ease the fuel situation for domestic and public users, leaders indicated.

Unaffected will be the big bituminous fields in Pennsylvania, Kentucky, Alabama and other states east of the Mississippi from which heavy industry draws the bulk of its fuel.

Negotiations with the Northern and Southern groups of operators, employing about 378,000 miners in those fields, are stalemated at White Sulphur Springs and Bluefield, W. Va., where the groups have been meeting. The Western operators have been negotiating in conjunction with the Northerners.

In those two bituminous areas about 15,000 miners continued today to work in nonunion pits and strip operations in the face of continuing violence and mass picketing, which, however, was on a much smaller scale than in the preceding eleven days of the full work stoppage.

Another outburst of gunfire, in which a coal trucker's home and parked truck were "shot up," was reported in Pennsylvania but no

Continued on Page 3, Column 8

President 'Through' in Strike; Peace Hope Lies With Ching

Mediation Director Is Expected to Map Talks First With Major Operators Then With Union in Moves to Ease Deadlock

By FELIX BELAIR Jr.
Special to The New York Times.

WASHINGTON, Sept. 30—President Truman will make no further attempt to intervene in the steel strike, the White House announced late today after the Chief Executive's return from Kansas City. A close associate of Mr. Truman, who would not be identified by name, said:

"The President is through—from now on they are on their own."

With the shutdown in steel at hand, one economist whose opinions go regularly to the White House compared the seriousness of the situation to the first hundred days of the New Deal. Federal agencies prepared to revise all forecasts of business conditions and employment to take account of a steel strike that would be felt throughout the industrial fabric.

The Presidential press secretary, Charles G. Ross, said the Government's effort to bring about a settlement of the pension dispute among 500,000 steel workers was in the hands of Cyrus S. Ching, director of the Federal Mediation and Conciliation Service.

When Mr. Ching left his office at 5 P. M. today he had just hung up the telephone after a conversation with the assistant mediation director, William N. Margolis, in Pittsburgh. He reported that Mr. Margolis had advised that there was no change in the situation as a result of all-day conferences. He received similar advices all day from his mediators in other steel centers.

Assuming that the strike is still under way early next week, Mr. Ching is reported to be determined to seek a way out of the continued deadlock by further conferences.

Continued on Page 3, Column 5

PARLEYS COLLAPSE

Murray Orders Men Out in Nation-Wide Tie-Up on Pensions Issue

SIDES ACCUSE EACH OTHER

CIO Chieftain Holds Industry 'Forced' Walkout—Fairless Blames Union Insistence

By A. H. RASKIN

PITTSBURGH, Saturday, Oct. 1—The national steel strike began at 12:01 A. M. today. Telegraphic orders from Philip Murray, president of the United Steelworkers of America, CIO, ordered 500,000 workers from their jobs after Federal mediation efforts had collapsed.

All signs pointed to a long stoppage as President Truman, who had won three postponements of the walkout since last July 15, let it be known that he had no thought of again stepping into the dispute.

The bitterness of the conflict over whether employers should assume the full cost of pensions and social insurance for their workers was reflected in statements issued a few hours before the midnight strike deadline by leaders on both sides. Each blamed the other for a tie-up that meant the slow choking of the manufacturing industry.

The shutdown affected 401,216 workers in the plants of thirty-seven basic steel producers and their subsidiaries. It also halted mining of iron ore by 12,117 miners in the Mesabi range of northern Minnesota. The other workers involved were scattered over a score of allied industries.

No Hope for Week-End

Hope for bringing the strike to an end over the week-end vanished when Federal conciliators, who spent all day yesterday in conference with negotiators for Mr. Murray's union and the United States Steel Corporation, decided to return to Washington while both sides did "some soul-searching."

William N. Margolis, assistant director of the Federal Mediation and Conciliation Service, and Peter Seitz, its general counsel, reported that they had never encountered a situation in which the parties were "so adamant and yet so affable." They expressed the hope that the company and the union would seek to work out their differences "in their own interest and in the interest of the nation."

Before the mediators withdrew, Cyrus S. Ching, director of the service, talked by long-distance telephone with union and management representatives. He instructed members of his staff assigned to major steel companies to return to the capital for discussion of the Government's next moves.

The strike cut off virtually all the country's output of steel. Only a handful of plants—some nonunion and some having continuing contracts with the union—remained in production. The daily wage loss to the workers will run to $6,500,000 a day. No accurate estimate of the potential loss to industry was obtainable.

Each Accuses the Other

The gulf between the union and the companies was reflected in the telegrams sent by Mr. Murray and in a comment issued immediately afterward by Benjamin F. Fairless, president of United States Steel.

Mr. Murray charged that the steel industry had "forced" the strike upon the union and the American people by "stubbornly and obstinately" refusing to accept the recommendations of President Truman's Steel Fact-Finding Board for employer-financed pensions and social insurance. He accused the companies of proceeding in "complete disregard of the national interest."

Mr. Fairless retorted that the strike call was attributable solely to the union's insistence that the recommendations of the Truman panel be considered "equivalent to those of a compulsory arbitration tribunal," despite the President's advance assurance that neither side would be bound by the board's findings. He accused the union of demanding that the company

Continued on Page 3, Column 1

McMahon Clears Lilienthal; Proposed Report Stirs Row

By JOHN D. MORRIS
Special to The New York Times.

WASHINGTON, Sept. 30—Circulation of a proposed report clearing David E. Lilienthal of accusations of "incredible mismanagement" as chairman of the Atomic Energy Commission stirred a harsh controversy today in the Joint Congressional Committee on Atomic Energy.

The confidential draft, distributed among committee members by the chairman, Senator Brien McMahon, Democrat, of Connecticut, stated that the country's atomic program was in good hands and in excellent shape despite some mistakes in administration. The importance of security by achievement, distinguished from security by concealment, was emphasized.

The proposed report was drawn up by the staff of the joint committee under the direction of Senator McMahon in consultation with Representative Carl T. Durham, Democrat, of North Carolina, the committee's vice chairman.

Its distribution, in printed galley-proof form, was immediately protested by Senator William F. Knowland, Republican, of California, in a letter to Mr. McMahon. The Californian said that it should have been first discussed with other committee members.

"It is my first experience in six years of service in the State Legislature and four years in the United States Senate when a report of this nature has been prepared and put into type without any prior consultation or discussion with the committee membership," he wrote. "The members of the joint committee and not the staff must make the decisions."

Mr. McMahon stated in reply that the proposed report was printed "not with any idea of finalizing it or to put it beyond your crit-

Continued on Page 4, Column 5

NAMED 'SCIENTIST X,' HE DENIES CHARGE

Dr. J. W. Weinberg of University of Minnesota Is Accused by House Committee

By The Associated Press.

WASHINGTON, Sept. 30—Ending a year-old mystery, the House Un-American Activities Committee today named a young Midwest university professor as the "Scientist X" it accused of giving wartime atomic secrets to a man it called a Communist spy.

The committee said that "Scientist X" was Dr. Joseph W. Weinberg of the University of Minnesota and formally recommended that the Justice Department prosecute him on perjury charges.

Dr. Weinberg promptly denied the accusation, saying it was a case of "mistaken identity."

The Justice Department said the Federal Bureau of Investigation had been investigating Dr. Weinberg "for a long period of time."

In Minneapolis, Dr. Weinberg, 32-year-old Assistant Professor of Physics, said:

"I am innocent. At no time have I participated in any way in disclosure of any secret or classified information or formula to any unauthorized person."

The young scientist also took a

Continued on Page 4, Column 6

World News Summarized

SATURDAY, OCTOBER 1, 1949

The 500,000 members of the United Steelworkers of America, CIO, were ordered out on strike by their leaders last night. An eleventh-hour conference of union and company representatives called by Federal mediators in a desperate effort to avert a nation-wide steel strike collapsed. Union and company representatives blamed each other for the strike. [1:8.] The White House said President Truman did not plan further intervention in the dispute. [1:6-7.]

About 102,000 of the 480,000 coal miners now on strike were ordered back to work Monday by union officials. The orders will affect 80,000 miners in the anthracite fields and 22,000 in bituminous fields west of the Mississippi River. However, no break in the deadlocked negotiations with the soft-coal producers over pension and welfare funds was indicated. [1:5.]

The news of the steel strike broke as the nation's economy appeared to be taking a more hopeful turn with unemployment falling. The Census Bureau reported that unemployment dropped from 3,689,000 in August to 3,351,000 in September for the second successive monthly decline. [1:6-7.]

The Senate approved two bills that authorize an estimated $150,000,000 in annual pay increases to 855,000 classified Federal employes and an additional $61,000,000 to 500,000 postal employes. [1:2.]

The House Un-American Activities Committee named a faculty member of the University of Minnesota as the "Scientist X" who allegedly had given atomic secrets to a man described as a Communist spy. The accused denied the charge. [1:7.]

The Joint Congressional Committee on Atomic Energy was stirred to controversy when it received a confidential draft of a proposed report to clear Chairman David E. Lilienthal of the United States Atomic Energy Commission of charges of "incredible mismanagement." [1:6-7.]

Immediate independence for Libya was urged in a resolution introduced by the Soviet Union before the Political and Security Committee of the United Nations General Assembly, which opened debate on disposition of the former Italian colonies. The Russian proposal also called for the evacuation from Libya within three months of all military personnel and equipment. The United States and Britain also favored Libyan independence, but not for at least three years. [1:1.]

Nationalist China's request for an early hearing on her charges that the Soviet Union had been aiding the Chinese Communists was also considered by the Political and Security Committee. The committee decided to defer the request to fifth place on its agenda. [4:1.]

In China, the Communists at the final session of the Political Consultative Conference in Peiping elected their leader, Mao Tze-tung, chairman of their new Central Government. [1:2-3.]

Washington rejected proposals for use of naval aid to free three United States freighters being detained off Shanghai by the Chinese Nationalists. [4:4.]

Quickly following Russia's example, Hungary and Poland denounced their treaties of friendship and mutual assistance with Yugoslavia. Poland ordered eight Yugoslav diplomats to leave Warsaw. [1:4.]

The historic airlift operations that began June 26, 1948, to supply blockaded Berlin ended with their 277,264th flight. [7:7.]

Index to other news appears on Page 14.

Unemployment Cut Second Month; Sawyer Hails Sign of Trade Gains

Special to The New York Times.

WASHINGTON, Sept. 30—Unemployment declined from 3,689,000 in August to 3,351,000 in September, according to the latest Census Bureau figures released today. This was the second successive decline in monthly unemployment figures.

Total civilian employment also dropped in the week ended Sept. 10, it was stated. The latest employment figure was placed at 59,411,000, about half a million lower than that in August.

The simultaneous decline in employment and unemployment was attributed chiefly to the return to school of many summer workers and was smaller than that seasonally expected, said Charles Sawyer, the Secretary of Commerce.

Secretary Sawyer said that the September labor force report was gratifying as "it further bolsters accumulating evidence that general business conditions are improving."

While unemployment figures dropped appreciably in August they still remained nearly double the 1,899,000 reported in September, 1948.

The number of workers in civilian jobs in August was estimated at 59,947,000, against 60,312,000 in September, 1948.

Agricultural employment fell to 8,158,000 in the week ended Sept. 10 from 8,507,000 in the week ended Aug. 13. According to reports the cotton and tobacco crops were slow in maturing this year. As a result the usual heavy demand for workers for the harvest season had not as yet developed to the customary extent by the September survey week.

The New York Times

PAGE ONE

1950-1959

"All the News That's Fit to Print"

The New York Times.

LATE CITY EDITION
Cloudy, mild today and tomorrow, followed by clearing and colder.
Temperature Range Today—Max., 50; Min., 34
Temperature Yesterday—Max., 40; Min., 34
Full U. S. Weather Bureau Report, Page 79

Section 1

NEWS INDEX, PAGE 79, THIS SECTION

VOL. XCIX..No. 33,601. Entered as Second-Class Matter. Postoffice, New York, N. Y. NEW YORK, SUNDAY, JANUARY 22, 1950. Including Magazine and Book Review. FIFTEEN CENTS

HISS GUILTY ON BOTH PERJURY COUNTS; BETRAYAL OF U. S. SECRETS IS AFFIRMED; SENTENCE WEDNESDAY; LIMIT 10 YEARS

TRUMAN, ACHESON DEMAND CONGRESS VOTE AID TO KOREA

Rayburn Says Bill Will Come to Floor Again, and It Is 'Going to Be Passed'

SPEEDY ACTION IS SOUGHT

Secretary of State Expresses 'Concern and Dismay'—Sees Threat to U. S. Policy

By JOHN D. MORRIS
Special to THE NEW YORK TIMES.

WASHINGTON, Jan. 21—President Truman today deplored the House of Representatives rejection of the Korean aid bill, and called for "speedy rectification."

In a statement released by the White House along with a letter in which Dean Acheson, Secretary of State, expressed "concern and dismay" over the development, the President said he would take up the matter with Congressional leaders and urge immediate action.

Even before he spoke out, however, Speaker Sam Rayburn told reporters that a bill would be brought to the floor again, and "the House is going to pass it."

The measure authorizing $60,000,000 of appropriations to continue the $120,000,000 economic aid program for the infant Korean Republic, was killed in the House Thursday by a surprise vote of 193 to 191. The Senate had passed a separate bill last year.

"Important Foreign Policy"

President Truman called for early reversal of the House action "in order that important foreign-policy interests of this country may be properly safeguarded."

He expressed his entire concurrence in the views expressed by Mr. Acheson in a letter to the President dated yesterday.

The Secretary said the House action, if not quickly repaired, would have "the most far-reaching adverse effects upon our foreign policy, not only in Korea but in many other areas of the world" where "our encouragement is a major element in the struggle for freedom."

Mr. Acheson said our conduct in Korea was regarded by the world "as a measure of the seriousness of our concern with the freedom and welfare of peoples maintaining their independence in the face of great obstacles."

He suggested that failure to provide further aid would imperil Korea's survival as a free nation and be "disastrous" for this country's foreign policy.

Dr. John Myun Chang, the Korean Ambassador, said tonight he was gratified and "very much encouraged" by the Truman and Acheson statements.

The envoy expressed "deep gratitude" for the statements and added the hope that the United States could find a way to continue aid to Korea, which, he said, is "absolutely essential to the recovery of its domestic economy."

Parley on Another Vote

Congressional leaders have already conferred with Mr. Acheson and other State Department officials on the question of obtaining another House vote on the question.

They are now seeking to determine the best way of doing so. To bring the defeated measure up for reconsideration would require a two-thirds majority vote. Consequently, it is believed that some other method must be found.

The prevailing view appeared to be that the quickest way would be to take the Senate-approved Korean aid bill to the House floor. It would have to be reported first by the Foreign Affairs Committee, after being amended there to conform with the House bill.

Speaker Rayburn, indicating that he favored this method, said an attempt could then be made to obtain Rules Committee clearance and, if this failed, the measure could be called up under the "by-passing" procedure that the House retained yesterday.

Senator Tom Connally, Democrat, of Texas, chairman of the Senate Foreign Relations Committee, voiced his readiness to help with the problem, if necessary, by putting through a bill linking Korean aid with continuation of the authority to provide economic assistance to Nationalist China.

He said this might be done by revising a bill sponsored by Senators H. Alexander Smith of New Jersey and William F. Knowland of California, Republicans, now pend-

Continued on Page 4, Column 1

The New York Times Five Cents Tomorrow

Because of continued increasing costs in all phases of the operation of this newspaper, the newsstand price of THE NEW YORK TIMES *on weekdays in New York City will be five cents beginning tomorrow. The new price of* THE TIMES *will be the same as that of other standard-sized newspapers in New York and generally throughout the country.*

FULL ASIA VICTORY IS SEEN IN MOSCOW

Lenin Memorial Orator Says Capitalism Cannot Halt the Revolutionary Movement

By HARRISON E. SALISBURY
Special to THE NEW YORK TIMES.

MOSCOW, Jan. 21—Top figures of the Soviet Government and the Communist party were told tonight that capitalism and imperialism were no longer capable of halting the mass revolutionary movement of millions of Asiatic peoples inspired by successes of communism in China and the Soviet Union.

This analysis of the contemporary situation in Asia was placed before leaders of the Soviet Union and Chinese Communist chiefs at the important annual memorial meeting held at the Bolshoi Theatre on the anniversary of Lenin's death twenty-six years ago.

The Lenin memorial oration is one of the year's most important Communist party declarations. Tonight as last year, it was given by P. N. Pospelov, editor of the party's newspaper Pravda.

[The Associated Press stated that among those reported present in the Bolshoi Theatre were Chinese Communist leader Mao Tse-tung and the regime's Premier and Foreign Minister, Chou En-lai. Mr. Mao received a special ovation at mention of his name by Mr. Pospelov.]

Chinese Leaders' Presence Cited

The leaders of the new Chinese Communist regime are in Moscow conferring upon the broadest kind of understandings with the Soviet leadership. Mr. Mao has been in Moscow for nearly five weeks. Last night he was joined by Mr. Chou, accompanied by a distinguished delegation including top figures in the new Northeast China Government established in Manchuria and most of the leading specialists of the new Chinese regime in trade, commerce and industry.

Mr. Pospelov's analysis of the revolutionary successes and possibilities in Asia was coupled with the sharpest denunciation of United States imperialists and a frank prediction that "capitalism will unavoidably be replaced by socialism."

The success of Communist construction in the Soviet Union, he declared, has become "an example for the people's democracies of Europe and Asia."

"The great victory of the Chinese people already has proved that imperialism is incapable of suppressing the forces of the people, that this struggle awakens and attracts into the struggle millions of toilers," he said. "The great teaching of Leninism shows the people of all countries the road of the fight against the unheard of calamities of imperialism, shows the road of liberation from the yoke of imperialism, the road to a new Socialist life."

He declared that the United

Continued on Page 5, Column 1

Bonn Halts French Trade Talks After Clash Over Policy on Saar

By HAROLD CALLENDER
Special to THE NEW YORK TIMES.

PARIS, Jan. 21—A diplomatic crisis between France and Western Germany developed suddenly today when the French learned that, after challenging France's policy in the Saar, the Bonn regime had suspended negotiations for the trade treaty with France that was to have been signed a week ago.

French officials were angered by these German actions, which they considered as endangering the faint beginnings of a French-German rapprochement in the field of economic relations.

[In Bonn, it was reported that Chancellor Konrad Adenauer, in a parting conference with High Commissioner John J. McCloy, had proposed the creation of an international statute for the Saar that would be similar to the Ruhr statute now in force.]

When asked by the French Foreign Office for an explanation of their suspension of the negotiations, Bonn officials replied that they did not mean to go back on the trade pact but they must postpone its signature because of internal difficulties raised by German farmers and because of "the positions taken on the Saar question."

French officials said this reply surprised them because they considered the treaty would contribute to development of intra-European trade and desired to sign it as soon as possible.

This move by Bonn was regarded here as a maneuver to force reconsideration of the status of the Saar. Such was considered the purpose likewise of the statement that Dr. Konrad Adenauer, Chancellor

Continued on Page 3, Column 5

BERLIN RAIL OFFICE IS RETURNED BY U. S. TO EAST GERMANS

Commandant Says He Yielded to Avoid New Hardships in the Western Sectors

HITS SOVIET 'PROVOCATION'

Difficulties Following Seizure Outweighed the Gain of 600 Rooms, He Asserts

Special to THE NEW YORK TIMES

BERLIN, Jan. 21—Maj. Gen. Maxwell D. Taylor, United States Commandant in Berlin, this afternoon ordered the State Railway Administration building in the American sector restored to East German custody. Western sector police were withdrawn at 5 o'clock.

At a press conference called simultaneously with the release of the building, General Taylor made it clear that the basis of his action was the reprisals already taken against the population of the Western sectors and the threats of further hardships through non-payment of wages to railway employes living in those sectors.

Confiscation of the Reichsbahn structure had been ordered, General Taylor said, as part of a program to obtain the maximum use of office and housing space in the United States sector of this badly damaged city; only forty of its 600 rooms had been used recently.

"Far from sympathizing with this purpose," his prepared statement said, "the Soviet authorities have seized upon the affair as an excuse to harass the residents of West Berlin, to threaten fresh reprisals against Reichsbahn workers and generally to disturb the peace of the city. They have not attempted to conceal their intention to discharge additional railway workers, and threaten to make further reductions in their West mark salary payments.

Claim Termed Absurd

"On Jan. 20, representatives of the Berlin press were given a tour of the Reichsbahndirektion building, where they verified the absurdity of the claim that the communications of the Reichsbahn were being interfered with. They found the usual communications personnel on the job, coming and going in the same way as during the Reichsbahn occupation. Furthermore, they verified the extent of the building space standing vacant.

"It was the American intention to put this space to use for the benefit of Berlin. Unfortunately, the unreasonable and provocative attitude of the Soviets and of the Reichsbahn makes it appear probable that the hardships which they intend to impose outweigh the benefits arising from the American plan.

"Having regretfully reached this conclusion, I am suspending the notice of custody and withdrawing the West sector police from the interior of the building.

"We now know the facts about it and shall watch to see whether the Reichsbahn puts it to a remunerative use in providing transportation service to the city.

"If our action accomplishes this, it will have served its purpose."

Obviously taken by surprise, Communist propaganda agencies were unprecedentedly brief in their comment tonight on General Taylor's move. The Soviet-controlled Radio Berlin said that the United States had succumbed to "thousands of protests by workers."

Continued on Page 12, Column 3

CHURCHILL WARNS OF SOCIALIST DRIFT, ASKS END TO CURBS

Defines Big Election Issue as More Regimentation or a Return to Freedom

LABOR CLAIMS FLOUTED

Conservative Leader Credits Full Employment to Loans From U. S. and Dominions

By RAYMOND DANIELL
Special to THE NEW YORK TIMES

LONDON, Jan. 21—Striking the first blow for the Conservatives in the election campaign, Winston Churchill called upon the nation's voters to set Britain free of Socialist controls and restrictions.

"The main reason why we are unable to earn our own living and make our way in the world is because we are not allowed to do so," he declared in a radio speech from his home at Westerham in Kent.

The former Prime Minister's radio address was described as a "political" but not an "election" speech. The fact is that the campaign does not officially begin until Feb. 3 when Parliament is dissolved.

As the first step toward its dissolution, taken in the orderly process of British electoral machinery, King George VI issued a proclamation today postponing the next meeting of Parliament until after Jan. 24, the date on which it had been called to reconvene. This means that this Parliament, elected in 1945, will not meet again.

It was a good Churchillian speech, which "pinked" the Laborites where it hurt, on spending, housing and the high cost of living, but possibly because of the high standard of oratorical leadership that the wartime leader had set, it fell a little flat on British ears.

The first five persons this correspondent talked to after its delivery found it "disappointing." But Mr. Churchill was under the handicap of sounding a keynote for his party before his party has made known its election program. That will be issued in the coming week.

It would have been a tactical blunder for him to anticipate any surprises that this Conservative manifesto will contain. So his address to the electorate tonight was necessarily primarily a critique rather than a statement of policy, but he did manage to get across the idea that between the Laborites and the Conservatives there is no dispute about the virtue of a country's whole labor force being usefully employed.

The choice before the people on

Continued on Page 30, Column 1

PRINCIPAL FIGURES IN THE HISS PERJURY TRIAL

Alger Hiss leaving Federal Building.

Mrs. Ada Condell, foreman of the jury.

Judge Henry W. Goddard, who presided. The New York Times

JURY OUT 24 HOURS

Verdict Follows a Call on Judge to Restate Rulings on Evidence

CHAMBERS STORY UPHELD

Defendant Is Impassive—His Counsel Announces That an Appeal Will Be Taken

By WILLIAM R. CONKLIN

Alger Hiss, a highly regarded State Department official for ten of his forty-five years, was found guilty on two counts of perjury by a Federal jury of eight women and four men yesterday.

Nearly twenty-four hours after receiving the case, the jury reported its verdict at 2:50 P. M. The middle-aged jurors had begun their deliberations at 3:10 P. M. on Friday after ten weeks of testimony in the second perjury trial.

By convicting Hiss on both counts, the jury found that he had betrayed his trust by passing secret State Department documents to Whittaker Chambers. The former courier for a Communist spy ring was the Government's key witness against the former official. The verdict meant that the jury believed Mr. Chambers and the corroborating evidence produced by the Government.

The convicted defendant faces maximum penalties of five years' imprisonment and a $2,000 fine on each count, a combined total of ten years and $4,000. Federal Judge Henry W. Goddard continued his bail at $5,000 and set Wednesday at 10:30 A. M. for sentencing. Sentence will be passed in the same thirteenth floor courtroom of the United States District Court where Hiss was tried.

Lapsing of Espionage Charge

The case of "The United States of America versus Alger Hiss" rested on a two-count perjury indictment. Thomas F. Murphy, Government prosecutor, had taxed Mr. Hiss with treason and espionage against his country. However, any possible prosecution for espionage had been ruled out by a three-year statute of limitations, which conferred immunity after March, 1941.

Hiss was thus brought to trial on one count of perjury for denying that he ever gave secret documents to Mr. Chambers. The second count charged perjury for denying that he had seen the ex-Communist after Jan. 1, 1937. The Government contended that the documents were passed in February and March, 1938.

By its verdict the jury upheld the Government's contention that Priscilla Hiss, 46-year-old wife of the defendant, had typed copies of the documents for Mr. Chambers on the Hisses' Woodstock typewriter.

Mr. Chambers had told the jury that he had been a paid functionary of the Communist party in Washington and had collected secret information for Russia from 1935 to April, 1938.

Basis Laid for Appeal

Claude B. Cross and Edward C. McLean, defense attorneys, would not say at first whether they would appeal the verdict. They had established a basis for an appeal by taking exception to a part of the charge of Judge Henry W. Goddard.

"There won't be any statement," Mr. McLean said. "I do not wish to discuss the possibility of an appeal now. There is just no statement." But later Mr. Cross said that "you can be sure the verdict will be appealed."

After the jury had convicted on both counts, Mr. Murphy asked that Hiss' bail of $5,000 be increased in conformity with the custom for "all convicted defendants." After Mr. Cross protested, Judge Goddard permitted Hiss to remain at liberty under the same bail. Mr. Cross said he would make some motions on Wednesday, the day set for sentencing.

Should defense attorneys file an appeal, it would act as an automatic stay of sentence. If an appeal should reach the United States

Continued on Page 58, Column 7

EARLY 'RIGHTS' VOTE APPEARS UNLIKELY

Items of 'Unfinished Business' May Get Precedence Despite House Action on Rules

Special to THE NEW YORK TIMES.

WASHINGTON, Jan. 21—Chances for consideration by the House of Representatives on Monday of the Administration's bill to establish a Federal Fair Employment Practices code were evaluated as practically nil at the Capitol today. Some proponents of the legislation had hoped a vote on it might be taken on that day.

Being the fourth Monday in the month, it will be in order for chairmen of committees that have favorably-reported bills pending before the Rules Committee for more than twenty-one days to move on the floor to proceed to their consideration. Such discharge motions

Continued on Page 37, Column 3

Senate to Sift R. F. C. Loans With View to Writing Curbs

By H. WALTON CLOKE
Special to THE NEW YORK TIMES.

WASHINGTON, Jan. 21—The stage has been set for a full-scale Congressional investigation of the lending policy of the billion-dollar Reconstruction Finance Corporation. As a result of the inquiry, Congress is expected to set forth, once and for all, the terms on which it wants the RFC's lending operations to function.

Irritated by recent big loans that the RFC granted to several corporations, as well as some that were made in the earlier days of the agency, members on both sides of the aisle in Congress have been demanding a clarification of policy.

Leading this group is Senator J. William Fulbright, Democrat, of Arkansas, who recently lost a battle with the RFC over a loan to the Kaiser-Frazer Corporation.

The Senator, who has not forgotten the rather sharp rebuff, has started the wheels of Congressional investigation turning. On Tuesday he will ask the Senate Banking and Currency Committee, headed by Senator Burnet R. Maybank, Democrat, of South Carolina, to inquire into the RFC's action in granting the following loans:

Kaiser-Frazer Corporation	$44,000,000
Northwest Air Lines	12,000,000
Waltham Watch Co.	6,000,000
Texmass Petroleum Co.	15,100,000

Financial observers here foresee nothing that would block the Senator's request for action. As head of the Senate Banking and Currency subcommittee on the RFC, he conducted a three-day inquiry into the loan policy of the agency last summer. It was at that time that the Senator questioned the wisdom of advancing additional funds to the Lustron Corporation, Columbus, Ohio, which is now in default on $37,500,000 of RFC loans.

Once the full committee ap-

Continued on Page 43, Column 3

MAYOR RIDICULES IDEA OF RESIGNING

Telephones From Florida That He Is Getting Rid of Virus and Will Return to Job

By JAMES A. HAGERTY

In a telephone message to THE NEW YORK TIMES from Key Largo, Fla., Mayor O'Dwyer declared yesterday that he had no intention of resigning.

In his telephone conversation, the Mayor appeared to be hearty of voice and very cheerful. Questioned about a report that he contemplated retirement, he said:

"It is utterly ridiculous. It touches my sense of humor."

The Mayor then laughed heartily and continued:

"I am down here to get the virus out of my system. I am going to stay till I've got it licked and I think I am well on the way to doing that. I feel much better. I want to get completely well so that I can return to the city and stay at my desk in City Hall to work uninterruptedly on my program."

The Mayor said that Dr. Edward M. Bernecker, who left Newark Airport by plane on Friday, had not arrived but was expected to reach Key Largo today. It is understood that he will have a series of talks with the Mayor and that

Continued on Page 37, Column 4

World News Summarized

SUNDAY, JANUARY 22, 1950

The jury of eight women and four men in the Alger Hiss trial yesterday found the former State Department official guilty of perjury on two counts. The jury reached this verdict nearly twenty-four hours after receiving the case and its decision meant that it had accepted the testimony of Whittaker Chambers, confessed former spy, over the denials by Mr. Hiss of having passed secret documents to Mr. Chambers. Federal Judge Goddard will pass sentence Wednesday. [1:8.]

Mayor O'Dwyer characterized as "utterly ridiculous" rumors that he might resign his office because of ill health. [1:7.]

Although some supporters of the Truman Administration's Federal Fair Employment Practices code had hoped that the House might vote on it tomorrow, there was little likelihood the measure would get to the House floor by that time. [1:5.]

Congress planned a sweeping inquiry into the lending policy of the Reconstruction Finance Corporation as a preliminary to fixing the terms on which the organization's lending may operate in the future. [1:6-7.]

President Truman urged "speedy rectification" in the House of its rejection by a narrow margin of the bill providing $60,000,000 for aid to Korea. Secretary of State Acheson asserted that failure to assist Korea would jeopardize her survival as a free nation. [1:1.]

The journey to Moscow of Communist China's Foreign Minister, Chou En-lai, was seen as an indication that the negotiations between the Chinese Communists and the Soviet Union had reached the decisive stage. Peiping vigorously denied Russia was "detaching" four north China areas as charged by Mr. Acheson. [7:1.]

The annual Lenin memorial meeting in Moscow was told that the mass revolutionary movement in Asia could not be stopped by capitalism. [1:2.]

Winston Churchill set the keynote for the campaign of the Conservative party for next month's general election by telling British voters that the "main reason why we are unable to earn our own living and make our way in the world is because we are not allowed to do so." Mr. Churchill said the choice was to regain freedom or plunge the nation deeper into socialism. [1:4.]

General Taylor, the United States commander in Berlin, ordered the seized Railway Administration building in the United States sector restored to East German custody. [1:3.]

Franco-German rapprochement was seen jeopardized as the result of an announcement by the West German republic that it was suspending trade talks with France. German officials cited France's attitude over the Saar as a reason for the suspension [1:2-3] and proposed an international Saar statute similar to that in the Ruhr. [3:1.]

The Allied High Commission, in a move intended as a public censure of the Bonn regime for "impudent" behavior, will demand that the Germans withdraw their announcement that gas rationing would end the end of this month. [2:3.]

Finland virtually rejected Moscow's demand that she extradite 300 "war criminals" who are said by the Russians to have found refuge among the Finns. [24:2.]

350,000,000-Gallon Water Loss In 24 Hours Largest Since Dec. 12

By PAUL CROWELL

The city's water storage reservoirs suffered a loss of 350,000,000 gallons in the twenty-four hours ended at 8 A. M. yesterday.

It was the first storage loss since Dec. 26 and the largest since Dec. 12. Officials of the Department of Water Supply, Gas and Electricity attributed the loss to a slightly increased consumption of water, coupled with the absence of appreciable rain or snowfall in the up-state watershed areas.

The city's reservoirs lost 103,000,000 gallons in the twenty-four hours ended at 8 A. M. on Dec. 27. In the twenty-four hours ended at 8 A. M. on Dec. 12 the storage loss was 693,000,000 gallons.

The reversal of the upward trend of water storage gave city officials serious concern and boosted to 1,121,000,000 gallons the aver-

Continued on Page 67, Column 1

The Water Situation

The following figures as of 8 A. M. yesterday give the number of gallons of water in the city's reservoirs. The difference in the two days is the net after intake and the day's consumption:

Friday	106,662,000,000
Yesterday	106,312,000,000
Net loss	350,000,000
Average daily storage gain needed to fill reservoirs by June 1	1,121,000,000
Watershed snowfall:	
Schoharie	.02 inch
Esopus	.04 inch
Croton	.02 inch

At present consumption there remains about ninety days' supply before pressure fails.

Catskill and Croton reservoirs at capacity hold 283,136,000,000 gallons.

"All the News That's Fit to Print"

The New York Times.

LATE CITY EDITION
A little rain and cold today. Cloudy, continued cold tomorrow.
Temperature Range Today—Max.,35; Min.,31
Temperature Yesterday—Max.,37; Min.,32
Full U. S. Weather Bureau Report, Page 55

VOL. XCIX...No. 33,611. Entered as Second-Class Matter. Postoffice, New York, N. Y.

NEW YORK, WEDNESDAY, FEBRUARY 1, 1950.

Times Square, New York 18, N. Y. Telephone Lackawanna 4-1000

RAG PAPER EDITION
SEVENTY-FIVE CENTS

TRUMAN ORDERS HYDROGEN BOMB BUILT FOR SECURITY PENDING AN ATOMIC PACT; CONGRESS HAILS STEP; BOARD BEGINS JOB

PRESIDENT SEEKS 70-DAY COAL TRUCE, FACT-FINDING BOARD

He Ignores Taft Law in Asking 5-Day Week at Old Wages Pending Study of Dispute

AVOIDS WORD 'EMERGENCY'

Operator Acceptance Is Seen Likely, but the Plan Holds Disadvantages for Lewis

Text of announcement by White House on coal, Page 22.

By JOSEPH A. LOFTUS
Special to The New York Times.

WASHINGTON, Jan. 31—President Truman moved into the soft coal dispute today with a proposal that John L. Lewis and the operators call a seventy-day truce and submit their arguments to a fact-finding board. He asked for an answer by 5 P. M. Saturday.

Under the truce "normal" production of coal would be resumed. This was understood to mean a return to the five-day work week by the members of the United Mine Workers, headed by Mr. Lewis. The wage scale of the expired union contract would be paid. A board of three would make recommendations in sixty days, but the recommendations would not be binding.

President Truman thus used the approach he used in the steel dispute last summer. This avoids use of the Taft-Hartley Law and its injunctive authority, although the President said in November that if he acted in the coal case he would use that law.

"Grave Concern" Voiced

The President's message to Mr. Lewis and the operators spoke of the "grave concern" about the dispute, but avoided Taft-Hartley words, such as "emergency" and "health and safety."

The dispute in the anthracite industry was omitted from the proposal.

The President said that in the final analysis the parties themselves must write their own agreement. "Voluntary action, not compulsion, in these matters is not only my personal conviction but the national policy," he declared.

Aware that the miners and operators were to meet at 2 P. M. tomorrow to try bargaining again, the President said he did not want to interfere with that. He told them that if they could reach an agreement to resume full production next Monday they should disregard his proposal and let him know about it by noon Saturday.

Mr. Lewis' attorneys are due in court at 10 A. M. tomorrow to answer a petition for an injunction filed by Robert N. Denham, general counsel of the National Labor Relations Board. Mr. Lewis and the other officers of the union filed affidavits in the case today. They denied violating the Taft-Hartley Law in the coal negotiations which began last May and accused the operators of refusing to bargain.

Surmise on Board Make-Up

The make-up of the fact-finding board, if the President's truce proposal goes into effect, is a matter of conjecture. When the proposal was under consideration at the White House in November the three men who had been asked if they were available were David L. Cole, who was a member of the fact-finding steel panel; John Dunlop, Harvard economics professor, and Willard Wirtz of Northwestern University, former chairman of the National Wage Stabilization Board.

Neither side would say tonight

Continued on Page 22, Column 2

Melchior Threatens To Quit Opera Here

Lauritz Melchior stepped into the Metropolitan Opera dispute last night by saying that he would not return next season "unless indicated plans change materially." He would make no comment on the possible return of Kirsten Flagstad, but, like Helen Traubel, he indicated resentment at not being approached sooner by Rudolf Bing, who will be the general manager for 1950-1951.

"I would have assumed," Mr. Melchior said, "that the natural courtesy of the management for the Metropolitan would dictate a call to any leading artist who had appeared regularly with the company for twenty-four years to determine his position with

Continued on Page 24, Column 2

By Winston Churchill: *The Second World War*

Volume III—The Grand Alliance

Book I—Germany Drives East

INSTALLMENT 6:

THE JAPANESE ENVOY

THE New Year had brought disturbing news from the Far East. The Japanese Navy was increasingly active off the coasts of Southern Indo-China. Japanese warships were reported in Saigon harbour and the Gulf of Siam. On January 31 the Japanese Government negotiated an armistice between the Vichy French and Siam. Rumours spread that this settlement of a frontier dispute in South-east Asia was to be the prelude to the entry of Japan into the war. The Germans were at the same time bringing increased pressure to bear upon Japan to attack the British at Singapore.

• • •

About this time several telegrams arrived from our Commander-in-Chief in the Far East urging the reinforcement of Hong Kong. I did not agree with his views.

Prime Minister to General Ismay 7 Jan 41

This is all wrong. If Japan goes to war with us there is not the slightest chance of holding Hong Kong or relieving it. It is most unwise to increase the loss we shall suffer there. Instead of increasing the garrison it ought to be reduced to a symbolical scale. Any trouble arising there must be dealt with at the Peace Conference after the war. We must avoid frittering away our resources on untenable positions. Japan will think long before declaring war on the British Empire, and whether there are two or six battalions at Hong Kong will make no difference to her choice. I wish we had fewer troops there, but to move any would be noticeable and dangerous.

Later on it will be seen that I allowed myself to be drawn from this position, and that two Canadian battalions were sent as reinforcements.

• • •

IN the second week of February I became conscious of a stir and flutter in the Japanese Embassy and colony in London. They were evidently in a high state of excitement, and they chattered to one another with much indiscretion. In these days we kept our eyes and ears open. Various reports were laid before me which certainly gave the impression that they had received news from home which required them to pack up without a moment's delay. This agitation among people usually so reserved made me feel that a sudden act of war upon us by Japan might be imminent, and I thought it well to impart my misgivings to the President.

Former Naval Person to President Roosevelt 15 Feb 41

Many drifting straws seem to indicate Japanese intention to make war on us or do something that would force us to make war on them in the next few weeks or months. I am not myself convinced that this is not a war of nerves designed to cover Japanese encroachments in Siam and Indo-China. However, I think I ought to let you know that the weight of the Japanese Navy, if thrown against us, would confront us with situations beyond the scope of our naval resources. I do not myself think that the Japanese would be likely to send the large military expedition necessary to lay siege to Singapore. The Japanese would no doubt occupy whatever strategic points and oilfields in the Dutch East Indies and thereabouts they covet, and thus get into a far better position for a full-scale attack on Singapore later on. They would also raid Australian and New Zealand ports and coasts, causing deep anxiety in those Dominions, which have already sent all their best-trained fighting men to the Middle East. But the attack which I fear the most would be by raiders, including possibly battle-cruisers, upon our trade routes and communications across the Pacific and Indian Oceans. We could by courting disaster elsewhere send a few strong ships into these vast waters, but all the trade would have to go into convoy and escorts would be few and far between. Not only would this be a most grievous additional restriction and derangement of our whole war economy, but it would bring altogether to an end all reinforcements of the armies we had planned to build up in the Middle East from Australasian and Indian sources. Any threat of a major invasion of Australia or New Zealand would of course force us to withdraw our Fleet from the Eastern Mediterranean, with disastrous military possibilities there, and the certainty that Turkey would have to make some accommodation, for reopening of the German trade and oil supplies from the Black Sea. You will therefore see, Mr. President, the awful enfeeblement of our war effort that would result merely from the sending out by Japan of her battle-cruisers and her twelve 8-inch-gun cruisers into the Eastern oceans, and still more from any serious invasion threat against the two Australasian democracies in the Southern Pacific.

Some believe that Japan in her present mood would not hesitate to court or attempt to wage war both against Great Britain and the United States. Personally I think the odds are definitely against that, but no one can tell. Everything that you can do to inspire the Japanese with the fear of a double war may avert the danger. If however they come in against us and we are alone, the grave character of the consequences cannot easily be overstated.

The agitation among the Japanese in London subsided as quickly as it had begun. Silence and Oriental decorum reigned once more.

Former Naval Person to President Roosevelt 20 Feb 41

I have better news about Japan. Apparently Matsuoka is visiting Berlin, Rome, and Moscow in the near future. This may well be a diplomatic sop to cover absence of action against Great Britain. If Japanese attack which seemed imminent is now postponed, this is largely due to fear of United States. The more these fears can be played upon the better, but I understand thoroughly your difficulties pending passage of [Lend-Lease] Bill on which our hopes depend. Appreciation given in my last Personal and Secret of naval consequences following Japanese aggression against Great Britain holds good in all circumstances.

• • •

Behind the complex political scene in Japan three decisions seem to emerge at this time. The first was to send the Foreign Secretary, Matsuoka, to Europe to find out for himself about the German mastery of Europe, and especially when the invasion of Britain was really going to begin. Were the British forces so far tied up in naval defence that Britain could not afford to reinforce her Eastern possessions if Japan attacked them? Although he had been educated in the United States, Matsuoka was bitterly anti-American. He was deeply impressed by the Nazi movement and the might of embattled Germany. He was under the Hitler

Continued on Page 31.

FRANCE PROTESTS SOVIET RECOGNITION OF HO CHI MINH RULE

Note to Russia Asserts Action Could 'Gravely Impair' Paris-Moscow Ties

U. S. AND BRITAIN INFORMED

Government of North Korea Announces Acceptance of Viet Nam Rebel Regime

By LANSING WARREN
Special to The New York Times.

PARIS, Jan. 31—France tonight delivered to the Soviet Embassy here a vigorous protest against Soviet recognition of Ho Chi Minh, the enemy of France in Indo-China. The note charged that the Soviet action was of a nature "gravely to impair French-Soviet relations."

In diplomatic circles here the Soviet Union's action was considered as a threat not only to the French position in Indo-China but as an effort to prevent the United States from building a policy of containment in Asia such as has been successful in Europe.

The text of the French note follows:

The French Government has learned through publication of a communiqué by the Tass Agency that the Government of the U.S.S.R. has taken the decision of recognizing as the Government of the Viet Nam the insurrectional government of Ho Chi Minh. Such a decision violates the principles of international law, since the only regular government of the Viet Nam is the government constituted by His Majesty Bao Dai, to whom the French Government has transferred the rights of sovereignty which it previously held.

In encouraging, as is the obvious intention of the Soviet Government, the insurrectional movement of Ho Chi Minh, this decision can only render more difficult the restoration of peace in Viet Nam. In taking the initiative which it has just announced, the Government of the U.S.S.R. is committing with regard to France an act whose character and consequences cannot be underestimated.

For all these reasons the French Government raises a solemn protest against a decision which is of a nature gravely to impair Franco-Soviet relations.

The note was delivered by Alexander Parodi, general secretary of the French Foreign Ministry, after Soviet Ambassador Alexandre Bogomolov, who was invited to the Quai d'Orsay, had replied he could not come today but would present himself tomorrow.

Copies of the French protest to

Continued on Page 11, Column 1

DISCUSSING PLANS FOR MAKING HYDROGEN BOMB

Members of the Joint Congressional Atomic Energy Committee talk with Sumner T. Pike, right, acting head of the Atomic Energy Commission, after President Truman gave his approval. Seated are Chairman Brien McMahon, Representatives Carl T. Durham, Chet Holifield and W. Sterling Cole. Standing are Senator John W. Bricker, Representatives Paul J. Kilday, Melvin Price, Carl Hinshaw and Charles H. Elston.

The New York Times (by George Tames)

HISTORIC DECISION

President Says He Must Defend Nation Against Possible Aggressor

SOVIET 'EXPLOSION' CITED

His Ruling Wins Bipartisan Support on Capitol Hill—No Fund Request Due Now

By ANTHONY LEVIERO
Special to The New York Times.

WASHINGTON, Jan. 31—President Truman announced today that he had ordered the Atomic Energy Commission to produce the hydrogen bomb.

The Chief Executive acted in his role of Commander in Chief of the Armed forces, ordering an improved weapon for national security. Thus, from the domestic standpoint, he removed the question of producing the super-weapon as an issue that might be argued on moral grounds.

As for international statecraft, Mr. Truman, by treating the hydrogen bomb as an addition to the American armory, also removed it as an issue that might be interpreted as an advanced threat or inducement in seeking international control of atomic weapons.

Nevertheless, Mr. Truman said that his perseverance in providing for national defense would be matched by his efforts to seek international control of atomic weapons.

New Phase of Atomic Age

In his announcement, Mr. Truman regarded the hydrogen bomb as a progressive outgrowth of United States production of the uranium-plutonium atomic bomb. He put it this way: the commission was "to continue its work on all forms of atomic weapons, including the so-called hydrogen or super-bomb."

His use of the word "continue" was understood to imply that with national security the over-riding consideration, the chief factor guiding his decision was whether it was practicable to make the weapon. Scientists have said that it is.

In effect, the President's decision, which won wide acclaim in Congress, marked the advent of a new phase of the atomic age and a surge ahead of Russia in the race to retain military ascendancy.

The bombs that visited destruction on Hiroshima and Nagasaki split the atom. The new bomb would fuse atoms instead, but with a power 100 to 1,000 times greater than the improved fission bombs that have been developed since the Japanese cities were struck.

The President's Statement

The President made his decision known in the following brief statement:

"It is part of my responsibility as Commander in Chief of the armed forces to see to it that our country is able to defend itself against any possible aggressor. Accordingly, I have directed the Atomic Energy Commission to continue its work on all forms of atomic weapons, including the so-called hydrogen or super-bomb.

Continued on Page 3, Column 2

STIKKER IS NAMED E. R. P. CONCILIATOR

Council in Paris Accepts Dutch Leader Supported by Britain —E. C. A. Goals Unmet

By HAROLD CALLENDER
Special to The New York Times.

PARIS, Jan. 31—Dr. Dirk U. Stikker, Foreign Minister of the Netherlands, was named today to the post of "political conciliator" of the European Marshall Plan Council instead of Paul-Henri Spaak, former Premier of Belgium, whose appointment was vetoed by the British Government. Paul G. Hoffman, Economic Cooperation Administrator, and W. Averell Harriman, ECA Ambassador in Europe, had desired that M. Spaak be chosen.

Dr. Stikker was elected by the Council. He was the candidate of the British who had first suggested Dr. Halvard M. Lange, Nor-

Continued on Page 14, Column 4

Truman Asks Utility Leader To Head Top Research Body

By JAMES RESTON
Special to The New York Times

WASHINGTON, Jan. 31—President Truman has offered the Government's top scientific job—chairmanship of the Research and Development Board in the Department of Defense—to William Webster of Boston, a vice president of the New England Electric System, it was learned today.

Mr. Webster, 49 years old, a graduate of the United States Naval Academy and former chairman of the Defense Department's Military Liaison Committee with the Atomic Energy Commission, would be largely responsible for preparing an integrated military research and development program so that weapons such as the new hydrogen bomb would take their proper place in a well-balanced defense policy.

The chairmanship of the Research and Development Board was held by Dr. Vannevar Bush from 1947 to 1948 and by Dr. Karl T. Compton, former president of Massachusetts Institute of Technology, from 1948 until Nov. 3, 1949. Since then the work of the board has been supervised by Dr. Robert F. Rinehart as deputy chairman.

Coincidental with his offer of the Government's principal scientific position to Mr. Webster, President Truman was reported to be working actively on selection of a successor to David E. Lilienthal as chairman of the Atomic Energy Commission. One person said to be under consideration is Carroll Wilson, present general manager of the AEC.

Mr. Lilienthal is reliably reported to have proposed that control of

Continued on Page 5, Column 3

IT'S A TRITON BOMB, MIGHTIEST POSSIBLE

Would Release Energy More Than Seven Times '45 Type —No Critical-Mass Limit

By WILLIAM L. LAURENCE

What President Truman referred to yesterday as "the so-called hydrogen bomb" is not a hydrogen bomb at all in the true scientific meaning of the term.

This, the most powerful superbomb that can be built on earth, it can now be revealed, actually is the triton bomb, in which the basic element used is tritium, a hydrogen isotope (twin) of atomic mass 3. It is an element hardly known to the public but well known to nuclear physicists. A triton is the nucleus of tritium, composed of one proton and two neutrons.

The term hydrogen, as used by scientists, refers strictly to the common form of hydrogen of atomic mass 1, a mass that cannot be made into a bomb.

While the process responsible for the vast amounts of energy released by the sun every second is

Continued on Page 4, Column 4

World News Summarized

WEDNESDAY, FEBRUARY 1, 1950

President Truman, acting in his capacity of Commander in Chief of the Armed Forces, yesterday directed the Atomic Energy Commission "to continue its work on all forms of atomic weapons, including the so-called hydrogen or super-bomb." The work, he said, would go forward "on a basis consistent with the over-all objectives of our program for peace and security" and "until a satisfactory plan for international control of atomic energy is achieved." [1:8.]

Congressional opinion heavily supported the President, and demands for speeding the work were made. The Atomic Energy Commission reported to Congress that atomic weapons now were being made by the "industrial type" of production and stockpiles were growing rapidly. [3:5.]

New defense safeguards were thrown about the atomic plants at Oak Ridge, Tenn., Los Alamos, N. M., and Hanford, Wash. Any plane approaching within 100 miles of the plants without prior identification and clearance will be intercepted by Air Force fighters. [1:8.]

The hydrogen bomb, it was disclosed, is really a triton bomb, the basic element of which is tritium, a hydrogen isotope. [1:7.]

William Webster has been asked to head the Research and Development Board of the Department of Defense as successor to Dr. Karl T. Compton, who resigned. [1:6-7.]

Dealing with the major domestic problem of coal, President Truman asked John L. Lewis and the operators to call a seventy-day truce and to submit the issues to a nonstatutory fact-finding board such as he had named in the steel dispute. The President asked for a full five-day week in the soft-coal mines during the truce. [1:1.] Leaders of more than 100,000 striking miners were divided over urging the men to return. Operators indicated an inclination to accept the plan. [22:5.]

This state paid $357,000,000 in jobless benefits last year, nearly twice the 1948 total, Albany reported. [21:1.]

A House committee reported, 17 to 1, a bill for economic aid to Korea and Nationalist China. [13:2.] The brutality of South Korean police was seen as a major problem of the Seoul Government. [13:4.]

France, in a strong note of protest, told Moscow that Soviet recognition of Ho Chi Minh in Indo-China "gravely" impaired French-Soviet relations. Washington called Moscow's action proof that the Ho regime was Communist. [1:4.]

Senator Connally said Britain's policy of extending her embargo on dollar oil to the Commonwealth was "an act of hostility to our economy." [15:2.]

Britain won a victory in the European Marshall Plan Council when Foreign Minister Stikker of the Netherlands was elected "political conciliator." [1:5.]

French Premier Bidault won five close votes of confidence on the budget. [14:3.]

This city's tentative realty value for tax purposes was set at $18,493,559,079. [1:6-7.]

Index to other news appears on Page 30.

City Realty Values Up for 6th Year; Assessment Total $18,493,559,079

By LEE E. COOPER

New York's taxable realty wealth has increased on the city's books for the sixth consecutive year, with the result that property owners are due to pay levies on the highest aggregate valuation in seventeen years, according to official figures made public yesterday.

In a report to Mayor O'Dwyer's office, William E. Boyland, president of the Tax Commission, set the total tentative assessed valuation of real estate in the five boroughs for 1950-51 at $18,493,559,079. This is $381,327,900 above the final valuation for 1949-50, which was $18,112,231,179.

The high mark in realty valuations here, including utility property and special franchises was reached in 1932, with $19,616,935,429.

The report showed a net rise for this year of $316,525,750 in "ordinary" real estate, to $16,120,113,875, and of $64,802,150 in the holdings of utility corporations, which were listed tentatively for the new tax year at $1,655,893,290.

Added to these sums was $717,551,914 for special franchises, the exact amount of which will not be set by the State Tax Commission for another month. The figure used by the city officials is based on the 1949-50 records.

Although no particular area was found by the field assessors to have increased generally in value—in contrast to last year when sharp gains were listed for the land around Stuyvesant Town and the United Nations site—there were three times as many rises as there were decreases in the city as a whole.

Largely for purposes of "equalization," to bring properties in line with neighboring valuations, in-

Continued on Page 20, Column 4

Air Defense Mapped For Atom Projects

By AUSTIN STEVENS
Special to The New York Times.

WASHINGTON, Jan. 31—The Air Force disclosed tonight that it planned to throw a protective aerial "wall" around key atomic installations of the country.

Under a plan worked out today at the Pentagon, the Air Force will insist on the positive identification of any airplane flying within 100 miles of three atomic plants and, failing to be advised of an aircraft's identity will send fighter planes aloft to observe its character and course.

The plan in effect is a revival of a wartime measure whereby in combat zones any aircraft picked up by radar or other means of detection was consid-

Continued on Page 3, Column 6

"All the News That's Fit to Print"

The New York Times.

LATE CITY EDITION
Drizzle and fog early today, fair later. Cloudy tomorrow.
Temperature Range Today—Max., 42; Min., 34
Temperature Yesterday—Max., 41; Min., 33
Full U. S. Weather Bureau Report, Page 51

Copyright, 1950, by The New York Times Company.

VOL. XCIX..No. 33,617. Entered as Second-Class Matter, Postoffice, New York, N. Y. NEW YORK, TUESDAY, FEBRUARY 7, 1950. Times Square, New York 18, N. Y. Telephone Lackawanna 4-1000 FIVE CENTS

TRUMAN INVOKES TAFT-HARTLEY ACT IN COAL STRIKE, NAMES FACT BOARD; 370,000 MINERS OUT, VOICING DEFIANCE

G. O. P. POSES ISSUE FOR '50 AS LIBERTY VERSUS SOCIALISM

FAIR DEAL IS TARGET

Republicans Want Cuts in Spending and Taxes, Revised Taft Law

BACK FOREIGN POLICY AID

But Hit Conduct of Program—Party Declaration Fails to Win United Support

Text of Republican party statement is printed on Page 20.

By W. H. LAWRENCE

Special to The New York Times.

WASHINGTON, Feb. 6—The Republican party policy makers today proclaimed "Liberty Against Socialism" to be the major domestic issue of the 1950 Congressional elections.

But the party failed to achieve complete unity, either in its denunciation of the Truman Administration's program at home and abroad, or on the alternatives which it promised.

In all-day separate and closed meetings members of the Republican National Committee and the House and Senate Republican conferences finally gave their approval to a "statement of principles and objectives" designed to serve as a national platform for the months between now and the November elections.

Party chieftains had hoped that the declaration would demonstrate party unity and purpose and bring a new flow of financial contributions to defray campaign expenses, but a group led by Senator Henry Cabot Lodge Jr. of Massachusetts, Senator Margaret Chase Smith of Maine, Representative Jacob K. Javits of New York and Representative James G. Fulton of Pennsylvania promptly made known its dissatisfaction.

"Fair Deal" Vigorously Opposed

As was to be expected, the party declaration approved by the majority was vigorous in its opposition to enactment of the most of the Fair Deal program put before Congress by President Truman.

On foreign policy questions it found a middle ground, advocating continuance of a bipartisan attitude but sharply criticizing the administration of foreign policy with particular reference to "secret agreements" made at Yalta and Potsdam "which have created new injustices and new dangers throughout the world."

An effort made by Werner Schroeder, Illinois national committeeman, to put the party on record as opposed to continuance of the bipartisan foreign policy, was overwhelmingly defeated in the national committee. Members said that a voice vote showed support for Mr. Schroeder from only one or two others.

The party statement declared:

"We advocate a strong policy against the spread of communism or fascism at home and abroad, and we insist that America's efforts toward this end be directed by those who have no sympathy either with communism or fascism."

It asserted that "basic American principles are threatened by the Administration's program for a planned economy modeled on the Socialist Governments of Europe, including price and wage control, rationing, socialized medicine, regional authorities and the Brannan Plan with its controls, penalties, fines and jail sentences."

The Republican program "to rebuild a prosperous and progressive America" included these major planks:

A return to a balanced budget

Continued on Page 20, Column 3

By Winston Churchill: The Second World War

Installment 11 of the excerpts from Mr. Churchill's memoirs of the war will be found today on Page 29

11,000 Crowd Arena For $1 Party Supper

Special to The New York Times.

WASHINGTON, Feb. 6 — The Republicans followed up their declaration of principles today with a box-supper party at Uline Arena. It was a noisy and crowded success. The scene was that of an old-fashioned political rally.

The crowd inside the building numbered about 11,000, it was estimated, with 2,000 more outside trying to get in. Only 7,000 supper boxes were on hand at the start.

Admission was $1.20 a person, the 20 cents being Federal tax. The guests good-naturedly seized upon the tax as an issue for impromptu and one-sided debate. Party officials stressed the price of their meal, comparing it with the Democrats' $100-a-plate fund-raising affairs.

There was a good deal of music, both professional and otherwise. Part of the celebration was broadcast over the American Broadcasting Company network, while various leaders made short speeches. The platform was studded with party stalwarts.

JAPAN SAID TO BACK GIVING BASES TO U.S.

Visit by Joint Chiefs Is Held to Have Convinced Most Party Heads on Move

By LINDESAY PARROTT

Special to The New York Times.

TOKYO, Feb. 6—Leaders of Japan's major political parties with the exception of the extreme left have become convinced as a result of the visit here by the Joint Chiefs of Staff that this nation should grant air, naval and army bases to the United States in return for a protective guarantee under the peace treaty. There are indications they believe that the view would be supported by a large majority of the post-war Japanese electorate.

The conviction of the Japanese leaders, the importance of which it is difficult to overstress, comes as a result of the emphasis they believe was placed by the Joint Chiefs on big American installations already existing here.

The three generals and one admiral who compose the Joint Chiefs left Japan today for Okinawa after visiting the naval base at Yokosuka, Army installations in the Osaka region and the large Air Force base at Itazuke in Kyushu. They were prevented from inspecting the newly built major air base at Misawa in northeast Honshu by weather conditions.

Though no information was forthcoming, either from the chiefs or local United States military authorities, the Japanese were inclined to believe the principal point of the visit was evaluation of these and other bases in

Continued on Page 11, Column 2

McCloy Warns the Germans Against a Revival of Nazism

At Opening of Amerika Haus in Stuttgart He Clarifies U. S. Policy, Declaring Its Chief Concern Is to Build Democracy

By DREW MIDDLETON

Special to The New York Times.

STUTTGART, Germany, Feb. 6—The United States will use all its power to fight a revival of nazism in Germany, John J. McCloy, United States High Commissioner, asserted today.

The western Germans were bluntly warned to concentrate on internal problems, avoid "agitation" on foreign issues and to build democracy toward "unification of all Germany."

Speaking before an audience of 1,600 in the Stuttgart Opera House, Mr. McCloy turned the dedication of this city's Amerika Haus, an information center, into what was at once a major declaration of United States policy in Germany and an admission that the progress of Germany toward democracy had been neither as fast nor as complete as some officials had believed.

Mr. McCloy flatly told the Germans they would not be allowed a political position endangering the peace of Europe and "there will be no German army or air force."

Later at a press conference he declared he was not contemplating any changes in the occupation statute that defines the Allied powers at present and did not talk about such changes on his recent trip to Washington.

Shortly after his speech the High Commissioner intervened sharply and perhaps decisively in the denazification scandal currently shaking the government of Wuerttemberg-Baden by publicly

Continued on Page 4, Column 3

The text of the McCloy address is on Page 4.

WORLD ARMS TALK URGED BY TYDINGS TO END 'NIGHTMARE'

Senator Asks Call by Truman to Ease Fears by Reducing All Weapons Down to the Rifle

By WILLIAM S. WHITE

Special to The New York Times.

WASHINGTON, Feb. 6—Senator Millard E. Tydings, Democrat, of Maryland, appealed to President Truman today to call a world conference for disarmament, in conventional as well as atomic weapons, to "end the world's nightmare of fear."

Mr. Tydings, a powerful figure as chairman of the Senate's Armed Services Committee and a member of its Foreign Relations Committee and the Joint Congressional Committee on Atomic Energy, asked the Senate to approve a resolution "authorizing and requesting" the President to summon such a meeting.

Lacking some such "fundamental" approach to peace, he asserted, "we are up against the possible extinction of all the human beings of this earth."

It would be "difficult" for Marshal Stalin or any other ruler, he argued, to "refuse an appeal by the President openly made on an honest and fair basis."

Senator Tydings' speech reopened a Senate debate on atomic policy, and weapons policy generally, which had been set off last week by Senator Brien McMahon, Democrat, of Connecticut, with the recommendation that this country at "almost any cost" seek an international arrangement neutralizing atomic and hydrogen weapons.

It appeared to reflect a considerable Congressional dissatisfaction at the fact that President Truman's recently announced decision to go ahead with the hydrogen bomb development was accompanied by no new approach to the Soviet Union toward atomic control.

Mr. Tydings contended that strict international inspection of

Continued on Page 2, Column 6

WEST GERMANS CUT SHIPMENT OF STEEL INTO RUSSIAN ZONE

Act After East Drops Far Below Pact Figure on Sending Grain to Western Areas

By JACK RAYMOND

Special to The New York Times.

FRANKFORT, Germany, Feb. 6—The West German Government has decided to curtail steel shipments from the Ruhr to the Soviet zone, it became known today.

The reason to be given the East zone regime will be that terms of the interzonal trade agreement are in danger of being broken by Soviet zone failure to provide adequate shipments of grain. It may be assumed that recent transport difficulties imposed by the Soviet zone regime had no little to do with it.

[Monday night the Russians again delayed traffic at Helmstedt without explanation, slowing down the entry of Berlin-bound trucks to the point where a waiting line was established again, The Associated Press said. By midnight, with the entry rate cut to four or five trucks an hour, there was a line of fifteen trucks, the first such

Continued on Page 6, Column 5

Widnall, Jersey Republican, Wins Thomas Seat in Congress by 2 to 1

Special to The New York Times.

HACKENSACK, N. J., Feb. 6—William B. Widnall, a Republican lawyer from Saddle River, tonight won a two-to-one victory in the special Seventh Congressional District election to choose a successor to J. Parnell Thomas, Republican, jailed for payroll padding.

Mr. Widnall received 31,754 votes against 15,370 for his Democratic opponent, former Mayor George T. English of East Paterson, a textile manufacturer.

The 42-year-old victor, a State Assemblyman from Bergen County, took the lead as soon as returns began to come in when the polls closed at 8 P. M. and maintained a wide margin from that time on.

A little more than two hours later Mr. English, who had predicted a "resentment vote" growing out of the Thomas scandal, conceded victory to Mr. Widnall.

"The victory is yours," he said at 10:10 P. M. in a telephone call to Mr. Widnall at the Republican campaign headquarters in Ridgewood. "My congratulations to you. Your support in the Seventh Congressional District apparently goes beyond partisan politics at this time."

On Mr. Widnall's invitation, Mr. English, accompanied by Mrs. English, then visited his opponent's headquarters, where a victory party was in the making. A momentary silence that greeted the Democrat and his wife when they walked in gave way immediately to a heavy burst of applause and cheers.

Mr. Widnall introduced his opponent to the gathering and read the message conceding victory. There was more applause and cheers.

The Republican said he hoped to offer a constructive program toward a better United States.

"It is my hope," he continued, "that this Republican victory is a forerunner of great Republican victories in November."

Mr. Widnall entered the primary fight for the candidacy without the

Continued on Page 26, Column 3

World News Summarized

TUESDAY, FEBRUARY 7, 1950

President Truman invoked the Taft-Hartley Act yesterday and named a three-man fact-finding board in the soft-coal dispute. The board was instructed to report not later than Monday, and if negotiations have not been resumed the President may seek an eighty-day injunction. It was the eighth time Mr. Truman had invoked the Taft-Hartley Act, which he strongly opposes, and the third time against the coal union. John L. Lewis made no comment. [1:8.] The miners, who went on a general strike, expressed defiance of an injunction. [1:5.]

Leaders of the CIO telephone union, who have called a nationwide strike for tomorrow, were voting on a Government proposal to delay action sixteen days while Federal mediators sought a peace formula. [1:6-7.]

In this city, a fact-finding board opened hearings on demands by the transit workers for a pay increase, shorter hours and other changes in working conditions. [1:6.] The Continental Paper Company announced it was closing its $16,000,000 Ridgefield Park, N. J., plant, which has been strike-bound seven months. [17:1.]

Concern was expressed over the growing danger to peace resulting from the inability of the United States and the Soviet Union to agree on atomic control. Senator Tydings introduced a resolution calling on the President to convoke a world conference for disarmament of conventional as well as atomic weapons under constant world-wide inspection. [1:3.] A Senate group heard pleas for a "tyranny-proof" United Nations police force to be set up with or without Soviet consent. [3:4.] Some United Nations observers held direct Washington-Moscow talks might prove of value. [3:2-3.]

The FBI told a Congressional committee that Dr. Fuchs, British atomic scientist who had worked on bomb research in this country, had transmitted "vital secret information" to the Russians and had a long record of "sympathy with Communist ideology." Dr. Fuchs is under arrest in Britain. [3:1.] A Justice Department official told the jury in the Coplon-Gubitchev espionage trial how a decoy message had led to the arrest of the defendants. [14:2.]

Republican policy conference, with distinct rumblings of discontent, adopted a statement proclaiming "liberty against socialism" the keynote of this year's Congressional elections. [1:1.] In New Jersey, William B. Widnall, Republican, was elected representative to succeed J. Parnell Thomas. [1:2-3.]

"We Americans are not here exclusively to feed the German people and promote economic recovery, but to help the Germans establish a political democracy, regain economic health, rejoin the democratic world and stamp out every vestige of nazism," United States High Commissioner McCloy said in Stuttgart. [1:3-4.] His blunt speech, which was welcomed by the British and French, was said to reflect accurately this country's new policy of straight talking. [5:3.]

Western Germany has decided to cut steel shipments to the Soviet zone. [1:4.]

Premier Bidault formed a new French Cabinet without any Socialist Ministers. [7:1.]

Index to other news appears on Page 23.

BITUMINOUS TIE-UP

Only 30,000 of 400,000 Diggers Stay on Job in Soft Coal Fields

TAFT ACT 'CLUB' ASSAILED

But Owners Hold Strikers Will Obey Writ to Work—Anthracite Mines Busy

By A. H. RASKIN

Special to The New York Times.

PITTSBURGH, Feb. 6—A general strike in the country's soft coal fields was the reply given by members of the United Mine Workers today to President Truman's request for voluntary restoration of "normal" coal production.

Two hundred and seventy thousand miners who had been working a three-day week put aside their tools and joined 100,000 others who have been on a "no-day week" for the last month. Their walkout left some 30,000 UMW members at work in bituminous mines that have signed new contracts with John L. Lewis, president of the union, and in a handful of mines west of the Mississippi.

News that President Truman had put in motion the machinery for an eighty-day injunction under the national emergency provisions of the Taft-Hartley Act brought fresh expressions of defiance from the strikers. In Pennsylvania and West Virginia, where the tie-up has been in effect for a full month, local union leaders asserted that their men did not intend to go back without a contract, even if Mr. Lewis ordered them to do so.

Sabotage Is Predicted

These statements were discounted by mine owners. They voiced certainty that the miners would go back on Mr. Lewis' signal when an injunction was issued. However, some operators said they expected many locals might be slow to return and that the injunction period would be marked by "sabotage, slowdowns and sporadic stoppages" in many areas.

The first hint that the union would instruct its members to comply with a back-to-work order

Continued on Page 19, Column 4

Ching Asks a 16-Day Delay In Call for Telephone Strike

Union, Polling Leaders Across Nation, Will Reply Today—Mediator Gravely Warns the 320,000 Set to Quit Tomorrow

A sixteen-day postponement of the threatened strike affecting 320,000 telephone workers hung in the balance last night. Acting on a proposal of Cyrus S. Ching, Federal Mediation and Conciliation Service director, the executive board of the Communication Workers of America, CIO, was being polled across the country on whether to accept the delay.

The walkout, scheduled for 6 A. M. tomorrow, would affect directly 100,000 telephone employes represented by the CWA. Another 220,000 telephone workers probably would refuse to cross picket lines. The postponement sought by Mr. Ching would delay the strike call until Feb. 24.

Before the union can answer Mr. Ching, nine members of the executive board must indicate their position to Joseph A. Beirne, president of the CWA.

These include, beside Mr. Beirne, John J. Moran, John Crull and A. T. Jones, all vice presidents of the national union; C. W. Werkau, secretary-treasurer, and four regional directors, Mrs. Mary Hanscom, Eastern region, Newark; Ray Hackney, Southwestern, St. Louis; Joseph Deirdoroff, Western, Denver, and Ray Dreyer, Central, Chicago.

Mr. Ching will receive the union leaders' decision in Washington this morning. He formulated his proposal for delay while in New York, where he sought vainly for a break in the deadlocked negotiations between the CWA and the American Telephone and Telegraph Company. The negotiations resume at 10 A. M. today in the New Yorker Hotel.

Mr. Ching warned of the grave impact should the strike take place. He told both union and company spokesmen that "many of the freedoms which both sides presently enjoy, and are enjoyed by employers and unions generally, will be endangered by a demonstration of an absence of sound and stable management-labor relations in the critical communications industry."

Despite this warning, after the

Continued on Page 18, Column 5

TRANSIT INQUIRY ON; QUILL LEADS FIGHT

Mayor's Committee Hearings Open With Union Vigorously Pressing Its Demands

By ALEXANDER FEINBERG

The Transport Workers Union, CIO, got its long-sought opportunity yesterday to start presenting to Mayor O'Dwyer's fact-finding board its case for higher wages and improved working conditions.

At the first all-day session of the board, the union restated its demands for a wage increase of 21 cents an hour across the board for all of the city's 43,000 transit workers, along with forty-eight hours' pay for a five-day, forty-hour week. Other salient points among its demands called for the setting up of a grievance committee with recourse to impartial arbitration, and improved pension, vacation and holiday benefits.

John F. O'Donnell, union counsel, introduced voluminous exhibits tending to show that New York's transit workers were the lowest paid of any in twelve major cities, several of them with municipally operated systems. Other exhibits sought to show that they were paid less than railroad employes and truck drivers.

Through still other exhibits he sought to make the contrasting point that New York took good care of its policemen, firemen and

Continued on Page 17, Column 4

WATER SUPPLY DIPS 3D SUCCESSIVE DAY

Officials Call On the Public to Reduce Consumption in 'Every Possible Way'

By CHARLES G. BENNETT

As water shortage in the city's Catskill and Croton reservoirs dipped by 134,000,000 gallons yesterday, the third successive day of storage losses, water officials issued an urgent appeal to the public to reduce water use "in every possible way."

The new appeal was underscored by the weekly consumption report. This showed that last week's water consumption averaged 868,000,000 gallons daily, an increase of 8,000,000 gallons daily over use in the previous week. It was the first week since mid-November that consumption had not declined or at least done no worse than in the preceding week.

Stephen J. Carney, Commissioner of Water Supply, Gas and Electricity, noted that in spite of the one-week rise, New Yorkers still had maintained an over-all average daily reduction of 324,000,000 gallons in water consumption since the "base" week, Oct. 2 to 8, 1949.

The new series of daily storage losses, coming at a time of the year when normally the reservoirs are rising, Mr. Carney said, make it imperative that the public make even further savings.

Mr. Carney said that he thought

Continued on Page 17, Column 2

Port Body Urges Helicopter Lines; Offers Field Atop Its Bus Terminal

By FREDERICK GRAHAM

The Port of New York Authority told the Civil Aeronautics Board yesterday that it strongly recommended mail, passenger and express service by helicopters in the metropolitan area. It offered to provide a landing area atop the new bus terminal it is building on Eighth Avenue between Fortieth and Forty-first Streets.

The recommendation and offer were made by Fred M. Glass, director of airport development for the bi-state agency, at the opening session of a CAB hearing to determine whether the New York area is to have helicopter shuttle service. The hearing was held in the assembly room of the Commerce and Industry Association, 233 Broadway.

In addition to the Port Authority, representatives of five communities in New Jersey, Connecticut and New York appeared before Ferdinand M. Moran, CAB examiner, to urge authorization of helicopter shuttle service.

Representatives of helicopter manufacturing companies also testified as to the types, performance and availability of their equipment. The sum of their testimony was that dependable helicopters were now flying and had been extensively tested both by the armed services and in commercial operations. They added that larger and better helicopters were coming along.

After explaining that the Port Authority was appearing at the hearing because of its obligation to promote the full, efficient and economical development of transportation in its area, Mr. Glass said:

"With our greater population and more intensified commercial life, the New Jersey-New York Port District, more than any other area in the country, requires the best transportation services. The helicopter, with its unique ability to take off and land on small spaces, and to move passengers and

Continued on Page 35, Column 3

RESORT TO THE LAW

President Acts Against Lewis, Chooses Inquiry Body Headed by Cole

ASKS A REPORT BY MONDAY

Injunction Move Is Due Then if the Operators and Miners Have Not Resumed Talks

By ANTHONY LEVIERO

Special to The New York Times.

WASHINGTON, Feb. 6—President Truman invoked the Taft-Hartley Act against John L. Lewis and the United Mine Workers today as the soft-coal strike became almost complete and virtually ended bituminous production.

Simultaneously the Chief Executive appointed an emergency board of three seasoned labor arbitrators to study the dispute and report to him on or before next Monday.

This move under the law allowed the mine owners and the miners six days in which to seek again a basis for negotiation. Failing that, the real showdown should follow next week. Under the Taft-Hartley Law, the Government is compelled to apply for a court injunction that would require the miners to go back to work for eighty days pending a renewed search for a settlement.

David L. Cole, a lawyer of Paterson, N. J., and a veteran arbitrator with experience in coal disputes, was appointed chairman of the board. The other members were William Willard Wirtz, a Professor of Law at Northwestern University and former chairman of the National Wage Stabilization Board, and John Dunlop, associate professor of economics at the Harvard School of Business Administration.

Board Holds First Meeting

The board members arrived here tonight and had a session with Peter Seitz, general counsel of the United States Conciliation Service, who briefed them on the background of the dispute. Then they held an organization meeting and planned to begin their proceedings tomorrow.

Through a spokesman, Mr. Lewis blanketed the President's dramatic action with a "no comment" and then lapsed into silence. What his course might be was a riddle. There was no assurance that he would cooperate with the board or that his miners would heed the eighty-day injunction, if the proceedings went that far.

All that appeared certain tonight was that Mr. Lewis had created an imposing dilemma for his old antagonist, President Truman, who has made the repeal of the Taft-Hartley Act a major political issue for this year's Congressional election.

Unlike his unsuccessful action of last Tuesday, when he issued a conciliatory statement and sought to bring the operators and the miners before an extralegal board, Mr. Truman today said nothing. He did what the law required—issued an executive order creating the board.

In the order, phrased in legal language, Mr. Truman expressed the opinion that if the strike were allowed to continue it "will imperil the national health and safety." He acted under Section 206 of the Taft-Hartley Act, which provides for Presidential action when a strike threatens to reach emergency proportions.

Action Forecast for Days

His action was announced by Charles G. Ross, White House press secretary. It had been forecast for several days, and a large number of reporters had gathered in the lobby of the Executive offices. Mr. Ross called them in a little after noon and said:

"The President at 11:35 this morning signed an Executive order creating a board to inquire into a dispute in the bituminous coal industry. This board is to report not later than Feb. 13. Of course, it could report earlier, but that is the terminal date."

Earlier the reporters got an intimation of this action from Speak-

Continued on Page 18, Column 1

"All the News That's Fit to Print"

The New York Times.

Copyright, 1950, by The New York Times Company.

LATE CITY EDITION
Sunny with pleasant temperatures today. Fair tomorrow.
Temperature Range Today—Max.,80; Min.,66
Temperature Yesterday—Max.,80.3; Min.,69
Full U. S. Weather Bureau Report, Page 55

VOL. XCIX..No. 33,758. Entered as Second-Class Matter. Post Office, New York, N. Y. NEW YORK, WEDNESDAY, JUNE 28, 1950. Times Square, New York 18, N. Y. Telephone Lackawanna 4-1000 RAG PAPER EDITION SEVENTY-FIVE CENTS

TRUMAN ORDERS U. S. AIR, NAVY UNITS TO FIGHT IN AID OF KOREA; U. N. COUNCIL SUPPORTS HIM; OUR FLIERS IN ACTION; FLEET GUARDS FORMOSA

114 RESCUED HERE AS LINER GROUNDS AFTER COLLISION

Excalibur, With Hole 15 Feet Wide in Side, Settles on Mud Flat Off Brooklyn

FIRES START ON FREIGHTER

One Person Slightly Injured—Responsibility for the Crash Still to Be Decided

By WILLIAM R. CONKLIN

Thirty-five minutes after a gay departure for a Mediterranean cruise, the American Export Line's Excalibur was disabled in a collision yesterday with a Danish freighter in the Narrows, but all her 114 passengers were taken off safely.

The confetti-speckled cruise ship left Pier 4, Jersey City, at noon for a forty-three-day voyage. At 12:35 P. M. the collision with the inbound Colombia occurred off Sixty-ninth Street, Brooklyn.

The impact crushed the bow of the freighter and tore a hole fifteen feet wide in the port side of the Excalibur forward of the bridge. Fire broke out in the Colombia's forepeak in a paint storeroom.

While passengers and both crews remained calm, water quickly flooded the forward holds of the cruise ship. The Excalibur settled with her bow on a midstream mud bank, with her screw lifted in the air.

Passengers Taken Off by Tugs

Passengers on the sinking ship donned bright orange life preservers and were taken off by two tugs of the Moran Towing Company. Except for one woman who bruised three fingers of her left hand, all passengers were uninjured. They were returned to Pier 4, and the ship line arranged for hotel accommodations for them.

No official on the scene would assess responsibility for the collision. The Coast Guard required both captains to file written reports on the crash today. Under usual procedure, a Coast Guard board of inquiry hears evidence and fixes blame. Unofficially, it was said that a misunderstanding of whistle signals was the probable cause of the accident.

Capt. S. N. Groves of Brooklyn, a veteran of twenty-five years at sea, commanded the Excalibur, a ship of 9,644 gross tons with a top speed of seventeen knots. The Colombia, owned by the United Steamship Lines of Denmark, was commanded by Capt. Christian Mikkelsen of Copenhagen. The freighter was operated by the Scandinavian-American Steamship Company of 25 Broadway. Carrying cotton, wool and lubricating oils, she was bound from Philadelphia to Pier 24 at Congress Street, Brooklyn.

When the collision occurred there was good visibility despite a light haze over the lower bay. Persons in Shore Road Park saw the collision clearly, half a mile off the Brooklyn waterfront.

As the Excalibur's forward holds filled, her nose dropped into a mud-bank and she swung to face upstream on the incoming tide.

2 Fireboats Help Freighter

The fireboats William J. Gaynor and Firefighter put lines on the 3,146-ton freighter to fight the fire on board. With the help of the ship's forty-two crewmen they subdued a fire in the forward hold. A collision bulkhead between that point and the forecastle prevented them from tackling another fire in the peak.

With Army, Navy, Coast Guard and Moran tugs helping, the burning vessel was moved into the north side of the Sixty-ninth Street ferry pier. John L. Holian, Deputy Fire Chief commanding the Marine Division, summoned a hook and ladder company to pour streams into the burning peak from the pier. Within an hour, the fire was extinguished.

Joseph H. Boggs, senior assistant purser of the Excalibur, said it was fortunate that the collision had occurred in shoal water.

"Immediately after the crash we

Continued on Page 29, Column 2

SANCTIONS VOTED

Council Adopts Plan of U. S. for Armed Force in Korea, 7 to 1

THE SOVIET IS ABSENT

Yugoslavia Casts Lone Dissent—Egypt and India Abstain

Mr. Austin's statement to the United Nations is on Page 6.

By THOMAS J. HAMILTON
Special to The New York Times.

LAKE SUCCESS, June 27—The Security Council adopted tonight a United States resolution recommending that members of the United Nations use armed force in repelling the invasion of southern Korea and restoring international peace and security.

The vote on the resolution, which amounted to Security Council authorization for President Truman's decision to send United States naval and air units to the defense of the Republic of Korea, was 7 to 1, with Yugoslavia voting against.

The representatives of India and Egypt did not vote because they had not received instructions from their Governments. The Soviet Union was absent.

Representatives of Britain, France, Nationalist China, Cuba, Ecuador and Norway announced this afternoon that they would vote for the United States resolution without change. However, the Council recessed at 5:12 P. M. to permit Sir Benegal Rau and Mahmoud Bey Fawzi, the representatives of India and Egypt, to try to reach their Governments by telephone.

The vote was finally taken at 10:45 P. M. after both said they had been unable to establish communication with responsible authorities. With Egypt and India again not participating, the Council then rejected, seven to one, a Yugoslav resolution proposing that the Council renew its appeal for compliance with the cease-fire resolution it adopted Sunday, and request the two sides to agree to United Nations mediation.

The Council then recessed again while Sir Benegal and Fawzi Bey again attempted to obtain instructions. Apparently Fawzi Bey did so, but neither he nor Sir Benegal made any further statement, and the Council adjourned at 11 P. M.

Both Security Council members and other delegates who crowded around their table showed their realization that a historic decision for the United Nations and the world was being taken tonight. Warren R. Austin, the United States representative, was determined to avoid postponing a decision until tomorrow, and the Indian and Egyptian representatives cooperated by not requesting a postponement because of their failure to receive instructions.

Mr. Austin said after the meeting that the immediate effect of the resolution "should be to stop

Continued on Page 7, Column 1

President Takes Chief Role In Determining U. S. Course

Truman's Leadership for Forceful Policy to Meet Threat to World Peace Draws Together Advisers on Vital Move

By ARTHUR KROCK
Special to The New York Times.

WASHINGTON, June 27—Some of those who participated in the meetings Sunday and Monday nights, at which the momentous decisions were taken to resist further Communist aggressions, beginning in the Far East, with the combat air and naval power of the United States, described the President to associates today as determined from the outset to adopt the forceful policy which was announced this morning.

As soon as the first meeting assembled, they said, Mr. Truman made it plain that these were to be the bases of his decision:

1. The situation created by Communist tactics at various points of the world, culminating in the attack of North Korea on South Korea, had been allowed to drift too long.

2. The entire Far East was deteriorating in a manner to threaten the peace of the world, a line had to be drawn at once, and the United States had to draw it.

3. National security was the primary interest, but embedded in this were world peace and the prestige and future effectiveness of the United Nations, which was the architect of the South Korean Government.

4. It was a time for courage, even boldness, and calculated risk, which other members of the United Nations would be invited to share as they saw fit.

5. It was not a time to give the slightest consideration to previous policies or to individuals associated with those policies. If, for example, the fundamental change in the Far Eastern sit-

Continued on Page 4, Column 3

U. S. FORCE FIGHTING

MacArthur Installs an Advanced Echelon in Southern Korea

FOE LOSES 4 PLANES

American Craft in Battle to Protect Evacuation —Seoul Is Quiet

By LINDESAY PARROTT
Special to The New York Times.

TOKYO, Wednesday, June 28—The United States is now actively intervening in the Korean civil war, an announcement from Gen. Douglas MacArthur's headquarters here made clear this morning.

[Gen. Douglas MacArthur announced Wednesday that the forces of South Korea now were holding the Communist Korean invaders, a United Press dispatch from Tokyo said. At the same time he reported that United States fliers had begun bombing and strafing missions against North Korean forces. Seoul was reported quiet.]

General MacArthur revealed that a "small advanced echelon" from his headquarters had been established in Korea, presumably cooperating with the United States Military Advisory Group, which has been in Korea since the republic was established there under President Syngman Rhee two years ago.

The MacArthur announcement stated that Far East air forces and elements of the naval forces under the general's command were "conducting" combat missions south of the Thirty-eighth Parallel—the dividing line between Communist North Korea and the United States-recognized Korean Republic. These operations, it was officially stated, are "in support of the Korean Republic," whose Government has now been reinstalled in the capital, Seoul, after isolation of the Northern armored spearheads that had penetrated to the outskirts of the city yesterday.

The announcement said that United States planes, which were providing air cover for the evacuation of women and children dependents of various United States missions, had shot down four North Korean fighters that were interfering with the operation of

Continued on Page 17, Column 3

Statement on Korea

By The Associated Press.

WASHINGTON, June 27—The text of President Truman's statement today on Korea:

In Korea the Government forces, which were armed to prevent border raids and to preserve internal security, were attacked by invading forces from North Korea. The Security Council of the United Nations called upon the invading troops to cease hostilities and to withdraw to the Thirty-eighth Parallel. This they have not done, but on the contrary have pressed the attack. The Security Council called upon all members of the United Nations to render every assistance to the United Nations in the execution of this resolution.

In these circumstances I have ordered United States air and sea forces to give the Korean Government troops cover and support.

The attack upon Korea makes it plain beyond all doubt that communism has passed beyond the use of subversion to conquer independent nations and will now use armed invasion and war.

It has defied the orders of the Security Council of the United Nations issued to preserve international peace and security. In these circumstances the occupation of Formosa by Communist forces would be a direct threat to the security of the Pacific area and to United States forces performing their lawful and necessary functions in that area.

Accordingly I have ordered the Seventh Fleet to prevent any attack on Formosa. As a corollary of this action I am calling upon the Chinese Government on Formosa to cease all air and sea operations against the mainland. The Seventh Fleet will see that this is done. The determination of the future status of Formosa must await the restoration of security in the Pacific, a peace settlement with Japan, or consideration by the United Nations.

I have also directed that United States forces in the Philippines be strengthened and that military assistance to the Philippine Government be accelerated.

I have similarly directed acceleration in the furnishing of military assistance to the forces of France and the associated states in Indo-China and the dispatch of a military mission to provide close working relations with those forces.

I know that all members of the United Nations will consider carefully the consequences of this latest aggression in Korea in defiance of the Charter of the United Nations. A return to the rule of force in international affairs would have far-reaching effects. The United States will continue to uphold the rule of law.

I have instructed Ambassador Austin, as the representative of the United States to the Security Council, to report these steps to the Council.

BID MADE TO RUSSIA

President Asks Moscow to Act to Terminate Fighting in Korea

CHIANG TOLD TO HALT

U.S. Directs Him to Stop Blows at Reds—Will Reinforce Manila

By ANTHONY LEVIERO
Special to The New York Times.

WASHINGTON, June 27—President Truman announced today that he had ordered United States air and naval forces to fight with South Korea's Army. He said this country took the action, as a member of the United Nations, to enforce the cease-fire order issued by the Security Council Sunday night.

Then acting independently of the United Nations, in a move to assure this country's security, the Chief Executive ordered Vice Admiral Arthur D. Struble to form a protective cordon around Formosa to prevent its invasion by Communist Chinese forces.

Along with these fateful decisions, Mr. Truman also ordered an increase of our forces based in the Philippine Republic, as well as more speedy military assistance to that country and to the French and Vietnam forces that are fighting Communist armies in Indo-China.

After he had started these moves that might mean a decided turn toward peace or a general war, the President sent Ambassador Alan G. Kirk to the Russian Foreign Office in Moscow to request the Soviet Union to use its good offices to end the hostilities. This was an obvious proffer of an opportunity for Russia to end the crisis before her own forces might get involved.

Door Opened for Russia

In the capital this was regarded as being at once a possible face-saving device for Russia in a show-down crisis and a feeler to determine her intentions.

The decisions amounted to a showdown in the "cold war" with Russia, in which this country has at last decided to begin shooting in a limited area. Yet all the decisions followed a carefully worked out formula of action within the framework of the United Nations, as well as unilateral moves that avoided any direct provocation of the Soviet Union.

Mr. Truman based the decision to fight for the South Koreans entirely on the Security Council resolution which called upon all members of the United Nations to help carry it out. And at the Pentagon it was explained that our air and naval forces would fight only below the Thirty-eighth Parallel line that divides South Korea from the Russian-sponsored North Korea.

"The Security Council called upon all members of the United Nations to render every assistance to the United Nations in the execution of this resolution," Mr. Truman stated. "In these circumstances I have ordered United States air and sea forces to give the Korean Government troops cover and support."

Russia Is Not Mentioned

Mr. Truman carefully avoided mentioning Russia in his statement. He pivoted today's great shift in United States foreign policy on a conclusion that the "cold war" had passed from an uneasy passive stage to "armed invasion and war." He blamed "communism."

"The attack upon Korea makes it plain beyond all doubt that communism has passed beyond the use of subversion to conquer independent nations and will now use armed invasion and war," he said. "It has defied the orders of the Security Council of the United Nations issued to preserve international peace and security. In these circumstances the occupation of Formosa by Communist forces would be a direct threat to the security of the Pacific area and to United States forces performing

Continued on Page 2, Column 2

MAINLAND ATTACKS ENDED BY FORMOSA

Chinese Nationalists Halt Air, Navy Forays in Accordance With Request by Truman

By The Associated Press.

TAIPEI, Formosa, Wednesday, June 28—The Chinese Nationalists today ordered their Air Force and Navy to cease attacks on the Communist mainland in accordance with a United States request.

President Truman had ordered United States warships to protect Formosa against Communist attack and at the same time asked the Nationalists to cease offensive operations.

Nationalist Foreign Minister George Yeh hailed the President's order for warship protection as "a most welcome sign of comradeship in the fight against communism."

Generalissimo Chiang Kai-shek and his Cabinet had met after the United States note was delivered to the United States Embassy. It was understood the note carried with it instructions to see that it was brought personally to Generalissimo Chiang's attention.

Mr. Yeh translated the text to the Generalissimo last night in the presence of United States Charge d'Affaires Robert Strong.

Mr. Strong was with Generalissimo Chiang for about twenty minutes. After his departure the latter consulted with Mr. Yeh, Premier Chen Cheng and other officials.

The decision was announced after Generalissimo Chiang conferred with Gen. Chou Chih-jou, Chief of the Joint General Staff and other top Nationalist commanders.

The Nationalists were believed to have agreed to Washington's re-

Continued on Page 3, Column 4

HOUSE VOTES 315-4 TO PROLONG DRAFT

Korea Crisis Breaks Deadlock —Bill Expected to Be Sent to White House Tonight

Special to The New York Times.

WASHINGTON, June 27—The House of Representatives today passed, by a vote of 315 to 4, an extension of the draft for another year.

The bill added authority for President Truman to call to active duty members of the National Guard and the reserve forces for periods not exceeding twenty-one months.

The Senate agreed to vote on the bill tomorrow afternoon. Swift passage is expected there so that the bill may reach President Truman for his signature tomorrow night.

As recently as yesterday the Senate and the House appeared to be in a hopeless deadlock over the manner in which the selective service system could be kept alive without much leeway for the President to put it to use. Today when

Continued on Page 16, Column 5

NORTH KOREA CALLS U. N. ORDER ILLEGAL

Declares Security Council's 'Cease Fire' Invalid Without Assent of China and Russia

Special to The New York Times.

HONG KONG, June 27—The North Korean Government issued a statement today saying that it regarded the cease fire order of the United Nations Security Council illegal for two reasons. It said these were, one, because the Democratic Peoples Republic of North Korea was not represented when its affairs were discussed and, two, because the Soviet Union and (Communist) China did not participate.

On the latter point it cited the United Nations Charter, which requires unanimity of five permanent members of the Security Council on questions of substance. China and Russia are both permanent members. [But the Communist rulers of China have not been recognized by the United Nations as representing that country.]

Drastic measures were taken in North Korea yesterday to organize

Continued on Page 18, Column 5

LEGISLATORS HAIL ACTION BY TRUMAN

Almost Unanimous Approval Is Voiced in Congress by Both Sides—House Cheers

By HAROLD B. HINTON.
Special to The New York Times.

WASHINGTON, June 27—President Truman's announcement today that United States air and sea power would be employed to expel the Communist invaders from South Korea evoked almost unanimous support in Congress. His statement was read by the majority floor leaders in both houses.

In the House of Representatives, the members rose to their feet and cheered as the reading was completed by Representative John W. McCormack, of Massachusetts. In the Senate, the reading by Senator Scott W. Lucas, of Illinois, brought immediate declarations of support from several Republican Senators.

Showing the same spirit of solidarity in the face of crisis, as the present situation was frequently described, Senate and House conferees agreed on legislation to ex-

Continued on Page 5, Column 1

City, T.W.U. in 2-Year Peace Pact; Mayor Signs Fare Rise Resolution

Officials of the Transport Workers Union, C. I. O., the members of the Board of Transportation and Mayor O'Dwyer signed at City Hall yesterday a memorandum of understanding seeking to guarantee two years of peace in the city-owned rapid transit system.

The accord closely followed recommendations made on May 31 by the Mayor's Transit Fact-Finding Board, granting an 11-cent-an-hour increase to 35,929 operating employes, a third week of vacation after ten years and an additional holiday each year. The cost of the changes recommended by the fact-finders amounts to $13,188,515 a year.

The union bound itself not to engage in any strike or other interference with transit operations and not to seek any basic changes in the accord before July 1, 1952. It agreed to resolve all disputes in accordance with the grievance machinery set up in the pact. The union obligated itself also to recognize the board's managerial authority and to "cooperate in the attainment of efficient operations."

The Board of Transportation agreed to retain competent industrial engineers to report on a program for achieving a five-day, forty-hour week for all employes now having a scheduled work-week in excess of forty hours.

Mayor O'Dwyer also signed yesterday afternoon a resolution of the Board of Transportation, effective Saturday, increasing fares on the city-owned surface lines

Continued on Page 28, Column 4

World News Summarized

WEDNESDAY, JUNE 28, 1950

United States air and sea forces were ordered by President Truman yesterday to give Korean troops "cover and support." Moving directly to meet Communist "armed invasion and war" in Asia, the President instructed the Seventh Fleet to "prevent any attack on Formosa," called on the Chinese Nationalists to halt all attacks on the mainland, ordered United States forces in the Philippines strengthened and moved to speed military assistance to those islands and to Indo-China. He instructed Ambassador Kirk in Moscow to urge the Soviet Union to help end hostilities. [1:8; map P. 2.]

Naval and air elements are "conducting" combat missions south of the Thirty-eighth Parallel of Korea in support" of the Seoul Government, General MacArthur announced. An advance echelon of his General Headquarters has been set up in Korea, he added. Conflicting reports of the fighting showed positions little changed during the day. [1:5; maps P. 17.] In Washington it was said that General MacArthur had sufficient forces to give the South Koreans air and sea preponderance. [13:3.]

This country's new Far East policy was set at conferences during which the President's positive program and leadership convinced his top aides that his decisions "were both inevitable and right." [1:3-4.] He brought unity to an Administration that had been split on many vital policy issues. [4:6-7.]

Governor Dewey, speaking as head of the Republican party, pledged full support to the President [4:3] and Congress was almost unanimous in its endorsement. [1:7.] The House, 315 to 4, passed a one-year extension of the draft with broad new powers for the President; the Senate will vote today. [1:4.] Senate Republicans, however, blocked a vote today on the foreign arms-aid bill. [14:3.] The National Security Resources Board has ready for introduction a sweeping bill authorizing the President to freeze prices, wages, manpower and materials. [15:2.]

The United Nations Security Council, with Russia absent and Yugoslavia voting no, approved a United States motion to permit member nations to send armed forces to help repel the Korean invasion. [1:2.]

British parties united in supporting President Truman's program. The Labor Government won confidence votes on its refusal to join talks on pooling Europe's heavy industry. [19:4.]

John S. Service, a key figure in Senator McCarthy's charges of communism in the State Department, has been cleared by the department's Loyalty Security Board. [22:3.]

Index to other news appears on Page 28.

Stocks Rally After Big New Losses In War Scare; Sales Near 5 Million

By ROBERT H. FETRIDGE

Securities markets the world over were subjected yesterday to wide fluctuations as the Korean situation approached a crisis of universal concern.

Calmer thinking emerged successful on the New York exchanges, but only after prices encountered terrific battering. Losses that at one time ranged to 5 points and even more in standard issues on the New York Stock Exchange were either trimmed or eliminated. Quotations were definitely on the recovery side at the close, with the final composite rate down only 0.75 point. As pictured by THE NEW YORK TIMES index, the market was midway between the highs and lows of the day at the final bell.

London was the worst sufferer among the major exchanges, while the Canadian markets followed the lead of New York.

It was a wild day on the trading floor of the Stock Exchange. Business almost reached the 5,000,000-share mark, the reporting ticker tape was constantly thrown behind actual transactions and at one time was twenty-seven minutes late. This necessitated "flash" prices on the ticker to keep brokerage offices at least abreast of the price changes in the key stocks.

The trend changed with such rapidity that selling orders were still being executed after the price direction changed for the better.

Continued on Page 41, Column 6

"All the News That's Fit to Print"

The New York Times.

LATE CITY EDITION
Some cloudiness early today, fair and warmer later. Mild tomorrow.
Temperature Range Today—Max.,75; Min.,60
Temperature Yesterday—Max.,66; Min.,57
Full U. S. Weather Bureau Report, Page 33

VOL. XCIX..No. 33,837. Entered as Second-Class Matter, Post Office, New York, N. Y. NEW YORK, FRIDAY, SEPTEMBER 15, 1950. Times Square, New York 18, N. Y. Telephone Lackawanna 4-1000 FIVE CENTS

U. N. FORCES LAND BEHIND COMMUNISTS IN KOREA; SEIZE INCHON, PORT OF SEOUL; MOVE INLAND; U. S. WILL PRESS FOR A JAPANESE PEACE TREATY

2 GARMENT UNIONS ASK 15% WAGE RISE IN POLICY REVERSAL

Nation-Wide Demand Drafted by Big A.F.L. and C.I.O. Units to Match Costs of Living

KOREAN WAR EFFECT CITED

Long Reluctance on Economic Grounds Dropped—Mills in Northeast Grant 10%

The two largest garment unions in the United States announced yesterday that they would seek an immediate, country-wide general wage increase of 15 per cent for their thousands of members.

In this city the International Ladies Garment Workers Union, A. F. L., held a special meeting of its general executive board to formulate wage policy for 425,000 members. Locally, the union has received no pay rise since 1948, and its 80,000 dressmakers have been at the same wage level since 1947.

By a coincidence a subcommittee of the general executive board of the Amalgamated Clothing Workers of America, C. I. O., meeting in Asbury Park, N. J., drafted a similar plan to be presented to the full board today for ratification. This union will try to win higher wages for 150,000 men's clothing workers and 80,000 others engaged in the making of shirts and cotton garments.

Both organizations, which are among the most powerful and responsible in the country in wage matters, based their new demands on the rise in living costs since the start of the Korean war. Amalgamated members received their last rise, $5, in 1947.

Turnabout in Attitude

In recent years the two unions, facing poor conditions in their industries, have pursued a cautious pace in moving on the wage question. Now with nearly full employment, rising prices for textiles and mark-ups on finished products, they have come to the conclusion that pay rises are both necessary and justified.

The Amalgamated, which has a total membership of 400,000—50,000 of whom are in New York—had operated on the theory that wage rises would force up clothing prices in a period of slack demand and increase unemployment among the union's members. However, it won increases in pension and medical benefits, involving no rise in employer payroll contributions.

Amalgamated officials estimated yesterday that their full 15 per cent demand would raise the cost of making a suit by less than $1. Average clothing pay ranges from $1.50 to $1.62½ an hour. The new demand would add 22½ to 24½ cents to those rates. Cotton wages run from $1.02 to $1.10. These would be brought up by 15 to 16½ cents an hour.

Unlike the Amalgamated, which bargains on a national level with employer associations, the Ladies Garment Workers will try to win its demands on a local basis. Word has already gone out to the union's 400 locals over the country to press for increases in talks for new contracts, under wage-reopening clauses and through requests for voluntary adjustments.

Agreement for Conference

Officials of the Amalgamated said that the United States Clothing Manufacturers Association had agreed to confer with the union's bargaining committee, but that no date had been set for the first meeting. Wage talks with shirt manufacturers will begin next week in this city and other shirt centers.

The move by the Ladies Garment Workers, fifth largest affiliate of the American Federation of Labor, represented the first such attempt by a major A. F. L. union. In the C. I. O., of which the Amalgamated is the fourth largest unit, the United Automobile Workers

Continued on Page 19, Column 2

Excess Profits Tax Now Asked by House

By JOHN D. MORRIS
Special to The New York Times.

WASHINGTON, Sept. 14—The House went on record today, 331 to 2, as favoring action this session on an excess profits tax that would be retroactive to July 1, or Oct. 1.

The vote came on a motion by Representative Herman P. Eberharter, Democrat of Pennsylvania, to amend the pending general tax-increase bill in such a way as to require the House Ways and Means and Senate Finance Committees to bring out a separate excess profits measure before adjournment. The opposition votes were cast by Representative E. E. Cox, Democrat of Georgia, and D. W. Nicholson, Republican of Massachusetts.

The directive will not be binding however, unless it is contained in the final draft of the general tax bill, which now goes to a House-Senate conference committee for adjustment of differences between versions originally passed by the two chambers.

As passed by the Senate, the bill contained a provision direct-

Continued on Page 20, Column 2

TAFT AND WHERRY OPPOSE MARSHALL

Favoritism to Chinese Reds Is Charged—Senate Puts Off Action Until Today

Special to The New York Times.

WASHINGTON, Sept. 14—A small band of Republican Senators gathered today in opposition to the bill to waive existing law and permit General of the Army George C. Marshall, a professional soldier, to serve as Secretary of Defense.

The Republican leaders, however, made no attempt to declare it an all-party issue, and the Senate's passage of the measure, probably tomorrow, was thus assured.

It had been intended to open debate tonight, but unexpected difficulties intervened in other aspects of the Administration's final "must" list for this Congress.

At length, soon after 9 P. M., Senator Scott W. Lucas of Illinois, the Democratic Senate leader, not only put over "the Marshall bill" until tomorrow but abandoned hope of bringing this Congress to a close, as had been planned, by Saturday night.

Preliminary action by the House of Representatives was expected tomorrow on the bill. The House Armed Services Committee will meet at 10 A. M. to give its approval. The House Rules Committee, which governs the legislative traffic in that chamber, will meet at 11 A. M. to give it a right of way for the floor.

The bill simply specifies that, the Military Unification Act notwithstanding, "General of the Army Gen. George C. Marshall" is to be permitted to serve as Secretary of Defense.

The act forbids the office to a

Continued on page 9, Column 3

SENATE UNANIMOUS FOR BIG ARMS FUND BUT VOTES AID CURB

Approval of 17 Billion Bars Economic Help if Ally Ships War Goods to Russia

MOVE IS AIMED AT BRITISH

Proposal Would Give Defense Secretary Authority Superior to That of E. C. A. Director

By WILLIAM S. WHITE
Special to The New York Times

WASHINGTON, Sept. 14—The Senate passed unanimously tonight an urgent and supplemental appropriation bill of $17,192,000,000. Nine dollars of every ten in it would go to strengthening the defense of the United States and its associates of the western world.

Added to this big measure was a rider intended to halt all Marshall Plan economic aid, but not military help, to any benefiting nation that shipped to the Soviet Union or any of its satellites any commodity or article deemed to be useful in the manufacture of "arms, armament, or military matériel."

This stipulation was offered by Senator Kenneth S. Wherry of Nebraska, the Republican Senate leader. It was approved by a voice vote, in which not a dissent was heard.

It would leave it to the Secretary of Defense to determine what commodities ought to fall under the ban. Once he had defined them, the Marshall Plan administrator, Paul G. Hoffman, would have no option but to cut off from that plan any offending country.

The stipulation was aimed mainly at the British, who long have been accused by the Republicans of sending to Russia or to Soviet friends articles that might be used in a war.

The effect was to put the Secretary of Defense in the great and delicate area of determining what would be useful to the Soviet war potential, far above the Marshall Plan agency, the Economic Cooperation Administration. Admittedly, it would give him a vast veto power over the trade practices of the European nations if he wanted to use it.

The prospective Secretary of Defense is the author of the Marshall Plan itself, General of the Army George C. Marshall.

The Senate's insistence upon this limitation over Mr. Hoffman has yet to meet the approval of the House of Representatives, as does the whole of the appropriations bill. That measure, when it passed the House in August, had been for $16,771,356,077, or some $421,000,000 less than it stood tonight as it came from the Senate.

The additions made by the Senate were largely military, to meet needs that had been indicated by the Korean war since August, but there were other new sums, too.

There was, for example, $60,000,-

Continued on Page 4, Column 3

Backbone of Attack On Taegu 'Broken'

Special to The New York Times

TAEGU, Korea, Sept. 14—Maj. Gen. Hobart Gay, commanding the United States First Cavalry Division, said today he believed "we have broken the backbone" of the North Korean attack on the key United Nations advance base at Taegu.

This, General Gay said, is the situation, at least, "at the moment," after four days of seesaw fighting north and west of the city. The Communists put an estimated three divisions into the attack, with a fourth behind the lines.

General Gay said he might have to change his mind but indications today were that the situation at Taegu had considerably bettered.

ATTLEE RISKS FATE ON STEEL QUESTION

Conservatives Offer Censure Motion on Labor's Decision to Implement Nationalization

Special to The New York Times.

LONDON, Sept. 14—The British Conservatives precipitated a Parliamentary crisis today by calling for a vote of censure after an announcement by the Labor Government that it intended to implement its authority to nationalize the country's steel industry.

The matter will be debated on Tuesday. If the Government, with its slim majority, is defeated it will resign and there will be a general election.

This is how the issue arose:

There is on the statute books a law enabling the Government to take over the steel industry next January and appoint a board to do it by October. The Opposition asked today what the Government proposed to do about it. George Strauss, the Minister of Supply, said the Government intended to carry out the law, which Parliament had enacted when Labor had a bigger majority than it has now.

Those were fighting words. They ended the political truce that Winston Churchill had proffered

Continued on Page 16, Column 5

ACTION BY TRUMAN

Right to Move Forces at Will in Islands Is Held U. S. Aim

MAY IGNORE SOVIET

Factors in Ending State of War With Germany Studied, He Says

By ANTHONY LEVIERO
Special to The New York Times.

WASHINGTON, Sept. 14—President Truman announced today that he had directed the State Department to begin a new effort to obtain a Japanese peace treaty. Behind the move was this country's resolve to produce a peace agreement, with or without Soviet participation.

[The Associated Press said Secretary of State Acheson had informed British Foreign Secretary Bevin and French Foreign Minister Schuman that the United States was ready to begin informal talks on development of a Japanese peace treaty.]

Our policy with respect to Japan, said the Chief Executive, was in harmony with our general aim to "end all war situations," including the deadlocks over Germany and Austria.

The President opened his news conference by reading a formal statement, announcing the new effort on the Japanese treaty, which would be made informally in discussions with members of the Far Eastern Commission. He said this would be done "in the first instance," leaving the implication that the U. S. would proceed further if the deadlock created by the Soviet Union in the commission persisted.

Informed sources said afterward that this country was determined to make some kind of peace settlement with Japan, without the Soviet Union if that country continues her obstructive tactics. The same sources said the United States would seek the right not

Continued on Page 15, Column 1

World News Summarized

FRIDAY, SEPTEMBER 15, 1950

United Nations forces have struck in strength against the North Koreans with landings on both coasts behind the enemy's lines. A major amphibious blow was at Inchon, the port of Seoul, where United States and British warships had shelled the area Wednesday. At least two other landings were on the east coast north of Pohang. Earlier, North Korean claims to have sunk landing craft were disputed. Along the United Nations defense perimeter in the south relatively light action was reported, except north of Taegu. [1:8; maps Pages 1 and 2.]

Observers with United States Marines on the way to a landing looked to a quick knock-out effect on the North Koreans. [1:6-7.]

The Commission on Korea reported to the United Nations Security Council that, six weeks before the invasion, American officers rejected South Korean warnings of an attack. The report blamed North Korea for an unprovoked aggression. [1:7.]

President Truman directed the State Department to try again to obtain a Japanese peace treaty and to seek some way to end the technical state of war with Germany. [1:5.] The State Department is studying a $250,000,000 economic aid program for South Asia and the Middle East. [4:5.]

Foreign ministers of the United States, Britain and France discussed the "serious situation" affecting Europe and Asia. The British and French ministers agreed to seek new instructions on rearming Western Germany. Britain and France feel no military aid should go to the Germans until the North Atlantic nations are armed. [1:6-7.] The North Atlantic Council will consider this subject at meetings opening today. [16:2.] Britain's Defense Minister predicted that a unified command would result from the talks. He disclosed that France planned to have ten divisions under arms next year and ten more later. [16:3-4.]

Britain's Labor government announced it would take over the steel industry in January. The Conservatives immediately demanded a no-confidence vote and the Commons will decide the issue next week. [1:4.]

The Senate unanimously passed a $17,192,000,000 money bill, mostly for defense, with a rider designed to end all Marshall Plan economic aid to nations shipping "arms, armament or military matériel" to the Soviet Union or its satellites. [1:3.]

The House sent the interim tax bill to conference, but voted 331 to 2 for Congress to stay in session until an excess profits tax was passed. [1:2.]

A Republican fight led by Senator Taft against enabling General Marshall to become Secretary of Defense delayed a Senate vote until today. [1:2.]

The A. F. L. and C. I. O. garment unions asked an immediate 15 per cent pay increase for their 655,000 members to meet higher living costs. [1:1.]

There will be no more dry days or water curbs in this city unless the situation again gets critical, but water must not be wasted, officials said. [27:8.]

NEWS BULLETINS FROM THE TIMES
Every hour on the hour
7 A. M. through Midnight
WQXR AM 1560
WQXR FM 96.3

Index to other news appears on Page 26.

3 Robbers Shoot 2 Payroll Guards, Flee With $23,436 in Madison Ave.

Three robbers shot down two armed payroll messengers as the victims stepped into the lobby of 625 Madison Avenue early yesterday and fled with $23,436.

There were no outside witnesses to the crime and no worthwhile clues. Two small blood stains near the curb outside 35 East Fifty-eighth Street, the service entrance through which the thugs escaped, were reported as of little value but an alarm describing the getaway car with the notation that it might be blood-stained was broadcast. One robber might have been accidently wounded by a companion, according to the police.

Fifty detectives were assigned to cover the East Side and to make a search through the city for the gunmen's car, and to check hospitals and offices of physicians for evidence of anyone treated for a gunshot wound. By last night detectives had questioned thirty persons, including a number employed in the vicinity of the crime, in their search for clues.

The thugs fired five shots as they ambushed the couriers, Harold F. O'Connor, 43 years old, of 883 Columbus Avenue, and Joseph E. Gilgar, 54, of 34-50 Twenty-eighth Street, Long Island City, Queens. Although Mr. O'Connor managed to get his pistol from his holster as the last of the attackers sped out the side door he did not return the fire.

Herman Siegal, an employe of a laundry service, entered the building soon after the shooting and sounded the alarm. An elevator operator and a porter, the only two building service workers on duty at the time, also heard the shots but the first policemen were arriving when they came up from the cellar.

Mr. Gilgar, critically wounded

Continued on Page 22, Column 3

U. N. TROOPS MAKE LANDINGS IN KOREA

The New York Times — Sept. 15, 1950

United States and South Korean forces landed at Inchon (1) and drove inland, while other South Korean troops landed near Pohang (4) and at another point on the east coast about twenty-five miles north of Pohang. A fourth landing was reported made at Kunsan (3) on the west coast. Earlier, United Nations naval planes had battered targets from Pyongyang (2) and southward (points are indicated by bomb devices). South Koreans already hold islands marked by stars. The diagonally shaded area is the United Nations' southern beachhead.

'This Is Our Sunday Punch,' Task Force Observer Says

By ROBERT C. MILLER
United Press Correspondent.

WITH UNITED STATES MARINES, at Sea, Friday, Sept. 15—This is the one we have been waiting for. Within a few hours ships of this blacked-out task force will begin a shore bombardment to pave the way for landing craft that will carry the Marines in for what we hope to be the final battle of the Korean war.

This is our Sunday punch. We will know by tonight whether it will knock out the North Koreans.

There are no excuses for this one—everything has been planned and worked out for weeks. The supplies are adequate, the men are trained and the plans drawn down to the merest detail.

Everything that can be done to insure the success of this operation has been done.

This ship is like a highly trained boxer during those dreadful last hours before the bell, when the long weeks of training camp ordeal are finished and there is nothing to do but wait.

We are crammed with men who have been stacked into every corner of this assault ship. In the holds are the deadliest weapons we possess to arm them for the attack.

Every marine aboard is a combat veteran who came to a South Korean port directly from the front lines. They were loaded at the same port at which they arrived

Continued on Page 4, Column 3

U. S. SHUNNED SIGNS ON KOREA, U. N. TOLD

Inquiry Report Says Republic Warned General an Invasion From North Was Near

Excerpts from findings of Commission are on Page 6.

By A. M. ROSENTHAL
Special to The New York Times.

LAKE SUCCESS, Sept. 14—The United Nations Commission on Korea reported today that six weeks before the start of the war United States officers denied South Korean warnings that invasion from the north was imminent.

From January, 1950, to May 12, the commission reported, defense officials of the Korean Republic had warned that the Communist army was strong and getting stronger and that it was just a

Continued on Page 7, Column 3

Bevin and Schuman Agree to Seek Instructions on Arming of Germans

By THOMAS J. HAMILTON

Foreign Minister Robert Schuman of France and Foreign Secretary Ernest Bevin of Britain agreed yesterday to ask their governments for instructions regarding a Western Big Three discussion of the rearmament of Western Germany.

This decision was hedged with many conditions, but it is believed that it may open the door—if only partly—to acceptance of Secretary of State Dean Acheson's contention that Western German soldiers are absolutely essential for the defense of Western Europe against Soviet aggression.

According to well-informed sources, M. Schuman and Mr. Bevin agreed to send cablegrams to their Governments on the German rearmament with certain blanks. If these blanks were filled satisfactorily, they would then be authorized to discuss the principle of Mr. Acheson's proposal on Monday, after the meeting today and tomorrow of the foreign ministers of the twelve countries that are parties to the North Atlantic Treaty.

It was understood that M. Schuman and Mr. Bevin were in effect suggesting that they be authorized to discuss Mr. Acheson's proposal if they obtained assurance regarding the three principal conditions fixed by M. Schuman and Mr. Bevin previously as a preliminary to any discussion of German rearmament:

1. The rearmament of the Western Allies must have priority.
2. Western German units must be

Continued on Page 14, Column 5

Text of foreign ministers' interim communiqué appears, Page 14.

3 LANDINGS MADE

Allies Strike at Western Port and Two Points North of Pohang

4TH PUSH REPORTED

Units of U. S. Marines Join Blow Behind the Front Lines of Foe

By The Associated Press.

TOKYO, Friday, Sept. 15—United Nations invasion forces landed today at Inchon, the port city for Seoul on Korea's west coast—150 miles behind the 130,000-man North Korean Army at the fighting front.

Covered by planes and warships, United States troops stormed ashore on the island of Wolmi, linked to Inchon by a causeway. South Korean Marines landed at Inchon.

In a simultaneous operation other United States forces landed immediately behind the Communist lines on the east coast. They made two landings—one two miles northeast of Communist-held Pohang, the other at Yongdok, more than twenty-five miles north of Pohang.

[Sources in Washington said the United States forces involved were units of the Second Marine Division.]

The west coast invasion, preceded by cruiser and destroyer bombardments and sweeping carrier plane strikes, swung the United Nations to the offensive for the first time since the Reds began the war last June 25.

Close to 38th Parallel

The invasion at Inchon, putting United Nations forces close to the Thirty-eighth Parallel which the North Koreans crossed June 25, was announced by the South Korean Commander in Chief, Maj. Gen. Chung Il Kwon.

He said that heavy pressure was quickly exerted by the invasion forces on the Communists near Kimpo airfield, Seoul's big air base. Kimpo is twelve miles northwest of Seoul and ten miles north of Inchon.

A report from Pusan said that still other United Nations forces had gone ashore at Kunsan, a west coast city 100 miles south of Seoul. The report came from Chin Soo, South Korean National Assemblyman, who said a warship bombardment had supported the landing.

One thousand South Korean commandos went ashore on the east coast near Pohang, striking at a coastal road that would bar the way to any retreat by the North Korean forces defending the port. The commandos quickly called for air support.

A big United States battleship was reported Thursday to be off the east coast in the Pohang-Yongdok sector.

Invasion Follows Naval Attack

The North Koreans had been expecting an invasion at Inchon since Rear Adm. John M. Hoskins, commander of Task Force 77, sent British and United States cruisers and destroyers close in to bombard Inchon Wednesday. The targets included Wolmi Island.

While their shells hit the area, carrier planes for the second straight day ranged 210 miles from Kunsan to Pyongyang, capital city of the North Koreans, hitting at airfields.

B-29's coordinated these blows, blowing up an underground arsenal north of Pyongyang and severing rail lines from Pyongyang for 100 miles south to Seoul and for 200 miles southeast to Kumchon.

[Gen. Douglas MacArthur's headquarters announced at noon today, Friday, that United Nations forces were again in the walled city of Kasan, ten miles north of Taegu, from which they had been forced to retreat last weeks. The United Press reported.]

The Pyongyang radio broadcast claimed shore guns had sunk three destroyers and four landing craft Wednesday. United States officials in Washington quickly said the three destroyers had suffered

Continued on Page 3, Column 8

"All the News That's Fit to Print"

The New York Times.

LATE CITY EDITION
Partly cloudy, warm today; showers tonight. Much cooler tomorrow.
Temperature Range Today-Max.,77; Min.,56
Temperatures Yesterday-Max.,81; Min.,58.9
Full U. S. Weather Bureau Report, Page 66

VOL. C..No. 33,885. Entered as Second-Class Matter. Post Office, New York, N. Y. NEW YORK, THURSDAY, NOVEMBER 2, 1950. Times Square, New York 18, N. Y. Telephone LAckawanna 4-1000 RAG PAPER EDITION SEVENTY-FIVE CENTS

ASSASSINATION OF TRUMAN FOILED IN GUN FIGHT OUTSIDE BLAIR HOUSE; PUERTO RICAN PLOTTER, GUARD DIE

WOULD-BE ASSASSIN OF PRESIDENT SHOT DOWN

Oscar Collazo lying at the bottom of the steps to the Blair-Lee House as White House guard is putting his revolver back in his holster. This picture was made by a photographer of The New York Times, who was waiting to accompany Mr. Truman to a dedication ceremony at Arlington Cemetery.

The New York Times (by Bruce Hoertel)

KOREAN REDS HIT U. S. UNIT; NOW USE JETS

REGIMENT TRAPPED

Foe Employing Rockets Against First Cavalry Division at Unsan

U. N. TROOPS FORCED BACK

Only 24th Division Makes Gain and Then It Is Told to Halt Its Advance

By LINDESAY PARROTT
Special to The New York Times.

TOKYO, Thursday, Nov. 2—North Korean Communists, reinforced by troops of the Chinese Red Army, savagely attacked today advance guards of the United States First Cavalry Division thrown into action near the west coast of Korea to reinforce the weakening South Korean troops.

The attack made north and west of Unsan, where the Communists had concentrated their strength during the last few days and had driven back South Korean spearheads by as much as thirty miles in some sectors. Using tanks, artillery and heavy mortar fire, the North Koreans cut off one regiment of the United States Cavalry Division. Other units of the division were reported to be attempting to fight their way through to reach the isolated troops.

The fighting was in progress between Unsan and Taechon, but a spokesman for the United States First Corps said the situation was too vague and confused to locate the positions to which the United States troops had been forced to retreat.

Admits Chinese Are Fighting

For the first time a corps spokesman officially admitted that "Chinese troops" were launching an assault.

"We don't know whether they represent the Chinese Government," he said, and added that it also was unknown whether or not Chinese reinforcements made up the bulk of the new strength that had enabled the shattered North Korean Army to take the offensive again—at least locally—against the United Nations move toward the Manchurian border.

The Communists launched their attack in the morning. According to reports from Korea, they used heavy rocket bombardment for the first time in the war. The latest accounts said the enemy had overrun several First Cavalry positions, capturing weapons and turning them against Americans who had been hurriedly brought up to the combat line after all but one United States division—the Twenty-fourth Infantry, farther to the west—had been out of the contact with the enemy and behind the Korean Republican spearheads driven in by the enemy counterattack.

This morning the North Koreans were reported to be within one half mile of Unsan.

Rockets Launched on Ground

The use of the rockets, fired from launchers on the ground, represented the second new weapon introduced on the North Korean side within the last two days. Yesterday for the first time the enemy flung jet-propelled fighter planes into combat.

Meanwhile, the ground advance of the Allied forces halted at Chongko, where the United States Twenty-fourth Infantry Division stood within eighteen miles of the border city of Sinuiju, reported to be the new capital of the North Korean Communist Government.

All along the rest of the front South Korean divisions were in retreat or on the defensive against enemy attacks strengthened by contingents of Chinese Communist soldiers trained in the Chinese Red Army.

Six enemy jet fighters made their appearance yesterday over Sonchon on the west coast, fought a brief dogfight with Mustangs of the United States Fifth Air Force and then flashed back toward the Manchurian border without casualties on either side. Observers said the jet-propelled planes resembled the Soviet model MIG-15, with swept back wings and a speed of 600 miles an hour. On the previous occasion jet planes were believed to have been seen over North Korea, but this was the

Continued on Page 3, Column 1

PLAYWRIGHT DIES

George Bernard Shaw
The New York Times

BERNARD SHAW, 94, DIES IN HIS HOME

Famous Irish Wit Had Been in Coma for Day—Broken Thigh Led to Final Illness

By The Associated Press.

AYOT ST. LAWRENCE, England, Thursday, Nov. 2—George Bernard Shaw, one of the modern age's greatest dramatists and its most caustic critic, died today at the age of 94. The white-bearded Irish-born sage, whose wit was renowned throughout the world for half a century, succumbed at 4:59 A. M. (11:59 P. M. Wednesday, Eastern standard time).

His death was announced to newsmen by his housekeeper, Mrs. Alice Laden. Wearing black, she appeared at the gates of the cottage, Shaw's Corner, and told the reporters: "Mr. Shaw is dead."

A few minutes after her announcement, Dr. Thomas Probyn, Shaw's physician, hurried into the house. Twenty minutes later, Shaw's longtime biographer, F. E. Loewenstein, told newsmen that the playwright died peacefully without regaining consciousness. Only two nurses were with him when death came.

The famed dramatist, who professed himself both a Communist and an atheist, was visited in his last hours by an Anglican clergyman, who said final prayers for the old sage's soul.

"It is wrong to say that he was an atheist," said the minister, the Rev. R. G. Davies. "He believed in God."

Shaw lapsed into his final coma yesterday morning at 3 o'clock (10 P. M. Tuesday, Eastern standard time) and never regained consciousness. Operated on seven weeks ago for a broken thigh suffered when he slipped and fell in his garden, he grew steadily weaker. A bladder ailment aggravated his condition.

Lights burned for two nights in Shaw's Corner, the red brick

Continued on Page 28, Column 2

LIE TERM EXTENDED AS U. N. SECRETARY FOR 3 YEARS, 46 TO 5

Assembly Vote Continues Him in Office Despite Bitter Attacks by Russians

ARAB BLOC, CHINA ABSTAIN

Australia Also Shuns Support—Final Move by Vishinsky to Block Step Fails

The text of Secretary Lie's address is printed on Page 3.

By THOMAS J. HAMILTON

Overriding last-ditch Soviet opposition, the General Assembly yesterday extended the term of Trygve Lie as Secretary General of the United Nations for another three years. The vote was 46 to 5, with only the five members of the Soviet bloc opposed.

However, Australia, Nationalist China and six members of the Arab bloc—Egypt, Iraq, Lebanon, Saudi Arabia, Syria and Yemen—abstained. Haiti was absent.

Mr. Lie, whose present five-year term will expire next Feb. 2, told the Assembly when it reconvened for the afternoon session that he interpreted the extension of his term as a vote of confidence and a reaffirmation of the independence and integrity of the position.

Mr. Lie did not refer to his stand in favor of United Nations action for the defense of South Korea, which had led the Soviet Union to veto his re-election. But he said that he had worked hard for the past five years to reconcile "the conflicting interests that divide the world" and that he would continue to do so.

Iraq Explains Abstention

Immediately after the vote Dr. Fadhil Jamali of Iraq explained that he had not been able to vote for the extension of Mr. Lie's term because he felt that, despite Mr. Lie's "many fine qualities," he had not been "entirely impartial" on the Palestine question. He added that "Mr. Lie did not react toward recent Jewish aggressions in Palestine with anything like the zeal which he displayed on the question of Korea."

"With due respect to Mr. Lie, we do not believe that he helped enough to make the United Nations bring about peace and justice to the Arabs of Palestine," Dr. Jamali said.

Nasrollah Entezam of Iran, President of the Assembly, who had given Dr. Jamali the floor to explain his vote, then pounded his gavel, declaring that this was not an explanation, and that Dr. Jamali could not "continue this way in attacking a person who is not present here and who has received the confidence of the General Assembly by forty-six votes in his favor."

Dr. Jamali then stepped down from the rostrum with the statement that "it would certainly have been a betrayal of Arab public opinion and sentiment if we had not abstained."

Sir Keith Officer, who then was recognized to explain Australia's abstention, said that Australia shared the view that Mr. Lie must not be punished for doing "his clear duty as regards the action of the United Nations in Korea," but that Australia had "genuine doubts" about the legality of the extension of Mr. Lie's term, which

Continued on Page 3, Column 5

CAPITAL STARTLED

Police Swiftly Cordon Blair House as Shots Attract Big Crowds

PHOTOGRAPHERS NEAR BY

Leap From Their Auto, Halted by Traffic Light, Into Action—Passers-by See Fight

By PAUL P. KENNEDY
Special to The New York Times.

WASHINGTON, Nov. 1—This city, which has heard the sound of assassins' guns before, reacted with electric suddenness today as shots exploded before the front door of President Truman's own residence.

Within a few moments after the firing had stopped in front of Blair House hundreds of spectators were straining at police cordons almost magically thrown up at the intersecting streets bounding the block in which the President's temporary residence is situated.

Street cars, which run along Pennsylvania Avenue in front of the White House and Blair House, were backed up three blocks from Jackson Place, which bounds the Blair House block on the east, and for as many blocks from Seventeenth Street, which bounds Blair House block on the west.

Automobile traffic snarls blocked the approach of a number of ambulances and police squad cars, and wailing sirens heightened the confusion.

Approaching the scene of the shooting from the outer fringe of the crowd, one picked up at least a dozen accounts of what had happened. The accounts grew less lurid toward the core of the trouble.

Rumors Fly Among Throngs

These reports were received from spectators, at least a half block from the Blair House, and from newspaper men scurrying from the scene to the nearest telephones. On the outer reaches of the crowd the rumor was that two or three persons had entered Blair House with submachine guns firing and that the President had been assassinated or wounded.

Even among the reporters and photographers directly in front of the Blair House, the early accounts were confusing. It was not until fully fifteen minutes after the firing that it was clearly estab-

Continued on Page 16, Column 6

PUERTO RICO'S HEAD LINKS TWO ATTACKS

Governor Says Nationalist Forces Sparked by Reds Shot at Truman, Himself

By The United Press.

SAN JUAN, Puerto Rico, Nov. 1—Gov. Luis Muñoz Marin said tonight that Puerto Rican Nationalists were being used by the Communists both in the attempt to assassinate President Truman and in the abortive revolt here, in which he also was a target.

"This further crime—the Washington attempt—further confirms me in my conviction that the Nationalists are having their lunacy, fanaticism and irresponsibility manipulated for the benefit of Communist propaganda and strategy," the Governor said.

"We all feel deeply relieved that no tragic consequences resulted from this criminal action.

"The people are profoundly

Continued on Page 19, Column 2

Assassins' Kin and Friends Are Rounded Up in Bronx

By MEYER BERGER

Thirteen Puerto Ricans—six women and seven men—were taken to the offices of the United States Secret Service at 90 Church Street last night for questioning about the attempt yesterday on President Truman's life in Washington.

Policemen said they were the families and friends of the two assassins. Unofficially, Oscar Collazo of 173 Brook Avenue, the Bronx, one of the men who fired a gun at Blair House, was described as treasurer of the New York City branch of the Puerto Rican Nationalists, bitter enemies of the United States.

Collazo, wounded, is in the Emergency Hospital in Washington. The second gunman, tentatively identified by Secret Service men as Griselio Torresola of 1259 Ward Avenue in the East Bronx, was killed by police bullets.

Mrs. Rose Collazo, 42 years old, the wounded man's wife, was one of those taken into custody. She was arraigned at 2 o'clock this morning in Federal Court before United States Commissioner Edward M. McDonald on a charge of having conspired with the two assassins and two unnamed persons to harm a member of the Government. Commissioner McDonald held her in $50,000 bail for a hearing next Thursday.

Following the arraignment Secret Service men took her to the Federal House of Detention.

At the request of Assistant United States Attorney Irving H. Saypol, Commisioner McDonald issued John Doe warrants for the two unidentified persons named in the conspiracy complaint.

Earlier Mrs. Collazo had told officials and newspaper men:

"I am Oscar Collazo's wife. He

Continued on Page 18, Column 3

PRESIDENT IS CALM AT DILL DEDICATION

Speaks, After Attempt to Kill Him, at Unveiling of Statue of British Field Marshal

By The Associated Press.

WASHINGTON, Nov. 1—Less than an hour after an attempt had been made to assassinate him, President Truman calmly dedicated a memorial to Britain's Field Marshal Sir John Dill at Arlington National Cemetery today.

"It is important to the peace of the world that peoples understand each other and have full faith in each other's sincerity," he said.

He made no reference to the gunfight in front of his Blair House residence. Many of the 600 dignitaries present at the unveiling wondered why Mr. Truman was surrounded by such an unusually heavy guard of Secret Service men.

The President in his address said that he welcomed "this opportunity to remind my countrymen that the maintenance of a perfect understanding between the people of Great Britain and the United States is of great impor-

Continued on Page 17, Column 2

PRESIDENT RESTING

Awakened by Shots, He Sees Battle in Which Three Are Wounded

HE KEEPS APPOINTMENTS

Documents Link 2 Assassins, Who Lived Here, to Puerto Rican Extremist Leader

By ANTHONY LEVIERO
Special to The New York Times.

WASHINGTON, Nov. 1—Quick-shooting White House guards cut down two assassins this afternoon when they attempted to invade Blair House in a Puerto Rican Nationalist plot to assassinate President Truman.

Tonight one assassin and one policeman were dead, and two policemen were wounded, one critically. The other assassin, seriously wounded, told the United States Secret Service that he and his companion had come down from New York two days ago to kill Mr. Truman.

On the body of the dead assassin Secret Service agents found a letter and a "memorandum," both cryptic but indicative of conspiracy. The missives were in the same handwriting and on the same stationery. They bore in the form of a signature, the name of Pedro Albizu Campos, leader of the Puerto Rican Nationalist extremists who carried out the uprising in Puerto Rico Monday.

U. E. Baughman, chief of the Secret Service, cautioned reporters, however, that he had no proof that Albizu Campos was the author of the two documents.

THE DEAD

COFFELT, Pvt. Leslie, of Arlington, Va., White House guard.

TORRESOLA, Griselio, of 1259 Ward Avenue, New York, assassin.

THE INJURED

COLLAZO, Oscar, of 173 Brook Avenue, New York, assassin; shot in the chest.

DOWNS, Pvt. Joseph, of Silver Spring, Md., White House guard, in critical condition with multiple wounds.

BIRDZELL, Pvt. Donald T., of Washington, White House guard; in "fair" condition with knees shattered by bullets.

All three wounded are expected to recover.

Taking his usual afternoon nap and roused by a fury of shooting, Mr. Truman looked down from an upstairs bedroom of Blair House. In the bright sun of Pennsylvania Avenue was terror and confusion. At the foot of the stoop leading into Blair House lay one of the assassins, alive, blood flowing from the middle of his chest and staining his blue shirt.

"A President has to expect those things," Mr. Truman said, later.

Truman Keeps to Schedule

Serene, a man of good conscience, for he had told the people of Puerto Rico unequivocally that they were free to work out their own political destiny, Mr. Truman punctiliously kept his remaining appointments of the day.

The outrage, however, made the Federal police agencies increasingly alert, and new safeguards were put around the President and his family. Meanwhile, the Secret Service began to trace back the plot through New York, to its apparent source in the island possession in the Caribbean, which is

Continued on Page 16, Column 2

Pope Affirms Dogma of Assumption Of Mary to Heaven 'Body and Soul'

By CAMILLE M. CIANFARRA
Special to The New York Times.

ROME, Nov. 1—Pope Pius proclaimed today the dogma of the Assumption into heaven of the Virgin Mary.

"We pronounce, declare and define to be a dogma revealed by God that the Immaculate Mother of God, Mary, ever virgin, when the course of her life on earth was finished was taken up body and soul into heaven," the Pope declared.

The Pontiff spoke ex cathedra as supreme pastor of the church and teacher of Roman Catholic doctrine during an open air ceremony of pomp and magnificence to an audience of thirty-six Cardinals and 480 Archbishops and Bishops in the grandiose setting of St. Peter's Square.

A throng of 200,000 faithful, including Holy Year pilgrims from so many countries that they could be said truly to represent the whole Catholic world, packed every inch of space of the oval-shaped square that had been transformed for the occasion into a vast Christian temple.

Beginning today 400,000,000 members of the Catholic religion must believe explicitly and without reservation—otherwise they will incur excommunication as heretics—the Catholic tradition of the Assumption now defined as a dogma or an article of faith. The Catholic Church holds that dogmas are truths revealed directly by God or through the apostles and contained in the two sole fonts of Catholic doctrine—the Bible and tradition.

As such they are irrevocably binding on all Catholics and may be defined by the Pope either alone as today or jointly with the Bishops in the Ecumenical Council repre-

Continued on Page 13, Column 1

Vatican texts on dogma and speech by Pope are on Page 12.

World News Summarized

THURSDAY, NOVEMBER 2, 1950

Two assassins, identified as Puerto Rican Nationalists, attempted to kill President Truman yesterday while he was taking an afternoon nap in Blair House. One assailant was killed and the other badly wounded in a gun fight outside the house with guards, one of whom died. Two policemen were seriously wounded. The President went to the window to see what had happened and was shooed to safety by alert agents. [1:8.] Later he dedicated a memorial in Arlington Cemetery honoring Sir John Dill, British Field Marshal. [1:7.]

Secret Service agents listed the two Puerto Ricans as Bronx residents, and last night six women and five men were taken to 90 Church Street for questioning. [1:6-7.] An hour before the Blair House attack an unidentified man threw two bottles of ignited gasoline into the Puerto Rican labor office in this city, but they did not explode. [17:7.] In Puerto Rico, which has been torn by Nationalist uprisings, the Government spurred its hunt for revolutionary leaders. [1:5.]

Washington, electrified by the attack, the sixth attempt on a President's life [16:8], crowded to the scene. Eyewitness reports were confusing and conflicting. [1:4]. An ironic twist to the assassination attempt was the fact that President Truman was a strong advocate of Puerto Rican independence. [16:1.]

Chinese and North Korean troops, using rockets and heavy guns, drove back United States troops in the Unsan area, trapping one regiment. Other United States forces were ordered to halt their advance 18 miles from the border. [1:1; map Page 2.]

India expressed "keen disappointment" in answering Communist China's rejection of her concern over the invasion of Tibet. [9:2.]

The United Nations General Assembly, 46 to 5, extended the term of Secretary General Lie for three years. Only the Soviet bloc voted no, while Australia, Nationalist China and the Arab states abstained. [1:3.]

France is ready to contribute half of forty divisions planned for Western Europe by 1953, Defense Minister Moch said. Secretary Acheson declared it was agreed there should be no German general staff, national army or war industries. [8:3.]

Pope Pius proclaimed as dogma the Assumption of the Virgin Mary into heaven. [1:2-3.]

George Bernard Shaw died at his home in England. He was 94 years old. [1:2.]

Theodore Roosevelt, Woodrow Wilson, Alexander Graham Bell, Dr. William C. Gorgas, Josiah Willard Gibbs and Susan B. Anthony were elected to the Hall of Fame. [34:3.]

The City Planning Commission approved a record $478,761,756 capital budget for 1951 and a $1,235,850,237 five-year program. [33:1.]

Index to other news appears on Page 32.

November Heat Record of 81° Set; Zoo and Parks Draw Big Crowds

By IRA HENRY FREEMAN

November came in like a lamb yesterday, a spring lamb.

On the fourth day of an unseasonably warm wave extending over the eastern third of the country, the temperature in this city climbed to 81 degrees at 1:15 P. M. It dropped one degree for an hour, but at 2:15 again reached 81, and the latter time was officially accepted as the record.

This was not only the warmest for any Nov. 1 but also higher than ever reached in November since the Weather Bureau began keeping records here in 1871. The previous record for Nov. 1 was 70 degrees in 1946, while the previous high for any November day was 80 on Nov. 6, 1948.

The coolest it got during the day was 59 degrees from 6 to 7 o'clock in the morning. That was two degrees above the normal maximum for Nov. 1, Col. James W. Osmun, chief assistant meteorologist in charge of the New York Weather Bureau, pointed out.

During the luncheon period when the mercury was rising 4 and 5 degrees an hour, throngs of office workers and shoppers on the midtown streets were uncomfortably warm. In Bryant Park the benches were jammed with men in shirt sleeves and girls in summer blouses.

Some air-cooled restaurants and offices turned the refrigeration back on temporarily. Women shoppers in Fifth Avenue and Fifty-seventh Street strolled along with their suit jackets over their arms. The retail clothing business, incidentally, was slackened temporarily by the weather, Thomas A. Terry, executive vice president of the Fifth Avenue Association, reported.

The brass Prometheus bringing

Continued on Page 22, Column 1

Campos Captured In San Juan Home

By The United Press

SAN JUAN, Puerto Rico, Thursday, Nov. 2—National policemen poured five heavy volleys of rifle and pistol fire into the home of Pedro Albizu Campos early today and captured the Nationalist party leader when he fled into the street.

The Puerto Rican Governor, Luis Muñoz Marin, earlier had accused the Nationalist extremist leader of responsibility for the assassination attempt made against President Truman yesterday. The would-be assassins were said to be members of the Nationalist party.

"All the News That's Fit to Print"

NEWS INDEX, PAGE 87, THIS SECTION

The New York Times.

Copyright, 1950, by The New York Times Company.

LATE CITY EDITION
Mostly fair and cold today. Fair and continued cold tomorrow.
Temperature Range Today—Max., 35; Min., 27
Temperatures Yesterday—Max., 42; Min., 32
U. S. Weather Bureau Report, Page 7; Sect. 5

Section 1

VOL. C..No. 33,930. Entered as Second-Class Matter, Post Office, New York, N. Y. NEW YORK, SUNDAY, DECEMBER 17, 1950. Including Magazine and Book Review. FIFTEEN CENTS New York City / 50 Mile Zone | Elsewhere / Twenty-five Cents

PRESIDENT PROCLAIMS A NATIONAL EMERGENCY; AUTO PRICES ROLLED BACK; RAIL STRIKE ENDS; ALLIES GIVE UP HAMHUNG; WU REJECTS TRUCE

U. N. 'TRAP' ALLEGED

Peiping Representative Says He Will Start Home Tuesday

BIDS U. S. QUIT KOREA

'Volunteers' to Withdraw if Formosa Also Is Yielded, He States

Text of press statement by Mr. Wu is printed on Page 12.

By A. M. ROSENTHAL
Special to The New York Times.

LAKE SUCCESS, Dec. 16—Communist China rejected today the United Nations plan for a cease-fire in Korea as a "trap," and Peiping's representatives here said they would leave for home on Tuesday.

The Chinese Communists warned that the great problems of the world could not be settled peacefully unless Peiping got a seat in the United Nations and a major voice in Asia. They made it clear that their conditions for peace in Korea remained United States withdrawal from the country and an end to American "aggression" in Formosa. On those conditions, they implied, Communist China would withdraw its "volunteer troops" from Korea.

Peiping's stand was outlined at a special press conference here called by its chief representative at the United Nations, the impassive Wu Hsiu-chuan. Before coming to the press conference Mr. Wu informed United Nations officials that he would leave for Peiping on Tuesday by air.

Wu Complains to Lie

Mr. Wu was reported to have told Secretary General Trygve Lie last night that his delegation had come to New York weeks ago to discuss Soviet charges of United States aggression against China and had not been invited to testify before the General Assembly's Political and Security Committee. The committee has opened debate on the item but recessed the discussion to take up the problem of Chinese intervention in Korea. Mr. Wu complained to Mr. Lie that there was no purpose in his staying if the committee did not discuss the Soviet charges, which are centered on Formosa and Korea.

The Secretary General immediately got in touch with the three-man cease-fire committee set up by the Assembly to sound out the United States and Communist China on the possibility of a cease-fire and efforts were said to have been made to persuade Mr. Wu to change his mind about leaving. But the Chinese still were planning to leave Tuesday.

Delegation May Stay

Some diplomats said that developments Monday would decide whether the Chinese Communists would leave. The Political Committee is to map its remaining work on Monday and the Chinese Communists may attend in the visitors' section. If the committee votes to resume talk on Formosa immediately, it was believed, the Chinese may stay for a while.

For its part, the cease-fire committee announced that it would present an interim report to the Assembly on Monday, and stressed the word interim. The committee released a statement saying that it intended to go ahead with its efforts for a Korean cease-fire. It was reported that the three diplomats—Lester B. Pearson of Canada, Sir Benegal N. Rau of India and Nasrollah Entezam of Iran—would now try to make direct contact with Chinese Communist leaders in Peiping.

The committee met with Mr. Lie today before the Wu press conference. In another room, a little while later, Mr. Lie met with Mr. Wu and introduced him to Mr. Entezam, who is president of the Assembly. Sometime over the weekend, there will be another — and

Continued on Page 12, Column 5

TURNING DOWN CEASE-FIRE PLAN

Wu Hsiu-chuan, right, outlining Communist China's stand at special press conference he called at Lake Success. With him are Miss Kung Pu-sheng and Chiao Kuan-hua.
The New York Times (by Ernest Sisto)

Paris and London Void Pacts In Arming Bonn, Soviet Says

By HAROLD CALLENDER
Special to The New York Times.

PARIS, Dec. 16—The Soviet Government handed to the French and British Ambassadors in Moscow yesterday a note accusing France and Britain of violating their treaties with the Soviet Union by sponsoring rearmament of the Germans.

[Text of the Soviet note to France and Britain, Page 18.]

The step was considered an effort to hamstring defense discussions due to begin in Brussels Monday among the Foreign and Defense Ministers of the North Atlantic Treaty nations.

The new note was a sequel to that of Oct. 18 to France, Britain and the United States in which Moscow said it would not "tolerate" measures of the Western powers aimed at reviving the German Regular Army.

The treaties that Moscow now charges were violated are Britain's pact with the Soviet Union of May 26, 1942, and France's similar treaty signed Dec. 10, 1944. The principal content of both treaties was an agreement not to make a separate peace with Germany or to make any alliance against either of the signatories.

Both treaties were made when the Soviet Union was aligned with but not formally allied with the Western powers in the war against Germany, and when both France and Britain sought to insure against a revival of German power, which then seemed to them the greatest possible future menace.

A warning of yesterday's note was given to the French by Jacques Duclos, French Communist leader, who, in a speech at Brest last Sunday, said that in accepting rearmament of the Germans "the French Government repudiates the signature of France and deliberately violates" the French-Soviet treaty.

M. Duclos specified that the vio-

Continued on Page 19, Column 1

RED CHINA'S ASSETS IN U. S. ARE FROZEN

Washington Takes Unilateral Action—Tightens Ban on Shipping to Mainland

By WALTER H. WAGGONER
Special to The New York Times.

WASHINGTON, Dec. 16—The United States, in actions believed to have fallen just short of a war declaration, froze Chinese Communist funds in United States territory tonight and prohibited United States ships from calling at Chinese ports.

These steps, taken less than twelve hours after President Truman had proclaimed a national emergency, completed an economic embargo characteristic of a state of war.

The State, Treasury and Commerce Departments acted in concert on the moves.

The United States took this action alone. That the Government had consulted other friendly powers was not denied, and the fact that the United States acted unilaterally indicated disapproval by the other nations.

The State Department said that the freezing of Communist China's assets and the barring of United States ships from her ports had been "forced upon us" by the in-

Continued on Page 16, Column 2

Nyack Area Fears the Thruway Means Razing of 250 Buildings

Special to The New York Times.

NYACK, N. Y., Dec. 16—Fear was widespread here today that the proposed Thruway crossing of the Tappan Zee would require the razing of 250 homes and other buildings and remove half the property in the village of South Nyack from local tax rolls.

Unpopular in this area from the time it was first contemplated, the Tappan Zee bridge project aroused fresh demonstrations of hostility as a relatively detailed map of the property needed for the bridge and approaches became available.

After examining the map, some residents asserted that the project would obliterate South Nyack almost as if it had been the target of an atomic bomb.

The villages of Nyack, South Nyack and Grandview, which are in the path of the Thruway, are planning a joint suit to enjoin the State Thruway Authority from proceeding with its plans. They are also arranging to send delegations to Governor Dewey and the Legislature to voice their demand for a change in plans.

Harold A. Williams, supervisor of the town of Orangetown, in which Grandview, South Nyack and Nyack are situated, received by messenger last night a copy of the new map from Bertram D. Tallamy, State Superintendent of Public Works and chairman of the Thruway Authority.

It showed the Rockland bridgehead of the Tappan Zee crossing in the northeast corner of Grandview. From that point the approach highway is sketched cutting diag-

Continued on Page 73, Column 3

BEACHHEAD IS CUT

U.N. Troops Forced Back to Narrowed Area as Foe Perils Lines

NAVY SHELLS REDS

MacArthur Aides Report Chinese Build-Up for Attack in West

By LINDESAY PARROTT
Special to The New York Times.

TOKYO, Sunday, Dec. 17—United Nations forces pulled back yesterday from the wrecked industrial city of Hamhung on the beleaguered northeast Korean beachhead to form a tight perimeter around the seaport of Hungnam. Off that port lay Allied warships to pour fire on advancing columns of Chinese Communists.

Hamhung was evacuated in mid-afternoon yesterday as Chinese troops began to pour into the city's northeastern suburbs. United States engineers blew bridges across the Tongsonchon River and smaller tributaries to delay the pursuit.

Reports this morning said the enemy occupied the city and in this area was about seven miles from the Hungnam beaches. Attacks from the northeast and northwest continued and at the deepest penetration the Reds were only three or four miles from the port.

The withdrawals came after heavy Chinese attacks on the northern and western faces of the United Nations area around the Hungnam beaches had made some penetrations south of Oro on a mountain highway down from the Changjin Reservoir and toward Chigyong where the Chinese were thrusting toward the important Yonpo airfield.

Indications were that the Communist invaders had massed ten to twelve divisions — more than 100,000 men — north and west of Hamhung in an attempt to drive

Continued on Page 3, Column 1

STRIKERS RETURN

Workers Heed Request of President—Freight Jam Is Melting

MAILS MOVING AGAIN

Pay Dispute Settlement Is Expected Quickly in Washington

By GEORGE ECKEL
Special to The New York Times.

CHICAGO, Dec. 16—Railroad transportation services were returning rapidly to normal today, as more than 10,000 switchmen ended their mushrooming three-day wildcat strike at the behest of President Truman.

The strikers were going back to work in fourteen of fifteen cities to which the walkout had spread. They did so without a settlement of the wage-hour dispute between the carriers and their union, the Brotherhood of Railroad Trainmen. The union, however, had not authorized the walkout.

[In Washington it was believed a quick settlement of the pay dispute underlying the strike would be effected, probably on terms long available to the union.

[In New York, mountains of mail and freight began to melt as virtually normal railroad service was restored.]

The last of the strikers to return were those at the Illinois Central yards in Birmingham, Ala. Strikers returned at the yards of the Southern Railroad in Birmingham a few hours earlier.

The Postoffice Department lifted its thirty-nine-hour embargo at 11:15 A. M., E. S. T., today, resuming "normal service" at once, and workers began the attack on mountains of backlogged Christmas parcels in the nation's key transport centers and transfer points as Chicago, St. Louis, Washington and Pittsburgh began to

Continued on Page 44, Column 1

World News Summarized

SUNDAY, DECEMBER 17, 1950

President Truman followed his Friday night message to the people that the nation was in grave danger by proclaiming yesterday a state of emergency. He delegated most of his own wartime powers to Charles E. Wilson, Director of the Office of Defense Mobilization, whose unparalleled controls over the country's economy will be subject only to Presidential veto. [1:8.] Shortly afterward, the Economic Stabilization Agency, in its first price-fixing action, ordered auto prices frozen at Dec. 1 levels. [1:6-7.]

In this city the declaration of emergency led to orders to twenty-two municipal departments that would have duties in the event of an attack to maintain around-the-clock vigil. [1:7.]

In response to the President's appeal to end their wildcat strike, railroad switchmen returned to work. [1:5.]

Shortly before leaving for Brussels, Secretary of State Acheson, acting with Mr. Truman's approval, proposed an emergency meeting of the foreign ministers of the twenty-one American republics to consider the strengthening of hemispheric defenses. [1:6-7.]

The United Nations' plan for a cease-fire in Korea was rejected by the Chinese Communist delegation as a United Nations "trap." The Chinese accused this country of "aggression" in Korea and Formosa, but indicated that if this "aggression" were terminated Peiping would be willing to advise the Chinese "volunteers" in Korea to quit fighting. [1:1.]

Two drastic steps directed against the Peiping regime were taken by Washington: all Chinese Communist funds in United States territory were frozen and all American ships were told to avoid Red China's ports. [1:2.]

Hamhung, in northeastern Korea, was abandoned to the enemy, as the defenders withdrew toward Hungnam. About 100,000 Chinese were reported pressing upon the shrinking beachhead. [1:4; maps, P. 2.]

Soviet Foreign Minister Vishinsky left Lake Success for home, expressing optimism and "wishes of peace, well-being and happiness" to the people of the United States. [5:1.] According to documents made public in Washington, Moscow's slave labor system has been a major factor in the economic organization of the Soviet Union. [20:1.] In new notes to France and Britain, the Soviet Government charged that London and Paris, by supporting the rearmament of Western Germany, were guilty of violating their agreements with Moscow not to participate in anti-Soviet alliances. [1:2-3.]

Prime Minister Attlee said there was no basis for the fear of wanton use of the atomic bomb by the United States. H warned Britons, however, that the future held disagreeable things in store for them, including a curb on improvements in their standard of living. [10:1.]

At the suggestion of Governor Dewey, Lieut. Gov. Joe R. Hanley has been named special counsel to the State Division of Veterans Affairs. [1:6-7.]

Recent Auto Rises Canceled By First Price-Freeze Edict

'Ceiling Regulation No. 1' of Economic Stabilization Agency Holds Schedules to Dec. 1 Levels—Wage Study Set

By CHARLES E. EGAN
Special to The New York Times.

WASHINGTON, Dec. 16—The first price freeze and roll-back actions to result from the present national emergency were announced today by the Economic Stabilization Agency.

Under orders effective at once prices of passenger automobiles are frozen as of Dec. 1, and companies that have increased quotations for their 1951 lines are ordered to "roll them back" to that date or face Federal penalties.

Today's order, which came soon after President Truman's action declaring a national emergency, was regarded here as a forerunner of a variety of similar edicts to issue from the agency beginning Monday.

[In Detroit, a Ford executive said the company would "conform promptly." The head of the automobile workers' union opposed "pin-prick" controls.]

The order was studied closely by representatives of business because they regarded it as setting a pattern for ensuing regulations. There was a general feeling that Dec. 1 would be selected as the terminal date for price increases and that ceilings declared by the Economic Stabilization Agency over the coming month would use quotations of that date as determining factors in industries affected.

The price action in the auto industry is based upon the authority granted under the President's declaration of a national emergency. It is the first order also to affect the economy since the Office of Price Administration exercised its powers in World War II.

According to officials the order was issued to enable the Economic Stabilization Agency to make a comprehensive analysis of the effect of cost increases upon the profit position of the companies affected and to ascertain whether cost increases actually incurred justified the recent price increases. If the study justifies the price advances, it was added, the agency will make whatever changes in

Continued on Page 59, Column 3

U. S. Urges Defense Parley By All American Republics

Special to The New York Times.

WASHINGTON, Dec. 16—The United States proposed today an emergency meeting of the foreign ministers of the twenty-one American republics for tightening the defenses of this hemisphere against the threat of international communism.

Secretary of State Dean Acheson instructed the United States representative to the Council of the Organization of American States to request such a meeting, and he said he was acting under the direction of President Truman.

In making his request known today, Mr. Acheson declared:

"The United States, having embarked on urgent mobilization for the common defense, wishes to consult its fellow members in the inter-American community with respect to the situation which we all face and on the coordination of the common effort required to meet it."

He asserted that "the aggressive policy of international communism, carried out through its satellites, has brought about a situation in which the entire free world is threatened."

The Secretary added that the United States, after consultations with leaders of Congress and the other American Governments, would propose a time and place for the meeting and set forth an agenda for consideration.

Edward G. Miller Jr., Assistant Secretary of State for Inter-American Affairs, said it was the hope

Continued on Page 33, Column 3

DISASTER SERVICES PUT ON ALERT HERE

Wallander Orders Agencies to Be in Condition of Readiness on 24-Hour-a-Day Basis

By DOUGLAS DALES

City agencies that would have functions to perform in the event of an enemy attack were ordered yesterday to be maintained in a condition of readiness on a twenty-four-hour-a-day basis.

The order was issued by Arthur W. Wallander, Civil Defense Director, with the approval of Mayor Impellitteri after the declaration of a state of emergency by President Truman.

Twenty-two municipal divisions, including the five borough presidents' offices, were directed by Mr. Wallander to maintain at least skeleton staffs throughout the day and night. Some of the departments affected already operate on a twenty-four-hour schedule be-

Continued on Page 39, Column 2

Hanley to Get $16,000 State Job; Dewey Makes Good His Promise

By WARREN WEAVER Jr.
Special to The New York Times.

ALBANY, Dec. 16—The appointment of Lieut. Gov. Joe R. Hanley as special counsel to the State Division of Veterans Affairs at an annual salary of $16,000 was announced today by Leo V. Lanning, director of the division. Mr. Hanley will take over the new post on Jan. 1.

Mr. Lanning said he had made the appointment "at the suggestion of Governor Dewey." Thus the Governor made good on a three-month-old pledge to give Mr. Hanley a state position, if the 74-year-old official should fail to win his Senatorial campaign against Senator Herbert H. Lehman.

The question of Mr. Hanley's future was one of the issues raised in the political storm that followed release Oct. 16 of the now famed Hanley letter, which was written Sept. 5. In the letter to Representative W. Kingsland Macy, the Lieutenant Governor wrote:

"I have an iron-clad, unbreakable arrangement whereby I will be given a job with the state which I would like and enjoy (I have been told what it is) at sufficient compensation to make my net income more than I now have."

Subsequently both the Governor and Mr. Hanley denied that any specific post had been discussed between them. Both men reported, however, that Mr. Dewey had expressed reluctance to lose Mr. Han-

Continued on Page 68, Column 1

TRUMAN SETS DRIVE

Gives Wilson Sweeping Powers, Asks 'Mighty Production Effort'

U. S. RALLIES TO CALL

Congress Speeds Action—Stand of President Praised in Europe

Texts of proclamation and executive order are on Page 30.

By ANTHONY LEVIERO
Special to The New York Times.

WASHINGTON, Dec. 16—President Truman proclaimed a state of emergency this morning and delegated many of his own war powers to Charles E. Wilson, the new Mobilization Director. Soon afterward the defense program moved into higher gear.

Today was a day of action in the White House, in Congress and elsewhere in the Government as officials moved to implement the President's declaration to the nation and the world last night that the United States would meet the challenge of communism.

The Economic Stabilization Agency canceled the price increases made by Ford, General Motors and Chrysler in the last few days, and this was merely the harbinger of many new controls that eventually will encompass the entire economy.

Industry evinced its readiness to accept any war production goals, striking railroad men returned to work, and the general response from the public indicated an acceptance of the austerity program suggested by the President.

Proclamation Is Signed

Mr. Truman had pleaded for unity, like past Presidents coping with crises, and as in 1917 and 1941 the country was rallying with vigor.

In the free countries of Western Europe Mr. Truman was applauded for his no-appeasement speech in which he pledged to create an "arsenal of freedom" to strengthen all free countries. From Russia, which the President blamed directly for the postwar troubles of the world, came a typical blast that this country was warmongering.

Mr. Truman took two actions this morning to start a drastic increase of the mobilization program. He signed the proclamation of emergency, which unleashed scores of additional executive powers, and issued an executive order granting virtually blanket authority to Mr. Wilson to carry out all aspects of war production and economic control he deemed necessary. This authority received by Mr. Wilson will be subject in the Executive Branch of the Government only to the veto of President Truman.

Threat to Freedoms Cited

In his proclamation President Truman declared that conquest of the world was the objective of "Communist imperialism." He said this now constituted a threat to the freedoms guaranteed by the Bill of Rights, to the free enterprise system and to other rights, like collective bargaining, that free people had chosen for themselves.

These were the elements of a "full and rich life" that could be lost by the triumph of the Communist way of life, Mr. Truman said, calling for "a mighty production effort" for defense.

Mr. Truman called for sacrifices, for cooperation by state and local officials, for loyalty to the principles on which the nation was founded, and faith in our friends

Continued on Page 28, Column 3

In order to continue the complete presentation of the news THE NEW YORK TIMES *was obliged to decline 192 columns of advertising for this issue.*

100TH ANNIVERSARY
"All the News
That's Fit to Print"
1851 1951

The New York Times.

LATE CITY EDITION
Fair today, increasing cloudiness tomorrow and mild both days.
Temperature Range Today—Max., 60; Min., 45
Temperatures Yesterday—Max., 65; Min., 48
Full U. S. Weather Bureau Report, Page 30

Copyright, 1951, by The New York Times Company.

VOL. C.No. 34,045. Entered as Second-Class Matter, Post Office, New York, N. Y. NEW YORK, WEDNESDAY, APRIL 11, 1951. Times Square, New York 18, N. Y. Telephone LAckawanna 4-1000 RAG PAPER EDITION SEVENTY-FIVE CENTS

TRUMAN RELIEVES M'ARTHUR OF ALL HIS POSTS; FINDS HIM UNABLE TO BACK U. S.-U. N. POLICIES; RIDGWAY NAMED TO FAR EASTERN COMMANDS

HOUSE VOTES U. M. T. ONLY AS A PROGRAM; MARSHALL WORRIED

Chamber Accepts Compromise Setting Up Commission to Draft Details of Plan

FUTURE LAW IS REQUIRED

Congress' Approval Is Needed to Start Universal Training—General Sees Risk in This

By JOHN D. MORRIS
Special to THE NEW YORK TIMES.

WASHINGTON, April 10—Concessions offered by advocates of Universal Military Training to save the program from outright rejection were approved today by the House of Representatives, but it remained to be seen whether the aim had been achieved.

General of the Army George C. Marshall, Secretary of Defense, meanwhile voiced the fear that current maneuvering in the House might "largely emasculate" the training features of the pending draft and training bill.

It was not clear, however, whether he was concerned over the main fight, expected later this week, over a proposal to eliminate all Universal Military Training provisions from the bill.

It was to head this off that the bill's managers headed by Representative Carl Vinson, Democrat of Georgia, offered the concessions that were approved today. The House accepted them on a voice vote.

Further Action Necessary

Consequently, as the bill now stands, little more than the principle of Universal Military Training is retained. A commission to draw up a detailed U. M. T. plan would be created. A "National Security Training Corps" would also be established, at least on paper.

But before anyone could be drafted to serve in the proposed corps, there would have to be another formal act of Congress, subject to Presidential approval or veto like any other bill, authorizing details of the training program.

At the same time, however, the revised bill retains safeguards against future pigeon-holing of U. M. T. in the House Rules Committee or elsewhere. The planning commission, which also would administer the program once Congress had authorized its institution, would be required to submit a detailed training plan to Congress within six months. The House and Senate Armed Services Committees would be required to report out a bill or resolution within forty-five days of receiving the plan. The measure then could be called up at any time.

Opponents Withhold Attack

In the House, bills ordinarily must be cleared by the Rules Committee before they can be considered on the floor. The Rules Committee bottled up a Universal Military Training Bill in the Eightieth Congress.

Opponents of any form of U.M.T. legislation did not fight the concessions approved in the House today, explaining that the proposals would make the bill less obnoxious although still unacceptable to them.

They were still hoping for approval of a substitute sponsored by Representative Graham A. Barden, Democrat of North Carolina, that would retain only what they regard as the "emergency" features of the pending draft measure. These include a three-year extension of authority to draft men 19 through 26 years of age for actual military service.

The Barden bill would eliminate authority to lower the draft age to 18½ as well as all long-range training features of the pending measure.

The Senate has already passed a draft and training bill adhering closely to the Administration's recommendations. It would authorize the drafting of men at the age of 18 and permit the President to put Universal Military Training

Continued on Page 18, Column 4

Tobey Asserts He Recorded R. F. C. Talks With Truman

President Said to Withdraw Fee Accusation—Niles Held Attempting to Aid Dawson

By C. P. TRUSSELL
Special to THE NEW YORK TIMES.

WASHINGTON, April 10—Senator Charles W. Tobey, Republican of New Hampshire, was represented tonight as having told the Senate (Fulbright) subcommittee investigating the Reconstruction Finance Corporation that President Truman had charged in a telephone conversation with him that members of Congress had accepted fees for obtaining R. F. C. loans for constituents.

The Senator was said to have reported also that in a later telephonic communication the President had said that he had been mistaken.

Both telephonic conversations were said to have been recorded on disks in Mr. Tobey's possession. The date, or dates, were not made public. The Senator declined to discuss the matter and members of the investigating group also were silent.

In another development in the R. F. C. inquiry, former Senator Burton K. Wheeler, Democrat of

Burton K. Wheeler
Associated Press

Montana, said today that he had asked Senator Tobey to "go easy on" Donald S. Dawson, White House aide, during the Senate investigation of the agency. Mr. Wheeler asserted that he acted at

Continued on Page 25, Column 3

Sterling Hayden Was a Red; 'Stupidest Thing I Ever Did'

Special to THE NEW YORK TIMES.

WASHINGTON, April 10—Sterling Hayden, motion picture actor and decorated former United States Marine, told the House Committee on Un-American Activities today that he had been a member of the Communist party from June to December of 1946.

"It was the stupidest and most ignorant thing I ever had done in my life," he said. "I went into it with an emotional and very unsound approach, but I don't mean to imply that I was dragged into it. I went in voluntarily."

Mr. Hayden, a native of Montclair, N. J., said there were thousands of others like him, who should come in and tell their stories.

He added that shortly after the invasion of South Korea his attorney had written to J. Edgar Hoover, director of the Federal Bureau of Investigation, giving his Communist case history and seeking a means of eliminating any prejudice against his recall to the service.

Under questioning for more than three hours, the former husband of Madeleine Carroll, screen star, told of a restless life that started with his quitting high school at the age of fifteen and going to sea, and winding up in Hollywood. A Capt. Warwich Tompkins, described by him as an "open and avowed Communist," ran through his story.

He identified Captain Tompkins as an employe of Amtorg, the of-

Continued on Page 14, Column 5

PRICE AIDE RESIGNS, CONDEMNS DI SALLE

M. E. Thompson, Ex-Governor of Georgia, Hits 'Kansas City Crowd' in Administration

Special to THE NEW YORK TIMES.

WASHINGTON, April 10—With bitter words for Price Stabilizer Michael V. DiSalle, and for the "Kansas City crowd" he said was in the saddle in the national Administration, M. E. Thompson, former Governor of Georgia, resigned today as a consultant to the Office of Price Stabilization.

Mr. Thompson, once a power in Georgia politics, and who asserted that he battled successfully against the States Righters there who tried to keep President Truman's name off the ballot in 1948, declared that he would not support the Democratic party in 1952 if the "Kansas City crowd" still held control.

"If this be political treason,

Continued on Page 20, Column 1

Navy Suspends Explosives Expert; State Department Then Bars Wife

Special to THE NEW YORK TIMES.

WASHINGTON, April 10—The Navy Department suspended Dr. Stephen Brunauer today as a "security risk," giving the 47-year-old high explosives expert thirty days in which to answer the charges.

The State Department meanwhile, suspended Mrs. Esther Caukin Brunauer, wife of the Navy scientist, pending the outcome of the investigation of her husband. The State Department made it plain in a statement that the action against Mrs. Brunauer was based not on information about her, but only as a result of the Navy suspension.

Both of the Brunauers were named by Senator Joseph R. McCarthy, Republican of Wisconsin, in the course of his charges last year of Communist infiltration of the Government.

The announcement of Dr. Brunauer's suspension, effective immediately, was made while he was on a trip to New England for the Navy. Questioned by reporters at LaGuardia Field, on his way back to the capital, he said:

"I do not know for what reason I was suspended. I think some one made a mistake. I telephoned Washington and a Navy spokesman said he did not know the reason for the suspension. I do not want to comment further on anything."

Mrs. Brunauer issued a stout denial of the McCarthy charges on March 13, 1950, defending herself and her husband against the allegations they were Communists.

The Navy announcement of its suspension of Dr. Brunauer followed the disclosure by the State Department that the action had already taken place. The Navy gave no details of the charges, but said that Dr. Brunauer would have thirty days to answer the charges and request a hearing.

The decision of Francis P. Matthews, Secretary of the Navy will be final, it was said.

Asked whether the suspension of Mrs. Brunauer in response to charges against her husband was

Continued on Page 16, Column 3

RISE IN SALES TAX EXPECTED TO PASS CITY COUNCIL TODAY

Finance Committee Studies Bill at Length—Fight Against Measure Goes On

RUML A FISCAL ADVISER

Mayor Declines Challenge to Debate With Hoving—Joseph Suggests State-Wide Levy

The finance committee of the City Council spent an inconclusive three-hour executive session at City Hall yesterday afternoon weighing the merits of the proposed increase in the retail sales tax from 2 to 3 per cent, but when the meeting ended nothing had changed the prospect that the tax rise would be approved.

It was indicated that today the committee, after further behind-closed-doors deliberations, would favor the sales impost rise by a vote of 8 to 2, or possibly 7 to 3, and that later today the full City Council would adopt the measure by something like 19 to 6.

If the tax bill clears the Council hurdles today, as is indicated, it is expected that the Board of Estimate, whose members are committed to it, will give its approval at tomorrow's regular meeting.

Ruml to Advise Controller

Meanwhile, Controller Lazarus Joseph announced the appointment of Beardsley Ruml, business consultant, financier and economist, as a special deputy controller to advise Mr. Joseph on fiscal matters. Mr. Ruml, whose appointment was for an "indefinite" tenure, will serve without pay.

Mr. Ruml was at one time connected with the Federal Reserve Board and also with the New York Stock Exchange. He is a

Continued on Page 32, Column 4

U. S. PRODS NATIONS

Suggests U. N. Members Send More Troops to Fight in Korea

3 AVENUES ARE LISTED

Contributions Sought From Nations Not Yet Committed

By A. M. ROSENTHAL
Special to THE NEW YORK TIMES.

UNITED NATIONS, N. Y., April 10—The United States has been quietly suggesting that members of the United Nations increase, or at least maintain, their contributions of troops for the Korean war effort.

Informed sources here report that for some time the United States has been keeping in touch with members of the world organization to see if non-United States representation in the international army could be increased.

[Chinese Communist troops in Korea clung to their positions along the Hwachon Reservoir in the face of daylong United Nations attacks. Eighth Army headquarters clamped a stringent security blackout on news from the front as a major battle seemed to impend in the reservoir area.]

So far there has been no general appeal to the United Nations members to contribute more troops; it has all been on a country-to-country basis. Diplomats said that there was no indication that a new general request for troops in Korea was in the making for the time being.

But on a longer-range basis, the question of more troops may be considered by the committee set up by the General Assembly on Feb. 1 to plan possible sanctions

Continued on Page 5, Column 3

World News Summarized

WEDNESDAY, APRIL 11, 1951

President Truman relieved General of the Army MacArthur of his command in the Pacific because the United Nations commander had been unable to give his "wholehearted support" to United States and United Nations policies. The Presidential ouster has forced the general from all his commands, including his role in the occupation of Japan. Lieut. Gen. Matthew B. Ridgway has been designated to take over all the Far Eastern commands. [1:8.]

The United States has been asking other United Nations members to increase, or at least maintain, their forces fighting in Korea and asking for troops from countries that have sent none. [1:5.]

Enemy resistance increased in the Hwachon Reservoir area of Korea. The Communists still held the dam although Hwachon itself appeared deserted. [3:1; map P. 2.] Mao Tse-tung was said to have been officially reported ill and Liu Shao-chi was said to be acting in his place at the head of the Chinese Communist regime. [9:2.]

Britain has suggested that the United States invite Communist China to the discussions on a Japanese peace treaty and send Peiping a draft of the proposed pact. The treaty, Britain holds, should include the return of Formosa to China. [1:6-7.]

The days of "easy and automatic" relations between the United States and Canada are over, Canada's External Affairs Minister declared. "There will be frictions" that can be settled easily, he said, if the United States recognizes that Canada's acceptance of Washington leadership does not mean she is "willing to be merely an echo of somebody else's voice." [1:6-7.]

A "severe, but not crippling" budget was presented to Britain by the Labor Government, which chose to increase taxes, already heavy, rather than cut social welfare funds. [1:7.]

The bill giving West German labor equal rights with management in the operation of the steel and coal industries was passed by the lower house. [14:2.]

The House passed and sent to the Senate a supplemental defense money bill 43 per cent below Administration requests [29:1] and cut from the draft bill a provision for Universal Military Training in favor of a Presidential commission to draw detailed plans. [1:1.] Defense Secretary Marshall ordered all three armed services to share equitably draftees of superior standing. [19:3.]

Mobilization Director Wilson called for an end to complacency, selfishness and partisanship if we are to beat down the "dreadful shadow" of history's most "absolute and ruthless" dictatorship. [23:1.] M. E. Thompson resigned as consultant to the Price Stabilizer in protest against "political" control and general wastefulness. [1:2.]

Organized baseball was ordered not to raise players' salaries above a club's 1950 highest. [33:2-3.] The Army halted certain pay rises for nonoperating rail workers until a special panel ruled in the case. [33:1.]

Senator Tobey was said to have disclosed that he had recorded telephone talks with President Truman about the Senate R. F. C. inquiry. [1:2-3.]

The Navy suspended Dr. Stephen Brunauer, a scientist, as a "security risk" and the State Department dropped his wife, Esther, until the husband's case was settled. [1:2-3.]

Index to other news appears on last page of this section.

DISMISSED BY THE PRESIDENT

General of the Army Douglas MacArthur

Britain Asks That Red China Have Role in Japanese Pact

By WALTER H. WAGGONER
Special to THE NEW YORK TIMES.

WASHINGTON, April 10—Britain has suggested to the United States that Communist China be brought into the negotiations for a Japanese peace treaty. The British proposal also specifically asked that the United States send a copy of its treaty draft to the Peiping regime for its consideration, and, further, that the treaty provide for the ultimate if not immediate return of Formosa to "China."

By "China" the British mean the regime of Mao Tse-tung, since that is the China now recognized by London.

These suggestions have been made in the course of recent conversations between the two Governments. They represent another difference of opinion that has developed between London and Washington on both the procedure for negotiating a Japanese treaty and the form the settlement should have.

The basis for the British request that Peiping be given a look at the United States treaty draft is to enable the Chinese Communists to reject the proposal if they want to, as the Soviet Union is expected to do.

At the same time, it is vigorously denied here that Britain will refuse to sign any treaty draft that Communist China rejects. Reports that such an "or else" position has

Continued on Page 8, Column 5

BUDGET INCREASES BRITONS' TAX LOAD

Income, Profit, Purchase, Auto and Gasoline Imposts Rise —Social Services Uncut

By RAYMOND DANIELL
Special to THE NEW YORK TIMES.

LONDON, April 10—The already heavily burdened British people were called upon today to pay even higher taxes to preserve their welfare state. Hugh Gaitskell, Chancellor of the Exchequer, introducing his first budget, told the House of Commons that there were only two ways of meeting the extra cost of rearmament. One, which brought cheers from the Conservative Opposition, was by reducing expenditures for social welfare.

The alternative he offered was a sharp rise in both direct and indirect taxes. This brought cheers

Continued on Page 10, Column 3

Canada Bars a 'Yes' Role to U. S.; Pearson Sees Unity Despite Friction

By The United Press

TORONTO, April 10—Lester B. Pearson, Canadian Secretary for External Affairs, said today that "easy and automatic" relations between Canada and the United States were a thing of the past.

In a speech apparently aimed at United States consumption, Mr. Pearson said that Canada was not willing to be "merely an echo of somebody else's voice" and reserved the right to criticize "our great friend, the United States."

Mr. Pearson said that Canada intended to prevent the United Nations from becoming "too much the instrument of any one country" and that it was time for the United States to stop telling Canada "that until we do one-twelfth or one-sixteenth, or some other fraction as much as they are doing, we are defaulting."

He said that there might be "angry waves which may weaken the foundation of our friendship" but that Canada would march forward with the United States "in the pursuit of objectives which we share."

"Nevertheless, the days of relatively easy and automatic relations with our neighbor are, I think, over," he added.

Mr. Pearson indicated that one of the "angry waves" that could weaken relations between Canada and the United States was the controversy over General of the Army Douglas MacArthur's statement on the war in Korea.

Later, in a second speech, Mr. Pearson made an indirect reference to General MacArthur when he said that a successful foreign policy must work toward goals accepted by the majority of the people, and it would have a better chance of "reaching these goals if we abandon what has been called 'hoop-la diplomacy' at Lake Success, at Ottawa, or, I hasten to add, at Tokyo."

He said that the free nations stood in danger of "nothing less

Continued on Page 6, Column 3

PRESIDENT MOVES

Van Fleet Is Named to Command 8th Army in Drastic Shift

VIOLATIONS ARE CITED

White House Statement Quotes Directives and Implies Breaches

Texts of statements and orders in MacArthur dispute, Page 8.

By W. H. LAWRENCE
Special to THE NEW YORK TIMES.

WASHINGTON, Wednesday, April 11—President Truman early today relieved General of the Army Douglas MacArthur of all his commands in the Far East and appointed Lieut. Gen. Matthew B. Ridgway as his successor.

The President said he had relieved General MacArthur "with deep regret" because he had concluded that the Far Eastern Commander "is unable to give his wholehearted support to the policies of the United States Government and of the United Nations in matters pertaining to his official duties.

General MacArthur, in a message to House Minority Leader Joseph W. Martin Jr. of Massachusetts, made public by Mr. Martin last Thursday, had publicly challenged the President's foreign policy, urging that the United States concentrate on Asia instead of Europe and use Generalissimo Chiang Kai-shek's Formosa-based troops to open a second front on the mainland of China.

The change in command is effective at once. General Ridgway, who has been in command of the Eighth Army in Korea since the death in December of Gen. Walton H. Walker, assumes all of General MacArthur's titles—Supreme Commander, United Nations Forces in Korea, Supreme Commander for Allied Powers, Japan, Commander-in-Chief, Far East, and Commanding General U. S. Army, Far East.

Commanded in Greece

The Eighth Army command will pass to Lieut. Gen. James A. Van Fleet whose most recent important command was as head of the American military mission in Greece, when that country was repelling a Communist-directed guerrilla attack under the Truman doctrine.

In ousting General MacArthur for his public disagreement with American policy designed to localize the Asiatic war, the President said:

"Full and vigorous debate on matters of national policy is a vital element in the Constitutional system of our free democracy.

"It is fundamental, however, that military commanders must be governed by the policies and directives issued to them in the manner provided by our laws and Con-

Continued on Page 3, Column 1

News Stuns Tokyo; MacArthur Is Silent

By The Associated Press

TOKYO, Wednesday, April 11—A small brown envelope with "flash" printed on it in red carried to General MacArthur today the news that he had been discharged from his commands by President Truman.

It was delivered by a senior aide, Col. Sid Huff, who said that the General received the news without comment. Colonel Huff indicated that the General had no forewarning that he was being relieved.

The General announced that he would have no statement immediately.

The message came as a Signal Corps communication about the time and Army radio announced the news.

General MacArthur got the word while at lunch with his wife, Senator Warren G. Mag-

Continued on Page 3, Column 4

100TH ANNIVERSARY
"All the News
That's Fit to Print"
1851 1951

The New York Times.

LATE CITY EDITION
Partly cloudy, mild today; cooler tonight. Rain likely tomorrow.
Temperature Range Today—Max., 70; Min., 56
Temperature Yesterday—Max., 70; Min., 47
Full U. S. Weather Bureau Report, Page 33

VOL. CI..No. 34,244. Entered as Second-Class Matter, Post Office, New York, N. Y. NEW YORK, SATURDAY, OCTOBER 27, 1951. Times Square, New York 18, N. Y. Telephone Lackawanna 4-1000 RAG PAPER EDITION SEVENTY-FIVE CENTS

CHURCHILL IS RETURNED TO POWER WITH A MARGIN OF 26 OVER LABOR; WASHINGTON EXPECTS VISIT SOON

TRUMAN PLEA TO PIER MEN IS UNHEEDED

TAFT LAW IGNORED

President Rejects Move by Industry After Talk With the Cabinet

BASES CALL ON DEFENSE

Insurgents Say No National Emergency Was Declared—Attack 'Unfair Verdict'

By GEORGE HORNE

President Truman appealed to New York waterfront strikers last night to return to work in behalf of the defense effort but the defiant strike committee immediately rejected the plea and called for widening of the costly stoppage.

The President, to whom Cyrus S. Ching, director of the Federal Mediation and Conciliation Service, had referred the dispute, discussed it with the Cabinet before making his decision not to accede to the demands of industrial leaders to invoke the procedure of the Taft-Hartley Act.

Mr. Truman said he had been informed that defense activity was being hampered and that "in the national interest" the employes ought to get back to their tasks.

The twelve-day strike started in a handful of locals on Oct. 15 and snowballed under pressure of roaming wildcat squads until it paralyzed the vast Port of New York, spread to Boston, halted work on military shipments and piled up cargoes estimated in value at nearly $300,000,000.

Demanded Pact Reopening

The intransigent strikers demanded reopening of a contract that had been negotiated through weeks of discussion with employers and was finally ratified by a 2-to-1 vote of the union's membership.

The new contract of the International Longshoremen's Association, A. F. L., and the New York Shipping Association, provided a 10-cent increase to make the basic hourly wage $2.10. It stipulated improvements in vacation terms, a single shape-up or work-call a day and other benefits which the majority of the union's 125-man wage committee approved and recommended.

Announcement of the plea from the White House was followed within ten or fifteen minutes by the insurgent rejection. John J. (Gene) Sampson, business agent of Local 791, spearhead local in the strike, said that the strikers would not accept the President's proposal since he had not seen fit to declare a national emergency.

The President could have invoked the Taft-Hartley Act despite the fact that the walkout involved an intra-union matter and not a labor-management dispute in which no contract existed. Moreover, he could have used a Wage Stabilization Board dispute procedure on a matter affecting national defense.

He had been urged by industrial and business associations and individuals in New York and New Jersey to apply the former procedure on the grounds that the stoppage was causing the lay-off of thousands of workers other than the 30,000 affected longshoremen and immobilizing ships, cargo and investments mounting into millions of dollars.

Two-Day Intercession Failed

Mr. Ching had sent the dispute to the White House following withdrawal of the Federal mediation agency after a boisterous and futile two-day intercession in New York.

Clyde M. Mills, No. 1 Ching aide and a trouble-shooter for the agency, had headed a commissioner's panel in New York in efforts to end the union's "family quarrel." The mediation men called it an "intolerable situation," a phrase that heightened the bitter feeling of recalcitrant strike leaders who described the Mills withdrawal announcement as unfair and tantamount to a verdict of guilt.

The text of Mr. Truman's statement follows:

"I have been informed by Mr. Charles E. Wilson, director of the Office of Defense Mobilization, that because of the work stoppages by the longshoremen the ports of New

Continued on Page 22, Column 3

Marciano Knocks Out Louis in 8th Round

Rocky Marciano, 27-year-old Brockton, Mass., boxer, became a leading contender for the world heavyweight championship when he knocked out Joe Louis, former holder of the title, in the eighth round of their scheduled ten-round bout in Madison Square Garden last night.

The defeat marked the end of the 37-year-old Louis' hopes of becoming the first ex-titleholder to regain the crown. Marciano dropped Louis for a count of eight before he sent him through the ropes with a right to the jaw at 2:36 of the eighth. Referee Ruby Goldstein disdained a count. It was Marciano's thirty-eighth triumph in a row, thirty-three of them by knockouts.

Louis showed no signs of weakening until the seventh round. He weighed 212½ pounds to Marciano's 187.

Details on Page 12.

FLATH'S VICE SQUAD UPSET BY MONAGHAN

Entire Personnel Transferred—Step May Foreshadow Clean Sweep of Plainclothes Men

By ALEXANDER FEINBERG

The entire personnel of the Chief Inspector's plainclothes squad, the top police unit assigned to the task of suppressing vice and gambling, was transferred yesterday by Police Commissioner George P. Monaghan.

Sixteen of the seventeen members of the squad were sent back to uniform a week after the retirement of August W. Flath as Chief Inspector and Mr. Monaghan's collateral declaration that all plainclothes squads would be reconstituted. The other member, formerly attached to the detective division, was reassigned there.

A year ago—on Sept. 29, 1950—Thomas F. Murphy, then Police Commissioner, on his fourth day in office ordered all of the 336 men in the plainclothes division back into uniform. He replaced them with selected patrolmen, "neither besmirched nor tainted," from the ranks of recruits and newly appointed policemen.

New Sweep Is Seen

Yesterday's action by Mr. Monaghan was believed to be the forerunner of a second clean sweep of all plainclothes personnel. In the shift, two acting lieutenants were reduced to sergeant, and an inspector, who headed the squad, a deputy inspector, an acting captain, two lieutenants and ten patrolmen were affected. Eight of the ten plainclothes men will take a loss of $240 a year in extra compensation.

Inspector Francis W. Lent, head of the squad under Chief Flath, who last week was succeeded by Chief Inspector Conrad H. Rothen-

Continued on Page 7, Column 3

KOREAN FOE DROPS DEMAND FOR TRUCE ON 38TH PARALLEL

But Enemy's Plan for 15-Mile U.N. Retreat From the Front Is Termed Unacceptable

REDS WOULD YIELD IN PART

Communists Propose to Move Out of Last Area They Hold South of Old Boundary

By LINDESAY PARROTT
Special to THE NEW YORK TIMES.

TOKYO, Saturday, Oct. 27—Although a Communist proposal for a fifteen-mile retreat by Allied forces in Korea was unacceptable to the United Nations Command, the negotiators for a truce were closer to geographical agreement on a cease-fire line today than at any time since the conferences started last July.

The enemy's proposal, providing for a United Nations withdrawal in the east and center, and for evacuation by the Communists of the last ground they hold in South Korea, was an abandonment of the Communist demand for a cease-fire based on the political boundary of the Thirty-eighth Parallel.

The plan was announced to Allied representatives at a ninety-minute meeting yesterday of subcommitteemen of both sides at their tent village near Panmunjom. There the United Nations on the day before had advanced its own proposal for a truce line and buffer zone close to the battle positions won by the Allied forces still grinding forward slowly into North Korea.

[The Associated Press said the third subcommittee session was held from 11 A. M. to 1 P. M. Saturday (9 to 11 P. M. Friday, Eastern standard time). The United Nations negotiators, Maj. Gen. Henry I. Hodes and Rear Admiral Arleigh A. Burke, failed to make any progress with the Communist representatives on the truce line issue. An afternoon session was scheduled for 3 o'clock.]

'Unilateral' Retreat Cited

Thus far, there has been no formal Allied rejection of the enemy proposal. But an official United Nations bulletin pointed out yesterday afternoon that the Chinese and North Korean plan required a "unilateral" withdrawal by United Nations forces from militarily important positions along virtually all of the present battle line.

Among these would be hard-won ground at "Heartbreak Ridge" and the "Punchbowl" in the rugged mountains of the peninsula's eastern watershed, and the "Iron Triangle" in the center. It was estimated that the retreat would extend along a 100-mile front, ceding almost all of the territory gained by Gen. James A. Van Fleet's summer and autumn offensives, staged since the armistice talks began.

In exchange, the Communists offered to yield the Ongjin Peninsula and an area around Yonan. There, tongues of land thrust down into the Yellow Sea below the Thirty-eighth Parallel.

But this territory generally is considered indefensible, except by a force that also could hold an enclave to the north above the old boundary, and the United Nations in the present campaign never has made any serious attempt to chal-

Continued on Page 2, Column 5

THE NEW PRIME MINISTER CONGRATULATED BY HIS WIFE

Winston Churchill as he appeared yesterday after late returns had assured his party of victory in the British elections
Associated Press Radiophoto

ATTLEE STEPS DOWN

King Then Calls on War Leader to Take Over at Time of Crisis

LABOR TOPS POPULAR VOTE

Party Polls 48.8% to Rival's 48.1 While Losing Out on Seats by 293 to 319

By RAYMOND DANIELL
Special to THE NEW YORK TIMES.

LONDON, Oct. 26—For the second time in both their lifetimes, George VI called upon Winston Churchill today to form a government at a time of national crisis.

A little earlier the King, who is convalescing from a serious operation, received Clement R. Attlee and accepted his resignation as Prime Minister because the verdict of the people of Britain had gone against the Labor party in yesterday's general election. Therefore, Mr. Churchill, leader of the Conservative party, now takes his place at the helm of the ship of state that Mr. Attlee has sailed according to Socialist navigation rules for the past six years, and with a depleted crew for nineteen months.

After the 1950 election Mr. Attlee's Labor Government never had a majority of more than seven. It seems now that Mr. Churchill in the skipper's role will not be much better off.

Over-all Margin Now 18

As matters stand now the Conservatives have a majority over all others of eighteen, and twenty-six more seats than the Labor party alone. The majority may increase or decrease but not enough to make any real difference.

There are only four constituencies remaining to be heard from in the present count. In addition there is a seat to be filled in a delayed election. If the Conservatives won all the remaining seats, which is unlikely, their over-all majority would be twenty-three. However, if these seats did not change the Conservative majority would be seventeen.

The present party standings follow:

Conservatives	319
Labor	293
Liberals	5
Independents	3

All of the Independents are Irish, two of them probably will not ever vote, and one of them leans toward Labor.

This accounts for 620 of the 625 seats in the House of Commons. Of the four constituencies remaining to be heard from, two have been held in the past by Conservatives, one by Labor and one by the Liberals.

Seat Held Safe for Labor

The 625th seat remains vacant because one of the candidates died during the campaign. It, however, is a safe seat for Labor and when the election is held it should add one more seat to Labor's strength in the House.

Mr. Attlee probably was right in ascribing his downfall to the way the Liberals voted. At party headquarters after he had taken leave of the King he said:

"I don't think there is any reason to dispute that our loss of seats has been due to the fact that when it came to the point more Liberals were Conservative than Labor."

How many more Liberals voted

Continued on Page 3, Column 2

MOSES SEEKS STEEL OF FOREIGN MAKERS

Would Meet Needs for Roads by Dealing Directly With Mills in Germany and Belgium

The quest of Robert Moses, City Construction Coordinator, for imported steel to fill the construction needs of traffic relief projects in the city has been frustrated thus far by soaring prices that far exceed the limitations of the public purse, he said yesterday.

Now he is seeking ways to get the essential metal directly from German and Belgian manufacturing bases without paying a middleman's profit to the importers in this country.

Mr. Moses pointed out that the Federal allocation system had seriously restricted domestic steel for city use.

The difficulties encountered in attempts to get foreign steel were

Continued on Page 34, Column 2

Gain for U. S.-British Ties Seen by Congress Members

By WILLIAM S. WHITE
Special to THE NEW YORK TIMES.

WASHINGTON, Oct. 26—The return of the Conservatives to power in Britain will improve British-American relations as far as both parties in Congress are concerned. The success of the ticket headed by Winston Churchill likewise will tend to ease the way for any future programs in aid of Britain, be they economic or military, other things being equal.

Washington generally expected Mr. Churchill to come to this country soon for consultation with President Truman on the coordination of United States and British foreign policy. The Prime Minister and the President are old friends, and their previous meetings having included the Potsdam conference of July, 1945.

There was much speculation here that Mr. Churchill would time his visit to coincide with the President's extended vacation at Key West, Fla., which starts Nov. 8.

Continued on Page 3, Column 7

U. S. WILL INCREASE ARMS TO YUGOSLAVS

Heavy Weapons Will Help Tito Resist Aggression—Pact to Be Signed Next Week

By WALTER H. WAGGONER
Special to THE NEW YORK TIMES.

WASHINGTON, Oct. 26—The United States and Yugoslavia will sign a military aid agreement in Belgrade next week to assure new and larger shipments of American arms to Marshal Tito's anti-Soviet armed forces.

The agreement will bring to a close negotiations between the two Governments that formally got under way here last June, with the visit of Col. Gen. Kuca Popovic, Chief of Yugoslavia's General Staff, and concluded with the inspection trip to Yugoslavia earlier this month by Gen. J. Lawton Collins, United States Army Chief of Staff.

Arms that can then be expected to start flowing to the only Government holding out in Eastern Europe against Russian domina-

Continued on Page 5, Column 4

MANY CHANGES SET BY CONSERVATIVES

'Denationalization' of Steel, Tax Revision and Broad Housing Program Listed

By CLIFTON DANIEL
Special to THE NEW YORK TIMES.

LONDON, Oct. 26 — Former Prime Minister Attlee said in his recent ill-starred election campaign that his Labor Government could not be expected to clear up in six years the mess of six centuries.

Next week the Conservatives will set about tidying up what they regard as the mess of Labor's six years. They have promised many changes, although not as many as the ideological differences between the two parties might indicate, and they have years of legislative work ahead of them.

Their program is not as ambitious as that of the 1945 Labor Government, which came to power with plans to remake the whole economic and social structure of Britain. Among the tasks that the Conservatives have set themselves are these:

1. To "denationalize" the iron and steel industry, the last enterprise taken under public ownership by the Labor Government last March.
2. To decentralize the administration of the Nationalized Coal Industry and of the state-owned railroad and road transport systems.
3. To build more houses, 300,000 a year being the stated target, and

Continued on Page 3, Column 4

World News Summarized

SATURDAY, OCTOBER 27, 1951

Winston Churchill, as the leader of the victorious Conservative party, was asked by King George VI to become the new British Prime Minister in place of Clement R. Attlee, who resigned. With four districts still unreported, the Conservatives had an over-all majority of eighteen and a majority of twenty-six over Labor in the newly elected Parliament. [1:8.]

Mr. Churchill and his aides will face many heavy tasks, including the fulfillment of their pledge to "denationalize" the iron and steel industry and to decentralize the administration of the nationalized coal industry and of the rail and road transport system. [1:7.] Mr. Churchill, reflecting the sober mood in which the Conservative victory was accepted on all sides, said, "We shall do our very best." [3:1.]

The majority of the remnants of the once mighty Liberal party backed the Conservatives and this support was the major factor in the Conservative capture of twenty-one of the twenty-four seats won from Labor. [3:8.]

Congressional members of both parties foresaw an improvement in British-United States relations, particularly in the field of foreign policies. [1:5-6.]

In Paris European observers also were optimistic of greater Allied unity as a result of the British election. [4:3.]

Yugoslavia will receive a larger amount of military aid from the United States under an agreement to be signed in Belgrade next week by representatives of the two countries. [1:6.]

In the Korean truce negotiations the Communists abandoned their demand that the demarcation line between the opposing armies be set along the Thirty-Eighth Parallel, but their newer proposal, calling for a fifteen-mile retreat by Allied forces, also was unacceptable to United Nations officials. [1:3.]

Allied fliers shot down two enemy jet planes and damaged three others in another air battle over Northwest Korea. [2:8; with map.]

The peace treaty signed at San Francisco was ratified by the lower house of the Japanese Diet, which also approved the security pact allowing the maintenance of a United States garrison in Japan. [2:1.]

President Truman, emphasizing the serious effect on the defense program of the wildcat dock walkout here, appealed to the strikers to return to work, but his plea was promptly rejected. [1:1.]

Thomas H. White, Cleveland industrialist, and his wife and daughter-in-law were killed when their private plane, piloted by Mr. White, crashed as it approached a landing at the Washington airport. [1:6-7.]

Index to other news appears on last page of this section.

Error in Race Placing at Jamaica Costs $15,655, Helps Cancer Fund

By JAMES ROACH

The Damon Runyon Fund for Cancer Research was the winner in the third race on the Empire City-at-Jamaica program yesterday—a horse race that the placing judges never will be able to forget.

The placing judges made a $15,655 mistake. Perhaps the fund will profit by as much as $10,000 from it.

A horse named Swing Cheer finished first, with Air Service second by a nose over Sao Paulo. The mutuel-ticket numbers, in order, were 11, 13 and 5. But the numbers didn't go up in the proper order on the result boards.

The three placing judges, in the unhappiest moment of their racing careers, reversed the place and show horses, and put up 11, 5 and 13.

They soon discovered their error, but not in time to prevent the flashing of the "official" sign, which set in motion the pay-offs. Apparently there were no complaints from any of the 19,353 racegoers. One reason: the photo was not put on public display. It showed that Air Service, on the outside, had beaten the on-the-rail Sao Paulo by six or eight inches.

Place payoffs on Sao Paulo were made at the rate of $5.10 for each $2. By the time the stewards had notified the Empire City Racing Association management of the error almost all of the payoffs had been made.

What to do?

James Butler, Empire City president, conferred with other officials. There was no precedent in New York racing for their problem.

The management had an "out" in that the first general rule of New York racing reads that "final decision of the racing officials upon the running and results of races shall be conclusive." The management didn't want that "out." It wanted to pay off those who had

Continued on Page 14, Column 1

Industrialist Flying to See Marshall Killed as Plane Crashes in Potomac

Special to THE NEW YORK TIMES.

WASHINGTON, Oct. 26—Thomas H. White, Cleveland industrialist; his wife, the former Miss Kathleen York, and his daughter-in-law, Mrs. Robert White, were killed here this morning when a plane piloted by Mr. White fell into the Potomac River while approaching National Airport. Mr. White was on his way to keep a luncheon appointment with General of the Army George C. Marshall, former Defense Secretary.

Mr. White, 57 years old, a grandson of the founder of the White Motor Company and White Sewing Machine Company, was piloting the plane, a single-engine Beechcraft Bonanza, from Hunting Valley Village, a Cleveland suburb, to Washington.

The plane had made a routine stop at Youngstown, Ohio, and was scheduled to arrive here at 10:15 A. M. The crash occurred at 10:12 A. M.

There was no immediate explanation as to the cause of the accident. Radio tower operators said that the plane, given landing clearance, was apparently making a normal approach when at about 200 feet altitude it suddenly nosed down and fell into the river's edge where the water was shallow.

Crash boats were at the scene within a few minutes and their crews recovered the bodies from the plane. The nose and engine of the plane were pushed into the passenger compartment.

The Civil Aeronautics Board, the Civil Aeronautics Administration and police began an investigation.

Mr. White's purpose in visiting General Marshall today was to talk with him about Nato, an Elkhound which the children of Norway recently presented to the General. General Marshall, long an acquaintance of Mr. White, said they had exchanged some correspondence about the dog. It was indi-

Continued on Page 34, Column 4

Churchill in Office: A Wartime Study

The energy, versatility and qualities of mind that Mr. Churchill brings to the Prime Ministership are vividly illustrated in today's installment of his war memoirs. His ideas on diplomacy, his attitude toward Americans, his views on how to handle the Russians are set forth in a series of wartime minutes.

See Page 21

"All the News That's Fit to Print"

The New York Times.

LATE CITY EDITION
Light snow this morning followed by clearing. Fair tomorrow.
Temperature Range Today—Max., 43; Min., 25
Temperatures Yesterday—Max., 40; Min., 33
Full U. S. Weather Bureau Report, Page 55

VOL. CI..No. 34,347. Entered as Second-Class Matter, Post Office, New York, N. Y. NEW YORK, THURSDAY, FEBRUARY 7, 1952. Times Square, New York 36, N. Y. Telephone Lackawanna 4-1000 FIVE CENTS

KING GEORGE VI DIES IN SLEEP AT SANDRINGHAM; ELIZABETH, QUEEN AT 25, FLYING FROM AFRICA; PRESIDENT AMONG WORLD LEADERS IN TRIBUTE

2½% INTEREST RATE FOR SAVINGS BANKS APPROVED BY STATE

85% of Institutions Expected to Adopt 'Permissive' Rule Lifting 17-Year Ceiling

NEW U. S. TAXES A FACTOR

Board Adjusts Payments on Commercial Deposits, Acts to Clear Extra Dividends

By GEORGE A. MOONEY

New York's thrifty received a new incentive yesterday.

Terminating a policy that dates to 1935, the State Banking Board acted to raise its ceiling on interest-dividends paid on savings and thrift deposits from a 2 per cent maximum to 2½ per cent. Eighty-five per cent of the state's 130 savings banks are expected to put the increase in effect at an early date.

Last night the Dime Savings Bank of Brooklyn became the first in this area to announce it would pay 2½ per cent for the current quarter ending March 31.

Trustees of the Roosevelt Savings Bank announced they would meet today to increase the rate from 2 to 2½ per cent on account balances and deposits for the three-month period starting Jan. 1.

Other savings banks and competitive commercial banks, where possible, are likely to take similiar action soon.

Responding to the higher level of prevailing rates, and especially to Federal taxes imposed at the beginning of this year, several savings banks asked permission some weeks ago to pay larger dividends. Under the new tax law, savings institutions are made liable for income taxes at the regular corporate rate on all earnings after surplus and reserves total 12 per cent of deposits.

Regulation Is "Permissive"

William A. Lyon, Superintendent of Banks, in announcing the board's action yesterday said the new 2½ per cent rate was "permissive."

"Banks are permitted under the regulation to pay any rate up to that maximum which directors and trustees believe to be advisable in the light of the earning power and the capital or surplus position of their institutions," he explained.

Two other important amendments also were made in General Regulation No. 3, the dividend and interest rate regulation, Mr. Lyon said. In the first of these, relating to commercial banks' special interest and thrift deposits, the board approved a limit on interest payments at the maximum rate of 2½ per cent on the first $10,000 of any account and setting a ceiling rate of 1½ per cent on that portion of any special and thrift account in excess of $10,000.

The largest individual account that may be accepted by savings banks is $10,000, the maximum

Continued on Page 55, Column 6

Truman 'Shows Off' New White House

By W. H. LAWRENCE
Special to The New York Times.

WASHINGTON, Feb. 6—Ducking nimbly around and under scaffolding, President Truman today took a few correspondents on a conducted tour of the White House, which is being reconstructed. He said it was still his hope that the First Family would be able to move into it early in April after three and one-half years in Blair House.

Mixing history and comment about the tribulations of a tenant who decides to get a house done over, Mr. Truman led the reporters through the building for forty minutes, answering questions and volunteering observations about nearly every room.

The hum of power saws as workmen went ahead with their jobs sometimes drowned his

Continued on Page 23, Column 1

1-Way Traffic Signs Due Soon in Times Sq.

By JOSEPH C. INGRAHAM

Conversion of Seventh and Eighth Avenues to one-way operation has been decided upon by Acting Traffic Commissioner T. T. Wiley despite objections of the New York City Omnibus Corporation.

Preparations for the new traffic pattern were well under way yesterday, with new guideposts rising in Times Square and the fittings all set to hold the one-way arrows. Work on the other sections of the one-way routes, which extend from Columbus Circle to below Canal Street, also was progressing. Seventh Avenue-Varick Street will handle southbound flow and Hudson Street-Abingdon Square-Eighth

Continued on Page 17, Column 5

CHARGES OF WASTE IN DEFENSE DENIED

Pentagon Aides Tell Senators of Savings—Admiral Calls Himself 'Oyster Fork Fox'

By HAROLD B. HINTON
Special to The New York Times.

WASHINGTON, Feb. 6—Officials of the Department of Defense underwent a period of criticism before a Senate Appropriations subcommittee today and did not seem to like it. They were appearing in support of defense budget estimates of more than $52,000,-000,000.

The principal witness was Vice Admiral Charles W. Fox, Chief of Naval Supplies, who told the Senators of the progress the Navy had made in simplifying the cataloguing of its supplies. When his presentation was interrupted by questions about allegations of waste and extravagance, the Pentagon contingent moved to the counter-offensive.

"I stand before you as Oyster Fork Fox," the admiral asserted, as the Senators and spectators laughed. "I am supposed to have bought 11,000,000 oyster forks for the Navy, and I had nothing more to do with it than you did."

He said that the Navy last

Continued on Page 4, Column 3

RED TRAPS FEARED IN FOE'S PROPOSAL FOR KOREA PARLEY

Communist Demand for Airing of Status of Formosa Viewed as Bar to U. N. Accord

TRUMAN CITED AS A GUIDE

Nam Il Argues Stand Taken by President on Blockading China Widens Issues

Text of Gen. Nam Il's statement is printed on Page 2.

By LINDESAY PARROTT
Special to The New York Times.

TOKYO, Thursday, Feb. 7—The United Nations Command began today a detailed study of the Communist proposal for a top-level political conference three months after the armistice in the Korean war to deal with related issues in the Far East.

This morning no hint of Allied reaction had come from the advance camp at Munsan, where the United Nations representatives took the Communist program after it had been delivered to them at a plenary session of the truce delegations at Panmunjom, or at the headquarters of the United Nations Commander, Gen. Matthew B. Ridgway, in Tokyo.

The enemy proposal was made by North Korean Gen. Nam Il, head of the Chinese and North Korean delegation, who drove to the meeting place in a big American limousine with whitewall tires. He nodded coldly to the senior United Nations representative, Vice Admiral Charles Turner Joy, and then launched into his prepared introductory remarks — considerably more extensive, it turned out, than the brief formal proposal for a governmental conference for "peaceful settlement of the Korean question and other questions related to peace in Korea."

Before the session adjourned it was agreed that a new plenary sitting should be held by the delegates of both sides after the United Nations study had been com-

Continued on Page 2, Column 6

World News Summarized

THURSDAY, FEBRUARY 7, 1952

King George VI died in his sleep at Sandringham Palace yesterday morning; his daughter was proclaimed Queen Elizabeth II. The King, who seemingly had recovered from an operation for the removal of a growth on his lung, had felt so well he had been out shooting the day before. [1:8.] The British people were stunned by their sudden loss. [1:7.]

King George became the British ruler in 1936 when his brother, King Edward VIII and later Duke of Windsor, abdicated. He saw little peace during his reign. Threats of war, armed conflict and the "cold war" marked his tenure. [10:1.] During the bombing of London he refused to take special precautions or leave Buckingham Palace. [13:7-8.]

The new Queen started for London by plane when she learned of her father's death. She had been touring East Africa with her consort, the Duke of Edinburgh. [1:6-7.] She is the first Queen to ascend Britain's throne since 115 years ago, when Queen Victoria was crowned. [1:5-6.] The Duke of Windsor sails from New York tonight, alone, to attend his brother's funeral. [14:8.]

President Truman, Secretary Acheson and others expressed the sorrow of the United States [1:5] as did former President Hoover, Mayor Impellitteri and others in this city. [14:5.] United Nations flags were flown at half-staff. [15:1.]

The Soviet Union, for the fifth time, vetoed Italy's membership in the United Nations. [1:4.] The Russians did not join forty-seven other countries in pledging funds for expanded technical assistance this year. [3:4.]

Allied officers studied the Communist proposal for a political conference three months after a Korean armistice. [1:3.]

West German leaders were unmoved by American and British pleas to cool their anger over French moves in the Saar and to not endanger plans for West Europe's defense. [6:3.]

A masked witness told a House committee he had seen Russians kill hundreds of Polish officers in Katyn Forest in 1939. [4:3.]

Defense Department heads, testifying on the military budget before a Senate group, vigorously defended their spending. [1:2.] Mobilization heads also were under attack for plans to spread defense contracts to unemployment areas. [39:4.]

The slow-down in the military aircraft production rate will have little immediate effect on consumer goods but will avoid more stringent curbs later, a survey showed. [31:3.]

Governor Byrnes of South Carolina blamed "Negro politicians of the North" for the Democratic party's shift from a State's Rights program. [21:1.]

This state authorized banks to pay up to 2½ per cent on savings and thrift accounts. [1:1.]

Columbia University will increase tuition fees up to 25 per cent next fall and adjust faculty salaries upward. [29:1.]

NEWS BULLETINS FROM THE TIMES
Every hour on the hour 7 A.M. through Midnight Except at 4 P.M. Today
WQXR AM 1560
WQXR FM 96.3

Index to other news appears on last page of this section.

THE NEW QUEEN AND THE LATE KING

ELIZABETH II

GEORGE VI Associated Press

SOVIET AGAIN BALKS ITALY'S U. N. ENTRY

Russia for Fifth Time Vetoes Application—Is Beaten on En Bloc Admission Bid

By THOMAS J. HAMILTON
Special to The New York Times.

PARIS, Feb. 6—Italy's application for membership in the United Nation's was vetoed by the Soviet Union tonight for the fifth time. Ten of the eleven members of the Security Council voted for a French resolution recommending the admission of Italy.

Jacob A. Malik, the Soviet representative, based his action on the refusal of the United States and other Western powers to accept a Soviet proposal for en bloc admission of fourteen applicants, including five Communist governments.

The Soviet resolution afterward was rejected by a vote of six to two. The United States, Brazil, Nationalist China, Greece, the Netherlands and Turkey voted against the resolution, while Pakistan joined the Soviet Union in supporting it. Britain, France and Chile abstained.

Mr. Malik accused the United States of blocking Italy's admission. He declared that "the Italian people will note that it is the United States, with the help of the United Kingdom" that had "provoked" the Soviet veto. He added that if the Western powers had wanted to get Italy admitted, they would have agreed to the Soviet proposal.

Gross Protests "Horsetrade"

Ernest A. Gross, the United States delegate, retorted that on the contrary the Italian people would hardly be grateful for being made a part of the proposed "horse-trade." He asked whether Mr. Malik really believed that Italy should be "put in the same basket" with such "a shadow state" as Outer Mongolia, one of the Communist candidates included in the Soviet resolution.

Mr. Gross also expressed regret that the new state of Libya, which came into existence on Christmas Day, 1951, had been included in the Soviet en bloc proposal—which presumably meant that it likewise would encounter a Soviet veto unless the Western powers agree to the Soviet mass entry proposal.

Mr. Malik replied that Outer Mongolia deserved to be admitted. He said that its participation in the war against Japan "along with that of the Soviet Union" saved 1,000,000 American lives. He said he based his statement on statements by the United States high command.

Reconsideration today of Italy's long-standing application was the result of a General Assembly resolution last fall requesting the Security Council to reconsider it in the light of Italy's responsibilities

Continued on Page 3, Column 5

Ruler Becomes Elizabeth II; Her Son, 3, Is Crown Prince

By CLIFTON DANIEL
Special to The New York Times.

LONDON, Feb. 6—Britain entered a new Elizabethan era today. Upon the death of King George VI, Princess Elizabeth Alexandra Mary, his elder daughter, automatically became Queen of the United Kingdom and the Dominions Overseas at the age of 25.

Tonight at the first meeting of her Privy Council she was formally styled Queen Elizabeth II.

[Text of the Privy Council's proclamation is on Page 14.]

Thus, for the first time in 115 years, a woman ascended the world's most exalted and stable throne. At the Gloucester Assizes, as in other law courts of the land, the judges marshal closed the court with words not heard since the end of Queen Victoria's sixty-three-year reign in 1901: "God save the Queen and my lords the Queen's justices."

For the first time in British history the sovereign was abroad in the Empire at the moment of accession.

Already bearing the full responsibility of the crown, the new Queen will return here by air from Kenya in Africa tomorrow accompanied by her consort, the Duke of Edinburgh.

They were to have boarded the liner Gothic at Mombasa tomorrow to sail for Ceylon, Australia and New Zealand on a five-month ceremonial tour deputizing for the late King, whose illness prevented him from going.

With the accession of the Queen, her son Prince Charles, three years and two months old, became the Crown Prince and heir to the

Continued on Page 14, Column 3

TRUMAN EXPRESSES SORROW OF NATION

Voices Sympathy for British Over Loss of King—Acheson and Others Pay Tribute

Special to The New York Times.

WASHINGTON, Feb. 6—President Truman and the nation paid tribute to King George VI today in extending this country's sympathy to the British people on his death.

"He played his part nobly and with full understanding of the responsibility which was his," the President said in a formal statement.

All official Washington responded in kind following the surprise and shock at the news of the monarch's passing early this morning. Highest officials in the Government and leaders of both House of Congress joined in expressions of sympathy and praise for the man who had been a steadfast friend of the United States, and, indeed, had been the first British King to visit the country.

Secretary of State Dean Acheson commented on the courage with which King George had borne his physical suffering and noted: "It is a characteristic English spirit and the King possessed it in abundance."

Envoy Calls on Acheson

Sir Oliver Franks, British Ambassador, accompanied by seven representatives of the British Commonwealth, called on Secretary Acheson shortly after noon to inform him formally of the King's death.

"A world personage who maintained the highest tradition of the English constitutional monarchy passes in the death of His Majesty King George VI," President Truman said in his statement.

"From his accession to the throne through all the ills which beset the world throughout the years of his reign—including the most disastrous war in history—he played his part nobly and with full responsibility which was his. His heroic endurance of pain and suffering during these past few years is a true reflection of the bravery of the British people in adversity.

"The King was ever conscious of his obligations as sovereign of a nation which through centuries has been the champion of personal liberty and those free institu-

Continued on Page 14, Column 5

LONDON IS STILLED AS BRITONS MOURN

All Amusements Closed, Lights Dimmed, Streets Nearly Empty After News Stuns People

By FARNSWORTH FOWLE
Special to The New York Times.

LONDON, Feb. 6—This was a silent city tonight, with bright lights dimmed and all places of entertainment closed, as Londoners went home shocked by the death of their King.

The news reached most office workers at noon when they went out for lunch and found venders of early editions of afternoon papers shouting "The King is dead!"

"What King?" was a typical first reaction. It was hard to believe that it was indeed their own monarch, even though it had been generally realized since the King's operation last September that he might not have many years to live. Only a week ago tonight he attended a performance of "South Pacific" at the Drury Lane Theatre.

The suddenness of the news contrasted with the memory of how the public had been prepared during the final illness of the King's father, George V, with a broadcast communiqué saying, "The King's life is moving peacefully to its close."

Flags at half-staff appeared on public buildings and many private ones by noon. Theatres, cinemas and night clubs all shut down, as did the Stock Exchange and other markets.

The laughter of London's usually cheerful office girls was muted as

Continued on Page 13, Column 6

Elizabeth Weeps at News of Death, But Is Calm in African Take-Off

By The United Press.

NAIROBI, Kenya, Feb. 6—Young Queen Elizabeth II left hurriedly for home by plane tonight only a few hours after her husband had broken the news to her of her father's death.

The 25-year-old former Princess, after having broken down in tears, was composed when she departed early tonight on the long flight to London.

With Prince Philip she left the hunting lodge where the royal couple had been staying and drove in a closed automobile eight miles to a small airport near the East African town of Nunyuki. She took off in an East African Airways C-47 for Entebbe in Uganda, where the British Overseas Airways craft that had flown her to Africa waited to take her back to Britain.

The royal couple landed at Entebbe airport at 9:10 P. M. (1:10 P. M., Eastern standard time), but news of her arrival was kept from the local populace to spare the new Queen a further ordeal.

A tropical thunderstorm at Entebbe delayed the departure of the Queen's plane for more than two hours, but it finally took off at 11:47 P. M. for Libya as the weather cleared.

[The plane made a stop at the Royal Air Force base at El Adem, Libya, landing there at 1:15 A. M., Thursday, Eastern standard time, The United Press reported.]

At El Adem and Malta the Royal Air Force had planes standing by to escort the Queen's plane over the Mediterranean. It is scheduled to reach London at 4:30 P. M. Thursday, Greenwich time (11:30 A. M., E. S. T.)

Crowds of silent, sorrowful persons of all races lined the main street of Nunyuki as the Queen's party passed through. The Queen, her face showing the strain of the

Continued on Page 13, Column 3

15-YEAR REIGN ENDS

British Monarch's Death at 56 Follows a Lung Operation Last Fall

PARLIAMENT HALTED

Churchill Conveys News to Commons—Attlee Suspends Party Strife

By RAYMOND DANIELL
Special to The New York Times.

LONDON, Feb. 6—In the early hours of this morning George VI died peacefully in his sleep at the royal estate at Sandringham. As night fell upon this mourning capital of a still great family of nations, his elder daughter was proclaimed Queen of this realm and its dependencies, head of the British Commonwealth and the Defender of the Faith, with the title of Elizabeth II.

She is flying home tonight from her tragically interrupted visit to East Africa with her consort, the Duke of Edinburgh, and is expected back tomorrow to assume her royal duties as the wearer of the crown that somewhat mystically binds the British Commonwealth together.

Like the Elizabeth of England's golden age, she takes the throne at the age of 25.

Operated On 4 Months Ago

The King's death occurred just a little more than four months after an operation for the removal of a growth in his right lung. This operation resulted in the loss of the lung. His recovery seemed assured and in recent days he had been seen publicly at the theatre and at London Airport when he bade good-by to his daughter, now the Queen, as she set out with Prince Philip, her husband, on a journey that was to take her to East Africa, Australia and New Zealand. Only yesterday he was out shooting, his favorite sport.

It was assumed that the King had died as a result of a heart attack, probably caused by coronary thrombosis.

Tributes to the late monarch poured into London from leading world figures and from persons of humbler station.

His death came in his 57th year. It was the beginning of the sixteenth year of an unhappy reign. He never wanted or expected the throne of Britain, but he ascended to it when his brother Edward VIII abdicated to marry "the woman I love," Wallis Simpson.

Six years of his reign were war years when he and Elizabeth, his Queen, who now becomes Queen Mother, endeared themselves to their people by their bravery and devotion to their predestined role.

When he was crowned King on May 12, 1937, he was King Emperor but the title of Emperor went with the granting of independence to India. His reign marked the end of an era of British power.

Parliament Is Suspended

His death also brought to an end this session of Parliament in the midst of a bitter and acrimonious debate on how far this country should go in aligning itself with United States policy in the Far East lest it be dragged into war. That debate, which began yesterday, was left in mid-air as Parliament put aside its controversies to swear allegiance to the new Queen and deferred its partisan arguments on controversial issues until a more seemly time.

At Sandringham when the King died there were his two grandchildren, whom he adored, Prince Charles and Princess Anne; Sir Alan Lascelles, his private secretary; Sir Harold Campbell, his Equerry, and Lady Hyde, Lady-in-Waiting to his Queen. Soon after his death had been discovered by a servant bringing early morning tea, Dr. James Ansell, "Surgeon Apothecary" to the royal household at Sandringham, was called. He said that the King had died in his sleep without pain.

The news of the King's death went out over the news tickers at 10:45 A. M. At 11:15 it was broad-

Continued on Page 13, Column 2

"All the News That's Fit to Print"

The New York Times.

LATE CITY EDITION
Mostly fair today and tonight. Chance of showers tomorrow.
Temperature Range Today—Max., 54; Min., 40
Temperatures Yesterday—Max., 53; Min., 41
Full U. S. Weather Bureau Report, Page 35

VOL. CI. No. 34,409. Entered as Second-Class Matter. Post Office, New York, N. Y. NEW YORK, WEDNESDAY, APRIL 9, 1952. Times Square, New York 36, N. Y. Telephone LAckawanna 4-1000 FIVE CENTS

TRUMAN SEIZES STEEL; STRIKE OFF; HE SCORES INDUSTRY AS RECKLESS; COMPANIES START FIGHT IN COURTS

TAFT SWEEPS ILLINOIS TEST BY MAJORITY

STASSEN IS SECOND

Eisenhower, Off Ballot, Is Third—Stevenson Write-In Is Light

KEFAUVER HAS STRENGTH

But Governor's Popular Vote for State Office Exceeds Tally for Tennessean

By RICHARD J. H. JOHNSTON
Special to The New York Times.

CHICAGO, Wednesday, April 9—Senator Robert A. Taft of Ohio, running far ahead of his opponents for the support of Illinois' fifty elected national convention delegates, emerged victor by a wide margin today in this state's Presidential preference primary election.

For President

Returns from 4,880 of 9,610 precincts gave:

REPUBLICANS

Sen. Robert A. Taft	366,977
Harold E. Stassen	61,252
Gen. Dwight D. Eisenhower	*50,877
Riley A. Bender	10,946
Gen. Douglas MacArthur	*3,092
Gov. Earl Warren	*119

(* Write-in.)

DEMOCRATS

Sen. Kefauver (4,576 pcts)	275,553
Gov. Stevenson (783 pcts)	*4,531

(* Write-in.)

The write-ins for Gov. Adlai E. Stevenson of Illinois were from downstate counties. Cook County, which includes Chicago, delayed write-in reports.

The tally for Senator Taft far exceeded the total votes of his rivals, Mr. Stassen, former Governor of Minnesota; General Eisenhower, a write-in candidate, and Mr. Bender, a Chicago Hotel operator.

The indications were that Mr. Taft was winning forty-eight of the state's fifty elected delegates. General Eisenhower appeared to have two.

Senator Estes Kefauver of Tennessee, unopposed for the Democratic Presidential nomination, rolled up a strong vote. However, Governor Stevenson ran ahead of the Tennessean in the total popular vote in his unopposed bid for the Gubernatorial nomination.

In the Illinois Republican Gubernatorial race, William G. Stratton, State Treasurer, outstripped his opponents.

For Governor

Returns from 5,366 of 9,610 precincts gave:

REPUBLICANS

William G. Stratton	297,409
Park Livingston	110,285
Richard Y. Rowe	95,184
W. N. Erickson (withdrawn from race)	36,287
Anthony A. Pelley	10,120

DEMOCRATS

Returns from 4,450 of 9,610 precincts gave:

Gov. Stevenson (unopp'sed)	356,209

On the basis of returns from about half of the state's 9,610 precincts in the Presidential popularity vote, it appeared that Mr. Taft would run 7 to 1 over Mr. Stassen

Continued on Page 20, Column 5

Mayor, 'Run Down,' Plans Florida Rest

Mayor Impellitteri announced yesterday at City Hall that on the advice of his physician he would leave the city late tomorrow afternoon by plane for a two-week vacation at Palm Beach, Fla.

According to the Mayor, his physician, Dr. James G. Robilotti, told him he was "run down" and "needed a rest." Mr. Impellitteri said that for about two months he had had a "recurring cold" from which he had not been able to recover completely, and he hoped the two-week sojourn in the South would provide a cure.

While in Palm Beach, the Mayor said, he will be the guest of City Commerce Commissioner and Mrs. Walter T. Shirley at the Shirley home in the Florida resort city.

Mr. Impellitteri said he would

Continued on Page 22, Column 4

WARREN DISAVOWS AN 'AGAINST' POLICY

Governor in Opening Speech Here Asks for Nomination of Sound Progressive

Gov. Earl Warren of California, making his first major address to a New York audience as a Republican Presidential contender, appealed last night for the nomination of a progressive candidate who would not "turn back the clock" in the nation's affairs, even if he could do so.

Governor Warren addressed an attentive gathering of more than 1,000 persons at the annual $100-a-plate dinner of the New York County Republican Committee in the Waldorf-Astoria Hotel. Governor Dewey, whose running mate in the 1948 Presidential campaign was Governor Warren, introduced Governor Warren without reference to the latter's 1952 ambition to head the slate, and Governor Warren in turn refrained from mentioning himself as a candidate.

Governor Warren, while attacking the Truman administration as graft-ridden and incompetent, summed up his philosophy by saying:

"We cannot rely upon an 'against' campaign to win the election in November. We must convince the American people that we are thinking in terms of forward action for their welfare. We must not be afraid of the word 'welfare.' We must not shrink from the known needs for social progress. We must have our own programs

Continued on Page 18, Column 6

COSTELLO RECEIVES 18 MONTHS, IS FINED $5,000 IN CONTEMPT

Judge Ryan Says He 'May Well Have Prevented Important Disclosures' to Senators

F. B. I. CHECKS ON 2 JURORS

Blaikie, to Whose Club Ousted Foreman Belongs, Charges 'Funny Politics' Go On

By CHARLES GRUTZNER

Frank Costello was sentenced yesterday to eighteen months in prison and fined $5,000—the heaviest penalty ever imposed here for contempt—by Federal Judge Sylvester Ryan, who declared that the gambler's balkiness before the Senate Crime Investigating Committee "may well have prevented important disclosures."

The bigtime racketeer, who has kept out of prison since he served ten months on a pistol-carrying conviction in 1915, remained free in $5,000 bail as the result of filing a notice of appeal with the United States Court of Appeals. A hearing will be held tomorrow to determine whether bail should be continued pending outcome of the appeal, expected to be heard next month.

Developments that followed quickly upon the sentencing of the well-dressed, gravel-voiced racket boss cleared up some of the mystery that had clouded the case since last Friday, when Judge Ryan had dismissed two jurors before giving Costello's fate into the hands of a jury reinforced by alternates.

Checking on Dismissed Jurors

United States Attorney Myles J. Lane announced that he and the Federal Bureau of Investigation were checking on Mrs. Helen Louise Mason, who had been jury foreman during four days of the trial, and Julius A. Fox, original Juror No. 9. The two jurors allegedly concealed from the court circumstances that may have prejudiced them in reaching a verdict.

The F. B. I., it was learned, is searching for a man who was brash enough and stupid enough to try to shake down Costello's attorney, Kenneth M. Spence, for $250 with a crude offer of jury-fixing. The bid for $250 had nothing to do with the dismissal of either juror.

Judge Ryan, who had withheld all details on Friday, instructed Mr. Lane yesterday to make public the record of conversations the judge had held in his chambers with Mrs. Mason, Mr. Fox and defense and prosecution attorneys. The record made it clear that Mrs. Mason was removed from the jury because of her political activity in the Democratic club headed by Robert Blaikie, Tammany leader who crossed party lines to support Rudolph Halley, former chief counsel to the Senate Crime Committee, in his successful race for City Council President last fall.

Mr. Fox was removed because of two civil actions for treble damages brought by the Office of Price

Continued on Page 23, Column 2

Pinay Wins 10 Tests On French Finances

By LANSING WARREN
Special to The New York Times.

PARIS, April 8—Premier Antoine Pinay, breaking through Opposition hostility and garnering support from both Gaullist and Popular Republican groups, won a victory today for his plan of financing France's budget.

The Premier, an independent, was successful in the National Assembly in a series of ten votes of confidence, which provided additional evidence of the shaping of a new right-wing majority in France.

The crucial vote was on the provision aiming to bring out hidden capital in France by an unconditional amnesty for all past tax delinquencies, which was adopted by 259 votes to 210. The program as a whole was approved by a vote of 311 to 206. Most of the other ballots gave the Government more than 400

Continued on Page 6, Column 8

FOE'S 'PHONY' ISSUE ON KOREA SCORNED

U. N. Accuses Reds at Parley of Setting Up Soviet Question for Airfield Bargaining

By LINDESAY PARROTT
Special to The New York Times.

TOKYO, Wednesday, April 9—The United Nations negotiators at Panmunjom accused the Communists today of introducing a "phony issue" in the negotiations for an armistice in Korea with the demand that the Soviet Union be included as a "neutral" nation to police a cease-fire.

The Allied representative on the committee of generals discussing conditions for the enforcement of a truce, Maj. Gen. William K. Harrison, told correspondents that the United Nations Command would not agree to the bargain hinted at by the Chinese and North Koreans. The enemy delegates had indicated that they might be prepared to withdraw the Soviet nomination if the Allies would agree to permit the construction and rehabilitation of airfields north of the Thirty-eighth Parallel during an armistice.

"They are trying to equate something for nothing," General Harrison said after an enemy spokesman, for the third time, had urged that the two outstanding questions be settled as a joint item.

General Harrison said he was convinced that the Russian issue had been raised "only to bargain

Continued on Page 2, Column 2

NEW PARLEY TODAY

Both Sides Will Confer With Steelman as Talks Shift to Washington

TO COOPERATE WITH U. S.

Union and Owners Promise to Run Mills After Truman Acts in Pay Deadlock

By A. H. RASKIN

The United Steelworkers of America, C. I. O., called off last night its national steel strike and directed its 600,000 members to stay at work under President Truman's seizure order.

The instructions were issued by Philip Murray, president of the union, even before the President had finished his radio speech announcing the takeover of the mills. The union leader expressed certainty that the workers would comply "as patriotic Americans."

High Government officials reported that they had assurances of industry cooperation in running the mills, even though the companies will fight the legality of the seizure in the Federal courts. A boycott by executive and supervisory personnel would have made it impossible for the Government to maintain steel production.

The industry, angered by the criticism Mr. Truman heaped on its position in the dispute over steel wages and prices, decided to wait until today before issuing formal comment. Privately company spokesmen denounced the seizure as "confiscation" and asserted that it could lead to the socialization of all American industry unless the courts upset the President's order.

Last-Minute Efforts Fail

The Federal takeover was ordered thirty minutes after frantic attempts to effect a last-minute agreement between the major steel producers and the union had collapsed in New York.

More than 400,000 steel workers already had been laid off and the fires were down in blast furnaces from Pittsburgh, Pa., to Pittsburg, Calif., when the President acted.

The Federal action warded off a full-fledged strike of the members of the steel union at 12:01 o'clock this morning, but the time required to reheat the furnaces will entail a minimum loss of 1,000,000 tons of steel this week.

Dr. John R. Steelman, Acting Director of Defense Mobilization, will make a new effort to settle the wage-price dispute at the White House this afternoon. He will be assisted by Nathan P. Feinsinger, Chairman of the Wage Stabilization Board, who sought unsuccessfully to effect an agreement in five days of talks with company and union officials here.

Two-Year Contract Proposed

Mr. Feinsinger, who gave up the New York conferences at 10 P. M., said he still hoped the suggestions he made would provide the basis for an eventual settlement. He disclosed that he had proposed that the parties agree on a two-year contract, instead of the eighteen-month pact originally recommended by the Wage Board.

Under the Feinsinger plan, the union would get the same wage increases and other benefits the board had proposed but they would be spaced over a longer period. This would assure the nation of a longer period of strike-free steel production and would give the companies a longer time before the union would be in a position to demand a new rise in wages.

The Wage Board's proposals called for a wage increase of 12½ cents an hour, retroactive to Jan. 1; a further increase of 2½ cents July 1 and a third increase of 2½ cents next Jan. 1. In addition, the board urged a union shop and fringe benefits that would cost 5.4 cents an hour this year and 3½ cents an hour more next year. Steel wages now average $1.88 an hour.

The union insisted that the industry accept all of the board's recommendations in a new eighteen-month contract. The industry countered with an offer of a pay increase of 9 cents an hour, retroactive to March 1 and 5.4

Continued on Page 14, Column 1

TAKES OVER STEEL INDUSTRY

Associated Press Wirephoto

President Truman speaking from the new White House communications room last night for the first time.

Sawyer, Taking Over Steel, Plans No Pay Changes Now

By JOSEPH A. LOFTUS
Special to The New York Times.

WASHINGTON, April 8—Charles Sawyer, Secretary of Commerce, who has become the nominal operator of most of the nation's steel industry, said tonight that he planned "no change of any kind at this moment" in the wages and working conditions of the industry's employes.

As to the legal justification for President Truman's seizure of the industry tonight, Mr. Sawyer said he understood the President had acted under his "general Constitutional powers, but I prefer not to bind the Attorney General."

"If the matter is taken to court the legal phases will be handled wholly by the Attorney General," he added. "He prepared the papers. I did not participate in it."

Reminded that the Attorney General, J. Howard McGrath, had just resigned, the Secretary said, "There's quite a department over there; a lot of competent men."

The Secretary held a news conference in his office a few minutes after Mr. Truman had finished his broadcast announcement that the Government was taking over the steel mills in order to continue production in the face of the impending strike.

Will Await Bargaining

Replying to questions about the wage increases recommended by the Wage Stabilization Board and rejected by the industry, Mr. Sawyer said he would "await the results of the collective bargaining negotiations Dr. [John R.] Steelman [Acting Director of Defense Mobilization] will carry on in accordance with the President's directive."

Pressed on whether present wage terms and conditions would continue, he declared: "I said for the time being they would; I don't commit myself for the long pull."

The Secretary answered without hesitation all questions fired at him, although qualifying some answers with statements that he was subject to the orders of the President and the legal interpretations of the Attorney General.

He issued a formal statement saying:

"I neither requested nor wanted this job, but when our men at the front are taking orders in the face of great danger those of us farther back can do no less.

"The President has given me what I realize is a difficult assignment. I accept it.

"I dislike as much as anyone to witness, let alone participate in, the seizure of property. We are, however, facing a situation of great peril where continued production of steel is essential to our national welfare.

"The President has made his decision and has given me certain work to do in that connection; and I shall do it.

"I hope that both industry and labor will accept the statements I make in good faith and will co-

Continued on Page 17, Column 3

TRUMAN SEES PERIL WORSE THAN SOVIET

In Point 4 Speech He Attacks Imperialism—Ties Liberty to Scientific Advance

Text of the President's address on Point Four, Page 4.

By FELIX BELAIR Jr.
Special to The New York Times.

WASHINGTON, April 8—President Truman told a national conference tonight that the Point Four concept of improving the lot of the neglected people of the earth would surely fail "unless scientific progress is linked with political freedom."

Mr. Truman declared he feared that the crescendo of imperialism in the recent history of the world might swell to even greater proportions, if it were not silenced now, than the menace of the Soviet Union today.

The President's speech was delivered at a night session of the National Conference on International Economic and Social Development by Dean Acheson, Secretary of State, who substituted for Mr. Truman to allow the President to make a speech to the nation on the steel situation.

"Mass suffering," the President

Continued on Page 4, Column 3

Two Hisses Termed Soviet Agents in '39

By CLAYTON KNOWLES
Special to The New York Times.

WASHINGTON, April 8—William C. Bullitt, former United States Ambassador to France and to Russia, asserted today that he was advised on the highest French authority late in 1939 that "two brothers named Hiss," both officers in the State Department, were "Soviet agents."

Testifying before the Senate Internal Security subcommittee, the ex-Ambassador said that this information was given to him by Edouard Daladier, then French Premier, who attributed it to the French Intelligence Service.

Mr. Bullitt said that at the time he did not know either Alger or Donald Hiss or that they were in the department. The former envoy added that he laughed at the

Continued on Page 15, Column 6

PRESIDENT IN PLEA

Address on Air Charges Industry With Greed for High Profits

SAWYER WILL RUN MILLS

Washington Judge Signs Order Setting Hearing for Today on Legality of Action

The President's broadcast and his Executive order, Page 16.

By CHARLES E. EGAN
Special to The New York Times.

WASHINGTON, April 8—President Truman tonight ordered seizure of the steel mills to avert a strike of their 600,000 workers. An order directing that the Government take over the mills was issued effective at midnight, one minute before the scheduled strike was to take place.

Under the terms of tonight's order, which the President said had been issued "in the public interest," Charles Sawyer, Secretary of Commerce, will take over the operation of the steel mills.

In moving against the giant of American industries the President was believed to have touched off one of the sharpest legal battles in a generation. The steel mill owners are insistent that the President does not have power, under the Constitution or under his emergency grants of authority, to take possession of the mills. Counsel for steel mills were prepared to challenge the President's action in a half dozen Federal district courts in the country tomorrow, according to reports.

[Federal Judge Walter M. Bastian signed an order early Wednesday in Washington calling a hearing for 11:30 A. M. on suits filed by two of the major steel companies—Republic and Youngstown Sheet and Tube—challenging the Government's seizure, The Associated Press reported.]

Steelman Sets Meeting

In compliance with the President's request, Dr. John R. Steelman, Acting Director of Defense Mobilization, telephoned representatives of the six big steel companies and Philip Murray, president of the United Steelworkers of America, C. I. O. Dr. Steelman asked the operators and Mr. Murray to come to Washington for a meeting with him at 3 P. M. tomorrow.

In addition, Dr. Steelman talked by telephone with Nathan Feinsinger, chairman of the Wage Stabilization Board, who has been in New York seeking to effect an agreement. Mr. Feinsinger will meet with Dr. Steelman at noon to give the Defense Mobilizer a complete report on the discussions that have been in progress in New York.

Also in response to the President's orders, Secretary Sawyer immediately designated the presidents of the steel companies as "operating managers" on behalf of the United States.

In a statement issued after the President's broadcast Mr. Sawyer

Continued on Page 16, Column 7

Phone Talks Stalled; Service Is Still Good

By STANLEY LEVEY

Substantial sections of the nation's communications systems still were beset by strikes yesterday, but telephone and telegraph service did not appear to be suffering much.

Attempts by Federal mediators to settle the telephone strikes begun Monday by 67,250 workers in forty-three states and the District of Columbia were unavailing. There were no such efforts in the six-day-old strike of 31,000 employes of the Western Union Telegraph Company, however, though the company reported further restoration of service. The issue in both cases is pay.

Chances that the Western Union strike would spread to New York were reduced last night when the striking union lost a National

Continued on Page 17, Column 6

Baruchs Praised at Site of Housing

Officials of City and U. S. Join in Tribute at Groundbreaking

City and Federal officials paid tribute yesterday to the Baruch family at a groundbreaking ceremony for Baruch Houses, the East Side's biggest public housing project. Tenancy is to begin in the summer of 1953.

Bernard M. Baruch and his brother, Dr. Herman B. Baruch, former Ambassador to the Netherlands, were at the ceremony. The project, bounded by Delancey, East Houston and Columbia Streets and Franklin D. Roosevelt Drive, is named for their father, Dr. Simon Baruch.

In behalf of the family Mr. Baruch expressed appreciation for "naming this great enterprise after my father." He was "deeply interested in the human side of people," the son said.

Robert Moses, City Construction Coordinator, told how Dr. Simon Baruch, a Confederate Army physician, was instrumental in setting up on the site in 1901 the city's first public bath, named for him. A bust of his noted son will be placed there, Mr. Moses said, adding: "Probably it's against his wishes, but we'll put it up anyway."

The speaker took time out for a

Continued on Page 25, Column 6

The New York Times (by Meyer Liebowitz)

Dr. Herman Baruch and Bernard M. Baruch with Diane and Irving Siegel, neighborhood children, after ground-breaking for the Baruch Houses on the lower East Side yesterday.

Halley Lists 'Waste' For 'Raucous' Critics

Specific illustrations of waste in the city government were offered yesterday by Rudolph Halley, President of the City Council, to support his argument that the only real cure for New York's recurring financial crises would be a complete overhaul of its system of administrative management.

In a speech at a luncheon arranged by the Citizens Budget Commission at the Roosevelt Hotel, Mr. Halley, self-styled "watchdog" of the city, gave these examples from the Department of Hospitals:

¶Bellevue Hospital ordered thirty-seven new refrigerators in 1948 at a cost of $35,183. They were delivered in 1948 and 1949. Last February they were not yet installed because they operated on alternating current while the hospital system used direct current.

¶A total of $45,000 of X-ray

Continued on Page 22, Column 5

"All the News That's Fit to Print"

The New York Times.

LATE CITY EDITION

Fair today; some cloudiness tonight. Becoming fair tomorrow.
Temperature Range Today—Max., 72; Min., 60
Temperatures Yesterday—Max., 81; Min., 58
Full U. S. Weather Bureau Report, Page 39

VOL. CI..No. 34,464. Entered as Second-Class Matter. Post Office, New York, N. Y. NEW YORK, TUESDAY, JUNE 3, 1952. Times Square, New York 36, N. Y. Telephone Lackawanna 4-1000 FIVE CENTS

SUPREME COURT VOIDS STEEL SEIZURE, 6 TO 3; HOLDS TRUMAN USURPED POWERS OF CONGRESS; WORKERS AGAIN STRIKE AS MILLS ARE RETURNED

SWIFT SENATE VOTE ON BONN ACCORDS IS ASKED BY TRUMAN

Message Calls Defense Moves in Europe 'Great Forward Stride' Toward Peace

ACHESON REPORTS TO U. S.

Both President and Secretary Declare Soviet Measures Will Not Deter the West

Truman message and Acheson address are on Page 8.

By WALTER H. WAGGONER
Special to The New York Times.

WASHINGTON, June 2—President Truman urged the Senate today to approve two agreements putting West Germany on a footing of equality among nations and binding an enemy of World War II to the free world's defense alliance.

Asking for "early and favorable" action on the two pacts, signed by the diplomats of the Western Governments in Europe last week, the President said in a message to the Senate that the documents taken together "constitute a great forward stride toward strengthening peace and freedom in the world."

Accompanying his message were the so-called peace contract with West Germany, an arrangement just short of a formal treaty, and an amendment to the North Atlantic Treaty that would extend its defense guarantees to the Bonn Government in return for reciprocal pledges. Both require approval by the Senate to become effective.

European Pact Also Sent

For the Senate's information, Mr. Truman also attached a number of other documents signed in either Paris or Bonn, the major one being the treaty constituting the six-nation European Defense Community that would bring West German troops into a European army.

[In Bonn, Germany, Dr. Kurt Schumacher, Social Democratic leader, began the Opposition's campaign against ratification of the defense arrangements. He said that under the present terms the Germans would bear the brunt of the burdens involved in those accords while the Western Allies would enjoy the benefits.]

Even before the President's message arrived, Senator Tom Connally, the Texas Democrat who heads the Senate Foreign Relations Committee, predicted that the Senate would give Mr. Truman the approval he sought.

The Senator's forecast was made on the basis of two hours of discussion, at a joint session of the Senate Foreign Relations and House Foreign Affairs Committees, with Secretary of State Dean Acheson.

Mr. Connally said that Mr. Acheson had assured the committees that "no secret or undisclosed commitments or guarantees" were made while he was on his European mission that produced the agreements.

Connally to Speed Action

The Senate's foreign policy spokesman said it was important that the treaties "go into effect as soon as possible" and he made it plain that he would do his part in speeding Senate action.

"In my view it is essential that Western Germany be accorded its proper place in the family of nations without delay so that we can proceed with the task of building the joint defense of the free world as rapidly as possible," he said in a statement.

Secretary Acheson, meanwhile, went directly to the American people for understanding and support of the new agreements, addressing the nation by radio and television this evening on the nature and necessity of the new line-up of allies.

As President Truman had done, Mr. Acheson stressed the "very great stake" held by the United States in helping support and

Continued on Page 8, Column 3

Red Leader Named Premier of Rumania

By The United Press.

BUCHAREST, Rumania, June 2—The National Assembly proclaimed Gheorghe Gheorghiu-Dej as new Premier of Rumania today to succeed Dr. Petru Groza, who was named President of the republic.

M Gheorghiu-Dej was named Premier by a unanimous vote. Dr. Groza, who had been Premier since March 6, 1945, was elected President of the Assembly, a post tantamount to President of the republic.

The Government changes followed a request from the former President, Dr. Constantin Parhon, that he be relieved of his functions so he could dedicate himself entirely to his scientific work.

The Assembly took no action regarding Mme. Ana Pauker.

[The Bucharest radio revealed last week that Mme. Pauker, Rumanian Foreign Minister, had

Continued on Page 13, Column 2

ALLIES TERM TRUCE UP TO FOE IN KOREA

Reds Are Told World Opinion Will Judge Refusal to Agree to New Poll of Captives

By LINDESAY PARROTT
Special to The New York Times.

TOKYO, Tuesday, June 3—Maj. Gen. William K. Harrison Jr., senior United Nations truce delegate, told the Communists today: "The entire future of the armistice negotiations is now up to your side."

He warned the Chinese and North Koreans that the "court of world opinion" would judge their refusal to entertain the United Nations proposal that prisoners of war should be questioned by an impartial body in the presence of Communist representatives after a truce to determine how many wished to return to their former command.

General Harrison spoke during a thirty-minute session in the gravest warning given so far that the world would hold the Communists responsible for a delay in the truce and the failure of prisoners to return to their homes.

Outlining the proposal for "rescreening" of the prisoners, made after the enemy had challenged the result of an Allied poll that showed fewer than half the total

Continued on Page 3, Column 3

EISENHOWER YIELDS PAY IN RETIREMENT; FREE TO CAMPAIGN

He Leaves Army Duties Today —Waives $19,541 a Year to Avert Any Criticism

DECORATED BY PRESIDENT

Truman Hails Him as Symbol of Nation's Aim—General to Leave for Abilene

By JAMES RESTON
Special to The New York Times.

WASHINGTON, June 2—General of the Army Dwight D. Eisenhower has asked to be placed on the Army's retired list without pay, starting tomorrow. This request, which the Army said today had been approved by Secretary of Defense Robert A. Lovett, will release the general from the Army's regulations against political campaigning.

The current military appropriations legislation does not permit officers under the age of 62 to retire with pay unless the Department of Defense finds that this would cause personal hardship or be bad for the service.

[In South Dakota and California the final primaries will be held Tuesday, with the Dakota contest between General Eisenhower and Senator Robert A. Taft of Ohio attracting major attention. On the Democratic side, Senator Estes Kefauver is seeking delegates in both primaries. The Missouri Republican convention completed the formalities of naming a twenty-six-member delegation.]

General Eisenhower wrote to Mr. Lovett on May 28, asking that no special certification be made in his case, because his name was "directly involved in the national political campaign." The general, who is 61, would have been entitled to $19,541 a year in pay and allowances if, like General of the Army Douglas MacArthur, he had remained on the active list.

From his European headquarters, General Eisenhower wrote:

"There are a number of delegates already pledged to seek my nomination as the Republican Presidential candidate and, in the normal course of events, I will be talking to some of these delegates prior to the National Convention. As an officer on the retired list, I would feel free to engage in such

Continued on Page 19, Column 1

Another Prisoner on Koje Is Killed; Clark Set to Use Force on Captives

By GEORGE BARRETT
Special to The New York Times.

KOJE ISLAND, Korea, Tuesday, June 3—The accidental firing by an Allied soldier of a heavy machine gun near a prison stockade on this island killed one North Korean captive and wounded another this morning.

This mishap followed a statement yesterday by the new Far East Commander, Gen. Mark W. Clark, that Allied camp authorities were prepared to use "maximum force" to restore uncontested control over Communist captives.

An Army spokesman said that the North Korean who was killed had been standing near the barbed wire of Compound 78 when the machine gun went off. Other prisoners dragged the body farther inside the enclosure and refused to surrender it to United Nations medical personnel. They also refused to yield the wounded man for hospitalization.

An Army spokesman said that Brig. Gen. Haydon L. Boatner, camp commander, expressed concern over the accidental shooting—the second within a week at Koje.

Meanwhile, the prisoners resumed their demonstrations inside the enclosures, to which the camp command had attempted to put an end. In Compound 76 captive North Koreans held a mock funeral, presumably commemorating the five prisoners who were killed there last Friday. They hung black crepe on a flagpole and draped an imitation coffin with paper wreaths while General Boatner looked on from outside the barbed wire.

In Compound 602, according to pooled dispatches, the prisoners again erected the flagpole knocked down yesterday in a tank-led raid by United Nations guards, after the flying of the North Korean emblem had been forbidden. General Boatner told correspondents: "It will not be there very long."

Making his first visit to the troubled prison island yesterday, General Clark made it clear that the new United Nations policy of firmness might have taken so much starch out of the "die-hard" Communists that not much real fight was left in them.

Gen. James A. Van Fleet, Eighth Army commander, who came with General Clark, compared the atmosphere in seventeen compounds with the captives' mood of only a few weeks ago and happily summed up the situation that way.

In a late development last night there was a sudden flare-up of resistance from Compound 60, when a group of North Koreans—there are about 200 prisoners in this compound on war crime charges—shouted taunts at a South Korean officer walking past the enclosure.

The South Korean listened at first to the taunting, but was fi-

Continued on Page 3, Column 2

TWO IMPORTANT STEPS YESTERDAY IN THE STEEL DISPUTE

Secretary of Commerce Charles Sawyer signing formal order returning nation's steel plants to owners.

Associated Press Wirephotos

Philip Murray, C. I. O. and steel union president, making call that sent 600,000 workers on strike.

REALTY TAX TO RISE 12 TO 15 POINTS HERE

Final Valuations Show Record City Rate of $3.08 Probably Will Soar to $3.21

By PETER KIHSS

A rise of twelve to fifteen points in the city's basic real estate tax rate of $3.08, already the highest in history, was forecast unofficially yesterday when the final valuations of taxable real estate and special franchises were set at $19,425,499,087 for the fiscal year beginning July 1.

The revised valuations were $58,392,794 less than the tentative valuations made public Feb. 1, but $648,742,541 above the final figure of $18,776,756,546 for the current tax year. The total was the second highest in the city's history, exceeded only by 1932's $19,616,915,429.

While no city official would go on record with a tax forecast, pending a revised estimate of general fund revenues due from Controller Lazarus Joseph on June 20, the pencils flew at City Hall to make some approximations based on Mayor Impellitteri's budget message of April 1.

Mayor's Estimate of Need

The Mayor had estimated then that the new $1,469,265,102 expense budget would need a yield of $622,804,788 from real estate taxes. The Mayor reported that this was practically the maximum that could be levied on real estate within constitutional limitations.

Dividing this proposed yield by the final realty valuations would give a basic tax rate of nearly $3.21 for each $100 of assessed valuation, or thirteen points above the rate that has prevailed this year and last. Above this come borough rates, which this year have varied from 18 to 21 cents.

Municipal fiscal experts indicated this $3.21 basic tax rate approximation might still vary slightly, depending on revisions in the general fund. But they noted that the original general fund estimate had included $12,500,000 from an overnight parking tax, which the Mayor has been unable to get.

The main hopes in fiscal quarters appeared to be for rises in other general fund sources that might at least make up the loss from the parking tax estimate. In round numbers, each point in the real estate levy yields not quite $2,000,000.

The final realty valuations were transmitted to the Mayor by William E. Boyland, president of the seven-member Tax Commission. They showed ordinary real estate at $16,846,784,544, up $553,300,800 from last year; real estate of utility corporations at $1,738,555,835, up $54,006,315, and special

Continued on Page 45, Column 7

600,000 Quit Steel Mills; Industry Offers to Bargain

By A. H. RASKIN
Special to The New York Times.

PITTSBURGH, June 2—The steel industry got its mills back today, but they were producing no steel. Six hundred thousand members of the United Steelworkers of America, C. I. O., quit work as soon as they learned that the Supreme Court had ruled against Government seizure of the steel plants.

Many did not wait even for formal strike orders from their union president, Philip Murray. They simply put aside their tools and streamed out of mills that normally produce 95 per cent of the country's steel. All who stayed were supervisors and maintenance men engaged in the orderly cooling of blast furnaces to prevent permanent damage to equipment.

[The text of Mr. Murray's strike order is on Page 22.]

Mr. Murray got word of the court's decision at luncheon in a hotel across from his Pittsburgh headquarters. He rushed back and wired all union locals to stop work.

His message said: "The act of the court leaves the members of the United Steelworkers of America without the benefit of a collective bargaining agreement. In the absence of a wage agreement, our members have no alternative other than to cease work."

Mr. Murray also called upon the major steel companies to renew contract negotiations on the basis of the wage increases and other benefits recommended by the Wage Stabilization Board.

In a joint reply tonight, six of the largest companies said they were prepared to sit down with the union at once but that bargaining would have to proceed in

Continued on Page 24, Column 2

CONGRESS HAILS END OF STEEL SEIZURE

Some Demand Constitutional Curb on President—Censure of Truman Is Hinted

By C. P. TRUSSELL
Special to The New York Times.

WASHINGTON, June 2—Congress generally hailed today the Supreme Court's 6-3 decision holding President Truman's seizure of the steel industry unconstitutional.

Many at the Capitol held to the view that Mr. Truman still had ample legal power to invoke the Taft-Hartley Act, which he has sought unsuccessfully to have repealed, and to let its injunctions against strikes settle the problem. There was much speculation as to whether the President now would invoke that law.

Prompt Congressional action to meet the problem of the steel walkout was in doubt, however.

Demands were made that the court's verdict be clinched, either by giving the President the powers he thought he had, or by writing into the Constitution a prohibition against the use of seizure powers without specific backing in law.

Committee Meets Tomorrow

A House Judiciary subcommittee that has on its docket a dozen or so measures to impeach Mr. Truman, to censure him or to give him powers or deprive him of them was scheduled to meet Wednesday. It appeared tonight that it might recommend a censure on top of today's court defeat.

On the Senate calendar today was a bill that would amend the Constitution to bar the President from seizing any private property except under specific law.

This measure was "passed over." Its sponsor, Senator Pat McCarran, Democrat of Nevada and chairman of the Senate Judiciary Committee, was across the Plaza hearing the Supreme Court's decisions.

Senator Homer E. Ferguson, Republican of Michigan, obtained the Senate's unanimous consent for the McCarran bill to remain on the calendar with no prejudice.

A single objection, under the rules of the calendar, could block a proposed Constitutional amendment under this procedure.

Another measure, sponsored by Senator Wayne Morse, Republican of Oregon, would provide Presiden-

Continued on Page 23, Column 3

NEXT MOVE IN CRISIS IS CALLED TRUMAN'S

President Could Use Taft Act or Appeal to Congress—No Word From White House

By ANTHONY LEVIERO
Special to The New York Times.

WASHINGTON, June 2—With steel workers walking out of mills all over the country in the wake of the decision of the United States Supreme Court today nullifying the President's seizure of the industry, the next move was held to be up to Mr. Truman.

There was no indication from the White House tonight, however, as to what he might do. Meanwhile, Mr. Truman and his advisers were studying the seven opinions of the high tribunal.

Two obvious steps were presumably being considered by Mr. Truman.

The first would be to invoke the Taft-Hartley Act, which would require the union men to return to work for eighty days while a fact-finding board investigated the wage dispute. The other move might be a renewal of the plea that Mr. Truman addressed to Congress soon after the seizure for specific statutory authority to deal with labor disputes in major industries in time of emergency.

In the courts and in Congress Mr. Truman has been severely criticized for not having used the Taft law that labor hates before he resorted to seizure. His answer has been that the steel workers had waited ninety-nine days while the Wage Stabilization Board studied the wage dispute. Further-

Continued on Page 23, Column 7

Speedy Action by a Teller Foils Hold-Up in East 42d Street Bank

A would-be bank robber who escaped although three armed guards were near by was foiled yesterday in an attempt to hold up the Irving Trust Company at 100 East Forty-second Street by an alert 27-year-old teller, described by his superiors in the bank as a "guy with real guts."

This was the story as it was pieced together from accounts by the police of the East Thirty-fifth Street station and H. G. Brownson, vice president in charge of the bank's Forty-second Street office at Pershing Square:

At 2:50 P. M., an hour and ten minutes before the bank's closing time, a man about 45 years old, dressed in a gray suit and wearing a dark felt hat, approached a teller's cage about 100 feet from the Forty-second Street entrance to the bank.

There were 125 employes on duty, including the armed guards, and fifteen persons on the bank floor, which is in the second story of the Continental Can Building.

The cage the man approached was occupied by Charles Lehanka of 460 Audubon Avenue, who has worked in the bank for a little more than a year.

Without a word, the man handed to Mr. Lehanka a two-page note. The writing was a combination of lettering and script and was done in pencil on unlined paper.

Mr. Lehanka read only the first couple of sentences of the 138-word message. They said: "Don't press the alarm button if you value your life. Give me all the folding money you have in that cage."

At this point, Mr. Lehanka made a swift and courageous decision. He dropped to the floor and pressed the bank alarm, which sounded at Police Headquarters

Continued on Page 26, Column 4

BLACK GIVES RULING

President Cannot Make Law in Good or Bad Times, Majority Says

VINSON IS DISSENTER

Rejects Idea Executive Is 'Messenger Boy' in Crisis—Steel Curbed

The majority opinion, Page 22; others in part, Pages 22 and 23.

By JOSEPH A. LOFTUS
Special to The New York Times

WASHINGTON, June 2—The Supreme Court of the United States ruled, 6 to 3, today that President Truman's seizure of the steel industry to avert a strike violated the Constitution by usurping the legislative powers reserved to Congress.

The President bowed promptly by directing Secretary of Commerce Charles Sawyer to release the properties to their private owners, and the United Steelworkers of America, C. I. O., went on strike.

As a result of the walkout the Government ordered a halt in deliveries of steel from retail warehouses to consumer goods producers in an effort to conserve steel for defense needs.

Authorities said the action was directed at preventing a drain on warehouses by buyers who usually got their steel at the mills. Manufacturers who ordinarily receive steel from warehouses will continue to do so, they added. No order was issued against steel exports.

The Supreme Court justices who voted to uphold District Judge David A. Pine's order dispossessing the Government were: Hugo L. Black, Felix Frankfurter, William O. Douglas, Robert H. Jackson, Harold H. Burton and Tom C. Clark.

Dissenting were: Chief Justice Fred M. Vinson and Justices Stanley F. Reed and Sherman Minton.

Founding Fathers' Action Cited

The court ruled in effect that when the President seized the steel mills he seized the lawmaking power, because only Congress could authorize the taking of private property for public use.

"The Constitution did not subject this law-making power of Congress to Presidential or military supervision or control," said the opinion of the court, written by Justice Black.

"The founders of this nation entrusted the lawmaking power to the Congress alone in both good and bad times," it added. "It would do no good to recall the historical events, the fears of power and the hopes for freedom that lay behind their choice. Such a review would but confirm our holding that this seizure order cannot stand."

Chief Justice Vinson, writing a vigorous dissent, declared that the President's action to keep steel flowing was warranted by the world emergency.

"History bears out the genius of the founding fathers, who created a Government subject to law but not left subject to inertia when vigor and initiative are required," the Chief Justice wrote.

Vinson Criticizes Majority

"As the district judge stated this is no time for 'timorous' judicial action," he declared. "But neither is this a time for timorous executive action."

Chief Justice Vinson said the majority of the court, not the minority, was seeking to amend the Constitution. He declared:

"The broad Executive power granted by Article II to an officer on duty 365 days a year cannot, it is said, be invoked to avert disaster.

"Instead, the President must confine himself to sending a message to Congress recommending action. Under this messenger-boy concept of the office, the President cannot even act to preserve legislative programs from destruction so that Congress will have something left to act upon."

The court, contrary to a widely

Continued on Page 23, Column 8

"All the News That's Fit to Print"

The New York Times.

ELECTION EXTRA
Fair, warmer today. Some cloudiness and turning cooler tomorrow.
Temperature Range Today—Max., 62; Min., 38
Temperatures Yesterday—Max., 52; Min., 39
Full U. S. Weather Bureau Report, Page 54

Copyright, 1952, by The New York Times Company.

VOL. CII No. 34,619. Entered as Second-Class Matter, Post Office, New York, N. Y. NEW YORK, WEDNESDAY, NOVEMBER 5, 1952. Times Square, New York 36, N. Y. Telephone LAckawanna 4-1000 FIVE CENTS

EISENHOWER WINS IN A LANDSLIDE; TAKES NEW YORK; IVES ELECTED; REPUBLICANS GAIN IN CONGRESS

G.O.P. HOUSE LIKELY

But the Senate Margin Hangs in the Balance of Two Close Races

LODGE TRAILING RIVAL

President Eisenhower May Lack a Working Majority in Congress

By JAMES RESTON

It appeared at 4:30 this morning that control of the United States Senate could be determined by the outcome of the Senatorial races in Michigan and Massachusetts.

At that time the Republicans appeared to have picked up five new seats and lost three others, thus enabling them to wipe out the two-seat advantage held by the Democrats at the end of the Eighty-second Congress.

To assure the power to organize the Senate and place their Republicans at the head of its important committees, however, Senator Henry Cabot Lodge Jr., Republican of Massachusetts, would have to overcome an advantage of more than 75,000 held by Representative John F. Kennedy, his opponent.

And Representative Charles E. Potter, Republican of Michigan had to retain the 47,000 lead he held over the Democratic incumbent, Senator Blair Moody of Michigan.

Morse May Be Vital

So close was the Senate race that there was a possibility that control of the upper chamber could be determined by the decision of Senator Wayne Morse of Oregon, who was elected as a Republican, but who broke with his party during the campaign, and announced that hereafter he was an "independent."

Though it appeared that the Republicans had won control of the House, one thing was certain: that President Dwight D. Eisenhower would not have a comfortable working majority in either house and would require all his gifts of persuasion to win consent for his policies on Capitol Hill.

Several factors in the Senate race were noteworthy:

¶Of the ten so-called isolationist or extremist Republicans who went before the voters yesterday, seven seemed fairly sure of victory. These were Senators Joseph R. McCarthy of Wisconsin; John W. Bricker of Ohio; William E. Jenner of Indiana; Edward Martin of Pennsylvania; Arthur V. Watkins of Utah, George W. Malone of Nevada and Hugh Butler of Nebraska.

Three other Republicans in this same category, however, were in serious trouble if they had not actually been defeated. They were:

Continued on Page 15, Column 1

Electoral Vote by States

	Eisenhower	Stevenson		Eisenhower	Stevenson
Ala.	—	11	Neb.	6	—
Ariz.	4	—	Nev.	3	—
Ark.	—	8	N. H.	4	—
Calif.	32	—	N. J.	16	—
Colo.	6	—	N. M.	4	—
Conn.	8	—	N. Y.	45	—
Del.	3	—	N. C.	—	14
Fla.	*10	—	N. D.	4	—
Ga.	—	12	Ohio	25	—
Idaho	4	—	Okla.	8	—
Ill.	27	—	Ore.	6	—
Ind.	13	—	Pa.	32	—
Iowa	10	—	R. Isl.	4	—
Kan.	8	—	S. C.	—	8
Ky.	—	10	S. D.	4	—
La.	—	10	Tenn.	11	—
Me.	5	—	Texas	24	—
Md.	9	—	Utah	4	—
Mass.	16	—	Vt.	3	—
Mich.	20	—	Va.	12	—
Minn.	11	—	Wash.	9	—
Miss.	—	8	W. Va.	—	8
Mo.	13	—	Wisc.	12	—
Mont.	4	—	Wyo.	3	—
			Total	442	89

*Trend.

EISENHOWER TAKES JERSEY BY 300,000

Senator Smith Is Re-elected—Bond Issues Supported in Record Balloting

By RUSSELL PORTER

With more than three-quarters of New Jersey's vote counted early this morning, Gen. Dwight D. Eisenhower appeared headed toward a plurality of close to 300,000 in the state over Gov. Adlai E. Stevenson. This far exceeded Governor Dewey's 1948 plurality of 85,669 over President Truman.

United States Senator H. Alexander Smith, Republican candidate for re-election, won a sweeping victory over his Democratic opponent, Archibald S. Alexander, though Mr. Smith ran behind the head of his ticket. His indicated plurality was about 200,000.

The returns were:

PRESIDENT

3,461 precincts out of 3,840:

Eisenhower	1,203,120
Stevenson	921,375

UNITED STATES SENATOR

3,399 precincts out of 3,840:

Smith	1,089,883
Alexander	903,533

The Republicans appeared to have retained their majority of nine to five in New Jersey's delegation in the House of Representatives.

Both bond issues on the ballot

Continued on Page 23, Column 2

STATE LEAD 850,000

General's Upstate Edge Tops Million—He Loses City by Only 362,674

PROTEST VOTE SEEN

Albany County, Other Areas in Democratic Column Switch

State Presidential Vote

CITY SUMMARY

	Eisenhower (Rep.)	Stevenson (Dem.-Lib.)
Manhattan	300,234	447,877
Bronx	241,545	393,052
Brooklyn	447,148	656,278
Queens	449,505	331,633
Richmond	55,981	28,247
Total	1,494,413	1,857,087
Upstate	2,413,299	1,147,510
Grand total	3,907,712	3,104,597

4,394 election districts out of 4,394 in the city reporting and 5,222 out of 5,954 upstate.

By JAMES A. HAGERTY

Gen. Dwight D. Eisenhower, Republican nominee for President, carried New York State with its forty-five electoral votes with a plurality of landslide proportions that will reach nearly 850,000.

With 33 election districts missing, all outside this city, General Eisenhower led Gov. Adlai E. Stevenson, his Democratic opponent, by an actual plurality of 846,020 and an indicated plurality of 840,034.

To carry his adopted state by this astounding plurality, General Eisenhower held Governor Stevenson down to an actual plurality of 362,674 in this city, far less than the supporters of the Democratic candidate expected.

With the 33 election districts missing, General Eisenhower carried the state outside the city by an actual plurality of 1,265,789 and, assuming that his vote held up in the missing districts, by an indicated plurality of about 1,270,000.

Governor Stevenson carried Manhattan by 147,633, the Bronx by 151,597 and Brooklyn by 209,130, all far below Democratic expectations. General Eisenhower carried Queens by 117,872 and Richmond by 27,834, well above

Continued on Page 24, Column 3

New President and Vice President

DWIGHT D. EISENHOWER

RICHARD M. NIXON

The New York Times

IVES IS RE-ELECTED BY RECORD MARGIN

Defeats Cashmore by Biggest Plurality of Any Republican—Harding Mark Topped

Vote for Senator

CITY SUMMARY

	Ives (Rep.)	Cashmore (Dem.)	Counts (Lib.)
Manh'n	303,040	322,157	88,797
Bronx	233,548	277,506	101,014
B'klyn	398,498	522,751	147,370
Queens	429,225	265,812	62,558
Rich'd	51,939	28,742	2,044
Total	1,416,250	1,416,968	401,783
Up-state	2,399,770	1,099,842	52,259
Gr Totl	3,816,020	2,516,810	454,042

4,394 election districts out of 4,394 in the city reporting and 5,854 out of 5,954 up-state.

By LEO EGAN

Senator Irving M. Ives won re-election in a three-cornered race yesterday by the largest plurality ever obtained by a Republican candidate in New York State, topping President Warren G. Harding's record-setting margin of 1,089,929 in 1920 by more than 200,000 votes.

The former majority leader of the State Assembly and co-sponsor of New York's law against racial discrimination in employment thus became the first Republican Senator to win re-election in New York since the late James W. Wadsworth performed that feat in the Harding landslide of 1920.

Not only did Senator Ives carry the normally Republican upstate area by a plurality that may reach 1,297,972, but he came within 718 votes of capturing normally Democratic New York City as well.

The complete Senate vote in the city gave Senator Ives 1,416,250 to 1,416,968 for Borough President John Cashmore of Brooklyn, the Democratic candidate. Thus Mr. Cashmore's plurality within the city was held to 718 votes.

With 5,854 of the 5,954 districts outside the city totaled, Senator Ives had an actual plurality of 1,299,928. On this basis, his final up-state margin should reach 1,300,000.

Dr. George S. Counts, the Liberal party candidate, polled 454,042 votes in the same districts tabulated for Senator Ives and Mr. Cashmore. On this basis his final vote could reach 460,000. Corliss Lamont, the American Labor candidate

Continued on Page 21, Column 2

NEW YORK TIMES news bulletins are broadcast over WQXR every hour.

Eisenhower Cracks South, Heads for Victory in Texas

By WILLIAM S. WHITE

Gen. Dwight D. Eisenhower, the Republican Presidential candidate, has smashed the traditionally Democratic Solid South in his national victory over Gov. Adlai E. Stevenson. He has carried outright Florida and Virginia, with their twenty-two electoral votes. This morning unofficial observers gave him the greatest Southern prize of all—Texas and its twenty-four electoral votes, the sixth biggest bloc in the United States.

Confirmation of this indicated loss would involve a Democratic disaster.

Apart from all this and from receiving the greatest popular ballot ever given a Republican in the South, General Eisenhower was first narrowly leading and then narrowly trailing this morning in Tennessee, which has eleven electoral votes. In Tennessee, the position was so close that the result probably will not be known until late this afternoon.

In Louisiana and South Carolina Governor Stevenson had slight leads after trailing often in the early returns.

Only the hardest of the hard core of the Old South has remained wholly faithful to the old Democratic tradition.

Mississippi, Arkansas, North

Continued on Page 22, Column 3

CONNECTICUT G. O. P. SEATS 2 IN SENATE

Benton and Ribicoff Concede to Purtell and Bush While Eisenhower Sweeps State

Special to THE NEW YORK TIMES.

HARTFORD, Conn., Wednesday, Nov. 5—Gen. Dwight D. Eisenhower swept to an amazing landslide victory in Connecticut yesterday, winning by a margin of nearly 130,000 votes over Gov. Adlai E. Stevenson in final returns from the 169 cities and towns in the state.

The victory astounded Republicans as well as Democrats. Prior to the election, Republican leaders had made cautious claims of victory by about 25,000 or 30,000 votes, while Democrats privately thought they had a chance to win the state.

The tremendous Eisenhower sweep carried two Republican United States Senators into office with him. Senator William A. Purtell of West Hartford defeated William Benton, Democrat, for the full six-year term by a margin of 90,286, and Prescott S. Bush, Greenwich banker, defeated Representative Abraham A. Ribicoff of Hartford, Democrat, by 30,373 votes. Mr. Ribicoff made a spectacular uphill run but was edged out by Mr. Bush's lead in the small towns that are traditionally Republican.

Final returns were:

PRESIDENT

169 precincts out of 169:

Eisenhower	610,989
Stevenson	481,482

UNITED STATES SENATOR

(For six-year Term)

169 precincts out of 169:

Purtell (R.)	575,445
Benton (D.)	485,159

(For Four-year Term)

Bush (R.)	559,586
Ribicoff (D)	529,212

The Eisenhower sweep enabled the Republicans to win five of the six seats from Connecticut in the House of Representatives, a gain

Continued on Page 23, Column 3

GENERAL APPEALS FOR UNITED PEOPLE

He Vows Not to Give 'Short Weight' as President—Thanks Rival for Pledge

By WILLIAM R. CONKLIN

A jubilant Gen. Dwight D. Eisenhower accepted his election as President early this morning with a pledge to the American people that he would not give "short weight" in the execution of his new responsibilities in Washington.

With his wife by his side, the Republican President-elect told 2,000 campaign supporters in the grand ballroom of the Commodore Hotel at 2:05 A. M. that it would take the support of a united people to carry his Administration to success in its efforts to build a "better future for America."

His remarks were carried by radio and television to all parts of the country.

He read a message he had sent a few minutes before to his defeated rival, Gov. Adlai E. Stevenson of Illinois, thanking him for his promise of assistance. General Eisenhower expressed hope that Americans of both parties would speedily forget campaign bitter-

Continued on Page 20, Column 2

RACE IS CONCEDED

Virginia and Florida Go to the General as Do Illinois and Ohio

SWEEP IS NATION-WIDE

Victor Calls for Unity and Thanks Governor for Pledging Support

By ARTHUR KROCK

Gen. Dwight D. Eisenhower was elected President of the United States yesterday in an electoral vote landslide and with an emphatic popular majority that probably will give his party a small margin of control in the House of Representatives but may leave the Senate as it is—forty-nine Democrats, forty-seven Republicans and one independent.

Senator Richard M. Nixon of California was elected Vice President.

The Democratic Presidential candidate, Gov. Adlai E. Stevenson of Illinois, shortly after midnight conceded his defeat by a record turnout of American voters.

At 4 A. M. today the Republican candidate had carried states with a total of 431 electors, or 165 more than the 266 required for the selection of a President. The Democratic candidate seemed sure of 69, with 31 doubtful in Kentucky, Louisiana and Tennessee.

General Eisenhower's landslide victory, both in electoral and popular votes, was nation-wide in its pattern, extending from New England—where Massachusetts and Rhode Island broke their Democratic voting habits of many years—down the Eastern seaboard to Maryland, Virginia and Florida and westward to almost every state between the coasts, including California.

General Wins Illinois

The Republican candidate took Illinois, Governor Stevenson's home state. In South Carolina, though he lost its electors on a technicality, he won a majority of the voters. And, completing the first successful Republican invasion of the States of the former Confederacy, the General carried Texas and broke the one-party system in the South.

The personal popularity that enabled him to defeat Senator Robert A. Taft of Ohio in the Republican primaries in Texas, and present him with the issue on which he defeated the Senator for the Republican nomination, crushed the regular Democratic organization of Texas that was led by Speaker Sam Rayburn of the House of Representatives and had the blessing of former Vice President John N. Garner.

The tide that bore General Eisenhower to the White House, though it did not give him a comfortable working majority in either the national House or the Senate (the Democrats may still nominally control the machinery of that branch), probably increased the number of Republican governors beyond the present twenty-five.

"My fellow citizens have made their choice and I gladly accept it," said Governor Stevenson at 1:46 A. M., Eastern standard time, and he asked all citizens to unite behind the President-elect. The defeated candidate said he had sent a telegram of congratulation to General Eisenhower.

At 2:05 A. M., from the Grand Ballroom of the Commodore Hotel, General Eisenhower said he recognized the weight of his new responsibilities and that he would not give "short weight" in their execution. He also urged "unity" and announced he had sent a telegram of thanks to the Democratic candidate for his promise of support.

The issues of the unusually vigorous campaign that was waged

Continued on Page 14, Column 3

Hill Battle Spurts in Korea; Allies Press 'Triangle' Fight

By LINDESAY PARROTT

Special to THE NEW YORK TIMES.

TOKYO, Wednesday, Nov. 5—The hard-fighting South Korean infantry, driving for the third time in three days up the slopes of the central Korean ridges, drove a penetration today into the Communist lines on the western flank of "Triangle Hill," a strategic position north of Kumhwa.

Early this afternoon, the Republic of Korea (R. O. K.) troops had captured one of the twin peaks that project from "Triangle"—named "Jane Russell Hill." The sharp, indecisive combat continued.

The attack on the twin peaks was tied in with a new drive against the central pyramid of "Triangle Hill." The South Koreans again thrust within yards of the crest.

The Chinese Reds struck again just to the east in a new attempt to capture the summit of "Sniper Ridge," flanking "Triangle" on the United Nations' right.

The crest of "Triangle" had been lost to the Chinese Communists after the United Nations limited objective offensive took it last month. The South Koreans pushed up southern slopes today to within fifty yards of the Reds' lines.

Some reports said the fighting again today was as furious as during the attacks Sunday and Monday, when the South Koreans desperately struggled to regain the positions.

Allied warplanes were out against the enemy guns. About fifty sorties had been flown by Fifth Air Force fighter-bombers before noon against Red artillery on high Papasan Mountain, the Communists' strongpoint just to the north of the central front.

At every opportunity, Allied guns pounded the Reds on the crest of "Triangle."

The Reds' guns dropped 5,000 rounds on the United Nations positions near "Heartbreak Ridge" and the "Punchbowl" in the mountainous eastern watershed, where the heaviest fighting of yesterday occurred. A North Korean battalion hit Allied defense positions on "Heartbreak" on the heels of the barrage, but the enemy failed to make a penetration.

On "Triangle Hill" and the twin peaks to the west of it, contact was light yesterday. At least temporarily, the South Koreans broke off attempts to storm two positions they had lost to the Chinese Reds' counter-attacks, after the United Nations limited objec-

Continued on Page 3, Column 3

M'Carthy Is Winner, But Is Last on Ticket

By RICHARD J. H. JOHNSTON

Special to THE NEW YORK TIMES.

MILWAUKEE, Wednesday, Nov. 5—Wisconsin went to the Republicans today for the third time in a national election since 1920.

The predicted Republican sweep of the state and capture of its twelve electoral votes became a certainty a few minutes after midnight.

Gen. Dwight D. Eisenhower, the Republican Presidential nominee ran second on the G. O. P. ticket with Gov. Walter J. Kohler Jr. leading the state in his bid for re-election.

As the returns neared the final count, Gen. Dwight D. Eisenhower's vote indicated he would emerge as leader of the G. O. P. slate in Wisconsin. With 2,036 of the state's 3,224 vtoing precincts reported, his vote was 554,369 to Gov. Adlai E. Stevenson's 356,218.

Gov. Walter J. Kohler, seeking

Continued on Page 22, Column 6

Stevenson Concedes the Victory As Weeping Backers Cry 'No, No'

By WILLIAM M. BLAIR

Special to THE NEW YORK TIMES.

SPRINGFIELD, Ill., Wednesday, Nov. 5—Gov. Adlai E. Stevenson conceded defeat early today to his Republican opponent. Gen. Dwight D. Eisenhower, and pledged the support "he will need to carry out the great tasks that lie before him."

The Governor came from the Executive Mansion to the Democratic Headquarters in the Leland Hotel to make his announcement before a jammed ballroom of supporters, many of whom broke into tears and cried, "No, no."

Governor Stevenson said:

"General Eisenhower has been a great leader in war. He has been a vigorous and valiant opponent in the campaign. These qualities will now be dedicated to leading us all through the next four years.

"It is traditionally American to fight hard before an election.

"It is equally traditional to close ranks as soon as the people have spoken. From the depths of my heart I thank all of my party, and all of those independents and Republicans who supported Senator Sparkman and me."

The Governor said he had dispatched to General Eisenhower in New York a telegram which he read. It said:

"The people have made their choice and I congratulate you. That you may be the servant and guardian of peace and make the dale of trouble a door of hope is my earnest prayer. Best Wishes.

Adlai E. Stevenson."

Governor Stevenson did have a grin, however, for the crowd and displayed his ever-present humor to reporters. Asked how about 1956, the next presidential election year, he echoed in a loud voice and with mock surprise "56! Examine that man's head."

As for his immediate plans, he

Continued on Page 16, Column 3

"All the News That's Fit to Print"

The New York Times.

LATE CITY EDITION

Cloudy, becoming fair this afternoon. Some cloudiness tomorrow.
Temperature Range Today—Max., 40; Min., 29
Temperatures Yesterday—Max., 29.6; Min., 14.5
Full U. S. Weather Bureau Report, Page 40

VOL. CII...No. 34,709. Entered as Second-Class Matter, Post Office, New York, N. Y. NEW YORK, TUESDAY, FEBRUARY 3, 1953. Times Square, New York 36, N. Y. Telephone Lackawanna 4-1000 FIVE CENTS

EISENHOWER FREES CHIANG TO RAID MAINLAND; BIDS CONGRESS VOID ALL 'SECRET' PACTS ABROAD; WOULD END CONTROLS; OPPOSES TAX CUTS NOW

EUROPE STORM TOLL EXCEEDS 1,400 DEAD AS FLOODS SUBSIDE

296 Die Along British Coast—Thousands Still Missing as Help Is Speeded

DUTCH COUNT 955 KILLED

Million in Netherlands Affected—Belgian Area Battered—Dunkirk Hard Hit

By TANIA LONG
Special to THE NEW YORK TIMES.

LONDON, Tuesday, Feb. 3—As the gales abated and the raging waters of the North Sea began to recede, three nations counted their dead today and assessed the damage resulting from their worst flood disaster in recent history.

Hard hit were Britain, the Netherlands and Belgium, where huge waves swept across large sections of the coast Saturday night and early Sunday, breaking through dikes and seawalls and swallowing entire towns and villages.

[The Associated Press said the known dead in the storm area totaled more than 1,400 early Tuesday. In the Netherlands, 955 persons drowned. The toll in Britain stood at 443, including 296 killed in floods along the east coast, 132 who lost their lives in the sinking of the ferry Princess Victoria in the Irish Sea and fifteen lost on a missing trawler. Belgium had twenty-two dead.]

Several thousand persons were still missing, and it was feared that the death roll would mount heavily as rescue squads, made up of policemen, military personnel and civilian volunteers, completed their search of the devastated areas. On Canvey Island in the Thames Estuary, for example, where there were 100 dead, 500 men, women and children were still unaccounted for. Several thousand persons were evacuated from Canvey, which suffered by far the greatest damage of any British community.

Mobilize Full Resources

When the whole magnitude of the disaster that struck most heavily at Britain and the Netherlands was realized, the full resources of the two countries were quickly mobilized to give aid in the emergency. At the same time, assistance was sped to the Netherlands from France, Belgium and Denmark, and the United States forces in Europe, which also had their casualties.

The Swiss Red Cross Society announced it would begin an immediate collection of money to aid the British and Dutch flood victims, and there were offers of assistance, financial or material, from many other European countries and the United States.

In the meantime, the two nations worst affected put into action emergency plans to deal with the thousands rendered homeless by the floods. In Britain, civil defense plans prepared against a possible atomic attack were put into operation to shelter and feed the dispossessed.

Government Sends Help

The Government ordered its storehouses opened and sent thousands of blankets, mattresses and other items to the distressed areas, while the women's voluntary services brought out their trucks and set into motion the Flying Food Convoys, organized during World War II and kept in reserve against the possible outbreak of another conflict.

While evacuation of many thousands was being carried on, engineers in Britain and the Netherlands began their battle to restore the broken dikes and sea walls. Using sandbags, logs and other material readily available, they filled the gaps in an effort to halt a further influx from the sea.

There was still danger that the combination of winds and high tides that caused the original disaster might bring further flood

Continued on Page 4, Column 5

Ships Arrive, Depart On Own in Tug Strike

Cargo and passenger vessels berthed and departed on their own power yesterday in New York, Philadelphia and Norfolk as the three-port strike of towboat crews continued without signs of a break.

Mild winds and calm waters here made it possible for most ships to dock or leave the harbor without the aid of tugs. A few inbound vessels, however, were held up at anchorage and several scheduled to leave were unable to do so.

Longshoremen shaped up and worked as usual. It had been feared that they might abstain from work in sympathy with the 3,500 strikers, who are members of Local 333 of the Marine Division of the International Longshoremen's Association, A. F. L.

One result of the strike was an interference with garbage dis-

Continued on Page 20, Column 4

A. F. L. ACTS TO END PIER UNION ABUSES

Breaking Traditional Policy, Its Council Orders Inquiry—Hogan Subpoenaes Ryan

By A. H. RASKIN
Special to THE NEW YORK TIMES.

MIAMI BEACH, Feb. 2—Acting to stamp out racketeering in its ranks, the American Federation of Labor made two sharp breaks today with its tradition of noninterference in the internal affairs of its affiliated unions.

Its executive council set up a committee of three federation vice presidents to consider means of cleaning up the gang-infested International Longshoremen's Association. The committee began its work at once and it was indicated that it would submit its report to the council within forty-eight hours.

[District Attorney Frank S. Hogan announced in New York Monday night that he had issued a grand jury subpoena for the appearance at 2 o'clock Tuesday afternoon of Joseph P. Ryan, president of the International Longshoremen's Association.]

The council also called on another affiliated union, the United Automobile Workers, to revoke the charter of a New York local headed by a convicted extortionist. If the automobile union refuses to comply, the council has the power to recommend that it be expelled from the federation at the next annual convention.

In a third action at the opening of its mid-winter meeting at the Monte Carlo Hotel here, the executive council set Feb. 24 as the date for resumption of formal peace talks between the A. F. L. and the

Continued on Page 20, Column 1

BRITAIN IS ANXIOUS

Makes Representations to U. S. on the Effects of Formosa Policy

PARLIAMENT AROUSED

Churchill Defers Debate Till Today, When Eden Will State Policy

By JAY WALZ
Special to THE NEW YORK TIMES.

WASHINGTON, Feb. 2—Britain has made representations to the United States about President Eisenhower's decision to allow the Chinese Nationalists to raid the China mainland.

Anthony Eden, British Foreign Secretary, who is to make a statement on the subject before the House of Commons tomorrow, communicated with the State Department today.

It is understood that he advised diplomatic officials here that the British Government believed the new order to the Seventh Fleet would greatly complicate the political situation both in Europe and in the Far East.

In his communication, Mr. Eden is believed to have argued that the new order would intensify the Chinese civil war, raise the fears of a general war in the Far East and thus make any general settlement in the Far East even more difficult.

Bradley Discounts Risk

General of the Army Omar Bradley, chairman of the Joint Chiefs of Staff, said tonight that President Eisenhower's new policy on Formosa did not increase greatly the chances of the United States' becoming involved in a "big war" in the Far East.

The Eisenhower Administration contends that the United States, while intending no aggressive move, cannot permit its Navy, as the President put it, "to serve as a defensive arm of Communist China" by continuing its neutralizing function between the Nationalists and the Communists.

Some diplomatic sources feel that Britain's concern over developments may reflect general uneasiness among United States Allies in Europe over the direction of United States foreign policy.

Among these were British Embassy officials, who withheld comment pending Mr. Eden's statement in Parliament tomorrow.

However, F. S. Tomlinson, an Embassy counselor, called on Assistant Secretary of State John M. Allison last Saturday to express "concern" over reports of President Eisenhower's decision about

Continued on Page 11, Column 2

The New York Times (by Bruce Hoertel)

DELIVERS FIRST STATE OF UNION MESSAGE: President Eisenhower addressing a joint session of Congress yesterday. In background are Richard M. Nixon, Vice President, and Speaker of the House Joseph W. Martin Jr.

RED BLOW STOPPED BY SOUTH KOREANS

650-Man Attack on the Eastern Front Repulsed — Sabres Down Two Enemy Jets

By The Associated Press.

SEOUL, Korea, Tuesday, Feb. 3—North Koreans launched a 650-man attack on the eastern Korean front today, but stout South Korean defenders repulsed the assault and pursued the Communists across the craggy No Man's Land in below-zero cold.

The Korean Communists attacked at 12:45 A. M. across one mile of the mountainous front. They threw three companies into this attack and mounted two diversionary attacks of platoon size to the east.

Moving up under cover of a 680-round artillery and mortar barrage, the main force drove within forty yards of the main South Korean defenses.

The bitterly resisting South Koreans mounted a counter-attack at 2 A. M., drove off the Reds and chased them back across the snow-clad hills. An Eighth Army staff officer reported an estimated fifty-five of the enemy were killed.

Sabres Down Two MIG's

Special to THE NEW YORK TIMES.

TOKYO, Tuesday, Feb. 3—Sabre jets of the United States Fifth Air Force shot down two Soviet-designed MIG jet fighters over northwest Korea yesterday, probably destroyed another and damaged two more, while fighter-bombers and high-velocity tank-mounted guns hammered at the enemy-entrenched line across the peninsula.

Twelve Sabres clashed with eight MIG's in dogfights that ranged from 50,000 feet to 500 feet altitude, and from the Yalu River to Changchon on the west coast. The two kills were credited to Col. James K. Johnson and Maj. Foster L. Smith.

Meanwhile, more than 100 fighter-bombers, continuing the pattern of saturation raids on selected targets, plastered a big enemy troop concentration and storage area south of Chinnampo, seaport of the North Korean Communist capital at Pyongyang and important communications hub on the main route to the western front. The planes leveled forty buildings, returning pilots said, and set off six large secondary explosions, indicating that ammunition storage areas had been hit.

Other fighter-bombers flying along the front lines knocked out

Continued on Page 3, Column 2

Capehart Moves to Retain Controls on Stand-By Basis

By CLAYTON KNOWLES
Special to THE NEW YORK TIMES.

WASHINGTON, Feb. 2—Opposition cropped up today in an influential Republican quarter to President Eisenhower's proposal to let price and wage controls die on April 30 without maintaining stand-by machinery to reimpose them if needed.

Senator Homer E. Capehart of Indiana, chairman of the Senate Banking and Currency Committee, introduced a bill to set up such machinery within a few minutes after the President made his position known in his State of the Union Message.

He did not challenge the President's belief that price-wage controls had outlived their present usefulness but he did question the possibility of enacting a controls law quickly if one should be needed again.

"It is the height of impracticability," Mr. Capehart said, "to expect that the Congress can do a proper job of legislating a good controls law into effect in a period of less than three months, and for such a law to begin properly functioning within seven months from the incidence of the request for the legislation."

He maintained that inaction during this enforced waiting period would promote hoarding, scare buying and indiscriminate spending, all of which contribute to inflation. He said this was precisely what happened after the outbreak of hostilities in Korea. Before a

Continued on Page 15, Column 4

CIVIL RIGHTS PLANS GET WIDE SUPPORT

Challenge to McCarthy Seen on Security Issues—Duel Over Immigration Looms

By WILLIAM S. WHITE
Special to THE NEW YORK TIMES.

WASHINGTON, Feb. 2—President Eisenhower appeared to please nearly all the political Center in Congress today by the civil rights, loyalty and immigration policies laid down in his State of the Union Message.

The Left Wing at some points and the Right Wing at other points were made far from happy, for varying reasons.

The prospect raised was that the President could count upon at least as much Democratic support as Republican support—and perhaps more—for his approach in these fields, which encompass some

Continued on Page 17, Column 1

CONGRESS PRAISES EISENHOWER TALK

But 7th Fleet Decision Brings Fear of War Extension and Deeper U. S. Involvement

By C. P. TRUSSELL
Special to THE NEW YORK TIMES.

WASHINGTON, Feb. 2—President Eisenhower's first message on the State of the Union, delivered personally today to a joint session of Congress in the packed House of Representatives chamber, got a rousing reception.

However, as the new President made his exit, arms linked with Senator Robert A. Taft of Ohio, Senate Majority Leader, whom he defeated for the Republican Presidential nomination, the speech appeared to leave in its wake a trail of issues that spelled Congressional controversy to come.

Although the President's speech brought praise from Democrats as well as Republicans, President Eisenhower's decision to end the United States Seventh Fleet's role as a barrier against raids by the Chinese Nationalists on the Communist-held mainland seemed to bring much concern to many Congressmen. It was difficult to determine whether the Republican view that the action would end the stalemate in Korea outweighed fear, expressed largely by Democrats, that it might extend the Korean conflict and involve the United States more deeply in Asia.

Resentment Expressed

Senators and Representatives repeatedly asked whether releasing Generalissimo Chiang Kai-shek's Formosa forces to attack the Chinese mainland would imply that the United States would have to back up such actions with American men and planes. This, they contended, would mean deeper involvement and perhaps another world war.

Influential Democrats in Congress expressed resentment over the section of the President's address in which he contended, in effect, that the present assignment of the Seventh Fleet, made by former President Truman, constituted a protection for the Communist mainland while other Communists were fighting United Nations troops, mostly American, in Korea.

Representative John W. McCormack, Democrat of Massachusetts and House Whip, called it "hitting below the belt." He charged that President Eisenhower, while asking for bipartisan foreign policy, was acting "to destroy it."

Opponents contended the Seventh Fleet decision would not

Continued on Page 17, Column 3

STATE OF THE UNION

President Sees No 'Logic or Sense' in Sea Patrol Helping Chinese Reds

HIS 'POSITIVE POLICY'

Reciprocal Trade Pacts, Aid to Europe Backed in Congress Message

Text of the State of the Union Message, Pages 14 and 15.

By ANTHONY LEVIERO
Special to THE NEW YORK TIMES.

WASHINGTON, Feb. 2—President Eisenhower today ended the United States Seventh Fleet's protective screening of Red China, thus permitting the Nationalist forces of Generalissimo Chiang Kai-shek on Formosa to attack the Communist-held mainland.

The President also called upon Congress to repudiate any secret concessions made to the Russians at the World War II conferences at Teheran, Yalta and Potsdam.

Roars of applause greeted General Eisenhower's twin enunciations of a "new, positive foreign policy," made in his first State of the Union Message delivered before a joint session of Congress.

The first Republican President to chart a course for the nation in two decades, General Eisenhower also dwelt on domestic affairs in his address, proposing a program that would turn the country toward a freer enterprise system and "natural"-economic law.

His Program Detailed

In outlining his policies for the new Administration the President made these points:

¶There no longer was any "sense or logic" in the use of the Seventh Fleet to shield Red China.

¶The Government "recognizes no kind of commitment contained in secret understandings of the past with foreign governments which permit * * * enslavement."

¶The training and arming of South Korean troops would be accelerated.

¶Aid to Europe would be continued with the Allies required to be full partners matching United States contributions according to their capabilities.

¶The new foreign policy would be the true product of bipartisanship and cooperation between the President and Congress and it would be coherent and global.

¶Incontrovertible evidence is at hand of Russian possession of atomic weapons and therefore civil defense preparedness is a "sheer necessity."

¶The reciprocal trade treaties should be continued. American investments abroad should be encouraged and customs procedures simplified.

¶The Secretary of Defense would take steps to obtain the maximum in national security at minimum cost.

¶The first order of domestic business should be to balance the budget, after which a reduction in taxation would be in order.

¶Wage-price controls should not

Continued on Page 15, Column 1

Southeast Britain's Coast Lifeless And Awash as Seen From Plane

By THOMAS F. BRADY
Special to THE NEW YORK TIMES.

LONDON, Feb. 2—A vast coastal region of southeastern Britain lay submerged by salt water today, as the Romans found it 2,000 years ago. Seen from the air the land was awash and lifeless.

This report was written after a survey flight in a little Consul plane over Essex and Suffolk, where the angry sea took several hundred lives Saturday night and Sunday. The scene from the air was a tragic disorder.

Miles of glistening gray water were broken by brown roofs of houses, telephone poles still tied together by wires, the gun barrels of an anti-aircraft battery, and, along the course of the Thames, reminders of industry and commerce—black oil tanks, stretches of raised railroad track, a long factory roof with a smokeless stack.

Above the Thames Estuary, thirty-five miles from London, the plane circled low over Canvey Island, where forty-eight hours earlier 13,000 persons had had their homes. Lower still a helicopter hovered, examining upper windows of houses for signs of life. The only other movement came from a big Army truck surging down a main street toward the submerged causeway to the mainland, leaving a white wake in the dirty water.

The plane's pilot, Capt. Theodore W. Morton, had been over Canvey early in the morning. Then a convoy of army trucks was splashing through the town getting out the last survivors. The trucks had towed rowboats, and other small boats had moved slowly in the canals between rows of brick houses. Captain Morton had seen one rescue—a man taken by a boat from the window of a house.

More than 100 bodies had been counted at Canvey by tonight, and 500 other persons were missing.

Today the wind was gone but its effect remained, in the breached seawall. Water six feet deep in parts of the town surged out through the breaks in the wall as the tide ebbed. It would surge back again with the flood tide.

Normally Canvey is separated from the mainland by a narrow stream, but today its housetops were isolated in the new swollen estuary of the Thames. The roofs

Continued on Page 4, Column 6

Convicted Communists Snub Offer To Go to Russia Instead of Prison

By EDWARD RANZAL

Thirteen secondary Communist leaders got the chance yesterday to go to Russia as an alternative to going to prison for criminal conspiracy to teach and advocate the overthrow of the United States Government by force and violence.

The offer was made by Federal Judge Edward J. Dimock.

Defense counsel and several of the defendants emphatically rejected the proposal, terming it "intolerable" and "unpalatable." Elizabeth Gurley Flynn, one of the thirteen, declared:

"We feel we belong here and have a political responsibility here. We feel we would be traitors to the American people if we turned our backs on them just to escape jail."

Judge Dimock also said he would not impose the maximum sentence of five years and $10,000 fine on the thirteen. However, United States Attorney Myles J. Lane recommended that the maximum sentence be imposed on each.

The actual sentencing was postponed until today by Judge Dimock after oral barrages by twelve of the thirteen defendants. At 4:40 P. M., after the court had been advised that in addition to the remaining defendant four defense attorneys would add to the voluminous record of the nine-and-a-half month trial, Judge Dimock adjourned court.

The first suggestion that Judge Dimock had an alternative plan came when the jurist asked Mr. Lane what he thought of the idea of permitting the defendants to go voluntarily to Russia rather than serve a prison sentence. Mr. Lane said he had no objection if the defendants first served their prison terms, then headed for the Soviet Union.

Then, after Miss Flynn had ad-

Continued on Page 8, Column 3

To Suburban Readers

The strike of newspaper deliverymen against suburban wholesalers has curtailed distribution of The New York Times outside New York City within a 50-mile radius.

Times may be obtained, however, at all newsstands within the New York City line. Suburbanites in New York during the evening are advised to get their copies before going home. Temporary mail subscriptions may be ordered for the duration of the emergency at no increase over the regular newsstand price by telephoning The Times. Information on how and where to get The Times is given at the end of The New York Times News Bulletins, which are broadcast every hour on the hour over WQXR, 1560 on the AM dial and WQXR-FM, 96.3 on the FM dial.

"All the News That's Fit to Print"

The New York Times.

LATE CITY EDITION
Fair, little temperature change today. Mostly fair tomorrow.
Temperature Range Today—Max., 42; Min., 29
Temperature Yesterday—Max., 44; Min., 33
Full U. S. Weather Bureau Report, Page 47

Copyright, 1953, by The New York Times Company.
VOL. CII..No. 34,740. Entered as Second-Class Matter. Post Office, New York, N. Y. NEW YORK, FRIDAY, MARCH 6, 1953. Times Square, New York 36, N. Y. Telephone LAckawanna 4-1000 FIVE CENTS

STALIN DIES AFTER 29-YEAR RULE; HIS SUCCESSOR NOT ANNOUNCED; U.S. WATCHFUL, EISENHOWER SAYS

WORST CITY CRISIS SINCE 1933 IS SEEN IN STATE TAX PLAN

Moore and McGovern Demand Payroll Levy and Transit Unit Mandated to Raise Fares

MAYOR CALLS DEMOCRATS

Estimate Board to Get Report on Views of County Leaders —Bus Reduction Directed

By PAUL CROWELL

The city Government is facing the most serious financial and political crisis to confront any Administration since 1933, when leading banking houses rescued a Democratic regime from fiscal disaster.

This was the consensus last night of top city officials to whom Lieut. Gov. Frank C. Moore and State Controller J. Raymond McGovern had indicated earlier in the day that a sound fiscal program for 1953-54 and succeeding years should include both a city payroll tax and a transit authority with a duty to increase fares to meet operating deficits of the municipal lines.

That the city Administration realized the political dangers inherent in the adoption of the suggested fiscal program was indicated later in the day when Mayor Impellitteri, without consulting the Board of Estimate, asked the five Democratic county leaders to confer with him at noon today at City Hall. Among those invited was Tammany leader Carmine G. De Sapio, the only member of the group who is at loggerheads with the Mayor on matters of patronage.

Leaders' Views Important

After a two-hour conference with Mr. Moore and Mr. McGovern at Mr. McGovern's office, 270 Broadway, the Mayor and Board of Estimate held an even longer closed meeting at City Hall, which will be resumed at 3 o'clock this afternoon. At today's session an important factor will be the attitude of the five Democratic county leaders, as reported by the Mayor, toward the proposals upon which the two state officials apparently are insisting.

In another municipal development, the Mayor's Transit Advisory Commission demanded that the eight privately owned bus companies involved in the recent bus strike and Michael J. Quill's Transport Workers Union, C. I. O., take immediate steps to wipe out excess bus lines and to reduce the number of buses on lines that were needed. City tax relief was made dependent on such action.

The conference with Mr. Moore and Mr. McGovern was a continuation of last Monday's talks at Albany on the city's $218,700,000 fiscal program, which in effect already had been rejected by the two state officials in their joint memorandum of Feb. 22.

At the outset of the meeting the

Continued on Page 19, Column 1

F.B.I. Agents Depict Rebuff by Monaghan

By LUTHER A. HUSTON
Special to THE NEW YORK TIMES.

WASHINGTON, March 5—Leland V. Boardman, special agent in charge of the New York office of the Federal Bureau of Investigation, asserted today that Police Commissioner George P. Monaghan had notified him that he would not make New York City policemen available to any Federal law enforcement agency for questioning and that they would respond only to summonses from a Federal grand jury.

This policy, Mr. Boardman said, was founded upon a purported agreement between the New York Police Department and the Criminal Division of the Department of Justice to block out F. B. I. investigators from cases involving police brutality in civil rights cases.

Another agent quoted Commis-

Continued on Page 14, Column 2

Eisenhower Plans to Pare Policy-Level Civil Service

Directive Will Repeal 2 That Truman Issued Anchoring Some Democrats in Their Jobs —Organization of Administration Object

By PAUL P. KENNEDY
Special to THE NEW YORK TIMES.

WASHINGTON, March 5—Several hundred persons face the possibility of losing Civil Service status and probably their Government jobs under an Executive Order to be issued by President Eisenhower next week.

In announcing the forthcoming order, James C. Hagerty, White House press secretary, said that all those affected would not necessarily lose their jobs. The announcement was generally interpreted, however, to mean that the Administration was preparing to clear out holdover Democrats in high policy-making and administrative positions in order to replace them with personnel of the Administration's own choosing.

President Eisenhower's order, which he directed to be drafted immediately, will repeal two Executive Orders of former President Truman in 1947 and 1948 in which certain persons on Schedule A of Civil Service rules would receive Civil Service protection against separation from the Government.

The President's order will emphasize that the rights of veterans, specified in the Veterans Preference Act of 1944 would be respected.

Schedule A is a list of positions to which appointments may be made without reference to Civil Service rules or regulations. The appointees may assume their positions without Civil Service examinations and their classifications are not subject to review by Civil Service Boards.

Mr. Hagerty said the "several hundred" persons to be affected by the order were employed in all departments and agencies of the Government. The order, he said, applied to people who had been put under Civil Service in the last twenty years.

The new Administration, since coming into office Jan. 20, Mr.

Continued on Page 15, Column 2

President May Take a Hand If Inquiries Imperil Amity

By C. P. TRUSSELL
Special to THE NEW YORK TIMES.

WASHINGTON, March 5—President Eisenhower indicated today that if the Senate investigation into the Voice of America, being conducted by Senator Joseph R. McCarthy, or other Congressional inquiries, reached a point of inviting international misunderstandings and difficulties he might intervene.

This, he emphasized at a news conference, would mean that he would have to desert his long-held conviction that the Congress had an inherent right to investigate as it pleased. He was still hoping, he said, to avoid a situation in which a spokesman for the Executive Branch of the Government would have to take issue with actions of the coordinate Legislative Branch.

The question that prompted these responses was based upon the hearings being conducted, largely before television, by the Judiciary subcommittee headed by Senator McCarthy, Republican of Wisconsin.

The group is inquiring into the management and personnel of the Voice, the Government's radio program for telling the story of America. Broadcasts are beamed to eighty-seven countries in nearly forty languages.

At yesterday's hearing Reed Harris, deputy director of the State

Continued on Page 14, Column 6

EISENHOWER PRAISES RESTRAINT IN PRICES

Asserts There Has Been Little Evidence of Gouging—More Controls Are Removed

By CHARLES E. EGAN
Special to THE NEW YORK TIMES.

WASHINGTON, March 5—President Eisenhower today complimented business for what he termed the admirable restraint it had shown in pricing policies since the removal of most price controls.

General Eisenhower said at his news conference that since the program of removing major segments of the economy from price regulation got under way Feb. 6, there had been little discernible evidence of attempts to gouge consumers.

The President's observations came immediately before an announcement from the Office of Price Stabilization that it had removed price ceilings on another wide range of items, including bread and bakery products, new and used cars, major household appliances, dry cleaning and diaper services.

Hopes for a New Climate

Another development was a Senate committee hearing at which Charles R. Sligh Jr., president of the National Association of Manufacturers, attacked proposals to establish stand-by controls authority. With such authority, the President could declare a ninety-day "freeze" of all prices and wages in event of all-out war or other critical emergency.

About the only major price increase that has occurred since the Office of Price Stabilization began implementing his orders for relaxation of price ceilings, the President said, has been an expected rise of 6 to 7 cents a pound in copper.

The absence of price gouging, the President added, confirms his belief that the American people are ready to be considerate and moderate. He added that he hoped a climate might be established—in labor-management relations, for instance—that would minimize harmful pressures on the economy

Continued on Page 15, Column 3

VISHINSKY LEAVING

Foreign Minister Called to Moscow to Report —Will Sail Today

U. N. TO LOWER FLAG

Lie Praises Premier as Statesman—Pearson Hails Fight on Nazis

By THOMAS J. HAMILTON
Special to THE NEW YORK TIMES.

UNITED NATIONS, N. Y., March 5—Soviet Foreign Minister Andrei Y. Vishinsky, who was reported to have been informed of the death of Premier Stalin before the public announcement by the Moscow radio, plans to leave for Moscow tomorrow.

Mr. Vishinsky and a party of Soviet officials are scheduled to sail aboard the French liner Liberté tomorrow at 4 P. M. Plans for the sailing were disclosed at Police Headquarters. The police said they had been informed that the party would travel in seven automobiles from Glen Cove, L. I., where the Soviet delegation to the United Nations has headquarters, to Pier 88, Hudson River at Forty-eighth Street. The liner will call at Plymouth and Le Havre.

Mr. Vishinsky has a heart condition and therefore avoids air travel whenever possible.

Valerian A. Zorin, Soviet representative to the United Nations, revealed this afternoon Mr. Vishinsky's plans to leave tomorrow. Mr. Vishinsky's decision was taken after he had received a telephone call from Moscow earlier in the day.

Disclosure by Consulate

There was no indication whether this telephone call had given any indication of Mr. Stalin's death. The news that Mr. Vishinsky had been informed prior to the public announcement came from a telephone inquiry at the Soviet Consulate at 680 Park Avenue.

Earlier inquiries at the headquarters of the Soviet delegation to the United Nations had brought repeated denials that Mr. Vishinsky was there. The consulate revealed, however, not only that Mr. Vishinsky was actually at the delegation headquarters but also that he had been informed of the news earlier.

According to United Nations protocol, the only flag that will fly at the United Nations flagpole tomorrow is the banner of the United Nations itself, and it will be at half-staff. The same procedure will be followed during the day of the funeral of Premier Stalin.

Informed of the death of Mr.

Continued on Page 13, Column 2

CONDOLENCES SENT

President Orders Terse Formal Note on Stalin Dispatched to Soviet

TRIBUTE IS OMITTED

Eisenhower Still Ready to Confer on Peace With the Kremlin

By JAMES RESTON
Special to THE NEW YORK TIMES.

WASHINGTON, March 5—President Eisenhower authorized John Foster Dulles, Secretary of State, tonight to send the United States' "official condolences" to the Soviet Government on the death of Premier Stalin.

Earlier the President had told reporters at his press conference that he could not tell what effect the illness of the Premier would have on the "cold war." A definite watchfulness is our policy for the moment, the President added.

The President announced the statement of condolences less than an hour after he had been informed of Mr. Stalin's death by James C. Hagerty, press secretary, at 3:25 P. M. The statement was as follows:

The President authorized the Secretary of State to send the following message to the American Embassy in Moscow: The Government of the United States tenders its official condolences to the Government of the Union of Socialist Soviet Republics on the death of Generalissimo Joseph Stalin, Prime Minister of the Soviet Union.

Dulles Informed by Hagerty

Mr. Hagerty notified Mr. Dulles, who was a guest at the British Embassy, immediately after the President had been informed.

The press secretary said the President's message would be transmitted to the Soviet Government by Jacob D. Beam, Chargé d'Affaires in Moscow.

The terse wording of the message was noted here, especially the phrase "official condolences." Diplomatic circles suggested that the wording was about as brief and formal as possible under diplomatic protocol.

They recalled, however, that the President previously had expressed condolences. In the first White House statement issued after word had been received of the serious illness of Mr. Stalin, General Eisenhower directed his words to the Soviet people rather than the Premier or the Government.

Indications were that the President's official condolences would stand in so far as the Government

Continued on Page 12, Column 5

PREMIER JOSEPH STALIN
A portrait released by Sovfoto, Soviet picture agency

Soviet Fear of an Eruption Discerned in Call for Unity

By HARRY SCHWARTZ

The fact that appeals for "monolithic unity" and "vigilance" have now become the main theme of Soviet domestic propaganda appears to be a clear indication that the present Soviet rulers fear Premier Stalin's death may result in an explosive resolution of the major tensions now repressed in the Soviet Union.

The unity theme dominates the official announcement of Stalin's death. It was first voiced in the initial communiqué regarding Stalin's illness issued by the highest Government and Communist party authorities. Unity and vigilance were the central ideas in the long leading editorials that appeared yesterday morning on the front pages of both Pravda and Izvestia.

Yesterday's Pravda editorial may also have given the first hint that Georgi M. Malenkov is leading in the succession race, but this hint seemed far from conclusive. The editorial mentioned by name only Lenin, Premier Stalin, and Mr. Malenkov, quoting the latter's speech last October when he said, "The prospects and ways of our progress are based on the laws of the national economy, on the science of the Communist social structure which have been evolved by Comrade Stalin."

The fact that Moscow has announced that Nikita S. Khrushchev will head the committee preparing

Continued on Page 12, Column 2

AMMUNITION SHORT, VAN FLEET ASSERTS

He Affirms Scarcity in Korea and Byrd Writes to Wilson Demanding Explanation

By HAROLD B. HINTON
Special to THE NEW YORK TIMES.

WASHINGTON, March 5—Gen. James A. Van Fleet, former Commander of United Nations ground forces in Korea, told the Senate Armed Services Committee today that he had been handicapped during the entire twenty-two months he had had the command by shortages of ammunition and manpower.

He specified hand grenades, and mentioned "other types" of ammunition as having been seriously short all the time and critically short on occasions.

The apparent contradiction of the General's testimony today with that of yesterday, in which he indicated there were no serious shortages of anything in Korea, was unexplained, except for the interpretation that yesterday he had been speaking for the present, whereas today he had been speaking for the past.

Praised by Symington

So much the general said before a public meeting of the committee. Senator Stuart Symington, Democrat of Missouri and former Secretary of the Air Force, praised General Van Fleet for his intelligence and courage in reporting these matters to the public. If other military figures would emulate the example, he declared, "we won't send our youth out to fight with these shortages, even if we have fewer television sets."

[In the Korean war action, Air Force Thunderjet fighter-bombers made a record 1,000-mile raid on a Communist industrial center on the northeast coast sixty miles from Siberia. Navy carrier bombers made heavy attacks in North Korea. Ground action was light.]

In a later closed session with the committee, General Van Fleet apparently amplified his discussion of the shortages. The amplification prompted Senator Harry F. Byrd, Democrat of Virginia, to write a letter to Charles E. Wil-

Continued on Page 2, Column 6

PREMIER ILL 4 DAYS

Announcement of Death Made by Top Soviet and Party Chiefs

STROKE PROVES FATAL

Leaders Issue an Appeal to People for Unity and Vigilance

Text of official announcement of Stalin's death, Page 8.

By HARRISON E. SALISBURY
Special to THE NEW YORK TIMES.

MOSCOW, Friday, March 6—Premier Joseph Stalin died at 9:50 P. M. yesterday [1:50 P. M. Thursday, Eastern standard time] in the Kremlin at the age of 73, it was announced officially this morning. He had been in power twenty-nine years.

The announcement was made in the name of the Central Committee of the Communist party, the Council of Ministers and the Presidium of the Supreme Soviet.

Calling on the Soviet people to rally firmly around the party and the Government, the announcement asked them to display unity and the highest political vigilance "in the struggle against internal and external foes." [No announcement was made of a successor to Premier Stalin.]

The Soviet leader's death from general circulatory and respiratory deficiency occurred just short of four days after he had been stricken with a brain hemorrhage in his Kremlin apartment.

Accompanying the death announcement was a final medical certificate issued by a group of ten physicians, headed by Health Minister A. F. Tretyakov, who cared for Mr. Stalin in his last illness under the direct and closest supervision of the Central Committee and the Council of Ministers.

Pulse Rate Was High

The medical certificate revealed that in the last hours Mr. Stalin's condition grew worse rapidly, with repeated heavy and sharp circulatory and heart collapses. His breathing grew superficial and sharply irregular. His pulse rate rose to 140 to 150 a minute and at 9:50 P. M., "because of a growing circulatory and respiratory insufficiency, J. V. Stalin died."

[The news of Mr. Stalin's death was withheld by Soviet officials for more than six hours.]

Pravda appeared this morning with broad black borders around its front page, which was devoted entirely to Mr. Stalin. The layout included a large photograph of the Premier, the announcement by the Government, the medical bulletins and the announcement of the formation of a funeral commission

Continued on Page 8, Column 2

Treaties Manifesto Shelved in Congress

By WILLIAM S. WHITE
Special to THE NEW YORK TIMES.

WASHINGTON, March 5—President Eisenhower's proposed United States declaration against "perversion" of the wartime Yalta and Potsdam agreements into instruments for enslaving peoples was put on the shelf in Congress today.

The announced Congressional reason was that the manifesto would be inopportune now in view of Premier Stalin's fatal illness, though the President himself indicated at his news conference that he thought this need not delay action. The Congressional developments came before the announcement of Mr. Stalin's death.

The Republican leaders in Congress could not take the resolution to the floor of either house

Continued on Page 6, Column 8

Pole Flies to Denmark in First Intact Russian MIG-15 to Reach West

Associated Press Radiophoto

A young Polish pilot seeking political asylum flew this Soviet-made MIG-15 into a Danish airport at Bornholm yesterday, making it the first fighter plane of its type acquired undamaged by the West. Name of pilot (center figure) was withheld.

Special to THE NEW YORK TIMES.

COPENHAGEN, Denmark, March 5—The first intact Russian-built MIG-15 jet fighter—the newest known type of Russian jet fighter—to land west of the Iron Curtain came down this morning at Roenne Airport on the Danish island of Bornholm. It came from a Polish Baltic base.

The 21-year-old Polish lieutenant who fled with the fighter gave himself up to Danish authorities as a political refugee and asked for asylum. Very little is known about his story. Danish authorities are keeping it secret for the time being.

The young Pole performed a fantastic maneuver in landing the jet fighter on the grass-covered airstrip at Roenne, only 1,200 meters (3,937 feet) long. Jet fighters normally require a 3,000-meter (9,843 feet) concrete runway to start and land.

At the farther end of the air-

Continued on Page 3, Column 2

"All the News That's Fit to Print"

The New York Times.

LATE CITY EDITION
Fair with little change in temperature today and tomorrow.
Temperature Range Today—Max., 72; Min., 52
Temperature Yesterday—Max., 70; Min., 53
Full U. S. Weather Bureau Report, Page 39

VOL. CII..No. 34,828. Entered as Second-Class Matter, Post Office, New York, N. Y. NEW YORK, TUESDAY, JUNE 2, 1953. Times Square, New York 36, N. Y. Telephone Lackawanna 4-1000 FIVE CENTS

2 OF BRITISH TEAM CONQUER EVEREST; QUEEN GETS NEWS AS CORONATION GIFT; THRONGS LINE HER PROCESSION ROUTE

AUTHORITY LEASES CITY TRANSIT LINES; FARE RISE IN SIGHT

Estimate Board Votes, 11-5, for 10-Year Pact Including Terms Asked by Joseph

EFFECTIVE DATE IS JUNE 15

New Agency Seeking Tokens From Mint, Indicating New Charge May Not Be 15c

Digest of lease signed by city and Transit Authority, Page 32.

By LEO EGAN

The Board of Estimate voted 11 to 5 yesterday to lease the city's $1,700,000,000 transit system to the newly created New York City Transit Authority for a period of ten years, during which the authority will be obligated to raise enough revenue from fares and incidental charges to meet operating costs.

By approving the lease, the board made it almost certain that the authority will raise transit fares by July 30 in an amount sufficient to overcome a prospective operating deficit of $47,000,000 for the fiscal year beginning July 1. A first step in this direction was taken by the authority within a few hours after the board acted when it decided to explore the possibility of obtaining from the United States Mint at Philadelphia an emergency supply of tokens, to be used on all three divisions of the rapid transit lines in the collection of a higher fare.

Casey Tells of Token Plans

The decision to request the Federal Government's help in obtaining enough tokens to put a fare change into effect by July 30, the statutory deadline, was announced by Maj. Gen. Hugh J. Casey, authority chairman, after a special authority meeting at the offices of the Board of Transportation, 370 Jay Street, Brooklyn.

Sidney H. Bingham, chairman of the Board of Transportation, will confer with the Director of the Mint at Philadelphia today on the possibility of obtaining 20,000,000 tokens, General Casey said. Subsequent additions to the supply would be obtained from private suppliers, he added.

To speed the negotiations with the Mint, the authority has requested Governor Dewey to intervene with the Secretary of the Treasury, General Casey said.

A design for the token was officially approved by the authority yesterday. It is a perforated coin, somewhat smaller than a dime.

By exploring the possibility of obtaining enough tokens for use on all three divisions, the authority indicated it might reject Mr. Bingham's recommendation for a 15-cent fare in favor of a smaller charge, perhaps 12 or 12½ cents a ride. The present fare is 10 cents.

A major justification for the Bingham recommendation was that it would involve use of tokens on only the I.R.T. division, which has electrically operated turnstiles. On the B.M.T. and IND divisions, which have mechanical turnstiles, two coins—a dime and a nickel—would be used to pay the fare.

General Casey emphasized in announcing the authority action that no decisions on a fare increase had been reached. It will not be possible to arrive at a conclusion, he said, until all pertinent facts are studied.

City Fiscal Problem Eased

The Board of Estimate's decision yesterday automatically relieved the city of the necessity of meeting the prospective operating deficit out of tax revenues in the new fiscal year that starts July 1. It likewise vested the city with power to collect $50,000,000 a year in additional taxes from real estate for general municipal purposes plus, for the next four years, enough to liquidate an accumulated deficit of $39,000,000 in the transit pension system.

Moreover, in accordance with special laws enacted by the Legislature earlier this year on the recommendation of Governor Dewey, transfer of the deficit-ridden transit system to the authority gives the city power at any time in the future to impose a one-half of 1 per cent payroll tax, payable in equal parts by employers and employes, estimated to raise $60,000,000 a year.

The city's budget for the new fiscal year, already approved by the Board of Estimate and City Council, contemplates full use of the additional real estate taxing powers, but no use of the payroll tax.

As had been forecast, Rudolph

Continued on Page 33, Column 2

Eisenhower Moves to Limit State Department to Policy

New Reorganization Plans Would Transfer Present Operating Functions to 2 Special Agencies, Information and Foreign Aid

By ANTHONY LEVIERO
Special to The New York Times.

WASHINGTON, June 1—President Eisenhower proposed today to restore the State Department to its traditional pre-war policy-making role and to transfer virtually all its operating functions to new organizations—the United States Information Agency and the Foreign Operations Administration.

A far-reaching reorganization of the State Department was projected by the President in two plans submitted to Congress today, with a promise of further changes to be sought early next year.

Today he stressed two objectives:

1. To divest the department of the functional tasks that had involved it in political controversy during the post-war era.
2. To make the Secretary of State supreme, next to the President, in the policy supervision of all foreign information and aid programs.

The controversial Voice of America and other information programs would be swept out of the State Department, the Mutual Security Agency and other agencies and concentrated in the new Information Agency. The Mutual Security Agency itself would become the nucleus around which would be built the new Foreign Operations Administration to take over various other programs for technical, economic and military assistance.

Of operating programs, all that would be left in the State Department would be the programs for the educational exchange of persons.

The two new agencies would have administrative autonomy, just as the Mutual Security Agency has today. But a new idea in Government organization was introduced. The directors of the two agencies not only would be subject to close

Continued on Page 24, Column 4

Text of message on propaganda and aid plans, Page 24.

MRS. HOBBY WARNS DOCTORS ON TASKS

Social-Economic Problems in the Field Must Be Solved by A.M.A. or Others, She Says

Mrs. Oveta Culp Hobby, Secretary of Health, Education and Welfare, declared at the annual meeting of the American Medical Association, which opened yesterday, that organized medicine must find solutions to the social-economic problems facing medicine today or the solution would be taken out of its hands. She expressed confidence that the American Medical Association "will meet this challenge."

Addressing the House of Delegates, policy-making body of the association, at the Waldorf-Astoria Hotel, Mrs. Hobby said the social and economic demands on the medical profession "are only the continuing challenge in this long history of constant adaptation to a changing society, but never have these problems been more onerous and critical than today."

The association opened its 102d annual meeting yesterday. For five days progress in all branches of medicine will be reviewed in 400 reports by leaders in their fields.

The sessions are being held in seven hotels and in Town Hall while 635 scientific and technical exhibits are being displayed on four floors of Grand Central Palace. The exhibits are open only to doctors and their guests.

Mrs. Hobby in her speech to the delegates said she agreed fully

Continued on Page 26, Column 5

HUMPHREY OPPOSES REVENUE LOSS NOW

He Calls Cut Gamble With U.S. Security—Asks House Unit to Extend Excess Profit Tax

By JOHN D. MORRIS
Special to The New York Times.

WASHINGTON, June 1—George M. Humphrey, Secretary of the Treasury, told Congress today that only "full mobilization" would justify tax increases to produce any more revenue than the Administration was now seeking.

The Government's chief fiscal officer so testified in opening the Administration's case before the House Ways and Means Committee for a six-month extension of the excess profits tax and the cancellation of automatic cuts in regular corporation and excise (sales) levies slated for next April 1.

The Administration, he said, wants those three phases of its tax program carried out in a single bill this year, though the committee has limited its present deliberations to extension of the excess profits law, which is due to expire June 30.

The Secretary asserted that losses in Federal revenue now would be an unsafe gamble with the country's security.

Mr. Humphrey also made the following points:

¶ That he was "very strongly opposed" to any change in the excess profits tax during the extension period.

¶ That he would fight any continuation of the levy beyond Dec. 31.

¶ That tax relief starting next

Continued on Page 47, Column 2

Harvard Elects Dr. N. M. Pusey, Midwest Educator, as President

Lawrence College Head, 46, Has 3 Degrees From University—Favors Humanities Study

By JOHN H. FENTON
Special to The New York Times.

CAMBRIDGE, Mass., June 1—Dr. Nathan Marsh Pusey, president of Lawrence College in Appleton, Wis., was elected the twenty-fourth president of Harvard by the Harvard Corporation today.

Dr. Pusey, who is a native of Council Bluffs, Iowa, and 46 years old, is a scholar in Greek history, and holds three degrees from Harvard: Bachelor of Arts, magna cum laude, 1928; Master of Arts, 1932, and Doctor of Philosophy, 1937. He prepared for college at Abraham Lincoln High School in Council Bluffs.

The Iowa educator will succeed Dr. James Bryant Conant, who will become president-emeritus of Harvard University on Sept. 1. Dr. Conant, now on leave, is serving as United States High Commissioner for Germany.

Dr. Pusey's election by the Harvard Corporation is subject to the confirmation of the Board of Overseers. This confirmation, customarily a formality, is scheduled to be voted on June 10, the day before the Harvard commencement. On only one occasion, in 1868, have the overseers refused the corporation permission to elect a president.

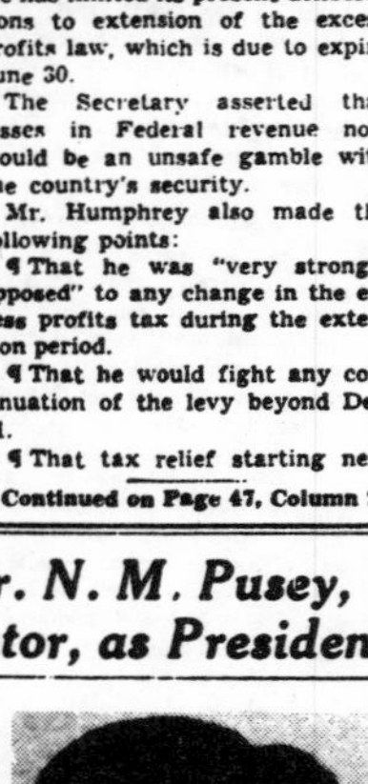

Associated Press
Dr. Nathan M. Pusey

The occasion of the only refusal was in the election of Dr. Charles W. Eliot, the original choice of the corporation, as the twenty-first president. The corporation prevailed after a delay of six months, and Dr. Eliot became president in 1869.

Dr. Pusey, reached by telephone at Appleton, said that he considered the corporation's action "a tremendous honor." But he de-

Continued on Page 27, Column 5

RHEE BOWS TO U.S.; SAYS KOREA AGREES TO EISENHOWER AIMS

Statement on Message From Washington Hints Opposition to Truce Plans Is Easing

By The Associated Press.

SEOUL, Korea, June 2—President Syngman Rhee disclosed today he had received a three-point message from President Eisenhower, and added: "We must accept anything that the United States President wants."

"Common sense and wisdom require that we cooperate with the United States at any cost," Dr. Rhee said, without saying what President Eisenhower had told him.

The statement of the 78-year-old leader of the Republic of Korea indicated that South Korean opposition to the secret proposal by the United Nations Command for bringing an armistice in Korea was lessening.

Dr. Rhee also said he was looking for some one to take the place of Maj. Gen. Choi Duk Shin as the South Korean delegate on the United Nations armistice negotiation team.

Dr. Rhee declined to elaborate on his apparently conciliatory statement. He spoke to correspondents at a parade of the British Commonwealth Division honoring the Coronation of Elizabeth II.

Nor did he make it precisely clear whether he was ready now to accept the Allied truce proposal, to which he and his Government had expressed vigorous opposition.

South Korea's acting Premier, Pyun Yun Tae, threatened yesterday a break with the Allies and a go-it-alone policy for South Korea but deferred action until after next Thursday's critical truce session.

The Communists are expected to reply to the Allied proposal at Thursday's meeting.

Rhee Said to Seek Treaty

By JAY WALZ
Special to The New York Times.

WASHINGTON, June 1—The Eisenhower Administration was reported today to have had a new request from President Syngman Rhee of South Korea for the pledge of a mutual defense pact and of military and economic help as a basis for the Seoul Government's support of present Allied truce proposals.

These conditions were said on good authority to be important features of a four-point program outlined in a letter forwarded to President Eisenhower through Ellis O. Briggs, United States Ambassador at Seoul.

The principal point in the still-secret United Nations proposal to the Communists for disposition of Korean war prisoners who refuse to return home was understood to be that final determination of the captives' fate would be up to the General Assembly of the United Nations.

Officially, the White House and State Department were silent on developments on Korea, and offered "no comment" even on reports that a letter from President Rhee might have been received.

Had Asked Pledge in Writing

The South Korean request for a mutual defense pact with the United States is not new. Dr. You Chan Yang, the Korean Ambassador here, has made repeated representations to the State Department for such a pledge of defense help in the event of future Communist aggression.

He has made the point that, while President Eisenhower has said publicly that the United States will never desert Korea, it would be more satisfying from the Korean standpoint to have "something down in black and white."

President Rhee's four points were reported to be (1) a pledge to sign a mutual defense pact with Korea; (2) a promise by the United States to provide military and financial help to Korea on a large scale; (3) withdrawal of all foreign troops on both sides as soon as a truce has started and prisoners have been exchanged, and (4) agreement that the United States would not stand in the way of South Korea in efforts to unite that country at some future time.

As far as the last point is concerned, sources felt South Korea did not have in mind the use of military force to bring together North and South Korea.

Meanwhile, some Capitol Hill leaders spoke out on recent Korean developments.

Senator William F. Knowland of California, who is chairman of the Senate Republican Policy Committee, said the United States should "risk" war with Russia to expand the fighting, if truce negotiations with the Communists collapsed at [illegible].

In anoth[illegible] Senator H. Alexan[illegible] Republican of New Je[illegible] he thought

Continued [illegible], Column 5

CROWDS DEFY RAIN

Face a Day of Showers After All-Night Vigil to Hail Their Sovereign

By RAYMOND DANIELL
Special to The New York Times.

LONDON, Tuesday, June 2—This is the day that all London, all Britain, all the Commonwealth and half the world have been awaiting. It is the day on which the crown of her forefathers is placed upon the head of this old country's radiantly lovely young Queen Elizabeth II whose reign, it is hoped, will usher in another golden age.

The weather for the day was uncertain. By early morning the wind still blew, but rains that fell during the night had ceased, at least temporarily. The weather forecaster, however, was not optimistic about the prospects for the day, which was chosen originally because rain had not fallen on June 2 for many years. The forecast was for cool weather and showers, with sunny intervals.

Last night's gusts and rain discomfited the hundreds of thousands of persons who squatted the whole length of the royal way but if these hardships dislodged any it was unnoticeable because there were others waiting to take their places.

Some of these squatters, lacking reserved seats in the stands to accommodate 250,000 persons, began staking out their claims as early as midnight Sunday.

Squatters Sit on Curbs

By noon yesterday they were sitting on the curbs at Trafalgar Square and were packed two and three deep on the sidewalks along the Mall leading from Admiralty Arch to Buckingham Palace. By dinner time last night the East Carriage Drive in Hyde Park was filled with men, women and even young children with raincoats, blankets, lunch baskets and inflatable mattresses prepared to defend their little vantage points until the Queen's ornate gilded coach, with its eight gray horses, one named Eisenhower, had passed late in the afternoon.

During the day Queen Mother Elizabeth, accompanied by Princess Margaret, visited the palace to see the Queen on the eve of her coronation. By the time they left, an hour later, the crowd outside Buckingham Palace numbered nearly 50,000. The police, who had let the crowd swarm over the roadway, had to make strenuous efforts to clear a path for their car.

Later Princess Margaret made a visit to Westminster Abbey, where she was received by the Earl Marshal. Again the police had trouble clearing a way for her to return home.

Even Oxford Street, that busy shopping center, was taken over by sidewalk squatters almost as soon as the big stores closed. Trafalgar Square, through which the Queen will pass three times on her way from Buckingham Palace to Westminster Abbey, out again and back to the palace, was filled with curbstone sitters even at midday. Some of them had been there twelve hours then with an additional twenty-four in front of them.

The litter they made of sodden

Continued on Page 8, Column 1

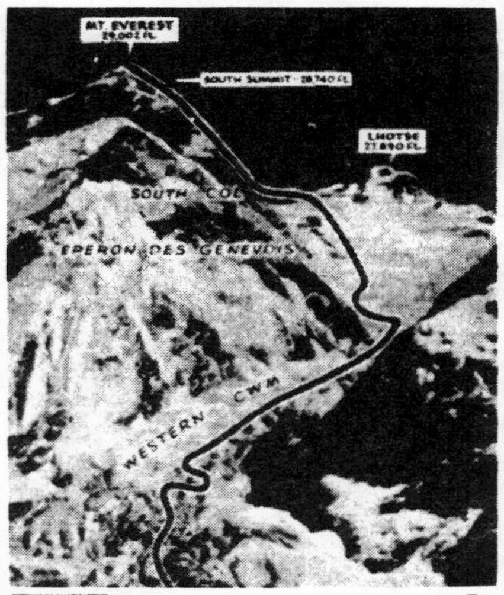

The New York Times June 2, 1953
AT THE TOP: Solid black line shows route of British expedition, the first to reach Mount Everest's summit.

Abbey, Bedecked and Aglow, Awaits the Coronation Hour

By TANIA LONG
Special to The New York Times.

LONDON, Tuesday, June 2—As one enters Westminster Abbey, where Elizabeth II is to be crowned in a few hours, a magnificent scene greets the eye. The austere gray interior has been converted into a rich and glowing setting for the young Queen's coronation. Carpeting and hangings in warm tones of blue and gold, banners of white embroidered with the royal coats of arms, and the deep rose of the throne and the royal chairs blend into a splendid symphony of color.

In the pale light of early morning a hush lies over the Abbey. Only a few of the great assemblage of 7,000 guests have arrived, and there is little movement in the vast edifice.

From the great west door, where the Queen will enter, a thick carpet of deep azure blue reaches through the nave to the choir stalls. Hangings of blue silk with royal emblems embroidered in gold are draped over the edges of the stands and balconies, giving warmth to the gray fabric of the church.

From the choir to the altar in that area known as the Coronation Theatre the floor is covered in rich gold pile, against which the deep rose-covered throne and chairs, and the opulent blue hangings on the walls stand out in sharp contrast.

Under a huge chandelier in the center of the Coronation Theatre and raised on a dais stands the throne. Five steps lead up to it. It faces the altar, and because the Queen will be facing away from the majority of the guests, its back is low so that they too may see the Queen's crowned head during the latter part of the ceremony.

The throne chair is late seven-

Continued on Page 6, Column 3

DULLES SAYS U.S. AIM IS TO GAIN FRIENDS

Report on Near East-Asian Trip Urges 'Impartial' Approach to Arab-Israeli Dispute

Text of Secretary Dulles' talk about recent trip, Page 4.

Special to The New York Times.

WASHINGTON, June 1—John Foster Dulles, Secretary of State, said tonight that it was the policy of the Eisenhower Administration to develop goodwill among the nations of the Near East and South Asia to thwart the Kremlin's desire to exploit their many differences.

To this end, he urged an "impartial" approach to Israeli-Arab disputes so as to win the support of both sides against the "common threat"—communism. He said the United States must make clear to all nations concerned with independence that the North Atlantic Treaty alliance was in no way related to a desire to help colonial powers keep or win back their colonies.

In a country-wide radio and television report on his twenty-day tour of the Middle East and South Asia, Mr. Dulles urged the strategic importance of that rich and populous area and said its problems could not be ignored without dangerous consequences.

'Primary Purpose' Stressed

The Secretary's half-hour address was carried over the radio and television networks of the American Broadcasting System and by the Du Mont television network, and the National Broadcasting Company radio network rebroadcast it. The Secretary gave a country-by-country account of the trip, on which he was accompanied by Harold E. Stassen, Director for Mutual Security. They made stops all the way from Egypt to Pakistan and India.

Mr. Dulles declared that the "primary purpose" of the trip "was to show friendliness and to develop understanding," and he added: "These people we visited are all proud peoples who have a great tradition and, I believe, a great future."

The Eisenhower Administration, he continued, plans to make "friendship—not fault-finding—the basis of its foreign policy."

Addressing himself to problems of the troubled Holy Land, Mr. Dulles said he had come back to Washington convinced that the Arabs were "more fearful of Zionism than of communism."

On the other hand, he added,

Continued on Page 5, Column 6

HIGHEST PEAK WON

New Zealander and a Guide Made the Final Climb to Top Friday

By Reuters.

KATMANDU, Nepal, Tuesday, June 2—The British expedition has conquered Mount Everest, a radio message flashed from Namche Bazar to the British Embassy here said today.

The message said Edmond Hillary, a New Zealand beekeeper and mountaineer, and Tensing Norkay, the famous Sherpa guide, had reached the hitherto unscaled summit from Camp Eight last Friday.

The news of this success had to be rushed by runner from the British expedition's base camp on Khumbu Glacier to the radio post at Namche Bazar.

It is understood here that this was the expedition's third attack on the last slopes leading to the summit, a first double attempt having failed.

Experts here said the success was largely due to the fine weather, combined with properly acclimatized climbers and the excellent organization and leadership of Col. H. C. J. Hunt.

Full details of the exploit are not expected to reach here for some days.

It is believed here that the news was transmitted specially to London by diplomatic channels so Queen Elizabeth could be told.

Queen Told at Palace

LONDON, Tuesday, June 2 (Reuters)—The Times of London reported the news of the scaling of Mount Everest in a copyrighted message today.

The news was published in a special edition of The Times on early sale among coronation crowds in London.

Queen Elizabeth, resting at Buckingham Palace, was told on the eve of her coronation that the British expedition had conquered the mountain. The news was brought to her as she spent a quiet evening "at home." The British climbers had succeeded in their plan to give her a world-shaking coronation present.

Mount Everest, the 29,002-foot giant, was the last main outpost of the world unknown to man.

The thirteen members of the expedition formed the eleventh team to try to conquer the mountain in the past thirty years. Many climbers have died in the high ice and snow of the Himalaya giant.

The Sherpa guide, Tensing Norkay, is a 42-year-old native veteran of more assaults on Mount Everest than any other man.

With 362 porters, twenty Sherpa guides and 10,000 pounds of baggage the expedition left the Nepalese base of Katmandu on March 10. Thus it took eighty days from start to finish.

The climbers carried three flags—the Union Jack, the United Nations flag and the Nepalese flag—to plant on the summit.

They made an approach to the "Goddess Mother of the Snows" from the south, or Nepalese, side.

It was the route reconnoitered by Sir Eric Shipton, who led a British

Continued on Page 14, Column 7

Notables File Past Empty Thrones On Way to Offer Homage to Queen

By C. L. SULZBERGER
Special to The New York Times.

LONDON, Tuesday, June 2—At 6 o'clock this morning the most distinguished men in Britain began filing past an empty throne. Within a few brief hours, seated upon it and wearing the heavy crown of St. Edward the Confessor, a young Queen will receive their homage.

For Britain and for her still vast empire, this is a significant moment. A new Elizabethan age of challenge and uncertainty has started.

Westminster Abbey, in its fullest splendor, with gold plate and regalia spread out on the altar, contains two thrones today. The first is that of King Edward I, a gnarled oaken chair having beneath it the Stone of Scone from the Scotland he had conquered.

Upon it the Queen is crowned. From it she will hear the acclaim of her subjects, the distant booming of her cannon and the solemn prayer of her primate, the Archbishop of Canterbury, exhorting:

"God crown you with a crown of glory and righteousness, that, having a right faith and manifold fruit of good works, you may obtain the crown of an everlasting kingdom by the gift of Him whose Kingdom endureth forever. Amen."

Only then, when she is fully consecrated and acclaimed, will the Queen, assisted by her lay and clerical peers, mount the royal throne on its dais.

Since the early dawn crept over the stirring city of London, pushing its light across gray Whitehall and through the soft rose and amber windows of this Holy Church of St. Peter, which is its rightful name, the Abbey has come to life for one of those great occasions when it nurtures monarchs.

Finely attired lords and ladies are sweeping to their places, bear-

Continued on Page 12, Column 3

Tito Abolishes Rank Of Army Commissar

By JACK RAYMOND
Special to The New York Times.

BELGRADE, Yugoslavia, June 1—President Tito abolished today the system of political commissars in the Yugoslav armed forces, asserting that present conditions no longer required them.

Not mentioned in Marshal Tito's order was the fact that this will undoubtedly make it easier for Yugoslavia to carry on with growing plans for integrating her military establishment with Western defense projects.

"It will be much easier to deal with Yugoslav military leaders now," said a Western military liaison expert here.

The political commissars, who wore uniforms and were equal in rank with military commanders in the Yugoslav Army, were introduced in imitation of Soviet military practice in the early days of partisan warfare against Germany.

Even after the break with the

Continued on Page 18, Column 3

"All the News That's Fit to Print"

The New York Times.

LATE CITY EDITION
Fair and quite warm today. Hot and humid tomorrow.
Temperature Range Today—Max., 89; Min., 68
Temperatures Yesterday—Max., 85; Min., 63
Full U. S. Weather Bureau Report, Page 21

VOL. CII..No. 34,846. Entered as Second-Class Matter. Post Office, New York, N. Y. NEW YORK, SATURDAY, JUNE 20, 1953. Times Square, New York 36, N. Y. Telephone Lackawanna 4-1000 RAG PAPER EDITION SEVENTY-FIVE CENTS

REDS INSIST U.N. RECAPTURE ALL RELEASED PRISONERS; TRUCE TALKS RECESS AGAIN

FOE WRITES CLARK

Questions if Allies Can Control South Korean Leaders and Army

Text of the Communist note to General Clark is on Page 3.

By LINDESAY PARROTT
Special to THE NEW YORK TIMES.

TOKYO, Saturday, June 20—Communist armistice delegates at Panmunjom demanded today that the United Nations recapture all 25,000 anti-Communist prisoners of the Korean war released by the order of Dr. Syngman Rhee, South Korean President.

The demand was made in the course of a twenty-five-minute meeting of the full truce delegations called for this morning by the senior Communist truce representative, Lieut Gen. Nam Il of North Korea.

The Communist high command sent a strong protest to Gen. Mark W. Clark, United Nations commander, asserting that the Allies, equally with Dr. Rhee, must bear "serious responsibility" for the incident. The message was signed by the top enemy commanders, Marshal Kim Il Sung, North Korean Premier, and Chinese Gen. Peng Teh-huai.

The Communist protest was an angry one, and it was significant that it was made directly to the Allied commander, not to the truce delegation. Yet it seemed to indicate that the enemy was not prepared to completely end the negotiations for an armistice.

The letter to General Clark repeated many of the old charges of American coercion and duplicity, but did not slam the door to further conversations.

[The Associated Press said that Pyun Yun Tae, Acting South Korean Premier, demanded Saturday in a letter to General Clark that all anti-Communist North Korean prisoners remaining in Allied stockades be turned over to the Republic for immediate release.

[Soon afterward, in Tokyo General Clark's United Nations headquarters made public a scorching letter to the South Korean President, saying General Clark could "not at this time estimate the ultimate consequences" of President Rhee's "precipitous and shocking" release of the 26,000 anti-Communist Korean war captives. General Clark accused Dr. Rhee of breaking a "persona commitment" not to take action.]

At the armistice conference, the Communists in effect demanded that the Allied command promise to control the fiery South Korean President from acting on his own. Pointedly, the Communists asked:

"Is the United Nations Command able to control the South Korean Government and Army? If not, does the armistice in Korea include the Syngman Rhee clique.

"If it is not included, what assurance is there for implementation of the armistice agreement on the part of South Korea?

"If it is included, then your side must be responsible for recovering immediately all the 25,952 prison-

Continued on Page 3, Column 4

Associated Press Wirephoto via Radio from Tokyo

HIS ATTEMPT TO ESCAPE FAILS: A U. S. Marine, right, escorts a wounded prisoner in the prisoner-of-war camp at Ascom City, near Inchon, where about 500 anti-Communists escaped. Marines and other troops prevented a larger break-out.

U. S. SEES POSITION IN KOREA AS GRAVE

Dulles Meets With Both Parties and Envoys of U. N. Allies in Atmosphere of Urgency

By WILLIAM S. WHITE
Special to THE NEW YORK TIMES.

WASHINGTON, June 19—The United States Government worked in haste today to save a Korean truce that some responsible men regarded as all but lost through South Korea's angry defiance of the United Nations.

The position was described authoritatively as the gravest since June 25, 1950—the day the Communists invaded the Republic of Korea.

There was hope, however, that if the Communists genuinely wanted peace they would not make capital of the defiance shown by Dr. Syngman Rhee, President of South Korea, to the United States and to its allies in the United Nations force that went to the rescue of his country three years ago.

All the possibilities seemed in the end to narrow to this one, even though there was some speculation that it might be feasible to take some sort of action to replace Dr. Rhee. Senator Walter F. George of Georgia, the senior Democratic member of the Senate Foreign Re-

Continued on Page 2, Column 5

U. N. OFFICERS FELT RHEE WAS BLUFFING

Warnings Unheeded, Prisoner Command Took No Steps to Prevent Mass Escape

By ROBERT ALDEN
Special to THE NEW YORK TIMES.

SEOUL, Korea, June 19—The United Nations Command was not prepared for the precipitate action taken by Dr. Syngman Rhee, President of South Korea, in freeing non-Communist prisoners of war.

According to an authoritative source in the Prisoner-of-War Command here, officials in Tokyo had been warned that such a measure might be taken by the Government of the Republic of Korea. However, the Prisoner-of-War Command was assured by higher headquarters that Dr. Rhee was "bluffing."

As a result, South Korean security guards were not replaced by American soldiers and other precautionary measures were insufficient.

However, the freeing of the prisoners came as no surprise to those who have been close to President Rhee these last few weeks. Nor was it a surprise to diplomatic circles in Pusan, the temporary South Korean capital.

They knew how defiant the President's attitude has been from the start, and they regard him as a rather unpredictable individual, apt to go off on a desperate tangent at almost any time.

Some Americans farther away from the scene, however, have had a tendency to underestimate what Dr. Rhee might do and to grasp at any straw that indicated that he was yielding ground in his fight. That was why the repeated threats to free the prisoners on the spot and the ample information available indicating that the South Korean Government was taking concrete steps along these lines were virtually ignored by those in a position to do something about it.

One reason for this reluctance to recognize the facts in the matter is that it is difficult for an American to understand Dr. Rhee's reasoning. The Korean leader feels that to accept a truce agreement, as drawn is tantamount to inviting self-destruction.

He is not only worried about the question of complete unification of the country. He has a great fear, for example, of allowing into the country Communist representatives and "pro-Communist" Indian guards.

President Rhee and those close

Continued on Page 3, Column 2

West Asks Soviet to Bar Firearms In Keeping Order in East Berlin

By WALTER SULLIVAN
Special to THE NEW YORK TIMES.

BERLIN, June 19—The three Western powers in Berlin urged the Soviet Union today to forbid the use of firearms by its troops and by the East German police in the Soviet sector of the city to prevent further bloodshed.

An announcement said Brig. Gen. Pierre Manceaux-Demiau, French Commandant in Berlin and this month's chairman of the Allied Kommandatura, had made repeated vain attempts to see high Soviet authorities to discuss the problem. It added that finally he had gone to Soviet headquarters in East Berlin to deliver in person a note stating the point of view of the Western Commandants.

Meanwhile, as the eastern part of the city continued to appear quiet, United States authorities delivered Otto Nuschke to Soviet officers. Herr Nuschke, East German Deputy Premier, was forced into the United States sector of Berlin by the rioters Wednesday.

Herr Nuschke, 70 years of age, was questioned thoroughly by both United States and West Berlin officials before being returned to the Soviet sector. According to an official announcement by the United States mission, he was asked whether he wanted political asylum in the West and said no.

The West Berlin police sought to determine whether he could be linked with "a kidnapping." Possibly this referred to the case of Dr. Walter Linse, anti-Communist leader, who was abducted from the United States sector last year.

East Germany's leading Communist newspaper, Neues Deutschland, conceded today that the work stoppages and disorders of the last few days had reached into the remote corners of that region. It expressed

Continued on Page 4, Column 4

AID BILL APPROVED AS DEMOCRATS SAVE MEASURE IN HOUSE

G.O.P. Split on Cutting Funds, but 280-108 Vote Prevails —4.9 Billion Authorized

By FELIX BELAIR Jr.
Special to THE NEW YORK TIMES.

WASHINGTON, June 19—The House of Representatives authorized today an appropriation of $4,998,732,500 for military, economic and technical aid to fifty-six free governments and dependencies resisting communism. The vote sending the measure to the Senate was 280 to 108, with one Representative merely voting "present."

Throughout the afternoon, a smoothly functioning bipartisan majority shouted down repeated attempts to cut the authorization items below the recommendations of the Foreign Affairs Committee. But it was the Democrats under Representative Sam Rayburn of Texas, the minority leader, who provided the margin of victory.

Republicans by the score deserted the leadership of Speaker Joseph W. Martin Jr. to vote for economy amendments. There was no record vote on any of the attempts to slash the measure and, although the foreign policy prestige of President Eisenhower had been thrown into the debate by the Republican leadership, it was the Democrats who gave him his vote of confidence.

On the final vote, 160 Democrats joined with 119 Republicans and an Independent, Frazier Reams of Ohio, to provide the 280 majority for the bill. A total of eighty-one Republicans and twenty-seven Democrats voted against the measure. Represenative Harold A. Patten, Democrat of Arizona, was the one who voted "present."

Members Rally to Vote

The high tide of opposition to the authorization—which is $476,000,000 less than the Administration had requested—came shortly before the final vote. Representative Hamer H. Budge, Republican of Idaho, offered an amendment to cut all the items by 10 per cent, but it was rejected by a standing vote of 152 to 101.

The same amendment had lost by a narrower margin a few minutes earlier when, on a count, the vote was put at 132 to 102. But when a vote by tellers was demanded, members burst from the cloakrooms on either side of the House to provide the extra votes.

An even earlier attempt to accomplish the same result and cut the authorization by $498,000,000 was made when Representative William M. Colmer, Democrat of Mississippi, sought to place a ceiling on the total authorization of $4,500,000,000. This move was rejected, 104 to 83.

The pattern of unrecorded voting on the amendments had been set shortly after the House met for business an hour before noon.

Representative Lawrence Smith, Republican of Wisconsin, proposed to cut $329,186,000 from the section providing military aid to Western Europe. The amendment would have eliminated military aid totaling $216,906,000 for Yugo-

Continued on Page 18, Column 4

4-Day Seamen's Strike Ends As Wage Demands Are Met

By GEORGE HORNE

The four-day-old seamen's strike, which immobilized 125 vessels and threatened to paralyze one-half of the nation's fleet of 1,500 ships, came to an end at 12:45 A. M. today.

National Maritime Union seamen, who struck on Tuesday when the operators refused to accede to wage demands, signed with the dry-cargo shipping employers at the headquarters of the Federal Mediation and Conciliation Service, winning wage rises ranging from 2 to 6 per cent. The settlement terms constituted a complete capitulation by the operators.

A few minutes earlier, the striking American Radio Association, also an affiliate of the Congress for Industrial Organizations, signed for a 6 per cent wage increase with a group of tanker operators.

Surrender of the employers in both cases had been foretold earlier in the day when a group of leading tanker operators submitted to the demands of the N. M. U. on the basis of similar wage rises and other terms. After this agreement was reached, it was a foregone conclusion that the rest of the industry would follow.

The mediators brought the N. M. U. into contact again with the Committee of Companies and Agents, Atlantic and Gulf Coasts, and it was apparent the costly hold-out of the companies was crumbling.

In its bargaining, the radio officer association also won its demands to gain full control over all radio telephones at sea, removing this equipment from the control of captains and other bridge officers. This was a major issue with the radio men.

All details of the fringe issues won by the seamen in their negotiations with the dry-cargo operators were not available, but mediators said they had matched those won earlier by the tanker men.

The new contract for the dry-cargo men will run for only a year, with a wage reopening in the fall. Union leaders called the wage terms "the best increases won by any industry this year." They were preparing to send out telegrams releasing the immobilized ships throughout the nation, including the superliner United States, tied up in New York.

Commissioners Harry Wimning and Sidney Sheiner, who have been serving under Frank Brown, regional director of the Federal Mediation and Conciliation Service, in seeking to settle the costly walk-

Continued on Page 22, Column 2

ROSENBERGS EXECUTED AS ATOM SPIES AFTER SUPREME COURT VACATES STAY; LAST-MINUTE PLEA TO PRESIDENT FAILS

SIX JUSTICES AGREE

President Says Couple Increased 'Chances of Atomic War'

Texts of related documents in case are printed on Page 7.

By LUTHER A. HUSTON
Special to THE NEW YORK TIMES.

WASHINGTON, June 19—President Eisenhower and the Supreme Court refused today to save Julius and Ethel Rosenberg from death in the electric chair.

The high court vacated the stay granted to the atomic spies on Wednesday by Justice William O. Douglas. It upheld the legality of the death sentence imposed by Federal Judge Irving R. Kaufman.

Less than an hour after the court had announced its verdict, President Eisenhower refused Executive clemency for the second time. He had denied a similar petition on Feb. 11.

"I can only say that, by immeasurably increasing the chances of atomic war, the Rosenbergs may have condemned to death tens of millions of innocent people all over the world," the President said. "The execution of two human beings is a grave matter. But even graver is the thought of the millions of dead whose deaths may be directly attributable to what these spies have done."

He was convinced, the President said, that the Rosenbergs had received "the fullest measure of justice and due process of law."

"When in their most solemn judgment the tribunals of the United States have adjudged them guilty and the sentence just, I will not intervene in this matter," the President declared.

Vinson Reads Court's Ruling

The prevailing opinion setting aside Justice Douglas' stay of execution was read by Chief Justice Fred M. Vinson and was concurred in by Associate Justices Stanley F. Reed, Robert H. Jackson, Harold H. Burton, Sherman Minton and Tom C. Clark.

Justices Douglas and Hugo L. Black dissented. Justice Felix Frankfurter announced neither a concurrence nor a dissent. In a brief separate opinion he said the questions raised were "complicated and novel" and that he felt the application of the Attorney General for revocation of the stay should not be disposed of until more time had been afforded for study and argument. He promised to set forth more specifically in due course the ground for this position.

Also read from the bench were a concurring opinion by Justice Clark, in which he was joined by Justices Vinson, Reed, Jackson, Burton and Minton, and a concurring opinion by Justice Jackson.

Continued on Page 8, Column 5

Their Death Penalty Carried Out

Julius Rosenberg

Ethel Rosenberg

Associated Press

Eisenhower Is Denounced To 5,000 in Union Sq. Rally

Sympathizers of Julius and Ethel Rosenberg bombarded judges with new appeals last night and staged rallies in a desperate last-minute flurry of efforts to save the condemned atom spies from the electric chair.

As time ran out for the doomed couple, lawyers and sympathizers tried every avenue of appeal and protest in a feverish evening that included:

¶An order by Police Commissioner George P. Monaghan to all police commands to maintain a special city-wide vigil against any disorder or violence in connection with the execution.

¶Three separate appeals to Federal Judge Irving R. Kaufman, who sentenced the Rosenbergs, to stay their execution. He rejected all.

¶Two separate appeals to two Federal Circuit Court judges to grant a stay. These also were denied.

¶A rally by an estimated 5,000 persons in Seventeenth Street, west of the north end of Union Square, where members of the New York Clemency Committee of the National Committee to Secure Justice in the Rosenberg Case denounced President Eisenhower as "bloodthirsty."

Final Pleas to Kaufman

Judge Kaufman, for whom the police ordered a reinforced fifteen-man guard at his Park Avenue apartment, was importuned by attorneys making frantic new legal maneuvers to save the Rosenbergs.

Daniel C. Marshall, a Los Angeles lawyer who had pleaded with the Supreme Court for a stay, begged Judge Kaufman to telephone the prison and delay the execution for one hour so that Mr. Marshall could elaborate his argument. But Judge Kaufman refused about twenty minutes before the executions began.

Milton H. Friedman, a lawyer representing the Rosenberg defense counsel, asked Judge Kaufman to stay the scheduled executions on the ground that they would constitute "an outrageous insult to world Jewry" if they were carried out on the Jewish Sabbath. Judge Kaufman rejected the plea, saying he had been assured the executions would not be within the Sabbath period.

Frank Scheiner, another lawyer representing the defense, asked Judge Kaufman to throw out the convictions of the couple on the same grounds argued yesterday before the Supreme Court. Judge Kaufman rejected this motion without any opinion.

Another defense lawyer, Arthur Kinoy, went to New Haven, Conn., in an unsuccessful effort to induce Judges Jerome N. Frank and Thomas W. Swan of the Federal Court of Appeals to block the executions.

'Prayer Meeting' Denunciations

In Seventeenth Street, more than 5,000 persons assembled for "a prayer meeting" for the Rosenbergs heard President Eisenhower denounced as "bloodthirsty."

He was linked with Attorney General Herbert Brownell Jr., Senator Joseph R. McCarthy, Republican of Wisconsin, and Senator William E. Jenner, Republican of Indiana, in "a plot" to destroy the rights and liberties of the American people.

A premature announcement at 8 P. M. that the Rosenbergs had been put to death created such a wave of hysteria at the

Continued on Page 6, Column 6

7 IN HAWAII GUILTY OF RED CONSPIRACY

Director of Bridges' Union and Six Others Convicted of Violating the Smith Act

Special to THE NEW YORK TIMES.

HONOLULU, June 19—A Federal jury today found Jack W. Hall, regional director in Hawaii for the International Longshoremen's and Warehousemen's Union, and six other defendants guilty of a Communist conspiracy to teach and advocate the overthrow of the United States Government by force and violence.

[Immediately after the verdict, stevedores halted work on all island docks in the possible forerunner of a general protest strike, The United Press reported. Within two hours after the verdict was announced Hall's union suspended negotiations on a new contract and longshoremen began walking off the job at Castle and Cook Pier 32. By 3:30 P. M., Hawaii time, all Honolulu docks were abandoned and stevedores had walked off the only two ships in the port of Hilo on the island of Hawaii.]

The all-male, multi-racial jury returned its verdict shortly before 1 P. M. Hawaii standard time (7 P. M., Eastern daylight time) after having deliberated for sixteen hours. Six men defendants clad in sports or aloha shirts and one woman heard the verdict read without any show of emotion as they stood behind the defense counsel's table.

A defense request for a poll of the jury revealed that the verdict was unanimous in each case.

The defense attorney, Richard

Continued on Page 5, Column 3

PAIR SILENT TO END

Husband Is First to Die —Both Composed on Going to Chair

By WILLIAM R. CONKLIN
Special to THE NEW YORK TIMES.

OSSINING, N. Y., June 19—Stoic and tight-lipped to the end, Julius and Ethel Rosenberg paid the death penalty tonight in the electric chair at Sing Sing Prison for their war-time atomic espionage for Soviet Russia.

The pair, first husband and wife to pay the supreme penalty here, and the first in the United States to die for espionage, went to their deaths with a composure that astonished the witnesses.

Julius, 35 years old, was first to enter the glaringly lighted, white-walled death chamber. He walked slowly behind Rabbi Irving Koslowe, a chaplain at Sing Sing, who was intoning the Twenty-third Psalm, "The Lord is my shepherd, I shall not want." As Rosenberg neared the brown-stained oak chair he seemed to sway from side to side.

Guards quickly placed him in the chair. He was clean-shaven, no longer wearing his mustache, and wore a white T-shirt. At 8:04 o'clock the first shock of 2,000 volts, with its ten amperes, coursed through his body. After two subsequent shocks his life ended at 8:06½ P. M.

Dr. H. W. Kipp and Dr. George McCracken applied stethoscopes to his chest, and Dr. Kipp said:

"I pronounce this man dead."

Wife Kisses Matron

Ethel Rosenberg, the 37-year-old wife, entered the death chamber a few minutes after the body of her husband had been removed. She wore a dark green print dress with white polka dots, and, like her husband, was shod in loafer-type cloth slippers. Her hair was close-cropped on top to permit contact of an electrode.

Just before she reached the chair the five-foot, 100-pound woman held out her hand to Mrs. Helen Evans, a matron. As Mrs. Evans grasped her hand, Mrs. Rosenberg drew her close and kissed her lightly on the cheek. Rabbi Koslowe, standing about ten feet from the chair, was intoning the Fifteenth and Thirty-first Psalms.

Mrs. Evans choked up at the final farewell and left the room quickly. Mrs. Lucy Many, a former matron who is now a prison telephone operator, also shook hands with the doomed woman.

Mrs. Rosenberg sat in the electric chair "with the most composed look you ever saw," one witness said.

She winced a bit as the electrode came in contact with her head, but her arms remained relaxed under their binding straps. Silent, she waited while the guards dropped a leather mask over her face. To her right stood Joseph P. Francel, the state executioner, in an alcove.

The first of three successive shocks was applied at 8:11½ P. M. After the third shock the two doctors applied their stethoscopes and found she was still alive. After two more applications of the cur-

Continued on Page 6, Column 8

Professor Loses Fulbright Award After Wife Balks at Red Inquiry

By FREDERICK GRAHAM

A Fulbright award granted last April to Dr. Naphtali Lewis of Brooklyn College to study in Italy during the next academic year has been canceled by the State Department, Senator Joseph R. McCarthy, Republican of Wisconsin, said here yesterday.

"I think it [the cancellation] is an excellent idea," the Senator asserted at the end of a thirty-seven-minute hearing of the Senate Permanent subcommittee on Investigations into the background of Dr. Lewis and his wife, Helen B. Lewis, who once held a teaching post at Brooklyn College.

The formal title of Fulbright award is the United States Educational Exchange Award. The awards are granted to educators and students for study abroad under the Fulbright Act, which is named for Senator J. William Fulbright, Democrat of Arkansas, who pioneered the program.

Senator McCarthy, who sat as a one-member subcommittee at the Federal Courthouse in Foley Square, said that the purpose of the inquiry was to learn whether Mrs. Lewis was now or ever had been a member of the Communist party.

Because she planned to go abroad with her husband for the study year at the expense of the Federal Government, Senator McCarthy declared that he believed it was very important to know if she was or had been a Communist. Unable to elicit an answer on that score from Mrs. Lewis, Senator McCarthy asserted that her refusal to answer on the ground it might tend to incriminate her was the same as saying that "I am a member of the party."

Mrs. Lewis steadfastly refused to answer questions as to whether she had held Communist cell meet-

Continued on Page 5, Column 6

"All the News That's Fit to Print"

The New York Times.

LATE CITY EDITION
Warm, humid, showers likely late today. Fair, not so warm tomorrow.
Temperature Range Today—Max., 88; Min., 68
Temperatures Yesterday—Max., 79; Min., 62
Full U. S. Weather Bureau Report, Page 25

VOL. CII..No. 34,883. Entered as Second-Class Matter. Post Office, New York, N. Y. NEW YORK, MONDAY, JULY 27, 1953. Times Square, New York 36, N. Y. Telephone Lackawanna 4-1000 FIVE CENTS

TRUCE IS SIGNED, ENDING THE FIGHTING IN KOREA; P.O.W. EXCHANGE NEAR; RHEE GETS U. S. PLEDGE; EISENHOWER BIDS FREE WORLD STAY VIGILANT

GEROSA AND STARK PICKED BY WAGNER TO COMPLETE SLATE

Bronx Contractor to Run for Controller, Brooklyn Clothier for Council President

DESAPIO PRAISES CHOICE

Tammany Head Sees Approval This Week by Party Leaders Opposed to Impellitteri

By PAUL CROWELL

Lawrence E. Gerosa, a Bronx contractor, and Abe Stark, a Brooklyn merchant, were selected as running mates yesterday by Manhattan Borough President Robert F. Wagner Jr., who was chosen last week by the Democratic organizations of Bronx and New York Counties as their candidate for Mayor.

Mr. Gerosa was named as a candidate for Controller and Mr. Stark for President of the City Council. The slate headed by Mr. Wagner will wage a primary contest against the ticket headed by Mayor Impellitteri, whose running mates are City Councilman Charles E. Keegan of the Bronx for Controller and Julius Helfand, assistant district attorney of Kings County, for Council President.

The Impellitteri-Keegan-Helfand ticket has the backing of the Democratic organizations of Brooklyn, Queens and Staten Island.

At the Biltmore Hotel Mr. Wagner said that Mr. Gerosa and Mr. Stark were his personal choices but that he expected the Bronx and Tammany Hall executive committees to approve them without hesitation.

Wagner Voices Confidence

"I was given a free hand in picking my running mates," Mr. Wagner said. "I chose them after consulting with representatives of civic organizations, labor and business and the Bronx and Manhattan county leadership.

"I am confident that the Bronx and New York County executive committees will approve my choices. Speaking for myself and my running mates I am sure that we will win the primary contest next September and go on to win the November election."

Carmine G. DeSapio, the leader of Tammany Hall, expressed confidence that the executive committees of the Bronx and Manhattan organizations would approve Mr. Wagner's selections at a meeting to be held early this week. He described Mr. Gerosa and Mr. Stark as "outstanding representative business men who will make a great contribution to public service."

Mr. Gerosa, who was born in Milan, Italy, Aug. 10, 1894, lives at 615 West 252d Street in the Riverdale section. He is married and has three children.

He was designated in 1945 by four of the five Democratic county leaders as a candidate for Controller on a ticket headed by former Mayor William O'Dwyer, but withdrew in favor of Lazarus Jo-

Continued on Page 20, Column 4

Clark Ready to Start Release Of Red Captives in Few Days

But Allied Commander Says It May Be Two or Three Weeks Before Americans Freed by the Communists Arrive in U. S.

By JAMES RESTON
Special to The New York Times.

SOMEWHERE IN KOREA, July 26—Gen. Mark W. Clark said tonight he was prepared to start shipping Communist prisoners of war to North Korea and Communist China within a "few days," but he thought it would be two or three weeks before American prisoners would reach the United States.

The United Nations commander told several reporters aboard his plane en route to the signing of the truce agreement at Munsan, Korea, that while the Communists had comparatively few prisoners to send back, United Nations procedures for handling captives were undoubtedly faster.

The United Nations Command now holds 68,000 North Koreans and 5,000 Chinese Communists who want to return to their native lands, and 8,000 North Koreans and about 15,000 Chinese Communists who have refused to return home.

In contrast, the Communists hold only 12,000 United Nations prisoners, of whom 3,000 are Americans.

Nevertheless, General Clark said, he thought it would be unwise for the Americans to expect that United States prisoners would be sent back as fast as the United Nations Command would return the Communists.

He said he expected the Communists to return the American captives at the rate of about fifty daily, while the Allies were in position to return as many as 1,500 Communists every day.

In accordance with plans that are now ready, General Clark asserted, the Communist captives would be put aboard small naval

Continued on Page 9, Column 2

Accord on plans for prisoners of war is on Page 7.

Eisenhower Accepts Aid Cut; Drive to Adjourn Advances

Special to The New York Times.

WASHINGTON, July 26—The drive for adjournment of Congress by Saturday appeared more certain of success today as the Eisenhower Administration privately indicated it could operate under the $4,562,664,000 foreign aid fund bill approved yesterday by the Senate Appropriations Committee.

The Administration decision, already conveyed to Senate leaders, was said to represent an understanding, reluctantly reached, that little improvement could be hoped for on the committee action, which restored half the $1,115,050,000 reduction made last week in the House of Representatives.

The Administration leaders in the Senate are being asked to do no more than "hold the line" when the Mutual Security money bill comes to the floor for debate, and possibly a vote, on Wednesday.

For the record, the Administration still sought passage before adjournment of the postal rate increase bill, designed to produce an additional $240,500,000 in revenue, but the pressure for the proposal did not seem very great.

Summerfield Is Doubtful

Postmaster General Arthur E. Summerfield, guest on the National Broadcasting Company's "Meet the Press" television interview, said tonight he thought Congress should stay in session to pass the bill but conceded he did not know whether it would.

"I know they've had a busy six months," he said.

The House Post Office and Civil Service Committee, which has been conducting hearings for two weeks, has given no indication when a postal bill will be reported. The House leadership tentatively has scheduled the measure for midweek consideration on the floor. There have been no Senate hearings.

With debate beginning tomorrow, quick Senate approval was forecast for a compromise bill providing for the admission to this country over the next three years of 209,000 refugees, many of them from lands now behind the Iron Curtain. The Administration originally had proposed permitting the entry of 240,000 above-quota immigrants in two years.

The compromise figure, worked out with Senator Pat McCarran, Democrat of Nevada, who will continue to oppose the legislation but will not obstruct its passage, falls below the 220,000 admissions in three years approved by the Senate Judiciary Committee.

House Votes Wednesday

The House will vote Wednesday on its version of the bill in which 240,000 refugees would be admitted over a three-year period. Conferees later will agree to a median figure on entries.

Apart from conference reports, which will be coming up for votes daily, the refugee bill is the last major piece of legislation awaiting

Continued on Page 13, Column 3

55 REPORTED KILLED IN CUBAN REBELLION

Batista Voids Constitutional Guarantees, Hits Partisans of Ex-President Prio

By R. HART PHILLIPS
Special to The New York Times.

HAVANA, July 26—Fifty-five persons were reported killed and many more wounded in a rebellion today at Santiago de Cuba and near-by Bayamo. Martial law was imposed in Santiago following the uprising and military authorities began to round up members of revolutionary groups.

President Fulgencio Batista and his Cabinet in a special session tonight suspended constitutional guarantees for a period of ninety days, according to an official note from the Presidential Palace. The action was taken to enable the Government to cope with revolutionary activities following the revolt earlier in the day.

"Mercenaries in the service of those who have been during the regime of Prio [former President Carlos Prio Socarras], in conjunction with Communist elements" were accused of the attacks on the military posts at Santiago and Bayamo in a joint statement signed by the Ministers.

Continued on Page 11, Column 2

TALK CONDITION SET

U.S. to Boycott Political Parleys After 90 Days if It Finds Foe Stalls

By W. H. LAWRENCE
Special to The New York Times.

WASHINGTON, July 26—The United States has agreed to join South Korea in walking out of the projected Korean political conference ninety days after it begins if this Government is convinced that the Communists are not negotiating in good faith and that further sessions would be futile.

But this Government has not promised to resume hostilities in Korea at that time, nor has it promised to give South Korea any moral or material support if that Government carries out its threat to attempt to unify divided Korea by military force.

The conditional pledge to quit the Korean political conference after ninety days—if this Government believes it is futile—has been given to Dr. Syngman Rhee, South Korean President, who has already announced publicly that his agreement to cooperate in the armistice extends for only ninety days after the political conference convenes. Under the truce terms the conference will convene within ninety days after the signing of the armistice.

The Communists have not been told heretofore of this American intention to quit the political talks in any specified period if they seem to this Government to be fruitless. The United States contends that a walkout from the political talks would not violate the armistice.

U. S. to Make Decision

This Government is not committed to walk out of the peace talks simply if Dr. Rhee and the South Koreans walk out. The United States will make its own decisions as to whether the political negotiations are being carried on in good faith.

There is not, so far as is known, any agreement by the other principal members of the United Nations to walk out at the same time that the United States might decide to leave the conference.

Observers here did not feel that the assurances given to Dr. Rhee were necessarily in conflict with the guarantees given the Communists by Lieut. Gen. William K. Harrison Jr., chief United Nations negotiator, that there would be no time limit on the political conference.

It was pointed out that the armistice agreement included no time limitation for success or failure of the political conference—but it also imposed no requirement on either the Communists or the Allies to continue negotiations if it

Continued on Page 3, Column 2

PRESIDENT IS HAPPY

But Warns in Broadcast That Global Peace Is Yet to Be Achieved

Texts of Eisenhower and Dulles talks are on Page 4.

Special to The New York Times.

WASHINGTON, July 26—President Eisenhower greeted the news of the Korean armistice tonight with prayers of thanksgiving but warned the nation that the Allies had won an armistice only on a single battleground and had not achieved peace in the world.

The President spoke over radio and television networks about an hour after the official cease-fire documents had been signed.

General Eisenhower said the United States and all the free world must not relax its guard, or fail to be vigilant against "the possibility of untoward developments."

After the President had spoken, Charles E. Wilson, Secretary of Defense, issued a statement warning against any relaxation in the country's defense program because of the truce. He advised, too, that it would be a "long time" before American troops could be withdrawn from Korea "with safety."

"We must not be misled into the same demobilization which followed World Wars I and II," he said. "Such a demobilization would inevitably again tempt an aggressor."

Dulles Sees U. N. Victory

John Foster Dulles, Secretary of State, described the armistice as a great victory for the United Nations because "for the first time in history an international organization had stood against an aggressor and has marshaled force to meet force."

President Eisenhower spoke from the White House, across Pennsylvania Avenue and about a block east from Blair House, where President Truman decided thirty-seven months ago to commit United States forces to the defense of South Korea, then being overrun by the Communist armies from the north.

The President said he hoped that the coming of peace to Korea would at last convince all nations of the wisdom of composing their differences by negotiation "rather than after "various resorts to brutal and futile battle."

He closed his brief speech by quoting from the final paragraph of Lincoln's Second Inaugural Address, which he said expressed the resolution and dedication of all Americans, now as in 1865.

These were Lincoln's words: "With malice toward none, with

Continued on Page 4, Column 2

The New York Times (by Fred J. Sass)

REPORTS ON TRUCE: President Eisenhower making nationwide television broadcast from the White House last night.

CEREMONY IS BRIEF

Halt in 3-Year Conflict for a Political Parley Due at 9 A. M. Today

Armistice text, on Pages 6, 7; Clark and Taylor statements, 9.

By LINDESAY PARROTT
Special to The New York Times.

TOKYO, Monday, July 27—Communist and United Nations delegates in Panmunjom signed an armistice at 10:01 A. M. today [9:01 P.M., Sunday, Eastern daylight time]. Under the truce terms, hostilities in the three-year-old Korean war are to cease at 10 o'clock tonight [9 A. M., Monday, Eastern daylight time].

[President Syngman Rhee of South Korea promised in a statement at Seoul Monday to observe the armistice "for a limited time" while a political conference tried to unify Korea by peaceful means, The United Press said.]

The historic document was signed in a roadside hall the Communists built specially for the occasion. The ceremony, attended by representatives of sixteen members of the United Nations, took precisely eleven minutes. Then the respective delegations walked from the meeting place without a word or handshake between them.

The matter-of-fact procedure underlined what spokesmen of both sides emphasized: That though the shooting would cease within twelve hours after the signing, only an uneasy armed truce and political difficulties, perhaps even greater than those of the armistice negotiations, were ahead.

Signers Are Expressionless

The representatives of the two sides were expressionless as they put their names to a pile of documents, providing for an exchange of prisoners, establishment of a neutral zone for the cease-fire and a later political conference that would attempt to settle the tragic Korean questions, unsolved by three years of fighting that caused hundreds of thousands of casualties.

According to the latest figures, revealed July 21 by the Department of Defense, the United States has suffered a total of 139,272 casualties. This included 24,965 dead, 101,368 wounded, 2,938 captured, 8,476 missing and 1,525 previously reported captured or missing, but since returned to military control.

Early this afternoon the Allied part in conclusion of the armistice agreement was completed at advance headquarters near Munsan, where Gen. Mark W. Clark, United Nations commander, put his name to the documents previously signed at Panmunjom.

General Clark signed in the presence of some of his high-ranking officers, Vice Admiral Robert P. Briscoe, commander of the naval forces in the Far East; Gen. Otto P. Weyland, head of the Far East Air Forces; Gen. Maxwell D. Taylor, Eighth Army commander; Lieut. Gen. Samuel Anderson of the Fifth Air Force, and Vice Admiral J. J. Clark, heading the Seventh Fleet.

Also present at Munsan was

Continued on Page 2, Column 5

DEFENSE CHIEFS SEE BILLION CUT IN ARMS

Wilson Tells Quantico Parley Our Gain in Might Makes Any Attack on Us 'Foolhardy'

By AUSTIN STEVENS
Special to The New York Times.

QUANTICO, Va., July 26—Defense officials attending the high-level defense conference at the Marine Corps base here predicted today that with any kind of "decent" Korean truce defense spending could be trimmed by as much as $1,000,000,000 in the next twelve months.

Secretary of Defense Charles E. Wilson told the conference that "we have attained a strength which should make any attack upon us foolhardy in the extreme, and we are increasing our strength daily."

The previously stated defense spending figure for the fiscal year that started July 1 was $43,200,000,000. Official announcement was made two days ago that W. J. McNeil, Assistant Secretary of Defense in charge of the budget, had told the conference, which included high military leaders, that cuts were expected in that figure. He did not indicate where the cuts were to be made.

In their prediction today the defense officials said that the post-truce reductions would not be greater than $1,000,000,000 in the year because so many fixed costs would continue.

The immediate economies would come in ammunition, trucks and other "consumption items" of war. Over-all military manpower gradually would be cut back from the present 3,500,000 by 200,000, perhaps more. One item mentioned today as an example was the immediate ending of combat pay, which is budgeted at $56,000,000.

However, defense officials stated, some other costs would rise. Assuming, for instance, that large numbers of United States troops would remain in Korea for some time, it was said, it would become necessary to build barracks and other semi-permanent structures.

The three-day highly secret conference called by Secretary Wilson to have the armed services present their situations and problems and also to get members of his new defense "team" to know

Continued on Page 9, Column 1

MARINES STOP REDS IN LAST-HOUR FIGHT

Chinese Foe's Dawn Attacks Hit U. S. Units on West and South Koreans in Center

By The United Press

TOKYO, Monday, July 27—Chinese Communist troops threw "last hour propaganda" attacks at Allied forces on the central and western fronts of the rain-swept Korean battle line today, only a few hours before the armistice was signed at Panmunjom.

An estimated two enemy companies smashed into United Nations lines at the bend of the Kumsong River on the central front. South Korean forces fought the Reds hand-to-hand for more than an hour.

Allied troops all along the 155-mile line across the peninsula were ordered to hold casualties to a minimum and not to pick fights with the Reds.

The Allied orders were issued as Chinese Red shock troops just before dawn attacked United States Marines on a western front outpost for the fourth consecutive day. The Reds hit the hillpost positions northeast of Panmunjom in forces up to 200 men.

First Marine Division officers said the first wave of the attack was turned off without casualty among the Americans. The marines

Continued on Page 2, Column 1

Arizona Raids Polygamous Cult; Seeks to Wipe Out Its Community

By GLADWIN HILL
Special to The New York Times.

SHORT CREEK, Ariz., July 26—Arizona authorities, under an unusual proclamation of insurrection, raided this remote farming hamlet on the state's northern border at dawn today and placed virtually the entire adult population under arrest in an effort to wipe out the nation's last remaining center of organized polygamy.

The defendants, thirty-six men and eighty-six women, constituted the principal membership of a professed Fundamentalist sect—disowned by the Church of Jesus Christ of Latter Day Saints (Mormon) in 1939—that has continued to practice the plural marriage renounced by the Mormon church in 1890.

Separated from the outside world by the towering cliffs and arid gorges of Arizona's wild and inaccessible "Strip" between the Grand Canyon and the Utah border, members of the cult, organized on a communal economic basis, allegedly have been maintaining as many as a half-dozen wives and thirty children, and have fostered child marriages.

In addition to 122 adults and child brides named in warrants held by a raiding force of 120 peace officers, the colony included some 263 children.

The state's avowed objective is to wipe out the community, imprison the adult ringleaders, and find new homes and lives for the children and for the numerous

Continued on Page 36, Column 1

U.N. Assembly Meets Aug. 17 To Plan Post-Truce Parley

Special to The New York Times.

UNITED NATIONS, N. Y., July 26—Promptly upon receiving formal notification of the signing of the Korean armistice, Lester B. Pearson of Canada, President of the General Assembly, issued a call tonight to member delegations for resumption on Aug. 17 of the suspended seventh Assembly session. The Assembly will decide details of the Far Eastern political conference scheduled to take place within ninety days of the signing of the truce agreement.

Official notification that the truce agreement had been signed was given orally to Secretary General Dag Hammarskjold and to Mr. Pearson by the permanent representative of the United States, former Senator Henry Cabot Lodge Jr., in the same committee room at headquarters here in which the Political and Security Committee held its lengthy debate on the Korean question some months ago.

Mr. Lodge then handed to Mr. Pearson a copy of the text of the communication, addressed to the Secretary General and issued by the United States Mission after word had been flashed from the Pentagon in Washington. It read:

"I have the honor to inform you that an armistice agreement has been entered into between the United Nations Command and the commanders of the Communist forces in Korea, i. e., the Korean People's Army and the Chinese People's Volunteers. The agreement was signed for the United Nations Command at 1000 hours [10 A. M.] on July 27, 1953, Korean time, and becomes effective at 2200 hours [10 P. M.], July 27, 1953, Korean time. [The actual signing was at 10:01 A. M., Korean time, or 9:01 P. M. Sunday, Eastern daylight time.]

"A report of the Unified Command transmitting the official text of the armistice agreement will be sent to you shortly."

Telegrams to the delegates, which had been prepared earlier, were dispatched to the delegations summoning them to report for the reconvened session in mid-August.

In a joint broadcast from the committee room, which followed that of President Eisenhower from Washington, all three of the United Nations principals repeated for radio and television audiences statements issued earlier.

"The whole world is thankful that the negotiations at Panmunjom have brought the fighting in Korea to an end by the signature of an armistice agreement," Mr.

Continued on Page 4, Column 5

Skeptical G.I.'s Finally Convinced; Most Take News With Little Elation

By GREG MacGREGOR
Special to The New York Times.

SEOUL, Korea, July 26—Tonight, on the eve of the armistice, front-line G. I.'s faced their last full night of fighting in the thirty-seven-month-old Korean war. Only a few minor clashes had taken place by early morning, and from all indications the war would be unofficially ended by dawn. No patrols were scheduled for tomorrow.

As news of the armistice filtered down to the men at the front, it left an atmosphere of mingled disbelief and temporary confusion in its wake. In many cases the soldiers flatly refused to accept the word of their own officers and noncommissioned officers. The men had had so many disappointments over cease-fire reports in the past that they were slow to accept the truth.

"It will never happen," a Marine private manning the line on the central front said with a laugh when his sergeant told him the war would end tomorrow.

Not until the Armed Forces Radio broadcast was picked up at 6 P. M. tonight by portable receivers along the front were the men willing to believe the news. Then the announcer's words struck like a bolt of lightning.

Some G. I.'s stared dumbly at each other and others broke out in howls.

"Didja hear that—didja hear that?" one might keep shouting over and over as he ran from his tent.

"Wait'll they sign it—who knows what's going to happen?" a skeptic

Continued on Page 2, Column 7

"All the News That's Fit to Print"

The New York Times.

LATE CITY EDITION
Considerable cloudiness today.
Partly cloudy, cold tomorrow.
Temperature Range Today-Max., 40; Min., 35
Temperatures Yesterday-Max., 56.4; Min., 47.7
Full U. S. Weather Bureau Report, Page 19

VOL. CIII..No. 35,101. Entered as Second-Class Matter, Post Office, New York, N. Y. NEW YORK, TUESDAY, MARCH 2, 1954. Times Square, New York 36, N. Y. Telephone Lackawanna 4-1000 FIVE CENTS

FIVE CONGRESSMEN SHOT IN HOUSE BY 3 PUERTO RICAN NATIONALISTS; BULLETS SPRAY FROM GALLERY

CAPITOL IN UPROAR

Woman, Accomplices Quickly Overpowered —High Bonds Set

By CLAYTON KNOWLES

Special to THE NEW YORK TIMES.

WASHINGTON, March 1 — Five members of the Congress of The United States were shot down on the floor of the House of Representatives today.

Their assailants, at least three Puerto Rican Nationalists, shouted for freedom of their homeland as they fired murderously although at random from a spectators' gallery just above the House floor. Possibly twenty-five shots were fired.

Bullets rained down from two German Lugers and other pistols of lesser caliber. They crashed through the table of the majority leader and chairs around it, and struck near the table of the Minority Leader beyond. The time was 2:32 P. M.

House members at first thought the sounds were those of firecrackers. But as their colleagues fell or took cover as they heard the slugs hit around them, all realized what was happening.

The wounded House members:

ALVIN M. BENTLEY, 35 years old, multimillionaire Michigan Republican, shot through lung, liver and intestine. Condition critical.

BEN F. JENSEN, 61, Republican of Iowa, shot in back. Condition serious.

CLIFFORD DAVIS, 56, Democrat of Tennessee, shot in the leg. Condition good.

GEORGE H. FALLON, 51, Democrat of Maryland, leg wound. Condition good.

KENNETH A. ROBERTS, 41, Democrat of Alabama, leg wound. Condition good.

Assailants Subdued

Within a matter of minutes, the episode, which threw the Capitol and most of official Washington into an uproar, was at an end. Gallery attendants, aided by spectators, Capitol police and even one House member, quickly overcame and disarmed the three gun wielders.

The three Puerto Ricans, all residents of New York, were booked at police headquarters on charges of assault with intent to kill. They gave their names and addresses as:

LOLITA LEBRON, 34, 315 West Ninety-fourth Street.

RAFAEL C. MIRANDA, 25, 120 South First Street, Brooklyn.

ANDRES CORDERO, or FIGUEROA, 29, of 108 East 103d Street.

A fourth Puerto Rican, also resident in New York, was arrested at a downtown bus station and booked on the same charge.

He was booked as Irving Flores, 27, also of 108 East 103d Street, described by Police Chief Robert Murray as a fourth member of the shooting party who had fled the Capitol successfully. When arrested, Flores still had a .45 caliber pistol.

Later, United States Commissioner Cyril S. Lawrence ordered all four held under $100,000 bonds each. He put off a preliminary hearing until March 10 to give them time to get counsel. Five counts of assault with intent to

Continued on Page 16, Column 1

HIDDEN OWNERSHIP OF RACEWAY STOCK BARED AT HEARING

Former Legislator, Intimate of O'Dwyer, Erickson Kin and Ex-Convict Are Identified

HOLDINGS PUT AT MILLION

Moreland Inquiry Opens Public Sessions, Gets Details of Yonkers Track Purchase

By EMANUEL PERLMUTTER

Politicians and persons with underworld backgrounds or friendships were found yesterday to have been the hidden owners of close to a million dollars' worth of stock in several New York harness racing tracks.

These disclosures were made as the Moreland Act Commission opened public hearings here on the scandal-ridden raceways. The proceedings are being held in the Criminal Court Building, 100 Centre Street.

Among those who were shown to have struck it rich secretly on the trotting tracks were former Assemblyman Elmer J. Kellam of Hancock, N. Y.; Irving Sherman, political intimate of former Mayor William O'Dwyer and admitted friend of gangsters; Frank J. Erickson, son of the convicted gambler, and Samuel J. Stirratt, an ex-convict with a long police record.

Additional testimony was introduced indicating that loans from racketeers had helped the original incorporators of the Algam Corporation to purchase Yonkers Empire City Race Track —now Yonkers Raceway—for $2,400,000 in 1949.

Named a Racing Steward

Mr. Kellam, who served in the Assembly from Delaware County between 1943 and 1950, admitted on the witness stand that he had transferred 10,000 shares in Mid-State Raceway, near Syracuse, to a "dummy" owner after he had been appointed as a state racing steward last year.

The former Republican legislator said that he became the beneficiary of the stock, which was listed in the name of Marvin Wynkoop of Downesville, N. Y., and that he intended to sell it but had been unable to do so because of the pressure of his duties as a steward at Roosevelt Raceway, Westbury, L. I. He described the duties of a steward as "protecting the public, to see if the races are on the level."

"Did you think it was proper for a steward to own stock in a track?" Bruce Bromley, the commission chairman, asked him.

Mr. Kellam, a sandy-haired, florid-faced man, shook his head apologetically. "I don't think it's good judgment," he conceded. "But I never performed any duties at a track where I was a stockholder."

Still Owns Track Stock

The witness said he now owned 9,500 shares in the upstate track. He said he assumed he still held the job as racing steward.

At this point, Harness Racing Commissioner George P. Monaghan, sitting as a member of the Moreland Commission, interrupted to point out that stewards served for one year and that they had to be reappointed each racing season.

The testimony involving Irving Sherman, who was referred to as the contact man for Frank Costello during Mayor O'Dwyer's administration, was given by Sam Sherman, a raincoat manufacturer, of 30 West Fifty-fourth Street. He is not related to Irving Sherman.

Sam Sherman testified that although he was the listed owner of 22,500 shares of stock and $50,000 worth of bonds in the Algam Corporation, holding company for the Yonkers track, Irving Sherman actually owned 80 per cent of the investment.

In October, 1953, soon after the Moreland Commission was appointed, Algam purchased 20,000 shares from him, Mr. Sherman said. He said the purchase price was $296,000, a total of $30 a share. Of this sum, he testified, he gave $145,000 to Irving Sherman, the remainder of the latter's share being tied up in litigation.

In addition, Mr. Sherman said, the 2,500 shares of voting stock that he and his secret partner owned were sold at the same time for $75,000 to M. Duke Manacher, a stockholder in Algam. He said he gave $60,000 of this sum to Irving Sherman.

The $50,000 worth of bonds

Continued on Page 12, Column 3

Jarka, Big Stevedore, Quits Port Under Fire

By A. H. RASKIN

The Jarka Corporation, one of the world's largest stevedoring enterprises, decided yesterday to stop operating in the Port of New York.

The company and its president, Frank W. Nolan, are awaiting trial in Special Sessions on charges of having paid out $119,859 in bribes to shipping executives for steering contracts to Jarka. The Waterfront Commission has been conducting an investigation to determine whether the company should be barred from doing business here.

The Jarka decision to withdraw its application for a stevedoring license was the highlight of another hectic day on the strife-swept waterfront. Other developments included:

¶A request by Charles T.

Continued on Page 11, Column 1

31 KILLED IN SUDAN IN NATIVES' CLASH AS NAGUIB ARRIVES

117 Hurt in Battle at Khartum Palace Between Tribesmen and Pro-Egyptian Group

Dispatch of The Times, London.

KHARTUM, the Sudan, March 1—The arrival in the Sudan today of Maj. Gen. Mohammed Naguib, Egyptian President, revived factional passions of this nascent state in a clash in which at least twenty-two persons were killed. [The Associated Press placed the toll at thirty-one.]

Among the dead were eight of the police force, including the British police commandant of Khartum, H. S. McGuigan, and the superintendent, Mustapha el Mahdi. One hundred seventeen were wounded, of whom thirty-two were seriously injured.

The factional struggle was of a primitive nature. The dead and wounded were seen to bear the marks of clubs and spears, not gunshot wounds.

[Meanwhile, a spokesman for the ruling junta in Egypt said in Cairo Monday that General Naguib owed his reinstatement as President to agitation begun by eight Communist army officers.]

The tragedy here was enacted outside the Governor General's palace, which stands on the site of the residency where Gen. Charles G. Gordon, then Governor General, died from the thrusts of tribesmen's spears during the historic Khartum siege in 1885. Inside the residency, General Naguib, Sir Robert Howe, Governor General, and Selwyn Lloyd, Minister of State of the British Foreign Office, were at lunch during today's events.

Parliament Opening Put Off

In view of the passions aroused by the rioting, the Governor General postponed a meeting of the Sudanese Parliament, scheduled for this afternoon, until March 10.

It seemed today as though the army of Mohammed Ahmed, the Mahdi, or Moslem leader who defeated General Gordon, were on the march again. The rioters massed outside the Khartum airport, turbaned and robed in shining white, with their hundreds of banners waving above the throng. They were supporters of the patron of the Sudanese independence movement, Sir Abdel Rahman el Mahdi, mainly Baggara tribesmen from the provinces who gathered to greet General Naguib with chanted slogans demanding independence for the Sudan.

"No Egypt, No Britain!" they cried as they surged up to Sudanese Defense Force troops who barred their way to the airport.

This was no unkempt rabble; their banners were of trim red, green and black stripes, superimposed with a white spear cutting a white crescent.

General Naguib left his aircraft at Khartum airport at 10 A. M. He was accompanied by Maj. Salah Salem, Egyptian Minister of National Guidance and Minister of State for Sudanese Affairs. Sir Robert, Ismail el Azhary, Prime Minister of the

Continued on Page 2, Column 2

UNITY PLEA OPENS CARACAS MEETING

Hemisphere Accord Founded on Sovereignty and Equality Is Urged on Delegates

By SAM POPE BREWER

Special to THE NEW YORK TIMES.

CARACAS, Venezuela, March 1—President Marcos Perez Jimenez of Venezuela opened the tenth Inter-American Conference today with a plea for closer unity among the American States on the basis of sovereignty and equality.

There is explosive material on the agenda in questions such as Communist infiltration in Latin America and rules for granting political asylum. Yet all indications today were that most of the delegates were in a conciliatory mood and that means would be sought to avoid heated clashes.

The elaborate security precautions taken for the conference seemed to grow in importance when word of the shooting in the United States Congress was received.

[Guatemala lost her first test at the parley on a procedural question, while at home President Jacobo Arbenz Guzman denied any Soviet intervention in the country's internal affairs.]

Speaking at the first session in the great modernistic assembly hall of University City, President Perez emphasized that the idea of continental unity had existed from the day the American nations won their independence.

"The existence of basic factors of a type common to all the continent, and the desire to obtain and preserve independence were the fundamental reasons for which there appeared almost simultaneously in the greater part of the peoples of America the idea of unity among them," he said.

He added, however, that "the unity of our peoples should be based on comprehension, the feeling of reciprocal assistance and mutual respect."

"We shall understand each

Continued on Page 9, Column 1

Nehru Decries U. S. Policy On Asia and the 'Cold War'

By ROBERT TRUMBULL

Special to THE NEW YORK TIMES.

NEW DELHI, India, March 1—Prime Minister Jawaharlal Nehru scathingly condemned virtually the entire United States policy in Asia and in the "cold war" today.

His most outspoken speech among many on this subject, delivered to the House of the People, the lower chamber of Parliament, was repeatedly interrupted by thunderous applause. He was given a prolonged ovation at its end.

Mr. Nehru was commenting on President Eisenhower's personal letter last week informing the Indian leader of Washington's intention to furnish military aid to Pakistan and simultaneously offering the same assistance to India.

Mr. Nehru scorned General Eisenhower's tender with the statement that "in making this suggestion, the President has done less than justice to us or to himself."

"If we object to military aid being given to Pakistan, we would be hypocrites and unprincipled opportunists to accept such aid ourselves," he added.

The Prime Minister told the cheering House that United States members of the United Nations cease-fire observer team in Kashmir should be removed. He said that "these American observers can no longer be treated by us as neutrals" in India's dispute with Pakistan over possession of the strategic northern state.

[At United Nations Headquarters a spokesman said no action would be taken pending an official communication from India. In Washington a State Department spokesman said India would have to complain to the United Nations if she wanted the United States members withdrawn.]

In his tersely formal reply to General Eisenhower, which he read out, Mr. Nehru coldly thanked the President for his "assurances," but dismissed them with this curt statement: "You are, however, aware of the views of my Government and our people in regard to this matter. We shall continue to pursue that policy."

The Indian note ignored the offer of arms.

Mr. Nehru, in his speech, took especially heated exception to the version of United States policy in Asia as quoted from testimony by Walter S. Robertson, Assistant Secretary of State, before a

Continued on Page 3, Column 2

Associated Press Wirephoto

SEIZED IN SHOOTING: Capitol police hold three Puerto Rican Nationalists after they fired from gallery seats into House chamber, wounding five Representatives. Prisoners, left to right, are Lolita Lebron, Rafael C. Miranda and Andres Cordero.

M'LEOD AUTHORITY IS CUT BY DULLES

Friend of McCarthy Loses Personnel Duties, Keeps His Security Office

Special to THE NEW YORK TIMES.

WASHINGTON, March 1 — The Eisenhower Administration stripped Scott McLeod today of his authority over State Department personnel. It left him in charge of security matters.

This action, which was announced on the authority of John Foster Dulles, the Secretary of State, was widely interpreted as a thrust by the Administration at the McCarthy wing of the Republican party.

Mr. McLeod is a close friend of Senator Joseph R. McCarthy, Republican of Wisconsin. He went to the State Department last January from the office of Senator Styles Bridges, Republican of New Hampshire.

He had served as administrative assistant to Senator Bridges and at one time was an agent of the Federal Bureau of Investigation.

Mr. McLeod made five speeches for the Republican party in the recent Lincoln Week series of partisan addresses, and there were Democratic protests that he was improperly using his office. A Republican member of the Civil Service Commission, George Moore, held informally that such political activity was forbidden by the Hatch Act, which limits the partisanship of certain Federal officials and employes.

However, the counsel of the State Department ruled that Mr. McLeod was not under the Hatch Act.

Policies Criticized

On Jan. 16, five former United States Ambassadors charged in an open letter that State Department personnel and security policies might be "laying the foundations for a Foreign Service competent to serve a totalitarian government rather than the Government of the United States as we have heretofore known it."

They did not mention Mr. McLeod by name, but both the personnel and security policies were under his direction.

In a speech on Feb. 18 in Larchmont, N. Y., Mr. McLeod described as "scandalous libel" any suggestion that he was attempting to destroy the diplomatic service by spreading fear among its people.

The State Department an-

Continued on Page 15, Column 1

McCarthy, Dirksen Suggest Labor Camps for Army Reds

By W. H. LAWRENCE

Special to THE NEW YORK TIMES.

WASHINGTON, March 1—Senators Joseph R. McCarthy and Everett M. Dirksen suggested today "disagreeable" labor camps for armed services personnel who were Communists or who invoked the Fifth Amendment when asked about Communist associations.

Their suggestion grew out of new disclosures by the Senate Permanent Subcommittee on Investigations of "contradictions" in the Army system of handling officers and enlisted men who are alleged Communists or admitted former Communists.

Senator McCarthy, Republican of Wisconsin, is chairman of the subcommittee, and Senator Dirksen, an Illinois Republican, is a member.

The subcommittee accepted an Army suggestion that it question Robert T. Stevens, Secretary of the Army, at a closed session on Thursday or next Monday. All advance indications on both sides were that it would be a "friendly" hearing and not a controversial showdown such as was threatened but called off last week.

With four Republicans and one Democrat present, the subcommittee today questioned in secret an Army private and a former private in considering a problem of fundamental importance to all the armed forces. Stated broadly, the subcommittee raised these questions:

¶Should admitted Communists,

Continued on Page 14, Column 2

EISENHOWER TARGET FOR FANATICS ALSO

Secret Service Men Detected Puerto Rican Plot Against President in November

Special to THE NEW YORK TIMES.

WASHINGTON, March 1—Puerto Rican extremists have been conspiring to harm President Eisenhower if they got the opportunity, according to the Federal Secret Service.

Henry Cabot Lodge Jr., chief of the United States delegation to the United Nations, was put under twenty-four-hour guard last November for the same reason.

U. E. Baughman, chief of the Secret Service, was asked tonight about the reports of a conspiracy against the President.

"Three or four months ago," he replied, "the Secret Service obtained information indicating the Puerto Rican Nationalists were still possibly interested in harming the President in their fight for independence."

This statement from the head of the agency charged with protecting the President reflected the close watch that the Secret Service had kept on the Nationalist movement ever since two of its members tried to kill President Truman on Nov. 1, 1950.

Truman Case Still 'Open'

Although one assassin was killed in the gun battle in front of Blair House and Oscar Collazo, his companion, is serving a life sentence, the Secret Service still carries the attempted assassination of Mr. Truman as an "open case." It does this because it has not given up the possibility of rounding up the conspirators who directed the assassins.

Mr. Baughman said that the Secret Service had obtained information about designs on President Eisenhower last November. That coincided with the threats on Mr. Lodge. It was indicated tonight that there was an apparent link between the threats to Mr. Lodge and the designs on the President.

A police guard was put around

Continued on Page 17, Column 2

U. S. Dismissed 355 In Subversive Cases

Special to THE NEW YORK TIMES.

WASHINGTON, March 1—The Civil Service Commission reported today that 355 Federal employes whose personnel files contained some allegations of subversive associations had been separated from the Government payroll between May 28 and Dec. 31, 1953.

The report was the first overall breakdown provided by the Administration to Congress since the controversy over the 2,200 persons said by President Eisenhower to have been separated as "security risks."

Philip Young, commission chairman, said the "security" separations totaled 2,224, of whom 983 were dismissed and 1,241 resigned. These figures included 211 dismissals and 231 resigna-

Continued on Page 13, Column 2

WITNESS DESCRIBES SHOOTING, CAPTURE

Reporter Sees Firing in House —Struck on Cheek by Chip Torn Loose by Bullet

By C. P. TRUSSELL

Special to THE NEW YORK TIMES.

WASHINGTON, March 1 — Until the shooting in the House of Representatives today things were somewhat dull.

So dull, in fact, that a short time before members had been summoned by bells to the floor to listen to the issue at hand, whether they wanted to or not. It concerned admittance of Mexican farm laborers.

The quorum bell was answered by 243 members, most of whom were still on the floor when the shooting started in what is called the Ladies' Gallery.

As a police reporter many years ago I was irked by eyewitnesses who had heard shots only as "backfiring automobiles," "blowouts" and "firecrackers." But this time I too thought that firecrackers were going off, and I thought it was a Latin demonstration.

But only for a moment. I saw two men and a woman, in the second row of the Ladies Gallery, pumping at pistols. The two men appeared to be aiming at the desk of Representative Charles A. Halleck of Indiana, the Republican Floor Leader.

The woman had her pistol high,

Continued on Page 16, Column 7

Atom Blast Opens Test in Pacific; No Hint of Hydrogen Plans Given

Special to THE NEW YORK TIMES.

WASHINGTON, March 1—The Atomic Energy Commission today announced the first in a new series of test explosions at its Pacific proving ground in the Marshall Islands.

No further announcement was expected until the series ended. A forty-two word statement told as much of the story as the commission wanted the public to know at this stage. It read:

"[Rear Admiral] Lewis L. Strauss, chairman of the United States Atomic Energy Commission, announced today that Joint Task Force Seven has detonated an atomic device at the A. E. C.'s Pacific proving ground in the Marshall Islands. This detonation was the first in a series of tests."

The language of Admiral Strauss' statement did not make clear whether the "atomic device" was of the fission or thermonuclear (hydrogen) type. There have been unofficial indications, however, that a variety of hydrogen weapons or devices will be tested during the next several weeks.

The most powerful of these is expected to be an actual hydrogen bomb with perhaps twice the explosive power of the experimental device that disintegrated an island of Eniwetok atoll on Nov. 1, 1952.

Representative W. Sterling Cole of upstate New York, the chairman of the Joint Congressional Committee on Atomic Energy, disclosed only two weeks ago that the first device had "completely obliterated" the island

Continued on Page 6, Column 5

"All the News That's Fit to Print"

The New York Times.

LATE CITY EDITION
Increasingly cloudy today. Rain tonight and tomorrow.
Temperature Range Today-Max., 45; Min., 31
Temperatures Yesterday—Max., 46; Min., 31
Full U. S. Weather Bureau Report, Page 43

VOL. CIII..No. 35,111. Entered as Second-Class Matter. Post Office, New York, N. Y. NEW YORK, FRIDAY, MARCH 12, 1954. Times Square, New York 36, N. Y. Telephone LAckawanna 4-1000 FIVE CENTS

ARMY CHARGES M'CARTHY AND COHN THREATENED IT IN TRYING TO OBTAIN PREFERRED TREATMENT FOR SCHINE

HALF OF DOCKMEN IN BROOKLYN JOIN OUTLAW WALKOUT

Huge Food Cargoes Reported in Danger of Spoiling—Trade Losses Mounting

COURT IS PICKETED AGAIN

Rally Backs a Tie-Up Until I. L. A. Is Certified—Jersey Strikers Pledge Return

By A. H. RASKIN

The outlaw dock strike got worse yesterday.

Half of the longshoremen in Brooklyn, the only section of the port that had been operating normally, joined the week-old walkout.

Importers notified the National Labor Relations Board that millions of dollars worth of fruit and vegetables were in danger of rotting on piers and in the holds of strike-stalled ships.

The tie-up turned into a blockade when Philadelphia locals of the old International Longshoremen's Association refused to unload passenger or cargo vessels diverted from New York. Rank-and-file leaders of the local stoppage sought to make the boycott coast-wide, but received no immediate assurances of help from other ports.

The Commerce and Industry Association reported that the turbulent dock labor situation was causing many large corporations to shunt their import and export schedules to other cities. The group predicted that 10 per cent of the lost trade never would be recovered.

The one bright spot in the waterfront picture was a promise by Jersey City strikers to go back to their jobs this morning. The promise was given by spokesmen for both of the warring dock unions—the I. L. A. and its American Federation of Labor rival—at a conference with Commissioner Lawrence A. Whipple in Jersey City.

Picket Line Is Crossed

The federation union, which has been opposing the walkout, mobilized 100 longshoremen to pierce an I. L. A. picket line at a Manhattan wharf of the United Fruit Company. Ignoring the jeers of several hundred members of the old union, five gangs of A. F. L. dock workers walked onto Pier 3, just north of the Battery, to unload coffee and miscellaneous cargo from Guatemala and Honduras. The cargo was aboard the freighter Lovland.

Two hundred and fifty I. L. A. strikers renewed the picketing of the United States Court House in Foley Square. It was the second time they had marched outside the building in protest against two anti-strike court orders.

One was an injunction forbidding the I. L. A. to strike or to interfere with waterfront truck movements. The other was a $100,000 contempt action against the union and three officers of its West Side locals.

The strike has been carried on in defiance of the two orders and in disregard of back-to-work appeals by Capt. William V. Bradley, president of the I. L. A. Strike leaders say the walkout will continue until the old union is certified as the sole bargaining agent for the port's 24,000 dock workers.

The threat to keep the port tied up for all the months that may

Continued on Page 43, Column 2

Wilson Aide Named Secretary of Navy

Associated Press Wirephoto

Charles S. Thomas, Assistant Secretary of Defense, after he was named the successor to Robert B. Anderson, right.

Special to THE NEW YORK TIMES.

WASHINGTON, March 11—Charles Sparks Thomas, Assistant Secretary of Defense, was nominated by President Eisenhower today to be Secretary of the Navy. Mr. Thomas, if confirmed by the Senate, will succeed Robert B. Anderson, who will become Under Secretary of Defense when Roger B. Kyes vacates the post on May 1. A successor to Mr. Thomas has not yet been chosen. The

Continued on Page 8, Column 4

'Direct' Warning to Reds Urged by U. S. at Caracas

By SYDNEY GRUSON

Special to THE NEW YORK TIMES.

CARACAS, Venezuela, March 11—The United States called on the Tenth Inter-American Conference today to issue a "simple, clear and direct" warning to the leaders of international communism to keep hands off the Americas.

The best way to do this, John Foster Dulles, United States Secretary of State, said, is to adopt the United States anti-Communist resolution without crippling amendments. These, he said, would "alter the heart" of the proposed denunciation of international communism as a threat to the hemisphere.

After a week of general debate the Communist issue was joined late today in the Political Committee when consideration of the resolution began. The Secretary made his third major speech on the question in an effort to block a series of crippling amendments submitted by Mexico.

Mr. Dulles sought to eliminate the fears of some delegates that the resolution could in his own words, "be interpreted as intervention or justifying intervention in the genuinely domestic affairs of an American state."

'Natural Historical Fears'

"This concern is, we believe, due to natural historical fears rather than to any language in the United States proposal," the Secretary said.

Delegates of Argentina, Guatemala and Mexico, all of whom spoke in the wind-up of the general debate this morning, had expressed this fear. The spokesmen for Guatemala, where the Communists have won high positions in the Government, have charged that the United States was seeking to cloak interventionist ideas in the guise of collective action against Guatemala.

Mexico's delegate spoke twice today, in the general debate and in answer to Secretary Dulles' rejection of Mexico's amendments. On both occasions Roberto Cordova of Mexico emphasized that his country was not trying to defend international communism but only the right of any people to choose their own form of government and political institutions.

Mexico, he said, would willingly subscribe to the United States proposal if his delegation were convinced that it did not represent a backward step regarding intervention. But later he brushed aside Mr. Dulles' assurances on this point and in fact took no note of the Secretary's announcement that the United States was itself proposing an addition to the declarative portion of the resolution to declare:

"This declaration of foreign policy made by the American republics in relation to the dangers originating outside this hemisphere is designed to protect and not to impair the inalienable right of each American state freely to choose its own form of government and economic system and to live its own social and cultural life."

As the resolution stood before,

Continued on Page 6, Column 4

SCHWABLE TELLS OF P.O.W. ORDEAL

Tells How His Mental Torture by Reds Almost Made Him Believe Germ 'Confession'

By ELIE ABEL

Special to THE NEW YORK TIMES.

WASHINGTON, March 11—Col. Frank H. Schwable described today how a mature man could be conditioned to accept as real the fictions he had invented to appease the Communists.

Taking the witness chair for the first time, the lean, nervous Marine aviator talked for six hours before a court of inquiry. He tried to explain how it felt to have his brain washed, how reality became a blur in the mind, how the judgment could be fogged and the will destroyed.

He did not quite believe his own story that the United States had waged bacteriological warfare in Korea, Colonel Schwable told the court, which is investigating his false "confession."

"I was never convinced in my own mind that we in the First Marine Air Wing had used bug warfare," he testified. "I knew we hadn't. But the rest of it [the fraudulent confession] was real to me—the conferences, the planes and how they would go about their missions."

Rear Admiral Thomas J. Cooper, who was questioning the

Continued on Page 5, Column 5

264 Exposed to Atom Radiation After Nuclear Blast in Pacific

By The Associated Press.

WASHINGTON, March 11—The Atomic Energy Commission said tonight that twenty-eight Americans and 236 natives were "unexpectedly" subjected to "some radiation" during the recent atomic test in the Marshall Islands but all those exposed were "reported well."

The commission announced on March 1 that the first of a series of nuclear tests had started in the Pacific proving grounds.

The commission announcement today said:

"During the course of a routine atomic test in the Marshall Islands, twenty-eight United States personnel and 236 residents were transported from neighboring atolls to Kwajalein Island according to plans as a precautionary measure.

"The individuals were unexpectedly exposed to some radiation. There were no burns. All are reported well.

"After completion of the atomic tests, they will be returned to their homes."

The commission made no immediate amplification of this announcement. However, it seemed probably that a "fall-out" of radioactive waste and activated moisture from a cloud drifting from the explosion probably descended on the Americans and natives on the atoll to which they had been moved.

Atomic test officials try to make careful forecasts of wind directions but sometimes miscalculate.

Exposure to mild radiation is not necessarily dangerous. Reporters last spring were within two miles of an atomic explosion at the Nevada proving grounds and later walked to "Ground

Continued on Page 8, Column 4

SENATE COMBINES STATEHOOD PLANS BY VOTE OF 46-43

Ignores Eisenhower's Wishes for Action on Hawaii Alone—Democrats Score Victory

By CLAYTON KNOWLES

Special to THE NEW YORK TIMES.

WASHINGTON, March 11—The Senate disregarded Administration wishes in voting today to put Hawaiian and Alaskan statehood proposals in a single bill.

The decision to join the proposals carried by a vote of 46 to 43 and came a day after President Eisenhower had urged separate consideration of the statehood measures. He had asked for immediate statehood for Hawaii alone. This is the Republican party position.

The Senate's vote was mainly along party lines, with the Democrats winning. However, the plan to combine the bills prevailed by the margin of the votes of three Republicans who broke with their party on the question. They were Senators William Langer of North Dakota, John M. Butler of Maryland and George W. Malone of Nevada.

Forty-two Democrats and the Senate's one independent, Wayne Morse of Oregon, cast the other votes for a combined bill.

Forty-one Republicans and two Democrats, Spessard L. Holland of Florida and Russell B. Long of Louisiana, opposed the merger plan.

Knowland to Back Bill

The issue in the three-day debate preceding the vote was whether statehood aspirations of Hawaii and Alaska would be hurt or helped by putting them together. Senator William F. Knowland of California, Republican Senate leader, contended it would hurt. Senator Clinton P. Anderson, Democrat of New Mexico and sponsor of the one-package proposal, asserted it would help.

The vote along party lines stemmed largely from the fact that Hawaii is normally Republican and might be expected to send a Republican delegation to Congress, while Alaska is Democratic at the polls and probably would send Democrats to the Congress.

After the Senate action, Senator Knowland, conceding a chance to pass a combined bill, said he would vote for it. So did other Republicans in opposition on the vote today. Senator Hugh Butler of Nebraska, Interior Committee chairman who fought the Anderson amendment, said the Senate "might fool some people by passing the bill now before us."

The Nebraska Republican alluded to the fact that a group of Southern Democrats, numbering fifteen to twenty, had supported the Anderson amendment in the hope of defeating both statehood proposals. Senator George A. Smathers, Democrat of Florida, frankly conceded during debate

Continued on Page 13, Column 3

SENATOR ATTACKS

Hits Back at Stevenson, Murrow and Flanders in Radio Broadcast

Special to THE NEW YORK TIMES.

WASHINGTON, March 11—Senator Joseph R. McCarthy struck back tonight at criticism of him by Adlai E. Stevenson, Edward R. Murrow and Senator Ralph E. Flanders.

The Wisconsin Republican said that Mr. Stevenson's assertion that only one alleged active Communist had been found in the Government in the last year was "absolutely false."

He called Mr. Murrow, Columbia Broadcasting System commentator, one of the "extreme Left Wing bleeding-heart elements of television and radio." He cited an article in The Pittsburgh Sun-Telegraph of Feb. 18, 1935, to charge that Mr. Murrow had been on the advisory council for a summer session of Moscow University, where overthrow of the existing social order was taught.

[Three and a half hours after Mr. McCarthy's broadcast, Mr. Murrow issued a statement in which he said that in 1935, in his capacity as assistant director of the Institute of International Education, he was a member of the advisory committee for a summer school in Moscow. He added, however, that "in actual fact the summer school was canceled by Russian authorities before it began."]

McCarthy Quotes Lincoln

Mr. McCarthy said he would rather stand with Abraham Lincoln, who said during Civil War times the danger to the United States was from within and not from without, rather than with Senator Flanders, a Republican of Vermont, who said the danger today is from without rather than from within.

Appearing on a question and answer radio broadcast with Fulton Lewis Jr., over the Mutual Broadcasting System, Senator McCarthy struck back at Messrs. Stevenson, Murrow and Flanders but made no mention of the implied criticism voiced by President Eisenhower at his news conference yesterday.

He also made no mention of his quarrel with the National Broadcasting Company and the Columbia Broadcasting System because they refused him free time for a reply to Mr. Stevenson and gave it instead to the Republican National Committee, which designated Vice President Nixon to make the official reply Saturday night.

Mr. Murrow had devoted a thir-

Continued on Page 11, Column 1

Cohn Scored When Woman Denies McCarthy's Charges

Mrs. Moss Counters Accusation as Red While Senators Decry 'Innuendo'—Crowd Applauds Hearing Scene

Special to THE NEW YORK TIMES.

WASHINGTON, March 11—Mrs. Annie Lee Moss, suspended Army Signal Corps employe, softly but flatly denied all Communist party activities or membership today.

The crowded caucus room of the Senate Office Building, where the Senate Permanent Subcommittee on Investigation was in session, rang with repeated applause as Democratic members struck at "convicting people by rumor and hearsay and innuendo."

The target of Democratic resentment was Roy Cohn, chief counsel for the subcommittee headed by Senator Joseph R. McCarthy, Wisconsin Republican. Mr. Cohn had countered Mrs. Moss' testimony by saying the subcommittee had still secret evidence that she was a Communist.

The Democrats, led by Senator John L. McClellan of Arkansas, demanded that he produce the evidence or refrain from public mention of it.

Senator McCarthy, in the original hearing at which the charges against Mrs. Moss were produced, had suggested she would "run the risk of indictment for perjury" when she appeared before the committee.

Senator McCarthy was absent from the committee room today when the scene over Mrs. Moss' testimony took place. He had gone to his office to prepare for his radio appearance later in which he answered criticism of him and the Republican party by Adlai E. Stevenson, the 1952 Democratic Presidential nominee.

No effort was made by the presiding officer, Senator Karl E. Mundt, South Dakota Republican, to check the crowd's applause or to interfere with the Democrats in their vigorous denunciation of Mr. Cohn's tactics.

Senator Mundt ordered Mr.

Continued on Page 10, Column 3

STEVENS A TARGET

Report Quotes Counsel As Saying Secretary Would Be 'Through'

The text of the Army's report is printed on Page 9A.

By W. H. LAWRENCE

Special to THE NEW YORK TIMES.

WASHINGTON, March 11—The Army reported today it had been subjected to direct threats by Senator Joseph R. McCarthy and his chief counsel, Roy Cohn.

The threats, the Army said, had been made in an effort to obtain preferential treatment for G. David Schine, now a private in the Army but formerly an investigator for the McCarthy subcommittee.

In a thirty-four-page report sent to each member of Senator McCarthy's Permanent Subcommittee on Investigations and some members of the Armed Services Committee, the Army declared the Wisconsin Republican and Mr. Cohn first had sought a direct commission for Private Schine.

Failing in that, the report said, they had then demanded for him an assignment in the New York area so he could study alleged subversive material in West Point textbooks.

In the period between Oct. 18 and Nov. 3, before Senator McCarthy began his open fight with the Army, John G. Adams, Army Counsel, reported he had told Mr. Cohn that it would not be in the national interest to give preferential treatment to Private Schine.

"Mr. Cohn replied that if the national interest was what the Army wanted, he'd give it a little and then proceeded to outline how he would expose the Army in its worst light and show the country how shabbily it is being run," the report declared.

Threat to Stevens Cited

The report quoted Mr. Cohn as threatening on one occasion to "wreck the Army" and make certain that Robert T. Stevens was "through" as the Secretary of the Army. At another time, the report said, "Mr. Cohn stated to Mr. Adams that he would teach Mr. Adams what it meant to go over his head."

The report is expected to spur growing demands for Mr. Cohn's ouster.

Senator McCarthy made it clear in answer that he would accept battle with "one or two" in the Army high command on the Cohn-Schine case. He said he had instructed his own committee staff to pull out of its files everything bearing on the case and give them to him so they could be "made available to the American public."

"I don't like to do it," he told a New York Times correspondent. "The deeper I get into it, I'm convinced the Army as a whole is damn clean. What some people in the Army do doesn't mean the entire Army."

He said he had sought at a luncheon with Charles E. Wilson, Secretary of Defense, yesterday

Continued on Page 9-B, Col 2

SENATE UNIT ASKS OUSTER OF CHAVEZ

Cites Election Irregularities in '52 but Does Not Accuse New Mexico Democrat

By WILLIAM S. WHITE

Special to THE NEW YORK TIMES.

WASHINGTON, March 11—A Senate showdown on a long-forecast Republican effort to unseat Senator Denis Chavez because of alleged election irregularities in 1952 drew near today. A Republican-controlled Senate subcommittee formally filed its expected report recommending that the New Mexico Democrat's seat be held vacant.

It also urged that the Senate find that "no member was elected from New Mexico in the 1952 general election."

The Republicans asserted that there had been no free expression of the will of the people, in part because of the alleged denial of the right of secret ballot. Senator Chavez nowhere was charged with fraud.

The Republican subcommittee chairman, Senator Frank A. Barrett of Wyoming, said there had been "no intention to cast aspersions" on Mr. Chavez. It simply had been impossible to determine whether Senator Chavez or his Republican opponent, Brig. Gen. Patrick J. Hurley, retired, actually had won, Mr. Barrett said.

Senator Chavez asserted the Republicans had delivered "a tremendous insult to the officials and people of New Mexico."

Democrats Are Confident

The Democrats, who had insisted on clearing the issue without further delay, plainly were confident he would be sustained. Disinterested observation seemed to support their confidence.

If Senator Chavez should be ousted and the Republican Governor of New Mexico, Edwin L. Mechem, should appoint a Republican as temporary successor, the Republican party would gain actual, as distinguished from its present nominal, control of the Senate.

The improbability of such an outcome, however, was reflected by the fact that there now were more Democrats in the Senate than Republicans and in the fact that it was the Democrats who were demanding decisive action.

The Democratic member of the subcommittee, Senator Thomas C. Hennings Jr. of Missouri, gave notice that he would file a dissenting report upholding Mr. Chavez' right to his seat.

The whole issue will go next week, probably on Tuesday, to the full Senate Rules Committee. The universal expectation in the Senate was that the full committee would sustain the Repub-

Continued on Page 14, Column 2

SHOWDOWN NEARS ON TAX EXEMPTION

Martin Admits Some Votes of Democrats Are Needed to Defeat Increase Plan

Special to THE NEW YORK TIMES.

WASHINGTON, March 11—The Administration will need the votes of some Democrats to win a showdown battle next week against higher personal income tax exemptions.

This was conceded by the Speaker of the House of Representatives, Joseph W. Martin Jr., Republican of Massachusetts. He said he realized some members of his party would break ranks on the issue but added:

"I am of the opinion that there will be enough responsible members of the Democratic party to more than offset what losses we may have."

His analysis was in response to a prediction by Representative Sam Rayburn of Texas, House minority leader, that the Democrats would win the fight for a $100 increase in present exemptions of $600 each for taxpayers and dependents.

Mr. Rayburn said after a caucus of House Democrats that he knew of none who would vote against the proposal. In that case, defection of half a dozen or so Republicans, depending on the absentee situation when the vote was taken, could bring victory for the Democrats.

Parliamentary preliminaries for the fight were completed this afternoon when the Rules Com-

Continued on Page 8, Column 6

Lasting Prevention of Polio Reported in Vaccine Tests

Dr. Salk Says Discovery Fights Off All 3 Kinds of Crippling Disease

By WILLIAM L. LAURENCE

Special to THE NEW YORK TIMES.

NEW ORLEANS, March 11—The latest tests on children with the anti-polio vaccine have revealed that the vaccine provides the body with lasting defensive powers against the three types of viruses causing the disease, it was reported tonight.

This was described as the long-sought answer to a vital question, making it practically certain not only that the vaccine will produce effective immunity against all the three types of polio but also that the immunity will be of the lasting type, possibly for the individual's lifetime.

This could mean that within the next three to five years polio, crippler of young and old alike, will join diphtheria, smallpox, typhoid and other formerly dreaded infectious diseases as plagues finally tamed and conquered by man.

The newest findings were described here tonight before the New Orleans Graduate Medical Assembly by Dr. Jonas E. Salk, of the Virus Research Laboratory, University of Pittsburgh School of Medicine.

Associated Press

Dr. Jonas E. Salk

Dr. Salk developed the vaccine against the three types of polio-producing viruses, using viruses that had been rendered incapable of producing the disease while they still retained their power to produce immunity.

Replying to remarks made this morning in Detroit by Dr. Albert

Continued on Page 22, Column 3

White Meets Backers of Young; Denies Central Compromise Bid

By ROBERT E. BEDINGFIELD

William White, president of the New York Central Railroad Company, had two important visitors in his offices at 230 Park Avenue yesterday: Clint W. Murchison and Sid W. Richardson.

They are the Texas millionaires who bought 800,000 shares of Central stock—one-eighth of the outstanding shares—last month from the Chesapeake and Ohio Railway Company to help their friend Robert R. Young in his attempt to wrest control of the $2,600,000,000 New York Central System from its present management.

Versions of the events leading to the meeting differed sharply.

Mr. White said Mr. Murchison had arranged it on his own motion. But the Texans said it had been requested by John J. McCloy, chairman of the Chase National Bank, of which Percy J. Ebbott is president.

Mr. Ebbott is a Central director. The Chase National Bank was the trustee for the 800,000 shares of Central stock before they were sold by the C. & O.

Mr. McCloy, through a spokesman, said last night that the request for the meeting had originated with Mr. Murchison. But a spokesman for Mr. Young insisted yesterday that the visit had been in response to an appeal from the Central forces for a Young representative to discuss settlement of their differences.

Mr. White branded as a "plain lie" intimations that the Central management might be seeking a compromise with Mr. Young.

Mr. White summoned reporters late yesterday afternoon to deny the "compromise" rumors that had spread through Wall Street and the Grand Central Terminal area after it was dis-

Continued on Page 36, Column 3

"All the News That's Fit to Print"

The New York Times.

LATE CITY EDITION
Clearing and continued cold today; fair tonight and tomorrow.
Temperature Range Today—Max., 45; Min., 32
Temperature Yesterday—Max., 44; Min., 32
Full U. S. Weather Bureau Report, Page 62

VOL. CIII. No. 35,131. Entered as Second-Class Matter. Post Office, New York, N. Y. NEW YORK, THURSDAY, APRIL 1, 1954. Times Square, New York 36, N. Y. Telephone Lackawanna 4-1000 FIVE CENTS

H-BOMB CAN WIPE OUT ANY CITY, STRAUSS REPORTS AFTER TESTS; U. S. RESTUDIES PLANT DISPERSAL

SOVIET IN BID TO JOIN NATO; U. S. SAYS 'NO'

OFFER BY MOLOTOV

He Urges West to Enter All-European Pact—Deplores 'Cold War'

Text of Soviet note to West on European security, Page 4.

By HARRISON E. SALISBURY

Special to The New York Times.

MOSCOW, March 31—The Soviet Union has proposed that the United States and West European states join a Soviet-sponsored general European security treaty. In return the Soviet Union is prepared to examine the question of assuming membership in the North Atlantic Treaty Organization.

The Soviet diplomatic move was contained in a note Vyacheslav M. Molotov, Soviet Foreign Minister, handed to Charles E. Bohlen, United States Ambassador, and his British and French diplomatic colleagues, Sir William Hayter and Louis Joxe.

There were qualifications and provisos, both written and implied, in Mr. Molotov's proposal, which was transmitted by the Western Ambassadors to Washington, London and Paris.

But the essence of what Mr. Molotov suggested was plain—that as soon as possible the "cold war," should be called off.

[The United States rejected the Soviet proposals. A State Department spokesman said the Soviet Government simply was continuing its effort to block the development of West European security. Paris sources called the Soviet note an attempt to spread confusion on the European Defense Community Treaty and to undermine the Atlantic alliance. British sources termed the Soviet suggestion of joining the alliance "just a Trojan horse."]

Defense Plan Main Target

The Soviet Foreign Minister made it plain that his immediate target was the European Defense Community.

But Mr. Molotov said the Atlantic alliance was another matter.

Mr. Molotov suggested that his proposed all-European organization and the Atlantic alliance be placed in balance. He proposed that all European powers, plus the United States, could join the Soviet-sponsored organization while the Soviet Union might become a member of the Atlantic alliance.

Mr. Molotov noted that the world was facing the peril of war in which atomic and hydrogen bombs threatened "incalculable disaster," including the annihilation of peaceful peoples, the wiping out of whole cities, of contemporary industry, culture and science, of "ancient centers of civilization" as well as "the great capitals of the states of the world."

Mr. Molotov asserted that in this moment all the world powers bore an especially great responsibility and said the Soviet Union

Continued on Page 5, Column 3

France Ousts Juin For Anti-Pact Talk

The New York Times

Marshal Alphonse P. Juin

Special to The New York Times.

PARIS, Thursday, April 1—Marshal Alphonse-Pierre Juin was disciplined by the French Cabinet at a special meeting early this morning for his speech against the European army treaty and for a snub to Premier Joseph Laniel. The

Continued on Page 7, Column 3

PRESIDENT BACKS FIRM ASIA POLICY

Supports 'United Action' Plan of Dulles—Senator Douglas Urges Facing War Risk

By WILLIAM S. WHITE

Special to The New York Times.

WASHINGTON, March 31—President Eisenhower made it plain today that this Government was deeply committed to "united action" against any Communist effort to overrun Southeast Asia.

He underwrote every word uttered by his Secretary of State, John Foster Dulles, in proclaiming that policy in a speech two nights ago.

[The Soviet Foreign Ministry in Moscow denied Mr. Dulles' assertion that Foreign Minister Molotov had agreed the Geneva conference would not be a five-power meeting.]

The President defined "united action" as primarily the responsibility of the free peoples directly under threat. He declared also that, speaking generally, the United States could put itself under no greater disadvantages than by spreading its ground forces and other forces about the

Continued on Page 12, Column 4

I. L. A. INSURGENTS REJECT PAY RISE, STALL PIER PEACE

Eisenhower, Putting Local Action First, Says U. S. Is Prepared to Cooperate

By A. H. RASKIN

Insurgent elements in the old International Longshoremen's Association yesterday killed a union-inspired move to end their strike, the longest and costliest in the port's history.

The union's sixty-two-member wage-scale committee spurned an employer pay offer and demanded a contract that would make the I. L. A. sole bargaining agent for the 24,000 workers on New York and New Jersey piers.

The shipping industry retorted that it could not legally sign such an agreement until the National Labor Relations Board decided whether the old union or its American Federation of Labor rival was entitled to speak for the dock workers.

The only remaining hope for a quick end to the twenty-seven-day tie-up was the possibility that the union might order the strikers back to the piers after the labor board in Washington had ruled on a new election. A ruling is expected before the end of this week.

At a City Hall conference with Deputy Mayor Henry Epstein, I. L. A. leaders authorized a statement that the sooner the board handed down its ruling the sooner the men would be back on the job. However, they shied away from any clear-cut promise that the strike would be called off as soon as the board acted.

President Watching Strike

In Washington, President Eisenhower said the Government was alert to the strike situation and was prepared to take whatever action might be necessary to cope with it, in cooperation with state and city authorities. The President added that the White House would be guided by this rule: Everything is handled locally as long as it can be.

The collapse of the back-to-work effort here speeded Federal plans to obtain a blanket injunction banning pickets and "loiterers" from the waterfront. Charles T. Douds, regional director of the National Labor Relations Board, laid the groundwork for such an injunction by issuing a sweeping complaint against the I. L. A. last night.

The complaint, described by members of Mr. Douds' staff as the most drastic ever issued by the board, accused the old union and its associates of having intimidated dock workers through mass picketing, blocking pier entrances, physical assaults, overturning automobiles, slashing tires and congregating in large groups" to harass non-strikers.

Labor board attorneys are expected to go into Federal Court today to ask for an injunction based on the Douds complaint. Its purpose would be to halt all picketing and other interference

Continued on Page 47, Column 4

NEW PLANS NEEDED

Defense Experts to Go to Work at Once on Factory Shifts

Special to The New York Times.

WASHINGTON, March 31—Dispersal plans for defense production plants in major cities will have to be redrawn in the light of today's hydrogen bomb disclosures.

Plans for dispersing defense production plants to date have been based upon a ten-mile radius of "immediate danger," which officials conceded was outdated.

Reliable sources indicated the Administration's defense planners were scheduled to go to work at once to draw a new set of criteria for plant dispersal.

The aim of the plant dispersal program is to get new key production plants outside probable target areas. To make this attractive, the Government offers builders of such plants accelerated tax amortization certificates permitting them to write off the cost of the plants for tax purposes in five instead of the normal twenty or more years.

Another plan, effective tomorrow, to insure control of materials and production in event of atomic or hydrogen-bomb attack, was announced by the Government today. Nominal account will be kept of available materials and production facilities so that an orderly but rapid expansion for military atomic production and construction will be possible in an emergency.

Eighty-nine Surveys Undertaken

The industry dispersal program is under the supervision of the Office of Defense Mobilization but is handled by the Area Development Division of the Business and Defense Services Administration within the Department of Commerce.

The Area Development group so far has organized committees to make dispersal plans in many key communities. Of eighty-nine committees that have undertaken such surveys, thirty-five have reported and their plans have been approved by the Office of Defense Mobilization. Among these is the committee for the New York City metropolitan area, which completed its work last month.

Officials predicted that the New York City survey, as well as the others, probably would have to be redone in the light of the facts learned about the destructiveness of the hydrogen bomb.

In announcing the new Defense Materials System, the Business and Defense Services Administration explained it would

Continued on Page 23, Column 2

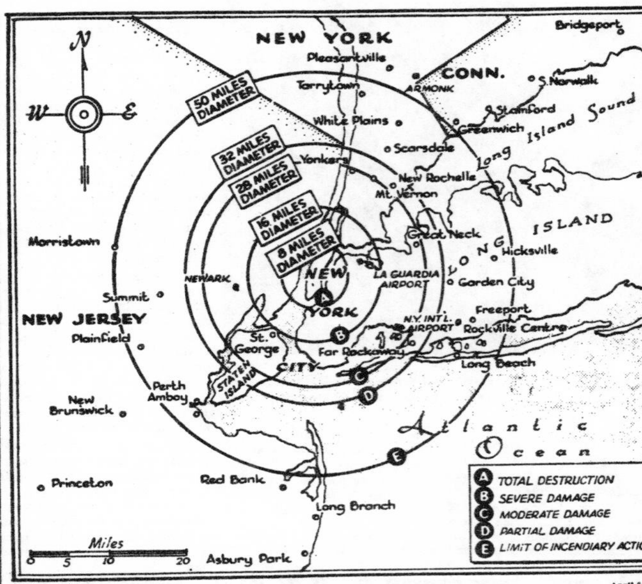

The New York Times April 1, 1954

Extent to which a hydrogen bomb explosion could devastate New York and its environs

VAST POWER BARED

March 1 Explosion Was Equivalent to Millions of Tons of TNT

Text of Strauss statement and conference transcript, Page 20.

By WILLIAM L. LAURENCE

Special to The New York Times.

WASHINGTON, March 31—The United States can now build a hydrogen bomb big enough to destroy any city.

In revealing this today, Rear Admiral Lewis L. Strauss, chairman of the United States Atomic Energy Commission, hinted that such a bomb could be delivered by plane.

The bomb tested at the Eniwetok proving grounds on March 1, Admiral Strauss announced, provided "a stupendous blast in the megaton range." He said it was "double that of the calculated estimate." A megaton is equivalent to 1,000,000 tons of TNT.

The explosive power attained in the test was reported by a member of the Joint Congressional Committee on Atomic Energy as twelve to fourteen megatons. This represents an explosive force 600 to 700 times that of the bombs that destroyed Hiroshima and Nagasaki.

No Limit to Bomb Size

Admiral Strauss made his statement at the President's news conference. He declared that the hydrogen bomb could be made as large as desired—"large enough to take out a city, to destroy a city."

"How big a city?," he was asked.

"Any city!"

"New York?"

"The metropolitan area, yes," he replied.

Admiral Strauss explained later that by "metropolitan area" he meant the heart of Manhattan and not the actual metropolitan area, which covers 3,550 square miles.

[Prime Minister Churchill, yielding to Opposition pressure, agreed to debate the Government's policy on the hydrogen bomb in the House of Commons Monday.]

Despite the hydrogen bomb's enormous power, Admiral Strauss said, the test was "at no time out of control." Furthermore, he gave the nation and the world the assurance given to him by scientists that it was "impossible for any such test or series of tests to get out of control."

Admiral Strauss' appearance at the President's press conference was at President Eisenhower's request. He made available to the American people portions of the report he had made to President Eisenhower yesterday on the hydrogen bomb tests in the Pacific.

The tests of hydrogen weapons on March 1 and 26, he said, have "added enormous potential to our military posture." He later amplified this remark with a statement that "the results of these

Continued on Page 21, Column 4

Senate Unit Votes Changes President Asked in Taft Act

By JOSEPH A. LOFTUS

Special to The New York Times.

WASHINGTON, March 31—The Senate Labor Committee approved a Taft-Hartley revision bill today with the Democrats crying "steamroller." The vote was 7 to 6 along party lines.

The bill deals only with President Eisenhower's recommendations, minus an Administration proposal to require Federally conducted elections among workers before a strike could be called.

Another Administration proposal, for standards to conserve union welfare funds, will be dealt with separately after an inquiry.

The House Labor Committee expects to report a bill on the same subject next week. It will contain many more revisions than the Senate bill.

Two provisions dealing with state powers were added to the Senate committee draft today just before the final vote to report a bill. They are certain to be fought vigorously.

One of these new sections deals with state emergencies. As finally approved, it reads:

"Nothing in this act shall be construed to interfere with the enactment and enforcement by the states of laws to deal in emergencies with labor disputes which, if permitted to occur or continue, will constitute a clear and present danger to the health or safety of the people of the state; provided, that no state shall be authorized by this subsection to take action in any labor dispute in which the Federal Government is acting pursuant to Sections 206 to 210, inclusive, of this act."

Sections 206 to 210 are the national emergency provisions of the Taft-Hartley Act. When these were invoked, state action would be superseded, but the

Continued on Page 34, Column 3

HOUSING BAN FOES CLAIM A 'VICTORY'

G.O.P. House Chiefs Foresee 33,000 Units in Fiscal '55 —Eisenhower 'Delighted'

Special to The New York Times.

WASHINGTON, March 31—What had been intended as a defeat for the Eisenhower Administration developed as a probable victory today as a parliamentary tangle over public housing legislation began unraveling.

President Eisenhower himself said he was delighted at the outcome.

Republican leaders of the House of Representatives already had claimed a victory by interpreting the mix-up, which occurred in the House yesterday, as meaning that the Public Housing Administration is free to go ahead with plans for construction of 33,000 to 35,000 new low-rent public housing units.

Today, the leaders moved to provide authority for an additional 35,000 units in the year starting July 1, 1955, by supporting an amendment to a general housing bill that comes before the House tomorrow.

Their aim is to give the President a legislative green light to carry out the first two years of his four-year program for 35,000 new units a year.

Action by Opposition

Yesterday's confusion in the House resulted from the attempt of public housing opponents, led by Representative Howard W. Smith, Democrat of Virginia, to kill the entire program by striking from a pending appropriations bill a "rider" allowing construction of 20,000 new units in the year starting next July 1.

The rider was eliminated from the bill on a point of order raised by Mr. Smith, who successfully challenged it as legislation on an appropriations bill in violation of House rules.

Killing the rider, according to Mr. Smith, would leave the Government without authority to start any new projects after next July 1. He based this position on an existing law, enacted as a rider on the same appropriations bill last year, limiting new construction to 20,000 units in the present fiscal year and prohibiting any further commitments without Congressional authorization.

As soon as Mr. Smith had com-

Continued on Page 34, Column 4

EISENHOWER SIGNS TAX CUT MEASURE

Excise Reductions Effective Today—President Voices Hope of Business Gain

By JOHN D. MORRIS

Special to The New York Times.

WASHINGTON, March 31—President Eisenhower signed the $999,000,000 excise tax reduction bill into law today. He voiced hope that the damage to Federal revenues would be offset to some degree by the resulting stimulation of business.

Federal sales taxes on a long list of items, from pocketbooks to household appliances, consequently will be reduced sharply as of 12:01 A. M. tomorrow. The savings are expected to be passed along to consumers, at least in part, by most of the industries affected. On a majority of the items covered, the tax cut amounts to 50 per cent.

Enactment of the bill adds an estimated $999,000,000 to the Federal deficit of $2,928,000,000 projected by President Eisenhower for the 1955 fiscal year, which starts next July 1.

On the ground that the Government could not afford such revenue losses in addition to those involved in other recent and pending tax cuts, the Administration had opposed any broad-scale reduction of excises at this time.

The President told his news conference that, nevertheless, he was accepting the bill wholeheartedly. From the beginning, he explained, there was a difference of opinion on the revenue effects. One school of thought, he noted, believes that the reductions can stimulate business to

Continued on Page 16, Column 7

10 Pupils Burned to Death in School Near Buffalo

Associated Press Wirephoto

Smoke and flames billow from frame annex of an elementary school in Cheektowaga, N. Y.

Special to The New York Times.

BUFFALO, March 31—Ten sixth grade pupils in the Cleveland Hill elementary school died today in a fire that trapped them in a room of the school's one-story frame annex on Mapleview Drive in suburban Cheektowaga. Twenty-two other persons, nineteen of them children, were burned or injured and taken to hospitals. The school has an enrollment of more than 1,200. Hundreds of pupils of the adjoining Cleveland Hill High School were sent home. The fire followed a blast that was described variously as an explosion and as "a

Continued on Page 24, Column 3

Reds in Mass Attack Against Dienbienphu

By TILLMAN DURDIN

Special to The New York Times.

SAIGON, Vietnam, March 31—Vietminh forces last night launched a new mass attack against the French defenses at Dienbienphu.

[The French High Command in Hanoi said three Vietminh divisions were assaulting Dienbienphu, The United Press reported.]

During a night of savage fighting the Communist-led Vietminh troops established a foothold within the French positions. However, they were pushed back this morning at some points by desperately resisting French Union contingents.

A late bulletin from French headquarters here said violent combat continued today. Bad weather yesterday facilitated the beginning of the Vietminh assault, but as the clouds cleared

Continued on Page 7, Column 1

Calm in Middle East Urged by President

By The United Press.

WASHINGTON, March 31—President Eisenhower called on Israel and the Arab states today to restrain their extremists and permit other nations to help them settle their disputes.

He declined to answer a question at his news conference as to whether he believed the bitter Arab-Israeli feud, which recently erupted into new violence, should be referred to the United Nations Security Council. However, he said the United Nations had the full support of the United States in its plan to seek harmony in the Middle East.

General Eisenhower said the United States had been giving strong support to the plan to develop the resources of the area, including the water resources of the Jordan River, and hoped the plan would be successful.

He said the Israeli-Arab issue was so charged with emotional

Continued on Page 2, Column 3

Color Film of First H-Bomb Test Is Previewed by Press in Capital

Special to The New York Times.

WASHINGTON, March 31—The world's most fearsome weapon, the fusion bomb, was shown in action for the first time here in public today before an audience of representatives of the press and other information media.

They saw a reproduction on color film of the phenomena that followed the explosion of the first full-scale hydrogen weapon on the Pacific proving grounds in the Marshall Islands in November, 1952.

The event marked the entry of mankind into the Hydrogen Age, taking the fateful step from the kiloton (thousands of tons) to the megaton (millions of tons) of explosive power in terms of TNT.

The film was released by the Atomic Energy Commission and the Department of Defense for public issuance by the Federal Civil Defense Administration. It was intended for general release at 6 P. M. April 7, and reviews of it were to be embargoed until then.

However, a descriptive review by a syndicated columnist appeared in newspapers a few hours after the showing. Because of this The Times is publishing its review now.

The test in November, 1952, was known as Operation Ivy and the device tested was known as Mike. At the time it was made the explosion was the greatest in history. Since then, however, it has been greatly exceeded by the test explosions on March 1 and 26.

The film opens with an introduction by President Eisenhower, who recites an excerpt from his historic address before the United Nations on Dec. 8, 1953, relating to the need of the peoples of

Continued on Page 23, Column 2

"All the News
That's Fit to Print"

The New York Times.

LATE CITY EDITION
Fair and cool today. Mostly sunny, continued cool tomorrow.
Temperature Range Today—Max., 63; Min., 52
Temperature Yesterday—Max., 69; Min., 61
Full U. S. Weather Bureau Report, Page 51

Copyright, 1954, by The New York Times Company.

VOL. CIII...No. 35,178. Entered as Second-Class Matter. Post Office, New York, N. Y. NEW YORK, TUESDAY, MAY 18, 1954. Times Square, New York 36, N. Y. Telephone Lackawanna 4-1000 FIVE CENTS

HIGH COURT BANS SCHOOL SEGREGATION; 9-TO-0 DECISION GRANTS TIME TO COMPLY

McCarthy Hearing Off a Week as Eisenhower Bars Report

SENATOR IS IRATE

President Orders Aides Not to Disclose Details of Top-Level Meeting

President's letter and excerpts from transcript, Pages 24, 25, 26.

By W. H. LAWRENCE
Special to The New York Times.

WASHINGTON, May 17—A secrecy directive by President Eisenhower resulted today in an abrupt recess for at least a week of the Senate's Army-McCarthy hearings.

Democratic and Republican Senators, some publicly and some privately, predicted that the investigation might never resume in earnest. However, there were other Senators who insisted that the investigation would go on to completion.

The recess was voted after Herbert Brownell Jr., the Attorney General, disclosed formally that criminal prosecutions might be instituted against those involved in the "preparation and dissemination" of an altered, condensed but still confidential Federal Bureau of Investigation report. This was offered in evidence last week by Senator Joseph R. McCarthy, Republican of Wisconsin.

Republicans outvoted Democrats 4 to 3 on the Senate Permanent Subcommittee of Investigation to recess the hearings until 10 o'clock next Monday morning. They acted amid charges and denials that the way was being prepared for a "whitewash."

Constitutional Division Cited

President Eisenhower cited the constitutional separation of powers between the Executive and Legislative branches in directing that details and conversations at a "high level" Administration meeting on Jan. 21 must be withheld from the committee.

Testimony already has been given that top White House, Justice and Defense officials had made plans at that conference to deal with Senator McCarthy.

The Presidential order served effectively to seal the lips of John G. Adams, the Army's regular counselor, about what Sherman Adams, the chief Presidential assistant, said to him in advising that a written report be prepared on how Senator McCarthy and his chief counsel, Roy M. Cohn, persistently sought preferential treatment for Pvt. G. David Schine.

Before his induction, Mr. Schine was an unpaid consultant to the McCarthy subcommittee, the same group that is now conducting the hearings under the temporary chairmanship of Senator Karl E. Mundt, Republican of South Dakota.

Senator McCarthy angrily denounced today's Eisenhower order as "an Iron Curtain." His ire was shared, but in more restrained terms, by all the Republican and Democratic members of the investigating committee.

The week's postponement of

Continued on Page 24, Column 1

Communist Arms Unloaded in Guatemala By Vessel From Polish Port, U. S. Learns

State Department Views News Gravely Because of Red Infiltration

Special to The New York Times.

WASHINGTON, May 17—The State Department said today that it had reliable information that "an important shipment of arms" had been sent from Communist-controlled territory to Guatemala.

It said the arms, now being unloaded at Puerto Barrios, Guatemala, had been shipped from Stettin, a former German Baltic seaport, which has been occupied by Communist Poland since World War II. The Guatemalan regime has been frequently accused of being influenced by Communists.

"Because of the origin of these arms, the point of their embarkation, their destination and the quantity of arms involved, the Department of State considers that this is a development of gravity," the announcement said.

A freighter arrived at Puerto

The New York Times May 18, 1954
Site of arms arrival (cross)

Embassy Says Nation of Central America May Buy Munitions Anywhere

Barrios last Saturday, the State Department reported, carrying a large shipment of armament consigned to the Guatemalan Government.

The State Department did not divulge the exact quantity of the arms, their nature or where they had been manufactured.

Reliable sources told The New York Times, however, that ten freight car loads of goods listed in the manifest as "hardware" had been unloaded from this ship and sent to the city of Guatemala since Sunday. Guatemala is 150 miles from Puerto Barrios. The

Continued on Page 10, Column 5

REACTION OF SOUTH

'Breathing Spell' for Adjustment Tempers Region's Feelings

By JOHN N. POPHAM
Special to The New York Times.

CHATTANOOGA, Tenn., May 17—The South's reaction to the Supreme Court's decision outlawing racial segregation in public schools appeared to be tempered considerably today.

The time lag allowed for carrying out the required transitions seemed to be the major factor in that reaction.

Southern leaders of both races in political, educational and community service fields expressed comment that covered a wide range. Some spoke bitter words that verged on defiance. Others ranged from sharp disagreement to predictions of peaceful and successful adjustment in accord with the ruling.

But underneath the surface of much of the comment, it was evident that many Southerners recognized that the decision had laid down the legal principle rejecting segregation in public education facilities.

They also noted that it had left open a challenge to the region to join in working out a program of necessary changes in the present bi-racial school systems.

Three of the most illustrative viewpoints were those expressed by Govs. James F. Byrnes of South Carolina and Herman Talmadge of Georgia, and Harold Fleming, a spokesman for the Southern Regional Council, the most effective interracial organization in the South.

Byrnes Sees Reversal

Governor Byrnes, who has vigorously defended the doctrine of separate but equal facilities in education, said that he was "shocked to learn that the court has reversed itself" with regard to past rulings on that doctrine.

However, Governor Byrnes, a former Associate Justice of the Supreme Court, noted that the tribunal had not yet delivered its final decree setting forth the time and terms for ending segregation in the schools.

Pointing out that South Carolina, a party in the litigation before the court, had until October to present arguments on how the Supreme Court should order the implementation of the decision, Governor Byrnes declared "I urge all of our people, white and colored, to exercise restraint and preserve order."

Governor Talmadge repeatedly has vowed there "will never be mixed schools while I am Governor" and has warned that school integration would lead to "blood-

Continued on Page 20, Column 1

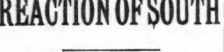

Associated Press Wirephoto

LEADERS IN SEGREGATION FIGHT: Lawyers who led battle before U. S. Supreme Court for abolition of segregation in public schools congratulate one another as they leave court after announcement of decision. Left to right: George E. C. Hayes, Thurgood Marshall and James M. Nabrit.

1896 RULING UPSET

'Separate but Equal' Doctrine Held Out of Place in Education

Text of Supreme Court decision is printed on Page 15.

By LUTHER A. HUSTON
Special to The New York Times.

WASHINGTON, May 17—The Supreme Court unanimously outlawed today racial segregation in public schools.

Chief Justice Earl Warren read two opinions that put the stamp of unconstitutionality on school systems in twenty-one states and the District of Columbia where segregation is permissive or mandatory.

The court, taking cognizance of the problems involved in the integration of the school systems concerned, put over until the next term, beginning in October, the formulation of decrees to effectuate its 9-to-0 decision.

The opinions set aside the "separate but equal" doctrine laid down by the Supreme Court in 1896.

"In the field of public education," Chief Justice Warren said, "the doctrine of 'separate but equal' has no place. Separate educational facilities are inherently unequal."

He stated the question and supplied the answer as follows:

"We come then to the question presented: Does segregation of children in public schools solely on the basis of race, even though physical facilities and other 'tangible' factors may be equal, deprive the children of the minority group of equal educational opportunities? We believe that it does."

States Stressed Rights

The court's opinion does not apply to private schools. It is directed entirely at public schools.

It does not affect the "separate but equal doctrine" as applied on railroads and other public carriers entirely within states that have such restrictions.

The principal ruling of the court was in four cases involving state laws. The states' right to operate separated schools had been argued before the court on two occasions by representatives of South Carolina, Virginia, Kansas and Delaware.

In these cases, consolidated in one opinion, the high court held that school segregation deprived Negroes of "the equal protection of the laws guaranteed by the Fourteenth Amendment."

The other opinion involved the District of Columbia. Here schools have been segregated since Civil War days under laws passed by Congress.

"In view of our decision that the Constitution prohibits the states from maintaining racially segregated public schools," the Chief Justice said, "it would be unthinkable that the same Constitution would impose a lesser duty on the Federal Government.

"We hold that racial segregation in the public schools of the District of Columbia is a denial

Continued on Page 14, Column 6

SOVIET BIDS VIENNA CEASE 'INTRIGUES'

Envoy Warns Austrian Chief on Inciting East Zone—Raab Denies Charges

By JOHN MacCORMAC
Special to The New York Times.

VIENNA, May 17—The Soviet Union warned Austria today to put an end to "hostile and subversive intrigues" against the Soviet occupation forces, or Soviet authorities would do it themselves.

Ivan I. Ilyichev, Soviet High Commissioner, reverted to a practice of early post-war days by summoning Chancellor Julius Raab and Vice Chancellor Adolf Schaerf to give them this warning. The Chancellor denied the Soviet charges.

Mr. Ilyichev said the Austrian Government had been guilty of staging actions hostile to the Soviet while the Austrian press had published daily slanderous and inciting announcements about the Soviet Union and Soviet occupation troops.

The cessation of Soviet control over the movement of freight, said the High Commissioner, was abused to smuggle militarist literature and provocative incitements into the Soviet zone with the connivance of the Austrian Minister of Interior.

When Soviet authorities ordered the removal of anti-Soviet placards in their zone, the minister instructed his subordinates to disregard the order and notes to disregard the order and the Government approved his action, said Mr. Ilyichev.

He added that the Government, and particularly the Minister of Interior, had tolerated militarist propaganda by former soldiers' organizations and dissemination of propaganda for another Anschluss (union) with Germany.

The High Commissioner reminded the Government leaders that since Austria had not ob-

Continued on Page 9, Column 3

City Colleges' Board Can't Pick Chairman

The Board of Higher Education was unable to elect a chairman at its annual meeting last night at Hunter College.

A spokesman said it was the first time "within memory of board officials" that such a situation had occurred.

Nineteen of the twenty-one members of the board, which governs the four municipal colleges, attended.

Two members nominated for the one-year-term were unable to attain the required majority of eleven votes. They were Joseph B. Cavallaro, who was up for re-election as chairman, and Dr. Harry J. Carman, who was restored to the board on March 2 by Mayor Wagner.

The election was laid over until June 15.

INDO-CHINA PARLEY WEIGHS TWO PLANS

French and Rebel Peace Bids Will Be Studied Jointly as a Basis for Settlement

By THOMAS J. HAMILTON
Special to The New York Times.

GENEVA, May 17—The Far East conference decided today to take up French and Vietminh proposals jointly as a basis for settlement of the war in Indo-China.

The secret session, which lasted three and a half hours, was generally recognized as the opening round in what may turn out to be a long process of negotiation. Another secret meeting will be held tomorrow.

Western delegates felt that Vyacheslav M. Molotov, Soviet Foreign Minister, was continuing to give the impression that in the end he might throw Moscow's influence on the side of an agreed settlement.

However, the West failed to obtain answers to the two fundamental questions that are expected to determine whether the negotiations here will have any chance of success: Will the Communists agree to a separate settlement for Laos and Cambodia, and will they agree to an armistice in Vietnam without at the same time requiring a political settlement?

The conference will address itself tomorrow to the issue of Laos and Cambodia. The two Indo-Chinese states are relatively free from Communist infiltration, and their leaders contend, with the support of the French, that the only thing that needs to be done is the withdrawal of the Communists.

The Laos-Cambodia and Vietnam issues were discussed inconclusively today after the delegates had devoted the first part of their meeting to the intricate dispute over evacuation of French Union wounded from Dienbienphu, seized by the Communist-

Continued on Page 2, Column 2

2 TAX PROJECTS DIE IN ESTIMATE BOARD

Beer Levy and More Parking Collections Killed—Payroll Impost Still Weighed

By CHARLES G. BENNETT

Two possible new revenue sources were definitely eliminated yesterday by the Board of Estimate in executive session. They were the proposed 1-cent-a-glass tax on beer and the suggestion to extend metered parking into hours now "free."

In a three-hour City Hall parley the board failed once more to decide on a new impost or imposts to balance the 1954-55 budget of $1,639,438,325. Mayor Wagner said after the meeting that the highly controversial 3 per cent sales tax on commercial services was "still one of the taxes at the top of the list."

Saying he felt the Board of Estimate was close to a decision on the knotty tax question, the Mayor added that "there's no decision to discard any tax" except the two mentioned above, and that at the same time "no tax is inevitable."

The board will wrestle with the tax question again in executive session on Thursday at 2:30 P. M. The Mayor said the City Council, which is holding up a bill to impose the sales tax extension, would be invited to send a delegation to the Thursday session.

Mr. Wagner asserted that he would like to see the Board of Estimate decide the tax question

Continued on Page 32, Column 5

MORETTIS' LAWYER MUST BARE TALKS

Jersey Court Orders Counsel to Racketeers in Bergen to Divulge Data to Grand Jury

By GEORGE CABLE WRIGHT
Special to The New York Times.

TRENTON, May 17—The New Jersey Supreme Court today ordered a lawyer who once had represented top Bergen County racketeers to divulge to a grand jury the substance of confidential talks with those clients.

The four-to-three decision reversed the rulings of two lower courts. Involved was the refusal more than a year ago of John E. Selser, Hackensack attorney, to answer four questions put to him by the Bergen County grand jury.

Mr. Selser told the jury that one of his clients, Willie Moretti, slain gambler, had given him the names of persons connected with Walter G. Winne who had received protection money from syndicate gamblers. Mr. Winne, superseded prosecutor of Bergen County, was acquitted last week of nonfeasance in office.

But the attorney balked when asked to reveal these and the names of other persons who, his clients alleged, had been paid protection money or who had received political contributions on the state and county level. He pleaded that his lips were sealed by the duty of "nondisclosure of confidential communications between client and attorney."

Represented Morettis, Others

Mr. Selser had represented Moretti, who was murdered in Cliffside Park in October, 1951, and his brother, the late Salvatore Moretti, for many years. He also was the attorney of record for Joe Adonis, Arthur Longano and James (Piggy) Lynch. The last four were among five men convicted and sent to prison in May, 1952, as the leaders of the Bergen gambling syndicate.

Mr. Selser appeared before the grand jury in February, 1953. The present court action was brought by the state after his refusal to answer the above questions on that occasion and two other questions. The latter pertained to testimony by John J. Dickerson, former Republican state chairman, before the same grand jury.

Mr. Dickerson had testified that Adonis and the two Morettis visited his home in November, 1950, and that Willie told him then that $225,000 in protection money had been paid to Harold

Continued on Page 36, Column 3

RULING TO FIGURE IN '54 CAMPAIGN

Decision Tied to Eisenhower—Russell Leads Southerners in Criticism of Court

By WILLIAM S. WHITE
Special to The New York Times.

WASHINGTON, May 17—Congress as a whole grappled gingerly today with the profound political implications of the Supreme Court's anti-segregation decision.

It became clear at once—and by both parties was accepted in private as inevitable—that the court's action would figure importantly in the coming Congressional election campaigns.

Publicly, however, the Republicans and the non-Southern Democrats on the whole maintained silence. The Southerners, all angry or sorrowing in one degree or another, were quickly articulate and split among themselves into at least three factions.

One Southern group, by all the indications not a large one, was openly defiant of the court, as typified by the comment of Senator James O. Eastland of Mississippi.

"The South," Mr. Eastland said, "will not abide by nor obey this legislative decision by a political court."

A second Southern group, while not openly challenging the court, began to threaten efforts to force an alteration of its view, as illustrated by the comment of

Continued on Page 20, Column 2

Churchill Asks Negotiated Peace With Guarantees for Indo-China

By DREW MIDDLETON
Special to The New York Times.

LONDON, May 17—Britain will seek effective international guarantees for any peace settlement in Indo-China, Prime Minister Churchill declared today.

Negotiation of an "acceptable" settlement at the Geneva conference remains the immediate task of the British Government, Sir Winston emphasized in a statement to the House of Commons.

Until the outcome of that conference is known, he added, "final decisions" cannot be taken by the Government about the establishment of a collective defense system in Southeast Asia and the Western Pacific.

Peace by negotiation emerged from Sir Winston's cautious statement as the only policy that the Cabinet was ready to apply to the problem of Indo-China. Observers were struck by the fact that, aside from the Prime Minister's reference to the necessity of backing a settlement there with guarantees, the British position was substantially the same as when the Geneva conference began.

[Indonesia is considering asking India and Burma to join her in a nonaggression treaty with Communist China as a means of offsetting United States plans for a Southeast Asian alliance.]

Sir Winston's adherence to negotiation is acceptable to both major parties in the Commons,

Continued on Page 4, Column 3

Costello Is Sentenced to 5 Years, Fined $30,000 in U. S. Tax Case

By EDWARD RANZAL

Frank Costello was sentenced yesterday by Federal Judge John F. X. McGohey to five years in jail and fined $30,000 for income tax evasion.

The dapper, 61-year-old gambler was remanded immediately. Later Judge Harold R. Medina in the United States Court of Appeals refused to set bail pending appeal. Costello, who listened to the sentencing in icy-calm manner, was taken to the Federal House of Detention, 427 West Street.

Besides the jail sentence and the fines, Judge McGohey also assessed Costello for court costs. Lloyd F. MacMahon, chief assistant United States Attorney, said the costs would be about $5,000, only a fraction of what it cost the Government in its investigation, which began in earnest in 1952.

Costello was convicted Thursday night by a Federal court jury of five women and seven men of three counts of a four-count indictment. They found the gambler guilty of evading a total of $51,095 in taxes from 1947 through 1949.

In 1947 Costello evaded $22,563; in 1948, $13,786, and in 1949, $14,746. He was acquitted of the charge of evading taxes in 1946. Costello's attorney, Leo C. Fennelly, told Judge McGohey that the acquittal on this count meant that the gambler was entitled to a refund for that year.

Before the sentencing Mr. MacMahon said that for years Costello had schemed to cheat the Government out of taxes. He added that the gambler had concealed at least $140,000 of his income from 1947 through 1949, more than half his income.

Mr. MacMahon contended that Costello, by devious means, had concealed the receipt of his income as well as the source by using cash in every transaction where it was possible.

Evidence at the six-week trial, the prosecution said, showed that from 1937 through 1945 Costello deliberately underestimated his income by at least $202,000. The statute of limitations, he added, bars prosecution for the earlier tax evasions.

"Costello has spent a lifetime making money on the shady side

Continued on Page 36, Column 4

'Voice' Speaks in 34 Languages To Flash Court Ruling to World

Within an hour after the Supreme Court decision on school segregation yesterday afternoon, the Voice of America sent a news broadcast by shortwave to Eastern Europe.

The decision came in time for the regularly scheduled "Worldwide English Broadcast" at 2 o'clock. The broadcast was written in English on the Voice's central desk and was sent by teletype to the thirty-four language desks.

There it was translated and sent out in various foreign tongues all over the world as broadcast time arrived for each.

"The Supreme Court has ruled unanimously," the Voice said in its broadcast, "that racial segregation has no place in American public education. It held that separation of students on a racial basis denies equal educational opportunities.

"Chief Justice [Earl] Warren, reading the court's findings, said that the doctrine of providing separate but equal facilities has no place in public education. Separation of children solely because of race, he said, generates feelings in their hearts and minds which might never be undone. * * *

"The ruling in effect outlaws all segregation in public schools throughout the United States. The court held that to separate students is a denial of the due process of law guaranteed by the Fifth Amendment to the Constitution and equal opportunity

Continued on Page 15, Column 4

"All the News That's Fit to Print"

The New York Times.

LATE CITY EDITION
Some cloudiness with a few showers today. Fair tomorrow.
Temperature Range Today-Max., 86; Min., 70
Temperatures Yesterday-Max., 88.3; Min., 68.8
Full U. S. Weather Bureau Report, Page 47

VOL. CIII No. 35,242. Entered as Second-Class Matter. Post Office, New York, N. Y. NEW YORK, WEDNESDAY, JULY 21, 1954. Times Square, New York 36, N. Y. Telephone LAckawanna 4-1000 FIVE CENTS

INDOCHINA ARMISTICE IS SIGNED; VIETNAM SPLIT AT 17TH PARALLEL; U. S. FINDS IT CAN 'RESPECT' PACT

McCARTHY ACCEPTS COHN RESIGNATION, TRANSFERS SURINE

Puts the Assistant Counsel on Own Payroll—Panel Defers Any Action on La Venia

CONFIRMS REST OF STAFF

Carr Among 22 Approved—Senator Calls Loss of Cohn 'Great Victory' for Reds

Texts of Cohn letter, McCarthy statement are on Page 10.

By ANTHONY LEVIERO

Special to The New York Times

WASHINGTON, July 20—Senator Joseph R. McCarthy yielded today to the insistent demand for a staff housecleaning from a majority of the members of the Senate Permanent Subcommittee on Investigations.

The results, as the subcommittee met over a steak luncheon in the old Supreme Court chamber in the Capitol, were these:

¶Senator McCarthy reluctantly accepted the resignation of Roy M. Cohn, the subcommittee's chief counsel, denouncing those who had sought it and saying the result was a "great victory" for communism.

¶Mr. McCarthy transferred the controversial assistant counsel, Don Surine, from the subcommittee staff to his personal payroll, also with a vigorous defense of him.

Action on La Venia Deferred

Both these changes were personal actions of Senator McCarthy as chairman taken before the subcommittee met. In this way he headed off inevitable defeat on a staff housecleaning demanded by a majority of four of the seven members of the subcommittee led by Senator Charles E. Potter, Republican of Michigan.

The subcommittee itself then voted unanimously to withhold "without prejudice" confirmation of Thomas La Venia in his position as office manager and investigator until further consideration of his personal record.

The subcommittee then voted to confirm twenty-two other employes of the subcommittee in their present jobs. Among them were two others who had come under fire during the thirty-six days of the Army-McCarthy hearings that ended on June 17.

One was Francis P. Carr, staff director, who had been named as a principal in the controversy but was removed from that category before the hearings ended.

Juliana Approved

The other was James N. Juliana, a staff investigator, who assumed full responsibility during the hearings for cropping an Army colonel out of a photograph introduced in evidence. As produced by the McCarthy side, this photograph showed only Robert T. Stevens, Secretary of the Army, and Pvt. G. David Schine.

There was no discussion by the subcommittee on whether to oust Mr. Carr, who said he was staying "unless I am voted out." Senator McCarthy said that all votes today were unanimous.

On Capitol Hill the staff changes were regarded as one of the few reversals ever suffered by Mr. McCarthy in his Senatorial career which began in 1946.

The action today was a direct

Continued on Page 10, Column 3

Miss Connolly Breaks Leg, Out of U.S. Play

By The Associated Press.

SAN DIEGO, Calif., July 20—Maureen Connolly, the tennis queen, was so seriously injured when she was crushed against a big cement truck while riding her horse here today that she will be unable to defend her national title next month at Forest Hills, Queens.

Surgery and X-rays determined that the small bone in her lower right leg was broken and that muscles and tendons of the calf were damaged by a deep gash.

This definitely ends her hope of winning the United States championship for the fourth straight time.

She will hardly be able to get around, doctors said, by the start of the tournament on Aug. 28.

"Little Mo," who will be 20 on Sept. 17, was wheeled into surgery within an hour after reaching the hospital.

She was conscious when she

Continued on Page 21, Column 2

House Inquiry Asked Into a House Inquiry

By C. P. TRUSSELL

Special to The New York Times.

WASHINGTON, July 20—The House of Representatives was urged today to investigate one of its investigations.

At issue was the inquiry into tax-free educational and philanthropic foundations that began in May.

Early this month the investigators decided to hold no more public hearings. At that point the witnesses, including two committee researchers, had been eleven to one in criticism of foundations. The foundations were given permission to file sworn statements in rebuttal.

A resolution was introduced in the House this afternoon by Representative Jacob K. Javits, Republican of Manhattan. It called on the Rules Committee,

Continued on Page 30, Column 7

SHOWDOWN TODAY ON T.V.A. CURB SET

Democrats Decide to Permit Vote on President's Order for Power Contract

By WILLIAM M. BLAIR

Special to The New York Times.

WASHINGTON, July 20—A band of Senate Democrats agreed tonight to a showdown vote tomorrow afternoon in their fight against President Eisenhower's order to the Atomic Energy Commission to carry out a private power contract.

They intimated, however, that if defeated they would renew what Senate Republican leaders have called a filibuster against the important atomic energy bill.

The President's order directed the commission to negotiate a contract with a private utilities group to supply the Tennessee Valley Authority with power.

The Senate recessed at 9:37 P. M. after Senator William F. Knowland, the Republican Floor Leader, had said he hoped for a vote in the power fight tomorrow and completion of the bill by the same time tomorrow night.

He announced that he had instructed the Sergeant at Arms to set up cots in the Senate wing of the Capitol in the event it was necessary to work through the night to complete the entire atomic energy bill.

The Democrats' decision at a strategy meeting ended temporarily seven days of unlimited talking in the Senate that stalled the Administration's program.

Backed up behind the atomic

Continued on Page 8, Column 2

EISENHOWER LOSES ON PUBLIC HOUSING BY VOTE OF 234-156

House Rejects Plan to Build 140,000 Units in 4 Years—35,000 in One Voted

By CLAYTON KNOWLES

Special to The New York Times.

WASHINGTON, July 20—The House of Representatives killed the last real hope today to enact President Eisenhower's public housing program at this session of Congress.

By a vote of 234 to 156, it rejected a proposal sponsored by Democrats to write the President's request for 140,000 public housing units over a four-year period into the compromise housing bill that emerged last week from Senate-House conference.

Arrayed against the proposal were 155 Republicans and 79 Democrats. Supporting the President's position in the vote were 105 Democrats, 50 Republicans and one Independent.

Soon after this test, the House approved, 358 to 30, terms of the omnibus compromise on housing. It contained provision for only 35,000 units in a one-year extension of the public housing program. Many asserted that this authorization was meaningless because of restrictions in the provision. Some said not 10,000 units could be built under it.

Action Regarded as Final

The House action, which promises to create a major political issue for the Congressional campaign, was as good as final even though the Senate still has to ratify the conference report. The original Senate bill carried the President's public housing program, but it was pared, almost beyond recognition, in conference.

The general belief was that the Senate would not even attempt to reinstate the President's program since today's vote was the second in which the House had rejected it. On April 2 the House, then considering the bill for the first time, turned down the 140,000-unit program, 211 to 176.

Representative Brent Spence, Democrat of Kentucky, made the motion to reinstate the President's program, on the ground that, without it, individuals of low income could only gravitate to the slums.

Representative Jesse P. Wolcott, Republican of Michigan, defending the proposition that a unit of slum housing must be razed before a unit of public housing could be built, declared:

"With these limitations, we conferees believe we have done a masterful job on public housing

Continued on Page 16, Column 4

CAPITAL CAUTIOUS

Accepts in Principle—Bars Any Guarantee Except by Alliance

Special to The New York Times.

WASHINGTON, July 20—The United States Government will issue a unilateral statement tomorrow accepting in principle the terms of the Indochina cease-fire accord. It also will acknowledge its "ability to respect" such terms under the United Nations Charter, diplomatic officials disclosed tonight.

The decision to state the United States Government's position on the agreement—probably by President Eisenhower at his regular news conference tomorrow—was disclosed after diplomatic intelligence established the terms contained a clause permitting a free exchange of populations between northern and southern Vietnam.

For a period of one year, according to this understanding, no effort would be made to prevent movement between the two areas. Diplomatic officials attached the greatest importance to this clause, which they considered would avert the swallowing up of the anti-Communist and predominantly Catholic population of parts of northern Vietnam by the Red regime.

Interruption Is Temporary

Of only slightly less importance is a provision in the agreement whereby the right of the free areas of the partitioned Indochina States to receive foreign military assistance would be interrupted only temporarily, so that no interference with their sovereignty would be entailed.

It was understood the temporary restriction on the receipt of military assistance from the United States and other free nations would end after a period of "disengagement" during which forces would be withdrawn from existing front-line areas.

Diplomatic officials conversant with its terms held that the cease-fire generally came within the terms of the seven principles that President Eisenhower and Prime Minister Churchill laid down three weeks ago.

These included division of the

Continued on Page 3, Column 5

Associated Press Radiophoto

AGREE ON TRUCE: Pierre Mendès-France, French Premier, as he appeared yesterday with Pham Van Dong, Vietminh Foreign Minister, left, at French headquarters in Geneva. Behind them are Guy de la Tournelle, wearing eyeglasses, and Georges Boris, aides to French leader.

Arrests Here Bare 'Sure Thing' Racing Fraud by Radio

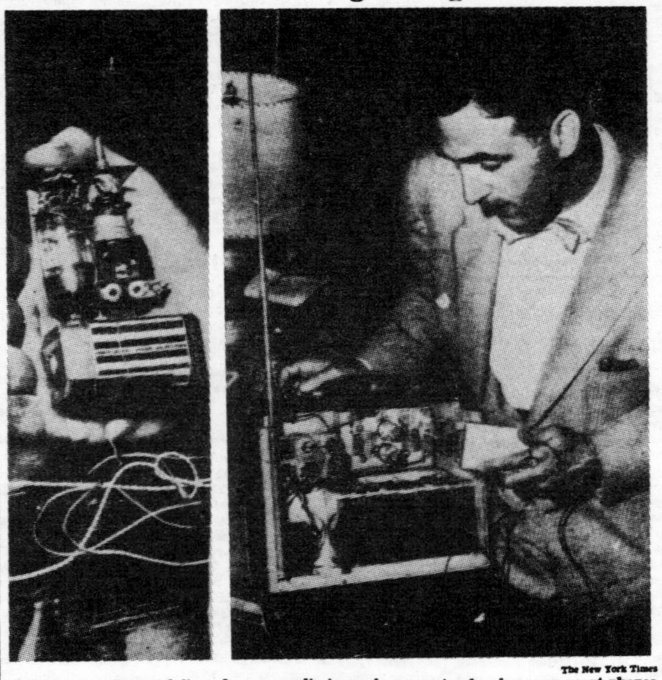

The New York Times

Pocket transmitter at left sends race results to receiver near track, whence an agent phones data to an associate posted near a betting parlor. This man, using transmitter built into suitcase at right, relays result to a better, who gets electronic impulses through concealed dimes on receiver shown in left hand above. Agent then bets on horse that won.

The police cracked down yesterday on a gambling ring that has been using Dick Tracy techniques, complete with purse-size transmitters and skin-shock radio receivers, to flash race results far in advance of official returns. Twenty-eight persons were rounded up in fast-hitting raids in Manhattan, Brooklyn and Queens. Fifty detectives and policemen, under the command of Supervising Assistant Chief Inspector James Nidds, fanned out through the three boroughs at 8 A. M. After the half-hour round-up, when the twenty-eight captives were paraded before Queens Assistant District Attorney Lawrence Peirez, a crime-comics story on the use of ingenious electronic devices was unfolded. Race-track plotters were pictured tapping

Continued on Page 23, Column 3

SENATORS TO PUSH GERMAN REARMING

Leading Republicans Will Urge Action This Year in Addition to Granting Sovereignty

By WILLIAM S. WHITE

Special to The New York Times.

WASHINGTON, July 20—Powerful Senate Republicans will advise the Eisenhower Administration that West German rearmament and sovereignty should be pushed this year.

They are prepared to suggest to the Administration that the United States-British plan to give sovereignty without the right to rearm, as an alternative to the faltering European Defense Community project, would not be realistic.

They will argue that implicit in sovereignty is the right of self-defense and that the two concepts cannot be separated validly, as John Foster Dulles, Secretary of State, has proposed to do.

Senator Homer Ferguson of Michigan, chairman of the Senate Republican Policy Committee, who is one of the leaders in this movement, expects some sort of Congressional resolution backing both German sovereignty and German rearmament to be offered before Congress adjourns this month or early next month.

Others, among them Senator William F. Knowland of California, Republican Senate floor leader, are taking a more reserved line pending a study by the State Department of the legal situation.

Mr. Dulles has adopted the position that the question of rearmament must be deferred un-

Continued on Page 5, Column 3

38 Jersey Forgeries Charged to Hoffman

Special to The New York Times.

TRENTON, July 20—The preliminary report of a handwriting expert released here today said that former Gov. Harold G. Hoffman apparently concealed his $300,000 defalcations by forging thirty-eight bank certifications in six years.

Attorney General Grover C. Richman made public the findings of Albert D. Osborne of Montclair, who for a month has been studying the signatures on the certifications from the South Amboy Trust Company.

The certifications of general state treasury funds deposited at the South Amboy bank cover a period from June 30, 1947, to Dec. 31, 1953. They all had the signature of George A. Kress, a vice president of the bank. No breakdown of the amount of

Continued on Page 48, Column 1

French Call Pact No Victory But See Gains for Europe

By HAROLD CALLENDER

Special to The New York Times.

PARIS, July 20—The terms of agreement for the truce in Indochina were regarded here as presaging a peace without victory. Some called it a peace that would confirm a defeat for the West in Asia and would mark the most notable loss in battle of French territories since Louis XV lost Canada in the eighteenth century.

But it was expected that this ill wind in Asia might blow some good for France and the Atlantic alliance in Europe.

The truce seemed likely to give great prestige to Premier Pierre Mendès-France, and to enable him to stay in office to seek a decision on the European army treaty and to press for a program to stimulate the French economy.

It appeared probable tonight that the Premier would submit the treaty to the National Assembly early in August with suggested modifications that would not require further action by the parliaments of the other signatories. The West German Chancellor, Dr. Konrad Adenauer, has indicated that he would consider changes that could be made without resort to parliaments.

New Unity a By-Product

Removal of the uncertainty that has surrounded the treaty for two years would clear up the question of West Germany's sovereignty and rearmament and permit in this sphere a unity among the United States, Britain and France that has not yet existed. Such a gain in Europe might be considered as offsetting to some extent the failure of Western policy in Indochina.

A severe blow to French prestige in Asia and probably in North Africa was foreseen in the truce. In North Africa that prestige is far more important than in Asia because France's African territories are more important to her. But M. Mendès-France's argument has been that France must cut her losses in Asia in order to conserve her strength in Europe; and if she revamps her economy, as he desires, the net result may be to increase her influence and even her prestige in Europe and Africa.

M. Mendès-France has urged that the failure to reconcile Vietnam with the French Union by a prompt grant of independence should not be repeated in North Africa, where nationalist movements now are menacing.

The truce in Indochina will mark the frustration of a prolonged Western effort to resist the conquest of Vietnam, Laos and Cambodia by a nationalist movement that was anti-Western and Communist-led. Against it were employed unsuccessfully a French army, a native force and United States aid that was to amount to $800,000,000 this year.

The truce will mark an advance of communism in the sense that

Continued on Page 3, Column 4

HANOI PREPARING FOR TRUCE PERIOD

French Study Plans Designed to Preserve Calm in Delta and Effect Evacuation

By HENRY R. LIEBERMAN

Special to The New York Times.

HANOI, Vietnam, July 20—Two kinds of preparations were being made here to cope with problems related to the surrender of North Vietnam to the Vietminh under a cease-fire. Hanoi will eventually be taken over by the Vietminh under a truce agreement.

French authorities were preparing security measures to "maintain calm" in this city of 340,000. Plans originally drawn up to evacuate French, foreign and a number of Vietnamese civilians under battle conditions were also being restudied in terms of a more leisurely evacuation.

It was being taken for granted today in this city, which is seven hours ahead of Geneva time, that the seven-and-a-half-year-old Indochinese war was drawing to a close.

Geneva reports aroused considerable interest in Hanoi but created no public excitement. In fact, despite a demonstration against partition yesterday by several thousand Vietnamese, there has been no major agitation

Continued on Page 2, Column 2

LONG WAR ENDING

2 Accords Completed—One on Cambodia Due Later Today

By THOMAS J. HAMILTON

Special to The New York Times.

GENEVA, Wednesday, July 21—Armistice agreements bringing the fighting in Vietnam and Laos to a halt were signed this morning by representatives of the French and Communist Vietminh forces.

A French spokesman said the armistice would take effect forty-eight hours later.

The signing ceremony, witnessed by representatives of the nine delegations participating in the Far Eastern conference here, began at 3:42 A. M. (9:42 P. M. Tuesday, Eastern daylight time). It brought to a close the eight-year struggle for Indochina.

The armistice in Cambodia will not be signed until later this morning. The Far Eastern conference will hold its final session this afternoon to complete work on the political settlement. Under it Laos and Cambodia will be neutralized and elections to create a unified government in Vietnam will be held within two years from the date of the armistice.

Pierre Mendès-France, French Premier, who had set July 20 as his deadline to obtain an armistice or resign, had missed it by a few hours. He canceled a radio speech to the French people and went to bed before the two agreements were signed at the Palais des Nations, former headquarters of the League of Nations, where conference sessions have been held since the Indochina negotiations began last May.

Rebels Get Northern Part

Under the Vietnamese agreement, Vietnam is to be divided into two parts, about equal in area and population, between the Communist-led Vietminh rebels who will hold northern Vietnam, north of a line along the Seventeenth Parallel, and the French-sponsored Government of Bao Dai.

The partition line thus is far enough north to preserve Hue, the ancient capital of Annam; Tourane, an important port and naval and air base, and the only major highway leading to Laos from the coast.

The French will not give up Hanoi and Haipong, in the Red River delta area, in the north, for approximately a year, which will give them time to evacuate personnel of the French expeditionary force in the territory remaining to them in the delta, plus civilians fearing persecution by the Communists.

Under the armistice agreements, the Communists recognize the Governments of Laos and Cambodia. However, regrouping areas for Communist troops were authorized in Laos. The forces of the Communist "resistance government" in Laos will be concentrated in two provinces near the frontier with Vietminh territory. [Some sources identified the two provinces as Samneua and Phongsaly.]

The Cambodian delegation held out against the provision, and prolonged sessions of the "drafting committee" of the Vietminh and Cambodian representatives

Continued on Page 2, Column 5

Reds Have Margin in Indochina Despite Even Split Under Truce

By TILLMAN DURDIN

Special to The New York Times.

GENEVA, July 20—In statistical terms, a balanced settlement on Indochina seems to have been reached.

The Communist Vietminh has gained the northern half of Vietnam, inhabited by about 12,000,000 persons. If the Vietminh forces evacuate other areas according to the terms, the southern half of Vietnam and the states of Laos and Cambodia will remain in non-Communist hands.

Approximately 10,000,000 Vietnamese, 4,000,000 Cambodians and 1,400,000 Laotians live in the territories to remain outside Communist control. Northern Vietnam is somewhat smaller, both in population and area, than the sum of the parts of Indochina due to be non-Communist.

However, the Communists will have advantages not reflected by comparative figures. The Vietminh rebels will have under their control the northern Vietnamese, who are more tough and vigorous than the southern Vietnamese and the easygoing Buddhists of Laos and Cambodia. North Vietnam will envelop northern and eastern Laos and will be in a commanding strategic position with relation to Vietnam's western neighbor.

The Vietminh will have a disciplined, well-organized government and a powerful army.

Continued on Page 3, Column 2

"All the News That's Fit to Print"

The New York Times.

LATE CITY EDITION
Fair and cold today and tonight.
Fair and milder tomorrow.
Temperature Range Today-Max., 40; Min., 25
Temperatures Yesterday-Max., 37.4; Min., 28.5
Full U. S. Weather Bureau Report, Page 51

VOL. CIV. No. 35,377. Entered as Second-Class Matter, Post Office, New York, N. Y. NEW YORK, FRIDAY, DECEMBER 3, 1954. Times Square, New York 36, N. Y. Telephone LAckawanna 4-1000 FIVE CENTS

FINAL VOTE CONDEMNS M'CARTHY, 67-22, FOR ABUSING SENATE AND COMMITTEE; ZWICKER COUNT ELIMINATED IN DEBATE

POPE IN COLLAPSE, BUT REST FOLLOWS A DIFFICULT NIGHT

Morning Announcement Tells of the 78-Year-old Pontiff's Battle Against Illness

KIN CALLED TO BEDSIDE

Trouble Laid to a Perforated Ulcer and Physicians Study Possibilities of Operation

By The Associated Press.

ROME, Friday, Dec. 3—The Vatican announced this morning that Pope Pius XII, gravely stricken, had survived the night. A spokesman said a more detailed bulletin would be issued later today.

The Pope suffered a severe collapse yesterday.

The first word this morning on his condition was given by Dr. Luciano Casimiri, spokesman for the Vatican press office, at 8:05 o'clock [2:05 A. M., Eastern standard time.]

"After a difficult night, the Holy Father is now resting," the spokesman said.

There were unconfirmed reports that the Pope had suffered a heart attack in the night, accompanied by more of the intense gastritis, nausea and hiccups for which he has been under treatment. There were indications also that the Pope's condition may be aggravated by a gastric ulcer.

His personal physician, Dr. Riccardo Galeazzi-Lisi, spent the entire night at his bedside, after making emergency X-rays yesterday and calling in a surgeon for consultation.

Grave Fears Felt

By ARNALDO CORTESI
Special to The New York Times.

ROME, Friday, Dec. 3—Pope Pius XII suffered a collapse at 3:30 o'clock yesterday afternoon due, it is believed, to a perforated ulcer.

The Pope fell into a coma and the gravest fears for his life were felt. He is 78 years old and has been weakened because for the last four days his feeding has been by artificial means.

Extreme unction was administered and Pius' nearest relatives—three nephews—were called to his bedside.

Five hours later, the Pope had overcome the crisis and his archiater, or chief physician, Prof. Riccardo Galeazzi-Lisi, said there was no immediate cause for alarm.

The Pope was stated to be resting as easily as could be expected under the circumstances, although breathing heavily and reduced to exhaustion.

It was learned that the possibility of an abdominal operation sometime today or in the next few days was being considered. The exact nature of the operation under consideration was not stated but it is understood that a noticeable swelling of the Pope's abdomen developed yesterday afternoon, accompanied by cramps and excruciating pain. Radioscopic and clinical tests were made late in the evening to ascertain both the exact nature of the Pope's ailment and whether he is in condition to undergo surgery.

From the time he fell seriously ill in January of this year, Pope Pius had refused to take the barium meal necessary if full X-ray examination of his stomach

Continued on Page 4, Column 1

Rio Conference Ends With Major Accords

By SAM POPE BREWER
Special to The New York Times.

PETROPOLIS, Brazil, Dec. 2—The twenty-one American republics ended tonight their first general economic conference with agreements on many major points and plans to hold another such meeting within two years.

Antonio Carrillo Flores, Minister of Finance of Mexico, said in the principal address at the closing session that public opinion of this hemisphere would find on studying results of the conference that its work "was not sterile."

Carlos Lleras Restrepo of Colombia introduced a dissenting note into the general air of agreement. He said at this final session that his country did not feel the conference had gone far enough toward increasing international banking facilities and stabilizing commodity prices. An

Continued on Page 16, Column 5

President Rejects Blockade Of China Now as Act of War

But He Pledges No Let-Up in Efforts to Free 13 Americans Jailed by Peiping—Holds Truce Obligates U. N. to Act

By JOSEPH A. LOFTUS
Special to The New York Times.

WASHINGTON, Dec. 2—President Eisenhower asserted today he was not going to be pushed emotionally into an act of war—such as a naval blockade of Communist China.

Neither, he said, is he going to let Peiping get away with the imprisonment of thirteen Americans on spy charges.

He insisted that the United Nations act for the release of at least eleven of the Americans because they were uniformed veterans of the Korean war and as such the United Nations was obligated to act in their behalf.

[At the United Nations, the United States said it wanted the world body to condemn the imprisonment by Red China of eleven American airmen shot down during the Korean war.]

"We are yet far from exhausting all of our resources" to liberate these men, the President said at his news conference: "I mention only one of those that is available to us."

He asserted that Red China deliberately timed its announcement of the imprisonment to divide the people of the United States as well as the United States from its allies. He added that the United States must be forever on its guard against this divide-and-conquer technique.

His personal feelings of anger, resentment and frustration were as great as any American's, he said, but he believed that restraint in public expression was the wiser course. To respond with patience rather than with truculence does not mean appeasement, he declared.

The President was clearly reading a lesson in the behavior of public officials to Senator Wil-

Continued on Page 2, Column 4

East Bloc Says Joint Army Will Counter Bonn in NATO

By CLIFTON DANIEL
Special to The New York Times.

MOSCOW, Dec. 2—In a declaration signed in the Kremlin tonight, eight European Communist regimes gave notice that if the Atlantic powers enlisted West Germany in their alliance, an East European defense organization would be created.

Representatives of eight governments concluding a four-day conference here said another meeting would be called to plan defense measures should the London and Paris agreements for West German armament and sovereignty be finally ratified.

The envisioned defense organization would have combined military forces under a joint command like that of the North Atlantic Treaty Organization. It would be in addition to the existing framework of treaties concluded long ago among the eight powers.

Communist China's complete approval of the declaration and the measures envisioned in it was signified at the final meeting by the representatives of the eight European powers today. China's endorsement was given by Chang Wen-tien, Peiping's Deputy Foreign Minister and Ambassador to Moscow.

Having in mind the combined strength of Communist China, the Soviet Union and seven other units in the East bloc conference, the delegates declared:

"Never before have the forces of peace and socialism been so mighty and so consolidated as now. Any attempt to attack, launch a war and interfere with the peaceful life of our peoples will meet with a shattering rebuff."

The declaration, bound in a red Morocco folder with ribbons

Continued on Page 5, Column 5

ATOM POWER SEEN AS COMMON IN 1976

Half of All Electric Plants Then Building Will Use It, G. E. Head Tells N.A.M.

By A. H. RASKIN

By 1976 atomic energy will be used to fuel half of all the electric generating plants then being built, it was predicted yesterday. This forecast was put before the National Association of Manufacturers by Ralph J. Cordiner, president of General Electric.

His estimate of the speed with which nuclear power would come into widespread use as a source of electric power was considerably more optimistic than most official calculations. Mr. Cordiner made his prediction as part of a plea to industrialists to shun "creeping conservatism" in their approach to business planning.

The head of the country's biggest electrical manufacturing company advised his fellow-executives to make their plans on a twenty-year basis, instead of limiting themselves to the ups and downs of the immediate sales market.

West Called Stronger

Other highlights at the second session of the association's fifty-ninth annual Congress of American Industry in the Waldorf-Astoria Hotel included:

¶An assertion by Gen. Walter Bedell Smith that the United States and its allies had built up a sufficient superiority over the Communist countries to "deter aggression and maintain peace." The former Under Secretary of State emphasized, however, that the balance of power was still "rather tenuous."

¶A report by a Dutch industrialist that five of his employes, who spent three months working in a Pennsylvania linoleum factory, had come home convinced that "America is a working man's world."

¶An attack by Charles R. Sligh Jr., N. A. M. board chairman, on union proposals for a guaranteed annual wage. He contended that wage guarantees would destroy business, rather than stabilize employment.

¶An assertion by Prof. Leo Wolman of Columbia University that the Taft-Hartley Act represented no substantial improvement over the old Wagner Act in curbing union power and preventing encroachment on management rights.

¶Election as N. A. M. president of Henry G. Riter 3d of Thomas A. Edison, Inc., and chairman of the board of Copperweld Steel. Mr. Riter, who was an investment banker before he became an industrialist, succeeds H. C. McClellan of Los Angeles.

General Smith, who quit the State Department two months

Continued on Page 24, Column 3

'Copter Saves 5 Plane Survivors Down 45 Hours on Mountainside

Two Perish in Crash of DC-3 in New Hampshire—Work of Stewardess Praised

By JOHN H. FENTON
Special to The New York Times.

BOSTON, Dec. 2—Five survivors of the crash of a Northeast Airlines plane were plucked by helicopter today from a bleak mountainside near the Maine-New Hampshire border. They had spent forty-five hours on the snow-covered spot in bitter cold.

The two others aboard the DC-3 died of injuries a few hours after the plane had fallen into a stretch of pine woods.

The dead were George McCormick, 37 years old, of Kingston, N. Y., co-pilot, and John McNulty, 39, of Boston, flight supervisor.

First to be rescued was the pilot, Capt. W. Peter Carey, 37, of Swampscott, Mass. He suffered severe head injuries. He and Miss Mary McEttrick, 23, of Boston, the stewardess, were flown here for medical treatment. Miss McEttrick suffered from shock and exposure.

The survivors praised Miss McEttrick for her coolness throughout the ordeal during which they huddled in the wrecked plane for nearly two days. Her cheerful attempts to make them com-

Associated Press Wirephoto
Stewardess Mary McEttrick in Berlin (N. H.) hospital.

fortable and her care of the injured prompted them to agree that "she's quite a girl."

Seventy-five Northeast employes, who were flown to Berlin,

Continued on Page 29, Column 4

EISENHOWER WARNS G. O. P. RIGHT WING; CHIDES KNOWLAND

Insists Party Must Follow a Progressive Course or Face Loss of Influence

Transcript and summary of the news conference, Page 18.

By WILLIAM S. WHITE
Special to The New York Times.

WASHINGTON, Dec. 2—President Eisenhower, reasserting leadership for his concept of a progressive Republican party, rebuked today the Senate Republican floor leader, William F. Knowland of California, and the party's right wing generally.

The President did not seek to disclaim the existence of a split in the party. He said instead that the party would not long be a force in American life unless it followed a course of progressivism.

As before, he defined this progressivism as a liberal attitude in the Government's relationship with the individual and a conservative attitude concerning the national economy and the individual's pocketbook.

It was the first time since he entered the White House two years ago that General Eisenhower publicly and without apology had criticized a leading member of his party in Congress. Always before, he had avoided such criticisms, relying frequently on the fact that the Constitution made Congress an independent branch of Government.

Even this time, the President somewhat softened his language toward the end, with the comments that while Senator Knowland sometimes made statements that certainly did not conform with the Administration's approach these normally affected method rather than principle.

China Blockade Urged

He made it clear, nevertheless, that distinctions in methods were important, suggesting that the methods of Senator Knowland might mean the difference between peace and war in Asia.

Senator Knowland, in the face of rejections from John Foster Dulles, Secretary of State, and the President himself, has been calling for a blockade of Communist China to force the liberation of United States citizens in Communist prisons.

Yesterday, moreover, Mr. Knowland broke with the Administration on another sensitive issue, coming out against a Senate censure of Senator Joseph R. McCarthy, Republican of Wisconsin.

The President said little about his differences with Senator Knowland over the McCarthy issue, observing only that it was up to the Senate to determine what was required for the preservation of its dignity.

On the point of the profound division within the Republican party over policy toward Red China, however, the President spoke extensively and voluntarily.

He took up Senator Knowland's

Continued on Page 18, Column 5

RANCOR CONTINUES

Welker Refuses to Let Flanders Apology Go Into the Record

By JAMES RESTON
Special to The New York Times.

WASHINGTON, Dec. 2—The McCarthy debate ended as it began in a spasm of rancor and vindictiveness that will divide the Senate and the country for a long time to come.

Though there were some light-hearted semantics at the close over whether Senator Joseph R. McCarthy was "censured" or "condemned," the underlying feeling among the principals ranged from uneasiness to sullen anger.

The junior Senator from Wisconsin himself produced almost the only hint of humor all day. Asked whether he thought the Senate had passed a resolution of "censure" or "condemnation," he replied:

"I wouldn't say it was a vote of confidence."

He then announced that he was "very happy to get this circus over" and would get back to "the job of digging Communists out of the Government" on Monday.

Controversy Continues

Even after the vote was over, the controversy went on.

Senator Ralph E. Flanders, Republican of Vermont, arose and said he wanted to apologize to the Senate for some remarks he had made about Senator McCarthy some months ago. He added that he had told the Wisconsin Senator that he proposed to do so and had asked him to remain in the chamber, but Senator McCarthy had declined.

Then Senator Flanders asked for unanimous consent to have the Congressional Record amended to show that he had apologized for some of his remarks. This was blocked by Senator Herman Welker, Republican of Idaho, who angrily refused to give consent.

The usual lavish courtesy of the upper chamber gave way to biting sarcasm at the close. When Senator J. William Fulbright, Democrat of Arkansas, said he would try to answer a question by Senator Welker, the latter remarked that he would be "very surprised if a distinguished Rhodes scholar could not answer any question."

The End of a Phase

The main significance of the special session was that it ended that phase of the McCarthy controversy in which the Senate of the United States was hesitant to take action against the Wisconsin Senator.

For most of the five years since Senator McCarthy launched his anti-Communist crusade, the Senate of the United States has led a double life—critical of the Senator in private, and afraid of his political power in public.

During most of this period there has been a kind of political paralysis among the anti-McCarthy faction, and it was never entirely clear who was for him and who was against him. This doubt has now been removed.

The Senator from Wisconsin will remain for a month as chairman of the Government Operations Committee. He will lose none of his rights. He will have the power of subpoena and he will wield his gavel.

What has changed is not Mr. McCarthy but his opponents. They are in the open now, willing and in some cases eager to match his criticisms with their own. In short, the balance of criticism, dominated for so long by Senator McCarthy, has been restored.

Behind this, too, is a decision by the Executive Branch of the Government to take a firmer position against his efforts to persuade Federal employes to give him documents they are not authorized to disclose.

So long as Congress hesitated to take action against Mr. McCarthy, the Executive itself was divided about how to defend its own classified files, but today's vote—regardless of what it is called—has stiffened the anti-McCarthy element in the Administration.

Thus, while he can exercise all

Continued on Page 16, Column 7

Associated Press Wirephoto
CONDEMNED ON TWO COUNTS: Senator McCarthy as he left the Senate floor last night after members adopted a resolution condemning his conduct. The vote was 67-22.

PRESIDENT ALERTS MAYORS ON ATTACK

Cities Are Front-Line Targets, He Warns—Asks Teamwork in Federal-Local Defense

By ELIE ABEL
Special to The New York Times.

WASHINGTON, Dec. 2—President Eisenhower warned today that United States cities were front-line targets for modern weapons "capable of such destruction as to appall the imagination."

The President called for closer municipal-Federal cooperation in civil-defense planning as he welcomed about 240 mayors, city manager and other local officials to a two-day conference in the State Department auditorium.

Val Peterson, Federal Civil Defense Administrator, expanded on the President's warning in a guarded discussion of radioactive "fall-out," a phenomenon that adds a new dimension to the terror of thermonuclear (hydrogen) bombs.

The idea that only city dwellers need to worry about bombing is obsolete today, Mr. Peterson said. If a hydrogen bomb is detonated on or close to the ground, he explained, tremendous amounts of earth and debris are sucked up into the fireball and made radioactive.

Although the heavy particles will not travel far, he said, the lighter ones may be swept along by winds of the upper air, at alti-

Continued on Page 19, Column 1

SENATORS CLEARED ON M'CARTHY MAIL

Inquiry Indicates Request for Check Was Handled by Staff as Routine Matter

By WILLIAM M. BLAIR
Special to The New York Times.

WASHINGTON, Dec. 2—A special Senate committee apparently will report to the Senate that a check of Senator Joseph R. McCarthy's mail in 1952 was handled as a routine matter by a subcommittee's staff members.

Senator Walter F. George, Democrat of Georgia, indicated as much to Senator McCarthy this afternoon as the special two-member committee completed its overnight inquiry into how the mail check was authorized.

"There's nothing to be gained from pursuing the matter further," Senator McCarthy told Senator George, who replied, "I don't think so."

Senator George and Senator Homer Ferguson, Republican of Michigan, spent the day in closed session to hear testimony from persons on the staff of the Senate subcommittee on Privileges and Elections, which had inquired into Senator McCarthy's finances in 1952.

Mr. Ferguson said that a written report would be filed with the Senate. The report is expected to be filed with the secretary of the Senate tomorrow.

The two Senators were named by the Senate last night to the

Continued on Page 15, Column 3

G.O.P. Weighs End of Rent Curb Outside of the Metropolitan Area

By LEO EGAN

Republican legislative leaders are giving serious consideration to relaxing state rent controls outside of the New York metropolitan area, which includes Nassau and Westchester counties as well as New York City.

Such a proposal could set the stage for a major clash between Governor-elect Averell Harriman, Democrat-Liberal, and Republican majorities in the Senate and Assembly.

The Democratic platform on which Mr. Harriman was elected favors tightening rather than relaxing rent control. Moreover, Mr. Harriman affirmed his full support of this position on several occasions during the campaign.

One proposal favored by some Republicans calls for decontrolling all rents outside of the New York metropolitan area. If this is politically impossible or unacceptable they favor decontrolling all one and two-family houses outside of the metropolitan area, leaving controls in effect only on apartments and tenements.

Both suggestions were formally advanced at a recent closed-door meeting of the Temporary State Commission on Rents and Rental Conditions, headed by Assemblyman Joseph F. Carlino of Long Beach, L. I.

As a result, Joseph D. McGoldrick, State Rent Administrator, was instructed by the commission to prepare a report and recommendations on both proposals covering the probable effect of such a relaxation of controls, the number of dwelling units involved, and the rate of vacancies to dwelling units affected at present.

Major up-state cities that would be affected by such a

Continued on Page 24, Column 5

REPUBLICANS SPLIT

Democrats Act Solidly in Support of Motion Against Senator

Excerpts from transcript of Senate debate, Pages 12, 13

By ANTHONY LEVIERO
Special to The New York Times.

WASHINGTON, Dec. 2—The Senate voted 67 to 22 tonight to condemn Joseph R. McCarthy, Republican Senator from Wisconsin.

Every one of the forty-four Democrats present voted against Mr. McCarthy. The Republicans were evenly divided—twenty-two for condemnation and twenty-two against. The one independent, Senator Wayne Morse of Oregon, also voted against Mr. McCarthy.

In the ultimate action the Senate voted to condemn Senator McCarthy for contempt of a Senate Elections subcommittee that investigated his conduct and financial affairs, for abuse of its members, and for his insults to the Senate itself during the censure proceeding.

Lost in a day of complex and often confused parliamentary maneuvering was the proposal to censure Senator McCarthy for his denunciation of Brig. Gen. Ralph W. Zwicker as unfit to wear his uniform.

This proposal was defeated by a parliamentary device that avoided a direct vote on the merits of the issue. Inquiry among influential Senators indicated they considered the Zwicker proposal a dilemma they wished to avoid.

Amendment Substituted

They said they wished to censure because the facts warranted it. If they failed to do so, they believed large elements of the public would feel the Senate took notice of offenses only against itself and not against ordinary citizens.

But also if they did censure for this, then Senator McCarthy could exploit the decision, contending he was being punished for his effort to expose former Maj. Irving Peress, the Army dentist who was promoted and honorably discharged, and who was denounced by Mr. McCarthy as a "Fifth Amendment Communist."

Mr. McCarthy's denunciation of General Zwicker, who was commanding officer at Camp Kilmer, N. J., when Dr. Peress was discharged, occurred when the Senator interrogated General Zwicker on the question of who had promoted Dr. Peress.

The direct test on the Zwicker issue was avoided by the substitution of the amendment to condemn Senator McCarthy for having insulted the Senate during his censure trial.

McCarthy Loses Three Tests

Thus in its final form the resolution of condemnation was in two parts, covering the offenses against the Elections subcommittee and its members in the first part, and against the Senate in the second. Three test votes were all lost by Mr. McCarthy before the final condemnation.

First was a motion to table the Zwicker proposal, made by Senator Styles Bridges, Republican of New Hampshire, the president pro tem of the Senate, who assumed the leadership of the effort to save Mr. McCarthy yesterday.

Such a motion, if it had succeeded, might have led to a situation that would have prolonged the debate.

But amid signs that the Zwicker issue would have tough sledding, Senator Wallace F. Bennett, Republican of Utah, served notice that if Mr. Bridges' move were defeated he would attempt to substitute for the Zwicker issue his amendment for abuse of the Senate. The significance of this was that an amendment by substitution would require no time out for debate.

Then the voting proceeded. The motion to table was defeated 55 to 33. Mr. Bennett's motion to substitute passed by 64 to 23 and in the next vote his amendment was adopted by the same tally.

The final vote placing Mr. Mc-

Continued on Page 14, Column 3

"All the News That's Fit to Print"

The New York Times.

LATE CITY EDITION
Partly cloudy today. Considerable cloudiness and milder tomorrow.
Temperature Range Today—Max., 41; Min., 30
Temperatures Yesterday—Max., 38; Min., 27
Full U. S. Weather Bureau Report, Page 55

VOL. CIV. No. 35,445. Entered as Second-Class Matter, Post Office, New York, N. Y. NEW YORK, WEDNESDAY, FEBRUARY 9, 1955. Times Square, New York 36, N. Y. Telephone LAckawanna 4-1000 FIVE CENTS

BULGANIN IS PREMIER AS MALENKOV RESIGNS, BUT KHRUSHCHEV IS VIEWED AS REAL LEADER; MOLOTOV, WARNING U. S., CLAIMS H-BOMB LEAD

EISENHOWER ASKS 7 BILLION PROGRAM TO BUILD SCHOOLS

Message to Congress Urges Federal-State-Local Plan for Grants and Loans

DEMOCRATS DECRY SCOPE

Leaders Denounce Proposal as 'Makeshift'—Demand Far Larger Expenditures

Text of the President's message is printed on Page 20.

By W. H. LAWRENCE
Special to The New York Times.

WASHINGTON, Feb. 8—President Eisenhower proposed today a three-year $7,000,000,000 Federal-state-local school construction program.

He asked Congress to make available $220,000,000 in Federal grants and about $900,000,000 in loans to meet a current deficit of more than 300,000 school classrooms.

The message went to a Democratic-controlled Congress. Leaders in the education field in both the Senate and the House called it inadequate and "makeshift."

Some critics declared the Presidential program would be ineffective in about one-fourth of the states, which have constitutional limitations on incurring or increasing debts.

Indirectly, President Eisenhower also suggested higher pay for school teachers, but his message advanced no concrete proposals on this. He said low pay was a factor in the shortage of teachers, which he declared was "less obvious but ultimately more dangerous than the classroom shortage."

"Because of the magnitude of the job, but more fundamentally because of the undeniable importance of free education to a free way of life, the means we take to provide our children with proper classrooms must be weighed most carefully," the President said, continuing:

"The phrase 'free education' is a deliberate choice. For unless education continues to be free—free in its response to local com-

Continued on Page 20, Column 1

President Appeals For Satellite People

Special to The New York Times.

WASHINGTON, Feb. 8—President Eisenhower urged tonight a continuing effort to "intensify the will for freedom in the satellite countries behind the Iron Curtain."

He spoke from the White House on a closed-circuit television program in behalf of the Crusade for Freedom, which operates Radio Free Europe and the Free Europe Press. The crusade hopes to raise $10,000,000 this year.

He took no cognizance of the resignation of Georgi M. Malenkov as Soviet Premier and his replacement by Marshal Nikolai A. Bulganin. His prepared text was left unchanged after the Moscow developments had become known.

The President emphasized that the masses imprisoned behind the Iron Curtain would remain potential deterrents to

Continued on Page 6, Column 6

MIGHT IS STRESSED

Foreign Minister Says Soviet Force Is on Par With West

Excerpts from Molotov speech are printed on Page 6.

Special to The New York Times.

MOSCOW, Feb. 8—Claiming superiority for the Soviet Union in hydrogen weapons, Foreign Minister Vyacheslav M. Molotov delivered to the United States today a warning of the strength of the world Communist forces.

His declaration reiterating the might of the Communist camp was made at a joint session of the Supreme Soviet, the national legislature of the Soviet Union. He spoke immediately following the change in Soviet Premiership that placed Marshal Nikolai A. Bulganin at the head of the Government.

[According to The Associated Press, the Soviet Parliament resumed its joint session at 2 A. M. Wednesday, New York time, and immediately began debating Mr. Molotov's speech.]

Laughter and applause greeted Mr. Molotov's taunts at, and defiance of, the United States, which he singled out as the leader of the "aggressive" Western coalition. He also called on the United States once again to evacuate Formosa.

Balance 'Quite Established'

In one of his most outspoken passages, Mr. Molotov declared that it must be understood that the balance of forces between the Soviet Union and the United States had been "quite established."

Comparing the two and taking into account the vast human and material resources of this country, the strength of its allies, and the justness of its cause, Mr. Molotov declared, "it will become clear that the Soviet Union is no weaker than the United States."

As for atomic strength, he said in an earlier passage that "the aggressive circles of the United States miscalculated again." They thought it would take ten or fifteen years for the Soviet Union to catch up with the United States, he asserted, but "the Soviet people have achieved such success that not the Soviet Union but the United States finds itself in the position of being behind."

In thus belittling and challeng-

Continued on Page 6, Column 4

Associated Press Radiophoto

CHANGE IN HIGH SOVIET COUNCILS: The scene yesterday in Supreme Soviet at Moscow after Marshal Nikolai A. Bulganin was elected to succeed Georgi M. Malenkov. Front row, from left, are Lazar M. Kaganovich, Marshal Bulganin, Nikita S. Khrushchev, Mr. Malenkov and Marshal Kliment E. Voroshilov. At far right in rear is Anastas I. Mikoyan.

MOSCOW SHAKE-UP

Malenkov Avows Guilt for Shortcomings in Agriculture

Texts of Malenkov statement and Khrushchev speech, Page 2.

By CLIFTON DANIEL
Special to The New York Times.

MOSCOW, Feb. 8—On nomination by Nikita S. Khrushchev, first secretary of the Communist party, Marshal Nikolai A. Bulganin became head of the Soviet Government today. He replaced Georgi M. Malenkov, who had been Premier since the death of Stalin March 5, 1953.

Reproaching himself for inadequate leadership, Mr. Malenkov offered his resignation this afternoon to the Supreme Soviet, national legislature of the Soviet Union.

[News of the resignation was published in a Late City Extra of The New York Times on Tuesday.]

Mr. Malenkov said he would fulfill "with greatest scrupulousness" the duties that would now be assigned to him. Those duties were not stated at once.

In resigning Mr. Malenkov took on himself the "guilt and responsibility" for the present state of Soviet agriculture, which has been roundly criticized by Mr. Khrushchev.

To Support Party Line

Mr. Malenkov also proclaimed his understanding of the Communist party line that forced development of heavy industry must be the basis for increasing agricultural production and all other branches of the Soviet economy. That line has recently been re-emphasized with new firmness by the Central Committee of the party and its propaganda organs.

The Central Committee's decision, taken in the last days of January on the initiative of Mr. Khrushchev, gave orders for still further efforts to increase Soviet agricultural output and Mr. Malenkov said today the decision had revealed to him his shortcomings as an administrator.

The change in the Premiership, accomplished in barely ten minutes of swift political action, left two major questions unanswered for the moment:

What will be Mr. Malenkov's future position and who will be Defense Minister of the Soviet

Continued on Page 2, Column 3

HOUSE, 394-4, BACKS DRAFT EXTENSION

Four-Year Continuance Finds the Democrats Unanimous—New Features Added

By C. P. TRUSSELL
Special to The New York Times.

WASHINGTON, Feb. 8—The House of Representatives voted 394 to 4 today to continue the draft for four years.

This extension, the fourth since 1940, was urged by President Eisenhower. The Administration concluded that the international situation generally required the maintenance of the United States armed forces of 2,850,000 officers and men. Such a force, experience had shown, could not be mobilized through voluntary enlistments.

The four who voted against draft extension were Republicans. Democrats supported the move unanimously. The four dissenters were Representatives Noah M. Mason of Illinois, Usher L. Burdick of North Dakota; Clare E. Hoffman of Michigan, and Wint Smith of Kansas.

The extension measure now goes to the Senate. There it is expected to win approval, with its opponents again on the Republican side. No one predicted that the extension would not be approved finally in Congress long before the present draft authorization expires June 30.

In granting the continuance of Selective Service the House added new features to the law. They included:

¶If the selective draft continued it should include all the benefits and allowance given to present draftees to aid their dependents. Also continued for four

Continued on Page 16, Column 4

SENATE UNIT VOTES FORMOSA TREATY

Committee Ballot Is 11 to 2—Whole Chamber May Adopt Pact by Tomorrow Night

By WILLIAM S. WHITE
Special to The New York Times.

WASHINGTON, Feb. 8—The Senate Foreign Relations Committee approved today the defense treaty with Nationalist China on Formosa. The vote was 11 to 2.

The committee's chairman, Senator Walter F. George, Democrat of Georgia, will take the pact to the Senate tomorrow in the hope that it can be cleared there by Thursday night.

Failing final action by then, there can be none before the week after next.

Beginning Friday, the Senate, by old custom, will have an unofficial holiday from all important business for ten days while Republican speakers celebrate the birthday of Abraham Lincoln.

Mr. George recognized the possibility of delay, though he spoke out against it as undesirable in the light of the changing of com-

Continued on Page 14, Column 3

Khrushchev Comes to Fore In Compromise on Bulganin

The following article is by a member of The Times staff who is a specialist on Soviet affairs.

By HARRY SCHWARTZ

Nikita S. Khrushchev appeared to have emerged yesterday as the most powerful single person in the Soviet Union, the heir to Stalin's mantle.

Stalin ruled the Soviet Union during most of his reign without holding any Government post, content to be general secretary of the Communist party.

It was as first secretary, the new name for general secretary, of the party that Mr. Khrushchev nominated Nikolai A. Bulganin to be Premier. But the largest ovation went to the first secretary, not to the new Premier.

Even before yesterday, Mr. Khrushchev had given abundant testimony that he, not some amorphous "collective leadership," is the leader.

It may be that his power is subject still to the majority of his colleagues in the Presidium of the Central Committee or to the will of the army leaders. But since last December the public image has been of a Mr. Khru-

Continued on Page 4, Column 5

This article is by a reporter of The Times who returned last fall after five years in Moscow.

By HARRISON E. SALISBURY

Marshal Nikolai A. Bulganin almost certainly is a compromise choice as Soviet Premier. He apparently represents a coalition of the party forces of Nikita S. Khrushchev and the army group headed by Marshal Georgi G. Zhukov.

The heralded showdown between Mr. Khrushchev and former Premier Georgi M. Malenkov has occurred more quickly than this observer had expected.

Apparently the army threw its backing to Mr. Khrushchev.

Regardless of the fire and vigor of Foreign Minister Vyacheslav M. Molotov's address yesterday, Soviet power in the international arena will remain weakened for a considerable time.

The crisis that resulted in the execution of Deputy Premier Lavrenti P. Beria left little outward signs of cracks in the Kremlin wall. However, it seemed certain the Soviet Government would be a longer time in over-

Continued on Page 4, Column 7

U. S. SEES STRUGGLE AS FAR FROM OVER

Experts on Moscow Conclude It Is Too Early to Decide About Effect of Change

By JAMES RESTON
Special to The New York Times.

WASHINGTON, Feb. 8—The United States Government, concentrating on its plans for blocking Communist expansion, refused to comment today on the battle of the dictators in the Soviet Union.

The capital hummed with speculation all day. But after hours of cooperative guesswork the official experts on the Soviet Union decided to let the events interpret the Moscow changes.

Ambassador Charles E. Bohlen's first official cablegram on the news came in at 7:49 A. M. It was discussed briefly by Secretary of State Dulles at his 9:15 staff conference.

Thereafter the official advisers on the Soviet Union were instructed to analyze the published facts. Their conclusions—far less dogmatic than most opinion in the capital—were as follows:

¶There is trouble in the Soviet "paradise." Premier Georgi M. Malenkov was dismissed not because everything was going well: the dramatic news was a sign, not of Communist strength, but of weakness.

¶Nikita S. Khrushchev, the Communist party boss, is probably the most powerful figure for the moment. But the fierce struggle over succession, always a problem in Russia, even in the time of the czars, is far from over.

¶It is too early to reach any

Continued on Page 7, Column 1

A. E. C. WON'T DROP DIXON-YATES PACT

2-1 Vote Disclosed by Board—Congress Plea Rejected

By WILLIAM M. BLAIR
Special to The New York Times.

WASHINGTON, Feb 8—By a 2 to 1 vote, the Atomic Energy Commission has turned down a Democratic demand that the Dixon-Yates private power contract be canceled.

The split vote, taken on Saturday, followed the lead of President Eisenhower, who asserted three days before the vote that he would not withdraw the controversial contract to feed private power into the Tennessee Valley Authority.

Lewis L. Strauss, A. E. C. chairman, and Dr. Willard Frank Libby, a new member, voted to stick by the contract. Thomas E. Murray voted for cancellation.

As Mr. Strauss disclosed the decision today, Mr. Murray went before the Joint Congressional Committee on Atomic Energy to renew his charge that the Dixon-Yates controversy had interfered with the commission's primary job of developing atomic weapons and peacetime uses of the atom.

His main concern, he testified, was "whether we will in the future maintain our present position of world leadership in the nuclear field." He concluded:

"The attention the commission today gives to making policy de-

Continued on Page 37, Column 6

Private Atom Reactor In This Area Planned

By PETER KIHSS

A plan for the nation's first nuclear reactor entirely owned and operated by private industry was announced here yesterday by the American Machine and Foundry Company. It would use radiations for confidential experiments for cooperating companies.

Gen. Walter Bedell Smith, retired, vice chairman of the foundry concern's board, said invitations to join the scheme had gone to companies in the fields of electronics, petroleum, food, pharmaceutical and chemical products, ceramics, rubber, metals, textiles, agriculture, machinery and others.

The project would occupy 250 acres somewhere in the New York area. A so-called swimming pool reactor would use uranium fuel surrounded by water serving as a moderator, cooler and shield.

The atomic furnace would

Continued on Page 19, Column 3

All Civilians Off Upper Tachen; First U. S. Ship Returns to Formosa

Associated Press Wirephoto via Radio From Taipei

American and Chinese military personnel, in the foreground, observe the evacuation operation on Upper Tachen Island

Special to The New York Times.

KEELUNG, Formosa, Wednesday, Feb. 9—The first United States Navy ship with Chinese Nationalist civilians evacuated from the Tachen Islands docked here this morning. She was an 8,000-ton transport with 3,816 civilians on board. Vice Admiral Alfred M. Pride, Commander of the United States Seventh Fleet, announced last night that the evacuation of civilians from Upper Tachen Island was completed at 5:17 P. M. yesterday. [In Washington, the Navy announced early Wednesday that the Seventh Fleet had reported that the last "organized group" of civilians had been evacuated from South Tachen Island, The

Continued on Page 14, Column 5

U. S. Plane Downed By Reds in Tachens

By The Associated Press.

WITH UNITED STATES SEVENTH FLEET, in the Tachens, Wednesday, Feb. 9—Red anti-aircraft batteries shot down a United States AD Skyraider plane twenty miles southwest of the Tachen Islands today, the Navy said.

The pilot and two crew members of the carrier-based plane were rescued by the destroyer Isbell, the Navy said.

WASHINGTON, Feb. 8 (AP)—The Navy said tonight that one of its patrol planes received three small holes in one wing from Chinese Communist antiaircraft fire during the Tachens evacuation today, but returned safely from its mission.

The Navy released a terse message from Vice Admiral Alfred M. Pride:

"Vice Admiral Pride learned during the night that three small holes were discovered in one wing during inspection after returning to base."

TUNIS LEADER AIDS PINAY ON CABINET

U.S. Bipartisan Idea Adapted by Premier-Designate

By LANSING WARREN
Special to The New York Times.

PARIS, Feb. 8—Premier-designate Antoine Pinay obtained some help today from the Tunisian Premier in his efforts to form a French Cabinet.

After their conference the Tunisian Premier, Tahar ben Ammar, said he had found that he and M. Pinay had similar ideas and that "I hope we shall continue the negotiations that were started with the Government of Mendès-France." M. ben Ammar declared that he was going full of optimism to Tunis to inform the Bey, Sidi Mohammed el Amin, about the consultations.

The statement will be used by M. Pinay in trying to convince the party groups that his Cabinet can handle the crisis in Tunisia.

In dealing with those groups today M. Pinay obtained support from M. Mendès-France's Radical group, but met a rebuff from the Socialists. The Radical executive body voted, 81 to 67, to participate in the Pinay Cabinet. This assures him of about two-thirds of the seventy-six Radical Deputies, who never vote in unison.

The Socialists, through Christian Pineau, former Minister of Finance, declined the invitation to join the Cabinet. M. Pinay had

Continued on Page 11, Column 3

"All the News That's Fit to Print"

The New York Times.

LATE CITY EDITION
Chance of some showers and mild today, tonight and tomorrow.
Temperature Range Today—Max., 65; Min., 47
Temperature Yesterday—Max., 66; Min., 43
Full U. S. Weather Bureau Report, Page 50

Copyright, 1955, by The New York Times Company.

VOL. CIV. No. 35,501. Entered as Second-Class Matter, Post Office, New York, N. Y. NEW YORK, WEDNESDAY, APRIL 6, 1955. Times Square, New York 36, N. Y. Telephone LAckawanna 4-1000 FIVE CENTS

CHURCHILL QUITS AS PRIME MINISTER; DECLINES DUKEDOM TO STAY AN M. P.; EDEN TAKES OVER LEADERSHIP TODAY

Associated Press Radiophoto

ON WAY TO RETIREMENT: Sir Winston Churchill moist-eyed as he arrived in auto yesterday at Buckingham Palace to tender resignation as Prime Minister to Queen Elizabeth.

BRITISH ERA ENDS

Aged Statesman Tells Queen of Decision—Cabinet Shifts Due

By DREW MIDDLETON
Special to The New York Times.

LONDON, April 5—Sir Winston Churchill resigned as Prime Minister today. Age has done what Britain's enemies and his political rivals could not accomplish.

Tomorrow Queen Elizabeth II will summon Sir Anthony Eden to Buckingham Palace and ask him to form a new Government. Sir Anthony's accession as Prime Minister will mark the passing of the Churchill era.

While shadows lengthened on the palace lawns, Sir Winston stood talking with the Queen at her study window. Their business was his resignation. When the audience ended he passed out of the palace, through cheering ranks of his countrymen.

The most important change in British political life since the end of World War II was announced from Buckingham Palace in a single sentence:

"The Right Honorable Sir Winston Churchill had an audience of the Queen this evening and tendered his resignation as Prime Minister and First Lord of the Treasury, which Her Majesty was graciously pleased to accept."

Transition to Eden Era

Thus Sir Winston, Knight of the Garter, Privy Councilor, Order of Merit and Companion of Honor, left the office he has held at two different times for a total of eight years, seven months and twenty-five days.

While Sir Winston, who is 80 years old, bowed beaming to crowds shouting "Good old Winnie!" in Downing Street tonight, political London bubbled with anticipation.

When Sir Anthony is asked by the Queen tomorrow to form a Government, all the Ministers will place their offices at his disposal. This will open the way to changes that, immediately or after the election, will change the Churchill Government into the Eden Government.

The decision on the date of a general parliamentary election is Sir Anthony's. Polls conducted by newspaper men in the House of Commons indicate that a great majority of the Members of Parliament expect the election will take place May 26.

If this date is chosen, the new

Continued on Page 11, Column 2

President Declares Allies Still Will Heed Churchill

By W. H. LAWRENCE
Special to The New York Times.

WASHINGTON, April 5—President Eisenhower declared today that leaders of the free world were bound to ask Sir Winston Churchill's counsel and advice, even in retirement. Democrats and Republicans joined the President in personal tributes to the retiring British Prime Minister.

There were formal statements from John Foster Dulles, Secretary of State; Vice President Richard M. Nixon, and from a host of Senate and House members.

The President went into the White House Rose Garden to record for newsreels and television cameras his personal tribute to his long-time associate in war and peace.

It is not usual for the head of the United States Government to express himself so feelingly when the head of another government resigns from office.

But Sir Winston's departure changed all the rules. The President spoke into the cameras in the obvious hope that the British statesman himself would see the pictures and hear the words.

"We have just had official word that my old and very dear friend, Sir Winston Churchill, has retired from his position as head of Her Majesty's Government in the United Kingdom," the President said.

"Naturally, an event such as this recalls to my mind many stirring incidents both of war and peace. I have greatly respected and valued my associations with a man so great as Winston Churchill.

"And now, if I dare, I should like to adress a word directly to Sir Winston.

"All of us in the free world

Continued on Page 11, Column 7

CHURCHILL BARS OFFER OF PEERAGE

Prefers to Stay Commoner, He Replies to Queen's Bid—Britons Acclaim Him

By BENJAMIN WELLES
Special to The New York Times.

LONDON, April 5—Sir Winston Churchill declined a dukedom today to remain in the House of Commons.

In an audience with Queen Elizabeth II in her study in Buckingham Palace, he tendered his resignation to his sovereign. The Queen accepted it and then offered him the highest titular dignity in the land. But Sir Winston, a grandson of the seventh Duke of Marlborough, humbly yet firmly declined it.

He had been a "House of Commons man" for almost fifty years, he recalled, and he preferred to remain one rather than accept a peerage and enter the House of Lords.

The decision showed that Sir Winston, after laying down the cares and responsibilities of high office, would continue as an elder statesman in the Commons, which he has loved—and which has intermittently loved him—during that half century.

Had Declined Earldom

It was not the first time Sir Winston had turned down the offer of a peerage to remain in the lower but more powerful legislative chamber. In the aftermath of victory in 1945 he was offered an earldom, but refused it.

The 28-year-old Queen and the 80-year-old statesman each knew what was in the other's mind when they met today. He knew in advance what she would offer and she knew what his reply would be. But Elizabeth and Sir Winston, both exemplars of tradition in a tradition-loving land, observed the forms and courtesies due between the sovereign and a retiring counselor and friend.

The last non-royal dukedom was given to the Marquess of Westminster in 1874, the year of Sir Winston's birth. There are now twenty-six dukes in the United Kingdom peerage, in addition to the royal dukes—Edinburgh, Cornwall, Gloucester, Kent and Windsor.

Sir Winston's refusal of the proffered peerage means that his name will remain as it is. His knighthood, acquired in 1953

Continued on Page 11, Column 5

DULLES SAYS U. S. WON'T START WAR

Holds Any Conflict in Formosa Area Would Be Reds' Doing—Restates Quemoy Stand

By DANA ADAMS SCHMIDT
Special to The New York Times.

WASHINGTON, April 5—Secretary of State Dulles said today that if there was war in the Formosa Strait it would be the Communist Chinese who started it.

The United States, he asserted, has made "perfectly clear" its desire for a cease-fire and peace in the strait. But the Chinese Communists, he declared, unfortunately do not seem to be much under the influence of the peace propaganda they disseminate.

The Secretary made his observations in reply to a request for an assessment of the prospects for war or peace in the Formosa Strait at the first news conference he has held since March 15.

"To answer that question would require me to read the minds of people to whom I have no access, that is, the Communist leaders in Peiping," Mr. Dulles replied.

The Secretary was asked about continuing demands in Congress that the United States make known now whether it will defend Quemoy and Matsu Islands against Communist attack. Mr. Dulles said he knew the answer to that one by heart. There was no commitment of any kind, sort or description, expressed or implied, he declared, binding the United States to the defense of anything except Formosa and the Pescadores.

'Very Difficult Ground'

The suggestion that the United States should announce how it proposed to fulfill its treaty commitments entered onto "very difficult ground," he said. He did not see how it could be done.

The Secretary observed that the United States also had a commitment to defend the United States of America but no one had yet asked for a commitment as to how that would be done.

Asked whether that meant the United States would not fight for the defense of Quemoy and Matsu for the sake of the morale of Chinese Nationalist troops in Formosa, he replied that it would not, "unless that was vital for the defense of Formosa and the Pescadores. It all comes back to that."

President Eisenhower has told Congress that he and he alone would make the decision whether the United States should help defend Quemoy and Matsu. He said his decision would depend on whether the invasion of the offshore islands was recognizable as a preliminary to invasion of Formosa or the Pescadores.

While Mr. Dulles was speaking to the press, Secretary of the

Continued on Page 7, Column 5

Vietnam Dissidents Give Warning to U. S.

By ROBERT ALDEN
Special to The New York Times.

SAIGON, Vietnam, April 5—The groups fighting Vietnam's Government warned tonight that continued United States support of Premier Ngo Dinh Diem might lead to civil war.

They said that as far as they were concerned the truce was ended and that "all responsibility for bloodshed—Vietnamese and foreign—would rest on Ngo Dinh Diem."

It was further charged that the United States had turned over four tanks to the Government. As far as can be determined, the United States does not have any tanks in Vietnam.

The Ngo Dinh Diem Cabinet voted today to stand firm in the face of the Opposition's threat. As the situation in Saigon grew more tense by the hour, officials made it known that the Government had

Continued on Page 12, Column 3

SOUTH AFRICA OUT OF UNESCO RANKS

Quits United Nations Agency Over Racial Issue

By LEONARD INGALLS
Special to The New York Times.

JOHANNESBURG, South Africa, April 5—South Africa has withdrawn from the United Nations Educational, Scientific and Cultural Organization.

Eric H. Louw, Minister of External Affairs, said today in Capetown that it had been decided to terminate his country's participation in the United Nations agency because of its "interference in South Africa's racial problems."

He reported that the South African Ambassador in Paris had been instructed to inform the director of the United Nations agency of the Union's action. The decision to withdraw, Mr. Louw said, was made recently.

The Minister announced also that South Africa would not participate in deliberations in May before the International Court of Justice on its administration of the territory of South-West Africa under the League of Nations mandate. The territory was incorporated by South Africa in 1949.

This step of incorporation was not approved by the United Nations, which sought to have South Africa accept trusteeship of South-West Africa under United Nations supervision. South Africa ignored the United

Continued on Page 2, Column 3

MANPOWER SLASH IN MARINES, NAVY BACKED WITH 'IFS'

Carney and Shepherd Call Reduced Budget Adequate if No Emergency Occurs

DEMOCRATS CONCERNED

But They Are Assured Corps' Ability to Strike Quickly in an Attack Won't Suffer

By C. P. TRUSSELL
Special to The New York Times.

WASHINGTON, April 5—Top uniformed officers of the Navy and Marine Corps supported the President's reduced armed services budget today. At points, they appeared to be salting loyalty to the Commander in Chief with reservations.

The $34,000,000,000 budget for the fiscal year starting July 1, it seemed, was all right as of now. It was evident, however, that if the 'international situation worsened, more money' would be requested in a hurry.

Those testifying before a Senate Appropriations subcommittee were Gen. Lemuel C. Shepherd Jr., Commandant of the Marine Corps, and Admiral Robert B. Carney, Chief of Naval Operations.

Meanwhile, more civilian heads of the armed services continued to support the reduced budget. They included Charles S. Thomas, Secretary of the Navy, and Harold E. Talbott, Secretary of the Air Force.

A spokesman for Robert T. Stevens, Secretary of the Army, is expected to back the other civilian leaders tomorrow. Mr. Stevens is out of the country.

Frank Answers Sought

Democrats of the subcommittee, which is headed by Senator Dennis Chavez, Democrat of New Mexico, continued to search for blunt answers from the uniformed officers as to how they felt about the military cuts.

The Democrats do not like proposed cuts in Marine Corps forces. General Shepherd was asked how he squared his support of a reduction in the armed forces with the mission of the Marine Corps to be the first to fight in case of an attack.

"It is manifest," he replied, "that reductions of the magnitude with which we are confronted [a cut from 215,000 to 193,-000] involve some sacrifice.

"However, we are determined that the sacrifice will not be made in readiness of our basic striking forces. The reduction will be absorbed primarily by disbanding certain reinforcing combat and logistic units and by reducing the manning levels of other supporting units.

"Operationally, the effect of these actions will be to diminish somewhat the staying power of

Continued on Page 14, Column 7

Harriman and Wagner Plan Own City-State Fiscal Study

Financing by a Private Foundation May Be Sought for Project Ignored by the Legislature, Mayor Announces

By CHARLES G. BENNETT

Governor Harriman and Mayor Wagner will go ahead soon with the appointment of a committee to make a long-range study of state-city fiscal relationships. It is possible that funds will be sought from a private foundation for the study.

Mayor Wagner announced this yesterday as he discussed the city's fiscal situation in an interview in his office, 63 Park Row, and later before 300 members of the Bond Club at a luncheon at 120 Broadway. He forecast that Republicans as well as Democrats would be invited to serve on the fiscal study committee.

The Mayor expressed hope that the committee would find a formula for taking the whole city-state financial problem "entirely out of politics." He predicted that the prestige of the study committee members would be so great that the state Legislature could not afford to ignore its suggestions.

At its session just ended, the Legislature failed to take any action creating a legislative commission to make the state-city financial study. Mayor Wagner, backed by the Governor, had called for such a survey in an effort to end the recurring crises that send the Mayor and his aides to Albany each year seeking state aid and authorization for new taxes.

At his interview yesterday Mayor Wagner commented that the city had had more cooperation than usual from the Legislature in approval of city bills.

At the same time he noted that the Legislature had helped to solve city fiscal woes for "this year only" and that the city financial measures did "not call

Continued on Page 21, Column 3

Canada Cuts Income Taxes In a Bid to Spur Prosperity

By RAYMOND DANIELL
Special to The New York Times.

OTTAWA, April 5—The Canadian Government decided tonight to cut taxes. The national debt will be increased in the interest of national prosperity. Indirect and direct personal and corporate income taxes were cut to increase purchasing power and investment capital, with the advance knowledge that the Government would be collecting less than it plans to spend.

This is in accord with the expressed Liberal policy of taxing for surpluses in good and prosperous times and accepting a deficit when business, agriculture and industry run into trouble. The Canadian economy is not in serious trouble, but unemployment, a slowing down in industry and a drop in farm income have raised danger signals.

Tonight, in presenting his first budget as Minister of Finance, Walter Harris, in spite of an unexpected deficit of nearly $150,-000,000 last year, proposed new tax cuts that will reduce the Government's revenues by about $207,000,000 in a full year based on normal expectations of increased prosperity.

Mr. Harris proposed a new schedule of rates to reduce the personal income tax by 12 to 13 per cent for 85 per cent of the country's taxpayers. There are 3,800,000 persons in this category in this country of 15,000,-000 inhabitants.

This, of course, will add to the country's national debt. This, Mr. Harris asserted, should be no cause for alarm. He was taking into account an expected rise in the country's gross national product of about 5 per cent. Mr. Harris said, in reducing the scale of taxes. With more wealth being produced, he said, it was possible to reduce

Continued on Page 12, Column 5

WEST BIG 3 BAR AUSTRIAN ACCORD WITH SOVIET ONLY

Joint Declaration Advises Both Vienna and Moscow Big 4 Approval Is Needed

Special to The New York Times.

WASHINGTON, April 5—The Western Big Three cautioned Austria and the Soviet Union today against making bilateral commitments on the terms of an Austrian state treaty.

The United States, Britain and France issued a joint declaration noting that conclusion of the long-pending pact was of concern to all of the Big Four powers as well as Austria.

If the Soviet Union should offer "proposals which hold clear promise of the restoration of freedom and independence to Austria, these would appropriately be discussed by the four Ambassadors in Vienna with the participation of the Austrian Government," the joint declaration said. It was made public simultaneously here and in London and Paris.

While it was not specifically directed to either the Moscow or Vienna Government, the statement was interpreted here as advice to both of the Western Big Three's attitude toward the Soviet-Austrian meeting scheduled for next week in Moscow.

West Wary on Concessions

The Western Big Three were understood to be particularly concerned lest Julius Raab, the Austrian Chancellor, make concessions to the Soviet Union that would be unacceptable to them.

Chancellor Raab and a delegation of Austrian officials will fly to Moscow Monday to discuss new ways of arriving at a treaty. The mission is being undertaken at the March 24 invitation of Vyacheslav M. Molotov, Soviet Foreign Minister.

One was a guarantee of Austrian independence that would prevent another Anschluss, or union, between Austria and Germany.

The other was an expression of Austria's willingness to guarantee that she would not join any military alliance or allow her territory to be used for foreign military bases.

The West has never opposed military neutrality for Austria and never has planned to include Austria in the North Atlantic alliance. The concern is more over a possible attempt by the Soviet Union to insist on unacceptable guarantee terms with respect to either or both of Mr. Molotov's points.

In the past, one of the main barriers to a pact restoring Austria's freedom and ending the four-power occupation has been the Soviet Union's insistence on the maintenance of occupation troops until a German treaty has been completed.

The text of today's three-power declaration follows:

"For many years the Governments of the United Kingdom, the United States and France have sought to conclude an Austrian state treaty. They have made ceaseless efforts thus to bring about the restoration of

Continued on Page 12, Column 3

RED CROSS EASES FUND DRIVE RULES

Permits Chapters to Join in Community Campaigns Under Some Conditions

By The Associated Press.

WASHINGTON, April 5 — The American National Red Cross announced today that it had relaxed its rules so that under certain conditions local chapters could participate in Community or United Fund raising drives.

Most Red Cross chapters have refused to become a part of fund-raising campaigns such as Community Chest and United Fund Drives. In these, welfare agencies are grouped. Each receives a percentage of the funds raised.

E. Roland Harriman, national Red Cross chairman, said the board of governors had adopted the policy yesterday.

With the changes, he said, "Red Cross chapters will be able to plan in a more direct and helpful manner with other agencies and community leaders in matters of united or federated fund raising."

The board said the United States Government had established the American National Red Cross as this nation's official volunteer agency under the Geneva conventions. It added that this "unique and official" status made certain conditions of fund-raising necessary.

Units Control Own Budgets

The board said each local Red Cross chapter would keep its rights:

¶To determine and control its budget and goal.

¶To conduct a roll-call for members and funds in the month designated by the board of governors.

¶To conduct emergency campaigns in disaster, war or other unforeseen need when authorized by the board of governors.

¶To issue a membership card to each person from whom contribution the Red Cross received $1 or more.

The amended policy keeps the provision that all chapters will "participate in annual campaigns for members and funds for the purpose of enrolling members and obtaining adequate voluntary contributions to finance the budgetary requirements of the chapters and the national organization."

Red Cross headquarters here said it would be possible for a local chapter to participate in a United Fund Drive and also conduct its own campaign later if needed to reach its goal.

Local chapters may work out their own program, headquarters said. They may get all their funds from the United Drive, merely retaining the "right" to their own drive.

Since most United Fund Drives

Continued on Page 24, Column 6

JERSEY SEIZES 62 IN HOT-ROD TRAP

Racers Caught on Unlighted Road Used as Speedway

Special to The New York Times.

CHATSWORTH, N. J., April 5—It's a rare man who can lay hands on a will-o'-the-wisp, especially if it's motor-powered. Yet that's what State Trooper Leonard Miller did under a bright moon last night.

For weeks now, nocturnal travelers through the lonely pine lands of Burlington County have been frightened almost off the highway by dabs of light whooshing past them at breakneck speed.

The police, who had their suspicions about the souped-up will-o'-the-wisps, were hard put to track them down. One night the reports came from here, the next from there. Always the apparitions appeared from unlighted stretches along Route 72, which runs from the center of the state to the coast. Among other attractions for hot-rodders it has a fourteen-mile stretch that is almost ruler-straight.

Last night the state troopers set a trap along a section that was without highway lamps but bright in the moonlight.

Trooper Miller, on watch near the Pennsylvania Railroad overpass, heard, at about 10:30 P. M., a buzz and then a roar. Out of the west came four blobs of light, spanning the two-lane roadway.

Trooper Miller stepped into the

Continued on Page 23, Column 5

3 Hefty Councilmen in Small Cab Say Rule on Front Seat Must Go

Six hundred and thirty-five pounds of City Councilmen found themselves uncomfortably squeezed recently into the back seat of one of the new small taxicabs. In front, the seat next to the driver beckoned, empty and inviting. Under the law, nothing could be done about it. The Councilmen had to stay put.

The Councilmen—there were three—decided "there ought to be a law." So now there probably will be.

The legislation authorizing use of the stock-car five-passenger cabs (driver and four fares, maximum) specifies that a passenger may legally ride in front with the driver only if there is a full complement of three in back. The law says nothing about the sizes and weights of these back-seat riders.

"Yesterday, a "Fat Man's Amendment" was introduced into the City Council to distribute the small-taxi fare weight more evenly.

The amendment, referred to the Council's General Welfare Committee, would permit a passenger to ride in front with either two or three passengers on the back seat. The sponsors of the amendment were Edward A. Cunningham, Bronx Democrat, and John J. Merli, Manhattan Democrat.

Mr. Cunningham, who weighs 225 pounds, was one of the three Councilmen who took the back-seat ride in discomfort. The others were James J. Murphy, Staten Island Democrat, weighing in at 216 pounds, and James J. Boland, Manhattan Democrat, a mere 200-pounder.

There was no ready explanation as to why Mr. Merli, who tips the beam at substantially less than 200 pounds, was a cosponsor of the amendment. Other Councilmen guessed that he was "just going along for the ride."

Councilman Cunningham noted, in explaining his bill after yesterday's Council session, that the proposed amendment would be of aid not only to overweight passengers but also to women burdened with bundles. Referring to the plight of Mr. Murphy, Mr. Boland and himself, Mr. Cunningham said:

"When three fat guys like us try to squeeze into the back seat of one of these small-sized cabs, it is a tight fit, and something has to give."

Since Mr. Boland was not at yesterday's Council session and Mr. Cunningham and Mr. Murphy left City Hall soon after the meeting, it was impossible to

Continued on Page 28, Column 5

"All the News That's Fit to Print"

The New York Times.

LATE CITY EDITION
Cloudy with some rain today. Chance of showers tomorrow.
Temperature Range Today—Max., 56; Min., 42
Temperature Yesterday—Max., 63; Min., 41
Full U. S. Weather Bureau Report, Page 59

VOL. CIV..No. 35,508. Entered as Second-Class Matter, Post Office, New York, N. Y. NEW YORK, WEDNESDAY, APRIL 13, 1955. Times Square, New York 36, N. Y. Telephone LAckawanna 4-1000 FIVE CENTS

SALK POLIO VACCINE PROVES SUCCESS; MILLIONS WILL BE IMMUNIZED SOON; CITY SCHOOLS BEGIN SHOTS APRIL 25

WORDS OF HOPE: Dr. Thomas Francis Jr., left, and Dr. Jonas E. Salk on speakers' platform at Ann Arbor, Mich., where they addressed scientists on effects of polio vaccine. Associated Press Wirephoto

TRIAL DATA GIVEN

Efficacy of 80 to 90% Shown—Salk Sees Further Advance

Abstract of report, summary of data on tests, Page 22.

By WILLIAM L. LAURENCE
Special to The New York Times.

ANN ARBOR, Mich., April 12—The world learned today that its hopes for finding an effective weapon against paralytic polio had been realized.

The triple anti-polio vaccine originated by Dr. Jonas E. Salk works. This was revealed in the long-awaited report on the mass field trials of 1954, largest of their kind in medical history.

In these tests the vaccine, designed to protect against the crippling effects of all the three types of virus known to produce paralytic polio, was administered to 440,000 children in forty-four states.

The report, a medical classic, was presented at a special scientific meeting at the University of Michigan by Dr. Thomas Francis Jr. It was he who had directed the evaluation of the vast mass of data provided by the tests, involving the correlation of 144,000,000 separate items of information.

Half Got Dummy Shot

Dr. Francis reported the vaccinations had been 80 to 90 per cent effective on the basis of results in eleven states.

In these states, which included New York, half of the children vaccinated got the Salk vaccine. The other half received a placebo, or dummy shot.

These results, Dr. Francis reported, were looked upon with "greater confidence" than the figures in other areas. In these the results indicated an effectiveness of 60 to 80 per cent against paralysis by any polio virus.

Dr. Salk reported at the meeting that new and more potent vaccines and more effective methods of administering them, were ready for the 1955 vaccinations.

Dr. Salk, who is a member of the faculty at the University of Pittsburgh's School of Medicine, said:

"Theoretically, the new 1955 vaccines and vaccination procedures may lead to 100 per cent protection from paralysis of all those vaccinated."

The new procedures he out-

Continued on Page 20, Column 2

STEVENSON COPIED PLAN ON FORMOSA, DULLES CHARGES

He Says Democrat Proposed as His 'Original' Ideas the Administration's Policy

SOME DIPLOMATS DIFFER

Know of No U.S. Moves in U.N. or With Allies Paralleling Views of 1952 Candidate

Special to The New York Times.

WASHINGTON, April 12—Secretary of State Dulles said today Adlai E. Stevenson advocated "as original ideas" the same steps toward peace in the Formosa Strait that the Administration was exploring.

The only major point of difference between the proposals made by the 1952 Democratic Presidential candidate in a Chicago speech last night and his own idea, Mr. Dulles said, lay in the degree of solicitude the United States should show toward Nationalist China.

"Mr. Stevenson speaks feelingly about our 'allies'," the Secretary of State said at his news conference this morning. "However, he forgets one ally, namely, the Republic of China.

"It is upon the loyalty and resources of that ally that the free world must primarily depend for the defense of Formosa. Yet Mr. Stevenson seems to assume that that ally can be ignored and rebuffed.

"Aside from this, Mr. Stevenson has in fact endorsed the main features of this Administration's program in relation to Formosa."

News to Some Diplomats

Mr. Stevenson's speech was on the whole more warmly received in the embassies of the major powers allied with the United States in Europe and Asia.

In these quarters, however, there was some puzzlement among some diplomats over Mr. Dulles' statement that the ideas advanced by Mr. Stevenson in his Chicago speech were "the very approaches which the Government has been and is actively exploring."

If the State Department was exploring with its allies a joint pledge for the united defense of Formosa combined with an effort to extricate the Chinese Nationalists from the Matsu and Quemoy Island groups, that was news to several senior diplomats today. Mr. Stevenson had urged such steps.

These diplomats did not know, either, of any active move by the United States and its allies calling on the United Nations General Assembly to "condemn any effort to alter the present status

Continued on Page 4, Column 3

Dulles Doubts Corsi Ability; Ex-Aide Charges Untruths

Associated Press Wirephoto
Edward Corsi at his Arlington, Va., home yesterday as he replied to charges made by Secretary of State Dulles.

Special to The New York Times.

WASHINGTON, April 12—It was open war today between John Foster Dulles, Secretary of State, and his former "old friend," Edward Corsi.

Mr. Dulles accused the New Yorker of making reckless charges, of trying to circumvent the law and of not being qualified to run the refugee relief program. Mr. Corsi charged the Secretary of State with "a whole string of falsehoods," adding that he was "terribly shocked and astounded that a man like Dulles for whom I had such respect could stoop so low."

Only four months ago Mr. Dulles had appointed Mr. Corsi his special assistant on refugee

Continued on Page 16, Column 6

HIGH COURT HEARS SOUTH WILL DEFY QUICK END TO BIAS

Gradual Approaches Urged for Integration of Schools—Negro Lawyers Opposed

By LUTHER A. HUSTON
Special to The New York Times.

WASHINGTON, April 12—Spokesmen for South Carolina and Virginia told the Supreme Court today that their people would not obey a decree ordering an immediate end to racial segregation in the public schools.

When Chief Justice Earl Warren asked S. E. Rogers, representing Clarendon County, S. C., if he were willing to say that an "honest attempt" would be made to conform to whatever decree the court might issue, Mr. Rogers said:

"Let's get that word 'honest' out of there. It would depend upon the kind of decree. The white people would not send their children to school with Negroes."

Archibald O. Robertson, who represented Virginia, said that Virginia would not defy the court, but that there were "subtle ways" of not complying with an order for an abrupt end to segregation. One would be for the voters to refuse to approve funds for an immediate integration of a school system.

Time Asked for South

J. Lindsay Almond Jr., Attorney General of Virginia, said that "forthwith enforcement of integration would be pre-emptive of the rights of a sovereign people." He asserted that the schools of his state "might have to close" if an abrupt end to segregation were ordered.

Throughout the second day of arguments on the type of decrees the court should issue to carry out its decision of last May 17 that public school segregation was unconstitutional, the Southern states pleaded for time to adjust their educational systems to the new order.

The states were not specific, however, as to the length of time they would need. Estimates ranged from a tentative five years to as high as the year 2045.

The lawyers for the Negro side, however, were specific. Thurgood Marshall, counsel for the National Association for the Advancement of the Colored People, submitted two proposed decrees. One would end all school segregation everywhere next September.

An alternate decree, which Mr. Marshall said was the least the Negroes should be asked to accept, would terminate separate schools for white and Negro pupils by September, 1956.

Mr. Marshall asserted that there could not be a "moratorium on the Fourteenth Amendment or local option" to enforce a constitutional decision of the court. The Fourteenth Amendment to the Constitution prohibits a state from denying to

Continued on Page 18, Column 5

281,853 ELIGIBLE FOR VACCINE HERE

City to Vote Fund Quickly for Equipment—Experts to Set Number of Shots

Mayor Wagner announced yesterday that a special appropriation of $100,000 would be made to speed the city's polio vaccination program.

Elated by the success of the Salk vaccine, city officials said they were ready to begin vaccination on April 25. Those eligible to receive free inoculations from the city are 281,853 school children. These include all first and second graders and those third and fourth graders who received dummy shots in last year's field trials.

In New York State, 725,000 children between 5 and 14 years of age will be vaccinated by June 1. In making this announcement, Dr. Herman E. Hilleboe, State Health Commissioner, said that if the dosage was reduced from three shots to two, the number of children immunized could be increased to 1,100,000.

In New Jersey, the inoculation of nearly 300,000 school children will begin on Monday, when the

Continued on Page 23, Column 3

Supply to Be Low for Time, But Output Will Be Rushed

By DAMON STETSON
Special to The New York Times.

ANN ARBOR, Mich., April 12—The Salk vaccine for poliomyelitis will be made available for the immunization of children as rapidly as possible, but it is expected to be in short supply temporarily. The National Foundation for Infantile Paralysis announced today that vaccine already purchased for 9,000,000 immunizations (three inoculations a child) would be turned over to state and territorial health officers.

This amount will be offered to all children who participated in last year's field trials but who did not actually receive vaccine. Children enrolled in the first and second grades of all public, private and parochial schools in the United States, Hawaii and Alaska also will be offered the vaccine.

Dr. Jonas E. Salk, who originated the vaccine, reported his belief that the maximum effect of the third (booster) inoculation could be achieved only if administered at least seven months after the primary inoculation of two shots.

Such a procedure would make it possible to give 13,500,000 children primary inoculations immediately upon approval of the vaccine by the National Institutes of Health. When the seven-month period had elapsed, additional vaccine would have been produced.

Dr. Salk also urged that all children who received inoculations during the 1954 field trials be given an additional booster dose in 1955. This is necessary, he said, because the three doses

Continued on Page 22, Column 6

6 VACCINE MAKERS GET U. S. LICENSES

Government Clears the Way for Quantity Production of Salk Preventive

By BESS FURMAN
Special to The New York Times.

WASHINGTON, April 12—The Federal Government today quickly gave a clear track to Salk polio vaccine.

It licensed six concerns to manufacture and distribute throughout the country the protective substance developed by Dr. Jonas E. Salk of the University of Pittsburgh.

The key action in the licensing was the signature of Oveta Culp Hobby, the Secretary of Health, Education and Welfare. Federal approval is required by the National Biologics Control Act. As she signed Mrs. Hobby said:

"It's a great day. It's a wonderful day for the whole world. It's a history-making day."

Licensed Concerns Named

The concerns approved to make and sell the product are:

Cutter Laboratories, Berkeley, Calif.; Eli Lilly Company, Indianapolis; Parke, Davis & Co., Detroit; Pittman-Moore Company, Zionville, Ind.; Sharp & Dohme, Philadelphia, and Wyeth Laboratories, Inc., Marietta, Pa.

Mrs. Hobby affixed her signature at 5:15 P. M. Had it been possible for her to sign at 4 P. M., the signing would have been what Washington calls a "full dress" ceremony for photographers and the press.

This press meeting was canceled because Mrs. Hobby had to wait for the final judgment of the Public Health Service on the vaccine evaluation study made public today by Dr. Thomas Francis Jr.

Thus it happened that only Surgeon General Leonard A. Scheele of the Public Health Service and a few other members of the departmental staff were present when Mrs. Hobby signed.

Earlier Dr. Scheele had said the delay had been because of "things running late out in Ann Arbor." He reminded that before licensing a new drug the Public Health Service must approve both safety and potency.

"The data on safety had all

Continued on Page 24, Column 4

FANFARE USHERS VERDICT ON TESTS

Medical History Is Written in Hollywood Atmosphere

Special to The New York Times.

ANN ARBOR, Mich., April 12—The formal verdict on the Salk vaccine was disclosed today amid fanfare and drama far more typical of a Hollywood première than a medical meeting.

The event that made medical history took place in one of the University of Michigan's most glamorous structures—Rackham Building. Television cameras and radio microphones were set up outside the huge lecture hall. Inside the salmon-colored hall a battery of sixteen television and newsreel cameras were lined up across a long wooden platform especially built at the rear.

At 10:20 A. M. Dr. Thomas Francis Jr., director of the Poliomyelitis Vaccine Evaluation Center and the man of the hour, was introduced. A short, chunky man with a close-cropped mustache, he was wearing a black suit, white shirt and striped gray tie.

He stepped behind a lectern decorated with a blue and gold banner bearing the seal of the university. He appeared small, hidden up to his breast pocket by the lectern, as he looked out toward his audience of 500 scientists and physicians. Cameras ground and spotlights played

Continued on Page 20, Column 4

SOVIET ARMED AID OFFERED AFGHANS

Moscow Said to Back Kabul in Dispute With Pakistan on North-West Frontier

By JOHN P. CALLAHAN
Special to The New York Times.

KABUL, Afghanistan (via Peshawar, Pakistan), April 11—The Soviet Ambassador was reported today to have offered help to Afghanistan's Premier. The aid was said to be military support if Pakistan or her Western allies "threaten aggressive interference" in Afghanistan's demand for a plebiscite in the adjoining North-West Frontier Province.

The Soviet Union borders on Afghanistan.

The report of the Soviet offer was made by an Afghan Government officer who has been observing the almost daily meetings since March 30 between Soviet Ambassador Mikhail V. Degtyar and Premier Sardar Mohammed Daud of Afghanistan.

It followed by a few hours a report, confirmed by foreign envoys, that King Mohammed Zahir Shah had informed the Ambassadors of the United States, Britain and Turkey that he was prepared to replace Premier Daud with his predecessor, Mahmoud Zahir if their Governments would assure Afghanistan of "full" support in event of attacks by "unfriendly powers."

Embassy spokesmen said Washington and London had been informed of the King's request and that they were awaiting replies. The Ambassadors of

Continued on Page 2, Column 3

YONKERS IS FACING LOSS OF STATE AID

Albany Threatens to Cut Off Grants Unless Schools Are Improved by Jan. 1

By LEONARD BUDER

The State Education Commissioner warned the City of Yonkers yesterday that it would lose its state grants to aid education unless it improved its public school system.

The Commissioner, Dr. Lewis A. Wilson, acted in response to an appeal made last year by a group of Yonkers residents who charged that the city's "starvation" budgetary allowances had produced "shocking" school conditions. He set Jan. 1 as the deadline for the Yonkers Board of Education to submit "sufficient evidence of an adequate program, both in respect to its educational offerings and its building needs for the ensuing year."

Commenting upon his action, Dr. Wilson said that his threat to withhold state aid to Yonkers was an "uncommon" but not an unprecedented move.

Yonkers this year is receiving $2,046,000 in regular state aid

Continued on Page 32, Column 5

CENSORSHIP MOVE DENIED BY WILSON

Secretary Defends His Curb on Giving Information

By ANTHONY LEVIERO
Special to The New York Times.

WASHINGTON, April 12—Charles E. Wilson, Secretary of Defense, defended today his directive for control of defense information, denying that it was "censorship."

He said in a news conference that the widespread publication of technical information in the hydrogen bomb age made national security a "greater problem than ever before in history."

He declared he would be willing to pay hundreds of millions of dollars to get the same kind of information about the Soviet Union as that country gets about the United States in its newspapers and periodicals.

The Secretary outlined a dilemma created by the great outpouring of technical information in a free and highly industrialized society. He said "our ...n folks" felt too much was being published as a result of ...es between corporations ...efense contracts and be... the armed forces, and of ...erprise of a free press historical tendency of to report all the latest ...nts.

...lson said the Adminis... as grappling with a problem the solution

...on Page 11, Column 1

Austro-Soviet Talk Toasted by Bohlen

By CLIFTON DANIEL
Special to The New York Times.

MOSCOW, April 12—In the presence of senior leaders of the Soviet state, Charles E. Bohlen, United States Ambassador, offered a toast this evening to the speedy restoration of Austria's independence and freedom.

Vyacheslav M. Molotov, Soviet Foreign Minister, said it was a good toast and raised his glass. So did Premier Nikolai A. Bulganin and Deputy Premiers Lazar M. Kaganovich, Anastas I. Mikoyan and Mikhail G. Pervukhin.

Drinking with them were Julius Raab, Chancellor of Austria, and other members of the Austrian delegation that arrived here yesterday. The Austrians opened negotiations with Mr. Molotov during the afternoon on the terms of a treaty intended to achieve

Continued on Page 8, Column 3

Eisenhower Gets Degree From Clark at The Citadel

Associated Press Wirephoto
President Eisenhower and Gen. Mark W. Clark, retired, review honor guard at The Citadel

By W. H. LAWRENCE
Special to The New York Times.

AUGUSTA, Ga., April 12—President Eisenhower declared today that military men of the present and future must be "apostles of peace" working to understand what makes humans and nations "tick." This was his advice to the corps of cadets at The Citadel, the military college of South Carolina, in Charleston. He received an honorary Doctor of Laws degree from retired Gen. Mark W. Clark, president of The Citadel, and reviewed the cadets en route here for an eight-day golfing vacation. Greeting the cadets and applauding thousands who lined Charleston's streets, the Presi-

Continued on Page 12, Column 4

T. V. A. Detractors Scored by Lilienthal

By JOHN N. POPHAM
Special to The New York Times.

CHATTANOOGA, Tenn., April 12—David E. Lilienthal made a blistering attack tonight on the economic and political detractors of the Tennessee Valley Authority, "from the White House down."

The former chairman of the authority said that as a one-time neighbor he felt impelled to return to the valley region to help warn its residents concerning the tactics of the enemies currently waging a "cold war" against the famous river resources agency.

Mr. Lilienthal guided the development of T. V. A. through a succession of national controversies from 1933 to 1946. Then he spoke for public power philosophies espoused by the Federal Government, in contrast with his role of accusing the present Administration of

Continued on Page 15, Column 3

"All the News That's Fit to Print"

The New York Times.

LATE CITY EDITION
Fair and seasonably warm today. Fair, quite warm tomorrow.
Temperature Range Today—Max., 86; Min., 67
Temperatures Yesterday—Max., 77.9; Min., 65.5
Full U. S. Weather Bureau Report, Page 28

Copyright, 1955, by The New York Times Company.

VOL. CIV. No. 35,616. Entered as Second-Class Matter. Post Office, New York, N. Y. NEW YORK, SATURDAY, JULY 30, 1955. Times Square, New York 36, N. Y. Telephone Lackawanna 4-1000 FIVE CENTS

U. S. TO LAUNCH EARTH SATELLITE 200-300 MILES INTO OUTER SPACE; WORLD WILL GET SCIENTIFIC DATA

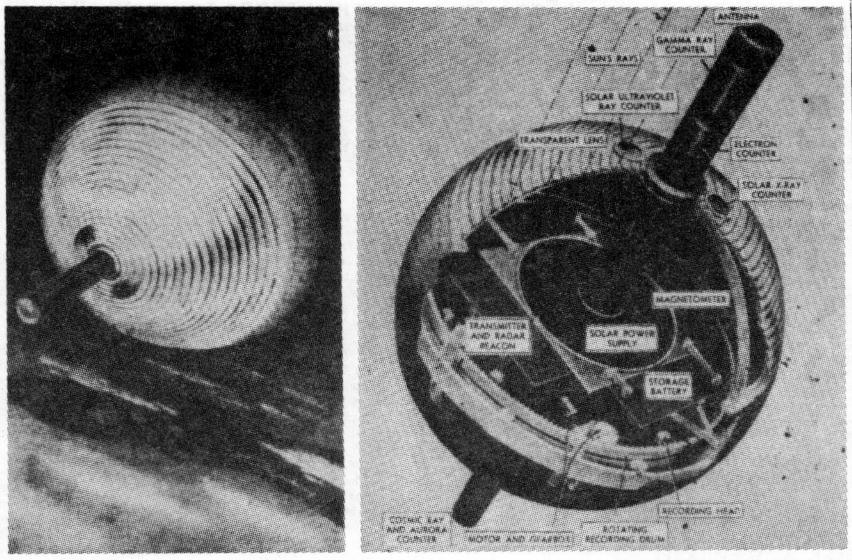

Associated Press Wirephoto (from Popular Science)

MAN-MADE SATELLITE: Artist's renditions of the earth-circling satellite, based on a concept of Prof. S. F. Singer of the University of Maryland. Professor Singer's specifications—diameter of about two feet, weight 100 pounds and speed 17,280 miles an hour—conform closely with those of the announcement from the White House.

PACE 18,000 M.P.H.

Rocket to Start Object Size of a Basketball in 1957 or 1958

Texts of press conference and documents, Pages 8 and 9.

By RUSSELL BAKER
Special to The New York Times.

WASHINGTON, July 29—This country plans to launch history's first man-made, earth-circling satellite into space during 1957 or 1958.

Tentative plans envision an unmanned globular object about the size of a basketball. The satellite will flash around the earth about once every ninety minutes at a speed of 18,000 miles an hour in a fixed path 200 to 300 miles above the ground.

These plans were announced this afternoon at an extraordinary White House news conference attended by a battery of prominent scientists.

James C. Hagerty, White House press secretary, joined the scientists in stressing the satellite's immense scientific value to all nations and minimizing its threat as a potential instrument of war.

All nations, including the Communist countries, will have complete access to all scientific data gathered beyond the earth's known frontier, Mr. Hagerty said.

American scientists also will give the world the plot of the satellite's orbit, or course through space, so that scholars of all countries may study it.

Data Available to All

If the object carries radio equipment for transmitting scientific data to the earth, other nations will receive the broadcasting frequencies so they can tune in.

The satellite will girdle the earth "entirely for scientific purposes," Mr. Hagerty said.

"Do you mean as distinct from war-making purposes?" he was asked.

"If you wish, yes," he replied.

The scientists said they were convinced that the satellite was now "feasible" with available technological methods and materials.

Once aloft, they said, it is expected to produce new information about the unexplored outer atmosphere that is necessary before human travel in space can be undertaken.

As the scientists depicted it, the satellite would be hurled into space under rocket power. The rocket, in several stages, would fall away piece by piece as each stage burnt out its fuel load.

At a point somewhere between 200 and 300 miles above earth, the satellite—or "the bird," as the scientists call it—would get one final mighty blast from the rocket's last stage.

This would send it hurtling into its orbit at a speed of 18,000 miles an hour. A man standing on earth could perhaps barely

Continued on Page 7, Column 1

TALBOTT QUITTING, PERHAPS AT ONCE, G.O.P. SOURCES SAY

But the White House Asserts 'There's Nothing Before Us' —Secretary 'Sits Tight'

ANOTHER INQUIRY LOOMS

Democrats Charge He Misled Them on Chrysler Stock by Giving It to Children

By ALLEN DRURY
Special to The New York Times.

WASHINGTON, July 29—Republican Senators high in Administration councils said tonight that the resignation of Harold E. Talbott as Secretary of the Air Force was "imminent."

The Senators, who declined to be quoted by name, said the resignation might be announced over the weekend. At the White House, the Presidential press secretary, James C. Hagerty, would say only, "There is nothing before us."

Mr. Talbott said he was "sitting tight" and "has no more idea than a jackrabbit" of resigning.

He said he would be at his office in the morning and that he was "going ahead and try and run the Air Force as I have tried to do through all of this."

[A possibility, at least, that the Secretary would resign was discerned by The Associated Press, which quoted him as having said later, "I will do nothing at any time to embarrass President Eisenhower, and I will do whatever the President wishes me to do."]

The embattled Cabinet officer, already under investigation for his activities in connection with business for a management consultant corporation in which he was a partner, appeared to be headed for still another inquiry.

Senators Differ With Him

This one would revolve around a promise he made at the time of his appointment in 1953 to divest himself of 2,000 shares of Chrysler stock.

The new investigation, it was indicated, might be instigated by Democratic members of the Senate Armed Services Committee, which handled the Talbott nomination two years ago. They charged today that he had "improperly misled" them at that time concerning his plans for the stock.

Mr. Talbott testified Wednesday before the Senate Permanent Subcommittee on Investigations that he had given the stock to his four children, two of them minors. The Secretary said he had made it clear to the Armed Services Committee that he might give the stock away instead of selling it outright. But members of that committee said today they had had no such understanding.

Senator Harry F. Byrd, Democrat of Virginia, with whom Mr. Talbott said he had had an informal understanding that he might give the stock to members of his family, said he had no recollection of such a conversation. The Senator said he had understood the stock would be sold.

Senator Richard B. Russell, Democrat of Georgia, chairman of the Armed Services Committee, said today it was his "distinct impression from what Mr.

Continued on Page 6, Column 7

Court Rejects Plea To Deport Bridges

Special to The New York Times.

SAN FRANCISCO, July 29—Federal Judge Louis E. Goodman today refused to strip Harry Renton Bridges, Pacific Coast labor leader, of his United States citizenship.

Judge Goodman, in the Government's fourth attempt to deport Mr. Bridges to his native Australia, ruled the prosecution had not proved its charges that the longshore leader had been a member of the Communist party before he was naturalized Sept. 17, 1945.

United States Attorney Lloyd H. Burke and Lynn J. Gillard and Robert H. Schnacke, assistant Federal attorneys, prosecuted the case. They said a decision to appeal would depend on the outcome of consultation with Department of Justice officials in Wash-

Continued on Page 10, Column 6

J. E. HOOVER SHUNS CITY POLICE POST

Declines Mayor's Bid to Be Commissioner—Wagner Is Said to Seek Outsider

By PAUL CROWELL

J. Edgar Hoover, director of the Federal Bureau of Investigation, has declined an invitation by Mayor Wagner to become the city's next Police Commissioner.

The offer of appointment to the $25,000 post now held by Francis W. H. Adams was made by the Mayor early this week through an unidentified emissary described at City Hall as a close friend of the F. B. I. chief.

Mr. Adams announced his resignation last Sunday but is remaining at his post until the Mayor appoints a successor.

The first announcement of Mr. Hoover's rejection of the Mayor's offer came from Washington. It was made by Louis B. Nichols, an assistant director of the F. B. I., after he had talked on the telephone with his chief. Mr. Nichols said Mr. Hoover was traveling "somewhere on the West Coast."

"Mr. Hoover has no plans to leave the F. B. I. and has declined Mayor Wagner's kind offer," Mr. Nichols said. He then telephoned the same announcement to William R. Peer, the Mayor's executive secretary. Mr. Peer passed the word along to the Mayor, who is spending the week-end at his summer home in Islip, L. I. The Mayor had no comment.

A report that Carmine G. DeSapio, head of Tammany Hall, was a guest at the Islip home, presumably to discuss the appointment of a new Police Commissioner, was spiked by the Mayor. Mr. DeSapio, he said, was not there and was not expected.

"I'll name the new Police Commissioner myself without consultation with anybody," the Mayor declared.

The Mayor did receive visits

Continued on Page 34, Column 6

CONGRESS CHIEFS ABANDON PLANS TO ADJOURN TODAY

House to Meet on Monday —Fuel Gas Bill Sidetracked —Public Housing Set Back

Special to The New York Times.

WASHINGTON, July 29—Congress was caught tonight in the traditional minor frenzy of the eleventh hour as the controlling Democrats labored urgently toward bringing this session to an end.

All hope for an adjournment by tomorrow night, as had long been planned, was abandoned.

The Senate was in position to finish its work by then but the House of Representatives had a solid docket of work still ahead.

Late in the day the House Democratic floor leader, Representative John W. McCormack of Massachusetts, officially announced that there would be a House meeting on Monday.

He prepared a calendar of business that will result in carrying Congress into next week.

The House quit for the night at 6:17 P. M. and will reassemble at 10:30 tomorrow morning.

Pressing to meet the original quitting date as nearly as they could, the Senate leaders officially cast aside until next year the most controversial single measure remaining on that side.

Defeat for President

This was a bill, passed 209 to 203 last night by the House, to exempt natural gas producers from Federal price control.

The decision was in a modified sense a blow to the President, who had expressed support in principle for the bill.

It was a much heavier blow, however, to the leading Democrats of Congress, including Sam Rayburn of Texas, Speaker of the House of Representatives, and the ailing Senate Democratic chieftain, Senator Lyndon B. Johnson of Texas.

While many Republicans had gone along with the bill, its essential backers were these and other Southern and Southwestern Democratic members of Congress from the gas-producing states.

Adamantly against the project was the great bulk of the Northern wing of the Democratic party in Congress; especially the members from urban consumer areas.

The President, too, was suffering setbacks, however provisional some might turn out to be. For the White House was understood to be appealing privately for some aspects of his program.

The House, with the encouragement of the Republican Administration leadership, by 217 to 188 knocked all public housing out of an omnibus housing bill.

The President had requested authority for the construction of 35,000 public housing units a year for two years.

One hundred fifty-one House Republicans voted with sixty-six Democrats to deny even this much public housing, though for complicated reasons not neces-

Continued on Page 6, Column 4

R.A.F. IS RETURNING 400 U.S. SABRE JETS

Set to Replace Fighters With British-Made Aircraft, to Be Paid For in Aid Funds

Special to The New York Times.

LONDON, July 29—Britain announced today she was returning 400 Sabre Jet fighters to the United States and replacing them with British-made Hawker Hunters.

The British jets will be paid for by the United States under the Mutual Defense Assistance Program. The contract for the planes totals $140,000,000. It was signed more than a year ago, but the Hunter has been haunted by production delays.

Today's announcement indicates both the United States and Royal Air Forces are confident that the Hunter's time of trial is over, and that the planes are being produced in satisfactory numbers.

"Several" Royal Air Force squadrons are already equipped with them, an Air Ministry spokesman said.

The Hunter, which is comparable in performance with the Sabre Jet, or North American F-86F, flies about 650 miles an hour in operational trim.

The 400 Sabre Jets are being replaced not because they are

Continued on Page 3, Column 3

Russians Already Striving To Set Up Space Satellite

By HARRY SCHWARTZ

The United States and the Soviet Union now appear to be in a race for the glory of making the first major step toward interplanetary flight—the launching of an earth satellite in space. Soviet determination to achieve this objective was announced last April 15 in the newspaper Vechernaya Moskva (Evening Moscow). The newspaper revealed then that a committee of top Soviet scientists, including the renowned physicist Prof. Peter Kapitsa, had been set up to devise a satellite in space somewhat similar to that outlined in Washington.

The announced objective of the Soviet space satellite was to photograph cloud and ice formations above the earth as an aid to weather forecasting.

[In Moscow, sources said Saturday that the Soviet Union was preparing to launch an earth satellite similar to the one planned by the United States, The United Press reported.]

Intense Soviet interest in achieving priority over all other nations in regard to all aspects of interplanetary flight has been evident for some years. The most authoritative Soviet statement of the practicability of such efforts was made in January, 1954, by the President of the Soviet Academy of Sciences, Alexander N. Nesmeyanov.

He said then: "Science has

Continued on Page 7, Column 4

A. E. C. CITES GAINS IN H-BOMB FIELD

Designs of New Arms Based on '54 Tests—Reactors for Plane Engines Advanced

Special to The New York Times.

WASHINGTON, July 29—Hydrogen weapons, apparently of several types, have been produced for the United States atomic arsenal in the first six months of this year.

The atomic energy commission disclosed this today in its eighteenth semiannual report. The design of the new weapons was based on the results of the spectacular 1954 hydrogen bomb tests in the Pacific.

The weapons advance was one of several major developments reported by the commission. Others were:

¶The commission's program for developing reactors for industrial and military electric power and for naval and aircraft propulsion "made greater strides during the first six months of 1955 than in any earlier half-year."

On the aircraft problem the

Continued on Page 15, Column 4

NO MILITARY ROLE FOR GLOBAL BALL

Device Cannot Survey Land Nor Can It Drop Bomb—Its Goal Is Defined

By ANTHONY LEVIERO
Special to The New York Times.

WASHINGTON, July 29—The earth satellite will have no practicable military application in the foreseeable future. However, it will help man come to a better understanding of the natural laws of the universe.

Research scientists in the Pentagon said the man-made satellite, whizzing around the earth with a tumbling motion, would give them valuable information. This could be applied to flight studies for the intercontinental ballistics missile, a dread atomic weapon now being developed for wars between the continents.

There are two important things that the satellite will not be able to do:

1. It will have no utility for gaining terrestrial data that might be used as part of President Eisenhower's Geneva plan for inspecting the military establishments of the United States and Russia.
2. It will not be able to drop nuclear weapons, or anything else for that matter, back on earth for use against a hostile country.

The first satellite may have a mouse aboard, but scientists said they could not foresee the time when human beings would be able to go into outer space as passengers.

The Return Expected

The greatest return the scientists expect from the first satellite will be knowledge of conditions in the outer atmosphere—for instance, the density of it at different altitudes, a field of knowledge with large gaps in it.

The first satellite also is expected to provide new information about:

¶The nature of the sun.

¶Solar radio noise.

¶Cosmic radiation.

¶Magnetic noises and their causes.

¶The aurora, or luminous, static-producing phenomenon that radiates from the north and south magnetic poles.

Defense Department research scientists pleaded with reporters to repress any tendency to exploit speculations that have been popularized in recent years by fiction writers. They said the possibility of human passengers in a man-made satellite and its use for military purposes were so remotely in the future that speculations about it were practically useless.

In stressing that all the data they will gain will be in abstract and basic science, the military

Continued on Page 7, Column 6

Three Ex-G.I. Turncoats Land in San Francisco and Are Jailed by Army

Associated Press Wirephoto

Capt. Walter R. Leahy, right, reads a summary of court-martial charges against the turncoats before formally taking them into custody. The prisoners are, from left, Otho G. Bell, William C. Cowart and Lewis W. Griggs.

By LAWRENCE E. DAVIES
Special to The New York Times.

SAN FRANCISCO, July 29—Three dishonorably discharged soldiers who renounced America two years ago for life in Communist China came home today to an emotional greeting from relatives and to an Army stockade. They promised to "gladly accept whatever punishment is coming to us." When the American President liner President Cleveland docked this afternoon after a trip from the Orient military policemen promptly arrested William C. Cowart, 22 years old, of Dalton, Ga.; Lewis W. Griggs, 22, of Jacksonville, Tex., and Otho G. Bell, 24, formerly of Hillsboro, Miss. They listened intently and soberly while Capt. Walter R. Leahy of the provost marshall's office at the San Francisco Presidio read a 400-word summary of court-martial charges based on their alleged

Continued on Page 10, Column 3

President Sees Party In Control 'Forever'

Special to The New York Times.

WASHINGTON, July 29—President Eisenhower said today that a properly unified Republican party could retain control of the national Administration "forever."

Addressing a Republican pre-adjournment breakfast rally, the President urged Republican legislators to get behind the principles he advocates.

He gave no sign whether he intended to lead the party again next year, but Republicans who have been urging him to run for re-election appeared encouraged.

Reporters were not invited to the meeting this morning. It was attended by all but a few of the Republicans in the Senate and House of Representatives, and members of the Cabinet and several members of the White House staff. James C. Hagerty, White House press secretary, gave a summary of

Continued on Page 6, Column 6

U. S.-Peiping Trade Of Shows Proposed

By THOMAS F. BRADY
Special to The New York Times.

PARIS, July 29—A Chinese Communist theatrical company and an American theatrical company have exchanged invitations to appear in each other's country.

The reciprocal invitations are subject to Government approval on both sides, but it is known that both Governments are aware of the project.

The participants, whose cultural olive branches may add another bit of greenery to the signs of post-"cold-war" spring, are the Peiping Opera, which is now touring Europe, and the Everyman Opera, which has presented George Gershwin's "Porgy and Bess" in most major European cities west of the Iron Curtain.

On the Chinese side the project has at least semi-official approval already. The invitation was extended by

Continued on Page 15, Column 5

Sofia Offers Israel Air Crash Damages

Special to The New York Times.

TEL AVIV, Israel, July 29—The Bulgarian Government has agreed to pay at least part compensation for the shooting down of an Israeli airliner Wednesday. Fifty-eight persons, including twelve New Yorkers, died in the crash.

A Foreign Office spokesman said today the Bulgarian promise was made yesterday in a note to Baruch Nir, Israeli chargé d'affaires in Sofia.

[Bulgaria will permit three Israeli aircraft investigators, who have been waiting in Greece, to go to the scene of the crash, Athens reported Friday.]

The Bulgarian note expressed the Sofia Government's "profound regret" and notified Israel of the appointment of a special Government commission to inquire into the circumstances of what it called "the deplorable accident." The Bul-

Continued on Page 2, Column 5

"All the News That's Fit to Print"

The New York Times.

LATE CITY EDITION
Heavy rain and high winds today; clearing tonight. Fair tomorrow.
Temperature Range Today—Max., 79; Min., 71
Temperatures Yesterday—Max., 78.6; Min., 67
Full U. S. Weather Bureau Report, Page 61

VOL. CV..No. 35,668. Entered as Second-Class Matter, Post Office, New York, N. Y. NEW YORK, TUESDAY, SEPTEMBER 20, 1955. Times Square, New York 36, N. Y. Telephone Lackawanna 4-1000 FIVE CENTS

PERON'S REGIME IS OVERTHROWN; JUNTA WILL MEET WITH REBELS; CROWDS HAIL FALL OF DICTATOR

GALES MOVE ON THE CITY; SOUTH IS HIT

DAMAGE IS SEVERE

New York Area Due to Feel the Effects of Hurricane Today

By PETER KIHSS

Hurricane Ione tore wide destruction in coastal North Carolina when it roared in from the Atlantic Ocean yesterday morning.

Then it slowed down and became a tricky problem that kept the entire Eastern Seaboard worried.

In Washington the United States Weather Bureau said at 3 o'clock this morning that the tropical twister was centered about twenty miles southeast of Norfolk, Va., with winds of over thirty-five miles an hour swirling outward 200 miles to the north and east.

Swirling northeastward at eight to ten miles an hour, it is expected to pick up speed and intensity as it swings out to sea. It was expected to be off the Delaware coast this morning and southeast of Long Island in the afternoon.

Ernest J. Christie, in charge of the Weather Bureau here, said at 3 o'clock this morning that New York City would feel the worst effects of the storm later today.

The center of the storm, he said, would pass southeast of the city during the day. New York City, on the northern fringe of the storm, would have heavy rain at times with wind velocities of forty to fifty miles an hour and gusts possibly up to sixty miles an hour. Clearing weather was forecast for tonight.

Forecasts Are Qualified

Hurricane force is seventy-five miles an hour or more, according to the Weather Bureau scale.

But meteorologists were qualifying all their forecasts, warning that Ione—whose name comes from the Greek word meaning "go"—was an erratic personality.

Ione, hatched last Wednesday east of Puerto Rico, did millions of dollars worth of damage as it roared overland across the coastal areas of North Carolina with winds up to 107 miles an hour.

Communications lines were down, roads and bridges washed out, crops destroyed, large areas of cities flooded and hundreds made homeless.

Reports of the damage were fragmentary, but mounting rapidly as communications were restored. Four persons were reported dead at New Bern, N. C., and three at Beaufort, N. C. The Red Cross said it was providing shelter for 1,800 persons in the state.

New Bern, a city of 15,000 persons, was jammed before the hurricane with hundreds of refugees from inland lowlands. Forty blocks of the city were flooded and for fifteen hours the community was without power, communications and drinking

Continued on Page 24, Column 1

Hilda Rips Tampico In 'Worst Disaster'

By The United Press.

MEXICO CITY, Sept. 19—President Adolfo Ruiz Cortines tonight ordered unlimited Government aid for storm-lashed Tampico as Hurricane Hilda sent a flood of "catastrophic proportions" over three-quarters of the port city.

The President said Tampico, cut off by winds and water from the outside world, was confronted with "the worst disaster in its history."

[The Associated Press said Monday that Gov. Horacio Teran reported the hurricane had killed twelve persons and injured 350 in Tampico. The Governor of Tamaulipas State said 90 per cent of the buildings in the city had been damaged and 15,000 were homeless. A state of emergency was ordered.]

A medical brigade of 200

Continued on Page 24, Column 7

CITY IS PREPARED FOR STORM'S FURY

Lines Kept Open From Center at Police Headquarters to Waiting Emergency Men

Residents of the metropolitan area battened down for Hurricane Ione yesterday while Government and welfare agencies made elaborate plans to mitigate the fury of wind, rain and high tides.

New York and surrounding communities, long forewarned, appeared to be prepared as never before to weather a big storm.

The focal point of relief, rescue and damage control activities was Mayor Wagner's board of planning and operations sitting at Police Headquarters.

A communications center in the line-up room, staffed by 114 policemen, maintained open lines to all city departments and welfare agencies. Representatives of each organization were posted there at nightfall ready to flash orders to emergency crews on stand-by throughout the city.

Police Commissioner Stephen P. Kennedy urged the public, in event of emergency, to telephone available information to the Police Department.

The Civil Defense Administration, on alert since Sunday night, had its 149 fire and rescue units ready for instant action. At 5 P. M. Robert E. Condon, City Director of Civil Defense, ordered his top personnel to remain on duty until further notice.

Two thousand Red Cross workers were standing by in the city and neighboring communities. The city's Department of Welfare was similarly prepared to staff 100 relief centers in the five boroughs.

In Albany three units of the New York National Guard, including the Forty-second Division stationed here, were alerted

Continued on Page 24, Column 5

HARRIMAN READY TO COMPETE IN '56, ADVISER DECLARES

Prendergast Says Governor Would Oppose Stevenson if Party Wanted Him

By WARREN WEAVER Jr.
Special to The New York Times.

ALBANY, Sept. 19—Governor Harriman will seek the Presidential nomination next year if "convinced the convention wanted him," the Democratic State Chairman said today.

The chairman asserted the Governor would do this even in the event of a floor fight with Adlai E. Stevenson.

Michael H. Prendergast, the Governor's chief political lieutenant, declared that under such conditions Mr. Harriman would take the nomination "regardless of whether Stevenson stepped aside or not."

This was the first public indication from within his official political family that Mr. Harriman's repeated expressions of support for Mr. Stevenson might be weakening in the face of insistence that he seek the nomination.

Charles Van Devander, the Governor's press secretary, said tonight there would be no comment from his office on the Prendergast statement. He said the Governor was in New York City. The Governor's aides in New York likewise said there would be no comment.

For the last year whenever Presidential politics were discussed, Mr. Harriman has said "I'm for Stevenson," smiled broadly and declined to discuss any other possibilities.

Says Democrats Can Win

Mr. Prendergast was the Governor's personal choice to succeed Richard H. Balch as head of the Democratic State Committee last July.

The Democratic chairman characterized as "a lot of nonsense" Republican assertions that no opponent could beat President Eisenhower.

"I don't give a damn who they run," Mr. Prendergast declared. "We can win next year with the right man, and I think Harriman is the right man. Regardless of who he says he's for, I'm representing the Democratic party—the rank and file of it—when I say I'm for Harriman."

Although Mr. Prendergast said he could not speak for the Governor, he described Mr. Harriman indirectly as a man who was thinking now in terms of his own candidacy, rather than Mr. Stevenson's or anyone else's.

"I know Mr. Harriman well enough to know that he is so definitely interested in a Democratic victory in 1956 that if he felt someone else, other than himself, were stronger and had a better chance of winning, he would be for him regardless," the state chairman declared.

Mr. Prendergast's analysis of the situation was made at a press conference. He called the session to announce that former President Harry S. Truman would speak at the state-wide Democratic candidate's rally here on Oct. 7.

The state chairman was generally deprecatory of Mr. Stevenson's chances. He said that the former Illinois Governor's announcement of his plans in November "isn't going to stampede anybody." He predicted that getting the nomination would be "no walkover for Stevenson."

Sees Swing to Harriman

On the contrary, Mr. Prendergast said, prospects that the national convention might look favorably on Mr. Harriman appear to be increasing daily.

"I think we're going into the convention with a lot of sentiment in our favor," he asserted. "Unless something unforeseen happens, I don't see how we can miss."

He later amended this to say he believed that the Governor has "a better than even chance of getting the nomination."

Mr. Prendergast was asked if the Governor had requested him to "soft-pedal" his Harriman-for-President campaign, inasmuch as Mr. Harriman was on record for Mr. Stevenson.

"No, he's said nothing about that," the chairman replied.

Mr. Prendergast also announced that he would open an upstate office for the State Committee in the Sheraton Ten Eyck Hotel here on Oct. 1. It will include offices for Miss Mary Louise Nice of Tonawanda, state committee vice chairman, and Carmine G. DeSapio, the party's national committeeman.

The Democratic leader said he was particularly glad to have

Continued on Page 23, Column 5

U. S. TIES HINTED

Will Grant Recognition to Insurgents as They Take Over Nation

By DANA ADAMS SCHMIDT
Special to The New York Times.

WASHINGTON, Sept. 19—Administration officials said tonight that the United States would undoubtedly recognize any new Argentine Government that showed it was in control of the country.

The State Department, insisting that any comment at this time would be a form of interference, declined to discuss the attitude the United States might take toward a new Argentine Government.

However, other officials of the Administration pointed out that the United States had followed the practice of recognizing Latin-American revolutionary governments as soon as they exercised full authority. In some cases there has been preliminary discussion with other Latin-American governments.

But the fact that relations between the United States and President Juan D. Perón were frequently strained during his nine years as President made it unlikely the United States would hesitate, these officials said.

Hostile Attitude Cited

For several years after President Perón had taken power his attitude toward the United States was hostile, thus playing upon popular antipathies toward the "Yankee imperialists." However, in recent years relations between Washington and Buenos Aires have been correct, although "hardly warm," in the view of one diplomatic student of Latin-American affairs.

President Perón has sought and obtained from the United States a number of loans that have helped his Government through the difficulties that followed the application of "Perónist economics." This consisted of building up industry at the expense of agriculture.

As to whether the United States has ever "supported" the Peronist regime, there are strong differences of opinion among officials. The prevailing view is that the United States Government's attitude has been carefully "objective."

While avoiding anything that would look like official interference, State Department officials told a Congressional committee after the unsuccessful June 16 rising in Argentina that they were seeking to use United States influence quietly to prevent persecution of the Roman Catholic Church.

Catholic groups in the United States at that time demanded that the United States openly

Continued on Page 2, Column 6

COMMAND VAGUE

Rebels Believed to Be in 3 Groups, With No Over-All Chief

By TAD SZULC
Special to The New York Times.

SANTIAGO, Chile, Sept. 19—Broadcasts from Argentina indicated today that the rebel forces were operating with at least three separate commands and that no over-all chief of the movement had yet emerged.

Admiral Issac Rojas was in charge of the naval operation along the Argentine coast and of the marine units ashore. There were contradictory reports as to the identity of the leaders of the insurgent army forces operating inland.

In a telephone interview from the headquarters of the rebel-directed Second Army in Mendoza, in the foothills of the Andes, a general who identified himself as the chief of staff of the revolutionary command said that Gen. Eduardo Leonardi was the top military leader of the movement.

He said that General Leonardi was in Cordoba, where attacks of the Government forces had been fought off for several days.

General About 52 Years Old

He described General Leonardi as a "respected" officer who had served at one time as an Argentine military attaché abroad. He said General Leonardi was about 52 years old. No other data about General Leonardi were available here.

A virtually independent command in Mendoza, embracing the provinces of Mendoza, San Juan and San Luis, was held by Gen. Julio Alberto Lagos.

In an earlier telephone interview General Lagos identified himself as the chief of the revolution. But his chief of staff said later that General Lagos meant he was merely in charge of the three western provinces.

The chief of staff said that the coordination among the various commands was still deficient and he refused to say what plans the rebels had to take over the Government of Argentina. He declined to say what form of revolutionary government was being contemplated.

He declared that communication among the various commanders was by radio and courier planes.

Broadcasts picked up in Santiago told the series of dramatic events that culminated today in the virtual surrender of the man who for twelve years had ruled Argentina as a dictator.

It came on the fourth day of the bloody rebellion against President Juan D. Perón by the Navy and sections of the Army as the insurgent fleet stood off

Continued on Page 2, Column 3

GEN. JUAN D. PERON

PEACE IS SOUGHT

Government Orders Its Forces to End Fight —Port Is Shelled

Texts of the Government and Perón statements, Page 3.

By EDWARD A. MORROW
Special to The New York Times.

BUENOS AIRES, Tuesday, Sept. 20.—The Government of President Juan D. Perón fell last night.

A four-man junta of army generals assumed command of the forces that had fought unsuccessfully to keep General Perón in power. He had been master of Argentina since Oct. 17, 1945, and its President for nine years.

[A loyalist military junta told the rebels that General Perón had officially resigned the Presidency, The Associated Press reported.]

The junta quickly entered into negotiations to end the four-day civil war. Army and Navy units had joined in the rebellion and forced the resignation of the President, the Cabinet and other authorities.

Among those who tendered their "irrevocable" resignations was the Minister of the Army, Gen. Franklin Lucero. On June 16 he had quelled a navy-led revolt.

There was no news about the whereabouts of President Perón tonight. Some reports had him in asylum at the Paraguayan Embassy in Buenos Aires. The embassy denied these.

Perón Statement Read

The low ceiling prevented any planes from leaving the city's army airport and seemed to cast doubt on other reports that the President had fled to Paraguay.

General Perón offered his resignation yesterday afternoon in a statement read for him over the state radio. He suggested that the Army take charge. He had made a somewhat similar offer to resign Aug. 31 but withdrew it after "protests" from his followers.

It was widely rumored that General Perón had committed suicide. There was no official announcement to this effect, and well-informed diplomats doubted the report.

[A rebel radio broadcast from Bahia Blanca said the Argentine Confederation of Labor was planning a general strike for dawn Tuesday in an effort to restore General Perón to power, The Associated Press reported.]

The Government ordered troops that still remained loyal to it to cease fighting. It asked the rebels to do likewise to prevent further bloodshed after the Navy had shelled the seaside city of Mar del Plata and the rebels had shown other signs of strength throughout the country.

Large sections of the Buenos Aires population braved a light rain this afternoon to stage joyful demonstrations in the city's streets. The Plaza de Mayo, scene of many mass Peronist demonstrations in the past, had a small number of the Presi-

Continued on Page 3, Column 5

MOSCOW TO INSIST ON BONN-RED TALK

Soviet Will Shun Any Voice in German Domestic Rifts in Treaty Due Today

By CLIFTON DANIEL
Special to The New York Times.

MOSCOW, Sept. 19—Measures to force West Germany to deal directly with the East German Communist Government were being planned today in Moscow.

Walter Ulbricht, East German Deputy Premier and Communist party chief, declared that in the future there would be no other way of settling questions in dispute between the two parts of Germany.

He said that under the treaty to be concluded with the Soviet Union here tomorrow the East German Government would control the border with West Germany and communications between West Germany and West Berlin.

"The sooner the politicians of Bonn and West Berlin realize that they cannot undermine the East German regime, the better it will be for the populace of West Berlin," Herr Ulbricht said ominously.

His implication seemed to be that the East German Government would be in a position to impose a new blockade on Berlin and that on such matters the Bonn Government would have to negotiate not with mere officials or technicians but with the East German Government itself.

Sovereign Status Due

Herr Ulbricht spoke during the negotiations with Soviet leaders on a treaty that will give to the East German regime the same sovereign status the Western Allies gave West Germany.

Upon conclusion of the treaty the Soviet Government will abolish the office of High Commissioner in Germany, Marshal Nikolai A. Bulganin, Soviet Premier, disclosed in a speech.

Henceforth, the Soviet Ambassador to East Germany will deal with United States, British and French representatives in West Germany on questions concerning Germany as a whole and on questions arising from four-power agreements, the Soviet Premier declared.

In addition, Marshal Bulganin said all laws, decrees and directives promulgated by the four-power Allied Control Council for Germany would be annulled on the territory of East Germany. Those regulations were enacted between 1945 and 1948, when the Soviet representative, Marshal Vassily D. Sokolovsky, withdrew and the Allied Control Council ceased to function.

The treaty between the Soviet Union and East Germany will provide that East Germany is free in all internal and foreign affairs, including relations with West Germany, Herr Ulbricht

Continued on Page 5, Column 3

FINNS AND SOVIET RENEW ALLIANCE

Moscow Agrees to Withdraw Its Military and Naval Forces Within 3 Months

Special to The New York Times.

MOSCOW, Sept. 19—Finland and the Soviet Union renewed their mutual defense alliance today for a period of twenty years.

At the same time the Soviet Government formally agreed to withdraw its military and naval forces from their base on Finnish territory within three months.

Those were the results of the Soviet-Finnish negotiations concluded here today and they gave "great joy" to the witty and lively old man who is President of Finland, Juho K. Paasikivi.

"I am here in Moscow for the seventh time for negotiations on affairs of state concerning Finland and the Soviet Union," the President said this evening at a party held in the Kremlin to celebrate the signing of the two agreements.

"But this is the first time that I return to our capital satisfied," he said. "Usually I have returned unsatisfied."

His audience laughed and applauded.

Exactly eight years ago today President Paasikivi was here on one of those unsatisfying missions. He signed a fifty-year lease that gave to the Soviet Union a naval and military base on the Porkkala Peninsula as provided by the truce agreement that ended the war between the two countries in 1944.

Tonight President Paasikivi observed that the Porkkala base now to be handed back to Finland was situated only twelve

Continued on Page 6, Column 3

Governor Calls for Federal Aid To Save Nation's Ailing Schools

But Royall Tells Conference That the Education System Should Be Contracted

By BENJAMIN FINE

A sweeping program of Federal aid to education, on both school and college levels, was advocated yesterday by Governor Harriman.

Speaking before 800 community, labor, business and school leaders at the New York State Conference on Education, the Governor said that nothing but Federal support could solve the critical problem in American education.

The two-day meeting at the Biltmore Hotel is a preliminary to the White House Conference on Education in Washington from Nov. 28 to Dec. 1. Major school issues are on the agenda, for both the New York and the Washington sessions.

Unexpectedly, the conference opened on a controversial note. The chairman of the New York State committee, Kenneth C. Royall, who was the keynote speaker, told the delegates they should be thinking of ways to contract, not expand, the educational system. Mr. Royall, who was Secretary of War under

Kenneth C. Royall

President Truman, said that too many young people were attending college who should not be there.

He deplored the "widespread feeling" among educators that every high school boy and girl should go to college. He urged

Continued on Page 25, Column 6

Democratic Farm Experts Call Republicans' Program Ruinous

By RICHARD J. H. JOHNSTON
Special to The New York Times.

CHICAGO, Sept. 19—The nation's farmers face a grim future unless action is taken immediately to relieve them of economic stress, a Democratic agricultural advisory committee said today.

Under the chairmanship of Claude R. Wickard, former Secretary of Agriculture, the fourteen-man committee met here in the Conrad Hilton Hotel to "explore all aspects of our agricultural problems."

This was the first meeting of the group that was formed to guide the Democratic farm policy fight. It was created on Aug. 31 at the behest of Paul M. Butler, chairman of the Democratic National Committee.

[Meanwhile, Democrats in Washington opened a drive to goad the Administration into unveiling its farm plans before Congress reconvenes in January. This was part of a Democratic effort to keep the offensive in building sagging farm prices and income into a major issue of the 1956 Presidential election.]

The advisory committee, which included another former Agriculture Secretary, Charles F. Brannan, as well as former Agriculture Department aides and five farmers, according to Mr. Wickard, had reached the conclusion that the Eisenhower Administration was neglecting the farmers' plight and ignoring distress.

While the committee went into executive session, Mr. Butler issued a statement on its aims and purposes. The statement bore down hard on the Republican Administration, which, he said, was both "ill-tempered and

Continued on Page 23, Column 4

U.N. Opening in Harmony Today; Chilean Next Head of Assembly

By THOMAS J. HAMILTON
Special to The New York Times.

UNITED NATIONS, N. Y., Sept. 19—A noncontroversial start is assured for the 1955 session of the United Nations General Assembly, which will convene tomorrow afternoon.

The only important business scheduled for tomorrow is the election of José Maza, a veteran Chilean diplomat, as President of the Assembly.

Some delegates believe that Vyacheslav M. Molotov, the Soviet Foreign Minister, will immediately put forward the standard Soviet demand for the seating of Chinese Communist representatives.

If he should do so, it would not cause more than a short flurry, since the United States is ready with its equally standard counter-proposal that the question of Chinese representation should not be taken up at the current session. The United States is known to have enough votes to assure the adoption of its resolution.

Dr. Joseph M. A. H. Luns, co-Foreign Minister of the Netherlands, will call the Assembly to order in the absence of the President of the 1954 session, Dr. Eelco N. van Kleffens, Dutch Minister to Portugal. The election of vice presidents and committee chairmen will take place Wednesday and the opening debate will begin Thursday.

Secretary of State Dulles will speak Thursday morning and Mr. Molotov on Friday. The two other Big Four Foreign Ministers, Harold Macmillan of Britain and Antoine Pinay of France, will not speak until next week.

In any event, the speeches by Mr. Dulles and Mr. Molotov are expected to set the keynote for

Continued on Page 12, Column 1

"All the News That's Fit to Print"

The New York Times.

LATE CITY EDITION
Condensation of U. S. Weather Bureau forecast: Mostly fair and somewhat milder today. Partly cloudy tomorrow.
Temp. range today: 42-25; yesterday: 35-23
Full U. S. Weather Bureau Report, Page 63

© 1956, by The New York Times Company.

VOL. CV..No. 35,831. Entered as Second-Class Matter, Post Office, New York, N. Y. NEW YORK, THURSDAY, MARCH 1, 1956. Times Square, New York 36, N. Y. Telephone LAckawanna 4-1000 FIVE CENTS

EISENHOWER SAYS HE WILL SEEK A 2D TERM; CONFIDENT OF HEALTH; BARS 'BARNSTORMING'; PRAISES NIXON BUT DOES NOT ENDORSE HIM

U.S. JUDGE ORDERS ALABAMA CO-ED TO BE REINSTATED

Bids School Admit Miss Lucy by Monday—Bars Contempt Action Against Trustees

CITES THEIR 'GOOD FAITH'

He Finds That Reaction Was Underestimated—Negro Says She Will Return

By WAYNE PHILLIPS
Special to The New York Times.

BIRMINGHAM, Ala., Feb. 29—The University of Alabama was ordered today to reinstate Autherine J. Lucy, its first Negro student, by Monday morning.

Miss Lucy, 26 years old, of Birmingham, was enrolled at the university Feb. 1 after a three-year court fight. She was suspended five days later after a series of campus disorders protesting her presence.

Federal Judge Hobart H. Grooms also vacated a contempt motion, sought by Miss Lucy, against the board of trustees and officials of the university. He said the trustees had acted in good faith in suspending Miss Lucy. If they had not done so, he ruled, "she might have suffered great bodily harm."

Miss Lucy sat tense and nervous today in the Federal District Court here as a succession of witnesses recounted the events leading to her suspension. Some said that if she returned to the campus she might be killed.

Feared for Life, She Says

She said on the witness stand that while she was a virtual prisoner in a classroom building held in a state of siege by a howling mob outside, she feared that she might be killed. She said she had prayed.

With deliberation and occasional flashes of dry wit she answered the questions of the university's attorney, Andrew J. Thomas. Beside her, when she sat at the counsel table, was a well-worn copy of the Bible.

After she heard the decision of Judge Grooms readmitting her, she said again that she would return to the campus.

"That girl sure has guts," her attorney, Thurgood Marshall, chief counsel for the National

Continued on Page 28, Column 1

TEAMSTERS UNION FACES SUSPENSION

Meany Weighs Tie to I. L. A. —Internal Strife Rises

By A. H. RASKIN

The International Brotherhood of Teamsters, most powerful unit in the merged labor movement, is facing possible suspension over its alliance with the exiled International Longshoremen's Association.

The possibility of punitive action by the parent federation arose yesterday amid fresh outcroppings of internal strife within the 1,300,000-member truck union. The uprisings were designed to prevent domination of the union by James R. Hoffa, international vice president and chairman of the Central States Conference of Teamsters.

The Detroit unionist announced Monday that the teamsters would deposit $400,000 to the credit of the I. L. A. to enable it to pay its debts and to participate in a joint organizing drive. The pier union was expelled from the American Federation of Labor in 1953 on charges of gang domination.

In Washington, George Meany, president of the united labor movement, announced that he had begun an investigation into the teamster-longshore pact. He pledged that he would take

Continued on Page 23, Column 3

Testimony Clashes At Gas Gift Inquiry

By RUSSELL BAKER
Special to The New York Times.

WASHINGTON, Feb. 29—Senate investigators were told today that John M. Neff had offered a $2,500 campaign contribution in Iowa for the chance to talk with Senator Bourke B. Hickenlooper about the natural gas bill.

However, Mr. Neff, an attorney for the Superior Oil Company of California, denied the story under oath. The conflicting testimony will be sent to the Department of Justice for possible perjury action.

The witness who testified that the offer had been made was Robert K. Goodwin, a Des Moines manufacturer and banker and Republican Committeeman for Iowa.

The two men, smiling wanly, confronted each other under the great glass chandeliers in the Senate caucus room, then

Continued on Page 13, Column 3

G.O.P. TAX CUT BILL VOTED AT ALBANY

Legislature Acts in Face of Veto Threat—Committees Propose Budget Slash

By LEO EGAN
Special to The New York Times.

ALBANY, Feb. 29—Republican majorities rammed their $50,000,000 income tax cut bill through both Senate and Assembly this afternoon. They did this despite warnings the bill would be vetoed by Governor Harriman, a Democrat.

In the Senate the vote was 35 to 23. In the Assembly it was 84 to 58. All the Democrats voted against the measure in both houses.

The Senate deliberately voted down the Governor's plan today. The vote was 36 to 22, one Democrat, Joseph Zaretski of Manhattan, voting with the Republicans in opposition. He explained he was opposed to any tax cut this year.

While the bill was under discussion, the Republican controlled Senate Finance and Assembly Ways and Means Committees proposed reductions totaling $23,528,072 in Governor Harriman's record high $1,494,700,000 state-spending program for next year.

Democrat Hits Action

Among the suggested cuts were the elimination of a $9,900,000 appropriation to give New York City a share in motor vehicle license fees and the elimination of a $2,400,000 item for state subsidies for child day-care centers, most of which would have gone to New York City.

Passage of the Republican income tax cut bill today represented an abrupt termination of negotiations between the Governor and legislative leaders for a compromise on this subject.

Assemblyman Eugene F. Bannigan, the Democratic minority leader, charged on the floor that Republicans were courting a veto of the tax-cut bill to justify a refusal to increase gasoline and Diesel fuel taxes. Such increases have been recommended by the Temporary Highway Finance Commission to support a $500,000,000 highway bond issue and an expanded highway construction program.

Lacking the two-thirds majorities needed in each House to repass a bill over the Governor's veto, the Republicans are expected to abandon their efforts for an income tax cut after today.

Mr. Harriman announced that he was still willing to resume compromise tax-reduction negotiations. But his offer is unlikely to be accepted.

The Republican bill as passed today would give all taxpayers a credit of 20 per cent on the first $100 of taxes due on April 15 and a 10 per cent credit on the next $400, with a limit of $60 to any one taxpayer. Governor Harriman had proposed a sub-

Continued on Page 25, Column 4

DULLES SUGGESTS SOVIET MAY FAVOR CUT IN ARMS COST

Tells Senate Unit, However, U. S. Will Not Be Misled Into Weakening Defenses

By ELIE ABEL
Special to The New York Times.

WASHINGTON, Feb. 29—Secretary of State Dulles suggested today that the Soviet Union might welcome some reduction in the present burden of armaments.

Testifying before a special Senate Foreign Relations subcommittee on disarmament, Mr. Dulles qualified this statement with assurances that the Administration would not jeopardize the nation's security by accepting at face value Soviet promises to disarm.

"We do not minimize the difficulties of dealing in these matters with a potential enemy who is untrustworthy and who in manifold ways has demonstrated that he is a past master of the art of evasion and secretiveness," the Secretary of State said.

"However, there is some reason to believe that the Soviet Union itself would welcome relief from the present burden of armament," he added.

Russians Called Dissatisfied

Mr. Dulles said this assessment was based on the "logic" of the present situation within the Soviet Union. He depicted the Russian people as being "in a state of very considerable dissatisfaction" with their low standard of living.

It would be logical for the Soviet leaders to agree to spend less on armaments so they could apply an increased share of their production to raising the living standards of their own people, Mr. Dulles said. In addition, the Soviet Union would thus have more to spend on its new program of economic aid to underdeveloped countries in South Asia and the Middle East, he added.

The Secretary of State, who leaves for Pakistan Friday afternoon to attend the council meeting of the Southeast Asian Collective Defense Treaty in Karachi March 6 to 8, appeared before a subcommittee headed by Senator Hubert H. Humphrey, Democrat of Minnesota, which is surveying the whole disarmament problem.

Senator Leverett Saltonstall, Republican of Massachusetts, asked Mr. Dulles whether "face-to-face" meetings with the Soviet leaders offered the best hope of achieving a disarmament accord.

"I don't know any other way," Mr. Dulles replied. "I don't get

Continued on Page 6, Column 3

Gronchi in Congress Discounts Arms Tie

By DANA ADAMS SCHMIDT
Special to The New York Times.

WASHINGTON, Feb. 29—President Giovanni Gronchi of Italy urged Congress today to lead the Western world away from military alliances and toward economic cooperation to counter Communist expansionism.

"The reorganization of the Western world is the central problem of the day," he declared in an address before a joint session of the Senate and the House of Representatives.

As an early step he proposed that the North Atlantic Treaty Organization be "brought into line" with today's realities, in which "military imbalance has been reduced," but in which, none the less, "the world is no more secure than it was one or two years ago."

The North Atlantic alliance,

Continued on Page 5, Column 3

PARIS ARMY CHIEF QUITS ON ALGERIA

Guillaume Out After Policy Dispute—Special Powers Asked by Government

By ROBERT C. DOTY
Special to The New York Times.

PARIS, Feb. 29—The French Government reorganized its high military command today and asked for special powers to deal with the Algerian revolt.

Gen. Augustin Guillaume was replaced as Chief of the General Staff following disagreement with his civilian chiefs over military policy in North Africa. He was succeeded by Gen. Paul Ely, a member of the high council of the armed forces.

Late today, Premier Guy Mollet submitted to Parliament a request for extensive powers in the fields of administration, economic and social affairs, and security for Robert Lacoste, Minister Residing in Algeria.

Details were not revealed, but the special powers were reported to include authority to reinstate the "state of urgency" in Algeria or even, if events should warrant it, full martial law.

Debate on this measure, probably early next week, was expected to present the left-of-center Republican Front Cabinet with its first serious political test. Some observers doubted that the National Assembly would grant the Government's request.

Neither here nor in Algeria has M. Mollet's appeal to the rebels to lay down their arms and accept the arbitration of new elections aroused any enthusiasm.

Conservatives, including most

Continued on Page 3, Column 2

9,000 Jam Court as Scofflaws Rush to Beat Amnesty Deadline

By JACK ROTH

The last day of the amnesty period for scofflaws found 9,000 persons in the Criminal Courts Building at 100 Centre Street yesterday. The worst jam in Manhattan Traffic Court history ensued.

About 6,000 persons waited in long lines in the lobby to pay their fines at the court clerk's windows. Three thousand of these were scofflaws. At one point the lines backed up a stairway leading to the second floor.

In addition, another 3,000 repentant drivers crowded about the Traffic Summons Control Bureau on the third floor. Tables were supplied in the corridors for the scofflaws to fill out forms.

Chief Magistrate John M. Murtagh called the amnesty a "great success" and estimated that of the 20,000 persons categorized as scofflaws all but about 6,000 had appeared.

He predicted that when all the scofflaw tickets of the amnesty period had been processed, the accounting would show that the city had collected nearly $750,000 in fines on long-ignored traffic summonses.

"Because of the last-minute influx of scofflaws," Mr. Murtagh said, "there will be a delay of perhaps a week before we can turn over the warrants to the police for the arrest of the remainder. We must make certain that none of the warrants apply to people who appeared at the last minute.

"But early next month the police will swing into action. Our goal is 100 per cent compliance with every summons issued since 1950."

He reiterated an earlier statement that this amnesty for scofflaws would be the last such grace period, because "motorists must be taught to answer summonses on time." There were two previous amnesties.

Concerning the last-minute rush, which was marked by confusion and grumbling, Mr. Murtagh admitted such great numbers had not been anticipated.

The confusion was caused by the fact that five patrolmen, suddenly called to keep the lines

Continued on Page 35, Column 3

2D SPOT IN DOUBT

Foes of Vice President Now May Push Drive to Block Him

By W. H. LAWRENCE
Special to The New York Times.

WASHINGTON, Feb. 29—President Eisenhower passed up today two opportunities to give an automatic immediate endorsement to renomination of Vice President Richard M. Nixon.

General Eisenhower said he properly could not speak out on the choice of a running mate until after the Republican National Convention itself had picked its Presidential nominee.

He mixed repetition of previous high praise for Mr. Nixon with what sounded at least like indirect criticism of the Vice President for his recent effort to continue a Republican party label on Chief Justice Earl Warren. The President said he personally would never admit that any Supreme Court justice continued to have a political designation while on the high court.

President Eisenhower's failure to call at once for Vice President Nixon's renomination undoubtedly will put new steam behind an effort already under way by some influential Republicans to select another running mate. These anti-Nixon men argue that the 1956 campaign involving a President who has suffered a heart attack will place new emphasis with voters on the Vice Presidential nominee.

Silent on Running Mate

In his radio-television address to the nation, the President made no mention at all of Mr. Nixon or any other possible running mate.

The omission by the President may not be meaningful, however. General Eisenhower is assured of renomination by acclamation, and the convention unquestionably will nominate any man he favors for Vice President. So he could speak up for Mr. Nixon even at the last minute and insure his renomination.

The Nixon question was raised in two ways immediately after the President had disclosed he would be available for renomination and re-election if the Republican party and a majority of the people wanted him.

He was asked directly whether he would again want Mr. Nixon as his running mate.

"As a matter of fact," President Eisenhower responded, "I wouldn't mention the Vice Presidency, in spite of my tremendous admiration for Mr. Nixon, for this reason: I believe it is traditional that the Vice President is not nominated until after a * * * Presidential candidate is nominated; so I think that we will have to wait and see whom the Republican convention nominates, and then it will be proper to give an expression on that point."

Respect 'Unbounded'

Asked whether, if nominated, he would have a personal preference for Mr. Nixon's renomination, the President responded:

"I will say nothing more about it. I have said that my admiration and my respect for Vice President Nixon is unbounded. He has been for me a loyal and dedicated associate, and a successful one.

"I am very fond of him, but I am going to say no more about it."

The indirect criticism came when President Eisenhower was asked his own reaction to the Vice President's characterization of Mr. Warren as a Republican Chief Justice.

The President said he would not comment, and never had, on a comment by someone else. He added:

"But I will say this: Once a man has passed into the Supreme Court he is an American citizen and nothing else in my book until he comes out of that court, and I believe that it would be—I would never admit that he was—longer had a political designation."

There has been sharp political controversy over the Vice President's recent contention in a New York speech that the Su-

Continued on Page 16, Column 5

Associated Press Wirephoto

EXPLAINS DECISION: President and Mrs. Eisenhower at the White House last night, before his TV-radio speech.

Butler Questions Fitness; Republicans Hail Decision

By JOHN D. MORRIS
Special to The New York Times.

WASHINGTON, Feb. 29—The physical fitness of President Eisenhower to serve another term was challenged sharply today within minutes of his announcement that he was willing to run. "The American people will never elect a President who, at 65, has had a serious heart attack and who is unable to be a full-time Chief Executive," Paul M. Butler, the Democratic National Chairman, declared.

While Mr. Butler raised the issue of health, other leaders of both parties publicly hailed the President's decision.

The texts of Butler and Hall statements are on Page 17.

The prevailing Democratic line was one of gratification that General Eisenhower considered his recovery sufficient to permit him to stand the rigors and pressures of four more years in the White House. But warnings of a hard campaign "on the issues," requiring vigorous activity by both candidates and ending in a Democratic victory, also came from leading party spokesmen.

Republicans responded to the announcement with enthusiasm that promised the President's renomination without a dissent by the national convention at San Francisco next August.

Predictions that the delegates would choose him by acclamation came from Vice President Richard M. Nixon and Senator Wil-

Continued on Page 17, Column 1

STEVENSON CALLS DECISION PROPER

Bids President 'Set Terms of Debate' on His Health —Sees 'Vigorous' Drive

By CLAYTON KNOWLES

Adlai E. Stevenson called upon President Eisenhower yesterday to "set the terms of the debate" on the issue of his health, now that he has declared his availability for a second term.

Most active of the Democratic candidates for the Presidency, the former Illinois Governor stressed that it was General Eisenhower who had "drawn the distinction between the private matter of his personal health and the public question of how the office of President shall be conducted."

In Washington, it was felt that President Eisenhower's decision would help Mr. Stevenson's chances for the Democratic nomination.

Mr. Stevenson said it was fitting that President Eisenhower, before whom he went to defeat in 1952, should be the candidate and thus defend the policies and record of his Administration.

This view, given in a brief statement, was echoed by other Democrats across the country and by leading Republicans, too, if with a noticeable change in inflection. And Mr. Stevenson noted also that the President must look forward to carrying the "burden of what will be a very vigorous campaign."

This was a point that other Democratic candidates, announced and unannounced, stressed as well.

In Albany, Governor Harriman asserted that the President "can no longer shift responsibility to associates and subordinates." Mr. Harriman asserted that the President must now answer for "surrender to the domination of one group in our country—the big interests"—and for policies abroad that have "undermined our prestige and shaken the confidence in us of the people of the free world."

And at Milwaukee, Senator Estes Kefauver, like Mr. Steven-

Continued on Page 19, Column 2

Two Senators Ask Inquiry on Benson

By WILLIAM M. BLAIR
Special to The New York Times.

WASHINGTON, Feb. 29—Two Senate Democrats suggested today that the special lobby investigating committee explore what they charged were efforts by the Secretary of Agriculture to influence Southern Senators to vote against rigid farm-price supports.

Senator Hubert H. Humphrey of Minnesota said that Ezra Taft Benson, the Secretary, appeared to have violated a law prohibiting lobbying with Federal appropriations. The situation is "close enough to make it appear necessary for our new committee on lobbying to look into it most carefully," he declared.

Senator Allen J. Ellender of Louisiana accused Mr. Benson of "trying to buy votes of

Continued on Page 12, Column 3

CAN 'LAST 5 YEARS'

President Finds 'Not Slightest Doubt' of Fitness for Duty

Conference transcript, Page 14; text of speech, Page 15.

By JAMES RESTON
Special to The New York Times.

WASHINGTON, Feb. 29—He said "yes."

Dwight David Eisenhower, the thirty-third President of the United States, agreed this morning to a second-term nomination. He explained why in a television-radio report to the nation tonight.

Speaking slowly and in a slightly hoarse voice, General Eisenhower said tonight: "After the most careful and devoutly prayerful consideration * * * I have decided that if the Republican party chooses to renominate me, I shall accept."

The 65-year-old President frankly told his party tonight, however, that because of his heart attack last Sept. 24, he must restrict his activities in the conduct of his office and in the Presidential campaign.

The President had raised personally the problems created by his heart attack at a crowded news conference this morning at which he said: "I assure you of this: My answer would not be in the affirmative unless I thought I could last out the five years."

Can Perform His Duties

And he told the nation tonight:

"As of this moment, there is not the slightest doubt that I can perform as well as I ever have all the important duties of the Presidency. This I say because I am actually doing so and have been doing so for many weeks."

Speaking of the Presidential campaign, General Eisenhower warned that "neither for renomination nor re-election would I engage in extensive traveling and in whistle-stop speaking—normally referred to as 'barnstorming.'" He added:

"I had long ago made up my mind, before I ever dreamed of a personal heart attack, that I could never, as President of all the people, conduct the kind of political campaign where I was personally a candidate. The first duty of a President is to discharge to the limit of his ability the responsibilities of his office."

General Eisenhower did not mention the Vice-Presidency in his radio address. He was cautious about committing himself

Continued on Page 15, Column 6

MARKET SURGES, THEN FALLS BACK

News Sets Off Buying Wave, but Stocks End Lower

By BURTON CRANE

Wall Street had its day of anticlimax yesterday. The President's announcement that he would seek re-election brought a boiling market of 3,900,000 shares, a ticker tape that ran nineteen minutes behind the floor for a time, an uprush of prices for a single hour—and a net loss on the day.

More stocks fell than rose. Seven of the ten most heavily traded issues closed lower. The New York Times combined average of fifty stocks fell 2.82 points to 322.88, a drop of more than 4/5 of 1 per cent.

Expectations that the President would announce his decision jammed the two galleries of the New York Stock Exchange well before its opening at 10 A. M. The east gallery was largely reserved for reporters, photographers and newsreel and television cameramen. The general public thronged the west gallery.

At the opening, the market was active and strongly higher, starting with gains of 1 and 2 points on good-sized blocks. United States Steel, for example, was up ⅞ on 10,000 shares. Volume continued heavy and

Continued on Page 47, Column 8

"All the News
That's Fit to Print"

The New York Times.

7:30 A. M. EXTRA
Condensation of U. S. Weather Bureau forecast:
Mostly sunny and warm today.
Mostly fair and warm tomorrow.
Temperature range today: 84—69.
Temperature range yesterday: 85.2—67.
Full U. S. Weather Bureau Report, Page 56.

© 1956, by The New York Times Company.

VOL. CV No. 35,978. Entered as Second-Class Matter. Post Office, New York, N. Y. NEW YORK, THURSDAY, JULY 26, 1956. Times Square, New York 36, N. Y. Telephone LAckawanna 4-1000 FIVE CENTS

ANDREA DORIA AND STOCKHOLM COLLIDE; 1,134 PASSENGERS ABANDON ITALIAN SHIP IN FOG AT SEA; ALL SAVED, MANY INJURED

STASSEN SUGGESTS EISENHOWER STATE IF HE IS FOR NIXON

Aide to End Pro-Herter Drive If the President Gives Nod to the Vice President

GETS NO G.O.P. BACKING

Says Hall Tries to Foreclose Choice of Delegates in Advance of Convention

By JAMES RESTON
Special to The New York Times.

WASHINGTON, July 25—Harold E. Stassen, the loneliest man in Washington, said today he would abandon his anti-Nixon campaign if President Eisenhower personally expressed a preference for Vice President Richard M. Nixon on the 1956 election ticket.

In the absence of such a statement from the President, the White House disarmament aide made it clear that he would continue to advocate the Vice-Presidential nomination of Gov. Christian A. Herter of Massachusetts.

The President has let it be known he was "delighted" that Mr. Nixon was available for the Vice-Presidential nomination. But he has not expressed a clear preference for him over other possible candidates.

Takes Aim at Hall

However, a reliable source informed The New York Times today that Governor Herter agreed to nominate Mr. Nixon for the Vice Presidency yesterday after a telephoned message from the White House saying that it was the President's wish that he do so.

Mr. Stassen was left today without the cooperation of Governor Herter or the public support of a single influential Republican politician.

Nevertheless, he took dead aim both at Mr. Nixon and the chairman of the Republican National Committee, Leonard W. Hall.

The 43-year-old Vice President, Mr. Stassen said, ran last in a private poll he (Stassen) conducted on eight potential Republican Vice-Presidential candidates. He did not say who was polled, or who did the polling, or what questions were asked—only that Mr. Nixon, Governor Herter and Mr. Stassen himself were among the eight.

He also wrote a letter in the middle of last night to Repre-

Continued on Page 8, Column 5

Jordanian Group Attacks U. N. Palestine Truce Unit

Villagers' Fire Wounds One Observer—Burns Scores Incident—Amman Puts the Blame on Israelis

By HOMER BIGART
Special to The New York Times.

JERUSALEM, July 25—Jordanian villagers attacked a team of United Nations military observers today near Jerusalem. Lieut. Col. E. H. Thalin of Sweden was seriously wounded by the Jordanian fire, United Nations sources said.

They reported that the villagers "went berserk" after an exchange of fire with Israelis in which several Jordanians were wounded. During the engagement the Israelis employed mortar fire. There were no Israeli casualties.

[Jordanian sources in Amman said Israeli fire had been responsible. The Amman report said ten Jordanians were wounded.]

Colonel Thalin was the third United Nations casualty in two days. Yesterday two Canadian officers were seriously wounded in a mine explosion on Mount Scopus.

Maj. Gen. E. L. M. Burns of Canada, United Nations truce supervisor, said tonight that he was "astonished and deeply concerned by the attack by the Jordanian villagers."

He had already made arrangements to confer tomorrow with Maj. Gen. Ali Abu Nuwar, Chief of Staff of the Jordanian Army, on measures to be taken by Jordan to reduce the number of provocative incidents along the Israeli frontier. Israeli's Premier, David Ben-Gurion, has threatened punitive action unless the provocations cease.

The current trouble spot on the frontier is in the Judean hills only five miles from Jerusalem where raw, new houses

Continued on Page 2, Column 3

DOWNTOWN TO GET 4TH NEW BUILDING

25-Story Structure Is Slated on Broad Street Site of R. C. A. Communications

By GLENN FOWLER

Another large office building is soon to rise in the downtown Manhattan financial district.

The building, the fourth large structure to be planned in the area within the last two years, will be twenty-five stories high. It will cover the block front on Beaver Street between Broad and New Streets, near Bowling Green.

It will stand on a plot of 48,000 square feet, running back 215 feet along Broad Street and 200 feet along New Street.

To be known as 60 Broad Street, the building will have an aluminum facade and a beacon light atop the roof. It will be fully air-conditioned, will have acoustic ceilings and will be equipped with operatorless elevators. Garage space will be provided in the basement. There will be 650,000 square feet of floor space above the ground floor.

The property on which the structure will be built is owned by R. C. A. Communications,

Continued on Page 41, Column 2

CONFEREES VOTE 3.7 BILLION IN AID

Reappropriated Fund Lifts Total to $4,006,570,000—Curb on Tito Supported

Special to The New York Times.

WASHINGTON, July 25—Conferees from the Senate and House of Representatives agreed today on a compromise foreign aid appropriation of $3,766,570,000.

This sum to carry the Mutual Security Program for another year would be increased by $240,000,000 of reappropriated money to a total of $4,006,570,000.

The bargain struck by the conferees amounted to a substantially even split between the $4,110,920,000 in new money originally allocated by the Senate and the $3,425,120,000 provided originally by the House.

President Eisenhower initially had asked for $4,900,000,000 for the fiscal year that opened July 1, although the appropriation for the fiscal year just ended was only $2,700,000,000.

Retained by the conferees was a rider in the Senate bill directing President Eisenhower not to give new military assistance funds to Communist Yugoslavia except for spare parts and replacements.

This stipulation was primarily the work of the Senate Republican leader, William F. Knowland of California. It did not affect $100,000,000 in military aid to Yugoslavia that already is "in the pipeline," nor did it

Continued on Page 12, Column 3

CRAFT RUSH TO AID

Terse Radio Messages of the Rescue Vessels Depict Operations

Help for the stricken liners Andrea Doria and Stockholm flowed almost instantly from all points of the compass to the spot at which they collided last night.

Ships large and small, Coast Guard vessels, luxury liners, Gloucester fishing boats, coastal steamers, all headed for the spot off Nantucket Lightship where the lives of some 2,500 persons were in danger.

It was 11:22 last night when the ships collided in a dense fog. The Andrea Doria, luxury liner of the Italian Line, shaken dangerously despite a double hull and other special safety features, sent out the first SOS less than a minute later.

The Coast Guard, with stations at Cape Ann, Cape Cod, Boston and other near-by points, sent out every available craft as soon as the position of the crash had been determined. Then came reassuring promises of help from the Ile de France and other craft within quick reach of the spot.

The Search and Rescue Division of the Coast Guard in New York received its first alert at 11:25 last night. It was then that the Coast Guard radio station at East Moriches, L. I. notified New York headquarters: "Andrea Doria and Stockholm collided 11:22 local time Lat. 40:30 N., Long. 69:53 W."

Coast Guard Cutters Aid

The East Moriches radio had picked up simultaneous SOS messages from the ships a minute or two before. The next hour was spent verifying positions and notifying all Coast Guard and merchant ships of the disaster and calling on them for help. The Coast Guard sent out ten cutters from New York, Boston and New London, Conn., and diverted three other ships cruising in that area.

The stark drama being played on the open ocean in darkness and fog was pictured in tense, taut radio messages recorded by the wireless room of The New York Times. They read:

12:21 A. M.—S. S. Stockholm says: Badly damaged. The whole bow crushed and No. 1 hold filled with water. Have to stay in our position. If you [Andrea Doria] can lower your lifeboats we can pick them up.

12:21 A. M.—S. S. Andrea Doria replied: You have to row to us.

12:38 A. M.—S. S. Cape Ann reports: Now between the two ships and her boats are ready. Has two lifeboats.

12:45 A. M. Coast Guard boat says: Ten miles away; have eighteen boats.

1:12 A. M. Andrea Doria says: Needs more lifeboats still.

1:13 A. M. Unidentified ship, when queried, says: We have twelve lifeboats.

Stricken Ship's Boats Useless

1:21 A. M. Cape Ann asks Doria: How close do you want our ship to come to you?

1:24 A. M. Cape Ann reports: We have two boats for Andrea. Now proceeding to get close to her.

1:26 A. M. Andrea Doria reports: Danger immediate, need lifeboats, as many as possible. Can't use our lifeboats.

1:30 A. M. Stockholm gives position: Lat. 40:34 N; Long. 69:45 W.

1:33 A. M. Cape Ann asks Andrea: Want Cape Ann to move in any closer than Cape Ann is now?

1:34 A. M. Ile de France says: We are nine miles from you. Will launch as many boats as possible.

1:43 A. M. Doria repeats earlier message: Here danger immediate. Need lifeboats, as many as possible. Can't use our lifeboats.

1:46 A. M. Unidentified ship radios Andrea: Two lifeboats on way over to you.

1:53 A. M. S. S. Manaqui radios both ships: Will arrive yours at 0900 G. M. T. (5 A. M., E. D. T.) Have two lifeboats.

1:54 A. M. Andrea replies: O. K. Thanks.

1:56 A. M. Unidentified Nor-

Continued on Page 15, Column 1

The New York Times

The 29,000-ton Italian Line vessel, the Andrea Doria, which carried 1,134 passengers

The 12,644-ton Swedish American liner Stockholm, largest liner ever built in Sweden

2D VESSEL IS SAFE

Ile de France In Today With Survivors From Crash Off Nantucket

By MAX FRANKEL

The trans-Atlantic liners Andrea Doria and Stockholm collided in a heavy Atlantic fog at 11:22 o'clock last night, forty-five miles south of Nantucket Island.

The Andrea Doria ordered her 1,134 passengers aboard to abandon ship. All were reported to have been rescued at 4:58 A. M. There was no immediate word, however, on the fate of her crew of 575.

At 5:15 A. M. today, however, the Ile de France reported from the scene that no more help was needed.

The French Liner estimated at 7 A. M. that she would arrive in New York shortly after 6 o'clock this afternoon with 1,000 survivors from the Andrea Doria. It was not clear to which ports the other survivors would be taken.

The Stockholm, although it had taken water through a crushed bow, was able to keep her 550 passengers and crew of 200 aboard. She was waiting for an escort to attempt to return to New York at a slow speed.

Many survivors of the Italian ship were said to have been seriously injured. The Stockholm said she had five "critical" cases aboard. Desperate and repeated calls for medical assistance were radioed from the score of rescue vessels in the area.

Deck Dips into Water

The Andrea Doria lay helpless in the thick fog. The black-and-white ship reported she was listing "very badly." She gave no other indication of the extent or nature of her damage nor was there word whether she could remain afloat.

The Stockholm reported at 6 A. M. that the Andrea Doria's main deck was dipping to the surface of the water.

The 29,000-ton Italian Line vessel apparently was listing so severely that she could launch no more than two of her lifeboats. Her lifeboats can carry 2,000 persons.

The French Ile de France, largest of the rescue vessels on hand, and the Stockholm apparently recovered the bulk of the Andrea Doria's passengers. At one time as many as 100 lifeboats probably were in the area. It was not clear how the passengers were loaded into the lifeboats.

At 4:58, the master of the Ile de France told the Stockholm: "All passengers rescued. "Proceeding to New York full speed."

The Ile de France left New York yesterday bound for Le Havre.

Since shortly after the collision, the Andrea Doria had run her lights and radio on emergency power and said she did not how much longer she could keep in touch with rescue craft. Her radio was so weak the Stock-

Continued on Page 14, Column 5

SHIPS' PIERS QUIET IN NEW YORK PORT

Crowds Expected at Andrea Doria's Docks—Relatives Begin Calling Lines

The sea diaster had not early today awakened the pier at West Forty-fourth Street where the Andrea Doria had been scheduled to dock later in the morning.

This pier, as well as the terminal at West Fifty-seventh Street, where the Stockholm had left just before noon yesterday in a gala sailing, remained dark and quiet.

However, unaccustomed night lights began blinking on at the Italian Line's office at 24 State Street before 4 o'clock when members of the company's staff began arriving.

They had been rounded up from their scattered homes around the Metropolitan area by officials of the line under Rosmino Pernigotti, assistant general manager of the company here.

The company officials were making plans to handle expected crowds at West Forty-fourth Street during the morning. Several thousand visitors were expected to begin gathering there by 8 o'clock, some not knowing about the collision.

It is an axiom in the harbor that every arriving passenger attracts five or more relatives and friends as welcomers, and the Italian Line officials were preparing to give them the tragic news and to forestall a rush by worried relatives on the line's downtown office.

Many of the relatives already knew of the crash at sea, and the office and pier of the com-

Continued on Page 14, Column 3

Many Notables Are Listed Aboard the Andrea Doria

Persons prominent in business, the theatre, politics, journalism and government were among the passengers aboard the Andrea Doria when she collided last night with the Stockholm. Two directors of the Standard Oil Company (New Jersey) were on the passenger list. They were Stewart Coleman, traveling with his family, and Marion W. Boyer, accompanied by his wife. Mr. Coleman, 57 years old, lives at 365 Barrett Road, Cedarhurst, L. I. Mr. Boyer, 54, lives in Greenwich, Conn.

Another passenger was Richardson Dilworth, Mayor of Philadelphia, and his wife. Mr. Dilworth, a lawyer by profession, is 57. He served as a Marine in both World Wars, and received the Purple Heart in World War I and the Silver Star in World War II.

Ruth Roman, Hollywood motion picture star, and her son, Richard Hall, were on the Andrea Doria. Miss Roman recently divorced Mortimer Hall, owner of a Los Angeles radio station.

Two refugees from behind the Iron Curtain, the dancers Istvan Rabovsky and his wife Nora Kovach, also were passengers. They are natives of Hungary. In May, 1953, they fled to the West from East Berlin, where they had gone for a dancing engagement. In 1954, they came to this country.

Also on board were Camille M. Cianfarra, Madrid correspondent of The New York Times, and his family. A native of New York, Mr. Cianfarra joined The Times in 1935 in Rome. He became a specialist in Vatican affairs, and has written two books about the Vatican. He became Madrid correspondent in 1951.

Others on board included Ferdinand M. Thieriot, circulation manager of The San Francisco

Continued on Page 15, Column 5

SHIP BUILT TO TAKE COLLISION SAFELY

Andrea Doria Hull Divided to Give Stability—Lifeboats Could Carry 2,000

The Andrea Doria was specially built to give her more stability in case of just such a collision as she had last night with the Stockholm.

The hull was subdivided into eleven watertight compartments extending the entire length of the ship. Bulkheads parallel with her engine rooms were designed to lessen the effect of a collision.

The ship carried lifeboats with a capacity of 2,000 persons. Some of these boats were made of light metal alloy and were hung from davits operated by motor-driven winches. Two of the boats were motor-driven and fitted with radios.

Luxurious to the last detail, the ship was completely fireproofed and radar-equipped.

The ship has two groups of turbines capable of generating 50,000 horsepower to turn its three blade propellors, each weighing sixteen tons. They are nineteen feet in diameter and turn 143 revolutions a minute.

The Andrea Doria and the Stockholm had been the prides of the Italian and Swedish merchant marines.

The Stockholm, when launched in 1948, was the largest passenger vessel ever to have been built in Swedish yards. The Andrea Doria, when launched in 1951, was the last word in modern design and comfort. Each was flagship of its line until supplanted by new vessels a few years later.

When she went into service as flagship of the Swedish American Line, the Stockholm had a capacity of 364 passengers and 150 officers and crew. Alterations in 1953 increased the capacity to nearly 600 passengers with a proportionate increase in the size of the crew.

The Stockholm had an over-all length of 510 feet and a beam of

Continued on Page 15, Column 6

The New York Times July 26, 1956

SCENE OF THE COLLISION: The liners Andrea Doria and the Stockholm stricken off Nantucket Island (cross).

Cause of the Crash Puzzles Radar Men

Experts on radar said today they could not explain how the collision between the Andrea Doria and the Stockholm could have taken place because both vessels were equipped with radar equipment.

They said that even with the "visibility nil" conditions reported in the vicinity each ship should have been able to observe the other for distances up to fifty miles.

The experts declared that, even without knowing precisely what systems the vessels carried, they almost certainly were flexible installations such as are standard on large passenger vessels. They should have been capable of two types of operation—generalized scanning all about the vessel, and a narrower type of observation of a restricted sector of the horizon. They should also have been

Continued on Page 14, Column 4

Eisenhower's Four Years

An Analysis of Agriculture Policy And Steps Taken to Meet Problems

This is the fifth of a series of articles analyzing the record of the Eisenhower Administration at the start of the Presidential election campaign.

By WILLIAM M. BLAIR
Special to The New York Times.

WASHINGTON, July 25—President Eisenhower has faced a number of stubborn dilemmas in the last four years but no other problem on the home front has been comparable to the one on farms.

Like the Communist problem overseas, it has absorbed his attention. From time to time it has been mitigated by his policies. Always, however, it has returned to plague him in one form or another.

In his home town of Abilene, Kan., in mid-1952 the President began formulating his program to reconcile freedom and prosperity for the American farmer. As he put it later, "full parity in the market place" and a minimum of Government regulation were his aims.

It has been a long, perplexing struggle for the President. But despite a notable effort, success has eluded him. The farmer still is tied up in Government controls and has considerably less cash in his pockets.

Every new Administration inherits the past. Thus twenty years of Democratic and often bipartisan farm policies have failed, despite high Federal subsidies, to solve the boom and bust ills that have beset agriculture in the midst of an expanding industrial economy and national prosperity.

Indeed, President Eisenhower and his embattled Secretary of Agriculture, Ezra Taft Benson, have blamed these policies and the last two wars for the surpluses that have resisted their remedies and have depressed farm prices.

From a peak of $15,943,000,000 in 1948, farm income fell to $12,851,000,000 in 1950, before the Korean war. It climbed to $14,801,000,000 in 1951, slipped to $14,051,000,000 in the Presiden-

Continued on Page 12, Column 1

Ailing Millikin Plans To Leave the Senate

By WILLIAM S. WHITE
Special to The New York Times.

WASHINGTON, July 25—Senator Eugene D. Millikin of Colorado, a powerful member of the Republican leadership, said a farewell today to the Senate.

He was compelled by long and agonizing illness to announce that he would not seek re-election in the fall.

The decision was a heavy blow to the Republican party generally, and to its conservative wing in particular.

Mr. Millikin as a well campaigner would have been a formidable favorite to keep his seat safe for the Republicans. Even as an ailing prospective campaigner he had been greatly feared by the Democrats.

His retirement seemed plainly to forward Democratic prospects for retaining control

Continued on Page 10, Column 3

"All the News That's Fit to Print"

The New York Times.

LATE CITY EDITION
Condensation of U. S. Weather Bureau forecast: Cloudy, cool with rain today. Fair and milder tomorrow.
Temperature range today: 58—48.
Temperature range yesterday: 55.4—45.4.
Full U. S. Weather Bureau Report, Page 42.

VOL. CVI..No. 36,071. Entered as Second-Class Matter, Post Office, New York, N. Y. NEW YORK, SATURDAY, OCTOBER 27, 1956. Times Square, New York 36, N. Y. Telephone Lackawanna 4-1000 FIVE CENTS

HUNGARIAN REVOLT SPREADS; NAGY TOTTERS; THOUSANDS IN ARMY FIGHT SOVIET TROOPS; U. S. CONSULTS ALLIES ON TAKING U.N. ACTION

STEVENSON ASKS EISENHOWER POLICY ON A COBALT BOMB

Inquires in Illinois Whether President Plans a Further Step in Nuclear Arms

Text of Stevenson speech will be found on Page 14.

By HARRISON E. SALISBURY

Special to The New York Times.

ALBUQUERQUE, N. M., Oct. 26—Adlai E. Stevenson challenged President Eisenhower today to state whether he proposed to develop the cobalt bomb or some more terrible weapon that might thrust the earth off its axis.

Mr. Stevenson suddenly renewed his nuclear offensive with an unexpected peroration to an address at Rock Island, Ill. He flew to Albuquerque later.

Tonight, in a speech here, he raised the question whether President Eisenhower had abandoned a move to halt hydrogen bomb tests "because his political opponents dared propose such a course."

The Rock Island audience of 1,300 filled the Fort Theatre, largest in the industrially depressed farm equipment center.

The Democratic Presidential nominee mentioned the cobalt bomb in a new indictment of General Eisenhower's policies and position on the hydrogen bomb.

Sees Fundamental Wrong

Mr. Stevenson asserted that he had evidence provided only yesterday by four scientists that already radiation "in certain areas of the world" had passed the danger point. Mr. Stevenson did not specify the areas.

Members of Mr. Stevenson's staff identified the scientists as Walter Selove, Brookhaven National Laboratories; Louis Osborn and R. M. Weinstein of the Massachusetts Institute of Technology, and Herman P. Epstein of Brandeis University.

Mr. Stevenson charged that the President was fundamentally wrong in basing national security on reliance upon the "deterrent effect of our lead in nuclear weapons." He recalled that ten years ago similar reliance had been placed upon the original atom bombs and that "to our surprise" the Russians had caught up with the United States in no time.

"And they'll do it again in the hydrogen field," he said. "Maybe they have already."

"What does Mr. Eisenhower propose then?" Mr. Stevenson

Continued on Page 14, Column 2

EISENHOWER ADDS TENNESSEE SPEECH

Expands Campaign Again—Check-Up Begins Today

By ALVIN SHUSTER

Special to The New York Times.

WASHINGTON, Oct. 26—President Eisenhower expanded his campaign plans again today. They now include a speech next week in Tennessee, one of the four Southern states he carried in 1952.

The White House announced that the President would add Memphis to a schedule that already included Texas, Florida and Virginia, the three other traditionally Democratic states that "liked Ike" four years ago.

In addition, he will speak in Oklahoma and Pennsylvania.

On Monday he will go to Miami, Jacksonville and Richmond; on Wednesday, Oklahoma City, Memphis and Dallas, and on Thursday, Philadelphia.

The decision to broaden the President's schedule came on the eve of his pre-election physical examination. The President will enter Walter Reed Army Medical Center shortly after noon. He will stay there until Sunday when the results of the "head-to-toe" examination will be made known. The President announced plans

Continued on Page 13, Column 1

U. N. Delegates Sign Atomic Energy Agreement Here

For United States, James J. Wadsworth

The New York Times (by Edward Hausner)

For Soviet Union, Georgi N. Zaroubin

STEVENSON LIKELY TO WIN IN VIRGINIA

Second Survey Finds States' Rights Bloc and Powell's Activity Hurt G. O. P.

A Times Team Report

Teams of New York Times reporters have recently surveyed political trends in twenty-seven closely contested states. They are now resurveying the most doubtful of those states. This is the first such resurvey. It comes from Clarence Dean, Tillman Durdin, Max Frankel, John D. Morris and William S. White.

By WILLIAM S. WHITE

Special to The New York Times.

RICHMOND, Va., Oct. 26—If visible trends and measurable data have their accustomed meaning, Adlai E. Stevenson should win Virginia's twelve electoral votes on Nov. 6.

On nearly every traditional basis of calculation, the Democratic Presidential nominee is ahead in the state, and should remain ahead at the decisive hour when the votes are counted on election night.

It is nevertheless necessary to put in a qualification that is both a cliché and a fact of political life in Virginia. This is that racial and other social currents run so deeply and are so unreadable that President Eisenhower might, after all, repeat his 1952 victory in this state—one of four Southern States that he carried.

A tragic, and in some degree hopeless, bitterness suffuses both the white and Negro races here. The issue of segregation versus integration is aflame, and it throws into doubt all the generally reliable political indexes.

Conclusions Indicated

These indexes, as far as they go, suggest the following conclusions:

¶The Eisenhower movement of 1952 has lost a good deal of its urgency; there is little now of the spirit of "crusade" in it. The social pressures for voting Republican are far less powerful than in 1952.

¶The President will lose some of his 1952 strength in every area of Virginia. Mr. Stevenson thus should be able to surmount the 80,000-vote plurality, out of a total of about 619,000, that General Eisenhower ran up here four years ago.

¶The third-party candidacy of T. Coleman Andrews, States' Rights Presidential aspirant, almost certainly will take more votes from President Eisenhower than from Mr. Stevenson.

This is the conclusion of a New York Times team that has just made a resurvey of this state. The team reported on Oct. 8 from Richmond that Mr. Stevenson seemed to have whatever edge there was then.

At that time there was some uncertainty about the most "Southern" part of Virginia. This

Continued on Page 13, Column 6

U.S. to Give Atom Agency 11,000 Pounds of Uranium

By LINDESAY PARROTT

Special to The New York Times.

UNITED NATIONS, N. Y., Oct. 26—President Eisenhower promised today to make available 11,000 pounds of Uranium 235 to the newly established International Atomic Energy Agency. The pledge was made in a message read this morning to the closing session of an eighty-two-state conference that debated and approved the statute of the new world organization.

Representatives of seventy of these states formally signed the statute just before noon at ceremonies in the newly decorated General Assembly Hall of the United Nations.

The President's message was read from the rostrum by Lewis L. Strauss, Chairman of the United States Atomic Energy Commission.

The message said in part:

"To enable the international atomic agency—upon its establishment by appropriate governmental actions—to start atomic research and power programs without delay, the United States will make available to the international agency, on terms to be agreed with the agency, 5,000 kilograms of a nuclear fuel, Uranium 235."

Text of Eisenhower's message is printed on Page 12.

This is one-quarter of the 20,000 kilograms (about 44,800 pounds) earmarked by the United States last February for use by friendly nations in the development of peaceful atomic programs.

In addition, the President pledged that the United States later would match the contributions of all other nations to the agency's nuclear materials "bank."

These additional supplies will become available between the establishment of the agency, after the ratification of the statute by eighteen powers, and July 1, 1960. They will be furnished on

Continued on Page 12, Column 3

CITY WARNS UNION ON SUBWAY STRIKE

Mayor Scores M.B.A. Threat as 'Political Blackmail'—Transit Board to Act

By RALPH KATZ

Mayor Wagner and the Transit Authority warned the Motormen's Benevolent Association yesterday against taking strike action on the city's subways.

In a telegram to Theodore Loos, president of the independent union, the Mayor asserted that he would not "tolerate" a strike. The authority said that if a strike vote was taken in violation of a Supreme Court injunction, "we shall take steps to meet it."

Both messages resulted from a report on Thursday by a union executive committee member that job action was planned for Nov. 5. The union official, who declined to permit the use of his name, said that the strike vote would be taken next Wednesday.

The union says it represents

Continued on Page 18, Column 6

Rioting in Singapore Takes Mounting Toll

Special to The New York Times.

SINGAPORE, Oct. 26—Rioting resulting from a strike of students spread to many parts of Singapore today. The official casualty toll reached seven dead and fifty-one injured.

The seriousness of the situation caused 27,000 police reserves and policemen to be held ready in the Federation of Malaya to be airlifted to Singapore if the violence in the Crown Colony got out of hand.

[More British troops were being moved into Singapore early Saturday as the number of dead rose to eleven, according to Reuters. Ninety-nine persons were officially listed as injured, and 219 have been arrested in two days of fighting.]

Malaya's Chief Minister,

Continued on Page 10, Column 3

WEST SEEKS WAY

France, Britain, Others Study How to Appeal Russian Intervention

By EDWIN L. DALE Jr.

Special to The New York Times.

WASHINGTON, Oct. 26—The State Department disclosed today that the United States was consulting with Britain, France and other friendly governments on "the feasibility and advisability of bringing the situation in Hungary before the United Nations."

This was revealed by Lincoln White, the State Department spokesman. Officials said later that the United States was making no proposals, but was exploring various possibilities.

The Governments being consulted, other than Britain and France, were not identified.

[In Paris, Foreign Minister Christian Pineau warned the West against attempts to exploit the uprisings in Poland and Hungary.]

Mr. White said that among the questions under consideration was that of the legality of the presence of Soviet troops in Hungary under the Warsaw pact. Statements by President Eisenhower and Secretary of State Dulles on this point have appeared to be in conflict.

Troop Use Questioned

The Warsaw Pact of May 14, 1955, is a Soviet version of the North Atlantic Treaty Organization. Under the pact's provisions, Soviet troops have remained in Hungary, a member nation, to "safeguard" her security.

The view in the State Department is that there is little doubt that the troops have a right to be there. But a question might be raised about the legitimacy of their use to put down an internal rebellion.

Even this raises a problem, however. The Soviet troops are being used at the request of the Hungarian Government. There is little effort in Washington to deny that United States forces abroad could be used in the same way if there were a Communist-led revolution in, say, Italy.

In 1944 and 1945, for example, British troops, on the request of the Athens Government, fought Communist rebels in Greece.

Furthermore, any possible United Nations approach is at the moment clouded by French threats to use force in Morocco and Tunisia to protect Europeans there.

The United Nations situation,

Continued on Page 5, Column 3

Reporter in Budapest Tells How Protest Grew Into War

Account From the Embattled City Says Soviet's Massed Tanks Slowed Revolt, Which the Massacre Then Rekindled

By JOHN MacCORMAC

Special to The New York Times.

BUDAPEST, Hungary, Oct. 26—What began here Tuesday as a demonstration turned that same night into a revolt and yesterday became a war that was still raging today.

It is war by Soviet troops and Hungarian political policemen against the mass of the Hungarian people. The war is being waged on behalf of the Soviet Union and in support of the Hungarian Communist Government, which would fall in ten minutes if it were not for the presence of Soviet tanks in Budapest.

The Soviet troops were called in by the Hungarian Government while it still was dominated by Erno Gero, who had succeeded Matyas Rakosi as First Secretary of the Hungarian Working People's (Communist) party. Imre Nagy, for whose appointment as Premier the insurgent masses had been calling, did not take office until after the invitation to the Soviet troops had been sent, although by doing so he countenanced it.

Mr. Gero's removal from power did not occur until Mikhail A. Suslov, a member of the Soviet Presidium, and Anastas I. Mikoyan, a Soviet First Deputy Premier, who had successively visited Hungary when the fall of M. Rakosi was imminent, arrived in Budapest yesterday for a brief visit.

As late as last night the insurgents still were calling for a democratic government headed by Mr. Nagy, but one that would accede to demands that no Communist regime anywhere had yet accepted. But they were saying that Mr. Nagy already had demonstrated he was no Gomulka. This was a reference to

Continued on Page 2, Column 3

Poles, Quiet, Watch Revolt in Hungary But Get Little News

By HENRY GINIGER

Special to The New York Times.

WARSAW, Oct. 26—For the first time in almost a week Poland was reported completely quiet today.

As the ferment that accompanied changes in the country's Communist leadership died down, considerable attention was turned to events in Hungary.

Warsaw newspapers announced that in response to an appeal by the Hungarian Red Cross a special plane flew to Budapest today with blood plasma and other supplies for the victims of the fighting there. Later it was understood the plane was unable to land in Budapest and returned here with its cargo.

Of the fighting itself there was virtually no news here. Communications between Warsaw and Budapest, by private phones at least, had been cut. Two regularly scheduled plane flights were canceled today.

From its "fragmentary information," Trybuna Ludu, the Polish Communist official organ, said this morning it had concluded that "the peaceful demonstration of the Hungarian

Continued on Page 3, Column 6

FIGHTING EXTENDS TO AUSTRIAN LINE

Hungarian Physicians Cross Border With Medical Plea in the Rebels' Behalf

By PAUL HOFMANN

Special to The New York Times.

VIENNA, Saturday, Oct. 27—Rebellion has spread to westernmost Hungary and has sent casualties and refugees across the border into Austria.

Shortly after 8 o'clock last night a Hungarian ambulance with three physicians appeared near the Austrian frontier village of Nicklesdorf on the main Vienna-Budapest highway and asked to see the Austrian authorities. The physicians said they were acting for the rebels and urgently requested medical supplies for their injured. They said seventy persons had been killed and 200 wounded in fighting in the Hungarian town of Magyarovar, seven miles east of the border.

The atmosphere in Vienna late yesterday was that of a city behind battle lines. Plasma and medical supplies were hurriedly assembled and Red Cross am-

Continued on Page 3, Column 4

Associated Press Radiophoto

SOVIET ARMORED VEHICLES PROWL STREETS OF BUDAPEST: A tank and a smaller vehicle moving yesterday along Kossuth Street in the embattled Hungarian capital. This picture was taken by a Western traveler, just before he left the city for Vienna. It was sent here by radio. The fighting that had started on Tuesday still continued.

NEW PEACE PLEA

Shake-Up of Regime and Revision of Tie to Moscow Vowed

By ELIE ABEL

Special to The New York Times.

VIENNA, Saturday, Oct. 27—The battle of Budapest was still in doubt early today, with Soviet troops on one side and a fiercely hostile Hungarian populace on the other.

The insurrection had spread over a large part of the country. The desperate regime of Premier Imre Nagy was struggling to maintain itself in a few scarred Government buildings along the Pest embankment with the aid of Soviet tanks and artillery.

The bulk of the Hungarian Army had given up the fight, according to reports reaching Vienna, and thousands of officers and soldiers had joined the insurrection, now in its fifth day.

[The Budapest radio said at dawn Saturday that Soviet and Hungarian troops had launched new attacks throughout Hungary against the rebels, The Associated Press reported from Vienna. The broadcast said fighting must continue because rebel elements had defied an ultimatum to surrender. No further word had been received up to 4 A. M., New York time.]

A Rebel Government

Rebel forces controlling the industrial town of Gyor in West Hungary, proclaimed their own "independent Hungarian Government." Western reporters managed to establish contact with this group from the Austrian frontier.

The anti-Communist Hungarians said they were expecting an early attack on Gyor by Soviet Army forces. The rebels told newsmen they had a number of tanks some of them captured and the rest surrendered voluntarily by Hungarian Army units.

The indication during the night was that Premier Nagy could count only on the support of the Hungarian Red Security Police and the Soviet Army. The weakness of his three-day-old Government was plain.

The Central Committee of the Hungarian Working People's (Communist) party made a fresh appeal for peace and order yesterday afternoon after an emergency meeting under the new First Secretary, Janos Kadar.

Communists' Program

The committee outlined a program virtually identical with that of the Polish United Workers (Communist) party led by Wladyslaw Gomulka. A new relationship with the Soviet Union will be worked out, the Hungarian committee promised, on the principles of "national independence, complete equality and non-interference."

The party leadership pledged that it would seek a withdrawal of Soviet forces from strongpoints as soon as order was restored, and offered an unconditional amnesty for all insurrec-

Continued on Page 3, Column 2

Sultan Strengthens Moroccan Cabinet

By THOMAS F. BRADY

Special to The New York Times.

RABAT, Morocco, Saturday, Oct. 27—A new Moroccan Cabinet of fourteen ministers, headed by Premier M'barek Bekkai, was sworn in at 3 A. M. today before Sultan Mohammed V. The Cabinet change gave predominance to the strongly nationalist Istiqlal (Independence) party.

The Sultan told his new Ministers they were chosen "to confront the difficulties" in which the country finds itself.

These difficulties are the result of the breach with France over the seizure of five Algerian nationalist rebel leaders from a Moroccan plane Monday night. The Algerians were the Sultan's guests and were on

Continued on Page 10, Column 3

"All the News That's Fit to Print"

The New York Times.

LATE CITY EDITION
Condensation of U. S. Weather Bureau forecast: Mostly fair today and tomorrow.
Temperature range today: 65—48.
Temperature range yesterday: 62.2—48.1.
Full U. S. Weather Bureau Report, Page 74.

VOL. CVI—No. 36,074. Entered as Second-Class Matter, Post Office, New York, N. Y. NEW YORK, TUESDAY, OCTOBER 30, 1956. Times Square, New York 36, N. Y. Telephone Lackawanna 4-1000 FIVE CENTS

ISRAELIS THRUST INTO EGYPT AND NEAR SUEZ; U.S. GOES TO U.N. UNDER ANTI-AGGRESSION PACT

Budapest Rebels Refuse to Yield Until Soviet Troops Leave

EISENHOWER BIDS SOUTH FIGHT BIAS ON A 'LOCAL BASIS'

In Miami He Stresses Roles of States—Hails Byrd in Speech in Virginia

Texts of Eisenhower speeches are on Pages 24 and 25.

By RUSSELL BAKER
Special to The New York Times.

RICHMOND, Va., Oct. 29—President Eisenhower, campaigning in the South today, urged that the problem of achieving racial equality be handled largely "on a local and state basis."

He told a Miami Airport audience he was convinced that progress today in equality of opportunity and equality before the law had "to be achieved finally in the hearts of men rather than in legislative halls."

The President was applauded lightly when he said that "there must be intelligent understanding of the human factors and emotions involved if we are to make steady progress in the matter rather than simply to make political promises never intended to be kept."

In the field of civil rights, he added, he had tried to bring "reason, good sense and good judgment to the performance of clear duty."

Makes 1,800-Mile Trip

Though he delivered three airport speeches in an 1,800-mile aerial campaign in Florida and Virginia, he touched on the civil rights issue only once.

That was in Miami, in the President's first speech today.

In Jacksonville, Fla., and Richmond, Va., where the southern tradition is stronger than in Miami, he did not discuss the racial theme. Nor did he refer directly in any of his speeches to the controversial school integration issue or the Supreme Court decision.

He concentrated instead on three matters: peace, prosperity and attacks on the Democratic ticket.

And at Miami General Eisenhower tried for the first time the handshaking style of campaigning developed to a high art by Senator Estes Kefauver.

Surrounded by several hundred rabid admirers on his way to his plane after speaking, he shook hands by the score with a zest rarely matched by Senator Kefauver and a folksiness as impressive as the Senator's own.

"Hi ya, folks," he said, and

Continued on Page 24, Column 4

Stevenson Says U. S. Gets 'Less Than Truth' on Strife

Charges President Endangered the Nation by 'Good News' From the Mideast—Boston Crowds Hail Candidate

By HARRISON E. SALISBURY
Special to The New York Times.

BOSTON, Oct. 29—Adlai E. Stevenson charged tonight that President Eisenhower had given the nation reassurances about the Middle East that had been "tragically less than the truth."

"The Government has not been telling us the whole truth," Mr. Stevenson said.

Texts of Stevenson statement and speech, Page 28.

The Presidential nominee addressed an overflow Democratic throng of more than 8,000 in Mechanics Hall in the climax of his drive for Massachusetts' sixteen electoral votes.

Mr. Stevenson's address was televised nationally by the American Broadcasting Company. After the telecast was completed, Mr. Stevenson appended one of his sharpest challenges to President Eisenhower's leadership. The Democrat declared:

"I deeply believe that we cannot afford another four years under a part-time leader of a party which will not plan, which will not create, which will not dare to see the vision of a new America and make that vision come true.

"As a campaigning politician there is none better. It is as a performing politician, as a President who knows how to control his own party, who knows how to grasp the reins of Government that he fails."

Several times Mr. Stevenson's partisan audience booed references to the President. The chorus of boos every time he mentioned Vice President Richard M. Nixon started the moment the crowd sensed that Mr.

Continued on Page 29, Column 3

FIGHTING PERSISTS

Russians Still Pulling Out, With Hungarian Units Taking Over

Text of editorial in Communist newspaper on Page 10.

By ELIE ABEL
Special to The New York Times.

VIENNA, Tuesday, Oct. 30—Soviet troops remained in control of Budapest this morning while the Government of Imre Nagy pleaded with the stubborn revolutionaries to lay down their arms.

But the rebels refused to give up the fight until Mr. Nagy had made good on his promise that the Soviet forces would evacuate the battered city, monitored reports from the Hungarian capital said.

This morning the Budapest radio broadcast the following communiqué:

"While Soviet forces are being withdrawn from Budapest, Hungarian police and armed youth units are maintaining order. Such armed groups as are still resisting will lay down their arms at 9 A. M. [3 A. M. New York time] and will then take part in maintaining order."

[Up to 5 A. M. New York time there had been no further reports on the situation in Hungary.]

Appeal Is Pressed

Earlier this morning the Budapest radio broadcast an appeal by Karoly Janda, Defense Minister, to the rebels to lay down their arms before 9 A. M.

In spite of the gradual Soviet withdrawal, fighting in Budapest flared up again last night. Soviet tank forces engaged in heavy combat in several parts of the city. Latest reports said artillery fire was heard in Budapest all night.

Rebels from eastern Hungary and from the region of Gyor in the west were understood to have joined the insurgents in the capital.

The rebel-held Miskolc radio in northeast Hungary, in a broadcast monitored here, urged anti-Communists in Budapest not to lay down their arms before the last Soviet soldier had left the country.

A general strike called by the rebel leaders appeared to be continuing in many parts of Hungary for the fifth day. Most factory workers, railroad men and miners stayed away from their jobs again this morning despite pressing appeals from Mr. Nagy's Government to resume work.

Nearly complete was an unofficial school strike. Instead of attending classes many teenagers in Budapest did courier work for the rebels and even

Continued on Page 10, Column 4

1950 PLEDGE CITED

White House Recalls Promise to Assist Victim of Attack

By DANA ADAMS SCHMIDT
Special to The New York Times.

WASHINGTON, Oct. 29—The United States will take the movement of Israeli forces into Egypt to the United Nations Security Council tomorrow morning.

The planned appeal to the United Nations was announced by the White House tonight after President Eisenhower had held an emergency meeting there with Secretary of State Dulles and six other high officials.

[An emergency meeting of the Security Council was set for 11 A. M. Tuesday.]

The White House statement follows:

"At the meeting, the President recalled that the United States under this and prior Administrations has pledged itself to assist the victim of any aggression in the Middle East. We shall honor our pledge.

"The United States is in consultation with the British and French Governments, parties with us to the tripartite declaration of 1950, and the United States plans as contemplated by that declaration that the situation shall be taken to the United Nations Security Council tomorrow morning.

Special Session in Abeyance

"The question of whether and when the President will call a special session of the Congress will be decided in the light of the unfolding situation."

The statement was read by James C. Hagerty, Presidential press secretary. He said it had the full authority of the President and the other conferees.

Others at the meeting, in addition to Mr. Dulles, were Charles E. Wilson, Secretary of Defense; Admiral Arthur W. Radford, Chairman of the Joint Chiefs of Staff; Sherman Adams, Assistant to the President; Herbert Hoover Jr., Under Secretary of State; Allen W. Dulles, director of the Central Intelligence Agency, and Wilton B. Persons, deputy assistant to the President.

The one-and-a-half-hour meeting at the White House took place immediately after the President's return by air from a campaign trip in Florida and Virginia.

The State Department said Americans "not performing essential services" would be asked to leave the Middle East. Among the first to leave was a group that flew from Israel to Athens.

Earlier, Secretary of State Dulles had initiated the joint steps with Britain and France.

The State Department an-

Continued on Page 3, Column 1

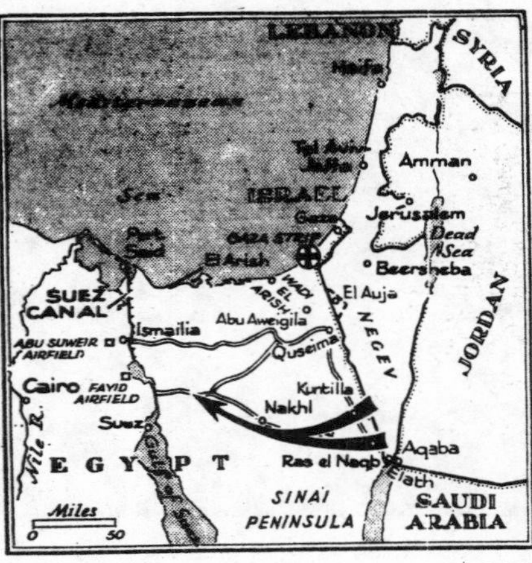

The New York Times Oct. 30, 1956

ISRAELIS OPEN DRIVE: The advance into Egypt was reported made at and below Kuntilla, with a thrust near the Suez Canal. There was a flare-up in Gaza area (cross).

Cairo Says Egyptian Units Have Engaged the Israelis

By The United Press.

CAIRO, Tuesday, Oct. 30—The Egyptian Army said today it had begun "liquidating" an Israeli force that had thrust deep into Egyptian territory toward the Suez Canal. Egyptian army headquarters announced that the Israeli force had suffered "heavy casualties" in the night-long fighting. It gave no precise figures.

"The enemy's plan to penetrate deep inside Egyptian territory failed," the Egyptian communiqué said. "Egyptian armed forces early this morning started liquidating the enemy forces."

[Iraq informed Egypt early Tuesday that Iraqi troops were ready to offer immediate assistance against the Israeli thrust, The Associated Press said. The offer was announced after an urgent morning meeting of Premier Nuri as-Said's Cabinet in Baghdad.]

Leaves Are Canceled

The high command of the Egyptian armed forces recalled all officers and enlisted men on leave to meet the Israeli threat. Orders broadcast by the Cairo radio said all must "report immediately to their units." Reservists were not affected.

The Egyptian communiqué identified the three frontier checkpoints where it said the Israeli raiders had been halted at Kuntilla, Nekhet and El Mimet. All are on the eastern side of the rocky Sinai Peninsula. [No additional details on the fighting were received up to 5 A. M.]

Suez Canal authorities in Cairo said the situation along the waterway was normal. They said no blackout has been imposed and no emergency alert sounded.

Continued on Page 6, Column 2

DEEP DRIVE MADE

Tel Aviv Declares Aim Is to Smash Egyptian Commando Bases

Text of Israeli statement will be found on Page 4.

By MOSHE BRILLIANT
Special to The New York Times.

TEL AVIV, Israel, Oct. 29—An Israeli military force thrust into the Sinai Peninsula of Egypt today. It was reported to have reached within twenty miles of the Suez Canal.

Army sources said the Israelis were west of the crossroads where the road to Kuntilla branches off from the Suez-Quseima highway.

The Israelis were said to have halted there and to have dug in.

A Foreign Ministry statement said the operation had been started "to eliminate the Egyptian fedayeen [commando squad] bases in the Sinai Peninsula."

Army sources said the Israelis had smashed the Egyptian position at Kuntilla and Ras el Naqb at the southern end of the international border. The forces then advanced more than seventy-five miles.

No fighting was reported on the northern end of the border or in the Gaza Strip, which is heavily populated.

'Too Big for a Reprisal'

Reports from the Sinai area described the fighting as "too big for a reprisal and too small for a war." Details of the fighting were not available tonight, but reliable sources said there had been no aerial bombardment of Egyptian positions.

It was not clear tonight whether the Israelis proposed to push on to the Suez Canal or withdraw to Israeli territory, as they have done after reprisal raids. A high official said: "I do not know. It depends on developments."

Yesterday the Israeli Government attributed its decision to call up reserves to what it said was a renewal of commando activities, to the Egyptian-Jordanian-Syrian military alliance negotiated last Wednesday, to Arab declarations that "their principal concern is a war of destruction against Israel" and to the movement of Iraqi forces to Jordan's border.

According to information here, the Egyptians have a considerable part of their Army in the Sinai Peninsula. Their land forces are reported equipped with the

Continued on Page 5, Column 5

POLAND'S LEADERS BACK HUNGARIANS

Support Demands for Exit of Soviet Troops—Call for End of Strife

By SYDNEY GRUSON
Special to The New York Times.

WARSAW, Oct. 29—The Polish Communist party, differing sharply once again with the Soviet Union, came out formally today in support of Hungarian demands for the withdrawal of Soviet troops from Hungary.

Yesterday the new leadership of the Polish United Workers (Communist) party rejected the Soviet allegation that foreign agents and counter-revolutionaries were responsible for the Hungarian tragedy. Today the Poles stood up again on the side of the Hungarians.

An appeal to those on both sides of the barricades in Hungary to halt fratricidal strife was issued by Wladyslaw Gomulka, the Polish party's First Secretary, and by Premier Jozef Cyrankiewicz.

Emphasizing the growing insistence here for independence in foreign as well as internal affairs, the party statement ignored the Soviet charges of Western interference in Hungary.

For the Poles the statement of solidarity was a means of publicly expressing their appreciation for Hungarian help when Poland was threatened by the Soviet leaders a week ago. Poland escaped Hungary's fate

Continued on Page 22, Column 1

Patrols in Budapest Are Trigger-Happy From Propaganda

By JOHN MacCORMAC
Special to The New York Times.

BUDAPEST, Hungary, Oct. 29—The seventh day of the Hungarian revolution has dawned with Soviet soldiers still patrolling the Budapest streets despite a promise by Hungary's new Government that they would be withdrawn. The Government had qualified its announcement yesterday with the condition "as soon as order has been completely restored."

As far as could be learned, armed resistance in Budapest has ceased, even in the Maria Theresa barracks in Ulloi Ut, which was holding out late yesterday. But that order can ever be completely restored in Budapest as long as the Russians are here seems unlikely because of the fears and propaganda with which the Soviet troops seem to be filled.

At 10 o'clock last night, for instance, a Soviet soldier guarding an area known as Szent Istvan Ut shot and seriously wounded Noel Barber, London Daily Mail correspondent. Mr. Barber had been making a tour of inspection to get the public's reaction to Premier Imre Nagy's announcement that there would be no further firing and that the insurrection had been recognized by his Government as

Continued on Page 15, Column 1

FRANCE ACCUSES FIVE OF TREASON

Files Formal Charges Against Algerians Seized in Plane—Sends Aide to Tunisia

By ROBERT C. DOTY
Special to The New York Times.

PARIS, Oct. 29—Five leaders of the Algerian rebellion, seized a week ago, were formally charged today with treason against France. The offense is punishable by death.

The five are Mohammed ben Bella, Mohammed Khider, Mustafa Lachraf, Monammed Boudiaf and Hossein Ait Ahmed, all members of the Algerian National Liberation Front, which has directed the two-year rebellion against France from headquarters in Cairo.

Their arrest Oct. 22, while aboard a Moroccan plane flying to a conference of North African leaders in Tunis, set off a wave of anti-French protest and violence. Arab anger was based on the theory that the five men were under the protection of Sultan Mohammed V of Morocco, with tacit French consent, at the time of their arrest.

[In the United Nations Security Council, France formally charged Egypt with gun-running for the Algerian rebels.]

As Algerians, the five seized rebel leaders are French citizens, hence subject to a treason

Continued on Page 10, Column 2

PRESIDENT GIVEN MINNESOTA LEAD

Resurvey Finds Him Moving Ahead in a Close Contest

A Times Team Report

Teams of New York Times reporters have recently surveyed political trends in twenty-seven closely contested states. They are now rechecking the most doubtful states. Following is a resurvey report from Leonard Buder, Donald Janson and W. H. Lawrence.

By DONALD JANSON
Special to The New York Times.

MINNEAPOLIS, Oct. 28—President Eisenhower appears to hold a tenuous lead in the race for Minnesota's eleven electoral votes.

A month ago New York Times reporters found the President and Adlai E. Stevenson running neck and neck in this state. The Eisenhower victory margin of four years ago—155,000 out of 1,379,000 votes cast—had buckled under the impact of defections by farmers who were caught in a cost-price vise.

The farm revolt remains strong today in some areas.

Continued on Page 28, Column 2

Russians Befriend One Hungarian City

By HOMER BIGART
Special to The New York Times.

GYOR, Hungary, Oct. 29—The small Soviet garrison of this industrial city has retired to a near-by wood, giving the townspeople free rein to rally and shout against the Nagy Government and demand democratic national elections.

The Russians here must be credited with sensible behavior. They abandoned their barracks a few days ago under no pressure and took to the wood.

There the Soviet officers are living with their wives and children in tents. They have not shot anyone. The townspeople show their gratitude by taking the Russians eggs and milk.

And although Gyor has

Continued on Page 12, Column 1

Associated Press Radiophoto

AMERICANS LEAVE ISRAEL: Wives and children of State Department personnel boarding Air Force transport plane last night at Lydda Airport near Jerusalem. They were flown to Athens. More dependents are to follow today.

Maria Callas Bows At Opening of 'Met'

By ROSS PARMENTER

Bellini's "Norma" has never been notably popular in this country. But last night, when it opened the Metropolitan Opera's seventy-second season, it established a compound record. Never have so many Americans tried to pay so much money to hear an opera.

The actual sum paid by those who managed to crowd into the opera house was $75,510.50. This exceeded by more than $10,000 the previous box-office record of $65,336, which was set with the opening night "Faust" in 1953. The larger sum, though, was not paid by a larger number of persons. After all, sell-outs have been customary on first nights, and fire regulations re-

Continued on Page 43, Column 4

CITY SCHOOL AIDES SPUR INTEGRATION

District Lines Are Shifted in Some Brooklyn Areas

By BENJAMIN FINE

Without any public announcement, the Board of Education has quietly begun a program to integrate white and Negro pupils in areas where a segregation pattern has existed in the past.

A score of schools in the Bedford-Stuyvesant area of Brooklyn have become interracial since the fall term opened. Children are taken from the all-Negro schools and put into the formerly all-white schools.

At the same time, fairly large groups of children—ranging from fifty to 200—have been taken from a number of all-white schools and placed in the all-Negro schools. In doing this, the board has amended or discarded the old district and school zoning regulations.

This step is part of a "positive program" on integration, Charles H. Silver, Board of Education president, said yesterday. The board has asked its forty assistant superintendents to do everything possible to place Negro and white children in the same schools.

The superintendents are doing

Continued on Page 30, Column 3

"All the News That's Fit to Print"

The New York Times.

© 1956, by The New York Times Company.

LATE CITY EDITION
Condensation of U. S. Weather Bureau forecast: Partly cloudy, little temperature change today and tomorrow.
Temperature range today: 65—51.
Temperature range yesterday: 68.3—53.
Full U.S. Weather Bureau Report, Page 46.

VOL. CVI—No. 36,078. Entered as Second-Class Matter. Post Office, New York, N. Y. NEW YORK, SATURDAY, NOVEMBER 3, 1956. Times Square, New York 36, N. Y. Telephone Lackawanna 4-1000 FIVE CENTS

BRITISH AND FRENCH PUSH TOWARD LANDING; ISRAELIS CAPTURE GAZA AND CONTROL SINAI

Hungary Protests to Soviet Against New Troop Moves; West Urges Action by U.N.; Tension Is Rising in Poland

STEVENSON OFFERS A PROGRAM TO END STRIFE IN MIDEAST

Calls for a Cease-Fire and Israel's Security—Detroit Crowd Boos President

Speech at Detroit and remarks at Cleveland, Page 20.

By HARRISON E. SALISBURY
Special to The New York Times.

DETROIT, Nov. 2—Adlai E. Stevenson offered tonight a program to restore peace in the Middle East, based on the security of Israel and restoration of the Western Alliance.

Mr. Stevenson submitted his program to an enthusiastic overflow audience at the Fox Theatre.

He charged that President Eisenhower did not know what had been happening in the Middle East and that "someone had misled him."

Mr. Stevenson's program called for these steps:

¶A cease-fire in the Middle East.

¶Restoration of the Western grand alliance of the United States, France and Britain.

¶Security for Israel against Arab attack.

¶Establishment of the principle of international concern for the Suez Canal and an end of one-man or one-country control.

¶An all-out attack on resettlement of 900,000 Arab refugees in Middle Eastern lands.

¶A joint program for improvement of economic conditions in the Middle East.

Mr. Stevenson's address was carried on a state TV network. Several thousand persons were unable to gain admission to the theatre.

Earlier today, Mr. Stevenson spoke in Cleveland's Public Square. A huge throng heard him demand United Nations action in behalf of the new Hungarian regime.

Democratic officials put the crowd at 65,000. Newspaper reporters estimated it at closer to 30,000. There was agreement, however, that it was larger than General Eisenhower drew in the same place and time three weeks ago.

Tonight Mr. Stevenson asserted that the first task in the

Continued on Page 20, Column 5

HUNGARIAN PREMIER Imre Nagy, Communist who took office during national anti-Soviet uprising, addressing nation by radio. Date when photograph was taken was not given.
Associated Press Radiophoto

NEW PLEA BY NAGY

Premier Asks That U.N. Defend Neutrality of Hungary

By JOHN MacCORMAC
Special to The New York Times.

BUDAPEST, Hungary, Saturday, Nov. 3—The Hungarian Government made three oral protests yesterday to the Soviet Ambassador in Budapest, complaining that Russian reinforcements were still pouring across the frontier.

[Soviet tanks sealed the main crossings of the Austrian-Hungarian border Friday. This was regarded as a preliminary to dealing sternly with the insurgents.]

Premier Imre Nagy also sent a new appeal to the Secretary General of the United Nations to guarantee Hungary's neutrality and to bring her case before the General Assembly.

Similarly Joseph Cardinal Mindszenty, primate of Hungary, appealed to the West for political support of the revolutionaries and relief for the needy.

Soviet Forces Approaching

Early today, forces at the command of the Revolutionary Council of the Hungarian Army occupied the Foreign Ministry. Other Army units cordoned off the Parliament Building and took up posts on and near all bridges spanning the Danube.

These measures were prompted by information that Soviet forces were approaching the capital.

In his plea to the Secretary General of the United Nations, Premier Nagy said that Hungary's first demand for the withdrawal of Soviet troops had been received favorably by Moscow. In spite of this, he went on, fresh Soviet troops were brought in to Hungary on Tuesday and Wednesday.

The Hungarian Government then denounced the Warsaw Pact, proclaimed Hungary a neutral state and demanded the withdrawal of all Soviet troops. Budapest also proposed the appointment of two joint Hungarian-Soviet committees, one political and one military, to discuss the terms and set the timetable for this withdrawal.

The Premier said that he had protested against any further influx of Soviet soldiers, pointing out to the United Nations that new Soviet units had entered

Continued on Page 15, Column 1

Israelis Are Mopping Up; Egypt Braces for Landing

12,000 Prisoners Taken

By HOMER BIGART
Special to The New York Times.

TEL AVIV, Israel, Saturday, Nov. 3—Israel's lightning conquest of Egypt's Sinai Peninsula and the Gaza Strip is complete except for minor mopping-up operations. The ancient Philistine capital of Gaza was the last town to fall.

In its drive, Maj. Gen. Moshe Dayan's tough Army had killed, captured or put to flight 30,000 Egyptian troops east of the Suez Canal.

With Israel's southern flank secure after only four days of operations, the Government faced with calm confidence reports that Jordan was being reinforced by Syrian troops and that the Syrian-Jordanian-Egyptian defense pact was about to become operative.

Gaza collapsed after a three-hour fight yesterday morning. A United Nations truce aide,

Continued on Page 3, Column 5

Cairo Defense Held Ready

By The United Press.

CAIRO, Nov. 2—Waves of British and French bombers and fighters blasted Cairo and outlying villages today. An Egyptian communiqué said 100 persons had been killed in one town alone.

Simultaneously, President Gamal Abdel Nasser announced that Egyptian forces in the Sinai desert had "completed their withdrawal safely."

"Now we are waiting for the British and French in the delta," he said. Only "suicide commandos" had been left in Sinai to harass the advancing Israeli forces, he added.

The communiqué asserted that fourteen British and French planes had been shot down in today's raids. An earlier communiqué had claimed three kills in the last twenty-four hours in addition to six reported downed yesterday morning. This would

Continued on Page 3, Column 2

BOMBING PRESSED

Planes Center Attacks on Army After Cairo Loses Airpower

By DREW MIDDLETON
Special to The New York Times.

LONDON, Nov. 2—The neutralization of the Egyptian Air Force, a primary condition to successful landing operations, was claimed tonight by British and French airpower.

More than a hundred Egyptian planes have been destroyed or damaged at airfields by bombers and fighters of Royal Air Force and French Air Force. A high proportion of these were Soviet-built MIG-15 jet fighter planes and Ilyushin-28 twin-jet bombers, R. A. F. sources said.

At the outset of the operations the Egyptian Air Force had ninety MIG's and fifty Ilyushins. Since not all of them were airworthy Wednesday when the attack began, the allies' claim to have neutralized Egypt's airpower appears valid.

Transit Camp Bombed

The British-French air attack is shifting away from air bases onto the Egyptian Army's central forces, now known to be moving slowly northward and northeastward away from the Cairo area.

British air reconnaissance reported the movement of tanks and infantry into the area around Port Said, one of the three sites chosen by the allies for occupation.

One target successfully attacked was a military transit camp, around which tanks and guns were concentrated, about fifteen miles northeast of Cairo in the El Khanka area.

[The British reported that the Egyptians had sunk seven ships in an effort to block the Suez Canal. It was not known in London whether the Egyptian effort had succeeded. No word of an allied landing in Egypt had been received up to 4 A. M., New York time.]

Information that the Syrian Government was placing its armed forces under the commander in chief of the Egyptian forces has not altered British or French planning for forthcoming operations.

As part of the psychological preparation for the allied landing operations the Cairo Radio, the Voice of Arabia, was silenced

Continued on Page 2, Column 3

Eisenhower Sees Victory, Leaves Campaign to Nixon

By RUSSELL BAKER
Special to The New York Times.

WASHINGTON, Nov. 2—President Eisenhower now is so confident of re-election Tuesday that he is treating Adlai E. Stevenson's driving campaign finish with a show of indifference. This was emphasized last night in Philadelphia when he indicated that, from his point of view, the campaign was over and that henceforth he would address the nation only in the nonpartisan role of President.

It was pointedly driven home today when the White House noted that Vice President Richard M. Nixon, rather than the President, had been selected to reply tonight to the Democratic nominee's attack on foreign policy.

James C. Hagerty, White House press secretary, said the President's discussion of the Middle Eastern and Central European crises Wednesday had been "nonpolitical." Mr. Stevenson's reply last night, he added, "was strictly political."

Mr. Hagerty's implication was that the President no longer intended to trouble with replies to Mr. Stevenson's "political" charges and that this chore now could be handled adequately by Mr. Nixon.

The President, he added, knew in advance the substance of the Vice President's speech. The White House staff had helped Mr. Nixon get "the facts to refute a lot of misstatements that Mr. Stevenson made last night," Mr. Hagerty said.

The White House also an-

Continued on Page 19, Column 6

PRESIDENT LEADS IN PENNSYLVANIA

Slim Edge Not Widened Yet by Crises Abroad—Clark's Margin for Senate Cut

A Times Team Report

Teams of New York Times reporters have now completed a survey of political trends in twenty-seven closely contested states. They have rechecked eight of those states—the most doubtful ones. Following is a final resurvey report by Leonard Buder, Donald Janson and Wayne Phillips.

By WAYNE PHILLIPS
Special to The New York Times.

PHILADELPHIA, Nov. 2—President Eisenhower is clinging to a lead in this state so insubstantial that it could be washed away by a heavy rain on election day.

Depending upon developments in the Middle East crisis, he may be able to increase that lead in the four days remaining before the election. But at the moment the world crisis has served only to create doubts in the minds of voters on both sides of the fence. Those doubts have not yet crystallized in favor of either candidate.

Two weeks ago a New York Times team found the Pennsylvania Democrats well organized and confident. They were fighting an uphill battle against the appeal of the President's personality, but the odds were on their side in a state that once was a bastion of Republicanism.

They appeared to have won the public—and some Republican newspapers, too—to their Senatorial candidate, Joseph S. Clark Jr. They had created a substantial indecision among the 1952 supporters of President Eisenhower, and had won over enough of them to give some hope of carrying the state for Adlai E. Stevenson.

For Mr. Stevenson this state is the keystone in any arch of triumph he may hope to build. Its thirty-two electoral votes, with various combinations of states, could carry him to a

Continued on Page 18, Column 2

TROOPS REPORTED CROSSING POLAND

Soviet Movement Is Said to Be to East Germany—Panic Buying in Warsaw

By SYDNEY GRUSON
Special to The New York Times.

WARSAW, Nov. 2—Reports reached Warsaw tonight of large-scale Soviet troop movements across Poland from Russia to East Germany. No details were available.

The purpose and the meaning of the troop movements were not disclosed. But even before they had been reported the situation in Poland had reached a point of extreme tension.

All through the day the Polish radio repeated its broadcast of an appeal by the Communist party's new leadership for "calm, discipline and a sense of responsibility" within the nation.

In Warsaw panic buying began. People bought up all the foodstuffs in the stores and then after withdrawing their money from the banks began to buy jewelry and valuables.

Word came from various parts

Continued on Page 14, Column 4

U. N. SPEAKERS ASK HELP FOR HUNGARY

Override Soviet Objections as Security Council Argues International Action

Excerpts from Security Council debate are on Page 16.

By LINDESAY PARROTT
Special to The New York Times.

UNITED NATIONS, N. Y., Nov. 2—The Western powers overrode Soviet objections today and called on the United Nations to take measures against Soviet military action in Hungary.

An emergency meeting of the Security Council heard all nations that spoke, except the Soviet Union, appeal for international action against the reinforcement of Soviet troops in Hungary, where rebel nationalists appear to have taken control. Imre Nagy, Hungarian Premier, asked the United Nations yesterday to guarantee the country's neutralism.

No decision was reached at the two-hour session of the Council tonight. The members will meet again tomorrow afternoon in an attempt to decide on a course of action.

The meeting was sparked by a new message from Mr. Nagy distributed to Council members tonight.

The letter, couched in terms similar to the one Mr. Nagy sent to the United Nations yesterday, charged that "large" Soviet military units had crossed the Hungarian border. Moving toward

Continued on Page 16, Column 5

PARIS ACTS TO BAR CEASE-FIRE NOW

Fears That Immediate Halt in Military Operations Would Save Nasser

By HAROLD CALLENDER
Special to The New York Times.

PARIS, Nov. 2—The French Government moved fast today to prevent a United Nations cease-fire in the Suez Canal Zone.

It feared a halt in military operation now would save Gamal Abdel Nasser, President of Egypt, whose regime the French and British seek to liquidate. In that case the French would feel deprived of a victory they regard as already within their grasp.

This was the explanation of the hurried trip to London during the day by Christian Pineau, French Foreign Minister, that was given by high political authorities here tonight.

In London, M. Pineau, Prime Minister Eden and Selwyn Lloyd, British Foreign Secretary, were reported to have agreed they would not accept a cease-fire at least until British-French troops had landed. They were expected to land tomorrow.

Action by U. N. Noted

The United Nations General Assembly voted early today for a cease-fire in the Middle East but the question was how it could be carried out.

[Prime Minister Eden rejected a Laborite demand that he order an immediate end to British attacks on Egypt. This was in response to Laborite pressure that he comply with the resolution of the United Nations General Assembly calling for a cease-fire.]

The fear that took posession of French officials was that Prime Minister Eden might agree to a premature cease-fire.

If so, he would do it, according to these officials, because he is harried by the British Labor party to call off the French-British military expedition to Egypt, and because he is pressed by Secretary of State Dulles, who is credited here with desiring a cease-fire before the United States election Tuesday.

It was even suggested that the United States Sixth Fleet, now in the Mediterranean, might be mandated by the General Assembly to occupy the Suez Canal zone, instead of the French-British forces now preparing to occupy it.

This fear arose because Lester B. Pearson, Canadian Secretary of State for External Affairs, proposed yesterday in New York that the General Assembly should authorise the immediate

Continued on Page 6, Column 4

ARABS SAID TO PUT TROOPS IN JORDAN

Syrian and Iraqi Forces Are Reported on March

By DANA ADAMS SCHMIDT
Special to The New York Times.

WASHINGTON, Nov. 2—Syrian and Iraqi troops are marching into Jordan, according to information telephoned from Cairo, the Egyptian Embassy press counselor announced tonight.

The official, Mohammed Habib, reported also that Lebanese workers had cut one of the pipelines that carry Arabian oil to the Mediterranean.

The report of the troop movements followed announcement by Syria, in a formal note to the State Department, that she had placed her armed forces under Egyptian command. This was done under terms of the Syrian-Egyptian defense pact, the Syrian Chargé d'Affaires, Mamun Jamui, informed the State Department.

"The Syrian armed forces are now taking orders from the Egyptian Commander in Chief, Gen. Abdel Hakim Amer," Mr. Jamui said, continuing, "Syria

Continued on Page 3, Column 3

COUNCIL HEARING ON QUINN SLATED

Mayor Backs Tenney Report on Official's Carting Job

By CHARLES G. BENNETT

The City Council will hold hearings soon to consider charges against Councilman Hugh Quinn, Queens Democrat.

In a report to Mayor Wagner on Thursday, Investigation Commissioner Charles H. Tenney found that Mr. Quinn had committed an "apparent" violation of the City Charter and had given grounds for his removal from office.

Yesterday Mayor Wagner said he agreed with the Investigation Commissioner's conclusions.

Council Majority Leader Joseph T. Sharkey, Brooklyn Democrat, said he would call the Councilmen together next week, probably Wednesday, to arrange for hearings in the Quinn case. A question for the Councilmen to determine, Mr. Sharkey said, is whether the hearings will be public or private.

The Council, under the Charter, is the judge of the qualifications of its members. It may expel a member by a two-thirds vote.

Mr. Sharkey said he thought

Continued on Page 42, Column 3

Nixon Hails Break With Allies' Policies

By WILLIAM M. BLAIR
Special to The New York Times.

HERSHEY, Pa., Nov. 2—Vice President Richard M. Nixon hailed tonight this country's break with Anglo-French policies as a "declaration of independence that has had an electrifying effect throughout the world."

Speaking with the full backing of President Eisenhower, he assailed Adlai E. Stevenson for charging that the Administration's foreign policy was a failure and that the President should have averted the Middle East crisis.

He said that the United Nations General Assembly vote gave "the lie to [Mr. Stevenson's] preposterous charge" that the United States stood alone "in an unfriendly world."

The General Assembly early

Continued on Page 18, Column 1

U. S. Protests Refusal by Soviet To Let Americans Quit Hungary

Special to The New York Times.

WASHINGTON, Nov. 2—The United States protested tonight to the Soviet Union against the action of Soviet troops who prevented a convoy of Americans from leaving Hungary.

A report of the incident from the United States Legation in Budapest reached the State Department in early evening. Deputy Under Secretary of State Robert Murphy called in Georgi N. Zaroubin, the Soviet Ambassador, at once.

Mr. Zaroubin told Mr. Murphy he would get in touch with his Government in Moscow about the matter.

A State Department spokesman said Mr. Murphy spoke 'energetically" to the Soviet Ambassador against the "interference with American official personnel."

According to the official report, the convoy consisted of dependents—wives and children—of diplomatic personnel at the American Legation. Lincoln White, State Department press officer, said the convoy returned safely to Budapest and would attempt to leave the city again tomorrow.

"We had a report from Budapest that a convoy of our legation dependents was turned back near the Austrian border this afternoon by Soviet tank blocks," said Mr. White. "They returned to Budapest safely."

According to Mr. White, Mr. Murphy told the Soviet envoy he "assumed the incident must be due to an error on the part of the Soviet military commander, although he could not imagine why Soviet forces were in that area."

The Ambassador said he had no information on this, Mr. White told reporters, but added "he would immediately communicate with his Government and that he assumed the matter would be straightened out."

Special to The New York Times.

BUDAPEST, Hungary, Nov. 2—A diplomatic convoy carrying out the wives and children of a United State legation staff in Budapest as well as French, British and American correspondents was turned back from the Austrian border by Soviet troops at 4:30 P. M. today.

"Polemics are useless," a Soviet officer told them. "It is requested that you turn around

Continued on Page 16, Column 8

Eisenhower Offers Relief to Hungary

Special to The New York Times.

WASHINGTON, Nov. 2—President Eisenhower late today offered $20,000,000 worth of food and medical supplies to relieve the suffering in Hungary resulting from the revolt against Soviet domination.

The White House announcement of this offer followed a conference between the President, Secretary of State Dulles, and Under Secretary of State Herbert Hoover Jr.

The aid would consist of $15,000,000 in surplus foodstuffs and $5,000,000 in specially purchased meats, oils, fats, and medical supplies.

The President urged the American people to continue sending their contributions to the American Red Cross, which is pouring relief supplies into

Continued on Page 16, Column 7

"All the News That's Fit to Print"

The New York Times.

LATE CITY EDITION
Condensation of U. S. Weather Bureau forecast:
Considerable cloudiness, seasonably cool today and tomorrow.
Temperature range today: 50—40.
Temperature range yesterday: 53.6—40.2.
Full U. S. Weather Bureau Report, Page 86.

NEWS SUMMARY AND INDEX, PAGE 95

© 1956, by The New York Times Company.

SECTION ONE

VOL. CVI . . No. 36,079. Entered as Second-Class Matter, Post Office, New York, N. Y. NEW YORK, SUNDAY, NOVEMBER 4, 1956. Including Magazine and Book Review. TWENTY-FIVE CENTS

SOVIET ATTACKS HUNGARY, SEIZES NAGY; U. S. LEGATION IN BUDAPEST UNDER FIRE; MINDSZENTY IN REFUGE WITH AMERICANS

U. N. Assembly Backs Call to Set Up Mideast Truce Force

STEVENSON HOLDS PRESIDENT LACKS 'ENERGY' FOR JOB

In Last Big Address, He Asks if Nation Is Prepared to Accept Nixon as Leader

Stevenson statement, Page 72; text of speech, Page 73.

By HARRISON E. SALISBURY
Special to The New York Times.

CHICAGO, Nov. 3—Adlai E. Stevenson charged tonight that President Eisenhower "now lacks the energy" to cope with world problems such as the present crisis in the Middle East.

He asked the nation whether it was prepared to accept Richard M. Nixon "as Commander in Chief to exercise power over peace and war."

"Every consideration," Mr. Stevenson said, "the President's age, his health and the fact that he cannot succeed himself make it inevitable that the dominant figure in the Republican party under a second Eisenhower term would be Richard Nixon."

This was the first time that Mr. Stevenson in direct fashion had raised the question of General Eisenhower's health, his physical strength and his ability to survive his full term if re-elected.

It placed—on the eve of the election—the question of General Eisenhower's age and his health directly in the forefront of the campaign.

Nixon Draws Boos

Mr. Stevenson's every reference to Mr. Nixon brought forth a hurricane of boos that was equaled only by several waves of boos for General Eisenhower's foreign policy and references to the asserted errors of John Foster Dulles, Secretary of State.

Mr. Stevenson's remarks, which were carried to the nation by television, were cut off the air on a chorus of boos for Mr. Nixon. The conclusion of his address ran over the allotted air time.

General Eisenhower is 66 years old. Mr. Stevenson had foresworn any discussion of the President's health, insisting that this was a matter for each individual voter.

However, in charging tonight that the crisis in world affairs had stemmed directly from the President's "part-time conduct" of his office, Mr. Stevenson took a look into the future.

The fact is, he asserted, General Eisenhower "in the next years would inevitably recede more and more from the picture."

The President, Mr. Stevenson

Continued on Page 73, Column 2

Major Sports News

FOOTBALL

Yale, Navy, Syracuse, Columbia and Army won major Eastern contests yesterday. Scores of leading games:

Amherst	6	Tufts	0
Army	55	Colgate	46
Columbia	25	Cornell	19
Georgia Tech	7	Duke	0
Illinois	7	Purdue	7
Michigan	17	Iowa	14
Michigan St.	33	Wisconsin	0
Minnesota	9	Pitt	6
Navy	33	Notre Dame	7
Ohio State	6	Northwest'n	2
Oklahoma	27	Colorado	19
Penn	28	Harvard	14
Princeton	21	Brown	7
Rutgers	20	Lafayette	19
Syracuse	13	Penn State	9
Tennessee	20	N. Carolina	0
T. C. U.	7	Baylor	6
U. C. L. A.	14	Stanford	13
W. Virginia	14	G. Wash'gton	0
Yale	19	Dartmouth	0

HORSE RACING

Summer Tan took the Gallant Fox Handicap in track record time at Jamaica.

Details in Section 5.

London, Paris Bar Truce; Eden Pledges Israeli Exit

U. N. Occupation Offered

By HAROLD CALLENDER
Special to The New York Times.

PARIS, Nov. 3—Britain and France rejected today the United Nations call for a cease-fire in the Suez area.

At the same time they made a counter-proposal designed to bring their independent military action under the authority of the United Nations. They thus sought to heal the breach between the two powers on the one hand and the United Nations and the United States on the other.

The United Nations General Assembly recommended the cease-fire Thursday by adopting a resolution introduced by the United States.

The two European powers de-

Continued on Page 18, Column 1

Prime Minister Speaks

By DREW MIDDLETON
Special to The New York Times.

LONDON, Nov. 3—The British Government will insure the withdrawal of Israeli forces from Egyptian territory once British and French troops have occupied

Eden's text and Gaitskell excerpts are on Page 28.

key points on the Suez Canal, Sir Anthony Eden declared tonight.

The objective of his policy of intervention in the Middle East is a lasting settlement in the area and a stronger United Nations, able "to act as well as to talk," the Prime Minister told

Continued on Page 28, Column 6

EISENHOWER PLANS TALKS TOMORROW

To Make 2 Short Speeches on TV—Mitchell Reports Advances by Labor

By CHARLES E. EGAN
Special to The New York Times.

WASHINGTON, Nov. 3—Politics held an active, if subordinate, role in White House operations on this Saturday before election.

While the President was closeted with advisers in discussions of events in the Middle East and Europe, his top aides found time:

¶To consult with Leonard W. Hall, chairman of the Republican National Committee, on campaign strategy.

¶To issue a special report by James P. Mitchell, Secretary of Labor, detailing aid given to workers by his department under the present Administration.

¶To give a preliminary outline of the President's two Election Eve television appearances on Monday.

Mr. Hall arrived at the White House at 11:30 this morning. He spent more than an hour there first with Sherman Adams, the Assistant to the President, and later with James C. Hagerty, White House press secretary.

Continued on Page 78, Column 4

DULLES IS GAINING AFTER OPERATION

Part of His Large Intestine Is Removed—He Will Stay in Hospital 2 Weeks

By EDWIN L. DALE Jr.
Special to The New York Times.

WASHINGTON, Nov. 3—John Foster Dulles, Secretary of State, underwent successful surgery today for removal of a perforated portion of his large intestine.

It was announced after the two-and-one-half-hour operation that Mr. Dulles had "left the operating table in good condition" and that he was "resting comfortably."

The announcement was made by a State Department spokesman, Lincoln White, at Walter Reed Army Hospital. It said Mr. Dulles, 68 years old, probably would be in the hospital for two to three weeks and that he "should be able to return to his desk in approximately six weeks." Mr. Dulles' pulse was reported to be 76, his blood pressure 126/75.

The surgery was performed by Maj. Gen. Leonard D. Heaton, commanding officer of Walter Reed, who had operated on President Eisenhower in June for ileitis. He was assisted today by

Continued on Page 78, Column 3

President Expected to Win; Democratic Congress Seen

New York Times Team Reports

Following are summaries of the apparent voting trends for President and the United States Senate and House of Representatives. They are based on the reports of New York Times teams that have surveyed twenty-seven closely contested states and of correspondents in twenty-one other states.

Presidential Race

By W. H. LAWRENCE

Surveys indicate that President Eisenhower and Vice President Richard M. Nixon will be re-elected on Tuesday by comfortable majorities of both the popular and electoral votes.

Reports from New York Times correspondents who have investigated political sentiment in the forty-eight states indicate these probable results:

For President Eisenhower — A minimum of twenty-seven states with 285 electoral votes, or nineteen votes more than required for a majority of the 531-member Electoral College.

For Adlai E. Stevenson — A minimum of seven states with seventy-six electoral votes.

Leaning toward President Eisenhower — Eight states with ninety-nine electoral votes.

Leaning toward Mr. Steven-

Continued on Page 69, Column 5

Congressional Races

By WILLIAM S. WHITE

The Democrats appear likely to hold Congress in Tuesday's national elections in spite of the prospect that President Eisenhower will retain the White House for the Republicans.

The outlook thus is for a continuation of the divided form of government that has guided the country since 1954.

A landslide for President Eisenhower would, of course, alter every present prospect. The weight of all current evidence suggests clearly, however, these approximate results:

¶The Democrats should at least retain their present thin margin of control in the Senate —49 Democrats to 47 Republicans.

¶There should be a Democratic House of Representatives again with no less than the

Continued on Page [illegible]

BID TO U. N. CHIEF

Canada's Motion That He Plan Suez Unit Adopted, 59 to 0

Texts of draft resolutions and debate excerpts, Page 29.

By KATHLEEN TELTSCH
Special to The New York Times.

UNITED NATIONS, N. Y., Sunday, Nov. 4—The General Assembly voted early today to ask the Secretary General to submit a plan for creation of a United Nations police force to obtain and supervise a cease-fire in the Middle East.

The policing proposal, sponsored by Canada, was adopted 57 to 0, at 2:17 A. M. at an emergency session of the Assembly.

Nineteen states abstained, among them Israel, France and Britain. The latter two earlier had rejected an Assembly call for a cease-fire and said they would keep on with their "police action" in Egypt to safeguard the Suez Canal.

The proposal, made by Lester B. Pearson, Canada's Secretary for External Affairs, calls on Secretary General Dag Hammarskjold to submit blueprints within forty-eight hours for an "emergency international United Nations force."

New Truce Plan Adopted

No details were suggested by Mr. Pearson, but such a police force presumably would have to include several thousand men. The Canadian spokesman has said he would recommend Canada's participation. His proposal, however, left all arrangements to the Secretary General.

Within minutes, the emergency session adopted a second resolution, co-sponsored by nineteen Asian and African countries. This renewed the cease-fire appeal made two days ago and asked Mr. Hammarskjold to report within twelve hours on whether the states had complied.

The second resolution was approved, 59 to 5, with twelve abstentions. Among the abstainers were France, Britain, Israel, Autralia and New Zealand.

[Washington indicated that the Administration, after initial anger at the British-French and Israeli moves, was taking a more moderate, hopeful and understanding attitude.]

Weary United Nations delegates approved the new proposals at an event-filled emergency session, at which the United States presented a new Middle East plan. This seeks a long-range settlement of the Palestine problem and also of the current Suez Canal dispute.

In warmly supporting the Ca-

Continued on Page 29, Column 8

Mideast Oil Lines Reported Blown Up

By SAM POPE BREWER
Special to The New York Times.

BEIRUT, Lebanon, Nov. 3—Pipelines carrying more than half a million barrels of oil daily from Iraq to the Mediterranean coast have stopped operating as a result of the fighting in Egypt.

Reports circulating here were that the Iraq Petroleum Company's three pumping stations in Syria known as T-2, T-3 and T-4 had been blown up and burned.

[At the United Nations an Egyptian spokesman was quoted by The United Press as having said all oil pipelines in every Middle East country except Saudi Arabia had been blown up or shut down.]

No oil installations in Lebanon were damaged up to tonight. Reports abroad to that effect are incorrect, according

Continued on Page [illegible]

SOVIET ROAD BLOCK IN HUNGARY: Soviet tank obstructs road near Magyarovar

Associated Press Radiophoto

ISRAELI PATROLS REACH SUEZ BANK

Penetrate Zone at 3 Points as Delay in British-French Landings Irks Regime

By HOMER BIGART
Special to The New York Times.

TEL AVIV, Israel, Sunday, Nov. 4—Israeli patrols reached the east bank of the Suez Canal yesterday.

A Government spokesman said Israeli columns had penetrated at three places the ten-mile buffer zone east of the canal that Britain and France wanted kept clear of warring Israeli and Egyptian forces.

Meanwhile, the Cabinet of Premier David Ben-Gurion studied reports that Syrian and Iraqi troops had entered Jordan. The developments in Jordan were being followed with "concern and alertness," according to a Foreign Ministry source.

[In Moscow, Marshal Kliment Y. Vorshilov, Soviet chief of state, told President Shukry al-Kuwatly of Syria at a farewell reception that the Soviet Union was prepared to give Syria the "necessary assistance "to reinforce her independence against foreign threats."]

2-Nation Plan Criticized

The Government spokesman offered no reason why the Israelis had entered the proscribed zone. But the Israelis are increasingly disturbed over the slowness of British and French forces in occupying the canal.

The announcement that Israelis were within ten miles of the canal at three points—opposite El Qantara in the north, Ismailia in the center and Suez at the southern terminus—may have been timed to coincide with reports here that the British-French invasion had been put off because of United States pressure.

The British-French proposals for an international police force to occupy the canal zone were regarded here as "unrealistic."

Until its announcement, the Israeli Government had indicated compliance with the British-French ultimatum.

But Israel has insisted that no firm deal was made with the French on where the advance would be halted.

Meanwhile, the Israelis reported, they were rapidly occupying all key points on the conquered Sinai Peninsula.

Lieut. Col. Moshe Pearlman, Government and Army spokesman, said that the whole area was "relatively quiet" and that the "entire peninsula in very short time will be in Israeli hands."

British Embassy sources said

Continued on Page 23, Column 4

British Bomb Raids On Egypt Continued In Landing Prelude

Texts of the communiqués are printed on Page 26.

By LEONARD INGALLS
Special to The New York Times.

LONDON, Nov. 3—British bombers turned their heaviest attack today from airfields in Egypt to ammunition dumps, barracks and armored weapons depots of the Egyptian Army.

There were indications that the landing by British and French forces in the Suez Canal Zone would be made by paratroopers and seaborne invasion units within the next forty-eight hours.

The Beirut radio, quoting an Egyptian communiqué, reported that a British-French force attempted to land at the southern entrance to the canal, but was driven off with heavy losses.

The Egyptians said they had sunk four British naval vessels and captured three troop landing craft at Suez with fire from shore batteries and torpedo boats. One British ship was said by the Egyptians to have been sunk by gunfire, and a British destroyer, a troop carrier and another British naval unit were said to have been sunk by torpedoes.

The Egyptians also reported they had shot down seventeen British-French planes over the Suez Canal area.

[There was little additional information on the military situation in announcements or dispatches from Cairo.]

An Admiralty spokesman said "there is no information in London to support the Egyptian

Continued on Page 17, Column 1

Nutting Quits Post; Churchill For Eden

The text of Churchill letter will be found on Page 24.

Special to The New York Times.

LONDON, Nov. 3—Anthony Nutting, Minister of State in the Foreign Office, resigned from the Government tonight because he strongly disagreed with its policy of armed intervention in Egypt.

The blow to the Government represented by the defection of one of its best-known and most effective young ministers at a critical juncture was balanced by a resounding declaration of support from Sir Winston Churchill.

Writing from his lair at Chartwell, the old lion of British politics blamed Egypt for provoking war with Israel, criticized the United States for failing to cooperate fully and

Continued on Page 24, Column 3

SOVIET VETO BARS ACTION IN COUNCIL

Censure Move in U. N. Over New Attack on Hungary Carried to Assembly

Excerpts from statements in Security Council, Page 35.

By LINDESAY PARROTT
Special to The New York Times.

UNITED NATIONS, N. Y., Sunday, Nov. 4—The Soviet Union early today vetoed a United States resolution proposing Security Council censure of the Russian military attack on Hungary.

Nine nations favored the United States proposal and one abstained, Yugoslavia.

The veto was at 5:15 A. M.

Henry Cabot Lodge Jr., United States representative, immediately moved for an emergency session of the General Assembly to take up the Hungarian crisis. The Assembly already was in permanent special session over the French-British intervention in the Suez Canal area.

Council's Will 'Thwarted'

Angrily, Mr Lodge told the Council that the will of the world organization had been "thwarted" by the Soviet veto and that the eleven-nation body had been prevented from fulfilling its responsibilities. In this "grave situation," he said, Assembly action was required.

The Council adopted the United States resolution for reference to the Assembly by a vote of 10 to 1. This ballot came at 5:21 A. M.

The Assembly meeting was set for 8 o'clock tonight.

The Council adjourned at 5:24 A. M.

The Council's action, marking the Soviet Union's seventy-ninth veto, was taken after the United States had called the group together at 3 A. M. to protest against the reoccupation of Budapest by Soviet troops. According to the latest reports here early today, the Hungarian capital was in the hands of Soviet troops after Russian tanks earlier had ringed the city.

The United States legation was understood to have been under fire. Mr. Lodge also reported that Joseph Cardinal Mindszenty and his staff had taken refuge in the legation.

The Security Council had adjourned shortly after midnight,

Continued on Page 35, Column 6

This section consists of 140 pages divided into three parts. The news summary and index will be found on Page 95. Society news begins on Page 90 and obituary articles will be found on Pages 86 and 87.

CAPITAL STORMED

Freedom Radios Fade From Air as Russians Shell Key Centers

By PAUL HOFMANN
Special to The New York Times.

VIENNA, Sunday, Nov. 4—Soviet troops started attacking Budapest and other Hungarian cities, towns and key military installations at dawn today.

At 9 A. M., local time (3 A. M. Eastern standard time) four hours after Budapest had been awakened by Russian artillery fire, overpowering Soviet tanks and infantry forces had stormed the Parliament Building and made Premier Imre Nagy and most members of his government prisoners.

Fighting in Budapest and many other parts of the country was continuing, but the prospects for the free Hungarian Government forces were nearly hopeless in the face of crushing Soviet superiority.

The Budapest radio and other Hungarian freedom stations went off the air one after another.

Before going silent, they directed desperate pleas to the West, especially to the United States, and to the United Nations for help to save the Hungarian people from "annihilation."

Mindszenty in U. S. Legation

Joseph Cardinal Mindszenty, Roman Catholic primate of Hungary, who had been freed from detention last week, and his secretary had taken refuge in the building of the United States Legation.

The United States legation, near the Parliament Building, was under fire at 9:30 A. M.

A fierce battle was raging in the immediate surroundings.

At 7 A. M. "several hundred" Soviet heavy tanks were reported attacking key Hungarian Army positions on the outskirts of Budapest and attempting to penetrate the city. The main thrust of the Soviet forces came apparently from the southeast.

Shortly before 7 A. M. the Budapest radio repeated Premier Nagy's announcement of the Soviet attack. It directed an appeal to Dag Hammarskjold, Secretary General of the United Nations. At the same time the M. T. I. Hungarian news agency reported:

"Russian troops have suddenly attacked Budapest and the entire country. They have opened fire on everyone in Hungary. It is a general attack.

"Janos Kadar [since Oct. 24 secretary of the Hungarian Communist party], Gyorgy Marosan and Sandor Ronai have formed a new Government and started crushing the counter-

Continued on Page 34, Column 6

Pravda Denounces Nagy for 'Reaction'

By Reuters.

LONDON, Sunday, Nov. 4—The Soviet Communist party newspaper Pravda attacked Premier Imre Nagy of Hungary today "in strong terms", according to the Moscow radio.

Pravda said: "The task of barring the way to reaction in Hungary has to be carried out without the slightest delay—such is the course dictated by events."

The broadcast quoted Pravda as saying: "Imre Nagy turned out to be, objectively speaking, an accomplice of the reactionary forces. Imre Nagy cannot and does not want to fight the dark forces of reaction."

Pravda asserted that it was Mr. Nagy who had requested bringing Soviet troops into Budapest, "as it was vital for the interests of the Socialist regime."

Continued on Page 15, Column 1

"All the News That's Fit to Print"

The New York Times.

LATE CITY EDITION
Condensation of U. S. Weather Bureau forecast: Some cloudiness today; cloudy tonight. Clearing, cooler tomorrow.
Temperature range today: 66—50.
Temperature range yesterday: 65.4—52.2.
Full U. S. Weather Bureau Report, Page 63.

VOL. CVI . No. 36,082. Entered as Second-Class Matter. Post Office, New York, N. Y. NEW YORK, WEDNESDAY, NOVEMBER 7, 1956. Times Square, New York 36, N. Y. Telephone LAckawanna 4-1000 FIVE CENTS

EISENHOWER BY A LANDSLIDE; BATTLE FOR CONGRESS CLOSE; JAVITS VICTOR OVER WAGNER

Suez Warfare Stopped Under British-French Cease-Fire

MAYOR CONCEDES

Javits, Swept In With the Eisenhower Tide, Wins Stiff Contest

Vote for Senator
CITY SUMMARY

	Javits (Rep.)	Wagner (Dem.-Lib.)
Manhattan ...	270,146	393,462
Bronx	218,895	374,810
Brooklyn	398,088	605,002
Queens	400,832	372,505
Richmond ...	49,694	32,881
Total	1,337,655	1,778,660
Upstate	2,362,618	1,478,238
Grand total	3,700,273	3,256,898

All E. D.'s of 4,607 in city and 6,522 of 6,525 upstate.

By DOUGLAS DALES

Attorney General Jacob K. Javits was swept to victory yesterday in the Eisenhower Republican landslide in his race against Mayor Wagner for the United States Senate.

Mayor Wagner conceded defeat in a statement at 1:22 A. M. after the trend to Javits' victory became unmistakable.

Mr. Wagner carried three boroughs in the city—Manhattan, Brooklyn and the Bronx—but lost in Queens and Richmond.

The city-wide complete totals gave Mr. Javits 1,337,655 votes to 1,778,660 for Mayor Wagner. The Mayor's total included 233,560 on the Liberal party line. The Liberal line attracted 404,769 votes in the city four years ago, when the party ran its own candidate for the Senate, George S. Counts.

The victor's margin was expected to reach 444,000 with the final results. With all city districts and 6,522 of 6,525 districts upstate reported, Mr. Javits had an edge of 443,375.

Mayor Wagner carried two of the fifty-seven upstate counties, Erie and Albany. Eisenhower carried both.

Everywhere outside the city, Mr. Javits ran substantially behind the President's vote. On the other hand, Mayor Wagner ran well ahead of Adlai E. Stevenson, the Democratic candidate for President.

In view of the size of the

Continued on Page 28, Column 2

PRESIDENT SCORES NEW HIGH IN STATE

Plurality Tops 1,500,000 as He Cuts Rival's City Edge

State Presidential Vote
CITY SUMMARY

	Eisenhower (Rep.)	Stevenson (Dem.-Lib.)
Manhattan ..	299,929	378,018
Bronx	256,909	343,656
Brooklyn ...	459,703	558,187
Queens	471,144	313,311
Richmond ..	64,236	196,653
Total	1,551,921	1,614,825
Upstate	2,766,183	1,127,403
Grand total	4,318,104	2,742,228

All E. D.'s of 4,607 in city and 6,522 of 6,525 upstate.

By LEO EGAN

President Eisenhower swept New York yesterday by a plurality that dwarfed all previous records.

With sixty-one of the state's 11,132 election districts still to report this morning, General Eisenhower's margin exceeded 1,500,000.

The previous record for a Presidential plurality in New York was established in 1920, when the late Warren G. Harding, Republican, defeated James M. Cox, Democrat, by 1,139,927.

All the missing districts are in Republican territory upstate.

Continued on Page 23, Column 1

An International Summary: The Mideast and Hungary

Following are summaries of the leading developments in the Middle East and Europe. The full foreign news report begins on the first page of the second part.

Cease-Fire Is On

Britain and France put a cease-fire into effect and halted their advance in Egypt. Prime Minister Eden told Commons that conditions had been established for an international police force under the United Nations to promote settlement of Middle Eastern issues.

Invaders Hold Canal

The invasion forces claimed control of the Suez Canal Zone. They took Port Said and drove south before the cease-fire became effective.

Egyptians Halt Fight

The Egyptians decided to hold their fire at the deadline in the hope that the United Nations resolution of Nov. 2, providing for withdrawal of all forces behind armistice lines, would be carried out.

Soviet May Send 'Volunteers'

Indications in Moscow were that Soviet "volunteers" who began applying for service with Egyptian forces might go to the Middle East despite the cease-fire. Moscow broadcast a Cairo appeal for aid.

Troop Withdrawal Asked

Asian and Arab states drafted a United Nations resolution calling on Britain, France and Israel to withdraw their troops from Egypt immediately. A special session of the General Assembly called for last night was postponed until this morning.

Hungarian Battle Persists

Stubborn Hungarian revolutionary forces are continuing to fight the Soviet army in Budapest, according to diplomatic reports received in Vienna. Women and children were said to be fighting alongside the men in a house-to-house struggle. The General Assembly scheduled a special session this afternoon to consider Soviet intervention in Hungary.

EISENHOWER SETS RECORD IN JERSEY

Margin of 700,000 Carries All 21 Counties—G. O. P. Wins 2 Hudson Seats

By GEORGE CABLE WRIGHT

President Eisenhower yesterday scored the greatest victory in New Jersey political history.

With most of the state's ballots tallied early this morning, his margin over Adlai E. Stevenson had soared above 700,000, almost double that of 1952. He became the first candidate in modern times to carry all twenty-one counties.

The returns were:

PRESIDENT
4,017 districts out of 4,155.

Eisenhower	1,522,971
Stevenson	821,067

The most startling aspect of his victory was the complete turnabout of Hudson County, for half a century a Democratic stronghold.

This county gave the President a majority of 76,554. In 1952 Mr. Stevenson had carried Hudson by 7,886 votes.

In fact, Republicans swept every county contest. When residents of Hudson awake this morning it is certain that many will find it hard to believe that for the next two years they will be represented in Congress by not one, but two, Republicans. There was no precedent there for that.

A third Democratic incumbent, Representative Harrison A. Williams Jr., went down to defeat in Union County.

Thus, the Democratic representation of six in the House was cut in half. All eight Republican incumbents were re-elected.

President Eisenhower became the first Presidential candidate to carry the solidly Democratic bailiwick of Jersey City since Warren G. Harding did it in 1920. Long the citadel of the late Frank Hague and now of John Kenny, it gave General Eisenhower a majority of 31,527 over Mr. Stevenson. In 1952 the Democratic candidate had carried the city by 8,251.

But the trouncing of the former Illinois Governor was by no means restricted to Hudson. Camden and Mercer Counties, which also went to Mr. Stevenson in 1952, likewise turned their backs to him this year.

Continued on Page 28, Column 5

BUSH RE-ELECTED IN CONNECTICUT

Plurality for Eisenhower of 303,036 Biggest in State in a Presidential Race

By RICHARD H. PARKE
Special to The New York Times.

HARTFORD, Nov 6—President Eisenhower scored an easy victory in Connecticut today. He carried to victory with him Senator Prescott S. Bush, the Republican incumbent.

The President's plurality of 303,036 votes over Adlai E. Stevenson, Democratic candidate, was the greatest margin the State ever has given a Presidential contender. The previous high figure was 136,138 votes, achieved by Praeident Coolidge in 1924.

The President, whose 1952 plurality of 129,363 was considered of landslide proportions, defeated Mr. Stevenson today by 708,995 votes to 405,959, according to complete but unofficial returns.

The Republican sweep was general throughout the state. It carried in Senator Bush by a plurality of 129,544 votes. He defeated his Democratic opponent, Representative Thomas J. Dodd, by 607,330 to 477,876.

The Republicans also retained

Continued on Page 28, Column 5

SENATE IN DOUBT

Democrats Lag in East on War Issue but Gain in the West

By WILLIAM S. WHITE

The Democrats and Republicans fought along a swaying electoral battle line early today for control of the oncoming Eighty-fifth Congress.

Not all the power of President Eisenhower's landslide victory had been enough to put his Republican Congressional colleagues in front.

The Senate race, in which the Republicans were attempting to overturn a present 49-to-47 Democratic margin of control, was an affair of hairbreadth drama.

Small net Republican gains for the House of Representatives were indicated. But whether these would continue or would be enough remained wholly in doubt.

The Republicans needed a net gain of 15 House seats, and the capture of 2 additional and now vacant seats that had been Republican.

The pattern of the Congressional contest was this: The East, more sensitive than other sections to the last-minute issue involved in the Middle Eastern and Central European war crises, on the whole was hitting the Democrats hard. The appeal of "don't change horses in midstream" was strong in this area. In the interior, however, Democratic organizational strength, farm discontent and other factors were turning up great Democratic strength.

Cooper Wins in Kentucky

The position on the Senate in some critical states was this:

KENTUCKY—A gain of one Republican seat in former Senator John Sherman Cooper's defeat of his Democratic challenger, Lawrence Wetherby, for the seat made vacant by the death of Senator Alben W. Barkley. The possibility of another gain for the Republicans in the fact that the assistant Democratic leader of the Senate, Earle C. Clements, was running behind Thruston B. Morton, a former assistant Secretary of State in the Eisenhower Administration.

NEW YORK—A Republican gain in the victory of Jacob K. Javits over Mayor Wagner for the seat being vacated by Senator Herbert H. Lehman, Democrat-Liberal.

OHIO—A Democratic gain in the defeat by Gov. Frank J. Lausche of Senator George H. Bender.

ILLINOIS—Senator Everett M. Dirksen, Republican, ran ahead of his Democratic opponent, Richard Stengel.

PENNSYLVANIA—Joseph S.

Continued on Page 3, Column 1

Coudert Wins in Close Contest; Vote in Queens 7th Rechecked

By CLAYTON KNOWLES

The Republicans emerged from a hard-fought Congressional campaign early today with a possible net gain of one in the state delegation to the House of Representatives.

At 4:20 A. M. a final decision rested on the outcome of the race in the Seventh district of Queens. Here Representative James J. Delaney, Democratic incumbent, claimed victory at 4:15 A. M. by forty votes, but a final tally was unavailable.

An hour and a half earlier, Delaney supporters were conceding the election of Joseph Stockinger, a Republican, but the contest was so close that all 217 districts were being rechecked.

The announced vote for 202 districts was 72,186 for Mr. Stockinger to 72,112 for Mr. Delaney, who ran with Liberal party backing.

The prospect that the Republicans would pick up a House seat in the state, giving them twenty-seven of a total of forty-three, arose when Representative Frederic R. Coudert Jr. staged an eleventh-hour triumph in the Manhattan Seventeenth District.

He prevailed once more over Anthony B. Akers, Democrat-Liberal who had come within 314 votes of defeating him in 1954. This time Mr. Coudert won, 68,862 votes to 66,207.

If Mr. Delaney should go to defeat, the Republicans will have seven of the twenty-two House seats filled in the city.

President Eisenhower's land-

Continued on Page 20, Column 6

PRESIDENT EISENHOWER

VICE PRESIDENT NIXON

G. O. P. MAKES BID TO CAPTURE HOUSE

Picks Up 9 Seats in East, but Drive Eases in West —Midwest to Decide

By JOHN D. MORRIS

Republicans got off to a fast start in their bid to recapture control of the House of Representatives, but appeared to lose steam early today as returns trickled in from the West.

As of 3 A. M., results from yesterday's Congressional races indicated a decided Republican trend, with some major upsets for the Democrats. However, with control of nearly two-thirds of the 435 seats still in doubt, victory for either party was far from certain.

The undecided contests were almost entirely in the Midwest, where the issue of declining farm income was a factor favoring the Democrats, and in the Far West.

G. O. P. Gains in East

Such returns as were available from those areas indicated possible Democratic gains in Iowa, California and South Dakota.

Eastward, where the only decisive tallies were available, Republicans had picked up nine seats held by Democrats in the Eighty-fourth Congress while holding their own in all other contests where returns were conclusive. One, in New York City, was subpect to a recount. Democrats had failed to capture any Republican seat except one that they took in the Maine election on Sept. 10.

Republican incumbents were easy victors in a number of contests that had promised to be close.

The most outstanding upsets were in New Jersey, where the Hudson county Democratic stronghold of the late Mayor Frank Hague of Jersey City unseated its two Democratic Representatives, T. James Tumulty and Alfred D. Sieminski, in the Thirteenth and Fourteenth Congressional Districts.

Mr. Sieminski lost to Norman H. Roth, Republican. Mr. Tumulty, a 300-pound legislator, was defeated by Vincent J. Dellay, Republican.

A third Democratic incumbent in New Jersey, Harrison A. Williams, lost to Florence P. Dwyer, Republican.

Republicans also picked up one D[illegible]cratic seat in Connecticut, one in Delaware, one in Pennsylvania, one in Indiana and

Continued on Page 3, Column 2

Stevenson Concedes Defeat and Wishes President Success

Stevenson and Kefauver talks appear on Page 13.

By HARRISON E. SALISBURY
Special to The New York Times.

CHICAGO, Wednesday, Nov. 7—Adlai E. Stevenson conceded the election of President Eisenhower in a statement made public at 12:25 A. M. Central standard time today (1:25 Eastern standard time).

In a telegram to President Eisenhower, the Democratic candidate expressed his understanding of "grave difficulties" that the Administration faced and wished all success to General Eisenhower in the years ahead.

Mr. Stevenson coupled his telegram of congratulations to the President with an appeal to his followers to carry forward in the crusade for what he called a "New America."

He called on America's leaders to recognize that the nation "wants to face up squarely to the facts of today's world."

"We don't want to draw back from them," Mr. Stevenson said. "We can't. We are ready for the test that we know history has set for us."

Mr. Stevenson in his statement took note of the troubled conditions of the world.

"Beyond the seas, in much of the world, in Russia, in China, in Hungary, in all the trembling satellites, partisan controversy is forbidden and dissent suppressed," Mr. Stevenson said.

Mr. Stevenson also took note

Continued on Page 13, Column 5

Electoral Vote by States

	Eisenhower	Stev'son		Eisenhower	Stev'son
Ala.	—	11	Nev.	3	—
Ariz.	4	—	N. H.	4	—
Ark.	—	8	N. J.	16	—
Calif.	32	—	N. M.	4	—
Colo.	6	—	N. Y.	45	—
Conn.	8	—	N. C.	—	14
Del.	3	—	N. D.	4	—
Fla.	10	—	Ohio	25	—
Ga.	—	12	Okla.	8	—
Idaho	4	—	Ore.	6	—
Ill.	27	—	Pa.	32	—
Ind.	13	—	R. Isl.	4	—
Iowa	10	—	S. C.	—	8
Kan.	8	—	S. D.	4	—
Ky.	10	—	Tenn.	11	—
La.	10	—	Texas	24	—
Me.	5	—	Utah	4	—
Md.	9	—	Vt.	3	—
Mass.	16	—	Va.	12	—
Mich.	20	—	Wash.	9	—
Minn.	11	—	W. Va.	8	—
Miss.	—	8	Wisc.	12	—
Mo.	—	13	Wyo.	3	—
Mont.	4	—			
Neb.	6	—	Total	457	74

EISENHOWER VOWS TO TOIL FOR PEACE

Hails Landslide Re-election as Proof Nation Wants 'Modern Republicanism'

Texts of the Eisenhower and Nixon talks on Page 12.

By RUSSELL BAKER
Special to The New York Times.

WASHINGTON, Wednesday, Nov. 7—President Eisenhower hailed his landslide re-election victory today as proof that his "modern Republicanism has now proved itself and America has approved of modern Republicanism."

He pledged in a victory statement early this morning to work with "whatever talents the good God has given me for 168,000,000 Americans here at home and for peace in the world."

Addressing a jubilant crowd of party workers at Republican election headquarters here and the nation, over television, the President declared that so long as the G.O.P. pursued the "ideals, the hopes and aspirations" of the people, it would continue to flourish.

"If it is anything less," he said, "it is only a conspiracy to seize power. And the Republican party is not that."

'Looks to the Future'

Thus, in his moment of triumph, General Eisenhower claimed a sweeping triumph for what his Administration's philosophers had styled the "new Republicanism" and what he himself termed this morning "modern Republicanism."

"Modern Republicanism," he said, "looks to the future and this means it will gain constantly new recruits." So long as it continued to remain "modern," he added, it would "continue to increase in power and influence for decades to come."

So long as it clings to its "modern" ideals, the President declared, it would "point the way to peace among nations and prosperity, advancing standards here at home in which everyone will share."

The President delivered his victory statement at 1:45 A. M., about fifteen minutes after this restive crowd gathered in the mammoth ballroom of the Sheraton-Park Hotel had heard Adlai E. Stevenson concede defeat in Chicago.

General Eisenhower had been waiting upstairs in a third-floor suite for three and a half hours,

Continued on Page 13, Column 1

41 STATES TO G.O.P.

President Sweeps All the North and West, Scores in South

By JAMES RESTON

Dwight David Eisenhower won yesterday the most spectacular Presidential election victory since Franklin D. Roosevelt submerged Alfred M. Landon in 1936.

The smiling 66-year-old hero of the Normandy invasion, who was in a Denver hospital recuperating from a heart attack just a year ago today, thus became the first Republican in this century to win two successive Presidential elections. William McKinley did it in 1896 and 1900.

Adlai E. Stevenson of Illinois, who lost to Mr. Eisenhower four years ago, thirty-nine states to nine, conceded defeat at 1:25 this morning.

At 4:45 A. M. President Eisenhower had won forty-one states to seven for Mr. Stevenson. His electoral lead at that time was 457 to 74 for Stevenson, and his popular vote was 25,071,331 to 18,337,434—up 2 per cent over 1952. Two hundred and sixty-six electoral votes are needed for election.

Victory in All Areas

This was a national victory in every conceivable way. It started in Connecticut. It swept every state in New England. It took New York by a plurality of more than 1,500,000. It carried all the Middle Atlantic states, all the Midwest, all the Rocky Mountain states and everything beyond the Rockies.

More than that, the Republican tide swept along the border states and to the South, carried all the states won by the G.O.P. there in 1952—Virginia, Texas, Tennessee and Florida—and even took Louisiana for the first time since the Hayes-Tilden election of 1876.

For the President and his 43-year old Vice Presidential running mate, Richard M. Nixon of California, who carried much of the Republican campaign, it was a more impressive victory than for the Republican party.

So close were many races for

Continued on Page 2, Column 3

CLARK LEADS DUFF IN PENNSYLVANIA

Democrat's Edge Dropping —President Takes State

By WILLIAM G. WEART
Special to The New York Times.

PHILADELPHIA, Wednesday, Nov. 7—Joseph S. Clark Jr., former Mayor of Philadelphia, was running ahead of Senator James H. Duff early today.

But his margin was ebbing as returns from rural areas and small towns began to offset the lead he piled up in large cities.

President Eisenhower won the state's thirty-two electoral votes by a plurality that was steadily mounting.

Mr. Clark expressed disappointment at the defeat of his party's standard-bearer. He attributed General Eisenhower's victory to his "personal popularity." Mr. Clark's campaign manager, Mayor Richardson Dilworth of Philadelphia, said the President's re-election was due to the "emotion caused by the war situation."

In the event the final tally in the Senatorial race is close, an estimated 50,000 absentee votes cast by servicemen and hospitalized veterans may decide the outcome. Under the law, absentee ballots are mailed to county

Continued on Page 13, Column 6

"All the News That's Fit to Print"

The New York Times.

LATE CITY EDITION
U. S. Weather Bureau report (Page 40) forecasts: Rain, drizzle early today; brightening later. Fair and warm tomorrow.
Temp. range: 64—54. (Yesterday's: 56.6—50.6)

VOL. CVI.. No. 36,252. NEW YORK, FRIDAY, APRIL 26, 1957. Times Square, New York 36, N. Y. Telephone Lackawanna 4-1000 FIVE CENTS

U. S. ORDERS 6TH FLEET TO MIDEAST, SAYS COMMUNISTS MENACE JORDAN; HUSSEIN PROCLAIMS MARTIAL LAW

EISENHOWER ASKS FULL DISCLOSURE OF LABOR FUNDS

Administration Calls for Laws to Wipe Out 'Abomination' of Union Racketeering

RANK AND FILE PRAISED

President and Mitchell Put Stress on Moves to Block 'Punitive' Legislation

Text of Eisenhower statement appears on Page 14.

By W. H. LAWRENCE
Special to The New York Times.

AUGUSTA, Ga., April 25—The Eisenhower Administration decided today to ask Congress for full public disclosure of union receipts and expenditures.

James P. Mitchell, Secretary of Labor, reported the interim legislative program for labor after a ninety-minute conference with President Eisenhower at the President's temporary office at the Augusta National Golf Club.

Mr. Mitchell said the legislative proposals had grown out of evidence of improper practices already developed by the Senate Select Committee on Improper Activities in the Labor or Management Field. The committee is headed by Senator John L. McClellan, Democrat of Arkansas.

Secretary Mitchell warned against a "headlong" rush "impelled by the hysteria of the moment to secure punitive legislation aimed at undermining or weakening the general body of organized labor."

A Request Renewed

He said the Administration proposals were designed to strengthen the rights of the union rank and file and to "help the American labor movement to clean house in those areas where they need help."

Specifically, the President and the Secretary of Labor renewed their three-year-old request to Congress that it pass laws providing for the registration, reporting and disclosure of funds deposited under welfare and pension plans.

In addition, Secretary Mitchell said the President also had approved a proposal that Congress authorize the Labor Department to make public the reports now filed with it concerning union funds in general under the Taft-Hartley Act. Those reports now are not made public.

Secretary Mitchell indicated that the Administration later might ask Congress for Federal review and audits of the union financial statements. These are

Continued on Page 14, Column 3

Associated Press Wirephoto

CONFER IN GEORGIA: President Eisenhower with James P. Mitchell, Secretary of Labor, in Augusta yesterday. They drew plans for laws dealing with labor unions.

M'CLELLAN WARNS OF 'GANGSTERISM'

Tells Publishers Momentum of Rackets Perils U. S.—Mrs. Luce Chides Press

Text of McClellan's speech will be found on Page 16.

The chairman of the Senate committee investigating union rackets said last night that it intended to continue its exposures of wrongdoing until Congress had enough information to "clean up the mess."

Senator John L. McClellan, Democrat of Arkansas, made his statement at a dinner of the Bureau of Advertising of the American Newspaper Publishers Association. He predicted that the investigation, which he said was still in its early stages, would produce legislation to protect union members, management and the public.

The committee chairman, speaking at the Waldorf-Astoria Hotel, warned that racketeering now had enough momentum to bring about a "gangsterism economy" and threaten liberty in the United States if it were not stopped.

'Shock Troops' of Diplomacy

Mrs. Clare Boothe Luce, former Ambassador to Italy, urged the press and public to support the American Foreign Service. Mrs. Luce spoke of the "shock troops of our diplomatic front lines" and termed them a vital instrument for the preservation of world peace.

The occasion, the Bureau of Advertising's forty-fourth annual dinner, marked the end of the seventy-first annual convention of the bureau's parent organization, the American Newspaper Publishers Association. It also marked the end of New York's annual Press Week.

As Senator McClellan spoke, preparations were made for a closed hearing on labor-management abuses in the United States Court House today. Three officials of one of the union locals under investigation were indicted by a New York County grand jury yesterday on charges of steal-

Continued on Page 16, Column 2

De Sapio Leadership Extolled by Wagner Before Party Chiefs

By CLAYTON KNOWLES

Ringing praise for Carmine G. De Sapio and predictions of a great victory for Mayor Wagner this fall marked speeches at the annual dinner of the New York County Democratic Committee last night.

The Mayor, a candidate for re-election, was lavish in proclaiming the "forceful, dynamic, political brilliance" of Mr. De Sapio, leader of the Tammany organization for the last eight years.

About 2,200 persons attended the $50-a-plate dinner, which was held at the Commodore Hotel.

In his text Mr. Wagner said also that Mr. De Sapio had set "an example of undivided allegiance to the principles of good government—of government devoted exclusively to the needs and the welfare of the people."

Called Friend of Decency

Extemporizing in delivery, he added that Mr. De Sapio had been the "stalwart friend of decency, honesty and integrity in government." He said he was "proud to call him my friend."

The extent of the accolade took on significance in view of the start next Monday of public hearings by the Republican-dominated legislative committee into the Joseph (Socks) Lanza parole case.

Lanza has Tammany connections. And there has been reference to aid sought from "the man with the glasses." Mr. De Sapio, who wears dark tinted glasses, has scoffed at the suggestion that the reference might have been to him.

In his own speech last night, Mr. De Sapio said that he still felt, as he had when he as-

Continued on Page 12, Column 4

PRESIDENT PLANS OIL IMPORT STUDY; SEES PERIL TO U. S.

Gets O.D.M. Report Warning of Rise in Foreign Fuel —Quotas May Result

By RICHARD E. MOONEY
Special to The New York Times.

WASHINGTON, April 25—President Eisenhower announced today he would order an investigation to determine whether imports of crude oil threatened national security. He asserted "there is reason for the belief" that such a threat exists.

The President, in Augusta, Ga., acted after receiving advice from Gordon Gray, Director of the Office of Defense Mobilization. Mr. Gray said that the trend of imports and forecasts for coming months had given reason to believe there was a threat. Mr. Gray released his and the President's memoranda at a news conference here.

If the President finds a threat to national security, he is required by law to take action that will reduce imports. This presumably would be done by placing them under quota limitations or by raising the tariff.

Independents Skeptical

General Eisenhower asked Mr. Gray to explore the possibility of limiting imports by voluntary action. This would be done while the Presidential investigation was under way.

Major importers might prefer voluntary restrictions, rather than legal quota limitations or higher tariff charges. But the independent producers in this country, with no overseas operations, feel efforts for voluntary curtailment are futile.

The question of import limitation has been introduced by the appeal of a number of independent companies. They contend that national security is being threatened because increased oil imports discourage exploration for new oil resources in this country—resources on which the United States would depend in time of war.

Voluntary Pact Sought

The Office of Defense Mobilization has tried for two years to get voluntary agreement among importers. Mr. Gray's certification to the President that a threat exists is the most forceful step that has been taken so far. In fact, it is the first such action under the law—Section 7 of the Trade Agreements Extension (Reciprocal Trade) Act of 1955.

The actual Presidential order for an investigation awaits the selection of a group to make the study, and the preparation of necessary papers.

The United States produced more than 2,600,000,000 barrels (forty-two gallons a barrel) of crude oil last year, or an average of more than 7,100,000 barrels a day. Refineries consumed a little more than 2,900,000,000 barrels.

On the basis of pure physical capacity, the nation's wells

Continued on Page 5, Column 4

KING SCORES CAIRO

Installs a New Cabinet —Vows Fight to the Finish on Reds

By OSGOOD CARUTHERS
Special to The New York Times.

AMMAN, Jordan, April 25—King Hussein proclaimed today a fight to the finish against a conspiracy to overthrow him. He imposed martial law and formed a new Government.

The 21-year-old monarch charged openly for the first time that the conspiracy was getting its support from Egypt.

Moving swiftly, the King placed the principal cities of Amman, Jerusalem, Ramallah, Nablus and Irbid under a total curfew. He also placed the Jordanian police force under direct command of the Army.

[The Associated Press reported from Amman that King Hussein had abolished Jordan's ten political parties.]

The monarch appeared to have emerged as a mature and grimly determined fighter, defending his throne against efforts by Egypt and Syria to turn Jordan into their anti-Western satellite.

His imposition of an armored fist on the Palestinian part of Jordan and his warning, in a pre-dawn broadcast, that "conspiracies might take away the remaining part of Arab Palestine" made clear that he would fight to prevent cession of the west bank and would be ready against possible Israeli attack.

Plans Carefully Laid

Events moved swiftly last night, but it was evident that the King's plans had been carefully laid. During the early evening the Government of Premier Hussein Fakhri Khalidi finally carried out an earlier decision to quit.

The Khalidi Government had been formed on the basis of support of all parties, including the National Socialists, the left-wing Baath (Resurrection) party and their pro-Communist supporters. That support was withdrawn the day before yesterday and these parties, encouraged by the Cairo radio, called the people out on a general strike and ineffective riots.

King Hussein was ready for these developments. He kept the rioters tightly confined and there was no bloodshed. In addition the monarch had a new Cabinet at his palace, ready and waiting to take over as soon as the Khalidi Government resigned.

The new Government is headed by Ibrahim Hashem, 69 years

Continued on Page 3, Column 3

The New York Times April 26, 1957

NAVAL MOVEMENT: Ships of the United States Sixth Fleet left Cannes (1) and Naples (2) to deploy in the eastern Mediterranean, perhaps from Egypt to Turkey (3), in a measure to help Jordan (4) remain independent.

Nasser Sees Syria's Leader On Mounting Jordan Crisis

By HOMER BIGART
Special to The New York Times.

CAIRO, April 25—In an atmosphere of deepening crisis, President Gamal Abdel Nasser conferred again tonight with President Shukri al-Kuwatly of Syria on what to do about Jordan. The Egyptian President is reported eager to avoid any break with King Hussein of Jordan.

But the formation of an avowedly pro-Western government in Amman has sharpened Egyptian suspicions of some grand strategic design by the Western powers to bring Jordan into the Baghdad Pact.

In an apparent effort to patch up relations with King Saud of Saudi Arabia, who has been backing Hussein, President Nasser will send a three-man mission to Riyadh tomorrow. Mr. al-Kuwatly will accompany the Egyptian team and it was reported that he would later go to Amman for a talk with King Hussein.

President Nasser's decision to send a special mission to Saudi Arabia came after he had received a message from King Saud, the contents of which were not disclosed. The Egyptian mission will consist of President Nasser's political adviser, Col. Ali Sabry, Sheikh Hassan el Bakouri, Minister of Works, and Anwar el Sadat, head of the Islamic Congress and publisher of the newspaper Al Gomhouria.

Chief Aides at Talks

Mr. al-Kuwatly arrived unexpectedly this morning from Damascus and for several hours Egypt tried to keep his arrival secret. The Cairo radio finally broke the news at 2:30 P. M. after Damascus had announced Mr. al-Kuwatly's departure for Egypt.

President Nasser and President al-Kuwatly conferred for three hours and met again tonight in another emergency session. The Egyptian Commander in Chief, Gen. Abdel Hakim Amer, and the Syrian Chief of Staff, Gen. Tewfik Nizam el-Din, attended both meetings.

Also present were Colonel Sabry, the Syrian Foreign Minister, Salah Bitar, and the Syrian Minister of Public Works, Fakhir Kayyali.

No communiqué was issued. Diplomatic sources speculated that neither President Nasser

Continued on Page 4, Column 1

MOSCOW ACCUSES U. S. OF MEDDLING

Broadcast Attacks 'Blatant Interference' in Jordan—Hussein Also Scored

By The Associated Press.

LONDON, April 25—Moscow accused the United States tonight of "blatant interference" in the internal affairs of Jordan.

An anonymous commentator on the Moscow radio's home service said the Jordanian situation remained tense amid an "atmosphere of deep internal political crisis."

The Moscow radio said the United States, "by means of behind-the-scenes machinations, is trying to set up a Jordanian Government that would adopt the aggressive Eisenhower Doctrine and give up the policy of protecting the national interests and [Jordan's] unity with other free Arab countries."

Later tonight, an Arabic-language broadcast from Moscow said, "One is surprised, to say the least, at what King Hussein said about international communism seeking to destroy Jordan." King Hussein, in interviews yesterday, attributed Jordan's troubles to international Communist propaganda and subversion.

U. S. Agitation Alleged

The commentator went on:

"We cannot but see in this statement an unsuccessful attempt to stir up suspicions against the Soviet Union. It is well known that the Soviet Union has never interfered in the internal affairs of Jordan. On the contrary, the Soviet Union has always firmly supported the struggle of the Jordanian people against all imperialists to build up their free and independent country.

"We must also point out that this statement is but a repetition of the false allegations that are being used by American propaganda to lay responsibility and consequences on others."

The broadcast said "the intervention of United States diplomacy in the internal affairs [of Jordan] is getting more open and brazen."

Dulles' Speech Criticized

By WILLIAM J. JORDEN
Special to The New York Times.

MOSCOW, April 25—The Soviet Union's leaders insisted tonight they were not trying to export the Communist revolution. They said they could not understand why Secretary of State Dulles insisted on advocating a policy of "liberation" from communism for the countries of Eastern Europe.

The Kremlin roundly castigated Mr. Dulles for the speech he made before a gathering of American editors three days ago. A statement criticizing his speech and attributed to "leading circles of the Soviet Union" was

Continued on Page 3, Column 3

A SHOW OF FORCE

British Also Say a Free Jordan Is Essential to Mideast Peace

By DANA ADAMS SCHMIDT
Special to The New York Times.

WASHINGTON, April 25—The United States deployed its military and political power today to assure the survival of an independent Jordan.

It sent the Sixth Fleet, with the aircraft carrier Forrestal, hurrying back from the western to the eastern Mediterranean so suddenly that 150 sailors were left stranded on leave in Paris.

[A British Foreign Office spokesman said that Jordan's independence and integrity were "essential elements" in maintaining Middle East peace.]

The United States also began to set out the political justification for any future intervention. This justification is, in the Administration's view, that Jordan is menaced by the forces of international communism.

A State Department declaration to this effect, following a similar statement by King Hussein of Jordan yesterday, seemed designed to make the Eisenhower Doctrine applicable in the struggle over Jordan.

Statement Expanded

The declaration expanded President Eisenhower's statement yesterday in Augusta, Ga., that preservation of Jordan's independence was "vital to the national interest."

Lincoln White, press officer of the State Department, read this statement:

"The statement issued in Augusta, Ga., represented a reminder to the world by the President that a finding had been made in the Joint Resolution of the Congress on the Middle East [the Eisenhower Doctrine] that the preservation of the independence and integrity of the nations of the Middle East was vital to the national interest of the United States and to world peace.

"This reminder was appropriate because of the threat to the independence and integrity of Jordan by international communism as King Hussein himself stated."

Generally, according to Administration experts, international communism works indirectly in Jordan through the left-wing and extremist nationalists.

Continued on Page 2, Column 4

U. N. CHIEF LOOKS TO COURT ON SUEZ

Hammarskjold Says It Could Settle Israeli Ship Issue

By THOMAS J. HAMILTON
Special to The New York Times.

UNITED NATIONS, N. Y., April 25—Dag Hammarskjold suggested today that the question whether Israeli ships had the right to use the Suez Canal be decided by the International Court of Justice.

The Secretary General of the United Nations asserted at a news conference that the "Governments concerned" could decide. He added, however, that "as a reasonably well-informed observer," he saw a possibility that the issue could be resolved under procedures set forth in the Egyptian declaration yesterday on operation of the canal.

The declaration provided that any unresolved differences among the signatories over the meaning of the Constantinople Convention of 1888, guaranteeing freedom of navigation, would be referred to the International Court.

Egypt apparently promised to accept compulsory jurisdiction. However, Israel and the United States, which were not parties to the convention, could not take the issue to the Court.

Further questions brought out the contradictory language of the convention, which provides that while the canal should be open to the shipping of all nations, both in war and peace, Egypt is entitled to take action to guard her security. Reminded that this right was qualified by

Continued on Page 4, Column 3

CITY BARS HOUSING AT CANCER CENTER

Relocation Problems Cited —Bridge Routes Filed

By CHARLES G. BENNETT

After months of hearings, the Board of Estimate yesterday rejected a proposal to build a $6,500,000 middle-income housing project in Yorkville.

The proposal had been made by the Memorial Center for Cancer and Allied Diseases, the Sloan Kettering Institute and the Rockefeller Institute for Medical Research.

The board acted on two other major items of city business.

It received and referred to city agencies the plans for Brooklyn and Staten Island approach routes to the Narrows Bridge and for the Queens and Bronx approaches to the Throgs Neck Bridge. Robert Moses, chairman of the Triborough Bridge and Tunnel Authority, submitted the plans.

The board approved $25,000 to put under way initial studies of the rehabilitation of the downtown area of Brooklyn, including the feasibility of a sports center that would serve as a home for the Brooklyn Dodgers baseball team.

In the case of the rejected Yorkville project, the sponsoring institutions had sought permission for nearly two years to construct two buildings. One would be for nurses and would contain 237 apartments. The other was for technical, research and professional personnel. It was to have 189 apartments.

The site for the proposed im-

Continued on Page 17, Column 5

Recording by Lanza Is Reported Missing

By LEO EGAN

A tape recording of one conversation between Joseph (Socks) Lanza and his wife and others at the Westchester County jail was reported missing yesterday.

The disclosure was made by Arthur L. Reuter, Acting State Commissioner of Investigation. The Commissioner is conducting one of two investigations into the dismissal of parole violation charges against Lanza, a convicted extortionist.

The missing recording was made a half-hour before Lanza's release on Feb. 20. He had been arrested as a parole violator on Feb. 5. His release followed the dismissal of the charges against him by Parole Commissioner James R. Stone.

Commissioner Stone subsequently resigned from the Parole Board while being questioned about his decision by

Continued on Page 15, Column 2

N. Y. U. Hospital Is Planned, With Research Chief Goal

This is a drawing of the new nineteen-story hospital building that will rise at New York University-Bellevue Medical Center. The architects are Skidmore, Owings & Merrill.

By ROBERT K. PLUMB

Plans for a new hospital to make the New York University-Bellevue Medical Center a pioneering scientific research institution were announced yesterday. The plans call for a nineteen-story building of white brick and glass just south of Thirty-fourth Street and east of First Avenue. But the plans tell only part of the story. For it is the intention of New York University medical men to use the new $20,000,000 institution to find out how to reduce the time lag between laboratory science and bedside medical practice. Other possible improvements in medicine may in part be "built into" the new hospital,

Continued on Page 18, Column 3

A.E.C. Aide Says Dr. Schweitzer Errs

By EDWARD L. DALE Jr.
Special to The New York Times.

WASHINGTON, April 25—The scientist member of the Atomic Energy Commission sharply disputed today the contention of Dr. Albert Schweitzer that nuclear weapons tests were creating "a danger for the human race."

Dr. Willard F. Libby, the commission member, wrote to Dr. Schweitzer "as a scientist, to present data bearing on a scientific fact." He made his letter public two days after a broadcast from Oslo of Dr. Schweitzer's warning.

After paying tribute to Dr. Schweitzer, humanitarian and winner of the Nobel Peace Prize, Dr. Libby said he feared Dr. Schweitzer's appeal was not based on the latest information on radioactive fall-out. Dr. Libby added: "I know you have the intellectual strength

Continued on Page 6, Column 4

"All the News That's Fit to Print"

The New York Times.

LATE CITY EDITION
U. S. Weather Bureau Report (Page 36) forecasts:
Some cloudiness, warm today.
Partly cloudy, humid tomorrow.
Temp. range: 88—70. Yesterday: 86.4—61.4.

VOL. CVI..No. 36,321. NEW YORK, THURSDAY, JULY 4, 1957. 10c beyond 100-mile zone from New York City FIVE CENTS

WIDE SHAKE-UP IN KREMLIN OUSTS MOLOTOV, MALENKOV, KAGANOVICH AS KHRUSHCHEV TIGHTENS REINS

PRESIDENT BARS BALLOT ON RIGHTS; WOULD HEAR FOES

Rejects Proposal by Russell to Hold Referendum, but Plans to Study Bill

CITES COURT'S DECISIONS

'Ready to Listen' to South's Arguments — Senator Welcomes the Offer

News conference transcript and summary, Page 13.

By WILLIAM S. WHITE
Special to The New York Times.

WASHINGTON, July 3—President Eisenhower made it plain today that he was taking another and a closer look at the implications of the Administration's civil rights bill in the wake of vehement Southern attacks on it.

At the same time, he rejected a proposal from the Southern opposition that the bill be submitted directly to the people in a national referendum.

He declared at his news conference, however, that he was "ready to listen" to any presentation of their side from the embattled Southerners.

Their chief spokesman, Senator Richard B. Russell, Democrat of Georgia, denounced the bill yesterday as so "cunningly contrived" that it could be questioned whether the President himself understood its full scope.

Opponents Map Strategy

Senator Russell was holding a strategy meeting at the Capitol with fellow Senators while the President was speaking. By coincidence, they themselves about that time were discussing the possibility of going to him in a group to offer their views.

Some were at first disposed not to attempt this course, lest it be interpreted as a sign of weakness.

Told later of the President's remarks, however, Senator Russell said:

"If the President wishes to talk to us on this matter, his wish—as would be the wish of any President of the United States—will be to us a command. I should be glad to meet with him in any circumstances he might prefer—alone or with others as he might wish."

From the Senate floor, Senator Russell charged yesterday that the Attorney General, Herbert Brownell Jr., had prepared a "deceptive piece of legislation" that would amount to "an unlimited grant of powers to the Attorney General to govern by injunction and Federal bayonet."

Bill Passed by House

As passed by the House of Representatives, the bill would:

¶Permit the Justice Department to intervene in behalf of any individual, with or without his consent, whose civil rights had been denied or were under threat of denial. This would be done by obtaining a Federal court injunction against the violator or imminent violator. If he refused to obey this writ, he could be held in contempt by a judge, sitting without a jury, and fined or imprisoned.

¶Set up a special civil rights division within the Justice Department.

¶Create a Federal civil rights commission to investigate and attempt to rectify cases of racial discrimination.

The civil rights advocates, Mr. Russell contended, are pretending that their main concern is to protect the right to vote, but in fact are seeking means to force racial integration in the South, in the schools and elsewhere, even to the point of possible use of Federal troops.

Russell Sees Pretense

The President at his news conference today showed that he had been disturbed by the comments of Senator Russell, with whom he had had many agreeable relationships.

During his military career, General Eisenhower often appeared before the Senate Armed Services Committee, of which Mr. Russell is chairman.

On Senator Russell's suggestion of a referendum, the President said he doubted that there was any constitutional basis for such a step; that Congress itself had the responsibility to enact legislation, and that in any case the issue would not make "a very good subject for a referendum, even if you could have one."

On Mr. Russell's general denunciation of the bill, however, President Eisenhower did

Continued on Page 26, Column 7

Eisenhower Raises Atomic Fuel Quota

By JOHN W. FINNEY
Special to The New York Times.

WASHINGTON, July 3—The White House more than doubled today the amount of nuclear fuel the United States would make available for atomic power plants at home and abroad.

President Eisenhower announced that he was allocating an additional 59,800 kilograms—or 131,560 pounds—of uranium 235 for peaceful purposes in domestic and foreign nuclear power projects.

Including its previous allocations, the United States has now pledged to make 100,000 kilograms—or 220,000 pounds—of uranium fuel available for peaceful purposes. At current atomic energy commission prices, the value of this fuel is $1,700,000,000.

The 100,000 kilograms will be

Continued on Page 12, Column 3

CITY BUILDING UNIT STUDIED BY STATE

Heck Announces Watchdog Inquiry—Step Welcomed by Mayor and Aides

By EMANUEL PERLMUTTER

The Republican-controlled legislative watchdog committee has begun an investigation of the New York City Department of Buildings.

This was disclosed yesterday by Assemblyman Oswald D. Heck, Republican Speaker of the Assembly. He said the committee was checking reports of "graft, corruption and extortion" in the department.

Confirmation was given by Senator William F. Horan, Republican of Tuckahoe, chairman of the Joint Legislative Committee on Government Operations, the official name of the watchdog unit.

Mr. Horan said the committee's staff was making "preliminary investigations into those and other matters."

Mayor Gives His Views

Mayor Wagner said his Administration welcomed the watchdog committee's investigation.

"I have said time and again that we would welcome any investigation of any city department," he declared. "We have nothing to hide. If there is wrongdoing no one is more impatient than I to root it out and take swift, decisive action.

"I have already asked those with complaints against the Department of Buildings to come in and state their complaints. I have promised full protection to all who cooperate in this fashion."

Charles H. Tenney, the City Investigation Commissioner who has begun his own inquiry into rumors that building inspectors were shaking down property-owners guilty of violations and those seeking building permits,

Continued on Page 37, Column 3

DEMOCRATS BACK EASING OF CURBS ON ALIEN QUOTAS

Key Legislators in Agreement on Compromise to Bring in 140,000 More in 2 Years

By JOHN D. MORRIS
Special to The New York Times.

WASHINGTON, July 3—Key Democrats in Congress have quietly reached substantial agreement on a compromise plan for easing restrictions on immigration.

The compromise, described as acceptable in nearly all major respects to legislators most interested in the problem, is embodied in a bill introduced last Thursday by Senator John F. Kennedy, Democrat of Massachusetts.

The measure has the backing of Lyndon B. Johnson of Texas, the Senate Democratic leader. Representative Francis E. Walter, Democrat of Pennsylvania, who holds the key to action by the House of Representatives, also participated in the unpublished negotiations that preceded its introduction. Sponsors look for his cooperation.

The bill would permit the entry over a two-year period of 140,000 to 150,000 regular immigrants and refugees who otherwise would be excluded.

Eisenhower Plan Included

While it includes features of President Eisenhower's immigration program, it stops short of making some basic changes that he had proposed in the McCarran-Walter Immigration and Nationality Act.

The President's recommendations, outlined Jan. 31 in a special message to Congress, asked authority to bring in 190,000 more persons a year.

The annual quota under present law is 154,857, of which 60,000 quota numbers expire unused each year. Total entrances, including unrestricted immigration from Western Hemisphere countries, amounted to 321,625 in 1956.

Democratic strategists hope to obtain Republican help in steering the Kennedy bill through Congress toward the end of the session without public hearings.

The tentative plan, similar to one that failed in the last hours of the 1956 session, is to attach the measure to a minor immigration bill passed by the House and now pending on the Senate calendar.

Tactic Failed Last Year

Senate passage of the combined bill would send it to a Senate-House conference committee for agreement on the final version.

The tactic failed last year when Representative Walter, chairman of the House Judiciary Subcommittee on Immigration, invoked a parliamentary technicality to keep a similar bill from going to conference.

This time, according to Senator Kennedy, Mr. Walter "has

Continued on Page 11, Column 1

G.O.P. Picks 3-War Marine To Oppose Jack in Borough

By RUSSELL PORTER

Melvin L. Krulewitch, 61-year-old lawyer and twice-wounded Marine Corps Reserve veteran of three wars, was designated yesterday as the Republican candidate for Borough President of Manhattan. He will oppose Hulan E. Jack, the Democratic incumbent in the November election.

Mr. Krulewitch, who is a major general in the Reserve, was the only Republican named for Borough President or District Attorney at meetings of the executive committees of the New York and Kings County Republican Committees.

The following three Democrats, who already had their own party designations, were endorsed by the Republicans for re-election as Borough President or District Attorney:

Borough President John Cashmore of Brooklyn.

District Attorney Frank S. Hogan of New York County (Manhattan).

District Attorney Edward S. Silver of Kings County (Brooklyn).

Both executive committees formally approved the recent designation of three Republican city-wide candidates by the five county leaders. These candidates are Robert K. Christenberry for Mayor, Mrs. Caroline K. Simon for President of the City Council and State Senator Walter G. McGahan of Queens for Controller.

Mr. Krulewitch's designation marked a departure from the Republican practice in the 1953 municipal campaign. At that time the Republicans picked a Negro, Elmer A. Carter, who lost to Mr. Jack, who is also a Negro.

Thomas J. Curran, the Republicans' New York County leader, said after yesterday's meeting that Mr. Carter, a member of the State Committee Against Discrimination, did not want to run for Borough President this year. According to Mr. Curran, Mr. Krulewitch was the only person mentioned for the post.

Mr. Krulewitch told Negro reporters yesterday that he had served with Negro troops at Iwo in the Pacific in World War II. "They were fine troops," he said.

The candidate is a tall, husky, clean-shaven man of military bearing. He wears dark horn-rimmed glasses and his hair is getting thin and gray. He has been a member of the Republican County Committee for eight years but has never run for public office. He has a law office on Madison Avenue and lives at 45 Gramercy Park North, in Mr. Curran's home district.

"Are you an Eisenhower Re-

Continued on Page 20, Column 7

U. S. IS GRATIFIED

State Department Says Ousters Show Strain in Soviet System

By JAMES RESTON
Special to The New York Times.

WASHINGTON, July 3—Official Washington tried hard to conceal its pleasure over the latest shake-up in the Soviet Union today but didn't quite succeed.

"No comment," said James C. Hagerty, White House press secretary, grinning broadly, and the grin was the most tangible and significant act in a day devoted mainly to gleeful speculation.

News of the official Soviet announcement of the dismissal of Vyacheslav M. Molotov, Lazar M. Kaganovich, Georgi M. Malenkov and Dmitri T. Shepilov was brought to President Eisenhower during a meeting of the National Security Council in the afternoon. Reports of developments were rushed to the White House from the State Department and the Central Intelligence Agency throughout the day.

Mr. Hagerty told the press in midafternoon that the Administration had advance indication of the ouster. He noted that Nikita S. Khrushchev, First Secretary of the Soviet Communist party, and Marshal Nikolai A. Bulganin, Soviet Premier, had recently postponed a visit to Czechoslovakia, and that an aerial demonstration over Moscow, to which Communist bloc leaders had been invited, had suddenly been canceled.

Beyond that, however, he would not comment.

White Reads Statement

The State Department was more explicit. In answer to reporters' questions, Lincoln White, press officer, read the following statement:

"It has long been known that the Soviet system operates under stresses and strains. Arbitrary and abrupt dismissals without public discussion of the issues are also characteristic of the system.

"The official Soviet press has at various times suggested there have been disagreements over basic policies in such fields as Government organizations, agriculture, heavy industry, consumer goods and satellite affairs.

"The serious nature of the divergence of views is clearly shown by the number and importance of the persons dismissed or shifted. We are naturally following these developments closely for the effect they may have on Soviet basic policy."

Effect on U. S. Policy Seen

The Soviet changes have come at a critical time in the development of United States foreign policy and is expected to have some influence on that policy, particularly as it affects Communist China and the Soviet Union.

Both the Executive and Legislative branches of the United States Government have been divided about how to deal with Moscow and Peiping. Some legislators and officials have favored making a major effort to reach a disarmament agreement with the Soviet Union and acquiescing in an accommodation with the Chinese Communists.

Others have been opposing this on the ground that the whole Communist world was in ferment. They have been going along reluctantly with the current United States policy in the disarmament talks in London, but insisting that the way to break up the Communist alliance between Moscow and Peiping was to maintain the economic pressure.

Secretary of State Dulles, who left for his Great Lakes retreat on Duck Island today, said only yesterday that he was opposed to making concessions to the Chinese Communists, and regarded dictatorial communism in both Peiping and Moscow as "a passing phase."

Today's developments in Moscow, coming on top of a noisy debate in Peiping over ideological questions, were expected to strengthen those who have contended that the thing to do was to keep the pressure on, not to grow weary of the long struggle, not to make risky conces-

Continued on Page 3, Column 4

The New York Times
Vyacheslav M. Molotov

Associated Press
Georgi M. Malenkov

Sovfoto
Lazar M. Kaganovich

U. S. MAY SPREAD 'CLEAN' BOMB DATA

President Weighs Proposal to Give Others Knowledge on Eliminating Fall-Out

By JACK RAYMOND
Special to The New York Times.

WASHINGTON, July 3 — President Eisenhower said today he was thinking of sharing with the Soviet Union and other countries the knowledge of how to produce "clean" hydrogen bombs.

Such a step would require legislation, he said. But he disclosed that he had asked his scientific advisers about the possibility of sharing, and they had suggested such a course might be adopted as soon as they had proved they could produce a bomb totally free of dangerous radioactive fall-out.

The President said that in the meantime he intended to invite foreign countries to make their own measurements of the percentage of radioactivity on the site of the next United States hydrogen bomb detonation.

This should serve as an appropriate test by doubters of the contention that even now only 4 per cent radioactivity results from the explosion of United States hydrogen bombs, the President declared.

U-235 Given to Others

President Eisenhower opened his news conference with an announcement that the United States was making more uranium-235 available in the peaceful uses of atomic power.

In response to questions about United States policy on disarmament and the effects on that policy of reduced radioactive fall-out in bomb explosions, the President emphasized:

¶The United States stands firm on its position at the London disarmament conference, agreeing to a temporary suspension of nuclear arms tests if it will lead to an end of bomb-making.

¶The United States disarm-

Continued on Page 12, Column 2

Moscow Ousters Termed Victory for 'Liberal' Policy

By HARRISON E. SALISBURY

Nikita S. Khrushchev, First Secretary of the Soviet Communist party, appears to have won a smashing victory for his "New Look" policies of easing tensions at home and abroad. This was the initial reaction of competent specialists in Soviet affairs to the dramatic decisions of the latest meeting in Moscow of the party's Central Committee.

With the firm support of the Soviet Army, the Communist party apparatus and the Government bureaucracy, Mr. Khrushchev has ousted from the Soviet ruling group a powerful bloc of Stalinist oppositionists.

Mr. Khrushchev's ability to remove from the party's Presidium and Central Committee such veteran party chieftains as Vyacheslav M. Molotov, Lazar M. Kaganovich and Georgi M. Malenkov was testimony to the power he had now mustered behind his leadership.

Indictment Is Stressed

Of great importance in international relations was the nature of the indictment placed against them, Mr. Khrushchev and his victorious Central Committee majority charged Mr. Molotov, Mr. Kaganovich, Mr. Malenkov and their supporters with persistent and deliberate efforts to sabotage every effort to ease international tensions, improve the life of Soviet citizens at home and destroy the vestiges of Stalinist excesses.

The communiqué announcing the expulsions contained a platform of the Khrushchev faction, which promised to continue striving for better international relations.

While the main force of the Khrushchev indictment was directed against Mr. Molotov, Mr. Kaganovich and Mr. Malenkov, they were not the only targets. In effect Mr. Khrushchev made a clean sweep.

He also ousted Dmitri T. Shepilov, the former Pravda editor and Foreign Minister who was identified with the "Young Turk" faction of the party. Mr.

Continued on Page 3, Column 2

SOVIET EXPECTED TO EASE BLOC TIE

Shift in Leadership Viewed as Move to Consolidate the Communist Orbit

By SYDNEY GRUSON
Special to The New York Times.

PRAGUE, Czechoslovakia, July 3—The changes in the Soviet Communist party's leadership, announced in Moscow tonight, may have ushered in a significant period of readjustment in relations between the Soviet Union and other Communist countries.

The changes, and the Pravda editorial accompanying them, were considered of such basic importance that people here and in Warsaw hesitated to comment until a more thorough study became possible. But among their first impressions were these:

¶Nikita S. Khrushchev had consolidated his position as the first among equals in the new Presidium of the Soviet party.

¶Mr. Khrushchev was bent on a determined effort to narrow the steadily widening gap between the Soviet party and some of the other Communist parties, particularly that of Communist China.

To Lessen Antagonism

The dismissal of Vyacheslav M. Molotov would be bound to lessen the sharp antagonism between Moscow and Belgrade, Yugoslavia, and the differences between Moscow and Warsaw as well. In both Belgrade and Warsaw Mr. Molotov had been considered the prime architect of a tough policy toward parties straying from the Soviet line.

The section of the Pravda editorial concerning the failure of "sectarians and dogmatists" [Stalinists] to understand the necessity of consolidating the Socialist camp was read here as aimed against Mr. Molotov.

Through the Pravda editorial the Soviet Union was assuming a posture that had already been taken up elsewhere in the Communist camp. Editorial strictures against Stalinists on the one hand and revisionists on the other echoed the "struggle on two fronts" adopted as the Polish party's major ideological line months ago.

One paragraph in Pravda particularly sounded like dozens of recent editorials of Trybuna Ludu, the newspaper of the Polish party's Central Committee. Pravda described "sectarians and dogmatists" as people "divorced from life" who have "backward conceptions."

"They do not see new situations," Pravda declared. "They stubbornly cling to obsolete forms and methods of work and reject that which is born by life. They would like to turn the party back to those incorrect methods of leadership rejected by the Twentieth Party Congress."

Thus at long last the Russians conceded that Marshal Tito had

Continued on Page 5, Column 7

Holiday Traffic Exodus Begins; 952 Police Cars Will Patrol City

Police Commissioner Stephen P. Kennedy yesterday declared "all-out war" on reckless drivers in a move to help law-abiding citizens survive the Fourth of July holiday week-end.

Fifty-two unmarked cars and 900 regular radio patrol cars were assigned to watch traffic from 4 P. M. yesterday until 8 A. M. Monday.

The holiday exodus began yesterday afternoon. It was estimated that 1,000,000 cars would carry 3,500,000 persons out of the city during the four-day week-end.

Most of the nation was promised generally fair and warm weather today with which to celebrate the 181st anniversary of the adoption of the Declaration of Independence by the Continental Congress.

The Weather Bureau said temperatures here — which climbed to 86.4 degrees at 6:40 P. M. yesterday — might reach 85 to 90 degrees today. Yesterday was the first day to exceed 80 degrees since last Friday. The outlook for tomorrow and Saturday is partly cloudy, warm and humid.

The National Safety Council estimated that 45,000,000 motor vehicles would be on the roads. It feared a possible record Independence Day toll of 535 highway deaths between 6 P. M. yesterday and midnight Sunday.

The council warned that eight of every ten fatal accidents occur in rural areas; speed is involved in seven out of ten, and drinking is a factor in almost half. Indiana and Iowa detailed National Guardsmen to aid road patrols; Kentucky and Georgia planned road blocks to check drivers, and New Mexico ordered jail for reckless drivers until their records could be checked.

In the city, 120 police cars will operate in a safety-chain plan, each patrolling back and forth on a single mile of the major parkways and highways. Six cars of the accident investigation unit will be on around-the-clock duty. Two police helicopters will help unsnarl traffic tie-ups.

The major delays yesterday affected traffic leaving the city over the George Washington Bridge. Between 5 and 6:30 P. M., cars on the West Side

Continued on Page 26, Column 3

3 STALINISTS OUT

Shepilov Also Dropped for Opposing Current Policies of Soviet

Texts of communiqué, Pravda editorial, Pages 2 and 4.

By WILLIAM J. JORDEN
Special to The New York Times.

MOSCOW, Thursday, July 4—The Soviet Communist party has accused Vyacheslav M. Molotov, Georgi M. Malenkov and Lazar M. Kaganovich of anti-party activities and has ousted them from the country's leadership.

They were removed both from the Presidium of the party's Central Committee and from the Central Committee itself. However, they remained as members of the party.

Dmitri T. Shepilov, who was said to have joined them in working against the majority, was also ousted from alternate membership in the Presidium, from the Central Committee and from his job as one of the party secretaries.

Three Linked With Stalin

The three Communist leaders, all known for their connections with Stalin, were accused of having tried to restore "methods of leadership that were condemned by the Twentieth Party Congress," an allusion to the system prevailing in Stalin's time. They were said to have tried to form an anti-party faction to achieve their aims.

The action against them was taken during an eight-day meeting of the Central Committee from June 22 through 29. The text of the committee's resolution was released by Tass, Soviet news agency, last night.

Of the former eleven members of the party Presidium only six remained. They are Nikita S. Khrushchev, Nikolai A. Bulganin, Kliment Y. Voroshilov, Anastas I. Mikoyan, Mikhail A. Suslov and Alexei I. Kirichenko.

Zhukov Is Elevated

Marshal Georgi K. Zhukov, the Defense Minister, and Miss Yekaterina A. Furtseva, the only woman on the Presidium, were among five alternate members who were raised to full rank. Four other regular members were newly added to the Presidium.

In addition to the four leading figures who were singled out for severe criticism and ousted from the Presidium, Mikhail G. Pervukhin and Maxim Z. Saburov also were dropped from the group.

Mr. Pervukhin was demoted to the position of alternate member of the Presidium, but nothing was known of Mr. Saburov's present position. He was not mentioned as having been dropped from the Central Committee itself.

Messrs. Molotov, Malenkov and Kaganovich were said to have opposed all the major policy moves of recent years that have come to be associated with the name of Mr. Khrushchev. The Central Committee's indictment

Continued on Page 2, Column 3

Italy Holds TV Aide In Give-Away Fraud

By PAUL HOFMANN
Special to The New York Times.

ROME, July 3—One of Italy's best-known television personalities was in prison today, charged with rigging give-away shows.

Giuseppe Ruggiero, 42 years old, never spoke a line before television cameras and never was introduced to watchers. But his sternly benevolent face is familiar to millions because it used to appear on the screen whenever something was to be won.

In his wordless way Signor Ruggiero was quite a performer. To the unseen audience he was fair play personified. As chief of the promotion department of the state broadcasting and television system Signor Ruggiero presided over the distribution of thousands of television sets, record players, refrigerators and automobiles.

Now he is accused of having

Continued on Page 37, Column 2

"All the News That's Fit to Print"

The New York Times.

LATE CITY EDITION
U. S. Weather Bureau Report (Page 59) forecasts:
Mostly fair and seasonable today and tomorrow.
Temp. range: 70—57. Yesterday: 67.7—55.9.

VOL. CVII . No. 36,404. | © 1957, by The New York Times Company. Times Square, New York 36, N. Y. | NEW YORK, WEDNESDAY, SEPTEMBER 25, 1957. | 10c beyond 100-mile zone from New York City | FIVE CENTS

PRESIDENT SENDS TROOPS TO LITTLE ROCK, FEDERALIZES ARKANSAS NATIONAL GUARD; TELLS NATION HE ACTED TO AVOID ANARCHY

WEST AGAIN BARS SOVIET PROPOSAL ON MIDEAST TALK

U. S. Says Latest Moscow Note 'Cynically Distorts' American Actions

Text of U. S. note to Soviet will be found on Page 5.

By DANA ADAMS SCHMIDT
Special to The New York Times.

WASHINGTON, Sept. 24—The United States, Britain and France rejected today the latest in a series of Soviet bids for recognition of the Soviet Union's role in the Middle East.

A brief United States reply delivered in Moscow today said a Soviet note of Sept. 3 was "offensive in tone and cynically distorts United States objectives and actions in the Middle East."

It accused the Soviet Union of setting in motion "a chain of events leading to the present dangerous situation" by shipping large quantities of arms into the area.

U. S. Affirms Doctrine

The note warned the Soviet Union that the United States Government intended to carry out the national policy laid down in the Eisenhower Doctrine, which "regards the preservation of the independence and integrity of the nations of that region as vital to world peace and as vital, therefore, to its own national interests."

The doctrine, proclaimed in a Joint Resolution of the House of Representatives and the Senate on March 9, 1957, also affirmed the President's authority to use United States forces to aid any Middle East state that asked for help against aggression by a power controlled by international communism.

The Soviet Union's note had accused the United States of seeking to overthrow the Syrian Government and of generally fomenting trouble in the Middle East.

3d Rejection of Soviet Bid

It had proposed, for the third time, a four-power declaration renouncing the use of force in the area. Earlier Soviet proposals for such a declaration, all rejected by the West, were made Feb. 11 and April 19.

As interpreted by United States experts on the Middle East, these notes were meant to convey the idea that the four powers should meet to negotiate a settlement of their rivalries in the Middle East. The first of the notes even went into detail with a proposal for an embargo on shipment of arms to the area.

Because the Soviet Union has asserted its presence in Syria, and because there seems to be little the Western powers can do to reverse developments in

Continued on Page 5, Column 3

London and Bonn Rule Out Any Currency Revaluation

Britain Tells Monetary Fund Session She Will Draw $500,000,000 in Stand-By Credit From Export-Import Bank

By EDWIN L. DALE JR.
Special to The New York Times.

WASHINGTON, Sept. 24—British and West German spokesmen and the Managing Director of the International Monetary Fund said today that the question of exchange rates for the pound and the mark was "definitely settled." There will be no change.

At the same time, Britain, through Peter Thorneycroft, Chancellor of the Exchequer, announced she would draw "over the coming weeks" the $500,000,000 stand-by credit she arranged last winter with the United States Export-Import Bank.

In his speech at the annual meeting of the fund, Mr. Thorneycroft indicated that Britain was drawing the money to demonstrate to speculators that she had the resources to defend the pound.

Both the British and the West Germans emphasized that the recent huge flow of gold and dollars out of Britain and into West Germany had been based solely on speculation, not on basic factors in their foreign trading accounts.

Per Jacobsson, the Fund's Managing Director, said: "The growing knowledge that there will be no alteration in the value of either the Deutsche

Continued on Page 8, Column 5

SOLDIERS FLY IN

1,000 Go to Little Rock —9,936 in Guard Told to Report

The texts of Executive orders on troops are on Page 16.

By JACK RAYMOND
Special to The New York Times.

WASHINGTON, Sept. 24—The Army ordered all Arkansas National Guardsmen to report for Federal duty tonight and rushed 1,000 airborne troops of the Regular Army into Little Rock to preserve order.

The Regulars were members of the 101st Airborne Division, which won fame in World War II under the command of Gen. Maxwell D. Taylor, now Chief of Staff of the Army.

Maj. Gen. Edwin A. Walker, a much-decorated combat commander with a reputation for toughness, was put in command of the Regular Army contingent and the federalized Guardsmen in Arkansas. He is the commander of the Arkansas Military District.

General Walker's mission is to make sure that no one frustrates Federal Court orders that nine Negro pupils be admitted to Central High School.

Wilson Carries Out Order

Charles E. Wilson, Secretary of Defense, carrying out President Eisenhower's mandate, earlier had called the entire Arkansas Army and Air National Guard, totaling 9,936 men, into Federal service.

The Secretary of Defense and Wilber M. Brucker, Secretary of the Army, acted two hours after President Eisenhower's executive order authorizing "all appropriate steps" to make school attendance possible for the Negroes who had been admitted to the high school.

However, an Army spokesman said that it was planned to make "the absolute minimum demonstration of force necessary."

Immediately after Secretary Wilson signed the federalization call to the Arkansas Guard at 2:25 P. M., Secretary Brucker telephoned the office of Gov. Orval E. Faubus in Little Rock.

At the same time he sent a telegram to the Governor, explaining that President Eisenhower "desires" the personnel of the Arkansas Army and Air National Guard organizations

Continued on Page 14, Column 2

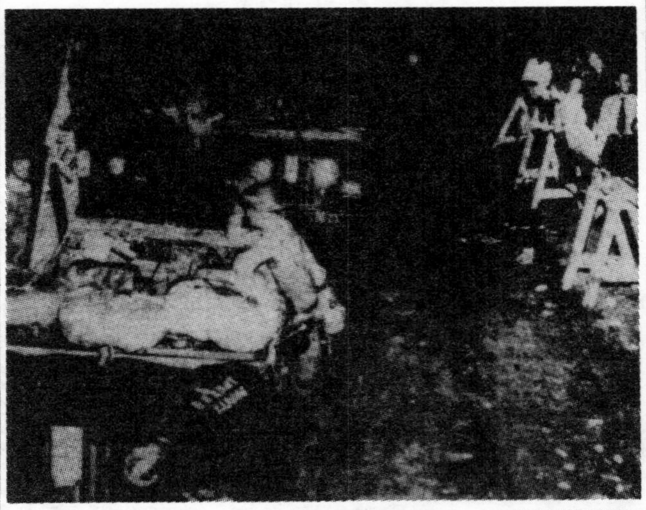

Associated Press Wirephoto

SOLDIERS IN LITTLE ROCK: Residents of Arkansas capital looking on last night as men of the 101st Airborne Division took positions outside the Central High School.

EISENHOWER ON AIR

Says School Defiance Has Gravely Harmed Prestige of U. S.

Text of President's address appears on Page 14.

By ANTHONY LEWIS
Special to The New York Times.

WASHINGTON, Sept. 24—President Eisenhower sent Federal troops to Little Rock, Ark., today to open the way for the admission of nine Negro pupils to Central High School.

Earlier, the President federalized the Arkansas National Guard and authorized calling the Guard and regular Federal forces to remove obstructions to justice in Little Rock school integration.

His history-making action was based on a formal finding that his "cease and desist" proclamation, issued last night, had not been obeyed. Mobs of pro-segragationists still gathered in the vicinity of Central High School this morning.

Tonight, from the White House, President Eisenhower told the nation in a speech for radio and television that he had acted to prevent "mob rule" and "anarchy."

Historic Decision

The President's decision to send troops to Little Rock was reached at his vacation headquarters in Newport, R. I. It was one of historic importance politically, socially, constitutionally. For the first time since the Reconstruction days that followed the Civil War, the Federal Government was using its ultimate power to compel equal treatment of the Negro in the South.

He said violent defiance of Federal Court orders in Little Rock had done grave harm to "the prestige and influence, and indeed to the safety, of our nation and the world." He called on the people of Arkansas and the South to "preserve and respect the law even when they disagree with it."

Guardsmen Withdrawn

Action quickly followed the President's orders. During the day and night 1,000 members of the 101st Airborne Division were flown to Little Rock. Charles E. Wilson, Secretary of the Defense, ordered into Federal service all 10,000 members of the Arkansas National Guard.

Today's events were the climax of three weeks of skirmishing between the Federal Government and Gov. Orval E. Faubus of Arkansas. It was three weeks ago this morning that the Governor first ordered National Guard troops to Central High School to preserve order. The nine Negro students were prevented from entering the school.

The Guardsmen were gone yesterday, withdrawn by Governor Faubus as the result of a

Continued on Page 14, Column 6

SOVIET ASSAILED BY LLOYD AT U. N.

Briton Suggests Arms Sent Arabs May Be Stocks for Future Bases

Excerpts from Lloyd's speech are printed on Page 4.

By THOMAS J. HAMILTON
Special to The New York Times.

UNITED NATIONS, N. Y., Sept. 24—Britain denounced today Soviet arms shipments to Arab countries. Selwyn Lloyd, British Foreign Secretary, suggested that the purpose might be to "pre-stock forward bases for the Soviet Union itself."

Mr. Lloyd told the General Assembly that Soviet arms had been delivered "on such a scale as to give some color to this suggestion." He added that Britain viewed the Syrian situation "with grave concern." In addition, he criticized Soviet policy throughout the area.

Mr. Lloyd devoted most of his speech to the Middle East and to disarmament. He did not say what action the Assembly should take on either subject.

However, he declared that Secretary of State Dulles, in

Continued on Page 4, Column 3

City Approves Plan By Wiley to Build Midtown Garages

By JOSEPH C. INGRAHAM

The Board of Estimate has approved in principle the program of Traffic Commissioner T. T. Wiley for garage construction in the heart of lower and mid-Manhattan.

The decision clears the way for a start on $24,000,000 of garages. It also settles a three-year dispute between Mr. Wiley and other city executives that has stymied off-street parking relief.

As a result, the first of the projects—a garage in the Herald Square area—will be on the board's calendar on Oct. 9. Eight other garages are to be centrally located in Manhattan and two in the busiest parts of the Bronx.

The Herald Square garage will be east of the Avenue of the Americas between West Thirty-fifth and Thirty-sixth Streets with entrances and exits on both streets. There will be space for 610 cars on eight levels accessible by ramps. Rates will be geared to "meet the heavy unsatisfied demand for short-time parking," Mr. Wiley said.

Rates proposed by the Commissioner would be 25 cents a

Continued on Page 25, Column 1

GOVERNORS URGE WHITE HOUSE TALK

Southerners Move to Set Up Mediation Machinery in Use of Federal Troops

By JOHN N. POPHAM
Special to The New York Times.

SEA ISLAND, Ga., Sept. 24—Southern Governors moved tonight to establish mediation machinery that would remove Federal troops from the South. The Governors acted a few hours after the President had federalized the Arkansas National Guard.

Gov. Luther Hodges of North Carolina, chairman of the Southern Governors Conference in session here, announced that two proposals would be submitted to the resolutions committee of the conference for formal consideration tomorrow.

One is a proposal of Gov. Frank G. Clement of Tennessee to establish an informal committee of Southern Governors to seek a meeting with President Eisenhower in a search for a solution to the Little Rock school integration crisis.

The other is a request to the President to hold off the use of Federal troops and to agree

Continued on Page 16, Column 2

Troops on Guard at School; Negroes Ready to Return

By BENJAMIN FINE
Special to The New York Times.

LITTLE ROCK, Ark., Sept. 24—Troops from the Army's crack 101st Airborne Division, carrying carbines and billy clubs, took posts around Central High School tonight. They were here to see that court-ordered integration is carried out.

With police sirens wailing and headlights flashing, Army trucks loaded with soldiers roared into position. The soldiers represented about a quarter of the contingent of 1,000 crack troops of the division that was ordered to Little Rock by President Eisenhower to prevent mob riots and violence.

The first group of 500 airborne soldiers came to the city this afternoon from Fort Campbell, Ky., and a second group of 500 arrived by plane this evening. The bulk of the two groups bivouacked for the night in areas away from the school.

General Issues Order

Maj. Gen. Edwin A. Walker, commander of the Arkansas Military District, issued a formal order to the people of Little Rock not to collect in crowds and to let Central High School be integrated peaceably.

With the arrival of Federal troops, including some Negro soldiers who were not expected to be on duty at the school, Negro students were ready to try again to enter the high school.

A mob of 1,000 persons yesterday forced the city and school authorities to withdraw nine Negro students who had attended integrated classes for 3 hours and 13 minutes. The students did not try to enter the school today.

Mrs. L. C. Bates, president

Continued on Page 15, Column 1

CONGRESS IS SPLIT ON USE OF TROOPS

Johnston Calls for Faubus to Resist President but Others Hail His Move

By JOHN W. FINNEY
Special to The New York Times.

WASHINGTON, Sept. 24—Congressional reaction to President Eisenhower's decision to use troops in the Little Rock integration crisis ranged from angry denunciation to outright praise today.

Southern Senators sharply criticized the President and suggested he had exceeded his legal authority. Northern Senators supported the President, but some of them expressed reservations that the action was rather belated.

Expects Faubus to Act

Senator Olin D. Johnston, Democrat of South Carolina, suggested that Gov. Orval E. Faubus of Arkansas "stand up for states' rights" and force a showdown with the President by calling out the Arkansas National Guard on his own.

Senator Johnston, a former Governor of South Carolina, said if he were Governor Faubus, "I'd proclaim a state of insurrection down there, and I'd call out the National Guard, and I'd then find out who's going to run things in my state."

Asked by reporters whether he believed Governor Faubus would take such steps, Senator Johnston said, "I think he will and I hope he will."

Aiken Defends Move

Senator John L. McClellan, Democrat of Arkansas, said he believed such use of military force by the Federal Government was "without authority of law."

He said he was "very apprehensive that such action may precipitate more trouble than it will prevent."

Senator Richard B. Russell, Democrat of Georgia and leader of Southern opposition to the Civil Rights Bill in the last session, said that President Eisenhower's use of troops might "put Negro children in the white schools," but that it would "have a calamitous effect on race relations and on the cause of national unity."

On the other side of the issue, Senator George D. Aiken, Republican of Vermont, said the President "is undoubtedly with-

Continued on Page 17, Column 3

U. S. Cutters Conquer Northwest Passage

3 Coast Guard Craft First of the Nation to Make Transit

By JOHN H. FENTON
Special to The New York Times.

BOSTON, Sept. 24 — Two Coast Guard cutters were saluted in Boston Harbor today at the end of a successful mission to find a practical Northwest Passage—a route around the top of the North American Continent.

A third cutter, the Spar, proceeded directly to her home port at Bristol, R. I., to be welcomed there as the first United States vessel to circumnavigate the continent.

The cutters Storis, from Juneau, Alaska, and the Bramble, from Miami, Fla., put in here for their welcoming. They will continue their homeward voyages later in the week.

The three cutters were the first United States vessels to make the passage.

The shrill sirens of water-spouting fireboats and the deeper-throated whistles of other craft sounded a "well done" as the two bulky cutters made their way up the harbor.

Ranking Coast Guard officers and civil officials joined with members of families of the crews in a dockside welcome as the cutters tied up at

Continued on Page 10, Column 1

U. S. Coast Guard

Coast Guardsmen on the stern of the Spar view her sister cutters, Bramble, left, and Storis, during the transit of Simpson Strait. This was a difficult part of the voyage.

Rebel Chief Seized In Algiers Gunfight

By THOMAS F. BRADY
Special to The New York Times.

ALGIERS, Algeria, Sept. 24—The chief of the nationalist terrorist organization in Algiers was in the hands of French parachute troops today. The rebel leader, Saadi Yacef, 29 years old, had eluded capture in the crowded Casbah for more than two years.

With him was 24-year-old Miss Zorah Drif, an Algerian revolutionary, who was condemned to death in absentia by a French military tribunal.

A parachute colonel told reporters this evening that Mr. Yacef and Miss Drif had surrendered at 5:30 A. M. after the terrorist chief had wounded a lieutenant colonel and a master sergeant of a Foreign Legion parachute regiment. The colonel then took reporters to a hideout high in the Casbah where he described how the

Continued on Page 4, Column 3

Price Index Up .2%; Sets Another High

By RICHARD E. MOONEY
Special to The New York Times.

WASHINGTON, Sept. 24—The United States Consumers' Price Index rose two-tenths of a per cent in August, setting another record. It was the twelfth consecutive monthly increase, but among the smallest of the twelve.

The Labor Department's Bureau of Labor Statistics reported today that the index rose in August to 121, using the price average in the 1947-49 period as a comparison base of 100. All the major categories of prices increased, but food and housing were the strongest factors.

The August index was 3.6 per cent higher than that of a year earlier. This meant that a typical city family paid $1.03 3/5 in August of 1957 for the goods and services that cost $1 in August of 1956.

The Commerce Department

Continued on Page 24, Column 3

Textile Union Gets 30 Days to Reform

By A. H. RASKIN

A scandal-tainted textile union was ordered yesterday to oust its two chief officers within thirty days or face possible suspension from the merged labor federation.

The ultimatum was given to the 40,000-member United Textile Workers by the executive council of the American Federation of Labor and Congress of Industrial Organizations.

It foreshadowed the fixing of a similar clean-up deadline today for the 1,400,000-member International Brotherhood of Teamsters and the 140,000-member Bakery and Confectionery Workers International Union.

The federation's Ethical Practices Committee has found all three unions guilty of violating the anti-racketeering provisions of the A. F. L.-C. I. O. constitution. The findings were based

Continued on Page 13, Column 3

"All the News That's Fit to Print"

The New York Times.

LATE CITY EDITION
U. S. Weather Bureau Report (Page 33) forecasts: Cloudy and cool today and tonight. Mostly fair tomorrow.
Temp. range: 65—53. Yesterday: 62.4—49.2.

VOL. CVII..No. 36,414.

NEW YORK, SATURDAY, OCTOBER 5, 1957.

10c beyond 100-mile zone from New York City

FIVE CENTS

SOVIET FIRES EARTH SATELLITE INTO SPACE; IT IS CIRCLING THE GLOBE AT 18,000 M. P. H.; SPHERE TRACKED IN 4 CROSSINGS OVER U. S.

HOFFA IS ELECTED TEAMSTERS' HEAD; WARNS OF BATTLE

Defeats Two Foes 3 to 1 —Says Union Will Fight 'With Every Ounce'

Text of the Hoffa address is printed on Page 6.

By A. H. RASKIN
Special to The New York Times.

MIAMI BEACH, Oct. 4—The scandal-scarred International Brotherhood of Teamsters elected James R. Hoffa as its president today.

He won by a margin of nearly 3 to 1 over the combined vote of two rivals who campaigned on pledges to clean up the nation's biggest union.

Senate rackets investigators and Hoffa critics in the union rank-and-file immediately opened actions to strip the 44-year-old former warehouseman from Detroit of his election victory.

A jubilant Hoffa exhibited, however, greater concern over the possibility that his union might be ousted from the American Federation of Labor and Congress of Industrial Organizations. He appealed for time to prove that he could make the teamsters "a model of trade unionism."

The parent organization has ordered the 1,400,000-member Teamsters Union to get rid of corrupt leadership by Oct. 24 or face suspension. Hoffa said he felt actions by the union at its week-long convention here should satisfy the federation.

Warns Union Will Fight

He made it plain to the 1,700 cheering delegates that he did not intend to go before the convention in the role of suppliant. He said expulsion would not destroy the teamsters. He warned that the union would fight "with every ounce of strength we possess" if it found itself outside.

In such a civil war the teamsters would start with a war-chest of $38,000,000 in the hands of the international union and much more at the disposal of its locals. The teamsters also could count on their strategic power over other unions through their control of trucks and warehouses.

The Hoffa victory brought warnings of repressive legislation from James P. Mitchell, Secretary of Labor, and Senator John L. McClellan, Democrat of Arkansas. The Senator heads the Select Committee on Improper Activities in the Labor or Management Field, which has accused Hoffa of gangster associations and questionable financial practices.

Winner on First Ballot

A three-hour roll-call gave Hoffa the $50,000-a-year union presidency on the first ballot. His machine, in full command of the convention since it opened Monday, registered 1,208 votes for Hoffa.

William A. Lee of Chicago, the union's seventh vice president, was second with 313 votes. Thomas J. Haggerty of Chicago, secretary-treasurer of Milk Wagon Drivers Union, Local 753, trailed with 140 votes.

The Hoffa forces then began providing the new leader a rubber stamp board. It elected five of thirteen vice presidents and would have elected the rest today if time had permitted completion of the cumbersome balloting procedure.

Hoffa repeatedly indicated his irritation that some of the old vice presidents marked for elimination had refused to give up without the formality of a roll-call.

Even before the voting, the McClellan committee subpoenaed the full records of the convention's credentials committee. A United States marshal served the subpoena this morning on Joseph Konowe of New York, the committee secretary. He was directed to turn over all

Continued on Page 6, Column 7

Associated Press Wirephoto

IN TOKEN OF VICTORY: Dave Beck, retiring head of the Teamsters Union, raises hand of James R. Hoffa upon his election as union's president. At right is Mrs. Hoffa.

COURSE RECORDED

Navy Picks Up Radio Signals—4 Report Sighting Device

By WALTER SULLIVAN
Special to The New York Times

WASHINGTON, Saturday, Oct. 5—The Naval Research Laboratory announced early today that it had recorded four crossings of the Soviet earth satellite over the United States.

It said that one had passed near Washington. Two crossings were farther to the west. The location of the fourth was not made available immediately.

It added that tracking would be continued in an attempt to pin down the orbit sufficiently to obtain scientific information of the type sought in the International Geophysical Year.

[Four visual sightings, one of which was in conjunction with a radio contact, were reported by early Saturday morning. Two sightings were made at Columbus, Ohio, and one each from Terre Haute, Ind., and Whittier, Calif.]

Press Reports Noted

Soviet newspapers reported several weeks ago that the Soviet satellites would broadcast on frequencies in the neighborhood of twenty and forty megacycles. More exact frequencies were given by Soviet scientists at a conference on rockets and satellites that took place here this week.

Presumably the Naval Research Laboratory, which is responsible for the United States satellite program under the National Academy of Sciences, immediately set up receivers on those frequencies.

The tracking system established in this country to monitor its own satellites uses 108 megacycles, since much more accurate positions can be obtained with the higher frequencies. The Russians at first agreed to use equipment "compatible" with that of the United States, but then announced the lower frequencies.

Deception Ruled Out

American scientists believe this was because of a shortage of Soviet receivers capable of handling the higher frequency. It was not thought to be designed to hide the satellite since the Soviet signals are within easy reach of American listeners.

This was demonstrated last night as amateur and commercial radio stations, as well as the Naval Research Laboratory, reported hearing them.

Teams of visual observers at 150 stations in the United States and other Western nations were alerted during the

Continued on Page 3, Column 6

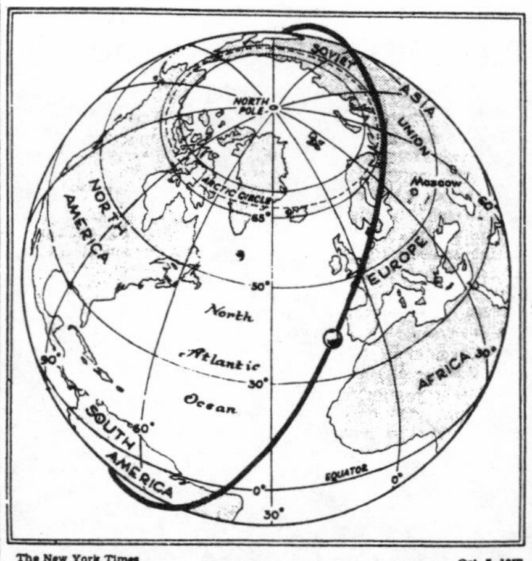

The New York Times — Oct. 5, 1957

The approximate orbit of the Russian earth satellite is shown by black line. The rotation of the earth will bring the United States under the orbit of Soviet-made moon.

560 MILES HIGH

Visible With Simple Binoculars, Moscow Statement Says

Text of Tass announcement appears on Page 3.

By WILLIAM J. JORDEN
Special to The New York Times.

MOSCOW, Saturday, Oct. 5—The Soviet Union announced this morning that it successfully launched a man-made earth satellite into space yesterday.

The Russians calculated the satellite's orbit at a maximum of 560 miles above the earth and its speed at 18,000 miles an hour.

The official Soviet news agency Tass said the artificial moon, with a diameter of twenty-two inches and a weight of 184 pounds, was circling the earth once every hour and thirty-five minutes. This means more than fifteen times a day.

Two radio transmitters, Tass said, are sending signals continuously on frequencies of 20.005 and 40.002 megacycles. These signals were said to be strong enough to be picked up by amateur radio operators. The trajectory of the satellite is being tracked by numerous scientific stations.

Due Over Moscow Today

Tass said the satellite was moving at an angle of 65 degrees to the equatorial plane and would pass over the Moscow area twice today.

"Its flight," the announcement added, "will be observed in the rays of the rising and setting sun with the aid of the simplest optical instruments, such as binoculars and spyglasses."

The Soviet Union said the world's first satellite was "successfully launched" yesterday. Thus it asserted that it had put a scientific instrument into space before the United States. Washington has disclosed plans to launch a satellite next spring. Oct. 4."

The Moscow announcement said the Soviet Union planned to send up more and bigger and heavier artificial satellites during the current International Geophysical Year, an eighteen-month period of study of the earth, its crust and the space surrounding it.

Five Miles a Second

The rocket that carried the satellite into space left the earth at a rate of five miles a second, the Tass announcement said. Nothing was revealed, however, concerning the material of which the man-made moon was constructed or the site in the Soviet Union where the sphere was launched.

The Soviet Union said its sphere circling the earth had opened the way to interplanetary travel.

It did not pass up the opportunity to use the launching for propaganda purposes. It said in its announcement that people now could see how "the new socialist society" had turned the boldest dreams of mankind into reality.

Moscow said the satellite was the result of years of study and research on the part of Soviet scientists.

Several Years of Study

Tass said:

"For several years the research and experimental designing work has been under way in the Soviet Union to create artificial satellites of the earth.

It has already been reported in the press that the launching of the earth satellites in the U. S. S. R. had been planned in accordance with the program of International Geophysical Year research.

"As a result of intensive work by the research institutes and design bureaus, the first artificial earth satellite in the world has now been created. This first satellite was successfully launched in the U. S. S. R. October four."

The Soviet announcement said that as a result of the tremendous speed at which the satellite was moving it would

Continued on Page 3, Column 5

Device Is 8 Times Heavier Than One Planned by U.S.

Special to The New York Times.

WASHINGTON, Oct. 4—Leaders of the United States earth satellite program were astonished tonight to learn that the Soviet Union had launched a satellite eight times heavier than that contemplated by this country.

Dr. Joseph Kaplan, chairman of the United States program for the International Geophysical Year, described the 184-pound weight as "fantastic." The heaviest American satellites are to weigh twenty-one and a half pounds.

The actual launching, nevertheless, did not take the American scientists by surprise. At the end of working sessions on the International Conference on Rockets and Satellites, which has been taking place here, some said they thought the pitching of a Soviet satellite into the sky was imminent.

The satellite must fly at a speed of about 18,000 miles an hour to counteract the force of gravity at an altitude of 560 miles. The initial announcement in Moscow did not make it clear whether or not the rocket that placed it in orbit was aimed north or south.

Its Direction in Doubt

This would determine whether or not the satellite's initial crossing of the United States was northbound or southbound. Since the earth rotates within the orbit the satellite should in one day traverse almost all nations of the world.

With an orbit inclined 65 degrees to the equator, its sweep would cover virtually the entire region between the Arctic circle and the Antarctic circle.

William A. Holaday, special assistant to the Secretary of Defense for guided missiles, said the launching was not evidence of Soviet technological superiority in missile and rocket developments.

Mr. Holaday noted that Project Vanguard, the United States satellite program, had been an "open" project as part of the International Geophysical year and there has been no

Continued on Page 3, Column 7

SATELLITE SIGNAL BROADCAST HERE

Impulse Carried on Radio and TV—First Reported by Long Island Station

By ROY SILVER

Radio signals from the first satellite launched yesterday by the Russians were broadcast to radio and television audiences here last night.

The first word that the signals had been received in this country was reported by RCA Communication, Inc. It said that its receiving station at Riverhead, L. I., had picked up what it believed to be impulse signals from the Soviet satellite.

The National Broadcasting Company and the Columbia Broadcasting System broke into their radio and television programs to enable their audiences to hear the pinging sound of the "moon's" signal. The British Broadcasting Corporation in London said it had tuned powerful receivers to the Soviet earth satellite frequencies. Reuter's radio station north of London reported hearing the signals.

RCA Communications, a subsidiary of Radio Corporation of America, said the first signal had been received at 8:07 P. M. on a frequency of 20.005 megacycles on the 15-meter wave length.

One hour and twenty-nine minutes later, at 9:36 P. M., the receiving station, situated about eighty miles from the city, reported that the satellite was making another round of the earth. Other approaches by

Continued on Page 2, Column 4

FAUBUS COMPARES HIS STAND TO LEE'S

Says He Will Remain Loyal to People of Arkansas—All Is Quiet at School

By HOMER BIGART
Special to The New York Times.

LITTLE ROCK, Ark., Oct. 4—Gov. Orval E. Faubus said today that he had made a decision as painfully difficult as the one that had confronted Robert E. Lee at the outset of the Civil War.

"Lee was offered command of the Federal Army in 1861," Governor Faubus recalled. "Lee decided to remain loyal to the people of his state.

"The Democratic party of the North wants me to go along with them on the integration issue. I will remain with the people of Arkansas."

Governor Faubus said he had come under no local pressure to change his stand on integration at Little Rock Central High School. It was a stand that forced President Eisenhower to send Federal troops into this city to uphold Federal Court decisions and to safeguard the nine Negro students registered at Central High.

Winthrop Rockefeller, chairman of the Arkansas Industrial Development Commission, broke silence today on the Little Rock integration crisis, declaring it had "damaged" the state's prospects for economic progress. He called events of the past month "tragic."

It was a quiet day in Little Rock. The nine Negro boys and girls attended school without incident. But no early solution to the crisis seemed likely.

There was no break in the impasse reached Tuesday night when a compromise plan for the

Continued on Page 18, Column 2

Flu Widens in City; 10% Rate Predicted; 200,000 Pupils Out

By ROBERT ALDEN

Asian influenza continued to spread through the city yesterday.

Commissioner of Hospitals Morris A. Jacobs reported that there were ten times more respiratory infections than during the comparable period a year ago.

Attendance in the city's schools fell again. The Board of Education said that close to 200,000 of the city's 941,000 pupils were not in their classrooms yesterday. On Thursday 160,000 pupils were absent.

The attendance estimates were based on a sampling of the schools by the board. The sampling showed that in some schools in the Harlem area—the section hardest hit by the epidemic—more than 50 per cent of the pupils were absent. The board estimated that the over-all city absence rate was 20 per cent.

3,000 Teachers Absent

About 3,000 teachers out of about 39,000 were not in their classrooms yesterday, compared with 2,700 absent on Thursday.

The city's acting Health Commissioner, Dr. Roscoe P. Kandle, said he expected that the total number of people affected by the highly infectious disease would run closer to 800,000 rather than 1,600,000 as predicted in some quarters.

It was estimated Thursday that 200,000 persons in New York had contracted the respiratory infection, and the total yesterday was believed to be somewhat higher.

Commissioner Kandle explained that any attempt to project the ultimate number of cases would involve conjecture

Continued on Page 8, Column 1

ARGENTINA TAKES EMERGENCY STEPS

State of Siege Proclaimed in Buenos Aires Region —Arrests Reported

By Reuters.

BUENOS AIRES, Oct. 4—A state of siege, suspending constitutional guarantees, was proclaimed tonight in Buenos Aires city and Province.

The Under Secretary of the Ministry of Interior, Garcia Puente, announced the state of siege at a news conference.

He said the emergency move suspended for thirty days the constitutional guarantees in the capital and the Province of Buenos Aires, but not in the remainder of the nation.

He said the measure was aimed exclusively "at defending the normal development of the Government's political plan, jeopardized through sabotage and social unrest."

The proclamation of the state of siege followed the arrest of scores of labor leaders during the day. The number arrested was estimated by observers as 100 to 300.

Bankers, telephone workers, oilworkers, seamstresses and other unions reported tonight that their leaders had been detained and were taken aboard

Continued on Page 4, Column 5

Ex-Premier Mollet Accepts Bid To Form a New French Cabinet

Socialist Leader Agrees With Reluctance and Without Giving Much Hope

By ROBERT C. DOTY
Special to The New York Times.

PARIS, Oct. 4—Former Premier Guy Mollet agreed reluctantly and without much hope today to try to form a new French Cabinet.

M. Mollet's pessimism, shared by many observers here, was based on the fact that both he and his party, the Socialists, still hold strongly to the policies that caused the defeat of the last two Cabinets, M. Mollet's own and that of Premier Maurice Bourgès-Maunoury, a Radical.

Thus the Socialists still support the views on economic and social questions, including the demand for extensive governmental decree powers in those domains, that brought M. Mollet's Government down last May after a record-breaking sixty-eight weeks in office. The average Cabinet's life span has been twenty-nine weeks.

At the same time the Socialists regard as a minimum of reform the program for limited

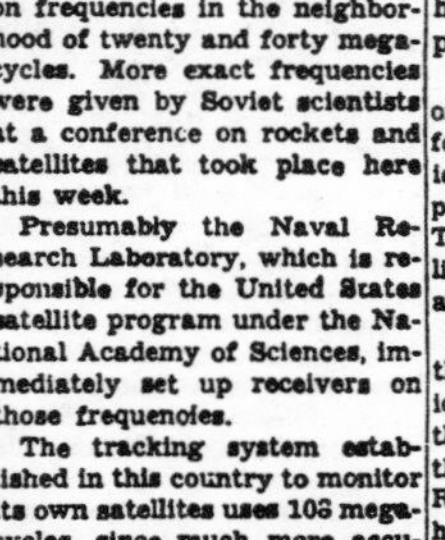

Associated Press

Guy Mollet

Algerian home rule outlined in the framework law that was defeated in the Assembly Monday.

In both cases, opposition from the Right-wing Independents constituted the margin of defeat.

If M. Mollet should find it impossible to muster a new major-

Continued on Page 5, Column 4

City Sifts Charge That Schupler, Brooklyn Councilman, Sold a Job

By PAUL CROWELL

The city is investigating a complaint that Councilman Philip J. Schupler accepted a $500 fee last year in exchange for a promise to get a job for a Brooklyn business man.

William R. Peer, executive secretary to Mayor Wagner, said yesterday that the inquiry was started several weeks ago after the complaint had been made by Sol L. Hoffman of 1934 Sixty-third Street, Brooklyn.

At the office of Investigation Commissioner Charles H. Tenney, who is making the investigation, it was said that no findings or conclusions had been reached.

The charge was denied by Mr. Schupler, a Democrat-Liberal, in a telephone interview. He said that he had received a $500 check from Mr. Hoffman in May, 1956, but that it was given to him as a campaign contribution. Mr. Schupler was then a candidate for re-election as a Democratic district leader. He was defeated in the primary election a month later.

Disclosure of the investigation brought from Robert K. Christenberry, the Republican candidate for Mayor, the charge that "corruption and scandal in our City Council is symptomatic of the Wagner administration."

In a formal statement commenting on the Schupler case Mr. Christenberry called upon the city's voters to support his

Continued on Page 15, Column 3

Warsaw Crushes New Protest; Clubs, Tear Gas Rout Students

By SYDNEY GRUSON
Special to The New York Times.

WARSAW, Oct. 4—Policemen and students clashed again in the streets of Warsaw tonight.

Security chiefs, seemingly nervous, threw a guard of several hundred workers' militia around the downtown headquarters of the ruling United Workers (Communist) party.

For the second successive night the police broke up demonstrations by firing tear gas and beating students and others with rubber truncheons.

What began last night as a protest against the closing of one newspaper was turning tonight into a general clamor against police brutality and the suppression of free speech. By midnight the city had calmed down and the people had left the streets.

Among those clubbed tonight was Franco Fabiani, permanent correspondent here of the Italian Communist paper L'Unità. He suffered two minor head wounds.

Signor Fabiani was caught in crowds charged by the police after about 3,000 students had met in the Polytechnic and adopted a resolution protesting both the closing of the newspaper Po Prostu and the "brutal interference" of the police at last night's meeting.

Tonight's trouble centered on the Polytechnic, the huge advanced technical school near the heart of Warsaw. It was

Continued on Page 5, Column 2

"All the News That's Fit to Print"

The New York Times.

LATE CITY EDITION
U.S. Weather Bureau Report (Page 95) forecast: Rain early today; cloudy later; rain late tonight and tomorrow. Temp. range: 65—55. Yesterday: 62.0—55.2.

NEWS SUMMARY AND INDEX, PAGE 95 — SECTION ONE

VOL. CVII—No. 36,443. — NEW YORK, SUNDAY, NOVEMBER 3, 1957. — 35c beyond 100-mile zone from New York City — TWENTY-FIVE CENTS

SOVIET FIRES NEW SATELLITE, CARRYING DOG; HALF-TON SPHERE IS REPORTED 900 MILES UP

Zhukov Ousted From Party Jobs; Konev Condemns Him

ORBIT COMPLETED

Animal Still Is Alive, Sealed in Satellite, Moscow Thinks

By The Associated Press.

LONDON, Sunday, Nov. 3—The Soviet Union announced today it had launched a second space satellite—this one carrying a dog. Radio signals indicated that the animal was living, the Russians said.

A satellite six times as heavy as the one sent up Oct. 4 now is circling the earth every hour and forty-two minutes at a height of 937 miles, Moscow said. This means that the speed is nearly 18,000 miles an hour for the 1,110-pound satellite.

The dog was reported hermetically sealed in a container equipped with an air-conditioning system.

Moscow Radio said data received from the second satellite indicated the "functioning of scientific instruments and control of the living activities of the animal are taking place normally."

First Trip Reported

The new satellite carries transmitting equipment and apparatus for measuring cosmic rays, temperature and pressure. It also carries equipment for reporting the condition of the dog.

It first passed over the Soviet capital at 11:20 P. M. Eastern Standard Time last night and then completed its first trip around the earth over Moscow at 1:05 A. M. today, the Soviet Union reported.

The announcement said the second satellite was "dedicated to the fortieth anniversary of the great October revolution," which the Communist world will celebrate in Moscow beginning next Thursday.

The new earth satellite is completing its orbit in about seven minutes more than the original Sputnik, still circling the earth.

Japan Receives Signals

Moscow said the second sphere was sending out two radio signals.

One, like the "beep" signal transmitted by the first satellite, is on a frequency of 20.005 megacycles. The other signal, at 40.002 megacycles, is a continuous note.

In Tokyo the Japan Broadcasting Corporation announced that radio signals from the second satellite were being heard.

The corporation picked up the signals twenty-three minutes after Moscow's announcement. The "beep" was at intervals of three-tenths of a second.

A three-stage rocket shoved the original satellite into its orbit. The first Moscow announcement of the second sphere did not explain how it had been sent up.

Although the announcement of the satellite's passing over Moscow indicated an interval of one hour and forty-five min-

Continued on Page 26, Column 2

SATELLITE SIGNAL RECEIVED AT M.I.T.

Scientists Believe That Orbit Repeats First Sphere—Trackers Are Alerted

By The United Press.

CAMBRIDGE, Mass., Sunday, Nov. 3—The first American pick-up of the new Soviet satellite's radio signal was reported early today to the Smithsonian Astrophysical Observatory.

Leon Campbell at the observatory said that the report was received from William S. Cooper of the Massachusetts Institute of Technology. Mr. Cooper said that he heard the signal at 2:02 A. M., between 20 and 20.5 megacycles.

Dr. J. Allen Hynek of the observatory staff said that the satellite apparently was in roughly the same path of 65 degrees as the first Soviet satellite.

The perigee (minimum altitude) probably is about 140 miles, the same as the first satellite, Dr. Hynek said. "It seems like a repetition of the orbit of the first satellite," he added.

The Soviet launching of the

Continued on Page 26, Column 4

ZHUKOV HUMBLED

He Admits 'Mistakes' —Accused of 'Cult' in Armed Forces

Text of Soviet communiqué is printed on Page 4.

By WILLIAM J. JORDEN
Special to The New York Times.

MOSCOW, Sunday, Nov. 3—Marshal Georgi K. Zhukov, dismissed a week ago as Defense Minister of the Soviet Union, has been removed from all his top posts in the Soviet Communist party.

The party's Central Committee announced last night that Marshal Zhukov had lost his place on the party's central policy-making group, the Presidium, as well as on the Central Committee itself. The principal charge against the hero of World War II was that he had tried to eliminate the Communist party's direction and control of the Soviet armed forces.

The Communist party newspaper Pravda reported this morning that Marshal Zhukov had admitted his "mistakes" during the Central Committee meeting at which he was expelled from the party leadership.

Anti-Stalin Phrase Used

He tempered that acceptance somewhat by telling his party comrades that he accepted their criticism of him as being "in the main correct." He also was said to have accepted the attack on his leadership of the armed forces as being of "comradely party assistance to me personally and to other military workers."

The barrel-chested, square-jawed soldier was charged with promoting his own "cult of personality" in the army. This is the phrase used here in reference to Stalin's one-man rule, which was vigorously condemned by the Twentieth Congress of the Communist party last year.

"With the help of sycophants and flatterers," the Central Committee said, "he was praised to the sky in lectures and reports, in articles, films and pamphlets, and his person and role in the Great Patriotic War [World War II] were overglorified."

The result, the Central Committee charged, was that the whole history of the war had been "distorted." It said that by building himself up Marshal Zhukov had belittled the efforts of the Soviet people, of the

Continued on Page 3, Column 1

Marshal Is Linked to Stalin In Blame for '41 Reverses

Konev Charges Ex-Chief Distorted History to Create Hero's Role

Special to The New York Times.

MOSCOW, Sunday, Nov. 3—Marshal Ivan S. Konev, long companion and subordinate of Marshal Georgi K. Zhukov, condemned the former Defense Minister today for "errors in military science."

Marshal Konev's attack was the first derogatory statement leveled against Marshal Zhukov on military grounds.

Soviet commander of the Warsaw Pact forces, Marshal Konev issued his condemnation in an article in today's Pravda, the Communist party organ.

The Konev article said that Marshal Zhukov was responsible along with Stalin for lack of preparedness in the Soviet Union to meet the imminent German attack in June, 1941. It belittled Marshal Zhukov's role in the victories at Stalingrad and Berlin and accused Marshal Zhukov of undue pride and of twisting historical fact.

Associated Press

Marshal Ivan S. Konev

Marshal Konev's attack on Marshal Zhukov was bitter and extensive. Marshal Konev noted that his former comrade in

Continued on Page 3, Column 4

SOVIET 'STRESSES' SEEN BY THE U.S.

Washington Expects Strain Behind the Iron Curtain From Zhukov Disgrace

State Department statement will be found on Page 6.

By RUSSELL BAKER
Special to The New York Times.

WASHINGTON, Nov. 2—The State Department said tonight that the downgrading of Marshal Georgi K. Zhukov showed the "strains and stresses" present in the Soviet Union and the countries dominated by the Soviet Communists.

In a brief formal statement, the department noted that Marshal Zhukov's "disgrace" followed only by a short time the expressed desire of Nikita S. Khrushchev, First Secretary of the Soviet Communist party, to send the military leader on a special mission to the United States.

The department said this, following so closely "similar action against" other one-time Soviet leaders, demonstrated the polit-

Continued on Page 7, Column 1

MEYNER'S VICTORY IS SEEN IN SURVEY OF JERSEY VOTERS

Democratic Governor Likely to Win Re-election Over Senator Forbes Tuesday

A Times Team Report

A team of New York Times reporters has just completed a survey of political trends and issues in New Jersey. Reports on the election campaign there come from George Cable Wright, Milton Honig, Alfred E. Clark, Leonard Buder, John W. Slocum and Layhmond Robinson.

By GEORGE CABLE WRIGHT

The curtain will descend tomorrow night on the New Jersey Governorship campaign. The contest—on the surface, at least — appears to have been enacted before a relatively bored audience.

Neither Gov. Robert B. Meyner, the Democratic incumbent, nor State Senator Malcolm S. Forbes, the Republican candidate, has exhibited the ability to rouse the voting public markedly from its apparent apathy.

Beyond the Hudson and the Delaware, however, far greater interest is being manifested in the contest.

The Eisenhower Administration has staked its prestige on the results of the balloting as never before in a state-wide race. Republicans and Democrats alike at the national level are eagerly awaiting the vote tally. Each party hopes to gain from it a trend in its favor.

Surprise Possible

The apparent lack of interest locally may well be misleading. It is not an uncommon trait of the state's electorate, as witness 1953, 1954 and 1956. In those years, the pre-election temper turned out to be a "sleeper." The voters, from Cape May to High Point, set their alarms for election morn and flocked to the polls.

As the present campaign progressed, it became increasingly evident that, in all probability, it would be decided on the basis of personality rather than on issues. This was verified by a team of New York Times reporters in the field.

On the basis of findings of The Times' survey team, victory for Mr. Meyner is definitely in-

Continued on Page 60, Column 6

President and Class Honor Academy

The New York Times (by Arthur Brower)

The President drinks from fountain he and other members of 1915 class gave to academy. Mrs. Eisenhower watches.

By W. H. LAWRENCE
Special to The New York Times.

WEST POINT, N. Y., Nov. 2 — President Eisenhower watched Army defeat Colgate today as the climax to a nostalgic reunion with his 1915 Military Academy classmates. Like any other old grad, the President leaped to his feet and cheered whenever Army threatened or scored—and he had many opportunities this afternoon as the West Point

Continued on Page 45, Column 1

A.F.L.-C.I.O. TARGET RESIGNS AS CHIEF OF TEXTILE UNION

Valente Voices Hope Group Will Stay in Federation —2 More Actions Taken

Special to The New York Times.

WASHINGTON, Nov. 2—The president of the United Textile Workers, Anthony Valente, resigned today. He said he was acting to help his union retain its membership in the American Federation of Labor and Congress of Industrial Organizations.

The 44,000-member union was one of three cited for corruption last month by the executive council of the parent labor organization. Mr. Valente was declared ineligible to hold office.

Tonight, the leadership of the union accepted the resignation of Mr. Valente and announced other steps to conform with demands by the A. F. L.-C. I. O. to "clean up" the textile workers operations.

Francis Schaufenbil, secretary-treasurer of the union, told reporters at the end of an all-day meeting of the organization's executive board that "we certainly hope" the actions taken would keep the textile workers in the parent body.

2 Other Measures

The board meeting was called today to answer charges brought by the A. F. L. C. I. O. council.

In addition to accepting Mr. Valente's resignation, the board took these two actions to comply with the council's demands:

1. It agreed to call a special convention "as soon as possible" to elect new officers. The session will be in Washington, New York or Philadelphia.
2. The board "rescinded" a $104,000 severance pay deal for Lloyd Klenert, resigned secretary-treasurer, and "has not obligated" the union on any financial arrangement with any other resigned officers. This was, presumably, a reference to Mr. Valente. Senate investigators have accused Mr. Valente and Mr. Klenert of buying their homes with union funds and using devious bookkeeping to cover their tracks.

Criticizes Members of Council

Mr. Valente resigned at a meeting of the Textile Workers Executive Board, called to answer the council's charges. Talking with reporters during a recess, he loosed bitter criticism against twelve of the twenty-nine members of the A. F. L.-C. I. O. council.

He said the twelve had pledged him their support, but "they reneged on their commitments." He did not name the twelve.

This development in the labor

Continued on Page 44, Column 3

DEMOCRATS COUNT ON PARTY VICTORY

Believe Wagner Can Win Without Liberal Votes in Mayoral Race

By LEO EGAN

Democratic leaders were counting confidently yesterday on obtaining enough votes on their party's line alone to insure the re-election of Mayor Wagner and his running mates next Tuesday. If they can do so it will be the first time since 1932 that a Democrat has received a majority of all the votes in a New York City Mayoral election.

Four years ago Mr. Wagner won by virtue of a split in the opposition between Harold Riegelman, Republican, and Rudolph Halley, Liberal and independent. Mr. Wagner received just over 45 per cent of the total vote cast.

This year the Liberal party is backing Mayor Wagner and his two city-wide running mates, Controller Lawrence E. Gerosa and City Council President Abe Stark. But Democratic leaders would like to be able to say they could have won without the Liberal endorsement.

Alex Rose, state vice chairman and spokesman for the Liberal party, referred to this Democratic attitude yesterday in appealing for a large Wagner-Gerosa-Stark vote on the Liberal party line.

"A large vote on the Liberal line is a vote with a special message to the city administration to be independent and is the best guarantee for a clean and effective administration on all levels of city government," he said.

"A large vote on the Liberal line will continue the Liberal party as the political conscience

Continued on Page 58, Column 2

Voters Will Settle 7 State Questions; Issues Are Listed

Special to The New York Times.

ALBANY, Nov. 2—Voters who go to the polls on Tuesday will have a chance to pass on six proposed amendments to the State Constitution and whether a constitutional convention should be held.

If performance runs true, only about half those voting will bother to answer the seven questions across the top of every ballot.

The type on the ballot is small and the questions do not always express in the limited space the impact of the proposition.

Following is a description of each proposal, what it would do and the arguments for and against it:

The ballot asks:

"Shall there be a convention to revise the Constitution and amend the same?"

Approval would mean the voters would elect delegates on a party basis in 1958 and those elected would hold a convention the following year, probably in the summer. The convention

Continued on Page 62, Column 4

Major Sports News

FOOTBALL

Navy beat Notre Dame in the nation's top college contest yesterday. Scores of leading games:

Alabama	14	Georgia	13
Amherst	19	Tufts	6
Army	53	Colgate	7
Auburn	13	Florida	0
Cornell	8	Columbia	0
Dartmouth	14	Yale	14
Delaware	23	Rutgers	19
Georgia T.	13	Duke	0
Harvard	13	Penn	6
Iowa	21	Michigan	21
Michigan St.	21	Wisconsin	7
Minnesota	34	Indiana	0
Missouri	9	Colorado	6
Navy	20	Notre Dame	6
N. C. State	19	Wake Forest	0
Ohio State	47	Northwestern	6
Oklahoma	13	Kansas St.	0
Oregon	27	Stanford	26
Oregon St.	39	Wash. St.	25
Penn St.	27	W. Virginia	6
Princeton	7	Brown	0
Purdue	21	Illinois	6
Syracuse	24	Pittsburgh	21
T. C. U.	19	Baylor	6
Tennessee	35	N. Carolina	0
Texas A.&M.	7	Arkansas	6
Vanderbilt	7	L. S. U.	0

HORSE RACING

Eddie Schmidt won the $86,900 Gallant Fox Handicap at Jamaica by half a length. Bold Ruler was first in the Benjamin Franklin Handicap.

HOCKEY

The Rangers routed the Boston Bruins, 5—0.

Details in Section 5.

This section consists of 136 pages divided into three parts. The news summary and the index will be found on Page 95. Society news begins on Page 90 and obituary articles will be found on Pages 88 and 89.

British and French, a Year After, Say Suez Invasion Was Justified

London Reconciled

By DREW MIDDLETON
Special to The New York Times.

LONDON, Nov. 2—In the view of some of those who planned the British-French invasion of Egypt, the situation obtaining in the Middle East a year later justifies that attempt to halt the march of Arab nationalism and its ally, Soviet communism, in the area.

A year ago the Soviet Union had one client and ally in the Middle East, Egypt. Today it has two, Egypt and Syria. The withdrawal of the British and French forces from Suez at the behest of the United Nations has been interpreted by Arab nationalism as a victory and has created a power vacuum into which Soviet imperialism has moved, it is noted.

The view that the invasion

Continued on Page 33, Column 3

Paris Still Bitter

By ROBERT C. DOTY
Special to The New York Times.

PARIS, Nov. 2—The week-end of the first anniversary of the British-French invasion of Egypt finds most Frenchmen, including those who planned the action, convinced that it was a good idea.

There is no tendency here to push such an idea aggressively. On the contrary, French high officialdom seeks to liquidate as speedily and unobtrusively as possible the remaining economic, political and diplomatic consequences of last fall's events. This is regarded as the logical prerequisite to a restoration of complete interallied confidence and effective action to repair the Western position in the Middle East.

Furthermore, the French-

Continued on Page 33, Column 1

Associated Press Radiophoto

CHINESE COMMUNIST LEADER GREETED IN MOSCOW: Mao Tse-tung, left, the chief of state and Communist party chief, as he arrived yesterday at the capital airport. Welcoming him were Nikita S. Khrushchev, center, Soviet Communist chief, and Premier Nikolai A. Bulganin. Mr. Mao will take part in commemorating the Bolshevik Revolution.

Mao Is in Moscow; He Hails Soviet Tie

By MAX FRANKEL
Special to The New York Times.

MOSCOW, Nov. 2—Mao Tse-tung, leader of Communist China, arrived in Moscow today. He is probably the most important of the gathering here to show the unity and might of international communism.

Virtually all the reigning heads of Communist nations and parties, with the notable exception of President Tito of Yugoslavia, will make the pilgrimage here to join in next week's celebrations of the fortieth anniversary of the Bolshevik Revolution.

Expected in addition to Mr. Mao, who is the Chinese Communist chief of state and party chairman, are Poland's party leader, Wladyslaw Gomulka, and Premier Jozef Cyrankiewicz; Premier Janos Kadar of Hun

Continued on Page 27, Column 5

"All the News That's Fit to Print"

The New York Times.

LATE CITY EDITION
U. S. Weather Bureau Report (Page 45) forecasts: Fair, breezy, less humid today; clear and cool tonight. Fair tomorrow.
Temp. range: 78—60. Yesterday: 79.3—64.8.

VOL. CVII..No. 36,654. © 1958, by The New York Times Company. Times Square, New York 36, N. Y. NEW YORK, MONDAY, JUNE 2, 1958. 10c beyond 100-mile zone from New York City. Higher in air delivery cities. FIVE CENTS

DE GAULLE NAMED PREMIER IN 329-224 VOTE; ASKS 6-MONTH DECREE RULE; LEFTISTS RIOT; ALGIERS IS DISPLEASED BY CABINET CHOICES

CRASHES KILL 344 ON 3-DAY HOLIDAY; RAIN CURBS TOLL

Auto Deaths Below Forecast —Temperature Climbs to 79.3 Degrees Here

By LAWRENCE O'KANE

Traffic fatalities climbed yesterday in the final, homebound hours of the Memorial Day week-end.

Bad weather over much of the nation dampened the outing spirits of many. But it also induced motorists to drive carefully.

By 2 A. M. today 344 persons had died in traffic accidents since 6 P. M. Thursday, according to The Associated Press. Altogether there were 554 accident deaths, including 122 drownings and eight-eight from miscellaneous causes.

In New York City, three persons were killed and 556 injured in 387 road accidents, according to Police Department figures covering the period from 8 A. M. Thursday to 4 P. M. yesterday. Only property was damaged in 487 other accidents.

Cautious Optimism

Late yesterday the National Safety Council began to express cautious optimism that traffic deaths would not exceed the peak three-day Memorial Day week-end toll of 369 recorded in 1955.

Last week the council had predicted 350 deaths for the 1958 holiday week-end, but after a series of multi-death accidents Saturday it began to voice fears of a new record.

The council said rain and slippery highways had restricted short-distance travel as picnics and beach outings were canceled. Showers and thunderstorms were reported yesterday from the Gulf states to southern New England. Squalls ranged the Great Lakes and tornado alerts were issued for parts of the South and Midwest.

Rain Avoids City

In New York City, the warmest day of the year sent hundreds of thousands to beaches and parks. Afternoon rains had been predicted, but failed to materialize. The threat kept crowds from swelling to record proportions, however, and chilly offshore winds kept most beachgoers out of the water.

The year's highest temperature here—79.3 degrees—was registered at 4:20 P. M.

Today is expected to be fair, but not as warm or humid as yesterday. Afternoon temperatures are expected to be in the 70's. The forecast for Tuesday is fair with pleasant temperatures and low humidity.

As yesterday drew to a close, city-bound traffic increased on highways and bridges and in tunnels. Most reports described the flow as heavy, but moving freely.

A 22-year-old airman was injured fatally early yesterday when his automobile struck a

Continued on Page 18, Column 2

Ernst Report on Galindez Clears Dominican Dictator

Inquiry for Trujillo Hints That Missing Columbia Scholar May Be Alive—Anti-Franco Activities Cited

By PETER KIHSS

Morris L. Ernst has filed a report in effect clearing Generalissimo Rafael L. Trujillo and his Dominican dictatorship of any role in the two-year-old disappearance here of Jesús de Galindez, a Basque scholar.

The New York lawyer's report, made after a ten-month investigation for the Dominican Republic, implied that the anti-Trujillo writer might be alive. It suggested that Dr. Galindez' disappearance March 12, 1956, might be related "to his substantial and perhaps carefully confused fiscal operations and his profound interest in Spain after Franco."

Dr. Galindez, a Spanish exile, had reported to the Department of Justice a total of $1,024,-418.24 in contributions he raised as agent for the anti-Franco Basque Government-in-exile from May, 1949, through January, 1956.

The Ernst report also rejected a theory that Gerald Lester Murphy, an American pilot who vanished in the Dominican Republic Dec. 3, 1956, might have flown Mr. Galindez to that country as a kidnap victim.

Mr. Ernst asserted that the Cuban Government had "reliable reports" that Mr. Murphy landed his plane in Cuba on March 13, 1956—before setting it down later that day in Miami.

The lawyer charged that Mr. Murphy had been "engaged in an illegal operation for hire." He recalled the pilot's reputed statements that he had flown arms and funds to Cuba for opponents of Cuban President Fulgencio Batista.

While formal comment by Government investigators in the United States was unavailable,

Continued on Page 14, Column 4

Hospital Deficits Increase With Advance in Medicine

By EMMA HARRISON

Voluntary hospitals in the New York area reported an operating loss of $23,500,000 for 1957, the United Hospital Fund disclosed yesterday. This is an increase of $3,550,000 over the 1956 figure of $19,950,000.

The operating loss for the seventy-four voluntary hospitals and convalescent homes is exclusive of the hospitals' receipts from philanthropic support and income from investment. But the figure also excludes hospital depreciation, interest on indebtedness and money spent on research and medical education, the fund noted.

The fund estimated the hospitals' net loss after all income at $6,000,000. This estimate includes an allowance of 5 per cent for plant depreciation.

However, operating income, including revenue from patients and from auxiliary activities such as nursing schools and cafeterias, went up 6.8 per cent to $176,000,000. Operating costs, meanwhile, climbed 8 per cent to $199,500,000.

Thus, with operating costs increasing partly because of better care for patients, the voluntary hospitals are faced with a paradox: The patients

Continued on Page 20, Column 2

187 MILLION URGED FOR CITY SCHOOLS

73 Projects Are Planned Over Three Budgets to House 74,740 Pupils

By GENE CURRIVAN

An extraordinary capital budget estimate of $187,600,000 for the city's school building program was announced yesterday. It would require financing in three successive budgets.

It includes seventy-three projects with an enrollment capacity of 74,740 pupils.

The proposed budget for next year is $108,200,000 for thirty-one projects.

Last year the Board of Education asked for $106,800,000 and received a little less than $96,000,000.

This year's unusual proposal was put forth by the Committee on Building and Sites headed by Charles J. Bensley. It may be predicated on the hope that a constitutional amendment giving the city the right to borrow $500,000,000 for spending on buildings will eventually be adopted. The amendment has been approved by the Legislature but must be reapproved at the next session and then sub-

Continued on Page 19, Column 4

JUNTA AIDE BITTER

'Not the Government We Hoped For,' Civil Leader Declares

By THOMAS F. BRADY
Special to The New York Times.

ALGIERS, June 1 — Léon Delbecque, vice president of the All-Algerian Committee of Public Safety, said tonight that the de Gaulle Cabinet was "not yet the Government of Public Safety we hoped for."

Looking at the list of ministers of Premier Charles de Gaulle, he said to reporters: "You call that a Government? Who is Minister of the Interior? A civil servant. Who is Minister of Foreign Affairs? A civil servant."

Emile Pelletier, the new Interior Minister, is a former Prefect. Maurice Couve de Murville, the Foreign Minister, is a career diplomat. Both are considered non-political "technicians."

Moderation Is Target

M. Delbecque was expressing the bitter disappointment that is felt among civilian insurgent leaders here at the liberal moderation shown thus far in General de Gaulle's assumption of power. No one associated with the Public Safety movement appears on the Cabinet list.

Although M. Delbecque did not appear to approve of career civil servants in the Cabinet, he expressed his confidence in Premier de Gaulle and said he regarded the Cabinet as a step toward the ultimate goal.

M. Delbecque denied a report that he had written Premier de Gaulle protesting against the make-up of the new Cabinet. The Algerian leader said he had written to the general every day for the last three days but did not indicate the contents except to say that he had informed General de Gaulle of the situation in Algeria. M. Delbecque added that he had not received any response.

Salan Aide Sees Victory

Col. Charles Lacheroy, spokesman for Gen. Raoul Salan, military ruler of Algeria, hailed General de Gaulle's assumption of power as a victory.

But outside the Government General Building, scene of regular mass demonstrations since the civil-military insurrection May 13, there was only a scattering of persons and no sign of rejoicing.

Asked why there was no celebration, Lucien Neuwirth, official spokesman for the Public Safety Committee, said: "Today is Sunday. People are at home." Last Sunday, however, the peo-

Continued on Page 3, Column 1

Associated Press Radiophoto

DE GAULLE STATES HIS TERMS: The general speaking in Paris yesterday to the French National Assembly before it approved the wartime leader as the nation's Premier.

U. S. IS 'GRATIFIED' AT FRENCH ACTION

White House Gives de Gaulle Warm Welcome—Capital Hopes He Can Visit Soon

By DANA ADAMS SCHMIDT
Special to The New York Times.

WASHINGTON, June 1—The White House welcomed Gen. Charles de Gaulle as Premier of France today in a warmly worded statement issued only two hours after the news of his investiture had reached Washington.

Administration officials said unofficially that they would be glad to see General de Gaulle visit the United States soon.

They said they assumed, however, that he would be too preoccupied with French internal affairs during his first six months to make such a trip unless it were required to prepare for a summit meeting with the Soviet Union.

The White House statement was issued from Gettysburg, where President Eisenhower is spending the week-end. It read as follows:

"We have been witnessing with sympathy and understanding the difficult days through which France has been passing, and we are gratified that the French crisis is now being resolved.

"General de Gaulle has assumed heavy responsibilities at a critical juncture in French history. Our thoughts go out to the great French nation, wish-

Continued on Page 6, Column 6

Red-Led Demonstrators Clash With Paris Police

By W. GRANGER BLAIR
Special to The New York Times.

PARIS, June 1—Communist-inspired riots erupted in Paris today a few hours before the National Assembly voted to install Gen. Charles de Gaulle as Premier. The outbreaks started at 3 P. M. in working-class quarters in northern, eastern and southern section of the city.

At almost the same moment the general rose to deliver his investiture speech in a jammed and tense Parliament ringed by armed security guards.

For the next three hours thousands of policemen, crowded into heavy vans, rushed to trouble spots to clash with about 10,000 demonstrators.

Many persons were injured—"several dozen," according to the police. The injured included twenty-five members of the security force. The police arrested 190 rioters.

Crowds Arrive From Suburbs

Besides Leftists ready for action in town, the mobs were replenished by Leftists from industrial suburbs. Even before they arrived, the police descended on key train, bus and subway exits to intercept them.

The first clash between security forces and rioters came in northern Paris near the Porte de Clignancourt. Several hundred demonstrators tried to force their way south toward the center of the city through four vanloads of policemen.

Both sides struck out with clubs. After fifteen minutes of confused fighting, the Leftists retreated northward.

These rioters, like their fellows elsewhere in the city, car-

Continued on Page 5, Column 1

DE GAULLE SHUNS ASSEMBLY DEBATE

Strides Out After He Makes Brief Statement — Anger and Fear Mark Session

By HENRY GINIGER
Special to The New York Times

PARIS, June 1—In anger, defiance, fear and resignation, the National Assembly held today one of the last sessions of France's present parliamentary Government.

The French Republic may go on—many Deputies fear its end—but it will not be the same one that France has known since it began functioning in 1947.

This was the consensus of those who were able to fight their way into the Assembly building on the Left Bank of the Seine to witness the strangest and most memorable session the Assembly has ever had.

That France had turned a page of her history was evident in the way the session ran its course. It took the Assembly a little more than four hours to accept Gen. Charles de Gaulle by a vote of 329 to 224 and during that time the man the Deputies were debating was not present.

General Scorns System

In the past, lesser aspirants to the Premiership—those willing to work within the established system General de Gaulle has always scorned—have made the investiture speeches, then have sat down alone on the front-center benches of the semi-circular chamber to follow the debate, take notes and answer questions put to them.

When General de Gaulle, looking tired and slightly hunched in his gray, double-breasted suit, finished his seven-minute speech, he strode out and was not seen again. From about 3:45 P. M. to shortly after 7:30, the Deputies seemed to be addressing a phantom or to be arguing with each other.

It appeared to many that for General de Gaulle the dialogue between him and the Republic representatives had ended with

Continued on Page 5, Column 4

GENERAL IS HEARD

Assembly Postpones Voting on Reforms Urged by Regime

Text of de Gaulle's speech to the Assembly, Page 4.

By ROBERT C. DOTY
Special to The New York Times.

PARIS, Monday, June 2—Gen. Charles de Gaulle has become Premier of France. The National Assembly voted last night, 329 to 224, to invest the 67-year-old leader of the wartime French liberation movement.

Approved at the same time was a fifteen-member Cabinet, including three former Premiers, representatives of seven parties on the Left, Right and Center, and five nonpolitical technicians. The most noteworthy of the latter was the choice of Maurice Couve de Murville, a career diplomat, as Foreign Minister.

General de Gaulle returns to power twelve years after renouncing the Provisional Presidency and at a moment when France faces the threat of civil war by civilians and military leaders dissatisfied with governmental efforts toward ending the rebellion in Algeria.

Terms Implicitly Accepted

By investing General de Gaulle as Premier, the Deputies implicitly accepted the terms he outlined in a seven-minute speech to the packed, breathless Assembly. He demanded:

¶Six months of full decree power, free from Parliamentary interference.

¶Immediate action to revise the Constitution in a manner to permit a popular referendum on sweeping reforms, transforming the Parliamentary regime into a Presidential one.

¶Authority to submit to a referendum reforms of the French Union, permitting a new basis of association with such overseas territories as Algeria and Central and West Africa. This was widely interpreted as opening the possibility even of full independence for some areas.

Breakdown of Vote

General de Gaulle had the almost solid support of the Center and Right wing, nearly half of the Socialist votes and more than half of the Radical votes. Voting against him were the Communists, the rest of the Socialists and Radicals, and scattered Deputies of other parties.

From Algiers came reports that the inclusion in the Cabinet of men of such liberal repute in colonial matters as former Premiers Antoine Pinay, an Independent, and Pierre Pflimlin, the Popular Republican who preceded General de Gaulle, had caused disappointment among ultra-colonialists in the dissident Committees of Public Safety there.

Soon after the Assembly vote was announced General de Gaulle met with President René Coty and the new Cabinet at Elysée Palace while a violent thunderstorm lashed the capital. During the meeting a bolt struck the palace.

At the end of the meeting,

Continued on Page 4, Column 6

Mahoney Wins Upstate Support As G.O.P.'s Choice for Governor

By DOUGLAS DALES

Support for State Senator Walter J. Mahoney of Buffalo as the Republican nominee for Governor spread eastward over the week-end. Heretofore backing for the Senate leader was concentrated in western New York.

In a joint statement, county chairmen of four Hudson Valley-Catskill counties declared that no suggested candidate and Senator Mahoney's experience in state government or his capacity to present issues in a forthright and intelligent fashion.

The statement was issued by Neal Brandow of Greene, Dr. Odgen Bush of Delaware, Harold Cole of Sullivan and Kenneth L. Wilson of Ulster.

These counties, with six others whose leaders or party organizations have endorsed Mr. Mahoney, will have 181 of the 586 delegates needed for nomination at the convention Aug. 25 and 26 in Rochester.

Previously the Buffalo Senator has been assured publicly of the backing of Erie, Niagara, Chautauqua, Oneida, Madison and Herkimer Counties. In addition, he has received private assurances of support in at least ten other counties, according to close associates.

Neither of the two other potential candidates—Nelson A. Rockefeller and Leonard W. Hall—has received comparable delegate support. Mr. Hall,

Continued on Page 18, Column 2

Soviet Fishing Fleet Off Canada Causing Concern in Washington

Vessels Anchored Near Grand Banks — Each Departing Craft Always Replaced

By ALLEN DRURY
Special to The New York Times.

WASHINGTON, June 1—A half-dozen Soviet fishing ships riding at anchor 100 miles off the east coast of Canada have the United States Navy and Air Force puzzled.

The vessels, stationed near an area marked off with buoys flying small Soviet flags, are in international fishing waters near the Grand Banks.

Moscow recently lodged a vigorous protest with the United States Embassy, charging that a United States military plane had flown over one of the vessels at masthead height. The accusation has been denied by a high Washington official. He told newsmen that planes in the area normally flew at several thousand feet altitude.

This official said the presence of the Soviet ships and buoys did not constitute any violation of international law, but the knowledge that the number of ships seldom varies and the fact that a departing

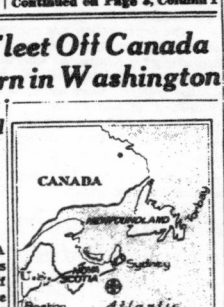

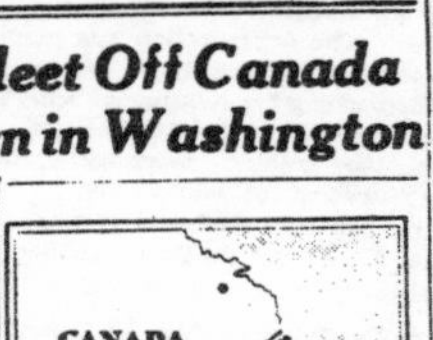

The New York Times June 2, 1958

Soviet fishing vessels are anchored 100 miles off east coast of Canada (cross).

vessel is always replaced are causing some concern.

According to this source, the United States Government recently received from Canada a photograph of one of the buoys made from a helicopter. The photograph appeared to indicate the buoy was a conventional type, with no signs of electronic gear that might be

Continued on Page 3, Column 4

Supporters of Foreign Aid Hope For Senate Passage This Week

Special to The New York Times.

WASHINGTON, June 1—Administration supporters hope to see the $3,068,900,000 authorization for foreign aid safely through the Senate this week. They will then concentrate on getting the five-year foreign trade extension through the House of Representatives.

The prospects for the first appeared somewhat brighter today than prospects for the second. Passage of the aid bill without major change may come by Thursday.

Passage of the trade bill may not come in the House until well into the following week, and then only with drastic changes that could provoke a Presidential veto if concurred in by the Senate.

Senate debate on the aid bill started last week with major speeches by the chairman of the Foreign Relations Committee, Senator Theodore Francis Green, Democrat of Rhode Island, and a top-ranking Republican, H. Alexander Smith of New Jersey. Much of the controversy, it was indicated, may center around an amendment authorizing aid to Communist-bloc nations.

This amendment would permit a broader interpretation of the Battle Act. That act now prohibits aid to Communist lands except when the President certifies to Congress that it is necessary for national de-

Continued on Page 16, Column 4

Tunisian Units Fire At 3 French Planes

By Reuters.

TUNIS, June 1—Tunisian troops fired today on three French planes that "violated Tunisian air space" in the Gabès region, a Government spokesman said tonight.

No further details were given and there was no immediate comment by French sources here.

The Tunisians reported yesterday that their troops had "apparently" hit a French plane that flew over Tunisian positions in the Gabès area. Gabès, the site of a French air base, is on Tunisia's east coast about 200 miles south of Tunis.

Government sources still withheld official comment on French political developments. But the

Continued on Page 4, Column 3

"All the News That's Fit to Print"

The New York Times.

LATE CITY EDITION
U. S. Weather Bureau Report (Page 60) forecasts: Mostly fair and continued warm today, tonight and tomorrow.
Temp. range: 86—68. Yesterday: 83.2—66.5.

VOL. CVII—No. 36,683. NEW YORK, TUESDAY, JULY 1, 1958. 300 beyond 100-mile zone from New York City. Higher in air delivery cities. K FIVE CENTS

ALASKA TO JOIN UNION AS THE 49TH STATE; FINAL APPROVAL IS VOTED BY SENATE, 64-20; BILL SENT TO EISENHOWER, WHO WILL SIGN IT

2 MORE AMERICANS ABDUCTED IN CUBA BY REBEL FORCES

44 From U. S. and Canada Now Held—Officials of Nickel Plant Latest

Special to The New York Times.

HAVANA, June 30 — Two more Americans were kidnapped today by the Cuban rebels, bringing to forty-four the number of North American servicemen and civilians seized since last Thursday.

Those kidnapped today are officers of the Nicaro nickel plant, on the north coast of Oriente Province.

Oriente is the center of operations of the rebels, led by Fidel Castro and his brother Raul, against the Government of President Fulgencio Batista. The rebels say they have carried out the kidnappings to bring pressure on the United States Government to halt military aid and assistance to the Batista regime.

Among the United States citizens seized — three of the victims are Canadians — are twenty-eight sailors and marines from the United States Naval Base at Guantanamo Bay, on the south coast of Oriente.

U. S. Denies Rebel Charge

Replying to a rebel charge that the base had been used by Cuban military planes operating against the insurgents, the United States Ambassador, Earl E. T. Smith, issued a statement yesterday saying that the base was not open to planes on combat operations.

The rebels told a sailor whom they did not abduct that his kidnapped colleagues would be released today.

United States officials have been in contact with the rebels in an attempt to negotiate the release of the naval and marine personnel as well as the ten Americans and two Canadians seized last Thursday. All twelve are employes of the Moa Bay Mining Company, on the north coast of Oriente. Two civilians, an American and a Canadian, were kidnapped last night.

Mine Is Not Guarded

The Americans seized today are Sherman Avery White and J. Andrew Poll, administrator general and assistant administrator general, respectively, of the Nickel Processing Company, which leases the Nicaro plant from the United States Government. They were carried off at 8:30 this morning by a group of eight rebels, according to the announcement of the United States Embassy.

No details are available, but it is supposed that the two officials went to the mine, about twelve miles from the small town of Nicaro, where 6,000 workers and officials live, to check on operations. Presumably they were abducted there. The entrance of the town is guarded by an army detach-

Continued on Page 3, Column 6

Russians to Attend Geneva Talk Today

By JOHN W. FINNEY
Special to The New York Times.

GENEVA, June 30—The Soviet Union agreed today to enter into technical talks with the West on the detection of tests of nuclear weapons. As a result, talks between scientists of four Western and four Communist nations will begin here tomorrow afternoon in a conference room in the Old League of Nations headquarters.

The Soviet agreement was announced by Dr. Yevgeni K. Fedorov, head of the Soviet delegation of scientists, following a two-hour conference with Dr. James B. Fisk, chairman of the Western scientific group.

Dr. Fedorov said at a news conference later it had been agreed that the talks would begin tomorrow and that discussions would be limited to

Continued on Page 5, Column 1

N. A. ROCKEFELLER ENTERS G.O.P. RACE FOR GOVERNORSHIP

Promises Strong Fight—Mahoney and Hall Top Him in Delegate Votes

Text of Rockefeller statement is printed on Page 36.

By CLAYTON KNOWLES

Nelson A. Rockefeller announced his candidacy for Governor yesterday. He said that if nominated he would "leave no stone unturned" to win election.

The announcement, expected for some weeks, brought the declared candidacies in Republican ranks to two.

Leonard W. Hall of Oyster Bay, L. I., former Republican national chairman, announced his candidacy several weeks ago and has been campaigning vigorously. State Senator Walter J. Mahoney of Buffalo has promised to announce his position "some time in August."

In promising an "aggressive campaign," Mr. Rockefeller declared that New York's status as the Empire State had been put in jeopardy by a "complacent administration" in Albany that evaded, rather than dealt with, serious fiscal and social problems.

New Approach Held Needed

His decision to make the race, he explained, was rooted in the "deep conviction that a new approach to government must be taken in New York State." He said "new energy and efficiency, vision, courage and imagination" would be needed to enable the state "to regain its traditional pre-eminence."

Mr. Rockefeller asserted that "a lifetime spent in administration, both in government and in private and philanthropic activities," qualified him to provide the "progressive, imaginative leadership" that state conditions required.

"If nominated, I will accept the challenge and wage an aggressive campaign on the issues," he said. "If elected, I shall serve with the full awareness of the responsibility such confidence places upon me."

A member of one of America's wealthiest families, the youthful-looking board chairman of Rockefeller Center, Inc., will celebrate his fiftieth birthday next Tuesday. He is the first Rockefeller to seek elective office.

A grandson of the late John D. Rockefeller, who founded the oil dynasty, he said his family

Continued on Page 36, Column 4

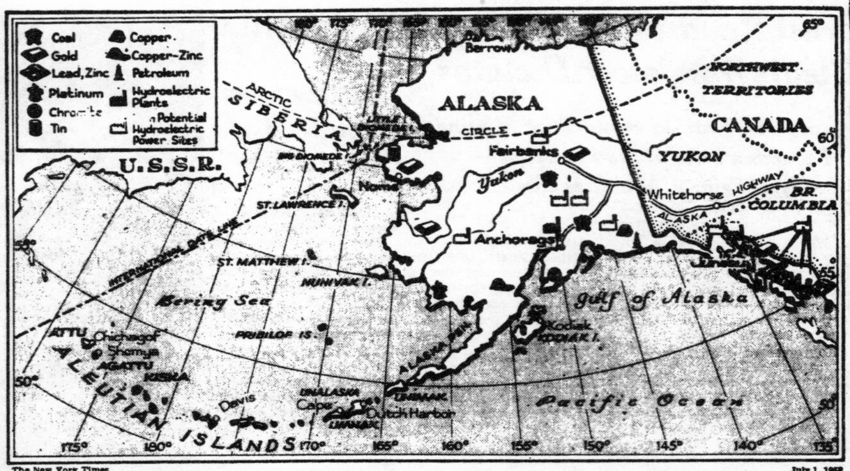

The New York Times July 1, 1958

ALASKA: Heavy lines define area approved for statehood. The symbols denote its present and potential resources.

OPPOSITION WILTS

A Bipartisan Coalition Defeats All Efforts to Amend Plan

By C. P. TRUSSELL
Special to The New York Times.

WASHINGTON, June 30—The Senate approved tonight the admission of Alaska as the forty-ninth state in the Union. The vote was 64 to 20.

Only President Eisenhower's signature, which is assured, and approval in a territorial referendum remain before statehood is formally achieved. Test votes indicate that the issue will carry by an overwhelming majority.

The Senate accepted the statehood bill passed by the House of Representatives word for word, beating down every effort to change it. Thus the bill goes directly to the White House.

Any change in the language would have sent the bill back to the House and invited further delays and possible death.

Final Senate action came after five days and evenings of battle, some of it bitter. The vote crossed party lines. The South fought admission, but not solidly. Senators from other sections of the country were also divided.

Stepovich in Gallery

Thirty-three Republicans and thirty-one Democrats voted in favor of admission. Opposed were seven Republicans and thirteen Democrats.

Gov. Michael A. Stepovich of Alaska sat tensely in the Senate gallery while the vote was being taken. When the result was announced he shouted:

"Thank God."

As well-wishers surrounded him he made a prediction.

"I believe that we will show the United States of America that we will be one of the greatest states in the Union within the next fifty years," he said.

It is expected that Alaska will assume full statehood by autumn or early winter. Its two Senators and one member of the House of Representatives could take their Congressional posts when the Eighty-Sixth Congress convenes next January.

Amendments Defeated

Before the final vote tonight, the Senate rejected by a vote of 62—22 a point of order entered by Senator James O. Eastland, Democrat of Mississippi.

He noted that Alaska Constitution provided that in the election of the first two Senators, one be given a six-year term and the other two or four years, to permit the staggering of Senatorial incumbencies.

Mr. Eastland said that this violated the United States Constitution's provision that all Senators be elected for six years.

But the Senate decided that this was not a valid objection and overrode it.

Senator John Stennis, Democrat of Mississippi, moved that the bill be referred to the Sen-

Continued on Page 16, Column 1

BEIRUT USES JETS TO CHECK REBELS

Bombards Force Imperiling Airport—U. N. Questions Suspected Syrians

By United Press International.

BEIRUT, Lebanon, June 30—The Government sent rocket-firing jet fighters against rebels in the hills only seven miles from Beirut International Airport today. At the same time, the Tripoli command reported it had cut the main rebel supply line into that city.

On their side, the rebels declared they had cut the main highway between Beirut and Damascus.

Druse tribesmen under the leadership of rebel chieftain Kamal Jumblatt were in the hills overlooking the airport. Jumblatt's army of 500 to 1,000 men appeared also to be poised for a night attack on Chemlan, fifteen miles southeast of the capital, which had been emptied of civilians.

[At the United Nations, Secretary General Dag Hammarskjold said United Nations observers in Lebanon had begun to question prisoners, "said to be Syrians," on their possible connection with the Lebanese uprising.]

A rebel spokesman said the Druse forces were astride the main highway to Damascus. There was no Government confirmation, but former Premier

Continued on Page 6, Column 3

DISMISSAL RULING CURBS PRESIDENT

High Court Holds He Lacks Power to Oust Wiener of War Claims Agency

By RUSSELL BAKER
Special to The New York Times.

WASHINGTON, June 30—The Supreme Court tightened today the limitation on the President's power to remove officials of Federal quasi-judicial bodies.

Where Congress has not defined justifiable causes for dismissal, the court held, it must be assumed that Congress does not want to hang a "Damocles' sword" over these officials by permitting the President to remove them solely to substitute "men of his own choosing."

The opinion, written for a unanimous court by Justice Felix Frankfurter, upheld Myron Wiener's contention that he was wrongfully dismissed from the War Claims Commission in 1953 so that President Eisenhower could administer the agency with personnel of his own selection.

1935 Ruling Recalled

The last significant Supreme Court ruling in the historic debate over Presidential power to dismiss was rendered in 1935. Then, in a case closely paralleling the Wiener case, the court ruled that the President could not dismiss an officer of a Federal regulatory agency for any reason except those stipulated in law.

In the 1935 case, Humphrey's Executor v. United States, President Roosevelt dismissed a member of the Federal Trade Commission on the ground that the "aims and purposes" of his Administration could be "carried out most effectively with personnel of my own selection."

The court overruled him, holding that a President could dismiss only for reasons speci-

Continued on Page 20, Column 2

Alabama Is Denied Access To Rolls of N. A. A. C. P.

Special to The New York Times.

WASHINGTON, June 30—A $100,000 contempt fine imposed by Alabama when the National Association for the Advancement of Colored People refused to disclose its list of members in the state was struck down today by the Supreme Court.

The court held unanimously that compulsory disclosure under the circumstances in Alabama would violate constitutional guarantees of free speech and association, Justice John Marshall Harlan, writing for the court, said:

"Inviolability of privacy in group association may in many circumstances be indispensable to preservation of freedom of

Text of the opinion will be found on Page 18.

association, particularly where a group espouses dissident beliefs.

"Petitioner [the N. A. A. C. P.] has made an uncontroverted showing that on past occasions revelation of the identity of its rank-and-file members has exposed these members to economic reprisal, loss of employment, threat of physical coercion and other manifestations of public hostility."

A Major Victory

The decision was a major victory for the N. A. A. C. P. in a fight to continue operations in the South. Its activities include helping to bring suits to end school segregation.

Seven Southern states have passed legislation aimed at the association or have acted against it through state courts. Included are several statutes to require disclosure of members' names and others to restrict any financial help to Negro plaintiffs in lawsuits.

The organization has carried most of the legal burden of pushing for compliance with the Supreme Court's decision of 1954 holding school segregation unconstitutional.

In 1956 Alabama accused the N. A. A. C. P. of failing to obey a law requiring out-of-

Continued on Page 18, Column 7

HIGH COURT BARS LITTLE ROCK PLEA

Suggests Appeals Bench Set Integration Stay Review Before School Term

Text of the opinion will be found on Page 19.

By ANTHONY LEWIS
Special to The New York Times.

WASHINGTON, June 30—The Supreme Court refused today to review on an emergency basis the order suspending school integration in Little Rock until January, 1961.

But the high court strongly suggested that the case be reviewed by the United States Court of Appeals for the Eighth Circuit before the next school term begins in September. That court "has recessed for the summer.

"We have no doubt," the Supreme Court said in a short unsigned order, "that the Court of Appeals will recognize the vital importance of the time element in this litigation, and that it will act upon the application for a stay or the appeal in ample time to permit arrangements to be made for the next school year."

Summer Review Asked

Lawyers of the National Association for the Advancement of Colored People had asked the Supreme Court to by-pass the Eighth Circuit and hear the case this summer to assure early and final review.

A notice of appeal from District Judge Harry J. Lemley's suspension decision has been filed with the Eighth Circuit. So has an application for a stay of the decision pending its appeal. Judge Lemley denied a stay.

If the Eighth Circuit were to grant the stay, the need for speed would be gone, from the N. A. A. C. P.'s viewpoint. Little Rock Central High School would open with a handful of Negro children among the whites, as this last year, while the appeal was argued.

Chief Justice Earl Warren read the order to a packed courtroom at the end of a busy and dramatic day—the last in the high court's 1957-58 term.

Twenty-one cases that had been argued earlier in the term were decided today—with forty opinions. The Chief Justice announced that the court had disposed of all its pending business before recess-

Continued on Page 19, Column 1

ALASKANS APPEAR STUNNED BY NEWS

Civil Defense Whistles in Anchorage Signal Vote to Crowds in the Streets

By LAWRENCE E. DAVIES
Special to The New York Times.

ANCHORAGE, Alaska, June 30—Alaskans were stunned today by the realization that Congress had finally invited them to become "first class citizens."

Here in the territorial metropolis, the center of much of the agitation for statehood, it took them a while to get their bearings.

Long after the civil defense whistles had blown, signaling the Senate's action preparing the way for a forty-ninth star on the flag, unbelieving crowds almost silently walked the streets amid the tooting of automobile horns.

Texas Car Is 'Shot'

Stores did business as usual. A woman traffic policeman rode her motorcycle down Fourth Avenue putting tickets on cars that were parked overtime.

Some amateur photographers gleefully "shot" a passing car bearing a Texas license plate, emblematic of a state that would have to give up its much-loved stories of bigness as Alaska completes the transition to statehood.

Rita Martin, queen of the annual Fur Rendezvous, climbed a fire truck ladder and pinned a huge silver star—the forty-ninth—to a 60-by-40-foot flag hurriedly draped over the front wall of the Federal Building.

Miss Orah Dee Clark, 83 years old, who in 1915 was the first school principal here, stood watching the star-pinning ceremony on an automobile-jammed street.

It was an emotion-packed moment for her. She had come to the territory in 1906, and to

Continued on Page 16, Column 2

Soviet Offers Talk On Yugoslav Credit

By United Press International.

LONDON, Tuesday, July 1—The Soviet Union proposed negotiations with Yugoslavia today on $285,000,000 in credits that the Kremlin had suspended.

The Moscow radio said the proposal was contained in a Soviet note sent to Yugoslavia June 28 and published today in Moscow newspapers.

In the note the Soviet Union said an earlier note to Yugoslavia had suggested revisions in existing economic agreements, including the postponement of one loan for several years. The Soviet Union received no reply to the suggestions, today's note said.

"The Soviet Government suggests that talks of representatives of both Governments should be held as soon as pos-

Continued on Page 2, Column 5

The New York Times

SEEKS NOMINATION: Nelson A. Rockefeller at news conference at which he discussed his candidacy for nomination for Governor of New York on Republican slate.

Narcotics Agent Warns Inquiry Mafia Seeks to Invade Industry

By JOSEPH A. LOFTUS
Special to The New York Times.

WASHINGTON, June 30—An expert on the Mafia told Senators today that the secret criminal organization was making a "concerted effort" to penetrate unions and management.

They are "the same people who are active in the narcotics traffic," Martin F. Pera, a Federal narcotics agent, told the Select Committee on Improper Activities in the Labor or Management Field.

Mr. Pera was the second witness as the committee laid the groundwork for extensive hearings on what the chairman, Senator John L. McClellan said, "appears to be a close-knit clandestine criminal syndicate."

The Arkansas Democrat, in his opening statement, said the committee "has become convinced that the relationship of the national criminal syndicate with legitimate labor and business is far more critical than has heretofore been revealed."

The first witness was Sgt. Edgar D. Croswell of the New York State police, who broke up a gangland meeting last Nov. 14 at the home of Joseph Barbara in Apalachin, N. Y. Barbara has a serious heart condition and will not testify.

Mr. Pera had barely touched on the labor-management angle when the committee recessed for the day. Photographs of him were barred because of the nature of his work.

The agent, who has worked on the narcotics problem in several foreign countries, told the committee about the origins of

Continued on Page 14, Column 6

Rayburn Bars G. O. P. Demand For Inquiry on Fox Testimony

By WILLIAM M. BLAIR
Special to The New York Times.

WASHINGTON, June 30—Speaker Sam Rayburn rejected today a Republican attempt to have the House of Representatives investigate the conduct of the subcommittee that has been investigating the relations of Sherman Adams and Bernard Goldfine.

The Democratic Speaker ruled out of order a resolution proposed by Representative Thomas B. Curtis, Republican of Missouri. Mr. Curtis argued that the testimony of John Fox of Boston, a lawyer and business man, should have been taken in executive session, in accordance with House rules.

His move was another effort by Republicans to smother the inquiry, which they contend has developed into a "smear" of Mr. Adams and others and to stem the political fears of Republican candidates up for re-election. Mr. Adams is the assistant to President Eisenhower.

Meanwhile, Mr. Fox announced that he had instructed his lawyers to file libel suits against Mr. Adams and four other persons for what he called "scurrilous" statements about his veracity. He said he would ask $1,000,000 damages from each.

Besides Mr. Adams, he named Roger Robb of Washington and Samuel P. Sears of Boston, lawyers for Mr. Goldfine, New England industrialist; Robert B. Choate, publisher of The Boston Herald and Boston Traveler; William J. Dempsey, counsel for the Boston Herald-Traveler Corporation, and the corporation itself.

As the political atmosphere

Continued on Page 14, Column 4

"All the News That's Fit to Print"

The New York Times.

LATE CITY EDITION
U. S. Weather Bureau Report (Page 39) forecasts:
Fair and pleasant today;
fair tonight and tomorrow.
Temp. range: 83—67. Yesterday: 83.0—70.0.

VOL. CVII . No. 36,722.

NEW YORK, SATURDAY, AUGUST 9, 1958.

10c beyond 100-mile zone from New York City. Higher in air delivery cities.

FIVE CENTS

NAUTILUS SAILS UNDER THE POLE AND 1,830 MILES OF ARCTIC ICECAP IN PACIFIC-TO-ATLANTIC PASSAGE

U. S. Navy, from Associated Press

TIME OF DECISION: Officers of the Nautilus choose a place to submerge below ice for undersea voyage across Arctic regions. Standing at the right in the conning tower of the submarine is her skipper, Comdr. W. R. Anderson.

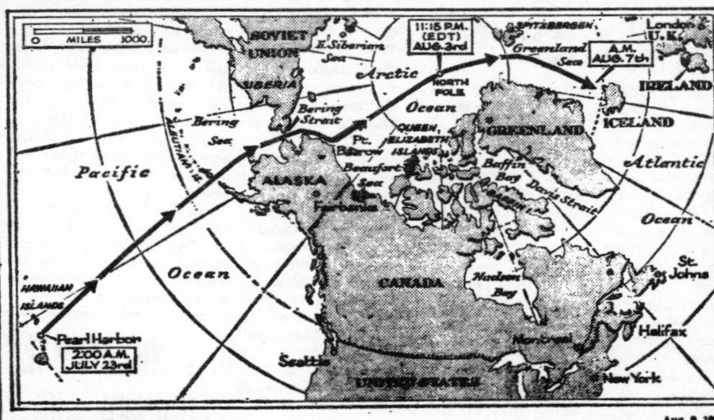

The New York Times — Aug. 9, 1958

NEW PASSAGE: Heavy line traces the Nautilus' route from Pacific to Atlantic Oceans

FOUR-DAY VOYAGE

New Route to Europe Pioneered—Skipper and Crew Cited

Text of Navy fact sheet, Page 6. The Citation, Page 7.

By FELIX BELAIR Jr.
Special to The New York Times.

WASHINGTON, Aug. 8 — History's first undersea voyage across the top of the world, a distance of 1,830 miles under the polar icecap, was disclosed at the White House today.

The trip was made in four days by the Nautilus, the world's first atomic submarine. The voyage pioneered a new and shorter route from the Pacific to the Atlantic and Europe — a route that might be used by cargo submarines. It also added to man's knowledge of the subsurface of the Arctic basin.

The voyage took the Nautilus under the North Pole. The overall trip began at Pearl Harbor July 23 and ended at Iceland Aug. 7.

Dives at Point Barrow

The Nautilus went under the icecap at Point Barrow, Alaska, and surfaced four days later at a point in the Atlantic between Spitzbergen and Greenland. She is now on her way to Western Europe.

The feat of the Nautilus, with 116 crewmen and scientific observers aboard, was revealed as President Eisenhower decorated the submarine's skipper, Comdr. W. R. Anderson, with the Legion of Merit. A Presidential Unit Citation—the first ever conferred in peacetime—went to the submarine, with a ribbon and special clasp in the form of a golden "N" to all who participated in the cruise.

The Presidential citation to Commander Anderson said that the Nautilus under his leadership had pioneered a submerged sea lane between the Eastern and Western Hemispheres. It added:

"This points the way for further exploration and possible use of this route by nuclear powered cargo submarines as a new commercial seaway between the major oceans of the world."

Skipper Tells Story

A few minutes after the award, Commander Anderson, admittedly "a little dazed" by the speed of events that brought him here overnight by helicopter and jet plane from Arctic waters, was telling his story of "Operation Northwest Passage."

News of the voyage reached the Capitol with electrifying effect. William F. Knowland of California, the Senate Republican leader, read a brief dispatch to the Senate and remarked:

"This should give us courage and remind us to have faith. It shows that this is no time to sell America short."

Senator Mike Mansfield of Montana, the Democratic acting

Continued on Page 6, Column 1

CHIEF OF U.N. GIVES A PLAN FOR MIDEAST

ASSEMBLY MEETS

Hears Call for Step-Up of Its Economic and Political Efforts

Hammarskjold and Munro statements are on Page 2.

By THOMAS J. HAMILTON
Special to The New York Times.

UNITED NATIONS, N. Y., Aug. 8—Secretary General Dag Hammarskjold proposed today that the United Nations step up its political and economic activities in the Middle East to stabilize the area.

The New York Times

CALL TO ACTION: Dag Hammarskjold addressing the General Assembly.

Mr. Hammarskjold took the floor at the opening of the General Assembly's emergency special session on the Middle East to put forward his program. He had intended to present this proposal if there was a meeting of heads of government within the framework of the United Nations Security Council.

The principal provisions of his plan are:

¶A declaration by the Arab states reaffirming their adherence to the principles of mutual respect for each other's territory, non-aggression and non-interference in each other's internal affairs.

¶The continuation and extension of present United Nations activities in Lebanon and Jordan.

¶Joint action by the Arab states, with the support of the United Nations, in economic development. This would include arrangements for cooperation between "oil-producing and oil-transiting countries" and joint utilization of water resources.

Session Is Adjourned

Mr. Hammarskjold's statement was the outstanding development of the opening session, which lasted thirty-five minutes. The Assembly adjourned until 10:30 A. M. Wednesday to give foreign ministers of some of the eighty-one member nations time to get here.

Contrary to the general expectation, Arkady A. Sobolev, Soviet delegate, did not demand the admission of Chinese Communist representatives. However, he took the floor to repeat his denunciation of the presence of United States forces in Lebanon and British forces in Jordan, and again demanded their immediate withdrawal.

Henry Cabot Lodge of the

Continued on Page 2, Column 3

U.S. LEADERS SPLIT ON MIDEAST AIMS

Eisenhower Action May Be Needed to Fix Policy for Assembly Debate

By E. W. KENWORTHY
Special to The New York Times.

WASHINGTON, Aug. 8—High-level differences of opinion have developed within the Administration over the strategy and tactics to be used in the United Nations debate on the Middle East crisis, officials indicated today.

The differences are being argued out thoroughly and amicably, and a concerted position will almost certainly be arrived at during the week-end, these officials said. Nevertheless, it was considered possible that President Eisenhower might have to make the final decision on the United States approach.

Dulles Remark Recalled

The differences were said to have become apparent soon after Secretary of State Dulles' news conference a week ago Thursday. At that conference he made it clear that the United States intended to meet the Soviet charge of United States and British aggression in Lebanon and Jordan with a counter-arraignment against the Soviet Union and the United Arab Republic on "indirect aggression."

Until the problems of indirect aggression are met directly and dealt with it will not be possible to create the atmosphere of political stability in the Middle East necessary for any attack on economic problems, Mr. Dulles said.

Almost immediately some

Continued on Page 3, Column 3

U. S. MAY REDUCE FORCE IN LEBANON

Token Removal of Marine Battalion Planned

By W. H. LAWRENCE
Special to The New York Times.

BEIRUT, Lebanon, Aug. 8—The United States tentatively plans to reload a marine battalion on ships next week in a "symbolic" gesture of withdrawal from Lebanon.

A responsible source said the decision to reduce the force on shore by about 2,000 men had been communicated to the Lebanese Government and to Gen. Fouad Chehab, armed forces commander and President-elect.

Before the marine unit is pulled out, a small detachment of Army engineers and truck personnel will be moved from Lebanon to the Turkish port of Iskenderun to improve facilities at the Atlantic alliance base at Adana, an important center of air striking power and supply for the United States operation in Lebanon.

The moves will have both political and military effects, it is believed. The political aims are both local and international.

Locally, leaders of the continuing insurrection against the Government of President Camille Chamoun have been insisting on speedy removal of United States troops as a condition for a cease-fire now that General Chehab has been elected. He will succeed Mr. Chamoun Sept.

Continued on Page 3, Column 2

Peronists Win Rule Of Argentine Labor

By JUAN de ONIS
Special to The New York Times.

BUENOS AIRES, Aug. 8—The Argentine Senate adopted today a controversial union organization law that virtually hands the labor movement back to Peronist control.

President Arturo Frondizi's Senate majority approved the text of a bill, passed by the Chamber of Deputies, without changing a word. It did so despite formal opposition to the measure by the Roman Catholic Church, business and professional organizations, nearly all of the press and the anti-Peronist labor unions.

The bill, which re-establishes the single General Labor Confederation, with the official right to speak for labor, awaits the President's signature only.

In eighteen of the bill's fifty-

Continued on Page 4, Column 7

HOUSE VOTES BILL TO AID EDUCATION IN SCIENCE FIELD

Student Loans Raised in Place of Scholarships by 900 Million Measure

By BESS FURMAN
Special to The New York Times.

WASHINGTON, Aug. 8 — The House of Representatives adopted today a four-year, $900,000,000 bill to aid science education.

No money was shorn from the bill. But the scholarship provision, on which a compromise had already been made with President Eisenhower, was deleted.

The scholarship funds were shifted to the bill's loan provisions. This was accomplished in a standing vote of 109 to 78, on a motion offered by Representative Walter H. Judd, Republican of Minnesota.

The loan provisions of the bill were increased from $40,000,000 in the first year to $60,000,000 and from $60,000,000 in each of the three succeeding years to $80,000,000.

The final adoption was by voice vote, after a motion to kill the bill by sending it back to committee had been defeated in a roll-call vote of 233 to 139. The motion was offered by Representative Ralph W. Gwinn, Republican of Westchester.

The legislation now goes to the Senate, which has already scheduled to consider on Monday its own broader science-aid bill, sponsored by Senator Lister Hill, Democrat of Alabama.

Scholarships in Senate Bill

The Senate bill includes a four-year program totaling $70,000,000 for college scholarships. If that survives on the Senate floor, some compromise on scholarships will have to be worked out by House and Senate conferees.

As adopted, the House bill would cost an estimated total of $147,000,000 in the first year of operation.

It would provide:

¶Loans averaging $600 to more than 90,000 needy students, of which the Federal Government would pay a total of $60,000,000.

¶One thousand fellowships of $2,000 each to train college teachers, with reimbursement to universities for additional costs to expand graduate schools.

¶Grants to the states for scientific teaching equipment and laboratory improvement, totaling $60,000,000.

¶Grants to states to improve testing and guidance programs, $15,000,000, and $6,000,000 to set up teacher-training institutes in this field.

¶Grants to institutions to set up short-term institutes for foreign language teachers, to pay half the cost of permanent foreign language centers and stipends for those attending. This was estimated at a total of $4,500,000.

¶For research under the United States Office of Education on better educational use

Continued on Page 5, Column 3

VETO THREATENED ON PENSIONS BILL

Social Security Rate Rise Backed by White House but State Plan Is Fought

By JOHN D. MORRIS
Special to The New York Times.

WASHINGTON, Aug. 8—The Eisenhower Administration raised the threat of a veto today against a bill to increase Social Security benefits.

The measure, approved by the House, calls for a 7 per cent increase in Old Age and Survivors Insurance benefits and higher Social Security taxes to finance it. Those provisions were endorsed by Arthur S. Flemming, Secretary of Health, Education and Welfare.

But the Administration is "strongly opposed," Mr. Flemming told the Senate Finance Committee, to provisions that would increase the Federal Government's share in the cost of state relief programs.

Would Recommend Veto

"Suppose we passed the House bill, would you recommend a veto?" asked Senator Paul H. Douglas, Democrat of Illinois.

"I would," Mr. Flemming replied.

Mr. Flemming was the first witness at the opening of two days of hearings on the measure, which is scheduled for Senate action before Congress adjourns. He told the Senators that his views were those of the Administration.

The bill calls for increases in monthly cash benefits under the insurance program starting

Continued on Page 5, Column 2

Glennan, Ohio Educator, Named To Direct New U. S. Space Unit

Case Tech President Served on A.E.C. Under Truman—Dryden Picked as Aide

Special to The New York Times.

WASHINGTON, Aug. 8—T. Keith Glennan, a Cleveland educator and former member of the Atomic Energy Commission, is President Eisenhower's choice to head the new civilian space agency.

Associated Press

T. Keith Glennan

The President sent Mr. Glennan's nomination to the Senate today along with that of Dr. Hugh L. Dryden as Deputy Administrator of the agency.

Mr. Glennan is president of the Case Institute of Technology. Dr. Dryden is director of the National Advisory Committee for Aeronautics.

The National Aeronautics and Space Administration was created by an Act of Congress signed by the President ten days ago.

Mr. Glennan's appointment is believed to be noncontroversial. There may be some objection to the choice of Dr. Dryden, however, and this could delay Senate confirmation of the nominees.

If the Senate does not act before Congress adjourns, both can be installed under recess appointments.

Members of the House Space Committee have criticized Dr. Dryden as presenting a program for the conquest of space that lacked "boldness, imagina-

Continued on Page 4, Column 3

Hogan Is Expected To Enter the Race For Senate Monday

By DOUGLAS DALES

A statement circulated yesterday by the New York Young Democratic Club indicated that District Attorney Frank S. Hogan had made up his mind to enter the race for the Democratic Senate nomination nearly a month ago.

Mr. Hogan yesterday scheduled a news conference for Monday noon to "issue a statement."

If, as expected, he then announces his entry, he will become the fifth declared candidate in the field.

Mr. Hogan's intentions were forecast in a summary of an interview conducted by a committee of the Young Democratic Club with Mr. Hogan on July 17. The summary was submitted to Mr. Hogan for revisions before its circulation among club members.

The summary indicated that Mr. Hogan was already making plans for the future operation of his office and that he expected to have a say in the selection of a successor.

His views on this were given as follows:

"When queried as to the

Continued on Page 14, Column 5

Rackets Unit Asks Prosecution for 13

By ALLEN DRURY
Special to The New York Times.

WASHINGTON, Aug. 8—Senate rackets investigators voted unanimously today to ask the Senate to approve contempt-of-Congress citations against thirteen witnesses.

They include the president of the Carpenters Union and the reputed heir to Al Capone's gangland empire.

The action was taken by the Select Committee on Improper Activities in the Labor or Management Field. It acted in a closed meeting between morning and afternoon public sessions at which it heard witnesses give further testimony on associates of James R. Hoffa, president of the International Brotherhood of Teamsters.

Senator John L. McClellan, Democrat of Arkansas, the com-

Continued on Page 5, Column 6

POLAR TRIP OPENS DEFENSE FRONTIER

U.S. Strategic Advantage Is Seen as Temporary—Soviet Effort Expected

By HANSON W. BALDWIN

A new ocean — the frozen wastes of the Arctic — has been opened to navigation and hence to naval utilization.

This is the meaning of the transpolar, under-ice voyage from Alaska to the Greenland Sea of the nuclear-powered submarine Nautilus.

The newest achievement of the Nautilus, which had already broken all records in submarine history, has immense strategic implications.

Last year the Nautilus made a five-and-one-half-day, 1,000-mile trip under the Arctic ice pack and clearly foreshadowed the shape of things to come.

The Arctic ice pack has hitherto prevented penetration of the Arctic Ocean except, with great difficulty, by foot or by air.

Ships Skirt Land

In certain seasons of the year when the ice pack recedes from the land, or thins out, surface ships have skirted the land masses bordering the Arctic, but their cruises have been short and difficult and they have never penetrated deep into the pack.

The submerged navigation of the Nautilus under the Pole and from Pacific to Atlantic means that utilization of the Arctic Ocean for military purposes is now possible for the first time in history.

Three military capabilities for Arctic submarine operations are immediately foreseeable.

Potentially the most important —in a strategic sense—is the utilization of the Arctic for the launching of guided missiles from submarines. The fleet ballistic missile, Polaris, a two-stage, solid-fuel rocket with a range of 500 to 1,500 miles, and a powerful thermonuclear warhead, is now under development. It has been designed for launching from a submerged submarine at considerable depths.

Nine nuclear-powered submarines, each much larger than the Nautilus and each capable

Continued on Page 6, Column 3

Nautilus' Skipper Helps to Mitigate A Snub to Rickover

By ANTHONY LEWIS
Special to The New York Times.

WASHINGTON, Aug. 8—The man largely responsible for construction of the world's first nuclear-powered submarine was not asked to the White House today to share her moment of triumph.

Some thought was given to inviting Rear Admiral Hyman G. Rickover to the ceremony for the Nautilus, White House officials said. But only "top brass" had been asked and it was decided no exception could be made for him.

The skipper of the Nautilus, Comdr. W. R. Anderson, proved in the circumstances to be as bold a navigator in Navy politics as in the waters under polar ice.

Commander Anderson went directly from the White House to Admiral Rickover's office in the Navy Building, a few blocks away. There he paid his personal respects on the slight, frail figure whose tough-minded drive made the Nautilus a reality.

For Admiral Rickover the of-

Continued on Page 7, Column 3

479 Get Jaywalking Summonses But Public Is Hailed on Response

By BERNARD STENGREN

Pedestrians waited for traffic lights and motorists waited for pedestrians yesterday as the police began enforcing New York's new safety law.

High officials of the Traffic and Police Departments said they were gratified at the extent of compliance by drivers and walkers.

Traffic Commissioner T. T. Wiley said:

"My hat is off to New York. The reaction is wonderful."

He spoke after a tour of midtown Manhattan during which turning trucks waited for pedestrians and cab drivers not only waited but also shouted warnings to pedestrians starting to cross against lights.

John J. King, assistant Chief Inspector and head of the Safety Division, said that although some persons had argued, most had stopped when patrolmen admonished them about jaywalking.

There were, however, exceptions. Between 8 A. M., when enforcement began, and 4 P. M., when the police day shift ended, 479 summonses returnable for $2 were issued to pedestrians.

These included 255 in Manhattan, ninety-three in Brooklyn, ninety-eight in Queens, thirty-one in the Bronx and two in Richmond—where there is only one "Don't Walk" signal.

Twenty-two motorists who failed to give the right of way to pedestrians received summonses for that infraction, which was added Thursday to violations subject to "rigid enforcement."

In Manhattan, five were is-

Continued on Page 15, Column 5

"All the News That's Fit to Print"

The New York Times.

LATE CITY EDITION
U. S. Weather Bureau Report (Page 77) forecasts:
Partly cloudy and mild today and tomorrow.
Temp. range: 72—59. Yesterday: 68.5—52.5.

VOL. CVIII..No. 36,783. © 1958, by The New York Times Company. Times Square, New York 36, N. Y. NEW YORK, THURSDAY, OCTOBER 9, 1958. 10c beyond 100-mile zone from New York City. Higher in air delivery cities. FIVE CENTS

POPE, 82, DIES AFTER 2D STROKE; MILLIONS OFFER THEIR PRAYERS; CARDINALS TO NAME SUCCESSOR

YANKEES WIN, 4-3, IN TENTH AND TIE BRAVES IN SERIES

McDougald's Homer Ignites 2-Run Rally and Starts Spahn to Defeat

DUREN VICTOR IN RELIEF

But Turley Collects Final Out After Losers Score and Get Two Men On

By JOHN DREBINGER
Special to The New York Times.

MILWAUKEE, Oct. 8—The Yankees kept going today in the 1958 world series. They did it by bringing down the Braves in ten innings to win the sixth game, 4 to 3.

Thus the Yankees, who only a few days ago trailed at three games to one, now are all square, with the seventh and deciding encounter coming up tomorrow.

Gil McDougald, with a home run in the tenth inning, brought to an end a heroic effort by the Milwaukee southpaw, Warren Spahn, to gain his third straight triumph of the series.

The blow broke a 2-all tie. In its wake the Bombers completed the rout of Spahn with singles by Elston Howard and Yogi Berra, a second tally coming home as Bill Skowron greeted the incoming Don McMahon with a single.

Braves Fight Back

The Yanks were ahead, 4—2, but the show was far from over for the crowd of 46,367. The Braves kicked up an uproar in the last of the tenth that just missed plunging the battle into another deadlock.

They routed Ryne Duren, whose blinding fast ball had baffled them in the four previous innings. They pushed across a run and got the tying run to third, with still another runner on first. But Casey Stengel, pulling out all the stops to maintain what was left of the lead, called on his other fireballing ace, Bob Turley.

Bullet Bob, who on Monday in New York had kept the Bombers in contention by winning the fifth game with a shutout, faced Frank Torre, a left-handed pinch hitter.

Torre sent a soft fly toward right and it looked every inch a single.

But McDougald, the Yankee second baseman and the hero apparent because of his homer, tore back on the grass. He leaped high in the air and pulled down the ball, which suddenly

Continued on Page 51, Column 5

MAN IN A BALLOON GIVES SPACE DATA

But Descends Prematurely After Going Up 19 Miles

By The Associated Press.

ALAMOGORDO, N. M., Oct. 8—An Air Force balloon exploring the fringe of space returned to earth early tonight after it had carried its pilot, Lieut. Clifton McClure 3d, to 99,600 feet.

The balloon, launched today, began an unexpected and unexplained descent late this afternoon. A spokesman at Holloman Air Force Base said "it must be an emergency or they wouldn't be bringing him down."

The balloon landed on the desert ranges west of here, near the San Andres Mountains about thirty miles away.

The Air Force sent a helicopter to the site of the landing to pick up the pilot and the instruments the gondola carried to the stratosphere.

[Failure of the cooling system forced the balloon down, United Press International reported. Lieutenant McClure walked out of the gondola and was taken to an Air Force hospital for a physical examination.]

At 11:05 A. M. Mountain standard time (2:05 P. M., New York time) the balloon reached an altitude of 99,600 feet—just 400 feet short of the planned goal. The balloon was launched at 5:58 A. M.

Lieutenant McClure started his descent about 4 P. M.

During his flight the 25-year-old jet pilot, who became a

Continued on Page 8, Column 3

Final Registration Is Starting Today

By LEO EGAN

The final registration period for this year's election starts today in New York City and Nassau and Westchester Counties. It will continue tomorrow and end on Saturday.

Democratic and Republican party officials are making strenuous efforts to persuade potential voters who have not registered yet to do so. Only those who are registered by Saturday night will be permitted to vote.

Those who registered for last year's municipal elections in New York City and Westchester are automatically registered for this year unless they have moved outside of their election districts. All others are required by law to register to qualify as voters.

In New York City 4,613

Continued on Page 31, Column 5

FAUBUS EXPANDS SCHOOL FUND PLEA

Letters With Seal of State Going Throughout Nation in Bid for Donations

Special to The New York Times.

LITTLE ROCK, Oct. 8—Gov. Orval E. Faubus opened a nation-wide appeal today for funds to help educate Little Rock's teen-agers in a system of private high schools.

The Governor said copies of a letter appealing for contributions would be mailed to persons who had written him pledging their support in his fight against school integration.

The letters will go out on official stationery displaying the official seal of the state. They will be signed by Governor Faubus and by Dr. T. J. Raney, president of the Little Rock Private School Corporation.

For the last ten days the corporation has been accepting donations for the operations of private high schools for Little Rock's white students.

No Date Announced

The corporation has not announced an opening date for its schools, although Dr. Raney has promised it would begin operation "as soon as we can get things rolling." The classes would be held in donated buildings.

Governor Faubus revealed the contents of his appeal letter in which he said donations would benefit "all freedom-loving citizens of this nation."

He said thousands of the letters would be printed. An extra staff of thirteen stenographers was at work filing addresses gleaned from the mail received by the Governor this fall. A secretary said there were between 20,000 and 30,000 pieces of mail and telegrams.

It was the first time that the Governor had asked for money in the fight to maintain segregated schooling in the state. But Mr. Faubus had earlier pledged his support to those who had appealed for financial support.

The Governor's Letter

The appeal letter said:

"The plan set up by action of the extraordinary session of the General Assembly provided for the use of state funds, to be allocated on a per-student basis, for the student's education in whatever school he chose to attend.

"At the request of the N. A. A. C. P. [National Association for the Advancement of Colored People] and the Justice Department, the Federal courts have enjoined all public officials, including school teachers, from using the state funds, as provided by law.

"The acts have been challenged in the courts of the state, where they have already been upheld as constitutional. At the present time the schools are closed through the injunctive process of the Federal courts.

"For this reason it appears necessary that the Little Rock Private School Corporation should proceed with its plan to set up private schools in private facilities, to be operated by private funds.

"It is urgent that the students re-enter school at the earliest possible date. We would, therefore, appreciate your assistance in providing contributions to

Continued on Page 28, Column 5

'PRIVATE' CLASSES DIRECTED TO STOP USING VIRGINIA AID

U. S. Judge Paul Says White Units Must Drop Public Teachers or Integrate

By ANTHONY LEWIS
Special to The New York Times.

HARRISONBURG, Va., Oct. 8—Federal District Judge John Paul ruled today that "private" classes set up to replace closed Virginia schools must stop using public funds and teachers or else end segregation themselves.

"It is the opinion of the court," Judge Paul said, "that these so-called private schools are an obvious evasion of the mandate of the Supreme Court."

His order affects Charlottesville, where 1,700 children have been shut out of a high school and an elementary school, and Warren County, where 1,000 students are out of the county's only high school.

A state anti-integration law requires the closing of any public school where white and Negro children are enrolled.

Court to Rule on Norfolk

About 10,000 children are out of school in Norfolk. Judge Walter E. Hoffman will consider that case on Friday of this week.

In Charlottesville, public school teachers have been giving classes in private homes and churches and lodge halls. A similar plan for Warren County is scheduled to start tomorrow.

Attorneys of the National Association for the Advancement of Colored People had asked Judge Paul in effect to make the two school boards reopen their schools. This was the burden of "motions for further relief" that they filed in the two cases.

Judge Paul said he did not think he had the right to direct the reopening of schools. He noted particularly that a suit to test the school closing law has been filed by state authorities in the Virginia Supreme Court of Appeals, and said he recognized the "propriety" of letting the issue be fought out there.

Asks State's Good Faith

But the judge said the state authorities, if they are in good faith, should not try to enforce the challenged acts until the results of the legal test are in.

"The state is not pursuing that course," he said. "It has closed these schools, and it is continuing to assist education in what are called private schools but are really public. All that has happened is that they've closed the school buildings but are continuing to operate the schools in other buildings.

"If the state is going to discontinue public education in these localities," he added, "it must be a complete abandonment and not a pretext."

Judge Paul's decision was based on the doctrine—re-emphasized by the Supreme Court in its Little Rock opinion last week—that no institution that

Continued on Page 27, Column 1

Announcement Of Pope's Death

By United Press International.

CASTEL GANDOLFO, Italy, Thursday, Oct. 9—Following is the official announcement of the death of the Pope:

The Supreme Pontiff, Pope Pius XII, is dead. Pius XII, the most esteemed and venerated man in the world, one of the greatest Pontiffs of the century, with sanctity passed away at 3:52 A. M., Oct. 9, 1958.

Eugenio Pacelli was born March 2, 1876, and elected Pope on March 2, 1939, with the name of Pius XII. He was therefore 82 years 7 months 7 days, and his pontificate was nineteen years 7 months and 7 days.

The Catholic Church and the whole world, for whose profit he spent his brilliant, intellectual energies, his heart and his actions, now gather in mourning around his body and memory, grateful for the immense and valid work he carried out to re-establish among men, children of God, the force of justice, law and peace.

Let the unanimous prayers for the repose of his lofty soul, which today passed into eternal bliss, rise from the hearts of all faithful and the entire Christianity.

U. S. ORDERS HALT IN QUEMOY ESCORT

Set to Resume Operations if Reds End Cease-Fire—Chiang Was Consulted

By E. W. KENWORTHY
Special to The New York Times.

WASHINGTON, Oct. 8—The United States announced today that its naval vessels in the Taiwan Strait had stopped escorting Chinese Nationalist convoys supplying Quemoy.

At the same time the United States made clear that it would resume the escort operations if the Chinese Communists resumed their artillery attacks on the Quemoy group.

Three days ago the Communists announced in a broadcast directed at the Nationalists that the bombardment had been ordered suspended for a week on condition that the United States stopped escorting Nationalist convoys.

Today the State Department said that the escort activity had been undertaken at the request of the Nationalist Government, and had been ordered "to the extent militarily neces-

Continued on Page 7, Column 5

President Completes His Staff, Naming Counsel as No. 2 Aide

Gerald D. Morgan

David W. Kendall

Associated Press

By FELIX BELAIR Jr.
Special to The New York Times.

WASHINGTON, Oct. 8—President Eisenhower completed the reorganization of the White House staff today by designating Gerald D. Morgan as No. 2 man in the chain of command. Mr. Morgan, who is 49 years old, has been special counsel to the President since February, 1956.

The announcement of the designation of Mr. Morgan was accompanied by the appointment of David W. Kendall, Washington attorney, to succeed Mr. Morgan as special counsel.

The promotion of another "old hand" on the White House staff served to emphasize President Eisenhower's continued main reliance on the staff system rather

Continued on Page 61, Column 1

COLLEGE IS CALLED

55 Princes of Church Rule Pending Vote in 15 to 18 Days

Special to The New York Times.

ROME, Thursday, Oct. 9—The death of Pope Pius XII today opened the interregnum, or regime of the Holy See's vacancy. It will last until a new Pontiff is elected by the Cardinals in a secret conclave, to be convened not sooner than Oct. 24 or later than Oct. 27.

During the next few weeks the Church will be governed by the Sacred College of Cardinals. As dean of this body, Eugene Cardinal Tisserant immediately instructed the Vatican Secretariat of State to notify all his colleagues that the Apostolic See had become vacant, and to summon them to Rome.

Later today, the French-born, bearded Cardinal, who is 74 years old, is to make the formal announcement of the Pope's death to the diplomats accredited to the Holy See and, through them or through apostolic nuncios in world capitals, to heads of state.

Fastest Travel Urged

Fifteen Cardinals were present in or near Rome early this morning. Of these, thirteen are Italians. The other two are Cardinal Tisserant and Gregory Peter XV, Cardinal Agagianian, a Russian-born Armenian who has risen to prominence in the Roman Curia, or central church administration.

Italian Cardinals heading Archdioceses in various parts of the country are due to reach the capital later today. Cardinals outside Italy are expected and indeed requested to come to Rome by the fastest possible means.

With aviation just entering the jet age, it may be foreseen that members of the Sacred College will gather here much quicker than after the death of Pius XI in 1939.

Will Meet Daily

As the "Senate of the Church," the Cardinals will hold a plenary meeting later today and will reconvene every day until they enter the conclave.

One of the first items on the agenda of the Cardinals' meeting later today will be the transfer of Pius XII's body from his death bed at Castel Gandolfo to Rome.

As if he had had a premonition, the late Pontiff in his apostolic constitution of 1945 concerning the vacancy of the Holy See inserted a provision contemplating the possibility of a Pope's death outside Rome. This had not occurred since the end of the eighteenth century.

The provision was that the Cardinals must see to it that the dead Pontiff is moved to St. Peter's Basilica in Rome in a "decorous and dignified manner."

Some of the powers of the Sacred College will be wielded in its name by the Cardinal Camerlengo, or chamberlain of the church. This dignitary will be elected by the cardinals in their first plenary meeting later today.

Now 55 Cardinals

The Sacred College now has fifty-five members, fifteen short of its full complement of seventy. Fifteen are in Rome. Most of the remaining forty will proceed here immediately for the exercise of the college's interim powers.

Most of these men are aged—in their seventies and eighties. Some are behind the Iron Curtain.

Jozsef Cardinal Mindszenty, Primate of Hungary, has been told that he will be allowed to go to Rome, but he has indicated that he probably will not do so, because he fears that the government might not readmit him.

The Cardinal is a refugee in the United States Legation in Budapest.

Others who may not reach Rome are Stefan Cardinal Wyszynski, Primate of Poland, and Aloysius Cardinal Stepinac, Primate of Yugoslavia. Cardinal

Continued on Page 24, Column 5

POPE PIUS XII

Associated Press

City Pays Homage On Receiving News Of Pontiff's Death

The news of the death of Pope Pius XII was received with varying manifestations in the New York area last night.

As the news became known in Times Square, many Roman Catholics paused and then continued on their way. A few inclined their heads briefly as they gave a prayer for the repose of the Pope's soul. Others made the sign of the cross unobtrusively.

Many Catholics walked to the nearest Roman Catholic church, some of which had been kept open beyond their usual 10 P. M. closing, aware that the Pope's death was imminent. There, prayers were said and impromptu services were held informally as the communicants offered prayers to the effect that Pope Pius' soul reach Heaven.

Some Churches Reopened

As some of the Catholic churches reopened their doors and their lights streamed out onto the sidewalks, patrolling policemen, many of whom had not heard of the Pope's death, stopped to investigate. Some of them stayed to pray.

Some persons, not all of Catholic faith, felt the hard-to-describe emotion experienced when the news of the death of one of the great world figures comes to them.

The Pope's death found Cardinal Spellman, Archbishop of the Diocese of New York aboard the Greek liner, Olympia, bound for New York from Cannes, France. He had been accompanying a group of 450 Catholics visiting the Holy Places of Europe. He received an audience with the late Pope several days ago.

The Chancery, at 452 Madison Avenue, headquarters of the

Continued on Page 21, Column 4

3 Countries Named To Security Council

By KATHLEEN TELTSCH
Special to The New York Times.

UNITED NATIONS, N. Y., Oct. 8—Italy, Tunisia and Argentina were elected to Security Council membership today. They will fill the vacancies that occur when the terms of Sweden, Iraq and Colombia expire at the end of 1958.

The three new members were elected at a session of the General Assembly. The voting by secret ballot was a formality since the three nations were unchallenged candidates.

The six nonpermanent seats on the Council are traditionally allotted to nations of six broad geographic areas. There have been exceptions, the latest in 1957, when Japan was elected to

Continued on Page 14, Column 8

ROME HEARS TOLL OF BELLS FOR PIUS

Some Citizens in Prayer Before St. Peter's Basilica as End Is Announced

By PAUL HOFMANN
Special to The New York Times.

ROME, Thursday, Oct. 9—When Rome's many church bells started tolling before dawn today to announce the death of Pius XII, a few persons were still praying in St. Peter's Square and in the city's churches that had remained open all night.

They had remained from the throngs gathered yesterday in the Square and at the churches.

Some crossed themselves at the announcement and fell to their knees to pray for the dead Pontiff's soul. Many were tearful. One elderly woman was heard to exclaim, "A saint has left us."

Attention Concentrated

At midnight thousands had still been thronging in front of St. Peter's Basilica. Among them were a group of pilgrims who had come from Germany in a dozen buses.

Although the streets and open squares of Rome had gradually emptied about 2 A. M., many Romans stayed up at their homes to follow transmissions of the Vatican radio from Castel Gandolfo.

Listeners said they were deeply impressed and moved by the post-midnight mass said at the dying Pope's beside by one of his former closest aides, Archbishop Domenico Tardini. The homely Roman accent with which the popular prelate flavors his Latin for once sounded solemn and grave as he recited the prayers of the dying.

After the end of the mass, the Vatican radio urged listeners to keep their sets tuned in and to pray for the Pontiff while waiting that "God's will be done."

The announcement to Rome of Pius XII's death was made in a brief bulletin by the Vatican radio at 3:56 A. M. (10:56 P. M., Wednesday, New York time.) Sacred music followed.

Pilgrims at Castel Gandolfo

Special to The New York Times.

CASTEL GANDOLFO, Italy, Oct. 8—Thousands of Romans and pilgrims gathered in this hill town today to be near the dying Pope and to pray for him.

With few exceptions they did not object to television cameras, batteries of klieg lights and clusters of newsmen in the narrow piazza in front of the pontifical palace.

The paraphernalia would have caused Pope Pius XII himself to smile indulgently and understandingly, a reporter told an officer when the Italian police attempted to clear part of

Continued on Page 24, Column 3

PONTIFF 19 YEARS

End Comes Quietly in Papal Bedroom at Summer Palace

By ARNALDO CORTESI
Special to The New York Times.

CASTEL GANDOLFO, Italy, Thursday, Oct. 9—Pope Pius XII, the 260th successor of the Apostle Peter on the Pontifical throne of Rome, died at 3:52 A. M. today (10:52 P. M. New York time, Wednesday).

The Pontiff's death came as millions prayed for him throughout the world.

The 82-year-old Pontiff did not regain consciousness after a cerebral stroke he suffered yesterday morning.

It was the second stroke he had suffered in forty-seven hours. The first occurred at 8:30 A. M. Monday and he seemed to be recovering from it.

The second stroke struck him at 7:30 A. M. yesterday. After it the Pope sank gradually until the moment of his death.

Death occurred in a simple and unadorned bedroom on the second floor at the back of the papal palace of Castel Gandolfo.

End Comes Quietly

The Pope was passing the summer there in the cooler atmosphere of the Alban Hills as he had done every year. He had planned to return to the Vatican at the end of November in time for the spiritual exercises before Christmas.

Pius XII had been Pope for nineteen years, seven months and seven days since his elevation to the pontificate March 2, 1939. He was born in Rome March 2, 1876. He was, therefore, elevated to the pontificate on his 63rd birthday and was a week more than 82 years and seven months of age when he died.

Since the Pope had been unconscious for many hours before his death he had left no last words in the generally accepted meaning of this term. The last recorded words that he uttered were: "Pray, pray, pray that this unhappy situation for the Church may end."

At the moment of his death Pius XII was completely paralyzed and incapable of any movement. He had been un-

Continued on Page 21, Column 1

WASHINGTON SEES LEBANON SECURE

Plans to Recall All Troops—Karami Said to Quit

By DANA ADAMS SCHMIDT
Special to The New York Times.

WASHINGTON, Oct. 8—United States troops will be "totally withdrawn from Lebanon" by the end of this month, the State Department announced today.

The department said this decision was based on improvement in "international aspects of Lebanon's security situation" and progress toward "more stable international conditions in the area."

[Reports from Beirut said Premier Rashid Karami had resigned after thirty-one of the sixty-six Deputies in Parliament said they would not support him. United States tanks were patrolling Beirut after a band disarmed three military policemen.]

State Department officials explained that Lebanon's security situation had improved mainly as a result of the election of a new President and the tapering off of the United Arab Republic's "indirect aggression" against Lebanon.

Interference in the life of Lebanon by infiltration of arms and men has apparently ceased, they said. Inflammatory broadcasts against the Government of Lebanon also have diminished, although broadcasts against the Government of Jordan have tapered off only a little, the officials reported.

In this connection the officials

Continued on Page 8, Column 1

"All the News That's Fit to Print"

The New York Times.

LATE CITY EDITION
U.S. Weather Bureau Report (Page 69) forecast: Mostly cloudy today; mostly fair tonight and tomorrow.
Temp. range: 56—44. Yesterday: 47.2—44.6.

VOL. CVIII..No. 36,803. © 1958, by The New York Times Company. Times Square, New York 36, N. Y. NEW YORK, WEDNESDAY, OCTOBER 29, 1958. 10¢ beyond 100-mile zone from New York City. Higher in air delivery cities. FIVE CENTS

CARDINAL RONCALLI ELECTED POPE; VENETIAN, 76, REIGNS AS JOHN XXIII; THOUSANDS HAIL HIM AT ST. PETER'S

Associated Press Radiophoto

THE NEW PONTIFF, Pope John XXIII, raising his hand in blessing yesterday on a balcony of St. Peter's Basilica. He appeared before throng an hour after he was elected.

PRESIDENT CALLS FOR VICTORY HERE TO AID HIS POLICY

Tells G. O. P. Workers That Democrats Lack Honest and Sane Principles

HE LAUDS ROCKEFELLER

Asks Special Aid to Keating —Meets Kean and Zeller —Talks at Sports Fete

By HARRISON E. SALISBURY

President Eisenhower yesterday attacked the "dominant wing" of the Democratic party as lacking "straightforward, honest, sound and sane principles, which make America great."

The President leveled the charge in urging Republican campaign workers here to make every effort to elect Nelson A. Rockefeller and Representative Kenneth B. Keating, the party's candidates for Governor and Senator.

The President spent the day in New York largely in political endeavors connected with the campaign. He spoke at two rallies of campaign workers and conferred with several candidates.

He traveled by bubble-topped car through midtown Manhattan streets. A persistent drizzle cut down street crowds. The police estimated that 30,000 persons saw the President.

Attends Football Dinner

The President spent just one minute less than twenty-four hours in the city. He arrived at La Guardia Airport at 11:14 P. M. Monday and departed last night at 11:13 o'clock after attending the first annual Football Hall of Fame dinner, sponsored by the National Football Foundation and the Football Hall of Fame at the Astor Hotel.

The President landed in Washington at 12:14 A. M. and went directly to the White House.

While the President's day was largely devoted to political tasks the partisan note was firmly sounded only once. This was during a brief talk he gave to workers at Republican campaign headquarters at the Roosevelt Hotel.

In making only one such call President Eisenhower generally followed the emphasis on an appeal to the independent, non-party voter that has been stressed by Mr. Rockefeller in his gubernatorial bid.

All Deny a Split

President Eisenhower did not repeat the harsh language he employed on the Pacific Coast in characterizing Democratic "radicals" or in calling for a "fumigation" of labor unions whose leaders had been found unworthy. Mr. Rockefeller has dissociated himself from these remarks of the President.

James A. Hagerty, the President's press secretary, vigorously denied that Mr. Rockefeller had indicated a negative attitude toward campaign efforts in New York City by the President.

Mr. Hagerty did say, however, that the state Republican committee had not, to his knowledge, requested the President to come to New York.

Mr. Rockefeller went out of his way to make clear that

Continued on Page 25, Column 1

Airliner Takes Dive To Avoid Collision

By The Associated Press

MIAMI, Fla., Oct. 28—A Panagra airliner with forty-five persons aboard dived to safety last night under a formation of an Air Force refueling tanker and two jet fighters.

The pilot of the airliner said that he was flying at an assigned altitude on a recognized airway when the incident took place over Wilmington, N. C., at 6:47 P. M.

The Air Force said that the tanker had a Civil Aeronautics Administration clearance within a 100-mile radius of Florence, N. C. The three Air Force craft were eighty-two miles from Florence when the incident took place.

The airliner was bound from New York to Peru, with stops at Washington and Miami.

The plane was manned by a

Continued on Page 19, Column 4

R.C.A. Yields in Trust Suit; Will Ease Patent Licensing

Consent Action to Aid Competitors and Inventors in Radio Field—Company Fined $100,000 in Monopoly Case

By EDWARD RANZAL

The Government's antitrust suits against the Radio Corporation of America ended yesterday in Federal court with a consent judgment and a fine.

R. C. A. declined to defend itself against the charges of criminal monopoly in the licensing of electronic radio equipment patents and was fined $100,000.

At the same time, the Government's civil action was ended with the consent judgment. Competitors will now be able to obtain R. C. A. electronic radio patents under a relaxed licensing agreement.

The decree also will assure patent owners of a competitive market for their inventions and will permit them to exploit the fruits of their own research, according to Victor R. Hansen, assistant attorney general in charge of the Antitrust Division.

A statement issued by David Sarnoff, chairman of the board, and John L. Burns, president of R. C. A., declared that the terms of the decree dealt primarily with apparatus for radio purposes and did not affect the company's activities in automation, electronic computers, medical electronics and other aspects of the new industrial field.

The criminal indictment was filed Feb. 1. R. C. A. pleaded no defense to the four counts—restraint of commerce in radio

Continued on Page 35, Column 3

Survey Finds Ohio Divided Over 'Right-to-Work' Issue

A Times Team Report

This is a report from a New York Times team that surveyed political sentiment in Ohio. Team members were Wayne Phillips, Edith Evans Asbury, Stanley Levey, Joseph A. Loftus and William G. Weart. Eleven pivotal states have been surveyed previously and other reports, including some state rechecks, will continue until the elections next Tuesday.

By WAYNE PHILLIPS

Special to The New York Times.

COLUMBUS, Oct. 27—With barely a week to go before the election, Ohio is a divided and confused state.

The presence on the ballot of a proposed "right-to-work" amendment to the State Constitution has become the dominant political issue, overshadowing contests for Governor and United States Senator.

The amendment would outlaw the union shop provision contained in 82 per cent of Ohio labor-management contracts. The provision makes union membership after a stated period a requisite of employment.

Members of a New York Times team, talking to voters from the Ohio River to Lake Erie, from the Pennsylvania to the Indiana border, found people thoroughly confused on how to vote on the amendment.

Unusual Interest in Off-Year

Republican Gov. C. William O'Neill appeared to be running behind his Democratic opponent, Michael V. DiSalle, former Mayor of Toledo and former Federal Price Administrator.

Senator John W. Bricker, a Republican, seemed to be safe in his bid for a third term unless the controversy over the "work" amendment brought out a disproportionately heavy Democratic vote.

If that happened, any of nine Republican-held Congressional seats might be in danger. Otherwise, the team saw little prospect of a change in the state's present Congressional line-up of seventeen Republicans and six Democrats.

Proponents of the amendment argue that it would help to clean up union corruption and make unions more responsive to the will of members. Opponents argue that it would destroy unions, reduce wages and undermine social benefits for which unions had fought.

The proposed amendment has created deep and bitter disputes

Continued on Page 26, Column 1

RECORD HIGH SET BY NATIONAL DEBT

Total at $280,851,429,657 Under Deficit Borrowing as Revenue Declines

By United Press International.

WASHINGTON, Oct. 28—The national debt, with larger spending and a decline in Government income as factors, has reached a record high, it was disclosed today.

The Treasury's daily financial statement showed that it was $280,851,429,657.13 on Oct. 23. Included are some non-Treasury securities the Government guarantees. The previous high was $280,821,613,238.96 on Dec. 31, 1955.

Based on the population of about 175,000,000, the new figure represents a debt of $1,604.87 for every man, woman and child in the nation. This per capita figure, however, is not a record. In the fiscal year 1946, before the post-war upsurge in the population, the per capita debt was $1,905.42. The debt then was $269,422,099,173.

The latest rise in the debt reflected recent Treasury borrowing to finance the record peacetime budget deficit of $12,000,000,000 expected for the current fiscal year. The deficit results

Continued on Page 39, Column 6

DULLES ASSAILS REDS' HALF-TRUCE AS POLITICAL STEP

Says Alternate-Day Shelling of Quemoy Results in 'Promiscuous Killing'

Transcript of the Dulles news conference is on Page 18.

By E. W. KENWORTHY

Special to The New York Times.

WASHINGTON, Oct. 28—Secretary of State Dulles said today that the intermittent shelling of Quemoy by the Chinese Communists had no military purpose and amounted to promiscuous killing for political ends.

Asked at his news conference what he thought of "the idea of having war every other day," Mr. Dulles replied:

"If you have a military purpose, you carry on your shooting for military objectives and your purpose is to destroy the capacity of your enemy to resist. When you do it only every other day and say, in between times, you can bring in supplies * * * that shows the killing is done for political purposes and promiscuously." [Question 5, Page 18.]

Red Conditions Recalled

The Chinese Communists have announced that they will not shell key military objectives on even-numbered days to enable the Nationalists to bring in supplies.

Mr. Dulles said he knew of no precedent for the alternate-day cease-fire, but he did have an explanation for what he called this "outlandish and rather uncivilized" procedure.

After seven weeks of trying to interdict resupplying of the islands, Mr. Dulles said, the Communists discovered that "the islands could not be cut off and made to wither on the vine."

"Therefore," he continued, "they had to confront a new situation. They knew that we could resupply the island, so in order to save face, they said, 'We will let you resupply the island every other day.'" [Questions 6 and 7.]

No General War Seen

In view of their failure to reduce the island or cut it off, Mr. Dulles said he doubted that the Chinese Communists would now "engage in a level of military effort which is likely to provoke a general war." [Question 7.]

Unquestionably, Mr. Dulles said, Peiping's real objective is not the offshore islands but Taiwan itself. The Communists, he indicated, hope to achieve that objective through a long-range propaganda campaign designed "to split the inhabitants of Taiwan away from cooperation with the Americans."

To that end, he suggested, the Chinese Communists are refurbishing the pre-World War II Japanese propaganda theme of a "co-prosperity sphere of Asia for the Asians."

The Chinese Communists, he declared, are now saying, "Let us work together and get rid of these Americans; they are the

Continued on Page 18, Column 4

DULLES IS GLOOMY ON A NUCLEAR BAN

Doubts Test Suspension Can Be Negotiated as Soviet Finds It Is 'Behind'

By DANA ADAMS SCHMIDT

Special to The New York Times

WASHINGTON, Oct. 28—Secretary of State Dulles said today that prospects for negotiating a ban on nuclear tests were dim because the Soviet Union had discovered it was "considerably behind" the United States in nuclear weapons development.

Soviet realization of inferiority grew out of the meetings of experts at Geneva last summer on technical means of controlling a suspension of nuclear tests, he said at his news conference.

As a result, he continued, the Soviet Union has "lost interest in the suspension" of tests, which is the subject of negotiations to begin in Geneva Friday. [Question 11, Page 18.]

The Secretary opened his conference by reading a statement denouncing Soviet "insincerity" on the test issue. This, he said, was "clearly exposed" by the Soviet rejection yesterday of the proposal of the United States and Britain to suspend tests for at least one year beginning Oct. 31.

After years of propaganda designed to show the Soviet Union's "high humanitarian purposes" and "concern for the effect of testing upon human

Continued on Page 6, Column 3

3 Russians and Briton Win Nobel Awards for Science

By WERNER WISKARI

Special to The New York Times.

STOCKHOLM, Sweden, Oct. 28—Three Soviet physicists and a British biochemist were named today as winners of Nobel Prizes in science. The 1958 physics prize is to be shared by Dr. Pavel A. Cherenkov, Prof. Ilya M. Frank and Academician Igor Y. Tamm, all members of the Physics Institute of the Soviet Academy of Sciences.

They were cited for research beginning in the Nineteen Thirties that is credited with having opened the way to recent discoveries of atomic particles, such as the antiproton, and with spurring the study of cosmic radiation.

[In Moscow, it was indicated that the three Soviet scientists would go to Stockholm to receive their prize.]

Briton Is Chemistry Winner

The 1958 chemistry prize goes to Dr. Frederick Sanger of Cambridge University's department of biochemistry. He was honored for developing a method for studying the structure of proteins and especially for isolating and identifying the components of the insulin molecule.

The prizes were announced this afternoon by the Royal Swedish Academy of Science, designated to make the annual awards under the will of Alfred Nobel, the Swedish inventor of dynamite. Each of the Nobel awards this year amounts to the equivalent of $41,420.

Like Tuesday's literature award to the poet and novelist Boris Pasternak, the physics prize constitutes a Soviet first. The only Soviet citizen to win a Nobel award before this year was Nikolai N. Semenov, who shared the 1956 chemistry prize with Sir Cyril Norman Hinshelwood of Britain.

Two Russians, Ivan P. Pavlov

Continued on Page 10, Column 3

Diefenbaker Sees Gain in Ties to U. S.

By RUSSELL PORTER

Prime Minister John Diefenbaker of Canada said last night that relations between Canada and the United States had improved in the last year, but that problems remained in the field of trade and economic affairs.

He urged that trade relations between the two countries be based on Canadian as well as American rights. Against the Soviet economic offensive, he declared, freedom cannot afford to allow the economic weakening of any free nation.

Mr. Diefenbaker spoke here at a dinner of the Pilgrims of the United States in his honor at the Waldorf-Astoria Hotel.

Secretary of State Dulles joined in the tribute to Mr. Diefenbaker and stressed the importance of Canadian-Ameri-

Continued on Page 16, Column 1

U.S. WON'T OPPOSE CHANGES IN NATO

However, Washington Aides Shun de Gaulle Plan for 3-Power Directorate

By JACK RAYMOND

Special to The New York Times.

WASHINGTON, Oct. 28—United States officials indicated today that the organizational structure of the North Atlantic alliance was as good as could be expected, but said they would not oppose some changes.

The proposal by Premier Charles de Gaulle of France for a United States-British-French political executive has found little sympathy here, regardless of whether the group is set up within NATO or outside it.

The proposal was contained in letters sent by the French leader to President Eisenhower and Prime Minister Harold Macmillan.

The chief reason for United States coolness toward the proposal is that most of the fifteen countries in the alliance have made clear that they are against it.

NATO Base Broadened

The majority, it was observed here, is composed of the small countries. They have, in recent years, forced changes that broaden rather than narrow the base of military and political responsibility in the organization.

The United States is interested in proposals for broadening the area of NATO responsibility. However, officials here are wary of any extension that would make NATO more than a "regional" organization as approved by the United Nations.

Nevertheless, peripheral problems, such as those developing in the Middle East, are recognized as having a great impact on the Western alliance. United States officials are prepared to discuss this.

At the same time it was made evident here that the United States wants to avoid participating in the formation of a Big Three political arrangement that commits this country to consultation on its world obligations.

The United States has agreed at past NATO meetings to discuss its affairs, but only as a matter of agreement rather than formal obligation.

Premier de Gaulle's proposal, which became known last week-

Continued on Page 6, Column 3

11 BALLOTS TAKEN

New Pontiff Elevates Conclave Secretary to Cardinalate

By ARNALDO CORTESI

Special to The New York Times.

ROME, Oct. 28—Angelo Giuseppe Cardinal Roncalli, Patriarch of Venice, was elevated to the Papacy this afternoon. He will be 77 years old Nov. 25.

He will sit on the throne of St. Peter as the 262d Supreme Pontiff of the Roman Catholic Church and will rule the Church as sovereign under the name of John XXIII. No Sovereign Pontiff has used the name John since 1334, when John XXII died.

The successor to Pope Pius XII, who died Oct. 9, was elected on the eleventh ballot by fifty-one Cardinals assembled in conclave since Saturday. He was named as the third day of the voting in a walled enclosure in the Vatican was drawing to a close.

The conclave that elevated him was one of the fifteen shortest held since the Papacy returned to Rome from Avignon, France, in the second half of the fourteenth century. Fifty-nine conclaves have been held since then.

Coronation Likely Nov. 9

Cardinal Roncalli became Supreme Pontiff at the very moment when he replied affirmatively on being asked by the Dean of the Sacred College of Cardinals whether he accepted his election. He uttered the Latin word "Accepto" ("I accept") a few minutes before 5 P. M. [11 A. M. New York time]. He was invested with the full powers of the Papacy from that instant, though his reign will be counted from the day of his coronation, expected to be Nov. 9.

One hour after his election, the new Pope appeared on the outer balcony of St. Peter's Basilica and gave his first blessing as a Pope to the thousands gathered in St. Peter's Square. Before and after the blessing the crowd sang hymns. The hymns sung were "Christus Vincit" (Christ Conquers) and the Te Deum.

New Cardinal Named

As the first act of his Pontificate, Pope John XXIII conferred the Cardinal's red hat on Msgr. Alberto di Jorio, who had acted as secretary of the conclave. The new Pope did so by removing his own Cardinal's biretta from his head and placing it on that of Msgr. di Jorio.

This was a return to tradition, since in the past all Popes were wont to reward the secretary of the conclave. However, Pius XII omitted to do so.

The new Pope also asked all Cardinals to remain in conclave until tomorrow morning, which they did.

That the Catholic Church again had a head was conveyed to watchers in St. Peter's Square by the white smoke emanating from a stovepipe above the roof of the Sistine Chapel, where the voting took

Continued on Page 14, Column 1

New Pontiff Faces Difficult Problems

By PAUL HOFMANN

Special to The New York Times

ROME, Oct. 28—Pope John XXIII was a successful Vatican diplomat before he became the new Supreme Pontiff of the Roman Catholic Church.

His great experience and skill in two distant fields of work for the church should enable the former Angelo Giuseppe Cardinal Roncalli to cope with the formidable problems confronting the Papacy at present, high ecclesiastics said tonight.

In choosing the Patriarch of Venice and former Apostolic Nuncio to France the Sacred College of Cardinals overcame with great wisdom its initial uncertainty whether to place on the Throne of St. Peter a "pastoral" or a "diplomatic" Pontiff, the churchmen remarked. The personality of

Continued on Page 15, Column 1

The New York Times

HIGH HOPES are expressed by President Eisenhower as he leaves the Astor Hotel here. With the President yesterday were Kenneth B. Keating, left, and Nelson A. Rockefeller, the Republican candidates for Senator and Governor.

"All the News That's Fit to Print"

The New York Times.

LATE CITY EDITION
U.S. Weather Bureau Report (Page 57) forecasts: Partly cloudy, warmer today; cloudy milder, chance of rain tomorrow.
Temp. range: 42—25. Yesterday: 35.3—27.9.

VOL. CVIII..No. 36,938. NEW YORK, FRIDAY, MARCH 13, 1959. 10 cents beyond 50-mile zone from New York City except on Long Island. Higher in air delivery cities. FIVE CENTS

HAWAII IS VOTED INTO UNION AS 50TH STATE; HOUSE GRANTS FINAL APPROVAL, 323 TO 89; EISENHOWER'S SIGNATURE OF BILL ASSURED

ADENAUER IS FIRM AGAINST TROOP CUT IN MIDDLE EUROPE

Gets Assurance in Talks With Macmillan That the British Seek No Disengagement

By SYDNEY GRUSON
Special to The New York Times.

BONN, Germany, March 12—Chancellor Konrad Adenauer restated to Prime Minister Harold Macmillan today West Germany's opposition to any reduction of Allied forces in Central Europe except within a general disarmament agreement.

The British leader came to Bonn today to give the Chancellor a personal report on his recent conversations in Moscow and to reassure the West Germans that Britain was not seeking the disengagement of Eastern and Western forces in Germany.

Nor, said a British Foreign Office spokesman, does London favor even a controlled limitation of forces if this would result in disequilibrium between the troops and armaments of East and West in Central Europe.

Trip Is Second of Three

Mr. Macmillan's trip here was the second of his three planned journeys to brief other Western leaders about his talks with Premier Nikita S. Khrushchev of the Soviet Union. Mr. Macmillan was in Paris earlier this week and he will cross the Atlantic for separate meetings with President Eisenhower and Prime Minister John Diefenbaker of Canada next week.

The first session between Mr. Macmillan and Dr. Adenauer, who were accompanied by their foreign ministers and two advisers each, lasted three hours. The talks were resumed tonight after a dinner in Mr. Macmillan's honor. They will continue tomorrow in the Chancellor's Palais Schaumburg offices.

The differences in outlook between the Prime Minister and the Chancellor were evident in their remarks at the airport on Mr. Macmillan's arrival.

Mr. Macmillan said the West was firm and united on the prin-

Continued on Page 3, Column 4

Governor Taking Charge Of Meeting City Tax Needs

Orders Report on Costs and Resources for Conference With Mayor Tomorrow —Wants an Agreement Next Week

By DOUGLAS DALES
Special to The New York Times.

ALBANY, March 12,—With his own program for higher state taxes out of the way, Governor Rockefeller has decided to take personal command of the Albany action needed to help New York City balance its budget for the fiscal year starting July 1.

The decision was made at a meeting with Republican legislative leaders today, called to discuss the conference to be held with Mayor Wagner Saturday morning on the city's budget problem.

The meeting will be held at the Executive Mansion and will be attended by Republican and Democratic legislative leaders.

In preparation for the meeting, Governor Rockefeller hastily named a task force to examine New York City's needs and the resources that might be tapped to meet them. A report has been asked by tomorrow night in time to be digested before the meeting with the Mayor.

The task force was designated at a meeting attended by Mr. Rockefeller, Tax Commissioner Joseph H. Murphy, Budget Director T. Norman Hurd, Majority Leader Walter J. Mahoney of the Senate and Majority Leader Joseph F. Carlino of

Continued on Page 16, Column 4

Snowfall of 5 to 10 Inches Delays All Transit in Area

By PETER KIHSS

With spring only nine days away, the city got its heaviest snowfall of the season yesterday—5.3 inches. It was perhaps nature's way of marking the seventy-first anniversary of the famous blizzard of '88.

On March 12, 1888, that storm hurled 16.5 inches of snow on the city, and in two more days brought the total to 20.9 inches.

Rockland and Fairfield Counties reported ten inches of snow yesterday; Westchester, seven to nine; Bergen, six to seven; Long Island, five to six; Elizabeth, N. J., 5.4, and New Brunswick, N. J., two to three.

Rain and warming temperatures turned the snow into slush in the city. Temperatures dropped during the night, however, and turned the slush to ice on some roadways. The less heavily traveled roads in the suburbs and upstate were reported especially dangerous.

The forecast for today was for partly cloudy and warmer. The temperature may reach the low forties and cause the ice and snow to melt.

Yesterday's storm was caused by two low-pressure areas moving in from the Midwest and from the Virginia coast. Snow fell throughout the Northeast. Depths ranged up to fourteen inches in Chautauqua County on Lake Erie, the Schoharie Valley west of Albany and in western Maryland.

Seven deaths were attributed to the storm in New York, New Jersey and Ohio.

The city's public schools had only 70 per cent attendance. Radio station WOR, which gathers and broadcasts news of

Continued on Page 22, Column 1

GOVERNOR NAMES COMMERCE HEAD

Appoints McHugh, President of New York Telephone—Utility Picks Successor

Governor Rockefeller completed his Cabinet in Albany yesterday with the appointment of Keith S. McHugh to head the Department of Commerce.

Mr. McHugh, who is 64 years old, will retire as president of the New York Telephone Company on April 30 to accept the appointment.

Governor Rockefeller said he was looking to Mr. McHugh to "invigorate" the department so that its full potential to stimulate business in the state would be realized.

Mr. McHugh is leaving a $150,000-a-year job for one that pays $18,500. However, within a year, he will qualify for a company pension as a forty-year man. A company spokesman said a pension arrangement would be worked out by the board of directors.

Meanwhile, the directors of the telephone company elected Clifton W. Phalen to succeed

Continued on Page 16, Column 2

CITY VOTES DEAL ON POWER PLANTS WITH CON EDISON

But Contract Is Changed to Permit New Bids When Final Auction Is Held

By PAUL CROWELL

Contracts for the sale of the city's three rapid-transit power plants to the Consolidated Edison Company at a gross price of $125,840,000 were approved unanimously by the Board of Estimate last night.

The vote was taken after the language of the contracts had been changed slightly to make certain that bidders other than Consolidated Edison could submit offers when the power plants were disposed of at public auction, as required by the City Charter.

The changes were made after Harvey M. Spear, counsel for unidentified "substantial New York interests," had complained that his clients might not be able to submit bids technically admissible under the terms of the agreements.

Clients Not Identified

Mr. Spear declined to tell the board the names of his clients, saying that they would be disclosed when bids were received.

Mr. Spear said his clients, while preferring to submit an offer to purchase the power plants for lease back to the Transit Authority, would also be prepared to submit a bid for purchase and operation.

The contracts approved by the board paved the way for transfer of the plants to Consolidated Edison by July 1, assuming that the company was the successful bidder.

The company's bid was for at least $99,382,871 in cash in addition to concessions that would bring the total minimum purchase price up to $125,840,000. The company also offered to supply the three divisions of the city subway system with power under a ten-year contract at uniform rates.

Company Supplies IND

The company now supplies all power for the IND division. The IRT and BMT divisions obtain power from the three city plants that are on Kent Avenue, Brooklyn, and West Fifty-ninth Street and East Forty-seventh Street in Manhattan.

By its vote the Board of Estimate authorized the Mayor to execute, subject to specified conditions, a contract for selling the three plants and one for purchasing power for the three divisions of the city subway system now operated by the Transit Authority.

The board also authorized the Commissioner of Marine and Aviation, Vincent A. G. O'Connor, to execute waterfront leases in connection with the transfer

Continued on Page 15, Column 2

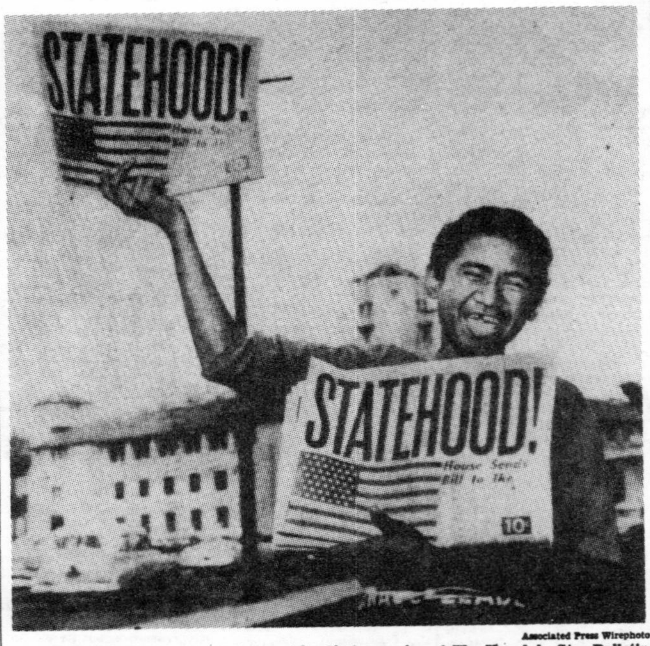

Associated Press Wirephoto

THE BIG NEWS: Chester Kahapea, 13, offering copies of The Honolulu Star-Bulletin yesterday in the Hawaiian capital. The flag on the front page contains fifty stars.

MEASURE SPEEDED

A Short-Cut Sends It Direct to President, Who Is 'Delighted'

By C. P. TRUSSELL
Special to The New York Times

WASHINGTON, March 12—The Territory of Hawaii was voted into the Union today as its fiftieth state.

The House of Representatives gave its approval by a vote of 323 to 89. Yesterday the Senate approved the Hawaii bill, 76 to 15.

President Eisenhower's approval is assured. The White House said today he was "delighted" and noted that "he has been urging it for some time."

Thus, after one of the fastest actions by Congress in years, only the mechanics of admitting a new state remain before Hawaii joins the Union.

The question arose as to whether the island territory some 2,000 miles from continental United States would seek to put its fiftieth star into the flag July 4 of this year when Alaska adds its forty-ninth. There is barely enough time to do so and island leaders doubted that it would be done.

Governor Gives Word

With the galleries filled, the House started its long roll-call in midafternoon. Among the spectators was the Governor of Hawaii, William F. Quinn. When the roll-call began he quietly left the gallery and went to the office of Sam Rayburn, Speaker of the House.

At the Speaker's office Governor Quinn telephoned Acting Gov. Edward E. Johnston at Honolulu and asked him to hold the line. When he was notified that the roll-call had recorded 219 ayes—a majority of the House—Governor Quinn set off a celebration in the islands by shouting:

"Sound the sirens, close the schools and get going."

A little later he added a note of caution:

"Keep the lid on a little, Ed."

Before Hawaii can attain statehood it must hold a referendum on whether it wants to assume the burdens at this time. Besides agreeing at the polls with provisions of the new law,

Continued on Page 13, Column 2

3 OF JOINT CHIEFS WILL BE RENAMED

Twining, Burke and White Slated for New Terms—Lemnitzer to Get Post

By HANSON W. BALDWIN
Special to The New York Times.

WASHINGTON, March 12—The reappointments of three members of the Joint Chiefs of Staff will be announced soon.

Those who will be reappointed to new two-year terms starting this summer are Gen. Nathan F. Twining, chairman of the Joint Chiefs of Staff; Gen. Thomas D. White, Chief of Staff of the Air Force, and Admiral Arleigh A. Burke, Chief of Naval Operations.

Gen. Lyman L. Lemnitzer, Vice Chief of Staff of the Army, will succeed Gen. Maxwell D. Taylor, present Army Chief of Staff, whose second two-year term ends June 30. General Taylor is expected to retire.

The second two-year term of Gen. Randolph McC. Pate, as Commandant of the Marine Corps, does not expire until next Dec. 31, and as far as is known his successor has not yet been selected. General Pate also expects to retire.

The names of Lieut. Gen. Merrill B. Twining, a brother of the chairman of the Joint Chiefs, and of Lieut. Gen. Edwin A. Pollock have been men-

Continued on Page 4, Column 2

U. S. and Canada List Seaway Tolls, Effective on April 1

By RICHARD E. MOONEY
Special to The New York Times.

WASHINGTON, March 12—The United States and Canada announced St. Lawrence Seaway tolls today, to take effect April 1.

They are identical to those proposed last June after negotiations by committees of both nations. The differences are primarily in definitions, mostly for the types of cargo that would qualify for the low rate applying to "bulk" shipments.

[Opposition to the toll setup came from port, rail, shipping and civic interests. They called the rates unrealistically low and the estimated revenue too high. The Port of New York Authority feared a loss of 3,500 waterfront jobs because of "unfair competition" resulting from the tolls.]

Railroads Competing

The Seaway links the Great Lakes and the Atlantic for deepwater ships. Part of it was opened last summer, and the full length is scheduled to be working soon.

Interests that would benefit from the new water route and those against whom it would compete had been fighting over the toll issue.

The fight was moving into a new phase. Major railroads are considering a 20 to 25 per cent reduction of rates they charge for transporting grain for export. This would enable them better to compete with the price for shipping via the waterway.

Seaway tolls are intended to

Continued on Page 10, Column 2

HOUSE UNIT CUTS JOBLESS AID BILL

Restricts Extension of U. S. Assistance to 3 Months Instead of One Year

Special to The New York Times.

WASHINGTON, March 12—The House Ways and Means Committee approved today a bill for a three-month tapering-off of emergency Federal aid to the unemployed.

The measure falls far short of earlier plans by Democratic leaders for a year's extension of the program beyond its present expiration date of March 31.

The effect would be to prevent an abrupt cut-off of payments to about 300,000 jobless workers expected to be drawing the emergency benefits at the end of this month.

Instead, these workers would stay on the rolls until they had exhausted the benefits to which they would have been entitled in the absence of a March 31 termination date.

The committee acted in closed session by what was reported as a one-sided voice vote. The House is expected to pass the bill early next week.

Democratic sources reported that the one-year extension plan had been set aside in the interest of assuring quick enactment of a bill. President Eisenhower and House Republican leaders had voiced strong opposition to the earlier Democratic proposal.

Another factor was the apparent lack of enthusiasm with which the proposed one-year

Continued on Page 18, Column 4

ROCKEFELLER ASKS A DRIVE ON CRIME

In Message to Legislature, He Urges Tighter Laws

By WARREN WEAVER Jr.
Special to The New York Times.

ALBANY, March 12—Governor Rockefeller called on the Legislature today to join him in prosecuting a war against organized crime "more vigorously than ever before."

The Governor sent a special message to the lawmakers, with a dozen recommendations for tightening the existing criminal law and making law-enforcement organizations more powerful and better trained.

In his election campaign last fall, Mr. Rockefeller was outspoken in his criticism of the increase in criminal activity during the Harriman Administration. He pledged swift action against racketeers and law violators if he should be elected.

Mr. Rockefeller urged today that the Legislature:

¶Make it a misdemeanor to defy a subpoena from the State Commission of Investigation or engage in obstructive or contemptuous conduct before the crime panel.

¶Set up a municipal police training council that would establish minimum training standards for all members of police forces.

¶Increase the statute of limitations for prosecution for tax evasion from two to six years, thus giving the state more time

Continued on Page 16, Column 2

There Are Times When Bad Weather Brings Out the Best in a Man

It was such a time yesterday at Vesey St. and Broadway

And a man came forward to lend a gallant, helping hand

Fulton Street Widening Dropped By Jack on Protest of Merchants

The highly controversial proposal to widen part of Fulton Street in lower Manhattan was withdrawn from further consideration yesterday by Borough President Hulan E. Jack of Manhattan.

The action by the Board of Estimate permitting Mr. Jack to drop the project constituted a victory for a group of Fulton Street merchants.

Opponents have fought the proposal as threatening hardship to "hundreds of business men and thousands of their employes." They have also argued that the widening would not materially relieve the area's traffic situation.

Mr. Jack said he favored studies of the possibility of both an eastbound and a westbound artery in lower Manhattan.

Pending such studies, he said, it would be better to withdraw the Fulton Street proposal. In the meantime, he added, he hoped all of those who have been involved in the widening dispute would have a better understanding of the problem.

The proposal that Mr. Jack withdrew called for widening Fulton Street on its south side from Broadway to Water Street. The project was intended as the first stage of an ultimate widening of Fulton Street from South Street to West Street.

Two major slum clearance cooperative housing projects totaling $61,000,000 in cost in the Rockaways, Queens, were approved by the board.

One was Hammels-Rockaway,

Continued on Page 22, Column 6

HAWAIIANS START 2 DAYS' FESTIVITY

Alaska Sends First 'Aloha' to Celebrating Islanders

By LAWRENCE E. DAVIES
Special to The New York Times.

HONOLULU, March 12—The kamaaina and the malihini celebrated today Congressional assurance that the nation was ready to welcome Hawaii as the fiftieth state.

That is to say, the oldtimer—the Hawaiian version of the Alaskan sourdough—joined with the newcomer—the Hawaiian counterpart of the Alaskan cheechako—in opening a two-day demonstration of gratitude over the prospective ending of territorial status for the islands.

The celebration got off to a restrained start. It picked up momentum as the day wore on toward a climax here on the island of Oahu with huge bonfire, aerial and offshore military pyrotechnics and hula dancing.

At the beginning everyone seemed to be waiting for someone else to show the way. Within a half-hour after word came from Washington of the action in the House of Representatives, however, the Waikiki area was clogged with horn-tooting automobiles. Bands and colorfully clad marchers took over at midafternoon.

Colored paper streamers were flung from downtown office buildings along King and Merchant Streets. Hands were thrust forward with a "happy statehood" salutation. Mayor Neal Blaisdell of Honolulu was so

Continued on Page 13, Column 1

"All the News That's Fit to Print"

The New York Times.

LATE CITY EDITION
U. S. Weather Bureau Report (Page 61) forecasts: Considerable cloudiness today and tonight. Chance of showers tomorrow.
Temp. range: 79—66; yesterday: 76.8—63.8.

VOL. CIX..No. 37,137.

NEW YORK, MONDAY, SEPTEMBER 28, 1959.

10 cents beyond 50-mile zone from New York City except on Long Island. Higher in air delivery cities.

FIVE CENTS

PRESIDENT AND KHRUSHCHEV IN AGREEMENT ON NEW BERLIN TALKS AND MORE EXCHANGES; EISENHOWER DEFERS VISIT; PREMIER LEAVES

TYPHOON DEATHS IN JAPAN AT 1,132; 1,457 ARE MISSING

Damage Tops $100,000,000 as Storm Heads North—927,700 Lose Homes

By The Associated Press.

TOKYO, Sept. 27—Battered Japan, struck by the worst typhoon in a quarter of a century, counted more than 2,500 dead or missing today.

As Typhoon Vera headed toward Soviet territory, the national police reported 1,132 known dead, 1,457 missing, 4,668 injured and 927,700 homeless. Damage was unofficially estimated at more than $100,000,000.

Officials feared the toll would rise when word was received from villages isolated by floods, landslides, washed-out roads and rail lines or broken telephone lines.

Nagoya Hit Hard

The harbor of the industrial city of Nagoya, one of the hardest hit, was described as a "sea of dead." Seven ocean-going ships lay grounded like beached whales in that area. The harbor was choked with debris. In other regions, parts of villages were swept away by floods.

Typhoon Vera, the fifth to strike Japan this year, formed in the southwest Pacific, off Iwo Jima. It struck Kii Peninsula in south-central Honshu Saturday night with maximum winds of 160 miles an hour.

The storm swept across the industrial heart of central Honshu over Mie, Nara, Gifu and Aichi prefectures and into the Sea of Japan.

The typhoon then moved up the Sea of Japan off the west coast of Honshu, crossed northern Honshu and southeastern Hokkaido, the northern-most island, and was last reported

Continued on Page 3, Column 4

STRIKE-BREAKING FACES STATE CURB

Registering of Job Agencies Asked in Panel Report

By RUSSELL PORTER

A state investigating committee recommended legislation yesterday to compel registration of professional strike-breaking agencies and public disclosure of their activities.

It also urged that all employment agencies be required to inform job applicants if they are to take jobs of striking workers.

The committee was appointed in 1958 by Isidor Lubin, then State Industrial Commissioner, to investigate concerns reported to be supplying out-of-state strikebreakers to New York employers.

Mr. Lubin's action followed charges by the International Typographical Union that the Macy chain of newspapers in Westchester County had imported to break a printers' strike.

Charges Strike Is Illegal

The Macy chain has charged the strike is illegal and that the union's demands violated the Taft-Hartley law.

Two other publishers were also involved in the investigation. They were the Griscom chain of weekly papers in Nassau County and The Lockport Union-Sun and Journal, a daily newspaper in Niagara County.

The committee in its report said it had discovered only one commercial agency engaged in supplying strikebreakers to newspapers.

It is said this firm was the Schleppey-Klein Agency, owned and operated by Bloor Schleppey of Zionsville, Ind., with the help of Miss Shirley Klein, now an executive of the Macy chain.

According to the committee, this agency is exclusively engaged in recruiting and supply-

Continued on Page 12, Column 3

Red Chinese Harass Indians on Frontier

By United Press International.

PAURI, India, Sept. 27—Chinese Communist troops from Tibet are taking over land previously considered India's and have reinforced their garrisons along the border, reports received here said today.

The reports said Chinese forces opposite the frontier of Uttar Pradesh were harassing Indian business men and confiscating their goods and money on the slightest pretext.

Traders and villagers said the Chinese had moved more troops into Tibetan areas facing Uttar Pradesh and had built new roads and six airstrips to supply them. Chinese planes frequently violate Indian airspace, they said.

The reports reached this

Continued on Page 3, Column 2

LAOTIANS RETAKE BORDER FORTRESS

Bastion Near North Vietnam Captured in Night Raid—Fighting Is Fierce

By GREG MacGREGOR
Special to The New York Times.

VIENTIANE, Laos, Sept. 27—Muong Het, a strongly defended rebel-held fortress about eight miles from the North Vietnamese border, was reported recaptured by Government troops at dawn today in one of the sharpest encounters of the current strife.

The thrust to retake the position, which was seized by the rebels Aug. 30, began yesterday, according to informed sources. It was estimated that about 300 "Lao-Viets," the name now used in Laotian military circles to describe non-North Vietnamese troops, had been encircled in Muong Het and forced to fight. Previous tactics adopted by both sides had been to withdraw in the face of heavy onslaught.

The size of the Government attacking force was not given. Casualties on both sides were described as heavy.

It was stated that Xieng Kho, another position in the northern part of Samneua Province near Muong Het, was still in enemy hands. Other positions along the border still held by the rebels were named

Continued on Page 2, Column 2

VIEWS UNCHANGED

But Both Sides Retain Reliance on Parleys to Solve Problems

By JAMES RESTON
Special to The New York Times.

WASHINGTON, Sept. 27—The main result of Premier Khrushchev's visit to the United States is that it produced agreement to talk some more. This, at least, is the general view here.

It avoided the danger of personal injury. It ended without any break in the policy of settling international differences by negotiation, and it extended the negotiating period well into the middle of President Eisenhower's last year in office.

The President and his guest reached few agreements, but apparently they were impressed with each other's determination to avoid war, and to continue talking to that end.

Arms Control Urged

If there was any change in the policies of the United States and the Soviet Union, it was in the emphasis on the principle of "the strictest comprehensive control" over any disarmament agreement.

This was Mr. Khrushchev's phrase in his television address to the American people tonight. This is the principle Washington has been trying to get Moscow to accept for years. The question now is whether this principle can now be applied in specific terms to all disarmament talks coming up or only to the Soviet Union's ambitious plan of "total disarmament."

The talks on the future of Germany and Berlin did not go well. They produced more heated conversation at Camp David than anything else.

Neither Side Budges

Neither side budged from the position it held in the nine weeks of fruitless negotiation at the Big Four foreign ministers' conference at Geneva this summer. And Mr. Khrushchev went away saying that his way of settling the problem was the only way he knew of reaching a settlement.

Nevertheless, there was agreement to reopen talks on the Berlin question if the other nations concerned agreed, and a curiously worded agreement to fix President Eisenhower's return visit to the Soviet Union "next spring."

There has been some talk

Continued on Page 20, Column 1

Associated Press Wirephoto
FAREWELL: President Eisenhower wishes Premier Khrushchev a safe voyage home on steps of Blair House in Washington. At right is Andrei A. Gromyko, Soviet Foreign Minister. Oleg A. Troyanovsky, an interpreter, is in the center.

Dodgers and Braves End in Tie; Pennant Play-Off Starts Today

The New York Times
Fred Haney

Associated Press Wirephoto
Walter Alston

The Dodgers and the Braves finished the National League season yesterday tied for the pennant. The two clubs will meet at Milwaukee this afternoon in the first of a three-game play-off series.

Manager Walter Alston's Dodgers defeated the Cubs, 7—1, and Manager Fred Haney's Braves downed the Phils, 5—2, in their final regularly scheduled games. The Giants, who had a chance for a tie in the event the Braves and Dodgers lost, bowed twice to the Cardinals.

Originally scheduled to open on Wednesday in Chicago with the White Sox, the American League pennant winner, as the home team, the world series will start either Thursday or Friday. There will be a one day rest after the play-off, with the second game scheduled for tomorrow in Los Angeles and the third game, if necessary, for Los Angeles on Wednesday.

Sandy Koufax will pitch for Los Angeles today. Lew Burdette will hurl for the Braves.

The play-off is the third in National League history. The Dodgers lost to the Cards in two games in 1946 and to the Giants in three in 1951.

Details on Page 40

RUSSIAN EXPECTS NO QUICK CHANGE

In Talks on Last Day He Says 'Effort and Patience' Are Needed to Erase Enmity

By WILLIAM J. JORDEN
Special to The New York Times.

WASHINGTON, Sept. 27—Premier Khrushchev said tonight it was "impossible to count on a sudden change" in United States-Soviet relations.

He said the main obstacle to an easing of tensions lay in certain influential forces in this country that opposed efforts to end the "cold war." He expressed confidence that common sense would prevail, but said "great effort and patience" would be required to erase the suspicions and enmity of recent years.

In his farewell appearances in this country, a news conference and a television speech, the visiting Premier repeated his assertion that it was the Soviet Union that was working hardest for better relations.

U. S. Desire for Peace Seen

Mr. Khrushchev said he had no doubt that President Eisenhower shared his desire for an improvement in relations. He declared, too, that he was sure the American people wanted peace as much as the Soviet people.

He accused those who questioned the sincerity of Soviet proposals of standing in the way of agreements. Progress is being frustrated by certain people in the United States, the Premier commented, but he did not name them or say more than that they were "still influential."

If Mr. Khrushchev was influenced in any way by his visit to the United States and his first-hand look at its wealth and variety, he gave no sign of it.

Soviet Progress Depicted

He said that what he had seen here had not shaken his "faith that the political, economic and social system in the Soviet Union is the fairest and most progressive." In fact, he spent most of the forty-five minutes of his television speech telling of the progress his country had made under the leadership of the Communist party.

Mr. Khrushchev's news conference, held earlier in the main ballroom of the National Press Club, was a light-hearted occasion unmarred by any display of temper such as marked his previous appearance there on Sept. 16, the day after his arrival in the United States.

Five minutes before the conference was to begin at 4 P. M.,

Continued on Page 19, Column 7

U.S.-Soviet Communique

Special to The New York Times.

WASHINGTON, Sept. 27—Following is the text of the joint United States-Soviet communiqué issued today:

The Chairman of the Council of Ministers of the U. S. S. R., N. S. Khrushchev, and President Eisenhower have had a frank exchange of opinions at Camp David.

In some of these conversations the United States Secretary of State Herter and Soviet Foreign Minister Gromyko, as well as other officials from both countries, participated.

The Chairman of the Council of Ministers of the U. S. S. R. and the President have agreed that these discussions have been useful in clarifying each other's position on a number of subjects. The talks were not undertaken to negotiate issues.

It is hoped, however, that their exchanges of views will contribute to a better understanding of the motives and position of each, and thus to the achievement of a just and lasting peace.

The Chairman of the Council of Ministers of the U. S. S. R. and the President of the United States agreed that the question of general disarmament is the most important one facing the world today. Both Governments will make every effort to achieve a constructive solution of this problem.

A Discussion of Germany

In the course of the conversations an exchange of views took place on the question of Germany, including the question of a peace treaty with Germany, in which the positions of both sides were expounded.

With respect to the specific Berlin question, an understanding was reached, subject to the approval of the other parties directly concerned, that negotiations would be reopened with a view to achieving a solution which would be in accordance with the interests of all concerned and in the interest of the maintenance of peace.

In addition to these matters, useful conversations were held on a number of questions affecting the relations between the Union of Soviet Socialist Republics and the United States. These subjects included the question of trade between the two countries. With respect to an increase in exchanges of persons and ideas, substantial progress was made in discussions between officials and it is expected that certain agreements will be reached in the near future.

The Chairman of the Council of Ministers of the U. S. S. R. and the President of the United States agreed that all outstanding international questions should be settled not by the application of force but by peaceful means through negotiation.

Finally, it was agreed that an exact date for the return visit of the President to the Soviet Union next spring would be arranged through diplomatic channels.

Grandchildren Key To President's Trip

By ANTHONY LEWIS
Special to The New York Times.

WASHINGTON, Sept. 27—Premier Khrushchev said today that it was because President Eisenhower's four grandchildren would accompany him to Russia that the President's projected Soviet visit had been postponed until next spring.

"I would like to reveal a secret," the Premier said at his news conference when he was asked the reason for the postponement. With a happy but sly smile, like a foxy grandpa, he told the story.

"Yesterday the President was kind enough to invite me to his farm, where I met his wonderful grandchildren," Mr.

Continued on Page 16, Column 2

Bonn Is Agreeable To Talks on Berlin

By SYDNEY GRUSON
Special to The New York Times.

BONN, Germany, Sept. 27—Government sources said tonight that West Germany would undoubtedly be agreeable to another foreign ministers' conference on the Berlin question.

News of the communiqué issued in Washington today by President Eisenhower and Premier Khrushchev arrived too late in European capitals for high-level government comment.

Although the Eisenhower-Khrushchev communiqué did not specify at what level the Berlin negotiations should be resumed, it was assumed here that the foreign ministers were meant and that the nine weeks of dis-

Continued on Page 19, Column 6

KHRUSHCHEV OFF WITH 21-GUN POMP

Nixon Bids Him Farewell at Airport—Both Stress Need for Negotiation

Remarks by Khrushchev and Nixon at airport, Page 17.

By W. H. LAWRENCE
Special to The New York Times.

ANDREWS AIR FORCE BASE, Md., Sept. 27—Premier Khrushchev took off for the Soviet Union at 10 o'clock tonight.

He flew in the giant TU-114 turbo-prop airliner that brought him here about noon Sept. 15. The flight to Moscow was scheduled to be non-stop.

Vice President Richard M. Nixon substituted for President Eisenhower in farewell ceremonies. With him were Secretary of State Christian A. Herter and Gen. Nathan F. Twining, Chairman of the Joint Chiefs of Staff.

The final ceremony at this air base about twelve miles from Washington included all the official honors usually paid a chief of state as Mr Khrushchev had been termed by the Soviet Foreign Ministry for this journey. Previously he had been considered a head of government.

Ceremonies At Airfield

Just before departure a twenty-one-gun salute from a 75-mm. howitzer boomed out after a fifty-six-piece Army band had played the anthems of the Soviet Union and the United States.

The ceremonies began shortly after 9:15 P. M., when Mr. Khrushchev arrived by car from Blair House, official guest house of the President, where he had had a quiet dinner with his family and fellow officials after a hectic day.

At the airfield he was greeted by a 128-member honor guard, including representatives of the Army, Air Force, Navy and Marines.

Mr. Nixon and Mr. Khrushchev did not, however, troop the guard, as the President and Mr. Khrushchev had done after the Premier's daylight arrival.

Mr. Khrushchev and Vice

Continued on Page 17, Column 1

NEWS INDEX

PEACE IS STRESSED

President Will Report His Views Today at News Conference

Khrushchev news conference and speech and U. S. news conference, Pages 18-19.

By HARRISON E. SALISBURY
Special to The New York Times.

WASHINGTON, Sept. 27—Premier Khrushchev brought his historic thirteen-day visit to a conclusion today by reaching a series of understandings with President Eisenhower designed to ease "cold war" tensions.

The extent of these understandings was not immediately revealed. However, they were of a scope that suggested that the Khrushchev-Eisenhower conversations had produced at least a limited armistice in the "cold war."

High Points Delineated

The high points of the discussions held by the Soviet and United States leaders, as outlined by a communiqué, by Mr. Khrushchev at a news conference and by United States statements, were:

¶An agreement that new talks will be held on the Berlin question. These talks may be held by the foreign ministers, or at a lower level, or possibly at a summit conference.

¶Discussion of a possible summit conference. Mr. Khrushchev said the Soviet Union felt that the time was ripe for such a meeting now and that Geneva might be a suitable place. The United States position on this point was not entirely clear.

¶An agreement for President Eisenhower to postpone his trip to the Soviet Union until spring or summer. Mr. Khrushchev said he had proposed the postponement because the weather would be better at that time.

¶An understanding to broaden the present program of exchanges between the United States and the Soviet Union and to undertake explorations of questions relating to trade.

¶An agreement to reopen the long-stalemated negotiations over the World War II Lend-Lease settlement.

¶A joint declaration that "all outstanding international questions should be settled not by the application of force but by peaceful means through negotiation."

The results of the three days

Continued on Page 16, Column 1

PRESIDENT URGED TO MEET SENATORS

Mansfield Asks Consultation on Khrushchev Talks

By WILLIAM M. BLAIR
Special to The New York Times.

WASHINGTON, Sept. 27—President Eisenhower was called upon today to consult as soon as possible with Senate Democratic and Republican leaders on his conversations with Premier Khrushchev.

Such a consultation would be a demonstration to Mr. Khrushchev and the world of the "basic unity of the American people," Senator Mike Mansfield, Democrat of Montana, declared in a statement.

The Senate's assistant Democratic leader asserted the conference also should be called "because if there is to be progress toward peace beyond the President's exchange of views with Prime Minister Khrushchev any actions to that end ultimately will require the advice and consent—the sanctions—of the Senate."

The President might also discuss the "significance" of his conversations with leaders of the House as well as of the Senate, Senator Mansfield said. He suggested that the meeting might be held at Camp David, the Maryland mountain retreat where the President and the So-

Continued on Page 17, Column 3

The New York Times

PAGE ONE

1960-1969

"All the News That's Fit to Print"

The New York Times.

LATE CITY EDITION

U. S. Weather Bureau Report (Page 61) forecasts: Fair today; mostly fair tonight. Partly cloudy and warm tomorrow. Temp. range: 74—54; yesterday: 69.1—52.5.

VOL. CIX. No. 37,358.

NEW YORK, FRIDAY, MAY 6, 1960.

10 cents beyond 50-mile zone from New York City except on Long Island. Higher in air delivery cities.

FIVE CENTS

SOVIET DOWNS AMERICAN PLANE; U.S. SAYS IT WAS WEATHER CRAFT; KHRUSHCHEV SEES SUMMIT BLOW

CAPITAL EXPLAINS

Reports Unarmed U-2 Vanished at Border After Difficulty

Text of the U. S. statement on plane is on Page 7.

By JACK RAYMOND
Special to The New York Times.

WASHINGTON, May 5—The United States said today an American weather-observation plane flown by a civilian apparently went astray near the Turkish-Soviet border Sunday when the pilot's oxygen supply failed.

This was the official explanation of the incident described by Premier Khrushchev when he said an American "invader" had been shot down over the Soviet Union.

According to the official statement, the pilot was in a heavily instrumented U-2 single-engine plane, chartered from the Lockheed Aircraft Corporation by the National Aeronautics and Space Administration.

The pilot was identified later as Francis G. Powers, 30 years old, a Lockheed employe.

Plane Used in Research

The plane was flying at an altitude close to 55,000 feet, making weather observations over the Lake Van area of Turkey as part of a world-wide research program begun in 1956, a spokesman for the civilian space agency said.

The spokesman emphasized that the plane was unarmed and carried no military equipment of any kind. He said it was marked with the letters N. A. S. A. in black on a gold-yellow band and with an N. A. S. A. seal, a globe inside calipers. [Premier Khrushchev said the plane shot down bore no identification marks.]

Can Text Radioactivity

The U-2, in addition to its use for weather observation, was developed by Lockheed originally for the Air Force in a secret program initiated in 1954 to study radioactivity resulting from nuclear tests.

The U-2 can maintain flight at altitudes up to 55,000 feet for as long as four hours. It is powered by a single Pratt & Whitney J-57 turbojet engine.

In the high-altitude sampling program, U-2 aircraft have taken samples of radioactive fall-out by exposing filter paper to the atmosphere.

The agency spokesman denied that the U-2 missing in Turkey carried any radioactivity-detection instruments.

The incident occurred in one

Continued on Page 7, Column 1

Associated Press Radiophoto

ANNOUNCES DOWNING OF U. S. PLANE: Premier Khrushchev speaking yesterday during opening session of the Supreme Soviet (parliament) at the Kremlin in Moscow.

PREMIER IS BITTER

Assails 'Provocation Aimed at Wrecking' May 16 Parley

Excerpts from Khrushchev's remarks are on Page 6.

By OSGOOD CARUTHERS
Special to The New York Times.

MOSCOW, May 5—Premier Khrushchev said today that a United States plane on a mission of "aggressive provocation aimed at wrecking the summit conference" invaded Soviet territory May 1 and was shot down.

The Premier, in the most blistering speech against American policies he had made since his meetings with President Eisenhower last autumn, declared that the incursion, as well as declarations by United States policy makers, cast gloom on the prospects for the success of the summit meeting in Paris eleven days hence.

He expressed anger over the fact that President Eisenhower had supported declarations against Soviet foreign policies by Vice President Richard M. Nixon, Secretary of State Christian A. Herter, Under Secretary of State Douglas Dillon and others.

He Seems to Bar Nixon

He surmised, Mr. Khrushchev said, that General Eisenhower, while wanting peace, was a victim of tight restrictions by "imperialists and militarists" around him.

Mr. Khrushchev expressed regret that the President wanted to limit the summit meeting to one week and he virtually rejected a proposal to sit at the table with Mr. Nixon if the Vice President was delegated to take over for General Eisenhower in case the session went over the time limit.

The most sensational section of Mr. Khrushchev's three-and-a-half-hour speech, made before the opening session of the Supreme Soviet, the nation's version of a parliament, was that concerning the charges of United States violations of Soviet airspace.

Foreign Policy to Fore

Mr. Khrushchev actually had been called upon to open the Supreme Soviet session to deal exclusively with sweeping new domestic policies that will affect every Soviet worker: gradual abolition of income taxes by 1965 and by next year, reduction of the work day to seven hours and an upward revaluation of the ruble.

However, the Soviet leader seized the occasion to discuss foreign policy and the summit conference. He apparently had determined to tell the Soviet people that recent Western actions and statements had darkened his previous optimism.

The Premier predicted to foreign diplomats earlier this week that his talk on foreign and domestic policies would contain major surprises. Indeed, his report of the plane incident came as a shock to Westerners and

Continued on Page 6, Column 4

U. S. ASKS DETAILS OF PLANE INCIDENT

Data Sought From Envoy in Moscow as Washington Reacts With Restraint

By WILLIAM J. JORDEN
Special to The New York Times.

WASHINGTON, May 5—Washington reacted with restraint today to Premier Khrushchev's announcement that a United States plane had been shot down Sunday on Soviet territory.

There were some angry words on Capitol Hill—including a suggestion that President Eisenhower refuse to go to the summit meeting with Mr. Khrushchev in Paris May 16. But the Administration would say little more than that additional information was being sought from Moscow.

A message went to Ambassador Llewellyn E. Thompson Jr. in Moscow this afternoon instructing him to request more details from the Soviet authorities.

Text Made Available Late

The text of Mr. Khrushchev's long speech to the Supreme Soviet became available to officials only late this afternoon. Their first reaction was that he seemed to be preparing the way for placing the blame for a summit failure on the Western powers.

He also seemed to be giving advance warning that the Allied leaders could expect little softness from him at the Paris meeting. The consensus was that the Khrushchev address was the latest move in pre-summit maneuvering, but that it had not altered measurably the outlook for the summit meeting.

Mr. Khrushchev said that the Governments of the United States, Britain and France did not seem to be looking forward

Continued on Page 7, Column 6

Soviet Will Revalue Ruble; Income Tax to End by '65

By MAX FRANKEL
Special to The New York Times.

MOSCOW, May 5—Premier Khrushchev proclaimed a complex fiscal reform today. The changes will bring a new and more costly ruble into Soviet circulation next year and an abolition of most personal income taxes by 1965.

The Premier pledged greater take-home pay to lower-paid industrial workers and office employes and said that this would be matched by increased stocks of consumer goods in the stores.

In fact, he promised a great new drive for the production of consumer goods once his ambitious seven-year economic plan is fulfilled in 1965.

Mr. Khrushchev proposed the currency revaluation and tax revisions to the Supreme Soviet, the national Parliament. Enabling legislation as requested by the Soviet leader is expected after a day or two of comment from the Deputies. It is expected to be some time, however, before everyone here, including experts, understands the ramifications of the program.

Unanimous Adoption Seen

There is little doubt that the changes will be unanimously adopted essentially as outlined by Mr. Khrushchev in a broadcast speech. He asked that all the arithmetic complications of the new formulas be tirelessly explained to the Soviet people, together with assurances that the country will gain by the changes and that no one will suffer.

Premier Khrushchev also promised that the currency reform would not affect the Soviet Union's foreign economic dealings or contracts. The official value of the ruble is four to $1. American tourists in the Soviet Union, however, receive a premium payment that brings them a total of ten rubles a dollar.

There was no suggestion in Moscow that the reform was a prelude to free convertibility of

Continued on Page 8, Column 3

ANKARA STUDENTS JOSTLE MENDERES

Turkish Premier Is Caught in Street Demonstration —Escapes Amid Jeers

By JAY WALZ
Special to The New York Times.

ISTANBUL, Turkey, May 5—Premier Adnan Menderes was jostled and jeered in Ankara today when he was caught by surprise in a student demonstration.

Anti-Menderes students mingled with a crowd of the Premier's supporters. They crowded around him shouting "Freedom! Freedom!" as he walked among them on his way to a political club.

One student clutched Premier Menderes' arm and asked, "How long do we suffer at your hands?" The Premier angrily called a policeman to take the young man away.

After a few minutes Mr. Menderes escaped unharmed in a small car that had been parked near by. It pushed through the throng to his own waiting automobile. President Celal Bayar and two Ministers saw the disturbance but were not involved.

Police and Cavalry Busy

About 300 policemen and a troop of cavalry dispersed the crowd, which witnesses estimated at about 3,000. A Government spokesman maintained that only 250 were demonstrators. The rest were bystanders, he said.

A few shots were fired into the air but no one was reported injured. The disturbance lasted for about an hour and a half.

Before the demonstrations in Ankara, a group of students allied with Mr. Menderes' Democratic party were waiting to greet him as he drove to the political club in Kizilay Square in the new section of Ankara. Soldiers lined his route along Ataturk Boulevard.

The anti-Menderes students had passed the word to infiltrate the throng, using the watchword "Five, Five, Five, K.," meaning "Be at Kizilay Square at 5:55 P. M."

The outbreak marked the

Continued on Page 4, Column 5

A. M. A. DENOUNCES EISENHOWER PLAN FOR CARE OF AGED

Says Proposal Takes False Tack That Most Over 65 Are Medically Indigent

OTHERS JOIN IN ATTACK

Goldwater Sees 'Socialized Medicine'—Labor Assails Measure as Unsound

By AUSTIN C. WEHRWEIN
Special to The New York Times.

CHICAGO, May 5 — The American Medical Association assailed today the Eisenhower Administration's health - care plan for the aged.

A statement issued through the association's headquarters here in the name of its president, Dr. Louis M. Orr of Orlando, Fla., said the Administration plan was "based on the false premise that almost all persons over 65 need health care and cannot afford it."

"This is not a fact," the statement declared.

"The truth is that a majority of our older people are capable of continuing a happy, healthy, and in many cases, productive life.

"Of the more than 15,000,000 persons in the nation over 65 years of age, only 15 per cent are on old age assistance.

Rejects 2 Proposals

"An undetermined number, although able to finance other costs, find it difficult to withstand the additional burden of the cost of illness.

"It is for these people that something should be done. Neither the Forand advocates nor the Administration proposal is tailored to meet these problems."

[In Washington, the Administration's proposal was attacked by Senator Barry Goldwater as "socialized medicine" and by the merged labor federation as unsound and politically inspired.]

The medical association's reference to "Forand" alluded to a bill sponsored by Representative Aime J. Forand, Democrat of Rhode Island. It would extend the Social Security system, and increase Social Security taxes, to provide medical care for persons over 65.

The Administration's proposal, offered yesterday, calls for Federal and state subsidies of insurance systems to be set up by the states. The estimated annual cost of $1,200,000,000

Continued on Page 32, Column 3

West Virginia Poll Finds Kennedy Gain

By W. H. LAWRENCE
Special to The New York Times.

CHARLESTON, W. Va., May 5 — Substantial voting gains for Senator John F. Kennedy were reported today in West Virginia.

Politicians and polls alike brought reports of a strong, well-financed and well-organized Kennedy drive to wrest victory from Senator Hubert H. Humphrey of Minnesota, considered the favorite in next Tuesday's Democratic Presidential preferential primary here.

One politician, who classified himself as neutral but formerly pro-Humphrey, admiringly called the Kennedy effort "a blitz." But what he and other politicians, including many in the Kennedy camp, questioned was whether the indicated gains in the southern coal fields were

Continued on Page 13, Column 1

RIBICOFF ASSAILS NEW HAVEN LINE

'This Is Not the Way to Run a Business,' He Says in Calling 4-State Parley

By RICHARD H. PARKE
Special to The New York Times.

GREENWICH, Conn., May 5—Gov. Abraham A. Ribicoff accused the New Haven Railroad today of "shabby and shoddy" bookkeeping, of wasting "great sums" and of employing "scare words, false issues, emotional appeals and misrepresentations."

"Clearly," he said, "this is not the way to run a business and especially a business which must count so heavily on public goodwill, public support, public respect and, yes, even public affection."

Governor Ribicoff delivered his attack in announcing that he was inviting the Governors of New York, Rhode Island and Massachusetts and the Mayor of New York to confer with him on the New Haven's future. No date has been set for the conference.

Tax Relief Proposed

Mr. Ribicoff said he would ask them to consider taking action on the recommendations in the report issued on the New Haven yesterday by the Connecticut Public Utilities Commission.

The report, which was also critical of the railroad management, proposed several measures to aid the line. They included a joint tax-relief program by the four states and an interstate authority that would cooperate with the railroad in providing commuter service in the New York area.

Governor Ribicoff, who discussed the railroad at a meeting here of the First Selectman's Association of Fairfield County, also said he was prepared to recommend a railroad

Continued on Page 20, Column 1

DILLON CONSULTS A. F. L.-C. I. O. AIDE IN ARAB SHIP CASE

Seeks Way to End Picketing Here as Mideast Boycott of U. S. Vessels Spreads

By DANA ADAMS SCHMIDT
Special to The New York Times.

WASHINGTON, May 5—Under Secretary of State Douglas Dillon conferred today with Arthur J. Goldberg, special counsel of the American Federation of Labor and Congress of Industrial Organizations, on possible ways of ending the picketing of the United Arab Republic ship Cleopatra in New York.

Union and State Department officials spoke of the possibility of working out a statement of United States policy that would lead the Seafarers International Union to call off its pickets.

But State Department officials were emphatic in pointing out that they had no means of forcing the United Arab Republic to give up its practice of blacklisting ships that put in at Israeli ports. This boycott precipitated the picketing.

Meanwhile, concern grew at the State Department over indications that the blockade of the Cleopatra and the Arab counter-blockade were reversing the trend toward better United States relations with the Arab world.

Blockade May Spread

"From almost every post we have had laments that the diplomatic efforts of years are being upset by this affair," an official of the department said.

If the blockade continues the impact on commerce would deepen and might next spread to airlines, he added.

The reports included the following points:

¶In Khartoum, capital of the Sudan, the press for the first time in two years assumed an anti-United States tone.

¶The Bombay Port Workers Union telegraphed President Eisenhower protesting the blockade of the Cleopatra and declaring that its continuance would result in a boycott of United States ships seeking to enter the Bombay port. This was the first sign that the counter-blockade might spread beyond the Arab world.

¶A Libyan Government official suggested informally to United States diplomats that "it would be better" if United States ships avoided Libyan ports while the Cleopatra was being picketed.

¶Consulates in a number of Arab ports reported that as the result of a knifing incident in which the eye of a member of the Cleopatra crew was injured it might be unsafe for American crewmen in Arab ports.

¶The American Export liner Excalibur, due today in Alexandria, the United Arab Republic port, was diverted by its owners to a destination not yet disclosed. The United States freighter Exchequer began un-

Continued on Page 2, Column 3

O'DWYER'S NIECE NAMED TO BENCH

Mayor Appoints Her Despite Bar Groups' Opposition

By LAYHMOND ROBINSON

Mayor Wagner named Joan O'Dwyer O'Neill, 33-year-old niece of former Mayor William O'Dwyer, a city magistrate yesterday, despite the objections of two of the three bar groups to whom he had submitted her name.

He reported, however, that five bar groups, including the third one asked to pass on her, had given her "unanimous approval."

The Mayor also made it clear that he regarded Mrs. O'Neill as qualified for the $16,000-a-year post on the Magistrate's Court, which basically has jurisdiction over minor crimes.

10-Year Term Slated

The appointment, which needs no further approval, is to fill out two months of a term of a magistrate who resigned. Mrs. O'Neill will then be appointed for a full ten-year term.

In commenting on the division of the bar associations over the designation, the Mayor said he had "always sought bar association approval for bench nominees," but had "never intended or pretended that such support had to be unanimous."

He emphasized that he regarded Mrs. O'Neill, "whom I know quite well," as qualified for the position.

The opposition to her appointment had stemmed largely from the feeling by some lawyers that Mrs. O'Neill had not

Continued on Page 14, Column 5

London in Gala Mood for Princess' Wedding Today

Associated Press Radiophoto

Princess Margaret and Antony Armstrong-Jones as they arrived yesterday at Clarence House, the Princess' home, after rehearsing for their wedding in Westminster Abbey.

By DREW MIDDLETON
Special to The New York Times.

LONDON, May 5—The Church of England stressed the spiritual aspects of tomorrow's royal wedding in a brave but unavailing attempt to modify the carnival mood that has gripped the heart of this dignified capital tonight. Outside Westminster Abbey crowds gaped at decorations hailing the marriage of Princess Margaret to Antony Armstrong-Jones. Inside, the Very Rev. Eric Symes Abbott, Dean of Westminster, emphasized that "here are two people—a man and a woman—for whom it is the greatest day of their lives." Westminster Abbey, the Dean observed,

Continued on Page 26, Column 3

23 Are Killed and Scores Injured As Twisters Hit East Oklahoma

By The Associated Press.

WILBURTON, Okla., May 5—At least twenty-three persons were killed by tornadoes that slashed across eastern Oklahoma tonight. At least eleven were killed and scores injured in this college town.

A witness, Mrs. Denny Jones, said the tornado hit Wilburton about 6:45 P. M. with a "freight-train" roar.

All communications were cut and travel and rescue efforts were hampered by torrential rains.

The highway patrol and newsmen listed the Wilburton victims as:

Gordon Mote, 70 years old; Mrs. James Reeves, wife of an instructor at Eastern Oklahoma A&M Junior College; a Mrs. Porter and a Mrs. McGee; James Parks, about 70; Mr. and Mrs. Mike Brady, both about 70; Truman Clark, about 45; Wildon Raines; Margie Bark, and one unidentified man.

Several of the older victims were killed when the twister leveled the Calvary Baptist Church where services were being held.

More than seventy-five persons were reported injured.

Ambulances raced over slick roads to hospitals at McAlester, Poteau, Hartshorne and Heavener.

A newsman on the scene said about 1,000 rescue workers rushed into the city of 2,000 in reply to a call for help.

Tornadoes killed five in the area around Moffett and Roland two small communities nestled against the Arkansas border near Fort Smith.

Sheriff Prentice Maddux of Fort Smith said four bodies

Continued on Page 62, Column 7

Harvey Firestone 3d Dies in Havana Fall

Special to The New York Times.

HAVANA, May 5—Harvey S. Firestone 3d plunged to his death from the twentieth floor of a Havana luxury hotel tonight, six hours after arriving here from Miami. The victim, who was 32 years old, was the son of Harvey S. Firestone Jr., chairman of the board of the Firestone Tire and Rubber Company.

[Cuban authorities ruled the death a suicide, The Associated Press reported.]

The Cuban police said David Morgan Firestone, 29, a cousin of the dead man, had told them that Harvey Firestone had attempted suicide on a previous occasion in the United States.

The victim had been crippled since birth by cerebral palsy.

Mr. Firestone arrived in Havana today accompanied by his

Continued on Page 62, Column 5

NEWS INDEX

"All the News That's Fit to Print"

The New York Times.

LATE CITY EDITION
U. S. Weather Bureau Report (Page 82) forecasts: Early showers, clearing later today; mostly fair tonight and tomorrow.
Temp. range: 78—62; yesterday: 77.0—61.5.

VOL. CIX..No. 37,370. NEW YORK, WEDNESDAY, MAY 18, 1960. 10 cents beyond 50-mile zone from New York City except on Long Island. Higher in air delivery cities. FIVE CENTS

SUMMIT CONFERENCE BREAKS UP IN DISPUTE; WEST BLAMES KHRUSHCHEV'S RIGID STAND; HE INSISTS ON EISENHOWER SPYING APOLOGY

PASSENGER GAINS AND CITY SUBSIDY END TRANSIT LOSS

Board Expects $4,000,000 Surplus June 30 Instead of Deficit of $116,000

By STANLEY LEVEY

Thanks to more riders and city subsidies, the Transit Authority expects to end the present fiscal year on June 30 with a surplus of $4,000,000, instead of a deficit of $116,000.

Most of the help from the city had been anticipated in planning for 1959-60. But the sharp upturn in passenger revenues had not.

While the agency was pleased with the development, it had no explanation for it yesterday beyond the suggestion that new buses and subway cars were responsible.

"We just have more riders," Charles L. Patterson, chairman of the authority, said happily.

The prospect of a big surplus apparently made firm a previous pledge by the authority that the present 15-cent bus and subway fare would be held at least until Jan. 1, 1962. On that date contracts between the agency and the Transport Workers Union expire.

City Subsidies Counted On

The projected $4,000,000 surplus was based on the records for the first nine months of the fiscal year. From last July 1 to March 31 the authority's revenues exceeded its expenses by $2,865,021. In the same period of the preceding year the agency had a $7,822,603 deficit and it finished that fiscal year with a total deficit of $10,200,000.

Last spring, when the authority drew up its 1959-60 operating budget, it expected to end the year with a deficit of $116,000. The officials knew then that they could count on the

Continued on Page 21, Column 3

2 NETWORKS FIGHT FREE TV DEBATES

But Would Give Candidates Time Under Own Plans

By TOM WICKER
Special to The New York Times.

WASHINGTON, May 17—Adlai E. Stevenson's idea for a series of television debates between the major Presidential candidates encountered stiff opposition today from the TV industry and the opposition party.

Dr. Frank Stanton, president of the Columbia Broadcasting System, and David C. Adams, senior vice president of the National Broadcasting Company, resisted Mr. Stevenson's proposal that the networks be required by law to grant free time to the candidates.

However, both said that their networks would make free time available voluntarily, under certain circumstances.

Bill Before Senate Unit

Mr. Stevenson's "great debate" plan is embodied in S. 3171, a bill pending before the Communications Subcommittee of the Senate Interstate and Foreign Commerce Committee. The group heard and questioned the former Governor of Illinois yesterday and Dr. Stanton today.

It also received today a written statement from Mr. Adams and took written testimony against the bill from Vice President Nixon, former President Herbert Hoover and Thomas E. Dewey, twice a Republican Presidential candidate.

Mr. Adams will be questioned at an afternoon session tomorrow. His statement today described S. 3171 as "the wrong way to go about doing the right thing." The bill, he said, is "discriminatory" and "confiscatory." It is not needed, he went on, because N. B. C. already proposes to "invite the major Pres-

Continued on Page 29, Column 3

U. S. Sues to Open Biloxi Beach to All

Special to The New York Times.

WASHINGTON, May 17—The Justice Department sued Biloxi, Miss., today in a move to open the Gulf coast beach there to Negroes.

Three weeks ago, on the week-end of April 23, a group of about forty Negroes tried to swim at the beach. They were chased by white men with clubs. It has been reported that Negroes are not permitted to swim anywhere on the twenty-six-mile beach.

Gunfire and street fights in Biloxi followed the episode. Two white men and eight Negroes were wounded by bullets. Several Negroes who had tried to use the beach were arrested and fined $25 each for "disturbing the peace."

The Justice Department suit was based on the fact that

Continued on Page 22, Column 1

KENNEDY SWEEPS MARYLAND'S VOTE

Gets 70% of Total in Routing Morse for Sixth Straight Primary Triumph

By W. H. LAWRENCE
Special to The New York Times.

BALTIMORE, May 17—Senator John F. Kennedy won a landslide victory in Maryland's Democratic primary today to enlarge his claim to the Presidential nomination.

The young Massachusetts contender polled about 70 per cent of the vote and picked up twenty-four first-ballot delegate votes at the national convention opening in Los Angeles July 11.

There was no contest in the Republican preferential primary.

Senator Kennedy overwhelmed Senator Wayne Morse of Oregon and Maryland politicians who had urged a vote for an uninstructed delegation to demonstrate support for the Presidential aspirations of Senator Stuart Symington of Missouri, Senator Lyndon B. Johnson of Texas and Adlai E. Stevenson of Illinois.

Returns from 1,354 of 1,356 precincts gave:

Kennedy	199,362
Morse	49,323

Mr. Kennedy jumped far ahead in the first precinct to report, and built his lead steadily in every section.

Mr. Morse took his worst beating in Baltimore, which casts about half the Democratic vote, trailing his rival by a plurality in excess of 73,000.

The Oregonian received about 17 per cent of the vote, or 50 per cent less than the expectation he voiced Sunday, when he conceded defeat in advance.

For Senator Kennedy this was his sixth straight primary victory and an impressive show of strength before his final

Continued on Page 30, Column 4

SOVIET SHIFT SEEN

'Warmed-Up Cold War' Awaited—Khrushchev Will Stop in Berlin

By SYDNEY GRUSON
Special to The New York Times.

PARIS, May 17 — Western diplomats here expressed the belief today that Premier Khrushchev's break with President Eisenhower signaled a major change in Soviet policy. One Frenchman suggested that this tended toward a "warmed-up cold war."

The change will become apparent quickly, these diplomats believe, perhaps even in a session of the Supreme Soviet, the parliament in Moscow, that Mr. Khrushchev is expected to summon on his return home.

Meanwhile, the Soviet Premier plans to stop in Berlin on his way back to Moscow. His meetings in Berlin with East Germany's Communist leaders are expected by Western diplomats to open some new phase in the Soviet campaign to resolve the Berlin issue.

Soviet-Bloc Parley Predicted

Soviet sources here said Mr. Khrushchev would also call together the Soviet Union's Eastern European allies to consider the consequences of the rupture with President Eisenhower and the failure of the Paris summit conference.

The Russians have been threatening to sign a separate peace treaty with East Germany and place access to West Berlin in East German hands unless the West negotiates a Berlin settlement.

Bits and pieces purporting to show the Soviet leader's plans and intentions were being dropped here all day by Communist sources. But nothing was forthcoming to answer clearly the major question bedeviling Allied diplomats:

What led the Soviet Premier to torpedo the summit conference before it ever got going?

Internal Pressures Seen

Two theses are being exchanged among the diplomats. They are essentially contradictory, but a common thread runs through them. It is that Mr. Khrushchev is under stronger pressure from his political opponents throughout the Communist bloc and not only in the Soviet Union than at any time since he won power.

The favored thesis was that Premier Khrushchev, arrived here Saturday with his position frozen, that a decision had been taken in Moscow beforehand to break up the conference by posing what were patently inacceptable conditions to the President of the United States.

The minority view was that something happened to force a policy switch on Mr. Khrushchev during the week-end.

Mr. Khrushchev made what was generally regarded as a conciliatory statement on arriving here Saturday but utterly abandoned that attitude the next day.

In that connection some

Continued on Page 15, Column 5

United Press International Radiophoto

TRANQUIL INTERLUDE: President Eisenhower and Prime Minister Macmillan stroll about the grounds of the villa in Marnes-la-Coquette, where the President lived in 1951 and 1952 as the commander of the North Atlantic Treaty Organization forces in Europe.

Radiophoto of The New York Times (by Erich Lessing—Magnum)

WIELDING THE AXE: Premier Khrushchev chops wood near Sézanne, France.

DEMOCRATS HINT 'BLUNDERS' PROBE

But Mansfield and Johnson Emphasize United Front During Crisis in Paris

By RUSSELL BAKER
Special to The New York Times.

WASHINGTON, May 17—Democratic Congressional leaders created a temporary united front behind President Eisenhower today for the duration of the summit crisis but hinted at possible investigations to come.

Senator Mike Mansfield of Montana, the Senate's deputy Democratic leader, said that questions about Administration "blunders" preceding the Paris conference "must be asked," but only "at the proper time."

While the President is still in Paris and the Soviet Union is threatening to create a fresh German crisis that could bring "all peoples to the edge of catastrophe" is not the right time, he told the Senate.

Lyndon B. Johnson of Texas, the Democratic Senate leader, agreed that first priority should be given to maintaining a united national front behind the President in the present period of uncertainty.

Johnson Bars Division

"If there have been mistakes, responsibility will be assessed coolly and objectively," he said. "But one mistake that we cannot afford to make right now is to weaken the free world by division within our own ranks."

Behind these speeches by the Senate's two Democratic leaders was the conviction that to permit a great national debate at this point might strengthen Premier Khrushchev's indictment of the United States Government and further embarrass President Eisenhower.

By tacit agreement with the leadership, most Congressional Democrats suspended criticism of the Administration and waited nervously for further developments in Paris.

Many Republicans were conceding today that even if the Administration got out of Paris without additional trouble, the party had been politically hurt for the election campaign ahead.

Moreover, the calm that Senators Johnson and Mansfield and Speaker Sam Rayburn have

Continued on Page 14, Column 5

The Western Communique

By The Associated Press.

PARIS, May 17—Following is a joint communiqué issued tonight by Britain, France and the United States:

The President of the United States, the President of the French Republic and the Prime Minister of the United Kingdom take note of the fact that because of the attitude adopted by the Chairman of the Council of Ministers of the Soviet Union it has not been possible to begin, at the summit conference, the examination of the problems which it had been agreed would be discussed between the four chiefs of state or government.

They regret that these discussions, so important for world peace, could not take place. For their part, they remain unshaken in their conviction that all outstanding international questions should be settled not by the use or threat of force but by peaceful means through negotiation. They themselves remain ready to take part in such negotiations at any suitable time in the future.

PRELATE IN CUBA DENOUNCES REDS

Archbishop Urges Fight—Stand Could Bring Death

By R. HART PHILLIPS
Special to The New York Times.

HAVANA, May 17—A pastoral letter attacking communism and urging Cuban Roman Catholics to combat this "enemy within our gates" has been issued by the Archbishop of Santiago de Cuba, Msgr. Enrique Pérez Serantes.

The letter, which the Archbishop ordered read in churches of his archdiocese of Oriente Province, was published in Havana today by Información and El Crisol, Cuba's only independent newspapers. The Government press and radio ignored the pastoral.

This letter has special significance since anti-communism has been declared by the Government of Premier Fidel Castro to be syhonymous with "counter-revolutionary activities," punishable by death before a firing squad or long imprisonment.

Castro's Ranks Split

The letter caused a sensation in the island, particularly since Archbishop Pérez Serantes has long been a close friend of Premier Castro and is credited with having saved the life of the revolutionary leader in 1953.

At that time, following an unsuccessful attack by Dr. Castro and a group of young revolutionaries on the Moncava army post of Santiago de Cuba, the Archbishop protected Dr. Castro and obtained assurances for his life from the authorities while others of the group were being hunted down and killed on sight.

Communism is a major issue in Cuba and has split the ranks of Premier Castro's own revolutionary followers. The issue has

Continued on Page 8, Column 3

LUMUMBA RISING AS A CONGO RULER

Defies Belgians as He Builds Power in Interior Region

By HOMER BIGART
Special to The New York Times.

STANLEYVILLE, Belgian Congo, May 17—Belgian authority is collapsing in part of the Congo.

Patrice Emergy Lumumba, Congolese nationalist leader, is taking over as virtual dictator of this city and much of the Stanleyville and Eastern Provinces.

Not even the arrival of Belgian troop reinforcements is likely to halt the rapid erosion of the colonial administration's authority. Forty-five days before Congolese independence the Belgian administration already seems subservient to the nationalists.

Ban on Meetings Defied

M. Lumumba saw reports of troops arrivals at the Kamina military base in Katanga Province as an "attempt to intimidate the voters and influence the election in favor of Belgian selected candidates." He said he had sent a telegram to King Baudouin of the Belgians demanding the recall of the troops. He did not seem unduly worried, however.

Yesterday, in a moment of painful humiliation for the Belgian settlers, M. Lumumba defied a ban on public meetings. He did it in the heart of the city that jailed him last October for inciting riots.

The incident marked the beginning of a triumphal tour by M. Lumumba of the region north of Stanleyville. There, in villages deep in the equatorial forest, he demanded and received assurances from Belgian officials that watchers from his party, the National Congolese Movement, would be allowed at

Continued on Page 5, Column 3

COLLAPSE FEARED FOR GENEVA TALK

Summit Breakdown Likely to Affect Nuclear-Test and Arms Discussion

By A. M. ROSENTHAL
Special to The New York Times.

PARIS, May 17—The East-West negotiations in Geneva on disarmament and on a nuclear test ban were collapsing today.

Premier Khrushchev's decision to boycott the summit meeting convinced Western diplomats that the chances for agreement on disarmament or the ending of nuclear tests had been blown to bits and would take considerable time to paste together again.

The West was going on the assumption that the Soviet Union would not immediately call off the two sets of negotiations.

Russians were saying that the Khrushchev tactics at the summit did not mean that the Geneva talks would be called off. But the opinion of diplomats here was that the political foundation for agreement had been smashed.

American sources said tonight that the prospects for both conferences had been pushed back, if not destroyed. Foreign Secretary Selwyn Lloyd of Britain said the breakdown at the summit need not wreck the two Geneva meetings.

The Western delegations were expecting the Soviet Union to take the issue of the U-2 reconnaissance plane to Geneva and make it their political centerpiece at the disarmament negotiations. Moscow has repeatedly said that the West is more interested in espionage than dis-

Continued on Page 15, Column 7

Jovial Khrushchev Has Rural Holiday

By OSGOOD CARUTHERS
Special to The New York Times.

PARIS, May 17—Premier Khrushchev spent a happy day outdoors in France today despite all the efforts of the Western leaders to get him indoors for a session of the summit conference.

With seeming abandon, the leader of the Soviet Union spent the day doing the things he wanted to do when he came to France on a state visit two months ago. Meanwhile, the tense and anxious leaders of the West waited for him to save the summit from catastrophe.

Mr. Khrushchev held sidewalk and barnyard news conferences. He dashed up to startled Frenchmen and shook their

Continued on Page 15, Column 3

CHARGES TRADED

Allies Leave the Door Open to New Talk—Soviet Scores U.S.

By DREW MIDDLETON
Special to The New York Times.

PARIS, May 17—The summit conference died tonight. The leaders of the West said Premier Khrushchev had killed it. The Russians blamed the United States.

President Eisenhower, Prime Minister Macmillan and President de Gaulle feel "complete disgust" at the attitude the Soviet delegation has taken here in the last two days, James C. Hagerty, White House press secretary, reported.

In a communiqué issued this evening, the three Western chiefs declared that the Soviet leader's attitude had made it impossible to begin examination of the problems that it had been agreed should be discussed.

Apology Was Demanded

Premier Khrushchev had refused to meet with the Western leaders, on the invitation of President de Gaulle, unless Presdnt Eisenhower apologized for United States espionage flights over the Soviet Union. This the President was not prepared to do.

The meeting, so long prepared and so anxiously awaited, expired in an atmosphere of gloomy foreboding. Diplomats of the three Western powers feared the world situation would deteriorate.

The Western leaders pledged their support to a settlement of all outstanding international issues by negotiation rather than by the use or threat of force. The United States, Britain and France remain ready for such negotiations "at any suitable time in the future," a communiqué said.

Soviet in Sharp Attack

A few minutes after the communiqué had been made public, a group of leading Soviet editors answered it with a sharp denunciation of the United States. The conference foundered, a Soviet statement said, because "aggressive actions" of the United States Government and the Administration's failure to accept responsibility had "torpedoed the conference which the peoples of the whole world were awaiting with such hopes."

The Western leaders will meet again tomorrow afternoon after a preliminary conference between their foreign ministers, Christian A. Herter, Selwyn Lloyd and Maurice Couve de Murville. These meetings, Western diplomats said, will review

Continued on Page 14, Column 1

KHRUSHCHEV STEP REKNITS NATO TIE

Allies Feel Premier Carried U-2 Exploitation Too Far

By ROBERT C. DOTY
Special to The New York Times.

PARIS, May 17—Soviet intransigence, applied this time to bringing the summit conference to a halt, has again served to restore the cohesion of the North Atlantic Treaty Organiation.

The conclusion of NATO secretariat officials of the United States and of smaller powers today was that Premier Khrushchev had again badly overplayed his hand in exploitation of Soviet grievances arising from the downing of the United States U-2 reconnaissance plane over the Soviet Union May 1.

The same officials were unwilling to predict the long-term effects on the Atlantic alliance of the events since Sunday. New, heavy Soviet pressure on Berlin—one of the possibilities—would reimpose severe strains on the military and political resources of NATO.

But for the present at least, resentment of Soviet tactics here has largely overshadowed Allied impatience with the

Continued on Page 14, Column 7

Vatican Paper Proclaims Right Of Church to Role in Politics

Special to The New York Times.

ROME, May 17—L'Osservatore Romano, the Vatican newspaper, declared today that the Roman Catholic hierarchy had "the right and the duty to intervene" in the political field to guide its flock. It rejected what it termed "the absurd split of conscience between the believer and the citizen."

The pronouncement was in a front-page editorial described by the Vatican Press Service as "authoritative." It was presented in a special make-up that L'Osservatore Romano usually reserves for semi-official statements emanating from its Vatican superiors, as distinct from its own editorial opinion.

The article clearly referred to the political situation in Italy, where some left-of-center elements in the dominant Christian Democratic party, which enjoys Vatican backing, have recently advocated collaboration with Left-Wing Socialists, against the advice of the Roman Catholic Episcopacy.

However, L'Osservatore Romano made it plain that the pronouncement was valid for Roman Catholic laymen everywhere. It deplored "the great confusion of ideas that is spreading, especialy in some nations, among Catholics with regard to the relations between Catholic doctrine and social and political activities, and between the ecclesiastical hierarchy and

Continued on Page 31, Column 1

NEWS INDEX

"All the News That's Fit to Print"

The New York Times.

LATE CITY EDITION
U. S. Weather Bureau Report (Page 54) forecasts: Cloudy, chance of showers today. Fair, cooler, less humid tomorrow.
Temp. range: 84—72; yesterday: 83.2—70.
Temp.-Hum. Index: high 70's; yesterday: 78.

VOL. CIX—No. 37,427. NEW YORK, THURSDAY, JULY 14, 1960. 10 cents beyond 50-mile zone from New York City except on Long Island. Higher in air delivery cities. FIVE CENTS

KENNEDY NOMINATED ON THE FIRST BALLOT; OVERWHELMS JOHNSON BY 806 VOTES TO 409

Security Council Authorizes U. N. Force to Aid Congo

PEACE UNIT VOTED

U. S. and Soviet Clash in Debate—Belgians Asked to Pull Out

Congolese texts, resolution, debate excerpts, Page 4.

By THOMAS J. HAMILTON
Special to The New York Times.

UNITED NATIONS, N. Y., Thursday, July 14 — The Security Council authorized Secretary General Dag Hammarskjold today to organize and send a United Nations force to the Congo.

The vote was eight in favor and none against, with Britain, France and Nationalist China abstaining.

The vote was taken at 3:03 A. M., nearly six and a half hours after the Security Council, at the request of Mr. Hammarskjold, began its urgent night session. The decision was delayed by bitter exchanges between the United States and Soviet representatives, Henry Cabot Lodge and Arkady A. Sobolev. The Council adjourned at 3:21 A. M.

Outcome Was Uncertain

The outcome remained uncertain until the last. It was known that Britain, France and Nationalist China would abstain. They objected to a provision in the resolution, which was introduced by Tunisia, calling for the withdrawal of Belgian troops from the Congo.

The withdrawal recommendation was included on the demand of the Soviet Union and the African states. However, word was passed during the long meeting that the Soviet Union and Poland had not received instructions on the Tunisian proposal, and would therefore abstain if the United States insisted upon a vote at this meeting.

This belief was strengthened after Walter Loridan, the Belgian representative, announced that Belgian troops would be withdrawn from the Congo when the United Nations force is able to provide "effective" maintenance of order.

Mr. Sobolev termed this statement unsatisfactory. He introduced amendments condemning Belgian "armed aggression" in the Congo, stating that the Belgian forces must be withdrawn "immediately," and limiting participation in the United Nations force to the other African states.

The first two amendments were rejected 7 to 2, with only the Soviet Union and Poland

Continued on Page 4, Column 3

Belgian Commandos Rout Congo Troops at Airport

Bunche Meets With Both Sides to Try to Halt Clashes—Congolese Open Fire on Convoy of Refugees

By HENRY TANNER
Special to The New York Times.

LEOPOLDVILLE, the Congo, July 13—Belgian commandos occupied Leopoldville's airport today and then clashed with Congolese troops. At least six Congolese and two Belgians were killed.

Belgian forces occupied the airport at midmorning. They went into action after Congolese soldiers had moved into the airport and had threatened to interfere with the evacuation of Belgian civilians by Sabena, the Belgian airline.

[Leopoldville was reported by press associations to be under the control of Belgian troops, but there was uncertainty over the extent of control. Congolese troops opened fire Wednesday night on a convoy of 300 Belgians heading for the airport. Reuters said the Congo Government had declared that a "state of war" existed with Belgium. The Congo has asked Ghana to send troops.

[In Brussels, the Belgian Government said it would keep troops at key points in the Congo.]

Dr. Ralph J. Bunche, United Nations Under Secretary, met with Congolese authorities and Ambassador Jean van den Bosch of Belgium this afternoon in an effort to halt the clashes.

Dr. Bunche was reported to have been called in by the Congolese to mediate a cease-fire between them and the Belgians. He left the United States Embassy, where he has an office, in the early afternoon with the blue United Nations flag flying

Continued on Page 3, Column 2

MOSCOW BIDS U. N. CONVENE AT ONCE ON RB-47 INCIDENT

Says Flights by U. S. Planes With Reconnaissance Aim Are Threat to Peace

By OSGOOD CARUTHERS
Special to The New York Times.

MOSCOW, July 13—The Soviet Union called today for an urgent meeting of the United Nations Security Council to discuss its charges of United States "aggressive actions."

The Soviet complaint derived from the shooting down of a United States RB-47 reconnaissance plane off the Soviet coast in the Barents Sea on July 1.

[In a statement from the summer White House at Newport, R. I., the United States backed a full investigation by the United Nations of the "wanton shooting down" of the plane.]

Moscow called for the United Nations meeting in a cablegram sent by Foreign Minister Andrei A. Gromyko today to the president of the Security Council, José A. Correa of Ecuador.

Hammarskjold Gets Copy

The message, a copy of which was sent to Secretary General Dag Hammarskjold, charged that the United States flights constituted "a serious threat to the preservation of peace."

The United States has denied that the RB-47 plane had violated Soviet territorial waters as alleged by the Kremlin.

The Soviet request came on the heels of a statement yesterday by Premier Khrushchev that his Government might take the matter of the plane before the Security Council.

He said he did not expect that the Security Council, which he described as an "instrument" of the United States, would take any action satisfactory to the Soviet Union. However, he said he thought it was necessary to raise the question there anyway if only to "discredit the dishonest judges once more."

Mr. Gromyko's cablegram, which he said would be followed by an explanatory letter, noted that the Security Council had discussed the previous plane incident, in which a U-2 reconnaissance jet was shot down deep inside Soviet territory on May 1.

The message asked the Security Council to "take such measures as appear necessary to put an end to these dangers

Continued on Page 6, Column 5

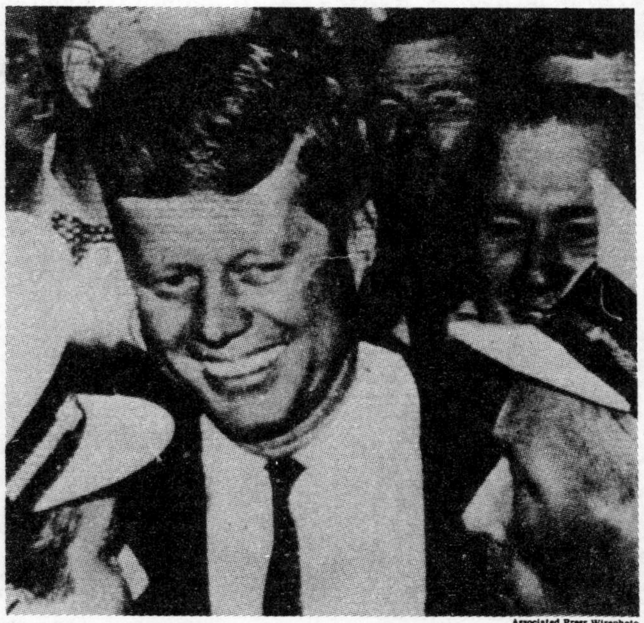

Associated Press Wirephoto

AFTER THE VICTORY: Senator John F. Kennedy of Massachusetts heads for rostrum at Los Angeles Memorial Sports Arena to address the Democratic National Convention.

LONG DRIVE WINS

Wyoming's Vote Puts Bostonian Over Top Before Acclamation

Kennedy's talk on Page 14; nominating speeches, 16.

By W. H. LAWRENCE
Special to The New York Times.

LOS ANGELES, Thursday, July 14—Senator John F. Kennedy smashed his way to a first-ballot Presidential nomination at the Democratic National Convention last night and won the right to oppose Vice President Nixon in November.

The 43-year-old Massachusetts Senator overwhelmed his opposition, piling up 806 votes to 409 ballots for his nearest rival, Senator Lyndon B. Johnson of Texas, the Senate majority leader. Senator Kennedy's victory came just before 11 o'clock last night [2 A. M. Thursday, New York time].

Then the convention made it unanimous on motion of Gov. James T. Blair Jr. of Missouri, who had placed Senator Stuart Symington of Missouri in nomination.

'We Shall Win'

Senator Kennedy, appearing before the shouting convention early today, pledged he would carry the fight to the country in the fall "and we shall win."

He thanked his defeated rivals for their generosity and appealed to all of their backers to keep the party strong and united in a tremendously important election. He spoke directly of Senators Johnson and Symington and the favorite sons, but made no reference to Adlai E. Stevenson.

The third session of the national convention adjourned after his speech. The next session will convene at 5 P. M. today.

Little Wyoming, well down the roll-call, provided the decisive fifteen votes that gave victory to Senator Kennedy. Two favorite-son states, Minnesota and New Jersey, waited in vain to give the on-rushing Kennedy bandwagon the final shove.

When Wyoming came in with its vote, the Kennedy total had mounted to 765 votes, or four more than the 761 votes required for nomination.

It was a tremendous victory for Senator Kennedy. Mr. Johnson, the Senate majority leader, had fought desperately to reverse a Kennedy tide that had been running for months. But Senator Johnson quickly telephoned his congratulations to

Continued on Page 14, Column 1

KISHI IS STABBED AT HOME IN TOKYO

Japan's Premier Is Reported Not Badly Hurt — Ikeda Chosen His Successor

By RICHARD J. H. JOHNSTON
Special to The New York Times.

TOKYO, Thursday, July 14—Premier Nobusuke Kishi was attacked by an assassin and stabbed in the thigh within an hour after his apparent successor had been elected by his party.

The Premier was attacked at a reception in his official residence. The attacker was identified by the authorities as Taizo Aramaki, a Rightist, about 45 years old.

Mr. Kishi was removed to a nearby hospital, where it was announced that his condition was not serious.

His assailant was arrested.

The police established the time of the attack as 2:30 P. M. This would be within forty minutes of Mr. Kishi's departure from Hibiya Hall in Downtown Tokyo, where the Liberal-Democratic party convention had been held.

The reception at the Premier's home was arranged to honor Hayato Ikeda, who, less than an hour before had been elected in the convention of the governing party as its new president, replacing Mr. Kishi who had resigned in the convention a short time before.

Mr. Ikeda, now Trade Minister, backs the Kishi policies.

The attack on the 63-year-old Premier was an ironic twist in the turbulent politics of recent months in Japan.

On June 23 he had announced

Continued on Page 11, Column 2

Peru Urges O.A.S. Debate Red Threat; U.S. Favors Parley

Special to The New York Times.

WASHINGTON, July 13 — Peru has suggested that the foreign ministers of the American nations meet soon to consider the Soviet threat to inter-American unity and democracy in the Western Hemisphere.

Informed sources said the Peruvian initiative was welcomed by the United States and that Washington would support the proposal. It is believed that the Peruvian suggestion will be considered at a meeting this week of the Council of the Organization of American States.

The Peruvian suggestion was circulated today among representatives of the twenty-one members of the O.A.S. It was also the subject of urgent consultation at embassies and in the State Department.

Peru's proposal was couched in careful diplomatic language, but its meaning was clear. The message stressed the necessity for the continued solidarity of the countries of this hemisphere. It called for the defense of the regional system in inter-American affairs and of democratic principles.

There was no specific refer-

Continued on Page 12, Column 5

JOHNSON PLEDGES HELP TO KENNEDY

He Assures Candidate of His Full Support and Issues a Call for Party Unity

By JOHN D. MORRIS
Special to The New York Times.

LOS ANGELES, July 13—Senator Lyndon B. Johnson accepted tonight "with all my heart" Senator John F. Kennedy's nomination for President.

The Texan, who had watched the convention proceedings by television in his suite at the Biltmore Hotel, issued a four-paragraph statement just as the first ballot ended. It had been prepared as Montana and some other Mountain States failed to provide expected shifts to the Johnson banner.

The statement follows:

"The delegates have made their decision and I accept it with all my heart.

"Senator Kennedy has my sincere congratulations, and my solemn assurance that in the coming months of this campaign, no one will be more dedicated than I—no one will work harder than I to make doubly sure of what all Democrats here and throughout the country know must come about for the good of the nation and the free world—that John F. Kennedy will be elected the next President of the United States.

"We have a winner—he has proved it here.

"Now, let our party unite behind our candidate—let us sweep the country this November, so that in January Demo-

Continued on Page 15, Column 6

Symington Heavy Favorite For Second Place on Ticket

By LEO EGAN
Special to The New York Times.

LOS ANGELES, July 13—Senator Stuart Symington became a heavy favorite for the Vice-Presidential nomination tonight following Senator John F. Kennedy's first-ballot nomination for President. The Missouri delegation was the first to swing into line behind Senator Kennedy after the New Englander had clinched the nomination for first place.

At the Kennedy headquarters in the Biltmore Hotel it was announced that the Presidential nominee would meet with those under consideration for Vice President and with party leaders from all sections of the country before going to bed.

Before the convention opened, he had promised the New York delegation, which was an important factor in his victory, that he would consult with its leaders before making a choice on second place.

Senator Symington parried questions about the Vice-Presidential nomination with the comment that the matter was entirely up to Senator Kennedy.

Good Word for Jackson

Although the Missouri Senator was regarded as the front runner for the Vice-Presidential nomination, two others were receiving serious consideration.

They were Gov. Orville L. Freeman of Minnesota, who had placed the New Englander in nomination, and Senator Henry M. Jackson of Washington State.

At a meeting of the Washington delegation today, Robert F. Kennedy, the Senator's brother and floor manager, said that Senator Jackson was his (Robert's) personal choice for the place but that political considerations might force his brother to turn elsewhere.

Governor Freeman had also been informed that those around Senator Kennedy had a high regard for him and that he would be acceptable as a Vice-Presidential candidate.

Up to the hour of Senator Kennedy's nomination, Senator Symington and Representative Charles A. Brown of Missouri, his campaign manager, were declaring that Senator Symington was not a candidate. But few delegates expected him to

Continued on Page 15, Column 6

STEVENSON GIVEN A WILD RECEPTION

His Nomination Touches Off Roaring Demonstration—It Lasts 25 Mintues

By WILLIAM M. BLAIR
Special to The New York Times.

LOS ANGELES, July 13—A wild, emotional demonstration for Adlai E. Stevenson shook the Democratic National Convention tonight.

As the name of the man who led the Democrats in 1952 and 1956 was placed before the convention, the galleries erupted in a screaming roar that dwarfed all that went before.

A rip-roaring nominating speech by Senator Eugene J. McCarthy, an "egghead" from Minnesota, set off the nearest thing to hysteria that this convention has seen.

Although the demonstrators obviously were full of enthusiasm, it was also obvious that the demonstration was at least partly contrived.

It took the convention chairman, Gov. LeRoy Collins of Florida, twenty-five minutes to slow down the stamping, shouting show to get seconding speeches.

Supporters Storm Floor

Stevenson supporters from outside the convention stormed the floor, some apparently gaining entrance by ruses, to call for the man who said he did not come West to seek the nomination.

Chanting, placard-waving demonstrators jammed the aisles while the galleries suddenly came alive with thousands of placards and hundreds of demonstrators going round and round in a deafening din.

The bobbing, weaving demonstrators on the floor, many of them young persons, caused many delegates to cover their ears. And many covered their heads with their hands as the Stevenson rooters bounced a giant, white papier-mâché ball through the air. The ball represented a snowball intended to dramatize the "Draft Stevenson" effort.

For the most part, the delegates appeared unmoved by the

Continued on Page 15, Column 2

HOGAN WILL PRESS A NEW JACK TRIAL

Fall Date to Be Asked Today in Borough Chief's Case

By PETER FLINT

A date for a new trial for Borough President Hulan E. Jack of Manhattan on charges of conflict of interest and conspiracy will be requested by District Attorney Frank S. Hogan today in the Court of General Sessions.

Since the court is now in summer recess, with only three of the nine judges sitting, the prosecutor is expected to ask for a date in the fall.

Mr. Jack's first trial ended last Thursday night when the jury failed to agree on a verdict after two days of deliberation and was discharged.

Mr. Jack's lawyer, Carson DeWitt Baker, said he would request an immediate trial. But he expressed the view that Mr. Hogan would "have his way as usual," and that the new trial probably would begin in October.

Mr. Baker also expressed "firm conviction" that the Borough President would continue his self-suspension from office until the case was resolved. Mr.

Continued on Page 25, Column 5

Union Forcing Plant To Return to City

By A. H. RASKIN

An arbitrator has ordered a New York clothing manufacturer to reopen his closed factory here and to pay the Amalgamated Clothing Workers union more than $200,000 in damages for having moved his work to Mississippi.

The employer, who lost a court fight to block arbitration, made it clear yesterday that he would resist the unusual award through new litigation.

The union is confident that recent decisions of the United States Supreme Court strengthening the power of arbitrators and limiting the right of judges to upset their awards will bar a successful challenge.

Jacob S. Potofsky, president of the Amalgamated, hailed the award as proof that "runaway

Continued on Page 55, Column 4

2 Planes Down Off Philippines; 86 of 88 Aboard Saved From Sea

Two Lost as U. S. Airliner Ditches—Island DC-3 Also Crashes, 30 on It Safe

By United Press International.

MANILA, Thursday, July 14—An American airplane and a Philippine passenger plane went down at sea in separate accidents today with a total of eighty-eight persons aboard. But eighty-six were reported safe after swift, dramatic rescue from shark-dangerous waters.

At least thirty-four Americans were aboard one of the planes, a Northwest Orient Airlines DC7-C on the last leg of a New York-to-Manila flight with fifty-one passengers and a crew of seven.

United States air force amphibious planes from Clark Field reported the rescue of fifty-six persons from the Northwest plane. One person was reported killed and one missing.

In the southern Philippines, 500 miles from Manila between the islands of Negros and Mindanao, a Philippines Airlines plane on an inter-island flight ditched in shallow water near land and all thirty passengers and crew members were picked up.

Passengers on the Northwest

The New York Times July 14, 1960

Sites of crash of U. S. plane (1) and Philippines plane (2)

airliner included Dr. Rodrigo L. Sarmiento, Filipino surgoen banished from the United States for the confessed killing of a Brooklyn nurse, Margaret Kabak. Dr. Sarmiento was among the survivors.

The Northwest plane, which had come from New York via Seattle, Anchorage, Tokyo and Okinawa, crash-landed near the little island of Jimalog, of the Potillo group about 150 miles northeast of Manila, after a propeller "ran away" and fell off and a wing caught fire.

Capt. David Rall, 53 years old of Seattle, deliberately put the plane down at sea after radioing at 4:20 A. M. [4:20 P. M.

Continued on Page 12, Column 4

Plan to End Strike On L.I.R.R. Offered

Governor Rockefeller's fact-finding board proposed an arbitration plan last night to bring an immediate end to the Long Island Rail Road strike.

The plan was rejected almost at once by the union's negotiating committee. It charged that most arbitrators had been "so brainwashed by the propaganda of the Association of American Railroads and the National Association of Manufacturers" that labor could not trust them.

The rejection will be reviewed by the 1,350 strikers at a meeting this morning, but union leaders said they would "bet a million dollars that the men will turn the idea down unanimously."

The company said the union's reaction made further study of the plan seem academic. It

Continued on Page 20, Column 2

NEWS INDEX

News Summary and Index, Page 29

F.H.A. INVESTMENT OPENED TO PUBLIC

Individuals Invited to Deal in U. S.-Insured Mortgages

By RICHARD E. MOONEY
Special to The New York Times.

WASHINGTON, July 13—The Government invited individuals today to invest in mortgages insured against loss by the Federal Housing Administration.

It was, in effect, an offer of a long-term investment that could earn the investor more than 5 per cent and would be paid off by the Government if the mortgage went into default. The yields of representative stocks and bonds currently are lower than 5 per cent.

Investment in an F. H. A.-insured mortgage would not be riskless. The investor would have to hold his investment until the mortgage was paid off, by the homebuyer or F. H. A., if he were to realize the full return. If he sold out before that, he might sell at a loss.

Besides being an attractive offer, and a break with policy of twenty-five years' standing, today's action was the Government's third stimulant to sagging activity in home building in as many months.

In April, the F. H. A. reduced

Continued on Page 55, Column 4

"All the News That's Fit to Print"

The New York Times.

LATE CITY EDITION
U. S. Weather Bureau Report (Page 54) forecasts:
Mostly fair and warm today, tonight and tomorrow.
Temp. range: 84—65; yesterday: 72.9—66.9.
Temp.-Hum. Index: 76; yesterday: 71.

VOL. CIX..No. 37,441. NEW YORK, THURSDAY, JULY 28, 1960. 10 cents beyond 50-mile zone from New York City except on Long Island. Higher in air delivery cities. FIVE CENTS

NIXON IS GIVEN NOMINATION BY ACCLAMATION AFTER GOLDWATER GETS 10 LOUISIANA VOTES; CANDIDATE PICKS LODGE FOR SECOND PLACE

SANITATION UNION QUITS IN PROTEST; GARBAGE PILES UP

5,000 March on City Hall as Wage Talks Break Off —Walkout May Go On

By LAYHMOND ROBINSON

Thousands of tons of refuse were left lying on city streets yesterday when angry sanitation workers suddenly stopped work to protest a breakdown in wage negotiations with the city.

The Sanitation Department reported that at least 4,000 of the 5,000 garbage collectors, street cleaners and incinerator employes on the day shift had failed to report for duty at 7 A. M. They may not report today, either.

Instead, the shouting, chanting city employes, augmented by 1,000 fellow workers who were on vacation or had days off, marched to City Hall.

They besieged the building for several hours, created a traffic jam and gave a 100-man police detail some anxious moments in holding the surging crowd behind barricades. However, there was no violence, though the police took the precaution of locking the doors of City Hall.

Meeting Collapses

Later in the day, a collapse of a hastily arranged meeting between union and city negotiators brought predictions that the walkout, which the union has denied is a strike, might last for some time.

Last night, as a result of the walkout, Traffic Commissioner T. T. Wiley announced that alternate-side parking rules would be lifted here today. Motorists may ignore signs that normally prohibit parking on Thursdays between 8 A. M. and 11 A. M. and 11 A. M. and 2 P. M. The department has not decided yet what it will do about parking regulations tomorrow.

City Demands Return

At the meeting between union and city negotiators, the spokesmen for the city, acting under instruction from the Board of Estimate, demanded that the men return to work before negotiations were resumed. Union negotiators rejected the demand and vowed to stay out until the city came up with a better offer on wages and fringe benefits.

The state's Condon-Wadlin Law prohibits strikes by Civil Service employes but Mayor Wagner would not say yesterday whether he viewed the stoppage as a strike, nor would he say whether the law would be invoked for the first time here.

Union members did not report for the night shift. The Sanitation Department said only a handful had showed up for night duty, which begins at 4 P. M. Usually about 700 men work the night shift in the summer.

The Sanitation Commissioner warned the men involved that they would be docked a day's pay for each day they refused

Continued on Page 11, Column 4

Stock Margin Rate Is Cut To 70% by Reserve Board

Officials Deny Reduction From 90% Is Aimed at Shoring Up the Market— Economic Significance Minimized

By TOM WICKER
Special to The New York Times.

WASHINGTON, July 27—The margin requirement for purchases of stocks was reduced from 90 to 70 per cent today by the Federal Reserve Board.

The reduction is effective tomorrow. It reflects the belief of the board of governors of the Federal Reserve that stock market credit is relatively stable at this time.

The margin requirement governs the minimum cash payment a stock buyer must make. As an example, today's action will reduce from $900 to $700 the amount of cash that must be put up for each $1,000 of stock.

The reduction also applies to short sales, in which a trader borrows stock and sells it in the hope of buying it back later at a lower price and thus making a profit.

The margin requirement is a device by which the Federal Reserve attempts to prevent excessive use of credit in the stock market. A spokesman said today the board of governors "just thinks 70 per cent will do it" under today's conditions.

The price of common stocks has declined recently. But the spokesman denied that today's action was an attempt to shore up prices or to stimulate credit and speculative activity.

He conceded, however, that since a trader could pick up more stock with the same amount of money, beginning tomorrow, the reduction might have an initial effect on the volume of transactions.

Despite the fact that the latest change before today's in margin requirements—an advance from 70 to 90 per cent on Oct. 16, 1958—came when the

Continued on Page 37, Column 1

CHIEFS CONSULTED

Bricker Is Expected to Place U.N. Aide in Nomination

By LEO EGAN
Special to The New York Times.

CHICAGO, Thursday, July 28 —Henry Cabot Lodge, delegate to the United Nations, was picked today by Vice President Richard M. Nixon to be his running mate.

Mr. Nixon revealed his preference a few hours after he himself had been nominated for President by the Republican convention.

Mr. Nixon came out of his room and made this announcement:

"I have reached a decision that I shall recommend to the convention Henry Cabot Lodge."

He said he would call Mr. Lodge at his New York home and ask if he would accept. He said he expected the decision to be affirmative.

Mr. Nixon made the announcement at 2:20 A. M. Central daylight time (3:20 A. M. New York time).

His decision all but assured Mr. Lodge's nomination for Vice President when the convention votes tonight on that post.

Mr. Nixon made the selection in consultation with leading Republicans in a meeting that began at his hotel about a half hour after the adjournment of last night's session of the convention.

Choice Not Unanimous

New York was represented at the meeting by L. Judson Morhouse, its Republican State Chairman.

The choice of Mr. Lodge was far from unanimous. However, Mr. Nixon insisted upon the Presidential nominee's right to choose his running mate.

Earlier yesterday, Mr. Nixon had listed the 58-year old former Massachusetts Senator as one of the four front runners for the vice-presidential nomination.

The three others were:

Senator Thruston B. Morton of Kentucky, the 52-year-old Republican National Chairman.

Representative Walter H. Judd of Minnesota, now 61 years old, who delivered the keynote address to the convention on Monday.

Robert B. Anderson, the 50-year-old Secretary of the Treasury, a former Texas Democrat who became an Eisenhower Republican in 1952.

To offset Midwest opposition to Mr. Lodge, an arrangement was reported to have been made to have former Senator John W. Bricker of Ohio place his name in nomination. And Representative Gerald Ford of Michigan, a

Continued on Page 12, Column 5

Associated Press Wirephoto
AFTER THE DELEGATES VOTED: Vice President and Mrs. Nixon at their hotel in Chicago last night with their daughters, Patricia, left, 14 years old, and Julie, 12.

UNITY IS STRESSED

Goldwater Withdraws and Asks Backing for the Nominee

Hatfield's speech, Page 12; Goldwater text, Page 14.

By W. H. LAWRENCE
Special to The New York Times.

CHICAGO, Thursday, July 28 —Vice President Richard M. Nixon swept to a first-ballot Republican Presidential nomination last night and the right to face Democratic Senator John F. Kennedy in the November election.

Early today, Mr. Nixon chose Henry Cabot Lodge, chief United States delegate to the United Nations, as his Vice-Presidential running mate.

Mr. Nixon received 1,321 votes on the polling of state delegations. Senator Barry Goldwater of Arizona received ten votes, cast by members of the twenty-six-vote Louisiana delegation even after the Arizonan had asked withdrawal of his name from consideration.

At the end of the roll-call, Louisiana moved to make Mr. Nixon's choice unanimous, but balked at changing its ten votes from the Goldwater to the Nixon column without a poll. When the roll-call vote was announced as 1,321 to 10, the Arizona delegation then moved to make the nomination unanimous, and this was done by acclamation.

Goldwater Asks Unity

The convention decision pits the 47-year-old Vice President against the 43-year-old Senator from Massachusetts. Mr. Nixon is the first Vice President in the history of the modern two-party system to win a Presidential nomination in his own right.

Senator Goldwater made the dramatic appearance of the night, calling upon all conservatives to back Mr. Nixon in November and avoid any party split or stay-at-home nonvoting attitude that would help Democrats "dedicated to the destruction of this country."

Withdrawing his own name from consideration for the Presidency, the Arizona Senator, an avowed conservative, said he had been campaigning for Mr. Nixon's nomination for the last six years and would fight for his election in November.

Lecture to Conservatives

"Let us put our shoulders to the wheel of Dick Nixon and push him over across the line," Senator Goldwater said.

He lectured conservatives sternly, telling them they must "grow up" and get to work "if we want to take this party back some day—and I think we can."

He said the Democratic party no longer was the party of Jefferson, Jackson and Wilson but now was ruled by "Bowles, Galbraith and Reuther." His references were to Representative Chester Bowles of Connecticut; Kenneth Galbraith, Harvard economist, and Walter P. Reu-

Continued on Page 12, Column 1

FRENCH 'SLIGHTS' ANGER ADENAUER

He Will Leave for Week-End Paris Talks Only Because His Hand Was Forced

By SYDNEY GRUSON
Special to The New York Times.

BONN, Germany, July 27—Chancellor Adenauer will fly to Paris for talks with President de Gaulle Friday, but in a furious mood and only because the French forced his hand.

Both Paris and Bonn announced the meeting this afternoon and said the main subject of the talks would be the political integration of Western Europe.

But the background to this laconic announcement was far more dramatic. The Chancellor had been infuriated by a number of what he considers slights to West Germany by France and had determined not to go through with the meeting this week-end.

The French, aware of his mood, let it be known last night to West German reporters in Paris and to some French newspapers that the meeting was on.

Apparently rather than permit a crack for all the world to see in the painfully restored French-German friendship, the keystone of his European policy,

Continued on Page 2, Column 5

British Earl Named Foreign Secretary In Cabinet Shuffle

By DREW MIDDLETON
Special to The New York Times.

LONDON, July 27 — Prime Minister Macmillan chose the Earl of Home as Britain's new Foreign Secretary today in a major reconstruction of the Conservative Government.

Selwyn Lloyd leaves the Foreign Office to become Chancellor of the Exchequer. A successful tenure there would improve Mr. Lloyd's prospects as the future Prime Minister.

Lord Home (whose name is pronounced Hume) is the first peer to be Foreign Secretary since Lord Halifax held the office twenty years ago. The official announcement of his appointment this evening brought to a climax the mounting criticism of the last five days.

Mr. Macmillan will be forced to defend his choice against the Labor party's censure in a House of Commons debate tomorrow night.

The objections to the appointment of Lord Home were based on two points. First, the critics said, the Foreign Secretary should be a member of the House of Commons and answerable in the House to any questions on foreign policy. Second, the objectors maintained, there was nothing in Lord Home's career to justify the appointment.

The first newspaper comment

Continued on Page 2, Column 2

NIXON BOLSTERS ROCKEFELLER TIE

New York Delegation Greets Him Warmly — Governor to Campaign Anywhere

By WARREN WEAVER Jr.
Special to The New York Times.

CHICAGO, July 27—At political sword points only a week ago, Governor Rockefeller and Vice President Nixon joined today in a powerful demonstration of concord.

Mr. Nixon made a special morning trip two miles up Michigan Avenue to visit his new-found supporters in the New York delegation. The delegation endorsed him unanimously, if belatedly, yesterday.

The Governor went to the Sheraton Towers lobby to greet Mr. Nixon, like classmates at a reunion. Beaming, he escorted him to the closed caucus. They posed for pictures with arms around each other.

Mr. Rockefeller said the Vice President's visit had given the New Yorkers "a final inspiration and emotional lift."

"We're with you all the way," he promised.

Mr. Nixon was hardly less enthusiastic about the Governor. He pleaded with the New York

Continued on Page 14, Column 5

13 Dead in Chicago Crash Of 'Copter on Airport Run

By The Associated Press.

CHICAGO, July 27—A helicopter carrying passengers between airports suddenly lost power and plunged in a mass of flames into a suburban cemetery tonight. All thirteen persons aboard were killed. Wreckage was scattered over a wide area.

A swath of clipped tree tops almost 600 feet long indicated that the pilot had tried to gain altitude.

Witnesses said the craft, an S-58, carrying eleven passengers and a crew of two, stopped in air, zigzagged a moment and then plummeted, shooting flames.

The helicopter, owned by Chicago Helicopter Airways, Inc., was on an eleven-minute trip from Midway Airport on the Southwest side to O'Hare International Airport on the Northwest side.

Falls Near River

It plunged into the Forest Home Cemetery north of Roosevelt Road near the Des Plaines River. The crash site is between suburban Maywood and Forest Park.

An officer of the helicopter company landed near the crash scene and said that the pilot of the downed craft was Capt. Robert Meyer, 37 years old. The names of the other victims were not immediately available.

However, a company spokesman said "no one of national importance was known to be aboard." He apparently referred to the fact the Republican National Convention is meeting in Chicago.

The helicopter, which has a capacity of fourteen, including

Continued on Page 55, Column 2

ROBERT KENNEDY EASES SPLIT HERE

Candidate's Brother Wins Prendergast's Approval of Independent Group

By CLAYTON KNOWLES

Robert F. Kennedy came to New York yesterday and brought Michael H. Prendergast around to an agreement that an independent citizens' committee could work effectively in the state for the election of Senator John F. Kennedy as President.

Mr. Prendergast, the Democratic state chairman, reversed his earlier opposition to such an auxiliary campaign unit during a two-and-a-half hour luncheon meeting with Mr. Kennedy, who is the manager of his brother's campaign for the Presidency.

Carmine G. De Sapio, Democratic national committeeman, who sat in on the session at the Hampshire House, was asked if he, too, was satisfied.

"One hundred per cent!" he said with emphasis.

The conference was one of five important meetings that Mr. Kennedy held during a busy day with representatives of virtually every shade of thinking within the Democratic party.

The session with Mr. Prendergast was of particular importance because Mr. Prendergast had understood originally in talks with Senator Kennedy that the campaign would be run strictly through the Democratic state organization.

Later, when the Senator agreed to establishing a Citizens for Kennedy committee here, Mr. Prendergast viewed the enterprise as competitive with the regular organization's work. He also viewed the individuals

Continued on Page 16, Column 1

Iran Cuts Cairo Tie In Dispute on Israel

By Reuters.

TEHERAN, Iran, July 27—Iran severed diplomatic relations with the United Arab Republic today and gave Cairo's Ambassador here twenty-four hours to get out of the country.

The severance was announced by Foreign Minister Abbas Aram after he had served the expulsion order on the Ambassador, Mahmoud Hammad.

Mr. Aram said the decision to oust Mr. Hammad was made after President Gamal Abdel Nasser attacked Shah Mohammed Riza Pahlevi of Iran yesterday in a speech at Alexandria. President Nasser assailed the Shah for his statement Saturday that Iran had recognized Israel.

The Iranian Foreign Minister described President Nasser as

Continued on Page 5, Column 1

The New York Times
PROTEST AT CITY HALL: Employes of the Department of Sanitation rally against the breakdown of wage talks

Key Issues in Congo Awaiting U.N. Chief

By HENRY TANNER
Special to The New York Times.

LEOPOLDVILLE, the Congo, July 27 — Secretary General Dag Hammarskjold is likely to be successful in paving the way for the peaceful entry of United Nations forces into Katanga Province, diplomatic observers here predict.

Mr. Hammarskjold is scheduled to arrive here tomorrow from Brussels. Katanga, which has declared its independence of the Congo, is expected to be the dominant issue in his consultations here. He will spend four or five days talking with Congolese, Belgian and United Nations officials.

Katanga is now controlled by Belgian forces that went there at the request of the provincial Premier, Moise Tshombe. Mr.

Continued on Page 3, Column 3

NEWS INDEX

Eisenhower Is Firm For Middle of Road

By DONALD JANSON
Special to The New York Times.

CHICAGO, July 27 — President Eisenhower emphasized today the superiority of a middle political course over right or left extremes.

He denounced the Socialist philosophy of a "fairly friendly European country" he said he had been reading about in the last few weeks.

"The experiment of almost complete paternalism" there, he said, has resulted in a sharp rise in the suicide rate, "more than twice our drunkenness," and a "lack of moderation discernible on all sides."

It was believed that he had alluded to Sweden. Her suicide rate is 19.9 for every 100,000 persons, compared with ten in

Continued on Page 14, Column 4

"All the News That's Fit to Print."

NEWS SUMMARY AND INDEX, PAGE 95

The New York Times.

LATE CITY EDITION
U. S. Weather Bureau Report (Page 95) forecasts:
Fair and warm today; fair tonight.
Chance of thunder showers tomorrow.
Temp. range: 83—68; yesterday: 82.3—63.4.
Temp.-Hum. Index: near 77; yesterday: 76.

SECTION ONE

VOL. CIX. No. 37,465.

NEW YORK, SUNDAY, AUGUST 21, 1960.

35c outside New York City, its suburban area and Long Island. 50c in 17 Western states, Canada; higher in air delivery cities.

THIRTY CENTS

NIXON ENDORSES NEW JAVITS PLAN FOR CARE OF AGED

Backs Contributory Medical Insurance Based on Aid From U. S. and States

MEANS TEST RULED OUT

Senator's Proposal Faces a Showdown With Kennedy's Social Security Set-Up

By TOM WICKER

Special to The New York Times.

WASHINGTON, Aug. 20—Vice President Nixon lent his support today to a new program of contributory health insurance as the Senate opened a politically charged debate on the issue of medical care for the aged.

The new plan was introduced and strongly advocated by Senator Jacob K. Javits, the New York Republican.

It will be offered, he told reporters later, as an amendment to the relief-payments bill approved by the Senate Finance Committee. It will also be offered as a substitute for the Social Security plan backed by the Democratic Presidential candidate, Senator John F. Kennedy of Massachusetts.

Mr. Nixon, the Republican nominee, made no statement on the matter. Senator Javits said he had his support and a Nixon spokesman later asserted that the Vice President had helped the Senator to prepare the insurance program.

Similar Plan Recalled

Mr. Javits noted that he had introduced a similar plan in the House of Representatives in 1949. Mr. Nixon and Christian A. Herter, now Secretary of State, were among the co-sponsors.

The Javits proposal is along the lines of the Eisenhower Administration's "medicare" voluntary insurance plan but offers considerably wider benefits. It is also more liberal in its not requiring a means test for beneficiaries and in being less costly for participants.

For these reasons, Senator Javits said he could not say he had the support of President Eisenhower. The Nixon spokesman said, however, that Arthur S. Flemming, Secretary of Health, Education and Welfare had also helped prepare the Javits program.

Saltonstall Backs Plan

Among Senator Javits' co-sponsors is Senator Leverett Saltonstall of Massachusetts, who introduced the Medicare scheme. Seven other Republicans also joined the New Yorker.

Their program would make about 11,000,000 persons over 65 years of age eligible for health insurance, but not those with incomes over $3,000 for individuals or $4,500 for couples. The Federal and state governments would share in the cost of the insurance.

Senator Javits put the annual

Continued on Page 44, Column 1

MEETING IN INDEPENDENCE: Senator John F. Kennedy with former President Truman at the Truman Library in the Missouri city. At rear is Senator Stuart Symington.

United Press International Telephoto

Kennedy Calls on Truman; Gets a Forecast of Victory

By W. H. LAWRENCE

Special to The New York Times.

INDEPENDENCE, Mo., Aug. 20—Former President Harry S. Truman joined Senator John F. Kennedy today in what he forecast would be a winning campaign for the Democratic Presidential nominee.

The former President conferred for forty minutes with the Massachusetts Senator, whose nomination he opposed when he boycotted the Democratic National Convention at Los Angeles.

Laughing in recollection of his upset victory in 1948 over Gov. Thomas E. Dewey of New York, Mr. Truman said he had "no use" for pollsters. He added that he put no stock in a recent Gallup poll that showed Vice President Nixon leading Senator Kennedy 50 to 44 per cent.

"The Democrats are going to win," Mr. Truman said.

Talked by Telephone

The Truman-Kennedy conference was their first meeting since the Democratic convention, but they had talked earlier by telephone. At that time Mr. Truman gave assurances that he would support the ticket actively.

The groundwork for this session had been laid ten days ago when Gov. Abraham A. Ribicoff of Connecticut came as Senator Kennedy's peacemaking emissary to talk with the former President.

From all appearances, the meeting was jovial and cordial, although Mr. Truman got a little edgy when he was reminded of the harsh things he had said about Senator Kennedy before his nomination.

He was reminded that he had expressed doubts that Senator Kennedy was ready for the Presidency because he was too young and inexperienced, and that he had also asserted that the convention had been "prearranged" to produce Senator Kennedy's nomination.

To most of these, the former

Continued on Page 46, Column 1

NIXON GIVES IDEAS ON RED CHALLENGE

Says Knowledge of Ideology Is Needed to Meet It—Report First in Series

By WILLIAM J. JORDEN

Special to The New York Times.

WASHINGTON, Aug. 20—Vice President Nixon released today a thirty-page analysis of the meaning of communism. It was the first of a series of reports setting forth the thinking of the Republican Presidential candidate on major issues facing the American people.

Mr. Nixon wrote that a "major weakness" in the struggle against "the militant aggressiveness of international communism" was a prevailing lack of understanding of the character of the challenge. He said that "nothing less than a knowledge in depth of the Communist idea is necessary if we are to deal with it effectively."

The Vice President offered his study of communism as an aid to the kind of knowledge he said was necessary. It did not pretend to be an original contribution to the vast collection of studies on Communist theory. Rather it was a summation of Mr. Nixon's thoughts on some of the main features of earlier studies.

Mr. Nixon said the American people recognized that "we must retain our present military and economic advantage over the Communist bloc." He said the United States would "keep the lead that we have gained" in rocket technology and space exploration.

Sees Battle of Ideas

"What we must realize," the Vice President wrote, "is that this struggle probably will not be decided in the military, economic, or scientific areas, important as these are. The battle in which we are engaged is primarily one of ideas. The test is one not so much of arms but of faith."

The Republican candidate then explored what he considered some of the main elements of Communist thought and attacked them variously as misleading, immoral or of demonstrated ineffectuality.

He stressed that the principal appeal of Communist ideas today was not to broad masses of people but "more often to an intelligent minority in newly developing countries who are trying to decide which system offers the best and surest road to progress."

Introducing his discussion of

Continued on Page 48, Column 1

Sports News

BASEBALL

The Yankees beat the Washington Senators, 9—5, yesterday with four runs in the eleventh inning — two on a homer by Bill Skowron. The victory kept the Yankees a game and a half ahead of the second-place White Sox. The White Sox defeated the Athletics, 3—0, on Herb Score's two-hit pitching. The Red Sox won from the Orioles, 8—6, in the afternoon. The Orioles won their night game, 6—0. In the National League, the first-place Pirates topped the Reds, 10—7.

HARNESS RACING

Hairos II, representing the Netherlands, won the $50,000 International Trot at Roosevelt Raceway. He paid $11.90 for $2. Crevalcore of Italy was second and Silver Song of the United States third.

HORSE RACING

Tompion, the 9-to-10 choice, won the $83,100 Travers Stakes at Saratoga. One-Eyed King took the Arlington Handicap at Chicago.

TENNIS

Rod Laver of Australia and Earl (Butch) Buchholz of St. Louis gained the final of the Newport Casino tournament.

Details in Section 5.

SOUTH FACES TEST IN SCHOOLS FIGHT

New Orleans Desegregation Ruling Sparks a Crisis—Election Adds Pressure

By CLAUDE SITTON

Special to The New York Times.

ATLANTA, Aug. 20—The deep South faces new steps toward desegregation of its public schools this fall under the complex pressures of a Presidential election year.

The area's response, according to the Southern Regional Council, may well affect both the election and the future pace of desegregation elsewhere.

The council, which is made up of white and Negro leaders in the South, released a study today of progress in the field since 1954, when the Supreme Court issued its decision on desegregation. The study also treated the outlook for this fall.

Its report noted that, after an initial surge of compliance in the border states, "desegregation has been a campaign fought by laws and lawyers over the careers of a few amazingly stanch Negro children."

As a result of a Federal court order directing New Orleans' schools to begin desegregation in September, the council said, "the deep South at last faces the demand that it comply with the law."

The outcome of that test will have far-reaching implications, the organization contended.

"Perhaps the truth has been," it said, "that desegregation cannot move more rapidly in the

Continued on Page 65, Column 3

Wagner Will Press Extra Registration

By DOUGLAS DALES

Mayor Wagner voiced regret yesterday at Governor Rockefeller's rejection of his plea for a special session of the Legislature to revise voter registration dates. He reaffirmed his intention to provide additional registration time.

The four days fixed by the Legislature for local registration, Oct. 12 through 15, conflict with Jewish religious observances. The Mayor had requested the special session to substitute Oct. 10 and 11 for Oct. 13 and 14.

Mayor Wagner said he could not understand why the Governor had turned down his request in view of its endorsement by the bipartisan Board of Elections, composed of two Democrats and two Republicans. He noted he had asked for the

Continued on Page 42, Column 4

DOMINICANS QUIT AMERICAS PARLEY; SANCTIONS VOTED

O. A. S. Ministers Condemn Trujillo Regime—Call for Severing of Relations

Text of O. A. S. resolution on Dominican Republic, Page 3.

By TAD SZULC

Special to The New York Times.

SAN JOSE, Costa Rica, Aug. 20—Dominican delegates abandoned the conference of the American foreign ministers today as it unanimously voted precedent-setting sanctions against the Dominican Republic.

The foreign ministers' meeting this afternoon as a general commission, approved by a roll-call vote a resolution "emphatically" condemning the Dominican Republic for "acts of aggression and intervention" against Venezuela, including an attempt to assassinate Venezuela's President, Dr. Romulo Betancourt.

The resolution also called for an immediate break in diplomatic relations with the Dominican regime by members of the Organization of American States and for "partial interruption of economic relations."

The afternoon action on the Dominican issue was final; the resolution now goes to the O. A. S. Council in Washington, which will ask member nations to carry out the terms.

New Sessions on Cuba

Next week the ministers will convene in new sessions to deal with Caribbean tensions and Soviet interests in Cuba.

The parting gesture of the Dominican delegation was to demand a fight against "American imperialism," apparently prompted by the firm position taken by the United States against the Dominican dictatorship of Generalissimo Rafael Leonidas Trujillo Molina.

As a result of a legal maneuver by Venezuela late last night, the conference members did not take any practical steps to provide for a peaceful transition to democracy in the Dominican Republic. Secretary of State Christian A. Herter had advocated the formation of a special mechanism to avert the danger of possible chaos if the Trujillo regime should crumble.

Herter States U. S. View

Speaking tonight at a formal closing session of this week's conference, Mr. Herter said that the United States, while supporting the resolution that was adopted, would have preferred to see the appointment of a special committee with power to foster true democracy in the Dominican Republic. The United States, he added adjusted its views "to maintain the solidarity and common approach of our community."

The Dominican Foreign Minister, Porfirio Herrera Baez, and several others in his delegation left San José late this afternoon for Panama en route to Ciudad Trujillo. They departed from their hotel through

Continued on Page 3, Column 1

Mali Alliance in Africa Splits; Senegal-Sudan Strife Feared

De Gaulle Invites Contending Premiers to Paris—Dakar Under Senegalese Rule

By HENRY GINIGER

Special to The New York Times.

PARIS, Aug. 20—The Mali Federation in West Africa broke up suddenly today. A civil war between its component states, Senegal and Sudan, was threatened.

The uneasy eighteen-month partnership between the former French territories, which are members of the French Community, broke down early this morning in Dakar when the Senegalese Government headed by Mamadou Dia announced its withdrawal.

The Senegalese thus struck back at the Mali Premier, Modibo Keita, who also is Premier of Sudan. Late last night Mr. Keita canceled Mr. Dia's defense and external-security powers and proclaimed a state of emergency.

Shortly after the Senegalese Government had declared its independence, Senegalese forces took over control of Dakar, the west-coast port that is Senegal's chief city. Mr. Keita was said

The New York Times Aug. 21, 1960

Senegal (1) broke her tie to the Sudan Republic (2).

to be virtually a prisoner in his palace.

Communications between Dakar and the outside world were cut about 4 A. M. and news reaching Paris was sketchy. Both Dakar and Bamako, capital of Sudan, were reported to be calm.

Acting swiftly early this evening to prevent an irreparable breach in the French Community, President de Gaulle

Continued on Page 8, Column 1

TWO SOVIET DOGS IN ORBIT RETURNED TO EARTH ALIVE AS SATELLITE IS RETRIEVED

ANIMALS UNHURT

Capsule Comes Down After 17 Circuits in 24-Hour Flight

By SEYMOUR TOPPING

Special to The New York Times.

MOSCOW, Aug. 20—Living creatures have returned safely to earth from an orbit in space for the first time in history, the Soviet Union announced today.

It said its "second cosmic space ship" landed on target today after circling the earth for twenty-four hours with its cargo of two dogs, some rats and mice, flies, plants, seeds and fungi.

On its eighteenth circuit of the earth at an altitude of about 200 miles, the five-ton space ship responded to a signal from the ground and began to descend, detaching the capsule containing the animals en route.

Announced by Tass

Tass, the Soviet press agency, said:

"The space ship's control system and braking device operated with great accuracy and ensured the ship's descent to the fixed spot. The deviation from the calculated spot amounted to some ten kilometers [6¼ miles].

"The space ship, weighing 4,600 kilograms (not counting the last stage of the carrier rocket), provided as it was with a special thermal shield, safely passed through the earth's atmosphere. The space ship and the jettisoned capsule containing the experimental animals landed safely."

[In Washington, T. Keith Glennan, head of the National Aeronautics and Space Administration, saluted the Soviet Union for "a fine job." He added, however, that he did not regard the accomplishment as "a major first" in space exploration but rather as "just another step" toward meeting "the problems we all face."]

Television in Cabin

The space ship was launched yesterday with what was described as a cabin equipped with "everything necessary for the future flight of a man."

In the cabin, under the lenses of television cameras, were the dogs Strelka and Belka (feminine forms of the words Little Arrow and Squirrel).

Tass said scientists on the ground watched the dogs on their television screens during the flight, observed their postures "and even saw one of the dogs take food."

Meanwhile, other apparatus was recording and transmitting the animals' heart beats, blood pressure, respiration and movements, and the functioning of equipment designed to maintain

Continued on Page 33, Column 1

Mrs. Powers Plans Appeal For Moscow's Clemency

Will Send a Letter Directly to Brezhnev—Wife of Pilot Is Unable to Leave 'Without Trying to Do Everything'

Special to The New York Times.

MOSCOW, Aug. 20—Mrs. Francis Gary Powers said today she would begin her fight to obtain clemency for her husband by appealing to President Leonid I. Brezhnev of the Soviet Union.

"I cannot leave Moscow without trying to do everything in the world for him," Mrs. Powers said. "But my impression on seeing Gary was that he did not think anything would help."

The wife of the U-2 pilot, who was shot down near Sverdlovsk May 1, spoke with reporters in her suite at the Sovetskaya Hotel.

She had been present yesterday in the Hall of Columns of Trade Union House when the Soviet's highest military tribunal found her husband guilty of espionage and sentenced him to a loss of freedom for ten years.

Mr. Powers will spend three years in prison, the court decreed. The remaining seven presumably will be in a penal colony, or working in a remote section of the Soviet under close supervision of the authorities.

Mrs. Powers, who is 25 years old, was pale but composed as she answered questions. She sat on a striped blue sofa beside her widowed mother, Mrs. Monteen Beck Brown.

Mrs. Powers and the pilot's parents, Mr. and Mrs. Oliver W. Powers, expect to deliver early next week a letter to the office of Mr. Brezhnev, President of the Presidium of the Supreme Soviet (Parliament).

Mikhail I. Grinyov, state-appointed defense attorney for the 31-year-old pilot, said this afternoon that Mr. Brezhnev prob-

Continued on Page 71, Column 4

Soviet Opposes U. N. Plan; Bunche Will Leave Congo

By JAMES FERON

Special to The New York Times.

UNITED NATIONS, N. Y., Aug. 20—The Soviet Union told Secretary General Dag Hammarskjold today it opposed the week-old United Nations technical assistance program in the Congo. Vasily V. Kuznetsov, a First Deputy Foreign Minister, also demanded the immediate withdrawal of

Statements at U. N. on the Congo appear on Page 16.

"armed groups from Canada" from the African republic "because they are allies of Belgium, which is guilty of aggression in the Congo."

[In Leopoldville, Premier Patrice Lumumba abandoned his demand for the withdrawal of all white United Nations troops.]

It was also announced here that Dr. Ralph J. Bunche, who has been in charge of all United Nations operations in the Congo, would be replaced shortly by Rajeshwar Dayal, India's High Commissioner to Pakistan. United Nations officials denied the change had been prompted by any diminishing effectiveness in Dr. Bunche's relations with Congolese officials.

They also denied the shift was prompted by rising tension between Gen. Carl Carlsson von Horn, head of the United Nations force, and Maj. Gen. Henry T. Alexander, head of the Ghanaian contingent.

The discord within the United Nations force in regard to the Ghanaian troops was brought out in documents made public by Mr. Hammarskjold. These included criticism by the Secretary General of actions of the Ghanaians and a reply by Gen-

Continued on Page 15, Column 1

Salt Inquiry Shows How Roy Cohn Lost

By CHARLES GRUTZNER

An account of how Roy M. Cohn and William Fugazy, the boxing promoters, lost a fight with Fortune Pope to control the supply of Dominican rock salt for this city is scattered through the files of the State Investigation Commission.

It depicts Joseph V. Spagna, who resigned Thursday as Purchase Commissioner, as the man who decided in favor of Mr. Pope, his friend of twenty-five years.

The state commission reported Wednesday that it had found contract-rigging, collusive bidding, bribery, shortweighting and other dishonesty in this city's annual purchase of $700,000 in rock salt for snow and ice removal. It accused Mr. Spagna of having rigged contract procedures to favor Mr. Pope, who had a financial inter-

Continued on Page 55, Column 1

LOYAL LAOS UNITS MARCH ON REBELS

Five Battalions Heading for Vientiane—Opposition to New Regime Growing

By JACQUES NEVARD

Special to The New York Times.

SAVANNAKHET, Laos, Aug. 20—Five battalions of loyal Laotian troops are moving on the rebel center of Vientiane from the north and south, it was learned here today from sources close to Maj. Gen. Phoumi Nosavan.

It was not known whether their orders were to attack the capital or to lay siege to it in an effort to starve the rebels into submission.

[About 200 American women and children have been evacuated from Laos to neighboring Thailand to escape the threats of civil war and floods. Planes flying from Vientiane to Bangkok completed the airlift of nearly 500 foreigners Saturday.]

Deputies Joining General

The original battalion of paratroopers headed by Capt. Kong Le, which seized Vientiane Aug. 9, was reported yesterday to have been joined by two companies of pro-Communist Pathet Lao rebels.

Meanwhile, General Phoumi Nosavan, pro-Western chairman of the "Committee to Counter the Coup d'Etat in Laos," was rapidly organizing a regime here in the south of Laos. Thus far twenty out of fifty-eight Deputies elected to the National Assembly last April have arrived and others are expected.

Under Laotian law thirty Deputies are required for a quorum and if that figure is reached it is expected that the Assembly will repudiate its action in voting against the Government of Premier Tiao Somsanith and setting up the present Vientiane regime of Prince Souvanna Phouma. It took the action under the guns of Captain Kong Le's troops with a mob howling outside the door of the National Assembly.

Three of the Deputies now here escaped from Vientiane by

Continued on Page 19, Column 1

Today's Sections

*Included in all copies in the New York metropolitan area and adjacent territory.

Index to Subjects

"All the News That's Fit to Print"

The New York Times.

LATE CITY EDITION
U. S. Weather Bureau Report (Page 93) forecasts: Cloudy, periods of rain today. Partly cloudy, colder tomorrow. Temp. range: 55—41; yesterday: 53.8—40.4.

VOL. CX..No. 37,546. NEW YORK, THURSDAY, NOVEMBER 10, 1960. FIVE CENTS

10 cents beyond 50-mile zone from New York City except on Long Island. Higher in air delivery cities.

KENNEDY'S VICTORY WON BY CLOSE MARGIN; HE PROMISES FIGHT FOR WORLD FREEDOM; EISENHOWER OFFERS 'ORDERLY TRANSITION'

DEMOCRATS HERE SPLIT IN VICTORY; LEHMAN ASSAILED

De Sapio Accepts Challenge for Party Control—Mayor Claims Leadership

Text of De Sapio statement appears on Page 43.

By LEO EGAN

Less than twenty-four hours after the polls closed, the political coalition that gave Senator John F. Kennedy New York's forty-five electoral votes began coming apart at the seams.

Its disintegration was signaled by Carmine G. De Sapio in a statement assailing former Gov. Herbert H. Lehman, key figure in the Democratic reform group, and Alex Rose, Liberal party master of strategy.

The statement accepted Mr. Lehman's election night challenge to a finish fight for control of the party organization in the city and state.

At the same time it appeared to rule out any chance of a Democratic-Liberal party coalition for next year's Mayoral election in New York City and for the Governorship election in the state in 1962 if Mr. De Sapio remains in control of the party machinery.

Kennedy's Delicate Problem

Mr. De Sapio, leader of Tammany and Democratic National Committeeman for New York, consulted Michael H. Prendergast, the Democratic State Chairman, and a number of party leaders in the city and upstate before issuing his statement.

The collapse of the coalition so soon after it achieved its goal gave President-elect Kennedy a delicate political problem before he takes office. At some stage soon he will have to decide whom in New York to consult about appointments for the new Administration.

Thus, in so far as New York is concerned, the election appeared to raise as many questions as it settled. Control of the Democratic party machinery is one of them. Among the others are: What is Mayor Wagner's political future? And what is Governor Rockefeller's?

When told of Mr. De Sapio's statement last night, Mayor Wagner commented that he in-

Continued on Page 43, Column 1

Registration Set-Up Called Faulty Here

By DOUGLAS DALES

Political leaders voiced dissatisfaction yesterday over the way permanent personal registration functioned here Tuesday in its first test in a Presidential election.

Charges were made that thousands of persons had been disfranchised because they were unable to convince election inspectors that they had registered and were eligible to vote.

How many voters may have been so affected was concededly a guess. But a check of the Supreme Courts in the five boroughs indicated that more than 1,300 persons had gone before the justices for orders directing the inspectors to permit them to vote.

"There was a minimum of 10,000 denied the right to vote," Abraham Gellinoff,

Continued on Page 43, Column 5

ASSEMBLY DELAYS U.N. CONGO DEBATE

Postpones It Indefinitely, 48-30, as Soviet Backs Step—U. S. Move Fails

By KATHLEEN TELTSCH
Special to The New York Times.

UNITED NATIONS, N. Y., Nov. 9—The General Assembly voted tonight to postpone the debate on the Congo indefinitely.

The 48-to-30 vote, with eighteen abstentions, was on a surprise move made by Ghana with the help of Guinea and Nigeria and the enthusiastic support of the Soviet bloc.

The United States tried to avoid the adjournment vote by asking for a suspension of the session until delegates could ponder the unexpected request.

Western sources said privately that Ghana's initiative appeared to have been prompted in part by the presence here of President Joseph Kasavubu of the Congo and the likelihood that the Assembly's Credentials Committee would agree to his request for the seating of a Congolese delegation of his supporters.

A Two-Hour Wrangle

Ghana, Guinea, India and five other states have joined in sponsoring a resolution that aims instead at having the Assembly seat a delegation designated by the deposed Congolese Premier, Patrice Lumumba.

The Assembly acted after a two-hour wrangle marked by two table-thumping demonstrations by the Soviet bloc and also by Ghana, both in protest against the efforts of Foreign Minister Pierre Wigny of Belgium to defend his country's position on the Congo issue.

The adjournment request was made by Alex Quaison-Sackey, Ghana's chief delegate. He appealed to the Assembly to hold off any further debate pending the efforts of a fifteen-member Asian-African commission to reconcile the clashing political factions in the Congo and restore some governmental stability.

He said that the commission probably would leave for the Congo in a week and that further acrimonious debate in the Assembly would only hamper the conciliation effort.

However, the adjournment as voted did not stipulate how long the debate should be suspended. United States sources said tonight that they understood this to mean that discussion could

Continued on Page 3, Column 1

WINNER'S PLEDGE

Family Is With Him as He Vows to Press Nation's Cause

Text of Kennedy's statement is printed on Page 36.

By HOMER BIGART
Special to The New York Times.

HYANNIS, Mass., Nov. 9—Senator John F. Kennedy accepted in solemn mood today his election as President.

He pledged all his energy to advancing "the long-range interests of the United States and the cause of freedom around the world."

He made this pledge inside the flag-decked Hyannis Armory at 1:45 P. M., an hour after Vice President Nixon, his Republican opponent, had conceded defeat.

His wife, Jacqueline, stood at his side as the 43-year-old President-elect faced 300 newsmen and massed batteries of TV cameras and gave his victory statement to the nation.

Behind him were arrayed the Kennedy family: his father, former Ambassador Joseph P. Kennedy; his mother, three sisters and three brothers.

No Sign of Jubilation

The Kennedys showed no evidence of jubilation. All wore expressions of solemnity. Mr. Kennedy's margin of victory was too slender to stir much elation. Some of his aides acknowledged disappointment over the startlingly narrow gap in the popular vote.

Mr. Kennedy, after responding to applause with a diffident bow and a smile, first read the telegram from Mr. Nixon conceding defeat and extending congratulations. The Senator had stayed up until 3:50 A. M. awaiting this concession and had gone to bed disappointed when the Vice President withheld it.

Replies to Nixon

Mr. Nixon wired the President-elect that all the nation would give him "united support" in the next four years.

Mr. Kennedy replied to Mr. Nixon:

"I know that the nation can continue to count on your unswerving loyalty in whatever effort you undertake, and that you and I can maintain our long-standing cordial relations in the years ahead."

Mr. Kennedy then read a congratulatory message from President Eisenhower.

In his message the President informed Mr. Kennedy that he would shortly receive suggestions from the President as to the change-over of responsibilities for national leadership.

To this Senator Kennedy had replied:

"I am grateful for your wire and good wishes. I look forward to working with you in the near future. The whole country is hopeful that your long ex-

Continued on Page 36, Column 7

United Press International Telephoto

THE MESSAGES WERE CONGRATULATORY: Senator John F. Kennedy displaying telegrams at Hyannis, Mass. With him are Mrs. Kennedy, his parents and Robert F. Kennedy, left, and R. Sargent Shriver, a brother-in-law.

KHRUSHCHEV NOTE SALUTES KENNEDY

Message of Congratulations Asks for Negotiations on Tensions in World

Text of Khrushchev message will be found on Page 42.

By The Associated Press.

MOSCOW, Nov. 9—Soviet Premier Khrushchev congratulated Senator John F. Kennedy today for his Presidential victory.

He expressed hope that Soviet-United States relations would "again follow the line along which they were developing in Franklin Roosevelt's time."

He urged negotiations aimed at easing the international situation.

[In Bonn, Chancellor Konrad Adenauer said he planned to go to Washington early next year for conferences with Mr. Kennedy.]

Mr. Khrushchev's statements in a congratulatory message to Mr. Kennedy coincided with Moscow's insistence that the policies of President Eisenhower had suffered a rebuff in the election.

The Soviet press contended that the election proved "the American people have blackballed the policy of the 'cold war' and the arms race, that they want changes and expect Washington to pursue a reasonable course in international affairs, a course dictated by life and the balance of forces now prevailing in the world." Mr.

Continued on Page 42, Column 4

Electoral Vote by States

	Rep.	Dem.		Rep.	Dem.		Rep.	Dem.
Alabama	..	5*	Louisiana	..	10	Ohio	25	..
Alaska	..	..	Maine	5	..	Oklahoma	8	..
Arizona	4	..	Maryland	..	9	Oregon	6	..
Arkansas	..	8	Mass.	..	16	Penna.	..	32
California	..	..	Michigan	..	20	Rhode Island	..	4
Colorado	6	..	Minnesota	..	11	So. Carolina	..	8
Conn.	..	8	Mississippi	**	**	So. Dakota	4	..
Delaware	..	3	Missouri	..	13	Tennessee	11	..
Florida	10	..	Montana	4	..	Texas	..	24
Georgia	..	12	Nebraska	6	..	Utah	4	..
Hawaii	..	..	Nevada	..	3	Vermont	3	..
Idaho	4	..	New Hamp.	4	..	Virginia	12	..
Illinois	..	27	New Jersey	..	16	Washington	9	..
Indiana	13	..	New Mexico	..	4	W. Virginia	..	8
Iowa	10	..	New York	..	45	Wisconsin	12	..
Kansas	8	..	No. Carolina	..	14	Wyoming	3	..
Kentucky	10	..	North Dakota	4	..	Total	185	300

*Five electors are pledged to Kennedy and six unpledged.
**Eight electors not pledged to vote for party candidates.

LIBERALS SUFFER SETBACK IN HOUSE

G. O. P. Picks Up 22 Seats to Aid Conservative Bloc

By JOHN D. MORRIS

The House of Representatives will have a more conservative tinge in the Eighty-seventh Congress.

Inroads into the present House Democratic majority of 283 to 154 scored by the Republicans in Tuesday's elections promised to strengthen their conservative coalition with Southern Democrats.

The liberal legislative program to be submitted early next year by the new Democratic President, John F. Kennedy, may consequently face handicaps in the new Congress, which convenes Jan. 3.

In the Senate, Republicans cut the Democratic margin by two seats, to 64 to 36. That chamber remains predominantly liberal in membership, although conservatives dominate key committee posts.

Gubernatorial Shifts

The Democrats achieved a net gain of one governorship and now control thirty-four of the fifty state houses. In twenty-seven gubernatorial contests the Democrats won fifteen and the Republicans twelve, with an exchange of party control in thirteen.

In the House races, nearly complete unofficial returns showed that the Democrats had elected 257 House candidates and the Republicans 175, with five contests still in doubt.

The Republicans captured twenty-nine seats held by Democrats and lost seven of their own, for a net gain of at least twenty-two. For a bare numerical majority of 219 they would have had to achieve a net gain of sixty-five.

Among the eleven states of the Old Confederacy the Republicans maintained their hold on seven seats of the Eighty-

Continued on Page 38, Column 4

NIXON WIRE GIVES HIS 'BEST WISHES'

Sends Kennedy a Message —500 in Capital Hail Him

By BILL BECKER
Special to The New York Times.

LOS ANGELES, Nov. 9—Vice President Nixon conceded today the Presidential election of his Democratic opponent, Senator John F. Kennedy.

About twelve hours after the polls had closed, the Vice President sent the following telegram to Senator Kennedy at Hyannis Port, Mass.:

"I want to repeat through this wire the congratulations and best wishes I extended to you on television last night. I know that you will have the united support of all Americans as you lead the nation in the cause of peace and freedom in the next four years."

Read by Aide

The telegram was read to newsmen by Mr. Nixon's press secretary, Herbert G. Klein, at 9:45 A. M., Pacific standard time (12:45 P. M., Eastern standard time).

The Vice President did not make a personal appearance. Mr. Klein said Mr. Nixon was resting with Mrs. Nixon and their two daughters in their suite at the Ambassador Hotel.

It was obvious that the Vice President had considered his remarks late on election night a virtual concession.

[A crowd of several hundred greeted Mr. Nixon as he arrived Wednesday night at Andrews Air Base, near Washington, after a flight of four and a half hours from Los Angeles.]

Mr. Nixon remained in seclusion most of the morning although Mr. Klein said he was up about 6 A. M. after little more than three hours of sleep. The secretary said Mr. Nixon

Continued on Page 42, Column 5

RESULTS DELAYED

Popular Vote Almost Even—300-185 Is Electoral Tally

By JAMES RESTON

Senator John F. Kennedy of Massachusetts finally won the 1960 Presidential election from Vice President Nixon by the astonishing margin of less than two votes per voting precinct.

Senator Kennedy's electoral vote total stood yesterday at 300, just thirty-one more than the 269 needed for election. The Vice President's total was 185. Fifty-two additional electoral votes, including California's thirty-two, were still in doubt last night.

But the popular vote was a different story. The two candidates ran virtually even. Senator Kennedy's lead last night was little more than 300,000 in a total tabulated vote of about 66,000,000 cast in 165,826 precincts.

That was a plurality for the Senator of less than one-half of 1 per cent of the total vote—the smallest percentage difference between the popular vote of two Presidential candidates since 1880, when James A. Garfield outran Gen. Winfield Scott Hancock by 7,000 votes in a total of almost 9,000,000.

End Divided Government

Nevertheless, yesterday's voting radically altered the political balance of power in America in favor of the Democrats and put them in a commanding position in the Federal and state capitals unknown since the heyday of Franklin D. Roosevelt.

They regained control of the White House for the first time since 1952 and thus ended divided government in Washington. They retained control of the Senate and the House of Representatives, although with slightly reduced margins. And they increased their hold on the state governorships by one, bringing the Democratic margin to 34—16.

The President-elect is the first Roman Catholic ever to win the nation's highest office. The only other member of his church nominated for President was Alfred E. Smith, who was defeated by Herbert Hoover in 1928.

Faces Difficult Questions

Despite his personal triumph, President-elect Kennedy is confronted by a number of hard questions:

¶In the face of such a narrow victory how can he get through the Congress the liberal program he proposed during the campaign?

¶Can so close an election produce any impetus for loosening the conservative coalition of Republicans and Southern Democrats which has blocked most liberal legislation in the House?

¶Will the new President be able successfully to claim a mandate for legislation such as the $1.25 minimum wage, Fed-

Continued on Page 35, Column 1

PRESIDENT SENDS WIRE TO KENNEDY

He Felicitates Senator and Orders Agency Chiefs to Cooperate With Him

By FELIX BELAIR Jr.
Special to The New York Times.

AUGUSTA, Ga., Nov. 9—President Eisenhower congratulated President-elect John F. Kennedy today on his election and then invited him to designate representatives to participate in all Federal policy discussions to assure an "orderly transition" to the new Administration.

The text of the President's telegram was withheld here at the request of Mr. Kennedy. But President Eisenhower is understood to have told the President-elect that he had instructed all heads of Federal departments and agencies to "cooperate fully" with Mr. Kennedy's representatives.

President Eisenhower arrived here for his customary fall holiday in midafternoon after a two-hour flight from Washington.

The President's message of congratulation to Mr. Kennedy was sent from the White House just before he took off for his favorite vacation retreat here at Augusta National Golf Club.

He also sent messages to the defeated Republican candidate, Vice President Nixon, and his running mate, Henry Cabot Lodge, as well as Vice President-elect Lyndon B. Johnson.

In his telegram to Mr. Nixon

Continued on Page 42, Column 7

ATOM BILL BEATEN IN FRENCH SENATE

Debre to Push Compromise on Nuclear Force Plan

By W. GRANGER BLAIR
Special to The New York Times.

PARIS, Thursday, Nov. 10—The Senate early today rejected President de Gaulle's project for an independent French nuclear striking force.

By a vote of 186 to 83, with seventeen abstentions, this conservative Upper House approved a procedural motion to table the national nuclear deterrent bill that had been passed to it by the National Assembly Oct. 27.

Although the Senate's action was a stinging blow to President de Gaulle and a sharp indication of mounting parliamentary opposition, it did not mean that the Government's measure would not eventually become law.

It was announced after the vote that Premier Michel Debré would call for the creation of a mixed committee of Senators and Deputies to work out a compromise measure. Should this conference committee fail to find a compromise, the Government would resubmit its measure to the Assembly for a second reading, and virtually certain approval. The measure would then become law with or without Senate's approval.

The Senate motion to table

Continued on Page 8, Column 1

10 Irish Soldiers Slain in Congo When U.N. Patrol Is Ambushed

By PAUL HOFMANN
Special to The New York Times.

LEOPOLDVILLE, the Congo, Nov. 9 — A patrol of eleven Irish soldiers of the United Nations force in the Congo was ambushed in the northern part of Katanga Province yesterday. The bodies of four men were sighted.

[The United Nations Command said that ten soldiers had been slain in the ambush, Reuters reported. The Irish Army announced in Dublin that one private had survived the attack. Reports received by the United Nations in New York said the surviving soldier was "badly wounded," according to United Press International.]

The patrol belonged to the Irish Thirty-third Battalion, which has headquarters in the industrial city of Albertville. The battalion, with a strength of about 550 men, is responsible for maintaining order in a vast area of North Katanga. The region has been the scene of intertribal warfare and clashes between Baluba tribesmen and the gendarmerie controlled by Moise Tshombe, President of Katanga.

United Nations officials here were unable to say who had attacked the Irish patrol. The ambush occurred south of Niemba, a village between Albertville and Kabalo. The zone is described as "Baluba country," but it is not known whether Baluba tribesmen were responsible for the assault.

Announcing the loss, a United Nations spokesman said it brought the toll of dead in the international force in the Congo to about thirty since the world organization's troops arrived

Continued on Page 2, Column 3

Vatican Calls Kennedy Election Proof of American Democracy

By ARNALDO CORTESI
Special to The New York Times.

ROME, Nov. 9—The election of Senator John F. Kennedy, a Roman Catholic, to the Presidency was received with keen satisfaction in the Vatican today.

During the campaign the Vatican remained neutral. Its newspaper, L'Osservatore Romano, abstained from all comment lest it be accused of siding with one candidate against the other.

Today the editor of the newspaper, former Italian Deputy Raimondo Manzini, said:

"Kennedy's victory strengthens the appreciation for the high democratic principles of freedom that guide American public life and assure access to the highest office to every citizen regardless of social class, race, or religion.

"The effective support given by large numbers of Protestant citizens to a Catholic considered suitable for the Presidency has been significant in this respect. Catholics are, of course, satisfied at the solemn confirmation of the principle that the office of President is open to a son of the Catholic Church, which enjoys such large prestige in the United States. Catholics have, however, always admired Nixon's irreproachable attitude of deferential respect for the Catholic hierarchy."

Senator Kennedy's victory was announced under large headlines by the whole morning press in Italy today. In most newspapers it took precedence over the results of the provincial and municipal elections that were held in Italy over the week-end.

Government circles received the news without astonishment

Continued on Page 38, Column 7

NEWS INDEX

"All the News That's Fit to Print"

The New York Times.

LATE CITY EDITION

U. S. Weather Bureau Report (Page 46) forecasts: Cold, chance of snow flurries today; fair and cold tonight and tomorrow. Temp. range: 35—22; yesterday: 40.1—30.

VOL. CX . . No. 37,583.

NEW YORK, SATURDAY, DECEMBER 17, 1960.

10 cents beyond 50-mile zone from New York City except on Long Island. Higher in air delivery cities.

FIVE CENTS

127 DIE AS 2 AIRLINERS COLLIDE OVER CITY; JET SETS BROOKLYN FIRE, KILLING 5 OTHERS; SECOND PLANE CRASHES ON STATEN ISLAND

STATEN ISLAND: Wreckage of Trans World Airlines Super Constellation in New Dorp

The New York Times

BROOKLYN: Rescue workers gather near ruins of United Air Lines DC-8 jet in Seventh Avenue at Sterling Place, in the Park Slope section

ETHIOPIAN REVOLT SAID TO COLLAPSE; SELASSIE HAILED

Envoys in U. S. and Britain Report Rebels Seized —Emperor in Asmara

Special to The New York Times.

WASHINGTON, Dec. 16 — The Ethiopian Embassy here reported today that the attempt by the Imperial Guard to overthrow Emperor Haile Selassie I had "ended in complete failure early this morning."

Ambassador Mikael Imru issued a statement saying that the army and air force, which had remained loyal to the Emperor, had captured Addis Ababa, the capital, and "overpowered and seized" the "disgruntled officers" of the Imperial Guard. The rebels had seized the city Wednesday.

[The Emperor arrived in Asmara, Ethiopia, Friday and received a tumultuous welcome from his loyal subjects there. He was told that the palace rebellion had failed.]

Prince Not Mentioned

The rebel group was reported at first to have been led by the Emperor's son, Crown Prince Asfa-Wossen. Later reports suggested that the Crown Prince might have acted "under duress."

The Ambassador's statement this noon made no mention of the part played by the Crown Prince and threw no light on his fate or his whereabouts.

Nor did the Ambassador say anything about his father, Ras Imru, the 68-year-old cousin of the Emperor, who was reported to have been appointed Premier of the government formed by the rebels.

The Ambassador stated that the loyal forces had been led by Maj. Gen. Merod Mengsha, Chief of Staff; Maj. Gen. Kebede Guebre, army commander,

Continued on Page 2, Column 4

New Pact to Expand Cuban-Soviet Trade

By MAX FRANKEL
Special to The New York Times.

HAVANA, Dec. 16 — Cuba and the Soviet Union plan to exchange goods valued at $168,-000,000 next year, the Ministry of Commerce disclosed here tonight.

The expanded trade dealings will be in addition to exchanges of sugar and other products for Soviet oil that had been agreed upon last February.

Although no details about the new arrangements were disclosed, it appeared almost certain that the Soviet Union would purchase considerably more Cuban sugar than it originally had planned.

Whatever the terms of the new trade agreement, it will

Continued on Page 6, Column 3

Dillon Appointed Secretary of Treasury; Kennedy's Brother Is Attorney General

By W. H. LAWRENCE
Special to The New York Times.

WASHINGTON, Dec. 16 — President-elect John F. Kennedy designated a Republican, Douglas Dillon, as his Secretary of the Treasury today and named his brother, Robert F. Kennedy, as Attorney General.

Mr. Dillon, now serving the Eisenhower Administration as Under Secretary of State, dis-

The texts of Kennedy's news conferences are on Page 14.

closed that he had sought the assent of President Eisenhower this morning and of Vice President Nixon earlier.

"Neither of them had any objection if I felt that this was something that would be in the national security interest of the country, and if we were to work toward a sound fiscal policy as is the case," Mr. Dillon said.

Both appointments long had been forecast. But the choice of Robert Kennedy, 35 years old, is expected to provoke a political storm. Senator Kennedy set a precedent by naming his brother to the Cabinet.

Second Republican Gets Post in New Cabinet— President Approves

Senator Kennedy said he would complete his Cabinet tomorrow by naming his Postmaster General from the family home at Palm Beach, Fla., where he is planning a prolonged holiday through Christmas and New Year's Day.

He left little doubt that his choice would be J. Edward Day, a California insurance executive, who flew in by jet from Los Angeles during the night and then flew South with the President-elect this afternoon.

The President-elect left Washington aboard his private twin-engine Convair, Caroline, at 4 P. M. Also aboard the airplane for the flight to Palm Beach were his brother, Robert, and two of Robert's children, Bobby and Joseph.

In two news conferences from the front stoop of his Georgetown home just after noon, Senator Kennedy announced first the choice of Mr. Dillon and then of his brother, Robert.

At the same time, he said Byron R. White, Denver attorney and former All-America football star at the University of Colorado, would be Deputy Attorney General. Harry J. Anslinger, Commissioner of Narcotics in the Treasury Department, has agreed to stay in that position, Senator Kennedy said.

Appointments Forecast

Highly placed Democrats forecast the following other major appointments by Senator Kennedy shortly:

¶Mrs. Elizabeth Smith, California's Democratic national committeewoman, as Treasurer of the United States, replacing Mrs. Ivy Baker Priest.

¶Fred Dutton of California as secretary of the Kennedy Cabinet. He is a former executive secretary to Gov. Edmund G. Brown of California.

Mr. Dillon, 51 years old, becomes the Cabinet's second Republican. He will serve with

Continued on Page 14, Column 6

PRO-WEST FORCES TAKE VIENTIANE

New Premier Enters Laos Capital as Fighting Ends

Because of communications difficulties, the following dispatch was filed jointly by correspondents in Vientiane.

VIENTIANE, Laos, Dec. 16—Prince Boun Oum, the new Premier of Laos, and the rightist pro-Western general, Phoumi Nosavan, drove into Vientiane at dusk today and announced the liberation of this shattered administrative capital.

At the same time, Capt. Peng, a cheerful Laotian tank officer, was busy cleaning from hold-out positions at the Vientiane airport the stubborn remnants of Capt. Kong Le's pro-Communist paratroops and guerrillas of the Communist-led Pathet Lao movement.

The seventy-six-hour battle for Vientiane ended at 5 P. M. local time [5 A. M., Friday, Eastern Standard Time].

Rightist Troops Hold City

By JACQUES NEVARD
Special to The New York Times.

VIENTIANE, Dec. 16—The troops of Gen. Phoumi Nosavan held the center of Vientiane this morning eighteen hours after they had captured it for a second time in a seesaw battle with tenacious pro-Communist defenders.

Mortar, machine-gun and small-arms fire could still be heard as tanks and armored cars cruised through the streets.

After a night lull the battle turned hot and fierce again. The heart of this usually somnolent

Continued on Page 4, Column 3

U. S. Offers NATO A Nuclear Arsenal And 5 Submarines

By DREW MIDDLETON
Special to The New York Times.

PARIS, Dec. 16—The United States offered Western Europe a mighty new nuclear armory today for defense against the Communist bloc.

Secretary of State Christian A. Herter announced what he termed a new concept for operation of medium-range ballistic missiles to the Ministerial Council of the North Atlantic Treaty Organization late this afternoon.

The offer was conditional upon agreement by the European allies on political control of the weapons, which were described by Mr. Herter as offering the best means for providing a common defense in the field of medium-range ballistic missiles.

The offer calls for commitment to the Atlantic alliance before the end of 1963 of five ballistic missile submarines armed with eighty Polaris missiles, the Secretary of State said. The step would enlarge the alliance's military capabilities and reaffirm the United States' commitment to Europe's defense, he said.

The United States would then expect other members of the

Continued on Page 13, Column 4

NEWS INDEX

WIDE U. N. POWER IN CONGO IS URGED

100-Day Blanket Authority Sought for Hammarskjold

By LINDESAY PARROTT
Special to The New York Times.

UNITED NATIONS, N. Y., Dec. 16—An urgent meeting of the General Assembly heard a proposal tonight to grant blanket emergency powers to Secretary General Dag Hammarskjold for 100 days to settle the growing crisis in the Congo.

Francisco Milla Bermudez of Honduras read the text of a proposed resolution that would give effect to the plan.

Because of the series of recurring emergencies in the new African state, he said, full interim powers for the Secretary General might be the best way to bring peace and order to the country under the terms of the Charter.

The Assembly adjourned at 10:35 P. M. to meet again at 10:30 A. M. tomorrow, with the United States delegate scheduled as the first speaker.

Latin-American sources said that some other Latin-American nations had been consulted on the Honduran proposal, though none joined in sponsoring the plan. Señor Milla Bermudez announced that he was prepared to consider changes in his text and would introduce it formally if others agreed.

The proposal would permit the Assembly to revoke the Secretary General's special authority if necessary or extend it beyond the 100-day period if Mr. Hammarskjold seemed to be succeeding.

The Honduran proposal was

Continued on Page 3, Column 6

A PILOT OFF ROUTE, U. S. OFFICIALS HINT

C.A.B. and F.A.A. Open Wide Inquiries—Tape Records of Flights to Be Studied

By RUSSELL PORTER

A preliminary investigation of the air disaster here yesterday suggested that the two planes collided because one was off its course.

An extensive inquiry was opened by the two Federal agencies concerned with civilian aviation, the Civil Aeronautics Board and the Federal Aviation Agency.

E. R. Quesada, Administrator of the Federal Aviation Agency, which is responsible for the operation of the airways, said last night that it was "very probable" that there had been a collision.

Alan S. Boyd, a member of the C. A. B., which investigates air accidents, was present when Mr. Quesada made his statement at New York International Airport. The two officials held a joint news conference.

They said that the investigation was just starting and little had been learned, but that the Trans World Airlines plane had fallen in three parts in Staten Island in a way indicating that it could not have been broken up by hitting the ground.

They said this made it appear likely there had been a collision, but there was as yet no positive evidence of a collision.

"All we know is that two planes crashed eleven miles apart," they said.

Shortly before the disaster, they said, the T. W. A. plane flew over the Linden, N. J., area

Continued on Page 10, Column 1

10 Brooklyn Houses Burn After Plane Hits a Church

By JOHN F. MURPHY

Ten four-story tenement buildings and an empty church were set afire when the United Air Lines DC-8 jet crashed and exploded in the populous Park Slope district of Brooklyn yesterday. More than 250 firemen and about fifty pieces of apparatus rushed to the seven-alarm blaze, which took more than two hours to bring under control.

There were several hundred persons in the buildings when the airliner plummeted through one tenement on Sterling Place and rammed into the Pillar of Fire Church across the street.

A rapid-fire series of small explosions followed, igniting roofs and spraying wreckage over a wide area.

Tenants Race From Homes

As soon as the plane crashed, women, children and elderly persons came pouring out of the buildings into the street, dressed in housecoats, sweaters and pajamas. They ran panic-stricken from the smoldering wreckage.

Aside from those on the plane who were killed, five persons on the ground died. These five presumably included three persons known to be missing. The police said even more bodies might be found beneath the fuselage.

The one victim identified was Charles J. Cooper, 34 years old, a sanitation worker, who had been shoveling snow. Those missing were Wallace E. Lewis, 90, the caretaker of the church at 123 Sterling Place; Joseph Colacano, 29, and John Opperisano, 35. Mr. Colacano Mr. Opperisano had been selling Christmas trees on the sidewalk.

The first fire alarm was sounded at 10:36 A. M. When

Continued on Page 9, Column 1

S. I. HOMES SPARED BY FALLING DEBRIS

Parts of Airliner Land in Backyards—No One on Ground Is Injured

By THOMAS BUCKLEY

Distances that can be paced off quickly—50 feet, 150 feet, 200 yards—were the measure of life and death on quiet streets on Staten Island yesterday.

Men, women and children saw the flaming wreckage of a Trans World Airlines Super-Constellation plunge toward them—and fall short. And although all forty-four persons on board were killed, no one on the ground was even scratched by the fall of the shattered airliner.

The flaming forward section of the craft, from which twenty-nine bodies were taken, smashed to earth on the northwest corner of Miller Army Air Field, less than 150 feet from the eight-room frame home of Edward Brody, at 324 Boundary Lane, Midland Beach. Dozens of other homes on tree-lined streets stood near by.

"I saw it coming right at us," Mrs. Brody said. "I ran upstairs to get my daughters,

Continued on Page 11, Column 1

Boy, 11, Only Survivor of Crash

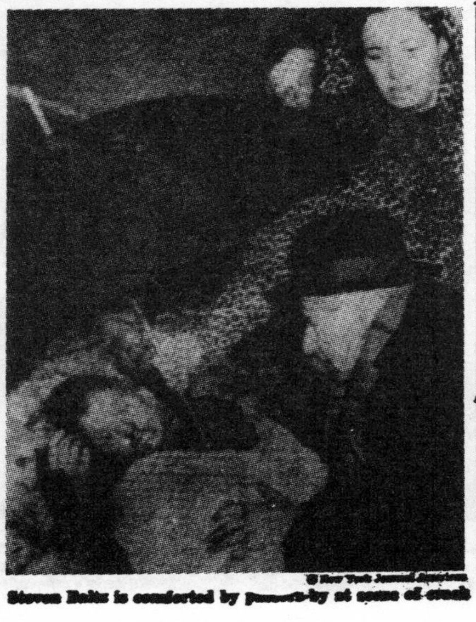

© New York Journal-American

Steven Baltz is comforted by passers-by at scene of crash

Condition Is Critical —Parents and Sister at His Bedside

By ROBERT CONLEY

An 11-year-old boy, flying here to meet his mother and sister, was the only survivor of yesterday's airliner collision.

He was thrown from the tail section of a United Air Lines jet and found in a Brooklyn snowbank, his clothes aflame.

The youngster, Steven Baltz of Wilmette, Ill., regained consciousness last night, but was still in critical condition early today with burns and broken bones.

His mother and sister were at his bedside when he awoke at Methodist Hospital in Brooklyn. They had flown here from Chicago ahead of him. His father, William S. Baltz, flew in late in the day and reached the bedside just after dark.

"He's coming along quite well, very well," the father said after

Continued on Page 11, Column 6

DISASTER IN FOG

DC-8 Plunges Into Park Slope Street, Missing School

By HOMER BIGART

Two airliners collided over New York harbor yesterday in fog and sleet, killing 127 passengers and crewmen. One plane crashed in Brooklyn, killing five more persons on the ground, and the other fell on Staten Island.

A United Air Lines DC-8 jet from Chicago plunged into the crowded Park Slope section of Brooklyn shortly after 10:30 A. M. All but one of its seventy-seven passengers and the crew of seven were killed. The survivor was an 11-year-old boy.

The plane demolished a church and killed a Department of Sanitation worker who was shoveling snow. Burning debris caused a seven-alarm fire, destroying ten brownstone apartment buildings, several shops and a funeral home. Nine persons were injured on the ground.

Three Unaccounted For

Three persons were unaccounted for, including the 90-year-old custodian of the Pillar of Fire Church, 123 Sterling Place, a Gothic structure that was leveled by flames.

At almost the same instant as the Brooklyn disaster, a Trans World Airlines Lockheed Super-Constellation crashed near Miller Army Air Field, New Dorp, S. I., eleven miles to the southwest.

This plane, out of Dayton and Columbus, Ohio, apparently exploded in the air just before the crash. All thirty-nine passengers and the crew of five were killed or fatally injured.

Parts of the plane fell in the Lower Bay and parts on the northwest corner of Miller Field.

Three victims were taken by Coast Guard helicopter to the Public Health Service Hospital

Continued on Page 8, Column 1

4 Cardinals Named; One Is an American

By ARNALDO CORTESI
Special to The New York Times.

ROME, Dec. 16—The Most Rev. Joseph Elmer Ritter, Archbishop of St. Louis, and three other prelates were named today by Pope John XXIII to become Cardinals Jan. 16.

The elevation of Archbishop Ritter will return the number of American Cardinals to six, as it was up to the death of John F. Cardinal O'Hara, Archbishop of Philadelphia, less than four months ago.

The present American Cardinals are Archbishops Francis Spellman of New York, James F. McIntyre of Los Angeles, Richard Cushing of Boston, Albert G. Meyer of Chicago and Aloysius J. Muench of Milwau-

Continued on Page 2, Column 1

"All the News That's Fit to Print"

The New York Times.

LATE CITY EDITION
U. S. Weather Bureau Report (Page 66) forecasts: Mostly fair, seasonably cold today and tonight. Fair, warmer tomorrow. Temp. range 38—25; yesterday: 35—31.

VOL. CX..No. 37,601. © 1961 by The New York Times Company. Times Square, New York 36, N. Y. NEW YORK, WEDNESDAY, JANUARY 4, 1961. 10 cents beyond 50-mile zone from New York City except on Long Island. Higher in air delivery cities. FIVE CENTS

U. S. BREAKS ITS DIPLOMATIC TIES WITH CUBA AND ADVISES AMERICANS TO LEAVE ISLAND; EISENHOWER CITES 'VILIFICATION' BY CASTRO

CONGRESS OPENS WITH CONFLICTS ON PROCEDURES

Filibuster Curbs Sought in Senate—Colmer's Purge Is Believed Certain

By RUSSELL BAKER
Special to The New York Times.

WASHINGTON, Jan. 3—The Eighty-seventh Congress convened today amid clashes in both houses over rules of procedure.

In the Senate, proponents of tighter curbs on the rules of debate opened a battle to make it easier to cut off filibusters. The skirmishes ended inconclusively with a decision to postpone further action until tomorrow.

In the House of Representatives, Speaker Sam Rayburn was reported to have completed arrangements for removing Representative William M. Colmer, Democrat of Mississippi, from the Rules Committee and replacing him with a member who would reinforce the Texas Democrat's leadership.

Pledges by Leaders

The Senate session was marked by a clash between Vice President Nixon and Richard B. Russell. The Georgia Democrat, leader of the Southern bloc, normally gets deference from the chair. Twice, however, Mr. Nixon used his gavel against him with authority.

In the House's traditional opening procedures, Mr. Rayburn and Charles A. Halleck of Indiana, the Republican minority leader, made pledges to work for responsible government.

Behind the scenes, however, a liberal-conservative fight for control of the Rules Committee continued unabated. Mr. Rayburn was assured of the necessary votes in the Democratic Committee on Committees to help purge Mr. Colmer.

This presumably would create a Rules Committee majority favoring critical parts of President-elect John F. Kennedy's program. Capitol observers described the Rayburn plan as "replacing a 'no' man with a 'yes' man."

Friction in Caucus

Meanwhile, Senate Republicans joined Democrats in a standing ovation for the new and only woman member on the Democratic side, Mrs. Maurine Neuberger of Oregon.

Mr. Nixon's duty on the rostrum was to administer the oath to each Senator elected in November.

A Senate Democratic caucus this morning brought more friction. As expected, Mike Mansfield of Montana was elected to succeed Vice President-elect Lyndon B. Johnson as majority leader, and Hubert H. Humphrey of Minnesota was named assistant leader.

Mr. Mansfield, however, created a surprise when he announced that he wanted the

Continued on Page 24, Column 3

Legislators Choose Mahoney, Carlino

By WARREN WEAVER Jr.
Special to The New York Times.

ALBANY, Jan. 3—Senators and Assemblymen descended on the capital tonight to prepare for the opening of the 1961 legislative session here tomorrow.

The Republican majorities in the Senate and Assembly held separate caucuses to choose their leaders and house-keeping officers for the next two years.

The Democrats chose their own nominees at separate sessions, but since the Republicans control both houses their nominations were equivalent to election.

There were no surprises. Senator Walter J. Mahoney of Buffalo was chosen temporary President of the Senate, the official title of the majority leader, a post he has held for the last seven years.

In the Assembly, Joseph F.

Continued on Page 14, Column 1

L.I.R.R. SEEKS AID TO AVERT 'CRISIS'

Says It Will Be Unable to Meet April Payroll—Two Rail Walkouts Cited

By CLARENCE DEAN

The Long Island Rail Road appealed yesterday for financial help to avert what it said was an impending crisis.

A statement by Thomas M. Goodfellow, president of the line, declared that unless the help was forthcoming the railroad would be unable to meet its payroll by the last week in April.

The present indications, Mr. Goodfellow said, are that the carrier's deficit by the end of this year will exceed $4,000,000.

If there is no financial help, Mr. Goodfellow said, three alternatives will arise: "a whopping fare increase," a cut in maintenance "to rock bottom" or "an arbitrary 12 per cent slash in the number of commuter trains." He declined to suggest specifically what kind of financial help the road wanted.

He attributed the railroad's predicament to unforeseen emergencies, chiefly a twenty-six-day strike on the Long Island last summer and a subsequent twelve-day shutdown of Pennsylvania Station as a result of a strike against the Pennsylvania Railroad.

For last October and Novem-

Continued on Page 67, Column 2

U. S. SAYS SOVIET AND RED VIETNAM AID LAOS REBELS

Asserts 180 Air Drops Were Made in Nineteen Days—President Sees Advisers

Text of the State Department statement is on Page 8.

By WILLIAM J. JORDEN
Special to The New York Times.

WASHINGTON, Jan. 3—The United States Government charged today that the Soviet Union and North Vietnam were guilty of "extensive participation" in military operations against the Government of Laos.

To bolster its charge, the State Department released a listing of Communist supply flights over Laos, serial numbers of Soviet planes engaged in the airlift, dates and places of air drops to the anti-Government rebels and other details.

The department said the two Communist powers had carried out more than 180 air sorties into Laos in the nineteen days from Dec. 15 through Jan. 2 to drop supplies and personnel to pro-Communist forces. It said that "substantial numbers" of North Vietnamese had been parachuted into Laos to help the rebels.

Elaboration Is Declined

A department spokesman would not elaborate on the numbers. Nor would he use the term "aggression" to describe the Communists' activities.

The charges against the Communist states were attributed to "hard evidence," however. Today's bill of particulars detailed earlier general charges of Communist intervention in Laos.

The catalogue of Communist involvement should be read, officials said, with the strong statement issued by the United States Government three days ago in mind. On Saturday the State Department warned that the Government would take "the most serious view" of intervention in Laos by the Chinese Communists, North Vietnamese "or others" in support of the anti-Government rebels.

Today's Government statement on Laos was issued soon after a special briefing on the Laos situation for President Eisenhower by his top diplomatic, military and intelligence advisers. It was the third White House conference on Laos in four days.

On Capitol Hill a group of House members also received an up-to-date report on developments in Laos. John M.

Continued on Page 8, Column 5

Associated Press Radiophoto

NO ENTRY: Portion of the crowd in front of the U. S. Embassy in Havana as Cubans sought visas yesterday. When they discovered that the visa section of the embassy had been closed, there were cries of protest and dismay.

REGIME IS SCORED

People Suffer Under 'Yoke of Dictator,' President Says

Texts of President's statement and notes are on Page 3.

By E. W. KENWORTHY
Special to The New York Times.

WASHINGTON, Jan. 3—The United States formally terminated diplomatic and consular relations with Cuba tonight.

President Eisenhower announced the break with the Government of Premier Fidel Castro in a statement issued at the White House at 8:30 o'clock.

The break came a day and a half after the Cuban Government had delivered a note to the United States Embassy in Havana demanding that the staff of the embassy and the consulate there be reduced to eleven persons within forty-eight hours.

The President said in his statement:

"There is a limit to what the United States in self-respect can endure. That limit has now been reached."

Normal Situation 'Impossible'

The action of the Castro Government, the President said, "can have no other purpose than to render impossible the conduct of normal diplomatic relations with that Government."

Therefore, the President said, he had instructed the Secretary of State to deliver a note to the Cuban Embassy here announcing the formal ending of relations.

The President added that "this calculated action on the part of the Castro Government is only the latest of a long series of harassments, baseless accusations and vilification."

President Eisenhower said in his statement that the friendship of the United States for the Cuban people "is not affected" by the breaking of diplomatic relations with the Castro regime.

Sympathy Expressed

"It is my hope and my conviction," the President said, "that in the not too distant future it will be possible for the historic friendship between us once again to find its reflection in normal relations of every sort."

"Meanwhile," the President said, "our sympathy goes out to the people of Cuba now suffering under the yoke of a dictator."

The United States requested the Government of Cuba, in turn, to withdraw "as soon as possible" the entire Cuban personnel in the Cuban Embassy in Washington and in all Cuban consular offices in the United States.

In a note to the Cuban Government, Secretary of State Christian A. Herter stated that it was requesting the Government of Switzerland to assume

Continued on Page 3, Column 1

Belgian Assembly Defeats Socalists; Violence Continues

By HARRY GILROY
Special to The New York Times.

BRUSSELS, Belgium, Jan. 3—The Belgian House of Representatives rejected today a motion to withdraw the proposed new law to raise taxes and tighten up the social security administration, against which 500,000 Socialist workers are striking.

Leo Collard, president of the Socialist party, and Achille van Acker, a former Premier, presented the motion. It was defeated by a vote of 121 to 83 with 1 abstention.

The House gave the Government three votes of confidence before adjourning at 8 P. M. until 2 P. M. tomorrow. The votes followed three critical speeches by Socialists and one by a Communist member on the conduct of public affairs and on the treatment of strikers.

The votes were taken in a calm parliamentary atmosphere that contrasted with an unruly session in which the measure was last discussed Dec. 23, and even more with the street demonstrations that turned up new

Continued on Page 12, Column 3

CASTRO'S CABINET DRAFTING A REPLY

Emergency Session Called After U. S. Acts—Premier Says 'Cuba Is Alert'

By R. HART PHILLIPS
Special to The New York Times.

HAVANA, Jan. 3—Premier Fidel Castro, President Osvaldo Dorticós Torrado and members of the Cuban Cabinet met in the Presidential Palace tonight at 10:30 to draft a reply to the United States' break in diplomatic relations with Cuba.

The reply will be delivered to the United States Embassy here soon, according to a statement by Dr. Carlos Olivares, Cuba's Foreign Under Secretary.

The Cabinet meeting ended without any announcement.

The Cuban people learned of the United States move tonight when the announcement was made over all radio stations.

The announcer said that "according to cables received President Eisenhower had broken off diplomatic relations with Cuba on the pretext of the order of the Revolutionary Government that he withdraw his 300 spies in the embassy from Cuba."

"Being discovered in his criminal plans of terrorism Eisenhower has responded with the habitual shamelessness of imperialism," the announcer declared.

The announcer said the radio would keep the people informed

Continued on Page 3, Column 5

U. S. Will Help Evacuate Its Citizens Living in Cuba

Special to The New York Times.

HAVANA, Wednesday, Jan. 4—The United States Embassy last night urged all Americans in Cuba to leave the island. A statement issued by the press attaché said that "all American citizens are urged to depart from Cuba immediately unless compelling reasons oblige them to remain."

The embassy has arranged for a ferry of the West Indies Fruit and Steamship Company to sail from Havana to West Palm Beach today and Friday to evacuate the Americans.

Additional extra flights to Miami from the José Marti International Airport will augment the facilities for departure today and tomorrow.

Cuba Guarantees Safety

The Castro regime, in a note delivered this morning to the United States Chargé d' Affaires, Daniel M. Braddock, pledged the "most absolute guarantees" for the safety of all American citizens in Cuba, including diplomatic or consular officials "as well as residents or tourists."

Meanwhile, thousands of Cubans who for months have been seeking visas to the United States were dismayed yesterday by the Cuban-United States crisis.

A long line of Cubans appeared as usual at the United States Embassy early in the morning after Premier Fidel Castro had ordered a cut in the embassy staff. They found the

Continued on Page 3, Column 6

KENNEDY AVOIDS ROLE IN DECISION

Rusk Turns Down Herter Move to Link Democrats to Break With Cuba

By JAMES RESTON
Special to The New York Times.

WASHINGTON, Jan. 3—The Eisenhower Administration took full responsibility tonight for the diplomatic break with Cuba.

Secretary of State Christian A. Herter yesterday informed Dean Rusk, who will succeed him in less than three weeks, of the President's decision, but he did not seek the advice of the leaders of the incoming Administration on what should be done.

Mr. Herter asked Mr. Rusk whether the incoming Democratic Administration wished to associate itself with the break. Mr. Rusk replied after consultations with President-elect John F. Kennedy that in the absence of complete information on all the relevant factors the new Administration did not feel that it could participate in the decision.

Both parties thus found themselves in an extremely delicate position. The Republicans were well aware of the fact that they were taking a decision that would greatly complicate the problems of the Kennedy Administration in the early days of its responsibility after the inauguration Jan. 20.

At the same time, they did not feel that they could avoid responsibility for reacting quickly to Premier Fidel Castro's demand that the United States diplomatic mission in Cuba should be reduced to eleven persons.

The Democrats were equally

Continued on Page 4, Column 3

I.T.T. Voices Hopes On H-Bomb Power

By GENE SMITH

Experiments that might lead to a "low-cost nuclear fusion process" were announced here yesterday by the International Telephone and Telegraph Corporation.

No details were given, but the experiments apparently deal with a concept that many nuclear experts have not considered promising. The company said the experiments had been conducted "for a number of years" but made no claim of success.

The problem of producing a controlled and sustained nuclear fusion, and thus harnessing the reaction of the hydrogen bomb, is the goal of many experiments being conducted both here and abroad.

Temperatures of millions of degrees Centigrade are neces-

Continued on Page 30, Column 3

Associated Press Wirephoto

WELCOME TO WASHINGTON: Lyndon B. Johnson, right, Vice President-elect, re[illegible] A. Ribicoff, successor as [illegible]. With them at [illegible] A. Smith 2d of [illegible]'s successor.

Hammarskjold Flying to Congo To Try to End Factional Strife

By JAMES FERON
Special to The New York Times.

UNITED NATIONS, N. Y., Jan. 3—Secretary General Dag Hammarskjold left for the Congo today in an attempt to end the civil disorders threatening the work of the United Nations force there.

His departure, which had been delayed a day to study disorders in Kivu Province, remained uncertain until two hours before he left because of the changing situation in Laos.

At New York International Airport, Mr. Hammarskjold said he did not intend to visit Laos on this trip but that he might return to the United Nations earlier than he had planned if the Laotian situation required his presence here.

The Secretary General was warmly applauded by a large crowd in the main lobby of the airline terminal. His plane left for Leopoldville at 5:55 P. M.

He will spend two days in the Congo and will talk with members of the eleven-nation United Nations Conciliation Commission, the Congo Government and United Nations force leaders. Technically, the visit is only a side trip on the way to South Africa, where the Secretary General will spend eight days studying racial segregation.

However, United Nations sources suggested that Mr. Hammarskjold's principal concern now was the "developing civil war" in the Congo. They felt that continuing strife between opposing Congolese factions could put the United Nations force in an untenable

Continued on Page 12, Column 5

Cuban U.N. Charge To Get Stern Reply

By LINDESAY PARROTT
Special to The New York Times.

UNITED NATIONS, N. Y., Jan. 3—The United States will follow up its break in relations with Cuba by sharply rejecting in the Security Council tomorrow Cuban charges of American "aggressive intentions."

Representatives of Western delegations here tonight expressed some surprise at the United States severance of relations. The American delegation, during the day, had been in contact with allied nations over the Cuban charges. It was understood, however, that the question discussed was largely whether opposition should be offered to Cuba's request to put the issue on the agenda.

The Council is to meet at 10:30 A. M. at the request of Foreign Minister Raul Roa of

Continued on Page 4, Column 4

NEWS INDEX

"All the News That's Fit to Print"

The New York Times.

LATE CITY EDITION
U. S. Weather Bureau Report (Page 81) forecasts: Increasing cloudiness today; chance of rain tonight and tomorrow. Temp. range: 54—40, yesterday: 52—43.

VOL. CX..No. 37,699. NEW YORK, WEDNESDAY, APRIL 12, 1961. 10 cents beyond 50-mile zone from New York City except on Long Island. Higher in air delivery cities. FIVE CENTS

SOVIET ORBITS MAN AND RECOVERS HIM; SPACE PIONEER REPORTS: 'I FEEL WELL'; SENT MESSAGES WHILE CIRCLING EARTH

HEAD OF RESERVE URGES PRICE CUTS TO RELIEVE SLUMP

Martin Asserts Reductions Would Mean More Jobs and Demand for Goods

By RICHARD E. MOONEY
Special to The New York Times.

WASHINGTON, April 11—The chairman of the Federal Reserve Board made a strong appeal today for price reductions as a means of solving the nation's economic problems.

"Throughout our country, we must not only increase our productivity but also pass some of the gains on to the consumer in the form of lower prices, rather than having all of it go exclusively to labor in higher wages or to management in higher profits," he said.

The chairman, William McC. Martin Jr., said that price cuts could stimulate buying demand that would "provide more jobs for those who are now unemployed, keep the economy moving to higher levels, and [provide] still greater job opportunities in the future."

Some Gains Reported

The Labor Department reported, meanwhile, a modest increase in the factory work week and factory pay for March.

Mr. Martin spoke at the annual meeting of the Association of Reserve City Bankers at Boca Raton, Fla. Copies of his talk were made available here.

It was not the first time that a voice from Washington had been raised in favor of price cuts. It is a point that gets lost, however, in the debates most often heard here, over what the Government should or should not do. In the form presented, it is simply an exhortation. Neither Mr. Martin nor the Kennedy Administration advocates price or wage controls.

Addressing himself to the domestic economy, Mr. Martin said that "at the moment we have pressing need to reduce unemployment and to promote economic growth at the maximum sustainable speed." The way to meet the need, he said, is "a judicious blend" of specific actions, monetary and fiscal policies, and wage-price policies.

Answers Critics of Policy

In such a setting, he said, interest rates need not rise so high nor fall so low as they have in past business cycles.

Mr. Martin used his speech to answer critics who have said that recent Federal Reserve strategy cannot work and has already failed. Seven weeks ago the reserve system abandoned its established policy of buying and selling only the shortest-term securities—Treasury bills—when it sought to impose its influence on credit conditions

Continued on Page 25, Column 5

Wide College Aid Is Adopted by State

By WARREN WEAVER Jr.
Special to The New York Times.

ALBANY, April 11—A higher-education program that will make $12,300,000 in new financial assistance available to college and university students in New York State this year was approved by Governor Rockefeller today.

He said the program gave assurance that "no young man or woman with the ability and desire for a higher education need be deprived of that opportunity for lack of funds."

The seven higher education measures that were signed included a bill that gave New York City permission to establish a city university to consist of the four municipal colleges and the community colleges in the five boroughs.

One of the bills provides

Continued on Page 48, Column 3

COUNCIL APPROVES OWN CHARTER BILL

Rebuffs Mayor by Spurning State Law Under Which He Named Commission

By CHARLES G. BENNETT

The City Council passed its own bill yesterday calling for the appointment of a commission to draft a new City Charter. The vote was 21 to 3.

Council officers immediately prepared to send the measure directly to Mayor Wagner for his signature or veto. This would be based on a contention by the Council's high command that since the bill merely calls for the appointment of a commission, it does not require Board of Estimate action.

The Council's stand constituted a challenge to the new state law under which Mayor Wagner already has appointed an eleven-member commission to revise the Charter.

Majority Leader Joseph T. Sharkey, who is also Democratic leader of Kings County, repeated his charge that Governor Rockefeller and Mayor Wagner had been "playing together" on Charter revision. Mayor Wagner supported the state bill.

Mr. Sharkey also said he "hoped and expected" that there

Continued on Page 26, Column 3

ISRAEL DEFENDS TRIBUNAL'S RIGHT TO TRY EICHMANN

Ex-Nazi Is More Confident as Jerusalem Hearing Enters Its 2d Day

By HOMER BIGART
Special to The New York Times.

JERUSALEM (Israeli Sector), Wednesday, April 12—The Attorney General of Israel, Gideon Hausner, resumed this morning his defense of the right of his country to try Adolf Eichmann for the murder of millions of Jews.

The defendant, as he entered his bulletproof glass cage on the second day of his trial seemed more confident. For the first time, he looked out at the audience. Then he sat down and engaged in an animated conversation with his German lawyer, Dr. Robert Servatius through a microphone in the glass cage. Eichmann smiled at his lawyer and seemed at ease.

On the first day of the trial, Eichmann, stonily impassive, heard his lawyer challenge the court's right to try the former Nazi leader on charges of delivering millions of Jews to Nazi annihilation camps.

The debate over Israel's right to try Eichmann was expected to continue through today's session. The court will not meet tomorrow, Holocaust Day, a day of mourning in Israel for the victims of Nazi terror.

Indictment Is Read

For seventy minutes Eichmann remained standing while the presiding judge, Justice Moshe Landau of the Israeli Supreme Court, read in Hebrew a fifteen-count indictment charging him with crimes against the Jewish people and crimes against humanity. The indictment was translated into German for Eichmann's benefit.

Rigidly erect, his head tilted back and his thin lips tightly compressed, the one-time chief of the Gestapo's Jewish Affairs Section betrayed no emotion during the opening day of trial.

His thin, hawklike visage with its large, sharply pointed nose was fixed intently on the proceedings. Not once did Eichmann turn to gaze on the throng of newsmen, foreign observers and Israeli citizens in the 750 seats in the Beit Haam (House of the People), the converted

Continued on Page 16, Column 1

Former Nazi Hears Indictment Read as Trial Begins in Jerusalem

Adolf Eichmann, charged with crimes against the Jewish people and against humanity, standing in special booth in Beit Haam courtroom yesterday. Justices at bench are, from left, Benyamin Halevi, Moshe Landau, Yitzhak Raveh.

Associated Press Radiophotos

Eichmann peers intently at tribunal during proceedings

U.S. IS DISTURBED BY DELAY ON LAOS

Soviet Lag on Cease-Fire and Increase in Supplies Regarded as Ominous

By WILLIAM J. JORDEN
Special to The New York Times.

WASHINGTON, April 11—Officials said today the United States Government was disturbed by Moscow's delay in accepting a Western plan for an immediate cease-fire in Laos.

A spokesman for the State Department said that continued delay would be regarded here as "a matter of very serious concern."

Adding to the worries of Administration leaders were intelligence reports of a general increase in the flow of Soviet-bloc military supplies to the Pathet Lao movement in recent days. This was regarded as an ominous sign of Soviet intentions in Laos.

Rusk Voices Hope

High officials continued to be hopeful, however, that Moscow would soon give a favorable answer to the cease-fire plan advanced by the British several weeks ago.

That hope was voiced on Capitol Hill today by Secretary of State Dean Rusk. The Secretary told Senators that he expected a Soviet answer "within a very few days."

The presumption here is that continued fighting in Laos contains the seeds of a possibly enlarged conflict and that the Soviet bloc does not want to

Continued on Page 12, Column 4

BRITISH CONSIDER TRADE UNITY STEP

Kennedy Hopes London Will Enter Common Market

By JAMES RESTON
Special to The New York Times.

WASHINGTON, April 11—President Kennedy now has the impression that the British Government is seriously thinking about joining the European Economic Community, or Common Market.

This impression is based on the fact that during the President's conversations with Prime Minister Macmillan here last week the British leader asked what the United States Government would think if Britain decided to reverse her policy and join the Western European nations now working toward economic and political integration.

Administration to Cooperate

President Kennedy's reply was that the United States would regard this as a major advance toward the unity of the West.

The President did not in any way imply that the United States was thinking of joining the Common Market itself, but he did stress his Government's determination to cooperate fully with its allies in the Organization for Economic Cooperation and Development.

On a recent trip to London it is known that George Ball, United States Under Secretary of State for Economic Affairs, urged upon Viscount Hailsham, the British Lord President of the Council, that Britain give the most serious consideration

Continued on Page 2, Column 3

ADENAUER IN U. S. TO SEE KENNEDY

Arrives for First Talks With President—Stresses Unity

Special to The New York Times.

WASHINGTON, April 11—Chancellor Adenauer of West Germany arrived here tonight for his first meetings with President Kennedy.

He alighted at Andrews Air Force Base from the Lufthansa jet airliner that brought him without stop from Bonn.

In an arrival statement the 85-year-old Chancellor said the German people had already developed "great confidence" in the new President of the United States. He said he was looking forward to establishing personal contact with Mr. Kennedy.

Dr. Adenauer pledged that his country's considerable energy and ability would be devoted to the cause of peace and freedom. He said that his Government realized that its share of responsibility for the future of the world grew "in proportion with our efficiency and capacity."

"Our times are filled with threats and dangers," the Chancellor said, "but I feel sure that the free people of the world will overcome those dangers if they are united and resolute."

The West German leader and his party, including his daughter, Frau Libeth Werhahn, were

Continued on Page 4, Column 5

FRANCE DECLARES ANTI-U.N. 'STRIKE'

De Gaulle Bars Any Role in Armed Ventures—Warns Algerians on Partition

By HENRY GINIGER
Special to The New York Times.

PARIS, April 11—France proclaimed today a virtual strike against the United Nations.

In one of the harshest indictments he has ever made against the organization, President de Gaulle said France "did not wish to participate either by her men or her money in any present or possible enterprise of this organization—or of this disorganization."

The President, in response to a question, confirmed his country's refusal to contribute to the costs of the United Nations force in the Congo. A Foreign Ministry spokesman said that in this context the President's statement referred to present or future military enterprises, although the word "military" did not occur in the text of the news conference.

On another issue, President de Gaulle offered a mixture of incentives for Algerian rebel cooperation with France. He warned anew that a "rupture" might result in the partitioning of Algeria to protect those Algerians who wished to remain under French control.

The President called for reform of the United Nations as well as of the Atlantic Alliance. He made it clear that the future of the alliance would be a major

Continued on Page 3, Column 5

187-MILE HEIGHT

Yuri Gagarin, a Major, Makes the Flight in 5-Ton Vehicle

Text of the Tass statement is printed on Page 22.

By United Press International.

MOSCOW, Wednesday, April 12—The Soviet Union announced today it had won the race to put a man into space. The official press agency, Tass, said a man had orbited the earth in a spaceship and had been brought back alive and safe.

A brief announcement said the first reported space man had landed in what was described as the "prescribed area" of the Soviet Union after a historic flight.

A Moscow radio announcer broke into a program and said in emotional tones:

"Russia has successfully launched a man into space. His name is Yuri Gagarin. He was launched in a sputnik named Vostok, which means "East."

Reports on Landing

Tass said that, on landing, Major Gagarin said: "Please report to the party and Government, and personally to Nikita Sergeyevich Khrushchev, that the landing was normal, I feel well, have no injuries or bruises."

He landed at 10:55 A. M. Moscow time [2:55 A. M. New York time].

Earlier, the major reported: "Flight is proceeding normally, I feel well."

After orbiting the earth the major applied a braking device, and the vehicle space landed in the Soviet Union, Tass said.

Major Gagarin, 27 years old, is an industrial technician, and married. He was reported to have received pre-flight training similar to that of the astronauts who will man the United States' first space ships.

Soared to 187 Miles

The announcer said the Sputnik reached a minimum altitude of 175 kilometers (109½ miles) and a maximum altitude of 302 kilometers (187¾ miles).

He said the weight of the Sputnik was 10,395 pounds, or slightly over five tons.

The announcement of the launching came at 2 A. M. New York time.

It said everything functioned normally during the flight.

Constant radio contact was maintained between earth and the sputnik, the Moscow radio said.

The announcer said the duration of each revolution around the earth was 89.1 minutes.

The title of the announcement was "The First Human Flight into the Cosmos."

The radio, which was quoting a Tass press agency statement on the launching, said that Maj.

Continued on Page 22, Column 1

Realtor Is Indicted In Expense Padding

By EDWARD RANZAL

The president of Pease & Elliman, Inc., a leading real estate concern here, was indicted yesterday on charges of income tax evasion through fraudulent claims for entertainment and travel expenses.

The indictment against the executive, Robert Neaderland, by a Federal grand jury was said to be the first of its kind in the Southern District of New York. It was expected to break ground for future prosecutions for overstatement of business expenses.

Mr. Neaderland, 53 years old, lives at 160 Central Park South. His company is one of the leading developers of apartments on the East Side. He is charged with attempting to evade $27,550 in income taxes in 1954 and 1955, according to

Continued on Page 30, Column 3

Population Center Moves West; Census Puts It at Centralia, Ill.

The New York Times April 12, 1961

United States center of population, which was near Portsmouth, Ohio, a hundred years ago, has continued moving west and by 1960 was just northwest of Centralia, Ill.

By The Associated Press.

WASHINGTON, April 11—The population center of the United States has moved again. Secretary of Commerce Luther H. Hodges announced today that the new center, based on the 1960 census, was near Centralia, Ill., fifty-seven miles west of its 1950 location.

In general, the population center is the point through which a straight line can be drawn in any direction dividing the country's population in half. As many people would live on one side of the line as on the other.

Mr. Hodges had another def-

Continued on Page 27, Column 3

Centennial of War Rocked by Dispute

By The Associated Press.

CHARLESTON, S. C., April 11—New Jersey accused the National Civil War Centennial Commission of "pathetic mismanagement" tonight and asked that President Kennedy remove Maj. Gen. Ulysses S. Grant 3d as chairman.

Joseph Dempsey, vice chairman of the Jersey Centennial Commission, made the charge at a news conference after General Grant had turned down the state's request for time to rebut a dinner speaker who had criticized its civil rights practices.

General Grant and Donald Flamm, Jersey chairman, engaged in an unscheduled standing debate at the crowded dinner at the Charleston Naval Base. General Grant, to loud applause, insisted that New

Continued on Page 36, Column 3

NEWS INDEX

White House Confirms Firing; Feat Hailed by U. S. Scientists

By JOHN W. FINNEY
Special to The New York Times.

WASHINGTON, Wednesday, April 12 — Pierre Salinger, White House press secretary, announced early today that "American tracking stations have confirmed the fact that the Soviet Union has launched a satellite today."

"We are keeping in close touch with the situation but have no additional comment at this time," he said.

The Soviet success in sending the first man into space left United States officials in a resigned mood of congratulations.

The United States has no chance of equaling the Soviet feat until perhaps late this year.

The Soviet announcement did not take them by surprise, since there had been advance information from United States tracking stations that a satellite had been launched.

James E. Webb, head of the National Aeronautics and Space Administration, described the feat as "a significant accomplishment" that "demonstrates great technical capacity."

"I hope that they can find it possible to make the benefits of this event available to the rest of the world," he said.

Dr. Hugh L. Dryden, deputy administrator of the space agency, commented, "This is something we have been expecting for some time."

"It is only the beginning of man's continued effort of manned exploration of space," he said, "and I think we should continue as rapidly as we can with our own program."

In appraising the achieve-

Continued on Page 24, Column 1

"All the News That's Fit to Print"

The New York Times.

LATE CITY EDITION
U. S. Weather Bureau Report (Page 74) forecasts: Mostly fair today. Fair tonight and tomorrow. Temp. range: 56—42; yesterday: 55—42.

VOL. CX..No. 37,705. NEW YORK, TUESDAY, APRIL 18, 1961. 10 cents beyond 50-mile zone from New York City except on Long Island. Higher in air delivery cities. FIVE CENTS

ANTI-CASTRO UNITS LAND IN CUBA; REPORT FIGHTING AT BEACHHEAD; RUSK SAYS U. S. WON'T INTERVENE

The New York Times April 18, 1961

CARIBBEAN STRIFE: Rebel forces attacking Cuba landed in Las Villas Province in the area of Bahia de Cochinos (1, and A on the inset map). Other anti-Castro landings were said to have taken place in area of Santiago de Cuba (2) and in Pinar del Rio (3).

PREMIER DEFIANT

Says His Troops Battle Heroically to Repel Attacking Force

The texts of Castro appeals are printed on Page 14.

By TAD SZULC

Special to The New York Times.

MIAMI, Tuesday, April 18—Rebel troops opposed to Premier Fidel Castro landed before dawn yesterday on the swampy southern coast of Cuba in Las Villas Province.

The attack, which was supported from the air, was announced by the rebels and confirmed by the Cuban Government.

After fourteen hours of silence on the progress of the assault, the Government radio in Havana broadcast early today a terse communiqué signed by Premier Castro announcing only that "our armed forces are continuing to fight the enemy heroically."

The announcement, made shortly before 1 A. M., said that within the next few hours details of "our successes" would be given.

The communiqué came amid a wave of rebel assertions of victories, new landings and internal uprisings. The rebel spokesmen were acclaiming important progress in new landings in Oriente and Pinar del Rio Provinces, but none of these reports could be confirmed.

Government Reports Battle

The Government communiqué said a battle had been fought in the southeastern part of Las Villas Province, where yesterday morning's landings occurred.

Although the communiqué was signed by Premier Castro, the Cuban leader has not spoken to his nation since the attack began. An earlier communiqué, issued yesterday, reported the rebel landings

In a communiqué issued last night, the Revolutionary Council, the top command of the rebel forces, said merely that military supplies and equipment were landed successfully on the marshy beachhead. The communiqué added that "some armed resistance" by supporters of Premier Castro had been overcome.

Premier Castro was reported to have escaped injury in an early-morning air raid yesterday near the beachhead.

The Revolutionary Council's announcement spoke of action in Matanzas Province, indicating that the rebels might have

Continued on Page 14, Column 1

ROA CHARGES U.S. ARMED INVADERS

Tells U.N. That C.I.A. Aided Attacks—'Aggression' Is Denied by Stevenson

Excerpts from Stevenson and Roa statements, Page 16.

By THOMAS J. HAMILTON

Special to The New York Times.

UNITED NATIONS, N. Y., April 17—Dr. Raul Roa, Foreign Minister of Cuba, charged today that his country had been invaded this morning "by a force of mercenaries, organized, financed and armed by the Government of the United States."

Dr. Roa told the General Assembly's Political Committee that the attack had been launched from points in Florida and Guatemala under the direction of the Central Intelligence Agency, which he called the "Gestapo." The Gestapo was the Nazi security police force.

He continued to use terms made familiar to nazism by calling Dr. José Miró Cardona, head of the anti-Castro Cuban Revolutionary Council, the "gauleiter." Gauleiters were regional party leaders under the Nazis.

Florida Launching Denied

Adlai E. Stevenson, chief United States delegate, said in reply that "the United States has committed no aggression against Cuba and no offensive has been launched from Florida or from any other part of the United States."

[In Guatemala, the Government denied that it had participated in any attack on Cuba.]

Just before the debate ended late this evening Dr. Roa charged that two jet planes from a United States carrier had escorted a Cuban rebel plane to safety this afternoon. He also alleged that forces from the United States Naval Base at Guantanamo had entered Oriente Province, where

Continued on Page 17, Column 1

Rusk Declares Sympathy Of Nation for Castro Foes

By JAMES RESTON

Special to The New York Times.

WASHINGTON, April 17—Secretary of State Dean Rusk expressed today the sympathy of the American people for those who struck against Castroism in Cuba, but emphasized "there is not and will not be any intervention there by United States forces."

The Administration did not deny that it was giving material support to the raiding parties, but this aid was undoubtedly on a much smaller

Transcript of Rusk's news conference is on Page 18.

scale than originally planned here and the landings in Cuba were much smaller than excited reports of "invasion" suggested.

No more than 200 to 300 men were involved in the week-end landings on the vast coastline of Cuba, according to reliable information reaching here.

In fact, the landings of the last forty-eight hours were not designed to get a lot of fighting men on the ground, but to provide supplies for the anti-Castro underground already operating there as a result of at least six other landings that have taken place over the last few months.

Refugees Assume Control

In the last ten days, the Cuban refugees have assumed control of the operations against Premier Fidel Castro. Accordingly, official Washington could not be sure of the fate of all the small parties that went ashore.

Secretary Rusk was extremely cautious in his remarks on the situation at his news conference this morning. What happens in Cuba, he said, is for the Cuban people to decide. He added, however, that the Administration was "not indifferent" to the intrusion of the "Communist conspiracy" into this hemisphere and promised to "work together with other governments of this hemisphere to meet efforts by this conspiracy to extend its penetration." [Opening statement, Page 18.]

On this point, considerable attention was being paid here

Continued on Page 18, Column 1

MOSCOW BLAMES U. S. FOR ATTACK

Izvestia Asserts 'American Hirelings' Invade Cuba—Khrushchev Confers

By SEYMOUR TOPPING

Special to The New York Times.

MOSCOW, April 17—The Soviet Union charged tonight that the United States was responsible for the landing in Cuba by what it described as "American hirelings."

Izvestia, the Soviet Government newspaper, contended that plans for landing anti-Castro forces in Cuba had been worked out and inspired by "American imperialists."

"On all continents voices now are crying out determinedly for an end to the armed aggression against Cuba and for the defense of the freedom and independence of the Cuban people," Izvestia said.

At his vacation retreat in Sochi on the Black Sea, Premier Khrushchev conferred on the Cuban crisis with Foreign Minister Andrei A. Gromyko. A formal Government statement is expected tomorrow.

Atmosphere Is Tense

An atmosphere of tension gripped the Soviet capital after the announcement at 4 P. M. by the Moscow radio that "an armed intervention against Cuba had begun."

It was felt by most Western experts that the Soviet reaction would be confined to strong diplomatic representations, complaints in the United Nations and a propaganda onslaught against the United States.

Some observers recalled that in a speech here July 10, Mr. Khrushchev had declared: "Figuratively speaking, if need be, Soviet artillerymen can support the Cuban people with their rocket fire, should the aggressive forces in the Pentagon dare to start intervention against Cuba."

The Soviet leader also had noted that the United States was no longer out of range of Soviet missiles.

Western experts said that Mr. Khrushchev's statement seemed to have more applicability to an invasion of Cuba by United States forces than to an attack of the type being under-

Continued on Page 17, Column 2

CHANTING CUBANS BACK CASTRO HERE

1,000 in Midtown March Dispersed by Police

Nearly 1,000 chanting, sign-bearing pro-Castro Cubans demonstrated last night outside the United Nations and the United States Mission to the United Nations and in the Times Square area.

Heavy police details had kept the crowds behind barriers most of the day and no violence erupted until a smaller group of pro-Castro Cubans blocked pedestrian traffic in Times Square. The police made two arrests and two policemen were injured during a brief scuffle with the demonstrators.

Many of the demonstrators carried Cuban flags and pictures of Dr. Castro as they marched from the United Nations Plaza along Forty-second Street to the corner of Eighth Avenue and Forty-third Street.

An emergency police signal brought ten radio cars and ten mounted policemen to that area. The crowd then broke up into four factions and departed in different directions.

A few minutes later, at 8 P. M., a smaller group of demonstrators formed on the sidewalk on Broadway between

Continued on Page 14, Column 5

SUPREME COURT UPHOLDS UNIONS AGAINST N. L. R. B.

It Upsets Board's Ruling That Contracts Illegally Force Membership

MAILERS' PACTS BACKED

New York Printers' Local and California Teamsters Win on Agreements

By ANTHONY LEWIS

Special to The New York Times

WASHINGTON, April 17—A series of decisions by the National Labor Relations Board designed to prevent the compelling of union membership was struck down today by the Supreme Court.

The court disposed of a group of major labor cases that will affect dozens of others pending in the lower courts and before the labor relations board. The court did the following things in its principal rulings:

¶It upheld, 6 to 2, contracts of the International Typographical Union with newspapers that provided that the foreman of the composing room or mail room must be an I. T. U. member and must handle all hiring in his operation.

¶By the same vote, it upheld a provision in I. T. U. contracts that made the I. T. U. "general laws" applicable unless in conflict with Federal or state laws.

¶By the same vote, it held there was nothing illegal in bargaining agreements that provided that casual workers, both union and nonunion, be hired through a union-operated hiring hall.

¶It killed, 7 to 1, an N. L. R. B. ruling making labor and management refund to employes all union dues collected under an agreement found to constitute an illegal closed shop.

Douglas Writes Opinion

Justice William O. Douglas wrote the opinion of the court in all the cases. There was an eight-man court because Justice Felix Frankfurter took no part in the decisions.

Two cases settled long disputes over standard contracts sought by the typographical union. The first of these involved the New York Mailers' Union 6, which is affiliated with the I. T. U., and The New York Daily News and The Wall Street Journal.

The contract specified that mail room foremen must be members of the I. T. U. and must do the hiring. The N. L. R. B. had ruled that the foremen clause was a coercive device to make sure that only union members were hired and that it was thus a violation of the Taft-Hartley Law.

Justice Douglas wrote today that first, the contract said no foreman should be disciplined by the union for carrying out the publisher's instructions, and he concluded that the foreman remained the employer's agent despite his union membership.

Second, Justice Douglas said, the court would "not assume" that the foremen clause would produce discrimination in favor of union members in the absence of actual proof of discrimination.

The N. L. R. B. was thus left free to bring a case to show that

Continued on Page 27, Column 3

U. S. Finds Soviet's Reply On Laos Is Unsatisfactory

Rusk Says Note Is Unclear on Timing and Verification of Cease-Fire—Calls Issue 'Very Critical'

By E. W. KENWORTHY

Special to The New York Times.

WASHINGTON, April 17—Secretary of State Dean Rusk said today that the new Soviet note on Laos did not satisfy the United States on the timing and verification of a cease-fire.

This, Mr. Rusk said at his news conference, is a "very critical matter" in any attempt to bring "the situation to a peaceful and satisfactory conclusion." [Introductory statement, Page 18.]

The Soviet note "clarifying" Moscow's first reply to the British proposals of March 23 was delivered to Sir Frank Roberts, the British Ambassador, yesterday. The British Embassy informed Mr. Rusk of the contents of the reply last night.

The British had proposed a three-step procedure—a call for a cease-fire by Britain and the Soviet Union, the co-chairmen of the 1954 Geneva Conference that brought the Indochinese war to an end; verification of the cease-fire by the three-nation International Control Commission, which observed the carrying out of the Geneva accord in Laos, and a fourteen-nation conference to set up a neutral, independent Laotian Government.

It was the British intention that these steps should take place in quick order. But Britain and the United States had made clear that there could be no conference until a cease-fire was in effect.

In one respect the Soviet note represented an advance over the earlier response, according to informed sources here. Previously Moscow had indicated that the cease-fire and the conference must take place simultaneously—or very nearly so.

In yesterday's note, these

Continued on Page 2, Column 3

GIZENGA OFFICERS ACCEPT MOBUTU AS ARMY'S CHIEF

Kasavubu Agrees to Reform Troops—Signs Accord on Congo-U.N. Cooperation

By HENRY TANNER

Special to The New York Times.

LEOPOLDVILLE, the Congo, April 17—Congolese Army headquarters announced tonight that field commanders operating under the control of the Leftist regime of Antoine Gizenga had recognized the authority of Maj. Gen. Joseph D. Mobutu as military commander in chief.

General Mobutu is the commander of the Central Government's forces.

The announcement said officers of the Gizenga regime had recognized General Mobutu during a conference at Bundoki, on the border of Eastern Province. The province is controlled by Mr. Gizenga.

The announcement also said a cease-fire had been ordered all along the border of Eastern and Equator Provinces.

Here in Leopoldville President Joseph Kasavubu and representatives of Secretary General Dag Hammarskjold signed an agreement on reorganization of the Congolese Army and the withdrawal of some foreign advisers.

Resolution 'Accepted'

The Congolese President and his Government "accepted" the Security Council resolution of Feb. 21 with the "understanding" that the United Nations, in implementing the resolution, respected the sovereignty of the Congo Republic.

The announcement on the military agreement did not say whether Gen. Victor Lundula, who has been commanding Mr. Gizenga's forces, took part in the conference.

Despite rumors of rivalry between him and Mr. Gizenga, General Lundula has consistently stressed his loyalty to his civilian superiors in Stanleyville, capital of Eastern Province.

General Mobutu left Leopoldville a week ago for the border area where the military conference took place. Talks between the two sides had continued intermittently for several weeks with and without his participation.

Kasavubu Plan Backed

In accepting the Security Council resolution the Leopoldville Government "recognized" the necessity for reorganizing the Congolese National Army. It reaffirmed President Kasavubu's earlier proposal that the reorganization take place with United Nations assistance, but under his personal authority as chief of state.

The agreement called for the United Nations to give assistance to the President so that "all foreign civil officials, military and paramilitary mercenaries and political advisers who have not been engaged under his authority" will be re-

Continued on Page 4, Column 3

HIGH COURT VOIDS CAFE'S NEGRO BAN

Holds Private Restaurant on State Land in Delaware Cannot Refuse Service

Special to The New York Times.

WASHINGTON, April 17—The Supreme Court held today that a privately operated restaurant situated in a publicly owned parking garage in Wilmington, Del., could not refuse to serve Negroes.

Six justices agreed on that result. The three others thought the case should have been sent back to the Delaware Supreme Court for clarification of its views on state law.

The decision is a significant one because of the light it throws on the established doctrine that only "official action" is covered by the Fourteenth Amendment. The Constitution does not prohibit racial discrimination by private persons or enterprises.

The court concluded that the Government of Delaware was sufficiently involved in this private enterprise, the restaurant, to bring it under the Constitution. In the view of observers here, the court broke at least some new ground in reaching that conclusion.

Justice Tom C. Clark wrote the opinion of the court. He was joined by Chief Justice Earl Warren and Justices Hugo L. Black, William O. Douglas and William J. Brennan Jr.

A separate concurring opinion, resting on quite different grounds, was filed by Justice Potter Stewart. Dissents suggesting that the court should

Continued on Page 26, Column 1

HAUSNER ATTACKS EICHMANN'S PLEA

Israeli Prosecutor Details His Charges After Ex-Nazi Says He Is Not Guilty

Text of decision and Hausner excerpts are on Page 23.

By HOMER BIGART

Special to The New York Times.

JERUSALEM (Israeli Sector), April 17—Attorney General Gideon Hausner began an attack today on Adolf Eichmann's plea of innocence at his trial for responsibility in the killing of millions of Jews.

Earlier in the day Eichmann lost a challenge to the court's jurisdiction and entered his not-guilty plea when the trial was resumed after the week-end recess. Eichmann's plea for a hearing on his kidnapping from Argentina was rejected by the court.

"In the sense of the indictment I am not guilty," Eichmann had told the three Israeli judges.

He made his statement of innocence in a precise but toneless voice in reply to charges that he had planned the annihilation of 6,000,000 European Jews for the Nazis during World War II.

From the qualified nature of his plea, it was clear that Eichmann's defense would be based on the contention that he was a mere cog in the machinery of genocide and that he was bound by higher orders when he delivered the Jews to death camps.

Standing rigidly erect and

Continued on Page 23, Column 7

Eisenhowers Are Welcomed Home to Pennsylvania

United Press International Telephoto

General and Mrs. Eisenhower in Harrisburg with Gov. David L. Lawrence of Pennsylvania

By The Associated Press.

HARRISBURG, Pa., April 17—Thousands of persons welcomed former President Dwight D. Eisenhower and Mrs. Eisenhower home to Pennsylvania today. The gathering was the state's official welcome for General Eisenhower, who left the White House Jan. 20. The former President, looking tanned and rested after a six-week vacation in California, was obviously touched. Gov. David L. Lawrence, a Democrat, headed the state and city officials on the platform. The Eisenhowers have a farm home in Gettysburg, thirty-five miles southwest of this capital city. It is the only home they have ever owned. They left for home by car after the ceremonies.

Jersey Votes Today In Primary Election

By GEORGE CABLE WRIGHT

Special to The New York Times.

TRENTON, April 17 — New Jersey residents will nominate major party candidates for Governor tomorrow, along with candidates for ten of twenty-one State Senate seats and for all sixty seats in the Assembly.

Also at stake will be the nominations for a number of county and local posts.

The polls will open at 7 A. M. and close at 8 P. M.

Interest will center on the balloting for the Republican nomination for Governor. A bitter three-way contest for the nomination came to a close tonight with television and radio appeals by the participants.

They are James P. Mitchell, the former Secretary of Labor, and State Senators Walter H. Jones of Bergen County and

Continued on Page 38, Column 1

Walker Is Relieved of Command While Army Checks Birch Ties

Special to The New York Times.

WASHINGTON, April 17—The Army said today that Maj. Gen. Edwin A. Walker had been relieved of his command in Germany while an investigation was made into reports that he had been indoctrinating his troops with the views of the John Birch Society.

The announcement said that Secretary of the Army Elvis J. Stahr Jr. had ordered General Walker transferred immediately from command of the front-line Twenty-fourth Division "pending the outcome of an official investigation."

The investigation will involve "certain published statements and actions of General Walker," the Army said.

General Walker was ordered transferred to the headquarters of the United States Army in Europe at Heidelberg, Germany, the Army said.

The announcement did not mention the Birch Society. However, officials acknowledged that the transfer and investigation had been prompted by allegations that the 51-year-old general had been urging the views of the Right-Wing group upon his troops for the last six months.

The Overseas Weekly, a privately owned newspaper distributed among American troops in Europe, reported last week that General Walker had instituted a special troop-indoctrination program using materials and publications of the society.

General Walker accused the newspaper yesterday of being "immoral, unscrupulous, corrupt and destructive." The newspaper stood by its original report and said that his charges

Continued on Page 24, Column 6

NEWS INDEX

"All the News That's Fit to Print"

The New York Times.

LATE CITY EDITION

U. S. Weather Bureau Report (Page 62) forecasts: Cloudy, warm, chance of rain late today or tonight and tomorrow. Temp. range: 61—46; yesterday: 70—47.

VOL. CX..No. 37,723.

NEW YORK, SATURDAY, MAY 6, 1961.

10 cents beyond 50-mile zone from New York City except on Long Island. Higher in air delivery cities.

FIVE CENTS

U. S. HURLS MAN 115 MILES INTO SPACE; SHEPARD WORKS CONTROLS IN CAPSULE, REPORTS BY RADIO IN 15-MINUTE FLIGHT

LAUNCHING: Rocket lifts the capsule

RETURN: Astronaut rides in one of helicopters carrying his Mercury capsule to the Lake Champlain

Associated Press Wirephotos

SAFE ABOARD: On the Lake Champlain's deck, Comdr. Alan B. Shepard Jr. views capsule he occupied

ASTRONAUT: Commander Shepard removes space suit.

IN FINE CONDITION

Astronaut Drops Into the Sea Four Miles From Carrier

Excerpts from radioed reports by Shepard, Page 8

By RICHARD WITKIN
Special to The New York Times.

CAPE CANAVERAL, Fla., May 5—A slim, cool Navy test pilot was rocketed 115 miles into space today.

Thirty-seven-year-old Comdr. Alan B. Shepard Jr. thus became the first American space explorer.

Commander Shepard landed safely 302 miles out at sea fifteen minutes after the launching. He was quickly lifted aboard a Marine Corps helicopter.

"Boy, what a ride!" he said, as he was flown to the aircraft carrier Lake Champlain four miles away.

Extensive physical examinations were begun immediately.

Tonight doctors reported Commander Shepard in "excellent" condition, suffering no ill effects.

Major U. S. Step

The near-perfect flight represented the United States' first major step in the race to explore space with manned space craft.

True, it was only a modest leap compared with the once-around-the-earth orbital flight of Maj. Yuri A. Gagarin of the Soviet Union.

The Russian's speed of more than 17,000 miles an hour was almost four times Commander Shepard's 4,500. The distance the Russian traveled was almost 100 times as great.

But Commander Shepard maneuvered his craft in space—something the Russians have not claimed for Major Gagarin.

All in all, the Shepard flight was welcomed almost rapturous-

Continued on Page 8, Column 1

JOHNSON TO MEET LEADERS IN ASIA ON U.S. TROOP USE

President Says Decision on South Vietnam Action Will Await Report

TALKS SET IN CAPITALS

Ngo Dinh Diem Is Expected to Seek American Units to Deter Red Attack

Transcript of news conference and summary, Page 14.

By WILLIAM J. JORDEN
Special to The New York Times.

WASHINGTON, May 5—President Kennedy said today that the assignment of United States armed forces to South Vietnam would be one of several important matters Vice President Lyndon B. Johnson would discuss on his coming trip to Asia. [Opening statement and Question 4, Page 14.]

The President confirmed that the possibility of sending United States troops to Southeast Asia was under study. He indicated that the final decision would depend on the results of Mr. Johnson's talks in Saigon with President Ngo Dinh Diem and others.

Mr. Kennedy said at a news conference that a special task force in the Government was working on problems related to helping South Vietnam maintain its independence. The question has been considered by the National Security Council as well, he said.

Vital Assignment

Mr. Johnson is expected to leave next Tuesday for the Far East. He also will meet with top Government officials in Bangkok, Thailand; Manila, and other capitals.

The President today described the Johnson mission as "an extremely important assignment."

It is widely assumed here that President Ngo will ask for the assignment of at least a token force of United States troops and regard it as a guarantee of United States' involvement should his country be attacked in force by the Communist North.

Mr. Kennedy did not touch on the matter today, but it is known that the Government is also considering the possibility of sending a similar token force to Thailand. The latter is allied to the United States in the

Continued on Page 3, Column 4

Talks Open in Laos On Truce Details; Meeting 'Friendly'

By JACQUES NEVARD
Special to The New York Times.

HIN HEUP, Laos, May 5—Military representatives of the pro-Western Laotian Government and the pro-Communist Pathet Lao rebels held a preliminary conference here today on machinery for continuing the cease-fire that became effective Wednesday.

The conference lasted one hour and five minutes and was described as "friendly."

According to a Laotian Army spokesman, Col. Oudom Sananikone, the meeting did not take up any political questions.

There appeared to be few tangible results of the talks, but Colonel Oudom Sananikone stressed that the meeting was a preliminary one.

He said that the first Pathet Lao request was that the next meeting take place at Namone, thirty-five miles north of here

Continued on Page 3, Column 2

2 BILLION AID PLAN FOR BRAZIL IS NEAR

U. S. Presses World-Wide Program of New Loans and Debt Deferments

By TAD SZULC
Special to The New York Times.

WASHINGTON, May 5—An international financial rescue package worth more than $2,000,000,000 is being prepared for Brazil. Negotiations, already well advanced, involve the United States, six Western European countries, Japan and the International Monetary Fund.

The agreements, which may be announced late next week, call for new loans totaling nearly $630,000,000. About $340,000,000 of this is to be provided by the United States. The remainder will take the form of a postponement in the repayment of much of Brazil's huge foreign debt.

This international financial operation, the largest ever involving a Latin-American country and one of the largest anywhere in postwar years, is designed to provide President Janio Quadros with extra time and resources to reorganize his economy.

Broad Effort in View

The United States is playing a key role in putting together the Brazilian package. It will also supply separate smaller loans to bolster the economies of Venezuela and Bolivia. Venezuela, which is facing serious budget difficulties, expects to receive soon an initial loan of $50,000,000.

Besides these emergency measures to assist the economies of individual Latin-American republics, the United States moved today to call a special inter-American conference to blueprint long-range economic and social development programs.

President Kennedy announced at his news conference that the United States' delegation to the Council of the Organization of American States had been in-

Continued on Page 17, Column 1

NIXON ASKS DRIVE TO OFFSET SOVIET

Bids Kennedy Rally America to a Fresh Foreign Policy

Excerpts from Nixon speech are printed on Page 2.

By AUSTIN C. WEHRWEIN
Special to The New York Times.

CHICAGO, May 5—Former Vice President Richard M. Nixon urged President Kennedy today to rally the American people for a new start in American foreign policy.

Mr. Nixon called for a "searching reappraisal of the free world's ability, particularly America's ability, to deal with the kind of aggression in which Communists are now engaging."

He further revealed that he had given President Kennedy the "assurance that I will support him to the hilt in backing positive action he may decide is necessary to resist Communist aggression."

[President Kennedy, meanwhile, sent his nuclear test-ban negotiator back to Geneva with an implied warning that the United States might not continue the talks much longer without some prospect of a safeguarded treaty.]

To meet such threats, the former Vice President said that the United States should be prepared to act alone if swift action were needed while machinery for collective action was being set up.

The lesson of Cuba and Laos, he said, is this:

"We must never talk bigger than we are prepared to act.

"When our words are strong and our actions are timid, we

Continued on Page 2, Column 3

Kennedy Plans Aid To Retrain Jobless And Spur Recovery

By PETER BRAESTRUP
Special to The New York Times.

WASHINGTON, May 5—The Kennedy Administration expects to ask Congress for at least $75,000,000 to provide retraining for the long-term unemployed. Other new anti-recession measures also are being considered.

The key question that President Kennedy has yet to decide is whether to break the Administration's self-imposed limit on Federal spending in an effort to stimulate the economy and spur employment.

The $75,000,000 program for retraining workers who have been laid off by technological change and by the decay of their own industries will not materially affect the budget. Nor will the President's orders to the Pentagon to channel more defense contracts to small

Continued on Page 19, Column 2

MAYOR IS UPHELD ON CHARTER LAW

But Court Reverses Ban on Action by Council, Opening Way to Rival Proposals

By RONALD MAIORANA

Mayor Wagner's right to appoint a Charter Revision Commission was upheld by Justice Irving Saypol yesterday in State Supreme Court.

However, Justice Saypol ruled invalid part of the law under which the Mayor had acted. This part excluded the City Council from Charter-revision activity.

Lawyers said the ruling appeared to make possible the enactment of the City Council's own plan for a Charter Revision Commission. Thus, it is conceivable, they said, that two competing Charters—one drawn by the Mayor's commission and the other by a commission created by the Council—could be submitted to the voters Nov. 7.

In a twenty-two-page decision that caused confusion at City Hall Justice Saypol ruled that the section of the state law that had the effect of bypassing the City Council was invalid because it was an improper delegation of legislative power. He said: "The newly enacted au-

Continued on Page 32, Column 1

Shepard Had Periscope: 'What a Beautiful View'

By JOHN W. FINNEY
Special to The New York Times.

CAPE CANAVERAL, Fla., May 5—"All systems go * * * Everything A-O.K. * * * Mission very smooth * * * What a beautiful view! * * * Coming in for a landing."

These were the reports of Comdr. Alan B. Shepard Jr. as he rode the capsule Freedom 7 115 miles up into space today in the United States' first step toward manned exploration of space. His "A-O.K," is a rocket engineer term meaning double O.K. or perfect.

In a calm, methodical way he reported back by radio on every detail of his fifteen-minute flight, even during the moments of greatest stress as his capsule accelerated from the launching pad and then quickly decelerated upon re-entering the earth's atmosphere.

And there were moments of excitement in his voice, such as when he viewed much of the Eastern Coast of the United States through a periscope from 115 miles up in space.

"What a beautiful view!" he exclaimed into a microphone inside his visored space helmet and then, according to instructions, he returned to scientific observations to report that the cloud cover was three- to four-tenths and was obscuring much of the coast up through Cape Hatteras.

Three-to-four-teenths cloud cover is a description used by

Continued on Page 10, Column 1

PRESIDENT TO ASK INCOME TAX CUTS

Drop Next Year Is Planned, Dillon Tells House Unit

By JOHN D. MORRIS
Special to The New York Times.

WASHINGTON, May 5—The Kennedy Administration plans to lay before Congress next year a tax reform program that will include reduction of individual income taxes.

Secretary of the Treasury Douglas Dillon told the House Ways and Means Committee of the plan today but gave no details. He made it clear, however, that taxpayers with high incomes would probably be among the chief beneficiaries of a proposed reduction in rates.

"I think those in high brackets deserve relief," he said.

Mr. Dillon was questioned for nearly three hours, mainly by Republican committee members, as he completed three days of testimony on tax-revision legislation being sought now by the Administration.

The pending proposals include $1,700,000,000 a year in special tax credits for business enterprises to encourage modernization and expansion of plant and equipment. Tax laws on foreign income, business expense accounts and stock dividends

Continued on Page 22, Column 8

NATION TO WIDEN ITS SPACE EFFORTS

Kennedy Wants More Funds—He Telephones Shepard to Offer Congratulations

Texts of Kennedy statement and call to Shepard, Page 11

By DAVID HALBERSTAM
Special to The New York Times.

WASHINGTON, May 5—An even greater effort in the exploration of space was promised today by President Kennedy.

On the day of this country's first manned space flight, he told a news conference he would make an additional request for appropriations for its space program this year.

"We are going to make a substantially larger effort in space," he declared. [Question 1, Page 14.]

Earlier in the day the President telephoned his personal congratulations to Comdr. Alan B. Shepard Jr., the nation's first space traveler, in a call from the White House to the aircraft carrier Lake Champlain.

The President also congratulated the commander's wife and his six fellow-astronauts.

Commander Shepard will visit Washington Monday. There will be a ceremony at noon on

Continued on Page 11, Column 7

Elizabeth Visits Pope in Vatican

Associated Press Wirephoto

Pope John XXIII in private audience with Queen Elizabeth

By ARNALDO CORTESI
Special to The New York Times.

ROME, May 5—Pope John XXIII received Queen Elizabeth II and Prince Philip in a private audience today with traditional pomp and ceremony. The meeting was marked by extreme cordiality. Addressing the Queen in French, the Pope said that relations between Britain and

Continued on Page 19, Column 4

14 Dead, 57 Hurt by Tornado; 2 Towns in Oklahoma Hard Hit

By The Associated Press.

POTEAU, Okla., May 5—A vicious tornado tore through two tiny eastern Oklahoma communities near here tonight, killing at least fourteen persons and injuring fifty-seven.

Ten were reported dead at Howe and four at Reichert. The death toll could go higher as rescue workers dug into the debris.

There was a report that a light plane—trying to avoid the massive storm cloud—crashed after a wing tore off. The highway patrol said that a woman who lived in the area reported she saw the plane go down west of [illegible] near Summerfield.

It was a grim anniversary for this rolling, wooded area some 200 miles southeast of Oklahoma City. Just one year ago twelve were killed when a twister destroyed most of the downtown area of Wilburton.

Tornadoes had plagued Oklahoma for two days, but until tonight there had been only one fatality from the scores of funnels sighted.

Two of the dead were babies. One father died with his 3-month-old son and a mother with her 14-month-old boy.

Tiny farms are scattered throughout the twister-pounded

Continued on Page 63, Column 6

Nation Exults Over Space Feat; City Plans to Honor Astronaut

By ROBERT CONLEY

The successful flight of America's first astronaut, Comdr. Alan B. Shepard Jr., roused the country yesterday to one of its highest peaks of exultation since the end of World War II.

The achievement brought relief from the strain of hearing about the Soviet Union's success in orbiting a man, feelings of new hope for the future from Maine to Hawaii and dancing in the streets at New York's Columbus Circle.

"Wonderful," "Tremendous," "The greatest thing that ever happened," thousands of persons said as the reaction took hold across the country.

Knots of people crowded sidewalks to watch television screens in store windows. Others jumped up to cheer, pounded friends on the back, ran into neighbors' houses or fell silent.

"He made it," a woman gasped in Chicago, then broke into tears. "He made it."

New York City laid plans for the "most fabulous" ticker tape welcome ever given—one that a city official said would be "even bigger than the one for Charles Lindbergh."

In Washington, Congressmen moved to bestow the nation's

Continued on Page 11, Column 5

NEWS INDEX

"All the News That's Fit to Print"

The New York Times.

LATE CITY EDITION
U. S. Weather Bureau Report (Page 80) forecasts: Considerable cloudiness today; occasional rain tonight, tomorrow. Temp. range: 72—59; yesterday: 71—49. Temp.-Hum. Index: middle 60's; yesterday: 66.

VOL. CXI. No. 37,859. © 1961 by The New York Times Company. Times Square, New York 36, N. Y. NEW YORK, TUESDAY, SEPTEMBER 19, 1961. 10 cents beyond 50-mile zone from New York City except on Long Island. Higher in air delivery cities. FIVE CENTS

HAMMARSKJOLD DIES IN AFRICAN AIR CRASH; KENNEDY GOING TO U.N. IN SUCCESSION CRISIS

MAYOR APPOINTS 9 CIVIC LEADERS AS SCHOOL BOARD

Group Is Due to Be Sworn Today but Injunction Is Sought to Bar Change

By PAUL CROWELL

Mayor Wagner named a new nine-member Board of Education yesterday to replace the present board, which goes out of existence tomorrow.

The new board, which like the old one is unsalaried, is scheduled to be sworn in at City Hall today at 3:30 P. M., but there may be a last-minute hitch.

Two members of the outgoing board moved in Supreme Court late yesterday to have the Legislature's recent action dismissing the old board declared illegal and to prevent Mayor Wagner, in the meantime, from swearing in the members of the new board this afternoon.

A legal representative of the city will appear at the Brooklyn court at 10 o'clock this morning to contest both the complaint and the appeal for an injunction against the Mayor.

'Red Letter Day'

For his own part, before the legal action was instituted, Mayor Wagner expressed the hope that the swearing-in ceremony scheduled for the new board members this afternoon would mark "a red letter day for the City of New York for all the days to come."

He expressed the belief that "this can be the best board our city has ever had, possibly the best board any city ever had."

The board has seven members from Manhattan, and one each from Brooklyn and Queens.

The board was chosen from a list of twenty-six recommended by an eleven-man panel set up by the state on Aug. 21. A special session of the Legislature had passed a law to dissolve the present board and pave the way for a new one.

Appointees Listed

The Mayor's appointees are:
Brendan Byrne, public relations man, 85-19 118th Street, Kew Gardens, Queens.
James B. Donovan, lawyer, 35 Prospect Park West, Brooklyn.
Lloyd K. Garrison, lawyer, 133 East Sixty-fourth Street.
John F. Hennessy, engineer, 144 East Thirty-ninth Street.
Morris Iushewitz, labor leader, 386 Park Avenue South.
Samuel R. Pierce, lawyer, 2225 Fifth Avenue.
Anna M. Rosenberg, public relations consultant, 1136 Fifth Avenue.
Max J. Rubin, lawyer, 101 West Fifty-fifth Street.
Clarence O. Senior, economist and sociologist, 15 Claremont Avenue.

In announcing the appointments, the Mayor said that he had chosen the board "without regard to politics."

"I do not even know the political affiliations of those I have selected," he said, "except in the cases where I have had previous personal knowledge." It was

Continued on Page 30, Column 6

New Group Seeks Funds to Purchase And Repair Slums

By MARTIN ARNOLD

A nonprofit organization has been set up here to offer inducements to private investors to buy and improve slum tenements.

The organization, headed by former Deputy Mayor Paul T. O'Keefe, would select the buildings, find buyers and repair, operate and maintain the tenements.

Private investors would own the buildings and would collect profits agreed upon between them and the organization.

8 to 10 Per Cent Profit

The profits usually would be 8 to 10 per cent. Many unimproved slum tenements now bring profits up to 25 per cent.

Laurance S. Rockefeller, son of the late John D. Rockefeller Jr., has agreed to invest up to $250,000 in tenements to get the program started.

Mr. Rockefeller will not be part of the organization. A spokesman said last night that Mr. Rockefeller had agreed to help the program because he felt it was "a way to get responsible private money that will be reasonably rewarded into such housing."

The Rockefeller spokesman and other supporters of the program emphasized that the project would not be charitable or philanthropic. Rather,

Continued on Page 25, Column 1

3 STATES TO GET U. S. TRANSIT AID

New Committee Wins Pledge of Support From 2 Bodies at Orientation Meeting

By LLOYD GARRISON
Special to The New York Times.

WASHINGTON, Sept. 18—The newly created Tri-State Transportation Committee won Government support today for its plans to improve transport and commuter service in the New York metropolitan area.

Committee members from New York, New Jersey and Connecticut met for more than three hours with representatives of the Housing and Home Finance Agency and the Bureau of Public Roads.

Dr. William J. Ronan, secretary to Governor Rockefeller, said the meeting had been called to explain the aims of the group and to seek Federal cooperation. He described the session as "very heartening." The committee did not ask for specific amounts of money, he added, but would undoubtedly seek financial support "sometime soon."

Government participants in the meeting indicated funds would be made available if requested.

Anxious to Aid

"This is the kind of program we would like to assist," said Morton J. Schussheim, assistant administrator for program policy at the Housing and Home Finance Agency. The agency is involved in transportation problems through its urban renewal program.

His enthusiasm was echoed by another Federal representative, Edward H. Holmes, assistant commissioner of the Bureau of Public Roads.

Dr. Ronan acted as regional spokesman at the meeting. The New Jersey delegation was led by Highway Commissioner Dwight R. G. Palmer and the Connecticut by Carl LaLumia, executive aide to Gov. John Dempsey.

Roger H. Gilman, on leave from the Port of New York Authority to serve as executive director of the committee, attended the meeting but departed immediately after it had ended.

The tri-state committee was established three weeks ago to study and make recommendations on improving commuter service and to attack also problems of motor traffic, air travel and freight transportation. Its

Continued on Page 18, Column 3

Militia Seizes 176 In Cuban Outbreak

Special to The New York Times.

HAVANA, Sept. 18—Militiamen in plainclothes who had mingled with the crowd arrested 176 persons last night after a demonstration had broken out during a religious procession near here.

Eighteen demonstrators were injured, three seriously, when the militiamen swung clubs they had hidden in their clothing.

The outburst occurred one week after a larger anti-Government demonstration before a Havana church. Seven were injured, one fatally, by the militia and many were arrested in that demonstration.

The new incident took place a few hours after 136 priests had been deported from Cuba

Continued on Page 13, Column 1

Associated Press Radiophoto

Rescue workers study wreckage of the Secretary General's plane in Northern Rhodesia

The New York Times

Secretary General Dag Hammarskjold

Adenauer Begins Efforts To Form Coalition in Bonn

By SYDNEY GRUSON
Special to The New York Times.

BONN, Germany, Sept. 18—Chancellor Adenauer began fighting for his political life today as a result of his party's heavy losses in the West German elections.

With the Christian Democratic Union's parliamentary majority wiped out yesterday, the 85-year-old Chancellor lost no time in seeking a coalition with the Free Democratic party led by Dr. Erich Mende. The Free Democrats made the biggest gain in the election.

Dr. Adenauer rejected the bid of Willy Brandt, West Berlin's Mayor, for a national coalition embracing the Social Democrats as well as the two other parties.

A coalition with the Socialists, the Chancellor said at a news conference, "would not correspond with our democratic feeling."

The big question was not whether Dr. Adenauer could set the terms for a coalition but whether he could survive the demands for his retirement and his replacement as Chancellor by Dr. Ludwig Erhard, the 64-year-old Minister of Economics.

There was considerable speculation that the Free Democrats would agree to Dr. Adenauer's continuing as Chancellor for a limited period—just long enough to carry the onus for accepting the hard decisions facing West Germany.

With the long, bitter campaign and the vote at last out of the way, a beginning was in sight for the long-awaited public discussion of these decisions.

The Free Democrats' news service, commenting on the election results, which left the party holding the balance of power, said:

"An epoch of German postwar history has ended. The coming months and years will destroy many illusions and place extraordinary demands on our people."

The statement reflected a continuing but decreasing reluctance to specify the demands. Two are accepted by almost all West German officials as inevitable: the acceptance of the Oder-Neisse border as Germany's frontier with Poland and some form of de facto recognition for Communist East Germany, with all that means to the loss of hope for the reunification of Germany.

No one here is yet sure whether the West Germans are

Continued on Page 3, Column 5

2D SOVIET ROCKET FIRED 7,500 MILES

Lands in Same Pacific Area as Shot Last Wednesday

By THEODORE SHABAD
Special to The New York Times.

MOSCOW, Sept. 18 — The Soviet Union fired a second rocket 7,500 miles into the central Pacific yesterday.

An announcement today by Tass, Soviet press agency, said that the dummy of the rocket's last stage had landed "in the immediate proximity" of the spot where the first rocket of the current series hit the water last Wednesday.

Today's brief Tass statement emphasized the accuracy of the Soviet shots. It referred to the "high-precision control system" of the rocket and called it "another big achievement of Soviet rocketry."

[In Washington, the Atomic Energy Commission announced that the Soviet Union on Monday exploded its thirteenth nuclear device since it resumed testing Sept. 1. The yield of the atmospheric explosion was "on the order of a megaton" and the site was "in the vicinity of Novaya Zemlya," the commission said.]

The present series of test shots was announced on Sept. 10. Ships and planes were advised to keep away from the target area, 1,000 miles southwest of Hawaii, during the

Continued on Page 8, Column 1

VIETNAM REBELS BURN CITY IN RAID

Regime Says 1,000 Reds Took Part in Attack

By The Associated Press.

SAIGON, Vietnam, Tuesday, Sept. 19—More than 1,000 Communist rebels attacked and burned the capital of Phuoc Vinh Province, sixty miles north of Saigon early yesterday, the Government said today.

It was believed to be the largest rebel assault so far in South Vietnam's civil war.

The province chief, an army major, and his deputy and a large number of Government civil guardsmen were killed.

About fifty wounded were rushed to Saigon hospitals after the rebels withdrew under attack.

The Government announcement said the Viet Cong guerrillas stormed the capital at 1 A. M. yesterday in a move to liberate rebels taken prisoner.

The Viet Cong held the town for several hours in pre-dawn darkness, burning and ransacking several provincial buildings.

One source estimated 1,500 Viet Cong took part in the attack, the first on a provincial capital.

It also marked a new height in violence in the areas north of Saigon where the rebels were said to be building strength.

Phuoc Thanh is a newly created province in a largely upland forest and rubber-growing

Continued on Page 3, Column 7

ACTING SECRETARY IS SOUGHT AT U. N.

Delegates Favoring Proposal to Appoint Mongi Slim—Assembly Meets Today

By THOMAS J. HAMILTON
Special to The New York Times.

UNITED NATIONS, N. Y., Sept. 18—On the eve of the opening of the United Nations General Assembly session, a move was developing to have Mongi Slim of Tunisia take over the coordination of the Secretariat until the election of a successor to Dag Hammarskjold.

The death of Mr. Hammarskjold saddened delegates to the General Assembly, which will open its sixteenth session tomorrow afternoon.

Delegates and members of the Secretariat mourned the death of an able diplomat who had helped bring about compromise solutions of dangerous issues in an age of nuclear stalemates.

Long Struggle Feared

There were grave forebodings of a long struggle over the choice of a Secretary General who would be acceptable to both the Soviet Union and the Western powers.

The interim plan gained momentum after Dr. Ali Sastroamidjojo of Indonesia, Mr. Slim's only competitor for President of the sixteenth session of the Assembly withdrew this afternoon on the understanding that the African-Asian group would support him for President next year.

Frederick H. Boland of Ireland, who was President of the fifteenth session, and a number of Asian, African and European delegates are understood to favor the plan, under which Mr. Slim would, in effect, become Acting Secretary General.

Mr. Boland will call the sixteenth session to order at 3 P. M. tomorrow. Its formal business will be limited to the election of Mr. Slim and the vice presidents and committee chairmen, who will serve under Mr. Slim as the Assembly's Steering Committee.

Soviet May Force Demand

The United States and some Western delegations declined to comment on the plan, which so far is still in the informal stage. However, other delegates expressed the belief that it would be accepted without opposition unless the Soviet Union decided to force an immediate showdown on its demand for the liquidation of the office of Secretary General and the substitution of a three-man directorate.

A Soviet spokesman said today that his delegation would press this demand, which was submitted to the General Assembly by Premier Khrushchev a year ago, at the impending session.

Although the Soviet delegate, Valerian A. Zorin, refused to join other members of the Security Council in praising Mr.

Continued on Page 16, Column 2

President to Assure U. N. U. S. Backs a Single Chief

By JAMES RESTON
Special to The New York Times.

WASHINGTON, Sept. 18—President Kennedy decided tonight to intervene personally in the constitutional crisis created at the United Nations by the death of Secretary General Dag Hammarskjold.

The White House announced that the President would address the General Assembly in New York, probably Friday. His purpose in doing so is to reassure the delegates and Secretariat that the United States supports the United Nations and is determined to do everything possible to maintain the executive authority of the office of the Secretary General.

The President's plan to address the United Nations was made known after he had paid a tribute to Mr. Hammarskjold, in which he said:

"I am hopeful that the members of the United Nations, recognizing his untiring labors, will attempt in the coming sessions and in the years to come to try to build the United Nations into the effective instrument for peace which was Dag Hammarskjold's great ambition."

Interim Plan Sought

As for the crisis at the United Nations, the United States believes that an interim arrangement must be made quickly, with the concurrence of the Soviet Union if possible, to enable the office of the Secretary General to carry out the past instructions of the world organization.

This is an urgent matter in the Congo, where United Nations troops in secessionist Katanga Province have been under fire and must be reinforced quickly.

Officials here and in New York were in constant consultation today about how this could be done in the face of the Soviet Union's opposition to the

Continued on Page 16, Column 1

KATANGA IMPERILS MAIN U. N. AIR BASE

Loss Would Be Second Big Defeat—Tshombe Units Claim Capture of 500

Special to The New York Times.

ELISABETHVILLE, the Congo, Sept. 18—United Nations troops guarding the big air base at Kamina, in Katanga Province, were reported under heavy fire today and in danger of being overwhelmed by their Katangan attackers.

[According to The Associated Press, Katangan military radio messages reported the capture of the Kamina base and the surrender of its 500 Irish and Swedish defenders.]

The loss of the air base would be the second major defeat for the United Nations in the six days of fighting here. This morning, the surrender of a garrison of 158 Irish troops was completed at Jadotville, sixty-five miles north of Elisabethville.

With the military situation deteriorating, United Nations forces here spent an anxious morning waiting for news of Secretary General Dag Hammarskjold. Word of his death brought sorrow to the already grim band of United Nations soldiers and officials.

Outside this capital of Katanga, the secessionist forces are more numerous than those

Continued on Page 14, Column 6

12 OTHERS KILLED

Lone Survivor Reports Explosions on Flight to Tshombe Talks

By DAVID HALBERSTAM
Special to The New York Times.

NDOLA, Northern Rhodesia, Sept. 18—Secretary General Dag Hammarskjold of the United Nations was killed today with twelve other persons in the crash of a plane carrying him to a meeting with President Moise Tshombe of Katanga Province. The meeting had been called in an effort to end the fighting in Katanga.

The bodies of the Secretary General and his staff were found about four miles from the Ndola airport in Northern Rhodesia. The plane had been scheduled to land at the airport last night.

[The Associated Press said that mistaken identity and tight security led it to report erroneously Sunday night that Mr. Hammarskjold's plane had reached Ndola.]

The site of the crash is close to the border of the Congolese province of Katanga. The Congo is an area that has demanded much of Mr. Hammarskjold's time and patience in the last fifteen months.

Crash Stuns U. N. Aides

The news of the crash stunned this area. Earlier today United Nations officials at Elisabethville seemed dazed as they kept hearing reports that Mr. Hammarskjold had not arrived in Ndola.

[The Associated Press reported that the lone survivor, Harold M. Julian, a United Nations security guard, said that a series of explosions had preceded the crash. He also said that the plane had turned away from a landing, apparently on Mr. Hammarskjold's orders.]

At near-by Kitwe, in Northern Rhodesia, President Tshombe was holding a news conference and was saying that he hoped to meet in a few minutes with the Secretary General and end the war when a newsman said:

"President Tshombe, Mr. Hammarskjold is dead. His body lies not far away in the wreckage of his airplane."

Mr. Tshombe's face reflected shock and horror in his eyes.

Tshombe Expresses Regret

"I regret it very much if what you say is true," he said. "He was a man who enjoyed the respect of many African nations and I had hoped to reach a settlement with him that would leave Katanga free."

Earlier in his news conference Mr. Tshombe had attacked United Nations policy in the Congo.

Mr. Hammarskjold's plane was a United Nations DC-6B. It left Leopoldville yesterday. Much concerning the crash remains inexplicable.

The Secretary General's plane apparently crashed after it had circled the Ndola airport twice and had been waved in. No one here could offer any explanation for the crash.

It was believed that the plane might have taken a circuitous route to avoid the Katanga area, which is patrolled by one Katanga jet fighter. This might account for the plane's late arrival here and it might account for some fatigue on the part of the pilot.

There apparently was only one survivor, a man who was found severely burned and in a delirious state near the plane. He was taken to a hospital.

Those who have been trying to end the Katanga fighting believe that Mr. Hammarskjold's death was a terrible blow to hopes for a truce.

Mr. Tshombe has refused to meet with United Nations officials in Elisabethville, the Ka-

Continued on Page 14, Column 1

French to End the Occupation Of Bizerte City, Starting Today

By THOMAS F. BRADY
Special to The New York Times.

TUNIS, Sept. 18—French and Tunisian representatives agreed today on a plan for the withdrawal of French troops from the city of Bizerte and its environs.

The withdrawal will start tomorrow morning and continue through Saturday.

Negotiations leading to the troop pullback began after a proposal by President Habib Bourguiba of Tunisia Sept. 7 to permit the French to maintain their naval-air base near Bizerte for the duration of the Berlin crisis if they would agree to a timetable for the eventual evacuation of the base.

The occupation of Bizerte and the surrounding area began July 20 when French forces moved against Tunisian troops and civilians who were barricading roads leading to the base entrance. Fighting had broken out July 19 after France defied a Tunisian demand for a promise to evacuate the base.

In return for ending of the city's occupation, the Tunisians have guaranteed to the French the right of circulation among the scattered military installations in the Bizerte region and freedom of movement through the entrance channel from the Mediterranean Sea to the Lake of Bizerte, on which the installations are situated.

The first concrete step toward a solution of the Bizerte dispute was an exchange of prisoners Sept. 10.

The second step was the agreement just achieved on a military withdrawal to the positions held before the July

Continued on Page 2, Column 3

NEWS INDEX

"All the News That's Fit to Print"

The New York Times.

LATE CITY EDITION
U. S. Weather Bureau Report (Page 90) forecasts:
Increasing cloudiness today.
Snow, rain tonight. Rain tomorrow.
Temp. range: 38—26; yesterday: 37—30.

VOL. CXI. No. 38,014. | NEW YORK, WEDNESDAY, FEBRUARY 21, 1962. | FIVE CENTS

10 cents beyond 50-mile zone from New York City except on Long Island. Higher in air delivery cities.

GLENN ORBITS EARTH 3 TIMES SAFELY; PICKED UP IN CAPSULE BY DESTROYER; PRESIDENT WILL GREET HIM IN FLORIDA

N.A.S.A. via Associated Press Wirephoto
READY: Lieut. Col. John H. Glenn Jr. walks to the van to take him to the launching site at Cape Canaveral, Fla.

N.A.S.A. via United Press International Telephoto
LIFT-OFF: The Atlas rocket booster bearing the Project Mercury spacecraft roars aloft with 360,000-pound thrust.

N.A.S.A. via Associated Press Wirephoto
RECOVERY: Crewmen of destroyer Noa secure capsule carrying astronaut before lifting it out of the Atlantic.

81,000-MILE TRIP

Flight Aides Feared for the Capsule as It Began Its Re-Entry

Transcript of conversations with Glenn, Pages 25 and 26.

By RICHARD WITKIN
Special to The New York Times.

CAPE CANAVERAL, Fla., Feb. 20—John H. Glenn Jr. orbited three times around the earth today and landed safely to become the first American to make such a flight.

The 40-year-old Marine Corps lieutenant colonel traveled about 81,000 miles in 4 hours 56 minutes before splashing into the Atlantic at 2:43 P. M. Eastern Standard Time.

He had been launched from here at 9:47 A. M.

The astronaut's safe return was no less a relief than a thrill to the Project Mercury team, because there had been real concern that the Friendship 7 capsule might disintegrate as it rammed back into the atmosphere.

There had also been a serious question whether Colonel Glenn could complete three orbits as planned. But despite persistent control problems, he managed to complete the entire flight plan.

Lands in Bahamas Area

The astronaut's landing place was near Grand Turk Island in the Bahamas, about 700 miles southeast of here.

Still in his capsule, he was plucked from the water at 3:01 P. M. with a boom and block and tackle by the destroyer Noa. The capsule was deposited on deck at 3:04.

Colonel Glenn's first words as he stepped out onto the Noa's deck were: "It was hot in there."

He quickly obtained a glass of iced tea.

He was in fine condition except for two skinned knuckles hurt in the process of blowing out the side hatch of the capsule.

The colonel was transferred by helicopter to the carrier Randolph, whose recovery helicopters had raced the Noa for the honor of making the pick-up. After a meal and extensive "de-briefing" aboard the carrier, he was flown to Grand Turk by submarine patrol plane for two days of rest and interviews on technical, medical and other aspects of his flight.

The Noa, nearest ship to the

Continued on Page 20, Column 1

CARLINO CLEARED IN SHELTER CASE BY ETHICS PANEL

Lane Scored in Unanimous Report, Which He Calls 'Cynical and Callous'

Text of concluding sections of report is on Page 50.

By WARREN WEAVER Jr.
Special to The New York Times.

ALBANY, Feb. 20—The Assembly Committee on Ethics and Guidance exonerated Speaker Joseph F. Carlino today of charges of conflict of interest made by Assemblyman Mark Lane.

In a unanimous report submitted to the Legislature, the bipartisan committee said:

¶Mr. Carlino did not "betray the public trust" by serving as a director of a company manufacturing home fall-out shelters while helping to pass school-shelter legislation last November.

¶He did not draft or support the shelter legislation "in any improper manner" for the benefit of the company, Lancer Industries, Inc.

¶The Speaker was not influenced in his official actions in behalf of the bill by the fact that he was a member of the board of directors of Lancer.

¶He did not receive any special benefit from the passage of the legislation.

Charges Unsubstantiated

"The committee concludes with respect to each and every accusation contained in the charges filed," the report said, "that Assemblyman Lane and those who testified in their support failed to submit credible evidence to substantiate them."

In submitting the report, the Ethics Committee requested that the full 150-member lower house vote "with respect to the conclusions reached herein" in the light of the fact that "the charges were directed against its [the Assembly's] highest ranking official."

Assemblyman Donald A. Campbell, Republican of Amsterdam, who is chairman of the committee, said he would move in the Assembly tomorrow for acceptance of the report. Mr. Carlino is expected to be absent during the debate and vote.

Assemblyman Lane, a Democrat of Manhattan, had charged that the Speaker was guilty of

Continued on Page 50, Column 1

Jersey Bus Strike Settled; Service Is Due Tomorrow

By PETER KIHSS

An agreement to end the New Jersey bus strike was reached last night. The agreement, subject to ratification by the striking employes, was announced by Gov. Richard J. Hughes. The pact will be submitted to the union members at their garages starting at 7 A. M. today.

Union and management men expressed hope that buses could begin operating tomorrow at 4:30 A. M.

The strike against Public Service Coordinated Transport started at 12:01 A. M. Monday and halted 2,511 buses providing 1,000,000 rides a day. The company's 200 routes serve all of New Jersey's twenty-one counties except Warren and Hunterdon and go into New York City and Philadelphia. The Newark subway system was also shut.

Carlin Gets Credit

Governor Hughes credited Mayor Leo P. Carlin of Newark with having "sparkplugged" the successful negotiations. Mayor Carlin flew back from a Miami Beach vacation yesterday and arranged the talks with both sides and with Daniel F. Fitzpatrick, a Federal mediator, and the Governor and himself. The meeting started in Newark at 8:30 P. M., and the agreement was announced at 11:28 P. M.

Earlier, David L. Yunich, president of Bamberger's New Jersey, had asserted that the strike was having a "devastating * * * almost catastrophic" effect on retail business in Newark and elsewhere in the state. A Camden department store reported sales had fallen nearly 50 per cent on Monday, although not that far yesterday.

Despite the drop in shopping, most commuters managed to get to work by alternate means and with a minimum of confusion.

The agreement reached last night provides for a wage increase of 10 cents an hour retroactive to Feb. 1 and extending to next Feb. 1; 4 cents more an hour from then until Aug. 1, 1963, and another 4 cents an hour from then until

Continued on Page 39, Column 3

ROSENTHAL WINS QUEENS ELECTION

But Democrat-Liberal Has Margin of Only 193 Votes —Machines Guarded

By CLAYTON KNOWLES

Benjamin S. Rosenthal, a Democrat-Liberal backed by President Kennedy, squeaked through to victory last night in a special Congressional election in Queens' Sixth District.

By the slim margin of 193 votes, Mr. Rosenthal, a lanky 38-year-old Elmhurst lawyer, edged past Thomas F. Galvin of Flushing, the Republican candidate, to win a three-way race. Emil Levin of Flushing, a Democrat running as an independent, finished far behind.

The unofficial final tally, delayed as the early vote was hastily rechecked for errors, was: Rosenthal, 16,032; Galvin, 15,839, and Levin, 4,216.

Republicans immediately challenged the result and, while Mr. Galvin did not immediately ask for a recount, he sent a telegram demanding that the voting machines be impounded. All voting machines, normally just

Continued on Page 48, Column 3

ROCKEFELLER BARS KOREA WAR BONUS

Voices Opposition in Face of Legislators' Backing

By LAYHMOND ROBINSON
Special to The New York Times.

ALBANY, Feb. 20—Governor Rockefeller expressed strong opposition tonight to a state bonus for veterans of the Korean war.

Mr. Rockefeller told the New York State Department of the American Legion that he could not "as a responsible leader of government" support the demand for a bonus. The veterans' group had been campaigning for a $100,000,000 bonus for the 482,000 Korean war veterans or their next-of-kin in the state.

The Governor said his stand was backed "unanimously" by the "Republican leadership of the state." This was a reference to the leaders of the Republican-controlled Legislature.

He said that demands for funds for education, mental health, narcotics control and other state services were too great to permit a diversion of money for a veterans' bonus.

Mr. Rockefeller thus took a position in direct opposition to that of most of the Republican and Democratic members of the Legislature, who have been pushing for the bonus. The issue

Continued on Page 51, Column 1

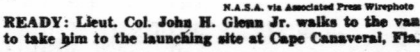

McNamara Reports Gains by Vietnamese

By JACK RAYMOND
Special to The New York Times.

WASHINGTON, Feb. 20—Secretary of Defense Robert S. McNamara returned to the capital today and reported improvement in the South Vietnamese effort against Communist insurgents.

He had presided at a meeting of United States military and civilian officials yesterday at the headquarters in Hawaii of Admiral Harry S. Felt, commander of United States forces in the Pacific. The meeting was the third in a series of monthly talks on the hostilities in South Vietnam.

A spokesman for Mr. McNamara said that the forces of South Vietnam, supported by the United States, "are hitting

Continued on Page 8, Column 5

KENNEDY PRAISES 'WONDERFUL JOB'

Tells Glenn Nation Is 'Really Proud of You'—Welcome at White House Planned

By TOM WICKER
Special to The New York Times.

WASHINGTON, Feb. 20 — President Kennedy phoned Lieut. Col. John H. Glenn Jr. today immediately after the astronaut's successful orbital flight and arranged to meet him at Cape Canaveral Friday morning.

The President also set in motion plans for bringing Colonel Glenn to Washington on Monday or Tuesday, for receptions at the White House and the Capitol and a parade down Pennsylvania Avenue

A television set in his office and an open telephone line to Cape Canaveral had kept Mr. Kennedy informed of Colonel Glenn's progress all through the day.

The astronaut's three orbits around the earth, Mr. Kennedy said in a statement, have embarked the United States on a "new ocean"—that of space.

"I believe the United States must sail on it and be in a position second to none," the President said within minutes of Colonel Glenn's safe emergence from his Mercury capsule.

Colonel Glenn, he said, is the "kind of American of whom we are most proud." Mr. Kennedy also praised "all those who participated" in making the astronaut's flight successful.

Then, at 4:10 P. M., Mr. Ken-

Continued on Page 23, Column 7

Leaders of Algeria Back Peace Terms

By THOMAS F. BRADY
Special to The New York Times.

TUNIS, Feb. 20—The Algerian nationalist Provisional Government met today and gave full approval to peace accords negotiated with the French by four members of the rebel regime.

One Algerian said afterward: "All twelve members of the Government are in unanimous agreement." This was a reference to five ministers who are prisoners in France, the four negotiators and three ministers who remained in Tunis during the secret talks last week on the French-Swiss border.

The negotiators were Belkacem Krim, M'Hammed Yazid, Saad Dahlab and Lakhdar Ben Tobbal. They met here today

Continued on Page 11, Column 1

The President's Statement

Special to The New York Times.

WASHINGTON, Feb. 20—Following is the text of President Kennedy's statement on Colonel Glenn's flight:

I know that I express the great happiness and thanksgiving of all of us that Colonel Glenn has completed his trip, and I know that this is particularly felt by Mrs. Glenn and his two children.

A few days ago Colonel Glenn came to the White House and visited me, and he is—as are the other astronauts—the kind of American of whom we are most proud.

Some years ago, as a Marine pilot, he raced the sun across this country—and lost. And today he won.

I also want to say a word for all those who participated with Colonel Glenn in Canaveral. They faced many disappointments and delays—the burdens upon them were great—but they kept their heads and they made a judgment, and I think their judgment has been vindicated.

We have a long way to go in this space race. We started late. But this is the new ocean, and I believe the United States must sail on it and be in a position second to none.

Some months ago I said that I hoped every American would serve his country. Today Colonel Glenn served his, and we all express our thanks to him.

ADENAUER WANTS PARLEY ON BERLIN

Suggests Foreign Ministers of Big Four Meet 'Soon'

By SYDNEY GRUSON
Special to The New York Times.

BONN, Germany, Feb. 20—Chancellor Adenauer suggested today that a Big Four foreign ministers' conference on Berlin should be convened "soon." He was speaking to the Parliamentary group of the Christian Democratic Union.

He said that it might be "expedient" to "take a pause" in the Berlin talks now going on between Andrei A. Gromyko, the Soviet Foreign Minister, and Llewellyn E. Thompson Jr., the United States Ambassador to Moscow.

Ambassador Thompson should not continue "negotiating" endlessly, Dr. Adenauer added. There have been four meetings in the last seven weeks between Mr. Gromyko and Mr. Thompson without any advance toward a Berlin settlement.

[A warning by Izvestia, the Soviet Government newspaper, that Moscow was ready to push through a separate peace treaty with East Germany if the United States did not alter its position in the talks raised the possibility of a renewal of the Soviet deadline on a peace pact.]

Dr. Adenauer's advocacy of a new conference of the United States, British, French and Soviet foreign ministers reflected his unhappiness with the course of the Gromyko-Thompson talks.

He is known to believe that Mr. Thompson has made what

Continued on Page 2, Column 3

URBAN PLAN VOTE PUT OFF IN SENATE

Administration Rebuffed on Forcing Issue to Floor

By RUSSELL BAKER
Special to The New York Times.

WASHINGTON, Feb. 20 — President Kennedy affronted the Senate's dignity today and got a political rebuff for it.

In a surprising repudiation of the Administration's voting form sheets, the elders turned on the White House and rejected a leadership move to get a quick floor test of the President's urban affairs proposal. The vote was 58 to 42.

Thus, the White House lost its chance to get a favorable Senate vote on the plan before the House could vote to kill it. The Democrats also lost their chance to get the Senate's Republicans clearly on record for or against the plan to create a Cabinet-level Department of Urban Affairs and Housing.

Today's test came on the dusty parliamentary question whether the Senate should take the plan away from the Government Operations Committee and bring it to an immediate floor vote. This is known as "discharging" the committee. It is an extraordinary procedure that is rarely used because it is repugnant to Senate traditions.

Today it became the instrument of the President's defeat.

The move to discharge the Government Operations Committee was undertaken with misgivings yesterday by Mike Mansfield of Montana, Senate Democratic leader. The reason was a sudden threat by the

Continued on Page 16, Column 4

COL. GLENN FLOWN TO ISLE FOR CHECK

He Feels Tired but Elated —Goes to Grand Turk for Report and Examination

By JOHN W. FINNEY
Special to The New York Times.

GRAND TURK ISLAND, Feb. 20—An elated but tired John H. Glenn Jr. returned to earth tonight and reported that he "couldn't feel better."

The 40-year-old astronaut also reported that he had felt no sickness or discomfort during his five-hour, three-orbit flight around the earth, even during the extended period of weightlessness.

Colonel Glenn landed at this small British possession at 9:11 P. M. in a Navy S-2-F submarine patrol plane. He was clad in light blue coveralls. He had co-piloted the plane from the carrier Randolph, where he spent several hours after being retrieved from the Atlantic ocean.

Around his ears were the marks of the earphones that he had worn while piloting a plane that traveled at about one-hundredth the speed of his Friendship 7 space capsule. And on his face was an excited enthusiastic smile.

Asked how he felt, the red-headed marine replied: "Fine, wonderful, I couldn't feel better."

And he was also hungry. His first comment on stepping into the small hospital arranged for him was: "First I want something to eat—I am hungry." A steak dinner was promptly or-

Continued on Page 23, Column 2

Moscow, Unmoved, Gives News of Orbit

By THEODORE SHABAD
Special to The New York Times.

MOSCOW, Feb. 20 — The Russians voiced congratulations tonight on hearing of Lieut. Col. John H. Glenn Jr.'s orbital space flight.

But they showed no enthusiasm on the successful launching and landing of the spacecraft Friendship 7.

These reactions were reported from Moscow University by United States exchange students who had been listening with Russians to radio reports of Colonel Glenn's progress.

"They congratulated us in friendly fashion but were oddly reserved," an American said.

Soviet radio and television were unusually prompt in reporting the flight. The first bul-

Continued on Page 23, Column 5

NEW YORK PAUSES TO 'WATCH' GLENN

Millions Rivet Attention on Astronaut in Flight

By NAN ROBERTSON

The thoughts of millions of New Yorkers were riveted for hours yesterday on one man alone in space.

Minute by minute, they followed the orbital flight of Lieut. Col. John H. Glenn Jr. three times around the earth, waiting in agonizing suspense for his safe return. The life of New York almost stood still during the dramatic countdown.

From then on until Colonel Glenn scrambled "hale and hearty" out of his capsule on the destroyer Noa, people carried on absent-mindedly and in spurts. Millions of working hours were lost during the day, but no one could have begrudged this. Employers and the employed alike were drawn irresistibly to radio and television sets.

The most spectacular display of interest occurred in Grand Central Terminal, where throngs of up to 9,000 persons massed before a huge television screen. The police described it as the largest static crowd in the station's history. The terminal manager said those who

Continued on Page 22, Column 6

NEWS INDEX

"All the News That's Fit to Print"

The New York Times.

LATE CITY EDITION

U. S. Weather Bureau Report (Page 95) forecasts: Sunny today; fair and cool tonight. Mostly fair and pleasant tomorrow.
Temp. range: 70—50; yesterday: 68—54.
Temp.-Hum. Index: 64; yesterday: 65.

NEWS SUMMARY AND INDEX, PAGE 95

VOL. CXII..No. 38,235.

NEW YORK, SUNDAY, SEPTEMBER 30, 1962.

35c beyond 50-mile zone from New York City, except on Long Island. 40c beyond 200-mile zone from New York City, higher in air delivery cities.

SECTION ONE

THIRTY CENTS

KENNEDY FEDERALIZES MISSISSIPPI'S GUARD; MOBILIZES TROOPS, ORDERS STATE TO YIELD; ADDRESSES NATION TODAY ON RACIAL CRISIS

PRESIDENT CALLS RUSK AND BRITON TO DISCUSS BERLIN

Lord Home and Envoys Will Fly to Capital Today as German Crisis Grows

By E. W. KENWORTHY
Special to The New York Times

WASHINGTON, Sept. 29—President Kennedy will meet here tomorrow with high United States and British officials to discuss the Berlin situation and other foreign policy questions.

The luncheon at the White House will be attended by Secretary of State Dean Rusk; the Earl of Home, the British Foreign Secretary; David K. E. Bruce, the United States Ambassador in London, and Sir David Ormsby Gore, the British Ambassador in Washington.

[Mr. Rusk said in New York that assertions by the Communists that they had no troops in Laos were "nonsense and the world knows it."]

Newport Trip Called Off

President Kennedy had planned to fly to Newport this afternoon and have luncheon there with the British and American officials. However, at 3 P.M. the White House said he had called off the trip.

Andrew T. Hatcher, associate press secretary, was reticent at the time about saying that the trip cancellation was related to the integration crisis in Mississippi.

The ministers and ambassadors will fly here tomorrow from New York, where they are attending sessions of the United Nations General Assembly.

The White House did not say what would be discussed. But officials here said it was obvious that Berlin and increasing tensions there would demand much of the meeting's attention.

High Administration officials have not disguised their deep concern over the lack of interest on the part of the Soviet Union in various proposals by the United States and Britain to reduce tension over Berlin.

For example, Soviet officials

Continued on Page 26, Column 1

Brandt, Rockefeller and Wagner Lead Steuben March

The New York Times

Mayor Willy Brandt of West Berlin joins Mayor Wagner and Governor Rockefeller at the head of about 25,000 marchers during annual Steuben Day parade up Fifth Avenue.

By DAVID BINDER

The Bavarians yodeled, the Cologners danced a two-step, the Rhinelanders sang, the Hamburgers cried "Hummel Hummel" and the bands played Berliner melodies as 25,000 German-Americans marched up Fifth Avenue yesterday. The occasion was the fifth annual Steuben Parade, honoring Baron Friedrich Wilhelm von Steuben, the general from Magdeburg who helped George Washington drill the Continental Army during the American Revolution. Mayor Willy Brandt of West Berlin was the honored guest. German touches were everywhere—in black corduroy carpenter costumes, gymnastic stunts

Continued on Page 52, Column 3

JOHNSON IS FINED

Barnett's Lieutenant Is Liable to a Penalty of $5,000 a Day

Text of court order finding Johnson guilty, Page 66.

By HEDRICK SMITH
Special to The New York Times

NEW ORLEANS, Sept. 29—Lieut. Gov. Paul B. Johnson Jr. of Mississippi was held in civil contempt of Federal court orders today in his state's integration crisis.

A three-judge panel of the United States Court of Appeals for the Fifth Circuit tried Mr. Johnson in absentia. He was found guilty of defying court orders forbidding any official interference with the desegregation of the University of Mississippi.

The court gave Mr. Johnson until 11 A.M. Tuesday to purge himself of contempt or face a fine of $5,000 a day. The fine is to start building up immediately, but no money is to be collected until Tuesday.

The opinion closely followed the language used in a contempt ruling yesterday against Gov. Ross R. Barnett except that Mr. Johnson is not initially subject to arrest.

Fine Might Increase

However, the court ruled that if Mr. Johnson became Acting Governor and refused to comply with its orders, he would face the same penalties as Mr. Barnett.

This means that, in such a situation, Mr. Johnson could face arrest and a fine of $10,000 a day unless he retreated and ordered Mississippi officials to comply with the court's desegregation orders.

Like Governor Barnett, Mr. Johnson did not appear at the court hearing.

There were no attorneys in court to represent him. However, the two attorneys for the state of Mississippi were in the courtroom—Charles Clarke of Jackson and John C. Satterfield of Yazoo City.

They entered no pleadings or arguments in Mr. Johnson's behalf. However, they submitted

Continued on Page 66, Column 1

Federal Troops Massing At a Base Near Memphis

Soldiers Landed by Army Helicopters for Possible Duty in Mississippi Crisis —Engineers Ordered Into State

Special to The New York Times.

MEMPHIS, Tenn., Sept. 29—Hundreds of Army troops and about 500 United States marshals were in the huge Memphis Naval Air Station near here tonight.

The Government kept flying men in during the day for a showdown next week with Gov Ross R. Barnett of Mississippi over the court-ordered desegregation of the University of Mississippi.

[President Kennedy ordered an Army Engineer battalion to move into Mississippi to set up a tent city for 700 United States marshals, according to United Press International.]

Large Army helicopters landed 200 to 250 soldiers during the day. Newsmen were barred from the air station, 18 miles north of Memphis, but they counted 16 helicopters as they landed and discharged troops.

The Pentagon in Washington admitted that the helicopters were here.

Earlier, about 400 men had been flown in by Navy transport planes. The armed soldiers were confined to the base.

Sailors leaving the base on weekend liberty told newsmen about the soldiers' being here.

The Department of Defense denied that any paratroop units had been sent to Memphis. So did Gen. C. W. G. Rich, commander of Fort Campbell, Army base in Kentucky. It was from here that 110 men of the 70th Battalion of Engineers were sent to the air station yesterday.

Gen. H. H. Howze, commander of Fort Bragg, Army base in North Carolina, would not confirm that paratroopers had been

Continued on Page 68, Column 5

ACTS AT MIDNIGHT

President Holds Talks With Gov. Barnett but to No Avail

Text of Kennedy proclamation is printed on Page 68.

By ANTHONY LEWIS
Special to The New York Times

WASHINGTON, Sunday, Sept. 30.—President Kennedy committed the full weight of the Federal Government at midnight last night to end Mississippi's defiance of the Union.

He called the state's National Guard into Federal service.

He sent troops of the United States Army to Memphis, Tenn., to stand in reserve if more force were needed.

And he issued a proclamation calling on the Government and people of Mississippi to abandon what had become the most serious challenge to Federal authority since the Civil War.

Addresses Nation Tonight

Tonight, the President goes on the air to explain the situation to the American people. He will speak over all national television and radio networks at 7:30 New York time.

The President took what one official called his "irrevocable steps" after three telephone conversations yesterday with Governor Ross R. Barnett of Mississippi.

In a statement issued at five minutes before midnight, the acting White House press secretary, Andrew T. Hatcher, said that in the conversations "the President was unable to receive from Governor Barnett satisfactory assurances that law and order could, or would, be maintained in Oxford, Miss., during the coming week."

Crisis Over Negro Student

Oxford is the seat of the University of Mississippi. Mississippi's defiance of Federal court orders to admit a Negro, James H. Meredith, to the university, has provoked the Federal-state crisis.

Mr. Hatcher said the action was being taken at that late hour—and telegrams dispatched to the guard commanders—so that the units "will be available for service Monday." Most Guardsmen are one-day-a-week soldiers, and it will take time to mobilize them.

The regular Army troops sent to Memphis comprised 900 military policemen, especially

Continued on Page 68, Column 1

KENNEDY WISHES BEN BELLA WELL

'Warmest Congratulations' Sent as U. S. Recognizes New Algerian Regime

By PETER BRAESTRUP
Special to The New York Times

WASHINGTON, Sept. 29—President Kennedy today sent "warmest congratulations" to Ahmed Ben Bella, Premier of independent Algeria's newly formed Government.

Mr. Kennedy, who as a Senator endorsed Algerian self-rule in 1957, wished Mr. Ben Bella "every success" and said that "my Government and my people share my earnest desire to foster and extend the cordial relations that exist between our two countries."

The President's message coincided with the State Department's announcement of formal diplomatic recognition of the newly established Government of Algeria.

New Premier to Visit Here

Yesterday Mr. Ben Bella announced his Cabinet and pledged a "neutralist and non-engaged" foreign policy in a speech before the week-old National Assembly. The Assembly subsequently approved the Cabinet list, 159 to 1 with 19 abstentions.

Secretary of State Dean Rusk sent congratulations to the Algerian Foreign Minister, Mohammed Khemisti, saying that he looked forward to a meeting "in the near future."

Informed sources said today that President Kennedy and Secretary Rusk would meet with Mr. Ben Bella sometime after the Algerian Premier's arrival in the United States, possibly late next week, to head

Continued on Page 4, Column 1

Norway Criticizes Paris Plan to Build National A-Forces

By HENRY GINIGER
Special to The New York Times

PARIS, Sept. 29—The four-day state visit by King Olav V of Norway ended today with a strong attack by the Norwegian Foreign Minister, Dr. Halvard M. Lange, on national atomic striking forces in Europe such as that planned by France.

King Olav took leave of President de Gaulle this morning before flying to Oslo. He had been warmly received and responded with the same warmth in a recorded message of thanks that was broadcast over the French radio and television.

It was left to Dr. Lange, who had accompanied the King, to underline the serious divergences between the Norwegian and French Governments on Western defense. He did so in a statement to the French News Agency.

Reliance Placed on the U. S.

Dr. Lange said the Western alliance must rest on confidence among its members, for "otherwise it has no sense." He said that Norway, placing her confidence in the United States' assumption of the burden and responsibility for the West's nuclear armament, was hostile to national atomic forces in Europe.

President de Gaulle has often said that France must assume responsibility for her defense, and he and his aides have left the widespread impression that they are not wholly confident of the United States' ability or willingness to defend Western Europe.

Dr. Lange said Western Europe should assume greater shares of the burden of conventional armaments and of help to underdeveloped nations, a

Continued on Page 23, Column 2

U.S. TELLS SOVIET TO OUST 2 AS SPIES

Says Aides at U. N. Bought Secrets From Sailor, Held Here in $100,000 Bail

By EMANUEL PERLMUTTER

The United States yesterday demanded the expulsion of two members of the Soviet delegation to the United Nations who were involved with an American sailor in an espionage plot.

In a sharply worded note to the Soviet mission, the United States said: "As host to the United Nations, the Government of the United States strongly protests the espionage activities directed against the internal security of the United States."

The Russians countered a few hours later with a note charging that Federal agents had illegally arrested, manhandled and questioned the two

Continued on Page 29, Column 1

Longshore Walkout Scheduled Tonight; Ships Rush to Sea

By EDWARD A. MORROW

A steady stream of ships sailed out of New York and other Atlantic and Gulf ports yesterday to avoid being caught in a longshoremen's strike that appeared certain to begin at 12:01 A.M. tomorrow.

Work on the piers continued at a record level as shipowners filed unusual weekend calls for labor with the Waterfront Commission.

The bistate agency said that 17,459 men had been hired to work 101 ships at 80 piers at time-and-a-half pay. On a normal Saturday the waterfront force is 2,000 to 3,000 men.

Sixty-two ships passed the quarantine station outbound yesterday. This number would have been even higher had not some operators decided to postpone the sailing of 12 ships until today to accept all the tonnage that could be moved off the piers before the deadline.

Cruise Liner Held Up

The 591 passengers aboard the Queen of Bermuda, which was scheduled to sail at 3 P.M. for Hamilton, Bermuda, found their cruise departure delayed until 8 A.M. this morning so the vessel could load cargo.

While the peak of the effort to get ships out has passed, a Sunday hiring record is expected to be broken today, a Waterfront Commission spokesman said.

The agency has received calls for 8,500 men to work 35 piers at double their regular pay of $3.02 an hour. The normal Sunday work force averages 1,000.

Federal mediators failed yes-

Continued on Page 44, Column 5

SUPREME COURT OPENS TOMORROW

Legislative Districting Still Among Major Problems—Goldberg to Be Sworn

Special to The New York Times

WASHINGTON, Sept. 29—The Supreme Court convenes Monday for a new term that promises to be one of high drama and significance.

Two issues that dominated the last term—legislative districting and prayers in the schools—will be back in new and difficult guises.

The court will consider such other controversial problems as restaurant segregation, contempt of Congress and censorship of books and movies.

Goldberg to Take Oath

The presence of two new justices on the bench will heighten interest. In a court that has so frequently been divided 5-to-4 in recent years, two changes in membership could shift the balance of judicial philosophies.

Arthur J. Goldberg, appointed to replace Felix Frankfurter on his retirement, is scheduled to take the oath of office Monday. Byron R. White succeeded Charles E. Whittaker last April, too late to permit any real appraisal of his views last term.

Seldom, if ever, have new members of the Supreme Court faced questions so intellectually challenging or with so great a potential impact on

Continued on Page 74 Column 3

GIANTS AND COLTS SPLIT TWO GAMES

Dodgers Clinch at Least a Tie for First Place

The league-leading Los Angeles Dodgers lost to the St. Louis Cardinals yesterday but remained a game ahead of the San Francisco Giants who split a double-header with the Houston Colts. The results assured the Dodgers of at least a tie for first place.

FOOTBALL

Army and Columbia won major college football contests in New York. Scores of leading games:

Army	9	Syracuse	2
Auburn	22	Tennessee	21
Boston Coll.	28	Villanova	13
California	22	San Jose St.	8
Colgate	23	Cornell	12
Columbia	22	Brown	20
Dartmouth	27	Mass.	3
Duke	21	S. Carolina	8
Ga. Tech	17	Florida	0
Harvard	27	Lehigh	7
Holy Cross	16	Buffalo	6
Iowa	28	Oregon St.	8
Minnesota	0	Missouri	0
Mississippi	14	Kentucky	0
Navy	20	W. & M.	16
Nebraska	25	Michigan	13
Notre Dame	13	Oklahoma	7
Ohio State	41	N. Carolina	7
Oregon	35	Utah	8
Penn.	13	Lafayette	11
Penn State	20	Air Force	6
Princeton	15	Rutgers	7
Stanford	16	Mich. St.	13
Washington	28	Illinois	7
Yale	18	Conn.	14

HORSE RACING

Kelso won the $115,200 Woodward Stakes as the Aqueduct meeting ended. Jaipur was a distant second to the favorite.

Details in Section 5

Principals in Naval Secrets Case

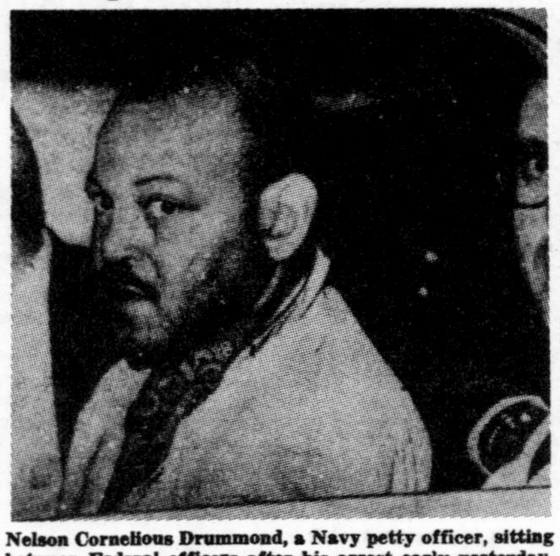

Nelson Cornelious Drummond, a Navy petty officer, sitting between Federal officers after his arrest early yesterday.

Ivan Y. Vyrodov, member of Soviet mission to the U. N.

Associated Press

Yevgeny M. Prokhorov, second secretary of mission.

U.N. Says Katanga Still Recruits Troops in Violation of Promise

BY SAM POPE BREWER
Special to The New York Times.

UNITED NATIONS, N. Y., Sept. 29—The United Nations has accused the Government of Katanga of continuing to recruit mercenaries in spite of repeated promises not to do so.

The charges were made in a letter from the chief United Nations officer in the Congo, Robert K. A. Gardiner, to President Moise Tshombe of Katanga Province, dated last Tuesday and made public here last night.

[In Elisabethville President Tshombe likened the United Nations charges to "the stories of sea serpents or the abominable snowman." He said such charges always precede an attack on Katanga.]

Mr. Gardiner said the Katangese gendarmerie "has been receiving reinforcements for some time both in the form of troops and material."

He said: "I am worried to see that in spite of your affirmations that there would be no more mercenaries serving the Katangese Gendarmerie, bodies of Europeans killed in combat between the National Congolese Army and the Gendarmerie have been found."

In further support of the charges, Mr. Gardiner said that the United Nations organization in the Congo had a complete file of the names, addresses and photographs of mercenaries who had arrived in Katanga in recent months. It also has copies of payrolls signed by the men, he said.

Mr. Gardiner charged that recruiting was still being carried on through newspaper advertisements, especially in

Continued on Page 8, Column 1

Traffic Overhaul at Lincoln Sq. Called Basic to Orderly Growth

By JOSEPH C. INGRAHAM

The city was urged yesterday to overhaul traffic patterns around Lincoln Center before approving any future construction.

The proposal for traffic relief was submitted in a report by Day & Zimmerman, Philadelphia consulting engineers.

The firm was hired by the city on April 23 to conduct a $30,000 study of the effects of future developments on traffic and mass transit, with "particular emphasis on the impact that the proposed Litho City housing development would impose."

Among the principal recommendations were the following:

¶Widening and rebuilding parts of the West Side Highway.

¶Changing the traffic pattern in local streets.

¶Adding crosstown express streets and rebuilding existing ones.

¶Changing the traffic pattern within the Lincoln Center for the Performing Arts.

The Litho City project, sponsored by Local 1, Amalgamated Lithographers of America, is planned along the Hudson River between 60th and 70th Streets.

Consisting of 17 buildings of 23 and 33 stories over the New York Central's freight yards, the project would tower above the western side of Lincoln Center.

The consultants stressed that their broad traffic study had been predicated largely on the Litho City project. They noted that the original plans had called for 6,000 apartments for 15,000 to 20,000 persons, but said

Continued on Page 85, Column 3

Today's Sections

Index to Subjects

"All the News That's Fit to Print"

The New York Times.

LATE CITY EDITION
U. S. Weather Bureau Report (Page 77) forecasts: Mostly sunny today. Fair tonight and tomorrow.
Temp. range: 75—54; yesterday: 74—52.

VOL. CXII. No. 38,237.

NEW YORK, TUESDAY, OCTOBER 2, 1962.

10 cents beyond 50-mile zone from New York City except on Long Island. Higher in air delivery cities.

FIVE CENTS

3,000 TROOPS PUT DOWN MISSISSIPPI RIOTING AND SEIZE 200 AS NEGRO ATTENDS CLASSES; EX-GEN. WALKER IS HELD FOR INSURRECTION

Associated Press Wirephoto

PRISONERS ARE MARCHED TO ARMORY IN OXFORD: Army men escort a group of prisoners to National Guard Armory. The group had participated in a disturbance and was apprehended after the soldiers were ordered to fire at the feet of the rioters.

United Press International Telephoto

WALKER IS STOPPED BY TROOPS: Former Maj. Gen. Edwin A. Walker is detained by soldiers near the courthouse in Oxford. He was turned over to U.S. marshals and is being held in $100,000 bail on charges stemming from his role in Sunday's campus riots.

SENATE REJECTS AID CUTS AND BAN ON HELP FOR REDS

Upholds Kennedy's Authority to Assist Nations That Do Business With Cuba

By FELIX BELAIR Jr.
Special to The New York Times.

WASHINGTON, Oct. 1—The Senate decided for the Administration today in preliminary votes on the foreign aid appropriation bill, due for passage tomorrow.

It voted, 47 to 28, against cutting $785,000,000 from the $792,400,000 of military and economic aid funds that its Appropriations Committee restored to the bill the House had cut heavily.

The effect of the vote was to hold the appropriation at $4,422,800,000, as recommended by its Appropriations Committee. The Administration had requested the full amount of the authorized ceiling of $4,-754,800,000 but the House cut this back to $3,630,400,000.

On a later vote, the Senate confirmed this action by rejecting a proposal by Senator Allen J. Ellender, Democrat of Louisiana, to adopt the House cut of $150,000,000 for military aid.

Votes Become Narrow

By increasingly narrow margins, however, it supported other Administration goals. For instance, it voted, 39-36 to continue the President's discretion to aid countries doing business with Cuba. Then it decided, 39-37, to give the President similar discretion to waive the ban on aiding Communist nations such as Yugoslavia and Poland.

All three proposals were sponsored by Senator William Proxmire, Democrat of Wisconsin.

They were intended, first, to cut back the separate money items in the bill to the low levels voted by the House. Second, they would have approved the House's ban on aiding any Communist countries or free nations that help the Castro regime or allow their ships to deliver cargo to Cuba.

Only with the help of Republican members was the Democratic leadership able to turn back the Proxmire attack on the President's discretionary powers. On the proposal to ban aid to nations shipping to Cuba, 12 Republicans voted with 27 Democrats to defeat the move, while 22 Democrats and 14 Re-

Continued on Page 16, Column 4

MOSCOW FOCUSING ON BLOC IN EUROPE

Rift With Chinese Believed Behind New Emphasis

By SEYMOUR TOPPING
Special to The New York Times

MOSCOW, Oct. 1—The Soviet Union has decided to pursue its program of rapprochement with Yugoslavia even at the risk of a further deterioration in relations with Communist China.

Diplomatic officials here have found evidence of this development in a comparative study of Soviet and Chinese Communist documents.

These officials believe that the ideological quarrel with Peking has caused Moscow to resolve to concentrate its resources on the consolidation of the European Communist economic bloc.

Pravda, the Communist party newspaper, published today an edited version of the communiqué issued by the Central Committee of the Chinese Communist party at the conclusion of its plenary session Friday.

The Soviet summary, which covered half a page in Pravda, omitted the strong attacks on President Tito of Yugoslavia for his so-called "modern revision-

Continued on Page 3, Column 1

Home Urges West to Help East's Coexistence Moves

By ARNOLD H. LUBASCH

The Earl of Home, Britain's Foreign Secretary, urged last night that the West pursue policies designed to help the Soviet bloc move toward genuine coexistence. He suggested that nuclear war was no longer a useful instrument of policy, that Communist doctrine was changing because of this and that Soviet society was changing even faster.

The West should recognize these facts, he said, and adapt its policies to them.

Lord Home's remarks were made at a dinner in the Waldorf - Astoria Hotel. The dinner was given by the Pilgrims of the United States, a friendship society devoted to cultivating understanding between this country and the nations of the British Commonwealth.

The organization, composed of 1,000 prominent persons, was founded in 1903. A sister organization across the Atlantic is known as the Pilgrims of Great Britain. The groups give dinners in honor of leading statesmen to promote understanding and brotherhood among nations.

Cites Soviet Ingenuity

Lord Home observed that the Russians exercise great ingenuity to reconcile their propaganda about peaceful coexistence with a program that permits limited force in certain regions to further the cause of Communist domination.

The West must be on guard against this technique, he said, and against the force that backs it up. He mentioned Berlin and South Vietnam as two areas of particular concern.

"I pray," he added, "that Cuba may never become a third."

Communist doctrine has begun to change, Lord Home

Continued on Page 2, Column 3

SPAAK REASSURES AFRICA ON TRADE

Tells Newer U.N. Members That Common Market Will Aid Their Development

By THOMAS J. HAMILTON
Special to The New York Times

UNITED NATIONS, N. Y., Oct. 1—Paul-Henri Spaak, the Foreign Minister of Belgium, assured underdeveloped countries today that they could count on the cooperation of the members of the European Economic Community in the fight for economic advancement.

In addition, Mr. Spaak appealed to the entire world to understand the "new Europe" and its goal of "world cooperation."

Mr. Spaak's policy statement in the General Assembly was addressed in the first instance to 18 newly independent African states, all former possessions of France, Belgium or Italy.

Some of the states have asked the European Economic Community, or Common Market, for status as associates.

The six members of the market — Belgium, France, West Germany, Italy, the Netherlands and Luxembourg—are negotiating with the African states in Brussels.

Success Is Predicted

Mr. Spaak predicted that these talks would be concluded successfully by the end of 1962.

He also predicted that the negotiations with Britain for her admission to the market would be successful. He said the market would then have about the same productive capacity as the United States, and more than the Soviet Union.

The Belgian Foreign Minister, who was one of the leaders in the formation of the Common Market, defended it against two charges: that it is a manifestation of "neo-colonialism," and that it is merely intended to provide economic support for the North Atlantic Treaty Organization.

Mr. Spaak devoted almost his entire speech to his explanation of the market's program. He received an ovation at the end, with African and Asian members joining.

The Belgian Foreign Minister emphasized that the exports of African associate members would be admitted duty-free to the Common Market countries, while the Africans would retain

Continued on Page 5, Column 2

Congo Flies Troops To End Kasai Revolt

By Reuters.

LEOPOLDVILLE, the Congo, Oct. 1—Reliable sources said today that the central Congolese Government was flying troops to Luluabourg to put down a new revolt by supporters of Albert Kalonji in South Kasai. Luluabourg is the Government army base nearest to the diamond-rich province.

The troop movement followed the declaration by the Government of a state of emergency in South Kasai. No immediate action was planned by the United Nations.

Mr. Kalonji, self - styled "king," virtually seceded from the central Government shortly after the Congo became independent two years ago. He escaped recently from a prison near Leopoldville and returned to his capital of Bakwanga.

A United Nations spokesman

Continued on Page 9, Column 3

KENNEDY MOVING TO END PIER TIE-UP

He Names Board of Inquiry as First Step in Obtaining Taft-Hartley Injunction

By JOHN D. POMFRET
Special to The New York Times

WASHINGTON, Oct. 1—President Kennedy took the first step today toward getting an injunction to end the Atlantic and Gulf Coast longshoremen's strike for 80 days.

Declaring that continuation of the strike would imperil the national health and safety, the President issued an Executive order naming a three-man board of inquiry to investigate the dispute and to report to him by Thursday.

[Meanwhile in New York, leaders of the nation's seven major maritime unions abandoned inter-union battling to plan support for the striking longshoremen. American seamen and officers started leaving their ships, while other unions made plans to avoid servicing foreign-flag ships entering Atlantic and Gulf ports.]

The strike, which began at 12:01 A.M. today, has tied up all ports from Searsport, Me., to Brownsville, Tex. About 75,-000 members of the Internation-

Continued on Page 78, Column 5

WALKER IS FACING 4 FEDERAL COUNTS

Flown to Medical Center in Missouri to Await Trial—Bail Put at $100,000

Special to The New York Times

OXFORD, Miss., Oct. 1 — Former Maj. Gen. Edwin A. Walker was arrested today on four charges, including insurrection, for his role in last night's rioting at the University of Mississippi.

The man who commanded Federal forces during the school integration crisis at Little Rock in 1957 was held in $100,000 bail.

Unable to put up the bail, he was flown to the United States Medical Center for Federal Prisoners in Springfield, Mo., to await his trial.

[Mr. Walker, accompanied by marshals, arrived at the medical center Monday night, The Associated Press said.]

"They don't have a thing on me," Mr. Walker said after his arrest. He dictated a message to Gov. Ross R. Barnett, which said:

"Mr. Walker hopes his efforts were in your behalf and in behalf of the stand for freedom everywhere. Do nothing based on my status that is not in support of your own objectives.

Continued on Page 27, Column 3

Columbia Study Scores Doctors; Says Quality of Care Lags Here

Financial Sanctions Under Blue Shield Suggested in Trussell Report

By FARNSWORTH FOWLE

The medical profession is "doing little" about the quality of medical care in the metropolitan area, the state was told yesterday in an experts' report.

The report warned that the first reaction of many laymen to poor medical care "is to demand firm and drastic government action—and indeed this may occur." It said that "strong medical, hospital, community and government leadership must be asserted in the public interest."

The conclusions were contained in the final volume of the Trussell-van Dyke Report, an independent study for the state by the Columbia University School of Public Health and Administrative Medicine. It was directed by Dr. Ray E. Trussell, chairman of the school, now on leave from the school while serving as New York City's Commissioner of Hospitals, and Frank van Dyke, an associate professor at the school.

The report called on the medical profession to welcome cur-

The New York Times

Dr. Ray E. Trussell

rent efforts of management and labor toward improving medical care.

"The organized purchasers of medical and hospital care can be the strongest arm of the community in upgrading standards, and it is to the best interest of organized medicine and hospitals to work with them,"

Continued on Page 42, Column 1

Mississippi Aides Blamed By U.S. Officials for Riot

By ANTHONY LEWIS
Special to The New York Times.

WASHINGTON, Oct. 1 — The Federal Government asserted today that the failure of Mississippi officials to keep their word led to the bloody rioting in Oxford, Miss., last night. Attorney General Robert F. Kennedy and other spokesmen said that Gov. Ross R. Barnett and his aides had repeatedly given assurances that they could and would maintain order when James H. Meredith, a Negro, entered the University of Mississippi last night.

Statements by Robert Kennedy and Eastland, Page 25.

Instead, the Federal spokesmen said, the state police were withdrawn at the crucial moment of the developing mob scene. Federal troops were then called in, but two men were dead and many were injured by the time they arrived.

Senator James O. Eastland, Democrat of Mississippi, read on the Senate floor this morning a report on the rioting. He said the report had been prepared by officials of the University of Mississippi.

Eastland Orders Inquiry

Tonight, Senator Eastland directed the Senate Judiciary Committee, which he heads, to make an investigation "of all events at the University of Mississippi since U.S. marshals and Army troops moved in."

The report read by Mr. Eastland this morning sought to put the blame for the rioting on "amateurism by untrained marshals." It said that the 300 marshals at the university last night had "provoked" the crowd of 2,500 persons gathered on the campus.

The university officials also

Continued on Page 25, Column 1

BARNETT CHARGES MARSHALS ERRED

Says 'Trigger-Happy' U. S. Officers Are Responsible for Campus Bloodshed

Text of Barnett statement appears on Page 25.

By HEDRICK SMITH
Special to The New York Times

JACKSON, Miss., Oct. 1—Gov. Ross R. Barnett tonight attributed the fatal rioting at the University of Mississippi last night to "inexperienced, nervous and trigger-happy Federal marshals."

The Governor made the statement in a recorded broadcast carried by the National Broadcasting Company. In a later recorded broadcast, carried by the Columbia Broadcasting System, Mr. Barnett directly assailed President Kennedy.

"The responsibility for this unwarranted breach of the peace and violence in Mississippi rests directly with the President of the United States." he said. "He ordered armed forces to invade Mississippi and their actions were directly responsible for violence, bloodshed and death."

People Are "Enraged"

In his earlier statement, the Governor said that the people of Mississippi "are enraged, incensed—and rightly so."

"Free men do not submit meekly to the kind of treatment Mississippians received," he said.

The Governor also said that the only solution to the Mississippi integration crisis was for the Federal Government to remove James H. Meredith, a 29-year-old Negro student, from the university.

"The Federal authorities alone have the power to stop bloodshed in Mississippi," he said.

Continued on Page 25, Column 5

Bidwell's Tax Trial Ends in Hung Jury

By DAVID ANDERSON

The tax-evasion trial of J. Truman Bidwell, former chairman of the New York Stock Exchange, ended early today with a hung jury.

The jury, which had been deliberating since 1 P.M., filed into the courtroom shortly after midnight and told Federal Judge Thomas F. Murphy that it was "hopelessly deadlocked."

Judge Murphy, who two hours earlier had rejected a similar report and had instructed the jurors to try once more, now said:

"I declare a mistrial. Unhappy as I am, I guess there is nothing else we can do."

The prosecutor, Assistant United States Attorney Stephen E. Kaufman, said the Government would now consider

Continued on Page 18, Column 3

NEWS INDEX

SHOTS QUELL MOB

Enrolling of Meredith Ends Segregation in State Schools

By CLAUDE SITTON
Special to The New York Times

OXFORD, Miss., Oct. 1—James H. Meredith, a Negro, enrolled in the University of Mississippi today and began classes as Federal troops and federalized units of the Mississippi National Guard quelled a 15-hour riot.

A force of more than 3,000 soldiers and guardsmen and 400 deputy United States marshals fired rifles and hurled tear-gas grenades to stop the violent demonstrations.

Throughout the day more troops streamed into Oxford. Tonight a force approaching 5,000 soldiers and guardsmen, along with the Federal marshals, maintained an uneasy peace in this town of 6,500 in the northern Mississippi hills.

[There were two flareups tonight in which tear gas had to be used, United Press International reported. A small crowd of students began throwing bottles at marshals outside Baxter Hall where Mr. Meredith was housed. They were quickly dispersed by tear gas. Soldiers also broke up a minor demonstration at a downtown intersection.]

200 Are Seized

The troops seized approximately 200 persons.

They were seized in the mobs of students and adults that besieged the university administration building last night and attacked troops on the town square this morning.

Among those arrested was former Maj. Gen. Edwin A. Walker, who resigned his commission after having been reprimanded for his ultra-right-wing political activity. He was charged with insurrection.

The university's acceptance of Mr. Meredith, a 29-year-old Air Force veteran, followed Gov. Ross R. Barnett's retreat from his defiance of Federal court orders that the Negro be enrolled.

The 64-year-old official, a member of the militantly segregationist Citizens Councils, had vowed he would go to jail if necessary to prevent university desegregation.

Mr. Meredith's admission marked the first desegregation of a public educational institution in Mississippi. It reduced the Deep South bloc of massive-resistance states to two —

Continued on Page 24, Column 6

CAMPUS A BIVOUAC AS NEGRO ENTERS

2,000 Troops Stand Guard —Meredith Eats Alone

By McCANDLISH PHILLIPS
Special to The New York Times

OXFORD, Miss., Oct. 1—The University of Mississippi campus was under military occupation today as James H. Meredith, its first Negro student, registered and attended two classes.

Two thousand of the more than 3,000 Army and National Guard troops here made the tree-studded, rolling campus look like a cross between a bivouac and a prisoner-of-war camp. More olive drab uniforms were evident on campus than student casual dress.

Mr. Meredith, who did not get his first meal on campus until supper was served to him privately tonight, was housed in an end room in Baxter Hall, a male residence dormitory. The room next door was occupied by Federal marshals.

The 29-year-old Negro was taken from his dormitory under guard at 7:45 A. M. and marched to the Lyceum, the administration building. There he was registered in 45 minutes—

Continued on Page 26, Column 1

"All the News That's Fit to Print"

The New York Times.

LATE CITY EDITION
U.S. Weather Bureau Report (Page 74) forecasts: Partly cloudy, breezy, cool today. Fair and cool tonight and tomorrow. Temp. range: 54—45; yesterday: 66—44.

VOL. CXII..No. 38,258. © 1962 by The New York Times Company. Times Square, New York 36, N.Y. NEW YORK, TUESDAY, OCTOBER 23, 1962. 10 cents beyond 50-mile zone from New York City except on Long Island. Higher in air delivery cities. FIVE CENTS

U.S. IMPOSES ARMS BLOCKADE ON CUBA ON FINDING OFFENSIVE-MISSILE SITES; KENNEDY READY FOR SOVIET SHOWDOWN

U.S. JUDGES GIVEN POWER TO REQUIRE VOTE FOR NEGROES

High Court Upholds Order Forcing the Registration of 54 in Alabama County

Special to The New York Times

WASHINGTON, Oct. 22 — The Supreme Court held today that Federal judges have the power to make state registrars put specific Negroes on the voting rolls.

Alabama had challenged an order by Federal District Judge Frank M. Johnson Jr. requiring the registration of 54 specific Negroes in Macon County, Ala. The order was upheld by the United States Court of Appeals for the Fifth Circuit.

Today the Supreme Court unanimously affirmed the disputed order. And it did so in a way that indicated once again its mood of impatience with Southern efforts to maintain denials of Negro rights.

One-Sentence Ruling

All that was before the court was an application for review of the Fifth Circuit decision. The usual alternatives would have been to deny the petition or to grant it and hear oral argument later.

Instead, the court granted review and then, summarily, affirmed the lower courts. It did so in a single sentence, with just one citation in the way of explanation.

The citation was to a decision in 1960 upholding a Federal Court order in a Louisiana voting case. There, a district judge had told Louisiana registrars to put back on their books 1,377 Negroes whose names had been removed in a purge by the segregationist Citizens Council.

Action by Congress

The Macon County case was one of the first brought by the Department of Justice under the Civil Rights Act of 1957. It is especially significant because the county is in the so-called Black Belt, with a predominantly Negro population.

In 1958, when the suit was started, virtually all of the 3,000 white persons of voting age in the county were registered. But only about 1,000 of the 12,000 potential Negro voters were actually eligible.

In a further move, the registrars resigned, and this was held to leave no defendants to be sued. Congress in 1960 handled this problem by providing

Continued on Page 24, Column 4

102 SAVED AT SEA AS PLANE DITCHES

Rescue Is Made off Alaska Minutes After Accident

By The Associated Press.

SITKA, Alaska, Oct. 22—A military-charter airliner ditched in the ocean near here today, but all 102 persons aboard were saved in a quick rescue operation.

The plane, a DC-7C of Northwest Airlines, was going from McChord Air Force Base in Washington to Anchorage, Alaska. It carried 95 passengers and a crew of seven.

The rescue was reported by Northwest and the Alaska Coastal-Ellis Airline at Sitka, which also reported that there apparently were no serious injuries.

The plane went down shortly after the Federal Aviation Agency at Anchorage got word that it was being ditched because of propeller trouble.

A Coast Guard plane alighted on the water nearby; the Air Force sent two rescue planes, and small boats from Sitka, about seven miles north of the

Continued on Page 6, Column 3

Chinese Open New Front; Use Tanks Against Indians

Nehru Warns of Peril to Independence —Reds Attack Near Burmese Border and Press Two Other Drives

Special to The New York Times

NEW DELHI, Oct. 22—Prime Minister Jawaharlal Nehru told the people of India tonight that the Chinese Communist attack was a threat to their liberty.

His grave warning followed word that the advancing Chinese had opened a third front in the Himalayas, near the Burmese border, and had used tanks for the first time. Five more Indian posts fell to the Chinese on the third day of savage fighting.

[A bid for negotiations for a peace accord was broadcast by the Chinese Communist radio early Tuesday, The Associated Press reported from Tokyo.]

In a broadcast, Mr. Nehru denounced the Peking regime as "a powerful and unscrupulous opponent, not caring for peace or peaceful methods."

"The time has come," he said, "for us to realize fully this menace that threatens the freedom of our people and the independence of our country."

Prime Minister Nehru said India would not abandon her economic development program and policy of nonalignment with international blocs, but called on the nation to switch "from the slow-moving methods of peacetime to those which produce results quickly."

"We must build up our military strength by all means at our disposal," he said.

The third front in the Himalayan fighting was opened early today when the Chinese attacked an Indian post at Kibitoo, on the border between

Excerpts from Nehru's speech will be found on Page 2.

Continued on Page 3, Column 1

U.S. Bids U.N. Bar China; Denounces Attack on India

By SAM POPE BREWER

Special to The New York Times

UNITED NATIONS, N. Y., Oct. 22—Adlai E. Stevenson told the General Assembly today that Communist China's "naked aggression" against India was new proof that it was unfit for membership in the United Nations.

The chief United States representative at the United Nations spoke as the Assembly took up the perennial question of admitting Peking.

Mr. Stevenson told the members that by their actions on the Indian frontier the Chinese Communists "again show their scorn for the Charter of this organization."

The Vice President of the Philippines, Emmanuel Pelaez, told the Assembly that there were more than 40,000,000 Chinese living outside China who would become "a Trojan horse" if the United Nations accepted the Communist Government.

Mr. Pelaez said that the Chinese abroad, 1,000,000 of them in the Philippines, would be used for subversion by the Peking Government. He said they could now be controlled because the Communist Government did not have the means to get at them.

On the fighting in India, Mr. Stevenson declared: "Should there be some among us who think that perhaps the whole thing is a mistake that will right itself before long, let me point out that when a nation moves its troops with tanks and armor, it is no mistake. It is a premeditated act. It is naked aggression. And it has been going on with gathering momentum for some three years."

He quoted Prime Minister

Continued on Page 5, Column 3

U.S. SAID TO EASE KATANGA POLICY

Reported Willing to Put Off Any Economic Sanctions —Congolese Disturbed

By LLOYD GARRISON

Special to The New York Times

LEOPOLDVILLE, the Congo, Oct. 22 — Authoritative sources said today that the United States was no longer insisting that Katanga Province strictly meet the deadlines of the United Nations plan to end its secession from the Congo.

This has alarmed Congolese officials. They say that the United States shift is reflected in United Nations policy.

The United Nations plan, introduced Aug. 2 by U Thant, Acting Secretary General, was said to have been conceived largely by the United States.

As outlined by Mr. Thant, the plan's first stage called for the following timetable:

Within thirty days a program was to be decided on for the reintegration of Katanga's army into the Congolese National Army. Sixty days were to be allowed for the program to be carried out.

Recall of Missions

All Katangese foreign missions were to be recalled immediately, and all Katanga's foreign currency reserves were to be put under the control of the central Government, with 50 per cent of these reserves rebated to Katanga.

Unification of the Congo's currency was to have begun within 10 days.

Katanga was to have started immediately to share 50 per cent of her tax revenues with the central Government.

Not one of these conditions has been met.

Last week Cyrille Adoula, Premier of the central Government, declared that "the deadline for the first stage has passed." He said that it was now time to consider the second stage — economic sanctions.

A shift in United States policy became apparent over the weekend after the departure of George C. McGhee, Under Secretary of State for Political Af-

Continued on Page 3, Column 6

Stocks Plunge Early On Crisis, but Rally

By RICHARD RUTTER

An already badly battered stock market was hit by massive selling yesterday as talk of a new international crisis spread in Wall Street.

The selling was of dimensions reminiscent of late May when the market experienced its worst break in a generation. Yesterday, the tape ran as much as 19 minutes late before a half-hearted recovery set in that cut losses by about one-third.

Both tape lateness and volume were the greatest since July 10. Two million shares were traded in the first two hours.

Stock markets in London, Frankfurt and Brussels, following Wall Street's lead, also took large losses.

The selling was directly ascribed to news in the morning about an air of crisis in Wash-

Continued on Page 49, Column 6

SHIPS MUST STOP

Other Action Planned If Big Rockets Are Not Dismantled

By JAMES RESTON

Special to The New York Times

WASHINGTON, Oct. 22 — President Kennedy drew the line tonight, not with Cuba, but with the Soviet Union. After almost a generation of trying to keep the "cold war" from reaching a direct confrontation between United States and Soviet power, a decision has been made to force Soviet missile bases from this hemisphere at the risk of war.

This is the official interpretation of President Kennedy's speech tonight, and the orders to American forces bear it out. On the highest authority, it can be said that these orders include the following:

¶Ships carrying to Cuba weapons capable of striking the continental United States must either turn back or submit to search and seizure, or fight. If they try to run the blockade, a warning shot will be fired across their bows; if they still do not submit, they will be attacked.

¶This applies not only to ships but to any planes suspected of carrying additional offensive weapons to Cuba. There is no evidence that there are nuclear warheads in Cuba, but long-range aircraft suspected of carrying these or any other offensive weapons, will be intercepted, and instructions have been issued to do everything possible to check all Communist-bloc planes en route to Cuba via Newfoundland or Africa.

Prepared to Risk War

Even this will not satisfy the new policy announced by President Kennedy. Not only must new offensive weapons be stopped, under the President's orders, but those already in Cuba must be dismantled, or the United States will take whatever additional action is necessary, beginning with a much more rigorous blockade of such things as Cuba's essential oil supplies, to force compliance.

If this leads to Soviet retaliation, such as a counter-blockade of Berlin, the United States is prepared to risk a major war to defend its present position in the former German capital. Accordingly, American forces, not only in Berlin and West Germany but all over the world, have been placed on emergency alert. The new policy has been defined in a private communi-

Continued on Page 19, Column 1

Associated Press Wirephoto

ANNOUNCES HIS ACTION: President Kennedy speaking to the nation last night on radio and television. He told of moves to keep offensive equipment away from Cuba.

Canada Asks Inspection of Cuba; Britain Supporting Quarantine

Diefenbaker Comments

By RAYMOND DANIELL

Special to The New York Times

OTTAWA, Oct. 22 — Prime Minister John Diefenbaker of Canada declared tonight the time had come for an impartial inspection of what is happening in Cuba by eight of the "nonaligned nations."

Interrupting debate of the Canadian economic crisis in the House of Commons, Mr. Diefenbaker described President Kennedy's speech on Cuba as "somber and challenging."

"Naturally," he said, "there has been little time to give consideration to positive action that might be taken. But I suggest that if there is a desire—and I am sure there is on the part of the U.S.S.R.—to have the facts, if a group of nations, perhaps the eight comprising the unaligned members of the 18-nation disarmament committee, were given the opportunity of making an on-site inspection of Cuba to ascertain what the facts are, a major step forward would be taken."

Meanwhile it was disclosed that Canada has barred the use of her airfields, including that

Continued on Page 21, Column 2

British Note Peril

By DREW MIDDLETON

Special to The New York Times

LONDON, Oct. 22—Qualified sources said today that approval for President Kennedy's military quarantine of Cuba could be expected from the British government.

A Foreign Office spokesman declared, "Revelation of the Soviet build-up in Cuba will come as a shock to the whole civilized world."

Official comment cannot be given until after Prime Minister Macmillan and his Cabinet have discussed the President's statement.

Initial reaction among diplomats was that the President had taken the most reasonable course to frustrate what military circles regard as evident danger to the United States: a Soviet nuclear capacity in Cuba.

The danger that war might result from a Soviet attempt to break what amounts to a military blockade of Cuba is acceptable. But one experienced airman expressed the general feeling this way: "War can come from any one of a number of causes,

Continued on Page 21, Column 1

TRAFFIC DELAYED AT BERLIN BORDER

Reds Start Intensive Check of Civilian Trucks an Hour Before Kennedy Speech

By SYDNEY GRUSON

Special to The New York Times

BONN, Oct. 22—The East German police began to slow down civilian traffic between West Berlin and West Germany late tonight.

About an hour before President Kennedy announced the United States countermeasures against the Soviet build-up in Cuba, the police started intensive examination of the papers of trucks moving into East German territory.

The connection, if any, between the two actions was not immediately clear. Similar harassment of civilian traffic has occurred periodically over the years. The immediate reaction was to consider tonight's harassment as part of the regular order of things, rather than as an advance countermeasure to the American moves against Cuba.

Nevertheless, there was deep anxiety that the Soviet Union would retaliate by causing trouble on the West's access lines to the city.

The outcome of tomorrow's meetings between Andrei A. Gromyko, the Soviet Foreign Minister, and East German Communist leaders was awaited with concern. Mr. Gromyko

Continued on Page 17, Column 3

Moscow Says U.S. Holds 'Armed Fist' Over Cuba

By SEYMOUR TOPPING

Special to The New York Times

MOSCOW, Tuesday, Oct. 23—In a broadcast before President Kennedy's speech on the missile build-up in Cuba, the Moscow radio said that the unusual activity in Washington indicated that the United States "once again was raising its armed fist over Cuba." The broadcast said there was "real hysteria" in Washington.

A Soviet reply to the United States note on Cuba that was given last night to Anatoly F. Dobrynin, the Soviet Ambassador to Washington, was expected to be delivered in 24 hours. It was expected that the reply would take the form either of a diplomatic communication or a message to President Kennedy from Premier Khrushchev.

Western observers said it appeared inevitable in view of recent Soviet statements that the reply would be a denial of any offensive Soviet intent and a charge of United States aggression against Cuba.

Veracity Questioned

The veracity of the Soviet Government was directly questioned in President Kennedy's speech, which was given after delivery of the note. The President said evidence had been obtained that Moscow was constructing offensive missile bases on Cuban territory.

The Soviet Government statement of Sept. 11, which warned the United States that an attack on Cuba would mean war, contended that the Soviet weapons supplied to Cuba were of a defensive nature.

Western observers said the crisis over Cuba would enter a critical phase when and if United States war vessels sought to halt and search a Soviet ship bound for Cuba.

A number of Soviet vessels carrying civilian goods and pos-

Continued on Page 18, Column 3

All Military Forces Mobilized by Castro

By The Associated Press.

KEY WEST, Tuesday, Oct. 23 —All of Cuba's military forces have been mobilized as a result "of the news from the United States," the Havana radio said today.

The broadcast said the order was issued by Premier Fidel Castro, who will address the nation later today.

"Our combat units rapidly placed themselves on a fighting basis," said the Havana broadcast.

"Hundreds of thousands of men were mobilized in the course of a few hours," added the broadcast, which followed by some hours President Kennedy's announcement of a naval blockade against Cuba.

During the evening, Havana appeared slow to react to President Kennedy's broadcast and

Continued on Page 20 Column 5

BIG FORCE MASSES TO BLOCKADE CUBA

Armada Is Under Orders to Open Fire if Necessary— All Troops Are Alerted

By JACK RAYMOND

Special to The New York Times

WASHINGTON, Oct. 22—American ships and planes began preparing tonight to impose a blockade of Cuba. United States forces are under orders to thwart any attempt to deliver offensive weapons to Havana.

A Defense Department spokesman said that a large force of ships and planes concentrating in the Caribbean area had instructions to use force if necessary, including sinking of ships, to carry out President Kennedy's orders for a "quarantine" of Cuba.

The Pentagon said also that United States military units throughout the world, including the garrison in Berlin and the nuclear-armed Strategic Air Command, had been placed "on alert."

Dependents of servicemen at the Guantanamo Bay Naval Base in Cuba have been evacuated, the department said.

Forces at Base Doubled

It added that the military forces there, which were previously put at 3,300 naval officers and men and several hundred Marines, have been doubled.

Air defense units in the United States, particularly radar warning stations, interceptor aircraft and ground-to-air missiles, "have been redeployed," the department spokesman said.

The orders for additional defense precautions were taken the spokesman continued, on the basis of aerial photographic evidence of long-range ballistic missile bases and the arrival of Soviet Ilyushin-28 bombers in Cuba.

The spokesman displayed some of the aerial photographs and pointed to some missiles sites that, he said, had been established only in the last 10 or 15 days.

He said some of the missile

Continued on Page 20 Column 1

PRESIDENT GRAVE

Asserts Russians Lied and Put Hemisphere in Great Danger

Text of the President's address is printed on Page 18.

By ANTHONY LEWIS

Special to The New York Times

WASHINGTON, Oct. 22 — President Kennedy imposed a naval and air "quarantine" tonight on the shipment of offensive military equipment to Cuba.

In a speech of extraordinary gravity, he told the American people that the Soviet Union, contrary to promises, was building offensive missile and bomber bases in Cuba. He said the bases could handle missiles carrying nuclear warheads up to 2,000 miles.

Thus a critical moment in the cold war was at hand tonight. The President had decided on a direct confrontation with — and challenge to — the power of the Soviet Union.

Direct Thrust at Soviet

Two aspects of the speech were notable. One was its direct thrust at the Soviet Union as the party responsible for the crisis. Mr. Kennedy treated Cuba and the Government of Premier Fidel Castro as a mere pawn in Moscow's hands and drew the issue as one with the Soviet Government.

The President, in language of unusual bluntness, accused the Soviet leaders of deliberately "false statements about their intentions in Cuba."

The other aspect of the speech particularly noted by observers here was its flat commitment by the United States to act alone against the missile threat in Cuba.

Nation Ready to Act

The President made it clear that this country would not stop short of military action to end what he called a "clandestine, reckless and provocative threat to world peace."

Mr. Kennedy said the United States was asking for an emergency meeting of the United Nations Security Council to consider a resolution for "dismantling and withdrawal of all offensive weapons in Cuba."

He said the launching of a nuclear missile from Cuba against any nation in the Western Hemisphere would be regarded as an attack by the Soviet Union against the United States. It would be met, he said, by retaliation against the Soviet Union.

He called on Premier Khrushchev to withdraw the missiles from Cuba and so "move the

Continued on Page 18, Column 1

KENNEDY CANCELS CAMPAIGN TALKS

He and Johnson Take Step to Concentrate on Crisis

By CABELL PHILLIPS

Special to The New York Times

WASHINGTON, Oct. 22—The White House announced tonight that President Kennedy and Vice President Johnson would make no further political appearances in the Congressional campaign because of the Cuban crisis.

The move by the Administration was considered evidence not only of the seriousness of the situation but also of the desire of the President to unify the country behind his blockade order and keep the issue out of partisan politics.

In this connection, the White House said the President personally informed former Republican Presidents Dwight D. Eisenhower and Herbert Hoover, as well as former Democratic President Harry S. Truman, of his decision.

And the White House announced that John J. McCloy, former disarmament adviser to the Kennedy Administration and a Republican, had been as-

Continued on Page 18, Column 7

"All the News That's Fit to Print"

The New York Times.

LATE CITY EDITION
U. S. Weather Bureau Report (Page 76) forecasts: Cloudy with chance of showers today; clear tonight. Fair, warm tomorrow. Temp. range: 80—63; yesterday: 67—58. Temp.-Hum. Index: high 60's; yesterday: 67.

VOL. CXII..No. 38,482. NEW YORK, TUESDAY, JUNE 4, 1963. TEN CENTS

POPE JOHN XXIII IS DEAD AT 81, ENDING 4½-YEAR REIGN DEVOTED TO PEACE AND CHRISTIAN UNITY

ARIZONA UPHELD OVER CALIFORNIA ON WATER RIGHTS

Supreme Court's 7-1 Ruling Caps 40-Year Fight on Use of the Colorado River

WIDE EFFECT FORESEEN

3 Justices Strongly Oppose Provision Allowing U. S. to Apportion Supplies

By WILLIAM M. BLAIR
Special to The New York Times

WASHINGTON, June 3—Arizona won in the Supreme Court today its 40-year struggle with California over how much water each state can take from the Colorado River.

The Court, voting 7 to 1, upheld a special master's recommendations on division of the water. The decision is of great economic significance to the Southwest, for the Colorado and its tributaries are the major water sources in that rapidly growing area.

The Court split, 5 to 3, however, on the majority ruling that the Secretary of the Interior had the power to apportion mainstream water among users in the lower basin states, particularly in periods of shortage.

Oppose Federal Role

The dissenters on this issue were Justices John Marshall Harlan, William O. Douglas and Potter Stewart. They sharply challenged the majority view that Congress intended a "single appointed Federal official" to have the authority to apportion mainstream waters, whether in shortage or surplus.

They found this delegation of power "extraordinary." And they argued that state law was intended to control apportionment among users within a single state and that this principle had been established by the Court in earlier water rights cases.

The majority opinion said California was entitled to 4,400,000 acre feet of water annually from the mainstream of the Colorado, Arizona 2,800,000 acre feet and Nevada 300,000 acre feet. An acre foot is the amount of water that will cover one acre to a depth of one foot—about 325,850 gallons.

The division was confined to the area's mainstream. The Court rejected California's effort to include the Colorado's tributaries, principally the Gila in Arizona, in any water allo-

Continued on Page 23, Column 1

AGENCY SHOP WINS COURT'S APPROVAL

Ruled Permissible by U.S. Law, Optional in States

By JOSEPH A. LOFTUS
Special to The New York Times

WASHINGTON, June 3—A labor contract requiring nonmembers to pay service fees to a union is permissible under Federal law, but may be prohibited by state law, the Supreme Court ruled today.

The agency shop, as this type of contract is called, was reviewed in two decisions. There was no dissent. Associate Justice Arthur J. Goldberg did not participate.

Where the state's prohibition is enforceable—in state courts or before the National Labor Relations Board—was a question reserved for later decision. That point was set for argument in the next term.

In two other labor decisions, the Court reversed damage verdicts won by individuals against unions in the state courts of Texas and Ohio. The vote in each was 6 to 2. Justices William O. Douglas and Tom C. Clark dissented. Justice Goldberg did not participate.

The central point in all four cases was the extent of state jurisdiction in the field of labor-management relations. Under the Court's doctrine of Federal pre-emption, the states have no jurisdiction except where Congress has specifically conceded it, or where the N.L.R.B. can afford no remedy, or where there is an overriding state in-

Continued on Page 24, Column 5

Douglas Upbraids Black From Bench

Special to The New York Times

WASHINGTON, June 3—Justice William O. Douglas made an unusually sharp attack today on a major opinion by his colleague on the Supreme Court, Hugo L. Black.

The tenor of Justice Douglas's extemporaneous remarks from the bench startled those in the courtroom. His strong language was the more surprising because the two men have served together for 24 years and have been regarded as extremely close in judicial philosophy.

Justice Douglas's dissent was in the Colorado River water case. Justice Black wrote the opinion of the court deciding generally against California's claims and in favor of Arizona's.

From the bench Justice

Continued on Page 22, Column 3

PRESIDENT DELAYS RIGHTS MESSAGE

Plans Conferences in Fight on Public Discrimination —G.O.P. Offers a Bill

By E. W. KENWORTHY
Special to The New York Times

WASHINGTON, June 3—President Kennedy decided tonight to delay for a week his civil rights message to Congress proposing legislation to outlaw discrimination in public accommodations.

He had hoped to get new legislative proposals to Congress tomorrow. He leaves on Wednesday for a Western trip and will stay out of Washington the rest of the week.

One factor in tonight's decision was that last-minute tinkering with the draft bills and the accompanying Presidential message was still going on. It was deemed wise not to rush so important a matter.

The President believed also that it would help the legislation to go ahead first with scheduled conferences. He will meet tomorrow, for example, with business executives with large holdings in the South. His brother, Attorney General Robert F. Kennedy, will meet other groups.

Democrats Briefed

The week will also be used to try to create a favorable climate at the Capitol. Democratic Congressional leaders, who were briefed on civil rights by the President today, will discuss the legislation with others in both parties.

The decision to delay the message was especially difficult for the President because 24 House Republicans introduced today their own legislation to bar racial discrimination in public accommodations. They were plainly intent on beating the Administration in offering a measure.

One of two main proposals in the Administration's legislation would deal with racial discrimi-

Continued on Page 27, Column 1

PUPIL TRANSFERS TO DIVIDE RACES VOIDED BY COURT

Supreme Bench Says Plan in Two Tennessee Areas Slows Desegregation

By ANTHONY LEWIS
Special to The New York Times

WASHINGTON, June 3—The Supreme Court held unconstitutional today a school desegregation plan that allows pupils to transfer out of schools where their race is in the minority.

Justice Tom C. Clark said that the plan was invalid because it based transfers "solely on racial factors" and led to "perpetuation of segregation." He spoke for a unanimous Court.

The transfer plan was at issue in cases from Knoxville, Tenn., and from Davidson County, adjoining Nashville. Similar provisions are in use in Memphis and in some Virginia communities.

Five other Southern states have statutes saying that no child may be compelled to attend a school where he would be in a racial minority. They are Alabama, Arkansas, Florida, Louisiana and North Carolina.

Broad Impact Likely

Thus today's decision can be expected to have a major impact on the South. It will remove the legal basis for a device widely used to cushion the effect of school desegregation.

In practice, the Tennessee provisions — and those in other areas — worked as follows:

School boards, in response to the Supreme Court's desegregation decision, abolished the former separate school maps for whites and Negroes. New school districts were drawn for a single, nonracial system.

But any white student who thereupon found himself in the district of "a school previously serving colored students" could automatically transfer to another school. So could a Negro zoned into a school formerly serving whites.

Transfers Made Easy

The plan also, significantly, permitted automatic transfers "when a student would otherwise be required to attend a school where the majority of students of that school or in his or her grade are of a different race."

A student in such a minority situation had only to ask and he would be transferred. Others who wanted to switch schools had to persuade the school board there was "good cause."

The provision was generally regarded as a way of assuring white families that their children would not be placed in a mostly Negro school. It was defended as necessary to reduce opposition to desegregation.

Negroes, on the other hand, said the transfer provision had made true integration of the schools impossible. They especially criticized the fact that there was no automatic right of a pupil to transfer from a school entirely or mostly of his

Continued on Page 25, Column 3

DC-7 With 101 Lost in Alaska; 95 Military Men and Kin Aboard

Vast Air-Sea Hunt Pressed for Chartered Craft After Radio Contact Breaks Off

By The Associated Press

JUNEAU, Alaska, June 3—A military-chartered airliner carrying 101 persons—men, women and children — vanished off southeastern Alaska today under circumstances suggesting sudden disaster.

The Northwest Airlines DC-7, a piston-engined aircraft, last radioed 30 to 40 miles at sea off Prince of Wales Island, requesting a change of altitude from 14,000 to 18,000 feet. Air traffic men trying to reply minutes later got no answer.

The last confirmed message from the plane was at 10:06 A.M., about two and a half hours after it had left McChord Air Force Base, Wash., with 95 military passengers, including dependents, and a crew of six.

An intensive search by planes and vessels was made in deteriorating weather.

The Coast Guard said later tonight that a Canadian plane had reported sighting what appeared to be wreckage near

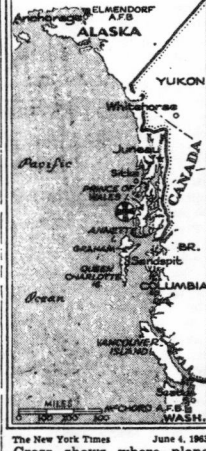

The New York Times June 4, 1963
Cross shows where plane last reported its position.

Graham Island, in northern British Columbia.

The only detailed information concerning the sighting came

Continued on Page 13, Column 1

Army May Release Ft. Tilden for Park

By CHARLES G. BENNETT

There is a "very, very good possibility" that the Army might make Fort Tilden available to the city for the Breezy Point park development, Mayor Wagner said yesterday.

"We learned last week," the Mayor said at an impromptu press conference, "that there is a good possibility that the Army might move its installations and Nike bases from there in the near future, and then we can start negotiations."

An Army spokesman said in Washington last night that the Army had been reviewing the situation but had not made any decision.

Fort Tilden is on 317 acres next to the 236-acre Jacob Riis Park. The city proposes ultimately to have in all 1,362

Continued on Page 43, Column 5

HAITIAN CONTACTS RESUMED BY U. S.

Duvalier Regime Regarded as Firmly in Power Even if Not Constitutional

By TAD SZULC
Special to The New York Times

WASHINGTON, June 3—The United States resumed "normal diplomatic business" with Haiti today after nearly three weeks of a suspension of contacts intended to underline Washington's disapproval of President François Duvalier.

The decision to return to normal relations and to remove a Navy task force from the vicinity of Haiti appeared to reverse last month's undisguised policy efforts aimed at Dr. Duvalier's removal.

At the peak of the Haiti crisis, the Kennedy Administration is known to have convinced itself that President Duvalier's regime was on the brink of collapse because of mounting United States pressures.

It was then expected that Dr. Duvalier would voluntarily give up office and leave Haiti on May 15. The United States regarded that date as the end of his legal term.

Marine Landing Envisaged

Accordingly, the Administration secretly prepared with at least three Latin-American governments a plan that might have involved a landing in Haiti by United States marines, it has been disclosed. An inter-American "police action" in support of a new regime in Haiti was also envisaged.

The details of this planned operation were disclosed by diplomats who participated in its preparation last month.

The operation was abandoned on May 15, however, after an all-night vigil here by officials of the Organization of American States. It then became clear that Dr. Duvalier did not intend to leave Haiti.

The State Department later that day instructed Ambassador Raymond L. Thurston in Port-au-Prince to suspend immediately his contacts with the Haitian Government. The move was made secretly and the Administration confirmed it indirectly only after it was published in press dispatches from Haiti.

Regime Still Held Illegal

Today, Lincoln White, the State Department spokesman, announced that the United States chargé d'affaires in Port-au-Prince, Glion Curtis Jr., was being instructed "to resume normal diplomatic business with the Government of Haiti."

Administration officials insisted that the lifting of the short-lived diplomatic sanctions did not imply any change in the United States view that the Duvalier regime was unconstitutional. It was made clear, however, that the United States had concluded that the Haitian Government was firmly in power.

Therefore, officials said, a re-

Continued on Page 6, Column 3

POST AWAITS VOTE

Archbishop of Milan a Possible Choice as New Pontiff

By PAUL HOFMANN
Special to The New York Times

ROME, June 3—Amid the drama of Pope John XXIII's final hours, Romans speculated whether his successor would be an Italian or a "foreigner."

At the same time, ecclesiastics and laymen debated whether the next Pontiff would show the conciliatory, progressive attitude of Pope John or lead the Roman Catholic Church back to a more conservative position.

An Italian prince of the church, Giovanni Battista Cardinal Montini, 65-year-old Archbishop of Milan, was widely mentioned as the leading candidate.

Cardinal Montini is regarded as a prominent representative of the "progressive" wing of the world episcopacy, which revealed its strength with the manifest encouragement of Pope John during the first session of the Ecumenical Council in the Vatican last autumn.

A Close Aide to Pius XII

As monsignor, the present Cardinal Montini was for many years a close aide to the late Pope Pius XII, Pope John's predecessor, in the Vatican Secretariat of State. The slim, ascetic-looking churchman, who is credited with a prodigious capacity for hard work, became Archbishop of Milan, one of the largest Catholic dioceses in the world, in 1954, but still was not a Cardinal when Pope Pius XII died in 1958.

The Archbishop of Milan then already had such a reputation that some commentators suggested that the Cardinals would depart from a 600-year-old tradition and elect a prelate who was not one of their number.

Instead the Cardinals elevated one of their number, Angelo Giuseppe Cardinal Roncalli, Patriarch of Venice, as Pope John XXIII he conferred on Archbishop Montini the red hat of Cardinal in his first consistory in December, 1958. Cardinal Montini was close to Pope John throughout his pontificate and if he is elected as his successor he is expected to continue his policies.

Cardinals Take Over Rule

Soon after Pope John died tonight, the Cardinals present in the Vatican started taking over the interim government of the church on behalf of the 82 members of the Sacred College of Cardinals. The Cardinals will rule jointly until their vote in conclave results in the election of the new Pope.

Prominent among conservative Italian Cardinals thought to be of papal timber is Giuseppe Cardinal Siri, Archbishop of Genoa. He is 57 years old.

The leader of the conservative wing at the Ecumenical Council, Alfredo Cardinal Ottaviani, a 72-year-old Vatican theologian and guardian of

Continued on Page 18, Column 6

Africans Complain Of Bias in Moscow

By SEYMOUR TOPPING
Special to The New York Times

MOSCOW, June 3—A sharp controversy has arisen between Soviet authorities and African students here who have complained of discrimination fostered by a Moscow newspaper article.

The article, published by Komsomolskaya Pravda, the newspaper of the Communist Youth League, purported to tell the experiences of a Russian girl who was sold into a harem by a Moslem student she had married.

African students here interpreted the article as a warning to Russian girls against association with them. It was published on Oct. 27 after a number of Africans had complained of being attacked by Russians because they had appeared publicly in the company

Continued on Page 5, Column 1

POPE JOHN XXIII
Associated Press

Washington Mourns Loss Of Great Force for Peace

By M. S. HANDLER
Special to The New York Times

WASHINGTON, June 3—President Kennedy paid high tribute today to the statesmanship and moral leadership of Pope John XXIII. The President said of the Pontiff: "His compassion and kindly strength have bequeathed humanity a new legacy of purpose and courage for the future."

Mr. Kennedy led official Washington in mourning the passing of Pope John as a great loss to mankind. Members of both houses of Congress and churchmen of various faiths joined in expressing the belief that the Pontiff had made an immense contribution to the reconciliation of all Christian faiths, to the reconciliation of his church with Judaism, and to the preservation of peace.

President Kennedy said the Pope had "brought compassion and understanding drawn from wide experience to the most divisive problems of a tumultuous age."

Statement by President

The President's statement said:

"The highest work of any man is to protect and carry on the deepest spiritual heritage of the race. To Pope John was given the almost unique gift of enriching and enlarging that tradition. Armed with the humility and calm which surrounded his earliest days, he brought compassion and understanding drawn from wide experience to the most divisive problems of a tumultuous age. He was the chosen leader of world Catholicism, but his concern for the human spirit transcended all boundaries of belief or geography.

"The ennobling precepts of his encyclicals and his actions drew on the accumulated wisdom of an ancient faith for guidance in the most complex and troublesome problems of the modern age. To him the divine spark which unites men would ultimately prove more enduring than the forces which divide. His wisdom, compassion and kindly strength have bequeathed humanity a new legacy of purpose and courage for the future."

The reference to Pope John's encyclicals marked the second time Mr. Kennedy had expressed such praise. At Boston College

Continued on Page 21, Column 7

WAGNER ORDERS FLAGS LOWERED

Leads City in Mourning and Picks 2 Representatives to Attend Pope's Funeral

Mayor Wagner yesterday ordered flags on all city buildings flown at half-staff until the burial of Pope John. The Mayor led the city in mourning the Pope.

"Pope John XXIII symbolized faith, goodness, courage and compassion," Mayor Wagner said, adding, "He appealed always to the best in the human heart and all humanity is uplifted by the noble example which he set."

Mayor Wagner also designated Commissioner of Public Events Richard C. Patterson Jr. and Thomas J. Deegan, chairman of the World's Fair executive committee, as official city representatives at the Pope's funeral.

Both are in Rome on other business.

Washington will not accord the Pope the flag tribute he will receive in New York. The State Department explained that flags in Washington are

Continued on Page 18, Column 4

St. Peter's Throng Silenced by Grief

Special to The New York Times

ROME, June 3—A vast throng in the piazza in front of St. Peter's Basilica heard the news of the death of Pope John this evening in sad and resigned silence.

Many knelt in quiet prayer and crossed themselves as other hundreds surged toward the bronze doors leading into Vatican City to watch as one of the two portals was swung shut as a traditional sign that the Pope was dead.

The Pope's death came only minutes after a choral offering brought to an end a mass celebrated for the Pontiff on the steps of the Basilica by Luigi Cardinal Traglia, pro-vicar of the Diocese of Rome.

More than 35,000 Romans, visitors, pilgrims, nuns and clergymen gathered to hear the mass, which started at 7 P.M. By the time the last sacred

Continued on Page 21, Column 2

NEWS INDEX

A LIBERAL PONTIFF

Church Council and Encyclical on Amity Marked Tenure

By ARNALDO CORTESI
Special to The New York Times

ROME, June 3 — Pope John XXIII, champion of world peace and a tireless fighter for the union of all Christian churches, died in the Vatican tonight while Cardinals and other prelates and several of his relatives prayed around his sickbed. He was 81 years old.

John XXIII was the 261st Pope to sit on the throne that was first occupied by the Apostle Peter.

In the four years, seven months and six days of his reign he conquered the hearts of people throughout the world. Few other Popes before him were so universally admired.

The Pope's death came at 7:49 P.M. (2:49 P.M. Eastern daylight time.)

After a long struggle the Pope developed peritonitis, brought on by a stomach tumor. The tumor was discovered last November.

Doctors Gave Up Hope

His doctors had given up hope at the onset of the peritonitis, an inflammation of the lining of the abdominal cavity. This was given as the cause of his death.

Much of the intervening period was passed in a state of coma or semicoma. The Pope was lucid most of yesterday, however, but in great pain, which he bore with remarkable fortitude. Early yesterday afternoon he suffered a "new crisis."

Before entering his last state of coma, he repeatedly said in Latin: "Into Thy hands, O Lord, I commit my soul."

The Pope had dedicated much of his pontificate to promoting Christian unity and the unity of all men as brothers with a common God.

Pope's Last Words

In his last words, addressed to the assembled Cardinals and prelates around his sickbed, the Pope said:

"Ut unum sint." They are Latin words meaning "That they may be one."

The words were originally spoken by Jesus after the Last Supper.

The night of May 25 the Pope suffered a hemorrhage that brought him close to death. A series of blood transfusions saved his life. He had been improving when peritonitis developed.

John XXIII was elected Pope Oct. 28, 1958. He was born in the village of Sotto il Monte in northern Italy Nov. 25, 1881. He was 81 years, six months and nine days old at his death.

Pope John passed his last days in his bedroom on the top floor of the Vatican Palace. A small crowd of ecclesiastics and laymen had congregated there when they were told that the Pope was near death.

Those at Bedside

Those around the bedside included Eugene Cardinal Tisserant, the bearded French dean of the Sacred College; Benedetto Cardinal Aloisi Masella, who as Cardinal Camerlengo, or Chamberlain, heads the interim administration of the Roman Catholic Church; the Pope's three brothers—Giuseppe, Alfredo and Zaverio Roncalli—and his widowed sister, Assunta; three nephews, several members of the Papal household, such as his sacristan, his confessor and his Master of the Chamber.

A larger crowd, including ambassadors and ministers, waited in an adjacent room.

Swiss guards kept all others out of the Papal apartment.

About 30 minutes before the Pope died it became clear from his labored breathing and his falling pulse rate that he was near death. The Pope's personal physician, Prof. Antonio Gasbarrini, warned Cardinal Aloisi Masella that the Pope had not long to live.

Mass for the Pope was said at an altar in an adjoining room

Continued on Page 18, Column 1

"All the News That's Fit to Print"

The New York Times.

LATE CITY EDITION
U.S. Weather Bureau Report (Page 50) forecasts: Sunny and cool today; clear tonight. Sunny and warmer tomorrow.
Temp. range: 74—55; yesterday: 70—55.
Temp.-Hum. Index: 70; yesterday: 69.

VOL. CXII . . . No. 38,500. | NEW YORK, SATURDAY, JUNE 22, 1963. | TEN CENTS

CARDINAL MONTINI ELECTED POPE; LIBERAL, 65, WILL REIGN AS PAUL VI; LIKELY TO CONTINUE JOHN'S WORK

United Press International Radiophoto

POPE PAUL VI in his first public appearance gives his blessing to the crowd that had gathered outside St. Peter's Basilica. Holding missal is Msgr. Salvatore Capoferri.

5TH VOTE DECISIVE

New Pontiff Gives His Blessing to Crowd—Coronation June 30

By ARNALDO CORTESI
Special to The New York Times

ROME, June 21 — Giovanni Battista Cardinal Montini, 65-year-old Archbishop of Milan, was elected Supreme Pontiff of the Roman Catholic Church today. He will reign as Pope Paul VI.

The man who had been described as the most likely prince of the church to succeed Pope John XXIII manifested his intention of continuing his predecessor's policies by confirming Amleto Giuseppi Cardinal Cicognani as Apostolic Secretary of State. Cardinal Cicognani held the post under John XXIII.

Pope Paul was elected on the fifth ballot conducted in the Sacred College of Cardinals. He and 79 other Cardinals from 29 nations — both figures were records — went into conclave Wednesday evening.

The news that the more than 500,000,000 Roman Catholics in the world had a new spiritual leader was given at 11:22 A.M. by a white puff of smoke from a stovepipe on the roof of the Sistine Chapel in Vatican City.

262d on Papal Throne

The new Pope, a native of the Lombardy region, who was 65 last Sept. 26, will be, according to Catholic tradition, the 262d occupant of the throne of St. Peter.

The coronation of Paul VI will take place in St. Peter's Basilica early in the morning of June 30, the day President Kennedy is to arrive in Rome during his 10-day tour of Europe. In the Western church the day is the Feast of St. Paul, the apostle who was the first in the church to bear the name. The last Pope to use it, Paul V, a Borghese, died in 1621.

An hour after his election, Pope Paul appeared on a balcony of St. Peter's Basilica to impart an apostolic benediction to a huge crowd. There were emotional scenes as most people dropped to their knees to receive the blessing. Some women wept and others held infants toward the Pope.

Acceptance at 11:15 A.M.

The conclave that elected Pope Paul lasted 41 hours. It ranks as the sixth shortest in the last four centuries. In the last century there have been only two that were shorter, the one that elected Pius XII in 1939, which lasted 30 hours, and the one that elected Leo XIII in 1878, which lasted 36 hours. Pope John was elected in 1958 on the 11th ballot on the third day.

Paul VI assumed all papal prerogatives and rights at 11:15 A.M. (6:15 A.M., Eastern daylight time) when, after protesting that he felt unworthy, he gave his acceptance to the dean of the Sacred College, Eugène Cardinal Tisserant. The coronation is a formality and the reign

Continued on Page 2, Column 1

Rome Believes New Pope Will Press for Reforms

Clear-cut Decision Seen

By PAUL HOFMANN
Special to The New York Times

ROME, June 21 — Pope Paul VI began his pontificate today amid general forecasts that it would bring an energetic continuation of the progressive course charted by Pope John XXIII.

The consensus in Rome was that the conclave, by elevating the 65-year-old Archbishop of Milan to the papacy, had made a clear decision for a liberal pontificate—and one hopefully expected to last a long time.

First responses from world centers showed international agreement with this evaluation.

The general belief here was that Pope Paul had been elected with the understanding that he would soon reopen the church's Ecumenical Council in the Vatican, suspended by the death of his predecessor. Ecclesiastics who had served in the past with the new Pontiff predicted that he would press for enactment

Continued on Page 3, Column 5

Choice Widely Hailed

By GEORGE DUGAN

The election of Giovanni Battista Cardinal Montini to succeed Pope John XXIII has met with worldwide acclaim.

Both Protestant and Jewish leaders said yesterday that the election of Pope Paul VI showed that the reform and renewal so close to the heart of Pope John would be emphasized in the days to come.

The new Pope, who was given the red hat of a cardinal by his predecessor, was deeply involved in the Ecumenical Council, which had been scheduled to reconvene on Sept. 8.

The election of Pope Paul aroused great interest in Washington, which is curious about the political effects the choice of a liberal will have on the European left. President Kennedy, who will visit the new Pope July 2, sent the Pontiff his "heartiest congratulations."

J. Irwin Miller, president of

Continued on Page 3, Column 3

18 UNION CHIEFS ACT TO END BIAS IN CONSTRUCTION

Bid Locals Admit Qualified Negroes as Apprentices and as Members

PROGRAM NOT BINDING

N.A.A.C.P. Aide Says Plan Sounds Good, but Notes It Must Be Implemented

Special to The New York Times

WASHINGTON, June 21—The presidents of the 18 building trades unions adopted today a program to eliminate racial discrimination in apprenticeship, union membership and assignment to job openings.

At the same time, they warned that they would fight any effort by the Government to determine qualifications necessary for admission into the industry and into union membership.

The building trades unions have been the most criticized segment of the labor movement on discrimination. The National Association for the Advancement of Colored People has long contended that most building trades locals practice systematic exclusion of Negroes. Recently, the association picketed construction projects in New York and Philadelphia.

Government Pressure

This activity and increased pressure on them by the Government to eliminate discriminatory practices prompted the building trades presidents to discuss the situation. Today's statement, adopted unanimously, was the result.

The union leaders said they recognized the Government's interest and its duty to correct economic injustice and pledged their "good faith to work toward the goal."

The program consists of the following points:

¶Local unions are urged to accept any applicant for membership who meets the required qualifications regardless of his race, creed, color or national origin.

¶If a local operates an exclusive hiring hall or a work referral system, applicants for employment are to be referred to work without discrimination as to race, creed, color or national origin.

¶Locals shall also accept and refer applicants for apprenticeship without discrimination.

Adoption of the statement does not automatically bind the local unions to abide by it.

A spokesman for the Building

Continued on Page 8, Column 1

Lawyers Promise Kennedy Aid in Easing Race Unrest

Leaders of Bar Agree to Form Working Group Across Nation—President to See Negro Officials Today

By MARJORIE HUNTER
Special to The New York Times

WASHINGTON, June 21—Many of the nation's leading lawyers promised President Kennedy at a conference today that they would help open the lines of communication between the races. But they were told by a participant at the conference that they faced "a long hot summer."

At a meeting in the White House, the lawyers acceded to a Presidential request that they set up a committee that would try to ease racial tensions and provide national and local leadership.

Today's meeting was one in a series that the President has held in recent weeks with religious leaders, businessmen, Governors and labor leaders. So far, the President has conferred with several thousand persons on civil-rights matters.

Heading the lawyers' racial communications committee will be Harrison Tweed of New York and Bernard G. Segal of Philadelphia. All of the 244 lawyers attending today's meeting were invited to serve on the committee.

Another committee, also dealing with racial communications, will be established by the American Bar Association. This was announced during the White House meeting by Sylvester C. Smith Jr. of Newark, N. J., the association's president.

Joining the President in meeting the lawyers in the East Room were Vice President Johnson and Attorney General Robert F. Kennedy. Of the lawyers present, 66 were from Southern states. There were 23

Continued on Page 8, Column 3

Wagner to Help Negroes Get More Building Jobs

By CHARLES G. BENNETT

Mayor Wagner said yesterday that he would appoint "in a day or two" a panel of three qualified persons to induce construction unions to take in more Negroes. The panel will be given a week to examine employment records, talk with all groups concerned and make recommendations.

At the same time the Mayor said he had been assured by Peter Brennan, president of the Building Trades and Construction Council, that "technically qualified" members of minority groups would be put to work "right away" if job opportunities existed.

The Mayor spoke at a news conference in City Hall a few hours after his return from two weeks in Hawaii and Tokyo. Beforehand he had conferred at Gracie Mansion with Mr. Brennan and with Harry Van Arsdale Jr., president of the Central Labor Council.

Asks Special Session

Mr. Wagner dashed from the City Hall news interview back to Idlewild Airport, where he had landed early in the morning, to fly to Lake Placid, N.Y., to attend the New York State Conference of Mayors.

At the Lake Placid conference last night, Mayor Wagner called on Mayors throughout the state to join him in a request to Governor Rockefeller and the legislative leaders to summon a special session to deal with racial discrimination.

New state laws, Mr. Wagner proposed, should include financial aid to municipalities to speed desegregation in jobs, housing, education and other fields.

At City Hall the Mayor said of Mr. Brennan's promise to bring more Negroes into construction jobs as fast as possible:

"During the week the panel is preparing its recommendations, my office staff will be

Continued on Page 9, Column 2

MAYOR TO OPPOSE RACE BY DE SAPIO

Indicates He May Campaign in 'Village' in an Effort to Block Comeback Drive

Mayor Wagner made it clear yesterday that he would actively oppose Carmine G. De Sapio's attempted political comeback.

The Mayor was asked at a wide-ranging City Hall news conference about Mr. De Sapio's announcement Wednesday that he would be a candidate for the Democratic leadership of the First Assembly District South. This Greenwich Village area was the base of his former statewide political power.

"This is a free country," the Mayor replied. Then he added grimly, "My position on Mr. De Sapio has not changed."

Pressed as to whether he would actually go into Greenwich Village to oppose a De Sapio comeback, Mr. Wagner said a Mayor did not generally have time to go into the districts in district campaigns. But he conceded that he had done so, and indicated he might do so again.

He was asked, "No one should expect any encouragement from you for Mr. De Sapio?"

"That is the understatement of the year," the Mayor shot back.

Then the Mayor said: "I'll wait until the campaign begins

Continued on Page 24, Column 3

JUDICIAL INQUIRY ON PROFUMO SET; LABOR ASSAILS IT

Macmillan Announces Study of Security Aspects, but Foes Call It 'Cover-Up'

By SYDNEY GRUSON
Special to The New York Times

LONDON, June 21 — Prime Minister Macmillan announced today that a judicial inquiry would be held into the security aspects of the Profumo scandal. The form of the inquiry was immediately criticized by the Opposition Labor party as a "cover-up."

Mr. Macmillan told the House of Commons that Lord Denning, as Master of the Rolls, the third-highest judicial official in Britain, would conduct the inquiry. The Prime Minister also gravely took note of continuing rumors about the involvement of "all sorts of people" in the affair.

Asked by Harold Wilson, Labor's leader, whether he was satisfied that nothing more remained to be disclosed, Mr. Macmillan replied:

"I know of no things which I have not told the House, but I have heard these terrible things being said now of all sorts of people which, if allowed to go on, will destroy not only one side of the House of Commons but the other side of the House of Commons."

Chamber Is Crowded

To a chamber unusually crowded for a Friday session, Mr. Macmillan said that the rumors "affect the honor and integrity of public life" in Britain "and if they were true such a situation might point to a security risk."

Pressing for the appointment of a select committee of Members of Parliament to conduct the inquiry, Mr. Wilson said that Lord Denning would have no power to compel the attendance of witnesses or compel proof.

"Is the Prime Minister aware that some of the evidence required will be collected from some of the most unmitigated liars in this country?" Mr. Wilson asked.

He also referred to the rumors. In a judicial inquiry, he said, they "cannot be dissipated and the men concerned enabled to clear their names, as they have every right to do."

Blackmail Linked to Case

The rumors are boundless on Fleet Street, the home of the British press, and in Westminster, the home of Parliament. Not even the royal family has escaped.

One of the rumors has linked blackmail to the case of Dr. Stephen Ward, 50-year-old society osteopath. Dr. Ward is in custody on charges of living off the earnings of prostitution.

He introduced Christine Keeler, 21-year-old self-styled model, to John Profumo when Mr. Profumo was Secretary of State for War and to Capt. Yevgeni E. Ivanov, a Soviet deputy naval attaché until his recall last December. Miss Keeler had simultaneous affairs with the two men.

Another rumor involves the identity of a man said to be

Continued on Page 7, Column 1

FRENCH NAVY ENDS NATO ATLANTIC TIE

Paris Announces Resuming of Unrestrained Control of Virtually Whole Fleet

By DREW MIDDLETON
Special to The New York Times

PARIS, June 21—France announced today that she would resume unrestrained control of virtually the whole of the nation's naval fighting force.

A curt bulletin issued by the semiofficial French Press Agency said that "the French Government has decided to withdraw from the NATO Fleet in the North Atlantic." The bulletin cited official sources.

The Government's decision was described here as a logical consequence of France's action in 1959. In that year she withdrew her Mediterranean fleet from the alliance's control.

Effect of New Move

Earlier this year the squadrons of that fleet were transferred from the Mediterranean base of Toulon to the North Atlantic base of Brest in Brittany.

As a consequence of today's announcement, the bulk of the powerful French forces hitherto earmarked for training and planning under the ultimate command of the Supreme Allied Commander Atlantic have now been withdrawn.

[In Washington officials were distressed by the French action. The Administration was embarrassed by its timing on the eve of President Kennedy's departure for Europe.]

Allied diplomats almost universally deplored the psychological shock that the action

Continued on Page 20, Column 5

World Labor Parley Bars South African

Special to The New York Times

GENEVA, June 21 — United States Government and American worker delegates voted today for the expulsion of a South African from the International Labor Organization conference.

The credentials of the South African, a worker delegate, were rejected by a vote of 135 to 3, with 57 abstentions. His credentials had been issued by his Government.

The member states of the 108-nation organization, a United Nations specialized agency, are represented by two government delegates, a representative of employer groups and a trade unionist. Each has separate voting rights. The worker repre-

Continued on Page 4, Column 5

HOUSE UNIT VOTES DEFENSE FUND CUT

Reduction of 1.9 Billion Is Protested by McNamara

By JACK RAYMOND
Special to The New York Times

WASHINGTON, June 21 — The House Appropriations Committee approved a $47,092,209,000 defense fund measure today, with only relatively small changes in the Administration's original request.

But even these changes drew an immediate protest from Secretary of Defense Robert S. McNamara. He said the cuts in airplane procurement money "would deny us necessary tactical support for our combat-ready Army divisions."

He charged also that other cuts would force a reduction in military personnel by some 60,000 men.

President Kennedy last January requested $49,014,237,000 in defense appropriations for the fiscal year 1964, beginning July 1. The committee cut the total by $1,922,028,000.

The committee noted that more than $500,000,000 of the cut represented bookkeeping shifts.

"The accompanying bill," the committee said in its report, based on four months of closed hearings, "will support programs which will promote the security of the United States and assure the continuation of the policy of military supremacy."

According to the report, the bill would provide armed forces totaling 2,695,000 officers and

Continued on Page 20, Column 2

TAX DISCLOSURE AROUSES OTTAWA

Minister Admits Plan Was Known to 3 Businessmen

By HOMER BIGART
Special to The New York Times

OTTAWA, June 21—Walter L. Gordon, the harassed Minister of Finance in the minority Liberal Government, gave fresh ammunition to his critics in Parliament today.

He admitted that the three Toronto businessmen who helped write his budget knew in advance of the withdrawal Wednesday of a controversial tax proposal. The tax had been aimed at halting the take-over of Canadian companies by foreigners.

The admission brought astonished gasps from Opposition benches in the House of Commons. Mr. Gordon had told the House yesterday that only Prime Minister Lester B. Pearson and the Cabinet knew of his decision to withdraw the tax.

The proposal would have placed a 30 per cent tax on the seller of a large block of shares in a Canadian company to a foreigner. Its withdrawal was announced while the stock markets of Canada were still open, and caused frenzied speculation. Members of the Opposition have demanded an investigation to determine whether the leakage of budget secrets permitted "insiders" to make windfall profits on the markets.

Mr. Gordon had been under fire all week for employing three financial experts from Toronto, two of whom had re-

Continued on Page 14, Column 7

Brezhnev Advances As Khrushchev Heir

By SEYMOUR TOPPING
Special to The New York Times

MOSCOW, June 21—Leonid I. Brezhnev, a member of the ruling Presidium of the Soviet Communist Party, emerged tonight after plenary meetings of the Central Committee as a likely political heir of Premier Khrushchev.

Mr. Brezhnev, who is 57 years old and a protégé of Mr. Khrushchev, has been appointed to the Secretariat of the Central Committee. The Secretariat is the chief executive body of the party.

Western analysts note that Mr. Brezhnev now holds an array of party and Government positions that make it appear that he is being groomed to assume the roles of Frol R.

Continued on Page 5, Column 3

STATE DEMOCRATS MAY SHIFT POWER

Change in Rules Proposed to Move Control Upstate

By RICHARD P. HUNT

State Democratic leaders are considering a reorganization plan that would for the first time give upstate Democrats a major, if not dominant, role in party affairs.

The plan, which is contained in a proposed set of rules of the state committee, implies that the traditional control of the party machinery by New York City Democrats will be limited or ended.

The rules have been proposed after a year of study by a nine-member committee appointed by William H. McKeon, the Democratic state chairman. They will be submitted for ratification at a state committee meeting in Albany on Tuesday.

The most important change proposed is the creation of a 38-member executive committee, which would be empowered to carry on the party's business in behalf of the full 300-member state committee.

Democrats from the 57 coun-

Continued on Page 24, Column 5

NEWS INDEX

The New York Times

PROMISES ACTION: Mayor Wagner at City Hall news conference where he announced plans to eliminate racial discrimination in the city's construction-industry unions.

"All the News That's Fit to Print"

The New York Times.

LATE CITY EDITION
U. S. Weather Bureau Report (Page 58) forecasts: Cloudy with scattered showers today; partly cloudy tonight and tomorrow.
Temp. range: 77—62; yesterday: 81—61.
Temp.-Hum. Index: 70 to 75; yesterday: 72.

VOL. CXII .. No. 38,568. NEW YORK, THURSDAY, AUGUST 29, 1963. TEN CENTS

200,000 MARCH FOR CIVIL RIGHTS IN ORDERLY WASHINGTON RALLY; PRESIDENT SEES GAIN FOR NEGRO

KENNEDY SIGNS BILL AVERTING A RAIL STRIKE

PRECEDENT IS SET

Arbitration Imposed by Congress—Vote in House 286-66

Text of Kennedy's statement will be found on Page 13.

By JOHN D. POMFRET
Special to The New York Times

WASHINGTON, Aug. 28 — Congress passed today a bill that prevented a national railroad strike scheduled for midnight. President Kennedy signed it immediately.

The House completed the Congressional action. It adopted by a standing vote of 286 to 66 the same joint resolution passed yesterday by the Senate. The measure provides for arbitration of the two principal issues in the railroad work rules dispute and bars a strike for 180 days.

The action was without Federal precedent. Never before in the history of peacetime labor relations has Congress imposed arbitration in a labor-management dispute.

The failure of the railroads and the five train operating unions to resolve their dispute, and the Congressional action this made necessary, is considered by many to represent a major failure for the collective bargaining system.

Many Are Reluctant

Even many Congressmen who voted for the measure, convinced that the economic consequences of a national railroad strike made action to head it off essential, did so with great reluctance. They said they feared that their action might set a precedent detrimental to collective bargaining.

An arbitration board was created by Congress to consider the two key issues. These are whether diesel locomotive firemen are necessary in freight and yard service and the size of train-service crews.

Congress ordered negotiations on the remaining issues on the theory that with the two main issues disposed of, the presumably less important matters could be settled by traditional collective bargaining.

But some well-informed Government sources do not believe the remaining issues will be

Continued on Page 13, Column 1

LODI KILLER SLAIN; 2D MAN GIVES UP

Ex-Convict Is Shot 7 Times in a Midtown Hotel

One of the killers of two New Jersey policemen was shot to death early yesterday by New York detectives during a violent struggle in his midtown hotel room. Sixteen hours later, the second man wanted in the slayings quietly surrendered.

The slain killer, 25-year-old Frank Falco, was asleep in his underwear when the police, using a passkey, entered his room at the Manhattan Hotel, Eighth Avenue and 44th Street. Although awakened with a revolver pressed to his throat, he fought desperately before being killed by seven bullets. He died snarling at the police and cursing them.

Thomas (Rabbi Tom) Trantino, 27, the second man, walked into the East 22d Street station house at 9:10 P.M., accompanied by a lawyer. He was neatly dressed and clean-shaven.

The men, both ex-convicts, had been the object of a grim police hunt since Detective Sgt. Peter Voto and Gary Tedesco, a police appointee, were gunned down early Monday morning in the Angel Lounge on Route 46 in Lodi, N. J. Mr. Tedesco was to have officially joined the Lodi force today.

A tip led the New York detectives to the hotel, where Falco had checked in at 8 P.M. Tuesday under the name of J. Rello of Newport, R. I.

Lieut. Thomas Quinn, a 53-year-old police veteran with 16 citations for bravery, entered Falco's 23d-floor room first, his

Continued on Page 35, Column 2

8 Dead in Utah Mine; Fate of 15 Unknown

Special to The New York Times

MOAB, Utah, Aug. 28 — Eight men were known dead today and 15 were trapped a half-mile underground in a potash mine rocked yesterday by a severe explosion.

Two survivors hoisted to the surface today reported that three men were dead, at least five were alive and the fate of 15 was unknown. Later, however, rescue workers deep in the mine spotted five more bodies that officials said might be the men whom the survivors first believed alive.

Rescuers were being hampered by deadly gas, extreme heat, water and mechanical failures. A communications breakdown added to their frustrations.

Donald Hanna, 27 years old, of Price and Paul McKinney,

Continued on Page 14, Column 3

U.S. SPURNS DENIAL BY DIEM ON CRISIS

Absolves the Army Again in Vietnam Pagoda Raids and Points Toward Nhu

By TAD SZULC
Special to The New York Times

WASHINGTON, Aug. 28.—The United States reaffirmed today its belief that the South Vietnamese Government had violated pledges on the Buddhist crisis and that Vietnamese military chiefs were innocent of responsibility for assaults on pagodas.

This was the reaction of the Administration to communiqués issued in Saigon in the last 24 hours by the Government of President Ngo Dinh Diem in the name of the Vietnamese Joint General Staff.

The communiqués charged that Washington's public statements on the crisis reflected "totally erroneous information."

[In Saigon, youths loyal to the secret police were reported to be warning the population against anti-Government demonstrations.]

Change Is Held Vital

With the Vietnam crisis already regarded by the United States as extremely grave, this public dispute seemed to push it toward an unpredictable showdown.

The quarrel over who smashed pagodas and who arrested leaders of the Buddhist protest movement is understood to affect deeply the Kennedy Administration's evolving policy of encouraging Vietnamese military chiefs to reach for power.

This policy, still tentative, is that a fundamental change is required in the structure of the Saigon Government, Washington sources explain. They say the goal is national harmony that would let Vietnam concentrate again on the war against the Communist guerrillas of the Vietcong.

Specifically, Washington is said to deem internal peace out of the question as long as Ngo Dinh Nhu, chief of secret police and brother of the President, retains his vast power.

Mr. Nhu is considered almost a symbol of the friction between Vietnam's Buddhists and the Roman Catholic Ngo family, which dominates the Government.

It is reported that in searching for an alternative to the regime—a course that was unthinkable here before the Buddhist crisis—the United States has almost openly been

Continued on Page 3, Column 4

U.S. PRESSES U.N. TO CONDEMN SYRIA ON ISRAELI DEATHS

Stevenson Deplores Killing of Youths—Thant Assures Council on Cease-Fire

Text of Stevenson statement appears on Page 2.

By KATHLEEN TELTSCH
Special to The New York Times

UNITED NATIONS, N. Y., Aug. 28 — Adlai E. Stevenson declared today that the recent slaying of two Israeli farmers by Syrians was "wanton murder" deserving the strongest condemnation by the Security Council.

The United States delegate, followed by the British representative, gave forceful support to Israel's charges arising from the Aug. 20 ambush killing of two 19-year-old Israelis at the Almagor farm settlement.

Mr. Stevenson rejected Syria's countercharges against Israel as "not corroborated" by United Nations investigations.

The United States policy statement drew a favorable reaction from Michael S. Comay of Israel, who said it encouraged him to expect the Council to take "firm and vigorous action."

Syrian Disapproves

However, there was disapproval from Dr. Salah el-Tarazi of Syria, who criticized Mr. Stevenson as "not particularly objective." He added that Mr. Stevenson in past years had not deplored Syrian losses with equal feeling.

The Council, resuming its airing of the new crisis, was told by the Secretary General, U Thant, that United Nations inspection showed "no evidence of a military build-up on either side" of the armistice line.

Mr. Thant reported that both parties were heeding the United Nations cease-fire achieved last Friday after the ambush and subsequent exchanges of shooting greatly increased tension in the area. Bullets collected at one shooting site were on exhibit in the Council chamber.

Both Mr. Stevenson and Roger W. Jackling of Britain urged Syria and Israel to accept the suggestion by the United Nations truce chief, Lieut. Gen. Odd Bull, for avoiding new eruptions along their border, including an exchange of prisoners. Mr. Comay indicated a favorable Israeli reaction.

Evidence Questioned

Dr. Tarazi, in his turn, insisted that Israel's allegations remained unproved and that some evidence could have been faked. He noted photographs of footgear found at the ambush scene and said Syrian soldiers did not wear such shoes.

He was supported by Sidi Baba of Morocco, who accused Israel of making a "great superficial fuss" over the Almagor incident to create a climate for pressuring the Arabs into signing a peace treaty.

The United States and Britain are understood to be drafting a resolution that would condemn the killings and rebuke Syria by implication, rather than by outright condemnation, as Israel has been asking. Similar formulas have been used in the past.

Such an indirect condemnation might be blocked by a veto from the Soviet Union, however, which in the past has rejected resolutions opposed by the Arabs.

Mr. Stevenson told the 11-nation Council that General Bull's information was admit-

Continued on Page 2, Column 3

2 Girls Murdered In E. 88th St. Flat

Two young women, one the daughter of a writer and the other of a prominent surgeon, were bound and stabbed to death yesterday in their apartment at 57 East 88th Street.

The victims, Janice Wylie, 21 years old, and Emily Hoffert, 23, had been slashed repeatedly. Three bloodstained kitchen knives were found in the five-room apartment, which the girls shared with another young woman. The suite had been ransacked.

The bodies were found on a bedroom floor by Janice's father, the writer Max Wylie, and by Patricia Tolles, 23, the third roommate.

Mr. Wylie, who lives nearby, at 55 East 86th Street, is a

Continued on Page 35, Column 5

Associated Press

VIEW FROM THE LINCOLN MEMORIAL: The scene during the march looking toward the Washington Monument

United Press International Telephoto

VIEW FROM THE WASHINGTON MONUMENT: Marchers assembling around Reflecting Pool at the Lincoln Memorial

CONGRESS CORDIAL BUT NOT SWAYED

Leaders of March Pay Calls of Courtesy at Capitol

By WARREN WEAVER Jr.
Special to The New York Times

WASHINGTON, Aug. 28—The civil rights demonstration that swept more than 200,000 people through the capital today appeared to have left much of Congress untouched — physically, emotionally and politically.

In the morning, 13 demonstration leaders drove quietly up Capitol Hill and paid courtesy calls on Congressional leaders of both parties. The atmosphere was cordial, but there were no conversions.

In the afternoon, about 75 Senators and Representatives went from Capitol Hill to the Lincoln Memorial to be introduced, sit on the steps and listen to Gospel singing and speeches on civil rights.

A few demonstrators violated marching orders and went up to the Capitol to visit legislators in their offices. A few Senators welcomed trainloads and busfuls of constituents in person.

Otherwise, there was really very little contact between the marchers and the group they were working hardest to impress. And there was very little evidence that the demonstration, however large and fervent, would play a material role in advancing civil rights legislation.

Senator Hubert H. Humphrey, one of the most enthusiastic of

Continued on Page 17, Column 1

'I Have a Dream . . .'

Peroration by Dr. King Sums Up A Day the Capital Will Remember

By JAMES RESTON
Special to The New York Times

News Analysis

WASHINGTON, Aug. 28—Abraham Lincoln, who presided in his stone temple today above the children of the slaves he emancipated, may have used just the right words to sum up the general reaction to the Negro's massive march on Washington. "I think," he wrote to Gov. Andrew G. Curtin of Pennsylvania in 1861, "the necessity of being ready increases. Look to it." Washington may not have changed a vote today, but it is a little more conscious tonight of the necessity of being ready for freedom. It may not "look to it" at once, since it is looking to so many things, but it will be a long time before it forgets the melodious and melancholy voice of the Rev. Dr. Martin Luther King Jr. crying out his dreams to the multitude.

It was Dr. King who, near the end of the day, touched the vast audience. Until then the pilgrimage was merely a great spectacle. Only those marchers from the embattled towns in the Old Confederacy had anything like the old crusading zeal. For many the day seemed an adventure, a long outing in the late summer sun—part liberation from home, part Sunday School picnic, part political convention, and part fish-fry.

But Dr. King brought them alive in the late afternoon with a peroration that was an anguished echo from all the old American reformers. Roger Williams calling for religious liberty, Sam Adams calling for political liberty, old man Thoreau denouncing coercion, William Lloyd Garrison demanding emancipation, and Eugene V. Debs crying for economic equality—Dr. King echoed them all.

"I have a dream," he cried again and again. And each time the dream was a promise out of our ancient articles of faith: phrases from the Constitution, lines from the great anthem of the nation, guarantees from the Bill of Rights, all ending with a vision that they might one day all come true.

Find Journey Worthwhile

Dr. King touched all the themes of the day, only better than anybody else. He was full of the symbolism of Lincoln and Gandhi, and the cadences of the Bible. He was both militant and sad, and he sent the crowd away feeling that the long journey had been worthwhile.

This demonstration impressed political Washington because it combined a number of things no politician can ignore. It had the force of numbers. It had the melodies of both the church and the theater. And it was able to invoke the principles of the founding fathers to rebuke the inequalities and hypocrisies of modern American life.

There was a paradox in the day's performance. The Ne-

Continued on Page 17, Column 6

PRESIDENT MEETS MARCH LEADERS

Says Bipartisan Support Is Needed for Rights Bill

Rights statement and Labor Day proclamation, Page 16.

By TOM WICKER
Special to The New York Times

WASHINGTON, Aug. 28—President Kennedy served tea and sympathy and blunt political advice late today to the tired but proud leaders of the march on Washington.

In an hour-long conference, the President told the 10 leaders that "very strong bipartisan support" would be needed to get civil rights legislation enacted this year.

In a statement issued immediately after the conference, Mr. Kennedy said that "the cause of 20,000,000 Negroes has been advanced" by the orderly demonstration, "conducted so appropriately before the nation's shrine to the Great Emancipator."

Earlier, in a Labor Day statement released in advance of the holiday, the President called on the nation to speed up its efforts to achieve equal rights for all in jobs, education and voting.

The main discussion between the march leaders and the President concerned prospects for civil rights legislation, the leaders said after the White House meeting. They talked with Mr. Kennedy around the long table in the Cabinet Room, where the leaders were served tea, coffee,

Continued on Page 16, Column 7

ACTION ASKED NOW

10 Leaders of Protest Urge Laws to End Racial Inequity

Excerpts from talks at rally are printed on Page 21.

By E. W. KENWORTHY
Special to The New York Times

WASHINGTON, Aug. 28—More than 200,000 Americans, most of them black but many of them white, demonstrated here today for a full and speedy program of civil rights and equal job opportunities.

It was the greatest assembly for a redress of grievances that this capital has ever seen.

One hundred years and 240 days after Abraham Lincoln enjoined the emancipated slaves to "abstain from all violence" and "labor faithfully for reasonable wages," this vast throng proclaimed in march and song and through the speeches of their leaders that they were still waiting for the freedom and the jobs.

Children Clap and Sing

There was no violence to mar the demonstration. In fact, at times there was an air of hootenanny about it as groups of schoolchildren clapped hands and swung into the familiar freedom songs.

But if the crowd was good-natured, the underlying tone was one of dead seriousness. The emphasis was on "freedom" and "now." At the same time the leaders emphasized, paradoxically but realistically, that the struggle was just beginning.

On Capitol Hill, opinion was divided about the impact of the demonstration in stimulating Congressional action on civil rights legislation. But at the White House, President Kennedy declared that the cause of 20,000,000 Negroes had been advanced by the march.

The march leaders went from the shadows of the Lincoln Memorial to the White House to meet with the President for 75 minutes. Afterward, Mr. Kennedy issued a 400-word statement praising the marchers for the "deep fervor and the quiet dignity" that had characterized the demonstration.

Says Nation Can Be Proud

"The nation, the President said, "can properly be proud of the demonstration that has occurred here today."

The main target of the demonstration was Congress, where committees are now considering the Administration's civil rights bill.

At the Lincoln Memorial this afternoon, some speakers, knowing little of the ways of Congress, assumed that the passage of a strengthened civil rights bill had been assured by the moving events of the day.

But from statements by Congressional leaders, after they had met with the march committee this morning, this did not seem certain at all. These statements came before the demonstration.

Senator Mike Mansfield of Montana, the Senate Democratic leader, said he could not say whether the mass protest

Continued on Page 16, Column 1

Capital Is Occupied By a Gentle Army

By RUSSELL BAKER
Special to The New York Times

WASHINGTON, Aug. 28 — No one could remember an invading army quite as gentle as the 200,000 civil rights marchers who occupied Washington today.

For the most part, they came silently during the night and early morning, occupied the great shaded boulevards along the Mall, and spread through the parklands between the Washington Monument and the Potomac.

But instead of the emotional horde of angry militants that many had feared, what Washington saw was a vast army of quiet, middle-class Americans

Continued on Page 17, Column 7

"All the News That's Fit to Print"

The New York Times.

LATE CITY EDITION
U. S. Weather Bureau Report (Page 58) forecasts: Cloudy, windy, chance of showers today and tonight. Cold tomorrow.
Temp. Range: 62—54; yesterday: 64—51.

VOL. CXIII...No. 38,654. NEW YORK, SATURDAY, NOVEMBER 23, 1963. TEN CENTS

KENNEDY IS KILLED BY SNIPER AS HE RIDES IN CAR IN DALLAS; JOHNSON SWORN IN ON PLANE

TEXAN ASKS UNITY

Congressional Chiefs of Both Parties Promise Aid

By FELIX BELAIR Jr.
Special to The New York Times

WASHINGTON, Nov. 22—Lyndon B. Johnson returned to a stunned capital shortly after 6 P.M. today to assume the duties of the Presidency.

The new President asked for and received from Congressional leaders of both parties their "united support in the face of the tragedy which has befallen our country." He said it was "more essential that ever before that this country be united."

Partisan differences disappeared in the chorus of assurances with which the Congressional leaders responded.

Mr. Johnson was described by those who talked with him as "stunned and shaken" by the assassination of President Kennedy.

Discusses U.S. Security

But he moved quickly from problems of national security and foreign policy to funeral arrangements for Mr. Kennedy.

Across the street from the West Wing of the White House, the President conferred with officials in his old Vice-Presidential offices in the Executive Office Building.

Senator George A. Smathers, Democrat of Florida, a personal friend of the dead President, was one of those who described Mr. Johnson as shaken.

"Everyone is," he added. "But the President is the more so because he was right there when the tragedy occurred."

While flying to Washington aboard the Presidential plane, Mr. Johnson arranged for a meeting with Cabinet members to ask that they remain at their posts. He made the same request of staff members in the executive office.

Meets With Harriman

"Calm and contained" was the way Senator J. W. Fulbright described the President's manner during a discussion of foreign-policy matters with Under Secretary of State W. Averell Harriman. The Arkansas Senator said the President had been working on "what looked like a statement"—presumably an assurance of continuity of the nation's foreign policy.

The new President's first conference was aboard the helicopter that flew him the 15 miles from Andrews Air Force Base

Continued on Page 11, Column 3

Henry Grossman

"This is a sad time for all people. We have suffered a loss that cannot be weighed. For me it is a deep personal tragedy. I know the world shares the sorrow that Mrs. Kennedy and her family bear. I will do my best. That is all I can do. I ask for your help—and God's."—President Lyndon Baines Johnson.

PRESIDENT'S BODY WILL LIE IN STATE

Funeral Mass to Be Monday in Capital After Homage Is Paid by Public

By JACK RAYMOND
Special to The New York Times

WASHINGTON, Nov. 22—The body of John F. Kennedy will lie in state in the rotunda of the Capitol Sunday and then will be borne to St. Matthew's Roman Catholic Cathedral for a pontifical requiem mass at noon Monday.

The President's body was returned to Washington today in the same Air Force jet that carried him to Texas. The airliner, with Mrs. Kennedy, the new President, Lyndon B. Johnson, and Mrs. Johnson aboard, arrived at Andrews Air Force Base at 5:58 P.M.

It was announced later that Mr. Kennedy's body would lie in the White House tomorrow from 10 A.M. to 6 P.M., during which time Government and diplomatic officials will pay their respects.

The coffin will be taken from the White House to the Capitol rotunda Sunday morning, where

Continued on Page 9, Column 3

PARTIES' OUTLOOK FOR '64 CONFUSED

Republican Prospects Rise—Johnson Faces Possible Fight Against Liberals

By WARREN WEAVER Jr.
Special to The New York Times

WASHINGTON, Nov. 22—President Kennedy's assassination threw the American political scene into turmoil today.

It removed at a single blow the man who would have been renominated for a second term in the White House by acclamation nine months from now.

It elevated into the Presidency and the leadership of the Democratic party an older, more conservative man still emerging from his Southern heritage.

It increased immeasurably for the leaders of the Republican party prospects of electing a President next November.

The shock of the President's death stilled the official voices of politics in the capital. But so profound was the potential effect on the government and leadership that private consideration could not be silenced.

Before, there had been facts and strong probabilities on the

Continued on Page 6, Column 3

LEFTIST ACCUSED

Figure in a Pro-Castro Group Is Charged—Policeman Slain

By GLADWIN HILL
Special to The New York Times

DALLAS, Tex., Nov. 22—The Dallas police and Federal officers issued a charge of murder late tonight in the assassination of President Kennedy.

The accused is Lee Harvey Oswald, a 24-year-old former marine, who went to live in the Soviet Union in 1959 and returned to Texas last year.

Capt. Will Fritz, head of the Dallas police homicide bureau, identified Oswald as an adherent of the left-wing Fair Play for Cuba Committee.

Oswald was arrested about two hours after the shooting, in a movie theater three miles away, shortly after he allegedly shot and killed a policeman on a street nearby.

He was arraigned tonight on a charge of murdering the police officer. The charge related to the Kennedy killing was made later.

Appears in Line-Up

After the arraignment, the suspect, a slight, dark-haired man, was taken downstairs to appear in a line-up, presumably before witnesses of the Kennedy assassination.

While being escorted, handcuffed, through a police building corridor, he shouted: "I haven't shot anybody."

Captain Fritz said Oswald was employed—the exact job was unknown—at the Texas School Book Depository, a warehouse from which the assassin's bullets came. The captain said some witnesses had placed Oswald in the building at the time of the assassination.

The sequence of events leading to his arrest was as follows:

As a citywide manhunt began during the hour following the assassination, an unidentified man notified police headquarters, over a police-car radio, that the car's officer had been

Continued on Page 4, Column 1

NEWS INDEX

Henry Grossman

John Fitzgerald Kennedy
1917-1963

Why America Weeps

Kennedy Victim of Violent Streak He Sought to Curb in the Nation

By JAMES RESTON
Special to The New York Times

WASHINGTON, Nov. 22—America wept tonight, not alone for its dead young President, but for itself. The grief was general, for somehow the worst in the nation had prevailed over the best. The indictment extended beyond the assassin, for something in the nation itself, some strain of madness and violence, had destroyed the highest symbol of law and order.

Speaker John McCormack, now 71 and, by the peculiarities of our politics, next in line of succession after the Vice President, expressed this sense of national dismay and self-criticism:

"My God! My God! What are we coming to?"

The irony of the President's death is that his short Administration was devoted almost entirely to various attempts to curb this very streak of violence in the American character.

When the historians get around to assessing his three years in office, it is very likely that they will be impressed with just this: his efforts to restrain those who wanted to be more violent in the cold war overseas and those who wanted to be

Continued on Page 7, Column 6

The City Goes Dark

By ROBERT C. DOTY

The center of New York, the restless night city, wore darkness and went in near silence after the murder of President Kennedy last night.

In and around Times Square, the normal, frenetic Friday night pulse slowed as near to a halt as it ever comes. Most legitimate and movie theaters, night clubs and dance halls closed their doors and darkened their marquees.

As dusk came, automatic devices turned on the huge, gaudy display signs that normally blot out the night. Then, one by one, the lights blinked out, turning the great carnival strip into what was almost a mourning band.

There were exceptions, of course. Restaurants, by decision of their trade associations, remained lighted and open as a

Continued on Page 5, Column 2

Gov. Connally Shot; Mrs. Kennedy Safe

President Is Struck Down by a Rifle Shot From Building on Motorcade Route—Johnson, Riding Behind, Is Unhurt

By TOM WICKER
Special to The New York Times

DALLAS, Nov. 22—President John Fitzgerald Kennedy was shot and killed by an assassin today.

He died of a wound in the brain caused by a rifle bullet that was fired at him as he was riding through downtown Dallas in a motorcade.

Vice President Lyndon Baines Johnson, who was riding in the third car behind Mr. Kennedy's, was sworn in as the 36th President of the United States 99 minutes after Mr. Kennedy's death.

Mr. Johnson is 55 years old; Mr. Kennedy was 46.

Shortly after the assassination, Lee H. Oswald, described as a one-time defector to the Soviet Union, active in the Fair Play for Cuba Committee, was arrested by the Dallas police. Tonight he was accused of the killing.

Suspect Captured After Scuffle

Oswald, 24 years old, was also accused of slaying a policeman who had approached him in the street. Oswald was subdued after a scuffle with a second policeman in a nearby theater.

The shooting took place at 12:30 P.M., Central standard time (1:30 P.M., New York time). Mr. Kennedy was pronounced dead at 1 P.M. and Mr. Johnson was sworn in at 2:39 P.M.

Mr. Johnson, who was uninjured in the shooting, took his oath in the Presidential jet plane as it stood on the runway at Love Field. The body of the President was aboard. Immediately after the oath-taking, the plane took off for Washington.

Standing beside the new President as Mr. Johnson took the oath of office was Mrs. John F. Kennedy. Her stocking was saturated with her husband's blood.

Gov. John B. Connally Jr. of Texas, who was riding in the same car with Mr. Kennedy, was severely wounded in the chest, ribs and arm. His condition was serious, but not critical.

The killer fired the rifle from a building just off the motorcade route. Mr. Kennedy,

Continued on Page 2,

Capt. Cecil Stoughton via United Press International

THE NEW PRESIDENT: Lyndon B. Johnson takes oath before Judge Sarah T. Hughes in plane at Dallas. Mrs. Kennedy and Representative Jack Brooks are at right. To left are Mrs. Johnson and Representative Albert Thomas.

Associated Press

WHEN THE BULLETS STRUCK: Mrs. Kennedy moving to the aid of the President after he was hit by a sniper yesterday in Dallas. A guard mounts rear bumper. Gov. John B. Connally Jr. of Texas, also in the car, was wounded.

"All the News That's Fit to Print"

The New York Times.

LATE CITY EDITION
U. S. Weather Bureau Report (Page 38) forecasts: Sunny and cool today; fair, milder tonight. Cloudy, milder tomorrow.
Temp. Range: 46—32; yesterday: 53—37.

VOL. CXIII..No. 38,656. NEW YORK, MONDAY, NOVEMBER 25, 1963. + TEN CENTS

PRESIDENT'S ASSASSIN SHOT TO DEATH IN JAIL CORRIDOR BY A DALLAS CITIZEN; GRIEVING THRONGS VIEW KENNEDY BIER

Associated Press Wirephoto

FAREWELL: Kneeling with her mother at John Fitzgerald Kennedy's coffin in the Capitol, Caroline touches the flag

Mrs. Kennedy Leads Public Mourning

By MARJORIE HUNTER
Special to The New York Times

WASHINGTON, Nov. 24 — Mrs. John F. Kennedy, firmly holding the hands of her two children, followed the coffin bearing the body of her husband as it left the White House today for the last time.

Her eyes swollen, she moved quietly to the edge of the steps of the North Portico and paused to watch the coffin placed in the caisson by military bearers.

Her son, John Jr., tugged at her hand and pointed to a black, riderless horse, part of the ceremonial procession. She leaned down and spoke to him.

Mrs. Kennedy wore a simple black suit and black lace mantilla. John Jr., who will be 3 years old tomorrow, and Caroline, who will be 6 on Wednesday, wore similar pale blue coats, white anklets and red shoes.

As the three stood there, framed against the black-draped doorway, there was an eerie silence. It was broken only by the occasional sound of hoofs of the restless gray horses that were to pull the caisson up Pennsylvania Avenue to the Capitol.

Mrs. Kennedy was composed, but appeared to be on the verge of tears as she and the children stepped into a black limousine for the slow ride to the Capitol. In the car, too, were President and Mrs. Johnson and Attorney General Robert F. Kennedy.

Still holding the hands of her children, Mrs. Kennedy followed the flag-draped coffin into the Capitol Rotunda. She stared straight ahead as the coffin was placed on the catafalque, a simple funeral bier draped in black broadcloth.

John Jr., wide-eyed and bewildered, was restless. Clutching a tiny flag, he was led away by a military aide.

Later, after the tributes had been spoken, Mrs. Kennedy walked slowly to the coffin, touched it with her fingertips, knelt and kissed it. Caroline was by her side. They were rejoined by John Jr. at the door.

Shortly after 9 o'clock tonight Mrs. Kennedy returned to the Capitol and again kneeled before the coffin and kissed it.

Mrs. Kennedy walked into the Rotunda on the arm of her husband's brother, Robert, who stopped at the rope holding

Continued on Page 2, Column 8

JOHNSON AFFIRMS AIMS IN VIETNAM

Retains Kennedy's Policy of Aiding War on Reds—Lodge Briefs President

By E. W. KENWORTHY
Special to The New York Times

WASHINGTON, Nov. 24 — President Johnson reaffirmed today the policy objectives of his predecessor regarding South Vietnam. He called upon all Government agencies to support that policy with full unity of purpose.

This was disclosed by White House sources after a meeting between President Johnson and Henry Cabot Lodge, United States Ambassador to South Vietnam.

The meeting lasted nearly an hour. It was described as being devoted to a full review of the conclusions reached by participants in a strategy conference on South Vietnam held in Honolulu last Wednesday.

In another move today that emphasized the President's desire to convey at home and abroad the impression of continuity, Mr. Johnson asked all members of the White House staff to remain at their jobs. This was announced by Pierre Salinger, White House press secretary.

Some Expected to Leave

Mr. Salinger said the President would leave up to the officials involved how long they wished to serve him.

Inevitably some of these officials—especially those from the universities and foundations—will decide to leave their posts after an interval.

But the President's request today would seem to insure that during the difficult days of adjustment and transition he would continue to have the benefit of the experience of key policy figures.

Attending the meeting between the President and Ambassador Lodge today were Secretary of State Dean Rusk, Secretary of Defense Robert S. McNamara, Under Secretary of State George W. Ball, John A. McCone, director of the Central Intelligence Agency, and McGeorge Bundy, special assistant to the President for national security affairs.

Secretaries Rusk and McNamara, Ambassador Lodge and Mr. Bundy all took part in the Honolulu conference.

As a result of the meeting, White House informants said, President Johnson laid down a

Continued on Page 5, Column 1

BUSINESS OF CITY WILL HALT TODAY

Mayor Says Only Essential Services Will Be Provided

Changes in events here are listed on Page 9.

By LEONARD INGALLS

Normal public, business and social activity in the city will be almost completely suspended today out of respect for President Kennedy.

Mayor Wagner announced yesterday that the city would continue in full mourning throughout the day. Only essential city services will be maintained, he said.

"Those city employees not engaged in activities imperative to the health, safety and welfare of our citizens are to be released from duty and their offices closed through Monday," Mr. Wagner said at City Hall.

Proclamation of the day as a legal holiday by Governor Rockefeller in observance of Mr. Kennedy's funeral permits banks and other institutions to close.

Classes at schools and colleges will be suspended. Department stores and specialty shops will be shut. Securities exchanges and commodity markets will not operate. Most places of entertainment will be closed. There will be no deliveries of mail and post offices will be shut.

Special memorial services for the murdered President have been scheduled at churches and synagogues.

At St. Patrick's Cathedral

Continued on Page 9, Column 1

Pope Paul Warns That Hate and Evil Imperil Civil Order

Special to The New York Times

ROME, Nov. 24 — Pope Paul VI, alluding to the assassination of President Kennedy, said today that it showed how much "capacity for hatred and evil still remains in the world."

Without mentioning Mr. Kennedy by name, the Pontiff spoke of "the crime that has aroused in these days the deploration of the whole world." He said it illustrated "how great the threat to civil order and peace still is."

The Pope was addressing thousands of people gathered in St. Peter's Square for his usual Sunday-noon benediction.

"We cannot, at this moment of prayer together, take our thoughts from the crime that has aroused in these days the deploration of the whole world," he said.

"After dwelling upon the man who is no longer with us and after comforting those who still live in mourning and grief, our thoughts show us how much the capacity for hatred and evil yet remains in the world, how great the threat to civil order and peace still is, and how great is the need for the grace

Continued on Page 4, Column 7

NEWS INDEX

JOHNSON SCORED BY CHINESE REDS

Views Called 'Reactionary' —Taiwan Aid Attacked

By United Press International

TOKYO, Nov. 24—Communist China bitterly criticized President Johnson today and termed him a supporter of the late President Kennedy's "trickery policy."

"Since the emergence of the Kennedy regime," the Chinese Communist press agency Hsinhua said, "Johnson has positively supported various reactionary policies of the Kennedy Administration and participated in formulating and promoting such policies.

"Johnson has supported Kennedy's trickery policy and has called for the maintenance of such a policy in a series of his speeches."

The Chinese Communists reported the assassination of President Kennedy in a four-paragraph dispatch eight hours after it occurred. But they made no comment.

Hsinhua said Mr. Johnson "was one of the central figures in the Kennedy Government and has made frequent trips abroad."

The Chinese statement added that Mr. Johnson believed "the United States, in making two-faced antirevolutionary plots, must maintain a strong position on the basis of strong force."

"He also looks toward Cuba with animosity and has called for the elimination of the Cuban revolutionary Government," it

Continued on Page 7, Column 6

CROWD IS HUSHED

Mourners at Capitol File Past the Coffin Far Into the Night

Texts of eulogies spoken in Washington, Page 4.

By TOM WICKER
Special to The New York Times

WASHINGTON, Monday, Nov. 25—Thousands of sorrowing Americans filed past John Fitzgerald Kennedy's bier in the Great Rotunda of the United States Capitol yesterday and early today.

Mr. Kennedy's body lay in state in the center of the vast, stone-floored chamber. Long after midnight the silent procession of mourners continued.

Some wept. All were hushed. As the two lines moved in a large circle around either side of the flag-covered coffin, almost the only sounds were the shuffle of feet and the quiet voices of policemen urging the people to "keep moving, keep moving right along."

By 2:45 A. M. today 115,000 persons had passed the bier.

Yesterday afternoon a crowd estimated at 300,000 lined Pennsylvania and Constitution Avenues to watch the passage of the caisson bearing the body of the 35th President of the United States, slain in the 47th year of his life by an assassin's bullet.

A Riderless Horse

Behind the caisson, following military tradition, came a riderless bay gelding, with a pair of military boots reversed in the silver stirrups.

The horse was Sardar, the thoroughbred that belongs to Mrs. John F. Kennedy.

Mrs. Kennedy, her two children, President and Mrs. Johnson and Mr. Kennedy's brother, Attorney General Robert F. Kennedy, rode in the first car of a 10-car procession that followed the caisson.

The procession moved at a funeral pace, to the sound of muffled drums, from the White House to Pennsylvania Avenue. It was a journey Mr. Kennedy had made formally four times.

At the Capitol, brief ceremonies of eulogy were held in the Rotunda before the admission of the waiting thousands who swarmed over the plaza and stretched in a long line up East Capitol Street.

At the conclusion of the cere-

Continued on Page 2, Column 1

World's Leaders to Attend Requiem Today in Capital

Mrs. Kennedy Will Walk Behind the Caisson to Mass at Cathedral

By JACK RAYMOND
Special to The New York Times

WASHINGTON, Nov. 24 — Mrs. John F. Kennedy, joined by world and national leaders, will walk behind the horse-drawn caisson that bears her husband's body from the White House to St. Matthew's Roman Catholic Cathedral tomorrow.

Following a requiem mass, John Fitzgerald Kennedy, the 35th President of the United States, will be escorted in a solemn state procession to Arlington National Cemetery to be buried with military honors.

The gravesite, on a beautiful grassy knoll, provides a sweeping view of the capital city and it is itself easily in view from the Memorial Bridge approach to the national burial ground.

The state funeral procession will begin at 10:30 A.M. at the Capitol, where the closed, flag-draped coffin of the President

Continued on Page 6, Column 8

Officials of Nearly 100 Lands in U.S.—They Will Meet Johnson

By MAX FRANKEL
Special to The New York Times

WASHINGTON, Nov. 24 — An emperor, a king, a queen, princes, presidents, premiers and ministers from every continent converged on Washington this evening to pay final tribute to

List of leaders expected at the funeral, Page 6.

President Kennedy and to make the acquaintance of President Johnson.

Representing nearly 100 nations, the foreign dignitaries will include the largest assembly of ruling statesmen ever gathered in the United States for any event.

Their arrival here, through the night, virtually overwhelmed an already tense and overburdened capital. Nonetheless, each visitor received the protocol deference and police protection of more normal

Continued on Page 6, Column 1

Millions of Viewers See Oswald Killing On 2 TV Networks

By JACK GOULD

The fatal shooting of Lee H. Oswald, who was held as the assassin of President Kennedy, was seen as it occurred yesterday by millions of television viewers.

The National Broadcasting Company telecast the dramatic happening live. Less than a minute later the Columbia Broadcasting System telecast it by means of tape, made as the shooting occurred.

C. B. S. headquarters recorded the pictures from Dallas as they were received here over a closed circuit. Officials, upon seeing the contents of the Dallas relay, put the tape out over the network instantly.

The incident marked the first time in 15 years of television around the globe that a real-life homicide had occurred in front of live cameras. The closest parallel occurred in October, 1960, when Inejiro Asanuma, Japanese political leader, was knifed on a public stage in

Continued on Page 10, Column 8

JOHNSON SPURS OSWALD INQUIRY

President Orders F. B. I. to Check Death—Handling of Case Worries Capital

By ANTHONY LEWIS
Special to The New York Times

WASHINGTON, Nov. 24— President Johnson directed the Federal Bureau of Investigation tonight to look into "every aspect" of the murder of Lee H. Oswald.

He spoke with the director of the F.B.I., J. Edgar Hoover, and ordered the redoubled investigation.

The action came as official Washington was showing increasing concern about the entire handling of the aftermath of President Kennedy's assassination.

Officials were convinced that Oswald was the assassin. But their concern was over the public impression of the criminal proceedings.

Tonight they were consider-

Continued on Page 11, Column 3

ONE BULLET FIRED

Night-Club Man Who Admired Kennedy Is Oswald's Slayer

By GLADWIN HILL
Special to The New York Times

DALLAS, Nov. 24 — President Kennedy's assassin, Lee Harvey Oswald, was fatally shot by a Dallas night-club operator today as the police started to move him from the city jail to the county jail.

The shooting occurred in the basement of the municipal building at about 11:20 A.M. central standard time (12:20 P.M. New York time).

The assailant, Jack Rubenstein, known as Jack Ruby, lunged from a cluster of newsmen observing the transfer of Oswald from the jail to an armored truck.

Millions of viewers saw the shooting on television.

As the shot rang out, a police detective suddenly recognized Ruby and exclaimed: "Jack, you son of a bitch!"

A murder charge was filed against Ruby by Assistant District Attorney William F. Alexander. Justice of the Peace Pierce McBride ordered him held without bail.

Detectives Flank Him

Oswald was arrested Friday after Mr. Kennedy was shot dead while riding through Dallas in an open car. He was charged with murdering the President and a policeman who was shot a short time later while trying to question Oswald.

As the 24-year-old prisoner, flanked by two detectives, stepped onto a basement garage ramp, Ruby thrust a .38-caliber, snub-nose revolver into Oswald's left side and fired a single shot.

The 52-year-old night-club operator, an ardent admirer of President Kennedy and his family, was described as having been distraught.

[District Attorney Henry Wade said he understood that the police were looking into the possibility that Oswald had been slain to prevent him from talking. The Associated Press reported. Mr. Wade said that so far no connection between Oswald and Ruby had been established.]

Oswald slumped to the concrete paving, wordlessly clutching his side and writhing with pain.

Oswald apparently lost con-

Continued on Page 10, Column 1

Copyright 1963—Dallas Times-Herald and Photographer Bob Jackson, from United Press International Telephoto

OSWALD IS SHOT: Lee Harvey Oswald cringes as Jack Ruby attacks him at Dallas jail. Policeman is J. R. Leavelle.

"All the News That's Fit to Print"

The New York Times.

LATE CITY EDITION
U. S. Weather Bureau Report (Page 48) forecasts: Sunny and pleasant today; clear, cool tonight. Sunny tomorrow.
Temp. Range: 82—62; yesterday: 81—62.
Temp.-Hum. Index: high 60's; yesterday: 71.

VOL. CXIII..No. 38,906. NEW YORK, SATURDAY, AUGUST 1, 1964. TEN CENTS

RANGER TAKES CLOSE-UP MOON PHOTOS REVEALING CRATERS ONLY 3 FEET WIDE; DATA GAINED ON LANDING SITE FOR MAN

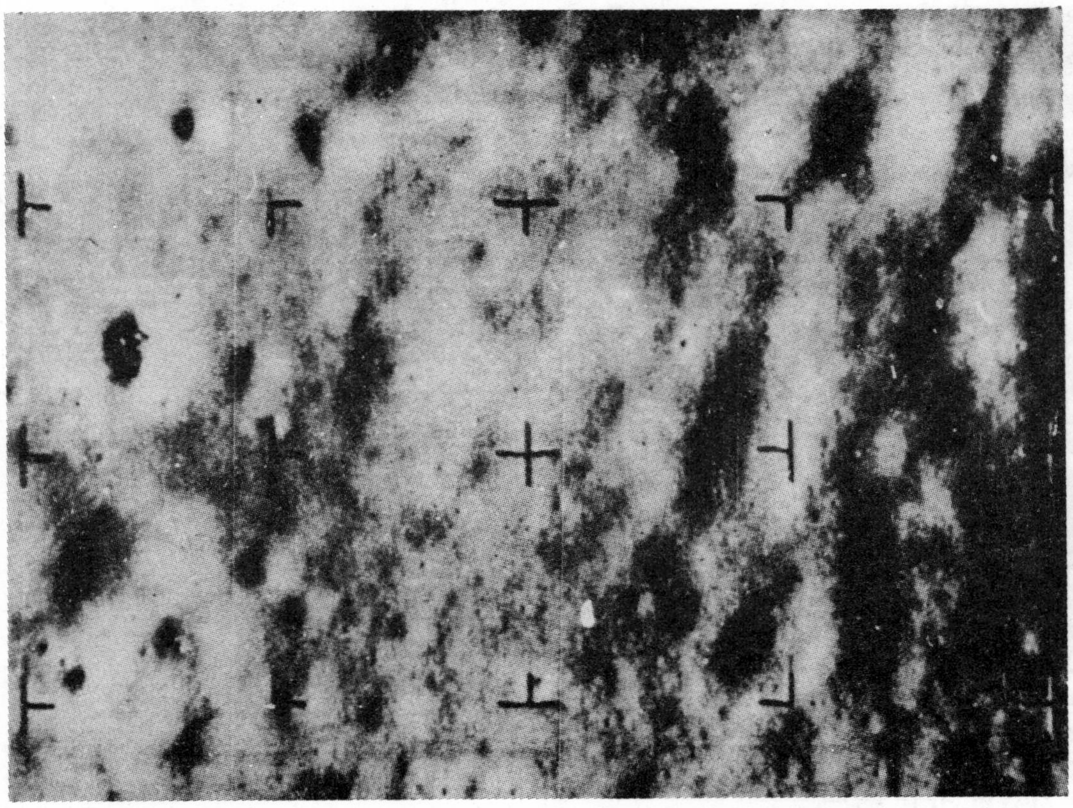

THREE MILES FROM THE MOON: This view of lunar surface was transmitted by the Ranger 7 spacecraft 3.2 seconds before it crashed. The lens gridmarks are scale references to calibrate amount of distortion. Smallest craters shown are about 30 feet in diameter and about 10 feet in depth.

Associated Press Wirephotos

1,000 FEET FROM THE MOON: Upper photo was the last. At right it merges into blur caused by static after the Ranger 7 crashed. Below, photo taken from 3,000 feet.

U.S. STEEL WEIGHS MIDTOWN PROJECT

$100 Million Industrial and Housing Complex May Be Built Above Rail Yard

By ROBERT E. BEDINGFIELD

The United States Steel Corporation has acquired the air rights over a 40-acre railroad yard in mid-Manhattan and is considering erecting a $100 million housing and industrial complex over the site.

U.S. Steel's board of directors has approved the purchase of Webb & Knapp's lease of the air rights over the New York Central Railroad's freight yard that lies between West 30th and West 37th Streets and extends from 10th to 12th Avenue.

Webb & Knapp realized about $7 million on the deal.

It is understood that the plan being considered calls for the construction of nine apartment buildings of about 30 stories each that would provide middle-income housing for 12,000 families. The project also envisages numerous adjoining industrial buildings of several stories each.

Plan Still Studied

Last night a spokesman for U.S. Steel confirmed that the directors had authorized the acquisition of the air rights from Webb & Knapp.

He said, however, that no definite plan had yet been decided for utilization of the area. If the corporation decides to go ahead with the proposed housing development, he added, it would be for the purpose of demonstrating the company's contention that steel is useful as a prime material in middle-income housing.

Webb & Knapp since Dec. 15, 1961, has held a leasehold on the air rights to the part of the Central yard that lies between West 30th and West 37th Streets and extends from 11th to 12th Avenue and from West 30th to West 33d Street between 10th and 11th Avenues.

Webb & Knapp will net $3 million on the deal since $4 million of the proceeds will be applied to the repayment of a note of that amount owed the steel company.

The proposed U.S. Steel plans

Continued on Page 34, Column 3

Wagner Rejects Demands For Civilian Police Board

By R. W. APPLE Jr.

Mayor Wagner refused yesterday to appoint an independent civilian police review board sought by civil rights leaders.

In a long statement released at City Hall, the Mayor omitted any mention of another key demand of Negro leaders—the suspension of Police Lieut. Thomas R. Gilligan, who shot and killed a 15-year-old Negro on the East Side on July 16.

Instead, Mr. Wagner proposed a seven-point program whose main thrust was economic,

Text of Wagner's statement is printed on Page 11.

calling for the creation of about 1,500 temporary and permanent city jobs for unemployed young people.

The Mayor also set up a committee to review the findings of Deputy Mayor Edward F. Cavanagh Jr., who had been directed earlier to review the actions of the Police Department's review board.

King Voices Regret

Mr. Wagner's statement was his first since he began last Monday a series of conversations with the Rev. Dr. Martin Luther King Jr., president of the Southern Christian Leadership Conference, following racial riots here two weeks ago.

Dr. King said in a telephone interview from Atlanta that he was "very sorry" the Mayor had not ordered the creation of an independent board to evaluate allegations of police brutality. He said he had pressed the issue again and again during his talks with Mr. Wagner.

L. Joseph Overton, president of the Unity Council of Harlem Organizations, condemned the Mayor's actions and demanded again the creation of a review board composed of persons associated with neither the city government nor the police.

"I believe the Mayor has made my position untenable," Mr. Overton said. "He has made it virtually impossible for me to guarantee continued peace on the streets of Harlem."

Mr. Overton's organization was set up in an attempt to restore order in Harlem after the riots touched off by the Gilligan incident. The council has insisted that only the creation of a review board would solve the city's racial crisis.

Police Commissioner Michael

Continued on Page 11, Column 5

M'KESSON TO CUT ANTIBIOTIC PRICE

Plans to Sell Tetracycline at Third of Present Cost—Pfizer Says It Will Sue

By MARTIN ARNOLD

The nation's largest wholesale drug distributor announced yesterday that it would manufacture and sell tetracycline at about one-third the price at which it is sold by other manufacturers in the United States.

Tetracycline is a broad-spectrum antibiotic that is effective against a variety of bacterial infections. Yearly sales in the country total about $100 million, or about a third of the total sale of antibiotics.

The announcement was made by McKesson & Robbins, which said that it would offer pills for about 6 cents each wholesale, or about $6 for 100 250-milligram tablets. A spokesman for the company said that other drug concerns that manufacture tetracycline in the United States sell it for "slightly more than $17 a hundred tablets wholesale."

Chas. Pfizer & Co., one of the discoverers of tetracycline, immediately announced that it would file suit against McKesson & Robbins for patent infringement.

There are a number of small distributing concerns that buy tetracycline abroad, notably in Italy, and sell it for a low price here.

The importance of the McKesson & Robbins move, observers point out, is that the company's product will be American made and therefore, justifiably or not, druggists and doctors will be less hesitant

Continued on Page 34, Column 6

PAKISTAN ACCEPTS LOAN FROM CHINA

$60 Million, Interest Free, to Be Used for Imports of Industrial Goods

Special to The New York Times

KARACHI, Pakistan, July 31 — Pakistan announced today that she would accept a "generous offer" by Communist China of a $60 million long-term, interest-free loan.

It is the first loan offered by Peking to Pakistan, which is allied with the West in the Central Treaty Organization and the Southeast Asia Treaty Organization, both aimed at preventing Communist aggression.

Commerce Minister Wahid-uz-Zaman, who recently returned from a tour of Communist China, said at a news conference in Rawalpindi that the loan would be used to pay for imports of machinery, cement and sugar mills.

Mr. Zaman said the Chinese Government would not even place a service charge on the loan.

United States loans offered to Pakistan are repayable in United States dollars in 40 years, including a 10-year grace period during which no payment is

Continued on Page 3, Column 2

Attitude on Soviet Is Upheld by Rusk In Policy Warning

By MAX FRANKEL
Special to The New York Times

WASHINGTON, July 31—Secretary of State Dean Rusk, in an oblique jab at Senator Barry Goldwater, said today that it was "unrealistic" to think the Soviet Union would "roll over and play dead" if its vital interests were threatened by the United States.

In answering several political questions at a news conference, Mr. Rusk said the Administration had "eminently demonstrated" that it was "just as tough and just as stubborn as is necessary" to protect its vital interests and those of the Western allies.

But he cautioned that the Soviet Union, too, would be stubborn in defending its interests. Therefore, he said, conflicts of interest must be approached with care and persistence to find ways in which the Communist and Western parts of the world can live together.

Mr. Rusk did not refer directly to Mr. Goldwater, the Republican candidate for President, or his views, but the Secretary's questioners did, leaving no doubt about the meaning of their inquiries.

Secretary Rusk said he

Continued on Page 2, Column 3

Johnson Is Said to Have Asked Kennedy to Manage Campaign

Offer Being Considered

By The Associated Press

WASHINGTON, Saturday, Aug. 1—President Johnson has asked Attorney General Robert F. Kennedy to manage his Presidential campaign, informed sources said today.

They said the offer was made Wednesday at the same time Mr. Johnson told Mr. Kennedy he was eliminating him from consideration as a Vice-Presidential candidate.

The offer reportedly is under consideration.

"I don't want to get into that," Mr. Kennedy said yesterday when asked about reports of the offer before he left for Hyannis Port, Mass., for the weekend. And Kennedy

Continued on Page 6, Column 2

Rusk Post Desired

By CABELL PHILLIPS
Special to The New York Times

WASHINGTON, July 31 — Attorney General Robert F. Kennedy would like to be Secretary of State now that the Vice-Presidency has been foreclosed to him.

This is the consensus of several close friends and associates of Mr. Kennedy after President Johnson's statement yesterday that the Attorney General and others of Cabinet rank had been eliminated from consideration for the second spot on the Democratic ticket.

Mr. Kennedy, his friends say, is exerting no pressure to obtain the State Department post. But they say he has let it be

Continued on Page 6, Column 5

PRESIDENT HAILS NEW LUNAR FEAT

Calls Ranger Flight 'Basic Step' to Manned Landing —Praises Scientists

By JOHN D. POMFRET
Special to The New York Times

WASHINGTON, July 31—President Johnson congratulated today the scientists and technicians responsible for the successful flight of Ranger 7 to the moon.

The President was in the White House living quarters when Dr. William H. Pickering, director of the Jet Propulsion Laboratory at Pasadena, Calif., telephoned to inform him that the shot was a success.

The President felicitated Dr. Pickering and Dr. Homer E. Newell, assistant administrator for space science and application of the space agency, then had the White House issue a statement praising those who participated in the flight.

Mr. Johnson called the flight "a basic step forward in our orderly program to assemble the scientific knowledge necessary for man's trip to the moon."

Guide in Planning Trip

"The pictures obtained of the lunar surface should prove extremely useful," the President said, continuing:

"They will be a guide in constructing the lunar excursion module and in planning the trip.

"We shall now be able to better map out our descent route. We'll be able to build our lunar landing equipment with greater certainty and knowledge of the conditions which our astronauts will encounter on the moon.

"I recognize that this great success has come only after a number of failures and partial failures in our efforts to send probes to the moon. This success should spur us on to added effort in the future.

"The fact that our Soviet competitors have had many unpublicized failures to the moon and the planets also confirms the complexity of today's success.

"On behalf of a grateful nation, let me again congratu-

Continued on Page 8, Column 3

Craft Hits Target Area; 4,000 Pictures Sent Back

Details of Lunar Region Seen Thousand Times Clearer Than Before—Feat Hailed as Leap in Knowledge

By RICHARD WITKIN
Special to The New York Times

PASEDENA, Calif., July 31—Ranger 7 radioed to earth today the first close-up pictures of the moon—a historic collection of 4,000 pictures one thousand times as clear as anything ever seen through earth-bound telescopes.

Scientists here were hailing the achievement, which exceeded all expectations, as by far the

Text of the news conference will be found on Page 10.

greatest advance in lunar astronomy since Galileo.

They said the pictures not only represented a great leap in man's knowledge of the moon, but also, on a more practical level, lent encouragement that the lunar surface was suitable for Project Apollo's manned lunar landings.

Taken in 17 Minutes

The still pictures were snapped and transmitted in the last 17 minutes before the spacecraft crashed into an area northwest of the Sea of Clouds

They meant in effect that the 240,000 mile distance to the moon had been shrunk by man's ingenuity to a mere half-mile in terms of what he could see of its topography. They showed craters three feet in diameter and a foot to a foot and a half deep.

The best earthbound telescopes, handicapped by the shimmering mantle of the atmosphere, can shrink the lunar distance only to 500 miles and reveal features no smaller than about one-mile across.

The startling disclosures of what Ranger 7 had wrought were made at a packed news conference here by a team of scientists headed by Dr. Gerard P. Kuiper of the University of Arizona.

The conference, televised nationally, was held in the auditorium of the Jet Propulsion Laboratory of the National Aeronautics Space Administration.

"This is a great day for science," the eminent astronomer said at the start, "and a great day for the United States.

"What has been achieved is truly remarkable. We have made progress in resolution [clarity of pictures] not by a factor of 10 . . . not by a factor of 100, which would have been remarkable, but by a factor of 1,000."

As a series of ten samples of the Ranger 7 photographs were flashed on a screen, Dr. Kuiper pointed out some of the more interesting features. Among the highlights of his recital and of answers both he and another member of the scientific panel made were these:

¶A few hours' quick study of Ranger 7's massive output had not revealed that there were any totally unforeseen problems on the moon. But the numberless new details opened a region of knowledge that would keep scientists in deep study for three or four years or more.

¶There was evidence that the white rays around some major craters were caused not by light fluffy material tossed up from the moon but by sizable rocks thrown off in the formation of these large craters. The rocks made numerous secondary craters deep enough to represent an extreme hazard for a manned lunar landing in the area. Such areas were to be avoided like poison, Dr. Kuiper said.

¶The tentative impression of the scientific team was that the lunar surface dust or other substance was not thick enough to swallow an astronaut landing craft. Dr. Eugene Shoemaker

Continued on Page 8, Column 1

NEWS INDEX

The New York Times.

LATE CITY EDITION
U.S. Weather Bureau Report (Page 66) forecasts: Variable cloudiness today; clear tonight. Fair and cool tomorrow.
Temp. Range: 86—65; yesterday: 81—57.
Temp.-Hum. Index: low 70's; yesterday: 73.

VOL. CXIII—No. 38,910. NEW YORK, WEDNESDAY, AUGUST 5, 1964. TEN CENTS

U.S. PLANES ATTACK NORTH VIETNAM BASES; PRESIDENT ORDERS 'LIMITED' RETALIATION AFTER COMMUNISTS' PT BOATS RENEW RAIDS

F. B. I. Finds 3 Bodies Believed to Be Rights Workers'

GRAVES AT A DAM

Discovery Is Made in New Earth Mound in Mississippi

By CLAUDE SITTON
Special to The New York Times

JACKSON, Miss., Aug. 4—Bodies believed to be those of three civil rights workers missing since June 21 were found early tonight near Philadelphia, Miss.

Federal Bureau of Investigation agents recovered the bodies from a newly erected earthen dam in a thickly wooded area about six miles southwest of Philadelphia, in east-central Mississippi.

The dam is several hundred yards off State Highway 21, near the Neshoba County fairgrounds.

Fulton Jackson, the county coroner, made a preliminary examination at the scene. The bodies were then sealed in plastic bags and brought by ambulance to the University of Mississippi Medical Center in Jackson, 70 miles to the southwest.

Pledge by Governor

Roy K. Moore, special agent in charge of the Jackson F.B.I. office, said physicians and fingerprint experts would seek to make positive identification and establish the cause of death.

[In Washington, authoritative sources said that President Johnson had telephoned Gov. Paul B. Johnson Jr. of Mississippi after having learned of the discovery of the bodies. However, this could not be confirmed immediately.]

Governor Johnson said in a statement:

"If these are the bodies of the three civil rights workers who have been missing several weeks, the investigative forces of the State of Mississippi will exert every effort to apprehend those who may have been responsible."

Area Searched Earlier

Mr. Johnson said he understood F.B.I. agents had searched the area once before and had noticed the new dam. Later, when they saw that the dam had collected no water despite heavy showers, they returned for a further investigation.

Excavation uncovered the bodies in the fill of the dam, the Governor said.

Sheriff L. A. Rainey, who had just returned from a vacation, visited the scene a short while after the discovery.

The missing men were Michael H. Schwerner, 24 years old, and Andrew Goodman, 20, both white and both from New York City, and James E. Chaney, 21, a Negro of Meridian, Miss.

All three had been taking part in the Mississippi Summer Project, a state-wide civil rights drive, which began on the week-

Continued on Page 37, Column 2

Scattered Violence Keeps Jersey City Tense 3d Night

400 Policemen Confine Most of Rioters to 2 Sections—Crowds Watch in Streets Despite Danger

By FRED POWLEDGE
Special to The New York Times

JERSEY CITY, Aug. 4—Scattered violence broke out again here tonight as roving groups of Negroes hurled crude Molotov cocktails in the streets. There was some gunfire but no injuries were reported.

About 400 city policemen contained most of the young riot-

Text of Whelan's statement will be found on Page 36.

ers to two predominantly Negro neighborhoods. There were at least — arrests.

Although it was dangerous to be on the streets on this third night of violence, many people watched from sidewalks and front porches as police cars, their red lights flashing, sped from one pocket of violence to another.

On Ocean Avenue the police trained spotlights on the roof of a three-story block of apartments. A man had been seen on the roof, and it was feared that he was armed with a rifle, tire bombs, or both. Yet on the sidewalk below, a woman walked her dog, apparently without concern, through throngs of helmeted policemen. From a front porch across the street, a baby cried.

Since the rioting started Sunday night, more than 30 persons have been injured, two of them with gunshot wounds. None of the wounds was critical. More than three dozen persons have been arrested.

Five hundred more Jersey City policemen stood ready to

Continued on Page 36, Column 1

JOHNSON SEEKING EXTREMISM PLANK

Favors a Stand Against Far Left and Right Without Naming Any Groups

Special to The New York Times

WASHINGTON, Aug. 4—President Johnson wants the Democratic platform to take a stand against extremism of the right and the left, without naming any particular organization.

Mr. Johnson, at the moment, plans to attend the party's national convention in Atlantic City only on Thursday night, Aug. 27, when he is scheduled to make his acceptance speech. But his wish on the platform is likely to be enough to make his views effective.

As yet, however, he has had no detailed discussions with the platform drafters.

The President is also planning to follow a somewhat unusual procedure in having himself placed in nomination. This is to be done by "co-nominators"— Governors Edmund G. Brown of California and John B. Connally Jr. of Texas.

These and other fairly well-advanced plans of the President have been learned from high Democratic sources.

However, on the question of most current interest, Mr. Johnson's choice for a Vice-Presidential candidate, no decision has yet been made.

Senator Hubert H. Humphrey

Continued on Page 14, Column 6

Rockefeller to Join Goldwater's Parley On Campaign Unity

Special to The New York Times

ALBANY, Aug. 4—Governor Rockefeller has accepted the invitation of Senator Goldwater to attend a meeting of Republican Governors at Hershey, Pa., on Aug. 12.

The invitation was extended by the Republican Presidential nominee in telegrams last Saturday to the 16 Republican Governors.

Mr. Rockefeller, who was a candidate for the Presidential nomination until after his defeat in the California primary, June 2, was one of Senator Goldwater's severest critics through the Republican National Convention last month in San Francisco.

Mr. Goldwater has called the Hershey gathering in an effort to promote unity within the Republican party behind his candidacy.

The prospects for success of

Continued on Page 16, Column 1

REDS DRIVEN OFF

Two Torpedo Vessels Believed Sunk in Gulf of Tonkin

By ARNOLD H. LUBASCH
Special to The New York Times

WASHINGTON, Aug. 4—The Defense Department announced tonight that North Vietnamese PT boats made a "deliberate attack" today on two United States destroyers patrolling international waters in the Gulf of Tonkin off North Vietnam.

The attack came two days after North Vietnamese torpedo boats attacked the Maddox, one of the destroyers in today's incident.

The destroyers and covering carrier-based aircraft fired on the vessels in today's attack, drove them off and apparently sank at least two of them, according to the announcement. The Pentagon said there were no United States casualties or damage.

The attack was made by an "undetermined number of North Vietnamese PT boats" during darkness about 65 miles from the nearest land, the Pentagon reported. It said the attack came at 10:30 P. M., North Vietnamese time, or 10:30 A. M., Washington time.

'Fabrication,' Reds Say

[The North Vietnamese regime said Wednesday that the report of another attack on United States ships was a "fabrication."]

The second attack was described in Washington as much fiercer than the first one, which was said to have lasted half an hour. The second battle was understood to have lasted about three hours in rough sea, with bad weather and low visibility.

"We are in a very serious situation," a Government official said.

The attack came shortly before the State Department made public a stern protest about the North Vietnamese attack Sunday on the Maddox, which was then patrolling about 30 miles off North Vietnam, also in international waters in the Gulf of Tonkin.

The protest over the first incident was announced shortly after noon here, when the

Continued on Page 3, Column 1

2 CARRIERS USED

McNamara Reports on Aerial Strikes and Reinforcements

By JACK RAYMOND
Special to The New York Times

WASHINGTON, Wednesday, Aug. 5—Secretary of Defense Robert S. McNamara said at a postmidnight news conference that the United States planes that attacked North Vietnam yesterday and today had come from the carriers Constellation and Ticonderoga in the Gulf of Tonkin.

He said that the attacks had been directed against the bases used by the North Vietnamese PT boats that attacked two United States destroyers in international waters yesterday.

The Secretary added that the naval planes, believed to have included propeller-driven as well as jet-powered craft, had also conducted strikes against "certain other targets directly supporting the operation of the PT boats."

The United States planes used conventional weapons.

Separate Targets

Mr. McNamara, who held his news conference shortly after President Johnson had addressed the nation on television, emphasized in his report that the PT boat bases and the supporting facilities in North Vietnam had been separate targets.

He offered a guess, based on incomplete reports, that in the exchange of fire between the attacking PT boats and the United States destroyers and aircraft in international waters, at least two and possibly four of the North Vietnamese Soviet-made PT boats had been sunk.

The Defense Secretary disclosed that at one point in the Vietnamese PT boat attack, the Maddox observed an unidentified aircraft on radar, but that there was no air attack and the radar image was soon lost.

The hostilities that provoked United States retaliation began Sunday with an attack by North Vietnamese PT boats on the United States destroyer Maddox in the Gulf of Tonkin.

Hanoi Not Attacked

The first United States reaction was a note of protest and warning. But, as announced by the President and the Secretary of Defense, the second PT boat attack on the destroyers Maddox and C. Turner Joy yesterday precipitated the counteraction.

The Secretary of Defense said at the news conference that the retaliatory strikes were still under way at that time.

He made clear, in response to questions, that no targets outside North Vietnam had been attacked by the United States warplanes. He specifically ex-

Continued on Page 4, Column 3

Associated Press Wirephoto

DECISION: President Johnson, in a nationwide broadcast, tells of action he ordered taken against North Vietnam.

The President's Address

Following is the text of the President's address on Vietnam last night, as recorded by The New York Times:

My fellow Americans:

As President and Commander in Chief, it is my duty to the American people to report that renewed hostile actions against United States ships on the high seas in the Gulf of Tonkin have today required me to order the military forces of the United States to take action in reply.

The initial attack on the destroyer Maddox on Aug. 2 was repeated today by a number of hostile vessels attacking two U.S. destroyers with torpedoes.

The destroyers and supporting aircraft acted at once on the orders I gave after the initial act of aggression.

We believe at least two of the attacking boats were sunk. There were no U.S. losses.

The performance of commanders and crews in this engagement is in the highest tradition of the United States Navy.

But repeated acts of violence against the armed forces of the United States must be met not only with alert defense but with positive reply.

Action 'Now in Execution'

That reply is being given, as I speak to you tonight. Air action is now in execution against gunboats and certain supporting facilities in North Vietnam which have been used in these hostile operations.

In the larger sense, this new act of aggression aimed directly at our own forces again brings home to all of us in the United States the importance of the struggle for peace and security in Southeast Asia.

Aggression by terror against the peaceful villages of South Vietnam has now been joined by open aggression on the high seas against the United States of America.

The determination of all Americans to carry out our full commitment to the people and to the Government of South Vietnam will be redoubled by this outrage. Yet our response for the present will be limited and fitting.

We Americans know—although others appear to forget—the risk of spreading conflict. We still seek no wider war.

I have instructed the Secretary of State to make this position totally clear to friends and to adversaries and, indeed, to all.

I have instructed Ambassador Stevenson to raise this matter immediately and urgently before the Security Council of the United Nations.

Congressional Resolution Asked

Finally, I have today met with the leaders of both parties in the Congress of the United States and I have informed them that I shall immediately request the Congress to pass a resolution making it clear that our Government is united in its determination to take all necessary measures in support of freedom and in defense of peace in Southeast Asia.

I have been given encouraging assurance by these leaders of both parties that such a resolution will be promptly introduced, freely and expeditiously debated, and passed with overwhelming support.

And just a few minutes ago I was able to reach Senator Goldwater and I am glad to say that he has expressed his support of the statement that I am making to you tonight.

It is a solemn responsibility to have to order even limited military action by forces whose over-all strength is as vast and as awesome as those of the United States of America.

But it is my considered conviction, shared throughout your Government, that firmness in the right is indispensable today for peace.

That firmness will always be measured. Its mission is peace.

FORCES ENLARGED

Stevenson to Appeal for Action by U.N. on 'Open Aggression'

By TOM WICKER
Special to The New York Times

WASHINGTON, Aug. 4—President Johnson has ordered retaliatory action against gunboats and "certain supporting facilities in North Vietnam" after renewed attacks against American destroyers in the Gulf of Tonkin.

In a television address tonight, Mr. Johnson said air attacks on the North Vietnamese ships and facilities were taking place as he spoke, shortly after 11:30 P.M.

State Department sources said the attacks were being carried out with conventional weapons on a number of shore bases in North Vietnam, with the objective of destroying them and the 30 to 40 gunboats they served.

The aim, they explained, was to destroy North Vietnam's gunboat capability. They said more air strikes might come later, if needed. Carrier-based aircraft were used in tonight's strike.

2 Boats Believed Sunk

Administration officials also announced that substantial additional units, primarily air and sea forces, were being sent to Southeast Asia.

This "positive reply," as the President called it, followed a naval battle in which a number of North Vietnamese PT boats attacked two United States destroyers with torpedoes. Two of the boats were believed to have been sunk. The United States forces suffered no damage and no loss of lives.

Mr. Johnson termed the North Vietnamese attacks "open aggression on the high seas."

Washington's response is "limited and fitting," the President said, and his Administration seeks no general extension of the guerrilla war in South Vietnam.

Goldwater Approves

"We Americans know," he said, "although others appear to forget, the risks of spreading conflict."

Mr. Johnson said Secretary of State Dean Rusk had been instructed to make this American attitude clear to all nations. He added that Adlai E. Stevenson, chief United States delegate, would raise the matter immediately in the United Nations Security Council. [The Council was expected to meet at 10:30 A.M. Wednesday.]

The President said he had informed his Republican Presidential rival, Senator Barry Goldwater, of his action and

Continued on Page 2, Column 3

Khanh Is Fighting Threat of a Coup

By SEYMOUR TOPPING
Special to The New York Times

SAIGON, South Vietnam, Aug. 4—Premier Nguyen Khanh struggled today to strengthen the political stability of his Government as his aides privately warned of plots to drive him from office. United States officials were concerned about the political deterioration in Saigon.

The malaise in the capital was attributed more to a clash of rival political and military personalities than to pressure from the Vietcong insurgents.

United States sources said reports from provinces indicated that conditions there were generally better than in Saigon.

Once again, rumors of a coup d'état were circulating in Sai-

Continued on Page 4, Column 7

Auto Collision Insurance Rates In State Increased 4.3 to 25%

By JOSEPH C. INGRAHAM

Higher auto damage insurance rates — with increases from 4.3 to 25 per cent—will go into effect today for private passenger car owners in the state.

The increases were disclosed yesterday by the National Automobile Underwriters Association, which said that sharp rises in auto thefts and in the cost of repairs had made them necessary.

The association said that although the statewide rise would be the lesser amount, the rates in most of the metropolitan areas had been increased as much as 25 per cent.

Physical damage insurance, which reimburses a car owner for loss of or damage to his own car, is optional. The rate revisions apply to collision insurance and to comprehensive coverage, which protects motorists against loss due to theft, fire, windstorm, glass breakage and other hazards.

While each of these coverages can be bought separately, the National Automobile Underwriters Association, rating organization for more than 400 companies here, lumps the vari-

Continued on Page 67, Column 2

NEWS INDEX

Salinger Appointed to the Senate

United Press International Telephoto

Pierre Salinger, left, with Gov. Edmund G. Brown of California after the announcement yesterday in Sacramento.

By WALLACE TURNER
Special to The New York Times

SAN FRANCISCO, Aug. 4—Pierre Salinger was appointed to the Senate today by Gov. Edmund G. Brown of California to fill the remaining five months of the term of the late Senator Clair Engle. Mr. Salinger is scheduled to be sworn in tomorrow about noon. He will be escorted to the rostrum by Senator Thomas H. Kuchel of California, the assistant Senate Republican leader. Governor Brown is to head a party of about 160 Democratic leaders who will be present in the Senate galleries when the new Senator takes his oath. Mr. Salinger, who was White House press

Continued on Page 16, Column 2

Congolese Battling Inside Stanleyville

By J. ANTHONY LUKAS
Special to The New York Times

LEOPOLDVILLE, the Congo, Aug. 4—Rebels of the "Popular Army" and Government troops battled tonight in the streets of Stanleyville, the chief city in the northern Congo.

Messages from the United States consul there said heavy fighting was going on early this evening in front of the consulate, about a mile from the center of the city.

At 6:15 P. M. Stanleyville time, the consul, Michael P. E. Hoyt, telegraphed that the army was "advancing across front lawn of consulate" and seemed to be "pushing rebels back."

Eight minutes later he wired that the army troops were "advancing rapidly and in numbers beyond consulate on road to Wanie Rukula." He said that

Continued on Page 3, Column 4

"All the News That's Fit to Print"

The New York Times.

LATE CITY EDITION

U. S. Weather Bureau Report (Page 45) forecasts. Cloudy, then fair today; fair and cooler tonight. Fair tomorrow. Temp. Range: 70—55; yesterday: 73—59.

VOL. CXIV . No. 38,964. | NEW YORK, MONDAY, SEPTEMBER 28, 1964. | Today's Issue Contains 96 Pages in Two Sections | TEN CENTS

WARREN COMMISSION FINDS OSWALD GUILTY AND SAYS ASSASSIN AND RUBY ACTED ALONE; REBUKES SECRET SERVICE, ASKS REVAMPING

F.B.I. IS CRITICIZED

Security Steps Taken by Secret Service Held Inadequate

By FELIX BELAIR Jr.
Special to The New York Times

WASHINGTON, Sept. 27—A sweeping revision of the organization and basic operating practices of the United States Secret Service was recommended today by the Warren Commission.

The commission sharply rebuked the Secret Service for failure to make adequate preparation for the visit of President Kennedy to Dallas last November. It reprimanded the Federal Bureau of Investigation for failure to supply the Secret Service with information concerning the presence of Lee Harvey Oswald in Dallas.

The commission deplored the fact that "there was no fully adequate liaison" between the F.B.I. and the Secret Service before the Dallas trip. It noted that some improvements had occurred since then but it insisted that, ultimately, Presidential protection required improvement in working arrangements of all Federal agencies concerned, including the Central Intelligence Agency, the State Department and the military intelligence branches.

Scrutiny Is Urged

The State Department was admonished to scrutinize more carefully requests for return to the United States of defectors

The report's appendix on Presidential protection will be printed in tomorrow's Times.

like Oswald "who have evidenced disloyalty or hostility to this country or who have expressed a desire to renounce their citizenship."

The brunt of the commission's indictment was directed at the century-old agency responsible for the safety of the President and his family. Its chief charge was that the Secret Service had not checked buildings along the route of the Presidential motorcade in Dallas nor asked the local police to do so.

The commission called for the appointment of a new special assistant to the Secretary of the Treasury with general supervisory authority over the Secret Service.

The commission found, however, that the conduct of the Secret Service agents in the Presidential motorcade "demonstrates that the President and the nation can expect courage and devotion to duty from agents of the Secret Service."

It acknowledged that whatever the human and material resources at the command of the Secret Service, a President can only be made as safe as he wants to be.

The report declared that its recommendations were "compelled by the facts disclosed in this investigation." It noted that

Continued on Page 15, Column 1

Harris & Ewing

THE WARREN COMMISSION: President's Commission on the Assassination of President Kennedy at commission offices at Veterans of Foreign Wars Building, Washington. From left: Representative Gerald R. Ford, Representative Hale Boggs, Senator Richard B. Russell, Chief Justice Earl Warren, Senator John Sherman Cooper, John J. McCloy, Allen W. Dulles, and J. Lee Rankin, commission counsel. Portraits are of President Johnson, President Kennedy and Joseph J. Lombardo, head of Veterans of Foreign Wars.

PANEL UNANIMOUS

Theory of Conspiracy by Left or Right Is Rejected

The text of the report begins on the first page of the second section.

By ANTHONY LEWIS
Special to The New York Times

WASHINGTON, Sept. 27—The assassination of President Kennedy was the work of one man, Lee Harvey Oswald. There was no conspiracy, foreign or domestic.

That was the central finding in the Warren Commission report, made public this evening. Chief Justice Earl Warren and the six other members of the President's Commission on the Assassination of President John F. Kennedy were unanimous on this and all questions.

The commission found that Jack Ruby was on his own in killing Oswald. It rejected all theories that the two men were in some way connected. It said that neither rightists nor Communists bore responsibility for the murder of the President in Dallas last Nov. 22.

Why did Oswald do it? To this most important and most mysterious question the commission had no certain answer. It suggested that Oswald had no rational purpose, no motive adequate if "judged by the standards of reasonable men."

A Product of His Life

Rather, the commission saw Oswald's terrible act as the product of his entire life—a life "characterized by isolation, frustration and failure." He was just 24 years old at the time of the assassination.

"Oswald was profoundly alienated from the world in which he lived," the report said. "He had very few, if any, close relationships with other people and he appeared to have had great difficulty in finding a meaningful place in the world.

"He was never satisfied with anything.

"When he was in the United States, he resented the capitalist system. When he was in the Soviet Union, he apparently resented the Communist party members, who were accorded special privileges and who he thought were betraying Communism, and he spoke well of the United States."

The commission found that Oswald shot at former Maj. Gen. Edwin A. Walker in Dallas on April 10, 1963, narrowly missing him. It cited this as evidence of his capacity for violence.

It listed as factors that might have led Oswald to the assassination "his deep-rooted resentment of all authority, which was expressed in a hostility toward every society in which he lived," his "urge to try to find a place in history" and his "avowed commitment to Marx-

Continued on Page 14, Column 1

JOHNSON NAMES 4 TO ACT ON REPORT

Commission Calls for Action to Increase the Security of the Presidency

By The Associated Press

JOHNSON CITY, Tex., Sept. 27—President Johnson appointed a four-man committee today to advise him "on the execution of the recommendations of the Warren Commission."

The commission, which investigated the assassination of President Kennedy, recommended action to tighten the protection of Presidents and to make the killing of a President or a Vice President a Federal crime.

[Mike Mansfield of Montana, the Senate majority leader, said in Washington that Congress, which has been aiming at adjournment at the end of this week, "should stay here and act, if the President sends us any recommendations."]

Members of the committee are Secretary of the Treasury Douglas Dillon, Acting Attorney General Nicholas deB. Katzenbach, John A. McCone, director of the Central Intelligence Agency, and McGeorge Bundy, Special Assistant to the President for National Security Affairs.

The President named no chairman for the committee, but it was understood that Secretary Dillon, as ranking member, would have general supervision over the group.

The group will presumably

Continued on Page 17, Column 3

A New Chapter Unfolds in the Kennedy Legend

By JAMES RESTON
Special to The New York Times

News Analysis

WASHINGTON, Sept. 27—The Warren Commission has fulfilled its primary assignment. It has tried, as a servant of history, to discover truth. But the assassination of President Kennedy was so symbolic of human irony and tragedy, and so involved in the complicated and elemental conflicts of the age, that many vital questions remain, and the philosophers, novelists and dramatists will have to take it from here.

The commission has not concluded the Kennedy mystery so much as it has opened up a whole new chapter in the Kennedy legend.

It has provided the greatest repository of Presidential political history, drama and fiction since the murder of Mr. Lincoln and since legend is often more powerful than history, this may be the commission's most significant achievement.

Now the central mystery of who killed the President has been answered by the commission only in the process of raising a new catalogue of mysteries. Now the main characters in the play have been surrounded by a host of new characters, each of whom appears briefly at a critical moment with some vital testimony, only to disappear without our really knowing much about who they are.

The whole story is full of the mystery of life. Lee Harvey Oswald's motive for murdering the President remains obscure. The distinguished members of the commission and their staff obviously gave up on it.

The "might-have-beens" are maddening. If only he had been given that visa to go to Cuba and thence to the Soviet Union just before the assassination! If he had not been allowed to come back from there in the first place! Who was "the neighbor" who got him the job in the Texas Book Depository, from where he shot the President? And what were the details of Oswald's attempted suicide in Moscow?

The wild accidents are equally intriguing. There is, for example, the case of Mrs. Bledsoe, who rented Oswald a room in Dallas and then, on a 10,000-to-1 chance, just happened to be on the bus he boarded when he was running away from the crime.

Then there are the consoling yearnings and kindnesses in the midst of tragedy: Ruth Paine, who was also "alienated" and "isolated," and frustrated like Oswald, but who nevertheless "befriended" Marina Oswald in her time of

Continued on Page 15, Column 6

'MYTHS' OF CASE DENIED IN DETAIL

Panel Says Misinformation on the Assassination Led to 'Distorted' Views

By PETER KIHSS

The Warren Commission rejected in detail yesterday a number of charges suggesting that Lee Harvey Oswald had not acted alone in the assassination of President Kennedy.

The commission said that "publicizing of unchecked information" had led to "myths" and "distorted" interpretations. While each inaccuracy could be explained, it went on, "the number and variety of misstatements issued by the police" in Dallas would have "greatly assisted a skillful defense attorney."

On the other hand, Mark Lane, chairman of a Citizens Committee of Inquiry here, contended that if the report contained all the available evidence, "Oswald would have been acquitted" of both the President's assassination and the murder of the Dallas patrolman, J. D. Tippit.

In a news conference, Mr. Lane, a former Assemblyman, said his group would continue its efforts to "answer the unanswered questions." He said it had more than 250 workers here, with other committees in England, France and Denmark, and interested groups on 20 college campuses. His group estimated that it had raised and

Continued on Page 16, Column 4

High Clerics to Ask Stronger Statement By Council on Jews

Special to The New York Times

ROME, Sept. 27—A powerful array of Roman Catholic prelates, including at least three American Cardinals, are preparing to speak out for a strong statement by the Ecumenical Council on the Jews, clerical sources said today.

The sources said that Richard James Cardinal Cushing, Archbishop of Boston, is known to have prepared an address to be given at the Council when the issue is debated.

The draft of the declaration was introduced last Friday by Augustin Cardinal Bea, the German Jesuit, who heads the Council's Secretariat for the Promotion of Christian Unity. It is considered by many Council Fathers—the voting prelates—and observers to be a "watered down" version of an earlier draft.

Other Cardinals Named

The earlier statement, among other things, made plain that the Jews of Christ's time and of today bore no responsibility for the Crucifixion. The weakened declaration declares only that Jews of today cannot be blamed.

Among those expected to attack the newer version are two other American Cardinals—Joseph Elmer Ritter, Archbishop of St. Louis, and Albert Gregory Meyer, Archbishop of Chicago.

Cardinal Spellman of New York has also said that he favors the more forceful state-

Continued on Page 7, Column 1

2 CITIES DENY REIN ON POLICE IN RIOTS

Civilian Review Units Hold F.B.I. Criticism Unfounded

By FRED POWLEDGE

Officials of civilian police advisory boards in Rochester and Philadelphia disagreed yesterday with a statement by the Federal Bureau of Investigation that boards such as theirs had "virtually paralyzed" the police during the summer riots.

The Rev. William H. Gray Jr., executive secretary of Philadelphia's eight-member review board, said: "It's over-simplifying the situation to say that the board has an effect on the rioting or the police behavior."

Ross J. Guglielmino, the executive director and legal counsel of the Rochester board, said he did not feel the F.B.I. criticism applied to Rochester.

What the F.B.I. Found

The two men commented in telephone interviews on a report released Saturday by President Johnson. The President had asked the F.B.I. to collect its investigations of summer riots in New York City, Rochester, Dixmoor, Ill.; Philadelphia, Seaside, Ore., Hampton Beach, N. H., and Jersey City, Paterson, and Elizabeth, N. J., and advise him if there were any pattern in the outbreaks.

The report, submitted by F.B.I. Director J. Edgar Hoover, concluded that the riots were not basically racial, although large numbers of Negroes took part; that they were not organized on a national basis, and that none of them was planned by any one group or individual.

Among the several points

Continued on Page 48, Column 1

Congress Will Act On Appalachia Aid And Medical Care

Special to The New York Times

WASHINGTON, Sept. 27—The fate of two key Administration programs—health insurance for the aged and aid to Appalachia—may be decided this week as Congress pushes toward adjournment.

"We could finish up Saturday; that's my most optimistic guess," Senator Mike Mansfield of Montana, the majority leader, said today. "But I have my fingers crossed."

The health insurance issue, currently in House-Senate conference, could delay adjournment until the following week, some legislative leaders believe.

Prospects for conference approval of some form of health insurance for the aged under Social Security have ranged from bright to gloomy in recent days.

The House passed a bill this summer to increase Social Security taxes as well as cash

Continued on Page 18, Column 4

NEWS INDEX

In this issue editorials appear on Page 28, obituaries on Page 29, TV and radio news on Page 47, and the News Summary and Index on Page 2.

CAMPAIGN IMPACT BELIEVED LIKELY

'Kennedy Legacy' Could Aid Democrats at the Polls

By TOM WICKER
Special to The New York Times

WASHINGTON, Sept. 27—The effects of the Warren Commission's report are sure to extend far beyond its conclusion that Lee Harvey Oswald, acting alone, killed President Kennedy last Nov. 22.

The massive document could have repercussions in the 1964 elections, on the present conduct of President Johnson, and ultimately on the availability to the public of Mr. Johnson and future Presidents.

It may produce major changes for the Secret Service, the agency now assigned to protect the President.

Other Agencies Affected

The assignments and powers of other agencies such as the Federal Bureau of Investigation and even the Central Intelligence Agency might be revamped and independent review of their activities and efficiency might be increased.

In the field of legislation, the report might produce—as recommended by the commission—a law making it a Federal crime to kill or attempt to kill a President, a Vice President or any officer next in line to the Presidency and the President-elect and Vice President-elect. Other legislation, particularly relating to security and investigative agencies and to the protection of Presidents, could also grow from the report.

Although the State Department was generally cleared of

Continued on Page 15, Column 5

G.I.'s Rescue Vietnam Captives; Uprising Stirs Mistrust of U.S.

By PETER GROSE
Special to The New York Times

SAIGON, South Vietnam, Sept. 27 — United States Army helicopters rescued 60 Vietnamese hostages today from a camp of rebel tribesmen in the central highlands.

The release of the prisoners met a Government condition for negotiations with the armed mountain tribesmen. It appeared to reduce the danger of a violent clash.

Nevertheless the revolt is having serious political consequences, involving growing suspicion between the United States mission and the Premier, Maj. Gen. Nguyen Khanh. The rebellion has intensified Saigon's feeling that the United States, which has supported General Khanh, is undergoing a change of policy.

[About five persons were reported shot dead when security forces fired on a crowd in Quinhon, 270 miles northeast of Saigon. Later a mob stormed a radio station and troops were called in to evict the demonstrators, Reuters reported.]

Officials around General Khanh say he no longer believes he can count on American help to stay in power and he feels he must seek firmer support from

Continued on Page 2, Column 1

Scientific Police Work Traced Bullets to Rifle Oswald Owned

By JOHN W. FINNEY
Special to The New York Times

WASHINGTON, Sept. 27—The Warren Commission's conclusion that Lee Harvey Oswald killed President Kennedy rests in large part on scientific evidence painstakingly established through modern technology.

On the basis of the scientific evidence alone it was possible to establish that the shots were fired by a rifle owned and possessed by Oswald, that the shots were fired from the sixth-floor window of a building in which Oswald worked, and that the fatal wound could have been caused by the bullets from the high-powered rifle.

These crucial points were established through scientific detective work that combined the techniques of handwriting, ballistics, and fiber and wounds analysis. Among the devices used were microscopes, spectroscopes, X-rays, surveying instruments and skulls filled with gelatin.

Even nuclear science was employed. Paraffin casts from Oswald's hands and face were put into a nuclear reactor at the Oak Ridge (Tenn.) National Laboratory in an unsuccessful attempt to see if radiation would show up traces of gunpowder. One major question left

Continued on Page 16, Column 5

NEW NUMBER FOR ORDERING WANT ads in The New York Times. OXford 5-3311. Fast. direct-line service to want ad takers.—Advt.

"All the News That's Fit to Print"

The New York Times.

LATE CITY EDITION

U.S. Weather Bureau Report (Page 76) forecasts:
Cloudy and cooler today; chance of rain tonight and tomorrow.
Temp. Range: 68—53; yesterday: 68 48.

VOL. CXIV. No. 38,982. NEW YORK, FRIDAY, OCTOBER 16, 1964. TEN CENTS

KHRUSHCHEV OUSTED FROM TOP POSTS; BREZHNEV GETS CHIEF PARTY POSITION AND KOSYGIN IS NAMED NEW PREMIER

Labor Party Is the Apparent Victor in British Election

JOHNSON DENIES JENKINS COVER-UP; SETS F.B.I. INQUIRY

Praises His Aide's Service, but Says He Requested Resignation From Post

By TOM WICKER
Special to The New York Times

WASHINGTON, Oct. 15—President Johnson said tonight that until late yesterday he had had no information of any kind that "had ever raised a question" about the personal conduct of Walter W. Jenkins, his friend and special assistant.

The President made the statement, his first public comment on the Jenkins case, as he flew back here from a day of campaigning in New York.

In effect, he was denying Republican allegations that he had covered up knowledge of Mr. Jenkins's two arrests on morals charges. The disclosure of these arrests yesterday has shaken the Johnson Administration and the Democratic Presidential campaign.

Mr. Jenkins's resignation as special assistant to the President was announced in New York last night after the disclosure of his police record.

Mr. Johnson also disclosed in his statement tonight that he had requested the resignation of Mr. Jenkins.

'Dedication' Is Cited

The text of Mr. Johnson's statement follows:

"Walter Jenkins has worked with me faithfully for 25 years. No man I know has given more personal dedication, devotion and tireless labor.

"Until late yesterday no information or report of any kind to me had ever raised a question with respect to his personal conduct. Mr. Jenkins is now in the care of his physician and his many friends will join in praying for his early recovery. For myself and Mrs. Johnson I want to say that our hearts go out with the deepest compassion for him and for his wife and six children—and they have our love and prayers.

"On this case as on any such case, the public interest comes before all personal feelings. I have requested and received Mr. Jenkins's resignation.

"Within moments after being notified last night, I ordered Director J. Edgar Hoover of the F.B.I. to make an immediate and comprehensive inquiry and report promptly to me and the American people."

The incident apparently is regarded by the Republicans as a major development in their

Continued on Page 20, Column 1

G.O.P. Hopes Rise, But Jenkins Effect On Race Is Cloudy

By EARL MAZO

The Walter W. Jenkins case inspired high hopes in the camp of Senator Barry Goldwater yesterday and dismay among supporters of President Johnson.

But by nightfall, reports from Moscow that Premier Khrushchev has been replaced led many political observers to speculate that the possible anti-Johnson impact of the Jenkins disclosure might be nullified by the effect of an international crisis upon the voters.

A leading Republican put it this way:

"That Lyndon Johnson is lucky. The arrest of his man Jenkins accented the whole Bobby Baker corruption mess, which is Barry Goldwater's strongest issue. But then comes this Khrushchev thing, taking the headlines and accenting Barry's greatest weak-

Continued on Page 21, Column 1

SLIM EDGE LIKELY

Wilson Aide Defeated in Campaign Marred by a Racial Issue

By SYDNEY GRUSON
Special to The New York Times

LONDON, Friday, Oct. 16—Britain apparently elected a Labor Government in yesterday's general election and sent the Conservatives, who have governed for 13 years, into opposition.

However, all indications pointed to the closest result since the Conservatives won with a majority of 17 in 1951. There is still a chance that Labor will not get a working majority.

With counting finished for the night, the standing of the parties from the results in 430 of the 630 constituencies was:

Labor—247
Conservative—181
Liberal—2

But this Labor lead of 66 House of Commons seats was misleading. Most of the results were from urban areas and the Conservatives are expected to cut deeply into the lead when counting in the rural Conservative strongholds resumes later this morning.

Labor Gains 52 Seats

The computers of the British Broadcasting Corporation and of Press Association, the cooperative newsgathering agency, both forecast an ultimate Labor majority over the Conservatives of 17.

Labor gained 52 seats, two from the Liberals and the rest from the Conservatives. The Conservatives lost 50 seats and took four from Labor.

Sir Alec Douglas-Home, the Conservative leader and Prime Minister, would not concede. He did not emerge from 10 Downing Street, his London office and residence, where he watched the election results on television.

So long as he did not concede, Harold Wilson, Labor's leader, refused to claim victory. Mr. Wilson would be Prime Minister in a Labor Government.

Patrick Gordon Walker, slated to be Foreign Secretary in a Labor Cabinet, lost the Smethwick constituency of industrial Birmingham to Peter Griffiths, a Conservative.

It was at Smethwick that a bitter campaign had been waged

Continued on Page 18, Column 1

Nikita S. Khrushchev
Relieved of political posts

Leonid I. Brezhnev
Named as the leader of the party

Associated Press

Aleksei N. Kosygin
Appointed as the Soviet Premier

MOSCOW IS QUIET

Pravda Says Change Won't Bring Return of Harsh Policies

By HENRY TANNER
Special to The New York Times

MOSCOW, Friday, Oct. 16 — Premier Khrushchev has been deprived of political power in the Soviet Union.

He was replaced by Leonid I. Brezhnev, 57 years old, as First Secretary of the Communist party and by Aleksei N. Kosygin, 60, as Premier.

Mr. Khrushchev, who is 70, even lost his seat in the Presidium of the Central Committee of the party, the third most important position he held in the leadership.

This indicated that he had fallen into disgrace.

[Dispatches did not mention if Mr. Khrushchev had been removed from the Central Committee itself. Under normal procedure such action would come at a meeting of the Soviet Communist party Congress.]

Adzhubei Reported Ousted

The changes were announced by Tass, the Soviet press agency, a few minutes after midnight.

The Tass statement did not contain a single word of praise for the ousted leader.

Unofficial but reliable sources later reported that Aleksei I. Adzhubei, Mr. Khrushchev's son-in-law, had been deposed as chief editor of the Government newspaper Izvestia.

Mr. Khrushchev's whereabouts was not known. Nor was it known whether he was at liberty or under surveillance. Western diplomats assumed, however, that the changeover had been made peacefully.

Diplomats Voice Assurance

Moscow's streets were quiet. There were no signs of movements by either the army or police. Some of the smaller Western embassies, which had been without a police guard for the last several months, reported yesterday that the policemen were back in front of the gates.

Western diplomats said they did not expect the new leaders to change basic Soviet policy toward the West.

Mr. Brezhnev and Mr. Kosygin can be expected to continue Mr. Khrushchev's policy of "peaceful coexistence" with the United States, the diplomats said.

The Soviet Communist party newspaper Pravda indicated today that the party would continue to carry out policies of de-Stalinization and economic improvements under its new leadership.

The paper printed the same bare announcement that had been carried in the English-

Continued on Page 14, Column 1

JOHNSON HAILED AT LIBERAL RALLY

Asserts 'Great Society' Is a Practical Goal—He Is Acclaimed Upstate

By HOMER BIGART

President Johnson received a frenzied ovation last night from 20,000 persons who packed Madison Square Garden for a Liberal party rally.

The President expounded to the Garden audience his vision of the "Great Society" and insisted it was a practical goal—"not some vague, dreamlike utopia."

He said he would present a series of proposals dealing with the total needs of a metropolitan area.

These proposals, he said, would be built on the cooperation of government with industry—"the same sort of cooperation that has built our national defense and allowed us to explore the stars."

Campaigns With Kennedy

The President went to the Garden after stumping the state with Robert F. Kennedy, the Democratic-Liberal candidate for the Senate, and receiving tumultuous welcomes from huge crowds on a 22-mile tour of Brooklyn.

Despite the Walter Jenkins scandal, no lessening of enthusiasm was apparent in the throngs that greeted the President in Brooklyn or jammed the Garden for the Liberal party's climactic demonstration.

Roaring applause greeted the President and Mrs. Johnson when they entered the Garden at 8:20 P.M.

The President read his speech in a matter-of-fact voice and the subject matter—the "Great Society"—inspired no cheers.

Interest Stimulated

But when he turned to the day's dramatic developments in the Soviet Union, the crowd's interest was stimulated. A crescendo of applause followed his remark: "We do not intend to bury anyone anywhere and we do not intend to be buried ourselves."

The President warned that this was no time for impulsive leadership. He said "an impulsive thumb can move up toward a button," resulting in the destruction of millions of lives in a matter of moments.

Recalling the Cuban missile crisis, he declared that President Kennedy "had the steadiest thumb, the greatest heart and

Continued on Page 22, Column 1

Cholesterol Studies Bring Nobel Award To Two Biochemists

By The Associated Press

STOCKHOLM, Oct. 15—The 1964 Nobel Prize in Physiology or Medicine was awarded jointly today to Prof. Konrad E. Bloch of Harvard University and Prof. Feodor Lynen of the University of Munich.

The two were honored for their discoveries concerning the mechanism and regulation of cholesterol and fatty acid metabolism. They will share prize money equivalent to about $54,000.

In its citation, the prize-awarding body, the Royal Caroline Institute, said the therapy against circulatory diseases and related disturbances in steroid hormone metabolism would in the future rest upon the work of today's Nobel Prize winners.

Dr. Bloch, a 52-year-old naturalized American born in Germany, is Higgins Professor of Biochemistry at Harvard. He was credited with "brilliant investigations" showing how cholesterol is built up from acetic acid.

Cholesterol, a fatty substance

Continued on Page 3, Column 1

THREATENED SUIT HALTS STATE LOAN

Deals to Borrow $17 Million Delayed by Challenge to Rockefeller Financing

By PETER KIHSS

Two state agencies have had to postpone the closing of deals to borrow $17.3 million because of a threatened court suit by Teamsters Joint Council 16 against financing methods of the Rockefeller administration.

The Governor's office declined yesterday to say why the closing had been held up. But a high state official said the purchasers of bond-anticipation notes required standard certificates assuring that they would not become involved in litigation, and he said that such statements could not be given because of the threatened teamsters suit.

Governor Rockefeller was reported to have sought through intermediaries to get the union council president, John J. O'Rourke, to drop the threatened suit. The Governor's view was said to have been that "thousands" of jobs of currently employed construction workers would be endangered if the financing were held up.

But Nicholas M. Kisburg, legislative and research director of the teamsters' council, said last night that the state could use $806 million to carry on construction through bond issues already approved by the voters but not yet invoked by the Governor.

Governor Rockefeller's office said that $13.8 million in bond-anticipation notes of the State Housing Finance Agency had first been sold to five buyers Oct. 8, with delivery scheduled for yesterday. Yesterday, the agency "postponed delivery of the notes," the Governor's office said.

Similarly, it said, $3.5 million in bond-anticipation notes of the State Dormitory Authority had been sold Oct. 8, but delivery had to be "postponed" on Wednesday

The purchasers of the Housing Finance Agency notes were

Continued on Page 31, Column 1

U.S. Surprised but Expects No Radical Shift in Policy

By MAX FRANKEL
Special to The New York Times

WASHINGTON, Oct. 15—The Administration was surprised but not alarmed by the change of leadership in Moscow today. Analysts of Soviet affairs were almost unanimous in the view that Premier Khrushchev had suddenly been forced to step down for reasons of personality and policy, not merely age and health.

But the survival and promotion of prominent Khrushchev lieutenants, officials said, seemed to preclude any radical policy changes in the near future, at least in East-West relations.

In New York, President Johnson said that the shift in the Kremlin "may or may not be a sign of deep turmoil or a sign of changes to come." He commented at the end of his prepared remarks at a Liberal party rally.

Peace Is the Mission

"For ourselves, the need is clear—we should keep steady on our goals," he said. "Peace is the mission of the American people and we are not about to be deterred. We will be firm and restrained. We can meet any test but our quest is always for peace."

In Milwaukee, Senator Hubert H. Humphrey expressed doubt that the Soviet change would bring about a "quick" meeting of Soviet and United States leaders. Talking to newsmen

Continued on Page 15, Column 1

STOCKS PLUMMET IN HECTIC TRADING

Changes in Kremlin Set Off Sharpest Drop in Prices Since Kennedy's Death

By RICHARD PHALON

Rumors of impending changes in the Kremlin swept Wall Street yesterday. By 1:30 P.M. a rolling tide of uneasiness had driven prices on the New York Stock Exchange to their deepest loss since the assassination of President Kennedy last Nov. 22.

Trading volume ran to 6.5 million shares, well below the record of 14.7 million shares churned up in the big market break of May 29, 1962, but much of it came in a concentrated burst after the noon hour. By 2:30 P.M. the tape lagged 27 minutes behind activity on the floor of the stock exchange.

Many brokers felt yesterday's market break followed a classic pattern. As one diagnosed it, the small investors were doing much of the selling. "They can't see anything, they can't touch anything and they're nervous. They're selling and the professionals are bargain-hunting," he observed.

Losses Cut in Half

The first tangible sign that bargain-hunters were on the move came at 2:30 P.M. when market losses were cut in half. By 3 P.M. reports that Premier Khrushchev was retiring were confirmed and the news spread rapidly across the floor of the stock exchange.

At the close of trading, the stock market was down 6.74 points as measured by the Dow-Jones industrial average. The New York Times combined average of 50 stocks closed with a loss of 5.79 points.

Despite the late rally, it was the biggest loss since Aug. 4 when the stock prices plummeted after the Gulf of Tonkin naval action.

Boardroom habitués at midtown brokerage houses glared at the dancing symbols on the big Trans-Lux tapes with a frowning concentration usually re-

Continued on Page 53, Column 7

Cole Porter Is Dead; Songwriter Was 72

By The Associated Press

SANTA MONICA, Calif., Oct. 15 — Cole Porter, the world-famed composer and lyricist, died at 11:05 P.M. today at a Santa Monica hospital, where he underwent kidney surgery last Tuesday. He was 72 years old.

Mr. Porter wrote the lyrics and music for his songs, and to both he brought such an individuality of style that a genre known as "the Cole Porter song" became recognized.

The hallmarks of a typical Porter song were lyrics that were urbane or witty and a melody with a sinuous, brooding quality. Some of his best-known songs in this vein were "What

Continued on Page 29, Column 1

Cards Win World Series, Defeating Yankees, 7 to 5

By JOSEPH DURSO
Special to The New York Times

ST. LOUIS, Oct. 15—The St. Louis Cardinals completed their melodramatic climb from the depths of the National League to baseball's pinnacle today when they defeated the New York Yankees, 7—5, and captured the World Series.

They won it in the seventh and final game before a roaring crowd of 30,346 persons in Busch Stadium after they had won the National League pennant in the final game of the regular season. And they won it in the same way—behind the fast-ball pitching of 28-year-old Bob Gibson, who struck out nine Yankees and survived three late home runs that knocked in all the Yankees' runs.

Five pitchers struggled against Gibson to withstand the Cardinals. But the Redbirds scored three runs in the fourth inning, three in the fifth and one in the seventh to bring St. Louis its first championship in 18 years and send the Yankees to their second straight loss of the World Series.

The Yankees had not lost two years in a row since 1921 and 1922, the first two times they played in the World Series. Since then, they had appeared in 25 Series in 40 years and won 20 of them until the Los Angeles Dodgers defeated them in four games last year.

Today they threatened until the last out to overpower the Cardinals in the winner-take-all game. Five home runs were struck, two by the Cardinals and three by the Yankees. Two were hit by the Boyer brothers—Ken of the Cards and Clete of the Yanks—while Lou Brock hit one for St. Louis and Mickey Mantle and Phil Linz for New York in the late innings.

But when Gibson got the Yankees' hitting star of the Series, Bobby Richardson, on a high pop-up to Dal Maxvill at second base in the ninth, the titanic struggle was over.

Busch Stadium erupted into shouting, chanting, singing, bugle-blaring and fireworks as fans emptied the grandstand

Continued on Page 44, Column 2

American Motors Struck by U.A.W.

By DAVID R. JONES
Special to The New York Times

DETROIT, Friday, Oct. 16—The United Automobile Workers struck the American Motors Corporation this morning after failure to reach a new labor agreement.

Edward L. Cushman, American Motors vice president and top labor negotiator, announced at 1:05 A.M. today that the parties had agreed to retain a profit-sharing plan in a new contract. But he said the strike deadline arrived before they could resolve other differences.

The strike affects about 23,000 workers at four plants in two Wisconsin cities. The company makes Rambler automobiles.

The walkout widened labor strife in the industry, where nearly 300,000 workers already have been made idle by an auto

Continued on Page 40, Column 1

The TFX Unveiled; McNamara Hails It

By RICHARD WITKIN
Special to The New York Times

FORT WORTH, Tex., Oct. 15—The TFX, the plane that launched 3,000 pages of Congressional inquiry, was rolled out the factory door into public view today.

The twin-jet plane, which has revolutionary movable wings and now is called the F-111, is scheduled to make its first flight by the end of the year.

The rollout ceremony was attended by a dais full of civilian and military dignitaries, headed by Secretary of Defense Robert S. McNamara.

Mr. McNamara has been at the center of the political storm that has enveloped the F-111 program since his office overruled the unanimous judgment

Continued on Page 11, Column 1

NEWS INDEX

"All the News That's Fit to Print"

The New York Times.

LATE CITY EDITION
U. S. Weather Bureau Report (Page 78) forecasts:
Sunny today; clear tonight.
Fair and milder tomorrow.
Temp. Range: 63—48; yesterday: 60—48.

VOL. CXIV.... No. 39,001. NEW YORK, WEDNESDAY, NOVEMBER 4, 1964. TEN CENTS

JOHNSON SWAMPS GOLDWATER AND KENNEDY BEATS KEATING; DEMOCRATS WIN LEGISLATURE

KENNEDY EDGE 6-5

Keating's Defeat Is Termed a 'Tragedy' by Rockefeller

New York Vote

PRESIDENT	
Johnson, Dem.	4,509,514
Goldwater, Rep.	2,089,113
11,330 of 12,439 E.D.'s rptg.	
SENATOR	
Kennedy, Dem.	3,479,976
Keating, Rep.	2,857,023
11,318 of 12,439 E.D.'s rptg.	

By R. W. APPLE Jr.

Robert F. Kennedy was elected to the United States Senate from New York yesterday in his first bid for elective office, overwhelming Republican Senator Kenneth B. Keating.

With more than 80 per cent of the vote counted, Mr. Kennedy held a 6-to-5 lead. Because most of the untallied vote was in heavily Democratic New York City, it appeared that the former Attorney General's plurality might reach 650,000.

Mr. Keating conceded defeat at 11:39 P.M. with the announcement at the Roosevelt Hotel that he had sent a congratulatory telegram to Mr. Kennedy.

Governor Rockefeller, standing beside the white-haired Rochester legislator, said Mr. Keating's defeat was "a tragedy for the state and nation."

Runs Behind Johnson

"Senator Keating, one of the great Senators in the history of New York, has been rolled under by a national landslide," the Governor added. "He waged a magnificent campaign."

Mr. Kennedy ran well behind President Johnson, who seemed to be headed for a record margin of 2.5 million votes or more in the state. The President won all of the state's 62 counties.

It thus appeared that about a million New York voters had split their ticket to cast votes for Mr. Johnson and Mr. Keating — but even this wasn't enough to make the Senate contest close.

A major surprise was the showing of the Liberal party, which had expected to deliver

Continued on Page 27, Column 4

The Election at a Glance

President

	Number of States*	Electoral Votes
Johnson	45	486
Goldwater	6	52

*Includes Dist. of Columbia

President—New York

Johnson	4,509,514
Goldwater	2,089,113

Incomplete

Senator—New York

Kennedy	3,479,976
Keating	2,857,023

Incomplete

The Senate

Newly Elected Senators		Make-up of New Senate	
Democrats	25	Democrats	65
Republicans	5	Republicans	30
In doubt	5	In doubt	5

The House

Democrats elected	261
Republicans elected	127
In doubt	47

JOHNSON CRUSHES RIVAL IN JERSEY

Lead Near 900,000, Topping Eisenhower's Record—Williams Re-elected

New Jersey Vote

PRESIDENT	
Johnson, Dem.	1,645,844
Goldwater, Rep.	853,708
4,001 of 4,603 E.D.'s rptg.	
SENATOR	
Williams, Dem.	1,474,523
Shanley, Rep.	891,425
4,001 of 4,603 E.D.'s rptg.	

By GEORGE CABLE WRIGHT

President Johnson won New Jersey's 17 electoral votes yesterday in the biggest political victory ever scored in the state.

With 91 per cent of the vote tallied, the President held a record lead of nearly 900,000 votes over his Republican opponent, Senator Barry Goldwater.

Until yesterday, the record plurality for a Presidential candidate in New Jersey was the 756,605-vote margin rolled up by President Eisenhower, a Republican, in 1956.

In sweeping at least 19, and possibly all of the state's 21 counties, Mr. Johnson carried to victory with him incumbent Democratic Senator Harrison A. Williams Jr. Democrats also captured a majority of the state's 15 seats in the House of Representatives for the first time since 1912.

In the present Congress, Republicans hold eight of the seats. On the basis of incomplete returns from yesterday's balloting, Democrats won at least 10 seats.

The Democratic candidate James J. Howard also held a narrow lead over his Republican opponent, Marcus Daly, in an

Continued on Page 32, Column 4

Connecticut Votes 2-1 for President; All Democrats Win

Connecticut Vote

PRESIDENT (Complete)	
Johnson, D.	825,416
Goldwater, R.	392,556
SENATOR	
Dodd, D.	779,252
Lodge, R.	425,376

By RICHARD H. PARKE

President Johnson led a sweeping Democratic victory in Connecticut yesterday.

His better than 2-to-1 margin over Senator Barry Goldwater eclipsed the previous record plurality in a Presidential race in the state. Mr. Johnson's plurality was 432,860. The earlier record had been set by President Dwight D. Eisenhower in 1956 when he defeated Adlai E. Stevenson by 306,758 votes.

Senator Thomas J. Dodd, the Democratic incumbent, also triumphed easily over his Republican opponent, former Gov. John Davis Lodge. But the 57-year-old Senator ran about 75,000 votes behind the President.

One result of President Johnson's landslide was the defeat of the state's only Republican Congressman, Representative Abner W. Sibal of the Fourth (Fairfield County) District. Mr. Sibal lost the normally Republican district to former Representative Donald J. Irwin, a

Continued on Page 32, Column 1

UPSET AT ALBANY

Carlino and Mahoney Defeated—Special Session Expected

By LAYHMOND ROBINSON

A surge of Democratic votes swept the Republicans from control of the State Legislature yesterday for the first time in more than a quarter of a century.

The massive victory gave the Democrats a probable working majority of a dozen seats in the Assembly and a half dozen in the Senate.

Not since 1935, in the sweep of Franklin D. Roosevelt's New Deal, had the Democrats had control of both the houses. Not since 1938 had they held control of the Senate.

Toppled from their powerful posts in stunning upsets were Assembly Speaker Joseph F. Carlino of Long Beach, L. I., and Senate Majority Leader Walter J. Mahoney of Buffalo.

Beaten by Outsiders

Both suffered defeat at the hands of virtually unknown Democrats.

Mr. Carlino, the top Republican figure in the lower house for six years and an Assemblyman representing Nassau's Second Assembly District for 20 years, was beaten by Jerome R. McDougal Jr., a car salesman making his first race for public office.

Senator Mahoney, often called the most powerful man in the Legislature, was unseated by John H. Doerr of Buffalo in Erie County's 55th Senate District.

Another high-ranking Republican who lost was Senator MacNeil Mitchell of Manhattan, the most influential New York City member of the two houses.

In some districts in the suburbs and in upstate counties, Democrats captured Assembly and Senate seats for the first time in this century.

Districting Fight Due

At the last session, the G.O.P. had a 10-vote edge over the Democrats in the Assembly, holding 85 seats to 65 for the Democrats. In the Senate they had a 33-25 edge.

Although the Democrats ended this G.O.P. domination, the battle for control could be resumed again in December.

The Governor is expected to call a special session of the Legislature then to adopt a new plan for reapportioning seats in the two houses.

This reapportionment session will be controlled by the present members, with the Republicans in control.

Members elected yesterday do not take their seats until the

Continued on Page 33, Column 3

LYNDON BAINES JOHNSON

The New York Times

HUBERT HORATIO HUMPHREY

TURNOUT IS HEAVY

President Expected to Get 60% of Vote, With 44 States

By TOM WICKER

Lyndon Baines Johnson of Texas compiled one of the greatest landslide victories in American history yesterday to win a four-year term of his own as the 36th President of the United States.

Senator Hubert H. Humphrey of Minnesota, Mr. Johnson's running mate on the Democratic ticket, was carried into office as Vice President.

Mr. Johnson's triumph, giving him the "loud and clear" national mandate he had said he wanted, brought 44 states and the district of Columbia, with 486 electoral votes, into the Democratic column.

Senator Barry Goldwater, the Republican candidate, who sought to offer the people "a choice, not an echo" with a strongly conservative campaign, won only five states in the Deep South and gained a narrow victory in his home state of Arizona. Carrying it gave him a total of 52 electoral votes.

Senator Plans Statement

A heavy voter turnout favored the more numerous Democrats.

In Austin, Tex., Mr. Johnson appeared in the Municipal Auditorium to say that his victory was "a tribute to men and women of all parties."

"It is a mandate for unity, for a Government that serves no special interest," he said.

The election meant, he said, that "our nation should forget our petty differences and stand united before all the world."

Mr. Goldwater did not concede. A spokesman announced that the Senator would make no statement until 10 A.M. today in Phoenix.

Johnson Carries Texas

But the totals were not the only marks of the massive Democratic victory. Traditionally Republican states were bowled over like tenpins—Vermont, Indiana, Kansas, Nebraska, Wyoming, among others.

In New York, both houses of the Legislature were headed for Democratic control for the first time in years. Heralded Republicans like Charles H. Percy, the gubernatorial candidate in Illinois, went down to defeat.

Former Attorney General Robert F. Kennedy, riding Mr. Johnson's long coattails, overwhelmed Senator Kenneth B. Keating in New York.

But ticket splitting was widespread. And in the South, Georgia went Republican; never

Continued on Page 22, Column 1

SOUTH REVERSES VOTING PATTERNS

Goldwater Makes Inroads, but More Electoral Votes Go to the President

By JOHN HERBERS
Special to The New York Times

ATLANTA, Nov. 3—President Johnson carried a majority of Southern states tonight by turning the normal voting patterns inside out.

The rural Deep South, solidly Democratic in the past, voted for Senator Barry Goldwater of Arizona on the Republican ticket. The states on the border of the region, which had gone Republican in recent Presidential elections, returned to the Democrats.

But so strong was the Goldwater tide in the Deep South that seven Republican Congressional candidates rode to victory on the Senator's coattails from districts that had been Democratic since Reconstruction.

The Republicans made their biggest gains in Alabama, where five candidates for Congress defeated Democratic opponents.

President Johnson carried Virginia, North Carolina, Florida, Tennessee, Arkansas and Texas with a total of 81 electorial votes. Senator Goldwater carried Louisiana, Mississippi, Alabama, Georgia and South Carolina with a total of 47 electorial votes.

South Carolina and Mississippi had not voted for Repub-

Continued on Page 24, Column 2

Democrats Are Assured Of Majorities in Congress

House Gain for Democrats

By JOHN D. MORRIS

Democrats strengthened their control of the House of Representatives in yesterday's elections, scoring substantial gains in all regions except the South.

With returns from Congressional races still incomplete early this morning, the trend indicated a Democratic pickup of at least 20 seats and possibly 30 or more.

The Republicans nevertheless scored spectacular breakthroughs in the South, winning five of Alabama's eight seats, one of Mississippi's five and at least one of Georgia's 10.

Those gains were more than offset, however, by the loss of both of their Texas seats and by heavy Democratic gains in other parts of the country.

The House division in the expiring 88th Congress is 257 Democrats and 178 Republicans. This credits five vacancies to the parties last holding the seats. Three were occupied by Democrats and two by Republicans.

With 218 needed for a major-

Continued on Page 21, Column 1

3 G.O.P. Senators Lose

By E. W. KENWORTHY

The Democrats appeared virtually certain today of maintaining a nearly 2-to-1 majority in the United States Senate.

At 3 A.M. the Democrats had won 25 of the 35 contests in yesterday's elections. These, added to their 40 holdovers, assured them of 65 seats when the Eighty-ninth Congress convenes in January.

The Republicans, at the same hour, had won only five seats—in Vermont, Nebraska, Delaware, Arizona and Hawaii—all of which were won by incumbent Senators. These, added to 25 holdovers, assured the Republicans of at least 30 seats.

The party line-up when Congress adjourned last month was 66 Democrats and 34 Republicans.

By 3 A.M. the Democrats had captured three seats from the Republicans.

In New York, Robert F. Kennedy, former Attorney General, a brother of President Kennedy,

Continued on Page 20, Column 1

STATE DEMOCRATS GAIN SIX IN HOUSE

Lindsay and Other Liberal Republicans Keep Seats

By WARREN WEAVER Jr.

Democrats swept through the New York Congressional delegation in yesterday's election, unseating six Republican Representatives and threatening the House seat of a seventh.

In the wake of the Johnson victory, the Democrats increased their strength in the delegation from 20 to 26 while the number of Republicans dropped from 21 to 14, with one district in doubt.

Although they failed to dislodge any of the three New York City Republican Congressmen, Democratic candidates scored victories elsewhere across the state. They took two seats in Nassau County, one in Westchester, one in the Hudson Valley and two in Western New York.

Among the chief Republican survivors was Representative John V. Lindsay of Manhattan, who won by a 65,000-vote margin in his East Side district.

Other Republicans to retain their seats were Representative Seymour Halpern of Queens, who like Mr. Lindsay had opposed Senator Barry Goldwater, and, Representative Ogden R.

Continued on Page 24, Column 3

G.O.P. Grip Broken In Suburban Voting

By JOHN SIBLEY

Traditional Republican bastions in the suburbs crumbled before the Johnson onslaught yesterday, and the President carried with him many local Democratic candidates in nearby New York and New Jersey communities.

Widespread ticket-splitting showed, however, that Republican suburbanites were not forsaking their party so much as they were renouncing its Presidential nominee, Senator Barry Goldwater.

Westchester County, for the first time since 1912, gave a plurality to a Democratic Presidential candidate. Rockland County went Democratic for the first time since Franklin D. Roosevelt carried the county in 1936 and for only the fourth time in 100 years.

Long Island's suburbs, too, went to the President. Mr. Johnson became the first Democratic Presidential candidate in modern

Continued on Page 33, Column 2

ROMNEY IS VICTOR; PERCY'S BID FAILS

Democrats Likely to Achieve Gain in Governorships

By JOSEPH A. LOFTUS

Democrats gave a good account of themselves in 25 contests for Governor yesterday, but it was a Republican who produced the spectacular.

Gov. George Romney, running aloof from Senator Barry Goldwater, set off a Michigan ticket-splitting spree to win re-election and thereby planted himself firmly in the thin front line of 1968 Presidential possibilities.

While Senator Goldwater gathered barely a third of Michigan's votes, the Governor defeated Neil Staebler with more than 55 per cent of the tally.

Strong Goldwater supporters "cut" Governor Romney, but the latter improved on his own 1962 vote totals in the labor-Democratic areas of Detroit and Flint-Saginaw.

The Republicans failed to capture a major prize, the Illinois governorship. The defeated nominee, Charles H. Percy, had figured in Presidential talk for the future.

Gov. Otto J. Kerner won a second term in Illinois despite the failure of Mayor Richard Daley's organization to deliver Chicago majorities as big as those Mr. Kerner won there four years ago.

Nationally the Democrats seemed likely to score a net

Continued on Page 24, Column 4

Summary of International News: Wilson Acts to Nationalize Steel

Following is a summary of foreign news. A full report begins on the first page of the second part.

Labor Offers Program

Britain's new Labor Government offered a program of controversial legislation to Parliament. Headed by a demand for renationalization of the steel industry, the proposals indicate one of the bitterest sessions in parliamentary history.

French Explain Aim

Foreign Minister Maurice Couve de Murville told the French Parliament that the United States and Europe should develop separate, but not necessarily hostile, policies. In Washington, officials predicted that a major crisis for Atlantic unity would arise at a NATO meeting in December.

Bolivian Troops Revolt

A military revolt broke out in Bolivia and appeared to be spreading across the country. A truce designed to open the way for efforts "to resolve the present crisis" facing the Government of President Victor Paz Estenssoro was announced. In neighboring Chile, Eduardo Frei Montalva was inaugurated as the country's 28th President. In Cuba workers will vote Dec. 2 for worker councils.

Soviet Voices Concern

The Soviet Union expressed concern to the United States over the situation along the Cambodian-South Vietnamese border. In Pnompenh, Prince Norodom Sihanouk said his nation was ready to retaliate against any further border incursions by South Vietnamese forces. In Saigon, United States officials raised the casualty toll in Sunday's bombardment of the Bienhoa air base to 76 Americans, of whom four were dead.

WHITE BACKLASH DOESN'T DEVELOP

Vote in Suburbs in North Is Strong for President

By ANTHONY LEWIS

Rich and poor, Protestant and Roman Catholic and Jew, farmer and city-dweller and suburbanite all showed marked shifts toward President Johnson in yesterday's extraordinary election.

Only in the Deep South did Senator Barry Goldwater score any significant gains for the Republican ticket over four years ago. Riding the crest of the racial issue there, he swung Mississippi, Alabama, Georgia, South Carolina and Louisiana to his party.

The white backlash, on which Mr. Goldwater had counted so strongly, failed to materialize in most parts of the North. Only among voters of Polish and other East European origins were there signs of this resentment toward Negroes, and even this phenomenon was scattered

Continued on Page 26, Column 1

NEWS INDEX

PRESIDENT SEES A UNITY MANDATE

In Victory Talk, He Pays Tribute to Predecessor

The text of Johnson's talk will be found on Page 22.

By CHARLES MOHR
Special to The New York Times

AUSTIN, Tex., Wednesday, Nov. 4—President Johnson said early this morning that his election was a "mandate for unity" and for a "government that provides equal opportunity for all and special privilege for none."

Mr. Johnson, obviously deeply moved by his landslide victory, told a crowd at the Municipal Auditorium here that it was a tribute to "the program begun by our beloved President John F. Kennedy."

Of the returns, Mr. Johnson said, "I doubt there have ever been so many people seeing so many things alike" on an Election Day.

Earlier, Mr. Johnson had said of Senator Barry Goldwater's refusal to concede that it was "purely a matter for the individual involved—whatever reasons he may have, I don't know."

He also said that the election was going "about as we expected."

Mr. Johnson appeared on the Municipal Auditorium stage with his wife and two daughters to a long ovation.

He said that "no words are

Continued on Page 22, Column 6

Salinger Is Losing; Johnson Wins State

By LAWRENCE E. DAVIES
Special to The New York Times

SAN FRANCISCO, Wednesday, Nov. 4—President Johnson captured California's 40 electoral votes in his triumph over Senator Barry Goldwater in yesterday's election.

On the basis of the incomplete count of ballots, however, the President's former press secretary, Senator Pierre Salinger, apparently lost his Senatorial battle to George Murphy, the Republican nominee.

Mr. Salinger late last night refused to concede defeat but said he "would be less than candid if I didn't say the vote doesn't look good." Some of his campaign strategists agreed that the results "looked bad" but declared they would await developments for a few hours before having anything definite to say.

Mr. Salinger, who has been

Continued on Page 34, Column 4

"All the News That's Fit to Print"

The New York Times.

LATE CITY EDITION
U. S. Weather Bureau Report forecasts: Mostly sunny, cool today; increasing cloudiness tonight and tomorrow. Temp. Range: 45—30; yesterday: 67—45.

VOL. CXV . . . . No. 39,372. © 1965 by The New York Times Company. Times Square, New York, N. Y. 10036 NEW YORK, WEDNESDAY, NOVEMBER 10, 1965. TEN CENTS

POWER FAILURE SNARLS NORTHEAST; 800,000 ARE CAUGHT IN SUBWAYS HERE; AUTOS TIED UP, CITY GROPES IN DARK

To Our Readers

Because of the power blackout, the mechanical facilities of The New York Times were put out of operation last night and early today. Through the courtesy of The Newark Evening News this issue of The Times was set into type and printed in The Evening News's plant from The Times's own news reports. The financial tables are those of The Evening News.

CITY IN DARKNESS: Except for scattered independent lighting this is how the city looked from the Jersey side.

The New York Times

ON A TRAIN GOING NOWHERE: Commuters waiting on subway in Times Square area. Picture was made in

Snarl at Rush Hour Spreads Into 9 States

10,000 in the National Guard and 5,000 Off-Duty Policemen Are Called to Service in New York

By PETER KIHSS

The largest power failure in history blacked out nearly all of New York City, parts of nine Northeastern states and two provinces of southeastern Canada last night. Some 80,000 square miles, in which perhaps 25 million people live and work, were affected.

It was more than three hours before the first lights came back on in any part of the New York City area. When they came on in Nassau and Suffolk Counties at 9 P.M., overloads plunged the area into darkness again in 10 minutes.

Striking at the evening rush hour, the power failure trapped 800,000 riders on New York City's subways. Railroads halted. Traffic was jammed. Airplanes found themselves circling, unable to land. But the Defense Department reported that the Strategic Air Command and other defense installations functioned without a halt.

National Guard Called Out

Five thousand off-duty policemen were summoned to duty here. Ten thousand National Guardsmen were called up in New York City alone. Other militiamen were alerted in Rhode Island and Massachusetts, as well as upstate New York.

The lights and the power went out first at 5:17 P.M. somewhere along the Niagara frontier of New York state. Nobody could tell why for hours afterward.

The tripping of automatic switches hurtled the blackout eastward across the state—to Buffalo, Rochester, Syracuse, Utica, Schnectady, Troy and Albany.

Within four minutes the line of darkness had plunged across Massachusetts all the way to Boston. It was like a pattern of falling dominoes—darkness sped southward through Connecticut, northward into Vermont, New Hampshire, Maine and Canada.

Sputtering at 5:27

At 5:27 P.M. the lights began sputtering in New York City, and within seconds the giant Consolidated Edison system blacked out in Manhattan, the Bronx, Queens and most of Brooklyn—but not in Staten Island and parts of Brooklyn that were interconnected with the Public Service Electric and Gas Company of New Jersey.

The darkness probed outward into northern New Jersey, up into Westchester and Rockland Counties, eastward into Long Island.

As far south as Washington, a Potomac Electric Power Company spokesman reported a power "dip" at 5:30 P.M., lasting less than a minute and virtually unnoticed in the nation's capital.

In Pennsylvania, the blackout spread through Pittsburgh and Reading into parts of Philadelphia and then into New Jersey along the coast above Atlantic City.

President Johnson, in Austin, Tex., ordered the full resources of the Federal Government thrown into an investigation by the Federal Power Commission. The Federal Bureau of Investigation, the Defense Department and other agencies were ordered to report "at the earliest possible moment."

Some Fear Sabotage

Asked whether there was any belief that sabotage might have been involved, Bill D. Moyers, the President's Press Secretary, would say only that "all of the resources of the Government" were being invoked in the investigation.

Later Mr. Johnson was advised that utility officials were "pretty well agreed upon the belief that there is substantially no chance of sabotage." Mr. Moyers said one theory was that the failure had been in automatic frequency control equipment.

Power companies, stripped of the protection of interconnected grids that would guard against minor failures, moved to isolate their areas to restore energy on their own. This was how the Ontario Hydro Electric Commission, a Government-owned utility, cut away after loss of power for six million persons. It began bringing power back at 6:15 P.M.

In New York City, the Ravenswood plant in Queens, which provides 1.8 million kilowatts out of the 7.6 million produced by the city's Consolidated Edison plants, began sending smoke up from its stacks, as auxiliary steam power began to build up for its generators.

At 7:15 P.M. smoke began curling up also from the Hudson Avenue station in Brooklyn. It was from Hudson Avenue that the first power was restored here: Five feeder cables of 27,000 volts each sent light back into Coney Island at 8:42 P.M.

An hour later Consolidated Edison reported 17 of the

(Continued on Page 2, Column 1 and 2)

Johnson Restates Goals in Vietnam

By The Associated Press

JOHNSON CITY, Tex., Nov. 9—President Johnson has restated broad American goals in Viet Nam and proclaimed Nov. 28 as "a day of dedication and prayer" for all members of the anti-Communist forces there.

The United States Government, he said, "remains ready without condition for the international discussions that can lead to lasting peace."

Mr. Johnson's proclamation, which followed a cue from Congress, was made public today though he actually signed it three days ago.

The Presidential document sidestepped one potential source of direct friction between Americans who support and oppose the Vietnam war.

Nov. 27 Suggested

Congress had suggested Nov. 27 as the day of prayer. However, a series of antiwar demonstrations, including a march on Washington, had been planned for that day.

Mr. Johnson, who had authority to fix the timing of the tribute to fighting forces in Vietnam, decided on the following day, a Sunday. In so doing, he is reported to have wanted to avoid a direct confrontation between backers and critics of American policy in Vietnam.

As the President has said on many occasions, he believes the great majority of Americans support his policy on Vietnam.

'Honored Tradition' Cited

The President proclaimed Nov. 28 "as a day of dedication and prayer, honoring the men and women of South Vietnam, of the United States, and of all other countries, who are risking their lives to bring about a just peace in South Vietnam."

He had this to say about American war aims:

"In assisting the people of South Vietnam to resist unprovoked aggression, the United States and other nations are carrying on the honored tradition of defending a people's right to freedom . . . the purpose of the United States in Vietnam is to help open the way for social justice in place of unprovoked aggression and peace instead of war."

Mr. Johnson noted that both the Senate and the House had passed resolutions saying "it would be fitting for the President to set aside a national day of remembrance dedicated to those Americans who are commiting their lives, blood and energies in the defense of world peace."

G.I.'s Score Big Victory

Vietcong Force Almost Wiped Out by U.S. Airborne Unit

By R. W. APPLE JR.
Special to The New York Times

BIENHOA, South Vietnam, Nov. 9—The toll of almost 400 Vietcong killed in a battle 30 miles northeast of Saigon yesterday marked a decisive victory for troops of the US 173d Airborne Brigade.

The American paratroopers, members of one battiation, fired into waves of enemy troops at point-blank range in the eight-hour battle.

The United States troops suffered substantial casualties in the battle in a dense tropical thicket, but only at the battle of Chulay had an American unit inflicted heavier losses on the Vietcong.

Most of the fighting tok place at such close range that American M-79 grenades, which explode only after they have traveled 12 yards, bouned harmlessly off the guerrillas.

Assaults Thrown Back

The Americans were surrounded several times, but each time they threw back enemy assaults and held their positions. The Vietcong, using flame throwers and molten-metal thermite grenades for the first time in the war, attacked until they were almost wiped out.

This afternoon, with the battle over, the United States troops were returned by helicopter to their base camp at the sprawling installation here.

Sunday night, two platoons from the 173d, moving through the underbrush on patrol in the jungle area where they had been operating since Nov. 5, found fresh footprints and heard the frightened cackling of chickens.

At 7:30 A.M. yesterday the two platoons moved out again, clawing their way through the brush in the jungle gloom, and began climbing a pair of rocky hills. Both platoons were from C Company of the First Battalion, 503d Infantry.

'Right on Their Patio'

Suddenly the platoon on the right, about 50 men, found itself in a circle of mud and thatch huts. The huts were invisible from the air because of the palmetto trees arching overhead and almost invisible from the ground because of the underbrush.

The company's commanding officer, Capt. Henry B. Tucker of Columbus, Miss., said later:

(Continued Page 5, Column 3)

Miss Liberty Shines Through Blackout

The Statue of Liberty maintained its illumination throughout last night's long blackout.

Residents of lower Manhattan saw clearly the floodlit base of the statue on Liberty Island and the lighted torch. Except for an occasional passing river craft, the statue appeared to be the only beacon of light in the harbor.

Power for statue's lights was supplied by the New Jersey Public Service Company.

U.S. Orders An Inquiry

President Calls for a Study of Power Failure in East

By JOHN D. POMFRET
Special to The New York Times

AUSTIN, Tex., Nov. 9—President Johnson ordered today an immediate and complete investigation of the power failure that blacked out a large section of the East.

The President issued the order in a memorandum to Joseph C. Swidler, chairman of the Federal Power Commission.

Within minutes after the investigation was ordered, Mr. Swidler sent telegrams to all power companies in the affected areas, requesting their assistance. He also telephoned Defense Secretary Robert S. McNamara and Attorney General Nichclas de B. Katzenbach, telling them to coordinate the inquiry with them.

During the evening Mr. Johnson talked by telephone with Governor Rockefeller and Mayor

(Continued Page 3, Column 3)

City's Glitter Goes But Not Its Poise

By FRED POWLEDGE

Broadway, Manhattan and the rest of the city lost their glitter last night. Yet New Yorkers, who are used to living in crises, seemed to take the blackout in stride.

By the thousands they calmly filed out of office buildings and stores soon after the blackout started.

They grabbed every taxicab in sight. Some cab drivers turned on their "off duty" signs and headed for home themselves. Then the New Yorkers grabbed every bus in sight.

Although many merchants feared looting and violence, the police reported little such trouble. Many New Yorkers even seemed merry. There was the same air of revelry that often accompanies a heavy snowstorm.

Time to Admire Skyline

Commuters stuck in Manhattan with the prospect of a long wait before getting to their homes found time to admire the unexpected sight of a moonlit Manhattan skyline, with stars, clouds and no neon.

Below ground, subway riders who waited in stalled trains sat quietly, resigned and good-humored.

At the Piccadilly Hotel on 45th Street in the heart of the theater district, a guest sat behind the desk helping the management dispense candles. No one seemed panicky, although a woman at the cigarette counter refused to sell anything to anyone who didn't have the correct change. Her cash register would not open.

Huckster Sells Flashlights

A huckster on Broadway sold flashlights, complete with batteries, for $1 apiece. A few doors away, in one of the shops that specializes in imported transistor radios and tape recorders a salesman got rid of dozens of flahlights at $3 each.

"It's a good quality flashlight," he said to someone who objected to the price. "It'll be working long after the current emergency is over."

After an initial period of darkness, little lights started appearing in windows. They were candles, retrieved from dusty desk drawers and kitchen cabinets, from the Bronx to Staten Island.

On street corners, New Yorkers gathered to listen to portable radios and wait for some form of transportation home.

Some did not wait. Thousands walked across the Queensboro and Brooklyn Bridges, where the stunning night views of the city were strangely missing. The Brooklyn Bridge has a pedestrian walkway, above the automobile roadway, but the Queensboro does not. The Queens bound pedestrians walked across the south lane of the auto roadway four and five abreast. Cars crawled along behind them.

Cross Streets Jammed

Although many offices and stores closed immediately after the blackout began, some essential services stayed open.

Hospitals, using emergency generator power supplies, stayed lighted. Newspapers did too, but the light came from candles.

Manhattan's crosstown streets became unbroken ribbons of white light as automobiles, the brightest sources of light, jammed the narrow roadways.

Police cars turned on their red blinking lights. Buses crawled down the streets, their interior lamps lighting the faces of crowded passengers.

A Woolworth's store on Lexington Avenue reported a "land-office business" in candles. People stood in lines that stretched into the street, waiting for a chance to buy a candle.

A street repair crew worked on, filling a hole in the pavement as their supervisor held a flashlight.

Bars filled quickly. The Astor Bar in Times Square, always a popular place, was more popular than ever. The candles planted in ashtrays seemed to produce more than enough light for drinkers.

Another bar in Times Square locked its doors, leaving contented drinkers with a good excuse to remain inside, but angering those who wanted to get in.

Brief Thought of Disaster

A young actress who lives in Greenwich Village was taking a bath when the lights went out. She said that her first thoughts were that "we were under attack," but that she quickly dismissed such an idea and poured herself a drink.

In Times Square, pedestrians

(Continued Page 3, Column 6)

Food Is Sent To Subways

10,000 Are Stranded Long After Most Are Led Out

By SAMUEL KAPLAN

Subway trains sputtered to a halt in tunnels, on elevated tracks and in stations yesterday, stranding about 800,000 rush hour riders—10,000 of whom were still stuck at midnight.

The Transit Authority and the Police Department worked into the early hours of the morning attempting to remove passengers from crowded, stalled cars.

At midnight, food was sent to the passengers who were still waiting to be escorted out along the narrow catwalks in dark tunnels and high above rivers and streets.

Despite the anxious condition, no panic was reported, although there was confusion and fear in some of the 600 trains when they first stalled on the city's tracks.

The most difficult evacuation took place on the Williamsburg

(Continued Page 2, Column 8)

Man, 22, Immolates Himself In Antiwar Protest at U.N.

By THOMAS BUCKLEY

A 21-year-old former seminarian soaked himself with gasoline and then set himself aflame in front of the United Nations at dawn yesterday, as a protest against "war, all war."

Guards from the world organization and city patrolmen beat out the flames that enveloped him as he sat cross-legged on First Avenue and then rushed him to Bellevue Hospital.

He was drifting near death in the emergency ward last night, with second and third-degree burns covering 95 per cent of his body. The hospital staff said he had almost no chance of surviving.

The youth, Roger Allen LaPorte, was a member of the Catholic Worker movement, a charitable and pacifist organization with headquarters at 175 Chrystie Street on the Lower East Side. He lived in a tenement apartment leased by the organization at 58 Kenmare Street, a few blocks away.

Mr. LaPorte's self-immolation was the second in seven days attributable, at least in part, to continued United States' involvement in the war in Vietnam. Last Monday, Norman R. Morrison, a 32-year-old Quaker from Baltimore, burned himself to death in front of the Pentagon in Washington.

U Thant, the Secretary General of the United Nations, which has been seeking a solution to the Asian conflict, and Arthur Goldberg, the chief United States delegate to the world body, reacted with shock and horror to Mr. LaPorte's action.

Questioned at a city reception, Mr. Goldberg said that while the youth had undoubtedly been impelled by "the highest principles and motives," his action was "terribly unfortunate and terribly unnecessary."

"Perhaps there has been a failure on our part," he went on. "Perhaps we are not sufficiently communicating to the people of the world our dedication, our attachment and complete commitment to the idea that peace is the only way for mankind in the nuclear age."

A spokesman said that Mr. Thant was "deeply grieved over this human tragedy, whatever the motivation might be. U Thant regards human life as very sacred."

Attended Union Sq. Protest

Friends of Mr. LaPorte said that he had been melancholy but not obviously emotionally disturbed since Saturday, when he attended the demonstration at Union Square at which five other youths burned their draft cards.

Robert Steed, a fellow member of the Catholic Workers, said that Mr. LaPorte had been unable to make up his mind to

(Continued Page 5, Column 1)

How City Met the Emergency: Off-Duty Men Are Mobilized

The city's emergency services were mobilized last night to deal with the sudden power blackout.

Five thousand off-duty policemen were summoned by a message broadcast over WNYC, the city's radio station. They joined the 7,000 who were on duty when the lights went out and who were held on for the emergency.

The Fire Department, too, brought in off-duty firemen because their overloaded telephone and telegraphic communications made it difficult to keep contact with scattered fire apparatus in the field.

The Fire Department radio was out of service from 5:30 p.m. to 8:30 p.m. and the dispatchers had to keep in touch with the firehouses and vehicles by telephone. They had the radio system back in operation at 8:30 and were able to communicate with men in the field from that hour.

Hospitals were generally able to carry on with the generating systems that they have for such emergencies. Operations were performed in some of them by lights provided by these auxiliary systems.

The switchboard in the Communications Bureau at Police Headquarters was swamped by calls from puzzled and frightened persons. So many calls came in for radio cars to help persons trapped in stalled elevators, in the subways and to deal with fires and other emergencies that no count was kept of their errands or destinations.

Looting Is Reported

Detectives were sent to West 123d Street in Harlem where they were told there had been looting. When they got there, they found one store window broken.

At Bellevue Hospital, the 2,300 patients were treated by several hundred nurses and doctors in candlelight. Although the city hospital has an auxiliary generating system, it is too small to service the massive enclave of buildings and was not used. However, in the operating and emergency rooms, the Fire Department set up emergency lights powered by small generators. One operation was finished just before the blackout occurred.

The major problems at Bellevue involved reassuring mentally disturbed patients and mixing medicines in dimly lighted pharmacies. Quantities of dry ice was obtained to keep blood plasma from spoiling.

Louis Lobo, who has been in an iron lung at Bellevue since 1962, was transferred to a Bird Resperator, which is operated by compressed air. No ill effects were reported.

Car Battery Used

One Bellevue employe brought in his car battery, set it up on a wheelchair and powered emer-

(Continued Page 2, Column 7)

"All the News That's Fit to Print"

The New York Times.

LATE CITY EDITION

U.S. Weather Bureau Report (Page 94) Forecast:
Light rain and snow, then clearing today; becoming cloudy tomorrow.
Temp. range: 46-37; yesterday: 48-42.

VOL. CXV..No. 39,408. NEW YORK, THURSDAY, DECEMBER 16, 1965. TEN CENTS

TWO GEMINIS FLY 6 TO 10 FEET APART IN MAN'S FIRST SPACE RENDEZVOUS; CREWS, FACE TO FACE, TALK BY RADIO

U.S. JETS SMASH BIG POWER PLANT OUTSIDE HAIPHONG

Cut Nation's Current 15%—Generators Supported Industries in Hanoi

By NEIL SHEEHAN
Special to The New York Times

SAIGON, South Vietnam, Dec. 15—United States jet fighter-bombers destroyed a large power plant today 14 miles from Haiphong, North Vietnam's chief port, in the first American air strike against a North Vietnamese target of major industrial importance.

A military spokesman said the planes, flown by Air Force pilots, had struck the Uongbi thermal power plant, northeast of Haiphong. The plant has a capacity of 24,000 kilowatts, about 15 per cent of North Vietnam's total electric-power output. It supplies some of the power needs of both Hanoi and Haiphong.

The center of the plant, housing steam turbines, generators and other sensitive equipment, was smashed at 11 A.M. with 12 tons of 3,000-pound bombs. A single flight of F-105 Thunderchief fighter-bombers—apparently four to six craft—made the raid.

Secondary Blasts Sighted

A spokesman said that the pilots had encountered bad weather and heavy antiaircraft fire but reported having destroyed the plant. Several secondary explosions—detonations of explosives on the ground—were observed during the raid.

This was the first time United States aircraft had struck so close to North Vietnam's two major cities—Hanoi and Haiphong. The closest previous strike was a recent raid against a firing site for Soviet-made surface-to-air missiles, 22 miles from Hanoi.

[Secretary of Defense McNamara, who arrived back in Washington shortly after midnight from the North Atlantic Alliance meeting in Paris, said the bombing of the power plant near Haiphong "is representative of the type of attack we have carried out and will continue to carry out," The Associated Press reported Thursday. Page 3.]

Many Homes Darkened

According to military spokesmen here, the destruction of the power plant was certain to affect North Vietnamese civilians much more directly than have previous strikes, almost all of which have been aimed at road, rail and river networks and military installations.

The power-station raid will probably cut off electricity in large numbers of civilian homes as well as significantly reduce the amount of power available for industries in the Hai-

Continued on Page 3, Column 1

Gemini 7 Crew

Lieut. Col. Frank Borman

Comdr. James A. Lovell Jr.

Major Steps From Launching to Rendezvous

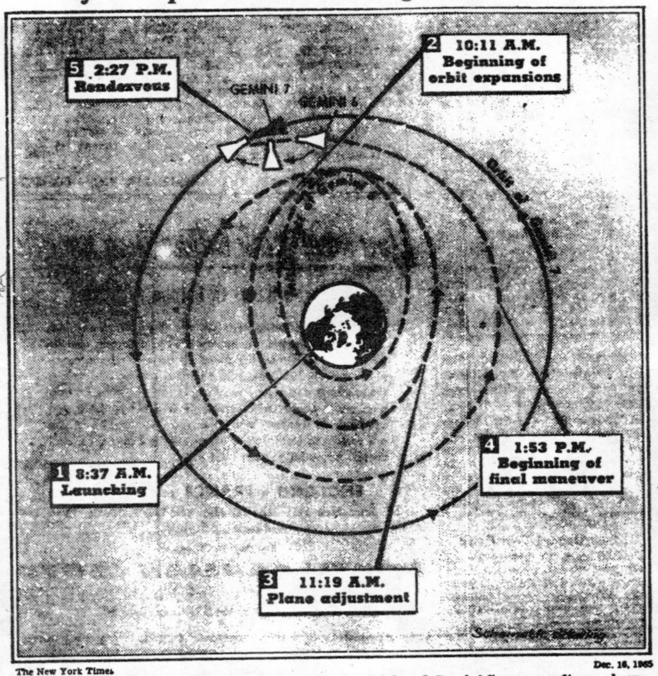

The New York Times Dec. 16, 1965

Major steps of yesterday's rendezvous of the Gemini 6 and Gemini 7 spacecraft are shown, from the launching of Gemini 6 to its meeting with Gemini 7, orbiting about 185 miles above the earth. At rendezvous two craft were nose to nose within 10 feet of each other.

Gemini 6 Crew

Capt. Walter M. Schirra Jr.

Maj. Thomas P. Stafford

Craft in Formation Orbit 185 Miles Up

Officials of Space Agency Are Jubilant at Success—Maneuver Is Vital to a Manned Landing on Moon

By JOHN NOBLE WILFORD
Special to The New York Times

HOUSTON, Dec. 15—Four American astronauts steered Gemini 6 and Gemini 7 today to man's first rendezvous in the vastness of outer space.

In a spectacular performance of space navigation, the astronauts brought their craft within six to ten feet of each other about 185 miles above the earth. The two capsules then circled the earth nearly two times on a four-hour formation flight before Gemini 6 broke away to a lower orbit.

The pilots of the pursuing Gemini 6 were Capt. Walter M. Schirra Jr. of the Navy and Maj. Thomas P. Stafford of the Air Force. Pilots of the Gemini 7 target ship were Lieut. Col. Frank Borman of the Air Force and Comdr. James A. Lovell Jr. of the Navy.

The crews came close enough to see into each other's cabins, trade gibes and inspect details on the exteriors of their funnel-shaped spacecraft. The Gemini 6 astronauts could see Commander Lovell's beard and could tell that Colonel Borman was chewing gum.

"We have company tonight!" radioed Colonel Borman from Gemini 7, which has been in orbit 11 days of its record 14-day mission. Gemini 6, launched from Cape Kennedy at 8:37 A.M., Eastern standard time, today, is expected to splash down near the Bahamas at 10:29 A.M. tomorrow.

Officials Jubilant

The success of the mission brought jubilation at the space center here.

"It's the biggest milestone since the flight of John Glenn," Christopher C. Kraft Jr., the flight director, said.

Colonel Glenn's Mercury flight on Feb. 20, 1962, was the first orbital mission by an American.

The two Geminis today proved that two spacecraft can find each other, rendezvous and presumably link up.

Such a maneuver is necessary if astronauts are to land on the moon and then return to their mother ship, which would be circling in a lunar orbit. Space officials are aiming for such a manned landing in 1969.

Today's rendezvous also opens the way to operations in which men and supplies can be ferried out to orbiting stations, such as the Air Force's planned Manned Orbiting Laboratory.

'Made It Look Easy'

"These crews made it look easy," said Dr. Robert Gilruth, director of the Manned Spacecraft Center here, praising all those who had made the mission a success.

Just before final rendezvous, there was an anxious moment of silence. Radio contact between the craft and the ground was lost. Then a relay tracking station off Hawaii reported in. The two Gemini had drawn within 120 feet of each other.

"There just seems to be a lot of traffic up here," Captain Schirra commented.

"Call a policeman," Colonel

Continued on Page 28, Column 1

AT LAST, GEMINI 6 HAS A PERFECT DAY

Even Sun Comes Out in Time to Dispel Last Doubt of Jubilant Ground Staff

By EVERT CLARK
Special to The New York Times

CAPE KENNEDY, Fla., Dec. 15—After twice having had its wings clipped by failure, the Gemini 6 finally climbed to its space rendezvous today in a most spectacular way.

For 15 years, missiles have flown from this sandy point of land. But no one today could recall a flight of greater beauty.

It left behind a sense of exhilaration missing since Mercury capsules took the first American astronauts into space four years ago.

On top of the triumph, plans were quickly made to have Gemini 6 splash down about 800 miles east of here at 10:29 o'clock tomorrow morning. The pilots will return here on Friday for the first of many days of debriefings.

A splendid sunrise had created the perfect backdrop and set the mood for the day. It dispelled a worrisome ground fog that had clung to the scrubby palmetto like the doubts that had hung over Gemini 6 in recent days.

Attitude Was Cautious

Through last night the memory of two recent false starts was so fresh that the attitude was one of caution and crossed fingers.

Yet today, from the beginning, a cockiness and almost a jubilance seemed to run through the pilots, the overworked ground crews and official observers.

It was typified by the reaction of James S. McDonnell, the 67-year-old engineer whose factory in Missouri makes the Gemini capsules.

He overslept. Awakened at 6:30 A.M., as the sun began to turn the high, scattered clouds the color of a tea rose, he looked at the sky and cried out: "You see! I told them I'd bring them good weather from St. Louis!"

It became a day for enthusiasm.

"She looks like a dream," Navy Capt. Walter M. Schirra

Continued on Page 28, Column 8

McNamara Warns NATO Of Chinese Atom Threat

By PETER BRAESTRUP
Special to The New York Times

PARIS, Dec. 15—Defense Secretary Robert S. McNamara urged the United States' Western European allies today to start worrying now about the threat posed by Communist China's growing nuclear strength.

At the same time, he pledged that the mounting United States effort in Vietnam would not require the withdrawal of "major combat units" from American forces in Western Europe.

Mr. McNamara addressed ministers of the 15-nation North Atlantic Treaty Organization in their year-end meeting, which began yesterday.

Behind Closed Doors

The Defense Secretary spoke behind closed doors. His remarks, like those of other speakers, were summarized by a delegation spokesman.

Mr. McNamara said that the Chinese Communists, having already detonated two test nuclear devices, would produce enough fissionable material in the next two years to start a small stockpile of atomic weapons.

Moreover, he continued, the Chinese, despite a "near-famine" economy, are spending 10 per cent of their gross national product on defense.

He said Peking's new mili-

Continued on Page 8, Column 3

JOHNSON AND AYUB CALL PEACE VITAL

Say Dispute With India Must Cease So Efforts Can Be Turned to Key Problems

By JOHN D. POMFRET
Special to The New York Times

WASHINGTON, Dec. 15—President Johnson and President Mohammad Ayub Khan of Pakistan said today that they agreed on the need for a peaceful resolution of all outstanding differences between India and Pakistan.

This is necessary, they said, "so that the energies and resources of the peoples of the subcontinent would not be wastefully diverted from their efforts to meet their vitally important social and economic problems."

The two leaders issued a joint communiqué at the conclusion of two days of meetings at the White House. It described the discussions as "frank, wide-ranging and productive."

Kashmir Main Issue

The main dispute between India and Pakistan is over Kashmir. This dispute led to a short war last summer.

There was no expressed agreement between the two Presidents on the specific lines along which the dispute over Kashmir should be settled.

They both were said to believe that the working out of such specific arrangements must await the outcome of further conferences that already have been scheduled.

President Ayub and India's Prime Minister, Lal Bahadur Shastri, are to meet Jan. 4 at the invitation of the Soviet Union to discuss their differences. They will confer at the Soviet Central Asian city of Tashkent.

Prime Minister Shastri and President Johnson will meet in Washington Feb. 1 and 2.

The United States cut off military aid and new economic

Continued on Page 6, Column 3

47-CENT FARE SEEN IN QUILL DEMANDS

Transit Authority Warns It Would Be Needed to Meet Union Pay Proposals

By EMANUEL PERLMUTTER

The Transit Authority said yesterday that if it granted the contract demands of its unions it would have to raise the 15-cent fare to 47 cents.

It asserted that a fare increase that great would lead to such a loss of riders that "the reduced use of the system would be financially catastrophic."

The authority has estimated that demands of the Transport Workers Union would cost it $680 million in a two-year contract.

"Adding an increased labor cost of $340 million annually to the T.A. budget would, in the absence of other sources of revenue, increase the present 3-cent deficit incurred for each passenger carried by 19 cents, creating a 22-cent operating deficit per ride," the authority asserted. "The fare would have to be increased to not less than 47 cents."

The authority said that granting the demands would also result in increasing the "basic wage rate per hour alone

Continued on Page 58, Column 4

Staggered Working Hours Urged to Cut Transit Jam

By JOSEPH C. INGRAHAM

The chronic morning and evening subway crushes can be eliminated by staggering working hours, according to a plan made public by Mayor Wagner yesterday. The success of the proposal hinges on whether employers and employes can be persuaded to alter their traditional 9-to-5 work pattern, the Mayor said.

Only the conclusions of the eight-volume, 200,000-word report, based on a six-year study that cost $200,000, were released by the Mayor. The study was directed by Prof. Lawrence B. Cohen of the department of industrial engineering of Columbia University.

Principal Finding

The principal finding was that "work staggering is a feasible way of relieving subway congestion into and out of Manhattan's central business district during the rush hours so that standing passengers might be reasonably comfortable."

Professor Cohen held that the idea was technically and economically feasible and, within limits, which he defined very generally, was sociologically acceptable to management and labor.

In Professor Cohen's view, rush-hour crowding would be markedly alleviated if a 25 per cent spread of the peak loads

Continued on Page 58, Column 3

NASA CUTS BACK SCIENCE PROGRAM

Orbiting Solar Observatory Canceled in Move to Hold Down Expanding Budget

Special to The New York Times

WASHINGTON, Dec. 15—The National Aeronautics and Space Administration, caught in a tight budgetary squeeze, canceled today one of its most ambitious scientific projects.

"Budgetary considerations" were cited by the agency in explaining a halt in further work on the Advanced Orbiting Solar Observatory. The observatory, capable of making detailed observations of the sun, had been planned for launching in 1969.

Behind the cryptic explanation was the deliberately unpublicized fact that the agency was faced with a budgetary dilemma. It has been attempting to finance its expanding program and still heed White House directives to hold down nonmilitary spending.

Some Delays Foreseen

The present expectation is that the civilian space budget for the fiscal year 1967, beginning next July 1, will be held by the White House to about $5.17 billion, equal to the appropriation for this year, and perhaps even less. This would be about $500 million less than the space agency considered necessary to maintain the momentum of its expanding program and sought from the White House.

Enough money will be provided in the budget next year to keep Project Apollo on its schedule of landing a manned expedition on the moon before 1970. But to keep within the budgetary confines imposed by the White House, there will have to be some curtailment in the

Continued on Page 30, Column 4

U.S. Said to Caution Latins on Moscow

By HENRY RAYMONT
Special to The New York Times

MONTEVIDEO, Uruguay, Dec. 15—The United States is warning Uruguay and other Latin-American countries against underestimating the continued aggressiveness and subversive potential of Soviet Communism, qualified sources said today.

The diplomatic initiative is directed against what United States authorities consider to be undue complacency among Latin-American leaders.

These authorities think that the split between Moscow and Peking has led to the assumption among Latins that pro-Soviet Communists no longer threaten republican institutions in the Western Hemisphere.

According to United States officials, this assumption ignores the deterioration in East-West

Continued on Page 17, Column 1

Somerset Maugham Is Dead at 91

Novelist, Short Story Writer, Playwright Succumbs in Nice

By The Associated Press

NICE, France, Thursday, Dec. 16—W. Somerset Maugham died early today at his Riviera villa, La Mauresque. The world-famous novelist, playwright and short-story writer was 91 years old.

Maugham fell last Friday and then suffered a stroke. He was taken to the British-American Hospital Saturday. After a medical consultation on Sunday, physicians gave him only hours to live.

He rallied slightly but weakened yesterday. When all hope was gone, he was taken from the hospital to die in his Moorish-style villa at nearby Cap Ferrat, his secretary and companion of many years, Alan Searle, said in announcing Maugham's death.

A prolific author, Maugham turned out 30 plays, 21 novels and 120 short stories. His masterpiece was "Of Human Bondage," published in 1915 when he was 41 years old. It centered

Continued on Page 50, Column 1

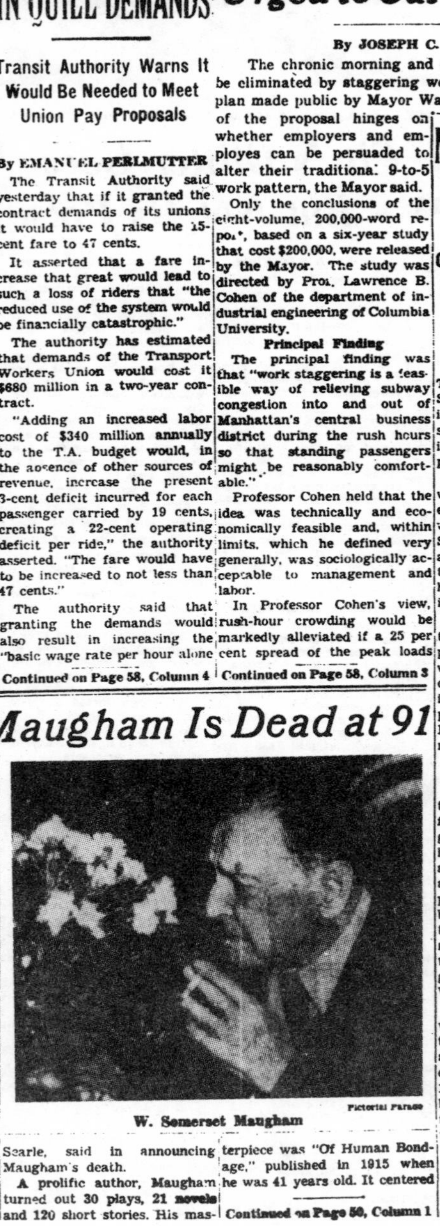

Pictorial Parade

W. Somerset Maugham

Johnson Calls Feat Step Toward Moon

By JACK RAYMOND
Special to The New York Times

WASHINGTON, Dec. 15—President Johnson hailed the Gemini satellite rendezvous today as a step toward the moon.

The President congratulated the astronauts and all those who had anything to do with the space feat.

"You have all moved us one step higher on the stairway to the moon," he said exuberantly.

The President conveyed his feelings in a message to James E. Webb, administrator of the National Aeronautics and Space Administration. He had watched the progress of the launching and flight anxiously throughout the day.

Bill D. Moyers, the President's press secretary, said Mr. Johnson watched the Gemini 6 launching over his bedroom television set. Then, throughout the

Continued on Page 29, Column 4

NEWS INDEX

News Summary and Index, Page 49

"All the News That's Fit to Print"

The New York Times

LATE CITY EDITION

Weather: Fair and warm today and tonight. Partly cloudy tomorrow. Temp. range: today 85-63; Wed. 81-62. Temp.-Hum. Index: mid-70's; Wed. 72. Full report on Page 93.

VOL. CXVI . No. 39,947 NEW YORK, THURSDAY, JUNE 8, 1967 — 10 CENTS

ISRAELIS ROUT THE ARABS, APPROACH SUEZ, BREAK BLOCKADE, OCCUPY OLD JERUSALEM; AGREE TO U.N. CEASE-FIRE; U.A.R. REJECTS IT

JOHNSON WILL USE CABINET TO COURT STATES' OFFICIALS

Aides Will Seek to Tighten Ties Between Governors and the White House

By WARREN WEAVER Jr.
Special to The New York Times

WASHINGTON, June 7—President Johnson has decided to use the members of his Cabinet as diplomatic agents in his campaign to improve relations between the Administration and state governments.

The President has approved a plan under which each member of the Cabinet would be assigned four or five states as his personal responsibility, with instructions to maintain personal contact between the Governors and the White House.

As part of the same effort, each of the 50 states will be given a "day" in Washington next fall and winter, when a planeload of its key officials will fly here to hold conferences all over the capital, capped by a meeting of the Governors with the President.

Bryant's Work Continued

Both projects reflect Mr. Johnson's continuing determination to build domestic as well as foreign bridges by working to sort out the tangled Federal-state relations that have been increasingly complicated by the administration of the Great Society programs.

Both are attempts to give some permanency to the contacts established during the last four months by Farris Bryant, the President's envoy to the states, on visits to 40 capitals with a squad of Federal experts.

Mr. Bryant, a former Governor of Florida who is now the director of the Office of Emergency Planning, plans to leave his White House post this summer, possibly to return to politics in his home state, and he is eager to help establish more permanent lines of communication before his departure.

As now envisioned, each Cabinet officer would visit all of

Continued on Page 29, Column 2

CONFEREES BLOCK A DRAFT LOTTERY

Compromise Bill Continues Deferment of Students

By United Press International

WASHINGTON, June 7—Senate and House negotiators reached agreement today on a new military draft bill that rules out, for the present, any lottery-like random selection system to determine the order of induction.

The bill was a compromise of differing bills that the Senate and House had passed. It would guarantee the continuance of educational deferments for college undergraduates and students enrolled in apprentice and job training programs.

Senator Richard B. Russell, Democrat of Georgia, who is chairman of the Senate conferees, said the Senate might act on the four-year draft extension bill tomorrow. House action must await approval by the Senate.

Congressional action will clear the way for President Johnson, under current discretionary powers, to reverse the order of induction and take 19-year-olds first from the Selec-

Continued on Page 3, Column 1

NEWS INDEX

News Summary and Index, Page 49

Rise in Debt Ceiling Rejected in House; Johnson Rebuffed

Special to The New York Times

WASHINGTON, June 7—The House of Representatives dealt the Johnson Administration a sharp setback today by rejecting a bill to increase the ceiling on the national debt $29-billion, to $365-billion.

The vote against passage was 210 to 197, with Republicans voting solidly to kill the bill. Enough Democrats, mostly Southerners, voted with them to turn the tide.

About six Northern Democratic "doves"—opponents of the war in Vietnam—also joined the opposition.

In all, 34 Democrats joined with 176 Republicans to defeat the measure.

Today's action raised the possibility—though a slim one—of financial chaos after June 30. At that time the debt limit reverts to its "permanent" ceiling of $285-billion, though the debt, at $330-billion, is already far above that level. The legal authority of the Treasury to pay its bills would be in doubt.

However, the Ways and

Continued on Page 30, Column 4

U.S. VOWS TO SEEK A DURABLE PEACE

Johnson Recalls Bundy for New Mideast Planning Unit —'Real Chance' Is Seen

By MAX FRANKEL
Special to The New York Times

WASHINGTON, June 7—President Johnson pledged today to do his best to help translate the new Middle Eastern situation into a more lasting settlement between Israel and her Arab neighbors.

Apparently hoping to exploit Israel's lightning military success—which has surprised but not displeased the White House—Mr. Johnson ordered the drafting of special policies for a "new peace" and set up new machinery to deal with the situation.

The President said that the United States, which had worked hard to avoid the war, felt that "there is now a real chance" to turn from "the frustrations of the past to the hopes of a peaceful future."

But Mr. Johnson said the handling of the crisis and the preparations for a lasting settlement would require the most careful consideration in the United States Government. To organize that effort he recalled McGeorge Bundy to temporary duty at the White House as executive secretary to a special subcommittee of the National Security Council.

Mr. Bundy will seek a temporary leave from the presidency of the Ford Foundation, which he assumed last year after serving as special assistant for

Continued on Page 19, Column 1

Dorothy Parker, 73, Literary Wit, Dies

By ALDEN WHITMAN

Dorothy Parker, the sardonic humorist who purveyed her wit in conversation, short stories, verse and criticism, died of a heart attack yesterday afternoon in her suite at the Volney Hotel, 23 East 74th Street. She was 73 years old and had been in frail health in recent years.

In print and in person, Miss Parker sparkled with a word or a phrase, for she honed her humor to its most economical size. Her rapier wit, much of it spontaneous, gained its early renown from her membership in the Algonquin Round Table, an informal luncheon club at the Algonquin Hotel in the nineteen-twenties, where some of

Continued on Page 38, Column 1

EBAN SEES THANT

Says Acceptance Is Based on Enemy's Reciprocal Action

Excerpts from debate at U.N. are printed on Page 18.

By DREW MIDDLETON
Special to The New York Times

UNITED NATIONS, N. Y., June 7—The Security Council unanimously adopted a Soviet resolution today calling on the combatants in the Middle East to "cease fire and all military activities" at 4 P.M., New York time today.

The Government of Israel shortly thereafter announced that she had accepted the call of the Council for a cease-fire, provided her Arab foes agreed.

In the evening, reports from the Middle East indicated rejection of the call by the United Arab Republic, Syria, Iraq, Saudi Arabia, Algeria and Kuwait. Jordan told Secretary General Thant that she would abide by the cease-fire, except in self-defense.

Says It's in Effect

Abba Eban, the Foreign Minister of Israel, told the Secretary General that a cease-fire was already in effect between Jordan and Israel.

In presenting the resolution, the Soviet delegate, Nikolai T. Fedorenko, made it clear that if Israel failed to heed the Security Council's demands, Moscow would consider severing diplomatic relations. The original Security Council resolution, adopted yesterday, simply called for a cease-fire.

But the reports from the Arab capitals indicate, diplomatic sources here said, that military operations will continue.

According to diplomats, the best hope lies in a draft resolution presented by George Ignatieff, the Canadian delegate. This proposes that the President of the Security Council and the Secretary General take measures to insure compliance with the resolutions.

Today's resolution demanded that the combatants "cease fire and all military activities on 7 June 1967 by 2000 hours Greenwich mean time." The resolution was adopted less than an hour before this time, which is 4 P.M. New York time, 10 P.M. in Jordan and Israel and 11 P.M. in the United Arab Republic and Syria.

The Council adjourned without voting on the Canadian draft largely because Milko Ta-

Continued on Page 18, Column 2

United Press International Radiophoto

OLD JERUSALEM IS NOW IN ISRAELI HANDS: Israeli soldiers in prayer at the Wailing Wall yesterday

Major Mideast Developments

On the Battlefronts

Israel claimed victory in the Sinai Desert after three days of fighting. Sharm el Sheik, guarding the entrance to the Gulf of Aqaba, fell after a paratroop attack, and the Israelis said the blockade of the gulf was broken. Other Israeli units were within 20 miles of the Suez Canal, and one Israeli report placed them in the eastern section of Ismailia, on the canal itself.

In Jerusalem, for the first time in 19 years, Israeli Jews prayed at the Wailing Wall as their troops occupied the Old City. Israeli troops captured Jericho, in Jordan, and sped northward to take Nablus, giving them control of the west bank of the Jordan.

The Egyptian High Command reported that its forces had fallen back from first-line positions in the Sinai Peninsula and were fighting fiercely from unspecified secondary positions. It announced that Egyptian troops had pulled back from Sharm el Sheik to join main defense units.

In the Capitals

In the United Nations, Israel accepted the call for a cease-fire, provided the Arabs complied. Jordan announced that she would accept and ordered her troops to fire only in self-defense. But Baghdad declared that Iraq had refused. There were indications that Syria, Algeria and Kuwait were also opposed.

In Cairo, an Egyptian official said the United Arab Republic would fight on.

In Moscow, the Soviet Union threatened to break diplomatic relations with Israel if she did not observe the cease-fire.

In Paris, the French proposed an international agreement for free passage in the Gulf of Aqaba similar to the one governing the Dardanelles in Turkey.

In Washington, President Johnson promised to seek a settlement that would assure lasting peace in the Mideast.

In London, the British urged the Israelis to halt before they aroused more turmoil in the Arab world and diminished the chances for a settlement.

Israelis Weep and Pray Beside the Wailing Wall

By TERENCE SMITH
Special to The New York Times

JERUSALEM, June 7—Israeli troops wept and prayed today at the foot of the Wailing Wall—the last remnant of Solomon's Second Temple and the object of pilgrimage by Jews through the centuries.

In battle dress and still carrying their weapons, they gathered at the base of the sand-colored wall and sang Hallel, a series of prayers reserved for occasions of great joy.

They were repeating a tradition that goes back 2,000 years but has been denied Israeli Jews since 1948, when the first of three wars with the Arabs ended in this area.

The wall is all that remains of the Second Temple, built in the 10th century before Christ and destroyed by the Romans in A.D. 70.

The Israelis, trembling with emotion, bowed vigorously from the waist as they chanted psalms in a lusty chorus. Most had submachine guns slung over their shoulders and several held bazookas as they prayed.

Among the leaders to pray at the wall was Maj. Gen. Moshe Dayan, the new Defense Minister. He told the troops:

"We have returned to the holiest of our holy places, never to depart from it again."

General Dayan, who was ap-

Continued on Page 17, Column 1

CAIRO ANNOUNCES A SINAI PULLBACK

Blames Foreign Aid to Foe, but Says Troops Fight On in Secondary Positions

By ERIC PACE
Special to The New York Times

CAIRO, June 7—An Egyptian military communiqué reported today that forces of the United Arab Republic had fallen back from some first-line positions on the Sinai Peninsula and were engaged in fierce fighting against Israeli troops from secondary positions.

Another statement of the High Command, broadcast four hours later by the Cairo radio, said Egyptian troops at Sharm el Sheik, guarding the entrance to the Gulf of Aqaba, had joined other Egyptian forces "now concentrated in the Sinai Peninsula."

There was no elaboration, but the communiqué, broadcast about 5:30 P.M., appeared to confirm Israeli reports that the Egyptians had been forced to retreat from Sharm el Sheik.

At night, the High Command reported that Israeli paratroops had dropped over the "second-line Egyptian front" but had been "completely wiped out."

The communiqué also said the Israelis had tried another drop at Sharm el Sheik after the

Continued on Page 17, Column 6

AQABA GULF OPEN

Dayan Asserts Israel Does Not Intend to Capture the Canal

By The Associated Press

TEL AVIV, June 7—Israel proclaimed victory tonight in the Sinai Peninsula campaign against the United Arab Republic. On the eastern front, both the Old City of Jerusalem and Bethlehem were captured from the Jordanians.

"The Egyptians are defeated," said Maj. Gen. Itzhak Rabin, the Israeli Chief of Staff. "All their efforts are aimed at withdrawing behind the Suez Canal, and we are taking care of that. The whole area is in our hands. The main effort of the Egyptians is to save themselves."

Israel Losses 'Not Great'

Describing the developments through the third day of this third Arab-Israeli war in 19 years, General Rabin made these claims:

¶Sinai, the Egyptian territory between Israel's Negev Desert and the Suez Canal, is taken.

¶Most of the Jordanian territory on the west bank of the Jordan River, including Jericho, is in Israeli hands, and most of Jordan's army has been captured.

¶Relative to what was done, the number of Israelis casualties was "not great."

The Israelis were reported to have swept to the Suez Canal.

[An Israeli delegation source at the United Nations said Israeli troops had seized that part of the canal city of Ismailia that is on the eastern side of the waterway. But this was denied by an army source in Tel Aviv, who said, according to Reuters, that the Israelis had not taken any point along the canal.

[Maj. Gen. Moshe Dayan, the Israeli Defense Minister, declared that there was "no intention" of taking the canal, United Press International reported.]

'Never to Depart'

After the fall of the Old City of Jerusalem, Defense Minister Moshe Dayan said that there the Israelis had reunited their capital and would never "depart from it again."

Israel reported that paratroops aided by naval units had captured Sharm el Sheik, commanding the entrance to the Gulf of Aqaba, and said the blockade that the Egyptians had mounted from that position had been broken.

"The Strait of Tiran is now open," General Rabin said.

Israel's chief of staff said his men had taken on the United Arab Republic, Jordan, Syria and Iraq, knocked out their air forces and overrun their armor and infantry.

"All this the armed forces of Israel did alone," he declared.

The general then turned over the briefing to Brig. Mordechai Hod, commander of the air force, who announced 441 Arab

Continued on Page 16, Column 1

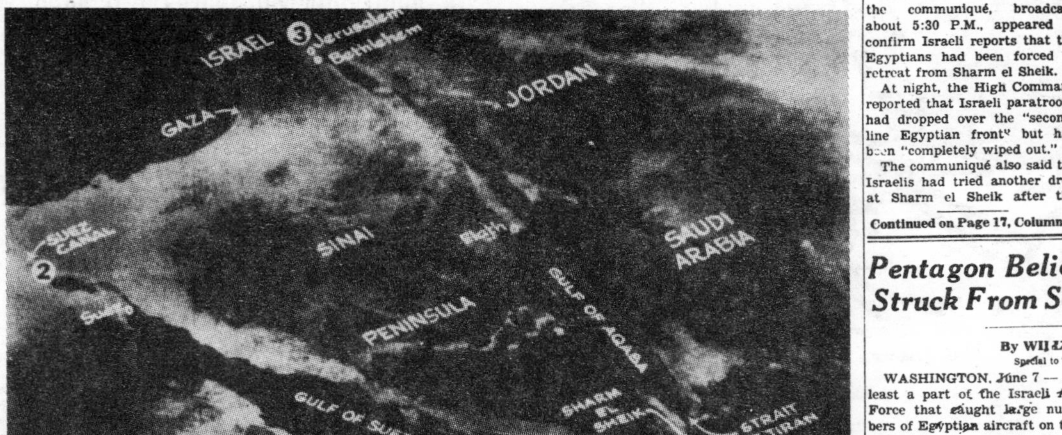

The New York Times — June 8, 1967

CONQUEST IN THE MIDEAST: Israeli troops took Sharm el Sheik (1), drove on to the Suez Canal (2) and seized control of the Old City in Jerusalem (3). Photo was taken in September, 1966, during the flight of Gemini II.

Pentagon Believes Israeli Jets Struck From Sea, Eluded Radar

By WILLIAM BEECHER
Special to The New York Times

WASHINGTON, June 7—At least a part of the Israeli Air Force that caught large numbers of Egyptian aircraft on the ground in the early hours of the war may have slipped through gaps in the United Arab Republic's radar net by flying in over the Mediterranean.

This possibility was raised today by Pentagon analysts. If correct, it would help to explain how Israeli pilots were able to surprise so many Egyptian jets before they could get into the air.

It might also serve to provide part of the explanation behind insistent Arab assertions that carrier-based United States and British jets participated in the raids.

The early blows to Arab, and especially Egyptian, air strength is credited by most military analysts as having been a decisive factor in the Israeli successes on land that followed.

"We know that some of the Israeli planes returned to their bases by way of the sea," one ranking officer said, "and we assume they may have approached from the seaward too."

The officer said it was obvious that Israel had excellent intelligence on weaknesses in the Egyptian radar system and exploited them.

Shortly after the raids, he went on, the Jordanian radio charged that Jordanian radar

Continued on Page 18, Column 8

"All the News That's Fit to Print"

The New York Times

LATE CITY EDITION

Weather: Fair and warm today, tonight and tomorrow. Temp. range: today 85-63; Thurs. 85-64. Temp.-Hum. Index: today 70 to 75; Thurs. 77. Full U.S. report on Page 89.

VOL. CXVI..No. 39,948 — NEW YORK, FRIDAY, JUNE 9, 1967 — 10 CENTS

EGYPT AND SYRIA AGREE TO U.N. CEASE-FIRE; ISRAEL REPORTS TROOPS REACH SUEZ CANAL; JOHNSON, KOSYGIN USED HOT LINE IN CRISIS

SENATE APPROVES A TIGHTENED RULE ON REDISTRICTING

33 States Ordered to Bring Population Variant Down to 10% by 1968 Election

By JAMES F. CLARITY
Special to The New York Times

WASHINGTON, June 8—The Senate approved today a bill requiring that by the 1968 election no state have a population variance of more than 10 cent between its largest and smallest Congressional districts.

The approval, which came in a surprise vote of 57 to 25, was a result of a fight by Senator Edward M. Kennedy, Democrat of Massachusetts, to amend a measure that would have permitted a variance of 35 per cent until the 1972 election.

The Kennedy amendment, which was soundly defeated in committee two weeks ago, is intended, according to the Senator, to make Congressional redistricting conform with the Supreme Court's one-man, one-vote ruling of 1964. The amendment also deleted language giving the states power to determine when the compactness of a district was "practicable."

An Altered Version

The measure, before it was amended today, was an altered version of a bill already passed by the House. The House bill provided for a population variance of 30 per cent, and was amended by the Senate Judiciary Committee to cover four additional states.

The version passed today, which now goes to a Senate-House conference, would apply to 33 states having variances of more than 10 per cent. Nine of these states are under Federal court orders to redistrict. The 17 states not covered by today's Senate action either elect Representatives at large or have variances lower than 10 per cent.

Mr. Kennedy's proposal was approved, first in a crucial 44-to-89 vote as an amendment, then in the final vote on the bill as amended, 57 to 25.

"We knew it would be close.

Continued on Page 26, Column 1

Arms Cost Stress Scored by Rickover

By EVERT CLARK
Special to The New York Times

WASHINGTON, June 8—Vice Adm. Hyman G. Rickover has denounced the cost-effectiveness approach to weapons development as an "ism," a "new religion" and a "fog bomb" that is keeping the nation from gaining technology that would save lives.

In Congressional testimony released today, the head of the nuclear-powered ship program attacked present management techniques in the Pentagon.

By Presidential order, many of these techniques—including the mathematical analysis of cost vs. effectiveness—are now being spread throughout the executive branch of

Continued on Page 2, Column 4

JURY FINDS LAXITY IN BUILDINGS UNIT

Graft, Shirking and Lack of Personnel Training Are Cited—Moerdler Agrees

By JACK ROTH

A New York County grand jury criticized yesterday long-standing conditions in the Buildings Department that it said had resulted in corruption among housing inspectors and landlords.

The jury also said the situation permitted some inspectors and their supervisors to quit work as early as 10:30 A.M. and go to bars and racetracks for the rest of the day.

The jury, in a presentment handed up to Supreme Court Justice Mitchell D. Schweitzer, charged that the department suffered from lack of financial and manpower resources.

It asserted that inspectors were not properly trained for their jobs, that they were unaware of their department's rules and regulations, that there was duplication in inspections, that electronic processing equipment was failing to do its job and that unauthorized persons had access to file rooms and private departmental offices.

The Buildings Commissioner,

Continued on Page 31, Column 1

ALL SINAI IS HELD

U.A.R. Loses 50 Tanks in Actions Termed Fiercest of War

By Reuters

TEL AVIV, Friday, June 9—Israeli troops have reached the bank of the Suez Canal and have taken control of the entire Sinai Peninsula, the Israeli radio reported this morning.

The radio broadcast the text of a message from the commander in the southern front, to the Chief of Staff, Gen. Yitzhak Rabin. The message said:

"Happy to inform you that our forces are stationed on the bank of the Suez Canal and the Red Sea. The Sinai Peninsula is in our hands. Greetings to you and to the whole defense forces of Israel."

Battle reports yesterday indicated that the remnants of two Egyptian armored divisions and four infantry divisions were trapped in the western part of that Sinai Desert.

50 Tanks Reported Wrecked

The news of Cairo's acceptance of the United Nations cease-fire coincided with an announcement by an Israeli spokesman that three battles in the desert yesterday had been "the fiercest in this war."

The Israelis said they had shot down eight Egyptian planes and destroyed at least 50 Egyptian tanks during the fighting.

Other tanks were wrecked and left on the road to Qunbara, about 30 miles north of Ismailia, about midway along the 100-mile Suez Canal.

Among the Egyptian planes downed were a Soviet-made Ilyushin bomber and several Soviet-built Sukhoi-7's. Israeli planes also struck Soviet-made missile sites in the Suez Canal zone during daylight raids, the spokesman added.

Despite the continuation of heavy fighting, the Israeli spokesman said that all escape routes for Egyptian armored units had been closed.

He added that Israeli forces had captured oilfields at Ras Sudar, south of the port of Taufiq on the western coast of the Sinai Peninsula. Israeli soldiers said the wells were afire

Continued on Page 17, Column 6

United Press International Cablephoto

AFTER THE BATTLE: Egyptian prisoners, prone on the sand, their hands behind their heads, are guarded in a compound by Israeli troops at El Arish in the northern Sinai Peninsula. El Arish was taken by Israel Tuesday.

A SHIFT BY CAIRO

Thant Notifies Council in Middle of Debate on Resolutions

Excerpts from the U.N. debate are printed on Page 16.

By DREW MIDDLETON
Special to The New York Times

UNITED NATIONS, N. Y., June 8—The United Arab Republic, the leader of the anti-Israel coalition, today accepted the Security Council's demand for a cease-fire in the Middle East provided Israel did the same.

Yesterday, the delegate of Israel said his country accepted the cease-fire provided Israel's foes agreed to it. Reports here yesterday indicated rejection by Cairo.

Syria gave notice tonight that she would also comply, informing the Secretary General after the Security Council recessed.

This afternoon, in his dry, precise voice Secretary General Thant read to the Council a brief letter from Mohamed Awad el-Kony, the Egyptian delegate, disclosing that President Gamal Abdel Nasser's Government had "decided to accept the cease-fire" called for in the two Council resolutions "on the condition that the other party ceases fire."

He Scraps Long Speech

Mr. el-Kony wrote the letter after a long telephone conversation with Cairo shortly before the Council meeting began. After the call, he scrapped a 20-page speech he had prepared and wrote the note to Mr. Thant.

The Israeli Foreign Minister, Abba Eban, hailed "the immediate prospect" of a cease-fire as "a notable step" and called on other Arab governments to follow the Egyptian lead.

Cairo's acceptance of the Council resolutions adopted unanimously on Tuesday and Wednesday raised rather than lowered the heat of the debate between the United States and the Soviet Union over the resolutions each submitted to the Council.

Arthur J. Goldberg, the United States delegate, saying he hoped for a peace "stable and just to all concerned," submitted a draft of a resolution calling for the "withdrawal and disengagement of armed personnel," the renunciation of force, "the maintenance of vital international rights" and the establishment of a durable peace in the area.

The Administration was said

Continued on Page 17, Column 1

EGYPTIANS TOLD OF TRUCE DECISION

Cairo Broadcast Is Terse —Syrians Also Announce Approval of Cease-Fire

By ERIC PACE
Special to The New York Times

CAIRO, Friday, June 9—The Government told the Egyptian people this morning that it had conditionally accepted a cease-fire in the war with Israel.

There was no immediate popular reaction because the Cairo radio waited until early morning before announcing, more than three hours after the fact, that the United Arab Republic had told Secretary General Thant of the United Nations that it would agree to a truce if Israel did so.

[The Damascus radio announced that Syria, too, had accepted the cease-fire, Reuters reported. Page 17.]

Cairo was blacked out as protection against possible Israeli air raids when the news came, but nocturnal strollers reported that policemen were already taking down at least some of the anti-Israeli banners that have festooned the city for the last few weeks.

An early edition of a popular Cairo newspaper, Al Akhbar, put the news on the front page but made no comment. There was also no elaboration from the radio, which broadcast a military communiqué saying that the battle against Israel was continuing at all points along the Egyptian front.

The terse announcement of the cease-fire contrasted with

Continued on Page 17, Column 2

Major Mideast Developments

In the Capitals

The United Arab Republic accepted a United Nations cease-fire. Israel had previously agreed to stop hostilities if her enemies were willing to go along.

In Damascus, after a series of militant vows to fight on, the Syrians announced that they would also accept the cease-fire.

President Johnson welcomed the cease-fire agreement and urged prompt action to solve the "many more fundamental" questions in the Middle East.

An emergency declaration on oil was being considered by the Johnson Administration after major oil companies reported that a worldwide transportation problem had resulted from the war.

The hot line between Washington and Moscow was used this week for the first time during a crisis.

On the Battlefronts

Before the cease-fire went into effect, Israeli planes and torpedo boats mistakenly attacked a United States communications ship about 15 miles off Sinai. The Pentagon reported that 10 Americans had been killed and 100 wounded. Israel sent an apology.

Israel reported that her troops had reached the bank of the Suez Canal and that the entire Sinai Peninsula was under her control. Earlier Israel reported three fierce desert battles in which at least 50 Egyptian tanks had been destroyed.

The United Arab Republic announced that its air force had inflicted heavy damage on Israeli armored columns trying to advance westward from El Arish in the Sinai Peninsula.

At the Strait of Tiran, a Soviet freighter bound for the Jordanian port of Aqaba was the first ship to pass since Israel declared the waterway open to shipping on Wednesday. Two Israeli ships prepared to follow.

JOHNSON PLEASED BY GAINS ON TRUCE

Looks to a Stable Peace—White House Discloses Use of the Hot Line

Texts of the Mansfield letter and Johnson reply, Page 18.

By MAX FRANKEL
Special to The New York Times

WASHINGTON, June 8—President Johnson welcomed spreading acceptance of a cease-fire agreement in the Middle East today, but urged all parties to move promptly toward the "many more fundamental questions" bearing on a stable peace.

While thus pressing for more than merely another frail armistice, the While House also disclosed that its hot-line connection with Moscow had been used for the first time this week in an international crisis.

The United States used the teletype link this morning when it heard of an attack on an American communications ship off the Sinai Peninsula. At the time, the source of the attack was not known.

The Soviet Government, whose warships have been observing the movements of the United States Sixth Fleet in the eastern Mediterranean, was advised that the carrier-based American planes were scrambling into action for the sole purpose of assisting the distressed vessel.

It was later learned that Israeli forces had attacked the American ship in error.

The announcement of quick exchanges to prevent misunder-

Continued on Page 18, Column 1

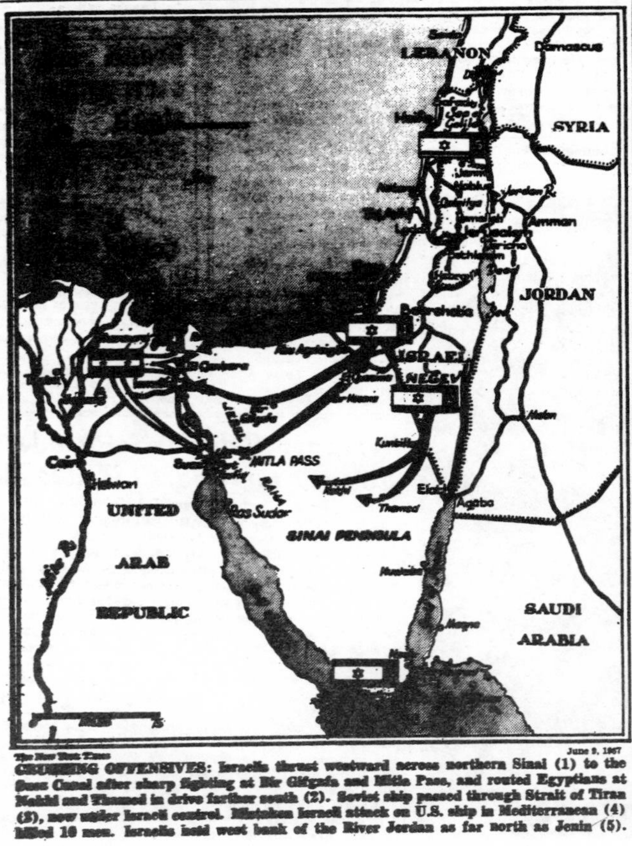

The New York Times — June 9, 1967

CRUSHING OFFENSIVES: Israelis thrust westward across northern Sinai (1) to the Suez Canal after sharp fighting at Bir Gifgafa and Mitla Pass, and routed Egyptians at Nakhl and Themed in drive farther south (2). Soviet ship passed through Strait of Tiran (3), now under Israeli control. Mistaken Israeli attack on U.S. ship in Mediterranean (4) killed 10 men. Israelis hold west bank of the River Jordan as far north as Jenin (5).

U.S. Planes Batter MIG Base in North

Special to The New York Times

SAIGON, South Vietnam, June 8 — American fighter-bombers knocked out a MIG base near Hanoi yesterday and wrecked a surface-to-air missile storage area 50 miles southwest of the capital, the United States Command reported today.

At the same time, new fighting broke out just south of the demilitarized zone at the border between North Vietnam and South Vietnam, where a fierce battle raged for control of three hills last month.

Navy carrier pilots attacked the Kep Airfield, 37 miles northeast of Hanoi, for the seventh time since April 24. A headquarters spokesman said the airfield is "closed tempo-

Continued on Page 8, Column 4

DONATIONS POUR IN FOR ISRAELI FUND

Many Give All They Have—Some Gifts in Millions

By M. S. HANDLER

"You have got it all now," said a brief letter containing a check for $25,000.

The message was from a professor at the Jewish Theological Seminary who said he had gladly stripped himself of his worldly goods and sent the proceeds to the United Jewish Appeal for the Israel Emergency Fund.

The owner of two gas stations arrived at the appeal's offices and turned over the deeds to the stations as his contribution to the multi-million fund drive.

Other Jews walked in with the cash-surrender values of their life insurance policies. Still others, deeply moved by the Arab-Israeli war, sold real estate and securities and sent the money to the fund's headquarters, on the Avenue of the Americas at 51st street.

These were some examples of the dramas being played out in the Jewish communities across the United States, U.J.A. officials said yesterday.

The contributions, appeal of-

Continued on Page 11, Column 1

ISRAEL, IN ERROR, ATTACKS U.S. SHIP

10 Navy Men Die, 100 Hurt in Raids North of Sinai

By WILLIAM BEECHER
Special to The New York Times

WASHINGTON, June 8—An American naval vessel was mistakenly attacked by Israeli planes and torpedo boats today in international waters about 15 miles north of the Sinai Peninsula. Reports tonight listed the toll as 10 dead and 100 wounded. Twenty of the wounded were hurt critically.

The vessel, the Liberty, was on a peaceful, though war-related mission. Pentagon sources said she had been dispatched from Spain to the war zone to provide additional communications to facilitate the evacuation of American citizens from the Middle East and North Africa.

Pentagon officials said it was too early to tell whether indemnification would be asked from Israel for the loss of life and the damage to the Navy ship.

President Johnson, in a letter to the Senate majority leader, Mike Mansfield, noted that the

Continued on Page 19, Column 1

Russians Continue To Harass 6th Fleet

By NEIL SHEEHAN
Special to The New York Times

ABOARD U. S. S. AMERICA, in the Eastern Mediterranean, June 8—Two Soviet warships, a destroyer and a small, highly maneuverable patrol craft, moved into the formation of this Sixth Fleet carrier task force group this morning and began systematically harassing the American ships.

The harassment was undertaken despite a warning to another Soviet destroyer yesterday from Vice Adm. William I. Martin, the Sixth Fleet commander. Admiral Martin warned the Soviet vessel to withdraw from the area of the American formation. He said the Soviet ship, while following the carrier

Continued on Page 15, Column 1

SOVIET SHIP SAILS INTO AQABA GULF

Passage Is First Since Israel Lifted Arab Blockade

By Reuters

ELATH, Israel, June 8—A Soviet freighter bound for the Jordanian port of Aqaba passed through the Strait of Tiran today, the first ship to do so since Israel declared the passage an international waterway yesterday.

Two outgoing Israeli freighters were preparing to be the first Israeli ships to pass through the strait since the Egyptians blockaded the Gulf of Aqaba on May 23.

A report from Sharm el Sheik, which dominates the strait, dis-

Continued on Page 17, Column 7

NEWS INDEX

"All the News That's Fit to Print"

The New York Times

LATE CITY EDITION

Weather: Snow likely today, tonight. Partly cloudy tomorrow. Temp. range: Today 35-31; Tuesday 41-32. Full U.S. report on Page 90.

VOL. CXVII . No. 40,177 NEW YORK, WEDNESDAY, JANUARY 24, 1968 — 10 CENTS

NORTH KOREA SEIZES NAVY SHIP, HOLDS 83 ON BOARD AS U.S. SPIES; ENTERPRISE IS ORDERED TO AREA

MILLS TURNS DOWN AIDES OF JOHNSON ON TAX SURCHARGE

Says They Did Not Convince Him They Had Done Their Best to Cut Spending

'ANOTHER LOOK' URGED

House Leader's Stand Hints at Delay Until March in Acting on New Levy

By EILEEN SHANAHAN

Special to The New York Times

WASHINGTON, Jan. 23 — Representative Wilbur D. Mills told the Administration "no" again today on the tax increase.

At the end of two days of hearings before the House Ways and Means Committee, of which he is chairman, the Arkansas Democrat told Administration officials that they had "not yet established" to his satisfaction that "you've done the best you can" to hold down Government spending.

Mr. Mills asked the officials to "take another look" at next year's planned Government spending of $147.4-billion, on the basis of the traditional administrative budget, while the committee turns its attention to another issue. That is the Administration's proposals to reduce the deficit in the United States' balance of international payments.

Date Left Undecided

Just how long the committee might take with the balance-of-payments program and when it might get back to the tax bill, Mr. Mills did not say. It seemed unlikely that the committee could resume consideration of the proposed 10 per cent tax surcharge before early March, at the soonest.

Meanwhile, the Gallup Poll reported that President Johnson faces a difficult task in trying to sell American voters on a tax increase at this time, and that the opposition comes as much from the rank and file of his own party as from others.

In addition to dealing with the balance-of-payments problem, Mr. Mills indicated that the committee might also consider, ahead of any new look at the tax surcharge, both the extension of excise taxes on automobiles and telephone service and a further step up in corporate tax collections.

Excise Action Favored

He said that an extension of the excise taxes "has to be done." Under present law they would go down on April 1 from 7 to 2 per cent on automobiles and from 10 to 1 per cent on telephone service.

In addition, he said it "might be possible, without a great deal of argument, to do some part" of what the Administration has asked to bring corporations closer to a pay-as-you-go tax basis.

Mr. Mills's reference to approval of only "part" of the corporate tax collection speed-up reflected his belief that the smallest corporations — those with tax liabilities of $25,000 or less — should probably not be put on a full pay-as-you-

Continued on Page 25, Column 1

Jersey Sues State On Price for PATH

By FRED P. GRAHAM

Special to The New York Times

WASHINGTON, Jan. 23 — New Jersey sued New York in the Supreme Court today in an unusual legal move designed to bar New York courts from approving an excessive land condemnation judgment against the Port of New York Authority.

In a suit filed directly in the Court, Attorney General Arthur J. Sills of New Jersey contended that the New York Court of Appeals violated an agreement between the two states when it ruled that the Port Authority should pay $30-million for the assets of the Hudson Rapid Tubes Corporation.

The assets, consisting of the Hudson & Manhattan Railroad

Continued on Page 30, Column 3

City Council Votes A One-Year Trial Of Group Cab Rides

By SETH S. KING

A year-long experiment in group taxi riding was approved yesterday by the City Council.

As soon as Mayor Lindsay signs the bill his task force on taxis will be allowed to organize and supervise such rides from the Eastern Airlines Shuttle Terminal at La Guardia Airport to four zones in Manhattan.

The Council also passed a bill eliminating a requirement that cab drivers be residents of the city.

It also adopted a resolution calling upon the Police Department's Hack Bureau to require each taxi to be equipped with an exterior switch, or similar device, instead of an interior switch, to operate its off-duty sign.

This was aimed at preventing a driver from suddenly turning on his off-duty sign with an interior switch when he saw a fare he did not want to pick up. The

Continued on Page 35, Column 1

JOHNSON PROGRAM INDICTED BY G.O.P.

In TV Reply, Party Charges His Policies Led to Riots, Crime Rise and Inflation

Excerpts from the statements will be found on Page 28.

By JOHN HERBERS

Special to The New York Times

WASHINGTON, Jan. 23—Republicans in Congress told the American people tonight that President Johnson's policies had led to riots, crime and inflation at home and loss of influence and prestige abroad.

In a one-hour telecast over the Columbia Broadcasting System from the auditorium of the new Senate Office Building, eight Senators and nine Representatives delivered a harsh indictment of the Administration's record and said that President Johnson had vastly underestimated the extent of discontent in the country.

America, they said, needs a new leader who would seek a military victory in Vietnam, take a strong stand against worldwide Communism, move decisively to stamp out crime and violence at home and hold down Government spending.

The broadcast, entitled "The State of the Union—the Republican Appraisal," was a reply to President Johnson's State of

Continued on Page 28, Column 3

PRESIDENT OFFERS PROJECT TO SPUR HIRING OF JOBLESS

$2-Billion Manpower Plea Stresses Industrial Effort to Assist 'Hard Core'

Text of President's message is printed on Page 24.

By MAX FRANKEL

Special to The New York Times

WASHINGTON, Jan. 23 — President Johnson asked Congress today for quick action to help him mount the first large-scale effort to induce private industry to train and hire the hard-core cases among the urban unemployed.

In the first of more than a dozen special messages covering his major legislative proposals for the year, the President urged the expansion of all Government manpower efforts by 25 per cent, from a budget of $1.65-billion in the current fiscal year, ending June 30, to $2.09-billion in the year starting July 1.

Total Is Expanding

He suggested spending the bulk of the $442-million increase on programs to find, train and employ the most disadvantaged citizens, most of whom have given up the search for work because of inadequate training, discrimination, discouragement and a general despair.

There are more than a million such persons, the Administration believes, including a still expanding total of 500,000 in 50 major cities. The President would try to place 100,000 of these in jobs in the next 18 months and aim for a target of 500,000 by mid-1971.

"It is a waste that an enlightened nation should not tolerate," Mr. Johnson said in his message. "It is a waste that a nation concerned by disorders in its city streets cannot tolerate."

National Organization

Existing manpower programs have not reached the hard-core jobless effectively, Mr. Johnson reported. Therefore he proposed the expansion of promising experiments with direct subsidies to private employers who incur the extra costs of training and making jobs available to hitherto unqualified persons.

He said he was creating a national organization of leading businessmen, headed by Henry Ford 2d, chairman of the Ford Motor Company, to enlist the cooperation of industry and to work with Government officials in the regions and cities.

At the same time, the President proposed a significant expansion of the year-old Government program to train the

Continued on Page 24, Column 1

3,600 Drugs Facing Relabeling To List Ailments They Combat

By United Press International

WASHINGTON, Jan. 23 — Virtually every drug originally manufactured in America between 1938 and 1962 will have to be relabeled to tell exactly what ailments it is effective against, the Government told the drug industry today.

Some of the 3,600 drugs — sold in as many as 18,000 different combinations — are going to be ordered off the market, and the advertising of nearly all the drugs will have to be changed, William W. Goodrich, assistant general counsel for the Food and Drug Administration, said.

He spoke at a two-hour conference of drug manufacturers called to explain the agency's study of the effectiveness of all prescription and nonprescription drugs marketed in that 24-year period.

The review had been ordered under the Kefauver-Harris Act of 1962, which requires that all drugs sold domestically be proved effective as well as safe for their intended uses. Prior to the new rules, the drugs had only to be found safe.

The first step toward removal from the market of a group of drugs was taken today with publication by the drug agency of a notice in The Federal Register that there was no evidence that the drugs rutin, quercetin, hesperidin or bioflavonoids "are effective for use in man for any conditions."

The listed drugs have been promoted for years as agents for the control of hemorrhage and in dietary food supplements.

Manufacturers of such drugs licensed by the drug agency and manufacturers of similar products — called "me too" products—were invited by the agency to a hearing Jan. 31 to discuss the ruling.

Robert Giles, a member of the Pharmaceutical Manufacturers Association, rose at the meeting to criticize Mr. Goodrich and other officials of the drug agency for public estimates that 10 per cent of the drugs under study would be found totally ineffective and ruled off the market.

In New York last month, Dr. James L. Goddard, Food and Drug Commissioner, estimated that 10 per cent of prescription and over-the-counter drugs would have to be withdrawn from the market because of the efficacy reviews.

Officials of the agency said

Continued on Page 32, Column 1

Associated Press

Pueblo, seized off North Korea and taken to Wonsan, is an intelligence collection vessel of the United States Navy

4 CREWMEN HURT

Rusk Says Efforts Are Under Way to Obtain Vessel's Release

U.S. statement and Pyongyang broadcast are on Page 15.

By NEIL SHEEHAN

Special to The New York Times

WASHINGTON, Jan. 23 — North Korean patrol boats seized a United States Navy intelligence ship off Wonsan today and took the vessel and her 83 crew members into the North Korean port.

The Defense Department, reporting the incident, said the ship had been in international waters about 25 miles off the eastern coast of North Korea when she was boarded by armed North Korean sailors at 1:45 P.M. (11:45 P.M. Monday, Eastern Standard time).

But North Korea, in a Pyongyang radio broadcast, asserted that the Pueblo had "intruded into the territorial waters of the republic and was carrying out hostile activities." The broadcast called the Pueblo "an armed spy boat of the United States imperialist aggressor force."

Matter of 'Utmost Gravity'

Secretary of State Dean Rusk called the seizure of the Pueblo "a matter of the utmost gravity." He said the United States was negotiating with North Korea "through the channels that are available to us to obtain the immediate release of the vessel and her crew."

The incident forced a sudden confrontation between the United States and an Asian Communist government that has long been calling for diversionary assaults against "United States imperialism" to distract American energies from the war in Vietnam.

The Defense Department said four crewmen of the Pueblo had been wounded, one critically. One report said a crew member had lost a leg. The Pentagon declined to say how the men had been wounded.

North Korean Report

Later—on Wednesday morning, Korean time—the North Vietnamese said at an armistice meeting in Panmunjom that several of the Pueblo's crew were "killed or wounded" in the incident, and a North Vietnamese broadcast monitored in Tokyo said the vessel resisted seizure. The Pentagon declined to comment.

The Pueblo carried 6 officers, 75 enlisted men and 2 civilians, whom the Defense Department identified as Navy civilian hydrographers performing oceanographic research.

Military sources said that the nuclear-powered aircraft carrier Enterprise and two destroyers

Continued on Page 14, Column 5

Danish Socialists Beaten in Election; Krag Will Resign

By ALVIN SHUSTER

Special to The New York Times

COPENHAGEN, Denmark, Jan. 23—The Social Democratic party, in power for the last 15 years, was defeated tonight in a huge protest vote.

The Danes, upset over rising prices and taxes, turned to the right in their national elections. Three non-Socialist parties won enough seats in Parliament to enable them to form a new government.

Premier Jens Otto Krag, the Social Democratic Premier, said he would resign tomorrow.

Emerging as victors today were the Radical Liberals, the Conservatives and the Agrarian Liberals. The three parties had indicated strongly before the election that if they won a parliamentary majority they would form a government.

Social Democrats Largest

Between them, with about 95 per cent of the votes counted, they had 101 seats, the Radical Liberals going from 13 to 28, the Conservatives from 34 to 38 and the Agrarian Liberals remaining unchanged at 35.

The Social Democrats will remain the largest single party in Parliament with 63 seats, a loss of six. The extreme leftist Socialist People's party, which had won 20 seats in the last elections in 1966, dropped to 11.

The voting was heavy. The final count may show that 90 per cent of the 3.3 million eligible voters cast ballots.

Mr. Krag appeared on television tonight and made a last-minute appeal to save his

Continued on Page 7, Column 1

RADIATION FOUND WHERE B-52 FELL

It Suggests Hydrogen Bombs Did Not Go Through Ice Off Greenland Base

By JOHN W. FINNEY

Special to The New York Times

WASHINGTON, Jan. 23—Air Force search teams were reported today to have detected small amounts of radiation from some or all of the four hydrogen bombs missing after a B-52 bomber crashed on the ice off northwest Greenland.

After two days of hunting with dog sleds and helicopters, teams from the Thule Air Force Base in Greenland still had not found the unarmed thermonuclear weapons. But the detection of the radiation was taken as an encouraging sign that the bombs were scattered across the surface and had not plunged through the ice with parts of the bomber into about 800 feet of water.

If the bombs are still on the surface, recovery operations will be easier. It was first thought that the bombs had sunk to the bottom of North Star Bay, about seven miles southwest of the Thule base, raising the problem of underwater recovery operations through the sea ice.

The radiation suggested that some of the bombs might have broken apart in the impact of the crash and during the subsequent explosion in the bomber as it careened several hundred feet across the ice. If the bombs have split and

Continued on Page 6, Column 4

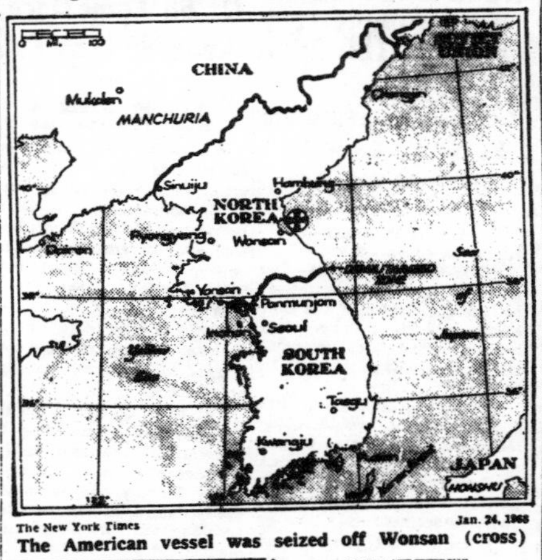

The New York Times — Jan. 24, 1968

The American vessel was seized off Wonsan (cross)

5,000 MEN MASSED AT KHESANH BY U.S.

Marines Rushed In as Foe Builds Up Force in Area—Supply Planes Fired On

By CHARLES MOHR

Special to The New York Times

KHESANH, South Vietnam, Jan. 23 — More than 5,000 United States marines have been concentrated at Khesanh amid indications that one of the major battles of the Vietnam war may be in the offing.

The marines were rushed in because of an increasingly obvious concentration of North Vietnamese troops in the area.

[Sixty-one enemy soldiers were reported killed by air strikes and artillery fire on Tuesday near Khesanh. In a battle on the Bongson plain, 128 Vietcong troops were reported killed by United States infantrymen.]

The nearness of the enemy forces made itself evident when the unmistakable sound of a bullet striking a fuselage rang out as a transport plane glided in to land at the Marine base here. The fat-bellied C-123 Loadmaster landed, safe despite the bullet hole.

The crew pushed pallets of 155-mm. artillery ammunition off the plane and then turned to four large wooden crates addressed to "Fifth Graves

Continued on Page 3, Column 1

RETURN OF PUEBLO ASKED BY U.S. AIDE

Immediate Action Sought at Meeting in Panmunjom of Armistice Group

By Reuters

PANMUNJOM, Korea, Wednesday, Jan. 24—The American commander of the United Nations Command demanded at a meeting of the Mixed Armistice Commission today that the Pueblo and her crew of 83 be returned immediately by North Korea.

Rear Adm. John V. Smith also told the chief North Korean delegate, Maj. Gen. Chung Kook Pak, that the United States reserved the right to demand compensation for the capture of the vessel by the North Korean Navy yesterday.

[The North Koreans said the ship "will remain in our hands," United Press International reported.]

General Pak said North Korean naval vessels fired at the Pueblo yesterday and "several of her crew members were killed or wounded." The Defense Department in Washington had said no one was killed.

Admiral Smith also protested what he said was an intrusion by a band of 31 North Korean agents into Seoul, the South Korean capital, Sunday night. The intrusion resulted in the death of 11 persons.

The meeting today in the demilitarized zone between North and South Korea was called by the United Nations Command Monday, before the Pueblo was taken, because of the infiltration incident.

The United Nations had asked that the meeting take place yesterday, but the North Koreans wanted it held today and

Continued on Page 14, C

U.S. Resumes Normal Relations With Greece's Military Regime

By PETER GROSE

Special to The New York Times

WASHINGTON, Jan. 23—The United States resumed "normal" diplomatic relations with Greece today, six weeks after King Constantine failed in his attempt to oust the military regime.

The State Department said that Ambassador Phillips Talbot had been instructed to make an official call on the Greek Foreign Minister, Panayotis Pipinelis, and thus signal the resumption of formal contacts between the two governments.

Shipments of large-scale military supplies from the United States remain embargoed, the department added, as they have been since last April when the junta seized power.

This is causing concern among Administration officials on a pragmatic basis, for they fear that the Greek forces in the North Atlantic Treaty Organization are being weakened by lack of heavy matériel.

Small arms, ammunition, spare parts and other maintenance stocks continue to be supplied to the Greek forces by the United States. This kind of military aid was not suspended after the April coup.

The department spokesman, Robert J. McCloskey, swept aside a maze of protocol and political considerations by stating, "The United States Government continues to regard King Constantine as the Greek chief of state—relations between the King and the Government in Athens are an in-

Continued on Page 8, Column 1

NEWS INDEX

News Summary and Index, Page 47

Seizure of Vessel Scored in Capital

By United Press International

WASHINGTON, Jan. 23 — North Korea's seizure of the United States intelligence-gathering ship Pueblo was condemned in Congress today as an act of war. Some lawmakers demanded a quick military response.

Senator Richard B. Russell, chairman of the Senate Armed Services Committee, said that the action was "a breach of international law amounting to an act of war."

The Georgia Democrat added that "it certainly behooves our Government to take a very strong position in demand... release of the ship and ... of the men."

Representative Bob...

"All the News That's Fit to Print"

The New York Times

LATE CITY EDITION

Weather: Clearing today, turning cold tonight. Fair, cool tomorrow. Temp. range: today 62-44; Thurs. 73-52. Full U.S. report on Page 92.

VOL. CXVII . No. 40,249

NEW YORK, FRIDAY, APRIL 5, 1968

10 CENTS

MARTIN LUTHER KING IS SLAIN IN MEMPHIS; A WHITE IS SUSPECTED; JOHNSON URGES CALM

JOHNSON DELAYS TRIP TO HAWAII; MAY LEAVE TODAY

President Spends a Hectic Day Here and in Capital —Sees Thant at the U.N.

By MAX FRANKEL
Special to The New York Times

WASHINGTON, April 4 — President Johnson postponed his trip to Hawaii at least until tomorrow after he heard of the death of the Rev. Dr. Martin Luther King Jr. tonight.

The news, which visibly shocked the President, came at the end of one of the most extraordinary days in perhaps the most extraordinary week of his Administration.

Mr. Johnson was to have flown from Washington at about midnight for a weekend of strategy conferences with his military and diplomatic leaders stationed in South Vietnam. On the way, he had planned a breakfast meeting in California with former President Dwight D. Eisenhower.

Instead, the President telephoned Mrs. King in Atlanta, made a brief appeal for calm on television and went to his office to follow the reports of unrest and disturbance given him periodically by Attorney General Ramsey Clark.

Cancels Dinner Appearance

Mr. Johnson also canceled an appearance before a Democratic party fund-raising dinner here —the final event of a hectic schedule that became ever more hectic as the day unfolded.

The President began the day by making final arrangements for the Hawaii meeting. It had been tentatively planned before his order Sunday to curtail the bombing of North Vietnam and the news yesterday that Hanoi was interested in establishing direct contact.

[The new United States peace moves are producing a quiet but bitter reaction in the South Vietnamese Government that is causing increasing concern among United States officials in Saigon. Page 14.]

But the diplomatic development, though not the principal subject of the Honolulu meetings, added special weight to his conversations with Gen. William C. Westmoreland, the American commander in South Vietnam, and other officials.

Mr. Johnson was careful not to arouse false hopes of peace, but he appeared encouraged and in buoyant spirt as he decided before noon to fly first to New York to attend the investiture of the Most Rev. Terence J. Cooke as Archbishop of New York.

Then, while in New York,

Continued on Page 12, Column 1

Hanoi Charges U.S. Raid Far North of 20th Parallel

By EVERT CLARK
Special to The New York Times

WASHINGTON, April 4 — North Vietnam charged in a broadcast today that United States planes had bombed a "populated area" in northwestern Vietnam far north of the 20th parallel. The Defense Department said it knew of no such raid but was investigating.

President Johnson has ordered that there be no attacks on North Vietnam north of the 20th Parallel as a step toward de-escalating the war.

[In South Vietnam, United States marines beat off an attack by about 400 North Vietnamese soldiers charging up a hill near Khesanh, killing 93, The Associated Press reported. Meanwhile, an American relief column was nearing the besieged base. Page 15.]

The Hanoi radio, in a broadcast monitored and translated here, said three waves of United States planes dropped more than 50 bombs on a "populated area" about 30 miles west of Laichau, capital of Laichau Province, this morning.

The nearest village to that

Continued on Page 15, Column 1

The New York Times April 5, 1968

Hanoi said that area near Laichau (cross) was target.

DISMAY IN NATION

Negroes Urge Others to Carry on Spirit of Nonviolence

By LAWRENCE VAN GELDER

Dismay, shame, anger and foreboding marked the nation's reaction last night to the Rev. Dr. Martin Luther King Jr.'s murder.

From the high offices of state to the man in the street, news of the moderate civil rights leader's violent death in Memphis yesterday drew, for the most part, stunned and sober statements.

Most major Negro organizations and Negro leaders, lamenting Dr. King's death, expressed hope that it serve as a spur to others to carry on in his spirit of nonviolence. But some Negro militants responded with bitterness and anger.

Roy Wilkins, executive director of the National Association for the Advancement of Colored People, said his organization was "shocked and deeply grieved by the dastardly murder of Dr. Martin Luther King."

"His murderer or murderers must be promptly apprehended and brought to justice," Mr. Wilkins said:

'A Man of Peace'

"Dr. King was a symbol of the nonviolent civil rights protest movement. He was a man of peace, of dedication, of great courage. His senseless assassination solves nothing. It will not stay the civil rights movement; it will instead spur it to greater activity."

Whitney M. Young Jr., executive director of the National Urban League, said:

"We are unspeakably shocked by the murder of Martin Luther King, one of the greatest leaders of our time. This is a bitter reflection on America. We fear for our country.

"The only possible answer now is for the nation to act immediately on what Dr. King has been fighting for—passage of the civil rights and anti-poverty bills and a true and just equality for all men. Those of us who have remained loyal to his concept of nonviolence have been dealt a mortal blow."

Mayor Richard G. Hatcher of Gary, Ind., a Negro, termed the death of Dr. King "every man's loss."

"Men who care for humankind and struggle for its salvation through reason and faith have lost a leader of monumental stature," he said. "A man of his magnitude will not soon pass this way again."

At his home in Stamford, Conn., the former baseball star Jackie Robinson called the

Continued on Page 26, Column 1

PRESIDENT'S PLEA

On TV, He Deplores 'Brutal' Murder of Negro Leader

Statements by Johnson and Humphrey are on Page 24.

Special to The New York Times

WASHINGTON, April 4— President Johnson deplored tonight in a brief television address to the nation the "brutal slaying" of the Rev. Dr. Martin Luther King Jr.

He asked "every citizen to reject the blind violence that has struck Dr. King, who lived by nonviolence."

Mr. Johnson said he was postponing his scheduled departure tonight for a Honolulu conference on Vietnam and that instead he would leave tomorrow.

The President spoke from the White House. At the Washington Hilton Hotel, where Democratic members of Congress had gathered to honor the President and the Vice President, Mr. Humphrey, his voice strained with emotion, said:

"Martin Luther King stands with our other American martyrs in the cause of freedom and justice. His death is a terrible tragedy."

The dinner was canceled 10 to 15 minutes after the Vice President spoke. Mr. Johnson, who was scheduled to appear at the dinner, canceled his plans to attend.

F.B.I. Inquiry Ordered

Attorney General Ramsey Clark ordered an immediate inquiry by the Federal Bureau of Investigation into the shooting of Dr. King in Memphis.

He said the purpose of the investigation would be to determine whether any Federal law had been violated.

One provision of the law that could be invoked makes it a crime to engage in a conspiracy to deprive a person of his civil rights.

In addition to F.B.I. agents, Department of Justice civil rights representatives were on the scene in Memphis and were in touch with the Attorney General.

Military sources said that no National Guard units had yet been Federalized and no Regular Army troops had been alerted yet for possible movement to cities where violence had broken out.

National Guard troops, such as the 4,000 men who have been called into Memphis, remain under state control until the responsible Governor requests help and the President

Continued on Page 24, Column 7

Associated Press

THE REV. DR. MARTIN LUTHER KING Jr.

GUARD CALLED OUT

Curfew Is Ordered in Memphis, but Fires and Looting Erupt

By EARL CALDWELL
Special to The New York Times

MEMPHIS, Friday, April 5— The Rev. Dr. Martin Luther King Jr., who preached nonviolence and racial brotherhood, was fatally shot here last night by a distant gunman who then raced away and escaped.

Four thousand National Guard troops were ordered into Memphis by Gov. Buford Ellington after the 39-year-old Nobel Prize-winning civil rights leader died.

A curfew was imposed on the shocked city of 550,000 inhabitants, 40 per cent of whom are Negro.

But the police said the tragedy had been followed by incidents that included sporadic shooting, fires, bricks and bottles thrown at policemen, and looting that started in Negro districts and then spread over the city.

White Car Sought

Police Director Frank Holloman said the assassin might have been a white man who was "50 to 100 yards away in a flophouse."

Chief of Detectives W. P. Huston said a late model white Mustang was believed to have been the killer's getaway car. Its occupant was described as a bareheaded white man in his 30's, wearing a black suit and black tie.

The detective chief said the police had chased two cars near the motel where Dr. King was shot and had halted one that had two out-of-town men as occupants. The men were questioned but seemed to have nothing to do with the killing, he said.

Rifle Found Nearby

A high-powered 30.06-caliber rifle was found about a block from the scene of the shooting, on South Main Street. "We think it's the gun," Chief Huston said, reporting it would be turned over to the Federal Bureau of Investigation.

Dr. King was shot while he leaned over a second-floor railing outside his room at the Lorraine Motel. He was chatting with two friends just before starting for dinner.

One of the friends was a musician, and Dr. King had just asked him to play a Negro spiritual, "Precious Lord, Take My Hand," at a rally that was to have been held two hours later in support of striking Memphis sanitationmen.

Paul Hess, assistant adminis-

Continued on Page 24, Column 1

HUMPHREY HINTS HE'LL ENTER RACE

Tells Unionists in Pittsburgh He Will Act Soon—Abel and Wirtz Back Him

By ROY REED
Special to The New York Times

PITTSBURGH, April 4—Two thousand labor representatives, including the head of the United Steel Workers union, clamorously urged Vice President Humphrey today to run for President.

The Vice President left little doubt that he would oblige them, but he indicated that he would wait until President Johnson returned from his Hawaii conference before making an announcement.

"I know what your request is, and I know what your thoughts are," he told the delegates to the Pennsylvania A.F.L.-C.I.O. convention. "I am most grateful. I am not one to walk away from a decision, and a decision will come in due time."

But nothing he does should interfere with President Johnson's peace mission, he said.

Several other political leaders urged Mr. Humphrey today to enter the race for the Democratic Presidential nomination. The most prominent among them was Secretary of Labor W. Willard Wirtz, who was addressing a union convention at Miami Beach.

I. W. Abel, president of the steelworkers Union, rose as Mr.

Continued on Page 32, Column 1

Johnson Shuns Role Of '68 'Lame Duck,' Kennedy Was Told

By JOHN HERBERS
Special to The New York Times

WASHINGTON, April 4—In his meeting with Senator Robert F. Kennedy yesterday President Johnson said he would remain out of the political fight this year because he did not believe it was appropriate for a "lame duck" President to try to pick his successor.

This and other details of the Johnson-Kennedy meeting were learned today from knowledgeable sources.

The meeting, which Senator Kennedy had requested in the interest of "national unity," was described as an extraordinarily friendly one, with both the Senator and the President speaking in a conciliatory manner.

President Johnson was pictured as the "elder statesman" of the party who had decided to remain aloof from this year's scramble for the Presidency in an effort to keep the party as strong as possible and retain his own dignity and effectiveness as President.

At one point, it was reported, the President said he did not want to make a spectacle of himself as a lame duck President attempting to dictate to the party who should be nominated at the national convention.

In this regard, he pointed out that in 1956 former President Harry S. Truman went to the

Continued on Page 31, Column 4

Scattered Violence Occurs In Harlem and Brooklyn

12 Are Arrested Here

By THOMAS A. JOHNSON

Sporadic violence erupted in Harlem and Brooklyn's Bedford-Stuyvesant section last night after news of Dr. Martin Luther King's assassination spread in the two predominantly Negro communities.

Mayor Lindsay, who went to Harlem in an effort to quiet the outbreaks, was caught in the midst of an unruly crowd and had to be hustled into a limousine by bodyguards.

Police reinforcements, including elements of the riot-trained Tactical Patrol Force, were rushed into both communities.

Two arrests were reported in Brooklyn and 10 in Harlem. A television crewman was said to have been injured by flying glass.

There were numerous instances of rock-throwing, looting and arson reported both in Brooklyn and in Harlem, starting around 11 P.M. and continuing early today.

Gangs of youth in both areas were reported roaming through the streets, now and then taunting policemen and firemen on duty.

The police fired several volleys of shots in the air to disperse crowds along Brooklyn's Fulton Street and Harlem's

Continued on Page 26, Column 2

Widespread Disorders

Disorders broke out in scattered parts of the nation last night after the slaying of the Rev. Dr. Martin Luther King Jr. The National Guard was called out or alerted in several cities.

In Washington, scattered but persistent looting and vandalism erupted, led for a time by Stokely Carmichael, former head of the Student Nonviolent Coordinating Commitee. All available policemen were being called to duty.

About 4,000 Tennessee National Guardsmen were ordered to duty in Nashville because of disorders.

In North Carolina, Gov. Dan K. Moore alerted the Guard in Greensboro at the request of Mayor Carson Bain. State Highway patrolmen were dispatched to Raleigh.

There were riotous outbursts

Continued on Page 26, Column 5

NEWS INDEX

Archbishop Cooke Installed; President Looks On

By EDWARD B. FISKE

The Most Rev. Terence J. Cooke was installed as the seventh Roman Catholic Archbishop of New York yesterday in a historic pageant attended by the President of the United States and highlighted by prayers for the success of his peace efforts in Vietnam.

"Let us pray with all our hearts that God will inspire our President," the 47-year-old Archbishop said in his homily at St. Patrick's Cathedral.

"In the last few days, we have all admired his heroic efforts in the search for peace in Vietnam. We ask God to bless his efforts with success. May God inspire not only our President, but also other leaders and the leaders of all nations of the world to find a way to peace."

Then the Archbishop, speaking from a white marble pulpit and surrounded by a blaze of purple, gold and scarlet robes, addressed himself directly to Mr. Johnson, who sat below him in a front pew.

The President, sitting with his hands clasped and his legs crossed, listened with obvious intensity to the Archbishop's words.

"Mr. President," he said, "our hearts, our hopes, our continued prayers go with you."

Mr. Johnson, accompanied by his daughter, Mrs. Patrick J. Nugent, led a festive congregation of about 5,000 cardinals, bishops, priests, laymen, nuns, civic leaders

Continued on Page 38, Column 1

The New York Times (by Neal Boenzi)

President Johnson and his daughter, Mrs. Patrick J. Nugent, right, listening during yesterday's ceremonies. At left are Mrs. John F. Kennedy and Lieut. Gov. Malcolm Wilson. Security personnel are in the row between them.

Archbishop Luigi Raimondi, Apostolic Delegate to the U.S., speaking after Archbishop Terence J. Cooke was enthroned

"All the News That's Fit to Print"

The New York Times

LATE CITY EDITION

Weather: Sunny and mild today; fair tonight. Sunny, mild tomorrow. Temp. range: today 50-35. Friday 62-46. Full U. S. report on Page 78.

VOL. CXVII..No. 40,250 NEW YORK, SATURDAY, APRIL 6, 1968 10 CENTS

ARMY TROOPS IN CAPITAL AS NEGROES RIOT; GUARD SENT INTO CHICAGO, DETROIT, BOSTON; JOHNSON ASKS A JOINT SESSION OF CONGRESS

SIEGE OF KHESANH DECLARED LIFTED; TROOPS HUNT FOE

Relief Column, Within Mile of Base, Presses Search —Helicopters Kill 50

By The Associated Press

KHESANH, South Vietnam, Saturday, April 6—The 76-day North Vietnamese siege of the Marine base at Khesanh was officially declared lifted yesterday.

United States marines and helicopter-borne Army troops today pushed toward what was described as North Vietnamese regimental headquarters south of the base.

The 20,000-man relief column reached the base and then fanned out on three sides in search of the vanishing enemy soldiers. Army helicopter units entered the base.

The sweep could take the Americans all the way to the Laotian border, less than 10 miles away, in the effort to root out the 7,000 men said to remain in an enemy force once estimated at 20,000. North Vietnam uses Laos as a staging area for attacks along South Vietnam's borders.

Gunships Attack Near Town

The United States command said that helicopter gunships of the First Cavalry Division (Airmobile), crisscrossing the skies ahead of the ground troops, killed 50 North Vietnamese late yesterday near the town of Khesanh, which is two miles south of the base.

Earlier, United States troops fought about 150 enemy soldiers four miles east of the town. Nine enemy soldiers and one American were reported killed.

The town was made an enemy command post after South Vietnamese troops and a small unit of United States marines abandoned it in January under a heavy siege.

Ten thousand civilians, mostly montagnard tribesmen, fled the town when fighting broke out. Many are in refugee camps in the coastal lowlands.

The relief column made no immediate attempt to enter the Khesanh base. Enemy gunners zeroed in on the outpost with 110 rounds of artillery and mortar fire.

Before the pressure on the

Continued on Page 2, Column 4

Hanoi Voices Doubt Over U.S. Sincerity

By Agence France-Presse

HANOI, North Vietnam, April 5—Hanoi protested today against what it called "savage bombings" of North Vietnam and "intensification of the war in South Vietnam" since President Johnson's announcement Sunday of restriction on attacks on the North.

Under the signature "Commentator," a pseudonym customarily indicating official authorship, an editorial in the party newspaper, Nhan Dan, questioned the sincerity of Mr. Johnson's avowed desire for peace.

[Despite the tone of the Hanoi editorial, Administration officials saw no indication that North Vietnam was backing away from talks with the United States. Page 5.]

The Nhan Dan editorial said: "The decision of the United

Continued on Page 3, Column 1

SOVIET ENDORSES ASSENT BY HANOI

Moscow Mentioned as Site of Talks With U.S.—China Urges Continued War

By RAYMOND H. ANDERSON

Special to The New York Times

MOSCOW, April 5 — The Soviet Government today endorsed the agreement by North Vietnam to start discussions with the United States toward a complete halt of bombing to open the door to full-scale negotiations.

The statement came amid speculation that Moscow might be the site for a meeting between United States and North Vietnamese representatives.

Premier Aleksei N. Kosygin is cutting short his trip to Iran and will return to Moscow Sunday, one day early.

[Communist China, however, termed President Johnson's peace overture a smokescreen and urged the North Vietnamese and the Vietcong to continue fighting.]

The United States Embassy denied that it had any knowledge of arrangements for a meeting here. The United States, it was understood,

Continued on Page 4, Column 3

PRESIDENT GRAVE

Sets Day of Mourning for Dr. King—Meets Rights Leaders

President's statement and his proclamation, Page 23.

By MAX FRANKEL

Special to The New York Times

WASHINGTON, April 5 — President Johnson asked today to address a joint session of Congress no later than Monday evening so that he could propose "constructive action instead of destructive action in this hour of national need."

Gravely imploring Americans to "stand their ground to deny violence its victory" in the reaction to the slaying of the Rev. Dr. Martin Luther King Jr., the President set out to arouse the nation's conscience and to win quick action on the long-stalled major items in his domestic program.

He proclaimed Sunday a national day of mourning for Dr. King, who was shot yesterday in Memphis and died later in a hospital.

Meanwhile, Congressional leaders said that Dr. King's murder could assure passage next week of a landmark civil rights bill.

Conference Canceled

To deal with the divisiveness that he said was "tearing this nation apart," Mr. Johnson canceled the already delayed conference he had planned for this weekend in Hawaii with American military and diplomatic officials stationed in South Vietnam.

Gen. William C. Westmoreland, the American commander in the war zone, was flying to Washington instead and will probably see Mr. Johnson tomorrow morning.

The President spent almost the entire day working "to avoid catastrophe." He met with moderate Negro leaders and members of Congress and of his Administration to find ways of containing the violence, arson and looting that threatened many big cities and that spread here to within a few blocks of the White House.

He also conferred all day with officials of the District of Columbia and gave them Federal troops this evening to help restore order.

Mr. Johnson's demeanor all

Continued on Page 23, Column 1

Associated Press

ON DUTY IN WASHINGTON: A soldier with a machine gun and another with a rifle, left, stand guard on the steps outside the Senate chamber. Flag was lowered to half-staff in tribute to the Rev. Dr. Martin Luther King Jr.

New York Volatile As Anger and Fear Set a Tense Mood

By MICHAEL STERN

A volatile mood of deep sorrow, fist-shaking anger and undefined fear settled on the city yesterday as it absorbed the impact of the death of the Rev. Dr. Martin Luther King Jr.

Many schools, colleges, offices and shops closed early partly out of respect for the memory of the slain civil rights leader, and partly because of reports that new outbreaks of violence would erupt.

The city's bustling waterfront grew still at noon as seamen and longshoremen stopped work as a tribute to Dr. King. The stoppage was announced by the International Longshoremen's Association and the National Maritime Union.

Seven thousand to eight thousand high school and college students released from classes assembled at a memorial rally for Dr. King at the

Continued on Page 26, Column 5

OUTBREAKS HERE RELATIVELY MILD

Negro Areas Are Quiet, but Bands of Young Vandals Roam Midtown Streets

By SYLVAN FOX

The streets of Harlem and Bedford-Stuyvesant were generally calm last night after a burst of violence and looting early yesterday in the wake of the assassination of the Rev. Dr. Martin Luther King Jr. in Memphis.

Mayor Lindsay, appearing on television at 11:30 P.M., praised New Yorkers for keeping the peace and said: "We can work together again for progress and for peace in this city and in this nation."

Earlier in the evening, bands of youths—mostly Negro teenagers—swarmed into mid-Manhattan, engaged in scattered violence and some looting and were dispersed by a massive show of police force.

The police arrested 27 adults in the Times Square area, most on minor charges, and nine youths were charged with juvenile delinquency. Two persons were reported seized at Columbus Circle, where seven shop windows were smashed and

Continued on Page 27, Column 1

7 Die as Fires and Looting Spread in Chicago Rioting

By DONALD JANSON

Special to The New York Times

CHICAGO, Saturday, April 6—Six thousand National Guard troops were called up yesterday as rioters pillaged stores along a two-mile stretch of Madison Street in the Negro West Side. Seven Negroes were killed and about 350 arrested, the police reported, as the violence and ransacking tapered off late last night.

Half of the armed guardsmen, in fatigues and riot helmets, began patrolling glass-littered West Side streets about 10 P.M. The rest stood by in armories.

About 100 city buses were damaged by bricks and rocks. Drivers, passengers, policemen, firemen, motorists and pedestrians were among at least 75 persons injured.

Mother Beaten

Mrs. Bernadine Laskow, mother of three children, was pulled from her car by Negro youths and beaten. Some white pedestrians who were in the Negro slum suffered the same treatment.

Dozens of automobiles that entered the 12-square-mile riot zone emerged with smashed windows and dented hoods. In some blocks all store windows were boarded or broken.

Cab drivers refused to enter

Continued on Page 23, Column 8

EUROPE DISMAYED; FEARFUL FOR U.S.

Murder of Dr. King Evokes Doubts Over Stability of the American Society

By ANTHONY LEWIS

Special to The New York Times

LONDON, April 5—The murder of the Rev. Dr. Martin Luther King Jr. evoked in Europe today a reaction of intense horror at the deed and of fear for the stability of American society.

In governments, in the press and among the public, there were expressions of sympathy that went beyond formalities. Dr. King was deeply admired in Europe and held up as a symbol of hope for America.

'A Common, Tragic Link'

All the concerns about the United States and its leadership that have grown here in recent years—concerns especially about the war in Vietnam and the violence in America—were fed by the killing of the civil rights leader in Memphis last night.

Everywhere in Europe, people linked Dr. King's death with the assassination of President Kennedy in 1963. That two men so admired here could so similarly be killed intensified doubts about the character of America today.

"From John Fitzgerald Kennedy to Martin Luther King,"

Continued on Page 28, Column 3

MANY FIRES SET

White House Guarded by G.I.'s—14 Dead in U.S. Outbreaks

Text of proclamation and Executive order, Page 22.

By BEN A. FRANKLIN

Special to The New York Times

WASHINGTON, April 5—President Johnson ordered 4,000 regular Army and National Guard troops into the nation's capital tonight to try to end riotous looting, burglarizing and burning by roving bands of Negro youths. The arson and looting began yesterday after the murder of the Rev. Dr. Martin Luther King Jr. in Memphis.

The White House announced at 5 P.M. that because the President had determined that "a condition of domestic violence and disorder" existed, he had issued a proclamation and an Executive order mobilizing combat-equipped troops in Washington. Some of the troops were sent to guard the Capitol and the White House.

Reinforcements numbering 2,500 riot-trained soldiers — a brigade of the 82d Airborne Division from Ft. Bragg, N. C.— were airlifted to nearby Andrews Air Force Base, to be held in reserve this weekend.

Guard Called In Other Cities

The National Guard also was called out in a half-dozen other cities in an effort to stem disorders or guard against them—Chicago, Detroit, Boston, Jackson, Miss., Raleigh, N. C., and Tallahassee, Fla.

The death toll from the violence stemming from Dr. King's assassination stood at a total of 14 tonight. Besides five deaths in Washington, they included seven in Chicago, one in Detroit and one in Tallahassee.

Mayor Walter E. Washington, who is a Negro, declared a 13-hour curfew, from 5:30 P.M. to 6:30 A.M. The Mayor's emergency order halted the sale of liquor and forbade the sale, transportation or possession of firearms, explosives or flammable liquids.

At midnight, the police reported five dead, all but one of them Negroes, in 28 hours of disorders in this city of about 800,000, 63 per cent of them Negroes. Four Negroes were killed today, including two suspected looters, one of them 14 years old, who were shot to death by policemen in separate isolated encounters across the Anacostia River, far from the areas of general disorders. The two other Negro deaths today were described as apparently the result of accidents.

The white man, George Fletcher, 28, of suburban Wood-

Continued on Page 22, Column 1

Clark Is Sure Killer Will Soon Be Seized

By MARTIN WALDRON

Special to The New York Times

MEMPHIS, Tenn., April 5—Attorney General Ramsey Clark said today that he was "confident" of a quick solution to the assassination here yesterday of the Rev. Dr. Martin Luther King Jr.

A source close to the intensive manhunt said that agents of the Federal Bureau of Investigation were close to making an arrest.

The Attorney General, who flew here this morning at the order of President Johnson with other top officials of the Justice Department, told a news conference that the F.B.I. was searching for the killer in several states.

He said that the killer, who was believed to have escaped in a white Mustang automobile,

Continued on Page 24, Column 1

The New York Times (by Barton Silverman)

MARCHING DOWN BROADWAY: Demonstrators protesting the slaying of the Rev. Dr. Martin Luther King Jr. crossing 23d Street on the way to City Hall yesterday. The march began after a memorial ceremony in Central Park.

Negroes Strive to Ease Tensions; False Rumors Raise City's Fears

Militants Join Effort

By THOMAS A. JOHNSON

At the height of the violence in Harlem early yesterday morning, about 30 young Negro militants fanned out from Jay's Bar and Grill on 125th Street near Eighth Avenue and tried to persuade other Negroes to stop breaking windows, looting and setting fires.

This particular group was made up of members of Harlem CORE, and they were only a part of the many hundreds of Negroes living in the violence-torn areas of Harlem and Brooklyn who worked actively to stop the disorders.

The volunteer peace-keepers tried to end the violence by a variety of methods and for a variety of reasons.

Some are church groups,

Continued on Page 26, Column 1

Racial Unrest Exaggerated

By MURRAY SCHUMACH

The city was flooded yesterday with wild and unfounded rumors that exceeded the amount of violence and heightened widespread fears of racial riots.

In some instances, the reports became so persistent that corporations allowed employes, particularly women, to leave for home early in the afternoon.

The untrue reports included subway disruptions, bombings, mass assaults and imposition of a citywide curfew. Almost any kind of holdup, apparently, was associated in the minds of some rumor-mongers with racial disturbances and was then exaggerated.

Barry H. Gottehrer, the head

Continued on Page 26, Column 6

NEWS INDEX

"All the News That's Fit to Print"

The New York Times

LATE CITY EDITION

Weather: Sunny, warm today; fair, continued warm tonight, tomorrow. Temp. range: today 88-62; Wed. 83-59. Temp.-Hum. Index 75; Wed. 74. Full U.S. report on Page 94.

VOL. CXVII..No. 40,311 — NEW YORK, THURSDAY, JUNE 6, 1968 — 10 CENTS

KENNEDY IS DEAD, VICTIM OF ASSASSIN; SUSPECT, ARAB IMMIGRANT, ARRAIGNED; JOHNSON APPOINTS PANEL ON VIOLENCE

MARCUS TESTIFIES DE SAPIO HAD ROLE IN A CON ED DEAL

Says Itkin Sought Delay of Permit to Aid Own Scheme With Ex-Tammany Head

By BARNARD L. COLLIER

Former Water Commissioner James L. Marcus testified yesterday that he had been asked to delay approval of a permit to Consolidated Edison while the former Tammany Hall leader, Carmine G. De Sapio, was trying to make a deal with the utility company.

Marcus testified that the request came last September from his business partner, Herbert Itkin, who was in turn trying to negotiate a deal with Mr. De Sapio.

The testimony was elicited from Marcus under cross-examination on the third day of a Federal bribery conspiracy trial that has been marked by the mention in Marcus's testimony of several prominent members of both the Republican and Democratic parties.

Marcus was asked if there was a time when he, as Commissioner of Water Supply, Gas and Electricity, had "done business" with Con Edison. His answer was yes.

Says Itkin Asked Delay

"Itkin came to me," he said, "and said that Con Ed wanted a permit to increase the voltage on one of their power lines for 20 miles." He added that his approval as Commissioner was needed.

"Itkin said I should hold up for a while because he was negotiating with Carmine De Sapio, who was negotiating with Con Ed."

Marcus said that Mr. Itkin asked him to delay the approval for "a few weeks."

At that point in the trial, which came at about 4:40 P.M., Herman Zoloto, a lawyer representing Henry Fried, a contractor, and Mr. Fried's company, S. T. Grand, Inc., shouted:

"You're way ahead of your story, Mr. Marcus!"

Judge Edward Weinfeld broke in and scolded Mr. Zoloto for "a highly improper re-

Continued on Page 41, Column 1

France Will Meet Tariff Deadline; Strikes Dwindling

By HENRY TANNER
Special to The New York Times

PARIS, June 5 — Maurice Couve de Murville told France's partners in the Common Market today that despite the nationwide strike now coming to a close, the Government would honor the July 1 deadline for the abolition of remaining tariffs in the European trade bloc.

Today workers in the nationalized railroad company, the Paris transit system, the post and telegraph offices and other public administrations voted to go back to work. Trains are expected to start running tomorrow on several major national lines and the Paris subways.

By the end of the week, it is expected, the nationwide strike, now in its 18th day, will be all but ended.

Mr. Couve de Murville, who is the new Minister of Economy and Finance, also reassured his countrymen

Continued on Page 15, Column 1

6 IN RACE GUARDED

Secret Service Given Campaign Security Task by President

Text of the Johnson speech is printed on Page 23.

By MAX FRANKEL
Special to The New York Times

WASHINGTON, June 5—For the second time in five years, Lyndon B. Johnson undertook today, amid national shock and outrage, to offer protection, prayer, comfort and assistance to his political rivals in the Kennedy family and then to try to heal the country's political and psychological wounds.

The President's first reaction to the shooting of Senator Robert F. Kennedy this morning was that "there are no words equal to the horror of this tragedy."

But tonight, in an emotional and at times even angry statement on television, he pleaded with all Americans to end the violence in their midst once and for all, to tolerate neither hatred nor the preaching of violence and to resolve to live under the law.

A Guard for Candidates

Mr. Johnson said he was appointing a commission of distinguished citizens to investigate both the circumstances and the causes of physical violence of all kinds in the United States, in the hope that the nation can learn "how we can stop it".

Earlier he had moved swiftly to provide protective Secret Service details to the six announced Presidential candidates of major parties, other than Vice President Humphrey, who already has such protection because of his office.

Meanwhile, in the House of Representatives, a vote of 317 to 60 cleared the way for the House to accept the Senate version of an anticrime bill, including controls over the interstate sale of hand guns. The vote rejected a move to send the legislation to a Senate-House conference.

Members of Commission

To the commission Mr. Johnson named Milton Eisenhower, former president of Johns Hopkins University; Archbishop Terence J. Cooke of New York; Albert Jenner, Chicago lawyer who worked for the commission that investigated the assassination of President Kennedy; former Ambassador Patricia Harris; Eric Hoffer, the longshoreman-turned-philosopher; Senators Philip Hart, Democrat of Michigan, and Roman L. Hruska, Republican of Nebraska; Representative Hale Boggs, Democrat of Louisiana, majority whip in the House; Representative William M. McCulloch, Republican of Ohio, and Federal Judge Leon Higginbotham of Philadelphia.

The President described himself as shocked, dismayed and deeply disturbed, as he knew all Americans were, by the shooting, which he described as the "latest spectacular example" of lawlessness and violence.

"So let us, for God's sake, re-

Continued on Page 23, Column 1

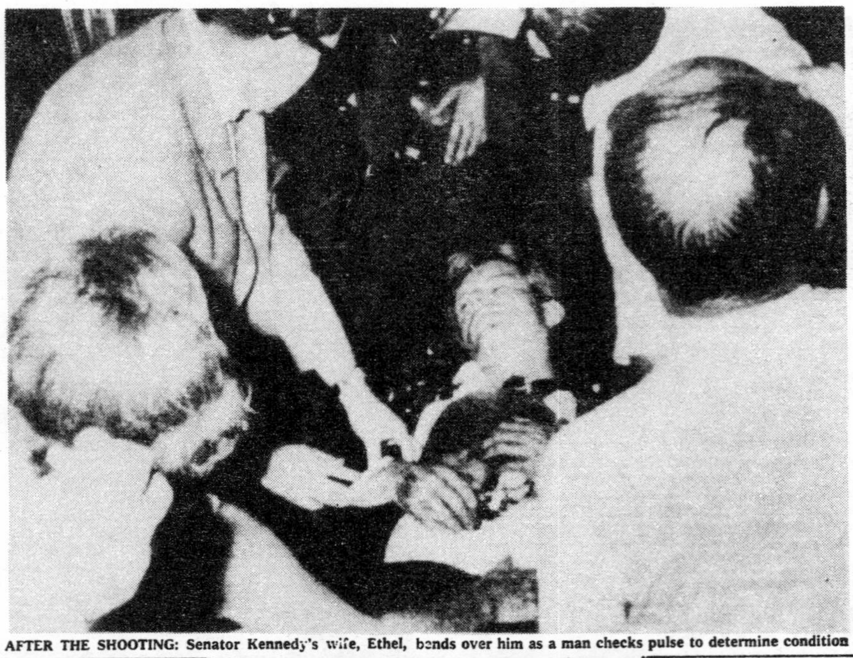

AFTER THE SHOOTING: Senator Kennedy's wife, Ethel, bends over him as a man checks pulse to determine condition

SURGERY IN VAIN

President Calls Death Tragedy, Proclaims a Day of Mourning

Texts of the medical reports appear on Page 22.

By GLADWIN HILL
Special to The New York Times

LOS ANGELES, Thursday, June 6—Senator Robert F. Kennedy, the brother of a murdered President, died at 1:44 A.M. today of an assassin's shots.

The New York Senator was wounded more than 20 hours earlier, moments after he had made his victory statement in the California primary.

At his side when he died today in Good Samaritan Hospital were his wife, Ethel; his sisters, Mrs. Stephen Smith and Mrs. Patricia Lawford; his brother-in-law, Stephen Smith; and his sister-in-law, Mrs. John F. Kennedy, whose husband was assassinated 4½ years ago in Dallas.

In Washington, President Johnson issued a statement calling the death a tragedy. He proclaimed next Sunday a national day of mourning.

The Final Report

Hopes had risen slightly when more than eight hours went by without a new medical bulletin on the stricken Senator, but the grimness of the final announcement was signaled when Frank Mankiewicz, Mr. Kennedy's press secretary, walked slowly down the street in front of the hospital toward the littered gymnasium that served as press headquarters.

Mr. Mankiewicz bit his lip. His shoulders slumped.

He stepped to a lectern in front of a green-tinted chalkboard and bowed his head for a moment while the television lights snapped on.

Then, at one minute before 2 A.M., he told of the death of Mr. Kennedy.

Following is the text of the statement from Mr. Mankiewicz:

"I have a short announcement to read which I will read at this time. Senator Robert Francis Kennedy died at 1:44 A.M. today, June 6, 1968. With

Continued on Page 20, Column 1

JERUSALEM POLICE CLASH WITH ARABS

Israelis Halt Procession on Anniversary of War—U.N. Council Meets on Fighting

Special to The New York Times

JERUSALEM, June 5—A silent Arab procession commemorating the first anniversary of the Arab-Israeli war erupted into a violent clash today when Isareli policemen intercepted the marchers at the edge of the walled Old City of Jerusalem.

The clash was the most violent aspect of a widespread protest in which Arabs shuttered shops and other businesses here and elsewhere on the west bank of the Jordan and in the occupied Gaza Strip. It came after a day-long battle yesterday across the Jordan between the Israelis and Jordanians, in which aircraft and artillery were used.

[The United Nations Security Council met Wednesday at the urgent request of Israel and Jordan to consider recurrent hostilities along their cease-fire line. It postponed debate, probably until Thursday. Page 3.]

In the west-bank towns of Nablus, Jenin and Tulkarm, all centers of Arab nationalism, the general strike was 100 per cent effective. All stores, cafes and offices were closed, public transportation ceased and the streets were virtually devoid of traffic and pedestrians.

Schools throughout the west bank and Gaza Strip had no

Continued on Page 2, Column 4

HANOI INSISTS U.S. HALT ITS BOMBING

Aides Call Talks Response to Johnson—Suspicion Voiced of a Plot Against Kennedy

By HEDRICK SMITH
Special to The New York Times

PARIS, June 5—North Vietnamese negotiators contended today that Hanoi had responded to President Johnson's restriction of American air attacks on the north by entering official talks here. They asserted that the next move, a total halt in bombing, was up to the United States.

The North Vietnamese argument, put forward in the seventh negotiating session between the two sides since May 13, produced one of the sharpest exchanges since the Vietnam talks began here.

The North Vietnamese made no direct comment on the shooting of Senator Robert F. Kennedy, but circles close to the delegation voiced suspicions in private, asking if the attack was not part of a conspiracy by the Johnson Administration. [Page 33.]

Near the end of today's session at the former Majestic Hotel, Hanoi's chief representative, Xuan Thuy, leaned across the negotiating table and asked the American delegates bluntly:

"When will the United States unconditionally cease the bombing and all other acts of war against the Democratic Republic of Vietnam so that other questions can be discussed?"

In response, W. Averell Har-

Continued on Page 8, Column 4

The New York Times (by George Tames)

ROBERT F. KENNEDY

NOTES ON KENNEDY IN SUSPECT'S HOME

Cite 'Necessity' to Murder Senator Before June 5, Anniversary of War

By PETER KIHSS

A notebook found in the Pasadena home of Sirhan Bishara Sirhan had "a direct reference to the necessity to assassinate Senator Kennedy before June 5, 1968," Mayor Samuel W. Yorty of Los Angeles said last night.

The date was the first anniversary of the six-day war, in which Israeli forces smashed those of the United Arab Republic, Syria and Jordan.

Sirhan, a 24-year-old Christian Arab, who has described himself as a Jerusalem-born Jordanian, is being held in the shooting of the New York Senator.

Justice Department records indicated that Sirhan came to the United States with his family in January of 1957 as immigrants, less than three months after the Suez war in 1956. Sirhan was 12 at the time.

The family quickly broke up in discord, the father staying in New York to work as a plumber and then going back to their former Palestine home, the mother taking five children to California, where a sixth child immigrated later.

Sirhan was described yesterday by Police Chief Thomas Reddin of Los Angeles as "very cool, very calm, very stable and quite lucid."

He was quoted as having said,

Continued on Page 21, Column 6

A Pall Over Politics

Murder Raises Grave Questions for Presidency Races Now and in Future

By TOM WICKER
Special to The New York Times

News Analysis

WASHINGTON, Thursday, June 6—The murder of Robert F. Kennedy shattered the 1968 Presidential campaign and lowered a pall of uncertainty over American politics now and in the years to come. For the immediate future, it may well have assured the nominations by the Democrats and Republicans of the present front-running candidates — Vice President Humphrey and Richard Nixon. It raised grave questions, however, about the personal dangers of political campaigning in the United States. It added a tragic new dimension to the near-martyrdom of the Kennedy family, which has now lost two sons to assassins' bullets.

It removed forever one of the most promising young political leaders in recent American history, one with particular appeal for the poor, the downtrodden and the alienated inhabitants of the Negro slums. That appeal had been proved in all of Robert Kennedy's primary victories this year.

These elements of society also revered the Senator's brother, President Kennedy, who was assassinated on Nov. 22, 1963. How they would react to Robert Kennedy's murder—both in the immediate future and for the long political pull—was a crucial question.

The murder added sorrowful emphasis to one of Robert Kennedy's major political themes—the necessity for orderly and just redress of grievances, in place of violent action.

Ultimately, Mr. Kennedy's death—the first assassination of an American Presidential candidate—might lead to changes in campaigning practices, even to the fundamental manner in which the nation chooses its President.

The most immediate effect, however, was that for the third—and most harrowing—time a shock wave of unexpected events had completely altered the shape of the 1968 campaign.

The first came on March 12 when Senator Eugene J. McCarthy of Minnesota won 42 per cent of the Democratic vote in the New Hampshire primary, and Mr. Kennedy immediately thereafter became an active candidate.

The second transformation

Continued on Page 25, Column 6

KUCHEL UNSEATED AS RAFFERTY WINS

Conservative Beats Senator in California's Primary

By LAWRENCE E. DAVIES
Special to The New York Times

LOS ANGELES, June 5—Dr. Max Rafferty, State Superintendent of Public Instruction, defeated Senator Thomas H. Kuchel in the Republican Senatorial primary in California yesterday, cutting short Mr. Kuchel's 15-year career in the Senate.

Returns from 20,714 of 21,301 precincts gave:

Rafferty	1,056,038	50%
Kuchel	985,097	47%

As the vote count continued today, it became apparent that the conservative Republicanism of Southern California had carried Dr. Rafferty to victory over the heretofore unbeatable Republican whip in the Senate.

Mr. Kuchel, an outspoken liberal-moderate who had made political extremists such as John Birch Society members his targets in recent years, was beaten by the voters in Los Angeles, San Diego and Orange Counties, after having led Dr. Rafferty last night and early today.

Dr. Rafferty, who has become

Continued on Page 23, Column 3

TRANSIT PACKAGE SUBMITTED TO CITY

M.T.A. Seeks Approval of 8 New Subway Routes

By EMANUEL PERLMUTTER

A $1.27-billion package of subway and commuter railroad additions and improvements was submitted to the Board of Estimate and Mayor Lindsay yesterday.

The program was presented by the Metropolitan Transportation Authority and the New York City Transit Authority with a request for speedy city agreement on the new routes and engineering designs.

The over-all plan, which would take 10 years to complete, consists of eight new subway routes, including a Second Avenue subway, and Long Island Rail Road connections to the East Side of Manhattan and to Kennedy International Airport.

City approval of the routes and designs is a first step before application can be made for $60-million set aside by the Legislature for the engineering design of the mass transportation program presented by the Metropolitan Transportation

Continued on Page 55, Column 1

Italy's Cabinet Quits As Parliament Opens

By ROBERT C. DOTY
Special to The New York Times

ROME, June 5—Premier Aldo Moro and his center-left coalition Government, which has ruled Italy for four and a half years, resigned tonight with the convening of the new parliament, the fifth since World War II.

President Giuseppe Saragat asked Mr. Moro and his ministers to remain in office as a caretaker government while the search for a new government, which may be arduous, goes on.

Resignation of the government with the convening of a new parliament is automatic. But any hope that the Moro

Continued on Page 14, Column 3

Big Board Weighs 4 Special Closings

By VARTANIG G. VARTAN

A securities industry panel recommended yesterday that the New York Stock Exchange, the American Stock Exchange and the over-the-counter market close down for four days over the next month to cope with the deluge of paperwork in brokerage offices.

The panel proposed closing the securities markets for three Wednesdays—June 12, 19 and 26—as well as Friday, July 5.

The board of governors of the New York Stock Exchange will meet this afternoon to consider the proposal. Wall Street sources said that in view of the critical situation the governors are expected to accept the pro-

Continued on Page 73, Column 1

Father of Suspect 'Sickened' by News

By TERENCE SMITH
Special to The New York Times

ET TAIYIBA, Israeli-Occupied Jordan, Thursday, June 6—Bishara Sirhan's hands trembled as he talked about his son Sirhan Bishara Sirhan, the accused assailant of Senator Robert F. Kennedy.

Mr. Sirhan dwelled on the tragedy of the shooting. He became angry as he talked, and finally said: "This news made me sick when I heard it. If my son has done this dirty thing, then let them hang him."

Mr. Sirhan's memories of his five sons are those of 10 years ago, when he last saw them and their mother. After years of fierce family quarrels, Bishara

Continued on Page 21, Column 4

NEWS INDEX

"All the News That's Fit to Print"

The New York Times

LATE CITY EDITION

Weather: Sunny, warm today; fair, seasonable tonight and tomorrow. Temp. range: today 89-73; Tuesday 91-72. Temp.-Hum. Index yesterday 81. Complete U.S. report on Page 90.

VOL. CXVII..No. 40,387

NEW YORK, WEDNESDAY, AUGUST 21, 1968 — 10 CENTS

CZECHOSLOVAKIA INVADED BY RUSSIANS AND FOUR OTHER WARSAW PACT FORCES; THEY OPEN FIRE ON CROWDS IN PRAGUE

13 INDICTED HERE IN RIGGING OF BIDS ON UTILITY WORK

Contracts Worth 49-Million Involved—14 Construction Companies Also Named

By MARTIN TOLCHIN

Fourteen major construction companies, 12 top corporate executives and one employe were indicted here yesterday on charges of rigging bids on utilities contracts totaling $49.8-million.

The defendants were accused of deciding among themselves who would be low bidder in the contracts with Consolidated Edison, the Brooklyn Union Gas Company, and the Empire City Subway Company—the latter a subsidiary of the New York Telephone Company.

The indictments charge that the defendants then accommodated the selected low bidder by submitting higher bids.

The companies included such important contractors as Lipsett, Inc., a leading demolition company that razed Pennsylvania Station, the Savoy Plaza Hotel and the Third Avenue El; the Slattery Contracting Company, which held the general contract for excavating the site of United Nations Headquarters and built subway spurs and the Lincoln Center reflecting pool, and the Thomas Crimmins Contracting Company, which did the excavation for numerous skyscrapers.

1959 Activities Covered

The companies received contracts to dig trenches for electrical conduits and gas mains and for paving work. The contracts totaled $49,788,165.

The four indictments, with a total of 28 counts, were an outgrowth of the investigation of James L. Marcus, former City Water Commissioner, who pleaded guilty in Federal court to receiving a $40,000 kickback on a city reservoir cleaning contract.

"Our interest in Marcus and [Herbert] Itkin led us to the inquiry that led to these indictments," Frank S. Hogan, New York County District Attorney, said.

He noted that the indictments alleged activities that began in 1959, "before the community at large was aware of Marcus and Itkin," and

Continued on Page 35, Column 3

OUTLOOK GUARDED FOR EISENHOWER

His Condition Still Critical Despite 'Favorable Trend'

By FELIX BELAIR Jr.
Special to The New York Times

WASHINGTON, Aug. 20 — Former President Dwight D. Eisenhower clung resolutely to life today, but with a fragile grip that his doctors acknowledged could loosen at any time.

The condition of the 77-year-old General of the Army still was listed as "critical" and the outlook for his survival as "guarded." His doctors have used this term to mean uncertain or unpredictable.

A bulletin issued at Walter Reed Army Medical Center about 11 A.M. mentioned the development of a "favorable trend" in the pattern of abnormal heart rhythm.

The episodes of rapid irregularity in the heartbeat persisted, the doctors reported, but they were isolated and did not involve the sustained fibrillating, or fluttering, reported prior to last night.

At the time of the morning

Continued on Page 13, Column 1

Democrats Debate Position on the War in Vietnam

The New York Times

Secretary of State Rusk defended the Administration's policies at the hearing.

Associated Press

Senator George S. McGovern of South Dakota was critical of the Administration.

The New York Times (by George Tames)

Kenneth P. O'Donnell, left, who was an aide to President Kennedy, talks with Senator J. W. Fulbright, standing right, at the platform hearing. The Senator spoke against the war.

NIXON INCREASES GALLUP POLL LEAD

Tops Humphrey, 45% to 29, and Maintains His Margin Over McCarthy, 42 to 37

Special to The New York Times

PRINCETON, N. J., Aug. 20—Richard M. Nixon stretched a slim mid-July edge over Vice President Humphrey to a 45-to-29 per cent lead in voter preference immediately following the Republican National Convention, according to the latest Gallup Poll.

Against Senator Eugene J. McCarthy—Mr. Humphrey's chief rival for the Democratic Presidential nomination—Mr. Nixon held a 42-to-37 per cent lead, almost the same margin he had in the previous test in mid-July.

Mr. Nixon's improved advantage over the Vice President was caused more by Mr. Humphrey's losses than by gains by Mr. Nixon. The Republican nominee was 5 percentage points higher than the preconvention survey, while Mr. Humphrey was 9 points lower.

Support for the independent candidacy of George A. Wallace of Alabama held up. He polled 18 per cent in the Nixon-Humphrey-Wallace test and 16 per cent in the Nixon-McCarthy-Wallace postconvention survey.

In interviewing between Aug. 8 and 11, the following question was asked of a representative sample of 1,526 adults in over 320 localities:

"Suppose the Presidential election were being held today. If Hubert Humphrey were the Democratic candidate, running against Richard Nixon, the Republican candidate, and George Wallace of Alabama were the candidate of a third party, which would you like to see

Continued on Page 34, Column 2

Guard Is Called Up To Protect Chicago During Convention

By DONALD JANSON
Special to The New York Times

CHICAGO, Aug. 20—Gov. Samuel H. Shapiro called up the National Guard today to keep order in the city during the Democratic National Convention.

At the request of Mayor Richard J. Daley, the Governor ordered 5,649 Illinois National Guardsmen to round-the-clock duty in Chicago beginning Friday to head off threats of "tumult, riot or mob disorder."

Meanwhile, an Army spokesman in Washington confirmed in a telephone interview that about 6,000 regular Army troops received rigorous riot-control training at Fort Hood, Tex., last week as a precautionary measure.

That exercise, he said, was called Operation Jackson Park, after the park in Chicago

Continued on Page 32, Column 2

Democrats to Seat Mississippi Rebels

By MAX FRANKEL
Special to The New York Times

CHICAGO, Aug. 20—Mississippi's regular delegation to the Democratic National Convention was barred from its seats tonight by an overwhelming vote of the Credentials Committee on the ground that it had failed to meet national standards to assure the full participation of Negroes in the political process.

A biracial delegation including many members who have fought many years for this moment will be seated in place of the regulars.

At the same time, the Credentials Committee rejected by various votes the delegate

Continued on Page 32, Column 6

KENNEDY BACKERS OFFER WAR PLANK

But McCarthy Group Balks at Compromise—Rusk Is for General Statement

Text of plank and excerpts from statement, Page 33.

By JOHN W. FINNEY
Special to The New York Times

WASHINGTON, Aug. 20—Supporters of the late Senator Robert F. Kennedy circulated in the Democratic platform committee today a compromise dovish plan on Vietnam calling for a halt in the bombing of North Vietnam, a cease-fire and negotiations between the Saigon Government and the National Liberation Front, the political arm of the Vietcong.

In the bitter fight developing within the platform committee, the proposed plank is designed to provide a common front for supporters of Senator Eugene J. McCarthy, Senator George S. McGovern and Senator Kennedy.

For the moment, however, some difficulty was being encountered in winning the approval of some McCarthy partisans, who were holding out for a plank that would be more critical of the Administration.

As the doves began to mount a concerted attack on the Administration's Vietnam policy, Secretary of State Dean Rusk was called in to defend the Administration position. Mr. Rusk,

Continued on Page 33, Column 2

NEWS INDEX

SOVIET EXPLAINS

Says Its Troops Moved at the Request of Czechoslovaks

By RAYMOND H. ANDERSON
Special to The New York Times

MOSCOW, Wednesday, Aug. 21 — Moscow announced this morning that troops from the Soviet Union and four other Communist countries had invaded Czechoslovakia at the request of the "party and Government leaders of the Czechoslovak Socialist Republic."

The announcement followed unofficial information here that Alexander Dubcek, the reform leader of the Czechoslovak party Presidium, had been overthrown.

In a statement authorized by the Soviet Government, the official press agency, Tass, declared at 7:30 A.M. Moscow time (12:30 A.M., New York time) that Czechoslovakia had come under a threat from "counterrevolutionary forces" involved in a collusion with foreign forces hostile to socialism.

Friendship Stressed

Tass said that troops from Bulgaria, East Germany, Hungary, Poland and the Soviet Union, acting from motivations of "inseverable friendship and cooperation," entered Czechoslovakia early this morning.

The troops will be withdrawn as soon as the threat to Czechoslovakia and neighboring Communist countries has been eliminated, according to Tass.

"The actions that are being taken are not directed against any state and in no measure infringe state interests of anybody," the statement said. "They serve the purpose of peace and have been prompted by concern for its consolidation."

"The fraternal countries firmly and resolutely counterpose their unbreakable solidarity to any threat from outside," the Soviet explanation continued. "Nobody will ever be allowed to wrest a single link from the community of Socialist states."

Polemics Resumed

The handwriting was on the wall for the Czechoslovak reform regime last Friday when the Soviet press abruptly resumed its bitter polemics against the country.

Czechoslovakia's seven-month-old experiment with democracy under Communist rule was explicitly doomed yesterday when the Soviet Communist party warned in an editorial that imperial intrigues must be "nipped in the bud."

Rumors swept Moscow yesterday that the Soviet party's Central Committee had met in secret session, presumably to endorse intervention. Official sources insisted, however, that

Continued on Page 14, Column 6

13 Points in Delta Are Shelled by Foe

By JOSEPH B. TREASTER
Special to The New York Times

SAIGON, South Vietnam, Wednesday, Aug. 21 — The Vietcong shelled 13 cities and military installations in the Mekong Delta this morning, extending their latest wave of attacks into South Vietnam's southern-most region.

Seven of the shellings were followed by ground attacks.

Initial reports were sketchy, but a United States military spokesman said that allied casualties and damage in all of the attacks appeared to be light.

To the north, allied troops are making an increasing number of forays into the southern

Continued on Page 4, Column 3

The New York Times — Aug. 21, 1968

FIVE-POWER INVASION: Soviet planes carried troops into Prague (cross). Ground forces of bloc crossed Czechoslovak borders that are indicated by heavy line.

Versions of the Two Sides

Following are the texts of the Prague radio announcement of the Soviet-bloc invasion of Czechoslovakia, as monitored in Washington, and of a Soviet statement distributed in New York by Tass, the Soviet press agency.

Czechoslovak Radio Broadcast

To the entire people of the Czechoslovak Socialist Republic:

Yesterday, on 20 August, around 2300 [11 P.M.], troops of the Soviet Union, Polish People's Republic, the G.D.R. [East Germany], the Hungarian People's Republic and the Bulgarian People's Republic crossed the frontiers of the Czechoslovak Socialist Republic.

This happened without the knowledge of the President of the Republic, the Chairman of the National Assembly, the Premier, or the First Secretary of the Czechoslovak Communist party Central Committee.

In the evening hours the Presidium of the Czechoslovak Communist party Central Committee [had] held a session and discussed preparations for the 14th Czechoslovak Communist party congress.

The Czechoslovak Communist party Central Committee Presidium appeals to all citizens of our republic to maintain calm and not to offer resistance to the troops on the march. Our army, security corps and people's militia have not received the command to defend the country.

The Czechoslovak Communist party Central Committee Presidium regard this act as contrary not only to the fundamental principles of relations between Socialist states but also as contrary to the principles of international law.

All leading functionaries of the state, the Communist party and the National Front: Remain in your functions as representatives of the state, elected to the laws of the Czechoslovak Socialist Republic.

Constitutional functionaries are immediately convening a session of the National Assembly of our republic, and the Presidium is at the same time convening a plenum of the Central Committee to discuss the situation that has arisen.

PRESIDIUM OF THE CZECHOSLOVAK COMMUNIST PARTY CENTRAL COMMITTEE.

Announcement by Moscow

Tass is authorized to state that party and Government leaders of the Czechoslovak Socialist Republic have asked the Soviet Union and other allied states to render the fraternal Czechoslovak people urgent assistance, including assistance with armed forces. This request was brought about by the threat which has arisen to the Socialist system existing in Czechoslovakia and to the statehood established by the Con-

Continued on Page 14, Column 2

Soviet Turns Back Clock

By JAMES RESTON

News Analysis

The Soviet invasion of Czechoslovakia has transformed world and American politics.

It occurred in the middle of the American Presidential election of 1968, as the Soviet invasion of Hungary took place during the Eisenhower-Stevenson Presidential election of 1956. The Soviet Union moved on Prague while the United States was preoccupied in Vietnam, as they moved on Budapest in 1956 while the British and French were preoccupied with the invasion of Suez. The latest move by Moscow startled Washington just as officials there were convening on new moves to reach an understanding with the Soviet Union on Vietnam.

Washington was prepared for a dramatic move by the Soviet Union against the new liberal regime in Prague, but not for anything quite so bold as an invasion by the Red Army.

It had been observing closely the increasingly violent attacks on the Czechoslovak Government in the Soviet press, and Under Secretary of State Charles E. Bohlen, former United States Ambassador to the Soviet Union and France, had warned of the possibility of a coup d'état, followed by Soviet military intervention in Czechoslovakia. But a direct invasion at this time was discounted.

In fact, the Johnson Administration, under attack on its Vietnam policy just before the Democratic Presidential nominating convention next week in Chicago, was discussing new moves to enlist the help of the Soviet Union for a compromise in Vietnam when the Red Army moved.

The first impression of the crisis was that this Soviet intervention in Czechoslovakia, like the first one at the end of World War II, would increase

Continued on Page 15, Column 1

TANKS ENTER CITY

Deaths Are Reported—Troops Surround Offices of Party

By TAD SZULC
Special to The New York Times

PRAGUE, Wednesday, Aug. 21—Czechoslovakia was occupied early today by troops of the Soviet Union and four of its Warsaw Pact allies in a series of swift land and air movements.

Airborne Soviet troops and paratroopers surrounded the building of the Communist party Central Committee, along with five tanks. At least 25 tanks were seen in the city.

Several persons were reported killed early this morning. Unconfirmed reports said that two Czechoslovak soldiers and a woman were killed by Bulgarian tank fire in front of the Prague radio building shortly before the station was captured and went off the air.

[Soviet troops began shooting at Czechoslovak demonstrators outside the Prague radio building at 7:25 A.M., Reuters reported. C.T.K., the Czechoslovak press agency, was quoted by United Press International as having said that citizens were throwing themselves in front of the tanks in an attempt to block the seizure of the city.]

Move a Surprise

The Soviet move caught Czechoslovaks by surprise, although all day yesterday there were indications of new tensions.

Confusion was caused in the capital by leaflets dropped from unidentified aircraft asserting that Antonin Novotny, the President of Czechoslovakia who was deposed in March by the Communist liberals, had been pushed out by a "clique." The leaflets said that Mr. Novotny remained the country's legal President.

At 5 A.M. the Prague radio, still in the hands of adherents of the Communist liberals, broadcast a dramatic appeal to the population in the name of Alexander Dubcek, the party

Continued on Page 14, Column 1

JOHNSON SUMMONS SECURITY COUNCIL

Calls Emergency Session After Seeing Soviet Envoy

By B. DRUMMOND AYRES Jr.
Special to The New York Times

WASHINGTON, Aug. 20—President Johnson met with the National Security Council in an emergency session tonight to discuss developments in Czechoslovakia after he received a visit from the Soviet Ambassador.

The Council meeting, which was held in the Cabinet Room in the West Wing of the White House, began at 10:15 P.M. and lasted for 55 minutes.

It was followed by a 15-minute meeting at the State Department between the Soviet Ambassador, Anatoly F. Dobrynin, and Secretary of State Dean Rusk.

There was no indication after either of the meetings of what course the United States would take in the crisis, which clearly came as a stunning surprise here.

During the recent weeks of tension around Czechoslovakia, the Administration has insistently maintained a hands-off attitude, arguing that any gestures of support from Washington would only complicate the Prague regime's status in the Communist camp. Any move to exploit the Soviet di-

Continued on Page 15, Column 1

"All the News That's Fit to Print"

The New York Times

LATE CITY EDITION

Weather: Rain today and tonight. Cloudy, showers likely tomorrow. Temp. range: today 52-48; Wed. 54-45. Full U.S. report on Page 93.

VOL. CXVIII . . No. 40,465

NEW YORK, THURSDAY, NOVEMBER 7, 1968

10 CENTS

NIXON WINS BY A THIN MARGIN, PLEADS FOR REUNITED NATION

The New York Times (by Neal Boenzi)

SHE KNEW IT ALL ALONG: President-elect Richard M. Nixon holding crewelwork, a facsimile of Presidential seal embroidered by his daughter Julie, who stands beside her fiancé, David Eisenhower. Mrs. Nixon and daughter Patricia completed the family group at the Waldorf-Astoria yesterday.

NIXON'S ELECTION EXPECTED TO SLOW PARIS NEGOTIATION

Allied Diplomats Suggest All Sides May Adopt a Wait-and-See Stance

By HEDRICK SMITH

Special to The New York Times

PARIS, Nov. 6 — Allied diplomats suggested tonight that Richard M. Nixon's election victory would add, at least temporarily, to the delays and complications of getting meaningful Vietnam peace negotiations under way.

The American, the North Vietnamese and the National Liberation Front delegations here had no comment on the election results.

But allied diplomats close to the talks suggested that the Republican victory would probably bring eventual changes in the American negotiating team, encourage delays by the South Vietnamese Government, and induce a wait-and-see attitude by all sides until Mr. Nixon's own approach to the talks became clearer.

The uncertainty about the future relationship between the outgoing Johnson Administration and Mr. Nixon is considered the primary complicating factor.

Eyes on Saigon

"Everybody has to see how Nixon and Johnson are going to handle this period," said one Western diplomat.

The Saigon Government is reported to feel that the Johnson Administration pressed it too rapidly toward expanded talks embracing the Vietcong. It now is expected to use the change-over period in the United States to play for time.

South Vietnamese officials here made no secret that they consider Mr. Nixon more sympathetic than Mr. Johnson to their position.

They have recently dropped hints that they expect no active negotiating on issues of substance until early next year.

Western diplomats now speculate that President Nguyen Van Thieu may delay sending a delegation to the talks here until he has learned Mr. Nixon's views.

But a more common opinion is that Saigon will send a delegation soon and then try to stall until the Republicans take office in January.

The Republican victory,

Continued on Page 13, Column 1

POLICE SEIZE 125 ON C.C.N.Y. CAMPUS

AWOL Soldier Taken From Student Center 'Sanctuary'

About 250 members of the Tactical Patrol Force moved onto the City College campus early today at the request of the administration and arrested more than 100 students and the AWOL soldier they had been guarding in a student center.

Under the direction of Police Commissioner Howard R. Leary, Chief Inspector Sanford Garelik and a number of other high police officials, the arrests were carried out without violence following a warning from the administration to vacate the building.

In all, about 125 persons were arrested, including supporters of the peace movement and Pvt. William Brakefield, who had been in the Finley Student Center, at 133d Street and Convent Avenue, since last

Continued on Page 4, Column 4

Soviet Bids U.S. Confer; Calls for 'Normalization'

By HENRY KAMM

Special to The New York Times

MOSCOW, Nov. 6—The Soviet Union greeted the election of a new President of the United States today with a call for the "normalization" of relations between Moscow and Washington for the sake of world peace.

The demand was put forward in a speech on behalf of the ruling Politburo of the Communist party by First Deputy Premier Kirill T. Mazurov as election returns in the United States showed that Richard M. Nixon had won the Presidency. The occasion was the traditional speech in the Kremlin on the eve of the anniversary of the Bolshevik Revolution.

To underline the importance Moscow attaches to relations with the United States, Mr. Mazurov raised the issue twice. Noting Soviet proposals for mutual limitations on nuclear weapons and delivery systems, the official said:

"It is relevant to recall in this connection that we have expressed readiness to conduct negotiations with the United States on the entire range of these problems. But their positive solution does not depend on the Soviet Union alone."

Review of Soviet Actions

After a review of Soviet actions on the international scene, Mr. Mazurov returned to Soviet-American relations. He said:

"We have always attached great importance to the normalization of relations between the Soviet Union and the United States, which would be important not only to both of our countries but also to world peace."

A public offer to enter into negotiations with the United States for an accommodation on vital issues was regarded as a Soviet reaction to the

Continued on Page 14, Column 1

POSITION ON SINAI DEFINED BY ISRAEL

Note to Jarring Links Issue of Boundaries to Security Needs and Tiran Rights

By DREW MIDDLETON

Special to The New York Times

UNITED NATIONS, N. Y., Nov. 6—Israel has told the United Arab Republic that her attitude toward the boundary problem will be governed by her security needs and the maintenance of full protection of Israeli navigation in the Strait of Tiran.

This is the first time that Israel has defined with any precision her interest in the Sinai Peninsula.

Western diplomats inferred that if Israel's security requirements were fulfilled, including protection of shipping in the Strait of Tiran, the Government would not reject an arrangement that returned a demilitarized Sinai to Egypt. The peninsula has been occupied by Israel since the Israeli-Arab war of June, 1967.

This information was in a memorandum that Foreign Minister Abba Eban gave yesterday to Dr. Gunnar V. Jarring, the United Nations intermediary. Mr. Eban went over the text of the memorandum with Dr. Jarring at meetings yesterday afternoon and last night.

Ambassador Jarring was asked to transmit the memorandum to Mahmoud Riad, the Egyptian Foreign Minister. The clarification of Israel's approach to the boundary problem apparently was intended to rebut Mr.

Continued on Page 2, Column 3

NEWS INDEX

REPUBLICANS GAIN SAFE ALBANY EDGE

Lead in Assembly Put at 77-73 and in Senate at 33-24 Unofficially

By JAMES F. CLARITY

Republican officials said yesterday that they expected to have clear majorities in both houses of the 1969 Legislature.

The Republicans, on the basis of unofficial but reliable vote-counts in the elections for the 150 Assembly and 57 Senate seats, will probably control the Assembly by 77 to 73, and the Senate by 33 to 24.

The official counts of several close Assembly races were not expected to affect lower house control, which the Republicans appeared almost certain to have wrested from the Democrats in Tuesday's election.

Official Count Delayed

The official count of the close races was expected to be completed early next week. The G.O.P. Senate majority was assured, regardless of the final count in a few close races.

But the Republicans' control of the Assembly, which they had lost in 1964, did not appear to give G.O.P. leaders assurance that their programs and legislation or those proposed by Governor Rockefeller would necessarily sail through the Legislature because of the majorities in both houses.

Among the Republicans who captured Democratic seats in the Assembly were several conservatives who, by combining with conservative Democrats, could obstruct, if not defeat, legislation they considered liberally oriented, or objectionable for other reasons.

Three of the newly elected Republican Assembly members

Continued on Page 40, Column 5

The Election at a Glance

President

Needed for Election—270 Electoral Votes

	Number of States*	Electoral Votes
Humphrey	14	191
Nixon	30	287
Wallace	5	45
In Doubt: Alaska, Missouri.	2	15

*Includes District of Columbia.

The Senate

Newly Elected Senators		Make-up of New Senate	
Democrats	18	Democrats	58
Republicans	15	Republicans	41
In Doubt	1	In Doubt	1

The House

Democrats Elected	243
Republicans Elected	192

Senate's Liberal Coalition Survives Gains by G.O.P.

By DAVID E. ROSENBAUM

Republicans made a net gain of at least four Senate seats in Tuesday's election, but the balance between liberals and conservatives did not appear to have changed substantially from the present Senate.

One Senate race remained in doubt last night. In Oregon, Wayne Morse, a Democrat, who served four terms, was running a close race with State Representative Robert W. Packwood, a Republican. Observers said it might be days before the outcome was certain.

Depending on the Oregon race, the Democrats will hold 58 or 59 seats in the new Senate to 41 or 42 for the Republicans. In the present Senate there are 63 Democrats and 37 Republicans.

Four conservative Republicans and one conservative Democrat were elected to seats that had been held by liberals or moderates. On the other hand, there was a shift in favor of liberals in at least two states.

Thus it appeared that a majority could still be formed from liberal Northern Democrats and moderate Republicans to pass legislation on such issues as civil rights and aid to education.

The Republicans' net gain of only four seats in the House of Representatives dashed the party's hopes of capturing control of that body.

In the Senate the Republicans picked up seats that had been held by Democrats in Arizona, Florida, Maryland, Ohio, Oklahoma and Pennsylvania. Democrats took Republican-held seats in California and Iowa.

Among the new conservatives was Barry Goldwater, the Republican Presidential nominee in 1964. He defeated Roy L. Elson for the Arizona

Continued on Page 29, Column 2

Election Tables

Tables reporting the vote in national, state and local contests in Tuesday's election are now scheduled for publication in The New York Times tomorrow.

The Times had expected to print them today, but breakdowns in the News Election Service's national and regional computers made a total recheck of the election results necessary. This recheck is expected to be concluded today.

A Loser Concedes and Tries to Smile

By R. W. APPLE Jr.

Special to The New York Times

MINNEAPOLIS, Nov. 6—It was probably Hubert Horatio Humphrey's last hurrah in Presidential politics.

He had tried once before, in 1960, and had been crushed by the superb organization of John F. Kennedy in the West Virginia primary. Now he had lost again, this time to the man whom John Kennedy had defeated, in an agonizingly close finish.

Transcript of the Humphrey statement is on Page 22.

The Vice President—a hearty, sentimental man, given to laughter and to tears—tried to smile as he stood on the stage in the Leamington Hotel's ballroom this morning and listened to his faithful followers shout, "We Want Humphrey!" But what he brought forth was more a grimace than a grin. "Thank you very much," he said in a quavering voice. "It's nice to know."

Mr. Humphrey went through

Continued on Page 22, Column 1

Associated Press

Vice President Humphrey with his wife after conceding

GOAL IS HARMONY

President-Elect Vows His Administration Will Be 'Open'

By ROBERT B. SEMPLE Jr.

President-elect Richard M. Nixon turned yesterday from the business of winning elections to the business of assembling an Administration.

Weary but thankful, he appeared before an elated band of supporters gathered in the ballroom of the Waldorf-Astoria at 11:35 A.M. He expressed his gratitude for their efforts and his admiration for the "gallant and courageous fight" of his opponent.

Transcript of Nixon's remarks will be found on Page 21.

He also extended the hand of friendship to the disappointed partisans of Mr. Humphrey's cause—particularly the young.

Near the end of his eight-minute talk, Mr. Nixon took note of the division in the nation and pledged, in these words, to bend every effort to restore racial peace and social harmony:

"I saw many signs in this campaign. Some of them were not friendly and some were very friendly. But the one that touched me the most was one that I saw in Deshler, Ohio, at the end of a long day of whistle-stopping, a little town, I suppose five times the population was there in the dusk, almost impossible to see — but a teen-ager held up a sign, 'Bring Us Together.'

"And that will be the great objective of this Administration at the outset, to bring the American people together. This will be an open Administration, open to new ideas, open to men and women of both parties, open to the critics as well as those who support us.

"We want to bridge the generation gap. We want to bridge the gap between the races. We want to bring America together. And I am confident that this task is one that we can undertake and one in which we will be successful."

Several hours later the campaign entourage began to disassemble, its members heading home for a brief but long-overdue rest. The candidate himself flew southward for a three-day vacation in Key Biscayne, a peninsula just south of Miami where he rested occasionally during the campaign.

Although he has been urged

Continued on Page 21, Column 1

ELECTOR VOTE 287

Lead in Popular Tally May Be Smaller Than Kennedy's in '60

By MAX FRANKEL

Richard Milhous Nixon emerged the victor yesterday in one of the closest and most tumultuous Presidential campaigns in history and set himself the task of reuniting the nation.

Elected over Hubert H. Humphrey by the barest of margins —only four one-hundredths of a percentage point in the popular vote—and confronted by a Congress in control of the Democrats, the President-elect said it "will be the great objective of this Administration at the outset to bring the American people together."

He pledged, as the 37th President, to form "an open Administration, open to new ideas, open to men and women of both parties, open to critics as well as those who support us" so as to bridge the gap between the generations and the races.

Details Left for Later

But after an exhausting and tense night of awaiting the verdict at the Waldorf-Astoria Hotel here, Mr. Nixon and his closest aides were not yet prepared to suggest how they intended to organize themselves and to approach these objectives. The Republican victor expressed admiration for his opponent's challenge and reiterated his desire to help President Johnson achieve peace in Vietnam between now and Inauguration Day on Jan. 20.

The verdict of an electorate that appeared to number 73 million could not be discerned until mid-morning because Mr. Nixon and Mr. Humphrey finished in a virtual tie in the popular vote, just as Mr. Nixon and John F. Kennedy did in 1960.

With 94 per cent of the nation's election precincts reporting, Mr. Nixon's total stood last evening at 29,726,409 votes to Mr. Humphrey's 29,677,152. The margin of 49,257 was even smaller than Mr. Kennedy's margin of 112,803.

Meaning Hard to Find

When translated into the determining electoral votes of the states, these returns proved even more difficult to read, and the result in two states—Alaska and Missouri—was still not final last night. But the unofficial returns from elsewhere gave Mr. Nixon a minimum of 287 electoral votes, 17 more than the 270 required for election. Mr. Humphrey won 191.

Because of the tightness of the race, the third-party challenger, George C. Wallace, came close to realizing his minimum objective of denying victory to the major-party candidates and then somehow forcing a bargain for his sup-

Continued on Page 20, Column 1

Johnson Vows Aid In Power Transfer

By NEIL SHEEHAN

Special to The New York Times

SAN ANTONIO, Tex., Nov. 6—In a telegram of congratulations this morning, President Johnson informed President-elect Richard M. Nixon that he would do "everything in my power to make your burdens lighter on that day when you assume the responsibilities of the President."

Even as Mr. Johnson's telegram was being transmitted to Mr. Nixon from the President's ranch 65 miles north of here, the machinery had been set in motion for an orderly transition from the old Administration to the new.

Lawson Knott, the administrator of the General Services

Continued on Page 20, Column 3

"All the News That's Fit to Print"

The New York Times

LATE CITY EDITION

Weather: Mostly sunny, cold today; fair, warmer tonight and tomorrow. Temp. range: today 30-20; Tuesday 34-24. Full U.S. report on Page 62.

VOL. CXVIII—No. 40,513 | NEW YORK, WEDNESDAY, DECEMBER 25, 1968 | 10 CENTS

3 MEN FLY AROUND THE MOON ONLY 70 MILES FROM SURFACE; FIRE ROCKET, HEAD FOR EARTH

PUEBLO CREWMEN GREETED ON COAST; CAPTORS ASSAILED

Relatives Weep and Scream —Captain Asserts North Koreans Are Inhuman

By BERNARD GWERTZMAN
Special to The New York Times

SAN DIEGO, Dec. 24 — The crew of the intelligence ship Pueblo returned to the United States today in time for Christmas with many of their families.

Led by Comdr. Lloyd M. Bucher, the 82 survivors arrived at the Miramar Naval Air Station outside this city and were met immediately by emotional, sometimes hysterical, greetings and embraces of wives, mothers, fathers and children.

The one man who did not return alive, Duane D. Hodges, was carried from one of the C-141 transports in a flag-draped coffin while the air station band played the Navy hymn.

Commander Bucher, apparently overwrought with emotion, spoke in a low voice as he told the more than 250 relatives, the 300 newsmen and the national television audience about the 11 months his crew spent in North Korean captivity.

Calls Captors Inhuman

He described North Korea as a land "completely devoid of humanity, completely devoted to enslavement of men's minds."

[In Washington, the Navy named Vice Adm. Harold S. Bowen to head a court of inquiry into the Pueblo incident.]

Commander Bucher said that, during the months in North Korea, "the thought that preyed on my mind was the embarrassment to my country because of the loss of one of its fine ships."

At a news conference held in the base theater at Navy Hospital here, Rear Adm. Edwin Rosenberg, the representative of the Commander in Chief, Pacific Fleet, in charge of the Pueblo's repatriation, repeated his past praise

Continued on Page 2, Column 1

Pope Paul Says Mass In a Huge Steel Mill

By ROBERT C. DOTY
Special to The New York Times

TARANTO, Italy, Wednesday, Dec. 25—Pope Paul VI celebrated Christmas midnight mass here for 15,000 workers and members of their families in a huge, echoing rolling mill.

The Pontiff chose the vast Italsider steel plant at this developing industrial center in the heel of the Italian boot as the place to express "the fraternal and radiant presence of Christ among workers throughout the world."

Even while the Pope said mass at an altar consisting of a four-ton slab of steel supported on two broad sections of steel pipe, work continued elsewhere throughout the 2,000-acre plant, the largest in Europe.

Blast furnaces poured plumes of flame into a rainy

Continued on Page 34, Column 1

VIOLATIONS MAR TRUCE IN VIETNAM

80 Incidents Are Reported —22 Enemy Soldiers and an American Killed

By B. DRUMMOND AYRES Jr.
Special to The New York Times

SAIGON, South Vietnam, Wednesday, Dec. 25—The allies and the Vietcong put separate cease-fires into effect yesterday to mark Christmas, but not all the guns fell silent.

At 9 o'clock this morning, the American military command said there had been at least 80 'incidents' involving military contact since the allied cease-fire, scheduled to run 24 hours, went into effect at 6 P.M. yesterday.

The enemy cease-fire began at 1 A.M. yesterday and was scheduled to run for 72 hours. Allied military spokesmen said there were at least eight incidents involving military contact during the first hours of that stand-down.

In about 30 of the incidents, casualties were suffered by one or both sides. The allied spokesmen said that over-all South Vietnamese losses had been light. United States losses were broken down as one soldier killed and 38 wounded.

At least 22 enemy soldiers died.

It was not known whether North Vietnamese troops in South Vietnam were complying with the Vietcong cease-fire order. During previous holiday

Continued on Page 5, Column 3

Col. Frank Borman

Maj. William A. Anders

Capt. James A. Lovell Jr.

Associated Press

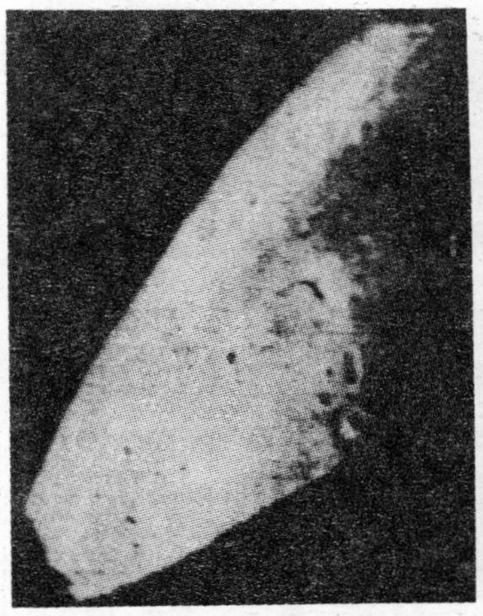

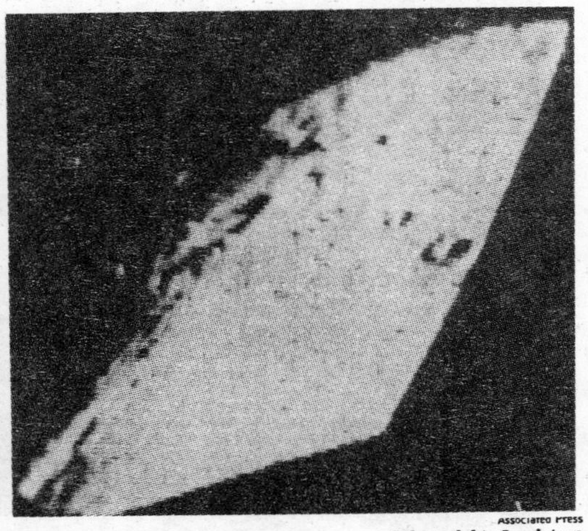

Associated Press

Moon pictures taken through the window of the Apollo 8 spacecraft that were telecast to earth last night. In picture at left of Sea of Crises area, the larger crater is 30 to 40 miles wide. The picture at right was last transmitted.

Astronauts Examine 'Vast, Lonely' Place; Read From Genesis

By JOHN NOBLE WILFORD
Special to The New York Times

HOUSTON, Wednesday, Dec. 25—The three astronauts of Apollo 8 yesterday became the first men to orbit the moon. Early today, after flying 10 times around that desolate realm of dream and scientific mystery, they started their return to earth.

They fired the spacecraft's main rocket engine at 1:10 A.M. to kick them out of lunar orbit

Excerpts from messages to and from Apollo, Page 36.

and to carry them toward a splashdown in the Pacific Ocean on Friday.

Through the static of 231,000 miles, as Apollo 8 swung around from behind the moon and started for earth, one of the astronauts dispelled any doubts, saying, "Please be informed there is a Santa Claus."

57-Hour Return Trip

It would be a 57-hour return trip from the most far-reaching voyage of the space age thus far—or of any other previous age. The astronauts had seen, as no other men had, the ancient lunar craters, plains and rugged mountains from as close as 70 miles.

At 4:59 A.M. yesterday, about 20 hours before the return trip, Col. Frank Borman of the Air Force, Capt. James A. Lovell Jr. of the Navy and Maj. William A. Anders of the Air Force, swept into an orbit of the moon by firing the spacecraft's main rocket. This occurred after they flew around the leading edge of the moon and were directly behind the earth's only natural satellite.

"We got it! We've got it!" exclaimed a mission commentator of the National Aeronautics and Space Administration as the spacecraft emerged from behind the moon 24 minutes later, and was clearly flying a safe and smooth orbit.

Businesslike Report

The calm and laconic Apollo explorers, however, were all business. Captain Lovell's first message to earth was simply:

"Go ahead, Houston. Apollo 8. Burn complete. Our orbit is 169.1 by 60.5—169.1 by 60.5."

The astronauts flew twice around the moon in the egg-shaped orbit, then dropped to a circular orbit nearly 70 miles above the ancient craters, plains and rugged mountains of the lunar surface.

As they beamed their first live television from orbit on Christmas Eve morning, they described the surface of the moon as a colorless gray, "like dirty beach sand with lots of footprints on it" and said it "looks like plaster of Paris."

At about 9:30 P.M. the astronauts began their second and last television show from lunar orbit. It ran some 30 minutes and showed the bright moon, in a pitch black sky, outside the spacecraft window.

Earth Like an 'Oasis'

Colonel Borman described the moon as a "vast, lonely and forbidding sight," adding that it was "not a very inviting place to live or work."

Captain Lovell saw the earth as a "grand oasis in the big vastness of space."

Major Anders was most impressed by "the lunar sunrise and sunsets."

As the telecast neared its end, Colonel Borman said "Apollo 8 has a message for you." With that, Major Anders began reading the opening verses from the Book of Genesis about creation of the earth.

"In the beginning," Major Anders read, "God created the heaven and the earth.

"And the earth was without form and void; and darkness was upon the face of the deep . . ."

Captain Lovell then took up with the verse beginning, "And God called the light day, and the darkness He called night."

Colonel Borman closed the reading with the verse that read:

"And God called the dry land Earth; and the gathering together of the water called He Seas: and God saw that it was good."

Sends Holiday Greetings

After that Colonel Borman signed off, saying:

"Good-by, good night. Merry Christmas. God bless all of you, all of you on the good earth."

Glynn S. Lunney, one of the flight directors here, told reporters earlier, "we have a completely 'go' spacecraft."

George M. Low, the spacecraft manager at the Manned Spacecraft Center, said he was "altogether happy" with the mission — the most ambitious and daring thus far in the nation's $24-billion Apollo project to land men on the moon next year.

Although the mission's object was not primarily scientific, Dr. John Dietrich of the space center's geology and geochemistry branch, said that the television pictures and astro-

Continued on Page 36, Column 1

FUEL DELIVERIES FALL SHORT HERE

City's Health Chief Warns of Danger to Sick—Flu Vaccine and Blood Low

By ARNOLD H. LUBASCH

A shortage of heat, vaccine and blood plagued the city yesterday as the Hong Kong flu epidemic continued, and the Health Commissioner warned that many sick people might die unless emergency fuel deliveries were made.

Mayor Lindsay, who said most drivers had stopped fuel deliveries for the holiday, joined Health Commissioner Edward O'Rourke in appealing for fuel deliveries today even though it was Christmas.

With the temperature dropping into the low twenties last night, hundreds of homes, apartment houses and commercial buildings remained without fuel, although oil companies sought to catch up on deliveries delayed by last week's strike.

The city's supply of flu vaccine ran out yesterday as efforts were made to arrange for further shipments before Jan. 2, when 40,000 more doses are scheduled to arrive.

A critical shortage of blood was reported by the Greater

Continued on Page 21, Column 1

Orbit Shows Lunar Interior Is 'Lumpy'

By WALTER SULLIVAN
Special to The New York Times

HOUSTON, Dec. 24—For the first time human beings took a close look today at the earth's nearest celestial neighbor, viewing it from many angles to seek out clues to the events that formed its awesomely rugged terrain.

Until now man has always been forced to look at the moon from a single direction at a great distance, although in the last few years spacecraft have provided glimpses of the far side and close-up views of the earth-facing side.

Today the three Apollo astronauts sailed serenely over the giant craters, looking down their throats, marveling at their crumbling walls and countless strange features that have long puzzled astronomers.

They reported seeing many freshly formed craters, indicating that the cataclysmic events that have pocked the moon and sprinkled it with rubble are continuing. Some of the craters, the astronauts said, looked as

Slight Wobbles Observed in Spacecraft's Course

though a giant pick had been hacking at a concrete surface, producing fine dust as well as other debris.

They became the first men to witness a lunar sunrise and found it a strange and unexpected experience. According to Capt. James A. Lovell Jr., about two minutes before sunrise a fine white haze appeared over the horizon where the sun was about to appear.

"It takes the fan shape," he said, "unlike the sunrise on earth, where the atmosphere affects it."

Meanwhile, analysis of the orbital flight by radio antennas on earth showed that, from time to time, the spacecraft wobbled slightly in its path. This confirmed earlier indications that the interior of the moon is "lumpy."

Some scientists, notably Dr. Harold C. Urey of the University of California, San Diego, a Nobel laureate, have suggested that the moon is like a giant raisin cake with lumps of dense iron embedded in material that is far less dense. Such a body could have been formed from a cloud of dust and smaller objects, including chunks of iron, during the formation of the solar system.

If the moon were uniformly dense and perfectly spherical, the gravitational field surrounding it would be perfectly symmetrical. It was this field that held the Apollo spacecraft in orbit. The fact that the spacecraft's road was slightly bumpy, so to speak, revealed an uneven distribution of mass within the moon. In particular, this was noted as the astronauts sailed over Copernicus, one of the largest and most spectacular craters on the moon. It was in darkness but was dimly illuminated by ghostly earthshine—sunlight reflected by the earth.

The lumpiness of the moon

Continued on Page 38, Column 1

At Least 22 Survive Pennsylvania Crash Of Plane With 45

Special to The New York Times

BRADFORD, Pa., Wednesday, Dec. 25—An Allegheny Airlines jetprop plane with 45 persons aboard crashed last night in rugged terrain during a heavy snowstorm while attempting to land at Bradford Regional Airport 15 miles south of here.

There were at least 22 survivors.

The twin-engine plane was Allegheny Flight 736, bound from Detroit to Washington. It had stopped in Erie, Pa., and had been scheduled to stop in Bradford and Harrisburg, Pa.

The wreck, about three miles southeast of the airport, was reported shortly before 9 P.M. by Allegheny Flight 734 out of Cleveland, which said it saw a fire.

It took rescue teams an hour to reach the scene on snowmobiles in freezing temperatures. Several inches of snow had fallen during the day in the heavily wooded area and

Continued on Page 62, Column 1

Christmas Day

Today is Christmas Day. Following is a list of services that are affected:

Public and Parochial Schools—Closed.

Post Office—Closed except for special delivery.

Stores—Most retail and department stores closed.

Banks—Closed.

Stock Exchanges—Closed.

Sanitation—No regular refuse collection.

Parking — Sunday parking regulations in force, permitting parking in alternate-side parking zones and at most parking meters.

Libraries—Closed except for the Main Reading Room of the Library at Fifth Avenue and 42d Street, which will be open from 1 to 10 P.M.

NEWS INDEX

A Reflection: Riders on Earth Together, Brothers in Eternal Cold

By ARCHIBALD MacLEISH

MEN'S conception of themselves and of each other has always depended on their notion of the earth. When the earth was the World—all the world there was—and the stars were lights in Dante's heaven, and the ground beneath men's feet roofed Hell, they saw themselves as creatures at the center of the universe, the sole, particular concern of God—and from that high place they ruled and killed and conquered as they pleased.

And when, centuries later, the earth was no longer the World but a small, wet, spinning planet in the solar system of a minor star off at the edge of an inconsiderable galaxy in the immeasurable distances of space — when Dante's heaven had disappeared and there was no Hell (at least no Hell beneath the feet)—men began to see themselves, not as God-directed actors at the center of a noble drama, but as helpless victims of a senseless farce where all the rest were helpless victims also, and millions could be killed in world-wide wars or in blasted cities or in concentration camps without a thought or reason but the reason—if we call it one—of force.

Now, in the last few hours, the notion may have changed again. For the first time in all of time men have *seen* the earth: seen it not as continents or oceans from the little distance of a hundred miles or two or three, but seen it from the depths of space; seen it whole and round and beautiful and small as even Dante—that "first imagination of Christendom"—had never dreamed of seeing it; as the Twentieth Century philosophers of absurdity and despair were incapable of guessing that it might be seen. And seeing it so, one question came to the minds of those who looked at it.

"Is it inhabited?" they said to each other and laughed—and then they did not laugh. What came to their minds a hundred thousand miles and more into space—"half way to the moon" they put it—what came to their minds was the life on that little, lonely, floating planet: that tiny raft in the enormous, empty night. "Is it inhabited?"

THE medieval notion of the earth put man at the center of everything. The nuclear notion of the earth put him nowhere — beyond the range of reason even—lost in absurdity and war. This latest notion may have other consequences. Formed as it was in the minds of heroic voyagers who were also men, it may remake our image of mankind. No longer that preposterous figure at the center, no longer that degraded and degrading victim off at the margins of reality and blind with blood, man may at last become himself.

To see the earth as it truly is, small and blue and beautiful in that eternal silence where it floats, is to see ourselves as riders on the earth together, brothers on that bright loveliness in the eternal cold—brothers who know now they are truly brothers.

"All the News That's Fit to Print"

The New York Times

LATE CITY EDITION

Weather: Rain, warm today; clear tonight. Sunny, pleasant tomorrow. Temp. range: today 80-66; Sunday 71-66. Temp.-Hum. Index yesterday 69. Complete U.S. report on P. 50.

VOL. CXVIII . No. 40,721

NEW YORK, MONDAY, JULY 21, 1969

10 CENTS

MEN WALK ON MOON

ASTRONAUTS LAND ON PLAIN; COLLECT ROCKS, PLANT FLAG

Voice From Moon: 'Eagle Has Landed'

EAGLE (the lunar module): Houston, Tranquility Base here. The Eagle has landed.

HOUSTON: Roger, Tranquility, we copy you on the ground. You've got a bunch of guys about to turn blue. We're breathing again. Thanks a lot.

TRANQUILITY BASE: Thank you.

HOUSTON: You're looking good here.

TRANQUILITY BASE: A very smooth touchdown.

HOUSTON: Eagle, you are stay for T1. [The first step in the lunar operation.] Over.

TRANQUILITY BASE: Roger. Stay for T1.

HOUSTON: Roger and we see you venting the ox.

TRANQUILITY BASE: Roger.

COLUMBIA (the command and service module): How do you read me?

HOUSTON: Columbia, he has landed Tranquility Base. Eagle is at Tranquility. I read you five by. Over.

COLUMBIA: Yes, I heard the whole thing.

HOUSTON: Well, it's a good show.

COLUMBIA: Fantastic.

TRANQUILITY BASE: I'll second that.

APOLLO CONTROL: The next major stay-no stay will be for the T2 event. That is at 21 minutes 26 seconds after initiation of power descent.

COLUMBIA: Up telemetry command reset to reacquire on high gain.

HOUSTON: Copy. Out.

APOLLO CONTROL: We have an unofficial time for that touchdown of 102 hours, 45 minutes, 42 seconds and we will update that.

HOUSTON: Eagle, you loaded R2 wrong. We want 10254.

TRANQUILITY BASE: Roger. Do you want the horizontal 55 15.2?

HOUSTON: That's affirmative.

APOLLO CONTROL: We're now less than four minutes from our next stay-no stay. It will be for one complete revolution of the command module.

One of the first things that Armstrong and Aldrin will do after getting their next stay-no stay will be to remove their helmets and gloves.

HOUSTON: Eagle, you are stay for T2. Over.

Continued on Page 4, Col. 1

VOYAGE TO THE MOON

By ARCHIBALD MACLEISH

PRESENCE among us,

wanderer in our skies,

dazzle of silver in our leaves and on our
waters silver,

O
silver evasion in our farthest thought—
"the visiting moon" . . . "the glimpses of the moon" . . .

and we have touched you!

From the first of time,
before the first of time, before the
first men tasted time, we thought of you.
You were a wonder to us, unattainable,
a longing past the reach of longing,
a light beyond our light, our lives—perhaps
a meaning to us . . .

Now
our hands have touched you in your depth of night.

Three days and three nights we journeyed,
steered by farthest stars, climbed outward,
crossed the invisible tide-rip where the floating dust
falls one way or the other in the void between,
followed that other down, encountered
cold, faced death—unfathomable emptiness . . .

Then, the fourth day evening, we descended,
made fast, set foot at dawn upon your beaches,
sifted between our fingers your cold sand.

We stand here in the dusk, the cold, the silence . . .

and here, as at the first of time, we lift our heads.
Over us, more beautiful than the moon, a
moon, a wonder to us, unattainable,
a longing past the reach of longing,
a light beyond our light, our lives—perhaps
a meaning to us . . .

O, a meaning!

over us on these silent beaches the bright
earth,
presence among us

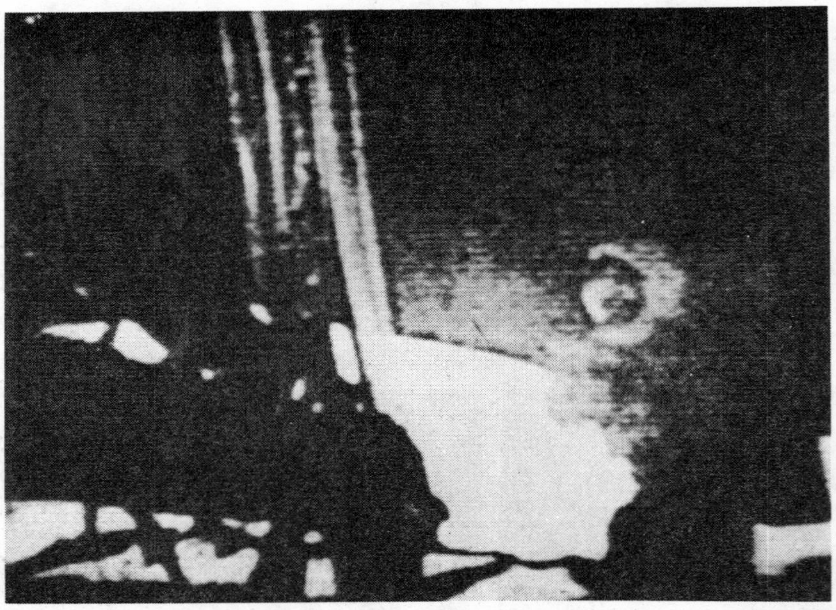

Neil A. Armstrong moves away from the leg of the landing craft after taking the first step on the surface of the moon

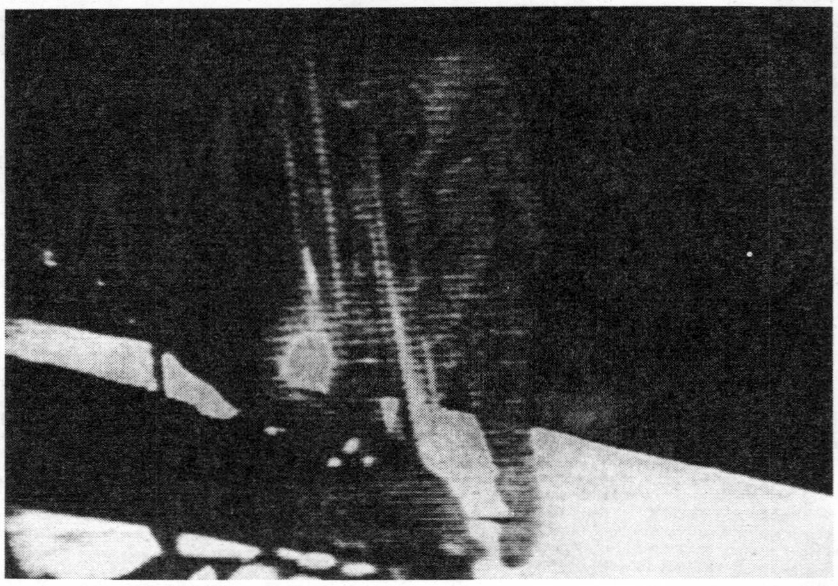

The New York Times from C.B.S. News

Col. Edwin E. Aldrin Jr. climbing down the ladder. The television camera was attached to a side of the lunar module.

Associated Press

Mr. Armstrong, right, and Colonel Aldrin raise the U.S. flag. A metal rod at right angles to the mast keeps flag unfurled.

A Powdery Surface Is Closely Explored

By JOHN NOBLE WILFORD

Special to The New York Times

HOUSTON, Monday, July 21—Men have landed and walked on the moon.

Two Americans, astronauts of Apollo 11, steered their fragile four-legged lunar module safely and smoothly to the historic landing yesterday at 4:17:40 P.M., Eastern daylight time.

Neil A. Armstrong, the 38-year-old civilian commander, radioed to earth and the mission control room here:

"Houston, Tranquility Base here. The Eagle has landed."

The first men to reach the moon—Mr. Armstrong and his co-pilot, Col. Edwin E. Aldrin Jr. of the Air Force—brought their ship to rest on a level, rock-strewn plain near the southwestern shore of the arid Sea of Tranquility.

About six and a half hours later, Mr. Armstrong opened the landing craft's hatch, stepped slowly down the ladder and declared as he planted the first human footprint on the lunar crust:

"That's one small step for man, one giant leap for mankind."

His first step on the moon came at 10:56:20 P.M., as a television camera outside the craft transmitted his every move to an awed and excited audience of hundreds of millions of people on earth.

Tentative Steps Test Soil

Mr. Armstrong's initial steps were tentative tests of the lunar soil's firmness and of his ability to move about easily in his bulky white spacesuit and backpacks and under the influence of lunar gravity, which is one-sixth that of the earth.

"The surface is fine and powdery," the astronaut reported. "I can pick it up loosely with my toe. It does adhere in fine layers like powdered charcoal to the sole and sides of my boots. I only go in a small fraction of an inch, maybe an eighth of an inch. But I can see the footprints of my boots in the treads in the fine sandy particles.

After 19 minutes of Mr. Armstrong's testing, Colonel Aldrin joined him outside the craft.

The two men got busy setting up another television camera out from the lunar module, planting an American flag into the ground, scooping up soil and rock samples, deploying scientific experiments and hopping and loping about in a demonstration of their lunar agility.

They found walking and working on the moon less taxing than had been forecast. Mr. Armstrong once reported he was "very comfortable."

And people back on earth found the black-and-white television pictures of the bug-shaped lunar module and the men tramping about it so sharp and clear as to seem unreal, more like a toy and toy-like figures than human beings on the most daring and far-reaching expedition thus far undertaken.

Nixon Telephones Congratulations

During one break in the astronauts' work, President Nixon congratulated them from the White House in what, he said, "certainly has to be the most historic telephone call ever made."

"Because of what you have done," the President told the astronauts, "the heavens have become a part of man's world. And as you talk to us from the Sea of Tranquility it requires us to redouble our efforts to bring peace and tranquility to earth.

"For one priceless moment in the whole history of man all the people on this earth are truly one—one in their pride in what you have done and one in our prayers that you will return safely to earth."

Mr. Armstrong replied:

"Thank you Mr. President. It's a great honor and privilege for us to be here representing not only the United States but men of peace of all nations, men with interests and a curiosity and men with a vision for the future."

Mr. Armstrong and Colonel Aldrin returned to their landing craft and closed the hatch at 1:12 A.M., 2 hours 21 minutes after opening the hatch on the moon. While the third member of the crew, Lieut. Col. Michael Collins of the Air Force, kept his orbital vigil overhead in the command ship, the two moon explorers settled down to sleep.

Outside their vehicle the astronauts had found a bleak

Continued on Pages 2, Col. 1

Today's 4-Part Issue of The Times

This morning's issue of The New York Times is divided into four parts. The first part is devoted to news of Apollo 11. and includes Editorials and letters to the Editor (Page 16). Poems on the landing on the moon appear on Page 17.

General news begins on the first page of the second part. The News Summary and Index is on the first page of the third part, which includes sports news, obituaries (Page 51) and transportation news and weather reports (Pages 50 and 52).

Financial and business news begins on the first page of the fourth part.

Following is the News Index for today's issue:

News Summary and Index, Page 35

The New York Times

PAGE ONE

1970-1979

"All the News That's Fit to Print"

The New York Times

LATE CITY EDITION
Weather: Cloudy but clearing today. Fair tonight. Cloudy, mild tomorrow. Temp. range: today 51-43; Tuesday 48-42. Full U.S. report on Page 85.

VOL. CXIX . . No. 40,989 — NEW YORK, WEDNESDAY, APRIL 15, 1970 — 10 CENTS

CREW OF CRIPPLED APOLLO 13 STARTS BACK AFTER ROUNDING MOON AND FIRING ROCKET; MEN APPEAR CALM DESPITE LOW RESERVES

Judge Blackmun of Minnesota Is Named To Supreme Court Seat by the President

Nominee, 61, Is Regarded as a Scholarly Jurist

By ROBERT B. SEMPLE Jr.
Special to The New York Times

WASHINGTON, April 14—President Nixon today nominated Harry Andrew Blackmun of Minnesota to the Supreme Court.

Judge Blackmun, a member of the United States Court of Appeals for the Eighth Circuit, is regarded in the legal profession as a scholarly and mildly conservative judge.

Mr. Nixon's third choice for the vacancy created by the resignation of Abe Fortas was announced by Ronald L. Ziegler, the White House press secretary, late this afternoon. The President did not appear and did not issue a statement.

Mr. Ziegler made the announcement while standing on the same small platform in the new White House press headquarters where Mr. Nixon last Thursday accused the Senate of hypocrisy and regional bias for refusing to approve his first two nominees for the vacancy.

United Press International
Judge Harry A. Blackmun in St. Louis yesterday.

The two men, both Southerners, were Clement F. Haynsworth Jr. and G. Harrold Carswell. The Senate rejected Judge Haynsworth last November and Judge Carswell last Wednesday.

A Prolonged Examination by Senate Panel Seen

Judge Blackmun will also require Senate confirmation, but early reaction to his nomination on Capitol Hill was inconclusive. On the basis of the Senate's recent performance, however, it seemed likely that Judge Blackmun would be subjected to prolonged and searching examination by the Senate Judiciary Committee. Until that time, there may be a reluctance on the part of many Senators to commit themselves.

Senator Sam J. Ervin Jr, Democrat of North Carolina and a senior member of the Judiciary Committee, refused to

Continued on Page 34, Column 3

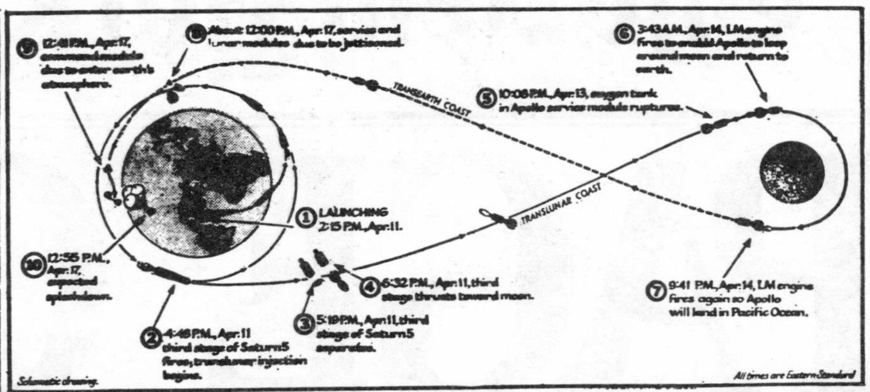

The New York Times — April 15, 1970
VOYAGE OF A STRICKEN SPACESHIP: Apollo 13, its hopes for America's third lunar landing dashed by a ruptured oxygen tank, arced around the moon last night on a course that would bring it back to earth on Friday.

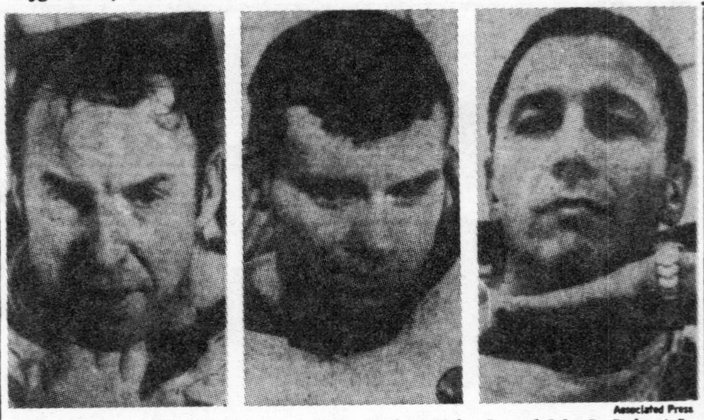

Associated Press
BEFORE FLIGHT: Capt. James A. Lovell Jr., Fred W. Haise Jr. and John L. Swigert Jr.

TARGET IS PACIFIC

Chance of Safe Return Deemed 'Excellent' Despite the Risks

Excerpts from conversations with spacecraft, Page 28.

By JOHN NOBLE WILFORD
Special to The New York Times

HOUSTON, Wednesday, April 15—With the lives of its three astronauts hanging in the balance, the crippled spaceship Apollo 13 swung around the moon last night and rocketed toward an emergency splashdown in the Pacific Ocean Friday.

After the craft looped the moon, a crucial four-minute and 24-second rocket firing sent the astronauts on a fast and more accurate course — a drastic change of plans caused by Monday night's massive power failure aboard the moon-bound spacecraft.

The rocket blast started at 9:41 P.M. Eastern standard time as the astronauts, depending on their attached lunar landing craft as a back-up return craft, pulled away about 6,000 miles from the right side of the moon.

"That was a good burn," Mission Control radioed after the lunar module's descent rocket shut down on schedule.

Though its success sent the first ripple of relief through Mission Control in 24 hours, Capt. James A. Lovell Jr. of the Navy and Fred W. Haise Jr. and John L. Swigert Jr., both civilians, were still a long way from home and not yet out of trouble.

A Race With Time

The three astronauts were calm, despite the fact that they were racing time, trying to reach the earth before their severely limited reserves of oxygen, electricity and water ran out.

Grim-faced flight directors here called it "the most critical situation" in the history of the American space program. But, barring any further trouble, they said the chances of the astronauts' safe return were "excellent."

A rising carbon-dioxide level in the spacecraft stirred new concern late last night for the astronauts' safety. The amount rose to the point where it triggered an alarm light, but Mission Control said it was prepared to have it go to twice that level to conserve the lithium hydroxide chemical used to cleanse the cabin atmosphere.

Laboratory tests have shown that triple the present level can be tolerated without signs of organic damage, space agency doctors said.

NASA scientists were de-

Continued on Page 28, Column 3

NIXON IS BRIEFED ON APOLLO CRISIS

Meets With Space Experts During Unannounced Visit to Center in Maryland

By RICHARD D. LYONS
Special to The New York Times

GREENBELT, Md., April 14—President Nixon, looking taut and tired, met with technical experts of the space agency here for 45 minutes this afternoon and was briefed about the past and future problems of the Apollo 13 mission.

Dr. John F. Clark, director of the National Aeronautics and Space Administration's Goddard Space Flight Center here, said that the President was deeply concerned and that he asked "many knowledgeable questions" about the mission's problems and "the contingencies that have been planned."

This center is the eyes, ears and touch of Apollo 13. It is here that all the information transmitted by the spaceship is collected from 17 tracking stations around the world and sent on to the Manned Spacecraft Center in Houston for analysis.

Unannounced Visit

Hatless and dressed in a tan raincoat, dark blue suit and blue striped tie, Mr. Nixon made an unannounced visit to the center, driving from the White House, 13 miles away, through a heavy rainstorm.

The President had been briefed by his aides three times during the night and early this morning about the sudden power loss in the Apollo 13 spaceship as it was heading toward the moon. According to Ronald L. Ziegler, the White House press secretary, Mr. Nixon was informed about 4 A.M. today that the corrective firing of the lunar module's engine would bring the space craft on a free return to earth.

"The President will be receiving reports throughout the day

Continued on Page 29, Column 7

RISE OF 30% URGED IN CITY REALTY TAX

G.O.P. Leaders in Albany Call On Mayor to Accept $440-Million Package

By RICHARD PHALON
Special to The New York Times

ALBANY, April 14 — Mayor Lindsay arrived here tonight for talks with Republican legislators on the city's financial problems facing the possibility that he might have to adopt a $440-million package of real estate tax increases.

The package, which some Republican leaders are urging as a part-answer to the $630-million the Mayor says he needs to balance the budget next fiscal year, would raise the real estate tax rate from $5.52 per $100 to around $7 per $100 of assessed valuation—an increase of almost 30 per cent.

City budget officials said about $200-million of the package would go into effect next year anyway through normal growth of assessed valuations and an expected increase in the equalization rate designed to iron out variations in assessment practices throughout the city.

The Mayor's mission here tonight is to persuade the Republican leaders that the city is entitled to more state aid on the basis of the tax effort it is already making and on the basis of the additional "do it yourself" revenue measures he has had introduced here in the closing days of the session.

Continued on Page 36, Column 4

Brezhnev Says Soviet Aim Is 'Reasonable' Arms Pact

By BERNARD GWERTZMAN
Special to The New York Times

MOSCOW, April 14—Leonid I. Brezhnev, the Soviet Communist party leader, said today that the Soviet Union would welcome "a reasonable agreement" with the United States on limiting strategic arms when the second round of Soviet-American talks begins in Vienna on Thursday.

But Mr. Brezhnev, making his second televised speech in two days from the Ukrainian city

Excerpts from Brezhnev talk are printed on Page 17.

of Kharkov, indicated doubt that the United States Government was sincere in wanting an accord.

Apparently alluding to Washington's decision to go ahead with new offensive and defensive missile systems, Mr. Brezhnev shook his fist and said that if anyone tried to gain military superiority over the Soviet Union "we will reply with the necessary increase in military might that guarantees our defense."

After loud and prolonged applause, Mr. Brezhnev added: "We cannot act otherwise."

His wide-ranging foreign policy speech covered the Middle East, Vietnam and Europe, in which he broke no new ground, and relations with China, which he said were being harmed by what he called continuing anti-Soviet war hysteria in Peking.

Last night's speech was devoted entirely to economic problems and reflected his view that the Soviet Union must adopt technological advances and rally the people to overcome its mediocre economic showing of recent years.

His critical words on how the

Continued on Page 17, Column 1

SENATE APPROVES TV CAMPAIGN CURB

Limit in Spending on Races for Federal Offices Voted Over G.O.P. Opposition

By JOHN W. FINNEY
Special to The New York Times

WASHINGTON, April 14 — Over Republican opposition, the Senate approved today campaign reform legislation designed to limit and perhaps reduce the mounting spending on political broadcasts over television and radio.

The legislation would place a ceiling on how much a candidate for Federal office could spend on television and radio broadcasts. In addition, it would reduce the rates at which broadcasting stations sell air time to political candidates.

The spending limitations were incorporated in legislation repealing the so-called "equal time" provision in the communications act, thus permitting the television and radio networks to provide free broadcast time for the Presidential and Vice-Presidential candidates in the 1972 elections without giving comparable time to every minor candidate. Whether or not this free time is to be used for debates, as it was in the 1960 Presidential elections, or for some other format is to be worked out by the candidates and the networks.

The campaign reform legislation, first proposed two years ago, passed the Senate with unexpected ease after only one day of debate. It now goes to the House, where, as in the Senate, the Democratic majority is expected to prevail over Republican opposition.

The legislation is designed to

Continued on Page 86, Column 6

Plight of 3 Crewmen Stirs World Interest and Prayer

By MARTIN ARNOLD

Suddenly, in the moment it takes an oxygen tank to spring a leak, the flight of Apollo 13 was no longer something everybody took for granted and was even slightly bored with.

For all around the world yesterday, during the Apollo 13 emergency, there was a surge of interest in the flight and there were prayers, and anguish also, for the three men who were fighting to get their crippled spaceship home.

The world-wide shift in interest in Apollo 13 was best summed up in two printed lines—one in an Italian newspaper, the other in a French paper.

Before the bad news broke, Milan's Il Giorno commented in a headline: "Too Perfect; the Public Is Getting Bored."

Yesterday morning, in Paris, Le Monde said: "The whole human race is participating with them in the agony of their return."

In the United States there was an outpouring of prayer, and here and there some expression of bitterness, too, that man was reaching toward space without having first solved the problems on earth.

Both the Senate and House passed resolutions yesterday asking all Americans to pray, at 9 o'clock Eastern standard time last night, for the safe return of their countrymen. And they urged businesses and communications media to pause briefly, if they could, for the prayers at that hour.

Special services and masses were called for in thousands of churches and synagogues around the country — at St. Patrick's Cathedral and St. Thomas Episcopal Church and Temple Emanu-El in New York City, for example.

Rabbi Abraham Gross, president of the Rabbinical Alliance of America, called on all clergymen to pray for the safe return of Apollo 13, and, in Baltimore, Frank Gunter Jr., Maryland chairman of the National Conference of Christians and Jews, asked all residents of the state to observe a minute of silent prayer at 4 P.M. yesterday.

In Montgomery, Ala., T.R. Hennessey, a retired Air Force

Continued on Page 29, Column 4

U.S. Arrests Russian Skipper In Alaska Gulf for Spilling Oil

By ROBERT M. SMITH
Special to The New York Times

WASHINGTON, April 14—A Coast Guard cutter sent a boarding party aboard a Soviet tanker in the Gulf of Alaska last night and there arrested the ship's master on charges of spilling a mile-long oil slick near Kodiak Island.

The master of the Soviet vessel, V. C. Sherstobitov, has been flown to Anchorage where he is awaiting arraignment under the Refuse Act of 1899. His ship, the 345-foot motor vessel Mozyr, is still standing by near Kodiak Island.

In response to questions about an unconfirmed report that became available here, the State Department said the Soviet captain had been arrested.

According to information obtained by telephone from the scene, the American boarding party—consisting of a young operations officer, a representative of the Bureau of Fisheries and a seaman-photographer—encountered no resistance.

The Americans spent several hours on board the Soviet vessel while Captain Sherstobitov waited for his fleet commander in Vladivostok to tell him whether he should go with the Americans.

Comdr. John H. Byrd Jr. of New London, Conn., was the captain of the Coast Guard cutter involved, the Storis. Commander Byrd was reached today by telephone on Kodiak Island—about 300 miles southwest of Anchorage—and provided this account:

"We were commencing patrol, and Coast Guard aviation units were also carrying out patrol, and they located a Soviet tanker refueling Soviet fishing vessels in U.S. territory

Continued on Page 74, Column 3

Adm. Moorer Named To Head Joint Chiefs

Special to The New York Times

WASHINGTON, April 14 — President Nixon today named Adm. Thomas H. Moorer, Chief of Naval Operations, to succeed Gen. Earle G. Wheeler as chairman of the Joint Chiefs of Staff, the nation's highest ranking military officer.

If confirmed by the Senate—and no obstacles to confirmation are foreseen here—Admiral Moorer will be the second Navy man to hold the post. Adm. Arthur W. Radford was chairman from 1953 to 1957, in the Eisenhower Administration.

Mr. Nixon also disclosed his intention to nominate Vice Adm. Elmo R. Zumwalt Jr., commander of naval forces in Vietnam and chief of the Naval Advisory Group, United States Military Assistance Command

Continued on Page 14, Column 4

Cambodia Appeals To World for Arms

By HENRY KAMM
Special to The New York Times

PNOMPENH, Cambodia, April 14—Premier Lon Nol issued an urgent appeal tonight for arms from any country that wanted to provide them.

[The State Department said the United States had received no request. Other sources expected one and predicted that it would be granted.]

In a broadcast statement in French and Cambodian, the Premier declared:

"The Salvation Government has the duty to inform the nation that in view of the gravity of the present situation, it finds it necessary to accept all unconditional foreign aid, wherever it may come from, for the salvation of the nation."

The Premier underlined the

Continued on Page 3, Column 1

NEWS INDEX

The New York Times (by Edward Hausner)
PRAY FOR ASTRONAUTS: Worshipers at a special mass at St. Patrick's Cathedral for the crew of Apollo 13

"All the News That's Fit to Print"

The New York Times

LATE CITY EDITION

Weather: Rain ending early today; clearing tonight. Fair tomorrow. Temp. range: today 66-49; Monday 62-53. Full U.S. report on Page 90.

VOL. CXIX..No. 41,009

NEW YORK, TUESDAY, MAY 5, 1970

10 CENTS

4 Kent State Students Killed by Troops

8 Hurt as Shooting Follows Reported Sniping at Rally

By JOHN KIFNER

Special to The New York Times

KENT, Ohio, May 4—Four students at Kent State University, two of them women, were shot to death this afternoon by a volley of National Guard gunfire. At least 8 other students were wounded.

The burst of gunfire came about 20 minutes after the guardsmen broke up a noon rally on the Commons, a grassy campus gathering spot, by lobbing tear gas at a crowd of about 1,000 young people.

In Washington, President Nixon deplored the deaths of the four students in the following statement:

"This should remind us all once again that when dissent turns to violence it invites tragedy. It is my hope that this tragic and unfortunate incident will strengthen the determination of all the nation's campuses, administrators, faculty and students alike to stand firmly for the right which exists in this country of peaceful dissent and just as strongly against the resort to violence as a means of such expression."

In Columbus, Sylvester Del Corso, Adjutant General of the Ohio National Guard, said in a statement that the guardsmen had been forced to shoot after a sniper opened fire against the troops from a nearby rooftop and the crowd began to move to encircle the guardsmen.

Frederick P. Wenger, the Assistant Adjutant General, said the troops had opened fire after they were shot at by a sniper.

"They were under standing orders to take cover and return any fire," he said.

This reporter, who was with the group of students, did not see any indication of sniper fire, nor was the scund of any gunfire audible before the Guard volley. Students, conceding that rocks had been thrown, heatedly denied that there was any sniper.

Gov. James A. Rhodes called on J. Edgar Hoover, director of the Federal Bureau of Investigation, to aid in looking into the campus violence. A Justice Department spokesman said no decision had been made to investigate.

At 2:10 this afternoon, after the shootings, the university president, Robert I. White, ordered the university closed for an indefinite time, and officials were making plans to evacuate the dormitories and bus out-of-state students to nearby cities.

Robinson Memorial Hospital identified the dead students as Allison Krause, 19 years old, of

Continued on Page 17, Column 1

Tarentum Valley Daily News via Associated Press

A girl screams as fellow student lies dead after National Guardsmen opened fire at Kent State

Associated Press

Ohio National Guardsmen advancing over the campus of Kent State University yesterday behind a screen of tear gas

HIGH COURT BACKS CHURCHES' RIGHT TO TAX EXEMPTION

Holds, 7 to 1, That Law Does Not Violate Ban on State Support of Religion

DOUGLAS CASTS DISSENT

Majority Rejects Plea of a Bronx Lawyer Over His Plot on Staten Island

By FRED P. GRAHAM

Special to The New York Times

WASHINGTON, May 4 — The Supreme Court ruled 7 to 1 today that laws that exempt church property from taxation do not violate the Constitution's prohibition against state support of religion.

The opinion was written by Chief Justice Warren E. Burger and was disputed only by Justice William O. Douglas. In it the Court upheld the constitutionality of New York State's exemption from real estate taxes of church property used solely for religious purposes.

The law had been challenged by Frederick Walz, a lawyer from the Bronx who purchased a 22-by-29-foot, weed-choked plot on Staten Island in 1967 and promptly sued the City Tax Commission over his $5.24 tax bill for a year.

'Establishment' Is Seen

Mr. Walz, who described himself as a "religious person, not a member of any religious organization," said that tax exemptions granted to church property raised his own tax bill and forced him to contribute to religious groups against his will.

He asserted that the result was an indirect state subsidy to churches, in violation of the First Amendment's prohibition against any "establishment of religion" by the Government.

The Supreme Court rejected that argument today, partly on the ground that no particular religion is singled out for favorable treatment and partly on the historical ground that church tax exemptions have been accepted almost without challenge in all states for most of the nation's history.

Chief Justice Burger's opinion conceded that the church exemption "necessarily operates to afford an indirect economic benefit." But he reasoned that the state might be less neutral toward churches if it taxed them and that it was faced with the delicate matter of deciding on each church's proper assessment.

Surprise and Concern

He concluded that some contact between churches and the state was inevitable and that it would be unfair to deny tax exemptions to religious groups while granting exemptions to nonsectarian charities that do similar good works.

The Supreme Court's decision to review Mr. Walz's appeal prompted widespread puzzlement in legal circles and concern among churchmen. The constitutionality of church tax exemptions was considered so well settled that the New York courts brushed off the challenge with brief orders declaring that it had no merit.

The American Civil Liberties Union backed Mr. Walz, and

Continued on Page 40, Column 5

3 in Bombing Plot Plead Guilty Here

By ARNOLD H. LUBASCH

Samuel J. Melville, Jane L. Alpert and John D. Hughey 3d pleaded guilty yesterday as the self-styled revolutionaries were about to stand trial on charges of conspiring to bomb Federal buildings here last fall.

After the case was convened amid stringent security measures in Federal Court, Judge Milton Pollack asked the bearded 34-year-old Melville why he wanted to plead guilty to three charges against him.

"I plead guilty to count one because I did conspire with others to destroy Federal property," Melville replied as he stood erectly in blue jeans and

Continued on Page 34, Column 1

WAR AND ECONOMY SPUR STOCK DROPS

Administration Economist Voices Apprehension as Market Falls 19.07

By TERRY ROBARDS

Uneasiness over the United States involvement in Cambodia and the bombing of North Vietnam, plus continuing uncertainty about the nation's business outlook, created a mood of deep pessimism on Wall Street yesterday and sent the securities markets into a tailspin.

Stock and bond prices fell sharply in response to selling by discouraged investors. The Dow-Jones industrial average, a gauge of price action on the New York Stock Exchange, plunged 19.07 points in its worst decline since the loss of 21.16 points Nov. 22, 1963, the day President Kennedy was assassinated.

In Washington, a leading Nixon Administration economist expressed apprehension about the situation. "The Administration is obviously concerned," said, declining to be publicly identified.

"An emotional reaction triggered by the stock market decline may mislead people concerning the basic strength of the economy and its favorable prospects," he asserted, adding that "the facts in the economic sense are pretty good."

His statements represented the first clear indication of anxiety by the Nixon Administration with respect to the stock market's behavior. They were issued before the close of trading and before it was clear that yesterday's nosedive would be

Continued on Page 69, Column 2

Report of Songmy Incident Wins a Pulitzer for Hersh

By PETER KIHSS

A report on the alleged Songmy massacre of Vietnamese civilians by United States soldiers won the 1970 Pulitzer prize in international reporting yesterday for Seymour Hersh, a free-lance reporter whose article was circulated through the Dispatch News Service.

A black playwright, Charles Gordone, won the drama prize for an Off Broadway play, "No Place to Be Somebody"—the first Off Broadway production so honored.

A musical composition on an electronic synthesizer won the music prize for the first time, the award going to "Time's Encomium," by Charles Wuorinen.

Ada Louise Huxtable, architecture critic of The New York Times, became the winner of the first Pulitzer prize for distinguished criticism. This was a new category, set up for criticism or commentary, and was divided in the judging, with Marquis W. Childs of The St. Louis Post-Dispatch taking the award for distinguished commentary.

The gold medal for meritorious public service went to Newsday of Garden City, L. I., for a three-year investigation and exposé of secret land deals and zoning manipulations by public and political party officeholders.

With 17 individuals named Pulitzer prize-winners in the 54th year of the awards, the laurels for history were carried off by former Secretary of

Continued on Page 48, Column 1

Study of LSD Spurs Suspicions Of Drug's Link to Birth Defects

By SANDRA BLAKESLEE

The first extensive, long-term study comparing the incidence of birth defects with parental use of LSD has concluded that the drug "must be seriously considered as a possible mutagen"—an agent that produces genetic changes in cells.

"Although we cannot rush in and say we have unequivocal evidence at this time that LSD use causes birth defects, we are on firmer ground, more suspicious, than ever before," said Dr. Cheston M. Berlin, a principal investigator in the study.

Dr. Berlin, a pediatrician at George Washington University School of Medicine, where the study was conducted, presented his findings at two recent scientific meetings. He elaborated on the results in an interview yesterday.

The issue of whether LSD (shorthand for lysergic acid diethylamide) is a mutagenic agent has not yet been resolved, Dr. Berlin said.

Such agents, or changers, act in some way to alter the normal configuration of the genetic material within the cells of an organism, often causing the organism to reproduce itself abnormally, producing birth defects.

If LSD is a mutagenic agent, Dr. Berlin said, evidence of its cellular interference might turn

Continued on Page 23, Column 1

ISRAELIS REPORT KILLING 21 ARABS

Toll in Guerrilla Battle at Jordan River Is Termed Largest Since '67 War

By RICHARD EDER

Special to The New York Times

JERUSALEM, May 4—Israeli military authorities announced today that an Israeli patrol surprised and killed 21 armed Palestinian infiltrators shortly after they crossed the Jordan River into Israeli-controlled territory last night.

At the same time the Israelis reported some tentative signs that intensive air strikes on Egyptian artillery positions west of the Suez Canal were beginning to ease the recent pressure on Israeli troops on the east bank.

Last night's encounter with the guerrillas involved the largest death toll reported by Israeli forces since the start of the struggle with Arabs infiltrating into territories occupied by Israel after the 1967 war.

According to the account provided by Israeli military authorities, the infiltrators, members of Al Fatah guerrilla organization, were pinned down by fire from the Israeli patrol just before midnight, not far from the banks of the Jordan River.

The infiltrators tried to take shelter in scrub and thornbushes, the account continued. Apart from firing one bazooka shot, it went on, they made no move to answer the Israeli fire, which went on heavily but intermittently all night and which, by sunup, had killed all but six of them.

When it began to grow light,

Continued on Page 8, Column 4

37 COLLEGE CHIEFS URGE NIXON MOVE FOR PROMPT PEACE

Warn Invasion of Cambodia Poses New Alienation Peril —Student Strikes Begin

By ROBERT D. McFADDEN

The presidents of 37 colleges and universities urged President Nixon yesterday to "demonstrate unequivocally your determination" to end promptly the United States military involvement in Southeast Asia.

In a letter to Mr. Nixon, the presidents said that "the American invasion of Cambodia" and the weekend bombing of North Vietnam had generated "severe and widespread apprehensions on our campuses."

"We share these apprehensions," the presidents said, adding:

"We implore you to consider the incalculable dangers of an unprecedented alienation of America's youth and to take immediate action to demonstrate unequivocally your determination to end the war quickly."

The signers, representing many of the nation's leading academic institutions, "urgently" requested a meeting with Mr. Nixon.

The letter was drafted by Dr. James M. Hester, the president of New York University, and bore the signatures, among others, of the presidents of Princeton University, Columbia University, the University of Notre Dame, Dartmouth College, the University of Pennsylvania and Johns Hopkins University.

Nationwide Strike Urged

In Washington, the leaders of the National Student Association and the former Vietnam Moratorium Committee called for a nationwide university strike of indefinite duration, starting today, to protest the war and to mobilize public opinion for a withdrawal of United States forces from Indochina. It would involve students, faculty members and administrators.

Antiwar groups at dozens of colleges and universities across the nation, meanwhile, began demonstrations and rallies to protest the Administration's policies.

There were strike pledges from at least 100 colleges and universities, and at some schools the strike began yesterday. Support for the strike was expressed in the editorials of many campus newspapers, along with a condemnation of what some called President Nixon's "illegitimate" decision to send troops into Cambodia.

At many schools, the strike was officially approved by college administrations. Most of

Continued on Page 18, Column 6

President Assailed By Fulbright Panel

By JOHN W. FINNEY

Special to The New York Times

WASHINGTON, May 4—The Senate Foreign Relations Committee complained today that the Nixon Administration, by sending American troops into Cambodia "without the consent or knowledge of Congress," was usurping the war-making powers of Congress.

The committee, which is headed by Senator J. W. Fulbright, also charged that over the years the executive branch had been "conducting a constitutionally unauthorized, Presidential war in Indochina." The charge was promptly rejected by the White House, which contended that President Nixon was relying upon his constitutional powers as Commander in Chief.

"The action which the

Continued on Page 4, Column 4

U.S. SAYS BIG RAIDS IN NORTH ARE OVER

Officials Stress That There May Be Smaller Strikes if Flights Are Periled

By WILLIAM BEECHER

Special to The New York Times

WASHINGTON, May 4—The Defense Department announced today it had "terminated" large-scale air raids mounted in recent days against three areas of North Vietnam.

But Pentagon officials stressed that smaller air strikes might be conducted in the future if American reconnaissance flights over North Vietnam were attacked.

For the first time, the Pentagon acknowledged that the raids north of the demilitarized zone over the weekend had been larger in scope than any since the bombing halt in November, 1968, and that so-called "logistics support" facilities for air defense had been struck in addition to antiaircraft gun and missile sites.

3 Areas Attacked

The Defense Department said that from 50 to more than 100 planes had been employed in each of the strikes near Barthelemy Pass, Bankarai Pass and in another area immediately north of the demilitarized zone. Barthelemy Pass, about 240 miles north of the demilitarized zone, is believed to be the farthest point north raided by American aircraft since November, 1968.

All three areas, officials said, are key conduits for the flow of men and matériel to enemy military units throughout Indo-

Continued on Page 15, Column 1

U.S. Officials in Saigon Reduce Their Hopes in Cambodia Drive

Red Leaders Elude Sweep

By TERENCE SMITH

Special to The New York Times

SAIGON, South Vietnam, May 4—Senior United States military and civilian officials here are beginning to scale down their definitions of success for the four-day-old American-South Vietnamese sweep into the Fishhook area of Cambodia.

One of their preliminary conclusions is that the success or failure of the sweep will have to be measured in terms of supplies captured and facilities destroyed, since the top enemy command and the vast majority of the 7,000 Communist soldiers who were believed to have been in the area appear to have fled.

Another preliminary conclusion is that additional forays into other parts of eastern Cambodia are virtually inevitable if lasting damage is to be inflicted on the North Vietnamese supply system. Strikes into eastern Laos, the officials say, are not to be ruled out.

The officials consider that substantial withdrawals of United States combat troops from Vietnam will almost certainly have to be deferred to

Continued on Page 16, Column 3

Big Base Area Discovered

Special to The New York Times

LANDING ZONE NORTH ONE, Cambodia, May 4—Soldiers from this northernmost American outpost in the drive against enemy sanctuaries in Cambodia today reached the site of what is believed to be the largest North Vietnamese base area discovered in the operation, which began last Friday.

The base area, referred to on tactical maps as "The City," is situated in rolling hills and jungles near the northwestern tip of Binhlong Province of South Vietnam. The area is about two miles south of this outpost, which was hastily set up yesterday as a blocking position 20 miles north of where American tanks first plunged into Cambodia along the southern edge of the Fishhook area.

[As the American soldiers advanced, North Vietnamese and Vietcong troops increased their pressure against Pnompenh by cutting the Pnompenh-Saigon highway 29 miles from the Cambodian capital. Page 16.]

A company of soldiers from this base camp was waiting tonight for reinforcements and

Continued on Page 16, Column 3

KOSYGIN ATTACKS NIXON FOR MOVING G.I.'S TO CAMBODIA

He Tells News Conference Action Raises Doubts on Bids for Negotiations

WARNS ON ARMS PARLEY

China Pledges Support to Indochinese People — U.S. in New Drive

Excerpts from Kosygin's text and Q. and A., Page 2.

By BERNARD GWERTZMAN

Special to The New York Times

MOSCOW, May 4—Premier Aleksei N. Kosygin today assailed President Nixon for having sent American forces into Cambodia. He warned that the action might lead to a "further complication" in the international scene and a worsening of Soviet-American relations.

[Communist China also denounced the United States on Cambodia and pledged support to the people of Indochina in their "patriotic struggle" against American forces. Page 3.]

[The Associated Press reported that thousands of American and South Vietnamese troops launched a new offensive into northeast Cambodia Tuesday, according to an announcement by the United States command The command said the attack was launched from a base 50 miles west of Pleiku, in the Central Highlands, near the Laotian border.]

Reading from a statement at the start of his first news conference in the Soviet Union in more than five years in office, Mr. Kosygin said the Cambodia intervention raised doubts about Mr. Nixon's sincerity in seeking an "era of negotiation."

He Sees Contradictions

"Is it possible to speak seriously," Mr. Kosygin said, "about the desire of the United States President for fruitful negotiations to solve pressing international problems while the United States is grossly flouting the Geneva Agreements of 1954 and 1962 to which it is a party, and undertaking one new act after another undermining the foundations of international security?

"What is the value of international agreements which the United States is or intends to be a party to if it so unceremoniously violates its obligations? It is impossible not to give serious thoughts to the fact that President Nixon's practical steps in the field of foreign policy are fundamentally at variance with those declarations and assurances that he repeatedly made both before assuming the Presidency and when he was already in the White House."

Attack Shocks Envoys

Western diplomats, who had expected a Soviet Government statement against the Cambodian action, were surprised that it was delivered by Mr. Kosygin in person, and were shocked by the personal attack on Mr. Nixon. Although Mr. Kosygin spoke in calm tones, the diplomats were taken aback by his characterization of President Nixon as a man whose words could not be trusted.

This seemed to indicate to the diplomats that a violent campaign would be started to enlist world opinion against Mr. Nixon.

Although the news conference was called to discuss Cambodia, in answer to a question on the Middle East, Mr. Kosygin said that Soviet military advisers were attached to the armed forces of the United Arab Republic to combat Israeli "aggression" and had certain

Continued on Page 3, Column 1

NEWS INDEX

"All the News That's Fit to Print"

The New York Times

LATE CITY EDITION

Weather: Sunny, cool today; clear, cool tonight. Fair, mild tomorrow. Temp. range: today 60-48; Monday 66-52. Full U.S. report on Page 85.

VOL. CXX..No. 41,156 NEW YORK, TUESDAY, SEPTEMBER 29, 1970 15 CENTS

NASSER DIES OF HEART ATTACK; BLOW TO PEACE EFFORTS SEEN; NIXON CANCELS FLEET EXERCISE

United Press International

VATICAN CITY: President Nixon with Pope Paul VI during special audience yesterday. Later, he flew by helicopter to U.S.S. Saratoga, with Sixth Fleet in the Mediterranean.

A GESTURE BY U.S.

President Terms Loss Tragic—He Joins Fleet Off Italy

By Reuters

ABOARD U.S.S. SARATOGA, in the Mediterranean, Tuesday, Sept. 29—President Nixon last night ordered cancellation of today's exercises of the United States Sixth Fleet in the Mediterranean because of the death of President Gamal Abdel Nasser of Egypt.

The President, who arrived aboard this aircraft carrier last night, had planned to watch a demonstration of Sixth Fleet firepower, including the launching and recovery of aircraft.

Officials said: "Upon hearing of the death of President Nasser, the President ordered the cancellation of the firepower demonstrations, which were to be held in conjunction with his visit to the Sixth Fleet."

They said that Mr. Nixon's conferences with Sixth Fleet commanders aboard the flagship Springfield would go on as scheduled.

The President flew to this carrier off the coast of Italy by helicopter after a day in which he had conferred in Rome with the President and the Premier of Italy and with Pope Paul VI.

'Tragic Loss'

The President in a statement said that the death of President Nasser was a tragic loss of an outstanding Arab leader.

"I was shocked to hear of the sudden death of President Nasser," Mr. Nixon said. "The world has lost an outstanding leader who tirelessly and devotedly served the causes of his countrymen and the Arab world.

"This tragic loss requires that all nations, and particularly those in the Middle East, renew their efforts to calm passions, reach for mutual understanding and build lasting peace.

"On behalf of the American people I extended deep sympathy to his family and to his people."

Stresses Role of Fleet

Earlier Mr. Nixon had told the men of the Saratoga that never had American military and diplomatic power been used more effectively than in the latest Middle East crisis.

Chatting with sailors who greeted his helicopter on the flight deck, Mr. Nixon spoke of "a hard two or three weeks," which he said had been capped by success. He referred to the Jordanian truce and recovery of the hostages from the hijacked airliners.

"The fact that we were successful is the fact that you were there," he told the sailors. He mentioned their

Continued on Page 19, Column 1

United Press International

President Gamal Abdel Nasser bidding good-by to King Hussein of Jordan after meeting in Cairo yesterday. From ceremony, he returned home where he died of heart attack.

ARAB-WORLD HERO

Vice President Sadat Takes Over as the Interim Leader

Obituary article will be found on Page 16.

By RAYMOND H. ANDERSON

Special to The New York Times

CAIRO, Tuesday, Sept. 29—President Gamal Abdel Nasser, leader of Egypt for 18 years and hero of much of the Arab world, died here yesterday.

The Government radio said the 52-year-old President was the victim of a heart attack.

The death was announced on Cairo's television and radio stations shortly before 11 P.M. by Vice President Anwar Sadat. An hour earlier, regular programs on television and radio were abruptly suspended and replaced with chanting of verses from the Koran. Official mourning was proclaimed for 40 days.

The President suffered the heart attack at 3 P.M. and died three hours later.

No obvious successor to Mr. Nasser was in sight, and no Egyptian seemed in a mood tonight to speculate about the matter.

Funeral Will Be Thursday

Vice President Sadat took over as interim ruler. He reported that emergency meetings had been held by the higher executive committee of the Arab Socialist Union, the political organization created by Mr. Nasser, and the Council of Ministers.

President Nasser's funeral will be held Thursday.

The impact of Mr. Nasser's death will be felt throughout the Arab world. Despite controversies and rivalries during his long years of power, he was the strongest figure of leadership among the Arabs.

Since the battlefield defeat of three Arab armies by Israel in June, 1967, Mr. Nasser was the leader who rallied the Arabs to rebuild their forces for a war of liberation if other means to recover the lands failed.

Favored Political Solution

But he repeatedly emphasized that he favored a political solution of the conflict with Israel if one could be achieved.

Although Mr. Nasser gained a reputation in his early years in power as a fire-breathing radical, in recent years he had become a force for moderation and pragmatism.

Even on the emotional issue of Israel, he was able to swing much of the Arab world behind his acceptance in July of a United States initiative for a cease-fire and he revived efforts for a negotiated settlement. The outlook for pursuing

Continued on Page 17, Column 1

50,000 FLEE BLAZE IN SAN DIEGO AREA

Brush Fire, 30 Miles Long, Is California's Biggest Yet —5 Die in Copter Crash

By United Press International

LOS ANGELES, Sept. 28—The largest brush fire in California history raged today through mountain canyons near the Mexican border, driving thousands of persons from their homes as the flames advanced.

In the San Gabriel Mountains to the north, a helicopter being used by the United States Forest Service to fight another fire crashed late today, killing the five persons aboard.

More than 50,000 persons were evacuated from small communities in San Diego County. The 200-acre fire there erupted in the Cleveland National Forest on Saturday when a falling tree severed a power line. At least 250 structures have been destroyed.

Decreasing winds tonight and a forecast of scattered showers in mountain areas raised hopes that the blaze could be contained tomorrow.

Arson Arrests Made

The enormous blaze, 30 miles from tip to tip, eclipsed in size the Matailaja fire of 1930, which burned 125,000 acres in Kern and Los Angeles Counties.

"We've barely kept up with the situation," said Arlen B. Cartwright of the State Division of Forestry. "The problem seems to come from the fact that fire nuts run around and see flames and smoke and this makes them want to set more fires—which they do."

Arson was suspected in two other major blazes in San Diego County, and five arrests were made in Los Angeles County.

More than 5,000 men worked 36-hour shifts on the fire lines and the neighboring county of San Bernardino was stripped of all but five of its fire engines.

Continued on Page 10, Column 2

Intrepid Wins Series, 4-1, And Keeps America's Cup

By STEVE CADY

Special to The New York Times

NEWPORT, R.I., Sept. 28—The longest series in 100 years of America's Cup challenges came to a desperately dramatic close today with Intrepid completing a 4-1 conquest of Gretel II.

Once again, the defender of yachting's most famous prize had to fight off almost constant pressure by the chunky Australian challenger.

Until a wind shift put Intrepid in clover starting the final leg of the 24.3-mile race, the action had been about as close as a boat race can produce. The cynics say watching two yachts is like watching grass grow, but the grass was on fire again today, as it was so often during this controversial series.

Stage Set for Upset

When Gretel II closed to within two boat lengths at the fifth mark, the stage was set for another upset of the kind the Australian sloop brought off last Thursday. Then the wind shifted from north to east, Intrepid hit it on the right tack and the suspense evaporated.

With the final windward leg turned into a race, the redesigned 1967 defender opened up and came home safely, 1 minute 44 seconds ahead.

As Intrepid swept majestically across the line about 250 yards ahead of her dangerous rival, the familiar dream of another successful Cup defense began unfolding. Horns, whistles and sirens aboard some 150 spectator boats and Coast Guard patrol vessels cut loose with a noisy salute to the American yacht—the second ever to defend the Cup twice.

A Triumphant Allusion

Bill Ficker, the 42-year-old Californian with the bald head and the bold starting-line maneuvers, shook hands with his young crew. They, in turn, hoisted a "Ficker Is Quicker" flag to the top of Intrepid's mast, a triumphant allusion to the tactical swiftness of their skipper.

In today's race, Ficker and his young stalwarts had to be quicker. Jim Hardy gave Gretel II a slight lead at the start but Ficker took it away early on the opening windward leg. He spent the rest of a cold, overcast afternoon desperately keeping the Aussies from breaking through in the fluky

Continued on Page 53, Column 1

U.S. Officials See Period Of Instability in Mideast

By TERENCE SMITH

Special to The New York Times

WASHINGTON, Sept. 28—United States officials, startled by the death of Gamal Abdel Nasser, tended to view it today as a blow to peace-making efforts in the Middle East.

A ranking State Department official described the Egyptian President's death as a "critical loss at a decisive moment in history."

The immediate reaction of officials here was that it would bring a period of instability in the Arab world and would therefore reduce the already-thin prospects for negotiating an early resolution of the Arab-Israeli dispute.

[In Moscow, Western diplomats expected the Soviet leaders to assure the United Arab Republic that President Nasser's death would not affect Soviet support for the Arab cause. Page 17.]

An hour before the Cairo radio announcement, a cable from Donald C. Bergus, the senior United States representative in Cairo, reported a rumor that the Egyptian leader was critically ill or perhaps dead. The message was being decoded as the public announcement came.

Six hours earlier Rodger P. Davies, the Acting Assistant Secretary of State for Near Eastern and South Asian Affairs, had told a closed session of the House Foreign Affairs Committee that the Nixon Administration was "leaning toward optimism" about the prospects of getting the United States-sponsored peace initiative in the Middle East back on the track.

The Senate was informed of the news by Senator John C. Stennis, Democrat of Mississippi, who interrupted a debate on election reform. He described Mr. Nasser, the leader in Cairo since 1952, as "superior to most anyone who might have been in power."

"I hope his death does not mean upheaval and turmoil in

Continued on Page 19, Column 1

THE ARAB WORLD IS GRIEF-STRICKEN

Moslems Fire Rifles Into Air as Sign of Mourning —Koran Read on Radio

By JOHN L. HESS

Special to The New York Times

BEIRUT, Lebanon, Sept. 28—The Arab world went into mourning tonight over the loss of its major international figure. Arab distress was heightened by the fear that instability would increase in the area and diminish the already slender prospect of peace.

Television stations went off the air and radio programs were replaced by chants and readings from the Koran. In Beirut, Moslems fired thousands of shots into the air as a sign of emotion for the loss of Gamal Abdel Nasser. Men walked in the streets in impromptu procession declaiming "Allah Akbar!"—"God is great."

Security forces raced to thwart rioting of the kind that followed President Nasser's offer of resignation after the six-day war of June, 1967.

Youths started bonfires of automobile tires and a crowd began collecting outside the United States Embassy.

[A senior Cabinet minister in Israel said that the Israelis now appeared to face an indefinite stalemate on peace negotiations. Page 18.]

Observers here said that President Nasser was the only Arab

Continued on Page 17, Column 7

John Dos Passos Is Dead at 74; Acclaimed for 'U.S.A.' Trilogy

Special to The New York Times

BALTIMORE, Sept. 28—John Dos Passos, the novelist of the post-World War I generation who wrote more than 30 books, including the trilogy "U.S.A.," died today in his apartment.

Mr. Dos Passos, who was 74 years old, had been troubled by a heart ailment in recent years and was released only Saturday from Good Samaritan Hospital. When not away on his extensive travels, he divided his time between his apartment here and a home in Westmoreland, Va.

Mr. Dos Passos is survived by his widow, the former Elizabeth Hamlin Holdridge; their daughter, Lucy, and a stepson, Christopher Holdridge.

A funeral service will be held Thursday at 10 A.M. at the William Cook-Brooks Funeral Home in the nearby town of Towson, Md.

Gil Friedberg-Pix

John Dos Passos

Fame From Early Books

By ALDEN WHITMAN

The life and writings of John Dos Passos were marked by a progression from left to right. "Every day I become more Red," he said in his youth. "My one ambition is to be able to sing 'The Internationale.'" But in middle and old age, he turned against his former ideas, berating liberals, Socialists and Communists with zeal. The one-time writer for The New Masses became a contributor to The National Review; the friend of Ernest Hemingway became that of William F. Buckley Jr.; and the supporter of William Z. Foster turned into the backer of Barry Goldwater.

His novels, too, marched rightward. The trilogy "U.S.A.," completed in 1936 and generally recognized as one of the hinges of modern fiction, was a painstakingly detailed and angry portrait of industrial America between 1898 and 1929. It concluded with the heroine's joining the Communist party in revulsion over what she believed were the injustices of the Sacco-Vanzetti case.

His subsequent trilogy, "District of Columbia," completed in 1949, acerbically chronicled what the author clearly viewed as the failure of the New Deal,

Continued on Page 47, Column 1

Malpractice Suits Reported Soaring

By LAWRENCE K. ALTMAN

Witnesses at a State Senate public hearing testified here yesterday that a steep rise in medical malpractice suits was forcing physicians to practice "defensive medicine," shirk hazardous modes of treatment that could be of benefit to patients, and pass along the costs of sky-rocketing insurance premiums to patients.

"One physician of every six has been sued for malpractice," State Senator Norman F. Lent told the hearing. And more than 10,000 Americans will initiate medical malpractice suits this year, Senator Lent, who is chairman of the Senate Committee on Health, added.

Because some insurance companies find medical malpractice insurance unprofitable, wit-

Continued on Page 32, Column 1

Anti-Arab Jet Plot Laid to Seized Pair

By MORRIS KAPLAN

An Israeli Army veteran and his wife, accused of trying to board a London-bound plane here with a live hand grenade and four loaded guns hidden in their clothing, were reported yesterday to have planned to hijack an Arab airliner and take it to Israel.

Law - enforcement sources said that the couple reportedly had planned to board a United Arab Airlines plane bound for Cairo at the London airport and divert the flight to Israel "in retaliation" for a recent attempted hijacking of an El Al airliner in London.

The sources said that the veteran, Avraham Hershkovitz, had worked as a "manager" here for the Jewish Defense

Continued on Page 12, Column 3

Arab Truce Observers Arrive In Generally Peaceful Amman

By ERIC PACE

Special to The New York Times

AMMAN, Jordan, Sept. 28—One hundred foreign Arab officers arrived here today to serve on the peace-keeping observer teams that will be deployed in Amman under the agreement reached yesterday in Cairo to end hostilities between the Jordanian Government and the Palestinian commandos.

The cease-fire instituted last Friday after nine days of civil

Text of Cairo agreement is printed on Page 18.

war seemed generally effective this morning. There were no fires along the capital's skyline, although a few bursts of firing resounded in the center of Amman and on Jebel Luweibida and Jebel Amman, two of the city's seven hills.

Western diplomats also reported that shelling or shooting was continuing in part of the Palestinians' Ashrafiyeh quarter, where many of the airline hostages had been held.

There was no sign that either the army or the commandos had abandoned their positions in Amman, as the Cairo agreement called for. The guerrillas are entrenched in a populous area around the Hussein Mosque at the heart of the city, where gunfire was occasionally heard during the day.

Despite a further provision of the Cairo agreement for a release of detainees, scores were still visible this morning at the army prison camp on the way to the airport. As their women peered in through the barbed-wire fence, they were seated in orderly rows, apparently being indoctrinated by their Jordanian Army captors.

The army appeared yesterday to be trying to finish its clean-up of Ashrafiyeh, once a commando stronghold. Aside from that, no wide-scale military operations were known to be under way. The general calm this morning followed radio broadcasts of the 14-point agreement signed by King Hussein

Continued on Page 18, Column 5

Fourth Group of Hostages Here After Seeing President in Rome

By ROBERT D. McFADDEN

Thirty - three travel - weary Americans, whose ordinary lives became the focus of international concern during three harrowing weeks while they were hostages in Jordan, arrived at Kennedy International Airport last night and were met by loved ones, friends and a clamoring throng of newsmen.

The passengers—26 men, 6 women and an infant—were the fourth group of Americans brought home safely from an ordeal that began with multiple hijackings Sept. 6. All but two of the 33 were released in Amman over the weekend and were flown home through Nicosia, Cyprus, and Rome.

Their faces were haggard but smiling and their clothes rumpled after a 12-hour flight from Rome, where they met briefly with President Nixon in the morning. They stepped off a chartered flight at the Trans World Airlines terminal shortly after 6 P.M. They were ushered quickly through Customs and led into a private room for a reunion with 175 relatives.

Nearly 1,000 friends greeted them in the corridors and public waiting rooms as they emerged.

Six Americans are still being held of the original group on three hijacked planes. They are someplace in Jordan.

Contrary to the confused receptions at three previous returning flights, passengers who were reluctant to talk were not besieged by newsmen thrusting cameras and microphones into

Continued on Page 18, Column 2

NEWS INDEX

"All the News That's Fit to Print"

The New York Times

LATE CITY EDITION

Weather: Partly sunny, mild today; fair tonight. Cloudy, mild tomorrow. Temp. range: today 49-35; Friday 40-26. Full U.S. report on Page 58.

VOL. CXX . . No. 41,286

NEW YORK, SATURDAY, FEBRUARY 6, 1971

15 CENTS

2 ASTRONAUTS WALK AND WORK FOR HOURS ON MOON'S SURFACE

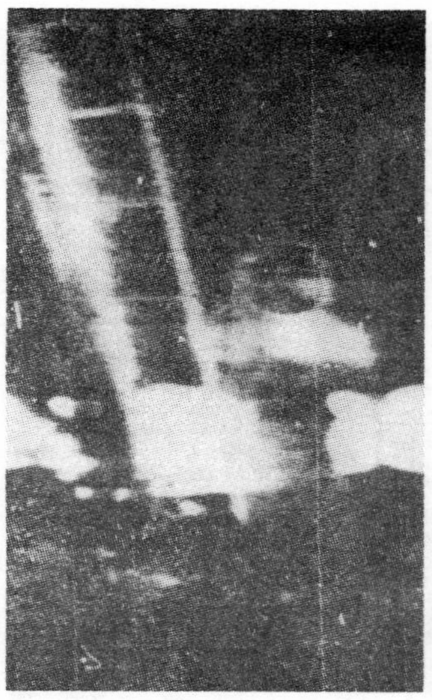

MAN ON MOON: Capt. Alan B. Shepard Jr. steps off module ladder onto lunar surface.

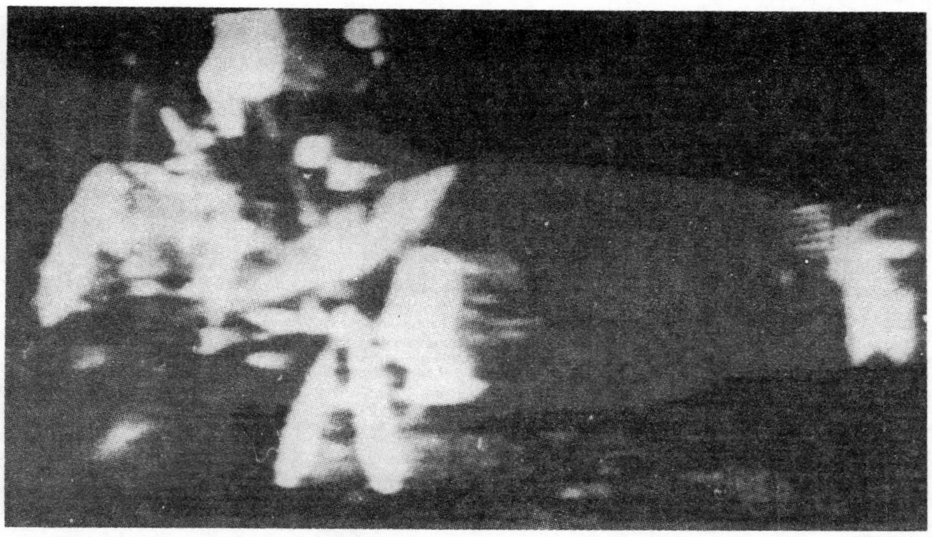

C.B.S. News

FOR THE RECORD: Captain Shepard, right, stands by the U.S. flag as Comdr. Edgar D. Mitchell snaps his picture. A TV camera transmitted the scene. At left, behind Commander Mitchell, are an umbrella-like communications antenna and, rear, the module.

2D WALK IS BEGUN

Hike to Crater Planned —Men Are to Rejoin Mother Ship Today

By JOHN NOBLE WILFORD

Special to The New York Times

HOUSTON, Saturday, Feb. 6—Two American astronauts walked the gentle slopes of Fra Mauro yesterday, setting up instruments, collecting rocks and probing subsurface reaches in search of clues to the moon's earliest history.

While earthbound scientists eagerly watched their every televised step, Capt. Alan B. Shepard Jr. and Comdr. Edgar D. Mitchell of the Navy, the Apollo 14 explorers, spent more than four and one-half hours outside their landing craft, Antares.

Shortly before 3:30 A.M. today, the men began their second moon exploration.

The 47-year-old Captain Shepard opened the hatch at 9:49 A.M. Eastern standard time yesterday and stepped out on the "porch" at the top of the ladder.

The hatch remained open for four hours and 40 minutes, until 2:29 P.M.

"It certainly is a stark place here at Fra Mauro," he remarked, looking out at the undulating hills and ridges, the gray and brown soil, the distant craters and the black sky above.

Nuclear-Powered Station

During the moon walk, Captain Shepard and Commander Mitchell established a nuclear-powered scientific station to record moonquakes, measure electrically charged particles and detect the composition and energies of solar wind. The first signals from the seismometers were of the astronauts' own footsteps.

The two men also "thumped" the ancient surface with small explosive charges that sent vibrations to depths of 70 feet for indications of the rubble-like structure below the surface. In addition, the astronauts gathered soil and rocks, two of which were as big as footballs.

It was the first of the two scheduled moon excursions by the two astronauts, who landed early yesterday in the Fra Mauro highlands for a planned 33½-hour visit.

Their explorations are considered the most intensive and ambitious made thus far on the moon. Scientists are especially interested in Fra Mauro because it may have rocks as old as the solar system itself.

Men Awaken Early

The second moon walk had originally been scheduled for 5:30 this morning, but the two astronauts awoke from a nap sooner than expected and received permission to begin their walk of up to five hours.

"We're up and running this morning," Commander Shepard reported at 12:23. "The shape of the crew is excellent."

A hike out to a boulder-rimmed crater about 2,000 feet from Antares was planned.

After the second walk, the astronauts are to fire the ascent engine of Antares at 1:47 P.M. to leave the moon and rejoin the command ship, Kitty Hawk.

Maj. Stuart A. Roosa of the Air Force, the third crew member, is piloting Kitty Hawk in a 70-mile-high lunar orbit.

Fra Mauro lies near the lunar equator at the eastern edge of the Ocean of Storms.

Continued on Page 12, Column 1

U.S. OFFICIALS FEEL NIXON HAS DECIDED ON STRIKE IN LAOS

Timing of South Vietnamese Drive Is Said to Depend on Pace of Build-up

By TERENCE SMITH

Special to The New York Times

WASHINGTON, Feb. 5—Strong indications emerged here today that the Nixon Administration had decided to go ahead with a strike by South Vietnamese troops against enemy supply lines in southern Laos.

The Administration's official spokesmen continued, for the seventh consecutive day, to refuse any public comment on the possibility of such a strike, but officials not directly concerned with the planning said they believed the White House had decided within the last 48 hours to go ahead.

Roads and Bridges Rebuilt

The timing of the strike, the officials said, would depend upon how quickly the nearly 30,000 allied soldiers massed along the Laotian border could complete "stage one" of the new operation, called Dewey Canyon II.

In the initial stage, which began early last Saturday, the troops have swept westward across the northernmost tip of South Vietnam, scouring the countryside for enemy troops, rebuilding roads and bridges and reoccupying long-deserted allied outposts such as Khesanh and Langvei.

According to reports from the field, this work was still under way today. [Page 4.]

Army engineers were working around the clock to rehabilitate the airstrip at Khesanh and strengthen the bunkers that 6,000 American Marines occupied during a 77-day siege at the outpost three years ago.

Secure Base Sought

Little enemy resistance has been encountered in the first stage of the operation, despite intelligence reports that up to nine regiments of North Vietnamese regulars were in the rugged mountains along the border.

According to a White House source, the operation was conceived as a two-stage project, with the final decision to go into Laos hinging, among other considerations, on the amount of fighting encountered in the first stage.

The military planners reportedly considered it necessary to establish a secure base in the northwestern corner of South Vietnam before deciding whether to begin the second stage of the operation.

At least one intelligence report indicated that American

Continued on Page 5, Column 1

A Laotian General Cool to Bigger War

By HENRY KAMM

Special to The New York Times

DONG HENE, Laos, Feb. 5—The commander of Laotian combat troops in the center of the panhandle of Laos said at his beleaguered forward command post today that the situation was critical and he did not expect to be able to hold out under mounting North Vietnamese pressure.

But the officer, Brig. Gen. Nouphet Deoheueng, said nobody had told him that less than 100 miles eastward in the northwest corner of South Vietnam, a large force of American and South Vietnamese troops was driving the enemy in his direction. His meagerly equipped, ragtag forces have received no reinforcements from the Laotian Government

Continued on Page 6, Column 4

JURY CALLS POLICE IN GAMING INQUIRY

Looks Into Charges That 30 Were Involved With Major Gambler in Brooklyn

By DAVID BURNHAM

A Brooklyn grand jury is investigating reports of corrupt links among more than 30 policemen and former policemen, a judge and a gambling empire allegedly operated by a Brooklyn figure with a long criminal record.

The investigation is based on evidence collected during the last year by the office of District Attorney Eugene Gold and the internal affairs division of the Police Department.

More than 50 known gamblers, policemen and former policemen already have been subpoenaed. One of the first subpoenas was handed on Thursday to Thomas Marino, 72 years old, reportedly the operator of the gambling ring.

In another development involving possible corruption, the State Supreme Court yesterday upheld the legality of the subpoenas for 14 policemen, in-

Continued on Page 14, Column 4

Court Upholds Patrolmen On Retroactive Pay Claim

By DAMON STETSON

State Supreme Court Justice Irving H. Saypol ruled yesterday that the Patrolmen's Benevolent Association had a valid contract with the city requiring a $100-a-month retroactive pay increase for 27,000 patrolmen.

The contract that the judge ruled "enforceable" ran from Oct. 1, 1968, to Dec. 31, 1970, so that the total of retroactive pay that the patrolmen claim is $2,700 each for the 27-month period.

The increase is based on a pay-parity provision in the contract saying the patrolmen should be paid at a rate of $3 for every $3.50 paid to sergeants.

Issue Not Settled

The issue, which has been in the courts for nearly a year and spurred a strike by the policemen last month, is still not settled, however.

A spokesman for Mayor Lindsay said that on advice of the Corporation Counsel, J. Lee Rankin, the city was going to appeal Judge Saypol's decision. The Mayor, the spokesman said, has asked the Corporation Counsel to expedite the appeal on the decision, which could cost the city hundreds of millions of dollars.

The appeal to the Appellate Division and then, perhaps, to the State Court of Appeals could take weeks or even months, lawyers said.

Edward J. Kiernan, president of the P.B.A., said the decision of Justice Saypol "reaffirmed my confidence in the court system."

Dissidents Noted

In an oblique reference to dissident members of the association who led last month's strike of policemen without P.B.A. sanction, Mr. Kiernan said the ruling should restore the faith of all policemen in the court structure. He recalled that the P.B.A. leadership had urged the strikers to get back on the job and trust the courts to deal fairly with the patrolmen's suit.

The policemen struck after the Court of Appeals ruled last month that a trial must be held to determine the validity of the contract.

John J. Loflin Jr., who represented the city in the trial be-

Continued on Page 14, Column 4

DEFECTIVE SWITCH POSED A PROBLEM

A Short Circuit That Could Have Aborted the Landing Required New Program

By RICHARD WITKIN

It took some ingenious rewriting of a computer program and about 60 rapid-fire punches on a cockpit keyboard to clear the way for the Apollo lunar landing yesterday.

The difficulty, described by officials as a "very serious" problem, was apparently in a cockpit switch that was producing intermittent short circuits.

The two astronauts aboard the lunar module were never endangered by the trouble. But it threatened to delay the landing attempt for one, two, or even three more lunar orbits. And there was an outside chance it could have canceled the landing attempt altogether.

Other Problems Cited

There were other technical aberrations that cropped up during the descent from lunar orbit to the Fra Mauro landing site, notably the distressing delay in proper functioning of the landing radar. However, it was the misbehaving switch that caused the day's biggest commotion.

The difficulty turned up at 1:30 a.m., less than three hours before the landing ship Antares was to start its final descent to the moon.

At the space agency's control center in Houston, engineers monitoring the operations of every spacecraft system saw a "spurious" number turn up on a console. The num-

Continued on Page 12, Column 2

Direct From Moon

Following are conversations between flight controllers in Houston and Capt. Alan B. Shepard Jr. and Comdr. Edgar D. Mitchell of the Navy, as recorded by The New York Times. The conversations occurred during the first moon walk yesterday, when the astronauts left the lunar lander, Antares.

ANTARES (9:49 A.M.)—Forward hatch the rest of the way open. O.K., forward hatch is open.

MITCHELL—I'll get your antenna as you go out.

SHEPARD — All righty, starting out the door.

HOUSTON—Shortly Shepard will be throwing the equipment conveyor belt.

MITCHELL — While he's working on the LEC [lunar equipment conveyor] let me comment that it certainly is a stark place here. I think it's made all the more stark by the fact that the sky is completely black.

SHEPARD—Starting down the ladder.

HOUSTON—Roger . . . O.K., Al, beautiful. We see you coming down the ladder now. It looks like you're about on the bottom step—and on the surface. How's that for an old man?

SHEPARD — O.K., you're right. Al is on the surface. It's been a long way, but we're here. Now I can see the reason we have a tilt is we landed on a slope. The landing gear struts appear to be about evenly depressed. Moving around, getting familiar with the surface. The surface in which the forward footpad landed is extremely soft. As a matter of fact, it's in a small depression. The soil is so soft that it comes up all the way to the top of the footpads.

HOUSTON—Roger.

SHEPARD—O. K., we'll move on over and take a look at Fra Mauro. Take a look at Cone Crater, which is right where it should be and is a very impressive sight.

HOUSTON—Antares, this is Houston. You are go for two-man EVA [extravehicular activity]. Over.

MITCHELL—Roger, Houston. Thank you.

SHEPARD—Continuing, we can see the boulders on the rim. It looks as though we have a good traverse route

Continued on Page 12, Column 6

WARNING!
NO U.S. PERSONNEL
BEYOND THIS POINT

Associated Press

NEAR THE LAOTIAN BORDER: G.I.'s posting a warning near Langvei in South Vietnam. U.S. ground forces are forbidden to cross into Laos, about 200 yards beyond the sign.

City Seeks New Unit To Finance Housing

By STEVEN R. WEISMAN

Mayor Lindsay yesterday announced a bipartisan drive to seek the creation of a city housing finance agency that would float $700 million in bonds to provide mortgages for 25,000 new and rehabilitated apartments here in two years.

The push to gain approval of the measure by the Legislature, Mr. Lindsay said, will be "the city's No. 1 state legislative priority."

Under the bill, bonds of the proposed New York City Housing Development Corporation would be backed up by the "moral obligation," rather than the full faith and credit, of New York City. In this manner, the corporation could be created without changing the city's debt limit, which is imposed by the

Continued on Page 16, Column 5

Unemployment Rate Down For First Time in 7 Months

By EILEEN SHANAHAN

Special to The New York Times

WASHINGTON, Feb. 5—The unemployment rate dropped somewhat in January, its first decline in seven months, the Labor Department reported today.

The actual number of people out of work rose, however, as it generally does in January, to 5.4 million, the largest number in 10 years.

The unemployment rate is adjusted to eliminate the effects of normal seasonal changes, a procedure designed to make the underlying trend clearer.

Secretary of Labor James D. Hodgson attributed "great significance" to the downturn in the unemployment rate in January, coupled with other developments in the labor market.

On the other hand, Harold Goldstein, the Assistant Commissioner of Labor Statistics, described the change as "marginally significant." Mr. Goldstein is a career civil servant, and the Bureau of Labor Statistics, where he works, is a traditionally nonpartisan division of the Labor Department.

The January statistics did present a somewhat confusing picture, partly because a routine revision in some of the statistics for last year changed the basis for comparison.

The unemployment rate for December, originally reported as 6 per cent, was revised upward to 6.2 per cent.

On the revised basis, the January rate was 6 per cent, a drop of two-tenths of a percentage point from the December level.

As it turned out, a drop of two-tenths of a percentage point would have been recorded if the revisions had not taken place. On the unrevised basis, the January rate would have been 5.8 per cent.

These revisions, which are made annually, incorporate the most up-to-date information on the adjustments in the raw figures that are needed to eliminate purely seasonal influences. The idea of revising the figures and the process by which they are revised are accepted as valid by all economists and statisticians in the field.

The differing interpretations of the figures made by Secretary Hodgson and Mr. Goldstein were unrelated to the revision in the seasonal adjustments, although some seasonal developments figured in the

Continued on Page 22, Column 1

NEWS INDEX

"All the News That's Fit to Print"

The New York Times

LATE CITY EDITION

Weather: Chance of showers today, tonight. Partly sunny tomorrow. Temp. range: today 74-94; Wed. 72-91. Temp. Hum. Index yesterday 82. Full U.S. report on Page 94.

VOL. CXX...No. 41,431

NEW YORK, THURSDAY, JULY 1, 1971

15 CENTS

SUPREME COURT, 6-3, UPHOLDS NEWSPAPERS ON PUBLICATION OF THE PENTAGON REPORT; TIMES RESUMES ITS SERIES, HALTED 15 DAYS

Nixon Says Turks Agree To Ban the Opium Poppy

By JOHN HERBERS

Special to The New York Times

WASHINGTON, June 30—President Nixon announced today that Turkey had agreed to eliminate within a year her production of opium poppies, which account for about two-thirds of the illegal heroin reaching the United States.

Mr. Nixon, in a brief announcement delivered in the White House press room, said that as a result of negotiations between the United States and Turkish Governments, Premier Nihat Erim had agreed to ban altogether the cultivation of opium poppies by June, 1972.

He said the joint announcement, made simultaneously in Washington and Ankara, "represents by far the most significant breakthrough that has been achieved in stopping the source of supply of heroin in our worldwide offensive against dangerous drugs."

Two weeks ago, Mr. Nixon sent a message to William J. Handley, the United States Ambassador in Turkey, saying that the time for talk had passed and the United States must have action by the Turkish Government in ending poppy cultivation.

Today, the President praised Premier Erim for "courageous, statesmanlike action" and said the United States would provide money and technical assistance in helping Turkish farmers shift to other crops.

Officials would not say how much American money would be involved, but the United States has made a $3-million commitment to Turkey on the heroin problem.

Secretary of State William P. Rogers, who helped work

Continued on Page 22, Column 1

PRESIDENT CALLS STEEL AND LABOR TO WHITE HOUSE

He Asks Both Sides to Meet With Him Tuesday Before Contract Talks Start

By PHILIP SHABECOFF

Special to The New York Times

WASHINGTON, June 30—President Nixon has called negotiators of the steel companies and steelworkers union to meet with him next Tuesday before they sit down to begin contract negotiations, a White House spokesman announced today.

It will be the first time that the President will have met with labor and management in any industry prior to nationwide contract negotiations, according to Ronald L. Ziegler, the White House press secretary.

Discussion Issues Listed

Mr. Ziegler said that the President had called the meeting to discuss general economic developments and trends in the world steel markets.

Earlier today, the chairman of the Federal Reserve Board, Arthur F. Burns, told a Congressional committee that the "first priority" should be given to a new Government move to try to moderate price and wage increases and expressed his concern over the spread of "inflationary psychology" in this country.

The Administration has repeatedly warned that excessive increases in steel wages and prices would severely retard efforts to control inflation. Hints have been dropped that import quotas that protect domestic steel from foreign competition will be eased or lifted if prices go too high.

President Nixon has been in-

Continued on Page 38, Column 1

Pentagon Papers: Study Reports Kennedy Made 'Gamble' Into a 'Broad Commitment'

By HEDRICK SMITH

The Pentagon's study of the Vietnam war concludes that President John F. Kennedy transformed the "limited-risk gamble" of the Eisenhower Administration into a "broad commitment" to prevent Communist domination of South Vietnam.

Although Mr. Kennedy resisted pressures for putting American ground-combat units into South Vietnam, the Pentagon analysts say, he took a series of actions that significantly expanded the American military and political involvement in Vietnam but nonetheless left President Lyndon B. Johnson with as bad a situation as Mr. Kennedy inherited.

"The dilemma of the U.S. involvement dating from the Kennedy era," the Pentagon study observes, was to use "only limited means to achieve excessive ends."

Moreover, according to the study, prepared in 1967-68 by Government analysts, the Kennedy tactics deepened the American involvement in Vietnam piecemeal, with each step minimizing public recognition that the American role was growing.

The expansion of that role, over three decades, is traced in the 3,000 pages of the Pentagon's study, which is accompanied by 4,000 pages of documents on the Vietnam era. Previous articles in The Times's presentation of this material have recounted President Johnson's movement to war in 1964 and 1965.

President Kennedy made his first fresh commitments to Vietnam secretly. The Pentagon study discloses that in the spring of 1961 the President ordered 400 Special Forces troops and 100 other American military advisers sent to South Vietnam. No publicity was given to either move.

Small as the numbers seem in retrospect, the Pentagon study comments that even the first such expansion "signaled a willingness to go beyond the 685-man limit on the size of the U.S. [military] mission in Saigon, which, if it were done openly, would be the first formal breach of the Geneva agreement." Under the interpretation of that agreement in effect since 1956, the United States was limited to 685 military advisers in Vietnam. Washington, while it did not sign the accord, pledged not to undermine it.

On May 11, 1961, the day on which President Kennedy decided to send the Special Forces, he also ordered the start of a campaign of clandestine warfare against North Vietnam, to be conducted by South Vietnamese agents directed and trained by the Central Intelligence Agency and some American Special Forces troops. [See text, action memorandum, May 11, 1961, Page 3.]

The President's instructions, as quoted in the documents, were, "In North Vietnam . . . [to] form networks of resistance, covert bases and teams for

Continued on Page 6, Column 1

The Times today resumes its series of articles on the Pentagon's secret study of the Vietnam war. The study was obtained through the investigative reporting of Neil Sheehan, and the articles were researched and written over three months by Mr. Sheehan and other staff members. The fourth and fifth articles, both by Hedrick Smith, are published today and form an account of decisions in the Kennedy Administration.

Three pages of documentary material covering the Kennedy policy begin on Page 3, and documents on the 1963 coup begin on Page 9. A summary of the three earlier articles, covering the Johnson Administration, appears on Page 15.

BURGER DISSENTS

First Amendment Rule Held to Block Most Prior Restraints

Decision, concurring opinions, dissents start on Page 17.

By FRED P. GRAHAM

Special to The New York Times

WASHINGTON, June 30—The Supreme Court freed The New York Times and The Washington Post today to resume immediate publication of articles based on the secret Pentagon papers on the origins of the Vietnam war.

By a vote of 6 to 3 the Court held that any attempt by the Government to block news articles prior to publication bears "a heavy burden of presumption against its constitutionality."

In a historic test of that principle — the first effort by the Government to enjoin publication on the ground of national security — the Court declared that "the Government has not met that burden."

The brief judgment was read to a hushed courtroom by Chief Justice Warren E. Burger at 2:30 P.M. at a special session called three hours before.

Old Tradition Observed

The Chief Justice was one of the dissenters, along with Associate Justices Harry A. Blackmun and John M. Harlan, but because the decision was rendered in an unsigned opinion, the Chief Justice read it in court in accordance with long-standing custom.

In New York Arthur Ochs Sulzberger, president and publisher of The Times, said at a news conference that he had "never really doubted that this day would come and that we'd win." His reaction, he said, was "complete joy and delight."

The case had been expected to produce a landmark ruling on the circumstances under which prior restraint could be imposed upon the press, but because no opinion by a single Justice commanded the support of a majority, only the unsigned decision will serve as precedent.

Uncertainty Over Outcome

Because it came on the 15th day after The Times had been restrained from publishing further articles in its series mined from the 7,000 pages of material—the first such restraint in the name of "national security" in the history of the United States—there was some uncertainty whether the press had scored a strong victory or whether a precedent for some degree of restraint had been set.

Alexander M. Bickel, the Yale law professor who had argued for The Times in the case, said in a telephone interview that the ruling placed the press in a "stronger position." He maintained that no Federal District Judge would henceforth temporarily restrain a newspaper on the Justice Department's complaint that "this is what they have printed and we don't like it" and that a direct threat of irreparable harm would have to be alleged.

However, the United States Solicitor General, Erwin N. Griswold, turned to another lawyer shortly after the Justices filed from the courtroom and remarked: "Maybe the newspapers will show a little

Continued on Page 15, Column 1

Soviet Starts an Inquiry Into 3 Astronauts' Deaths

By BERNARD GWERTZMAN

Special to The New York Times

MOSCOW, June 30—The Soviet authorities appointed a special commission tonight to investigate the deaths of their three astronauts who perished this morning when their Soyuz 11 craft was returning to earth after the longest manned space flight in history.

News of the astronauts' deaths shocked many Soviet people. And Western specialists predicted that their deaths would retard development of the Salyut space station program. The three astronauts had spent more than three weeks working and exercising aboard the Salyut craft, described as the world's first space laboratory.

[In the United States, American officials said the Soviet space disaster had probably been caused by a failure in the oxygen supply. They also said the accident should not delay United States space flights. Articles on Page 30.]

Tonight, the Soviet people seemed caught up in the human aspects of the disaster and the mystery of what caused the deaths of Lieut. Col. Georgi T. Dobrovolsky, the flight commander, Vladislav N. Volkov, the flight engineer, and Viktor I. Patsayev, the test engineer.

Were their deaths caused by the weakened state of their bodies after nearly 24 days of weightlessness? Were they

Continued on Page 30, Column 3

U.S. and Diem's Overthrow: Step by Step

The Pentagon's secret study of the Vietnam war discloses that President Kennedy knew and approved of plans for the military coup d'état that overthrew President Ngo Dinh Diem in 1963.

"Our complicity in his overthrow heightened our responsibilities and our commitment" in Vietnam, the study finds.

In August and October of 1963, the narrative recounts, the United States gave its support to a cabal of army generals bent on removing the controversial leader, whose rise to power Mr. Kennedy had backed in speeches in the middle nineteen-fifties and who had been the anchor of American policy in Vietnam for nine years.

The coup, one of the most dramatic episodes in the history of the American involvement in Vietnam, was a watershed. As the Pentagon study observes, it was a time when Washington—with the Diem regime gone—could have reconsidered its entire commitment to South Vietnam and decided to disengage.

But at least two Administration officials advocated disengagement but, according to the Pentagon study, it "was never seriously considered a policy alternative because of the assumption that an independent, non-Communist SVN was too important a strategic interest to abandon."

The effect, according to this account, was that the United States, discovering after the coup that the war against the Vietcong had been going much worse than officials previously thought, felt compelled to do more—rather than less—for Saigon. By supporting the anti-Diem coup, the analyst asserts, "the U.S. inadvertently deepened its involvement. The inadvertence is the key factor."

According to the Pentagon account of the 1963 events in Saigon, Washington did not originate the anti-Diem coup, nor did American forces intervene in any way, even to try to prevent the assassinations of Mr. Diem and his brother Ngo Dinh Nhu, who, as the chief Diem political adviser, had accumulated immense power. Popular discontent with the Diem regime focused on Mr. Nhu and his wife.

But for weeks—and with the White House informed every step of the way—the American mission in Saigon maintained secret contacts with the plotting generals through one of the Central Intelligence Agency's most experienced and versatile operatives, an Indochina veteran, Lieut. Col. Lucien Conein. The colonel, who is now in retirement, first landed in Vietnam in 1944 by parachute for the Office of Strategic Services, the wartime forerunner of the C.I.A.

So trusted by the Vietnamese generals was Colonel Conein that he was in their midst at Vietnamese General Staff headquarters as they launched the coup. Indeed, on Oct. 25, a week earlier in a cable to McGeorge Bundy, the President's special assistant for national security, Ambassador Lodge had occasion to describe Colonel Conein of the C.I.A.—referring to the agency, in code terminology, as C.A.S.—as the indispensable man:

"C.A.S. has been punctilious in carrying out my instructions. I have personally approved each meeting between General Don [one of three main plotters] and Conein who has carried out my

Continued on Page 12, Column 1

CHOU TIES U.N. SEAT TO TAIPEI'S OUSTER

Also Says Peking Must Have Permanent Council Post if It Is to Be Member

By TAKASHI OKA

Special to The New York Times

TOKYO, June 30 — Premier Chou En-lai of China said in an interview published here today that for his country to join the United Nations it was necessary not only that all membership rights be "restored," including a permanent seat on the Security Council, but that the Nationalists be ousted from the United Nations.

Mr. Chou made the comment in a meeting with Yoshikatsu Takeiri, chairman of Komeito, the Clean Government party, who is visiting Peking with eight of his followers. The Premier's comments were published today in the party newspaper Komei Shimbun as well as in other major Japanese newspapers.

'What Steps Are Necessary'

Mr. Chou's comments, which are consistent with the line Peking has taken on prospective United Nations membership, apparently weakened attempts by the United States, Japan and other interested members of the United Nations to safeguard at least a General Assembly seat for the Nationalists while admitting the Chinese Communists to the Security Council as well as the Assembly.

"What steps do you think are necessary in order to get China back into the United Nations?" Mr. Chou was asked,

Continued on Page 32, Column 4

Jim Garrison Is Arrested; U.S. Says He Took Bribes

By ROY REED

Special to The New York Times

NEW ORLEANS, June 30—District Attorney Jim Garrison was arrested by Federal agents today and charged with taking bribes to protect illegal pinball gambling in New Orleans.

The Justice Department said that the last payment, $1,000, was delivered to Mr. Garrison at his home last night in marked $50 bills. The payment, the department said, was handed to him by a once-trusted confidant who had secretly gone to work for the Government's agents.

Mr. Garrison, 50 years old, who attempted to prove a conspiracy in the 1963 assassination of President Kennedy, was taken into custody at his home. He was fingerprinted and placed under $5,000 bond by a Federal magistrate.

The Justice Department said that Mr. Garrison had taken up to $1,500 a month in bribes.

According to the Government, Mr. Garrison had received the bribes from pinball operators since 1962.

"I've never accepted a dollar in my life," the District Attorney told reporters as he walked into the French Quarter Courthouse to face the magistrate.

Mr. Garrison was one of 10 men arrested. The others in-

Continued on Page 55, Column 3

Cousin Asserts Jerome Johnson Told of Job With Italian League

By BARBARA CAMPBELL

A cousin of Jerome A. Johnson, who was shot to death at the site of a rally in Columbus Circle after allegedly firing three bullets into Joseph A. Colombo Sr., said yesterday that Johnson told him "several months ago" he was working for the Italian-American Civil Rights League as a photographer.

This was corroborated by a close friend of Johnson's, who said the 24-year-old slain man had also told him on a May 15 visit to California that he was working for the league.

About three months before the shooting, Johnson gave his cousin a telephone number where he could be reached and a check by The New York Times disclosed yesterday that the number had been recently changed. The operator said the number had been switched to a new number, that of the Italian-American League.

This latest development raised a series of questions for investigators. If Johnson was working for the league, was he known there? Was he an employe or a hanger-on, perhaps a temporary called in on occasions?

Chief of Detectives Albert A. Seedman said last night only that the telephone-number switch, if true, "certainly puts

Continued on Page 53, Column 1

THE STATES RATIFY FULL VOTE AT 18

Ohio Becomes 38th to Back the 26th Amendment

By R. W. APPLE Jr.

Special to The New York Times

WASHINGTON, June 30—The 26th Amendment to the Constitution, lowering to 18 years the minimum voting age in local and state as well as Federal elections, was ratified tonight.

Ohio became the 38th state to approve the Amendment when the state's House of Representatives, meeting in extraordinary evening session, gave its assent, 81 to 9. The Ohio Senate had approved the measure yesterday, 30 to 2.

The ratification of at least 38 states, or three-quarters of the total, is required for constitutional amendments.

An atmosphere of near-panic attended Ohio's climactic vote. The Republican Speaker of the House, Charles F. Kurfess, had planned to let a number of members, both Republicans and Democrats, speak on the issue before calling for a vote.

But after only three short speeches, the Republican floor leader, Robert E. Leavitt, interrupted to warn:

"I've just been informed that the Legislature of Oklahoma

Continued on Page 43, Column 1

Conferees Cut Military Pay Rise As Authority to Draft Runs Out

By DAVID E. ROSENBAUM

Special to The New York Times

WASHINGTON, June 30—The Nixon Administration won a major budgetary victory today in the House-Senate conference on the draft extension bill.

The conference agreement also appeared to represent a setback for supporters of an all-volunteer Army, who had sought larger pay increases than those cleared by the conferees.

The conferees accepted a figure for military pay and allowances that was more than $900-million below what the Senate and House had approved. The raises voted by the conferees would cost about $1.8-billion in the fiscal year starting tomorrow and would go into effect Oct. 1.

The figure approved by the conference was still $800-million above what President Nixon sought in his budget, but the House and Senate had passed increases of about $1.7-billion over the budget.

The Nixon Administration had argued that so large an increase would force severe and possibly dangerous reductions in other parts of the defense budget.

The Government's basic authority to draft men into the military expires at midnight tonight.

The conferees completed action on all provisions of the draft bill today except the Senate-passed amendment that calls for the withdrawal of United States troops from Indochina within nine months if prisoners of war are first

Continued on Page 29, Column 1

ACTION BY GRAVEL VEXES SENATORS

But No Disciplinary Action Against Him Is Expected

By JOHN W. FINNEY

Special to The New York Times

WASHINGTON, June 30—Many Senators privately expressed dismay, shock and chagrin today at Senator Mike Gravel's release of parts of the Pentagon's secret study of the Vietnam war. But it appeared that no disciplinary action would be taken against the Alaska Democrat.

Last night Senator Gravel tried to read the documents to the Senate in an all-night speech and, when he was blocked for lack of a quorum, proceeded to call an impromptu meeting of his Senate Public Works subcommittee. He read from the study for three and one-half hours, with his voice sometimes breaking into sobs, and tears occasionally rolling down his face.

His action incurred the displeasure of many of his colleagues, who felt that it reflected on the dignity and composure of the Senate. But in the clubby atmosphere of the Senate, there was a widespread reluctance, extending down from the leadership, to take any formal disciplinary

Continued on Page 16, Column 2

False Advertising Laid to H&R Block

By JOHN D. MORRIS

Special to The New York Times

WASHINGTON, June 30—H & R Block, Inc., which says it prepares income tax returns for eight million American annually, was accused by the Federal Trade Commission today of false advertising and illegally using confidential information supplied by customers.

The commission published similar but separate citations against H & R Block and the Beneficial Corporation, which offers income tax services on a smaller scale through a subsidiary, the Beneficial Management Corporation. In radio and television advertisements, the name

Continued on Page 37, Column 2

NEWS INDEX

"All the News That's Fit to Print"

The New York Times

LATE CITY EDITION

Weather: Variable cloudiness, mild today; fair tonight and tomorrow. Temp. range: today 70-78; Monday 71-75. Full U.S. report on Page 81.

VOL. CXX ... No. 41,506 NEW YORK, TUESDAY, SEPTEMBER 14, 1971 — 15 CENTS

9 HOSTAGES AND 28 PRISONERS DIE AS 1,000 STORM PRISON IN ATTICA; 28 RESCUED, SCORES ARE INJURED

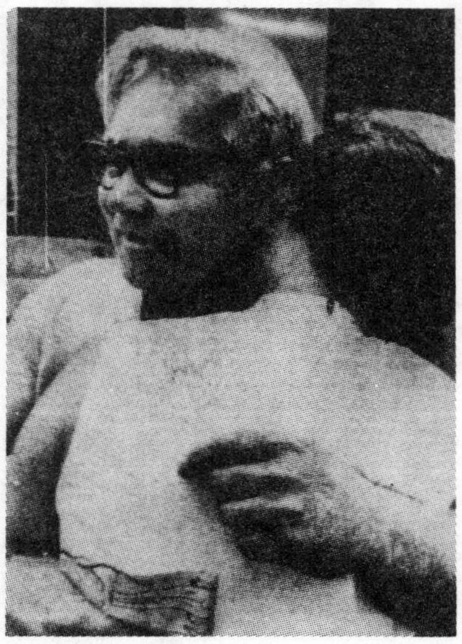

The New York Times

Elmer Huehn, released hostage, being greeted by his wife

Associated Press

Guard, who had been held, still dazed after being released

The New York Times/Michael Evans

Relatives of hostages in Attica prison after being told that at least 15 of the men being held had been set free

'LIKE A WAR ZONE'

Air and Ground Attack Follows Refusal of Convicts to Yield

By FRED FERRETTI

Special to The New York Times

ATTICA, N. Y., Sept. 13—The rebellion at the Attica Correctional Facility ended this morning in a bloody clash and mass deaths that four days of taut negotiations had sought to avert.

Thirty-seven men — 9 hostages and 28 prisoners — were killed as 1,000 state troopers, sheriff's deputies and prison guards stormed the prison under a low-flying pall of tear

Text of Oswald's statement is printed on Page 28.

gas dropped by helicopters. They retook from inmates the cellblocks they had captured last Thursday.

In this worst of recent American prison revolts, several of the hostages — prison guards and civilian workers — died when convicts slashed their throats with knives. Others were stabbed and beaten with clubs and lengths of pipe.

Most of the prisoners killed in the assault fell under the thick hail of rifle and shotgun fire laid down by the invading troopers.

Doctor Fears More Deaths

A volunteer doctor who worked among the wounded after the assault said the prison's interior was "like a war zone." Standing in front of the prison in a blood-stained white coat, he said that many more of the wounded "are likely to die."

Late today a deputy director of correction, Walter Dunbar, said that two of the hostages had been killed "before today" and that one had been stabbed and emasculated.

Of the remaining seven, five were killed instantly by the inmates and two died in the prison hospital.

Mr. Dunbar said that in addition to the 28 dead inmates, eight other convicts of the total of 2,237 were missing. Two of the dead prisoners, he said, were killed "by their own colleagues and lay in a large pool of blood in a fourth-tier cellblock."

Oswald Orders Attack

He said he considered the state's recapture of the prison an "efficient, affirmative police action."

The action was ordered with "extreme reluctance" by State Correction Commissioner Russell G. Oswald after consultation with Governor Rockefeller. It followed an ultimatum to the more than 1,000 rebellious prisoners that they release the hostages they held and return to their cells.

Most of the 28 hostages rescued by the invaders and scores of prisoners were treated for wounds and the effects

Continued on Page 28, Column 2

Associated Press

GAVE ORDER: Russell G. Oswald, State Correction Commissioner, after action.

4 Days of Attica Talks End in Failure

By TOM WICKER

Special to The New York Times

ATTICA, N. Y., Sept. 13—At 9:43:28 this morning the power went off in the small littered steward's room on the second floor of the Attica Correctional Facility's administration building.

The hands of an electric clock on the wall pointed to that second for almost two hours, while state policemen and other officers put a bloody end to a massive uprising by about 1,500 inmates —mostly black and Puerto Rican.

To the 17 men in the room, the hands marked the moment of truth—the second when the end came for four days of emotional and exhausting effort to avoid the bloodshed that every one of them feared from the beginning. For 28 of the prisoners with whom they had vainly "negotiated" and for nine of the hostages the prisoners had been holding, death had been signaled.

At 9:48 A.M., five minutes after the lights went out, armed troopers moved behind fire hoses down the littered, gasoline-smelling corridor the 17 men and their colleagues had used in a series of harrowing visits to the prisoners' stronghold in Cellblock D and its exercise yard.

Other assaulting forces came over the walls that surrounded the exercise yard. By about 11 A.M., the prison authorities said that the institution was virtually "secure," although some cell block areas remained to be finally cleared. Active resistance had ceased.

Some members of the unusual group of 17 citizen "observers," summoned by the prisoners and authorized by the state authorities to try to find a peaceful solution, had believed all along that none could be devised. Others had hoped to the last. All had drained themselves emotionally and physically, when failure put an end to their efforts and to the lives of 37 men.

Gazing out the window of the steward's room at the helmeted troopers and the drifts of gas floating across the prison grounds, two of the 17-member group, Representative Herman Badillo of New York City and this correspondent, assured each

Continued on Page 29, Column 1

ROCKEFELLER SEES A PLOT AT PRISON

'Revolutionary Tactics' Led to Uprising, He Says—Investigation Planned

By WILLIAM E. FARRELL

Governor Rockefeller said yesterday that the uprising at Attica Prison was brought on by the "revolutionary tactics of militants" and that he had ordered "a full investigation of all the factors leading to this uprising, including the role that outside forces would appear to have played."

The Governor's comments were contained in a statement issued by his office here following one of the most critical moves of his 13 years in office —his sanctioning of the decision of State Commissioner of Correction Russell G. Oswald to storm the prison.

The action taken by the state was the subject of a telephone conversation yesterday afternoon between the Governor and President Nixon in which the President expressed support for the Governor's response to the prisoner rebellion, and in particular for his refusal to grant the amnesty demand.

Spokesmen for the Governor and the President agreed on the substance of the conversa-

Continued on Page 30, Column 1

A Hostage Says Threats Left Him 'Scared Silly'

By JOSEPH LELYVELD

Special to The New York Times

ATTICA, N. Y., Sept. 13—"I laid there on the floor and knew I was going to bleed to death right there."

As he said this, the only signs that Ron Kozlowski had been one of the hostages whose throats had been slit in the first fierce instants of the assault on the rebellious prisoners here were a small two-inch bandage at the base of his neck and a visible shakiness in his knees.

"They told us, 'As soon as the first shot is fired, you white blankety-blanks have had it.' I was scared silly up there. I really was. I didn't want them to shoot."

Mr. Kozlowski, a 23-year-old accounts clerk at the prison, said he was one of a small group of hostages who were led this morning, bound and blindfolded, out of the jerrybuilt pen in the center of the prison yard where all the hostages had been held for four days. The 30 others left in the pen were also bound and blindfolded soon after State Correctional Commissioner Russell G. Oswald delivered the ultimatum to the more than 1,000 rebellious prisoners.

First, Mr. Kozlowski said, his group was taken to a pit that was doused with gasoline and told they would be burned alive

Continued on Page 29, Column 3

BUSINESS FAVORS U.S. PANEL TO RULE PAY-PRICE POLICY

Leaders Urge President to Give the Private Sector Only an Advisory Role

MEET AT WHITE HOUSE

Oppose Curb on Profits in Phase Two of Program—Nixon Offers No Plan

By ROBERT B. SEMPLE Jr.

Special to The New York Times

WASHINGTON, Sept. 13 — Spokesmen from the business community told President Nixon today that the next phase of the new economic strategy should be managed by the Federal Government, with the private sector playing essentially an advisory role.

Last Friday, union leaders who met with the President recommended the creation of a tripartite board representing labor, management and the general public to control wages and prices, without governmental interference, after the current 90-day freeze.

Confer Two Hours

This morning Mr. Nixon met for nearly two hours with 11 corporate executives and leaders of business associations in the second of a series of meetings designed to solicit ideas from various interest groups on what ought to be done to manage the economy after the current wage-price-rent freeze expires at midnight, Nov. 13.

Meanwhile, Secretary of the Treasury John B. Connally indicated that price controls in some form would be continued after the expiration of the freeze.

At today's meeting, according to the public statements of some participants and the private comments of others, most of the businessmen present told Mr. Nixon that the basic decisions on wage and price policy should remain with some kind of Government board.

They felt, however, that business, labor, agriculture and other groups should be consulted extensively before such decisions were made.

Typical Comment

It was not totally clear whether the business group thought that the private sector should have veto power over the decisions made by the Government board. But sources said that the consensus of the group was that business, labor and other groups should restrict themselves to offering suggestions and making recommendations, leaving ultimate wage-price decisions in the Government's hands.

A typical comment came from James M. Roche, chairman of General Motors, who was asked to address himself to labor's suggestion that a tripartite board draw up its own rules on what specific wages and prices should be controlled, rather

Continued on Page 26, Column 4

Common Market Agrees To Resist U.S. on Dollar

6 Finance Ministers Ask America to Devalue

By CLYDE H. FARNSWORTH

Special to The New York Times

BRUSSELS, Sept. 13—The European Common Market, in an assertive mood, temporarily buried its internal quarrels today to confront the United States with a uniform set of demands, including devaluation of the dollar, to resolve the monetary crisis.

Finance ministers of the six member countries of the trade

Text of the finance ministers' agreement is on Page 25.

bloc took the position that the United States would not get the multilateral upward revaluation of major foreign currencies that it is seeking until it agreed to eliminate its import surcharge and raise the official price of gold.

Stand Is Prepared

The six nations, which will probably be joined by other European powers (including Britain) and by Japan as well, were preparing the stand they will take at key monetary meetings later this month in London and Washington.

Observers said the effect of today's decision was to throw the ball back at President Nixon, who imposed the surcharge on Aug. 15 as a weapon to force currency valuations upward, a greater sharing of de-

Continued on Page 25, Column 5

Basic Payments Deficit Hits $9-Billion Rate

By PHILIP SHABECOFF

Special to The New York Times

WASHINGTON, Sept. 13 — Paul A. Volcker, Under Secretary of the Treasury, disclosed publicly today that the United States' basic balance-of-payments deficit reached an annual rate of $9-billion in the first half of 1971.

It had been reported earlier that the basic deficit was so large that Mr. Volcker had shocked representatives of the group of 10 major trading nations at a meeting in Paris last week when he described its dimensions.

A $9-billion deficit for the year would be almost three times higher than the highest previous such deficit in recent American history.

Panel Hears Testimony

The basic balance of payments refers to all trade and monetary transactions with foreign countries except for erratic short-term capital flows. It is often regarded as the best measure of a country's true international payments position.

Mr. Volcker told the International Trade Subcommittee of the Senate Finance Committee today, "At the heart of this deterioration in our basic accounts was a severe decline in our merchandise trade balance."

In the years 1960-1969 the

Continued on Page 25, Column 1

NIXON PANEL ASKS FREE TRADE MOVES

Urges Negotiations to End All Barriers in 25 Years—Labor Members Dissent

By EDWIN L. DALE Jr.

Special to The New York Times

WASHINGTON, Sept. 13—A Presidential commission, calling for a "new realism" in the nation's foreign economic and trade policy, said today that "the time has come to begin immediately a major series of international negotiations" with the long-term aim of "elimination of all barriers to international trade and capital movements within 25 years."

The basic thrust of the report of the 27-member Commission

A summary of the panel's recommendations, Page 24.

on International Trade and Investment Policy was in the direction of freer trade here and abroad. The two members from organized labor dissented from the entire report, calling for controls on the inflow of goods and the outflow of capital and technology.

The report, consisting of 307 pages and 147 recommendations, was presented to President Nixon today by the commission chairman, Albert L.

Continued on Page 24, Column 1

Knowles Will Head Rockefeller Fund; Lost Out on U.S. Job

By M. A. FARBER

Dr. John H. Knowles, the 45-year-old Massachusetts hospital administrator who was a controversial candidate for the nation's top health post in 1969, was named president of the Rockefeller Foundation yesterday.

He will succeed Dr. J. George Harrar next July as head of the second wealthiest foundation in the country, a multipurpose philanthropic enterprise with assets of more than $800-million and activities throughout the world. The Ford Foundation has assets of more than $2.5-billion.

Dr. Harrar, an early leader in the "green revolution" in food production in developing nations, will reach the Rockefeller Foundation's mandatory retirement age of 65 next December.

Dr. Knowles, an outspoken liberal on social as well as specifically medical issues, has been general director of the Massachusetts General Hospital in Boston since 1962.

In 1969 Dr. Knowles was proposed by Robert H. Finch as Assistant Secretary for Health and Scientific Affairs, in the Department of Health, Education and Welfare. Mr. Finch, who is now on the White House staff, was then Secretary of the

Continued on Page 37, Column 3

Associated Press

BID FAREWELL TO HUSBAND AND FATHER: Nina Khrushchev paying her last respects as rain fell yesterday in Novodevichye Monastery's Cemetery in Moscow. Daughters, Yelena, right, and Rada, behind mother, stand with friends and relatives at flower-covered bier. Cemetery is three miles from Kremlin. Dispatch is on Page 10.

NEWS INDEX

News Summary and Index, Page 43

"All the News That's Fit to Print"

The New York Times

LATE CITY EDITION

Weather: Cloudy today and tonight. Partly sunny and milder tomorrow. Temp. range: today 60-67; Monday 58-62. Full U.S. report on Page 82.

VOL. CXXI . . No. 41,548 NEW YORK, TUESDAY, OCTOBER 26, 1971 — 15 CENTS

U.N. SEATS PEKING AND EXPELS TAIPEI; NATIONALISTS WALK OUT BEFORE VOTE; U.S. DEFEATED ON TWO KEY QUESTIONS

United Press International

Tanzanian and Albanian delegations applaud defeat of "important question" resolution

WASHINGTON CALM

Officials Uncertain of Effect of Defeat on Future Relations

Special to The New York Times

WASHINGTON, Oct. 25—Official Washington reacted with outward calm tonight to the crushing American defeat in the United Nations on the China issue. But there was uncertainty as to the effect the historic vote would have on future United States relations with Taiwan, the United Nations and the Peking Government.

Although the defeat was a distinct public setback for the Administration, most knowledgeable officials here had concluded in the last 48 hours that the weeks of arm twisting and private pressure in foreign capitals would fail to save Taiwan's seat and were therefore not surprised by the outcome.

At the time the vote was being held on the "important question," many prominent Administration and Congressional figures were unaware that it was taking place. On this Veterans Day holiday, most people here had assumed that the crucial voting would not take place until tomorrow. And with a heavy rain falling all day in Washington, many officials had retired early.

No television station in Washington carried the initial phases of the debate live tonight, contributing to the lack of awareness. Washington's public television station, WETA, carried the later parts of the debate, after the crucial vote.

U.S. Withholds Comment

Even James C. H. Shen, the Ambassador of Nationalist China, was caught by surprise by the vote tonight. He was in New Haven for a speaking engagement at Yale and had gone to sleep without knowing of the events at the United Nations. When awakened by a reporter's call, he said he would have no comment.

Both the State Department and the White House said there would be no immediate official comment, but privately some officials wondered aloud about the significance of what they called the most important defeat ever suffered by the United States in the world organization.

Senator James L. Buckley, Conservative-Republican of New York, reacted sharply. He said he had asked his staff to prepare legislation for "a major reduction" in the American financial contribution to the United Nations, which runs about one-third of the annual $200-million budget.

"The action taken by the General Assembly tonight," he said, "may well be recorded as the beginning of the end of the United Nations, as marking

Continued on Page 10, Column 6

United Press International

Liu Chieh, right, Nationalists' chief U.N. delegate, and delegation walk out of the hall

SESSION IS TENSE

Washington Loses Its Battle for Taipei by 76 to 35

By HENRY TANNER

Special to The New York Times

UNITED NATIONS, N. Y, Tuesday, Oct. 26—In a tense and emotion-filled meeting of more than eight hours, the General Assembly voted overwhelmingly last night to admit Communist China and to expel the Chinese Nationalist Government.

Moments before the vote, Liu Chieh, the Chinese Nationalist representative, announced from the rostrum that his Government would take no further part in the proceedings of the Assembly. He received friendly applause from most delegations, and then led his delegation out of the hall.

Texts of U.N. resolutions will be found on Page 10.

The vote, which brought delegates to their feet in wild applause, was 76 in favor, 35 opposed, and 17 abstentions. The vote was on a resolution sponsored by Albania and 20 other nations, calling for the seating of Peking as the only legitimate representative of China and the expulsion of "the representatives of Chiang Kai-shek."

Voting Is Sudden

Thus, the United States lost—in the 22d year—its battle to keep Nationalist China in the United Nations. This development, which came with dramatic suddenness, was denounced by the chief American delegate as a "moment of infamy."

The key decision that signaled the United States defeat came an hour and a half earlier, when the Assembly voted, 59 to 55 with 15 absentees, to reject the American draft resolution that would have declared the expulsion of the Nationalists an "important question" requiring a two-thirds majority for approval.

The United States had successfully used such a resolution since 1961 to keep the Chinese Communists out and the Chinese Nationalists in. Before that time, a simple majority would have admitted Peking, but no majority could be mustered.

Pandemonium Breaks Out

Last night as the electrical tally boards flashed the news that the "important question" proposal had failed, pandemonium broke out on the Assembly floor. Delegates jumped up and applauded.

The American delegation, also in the front row, sat in total dejection. George Bush, the United States delegate, who had

Continued on Page 10, Column 2

Peking's Backers Jubliant Over Vote

By TAD SZULC

Special to The New York Times

UNITED NATIONS, N. Y., Oct. 25—Salim Ahmed Salim, the young chief delegate from Tanzania, jumped to his feet tonight and led his colleagues in a victory jig in front of the Tanzanian seats in the front row of the General Assembly hall.

At the opposite end of the hall, where the United States delegation occupies a front-row seat, George Bush, the American chief delegate, slumped dejectedly in his chair.

It was exactly 9:47 P.M. and the United Nations General Assembly had just finished its roll-

Continued on Page 10, Column 2

LINDSAY DEFENDS KNAPP HEARINGS

Tells P.B.A. Head the Inquiry is in 'The Best Interest' of Everyone on Force

By DAVID BURNHAM

Mayor Lindsay said yesterday that while the Knapp Commission hearings meant "discomfort and shock" for many policemen and citizens, dealing decisively with police corruption was in "the best interest of every member of the police force."

Mr. Lindsay made the statement in a letter to Edward J. Kiernan, president of the Patrolmen's Benevolent Association.

The Mayor also said he intended to use the recommendations of the Knapp Commission, expected in a written report by the end of the year, "as the basis for a major campaign to build public confidence in the Police Department and the integrity of our law enforcement processes."

The Mayor's letter was in response to charges made last week by Mr. Kiernan that the Knapp Commission's hearings

Continued on Page 31, Column 5

Powell Is Seeking To Avoid Clashes Over Court Seat

By JAMES M. NAUGHTON

Special to The New York Times

WASHINGTON, Oct. 25 — Lewis F. Powell Jr., the third Southern conservative nominated to the Supreme Court by President Nixon, is attempting to avoid the collisions over ethics and racial attitudes that contributed to the Senate's rejection of his two predecessors.

Mr. Powell, aware that his life, professional record and judicial philosophy are about to undergo rigorous examination, discussed his background with unusual candor in an interview at his Richmond law office this weekend.

He pledged to do "whatever is necessary and proper" to separate himself from corporate directorships and financial holdings that might constitute potential conflicts of interest.

Mr. Powell sought to place in what he regards as the proper context the comparatively minor chinks that have appeared in his image as a racial moderate — membership in two segregated clubs in Richmond and authorship of a brief filed by

Continued on Page 22, Column 4

Pakistanis Report 501 of Foe Killed In Eastern Area

By MALCOLM W. BROWNE

Special to The New York Times

KARACHI, Pakistan, Oct. 25—The Government reported tonight that its forces had killed 501 "enemy troops"—defined as "Indians and Indian agents"—in heavy fighting in East Pakistan.

The Government, here in Pakistan's western wing, uses the term "Indian agents" to refer to all of its adversaries in East Pakistan, including the Pakistanis there who have been battling for Bengali independence since March with Indian support.

U.N. Observers Suggested

Today the Government said some of the bodies bore identification tags of the Indian Army. If the casualties are indeed Indians and if the toll even approaches the figures given, that would indicate that the fighting had reached its greatest intensity since the brief Indian-Pakistani conflict in 1965.

[In New Delhi, Defense Minister Jagjivan Ram reiterated that India would not pull her troops back from her borders "as long as the Pakistani threat continues." Page 17.]

Meanwhile, the Government announced that President Agha Mohammad Yahya Khan had asked for the intercession of Secretary General Thant of the United Nations in the dispute.

According to the Pakistani radio, President Yahya Khan proposed that United Nations observers be posted on both sides of the border between East Pakistan and India to supervise a mutual withdrawal

Continued on Page 17, Column 1

BREZHNEV IN PARIS, BACKED ON TALKS

Pompidou Agrees to a Quick Start on Preparations for Europe Security Parley

By HENRY GINIGER

Special to The New York Times

PARIS, Oct. 25—President Pompidou and Leonid I. Brezhnev, leader of the Soviet Communist party, agreed quickly today to begin active preparation for a European security conference.

The agreement was made known at a state dinner in Versailles that marked the end of the first day of a six-day visit by Mr. Brezhnev. The Soviet leader was received this afternoon with the honors of a chief of state, and only a few discordant notes marred the friendly atmosphere of Mr. Brezhnev's first visit to a Western country since he became party leader in 1964.

[In Washington it was reported that Mr. Brezhnev had signaled Western leaders that he had officially assumed over-all responsibility for Moscow's relations with the United States and Western Europe. Page 5.]

In toasts this evening, Mr. Pompidou and Mr. Brezhnev spoke in similar terms of the need to end hostility between blocs.

Mr. Brezhnev said that France and the Soviet Union were close "on a fundamental problem—that of ending the division of the world into political-military blocs." Mr. Pompidou declared such blocs carried within them "the certainty of

Continued on Page 6, Column 4

CHOW SAYS PEKING WILL SUBVERT U.N.

Nationalist Minister Sees Change to 'Maoist Front' As Result of Defeat

By SAM POPE BREWER

Special to The New York Times

UNITED NATIONS, N.Y., Oct. 25—Nationalist China's Foreign Minister, Chow Shu-kai, walked with his delegation out of the United Nations tonight and declared bitterly that Communist China, in his nation's place, would subvert the world organization.

"Once it has been seated both in the General Assembly and in the Security Council," Mr. Chow said of Peking, "it will surely transform the United Nations into a Maoist front and a battlefield for international subversion."

Mr. Chow, grave but unflinching in the glare of batteries of television lights, stood with Taiwan's delegate, Liu Chieh, at his side in a hallway outside the General Assembly Hall, where the overwhelming defeat for his Government had been voted. He declared:

"There are those who think that participation of the Communist regime will enhance the prospect of peace. The idea is to subject the aggressive regime to the discipline of international public opinion. This is dangerous nonsense—it is like tying a tiger with a straw rope."

Asked if he had had a foreboding of defeat when he wrote the document, Mr. Chow said, quietly: "When you are fighting a war, you prepare for

Continued on Page 11, Column 1

U.N. Roll-Calls on China

Special to The New York Times

UNITED NATIONS, N. Y., Oct. 25—Following are two roll-call votes taken in the General Assembly tonight on seating Communist China and expelling Nationalist China.

On Two-Thirds Requirement

Resolution declaring the expulsion of Nationalist China an "important matter" and thus requiring a two-thirds vote rather than a simple majority for passage.

IN FAVOR—55

Argentina	Ghana	New Zealand
Australia	Greece	Nicaragua
Bahrain	Guatemala	Niger
Barbados	Haiti	Panama
Bolivia	Honduras	Paraguay
Brazil	Indonesia	Philippines
Cambodia	Israel	Portugal
Cent. Afr. Rep.	Ivory Coast	Rwanda
Chad	Jamaica	Saudi Arabia
China	Japan	South Africa
Colombia	Jordan	Spain
Congo (Kinsh.)	Lebanon	Swaziland
Costa Rica	Lesotho	Thailand
Dahomey	Liberia	United States
Dominican Rep	Luxembourg	Upper Volta
El Salvador	Madagascar	Uruguay
Fiji	Malawi	Venezuela
Gabon	Mauritius	
Gambia	Mexico	

OPPOSED—59

Afghanistan	Ethiopia	Norway
Albania	Finland	Pakistan
Algeria	France	Peru
Bhutan	Guinea	Poland
Britain	Guyana	Rumania
Bulgaria	Hungary	Sierra Leone
Burma	Iceland	Singapore
Burundi	India	Somalia
Byelorussia	Iraq	So. Yemen
Cameroon	Ireland	Soviet Union
Canada	Kenya	Sudan
Ceylon	Kuwait	Sweden
Chile	Libya	Syria
Congo (Brazza)	Malaysia	Tanzania
Cuba	Mali	Trinidad-Tobago
Czechoslovakia	Mauritania	Uganda
Denmark	Mongolia	Ukraine
Ecuador	Nepal	Yemen
Egypt	Nigeria	Yugoslavia
Eq. Guinea		Zambia

ABSTENTIONS—15

Austria	Italy	Qatar
Belgium	Laos	Senegal
Botswana	Malta	Togo
Cyprus	Morocco	Tunisia
Iran	Netherlands	Turkey

Absent—Maldives, Oman.

On Seating Peking

Resolution to seat Communist China and expel Nationalist China.

IN FAVOR—76

Afghanistan	Guyana	Portugal
Albania	Hungary	Rumania
Algeria	Iceland	Rwanda
Australia	India	Senegal
Belgium	Iran	Sierra Leone
Bhutan	Iraq	Singapore
Botswana	Ireland	Somalia
Britain	Israel	So. Yemen
Bulgaria	Italy	Soviet Union
Burma	Kenya	Sudan
Burundi	Kuwait	Sweden
Byelorussia	Laos	Syria
Cameroon	Libya	Tanzania
Canada	Malaysia	Togo
Ceylon	Mali	Trinidad-Tobago
Chile	Mauritania	Tunisia
Cuba	Mexico	Turkey
Czechoslovakia	Mongolia	Uganda
Denmark	Morocco	Ukraine
Ecuador	Nepal	Yemen
Egypt	Netherlands	Yugoslavia
Eq. Guinea	Nigeria	Zambia
Ethiopia	Norway	
Finland	Pakistan	
France	Congo (Brazza)	
Ghana	Peru	
Guinea	Poland	

OPPOSED—35

Australia	Gambia	Nicaragua
Bolivia	Guatemala	Niger
Brazil	Haiti	Paraguay
Cambodia	Honduras	Philippines
Cent. Afr. Rep.	Ivory Coast	Saudi Arabia
Chad	Japan	South Africa
Congo (Kinsh.)	Lesotho	Swaziland
Costa Rica	Liberia	United States
Dahomey	Madagascar	Upper Volta
Dominican Rep.	Malawi	Uruguay
El Salvador	Malta	Venezuela
Gabon	New Zealand	

ABSTENTIONS—17

Argentina	Greece	Mauritius
Bahrain	Indonesia	Panama
Barbados	Jamaica	Qatar
Colombia	Jordan	Spain
Cyprus	Lebanon	Thailand
Fiji	Luxembourg	

Absent—China, Maldives, Oman.

End of China's Isolation

Peking Victory Held Likely to Speed Series of International Realignments

By MAX FRANKEL

Special to The New York Times

WASHINGTON, Oct. 25—With the vote at the United Nations tonight, China burst fully and finally from the isolation first imposed on her by the United States a generation ago and periodically preferred by her own Communist Government.

News Analysis

Though Washington was calm or simply asleep at the symbolic moment, its rear-guard effort to save Taiwan in the world organization only heightened the drama of Peking's entry onto the world stage and deepened some of the resentments in conservative circles here.

President Nixon will undoubtedly show some sympathy for those resentments. He considers his projected journey to China as far more significant than most actions of the United Nations, and he sincerely hoped that his gesture would win a more gentle handling for the Chinese Nationalists.

But there was obviously a pent-up desire among many nations to make whole and unambiguous this final reversal of American policy. This will complicate the President's task in defending his new China policy and the irritations are bound to be reflected in Washington's relations with the United Nations.

There is universal agreement here, however, that whatever the consequences inside the world organization, tonight's voting and walkout by the Nationalists will further accelerate a whole series of realignments and shifts on the international scene.

Several important trends had already combined to determine

Continued on Page 10, Column 7

NEWS INDEX

By Lyndon B. Johnson: First Steps Toward Peace

INSTALLMENT X

Following is the 10th of 11 installments of excerpts from Lyndon Baines Johnson's memoirs of his Presidential years, which will be published by Holt, Rinehart & Winston on Nov. 1 under the title "The Vantage Point: Perspectives of the Presidency, 1963-1969":

Wednesday, April 3, 1968, began like most days in the White House. I was up early and read through the morning papers over breakfast. I listened to the radio news and glanced again at the front pages. One item, which I had heard broadcast the previous afternoon, was receiving considerable attention. In a speech on Tuesday Senator J. William Fulbright had told the Senate that the partial bombing halt I had ordered three nights before added up to only "a very limited change in existing policy." He forecast that the halt would not move Hanoi in the direction of peace talks.

I was surprised by Fulbright's reasoning and by his timing. We had stopped bombing over more than three-fourths of North Vietnam, an area where 9 out of every 10 North Vietnamese lived. That was much more than a "limited change" in our actions. Moreover, I believed Hanoi was perfectly able to judge the significance of our move without advice from Americans.

In the Senate discussion following Senator Fulbright's speech, Majority Leader Mike Mansfield and other Senators spoke up strongly in defense of our action and disputed Fulbright's charges. Senator Mansfield recalled the long talk he and I had had on the evening of March 27 and he disclosed that I had informed him on that occasion that we were going to stop bombing north of the 20th parallel.

To my mind, the principal issue was not where the precise line marking the no-bombing area was drawn but rather how Hanoi would react to our self-imposed restriction. The key question in the Senate discussion, I believed, was raised by Senator Frank Lausche of Ohio: "How can Ho Chi Minh give any affirmative action when the Senator from Arkansas and others attack the Government before Ho can respond?"

While Fulbright's allegations dominated the news stories and headlines, Lausche's pertinent question received scant attention. I saw it mentioned only once, in The New York Times on April 3, and then only in the 30th and last paragraph on Page 14.

These reflections put me in a bad mood as I prepared to leave for the

Continued on Page 34, Column 1

"All the News That's Fit to Print"

The New York Times

LATE CITY EDITION

Weather: Cloudy and co[illegible] day, colder tonight. Sunn[illegible] Temp. range: today 4[illegible] 52-63. Full U.S. report on Page 82.

VOL. CXXI...No. 41,600

NEW YORK, FRIDAY, DECEMBER 17, 1971

15 CENTS

INDIA ORDERS CEASE-FIRE ON BOTH FRONTS AFTER PAKISTANIS' SURRENDER IN THE EAST

CONGRESS BREAKS FOREIGN AID JAM; SEEKS TO ADJOURN

House Rejection of Vietnam Amendment Sets Stage for Conferees' Accord

By JOHN W. FINNEY

Special to The New York Times

WASHINGTON, Dec. 16 — Congress apparently broke today the impasse on foreign aid legislation that has been holding up adjournment as the House unexpectedly met Senate demands for a vote on an amendment on Vietnam troop withdrawal.

The House rejected, by a vote of 130 to 101, the withdrawal amendment offered by the Senate majority leader, Mike Mansfield, and incorporated by the Senate in the foreign aid authorization legislation. But the net effect of the House action was to reopen Senate-House negotiations on the foreign aid legislation that had been deadlocked for weeks in a conference committee.

With the foreign aid issue apparently on the way to resolution, Senate and House leaders were optimistic that the first session of the 92d Congress could adjourn by tomorrow.

Ryan Breaks Impasse

With Senate and House leaders caught up in a power struggle over foreign aid, the impasse was broken in a surprise move by Representative William Fitts Ryan, Democrat of Manhattan.

Independently of the Congressional leaders who were meeting in the Senate Appropriations Committee room seeking a way to continue the foreign aid program, Mr. Ryan unexpectedly stood up on the House floor to offer a motion instructing the House conferees to accept the Mansfield amendment.

He had found a provision in the House rules permitting such a motion to be made if a Senate-House conference committee had been deadlocked for 20 days.

Motion to Table

A surprised Representative, Thomas E. Morgan of Pennsylvania, chairman of the House Foreign Affairs Committee, promptly moved to table, or lay aside, the Ryan motion, a move that carried by the 29-vote margin.

Technically, the House did not have the specific vote on the Mansfield amendment that Senate conferees had been demanding in the conference on the foreign aid legislation. It was the refusal of the House conferees to yield to this demand by Senator Mansfield

Continued on Page 45, Column 4

Monthly Record Set For Housing Starts

By JACK ROSENTHAL

Special to The New York Times

WASHINGTON, Dec. 16 — Home building reached a monthly high in November, practically insuring that 1971 will be a record year, George Romney, Secretary of Housing and Urban Development, announced today at an odd, hastily called news conference.

The seasonally adjusted annual rate of housing starts in November was 2,316,000 units, Mr. Romney said, the highest figure ever. The actual 1971 figure is now likely to approach 2.1 million units, probably the highest ever.

The November figure compares with a downward revised October figure of 2,008,000 units and with 1,693,000 units for November, 1970.

The gain in housing starts,

Continued on Page 69, Column 5

REVAMPING URGED FOR BANK SYSTEM

Hunt Commission Proposes Change in U.S. Regulation of Money Institutions

By H. ERICH HEINEMANN

Special to The New York Times

WASHINGTON, Dec. 16 — The nation's financial structure and the Federal agencies that regulate it require a complete overhaul, a Presidential commission has concluded.

If adopted, the commission's recommendations should result in sharper competition, possibly lower prices for consumers and — over time — the gradual disappearance of the present sharp legal distinctions between different types of financial institutions.

The group is formally called the Presidential Commission on Financial Structure and Regulation and informally known as the Hunt Commission (for its chairman, Reed O. Hunt, retired chairman of the Crown Zellerbach Corporation). The commission is due to present its report to the White House in a few days. A copy of its recommendations, but not the report itself, was obtained today.

The key problem that led

Continued on Page 65, Column 1

WEST TO FIGHT ON

Yahya Calls for Help, but Vows to Battle 'Alone if We Must'

By MALCOLM W. BROWNE

Special to The New York Times

RAWALPINDI, Pakistan, Dec. 16—President Agha Mohammad Yahya Khan acknowledged tonight that his forces in East Pakistan had been overwhelmed but pledged to continue the war against India until final victory.

In a radio speech to the nation, he also urgently called for

Text of Yahya's speech will be found on Page 17.

help from the community of nations in Pakistan's struggle, but added: "We shall fight alone if we must."

Later, Pakistan formally acknowledged that India now controls what had been East Pakistan.

A communiqué issued here in West Pakistan said:

"Latest reports indicate that following an arrangement between the local commanders of India and Pakistan in the Eastern theater, fighting has ceased in East Pakistan, and Indian troops have entered Dacca."

No Details Are Given

The communiqué said nothing more about East Pakistan and gave no details of the "arrangement."

But it indicated that fighting in West Pakistan was continuing.

For the first time since the war began, military and diplomatic spokesmen failed to hold their daily evening briefing and correspondents here had no access to Pakistani officials.

The air war in the west was apparently still in progress. Indian air raids were reported on Karachi, Sialkot and other cities with significant numbers of civilian casualties.

The President implied that he had by no means accepted the separation of East Pakistan from the West, despite Pakistan's military defeat there.

"No sacrifice will be too great to preserve this Islamic homeland of the 120 million people of Pakistan," he said.

He also said: "To all our friends we say: stand by us and rest assured that the people of Pakistan and their armed forces will not cease their struggle

Continued on Page 17, Column 4

SIGNING THE SURRENDER AGREEMENT: Lieut. Gen. Jagjit Singh Aurora, left, commander of India's eastern forces, and Lieut. Gen. A. A. K. Niazi, Pakistani commander in East Pakistan, during surrender ceremony in Dacca yesterday.

United Press International

DACCA CAPTURED

Guns Quiet in Bengali Area but War Goes On at Western Front

By CHARLES MOHR

Special to The New York Times

NEW DELHI, Dec. 16—India today ordered a complete cease-fire in the war with Pakistan after seizing Dacca, the East Pakistani capital, and accepting the surrender of Pakistan's forces there.

With guns stilled by the surrender in the East, the cease-

Statements by Mrs. Gandhi appear on Page 16.

fire on the western front, more than a thousand miles away, was set—without any agreement from Pakistan—to begin at 8 P.M. tomorrow, Indian time (9:30 A.M. Friday, New York time).

After 14 days of bitter warfare over the status of the Bengalis in East Pakistan, Prime Minister Indira Gandhi of India said, "It is pointless in our view to continue the present conflict."

Pakistani Shortages Seen

But President Agha Mohammad Yahya Khan of Pakistan asserted in a nationwide radio broadcast that the war was still on "and we will continue to fight."

Pakistan is believed by independent observers, however, to have grave supply-line problems, so that her stockpiles of fuel and ammunition may not permit a prolonged war.

A major tank battle—the largest of the war—has erupted on the western front near the little Pakistani town of Shakargarh, in the Punjab. Indian officials said India had lost 15 tanks and claimed the destruction of 45 Pakistani tanks.

Even as India celebrated her quick victory in the East, China accused her of violating the border between the Indian protectorate of Sikkim and Tibet, terming the action "a grave encroachment" on Chinese territory.

Chinese Charge Denied

Indian officials said there had been no fighting on the Chinese border, and a Foreign Ministry spokesman described the accusation by Peking—a supporter of Pakistan—as "totally without foundation." Nonetheless, the protest raised apprehensions here that the conflict might be widened.

India's offensive in East Pakistan, which began in the early hours of Dec. 4, ended at 4:31 P.M. today in the total surrender of the four divisions of West Pakistani troops there.

The surrender agreement was signed in Dacca by Lieut. Gen. Jagjit Singh Aurora, who commands India's eastern forces, and Lieut. Gen. A. A. K. Niazi,

Continued on Page 16, Column 1

BHUTTO SUGGESTS ACCORD ON BENGAL

Pakistani Urges Cease-fire and Negotiations With Both Indians and Insurgents

By HENRY TANNER

Special to The New York Times

UNITED NATIONS, N. Y., Dec. 16 — Pakistan's Deputy Prime Minister and Foreign Minister, Zulfikar Ali Bhutto, declared today that Pakistan should accept a cease-fire with India and should prepare to negotiate a permanent settlement with the insurgents in East Bengal as well as with the Government of India.

Mr. Bhutto, in an interview, also said that Pakistan, which is now ruled by a military government, should return to civilian democratic government "very soon." His remarks appeared to put him at odds with President Agha Mohammad Yahya Khan of Pakistan, who pledged today in a speech to continue the war against India.

Mr. Bhutto announced that he would return to Pakistan in a few days to start laying the groundwork for sweeping internal and external reform as well as for negotiation with the insurgents.

Mr. Bhutto, who is the leading civilian figure in West Pakistan, stressed that he did not concede the final loss of East Pakistan.

The Security Council, meanwhile, was close to agreement when it adjourned tonight on a resolution calling for an im-

Continued on Page 17, Column 1

The Surrender Document

By Reuters

NEW DELHI, Dec. 16—Following is the text of the instrument of surrender signed today by the Pakistani and Indian commanders in East Pakistan:

The Pakistani Eastern Command agree to surrender all Pakistani armed forces in Bangladesh to Lieut. Gen. Jagjit Singh Aurora, general officer commanding in chief of the Indian and Bangladesh forces in the eastern theater.

This surrender includes all Pakistani land, air and naval forces as also all paramilitary forces and civil armed forces.

These forces will lay down their arms and surrender at the place where they are currently located to the nearest regular troops in the command of Lieut. Gen. Jagjit Singh Aurora.

Pakistani Eastern Command shall come under the orders of Lieut. Gen. Jagjit Singh Aurora as soon as this instrument has been signed. Disobedience of orders will be regarded as a breach of the surrender terms and will be dealt with in accordance with accepted laws and usages of war.

The decision of Lieut. Gen. Jagjit Singh Aurora shall be final should any doubt arise as to the meaning or interpretation of surrender terms.

"Lieut. Gen. Jagjit Singh Aurora gives his solemn assurance that personnel who surrender shall be treated with dignity and respect that soldiers are entitled to in accordance with the provisions of the Geneva convention and guarantees safety and well-being of all Pakistan military and paramilitary forces who surrender.

Protection will be provided to foreign nationals, ethnic minorities and personnel of the West Pakistan region by the forces in the command of Lieut. Gen. Jagjit Singh Aurora.

CHINESE CHARGE INDIAN INCURSION

Protest May Foreshadow Use of Military Pressure in Support of Pakistan

By TILLMAN DURDIN

Special to The New York Times

HONG KONG, Dec. 16—China, in a formal Government statement today on the Indian-Pakistani war, predicted a turbulent future for India. At the same time, the Chinese pointed toward a possible trouble zone by filing a strong protest in New Delhi over alleged Indian incursions from Sikkim into Tibet.

The statement and the protest were reported here in quick

Text of Chinese statement is printed on Page 18.

succession tonight from Peking by Hsinhua, the Chinese press agency.

The protest could foreshadow military pressure from China, a strong supporter of Pakistan, along sections of the eastern Himalayan border between India and China.

The 1,600-word statement warned India that "he who plays with fire will be consumed by fire" and asserted that "henceforth there will be no tranquillity" for the Indian people.

Calling attention to India's own problems with minority nationalities, which it likened to the Bengali situation in East Pakistan, the statement said: "It may be asked how

Continued on Page 18, Column 2

Nixon Pledges to Seek Release Of Skipper of Ship Cuba Seized

Mr. Nixon consoles wife of José Villa, ship's captain

Associated Press

By JAMES M. NAUGHTON

Special to The New York Times

KEY BISCAYNE, Fla., Dec. 16 — President Nixon pledged today that he would do what he could to seek the release of José Villa, the captain of a Miami-based freighter attacked by a Cuban gunboat and seized yesterday in the Bahamas.

The President met with Captain Villa's wife, Isabel, and three children for 10 minutes at the Florida White House. The family of the captain, a Cuban exile who is now a naturalized United States citizen, had gone there to deliver a letter plead-

ing for Mr. Nixon's intervention.

Ronald L. Ziegler, the White House press secretary, that after the meeting that the Administration deplored the Cuban attack as an "unconscionable act" and that the United States had asked the Swiss Embassy in Havana to demand the "immediate" release of Captain Villa.

Earlier, before the captain's family saw the President, Mr. Ziegler used milder terms to

Continued on Page 12, Column 3

City Speeds Repair On Garbage Trucks

By PAUL L. MONTGOMERY

Sanitation Department officials here believe they are on the way to solving one of their most persistent problems—the inordinate number of collection trucks awaiting repairs in the department's shops.

The solution, something of a revolution in city administration, is embodied in a single sheet of statistics distributed to department mechanics this week. It lists the times the mechanics will be expected to spend to complete 18 routine tasks.

The revolution is that the times listed are an average of 46 per cent less than those that had prevailed.

The new productivity standards, reached after consultation with the mechanics' union, are frequently mentioned by city officials as an example of

Continued on Page 72, Column 1

Walsh at Hearing: Forgot Graft Report

By DAVID BURNHAM

Former First Deputy Police Commissioner John F. Walsh admitted in sworn testimony yesterday that he had received a report of widespread police corruption in the Bronx at least six months before any police investigation was begun.

Mr. Walsh, the second-ranking New York police official for almost 10 years, told the Knapp Commission that the detailed report he had received on corruption among plainclothes men enforcing the gambling laws "left my mind."

Months later, without any orders to initiate it from Mr. Walsh, an investigation was begun by police officials in the Bronx that eventually led to criminal indictments against 10 policemen and department charges against 11 others, in-

Continued on Page 46, Column 1

The March Into Dacca: Last Clash and Victory

2 Men at a Table

By SYDNEY H. SCHANBERG

Special to The New York Times

DACCA, Pakistan, Dec. 16—On a broad grassy field in central Dacca known as the Race Course, the Pakistani forces formally surrendered today, 13 days after the Indian Army began its drive into East Pakistan.

It was at the Race Course on March 7 that Sheik Mujibur Rahman, in a speech to thousands of Bengalis, called for the end of martial law and the transfer of power to his autonomy-minded Awami League, which had won a majority in national elections.

Today there were no speeches—just two men sitting at a single table on the grass—Lieut. Gen. Jagjit Singh Aurora, chief of India's Eastern Command, and Lieut. Gen. A. A. K. Niazi, commander of the 70,000 Pakistani troops in East Pakistan—who signed the formal papers of Pakistani surrender in the East.

The final hours of the Indian drive, which ended with the ceremony at the Race Course, were punctuated by artillery and machine-gun fire as the troops pushed across the Lakhya River, just outside Dacca proper.

Seven Western journalists, in-

Continued on Page 16, Column 3

Joy and Marigolds

By JAMES P. STERBA

Special to The New York Times

DACCA, Pakistan, Dec. 16—Shouting "Joi Bangla!" and waving the Bangladesh flag, Indian troops in trucks and buses poured into the Pakistani military camp north of town today just after the Pakistanis had accepted an ultimatum to surrender.

Indian soldiers with marigolds in their gun barrels passed armed Pakistani soldiers in great traffic jams within the camp. Pakistani officers saluted Indian officers. Officers of both armies, many of whom attended the same schools under the British, shook hands and asked about mutual friends.

In Dacca itself, there were spontaneous eruptions of joy and celebration in the streets. Bengalis kissed Indian Punjabi soldiers, tossing flowers at them and at the rebels who accom-

Continued on Page 16, Column 7

NEWS INDEX

Mrs. Gandhi Writes President: U.S. Could Have Averted War

By FOX BUTTERFIELD

Special to The New York Times

NEW DELHI, Dec. 16—Prime Minister Indira Gandhi has written to President Nixon, in a letter released today, that the war between India and Pakistan could have been avoided if the United States had used its

Text of Mrs. Gandhi's letter is printed on Page 17.

"power, influence and authority" to achieve a political solution to the crisis in East Pakistan.

Mrs. Gandhi wrote that despite advice that she gave in August to Henry A. Kissinger, the President's adviser on national security affairs, only "lip service was paid to the need for a political settlement, but not a single worthwhile step was taken to bring it about."

Mrs. Gandhi said she was writing at a time of deep anguish over the "unhappy turn which relations between India and the United States have taken." The letter was sent to Mr. Nixon yesterday.

Relations between the two countries, which have been strained because the United States did not denounce Pakistan for her repression of the Bengali movement for autonomy last spring, deteriorated sharply this week with the news that the nuclear-powered aircraft carrier Enterprise and seven other American Navy ships were heading for the Bay of Bengal.

"India was deeply hurt," Mrs. Gandhi wrote, "by the innuendoes and insinuations that it was she who had precipitated

Continued on Page 17, Column 3

"All the News That's Fit to Print"

The New York Times

LATE CITY EDITION

Weather: Rain today; mostly cloudy tonight. Fair and milder tomorrow. Temp. range: today 51-55; Monday 53-66. Full U.S. report on Page 82.

VOL. CXXI .. No. 41,744 © 1972 The New York Times Company NEW YORK, TUESDAY, MAY 9, 1972 15 CENTS

NIXON ORDERS ENEMY'S PORTS MINED; SAYS MATERIEL WILL BE DENIED HANOI UNTIL IT FREES P.O.W.'S AND HALTS WAR

Governor Reported Irked By Nixon's Abortion Views

Rockefeller Indicates Plan to Veto Bill Stands Despite President's Support for Repeal of Present State Law

By JAMES F. CLARITY

Special to The New York Times

ALBANY, May 8 — Governor Rockefeller was reliably reported today to be angered by President Nixon's intervention in the issue of elective abortions, now pending in the Legislature.

One of the highest elected Republican officials in the state described Mr. Rockefeller as "very upset" about the President's action.

The Governor's office said that despite the President's announced support for repeal of the state's liberal abortion law, Mr. Rockefeller would veto the repeal if it was approved by the Legislature. Relations between the Governor and the President, which had improved greatly in the last several months, with Mr. Rockefeller agreeing to serve as the President's campaign manager in the state, now seem strained, at least on this one issue.

The Assembly was expected to debate the repeal legislation tomorrow.

Evidence of the Governor's pique was clear in the statement his office issued in response to requests for comments on the President's action: "We are referring all calls to the White House on this."

Mr. Nixon intervened in the state issue in a letter to Cardinal Cooke. The letter, made public Saturday, made clear the President's support for repeal of the New York law, which permits elective abortions through the 24th week of pregnancy.

The day before the letter was made public, Mr. Nixon had rejected recommendations for lib-

Continued on Page 26, Column 2

PAY BOARD TRIMS EAST COAST RAISE OF LONGSHOREMEN

Votes, 6-1, to Permit Rises of 9.8 to 12% Instead of 15 —Fitzsimmons Dissents

By EDWARD COWAN

Special to The New York Times

WASHINGTON, May 8—The Pay Board directed East and Gulf Coast shippers and longshoremen tonight to roll back their agreed wage increase of 70 cents an hour to 55 cents.

About 49,000 longshoremen will be allowed increases ranging from 9.8 per cent to 12 per cent under the decision, which scaled back an agreement that had contemplated an increase calculated by the board at 15 per cent.

George H. Boldt, chairman of the seven-member board, said that he expected the International Longshoremen's Association "to look it over, be disappointed and go along with what's now the law of the land."

Boldt Declines to Predict

However, Judge Boldt, in a brief corridor meeting with newsmen, declined to prognosticate when asked if he thought the dock workers would strike.

Judge Boldt issued a brief summary of the decision after a difficult four-hour board meeting that ended with a vote of 6 to 1. The dissenter was Frank E. Fitzsimmons, president of the International Brotherhood of Teamsters, who is the only labor leader still on the board.

Four other union leaders quit the board in March after it scaled back the longshore settlement on the West Coast to 14.9 per cent from a proposed 20.9 per cent. Only Mr. Fitzsimmons remained.

President Nixon then reconstituted what had been a 15-member tripartite group as a panel of seven public members.

In New York, Thomas G. Gleason, president of the Inter-

Continued on Page 17, Column 1

VIETNAM ADDRESS: President Nixon speaking last night Associated Press

The New York Times/May 9, 1972

NEW TARGETS: Ports (underlined), rail lines from China

SPEAKS TO NATION

He Gives the Ships of Other Countries 3 Days to Leave

By ROBERT B. SEMPLE Jr.

Special to The New York Times

WASHINGTON, May 8 — President Nixon announced tonight that he had ordered the mining of all North Vietnamese ports and other measures to prevent the flow of arms and other military supplies to the enemy.

Mr. Nixon told a nationwide television and radio audience

The text of Nixon's speech is printed on Page 18.

that his orders were being executed as he spoke.

From the President's somber and stern speech and from explanations by other Administration officials, the following picture of the American action emerged:

¶All major North Vietnamese ports would be mined, ships of other countries in the harbors, most of which are Russian, would have three "daylight periods" in which to leave. After that the mines will become active and ships coming or going will move at their own peril.

¶United States naval vessels will not search or seize ships of other countries entering or leaving North Vietnamese ports, thus avoiding a direct confrontation with the Russians.

¶American and South Vietnamese ships and planes would take "appropriate measures" to stop North Vietnam from unloading matériel on beaches from unmined waters.

¶United States and South Vietnamese forces would interdict, presumably by bombing, the movement of matériel in North Vietnam over rail lines originating in China.

There was much confusion tonight about whether the United States and South Vietnam had proclaimed a blockade. The President did not use the word and Pentagon spokesmen denied that a blockade existed in the technical sense. But some observers felt that the practical effect on North Vietnam of the President's actions would be the same as a blockade.

[In Saigon, the United States command announced Tuesday that Navy planes had completed the initial phases of the mining operations in North Vietnamese harbors ordered by President Nixon.]

Two Basic Conditions

Mr. Nixon said the mining, the attacks on the rail lines within North Vietnam, and the efforts to interdict the movement of supplies by water would cease the moment the enemy agreed to two basic conditions: the return of American prisoners of war, and an internationally supervised cease-fire.

"Then," he said, "we will stop all acts of force throughout Indochina and proceed with the complete withdrawal of all forces within four months."

The White House would not say tonight whether, in these words, Mr. Nixon was in effect making the North Vietnamese a new peace proposal.

But observers here noted that he mentioned no political requirements for American withdrawal. Until now he has always insisted on some form of

Continued on Page 18, Column 5

Ruling Party Leads In Italian Election; Neo-Fascists Gain

By PAUL HOFMANN

Special to The New York Times

ROME, Tuesday, May 9—The governing Christian Democrats achieved a remarkable comeback in Italy's general elections Sunday and yesterday, receiving a clear mandate to continue leading the Government as they have been doing since 1945.

At the same time, however, the neo-Fascists advanced and the Communists won gains in the Chamber of Deputies and suffered losses in the Senate. With most of the votes counted early today, increasing polarization between left and right in Italian politics became apparent.

The Christian Democrats apparently raised their share of the total popular vote close to 40 per cent again and were confirmed once more as the nation's strongest political force.

But no party was anywhere near winning a majority in the 630-seat Chamber or among the 315 elected members of the Senate. The prospects, therefore, appeared to be for another period of coalition governments and, possibly, protracted instability.

Italian commentators attributed the rightist gains and

Continued on Page 3, Column 1

CONGRESS IS SPLIT ON NIXON'S ACTION

Republicans Acclaim His Leadership—Democrats Call Him Reckless

By JOHN W. FINNEY

Special to The New York Times

WASHINGTON, May 8—President Nixon was alternately praised tonight by members of Congress for his firm leadership and accused of setting the nation on a dangerous confrontation with the Soviet Union that could lead to world war.

Republicans praised him on both political and military grounds for his decision to mine North Vietnam's harbors.

Representative Gerald R. Ford, the House Republican leader, described Mr. Nixon as "generous in his bid for peace but firm in his determination that we will not surrender."

"The only way left to end the Vietnam war is to deprive the enemy of the supplies he needs to continue the invasion," Mr. Ford said.

Senator Robert P. Griffin of Michigan, the assistant Republican leader in the Senate, said "it was strong medicine but necessary."

Democrats, however, used

Continued on Page 19, Column 1

President Urges Soviet To Avoid Confrontation

By BERNARD GWERTZMAN

Special to The New York Times

WASHINGTON, May 8—President Nixon's speech tonight appealed to the Soviet Union not to let its support of Hanoi lead it to a confrontation with the United States over his decision to try to cut off supplies to North Vietnam.

In carefully chosen language, Mr. Nixon appeared anxious to avoid turning the Vietnam war into a direct Soviet-American clash.

But some diplomats feel the mining of North Vietnam's ports has raised the possibility of cancellation of Mr. Nixon's scheduled trip to Moscow two weeks from today and even of a military confrontation if Soviet naval forces try to thwart Mr. Nixon's actions.

Dobrynin Informed

Officially, the Nixon Administration said tonight that plans for Mr. Nixon's visit to the Soviet Union were still going ahead. But a high official added that the chances that it would take place had sharply lessened because of the tensions sure to be raised as the result of the effort to prevent supplies from arriving in North Vietnam.

Anatoly F. Dobrynin, the Soviet Ambassador to the United States, was informed of Mr. Nixon's speech about an hour beforehand at a White House meeting with Henry A. Kissinger, President Nixon's adviser on national security.

Mr. Dobrynin was also the Soviet envoy in October, 1962, when President John F. Kennedy ordered a quarantine of offensive Soviet weapons being shipped to Cuba. This led to the so-called Cuban missile crisis,

Continued on Page 19, Column 5

HANOI SAYS RAIDS STRUCK AT DIKES

But U.S. Asserts Military Installations Were Hit in Attacks on North

By CRAIG R. WHITNEY

Special to The New York Times

SAIGON, South Vietnam, Tuesday, May 9—United States Navy fighter-bombers struck at North Vietnamese storage facilities, barracks and training facilities in an area about 15 miles west of Hanoi yesterday in the closest strikes to the North Vietnamese capital since April 16, the American command announced.

The command's announcement said the planes attacked "military heartland targets" that "are helping to support the Communist invasion" of South Vietnam.

The Hanoi radio, in a broadcast at noon, said American planes "deliberately struck at the dike system in Namha Province" southeast of Hanoi.

[The United States command denied that American jets had bombed the dikes, United Press International reported.]

The dikes support an elaborate system of irrigation and

Continued on Page 19, Column 7

HIGH MEAT PRICES LAID TO RACKETS

City Consumers Squeezed by 15% Inflation of Costs, Law Officials Report

By LACEY FOSBURGH

The infiltration of organized crime into key positions in the New York City meat industry has artificially inflated the retail prices for fresh meat in supermarkets by 15 per cent, according to information developed by the Manhattan District Attorney's Office and other law-enforcement agencies here and in Washington.

Consumers buying meat in the New York-New Jersey area, they say, are putting at least a million dollars a week directly into the coffers of organized crime.

Years of Collusion Alleged

Racketeers — both in the industry and in the unions that service it — have reportedly been in collusion for at least two years "systematically" extorting "week by week, month by month," as one source put it, "vast sums of money" from the supermarket chains and the wholesale suppliers.

"This is the price they pay to stay in business," another source said, "the price of labor peace."

This picture of extortion, bribery and the ultimate victimization of the consumer

Continued on Page 66, Column 1

State Senate Votes To Liberalize Curbs In Rape Testimony

By ALFONSO A. NARVAEZ

Special to The New York Times

ALBANY, May 8—The Senate gave overwhelming approval today to a bill modifying the extent to which a rape victim's testimony must be corroborated to convict an alleged attacker.

The measure, which passed by a vote of 56 to 1, removes the need for testimony corroborating the identity of the alleged assailant and the fact that penetration actually took place. The bill, passed with no debate, now goes to the Governor, who is expected to sign it.

In other action today as the Legislature continued its push for adjournment:

¶Three city officials—Controller Abraham D. Beame, City Council Majority Leader Thomas J. Cuite and the Council's finance chairman, Mario Merola—met here with state budget officials on legislation affecting the city's proposed $9.9-billion budget. The meet-

Continued on Page 27, Column 1

New Vega Recall

The General Motors Corporation yesterday recalled 350,000 of its 1971 and 1972 Vegas to correct a safety defect. It was the second major recall of Vegas in a month. Details on Page 16.

Local School Units Defended by Mayor

By LEONARD BUDER

Mayor Lindsay declared yesterday that the city's decentralized school boards had brought "a new vigor to the whole process of achieving quality public education."

Mr. Lindsay said that while it is "much too soon to make a final judgment on decentralization" he felt that "the community school boards have made important advances since the inception of decentralization a little less than two years ago."

The Mayor made the statement in commenting on the assertion Sunday by Dr. Kenneth B. Clark, a member of the State Board of Regents, that school

Continued on Page 58, Column 5

The New York Times/William E. Sauro

CITY OFFICIALS IN ALBANY: Foreground, from left: Controller Abraham D. Beame and Councilmen Thomas J. Cuite, majority leader, and Mario Merola, finance committee chairman. City budget was topic. Rear, from right, State Senator John J. Marchi, Assemblyman Alexander Chananau, almost hidden; Senator Warren M. Anderson.

4 Armed Arab Hijackers Hold Jet and 101 Hostages in Israel

By The Associated Press

TEL AVIV, May 8—Despite a tip-off and a security search, four armed Arabs hijacked an Israel-bound Belgian Sabena jetliner carrying 101 persons today.

After landing in Tel Aviv, they threatened to blow up the plane and its passengers unless Israel freed 300 Palestinian guerrilla prisoners and flew them to Cairo. A senior Israeli Army officer told the hijackers that freeing hundreds of prisoners within a few hours was impossible.

The Israelis, speaking to the hijackers by radio, were reported to have offered to free 15 or 20 military prisoners of war "as a gesture of goodwill."

The gunmen, who seized the plane after it left Vienna, set a deadline of 10 P.M. Tel Aviv time to make a deal, but the deadline passed with no explosion or other evident action.

As negotiations were being carried on by radio, the pilot, Captain Reginald Levy, said that the plane was unfit to take off. The hijackers said that it must be made ready to leave at 5:30 A.M. or that it would be blown up. They later extended the deadline again but stipulated no time.

The Arabs also demanded to talk with a representative of the International Committee of the Red Cross.

"If the plane is not refueled I think they will blow it up," Captain Levy said by radio. "They are serious."

The police in Brussels said that they had been told by tele-

Continued on Page 7, Column 1

NEWS INDEX

"All the News That's Fit to Print"

The New York Times

LATE CITY EDITION

Weather: Cloudy, mild with chance of showers today, tonight, tomorrow. Temp. range: today 59-73; Monday 57-74. Full U.S. report on Page 86.

VOL. CXXI . No. 41,751 | NEW YORK, TUESDAY, MAY 16, 1972 | 15 CENTS

WALLACE IS SHOT; CONDITION SERIOUS; A SUSPECT SEIZED AT MARYLAND RALLY

Associated Press

AFTER SPEECH: Gov. George C. Wallace takes off jacket and goes to shake hands. At front is Secret Service agent.

C.B.S. News via United Press International

DURING SHOOTING: Man at right with light hair and sun glasses holds gun as person in crowd tries to shake his arm

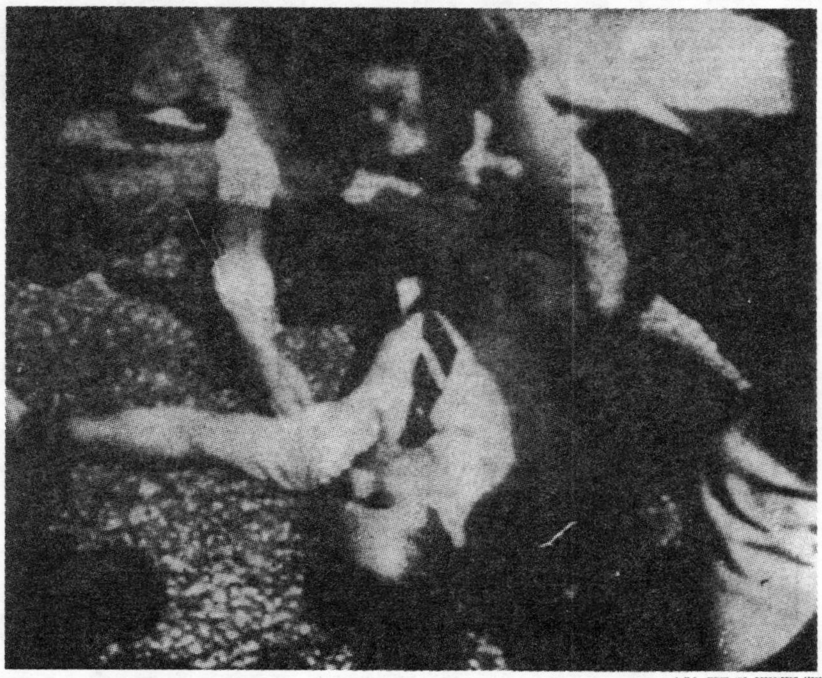

C.B.S. News via Associated Press

KNEELING OVER HUSBAND: Mrs. Cornelia Wallace bending over the Governor after he was shot at close range

3 MORE WOUNDED

Legs of Governor Are Paralyzed but Hope Is Voiced by Doctor

By R. W. APPLE Jr.

Special to The New York Times

LAUREL, Md., Tuesday, May 16—Gov. George C. Wallace of Alabama, seemingly on the verge of his greatest electoral triumphs, was shot and gravely wounded yesterday afternoon as he campaigned for President at a shopping center in this suburb of Washington.

Late last night, after the 52-year-old Governor emerged from almost five hours of emergency surgery at the Holy Cross Hospital in nearby Silver Spring, Md., one of his surgeons said that he expected Mr. Wallace "to make a full recovery."

The surgeon, Dr. Joseph Schanno, said that Mr Wallace had suffered at least four wounds and the doctors had removed one bullet. He said that another bullet was lodged near the spine and that the Governor's legs were paralyzed as a result.

Will Continue Campaign

The Governor's wife, Cornelia, said she was "very happy that he's alive and has a sound heart and a sound brain." Billy Joe Camp, his press secretary, reported this morning, after Mrs. Wallace had talked with the Governor, that he would continue his Presidential campaign and "will be at the Democratic convention as a strong, viable candidate."

The state and local police arrested a suspect, who was identified by the Justice Department as Arthur Herman Bremer, a 21-year-old white man from Milwaukee. The department said that the Secret Service had taken custody of a .38-caliber, snub-nosed, five-shot revolver allegedly used by Mr. Bremer in the shooting. Later, Federal and state charges were filed against him.

Held in $200,000 Bond

Mr. Bremer was taken before United States Magistrate Clarence Goetz in Baltimore last night and was ordered held under $200,000 bond.

Three persons who were with Governor Wallace as he plunged into the crowd at the Laurel Shopping Center were also hit by the four or five bullets fired by the attacker.

The shooting occurred after the Governor, having finished a speech here, shed his coat and stepped from behind the protection of his bullet-proof speaking stand.

A young man wearing sunglasses and a red, white and blue shirt bedecked with Wallace buttons thrust his right hand between two other people

Continued on Page 34, Column 1

Saigon's Forces Reoccupy Bastogne Base Near Hue

By MALCOLM W. BROWNE

Special to The New York Times

SAIGON, South Vietnam, Tuesday, May 16 — South Vietnamese troops, led by a platoon of 30 soldiers flown in by helicopters, reoccupied Fire Base Bastogne yesterday on the southwesterly approaches to Hue.

The five helicopters carrying the soldiers reportedly encountered no enemy fire as they landed at the base, which the South Vietnamese abandoned April 28 under heavy attack. The base had fallen after the North Vietnamese who had besieged it for more than three weeks sent commandos storming in to penetrate the barbed-wire defenses.

But after routing the defenders at the end of April, the North Vietnamese did not move their long-range 130-mm. artillery into Bastogne to shell Hue, the former imperial capital of Vietnam on the coast 15 miles away.

[The United States command announced the arrival of the carrier Saratoga off the Vietnamese coast Monday, bringing to six the number of attack carriers there. United Press International reported. The United States Seventh Fleet was now said to have 60 ships in the area.]

[In Washington, Secretary of State William P. Rogers angrily defended the mining of North Vietnam's harbors and said that if the Johnson Administration had taken the step earlier, the war might have ended long ago. Page 14.]

Allied officers in the Hue area said that if the re-entry into Fire Base Bastogne appeared to have been easy, this was only because it had capped more than a week of slow, hard fighting and several more days of heavy air and artillery bombardment.

South Vietnamese spokes-

Continued on Page 14, Column 3

PRESSURE GROUPS ANGER ROCKEFELLER

He Asserts Judges Blocked Court Reform and Lawyers Stymied 'No-Fault' Bill

By JAMES F. CLARITY

Special to The New York Times

ALBANY, May 15—Governor Rockefeller charged today that "inordinate pressures" placed on legislators by judges and lawyers had blocked two of his "vital programs"—court reform and no-fault insurance—in the 1972 Legislature.

Mr. Rockefeller, commenting on the action of the Legislature three days after it had adjourned for the year, said the

The no-fault insurance bill was defeated through the lobbying efforts of one small group of men—the New York State Trial Lawyers Association. Article on Page 31.

judges had stymied most of his court-reform program. The lawyers, Mr. Rockefeller said, had blocked the no-fault automobile accident insurance bill he had supported.

The Governor pledged to continue to fight for passage of the two programs next year. He said undue pressure had also been exerted on the legislators to repeal the state's liberalized abortion law. The Governor vetoed the repeal measure Saturday.

"My pledge is to make an all-out fight for no-fault automobile insurance and court reform in 1973," Mr. Rockefeller said at a news conference in the Red Room of the Capitol. "Some headlines have interpreted the failure of the Legislature to enact these two vital programs as a setback for me. The truth is that they marked a setback for the people of New York State.

"At no time," the Governor

Continued on Page 30, Column 3

Court Exempts the Amish From Going to High School

By FRED P. GRAHAM

Special to The New York Times

WASHINGTON, May 15—The Supreme Court ruled 7 to 0 today that the Amish religious sect is exempt from state compulsory education laws that require children to attend school beyond the eighth grade.

The Amish—the rural "plain people" who cling to a horse-and-buggy way of life—believe that education beyond the eighth grade teaches worldly values at odds with the simple life required by their creed.

With this in mind, the Court held that state laws requiring children to attend school until they are 16 years of age violate the constitutional rights of the Amish to free exercise of religion.

The decision specifically applied to Wisconsin, but it was written in terms broad enough to apply to all states that require attendance in public or private schools beyond the eighth grade. Mississippi and South Carolina are the only states that do not have compulsory school attendance laws.

The opinion, written by Chief Justice Warren E. Burger, was the first by the Court holding a religious group immune from compulsory attendance requirements.

The Court stressed the 300-year resistance of the Amish to modern influences and served notice that faddish new sects or communes that reject formal education would probably not be granted similar exemptions.

"It cannot be overemphasized," Justice Burger wrote, "that we are not dealing with a way of life and mode of education by a group claiming to have recently discovered some 'progressive' or more en-

Continued on Page 28, Column 1

NEWS INDEX

Hogan Drops Jay Kriegel Case; Reports He Can't Prove Perjury

By DAVID BURNHAM

The question of whether one of Mayor Lindsay's closest aides, Jay L. Kriegel, committed perjury during his testimony before the Knapp Commission will not be presented to a grand jury, District Attorney Frank S. Hogan announced yesterday.

Mr. Hogan said his office was dropping the case because "the people would not be able to establish beyond a reasonable doubt that there was a willful, irreconcilable inconsistency" between Mr. Kriegel's testimony before the Knapp Commission on June 17, 1971, and Dec. 20, 1971.

The commission was created by Mayor Lindsay—on the recommendation of a special committee that included Mr. Hogan—to investigate allegations of widespread police corruption and of failure by officials in the Lindsay administration to follow up on information about cases of corruption brought to their attention.

Mr. Hogan, in a two-and-a-half-page statement, said another reason for not proceeding with the case was that "there is substantial doubt concerning the authority of the Knapp commission to administer the oath" at the December hearings.

Whitman Knapp, the chairman of the commission, said in

Continued on Page 28, Column 3

GUNMAN'S ATTACK CLOUDS CAMPAIGN

Uncertainty Created Both by Wallace's Status and Impact of Shooting

By MAX FRANKEL

Special to The New York Times

WASHINGTON, May 15—The bullets that felled George C. Wallace on the eve of his greatest achievements in national politics will also upset both the conduct and the calculations of the 1972 Presidential campaign.

If he could recover in time to resume some form of campaigning, and his press secretary says he will, the Alabama Governor may find an even more aroused constituency rallying to his cause. And some degree of sympathy vote may further swell his expected victories tomorrow in the Democratic primaries of Michigan and Maryland.

The Governor had 210 delegate votes of the 1,509 needed for nomination when he was struck down.

If he is forced out of the campaign, there is no one now in sight to pick up the banner of populism, tinged with an overtone of segregation, that brought the Governor 9.9 million votes, or 13.5 per cent of the total cast for President, in 1968 and seemed to promise him an equally strong following this year.

No one has ever quite

Continued on Page 34, Column 7

Shooting Suspect Shouted: 'Hey, George! Over Here!'

By WARREN WEAVER Jr.

Special to The New York Times

LAUREL, Md., May 15 — George C. Wallace was shot while standing at the new crossroads of middle America today, between the drive-in bank and variety store of a suburban shopping center.

The suspected assailant, a young white man, called the Alabama Governor over to him after Mr. Wallace had stepped from behind his bullet-proof speaking stand and came down to shake hands with the crowd of about 1,000.

"Hey, George! Hey, George! Come over here! Come over here!" the man shouted insistently, according to several witnesses. The man had been standing against the ropes that cleared a space for security guards and reporters between the crowd and the small parking lot speaking stand.

Mr. Wallace heard the shouts and veered to his left, working his way down the line of admirers. He came first to Mrs. Brigitte Howkins of Hyattsville, a plump matron, who reached over a man, took Mr. Wallace's hand and said: "Good luck, Governor Wallace."

"He smiled at me," Mrs. Howkins recalled later, "dropped my hand and reached out for another when the man who had been standing on my right lifted his right arm and suddenly there were shots."

Mr. Wallace fell to the asphalt parking surface and lay on his back in the brilliant sunshine. Witnesses said he was bleeding from the chest and appeared also to have been struck in the right arm.

Val Hymes, a columnist for several Maryland newspapers, saw the Governor sprawled on the pavement, a large red splotch spreading across his shirt front. "I thought at first he was dead," she said.

Mrs. Wallace ran to his side,

Continued on Page 34, Column 4

Kennedy Guarded By Secret Service

By BEN A. FRANKLIN

Special to The New York Times

WASHINGTON, May 15—Shortly after Gov. George C. Wallace of Alabama was shot today, President Nixon ordered Secret Service protection for Senator Edward M. Kennedy of Massachusetts, Representative Shirley Chisholm of Brooklyn and Representative Wilbur D. Mills of Arkansas.

Senator Kennedy, who has declared repeatedly that he is not a candidate for President, accepted the offer, and an unspecified number of agents were guarding his home tonight in nearby McLean, Va. Agents joined Mrs. Chisholm in Detroit, where she was stay-

Continued on Page 35, Column 1

MILWAUKEE MAN HELD AS SUSPECT

Seized on Weapons Charge Last October in Wisconsin —Many Paradoxes Seen

By JAMES T. WOOTEN

Special to The New York Times

WASHINGTON, May 15—The young white man arrested as a suspect today in the shooting of Gov. George C. Wallace is a 21-year-old resident of Milwaukee who pasted Wallace bumper stickers on his car and his apartment door and was exuberantly cheering the Democratic Presidential candidate only moments before the shots rang out.

Those apparent contradictions are but a small part of the paradoxical picture now being sketched of Arthur Herman Bremer, the man accused by Federal authorities today of having tried to kill the Alabama Governor at a shopping center in Laurel, Md.

It was reported that he was arrested on a charge of carrying a concealed weapon last Oct. 18 and was subsequently convicted of disorderly conduct.

A Justice Department spokesman said that the .38-caliber snub-nosed revolver allegedly used at Laurel had been purchased in Milwaukee Jan. 13 and fired five times today.

From descriptions supplied

Continued on Page 34, Column 3

"All the News That's Fit to Print"

The New York Times

LATE CITY EDITION

Weather: Mostly sunny, mild today. Fair and mild tonight, tomorrow. Temp. range: today 54-71; Friday 46-67. Full U.S. report on Page 58.

VOL. CXXI ... No. 41,762 NEW YORK, SATURDAY, MAY 27, 1972 — 15 CENTS

U.S. AND SOVIET SIGN TWO ARMS ACCORDS TO LIMIT GROWTH OF ATOMIC ARSENALS; TRADE PACT DELAYED, TALKS TO GO ON

Joint Commission Set Up To Resolve Trade Issues

By ROBERT B. SEMPLE Jr.
Special to The New York Times

MOSCOW, May 26—The United States and the Soviet Union announced the formation of a joint commission today to devise a comprehensive trade agreement that has proved impossible to reach during President Nixon's visit to Moscow.

The announcement, not altogether unexpected, represented an admission by both sides that the two countries had been unable to reconcile differences on the trade issue, and it constituted the first disappointment of the Moscow summit meeting.

Under the terms of the agreement, announced to reporters here by Peter M. Flanigan, Assistant to President Nixon, the joint commission will have these assignments:

¶To negotiate an over-all trade agreement including reciprocal "most favored nation" treatment—meaning, essentially, that imports from the Soviet Union will receive the same tariff advantages given most other United States trading partners.

¶To devise arrangements under which credits will be provided to finance sales by each nation to the other.

¶To negotiate provisions for the establishment of business offices in each country by concerns in the other.

¶To set up an arbitration mechanism for settling commercial disputes arising from trade.

President Appears Tired

The President himself appeared tired yet exhilarated after his first five days in the Soviet Union. At a dinner he gave this evening for Leonid I. Brezhnev, general secretary of the Soviet Communist party, Mr. Nixon raised his glass, and said:

"We look forward to the time when we shall be able to welcome you in our country and in some way respond in an effective manner to the way in which you have received us so generously in your country."

In effect, today was Mr. Nixon's last day of official meetings with Soviet leaders. He will pay a ceremonial visit to Leningrad tomorrow, rest for most of Sunday before delivering a televised address to the Soviet people that evening, and will participate in a reception Monday before flying to Kiev.

Yet the final day ended on what was seen by both sides as an immensely positive note, reflected not only in the arms agreement but in the words of the dignitaries here.

Mr. Nixon, in his toast tonight, called the arms accord not only an "enormously important agreement" but also an "indication of what can happen in the future as we work toward peace in the

Continued on Page 9, Column 6

U.S. TRADE DEFICIT BIG AGAIN IN APRIL

Imports Exceeded Exports by $699-Million, Second Largest Gap on Record

By EDWIN L. DALE Jr.
Special to The New York Times

WASHINGTON, May 26—The United States recorded another huge deficit in its foreign trade in April, the Commerce Department reported today. Imports exceeded exports by $699-million, the second largest deficit for a month on record. The high was set last October, at $821-million.

In the first four months of the year the total trade deficit was $2.2-billion, almost guaranteeing that the year as a whole will see a larger deficit than last year's $2-billion, which was the first trade deficit in this century.

However, officials continue to expect some improvement as 1972 proceeds and the delayed effects of devaluation of the dollar begin to be felt.

Exports in April, seasonally adjusted, were $3.760-billion, down from $3.891-billion in March and the lowest export total of the year so far. A drop in exports of large jet aircraft was partly responsible.

Imports in April were $4.46-billion, down slightly from the figure of $4.475-billion in March. Both figures were above April a year ago—indicating a continued expansion of trade—but the rise in imports was much bigger than that for exports.

For the first four months of the year, exports were running

Continued on Page 35, Column 1

Lindsay Aide Says Council Must Raise Taxes on Property

By FRANCIS X. CLINES

Mayor Lindsay's office insisted yesterday that the City Council had no choice but to approve up to $89-million in higher property taxes to close an expected budget gap, regardless of the continuing opposition of Council members.

Councilman Matthew J. Troy Jr., the leader of the tax revolt, agreed with Deputy Mayor Edward K. Hamilton that there was such an obligation in the City Charter's mandate to approve real-estate taxes by June 25. But he said he would violate it rather than vote aye.

"I'm prepared to go to jail," Mr. Troy declared.

The Mayor's press spokesman, Thomas Morgan, immediately commented: "We've alerted the Corrections Department to prepare a padded cell with a view."

Thus, a farcical tone was added to the considerable confusion as the Mayor's office tried to decide what to do next in completing a balanced budg-

Continued on Page 12, Column 5

NEWS INDEX

United Press International

AFTER SIGNING: President Nixon and Leonid I. Brezhnev exchange treaty copies at Kremlin. In center, Soviet President Nikolai V. Podgorny.

FOE PUSHES FIGHT IN TWO KEY AREAS

Losses Heavy, but Enemy Clings to Small Gains at Kontum and Hue

Special to The New York Times

SAIGON, South Vietnam, Saturday, May 27—North Vietnamese soldiers hurled themselves against Government defenses in the Central Highlands city of Kontum and near the northern city of Hue through the day yesterday.

They suffered many casualties and lost 16 tanks, 13 at Kontum and three near Hue, according to American and South Vietnamese military spokesmen. But at nightfall they reportedly continued to hold small pockets of ground taken from the South Vietnamese.

In Kontum, North Vietnamese infiltrators still occupied pockets in the southeastern and northeastern parts of town and continued to keep the airport closed to traffic, according to American sources.

In the northernmost part of South Vietnam, Communist forces were said to hold small bulges of territory about 20 miles northwest of Hue, having penetrated Government defenses along the Mychanh River.

Informed sources said that at one point four North Vietnamese tanks rolled into a de-

Continued on Page 6, Column 2

A First Step, but a Major Stride

By MAX FRANKEL
Special to The New York Times

News Analysis

MOSCOW, Saturday, May 27—The nuclear age gained its first strategic arms limitation treaty in the Kremlin last night. Its awkward name—commonly shortened to SALT—is needed because the accord involves no disarmament. Its purpose is to freeze the balance of terrifying weapons and to make sure the terror works by preventing any effective defense against them.

It is a major step forward in the already long history of nuclear arms negotiation. But it is also only a beginning.

Both President Nixon and the Soviet Party chief, Leonid I. Brezhnev, vowed to press ahead toward further limitations and perhaps eventually even some reductions in arms. So this treaty is likely to be known as SALT I.

It is a beginning, achieved after seven years of effort and 30 months of negotiation in one of those fleeting moments when the two superpowers felt themselves strategic equals, despite inequality in the quality and number of their arms, and when their two leaders felt themselves strong enough politically to make the agreements stick.

The arms race will go on, not only in the regular army, navy and air force weaponry that is unaffected by the accord but also in the quality of nuclear warheads—that is, their size and accuracy and evasive skills—and in the arts of antisubmarine warfare and even in the technology of the missile defense systems that the treaty is to limit severely at inadequate levels.

Indeed, under certain conditions or political pressures, the treaty itself may stimulate further competition in these uncovered areas. And because the accord renounces those weapons that both sides think they now possess in sufficient number, it may not even save much money in future budgets.

The United States had no plans to augment the land and submarine missiles and antimissile installations covered by the treaty. The energetic Soviet build-up of recent years was presumably intended primarily to reach a comfortable level before the freeze.

The significance of the treaty lies in that it makes the freeze legally binding. It becomes an important weapon for political

Continued on Page 9, Column 7

LAIRD DISCOUNTS BIG ARMS SAVINGS

Reaction to Pact in Capital Mostly Favorable but Some Conservatives Are Critical

By JUAN M. VASQUEZ
Special to The New York Times

WASHINGTON, May 26—Defense Secretary Melvin R. Laird today hailed the United States arms agreements with the Soviet Union but warned against the expectation of major cost savings.

Returning to the capital after several days of discussions with Atlantic alliance defense ministers in Brussels, Mr. Laird declared that the agreements to limit strategic arms "will enhance the national security of the United States."

He asserted, however, that "we still need to keep up our guard" and that the United States must "maintain a technological superior position."

He added, "There will be no savings as far as the request for offensive strategic weapons which have been presented to the Congress in the 1973 budget."

Specifically, he cited the Air Force B-1 bomber program and submarine construction as areas in which Congress might seek reductions, according to reports he had heard. "That just cannot be," he said.

Mr. Laird, a former Congressman from Wisconsin, told

Continued on Page 10, Column 3

Court Throws Out Jersey Law Barring Primary Cross-Voting

Special to The New York Times

NEWARK, May 26—New Jersey's primary election law prohibiting enrolled voters from casting ballots in other party contests was declared unconstitutional today by a three-judge Federal panel.

The decision specifically threw out the provisions that require enrolled voters to sit out two consecutive primary elections before switching parties. The court declared this waiting period "unreasonable and excessive."

The court directed Attorney General George F. Kugler Jr. to notify local election boards that they must permit voters to choose in which primary they want to vote on June 6 without reference to their party enrollment.

A spokesman for the Attorney General said he would not comment on whether the decision would be appealed until he had had time to study it.

If the decision stands for the coming primary, it could affect the outcome of the contests for 109 Democratic convention delegates between Senators Hubert H. Humphrey and George McGovern. Republican voters could tip the scales in favor of the man they consider the weaker candidate against President Nixon, who is unopposed on the Republican primary ballot.

The Democratic state chairman, Salvatore A. Bontempo, said he did not know how the decision would affect the primary balloting but said he was

Continued on Page 22, Column 2

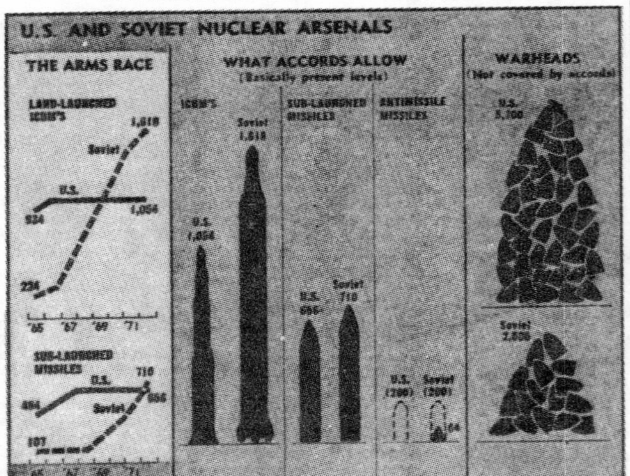

Photograph from Gamma/Photoreporters — The New York Times/May 27, 1972

MISSILE IN SILO: Above photograph, from a Czech source, is said to show a Soviet emplacement. Soviet arms totals on chart include weapons that are under construction.

Von Braun Will Leave NASA For Job in Aerospace Industry

By HAROLD M. SCHMECK Jr.
Special to The New York Times

WASHINGTON, May 26—Dr. Wernher von Braun, one of the chief architects of man's first landing on the moon, is retiring from the National Aeronautics and Space Administration.

The German-born rocket expert, who has worked for the United States Government since the end of World War II, will leave the space agency July 1 to become corporate vice president for engineering and development of Fairchild Industries, a major aerospace company.

"Dr. von Braun's decision to retire from NASA is a source of great regret to all of us at the agency," said Dr. James C. Fletcher, NASA's administrator.

"For more than a quarter of a century, he has served the United States as the leader in space rocket development," Dr. Fletcher said in the announcement. "His efforts first put the United States in space with Explorer 1. As director of the Marshall Space Flight Center for over 10 years, he directed the development of the world's most powerful rocket, the Saturn 5—which has taken 10 American astronauts to the surface of the moon."

Two of those astronauts, Neil A. Armstrong, the first man to set foot on the moon, and Edwin E. Aldrin Jr., his companion on the historic Apollo 11 moon landing, have al-

Continued on Page 59, Column 1

CEILINGS ARE SET

Nixon and Brezhnev Pledge to Abide by Treaty at Once

By HEDRICK SMITH
Special to The New York Times

MOSCOW, Saturday, May 27—President Nixon and the Soviet Communist party leader, Leonid I. Brezhnev, signed two historic agreements last night that for the first time put limits on the growth of American and Soviet strategic nuclear arsenals.

In a brief televised ceremony in the Great Hall of the Kremlin, the two leaders put their

Arms accord texts, Page 8, and toasts on Page 9

signatures to a treaty that establishes a ceiling of 200 launchers for each side's defensive missile systems and commits them not to try to build nationwide antimissile defenses. The treaty, which is to run indefinitely, requires ratification by the Senate in Washington, but both sides pledged to abide by it at once.

Applause After Signing

They also signed an interim accord on offensive systems that freezes land-based and submarine-based intercontinental missiles at the level now in operation or under construction.

After signing the two accords, Mr. Brezhnev and Mr. Nixon walked toward each other, smiling broadly, and shook hands vigorously amidst applause from a gathering of senior officials, including negotiators who had worked through the day to put the final touches on the agreement.

Mr. Nixon then said:

"We want to be remembered by our deeds, not by the fact that we brought war to the world, but by the fact that we made the world a more peaceful one for all peoples of the world."

Can Improve Quality

Mr. Kosygin said in reply:

"This is a great victory for the Soviet and American peoples in the matter of easing international tension. This is a victory for all peaceloving people, because security and peace is the common goal."

Later, American officials reported that the two leaders had resolved several deadlocks in their talks here this week.

In a toast at a dinner he gave for the Soviet leaders at Spaso House, the American Ambassador's residence, the President hailed the agreements as "enormously important."

Gerard C. Smith, the chief American negotiator, told reporters that today's two agreements were "not the end of the road by any means, but they

Continued on Page 8, Column 1

"All the News That's Fit to Print"

The New York Times

LATE CITY EDITION

Weather: Rain today; showers likely tonight. Fair and milder tomorrow. Temp. range: today 68-74; Thursday 66-76. Temp.-Hum. Index yesterday 71. Full U.S. report on Page 70.

VOL. CXXI . No. 41,796

NEW YORK, FRIDAY, JUNE 30, 1972

15 CENTS

SUPREME COURT, 5-4, BARS DEATH PENALTY AS IT IS IMPOSED UNDER PRESENT STATUTES

Party Panel Strips McGovern of 151 California Delegates

SENATOR SET BACK

He Deplores Move by Coalition of Rivals—State Law Ignored

By WARREN WEAVER Jr.

Special to The New York Times

WASHINGTON, June 29—The Democratic National Convention's Credentials Committee stripped Senator George McGovern today of 151 delegates he thought he had won in the California primary, disregarding state law in a display of political power.

Accomplished by a coalition of his rivals for the Presidential nomination, the move abruptly slowed the momentum of the South Dakotan's campaign and heavily clouded his prospects for tying up the nomination before the convention meets July 10.

The committee ended nearly four hours of debate by voting, 72 to 66, to divide the 271-member California delegation among all the Presidential candidates who competed in the June 6 primary, instead of following the California statute, which allots all the delegates to whoever gets the most votes.

Move Called 'Outrageous'

In an unusually bitter news conference at the Capitol, Senator McGovern called the committee decision "an incredible, cynical, rotten political steal" and "an outrageous way to treat the American people."

Informed at a National Press Club luncheon about the committee action, Senator Hubert H. Humphrey said that his chances for the nomination had been "markedly improved."

"I'm not going to say any more—I've got the votes," the Minnesotan said.

Authoritative sources said, meanwhile, that Senator McGovern, if he ultimately won the nomination, viewed Senator Edward M. Kennedy of Massachusetts as his first choice for a running mate. [Details on Page 20.]

Appealed Is Planned

The Credentials Committee decision will be appealed to the convention when it opens in Miami Beach, but it may prove difficult for the McGovern forces to reverse because the 151 delegates at issue—or perhaps the entire 271 from California—will not be able to vote on their own case.

This dramatic reversal for Senator McGovern was achieved by a tight, well-disciplined coalition of committee members who were either uncommitted or favored Senator Humphrey, Senator Edmund S. Muskie of Maine, Senator Henry M. Jackson of Washington or Gov. George C. Wallace of Alabama.

The development provoked angry protests from Mr. McGovern's supporters, who main-

Continued on Page 20, Column 3

Press Loses Plea to Keep Data From Grand Juries

Special to The New York Times

WASHINGTON, June 29—The Supreme Court held 5 to 4 today that journalists have no First Amendment right to refuse to tell grand juries the names of confidential sources and information given to them in confidence.

The decision overturned a lower Federal court ruling on behalf of Earl Caldwell, a reporter for The New York Times

Excerpts from Supreme Court action are on Page 15.

in San Francisco, who had refused to enter a Federal grand jury room to be questioned on information given him by the Black Panther party.

In two related cases, the Court held that Paul M. Branzburg, an investigative reporter for The Louisville Courier-Journal at the time his case arose, and Paul Pappas, a television newsman in New Bedford, Mass., must tell state grand juries names and other information given them in confidence or face imprisonment for contempt.

The sweeping decision by Justice Byron R. White, supported by President Nixon's four appointees, contained a firm rejection of the theory that the First Amendment shields newsmen under certain circumstances from having to testify when the result would be to cut off news sources and deprive the public of news.

This theory has never been considered before today by the Supreme Court. But in recent years, as a wave of subpoenas issued from grand juries for newsmen's notes, radio stations' tapes and television companies' films, some lower courts began to construe the First Amendment as giving journalists some protection against being compelled to disclose confidences.

The courts usually reasoned that if forcing a newsman to testify would cut off future information, he should be excused unless the Government could show a compelling need for his testimony.

"We cannot accept the argu-

Continued on Page 15, Column 4

NIXON DISCLOSES VIETNAM PARLEY RESUMES JULY 13

He Says U.S. Is Returning on Assumption Hanoi Will Negotiate Constructively

By ROBERT B. SEMPLE Jr.

Special to The New York Times

WASHINGTON, June 29 — President Nixon disclosed tonight that the United States and North Vietnam would resume the Paris peace talks on the Vietnam war on July 13.

In a nationally televised news conference—his first in more

Transcript of Nixon news conference is on Page 2.

than a year—Mr. Nixon said the United States was returning to the negotiating table "on the assumption that the North Vietnamese are prepared to negotiate in a constructive and serious way."

He said that if both sides were prepared to engage in serious talks the war could be ended by next year. He also left open the opposite possibility—that the North Vietnamese might not proceed "on that basis," in which case he vowed to continue American bombing and other forms of military pressure. [Question 1, Page 2.]

Talks 'Without Conditions'

Though Mr. Nixon seemed pleased to anounce the resumption of the talks, which were suspended by the United States on May 4, he gave no hint in his remarks that his intense diplomacy in Moscow and Peking in recent weeks had produced assurances that Hanoi was now prepared to move closer to the American position. The most he could or would say was that both sides had agreed to resume negotiating "without conditions."

The President also used the news conference to offer an unusually strong defense of his bombing policy and to give that policy an expanded rationale. In previous statements he has described the bombing as an essentially military tactic designed to protect the shrinking American ground forces in Vietnam and to compensate for the North Vietnamese attacks launched at the end of March.

Tonight he emphasized that

Continued on Page 3, Column 5

Associated Press

SPARED: Elmer Branch, 19, sentenced to die for nonfatal assault, in Huntsville, Tex., jail. He was one of condemned men whose sentences were upset by Supreme Court.

COURT SPARES 600

4 Justices Named by Nixon All Dissent in Historic Decision

By FRED P. GRAHAM

Special to The New York Times

WASHINGTON, June 29—The Supreme Court ruled today that capital punishment, as now administered in the United States, is unconstitutional "cruel and unusual" punishment.

The historic decision, came on a vote of 5 to 4.

Although the five Justices in the majority issued separate opinions and did not agree on

Excerpts from Court decision on death penalty, Page 14.

a single reason for their action, the effect of the decision appeared to be to rule out executions under any capital punishment laws now in effect in this country.

The decision will also save from execution 600 condemned men and women now on death rows in the United States, although it did not overturn their convictions. Most will be held in prison for the rest of their lives, but under some states' procedures some of the prisoners may eventually gain their freedom.

Eighth Amendment Cited

The decision pitted the five holdovers of the more liberal Warren Court against the four appointees of President Nixon, who dissented. The ruling came as the Supreme Court handed down its final decisions of the year and recessed until Oct. 2.

Three Justices in the majority, William O. Douglas, William J. Brennan Jr. and Thurgood Marshall, concluded that executions in modern-day America necessarily violate the Eighth Amendment's prohibition against "cruel and unusual punishments."

The other two in the majority, the two "swing men" of the Court, Justices Potter Stewart and Byron R. White, reasoned that the present legal system operates in a cruel and unusual way, because it gives judges and juries the discretion to decree life or death and they impose it erratically.

As Justice Stewart put it, the death penalty is "so wantonly and so freakishly imposed" that those who are sentenced to death receive excessively harsh treatment.

View of Chief Justice

"These death sentences are cruel and unusual in the same way that being struck by lightning is cruel and unusual," he said.

As the dissenters pointed out, this alignment means that no death sentence can pass muster before the present Supreme Court unless it satisfies the objections voiced by Justices Stewart and White.

Chief Justice Warren E. Burger suggested that legislatures could attempt to do this in two ways. One is to state in statute books in detail the conditions under which a judge or jury can impose the death penalty—such as rape accompanied by a vicious assault, or a convict's murder of a prison paguard.

The second would be to revert to the practice of more than a century ago, and impose mandatory death sentences for

Continued on Page 14, Column 4

Gravel Is Denied Immunity In Case of Pentagon Papers

By ROBERT M. SMITH

Special to The New York Times

WASHINGTON, June 29—The Supreme Court ruled today, by a 5-to-4 vote, that Congressional immunity did not prevent a grand jury from asking Senator Mike Gravel or his aides certain questions about his version of the Pentagon papers—including the question where had he obtained the papers.

In a second case that turned on the same constitutional issue, the Court held, 6 to 3, that legislative privilege did not shield Daniel B. Brewster, a former Democratic Senator from Maryland, from prosecution on bribery charges.

Both decisions were handed down, with several others, on the last day of the Court's current term. The Gravel decision was written by Justice Byron R. White, who was joined by the four men President Nixon named to the Court—Chief Justice Warren E. Burger and Associate Justices Harry A. Blackmun, Lewis F. Powell Jr. and William H. Rehnquist.

Senator Gravel, Democrat of Alaska, reacted by issuing a

Continueu on Page 16, Column 4

FUND MISUSE LAID TO 4 L.I. UNIONISTS

U.S. Says They Used Money in Labor-Industry Pool to Pay Ball Team's Debt

By DAVID K. SHIPLER

Four officials of a Long Island construction union were charged yesterday with using employer funds to pay off a union debt of $11,245.

The charges, filed by the Federal Organized Crime Strike Force in Brooklyn, came just hours after city officials discharged a veteran inspector in the Buildings Department who was accused of taking a $100 bribe from the owner of a Park Avenue cooperative apartment.

The two cases, while unrelated, continued to focus attention on the widespread corruption in the construction industry described early in the week by a New York Times report. According to the articles in The Times, based on a six-week investigation, builders pay at least $25-million a year here in bribes to inspectors, policemen, union

Continued on Page 28, Column 1

PRESIDENT WIDENS FOOD PRICE CURBS

Applies Controls to Produce After It Leaves the Farm —Seafood Also Covered

Special to The New York Times

WASHINGTON, June 29—President Nixon extended controls today to the retail and wholesale prices of such unprocessed food products as eggs, fresh vegetables, fresh fruits and all raw seafood products.

But he stopped short of the far more drastic step of placing direct controls on the prices farmers receive for these products.

The action was the President's second effort this week to impose some restraint on rising food prices, which could be a crucial issue next fall in the Presidential campaign. His reluctance to act directly on farm prices, however, appeared to reflect his concern about antagonizing the farm vote in an election year, as well as fears among some officials that direct controls might be difficult to enforce and might result in shortages.

Officials conceded at a White House briefing that the action might have little immediate effect on prices. But they expressed hope that it would exert pressure on mark-ups and profit margins at each stage of the food distribution chain that, in time, could stem the

Continued on Page 10, Column 2

Nixon Backs Death Penalty For Kidnapping, Hijacking

By WILLIAM ROBBINS

Special to The New York Times

WASHINGTON, June 29—President Nixon said tonight he hoped that the Supreme Court's decision restricting the death penalty "does not go so far as to rule out capital punishment for kidnapping and hijacking."

Asked about the Court's 5-to-4 decision, issued today, Mr. Nixon said that "any punishment is cruel and inhuman which takes the life of man or woman." He added that the death penalty had actually saved lives by deterring such major crimes as kidnapping. [Question 15, Page 2.]

The President acknowledged, however, that he had not had time to study all nine opinions. He said that he had read only the opinion of Chief Justice Warren E. Burger, which was a dissent from the majority ruling.

The words of the Chief Justice as well as those of another dissenter, Justice Powell, clearly bar capital punishment under both Federal and state laws as presently written.

"Not only does it [the ruling] invalidate hundreds of state and Federal laws," Justice Powell wrote in his dissenting opinion, "it deprives those jurisdictions of the power to legislate with respect to capital punishment in the future, except in a matter consistent with the cloudily outlined views of those Justices who do not purport to undertake total abolition."

And Chief Justice Burger himself said: "It is clear that if state legislatures and the Congress wish to maintain the availability of capital punishment, significant statutory changes will have to be made."

On other domestic questions, the President did the following:

¶He declined to say whether Vice President Agnew would be his choice as a running-mate in the next election.

¶He voiced support for legislation specifically restricting the possession of handguns.

¶He said former Secretary of

Continued on Page 14, Column 5

U.S. Copters Ferry 1,000 To Quangtri Battleground

By MALCOLM W. BROWNE

Special to The New York Times

SAIGON, South Vietnam, Friday, June 30—About 1,000 South Vietnamese marines were flown by United States helicopters yesterday into an area between the city of Quangtri and the South China Sea to join in the drive to retake the Communist-held province.

With the South Vietnamese offensive in the northernmost part of the country broadened, heavy fighting was reported from the area today. The thrust was begun Wednesday by a task force of more than 10,000 South Vietnamese marines and paratroopers.

During the night, South Vietnamese troops reported that they killed 225 enemy soldiers in various enemy sectors. Two enemy tanks were reported destroyed by artillery fire near Hailang, in the southern part of Quangtri province, where the bulk of the South Vietnamese tank force was fighting.

The helicopter-borne assault yesterday brought two battalions of South Vietnamese marines into two landing zones in a region east of the city of Quangtri. That city was abandoned to Communist forces on May 1 and the present drive is intended to oust the North Vietnamese from the whole province within three months.

The main South Vietnamese force, which began a northward drive Wednesday from positions along the Mychanh river line, northwest of the city of Hue, consists of elements of South Vietnamese marine and airborne divisions.

A United States Navy spokesman said that American marine helicopters took four hours to complete the landings. While a South Vietnamese spokesman said there had been no enemy opposition, another American spokesman said enemy ground fire had been encountered in both of the landing zones east of the city.

After heavy naval bombard-

Continued on Page 3, Column 4

$502,000 Hijacking Laid to Jobless Man

By JERRY M. FLINT

Special to The New York Times

DETROIT, June 29—Martin Joseph McNally, 28 years old, was arrested last night in front of his home in Wyandotte, Mich., outside Detroit, by agents of the Federal Bureau of Investigation and charged with air piracy in connection with an airline hijacking in the Midwest last week in which $502,000 ransom was paid. He was held today in $100,000 bond.

The hijacker bailed out over Peru, Ind., but dropped the money, which was later recovered.

Government attorneys said Mr. McNally; an unemployed

Continued on Page 9, Column 2

Parole in Capital Offenses Less Likely, Officials Say

By MARTIN ARNOLD

Governors and high state officials said yesterday that the Supreme Court's ruling that capital punishment was unconstitutional could profoundly change the structure of criminal penalties in the country.

Officials in many areas said it might become much more difficult, if not impossible, to get parole in cases that were until yesterday capital offenses. Thus, when a person is sentenced to life in prison, it may mean just that, they said.

Gov. Preston Smith of Texas said that the state legislature would be called upon to pass mandatory life prison sentences for certain crimes, barring any parole.

Gov. Jimmy Carter of Georgia said:

"This decision clears the way for us to re-examine all our laws in Georgia. I still don't think seven years is long enough for a man to serve in prison who has committed premeditated murder and is given a life sentence."

Gov. Ronald Reagan of California said he believed that the ruling would allow his state to reinstate the death penalty in certain cases — "cold-blooded, premeditated, planned murder"—if the voters approved a death penalty referendum that will be on the ballot in November.

Brendan Ryan, St. Louis Circuit Attorney, said: "We will have to re-examine our statutes and perhaps make a life sentence really mean life. Perhaps we should now redefine our homicide laws so as to make some eligible for parole after a given time, but others only parolable through executive clemency, if at all."

Prof. Yale Kamisar of the University of Michigan Law School, considered one of the nation's leading constitutional authorities, expressed surprise and delight with the ruling, but was fearful that there would be a reaction against it.

"There will be increased attention given life sentencing."

Continued on Page 15, Column 1

Senate Votes Antipoverty Bill, Including Plan for Legal Aid

By The Associated Press

WASHINGTON, June 29—The Senate passed a $9.6-billion antipoverty bill today that included a provision to put the Legal Services program for the poor under an independent corporation.

The bill, passed by a vote of 74 to 16 after a week of debate, authorizes funds for two additional years for programs designed to help 26 million Americans officially defined as poor.

The Senate vote sent the legislation back to the House, which passed a somewhat different version last February.

The conference to try to settle the differences between the two measures will be held after Congress returns July 17 from its recess for the Democratic National Convention.

The bill authorizes sums well beyond President Nixon's recommendations for many programs of the Office of Economic Opportunity, the antipoverty agency. And the bill does not give the President the completely free hand he sought in handling or transferring the programs.

In addition, Administration officials indicated that they still found unacceptable the form of the Legal Services Corporation set out in the bill.

For these reasons, there is reason to believe that Mr. Nixon

Continued on Page 18, Column 4

NEWS INDEX

"All the News
That's Fit to Print"

The New York Times

LATE CITY EDITION

Weather: Sunny and milder today; fair and mild tonight, tomorrow. Temp. range: today 58-77; Tuesday 57-74. Temp.-Hum. Index yesterday 67. Full U.S. report on Page 90.

VOL. CXXI . . . No. 41,864 | © 1972 The New York Times Company | NEW YORK, WEDNESDAY, SEPTEMBER 6, 1972 | 15 CENTS

9 ISRAELIS ON OLYMPIC TEAM KILLED WITH 4 ARAB CAPTORS AS POLICE FIGHT BAND THAT DISRUPTED MUNICH GAMES

United Press International

A copter making a test run before picking up Arabs involved in the attack on Israelis. At rear is the Olympic Tower. Sign in German says, "Olympic Village, Gate 6."

MRS. MEIR SPEAKS

A Hushed Parliament Hears Her Assail 'Lunatic Acts'

By TERENCE SMITH

Special to The New York Times

JERUSALEM, Sept. 5—Her voice heavy and trembling with emotion, Premier Golda Meir today denounced "these lunatic acts of terrorism, abduction and blackmail, which tear asunder the web of international life."

Speaking to a hushed and somber parliament before the fate of the Israeli hostages held captive in Munich was known, she said, "It is inconceivable that the Olympic events should continue as long as our citizens are under the threat of being murdered in the Olympic Village."

She called on all the nations participating in the Olympics to do "whatever is necessary" to rescue the nine Israelis taken hostage by Arab guerrillas in an early-morning attack in which two other Israelis were killed.

[Official sources in Jerusalem said early Wednesday that the Cabinet would meet later in the morning and that there would be no statement on the deaths of the hostages until then.]

Cabinet Still Firm

Although she was not explicit, Mrs. Meir left the impression that Israel would continue to refuse the guerrillas' demands for the release of 200 Palestinian commandos held in this country. Cabinet sources said the Government remained committed to its hard-line policy of neither dealing with nor making concessions to the guerrillas.

Most Israelis seemed stunned by the news of the bizarre attack on the Israeli athletes, which was first reported here on a radio broadcast at 9 A.M. (3 A.M. Tuesday, New York time). Although Israeli citizens traveling abroad have been attacked by Palestinian guerrillas before, the Olympics seemed to many an unlikely setting.

"The games were going so well," one Jerusalem news dealer said, "and now this."

In parliament, where the members had gathered in an extraordinary session to confirm the Justice Minister, the attack was the sole topic of conversation.

Cabinet Ministers and members of parliament sat in the building's modern, sun-washed dining room waiting for additional news from Munich. Each hour on the hour, the large room grew silent and the ministers gathered four deep around a radio as the Israeli radio summarized the developments.

The tension was greatest at

Continued on Page 20, Column 2

West German policemen talking with a spokesman, right, for Arabs who invaded Israeli quarters at Olympic Village

Associated Press

A West German Army ambulance passing through the heavily guarded gate at the military airfield in Fürstenfeldbruck, near Munich, after the commandos and the hostages landed in three helicopters.

A 23-HOUR DRAMA

2 Others Are Slain in Their Quarters in Guerrilla Raid

By DAVID BINDER

Special to The New York Times

MUNICH, West Germany, Wednesday, Sept. 6—Eleven members of Israel's Olympic team and four Arab terrorists were killed yesterday in a 23-hour drama that began with an invasion of the Olympic Village by the Arabs. It ended in a shootout at a military airport some 15 miles away as the Arabs were preparing to fly to Cairo with their Israeli hostages.

The first two Israelis were killed early yesterday morning when Arab commandos, armed with automatic rifles, broke into the quarters of the Israeli team and seized nine others as hostages. The hostages were killed in the airport shootout between the Arabs and German policemen and soldiers.

The bloodshed brought the suspension of the Olympic Games and there was doubt if they would be resumed. Willi Daume, president of the West German Organizing Committee, announced early today that he would ask the International Olympic Committee to meet tomorrow to decide whether they should continue.

Policeman Killed

In addition to the slain Israelis and Arabs, a German policeman was killed and a helicopter pilot was critically wounded. Three Arabs were wounded.

There were some reports that two of the hostages said to have been killed might still be alive. "It is a dim hope," said Dr. Bruno Merk, the Interior Minister of Bavaria, "but I am skeptical on this point."

The bloodbath at the airport that ended at 1 A.M. today, came after long hours of negotiaton between German and Arabs at the Israeli quarters in the Olympic Village where the Arabs demanded the release of 200 Arab commandos imprisoned in Israel.

Finally the West German armed forces supplied three helicopters to transport the Arabs and their Israeli hostages to the airport at Fürstenfeldbruck. From there all were to be flown to Cairo.

A Boeing-707 provided by the Lufthansa German Airlines was waiting.

Two of the terrorists, carrying their automatic rifles, walked about 170 yards from the helicopters to the plane. And then they started back to pick up the other Arabs and the hostages.

Positions Cited

As the Arabs were returning, German sharpshooters reportedly opened fire from the darkness beyond the pools of light at the airport. The Arabs returned fire.

The torment of the entire event was heightened by confusion created in the public mind by contradictory reports from German and Olympic officials after the gunfire erupted at the airport.

Dr. Merk, in a press conference at 3 o'clock this morning said:

"In this situation our task and goal to free the hostages was made more difficult by the lack of agreement from Israel to free prisoners or to get guarantees from the Arabs not to take action against the hos-

Continued on Page 18, Column 1

752 Air-Conditioned Cars Ordered for City Subways

By EDWARD RANZAL

Mayor Lindsay announced yesterday that 752 new air-conditioned subway cars had been ordered for $210.5-million. He said the contract was the largest ever signed in the country for the purchase of passenger railroad cars.

The first group of cars, which will be manufactured by the Pullman - Standard Company, are to be delivered by 1973.

The cars will provide a quieter ride than present equipment, according to Dr. William J. Ronan, chairman of the Metropolitan Transportation Authority.

The new equipment, which will be used on the IND and BMT lines, will enable the authority to phase out more than 1,200 pre-World War II cars, which are smaller than the new ones. A study is being made, Dr. Ronan said, to produce an air-conditioned unit that can be used in cars in the smaller tunnels of the IRT system.

20% of Fleet by '75

Each car will cost more than $273,000. The city will provide one-third of the total funds—the money has been provided in the city's 1972-73 capital budget—and the Federal Urban Mass Transportation Administration will supply the rest.

By 1975 more than 20 per cent of the city's fleet of nearly 7,000 subway cars will consist of new air-conditioned cars.

The first order will be for 454 cars at a cost of $127.4-million. Some of them will be delivered in

Continued on Page 91, Column 2

Berrigan and a Nun Get Prison Terms In Letter Smuggling

By JOHN KIFNER

Special to The New York Times

HARRISBURG, Pa., Sept. 5—The Rev. Philip F. Berrigan—cleared of charges that he led a plot to kidnap President Nixon's adviser on national security affairs, Henry A. Kissinger—was sentenced in Federal District Court here today to four concurrent two-year terms for smuggling letters out of the Lewisburg Penitentiary.

Sister Elizabeth McAlister, also cleared of the plot charges, was sentenced to one year in jail and three years' probation for smuggling letters.

Moments after the sentences were announced, Government attorneys moved to dismiss the first three substantive counts of their indictment, confirming that the Justice Department would not seek a retrial of the controversial "Harrisburg Seven" case.

The Government charged Father Berrigan, Sister Elizabeth, two other Roman Catholic priests, a former priest, a former nun and a Pakistani scholar with conspiracy to kidnap Mr. Kissinger as ransom to force a halt to the bombing in Viet-

Continued on Page 16, Column 1

PARLEY REJECTS HIJACKING TREATY

U.S.-Canadian Project for Penalizing Nations Aiding Air Pirates Rebuffed

By ROBERT LINDSEY

Special to The New York Times

WASHINGTON, Sept. 5—Delegates to a 17-nation conference here rejected today United States-Canadian efforts to negotiate an international antihijacking treaty based on a draft proposed by the two nations.

The move for nonacceptance was led by France and Britain and supported by the Soviet Union and Egypt.

Faced with what appeared to be certain defeat of the proposed treaty if it came to a vote, the two North American nations acquiesced in a French proposal to start writing a new treaty from scratch, after debates on what "principles" should be included.

The delegates have eight working days left before the conference is scheduled to end.

Today's rejection was a significant setback for the United

Continued on Page 91, Column 2

Nixon Tightens Security In U.S. Against 'Outlaws'

By TAD SZULC

Special to The New York Times

WASHINGTON, Sept. 5—President Nixon said today that "extra security measures" would be taken in the United States to protect American citizens as well as visiting Israelis from possible attacks by Palestinian guerrillas.

Mr. Nixon, speaking to newsmen in San Francisco, left it unclear, however, whether the new protection would cover prominent American Jews or only those whom he described as "Americans of Israeli background, American citizens."

Speaking before the gunfight at a military airport in Munich, in which the Israeli hostages were killed, Mr. Nixon discussed the capture of Israeli Olympic team members by Palestinian guerrillas and the slaying of two Israelis. He said:

"Since we are dealing with international outlaws who are unpredictable, we have to take extra security measures to protect those who might be the targets of this kind of activity in the future. That might include Americans of Israeli background, American citizens."

Late tonight, after word was received in Washington of the death of the Israeli hostages and West German policemen,

Secretary of State William P. Rogers issued this statement on behalf of the Administration:

"There are no words which can fully express our reaction to today's tragedy at the Olympic Games. I know I speak for all Americans in extending the deepest sympathies of the

Continued on Page 18, Column 4

Reports First Said Israelis Were Safe

Contradictory reports last night about the fate of the Israeli hostages seized by Arab terrorists in the Olympic Village threw the public into confusion all over the world.

Throughout the day, as the tragedy in Munich unfolded, millions of viewers throughout the world watched on live television, which employed circuits that had been intended for the Games. But in the evening, when the events reached their climax, viewers could get no definitive word for hours on how the hostages fared.

At first the West German Government's official spokesman, Conrad Ahlers, announced

Continued on Page 20, Column 1

GAMES SUSPENDED; RITES IN ARENA SET

Halt Is the First Since 1896, When the Classic Resumed —Egypt Team in Forfeit

By NEIL AMDUR

Special to The New York Times

MUNICH, West Germany, Wednesday, Sept. 6 — The Olympic Games were suspended yesterday for the first time since competition in the modern era began in 1896.

Late-afternoon and evening events were called off in the wake of an attack staged by Arab guerrillas before dawn on the Olympic Village in which two Israelis were killed and nine others taken hostage. The hostages were later killed.

After the attack, Mark Spitz, the American swimmer who won seven gold medals at the Munich Olympics and who is Jewish, flew hurriedly to London on his way back to the United States. There were fears before his departure that he too might become a victim. [Page 20.]

The announcement of the suspension, made by the International Olympic Committee, also said that a memorial service would be held for the victims

Continued on Page 18, Column 7

Elizabeth City Hall Under Investigation

By RONALD SULLIVAN

Special to The New York Times

TRENTON, Sept. 5—Law enforcement authorities reported here today that the administration of Mayor Thomas J. Dunn of Elizabeth was the target of a Union County grand jury investigation of alleged municipal corruption.

Mayor Dunn, a Democrat running for a third term, said in an interview that he had "no knowledge of any investigation involving me or my administration." But he said he volunteered last spring to go before a Union County grand jury.

According to official sources, the grand jury is investigating charges of payoffs and kickbacks involving city officials, contracts and businessmen. City license officials have already been subpoenaed, as have a number of city records and contracts.

Karl Asch, the county prosecutor, refused to comment on the nature of the reported investigation. He did say his staff had been instructed to seek indictments before the Nov. 7 elections.

Last week two of Mr. Dunn's three mayoral opponents were indicted in separate matters by a Union County grand jury.

Matthew J. Nilsen, a Republican freeholder in the county, was indicted on charges of atrocious assault in August in a case involving an alleged extortion.

In the other indictment, Michael J. DeMartino, a Democratic City Councilman in Elizabeth, was charged with misconduct in office in a case involving a $3,000 bribe in 1968.

Mayor Dunn recently endorsed President Nixon for reelection. Political observers in Union County noted that the indictments of two of his opponents were sought by a Republican prosecutor, and were seen as aiding the Mayor's re-election chances.

However, Mr. Asch, who has obtained indictments against prominent Union County political figures in recent months, contended today that his anticorruption drive was "absolutely nonpolitical" and that the investigation of the Dunn

Continued on Page 69, Column 6

NEWS INDEX

"All the News That's Fit to Print"

The New York Times

LATE CITY EDITION

Weather: Cloudy, rain likely today and tonight. Cloudy, cool tomorrow. Temp. range: today 48-60; Tuesday 45-61. Full U.S. report on Page 93.

VOL. CXXII . . No. 41,927 — NEW YORK, WEDNESDAY, NOVEMBER 8, 1972 — 15 CENTS

NIXON ELECTED IN LANDSLIDE; M'GOVERN IS BEATEN IN STATE; DEMOCRATS RETAIN CONGRESS

President Loses in City By 81,920-Vote Margin

By FRANK LYNN

President Nixon swept New York State yesterday, but lost to Senator McGovern in New York City by a total of 81,920 votes.

Mr. Nixon's statewide plurality was expected to be about a million votes.

With 11,521 of the 12,948 districts in the state reporting, the tally was:

Nixon	3,712,113
McGovern	2,539,326

With all of the 4,219 districts in the city reporting, the tally was:

Nixon	1,259,244
McGovern	1,341,164

The President's strong showing in the state rivaled the 1956 victory of President Dwight D. Eisenhower, who first brought Mr. Nixon to the national ticket 20 years ago.

The Nixon victory did not appear to carry too far down the Republican line. The Legislature remained Republican, but with no indication of substantially increased Republican majorities.

Three Republican candidates for the Court of Appeals held slight leads but returns were still inconclusive.

The President's capture of the state was only the third time a Republican Presidential candidate had won New York since 1928.

Dozens of sample districts showed last night that the President substantially improved his 1968 showing in virtually all ethnic groups and geographic areas in the state and city.

In many cases, particularly in the cities, Mr. Nixon surpassed Governor Rockefeller's victory margins of two years ago.

In New York City, Senator McGovern carried districts that were predominantly black, Puerto Rican and Jewish. But in the Jewish areas, Mr. Nixon doubled his showing of four years before. In a middle class

Continued on Page 36, Column 2

MANY VOTES SPLIT

G.O.P. Loses Senate Seats in 6 States and Picks Up 4 Others

By R. W. APPLE Jr.

The Democratic party withstood President Nixon's landslide yesterday to retain control of both houses of Congress.

With voters in all parts of the nation splitting their tickets in huge numbers, the Democrats brought off a series of startling upsets in Senate contests to gain at least two seats, similar to their feat in the face of Dwight D. Eisenhower's sweep of 1956.

The Democrats captured previously Republican Senate seats in six states—Delaware, Iowa, Kentucky, Maine, Colorado and South Dakota. Those pickups more than offset Republican gains in the two Southwestern states of Oklahoma and New Mexico and the two Southern states of Virginia and North Carolina.

Two Races Open

Two Senate races remained in doubt this morning—in Alaska and Nebraska. Both seats were held by the Republicans in the last Congress.

The figures for the House were far less complete, but the Republicans were not making the gains they needed to take control. It appeared that they would pick up somewhere in the neighborhood of a dozen seats; they had already gained seven.

At present, the Senate lineup is 54 Democrats, 44 Republicans, one Conservative-Republican and one independent who votes with the Democrats. In the House it is 255 Democrats, 177 Republicans and three vacancies.

Mr. Nixon's coattails proved relatively short this year, as they had in 1968. In state after state, he swept to massive vic-

Continued on Page 34, Column 7

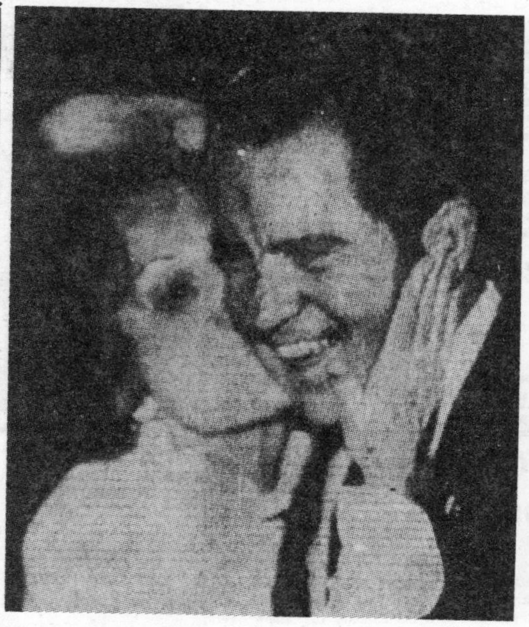

C.B.S. News

Associated Press

President and Mrs. Nixon and Vice President Agnew at the Republican celebration in Washington early today

MARGIN ABOUT 60%

Massachusetts Is Only State to Give Vote to the Dakotan

By MAX FRANKEL

Richard Milhous Nixon won re-election by a huge majority yesterday, perhaps the largest ever given a President.

Mr. Nixon scored a stunning personal triumph in all sections of the country, sweeping New York and most other bastions of Democratic strength.

He was gathering more than 60 per cent of the nation's ballots and more than 500 electoral votes. He lost only Massachusetts and the District of Columbia.

The victory was reminiscent of the landslide triumphs of Franklin D. Roosevelt in 1936 and Lyndon B. Johnson in 1964, although it could fall just short of their record proportions.

Tickets Are Split

Despite this drubbing of George Stanley McGovern, the Democratic challenger, the voters split their tickets in record numbers to leave the Democrats in control of both houses of Congress and a majority of the nation's governorships. Mr. Nixon thus became the first two-term President to face an opposition Congress at both inaugurals.

The turnout of voters appeared to be unusually low, despite jams at many polling places. Projections indicated a total vote of 76 million out of a voting-age population of 139.6 million, or only about 54 per cent. If accurate, that would be the lowest proportion since 51.4 per cent in 1948. The percentage had been over 60 per cent in every election since then.

May Claim Mandate

The President seemed certain, however, to claim a clear mandate for his policies of gradual disengagement from Vietnam, continued strong spending on defense, opposition to busing to integrate the schools and a slowdown in Federal spending for social programs. These are the issues he stressed through the campaign.

The 59-year-old Mr. Nixon, who will be 60 before inauguration on Jan. 20, could also claim a resounding personal vindication against the strong charges of corruption brought against him personally by the opposition.

By coincidence, the greatest triumph of his 26 years in national politics came on the 10th anniversary of his defeat for Governor of California—the time he told newsmen they would not have Nixon to kick around anymore.

McGovern Concedes

Mr. McGovern, 50, conceded defeat before midnight in the East with a telegram of support for the President if he leads the nation to peace abroad and justice at home.

The South Dakotan took credit for helping to push the Administration nearer to peace in Indochina and assured his cheering supporters at the Sioux Falls Coliseum that their defeat would bear fruit for years to come.

The President responded in a brief address from the White

Continued on Page 34, Column 1

Nixon Has a Big Plurality In Jersey and Connecticut

Case an Easy Winner

By RONALD SULLIVAN

President Nixon won the overwhelming victory predicted for him in New Jersey in yesterday's Presidential election, defeating Senator George Mc Govern by a 2-to-1 margin.

At the same time, Senator Clifford P. Case, the liberal Republican, won a fourth term and one of the biggest Senate election victories in New Jersey's history, defeating Paul J. Krebs, the Democratic candidate.

However, incumbent Democratic Representatives survived the G.O.P. onslaught at the top of the ballot in what political leaders described as a remarkable display of ticket-splitting.

The Presidential tally, with 4,142 districts of 5,212 reporting, was:

Nixon	1,440,420
McGovern	862,582

The tally in the race for the Senate, with 3,657 of 5,212 districts reporting, was:

Case	1,112,754
Krebs	627,352

With both Mr. Nixon and Senator Case piling up 2-to-1 margins throughout the state, Republican leaders predicted that the President's margin would rival the 800,000-vote plurality achieved by Dwight D.

Continued on Page 37, Column 3

Hartford Assembly G.O.P.

By LAWRENCE FELLOWS

Special to The New York Times

HARTFORD, Nov. 7—President Nixon carried Connecticut today in a landslide victory.

The President swept the state's eight electoral votes with a plurality of 252,289, approaching the 306,758-vote margin by which the late President Dwight D. Eisenhower carried the state in 1956.

The Republicans also took control of the General Assembly, winning the State Senate by 23 to 13 and the House of Representatives by 93 to 58.

But widespread ticket-splitting enabled three of the four incumbent Democratic Representatives to keep their seats in Washington.

With all of the 169 towns in the state reporting, the Presidential tally was:

Nixon	799,249
McGovern	546,960

Representative John G. Schmitz of California, the

Continued on Page 37, Column 7

Olympic Fund Barred

Voters in Colorado cut off public funds for the 1976 Winter Olympics yesterday. Without the tax money, the International Olympic Committee was all but forced to move the games to another site. Page 31.

M'GOVERN TO BACK MOVES FOR PEACE

But Says He Will Continue to Oppose Policies He Had Deplored in Campaign

By JAMES M. NAUGHTON

Special to The New York Times

SIOUX FALLS, S.D., Nov. 7 — Senator George McGovern conceded defeat of his Presidential candidacy here tonight but said that he would "shed no tears" because of the effort his campaign had made to draw the nation close to peace.

The Democratic nominee told 1,200 cheering enthusiasts at 10:40 P.M., Central standard time, that he had sent a telegram to President Nixon pledging support for "peace abroad and justice at home."

Text of McGovern's comments appears on Page 3

He said the President had his "full support" in efforts toward such goals.

But he added in his speech, which was televised, that he would, as the leader of the "loyal opposition," continue to oppose any policies that he had deplored during his long campaign.

"Now, the question is to what standards does the loyal

Continued on Page 3, Column 3

The Election at a Glance

President

Needed for Election—270 Electoral Votes

	*Number of States	Electoral Votes
Nixon	49	521
McGovern	2	17

The Senate

Newly Elected Senators		Make-up of New Senate	
Democrats	16	Democrats	57
Republicans	15	Republicans	41
In Doubt	2	In Doubt	2

The House

Democrats Elected	218
Republicans Elected	154
In Doubt	63

*Includes District of Columbia.

NIXON ISSUES CALL TO 'GREAT TASKS'

At Victory Celebration, He Vows to Make Himself 'Worthy' of Victory

By ROBERT B. SEMPLE Jr.

Special to The New York Times

WASHINGTON, Wednesday, Nov. 8 — President Nixon summoned the nation last night "to get on with the great tasks that lie before us" and, in a later statement to a crowd of cheering supporters, pledged to make himself "worthy of this victory."

Mr. Nixon made two statements, both televised.

The first of these was a brief statement from his desk in the Oval Office of the White House in which he pledged himself to secure not only "a peace with honor in Vietnam" but also "a new era of peace" throughout the world; to "prosperity without war and without inflation" at home, and to an America in which all citizens will have "an equal chance."

Text of Nixon's remarks is printed on Page 34

"I would only hope," he said, "that in these next four years we can so conduct ourselves in

Continued on Page 34, Column 3

Victory, 10 Years Later

Spectacular Nixon Vote Considered Vindication in Light of Past Defeats

By JAMES RESTON

News Analysis

It was a spectacular personal victory for Richard Nixon, 10 years to the day, and almost to the hour, after his most humiliating defeat by Pat Brown in the 1962 election for the governorship of California.

Beaten by John Kennedy by the narrowest of margins in the Presidential election of 1960, beaten again for the control of his own state in 1962, finished with American politics by his own angry proclamation exactly a decade ago, here he is now, not only vindicated but triumphant in one of the most decisive victories in the history of American Presidential politics.

In a few days before he will take the oath of office for a second term as President of the United States (Jan. 9), he will be 60 years old. His thirties were a political surprise, even to himself, his forties were an agony of controversy and self-doubt, his fifties were a struggle and at the end a triumph. What now will he do with his sixties? This is the question that even his most intimate associates in Washington cannot answer.

In the world, he has to achieve not only the cease-fire, but the peace he has promised in Vietnam, the "reconciliation and cooperation" with Peking and Moscow that were so central to his victory, the truce in the savage struggle between Israel and the Arab states, and some kind of new economic and political relationship with Japan and the Common Market countries of Europe, who are now challenging the American economic leadership of the modern world.

At home, Mr. Nixon has to deal also now with the minorities who failed to support him in the election: the poor and the blacks who have been left behind in the general prosperity of the nation, the young in the universities who have been over-run but not persuaded or

Continued on Page 34, Column 3

Reid Wins as Democrat; Bella Abzug Easy Victor

By RICHARD L. MADDEN

Representative Ogden R. Reid, a former Republican, was reelected yesterday as a Democrat in Westchester County, and Representative Bella S. Abzug, a one-term Democrat, won a decisive re-election in Manhattan.

In another key Westchester race, Representative Peter A. Peyser, a freshman Republican, claimed victory over his predecessor in the House, Richard L. Ottinger, a Democrat-Liberal, who was seeking to recapture his former seat.

Mrs. Abzug defeated by about a 2-to-1 margin Mrs. Priscilla M. Ryan, a Liberal and widow of the late Representative William F. Ryan, who had defeated Mrs. Abzug in the Democratic primary in the 20th Congressional District last June.

With about 85 per cent of the vote reported in Westchester, but with large numbers of absentee ballots still to be counted, Mr. Reid led Carl A. Vergari, a Republican-Conservative and the county's District Attorney, by more than 8,000 votes.

Despite the strong vote for President Nixon in the state, incumbent Democratic Representatives generally appeared to be withstanding the Republican tide. One exception was Representative John D. Dow, of Newburgh, a liberal Democrat who had strenously opposed the war in Vietnam.

Mr. Dow, who lost his House seat in the generally conservative Rockland-Orange county area in 1968 and won it back two years ago, was substantially trailing Assemblyman Benjamin A. Gilman, a Middletown Republican.

Representative Otis G. Pike, a six-term Democrat from Suffolk County, won a three-way fight for re-election and another prime target of the Republicans, Representative James M. Hanley of Syracuse, defeated his Republican-Conservative opponent, Leonard C. Koldin.

Representative Lester L. Wolff, a four-term Democrat whose new Nassau County district now takes in part of Queens, led Assemblyman John

Continued on Page 36, Column 6

Mrs. Smith Defeated For Senate in Maine

By BILL KOVACH

Special to The New York Times

PROVIDENCE, R. I., Wednesday, Nov. 8—The 34-year Congressional career of Senator Margaret Chase Smith, the Senate's only woman member, ended last night in a major upset as Democrats showed unexpected strength in New England Senate and Gubernatorial races.

William D. Hathaway, the Democrat who gave up his Second District Congressional office to challenge the 74-year-old Mrs. Smith despite her near-legendary standing in Maine, won the seat in a hard-fought contest.

Mr. Hathaway's stunning victory was part of a Democartic surge that overcame the general New England sweep by President Nixon, and reflected stubborn ticket-splitting by

Continued on Page 21, Column 1

A Rockefeller Loses West Virginia Race

By BEN A. FRANKLIN

Special to The New York Times

CHARLESTON, W. Va., Wednesday, Nov. 8—Secretary of State John D. Rockefeller 4th suffered a sharp defeat yesterday in a bid for the West Virginia governorship. The loss appeared, at least, to have postponed a possible role for him in national Democratic politics in 1976.

Mr. Rockefeller's well-financed candidacy had depended heavily on proposals on the environment in this the second-ranked coal-mining state. These also suffered a setback through his defeat in a race that eclipsed all others here.

Gov. Arch A. Moore Jr., a Republican former Congressman who is the first Governor here who has been constitutionally able to succeed to a second

Continued on Page 23, Column 1

Summary of Other News

Following is a summary of major nonelection news. A full report begins on the first page, second part.

Canarsie School Boycott

Leaders of Canarsie parents who have kept their children out of school for two weeks declared yesterday that "the boycott is over" and called on parents to return their children to school. But the prospect of full classes today remained in doubt since more than 1,000 parents shouted down the same call Monday night.

Bid by Vietcong

Agents of the National Liberation Front have made several recent contacts with Saigon's anti-Government, non-Communist opposition, according to opposition sources.

Britons Protest Price Rises

British Government offices were swamped with complaints of price increases on the first full day of Prime Minister Heath's anti-inflation freeze. But a check of London shops found no wide pattern of violations. Most of the increases involved noncontrolled items.

Soviet Parades Its Arms

The Soviet Union, marking the 55th anniversary of the Bolshevik Revolution, paraded its military might in low-key fashion. The unusually deliberate movements of Leonid I. Brezhnev, the party leader, reinforced speculation that he had been ill.

NEWS INDEX

"All the News That's Fit to Print"

The New York Times

LATE CITY EDITION

Weather: Mostly cloudy, seasonably cold today, tonight and tomorrow. Temp. range: today 34-42; Tuesday 37-42. Full U.S. report on Page 78.

VOL. CXXII ... No. 41,976 — NEW YORK, WEDNESDAY, DECEMBER 27, 1972 — 15 CENTS

TRUMAN, 33D PRESIDENT, IS DEAD; SERVED IN TIME OF FIRST A-BOMB, MARSHALL PLAN, NATO AND KOREA

HARRY S. TRUMAN, 1884-1972

Funeral to Be Tomorrow In Independence Library

By B. DRUMMOND AYRES Jr.

Special to The New York Times

KANSAS CITY, Mo., Dec. 26—Harry S. Truman, the 33d President of the United States, died this morning. He was 88 years old.

Mr. Truman, an outspoken and decisive Missouri Democrat who served in the White House from 1945 to 1953, succumbed at 7:50 A.M., central standard time, in Kansas City's Research Hospital and Medical Center.

He had been a patient there for the last 22 days, struggling against lung congestion, heart irregularity, kidney blockages, failure of the digestive system and the afflictions of old age.

In the more than seven years he was President, from the time Franklin Delano Roosevelt's death suddenly elevated him from the Vice-Presidency until he himself was succeeded by Dwight David Eisenhower, Mr. Truman left a major mark as a world leader.

He brought mankind face to face with the age of holocaust by ordering atomic bombs dropped on Japan, sent American troops into Korea to halt Communist aggression in Asia, helped contain Communism in Europe by forming the North Atlantic Treaty Organization and speeded the postwar recovery of Europe through the Marshall Plan.

His domestic record was somewhat less dramatic, for his proposals and ideas were often premature. He ended up on the losing side of fights other Presidents later won — Federal health care, equal rights legislation, low income housing.

His other legacies were perhaps less tangible but no less remembered — the morning walk, the "give 'em hell" campaign that nipped Thomas E.

An obituary article appears on Pages 46-49. An appraisal by the late Dean Acheson, written in 1964, will be found on Page 45.

Dewey at the wire, the desk plaque that proclaimed "The buck stops here!" and the word to the timid and indecisive: "If you can't stand the heat, you better get out of the kitchen."

Toward the end of his struggle for life, the former President weakened steadily. Early yesterday, his doctors warned that death might come "within hours."

When it came, the doctors announced that the cause was "a complexity of organic failures causing a collapse of the cardiovascular system."

A state funeral will be held Thursday in nearby Independence, Mr. Truman's home

Continued on Page 44, Column 1

United Press International

The Truman home in Independence, Mo., yesterday

National Day of Mourning Proclaimed by President

By JACK ROSENTHAL

Special to The New York Times

WASHINGTON, Dec. 26—President Nixon today declared Thursday a national day of mourning for former President Harry S. Truman and made plans to pay his personal respects tomorrow in Independence, Mo.

In a proclamation issued before leaving the vacation White House in Key Biscayne, Mr. Nixon ordered all Federal of-

Text of Nixon's proclamation will be found on Page 44.

fices to close Thursday and urged that the nation pay homage to the late President in worship services.

As he returned to Washington, Mr. Nixon announced that he and Mrs. Nixon would fly to Independence tomorrow to lay a wreath at the Truman Presidential Library, where Mr. Truman's body will lie in state. Officials said that the Nixons hoped to have the opportunity to offer their condolences in person to Mrs. Truman.

The Nixons plan to return to Washington after the wreath-laying, indicating that they will not attend the funeral in Independence on Thursday.

The reason, it appeared, was the desire of the Truman family to have a private funeral.

It was announced in Austin, Tex., that former President and Mrs. Lyndon B. Johnson and members of their family would also go to Independence tomorrow to pay their final respects. They planned to return to Texas in the late afternoon.

All stock exchanges will be closed Thursday. Most banks, with the exception of those in Connecticut, will be open. Post offices will be closed, and there will be no regular delivery of mail. [Details on Page 59].

A memorial service for Mr. Truman here will be held in the Washington Cathedral, for Federal and foreign dignitaries. No date has been set, but the State Department said it would be within two weeks.

As a Senator and as Vice-Presidential candidate in 1952, Mr. Nixon had been bitterly critical of Mr. Truman, but today, the President voiced warm and unstinting praise.

In a statement issued an hour after word of Mr. Truman's death reached the vacation White House in Florida, Mr. Nixon said:

"Harry S. Truman will be remembered as one of the most courageous Presidents in our history, who led the nation and the world through a critical period with exceptional vision

Continued on Page 44, Column 2

U.S. SAYS BOMBING IS BACK AT LEVEL PRECEDING PAUSE

Warplanes From Thailand, Guam and Carriers Take Off for North Vietnam

HALT LASTED 36 HOURS

Hanoi Reports 8 B-52's Shot Down in Day—Pentagon Calls Loss Rate Normal

By JOSEPH B. TREASTER

Special to The New York Times

SAIGON, South Vietnam, Wednesday, Dec. 27—With its 36-hour pause in the bombing of North Vietnam ended, the United States command said yesterday that the planes were once again operating as they had last week, when the raids were the heaviest of the war.

Maj. Jere K. Forbus, a spokesman for the command, announced yesterday afternoon that the Christmas pause in bombing had ended three hours earlier, at 1 P.M. (midnight Monday, New York time). At that time, warplanes started taking off from aircraft carriers in the South China Sea and from bases in Thailand and Guam.

Informed officers had said before the pause that about 100 B-52's and several hundred smaller fighter-bombers had been participating in the attacks.

57 Listed as Missing

Many officers in Saigon said yesterday that despite denials from the Pentagon, B-52 losses since the raids began Dec. 18 have been much higher than had been expected.

As of last evening the command had acknowledged having lost 11 of the heavy eight-engine bombers, which each carry more than 24 tons of bombs and which usually fly in formations of three. The command has also reported six fighter-bombers down.

Altogether, the command says, 57 American airmen are missing in action. Hanoi says it has captured more than 100.

The Hanoi radio said today that eight more B-52's and an F-4 Phantom fighter-bomber were shot down yesterday. The North Vietnamese now maintain that they have destroyed a total of 62 American aircraft, including 26 of the heavy bombers, which are valued at $8-million each, since the raids began Dec. 18.

[The Pentagon had no comment on the Hanoi radio report, but it said earlier that the loss rate of B-52's was not materially greater than in raids last spring though now "there are more B-52's involved."]

'Brutal and Barbaric Act'

In a statement condemning the resumption of the bombing, the North Vietnamese Foreign Ministry said over the Hanoi radio this morning that many B-52's and "scores of other aircraft" struck urban and suburban areas in Hanoi, Haiphong, Thai Nguyen — the site of the nation's principal steel mill—and other cities last night.

"This is a brutal and barbaric action aimed at killing civilians, an act that surpasses Hitler's war crimes in scope and intensity," the Foreign Ministry

Continued on Page 10, Column 1

Jury Begins Investigation Into Drug Losses by Police

Judge Threatens Murphy With Contempt for Refusal to Cooperate in Inquiry as Two Officers Fail to Appear

By EMANUEL PERLMUTTER

A grand jury began taking testimony yesterday in the recently disclosed theft of 300 pounds of heroin and cocaine from the Police Department, and a judge threatened Police Commissioner Patrick V. Murphy and two of his aides with contempt for refusing to cooperate with the jury.

Gene L. Grupposo, the police property clerk, testified before the jurors in the morning in the Manhattan Criminal Court Building. However, Assistant Chief Inspector John Guido, who is in charge of the inspection division, and Inspector Howard A. Metzdorff of the internal affairs division, were not present to testify when their names were called.

The subpoenaing of the policemen by the grand jury was a rebuff to Maurice H. Nadjari, the special state prosecutor, and to Governor Rockefeller. Last October, the Governor had directed Commissioner Murphy to send information about possible criminal-justice corruption only to Mr. Nadjari. The city's District Attorneys and Mr. Nadjari are fighting over who should investigate the narcotics thefts.

A subpoena had been served on Commissioner Murphy last Friday, calling for the three witnesses to appear before the grand jury yesterday. Mr. Murphy was also directed to turn over to the jurors department records on the stolen narcotics that had been held as evidence by the police.

Frank Rogers, a special assistant district attorney who is in charge of prosecution in the 12 narcotics courts in the city, is supervising the citywide grand jury that is investigating the drug thefts as well as other narcotics cases.

At the request of Mr. Rogers, Supreme Court Justice Sidney A. Fine issued the subpoenas last week.

In a hearing yesterday before Justice Fine, Mr. Rogers contended that the grand jury

Continued on Page 25, Column 6

CITY AIDES TO LOSE APPROVAL POWER ON NEW BUILDING

Owners to Be Responsible Under Antigraft Plan—Delays Seen Curbed

By ROBERT E. TOMASSON

In a major move aimed at reducing "graft-inducing situations" in the construction industry, the city will shift authority for initial building approval next month from its 75 plan examiners to individual owners, architects and engineers.

The "sharp departure from tradition" was announced by Joseph Stein, Commissioner of the Department of Buildings, who said the move was taken in response to the industry's complaint of excessive delays in obtaining building permits that "created graft-inducing situations to obtain expeditious approval."

Instead of the months that were often required to obtain the necessary building permits, they will be issued within days under the new system, Commissioner Stein said.

Builder Cites 'Ways'

Owners will still be held accountable for meeting requirements of the building code, Mr. Stein said, but will no longer have to suffer delays because of objections raised by individual examiners.

Building plans have often had to be submitted several times before their approval, and there has been widespread talk in the industry that there "were ways," as one major builder phrased it yesterday, to expedite approval.

One alleged widespread abuse was the consideration of plans out of sequence in which they were submitted.

In a series of articles in The New York Times last summer, it was estimated that the construction industry paid out at least $25-million in bribes annually to officials and others in connection with virtually every phase of building.

Rise of the 'Expediter'

The complexity of the city's 371-page building code has given rise to creation of the position of men known in the trade as "expediters" whose essential function is to cultivate plan examiners.

One chief executive of a large construction firm here said yesterday that plan approval was often obtained "on what amounts to a scale system, with so much graft for each apartment" in a proposed project.

John Tudda, an architect whose firm has functioned as a consultant to expedite city approval on projects including the Ruppert Brewery Urban Renewal site in the Yorkville area of Manhattan and Lincoln

Continued on Page 18, Column 4

School Board Plans Offer To Buy Scribner Contract

By GENE I. MAEROFF

The Board of Education was drafting a letter yesterday that it intends to send to School Chancellor Harvey B. Scribner, outlining a proposal to buy up his contract. A board member, who declined to be identified, said that there "had been no dissent" at a meeting Friday at which the five members decided to offer to pay Dr. Scribner for the remaining six months of his three-year contract and relieve him of his $53,000-a-year post.

Dr. Scribner, who was reported to be out of town and unavailable for comment, announced at a news conference Thursday that he intended to leave his post June 30. He blamed his decision on a "confidence gap" that he said had developed between him and the Board of Education.

The names of possible successors have not been mentioned by the board, but speculation centered on Irving Anker, the deputy chancellor.

Once Headed System

Mr. Anker headed the 1.1-million-pupil New York City school system on an interim basis in 1970, before Dr. Scribner assumed the job. Mr. Anker is seen as someone who could again serve on an acting basis until a permanent chancellor is named.

Should Dr. Scribner refuse to accept a settlement, the board—if it continues to seek his removal—would have to bring departmental charges against him, which is regarded as an unlikely possibility.

"We would rather not have to think about this aspect," one board member said yesterday.

Prior to his announcement last week, Dr. Scribner's reappointment was by no means assured, but he was regarded as still being in contention.

However, he apparently

Continued on Page 27, Column 3

GRAND JURY GETS POLICE SHOOTING

Defendant Is Central Figure in $500 Bail Dispute Involving Two Judges

By RALPH BLUMENTHAL

A grand jury here began an investigation yesterday of the holdup shooting of a patrolman—a case that has stirred controversy because of the release of the suspect in $500 cash bail.

Among the first to testify was another man shot in the holdup. He said he had told the grand jury he could identify the holdup man.

The witness, Edward M. Blagden, then returned to his hospital bed, from where he made public an open letter berating Criminal Court Judge Bruce McMarion Wright for having released the suspect in $500 cash bail.

Judge Wright indicated yesterday that the case was under review by the Appellate Division and a spokesman said the judge was under the division's orders not to discuss the matter publicly.

Other judicial authorities, meanwhile, said they had no jurisdiction and indicated they were not now preparing any

Continued on Page 25, Column 1

Appraisal of the Arts

The second half of an assessment of the year in art and culture by nine critics for The New York Times appears on Page 29.

Study Finds Incomes More Unequal

By PHILIP SHABECOFF

Special to The New York Times

WASHINGTON, Dec. 26—A changing population and a changing industrial structure are producing a persistent trend toward inequality in the distribution of income among wage and salary earners in the United States, a study published by the Labor Department has found.

The trend is toward a concentration of an increasingly large share of average wage and salary income among people in jobs and professions that already bring higher pay, and it is likely to continue for some time, Peter Henle, author of the study, says.

The study, in the department's current Monthly Labor Review, departs from the widely accepted view that there has been little change in the distribution of income in America since World War II.

Most studies of income distribution examine family incomes, which include such nonearned incomes as welfare and Social Security payments. Family incomes also reflect the growing trend toward more than one wage earner per family.

The study by Mr. Henle, senior specialist on labor for the Library of Congress, examines only the money earnings, wages and salaries of male workers, so as to obtain a view of shifts in the distribution of payments for work performed.

Male Workers Studied

In the period examined, 1958-1972, average earned income was steadily rising throughout the economy as a whole. But in the distribution of that income Mr. Henle found "a slight persistent trend toward inequality." This trend toward inequality was found between various occupations and industries and was also found within several occupations and industries.

For example, using unpublished data from the Bureau of the Census, Mr. Henle found that from 1958 to 1970 the share of aggregate wage and salary income earned by the lowest fifth of male workers declined to 4.60 per cent from 5.10. At the same time, the share of the highest fifth of male wage and salary earners rose to 40.55 per cent from 38.15.

This trend did not necessarily affect the very highest-paid and lowest-paid workers on the earned income scale, Mr. Henle said. For example, he noted that, while there had been a marked increase in the number of professionals earning $40,000 to $50,000 a year, there had been little change in the number of executives earning $200,000 or more.

Denies 'Scheme Against Poor'

In a telephone interview, he stressed that the inequality in income distribution was not caused by any "nefarious scheme against poor people." Rather, the trend reflects a tendency in the economy to produce more higher-paying jobs without reducing the number of lower-paid workers, he said.

One reason has been a heavy flow of young people into the labor force as a result of the

Continued on Page 22, Column 4

NEWS INDEX

Tug of War Strains West Side Housing

By DEIRDRE CARMODY

An empty brick-strewn lot on the Upper West Side, first scheduled for middle-income housing and now slated for low-income housing, has become the symbol of controversy between groups in the neighborhood that are dedicated to preserving the ethnic and economic mix in the area but that cannot agree on how to do it.

The site, on Columbus Avenue between 90th and 91st Streets, is also a symbol of the pitfalls of the ambitious West Side Urban Renewal Project, which celebrates its 10th anniversary next month.

It is caught in a tug-of-war between those who believe there is an urgent need for middle-income housing to keep the area from becoming a slum and those who say that the urgent need is for low-income housing to relocate the hundreds of residents who have been uprooted by the urban-renewal project.

One of the major complainants about the housing change from middle-income to low-income is Trinity School, which is directly across 91st Street from the lot. The private coeducational school, which has been on its present site since 1893, has filed suit against the city in Federal Court for allegedly having reneged on an agreement with the school that provided for a middle-income apartment house on the site across the street.

According to school officials, Trinity has long considered moving the entire institution to Pawling, N. Y., where it owned land. As the area around the school became shabbier and increasingly less attractive to prospective parents (who today pay from $1,600 for a first-grader to $2,500 for a 12th-grader), the decision to move became more imminent.

By the mid-nineteen sixties the area, in the words of the lawsuit, was "deteriorated, substandard unsanitary" with "delapidated and crumbling structures" and a high incidence of crime.

At this time, however, the city was completing its fourth revision of the West Side Urban Renewal Project, which envisioned the refurbishing of the area from 87th Street to

Continued on Page 16, Column 4

Navy Buys $1.7-Million in Stock Of Ailing Defense Plant on L.I.

By DAVID A. ANDELMAN

Special to The New York Times

HAUPPAUGE, L.I., Dec. 26—The Navy has purchased all 17,414 shares of preferred stock in the Gap Instrument Corporation here as a means of helping the company, which has been experiencing heavy cost overruns. This has made the Department of Defense the largest single stockholder in the company.

The arrangement, believed to mark the first time that the Department of Defense has purchased stock in a private corporation, provides that no dividends be paid on the $1.7-million in nonvoting, nonconvertible shares and that the stock be redeemed beginning in 1976 but only out of the company's after-tax profits.

The company has not shown a profit in the last four years, and in 1968 showed a profit of only $10,700.

Last week, Senator William Proxmire criticized the Navy for acting as "Grumman's banker" because the Navy delivered a $26-million loan at 6⅞ per cent interest to that aerospace company for the F-14, a plane that has also experienced cost overruns.

Gap first ran into trouble nearly three years ago on a contract to manufacture 31 fire-control consoles for Navy destroyers. The company had

Continued on Page 20, Column 4

"All the News That's Fit to Print"

The New York Times

LATE CITY EDITION

Weather: Rain late today, tonight becoming light snow early tomorrow. Temp. range: today 40-45; Saturday 40-44. Full U.S. report on Page 59

SECTION ONE

VOL. CXXII . . No. 42,008 NEW YORK, SUNDAY, JANUARY 28, 1973 — 75¢ beyond 50-mile zone from New York City, except Long Island. Higher in air delivery cities. — 50 CENTS

VIETNAM PEACE PACTS SIGNED; AMERICA'S LONGEST WAR HALTS

Nation Ends Draft, Turns to Volunteers

Change Is Ordered Six Months Early—Youths Must Still Register

By DAVID E. ROSENBAUM

Special to The New York Times

WASHINGTON, Jan. 27—Defense Secretary Melvin R. Laird announced today that the military draft had ended.

As a result of the announcement, men born in 1953 and afterward will not be subject to conscription, and men born before 1953 but not yet drafted will have no further liability to the draft.

These men will be the first in two generations to have no prospect of being drafted. Except for a brief hiatus in 1947 and 1948, men have been conscripted regularly since 1940.

President Nixon's authority to conscript troops into the military expires June 30. Since no one has been drafted since December, the President achieved his goal of turning the military into an all-volunteer force six months ahead of the deadline.

The President and Mr. Laird had promised repeatedly that the June 30 deadline would be met. But Mr. Laird had held out the possibility that as many as 5,000 men would be drafted this year from March through June.

Message From Laird

But, in a message to senior defense officials that was made public today, Mr. Laird said:

"With the signing of the peace agreement in Paris today, and, after receiving a report from the Secretary of the Army that he foresees no need for further inductions, I wish to inform you that the armed forces henceforth will depend exclusively on volunteer soldiers, sailors, airmen and marines.

"The use of the draft has ended."

Although no one will be drafted, the Selective Service machinery will most likely remain on the books for standby use in an emergency. Men will continue to have to register for the draft when they turn 18, and young men will still be assigned lottery numbers based on their birthdays.

Congress has mandated, however, that the Government call up Reserves and National Guardsmen before it turns to a reinstatement of the draft to meet future emergencies.

A spokesman for the Selective Service System said that men who had refused to report for induction would still be subject to criminal prosecution. But, he said, men with induction postponements that were due to expire before June 30 will not be drafted.

"We will draft nobody," the spokesman said.

Hopes Senate Will Act

Mr. Laird's single qualification about ending the draft applied to doctors and dentists. The Nixon Administration has asked Congress to approve sizable bonuses for doctors and dentists in an effort to attract enough volunteers in those professions.

The House of Representatives passed such legislation last year, and Mr. Laird said in his message today:

"I am particularly hopeful that the Senate will promptly follow the lead of the House and enact legislation giving added incentives for service from members of the health professions, so that the requirements for health services personnel can also be put on a volunteer basis."

The House is almost certainly willing to pass the bill again this year, but Representative F. Edward Hébert, chairman of the House Armed Services Committee, has said that his committee will not act until the Senate passes the legislation.

Mr. Laird also urged Congress to approve bonuses to attract men to the National Guard and

Continued on Page 28, Column 1

In the morning ceremony at the Hotel Majestic in Paris were, from the left, the Vietcong, North Vietnamese, South Vietnamese and U.S. delegations

Associated Press, United Press International and C.B.S. News

Signing, from left, William P. Rogers for U.S., Nguyen Duy Trinh for Hanoi, Mrs. Nguyen Thi Binh for the Vietcong, Tran Van Lam for Saigon

Hanoi Lists of P.O.W.'s Are Made Public by U.S.

By BERNARD GWERTZMAN

Special to The New York Times

WASHINGTON, Jan. 27—The State Department tonight released the list of American civilians acknowledged by North Vietnam as having been captured in South Vietnam during the Vietnam war. The list left about half the 51 American civilians believed missing or captured unaccounted for.

The list that the North Vietnamese turned over to American officials in Paris today named 27 American civilians as prisoners of the Vietcong, and listed seven other Americans as having died in captivity.

At the same time, the Defense Department began releasing, in batches, the names of the military prisoners in Communist hands who were on the list turned over in Paris along with the civilians.

2 Diplomats Listed

The United States, in Paris, provided a list of 26,000 Communist prisoners held by South Vietnam in exchange. The lists were turned over following the formal signing of the Vietnam cease-fire agreement.

Frank A. Sieverts, the State Department official charged with prisoner affairs, said that Hanoi apparently did not in-

Continued on Page 26, Column 1

The Toll: 12 Years of War

Military

United States—45,933 killed, 303,616 wounded, 587 captured, 1,335 missing (up to Jan. 13, 1973).

South Vietnam—183,528 killed and 499,026 wounded.

North Vietnam and Vietcong—924,048 (an estimate by Saigon; figures on wounded not available.)

Civilian

415,000 South Vietnamese killed and 935,000 wounded in combat (1965 through 1972).

31,463 South Vietnamese killed and 49,000 abducted as result of Vietcong actions against civilians.

20,587 killed by Saigon actions against civilian Vietcong.

North Vietnamese—Casualties not known.

A Reluctant G.I.'s Life and Death

By JON NORDHEIMER

Special to The New York Times

ST. JOSEPH, Mo.—The house on Penn Street where Charley Stockbauer used to live sits near a historic crossroads of America.

It was from St. Joseph that the pioneers who won the West a century ago set out across the prairie in rough wagons drawn by mules and oxen and gritty conviction.

They came here by railroad and steamboat in the waning days of winter and huddled in muddy encampments on the gray bluffs above the Missouri River, waiting with mounting excitement for the floodwaters to recede from the Kansas plain.

As with most American school children, the seeds of patriotism were planted deep in Charley Stockbauer, and he grew to manhood in St. Joseph surrounded by the ghosts of 19th-century heroes and the legends of the days when men strode boldly toward an uncertain horizon, enduring hardship and fear on the impulse of duty or national destiny.

Values Questioned

These values are still enshrined, but they have been questioned as never before by Charley Stockbauer's generation during the turbulent years when the vagaries of the war in Vietnam challenged traditional American attitudes about sacred abstractions such as patriotism.

Charley Stockbauer was a confused and reluctant warrior in a conflict that almost nobody fully understands, and that confusion and reluctance are mirrored here in the town that was his home before he died in Vietnam. Patriotism has not died in St. Joseph, but here, as elsewhere across the country in these days when the war has at last come to an end, there is a reticence about it all, a nervous hesitance about parading the flag.

The myths and the legends persist. Buffalo Bill and Wild Bill Hickok were raw-boned riders from the Overland Pony Express, and the mail they carried westward started out from a brick building that still stands on Penn Street. Indian fighters purchased, with leather pouches

Continued on Page 24, Column 2

Today's Sections

Index to Subjects

*Included in all copies distributed in New York City and the suburban area.

Nation Celebrates Peace In Prayer and Muted Joy

By MICHAEL KNIGHT

President Nixon, like millions of other Americans, watched the signing of the Vietnam cease-fire agreement on television yesterday and then, like many others, took part in a modest and somber celebration of the end of a tragic war.

The President, relaxing in his home at Key Biscayne, Fla. had proclaimed 7 P.M. yesterday as a "national moment of prayer and thanksgiving" and the 24-hour period thereafter as a day of prayer.

Throughout the country, in cities and in hamlets, church bells tolled, fire companies sounded their horns, and small, quiet gatherings were held in homes and in public places.

Some Voice Caution

Some of those who celebrated the end of the American war did so cautiously. The executive secretary of the Washington, D. C., Council of Churches said, "The reason many of us are not throwing our hats in the air is that we are just so stunned and ashamed because the war went on so long, so needlessly."

In Elmira, N. Y., Mrs. Lucielle Cesari did not turn on the lights of a Christmas tree in her yard, lights she had lit every night for five years in a "vigil" remembering the war.

In Longmeadow, Mass., a bell forged by Paul Revere, the silversmith and patriot, was sounded in its steeple at the First Church of Christ. The bell was first sounded to signal the end of the War of 1812.

In Key Biscayne, the President attended a special service at the Key Biscayne Presbyterian Church about a mile from his home.

The minister, the Rev. John A. Huffman, Jr., borrowed from a song by two antiwar activists,

Continued on Page 20, Column 3

United Press International

President and Mrs. Nixon and their daughter, Mrs. David Eisenhower, attending a memorial service in Key Biscayne Presbyterian Church, near the Florida White House.

CEREMONIES COOL

Two Sessions in Paris Formally Conclude the Agreement

By FLORA LEWIS

Special to The New York Times

PARIS, Jan. 27—The Vietnam cease-fire agreement was signed here today in eerie silence, without a word or a gesture to express the world's relief that the years of war were officially ending.

The accord was effective at 7 P.M. Eastern standard time.

Secretary of State William P. Rogers wrote his name 62 times on the documents providing—after 12 years—a settlement of the longest, most divisive foreign war in America's history.

The official title of the text was "Agreement on Ending the War and Restoring Peace in Vietnam." But the cold, almost gloomy atmosphere at two separate signing ceremonies reflected the uncertainties of whether peace is now assured.

The conflict, which has raged in one way or another for over a quarter of a century, had been inconclusive, without clear victory or defeat for either side.

Involvement Gradually Grew

After a gradually increasing involvement that began even before France left Indochina in 1954, the United States entered into a full-scale combat role in 1965. The United States considers Jan. 1, 1961, as the war's starting date and casualties are counted from then.

By 1968, when the build-up was stopped and then reversed, there were 529,000 Americans fighting in Vietnam. United States dead passed 45,000 by the end of the war.

The peace agreements were as ambiguous as the conflict, which many of America's friends first saw as generous aid to a weak and threatened ally, but which many came to consider an exercise of brute power against a tiny nation.

Built on Compromises

The peace agreements signed today were built of compromises that permit the two Vietnamese sides to give them contradictory meanings and, they clearly hope, to continue their unfinished struggle in the political arena without continuing the slaughter.

The signing took place in two ceremonies. In the morning, the participants were the United States, North Vietnam, South Vietnam and the Vietcong. Because the Saigon Government does not wish to imply recognition of the Vietcong's Provisional Revolutionary Government, all references to that government were confined to a second set of documents. That set was signed in the afternoon,

Continued on Page 24, Column 7

BATTLES CONTINUE AFTER CEASE-FIRE

U.S. Copter Sent to Pick Up Vietcong Officers Said to Have Been Shot Down

By FOX BUTTERFIELD

Special to The New York Times

SAIGON, South Vietnam, Sunday, Jan. 28—A cease-fire officially went into effect throughout Vietnam at 8 A.M. today, but widespread fighting continued and there were reports that an unarmed American helicopter sent to pick up a Vietcong delegation and bring it to Saigon had been shot down over Tay Nin Ninh Province.

The helicopter, which was painted white and which is normally used for medical evacuation flight, was to bring the Vietcong's delegation to the four-power Joint Military Commission that will oversee the cease-fire. There was no immediate word on the fate of the crew.

[North Vietnam issued a statement Sunday informing its people of the cease-fire, saying, "Today, the 28th of January, war completely ends in both zones of our country," Reuters reported from Hong Kong.]

334 Incidents Reported

The South Vietnamese command reported this morning that in the 24 hours ending at dawn, North Vietnamese and Vietcong troops initiated 334 incidents throughout the country. According to Government officers, that is the highest number since they began keeping a record. However, more Communist troops were probably involved during the 1968 Tet offensive, they said.

Only an hour and a half before the cease-fire began, Communist gunners struck Tan Son Nhut airport on the outskirts

Continued on Page 18, Column 1

Other News About Accords

CAMBODIA—The exiled Cambodian head of state said in Peking that his guerrilla forces would fight on despite the cease-fire in Vietnam. Cambodia announced a suspension of offensive activities tomorrow. [Page 26.]

TRUCE OBSERVERS—Teams of officers from Poland and Canada left for Vietnam to join with others expected from Hungary and Indonesia. [Page 24.]

INTERNATIONAL CONFERENCE—The United States proposed Feb. 26 as the date for 12-nation meeting on guaranteeing peace. [Page 16.]

LAOS—The head of the pro-Communist negotiating team returned from Hanoi and gave no indication that a cease-fire could be arranged quickly in Laos. [Page 21.]

"All the News That's Fit to Print"

The New York Times

LATE CITY EDITION

Weather: Partly sunny today; fair tonight. Chance of rain tomorrow. Temp. range: today 50-64; Monday 45-68. Full U.S. report on Page 86.

VOL. CXXII . . . No. 42,101 NEW YORK, TUESDAY, MAY 1, 1973 — 15 CENTS

NIXON ACCEPTS ONUS FOR WATERGATE, BUT SAYS HE DIDN'T KNOW ABOUT PLOT; HALDEMAN, EHRLICHMAN, DEAN RESIGN; RICHARDSON PUT IN KLEINDIENST POST

Elliot L. Richardson, named Attorney General, yesterday

United Press International

President Nixon in White House press room after address

2 AIDES PRAISED

Counsel Forced Out —Leonard Garment Takes Over Job

By R. W. APPLE Jr.

Special to The New York Times

WASHINGTON, April 30—Four top Nixon Administration officials resigned today as a consequence of the Watergate case, one of the most widespread scandals in American Presidential history.

H. R. Haldeman, the austere and secretive White House chief of staff, and John D. Ehrlichman, the President's chief adviser on domestic affairs, maintained their innocence in letters submitting their resignations. Both said their ability to carry out their daily duties had been undermined.

Texts of Nixon announcement and resignations, Page 30.

The President chose Elliot L. Richardson, the Secretary of Defense, to succeed Richard G. Kleindienst as Attorney General and placed Mr. Richardson in charge of the Watergate investigation.

Mr. Kleindienst said he had quit because close friends had become Watergate suspects and "impartial enforcement of the law" ruled out such "intimate relationships."

Dean's Departure Asked

Mr. Nixon also announced that he had "requested and accepted" the resignation of John W. Dean 3d, the White House counsel, who had threatened to implicate superiors. Leonard Garment, a special Presidential consultant, was named to replace Mr. Dean temporarily.

No replacements for the two key aides were named, and the President gave no hint as to whom he might choose.

In a related development, the United States Information Agency announced tonight that Gordon Strachan had resigned as general counsel "after learning that persons with whom he had worked closely at the White House had submitted their resignations today." The statement said Mr. Strachan "stressed that he had no complicity in the Democratic National Committee break-in or in any alleged attempt to cover it up."

Mr. Haldeman's and Mr. Ehrlichman's departures strip the White House of its central operating mechanism at a time when far-reaching decisions must be made on inflation, Indochina policy and American relations with Europe.

The actions were announced

Continued on Page 30, Column 1

NEW DATA CITED

President Tells How He Changed Mind About Charges

By JOHN HERBERS

Special to The New York Times

WASHINGTON, April 30 — President Nixon told the nation tonight that he accepted the responsibility for what happened in the Watergate case even though he had had no knowledge of political espionage or attempts to cover it up.

The President went on nationwide television and radio to discuss the case after he received the resignations of three top staff members who have been implicated—H. R. Haldeman, John D. Ehrlichman and John W. Dean 3d. He also accepted the resignation of Attorney General Richard G. Kleindienst.

The text of Nixon's speech is printed on Page 31.

Wrongdoing Alleged

While the President accepted the responsibility and pledged every effort to achieve justice in the case, he alleged wrongdoing or cover-up attempts on the part of those he had delegated to run his 1972 Presidential campaign and those he appointed to investigate the matter during the campaign.

And he implied that his own election officials, in the Watergate espionage, were attempting to stop wrongdoing by the Democrats.

Mr. Nixon also said that hereafter the investigation of the Watergate matters would be delegated to his new Attorney General, Elliot L. Richardson, while he, the President, turned his attention to grave foreign and domestic matters. He added that he would leave it up to Mr. Richardson whether to appoint a special prosecutor.

Weeks of Tension

The speech, which came after weeks of growing tension at the White House as developments in the Watergate scandal implicated Administration figures, was an emotional appeal to save the integrity of the Presidency for the 1,361 days, by Mr. Nixon's count, that remain in his term. This was the 100th day of his second term.

"Tonight I ask for your prayers to help me in everything that I do," Mr. Nixon said at the end. "God bless America, and God bless each and every one of you."

He accepted responsibility for Watergate with these words:

"In any organization the man

Continued on Page 31, Column 5

Biaggi Testimony to Jury Ordered Released in Full

U.S. Judge Criticizes Candidate's Petition —Delays Disclosure Pending Appeal —Troy Out as Campaign Chief

By JOHN CORRY

A Federal judge yesterday ordered the release of Mario Biaggi's testimony before a grand jury but held up the order when the mayoral candidate's lawyer said he would appeal to block disclosure.

In issuing the order, Judge Edmund L. Palmieri denied a motion by the Bronx Congressman for a panel of three judges to look over his testimony and state whether he had taken the Fifth Amendment "solely" on questions about his personal finances.

In the past, Mr. Biaggi had told leaders of the Conservative party that he had answered all the questions put to him by the grand jury.

Excerpts from court testimony appear on Page 35.

"Upon reflection," said Judge Palmieri in explaining why he ordered the minutes disclosed, "this court can only conclude that this blatantly unsanctioned petition [by Mr. Biaggi] was made with an expectation of its denial by the court, and for the purpose of publicly exploiting the court's denial of the motion."

Judge Palmieri said that he agreed with United States Attorney Whitney North Seymour Jr., who had asked for full disclosure of the testimony, that Mr. Biaggi's motion constituted an abuse of the court.

"What we have here is tantamount to a manipulation of legal procedures so that the truth can either be successfully concealed or at the very least made to appear different from the underlying facts," the judge said.

Appeal Set for Today

Mr. Biaggi's lawyer, Arthur H. Christy, said he would appeal the decision today to the United States Circuit Court of Appeals. Court sources reported that an appeal would probably be heard later this week or early next week.

Asked outside the court if Mr. Biaggi had told him to appeal, Mr. Christy said, "I follow the instructions of my client."

The political impact to the decision came quickly. Mr. Biaggi dismissed City Councilman Matthew J. Troy Jr. as his mayoral campaign manager. Mr. Troy said he had been preparing to quit anyway.

Simultaneously, leaders of the Conservative party, which has endorsed Mr. Biaggi for Mayor, were thrown into an argument.

Some of the leaders said they

Continued on Page 34, Column 5

ROGERS DEFENDS CAMBODIA RAIDS

Facing Fulbright Committee, He Says the Constitution Justifies the Bombing

By BERNARD GWERTZMAN

Special to The New York Times

WASHINGTON, April 30 — Secretary of State William P. Rogers said today that the continued American bombing in Cambodia was legally justified by the Constitution and was "a meaningful interim action" to force the Communist-backed insurgents there to agree to a cease-fire.

Mr. Rogers, testifying before the Senate Foreign Relations Committee, presented the Administration's long-awaited legal justification for the Cambodian bombing, an issue that has aroused considerable criticism from members of the committee, including its chairman, Senator J. W. Fulbright.

Text of Rogers memorandum will be found on Page 10.

They have argued that President Nixon has no legal basis for the bombing, now that all American troops have been withdrawn from South Vietnam.

Though the committee members generally accorded Mr. Rogers friendly treatment, his arguments, both in his comments to the committee and in a 13-page legal memorandum, failed to sway the most vocal critics such as Senators Ful-

Continued on Page 11, Column 1

Egyptian Air Bases Reported Equipped For Libyan Planes

Special to The New York Times

BEIRUT, Lebanon, April 30—Diplomatic sources report that ground equipment has been installed at some Egyptian air bases for French-built fighter-bombers from Libya and British-built planes from other Arab countries, and that it has been tested by the aircraft during brief visits.

Israel has been charging that French-built Mirage jets from Libya and British-built Hunter interceptors from Iraq have been transferred to Egyptian bases, but there has been no comment in Cairo. A French Government spokesman said last week that French inquiries about the charges had brought denials from Libya and Egypt.

According to informed diplomats here, however, several embassies are known to have reported to their governments that ground equipment for Mirages was installed several weeks ago. These embassies are said to believe that the

Continued on Page 6, Column 1

CONTROLS VOTED FOR ANOTHER YEAR

President Reluctantly Signs Compromise Bill Extending Wage and Price Curbs

By EDWARD COWAN

Special to The New York Times

WASHINGTON, April 30—With the reluctant support of the Administration, both houses of Congress approved today, and President Nixon signed, a compromise bill extending for another year the President's authority to regulate wages and prices.

Mr. Nixon signed the bill tonight, just after making a nationwide television and radio speech. The existing law, called the Economic Stabilization Act, was scheduled to expire at midnight.

The vote in the House was 267 to 115, a larger margin for passage than appeared likely before the Easter recess. The voice vote in the Senate was unrecorded.

Voting for the bill were 153 Democrats and 114 Republicans; opposed were 58 Democrats and 57 Republicans.

Meanwhile, the Department of Agriculture reported that prices received by farmers fell by 1.5 per cent in April, the first decline in a year. [Page 55.]

Mr. Nixon had sought a simple one-year extension of the act. But with the public frus-

Continued on Page 17, Column 1

Ellsberg Judge Demands Affidavits on Bugging Tie

By MARTIN ARNOLD

Special to The New York Times

LOS ANGELES, April 30 — The judge in the Pentagon papers trial today ordered four figures connected to the Watergate affair to produce affidavits concerning any link between that break-in and the trial here.

Federal District Judge William Matthew Byrne Jr. said that he was not foreclosing the possibility of summoning the four men here to testify, although he denied, for now, a defense request for an immediate hearing.

The affidavit order was directed to John W. Dean 3d, former special counsel to President Nixon; L. Patrick Gray 3d, former acting director of the F.B.I., and G. Gordon Liddy and E. Howard Hunt Jr., conspirators in the Watergate bugging.

Judge Byrne indicated that he also would probably require affidavits and perhaps testimony from former Attorney General John N. Mitchell, Richard G. Kleindienst, the present Attorney General; John D. Ehrlichman, until today the President's chief for domestic affairs; H. R. Haldeman, Mr. Nixon's chief of staff who also resigned today; Charles W. Colson, former Presidential special counsel, and Robert C. Mardian, former Assistant Attorney General.

Today's court session began with the judge announcing from the bench that about a month ago he met with Mr. Ehrlichman and President Nixon, "for approximately one minute or less," at Mr. Ehrlichman's suggestion.

At that time, he said, he was offered a new Government position, but he said he told Mr. Ehrlichman that he could not consider it "until this case is concluded." He did not say what the position was, but his name has been mentioned as a possible director of the Federal Bureau of Investigation.

Then, in response to demands from two defense lawyers,

Continued on Page 33, Column 6

SHAKE-UP LAUDED BY CONGRESSMEN

But Many Warn That Step Is Not Enough to Restore Faith in Administration

By JAMES M. NAUGHTON

Special to The New York Times

WASHINGTON, April 30 — Members of Congress joined in widespread, bipartisan praise today for President Nixon's shake-up of his Administration's high command.

But many Senators and Representatives coupled their commendations with warnings that a housecleaning of the White House staff would not be sufficient to restore faith in the Nixon Administration or the Government as a whole.

Furthermore, Representative John E. Moss of California urged House Democratic leaders to open a formal inquiry into the possible impeachment of President Nixon.

The suggestion by the longtime Democratic Congressman—which key leaders of both parties in the House described as "premature" — was the most severe reaction on Capitol Hill to the latest developments in the Watergate conspiracy case.

At Huron, Ohio, the nation's Democratic Governors joined in the call for appointment of a special prosecutor in the Watergate case.

Mark O. Hatfield, Republican

Continued on Page 33, Column 6

Kissinger Is Going to Moscow For Talks on Brezhnev's Visit

Special to The New York Times

WASHINGTON, April 30 — Henry A. Kissinger will fly to Moscow this week for talks with Leonid I. Brezhnev, the Soviet Communist party leader, on plans for Mr. Brezhnev's expected visit to the United States late in June.

While in Moscow with his top staff aides, Mr. Kissinger will also discuss Vietnam, arms control negotiations, trade questions and other matters with Mr. Brezhnev and other top officials, a senior Administration official said.

The White House, in making the announcement, limited itself to saying that Mr. Kissinger would leave Thursday for four to five days in Moscow "for an exchange of views on a wide range of bilateral problems and matters of mutual interest."

But a senior Administration official said that the primary mission of the President's adviser for national security would be to discuss the details and likely agenda for Mr. Brezhnev's visit to the United States, which will return Mr. Nixon's visit to the Soviet Union last spring.

No date for Mr. Brezhnev's trip has been announced, but an Administration official said that both sides were planning on late June—around June 25.

It will be Mr. Brezhnev's first journey to the United States and the first by a top Soviet

Continued on Page 4, Column 4

Nixon Asks Tax Law Shift To Ease Filing on Income

By EILEEN SHANAHAN

Special to The New York Times

WASHINGTON, April 30 — The Nixon Administration proposed today changes in the tax laws and tax forms that would make it easier for millions of individuals to figure out their Federal income taxes.

The Administration's proposals contained little, however, that appeared likely to satisfy the demands of those who have been calling for reform of the tax laws.

Summary of proposed changes is printed on Page 34.

All the basic provisions of the laws that reduce taxes for those who invest in business or property — the provisions relating to capital gains, depreciation, the depletion allowance and so on — would remain untouched under the Administration's plan.

The Administration did, however, recommend enactment of two new provisions that would limit the ability of wealthy individuals to combine different preferential sections of the tax laws in ways that permit them to escape all or most Federal income tax.

The proposals were submitted to the House Ways and Means Committee by the Secretary of the Treasury, George P. Shultz, in the form of a 175-page booklet called "Proposals for Tax Change."

The committee chairman, Wilbur D. Mills, Democrat of Arkansas, said he thought the proposals did not go far enough and criticized particularly the lack of any proposed changes in the taxation of capital gains and in the estate and gift taxes.

The plan for simplifying the

Continued on Page 35, Column 7

NEWS INDEX

News Summary and Index, Page [illegible]

End of Era in Nixon Presidency

By ROBERT B. SEMPLE Jr.

Special to The New York Times

News Analysis

WASHINGTON, April 30 — The resignations of H. R. Haldeman and John D. Ehrlichman from President Nixon's senior staff clearly mark the end of one era of the Nixon Presidency and the beginning of another. Things simply will not be the same. The question is how much different they will be.

The few men who remain in the President's suddenly shrunken entourage do not believe that the scandals of the moment will have much impact on Mr. Nixon's own personality. His habits are well entrenched, and any future White House operation will reflect the style of its master.

But there are some here now, in the White House and on Capitol Hill, who hope that Mr. Nixon will seize what they sense to be a rare opening to redesign his relationships with Congress, the bureaucracy, and even the press.

They hope to increase his access to others and theirs to him, to replace the closed corporation that the White House had become with the "open Presidency" to which he once aspired, and to return to his own first principles by decentralizing some of the power that has steadily flowed from the Government agencies to a few decision-makers in the White House.

Mr. Haldeman and Mr. Ehrlichman helped design that system, ran the system and, in time, came to symbolize the system. Their Teutonic names and mutual zeal for efficient execution gave rise to many jokes. Their enemies called them Hans and Fritz; their friends simply teased them.

In Mr. Ehrlichman's office on the second floor of the White House is a copy of Daniel P. Moynihan's "Understanding Poverty," which carries this inscription: "For John Ehrlichman. Achtung! D.P.M."

But their power was no joke. They were men with long ties and easy access to the President, men of loyalty, men who transmitted Mr. Nixon's orders to the bureaucracy and to whom, with few exceptions, Mr. Nixon's Cabinet members were forced to report before winning humble access to the Oval Office.

In all areas other than for-

Continued on Page 33, Column 4

"All the News That's Fit to Print"

The New York Times

LATE CITY EDITION

Weather: Partly cloudy today; cool tonight. Partly sunny tomorrow. Temp. range: Today 57-69; Friday 55-75. Full U.S. report on Page 66.

VOL. CXXII ... No. 42,112 NEW YORK, SATURDAY, MAY 12, 1973 15 CENTS

PENTAGON PAPERS CHARGES ARE DISMISSED; JUDGE BYRNE FREES ELLSBERG AND RUSSO, ASSAILS 'IMPROPER GOVERNMENT CONDUCT'

White House Says Attacks Will Continue in Cambodia

By BERNARD GWERTZMAN

Special to The New York Times

WASHINGTON, May 11 — The White House said today that the United States would continue with "the right policy" of bombing in Cambodia in support of President Lon Nol's government, despite the vote yesterday in the House of Representatives blocking the transfer of military funds for such raids.

Ronald L. Ziegler, the White House press secretary, made the statement and also announced — jointly with North Vietnam—that Henry A. Kissinger and Le Duc Tho, Hanoi's chief negotiator, would resume talks on Thursday in Paris to seek ways of achieving "strict implementation" of the three-and-a-half-month-old cease-fire agreement.

In its insistence on the bombing program, the Nixon Administration is apparently heading for a possible constitutional conflict with Congress, if the Senate, as expected, supports the House action next week.

The Senate majority leader, Mike Mansfield, told reporters today: "If the will of the Congress and the intention of the Congress — the representatives of the people—are not adhered to, then we will face a true constitutional crisis. One thing this country cannot afford at this time is a constitutional crisis."

To those who urged that any action be postponed until after Mr. Kissinger completed his talks with Mr. Tho, Mr. Mansfield said: "My sympathies are with Mr. Kissinger. But I don't think we should delay exercising our responsibilities."

Yesterday the House voted, 219 to 188, to block the transfer of funds for continued bombing in Cambodia. This was the first time that the House had supported an end-the-war amendment.

"We, of course, observed the vote in the Congress yesterday," Mr. Ziegler said. "We will continue with the policy which we feel is the right policy, and that is to provide support to the Government of Cambodia at their request. If at some time in the future the funds are not available, then the Congress will have to assume the responsibility in that matter."

Mr. Ziegler repeated that

Continued on Page 4, Column 3

Sudan Puts Off Trying 8 Who Killed U.S. Envoys

By HENRY TANNER

Special to The New York Times

CAIRO, May 11—President Gaafar al-Nimeiry of the Sudan has decided to postpone indefinitely the trial of the eight Palestinian guerrillas who killed three diplomats, two Americans and a Belgian, while holding the Saudi Embassy in Khartoum last March 2, informed Sudanese sources said here today.

After the slayings General Nimeiry and other leading officials publicly pledged an early trial. They said that the guerrillas would be charged with murder, a capital offense in the Sudan.

Now the same officials say that the Israeli force that thrust into the heart of Beirut, the Lebanese capital, last month and killed three leading members of the Palestinian resistance made it impossible for General Nimeiry—or any other Arab statesman—to convict Palestinian guerrillas of a crime that in Arab eyes was as much a patriotic deed as the raid into Beirut was in Israeli eyes.

The recent fighting between Lebanese troops and Palestinians is another reason why no public trial of the eight guerrillas should be held, Sudanese officials say. The trial, they maintain, would be interpreted throughout the Arab world as another instance of "fratricide."

The outlook now is for a lengthy confinement of the eight without trial, informed sources say.

General Nimeirys decision is likely to renew friction between the Sudan and the United States, which resumed diplomatic relations less than a year ago.

The State Department is known to have served notice that no new ambassador will be sent to Khartoum unless the slayers of Ambassador Cleo A.

Continued on Page 11, Column 3

2-GERMANY PACT IS VOTED IN BONN

Parliament Also Approves Joining United Nations

By DAVID BINDER

Special to The New York Times

BONN, May 11—The treaty that will establish formal relations between the two Germanys after more than two decades of hostile nonrecognition was ratified by the lower house of the West German Parliament today by a vote of 268 to 217.

By a second vote, 365 to 121, the lower house also gave its approval to the prospective entry of West Germany into the United Nations along with East Germany.

The treaty, regarded as the crowning achievement of Chancellor Willy Brandt's policy of normalizing relations with Eastern Europe, was concluded last November. It is expected to go into effect later this month after the ratification process is completed here and in East Germany.

The upper house of the West German Parliament is expected to approve the treaty next week and send it to President Gustav Heinemann for signature. Ratification by the East German Parliament is also expected next week, with ceremonial approval by the State Council to follow.

The treaty will greatly enlarge the opportunities for the Germans of the two states to

Continued on Page 10, Column 1

GRAY CALL TO NIXON

Said to Inform Inquiry It Came 3 Weeks After Watergate

By ANTHONY RIPLEY

Special to The New York Times

WASHINGTON, May 11 — L. Patrick Gray 3d has told Senate investigators that he talked by telephone with President Nixon about three weeks after the Watergate burglary last June 17 to express concern over White House obstacles in his path and confusion that was hampering his investigation, committee sources said today.

Mr. Gray, at the time acting director of the Federal Bureau of Investigation, was concerned over the action of White House aides, these sources said.

The sources would not comment on how Mr. Gray said the President reacted to the telephone complaint. The sources did not specify the nature of the obstacles that Mr. Gray said he had faced.

Talks To Prosecution

Mr. Gray, who resigned as acting director of the F.B.I. in the wake of the Watergate scandals, was questioned by the Senate investigators last night. He spent most of today talking to the prosecution team from the Justice Department but apparently did not appear before the grand jury, which gathered at 4:30 P.M. in the Federal courthouse.

There were a flurry of news reports tonight that Mr. Gray had told the President of an attempt to impede the Watergate investigation. Mr. Gray received "no reaction" from the President, according to The Baltimore Sun.

Committee sources here said such reports were "out of focus" and did not fully reflect Mr. Gray's position.

Sought to End Confusion

"There was confusion," one source said. "Gray felt things should be straightened out so that he could carry out this investigation."

In past statements to friends and testimony before Congress, Mr. Gray has repeatedly described his troubles with the White House staff.

Mr. Gray said that the President's counsel, John W. Dean 3d, had sat in while F.B.I. agents were interviewing persons at the White House and that Mr. Dean had "probably" lied to agents. Mr. Gray also said that he had turned over raw F.B.I. investigation files to Mr. Dean. At the time the Presidential counsel was conducting a separate investigation of the

Continued on Page 15, Column 1

United Press International

Judge William Matthew Byrne Jr., above, threw out the Pentagon papers case and, left, defendants were freed. They are Anthony J. Russo Jr., left, and Dr. Daniel Ellsberg.

NEW TRIAL BARRED

But Decision Does Not Solve Constitutional Issues in Case

By MARTIN ARNOLD

Special to The New York Times

LOS ANGELES, May 11—Citing what he called "improper Government conduct shielded so long from public view," the judge in the Pentagon papers trial dismissed today all charges against Dr. Daniel Ellsberg and Anthony J. Russo Jr.

And he made it clear in his ruling that the two men would not be tried again on charges of stealing and copying the Pentagon papers.

The text of Judge Byrne's decision is on Page 14.

"The conduct of the Government has placed the case in such a posture that it precludes the fair, dispassionate resolution of these issues by a jury," he said.

David R. Nissen, the chief prosecutor, said, "It appears that the posture is such that no appeal will be possible."

Defendants Not Vindicated

But the decision by United States District Court Judge William Matthew Byrne Jr. did not vindicate the defendants; it chastised the Government. Nor did it resolve the important constitutional issues that the case had raised.

The end of the trial, on its 89th day, was dramatic. The courtroom was jammed; the jury box was filled with news reporters; defense workers in the Ellsberg-Russo cause, mostly young people, sat in chairs lining the courtroom wall.

Dr. Ellsberg and Mr. Russo, surrounded by their lawyers, stared intently as Judge Byrne quickly read his ruling.

The Government's action in this case, he said, "offended a sense of justice," and so "I have decided to declare a mistrial and grant the motion for dismissal." The time was 2:07 P.M.

The courtroom erupted in loud cheering and clapping. The judge, barely hiding a smile, quickly strode out the door behind his bench.

Tension had been building

Continued on Page 14, Column 5

Air of Expectancy, Then Tears, Shouts, Embraces

By JUDITH KINNARD

Special to The New York Times

LOS ANGELES, May 11—Her tears of joy had dried, but cheers still filled the courtroom when Patricia Ellsberg embraced one of many friends and said:

"I could never believe the scene of waiting for the jury to come in. I just knew it would never happen."

Federal District Court Judge William Matthew Byrne Jr. had just closed the Pentagon papers trial with a broad decision that harshly admonished the Government for misconduct.

Dr. Ellsberg, looking gaunt as much from loss of weight as from the pressure of the last two years, spoke to a cheering crowd on the steps of the courthouse after the verdict.

Almost crushed by newsmen as he stood with his arm around his wife, he said: "This trial is not over until that bombing is over in Cambodia." And he added that he intended to sue for damages specific individuals in the Government, perhaps the President himself.

Like every other major decision in the case since it went to trial in January, the final dramatic ruling came amid an air of expectancy that had pervaded the proceedings all week.

By 7 A.M., when the smog had already descended on Los Angeles, spectators had begun lining up in the corridor outside the dark brown door to the courtroom for the limited passes for access to the trial, which ended almost two years after Dr. Daniel Ellsberg and Anthony J. Russo Jr. were indicted.

Photographers waited for the judge, whose latest pictures, showing shorter and fuller hair, were taken three

Continued on Page 14, Column 2

A New Grand Jury Reported Planning To Summon Biaggi

By NICHOLAS GAGE

Representative Mario Biaggi, who appeared twice before a Federal grand jury in 1971, will be called before another jury for further questioning, authoritative sources said yesterday.

On Thursday night Mr. Biaggi admitted that he had refused to answer questions before the 1971 jury after repeatedly denying it for several months.

The Bronx Representative had been scheduled to be called before a Federal grand jury on April 27, but the appearance was postponed pending resolution of the court battle—that was just then beginning—over release of his 1971 testimony. That testimony is to be released today.

The United States Attorney's office has received new infor-

Continued on Page 16, Column 3

CONNALLY TO TAKE LEAVE FROM FIRM

New Adviser to President Will Also Resign From All Corporate Boards

By JOHN HERBERS

Special to The New York Times

WASHINGTON, May 11—John B. Connally announced today that he would take a leave of absence from his law firm and resign from all corporate boards during the time he will serve as special adviser to President Nixon.

Mr. Connally's announcement, issued by his office in Houston, came after disclosure that the firm in which he is a senior partner is representing the Gulf Resources and Chemical Corporation, now under investigation by a Federal grand jury in connection with campaign contributions sent to the Committee for the Re-election of the President. The disclosure was made today in Newsday and other newspapers.

"I am today taking a leave of absence from my law firm for the period during which I will serve as a special adviser to the President," said the former Secretary of the Treasury and former Texas Governor.

"I am also resigning from all corporate boards on which I serve," he continued. "Notwithstanding that my service will be on an intermittent and voluntary basis and without any operational role, I will not engage in any legal practice nor participate in any dividends or revenues or as a partner of the firm during this advisory pe-

Continued on Page 15, Column 5

Congress Ascending

Watergate Seen as Altering Balance Between Executive and Capitol Hill

By JAMES M. NAUGHTON

Special to The New York Times

WASHINGTON, May 11—The White House is slipping and Congress is rising as the balance of power in Washington is being altered perceptibly by the Watergate conspiracy case.

For the first time in six years the House of Representatives went on record yesterday, by a vote of 219 to 188, in opposition to White House policies in Indochina. For the second time in five weeks, the Senate declared yesterday, 66 to 24, that the White House was obligated to adhere to the directions of Congress on Government spending.

News Analysis

"Both houses are beginning to see eye to eye on Congressional responsibility," the Senate Democratic leader, Mike Mansfield, said today in an interview.

A senior associate of President Nixon predicted privately today that the White House and the Nixon Cabinet would abandon their attitude of disregard for those on Capitol Hill and become, in the official's words, "more receptive" to Congressional viewpoints.

The change is only beginning to be visible. Much of it is atmospheric. It remains for Congress, long a slumbering giant, to take steps to "even the balance," as Mr. Mansfield put it, but he and others are becoming

Continued on Page 13, Column 1

NIXON AGAIN ASKS LEGAL AID TO POOR

Independent Agency Would Replace O.E.O. Unit

By LINDA CHARLTON

Special to The New York Times

WASHINGTON, May 11—President Nixon resubmitted to Congress today, in slightly revised form, his proposals for providing free legal assistance to the poor through the creation of an independent Legal Services Corporation.

A program to make available legal aid in civil matters to those unable to afford it otherwise is now a part of the Office of Economic Opportunity, which is scheduled to go out of existence July 1. Efforts to establish the program as an independent entity date back more than two years through a history of disagreement, compromise and veto. Today's bill is apparently a compromise reached after much internal Administration battling.

The new proposal would create an independent, federally funded Legal Services Corporation with an 11-member board of directors appointed by the President—a focal point of controversy in previous versions—but subject to confirmation by the Senate. Not more than six members could be of the same political party, and a majority would be lawyers.

It also includes very specific

Continued on Page 31 Column 3

Norton Simon Bought Smuggled Idol

By DAVID L. SHIREY

Norton Simon, the West Coast industrialist and art collector, said yesterday that he had paid $1-million for a bronze sculpture of a Hindu deity that Indian Government officials say was stolen from a South Indian temple and smuggled out of India.

"Hell, yes, it was smuggled," said Mr. Simon in a telephone interview. "I spent between $15-million and $16-million over the last two years on Asian art, and most of it was smuggled. I don't know whether it was stolen."

Indian Government officials, who have for two years been seeking the return of the 44-inch sculpture representing the deity Siva, known in its region of discovery as Nataraja, say that it was one of several stolen from a temple in Sivapuram, in southern India and smuggled out of the country. They also say that the original works were replaced in the temple by modern fakes.

Continued on Page 20, Column 1

The New York Times/Meyer Liebowitz

The bronze statue of the Hindu deity Siva, dancing

86th St. Toonerville Tale: 3 Flee From a Police Van

By LESLEY OELSNER

Three prisoners, two of them handcuffed together, leaped from the back of a police van yesterday and ran off along West 86th Street to freedom.

The van continued on its precinct-to-precinct morning rounds and then, 40 minutes later, at 79th Street and Lexington, two more prisoners jumped out. This time bystanders shouted and policemen jumped from the vehicle, quickly capturing the fugitives—and learning for the first time of the disappearance of the three others.

Capt. Alexander Davis of Manhattan North, said, "How's that for a Toonerville tale?"

Captain Davis, who is in charge of investigating how the escapes occurred, reported late yesterday afternoon that the fugitives—all alleged robbers—were still at large. "Four or five detectives," he said, as well as the police officer who had arrested them the night before, Daniel Traynor of the 28th Precinct, were looking for the men.

The route to freedom, the captain said, appeared to have been facilitated by a defective lock on the van door.

The van began its trip early yesterday at the 28th Precinct station at 229 West 123d Street. It was to go from precinct to precinct picking up men who had been arrested the night before and then take them to the Criminal Courts Building at 100 Centre Street.

Among the men it picked up at the 28th were the three escapees—Edward McBride, 24 years old, of 215 West 101st Street, and Vincent Perry, 19, and Tony Grant,

Continued on Page 21, Column 1

NEWS INDEX

"All the News That's Fit to Print"

The New York Times

LATE CITY EDITION

Weather: Very hot again today; very warm tonight. Hot tomorrow. Temp. range: today 78-98; Wed. 76-95. Temp.-Hum. Index yesterday 83. Full U.S. report on Page 66.

VOL. CXXII..No. 42,222

NEW YORK, THURSDAY, AUGUST 30, 1973

15 CENTS

JUDGE SIRICA ORDERS NIXON TO YIELD TAPES TO HIM FOR A DECISION ON GRAND JURY USE; PRESIDENT DECLARES HE 'WILL NOT COMPLY'

PEKING DISCLOSES 5-DAY CONGRESS OF CHINESE PARTY

Meeting Ousted Lin, Named Central Committee and Adopted a Constitution

By TILLMAN DURDIN

Special to The New York Times

HONG KONG, Aug. 29 — China disclosed today that the 10th Congress of her Communist party was held in Peking last Friday through yesterday.

The announcement was made in a dispatch of Hsinhua, the

Text of the communiqué is printed on Page 14.

official press agency. It said the Congress formally expelled Defense Minister Lin Piao and Chen Po-ta from the party. Mr. Lin was designated Chairman Mao Tse-tung's successor during the last Congress in 1969, and is reported to have been killed in 1971 after attempting to assassinate Chairman Mao. Both he and Mr. Chen, a former Politburo member, were denounced as renegades and traitors.

Political Report by Chou

The Congress also adopted a revised party constitution, selected a new Central Committee and approved a political report delivered by Premier Chou En-lai.

It is assumed that the new Central Committee will hold its first meeting in a day or two and name members of the all-important Politburo and the standing committee of the Politburo. These bodies run China on a day-to-day basis.

The Central Committee members were reported to include the old, middle-aged and young, which the communiqué said showed that the party "has no lack of successors."

Mao Presided

The Congress, at which Chairman Mao presided, was the briefest in the history of the Chinese party.

Attended by 1,249 delegates, the Congress was held in the greatest secrecy and confounded foreign newsmen and diplomats in Peking.

Obviously, hard decisions on sharing of power and position between factions had to be made before the Congress was held and this probably delayed its convening. The result is an apportioning of positions between the civilian moderates, represented by Premier Chou, and important career party members, military leaders and the so-called leftists generally associated with Chiang Ching, Mr. Mao's wife.

The 10th Congress appeared to have been even more of a

Continued on Page 14, Column 1

180,000 Hit by Blackout In Four Areas of Queens

By FRANK J. PRIAL

About 180,000 Queens residents were left without electrical power last night when a group of Consolidated Edison Company cables burned out at 6:15 P.M. The blackout, the first major power failure of the summer, also darkened passenger terminals and hangars at La Guardia Airport.

The cables, and the entire Con Edison network, had been running at full capacity because of the unrelenting, record-breaking heat. Yesterday New Yorkers plodded through their second day of above 90-degree temperatures and high humidity, and there was no relief in sight.

High for the day was 95 degrees at 2:35 P.M., three degrees below Tuesday's high of 98, the record for the summer—so far.

The burned-out cables, 27,000-volt feeder lines supplying all of Jackson Heights and parts of Corona, Woodside and Elmhurst, as well as the airport, had been strained by a day of fires and breakdowns.

At about 11:30 P.M., at least 5,000 Con Edison customers were left without power on Staten Island, when seven feeder cables were knocked out in the Great Kills and Richmondtown sections. Full power was restored to 795 customers in Richmondtown after 65 minutes. Scattered areas of Great Kills were still blacked out at 2:30 A.M.

The power failure in Queens came just as Con Edison was about to end its second day of a 5 per cent system-wide power reduction. The cutback, which also affected the rest of the state's power companies, which are members of the New York State Power Pool, lasted from 10 A.M. to 6:25 P.M.

Throughout the day, the situation had been more serious in Jackson Heights than anywhere else in the Con Edison area, and the company had asked its Jackson Heights customers to be particularly careful about using power when they came home from work last night.

Four of eight feeder cables serving the area had burned out at about 3 A.M. yesterday. One

Continued on Page 27, Column 1

Official Temperatures

	Wed.	Tues.		Wed.	Tues.
2 A.M.	81	79	2 P.M.	94	95
3 A.M.	80	79	3 P.M.	94	97
4 A.M.	78	79	4 P.M.	94	98
5 A.M.	77	79	5 P.M.	93	98
6 A.M.	77	77	6 P.M.	92	96
7 A.M.	76	77	7 P.M.	89	93
8 A.M.	78	78	8 P.M.	88	90
9 A.M.	81	81	9 P.M.	86	87
10 A.M.	85	84	10 P.M.	86	87
	Wed.	Tues.	11 P.M.	85	86
11 A.M.	87	87	Midnight	84	84
Noon	90	89		Thurs.	Wed.
1 P.M.	92	92	1 A.M.	84	82
			2 A.M.	83	81

The Soviet Dissidents

Moscow Showing It Will Maintain Ideological War and Internal Curbs

By THEODORE SHABAD

Special to The New York Times

MOSCOW, Aug. 29—The sudden upsurge in news of dissidence from Moscow has brought into sharp focus the Soviet leaders' determination to pursue their policy of improved relations with the West without giving an inch to domestic pressures for liberal reforms.

News Analysis

There appear to be some elements of coincidence in the timing of the current trial of two dissidents and the rash of moves and countermoves in the cases of two of the most outspoken advocates of change in the Soviet system—Andrei D. Sakharov, the physicist, and Aleksandr I. Solzhenitsyn, the novelist.

But the pattern of events of the last two weeks also fits in neatly with the intensification of ideological warfare that has become increasingly evident in the Soviet Union since the meeting between President Nixon and Leonid I. Brezhnev, the Soviet Communist party chief.

It seems a far cry from the smiles-and-sweetness atmosphere that was being conveyed by the Soviet mass media in those June days to the rapid-fire sequence of recent Soviet denunciations of supposedly subversive threats, foreign and domestic.

First, after a moratorium of several months coinciding with the summit period, the United States again became fair game in the Soviet media. Radio listeners were warned against writing to the Voice of America, which was presented as an intelligence-gathering organization, and "Sesame Street" was described as the kind of program that should be kept off Soviet living room screens in

Continued on Page 9, Column 1

APPEAL UNCERTAIN

White House Hints at Possible Defiance of Court Ruling

By JOHN HERBERS

Special to The New York Times

SAN CLEMENTE, Calif., Aug. 29—The White House said today that President Nixon would not comply with Judge John J. Sirica's order to turn over his Watergate tape recordings to the court.

In a terse statement issued by its press office, the White House said the President was considering the possibility of appeal or "how otherwise to sustain the President's position."

This left open the clear possibility that the President might simply refuse to obey the order without first resorting to appeal.

Compromise Ruled Out

White House spokesmen would not elaborate on the statement, but it was plain that it was another assertion by President Nixon that he would not compromise on the issue.

In his news conference last Wednesday, Mr. Nixon said his right to withhold the tapes as a point of executive privilege was absolute.

"Let me explain the principle of confidentiality exists or it does not exist," he said. "Once it is compromised or it is known that a conversation that is held with the President can be subject to a subpoena by a Senate committee, by a grand jury, by a prosecutor, and be listened to by anyone, the principle of confidentiality is thereby irreparably damaged."

Confidentiality Needed

To conduct the affairs of the Presidency, in both foreign and domestic matters, Mr. Nixon said, "he must be able to do so with the principle of confidentiality intact."

The President seems more determined now to resist compromise on the tapes than he was a few weeks ago. Last month, Gerald L. Warren, the deputy White House press secretary, said Mr. Nixon would

Continued on Page 21, Column 6

Union Aides Indicted

Peter Ottley, president of the 20,000-member Local 144 of the Hotel, Hospital, Nursing Home and Allied Service Employes Union, and Peter Byrne, its secretary-treasurer, were indicted here yesterday by a Federal grand jury on charges of embezzling union funds. Page 44.

The New York Times/George Tames

Judge John J. Sirica, who ruled on the Presidential tapes, in his chambers

NIXON'S LAWYERS ASSAIL COMMITTEE

In Paper Filed in Court, His Counsel Rejects Demand of Senators for Tapes

Special to The New York Times

WASHINGTON, Aug. 29 — President Nixon's lawyers charged today that the Senate Watergate committee had conducted a "criminal investigation and trial" that exceeded the authority granted to Congress by the Constitution.

In papers filed in Federal District Court, the White House attorneys rejected the committee's demand for tape recordings of Nixon conversations on the ground that the Senators were illegally attempting to determine "whether or not criminal acts have been committed and the guilt or innocence of individuals."

The President's lawyers also contended that the court had no jurisdiction over their client, either as an individual or as President, and that Mr. Nixon "owes no duty," in either capacity, to the Senate committee to provide it with recordings of his confidential meetings or other related documents.

In a legal countermove, the Senate committee filed with Chief Judge John J. Sirica a motion for summary judgment in the same case, a request that the judge enforce two subpoenas already served on the President with a minimum of further court proceedings.

The motion by the commit-

Continued on Page 21, Column 3

Judge Sirica's Order

This matter having come before the court on motion of the Watergate special prosecutor made on behalf of the June, 1972, grand jury of this district for an order to show cause, and the court being advised in the premises, it is by the court this 29th of August, 1973, for the reasons stated in the attached opinion,

Ordered that respondent, President Richard M. Nixon, or any subordinate officer, official or employe with custody or control of the documents or objects listed in the grand jury subpoena duces tecum of July 23, 1973, served on respondent in this district, is hereby commanded to produce forthwith for the court's examination in camera, the subpoenaed documents or objects which have not heretofore been produced to the grand jury; and it is

Further ordered that the ruling herein be stayed for a period of five days in which time respondent may perfect an appeal from the ruling; and it is

Further ordered that should respondent appeal from the ruling herein, the above stay will be extended indefinitely pending the completion of such appeal or appeals.

JOHN J. SIRICA
CHIEF JUDGE

White House Reply

As Mr. Wright pointed out in his oral argument before the court, in camera inspection of these tapes is inconsistent with the President's position relating to the question of separation of powers as provided by the Constitution and the necessity of maintaining the precedent of confidentiality of private Presidential conversations for this President and for Presidents in the future.

The President consequently will not comply with this order.

White House counsel are now considering the possibility of obtaining appellate review or how otherwise to sustain the President's position.

A HISTORIC RULING

President First Since Jefferson Directed to Give Up Records

By WARREN WEAVER Jr.

Special to The New York Times

WASHINGTON, Aug. 29—President Nixon was ordered today by Judge John J. Sirica to make tape recordings of White House conversations involving the Watergate case available to him for a decision on their use by a grand jury.

Presidential aides announced, however, that Mr. Nixon "will

Text of Judge Sirica's opinion will be found on Page 20.

not comply with the order."

A White House statement said that the President's lawyers, led by Prof. Charles Alan Wright, were considering appealing the decision by Judge Sirica, who is chief judge of the United States District Court here, but it also hinted that they might find some other method of sustaining the President's legal position.

If faced with a refusal by Mr. Nixon to accept the court's ruling or to challenge it by an appeal, Archibald Cox, the special prosecutor, might initiate contempt proceedings or begin an appeal of his own, based on the court's refusal to give him the tapes directly.

Serious Consequences

It was only the second time in the nation's history that a court had required a President, against his will, to produce his personal records as evidence, and the decision was certain to have serious political, governmental and legal consequences, both immediate and long-range. The first case involved President Jefferson.

At San Clemente, where President Nixon is vacationing, officials announced that he would not comply with the court order on the ground that inspection of the tapes by a judge "is inconsistent with the President's position relating to the question of separation of powers as provided by the Constitution and the necessity of maintaining precedents of confidentiality of private Presidential conversations . . ."

The White House statement said that the President's lawyers were considering an appeal "or how otherwise to sustain" Mr. Nixon's legal position.

The last phrase raised the possibility that the President might ignore the order rather than appeal it, thus precipitating another constitutional clash between the executive and judicial branches.

Authority Upheld

Judge Sirica said that he was "simply unable" to decide whether the President's refusal to release the tapes and related documents was valid without inspecting the recordings himself. He upheld the authority of the court to take such action.

If he finds evidence relating to criminal activity in the tapes, and it can be successfully separated from the privileged statements dealing with the President's official duties, the judge said, he will excise the privileged portions and pass the unprivileged portions along to the Watergate grand jury. Archibald Cox, the special prosecutor, is presiding over the panel.

"If privileged and unprivi-

Continued on Page 21, Column 1

Nadjari Studying Charge Of Plan to Bribe a Justice

By C. GERALD FRASER

Special Prosecutor Maurice H. Nadjari's office disclosed yesterday that it was investigating an alleged conspiracy to pay a $50,000 bribe to a State Supreme Court justice.

Although details of the conspiracy were not disclosed, sources close to the investigation said that it grew out of a case involving the Citizens Casualty Company of New York, which was declared insolvent in 1970 after fighting a long court battle to stay in business.

In that battle, the company, whose lawyer was Representative Mario Biaggi, won a brief victory before Acting Supreme Court Justice Adolph C. Orlando, an interim appointee, who is now sitting in the Court of Claims. But Judge Orlando was reversed and the company was ordered dissolved.

Biaggi Received $240,000

Mr. Biaggi was paid $240,000, but was later ordered to return $100,000 of the fee. The court order said that the $100,000 was contingent on Mr. Biaggi's winning complete victory for the company while Mr. Biaggi maintained that he was obligated only to win the aspect of the case that came before Judge Orlando.

Yesterday in State Supreme Court, Justice John M. Murtagh refused to quash a subpoena issued by Mr. Nadjari to the Century National Bank and Trust Company. Joseph A. Phillips, the chief assistant special prosecutor, said that bank records would be able to shed light on "the sources of moneys used to pay the bribe and to account for moneys obtained as a result of the case."

Mr. Phillips told Justice Murtagh yesterday that "in the course of that investigation, the evidence developed by the grand jury indicates that the principal officers of the Century Bank have information and evidence" relating to the alleged bribery.

Inquiry Leads to Bank

In this way, the special prosecutor got into transactions involving the Century National Bank and Trust Company of 1372 Broadway.

In an affidavit filed yesterday, Mr. Phillips said: "As a result of the alleged bribe, the conspirators obtained substantial sums of moneys due to the determination of the case."

And he said to Justice Murtagh: "Where did the money as a result of the bribe go? . . . all of the leads we have produced point to Century National Bank."

The executive officers of the bank are Vincent F. Albano, Republican county chairman,

Continued on Page 53, Column 3

Sadat and Qaddafi Act on Unification

By HENRY TANNER

Special to The New York Times

CAIRO, Aug. 29—President Anwar el-Sadat of Egypt and the Libyan leader, Col. Muammar el-Qaddafi, tonight proclaimed the "birth of a new unified Arab state" but made it emphatically clear that actual unification of their two countries was still a long way off.

A declaration issued in the name of the two leaders satisfied every point of the Egyptian Government's wish for a slow, gradual approach that could be broken off at any stage. It fell far short of the immediate full union that Colonel Qaddafi had urgently demanded.

Mr. Sadat and Colonel Qaddafi agreed in August, 1972, to work toward "complete unity." The process, to take a year,

Continued on Page 5, Column 1

United Press International

BEREAVED BY EARTHQUAKE: A woman and the only one of her four children who survived sit in ruins of home in Orizaba, Mexico. Incomplete reports put the toll of Tuesday's quake at more than 600. Details, Page 12.

"All the News That's Fit to Print"

The New York Times

LATE CITY EDITION

Weather: Partly sunny today; fair tonight. Partly sunny tomorrow. Temp. range: today 53-75; Saturday 53-73. Additional details on Page 91.

SECTION ONE

VOL. CXXIII..No. 42,260 — NEW YORK, SUNDAY, OCTOBER 7, 1973 — 75¢ beyond 50-mile zone from New York City, except Long Island. Higher in air delivery cities. — 50 CENTS

ARABS AND ISRAELIS BATTLE ON TWO FRONTS; EGYPTIANS BRIDGE SUEZ; AIR DUELS INTENSE

Associated Press

REDS, ORIOLES WIN PLAYOFF OPENERS: Johnny Bench after his homer won National League game for Cincinnati from New York, 2-1. Sparky Anderson, manager, is at lower left. Baltimore beat Oakland, 6-0, in the American League. Details in Section 5.

U.S. ASKS A HALT

Pleas by Kissinger to Prevent the Fighting Prove Fruitless

By BERNARD GWERTZMAN

Special to The New York Times

WASHINGTON, Oct. 6—The United States appealed to Israel and Egypt today to halt the fighting.

Secretary of State Kissinger, who was in New York, was caught by surprise when the crisis developed. He made a last-minute effort by telephone with Foreign Minister Abba Eban of Israel and Foreign Minister Mohammed H. el-Zayyat of Egypt to prevent the fighting from breaking out, but it proved fruitless.

Both men had had routine talks with Mr. Kissinger in the last two days without giving any indication that fighting was about to erupt, Administration officials said.

Kissinger Urges 'Restraint'

On instructions from President Nixon, who was in Key Biscayne, Fla., for the weekend, Mr. Kissinger "urged restraint to avoid the undermining and violation of the cease-fire" in effect since August, 1970, "and to avoid any escalation and continuation of the fighting," Robert J. McCloskey, a State Department spokesman, said in New York before Mr. Kissinger returned to Washington this afternoon..

In addition, Mr. Kissinger sent cables to King Faisal of Saudi Arabia and King Hussein of Jordan, both friendly to the United States, expressing the hope that they would "use their good office to urge restraint where they have the influence to do so," Mr. McCloskey said.

Call to Waldheim

Mr. Kissinger telephoned Secretary General Waldheim of the United Nations and Sir Lawrence McIntyre of Australia, this month's President of the Security Council, to discuss possible Council action. He also called the Soviet Ambassador, Anatoly F. Dobrynin, in Washington, Mr. McCloskey said, presumably to urge Soviet restraint as well.

The crisis struck Washington without much warning. American intelligence had routinely reported signs of military build-ups in Egypt and Syria in recent weeks, but the analysts believed these were either

Continued on Page 14, Column 1

United Press International

Army boots slung over his shoulder, an Israeli reservist reports for duty in Tel Aviv

SYRIANS IN CLASH

Fighting Along Canal and Golan Heights Goes On All Night

By ROBERT D. McFADDEN

The heaviest fighting in the Middle East since the 1967 war erupted yesterday on Israel's front lines with Egypt along the Suez Canal and Syria in the Golan heights.

Official announcements by Israel and Egypt agreed that Egyptian forces had crossed the Suez Canal and established footholds in the Israeli-occupied Sinai Peninsula.

A military communiqué issued in Cairo asserted that Egyptian forces had captured most of the eastern bank of the 100-mile canal. An Israeli military communiqué said the Egyptians had attempted to cross the canal at several points by helicopters and small boats and had succeeded in laying down pontoon bridges at two points. Armored forces were pouring across them into Sinai, it said.

Fighting All Night

A communiqué issued early today in Tel Aviv said fighting had raged all night along the canal's eastern bank and along the entire cease-fire line with Syria.

Each side accused the other of having started the fighting. But military observers posted by the United Nations reported crossings by Egyptian forces at five points along the Suez, and said Syrians had attacked in the Golan heights at two points.

Israeli and Syrian artillery dueled in the Golan heights, and on both battlefronts there were air clashes. The Cairo radio said Egyptian forces had shot down 11 Israeli planes and lost 10 of their own in battles over the Sinai and the Gulf of Suez. The Israeli spokesman did not comment on losses but said Israeli planes had shot down 10 Egyptian helicopters carrying troops into the southern Sinai.

Shelling by Syrians

In Damascus, the military command said that Syrian pilots and ground fire had shot down 10 Israeli aircraft in renewed action over the Golan heights this morning.

Syrian artillery was reported by the Israelis to have shelled a number of settlements in the occupied Golan heights and the Hula Valley area.

The Damascus radio said that Syrian forces had reoccupied Mount Hermon in the Golan heights for the first time since 1967, and said Syrian troops were fighting on the ground with Israeli forces along the entire cease-fire line.

An Israeli spokesman said today that Israeli planes had sunk an Egyptian vessel and that the navy had sunk three troop-carrying Egyptian craft during the night.

Gunboats Reported Sunk

As fighting continued into the night, Syrian and Israeli gunboats clashed in the Syrian harbor of Latakia, 110 miles north of Beirut. An Israeli communiqué said that five Soviet-built Syrian vessels were sunk by Israeli sea-to-sea missiles being used for the first time.

In Damascus, however, a military spokesman said that Syrian forces had sunk four Israeli naval vessels and shot down two Israeli helicopters in the sea battle.

No military action involving Jordan or Lebanon was reported, but King Hussein of Jordan placed his armed forces on full alert and conferred by telephone with President Anwar el-Sadat of Egypt and President Hafez al-Assad of Syria. Jordan was a belligerent in the 1967 war won by Israel.

The Government radio stations in Cairo and in Damascus

Continued on Page 2, Column 3

CAB DRIVER SLAIN IN TENSE BOSTON

Found Stabbed to Death in Roxbury Area Following Two Previous Killings

By JOHN KIFNER

Special to The New York Times

BOSTON, Oct. 6—The body of a young white taxi driver who had been stabbed to death was found today in the predominantly black Roxbury neighborhood as this uneasy city tried to come to grips with its racial fears.

The police identified the driver as Kirk Miller, a student at Clarkson College, who was working for the Boston Cab Company. His body was found hidden in some bushes in a vacant lot in Roxbury.

Detectives said that he had multiple stab wounds in his back and head. They said that they "had to assume" that robbery was a possible motive although they could not discount other factors. They said that no money was found on the body.

Mr. Miller was discovered by his sister Sally and a friend, Jeffrey Carter.

Tuesday night, a young white woman was burned to death by six youths in Roxbury, and less than 48 hours later an elderly white man was slain near a housing project. There

Continued on Page 77, Column 3

Tax Agents Compile Data On Net Worth of Agnew

By MARTIN WALDRON

Special to The New York Times

BALTIMORE, Oct. 6—Agents of the Internal Revenue Service are apparently compiling a statement on Vice President Agnew's net worth as part of the continuing investigation into his financial affairs.

Although the purpose of the revenue service's investigation is not known, the service often uses the technique of the net worth audit in an attempt to show that a defendant accused of evading taxes is worth more than the amounts on which he paid taxes.

Earlier this week, the Federal grand jury investigating Mr. Agnew indicted N. Dale Anderson, who succeeded Mr. Agnew as Baltimore County Executive, on income tax charges after revenue agents compiled a net worth statement on Mr. Anderson.

By law, the revenue service is prohibited from commenting on individual income tax reports or on investigations it may have under way.

But in the last few weeks its agents have been collecting data dealing with Mr. Agnew's affairs, even minor transactions, according to sources knowledgeable about the investigations.

On Oct. 3, agents from the Charlotte, N. C., intelligence office of the service subpoenaed records in Asheville, N. C., showing a gift of four yards of homespun cloth worth $16 to Mr. Agnew in 1967 at the time of the Southern Governors Conference, the sources said.

Such gifts are sometimes considered as income for tax purposes.

In making a case charging income tax evasion against an individual, the revenue service sometimes alleges failure to pay tax on specific income items, which it then seeks to prove were received by the individual.

The revenue agents and agents of the Federal Bureau of Investigation are apparently checking every financial transaction that the Vice President

Continued on Page 33, Column 1

U.N. COUNCIL AIDES CONFER ON CRISIS

President of Body Seeks Views on Calling Meeting to Deal With Fighting

By ROBERT ALDEN

Special to The New York Times

UNITED NATIONS, N. Y., Oct. 6—The President of the Security Council, Sir Laurence McIntyre of Australia, opened formal consultations tonight with other members of the Council to seek their views on calling a Council meeting to deal with the fighting in the Middle East.

The Western powers generally favored calling such a meeting, but not prematurely. They said that a premature meeting would result in little more than invective, claim and counterclaim.

Another proposal the Council members were discussing was for the President of the Council to appeal to both sides in the Middle East to halt the fighting. While Western powers generally supported such an appeal, the Chinese and the Russians held back endorsement; the French said they would have to study the idea.

Neither the Israelis nor the Arab states called for an urgent meeting of the Council today, though the Egyptian Foreign Minister, Dr. Mohammed H. el-Zayyat, said he wanted to

Continued on Page 8, Column 1

Israelis and Egyptians Tell Of Beginnings of Conflict

Jerusalem's Report

By TERENCE SMITH

Special to The New York Times

JERUSALEM, Sunday, Oct. 7—Heavy fighting erupted yesterday between Israeli and Arab forces along the Suez Canal and Golan heights cease-fire lines, a military spokesman announced.

The forces were still fighting early this morning in what Defense Minister Moshe Dayan described as "all-out war."

Mrs. Meir's address, Page 5; Dayan excerpts, Page 6.

The fighting began at 2 P.M. yesterday, Israeli time (8 A.M. New York time). Egyptian forces managed to cross the Suez Canal during the afternoon and establish bridgeheads at several points on the Israeli-held eastern bank, but Israeli military spokesmen said last night that Israeli forces had moved into position to block them.

On the occupied Golan heights, a large-scale Syrian force including armor and artil-

Continued on Page 4, Column 1

Cairo Communiques

By HENRY TANNER

Special to The New York Times

CAIRO, Oct. 6 — The Egyptian Government announced today that Israeli ground, sea and air forces attacked Egypt and Syria early this afternoon along the entire length of their front lines with Israel.

In a succession of communiqués read on the Government-controlled Cairo radio, Egypt said that her forces had crossed the Suez Canal in several places and had placed Egyptian flags on the Israeli-held eastern bank.

The radio said that the Egyptians had crossed the canal—the cease-fire line since the 1967 war—after repelling Israeli landing attempts on the Egyptian-held western bank.

The radio interrupted its regular program just after 2 P.M., Cairo time (8 A.M., New York time) saying that the Israeli action had started at 1:30 local time with air attacks on Ain Sukhna, 30 miles south of the town of Suez on the Egyptian shore of the Red Sea, and

Continued on Page 7, Column 1

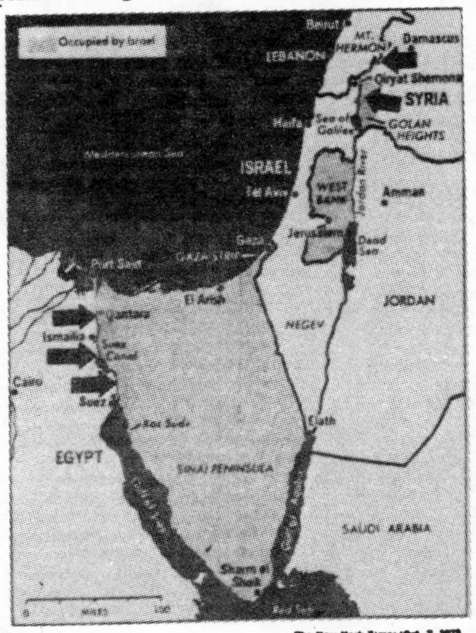

The New York Times/Oct. 7, 1973

Heavy arrows (upper right) indicate drive by Syrians and (lower left) crossing of Suez Canal by Egyptians.

Queens Sports Center Proposed

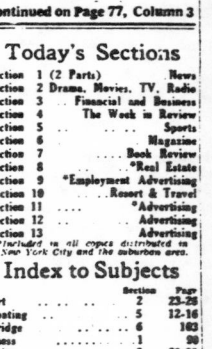

Race track is flanked by Northern Boulevard at right and Skillman Avenue, left. Hotel rises at center, next to stadium. Queensboro Bridge leads to Manhattan.

By EMANUEL PERLMUTTER

Creation of a $275-million sports complex on air rights over the Sunnyside, Queens, railroad yards of the Penn Central was proposed yesterday by the State Racing and Wagering Board.

The project, which would be competitive with the proposed athletic complex in the New Jersey Meadows, would include two race tracks, an 80,000-seat stadium for football and other entertainments, a 1,000-room resort and convention hotel and parking for 20,000 cars.

No housing or other buildings would have to be demolished for the project since it would be built on a platform over the 300-acre yard site, which is less than a mile east of the Queensboro Bridge at the junction of Queens and Northern Boulevards and just a few minutes from Times Square by subway.

Under the proposal, the project would be financed by a bond issue and proceeds from the sale of Aqueduct Race Track. The air rights would be purchased by the Metropolitan Transportation Authority from the Penn Central and leased to the State Urban Development Corporation, which would build the necessary facilities.

Emil Mosbacher Jr., chairman of the Racing and Wager-

Continued on Page 49, Column 1

Gas Pipeline Contest Develops in Alaska

By GLADWIN HILL

Special to The New York Times

PRUDHOE BAY, Alaska, Sept. 29 — Another Alaskan pipeline dispute is brewing.

While the oil companies with the big petroleum deposits here on the North Slope await a final Congressional go-ahead to build a controversial 789-mile pipeline to Alaska's south coast, a consortium of United States and Canadian concerns is pushing plans to tap the region's rich natural gas reserves via a different but equally controversial 2,000-mile route.

Current exploratory activities of the gas consortium, pointing toward a possible major incursion into the Arctic National

Continued on Page 74, Column 3

Today's Sections

Index to Subjects

"All the News That's Fit to Print"

The New York Times

LATE CITY EDITION

Weather: Partly sunny today; cool tonight. Fair and milder tomorrow. Temp. range: today 54-68; Wed. 58-75. Additional details on Page 90.

VOL. CXXIII... No. 42,264 © 1973 The New York Times Company NEW YORK, THURSDAY, OCTOBER 11, 1973 15 CENTS

AGNEW QUITS VICE PRESIDENCY AND ADMITS TAX EVASION IN '67; NIXON CONSULTS ON SUCCESSOR

U.S. Believes Moscow Is Resupplying Arabs by Airlift

Soviet Could Spur Move to Aid Israel

By JOHN W. FINNEY

Special to The New York Times

WASHINGTON, Oct. 10—Administration officials said today that they believed the Soviet Union was airlifting military equipment to resupply the forces of Egypt and Syria.

The State Department said that if the Russians were in fact engaged in a huge resupply effort, this would put a "new face" on the Middle East conflict. Speaking for the department, Robert J. McCloskey said, however, that he was "not in a position to confirm that any of this is taking place at this time."

But other officials, apparently acting upon instructions laid down by the State Department, readily volunteered information. They did so, however, on a basis that precluded their identification.

The fact that officials who until today had been extremely reluctant to discuss any detail of the Middle East war were now willing to talk openly about indications of a Soviet resupply effort prompted immediate speculation that the Nixon Administration might be laying the groundwork for resupplying the forces of Israel.

There were reports that Israel was flying military supplies from the United States and from American bases in Britain and West Germany, but it was not clear whether the supplies referred to had previously been ordered. Asked about the reports, the Defense Department refused to confirm or deny them.

The exact nature of the reported Soviet airlift remains unclear, United States officials said. All that is known, according to officials, is that in the last day or so, an unusually large number of Soviet transports have been observed landing at Egyptian and Syrian airports. The presumption is that the planes are carrying military equipment.

The airlift, officials reported, was being staged primarily from Hungary, with the planes

Continued on Page 18, Column 1

A 10-Mile Egyptian Gain

By HENRY TANNER

Special to The New York Times

IN THE SINAI PENINSULA, Oct. 10 — Egyptian soldiers, tanks and equipment are continuing to pour across the Suez Canal, a group of Western correspondents confirmed from the battle area today.

On a three-and-half-mile tour into the Sinai Peninsula, this correspondent also saw evidence that Egyptian forces had reached positions 10 miles or more east of the canal in some parts of the sector.

[In the air war the Egyptians said they had shot down six more Israeli planes. Egyptian aircraft were said to have attacked Israeli command headquarters, units and administrative installations on the northern Sinai coast.]

The Egyptian soldiers in the area toured by the correspondents were in high spirits, often jubilant, and seemed oblivious to Israeli artillery shells bursting near them.

"Don't worry, God is with us!" one of three young soldiers shouted laughingly to the correspondents, who ducked for cover when a shell burst too close for comfort. The Egyptians remained where they were, standing atop a ridge.

Shells fell every few moments but caused no casualties during a half-hour visit to the particular sector. An Egyptian officer said they were from an Israeli battery 15 miles away that was trying to hit a military bridge.

More than 50 trucks interspersed with antiaircraft guns were lined up in open country on the west bank, waiting for their turn to cross the canal. Waved onto the bridge by a young soldier with a yellow flag, they moved quickly, often with three or four vehicles on the bridge simultaneously.

On one truck two young soldiers were dancing. Others clapped their hands rhythmically.

The elation and excitement of returning to Egyptian territory occupied for more than six years by Israel was everywhere.

The loose boards and pontoons that made up the bridge

Continued on Page 18, Column 5

Israel Claiming Heights

By CHARLES MOHR

Special to The New York Times

TEL AVIV, Thursday, Oct. 11—Israel said last night that the Syrian Army on the Golan heights had been driven back to the 1967 cease-fire line, but Israeli forces fighting the Egyptians clearly seemed to have suspended a counterattack aimed at pushing them from the eastern bank of the Suez Canal.

Text of Mrs. Meir's address is printed on Page 19.

A highly informed source said that Israel estimated the Egyptian invasion force at five divisions, which could be close to 75,000 men. The force, he said, crossed with about 600 tanks, and 300 to 400 of these may still be operational.

The Israeli Air Force bombed two air fields in the Nile delta as well as a naval headquarters, fuel installation and power plant in Syria in a day of slackening air action.

The Israeli command announced this morning that for the first time in the war Israeli forces had struck against the opposite bank of the Suez Canal. The command spokesman said that an Israeli force of unannounced size had raided convoys and rear echelon installations of the Egyptian Army.

The wording of the communiqué indicated that the operation was not an attempt to gain a foothold on the other side and that the raiding force

Continued on Page 19, Column 3

CONGRESS TO VOTE

Opposition Is Hinted if Choice Is Possible 1976 Candidate

Special to The New York Times

WASHINGTON, Oct. 10—President Nixon began his search today for a successor to Vice President Agnew amid indications that he will face stiff resistance from Congress if he chooses anyone who might qualify as a strong Republican candidate in 1976.

The Senate majority leader, Mike Mansfield, Democrat of Montana, said the choice of either John B. Connally, the former Treasury Secretary and Texas Governor, or Gov. Ronald Reagan of California—both presumed contenders for the Republican Presidential nomination in 1976—would provoke a fight from Senate Democrats.

Similar warnings had come from Democratic leaders in the House.

Quick Action Indicated

Mr. Nixon's first moves today indicated that he wished to move quickly but with some show of bipartisan consultation. Senator Mansfield said after meeting the President that Mr. Nixon had indicated he would submit the name of his nominee to Congress "at the end of this week or the first of next week."

"President Nixon intends to move expeditiously in selecting a nominee and he trusts the Congress will then act promptly to consider the nomination," Ronald L. Ziegler, the President's press secretary, announced shortly after word that the President had accepted Mr. Agnew's resignation spread through the White House.

Mr. Nixon then began meeting with Congressional leaders of both parties and with George Bush, chairman of the Republican National Committee, to reach an understanding on the procedures he will follow in selecting a Vice President ac-

Continued on Page 34, Column 2

Associated Press

Spiro T. Agnew speaking to reporters after appearing at court in Baltimore yesterday

Agnew Plea Ends 65 Days Of Insisting on Innocence

By BEN A. FRANKLIN

Special to The New York Times

BALTIMORE, Oct. 10—Vice President Agnew ended today 65 days of defiant insistence that he was innocent of any wrongdoing by pleading no contest to a charge of cheating the Government of $13,551.47 on his Federal income tax payment for 1967, his first year as Governor of Maryland. Then he resigned his Federal office.

Richardson, Agnew, Hoffman statements on Page 35.

At a dramatic, surprise appearance here before United States District Court Judge Walter E. Hoffman after two days of secret negotiations, Mr. Agnew was confronted in open court by Attorney General Elliot L. Richardson.

The Attorney General said in a prepared statement that the Government's evidence against the former Vice President went far beyond the six-year-old tax violation. But he said that "critical national interests"—the avoidance of the "serious and permanent scars" upon the nation that would have been inflicted by months or years of a criminal prosecution of a sitting Vice President, together with the new and allied dispute over newsmen's sources—justified the agreement with Mr. Agnew. Judge Hoffman then approved the agreement.

Under it, Mr. Agnew in a 40-minute court appearance waived all his rights as a defendant—the right to be indicted and to an arraignment—and was sentenced on the spot to pay a $10,000 fine and to three years of probation. He was admonished by Judge Hoffman to violate no state or Federal laws on pain of having his avoidance of a prison term reconsidered.

A long list of other charges, involving perhaps $100,000 in payoffs by Maryland contrac-

Continued on Page 35, Column 1

EVIDENCE SHOWS GIFTS TO AGNEW

Cites Requests and Receipt of Over $100,000—Denial Also Entered in Record

By ANTHONY RIPLEY

Special to The New York Times

BALTIMORE, Oct. 10—Spiro T. Agnew, in three elective offices including the Vice-Presidency, asked for and accepted cash payments totaling more than $100,000, according to the evidence gathered against him by the United States Attorneys in Baltimore.

That evidence, denied by Mr. Agnew, was entered by Attorney General Elliott L. Richardson in Federal District Court today as part of the agreement between the Justice Department and Mr. Agnew's lawyers.

Charge and jury information are on Pages 36, 37 and 38.

It became a permanent part of the record in the case, along with Mr. Agnew's denial and other terms of the agreement that included his resignation and a plea of no contest to a tax charge.

The 40-page document told of

Continued on Page 28, Column 1

Mets in World Series; Defeat Reds for Flag

By JOSEPH DURSO

The New York Mets completed their six-week odyssey from last place to the National League pennant yesterday when they overpowered the favored Cincinnati Reds, 7-2, in a tumultuous game that rocked and almost ruined Shea Stadium.

In a riotous scene that brought back memories of their "miracle" of 1969, they decided the issue with four runs in the fifth inning of a 2-2 game.

But then, in a swirling scene, thousands of persons in the crowd of 50,323 stormed the field after delaying the game in the ninth inning and clawed huge chunks of fence, sod and fixtures from the arena.

Professional sports may have had more clamorous moments. But New York baseball has had none since the Mets won the World Series four years ago after eight seasons as the comic relief of the leagues.

Their rise this summer carried them from medical history to baseball history, and their public responded yesterday by mobbing Willie Mays, Pete Rose and the 340 police officers struggling to prevent panic.

Repairs on the stadium were started immediately after the crowd had dispersed shortly after 5 o'clock, while the Mets celebrated their victory in champagne and prepared for the next milestone.

They will open the World Series on Saturday in the home park of the Oakland A's or Baltimore Orioles, who will decide the American League pennant this after-

Continued on Page 61, Column 4

NEWS INDEX

News Summary and Index, Page 67

I.R.S. Sees Nothing to Prevent New Tax Cases Against Agnew

By EILEEN SHANAHAN

Special to The New York Times

WASHINGTON, Oct. 10—Former Vice President Agnew's plea of "no contest" today in the income-tax evasion case against him could mark only the beginning of difficulties for him with the Internal Revenue Service.

An official spokesman for Internal Revenue said that so far as the agency is aware, there was nothing in the agreement leading to Mr. Agnew's resignation that would prohibit Internal Revenue from attempting to collect taxes on every payment to Mr. Agnew that could be documented as having been made but not reported on his tax returns.

The charge of tax evasion to which Mr. Agnew pleaded "nolo contendere" involved $29,500. But a document released by the Justice Department detailing the evidence against the former Vice President alleges payments from contractors and others totaling as much as $100,000. The precise figure is not clear, because some of the allegations of illegal payments are stated in terms of percentages of the value of construction contracts awarded, and the figures for the contracts themselves are not given.

The Internal Revenue spokesman said, however, that it was common in tax-evasion cases for a charge of criminal tax-evasion to be made involving

Continued on Page 33, Column 3

Judge Orders Fine, 3 Years' Probation

By JAMES M. NAUGHTON

Special to The New York Times

WASHINGTON, Oct. 10—Spiro T. Agnew resigned as Vice President of the United States today under an agreement with the Department of Justice to admit evasion of Federal income taxes and avoid imprisonment.

The stunning development, ending a Federal grand jury investigation of Mr. Agnew in Baltimore and probably terminating his political career, shocked his closest associates and precipitated an immediate search by President Nixon for a successor.

"I hereby resign the office of Vice President of the United States, effective immediately," Mr. Agnew declared in a formal statement delivered at 2:05 P.M. to Secretary of State Kissinger, as provided in the Succession Act of 1792.

Minutes later, Mr. Agnew stood before United States District Judge Walter E. Hoffman in a Baltimore courtroom, hands barely trembling, and read from a statement in which he pleaded nolo contendere, or no contest, to a Government charge that he had failed to report $29,500 of income received in 1967, when he was Governor of Maryland. Such a plea, while not an admission of guilt, subjects a defendant to a judgment of conviction on the charge.

Tells Court Income Was Taxable

"I admit that I did receive payments during the year 1967 which were not expended for political purposes and that, therefore, these payments were income taxable to me in that year and that I so knew," the nation's 39th Vice President told the stilled courtroom.

Judge Hoffman sentenced Mr. Agnew to three years' probation and fined him $10,000. The judge declared from the bench that he would have sent Mr. Agnew to prison had not Attorney General Elliot L. Richardson personally interceded, arguing that "leniency is justified."

In his dramatic courtroom statement, Mr. Agnew declared that he was innocent of any other wrongdoing but that it would "seriously prejudice the national interest" to involve himself in a protracted struggle before the courts or Congress.

Mr. Agnew also cited the national interest in a letter to President Nixon saying that he was resigning.

"I respect your decision," the President wrote to Mr. Agnew in a "Dear Ted" letter made public by the White House. The letter hailed Mr. Agnew for "courage and candor," praised his patriotism and dedication, and expressed Mr. Nixon's "great sense of personal loss." But it agreed

Continued on Page 33, Column 1

Agnew-Nixon Exchange

October 10, 1973

Dear Mr. President:

As you are aware, the accusations against me cannot be resolved without a long, divisive and debilitating struggle in the Congress and in the courts. I have concluded that, painful as it is to me and to my family, it is in the best interests of the nation that I relinquish the Vice Presidency.

Accordingly, I have today resigned the office of Vice President of the United States. A copy of the instrument of resignation is enclosed.

It has been a privilege to serve with you. May I express to the American people, through you, my deep gratitude for their confidence in twice electing me to be Vice President.

Sincerely,
SPIRO T. AGNEW

October 10, 1973.

Dear Ted:

The most difficult decisions are often those that are the most personal, and I know your decision to resign as Vice President has been as difficult as any facing a man in public life could be. Your departure from the Administration leaves me with a great sense of personal loss. You have been a valued associate throughout these nearly five years that we have served together. However, I respect your decision, and I also respect the concern for the national interest that led you to conclude that a resolution of the matter in this way, rather than through an extended battle in the courts and the Congress, was advisable in order to prevent a protracted period of national division and uncertainty.

As Vice President, you have addressed the great issues of our times with courage and candor. Your strong patriotism, and your profound dedication to the welfare of the nation, have been an inspiration to all who have served with you as well as to millions of others throughout the country.

I have been deeply saddened by this whole course of events, and I hope that you and your family will be sustained in the days ahead by a well-justified pride in all that you have contributed to the nation by your years of service as Vice President.

Sincerely,
RICHARD NIXON

"All the News That's Fit to Print"

The New York Times

LATE CITY EDITION

Weather: Mostly sunny, mild today; cloudy, chance of rain tonight. Temp. range: today 56-73. Friday 51-71. Additional details on Page 70.

VOL.CXXIII....No.42,266 | NEW YORK, SATURDAY, OCTOBER 13, 1973 | 15 CENTS

GERALD FORD NAMED BY NIXON AS THE SUCCESSOR TO AGNEW

Appeals Court Agrees President Should Give Up Tapes

Israelis Drive Syrians Back Within 18 Miles of Damascus

Capture of Capital Thought Unlikely

By CHARLES MOHR

Special to The New York Times

EL QUNEITRA, on the Golan Heights, Oct. 12—Parts of the Syrian Army appeared to be in full retreat today as the Israeli Army advanced to within 18 miles of the Syrian capital of Damascus.

But an Israeli officer said: "We won't be having dinner together tomorrow in Damascus."

[In Tel Aviv, a well-informed Israeli source said that "the latest thinking is that we will not capture Damascus, which would be a terrible headache." An Israeli military spokesman said that Israeli forces had encountered Iraqi troops in the Golan heights for the first time.]

In at least one area of the Syrian front, northeast of the town of El Quneitra, it was apparent that Syrian forces were in retreat, although still fighting delaying actions.

Reporters following the Israeli Army—and clocking distances on the odometers of their rented sedans—could see that the Israeli forward elements were at least 30 kilometers, or 18 miles, past the old 1967 cease-fire line—and thus about 30 kilometers from Damascus.

It was apparent to neutral foreign observers that, in this one area at least, the main Syrian line of resistance had been smashed. The heavy fortifications constructed by Syria on the 1967 cease-fire line were abandoned and many of its bunkers damaged or destroyed.

Great plumes of brown dust rose in the air as Israeli tank companies moved forward over the rolling, hill-dotted terrain east of the cease-fire line.

A heavy Syrian artillery barrage came in on an area about four miles within Syria this afternoon, but journalists had no clear idea what was happening at the spearhead of the Israeli advance and how determined Syrian resistance was in the most forward areas.

On a brief visit to what is now the Israeli rear area on the route of advance, there were

Continued on Page 14, Column 5

3 Freighters Sunk

By JUAN de ONIS

Special to The New York Times

DAMASCUS, Syria, Oct. 12 — Syrian air defenses today shot down 35 Israeli planes that attacked military air bases around this capital and other targets, according to a military spokesman.

Three freighters, one Soviet, one Japanese and one Greek, were sunk during attacks by Israeli missile boats on the ports of Latakia and Tartus, an official announcement said today. The Syrian spokesman said eight of the attacking Israeli craft were sunk by Syrian missile boats.

[In Cairo, military communiqués said that Egyptian forces were continuing to pour across the Suez Canal. Page 15.]

On the ground, "fierce fighting" continued all along the Syrian front, said the spokesman. He said more than 40 Israeli tanks and 20 armored vehicles had been destroyed. There was no figure on Syrian losses.

The front, along the occupied Golan Heights, was 24 miles southeast of this city of 840,000 people, which was calm tonight under a nearly full moon.

Traffic in the blacked-out streets consisted mainly of

Continued on Page 15, Column 1

To Our Readers

Distribution of this issue of The New York Times was delayed by work stoppages by the printers' union in defiance of a court order. The stoppages also made it necessary to reduce coverage of the news. Details, Page 24.

United Press International

Fumes and smoke rise as Israeli artillerymen, on the Syrian border, fire 155-mm. guns

JUDGES RULE 5-2

Historic Decision Finds President Not Above Law's Commands

By LESLEY OELSNER

Special to The New York Times

WASHINGTON, Oct. 12—In what it called an "unavoidable" and "extraordinary" ruling, the United States Court of Appeals held tonight that President Nixon must turn over to the Federal District Court here the disputed White House tape recordings possibly bearing on Watergate crimes.

By a 5-to-2 vote, the appeals court said that the District

Excerpts from court opinions will be found on Page 21.

court could then give the Watergate grand jury any relevant material, unless it felt that there was some public interest to be served by withholding "particular" statements or information.

"Though the President is elected by nationwide ballot, and is often said to represent all the people, he does not embody the nation's sovereignty," the court said. "He is not above the law's commands."

Order Is Upheld

Participants in today's decision were David L. Bazelon, chief judge, and J. Skelly Wright, Carl McGowan, Harold Leventhal, Spottswood W. Robinson, 3d, George E. MacKinnon and Malcolm R. Wilkey.

The court's ruling, issued at 6 P.M. through the clerk's office on the fifth floor of the Federal Courthouse here, thus substantially upheld the order last August of Federal District Judge John J. Sirica, although it appeared to take an even tougher stance against the President than Judge Sirica had.

The appellate court made its ruling in response to requests by both Mr. Nixon and Archibald Cox, the special Watergate prosecutor, to reverse Judge Sirica. Mr. Cox, who had initiated the proceedings when he had a subpoena issued for the tapes, asked the appeals court to order that the tapes be turned over directly to the grand jury.

Mr. Nixon, for his part, asked

Continued on Page 20, Column 4

United Press International

Gerald R. Ford with President, after Mr. Nixon nominated him for Vice President

MOVE IS SURPRISE

House G.O.P. Leader Would Be the 40th Vice President

By JOHN HERBERS

Special to The New York Times

WASHINGTON, Oct. 12 — Gerald Rudolph Ford of Michigan, the 60-year-old minority leader of the House of Representatives, was nominated by President Nixon tonight to be the 40th Vice President of the United States.

Mr. Nixon, making the surprise announcement on national television and radio shortly after 9 P.M., said that he would

Texts of Nixon and Ford remarks are on Page 19.

send the nomination to Congress tomorrow. Because of Mr. Ford's long service in that body, 25 years, he was expected to be easily confirmed.

Under the 25th Amendment, ratified in 1967 and never used before tonight, the nomination must be approved by simple majorities of both the House and the Senate before he can take office.

Mr. Ford's selection came two days after Spiro T. Agnew, who had served in the office almost five years, resigned, pleaded no contest to income tax evasion, was fined $10,000 and was placed on probation for three years.

Move Toward Unity

In a brief announcement speech in the East Room of the White House, Mr. Nixon made it clear that he had chosen a respected memb of Congress for the post because he considered it essential for national unity to select a person who would not be the subject of a protracted and bitter fight in Congress.

It was learned that Mr. Nixon had given strong consideration to former Treasury Secretary John B. Connally but that leaders in the Democratic-controlled Congress had served notice they would oppose him. They opposed Mr. Connally because he recently switched to the Republican party and because it would have appeared that Mr. Nixon was setting him up for the Presidency in the 1976 elections.

Mr. Ford, the President said, "has earned the respect of both Democrats and Republicans."

'Unwavering' on Vietnam

"He is a man also who has been unwavering in his support of the policies that brought peace with honor for America in Vietnam and in support of the policies for a strong national defense," Mr. Nixon said.

Several score Congressional leaders, Cabinet members and other high Government officials burst into cheers and surrounded the baldish, tanned Republican and offered congratulations even before Mr. Nixon uttered his name. They knew he was the nominee when Mr. Nixon said his choice "is a man who has served for 25 years in the House of Representatives with great distinction."

Mr. Ford, the President said, met the three criteria he had set for the nominee—that "the

Continued on Page 19, Column 1

Amtrak Will Double Fleet Of 'Corridor' Metroliners

By EDWARD C. BURKS

Amtrak, the nationwide rail passenger system, announced yesterday that it would virtually double its fleet of Metroliner cars and extend high-speed Metroliner service from New York to Boston.

It signed contracts in Washington for new equipment valued at $63.5-million including the following:

¶Fifty-seven new Metroliner-type coaches, capable of operation in trains pulled by either electric or diesel locomotives, for service in the Washington-New York-Boston "Northeast Corridor."

¶Eleven new 6,000-horsepower electric locomotives (added to 15 ordered earlier this year) to replace the famed but ancient Penn Central GG-1 electrics that have operated in the corridor since the nineteen-thirties.

¶Seventy new diesel passenger locomotives for other Amtrak routes around the nation.

In Philadelphia, Judge John P. Fullam, who is in charge of the Penn Central Railroad's bankruptcy case in Federal District Court, said he believed there was no immediate need for the carrier to cease its operations. [Details Page 47.]

With the award of yesterday's contracts, Amtrak has now committed more than $110-million this year to new locomotives and passenger cars.

Started in 1969, the high-speed Metroliner service between New York and Washington has been expanded to a train every hour in each direction from early morning until evening on weekdays.

There are somewhat fewer services on the weekends. In addition, some Metroliners go on through New York as far as New Haven.

Although very-high speed service on the New York-Boston line must await the day of extensive track realignment on the curving route, new equipment ordered yesterday can substantially reduce present running times, according to Amtrak.

Bryan Duff, Amtrak's news director, said that the first of the new Metroliner-type coaches with airliner interiors should be delivered in 15 months. They are to be built by the Budd Company at Red Lion, Pa.

The 61 Metroliner cars now in operation are self-propelled and equipped with pantographs on the roof. Their use is thus limited to the relatively short stretches in this country with overhead catenary installations.

The new cars will have the

Continued on Page 70, Column 5

CHOICE IS PRAISED BY BOTH PARTIES

Widespread Enthusiasm Is Expressed in Congress—Fast Confirmation Seen

By RICHARD L. MADDEN

Special to The New York Times

WASHINGTON, Oct. 12—Congressional Democrats and Republicans received President Nixon's choice of Gerald R. Ford to be Vice President with widespread enthusiasm tonight.

The reaction indicated that the nomination of Mr. Ford of Michigan, who has been the House Republican leader since 1965, would be confirmed relatively quickly by both houses, barring some unforeseen development.

However, it was expected that the Senate would take more time than the House in considering the nomination.

"My own feeling is Gerry will probably be confirmed," said Speaker Carl Albert of Oklahoma, he added:

"I think I was the first in Congress to tell the President that Gerry would be the easiest candidate to sell to the House. He's a very fine man to work with. I think he earned this."

Senator Robert C. Byrd of West Virginia, the Democratic majority whip and member of the Senate Rules Committee, which will probably handle Mr. Ford's nomination, said he did not think it would be proper

Continued on Page 19, Column 5

P.S.C. Certifies Shortage Of Fuel Oil on Long Island

First in the State

By DAVID A. ANDELMAN

The State Public Service Commission certified yesterday that a major shortage in home and industrial fuel oils existed for Long Island—the first region in the state to be declared an "oil insufficient area."

According to the certification, between now and Jan. 15 Long Island will face a shortage of at least 150.1 million gallons of No. 2 home heating oil and 39.5 million gallons of Nos. 4 and 6 industrial fuel oils.

The certification was made to Henry L. Diamond, the State Environmental Conservation Commissioner, who must now decide whether to lift the regulations prohibiting use of high-sulphur fuel oil to ease the anticipated shortage.

Yesterday's certification applies only to fuels distributed through Northville Industries, the largest distributor on Long Island, but reportedly not the only one finding supplies short.

As a result, a senior official of the Public Service Commission noted, "there may be other

Continued on Page 36, Column 3

Federal Controls Ordered

By The Associated Press

WASHINGTON, Oct. 12—The Nixon Administration reluctantly adopted today a mandatory allocation program governing the wholesale distribution of home heating oil.

At the same time, Congress moved steadily closer to forcing a mandatory program for all petroleum products.

The Administration's limited program, which will take effect Nov. 1, requires suppliers to distribute home heating oil, jet fuel, kerosene, diesel fuel, range oil, stove oil and gas oil to their customers in proportion to purchases made in the calendar year 1972.

On Oct. 2, the Administration imposed a similar allocation program on propane gas, but so far there is no Government control over the distribution of crude oil or of gasoline and other petroleum products.

Legislation now before Congress would require mandatory allocation of all petroleum products and crude oil.

The House Rules Committee

Continued on Page 36, Column 5

Agnew Prosecution Took Pains To Prepare a 'Locked-Up Case'

By AGIS SALPUKAS

Special to The New York Times

BALTIMORE, Oct. 12—It started modestly.

When George Beall, the United States Attorney for Maryland, asked that a grand jury be impaneled last Dec. 4, he recalled in an interview today, the thought was: "If we ended up bringing criminal charges against a couple of building inspectors in Baltimore it would have been justified."

And the inquiry remained focused on lesser political figures, with no hint that it would lead higher, until the beginning of June when several key witnesses began to seek favored treatment from the prosecutors by telling them what they knew about making payments to the then Vice President Agnew.

By the beginning of July, Mr. Beall was convinced that the case against the Vice President was serious and on July 3 he called Attorney General Elliot L. Richardson to inform him of the explosive turn of events.

Mr. Beall comes from a long line of prominent Republicans in Maryland. He is the son of J. Glenn Beall, the former Republican United States Senator, and the brother of J. Glenn Beall Jr., who won election to the Senate in 1970. Today he recalled his feelings at that point last summer when he realized the implication of the inquiry.

"I was turning somersaults," he said as he sat at his neat

Continued on Page 18, Column 2

Israel Is Accused in U.N. Of Sinking a Soviet Ship

By ROBERT ALDEN

Special to The New York Times

UNITED NATIONS, N. Y., Oct. 12—The Soviet Union accused Israel today of "barbarous" attacks on nonmilitary targets and demanded that they be stopped at once.

Yakov A. Malik, the Soviet delegate, read to the Security Council a dispatch from Tass, the Soviet press agency, that said the Soviet merchant ship Ilya Mechnikov had been sunk in Tartus, a Syrian port, by an Israeli attack.

Tass demanded "an immediate stop to the bombings of peaceful towns in Syria and Egypt, and the strict observance by Israel of the norms of international law."

"The continuation of criminal acts by Israel will lead to grave consequences for Israel itself," the Tass article added.

Yosef Tekoah, the Israeli representative, said his information on the basis of a news dispatch was that the Soviet merchant ship had been damaged as a result of a naval battle that took place between Syrian and Israeli naval vessels outside the port. He termed the damage "unfortunate."

Reports from Damascus said that the ship had subsequently been sunk, as had a Greek and a Japanese merchant ship during attacks made by Israeli missile boats on the ports of Tartus and Latakia.

"We regret the sinking of

Continued on Page 14, Column 2

Rival Stadium Plans Stir a Bistate Furor

By FRANK LYNN

A bitter behind-the-scenes struggle has developed between New York and New Jersey over a proposed Sunnyside, Queens, sport complex that has the strong backing of Governor Rockefeller and that could effectively kill a similar New Jersey race track and football stadium.

High New York State sources said that the Governor had approved the announcement of the Queens sports complex last Saturday that forced postponement of the sale of a $280-million bond issue to finance the New Jersey race track and stadium for the New York Football Giants in the Hackensack Meadows.

"We were signaling investors of New York's interest in its

Continued on Page 24, Column 5

NEWS INDEX

"All the News That's Fit to Print"

The New York Times

LATE CITY EDITION

Weather: Chance of showers later today, tonight. Milder tomorrow. Temp. range: today 36-46; Friday 43-49. Additional details on Page 62.

VOL. CXXIII . . . No. 42,406

NEW YORK, SATURDAY, MARCH 2, 1974

20¢ beyond 50-mile radius of New York City, except Long Island. Higher in air delivery cities.

15 CENTS

FEDERAL GRAND JURY INDICTS 7 NIXON AIDES ON CHARGES OF CONSPIRACY ON WATERGATE; HALDEMAN, EHRLICHMAN, MITCHELL ON LIST

John N. Mitchell
Former Attorney General

H. R. Haldeman
Headed White House staff

John D. Ehrlichman
Was Presidential adviser

Charles W. Colson
Former White House lawyer

Robert C. Mardian
1972 campaign coordinator

Kenneth W. Parkinson
Lawyer for campaign unit

Gordon C. Strachan
Assisted Mr. Haldeman

COLSON IS NAMED

A Question of Veracity of the President Is Indirectly Raised

By ANTHONY RIPLEY
Special to The New York Times

WASHINGTON, March 1—A Federal grand jury today indicted seven men, all former officials of President Nixon's Administration or of his 1972 reelection campaign, on charges of covering up the Watergate scandal.

Never before have so many close and trusted advisers of an American President faced criminal accusations in a single indictment.

All were charged with conspiracy — a conspiracy, the grand jury said, that continued

Five pages of Watergate material with indictment text begin on Page 14.

"up to and including" today; six were charged additionally with obstruction of justice; two with perjury and three with false statements to the Federal Bureau of Investigation, the grand jury or both.

The indictment accused one defendant, H. R. Haldeman, the former White House chief of staff, of lying when he quoted the President as saying "it would be wrong" to raise hush money for the perpetrators of the original Watergate burglary—a break-in June 17, 1972, at the Democratic National Committee headquarters.

Endorsed Statement

This indirectly raised a question about Mr. Nixon's veracity because he endorsed Mr. Haldeman at a news conference last Aug. 22. The President recalled a meeting at the White House at which clemency for the Watergate defendants and financial support for their families was discussed. Mr. Nixon said he had told his White House counsel, John W. Dean 3d, "John it, is wrong, it won't work."

With the indictment, the grand jury handed to Chief Judge John J. Sirica of the Federal District Court here a sealed report, accompanied by a bulky briefcase reportedly containing information about Mr. Nixon's role in the Watergate affair.

This information was presumably intended for the House Judiciary Committee, which is considering a motion to impeach the President and put him on trial before the Senate.

The defendants and the charges against them are as follows:

John N. Mitchell, former Attorney General and director of Mr. Nixon's 1968 and 1972 Presidential campaigns—conspiracy, obstruction of justice, false statements to the F.B.I., false statements to the grand jury and perjury.

Mr. Haldeman—conspiracy, obstruction of justice and perjury.

John D. Ehrlichman, former assistant to the President for domestic affairs—conspiracy, obstruction of justice, false statements to the F.B.I. and false statements to the grand jury.

Charles W. Colson, former special counsel to the President—conspiracy and obstruction of justice.

Robert C. Mardian, former aide to Mr. Mitchell in the 1972 campaign—conspiracy.

Kenneth W. Parkinson, attorney for the Committee for the Re-election of the President—conspiracy and obstruction of justice.

Gordon C. Strachan, former aide to Mr. Haldeman—conspiracy, obstruction of justice and false statements to the grand jury.

The key conspiracy count

Continued on Page 16, Column 1

Heath, Trailing Labor Party In Britain, Declines to Resign

Special to The New York Times

LONDON, March 1—Prime Minister Heath, deprived of his majority in Parliament by Britain's voters, declined to resign tonight. His action raised the prospect that Mr. Heath's Conservatives, outnumbered by the Labor party in the House of Commons, would try to remain in power.

Thus Britain faced one of the gravest crises in her modern political history. The last time when neither main party won an over-all majority was in 1929.

There was no official word. But sources close to Mr. Heath said that he had told Queen Elizabeth tonight that he wanted to stay in office despite his party's failure to win an over-all majority in the general election yesterday.

Wilson Prepared to Govern

A few hours earlier, Harold Wilson, the leader of the Labor party, said that he was prepared to form a new Cabinet. Labor also failed to win a majority, but it holds five more seats than the Conservatives.

With the virtual stalemate between the two big parties, the balance of power in the new House would be held by smaller ones, including the Liberals, Scottish and Welsh Nationalists and the Members from Northern Ireland.

If Mr. Heath carries on with a minority government, despite his campaign bid for a "fresh mandate" and a "strong" majority, the question is for how long. He could go down to defeat quickly in the new House of Commons if a majority voted "no confidence" on some issue that arose for debate.

If that occurred, it is expected that he would ask the Queen to call for Mr. Wilson to form a new Government. Any call for a new election is regarded as unlikely until sometime later after the party leaders have a chance to try to win support in the House.

It was Mr. Heath, on Feb. 7, who used his power as Prime Minister to order Parliament dissolved and to call yesterday's election.

His goal was a mandate to settle a strike in the Government-owned coal mines that had crippled the country's production and forced it onto a three-day work week. Yesterday that mandate from the voters eluded him.

Tonight this was the standing of the parties in the new House of Commons, compared with their standings in the old one:

	New	Old
Labor	301	287
Conservative	296	322
Liberal	14	11
Others	23	10
Undecided	1	..

Mr. Heath, after a day of meetings with his advisers at 10 Downing Street, emerged shortly after 7:30 P.M. local time (3:30 P.M., New York time) for his meeting with the Queen, who had interrupted a visit to Australia to return here.

Statement Is Issued

A statement from 10 Downing Street said:

"The Queen has granted the Prime Minister's request to her to grant him an audience at 7:45 P.M. so that he can report on the current political situation."

If Mr. Health had submitted his resignation, the announcement would have come quickly. But it was clear that he had

Continued on Page 10, Column 1

British Pound Plunges

The value of the British pound fell 1.85 cents and prices of stocks went down 24 points in hectic trading in London yesterday in reaction to the setback for Britain's Conservative Government. Details on Page 41.

MITCHELL JUDGE HALTS TRIAL HERE

Weighs Motion for Mistrial Over 'Apparent Excesses' in Prosecutor's Speech

By RALPH BLUMENTHAL

Federal Judge Lee P. Gagliardi abruptly suspended yesterday the conspiracy-perjury trial of John N. Mitchell and Maurice H. Stans for what he called "apparent excesses" by the chief Government prosecutor in his opening statement.

Judge Gagliardi said that he would rule Monday on demands by defense attorneys for a mistrial. He ordered the prosecutor, Assistant United States Attorney James W. Rayhill, to submit a "documented response" with his "excuses."

While neither side would comment on the surprising development, some observers in the court believed it unlikely that the judge would decide to discharge the newly picked jury, which had been carefully isolated from news of yesterday's Watergate indictments naming Mr. Mitchell along with six others.

Conspiracy Charged

The historic trial was interrupted just after the Government had told the jury that it would prove that the defendants had conspired to quash a Federal investigation of Robert L. Vesco, the fugitive financier, in exchange for his secret $200,000 cash contribution to President Nixon's reelection campaign, that the defendants covered up the scheme and lied, about it when questioned under oath.

At the close of his hour and 50 minutes presentation in the fifth-floor courtroom in the

Continued on Page 18, Column 6

Nixon Urges Quick Trials, Cautions on Prejudgment

By JOHN HERBERS
Special to The New York Times

WASHINGTON, March 1 — President Nixon expressed the hope today that trials arising out of the new Watergate indictments "will move quickly to a just conclusion." He also cautioned the nation to remember that the accused are presumed innocent unless proved guilty.

"The indictments indicate the judicial process is finally moving toward resolution of the matter," Gerald L. Warren, the White House deputy press secretary, said in a statement approved by Mr. Nixon. The statement, read to newsmen, added:

"It is the President's hope that the trials will move quickly to a just conclusion. The President is confident that all Americans will join him in recognizing that those indicted are presumed innocent unless proof of guilt is established in the courts."

The statement also declared that the President had "always maintained that the judicial system is the proper forum for the resolution of the questions concerning Watergate."

Two of the seven men accused in today's indictment, Charles W. Colson and Kenneth W. Parkinson, issued personal statements of innocence and predicted their eventual exoneration on the charges. The other five relied on their attorneys to issue brief statements of innocence. [Details, Page 16.]

Word of the Watergate indictments reached the Oval Office today via the news tickers, and the President—busy with policy meetings, ceremony and entertaining of Congressmen—reacted with his brief formal statement a short time later.

Gen. Alexander M. Haig Jr. and Ronald L. Ziegler, the President's chief assistants, informed Mr. Nixon of the charges against his former high associates just as the President was ending a meeting with his economic and energy advisers and was preparing to welcome the Mayor of Meridian, Miss., Tom Stuart, who had gotten 20,000 names on a petition in

Continued on Page 17, Column 3

SIRICA SAID TO GET FINDINGS ON NIXON

Grand Jury Reported to Ask Him to Give Evidence on Watergate to House

By JAMES M. NAUGHTON
Special to The New York Times

WASHINGTON, March 1—The Watergate grand jury reportedly asked Chief Judge John J. Sirica of the United States District Court today to give the House impeachment inquiry evidence relating to President Nixon's role in the Watergate case.

The grand jury issued a sealed "report" to the judge, and investigative sources said that they understood the document contained a description of the grand jury's findings about Mr. Nixon's possible involvement in the Watergate cover-up.

Moments later, the special Watergate prosecutor's office gave Judge Sirica a large briefcase said to contain a mass of documents and other evidence sought by the House Judiciary Committee for its investigation of the President's conduct in

Continued on Page 17, Column 1

The Scene in Sirica's Court: A Historic 13 Minutes

By LINDA CHARLTON
Special to The New York Times

WASHINGTON, March 1—At 10 A.M. today, Judge John J. Sirica was sitting in his chambers, reminiscing about his 16 years on the bench, whiling away the time until he could put a black robe over his gray suit and walk into Courtroom 2 to preside over history.

He arrived to be greeted with the shuffle of a crowd rising to its feet as a court functionary intoned ceremonial phrases, ending with the prayer for the country and for "this honorable court." Some 13 minutes and surprisingly few words later, it was over.

The small, wood-paneled courtroom, with a checkerboard cork floor, an American flag and seal and two maroon ceramic water pitchers as the only decorations, was filled—with lawyers, Watergate task force staff members and reporters. The long line of would-be spectators that had started forming two hours before the 11 A.M. hearing was exiled to the corridor.

The prosecution's table was crowded with lawyers and papers. At the defense table, on the right side of the courtroom, sat a lone figure, Paul Murphy of the law firm of Hundley & Gacheris, representing John N. Mitchell.

The focus of attention was a group of 21 distributed

Continued on Page 18, Column 3

RED CROSS VISITS 65 ISRAELI P.O.W.'S

Sees Prisoners in Syria—Kissinger Confers With Assad in Damascus

By BERNARD GWERTZMAN
Special to The New York Times

DAMASCUS, Syria, March 1—Israeli prisoners held by Syria, long the focus of a dispute that prevented troop-pullback negotiations, received their first visit from Red Cross inspectors today.

The visit was arranged as part of the latest round of Middle East diplomacy, which carried Secretary of State Kissinger today from Egypt to Israel and then to Syria. He immediately began talks here with President Hafez al-Assad to convey ideas on troop disengagements that he had just received from Premier Golda Meir and other top Israeli officials.

At the end of the session between President Assad and the Secretary of State, both American and Syrian spokesmen indicated that talks on the separation of forces would continue after Mr. Kissinger left here tomorrow on his way to return to the United States. There was no announcement that any firm agreement had been reached on how negotiations between Israel and Syria would take place.

The Syrian spokesman said that Mr. Assad had not accepted the Israeli ideas presented to him by Mr. Kissinger and had offered one in return, which Mr. Kissinger "will study

Continued on Page 4, Column 3

Two-Way Radios in Taxis To Help City Fight Crime

By WILL LISSNER

The city officially began a program yesterday to put on the streets thousands of cruising taxicab drivers trained in the observation and reporting of crime and who are in radio communication with the police.

The new auxiliary arm of the police is the Civilian Radio Motor Patrol, which, Mayor Beame said, already has 500 crime watchers at work — 350 in the Bedford Park section of the Bronx and 150 in communities in Brooklyn operating from a Sheepshead Bay base.

Many taxicabs are dispatched by radio, the dispatcher having the transmitter and the cab the receiver. These one-way systems cannot be used in this program. The patrol system in use links the dispatcher and the driver by a two-way radio.

Under the system, telephone lines link the dispatcher to the switchboard operator in the police station. When necessary, the desk sergeant can then talk directly to the taxicab driver.

Two similar networks are to be opened soon in Queens, one in Long Island City and one in Richmond Hill, according to Stanley Bakalar, president of the Associated Radio Metered Taxi Owners Council.

"Eventually Manhattan and Staten Island will be covered, too," he added.

"This is another example of how we can use the city's greatest asset—its citizens—in attacking its number one problem, crime," Mayor Beame said. He and Police Commissioner Michael J. Codd and a group of Bronx officials joined in inaugurating the system at a ceremony at the Bedford Park station in the Bronx.

The program costs the city only the services of the coordinator, Lieut. John Higgins, and the training officers. In the Bronx the cost of installing the tie-lines between the taxi dispatchers and the police was paid for by the First National City Bank and the $12 monthly service charge for the tie-line phones is paid by the taxi cooperatives—the All City Radio Taxi Association and the Bronx Two-Way Radio Metered Taxi Company. Each taxi will display a yellow and black decal announcing its participation in "Civilian Radio Patrol, Community Service."

The city's police have a number of programs in operation using civilians to supplement the department's professional manpower. A primary one is the Auxillary Police, whose members patrol the streets and perform other police functions under the supervision of police officers.

Another is the Blockwatcher Program, in which civilians act as the eyes of the police on their own block.

NEWS INDEX

The New York Times/Marilyn Church

Assistant U.S. Attorney James W. Rayhill, standing, making his opening statement to the jury in the trial of John N. Mitchell, seated foreground, and Maurice H. Stans. Judge Lee P. Gagliardi is at upper left.

"All the News That's Fit to Print"

The New York Times

LATE CITY EDITION

Weather: Sunny, mild today; cool tonight. Sunny, pleasant tomorrow. Temp. range: today 66-83; Friday 73-93. Highest Temp.-Hum. Index yesterday: 81. Details on Page 62.

VOL. CXXIII . . No. 42,546

NEW YORK, SATURDAY, JULY 20, 1974

20c beyond 50-mile radius of New York City, except Long Island. Higher in air delivery cities.

15 CENTS

TURKEY LANDS AN ARMED FORCE IN CYPRUS; DROPS PARATROOPERS INTO NICOSIA SECTOR

Doar Urges Committee to Vote for Nixon's Impeachment

5 MAJOR CHARGES

G.O.P. Counsel Backs Appeal to Committee for Senate Trial

By JAMES M. NAUGHTON
Special to The New York Times

WASHINGTON, July 19—The House Judiciary Committee's senior counsels to both the Democrats and Republicans urged the committee today to recommend a Senate trial of President Nixon on one or more of five central impeachment charges.

John M. Doar, the special counsel to the Democrats, told the committee as it began im-

Text of proposed articles of impeachment, Pages 17, 18.

peachment deliberations that he could not remain "indifferent" if President Nixon or any other President committed the "terrible deed of subverting the Constitution."

The special Republican counsel, Albert E. Jenner Jr., endorsed Mr. Doar's conclusions by admonishing the committee to live up to the standards set by the nation's founders.

29 Potential Articles

Mr Doar submitted to the panel 29 potential articles of impeachment—some drafted by the committee staff and others proposed by committee members—that represented various approaches to the following five fundamental allegations against Mr. Nixon:

¶Obstruction of justice in the Watergate and related scandals.

¶Abuse of Presidential power in dealings with Government agencies.

¶Contempt of Congress and the courts through the defiance of subpoenas for evidence.

¶Failure to adhere to an explicit constitutional duty to "take care that the laws be faithfully executed."

¶Denigration of the Presidency through underpayment of Federal income taxes and use of Federal funds to improve personal property.

Harsh Judgments Suggested

Along with the 29 potential charges against Mr. Nixon, Mr. Doar submitted a thick volume outlining a summary of the inquiry's key findings and suggesting harsh judgments about the President's conduct both before and after the 1972 Watergate burglary. [Page 19.]

The proposed impeachment articles drafted at Mr. Doar's direction contained language accusing the President of "having made it his policy to cover up and conceal responsibility" for the Watergate break-in at Democratic headquarters in June, 1972. Mr. Nixon was said to have furthered the alleged conspiracy through such means

Continued on Page 18, Column 4

Prince Juan Carlos de Borbón signing Spanish-American declaration in first official act as chief of state. At ceremony was Adm. Horacio Rivero, right, U.S. Ambassador.

United Press International

FRANCO DELEGATES POWERS AS RULER TO JUAN CARLOS

Gravely Ill Spanish Leader, 81, Issues Decree That Delegates Authority

By HENRY GINIGER
Special to The New York Times

MADRID, July 19—The ailing Generalissimo Francisco Franco, his condition suddenly worsened, delegated his powers as ruler of Spain today to his designated successor, Prince Juan Carlos de Borbón.

From the clinic where he has been under treatment for phlebitis for 10 days, the 81-year-old chief of state issued a decree that interrupted for the first time his 35 years of dominion over his people, in favor of the 36-year-old heir to a throne that has been vacant since 1931.

The six doctors treating General Franco, after talking at noon of a "setback" caused by "gastric complications," acknowledged tonight that he had vomited blood early this morning. The bulletin at 8:30 P.M. said the bleeding had been checked and that all body functions continued within normal limits. It was believed that anticoagulants, administered to inhibit blood clots in the leg, had caused internal hemorrhaging.

Pio Cabanillas, Minister of Information, said tonight that the news from the general's bedside was satisfactory. He praised the calm of the Spanish people but throughout the day and evening members of the Franco family and dignitaries of the Government indicated their alarm by streaming in general's wife, Carmen, has been staying in a room adjoining his.

General Franco acted under Article 11 of Spain's Organic Laws, which states that in case of absence or illness of the chief of state, the royal heir will assume his duties. But there was a strong feeling in the excited Spanish political world that the end of a long and often bitter era was at hand and that a new chapter in Spanish history was about to open.

Speculation about a possible momentous change, eagerly awaited by some Spaniards, feared by others, had begun the moment General Franco entered the modern hospital named for him in northern Madrid on July 9. There had been frequent meetings between the general, the prince and other officials concerning a temporary delegation of power. But optimistic medical bulletins, backed by photographs published for the first time yes-

Continued on Page 3, Column 4

Premier Bulent Ecevit announcing invasion in Ankara

United Press International

CLASHES REPORTED

Capital's Airport and Northern Port Are Bombed

By NAN ROBERTSON
Special to The New York Times

ANKARA, Turkey, Saturday, July 20—Premier Bulent Evevit announced today that Turkey had invaded Cyprus by sea and air.

The attack came after intensive diplomatic activity involving officials of Turkey, Britain and the United States had broken down. The crisis grew out of the overthrow Monday of the elected Cypriote Government of Archbishop Makarios by the Greek-officered Cypriote National Guard.

The Turkish Premier, his voice trembling with emotion, announced the invasion after meeting with Under Secretary of State Joseph Sisco of the United States at 2 A.M. today, Ankara time (7 P.M., Friday, New York time). Mr. Sisco had flown here from Athens last night to try to avert war.

Bombing Reported

[Turkish forces strafed and bombed the northern port of Kyrenia and dropped paratroopers into Turkish-Cypriote areas near Nicosia, the capital, Reuters reported.

[Turkish planes bombed Nicosia airport and a Cypriote National Guard camp south of the capital. Other Turkish jets dropped bombs and rockets on a camp of the small Greek army contingent in Cyprus on the western side of Nicosia.

[Machine-gun fire and explosions were heard from many directions around the capital, and Turkish Air Force planes flew overhead.

[The Cyprus radio broadcast an appeal to all Greek Cypriot with weapons to resist the Turkish invaders, and the Turkish Cypriote radio said that a Greek Cypriote gunboat had been sunk off Kyrenia.

[In San Clemente, Calif, President Nixon conferred late last night with Secretary of State Kissinger as soon as he received news that Turkish troops had landed in Cyprus, Reuters reported. The Presidential press secretary, Ronald L. Ziegler, said that "we are following the situation" but made no other comment.]

[The Pentagon ordered the United States carrier Forrestal and other naval vessels toward Cyprus in case American citizens in the area needed to be evacuated, The Associated Press reported.]

Premier Ecevit said that the decision to intervene in Cyprus

Continued on Page 8, Column 1

House Unit Releases Data On I.T.T. and Milk Affair

Antitrust Suit Inquiry

By E. W. KENWORTHY
Special to The New York Times

WASHINGTON, July 19—The House Judiciary Committee published today voluminous documentation on the tangled web known as "the I.T.T. affair."

But no document substantiated conclusively an allegation that the Nixon Administra-

Excerpts from the committee evidence and White House responses on milk and I.T.T., Pages 12-16.

tion's settlement of an antitrust suit against the International Telephone and Telegraph Corporation was in return for the conglomerate's pledge of up to $400,000 for the Republican National Convention in 1972.

The settlement permitted the corporation to retain the Hartford Fire Insurance Company.

The allegation was at the core of the committee's inquiry as it pursued evidence of impeachable offenses, as it was at the core of the Senate Judiciary Committee's resumed hearings in March-April, 1972, on the nomination of Richard G. Kleindienst to be Attorney General.

In the 980 pages of the House committee's volume No. 5 of

Continued on Page 19, Column 1

Price Supports Studied

By WILLIAM ROBBINS
Special to The New York Times

WASHINGTON, July 19—President Nixon disclosed his decision to raise milk-price supports in 1971 after listening to an exposition by John B. Connally on political and economic considerations and on dairy cooperatives' potential for campaign funding, a new transcript released by the House Judiciary Committee showed today.

The President's decision became clear, according to the document, early in a White House discussion on the afternoon of March 23, 1971, after Mr. Connally, then Secretary of the Treasury, had said that Congress would probably raise milk-price supports if the Administration did not and told Mr. Nixon:

"If you do [veto the increase], you've cost yourself the money—you've lost your political advantage."

A short while later, the transcript shows, Mr. Nixon said: "Under the circumstances, I think the best thing to do is to just uh, relax and enjoy it."

Mr. Nixon, Mr. Connally and other aides then discussed a delay in making a public an-

Continued on Page 19, Column 3

CONSUMER PRICES UP 1% FOR MONTH

Yearly Increase 11.1%—Rise in Food Slows—Real Earnings Down

By EILEEN SHANAHAN
Special to The New York Times

WASHINGTON, July 19 — Consumer prices rose by 1 per cent in June, despite a slowdown in the pace of the rise of food prices, the Labor Department reported today.

The June rise brought the index to a level that was 11.1 per cent higher than in June a year ago.

In the New York-Northeastern New Jersey-Long Island area, prices rose nine-tenths of 1 per cent from the prior month and 10.6 per cent from a year ago, according to the Bureau of Labor Statistics.

The yearly increase was the largest in 27 years, said Herbert Bienstock, regional head of the bureau.

Meat Prices Down

Nationally, although there was a decline in the prices of some food items, particularly meats, the drop was less than is normally expected in June. Thus, the Labor Department's seasonally adjusted statistics, which eliminate the effects of normal seasonal changes in an attempt to focus on basic trends, showed a rise of three-tenths of 1 per cent in food prices.

The food price trend was the best for this year except for April, when seasonally adjusted food prices declined.

The prices of all commodities other than food in the index,

Continued on Page 36, Column 2

U.S. Says Soviet Alerted Seven Airborne Divisions

By JOHN W. FINNEY
Special to The New York Times

WASHINGTON, July 19—Defense Department officials said today that the Soviet Union had put seven airborne divisions on alert.

American officials said that the eventual Soviet military intentions remained unclear and the Administration chose to make no announcement of the Soviet action and ordered no reciprocal alert for American forces.

[In Moscow qualified analysts said that there were indications that the Soviet Union might have placed one division on alert, and probably not more than that.]

Diplomatically, the United States applied pressure today on both the Greek and Turkish Governments in an effort to avoid a military clash between the two Atlantic alliance allies.

Undersecretary of State Joseph Sisco flew into Athens for meetings with Greek civilian and military leaders, and then rushed to Ankara for more talks there.

And in Washington, the State Department announced that Secretary of State Kissinger would meet on Monday with Archbishop Makarios. At the same time, American officials said that the United States Embassy in Athens recently sent a cablegram to Mr. Kissinger that detailed the direct involvement of the Greek junta in the Cyprus coup. [Page 8.]

Discussing the Soviet alert, some officials speculated that Moscow was trying to demonstrate its support if Turkey made any move to intervene militarily on Cyprus. According to well-placed officials, there were indications that the Soviet Union had suggested to the Ankara Government that it could count on Soviet support.

As analyzed by Defense Department officials, the Turkish Government was following a deliberate, step-by-step strategy of seeming to indicate a willingness to take military action if no political solution could be reached.

The prevailing Pentagon view, however, was that the Turkish Government was not intent on rushing troops to Cyprus and had little military capability to carry out such action.

Turkey has a small number of amphibious craft, most of those small, open boat not suitable for carrying troops across long stretches of open water. As a result, officials believed Turkish forces would have considerable difficulty mounting an invasion against any resistance from pro-Greek forces on

Continued on Page 8, Column 7

Justices' Ruling on Tapes May Follow Vote by Panel

By WARREN WEAVER Jr.
Special to The New York Times

WASHINGTON, July 19—The Supreme Court may be unable or unwilling to hand down a decision in the Nixon tapes case until after the House Judiciary Committee has voted late next week whether to recommend the impeachment of President Nixon.

Whichever way the Justices decide, their ruling is expected to have a substantial impact on the impeachment proceedings, either upholding the President's unlimited concept of his authority or requiring him to surrender evidence that might further incriminate him and his former colleagues.

The case was argued on July 8, and Court officials said today that a decision could not be expected until next Tuesday at the earliest. One source predicted that the decision might not be handed down next week, which would postpone it until after the Judiciary Committee voting is over.

"I can't exclude that possibility, although I'm not signalling it," Barrett McGurn, the Court information officer, said.

Congressional leaders believe that a Supreme Court ruling against the President could influence several undecided Republican members of the committee to vote for impeachment. In turn, the number of Republicans who support impeachment at the committee level is expected to have considerable influence on the size of the Republican vote in the House.

Conversely, if the Justices support President Nixon's refusal to surrender 64 more White House tapes to Federal District Judge John J. Sirica and order Mr. Nixon's name stricken from the Watergate cover-up indictment, the decision could stiffen committee re-

Continued on Page 19, Column 5

Brasco Convicted of Conspiracy To Take Truck-Contract Bribes

By ARNOLD H. LUBASCH

Representative Frank J. Brasco was convicted last night of conspiracy to take bribes to get a Post Office contract for a Mafia-controlled truck company.

The 41-year-old Brooklyn Democrat, whose first trial on the conspiracy charge resulted in a hung jury, bowed his head but maintained his composure when the guilty verdict was announced at the end of the month-long second trial in Federal District Court here.

His wife, Linda, who sat in the front row of the courtroom throughout the trial, moved quickly to Mr. Brasco's side and put her arms around his shoulders after the jury of five men and seven women reached the verdict following almost eight hours of deliberations.

Judge John M. Cannella set Oct. 2 for sentencing Mr. Brasco, who faces up to five years in prison and a maximum fine of $10,000.

The short, solidly built Congressman, who served as an assistant district attorney in Brooklyn before he was elected to Congress in 1966, will appeal the verdict, according to his lawyer.

Mr. Brasco declined to comment when asked if he would withdraw from his current race for re-election in the 11th Con-

Continued on Page 11, Column 1

3d City Audit Is Believed To Be Most Devastating

By MAURICE CARROLL

Mayor Beame called back yesterday the top team that served him when he was City Controller to try to blunt the impact of still a third audit report from his successor. At City Hall the latest report was said to be "even more devastating" than the first two, which have caused the Mayor profound embarrassment.

The third report deals with the management of $6.7-billion in pension funds. It is due to be made public next week by Controller Harrison J. Goldin, whose aides carefully guarded preliminary draft copies yesterday.

From what the Beame aides have been able to ferret out, the report "comes down hard on bad management," according to one Beame sympathizer in City Hall.

Some sources said the report would cite failure to reconcile city records with bank records by several hundreds of thousands of dollars, would criticize the use of handwritten ledgers—instead of computers—to keep track of investments and would urge that a more seasoned team be put in charge of pension investments.

It would say, these sources suggested, that the investment pattern under Mr. Beame had been unimaginative and unproductive and that opportunities to earn money for the retirement funds had been missed.

If so, that will be an ironic comment, because one of Mr. Beame's boasts as Controller was that he had begun exchanging low-yield city bonds held by the pension funds for high-interest stocks, taking a short-term loss on the exchange to increase the long-run yield.

Mr. Beame, whose mayoral campaign featured the slogan "If you don't know the buck, you don't know the job," was jolted personally as well as politically by the earlier reports.

Proud of his record and well aware of the source of his political reputation, Mr. Beame was upset by the two previous reports, which charged:

¶There was $5.4-million less in a vault holding security deposits from people doing work for the city than the dog-eared, handwritten ledgers said should be there. Mr. Goldin

Continued on Page 32, Column 2

Ziegler Condemns A 'Kangaroo Court'

By PHILIP SHABECOFF
Special to The New York Times

SAN CLEMENTE, Calif., July 19—In its harshest attack yet on the House Judiciary Committee, the White House accused the committee's counsel today of conducting a "kangaroo court" and challenged the right of its chief counsel to present articles of impeachment against President Nixon.

Ronald L. Ziegler, the White House press secretary, charged that the committee had made "a total shambles out of what should have been a fair proceeding."

Talking to reporters outside the President's office here, Mr. Ziegler accused the chairman of the committee, Peter W. Rodino Jr. of New Jersey, of "falsely presenting a picture of fairness."

Later, at a news briefing,

Continued on Page 19, Column 5

U.N. Calls Session Today About Cyprus

By Reuters

UNITED NATIONS, N.Y. Saturday, July 20—The Turkish troop landing in Cyprus will top the agenda at a Security Council meeting scheduled for 11 A.M. today.

One Western diplomat predicted a cease-fire call would be the logical first order of business.

The Security Council had been scheduled to meet today to consider a resolution calling for the withdrawal of the Greek Army officers serving with the Cyprus National Guard that toppled the Makarios Government last Monday.

By KATHLEEN TELTSCH
Special to The New York Times

UNITED NATIONS, N.Y., July 19—Archbishop Makarios, the deposed President of Cyprus appealed to the United Nations

Continued on Page 8, Column 4

Soyuz Returns Safely

Two Soviet astronauts returned to earth safely after rehearsing docking techniques for next year's Soviet-American space mission. Page 62.

NEWS INDEX

"All the News That's Fit to Print"

The New York Times

LATE CITY EDITION

Weather: Partly cloudy today; cool tonight. Fair, pleasant tomorrow. Temp. range: today 65-78; Thursday 64-85. Highest Temp.-Hum. Index yesterday: 75. Details on Page 66.

VOL. CXXIII.. No. 42,566

NEW YORK, FRIDAY, AUGUST 9, 1974

20c beyond 50-mile radius of New York City except Long Island. Higher in air delivery cities

15 CENTS

NIXON RESIGNS

HE URGES A TIME OF 'HEALING'; FORD WILL TAKE OFFICE TODAY

'Sacrifice' Is Praised; Kissinger to Remain

By ANTHONY RIPLEY

Special to The New York Times

WASHINGTON, Aug. 8—Vice President Ford praised President Nixon tonight for "one of the greatest personal sacrifices for the country and one of the finest personal decisions on behalf of all of us as Americans."

Mr. Ford, who will take office as the 38th President at noon tomorrow, vowed to continue Mr. Nixon's foreign policy and announced that Secretary of State Kissinger had agreed to stay on in the new Administration.

"I pledge to you tonight, as I will pledge to you tomorrow and in the future, my best efforts in cooperation, leadership and dedication to what's good for America and good for the world," he said.

The Vice President, who never sought the nation's highest office and disclaimed any intention of seeking it after Mr. Nixon's term, will take the oath of office in a private ceremony at the White House.

Thus will he become the first man to serve as President without being chosen by the American people in an election. Tomorrow night he will address the nation on radio and television. It is expected that he will speak at 6 P.M.

All day today the signs of the historic change were in the air, sensed by the crowds that gathered along Pennsylvania

Text of Mr. Ford's remarks appears on Page 2.

Avenue near the White House. Applause rang out from the crowds when Mr. Ford appeared briefly.

After watching Mr. Nixon on television tonight with his family, the Vice President stepped outside into a slight drizzle at his suburban split-level home in nearby Alexandria, Va., to face television cameras and photographers assembled in the street and about 100 cheering neighbors.

Speaks Outside Home

Speaking without notes or a prepared text, Mr. Ford pledged to continue the Nixon foreign policy and called the Secretary of State "a very great man" whom he has known for many years.

On domestic policy, he said that he had been "very fortunate in my lifetime" to have adversaries in Congress but said that he did not think he had "a single enemy" there.

President Nixon had cited in his resignation address his lack of support in Congress as one of the major reasons for his resignation.

Mr. Ford said, "The net result is that I think tomorrow I can start out working with Democrats and with Republi-

Continued on Page 4, Column 3

SPECULATION RIFE ON VICE PRESIDENT

Some Ford Associates Say Selecting a Successor Could Take Weeks

By CHRISTOPHER LYDON

Special to The New York Times

WASHINGTON, Aug. 8 — Potentially the most revealing and most important decision of Gerald R. Ford's Presidential debut — his choice of a successor in the Vice Presidency — was a much-discussed mystery here today.

Close friends of Mr. Ford continued to feed speculation about more than a dozen possible candidates. But none of the friends claimed to have discussed the Vice-Presidential question with Mr. Ford or to be speaking for him on it. A number of Ford associates thought he might hold off the decision for days or even weeks.

"Everybody's on tenterhooks up here," a Senator remarked this afternoon in a telephone interview from the Republican cloakroom, "but I think they're wasting their time. It's going to be a week or two. So far I'd say he's a loner on this issue."

Former Defense Secretary Melvin R. Laird, a Ford counselor in the House for more than a decade, was being quoted again today as saying he believes that Nelson A. Rocke-

Continued on Page 4, Column 1

The New York Times/William E. Sauro

Vice President Ford meeting with newsmen last night

United Press International

President Nixon on TV as he announced his resignation

POLITICAL SCENE SHARPLY ALTERED

G.O.P. Prospects Improved, Ford in Good Spot for '76 and Watergate Fades

By R. W. APPLE Jr.

Special to The New York Times

WASHINGTON, Aug. 8—President Nixon's resignation drastically altered the American political landscape.

It improved Republican prospects for the Congressional elections in November, thrust Vice President Ford into the favorite's role for the 1976 Presidential election, ended the Watergate agony that has served to bind together the heterogeneous Democratic party and removed from the political stage the man who was the dominant Republican for the last 15 years.

In a larger sense, it seemed to presage an era of more open government, of more cooperation and less antagonism between Capitol Hill and the White House and of decline of the White House staff as an independent power center.

Lives Are Altered

A kind of "honeymoon" between the executive and legislative branches was widely predicted by Congressional leaders today. Congressmen who knew Mr. Ford for years as a Capitol Hill colleague said that they expected to work closely with him.

At least in the beginning, pragmatic conservatism is expected to remain the dominant ideological tone in the executive branch.

How that will be translated into policies, and how those policies will shape the political dialogue, will not be clear for weeks. But experts in the two fields forecast an essentially unchanged foreign policy and a similar, but more carefully and consistently applied, economic policy.

By his decision, Mr. Nixon

Continued on Page 6, Column 4

Rise and Fall

Appraisal of Nixon Career

By ROBERT B. SEMPLE Jr.

The central question is how a man who won so much could have lost so much. How could a public figure who so well perceived the instincts of the majority of his countrymen have misused the powers and duties those same countrymen so eagerly ceded him?

The historians will be kept busy on these questions, but for those who spent their time observing Mr. Nixon for the last six years the answer may well be found in a phrase he often applied to himself. "At bottom," he used to say, "I am a political man."

By his own description, he was a man of action rather than contemplation, a tactician rather than a theologian, a student of technique who seemed always impatient with substance, a figure whose exceptional antennae seemed to dwarf and even hide what lay at the core.

To his enemies, he was both manipulative and synthetic; to his friends, a pragmatist unencumbered by inflexible principles; to those who watched him, a man who learned to run before he had learned to walk and who, on reaching his destination, was not always certain what to do when he got there—except, perhaps, to keep going.

That image has only been reinforced and deepened by the transcripts of three conversations with H. R. Haldeman on June 23, 1972, six days after the Watergate break-in, which were released on Aug. 5, and the edited transcripts of White House conversations published April 30. Whatever history's judgment of those tapes, this much was clear: Faced with mounting evidence of deception and wrongdoing in his own official family, he sought not to confront the issue but to manipulate it until he himself became part of the deception.

Mr. Nixon used the words "I am a political man" proudly, as if to challenge the moralists, but in the end they became his epitaph—a possible explanation for both his success and failure.

For if the words implied the presence of a talent for finding opportunities for political prof-

Continued on Page 11, Column 1

JAWORSKI ASSERTS NO DEAL WAS MADE

Says Nixon Did Not Ask for and Was Not Given a Way to Avoid Prosecution

By RICHARD D. LYONS

Special to The New York Times

WASHINGTON, Aug. 8—Leon Jaworski, the special Watergate prosecutor, said tonight after President Nixon's resignation speech that no deals had been either made or offered that would have given Mr. Nixon immunity from prosecution on any charges that might stem from the Watergate scandal.

"There has been no agreement or understanding of any sort between the President or his representatives and the special prosecutor relating in any way to the President's resignation," Mr. Jaworski said in a statement issued by his office.

Mr. Jaworski's words, plus the fact that the President made no mention of the immunity issue in his address to the nation, left open the possibility, at least for the moment, that Mr. Nixon might be charged and stand trial.

No Immunity Sought

Mr. Nixon did not ask for any immunity assurances from Mr. Jaworski before the resignation speech, the prosecutor said, adding that none had been offered.

As Mr. Jaworski put it, "The special prosecutor's office was not asked for any such agreement or understanding and offered none."

"Although I was informed of the President's decision this afternoon, my office did not participate in any way in the President's decision to resign," the statement concluded.

Mr. Jaworski met earlier today with Gen. Alexander M. Haig Jr., the White House chief of staff, but that meeting was said to have been only for the purpose of informing the special prosecutor of what the President would say later in the evening.

The meeting did not take place in the White House, presumably because Mr. Jaworski would have been recognized there, and his visit would have excited speculation.

Earlier today, there were moves in both houses of Congress to grant Mr. Nixon immunity from prosecution, but

Continued on Page 2, Column 4

The 37th President Is First to Quit Post

By JOHN HERBERS

Special to The New York Times

WASHINGTON, Aug. 8—Richard Milhous Nixon, the 37th President of the United States, announced tonight that he had given up his long and arduous fight to remain in office and would resign, effective at noon tomorrow.

At that hour, Gerald Rudolph Ford, whom Mr. Nixon nominated for Vice President last Oct. 12, will be sworn in as the 38th President, to serve out the 895 days remaining in Mr. Nixon's second term.

Less that two years after his landslide re-election victory, Mr. Nixon, in a conciliatory address on national

Text of the address will be found on Page 2.

television, said that he was leaving not with a sense of bitterness but with a hope that his departure would start a "process of healing that is so desperately needed in America."

He spoke of regret for any "injuries" done "in the course of the events that led to this decision." He acknowledged that some of his judgments had been wrong.

The 61-year-old Mr. Nixon, appearing calm and resigned to his fate as a victim of the Watergate scandal, became the first President in the history of the Republic to resign from office. Only 10 months earlier Spiro Agnew resigned the Vice-Presidency.

Speaks of Pain at Yielding Post

Mr. Nixon, speaking from the Oval Office, where his successor will be sworn in tomorrow, may well have delivered his most effective speech since the Watergate scandals began to swamp his Administration in early 1973.

In tone and content, the 15-minute address was in sharp contrast to his frequently combative language of the past, especially his first "farewell" appearance—that of 1962, when he announced he was retiring from politics after losing the California governorship race and declared that the news media would not have "Nixon to kick around" anymore.

Yet he spoke tonight of how painful it was for him to give up the office.

"I would have preferred to carry through to the finish whatever the personal agony it would have involved, and my family unanimously urged me to do so," he said.

Puts 'Interests of America First'

"I have never been a quitter," he said. "To leave office before my term is completed is opposed to every instinct in my body." But he said that he had decided to put "the interests of America first."

Conceding that he did not have the votes in Congress to escape impeachment in the House and conviction in the Senate, Mr. Nixon said, "To continue to fight through the months ahead for my personal vindication would almost totally absorb the time and attention of the President and the Congress in a period when our entire focus should be on the great issues of peace abroad and prosperity without inflation at home."

"Therefore," he continued, "I shall resign the Presidency effective at noon tomorrow. Vice President Ford will be

Continued on Page 3, Column 1

The Other Major News

Wholesale Prices Up

A new upward surge of farm prices joined a big jump in industrial prices to produce the year's largest monthly increase in the wholesale price index. The rise for July was 3.7 per cent, seasonally adjusted, and 3.9 per cent before adjustment. Page 45.

Election Bill Voted

The House approved by a vote of 355 to 48 a broad campaign-finance reform bill. The measure would set limits on political contributions, restrict candidate spending and provide subsidies for Presidential primaries, conventions and elections. The bill now goes to a House-Senate conference committee. Page 36.

Cyprus Talks Open

The foreign ministers of Greece, Turkey and Britain met in Geneva to try to work out an effective cease-fire on Cyprus and to tackle the political problems behind the fighting there. Page 16.

On Cyprus, acting President Glafkos Clerides named a moderate Cabinet stripped of any militant proponents of union with Greece.

Mr. Clerides, who will occupy the key posts of Foreign Affairs and Interior, left for Athens on his way to Geneva for the talks on a political settlement. Page 16.

10 Police Accused

Ten New York City police sergeants were arrested for allegedly participating in a "club" that collected more than $250,000 over a decade from legitimate businesses and illegal rackets operations in Queens. Page 68.

Meskill Named Judge

Gov. Thomas J. Meskill of Connecticut was nominated by President Nixon to a seat on the Federal bench. Mr. Meskill, a Republican, stunned the state Republican party earlier this year by declining to run for a second term amid reports that he had been offered a judgeship. Page 38.

A Tiny G.O.P. Bastion Feels Loss and Relief

By PRANAY GUPTE

Special to The New York Times

SHELTER ISLAND, L.I., Aug. 8—Six years after he put it on his car, Evans K. Griffing sadly stripped off his bold, red-lettered bumper sticker today — the one that said "NIXON."

Mr. Griffing felt a sense of loss. So did hundreds of people in this conservative community 100 miles east of New York City.

In 1968 and 1972, Suffolk County gave Richard M. Nixon the largest single election plurality of any county in the United States. Today all that had changed on Shelter Island.

As the hour of the President's resignation announcement approached, many islanders expressed both a feeling of hurt at having been "betrayed" by Mr. Nixon and relief that he was leaving office.

"We tried to stay by him till the very end," said Thomas L. Jernick, the Town Supervisor. "But when he disclosed on Monday that he had covered up his role in Watergate, we couldn't support him any more. He lied to us, and for a President of the United States to lie is inexcusable."

"We really believed in Mr. Nixon" was a phrase used again and again by dozens of islanders today.

At the same time they spoke hopefully of the Ford Administration and of moving urgently to tasks long neglected—ending the nation's political turmoil and easing its economic distress.

Shelter Island has 1,800 year-round residents, most of whom are registered Republicans.

Only last June interviews with islanders indicated that whatever else Watergate had done, it apparently had not diluted Shelter Island's faith in Mr. Nixon. People said at the time that they felt the President was being vilified by the media

Continued on Page 7, Column 6

Only Nixon Is Serene At Sad White House

By PHILIP SHABECOFF

Special to The New York Times

WASHINGTON, Aug. 8—On his 2,027th and penultimate day as President of the United States, with his staff and family unable to conceal their anguish, Richard M. Nixon went composedly through the schedule of a busy President.

He met with his Vice President and the bipartisan leadership of Congress. He appointed Federal judges, accepted resignations from executive agencies and signed several laws.

He vetoed as inflationary an appropriation bill for the Department of Agriculture and the Environmental Protection Agency.

He also announced, over national television, that tomorrow he would resign his high office.

Mr. Nixon did not loosen his self control even when he talked of his "regret" and his "sadness" at leaving the Presidency. His delivery, with its familiar half-smiles, did not reflect the momentous message he had for his audience: that at noon tomorrow he would become the first healthy, living American President to leave office before his term expired.

At 12:30 this afternoon, the White House press secretary, Ronald L. Ziegler, announced that the President would address the nation at 9 P.M.

Mr. Ziegler did not say what the speech would be about. He did not have to. He choked on his words several times and was struggling visibly to keep himself under control as he left the rostrum of the packed but hushed briefing room at the White House.

The young women who work in the press office went through the motions of their jobs while tears streamed down their faces.

But the President himself, according to his appointments

Continued on Page 3, Column 6

NEWS INDEX

"All the News That's Fit to Print"

The New York Times

LATE CITY EDITION

Weather: Partly sunny today; cool tonight. Partly sunny tomorrow. Temp. range: today 65-78; Friday 68-84. Highest Temp.-Hum. Index yesterday: 78. Details on Page 58.

VOL. CXXIII ... No. 42,567 — NEW YORK, SATURDAY, AUGUST 10, 1974 — 15 CENTS

[illegible] beyond 50-mile radius of New York City, except Long Island. Higher in air delivery cities.

FORD SWORN IN AS PRESIDENT; ASSERTS 'NIGHTMARE IS OVER'

Nixon Bids an Emotional Farewell to Washington

Gerald R. Ford takes the Presidential oath, administered by Chief Justice Warren E. Burger. Mrs. Ford attends the White House ceremony. Associated Press

TEARS AT PARTING

Ex-President Warns Against Bitterness and Revenge

By JAMES T. WOOTEN
Special to The New York Times

WASHINGTON, Aug. 9 — Richard M. Nixon, his face wet with tears, bade an emotional farewell to the remnants of his broken Administration today, urging its members to be proud of their record in government and warning them against bitterness, self-pity and revenge.

"Always remember, others may hate you," he told mem-

The text of Nixon's speech is printed on Page 4.

bers of his Cabinet and staff in a final gathering at the White House, "but those who hate you don't win unless you hate them—and then you destroy yourself."

Shortly thereafter, for the last time as President of the United States, he strode up the ramp of the plane that had taken him to the capitals of the world and was flown home to California, where his career in American politics began nearly thirty years ago.

It was 11:35 A.M. here when President Nixon's letter of resignation was delivered to the office of Secretary of State Kissinger. This is what it said:

"Dear Mr. Secretary: I hereby resign the office of President of the United States. Sincerely, Richard Nixon."

Greeted by 5,000

Soon after his departure, while the giant jet was soaring high above the heartland of the country, Gerald R. Ford was sworn in here as the nation's President.

Despite that new status, 5,000 people greeted his arrival in his native state at El Toro Marine Base. They cheered and applauded when, with his wife, Pat, standing nearby, Mr. Nixon stepped to a waiting microphone, squinted into the brilliant midday heat and said, "We're home."

After a few more remarks, a helicopter whisked the former President, Mrs. Nixon, their daughter Tricia and her husband Edward F. Cox, to La Casa Pacifica, the sprawling seaside villa near San Clemente.

Mr. Nixon's day began in the mist and rain of a humid Washington morning, when Manolo Sanchez, his long-time valet, laid out the clothes he would wear during the final hours of

Continued on Page 4, Column 1

A Plea to Bind Up Watergate Wounds

By MARJORIE HUNTER
Special to The New York Times

WASHINGTON, Aug. 9—Gerald Rudolph Ford became the 38th President of the United States today, declaring that "our long national nightmare is over."

Calling upon the nation to "bind up the internal wounds of Watergate," he said, "Our Constitution works. Our great Republic is a government of laws and not of men. Here the people rule."

And then, his voice filled with emotion, he urged the nation to pray for his predecessor

The text of Ford's address will be found on Page 3.

and friend of a quarter century, Richard Milhous Nixon.

"May our former President, who brought peace to millions, find it for himself," he said.

Mr. Ford assumed the powers of the Presidency at 11:35 A.M., the moment that Mr. Nixon's letter of resignation was handed to Secretary of State Kissinger.

Then, at 12:03 P.M., he was administered the oath of office in the historic East Room of the White House by Chief Justice Warren E. Burger before an overflow crowd of friends, the Cabinet and former Congressional colleagues from both parties.

Wife Holds Bible

It was in that same room, scarcely two hours earlier, that Mr. Nixon said an emotional good-by to his Cabinet and top aides.

Raising his right hand, Mr. Ford rested his left hand on a Bible held by his wife and opened to one of his favorite passages, the fifth and sixth verses of the third chapter of Proverbs: "Trust in the Lord with all thine heart; and lean not unto thine own understanding. In all thy ways acknowledge Him, and He shall direct thy paths."

Then, in a firm voice, he took the oath of office: "I, Gerald R. Ford, do solemnly swear that I will faithfully execute the office of President of the United States and will to the best of my ability preserve, protect and defend the Constitution of the United States."

As the heavy applause ended, the 61-year-old President began perhaps the most moving speech of his career. Speaking in his flat, Middle Western tone, but with what appeared to be a new sense of self-assurance, he said that he was assuming the Presidency under circumstances never before experienced by Americans.

Minds Are Troubled

"This is an hour of history that troubles our minds and hurts our hearts," he said.

"Therefore," he continued, "I feel it is my first duty to make an unprecedented compact with my countrymen. Not an inaugural address, not a fireside chat, not a campaign speech. Just a little straight talk among friends. I intend it to be the first of many."

As the first American to assume the office after the resignation of a President, Mr. Ford said that he was "acutely aware that you have not elected me as your President by your ballots."

"So I ask you to confirm me as your President with your prayers," he added.

He declared that he had not gained office by secret promises, that he had not campaigned either for the Presidency or the Vice-Presidency.

"I have not subscribed to any partisan platform," he said. "I am indebted to no man and only to one woman, my dear wife."

This was reminiscent of the earlier "I am my own man," a declaration that he repeated frequently in recent months as he sought to remain loyal to Mr. Nixon and at the same time hold himself above the spreading taint of the Watergate affair.

He said that while he had not sought the responsibility, he would not shirk it. He said that those who nominated him and confirmed him just eight months ago as Vice President were his friends from both parties.

"It is only fitting then that I

Continued on Page 3, Column 1

G.M. to Raise Prices 9.5% On 1975 Cars and Trucks

Special to The New York Times

DETROIT, Aug. 9—The General Motors Corporation announced today that it would raise prices of 1975 model cars and trucks by an average of $480 or 9.5 per cent.

The price increase will include about $130, or 2.5 per cent for government-required pollution control equipment—catalytic converters, while $350, or 7 per cent, will be to cover added labor and material costs, the corporation said.

Mack W. Worden, G.M. vice president, made the announcement in a letter sent to dealers Thursday and released publicly today. G.M. is traditionally the price pace-setter for the auto industry. The increases it sets are expected to be matched by its competitors.

Ford Sending Notices

The Ford Motor Company has already told its dealers it is sending them advanced billing notices of an average 8 per cent increase above the 1974 prices, which is calculated to mean an increase ranging from about $225 to $800, depending on the model.

Chrysler Corporation officials have indicated their price increases will be in the same area.

A Chrysler spokesman said today that next week "we are going to begin mailing tentative price bulletins on 1975 trucks. They will be in the same ball park as the G.M. and Ford increases. But that is as much as we are going to say at the present time."

Mr. Worden, in charge of the G.M. marketing staff, said that "based on past practice we would expect the Bureau of Labor Statistics will recognize "the catalytic converter's added value and not consider it a price increase in their published data."

Mr. Worden told the dealers G.M. recognized the increases were "substantial" but said the corporation had "no alternative in light of rapidly rising labor and material costs over which we have only limited control and the necessity of complying with 1975 emission standards, which have been mandated by the Government."

As for the other auto com-

Continued on Page 26, Column 4

PAPERS AND TAPES ISSUES IN CAPITAL

Impoundment of Nixon Data in White House Is Urged by Some in Congress

By RICHARD D. LYONS
Special to The New York Times

WASHINGTON, Aug. 9—On the heels of Richard M. Nixon's resignation, some members of Congress were urging impoundment of Presidential documents still in the White House. A few even demanded that the Watergate investigations be continued.

But Representative Peter W. Rodino Jr. said after a morning discussion of whether his House Judiciary Committee should make another attempt to obtain the 147 subpoenaed Presidential tape recordings that "we're not an investigative body."

"Our inquiry is at an end," the New Jersey Democrat said in expressing what seemed to be the feeling of the majority of the membership of both houses of Congress.

Yet the disposition and even ownership of the vast amount of Presidential records, some of which could be used as evidence in forthcoming trials, was a recurring question that remained unresolved.

As Representative Jonathan

Continued on Page 7, Column 6

Friedmann Case Ends

The third and last person charged with the 1972 murder of Wolfgang Friedmann, Columbia University law professor, pleaded guilty to robbery last night. The others had earlier pleaded guilty to robbery. As a result, none of those who have admitted robbing the professor will be convicted of murdering him. Page 33.

Aide Doubtful That Ford Would Give Nixon Pardon

By LESLEY OELSNER
Special to The New York Times

WASHINGTON, Aug. 9—The new White House press secretary, J. F. terHorst, suggested today that President Ford was not likely to grant a pardon to former President Nixon. The press secretary was asked at a briefing this afternoon about the prospects of a pardon.

He replied that he had not spoken to Mr. Ford about the question directly, but that the President had apparently stated his position on the matter last fall, during the Senate confirmation hearings into his nomination as Vice President.

"I do not think the public would stand for it," Mr. Ford said then.

Mr. Nixon's prospects for avoiding criminal prosecution thus remained in doubt, with the office of the special Watergate prosecutor saying only that a decision on whether to prosecute had not been made.

Mr. Nixon lost whatever immunity from prosecution that he may have had when he resigned today. According to Mr. terHorst, Mr. Nixon did not try to pardon himself before leaving office, nor did he grant pardons to anyone else.

Some Republican members of Congress urged today that Mr. Nixon not be prosecuted, saying that he had already suffered enough. But even among Republicans, the sentiment was not unanimous.

Senator Edward W. Brooke, Republican of Massachusetts, submitted a resolution to the Senate yesterday expressing the "sense" of the Congress

Continued on Page 5, Column 2

4 NAMED TO HELP FORD'S TRANSITION

All on New Panel Served in House—President Vows Open Administration

By JOHN HERBERS
Special to The New York Times

WASHINGTON, Aug. 9—Immediately after he was sworn in today as the nation's 38th President, Gerald R. Ford took control of the Presidency and moved to give it a character and shape different from that of his predecessor, Richard M. Nixon.

After declaring in his inaugural speech that "here the people rule," President Ford named a four-member committee composed of former elected officials to oversee the transition and make recommendations for staff changes.

The four are William W. Scranton, former Governor of Pennsylvania; Donald M. Rumsfeld, Ambassador to the North Atlantic Treaty Organization and a former Republican member of Congress from Illinois; Rogers C. B. Morton, Secretary of the Interior and a former

Continued on Page 5, Column 3

President and Kissinger Confer With the Envoys of 60 Nations

By BERNARD GWERTZMAN
Special to The New York Times

WASHINGTON, Aug. 9—President Ford undertook to convince foreign governments today that he would pursue the same foreign policy objectives that brought wide respect to Richard M. Nixon.

Two hours after taking the oath as President, Mr. Ford, assisted by Secretary of State Kissinger, who will retain his office, began meeting with about 60 envoys—some in groups and some individually—in brief sessions that lasted into the early evening.

The substance of what was said was, in general, a reaffirmation of well-known American policy positions. But Mr. Ford and Mr. Kissinger believed the exercise to be necessary to emphasize that there would be no significant change during the transition period in which Mr. Ford, who is less experienced in foreign affairs than his predecessor, makes his leadership felt.

Priority was given to a group meeting in the Roosevelt Room of the White House with members of the North Atlantic Treaty Organization. In a pattern followed in the other sessions, Mr. Kissinger and members of his staff met with 13 envoys for about 20 minutes

Continued on Page 6, Column 6

Gains of Watergate

Positive and Hopeful Results Found As the Transition Is Made Smoothly

By CLIFTON DANIEL
Special to The New York Times

WASHINGTON, Aug. 9—Watergate has now joined Teapot Dome, Credit Mobilier and the Whisky Ring in the lexicon of political infamy. Yet, in millions of minds it also symbolizes the finest hour of American democracy. A President has been deposed, but the Republic endures. Its institutions have survived, and some are saying they have been strengthened as well. Even the Presidency, which Richard M. Nixon professed to be so anxious to protect, shows no signs of debility. The man in the White House is as powerful today as he was yesterday, although his name has changed from Nixon to Ford.

News Analysis

He is just as powerful, although, as the new President said today, he is "acutely aware" that he was not elected by the votes of the people, whereas his predecessor had the largest popular majority in history.

Under the United States Constitution, removal of the President requires drastic surgery, not just a shift in the political balance, as it does in the parliamentary democracies.

However, the surgery performed on the American Government this week, while agonizing and painful, has done a minimum of visible damage to the body politic.

Mr. Nixon himself has said that one way to judge a country is to see how it effects a transfer of power. Today's transfer was effected without missing a heartbeat.

"Our Constitution works," President Ford proclaimed, after taking the oath of office. "Here the people rule."

"All in all," William P.

Continued on Page 7, Column 3

President Nixon at ceremony where he bade his Cabinet and staff good-by. At left is his daughter Julie Eisenhower. The New York Times/Mike Lien

"All the News That's Fit to Print"

The New York Times

LATE CITY EDITION

Weather: Warm, partly sunny today; partly cloudy tonight, tomorrow. Temp. range: today 62-78; Sunday 58-77. Highest Temp.-Hum. Index yesterday: 72. Details on Page 66.

VOL. CXXIII . . No. 42,597 — © 1974 The New York Times Company — NEW YORK, MONDAY, SEPTEMBER 9, 1974 — Higher in air delivery cities. — 20 CENTS

FORD GIVES PARDON TO NIXON, WHO REGRETS 'MY MISTAKES'

U.S.-Bound Plane With 88 Crashes in Sea Off Greece

All on T.W.A. Flight From Tel Aviv Are Believed Dead—Wreckage Is Sighted

By The Associated Press

ATHENS, Sept. 8 — A Trans World Airlines jet bound for the United States with 88 persons aboard crashed today in the stormy Ionian Sea off Greece. The Greek Civil Aviation Authority said there appeared to be no survivors.

T.W.A. said that the Boeing 707 fell from an overcast sky after the pilot reported that an engine had failed.

Flight 841 originated in Tel Aviv, stopped in Athens and was scheduled to make stops in Rome and New York.

The airline's Tel Aviv office said 49 passengers boarded the plane there for Rome and the United States. They included 17 Americans, including a baby, 13 Japanese, four Italians, four French, three Indians, two Iranians, two Israelis, two Sri Lankans, an Australian and a Canadian.

The nationalities of 30 other passengers and the nine crew members were not immediately known. [Reuters reported a total of 37 Americans aboard.]

[In Beirut, it was reported that a Palestinian youth organization said it had placed a guerrilla aboard the plane with a bomb. In New York, however, a spokesman for T.W.A. said sabotage was "highly unlikely."]

"All that can be seen by our overflying planes are remnants of the wreckage and bodies floating on the surface," said a Greek aviation official. "The stormy sea in the area is making it difficult for our ships to approach.

"Only when our ships can get nearer will we be able to

Continued on Page 6, Column 1

The New York Times/Sept. 9, 1974

State Panel Charges City Fails to Pursue Fugitives

By SELWYN RAAB

The State Commission of Investigation disclosed yesterday that the backlog of missing bail jumpers and probation violators in the city had risen during the last three years from 82,000 to 130,000.

After sifting through voluminous police and court records, the commission largely blamed the Police Department's warrant division for the 50 per cent increase since 1971 in unexecuted warrants for criminal defendants who fail to appear in court. The police division is primarily responsible for capturing such fugitives.

Sharply criticizing the performance of the division over the last three years, the investigation commission said in a report that it had found that warrant officers rarely worked at night or on weekends and that a typical attempt to track down a fugitive consisted of no more than one or two visits to an often fictitious home address given by the suspect.

The commission described the problem of fugitives here as "critical to the public safety" and called for a major reorganization of the warrant division.

"At the present time the people of New York City are unnecessarily subjected to the risk of grave harm from known criminals because of ineffective warrant enforcement," the commission declared in its report.

In response to the findings, Police Commissioner Michael J. Codd said he was "concerned" by the growing backlog, and he hinted there might be a reorganization of the warrant division.

He also announced the assignment of First Deputy Com-

Continued on Page 21, Column 1

CANDIDATES SKIRT LAWS ON FINANCING

Evidence Shows Big Money Played a Major Role—Voting Is Tomorrow

By FRANK LYNN

Big money—from family fortunes and large contributors—played a major role in the Democratic primary campaigns despite new state and Federal

Ballot and candidate list appear on Page 28.

campaign-finance laws that were supposed to have reduced its influence.

The question of how much money was spent and where it came from was being discussed as the primary campaigns drew to a close. The polls will be open tomorrow in the city from 6 A.M. to 9 P.M. and in the rest of the state from noon to 9 P.M.

Interviews with campaign aides and campaign financial reports show that there was considerable evidence of circumventing of the new laws in fact and in spirit, possible unrecorded cash contributions and spending and even "laundering" of campaign contribu-

Continued on Page 28, Column 1

Knievel Safe as Rocket Falls Into Snake Canyon

By JON NORDHEIMER

Special to The New York Times

TWIN FALLS, Idaho, Sept. 8—Evel Knievel failed today in an attempt to rocket 1,600 feet across the Snake River Canyon when a tail parachute deployed prematurely on the take-off of his vehicle.

The vehicle, which Mr. Knievel calls the Sky-Cycle X-2, went streaking to about 1,000 feet above the river before floating into the canyon to make a nose-down crash landing on a rocky bank at the river's edge.

Mr. Knievel was pulled from the craft several minutes later by a rescue team. He had superficial cuts and scrapes of the face and legs.

The flight aborted almost as soon as steam exploded from a rear nozzle of the 13-foot-long craft and propelled it along a 108-foot launching track aimed at the cloudless sky.

A drogue parachute designed to slow the rocket at an altitude of 2,800 feet deployed while the vehicle was still on the ramp, whipping in a blast of steam.

Once the vehicle lifted off the ramp, it turned belly up and the main chute, attached to the drogue, was automatically deployed at about 1,000 feet.

A large crowd along the canyon's south rim gasped as a 15-mile-an-hour wind blew the vehicle back toward them, rocking gently in the air nose-down like a red, white and blue Christmas ornament.

For several seconds, it appeared that Mr. Knievel, who could be seen struggling inside the open cockpit, might crash into the crowd on the rim of the canyon.

But the vehicle dropped onto a boulder-strewn ledge, bounced twice on its bottom and came to rest about 20 feet from the water's edge.

The vehicle was obscured from sight from the plateau 540 feet above, and some cries of anguish were heard in the crowd when several minutes went by and there was no sign of the stuntman.

But a helicopter picked him

Continued on Page 58, Column 5

Chris Evert Beaten

Evonne Goolagong of Australia defeated Chris Evert in the semifinals of the United States Open tennis at Forest Hills, Queens, yesterday, 6-0, 6-7, 6-3, and will meet Billie Jean King in the final today. Details, Page 45.

'PAIN' EXPRESSED

Ex-President Cites His Sorrow at the Way He Handled Watergate

By EVERETT R. HOLLES

Special to The New York Times

SAN CLEMENTE, Calif., Sept. 8—President Ford's pardon for Richard M. Nixon evoked today from the former President an expression of "regret and pain at the anguish my mistakes over Watergate have caused the nation and the Presidency."

Within 10 minutes after the Presidential pardon was announced in Washington, Mr. Nixon's statement was released at his Casa Pacifica estate, citing his sorrow in allowing Watergate to become "a national tragedy."

"That the way I tried to deal with Watergate was the wrong way is the burden I shall bear for every day of the life that is left in me," he said.

Hopes Burden Is Lifted

In a subsequent statement, given in response to reporters' questions, an aide quoted Mr. Nixon as saying that, in gratefully accepting the Presidential pardon, he hoped Mr. Ford's "compassionate act would contribute to lifting the burdens of Watergate from our country."

When the Nixon statement was released by his adviser and former White House press secretary, Ronald L. Ziegler, Mr. and Mrs. Nixon were already on the way to a new haven of seclusion away from the heavily guarded Casa Pacifica.

They left at 7 A.M., Pacific Coast time, in a large black limousine accompanied by Secret Service agents and Mr. Nixon's military aide, Lieut. Col. Jack Brennan, reportedly for the Palm Desert estate of Walter H. Annenberg, Ambassador to Britain.

A close friend of the Nixons said the former President planned to play golf on the Annenberg private 18-hole course.

[In New York, Mr. Nixon's daughter, Julie Nixon Eisenhower, said that her father had gone to the Annenberg estate "for a rest," The Associated Press reported.]

Mr. Ziegler and Mr. Nixon's appointments secretary, Stephen

Continued on Page 24, Column 1

Richard M. Nixon in a photo made earlier this year

Associated Press

President Ford speaking at the White House yesterday

The Statement by Nixon

I have been informed that President Ford has granted me a full and absolute pardon for any charges which may be brought against me for actions taken during the time I was the President of the United States. In accepting this pardon, I hope that his compassionate act will contribute to lifting the burden of Watergate from our country.

Here in California, my perspective on Watergate is quite different than it was while I was embattled in the midst of the controversy while I was still subject to the unrelenting daily demand of the Presidency itself.

Looking back on what is still in my mind a complex and confusing maze of events, decisions, pressures, and personalities, one thing I can see clearly now is that I was wrong in not acting more decisively and more forthrightly in dealing with Watergate, particularly when it reached the stage of judicial proceedings and grew from a political scandal into a national tragedy.

No words can describe the depths of my regret and pain at the anguish my mistakes over Watergate have caused the nation and the Presidency, a nation I so deeply love and an institution I so greatly respect.

I know that many fair-minded people believe that my motivation and actions in the Watergate affair were intentionally self-serving and illegal. I now understand how my own mistakes and misjudgments have contributed to that belief and seemed to support it. This burden is the heaviest one of all to bear.

That the way I tried to deal with Watergate was the wrong way is a burden I shall bear for every day of the life that is left to me.

Proclamation of Pardon

Richard Nixon became the thirty-seventh President of the United States on January 20, 1969, and was re-elected in 1972 for a second term by the electors of forty-nine of the fifty states. His term in office continued until his resignation on August 9, 1974.

Pursuant to resolutions of the House of Representatives, its Committee on the Judiciary conducted an inquiry and investigation on the impeachment of the President extending over more than eight months. The hearings of the committee and its deliberations, which received wide national publicity over television, radio, and in printed media, resulted in votes adverse to Richard Nixon on recommended Articles of Impeachment.

As a result of certain acts or omissions occurring before his resignation from the office of President, Richard Nixon has become liable to possible indictment and trial for offenses against the United States. Whether or not he shall be so prosecuted depends on findings of the appropriate grand jury and on the discretion of the authorized prosecutor. Should an indictment ensue, the accused shall then be entitled to a fair trial by an impartial jury, as guaranteed to every individual by the Constitution.

It is believed that a trial of Richard Nixon, if it became necessary, could not fairly begin until a year or more has elapsed. In the meantime, the tranquility to which this nation has been restored by the events of recent weeks could be irreparably lost by the prospects of bringing to trial a former President of the United States. The prospects of such trial will cause prolonged and divisive debate over the propriety of exposing to further punishment and degradation a man who has already paid the unprecedented penalty of relinquishing the highest elective office in the United States.

NOW, THEREFORE, I, Gerald R. Ford, President of the United States, pursuant to the pardon power conferred upon me by Article II, Section 2, of the Constitution, have granted and by these presents do grant a full, free, and absolute pardon unto Richard Nixon for all offenses against the United States which he, Richard Nixon, has committed or may have committed or taken part in during the period from January 20, 1969, through August 9, 1974.

IN WITNESS WHEREOF, I have hereunto set my hand this 8th day of September in the year of our Lord nineteen hundred seventy-four, and of the independence of the United States of America the 199th.

Jaworski Won't Challenge Pardon, Spokesman Says

By JOHN M. CREWDSON

Special to The New York Times

WASHINGTON, Sept. 8 — Leon Jaworski, the Watergate special prosecutor, apparently has no plans to challenge the validity of the unconditional pardon that President Ford bestowed today on Richard M. Nixon, according to a spokesman for Mr. Jaworski.

The special prosecutor "accepts the decision," said John Barker, the spokesman. "He thinks it's within the President's power to do it. His feeling is that the President is exercising his lawful power, and he accepts it."

Mr. Barker added that Mr. Jaworski had not been consulted in advance on the decision by either Mr. Ford or White House lawyers, and learned of the President's position less than an hour before it was announced.

Some lawyers, including Senator Edmund S. Muskie, Democrat of Maine, questioned the legal and constitutional validity of a Presidential pardon conferred before an indictment had been brought or a conviction obtained.

"It could be challenged," declared Mr. Muskie, adding "there are those who say that it ought to be challenged, lest the precedent be established in an undesirable way."

But the remarks by Mr. Barker and by other lawyers familiar with the Watergate prosecutions indicated strongly that Mr. Jaworski was little inclined to test the pardon by seeking to indict Mr. Nixon, which one authority described as "the way to do it."

The principal Watergate grand jury voted earlier this

Continued on Page 25, Column 6

Some Mixed Reactions in Foley Square

By PAUL L. MONTGOMERY

A few hours after President Ford's pardon of his predecessor was announced yesterday, Mr. and Mrs. Wilson Wainwright of Olean, N.Y., were strolling in Foley Square in lower Manhattan, looking at the public buildings.

"It's going to make a lot of people mad, but I can see why he did it," Mr. Wainwright said. "It wouldn't look right to the rest of the world to have a President of the United States in jail."

Mr. Wainwright, here on a late-summer vacation, was asked if he had any doubts about former President Richard M. Nixon's guilt.

"None that I can see," his wife, Judy, replied. "I guess some people would say it would have been better to pardon him after the courts decided."

Nearby, at 100 Centre Street, the afternoon session of the arraignment part of Criminal Court was about to begin. In the dingy, crowded room, lawyers and policemen, and defendants and their families lounged on the oak benches, waiting for the judge to return from lunch.

Hal Mayerson and Peter Davis of the Legal Aid Society, which represents indigent defendants, had been discussing the pardon during the break.

"It's a bit unseemly to pardon someone before they're prosecuted," Mr. Davis said. "It doesn't do much for the concept of equal justice under law."

"How about all the young men who refused to serve in an illegal, immoral and vicious war?" Mr. Mayerson asked. "Is he going to pardon them, too? It's like Peter was saying, maybe they should give Nixon a pardon if he does 18 months of alternate service."

Mr. Mayerson looked around the room.

"Seriously, though, it's outrageous," he continued. "You get a lady here who's going to jail for stealing a blouse, or some guy in on assault because he got tired of living with the rats and hit somebody. And here's one of the biggest plun-

Continued on Page 28, Column 6

Nixon Tapes Must Be Kept 3 Years for Use in Court

By R. W. APPLE Jr.

Special to The New York Times

WASHINGTON, Sept. 8 — Richard M. Nixon and the Ford Administration have reached an agreement under which the former President will ultimately be permitted to destroy the White House tape recordings that led to his downfall.

The agreement, announced today by the White House, also provides that all of Mr. Nixon's Presidential papers and tapes will be preserved for three years for possible use in court cases arising out of the Watergate scandals.

Mr. Nixon signed the agreement in San Clemente, Calif., on Friday; it was countersigned yesterday by Arthur F. Sampson, head of the General Services Administration.

Philip W. Buchen, counsel for President Ford, said at a White House briefing this afternoon that Mr. Ford instructed him about 10 days ago to resolve the controversy over the White House files so the Administration would not find itself "enmeshed for a long time" in jurisdictional disputes.

Although Mr. Buchen denied

Continued on Page 28, Column 1

NEWS INDEX

NO CONDITIONS SET

Action Taken to Spare Nation and Ex-Chief, President Asserts

By JOHN HERBERS

Special to The New York Times

WASHINGTON, Sept. 8—President Ford granted former President Richard M. Nixon an unconditional pardon today for all Federal crimes that he "committed or may have committed or taken part in" while in office, an act Mr. Ford said was intended to spare Mr. Nixon and the nation further punishment in the Watergate scandals.

Mr. Nixon, in San Clemente, Calif., accepted the pardon, which exempts him from indictment and trial for, among

Text of the Ford statement is printed on Page 24.

other things, his role in the cover-up of the Watergate burglary. He issued a statement saying that he could now see he was "wrong in not acting more decisively and more forthrightly in dealing with Watergate."

'Act of Mercy'

Philip W. Buchen, the White House counsel, who advised Mr. Ford on the legal aspects of the pardon, said the "act of mercy" on the President's part was done without making any demands on Mr. Nixon and without asking the advice of the Watergate special prosecutor, Leon Jaworski, who had the legal responsibility to prosecute the case.

Reaction to the pardon was sharply divided, but not entirely along party lines. Most Democrats who commented voiced varying degrees of disapproval and dismay, while most Republican comment backed President Ford.

However, Senators Edward W. Brooke of Massachusetts and Jacob K. Javits of New York disagreed with the action. [Page 25.]

Dangers Seen in Delay

Mr. Buchen said that, at the President's request, he had asked Mr. Jaworski how long it would be, in the event Mr. Nixon was indicted, before he could be brought to trial and that Mr. Jaworski had replied it would be at least nine months or more, because of the enormous amount of publicity the charges against Mr. Nixon had received when the House Judiciary Committee recommended impeachment.

This was one reason Mr. Ford cited for granting the pardon, saying he had concluded that "many months and perhaps more years will have to pass before Richard Nixon could obtain a fair trial by jury in any jurisdiction of the United States under governing decisions of the Supreme Court."

"During this long period of delay and potential litigation, ugly passions would again be aroused, our people would

Continued on Page 24, Column 4

terHorst Quits Post To Protest Pardon

Special to The New York Times

WASHINGTON, Sept. 8—J. F. terHorst, whose appointment as White House press secretary was the first in President Ford's new Administration, resigned tonight in what he said was a protest over the granting of an unconditional pardon to former President Nixon.

In a statement released by the White House tonight, Mr. Ford said that he deeply regretted Mr. terHorst's decision.

"I understand his position," the statement said. "I appreciate the fact that good people will differ with me on this very difficult decision. However, it is my judgment that it is in

Continued on Page 25, Column 1

"All the News That's Fit to Print"

The New York Times

LATE CITY EDITION

Weather: Sunny, warmer today; cold tonight. Chance of rain tomorrow. Temperature range: today 31-47; Thursday 29-38. Details on Page 74.

VOL. CXXIV..No. 42,699 · NEW YORK, FRIDAY, DECEMBER 20, 1974 · Price higher in air delivery cities. · 20 CENTS

ROCKEFELLER SWORN IN AS VICE PRESIDENT AFTER CONFIRMATION BY HOUSE, 287 TO 128

Congress Votes $1-Billion For Jobs for Unemployed

By DAVID E. ROSENBAUM

Special to The New York Times

WASHINGTON, Dec. 19 — The House and Senate gave final approval tonight to legislation appropriating $1-billion for jobs for the unemployed next year.

The money was part of a $5-billion appropriations bill that also allocates money for increased unemployment compensation.

President Ford supports the measure and is considered certain to sign it.

It was estimated that the measure would provide 100,000 jobs nationwide at an average salary of $7,500.

More than $2-billion would become available for unemployment compensation, with the exact amount depending on the number of persons out of work next year.

Under the bill, $875-million would be distributed to states and communities to provide public service jobs for the unemployed in such areas as health, education, recreation and sanitation.

The measure specified that $125-million would be distributed through the Economic Development Administration to stimulate public works projects in depressed areas.

Based on the September unemployment statistics and an appropriation of $1-billion, the Labor Department calculated that New York State would get $107-million, of which New York City would get $61-million; New Jersey would get $48-million, and Connecticut $18-million. [Page 4.]

The Senate had authorized $4-billion and the House $2-billion for the public service jobs program. But the authorization figures merely set ceilings on the amount of money that might be made available. The appropriation determines the amount available to be spent.

Meanwhile, today, the Democrats on the House Ways and Means Committee, which has jurisdiction over many of the important economic measures to be considered next year, created six subcommittees and appointed chairmen.

It was the first time the panel formed subcommittees since 1957.

The committee Democrats de-

Continued on Page 10, Column 2

CITY AND UNIONS SEEK RETIREMENT ON ELECTIVE BASIS

510 Workers Who Were to Be Let Go Today Get a Month's Reprieve

By FRED FERRETTI

The city and a group of leaders representing the municipal unions agreed yesterday to seek voluntary retirements of city employes aged 63 to 70 to save the jobs of 860 younger employes. The latter are scheduled to be dismissed in the budget-cutting layoffs recently announced by Mayor Beame.

The agreement is an alternative to an earlier plan, which would have forced the retirement of 860 older Civil Service employes to save the jobs of the younger employes — a plan that on Wednesday was declared illegal by the United States Secretary of Labor, Peter J. Brennan.

First Deputy Mayor James Cavanagh, in announcing the alternative, said that to give union actuaries time to find prospective volunteers, 510 employes scheduled to be dismissed today would get a month's reprieve.

The 510 represented part of the first wave of 1,510 municipal layoffs announced by Mr. Beame on Nov. 22 in an effort to decrease the deficit in the city's $11.1-billion budget.

The Second Wave

On Dec. 11 the Mayor called for the discharge of 6,425 more city employes, consisting of 2,200 permanent Civil Service workers, 1,525 appointed provisionals and 2,700 workers aged 65 or older who the Mayor said would not receive renewals of their work extensions and would have to retire by next June 30. In the group of 2,200 were teachers, policemen, firemen and sanitation workers and 350 other permanent Civil Service employes.

The 350, like the first group of 510, are in the New York City Employes Retirement System, one of the city's five pension programs. It was these 860 employes, mostly young members of minority groups and women, who were scheduled to be dismissed and on whom a week's effort was expended in attempts to save their jobs.

After Victor Gotbaum, executive director of the 110,000-member District 37, American Federation of State, County and Municipal Employes, and other union leaders denounced the dismissals, the Mayor met with them and announced a plan to

Continued on Page 25, Column 1

The New York Times/George Tames

Nelson A. Rockefeller being sworn in as Vice President last night by Chief Justice Warren E. Burger. In background from left are Senators Hugh Scott, Jacob K. Javits, Robert C. Byrd, James L. Buckley and Howard W. Cannon.

SENATE CEREMONY

He Tells of 'Gratitude for the Privilege of Serving Country'

By LINDA CHARLTON

Special to The New York Times

WASHINGTON, Dec. 19 — Nelson Aldrich Rockefeller was sworn in tonight as the 41st Vice President of the United States.

He was sworn in by Chief Justice Warren E. Burger in a televised ceremony in the Senate chamber.

Mr. Rockefeller became Vice President one day short of four months after his nomination by President Ford. He was escorted to the Senate by Mr. Ford.

Transcript of the ceremony appears on Page 16.

Members of Mr. Rockefeller's family, Congress, the Cabinet and New York State dignitaries were among those who witnessed the ceremony.

He took the oath of office with his hand on a family Bible at 10:12 P.M.

The former New York Governor, only the second man to become Vice President without a public vote, took office after the House completed Congressional approval of his nomination by a vote of 287 to 128. The Senate approved him by a vote of 90 to 7 last week.

Ford Is Pleased

Immediately after the confirmation vote, the White House issued the following statement by President Ford:

"I am delighted that Nelson Rockefeller has been duly confirmed today to be the 41st Vice President of the United States. I congratulate him and look forward to his participation and assistance in the Administration. I commend the House of Representatives for its confirmation vote today, and the Senate for its vote earlier. Members of the 93d Congress have rendered a service to the nation by filling the constitutional office of the Vice President before adjournment. All Americans will benefit from the distinguished and devoted public service of the new Vice President."

Oath and Speech

At just past 10:11 P.M., Mr. Rockefeller raised his right hand to take the oath: "I, Nelson Aldrich Rockefeller, do solemnly swear that I will support and defend the Constitution of the United States . . ."

When the applause had subsided, Mr. Rockefeller read a short speech to the crowded chamber illuminated by five banks of television lights.

"I feel," he said, "a great sense of gratitude for the privilege of serving the country I love."

He went on to thank all those involved in his nomination—the President, Congress, Betty Ford for "her great warmth and her courage."

"And if you'll forgive me for a personal note, my love and

Continued on Page 16, Column 1

Cuomo Selected by Carey As His Secretary of State

By FRANCIS X. CLINES

Governor-elect Hugh L. Carey announced yesterday that Mario M. Cuomo, a longtime friend, would be appointed Secretary of State, and that Raymond T. Schuler, the incumbent Secretary of Transportation, would be retained in the new administration, which takes office Jan. 1.

Mario M. Cuomo

Mr. Cuomo, who ran unsuccessfully this year for the Democratic nomination for Lieutenant Governor, will have the responsibilities of his post expanded to include special advisory and trouble-shooting duties, Mr. Carey announced. These include the inquiry into nursing home abuses Mr. Carey charged him with earlier this week, plus executive responsibilities in programs for judicial selection, income disclosure for public officials and the current review of the New York City Charter.

Commissioner Schuler, like Mr. Cuomo, is a Democrat. He has 18 years of career service in the state bureaucracy and was appointed Commissioner two years ago by former Gov. Nelson A. Rockefeller. Under his control, the transportation agency has started to shed its traditional highway-oriented direction and to stress the need for mass transit.

Mr. Cuomo, who is 42 years old, practices law in Brooklyn and lives in Queens with his wife, Matilda, and five children. He is also a law professor at St. John's University Law School. He had been reported concerned about moving to Albany and yesterday he said that in the light of the expanded role being created for Secretary of State, he was not sure whether he would be living upstate. The Department of State, which has headquarters in Albany, oversees the licensing and registration procedures for professions and technical jobs.

Mr. Cuomo said the Governor-elect had emphasized that the post—which politicians in recent years had come to consider a Governor's symbolic Italian-American chamberlain—would not be "an ethnic position."

Mr. Cuomo first came to pub-

Continued on Page 25, Column 2

Nominee Takes His Oath On the Old Family Bible

By RICHARD L. MADDEN

Special to The New York Times

WASHINGTON, Dec. 19—In a simple but well-organized ceremony in the Senate chamber, Nelson A. Rockefeller held a black family Bible in his left hand tonight and took the oath of office as Vice President.

The oath was administered by Chief Justice Warren E. Burger amid a blaze of lights to accommodate television cameras, the first time they had been allowed in the room. It brought the 66-year-old Mr. Rockefeller within a heartbeat of the Presidency, a job he had been denied three times by the Republican party.

The Bible was the same one that Mr. Rockefeller had used four times when he was sworn in at Albany as Governor of New York, and in it was a note from his father, John D. Rockefeller, Jr., which said:

"This was my mother's Bible, which always lay on the table in the library at 4 West 54th Street, New York. April 1, 1946."

The 25-minute ceremony was a combination of a solemn oath, a brief speech of gratitude, formal expressions of good wishes from Senate leaders and finally hearty applause and handshakes from Representatives who had confirmed Mr. Rockefeller's nomination two hours earlier and from Senators who had done the same last week, as well as some who had

Mr. Rockefeller, wearing a dark blue suit, blue-and-white-striped shirt and dark blue tie, stumbled briefly as he took the first step down to the well of the Senate on entering the chamber. But he recovered his balance quickly, grinned and waved as he strode toward the

Continued on Page 17, Column 1

Outlook for Rockefeller

Long Experience in Running Things Is Expected to Reinforce President

By R. W. APPLE Jr.

Special to The New York Times

WASHINGTON, Dec. 19—Even before Nelson A. Rockefeller was sworn into office, the Washington sharpshooters were reminding him that the principal assignment of most Vice Presidents has been to stay reasonably healthy. In his whimsy for today, for example, Art Buchwald wrote of the Vice President who had to pretend he was the March of Dimes poster child's father just to get into the President's office.

News Analysis

But the fact is that Mr. Rockefeller has the best chance of anyone who has held the Vice-Presidency in recent times to make a real impact on government and politics, despite all the continuing constraints of the No. 2 job.

This is so for two basic reasons.

First, Mr. Rockefeller himself brings to the job a depth of executive experience—years and years of running things, not just talking about them—that is unmatched in this century. He is by disposition and by training an operator, and as one Senator said, "he will find some way to operate."

Second, Mr. Rockefeller joins a President who came to office with no electoral mandate in a time of national crisis, a President who needs reinforcement in a way unique in American political history. That was one of the reasons that Mr. Ford chose him.

Not that it is going to be easy.

Continued on Page 17, Column 3

6 SUGAR REFINERS INDICTED BY JURY

Price-Fixing Conspiracies Alleged in Three Markets in West and Midwest

By HENRY WEINSTEIN

Special to The New York Times

SAN FRANCISCO, Dec. 19—Six major sugar refining companies were indicted today by a Federal Grand Jury on charges of illegal price fixing after an 18-month investigation.

The companies indicted were the Great Western Sugar Company of Denver, the American Crystal Sugar Company, formerly of Denver; the Holly Sugar Corporation of Colorado Springs, Colo.; California and Hawaiian Sugar Company of San Francisco; the Amalgamated Sugar Company of Ogden, Utah; and the Union Sugar Division of the Consolidated Foods Corporation of Chicago. Also named as civil defendants were the National Sugar Beet Growers Federation of Greeley, Colo.; and Utah-Idaho Sugar Company of Salt Lake City, Utah.

The indictments and three companion civil antitrust suits covered acts allegedly committed through the end of 1972. Since then sugar prices have soared, and Robert J. Staal, assistant United States Attorney, stated here today that "the current pricing practices of the sugar industry are still under investigation."

Last month the staff of the Council on Wage and Price Stability said the United States sugar industry had "reaped very large windfall gains" this year from rapidly increasing sugar prices. Mr. Staal declined to state whether a grand jury

Continued on Page 62, Column 4

TEN ECONOMISTS FAVOR STIMULUS

Group Meets With Ford's Top Advisers — Details of Some Views Differ

By EDWIN L. DALE Jr.

Special to The New York Times

WASHINGTON, Dec. 19—Government stimulus for the sliding economy was reported favored by a group of 10 leading private economists at an unpublicized meeting at the White House today.

Participants at the meeting declined to discuss individual views in detail. However, some of the views are well known. But one participant did say, "I can't think of anyone who didn't favor stimulus in some form." The group's members, however, were reported to have differed on numerous important details, including the type of stimulus and how large it should be.

President Ford was not present, but nearly all his chief economic advisers were. Alan Greenspan, chairman of the Council of Economic Advisers, presided.

According to reports, the Government members mainly listened and asked questions and made no attempt to achieve a consensus. Mr. Greenspan had previously pledged to solicit

Continued on Page 54, Column 1

City's Fire Alarm Boxes Are Called Undependable

By JOHN DARNTON

The city's fire-alarm boxes, connected to a deteriorating network of cables laid more than half a century ago, are becoming dangerously unreliable, according to Fire Department dispatchers, maintenance men and fire fighters.

While some of the old mechanical "pull" boxes have failed in recent months, the new voice-alarm boxes that are replacing them at the rate of 60 a month have developed technological problems of their own. All of these Emergency Response System boxes installed in the city so far—over 1,000—will be replaced by their manufacturer because they have been found to "transmit themselves" during electrical storms.

The scope of the fire-box problem, as the city enters its heavy fire-fatality season, is indicated by the aftereffects of one severe ice storm a year ago. The storm knocked out 2,500 of the department's 15,840 street and building boxes. Most of them were in Queens and many were out of service for weeks.

Since the storm of Dec. 17, 1973, "silent sentries"—alarm boxes that do not work—have been implicated in at least two deaths here so far.

The problem appears most severe in Queens, where aerial cables that have lost their insulation come into contact with tree branches, sometimes grounding entire circuits. In Queens, some circuits carry as many as 80 boxes, contrary to the generally accepted standard of allowing 20 to 30 boxes on a circuit.

But the problem appears in the other boroughs, such as

Continued on Page 38, Column 1

Export Bank Credit Curbs Are Said to Anger Moscow

By BERNARD GWERTZMAN

Special to The New York Times

WASHINGTON, Dec. 19—The Soviet Union has followed up yesterday's disavowal of a deal on emigration for trade benefits with a private denunciation of Congressional adoption of a ceiling on Export-Import Bank credits to Moscow.

United Press International

According to State Department officials, Ambassador Anatoly F. Dobrynin told Secretary of State Kissinger yesterday that Moscow was angry at what it regarded as the failure of the United States to live up to its side of détente.

Without stating whether the Soviet Union would step up emigration in return for the modest trade benefits approved by Congress, Mr. Dobrynin reportedly was caustic in his complaints, particularly about the credit limitation.

Some officials said that because the additional credits—a ceiling of $300-million over four years, limited to $75-million a year—were lower than Moscow had expected, there was some question whether the Kremlin would go ahead with the informal arrangement to ease emigration restrictions in return for trade concessions. Despite the Soviet denial, the officials insist that such an arrangement exists.

The consensus was that it

Continued on Page 13, Column 1

Man, 98, Strangled In Brooklyn Robbery

By JOSEPH B. TREASTER

A 98-year-old former yeshiva principal was choked to death with his yarmulke early yesterday morning by thieves who climbed into his ground-floor apartment in the Crown Heights section of Brooklyn as he slept, the police said.

The victim, Nathan Friedler, who was described by neighbors as "a nice, quiet old man," was found tied on his bed, spread-eagled with neckties to the four corner posts. He was found by his daughter, Mrs. Sigmund Schwartz, as she brought him breakfast at about 8 A.M. from her own apartment in the same building at 899 Montgomery Street. The skull cap had been

Continued on Page 74, Column 4

Publisher Suspends Luciano Paperback

By NICHOLAS GAGE

New American Library is suspending its plans to publish a paperback edition of "The Last Testament of Lucky Luciano," for which it was going to pay $800,000, according to a company spokesman.

The spokesman, Harold Rosenthal, said the decision was reached following a meeting Wednesday in Boston with executives of Little, Brown & Co., the book's primary publisher.

The New York Times disclosed last Tuesday that an examination of the book, including research into papers and documents concerning Mr. Luciano and more than 20 interviews, produced information that questioned the publisher's

Continued on Page 29, Column 7

Watergate Argument

The chief prosecutor at the Watergate cover-up trial began his final argument to the jury yesterday after 46 days of testimony. The prosecutor, James F. Neal, mocked and scorned the five defendants. Page 18.

NEWS INDEX

"All the News That's Fit to Print"

The New York Times

LATE CITY EDITION

Weather: Continued mostly cloudy, cool today, tonight and tomorrow. Temperature range: today 46-58; Tuesday 45-53. Details on Page 81.

VOL. CXXIV ... No. 42,830 | © 1975 The New York Times Company | NEW YORK, WEDNESDAY, APRIL 30, 1975 | Price higher in air delivery cities. | 20 CENTS

MINH SURRENDERS, VIETCONG IN SAIGON; 1,000 AMERICANS AND 5,500 VIETNAMESE EVACUATED BY COPTER TO U.S. CARRIERS

United Press International

A crewman from an American helicopter helping evacuees to the top of a building in Saigon for flight to a U.S. carrier

U.S., GREECE AGREE TO END HOME PORT FOR THE 6TH FLEET

Air Base of Americans at Athens Is Also Closed, but Some Facilities Remain

By United Press International

ATHENS, April 29—United States and Greek officials announced today the termination of the home-port arrangement for Sixth Fleet ships at the port of Eleusis near Athens and the closing of the American air base at Athens airport.

The announcement came in a joint statement at the end of a second round of talks on the status of United States military facilities in Greece.

The Greek Government threatened to close all United States bases and it withdrew from the North Atlantic Treaty Organization's military command after the invasion of Cyprus by Turkey last July.

"Certain United States facilities which contribute to Greek defense needs will continue to operate on the Greek Air Force base at Hellenikon," today's statement said.

The statement said that the second phase of the talks, held April 7 to 29 by the two delegations under the United States Embassy Minister, Monteagle Stearns, and Ambassador Petros Kalogeras of Greece also discussed the status of other facilities.

"Agreement is also expected on the elimination, reduction and conservation of other United States facilities in Greece," it said.

The two delegations said that they made progress on the review of the privileges, immunities and exemptions of American personnel in Greece.

The two Governments said

Continued on Page 4, Column 4

G.M.'s Profits Fall

First-quarter profits of General Motors declined 50.8 per cent from the depressed 1974 quarter. Page 53.

HEAVY USERS FACE CON ED INCREASE

P.S.C. Also Orders Cuts for Smaller Consumers

By WILL LISSNER

The state's Public Service Commission ordered the Consolidated Edison Company yesterday to raise its rates for those customers who accounted for the heaviest summer power demands and to cut the rates for customers whose usage did not create excess power demand.

The change — technically a revision of the rate structure approved last November to give the utility $338.7-million more a year — will not mean any extra revenue for the company. Nor will it affect the rates for the great majority of customers, the 2.5 million small residential and commercial users.

Instead, yesterday's order makes revisions in bills that will take less than $20-million from some customers and give it to others, a relatively small amount compared with its total annual billings for electricity of $2.10-billion. It affected less than 500,000 of its 2.9 million customers in New York City, Westchester County and part of Nassau County.

But the order was significant because it introduced into energy ratemaking the philosophy that the customers who are responsible for excess costs should be required to bear more

Continued on Page 34, Column 5

Abram Offers Bills To Curtail Abuses Of Nursing Homes

By ALFONSO A. NARVAEZ
Special to The New York Times

ALBANY, April 29—Morris B. Abram proposed today a series of changes in the laws governing nursing homes to "deal with the most serious immediate problems" uncovered during his month-long investigation.

The proposals were contained in a package of 11 bills submitted to Governor Carey and legislative leaders by Mr. Abram, head of the Moreland Act Commission investigating the nursing-home industry.

Among other things, they would authorize nursing-home residents to file class-action suits for deprivation of their rights and would entitle them to receive a minimum of 25 per cent of the daily reimbursement rate paid by government regulations for each day of a violation.

[In Washington, Senator Frank Moss, Democrat of Utah and chairman of the long-term care subcommittee of the Special Committee on Aging, introduced a package of 36 bills for nursing home reform. Among them were measures to make long-term care more readily available to all older Americans, improve inspection and enforcement procedures and provide training for nursing-home physicians, nurses,

Continued on Page 81, Column 3

CAMBODIA ORDERS FOREIGNERS OUT

Planned 250-Mile Road Trip to Border Is Protested by Paris as Debilitating

By FLORA LEWIS
Special to The New York Times

PARIS, April 29—The French Government said today that the people who have been isolated in its Phnom Penh embassy since the Cambodian Communists took over two weeks ago had been ordered expelled "in the worst possible conditions."

There are 610 refugees in the embassy. They are to be sent out by truck to the town of Poipet on the Thailand border, beginning tomorrow.

Foreign Minister Jean Sauvagnargues told newsmen after having conferred with President Valéry Giscard d'Estaing;

"We fear these extremely precarious evacuation conditions will be beyond the strength of some whose health is poor."

"We continue to insist that the plane that we have held in Vientiane for evacuation of the ill be allowed to land in Phnom Penh."

However, a Foreign Ministry spokesman said that so far there has been no response to

Continued on Page 17, Column 6

74 Saigon Planes Fly 2,000 to Thailand

By DAVID A. ANDELMAN
Special to The New York Times

BANGKOK, Thailand, April 29—At least 74 South Vietnamese Air Force planes fleeing the country streamed into U Taphao air base in southern Thailand without warning this afternoon.

The pilots and passengers—2,000 people—requested asylum, American and Thai Foreign Ministry officials said.

About 30 of the planes were F-5 jet fighters and there were reports that at least one had crashed on a highway near the base as it was making its approach.

The planes began arriving at the huge naval and air base on the Gulf of Siam at about the time that the American evacuation of South Vietnam was ending and the planes were still landing as night fell.

The aircraft were said to include C-47 transports and the C-130 cargo planes that the American military has been using to ferry refugees from South Vietnam to Guam and the Philippines. However, all the aircraft were understood to be Vietnam Air Force planes, originally supplied by the United States.

A Thai Foreign Ministry spokesman said that American authorities at U Taphao had been asked to turn over the aircraft to the Thai Government, which would return them to "the new South Vietnamese government." The pilots and passengers, the Thai spokesman said, "must leave Thailand."

"They just landed first and asked permission afterwards," said an astounded Thai Foreign Ministry official. Other Government sources said that apparently no efforts were made to prevent the planes from landing and no aircraft went up to intercept the fighters as they roared in.

American Embassy officials in Bangkok declined to comment on the Thai request that the planes be returned and their status was unclear. An unresolved question here appeared to be whether the planes were still American property or belonged to whatever government continued in Saigon. The planes could be worth $200-million, one official said.

No details were available on the status of the refugees or

Continued on Page 16, Column 6

2d Key Met Museum Aide Quits In Dispute Over Hoving Methods

By GRACE GLUECK

With an attack on Thomas P. F. Hoving's administration at the Metropolitan Museum of Art alleging its inability to function "in any way that creates or preserves trust, confidence and decency," Anthony M. Clark, chairman of the museum's department of European paintings, has resigned.

Mr. Clark's resignation, one of several that have occurred among senior curatorial personnel at the museum in recent years, represents the first open challenge to Mr. Hoving's administration.

The resignation, effective June 30, follows that of John Walsh, the vice chairman and curator of this key department a month ago. Mr. Clark would not speak for Mr. Walsh, who is abroad, but it is understood that their basic grievances are similar.

"I can't work with or for the present administration at the Met," said Mr. Clark, who had been director of the Minneapolis Institute of Arts for 10 years before his appointment to the Metropolitan in 1973. "I believe that its relation to art has become incidental, wrong and even risky. It's also hell on professionals."

In a statement last night, Mr. Hoving said that he was

Continued on Page 24, Column 1

NEWS INDEX

News Summary and Index, Page 43

United Press International

President Ford and Secretary of State Kissinger returning to White House to resume talks on Vietnam. They had just said good-by to King Hussein of Jordan after visit.

FORD UNITY PLEA

President Says That Departure 'Closes a Chapter' for U.S.

By JOHN W. FINNEY
Special to The New York Times

WASHINGTON, April 29—The United States ended two decades of military involvement in Vietnam today with the evacuation of about 1,000 Americans from Saigon as well as more than 5,500 South Vietnamese.

The emergency helicopter evacuation was ordered last night by President Ford after the Saigon airport was closed

Ford statement and excerpts from Kissinger's, Page 17.

because of Communist rocket and artillery fire. The 1,000 Americans were the last contingent of a force that once numbered more than 500,000.

They were carried by a fleet of 81 American helicopters to carriers in the South China Sea.

The helicopters removed the 5,500 South Vietnamese citizens because their lives were presumed to be in danger with a Communist take-over of South Vietnam. Over the last two weeks, a total of about 55,000 South Vietnamese have been removed. Most of them will come to the United States. The helicopter flights ended the United States evacuation of South Vietnamese.

Last Marines Evacuated

The final withdrawal of Americans was completed at 7:52 P.M., about two hours after the White House had announced the evacuation was completed, when 11 marines were taken by helicopter from the roof of the American Embassy in Saigon. Officials said that the marines, the last of a security guard sent in to protect the evacuation, were safely removed although small-arms fire had broken out around the deserted embassy.

President Ford, in a statement issued by the White House, said the evacuation "closes a chapter in the American experience." In a plea for national unity in the post-Vietnam period, the President said:

"I ask all Americans to close ranks, to avoid recrimination about the past, to look ahead to the many goals we share and to work together on the great tasks that remain to be accomplished."

Appeal by Kissinger

At a news conference, Secretary of State Kissinger appealed to North Vietnam not to storm Saigon by force because the United States believed the new South Vietnamese Govern-

Continued on Page 17, Column 1

DEFENSE ENDS

General Tells His Troops to Turn in Their Weapons

By The Associated Press

SAIGON, South Vietnam, Wednesday, April 30—President Duong Van Minh announced today the unconditional surrender of the Saigon Government and its military forces to the Vietcong.

Columns of South Vietnamese troops pulled out of their defensive positions in the capital and marched to central points to turn in their weapons.

Within two hours, Communist forces began moving into Saigon. A jeep flying the Vietcong flag and carrying eight cheering men in civilian clothes armed with an assortment of weapons drove along the street a block from the United States Embassy compound.

This action followed by hours the ending of the American involvement in Vietnam through the evacuation of most of the approximately 1,000 Americans still here.

[In Washington, the White House said that President Ford had "no comment" on the surrender of Saigon, but a White House spokesman said the surrender was considered 'inevitable.' Page 16]

3 Decades of Fighting

The surrender announcement, made in a broadcast to the nation, signaled the end of three decades of fighting. It came 21 years after the 1954 Geneva accords divided Viet-

The text of President Minh's statement is on Page 16.

nam into North and South and a little more than two years after the Vietnam cease-fire agreement was signed in Paris on Jan. 27, 1973. The last American troops left the country in March of that year.

President Minh, who took office on Monday to lead South Vietnam into peace negotiations, said in his brief radio address:

"I believe firmly in reconciliation among Vietnamese to avoid unnecessary shedding of the blood of Vietnamese. For this reason, I ask the soldiers of the Republic of Vietnam to cease hostilities in calm and to stay where they are."

The President also asked the "brother soldiers" of the Vietcong to cease hostilities and added:

"We wait here to meet the Provisional Revolutionary Government of South Vietnam to discuss together a ceremony of orderly transfer of power so as to avoid any unnecessary

Continued on Page 16, Column 1

Saigon Copter Lands on Another In Stampede to U.S. Ship's Deck

By The Associated Press

ABOARD U.S.S. BLUE RIDGE, in South China Sea, April 29—Scores of South Vietnamese helicopters filled with military men and civilians fled Saigon today and headed out to sea to search for the carriers of the United States Seventh Fleet.

Seven of the helicopters arrived unexpectedly above this vessel carrying Americans and Vietnamese evacuated from South Vietnam. The seven copters made a dash for the helipad at the rear of the ship.

One pilot dropped his helicopter on the blades of another that had just landed and chunks of metal ripped through the air. The top helicopter, with its load of women and children, nearly toppled into the sea, but they were rescued and there were no injuries.

United States sailors heaved the two damaged choppers overboard to clear the landing pad. For the Vietnamese it was a last-ditch chance to survive.

As other Vietnamese helicopters landed their passengers were pulled free. American sailors ripped the doors off the craft to make them sink and the pilots then jettisoned them in the sea to make room for other arrivals circling overhead. Two small craft rescued the swimming pilots.

The American evacuation was reported orderly, although it was delayed several times because of weather and pilot fatigue.

The Blue Ridge is the command and communications vessel of the 40-ship Seventh Fleet armada waiting off the coast of South Vietnam to evacuate Americans and other foreigners

Continued on Page 17, Colum

"All the News That's Fit to Print"

The New York Times

LATE CITY EDITION

Weather: Partly cloudy and less humid today through tomorrow. Temperature range: today 64-80; Sunday 63-82. Details on page 30.

VOL. CXXV ... No. 43,262

NEW YORK, MONDAY, JULY 5, 1976

25 cents beyond 50-mile zone from New York City, except Long Island. Higher in air delivery cities.

20 CENTS

Nation and Millions in City Joyously Hail Bicentennial

ISRAELIS RETURN WITH 103 RESCUED IN UGANDA RAID

Toll Is Put at 3 Hostages, 7 Hijackers, Army Officer and 20 of Amin's Men

FORD LAUDS OPERATION

Freed Captives Are Received Joyously at Airport After Their 7-Day Ordeal

By TERENCE SMITH

Special to The New York Times

JERUSALEM, July 4—An Israeli commando unit that last night conducted a daring raid on the Entebbe airport in Uganda flew home today with the hostages it released.

Military officials said that 103 hostages had been flown to Israel. They said that four Israelis, seven of the 10 hijackers and about 20 Uganda soldiers had been killed.

Text of the Rabin address will be found on page 2.

Some of the hostages arrived exhausted, some exuberant, to a noisy, joyous reunion here with family and friends. A majority of those freed last night were Israelis.

[President Ford sent a message of congratulation to Prime Minister Yitzhak Rabin, voicing "great satisfaction" that the passengers of the hijacked plane had been saved and "a senseless act of terrorism thwarted." Page 2. President Idi Amin of Uganda condemned the Israeli action.]

Back at Same Airport

A week to the day after they set off on an Air France airbus, the Israeli passengers and French crew members were back at the same airport where they had originally started their trip. They were weeping, laughing and literally falling into each other's arms with relief.

Their return here brought to an end seven days of terror that culminated in the spectacular rescue operation, in which Israeli airborne troops traveled 2,500 miles to pluck the hostages from the gunpoints of their captors at the Entebbe airport.

Rabin Addresses Parliament

The success of the operation, which surprised most Israelis, electrified the country. Flags were brought out, people rejoiced openly in the streets, and in the sky over Jerusalem, a skywriter wrote in Hebrew: "Kol hakavod zahal," or "All honor to the army."

Addressing a specially convened session of the Israeli Parliament, Prime Minister Yitzhak Rabin declared: "This operation will become a legend. It is Israel's contribution to

Continued on Page 3, Column 4

Preceded by a fireboat, the Coast Guard training ship Eagle leads the armada of ships past the Battery up the Hudson for the naval review

The New York Times/Edward Hausner

French Officials See Signs Amin, Hijackers Colluded

Special to The New York Times

PARIS, July 4 — Officials and released hostages said here today that they had substantial evidence that President Idi Amin had been in collusion with the hijackers of an Air France airbus in the seizure of the plane as well as after it landed in Uganda.

Although the officials refused to be quoted publicly, one said that negotiations got "much tougher" last night after President Amin returned to Uganda from a meeting of the Organization of African Unity in Mauritius.

A highly placed French source said that President Amin had refused to allow Pierre Renard, the French Ambassador to Uganda, or a special French envoy to deal with the hijackers directly.

While President Amin was out of the country, messages from Israel had to be passed by French Government representatives through the Somalian Ambassador, Hashi Abdullah Farah, to the hijackers. Messages back to the Israelis followed the same route.

Uganda Guards

When Gen. Amin returned from Mauritius yesterday, he resumed the role of mediator. He told the French Ambassador that demands for the release of 53 pro-Palestinian prisoners in Israel, Kenya and Europe must be met by early today or all the hostages would be killed.

Officials here pointed out that on the list of prisoners were five Ugandans held in Kenya on charges of attempting to assassinate President Jomo Kenyatta.

They also noted that during the first 24 hours after the aircraft reached Entebbe, the hijackers withdrew to rest and Ugandans guarded the hostages.

Other evidence pointing to the Uganda President's involvement with the terrorists was included in comments by French diplomats and the reports of hostages freed earlier by the terrorists. At the time of the Israeli rescue operation nearly all of the hijackers' captives were Israelis or dual nationals.

Among the passengers released last week were Michel Cojot and his 12-year-old son, Olivier. Mr. Cojot, a French management consultant, served as interpreter for the hostages, and negotiated on their behalf for small conveniences during the ordeal.

'Not Shadow of Doubt'

Mr. Cojot said that he had "not a shadow of a doubt" that the Uganda President knew of the hijack plan in advance and had prepared for the action.

He said that the airbus, a new European-built plane with a normal four-hour flying capacity, flew non-stop to Entebbe after a refueling stop in Benghazi, Libya — a six-hour flight. "We couldn't possibly have made any other airport by then," he said. "The hijackers were obviously certain they

Continued on Page 4, Column 2

CARTER TO BEGIN TALKS ON TICKET

Will See Muskie Today and Other Possible Running Mates Soon After

By CHARLES MOHR

Special to The New York Times

PLAINS, Ga., July 4—Jimmy Carter has asked Senator Edmund S. Muskie to visit him here tomorrow and discuss the Maine Senator's qualification to serve as Mr. Carter's running mate on the 1976 Democratic ticket.

Mr. Carter told reporters gathered at the driveway of his home in this small Georgia town this morning that he expected to talk to at least four other persons about the Vice-Presidential nomination between now and the Democratic National Convention, which convenes July 12.

The former Georgia Governor, who is assured of the Presidential nomination, said that it would be wrong to assume that there was any special significance in the fact that Senator Muskie was the first to be invited to meet with him. And, indeed, few political observers seem to feel that Mr. Muskie is a front-runner for the job. He was the Vice-Presidential nominee in 1968 and an unsuccessful candidate for the Democratic Presidential nomination in 1972.

A highly knowledgeable source said that the three men

Continued on Page 16, Column 4

A Day of Picnics, Pomp, Pageantry and Protest

By JOHN L. HESS

The nation celebrated its 200th birthday yesterday with pageantry and prayer, with games and parades, with picnics and fireworks, with the peal of bells and the chant of protests.

It began with a flag-raising atop Mars Hill Mountain in Maine, where dawn reached the continent, and moved on to Fort McHenry, in Baltimore Harbor, where it was greeted by the rocket's red glare of the national anthem. The activities were to end nearly a day later with an indigenous festival in American Samoa.

At 2 P.M., Eastern daylight time, descendants of the Revolutionaries laid hands symbolically on the Liberty Bell in Philadelphia, and bells rang in the 50 states and in American communities overseas. At Independence Hall, President Ford read the day's keynote address.

This being an American festival, many new records were claimed: the largest cherry pie (60 square feet), at George, Wash.; the largest cake (69,000 pounds), at Baltimore; the largest fireworks display, in Washington, D.C.; the largest gathering of sailing ships, in New York Harbor.

Yet many sponsors of celebrations were disappointed at the turnouts. The Philadelphia parade, planned for 70,000 marchers, drew about half that

Continued on Page 18, Column 1

PRESIDENT TALKS

Philadelphia Throngs Told U.S. Is Leader—Liberty Bell Rings

By JAMES T. WOOTEN

Special to The New York Times

PHILADELPHIA, July 4 — With its famous bells ringing, bands blaring, choirs singing and fireworks exploding, this city today staged a joyous, cacophonous commemoration of that day two centuries ago when the representatives of the 13 English colonies met here to renounce their allegiance to the British Crown.

At least one million people were in Philadelphia for the centerpiece of the Bicentennial observances.

President Ford came here from Valley Forge to recall that first Fourth of July as "the beginning of a continuing adventure," unfinished, unfulfilled, but still unchallenged as a model of social and political achievement.

"The world is ever conscious of what Americans are doing, for better or for worse," he said at Independence Hall, "because the United States remains today the most successful realization of humanity's universal hope.

Says Nation Leads

"The world may or may not follow, but we lead because our whole history says we must."

Then, after he left for New York City, the Liberty Bell, that faulted but venerated symbol, was softly sounded with a rubber mallet as millions across the nation watched on television. In clamorous response, hundreds of other bells rang out in Philadelphia's steeples and towers.

Meanwhile, several miles from the official observances, more than 30,000 other Americans, most of them members of two radical coalitions, staged their own peaceful Bicentennial celebration. Mayor Frank L. Rizzo had warned of potential disorders, but there were none.

At the main celebration, blue-shirted policemen cordially gave

Continued on Page 18, Column 5

PANOPLY OF SAILS

Harbor Armada Led by Tall Ships in Salute to Fourth

By RICHARD F. SHEPARD

Buoyed by panoramic spectacles that included a unique armada of tall-masted ships, a massive fireworks display and a series of festivals that took over downtown Manhattan, millions of New Yorkers and visitors in a happy mood observed the nation's Bicentennial yesterday.

It was a day of mammoth presentations.

Uncounted crowds lining the waterfront of the magnificent but underused harbor saw a virtually unbroken bridge of small craft that reached from the shores of Brooklyn to the coast of New Jersey.

More than 225 sailing ships under 31 flags paraded up the Hudson, a river that foretold their doom in 1807 when Robert Fulton's smoky little Clermont started steamboat service on it.

International Review

A 22-nation fleet of 53 naval units gray and grim—even ships festooned with pennants—lined the upper Bay and the Hudson for the International Naval Review, which had Vice President Rockefeller as the chief United States official present.

President Ford flew onto the hulking 79,000-ton aircraft carrier Forrestal, the host ship of the review, and later went by helicopter to the U.S.S. Nashville, anchored in mid-Hudson. He watched the sailing ships and was stranded for 40 minutes by a sudden squall before taking off again, headed for Washington, without having set foot ashore in the city.

As night fell, hundreds of thousands jammed onto the shore of lower Manhattan—some dangling from trees like so many Christmas decorations—to watch the dazzling fireworks explode over the harbor and the Statue of Liberty. When it was over, the tide of the departing throngs sometimes swept people out of con-

Continued on Page 20, Column 3

The New York Times/Teresa Zabala

President Ford waves to the crowd at Valley Forge, Pa., where he signed a bill making it a national historical site. He stands on a covered wagon that represented Michigan, his home state, in the Bicentennial wagon train.

Ethnic Diversity Adds Spice to the Holiday

The New York Times/Roger W. Strone

City Hall is the scene of street dancing and music in July 4th in Old New York Festival

By FRED FERRETTI

New Yorkers and their friends poured into lower Manhattan yesterday and compressed 200 years of their history and varied ethnic heritages into a day-long birthday party crammed with prayer, martial music, high spirits and good fellowship.

It was the tall ships and the warships that drew them there, but it was Dr. Quackenbush's Traveling Medicine Show, Delancy's Loyalist Red Coat Brigade, Fraunces Tavern, Oscar Brand, falafel and pizza and egg rolls, and John Philip Sousa that kept them there.

Not even a succession of torrential downpours late in the afternoon could drive them away. They watched George III beheaded at Federal Hall National Memorial, listened to Terence Cardinal Cooke pray at Castle Clinton, watched the Turks take over Wall Street for

Continued on Page 22, Column 4

O, Say, It Was a Glorious Patchwork-Quilt of a Fourth

By McCANDLISH PHILLIPS

The Fourth of July celebration in New York City yesterday was as American as a patchwork quilt—full of a joyous order-in-disarray and a series of brilliantly improbable juxtapositions.

It was an exercise in percussion, procession, demonstration, declamation, detonation, commemoration, vociferation, trivialization, solemnization and, for some, indigestion.

The free and independent citizens of New York City got themselves into a good many unusual postures as they scrambled for perspective on events, sometimes at the price of mild peril.

In parks and on piers, on fences, balconies, ramps, rooftops, chimneys, ledges, abutments and the ladders of water storage tanks, they sat, stooped, stood and clung, chiefly to watch great ships come sailing out of the distant past and go up the hazy Hudson like a vision.

It was a great day for family portraits to be taken with the most senior member of the American family. The process began early in the day in front of the Federal Hall National Memorial on Wall Street, on the site where George Washington took the oath as President on April 30, 1789.

Washington's statue dominates the steps leading up to the eight columns of the hall, and the base of the pedestal is a stage large enough for at least half a dozen persons to stand on.

As soon as one group posed and left, the next moved up to be photographed with the unblinkingly obliging founding father.

Seven small children in bright summer colors nearly ringed the great figure, standing under his outstretched right hand their heads reaching to half the height of the pedestal. They looked very serious for the moment or so they stood there.

Though few noticed it, Christopher Columbus was in town. Not the old boy him-

Continued on Page 20, Column 5

NEWS INDEX

"All the News That's Fit to Print"

The New York Times

LATE CITY EDITION

Weather: Chance of rain late today, tonight. Partly sunny tomorrow. Temperature range: today 72-86; Tuesday 66-90. Details on page 65.

VOL. CXXV . . No. 43,278

NEW YORK, WEDNESDAY, JULY 21, 1976

25 cents beyond 50-mile zone from New York City, except Long Island. Higher in air delivery cities.

20 CENTS

VIKING ROBOT SETS DOWN SAFELY ON MARS AND SENDS BACK PICTURES OF ROCKY PLAIN

Associated Press

A composite photo showing a 300-degree panorama of the surface of Mars, made by a camera on the Viking 1 landing craft just after touchdown on the planet yesterday morning. Parts of the craft are visible in foreground.

Ford Gains 10 Delegates And Needs Only 18 More

By JAMES M. NAUGHTON

Special to The New York Times

WASHINGTON, July 20—President Ford gained substantial delegate strength today to pull within 18 votes of the total needed to gain a first-ballot nomination at the Republican National Convention.

Amid conflicting claims from the rival Republican camps, The New York Times determined from the best available information and a canvass of the delegates involved that Mr. Ford had a net gain of 10 delegates while Ronald Reagan had a net increase of one.

The new tally by The Times listed 1,112 delegates for Mr. Ford—18 short of the 1,130 needed for nomination — and 1,064 for Mr. Reagan, with 83 still uncommitted. Thirteen of the 83 said they were leaning to Mr. Ford and three to Mr. Reagan.

James A. Baker, a deputy chairman of the President Ford Committee, claimed the conversion of several delegates and proposed to certify the President's strength by making public the identities of all Ford delegates once they constitute a convention majority.

The proposal to list the delegates by name and address was the latest move in a war of nerves between supporters of the President and of Mr. Reagan.

Mr. Baker dismissed as "blowing smoke" the largely unsubstantiated claim yesterday by John P. Sears, the Reagan campaign manager, to 1,140 delegates for the former California Governor—10 more than needed for nomination.

Mr. Sears retaliated later to-

Continued on Page 22, Column 1

U.S. AGENCY FINDS DRUG TESTING LAX

Says F.D.A., Makers and Others Expose the Public to Needless Risks

By RICHARD HALLORAN

Special to The New York Times

WASHINGTON, July 20—Congressional investigators have issued a blistering indictment of the Food and Drug Administration, pharmaceutical makers, doctors and research scientists, charging them with exposing humans to unnecessary risks in testing new drugs.

The General Accounting Office also reported that the testing procedures could result in F.D.A. approval of a new drug for public use based on "inaccurate and unreliable data."

The Congressional investigating unit disclosed instances of "alarming adverse reactions" to new drugs that went unreported and the death of eight soldiers in an Army test of a drug intended to prevent malaria.

Despite continued controversy over many aspects of the regulation of prescription drugs in recent years, the general ac-

Continued on Page 8, Column 1

Rao Indictments Obtained By Nadjari Are Reinstated

By MAX H. SEIGEL

The Appellate Division in Brooklyn yesterday reinstated perjury indictments obtained by Maurice H. Nadjari against Judge Paul P. Rao Sr. of United States Customs Court; his son, Paul Jr., and another lawyer, Salvatore Nigrone.

The indictments had been dismissed last Dec. 2 by the late Justice John M. Murtagh of State Supreme Court on the ground that undercover agents had made statements to the grand jury that "were highly prejudicial to the defendants." Justice Murtagh also had questioned whether the evidence before the grand jury was legally sufficient to establish the offense charged.

Several weeks after the dismissal of the indictments, which involved a manufactured "robbery" case, Governor Carey cited the Rao reversal —and others that had occurred less than a month earlier—in announcing his intention to dismiss Mr. Nadjari as the special state prosecutor looking into the criminal-justice system in New York City.

In its 4-to-1 decision reinstating the indictments, the Appellate Division majority said that it acted "on the law" without going into the actual merits of the case.

The majority found that Justice Murtagh had said improperly that he was dismissing the indictments "in the interests of justice" while he had actually ordered the dismissal

Continued on Page 67, Column 1

Long Offers 2d Vote In Tax-Aid Dispute

By EILEEN SHANAHAN

Special to The New York Times

WASHINGTON, July 20—Russell B. Long, chairman of the Senate Finance Committee, promised today to give the panel a new opportunity to vote for or against each of 73 provisions of the pending tax bill, most of which benefit just one company or industry.

Senator Long made the commitment after an unusually heated session of the committee during which Senator Edward M. Kennedy was, in effect, called a demagogue by one Republican member and accused of not knowing what he was talking about by another.

Mr. Kennedy, Democrat of Massachusetts, has emerged as a leading foe of the kind of narrow-interest tax legislation

Continued on Page 42, Column 4

Associated Press

Foot pad of the Viking 1 resting on Mars. Center of this picture is five feet from camera and the rock at center is approximately four inches across.

South African Black Is Reported Killed In Renewed Rioting

By JOHN F. BURNS

Special to The New York Times

JOHANNESBURG, July 20—At least one black man was reported killed tonight when police reinforcements were rushed to the coal-mining center of Witbank, 75 miles east of here, which was in the grip of the most serious rioting since the widespread anti-Government upheavals last month.

Reports from the scene said that about 3,000 black youths had poured out of black townships and attacked people and buildings in areas occupied by Indians and people of mixed descent, who are called colored here.

Few details were available, and it was unclear how the reported death had occurred. However, the riot policemen, armed with automatic rifles, were acting under standing Government orders to suppress fresh outbreaks of violence with all necessary force.

The possibility of a chain reaction was raised by a police report of at least one outbreak elsewhere. At midnight, rioters were said to have set fire to several buildings in Khutsong. a black township near Carletonville, a mining town southwest of Johannesburg.

The death would be the first since the end of the rioting

Continued on Page 4, Column 7

GOLD PLUNGES 12% IN WEEK TO $107.75

Slump Hurts South Africa —Heavy Soviet Selling Is Seen as Part of Cause

By PETER T. KILBORN

Special to The New York Times

LONDON, July 20 — The turmoil that has been swirling through many nations' currencies has now swept into gold, long a major component, along with the dollar, of the world's monetary reserves.

In only five business days, the price of gold has tumbled nearly 12 percent, from $122 an ounce last Wednesday to $107.75 at its close today in London. Today alone it fell nearly $6.

The drop has been so abrupt, gold experts here said, that South Africa, the world's leading producer of gold, now faces political as well as economical consequences unless the price recovers quickly.

"If you take the gold out of South Africa," said Richard Lockwood, a mining expert for a brokerage firm in London, "you've got one of the worst economies in the world."

Experts also expected difficulties for the Soviet Union, another major producer. Ironically, they said, the Russians helped bring on the decline in

Continued on Page 47, Column 5

Attica Is Termed as Bad As Before 1971 Rebellion

By FRED FERRETTI

Special to The New York Times

ATTICA, N.Y., July 20 — The chief of a State Commission of Correction team sent into the Attica prison last week following the most recent outbreak of violence there described conditions within the facility today as "just as bad, perhaps worse" than in September 1971, just before an inmate rebellion that resulted in the deaths of 43 persons.

"What we have is a combat situation," said Scott Christianson, director of the Correction Commission's State Prison Unit, following five days of investigation and interrogation of inmates and guards. "The environment is so physical, so potentially dangerous, the power of both the inmates and the guards is so awesome, that it can go off at any time. Both sides have the power of death in their hands."

The superintendent of the prison, Harold J. Smith, conceded in an interview that an inmate rebellion could happen again. "Yes, it could," he said, "I'd be a damn fool to say otherwise."

The Correction Commission has reported formally to Governor Carey that a set of parallels exists between the situation here today and what it was in Attica just before Sept. 9, 1971, when the prisoners revolted. The prison was subsequently recaptured by state troopers who stormed it.

The new report urged the

Continued on Page 65, Column 1

Nitrogen, Key to Life, Is Found

By WALTER SULLIVAN

Special to The New York Times

PASADENA, Calif., July 20—The first definitive analysis of the Martian atmosphere has disclosed the presence of a small component of nitrogen. Until now the absence of any evidence of that gas stood as a major obstacle to speculation that life might exist on the planet.

The analysis has also provided long-sought clues to the history of Mars, including the possibility that enough water is hidden beneath its surface to cover the planet one mile deep.

The chief surprise has been Viking's discovery that argon, an inert gas, constitutes far less of the Martian atmosphere than scientists previously believed. Whereas estimates of the argon level on Mars had been as high as 30 percent, data from Viking indicate that it is only about 3 percent, compared with about 1 percent in the Earth's atmosphere.

The analysis also put the level of nitrogen at about 3 percent.

This and other detailed determinations should bear on such questions as the history of the Earth's known atmosphere, including the proposal that the atmosphere of both Earth and Mars were formed in eruptions very early in each planet's history.

Such an early formation of the atmosphere would mean, as well, the early appearance of oceans or smaller water bodies suitable for the evolution of life.

Higher Ratio Suggested

When the Soviet Union's Mars 6 plunged into the Mars atmosphere in its unsuccessful landing attempt in 1974 it was thought that perplexing features of its data transmissions could be explained if 30 percent of the Martian air consisted of argon. The possibility of so large a percentage also offered an explanation for observations made near one of the Martian poles a few days ago by the Viking mother ship that cast loose the lander today.

Today's measurement, which is considered definitive, put the argon level at about 3 percent.

The lower abundance of argon is good news for those experimenters hoping to learn the composition of Mars's surface materials. Their instrument aboard the lander will determine such compositions with a gas chromatograph mass spectrometer that could have been rendered useless by an atmosphere rich in argon.

The project's scientists believe that today's measurements will help clarify whether, as some of them believe, there is still enough water hidden beneath the surface of Mars to cover that planet to a depth of one mile.

The abundance of argon in the air of Mars today is a critical index of the atmosphere's history. If volcanic eruptions and other processes generated the same atmospheric constituents as those produced by such activity on Earth the present abundance of argon could, it was argued, have been as high as reported by the Russians.

The reasoning is that since

Continued on Page 12, Column 4

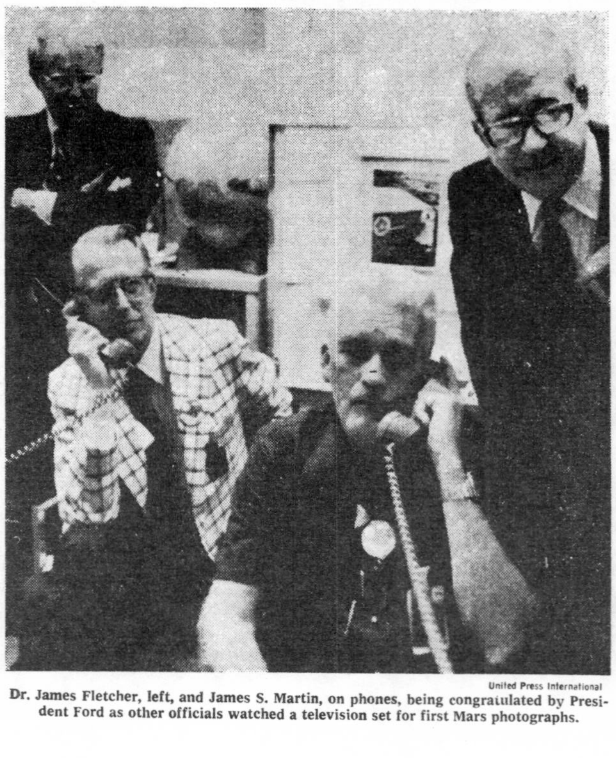

United Press International

Dr. James Fletcher, left, and James S. Martin, on phones, being congratulated by President Ford as other officials watched a television set for first Mars photographs.

3¼-HOUR DESCENT

Scientists Are Jubilant as News Is Flashed, Taking 19 Minutes

By JOHN NOBLE WILFORD

Special to The New York Times

PASADENA, Calif., July 20—An explorer from Earth, the robot craft Viking 1, made the first successful landing on Mars today and transmitted spectacular photographs of a rocky, wind-scoured desert plain, the site for the first direct search for life on another world.

The squat, three-legged Viking landing craft came to rest, upright and intact, on the Chryse Plain of Mars at 7:53 A.M. Eastern daylight time after a voyage of 11 months and nearly half a billion miles. The final and most suspenseful step, the craft's descent to the surface from its mother ship in Mars orbit, took 3 hours 13 minutes.

Then, Touchdown

Responding to automatic computer commands, the lander's rockets fired, its parachute unfurled, protective shielding broke away, more rockets were fired—and then, touchdown. It was 19 minutes, because of the great distance between Mars and Earth, now more than 212 million miles, before confirmation of the safe landing reached the control rooms here at the Jet Propulsion Laboratory.

"Touchdown!" announced Richard Bender, one of the flight controllers. "We have touchdown. We have several indications of touchdown."

It was an emotional moment for the scientists and engineers of the $1 billion Viking project, many of whom had spent eight years preparing for this day.

Applause and Amazement

There was applause in the control room and throughout the laboratory. There were broad smiles and moist eyes. There were soft expressions of numbed amazement at what they had wrought.

With the Viking landing begins the first surface exploration of Mars (two Soviet landings failed to produce usable data). The planet has fascinated man for centuries and been the object of legend and endless scientific speculation.

In eight days, if all continues to go according to plan, a mechanical arm on the lander is to reach out and scoop up soil samples for chemical and biological analysis by onboard instruments. This will mark the beginning of the mission's search for signs of possible life on Mars.

Though Mars is no longer seriously thought of as an

Continued on Page 12, Column 1

NEWS INDEX

"All the News That's Fit to Print"

The New York Times

LATE CITY EDITION

Weather: Sunny today; clear, mild tonight. Sunny, warmer tomorrow. Temperature range: today 63-83; Wednesday 64-80. Details, page 70.

VOL. CXXV . No. 43,307

NEW YORK, THURSDAY, AUGUST 19, 1976

25 cents beyond 50-mile zone from New York City, except Long Island. Higher in air delivery cities.

20 CENTS

FORD TAKES NOMINATION ON FIRST BALLOT; REVEALS VICE-PRESIDENTIAL CHOICE TODAY

2 AMERICANS SLAIN BY NORTH KOREANS IN CLASH AT DMZ

4 U.S. Soldiers and 5 South Koreans Hurt in Assault by Communists With Axes

Special to The New York Times

SEOUL, South Korea, Thursday, Aug. 19 — North Korean soldiers, wielding axes and metal pikes, attacked a group of American and South Korean soldiers in the demilitarized zone yesterday, killing two American officers and wounding four American enlisted men and five South Korean soldiers.

The attack took place as the American and South Korean soldiers were trimming branches from a tree at the Panmunjom truce site near an allied checkpoint at the south end of the "Bridge of No Return," over which prisoners were exchanged after the Korean War.

According to the United Nations Command, the American and South Korean work group was performing a routine task when two North Korean officers and some soldiers approached and, after some discussion, demanded that the Americans and South Koreans stop trimming the tree.

Order to 'Kill' Overheard

Shortly afterward a truck carrying North Korean soldiers drove up and one of the officers was heard to tell the soldiers to "kill" the Americans and South Koreans. Then, according to the United Nations Command's account, the North Koreans rushed the Americans and South Koreans with axes, metal pikes and ax handles.

[In Kansas City, President Ford in a statement Wednesday condemned the attack as "brutal and cowardly" and warned that the North Korean Government would be responsible for "the consequences." Page 14.]

The North Koreans charged in a radio broadcast last night that "U.S. imperialist troops" armed with "lethal weapons" had pounced on North Korean soldiers who had protested the trimming of the tree, which the broadcast said was in an area under North Korean control.

The broadcast made no mention of any casualties on either side in the clash. A Japanese news agency quoted military sources as having said that three North Koreans had been killed in the clash, but the report could not be confirmed and

Continued on Page 14, Column 5

Burmah Oil's U.S. Aid Bid Studied for Possible Fraud

By TERRY ROBARDS

The Securities and Exchange Commission, the Federal Maritime Administration and at least one Congressional committee are investigating whether the Burmah Oil Company, a major British concern, illegally received commitments for Federal guarantees or subsidies to build at least eight huge tanker ships in this country.

Hundreds of millions of dollars in shipbuilding projects and thousands of American shipyard jobs may be in jeopardy because of the possibility of fraud in applying for the Government backing, which is illegal for foreign companies under Federal law.

The ships are under construction at the Quincy, Mass., yards of the General Dynamics Corporation, which received the shipbuilding contracts from Burmah affiliates or subsidiaries. A major portion of the $1.06 billion in these contracts is understood to be in question.

At issue is whether the ships have any right to American subsidies or loan guarantees, since Burmah is not an American company. Federal law specifies that only domestic concerns can receive such Government backing.

Commitments for this backing have been made to a group of companies related to Burmah and set up for the express purpose of trying to fulfill the requirements for American citizenship.

Robert J. Blackwell, Assistant Secretary of Commerce for Maritime Affairs and head of the Maritime Administration, said in a telephone interview from Washington last night that the agency "has no information to indicate that there was fraud of any type or wrongdoing" in the Burmah applications.

However, Mr. Blackwell also said that some of the original applications filed by the Burmah affiliates had been "more or less aborted" because the companies could not fulfill some of the conditions specified by his agency.

He added that the structure of the corporate entities involved in the shipbuilding contracts was being changed in an effort to assure compliance

Continued on Page 60, Column 1

PLAN IS OUTLINED FOR 1978 FREEDOM IN AFRICAN AREA

South-West Africa Proposal for a Multiracial Regime Ignores the Guerrillas

By JOHN F. BURNS

Special to The New York Times

JOHANNESBURG, Aug. 18 — Faced with a United Nations ultimatum that expires at the end of the month, a constitutional committee in South-West Africa today announced plans for a multiracial government to lead the territory to independence from South Africa by Dec. 31, 1978.

The announcement, made with the tacit approval of the

Text of committee statement is printed on page 4.

South African Government, represented the second major move within a week to relieve international pressure on South Africa. On Friday, South Africa announced its support for the United States effort to promote a negotiated settlement of the Rhodesian crisis.

South Africa once vigorously opposed a surrender of power by the white minorities on its borders. However, its current view is that supporting moves toward majority rule outside its own borders will gain it time in which to persuade the world that white rule in South Africa, adjusted to relieve black grievances, is indispensable.

No Mention of Rebels

The statement on South-West Africa, issued in Windhoek, the territorial capital, made no mention of the South-West Africa People's Organization, recognized by the United Nations as the representative of the territory's 800,000 inhabitants. The group, which has been carrying on a guerrilla war, has been not participating in the discussions.

Nor did the statement make any reference to elections. The ultimatum issued by the Security Council called for United Nations-supervised elections in the territory, which South Africa has continued to govern in defiance of a decision by the International Court of Justice holding its occupation to be illegal.

However, the committee, representing 11 ethnic groups, appealed to all nations to counter any attempt at solving the territory's problems violently. This was seen as a reference to the South-West Africa People's Or-

Continued on Page 4, Column 4

The New York Times/Teresa Zabala

President Ford before his nomination yesterday

2 RIVALS MEET

Reagan Not Running for No. 2 Spot but Doesn't Bar Draft

By R. W. APPLE Jr.

Special to The New York Times

KANSAS CITY, Mo., Thursday, Aug. 19 — Gerald Rudolph Ford, who struggled for seven grueling months to avoid rejection by his party, was nominated in his own right early this morning at the 31st Republican National Convention on the first and only ballot.

The party sent Mr. Ford, a political insider who has held elective office for 28 years, into combat against Jimmy Carter, the political outsider chosen by the Democrats, after Gov. William G. Milliken of Michigan hailed him as the nation's "present and future President."

Unlike most Presidents, Mr. Ford, who inherited the White House after Richard M. Nixon resigned, will enter the general election campaign as the underdog.

West Virginia Clinches

West Virginia, the scene of intensive combat for the loyalties of delegates, gave the President 20 votes—as promised by Gov. Arch A. Moore Jr. for months—and put him over the top at 12:29 A.M. Central daylight time.

In the gallery at the south end of the hall, Betty Ford rose to her feet and waved her hands above her head in evangelistic style. Then she and her three children hugged and kissed each other.

The final count gave Mr. Ford 1,187 votes and Ronald Reagan 1,070. John J. Walsh Jr., an Illinois alternate from River Forest, abstained, and Ralph DeBlasio, a Greenwich Village district leader, voted for Commerce Secretary Elliot L. Richardson.

Despite a scattering of "noes," mainly from the pro-Reagan Texas delegation, Representative John J. Rhodes of Arizona, the convention's permanent chairman, declared Mr. Ford nominated by acclamation.

27-Minute Meeting

Mr. Ford then drove to Mr. Reagan's hotel for a 27-minute meeting with his vanquished adversary. They discussed the Vice Presidency. Mr. Reagan said at a subsequent news conference that he stood by earlier statements that he would not run with the President, but it was unclear whether he had been asked.

The Californian said he would not permit his name to be put in nomination for the Vice Presidency, but he left open the door for a draft by the delegates, many of whom appeared to want a Ford-Reagan ticket. The President, who was to announce his choice later today, smiled as Mr. Reagan responded to questions about a draft.

Describing the former Governor as "the most effective campaigner in America" and

Continued on Page 26, Column 1

FILIPINOS DESCRIBE HOW DISASTER HIT

Amid Debris on Mindanao, They Tell How Quake and Tidal Wave Swept Area

By ALICE VILLADOLID

Special to The New York Times

DINAIG, the Philippines, Aug. 18—The coastal strip near this town, an hour's drive from Cotabato City, was once a scenic spot. Today it is littered with twisted roofing, uprooted coconut trees, battered furniture and other debris left by the earthquake and tidal wave that struck at dawn yesterday on the island of Mindanao.

The area was one of the worst hit in the quake, which the National Disaster Coordinating Center said left 3,131 dead and 3,117 missing. The head of the center said the death toll might reach 5,000. More than 28,000 were left homeless by the quake and 18-foot-high waves, and 688 were listed as injured.

One victim described the start of the disaster this way: "When the earth began shak-

Continued on Page 3, Column 1

Deportation Faced By Danish Widow Of Stabbing Victim

By JOYCE MAYNARD

The Danish widow of an actor fatally stabbed in Greenwich Village last June is threatened with deportation on the ground that she does not meet United States residency requirements because, in the words of immigration officials, "the marriage no longer exists."

The woman, Sus McCready, had been married 11 months and was awaiting approval of her petition for a green card signifying permanent residency when her husband, Tom, was killed.

"I try to be a hopeful person but they get me over and over and over," said Mrs. McCready in a steady voice, sitting on a single bed in the studio apartment where she moved shortly after the murder, with a few plants and some recordings and a man's rumpled brown hat on a table.

Four days after the murder, Mrs. McCready received a bill for $982 from the hospital emergency room where her husband was treated.

"There are so many papers

Continued on Page 49, Column 4

PRESIDENT URGED TO NETTLE CARTER

Advisers Feel Sharp Attacks on Integrity Will Rattle Democratic Opponent

By JAMES RESTON

Special to The New York Times

KANSAS CITY, Mo., Aug. 18 —President Ford is being urged by some of his closest advisers to follow a strategy of provocation against Jimmy Carter in the Presidential campaign.

"You just watch us," one of them said today. "We're going to wipe that smile off his face."

This proposed strategy rests on the assumption that the Democratic nominee is vague, self-righteous and short-tempered, and that he can be rattled by sharp attacks on his integrity and credibility.

With this in mind, the President's advisers are proposing that he put former Gov. John B. Connally of Texas in charge of the Republican campaign. Mr. Connally has a reputation as a master of political ridicule and sarcasm.

It is not clear that President Ford has agreed to this line of attack on Mr. Carter. His staff has been looking at some of the speeches made here to the delegates, but there is no evidence that the President himself has been directing the

Continued on Page 30, Column 7

Reagan's Backers Stage Noisy Last-Ditch Parade

By JAMES T. WOOTEN

Special to The New York Times

KANSAS CITY, Mo., Thursday, Aug. 19—Jubilantly parading as enthusiastically as winners, Ronald Reagan's supporters celebrated his proposed candidacy at the Republican National Convention here last night with a rowdy, raucous, unscheduled demonstration that lasted 43 minutes and defied several attempts to stop it.

Moments later, equally ardent backers of President Ford responded when his name was formally placed in nomination with a shorter but similarly well-organized show of support that filled the air of Kemper Arena with hundreds of beach balls.

The Reaganites' histrionics, however, seemed finally to go beyond the control of the Californian's floor leaders and the candidate himself eventually conceded that they were "running too long."

Armed with plastic horns and the lingering frustrations of a long campaign, the Reaganites raised the roof of the Kemper Arena, dancing in the aisles of the Convention floor and around the edges of the jammed balconies.

With the Californian's name officially entered as a candidate by his campaign chairman, Senator Paul Laxalt of Nevada, his supporters were unwilling to halt the demonstration despite the gaveling of the convention chairman, Representative John J. Rhodes.

"This is the longest demonstration of my seven con-

Continued on Page 26, Column 3

Sears Says Twists of Fate Hurt Reagan's Chances

By JON NORDHEIMER

Special to The New York Times

KANSAS CITY, Mo., Aug. 18 —It was the little things—the unpredictable turns of fortune that make American politics at once so fascinating and so frustrating — that gravely wounded Ronald Reagan's chances for the Republican nomination, the former California Governor's campaign manager, John P. Sears, said today.

"It's been true at many points in this campaign that very small items have had very large significance," Mr. Sears told a news conference hours before the Republican National Convention met to confer its nomination for President.

The vote of the Mississippi delegation yesterday afternoon not to support Mr. Reagan's crucial floor fight last night for a rules change was the final unexpected twist that helps change history, Mr. Sears said philosophically.

Mistakes. Misunderstandings. Misinterpretation. A lost vote here and there. They all added up, he said, to bring the Reagan campaign to a point where victory after nine hotly contested months of campaigning seemed beyond reach.

In a 30-minute news conference marked by Mr. Sears's candor and crackling wit, and

Continued on Page 29, Column 3

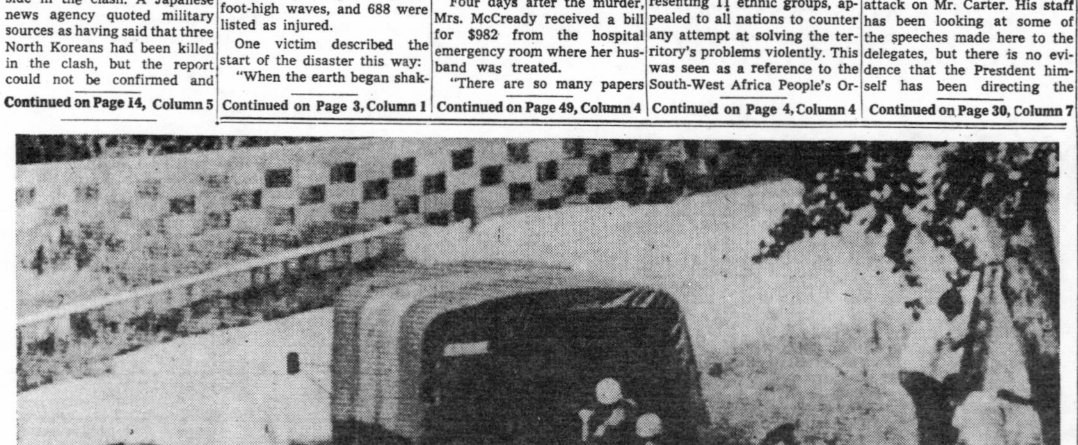

United Press International

North Korean troops attacking a United Nations work party in the demilitarized zone, killing two U.S. officers. Photo was made by a U.S. soldier.

Calls Swamp Police 911 Emergency Line

By PRANAY GUPTE

The 911 emergency telephone number system is being flooded by a record number of calls, and the police, citing dwindling manpower, say they cannot handle the calls as fast as they would like. This includes, they say, incidents involving what officials acknowledge are increasing activities by youth gangs.

"We need more people to handle 911 calls," Inspector Charles F. Peterson, commanding officer of the Police Department's communications bureau, said yesterday. "And we need an army to deal with these roving bands of youths."

He was responding to charges by some civic groups that the police were inefficient and tardy in responding to three recent incidents in Manhattan, Brooklyn and Staten Island in which rampaging youths terrorized residents, shopkeepers, pedestrians and even passengers in taxis.

Such charges are currently being investigated by Police Commissioner Michael J. Codd.

A spokesman indicated last night that the investigation could produce changes in the way emergency calls were acted upon by radio-car dispatchers in the 911 communications center at police headquarters.

Commissioner Codd and Inspector Peterson had met yesterday afternoon with John E. Zuccotti, the First Deputy Mayor, to discuss the recent incidents involving youth gangs. At that meeting the police officials were reported to have renewed their request for more manpower.

They told Mr. Zuccotti that the number of personnel direct-

Continued on Page 60, Column 2

NEWS INDEX

"All the News That's Fit to Print"

The New York Times

LATE CITY EDITION

Weather: Showers likely today and tonight. Partly cloudy tomorrow. Temperature range: today 63-73; Thursday 60-79. Details, page D17.

VOL. CXXV .... No. 43,329 NEW YORK, FRIDAY, SEPTEMBER 10, 1976 — 25 cents beyond 50-mile zone from New York City, except Long Island. Higher in air delivery cities. — 20 CENTS

MAO TSE-TUNG DIES IN PEKING AT 82; LEADER OF RED CHINA REVOLUTION; CHOICE OF SUCCESSOR IS UNCERTAIN

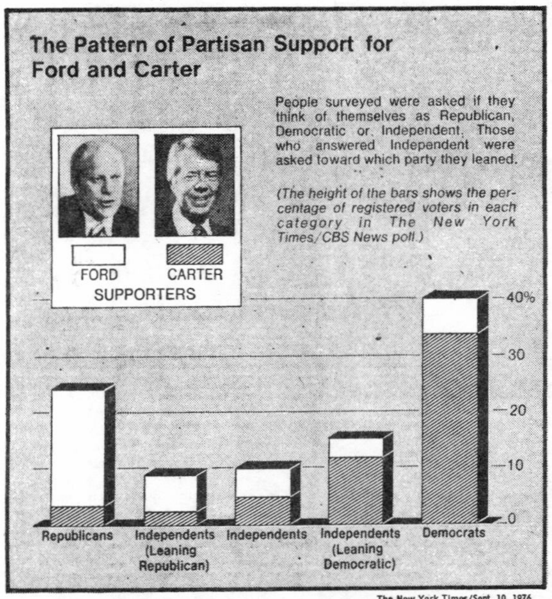
The Pattern of Partisan Support for Ford and Carter
People surveyed were asked if they think of themselves as Republican, Democratic or Independent. Those who answered Independent were asked toward which party they leaned.
(The height of the bars shows the percentage of registered voters in each category in The New York Times/CBS News poll.)
FORD
CARTER
SUPPORTERS
40%
30
20
10
0
Republicans
Independents (Leaning Republican)
Independents
Independents (Leaning Democratic)
Democrats
The New York Times/Sept. 10, 1976

This chart shows that President Ford's support is predominant among Republicans and that Jimmy Carter's support rises steadily along the Democratic end of the spectrum. For example, 22 percent called themselves Republicans. Among these Ford had roughly a seven-to-one advantage.

Poll Shows Ford Trailing in Bid For 2 Voter Groups G.O.P. Needs

By R. W. APPLE Jr.

President Ford is trailing Jimmy Carter among self-described independents and moderates, the two elements of the electorate without whose strong support Republican nominees have been unable to win Presidential elections in the post-World War II era.

With less than two months remaining until Election Day, the President's strength is concentrated in groups that lack the voting power to elect a President—the well-to-do, the Republicans, the white Protestants, the conservatives. In almost every other segment of the electorate, Mr. Ford is running well behind his Democratic opponent, Mr. Carter.

Those are two of the central conclusions that emerge from the first national poll taken by The New York Times and CBS News since the two party conventions—a survey of 1,703 registered voters, selected at random, who were interviewed by telephone during the week that ended Sept. 5, immediately before the formal start of the general election campaign on Labor Day.

The New York Times/CBS News poll was not designed to predict the outcome of the election but to analyze the thinking of the electorate as it stood early this month. Nonetheless it reflected the same over-all standing of the candidates as recent surveys by the Gallup and Harris organizations, with Mr. Carter leading the President by a margin of roughly 4 to 3.

Insofar as issues determine how people cast their votes for President, the poll indicated, President Ford is suffering from the continuing deep divisions in the country over two issues he inherited from his discredited predecessor — the

Continued on Page A19, Col. 3

AGREEMENT REACHED ON TAX REVISION BILL

Conferees Adopt First Reform of Estate Levies in 35 Years

By EDWIN L. DALE Jr.

Special to The New York Times

WASHINGTON, Sept. 9 — House and Senate conferees agreed tonight on all provisions of the sweeping tax revision bill after adopting the first major reform of the nation's system of estate taxes in 35 years.

The final version of the bill, it was estimated, would give the Treasury $1.6 billion more in revenues in the fiscal year 1977, thus meeting the demands of the new Congressional budget control process and greatly augmenting the bill's chances for passage.

The revenue increase would rise to $2.4 billion five years from now, offset in part by revenue losses from the new estate tax reform.

The bill has hundreds of provisions, among them a significant increase in taxes on wealthy taxpayers who avail themselves of various tax "shelters."

It also would impose tax penalties on United States companies complying with the Arab boycott of Israel.

The estate tax reform would provide

Continued on Page D17, Col. 5

Ford Asserts Rival Would Create Peril To Defense of U.S.

By JAMES M. NAUGHTON

Special to The New York Times

WASHINGTON, Sept. 9—President Ford said today that Jimmy Carter's plans to reduce Pentagon spending and troop levels overseas would make it "impossible to have a defense adequate to maintain our freedom and the freedom of our friends."

Addressing the national convention of B'nai B'rith one day after Mr. Carter did, the President departed from a prepared text to read notes sharply critical of the national security positions of his Democratic challenger.

Says Carter Invites Crisis

Mr. Ford contended that the former Georgia Governor's proposals would, among other things, require the United States to rely on "a nuclear strategy of massive retaliation" and thus "invite a major crisis with our allies, including Israel."

Mr. Carter, meanwhile, took issue with Mr. Ford's remarks yesterday, in which the President embraced proposals for a constitutional amendment to limit abortions. The Democratic nominee said that he thought the sensitive abortion issue could backfire on any Presidential candidate who attempted to exploit it.

Even Mr. Ford's running mate, Senator

Continued on Page A21, Col. 1

Radar Images From Venus Depict Vast Area of Possible Lava Flow

By JOHN NOBLE WILFORD

American astronomers who have obtained the first detailed radar images of a large portion of the surface of Venus say they revealed a possible lava flow the size of Oklahoma, an impact basin much like those on the moon and evidence of mountain-building processes similar to those that have shaped the Earth.

Since Venus is completely enveloped by thick clouds, the radar images represent the first relatively clear picture of what the planet's surface looks like. The images covered an area of about four million square miles in the northern latitudes of Venus.

The most distinctive feature in the north of Venus, as shown by the radar, is a very bright Oklahoma size area that the scientists said looked like a broad lava field. It appears to be a sharply defined feature overlaying an older surface.

The scientists said that the area did not have a shape that might have been created by the impact of a meteorite, but instead seemed to be a result of processes internal to Venus, such as a volcanic eruption of lava. The feature has been tentatively named Maxwell, for James Clerk Maxwell, the 19th-century Scottish physicist.

Maxwell's surface appears extremely rough and apparently contains long paral-

Continued on Page A18, Col. 5

KISSINGER IS CAUTIOUS

Discerns No Setback for U.S. Relations With China, but Sees Hazards in a Change

By BERNARD GWERTZMAN

Special to The New York Times

WASHINGTON, Sept. 9—Secretary of State Henry A. Kissinger said today that he did not think Mao Tse-tung's death would set back Chinese-American relations, but he cautioned that "when any historical figure disappears it is extremely difficult to predict everything his successor will do."

At a brief news conference Mr. Kissinger reflected Washington's uncertainty about the future in light of Mao's death. Officially, Secretary Kissinger and President Ford expressed confidence that the trend toward improved relations started by the Chinese leader and President Richard M. Nixon in 1972 would continue.

[In Moscow, diplomatic observers said the death of Chairman Mao raised the possibility of a relaxation of tensions between the Soviet Union and China. Page A17.]

Kissinger Met Mao Five Times

The Secretary of State, who has met Mao five times since 1971, tempered the official optimism with the caution that because China was probably on the verge of major changes, the eventual trend of its policy could not be predicted with assurance.

"We have to remember that when a towering figure disappears from the scene, not even his successors can know exactly what the shape of events will be and it is premature to speculate as to what the future evolution should be," he said in answer to a question.

Mr. Kissinger, in a signal to Chinese leaders, said that since the opening to China, it and the United States had "created a durable relationship based on mutual confidence and perception of common interests."

Pledge to Adhere to Communiqué

"We for our part will continue to cement our ties with the People's Republic of China in accordance with the Shanghai Communiqué issued at the end of Mr. Nixon's visit and calling for normalization of relations.

Earlier in the day the Secretary told newsmen that "we consider our opening to the People's Republic of China one of the most important foreign policy actions of the recent period and we don't really expect any change on the Chinese side, but the methods and the nuances

Continued on Page A17, Col. 6

United Press International

Mao Tse-tung is shown in 1969 at the Ninth Party Congress, proclaiming the triumph of his Cultural Revolution over disgraced President Liu Shao-chi.

Political Uncertainty in China

Natural Disasters and Reports of Indiscipline Leave Analysts Fearful of Forecasting Events

By FOX BUTTERFIELD

Special to The New York Times

HONG KONG, Sept. 9—The death today of Chairman Mao Tse-tung comes at a time when China's political situation seems more uncertain than at any point since the end of the Cultural Revolution.

News Analysis

Over the last 18 months four other members of the nine-man standing Committee of the party's Politburo, China's highest decision-making body, have died, including Prime Minister Chou En-lai. Since last winter Peking has been preoccupied with a divisive political campaign, there have been growing reports of a breakdown in public discipline, and there have even been some isolated incidents of violent conflict.

There have also been other misfortunes for China. Last July parts of Northern China were devastated by the world's worst earthquake in a decade, and both northeast and southwest China have recently been hit by strong tremors.

No analysts here believe that the Communist regime is likely to be seriously jeopardized by these troubles. But few of them would dare to forecast the shape of events.

The most likely course of events in China after the funeral, some analysts believe, is that a transitional collective leadership, following current party ranking, will emerge centered on the new Prime Minister, Hua Kuo-feng.

The tall, burly, crewcut Mr. Hua, a career party administrator, seems to have swiftly strengthened his grip on the levers of leadership in Peking. He headed relief efforts after July's earthquake and last week, in a major speech, he called for the strict restoration of law and order against "class enemies."

Background and Philosophy Cloudy

Little is known about Mr. Hua's personal background or political philosophy. But judging from his few public statements, he seems to share the pragmatism of his late predecessor, Chou, and yet to be keenly aware of the need to use some of the language of Chairman Mao's more radical followers, lest the party be further split.

Whoever emerges as the dominant figure, if anyone, it is possible Peking may not actually fill Mao's place as party chairman in the immediate future. For one thing, it would be a symbolic recognition that no one was capable of succeeding Mao. North Vietnam has never filled Ho Chi Minh's post as party chairman.

Moreover, Peking's leaders may find it

Continued on Page A16, Col. 3

PARTY IN UNITY PLEA

Appeal to People Is Coupled With Delayed Disclosure of Chairman's Death

By Reuters

PEKING, Sept. 9—Mao Tse-tung, the pre-eminent figure of the Chinese Communist revolution and the leader of his country since 1949, died today at the age of 82.

His death, at 12:10 A.M. after a long illness, left uncertain the question of who

Obituary article appears on pages A13-15; text of announcement, page A16.

was to succeed him. There is no designated heir, nor is there anyone among his subordinates who commands the awe and reverence with which he was regarded among the 800 million Chinese.

The party leadership delayed the announcement of Chairman Mao's death for about 16 hours until 4 P.M. [4 A.M. Thursday New York Time]. The announcement included an appeal to the people to uphold the unity of the party that he had headed.

Plea to Follow Mao's Policies

It said China must "continue to carry out Chairman Mao's revolutionary line and policies in foreign affairs resolutely."

It urged the people to "deepen the criticism" of former Deputy Prime Minister Teng Hsiao-ping, who was toppled in the power struggle that followed the death in January of Mao's closest comrade in arms, Prime Minister Chou En-lai.

After the disgrace of Mr. Teng, Hua Kuo-feng, regarded as a centrist, was made Prime Minister and First Deputy Chairman of the party.

Funeral music followed today's announcement broadcast over the Peking radio, and 2,000 people gathered in the vast Tien An Men Square, many wearing black armbands, some weeping. Flags fluttered at half staff.

'Internationale' Heard Across City

"The Internationale," the world Socialist anthem, echoed over the city from loudspeakers at dusk as bicyclists made their way home from work.

Eight days of memorial ceremonies were scheduled to begin Saturday and end Sept. 18 with the entire nation standing in silent tribute for three minutes but with trains, ships and factories sounding sirens.

The announcement said that no foreign leaders would be invited to Peking during the period of mourning.

Chinese embassies abroad, it said, would express gratitude to foreigners wishing to come, but would "inform them of the decision of the Central Committee of our party and the Government of our country not to invite foreign governments, fraternal parties or friendly personages."

It was believed the actual cremation or burial would be attended only by the

Continued on Page A16, Col. 1

Panel on Paperwork Assembling A Litany of Constant Redundancy

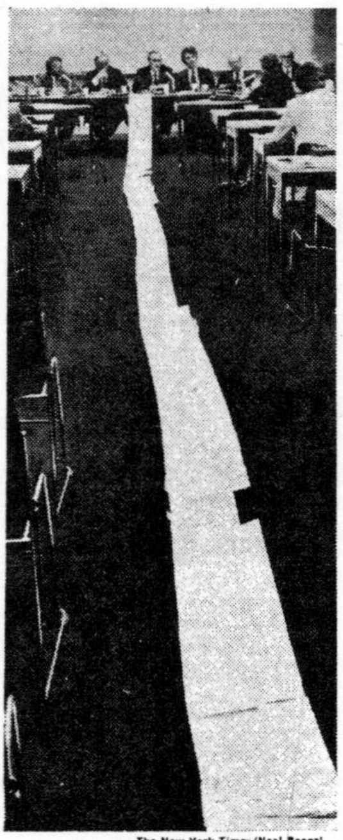

The New York Times/Neal Boenzi

The Commission on Federal Paperwork at the World Trade Center yesterday with a 45-foot string of forms that represents one year's paperwork on a single child on Aid to Dependent Children.

By MOLLY IVINS

The Commission on Federal Paperwork convened in New York City yesterday to communicate on the feasibility of implementing a restriction in the ongoing paperflow.

The commission, which reports to both the Congress and the President, has been assigned the almost insuperable task of doing something about the sea of forms, applications and reports that threatens to engulf everyone.

The members of the commission seem almost awed by the dimensions of the paperwork problem: They estimate that paperwork and red tape cost the nation's economy $40 billion a year, not counting paper clips. But they are making inroads on the problem.

They have a way to go, as was shown by Philip Toia, Commissioner of New York State's Department of Social Services, who arrived trailing a 45-foot-long string of forms—the result of one year's paperwork on a single child in the program of aid to dependent children.

Clients Ping-Ponged

The commission has been holding a series of hearings around the country, and this one focused on the paperwork in income maintenance programs.

James Reed, director of the Monroe County Department of Social Services, explained his department's procedure for Supplemental Security Income recipients. It was a five-minute litany of recipients getting ping-ponged between agencies, punctuated by requirements to fill out 22-page forms.

Tales of the labyrinthine inner workings of assorted New York welfare de-

Continued on Page B18, Col. 1

INSIDE

Spending Limit Voted

Congress has voted to limit spending to about $413 billion, $13 billion more than President Ford has projected, in the fiscal year 1977. Page A18.

British Strike Threat

The British Government and its allies in the labor movement held meetings in an effort to prevent a strike that could damage the economy. Page D1.

Medicaid Law

A new state law intended to prohibit kickbacks by clinical laboratories may actually have legalized the practice, city health officials said. Page B2.

Borman Son Denies Bribe at West Point

By CHARLES KAISER

Special to The New York Times

WEST POINT, N. Y., Sept. 9—Lieut. Frederick P. Borman, a 1974 West Point graduate, categorically denied tonight that he had received $1,200 to change his vote on an honor-code board.

"It's completely false," Lieutenant Borman said of the allegation, part of an affidavit sworn to by two cadets who had been accused of cheating at the United States Military Academy here.

[Lieutenant Borman's father, Frank Borman, the former astronaut who is president of Eastern Airlines, said in an interview with The Associated Press that he had no intention of stepping down as chairman of a five-member special West Point review panel appointed by the Secretary of the Army.

[Robert K. Koster, another cadet accused of cheating in affidavits signed by other cadets, said he had resigned from the Academy. He is the son of Maj. Gen. Samuel W. Koster, a former West Point superintendent who stepped down from his position after charges that, when he commanded the American Division in Vietnam, he had helped to cover up the alleged massacre by American soldiers at My Lai.]

Lieutenant Borman said that he had

Continued on Page A11, Col. 1

"All the News That's Fit to Print"

The New York Times

LATE CITY EDITION

Weather: Partly sunny today; cool tonight. Fair and cooler tomorrow. Temperature range: today 42-58; Tuesday 33-50. Details on page 82.

VOL. CXXVI . . No. 43,383 — © 1976 The New York Times Company — NEW YORK, WEDNESDAY, NOVEMBER 3, 1976 — 25 cents beyond 50-mile zone from New York City, except Long Island. Higher in air delivery cities. — 20 CENTS

CARTER VICTOR IN TIGHT RACE; FORD LOSES NEW YORK STATE; DEMOCRATS RETAIN CONGRESS

Moynihan Defeats Buckley For New York Senate Seat

By MAURICE CARROLL

Daniel P. Moynihan won election to the United States Senate yesterday and shouted jubilantly to a jostling crowd in his headquarters, "It's time we made some claims on the national Government."

Mr. Moynihan topped a cautious campaign that counted on the normal Democratic sympathies of New York voters by easily defeating James L. Buckley, the Conservative-Republican incumbent.

With 12,407 of 13,844 districts reporting, the vote for Senator was:

Moynihan	2,973,200
Buckley	2,517,292

His long gray hair toppling over his forehead and perspiration gleaming on his roundish face, Mr. Moynihan told several hundred supporters in his jammed storefront office on the Avenue of the Americas: "New York was on the ballot—and New York won."

It took almost 10 minutes for Mr. Moynihan to squeeze through the cheering crowd and step to the platform to claim victory.

Six years ago, the cheers had been for Mr. Buckley, who won an unexpected victory as a third-party candidate. But last night, Mr. Moynihan reconstituted much of the traditional Democratic vote—with the exception of some parts of the black community and some liberals disgruntled over his narrow primary-election victory—and it was his turn to congratulate Mr. Buckley for "gracious" concession.

Then Mr. Moynihan headed for a series of celebrations, but today, his wife, Liz, said, he will go to Harvard to teach his customary class there. He did not interrupt his academic chores during the campaign and will not today, she said.

Mr. Moynihan led by 2-to-1 margins in the traditional Democratic territory in

Continued on Page 19, Column 3

Atlantic City Casinos Approved

By MARTIN WALDRON

New Jersey voters yesterday approved Las Vegas-style casinos for Atlantic City, the first on the East Coast, and residents of the shore resort began celebrating as many bars handed out free drinks.

With 4,991 districts of 5,569 reporting, the vote was:

Yes	1,305,800
No	1,015,126

In the state's Congressional contests, Senator Harrison A. Williams Jr., a Democrat, easily won re-election to a fourth term, while Representative Henry Helstoski, a six-term Democrat from the Ninth District who is under indictment on Federal extortion charges, was defeated. Thirteen other incumbents—10 Democrats and three Republicans—won, as did Joseph A. LeFante, also a Democrat, who succeeded the retiring Dominick V. Daniels in Hudson County.

Two years ago, New Jersey voters defeated by more than 400,000 votes an amendment to the State Constitution that would have allowed casinos anywhere in the state.

Promoters of casinos, including Atlantic City's legislative delegation, scheduled a meeting for 9 A.M. today to begin drafting a law to implement the constitutional amendment voted on yesterday.

The Council of Churches and United States Attorney Jonathan L. Goldstein, who was the most vocal opponent of casinos, had predicted that if Atlantic City got casinos, other areas of the state would demand them also.

Mr. Goldstein also warned that gambling casinos were a magnet for organized crime, and said that loan sharks and prostitutes would flock to Atlantic City if casinos were opened there.

In the midst of the noisy crowd in the headquarters of the Committee to Rebuild Atlantic City, an organization of businessmen and public officials who led the drive for the casinos, Mayor Joseph

Continued on Page 28, Column 1

Weicker Wins a 2d Term Easily

By MICHAEL KNIGHT

Special to The New York Times

HARTFORD, Nov. 2—United States Senator Lowell P. Weicker Jr. scored an impressive re-election victory today over Gloria Schaffer, the state's top Democratic vote-getter and the only woman running for the Senate this year.

With all of the state's 169 towns and cities reporting, the unofficial vote was:

Weicker	787,568
Schaffer	559,109

Despite an intensive effort, Mrs. Schaffer, who is Connecticut's Secretary of State, was unable to generate much excitement during the campaign or close the gap between herself and Senator Weicker, the maverick first-term Republican who earned a nationwide reputation in 1973 as a member of the Senate Watergate committee.

The clear-cut result in the senatorial race was in marked contrast to the voting in the Presidential contest in this state, where President Ford defeated Jimmy Carter by a narrow margin.

Mrs. Schaffer won handily, and sometimes even overwhelmingly, in many of the state's ethnic neighborhoods. She carried the black districts of normally Republican Stamford, for example, the Italian and Polish areas of industrial New Britain and the Italian, Irish and black districts of Hartford.

In the Congressional races, all of the state's four Democratic and two Republican United States Representatives won re-election by wide margins. The Representatives from the three western districts—Stewart B. McKinney and Ronald A. Sarasin, Republicans, and Anthony Toby Moffett, a Democrat—had faced the possiblity of an upset.

The Republicans gained seven seats in

Continued on Page 29, Column 1

Jimmy Carter leaves voting booth in Plains, Ga. — United Press International

Walter F. Mondale waiting to vote in Afton, Minn. — Associated Press

Election At a Glance

PRESIDENT

Needed to Win—270 Electoral Votes

	Number of States*	Electoral Votes
Carter	23	272
Ford	23	160

THE SENATE

33 of 100 Members to Be Elected

Newly Elected Senators

Democrats	20
Republicans	8
Independent	1
In Doubt	4

Makeup of the New Senate

Democrats	61
Republicans	37
Independent	1
In Doubt	1

THE HOUSE

All 435 Seats to Be Filled

Democrats Elected	255
Republicans Elected	120
In Doubt	60

*Includes District of Columbia

A guide to election news, page 17.

METZENBAUM BEATS TAFT IN SENATE RACE

Democrat Wins Ohio Contest That Was Clear Test of Philosophies

By WILLIAM K. STEVENS

Special to The New York Times

CLEVELAND, Wednesday, Nov. 3—Robert Taft Jr., bearer of one of the most famous names in national Republican politics, lost his seat in the United States Senate yesterday to former Senator Howard M. Metzenbaum, a Democrat.

The contest between the two was a clear-cut test of orthodox Republican conservatism against classical Democratic liberalism.

With 11,138 of the 13,104 polling places reporting, the tally was:

Metzenbaum	1,637,778
Taft	1,537,830

Mr. Metzenbaum rolled up a sufficient margin of votes in Cuyahoga County (Cleveland) to offset Senator Taft's strength downstate. With 1,700 of 1,727 polling places in the county reporting, the Democrat held a 122,000-vote lead there.

The campaign was a rematch of a 1970 race in which Mr. Taft narrowly defeated Mr. Metzenbaum to win his first Senate term. In losing that election six years ago, Mr. Metzenbaum won 49 percent of the vote.

He also won statewide recognition and sufficient stature within the party to be appointed to the Senate by former Democratic Gov. John J. Gilligan in 1974. Mr. Metzenbaum subsequently ran that year

Continued on Page 24, Column 5

8 Senators Lose Seats, but Lineup Of Parties Stays About the Same

By DAVID E. ROSENBAUM

At least eight incumbent Senators were defeated yesterday, and a ninth was in a close struggle for re-election.

Nonetheless, the Democrats did no worse than retain their current 61-to-38 majority in the Senate, with one seat held by an independent, and they may have picked up one seat.

In the House, the Democrats' 2-to-1 majority was not substantially changed.

The Democratic Senators who lost were Vance Hartke of Indiana, Joseph M. Montoya of New Mexico, Frank E. Moss of Utah and Gale W. McGee of Wyoming.

The other losers were James L. Buckley, Conservative-Republican of New York, and Bill Brock of Tennessee, J. Glenn Beall Jr. of Maryland and Robert Taft Jr. of Ohio, all Republicans.

Senator John V. Tunney, Democrat of California, was in a close race with S. I. Hayakawa, a Republican, who had been president of San Francisco State College.

Fourth-Term Bids Lost

Senator Moss and Senator McGee, both committee chairmen, were defeated in their attempts at fourth terms in the Senate. Mr. Moss lost to Orrin E. Hatch, a lawyer who has never held public office. Mr. McGee lost to a State Senator, Malcolm Wallop. Mr. Hatch and Mr. Wallop are much more conservative than the incumbents.

But, in Ohio, Mr. Taft was beaten by a liberal, Howard W. Metzenbaum, a former Senator whom Mr. Taft beat in 1970.

Senator Robert T. Stafford, Republican of Vermont, won a close victory over Gov. Thomas P. Salmon, his Democratic challenger.

Eight senators, four Republicans and four Democrats, are retiring, but neither party was able to take advantage of the situation to gain in total strength.

Republicans John C. Danforth and John H. Chaffee took Senate seats in Missouri and Rhode Island that are held by retiring Democrats Stuart Symington and John O. Pastore.

Democrats Apparent Winners

But Democrats apparently captured seats in Arizona and Nebraska that are held by Republicans. Dennis DeConcini, a Democratic county prosecutor, was leading in the race for the Arizona seat of Paul J. Fannin, and Mayor Edward Zorinsky was ahead in the race for Roman L. Hruska's race in Nebraska.

In Pennsylvania, Representative H. John Heinz 3d held the seat for the Republicans by narrowly beating Representative William J. Green. Hugh Scott, the Republican leader, is the incumbent.

Senator Philip A. Hart's seat in Michigan was retained for the Democrats by Representative Donald W. Riegle Jr., who defeated Representative Marvin L. Esch, a Republican.

In Montana, Representative John Melcher, a Democrat, easily won the seat now held by Mike Mansfield, the Democratic leader.

The eighth Senate vacancy was that created by the retirement of Hiram L. Fong, Republican of Hawaii. Returns from Hawaii were reported late, but it was widely believed that Representative Spark M. Matsunaga, a Democrat, would win.

In the House, nearly all of the 79 freshmen Democrats, who were the principal targets of the Republicans during the campaign, managed to win re-election.

With half of the House races already

Continued on Page 17, Column 3

GEORGIAN WINS SOUTH

Northern Industrial States Provide Rest of Margin in the Electoral Vote

By R. W. APPLE Jr.

Jimmy Carter won the nation's Bicentennial Presidential election yesterday, narrowly defeating President Ford by sweeping his native South and adding enough Northern industrial states to give him a bare electoral vote majority.

Three of the closely contested battleground states slipped into Mr. Carter's column shortly after midnight—New York, Pennsylvania and Texas. The President-designate lost New Jersey and Michigan, Mr. Ford's home state, while Ohio, Illinois and California were still up for grabs.

New York teetered between the rivals for hours, contrary to all expectations, before delivering a small majority to Mr. Carter—a majority that gave the Democrat a bonanza of 41 electoral votes.

When Mr. Carter finally carried Hawaii by a far narrower margin than customary for Democratic candidates in that Democratic stronghold, it gave the Georgian 272 electoral votes in 23 states, two more than a majority. Mr. Ford had 160 electoral votes in 23 states, and five states were still in doubt.

A Southern Victor

Mr. Carter was the first man from the Deep South to be elected President in a century and a quarter, and Mr. Ford, the nation's first appointive President, was the first incumbent to lose a Presidential election since Herbert Hoover.

Although the President dominated the Plains and Mountain regions, he lost several middle-sized states that he had counted upon. Among them were Louisiana and Mississippi on the Gulf Coast, and Wisconsin, which went to the Democrats for only the second time in a quarter-century as the result of an outpouring of votes from industrial Milwaukee and liberal Madison.

Mr. Carter owed large debts to Mayor Frank L. Rizzo of Philadelphia, who produced the 250,000-vote margin Mr. Carter needed to carry Pennsylvania; to Robert S. Strauss, the Democratic national chairman, who worked tirelessly to put together the Texas operatic , and to the South and the Border states as a whole. The Georgian won every Border state and every Southern state except Virginia, which seemed headed for the Ford column.

Division of Popular Vote

The popular vote, which was swelled by a relatively heavy turnout to roughly the same level as four years ago, appeared likely to split 51 percent for Mr. Carter, 48 for Mr. Ford and 1 for others.

With 81 percent of the nation's precincts reporting, the vote was:

Carter	33,684,344—51 percent
Ford	31,665,958—48 percent

In the metropolitan area, Mr. Carter lost both New Jersey and Connecticut, as his backers had feared he would.

All 25,000 voting machines in New York were ordered impounded by State Supreme Court Justice Edward S. Conway. Acting at the request of state Re-

Continued on Page 17, Column 1

Summary of Other Major News

Articles on the first page of the second part of this issue are:

Indian Amendments Pass

The lower house of India's Parliament passed a sweeping set of constitutional amendments that will shift the balance of power in the Government.

No Accord on Rhodesia

Prime Minister Ian D. Smith of Rhodesia and African nationalist leaders failed to agree on a date for independence of the territory.

Burundi Chief Ousted

Burundi's armed forces deposed the President of the small central African country without violence, according to an official broadcast.

Park Tong Sun Disputed

The Gulf Oil Corporation has disputed a statement by Park Tong Sun that he received $1 million a month from his relationships with the oil company.

State U. Social Clubs

National sororities and fraternities will be allowed on the campuses of the State University of New York after a 23-year ban.

Ouster Held Illegal

The Supreme Court in effect affirmed that a company acted illegally in dismissing an employee for refusing on religious ground to work Saturday.

Pro-Statehood Candidate Stages Puerto Rican Upset

By DAVID VIDAL

Special to The New York Times

SAN JUAN, P.R., Wednesday, Nov. 3—In a staggering upset, San Juan Mayor Carlos Romero Barcelo of the pro-statehood New Progressive Party snatched the governorship of Puerto Rico from the incumbent, Rafael Hernández Colón, sending the Popular Democratic Party to only its second defeat since 1940.

The Governor, speaking to weeping campaign workers, conceded defeat and asked the party faithful "to heed this decision, if confirmed by the final official results, as the will of the people of Puerto Rico."

"That is how I accept it," he said, in a brief statement. He also called for unity but added: "The campaign for 1980 begins tomorrow."

The election was all the more surprising because the New Progressives were also on their way to assuming control of both houses of the Puerto Rican legislature as well as retaining the powerful post of mayor of San Juan.

The results reflected less a mandate for statehood than they did voter discontent with the administrative and economic problems under Mr. Hernández Colón's leadership.

In another surprise, the two parties favoring independence were running behind their 1972 pace.

With 66 of 113 precincts reporting, the tally was:

New Progressive Party	312,055
Popular Democratic Party	297,632
Puerto Rican Independence Party	33,170
Puerto Rican Socialist Party	4,604

A measure of the trend was seen in Barranquitas, considered a stronghold of the Popular Democrats because it was the birthplace of the father of Luis Muñoz Marín, founder of the Popular Democratic Party and of the Commonwealth. The 78-year-old leader came out of political seclusion to campaign there personally over the weekend. The party was losing there, however, as it was in Mayaguez, called the capital of the Popular Democrats.

In 1972, when 84.14 percent of the electorate voted, the Popular Democratic Party won by 85,631 votes, taking 51.2 percent as against 44.01 percent for the New Progressives. Other parties divided the rest.

Although each major party had pre-election polls indicating it would win this year, other polls had shown a high number of undecided voters.

That there was any doubt at all of a Popular Democratic victory was significant and indicated the changing nature of the electorate, of its perception of the party and of the party itself.

For years, islanders had grown accustomed to more and more prosperity under the "bread, land, and liberty" slogan of

Continued on Page 22, Column 5

"All the News That's Fit to Print"

The New York Times

LATE CITY EDITION

Weather: Sunny, hot today; warm tonight. Fair, hot, humid tomorrow. Temperature range: today 70-90; yesterday 73-93. Details, page 30.

VOL.CXXVI ... No.43,636 © 1977 The New York Times Company NEW YORK, THURSDAY, JULY 14, 1977 35 cents beyond 50-mile zone from New York City. Higher in air delivery cities. A 20 CENTS

POWER FAILURE BLACKS OUT NEW YORK; THOUSANDS TRAPPED IN THE SUBWAYS; LOOTERS AND VANDALS HIT SOME AREAS

State Troopers Sent Into City As Crime Rises

Some Civilians Assist Police – '65 Blackout Peaceful in Contrast

By LAWRENCE VAN GELDER

Thousands of looters, emboldened by darkness and confusion, ranged through the city last night and early today in a wave of lawlessness.

Amid shattering glass, wailing sirens, and the clang of trashcans used to demolish metal storefront barricades, thieves and vandals ravaged store after store.

Governor Carey ordered the state police into the city to assist the local police.

At the same time, other people left their homes to help direct traffic in the suddenly darkened streets. Often armed with flashlights, they took up their impromptu stations at intersections and guided drivers and pedestrians.

Hundreds of Arrests

By 2 o'clock this morning, the police reported a total of 880 arrests, almost all for looting in Manhattan, the Bronx, Brooklyn, and Queens. In downtown Brooklyn and in East Harlem, where looting and rock and bottle-throwing were reported, several policemen were listed as casualties.

"It's a lot different from 10 years ago," said Daisy Voight, referring to the blackout of 1965 as she emerged from a meeting in Harlem. "Last time people were helpful. This time people are scared. They are running for buses or bars. Everybody's afraid to go out."

In Brooklyn, standing guard at an ice cream store in the downtown area at Fulton Street near Adams, the owner watched youths racing by.

"They're crazy," he shouted. "They're taking their shoes and breaking windows. They're animals. They should be put in jail and throw the key away. The cops are doing the best they can. There are about 500 kids in the street."

So accelerated was the police effort against the onslaught of looters in Brooklyn that officers bringing prisoners into the central booking facility in the 84th precinct stationhouse, at 301 Gold Street, did not wait as usual to fill out papers.

As quickly as they could, the hard pressed police—regular patrols augmented by colleagues who had responded to appeals to report to work—deposited their prisoners and returned to the battle ground.

Mayor and Officers Meet

At 1:40 A.M. after meeting at Police Headquarters with his major commissioners to review the blackout situation, Mayor Beame characterized the looting as "sporadic." The Mayor said the police were "addressing all problems."

Vandalism and looting were reported in

Continued on Page B

The New York Times/D. Gorton

A view of the darkened New York City skyline taken from New Jersey during blackout last night.

Some Led Others by Flashlight, Some Knocked on Doors to Help

By DEIRDRE CARMODY

It is the New Yorker's real badge of pride — not the little red-apple lapel pins — that whatever else can be said about them, one truth is undeniable: New Yorkers know how to cope when trouble strikes their city.

And cope they did last night.

Some rushed undaunted into chaotic intersections and began to direct traffic. Those who had flashlights led others, Pied Piper-like, up darkened stairwells in buildings where elevators were dormant.

In the Excelsior apartment building, at 57th Street and Seventh Avenue, Roy Svendson, the manager, and members of his staff knocked on every apartment door and asked if anyone needed oxygen. They found only one lady who did, but their very helpfulness bolstered spirits and subdued a bit of the terror those who lived alone were beginning to feel.

In the cavernous waiting room of Grand Central Terminal, hundreds of people coped by simply waiting until the trains would be ready to run again. They were somber and bored and tired and hot, but they sat there and waited.

At one point, a bagpiper came through and played for about five minutes near the big clock that remained stubbornly at 9:35. Some people held flashlights by the telephone booth so that others could dial home and reassure the people there that they were safe, albeit bored.

"Where are all those kids now with the transistor radios," muttered one passerby.

On the corner of Madison Avenue and 65th Street, a woman in a bare-backed dress and a slouched straw hat, looking the personification of East Side dinnertime chic, raced into the intersection and began to direct traffic. Dramatically but efficiently, she spread her arms. Suddenly the

Continued on Page B

Westchester Dark; Long Island's Power Interrupted Briefly

By TOM GOLDSTEIN

Although all of Westchester County was without power last night, no serious traffic or crime problems were reported.

"All's quiet," said Charles G. McLaughlin, chief of Rye Police Department. "We have a nice quiet community under any circumstances."

Hammering rainstorms hit certain parts of the county, temporarily clogging traffic. Most of the nearly 900,000 county residents who were out headed home.

On Long Island, which is served by the Long Island Lighting Company, a spokes-

Continued on Page B

Lightning Bolt: How It Struck

By JOHN NOBLE WILFORD

The blackout had its beginning in the thunderclouds that gathered last night over Westchester County. Lightning struck in the vicinity of Consolidated Edison's Indian Point Nuclear Power Plant 3, and major power transmission lines were short-circuited.

This tripped relays, shutting down transformers and other power plants throughout the New York metropolitan area, according to Con Ed officials.

Norman Terrevi, assistant vice president for transmission operations for Con Edison, said that several "massive lighting bolts" struck the 345,000-volt power lines several times. Those hit were major feeder lines running from Pleasant Valley in Dutchess County to New York City.

Reports from Indian Point indicated that there was no damage to the nuclear power plant and no threat of radiation leakage. However, state troopers had the area blocked off. People in the area reported seeing the sky light up around Buchan, near Indian Point, at 10:45 P.M. The strange light and a "whirling sound" lasted 10 seconds, witnesses reported.

Joyce Tucker, Con Edison's acting vice

Continued on Page B

Westchester Is Also Darkened After Lightning Hits Line

By ROBERT D. McFADDEN

A power failure plunged New York City and Westchester County into darkness last night, disrupting the lives of nearly nine million people.

Spokesmen for the Consolidated Edison Company said that power for all of its 2.8 million customers would not be restored until late this morning.

By 2 A.M., the utility had restored power to 150,000 customers in the Jamaica, Flushing, Queens Village and Kew Gardens sections of Queens, and to 50,000 customers in the Pleasantville area in Westchester County.

Though not as big as the nine-state blackout that hit the Northeast in November 1965, last night's power failure was in some respects an uglier experience. There was widespread looting in Manhattan, the Bronx and Brooklyn, and four hours after the blackout began, the police had arrested nearly 900 people.

Several thousand subway riders were trapped in trains between stations—but nowhere near the masses stranded 12 years ago during the rush hour.

Uprising in Bronx Jail

Thousands more were trapped last night in elevators. Homes and apartments went black. People stumbled and streamed from theaters, restaurants and late-closing shops and office buildings. In some sections, crowds milled in the streets into the early morning hours.

Prisoners in the House of Detention in the Bronx briefly took over a guard house after setting fires on four floors. The backup power in two major hospitals failed. Fires erupted in various sections of the city.

Kennedy International and LaGuardia Airports both closed, and flights were diverted to Newark, Boston and other cities.

As the ordeal continued through the night and into the morning, there were no reports of deaths or serious injuries.

The blackout struck the city shortly after 9:30 P.M. in stages, after lightning hit a major Consolidated Edison electrical transmission line in northern Westchester County. Like dominoes toppling through Westchester and the city, circuit breakers on successively overloaded transmission lines went off automatically.

Early this morning Charles F. Luce, the chairman of Con Edison, noted that the utility's entire system of circuit breakers would have to be reset and all power lines and generators inspected, a task that he said would take until at least 8 A.M.

"When we are sure everything is set to go, we can bring the power back slowly," he said. Another utility spokesman said that the restoration would have to proceed cautiously to avoid another systemwide shutdown.

The blackout came only three days after Mr. Luce said on television that there was no immediate danger of a major blackout

Continued on Page B

To Our Readers

This is a special blackout edition of The New York Times. Regular pages of the paper's City Edition, prepared before the electrical power failed, appear inside the paper, starting on the first right-hand page. News and pictures of the blackout appear on the first two pages.

When the power failed, only a handful of copies of The Times had come off the presses in New York. Pages were taken to the plant of The Record in Hackensack, N.J., where they were photographed. Offset printing took place at The Times's satellite plant in Carlstadt, N.J.

For mechanical reasons, the size of the newspaper was limited to 40 pages, and the most important news pages were selected. Therefore, the "continued" guidelines for some articles give incorrect page numbers, as do some references in the News Summary and Index.

This page and the one following were prepared using copy and photographs provided by The Times, at The Record's plant. The Times expresses its appreciation to The Record.

Riders Safely Flee the Subway Though Some Swelter Hours

By RALPH BLUMENTHAL

Thousands of home-bound travelers were trapped in subway tunnels and along suburban railroad lines by last night's blackout.

There were no initial reports of panic, however, and although many trains remained stranded in sweltering tunnels at least two hours after the blackout began, many others were able to coast into stations and discharge passengers with ease.

In a subway tunnel at Broadway at 19th Street, for example, Officer Thomas Duffey of the Transit Authority Police guided 1,500 passengers out of a train without incident.

But George Thune, a Long Island Rail Road aide, said passengers on 12 to 14 commuter trains backed up and stranded by the power loss in Jamaica, Queens, were still awaiting buses at 11 P.M.

Trains drawing power from the Long Island Lighting Company, which was unaffected by the blackout, were able to get through, as were diesel trains on the nonelectrified portion of the line in Eastern Long Island.

Outside Grand Central Terminal, cabdrivers called out "Yonkers and Westchester," attracting a steady stream of commuters. Inside the station at 11 P.M., passengers waited in the subway aboard a Lexington Avenue downtown express.

The Times Square subway concourse was crowded with people waiting for news and snacking on donuts and fried chicken from subway stands.

The Transit Authority said that the impact on the system was lightened by quick action by transit officials and workers.

"At 9:30 sharp we began getting power surges and A.C. power failures, which took the form of signal blackouts," Jacques Nevard, an authority official, said. "Motormen started calling the train masters. The train masters have dispatchers in a ring around them, and some time between 9:30 and 9:34 they put out the word by radio to the motormen to move immediately to the closest station.

"They anticipated we may be in for a failure, so they took the precaution of ordering all trains moving to stations. As a result of approximately 150 trains normally operating at that time, only seven, as of reports of 11:30 P.M., were caught between stations."

The seven stuck trains listed by Mr. Nevard were an IRT train north of 125th Street and Lexington Avenue, an AA local on Cen-

Continued on Page B

Bellevue Patients Resuscitated With Hand-Squeezed Air Bags

By LAWRENCE K. ALTMAN

Doctors and nurses at Bellevue Hospital had to squeeze bags of air with their hands to resuscitate patients in respiratory failure after the municipal hospital's emergency backup power supply failed at 10:10 P.M. last night.

Bellevue was one of a number of hospitals in the blacked-out area whose emergency generators — ordered after the power failure of 1965 — were unable to supply power.

About 15 Bellevue patients were on mechanical respirators in six intensive care units when the power failed. But as of midnight, officials said there had been no deaths in the hospital as a result of the power failure.

Doctors resorted to squeezing the airbags by hand to breathe for the patients. Airbags were the only form of resuscitation available before mechanical respirators became the standard form of treatment in recent years.

At 11:50 P.M., Bellevue officials closed the emergency room and referred all prospective patients to other hospitals. Bellevue was described as dark with islands of lights.

A visitor to Bellevue found the scene confused but without panic as doctors and nurses, working with flashlights, occasionally bumped into beds and intravenous feeding equipment.

"There's no real cause for concern because we can bag-breathe [for the patients] for hours," one physician said.

At Bellevue, there were no women in labor, and no patients undergoing surgery at the time the backup power supply failed.

Bellevue's diesel auxiliary generator responded immediately to the Con Edison power failure, but the backup supply went out a few minutes later, according to Felix Calabrese, associate executive director of the hospital.

Emergency backup generators to supply hospitals with power were made mandatory by legislation after the 1965 blackout. Such units were intended to supply enough power to keep life-supporting mechanical equipment running during a power failure.

After the Bellevue emergency system failed, police and fire officials took auxiliary power units to Bellevue and Metropolitan Hospitals to help keep such equipment running.

At the New York Hospital-Cornell Medical Center, New York University Hospital, the Veterans Administration Hospital at 24th Street, and other hospitals, officials reported that the backup generators were meeting critical needs.

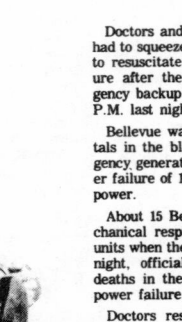

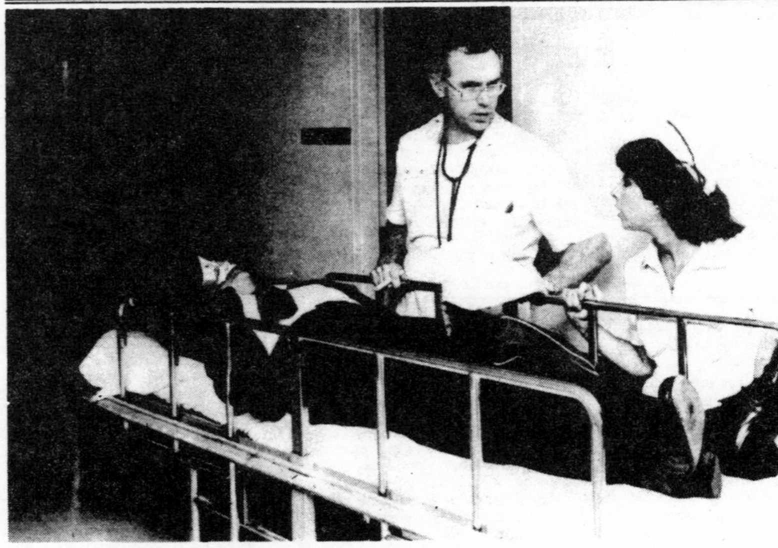

The New York Times

A doctor and a nurse aiding an injured motorist in the darkened emergency room of Bellevue Hospital last night.

"All the News That's Fit to Print"

The New York Times

CITY EDITION

Weather: Cold, snow late today into tonight. Partial clearing tomorrow. Temperature range: today 27-36; yesterday 44-49. Details, page D14.

VOL. CXXVII....No. 43,881 — NEW YORK, THURSDAY, MARCH 16, 1978 — 25 cents beyond 50-mile zone from New York City. Higher in air delivery cities. 20 CENTS

ISRAELIS SEIZE A 63-MILE 'SECURITY BELT' IN LEBANON AND SAY TROOPS WILL REMAIN; WASHINGTON SEES 'IMPEDIMENTS TO PEACE'

Senate Backers Of Canal Treaty Sure of Victory

Say They Have Votes to Win Roll-Call Today

By ADAM CLYMER

Special to The New York Times

WASHINGTON, March 15—Senate supporters of the Panama Canal treaties said today that they had enough votes to win tomorrow's crucial roll-call on the first of the pacts.

On the eve of one of the most important foreign policy votes in many years, Senator Howard H. Baker Jr., the minority leader, told reporters he now believed that the treaty guaranteeing the neutrality of the canal after American control ends in the year 2000 would be approved. And the effective leader of the opposition, Senator Paul Laxalt, Republican of Nevada, characterized the situation as "not so good."

In a day of intense lobbying, beginning when Vice President Mondale appeared unannounced at the office of Senator Wendell H. Ford, Democrat of Kentucky, at 7:15 A.M., none of the uncommitted senators, including Mr. Ford, announced that they would vote against the treaty.

Two New Votes in Favor

Two uncommitted senators, Edward W. Brooke, Republican of Massachusetts, and Dennis DeConoini, Democrat of Arkansas, said they would vote for the neutrality treaty. Mr. Brooke, however, said he might vote later against the treaty turning over he canal and he canal zone to Panama.

The backing of Mr. Brooke and Mr. DeConcini, plus the expected support of Senator Bob Packwood, Republican of Oregon, gave the treaty supporters 65 votes they could count on. hey would not say where they expected to get the two more votes they needed to make up the 67 required for approval.

There were still four uncommitted senators available and at least the chance of shaking one or two antitreaty senators loose. One of the the uncommitted, Senator Henry Bellmon, Republican of Oklahoma, was to announce his stand tomorrow at 9 A.M., and Senator Edward Zorinsky,

Continued on Page A3, Column 1

CAPITAL SYMPATHETIC

U.S. Officials Relieved That Heavy Combat Activity Is Apparently Over

By BERNARD GWERTZMAN

Special to The New York Times

WASHINGTON, March 15—Israel's invasion of southern Lebanon evoked a sympathetic response from the United States today, but Secretary of State Cyrus R. Vance conceded that the Israeli attack and the Palestinian raid that inspired it had raised "impediments to the peace process."

The general mood at the highest levels of the Administration was relief this afternoon that the main fighting seemed at an end.

The evidence that the Israelis were confining their ground operations to a six-mile-deep belt along the border reduced the likelihood that the Syrians would enter the conflict and spread the warfare; one high official said.

Begin Statement Causes Worry

In Beirut, however, Syrian and Lebanese officials appealed for international help in obtaining Israeli withdrawal. [Page A17.] In Cairo, Foreign Minister Mohammed Ibrahim Kamel denounced the Israeli action as "organized genocide" and said that it harmed Egyptian peace efforts. [Page A17.]

American officials said that with Prime Minister Menachem Begin due in Washington next Monday for talks with President Carter on Tuesday and Wednesday, the chances for diplomatic progreess, already dim, were now more remote.

A new problem has now arisen, officials said, over a statement by Mr. Begin today that Israeli forces would remain in the belt of Lebanese territory until an agreement was reached to prevent the Palestinians from returning to the area.

The United States, a strong backer of Lebanon's sovereignty and integrity, wants the Israelis to withdraw as soon as possible and the withdrawal issue undoubtedly will now become a major topic during Mr. Begin's talks with Mr. Carter, officials said.

Late this afternoon, Ambassador Simcha Dinitz of Israel conferred for 90 minutes with Alfred L. Atherton Jr., the Administration's top Middle East negotiator, to discuss the Israeli presence in

Continued on Page A17, Column 6

Associated Press

Israel's Prime Minister, Menachem Begin, left, arriving at the border with Lebanon yesterday for a close look at the action. Defense Minister Ezer Weizman is at center, wearing flight jacket and sunglasses.

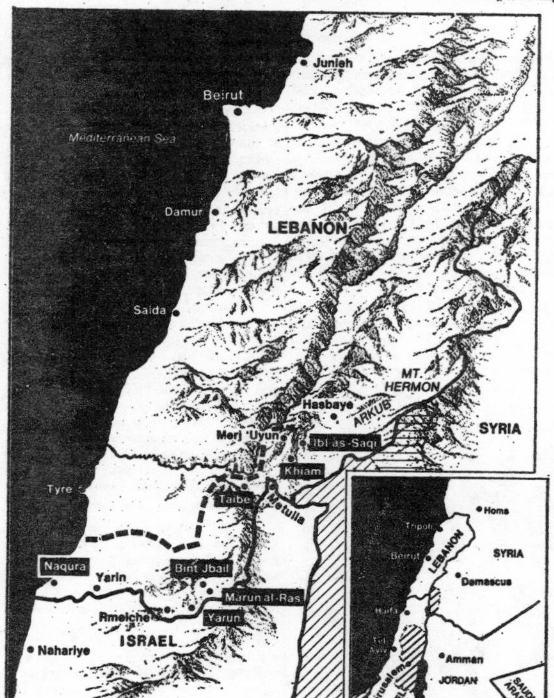

The New York Times/John Leinung/March 16, 1978

Israelis established "security belt" in southern Lebanon after capturing Palestinian strongholds [marked by panels]. Israeli gunboats attacked Tyre, and jets ranged from there up the coast to Beirut area.

Guerrillas Join Civilian Retreat From Attackers

By MARVINE HOWE

Special to The New York Times

TYRE, Lebanon, March 15 — Many Palestinian and Lebanese families fled in panic today from population centers in southern Lebanon that had been bombarded by Israeli fighter-bombers, gunboats and artillery.

"We're going north, anywhere, to get away from the shelling," said Mohammed Ahmed al-Mohammed, a Lebanese farmer, as he and his family of 12 set out on foot along the Tyre-Nabatiye road carrying only small bundles of blankets and clothing.

While young Lebanese and Palestinian guerrillas in the towns and villages spoke of their "fierce resistance," it was clear they were retreating in face of the heavy Israeli odds.

"We are not going to let ourselves be annihilated," said a member of the Palestine Liberation Organization's southern military command at Saida. "We cannot destroy the Israeli forces, but we can inflict as many casualties as possible and then make a tactical withdrawal."

The Palestinian military spokesman confirmed reports that the joint Palestinian-Lebanese leftist forces had lost their principal positions in the border area: Khiam, Ibl es Saqi and Taibe in the east, Bint Jbail and Marun al-Ras in the center and Naqura and Alma 'al-Chaab in the southwest.

The city of Tyre was a prime target as the main port of entrv for arms sup-

Continued on Page A16, Column 3

MAJOR FIGHTING ENDS

Forces Rout the Palestinians in Border Strongholds —Planes Bomb Bases

By WILLIAM E. FARRELL

Special to The New York Times

JERUSALEM, March 15—Israeli forces routed Palestinian guerrillas today from at least seven strongholds in southern Lebanon, and Prime Minister Menachem Begin said the troops would remain until an agreement was reached to insure that the area could never again be used for raids against Israel.

With land, sea and air operations continuing from the Mediterranean to the foothills of Mount Hermon, Israelis occupied what Lieut. Gen. Mordechai Gur, the Chief of Staff, called a "security belt" along the 63 miles of its northern border, with a depth of four and a half to six miles. Late tonight, General Gur said the major fighting was over.

Mr. Begin's remarks about how long Israelis would remain in Lebanon were echoed by Defense Minister Ezer Weizman, who told reporters:

Israeli Withdrawal Demanded

"We shall continue to clear the area—prevent the area from being attack positions against us as long as we find it necessary."

The suggestion of a prolonged Israeli presence in southern Lebanon seemed likely to provoke international controversy. Even as the military drive continued, calls were being raised for Israel to withdraw.

The ground offensive, the largest that Israel has ever carried out against Palestinians, was accompanied by air strikes against Palestinian enclaves and camps far north of the Israeli border, including at least two in the vicinity of Beirut.

The Israeli Army spokesman announced that Israeli planes had bombed a Palestinian base near Damur, about 20 miles south of Beirut, which he said had been the staging area for the Arab raiders who infiltrated into Israel on Saturday and seized a bus.

Syrians Said to Fire on Planes

The seizure touched off a wild ride on the Haifa-Tel Aviv highway, with shooting and an explosion that led to the death of 35 Israelis and an American and the injury of more than 70 persons.

The army spokesman said that Israeli planes had struck targets at the Mediterranean port of Tyre and at a site near Beirut that the spokesman described as a Palestine Liberation Organization training and supply base "for terrorist naval units and for their equipment."

In the raid at Damur, the spokesman said the Israeli planes had been fired on by a Syrian guerrilla unit. The Israeli planes did not fire back at the Syrians, he said, and returned safely to base.

The Syrians have a large military

Continued on Page A16, Column 4

Soviet Reportedly Cool to Linking Cuban, Somali Pullout in Ethiopia

By RICHARD BURT

Special to The New York Times

WASHINGTON, March 15—Contrary to what reporters were told at the State Department last week, the Soviet Union has given little sign that it is prepared to link the end of Somali-Ethiopian fighting with cuts in Cuban forces in Ethiopia, government officials said today.

They said Ambassador Anatoly F. Dobrynin, at a meeting with Secretary of State Cyrus R. Vance on Saturday, declined to commit Moscow on the future of either its own advisers or the Cuban forces.

The previous evening, reporters were told that Moscow said the Cuban forces, estimated at 12,000, would be reduced once Somalia ended its occupation of Ogaden, an ethnic Somali region of Ethiopia. The reporters were also told that the Soviet Union had agreed to have neutral observers monitor a cease-fire. The information was supplied as "deep background," meaning that it could not be attributed.

Pullout Up to Cuba and Ethiopia

Today, a high-ranking State Department official said the information had been based on a previous "direct conversation" between Mr. Vance and Mr. Dobrynin. However, at their Saturday meeting, the Soviet envoy said the withdrawal of Cuba's forces from Ethiopia had to be taken up with those two governments, the official said..

The State Department spokesman, Hodding Carter 3d, announced that the Somali pullout, begun last week, was now complete, and he called on Moscow to facilitate the withdrawal of the Cuban troops and of the 1,000 Soviet advisers in Ethiopia.

Privately, State Department and White House officials said the Russians had been unwilling to discuss concrete plans for withdrawing the Cubans or establishing a truce-observation group.

"We have no evidence from Moscow or anywhere else that the Soviets are inclined to be cooperative on the Horn," said one White House official.

Officials expressed doubts over the likelihood of an early reduction in the

Continued on Page A6, Column 1

6 Guilty in Attack At Washington Sq.

By GREGORY JAYNES

Six of nine young men charged with taking part in a 1976 rampage in Washington Square Park that left one man dead and 13 persons injured were found guilty yesterday—three of manslaughter and three of lesser charges.

The verdict was delivered, after a nine-week trial and six days of deliberation, while a number of the defendants' parents wept in a closed courtroom in State Supreme Court in Manhattan. Parents of the three men found not guilty also cried.

Sentencing was scheduled for April 19 before Justice Robert Haft, in whose court the trial was held. Those convicted of manslaughter could be sentened to as much as 25 years.

Calling the crime "one of great social severity," Assistant District Attorney John Moscow, the prosecutor, said tht "the people will ask for imprisonment for all" those convicted.

During the trial, Mr. Moscow argued that the nine defendants had planned the atck on Washington Square to clear the park of blacks and Hispanic persons.

Of the nine defendants, one, Robert

Continued on Page B6, Column 1

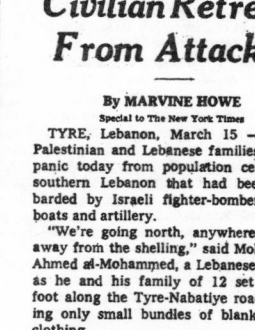

United Press International

Palestinian refugees fleeing from Damur, Lebanon, following Israeli air strikes yesterday

INSIDE

Parking Rules Reinstated

Alternate-side-of-the-street parking regulations are reinstated to let sweepers get at a 62-day accumulation of slushy litter. Page B1.

Soviet Curbs Rostropovich

The Soviet Union revoked the citizenship of the expatriate cellist Mstislav Rostropovich and his wife, Galina Vishnevskaya. Page A10.

Death-Penalty Debate

The emotional debate over capital punishment has shaken legislators in Albany, splitting some from their families and constituents. Page B12.

Rise in Fuel Prices Urged

Presidential action to raise fuel prices if Congress fails to enact the energy program was urged by G. William Miller the Federal Reserve chief. Page D1.

News Summary and Index, Page B1

"All the News That's Fit to Print"

The New York Times

LATE CITY EDITION

Weather: Rain, windy today, tonight; partly sunny and milder tomorrow. Temperature range: today 47-55; yesterday 40-62. Details, page B6.

VOL. CXXVII....No. 43,915 | NEW YORK, WEDNESDAY, APRIL 19, 1978 | 20 CENTS

25 cents beyond 50-mile zone from New York City. Higher in air delivery cities.

SENATE VOTES TO GIVE UP PANAMA CANAL; CARTER FORESEES 'BEGINNING OF A NEW ERA'

Associated Press

President Carter shaking hands with Gabriel Lewis, Panama's Ambassador to the U.S., after Senate vote

NARROW 68-32 VICTORY

Two-Thirds Majority Gained With One Vote to Spare, as in Earlier Success

By ADAM CLYMER

Special to The New York Times

WASHINGTON, April 18—The Senate voted today to turn over the Panama Canal to Panama on Dec. 31, 1999, moving to establish a new spirit of relations with Latin America and saving President Carter from a grave political defeat.

With one vote to spare, the Senate voted to approve a treaty giving up a

Text of Senate reservation, page A16.

symbol of American power and engineering that gripped the minds of so many of their constituents..

The vote of 68 to 32, one more than the two-thirds majority required by the Constitution, was identical to one by which the Senate approved a treaty on March 16 that guarantees the neutrality of the canal. The outcome was in doubt until just before the historic roll-call at 6 P.M.

New Battle Looms

Today's vote settles an issue that has existed since Panama seceded from Colombia in 1903 and entered into a treaty with the United States. It also effectively ended a 13-year negotiating process, although some financial details remain to be resolved by both Houses of Congress, probably next year.

That is expected to be the next battleground. Under an amendment agreed to last night formal ratification will be delayed until the implementing legislation is approved or until March 31, 1979, whichever comes earlier. Six months after the formal ratification, the United States will surrender large parts of the Canal Zone and a gradual Panamanian takeover will begin.

In television remarks after the vote, President Carter said, "This is a day of which Americans can always feel proud; for now we have reminded the world and ourselves of the things that we stand for as a nation."

'Mutual Respect and Partnership'

"These treaties can mark the beginning of a new era in our relations not only with Panama but with all the rest of the world," he said. "They symbolize our determination to deal with the developing nations of the world, the small nations of the world, on the basis of mutual respect and partnership."

Mr. Carter said Panama's Ambassador, Gabriel Lewis Galindo, had informed him that the country's leader, Brig. Gen. Omar Torrijos Herrera, would accept the treaties with the Senate's changes. He added that he had been invited to visit Panama and "I would like very much to accept."

The victory was critical for President Carter, who had repeatedly told wavering senators that his ability to conduct foreign affairs hung in the balance. But the

Continued on Page A16, Column 1

ITALIANS FAIL TO FIND MORO'S BODY IN AREA CITED BY ABDUCTORS

Searchers Sent to Mountain Lake Report Unbroken Ice Cover and No Tracks in the Snow

By HENRY TANNER

Special to The New York Times

ROME, April 18—Italian security forces on skis and in helicopters today staged a vain search for the body of Aldo Moro, the political leader, after his kidnappers had said in a statement that he was dead and that his body had been thrown into a mountain lake about 75 miles northeast of here.

The searchers at Lake Duchessa, 5,000 feet high in the Abruzzi Mountains, found the lake covered with a blanket of ice and no human tracks on the steep snow-covered slopes around it.

Toward evening, officials of Mr. Moro's Christian Democratic Party said they had reached the tentative conclusion that the terrorists' statement was a diversionary maneuver, perhaps to make it easier to move Mr. Moro from one hiding place to another.

Statement Found in Garbage Can

There was little doubt about the authenticity of the statement in which the Red Brigades, the terrorist group, announced Mr. Moro's execution by means of suicide. The statement was found in a garbage can in the center of Rome by a staff member of the newspaper Il Messaggero after it had received an anonymous phone call. Contrary to earlier messages from the Red Brigades, this one was not simultaneously distributed in Milan, Turin and Genoa.

Today marked the 30th anniversary of Christian Democratic government in Italy. The party's first Cabinet was formed on April 18, 1948, by Alcide de Gasperi. A spectacular move by the publicity-conscious kidnappers had therefore been expected.

The terrorists' statement, titled "The Trial of Aldo Moro," took note of the

Continued on Page A10, Column 4

High Court Bars Networks' Right To Nixon Tapes

Indicates U.S. Agency Could Allow Release

By WARREN WEAVER Jr.

Special to The New York Times

WASHINGTON, April 18—The Supreme Court today refused to give broadcasters and recording companies the right to copy, broadcast and sell excerpts from the White House tapes that led to the resignation of President Nixon and the criminal conviction of four of his aides.

Dividing 7 to 2, the Justices concluded that the networks had no constitutional right that was enforceable in the courts to reproduce and circulate the taped material because Congress had established a system for access to the tapes.

Texts of the taped material were printed in full at the time of the Watergate trial. The Court majority indicated today that anyone seeking sound reproductions of the tapes could apply to the General Services Administrator for permission under the Presidential Recordings Act of 1974.

No Guidelines for Access

The decision involved only the 30 tapes, covering about 22 hours of White House conversations, that were played at the Watergate trial. Eventually, as a result of the procedures that could be adopted under the recordings act, the tapes may become available for copying and broadcast. But uncertainty as to the procedure to be used, which will require further lower court consideration, makes any action in the near future unlikely.

The Court declined to give the administrator any guidelines for regulating public access to the tapes in the interests of privacy or executive privilege, saying the case before it did not require such a ruling.

In separate dissenting opinions, Associate Justices Thurgood Marshall and John Paul Stevens said that they believed Congress had intended that the tapes be made fully available to the public, includ-

Continued on Page A20, Column 3

New Chancellor Would Reward Schools That Improved Reading

By MARCIA CHAMBERS

Frank J. Macchiarola, the New York City public-school system's next Chancellor, said yesterday that he hoped to find a way to give extra money to schools that improved pupils' reading scores.

At the same time, he was critical of the state and Federal systems that first funnel compensatory funds to poverty areas where pupils often read below grade level and then may cut off the school districts if the areas improve economically or scholastically. A school may improve, Mr. Macchiarola said, but there is often a dangerous regression once the funds are removed.

At his first news conference and in an interview following his designation Monday as Chancellor, Mr. Macchiarola drew the broad outlines of his educational and fiscal philosophy and the direction he hopes the nation's largest school system will take during his tenure.

Dr. Macchiarola, the 37-year-old vice president for institutional advancement at the Graduate School of the City University, and the man who won Mayor Koch's endorsement for Chancellor, said his first priority would be to get everyone in the schools to understand "that we can do the job."

In an interview, he said excellence had to be rewarded not only to stress achievement, but, also to demonstate that many public schools were working well. Then, he said, middle-class parents will want to send their children to the city's schools.

"I think when somebody does a job you've got to pat that person on the back, and say well done," Mr. Macchiarola said. "The scale of excellence and the scale of failure is a very minuscule portion of our focus. I want to broaden that scale so that the category of excellence is one that we focus on. If you try to hit that level, inevitably others aspire to it."

Cites Success in Brooklyn

He said that an incentive system that gives financial rewards to schools that improve their reading scores had been success in District 22, in Brooklyn, where, until his taking office as Chancellor, he serves as president of the school board.

The reward was based on the ranking a school achieved on the annual citywide reading examination. Mr. Macchiarola agreed with some parents' criticism that the citywide test was given too much importance in pupil evaluation, but he said it was one measure "and not the only measure" for helping him "determine who is doing the job and who is not doing the job."

In the interview, Mr. Macchiarola said

Continued on Page B5, Column 3

PANAMANIAN LEADER ACCEPTS CANAL PACTS

Torrijos Says Approval by Senate Is Great Triumph for Nation

By ALAN RIDING

Special to The New York Times

PANAMA, April 18—Panama's leader, Brig. Gen. Omar Torrijos Herrera, accepted the new canal treaties as amended by the United States Senate tonight and declared their approval to be "one of the greatest and most awaited triumphs" in this country's history.

As firecrackers exploded and sirens wailed across Panama City, General Torrijos told a nationwide radio and television audience moments after the Senate vote, "I feel proud that I have fulfilled my mission."

Clearly seeking to stir up enthusiasm after weeks of mounting opposition to the treaties, the Government urged the people to celebrate the victory in the streets, and excited crowds gathered in the May 5 Plaza close to the United States-controlled Canal Zone.

The 48-year-old general, who has ruled Panama since 1968, declared tomorrow a national holiday and announced that some 100 political exiles could immediately return to Panama and that banned political parties might soon be legalized.

The new treaties, the result of 13 years of negotiations, recognize Panama's jurisdiction over the 553-square-mile Canal Zone and provide for the handing over of the canal itself on Dec. 31, 1999. Pana-

Continued on Page A16, Column 4

United Press International

Italian security forces preparing to fly to Lake Duchessa from Valle del Salto in search for Aldo Moro

Yanks Deny Abuses On Stadium's Lease

Al Rosen, president of the New York Yankees, said yesterday that a "thorough review" by the club's fiscal experts had shown "no evidence of impropriety" in its financial dealings with New York City, which rebuilt and owns Yankee Stadium.

He said that officers of the club remained "willing to meet with any responsible official who claims to have tangible evidence that there has been a violation of our lease."

The comments, in a statement and interview at the Stadium, came a month after Comptroller Harrison J. Goldin opened an investigation into "maintenance costs" at the Stadium. Under the terms of the lease, the Yankees were able to reduce the rent due to the city by more than $1.5 million the team said it paid in maintenance costs.

Yankee front-office executives conceded that the allegation by Comptroller Goldin that $65 of the cost of a commercial by Catfish Hunter, Yankee pitcher, in 1976, had been mistakenly charged to the city as a maintenance cost. But they added that this had been corrected when

Continued on Page D16, Column 1

Basic Provisions of Treaties

WASHINGTON, April 18—Following are the basic provisions of the two treaties that provide for turning over control of the Panama Canal to Panama by the year 2000 and for the permanent neutrality of the canal thereafter.

Panama Canal Treaty

THE CANAL: Panama will assume "full responsibility for the management, operation and maintenance of the canal" on the termination of the treaty at noon Dec. 31, 1999. Until then the canal will be operated by a new United States agency, Canal Commission, whose board will include five Americans and four Panamanians.

THE CANAL ZONE: Panama will assume jurisdiction of the 533-square-mile zone when the treaty comes into force, but the zone will be integrated into Panama over 30 months.

DEFENSE: The United States will continue to have primary responsibility for the defense of the canal until expiration of the treaty in 1999, but will establish with Panama a combined board of officers for consultation and cooperation on defense matters.

SEA LEVEL CANAL: Under the treaty, the United States will agree to negotiate only with Panama for construction of a sea-level canal across Central America, and Panama will agree not to undertake such a project except with the United States.

RESERVATIONS: The Senate adopted a measure yesterday allowing the United States to use its forces unilaterally if necessary. But another reservation specifies that any intervention would be only to keep the canal open, not to interfere in Panama's internal affairs. Another measure adopted by the Senate would nullify the mutually exclusive comitment on a new canal.

Neutrality Treaty

DEFENSE: After the treaty comes into effect on Dec. 31, 1999, the United States and Panama will each have the right to defend the canal against threats to its neutrality or to the peaceful transit of ships.

TRANSIT: Panama pledges to keep the canal open to "peaceful transit" by all nations, including warships.

RESERVATIONS: A measure adopted by the Senate last month in effect gives the United States the right to take "such steps as it deems necessary," including the use of force to reopen the canal or restore its operations, should this become necessary. Another measure adopted by the Senate keeps the possibility of maintaining United States troops or bases in Panama after 1999 if Panama and the United States decided it was necessary.

AMENDMENT: Interprets the treaty to mean that Panamanian and American vessels, in an emergency, could "go the head of the line."

Ex-Diplomat to Head Met Museum

By GRACE GLUECK

After more than a year's search, the trustees of the Metropolitan Museum of Art have elected the museum's first full-time salaried president. He is William B. Macomber Jr., a 57-year-old retired diplomat whose last post was Ambassador to Turkey from 1973 to 1977.

The choice of Mr. Macomber, by unanimous vote of the board, surprised the museum world, because he is not known in the art field nor had his name been among the many reported to be in contention.

Under a reorganization of the museum's administrative structure voted by the board last March, Mr. Macomber as president will be in charge of management and finances while a subordinate director will be in charge of curatorial and artistic matters. The director, who will succeed Thomas Hoving, has not yet been chosen.

Mr. Macomber, whose salary was not disclosed, succeeds Douglas Dillon, who had served as unsalaried president since 1969 and now becomes board chairman.

Yesterday Mr. Dillon said that Mr. Macomber's extensive Washington background, which includes a stint as chief administrative officer of the State Department from 1969-1973 and as Assistant Secretary of State for Congressional Relations from 1957 to 1962 and from 1967 to 1969, would be "very useful in dealing with political figures in the city, in Albany and in Washington."

And he termed Mr. Macomber's lack of experience in the art world "a plus factor rather than a minus," adding, "We didn't want someone who'd second-guess or dominate the director and

Continued on Page C22, Column 3

INSIDE

Stocks Drop; Dow Off 6.85

The stock market declined moderately after three sessions of soaring prices and hectic trading as traders cashed in gains. The Dow was off 6.85. Page D1.

Setbacks for Carter Tax Plan

President Carter's income tax plan suffered setbacks when a House panel rebuffed proposals on medical expenses and charitable deductions. Page D1.

"All the News That's Fit to Print"

The New York Times

LATE CITY EDITION

Weather: Mostly sunny, milder today; fair tonight. Sunny, mild tomorrow. Temperature range: today 50-70; yesterday 53-65. Details, page B10.

VOL. CXXVII ... No. 43,936

NEW YORK, WEDNESDAY, MAY 10, 1978

25 cents beyond 50-mile zone from New York City, higher in air delivery cities.

20 CENTS

MORO SLAIN, BODY FOUND IN ROME; WEST'S LEADERS ASSAIL TERROR

Vance Offering To Sell Israel 20 More F-15's

He Informs Congress of Possible Solution to Jet Controversy

By BERNARD WEINRAUB

Special to The New York Times

WASHINGTON, May 9—Secretary of State Cyrus R. Vance offered Congress an informal compromise today in an effort to ease opposition to the Administration plan to sell advanced military jets in a package to Saudi Arabia, Egypt and Israel. Mr. Vance proposed that Israel be offered the opportunity to purchase additional planes beyond the package and that assurances be obtained from Saudi Arabia that its planes would be used solely for defense.

Mr. Vance made his offer at a private meeting with members of the Senate Foreign Relations Committee.

Administration sources said that Mr. Vance had tentatively offered to sell 20 additional F-15 fighters to Israel, to be delivered in 1983 and 1984. The extra F-15's in addition to 15 in the current package and 25 sold earlier, would give Israel a total of 60 of the high-performance planes, the same number that the United States proposes to sell to Saudi Arabia by 1984.

Way Is Open to a Compromise

Although Administration and Congressional sources were reluctant to discuss details of the Vance offer, which was not totally fixed yet, it was evident that the Administration's plans had opened the way for a potential compromise.

"I believe we're on a road which could lead to a settlement," said Senator Jacob K. Javits, Republican of New York, one of the Foreign Relations Committee's key opponents of the package sale. "But it's a long road and we're far from home. The Administration has made proposals. We asked a lot of questions. We're thinking about it."

Two major themes dominate the Administration's compromise. One is the number of additional planes to be sold to the Israelis beyond the current package offer. The second is the Administration's willingness to give written assurances that Saudi F-15's will not be equipped with air-to-surface weapons and will not be based at sites close to Israel.

By late today, several opponents of the Administration's arms package made it clear that the number of additional planes for Israel remained an issue of discussion.

Moreover, Administration assurances involving the use of Saudi F-15's solely

Continued on Page A7, Column 1

LAW ALLOWING CITIES TO EXCEED TAX LIMIT UPSET IN NEW YORK

Appeals Court Action Also Affects School Districts—Puts Buffalo and Rochester Into Deficit

By STEVEN R. WEISMAN

Special to The New York Times

ALBANY, May 9—The State Court of Appeals today struck down a two-year-old law that allowed localities to collect property taxes above state constitutional ceilings to pay for pensions, Social Security and other costs.

The unanimous decision by the state's highest court effectively throws into deficit the budgets of the cities of Buffalo, Rochester and the school districts of those two cities as well as the budgets of 48 other school districts across the state. It raises the possibility that residents and businesses in the areas involved may file claims for illegally collected back taxes.

According to the office of State Comptroller Arthur Levitt, the affected localities collected an aggregate of $110 million this year in excess of the property tax ceiling.

Legislative experts said that unless alternative sources of revenue were devised, the localities might have to cut spending deeply as early as July 1, when their new fiscal years begin, to bring their budgets into balance.

Legislative Leaders Meet

Aides to the legislative leaders began meeting this afternoon to review the possibility of authorizing new state aid, or new types of local levies, for the localities. Faced with the complexity of the issue, plus the unpleasant possibility of imposing new taxes in an election year, the Legislature is likely to put off moving until next month, perhaps in a special session after its regular session adjourns in two weeks.

In its unsigned opinion, the Court of Appeals noted that it had in 1974 thrown out a law permitting localities except New York City to tax above their constitutional limits for pension and other costs.

The new law, enacted in 1976, permitted the localities to go ahead anyway because they were facing a fiscal "emergency." It also sought to redefine the local property tax as a state property tax, but the court today said it viewed these tactics as creating a statute whose flaws were "indistinguishable" from the old one.

In its decision, the Court of Appeals rejected the localities' contention that they had been facing a "fiscal crisis"

Continued on Page D15, Column 5

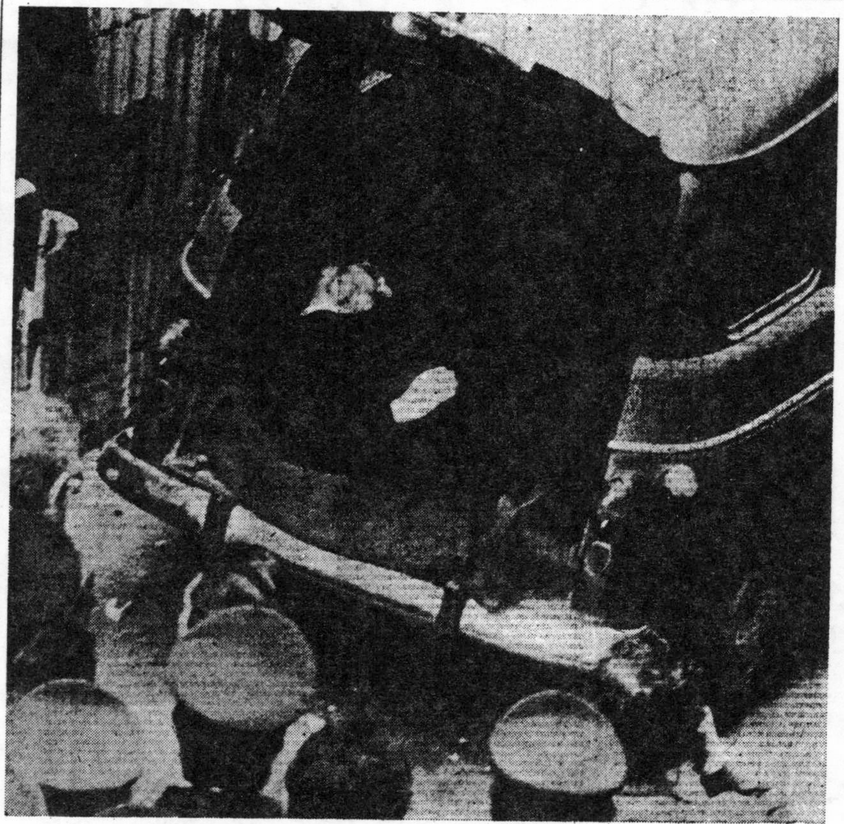

United Press International

The body of Aldo Moro lies in the back of a car parked on Via Caetani in the center of Rome

HE IS SHOT 10 TIMES

Ex-Premier Is Discovered in Car on Downtown Street 54 Days After Abduction

By HENRY TANNER

Special to The New York Times

ROME, May 9—The bullet-riddled body of former Prime Minister Aldo Moro was abandoned by his kidnappers today in a parked car in the historic center of Rome, a short distance from the headquarters of both the Communist and Christian Democratic parties, whose alliance the terrorist Red Brigades are fighting to destroy.

The discovery of the body behind the back seat of a burgundy red French Renault R-4 came 54 days after Mr. Moro, who was expected to be the next president of Italy, was abducted in a hail of gunfire in a street near his suburban home by urban guerrillas belonging to the Red Brigades.

Policemen raced to Via Caetani shortly after 1 P.M. today after intercepting an anonymous phone call to one of Mr. Moro's secretaries. The caller said, "In Via Caetani there is a red car with the body of Moro," and hung up, officials at Rome police headquarters said.

The kidnapping of Mr. Moro led to a nationwide manhunt by thousands of policemen and soldiers. Roadblocks were set up throughout the Rome area and a number of suspected terrorists were arrested in extensive house-to-house searches.

Body in Luggage Compartment

Mr. Moro was killed sometime early yesterday, according to first estimates by the police. He had at least 10 bullet holes in his chest. The cuffs of his trousers were full of sand as if he had been walking on a beach or been dragged across rough soil shortly before his death, the police said.

He was dressed in the clothes he had worn on the day of his abduction: a navy blue suit, a heavy overcoat, striped shirt and dark tie. He was found lying in the luggage compartment of the small car, his head leaning against the back of the rear seat. His face had been covered by a blanket. Next to his body was a plastic bag containing his watch, razor and other personal effects.

Mr. Moro was killed before being placed in the car, according to police sources, who said that there were no bullet holes in his overcoat. He was lying in a pool of blood.

The news of the discovery of Mr. Moro's body spread rapidly through Rome after radio stations broke into their programs with bulletins at about 1:30.

There were no crowds in front of the Communist headquarters, but in front of the offices of the Christian Democrats throngs of grieving men and women shouted their anger. "Moro is alive!" some cried. Others shouted, "Death to

Continued on Page A16, Column 1

Europeans Pay Homage to Moro, Call for Defense of Democracy

By FLORA LEWIS

Special to The New York Times

PARIS, May 9—Throughout Western Europe today, leaders paid homage to Aldo Moro, expressing horror at his death, which several considered an attack on the institutions of democracy itself. Several leaders called for a common front to fight terrorism and defend democratic regimes.

Some governments, including the Dutch and Norwegian, explicitly supported the stand of the Italian Government in having refused to accept terrorist conditions or make compromises to obtain the release of the Christian Democratic leader. Despite the sorrow and shock at the murder of a man, there was a general feeling that the very base of democratic government had been at stake.

Legislatures and international organizations, including the European Parliament and conferences of Common Market agricultural ministers and the World Health Organization, interrupted or even suspended their sessions to honor and to mourn Mr. Moro.

Killing Denounced by Carter

In Washington, President Carter called the murder of Mr. Moro "a contemptible and cowardly act."

The only word from Eastern Europe so far was a brief dispatch by Tass, the official Soviet press agency, reporting the death without comment. Previously the Soviet agency had suggested that the kidnapping was a plot by both left-wing and right-wing extremists to provoke chaos in Italy, and Italian press reports that the terrorists had been armed by Communist countries were indignantly denied.

The official Chinese press agency, Hsinhua, reported the death of Mr. Moro without comment, citing reports from Western news agencies and summarizing major developments in the kidnapping case.

Spanish and French Communists denounced the killing, in shaded terms reflecting the different positions of their parties.

The Spanish Communist Party said it was a "crime against Italian democracy and democracy in all of Europe," suggesting that the assassination was a reprisal against Mr. Moro's role in bringing the Italian Communist Party closer to a role in the Government. "It only serves the darkest forces of reaction and imperialism," the Spanish Communists said, using a phrase that they sometimes rely on in reference to the East as well as the West.

The French Communist leader, Georges Marchais, expressed his view in a telegram to the Italian Communist Party leader, Enrico Berlinguer, deploring the

Continued on Page A16, Column 1

LIMIT ON ABORTIONS ADVANCES IN ALBANY

Bill Requiring Parental Notification for Minors Is Passed by Senate

By SHEILA RULE

Special to The New York Times

ALBANY, May 9—The Republican-controlled State Senate tonight passed a measure that generally requires notification of the parents of a teen-age girl before the girl can have an abortion.

Democrats denounced the measure as an attempt to legislate family relationships.

The measure requires that, if a physician does not have the parents' consent, he have proof that he had sent the parents notification by registered mail five days before the scheduled operation.

The bill, according to its sponsor, would not give objecting parents the power to veto the abortions.

After a lengthy and at times emotional debate, the Senate passed the measure 36 to 19. But the bill's fate in the Democratic-controlled Assembly is uncertain. A close vote is expected in that house's Health Committee when it considers the bill next week.

The Senate sponsor, Frank Padavan, Republican-Conservative of Queens Village, two years ago sponsored tougher parental-consent legislation that passed both houses but was later vetoed by Governor Carey.

With the Senate having recently gone through a protracted battle over the

Continued on Page B20, Column 1

Lettuce: Wet Winter, High Prices

By ROBERT LINDSEY

Special to The New York Times

LOS ANGELES, May 9—As two women stood frowning before a mound of 99-cent lettuce in a suburban supermarket here the other day, one turned to the other and said, "Unbelievable, isn't it?"

The other replied, "It sure is. Three months ago I said I'd make salad for 100 people for a church party tonight."

Such reports probably will not relieve the frustration of Easterners who recently have had to pay as much as $1.49 a head for iceberg lettuce, much of it tarnished and wilted. But the supermarket encounter demonstrated that even in California, the nation's salad bowl, people are shocked by the price of produce this spring.

Lettuce prices in many parts of the country are beginning to edge down from a peak of two weeks ago. But, according to crop experts, the weeks ahead will still bring prices higher than the 30 to 40 cents typical of the spring season in recent years.

The problem began in California, which grows more than 40 percent of the nation's fresh produce and more than 40 percent of the spring crop. This year the state's vegetable farms are operating at much less than full capacity.

North from the Imperial Valley on the Mexican border to the Salinas and Santa Clara Valleys, and up through the great San Joaquin Valley, a 500-mile spine of agriculture that is one of the richest sources of food in the world, farmers are still trying to recover from one of the state's wettest winters ever.

After a two-year drought that was one of the worst in a century, rains began to fall in December, and with

Continued on Page D15, Column 5

An Embittered Family Excludes Leaders of Italy From Funeral

By INA LEE SELDEN

Special to The New York Times

ROME, May 9—The family of Aldo Moro told Italian political leaders and members of the slain leader's Christian Democratic Party today that they would not be welcome at his funeral.

A statement issued by the family asked that there be no public expressions of mourning. It repeated a wish expressed by Mr. Moro in one of his letters toward the end of his 54-day captivity in what his abductors, the Red Brigades, termed a "people's prison."

"The family desires that the state authorities and the political leaders respect the will of Aldo Moro," the statement said. "This means no public demonstrations or speeches, no national mourning, no state funeral or medals to his memory."

'Those Who Loved Me'

Mr. Moro had asked in one of his many letters that neither state authorities nor politicians attend his funeral, and added:

"I ask to be followed only by those who loved me and are thus worthy of coming with me with their prayers and with their love." The letter was addressed to the party secretary, Benigno Zaccagnini, but intended for all the members of the Christian-Democratic Party and others who had opposed an exchange of prisoners as requested by the Red Brigades for Mr. Moro's release.

Today, Eleonora Chiavarelli Moro, the widow, left her house to visit the morgue. With her were two of her daughters, her

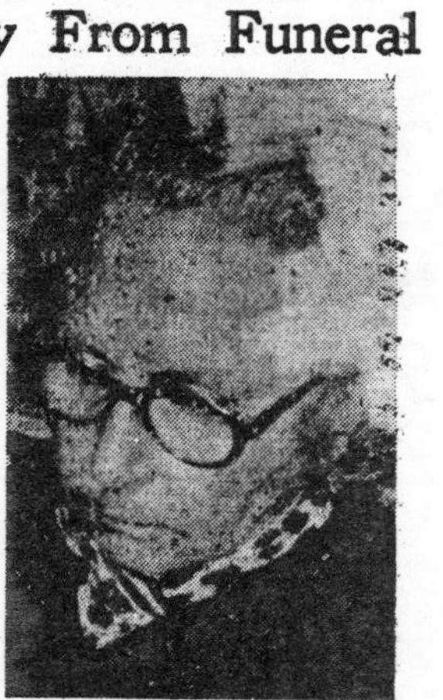

Associated Press

Eleonora Moro leaving church in Rome after prayers, on Sunday.

son, her sister and brother-in-law and her son's fiancée.

When the family reached the room containing Mr. Moro's body, Mrs. Moro went in alone, touched the sheet covering the body, and dropped to her knees to pray.

"The family is not just embittered," said a confidant of Mr. Moro, adding that they wanted to make the political forces feel the brunt of their bitterness.

"They feel," he said "you didn't want

Continued on Page A16, Column 1

INSIDE

Massive A.M.C. Car Recall

The E.P.A. is ordering American Motors to recall nearly all its 1976 model cars to remedy a possible pollution-control defect. Page A18.

Joan Little Loses Appeal

New York State's Court of Appeals ordered the return of Joan Little to North Carolina from where she escaped last October. Page A23.

Associated Press

AWASH IN ESCAMBIA BAY: Water pours through the National Airlines jet that crashed while approaching Pensacola, Fla., Monday night. Three were killed but 55 survived, some saved by a passing tug. Page A18.

"All the News That's Fit to Print"

The New York Times

LATE CITY EDITION

Weather: Sunny, warm today; fair tonight. Sunny, warm tomorrow. Temperature range: today 69-84; yesterday 75-90. Details, page B17.

VOL. CXXVII .... No. 43,986 Copyright © 1978 The New York Times NEW YORK, THURSDAY, JUNE 29, 1978 25 cents beyond 50-mile zone from New York City. Higher in air delivery cities 20 CENTS

HIGH COURT BACKS SOME AFFIRMATIVE ACTION BY COLLEGES, BUT ORDERS BAKKE ADMITTED

PRESIDENT TO ISSUE ORDER TO LIBERALIZE RULE ON SECRET DATA

Change in Procedure on Classified Documents Designed to Exhibit Interest in Open Government

By MARTIN TOLCHIN

Special to The New York Times

WASHINGTON, June 28 — President Carter plans a sweeping liberalization of the procedures governing the classification of Government documents.

He intends shortly to issue an executive order that will sharply limit the extent and duration of classifications, such as "confidential," "secret" and "top secret," and reduce the number of agencies that have classification authority.

The executive order will also provide that declassification procedures consider "whether the public interest in disclosure outweighs the damage to national security that might be reasonably expected from disclosure," according to the document, a copy of which was obtained by The New York Times.

The White House intends to present the executive order as a demonstration of the President's commitment to open government. Although civil liberty groups praised the new procedure, they said they did not believe the new policy would offset what they regarded as the Administration's commitment to secrecy in other areas.

Three Cases Cited

They cited the cases against Frank Snepp, a former agent of the Central Intelligence Agency who wrote a book critical of the agency, and the prosecutions of David Truong and Ronald Humphrey for theft.

"Nothing that they could do in the executive order could outweigh the harm to free debate on national security issues brought about by the Snepp and Truong cases," said Morton Halperin, director of the Center for National Security Studies, who helped to formulate the new procedures.

Mark Lynch, a staff attorney for the American Civil Liberties Union who specializes in government secrecy, said that the new procedures "could be very useful" because "they'll have to think harder about what they're doing."

He agreed with Mr. Halperin, however,

Continued on Page A16, Column 3

Associated Press

Gerard C. Smith

South Africans Reported Ready For Nuclear Ban

By JOHN F. BURNS

Special to The New York Times

JOHANNESBURG, June 28—American efforts to persuade South Africa to sign the treaty banning the spread of nuclear weapons reportedly reached an advanced stage today as high-level officials of the two Governments ended talks in Pretoria on the nuclear issue.

Sources close to the talks disclosed tonight that Gerard C. Smith, President Carter's ambassador at large in charge of efforts to prevent the spread of nuclear weapons, had been in the South African capital of Pretoria since Sunday for discussions with Foreign Minister Roelof F. Botha and other senior officials, including Abraham J. Roux, chairman of the South African Atomic Energy Board.

[Reports from Washington indicated, meanwhile, that South Africa was considering signing the treaty and was prepared to accept stricter international controls to prevent its atomic energy program from being used to develop weapons.]

Details Not Disclosed

Neither side in the Pretoria talks would divulge any details of what went on or say whether an agreement was in prospect. However, it is known that Mr. Smith, a 68-year-old veteran of arms-limitation talks, arrived here with the aim of gaining South African accession to the nuclear treaty in return for a pledge of continued cooperation between the two Governments in the peaceful applications of nuclear energy.

The talks in the South African capital are the culmination of secret negotiations that began last year, after a diplomatic flurry over fears that South Africa was preparing to test a nuclear explosive. The

Continued on Page A6, Column 3

BELL HAILS DECISION

Calls Ruling a 'Great Gain'— Plaintiff Is 'Pleased' and Others Express Relief

By LINDA GREENHOUSE

Special to The New York Times

WASHINGTON, June 28—Among the entire spectrum of people and groups with a stake in the Bakke decision, there were degrees of satisfaction and relief today.

From Allan P. Bakke himself, who will enter medical school next September at the age of 38, to the civil rights organizations that opposed his challenge to the special minority-admissions program, people drew from the 154 pages of Supreme Court language the conclusions they most wanted to find. Mr. Bakke said he was "pleased" with the decision.

Attorney General Griffin B. Bell told reporters at the White House that he and President Carter regarded the decision as "a great gain for affirmative action."

"This is what we thought the law was," the Attorney General said.

Benjamin L. Hooks, executive director of the National Association for the Advancement of Colored People, called the decision a "clear-cut victory for voluntary affirmative action," not only in education but also in other areas.

'Quotas Are Flatly Illegal'

Arnold Forster, general counsel of the Anti-Defamation League of B'nai B'rith, said his organization was "comforted that, once and for all, the United States Supreme Court has held that racial quotas are flatly illegal."

Among educators, the reaction was almost one of relief that their worst fears had not come to pass and that most existing college admissions policies could continue unchanged. [Page A23.]

Whether the decisions in Regents of the University of California v. Bakke will go down in history as "an act of judicial statesmanship," in the words of Prof. Alan Dershowitz of Harvard Law School, the nine Justices in their six opinions did seem to be offering something for everyone in a case that has been scrutinized as closely and argued as bitterly as any to reach the Court in recent decades.

The Court both ordered Mr. Bakke's admission to medical school and upheld the use of race as a factor in university admissions programs.

Black Leader Sees Threat

At a news conference of black leaders in New York City, Jesse Jackson, chairman of Operation PUSH, warned that the part of the decision striking down the minority-admissions program at the medical school of the University of California at Davis might be received by other universities as a signal to cut back on even those affirmative action programs that quite clearly have the approval of a majority of the Supreme Court.

But other civil rights leaders chose to focus on the part of the opinion establish-

Continued on Page A23, Column 6

Associated Press

Allan P. Bakke returning to home in Los Altos, Calif., after work yesterday

A Plateau for Minorities

Most College Programs Expected to Continue, But Ruling Is Seen as Brake on Rights Efforts

By JOHN HERBERS

Special to The New York Times

WASHINGTON, June 28—The United States Supreme Court's split decision in the Allan P. Bakke case means, according to the consensus on both sides, that the great majority of affirmative action programs, public and private, will continue, as will the debate and lawsuits over what constitutes a proper racial balance.

News Analysis

For that, the leaders of the nation's minorities expressed pleasure and relief today at the 5-to-4 decision, which said that race may be considered in deciding who is admitted to colleges.

The rigid affirmative action program of the medical school of the University of California at Davis, which the Court struck down, was considered extreme in that it set aside 16 of 100 places for members of minority groups. Many other programs for enrolling minorities are more flexible and seem to fall within the boundaries set in today's decision.

A Retreat Is Seen

However, as Julian Bond, the Georgia civil rights leader and state legislator, said, affirmative action efforts reached a plateau today, and there was some fear that the decision would cause a decline in attempts to broaden educational and employment opportunities for blacks and other minorities.

Associate Justice Thurgood Marshall expressed the opinion, widely held among minority leaders, that the nation has been retreating from a commitment to racial justice made in the 1960's, in a parallel to what happened in the 19th century after the Reconstruction period.

"I fear that we have come full circle," he wrote, pointing out that "several affirmative action programs" were voided in that period by the Supreme Court. He cited the decision in Plessy v. Ferguson, which upheld segregation in public education, and said, "Now we have this Court again stepping in, this time to stop affirmative action programs of the type used by the University of California."

Although the majority decision appeared to please a broad spectrum of people on both sides of the issue, Justice Marshall put his finger on a deep division remaining in this country between blacks and whites.

The division concerns whether the nation should give special preference to a people who in a unique way were subjected to a basic denial of human rights, beginning with slavery.

"It must be remembered," he wrote, "that during most of the past 200 years, the Constitution as interpreted by this Court did not prohibit the most ingenious and pervasive forms of discrimination against the Negro. Now, when a state acts to remedy the effects of the legacy of discrimination, I cannot believe that this same Constitution stands as a barrier."

Associate Justice Lewis F. Powell Jr., who wrote the main opinion, made it clear that special preference for blacks was not what the majority had in mind when it said race could be considered in an admissions policy. He spoke of the need for diversity, for Asians, Mexican-Americans, people from rural as well as urban areas.

"The file of a particular black applicant may be examined for his potential contribution to diversity without the factor of race being decisive when compared, for example, with that of an applicant identified as an Italian-American if the latter

Continued on Page A22, Column 3

GUIDANCE IS PROVIDED

Medical School Racial Quota Voided, but Advantage for Minorities Is Allowed

By WARREN WEAVER Jr.

Special to The New York Times

WASHINGTON, June 28—The Supreme Court by 5-to-4 vote affirmed today the constitutionality of college admission programs that give special advantage to blacks and other minorities to help remedy past discrimination against them.

But the Justices also ruled that Allan P. Bakke must be admitted to the University of California Medical College at

Excerpts from opinions, Pages A20, A21.

Davis, determining that the college's affirmative action program was invalid because it was inflexibly and unjustifiably biased against white applicants like him.

In today's opinion, the Court provided some guidance for educators trying to insure that their programs will pass judicial muster, and future cases will almost certainly shed some more light on what constitutes permissible affirmative action.

Most Significant Since '54

Both decisions involved 5-to-4 votes, with Associate Justice Lewis F. Powell Jr. joining four other Justices to force the admission of Mr. Bakke, then shifting to join the four remaining Justices in support of the constitutionality of carefully tailored flexible affirmative action plans.

Although the two-sided ruling aroused some confusion and controversy, it was generally regarded as the most significant civil rights pronouncement the high court had made since it outlawed public school segregation in 1954.

It was not initially clear whether the Bakke decision would affect future Supreme Court rulings on affirmative action in employment. Such hiring plans tend to incorporate fixed arbitrary formulas for blacks, women and others, somewhat akin to the Davis admissions program that was invalidated today, but the high court has generally approved them in the past.

Two Groups in Voting

Generally, however, civil rights advocates felt they had won a major victory by preserving the constitutionality of admissions plans to professional schools that favor minority group members, who had been all but barred from such education until recent years.

One group of Justices—William J. Brennan Jr., Byron R. White, Thurgood Marshall and Harry A. Blackmun—maintained that the special Davis admissions program was permissible because the Government could use racial classifications as long as it has the benign purpose of remedying past discrimination. They voted, as a result, to deny Mr. Bakke entrance.

A second group of four—Chief Justice Warren E. Burger and Associate Justices Potter Stewart, William H. Rehnquist and

Continued on Page A22, Column 1

2 U.S. NEWSMEN GET SOVIET LIBEL CHARGE

TV Agency Files Suit Stemming From Dispatches About Dissident

By DAVID K. SHIPLER

Special to The New York Times

MOSCOW, June 28—Two American reporters were formally accused in a Moscow court today of having libeled Soviet state television by writing articles about an imprisoned dissident's televised "confession" that his friends and relatives believed had been fabricated.

It was the first time that Western diplomats and correspondents could remember the Soviet Government's taking legal action against foreign journalists for their dispatches.

The two reporters, Craig R. Whitney of The New York Times and Harold D. Piper of The Baltimore Sun, appeared in court in answer to a summons and were presented with copies of the claim against them by Lev Y. Almazov, chairman of the Moscow City Court.

Written Response Is Due Tomorrow

Judge Almazov set noon Friday as a deadline for a written response to the charge, and July 5 as a trial date. A guilty finding, according to Article 7 of the Civil Code, may result in a court order to publish a retraction and, failing that, a fine.

The claim, brought by the Soviet Government's broadcasting agency, asked that the two reporters "be held answerable for publishing in the foreign press slanderous information denigrating the honor and dignity of the members of the staff of the State Committee for Television and Radio of the U.S.S.R. and that they be caused to publish a retraction in the press."

It was not explained how a Soviet court could claim jurisdiction over newspapers

Continued on Page A13, Column 1

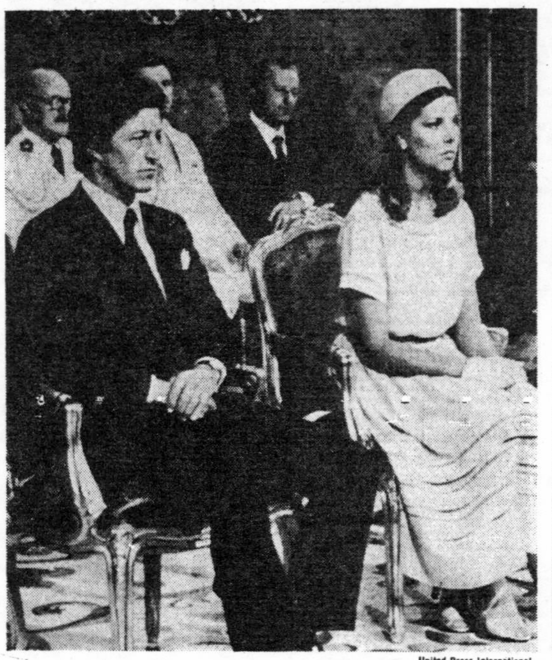

United Press International

WED IN MONACO: Princess Caroline and Philippe Junot during civil marriage ceremony at palace in Monaco. They exchanged vows in same room where Prince Rainier and Grace Kelly were wed in 1956. Page C10.

INSIDE

Blackout Cost Tallied

New York City's blackout last July cost at least $310 million, a study by the Library of Congress research service found. Page B9.

Levitt Disputes Vouchers

Arthur Levitt charged that the Port Authority let directors accused of falsifying expense vouchers alter them retroactively. Page B6.

Boy, 15, Who Killed 2 and Tried To Kill a Third Is Given 5 Years

By CHARLES KAISER

A 15-year-old Harlem youth who admitted killing two subway passengers and attempting to kill a subway motorman in one eight-day period last March has been sentenced to a maximum of five years in prison.

Under the terms of the sentence, imposed by Judge Edith Miller in Family Court—it was the maximum she could impose under state law—the youth will be required to spend at least 18 months in a "secure facility." After that he could be moved to a "residential facility" or kept in the secure facility, at the option of the state's Division for Youth.

Robert H. Silberling, head of the District Attorney's juvenile offense bureau, said that the state could, at its discretion, choose to keep the youth confined beyond the court-imposed five-year sentence. But when he reached the age of 21, Mr. Silberling said, he would have to be released.

Morgenthau Comments

"We've urged longer sentences," said District Attorney Robert M. Morgenthau of Manhattan, who cited the case yesterday in renewing a call for revision of the state's juvenile-offender laws. "I don't think the present law provides for adequate sentences for violent offenders. There has to be a provision for longer sentences for unusual cases like this one."

According to police and court officials, what makes the case unusual is the violent nature of the slightly built youth who they say has threatened to kill the detectives who arrested him, the prosecutors assigned to the case and Judge Miller herself. The police said he had also stabbed a fellow inmate at the Spofford Juvenile Center in the neck with a fork, saying: "I'll kill you if you sit down next to me."

"He's a kid who showed no remorse whatsoever," said Detective Sgt. Thomas Brady, who helped supervise the investigation that led to the youth's arrest.

Special Units Formed

Crimes by youthful repeat offenders, especially against the elderly, have generated controversy over what have been called lenient sentences sometimes handed out by judges. A highly publicized series of such crimes two years ago led to the formation in November 1976 by the Police Department of senior-citizen robbery units in all five boroughs.

Last year Mayor Koch's advocacy of the death penalty for heinous crimes was a major issue in the mayoralty campaign. Some people believe that Mr. Koch's support for the death penalty provided his margin of victory over Mario M. Cuomo

Continued on Page B7, Column 1

"All the News That's Fit to Print"

The New York Times

LATE CITY EDITION

Weather: Foggy, a chance of showers today and tonight. Fair tomorrow. Temperature range: today 80-71; yesterday 80-70. Details on page D8.

VOL.CXXVII . . . No.44,025

NEW YORK, MONDAY, AUGUST 7, 1978

25 cents beyond 50-mile zone from New York City. Higher in air delivery cities.

20 CENTS

POPE PAUL VI IS DEAD OF A HEART ATTACK AT 80; GUIDED THE CHURCH THROUGH ERA OF CHANGE

Begin and Vance Consult in Israel On Reviving Stalled Mideast Talks

But Decision to Reschedule Foreign Ministers' Session Awaits Secretary's Meeting in Egypt With Sadat

By BERNARD GWERTZMAN

Special to The New York Times

JERUSALEM, Aug. 6 — Secretary of State Cyrus R. Vance and Prime Minister Menachem Begin of Israel met for more than four hours today in what they agreed were "serious, good and useful" talks.

But a decision on reviving the newly stalled Middle East peace negotiations awaited Mr. Vance's meeting with President Anwar el-Sadat in Egypt tomorrow and Tuesday.

Mr. Begin was evidently pleased that, for the moment at least, not he but Mr. Sadat was being perceived in the West as responsible for the breakdown in negotiations. He said that if the atmosphere was as good in Alexandria, at Mr. Vance's talks with Mr. Sadat, as it had been here today, "there will be a success" and the negotiations could resume.

Talking to reporters at the end of the day, however, the Prime Minister seemed to stand firm on previous Israeli proposals that led Mr. Sadat to break off direct talks and cancel a planned meeting of foreign ministers. And he said that Mr. Vance had not asked him to change his position.

"We were not approached to change," Mr. Begin said. "The whole problem is President Sadat's agreement to the tripartite meeting." He said he had told Mr. Vance that Israel remained ready to participate in the Egyptian-Israeli-American meeting of Foreign Ministers that had originally been planned this week as a follow-up to one held last month at Leeds Castle, near London.

"Everything hinges on President Sadat's reply" to Mr. Vance, the Israeli leader said. He added that no Israeli government could agree to what he called Mr. Sadat's precondition that direct talks take place only if Israel agrees ahead of time to withdrawal from all the territories occupied in the 1967 war.

Mr. Vance said he shared Mr. Begin's hope that the talks could be resumed, because "it's important to all of us; it's important to the world." But the Secretary of State and American officials — though Mr. Vance's prime goal on this trip is to persuade Mr. Sadat to remain involved in negotiating a Middle East peace settlement — refused to join in Mr. Begin's evaluation that all depended on President Sadat.

Israeli Flexibility Seen Necessary

American officials said again privately that for a breakthrough to take place, Israel would have to be more forthcoming on the key question of whether it is willing to withdraw from substantial parts of the West Bank of the Jordan River and the Gaza Strip. These two areas, which were occupied by Israel in 1967, are inhabited by more than a million Palestinians.

Mr. Begin, who has been ill, seemed relaxed and ebullient in his morning and late afternoon sessions with reporters. He appeared pleased that the latest turn of events had deflected American pressure for compromise away from him and to-

Continued on Page A4, Column 3

Carter Striving To Ease Strains With Congress

By TERENCE SMITH

Special to The New York Times

WASHINGTON, Aug. 6 — Like the suitor of a reluctant maiden, Jimmy Carter has been pursuing Congress in recent weeks with everything from flattery to invitations to the White House.

He has had Congressmen over in droves for working breakfasts, private luncheons, buffet dinners, tennis games and private film showings in the White House theater. In all, more than 350 of the 535 senators and representatives have trooped through the Executive Mansion in the last month.

More than mere sociability lies behind the Presidential invitations. Mr. Carter and his top aides are engaged in their most concentrated effort to date to improve the Administration's tattered relations with Capitol Hill.

House Recess Is Near

The courtship takes on a special urgency as the House approaches its Aug. 16 recess with several major Carter legislative programs still to be acted upon, including those concerning energy, Civil Service reform and taxes.

The courtship is also meant to reverse the deterioration of the President's relations with the House Democratic leadership before it is too late. That crucial relationship reached a new low last week

Continued on Page D10, Column 1

MANY VOICE SADNESS

World Remembers Leader for His Firm Guidance and Peace Efforts

Across the nation and the world, the powerful and the average parishioner yesterday mourned the man who for 15 years had been the spiritual leader of the Roman Catholic Church.

As Pope Paul VI was remembered by political and church leaders as a man who worked for world peace and guided the church during a time of social and religious unrest, the solemn hymns usually reserved for the mournful season of Lent were heard in some churches in New York. Plans were being made for special memorial masses, and some of the world's 550 million Catholics gathered to pray for the Pope, who died yesterday at his summer retreat at Castel Gandolfo.

President Carter said in a statement issued by the White House, "I was deeply saddened to learn of the death of Pope Paul VI, a man whose life and works have served personally as a great source of moral inspiration."

Remembered for Vatican II

Archbishop John Quinn of San Francisco, president of the National Conference of Catholic Bishops and the United States Catholic Conference, said: "One of the century's greatest popes has closed the long day of his earthly life. With superb skill, Paul VI brought the Second Vatican Council through three major sessions to its fruitful conclusion."

The Rev. Dario Pedroza, executive secretary of the Bishop's Commission for Evangelism and Catechism in Mexico, hailed the Pontiff's "valiant and faithful attitude toward the principles of the church and evangelism."

He added, as did many Catholic clerics, "The church is an institution that runs without dependence on any single person."

Cooke Offers Prayer

Terence Cardinal Cooke, who was named Bishop of the Archdiocese of New York by Pope Paul a decade ago, knelt at one side of the altar in St. Patrick's Cathedral and said in prayer at an evening mass, "May he now share in the joy of the Risen Lord, in the company of the Apostles, and of all those holy shepherds in whose footsteps he walked so valiantly and so selflessly."

And a statement by Governor Carey said, "His holiness Pope Paul devoted his life and his ministry to seeking world peace, to stabilizing the unity of the

Continued on Page A15, Column 1

©Karsh, Ottawa

POPE PAUL VI

ELECTION TO BE HELD

Cardinals Are to Convene in About Two Weeks to Choose Successor

By HENRY TANNER

Special to The New York Times

ROME, Aug. 6 — Pope Paul VI, the 262d occupant of the Throne of St. Peter, died peacefully tonight at the age of 80 after a heart attack in his summer residence at Castel Gandolfo.

The death of Giovanni Battista Montini — who had served as Pope Paul VI since June 21, 1963, had presided over major changes in the liturgy and organization of the Roman Catholic Church and had broken new ground in relations with

Pontiff's obituary begins on page A12.

Protestant and Eastern Orthodox Christians — was announced at the Vatican by the Rev. Pierfranco Pastore, acting head of the press service.

"With profound anxiety and emotion I must inform you that Pope Paul VI passed away at 2140 this evening, Aug. 6, 1978, at the papal summer residence of Castel Gandolfo," Father Pastore told reporters in the briefing hall of the Vatican press center. That time is 9:40 P.M., or 3:40 P.M. New York time.

Cardinal Assumes Role

Jean Cardinal Villot, the Vatican's Secretary of State, assumed the temporal and juridical but not the spiritual powers of the pontificate upon Pope Paul's death.

Cardinal Villot will summon the conclave of cardinals that will elect a new pope. Under a rule instituted by Pope Paul that limits voting rights to prelates under 80 years of age, 116 cardinals will be entitled to vote. Fourteen cardinals are over 80, church sources said.

The conclave will begin 15 to 18 days from now. Cardinal Villot's interregnum will last until the coronation of the new pope. The election may take several weeks.

During his reign, Pope Paul sought to mediate between the progressive and conservative forces within the church. This was true especially in his first years, when the progressive impetus given by Vatican II was at its strongest and provoked conservative counterpressures.

The Pope staked out new positions on ecumenism and carried out the sharpest liturgical changes in centuries, including abandonment of the Latin mass in favor of use of local languages. But fearing severe damage to the church, he resisted pressures to change traditional teachings on birth control, priestly celibacy and exclusion of women from the priesthood.

Bells Ring Death Knell

At Castel Gandolfo, a small town 15 miles southeast of Rome, the bells of St. Thomas Aquinas, Pope Paul's church, rang the death knell.

Outside the Pope's residence a crowd of tourists and local citizens had been waiting through the early evening. When the bells rang, many of them fell to their knees in prayer.

The lights in the square were turned off for a few minutes.

The first indication of a serious deterio-

Continued on Page A14, Column 3

Compassionate Conservative

Paul VI Was a Firm Guardian of Church Doctrine And a Champion of the Hungry and the Oppressed

By KENNETH A. BRIGGS

An Appraisal

In contrast to Pope John XXIII, his predecessor, Paul VI was not naturally gregarious and innovative. He was the consummate bureaucrat in his Vatican career and not given to striking out in new directions.

If there had been no Second Vatican Council, begun under John XXIII and completed during his own reign, it is unlikely that Paul VI would have proposed such an updating of the church. But the modernizing was already well under way when he began his reign.

Paul's contribution was a product of his superior intellect, applied in the delicate application of so many Vatican II reforms. It was felt also in his unassuming presence, in which many world leaders found a poignant, peaceful respite.

Enormous Spiritual Quality

To those who met him across ideological and religious boundaries, Paul VI was first and foremost a man of surpassing spiritual quality.

He was a progressive exponent of human rights, a position that contrasted with his conservatism on church doctrine. He appealed for commitment to conventional Catholic principles as ardently as he championed the cause of the poor, the hungry and the oppressed.

To those who follow the proceedings of the church, he was much more. He performed the arduous and often thankless role as caretaker over a church that was in the midst of a tumultuous change.

In terms of particular actions, Pope Paul may be best remembered for his 1967 encyclical that underscored the church's opposition to artificial means of birth control. It caused a storm of protest, particularly in the United States, and is often cited as a major reason for the large-scale decline in mass attendance that followed in America.

For the Pope it was a matter of unshakable faith in historical Catholic reasoning rather than a question that should be rethought according to modern psychological, demographic or theological factors. He listened to the case for loosening the ban, brought forcefully by those appointed to study the problem, then made his decision.

Question of Women as Priests

The same pattern accompanied his decision in 1977 to approve a statement by the Congregation for the Doctrine of the Faith, which upheld the church's policy of refusing to ordain women to the priesthood. Since a priest must bear the image of a man because Christ was a man, he said, female priests were unthinkable.

Though these decisions often left progressives in the church disgruntled, his pleas for the downtrodden and his capacity for self-sacrifice won him a spiritual following that included all elements of the church.

His humility was epitomized when he offered himself in exchange for hostages held captive in Mogadishu, Somalia. In a political world rife with cynicism, his offer bore the stamp of sincerity.

He faithfully put in effect many of the changes that Vatican II called for. He

Continued on Page A14, Column 1

United Press International

Secretary of State Cyrus R. Vance listens as Prime Minister Menachem Begin of Israel discusses talks in Jerusalem

New York Hospitals Learning Economics Lessons

By RONALD SULLIVAN

The hospital's physicians were assembled for grand rounds, a hallowed monthly teaching forum at large medical centers. But Dr. Thomas C. Chalmers, the president of Mount Sinai Medical Center and the dean of its School of Medicine, did not have a fascinating disease to discuss, nor an unusual medical case history to present to the white-coated physicians gathered quietly in the hospital's auditorium.

Instead, he talked about a 60-year-old patient who had stayed at Mount Sinai for 17 days and who had run up a bill of $6,668, a considerable share of which represented what he said were questionable or downright unnecessary hospital tests.

"If we don't stop runaway costs ourselves," Dr. Chalmers told his fellow physicians, "then government will come in with a meat ax and destroy the quality of medical care we have achieved."

A decade ago, when there seemed no end to the financial largesse pouring out of government-financed programs such as Medicaid and Medicare, virtually every kind of hospital procedure or grandiose expansion was approved without much thought given to the high costs involved.

Now, however, both state and Federal governments are cutting back on inflationary hospital costs. In New York City, respected medical centers in the world, the state is intent on shrinking a redundant hospital system with too many beds that will spend nearly $4 billion this year, more than two-thirds of it public funds.

In the last three and a half years, 24 hospitals have closed in New York City, many of them small, privately run facilities that health officials regarded as expendable. Increasingly, however, the city's continuing fiscal crisis, combined with the state's determination to eliminate 5,000 more hospital beds in the city,

Continued on Page B2, Column 1

INSIDE

3 New York Beaches Reopened

Coney Island and two other beaches were reopened after a cleanup, as an oil slick from a foundered barge drifted farther out to sea. Page B3.

Black Leader Assails Congress

Vernon E. Jordan, head of the National Urban League, called Congress "callous" and said it was sabotaging the social progress of minorities. Page D10.

Deadline Passes in Portugal

The deadline for a solution to Portugal's governmental crisis passed amid signs that the President would choose his own Prime Minister. Page A3.

Edward Durell Stone Dead at 76; Designed Major Works Worldwide

By The Associated Press

Edward Durell Stone, one of the nation's premier architects, whose designs include such public buildings as the United States Embassy in New Delhi and the Kennedy Center in Washington, died yesterday in New York City. He was 76 years old.

Mr. Stone died at Roosevelt Hospital after a brief illness, a family friend said.

Edward Durell Stone was born in Fayetteville, Ark., on March 9, 1902. He attended the University of Arkansas, and worked as an architectural apprentice at the office of Henry R. Shepley, a distinguished Beaux-Arts architect in Boston.

Started With Coveted Prize

From 1925 to 1927 Mr. Stone — who never received a college degree until his later years, when an honorary doctorate was conferred upon him by Arkansas — attended the architecture schools of Harvard and the Massachusetts Institute of Technology. In 1927 he was awarded the Rotch traveling scholarship, a coveted architectural prize that permitted him to spend two years of expense-paid travel abroad.

He went to Europe, where he had his first glimpse of modern architecture, and shortly after his return in 1929 settled in New York and took a job with the consortium of architects designing Rockefeller Center. There he worked on what was to be considered his first major early achievement — the design of the interiors of Radio City Music Hall.

First House in Mt. Kisco

Mr. Stone became deeply involved in the growing modern movement in New York, and in 1933 designed his first house, a starkly modern concrete and glass-blocked estate for Richard H. Mandel in Mount Kisco, N.Y. The boxy white house with strip windows and a semicircular glass-block dining area attracted wide attention, and Mr. Stone was soon called to design a compound for Mr. and Mrs. Henry R. Luce at Mepkin Plantation in South Carolina.

His next major commission was the Museum of Modern Art, and at the same time Mr. Stone designed a house in Old Westbury, L.I., for A. Conger Goodyear, the museum's president. The house's strong horizontal lines and large roof overhangs displayed a certain Frank Lloyd Wright influence that was to become even more marked in Mr. Stone's later buildings.

"All the News
That's Fit to Print"

The New York Times

LATE CITY EDITION

Weather: Mostly cloudy, chilly today; cloudy, damp tonight and tomorrow. Temperature range: today 27-38; yesterday 39-49. Details on page B10.

VOL.CXXVIII..No.44,043 Copyright © 1978 The New York Times NEW YORK, TUESDAY, NOVEMBER 21, 1978 25 cents beyond 50-mile zone from New York City. Higher in air delivery cities. 20 CENTS

400 ARE FOUND DEAD IN MASS SUICIDE BY CULT; HUNDREDS MORE MISSING FROM GUYANA CAMP

United Press International
Chairman Hua Kuo-feng

2 Peking Wall Posters Raise New Questions On the Status of Hua

By FOX BUTTERFIELD
Special to The New York Times

HONG KONG, Nov. 20 — Two wall posters calling for a full public investigation into the suppression and cover-up of the major anti-Government demonstration in Peking in 1976 appeared in the Chinese capital today, raising questions about the status of Hua Kuo-feng, Chairman of the Chinese Communist Party.

The posters said an inquiry was necessary so that "those responsible" for the suppression and cover-up could be brought to justice." According to diplomats in Peking, the posters demanded that the committee of investigation be made up of all major organs of the party and state.

Mr. Hua's present standing is closely linked to the incident, which took place in Tien An Men Square in central Peking on April 5, 1976 and was ostensibly in memory of the recently deceased Prime Minister Chou En-lai. At the time, Teng Hsiao-ping was blamed.

Two days later, "on the proposal" of Mao Tse-tung, Mr. Teng was purged and Mr. Hua was named party Chairman and Prime Minister. Mr. Teng, now again a Deputy Prime Minister, was reinstated in 1977 after the death of Mao and the arrest of his radical followers.

Yesterday, another poster put up in

Continued on Page A5, Column 1

SHORTAGES GROWING IN NO-LEAD GASOLINE OF HIGHER OCTANES

Although Overall Supply Appears Adequate, Some Companies Lag on Premium Grades

By ANTHONY J. PARISI

Shortages of premium unleaded gasoline are cropping up around the country, arousing fears among motorists of a general shortage of fuel for their automobiles.

Although supplies of gasoline appear adequate over all, some companies have been unable to keep up with the keen demand for high-octane unleaded gasoline, which provides superior performance for some automobiles. Some service stations have begun to turn away customers, who then find themselves waiting on longer and longer lines at stations that still have sufficient supplies on hand.

The Shell Oil Company, which has had to shut down two of its key refineries, was the first to report such shortages. Now Mobil stations are having problems, too, and other companies say their supplies are getting tighter by the day.

Some Rationing at Stations

To spread limited supplies among as many customers as possible, some stations have even begun to ration premium unleaded fuel — the first widespread example of gasoline rationing since the Arab oil embargo of 1973-74. The Bronxville Service Station in suburban Westchester County, for example, has been limiting purchases of Mobil Super unleaded to 10 gallons at a time — when it can get supplies. Yesterday it had no premium gasoline of any kind.

The shortages have appeared just as the Department of Energy is preparing to remove controls from gasoline prices. Yesterday, the department's Economic Regulatory Administration published an environmental impact statement on gasoline decontrol, recommending that the Government proceed with the plan despite concerns that the price of unleaded gasoline may skyrocket as a result.

One reason for the shortage is that motorists whose cars require unleaded gas have grown impatient with how their cars perform using regular grades of lead-free fuel. Almost a third of all the

Continued on Page D5, Column 4

Bodies lie strewn about vat containing drink laced with cyanide at the Jonestown headquarters of the People's Temple

Associated Press

Defectors From Sect Depict Its Rehearsals for Suicide

By ROBERT LINDSEY
Special to The New York Times

LOS ANGELES, Nov. 20 — "He has mass suicide drills, where he tells all the people, hundreds of people, to drink a certain drink, and he says, 'That's fatal, you're all going to die in 45 minutes, I want to see how you feel about dying for socialism.' "

And, said Timothy Stoen, a San Francisco lawyer and former aide to the Rev. Jim Jones, the founder of the People's Temple, when Mr. Jones ordered his followers in his Guyana commune to drink the liquid, "everybody drank."

"It was like he wanted to believe he was God," said Anna Mobley, a member

for four years. "He would get you so tired it would make you lose your mind."

"He had something they called the 'blue-eyed monster,' a thing they did to children," another former member said. "They took children into a dark room and attached electrodes to them and then shocked them and told them never not to smile at Jim Jones."

"He sent spies to our home and said that if we didn't sell all our property, we would die," said Wade Medlock, the owner of a Los Angeles maintenance company, who turned over two of his homes to the cult under threats.

The remarks were made at a meeting of a group called the Human Freedom Foundation, which was set up here last summer by two psychics, Maria Papapetros and Jenita Cargile, after former cult members had sought them out for counseling on how to "deprogram" themselves. A recording of the meeting was made available to The New York Times.

According to former members, the cult was run as a police state by Mr. Jones, who was said to have enforced discipline by beatings and death threats; pursued bizarre sexual activities, and indoctrinated members in his personal brand of agrarian socialism.

According to Mr. Stoen, Mr. Jones first

enticed members with a doctrine of selflessness and a simple Christian faith of social equality that found support among blacks and upper middle-class whites who had become alienated in the 1960's.

Once he got "control of their minds, he would accept no dissent and told members that a defector had no right to live," Mr. Stoen said. He is a former deputy district attorney in Mendocino County who had been attracted by Mr. Jones's views in the late 1960's and became one of his lieutenants as the cult spread to San Francisco and Los Angeles and ultimately to the settlement in Guyana.

He said that as a sect official he had transferred more than $5 million to foreign bank accounts and said he believed the church's assets probably totaled much more.

Mr. Stoen said "people who disagreed would get phone calls at 3 A.M. with heavy breathing" or cult officials would find a drunk and pay him to read a script containing threats over the telephone. The children of parents who decided to leave the sect were often seized and kept in Guyana under guard.

Mr. Jones, he continued, had a "relationships committee" that had to approve

Continued on Page A16, Column 4

LEADER OF SECT DIES

Parents Reported to Give Children Poison Before Dying Beside Them

By JON NORDHEIMER
Special to The New York Times

GEORGETOWN, Guyana, Nov. 20 — In a scene that dashed the senses, Guyanese forces today picked their way through an open-air pavilion choked with the bodies of 405 men, women and children in an American cult group who apparently committed suicide on the orders of their leader.

Wearing gaily colored clothes, the bodies were clustered in family groups, side-by-side in deathly embrace, all but three dead from drinking a concoction made of Kool-Aid and cyanide.

The setting was the jungle church of the People's Temple, the group that has been blamed for the slaying of Congressman Leo J. Ryan and four other Americans on Saturday.

Survivor Describes Scene

A surviving cult member gave the first newsmen to reach the scene today an account that was as incredible as it was filled with horror, a story of death plots and madness, of parents spooning a poisonous punch into the mouths of their babies before drinking it themselves.

And on the altar of the pavilion, surrounded in death by his followers as he had been surrounded by them in life, was the body of James Warren Jones, also known as the Rev. Jim Jones, the charismatic leader of the People's Temple, who had promised his racially integrated flock a utopia in the South American wilds. Instead, he gave them death.

"The time has come to meet in another place," he was said to have told the cultists he had assembled around him shortly after learning of the failure of a plan to kill the entire group of newsmen and parents of cultists who had flown deep into a lonely jungle airport with Congressman Ryan, according to the survivor, Odell Rhodes, 36 years old, from Detroit.

400 Are Still Missing

And then, according to the survivor's account, cyanide was dumped into a huge soup kettle, and the liquid was fed first to the babies, then to the children old enough to drink it themselves, and finally swallowed by the adults, many of whom were older people who had turned their Social Security checks and their lives over to the custody of Mr. Jones.

The leader, who at different times had described himself as the reincarnation of Christ and Lenin, died of a bullet wound in the head, according to the Guyanese police.

Nothing is known about the whereabouts of the remaining 400 or more cultists, who either fled into the jungle to escape death, or have elected to die deeper inside the canopied rain forest, where flesh-eating piranha and electric eels move in the murky jungle streams and insects swarm in the midday heat.

Cult Was Drilled in Suicide

It was learned that the cult was routinely drilled in suicide by Mr. Jones, who had a vision of a need to destroy the community if it was ever attacked.

Apparently, Mr. Ryan, who had been asked to investigate claims by his California constituents that members of the cult were being held in virtual bondage on the commune, and the party that accompanied him last Saturday, were seen as a grave danger.

Mr. Jones had decided to kill Mr. Ryan and the two dozen or so people who ac-

Continued on Page A17, Column 1

Bally Corp. Plan to Build Casino On Historic Site Backed by Jersey

By DONALD JANSON
Special to The New York Times

ATLANTIC CITY, Nov. 20 — New Jersey officials indicated today that they would permit the Bally Manufacturing Corporation, the world's leading manufacturer of slot machines, to demolish the historic Blenheim Hotel rotunda on the Boardwalk to make way for a casino.

The "preliminary" finding by the State Department of Environmental Protection is the latest step in changing the face of Atlantic City, with the classic resort hotels of the city's heyday yielding to a new line of modern casino hotels. Keeping the Moorish rotunda of the Blenheim intact — the main wing has been demolished — is the focal point of a determined drive by preservationists.

Last May 26 Resorts International opened the city's first casino in the old Haddon Hall Hotel after radically altering the structure and renaming it the Resorts International Hotel.

Since then 32 companies, including most of the major concerns operating casinos in Nevada, have either acquired potential casino sites in Atlantic City or announced plans to do so.

One company, Caesars World, operator of Caesars Palace in Las Vegas, has acquired two Boardwalk sites and has a casino under construction on one of them. Steel girders are up on the site of the Howard Johnson Regency Hotel, which will be incorporated into the new casino hotel.

Caesars hopes to open the city's second casino by next Memorial Day. It has also acquired, for possible construction of another casino, the site of the Traymore Hotel, a Boardwalk landmark that was demolished six years ago.

Bally hopes to be third to open an At-

lantic City casino. Its target date is July. It acquired three adjacent, historic hotels and wants to demolish all three eventually.

Last month Bally did demolish the Marlborough, a Queen Anne 1902 wooden structure that was one of first in the city to provide a private bath with every room.

In addition Bally is ripping out the interior of the Dennis, built in 1900 in the French Chateau style, and renovating it. The Dennis is the oldest hotel name on the beachfront today.

Last week 326 pounds of dynamite top-

Continued on Page B7, Column 2

INSIDE

Carter Aides Named in Inquiry
A grand jury is studying charges that White House aides considered dropping the Vesco extradition case in return for $10 million in stock. Page B11.

Trucking Restriction Dropped
The Interstate Commerce Commission dropped a 40-year-old rule that barred companies that truck their own goods from hauling goods of others. Page D1.

ROTHKO 1903-1970 MURALS THRU DEC. 2
AT THE PACE GALLERY 32 EAST 57 ST NY ADVT.

© 1978, The San Francisco Examiner
CULT LEADER: Jim Jones in Jonestown before shootings. Guyana revealed references from prominent Americans. Page A16.

Bodies of five Americans lie at ambush site in Port Kaituma, Guyana. From left, in foreground: Representative Leo J. Ryan; Don Harris, reporter for NBC: Gregory Robinson, photographer for The San Francisco Examiner, and Patricia Parks, believed to be a member of the commune. At rear is Robert Brown, an NBC cameraman.

"All the News That's Fit to Print"

The New York Times

CITY EDITION

Metropolitan area weather: Mild today; colder tonight, tomorrow. Temperature range: today 51-30; yesterday 45-30. Details on page 39.

VOL. CXXVIII . . . . No. 44,068

— NEW YORK, SATURDAY, DECEMBER 16, 1978 —

25 cents beyond 50-mile zone from New York City. Higher in air delivery cities.

20 CENTS

U.S. AND CHINA OPENING FULL RELATIONS; TENG WILL VISIT WASHINGTON ON JAN. 29

Israel Rejects New Peace Proposal; U.S., Irritated, Charges Distortion

Cabinet Backs Begin Stand

By PAUL HOFMANN

Special to The New York Times

JERUSALEM, Dec. 15 — The Israeli Cabinet decided today to reject the latest proposals by Egypt for a peace treaty as well as the "attitude and interpretation" of the United States regarding the proposals.

At the end of a special four-hour meeting, Prime Minister Menachem Begin,

Text of Israeli decision, page 3.

looking grim, said to reporters:

"The consultations, the negotiations will resume — we cannot say when."

[An official in the Egyptian Foreign Ministry denied Israeli charges that Cairo had made new demands during Secretary of State Vance's trip. Page 4.]

No Hope for Treaty by Deadline

The endorsement by the Cabinet of Prime Minister Begin's stand in talks with Secretary of State Cyrus R. Vance here Wednesday and yesterday quashed any remaining hope that the proposed Egyptian-Israeli peace treaty might be signed by this Sunday, the original deadline.

Foreign Minister Moshe Dayan warned in an interview broadcast tonight that there was a possibility the draft peace treaty might not be signed at all, and that negotiations between Israel and Egypt would have to start all over again.

The Cabinet's refusal to go along with the United States Government's view

Continued on Page 5, Column 1

Vance Reports to President

By BERNARD GWERTZMAN

Special to The New York Times

WASHINGTON, Dec. 15 — The Carter Administration accused Israel today of deliberately distorting the nature of new peace proposals taken to Jerusalem this week by Secretary of State Cyrus R. Vance in his effort to complete an Egyptian-Israeli treaty.

Obviously irritated by the Israeli Cabinet's decision to reject the proposals, announced today by Prime Minister Menachem Begin, officials accompanying Mr. Vance on his Air Force plane from Cairo to Washington, gave reporters a highly detailed briefing intended to rebut Mr. Begin's statements.

Vance Goes to White House

Mr. Vance, who arrived at Andrews Air Force Base late this afternoon, went by helicopter directly to the White House to report to President Carter on the trip to Cairo and Jerusalem.

There was no official statement by the White House after the Vance-Carter meeting. But the State Department was instructed to draft a "white paper" to put on record the complaints against the Israelis.

Relations between Washington and Jerusalem were again under severe strain, and Mr. Vance was described as "saddened" and annoyed by the Israeli Cabinet's decision, which left little room for any early progress.

The immediate reaction of American officials in the Vance party was that a

Continued on Page 3, Column 1

Associated Press

President Carter making announcement last night

United Press International

Deputy Prime Minister Teng Hsiao-ping

LINK TO TAIWAN ENDS

Carter, in TV Speech, Says 'We Recognize Reality' After 30-Year Rift

By TERENCE SMITH

Special to The New York Times

WASHINGTON, Dec. 15 — President Carter announced tonight that the United States and China would establish diplomatic relations on Jan. 1.

The President also said that Teng Hsiao-ping, the powerful Deputy Prime

Text of Carter statement, page 8.

Minister, would visit this country later in January. In a press briefing, reporters were told that Mr. Teng will visit the United States Jan. 29. It will be the first such visit by a high-level Chinese official since the Communists took power on the mainland in 1949.

In a dramatic, nationally televised speech, Mr. Carter also announced that the United States would terminate diplomatic relations with Taiwan as well as the mutual defense treaty with the Chinese Nationalists. In four months, the United States will also withdraw its remaining military personnel from Taiwan, the President said, but in remarks addressed especially to the people of the island, he pledged that the United States would remain interested in the peaceful resolution of the issue.

'Recognizing Simple Reality'

"We do not undertake this important step for transient, tactical reasons," Mr. Carter said. "In recognizing that the Government of the People's Republic of China is the single Government of China, we are recognizing simple reality."

"Normalization — and the expanded commercial and cultural relations it will bring with it — will contribute to the well-being of our own nation and will enhance stability in Asia," the President said.

In reassuring the people of Taiwan, Mr. Carter said he had taken care in reaching the agreement to make sure that the normalization of relations with the mainland "will not jeopardize the well-being of the people of Taiwan.

Certain Ties to Be Maintained

"We will continue to have an interest in the peaceful resolution of the Taiwan issue," Mr. Carter said. He added that the United States would maintain "our current commercial, cultural and other relations with Taiwan through nongovernmental means."

Mr. Teng's visit, Mr. Carter said, "will give our Governments the opportunity to consult with each other on global issues and to begin working together to enhance the cause of world peace."

The two countries will exchange ambassadors and establish embassies on March 1.

The President made special mention of the "long, serious negotiations" with China carried on before him by Presidents Richard M. Nixon and Gerald R. Ford. The results, he said, "bear witness to the steady, determined, bipartisan effort of our own country to build a world in which peace will be the goal and the responsibility of all countries."

Earlier in the evening, Administration officials confirmed that Treasury Secre-

Continued on Page 8, Column 1

CLEVELAND RACING DEFAULT DEADLINE

Bankers Grant Brief Extension — City Bond Credit Rating Cut

By REGINALD STUART

Special to The New York Times

CLEVELAND, Dec. 15 — City officials scheduled a meeting for 11 o'clock tonight to decide whether to accept Mayor Dennis J. Kucinich's sweeping fiscal rehabilitation plan for the city or find some other means of avoiding default on $15.5 million in loans that were due today.

At the same time, banker-creditors, whom the city had contracted with to repay the short-term loans, extended their hours until midnight to see if the city would either pay the debts or come up with a plan that would persuade them to renew the loans.

Mayor Assails Bank and Council

Meanwhile, Moody's Investors Service, the municipal bond credit-rating company, lowered the city's bond rating today to Caa. That was the lowest rating reached three years ago by New York City during its financial crisis. A Caa classification defines such bonds as being in default or having "present elements of danger with respect to principal or interest."

The chances for success of the Mayor's plan, which has drawn strong opposition from City Council leaders and at least two of the six lenders, were further diminished tonight when the Mayor ac-

Continued on Page 11, Column 1

China Tie Reflects Carter's Feeling That Country Was Ready for Move

By HEDRICK SMITH

Special to The New York Times

WASHINGTON, Dec. 15 — President Carter's dramatic announcement that he was taking this country into a new era of diplomatic relations with China reflects the confident political calculation that the country-at-large is now ready for this step and the hopeful diplomatic calculation that it will not jeopardize the imminent new strategic-arms agreement with the Soviet Union.

High Administration officials revealed that the breakthrough had come quicker than expected and had been pushed by the Chinese. Although the White House found the timing awkward, because of the delicate stage of negotiations with Moscow on an arms accord, Washington felt that the Chinese initiative could not be turned down.

In another way, however, the breakthrough could not have come at a more opportune moment for an Administration frustrated by the latest impasse in the Middle East talks and beset by the political upheaval in Iran and the potential tremors elsewhere in the Near East.

The move appeals to the historic American fascination with the Orient since the days when clipper ships carried missionaries and merchants to distant China from the salty harbors of Massachusetts. In the modern calculus of global power politics, the tie with China offers new leverage in the triangular relationship with the Soviet Union, as well as a counter to recent Soviet gains in Afghanistan and the Horn of Africa.

As rumors swept the city tonight before

Continued on Page 8, Column 5

Koch Gets 3 Billion School Budget; Smaller Classes Among Objectives

By MARCIA CHAMBERS

The New York City School Chancellor, Frank J. Macchiarola, submitted a $3 billion expense budget to Mayor Koch yesterday that calls for smaller classes, intensified remedial instruction and additional personnel to combat truancy, vandalism and internal mismanagement.

To finance these additional programs, the Chancellor said he had to find $130 million in the budget from sources not yet committed to the public school system's anticipated revenues. The system's costs are roughly a third of the city's overall expense budget. He said that following the Mayor's lead he intended to try to get the necessary funds from the state and Federal Governments.

The Chancellor plans to have an all-day meeting on Monday with Federal officials in an attempt to obtain changes in Federal law that would give the school system more say in how and where remedial funds can be spent. Then, Mr. Macchiarola said, he intends to talk to Albany lawmakers, who are under a court ruling to revise the state-aid allocation formula for the financing of public schools.

If the city school district — the biggest in the country, with nearly a million students — "gets its fair share of state funding," he said, "we would get triple the

The Mayor's consultant on the City University has endorsed $160 million in priority construction projects. Page 25.

amount we get now." He said that would be more than enough for the new programs.

In an obvious criticism of his predecessor, Irving Anker, Mr. Macchiarola said in his budget message to the Board of Education that "additional funds will be required in order to begin the programing that has been neglected — not without severe effect — in recent years." Mr. Macchiarola's proposed 1979-80 budget is virtually the same as the Anker budget proposal last year. The Board of Education will hold a public hearing on the

Continued on Page 28, Column 1

China: The Long Wait

By FOX BUTTERFIELD

Special to The New York Times

HONG KONG, Saturday, Dec. 16 — President Carter's announcement last night that the United States and China are finally normalizing diplomatic relations comes nearly seven years after Richard M. Nixon pledged in the Shanghai Communiqué of February 1972 to work toward that goal.

News Analysis

The major obstacle to progress on restoring relations has been America's long-time military and diplomatic commitment to the Chinese Nationalist regime on Taiwan, a problem compounded by the continued strong support for Taiwan among many in the United States.

After the initial euphoria that accompanied Mr. Nixon's epochal trip to China, relations between the two nations seemed to languish for several years as events gave Taiwan a series of reprieves. First, Mr. Nixon's plans to improve ties were hampered by the Watergate scandal. Then President Gerald R. Ford was caught by the debacle of Vietnam's collapse. And more recently Mr. Carter himself was sidetracked by the Panama Canal negotiations, the Middle East problems and talks to limit the spread of nuclear weapons. Fears were raised that Washington was frittering away a critical opportunity to strengthen America's interests in Asia.

Recent Improvement in Relations

But in recent months, largely at China's initiative, relations began to improve rapidly. Since the summer, in fact, the two countries have been drawing together in a process that looked like normalizing without the final actual step.

Two factors impelled this change: China's increased fears of being encircled by the new alliance between the Soviet Union and Vietnam, and its desire for expanded trade and technology to

Continued on Page 8, Column 5

United Press International

Mayor Dennis J. Kucinich of Cleveland, foreground, was accused at City Council debate of not acting to prevent default

Taiwan Leaders Confer Hurriedly After Learning of U.S.-China Step

Special to The New York Times

TAIPEI, Taiwan, Saturday, Dec. 16 — Leaders of the Chinese Nationalist Government were abruptly summoned into emergency meetings here early today, a few hours before the announcement in Washington that the United States was establishing diplomatic relations with Peking.

The United States, it appeared, gave only a few hours' notice to Taiwan that it was withdrawing its recognition of the Government of President Chiang Ching-kuo.

U.S. Decision a Heavy Blow

President Chiang first called several Cabinet ministers to his office to brief them on the developments. Then, official sources said, an emergency meeting of the central committee of the Kuomintang, the governing party, was scheduled to consider the most serious blow it has suffered in the three decades since Chiang Kai-shek led his defeated followers here from the mainland.

More than 50 countries have broken relations with Taiwan since the Chinese Nationalists were replaced at the United Nations in 1971 by the Communist regime. But the American decision comes as a particularly heavy blow since the United States, the last world power to recognize the Nationalists, has supported them since 1954 with a mutual-defense treaty.

Since President Richard M. Nixon's visit to China in 1972, the Nationalists have expected that the United States would eventually break relations. The timing, however, was apparently a surprise.

It comes during a heated parliamentary election campaign on Taiwan, when some rightist candidates have been warning that it faces a possible "betrayal" by the United States. Others, however, have campaigned on the slogan that the fate of Taiwan should be decided by the island's 16 million people.

One candidate said: "We should not repeat the history in Vietnam. Taiwan's fu-

Continued on Page 8, Column 1

INSIDE

Saudis Moderate on Oil Prices

On the eve of a meeting of oil-exporting countries, Saudi Arabia's delegate called for moderation in determining an increased price of oil. Page 29.

Cults' Funds Reported Gone

A U.S. official said a Zurich bank had told the Justice Department that as much as $8 million in People's Temple funds had been removed. Page 12.

"All the News That's Fit to Print"

The New York Times

LATE CITY EDITION

Weather: Snow likely and cold today; snow changing to sleet or rain tonight. Temperature range: today 28-35; yesterday 25-41. Details on page B9.

VOL.CXXVIII No.44,100

NEW YORK, WEDNESDAY, JANUARY 17, 1979

25 cents beyond 50-mile zone from New York City. Higher in air delivery cities.

20 CENTS

SHAH LEAVES IRAN FOR INDEFINITE STAY; CROWDS EXULT, MANY EXPECT LONG EXILE

New York City Gets Passing Grade On $100 Million Notes It Will Sell

By ANNA QUINDLEN

The city prepared to go ahead this month with its proposed $100 million note sale after the notes received a passing, but not superior, grade yesterday. The note sale will be the city's first foray into the public borrowing market in nearly four years.

The fiscal rating is expected to be one piece of evidence of economic recovery Mayor Koch takes with him when he testifies before the Senate Banking Committee. The committee's chairman, William Proxmire, announced yesterday that he would hold hearings Feb. 7 on the city's financial condition.

The MIG-3 rating given to the notes by Moody's Investor Service yesterday was lower than city officials had hoped for, but it was still an improvement over its last investment grade, the lowest ranked MIG-4. That rating quashed a scheduled note sale in November 1977. Moody's noted in a statement that while repayment of the short-term notes seemed secure, the "chronic financial weakness" of the city made a higher rating impossible at this time.

Moody's defines MIG-3 as an investment of "favorable quality, but lacking the undeniable strength" of the two higher classifications. The letters MIG stand for Moody's Investment Grade.

'A Climate of Uncertainty'

"Reliability of pledged revenues in the quality of the mechanism to assure payment of notes provides basic security," Moody's said in issuing its grade.

"The chronic financial weakness of the issuer (continual budget balancing efforts, persistent revenue shortages, magnitude of fixed costs) still creates an overall climate of uncertainty. The balancing of this year's budget indicates financial progress."

"I'm obviously pleased that our credit rating is better," said Mayor Koch when the rating was announced, a day after the unveiling of his own plan to close the city's budget gap. "If your credit rating is better it means more people have faith in you."

Mr. Koch and Deputy Mayor Philip L. Toia said they expected the city to go ahead with the sale, although neither would speculate on how high a rate of interest the city might have to pay in the current market on such notes. The notes will be offered by a consortium of underwriters to the public in $10,000 and $25,000 denominations.

Deficit Dispute Blamed

However, Jackson Phillips of Moody's said he did not think the city would proceed with a sale if the interest rate on the notes went above the 9.5 per cent it currently pays on loans from banks. "I hear

Continued on Page B4, Column 5

New York State to Try New Negotiation Plan

By RICHARD J. MEISLIN

Special to The New York Times

ALBANY, Jan. 16 — Governor Carey's administration and New York's largest public-employees union agreed today to adopt an experimental bargaining method in which each side would negotiate to its "last, best offer" and an impartial arbitration panel would be forced to choose one proposal or the other.

The union, the Civil Service Employees Association, guaranteed as part of the agreement that its members would not strike and agreed to require the arbitration panel to give "substantial weight" to the "ability of the state to pay the cost of any economic benefit without requiring an increase in present taxes." The agreement covers 107,000 state workers, whose contracts expire March 31.

It will be the first use of binding arbitration to resolve impasses in negotiations between the state and its workers, which in the past have been subject to the state's Taylor Law requirements for state mediation and fact-finding and for legislative resolution.

If the new method, known as "last-offer

Continued on Page B5, Column 1

Battle Intensifies Over Authority Of President to Control Agencies

By MARTIN TOLCHIN

Special to The New York Times

WASHINGTON, Jan. 16 — President Carter's fight to control inflation is intensifying a constitutional conflict between his authority to develop national policies and Congress's power to mandate the independence of Government regulators.

In a direct challenge to the President's authority several environmentalist groups have brought a Federal court action asking that White House economic advisers be prohibited from interfering with the Interior Department's formulation of strip-mining regulations. The enforcement of the regulations was delayed for six months last week after the economic advisers expressed fears that they might be inflationary.

In recent years, Congress, suspicious of past Presidential abuses, has given no fewer than 60 agencies in the executive branch the authority to issue regulations on specific and distinct areas without reference to broader concerns. The mandates include authority to clean up the air and water, protect consumers and improve workplace health and safety, all of which affect Presidential concerns such as inflation, the energy gap and economic growth.

The White House View

The powers of such long-time regulatory agencies as the Interstate Commerce Commission and the Federal Communications Commission, whose independence from Presidential intervention is well established, are not in dispute.

But the White House does challenge the theory that executive branch agencies should perform their new regulatory functions without Presidential direction. It contends that the President's power to appoint and dismiss Cabinet officers carries an implicit authority to direct the agencies' actions.

Critics, mainly single-interest groups that have fought to get regulations through Congress, maintain that Congress intended that these Cabinet officers

Continued on Page D17, Column 1

West German Retailer Seeks 42% of A.& P. In a $75 Million Deal

By BARBARA ETTORRE

A major West German food retailer announced plans yesterday to acquire 42 percent of the Great Atlantic and Pacific Tea Company, the supermarket giant whose initials have long been a household term in American retailing.

The Tengelmann Group, a privately owned company, said that it planned to buy some A.& P. shares from the John A. Hartford Foundation, which has held a major interest in the chain for many years, and from several other major shareholders.

The 42 percent interest would mean effective control of A.& P. for the German company and would represent an investment of more than $75 million. Trading of A.& P. stock on the New York Stock Exchange was halted yesterday afternoon at 6⅞, up ⅛. The plan would involve a purchase of approximately 10 million of the 25 million A.& P. shares outstanding.

Jonathan L. Scott, chairman and chief executive officer of A.& P., said in a statement that the company "welcomes this expression of investment confidence." He continued, "We at A.& P. look

Continued on Page D4, Column 1

INSIDE

Vietnam Troops Lose Port

In their first reverse in Cambodia, Vietnamese troops were driven out of Kompong Som, a key port, according to Western analysts. Page A3.

52 Convicts Get Clemency

Freedom or parole eligibility was granted by Tennessee's governor while hearings on the alleged sale of clemency continued. Page A14.

Shah Mohammed Riza Pahlevi and his wife, Empress Farah, as they prepared to leave Teheran yesterday

United Press International

On Streets: Cheers, Roses and a Mink Coat

United Press International

Statue of the Shah's father, Riza Shah, being toppled shortly after Shah left

One Man in Crowd Hailing Shah's Departure Asks, 'Am I Dreaming?'

By ERIC PACE

Special to The New York Times

TEHERAN, Iran, Jan. 16 — "Shah raft! Shah raft!" The joyful shout announced: "The Shah is gone!"

As soon as the news broke on the Teheran radio, the cry began sounding along Vesel-e-Shirazi Street. Cheering crowds formed and happy women tossed candy and rosewater at them. Farokh Marvasti, an electrical engineer, had a dazed smile. "Am I dreaming?" he said. "What I have always hoped for has come true: The whole system of monarchy is collapsing here after 2,500 years."

"Salute to the mother of martyrs!" the throng of black-veiled women chanted at a rally in the Dehkade Vanek section of this sprouting, traffic-clogged city of five million. They waved their fists toward Zahra Rezai, who is revered by Islamic militants as the mother of four Islamic anti-Government "guerrillas" who died at the hands of the Shah's Government, one in prison and three in shootouts. "I never thought the Shah would leave so soon," Mrs. Rezai said, weeping. "I am glad the lives of my children were not wasted and now our country will have peace."

For the throng of hundreds of thousands that surged through the boulevard it was a day of reveling and roses, roses that marchers tossed in the air as they chanted: "O the anti-Islamic Shah!" "His return is impossible!" "The Shah has become a fugitive!"

Some demonstrators tried and eventually succeeded in pulling the equestrian statue of Riza Shah, the present Shah's father, from its pedestal on Sepah Square; it took a lot of pulling. On Pahlavi Avenue others toppled a statue of his son from its pedestal.

"May God help you," the militant Islamic clergyman known as Mullah Doost Mohammed said as he tried to comfort a strong-jawed woman, Nemati Roshan, who was weeping uncontrollably after the rally in Dehkade Vanek.

"Damn the Shah!" Mrs. Roshan had yelled when the rally was at its peak. Now she was sobbing as she told the

Continued on Page A8, Column 5

Iran, a Country Adrift

By R.W. APPLE Jr.

Special to The New York Times

TEHERAN, Iran, Jan. 16 — The din of triumph that echoed through Teheran today expressed the spirit of the moment. But the spirit of the future may have been more truly expressed by a phrase uttered at the same time near Paris by a resolute 78-year-old man who has made a revolution. The depature of Shah Mohammed Riza Pahlevi, said Ayatollah Ruhollah Khomeini, was "only a first step" toward his goals.

News Analysis

In the sense that little could be accomplished while the Shah remained here, his flight to Egypt and, later, to the United States removed a great obstacle to the resolution of Iran's yearlong political crisis. It also removed the man by whom and around whom the country's life has been organized since the start of World War II.

No one is really in charge here now — a situation symbolized by banknotes, held aloft by celebrants, from which the Shah's portrait had been excised. With what is probably the permanent departure of the Shah, the heir to Iran's proud 2,500-year imperial history, Ayatollah Khomeini has become the cardinal political figure. He has not yet established full control, but he more than anyone else commands the affection of the masses.

The central question tonight was this: Having brought down the Shah, with whom he has feuded for 15 years, will he demand that the struggle continue until an Islamic republic can be established with him as the strongman, or will he mute his militancy and compromise with the struggling social democratic Government of Prime Minister Shahpur Bakhtiar?

From the answer to that question will flow the answers to many others, both do-

Continued on Page A8, Column 3

Associated Press

In Aswan, Egypt, President Sadat took Shah on canopied ferry to hotel on Nile

RULER GOES TO EGYPT

He Voices Hope Bakhtiar's Government Can Make Amends for Past

By NICHOLAS GAGE

Special to The New York Times

TEHERAN, Iran, Jan. 16 — Shah Mohammed Riza Pahlevi left Iran today, driven from the country he has ruled for 37 years by a popular upheaval that gathered force until it undermined his throne.

A year of demonstrations and crippling strikes culminated in a brief farewell ceremony near the imperial pavilion at Mahrabad Airport, before the Shah's departure for Aswan, Egypt, where he was to be a guest of President Anwar el-Sadat. Tears appeared to be welling in the ruler's eyes.

"I hope the Government will be able to make amends for the past and also succeed in laying the foundation for the future," he said.

Changes Aroused Resentment

The Shah had laid ambitious plans to carry his country from feudalism to the front ranks of the industrial states within a generation. But his ambitions aroused resentment at various levels of the society.

The demonstrators who took to the streets to bring down the Shah complained most loudly about the arbitary manner in which he pressed his programs, the corruption in ruling circles and the harsh measures used to suppress opposition from the religious community and liberal political groups.

In the end, the 59-year-old Shah had accumulated so much hostility from so many quarters that his throne could be saved neither by his lavishly equipped armed forces nor by the United States, which had regarded him as a key ally.

Long Exile Thought Likely

He described his departure today as an extended vacation, but it was believed by his opponents in Iran and by government officials here and in other countries that the trip marked the beginning of a long and perhaps permanent exile.

It was at 1:24 P.M. that the royal jet, a silver-and-blue Boeing 707 named Shahin (Falcon), took off from the airport for Egypt.

[The Shah took the controls himself, The Associated Press reported, and flew the plan over Teheran and on to Egypt.]

As the jet flew over the capital, its citizens were unaware that the year of riots, which are believed to have caused the loss of more than 2,000 lives, had finally succeeded in driving out the Shah.

But within 15 minutes the news had spread throughout Teheran and hundreds of thousands of people poured out of their homes shouting "Shah raft!" — "The Shah is gone!"

The streets, nearly empty during recent days of strikes and gasoline shortages, were quickly clogged with automobiles that added the sound of their horns to the din, as people embraced, wept and

Continued on Page A8, Column 1

Other Iran News

Arriving in Aswan, Egypt, Shah Mohammed Riza Pahlevi was escorted by President Anwar el-Sadat to a secluded hotel on an island in the Nile. Page A8.

In Paris, Ayatollah Ruhollah Khomeini, the exiled leader of the Shah's religious opposition, congratulated the Iranian people for forcing the Shah's departure through their increasingly violent demonstrations over the last year. Page A8.

In Washington, the Carter Administration made no formal comment on the Shah's departure, which it had encouraged, but officials said privately that the Government of Prime Minister Shahpur Bakhtiar probably had no better than a 50-50 chance of survival. Page A10.

Also in Washington, the Iranian envoy and friend of the Shah, Ardeshir Zahedi, declared himself the "Ambassador of the Shah" and said he would continue as an attempt by six employees to bar him from his embassy failed for lack of support. Page A10.

At the United Nations, Iranian diplomats closed their mission all day in what they described as solidarity with the Iranian people on the occasion of the Shah's departure. Page A10.

In Lubbock, Tex., Crown Prince Riza Pahlevi welcomed his brother and two sisters, who arrived a few hours before their father left Teheran. Page A10.

On Beekman Place in New York, neighbors of Princess Ashraf Pahlevi, the Shah's twin sister, said they thought a visit by the Shah was likely. Page B3.

"All the News That's Fit to Print"

The New York Times

LATE CITY EDITION

Weather: Mostly sunny, cool today; clear, cold tonight. Sunny tomorrow. Temperature range: today 32-48; yesterday 37-49. Details on page C12.

VOL.CXXVIII . . . . No.44,169 — NEW YORK, TUESDAY, MARCH 27, 1979 — 20 CENTS

25 cents beyond 50-mile zone from New York City. Higher in air delivery cities.

EGYPT AND ISRAEL SIGN FORMAL TREATY, ENDING A STATE OF WAR AFTER 30 YEARS; SADAT AND BEGIN PRAISE CARTER'S ROLE

OPEC PARLEY WEIGHS NEW OIL PRICE RISES AND CUTS IN OUTPUT

Saudis Say They Will Try to Resist Big Increases — Carter Puts Off Decisions on Energy

By PAUL LEWIS
Special to The New York Times

GENEVA, March 26 — Pressure for another large increase in world oil prices built up today at the opening of a meeting of oil ministers of the 13 member nations of the Organization of Petroleum Exporting Countries.

The advocates of a sharp new oil price rise, of anywhere from 20 to 35 percent from current levels on April 1, also urged other oil producers to reduce output. The aim would be to keep world markets tight as Iran resumes exports to insure that the new price levels stick.

But Saudi Arabia, the world's largest oil exporter, resisted pressure for price jumps, pointing out that they could do severe damage to the economies of both the developing and the industrialized world. "There is worry particularly about the effects of price changes on developing countries," OPEC's secretary general, René Ortise, said.

Effort to Reduce Increases

Sheik Ahmed Zaki Yamani, Saudi Arabia's oil minister, interviewed after tonight's session, said the ministers faced a "deadlock," with the Saudis feeling that the increases demanded by Iran and Libya were "too steep." Observers here interpreted his stance as an effort to cut probable increases to more moderate levels.

The ministers have not yet voted themselves the power to take any pricing action at the current two-day session but are expected to do so tomorrow. A simple majority vote would grant the meeting such authority.

On the question of possible punitive cutbacks in supplies, reflecting displeasure with some consuming nations' positions on the Palestinian question, Iraqi representatives said such moves were possible, particularly against Egypt. But they carefully noted that no such moves were planned by OPEC, although the "oil weapon" could re-emerge if conditions returned to the situation of 1973.

Carter Decisions Deferred

In Washington, meanwhile, Administration officials said that President Carter's decisions on various energy proposals, expected Thursday, would be deferred, apparently because key White House officials had not been able to devote enough time to the controversial plans. [Page D12.]

When Sheik Yamani entered the OPEC

Continued on Page D12, Column 3

United Press International

Leaders join hands after signing pact. President Anwar el-Sadat signed first, followed by Prime Minister Menachem Begin. President Carter was witness.

CEREMONY IS FESTIVE

Accord on Sinai Oil Opens Way to the First Peace in Mideast Dispute

By BERNARD GWERTZMAN
Special to The New York Times

WASHINGTON, March 26 — After confronting each other for nearly 31 years as hostile neighbors, Egypt and Israel signed a formal treaty at the White House today to establish peace and "normal and friendly relations."

On this chilly early spring day, about 1,500 invited guests and millions more watching television saw President Anwar el-Sadat of Egypt and Prime Minister

Transcripts of statements at signing are on page A11. Texts of treaty and Camp David accords are on pages A12, A13 and A14.

Menachem Begin of Israel put their signatures on the Arabic, Hebrew and English versions of the first peace treaty between Israel and an Arab country.

President Carter, who was credited by both leaders for having made the agreement possible, signed, as a witness, for the United States. In a somber speech he said, "Peace has come."

'The First Step of Peace'

"We have won, at last, the first step of peace — a first step on a long and difficult road," he added.

All three leaders offered prayers that the treaty would bring true peace to the Middle East and end the enmity that has erupted into war four times since Israel declared its independence on May 14, 1948.

By coincidence, they all referred to the words of the Prophet Isaiah.

"Let us work together until the day comes when they beat their swords into plowshares and their spears into pruning hooks," Mr. Sadat said in his paraphrase of the biblical text.

Mr. Begin, who gave the longest and most emotional of the addresses, exclaimed: "No more war, no more bloodshed, no more bereavement, peace unto you, shalom, saalam, forever."

"Shalom" and "salaam" are the Hebrew and Arabic words for "peace."

A Touch of Humor by Begin

The Israeli leader, noted for oratorical skill, provided a dash of humor when in the course of his speech he seconded Mr. Sadat's remark that Mr. Carter was "the unknown soldier of the peacemaking effort." Mr. Begin said, pausing, "I agree, but as usual with an amendment" — that Mr. Carter was not completely unknown and that his peace effort would "be remembered and recorded by generations to come."

Since Mr. Begin was known through the

Continued on Page A10, Column 1

Mood of Peace Seems Somber And Uncertain

By BERNARD WEINRAUB
Special to The New York Times

WASHINGTON, March 26 — Shortly after 6 A.M. today, President Anwar el-Sadat arose in the residence of the Egyptian Ambassador and began wandering around the five-bedroom house.

He scanned the morning newspapers, pedaled a stationary exercise bicycle, nibbled a slice of unbuttered toast, sipped a glass of orange juice and, by 7 A.M. turned on the television to watch the morning news.

Less than one mile away, in a guarded ninth-floor suite at the Washington Hilton Hotel, Prime Minister Menachem Begin of Israel peered out the windows at the traffic moving along Connecticut Avenue.

He turned away and, carrying a cup of tea, walked to a writing desk and began working on the emotional speech that he would deliver in mid-afternoon at the White House ceremony ending 30 years of war between Israel and Egypt.

It was the start of a day marked by paradox — a triumphal day of peace that seemed curiously somber, a day of celebration blurred by protests in the heart of Washington, a bright day shadowed by uncertainty.

"There is, you know, a sense of trepi-

Continued on Page A9, Column 1

Photographs for The New York Times by TERESA ZABALA

Treaty Impact Still Unknown

'Hopes and Dreams' but 'No Illusions' for Carter

By HEDRICK SMITH
Special to The New York Times

News Analysis

WASHINGTON, March 26 — The elusive, unprecedented peace treaty that Egypt and Israel signed today has enormous symbolic importance and the potential for fundamentally transforming the map and history of an entire region, but the agreement faces an uncertain future.

Israel has now won what it has sought since 1948 — formal recognition and acceptance from the most powerful Arab state and the ultimate prospect of exchanging ambassadors and entering into a full range of normal relations.

For all the violent denunciations that this historic breakthrough aroused in the Arab world, the best diplomatic estimate here is that the treaty has markedly reduced the risk of a major war in the Middle East for a considerable time by removing Egyptian strength from the active Arab arsenal.

And it has demonstrated American capacity to influence events in the Middle East despite the setbacks Washington has suffered since the overthrow of the

Continued on Page A10, Column 5

Judge Bars Hydrogen Bomb Article After Magazine Rejects Mediation

By DOUGLAS E. KNEELAND
Special to The New York Times

MILWAUKEE, March 26 — A Federal District Court judge here, acting only after his suggestion for an attempt at out-of-court settlement was turned down, granted the Government's motion for a preliminary injunction today to keep The Progressive magazine from publishing an article about the hydrogen bomb.

In so doing, Judge Robert W. Warren became the first Federal judge ever to issue an injunction imposing prior restraint on the press in a national security case.

The magazine's attorneys said they would file an appeal shortly with the United States Court of Appeals for the Seventh Circuit in Chicago.

Court's 'Awesome Responsibility'

Before announcing his decision this afternoon, Judge Warren, a former Wisconsin Attorney General, acknowledged that he considered it an "awesome responsibility."

"Stripped to its essence, then," he said, "the question before the court is a basic confrontation between the First Amendment right to freedom of the press and national security."

The judge said "a mistake in ruling against The Progressive will seriously infringe cherished First Amendment rights." However, he added, "a mistake

Continued on Page B12, Column 3

INSIDE

Michigan State Wins

Michigan State became the National Collegiate basketball champion by defeating Indiana State, 75-64, at Salt Lake City. Page C13.

H.R.A. Administrator Quits

Blanche Bernstein, the Human Resources Administrator, resigned rather than accept Mayor Koch's offer to stay in the job without power. Page B1.

Palestinians, Reacting to the Pact, Go on Strike and Denounce Egypt

Special to The New York Times

BEIRUT, Lebanon, March 26 — Vowing revenge, staging strikes and protest marches and calling for punitive measures against Egypt, Palestinians and other Arabs reacted angrily today against the signing of the Egyptian-Israeli peace treaty in Washington.

Yasir Arafat, chairman of the Palestine Liberation Organization, vowed to chase Americans out of the Middle East and to "chop off the hands" of President Carter, President Anwar el-Sadat of Egypt and Prime Minister Menachem Begin of Israel. He spoke to a group of guerrilla recruits at the Sabra Palestinian camp here as effigies of the three signers were burned.

The inhabitants of Lebanon's 15 Palestinian camps protested the signing today by refusing to work, as did many Lebanese Moslems. Similar protests were staged in the occupied West Bank of the Jordan River and the Gaza Strip, and in the Arab Old City of Jerusalem a grenade exploded tonight, wounding five tourists.

Iran Government Condemns Pact

In Teheran, the Iranian Government condemned the treaty, and 30 Arab students took over the Egyptian Embassy there. Protesters also stormed the Egyptian Embassy in Kuwait, where 250,000 Palestinians live, forming the largest foreign community in that small country. In Damascus, Syria, demonstrators occupied the offices of the Egyptian airline, Egyptair.

Meanwhile, foreign and finance ministers of Arab League countries gathered today in Baghdad, Iraq, for a meeting tomorrow on possible economic and political measures against Egypt. The countries had vowed last November to hold such a meeting if the Egyptian-Israeli peace treaty was signed, but Saudi Arabia, Egypt's principal foreign backer, has been trying to exercise a moderating influence.

King Hussein of Jordan flew to Damascus and Baghdad during the day in what was believed to be an effort to coordinate the positions of hard-liners and moderates at tomorrow's Arab meeting.

Gromyko Comments on Treaty

In Damascus, Foreign Minister Andrei A. Gromyko of the Soviet Union ended a three-day visit to Syria today by joining with President Hafez al-Assad in denouncing the peace treaty, saying it appeared bound to increase tension in the Middle East. A joint Soviet-Syrian communiqué said the treaty was aimed at perpetuating the Israeli occupation of Arab lands, the annexation of Arab East-

Continued on Page A10, Column 5

"All the News That's Fit to Print"

The New York Times

LATE CITY EDITION

Weather: Cloudy and hazy today; showers likely today, tomorrow. Temperature range: today 53-73; yesterday 52-75. Details on page 10.

VOL.CXXVIII . No.44,173

NEW YORK, SATURDAY, MARCH 31, 1979

25 cents beyond 50 mile zone from New York City. Higher in air delivery cities.

20 CENTS

U.S. AIDES SEE A RISK OF MELTDOWN AT PENNSYLVANIA NUCLEAR PLANT; MORE RADIOACTIVE GAS IS RELEASED

The New York Times / Teresa Zabala

Elementary-school children arriving at the West Shore School in Dillsburg, Pa., after they were evacuated from Middletown, site of nuclear plant

Teamster Talks Recess, and Gap Is Called Sizable

Mediator, Differing With Optimistic Report, Sees 'Tense, Difficult Spot'

By PHILIP SHABECOFF

Special to The New York Times

ARLINGTON, Va., Saturday, March 31 — Negotiations between the Teamsters and the trucking industry recessed early this morning with "substantial differences still separating the parties," according to Wayne L. Horvitz, the director of the Federal Mediation and Conciliation Service.

"We are at a tense and difficult spot right now," Mr. Horvitz said in announcing that talks would resume tomorrow morning. He added that "reports we are awfully close to a settlement are not true."

Earlier, sources close to the negotiations reported that the two sides had tentatively agreed to a wage increase of $1.50 an hour over three years plus increases in benefits totaling $30 a week over the same period.

Problems Still Unsolved

Mr. Horvitz said that there were problems still to be resolved in both economic and noneconomic areas.

Government officials said earlier in the day that they were optimistic about the prospects for a peaceful conclusion to the negotiations with a settlement that would within President Carter's wage guidelines.

In theory, the guideline would limit annual wage increases to 7 percent. However, to remove what it called inequities and to pave the way for a settlement, the Administration adjusted the guideline so that increases well over 7 percent would be technically in compliance.

26 to 30 Percent Increase

In fact, sources close to the negotiations said that they expected a total wage and benefit package providing an increase of from 26 to 30 percent over the three-year contract. A 7 percent wage guideline, when compounded, would permit a wage and benefit increase of 22.5 percent over three years.

The average wage paid to the 300,000 truckdrivers and other workers covered by the master freight agreement is estimated at about $9.50 an hour. Adminis-

Continued on Page 45, Column 1

BRITISH TORY IS SLAIN IN PARLIAMENT YARD, APPARENTLY BY I.R.A.

Bomb in Car Kills a Close Adviser to Mrs. Thatcher — 2 Groups Claiming Responsibility

By WILLIAM BORDERS

Special to The New York Times

LONDON, March 30 — A leading Member of Parliament was killed this afternoon when a bomb apparently set by Irish terrorists exploded in his car as he was driving out of the Parliament grounds.

The blast, which brought other members rushing from the House of Commons, occurred on an underground ramp in the main courtyard of the building, less than 50 yards from the clock tower. Its victim, Airey M.S. Neave, who was one of the closest advisers to Margaret Thatcher, the Conservative Party leader, died at a nearby hospital 40 minutes later without regaining consciousness.

His murder, for which two separate factions of the Irish Republican Army claimed responsibility tonight, cast a pall over the election campaign that has just begun in Britain, and it deeply shocked a nation unaccustomed to violence against its elected leaders.

'This Terrible Outrage'

Prime Minister James Callaghan, saying he was "appalled at this abhorrent act," promised that "no effort will be spared to rid the United Kingdom of the scourge of terrorism." All over London this evening, homebound workers stopped to read newspaper headlines about Mr. Neave's murder, shaking their heads and murmuring about what one of them called "this terrible outrage."

The bombing came just eight days after Britain's Ambassador to the Netherlands, Sir Richard Sykes, was shot to death in The Hague. Anonymous callers said later that the Provisional wing of the I.R.A. was responsible for his murder.

Mr. Neave, a much-decorated hero of World War II who had been in Parliament for 25 years, was the member of Mrs. Thatcher's shadow Cabinet responsible for the affairs of Northern Ireland. He knew, according to his friends, that the job made him a natural target for the terrorists who are trying to drive the British out of that province.

He was, nevertheless, outspoken on the

Continued on Page 4, Column 3

CHILDREN EVACUATED

But Governor Says Later Further Pullouts Are Not Thought Likely

By RICHARD D. LYONS

Special to The New York Times

MIDDLETOWN, Pa., March 30 — Gov. Dick Thornburgh advised pregnant women and small children today to stay at least five miles away from the crippled Three Mile Island nuclear power plant as radioactivity continued to leak and another burst of contaminated steam had to be released for safety reasons.

Tonight, at a Harrisburg news conference, Government nuclear experts said there was no immediate threat to public health, but Governor Thornburgh said his suggestion for the women and children "remains in force until tomorrow."

Earlier in the day several thousand schoolchildren were evacuated from the plant area, 10 miles southeast of Harrisburg, and other people began leaving on the Governor's advice. More than 150 pregnant women and young children were at a shelter in Hershey, for example.

No Evacuation Order

As for others in the area, the Governor said tonight: "No evacuation order is necessary. My earlier advice that people try to remain indoors expires at midnight."

The highest levels of radioactive material yet vented were let go from the facility today, and one official of the Nuclear Regulatory Commission, Dennis Crutchfield, said that up to one-fourth of the fuel rods, or 9,000 of the 36,000 fuel elements, may have been damaged since Wednesday.

Further, Government and nuclear

Continued on Page 8, Column 3

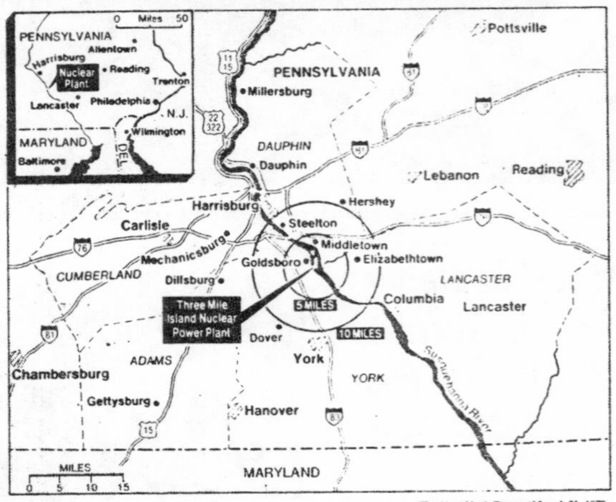

The New York Times / March 31, 1979

Gov. Dick Thornburgh of Pennsylvania urged young children and pregnant women to avoid the area within five miles of the Three Mile Island plant until sometime today. His request to those within 10 miles to stay indoors expired at midnight. Earlier, residents of Lancaster, Adams, Cumberland and Dauphin counties were alerted to possible evacuation, an alert that was canceled.

CONGRESS IS BRIEFED

Carter Aide at Scene Says Danger to the Public Is Believed Remote

By DAVID BURNHAM

Special to The New York Times

WASHINGTON, March 30 — The Nuclear Regulatory Commission told Congress today that the risk of a reactor core meltdown had arisen at the crippled Three Mile Island atomic power plant at Middletown, Pa., an event that could necessitate a general evacuation of the surrounding area.

A core meltdown — a melting of the reactor's stainless steel fuel rods or the enriched uranium pellets within them — is second only to an explosion in terms of seriousness of a nuclear accident.

At a televised news conference in Middletown tonight, Gov. Dick Thornburgh said that no general evacuation was deemed necessary, and Harold Benton, an N.R.C. official sent to the scene as President Carter's representative, said, "There is no imminent danger to the public." He called the possibility of a core meltdown "very remote."

Bubble of Hydrogen Forms

Earlier, officials said that a large pressurized hydrogen bubble had formed in the top of the reactor's sealed core vessel, which is supposed to be full of water for cooling the fuel rods. They said that unless the bubble was removed carefully, it could expand and leave the top of the fuel rods out of the cooling water, allowing them to overheat, melt and release large amounts of radioactivity.

While calling the situation stable for the moment, they noted that both methods under discussion for removing the bubble — letting it sink to the bottom of the vessel by drawing off water, or trying to break it up with steam — involved risks of further exposure of the fuel rods and a possible meltdown.

At the request of Gov. Thornburgh, young children and pregnant women began evacuating an area within five miles of the plant today. In addition, 23 schools were closed, and 15 mass-care centers were established as a precaution in counties surrounding the Middletown area.

Evacuation Plan Developed

In Washington and elsewhere, concern mounted over what has become the nation's most serious commercial nuclear reactor accident.

At the White House, President Carter was briefed by the National Security Council, and Jody Powell, the President's Press Secretary, said that a contingency

Continued on Page 8, Column 1

Delay on U.S. Debt Ceiling Hurts Treasury and Financial Markets

By JOHN H. ALLAN

The delay by Congress in raising the legal ceiling on the national debt is disrupting financial markets across the country.

Although most observers are confident that the fiscal drama will be settled by Congressional action on Monday, the Treasury had to scramble yesterday to make sure it had enough money to last until then.

To keep its debt under the ceiling and to gather in all its tax payments being held by banks, the Treasury announced a comprehensive program.

It postponed plans to borrow $6 billion on Monday, and it also suspended sales of Government savings bonds. Banks were called on for any tax receipts they are holding, and the Treasury arranged to borrow $3 billion from the Federal Reserve. It also asked the Federal Reserve to make its monthly Government payment from earnings — about $700 million — on Monday instead of Tuesday.

In addition, the Treasury said that, starting Monday, it would not make interest payments on its trust funds for Social Security and Civil Service. If Congress raises the debt ceiling on Monday, however, the payments would be resumed quickly.

The temporary ceiling on the debt, now $798 billion, will revert at 12:01 A.M. tomorrow to its "permanent" level of $400 billion. The reversion does not invalidate the $398 billion difference, but it prevents the Treasury from borrowing more and it means the Government must pay off its debt as it matures.

The debt ceiling limits the amount of money the Government can borrow at

Continued on Page 30, Column 4

Within Sight of Stricken Plant, A Town's Main Street Is Empty

By B. DRUMMOND AYRES Jr.

Special to The New York Times

GOLDSBORO, Pa., March 30 — At 5:15 P.M. today on Main Street here, the only living thing in sight was a brown-and-white dog, wandering aimlessly, oblivious to the radiation that was leaking from the crippled nuclear power plant just across the muddy Susquehanna.

"Almost everybody's gone," Annette Baker said, emerging from Reeser's grocery and casting a wary eye toward the plant's huge cooling towers, looming ominously above Goldsboro less than half a mile away. "Normally at this time of day, the people are around, coming home. I don't mean this place is a traffic jam or anything like that. We've only got 600 or so people. But this . . ."

'You Just Don't Know When'

She gestured toward the empty town square and the surrounding houses and stores, every window and door tightly shut despite an unseasonable afternoon temperature in the 70's.

"You live with that plant over there for years and years and don't think much about it," Terry Heidler, a print shop operator, said during a quick visit to Reeser's. "But it's like living with a rattlesnake. Sooner or later it's going to bite you. You just don't know when."

The people of Goldsboro, like the 20,000 or so other Pennsylvanians living within a five-mile radius of the Three Mile Island power plant, began pulling out Wednesday within an hour or so of the malfunction that caused what appears to be America's worst nuclear accident.

Most went to the homes of relatives of friends in other counties. At first, there was only a trickle. But this morning, when the authorities advised that pre-school children and pregnant women definitely should abandon the area, the trickle became a stream, then a river.

Switchboards Tied Up

There were jammed gasoline stations. There were panicky phone calls that so cluttered up switchboards that hours went by when nothing could be heard but the buzz, buzz, buzz of a busy signal.

"This is really like '1984,'" a local radio announcer commented, searching frantically for a metaphor that would somehow put the unthinkable into perspective. He got it wrong — Big Brother wasn't really involved — but somehow the message came through.

"People have really been shaken by this," Goldsboro's Mayor, Kenneth Myers, said. "We're prepared to

Continued on Page 7, Column 4

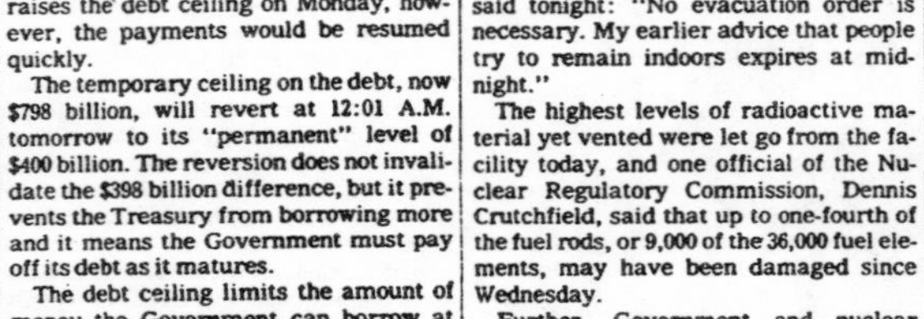

The New York Times / Keith Meyers

Duane and Marian Shuttlesworth leave Middletown with daughter, Rebecca

United Grounds Jets As Union Walks Out

By RICHARD WITKIN

United Airlines, the nation's largest carrier, was grounded today by a strike of 18,600 mechanics and other ground workers after they voted down a new contract tentatively agreed to by their union officers.

The union, the International Association of Machinists and Aerospace Workers, notified the company at midday yesterday that the strike would get under way today at 12:01 A.M. And early last evening, United announced that it had canceled all of its 1,600 daily flights from today through April 8.

The airline said that flights that were under way at 12:01 this morning would continue to their first stop; the crew on each flight with more than one stop was to decide whether to continue to the final destination.

There was no indication when negotiations might be resumed. The airline's switchboards were ablaze yesterday as customers with reservations sought help

Continued on Page 28, Column 1

INSIDE

Arabs Deadlocked on Egypt

Despite Saudi offers of concessions, an Arab conference stayed deadlocked over what to do about Egypt's signing of the treaty with Israel. Page 2.

New Sea Creatures Found

Ten-foot-long, wormlike animals that may constitute a new phylum have been discovered on the floor of the sea in the Galapagos Islands. Page 26.

Conflicting Reports Add to Tension

By BEN A. FRANKLIN

Special to The New York Times

HARRISBURG, Pa., March 30 — When an air raid siren shrieked what turned out to be an unauthorized alert near the state Capitol here before noon today, setting off an unscheduled midday traffic jam of jittery state employees, it was only the most dramatic result of three days of conflicting and sometimes flatly contradictory statements about the nuclear emergency at the Three Mile Island atomic plant near Middletown in south-central Pennsylvania.

The alert was variously said to have been a malfunction or to have been sounded by a Civil Defense official who misinterpreted Gov. Dick Thornburgh's widely misreported early-morning decision to prepare for, but not to carry out, a mass evacuation.

Mr. Thornburgh acted after receiving reports of what he called an "uncontrolled" release of radioactivity from the nuclear plant. And again, as has happened so often since details of the accident were announced Wednesday, the public was receiving information that was at loggerheads with other reports.

While the Governor, after four hours' sleep, said he was preparing to act "in the interest of taking every precaution" against radiation injuries, the power plant's top nuclear engineer, citing radiation readings far lower than those re-

Continued on Page 8, Column 1

"All the News That's Fit to Print"

The New York Times

LATE CITY EDITION

Weather: Mostly cloudy, mild today; showers tonight. Showers, tomorrow. Temperature range: today 52-68; yesterday 54-70. Details on page A27.

VOL.CXXVIII No.44,207

NEW YORK, FRIDAY, MAY 4, 1979

25 cents beyond 50-mile zone from New York City. Higher in air delivery cities.

20 CENTS

CONSERVATIVES WIN BRITISH VOTE; MARGARET THATCHER FIRST WOMAN TO HEAD A EUROPEAN GOVERNMENT

United Press International

Margaret Thatcher leaving polling station after casting her vote in London yesterday

BIG SWING INDICATED

Tory Leader Given a Clear Mandate to Change the Country's Course

By R. W. APPLE Jr.

Special to The New York Times

LONDON, Friday, May 4 — Margaret Thatcher and the Conservative Party won a decisive victory in Britain's general election yesterday.

Mrs. Thatcher, an Oxford-educated chemist and lawyer who entered Parliament in 1959, won a substantial majority and a clear mandate to reverse the nation's course. She promised during her campaign to restrain the trade unions, to cut personal income taxes and to bolster the armed forces.

She will become the first woman Prime Minister of a major European nation.

Voting Pattern Shifts

Projections by the television networks and by the Press Association suggested that the Tories would hold a majority over all other parties of approximately 35 to 40 seats. But the voting pattern was not as uniform as in past elections, and the ultimate majority might therefore be somewhat smaller.

With results declared in 200 of 635 constituencies, the totals were as follows:

Conservatives	82
Labor	116
Liberals	1
Scottish Nationalists	1
Others	0

The totals reflected a gain of eight seats for the Conservatives, a loss of two for Labor and no change for the Liberals. The Scottish Nationalists had lost four seats and there was a loss of two for other parties.

Jeremy Thorpe, who had represented North Devon for 20 years, was beaten by 8,000 votes. His highly publicized legal difficulties — his trial on charges of conspiracy and incitement to murder opens Tuesday — apparently proved too large an obstacle to overcome.

For Prime Minister James Callaghan and the Labor Party, the brightest spots were Scotland and Northern England, where the Conservative tide was running much less strongly. Denis Healey, the Chancellor of the Exchequer, suggested that Labor could still be saved by regional voting inconsistencies.

In the London area, the swing approached 7 percent, but in Manchester it was running at only about 2 percent.

Constituencies whose results were reported in the first few minutes after midnight suggested that the Liberal Party was doing reasonably well. However, the Scottish National vote seemed to be collapsing, and the party appeared to be in danger of losing all but one of the 11 seats it held before the voting.

Counting was slow in two of the most closely watched contests, those involving the Foreign Secretary, Dr. David Owen, at Plymouth Devonport, and Mr. Thorpe, at Devon North.

The first three Labor seats to fall to the Conservatives were two in the vital belt

Continued on Page A10, Column 1

The New York Times/George Tames

Senator Abraham A. Ribicoff

Ribicoff Decides He Won't Seek A Fourth Term

By STEVEN R. WEISMAN

Special to The New York Times

WASHINGTON, May 3 — Senator Abraham A. Ribicoff of Connecticut announced today that he would retire from the Senate after his current term of office — his third — expires next year.

His decision startled his political colleagues, as well as his staff aides, and immediately set off a scramble to succeed him. At least three Democrats and three Republicans in Connecticut indicated their interest in running for his seat. [Page B4.]

Mr. Ribicoff, a 69-year-old Democrat, has become Connecticut's most influential elected official in modern times, and his departure from Washington would bring to a conclusion an extraordinary public career that has included service as a United States Representative, Governor, Cabinet member under President John F. Kennedy and, since 1963, United States Senator.

Today he dismissed any suggestion that he would accept either a Cabinet post or an ambassadorship after he retired.

"As Mike Mansfield said, 'There is a time to stay and a time to go,'" Mr. Ribicoff told reporters this morning, referring to the former Senate majority leader, who is now Ambassador to Japan.

"I've watched them come and go," Mr.

Continued on Page B4, Column 1

PRODUCER PRICES UP BY 0.9% FOR APRIL; FOOD DOWN A LITTLE

Rises Expected to Keep Consumer Costs High and Further Harm Carter Fight on Inflation

By STEVEN RATTNER

Special to The New York Times

WASHINGTON, May 3 — Producer prices rose by nine-tenths of 1 percent in April, and, despite a slight slowing from March, signs pointed to at least another month of substantial increases, according to Labor Department figures released today.

The increase would have been greater if food prices had not fallen slightly last month. The overall increase in prices at the producer level was the smallest for any month since last November. Food prices have been rising rapidly, and Carter Administration officials were particularly relieved by last month's abatement.

The Government now computes producer prices for finished goods ready for shipment to retailers to compile a more accurate economic indicator than the former Wholesale Price Index, which has been abandoned. But producer prices are roughly equivalent to wholesale prices.

Period of Weeks or Months

Producer price increases do not directly affect consumers but gradually work their way over a period of weeks or months to the retail level. Accordingly, last month's rise in the Producer Price Index suggests that high rates of consumer price increases will continue.

The increases would, in turn, further jeopardize President Carter's anti-inflation program, which seeks to hold wage increases to 7 percent annually. Meanwhile, consumer prices rose at a 13 percent rate in the first three months of the year. The April rise in producer prices translated into a compound annual inflation rate of 11.5 percent.

The rises last month in wholesale prices were paced by sharply higher prices for fuel, plastics, cars and leather. Home-heating oil, for example, rose by 6.7 percent in the month alone. Gasoline prices increased by 4.4 percent. The increases in energy prices reflects the worldwide shortage of oil as a result of the shutdown earlier this year of Iranian oil production and the price increases by the Organization of Petroleum Exporting Countries.

Perhaps more worrisome was the news that the increases in energy prices appeared to have begun to filter

Continued on Page D14, Column 5

Terrorists Bomb the Rome Offices Of the Christian Democratic Party

By HENRY TANNER

Special to The New York Times

ROME, May 3 — A group of urban guerrillas raided the Rome area headquarters of Italy's dominant Christian Democratic Party today, wrecked two floors with bombs, killed one policeman, wounded two others and escaped.

The attack, the largest terrorist operation since Red Brigade terrorists kidnapped former Prime Minister Aldo Moro last year, killing five bodyguards and subsequently Mr. Moro, came on the eve of a general election campaign.

The raiders spray-painted the walls of the party headquarters with the initials of the Red Brigades and with its emblem, a five-pointed star. They also left behind this inscription: "We shall transform the fraudulent elections into a class war."

Fears were expressed that there would be a wave of terrorist attacks during the campaign for the elections that are scheduled for June 3 and 4.

Shaken by the magnitude of today's attack, former President Giuseppe Saragat and other political figures called for stronger antiterrorist measures. Some suggested that martial law was needed, as they had done when Mr. Moro was abducted on March 16, 1978. His body was found nearly two months later.

"Political terrorism," Mr. Saragat said, "is turning into full-scale civil war and must be confronted not only by the police but also by the armed forces of the republic."

The Red Brigades, the most feared of Italy's terrorist groups, have as their aim the destruction of the Italian state and society as a step toward a revolutionary takeover. They accuse the Communist Party of having sold out to the bourgeoi-

Continued on Page A4, Column 3

'Genuine' Tory Taking Charge

Margaret Roberts Thatcher

By WILLIAM BORDERS

Special to The New York Times

LONDON, May 3 — To Margaret Thatcher, "free choice is ultimately what life is about," and she likes to illustrate what she means in political terms with this example: "If somebody comes to me and asks, What are you going to do for us small businessmen? I say, the only thing I'm going to do for you is make you freer to do things for yourselves. If you can't do it then, I'm sorry. I'll have nothing to offer you."

Woman in the News

Judging by what she has been saying over the years, in public and in private, that is the center of Mrs. Thatcher's political philosophy, — what she calls "a positive creed, to promote, not destroy, the uniqueness of the individual."

In the election campaign Mrs. Thatcher sketched a vision of a Britain that would be rebuilt, on the strong base of that kind of individualism, to the economic strength it used to know, "so that once again the products stream from our factories and workshops while the customers of the world scramble over each other to buy them." She also promised a government that "would stop trying to step in and take decisions for you that you should be free to take on your own."

Now, the British people, having chosen as their leader the first woman to head a modern European government, will have a chance to put to a practical test what she terms the genu-

Continued on Page A11, Column 1

CALIFANO REASSESSES RADIATION HAZARDS

He Now Says Some Cancer Deaths From Accident Are Possible

By CHARLES MOHR

Special to The New York Times

WASHINGTON, May 3 — Joseph A Califano Jr., Secretary of Health, Education and Welfare, said today that radiation exposure from the Three Mile Island reactor accident was higher than earlier measurements had indicated. As a result, he said, statistical probability indicates that at least one to 10 cancer deaths caused by radiation could be expected among the two million people living within 50 miles of the Pennsylvania power plant.

He also said that the radiation could be expected to cause as many as 10 additional nonfatal cancers.

Mr. Califano, who testified a month ago that no deaths would result from the exposure, said today that subsequent measurements showed radiation levels had been nearly twice as high as earlier estimates. He also said that the estimates were expected to rise further.

His testimony, before the Subcommittee on Energy, Nuclear Proliferation and Federal Services of the Senate Government Affairs Committee, took note of the contention of some scientists that assumptions about low-level radiation as a cause of cancer might be 10 times too low.

Under normal conditions, the number of cancer deaths in a population of two million would be 325,000.

Meanwhile, the Nuclear Regulatory Commission reported that the Oyster Creek Plant at Forked River, N.J., was shut down automatically yesterday during a test of the reactor's pressure-reading instruments. [Page B3.]

And the Nuclear Regulatory Commission, considering the status of a Maine reactor that was among five closed in

Continued on Page A19, Column 4

The New York Times/John Sotomayor

Bird watchers stalking their "prey" early yesterday morning in Central Park

For Central Park Bird Watchers, Thrills Take Flight Every Spring

By ROBIN HERMAN

Why don't bird watchers get "warblers' neck" in Central Park? Why does the Police Department assign a patrolman to watch the bird watchers? And have you ever seen a rock dove?

Bird watchers don't get warblers' neck from craning to see warblers in the treetops because the hills in Central Park put bird watchers at eye level with the tops of the trees. The Police Department assigns an officer to watch bird watchers because many of them carry expensive field glasses that make them likely targets for muggers. And if you think you have never seen a rock dove you probably have because they are otherwise known as pigeons and Central Park is full of them.

Fifty New Yorkers who went "birding" yesterday at 7 A.M. along the Central Park Ramble spotted nearly 40 species of birds in an hour and a half, including multitudes of rock doves bobbing and cooing on the paths and outcroppings. The real prizes, however, were the visiting warblers who stop in Manhattan this month for a drink and a

Continued on Page B3, Column 2

INSIDE

Giants Pick Quarterback

The Giants' first pick in the National Football League draft was Phil Simms, a quarterback from Morehead State in Kentucky. Page A21.

Islanders Tie Series

Bob Nystrom's goal in overtime gave the Islanders a 3-2 victory over the Rangers, tying their playoff series at two games apiece. Page A21.

News Summary and Index, Page B1

In Her Own Words

Comments by Margaret Thatcher since taking the party leadership in 1975:

Limitation of government doesn't make for a weak government — don't make that mistake. If you've got the role of government clearly set out, then it means very strong government in that role. Very strong indeed. You weaken government if you try to spread it over so wide a range that you're not powerful where you should be because you've got into areas where you shouldn't be.

•

Overtaxation is transparently foolish. Most of us are willing to work for our families and neighbors but not for the Chancellor of the Exchequer. In a free country people will work hard if it pays them to do so. At present, taxes are so high that for many it is not worthwhile working hard, and for some it is not worthwhile working at all. The first step to recovery, therefore, is to lower taxes on earnings.

•

There are two ways of making a cabinet. One way is to have in it people who represent all the different viewpoints within the party, within the broad philosophy. The other way is to have in it only the people who want to go in the direction in which every instinct tells me we have to go. As Prime Minister I couldn't waste time having any internal arguments.

•

The power of trade unions over individual members is far too great. We shall have to stand up against those elements who are prepared to use their present freedom in society to destroy society. . . . A strong trade-union movement is an integral part of modern industrial society, but it must not ride roughshod over the rest of that society.

•

On immigration from the Commonwealth: Small minorities can be absorbed — they can be assets to the majority community — but once a minority in a neighborhood gets very large, people do feel swamped. They feel their whole way of life has been changed.

•

On male colleagues: I'm not conscious of them as men at all. Don't mistake me: I see A as taller than B; I see X as more handsome than Y. What woman wouldn't? What man wouldn't have such perceptions about women? But I don't see me and my colleagues in an "I'm a woman, you are men" relationship.

"All the News That's Fit to Print"

The New York Times

LATE CITY EDITION

Weather: Cloudy, chance of showers today and tonight. Sunny tomorrow. Temperature range: today 54-66; yesterday 62-67. Details on page 8.

VOL.CXXVIII . . . No.44,229 | Copyright © 1979 The New York Times | NEW YORK, SATURDAY, MAY 26, 1979 | 25 cents beyond 50-mile zone from New York City. Higher in air delivery cities. | 20 CENTS

272 DIE AS JET CRASHES ON TAKEOFF IN CHICAGO AFTER LOSING ENGINE; WORST U.S. AIR DISASTER

ISRAEL LOWERS FLAG, GIVES TOWN IN SINAI BACK TO EGYPTIANS

Inhabitants of El Arish, Conquered in 1967, Cheer, Weep and Jeer at Withdrawal Ceremony

By CHRISTOPHER S. WREN
Special to The New York Times

EL ARISH, Egypt, May 25 — Egyptians cheered, prayed and wept as this town, capital of the Sinai Peninsula, was handed back to Egypt today, after 12 years under Israeli occupation.

The dusty coastal town, separated from the Mediterranean by groves of stately palms amid dunes, became the first still-inhabited Arab town conquered in the 1967 war to be relinquished.

The pullout marked the beginning of Israel's promised withdrawal from Sinai under the peace treaty signed with Egypt March 26 in Washington.

The return of El Arish and a coastal strip westward is the first step of a process that will return to Egypt nearly three-fourths of Sinai within nine months. Israel has agreed to withdraw within three years from the remainder of Sinai, to the border that prevailed before the 1967 war.

Two Sides Meet at Beersheba

As the transfer took place, Egyptian and Israeli negotiators met at Beersheba to begin negotiations on a solution to the question of autonomy for Palestinians of the West Bank and Gaza. Secretary of State Cyrus R. Vance, who attended, urged both sides, whose positions were far apart, to show "maximum restraint and farsightedness." [Page 3.]

The turnover ceremony was held in the asphalt parking lot of a former Israeli Army canteen and rest stop a mile and a half east of town. More elaborate festivities are planned tomorrow when President Anwar el-Sadat comes to El Arish.

Egyptians Whistle and Chant

As the blue and white Israeli flag was lowered to bugle accompaniment today, more than a thousand residents watching from across a road began to clap, whistle and chant.

Hundreds of young men ran toward the barbed wire of the compound where the half-hour ceremony was taking place. Armed Israeli troops in combat gear chased them back in jeeps. Four armored half-tracks sent to assist the soldiers sent up plumes of dust.

When the red, white and black Egyptian flag was run up the pole, the nearly hysterical spectators cheered wildly and surged forth again amid cries in Arabic: "God is great!" and "Long live Egypt!"

There was scuffling between some Egyptians and Israeli soldiers, who seemed unprepared for the outburst. Although the scene briefly turned ugly, violence was averted as Egyptian military policemen rushed in to calm the people.

When the Israelis got into their trucks and jeeps and began driving to their new lines a few miles east of town, some

Continued on Page 4, Column 1

Associated Press

Firemen searching through the smoldering wreckage of an American Airlines jet that crashed on takeoff yesterday at Chicago's O'Hare International Airport

NO SURVIVORS FOUND

Los Angeles-Bound DC-10 Narrowly Misses Tract of Mobile Homes

By DOUGLAS E. KNEELAND
Special to The New York Times

CHICAGO, May 25 — An American Airlines jetliner lost an engine and crashed shortly after takeoff from O'Hare International Airport this afternoon, killing all 272 persons aboard. It was the worst disaster in United States aviation history.

Flight 191, a DC-10 bound for Los Angeles at the beginning of the Memorial Day weekend, rose to the northwest from Runway 14 just after 3 P.M., central daylight time. Then, witnesses said, the plane appeared to suffer difficulties with an engine on the left wing, rolled to the left, stalled and plunged into the small abandoned Ravenswood Airport, narrowly missing a mobile home court.

Several witnesses said the engine exploded, and others reported seeing a "huge cylinder" fall from the plane to the runway and burst into flames.

No Survivors Reported

American Airlines officials said there were apparently no survivors of the crash, which scattered debris over an area about 100 by 200 yards. The crash sent up flames and black smoke that could be seen 15 miles away in Chicago's downtown Loop area, and fiery remnants struck some of the mobile homes nearby, severely damaging three of them. Two persons who were apparently working on the ground near the crash site were injured.

The plane narrowly missed a Standard Oil Company gasoline storage facility a block away.

Fire trucks, ambulances and police vehicles from the city and surrounding suburbs rushed to the area and poured water on the flames from the nearly unrecognizable wreckage of the shattered DC-10.

Late this afternoon, ambulances began removing bodies of the victims to a temporary morgue set up in an aircraft hangar. By 11 P.M., 250 bodies had been removed from the wreckage, and Douglas Dreifus, a Federal investigator, said the rest would not be removed before daylight.

Worst Previous U.S. Crash

The worst previous air disaster in the United States occurred last September, when 144 persons died in the collision of a jetliner and a small private plane over San Diego.

William Nickerson, 52 years old, of Elk Grove Village, where the plane crashed, said he saw the DC-10 take off with the left engine smoking. Almost immediately, he said, the engine fell from the plane and the massive jet lost altitude and crashed, sending flames shooting 125 feet into the air.

Danny Niemann, 25, an employee of a

Continued on Page 7, Column 1

FLORIDA EXECUTES KILLER AS PLEA FAILS

Spenkelink, Electrocuted, Is First to Die Since Gilmore in 1977

By WAYNE KING
Special to The New York Times

STARKE, Fla., May 25 — The state of Florida trussed John Arthur Spenkelink immobile in the electric chair this morning, dropped a black leather mask over his face and electrocuted him.

"He simply looked at us and he looked terrified," said Kris Rebillot, a reporter who was one of 32 persons who watched through a window from an adjoining room. "It was just a wide, wide, wide stare."

The execution was carried out a few hours after the last plea in an extended legal battle. It was the first execution in the United States since Gary Mark Gilmore faced a Utah firing squad voluntarily on Jan. 19, 1977, and the first since 1967 in which the condemned person was put to death against his will.

No Final Statement — His Wish

Mr. Spenkelink made no final statement. The prison authorities said that had been his wish.

The prisoner was given three surges of electricity. The first, 2,500 volts, was administered at 10:12 A.M. Mr. Spenkelink jerked in the chair and one hand clenched into a fist.

Then came the second, and the third, by two executioners in black hoods. A doctor stepped forward after the third surge, pulled up the prisoner's T-shirt

Continued on Page 6, Column 2

Flattened Debris and 'Bodies All Over'

By WILLIAM ROBBINS

CHICAGO, May 25 — "The plane just lost power and slowly rolled over on its side," George Owens, a witness to the worst domestic air crash in history, said today shortly after the fiery disaster at O'Hare International Airport here.

Then, he said, he "saw a huge fireball."

Hours after the crash of American Airlines Flight 191, which had just taken off for Los Angeles, smoke was still pouring from the wreckage, which was too hot for removal of many of the bodies of the victims. Red and yellow stakes marked the few charred bodies that firemen could reach. It was nearly 6 P.M. before the first bodies were moved to a nearby hangar.

One of the first physicians to arrive at the scene was Dr. Robert Loguersio. "There were bodies all over," he said. "There were a lot of corpses on the scene. Obviously there was nothing I could do. Obviously there were no live injuries."

Helplessly, the police and firemen could only mill around the scene, keeping onlookers back and out of possible danger.

Wreckage Carried Off

But immediately after the crash, and before the police could cordon off the site, some small boys arrived and began to carry off bits of wreckage. One was seen walking off with what looked like a fan belt in his hand.

The wreckage of the plane was spread over part of a small abandoned airport, one of the few open areas in the populated region surrounding O'Hare. It ignited three mobile homes situated in a neatly landscaped park at the edge of the field.

A resident of one of the mobile homes, Marie Nikopoulos, had been stretched out on a couch, watching television, when she heard a "big bang."

"It threw me off the couch," she said, "and the force knocked dishes off the shelves and my chandelier fell. I ran and opened the front door and saw part of the plane burning in the street. Thick black smoke filled the neighborhood and turned it pitch black. You couldn't see a foot in front of you."

Residents Ordered Out

Soon officials arrived and ordered the residents out for fear the fires might spread.

One witness, Winnann Johnson, saw what was later determined to have been an engine fall from the wing.

"I saw this silver cylinder thing fall from the plane onto the runway," she said. "It burst into flames and then smothered real quickly."

Larry Roderick saw the flight from about the same vantage point. "The left engine was smoking badly on takeoff," he said. "Then there seemed to be an explosion. There was a burst of flame and the engine fell. The plane appeared to make a steep climb. Then it swung over to the left and plunged to the ground."

President, Angered Over Setbacks, Urges Leadership From Democrats

By TERENCE SMITH
Special to The New York Times

WASHINGTON, May 25 — President Carter, stung by a series of defeats on Capitol Hill, lashed out today at the "demagoguery and political timidity" that he said had made the American people doubt the courage and effectiveness of their political leaders.

Displaying more passion and anger than he normally allows himself on a public forum, the President lectured about 200 members of the Democratic National Committee at their spring meeting here on the need for Congress and the party to confront the difficult choices that face the nation on energy and the economy.

"The American people are looking to us for honest answers and clear leadership," Mr. Carter said. "What they see is a Government which seems incapable of action at all."

In a long answer to a question from the floor, the President also all but declared his candidacy for re-election.

"I haven't made my announcement of

Excerpts from Carter remarks, page 8.

what I'm going to do in 1980," he said, "but I have never backed down from a fight, and I have never been afraid of public opinion polls. And if and when I decide to run, it will be in every precinct in this country, no matter who else ran, and I have no doubt it will be successful."

Mr. Carter also had some thinly veiled criticism for Senator Edward M. Kennedy and the five Democratic Representatives who announced their opposition to the President's re-election earlier this week. "Press conferences will not solve the serious problems we face in energy, in inflation, in maintaining peace in a troubled world," Mr. Carter said.

At a news conference on Monday, Representatives Edward P. Beard of Rhode Island, John Conyers Jr. of Michigan, Richard M. Nolan of Minnesota, Richard L. Ottinger of Westchester and Fortney H. Stark of California announced that they were organizing a campaign to dump Mr. Carter from the Democratic ticket and replace him with Senator Kennedy, who has criticized the President's domestic policies at several meetings with the press in the last fortnight.

Mr. Carter's tone ranged from anger to

Continued on Page 8, Column 5

Gas Lines Touch Off Arguments; Price Hits a Record in Manhattan

By ALAN RICHMAN

Gasoline shortages caused arguments at service stations on Long Island yesterday and forced the posting of police officers to direct a line of waiting motorists in Manhattan. Meanwhile, prices rose to record levels — 56.5 cents a half-gallon at a Getty station in lower Manhattan.

The frantic activity was expected to end soon, because many stations indicated they would run out of gas before Monday night, the end of the Memorial Day weekend.

"My particular situation is that the company is running a day behind in deliveries," said Tim. Sullivan, owner of a Sunoco Station at the corner of 220th Street and Horace Harding Boulevard in Bayside, Queens. Mr. Sullivan, who usually sells 1,800 gallons a day, received a 3,000-gallon delivery yesterday morning and sold out by 3:30 yesterday afternoon.

At a Hess station in Manhattan offering regular gasoline for 82.9 cents a gallon, automobiles were lined up from the entrance on 10th Avenue down 44th Street to the corner of 11th Avenue.

Arguments started not only between drivers waiting in line and those pulling in front of the line, but also between drivers waiting in line and those attempting to leave the station. Finally, the Midtown North police precinct dispatched two officers, who spent the rest of the day asking "Leaded or unleaded?" and directing cars to appropriate pumps.

Mostly a Battle of Words

"There's been nothing worse than verbal altercations with some bumping into one another," explained Officer Tony Graffeo, who ordinarily drives a patrol car. "We call that a West Side conversation. Anything short of shooting on the West Side is a friendly discussion."

On Long Island, fist fights started at several stations and Matthew Troy, executive director of the Long Island Gasoline Retailers Association, warned that association members might close for the weekend if drivers did not "behave themselves."

Mr. Troy reported, as of midafternoon yesterday, 50 incidents of verbal abuse by motorists against gas station owners and

Continued on Page 22, Column 5

INSIDE

Inflation in Double Digits Again

The Consumer Price Index rose 1.1 percent in April, making for an annual rate of 13.9 percent. April prices were up 10.4 percent from 1978. Page 38.

E.P.A. Rules on Coal Burning

The Environmental Protection Agency introduced rules on coal emissions by power plants that will please neither industry nor environmentalists. Page 6.

An Ayatollah Shot in Teheran

An Iranian religious figure believed to be a member of the secret, ruling Revolutionary Council was shot and wounded near his home. Page 2.

Spanish Army Officers Killed

A lieutenant general in the Spanish Army, two colonels and their driver were killed by Basque terrorists who ambushed their car in Madrid. Page 5.

Associated Press

The Israeli flag being lowered and the Egyptian flag being raised yesterday in the Sinai town of El Arish

The New York Times

PAGE ONE

1980-1989

"All the News That's Fit to Print"

The New York Times

LATE CITY EDITION

Weather: Cloudy, sporadic rain today; rain ending tonight. Sunny tomorrow. Temperature range: today 55-65; yesterday 63-74. Details on page B6.

VOL. CXXIX .... No. 44,590 NEW YORK, WEDNESDAY, MAY 21, 1980

30 cents beyond 50-mile zone from New York City. Higher in air delivery cities.

25 CENTS

BUSH WINS MICHIGAN, SLOWING REAGAN BID TO LOCK UP VICTORY

CALIFORNIAN LOSES A KEY AIDE

Ex-Governor Sought Delegates in 2 Primary Fights to Top 998 Needed for Nomination

By ADAM CLYMER

George Bush checked Ronald Reagan's march to a delegate majority yesterday, defeating the former California Governor in the Michigan Republican primary and apparently postponing for a week Mr. Reagan's amassing the 998 convention votes needed for nomination.

The two also competed in the Oregon primary. But the solid Bush margin in Michigan, with 82 delegates, made it all but certain that Oregon, with 29, could not give Mr. Reagan the needed total last night, though it seemed sure that he would clear that numerical hurdle next week.

Even as Mr. Reagan faltered in Michigan, his campaign also suffered the resignation of Anderson Carter, his field director, the politician on the staff with the most experience in recent campaigns. In announcing that he would leave in a few days, Mr. Carter gave no reason, but some campaign sources said that he was unhappy with the dominance of other aides whom he considered inexperienced.

Leads Throughout Michigan

In a very light turnout, Mr. Bush ran well ahead of Mr. Reagan in all parts of Michigan, taking about 57 percent of the popular vote.

With more than half the returns in, Mr. Bush was winning 53 Michigan delegates to Mr. Reagan's 29.

Campaigning last night in Cleveland, the former Congressman, diplomat and Director of Central Intelligence exulted over his victory, saying: "It means I shouldn't be written off. I've been trying to make that point over and over again, and the Michigan vote states very clearly that people want a look at my candidacy."

The Democrats held a meaningful primary only in Oregon, where 39 delegates were at stake between President Carter and Senator Edward M. Kennedy of Massachusetts. The Michigan party picked

Continued on Page A26, Column 2

50,000 Warned of Volcano Flood Threat

Scientists See Danger In Overflow of Lake Dammed by Debris

By WALLACE TURNER

Special to The New York Times

VANCOUVER, Wash., May 20 — Officials said today that about 50,000 people living in Washington cities along the lower Columbia River were threatened by a flash flood that might develop in the aftermath of the eruption of Mount St. Helens.

"I think an overflow is imminent," said Dwight Crandell, one of the United States Geological Survey scientists monitoring the eruption. The threat of flooding was created when the outlet of Spirit Lake, on the mountain's shattered north flank, was plugged by dirt, rock, trees and volcanic ash from the explosion on Sunday morning. The outlet is the source of the Toutle River, the valley of which was the scene of mudflows, flooding, and flows of superheated volcanic ash.

"The best we would hope for," Mr. Crandell said, "is for the water to spill over the top and go quietly down the river. The worst would be for the whole thing to come crashing down."

Much of Valley in Path

A total, rapid deterioration of the earth plug, which scientists say is 200 feet high and 1.5 miles wide, would mean a disastrous flood that would careen down the Toutle River Valley to the Cowlitz River at Castle Rock, Wash., and then inundate much of Kelso and Longview, Wash., before pouring into the Columbia River.

The cloud of gas and particles of volcanic debris that resulted from the eruption moved east today, widening into an arc from Maine to Georgia. The cloud was not visible in New York, and environmental officials said it did not present any health hazard.

98 Reported Missing

Whether there will be any long-term health effects from the fallout is not known without more detailed analysis of the content of the cloud, but scientists say that the eruption is not likely to bring any significant changes in weather patterns, and they expect only negligible effects to be felt at ground level. [Page A20.]

The names of six persons killed in Washington were released today by the authorities, who also said that two unidentified bodies had been discovered and that they were trying to locate 98 other persons who had been reported missing.

Continued on Page A20, Column 2

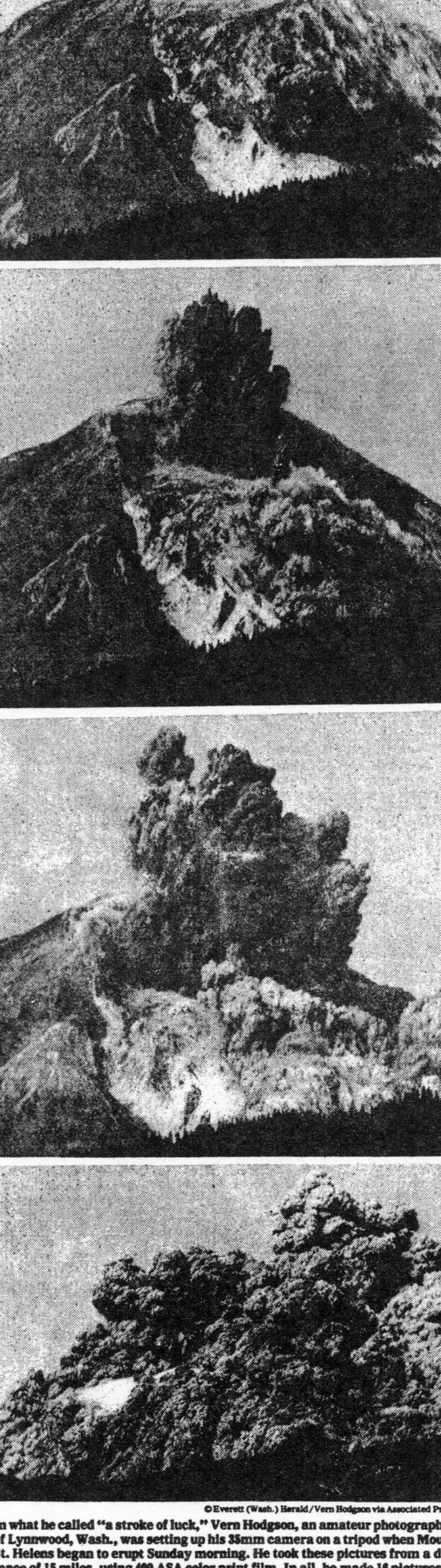

© Everett (Wash.) Herald/Vern Hodgson via Associated Press

In what he called "a stroke of luck," Vern Hodgson, an amateur photographer of Lynnwood, Wash., was setting up his 35mm camera on a tripod when Mount St. Helens began to erupt Sunday morning. He took these pictures from a distance of 15 miles, using 400 ASA color print film. In all, he made 16 pictures in about four minutes, shifting from a 75-150mm zoom lens with an extender, making it the equivalent of a 300mm lens, to a 50mm lens and finally a 25mm wide-angle lens as the cloud from the eruption widened to about 20 miles.

The New York Times/May 21, 1980

Dissipating cloud of fallout from eruption reached Eastern States last night

Accord Is Reported on Evacuation Of Last 710 Love Canal Families

By ROBIN HERMAN

Special to The New York Times

ALBANY, May 20 — New York State and Federal officials were reported tonight to have reached agreement on evacuating the 710 remaining families in the Love Canal area of Niagara Falls, N.Y., but were snagged on whether the relocation should be permanent or temporary.

Governor Carey told Federal officials this afternoon — including Vice President Mondale and members of the New York delegation in Congress — that short-term assistance was unacceptable and that the Federal Government should offer the residents of the chemically polluted area the option of permanent relocation.

Love Canal residents were calmer yesterday after the release of two Federal officials held in a protest the night before. Page B1.

A deputy assistant to the President for intergovernmental affairs, Eugene Eidenberg, said in Washington early tonight that he had been in consultation with Governor Carey but that no final decision had been reached.

Sources close to the negotiations reported, however, that the decision to relocate had been made, and that an announcement awaited only a resolution of details. It was not immediately clear when the evacuation would begin.

State and Federal officials had not

Continued on Page B4, Column 1

CONFEREES' ACCORD ON BUDGET SNAGGED

5 Liberal House Democrats Balk at $6.1 Billion Rise for Military

By MARTIN TOLCHIN

Special to The New York Times

WASHINGTON, May 20 — House and Senate budget conferees reached a tentative agreement to break an impasse in a dispute involving guns versus butter this evening but it quickly collapsed when five liberal House Democrats balked at accepting $154 billion in military spending for the fiscal year 1981.

"They made a firm offer and we accepted it," Senator Ernest F. Hollings, chairman of the Senate Budget committee, said of the House conferees' proposal to increase military spending by $6.1 billion from the $147.9 billion proposed by the House.

"They reneged on it," the South Carolina Democrat told reporters.

The Senate has passed a budget resolution calling for military spending of $155.7 billion. Although the Senate conferees had indicated earlier in the day that they would not accept any figure below $155.4 billion, they relented and agreed to the House conferees' proposal for spending of $154 billion, which would represent an increase of about 5 percent over 1980 after accounting for inflation.

The compromise proposal resulted from an hour-long meeting between Mr. Hollings and Representative Robert N.

Continued on Page A33, Column 2

INSIDE

Decision on Cubans' Status

The White House said arriving Cubans would be treated as applicants for asylum, so Congress need not be consulted on the number admitted. Page A24.

New York to Get U.S. Funds

New York State will get the Federal money it needs to make $40 million in Medicaid payments to New York City hospitals and nursing homes. Page B3.

Miami Police Inquiry Is Set

The Attorney General announced that a team of Federal prosecutors and agents would study alleged abuses by the Miami police. Page A22.

QUEBECERS DEFEAT SOVEREIGNTY MOVE BY A RATIO OF 3 TO 2

A TRUDEAU VICTORY

Many French Canadians Join English-Speakers to Back Federalism

By HENRY GINIGER

Special to The New York Times

MONTREAL, May 20 — In a historic referendum, Quebec voted overwhelmingly today to reject a move to put this predominantly French-speaking province on the road out of the Canadian federation.

Federalist forces, led by Prime Minister Pierre Elliott Trudeau of Canada and Claude Ryan, leader of the Quebec Liberal party, who had cautioned against breaking up Canada and had promised constitutional changes, took 59 percent of the vote compared with 41 percent for the "yes" side led by the provincial Premier, René Lévesque.

Mr. Lévesque did not even obtain a majority of French speakers, who make up 80 percent of the province's 6.2 million people. About 54 percent of the Quebec French refused to heed his appeal for solidarity and joined with more than 80 percent of the non-French minority, mainly English-speakers, to produce the decisive federalist victory.

Lévesque Close to Tears

Close to tears, Mr. Lévesque appeared before his supporters tonight and promised "a next time." He said the vote, "an upsurge of old Quebec," had to be accepted, but he warned Mr. Trudeau that "the ball was in his court now" and that he had to make good his promises of constitutional change.

One of the heaviest turnouts in Quebec's electoral history, about 80 percent of the 4.3 million registered voters, indicated the public interest in the province's first occasion to exercise the right of self-determination for its political future.

With the count almost complete, the vote for the "no" side was 2,140,814, or 59.4 percent, while the "yes" vote was 1,475,509, or 40.6 percent.

Voters appeared unwilling to take the risk of separating their province from Canada, thus heeding the warnings of Mr. Trudeau and Mr. Ryan. At the same

Continued on Page A9, Column 1

U.S. Scolds Paris For Secretiveness On Soviet Parley

Also Criticizes the British for Reneging Over Iran

By BERNARD GWERTZMAN

Special to The New York Times

WASHINGTON, May 20 — The United States criticized France today for failing to consult before the French-Soviet meeting in Warsaw and criticized Britain for reneging on a Common Market commitment to block exports to Iran under contracts made since the takeover of the American Embassy.

After holding back on criticism of the French move for two days and expressing satisfaction with the Common Market steps to impose sanctions as of Nov. 4 — a move that nevertheless fell short of an earlier European pledge to cancel all trade except food and medicine — the Carter Administration found itself today in public dispute with two of its major allies.

Britain's abrupt decision against imposing the retroactive sanctions made the united front that Western Europe had presented on the Iranian crisis collapse. In Paris, French officials acknowledged that the talks yesterday in Warsaw between President Valéry Giscard d'Estaing and Leonid I. Brezhnev, the Soviet leader, had achieved no major breakthrough, but they insisted that the meeting had at least kept lines of communication open. [Pages A16 and A14.]

Muskie Criticizes France

Secretary of State Edmund S. Muskie said at a news conference that France, by failing to consult with its allies about the Warsaw talks, was reasserting its independence at the cost of allied solidarity and unity.

The criticism of Prime Minister Margaret Thatcher's Government was the first by the Carter Administration. It was issued by the State Department late in the day after Britain announced that it would not carry out the Common Market decision it had participated in making on Sunday.

That decision, a compromise between those who wanted sanctions to include

Continued on Page A16, Column 1

South Korean Government Resigns As a TV Station Is Burned in Riots

By HENRY SCOTT STOKES

Special to The New York Times

SEOUL, May 20 — The South Korean Cabinet of Prime Minister Shin Hyon Hwack resigned today "to take responsibility for failure to maintain domestic calm" as riots continued in the provincial city of Kwangju.

Reports from Kwangju, a stronghold of Kim Dae Jung, the arrested opposition leader, said that a television and radio station was burned as 30,000 demonstrators, mainly students and workers, marched in groups and that some battled a division-strength army unit that was rushed to the city when troubles began there. At least five people were killed and 70 injured in clashes in Kwangju yesterday.

Seoul, situated only 25 miles from the strategic border with North Korea, was calm. But the full martial law imposed Saturday night, which gave Lieut. Gen. Chon Too Hwan, the head of the country's intelligence apparatus, virtual control of the country, appeared shaky in other provincial cities such as Mokpo, Chongju and Yosu.

Political Liberalization Asked

The imposition of full martial law followed several days of protests by university students in Seoul demanding an end of the limited form of martial law previously in force and a more rapid rate of progress toward a democratic governmental structure.

After the student leaders called off the demonstrations on Friday in response to pleas by the Government, troops raided a gathering of student leaders on Saturday. Hundreds of people have been arrested, including Kim Dae Jung, a persistent critic of the regime of the late President Park Chung Hee, and former Prime Minister Kim Jong Pil, the head of the majority Democratic Republican Party.

The leader of the opposition New Democratic Party, Kim Young Sam, another longtime opponent of President Park's regime, is under virtual house arrest here with about 100 soldiers surrounding his home.

Many South Koreans regard the weekend's events as, in effect, a coup by General Chon, who has shielded his actions with an argument that they were called for by President Choi Kyu Hah. This explanation was given credence by some South Korean officials but rejected by others, as confusion and concern spread in Seoul today after the Cabinet's resignation.

In another development in Seoul, the Supreme Court today rejected an appeal

Continued on Page A8, Column 2

157 ELDERLY WOMEN DIE IN JAMAICA FIRE

14 Missing at Kingston Institution — Question of Arson Raised

By United Press International

KINGSTON, Jamaica, May 20 — Fire swept through a two-story wooden home for poor and elderly women here early today, and officials said at least 157 were killed and 14 others were missing.

Of the 204 women asleep in their beds when the fire broke out about 1 A.M., only 33 were reported safe and accounted for hours after the blaze had been brought under control.

Prime Minister Michael N. Manley told Jamaicans in a radio broadcast that security officials thought arsonists could have started the blaze, but the city's fire chief said there was no proof of that. He suggested that an electrical short could have started the fire.

The fire chief, Allan Ridgeway, said the fire consumed the building so quickly that his men had to stand helplessly by, watching a few women jump through windows and listening to the screams of those trapped inside. Those who jumped were seriously injured.

The building collapsed four minutes

Continued on Page A3, Column 1

"All the News
That's Fit to Print"

The New York Times

LATE CITY EDITION

Weather: Partly sunny today; mostly cloudy and cold tonight and tomorrow. Temperature range: today 28-38; yesterday 36-43. Details on page D21.

VOL.CXXX . . . No. 44,835 NEW YORK, WEDNESDAY, JANUARY 21, 1981

30 cents beyond 50-mile zone from New York City. Higher in air delivery cities.

25 CENTS

REAGAN TAKES OATH AS 40TH PRESIDENT; PROMISES AN 'ERA OF NATIONAL RENEWAL'

MINUTES LATER, 52 U.S. HOSTAGES IN IRAN FLY TO FREEDOM AFTER 444-DAY ORDEAL

'ALIVE, WELL AND FREE'

Captives Taken to Algiers and Then Germany — Final Pact Complex

By BERNARD GWERTZMAN
Special to The New York Times

WASHINGTON, Wednesday, Jan. 21 — The 52 Americans who were held hostage by Iran for 444 days were flown to freedom yesterday. Jimmy Carter, a few hours after giving up the Presidency, said that everyone "was alive, was well and free."

The flight ended the national ordeal that had frustrated Mr. Carter for most of his last 14 months in office, and it allowed Ronald Reagan to begin his term free of the burdens of the Iran crisis.

The Americans were escorted out of Iran by Algerian diplomats, aboard an Algerian airliner, underscoring Algeria's role in achieving the accord that allowed the hostages to return home.

Transferred to U.S. Custody

The Algerian plane, carrying the former hostages, stopped first in Athens to refuel. It then landed in Algiers, where custody of the 52 Americans was formally transferred by the Algerians to the representative of the United States, former Deputy Secretary of State Warren M. Christopher. He had negotiated much of the agreement freeing them.

They then boarded two United States Air Force hospital planes and flew to Frankfurt, West Germany early this morning. They will stay at an American military hospital in nearby Weisbaden, where they will be visited by Mr. Carter, as President Reagan's representative, later today. They will stay in Wiesbaden for a week or less to "decompress," as one official described it.

The 52 Americans were freed as part of a complex agreement that was not completed until early yesterday morning, when the last snags holding up their release were removed by Mr. Carter and

Continued on Page A3, Column 5

Teheran Captors Call Out Insults As the 52 Leave

By JOHN KIFNER
Special to The New York Times

TEHERAN, Iran, Jan. 20 — The 52 American hostages began to roll down the runway to freedom today minutes as President Reagan was finishing his inaugural address.

As the Algerian 727 lifted off from Mehrabad Airport, ending 444 days of captivity for the Americans, they could see, most of them probably for the last time, a full moon picking out the sharp white peaks of the Elburz Mountains to the north. The time was 8:55 P.M., 12:25 P.M., New York time.

"God is great! Death to America!" cried the young Islamic militants who kept custody of the hostages to the last minute, hustling them to the stairs of the airplane.

They Soon Are 'Former Hostages'

The American diplomats, Marine guards and the other hostages stepped one at a time from a bus, whose windows were covered with checked curtains, into a clear cold night. As they touched the tarmac, two young militants, the hoods of their parkas up against the chill, took them just above the elbows and propelled them through the shouting crowd toward the Algerian plane with its red stylized bird emblazoned on the tail.

Looking dazed, some with long hair and beards that contrasted with the neat trims of their official days before the embassy takeover Nov. 4, 1979, they stumbled into the first-class section of the plane. Now they were what a bulletin on Pars, the state press agency, would describe later as "former hostages."

"They seem stunned, as if they cannot believe they are going free," Ahmad Azizi, the Government's director of hostage affairs, remarked to an Iranian state television crew covering the departure.

At 8:20, the doors were sealed, Pars reported, and the engines began to whine. A

Continued on Page A8, Column 1

United Press International

11:57 A.M.: Ronald Reagan being sworn in as 40th President by Chief Justice Warren E. Burger. Nancy Reagan held the Bible and Senator Mark O. Hatfield witnessed the ceremony.

Pars via Associated Press

12:25 P.M.: Sgt. Joseph Subic Jr. propelled by militants to waiting plane at airport in Teheran

FREEZE SET ON HIRING

Californian Stresses Need to Restrict Government and Buoy Economy

By STEVEN R. WEISMAN
Special to The New York Times

WASHINGTON, Jan. 20 — Ronald Wilson Reagan of California, promising "an era of national renewal," became the 40th President of the United States today as 52 Americans held hostage in Iran were heading toward freedom.

The hostages, whose 14 months of captivity had been a central focus of the Presidential contest last year, took off from Teheran in two Boeing 727 airplanes at 12:25 P.M., Eastern standard time, the very moment that Mr. Reagan was concluding his solemn Inaugural Address at the United States Capitol.

The new President's speech, however, made no reference at all to the long-awaited release of the hostages, emphasizing instead the need to limit the powers of the Federal Government, and to bring an end to unemployment and inflation.

'Government Is the Problem'

Promising to begin immediately to deal with "an economic affliction of great proportions," Mr. Reagan declared: "In this present crisis, government is not the solution to our problem; government is the problem." And in keeping with this statement, the President issued orders for a hiring "freeze" as his first official act. [Page B6.]

Wearing a charcoal gray club coat, striped trousers and dove gray vest and tie, Mr. Reagan took his oath of office at 11:57 A.M. in the first inaugural ceremony ever enacted on the western front of the United States Capitol. The site was chosen to stress the symbolism of Mr. Reagan's addressing his words to the West, the region that served as his base in his three Presidential campaigns in 1968, 1976 and 1980.

Oldest to Assume Presidency

The ceremony today, filled with patriotic music, the firing of cannons and the pealing of bells, marked the transfer of the Presidency back to the Republicans after the four-year term of Jimmy Carter, a Democrat, as well as the culmination of the remarkable career of a conservative former two-term Governor of California who had started out as a baseball announcer and motion picture star.

At the age of 69, Mr. Reagan also became the oldest man to assume the Presidency, and in five months he will become the oldest man to serve in the office.

Mr. Carter, looking haggard and worn after spending two largely sleepless nights trying to resolve the hostage crisis

Continued on Page B8, Column 2

Anxious Families and Towns Erupt Into Long-Postponed Celebrations

Black Star/John Troha for The New York Times

Anita Schaefer, wife of a hostage, embraced Mr. Carter at airport.

By JOSEPH B. TREASTER

Saying his final farewells at Andrews Air Force Base yesterday, Jimmy Carter spotted Anita Schaefer, the wife of one of the hostages, and exuberantly embraced her.

"Tom is in the air," Mr. Carter said, speaking of her husband, Col. Thomas E. Schaefer of the Air Force, who was the senior military officer at the United States Embassy in Teheran.

"Really, truly, Mr. President," she whispered.

"Really, truly — at long last," he said, "Tom is safe. I'll be with him tomorrow morning in Germany."

"Oh, thank God, Mr. President."

Then they both cried. And they embraced again.

The First Glimpse

As the hostages arrived in Algiers, relatives strained close to television screens for the first glimpse of their loved ones out of captivity in more than 14 months.

"There's Billy," cried Letezia Gallegos, as her brother, Sgt. William Gallegos of the Marines, stepped down the ramp. His mother, Theresa, broke into deep sobs.

News that the plane carrying the hostages had taken off from Teheran came to Penelope Laingen, the wife of L. Bruce Laingen, the embassy's chargé d'affaires, as she sat in a reserved seat at the inauguration of President Reagan. A military policeman shouted the word for everyone to hear.

Some had gotten the word from radio and television broadcasts, and still others, like Marjorie Moore, the wife of Bert C. Moore, the administrative consul, received phone calls from the State Department.

Most of the homes of the hostages' families, torn by doubt, fear and anger for so long, exploded with joy. They cried

Continued on Page A5, Column 1

A Hopeful Prologue, a Pledge of Action

By HEDRICK SMITH
Special to The New York Times

News Analysis

WASHINGTON, Jan. 20 — For a President who has promised Americans a new beginning, an era of national renewal at home and restored strength and stature abroad, the release of the American hostages in Iran was exquisitely timed.

The extraordinary deadline diplomacy that put the 52 captured Americans into the air over Iran minutes after the howitzers thundered a new leader into office provided a graceful exit for Jimmy Carter, a hopeful prologue for Ronald Reagan and relief for a nation weary from 14 months of humiliation and seeming impotence.

Almost unavoidably the human drama in Iran overshadowed an Inaugural Address that was less an inspirational call to national greatness than a plain-spoken charter of Mr. Reagan's conservative creed, less a sermon than a stump speech, less a rallying cry than a ringing denunciation of overgrown government and a practical pledge to get down to the business of trimming it at once.

For all the new President's vaunted reputation as one of the nation's most polished political orators, his Inaugural Address offered surprisingly few rhetorical flourishes beyond the populist tribute to ordinary Americans that "those who say that we are in a time when there are no heroes, they just don't know where to look."

Although Mr. Reagan made no direct mention of the hostages, their release was on everyone's lips. Moments before Mr. Reagan took his oath of office, word that the hostages were about to be flown out of Iran swept through the crowd stretched out before the Capitol, and though that news was premature, it provided the perfect symbolic backdrop for

Continued on Page B7, Column 1

More News And Pictures

The Inauguration

The Hostages

Summary and Index, Page A2

"All the News
That's Fit to Print"

The New York Times

LATE CITY EDITION

Weather: Mostly sunny, mild today; fair tonight. Chance of showers tomorrow. Temperature range: today 48-72; yesterday 56-65. Details on page C9.

VOL.CXXX . No. 44,904

NEW YORK, TUESDAY, MARCH 31, 1981

30 cents beyond 50-mile zone from New York City. Higher in air delivery cities.

25 CENTS

REAGAN WOUNDED IN CHEST BY GUNMAN; OUTLOOK 'GOOD' AFTER 2-HOUR SURGERY; AIDE AND 2 GUARDS SHOT; SUSPECT HELD

Bush Flies Back From Texas Set to Take Charge in Crisis

By STEVEN R. WEISMAN
Special to The New York Times

WASHINGTON, March 30 — Vice President Bush, cutting short a trip to Texas, returned to the White House this evening to take charge of the crisis in the Government and to assume the responsibilities of the Presidency if President Reagan's injuries prevented him from serving in the office.

It was unclear tonight how long Mr. Bush would remain in charge of Government functions, however. At George Washington Univerity Hospital, the dean of clinical affairs said that President Reagan was "alert" and that he "should be able to make decisions by tomorrow." But he said Mr. Reagan might have to remain in the hospital for two weeks.

"I can reassure this nation and a watching world that the American Government is functioning fully and effectively," Mr. Bush said this evening after presiding over a half-hour Cabinet meeting in the White House situation room, where participants also heard the televised news conference reporting on Mr. Reagan's condition.

'Officers Fulfilling Obligations'

"We've had full and complete communications throughout the day, and the officers of the Federal Government have been fulfilling their obligations with skill and with care," Mr. Bush continued. He added that "all our prayers" and "all our hope" were extended for the recovery of the two wounded law enforcement men and for James S. Brady, the White House press secretary.

White House spokesmen said this evening that no steps had been taken to install Mr. Bush as Acting President under the terms of the 25th Amendment to the Constitution, which provides for succession in case of Presidential disability.

Mr. Bush was scheduled to fill in for the President tomorrow, however, at a series of previously scheduled functions, including a Cabinet meeting, a session with Congressional leaders, and a lunch with the Prime Minister of the Netherlands, Andreas A. M. van Agt. He prepared to

Americans were saddened and outraged by news of the shooting of the President. In the business community, activity came to a standstill; stock trading was halted. Pages A5 and D1.

spend the night at his own official residence in northwest Washington, a few miles from the White House.

Contradictory Statements

There were contradictory statements in the afternoon and evening about who was in charge of the Government.

Shortly after 4 P.M., Secretary of State Alexander M. Haig Jr., who rushed to the White House minutes after the attack, announced he was in control pending the return of the Vice President to Washington. Mr. Haig also said he was in charge because the newly created system of "crisis management" was in effect, and he suggested that it was his role to serve as crisis-management coordinator until the

Continued on Page A5, Column 2

Suspect Was Arrested Last Year In Nashville on Weapons Charge

John W. Hinckley Jr. in photo made Jan. 21 for his driver's license.

Associated Press

By PHILIP TAUBMAN
Special to The New York Times

WASHINGTON, Tuesday, March 31 — The 25-year-old son of a Denver oil executive was overpowered by police officers and Secret Service agents yesterday at the scene of an attack on President Reagan. He was charged with the attempted assassination of the President and the shooting of three other persons.

The suspect was identified as John W. Hinckley Jr., who was said to have been in psychiatric care recently. He was arrested in Nashville last Oct. 9 for possession of concealed weapons, according to Nashville police records, and was released after paying a fine of $62.50. President Carter had arrived in Nashville a few hours earlier that night to speak at Opry Land.

Yesterday, in the tumult that followed the firing of a series of shots at Mr. Reagan's party, Mr. Hinckley was grabbed and pushed against a wall outside the Washington Hilton Hotel. Secret Service agents said that a Harrington Richards .22-caliber pistol was recovered from him, and he was quickly taken away in a District of Columbia police car.

Mr. Hinckley, described as a blue-eyed, sandy-haired man about 5 feet 10 inches tall, was turned over by the police to the Federal Bureau of Investigation and was arraigned early this morning in Federal District Court here.

He was ordered held without bail by Federal Magistrate Arthur L. Burnett on a charge that he "knowingly and intentionally" attempted to kill President Reagan and assaulted a Secret Service

Continued on Page A2, Column 4

Witnesses to Shooting Recall Suspect Acting 'Fidgety' and 'Hostile'

By RICHARD D. LYONS
Special to The New York Times

WASHINGTON, March 30 — "I spotted him walking rapidly up and down outside the back door of the hotel," John M. Dodson said. "He looked fidgety — agitated — a little strange, and I said to myself 'What if he takes a shot at the President?' "

Mr. Dodson, a computer specialist, was not the only person to take note of the behavior of the blond young man outside the Washington Hilton where President Reagan was making a speech. Walter C. Rogers, a reporter for Associated Press Radio, said the young man had been hostile to the group of reporters he had penetrated. And another witness, Samuel Lafta, an iron worker from Warren, Mich., said that a police lieutenant had stared at the young man several times.

But, nothing was done until the shots that wounded the President, his press secretary and two guards rang out. Then, the young man was overwhelmed by police officers and Secret Service agents.

Mr. Dodson, who works for the Pinkerton Detective Agency was standing on the seventh floor of the Universal North

Continued on Page A4, Column 3

Other News

Polish Strike Suspended

A nationwide strike threatened for today was averted after leaders of Solidarity reached a tentative settlement with the Polish Government. Page A9.

Indonesians Storm Hijacked Jet

Four of five hijackers were slain and 55 hostages freed when commandos in Bangkok retook an Indonesian airliner held since Saturday. Page A8.

ABC News

President Reagan leaving the Washington Hilton. At right is James S. Brady. As Mr. Reagan waved to the crowd . . .

Associated Press

. . . the gunman fired, hitting the President below his left arm. In photo made over roof of Presidential car . . .

Associated Press

. . . Secret Service agents are seen pushing Mr. Reagan into the vehicle, which immediately sped to a hospital.

NBC News

Circle at right shows gun held by suspect. Legs of Timothy J. McCarthy, the wounded agent, are visible at center.

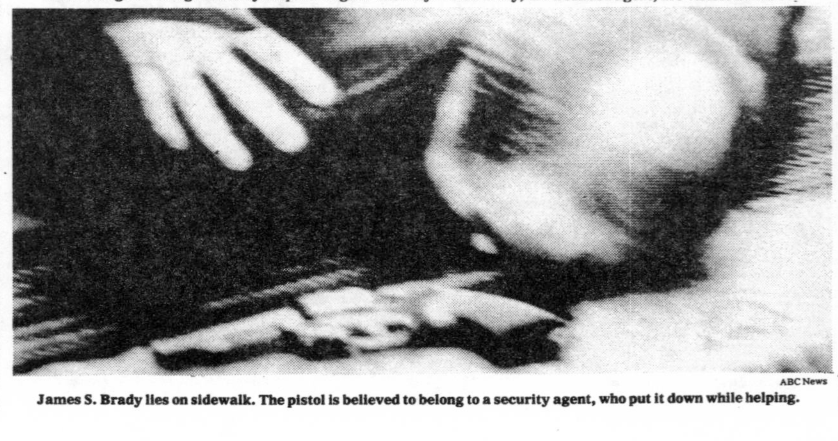

ABC News

James S. Brady lies on sidewalk. The pistol is believed to belong to a security agent, who put it down while helping.

LEFT LUNG IS PIERCED

Coloradan, 25, Arrested — Brady, Press Chief, Is Critically Injured

By HOWELL RAINES
Special to The New York Times

WASHINGTON, Tuesday, March 31 — President Reagan was shot in the chest yesterday by a gunman, apparently acting alone, as Mr. Reagan walked to his limousine after addressing a labor meeting at the Washington Hilton Hotel. The White House press secretary and two law-enforcement officers were also wounded by a burst of shots.

The President was reported in "good" and "stable" condition last night at George Washington University Hospital

Statements in capital, pages A5 and A7.

after undergoing two hours of surgery. "The prognosis is excellent," said Dr. Dennis S. O'Leary, dean of clinical affairs at the university. "He is alert and should be able to make decisions by tomorrow."

The hospital spokesman said surgeons removed a .22-caliber bullet that struck Mr. Reagan's seventh rib, penetrating the left lung three inches and collapsing it.

A rapid series of five or six shots rang out about 2:30 P.M. as Mr. Reagan left the hotel. A look of stunned disbelief swept across the President's face when the shots were fired just after he raised his left arm to wave to the crowd. Nearby, his press secretary, James S. Brady, fell to the sidewalk, critically wounded.

Eyewitnesses said six shots were fired at the Presidential entourage from a distance of about 10 feet. The assailant had positioned himself among the television camera crews and reporters assembled outside a hotel exit.

The authorities arrested a 25-year-old Colorado man, John W. Hinckley Jr., at the scene of the attack. He was booked on Federal charges of attempting to assassinate the President and assault on a Federal officer, and early this morning he was ordered held without bail by Federal Magistrate Arthur L. Burnett.

According to police records, Mr. Hinckley was arrested in Nashville last fall on weapons charges on a night when President Carter was speaking there.

Scene of Turmoil

Within minutes after the attack yesterday afternoon, Americans were witnessing for the second time in a generation television pictures of a chief executive being struck by gunfire during what appeared to be a routine public appearance. For the second time in less than 20 years, too, they watched as the nation's leaders scrambled to meet one of the sternest tests of the democratic system.

Mr. Reagan, apparently at first unaware that he had been wounded, was shoved forcefully by a Secret Service agent into the Presidential limousine,

Continued on Page A3, Column 3

A Bullet Is Removed From Reagan's Lung In Emergency Surgery

By ROBERT REINHOLD
Special to The New York Times

WASHINGTON, March 30 — President Reagan was treated for a partly collapsed lung today, but the bullet that entered his left side and lodged in the tissue of his left lung did not do much further damage, according to doctors who operated on him. Surgeons removed a .22-caliber bullet from the President's lower left lung.

Neither Mr. Reagan's heart nor such vital blood vessels as the aorta were affected, Dr. Dennis S. O'Leary, dean for clinical affairs at George Washington University, said at a briefing this evening. "The bullet was never close to any vital structure," he said. He called Mr. Reagan's prognosis "excellent."

Emergency surgical procedures, which took about two hours, found no bleeding or damage in the abdominal area. Mr. Reagan received five units, or two and a half quarts, of blood in a transfusion before surgery. His vital signs were stable throughout his ordeal.

The adult body contains five to six quarts of blood. The hazard of blood loss relates to how rapidly the blood is lost and whether the volume of the blood sup-

Continued on Page A7, Column 1

"All the News That's Fit to Print"

The New York Times

LATE CITY EDITION

Weather: Mostly sunny, windy today; mostly clear tonight. Sunny tomorrow. Temperature range: today 35-50; yesterday 43-58. Details are on page B8.

VOL.CXXX . . No. 44,919

NEW YORK, WEDNESDAY, APRIL 15, 1981

30 cents beyond 50-mile zone from New York City. Higher in air delivery cities.

25 CENTS

COLUMBIA RETURNS: SHUTTLE ERA OPENS

First Re-usable Spaceship Glides to Landing in Desert; Commander Calls Flight 'Tremendous, Start to Finish'

Goal: 2d Trip in 6 Months And 100 in Ship's Lifetime

By WALTER SULLIVAN
Special to The New York Times

EDWARDS AIR FORCE BASE, Calif., April 14 — With the nearly flawless completion of the voyage of the shuttle Columbia, space agency officials began today to draw up firmer plans for the future of man in space, a future that they had always envisioned with a clarity that left their critics scoffing.

The triumph of the Columbia is expected to lead to flights with far-reaching commercial, scientific and military applications.

An agency official said at a briefing this afternoon that the Columbia would probably begin its return flight to Cape Canaveral, Fla., riding piggyback on a Boeing 747 jet in about a week.

He said that the "optimistic" estimate was that the shuttle would fly again under its own power in "less than six months" on a four-day flight from which it might be able to turn around and return to space in four months. Ultimately officials envision the shuttle being able to turn around in a matter of weeks. Each shuttle would have a life of 100 missions.

Apparently responding to the space program's critics, Christopher C. Kraft Jr., director of the Johnson Space Center in Houston, in a message relayed to the astronauts just before they left the shuttle, said: "We just became infinitely smarter."

What uncertainty remaining today centered on questions about just how quickly the spaceship could be readied for another flight. Specialists still have to determine the extent of the damage to the tiles that protect the ship from the searing heat of re-entry into the atmosphere. There was also some question about the suitability for quick re-use of the launching pad at Cape Canaveral, which was significantly damaged at liftoff on Sunday. [Page A23.]

Donald K. Slayton, orbital flight test manager and a former astronaut, said that a preliminary inspection revealed no more tiles missing than had been seen earlier on television from space. He said, "minimum work" would be required to replace them. But he added that a more detailed inspection would follow.

The shuttle's success is sweet vindication of American know-how, but social scientists say the psychological uplift will pass. News analysis, page A22.

If close inspection of the tiles here and later when the Columbia is airlifted back to Florida reveals no fundamental problems, the "optimistic" estimate of a launching in the fall would prove true, with the third test mission in the spring and the fourth and final one later in 1982. One of the last two test missions, both of which are to last for seven days, would orbit while opened to the sky, rather than flying upside down to scan the earth.

The first operational, or nonexperimental, flight would take place by the end of that year.

The payload for that flight, as now planned, will be a TDRS or Tracking and Data Relay Satellite to be gently released into earth orbit. Among other roles, this

Continued on Page A22, Column 1

A Speck Pierces Horizon

By ROBERT LINDSEY
Special to The New York Times

EDWARDS AIR FORCE BASE, Calif., April 14 — First came the sonic boom announcing that it was near: two loud shocks that reverberated like cannon blasts across the desert floor.

Over the public address system, the voice of Mission Control read out the orbiter's speed and altitude, now rapidly declining: "Columbia, you're right on the money, right on the money,"

"Where is it, where is it?" perhaps 10,000 voices asked at once from the edge of Rogers Dry Lake.

Dropping to the Desert

Then, the sharpest eyes on the ground, squinting upward, saw it: a tiny, moving speck high over the horizon, dropping fast through a dusty, luminescent haze that rose from the surface of the parched dry lake like a cloudy mist. Suddenly, the tension broke.

"There it is!" the first voice said, and then others. The spectators, in clusters and large crowds, some who had been up all night waiting, broke into cheers as the space shuttle orbiter Columbia glided gracefully toward the hard-packed, cream-colored desert runway.

"Incredible!" shouted Joseph Lyon, who sells plywood for a living. "Can you believe it?" he asked, as he recorded the Columbia's descent with his portable home video recorder.

The Columbia, perhaps only 60 seconds after it had first been seen from the desert gallery, touched down, and the spectators continued to cheer.

The craft then rolled to a stop and seemed, from a distance, to become mired in a shimmering lake, a desert mirage that gave the illusion that the prehistoric dry lake was no longer dry.

Even before the Columbia had stopped its landing roll, a convoy of 21 service vehicles whose operators had been been training for that moment for almost three months, was moving in a phalanx toward the craft, stirring up a cloud of dust like a battalion of tanks moving over the Sahara before battle.

"It's a great day for the country," Albert Wheelon, an aerospace executive in the crowd said when he spotted a friend. "America's confidence ought to be up 100 percent."

It was a thought expressed repeatedly in the crowd of spectators, estimated by the National Aeronautics and Space Administration at more than 250,000, who had come here to watch a spaceship for

Continued on Page A23, Column 1

'Welcome Home, Columbia'

—Joseph Allen, Mission Control Communicator, 1:21 P.M.

HOUSTON: Columbia, we show you crossing the coast now.

CAPT. ROBERT L. CRIPPEN: What a way to come to California!

HOUSTON: Columbia, you're out of 130K [130,000 feet] on the tracking, 6.4 Mach, looking good.

Mach 6, 124,000 feet, range 177 miles.

JOHN W. YOUNG: John Young rolling, using manual control now.

HOUSTON: Mach 4.4, 107,000 feet, range 112.

Roll reversal complete. Control looks good.

Ejection seats can be used now, below 100,000.

You're coming right down the chute.

Rudder active now, looking good. Range 73 miles.

We now have a live television picture from the long-range optics at Dryden Flight Research Center.

Columbia, you're coming right down the track. The tracking data, map data and preplan trajectory are all one line on our plot boards here.

YOUNG: Roger, we concur.

HOUSTON: Columbia, we show you very slightly high in altitude, coming down nicely.

Mach 1 at 51,000 feet, range 28 miles.

Columbia, you're going subsonic now out at 50K, looking good.

YOUNG: Roger that.

HOUSTON: Columbia getting ready to start the big sweeping turn into the runway.

Columbia, you're really looking good, right on the money, right on the money.

25,000 feet, 1.6, range 13 miles; 22,000 feet. Control looking very smooth, speed brake at——. We have a television picture now.

You're right on the glide slope, Columbia. Right on glide slope, approaching center line, looking great.

That's TV from the chase plane. 16,000 feet.

Air speed 271 knots.

5,290.

2,500 feet.

50 feet, 40, 30, 20, 10, 5, 4, 3, 2, 1. Touchdown.

Welcome home, Columbia! Beautiful, beautiful.

More from the dialogue, page A23.

The New York Times/Jim Wilson

The Columbia, accompanied by two escort planes, descending toward a landing at Edwards Air Force Base

NBC News

The shuttle's rear wheels touch the runway on Rogers Dry Lake. Craft was traveling about 215 miles an hour.

CBS News via Associated Press

John W. Young, left, and Capt. Robert L. Crippen walking away from their craft after landing safely in the desert

FLIERS EMERGE ELATED

Crippen Says That Nation Is 'Back in the Space Business to Stay'

By JOHN NOBLE WILFORD
Special to The New York Times

EDWARDS AIR FORCE BASE, Calif., April 14 — The space shuttle Columbia rocketed out of orbit and glided to a safe landing on the desert here today to conclude the successful first demonstration of a bold new approach to extraterrestrial travel, the re-usable winged spaceship.

Heralding its triumphant return with a sharp double sonic boom, one of technology's fanfares, the 122-foot-long Columbia appeared in the clear blue sky, soared over the base, looped back and touched its wheels down in the wash of a mirage on the hard-packed clay of a dry lake bed. Touchdown came at 1:21 P.M., Eastern standard time.

"Welcome home, Columbia!" was the simple message from Joseph Allen in Mission Control.

215 Miles an Hour

Capt. Robert L. Crippen of the Navy and John W. Young brought the 80-ton gliding vehicle with its stubby delta wings to a smooth landing at a speed of 215 miles an hour, about twice the velocity of a jetliner landing.

Never before had a space vehicle returned to the earth in such a way so that it could be flown again. The Columbia and its three sister ships now under construction are each designed for as many as 100 flights to and from the space frontier.

"It was really a tremendous mission from start to finish," said Mr. Young, the commander, in a brief post-landing appearance before officials of the National Aeronautics and Space Administration.

Right on Course in Approach

Moments earlier, the Columbia had come over the California coast, and Mission Control reassured the astronauts that "we've got good data, looking good."

At 1:09, the astronauts were advised, "You've got perfect energy, perfect ground track," meaning that they were on target and slowing for the kind of landing they had practiced so many times.

"What a way to come to California!" Captain Crippen exclaimed.

The Columbia was launched Sunday morning at the Kennedy Space Center in Florida and orbited the earth 36 times over a period of 54 hours and 22 minutes. It was the first orbital test of the shuttle and the first time American astronauts had ventured into space in nearly six years.

"I think we're back in the space business to stay," Captain Crippen said.

The development of the shuttle, a hybrid spacecraft-airplane, has cost almost $10 billion since the project was initiated

Continued on Page A21, Column 1

Other News

Bloc Maneuvers Said to End

Reagan Administration officials say that unusual military activity by Warsaw Pact forces in and around Poland has virtually ended. Page A8.

Fighting Traps Beirut Premier

Artillery and mortar fire between Syrian and Lebanese Christian forces exploded around Parliament, trapping the Prime Minister inside. Page A3.

Aid Planned for Banks

Federal regulators plan to draft legislation soon to help financially troubled savings and loan associations and other institutions. Page D1.

Bradley Wins Third Term

Mayor Tom Bradley of Los Angeles was re-elected, becoming the first Mayor in the city's history to win a third term without a runoff. Page A13.

"All the News That's Fit to Print"

The New York Times

LATE CITY EDITION

Weather: Increasing cloudiness today; chance of showers tonight and tomorrow. Temperature range: today 54-71; yesterday 42-72. Details on page C18.

VOL.CXXX . No. 44,948 | Copyright © 1981 The New York Times | NEW YORK, THURSDAY, MAY 14, 1981 | 30 cents beyond 50-mile zone from New York City. Higher in air delivery cities | 25 CENTS

POPE IS SHOT IN CAR IN VATICAN SQUARE; SURGEONS TERM CONDITION 'GUARDED'; TURK, AN ESCAPED MURDERER, IS SEIZED

MADE THREAT IN '79

Alleged Assailant Wrote a Letter Saying He'd Kill John Paul on Trip

By R. W. APPLE Jr.

Special to The New York Times

ROME, Thursday, May 14 — The first reports said only that he spoke no Italian, that he was young and that he had dark hair.

But within a matter of minutes, a picture of the man accused of shooting Pope John Paul II in St. Peter's Square yesterday afternoon began to emerge, a picture of a militant Turkish terrorist, already convicted of one murder, who escaped from a maximum security prison in 1979 and then threatened in a letter to assassinate the Pope.

The Turkish Ambassador in Washington, Sukru Elekdag, said after the news of the shooting had flashed around the world, "The Turkish police have been under instruction to shoot him on sight."

Said He Was a Student

Moments after he was wrestled to the ground by pilgrims who had been standing near him, the alleged assailant told the Italian police that his name was Mehmet Ali Agca. He gave his age as 23 and said he was Turkish. He said also that he was a student at the University for Foreigners in Perugia in central Italy, but the records of the university showed that he had attended Italian-language classes there for only one day last month.

Mr. Agca was described by the police and by bystanders as a dark-haired young man, clean-shaven, with an angular face. He was wearing an open-neck white shirt under a lightweight jacket.

Mr. Agca was convicted in February 1979 of having murdered Abdi Ipekci, the editor of the independent Turkish daily newspaper Milliyet. He was jailed. But in late November, he escaped from the military prison where he was being held, and he had apparently been in hiding ever since.

When he fled from the prison, Turkish authorities say, he left behind a letter, addressed to Milliyet, threatening the life of the Pope. If the Pontiff did not cancel his visit to Turkey, which was then imminent, Mr. Agca wrote, he would shoot him in revenge for the attack by Moslem extremists on the Grand Mosque in Mecca earlier that year.

Blame Put on U.S. and Israel

The attack was considered a desecration of the Islamic holy place by Moslems, and Mr. Agca charged that the incident was of American or Israeli origin. His letter denounced the Pontiff as "the masked leader of the Crusades."

A partial text of the letter, made available by the Turkish police, reads as follows:

"Western imperialists who are afraid of Turkey's unity of political, military and economic power with the brotherly Islamic countries are sending Crusader

Continued on Page A3, Column 5

United Press International · The Vatican

Pope John Paul II, with blood on his left hand, being comforted by aides moments after being shot yesterday as he rode through St. Peter's Square at the Vatican

2 BULLETS HIT PONTIFF

Part of Intestine Removed in 5-Hour Operation— Hand Also Injured

By HENRY TANNER

Special to The New York Times

ROME, Thursday, May 14 — Pope John Paul II was shot and seriously wounded yesterday as he was standing in an open car moving slowly among more than 10,000 worshipers in St. Peter's Square.

The police arrested a gunman who was later identified as an escaped Turkish murderer who had previously threatened the Pope's life in the name of Islam.

The Pontiff, who was struck by two pistol bullets and wounded in the abdomen, right arm and left hand, underwent 5 hours and 25 minutes of surgery in which parts of his intestine were removed. A hospital bulletin at midnight said he was in "guarded" condition, but the director of surgery expressed confidence that "the Pontiff will recover soon."

By morning the Pope was reported conscious and still in guarded but stable condition.

Pope Falls Into Aides' Arms

The attack occurred as the Pope, dressed in white, was shaking hands and lifting small children in his arms while being driven around the square. Suddenly, just outside the Vatican's bronze gate, there was a burst of gunfire.

One hand rising to his face and blood staining his garments, the Pope faltered and fell into the arms of his Polish secretary, the Rev. Stanislaw Dziwisz, and his personal servant, Angelo Gugel.

The 60-year-old Pope, the spiritual leader of nearly 600 million Roman Catholics around the world, was rushed by ambulance to Gemelli Hospital, two miles north of the Vatican, for surgery.

'How Could They Do It?'

The Pope was conscious as he was taken to the operating room and seemed to speak of the attack on him as the work of more than one person.

"How could they do it?" a nurse quoted the Pope as asking.

The gunman fired four times in the attack, the police said. Two tourists, an American and a Jamaican, were wounded by two of the bullets. Ann Odre, 60, of Buffalo, was struck in the chest; she underwent surgery and was listed in critical condition. Rose Hill, 21, of Jamaica, was slightly wounded in an arm.

The gunman, who the police said was armed with a 9-millimeter Browning automatic, was set upon in the square by bystanders, who knocked the pistol out of his hand. He was then arrested, taken away and later identified as Mehmet Ali Agca, 23. Despite reports that another man had been seen fleeing from the square, the police said they were convinced that the gunman had acted alone.

The police quoted Mr. Agca as having told them, "My life is not important."

He was said to have arrived in Italy

Continued on Page A3, Column 3

Amid Prayers, World Voices Its Indignation

Prayers, shock and indignation resounded around the world yesterday after the shooting of Pope John Paul II.

President Reagan, recovering from wounds inflicted six weeks ago by a gunman, said he would pray for the Pope. In a message Mr. Reagan said, "All Americans join me in hopes and prayers for your speedy recovery."

Queen Elizabeth II said she was horrified. President-elect François Mitterrand of France spoke indignantly of "this new manifestation of destestable violence."

In Poland, the Pope's native land, television broadcasts were interrupted with news bulletins. Stanislaw Kania, head of the Communist Party, and other leaders offered "the best wishes for a speedy recovery necessary for the mission in service of humanist ideals of peace for the benefit of mankind." In Warsaw, people gathered somberly on street corners and around television sets in hotel lobbies, and wept during church services.

Americans shared in the grief at services in cathedrals, parochial schools and neighborhood churches.

In New York, more than 2,500 people, including Mayor Koch, jammed St. Patrick's for a mass led by Terence Cardinal Cooke. Protestant and Jewish leaders leaders joined in appeals for prayers.

The Connecticut Senate reversed itself and approved a bill calling for mandatory one-year jail sentences for illegal possession of a handgun.

"Regardless of what religion you are, he is a man of God," said Maria Lougee, a waitress on Ninth Avenue, who cried when she learned of the shooting. "Who could do something like that?"

For many, the shooting of President Reagan remained fresh in their minds. "When you shoot a President, you shoot a country," said the Rev. Miles Riley of the Archdiocese of San Francisco. "When you shoot a Pope, you shoot the church. We all felt shook, we all felt wounded."

The world, nation and region respond with shock. Pages A4-A6.

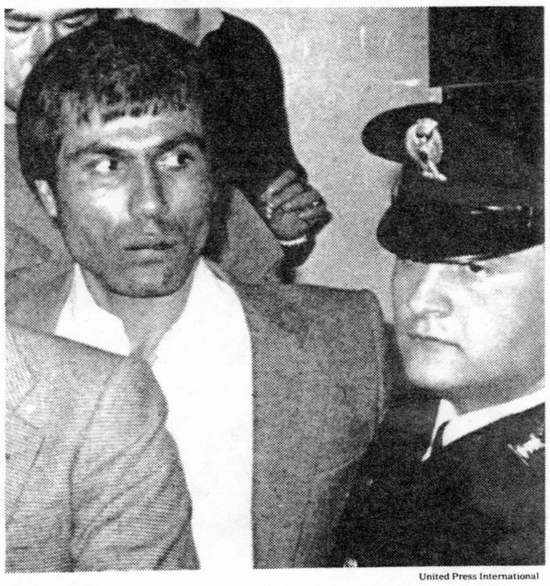

United Press International

Man identified as Mehmet Ali Agca, a 23-year-old Turkish citizen, is led away

For New York, Tearful Memories

By LESLIE BENNETTS

In the rectory basement at St. Charles Borromeo Church in Harlem, the women in the Senior Citizens Group wept quietly over the crepe paper banner they were making for a dance and recalled how the Pope leapt from his car to kiss the ground in front of their church.

At the school next door, students were wide-eyed and solemn as they chanted Hail Marys and prayed for the Pope's recovery.

And in the Bronx, where the Pope had stopped on Morris Avenue on his trip to New York in 1979, worried neighborhood residents gathered on the sidewalk to exchange rumors about his condition.

Many Remember His Visit

But for those New Yorkers with personal memories of the Pope's visit to their own school or street, the news came as a particular shock. "How could somebody shoot the Pope?" wondered Lynda Anderson, a 10-year-old student at St. Charles Borromeo, who had presented the Pope with a bouquet of roses.

Her incredulity was shared by those much older than she, many of whom had found the Pope's visit one of the great thrills of their lives. "It could not have been more wonderful," said Juanita Taylor, a retired nurse who overheard yesterday's bad news on the street and hurried to the church. "I don't think it would have been much different if Jesus Christ himself had come here. All I can do now is pray."

At the Senior Citizens' meeting, Emily Allred sighed and wiped a tear from her cheek. "He left some sort of feeling with us when he was here," she said. "It worked inwardly on us. If you could have seen him jump from his car and kiss the earth, it was one of the most fantastic things that ever happened in Harlem. He's a wonderful leader."

Many people commented on the helplessness of world leaders to defend themselves against deranged individuals. "So many people are walking around who are sick and need help," said Gwendolyn Burwell, a church volunteer. "I imagine this was a person who wanted to be seen or heard, and this was the only way he thought he could be heard."

Memories of the Pope's presence and

Continued on Page A6, Column 1

A Firm Papacy For the People

Pope Strives to Deliver His Message Worldwide

By KENNETH A. BRIGGS

News Analysis

From the day that Karol Cardinal Wojtyla stepped confidently onto the balcony of St. Peter's Basilica as the newly elected Pope John Paul II, he has boldly challenged the church and the world. Striving to make Christianity a renewed force, he has taken his message from St. Peter's Square around the globe, traveling widely with little apparent regard for his personal safety.

The "Popemobile," an open vehicle such as the one he was riding in when he was shot yesterday, has become a symbol of his mobility. Before his weekly audiences in the square, he stands in the vehicle as it winds through the crowds. The act is a byproduct of his instinctive showmanship and his irrepressible desire to bring the church to the people.

Whether his efforts have been applauded or criticized, John Paul has made the world pay attention to the church. He is a subject of great contentiousness as a leader, but he has remained personally popular to all sides in disputes and has gained a reputation for bending decorum and playing to crowds.

The Pope has undertaken nine major trips in his mission of evangelization, a concept that includes not only the preaching of the Gospel as an alternative to ideologies such as Marxism but also the advocacy of the rights of the poor and oppressed. Repeatedly he has warned Roman Catholics against using violence to erase injustice. "Violence," he said during his trip to Brazil, "kills what it intends to create."

John Paul II, a laborer in Poland in his youth, has won the world's affection and respect as Pope. Page A7.

Elected to the papacy on Oct. 16, 1978, he promised "a ministry of love," and he has plunged into the world scene with a sense of fearless resolve and tireless devotion.

On his trips, he has thrived on schedules that most of his aides find exhausting. Though an intensely private man, he has a knack for stirring crowds — wandering into their midst, donning the hats worn by local people, often speaking in the local language and reaching out to touch hands.

Some of his aides have been nervous

Continued on Page A5, Column 4

Infection Is Main Risk In Pontiff's Recovery; New Surgery Required

By LAWRENCE K. ALTMAN

The medical information on the shooting of Pope John Paul II, although incomplete, showed that the most serious damage was done to the intestines.

Three sections of the bowel, or intestines, were removed in surgery, which was termed successful, at the Gemelli Hospital in Rome.

A second operation will be needed to reconnect portions of the bowel that were surgically severed in a procedure called a temporary exclusion colostomy, which allows removal of bodily wastes through an opening of the colon part of the bowel outside the body.

The Pope received about six pints of blood, the equivalent of about 60 percent of his total blood volume.

Surgical repair of the bowel is common in gunshot wounds to the abdomen, and a temporary colostomy is often necessary in such injuries. Recovery is often complete, provided complications do not develop.

"The main risk now is infection," a hospital spokesman said.

In addition to the bullet that "went through the abdominal cavity," the Pope suffered two minor gunshot wounds in his right arm and one in his left hand, ac-

Continued on Page A2, Column 5

Other News

Reagan Tax Compromise Seen

President Reagan is prepared to compromise on the size of his tax cuts, an aide said, because of the financial markets' unsettled conditions. Page D1.

Social Security Plan Assailed

The Reagan Administration's plan to trim Social Security benefits aroused wide protest and the first hint of serious Congressional opposition. Page B15.

U.S. Envoy Returns to Beirut

Philip C. Habib, President Reagan's special envoy, arrived from Jerusalem with a plan for easing the crisis over Syrian missiles in Lebanon. Page A17.

U.S. Holds Soviet Cargo

Federal agents, suspecting violations, boarded a Soviet jetliner in Washington and seized gear, some of which was properly licensed for export. Page A9.

Reagan's Son Cited Ties

Michael Reagan, elder son of the President, referred to his father in letters seeking military contracts, an official of his company said. Page A24.

Plans for Battery Park Shown

Plans for the long-delayed Battery Park City commercial complex call for office buildings, plazas, restaurants, gardens and a skating rink. Page B1.

"All the News That's Fit to Print"

The New York Times

LATE CITY EDITION

Weather: Mostly sunny today; clear tonight. Mostly sunny tomorrow. Temperature range: today 76-99; yesterday 74-94. Details on page B8.

VOL.CXXX . . . No. 45,003 | NEW YORK, WEDNESDAY, JULY 8, 1981 | 30 cents beyond 50-mile zone from New York City. Higher in air delivery cities. | 25 CENTS

REAGAN NOMINATING WOMAN, AN ARIZONA APPEALS JUDGE, TO SERVE ON SUPREME COURT

Associated Press

Judge Sandra Day O'Connor at news conference yesterday in Phoenix

REACTION IS MIXED

Senate Seems Favorable but Opposition Arises on Abortion Stands

By STEVEN R. WEISMAN

Special to The New York Times

WASHINGTON, July 7 — President Reagan announced today that he would nominate Sandra Day O'Connor, a 51-year-old judge on the Arizona Court of Appeals, to the United States Supreme Court. If confirmed, she would become the first woman to serve on the Court.

"She is truly a 'person for all seasons,'" Mr. Reagan said this morning, "possessing those unique qualities of temperament, fairness, intellectual

Remarks on Court post, page A12.

capacity and devotion to the public good which have characterized the 101 'brethren' who have preceded her."

White House and Justice Department officials expressed confidence that Judge O'Connor's views were compatible with those espoused over the years by Mr. Reagan, who has been highly critical of some past Supreme Court decisions on the rights of defendants, busing, abortion and other matters.

Some Quick Opposition

From the initial reaction in the Senate, it appeared her nomination would be approved. However, her record of favoring the proposed Federal equal rights amendment and having sided once against anti-abortion interests while she was a legislator provoked immediate opposition to her confirmation by the National Right to Life Committee, Moral Majority and other groups opposed to abortion.

At a brief news conference in Phoenix, Judge O'Connor declined to explain her views, saying that she intended to leave such matters to her confirmation hearings before the Senate Judiciary Committee. [Page A12.]

Mr. Reagan, himself an opponent of abortions, said in response to a question that he was "completely satisfied" with her position on that issue.

No Radical Shift Expected

White House officials were hopeful that Judge O'Connor's appointment could be historic not only because she is a woman but also because her presence on the Court, as a replacement for Associate Justice Potter Stewart, who was often a swing vote between ideological camps on the Court, could shift the Court's balance to the right.

However, an examination of the Court's voting patterns suggests no radical shift is likely even if she does vote with the more conservative Justices. [News analysis, page A13.]

It is the additional hope of Mr. Reagan's aides to make the Court even more conservative in the years ahead, when more vacancies are possible.

Judge O'Connor was appointed to

Continued on Page A12, Column 2

'A Reputation for Excelling'

Sandra Day O'Connor

By B. DRUMMOND AYRES Jr.

Special to The New York Times

WASHINGTON, July 7 — Judge Sandra Day O'Connor's place in history is already secure, based on today's announcement that she will be President Reagan's nominee as the first woman on the United States Supreme Court.

Woman in the News

But if her past is prologue, after her Senate confirmation Judge O'Connor might well go on to leave even larger "footprints on the sands of time," as Mr. Reagan, quoting Longfellow, described the mark of United States Justices. Thus far in her 51 years, Judge O'Connor has compiled an impressive list of academic, civic, political and legal achievements.

"She's finished at the top in a lot of things," said Mary Ellen Simonson of Phoenix, who was a legislative aide when Mrs. O'Connor was majority leader of the Arizona State Senate, the first woman in the nation to hold such a leadership position.

"She has a reputation for excelling," Mrs. Simonson continued. "As a result she's been one of the state's leading role models for women. Now she's a national role model."

Judge O'Connor, who currently sits on the Arizona Court of Appeals, the state's second highest court, refused this afternoon to discuss "substantative issues" when she met with reporters in Phoenix. And, because of her short, 18-month tenure on the appeals court and its somewhat limited docket, she has faced few of the nettlesome issues routinely taken up by the United States Supreme Court. Nevertheless, her past and her acquaintances provide some insights into her mind and personality.

She is said, by friend and foe alike, to be notably bright, extremely hardworking, meticulous, deliberate, cautious and, above all, a Republican conservative.

"But she has an open mind when it comes to her conservatism," said a longtime friend, Sharon Rockefeller, wife of Gov. John D. Rockefeller IV of West Virginia. "I can't conceive of her closing off her mind to anything."

A leading Democratic politician in

Continued on Page A13, Column 5

Baker Vows Support for Nominee

By FRANCIS X. CLINES

Special to The New York Times

WASHINGTON, July 7 — Anti-abortion groups today denounced President Reagan's decision to nominate Judge Sandra Day O'Connor to the Supreme Court, but initial reaction in the Senate, which will vote on confirmation, was favorable.

"I commend the President for the courage of his decision," said Howard H. Baker Jr., the Senate Republican majority leader. "I am delighted with his choice, and I pledge my full support for her confirmation by the full Senate."

The National Right to Life Committee, an amalgam of anti-abortion lobbying groups in the 50 states, said that it would mobilize its members to "prevail upon senators to oppose this nomination." The committee said that Judge O'Connor was "pro-abortion" as a member of the Arizona State Legislature.

Dr. Carolyn Gerster, a vice president of the National Right to Life Committee, said that the nominee, as a legislator, voted in 1974 not to allow an anti-abortion resolution out of caucus, thus killing it. The resolution asked Congress to pass a Constitutional amendment protecting the fetus except when the mother's life was in danger, and allowed abortions in the case of rape.

Dr. Gerster based her statement of Judge O'Connor's record on that and other votes, which were characterized as "pro-abortion," on newspaper accounts and the recollections of other legislators, she said. Before 1975, the State Legislature kept no records of

Continued on Page A12, Column 1

Rupturing of Reservoir Pipelines Imperils Newark's Water Supply

Chain Reaction Set Off as Valve Is Opened — Vandalism Suspected

By ROBERT HANLEY

Special to The New York Times

PEQUANNOCK TOWNSHIP, N.J., July 7 — A valve at an aqueduct was opened here today, apparently by vandals, starting a chain reaction that burst two huge pipelines and cut off Newark from its main water supply.

The New York Times / July 8, 1981

"It's an imminent catastrophe," said James F. Conley, the chief engineer of Newark's Division of Water Supply.

Mr. Conley said that unless the city could activate two existing pipeline interconnections with three other water supply systems and could build two new ones, parts of Newark "will be out of water" in five days.

Other Communities Affected

The pipelines that ruptured, he said, normally carry about 75 million of the 120 million gallons a day used by 600,000 people in Newark and parts of Elizabeth, Bloomfield, Belleville and Wayne.

Those four other communities, all of which purchase some of their water from Newark, began planning for alternative supplies.

Mayor Kenneth A. Gibson of Newark declared a water emergency in the early afternoon, prohibiting all nonessential uses of water, including lawn watering, car washing and opening of hydrants for any purposes other than firefighting.

Douglas Eldridge, a spokesman for the Mayor, said officials did not expect any declines in water pressure or other serious difficulties in the next day or two. He said some discolored water could come from taps because of adjustments being made on the distribution system following the huge loss of water.

But officials said that if the city could not restore a steady water source within five days, parts of Newark would run out of water. A heat wave that pushed temperatures today into the mid-90's and may see higher readings tomorrow is expected to increase water use and has heightened the officials' concern.

A 1,200-foot section of the two pipelines was torn away after they ruptured, sending tens of millions of gallons of water down a hillside here from about 4 A.M. today until the aqueduct's main supply valves at the Charlotteburg Reservoir were shut off sometime after 5 A.M., Mr. Conley said.

The cascading water, estimated at 40

Continued on Page B2, Column 4

U.S. FRAMES POLICY ON HALTING SPREAD OF NUCLEAR ARMS

American Reliability as Seller of Technology Stressed — Use Must Be Peaceful

By TERENCE SMITH

Special to The New York Times

WASHINGTON, July 7 — The Reagan Administration plans to announce shortly that while it is committed to halting the spread of nuclear weapons abroad the United States will be a "clearly reliable and credible" supplier of nuclear technology for peaceful purposes.

This policy is contained in an eight-point set of guidelines that has been prepared by the State Department and submitted to the White House. The White House is expected to issue the list before a meeting in Ottawa July 20-21 of the leaders of seven industrial nations. The spread of nuclear weapons will be one of the items on the agenda.

Although the guidelines are couched in the most general of terms, Administration officials say, they reflect a stronger commitment to halting the spread of nuclear weapons than was contained in Mr. Reagan's campaign statements last year and in a transition paper prepared by his advisers in December.

A Bigger Nuclear Umbrella

As described by Administration officials who have seen the guidelines, there are several principal points:

¶The goals of stopping the spread of nuclear weapons must be strongly reaffirmed.

¶A determined effort should be made to reduce the motivation of other countries to obtain nuclear weapons and an acknowledgement should be given that security considerations are often a basic factor in that decision. To this end, officials said, the United States would be prepared to sell conventional arms and consider extending its own nuclear umbrella.

¶The 1968 Nonproliferation Treaty, by which the nuclear powers undertook not to help others make or acquire nuclear weapons, and the 1967 Treaty of Tlatelolco, Mexico, which established a nuclear-free zone in Latin America, must be emphatically supported.

¶The International Atomic Energy Agency and its system of safeguards against the conversion of nuclear power and research facilities to weapons purposes should be strongly supported.

¶The United States should cooperate with other supplier countries to prevent the transfer of sensitive technology and material to nonnuclear countries where such transfers carry a risk of weapons production.

¶A high level of intelligence activities, including the possible upgrading of

Continued on Page A8, Column 1

New Pact Ends 7-Day Strike Of Garbage Haulers in Jersey

By ALFONSO A. NARVAEZ

Special to The New York Times

WEST PATERSON, N.J., July 7 — A seven-day strike against private garbage haulers in 108 northern and central New Jersey communities ended today when 1,400 drivers and loaders accepted a three-year contract that gives them a 50 percent pay increase.

Garbage trucks in the 12 affected counties will begin rolling early tomorrow. and Picket signs that had blocked municipal sanitation employees will come down from entrances to landfills.

The new contract was accepted after a long and confusing day in which the union members first rejected an agreement hammered out by negotiators in an 18-hour session at the Sheraton Heights Hotel in Hasbrouck Heights.

$155-a-Week Raise

When that proposal was rejected, the negotiators immediately went into new talks.

The union then approved a proposal that gives the drivers the $155-a-week raise over three years that was contained in the proposal they rejected, but adds three days of sick leave a year and guarantees that double time for work on the sixth day will go to workers with seniority. The drivers currently earn $310 a week for an average six-day, 48-hour week, and the loaders get about $50 less.

The union also won an additional paid holiday, four weeks of vacation after 15 years and $56 in increased health and welfare benefits.

The agreement provides for an immediate increase of $55 a week, then $35 a week on Jan. 1, 1982, $20 a week on July 1, 1982, and $45 more on July 1, 1983.

The cost of the package to residents and communities in the affected area has not yet been calculated. However, during the negotiations, the State Attorney General, James J. Zazzali, assured the owners — members of the New Jersey State Municipal Contractors Association and the Solid Waste Industry Association — that their requests for rate increases would be handled expeditiously.

The membership did not vote on the final package. The leaders of the union,

Continued on Page B4, Column 1

Sun-Powered Airplane Crosses Channel

Special to The New York Times

MANSTON, England, July 7 — After several earlier unsuccessful attempts, the first solar-powered airplane succeeded today in crossing the English Channel.

It took an atypically sunny English summer afternoon and a five-and-a-half-hour flight, but late this afternoon, the Solar Challenger dropped slowly onto the concrete landing strip of Manston Royal Air Force Base, on the southeastern coast of England.

Designed by Paul MacCready, who also designed the first human-powered plane to cross the Channel, the 210-pound Solar Challenger is powered by 16,000 photovoltaic cells on the wings that convert solar energy to electricity, which drives the motor.

No Battery Power

Other airplanes have flown on solar power, but only the Solar Challenger has been able to do so without the help of storage batteries. The project was paid for largely by DuPont and employed many high-strength, low-weight materials made by that company.

Starting from an airport at Cormeilles-en-Vexin, 25 miles northwest of Paris, the spidery plane, which has a wingspan of 47 feet, made the 165-mile journey at an average speed of about 30 miles per hour and a cruising altitude of 11,000 feet.

Standing in the deep grass along the main east-west runway at Cormeilles, a small crowd of about 30 persons had gathered to cheer on the tiny, transparent aircraft and its pilot. They watched the delicate plane corkscrew slowly and almost silently into the sky above the airport. The 2.7 horsepower electric motor produced only a slight buzz.

At an altitude of about 2,000 feet, Stephen Ptacek, the 28-year-old pilot from Golden, Colo., headed northwest in the direction of the Channel. In two or three minutes, he disappeared from sight.

Mr. Ptacek was greeted at the Man-

Continued on Page B4, Column 1

Associated Press

French policemen watch as Solar Challenger begins flight to England

Prelate, 52, Chosen By the Pope to Lead The Polish Church

By JOHN DARNTON

Special to The New York Times

WARSAW, July 7 — Bishop Jozef Glemp of Warmia was named today by Pope John Paul II as Archbishop of Gniezno and Warsaw and the Primate of Poland, succeeding Stefan Cardinal Wyszynski, who died on May 28.

The new head of the Church in this overwhelmingly Roman Catholic nation said he would continue the policies begun by his predecessor of dialogue and cooperation with both the Government and the Solidarity labor union.

"I am convinced I must follow the road laid out by Cardinal Wyszynski," he said in an interview. "The work of the Primate is not political. It is pastoral. But if we in the church are to do our duty, we must not remain above social issues. If the Solidarity and other social movements want to follow the truth and the light, we will give them our protection. It is in line with the proper role of the church."

Archbishop Glemp, 52 years old and a specialist in both canon and civil law, said he believed in working closely with the Conference of Bishops and would strive for collegial rule. Cardinal Wy-

Continued on Page A6, Column 1

INSIDE

9 More Executed in Iran

Iran executed nine opponents in its drive against "counterrevolutionary" elements. It also ordered Reuters to close its Teheran bureau. Page A3.

Upset in Mississippi Vote

Wayne Dowdy, a Democrat, apparently won a Congressional election in Mississippi, beating a strong supporter of President Reagan. Page A18.

"All the News That's Fit to Print"

The New York Times

LATE CITY EDITION

Weather: Chance of drizzle today and tonight. Partly cloudy tomorrow. Temperature range: today 51-63; yesterday 59-68. Details, page D24.

VOL.CXXXI.. No. 45,094 Copyright © 1981 The New York Times NEW YORK, WEDNESDAY, OCTOBER 7, 1981 20 cents beyond 50-mile zone from New York City. Higher in air delivery cities. 25 CENTS

SADAT ASSASSINATED AT ARMY PARADE AS MEN AMID RANKS FIRE INTO STANDS; VICE PRESIDENT AFFIRMS 'ALL TREATIES'

Israel Stunned and Anxious; Few Arab Nations Mourning

Worry in Jerusalem

By DAVID K. SHIPLER
Special to The New York Times

JERUSALEM, Oct. 6 — Israel, which had such a high stake in the survival of President Anwar el-Sadat, reacted with stunned anxiety today to news of his assassination in Cairo.

A fear for the peace treaty between Egypt and Israel dominated all emotions. So thoroughly had the Egyptian leader come to personify that peace, and so deeply had Israelis distrusted the motives of other Egyptians, that his death today swept away confidence as swiftly as his historic visit to Jerusalem in 1977 had brought hope.

"The very fact that one bullet can cancel an agreement," said Geula Cohen, who heads the Tehiya Party in Parliament, "is a sign that not only the withdrawal, but all these procedures, must be stopped. There is no doubt that this incident confirms all that we have been saying; there is no stability in this region and one cannot make an agreement which is dependent on a nondemocratic regime and one man."

Question About Treaty

Even in the likelihood that Mr. Sadat's successor will adhere to the treaty's precepts, serious questions are bound to linger for some time, and the Government of Prime Minister Menachem Begin is certain to face rising political difficulties domestically in completing the return of Sinai to Egypt, scheduled for April 1982.

This afternoon, voices on the right were raised in demands that all prepa-

Continued on Page A9, Column 5

Jubilation in Beirut

By JOHN KIFNER
Special to The New York Times

BEIRUT, Lebanon, Oct. 6 — There was no mourning in most of the Arab world today for President Anwar el-Sadat of Egypt, whose separate peace with Israel had led to his isolation.

Public jubilation was reported in Syria, Iraq and Libya, and the streets of mostly Moslem, leftist-dominated West Beirut echoed with gunfire in celebration of the assassination. Most public statements attributed Mr. Sadat's death to discontent with the Egyptian-Israeli peace accord.

However, the Sudan, Egypt's closest friend in the Arab world, condemned the assassination and said it stood with the Egyptian Government against all forms of conspiracy and aggression.

Hope for Arab Unity Expressed

There was little public comment in Saudi Arabia. At the United Nations, Gaafar M. Allagany, the acting head of the Saudi mission, expressed sorrow "that this had to happen at a crucial stage." Noting Saudi opposition to Mr. Sadat's policies, he said, "We hope that our sister country will rejoin the Arab states."

An aide to Yasir Arafat, the leader of the Palestine Liberation Organization, said here on hearing of the shooting of Mr. Sadat, "We shake the hand that fired the bullets."

The aide, Saleh Khalef, better known by the code name Abu Iyad, said that "all attempts at dialogue" with Mr. Sadat had failed and that "it was inevi-

Continued on Page A9, Column 1

As President Sadat watched parade with Vice President Hosni Mubarak, left, and Defense Minister Abu Ghazala . . .
Associated Press

. . . uniformed men, apparently part of the assassination team, approached the reviewing stand. Moments later, . . .
CBS News

Egypt After Sadat

Washington's Policies Facing New Problems

By BERNARD GWERTZMAN
Special to The New York Times

WASHINGTON, Oct. 6 — The assassination of President Anwar el-Sadat of Egypt created a new series of problems for future American policy in the Middle East at a time when the Reagan Administration was already worried about the spread of disorder in the region.

Administration officials, concerned about the chaos in Lebanon, the increased subversive activity of Libya and the Soviet inroads in Afghanistan, Southern Yemen and Ethiopia, had viewed Mr. Sadat as a solid, pro-American anchor of stability in the Middle East. With his death, there is now apprehension about the situation in Egypt as well.

At the White House, President Reagan said the United States had lost "a close friend" and "a champion of peace." But the Administration refrained from any public assessment of the possible repercussions of the assassination. [Page A12.]

The mood in Washington was one of shock and sadness at the loss of a leader who had done what would have seemed impossible a decade ago. He replaced the Prime Minister of Israel as the favorite Middle East statesman in Washington.

On virtually every Middle East, African and world issue, the Reagan Administration and Mr. Sadat saw eye to eye. With the expectation that Mr. Sadat would be in control of Egypt's policies

News Analysis

Continued on Page A9, Column 2

Cairo Regime's Plans Now Question Marks

The following article is by William E. Farrell, who has reported on Anwar el-Sadat's diplomacy from Jerusalem as well as Cairo.

Special to The New York Times

CAIRO, Oct. 6 — Anwar el-Sadat's rule in Egypt was that of one man who skillfully engineered, in his 11 years in power, the means of controlling every important facet of Egyptian life.

Although he was dismissed by many as a somewhat feckless interim leader when he became President after the death of Gamal Abdel Nasser, Mr. Sadat gradually showed that he had staying power, political skill and an ability that transformed him into a world statesman when he paid his historic visit to Jerusalem in the search for peace.

Now, with his sudden, violent death, many questions about the future of Egypt and its role in the world are beginning to be raised in this saddened capital and in many other countries.

Over the years, Mr. Sadat controlled his political party, the National Democratic Party; he supervised the Egyptian press, which lauded him; he was commander of the military, a key factor in his rule, and he had a facility for taking the pulse of Egypt's masses — about 43 million people. Some 67 percent of them are illiterate, but he was able to reach them by television and radio. He often did, in long speeches that had a pedagogical tone.

Some Egyptians opposed Mr. Sadat,

Continued on Page A8, Column 5

AT LEAST 8 KILLED

Speaker of Parliament Is Interim President — Election in 60 Days

By WILLIAM E. FARRELL
Special to The New York Times

CAIRO, Oct. 6 — President Anwar el-Sadat of Egypt was shot and killed today by a group of men in military uniforms who hurled hand grenades and fired rifles at him as he watched a military parade commemorating the 1973 war against Israel.

Vice President Hosni Mubarak, in announcing Mr. Sadat's death, said

Mubarak speech excerpted, page A9.

Egypt's treaties and international commitments would be respected. He said the Speaker of Parliament, Sufi Abu Taleb, would serve as interim President pending an election in 60 days.

The assassins' bullets ended the life of a man who earned a reputation for making bold decisions in foreign affairs, a reputation based in large part on his decision in 1977 to journey to the camp of Egypt's foe, Israel, to make peace.

Sadat Forged His Own Regime

Regarded as an interim ruler when he came to power in 1970 on the death of Gamal Abdel Nasser, Mr. Sadat forged his own regime and ran Egypt singlehandedly. He was bent on moving this impoverished country into the late 20th century, a drive that led him to abandon an alliance with the Soviet Union and embrace the West.

That rule ended abruptly and violently today. As jet fighters roared overhead, the killers sprayed the reviewing

Of humble origin, Anwar el-Sadat became a statesman known for daring actions. Obituary, pages A8 and A9.

stand with bullets while thousands of horrified people — officials, diplomats and journalists, including this correspondent — looked on.

Killers' Identity Not Disclosed

Information gathered from a number of sources indicated that eight persons had been killed and 27 wounded in the attack. Later reports, all unconfirmed, put the toll at 11 dead and 38 wounded.

The authorities did not disclose the identity of the assassins. They were being interrogated, and there were no clear indications whether the attack was to have been part of a coup attempt.

[In Washington, American officials said an army major, a lieutenant and four enlisted men had been involved in the attack. The major and two of the soldiers were killed and the others captured, the officials said.]

The assassination followed a recent crackdown by Mr. Sadat against religious extremists and other political op-

Continued on Page A8, Column 1

. . . after the attack, victims lay sprawled on the floor of the stand.
CBS News

Who Murdered President Sadat?

In the confusion swirling around the assassination of Egypt's President, Anwar el-Sadat, little information was made public in Cairo about the killers. Egyptian authorities were known to have several uniformed men in custody last night, but the Egyptians gave no details about the number or identity of the attackers or the reasons for the attack.

"Islamic fundamentalists" within the Egyptian Army was the characterization offered by Secretary of State Alexander M. Haig Jr. to a group of senators late yesterday afternoon. He also mentioned discontent among some Egyptian officers with the peace treaty that Mr. Sadat signed with Israel.

Reagan Administration officials said their information was that six uniformed men had taken part in the shooting, that three were killed and that the others were captured. They said that at least one was linked to the Takfir Wahigra Society, a radical right-wing Islamic group whose name translates as Repentance and Atonement. Its past actions include the slaying of the Egyptian Minister of Religious Affairs in 1977.

In Beirut, a handful of organizations stepped forward to claim responsibility for the killing, with representatives calling news agencies with their statements. But Reagan Administration officials said they doubted that any of them had been involved in the killing. Details are on page A12.

Other News

'Safety Net' Bill Passes

The House of Representatives approved spending $87.3 billion for social programs, despite President Reagan's threat to veto the bill. Page B10.

Ulster Prison Rule Is Eased

Britain gave inmates in Northern Ireland the right to wear their own clothing but stopped short of meeting the hunger strikers' demands. Page A3.

Runoff Due in Atlanta

Andrew Young, the former diplomat, and a State Representative, Sidney Marcus, won places in a mayoral runoff in Atlanta. Page A20.

Lindbergh Papers Unsealed

Evidence in the kidnapping-murder of the infant son of Charles A. Lindbergh 49 years ago will be opened to review by scholars and others. Page B1.

Classified AdsB18-27 Auto ExchangeD24-27

The Scene Of the Assassination In Cairo

Sadat Residence

Nile

Mile
0 1

Men in military uniforms stepped from a truck and fired on President Sadat, who was in the center of the reviewing stand. The wounded president was carried to the back of the stand and flown south by helicopter to Maadi Military Hospital.

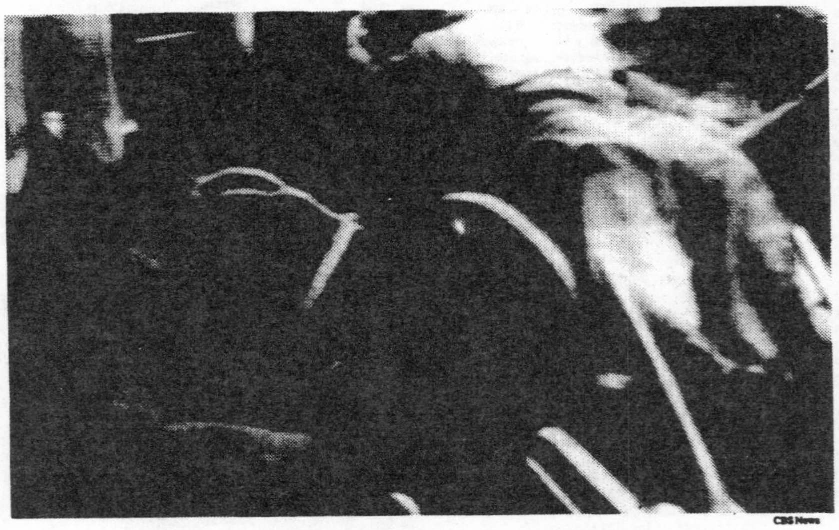

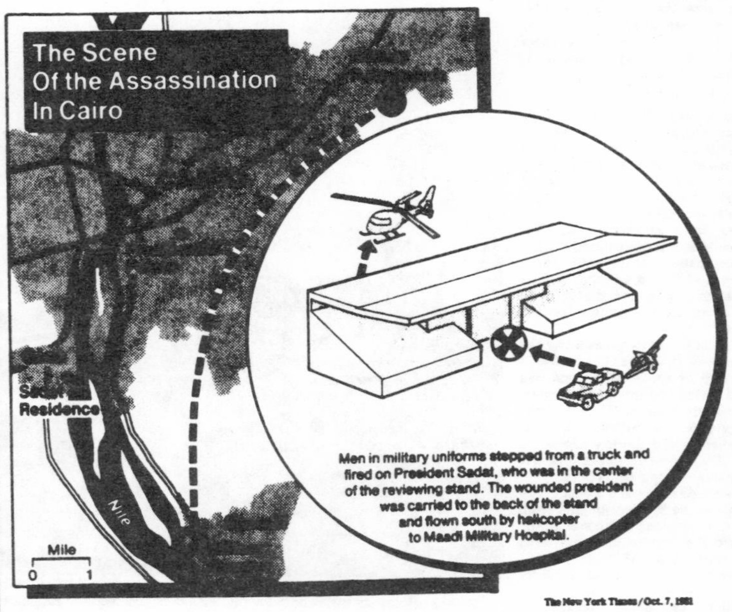

The New York Times/Oct. 7, 1981

Dear Vic: What could possibly be uncivil about liberties? Chet.—ADVT.

"All the News
That's Fit to Print"

The New York Times

LATE CITY EDITION

Weather: Increasing cloudiness today; rain likely tonight, tomorrow. Temperature range: today 29-40; yesterday 28-38. Details, page C21.

VOL.CXXXI . . . No. 45,162 | NEW YORK, MONDAY, DECEMBER 14, 1981 | 25 CENTS

20 cents beyond 50-mile zone from New York City. Higher in air delivery cities.

POLAND RESTRICTS CIVIL AND UNION RIGHTS; SOLIDARITY ACTIVISTS URGE GENERAL STRIKE

Judge Reduces Westway Suits To Single Issue

Landfill's Effect on Fish Still to Be Considered

By ROBIN HERMAN

A Federal judge has whittled down the longstanding legal attacks on the Westway highway project to a single issue — the fate of fish in the Hudson River — and he will set a hearing date today for arguments on that obstacle.

The judge, Thomas F. Griesa of Federal District Court in Manhattan, has dismissed all objections to the highway contained in two remaining lawsuits except for questions on the effect the landfill for the project would have on aquatic life.

John Marino, the state's Assistant Transportation Commissioner for New York City, said that the judge's action was "a very positive development" and that it reflected the Carey administration's interest in seeing the highway built.

As for environmentalists' concern about aquatic life — especially striped bass — Mr. Marino said yesterday: "When was the last time you had striped bass from the Hudson? That's our comment on it. I don't expect that in the end this will be a serious issue. The way is clear for Westway. It's a go-ahead."

Most Objections Dismissed

The judge, meeting in private on Friday with both the plaintiffs and the state and Federal defendants, dismissed altogether a suit brought in 1974 by Action for Rational Transit, an anti-Westway group, which was attempting to block the project. The suit contended chiefly that the highway would violate Federal clean-air standards.

Also, according to both sides, Judge Griesa dismissed most objections made in a 1977 suit brought by the Sierra Club and other environmental and civic groups. That suit challenged the dredge-and-fill permit for the project granted by the Army Corps of Engineers.

The suit charged that the Government had not adequately examined alternative routes, the trade-in of the Federal Westway funds for mass-transit funds or the possibility that the landfill on which the highway would be built could threaten New Jersey with flooding. It also questioned whether the river's aquatic life had been considered in the environmental impact statement. The highway's official cost is $1.7 billion, but it is expected to exceed that figure by millions of dollars.

After a hearing, possibly next month, on the aquatic-life question, Judge Griesa has said he will issue a written decision on all claims. At that time, the two groups of plaintiffs can appeal the earlier dismissals, which the judge made orally.

Albert Butzel, the lawyer representing the Sierra Club, said yesterday that,

Continued on Page B10, Column 3

HAIG WARNS SOVIET

He Says U.S. Is 'Seriously Concerned' and Backs New Warsaw Talks

By BERNARD GWERTZMAN

Special to The New York Times

BRUSSELS, Dec. 13 — Secretary of State Alexander M. Haig Jr. said today that the United States was "seriously concerned" about the imposition of martial law in Poland, and he renewed the West's warning to the Soviet Union not to interfere in the crisis.

After talking by phone with President Reagan, who was then at Camp David, Md., Mr. Haig said at a news conference here that the United States was urging

News conference excerpts, page A19.

the Polish Government to resume negotiations and to pursue a policy of compromise with the Solidarity trade union to prevent an outbreak of civil strife that could worsen the situation.

Mr. Haig said Polish authorities had assured the United States Embassy this morning that "there will be no return" to the situation that existed in Poland prior to establishment of the independent union in 1980. In addition, he said Western intelligence agencies had not detected any Soviet military moves "which would be a source of alarm."

"But we continue to watch the situation very carefully," he said.

'Very Serious' Consequences

If the Soviet Union intervened in Poland, Mr. Haig said, "the consequences would be very serious and long lasting." Western officials have previously said that, in that event, all trade with the Soviet Union would be suspended and political relations would be sharply curtailed.

President Reagan, arriving back at the White House, was asked about the danger of Soviet intervention and said that the United States had several times "made it plain how seriously we would view interference" by the Soviet Union. The Polish Ambassador and the Soviet Deputy Chief of Mission were summoned to the State Department for discussions on the situation. [Page A15.]

Mr. Haig was scheduled to leave Brussels this morning for a seven-day trip to Israel, Turkey, Pakistan, India, Egypt and Morocco. But after talking by phone with Vice President Bush and with various foreign ministers, Mr. Haig decided at the last minute to scrap his travel plans. Reporters traveling with him

Continued on Page A19, Column 4

Sipa Press/Black Star

Police in Wroclaw surround the Solidarity offices and keep crowds away. Photo was made from inside the building. Wroclaw, formerly Breslau, is an industrial city 190 miles southwest of Warsaw, near the Czechoslovak border.

Communism and Better Life: Poles Found Wait Too Long

John Darnton, who has been chief of The New York Times bureau in Warsaw since September 1979, reports in the following article on the problems underlying the crisis in Poland.

Special to The New York Times

WARSAW — Behind the workers' revolt that began with strikes in the summer of 1980 and grew to a revolution on the shoulders of the Solidarity union, the operation of which was suspended when martial law was declared, lies a story of failure. It is the failure of Communism, in the eyes of the workers, to deliver on its promise of a better life.

The revolt sprang from an unspoken consensus among Poles that despite more than three decades of sacrifice and toil, conditions of everyday life were scarcely improving and that the Communist system had failed most dramatically in precisely those areas, in the realm of social welfare, where its ideology called for greater exertion and improvement.

Appalling dirt and safety conditions in factories, cramped and unavailable apartments, substandard and sloppy health care, lines in front of meat shops — food shortages in general despite a stringent rationing system — these were the distinguishing traits of what the Government referred to as "people's Poland." They were glossed over, ignored or denied by successive governments that pressed instead for higher production statistics in heavy industry.

They certainly did not keep pace with expectations and, compared with the West, which more and more Poles were visiting when restrictions were loosened as the cold war period came to a close, Poland was failing behind.

'My Life Doesn't Count'

"All my adult life I've been told that my life doesn't count, that I'm sacrificing myself for my children," said one well-known Polish journalist, speaking privately. "Well, now I'm 48. My son is 19. His life is no better than mine and he's being told he must sacrifice himself for his children. What's life all about, anyway?"

Satisfying the basic needs of the population was given low priority when it came to allocating investment in the national budget, but it was given lip service in public propaganda and high-

Continued on Page A18, Column 1

Army's Rule: Two Targets

General Hits at Foes In Party and Solidarity

By DAVID BINDER

Special to The New York Times

WASHINGTON, Dec. 13 — Poland's soldier-leader, Wojciech Jaruzelski, has struck at what he perceives as the two main roots of his country's current troubles: the radical "confrontationists" of the Solidarity labor movement and the still influential members of the Communist Party's old guard.

News Analysis

His martial law decree, accompanied by the detention of Solidarity leaders and former party leaders and an internal communications blackout, has eliminated the cadres and the instruments that might have been used to rally supporters against his rule.

A 56,000-Member Force

The state of emergency was long in the making, in the estimate of Administration specialists on Polish affairs, and was foreshadowed not only by large-scale maneuvers of Soviet troops on Poland's borders earlier in the year, but also by the brief mobilization of the Polish Internal Defense Forces last September.

The Internal Defense Forces are heavily equipped paramilitary security troops with 56,000 members. They are trained for riot control, and are deployed in three contingents, one in War-

Continued on Page A19, Column 1

WALESA NEGOTIATES

New Army Council Bans Rallies and Sets Wide Grounds for Arrests

By JOHN DARNTON

Special to The New York Times

WARSAW, Dec. 13 — Poland's new military leaders issued a decree of martial law today, drastically restricting civil rights and suspending the operations of the Solidarity union. The union's activists reacted with an appeal for an immediate general strike to protest.

A proclamation broadcast by the newly formed Martial Council for National Redemption, now the top authority in the country, also banned all kinds

Premier's address, page A16.

of public gatherings and demonstrations and ordered the internment of citizens whose loyalty to the state was under "justified suspicion."

The military rule was announced in a dramatic broadcast at dawn by Gen. Wojciech Jaruzelski, the Prime Minister and Communist Party leader, who said a strict regime was necessary to save Poland from catastrophe and civil war. Hours before, Solidarity leaders meeting in Gdansk had proposed holding a national referendum on forming a non-Communist government.

No Reports of Violence

Following a provision in the constitution, General Jaruzelski, declared a "state of war," equivalent to a state of emergency in other countries.

There were no immediate reports of any violence, but opposition to the military move seemed in the offing. Union activists, in dozens of leaflets being circulated in the streets, called for an immediate general strike.

Many Solidarity activists were in detention following coordinated police raids across the country after midnight last night. So were several former leaders of Poland's Communist Party.

Among the detained were some of the top leaders and advisers of the Solidarity union who had assembled in Gdansk to work out strategy in the latest confrontation with the Government.

Walesa Flown to Warsaw

Lech Walesa, Solidarity's chairman, who became an international figure by his role in the workers' uprising of last summer, was meeting with Government officials at a site outside Warsaw today, Jerzy Urban, a Government spokesman, said at a news conference.

Mr. Walesa was flown to Warsaw in a Government plane at 4 A.M. to begin talks with Stanislaw Ciosek, the Minister of Trade Union Affairs, according to the Interpress information agency. Mr. Urban said that Mr. Walesa had not been detained at any point.

Mr. Urban also stressed that Soli-

Continued on Page A16, Column 1

Budget Cuts, Weak Market Hurt Gasohol

By DOUGLAS MARTIN

Special to The New York Times

DES MOINES — Interest in gasohol, which has attracted more Government encouragement in recent years than any other energy source, has been fading — the result of an oversupply of crude oil and the Administration's efforts to curb Federal spending.

Enthusiasm for gasohol, a mixture of gasoline and alcohol, was born amid farmers' anger over the restrictions on grain sales to the Soviet Union and consumers' concern about the shutdown of Iran's oil fields. The fuel seemed a way for America to cultivate its way out of the energy crisis, drawing on this nation's unrivaled agricultural strength. Most commercial gasohol is a 90-10 mixture of refined gasoline and ethanol derived from corn.

Pledge of Subsidies

The Carter Administration and Congress responded to the apparent groundswell by pledging subsidies for gasohol exceeding $30 billion by 1992, making it, gallon for gallon, by far the most heavily subsidized fuel.

But over the past few months, the White House has moved vigorously to slash funding for gasohol plants, large

Continued on Page D5, Column 5

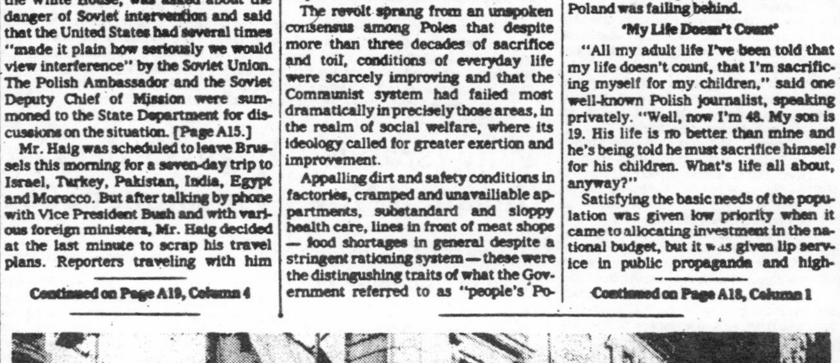

The New York Times/Dith Pran

Demonstrators marching past the Polish Consulate on 37th Street near Madison Avenue. Similar protests against the military takeover in Poland were held in Paris, Vienna, London, Rome, Brussels and other European cities.

Biotechnology: Better Breeds and Crops

By HAROLD M. SCHMECK Jr.

The first major products from the young industry using the techniques of gene-splicing are expected to go on world markets next year, a development that some experts believe will usher in a new era in the prevention and treatment of disease.

Agriculture will probably be the first to benefit from such products, including vaccines against foot-and-mouth disease and scours, two economically serious diseases that afflict cattle.

Two important medical products now undergoing extensive clinical tests are expected to follow, probably in 1983 in the United States: human insulin and human growth hormone produced in bacteria that have been adapted for the purpose by gene-splicing techniques. Animal growth hormone produced by the same techniques is also being developed for agricultural use.

The predicted uses of gene-splicing techniques include such diverse products as industrial enzymes, food additives, medical and veterinary test chemicals and drugs, as well as improved plant species.

The long-range potential uses for the chemical, mining, energy and forest products industries, and for agriculture, dwarf all the prospective uses for medicine. Except for products related to health and food, however, the emergence of competitive major industrial

Continued on Page D13, Column 1

The New Genetics

Biology at a Turning Point

Second of three articles.

Other Developments

Warsaw mood — Every hour on the hour beginning at 6 A.M., Poles listening to their radios heard Prime Minister Wojciech Jaruzelski speak in solemn tones about having placed the country under martial law. The interludes were filled with music. More cars were on the streets than is usual for a Sunday, particularly in a period of acute gasoline shortage. All telephones had stopped functioning, presumably to keep those who might wish to resist from coordinating actions. Page A17.

Washington concern — The Reagan Administration called in the Polish Ambassador and the Soviet Deputy Chief of Mission for discussions. Several allied diplomats were also called to the State Department. President Reagan returned ahead of schedule from a weekend at Camp David to be briefed on Poland by Administration officials. Page A15.

Soviet silence — The Soviet Union made no official comment on the declaration of martial law in Poland. The Polish developments were reported in a series of brief and largely factual dispatches by the official news agency Tass. Page A19.

Papal appeal — Pope Paul John II asked his fellow Poles to pray for peace and to do everything in their power "to peacefully build a peaceful future." Page A14.

German reaction — Chancellor Helmut Schmidt of West Germany, visiting a small East German town, seemed intent on demonstrating through his presence that there was no reason for the West to dramatize the situation in Poland. Page A20.

Polish-American reaction — Tens of thousands of Polish-Americans across the nation voiced outrage and despair. In the New York metropolitan area and in Chicago, Philadelphia and other centers of Polish-American life, the outpouring was emotional but nonviolent as workers, scholars, writers, clergymen and diplomats spoke of their homeland. With a communications blackout severing their contacts with friends and relatives in Poland, there was also widespread concern over loved ones and acquaintances. Page A17.

INSIDE

U.S. Wins Davis Cup

John McEnroe defeated José-Luis Clerc in five sets to give the United States a victory over Argentina in the final of the Davis Cup. Page C1.

Sakharovs: Weak but Elated

The Soviet dissident Andrei D. Sakharov and his wife were said to be emaciated but in high spirits at the success of their hunger strike. Page A3.

"All the News That's Fit to Print"

The New York Times

Late Edition

Weather: Rain ending today, mostly cloudy and cool; cloudy and cooler tonight. Partly cloudy and mild tomorrow. Temperatures: today 61-66, tonight 54-56; yesterday 55-60. Details, page B10.

VOL. CXXXI . . No. 45,337 NEW YORK, MONDAY, JUNE 7, 1982 30 CENTS

BIG ISRAELI FORCE INVADES SOUTH LEBANON; SHARP FIGHTING WITH GUERRILLAS REPORTED

Limited Summit Agreement Set on Trade and Currency

By RICHARD EDER

Special to The New York Times

VERSAILLES, France, June 6 — The eighth summit conference of the industrialized nations reached limited agreement today on two contentious subjects — East-West trade and the handling of currency fluctuations — and produced something of a breakthrough on North-South relations.

The agreements themselves were the subject of some disagreement: whether they bridged or merely papered over fundamental differences. Prime Minister Margaret Thatcher of Britain described the atmosphere as one of unanimity. Prime Minister Pierre Elliott Trudeau of Canada called it "difficult."

The conference was, in any case, shaded and sometimes interrupted by the fighting in the Falklands and Israel's invasion of Lebanon. Today's final hard bargaining on East-West trade was interrupted by the announcement by President François Mitterrand of France of the Israeli move, and the assembled leaders approved a statement expressing shock.

The accord fell short of American hopes and was seen as having little world impact. News analysis and economic analysis, with text of the communiqué, page D6.

The Falkland crisis, apart from producing an embarrassing flip-flop over the United States vote in the Security Council, caused Mrs. Thatcher to fly back to London tonight after the state dinner in the Versailles chateau's Hall of Mirrors.

She thus missed the musical masque and ballet and other festivities organized by France to make this the most glittering summit conference, whether or not it will have turned out to be the most productive.

The seven nations — the United States, Japan, Britain, France, West Germany, Italy and Canada — agreed to a compromise on the East-West trade issue. It fell short of American hopes for abolition of government-subsidized financing for such trade. Instead, it calls for "caution" in financial dealings with the Soviet bloc, and it says there is a need for "commercial prudence in limiting export credits."

The Reagan Administration had

Continued on Page D7, Column 1

Associated Press

President Reagan at economic meeting yesterday in Versailles.

United Press International

An armored personnel carrier, part of the Israeli invasion force, breaks through the border with southern Lebanon.

THOUSANDS ATTACK

Some Syrian Units in Area Said to Have Clashed With Raiding Force

By THOMAS L. FRIEDMAN

Special to The New York Times

BEIRUT, Lebanon, Monday, June 7 — The Israeli Army invaded southern Lebanon by land, sea and air Sunday in an attack aimed at destroying the main military bases of the Palestine Liberation Organization.

More than 250 Israeli tanks and armored personnel carriers, as well as thousands of infantrymen, rolled past the observation posts of the United Nations peacekeeping troops in southern Lebanon at 11 A.M. (5 A.M., New York time) and fanned out across the frontier, according to a United Nations spokesman in Beirut.

By late Sunday evening the Israelis had taken several P.L.O. outposts in the craggy hills of southern Lebanon and were engaged in fierce firefights with the Palestinians for control of scores of other strongholds along the 33-mile front, stretching from the port city of Tyre to the foothills of Mount Hermon, the United Nations spokesman said.

Main Targets Besieged

In the first day of the invasion the Israelis besieged all their main targets — Tyre, Beaufort Castle, Nabatiye and Kawkaba — but the Palestinians stood their ground and did not flee north. The number of casualties was not known.

Israel said this morning that Beaufort Castle, a Crusader stronghold overlooking the border that the Palestinians have used as a communications and artillery base, was captured during the night by an Israeli infantry battalion. But the Palestinians denied that the castle had fallen.

It appeared that at least a few elements of Syria's force of about 25,000 men in Lebanon had become involved in confrontations with the Israelis.

The state-run Beirut radio reported Sunday night that Syrian artillery north of Hasbeya was exchanging fire with the Israelis on the eastern route of their advance. This could not be confirmed. In Damascus, a Syrian military spokesman said Israeli forces had come into contact with Syrian troops in three places, but it was not clear whether fighting had occurred. [Page A12.]

The Israel radio broadcast a state-

Continued on Page A12, Column 1

U.N. COUNCIL ASKS ISRAELI PULLBACK

But Delegate, Hinting Refusal, Notes 'Limit of Endurance'

By BERNARD D. NOSSITER

Special to The New York Times

UNITED NATIONS, N.Y., June 6 — The Security Council unanimously demanded tonight that Israel pull its invading forces out of Lebanon. There was, however, no indication that Israel would pay any more attention to this order than to the unanimous Council demand Saturday night for a cease-fire.

Instead, Yehuda Z. Blum, the Israeli delegate, taunted the Council's 15 members for "evincing not the slightest interest" in scores of terrorist acts he attributed to the Palestine Liberation Organization. "How many Israelis have to be killed by terrorists for this Council to be persuaded that the limits of our endurance have been reached?" he asked rhetorically. "Israel cannot expect this body even to deplore P.L.O. barbarism against Israel's civilian population, let alone take any steps with a view towards curbing that barbarism."

Leaders of the major industrial democracies expressed shock at Versailles over Israel's move. Page A14.

Tonight's text, a compromise drafted by Ireland after a day of discussion behind closed doors, directed Israel to withdraw its forces "forthwith and unconditionally." The Soviet Union insisted on that last phrase.

At the demand of the United States, the resolution calls on Israel and the Palestinians to halt all military action "within Lebanon and across the Lebanese-Israeli border." That language was designed to cover P.L.O. shelling into Israel as well as Israeli strikes. The document directs both sides to report

Continued on Page A14, Column 5

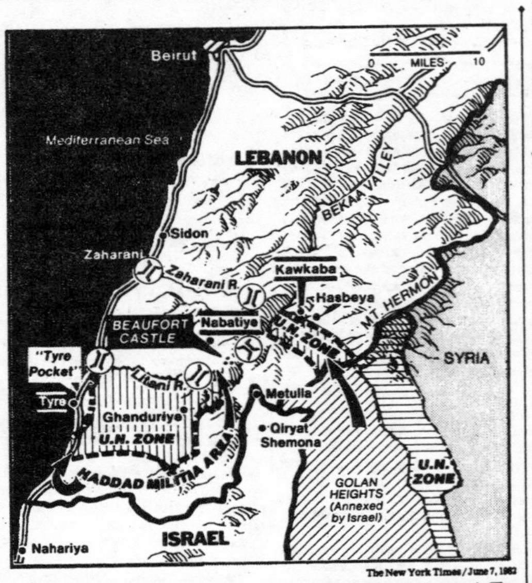

The New York Times / June 7, 1982

Israeli tanks and troops moved into Lebanon in three columns (arrows). The land assaults, together with air and sea attacks, were aimed at the main Palestinian strongholds — Tyre, Beaufort Castle, Nabatiye and Kawkaba. Warships destroyed the Qasmiye Bridge spanning the Litani River north of Tyre, cutting the main Palestinian supply line. Towns shown in northern Israel were among those shelled last week by Palestinian forces.

Britain Confirms the Landing Of 3,000 Soldiers From QE2

By R.W. APPLE Jr.

Special to The New York Times

LONDON, June 6 — British troops besieging the Argentine garrison at Stanley in the Falkland Islands have been reinforced by 3,000 fresh infantrymen from the liner Queen Elizabeth 2, the Defense Ministry announced tonight.

The arrival of the Fifth Infantry Brigade, including a battalion each of Scots and Welsh Guards and Gurkha Rifles, raises British strength on East Falkland Island to about 8,000. About 5,000 paratroops and Royal Marine commandos went ashore last month, and most are drawn up opposite the 7,000 Argentine defenders of Stanley, the Falklands capital.

In Buenos Aires today, Argentina said its planes and artillery had bombarded the British positions surrounding Stanley. Senior military officers said they expected the British to launch a major assault on the Argentine garrison at any moment. [Page A6.]

There were hints in London that the long-awaited assault on Stanley had already begun in a report from Michael Nicholson of Britain's Independent Television News.

"The British push is really on," he said in a broadcast this evening. "There are under way at this moment operations which I can only describe as extraordinarily daring which cannot be revealed until they are completed, but which, almost certainly if they are successful, will surely bring the end of this war that much closer."

Mr. Nicholson reported that the Gurkhas, composed entirely of Nepalese volunteers, were operating on their own, "crisscrossing East Falkland" in a search for Argentine units lurking in the interior, between the British base at San Carlos Bay and their forward headquarters near Mount Kent.

According to unofficial sources, the Fifth Brigade transferred from the Queen Elizabeth to the assault ships In-

Continued on Page A8, Column 3

Why Israelis Invaded Now

Heavy P.L.O. Shelling Said to Tip the Scale

The following dispatch has been subjected to military censorship.

By DAVID K. SHIPLER

Special to The New York Times

News Analysis

JERUSALEM, June 6 — Israel's invasion of Lebanon came today as the culmination of months of military and political calculation in which Prime Minister Menachem Begin repeatedly allowed the troops to be massed and the saber to be rattled, only to pull back at what seemed like the last moment.

Until today the crucial factors favoring a major assault never quite lined up, and the risks seemed greater than the potential benefits.

This time, however, Mr. Begin decided to make the military gamble and to pay the political costs that he and his advisers know exist. The crucial reason was the intensive shelling of northern Israel by forces of the Palestine Liberation Organization, which began Friday afternoon after Israeli air strikes on Palestinian bases near Beirut.

P.L.O. Has Become an Army

The Israeli command described the air raids as retaliation for the shooting Thursday of Israel's Ambassador to Britain, Shlomo Argov, who was critically wounded in London. Five suspects, all traveling on passports from Arab countries, were captured. The P.L.O. denied any responsibility for the attack.

The Palestinian shelling, with artillery and rocket launchers, was the most severe ever directed against Israeli towns and kibbutzim by the P.L.O.,

Continued on Page A13, Column 1

Begin Orders Israelis to Push Palestinians 25 Miles to North

The following dispatch has been subjected to military censorship.

Special to The New York Times

JERUSALEM, Monday, June 7 — Prime Minister Menachem Begin said Sunday that the Israeli Army had been ordered to push the Palestinian forces northward to a distance of 25 miles from the Israeli border, to place their artillery beyond the range of Israeli territory.

Mr. Begin made his statement in a letter to President Reagan, excerpts of which were reported on the Israeli radio. The Cabinet, after an emergency session, issued a statement saying Israel would not attack any Syrian forces in Lebanon or Syria unless the Syrians engaged the Israelis.

The Damascus radio said the Syrian Army was battling the Israelis near Hasbeya, 10 miles north of the border. The Israeli military spokesman said there had been no verification that any such clashes with the Syrians had occurred.

Reagan Urged Restraint

Mr. Begin's letter to President Reagan, disclosing the orders to the army to push the Palestine Liberation Organizaton 25 miles north of the border, came after the President sent a letter to the Israeli leader. That letter, delivered Sunday morning, requested Israeli restraint.

In his reply, as reported by the Israeli radio, Mr. Begin said that "the terrorists aim their weapons only at the civilian population." He went on: "The aim of the enemy is to kill Jews, men, women and children. Is there any people in the world that would accept such a situation?"

The invasion operation, called "Peace for Galilee," would not be aimed at acquiring any Lebanese territory and was not being undertaken against Lebanon, according to Mr. Begin's letter. It was begun after months of sporadic terrorist attacks on Israelis here and abroad, attacks that Israel regarded as violations of the cease-fire that had been negotiated across the Lebanese-Israeli border last July.

As Israeli armored columns swept through the lines of the United Nations peacekeeping forces, a United Nations spokesman in Jerusalem reported, several United Nations units were caught in crossfire. By Sunday evening, one

Continued on Page A12, Column 3

Floods Rampage in Connecticut; 8 Believed Dead

By ROBERT D. McFADDEN

Torrential weekend rains and overflowing rivers swamped wide areas of Connecticut yesterday with the state's worst floods in decades.

The state police said that eight persons were dead or missing in the storm. More than 1,300 others were removed from their homes as floodwaters invaded residential areas, washed out roads and earthen dams and disrupted electric and telephone service and public transportation for tens of thousands of residents.

The floods, accompanied by 5 to 8 inches of pounding rain, struck a wide swath of the state, from Westport and other Fairfield County communities on the west to Waterford and New London on the east. At least 38,000 homes were hit by power blackouts, and 6,000 telephones were knocked out.

Nearly all trains in the state, including those operated by Amtrak between New York and Boston, were halted as Conrail and Amtrak used buses to carry passengers. Commuters and long-distance travelers were expected to face further delays today. Many communities in flooded areas canceled school for today.

The rest of the New York metropolitan area was relatively unscathed. But on eastern Long Island, up to 9.79 inches of rain also triggered heavy weekend flooding. Many traffic accidents were reported, and a stretch of Long Island

Continued on Page B4, Column 1

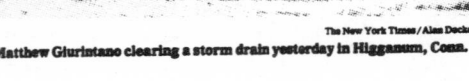

The New York Times / Alan Decker

Matthew Giuintano clearing a storm drain yesterday in Higganum, Conn.

INSIDE

Defeat for Schmidt's Party

The Social Democrats were defeated in state elections in Hamburg in what was considered a direct blow to Chancellor Helmut Schmidt. Page A9.

'Nine,' 'Nickleby' Win Tonys

"Nine," based on "8½," won the Tony award for musicals. The Royal Shakespeare Company's "Nicholas Nickleby" won for plays. Page C11.

"All the News
That's Fit to Print"

The New York Times

Late Edition
Weather: Sunny today with light southeasterly winds; clear and mild tonight. Cloudy with a chance of rain tomorrow. Temperatures: today 81-83, tonight 63-67; yesterday 54-72. Details, page D24.

VOL.CXXXI. No. 45,345

NEW YORK, TUESDAY, JUNE 15, 1982 30 CENTS

BRITAIN ANNOUNCES ARGENTINE SURRENDER TO END THE 10-WEEK WAR IN THE FALKLANDS

Israelis Cut Off West Beirut, Trapping P.L.O. Leaders

ACTION IN LEBANON

Tank Units Push Through the Christian Suburbs Around the Capital

By THOMAS L. FRIEDMAN
Special to The New York Times

BEIRUT, Lebanon, June 14 — Israeli tank columns completely cut off Moslem western Beirut today, trapping the military and political leadership of the Palestine Liberation Organization.

At the same time, other Israeli armored units, greeted by rice and flowers from sympathetic Lebanese Christians, began driving still deeper into Lebanon, apparently in an effort to push Syrian troops northeast of the capital into the Bekaa Valley.

There is a concentration of Syrian troops in the Khalde junction area on the coastal highway south of Beirut near the airport, and fighting was reportedly continuing there today between Israeli forces and Palestinians and Syrians.

The Israeli radio quoted Israel's Chief of Staff, Lieut. Gen. Rafael Eytan, as saying that Israeli troops had trapped guerrilla forces in Beirut and that the troops' mission was to smash the P.L.O.'s political and military nerve center there. [Page A18.]

Lebanese Leader Forms Council

The Israeli siege of guerrilla forces in Beirut came as the Lebanese Government announced the formation of a six-member Council of National Salvation to deal with the political repercussions of the Israeli invasion.

The committee, which was to contain the leading Christian and Moslem militia commanders, was formed by President Elias Sarkis and Prime Minister Shafik al-Wazzan to determine the Government's response to Israeli conditions for withdrawal.

Israel's withdrawal terms were delivered this evening to Mr. Sarkis at the presidential palace in Baabda by the special United States envoy, Philip C. Habib. Mr. Habib arrived by car from Damascus, to which he had flown earlier today from Jerusalem.

Mr. Habib declined to make any statements to the press, but Israel's conditions are reportedly the creation of a demilitarized zone stretching 25 miles north of its border to prevent attacks by Palestinian guerrillas and the withdrawal of the 30,000 Syrian peacekeeping troops from Lebanon.

Leftist Rejects Council

A meeting of the national council to consider the conditions, scheduled for this afternoon, was canceled after one proposed member, Walid Jumblat, leader of the leftist Moslem National Movement, said he would not have anything to do with the group as presently constituted.

Mr. Jumblat, who is under virtual house arrest by Israeli invasion forces occupying his mountain village of Mukhtara south of Beirut, said through a spokesman that the board should be "more comprehensive."

The other proposed council members are Bashir Gemayel, a Chrisian Phalangist militia commander; Nabih Berri, head of Lebanon's Shiite Moslem Party; Nasri Maalouf, another leading Christian political leader; Foreign

Continued on Page A18, Column 1

Associated Press
Israeli soldier atop armored vehicle in position overlooking western Beirut.

In Lebanon, White Flags Fly Amid the Misery and Rubble

By DAVID K. SHIPLER
Special to The New York Times

SIDON, Lebanon, June 14 — Along the battered Lebanese coast, in the wake of the invasion, white flags still fly.

They flutter from the antennas of cars without windows or windshields. They hang from bamboo poles stuck into the shell-pocked roofs and verandas of concrete houses. Even some pedestrians carried torn strips of white cloth to signify their neutrality, their surrender to the storm of war.

The Israeli Army warned residents of Lebanon's picturesque coast to leave their homes before the bombing and shelling began, and many followed the instructions on leaflets dropped from planes.

Battles Silently Traced

But when the fighting was over and they returned home from the beaches and the orange groves and the banana plantations where they had camped for days without food or water, what they saw took the strength out of them.

In Tyre, a stronghold and command center of the Palestine Liberation Organization, not a single building was untouched by the flying shrapnel.

Some high-rise apartments had collapsed like houses of cards, some villas were chewed into piles of dust and rubble.

Many other buildings revealed the course of battle: pits and chips around the doors and windows as Israeli troops fired at guerrillas, then a single gaping hole in a wall where a heavier weapon finished off the resistance.

The Israeli military governor of the town, Maj. Joseph Dana, who in civilian life is a lecturer in Arabic at Haifa University, estimates that 30 percent of all buildings in the town were destroyed.

In Sidon, farther up the coast toward Beirut, the damage was less ex-

Continued on Page A18, Column 4

A MIDEAST WARNING

Soviet Conveys Concern Over Military Activity Near South Border

By JOHN F. BURNS

MOSCOW, June 14 — The Soviet Government warned Israel today not to forget that the Middle East was close to the Soviet Union's southern borders and that developments in that area "cannot help affecting the interests of the U.S.S.R."

The warning was coupled with a demand, apparently directed at the United States, for "urgent effective measures" to halt Israel's "criminal

Text of Soviet statement, page A20.

act of genocide" against Palestinians and to bring about a withdrawal of Israeli troops from Lebanon.

The statement, issued through the official press agency Tass, said in part:

"The Soviet Union takes the Arabs' side not in words but in deed and presses to get the aggressor out of Lebanon.

"The present-day Israeli policy makers should not forget that the Middle East is an area lying in close proximity to the southern borders of the Soviet Union and that developments there cannot help affecting the interests of the U.S.S.R. We warn Israel about this."

Implications of Soviet Action

The statement was evidently intended to arouse concern that American inability to arrange an early cease-fire between Israeli forces and Palestinian guerrillas could provoke direct Soviet intervention.

Theoretically, Soviet options would include an emergency airlift of arms to Palestinian guerrillas by way of Syria, which has signed a Treaty of Friendship and Cooperation with Moscow, or a new supply of weapons to the Syrian forces.

As if to underscore the Soviet warning, a Soviet general was reported to have begun talks in the Syrian capital.

Sources in Damascus identified the officer as Col. Gen. Yevgeny S. Yurasov, a first deputy commander of the air defense system. The sending of the general to Syria suggested that the

Continued on Page A20, Column 1

United Press International
Prime Minister Margaret Thatcher after addressing Parliament.

Bus-Only Lanes To Be Increased To Speed Travel

By ARI L. GOLDMAN

Mayor Koch announced yesterday the creation of a system of 10 "red zone" lanes for buses in Manhattan to help relieve traffic congestion, increase bus speeds and reduce what has long been the bane of bus travelers — bus bunching.

Along the pavement at each of the 10 thoroughfares in the program, a bright red eight-inch thermoplastic strip will remind motorists of heavy fines if they park, stand or travel in the bus lane.

"Don't Even Think of Parking Here," a sign along the routes will read. Other signs will warn that fines of at least $100 will be imposed on violators. Only cars preparing to make right turns will be permitted to travel in the lanes, and then only for short distances.

Next Tuesday, the first of the red zone lanes will go into effect, on Third Avenue from 36th to 58th Streets from 7 A.M. to 7 P.M. The others, which will be added over the course of the summer, will be in effect at various times on major thoroughfares in both midtown and lower Manhattan. Fourteen miles of city streets will be affected.

The other streets to get red zone lanes will be: Eighth Avenue from 42d to 57th Streets between 4 P.M. and 7 P.M.; Avenue of the Americas from 40th

Continued on Page B6, Column 1

TRIUMPH BY LONDON

Commander Says Enemy Troops Are Assembled 'for Repatriation'

By R. W. APPLE Jr.
Special to The New York Times

LONDON, Tuesday, June 15 — Argentine forces in the Falkland Islands have surrendered, halting the war in the South Atlantic, Prime Minister Margaret Thatcher's office announced early this morning.

A spokesman quoted Maj. Gen. Jeremy Moore, the commander of British land forces in the archipelago, as saying that enemy troops were being rounded up for eventual repatriation to Argentina. The surrender came at 1 A.M. British time, (8 P.M. Monday New York time), the official announcement said.

There was no confirmation of the surrender from Buenos Aires by early this morning, but the Argentine high command announced Monday afternoon that an unofficial cease-fire had gone into effect on the Falklands. [Page A14.]

'God Save the Queen'

General Moore radioed from his command post on Mount Kent: "Falkland Islands once more under Government desired by their inhabitants. God Save the Queen." It had taken the British three weeks and four days of fighting on the ground to retake the islands following their landings at San Carlos Bay.

The Prime Minister signaled that the end of the conflict, or at least this phase of it, was at hand in a statement to Parliament Monday night in which she said that Argentine forces in Stanley, the last major enemy stronghold in the Falklands, had begun throwing down their arms and hoisting white flags.

As the House of Commons erupted in prolonged cheers, the Prime Minister disclosed that the deputy commander of British land forces, Brig. John Waters, was negotiating surrender terms with the commander of the 6,500 Argentine defenders of the town, Brig. Gen. Mario Menéndez. The surrender terms, she added, would cover both East Falkland, the island on which Stanley is situated, and West Falkland, where two small Argentine forces are based.

Crowds Hail Victory

Within minutes of her statement to the House, crowds gathered outside Mrs. Thatcher's residence at 10 Downing Street, singing "Rule Britannia." When she returned from the House, they cheered her and she said, "What matters is that it was everyone together — we all knew what we had to do and we went out there and did it."

Although it remained possible that fighting would continue on or around

Continued on Page A15, Column 1

1,600 Are Arrested In Nuclear Protests At 5 U.N. Missions

By PAUL L. MONTGOMERY

Offering daisies to policemen or chanting prayers for peace, more than 1,600 nonviolent demonstrators for disarmament were arrested in midtown Manhattan yesterday as they tried to block the entrances of the United Nations missions of five countries that have atomic weapons.

In an assembly-line operation that began at 7:30 A.M., the police carried the unresisting demonstrators to rented city buses to be booked for disorderly conduct. Some who had been arrested in the morning were back later in the day, encouraging their friends or sitting down again for another arrest.

The Police Department, which had 3,000 extra officers at the demonstration sites, said the total booked was a record for a civil disobedience campaign in the city. Patrick J. Murphy, the department's chief of operations, said, "almost everybody was very well-behaved — it was a textbook exercise."

The demonstrations, for which the participants were rehearsed and the police were briefed in advance, were a continuation of the protest that brought

Continued on Page A23, Column 1

United Press International
Yasir Arafat, left, leader of the Palestine Liberation Organization, and an aide yesterday in Beirut.

U.S. Is Easing '68 Antitrust Guidelines on Mergers

By ROBERT D. HERSHEY Jr.
Special to The New York Times

WASHINGTON, June 14 — The Government, seeking to reduce uncertainty about the types of corporate mergers that it will allow, today published a new set of enforcement guidelines "more lenient" than previous antitrust policy.

Nevertheless, the Justice Department and the Federal Trade Commission, which share antitrust responsibility, said they did not believe that their long-awaited statements would lead to any significant increase in mergers, which have diminished recently.

Attorney General William French Smith described the new guidelines as an "evolutionary change — not a revolutionary change" from actual practices in recent years. William F. Baxter, the Assistant Attorney General in charge of the antitrust division, said that, "in general, the new guidelines would have to be regarded as more lenient." But he added that he did not expect them to encourage more corporate combinations than guidelines that have existed since 1968. Antitrust experts said the new guidelines were more than

Continued on Page D6, Column 4

INSIDE

Sports Pages

The New York Times today introduces Sports Pages, an expanded and redesigned sports section appearing Tuesday through Saturday. It will include added news as well as new columns and features. Today's section begins on page D25.

U.S. Enters Dollar Market

As the dollar reached new highs against the devalued French franc, the Administration intervened in trading to try to restore order. Page D1.

Ruling Due on Copying TV

The Supreme Court agreed to decide whether use of home video recorders to tape television broadcasts violates Federal copyright law. Page D1.

U.S. Challenged in Space

A lack of planning and foreign competition were reported to threaten United States leadership in nonmilitary space technology. Page C1.

17 Fakes at Met Museum

The Metropolitan Museum has discovered that 17 gold vessels it had been believed to be ancient Egyptian are modern fakes. Page C9.

"All the News That's Fit to Print"

The New York Times

Late Edition

Weather: Overcast and mild today with scattered rainshowers likely through tonight. Cloudy, chance of rain tomorrow. Temperatures: today 73-77, tonight 61-63; yesterday 65-81. Details on page B10.

VOL. CXXXI . No. 45,437

NEW YORK, WEDNESDAY, SEPTEMBER 15, 1982

30 CENTS

GEMAYEL OF LEBANON IS KILLED IN BOMB BLAST AT PARTY OFFICES

Hussein Praises Reagan's Mideast Plan

KING OFFERS HELP

But Jordanian Asserts He Lacks the Authority to Enter Peace Talks

By BERNARD GWERTZMAN

Special to The New York Times

WASHINGTON, Sept. 14 — King Hussein of Jordan, in his first public comment on President Reagan's Middle East peace plan, said in an interview that it was "a very constructive and a very positive move." He added that he would play "a very active part" in trying to bring about a federation between Jordanians and the Palestinians.

But in the interview, aired by the British Broadcasting Corporation on Monday night, the King said he did not

Transcript of interview, page A10.

have an Arab mandate to join talks with Israel, Egypt and the United States on Palestinian self-rule.

He said the Arab leaders who met in Fez, Morocco, last week did not alter the 1974 Arab League decision to give the Palestine Liberation Organization, not Jordan, responsibility for negotiations dealing with the Palestinians living in territories occupied by Israel.

'A Very Active Part'

Although the 1974 decision still holds, he said, "I am going to play a very active part in helping, pushing forth every possible attempt for the establishment of a just and durable peace."

King Hussein, in describing his ideas for an eventual settlement of the Palestinian issue, put forth a plan that was very similar to the one proposed by President Reagan in his address on the Middle East on Sept. 1.

In that speech, Mr. Reagan said the United States favored some kind of "association" between Jordan and the Palestinians. He said the United States rejected the idea of Israeli sovereignty over the the West Bank and the Gaza Strip, but would not support an independent Palestinian state in the occupied territories.

Israel captured the West Bank from Jordan and Gaza from Egypt in the 1967 war.

The Fez communiqué repeated the traditional Arab demand for the establishment of an independent Palestinian

Continued on Page A10, Column 1

The New York Times / George Tames

Bashir Gemayel during a visit to Washington a year ago.

8 REPORTED SLAIN

President-Elect Was 34 — No Group Reports Making the Attack

By COLIN CAMPBELL

Special to The New York Times

BEIRUT, Lebanon, Wednesday, Sept. 15 — President-elect Bashir Gemayel was killed Tuesday when a bomb shattered the headquarters of his Lebanese Christian Phalangist Party in east Beirut. The Government said he would be buried today.

Mr. Gemayel, 34 years old, who was to have been inaugurated Sept. 23, was said to have died as he was about to address 400 of his followers at a weekly meeting. The state radio said the blast left at least 8 dead, among them other Phalangist leaders, and more than 50 wounded.

Prime Minister Shafik al-Wazzan deplored the killing in a statement, describing it as "a link in a chain of criminal conspiracies against Lebanon at a time when it started to restore its strength."

New Fighting Is Feared

No one took responsibility immediately for the bombing. It raised widespread fears that it would be followed by new fighting between Lebanon's Christian and Moslem militias.

Mr. Gemayel, who had been the commander of the Christian militias, was elected President Aug. 23 at a special session of Parliament that was boycotted by many Moslem legislators. To them, many other Moslems and some Christian groups, he was an enemy and an agent of Israel, whose invading troops made his election possible. [In Israel, there was no immediate official comment on the assassination.]

Until Sept. 23, the current President, Elias Sarkis, will continue as chief of state. Government sources said he could call new elections before then or appoint a presidential council to exercise presidential power until new elections could be called. Since the President in Lebanon is by tradition a Maronite Catholic, the council would also be headed by one.

400 Pounds of Explosives

The sources said another possibility was an extension of the Sarkis term, but this would require a change in the Constitution. The Lebanese President is not allowed under current law to succeed himself.

The blast, involving the detonation of what Phalangist and Government sources estimated to be more than 400 pounds of high explosives, occurred at 4:10 P.M. Tuesday. There was no immediate explanation for how so large an amount of explosive could have been introduced into the building.

For several hours reports circulated that Mr. Gemayel had survived.

There were reports that he had said "God be praised" as he left the scene for treatment of leg bruises at the nearby French-run Hôtel Dieu hospital. Those accounts were broadcast by the Phalangist radio, which quoted wit-

Continued on Page A8, Column 4

Slaying Is Denounced by Reagan; U.S. Fears New Burst of Fighting

Special to The New York Times

WASHINGTON, Sept. 14 — President Reagan said tonight that the "cowardly assassination" of President-elect Bashir Gemayel of Lebanon was a "shock to the American people and to civilized men and women everywhere."

In an unusually sharp statement, Mr. Reagan added, "We condemn the perpetrators of this heinous crime against Lebanon and against their cause of peace in the Middle East."

The White House statement, issued late tonight, expressed deepest sympathy to the Gemayel family, and said, "The tragedy will be all the greater if men in countries friendly to Lebanon permit disorder to continue in this war-torn country."

'U.S. Stands By Lebanon'

Mr. Reagan added that the "U.S. Government stands by Lebanon with its full support in its hour of need."

American officials said earlier that the assassination raised the possibility of new fighting in that country between Mr. Gemayel's Christian Phalangist forces and Moslem leftists.

New internal strife would also raise the possibility that Syrian and Israeli forces, confronting each other in Lebanon, might enter the conflict, destroying hopes for restoring stability.

The Israelis had strongly supported Mr. Gemayel, who was an avowed enemy of Syria. Just today, the Israeli Ambassador, Moshe Arens, called on Secretary of State George P. Shultz to say Israel wanted American assistance in obtaining a peace treaty with Lebanon.

It is the American hope that Elias Sarkis, the Lebanese President, whose term of office officially ends in nine days, will remain in office pending a new consensus choice as President.

The special American Middle East envoy, Morris Draper, arrived in Israel today on his way to Lebanon to help negotiate the withdrawal of Syrian and Israeli forces and the strengthening of the Lebanese Government. His mission is even more precarious now, officials said, given the uncertain future in Lebanon.

There was no fundamental difference between Mr. Sarkis and Mr. Gemayel on the withdrawal of foreign troops from Lebanon, American officials said. They expressed hope that Mr. Sarkis

Continued on Page A9, Column 1

Haig, at U.J.A., Criticizes Reagan's Mideast Plan

By BERNARD D. NOSSITER

Former Secretary of State Alexander M. Haig Jr. attacked President Reagan's Middle East plan yesterday, describing the proposal for a freeze on Israeli settlements in the occupied West Bank as "a very serious mistake."

Mr. Haig also said the Administration's plan for autonomy for the Palestinians in association with Jordan threatened a "gutting session" between Israel and the United States.

"The peace process will only move forward if there is a spirit of cooperation between Israel and the United States," Mr. Haig said. "That has been shaken in recent days."

It was the first time Mr. Haig is known to have criticized the Administration in which he served until June. He spoke without a text to 300 officials of the United Jewish Appeal at the Hilton Hotel in Manhattan.

Mr. Haig made no direct reference to the speech Sept. 1 in which Mr. Reagan announced the Middle East plan, or to his successor, George P. Shultz, who is regarded as the architect of that

Zion Ozeri

Alexander M. Haig Jr. yesterday.

speech. When Mr. Haig was asked to comment on the Reagan plan, he smiled and said it would be inappropriate to "parse the pros and cons." But he added that his own remarks contained "some pertinent observations."

The United Jewish Appeal raises funds for needy Jews around the world. It has not taken a formal position on Mr. Reagan's peace plan, but the frequent applause yesterday indicated strong agreement with Mr. Haig's criticism. Mr. Haig, who reportedly received $25,000 for his 45-minute appearance, serves as a consultant for United Technologies, a leading military contractor, and is a senior fellow at the Hudson Institute, a research center.

Mr. Haig received a standing ovation by concluding, "When we are true to Israel, we are true to ourselves."

He had earlier said, "When by our policies we can't deal effectively with our friends in Israel, we are undercutting our effectiveness throughout the Arab world."

Mr. Haig also asserted that "had the credibility" of Israel's invasion of Lebanon "been left undisturbed, the Palestine Liberation Organization would have left weeks earlier, and there would have been less bloodshed."

That was apparently an allusion to

Continued on Page A12, Column 4

The New York Times / Dan [illegible]

Grace Kelly, the actress: In "The Country Girl," 1954, for which she won an Oscar. Princess Grace of Monaco: At a tribute in Philadelphia this year.

Princess Grace Is Dead After Riviera Car Crash

By CLYDE HABERMAN

Princess Grace of Monaco, whose stately beauty and reserve gave her enduring Hollywood stardom even long after she ended her film career, died yesterday in Monte Carlo of injuries suffered when her car plunged off a mountain road Monday. She was 52 years old.

The Princess, the former Grace Kelly, died of a cerebral hemorrhage, a palace spokesman said in Monaco.

Princess Grace was driving her British Rover 3500 on a snaking road at Cap-d'Ail in the Côte d'Azur region when she lost control and plunged down a 45-foot embankment. The car burst into flames, and the Princess suffered multiple fractures, including a broken thighbone, collarbone and ribs.

Initial reports gave no sense that her life was in jeopardy. But a Monaco Government announcement yesterday said that her health had "deteriorated during the night."

"At the end of the day all therapeutic possibilities had been exceeded," the announcement said.

With her in the car was Stephanie, 17, her youngest child by Prince Rainier III of Monaco. Stephanie was under observation at a hospital where she had been treated for shock and bruises.

Reagan Praises 'Gentle Lady'

Princess Grace's death brought expressions of grief from former Hollywood colleagues and from residents of her hometown, Philadelphia. President Reagan called her "a compassionate and gentle lady." In Philadelphia, a spokesman for John Cardinal Krol said the Cardinal, who was a close friend, would offer a memorial mass for her at noon Friday.

Alfred Hitchcock, who directed Grace Kelly in three films and was certainly in a position to judge, once said she had "sexual elegance." And it was that very elegance that probably made its most lasting impression on movie audiences of the 1950's.

Whether playing the heiress in "To Catch a Thief" or the Quaker pacifist in "High Noon" or the amusedly detached career girl — a term still in vogue when "Rear Window" was made — Grace Kelly carried herself with straight back and clipped-voice self-assurance. Yet just beneath the frosty exterior lay a sensuality and warmth that cracked the formidable reserve.

It was this delicate balance of contrasts that helped give her legendary status — a remarkable achievement for an actress whose career encompassed only 11 films. She made more of that

Continued on Page C24, Column 1

Primaries Won By Ex-Governor, Two Incumbents

By ADAM CLYMER

A former Massachusetts Governor trying a comeback and two important members of Congress won key tests yesterday as 12 states and the District of Columbia held primary elections.

But another incumbent, Senator Howard W. Cannon of Nevada, was locked in a tight race with Representative James D. Santini as he sought the Democratic nomination for a fifth term.

In Massachusetts, former Gov. Michael S. Dukakis, attacking his successor's administration as corrupt and too supportive of President Reagan, defeated the incumbent, Gov. Edward J. King, for the Democratic nomination for Governor, just as Mr. King did four years ago when Mr. Dukakis was the incumbent. In the heavily Democratic Bay State, Mr. Dukakis will be favored over the Republican nominee in November, John W. Sears, a former Boston City Councilor.

In Vermont, Senator Robert T. Stafford, the Republican chairman of the Committee on the Environment and Public Works, defeated two conservative foes trying to end his 11-year Senate career. The two, Stewart M. Ledbetter and John McClaughry, argued that Mr. Stafford had become more interested in Washington than in Vermont.

With 93 percent of the precincts reporting, Mr. Stafford was safely ahead with 23,815 votes, or 46 percent of the

Continued on Page B11, Column 4

I.B.M. Accuses 3 Executives Of Stealing Computer Secrets

By ANDREW POLLACK

The International Business Machines Corporation, following its second undercover investigation in recent months, said yesterday that it had dismissed three of its executives and had sued them on charges of stealing corporate secrets.

The key figure in the month-long I.B.M. investigation, conducted by the company's own security officers, was the president of a small Cleveland computer company who pretended to negotiate a business deal with the I.B.M. executives. While he negotiated, he secretly taped the conversations on recording equipment supplied by I.B.M.

One of the executives had approached the Cleveland company, Tecmar Inc., and had offered to sell designs for products that would enhance I.B.M.'s new and fast-selling personal computer, according to court papers. In some cases, they would compete with still-secret products I.B.M. itself is planning to introduce, the affidavits filed in connection with the lawsuit stated.

The president of the Cleveland company, Martin A. Alpert, reported the approach to I.B.M. and agreed to cooperate when I.B.M. suggested the tape-recording plan.

In one excerpt from the transcript quoted in the court papers, William W. Erdman, an I.B.M. product manager and one of the defendants, said to Mr. Alpert: "I guarantee you that we know more about the way I.B.M.'s going to put it [personal computer products] together than I.B.M. knows, because when the guys that we're talking about leave, a good deal of knowledge leaves with them."

The three men sued in the civil action included two high-level engineers who were heavily involved in the design of I.B.M.'s personal computer and follow-up products. Also sued was Bridge Technology Inc., a White Plains company that I.B.M. asserts was established by the three executives to market their products. The three executives were dismissed by I.B.M. on Monday.

Mr. Erdman, reached yesterday at his home in Stamford, Conn., said he

Continued on Page D7, Column 1

INSIDE

Doctor Shot to Death

A physician was fatally shot as he sat in his car near his Gramercy Park office. The victim, Dr. Philip Wald, 53, was shot once in the head. Page B6.

Tuition Credit Compromise

President Reagan, returning to the theme of social issues, backed legislative compromises aimed to advance a tuition tax credit bill. Page A20.

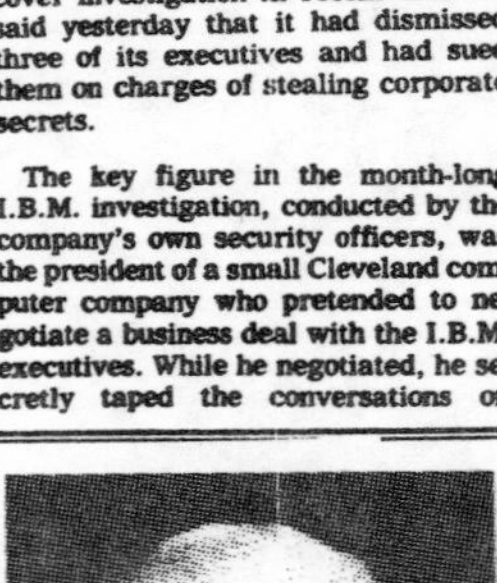

Thomas Victor

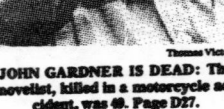

JOHN GARDNER IS DEAD: The novelist, killed in a motorcycle accident, was 49. Page D27.

"All the News That's Fit to Print"

The New York Times

Late Edition
Weather: Increasing cloudiness, southerly winds today, cloudy, not as cool tonight. Partly cloudy, milder tomorrow. Temperatures today 53-57, tonight 43-47, yesterday 39-52. Details, page D28.

VOL.CXXXII . . No. 45,494 — Copyright © 1982 The New York Times — NEW YORK, THURSDAY, NOVEMBER 11, 1982 — 30 CENTS

BREZHNEV IS DEAD IN SOVIET AT AGE 75; NO IMMEDIATE WORD ON A SUCCESSOR; U.S. FORESEES NO EARLY POLICY SHIFTS

Mexico Agrees to Austerity Terms For $3.84 Billion in I.M.F. Credit

By ALAN RIDING
Special to The New York Times

MEXICO CITY, Nov. 10 — The Government announced today that it had reached a long-awaited agreement with the International Monetary Fund on an austerity program aimed at easing the crisis caused by the nation's huge foreign debt.

Under the agreement, Mexico would receive $3.84 billion worth of credit from the I.M.F. over the next three years, but the Government must slash public spending, raise taxes and curb imports to qualify for the funds.

The austerity program could stabilize the Mexican peso, which has lost 70 percent of its value since February. But Government officials said today that it would also bring an economic slowdown and thus higher unemployment and a sharp drop in living standards.

"This agreement enables us to avoid defaulting on our foreign debt of $78 billion," Finance Minister Jesús Silva Herzog said at a news conference today. He added that the Government now hoped to obtain fresh credits from private financial institutions abroad. Many of them have already lent millions of dollars to Mexico, whose foreign debt is the highest in the world.

Deep Concerns Abroad

Mexico's crisis had sent shudders through the world banking system, raising the specter of major defaults by developing countries whose economies have been undermined by the fall in commodity prices and the recession in the industrial world.

The crisis has made major banks in the industrial world reluctant to extend new loans to developing countries — loans they seek to help meet payments on their existing debt. The I.M.F. agreement eases that problem in Mexico's case by requiring an austerity program that makes this country more creditworthy in the eyes of financial institutions in the industrial world.

Argentina and Brazil, which face debt repayment problems similar to Mexico's, also received help today. The I.M.F. gave approval to a $2.1 billion credit for Argentina as the first step in a program to help that nation catch up with payments on its nearly $40 billion in foreign debt. The Argentine Government had agreed earlier to an austerity program required by the I.M.F.

Separately, six leading American banks made $600 million in emergency loans to Brazil to help that country meet debt payments abroad until it can obtain longer-term credits, banking sources said. Brazil's foreign debt is nearly as large as Mexico's.

The agreement with Mexico, the sub-

Continued on Page D3, Column 1

JOBS LEGISLATION IS GAINING SUPPORT

Reagan May Back One Plan — Two Houses Prepare Bills

By MARTIN TOLCHIN
Special to The New York Times

WASHINGTON, Nov. 10 — Bipartisan support for a public works program that would provide jobs for the unemployed solidified in Congress today. There were indications that President Reagan might support a limited jobs program.

Responding to what they regarded as a mandate in last week's Congressional elections, Democrats and Republicans vied to claim authorship of jobs legislation, and they began a bidding contest to determine who could come up with a program that would put the most people to work at the least expense.

Reagan Studies Lewis Plan

Both House Democrats and Senate Republicans were drafting public works legislation that would provide more Federal funds for construction and repair of highways and bridges, sewers, dams and public buildings. Both sides expressed hope of bipartisan agreement on such legislation in the lame-duck Congressional session that starts Nov. 29.

The President studied a more limited proposal submitted by Drew Lewis, Secretary of Transportation, which included only the rehabilitation of highways, bridges and mass transit, to be financed by an increase in the gasoline tax. Mr. Lewis initially submitted his

Continued on Page A19, Column 6

Richmond Sentenced To a Year and a Day And Fined $20,000

By JOSEPH P. FRIED

Former Representative Frederick W. Richmond of Brooklyn was sentenced yesterday to a year and a day in prison and fined $20,000 for income-tax evasion, marijuana possession and making an illegal payment to a government employee.

He had pleaded guilty to these charges and agreed to resign from Congress and not seek re-election in a plea bargaining with Federal prosecutors on Aug. 25. They agreed not to prosecute him for other matters that they had also been investigating.

Judge Is Typically Informal

No date was set for him to begin serving his term, although he will probably have to begin doing so in a few weeks, officials said.

As Chief Judge Jack B. Weinstein of Federal District Court in Brooklyn pronounced the sentence, Mr. Richmond, who will be 59 years old Monday, gazed somberly at the judge from across a polished wood conference table, at which the participants in the case were seated.

Judge Weinstein normally conducts

Continued on Page B9, Column 1

WASHINGTON REACTS

Clark Informs Reagan — Official Says President May Go to Funeral

By HEDRICK SMITH
Special to The New York Times

WASHINGTON, Thursday, Nov. 11 — The Reagan Administration expects no dramatic change in Soviet policies and no firm, quick resolution of the Soviet leadership succession in the period just after Leonid I. Brezhnev's death. The United States has already taken steps to inform Moscow that American policy will remain steady.

A high White House official said President Reagan was awakened and informed of the news at 3:25 A.M. by his national security adviser, William P. Clark. The official said the President and his top advisers would meet at 8 A.M. to assess the situation.

Military Buildup Under Brezhnev

The official said there was "some possibility" that President Reagan himself might attend Mr. Brezhnev's funeral. The Administration, having anticipated Mr. Brezhnev's death because of the Soviet leader's long illnesses, had made contingency plans for Vice President Bush to attend, but Mr. Bush left for Africa late Wednesday.

Mr. Brezhnev's 18-year rule was a period of great Soviet military buildup, and just two weeks ago the 76-year-old Soviet leader re-emphasized that policy in a major speech to top military commanders in which he pledged further increases in arms spending.

The fact that he was flanked by other top leaders, including his two ranking potential successors, was taken as a sign that these policies would be continued under new leadership.

In other areas as well, including arms negotiations with the United States and

Continued on Page D21, Column 1

Photoreporters

Leonid Ilyich Brezhnev

Polish Strike Call Goes Unheeded In Face of Government Warnings

By JOHN KIFNER
Special to The New York Times

WARSAW, Nov. 10 — A national strike called for today by the underground leaders of the Solidarity movement appeared to have been generally unsuccessful in the face of a carefully orchestrated Government campaign backed up by a display of police power.

As darkness fell, caravans of armored vehicles of the riot police fired tear gas and water cannons at any groups on the streets near the Old Town section of the capital, then took up positions at traffic circles and intersections to prevent crowds from forming.

A march through the center of Warsaw did not materialize and it appeared that there had been only spotty response to the strike call intended to protest the recent banning of Solidarity. However, in Nowa Huta, the steel center, there were clashes between demonstrators and the police. [Page A13.]

"There was not a single major strike," Jerzy Urban, a Government spokesman, said. "The day has been a full defeat for the underground and its foreign supporters."

The apparent failure of the strike call — the first stage in a planned series of demonstrations — seemed a blow to the

Continued on Page A12, Column 3

The New York Times/D. Gorton

At the Vietnam War Memorial, veterans were reunited as they found the names of comrades killed on the same day.

Tribute to Vietnam Dead: Words, a Wall

By FRANCIS X. CLINES
Special to The New York Times

WASHINGTON, Nov. 10 — President Reagan stopped by the National Cathedral to listen for a while to the reading of the names of the Vietnam war dead this evening.

His motorcade sounded fast and faroff heading northwest to the cathedral in the dusk as Tom Toohey, unheeding in another part of town, stepped up to the glossy dark wall of the war's freshly completed memorial with its long listing of its dead, touching it for "the name," he emphasized, of "one good lieutenant."

"There," said Mr. Toohey, his fingers brushing the name of Richard H. Housh. "A real good lieutenant. I saw him jump up with his pump shotgun one time and blow away four guys coming at us. He was somebody else, one good lieutenant."

Ceremony by Candlelight

While the President journeyed to one part of the capital's weeklong commemoration of the Vietnam dead, the continuous reading of their names in a candlelighted chapel at National Cathedral, Mr. Toohey and hundreds of other Americans continued to arrive at the wall even after darkness fell tonight, the eve of Veterans Day. They bore the slow grief of the Vietnam time and indulged the simplest sort of human memorial, the act of touching stone, feeling the cold, stony texture of the engraved names of the dead that showed up by flashlight and in the wavering glow of matches struck in the dark.

Official Washington has built a week of ceremony around the opening of the simple memorial that hugs a part of the Washington earth. The first senators have already come to pose for photographs, according to attendants.

But it is already clear that the wall has touched a much more basic and human strain of response, the simple act of touching the wall as much as reading the names. Bearded veterans wearing old fatigue jackets and battle medals can be seen reaching toward the names of remembered dead war-

Continued on Page B15, Column 1

Spy in Britain Given 35 Years for Selling Secrets to the Soviet

By JON NORDHEIMER
Special to The New York Times

LONDON, Nov. 10 — A British linguistics expert pleaded guilty today to charges of passing secrets to the Soviet Union on the activities of a classified electronics listening post.

The expert, Geoffrey Arthur Prime, 44 years old, was sentenced to 35 years in prison by Lord Lane, the Lord Chief Justice, who said that Mr. Prime's treason had caused "incalculable harm" to the security interests of Britain and its allies.

According to United States sources, British intelligence officials have determined that the case represented one of the most potentially damaging penetrations of Western intelligence since World War II.

"The legal phase of the case is over, but the assessment of the intelligence implications has really only just begun," said one American intelligence official.

Details on the information supplied by Mr. Prime to the Russians in the 14 years he was in their pay were not included in the brief outline of the case presented by the prosecution today. The Attorney General, Sir Michael Havers, said the defendant's activities involved materials "prejudicial to the national

Continued on Page A8, Column 1

DEATH IS 'SUDDEN'

Cause Is Not Revealed, but Leader Had Long Been in Poor Health

By JOHN F. BURNS
Special to The New York Times

MOSCOW, Thursday, Nov. 11 — Leonid I. Brezhnev, the Soviet leader for 18 years, died yesterday, the state television announced this morning.

The announcement, carried simultaneously on radio and television and on the official press agency Tass, said: "The Central Committee of the Communist Party of the Soviet Union, the Presidium of the U.S.S.R. Supreme Soviet and the Council of Ministers of the U.S.S.R. inform with deep sorrow

Leonid Brezhnev was a canny leader who tried to make his country the military equal of the United States. An obituary, Page D22.

the party and the entire Soviet people that Leonid Ilyich Brezhnev, general secretary of the C.P.S.U. Central Committee and president of the Presidium of the U.S.S.R. Supreme Soviet, died a sudden death at 8:30 A.M. on Nov. 10, 1982.

"The name of Leonid Ilyich Brezhnev, a true continuer of Lenin's great cause and an ardent champion of peace and Communism, will live forever in the hearts of the Soviet people and the entire progressive mankind."

Cause of Death Not Given

The two-minute announcement was read twice on television by a dark-suited announcer. As he spoke the screen displayed a recent photograph of Mr. Brezhnev bordered by orange bands.

Mr. Brezhnev was 75 years old. The announcer gave no indication of the cause of Mr. Brezhnev's death. Nor did he give any suggestion of Mr. Brezhnev's successor as general secretary of the party or president of the Presidium of the Supreme Soviet.

Mr. Brezhnev had been in poor health for several years, apparently because of heart and respiratory problems. His last public appearance was on Sunday, when he stood for two hours atop the Lenin mausoleum in Red Square reviewing the annual military parade marking the 65th anniversary of the Bolshevik Revolution.

No Obvious Successor

Later he spoke at a Kremlin reception attended by Soviet dignitaries and the diplomatic corps.

Westerners at the parade were surprised that Mr. Brezhnev stayed so long in the subzero weather. Clad in a heavy overcoat and fur hat and with tinted sunglasses to shield the sun's glare, he stayed atop the mausoleum with other Politburo members more than twice as long as he did in 1981, when the weather was milder.

However, Soviet television offered

Continued on Page D21, Column 1

INSIDE

Shuttle Launching Set
The fifth launching of the space shuttle, scheduled for today, marks a critical transition from flight testing to the hauling of orbital freight. Page B38.

State's Bond Rating Drops
Standard & Poor's cut the rating on New York State bonds to the lowest level ever, noting the state's difficulty in balancing its budget. Page B1.

Kohl Speaks of Promises
Helmut Kohl, West Germany's new Chancellor, said his Government would keep its promises to the United States. Page A11.

"All the News That's Fit to Print"

The New York Times

Late Edition

Weather: Mostly cloudy, humid, chance of showers today; cloudy, chance of showers tonight. Clearing tomorrow. Temperatures: today 78-83, tonight 67-73; yesterday 67-83. Details on page 33.

VOL.CXXXII . . No. 45,714 NEW YORK, SUNDAY, JUNE 19, 1983 — $1.50 beyond 75 miles from New York City, except on Long Island. — ONE DOLLAR

Associated Press

Pope John Paul II at the Jasna Gora monastery in Czestochowa, Poland.

Pope Hails the 'Solidarity' of Poles And Gets a Tumultuous Ovation

By JOHN KIFNER

Special to The New York Times

CZESTOCHOWA, Poland, June 18 — Pope John Paul II, addressing a crowd estimated at more than a million people here, hailed the Polish people today for their acts of "solidarity" with those who were interned or dismissed from work under martial law. His remark drew a tumultuous ovation.

Although the Pope did not use the word solidarity to refer to the outlawed union of that name, his reference was unmistakable. The crowd rose in applause, with many people raising their arms in a V-for-victory sign signifying resistance, and they shook their red and white Solidarity banners.

Earlier in this increasingly politically charged visit, the Pope said on arriving here that the 1980 workers' uprising that led to the creation of Solidarity had "touched hearts and consciences" all over the world.

It was the Pope's strongest direct reference to the events surrounding the creation of the union since he arrived in his homeland Thursday on an eight-day trip.

The Pope flew to the Jasna Gora monastery here by helicopter this afternoon after visiting the monastery in Niepokalanow that was founded by the Rev. Maksymilian Kolbe, who gave his life for a fellow Pole at Auschwitz and who was elevated to sainthood last fall. [Page 12.]

Speaking soon after his arrival in Czestochowa, the Pontiff said the events of 1980 marked a time "when the Polish worker stood up for himself with the Gospel in his hand and a prayer on his lips."

The commitment of Poles to that struggle, he said, was "a testimony that amazed the whole world."

Gdansk Strikes Are Recalled

"The pictures that went around the world in 1980 touched hearts and consciences," the Pope said, referring to the August 1980 strikes that began at the Gdansk shipyard. The walkouts were settled under an agreement with the Government that permitted the creation of the first independent union in the Soviet bloc.

John Paul's first address here today was directed to members of the Baltic diocese of Szczecin. His later remarks, in which he used the word solidarity, were at a mass for Polish youths.

At that service, the Pope spoke of solidarity twice, first in reference to "historical experiences" that "tell us how much the immorality of certain periods cost the whole nation." In such circumstances, he suggested, there is a need for "love of neighbor," which he de-

Continued on Page 13, Column 1

CUBAN COMMANDER IN NICARAGUA POST

U.S. Says Intelligence Report Places Him on Duty There

By LESLIE H. GELB

Special to The New York Times

WASHINGTON, June 18 — Cuba's top military combat commander has been working in Nicaragua for about a month and has been "secretly assigned to duty" there, according to an intelligence report disclosed by a Reagan Administration official.

The commander was identified as Gen. Arnaldo Ochoa Sánchez, who as a brigade commander was said to have been instrumental in negotiating, organizing and leading the Cuban military buildup in Angola in 1976 and in Ethiopia in 1977. He is now deputy to Raúl Castro, Minister of the Armed Forces.

No Independent Confirmation

The report is based primarily on Central American military sources who, two officials said, have been reliable in their accounts of Cuban activities in Nicaragua.

These sources, according to the report, believe General Ochoa is organizing a "large-scale Cuban move into Nicaragua." One of the sources even said he would be chief of all Nicaraguan and Cuban armed forces.

Over the last few days, calm has returned to two Nicaraguan border towns where heavy fighting was reported last week between Nicaraguan forces and Honduran-based rebels. But a visit to the area turned up evidence that the insurgents caused extensive damage to farms and warehouses. [Page 10.]

Administration officials acknowledged that apart from the Central American sources, they had no independent confirmation that General

Continued on Page 10, Column 3

Shuttle Rockets to Orbit With 5 Aboard

Physicist Is First U.S. Woman in Space — Satellite Launched

By JOHN NOBLE WILFORD

Special to The New York Times

CAPE CANAVERAL, Fla., June 18 — Four men and a woman, the first American woman to go into space, rocketed into orbit today aboard the space shuttle Challenger and then launched the first of two satellites in the successful beginning of a busy six-day mission.

The winged spaceship lifted off on schedule at 7:33 A.M. after one of the smoothest countdowns of the shuttle program. It carried two communications satellites, an assortment of scientific experiments and a West German satellite that is to be released and then retrieved in a critical test of the shuttle's 50-foot mechanical arm.

Deployment of Missiles

On future missions astronauts expect to release small satellites with the mechanical arm and to rendezvous with ailing satellites to retrieve them for repairs in orbit or back on the earth.

One of the communications satellites, Canada's Anik C, was launched from Challenger's cargo bay late this afternoon and, with a boost from its own small rocket, sent spinning into the darkness of space on a course toward a 22,300-mile-high orbit. The other satellite, Indonesia's Palapa B, is set to be similarly launched Sunday morning to complete the mission's primary objectives.

But what set this flight apart from the 36 other manned American space missions over the last 22 years was not the cargo but the occupant just behind the two pilots. She was Dr. Sally K. Ride, a 32-year-old physicist who has been in astronaut training since 1978. She is the third woman to fly in space, but the first on an American mission.

2d Flight for Crippen

A crowd estimated at 250,000 stood in the bright morning sun to watch the seventh shuttle launching, and many of them wore "Ride, Sally Ride" T-shirts.

In his weekly radio address, President Reagan said that Dr. Ride's flight was "another example of the great

Continued on Page 20, Column 1

NASA via Associated Press

The space shuttle Challenger lifting off the launching pad at Cape Canaveral, Fla. Inset: Dr. Sally K. Ride, the first American woman to fly in space, at work as the crew prepared to deploy a communications satellite.

Cool, Versatile Astronaut

Sally Kristen Ride

By WILLIAM J. BROAD

Woman in the News

The celebration over sending the first American woman into orbit has tended to overshadow the fact that Dr. Sally K. Ride is to be the first person to perform one of the most significant tasks of the space age.

Reaching into the void with a 50-foot robotic arm, she plans to capture a satellite as it hurtles about the earth and, using mechanical might conferred by gears and motors, bring it safely to rest in the cargo bay of the space shuttle.

Her aerial exercise points to the not-so-distant future when it could be routine to grasp satellites, mine asteroids, build space stations — in short, to clutch and shape instead of just to pass through space as an awestruck visitor. It marks a new stage in the taming of the high frontier.

Even before liftoff, Dr. Ride had achieved world renown as the woman designated to break the all-male barrier in the American space program. There are now eight women in the astronaut corps.

Important Future Role

Dr. Ride will also play an important role in preparation for future missions. She will act as a liaison agent between the Government and private companies when clients from aerospace and military industries contract for space aboard the shuttle.

In the course of 32 years, Dr. Ride has devoted herself to the conquest of tennis, Shakespeare, physics and now the intricacies of space flight. Her diverse background, at odds with the narrow path of the speed-loving test pilots who pioneered the space program, has prepared her in an unusual way for the historic mission.

Sally Kristen Ride was born May 26, 1951, to Dale B. and Joyce Ride. Growing up in the Los Angeles neighborhood of Encino, she used to stretch

Continued on Page 20, Column 1

VOLCKER RENAMED BY REAGAN TO RUN FEDERAL RESERVE

WIDE SPECULATION ENDED

President's Declaration Cites Chairman's Record in Fight to Bring Down Inflation

By STEVEN R. WEISMAN

Special to The New York Times

WASHINGTON, June 18 — Ending months of speculation that has roiled the financial markets, President Reagan announced today that he would reappoint Paul A. Volcker to another four-year term as chairman of the Federal Reserve Board.

Taking time from his regular Saturday radio address for what he said was "a news flash," Mr. Reagan told listeners that he telephoned Mr. Volcker this morning and asked him to accept the reappointment.

"He's agreed to do so," the President said. "And I couldn't be more pleased. He is as dedicated as I am to continuing the fight against inflation. And with him as chairman of the Fed, I know we'll win that fight."

Credited for Cutting Inflation

Mr. Volcker's tight money policies in 1981 and 1982 were credited by most economists with helping to bring down the nation's inflation rate, and by critics with causing the recession.

The chairman issued a statement saying he was "gratified and honored by the expression of confidence by the President."

"As I have said on a number of occasions, I do believe we now have a rare opportunity to achieve sustained growth on a firm foundation of stability," Mr. Volcker added. "I am sure I can speak for the entire Federal Reserve System as to our commitment to work toward that objective."

The reappointment of Mr. Volcker appears to mean a stronger recovery this year and continuing into 1984. Economic analysis, Page 26.

Mr. Volcker was appointed chairman by President Carter in 1979. His appointment to a new term beginning Aug. 6 is subject to approval by the Senate, but he was not expected to have much difficulty winning confirmation.

Support From Eagleton

In the regular Democratic response to Mr. Reagan's address, Senator Thomas F. Eagleton of Missouri, said, "I vigorously support President Reagan's reappointment of Paul Volcker."

Another Democratic Senator, Gary Hart of Colorado, who is seeking his party's Presidential nomination, issued a statement saying that "to the degree this represents a continuation of the policies of the past two years," the selection "could be a disaster for our economy and for the unemployed."

"But it actually matters little whom President Reagan appoints to head the Federal Reserve Board if the Reagan Administration's economic policies don't change," Mr. Hart added.

Senator John Glenn of Ohio, another

Continued on Page 26, Column 1

New China / United Press International

CHINA NAMES PRESIDENT: Li Xiannian, left, a veteran of the revolution, accepting the post in Peking. At right is Peng Zhen, new chairman of Parliament. The presidency had been vacant for years. Page 9.

Debate Grows Over Adoption Of National Industrial Policy

By KAREN W. ARENSON

The ills of the American economy are obvious — high interest rates, high unemployment, low productivity, uncompetitive plants.

The cures are not so evident. In recent decades, Americans have successively taken, and then discarded, a variety of economic medicines, from Keynesianism to monetarism to supply-side economics.

Now, a new prescription — industrial policy — is sweeping intellectual and political circles. It is an idea that has been spurred by the success of the Japanese economy, and by the crucial role played by Japanese industrial policy and its centerpiece, the Ministry of International Trade and Industry.

The issue is prompting much debate. To supporters, a national industrial policy, aimed at helping particular industries, holds the key to reshaping America's economy and setting the course for future growth. To others, it is simply the latest brand of snake oil or voodoo economics.

The issue is attracting high-powered attention. In the past year, the Council on Foreign Relations, the Aspen Institute, Harvard University, Columbia Law School and the Federal Reserve Bank of Kansas City have all scheduled symposiums on the topic, with participants from politics and the academic world, unions and business.

In addition, industrial policy is expected to be an important issue in the 1984 Presidential race, provided the economy continues to have visible problems as the recovery progresses. Several Democrats have endorsed the concept, and industrial policy bills are beginning to appear in Congress.

The Republicans, on the other hand, are hoping that recovery will make the discussion moot, that the worst of the economy's troubles will disappear with the recession.

Industrial policy remains an elusive concept. It encompasses ideas, some of them contradictory, ranging from the establishment of an industrial development bank to support winning industries, to an industrial conversion agency to rehabilitate losing industries and their workers. Many proposals prescribe some type of three-way bargain-

Continued on Page 38, Column 1

Kean Orders 3d Dioxin Site Shut

By DOUGLAS C. McGILL

Special to The New York Times

CLIFTON, N.J., June 18 — Governor Kean said today that preliminary tests had discovered dangerous levels of dioxin in the soil at a chemical plant near an elementary school in a mostly residential area here.

He ordered the closing of a section of the plant, which is operated by the Givaudan Corporation, pending the results of further tests and an examination of employees who may have been exposed to the toxic chemical. The area to be closed is 160 feet long and 30 feet wide and contains 14 small buildings.

The Givaudan plant, at 125 Delawanna Avenue, is the third industrial area in New Jersey where dioxin contamination has been found. However, it is the first operating plant found to be contaminated, and the first whose daily business will be affected by a gubernatorial order.

Earlier this year, the New Jersey Department of Environmental Protection checked industrial records and identified 11 areas in the state where dioxin contamination might be found. The owners of the eight remaining areas are cooperating with the state to test for dioxin.

The two other areas, both of which were abandoned industrial plants, were in Edison and in the Ironbound section of Newark.

The Governor, at a news conference at Clifton's City Hall today, emphasized that there was "absolutely no evidence of off-site contamination" in Clifton. He added that "a number of precautionary steps have been taken to assure protection of public health."

The steps included covering contami-

Continued on Page 28, Column 1

Today's Sections

Index to Subjects

INSIDE

Affirmative Action Gauged

A Labor Department study says affirmative action has raised minority employment in companies dealing with the Government. Page 16.

P.L.O. Guerrillas Clash

New fighting was reported between Palestine Liberation Organization units in Lebanon, scene of a month-old mutiny against Yasir Arafat. Page 6.

"All the News That's Fit to Print"

The New York Times

Late Edition
Weather: Mostly cloudy, warm today, light southwesterly winds; clear tonight. Sunny, more humid tomorrow. Temperatures: today 83-85, tonight 67-73; yesterday 69-84. Details, page B17.

VOL.CXXXII . . No. 45,789
Copyright © 1983 The New York Times
NEW YORK, FRIDAY, SEPTEMBER 2, 1983
60 cents beyond 75 miles from New York City, except on Long Island
30 CENTS

U.S. SAYS SOVIET DOWNED KOREAN AIRLINER; 269 LOST; REAGAN DENOUNCES 'WANTON' ACT

Begin's Party Chooses Shamir as New Leader

Associated Press
Yitzhak Shamir

By DAVID K. SHIPLER
Special to The New York Times

JERUSALEM, Friday, Sept. 2 — Yitzhak Shamir, the 68-year-old Foreign Minister of Israel, was elected early this morning to succeed Prime Minister Menachem Begin as leader of the governing Herut Party. This placed him in a favorable position to become the next Prime Minister if he can hold together Mr. Begin's coalition of right-wing and religious factions.

A former guerrilla who led the underground Stern Gang against the British in Palestine, Mr. Shamir could be expected to continue Mr. Begin's major hard-line policies, including the active program of Jewish settlement on the West Bank. In 1979 he opposed the peace treaty with Egypt.

The Foreign Minister was elected at a late-night caucus of Herut's central committee, where 745 of about 900 members voted in secret ballots. The counting at the meeting in Tel Aviv went on until nearly 2 A.M. Seven votes were invalidated.

Mr. Shamir received 436 votes to 302 for the only other contender, Deputy Prime Minister David Levy, a 45-year-old Moroccan-born Jew who rose from poverty in a Jordan Valley development town.

Had Support of Old Guard

Mr. Levy is considered somewhat more moderate and more interested in domestic social issues than Mr. Shamir, but is inexperienced in foreign affairs and military matters. Because he is young, he is still likely to be regarded as a potential leader of the party.

Former Defense Minister Ariel Sharon had withdrawn from the contest in favor of Mr. Shamir and was reported to have said that he would not serve in any government led by Mr. Levy.

Mr. Shamir had the support of the party's old guard, most of whom had fought in the underground against the British and were said to feel that Mr. Levy was not as ideological as they would have liked.

In Search of a Majority

Prime Minister Begin has said that he plans to submit his formal resignation as Prime Minister and as leader of the party within the next few days. He delayed it to give his party time to choose a new leadership.

Now Mr. Shamir's task will be to get the agreement of enough coalition partners to make up a majority in the Parliament. This should be completed by early next week.

In an acceptance speech, the new party head said he would keep the Prime Minister's job in trust for Mr.

Continued on Page A3, Column 1

U.S. Positioning 2,000 Marines Off Beirut Coast

By WILLIAM E. FARRELL
Special to The New York Times

WASHINGTON, Sept. 1 — President Reagan today ordered a 2,000-member Marine force into the Mediterranean to position itself off Beirut so "that all necessary measures" could be taken to "assure the safety" of the 1,370 marines already on shore.

Pentagon officials said the additional marine contingent would sail Friday from Mombasa, Kenya, and anchor off Lebanon in about a week. The officials said there were no plans now to send the additional marines ashore.

The announcement of the President's decision was made in California, where Mr. Reagan is vacationing, by Larry Speakes, the White House spokesman. It came during a week when two marines were killed and 14 wounded in Beirut as leftist Moslem militiamen battled the Lebanese Army.

While the army succeeded on Wednesday in taking control of major points of West Beirut from the militiamen, reports from Lebanon said fighting continued today as soldiers hunted snipers still in place on roofs and in buildings.

There was scattered shelling of Christian East Beirut areas by militiamen in the hills, and shells reportedly

Continued on Page A2, Column 3

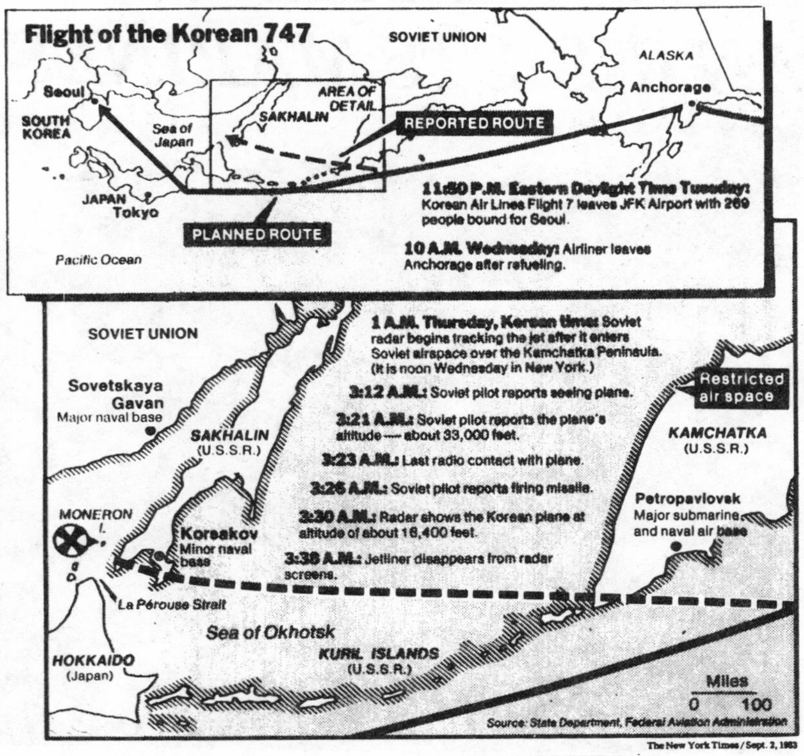
Flight of the Korean 747
SOVIET UNION
ALASKA
Anchorage
Seoul
SOUTH KOREA
Sea of Japan
AREA OF DETAIL
SAKHALIN
REPORTED ROUTE
JAPAN
Tokyo
PLANNED ROUTE
Pacific Ocean
11:50 P.M. Eastern Daylight Time Tuesday: Korean Air Lines Flight 7 leaves JFK Airport with 269 people bound for Seoul.
10 A.M. Wednesday: Airliner leaves Anchorage after refueling.
SOVIET UNION
1 A.M. Thursday, Korean time: Soviet radar begins tracking the jet after it enters Soviet airspace over the Kamchatka Peninsula. (It is noon Wednesday in New York.)
3:12 A.M.: Soviet pilot reports seeing plane.
3:21 A.M.: Soviet pilot reports the plane's altitude — about 33,000 feet.
3:23 A.M.: Last radio contact with plane.
3:26 A.M.: Soviet pilot reports firing missile.
3:30 A.M.: Radar shows the Korean plane at altitude of about 16,400 feet.
3:38 A.M.: Jetliner disappears from radar screens.
Sovetskaya Gavan
Major naval base
SAKHALIN (U.S.S.R.)
Restricted air space
KAMCHATKA (U.S.S.R.)
MONERON I.
Korsakov
Minor naval base
Petropavlovsk
Major submarine and naval air base
La Pérouse Strait
Sea of Okhotsk
HOKKAIDO (Japan)
KURIL ISLANDS (U.S.S.R.)
Miles
0 100
Source: State Department, Federal Aviation Administration

The New York Times / Sept. 2, 1983

MOSCOW CONFIRMS TRACKING OF PLANE

But Tass Statement Is Silent About an Attack on Airliner

By JOHN F. BURNS
Special to The New York Times

MOSCOW, Sept. 1 — After nearly 24 hours of silence, the Soviet Union confirmed tonight only that its jet fighters in the Far East had intercepted and warned "an unidentified plane" intruding into Soviet airspace. But it made no mention of any attack on the plane.

The statement, by the Government press agency Tass, was the first acknowledgment that Moscow knew about the South Korean airliner that the United States said was shot down off southern Sakhalin.

[In Washington, the State Department said Foreign Minister Andrei A. Gromyko had sent a message along the lines of the Tass statement, saying that the plane had violated Soviet airspace, but seeming to disclaim responsibility for the downing of the craft. Mr. Gromyko added that search planes had found "signs of a possible crash" near Moneron Island, off southwest Sakhalin.

[John Hughes, the department spokesman, said the United States "finds this reply totally inadequate and reiterates its demand for a satisfactory explanation."]

Earlier in the day the Soviet Foreign

Continued on Page A4, Column 4

President Demands Explanation For 'Horrifying Act of Violence'

By STEVEN WEISMAN
Special to The New York Times

SANTA BARBARA, Calif., Sept. 1 — President Reagan expressed revulsion today at the reported downing of a South Korean passenger airplane off the Soviet coast. He declared angrily that the Russians had "totally failed to explain how or why this tragedy has occurred."

He also decided to cut short his vacation here by three days to return to the White House Friday for a National Security Council meeting to discuss responses to the incident. In addition, Mr. Reagan asked Republican and Democratic Congressional leaders to meet with him at the White House, possibly Saturday, to discuss the situation.

Shultz Also Denunciatory

"I speak for all Americans and for the people everywhere who cherish civilized values in protesting the Soviet attack on an unarmed civilian passenger plane," Mr. Reagan said. "Words can scarcely express our revulsion at this horrifying act of violence.

"The United States joins with other members of the international community in demanding a full explanation for this appalling and wanton misdeed," Mr. Reagan said. "The Soviet statements to this moment have totally failed to explain how or why this tragedy has occurred. Indeed, the whole incident appears to be inexplicable to civilized people everywhere."

In Washington this morning, Secretary of State George P. Shultz also issued a strong statement, expressing revulsion at the reported downing of the plane. Mr. Shultz, speaking at a news conference at the State Department, also said that he had not yet talked by telephone to Mr. Reagan.

Larry Speakes, the chief White House spokesman, said the National Security Council meeting was expected to concern "ways in which the United States may join with Korea and Japan to express effectively the disgust that the entire world feels at the utter barbarity of the action of the Soviet Government in shooting down an unarmed, nonmilitary passenger plane and their refusal thus far to acknowledge either the responsibility or their sorrow for this action."

Mr. Reagan's strong reaction to the incident was the culmination of a day in which he had been briefed by telephone by William P. Clark, the director of the National Security Council, and Edwin Meese 3d, the White House counselor. Both have been working at a resort

Continued on Page A5, Column 6

A FRUITLESS SEARCH

President Calls Meeting of National Security Council for Today

By ROBERT D. McFADDEN

A South Korean airliner missing with 269 people on a flight from New York to Seoul was shot down in the Sea of Japan by a Soviet jet fighter near a Soviet island off Siberia, the United States said yesterday.

There were no known survivors of the attack, in which a heat-seeking missile was said to have been fired

Statements by U.S., page A5.

without warning at the airliner by an interceptor that had tracked it over Soviet territory for two and a half hours.

President Reagan expressed "revulsion" over what he called "a horrifying act of violence." He cut short his California vacation and called a National Security Council meeting in Washington today to discuss possible reprisals.

U.N. Meeting Requested

Members of Congress and other American officials erupted in a fury of outrage, and the United States and South Korea requested a United Nations Security Council meeting on the incident. The Council was expected to begin debate today.

There was no clear explanation for the reported attack, which occurred amid several puzzling circumstances. There was an unconfirmed report that the airliner had experienced radio trouble. Soviet officials said it was flying without lights. And United States authorities acknowledged that it was far off course, despite carrying what South Korean officials called sophisticated navigational equipment.

As American, Soviet and Japanese ships and planes searched frigid seas north of Japan and reportedly found traces of fuel where the jet apparently went down, Secretary of State George P. Shultz demanded an explanation from the Soviet Union and told reporters, "The Soviet pilot reported that he fired a missile and the target was destroyed." [Page A5.]

Soviet Explanation Rejected

A Soviet explanation late yesterday was rebuffed by the State Department as "totally inadequate." The Soviet statement did not acknowledge that a Soviet plane had shot down the airliner and did not accept responsibility for the incident, the State Department said.

The State Department spokesman, John Hughes, said a message from the Soviet Foreign Minister, Andrei A. Gromyko, asserted only that a plane

Continued on Page A4, Column 1

Heart Attack Kills Sen. Jackson

By LES LEDBETTER

Senator Henry M. Jackson, Washington State's senior Senator and a 44-year veteran of Congress and national politics, died in Everett, Wash., Thursday night after a massive heart attack. He was 71 years old.

Senator Jackson was taken to Providence Hospital in Everett shortly before 11 P.M., Eastern daylight time, after suffering a heart attack in his home, according to a broadcast account by Mayor Bill Moore of Everett, a family friend. He died a short time later.

The heart attack came 12 hours after the Senator held a news conference in Seattle on the destruction of a Korean Air Lines jet, apparently by the Russians.

Senator Jackson, who was a Presidential contender twice, was a power in the Democratic party and in the Senate who was known for consistency over the decades despite the prevailing political winds.

His power and prestige were so established in Washington circles that Presidents of both parties and all ideologies sought his counsel and his support for their military and international policies.

The ranking Democratic member of the Senate Armed Services Committee, he was conservative on dealing with the Soviet Union and hawkish on arms buildup.

He was a lifetime liberal in matters dealing with civil rights and organized labor. He was also a strong supporter of Israel, tying Soviet immigration policies toward Jews to any deals with that nation. And he was an outspoken advocate for Boeing, his state's largest employer.

Some observers even complained

Continued on Page B9, Column 5

Strategic Soviet Region

Area Where Russians Say Plane Intruded Is Critical Part of Their Far East Defenses

By DREW MIDDLETON

Military Analysis

Soviet sensitivity over foreign radar penetration of defenses guarding La Pérouse Strait south of Sakhalin may have been the motivation for the reported destruction of a South Korean airliner by a jet fighter, according to American officers. In war the strait would be the direct route for the deployment of the Soviet Pacific Fleet into the northwest Pacific, the officers said.

Over the last 27 months United States and Japanese intelligence services have reported the expansion of Soviet military power on Sakhalin, on the Siberian mainland and on the island of Etorofu of the Kuril island chain. Etorofu lies 150 miles northeast of Hokkaido, the northern Japanese island. The entire area, one officer said, is of major importance to Soviet strategic planning.

A squadron of MIG-23's was deployed on Etorofu about a month ago, according to intelligence sources.

American and NATO intelligence analysts rejected the idea that the shooting down of the Boeing airliner could have been the impulsive act of a Soviet pilot. They cited the rigid, centralized command system of Soviet forces and said an attack on a civilian airliner, even when it was in Soviet airspace, could not have been carried out without the approval of a higher headquarters.

They noted that the elapsed time between the first Soviet radar sighting of the airliner and the attack was sufficient for an exchange of messages between the local commander and headquarters either in Vladivostok, headquarters of the Pacific Fleet, or in Moscow.

Air Force sources were puzzled by the fact that the stricken South Korean

Continued on Page A7, Column 1

INSIDE

Software Copyright Upheld

In a key victory for computer and software makers, a Federal appeals court ruled that all computer programs can be copyrighted. Page D1.

When Parents Kill the Child

The story of Renee Nicely and Allen Bass and their 3-year-old son, Shawn Nicely, whom they beat to death early one Sunday morning. Page B1.

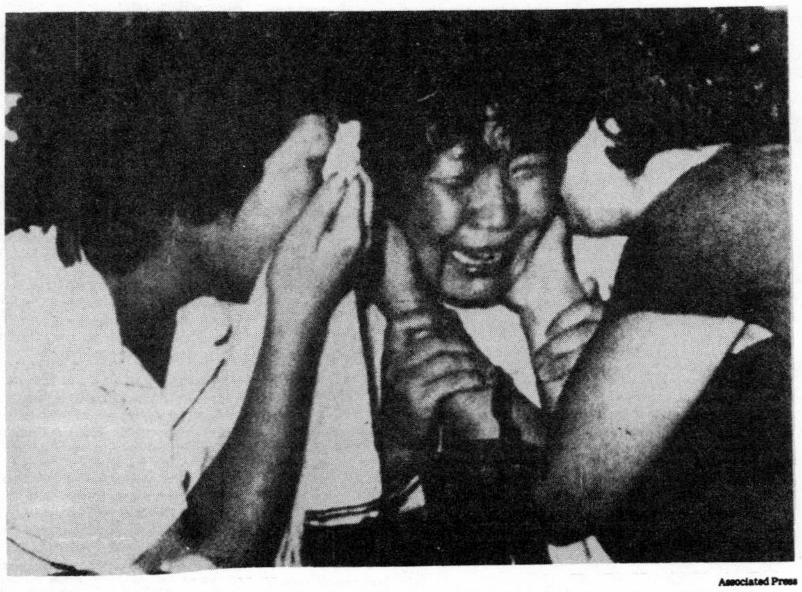

Associated Press
Sisters of a passenger weeping as South Korean official announced in Seoul that plane was probably shot down.

"All the News
That's Fit to Print"

The New York Times

Late Edition

Weather: Rain ending in the afternoon, cool, southeasterly winds today; remaining cloudy tonight and tomorrow. Temperatures: today 53-57, tonight 40-45; yesterday 48-59. Details, page D12.

VOL.CXXXIII . . No. 45,841 NEW YORK, MONDAY, OCTOBER 24, 1983 — 30 cents beyond 75 miles from New York City, except on Long Island — 30 CENTS

BEIRUT DEATH TOLL AT 161 AMERICANS; FRENCH CASUALTIES RISE IN BOMBINGS; REAGAN INSISTS MARINES WILL REMAIN

Associated Press

Rescuers removing a wounded marine on a stretcher from the rubble of the bombed-out building that housed a U.S. Marine battalion in Beirut.

ATTACK IS ASSAILED

U.S. Says Terrorists Tied to Iran May Have Set Off the Lethal Blast

By FRANCIS X. CLINES

Special to The New York Times

WASHINGTON, Oct. 23 — President Reagan, voicing outrage over the "despicable" destruction of the Marine Corps headquarters in Lebanon, called on the nation today to be more determined than ever to keep a force in that country and resist "the bestial nature of those who would assume power."

The President, plunging into a day of emergency strategy meetings on the bombing, denounced the unidentified forces behind the attack and said the

Reagan statement, page A8.

nation "must be more determined than ever that they cannot take over that vital and strategic area of the earth."

Administration officials, emphasizing that there would be no change in the United States' military role in Lebanon, said there was "circumstantial evidence" that fanatiç terrorists aligned with Iran may have been responsible for the truck bomb that razed the four-story Marine Corps headquarters in Beirut, leaving 161 dead and 75 wounded.

The White House spokesman, Larry Speakes, said this evening that the Administration was also "looking into" Syria's possible role in the incident, but he did not cite any evidence.

No Dramatic Moves Anticipated

Official spokesmen stressed that no dramatic countermoves by the military were anticipated.

In the aftermath of the attack, legislators from both parties said the Administration must redefine and clarify the role of its troops and their long-range mission in the Middle East. [Page A8.]

The troops, who were fired on by snipers even as they rescued the wounded at the Marine headquarters, have been drawing sniper fire from areas near their base at the Beirut airport for weeks. There have been re-

Prime Minister Pierre Mauroy of France condemned the Beirut attacks and said French forces would stay in Lebanon. Page A7.

ports that Palestinian guerrillas who have returned to the Beirut area were responsible.

The bombing put the Administration at crisis alert, with Secretary of State George P. Shultz postponing a trip Monday to Brazil and El Salvador.

"There is much that points to the direction of Iran," Secretary of Defense Caspar W. Weinberger declared after the first of two emergency briefings of the President by his national security advisers. The White House said, however, that the Administration had no conclusive findings and that the President had ordered additional intelligence investigations.

The President directed the Marine Corps commandant, Gen. P. X. Kelley, to go to Beirut to inspect the scene and

Continued on Page A8, Column 2

BUILDINGS BLASTED

Truck Loaded With TNT Wrecks Headquarters of a Marine Unit

By THOMAS L. FRIEDMAN

Special to The New York Times

BEIRUT, Lebanon, Oct. 23 — A suicide terrorist driving a truck loaded with TNT blew up an American Marine headquarters at the Beirut airport today, killing at least 161 marines and sailors and wounding 75.

In an almost simultaneous attack, another bomb-laden truck slammed into a French paratroop barracks two miles away.

According to Lebanese Civil Defense authorities, at least 27 French paratroopers were killed, 12 were wounded and 53 were reported missing and believed buried in rubble. Official Defense Ministry figures issued in Paris listed 12 French soldiers dead, 13 wounded and 48 missing.

It was the highest number of American military personnel killed in a single attack since the Vietnam War.

The identity of the attackers still had not been determined tonight.

Vehicle Smashes Barriers

According to a Pentagon spokesman, a Mercedes truck filled with some 2,500 pounds of TNT broke through a series of steel fences and sandbag barricades and detonated in the heart of the Marines' administrative headquarters building shortly after dawn. The explosion collapsed all four floors of the building, turning it into a burning mound of broken cement pillars and cinder blocks.

Although a marine sentry was able to fire about five shots at the suicide driver and another marine threw himself in front of the speeding, explosive-filled truck, neither could block its entry into the headquarters building, where it exploded in a fireball that left a crater 30 feet deep and 40 feet wide.

In a haunting scene late tonight, rescue workers using blow torches, pneumatic drills and cranes worked furiously under floodlights to pry out the dead and wounded still crushed beneath the smouldering debris. Marine spokesmen said there might have been as many as 300 men sleeping in the building — which doubled as a bunk house — at the time of the blast.

'Carnage' Like That in Vietnam

"I haven't seen carnage like that since Vietnam," the Marine spokesman, Maj. Robert Jordan, said shortly after emerging from the rescue operation with his forearms smeared with blood.

Today's blast brought to 184 the number of Americans killed in Lebanon since the bombing of the American Embassy here in April.

Rescue workers were hindered in their movements by unidentified snipers who intermittently fired shots into the Marine compound from the nearby southern suburbs of Beirut. The marines occasionally returned the fire.

Less that two minutes after the attack on the Marine compound, a truck laden with explosives slammed into a building used by the French as a headquarters for one of their 110-man companies in the southern Beirut suburb of

Continued on Page A6, Column 1

MARINES' SECURITY RAISES QUESTIONS

Reagan Sends Commandant to Lebanon to Investigate

By CHARLES MOHR

Special to The New York Times

WASHINGTON, Oct, 23 — After a car bomb blew up the United States Embassy in Beirut on April 18, killing 63 people, the Marine force at the Beirut airport took steps to strengthen security measures against a similar incident, Marine Corps officers said today.

The embassy bombing, and at least seven other serious car bombings this year in Beirut, gave warning of a common tactic. But a determined terrorist overwhelmed the new airport defenses, raising questions about why the security measures were inadequate.

Larry Speakes, the chief White House spokesman, said tonight that President Reagan had ordered the Marine Commandant, Gen. P. X. Kelly, to go to Beirut to determine what security measures could be taken to improve protection for the marines in Lebanon.

'Unbelievable,' Kennedy Says

Senator Edward M. Kennedy, Democrat of Massachusetts, a member of the Armed Services Commitee, asked for an investitation by the committee into what he called the "unbelievable breakdown in security that allowed it to happen."

In testimony before the Senate Foreign Relations Committee in September, General Kelly said in answser to a question that the area of responsibility given the marines in the multinational force dictated their position and that the Marines Corps was satisfied with

Continued on Page A12, Column 3

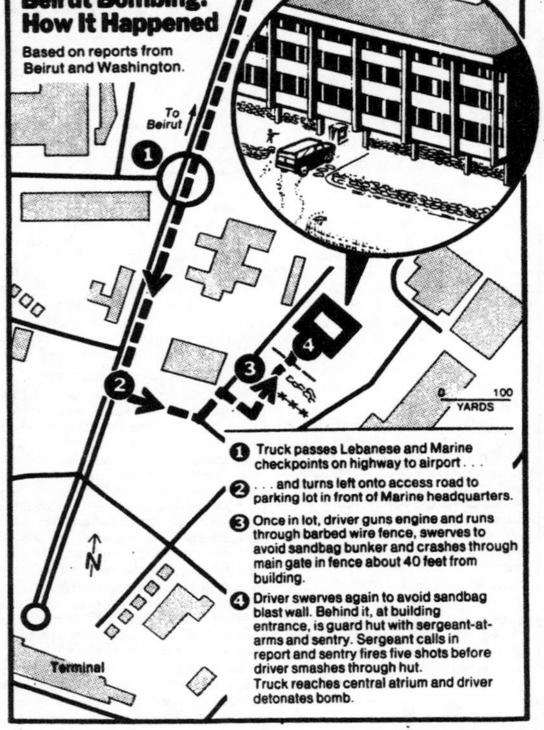
Beirut Bombing: How It Happened
Based on reports from Beirut and Washington.
To Beirut
1
2
3
4
0 100 YARDS
N
Terminal
1 Truck passes Lebanese and Marine checkpoints on highway to airport . . .
2 . . . and turns left onto access road to parking lot in front of Marine headquarters.
3 Once in lot, driver guns engine and runs through barbed wire fence, swerves to avoid sandbag bunker and crashes through main gate in fence about 40 feet from building.
4 Driver swerves again to avoid sandbag blast wall. Behind it, at building entrance, is guard hut with sergeant-at-arms and sentry. Sergeant calls in report and sentry fires five shots before driver smashes through hut.
Truck reaches central atrium and driver detonates bomb.

The New York Times/Oct. 24, 1983

'DON'T LEAVE US,' TRAPPED MEN CRY

Survivors Recount the Horror of Scene at Marine Base

Special to The New York Times

BEIRUT, Lebanon, Oct. 23 — Gunnery Sgt. Herman Lange was one of the first marines to get down to the bombed Marine headquarters from a nearby barracks.

"Bodies were lying around all over," he said. "Other people were trapped under the concrete. I could hear them screaming: 'Get us out. Don't leave us.' I just started digging, picking men out and taking them away on a jeep. It was total devastation."

The blast at the Marines' headquarters building, which housed the Battalion Landing Team and was known by the marines as the BLT, was so massive it dug a crater in the heart of the building 30 feet deep and 40 feet across. In the crater, piles of reinforced concrete, marines still in their cots, files, air conditioners, clothes and crates all intermingled.

Playing Cards and Deodorant

Classified papers were blown all over the area and the marines who survived scrambled to pick them up. The pile of rubble was peppered with personal items — a can of deodorant, a jack of hearts from someone's deck of playing cards and a United States quarter, twisted out of shape by the blast. "It felt just like an earthquake," said Staff Sgt. Alfonso Hernandez.

"I was sleeping in my rack in a tent about 200 yards away," Sergeant Hernandez said. "We were all thrown out

Continued on Page A7, Column 1

Questions on Mission

By BERNARD GWERTZMAN

Special to The New York Times

News Analysis

WASHINGTON, Oct. 23 — The devastating attack on the American marines in Lebanon today stunned the Reagan Administration and put it under new pressure to come up with a clearer explanation of why the marines are there.

Tonight the White House, seeking to justify the presence of the marines in Lebanon, said they had to remain there and not yield to "international terrorism." If they were withdrawn now, the White House said, "the civilized world" would suffer.

In the 13 months since the marines were sent to the Beirut area, the reasons for their presence there have shifted with the situation. At first they were dispatched to bolster the morale of the Lebanese people and Government and to be ready to help police areas that the United States had expected would be evacuated by the Israeli, Syrian and Palestinian forces.

But more recently, as the hopes for an early withdrawal of these forces faded, the marines, augmented by United States Navy ships, have become in effect a protector of the Lebanese Army, fighting off efforts by Syrian-backed Druse and Shiite factions to undermine the Lebanese Government. But even this role was ambiguous because the Administration would not sanction an all-out military role for the marines for fear of alienating Congress and friendly Arab nations.

Today President Reagan, clearly frustrated by the Marine casualties, vowed even before he had met with his National Security Council that the United States would not be driven out of Lebanon.

Yet after the morning meeting of the

Continued on Page A9, Column 1

United Press International

French paratrooper holding trapped comrade's hand at site of second blast.

Other News

Stirring Marathon Victory

Rod Dixon of New Zealand took the lead in the final mile to win the men's title. Grete Waitz won a fifth women's crown. SportsMonday, page C1.

Grenada Warns of Invasion

Grenada's radio issued a warning to the island's residents to expect an imminent invasion from the country's Caribbean neighbors. Page A4.

Mixed Signals for Bonn

The antimissile protests in West Germany conveyed signs of both disquiet and reassurance for Bonn and its allies. News analysis, page A3.

Augusta Suspect 'Troubled'

The suspect charged with taking hostages while President Reagan played golf was a 'troubled' man who may have been drinking. Page A14.

Food Tests Reviewed

A Louisiana laboratory's tests of chemicals for consumer use are being reviewed because a test on a coffee chemical was "sloppy." Page D12.

DeLorean Tape Shown

CBS News won a court battle and televised a videotape of the scene culminating in the arrest of John Z. DeLorean on drug charges. Page A16.

"All the News That's Fit to Print"

The New York Times

Late Edition

Weather: Mostly cloudy and cool, brisk northeasterly winds today; remaining cloudy and cool tonight and tomorrow. Temperatures: today 49-51 tonight 41-43; yesterday 46-53. Details, page C20.

VOL.CXXXIII . No. 45,843 Copyright © 1983 The New York Times NEW YORK, WEDNESDAY, OCTOBER 26, 1983 60 cents beyond 75 miles from New York City, except on Long Island 30 CENTS

1,900 U.S. TROOPS, WITH CARIBBEAN ALLIES, INVADE GRENADA AND FIGHT LEFTIST UNITS; MOSCOW PROTESTS; BRITISH ARE CRITICAL

Toll Climbs In Bombing In Lebanon

216 Americans Dead, 20 to 30 Missing

By THOMAS L. FRIEDMAN

Special to The New York Times

BEIRUT, Lebanon, Oct. 25 — Gen. Paul X. Kelley, the United States Marine commandant, arrived here from Washington today as the Marine contingent was placed on its highest state of alert.

Late in the day, it was announced that the number of American military personnel killed in Sunday's bombing of the Marine headquarters had risen to 216, with 20 to 30 bodies still believed buried in the rubble of the headqurters building at the Beirut airport.

The alert was ordered after an early morning intelligence warning was passed to the marines by the Lebanese Army saying that three vehicles reportedly carrying high explosives were circling the area and might strike at the Marine compound.

[Vice President Bush left Washington for Beirut, where he will meet with President Amin Gemayel and visit with the Marine force, The Associated Press reported. Mr. Bush, whose trip was announced after his departure, is expected to return Wednesday night, a White House spokesman said.]

Removal of Barrier Reported

In another development, a marine officer familiar with the bombed compound said that two long, thick pipes that had been placed as barriers in front of the entryway of the headquarters to protect against car-bomb attacks had been removed several days before Sunday's attack.

This evening, a Marine spokesman, Maj. Robert Jordan, said he could not say for certain whether the pipes, which had apparently been installed months ago, had been in their position at the time of the attack.

General Kelley came to the Lebanese capital to review security measures at the Marine compound and to meet with the members of the American contingent in the multinational force here.

Replacements Arrive

Hours before General Kelley reached Beirut, 300 more marines arrived by plane from the United States to replace their fallen comrades.

General Kelley toured the ruins of the Battalion Landing Team headquarters, while marines and Lebanese civil defense workers continued to excavate bodies from the jagged wreckage of the

Continued on Page A8, Column 1

United Press International

President Reagan, accompanied by Prime Minister Eugenia Charles of Dominica, holding a news conference on the Grenada invasion. Listening were Secretary of State George P. Shultz, Defense Secretary Caspar W. Weinberger and, behind them, David R. Gergen, the White House communications director.

Key Events in Caribbean Invasion

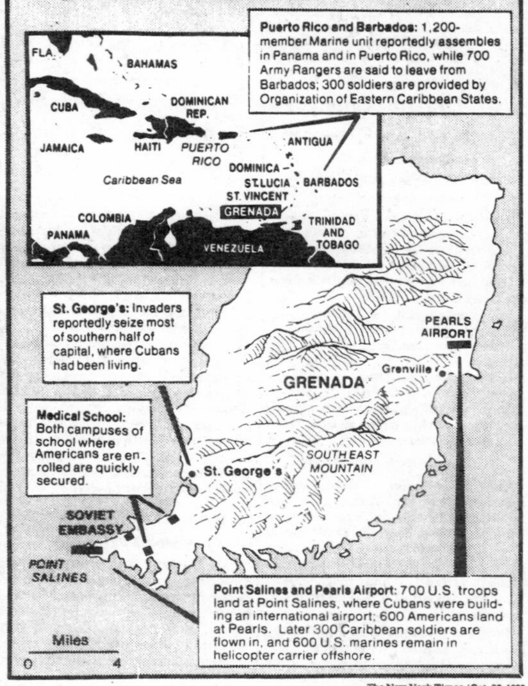
Puerto Rico and Barbados: 1,200-member Marine unit reportedly assembles in Panama and in Puerto Rico, while 700 Army Rangers are said to leave from Barbados; 300 soldiers are provided by Organization of Eastern Caribbean States.
FLA.
BAHAMAS
CUBA
DOMINICAN REP.
JAMAICA
HAITI
PUERTO RICO
ANTIGUA
DOMINICA
Caribbean Sea
ST.LUCIA
BARBADOS
ST. VINCENT
GRENADA
COLOMBIA
PANAMA
TRINIDAD AND TOBAGO
VENEZUELA
St. George's: Invaders reportedly seize most of southern half of capital, where Cubans had been living.
PEARLS AIRPORT
Grenville
GRENADA
Medical School: Both campuses of school where Americans are enrolled are quickly secured.
SOUTH EAST MOUNTAIN
St. George's
SOVIET EMBASSY
POINT SALINES
Point Salines and Pearls Airport: 700 U.S. troops land at Point Salines, where Cubans were building an international airport; 600 Americans land at Pearls. Later 300 Caribbean soldiers are flown in, and 600 U.S. marines remain in helicopter carrier offshore.
Miles
0
4

The New York Times / Oct. 26, 1983

Airports Seized, Drive on Capital Faces Stiff Fire

By MICHAEL T. KAUFMAN

Special to The New York Times

BRIDGETOWN, Barbados, Oct. 25 — An assault force spearheaded by United States troops invaded Grenada before dawn today and soon seized both of the island's airfields. But the advance of the invaders, who included contingents from seven Caribbean nations, was reportedly slowed in the afternoon by heavy fire in the capital.

According to military and intelligence sources in the Caribbean, the initial landings were made by helicopter. Fire from armed Cubans met those landing at a jet runway being completed by Cuban workers at Point Salines, four miles south of St. George's, the capital.

In the initial contact, 12 Cubans were killed and 24 captured, according to officials of the Barbados Government, one of the contributors of troops to the invading force.

Russians Reported Seized

The United States contingent consisted of marines and army rangers. At least one marine was reported here to have been killed; in Washington the Defense Department put the number of Marine dead at two.

Radio stations here reported that 30 Soviet advisers to the Grenadian Government had been seized. But officials here said they could not confirm that report.

By this afternoon, a source who had returned from Grenada reported that the invading force had established a perimeter that included the southern half of St. George's. The part of the city held by the multinational force included the deep-water harbor, the Prime Minister's residence and the Grenada Beach Hotel, the former Holi-

Continued on Page A17, Column 3

2 AMERICANS KILLED

Cubans Clash With Force — 30 Soviet Advisers Are Reported Safe

By HEDRICK SMITH

Special to The New York Times

WASHINGTON, Oct. 25 — President Reagan announced today that he had ordered a predawn invasion of Grenada by nearly 1,900 marines and Army airborne troops.

He said the invasion was intended to protect American citizens and to help restore democratic institutions on the Caribbean island.

The Defense Department said two Americans had been killed.

Four hours after the American landings began, the President said the

Reagan statement, page A16; Shultz news conference, page A18.

operation was launched in response to an urgent request from some members of the Organization of Eastern Caribbean States, some of which provided 300 troops for the operation.

'No Choice But to Act'

The United States, President Reagan told a 9 A.M. news conference, "had no choice but to act strongly and decisively" to oppose "a brutal gang of leftist thugs" that had violently seized power on Oct. 12, later executed Prime Minister Maurice Bishop and other Cabinet ministers, recently imposed a "shoot on sight" curfew and shut down the international airports this weekend when some of the 1,000 Americans on the island wanted to leave.

The President said American forces had quickly "secured" the island's two airports. This afternoon, Secretary of State George P. Shultz said American troops had identified and were assuring the safety of 30 Soviet military advisers on the island and had also taken over part of the island's medical school, where more than 500 Americans are studying.

'Pockets of Resistance'

Mr. Shultz said American forces had encountered "pockets of resistance" around the capital city of St. George's and were also fighting some of the 600 armed Cuban construction workers building an airfield near Point Salines. But he gave no details. A Cuban broadcast, quoted by The Associated Press, said that "at nightfall the heroic resistance of our constructors and collaborators continued."

Tonight, at an urgent meeting of the United Nations Security Council called to discuss the situation in Grenada, the United States clashed sharply with Latin American countries critical of the invasion. [Page A18.]

Extremely tight secrecy surrounded the invasion and only at 9 P.M. did the Pentagon release its first combat communiqué, reporting that two American troops had been killed and 23 wounded

Continued on Page A16, Column 1

U.S. WAS WARNED BY MRS. THATCHER

She Urged Caution on Reagan — London Played No Role

By BARNABY J. FEDER

Special to The New York Times

LONDON, Oct. 25 — Prime Minister Margaret Thatcher said today that the British Government had urged President Reagan to reconsider his plans to launch an invasion of Grenada after learning of them Monday, and that no British ships or forces had taken part.

The announcement in the House of Commons that Grenada, a member of

The Soviet press called the invasion an "act of undisguised banditry." Cuba said its workers in Grenada had been ordered not to give up under any circumstances. Page A17.

the Commonwealth, had been invaded by an ally despite the Government's expressed misgivings led to harsh criticism of both the British Government and President Reagan by opposition parties and some of Mrs. Thatcher's own Conservatives.

France described the invasion as "a surprising action in relation to international law" and said it had not been informed of the action. [Page A17.]

Opposition Speaks of Deception

Sir Geoffrey Howe, the Foreign Secretary, underwent 45 minutes of tumultuous questioning when called upon to explain the events that had begun to unfold hours after he assured the House on Monday that there was no reason to anticipate any military intervention in Grenada.

Denis Healey, the Labor Party's spokesman on foreign affairs, said the United States and some Commonwealth nations in the Caribbean had deceived Britain about their plans.

"None of the objectives stated by President Reagan justifies the invasion of an independent state," Mr. Healey said.

The Government, however, refused to condemn the invasion. Mrs. Thatcher said, "We understand that what weighed heavily with the United

Continued on Page A17, Column 1

Associated Press

Gen. Hudson Austin, head of Grenada's military junta.

Agony of Lebanon Is Felt in Connecticut

By SUSAN CHIRA

Special to The New York Times

NAUGATUCK, Conn., Oct. 25 — Schoolchildren passed around Dwayne Wigglesworth's picture and talked about why people were killing one another in Lebanon. Older men talked about why the young always had to die, and young boys talked about whether they would have to fight, too.

Lance Corporal Wigglesworth, 19 years old, died Sunday in Beirut, a victim of the terrorist bombing against the Marines. Today, as word of his death spread, people here thought of how they could comfort members of his family, who live in this town of nearly 30,000. Neighbors and strangers called the Wigglesworth home, offering help or bringing food.

The fighting in Beirut came home to this town Monday morning, when three marines in dress blues knocked on the door of the Wigglesworths' home to tell them what they had been praying not to hear.

"The first reaction is anger, hatred, all the frustration," said Henry Wigglesworth, Corporal Wigglesworth's father. "There are a lot of whys, a lot of questions, and we haven't had the answers yet to give anybody else."

The Wigglesworths have seven other sons and one daughter. Robyn, 21, is a marine stationed in Japan. Gary, 22, is in the Army, stationed at Fort Bragg, N.C.

Gary and Dwayne spent the last month before Corporal Wigglesworth was sent to Beirut "fishing and enjoying each other," their father said.

Today Robyn arrived home to be with his family, and Corporal Wigglesworth's death was the topic of conversation at shoe stores and stationers, at schools and at City Hall.

"It's not only people outside that we don't know getting killed," said Paul DeFranzo, 18. "It's somebody from your own hometown. It makes you think even harder."

"I feel sorry for people who have to suffer because it's in the family," said Robin Henao, a 13-year-old seventh grader at the Hillside Middle School. Her teacher passed Corporal Wigglesworth's picture around her social studies class and read them news of Lebanon from the newspaper.

Five flags surrounded the war me-

Continued on Page A7, Column 1

An Invasion Prompted by Previous Debacles

By BERNARD GWERTZMAN

Special to The New York Times

News Analysis

WASHINGTON, Oct. 25 — Behind President Reagan's decision to invade Grenada today was his concern that the island not become either "another Iran," where Americans were held hostage for 444 days, or "another Beirut," where the United States was powerless on Sunday to prevent the death of more than 200 marines, Administration officials said.

But in addition to these reasons, which Secretary of State George P. Shultz insisted were the paramount ones, there was additional motivation, officials said: to rid the Caribbean of a potential outpost for Cuba and the Soviet Union and to stop what the Administration perceived as a drift toward more radicalism in the region.

Some officials said the White House could not afford "another Nicaragua," the Cuban ally in Central America, while others said a more real concern was that there not be "another Suriname," the former Dutch colony in northern South America that was taken over by leftists last year in a coup.

The move also demonstrated the determination of this Administration not to appear passive in the face of foreign crisis. A French diplomat, who derided the Grenada invasion, said the President looked as if he was "flailing around," striking at the Grenadians out of his frustration at not being able to hit Damascus, Havana or Moscow.

White House officials defended the President as being suitably cautious, but unwilling to run the risk of being compared to his predecessor, Jimmy Carter, whose handling of the hostage crisis in Iran may have caused him to lose the election to Mr. Reagan.

The invasion, however, has produced a new series of international problems for the Administration, already faced with a difficult crisis in Lebanon. Launching the action without advance consultation with Congress, and without the cooperation of its key North Atlantic Treaty Organization and Latin American allies, the Administration

Continued on Page A17, Column 2

Days of Crisis for President: Golf, a Tragedy and Secrets

By FRANCIS X. CLINES

Special to The New York Times

WASHINGTON, Oct. 25 — At midday Saturday, as President Reagan was in the midst of a round of golf at the Augusta National Golf Course in Georgia, he had under active consideration a secret request from Caribbean nations to join in the invasion of Grenada.

The President, already a legend in the Administration for keeping his own counsel, had begun the most secretive and momentous week of his incumbency with a golf club in his hands.

One of his golfing partners, Secretary of State George P. Shultz, was receiving the latest details of Grenada plans going on back in Washington, and discussing them with the President on the golf course, according to White House officials.

At the same time, the President's national security adviser, Robert C. McFarlane, was monitoring the situation nearby as the President stroked away.

On Sunday morning, the Grenada issue was further laid out in Administration study papers as Mr. Reagan made a sudden return home and appeared standing in the rain outside the White House, grief-stricken and mourning the marines who had died in the shocking Beirut explosion a few hours earlier.

The national security meetings that followed were ostensibly devoted entirely to the Lebanon crisis, but today it became clear that they also advanced the Grenada invasion decision

Continued on Page A22, Column 3

INSIDE

Civil Rights Dismissals

In an unexpected move, President Reagan removed three Democratic critics from the United States Commission on Civil Rights. Page A24

Indian Pt. [illegible]

A panel told the [illegible] Commission [illegible] improvements [illegible] the Indian [illegible] Page B2.

"All the News That's Fit to Print"

The New York Times

Late Edition

Weather: Mostly cloudy, chance of morning showers today; partly cloudy tonight. Partly cloudy, mild tomorrow. Temperatures: today 51-53, tonight 41-43; yesterday 30-47. Details, page 54.

VOL.CXXXIII . . . No. 45,951 | NEW YORK, SATURDAY, FEBRUARY 11, 1984 | 30 CENTS

80 cents beyond 75 miles from New York City, except on Long Island

ANDROPOV IS DEAD IN MOSCOW AT 69; REAGAN ASKS 'PRODUCTIVE' CONTACTS AND NAMES BUSH TO ATTEND FUNERAL

LILCO WITHDRAWS FROM PARTNERSHIP IN UPSTATE PLANT

Misses $1.1 Million Payment for Building Nuclear Unit, Citing Financial Woes

By MATTHEW L. WALD

The Long Island Lighting Company defaulted yesterday on its partnership agreement with four other New York State utilities that are building the Nine Mile Point 2 nuclear power plant on the shore of Lake Ontario.

The company said that it had missed a $1.1 million payment due Thursday and that it would spend no more on the plant, which is still at least two years from operation, at an estimated cost of $4.2 billion for completion.

Lilco has invested about $500 million in the project since 1975, when it agreed to buy 18 percent of the reactor. This year its share would have been $180 million.

The utility is struggling to raise cash because of its troubles with the Shoreham reactor, which it is building alone on Long Island.

Mismanagement Charged

In another blow yesterday, the staff of the state's Public Service Commission recommended that Lilco, not its customers, should bear $1.5 billion of the reactor's cost of approximately $4 billion because of "serious mismanagement and inefficiency throughout the project." [Page 31.]

Governor Cuomo said he would meet with legislative leaders next week and "provide them with a comprehensive agenda for action including the problem of Shoreham and all other current energy concerns."

Lilco's four partners in the Nine Mile Point project had no comment yesterday on what they would do next to pick up the cost of the project and said they

Continued on Page 31, Column 3

400 Americans Are Evacuated From Lebanon

By THOMAS L. FRIEDMAN

Special to The New York Times

BEIRUT, Lebanon, Feb. 10 — With only a few hours' notice, more than 400 American citizens, protected by United States marines and Druse militiamen, were evacuated from Beirut today. Britain also evacuated hundreds of its citizens, and Italy prepared to do so.

The American Embassy had received many appeals from American citizens for transport out of Beirut, where they have been trapped by fighting. It announced this morning that "because of the unsettled conditions in Lebanon" it would evacuate any Americans or Lebanese in the process of taking up American citizenship.

On Thursday the embassy said it did not regard such a move as justified, and political sources close to the Americans said there was concern that an evacuation might upset negotiations aimed at keeping President Amin Gemayel in power.

Waiting for the Weather

Asked today why the embassy had waited to decide on an evacuation, its spokesman, John Stewart, said, "We were waiting to see if the weather was good."

In military action today, Israeli jets attacked targets in hills 12 miles east of Beirut in their first raids in Lebanon since Moslem militiamen took over West Beirut. The Israeli command said the raids, which came a day after rockets were fired into northern Israel from southern Lebanon, were against Palestinian guerrilla positions. [Page 5.]

[In Washington, a senior Reagan Administration official expressed optimism that the withdrawal of United States marines from the Beirut airport would begin "in a matter of days" and would be completed within a month. Page 5.]

According to the registration list, 410 Americans, Lebanese and diplomats from Egypt, Japan and South Korea were airlifted out of West Beirut by

Continued on Page 5, Column 4

QUICK SIGNAL SENT

Shultz Emphasizes U.S. Is Ready for Effort to Improve Relations

By BERNARD GWERTZMAN

Special to The New York Times

WASHINGTON, Feb. 10 — President Reagan and Secretary of State George P. Shultz told Soviet leaders today that during this period of transition in Moscow the United States wanted to reaffirm its desire "for a constructive and realistic dialogue" with the Soviet Union.

Although some thought was given to having Mr. Reagan lead the American delegation to the funeral of Yuri V. Andropov, the White House said late today that Vice President Bush would head the delegation. [Page 7.]

In Santa Barbara, Calif., Larry Speakes, the White House spokesman, said that Mr. Reagan, in a message of condolences, called on the Kremlin to "join in peaceful purpose for all mankind."

Prompt Signal to Moscow

Mr. Shultz appeared before reporters in Washington to read an Administration statement that incorporated some of Mr. Reagan's message and some additional thoughts. The purpose of the publicity given the Administration's messages, State Department officials said, was to send a prompt signal to the Soviet leaders that Washington was more ready than ever for a significant improvement in relations, in keeping with the Administration's conciliatory policy of the last month.

Mr. Shultz was reported to have favored Mr. Reagan's going to the funeral, although other senior officials saw more merit at this time in Mr. Bush and Mr. Shultz heading the delegation, as they did at the funeral for Leonid I. Brezhnev in November 1982. In a telephone conversation with Mr. Reagan this morning, Mr. Shultz laid

Continued on Page 7, Column 1

Woodfin Camp / Lehtikuva Oy

Yuri Vladimirovich Andropov

Policy After Andropov

No Drastic Changes Expected in Moscow

By SERGE SCHMEMANN

Special to The New York Times

MOSCOW, Feb. 10 — Yuri V. Andropov's death put an end to the shortest period of rule in Soviet history, if Georgi M. Malenkov's week as titular Communist Party chief after Stalin's death can be overlooked.

But neither the worsening Soviet-American chill that marked Mr. Andropov's 15 months as leader nor the changes he set in motion through the Soviet Union's ponderous economic system and bureaucracy are considered likely to be altered anytime soon, no matter who succeeds him.

Ending the Stagnation

The chief reason, most diplomats agree, is that Mr. Andropov's economic experiments, his crackdown on corruption, and even his hard line in foreign relations found the support of a populace yearning for a tough "khozyain," or boss — and, more important, the support of powerful men and institutions.

Power brokers like Defense Minister Dmitri F. Ustinov, now arguably the most powerful man in the Politburo, or

Continued on Page 8, Column 2

Washington Foresees Continuing Conflicts

By LESLIE H. GELB

Special to The New York Times

News Analysis

WASHINGTON, Feb. 10 — The passing of a major political leader sometimes creates a sense of opportunity. But as seen by a range of Reagan Administration officials, Yuri V. Andropov's death offers not so much a chance for breakthroughs as a time for gestures that might lead to breakthroughs later on.

There is little evidence that anything fundamental has changed in either Moscow or Washington with Mr. Andropov's passing. Essentially, the same people have been running Soviet foreign policy for five or six years. Mr. Andropov was ill for almost one year of his 15-month tenure. His predecessor, Leonid I. Brezhnev, seemed inactive for his last three years. Soviet policy has been much the same throughout.

Profound Differences

Nor is there much evidence that President Reagan is prepared to propose new compromises that might help break the impasses over the Soviet intervention in Afghanistan or the Lebanon situation or the talks on nuclear arms. All that can be seen thus far is a

Continued on Page 8, Column 2

BURIAL ON TUESDAY

Chernenko to Lead Rites — Role May Be a Hint on the Succession

By JOHN F. BURNS

Special to The New York Times

MOSCOW, Feb. 10 — The Soviet leadership announced today that Yuri V. Andropov died Thursday, less than 15 months after he succeeded Leonid I. Brezhnev as General Secretary of the Communist Party. He was 69 years old.

The two-paragraph announcement was read on radio and television at 2:30 P.M. (6:30 A.M. New York time) and was repeated throughout the day. It was followed by a series of bulletins on the causes of death and on arrangements for a funeral on Tuesday.

Konstantin U. Chernenko, 72 years old, a Brezhnev protégé who served as the second-ranking secretary, will lead the funeral commission. Foreign diplomats took this as an indication that he might succeed Mr. Andropov.

[Governments in Western Europe and Japan expressed regret and some indicated they would send high officials to the funeral. In Poland, the press mourned the Soviet leader, but people in the street reacted with sarcasm or indifference. Page 10.]

Absent for Six Months

The Soviet leadership said official mourning would last from Saturday until the burial in Red Square.

Mr. Andropov's death, from a chronic kidney ailment that had kept him from public functions for six months, left vacant several key positions. In addition to being party leader, he was chairman of the Presidium of the Supreme Soviet, the equivalent of

As Soviet leader, Yuri V. Andropov encountered major problems with the West and with a stagnating economy at home. An obituary, page 9.

head of state, and chairman of the Defense Council, with authority over the armed forces.

The official announcement said Mr. Andropov died at 4:50 P.M. on Thursday "after a long illness," identified by the medical bulletin as having involved nephritis, diabetes and hypertension "complicated by a chronic kidney deficiency."

The medical statement said he had been receiving treatment on an artificial kidney machine for 12 months, but had suffered a deterioration in his condition toward the end of January.

The pronouncements did not say where Mr. Andropov died. He had been reported hospitalized at a special clinic

Continued on Page 6, Column 1

United Press International

Britons boarding Royal Navy helicopters as foreign civilians, including Americans, began to leave Beirut.

The Chief Mourner in Moscow

Konstantin Ustinovich Chernenko

Special to The New York Times

Man in the News

MOSCOW, Feb. 10 — The appointment of Konstantin U. Chernenko today to head Yuri V. Andropov's funeral commission marked at least a partial triumph for a veteran Communist who only 15 months earlier seemed to have reached the end of his political career.

Whether the appointment suggested that Mr. Chernenko had been tapped to succeed Mr. Andropov, or whether it was given him on the strength of his position as the second-ranking secretary, was likely to become clear only when the Central Committee named a new General Secretary.

But the fact that Mr. Chernenko would be the one to supervise the burial of his former rival was in itself a feat of political survival not without an element of irony.

Mr. Chernenko, now 72 years old, had been the closest aide to Leonid I. Brezhnev and the clear choice of Mr. Brezhnev's entourage to succeed the late leader. But Mr. Andropov had outmaneuvered them all, and on Nov. 12, 1982, Tass, the official press agency, announced that Mr. Chernenko himself had nominated his rival to become the new Soviet chief.

This act of party loyalty apparently paid off. While many of Mr. Brezhnev's political allies found themselves retired or disgraced in the shuffles and crackdowns instigated by the new regime, Mr. Chernenko settled into a reasonably prestigious job. Although relieved of his post as chief of the Central Committee's General Department, with broad responsibility over the day-to-day work of

Sketches of other leaders mentioned as possible successors, page 8.

the party and its personnel, he was handed the late Mikhail A. Suslov's stewardship over ideology and culture.

In that role, Mr. Chernenko made the keynote speech at a Central Committee meeting last spring and con-

Continued on Page 8, Column 1

Gamma-Liaison / Alain Mingam

Followed his patron, Leonid I. Brezhnev, up the party ladder.

Producer Prices Up 0.6% in Month, Led by Food

By JONATHAN FUERBRINGER

Special to The New York Times

WASHINGTON, Feb. 10 — Producer prices for finished goods, driven up by a sharp rise in food prices, climbed six-tenths of 1 percent in January, the Labor Department reported today. It was the largest monthly rise in more than a year.

The increase, which was as much as the Producer Price Index rose for all of 1983, surprised some economists but was not, several said, a cause for alarm. "This is not a fundamental turn," toward broadly higher inflation, said Otto Eckstein of Data Resources Inc.

"It just shows there is only so much luck you can have with fruit and vegetable prices and oil prices," he added, a reference to the slight increases in food prices and sharp declines in energy prices largely responsible for last year's almost stable index.

Over all, food prices rose 2.7 percent, the largest one-month jump since August 1980. In December, food prices rose seven-tenths of 1 percent. Pork, beef, veal and fish prices were up because of the cold weather, which killed cattle or kept their weight down and disrupted the delivery of hogs. Poultry prices rose because of the loss of hundreds of thousands of chickens to avian flu, which also pushed up egg prices.

Because changes in producer prices of fresh food flow through quickly to retail prices, much of the January increase reported today may already be reflected in what consumers are paying at the store.

On the other hand, energy prices declined 1.2 percent in the Janaury index, the sixth drop in the last seven months, and prices of other goods held rela-

Continued on Page 41, Column 5

INSIDE

Diet May Cut Cancer Risk

The American Cancer Society issued new diet guidelines and urged Americans to avoid obesity to reduce the risk of cancer. Page 12.

British Skaters Take Lead

Jayne Torvill and Christopher Dean were given three perfect scores in ice dancing as skating began at the Olympic Winter Games. Page 21.

"All the News That's Fit to Print"

The New York Times

Late Edition

Weather: Morning fog and drizzle, afternoon rain, mild today; rain, fog tonight. Gradual clearing, mild tomorrow. Temperatures: today 49-51, tonight 41-43; yesterday 36-45. Details, page C10.

VOL.CXXXIII . . . No. 45,954 | NEW YORK, TUESDAY, FEBRUARY 14, 1984 | 30 CENTS

30 cents beyond 75 miles from New York City, except on Long Island

CHERNENKO IN TOP SOVIET POST; VOWS TO RETAIN ARMS BALANCE, WARNS AGAINST 'ADVENTURISTS'

Associated Press, Tass

Konstantin U. Chernenko, above at left, with Politburo members at the House of Unions in Moscow where Yuri V. Andropov lies in state. From the right are Dmitri F. Ustinov, Andrei A. Gromyko and Nikolai A. Tikhonov. Below: President Reagan signing book of condolences yesterday at the Soviet Embassy in Washington.

NOTABLE COMEBACK

New Chief, 72, Succeeds the Rival Who Foiled Him in '82 Contest

By JOHN F. BURNS

Special to The New York Times

MOSCOW, Feb. 13 — Konstantin U. Chernenko was chosen by the Communist Party's Central Committee today to succeed Yuri V. Andropov as its General Secretary.

His assumption of the post automatically made Mr. Chernenko the Soviet Union's pre-eminent leader. At 72 years of age, he is the oldest of the men named to lead the party since the Bolshevik Revolution in 1917.

Mr. Chernenko immediately made a wide-ranging speech to the Central Committee in which he praised Mr. An-

Excerpts from speech, page A11.

dropov for the "tremendous prestige and respect" he had gained among the Soviet people and endorsed many of Mr. Andropov's domestic policies.

Selection Termed Unanimous

On relations with the United States, he said that while the Soviet Union remained committed to peaceful co-existence and elimination of the threat of nuclear war, it would insure that it had enough arms "to cool the hotheads of militant adventurists."

"We need no military superiority," he said. "We do not intend to dictate our will to others. But we will not permit the military equilibrium that has been achieved to be upset. And let nobody have even the slightest doubt about that: We will further see to it that our country's defense capacity be strengthened, that we should have enough means to cool the hot heads of militant adventurists."

An official announcement said that the 12 members of the ruling Politburo had unanimously recommended the appointment of Mr. Chernenko and that the Central Committee, which has about 300 members, had also been unanimous in approving the nomination.

An Aide to Brezhnev

The appointment marked what appeared to be a remarkable political comeback for Mr. Chernenko, a Russian peasant's son from Siberia who left school at the age of 12 and worked his way through party ranks to the Kremlin as an aide and protégé of Leonid I. Brezhnev. He was the losing candidate 15 months ago when Mr. Andropov was named party leader in succession to Mr. Brezhnev and in the months

Continued on Page A11, Column 1

U.S. TELLS JORDAN OF ITS COMMITMENT DESPITE PULLBACK

Reagan Assures Hussein That American Support Against Syrians Will Continue

By STEVEN R. WEISMAN

Special to The New York Times

WASHINGTON, Feb. 13 — President Reagan assured King Hussein of Jordan today that his decision to pull back the marines from Beirut did not imply a weakening of his commitment to Jordan and Lebanon in their struggles against Syria.

Mr. Reagan's assurances came at a meeting with the King at the White House that marked the beginning of a round of discussions on the turbulent situation in the Middle East. The President is to follow up the session today with a meeting Tuesday with both King Hussein and President Hosni Mubarak of Egypt.

Mr Mubarak and the King had dinner together Sunday night, but an American official said he did not regard their getting together as "historic" or "ice breaking." The two leaders had met twice before and the Administration has said their presence in town together is a coincidence.

'Terrorism Cannot Be Tolerated'

In his statement after the talk with King Hussein, Mr. Reagan criticized nations he said have supported terrorism in the Middle East. He did not single out any nations, but both he and the King have in the past charged that Syria had supported terrorist attacks against Jordan, the United States and others.

"We also agree that terrorism cannot be tolerated and that the leaders of all states must stand together against this new barbarism that threatens civilization," Mr. Reagan said. "States that condone terrorism undermine their own legitimacy."

The King, who is making an unofficial visit here after a medical checkup in Cleveland and a holiday in Colorado, thanked Mr. Reagan and said, "On all subjects, sir, that you were kind enough to address, I could not in all honesty say that I could have presented my views differently."

Support for U.N. Resolution

In a briefing after the meeting, an Administration official said the session was marked by expressions of friendship and like-mindedness, particularly on the need to oppose Syrian influence and to achieve progress in returning some autonomy to the Palestinians on the West Bank of the Jordan River.

Once more, the official said, Mr. Reagan told King Hussein that he supported United Nations Security Council Resolution 242, as well as his own peace initiative of Sept. 1, 1982. The King is known to be fearful that these initiatives will be de-emphasized in the

Continued on Page A8, Column 1

The New York Times

Elizabeth Hanford Dole

F.A.A. SET TO HIRE MORE INSPECTORS

Mrs. Dole Plans 30% Increase for Airline Safety Checks

By RICHARD WITKIN

Secretary of Transportation Elizabeth Hanford Dole, noting the recent temporary groundings of three small airlines for safety reasons, announced yesterday that the airline inspector force of the Federal Aviation Administration would be increased by more than 30 percent.

Mrs. Dole also said she had recommended to the White House that Adm. Donald D. Engen, retired, now on the National Transportation Safety Board, be nominated to head the aviation agency, which is part of her department.

The Reagan Administration has been criticized in Congress in recent months because of cutbacks made in the airline inspector force. The number dropped from 638 in 1981 to 534 last year, and another 7 percent cut had been set for the current fiscal year.

Under the turnaround announced by Mrs. Dole yesterday, 166 new inspectors would be added to the 508 now authorized. That would bring the total to 674, the number authorized in 1981.

Mrs. Dole, speaking at the National Press Club in Washington, did not say how the financing of the increased force would be arranged. Later an F.A.A. spokesman, Dennis Feldman, said: "We have to begin the process immediately of hiring the additional inspectors. And we'll have to absorb the increase within our present fiscal 1984

Continued on Page D27, Column 1

U.S. Says the Chernenko Speech Hints Door May Be Open to Talks

By BERNARD GWERTZMAN

Special to The New York Times

WASHINGTON, Feb. 13 — The United States said today that it welcomed some apparently conciliatory comments in the speech by the new Soviet leader, Konstantin U. Chernenko. American officials said the comments suggested that the door might be open to reviving a dialogue.

Senior Reagan Administration officials said Mr. Chernenko's speech, which he gave after being chosen as the new General Secretary of the Communist Party, broke no major new ground. But they said it appeared to respond indirectly to President Reagan's call for a new "constructive dialogue."

Late this afternoon, President Reagan arrived at the Soviet Embassy in Washington and signed the condolence book for Yuri V. Andropov that was opened to the public this morning. The White House said Mr. Reagan signed this message:

"Please accept my condolences on the death of Chairman Andropov and convey my sympathy to his family."

The White House said Mr. Reagan had signed a similar book after the death of Leonid I. Brezhnev in 1982.

In responding to Mr. Chernenko's speech, State Department officials glossed over his tough-sounding words. Instead they focused on his comments about Soviet readiness to "cooperate with" countries that were prepared to help lessen tensions "through practical deeds."

From the context of his remarks, he could have been placing responsibility on the United States to come up with "practical deeds," a position voiced earlier by Mr. Andropov in responding to Mr. Reagan's overture.

But the State Department chose to put a more positive interpretation on Mr. Chernenko's remarks by making it appear that it was the Soviet Union that was ready to offer "practical deeds."

The senior Administration officials said they expected Mr. Chernenko to move cautiously in foreign affairs and rely, perhaps more than had any previ-

Continued on Page A13, Column 1

A Bolshevik Of Old Mold Rises to Top

By SERGE SCHMEMANN

Special to The New York Times

MOSCOW, Feb. 13 — In selecting Konstantin Ustinovich Chernenko to be the next leader of the Soviet Union, his comrades on the Politburo went for a Bolshevik from the old mold.

Mr. Chernenko is widely regarded here as an ideologue, low on formal education or managerial experience but high on old-fashioned propaganda and party loyalty.

If Yuri V. Andropov began his 15-month tenure saying that tired slogans would no longer suffice, Mr. Chernenko began his with a handful of slogans: "Our party's principled stand on these issues is clear, pure and noble," "The party, which is selflessly devoted to the masses, enjoys full trust of the masses," "The inexhaustible strength of Soviet Communists is in cohesion of their ranks."

The occasion, of course, was one that demanded some ceremonial platitudes. Mr. Andropov had not yet been buried and Mr. Chernenko had just been selected General Secretary of the Soviet Communist Party, and the theme of speeches on such occasions is invariably the unity, strength and inevitable triumph of the party.

But Mr. Chernenko's remarks fit neatly into the pattern of all his major pronouncements since he came to prominence as Leonid I. Brezhnev's closest ally on the Politburo.

It was a style probably derived from his years working in agitation and propaganda, or "agit-prop," in Siberia and Moldavia and on the party's Central Committee. But it also reflected a

Continued on Page A11, Column 3

U.S. Captures Giant Slalom And Takes First Gold Medal

By JOHN TAGLIABUE

Special to The New York Times

SARAJEVO, Yugoslavia, Feb. 13 — The United States, which had won only one medal in the first four days of full-scale competition at the XIV Olympic Winter Games, picked up two more today when Debbie Armstrong won the gold and Christin Cooper the silver in the women's giant slalom.

The race marked the first time that Americans had ever taken the first two places in an Olympic skiing event. It also brought the first Olympic skiing gold medal to the United States since Barbara Ann Cochran won the women's slalom in 1972 at Sapporo, Japan.

Meanwhile, the United States' medal hopes brightened on another front. Scott Hamilton of Denver was in the lead after the first of three days of competition by male figure skaters.

In women's speed skating, Karin Enke of East Germany won her third medal of the Games, and her second gold, by setting an Olympic record in the 1,000-meter race. The only other event in which medals were awarded today was the men's 15-kilometer cross-country ski race, won by Gunde Svan of Sweden.

The women's giant slalom, two

Continued on Page B8, Column 1

Associated Press

Debbie Armstrong celebrating her gold medal in the giant slalom — the first for the United States at Sarajevo.

Salvador Is Faulted On Diversion of Aid In Auditors' Report

By RAYMOND BONNER

Special to The New York Times

WASHINGTON, Feb. 13 — The Salvadoran Government lacks an effective mechanism for preventing the diversion of United States aid money, according to a confidential report prepared for the Agency for International Development.

One result, according to the report, is that a Salvadoran importer can "obtain foreign exchange for transfers to his offshore account." In addition, the report found that some Salvadoran businessmen were reporting "that either political influence or payoffs are necessary to obtain timely financing for imports."

The 100-page report was prepared by Arthur Young & Company, a private consulting company under contract to A.I.D., and completed in June 1983.

At a Congressional hearing late in January, Representative Michael D. Barnes, Democrat of Maryland and chairman of the House Foreign Affairs subcommittee on Latin American, referred to the report and said it showed "rampant corruption and mismanagement" in the use of United States aid to El Salvador.

He asked that the report be made public, but Administration officials re-

Continued on Page A9, Column 1

INSIDE

Iranian and Iraqi Shelling

Iran and Iraq attacked towns on each other's borders for a second day, and Iran said it had launched a major offensive into northeast Iraq. Page A6.

Alumni Donations Set Mark

Graduates of colleges in New York, New Jersey and Connecticut are sending donations in record amounts, college fund-raisers report. Page B2.

Index to Subjects

"All the News That's Fit to Print"

The New York Times

Late Edition

Weather: Sunny and cool, brisk westerly winds today; cloudy, showers possible tonight. Sunny again tomorrow. Temperatures: today 63-67, tonight 45-50; yesterday 55-69. Details, page C22.

VOL. CXXXIII . . No. 46,039 NEW YORK, WEDNESDAY, MAY 9, 1984

60 cents beyond 75 miles from New York City, except on Long Island.

30 CENTS

OHIO AND INDIANA ARE WON BY HART, BUOYING HIS DRIVE

HE LOSES 2 STATES

Mondale Takes Maryland and North Carolina to Hold Delegate Lead

By HOWELL RAINES

Gary Hart won the Presidential primaries in Ohio and Indiana yesterday, denying Walter F. Mondale the victories he needed to bring the battle for the Democratic nomination to an early close.

By winning the primaries in North Carolina and Maryland, Mr. Mondale sustained his commanding lead in the competition for delegates. He has about two-thirds of the 1,967 needed for nomination.

But by narrowly achieving his first primary victories since the voting in Connecticut on March 27, Mr. Hart prevented the former Vice President from gaining the big prize of the day, Ohio. Democratic strategists and party leaders had agreed that if Mr. Mondale could add a victory there to his triumph in the Texas caucuses last Saturday, he could have sewn up the nomination, for practical purposes.

Showdown on June 5

Now, Mr. Hart said last night, the nomination battle will continue toward a showdown on the final day of the campaign season on June 5, when California, New Jersey and three other states hold primaries. Mr. Hart's strategy calls for weakening Mr. Mondale with a series of defeats in the late primaries and then overtaking him at the Democratic National Convention in July.

With his performance, Hart aides said the Colorado Senator "bought time" to execute his strategy. Mr. Hart sounded the same theme in an appearance before supporters in Washington. He said the Ohio results showed that "the Democrats of this nation are not prepared to have this contest and this debate end at this time."

Mr. Mondale conceded shortly before midnight, ending an evening in which Mr. Hart held a narrow but steady lead of one to two percentage points in Ohio and Indiana.

Mondale Blames Himself

Mr. Mondale blamed himself for failing to reach the voters, just as he did in his initial upset defeat this year in the New Hampshire primary.

"I think I did not make my case," Mr. Mondale said in Washington. "The contrasts were not drawn as they should have been." He added, however, that he remained "confident" of winning the nomination.

The Rev. Jesse Jackson placed third in Ohio, Indiana and North Carolina and, in late returns from Maryland,

Continued on Page B10, Column 1

United Press International

PRIME LOAN RATE IS RAISED BY BANKS ½ POINT, TO 12½%

White House Says Monetary Rein of Federal Reserve Is Threat to the Recovery

By GARY KLOTT

The nation's leading banks raised their prime lending rate half a percentage point yesterday, to 12½ percent, the third such increase in two months.

The rise in the key interest rate to its highest level in 18 months brought sharp criticism by the White House of the Federal Reserve Board, which is the nation's central bank.

Larry Speakes, chief White House spokesman, said the Federal Reserve had been unduly restricting the supply of money to the national economy, thus driving up the cost of money — interest rates — and threatening to choke off the economic recovery. [Page D6.]

Economists said the rise in the prime rate, which is set by the banks, underscored the recent sharp run-up in interest rates caused by a surge in borrowing by both businesses and individuals as economic expansion continues at a stronger-than-expected pace.

Blow to Third-World Nations

Despite the comment by Mr. Speakes, the increase in the prime rate was not widely viewed among bankers as immediately threatening the general economic recovery. But it will complicate the problems of the many third-world nations whose vast debt payments are tied to the prime rate.

Further, the recent rise in mortgage and consumer loan rates has raised concerns that housing and auto sales — which are particularly sensitive to interest rate changes — will weaken.

Economists, who have been surprised by the enduring strength of the economy, said yesterday that additional rate increases were likely. "We have been anticipating further rate increases as long as the economy continues to be this strong," said Leif H.

Continued on Page D8, Column 3

MOSCOW WILL KEEP ITS TEAM FROM LOS ANGELES OLYMPICS; TASS CITES PERIL, U.S. DENIES IT

MAJOR EFFECT SEEN

If Soviet's Allies Follow, Quality Would Suffer More Than in 1980

By FRANK LITSKY

The absence of a Soviet team would drastically diminish the quality of competition at the 1984 Olympic Games in Los Angeles. If other Soviet bloc nations also stay away, many of the most successful and famous athletes in international sports will be absent — far more than when the United States withdrew from the 1980 Moscow Olympics.

The chairman of the Los Angeles Olympic Organizing Committee, Paul Ziffren, acknowledged today that the Olympic Committee faced a loss of income because of the Soviet withdrawal from the 1984 Games. But he said "adjustments" would be made in income and expenses to insure that the Games "are operated at a reasonable profit." [Page A17.]

The withdrawal of the Soviet Union from Los Angeles, if it is not reversed, would remove such gold-medal favorites as Sergei Bubka, the world's leading pole vaulter; Tamara Bykova, the world record-holder outdoors and indoors in the women's high jump; Vladimir Salnikov, winner of two swimming gold medals in 1980, and Anatoly Pisarenko, the world champion and world record-holder in super-heavyweight weight lifting.

Gymnastics Champions Affected

It would eliminate Dmitri Belozertchev and Natalia Yurchenko, the world overall gymnastics champions. It would leave at home the men's and women's basketball teams that ranked as favorites with the American teams and men's and women's volleyball teams that won gold medals in 1980.

A withdrawal by Eastern European countries allied to the Soviet Union would also eliminate East Germany, which has moved ahead of the Soviet Union in track and field and swimming. There will be 24 gold medals for

Continued on Page A17, Column 3

United Press International

Mayor Tom Bradley of Los Angeles said he rejected reasons given for the Soviet decision.

PROTESTS ARE ISSUE

Russians Charge 'Gross Flouting' of the Ideals of the Competition

By JOHN F. BURNS

Special to The New York Times

MOSCOW, May 8 — The Soviet Union announced today that it would not take part in the Olympic Games in Los Angeles this summer.

A statement issued by the Soviet National Olympic Committee said the particpation of Soviet athletes was impossible because of "the gross flouting" of Olympic ideals by United States authorities. In particular, the statement, distributed by the press agency Tass, cited plans by groups to stage anti-Soviet demonstrations during the Games and the American refusal to ban such protests.

[The Reagan Administration said the Soviet decision was "a blatant political action for which there was no real justification." The Soviet charges were heatedly denied by White House and State Department officials, as well as by several members of Congress. Page A16.]

Boycott by U.S. Recalled

In 1980, the United States led nearly 60 other nations in boycotting the Moscow Olympic Games to protest the Soviet military intervention in Afghanistan. The Soviet statement today and others in recent months have carefully avoided any suggestion that revenge might be a factor in a decision not to go to the Games in Los Angeles.

At the time of the Moscow Games, and repeatedly since, Soviet sports officials have said they oppose sports boycotts in principle.

The American boycott of the 1980 Olympics in Moscow appeared to be a factor behind the Soviet decision. News analysis, page A16.

Apparently to maintain consistency with that position, they have taken to saying in recent months that although they would not boycott the Olympics in Los Angeles, they might not send a team, a distinction that they have not further explained. The announcement today did not use the word "boycott."

Other Nations May Follow

The Soviet announcement raised the strong possibility that several Eastern European nations, as well as Cuba, Vietnam and other countries allied with Moscow, will also stay away from the Los Angeles Games.

A common front on the issue was suggested when 12 Communist nations met in Moscow early last month to discuss the issue, and subsequent statements

Continued on Page A16, Column 1

SOVIET PUTS LIMITS ON SAKHAROV WIFE

Husband Starts Hunger Strike to Get Treatment for Her

Special to The New York Times

MOSCOW, May 8 — Yelena G. Bonner, the wife of Andrei D. Sakharov, is under investigation for "defaming the Soviet system" and has been barred from leaving the city of Gorky, a friend of the couple said today.

The friend said Dr. Sakharov, the dissident physicist who was banished to Gorky four years ago, has begun a hunger strike to demand medical treatment for his wife abroad.

The friend, Irina G. Kristi, a mathematician who managed to talk to Dr. Sakharov and his wife Sunday for three minutes in Gorky, said the couple told her Miss Bonner had been put under investigation and barred from leaving the city. She said Miss Bonner had also been threatened with charges of treason.

Dr. Sakharov, Mrs. Kristi said, began a hunger strike last Wednesday to seek help for his wife, who has had several heart attacks. Mrs. Kristi quoted Dr. Sakharov as saying of his wife that he would "fast to the very end if they do not let her go abroad for medical treatment."

Mrs. Kristi said that Dr. Sakharov and his wife were outside their building when she reached their home on Sunday, and that she managed to talk with them for three minutes before the police seized her.

Mrs. Kristi said Miss Bonner told her that an investigation had been opened

Continued on Page A7, Column 1

Soldier in Quebec Opens Fire At Legislature, Killing Three

By DOUGLAS MARTIN

Special to The New York Times

QUEBEC, May 8 — A Canadian soldier who said his goal was to assassinate Quebec government officials burst into the Quebec National Assembly today, firing volleys of shots with a submachine gun. Three people were killed and 13 wounded.

"I came here to kill," the soldier shouted as he entered the Assembly building.

For a tense four and a half hours the soldier, later identified by military authorities as J. P. L. Denis Lortie, a 38-year-old corporal in the Royal 22d Regiment, held the Assembly's sergeant-at-arms hostage.

The police negotiated with Corporal Lortie by telephone as he and his hostage appeared to roam around the otherwise empty building.

Hostage Rescued Unharmed

Finally, at 2:25 P.M., the police, including a specially trained crisis team from Montreal, overwhelmed the soldier and rescued the hostage unharmed.

The soldier was dressed in military fatigues, a flak jacket and a beret. In addition to the submachine gun, he had two handguns and a hunting knife.

Little was known about the soldier. Military authorities said he was assigned to a base near Ottawa where he was a supply corporal, a job that might have given him access to weapons. The base, in effect, serves as a bunker for the Prime Minister and other Canadian leaders in the event of a nuclear war. Called Carp, it is some eight miles southwest of Ottawa.

Corporal Lortie's declared motiva-

Continued on Page A6, Column 1

Reagan Speech Tonight

President Reagan scheduled a speech on his Central America policy for 8 o'clock tonight. It will be broadcast by the television networks.

ATTACK REPORTED ON QADDAFI HOME

Libyan Leader Said to Survive an Assault by 20 Gunmen

By WERNER WISKARI

At least 20 gunmen yesterday reportedly attacked a barracks usually used as a residence by Libya's leader, Col. Muammar el-Qaddafi. After several hours of fighting, their attack was ended by Libyan troops, according to reports reaching the West from diplomats and an Italian journalist in Tripoli, the Libyan capital.

Information on the attack was sketchy and in some respects contradictory. But a diplomat said in Rome late in the day, according to The Associated Press, that Colonel Qaddafi had apparently survived another of the several attempts that have been made to overthrow him since he seized power in 1969 as the leader of a coup that ended the Libyan monarchy.

The journalist, representing the Italian news agency Ansa, said the episode began at 7 A.M. with 20 to 30 gunmen attacking the barracks on the southern outskirts of Tripoli with rocket-propelled grenades and automatic fire. He said it was not clear whether Colonel Qaddafi was inside at the time.

Nor was it established who the gunmen were and where they had come from, although people describing

Continued on Page A12, Column 1

INSIDE

Democrats' Budget Loses

The Senate rejected, in a tie vote, a Democratic plan that would have cut projected deficits by $204 billion over the next three years. Page A28.

Trials Sought in Papal Case

A prosecutor recommended that three Bulgarians and four Turks be tried in connection with the attack on Pope John Paul II in 1981. Page A4.

United Press International

POPE CELEBRATES MASS IN PAPUA NEW GUINEA: Pope John Paul II giving communion to a Catholic tribesman in Mount Hagen, Papua New Guinea. Mass was celebrated in pidgin English for 100,000 people. Page A3.

Lila Wallace, Who Bestowed Reader's Digest Wealth, Dies

Lila Acheson Wallace, the co-founder and longtime co-chairman of Reader's Digest whose philanthropic donations totaled scores of millions of dollars, died of heart failure yesterday morning at her Mount Kisco, N.Y., home. She was 94 years old and had been in declining health for some time.

The shy, strong-willed daughter of a Presbyterian clergyman, Mrs. Wallace for years wielded extensive, though indirect, influence over the Reader's Digest publishing combine through her husband, DeWitt Wallace. Mr. Wallace, who founded the magazine with his wife in 1922, died in 1981 at the age of 91.

When Mrs. Wallace chose to exercise leadership at the Digest directly, she sometimes told associates simply, "Do your best."

Mrs. Wallace took enormous interest in, and pains over, her numerous philanthropies. They ranged from large gifts to The Juilliard School of Music and the New York Zoological Society, to restoring a mansion on the Hudson River, temples at Abu Simbel in Egypt and the painter Monet's house and grounds at Giverny, France, to providing daily fresh flowers in the Metropolitan Museum of Art's Great Hall.

Once, several years ago, while appreciatively sipping a martini from a 4,000-year-old gold Egyptian cup at her Mount Kisco home, Mrs. Wallace told visitors: "If I displayed this cup, I might look at it once or twice a week. By using it, I get pleasure from it continually."

She also brought her energy and attention to detail to purchases of art, made in the magazine's name, that grew into a multimillion dollar collection. She once told an interviewer that she bought paintings not with regard to

Continued on Page B9, Column 1

The New York Times, 1972

Lila Acheson Wallace

"All the News That's Fit to Print"

The New York Times

Late Edition
Weather: Partly sunny today; cloudy, showers possible tonight. Partly sunny after lingering showers tomorrow. Temperatures: today 60-63, tonight 50-53; yesterday 57-72. Details, page C24.

VOL.CXXXIV.. No. 46,215

Copyright © 1984 The New York Times

NEW YORK, THURSDAY, NOVEMBER 1, 1984

30 cents beyond 78 miles from New York City, except on Long Island.

30 CENTS

GANDHI, SLAIN, IS SUCCEEDED BY SON; KILLING LAID TO 2 SIKH BODYGUARDS; ARMY ALERTED TO BAR SECT VIOLENCE

U.N. SAYS LEBANESE AND ISRAELIS PLAN TALKS ON PULLOUT

A Meeting of Military Teams Reported Set for Monday in South Lebanon Town

By JAMES FERON
Special to The New York Times

UNITED NATIONS, N.Y., Oct. 31 — The United Nations announced today that Israeli and Lebanese military teams would begin talks Monday in southern Lebanon on the subject of Israeli withdrawal from that region.

The conference, which is to take place at Naqura, headquarters of the United Nations Interim Force in Lebanon, also will deal with the security of Israel's northern border, which Israel has long demanded as a precondition for any withdrawal.

United Nations officials declined to discuss the agreement, indicating that to do so might jeopardize any prospect of success. Syria, which also occupies part of southern Lebanon, will not take part in the talks.

Apparently a Breakthrough

But a source familiar with the negotiations that prepared the way for the conference said that "the Israelis and the Lebanese want to get on with it and the Syrians don't want to get in the way." Diplomats here said Lebanon would almost certainly not have agreed to the negotiations without having consulted Syria.

The terse announcement appeared to represent a breakthrough in efforts by both Israel and Lebanon to end an occupation that has been costly to both. The Israelis invaded Lebanon in 1982 in an operation they said was intended to secure their northern border against attacks by Palestinians.

U.N. Role Not Specified

It was understood that the Israeli and Lebanese military teams probably would include senior staff officers. Israeli newspapers said today that the talks would be conducted directly by the two sides, but there was no confirmation of that here.

The United Nations role, similarly, was not spelled out. But the organization's involvement renewed speculation here that the role of the United Nations force in Lebanon might be expanded. Such a decision would require

Continued on Page A8, Column 1

Rebel Asserts C.I.A. Pledged Help in War Against Sandinistas

By JOEL BRINKLEY
Special to The New York Times

WASHINGTON, Oct. 31 — A senior director of the largest Nicaraguan rebel force says the Central Intelligence Agency recruited him to serve as a director two years ago and told him, "We are going to help you change the Government in Managua and do it within a year."

The officer, speaking in an interview, said the C.I.A. paid his family's expenses for more than a year and coached him and other rebel leaders on what to say in public so they would not anger members of Congress, who had to approve financing for the contras, as they are called.

In interviews at his home in Key Biscayne, Fla., the officer, Edgar Chamorro, one of seven directors of the Nicaraguan Democratic Force, gave a detailed description of the relationship between the group and the C.I.A.

He said he was telling the story now, contrary to orders he and other rebel officers received from the C.I.A., partly because he now believes that the United States is not likely to renew aid to the rebels. Aid was ended last spring.

Mr. Chamorro also said: "I resent some of the things the C.I.A. did the

Continued on Page A14, Column 1

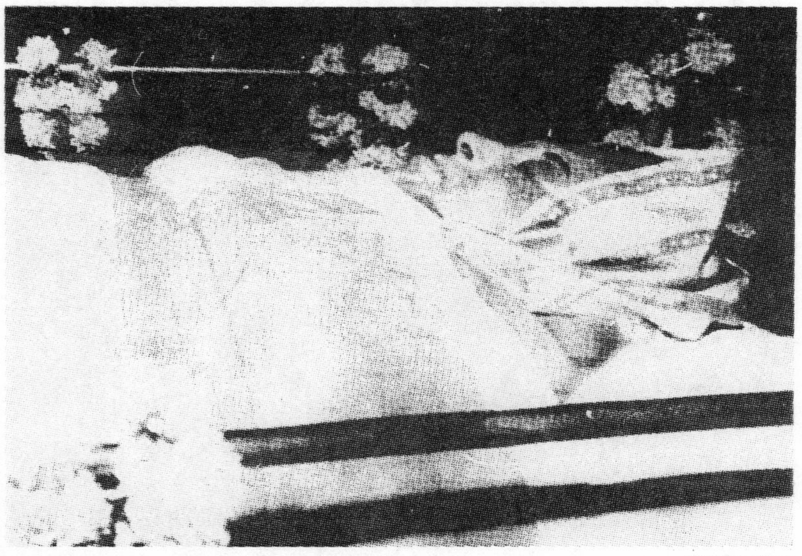

HEALTHCHECK: A BRAND-NEW ALL-ADVERTISING supplement on health, fitness, nutrition and personal well-being. Sunday, January 13 ... in The New York Times. Advertisers call (212) 556-1449—ADVT.

FOR A LIMITED TIME: HOME OR OFFICE delivery of The Times costs less than the newsstand price in most cities. Call toll-free, 1-800-631-2500 for details—ADVT.

The body of Indira Gandhi outside the All-India Institute of Medical Sciences before being taken to her residence.
Agence France-Presse

Son in Charge In New Delhi
Rajiv Gandhi

By SANJOY HAZARIKA
Special to The New York Times

NEW DELHI, Oct. 31 — Rajiv Gandhi, who was chosen today to become India's new Prime Minister after the assassination of his mother, Indira, was propelled into public life after his younger, more politically ambitious brother, Sanjay, died in a stunt plane crash in 1980.

At the time, Sanjay was regarded as his mother's likely successor and, after Mrs. Gandhi, the most powerful politician in the country. Sanjay's death left a vacuum that Mrs. Gandhi and her followers urged Rajiv to fill.

Rajiv, who is now 40 years old, apparently reluctantly resigned his job with Indian Airlines and agreed to contest an electoral race to fill Sanjay's seat in Parliament the next year. He won the election by a large margin, promising to rid Indian politics of corruption and venality, a campaign that earned him the nickname "Mr. Clean."

Better Known as Indira's Son

Yet as a freshman Member of Parliament, Rajiv was still better known as Mrs. Gandhi's unassuming elder son. After his election he began helping his mother — screening appointments, advising her on reorganizing the affairs of her ruling but decaying Congress Party and receiving petitions. Recognizing him as a major influence on his mother, party leaders began to cultivate him.

Mrs. Gandhi, who increasingly turned to him for support and advice after Sanjay's death, is also known to

Man in the News

Continued on Page A24, Column 3

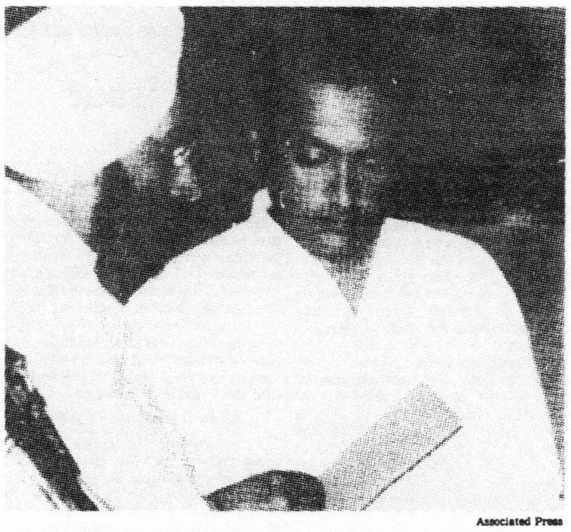

Rajiv Gandhi being sworn in as Prime Minister by President Zail Singh.
Associated Press

For India, Huge Void
Ability of Son Seen As Major Question

The writer of this dispatch, William K. Stevens, has been The Times's New Delhi correspondent since 1982.

Special to The New York Times

NEW DELHI, Oct. 31 — So thoroughly had Prime Minister Indira Gandhi dominated Indian politics over the last two decades that even some of her critics said she was what held the fractious country together.

News Analysis

Many called her Madam, Madamji, Mrs. G., Indiraji, Amma (Mother) or just "She." Not everyone thought of her in kind terms, but all knew who "She" was,

Facts and figures: a profile of India, in charts, page A22.

and her assassination leaves an incalculable void in the life of the country. Her sudden disappearance from the public scene represents a considerable challenge to the future of the Indian experiment in democracy.

Hours after her death, her 40-year-old son, Rajiv Gandhi, was sworn in as her successor. His abilities and performance are perhaps the biggest uncertainty for many people as the nation tries to adjust to the events of today.

Charan Singh, another former Prime Minister, who failed to hold an opposition Government together in 1979 and 1980, thereby paving the way for Mrs. Gandhi's return from three years out of power, expressed as much horror as anyone else when he heard the news of Mrs. Gandhi's assassination.

'Dynastic Rule' Feared

But when he heard about Rajiv Gandhi's rapid elevation, he said it confirmed his fear that "democracy is being gradually eroded in the country in order to establish a dynastic rule."

Whether that interpretation turns out to be correct, or whether Mr. Gandhi's swift installation as Prime Minister will exercise a stabilizing influence, is not clear.

What seems clearer is that Mr.

Continued on Page A19, Column 3

ATTACKS IN 8 CITIES

New Leader Tells Nation 'Maximum Restraint' Is Vital in Crisis

By WILLIAM K. STEVENS
Special to The New York Times

NEW DELHI, Thursday, Nov. 1 — Prime Minister Indira Gandhi was shot and killed at her home Wednesday by two gunmen identified by police officials as Sikh members of her personal bodyguard. Mrs. Gandhi's only surviving son, Rajiv, was sworn in Wednesday night as her successor.

Mrs. Gandhi was killed by at least eight bullets fired at close range from a submachine gun and a pistol by two men, according to police officials. One of the men was said to have been killed by other guards on the scene. The other was reported captured.

If Mrs. Gandhi was killed by Sikhs, it would be the second time since independence that an Indian leader had been the victim of a killing motivated by religious hatred. Mohandas K. Gandhi, who was not related to Mrs. Gandhi, was killed in 1947 by Hindu extremists opposed to partition.

The shooting occurred as Mrs. Gandhi, dressed in an orange-colored

The United States and the Soviet Union both assailed the assassination. Page A23.

Fierce condemnations also came from political and religious leaders in all parts of the world. Page A23.

sari, was walking from her house to her office in the same compound shortly before 9:30 A.M. (11 P.M. Tuesday, New York time). She was pronounced dead at a nearby hospital.

The assassination plunged this country, one-third the size of the United States and with more than 685 million people, into a major political crisis. As word of the assassination spread, Hindus began attacking Sikhs in the streets of the capital and in at least seven other cities. [Page A18.]

Apparently in anticipation of disorder, the army was put on alert. All military personnel on leave were called back to their posts. Approaches to New Delhi were sealed off, as were the approaches to the hospital and Mrs. Gandhi's residence.

Street violence was reported in at least six areas of New Delhi today.

Funeral Is Saturday

In his first radio broadcast to the nation as Prime Minister, Mr. Gandhi, 40 years old and previously the ranking general secretary of his mother's party, appealed for "maximum restraint" in view of the violence that was already beginning.

Mrs. Gandhi, a Hindu, had at age 66 led India for all but 3 of the last 18 years and was regarded as a major international figure. The Government announced that her funeral would be held Saturday and that she would then be cremated. Many world leaders are expected to attend the funeral.

Today, some mourners burst through barricades and surged to within 30

Continued on Page A18, Column 1

Father and Daughter: A Remembrance

By A. M. ROSENTHAL

In India's great years of hope, when Jawaharlal Nehru was Prime Minister and the people called him their beloved jewel, the young woman was almost always with him, usually not at his side, but a few steps behind.

Indira, Nehru's only child, appeared with him at receptions and meetings in New Delhi, smiling, nodding, holding her hands together gently to her forehead in greeting, murmuring a word now and then.

Boosts Up the Ladder

In villages far from New Delhi she walked behind him down dusty roads. She sat motionless on platforms while he talked to city crowds of hundreds of thousands, millions sometimes, usually scolding them for their faults, a father quite loving but quick to anger.

She was close to him and he favored her. He gave her boosts up the political ladder within his Congress Party. Then, in 1964, Jawaharlal Nehru died, and two years later, Indira Gandhi was Prime Minister.

And now she is dead herself, one more victim of the religious hatreds of India against which her father used to harangue the crowds. Now she is dead

and her son Rajiv is Prime Minister. Rajiv, whom she had selected as her heir when her first choice, her younger son, Sanjay, died in a wild, senseless airplane stunt over New Delhi, almost within sight of his mother's offices.

Because of Indira Gandhi's open and obvious preparation to turn over rule to one of her sons, the theory of Indian dynasty has been growing and now will become written into history. Father to child to grandchild, just like the old Indian rajahs.

It is a neat theory, fitting comfortably into the stereotypes of India, but at best it is only half true — and it will take time to discover whether even that half holds.

For the fact is that there is no evidence that Jawaharlal Nehru ever really thought in dynasty terms, of turning over office to Indira.

There was a closeness between them, but also a certain aloofness. For years — the years he spent in fighting for Indian independence and the years in prison that were part of that struggle — he was remote, a father she knew mostly from his jail cell letters. Then her mother, the lonely, sad, often neglected Kamala, died and Indira went off to school abroad, far from home and father.

All this was in the 1920's and 30's, and

Continued on Page A19, Column 1

INSIDE

Forecast Index Rises
The index of leading indicators, used to predict economic change, rose modestly in September, after three consecutive declines. Page D1.

Charges in Priest's Death
Poland said murder charges would be filed soon against three security officers arrested in the killing of a pro-Solidarity priest. Page A15.

Suit on Loan Bias Settled
The Household Finance Corporation settled a suit charging loan discrimination against welfare recipients, women and the unmarried. Page D32.

The Inquiry Report On the Vatican Plot

Mehmet Ali Agca, the man convicted of shooting Pope John Paul II, told Italian investigators that a second gunman had instructions to carry out the assassination if Mr. Agca was unable to get off at least five shots, according to a judicial report filed yesterday in Rome.

Key sections of the report, prepared by Judge Ilario Martella, begin on page D30.

Prime Minister Indira Gandhi with her son, Rajiv, who has succeeded her.
United Press International

"All the News That's Fit to Print"

The New York Times

Late Edition
Weather: Mostly sunny and cool today, northwesterly winds; mostly clear tonight. Mostly sunny, mild tomorrow. Temperatures: today 50-53, tonight 33-37; yesterday 42-59. Details. page A24.

VOL. CXXXIV . . No. 46,221 | NEW YORK, WEDNESDAY, NOVEMBER 7, 1984 | 50 cents beyond 75 miles from New York City, except on Long Island. | 30 CENTS

REAGAN WINS BY A LANDSLIDE, SWEEPING AT LEAST 48 STATES; G.O.P. GAINS STRENGTH IN HOUSE

Two Parties Still Split Control on Capitol Hill

House Power Battle

By STEVEN V. ROBERTS

Republicans cut into the Democratic majority in the House of Representatives last night, but their drive to shake the control of Democratic leaders seemed to fall short.

If last night's trends hold when the final votes are tallied, the House would continue to pose a major obstacle to President Reagan's legislative agenda, despite his overwhelming re-election victory.

Representative Thomas P. O'Neill Jr., the Speaker of the House, estimated that the Democrats would lose 10 to 12 seats from their majority of 99. In a television interview, he attributed the Democrats' strong showing to widespread desire in the country check Mr. Reagan's more conservative proposals.

G.O.P. Needed 25 Seats

"I believe they wanted the Democrats in there as a safety net," he said. Speaking of President Reagan, Mr. O'Neill said, "He really hasn't had coat tails."

The Republicans needed a gain of about 25 seats to give them a chance to form the sort of coalition with conservative Democrats that enacted many of Mr. Reagan's proposals during the first two years of his Presidency.

In many states, Democratic Representatives survived the Reagan landslide by distancing themselves from the national ticket and stressing their personal records of service to their constituents.

In North Carolina and Texas, the Republicans had a chance to make sweep-

Continued on Page A23, Column 1

Helms Senate Victor

By MARTIN TOLCHIN

Senate Republican candidates grasped President Reagan's coattails yesterday, but early returns indicated that they would be unable to solidify their control of the Senate.

Mr. Reagan, who spent the final week of his campaign appearing in behalf of Senate Republican candidates, seemed unable to translate his dramatic victory into significantly increasing the Republican margin in the Senate. But Democrats were similarly unable to make significant inroads into the Republican margin.

Should this pattern prevail, Mr. Reagan could expect to encounter the same resistance to some of his programs that he experienced in the last two years.

Helms Wins Bid

In the most acrimonious, expensive and closely watched Senate race, Senator Jesse Helms, Republican of North Carolina, leader of the New Right and a foe of abortion and supporter of organized school prayer, defeated Gov. James B. Hunt Jr., a moderate Democrat. The two had exchanged invectives right up to election day.

In Iowa, Senator Roger W. Jepsen, a Republican, was defeated by Representative Tom Harkin, a Democrat, in another campaign in which both candidates engaged in intensive negative campaigning.

Republicans appeared to have won an upset victory in Kentucky, where A. Mitchell McConnell, Jefferson County Judge, was narrowly leading Senator Walter D. Huddleston, a Democrat, although The Associated Press reported

Continued on Page A23, Column 3

The New York Times/Paul Hosefros

President and Mrs. Reagan claiming victory last night in Los Angeles.

MANDATE CLAIMED

Mondale Concedes Loss — Democrats Seek to Avert Realignment

By HOWELL RAINES

Ronald Wilson Reagan won a second term as President yesterday in an election that Republican leaders hailed as a sweeping personal triumph and a mandate for his policies.

Mr. Reagan secured clear landslide victories in both popular and electoral votes as he defeated Walter F. Mondale, the Democratic nominee, in at least 48 of the 50 states.

However, it remained unclear whether the powerful tide of support for Mr. Reagan ran deeply enough to carry enough Republican Congressional candidates into office to secure the "historic electoral realignment" that the President asked the voters to deliver.

Transcripts of speeches, page A21.

With more than two-thirds of the popular vote counted, Mr. Reagan led Mr. Mondale by about 59 percent to 41 percent.

The President waited until after midnight, Eastern time, to claim the election that continued his tenure as the oldest man to occupy the White House.

Entering the ballroom of the Century Plaza Hotel in Los Angeles to the strains of "Hail to the Chief," Mr. Reagan received a tumultuous welcome from a crowd that chanted, "Four more years."

"I think that's just been arranged," said Mr. Reagan with a grin.

Policy Extension Planned

He said he would use his mandate to extend the economic and military policies of his first term. But, as if answering criticisms made by Mr. Mondale, he said he would also devote his second term to limiting nuclear weapons and to "lifting the weak and nurturing the less fortunate."

"You know, so many people act as if this election means the end of something," Mr. Reagan concluded in an indirect reference to the fact that this was the last election night of his career. "To each one of you I say, it's the beginning of everything," Mr. Reagan said. Then he stirred full-throated cheers by repeating an informal slogan of his campaign, "You ain't seen nothing yet."

Mondale Affirms Principles

Mr. Mondale, looking somber and drained, conceded shortly after 11:20 P.M., Eastern time. After complimenting the President on his victory, Mr. Mondale affirmed his commitment to the principles he had championed in a long, grinding campaign.

"Let us continue to seek an America that is just and fair," Mr. Mondale said. "Tonight especially I think of the

Continued on Page A20, Column 1

Economy the Key Issue

By HEDRICK SMITH

News Analysis

For all the careful orchestration of campaign rallies and political commercials, the televised debates, the partisan clashes over fine points of foreign and military policy, it was the economy that set the basic pattern for President Reagan's stunning re-election sweep yesterday and that fueled Republican gains in Congress.

In a very real sense the election returns followed the well-established script of the Reagan Presidency to make economic policy the central issue of American politics, according to a New York Times/CBS News Poll of 5,051 people as they left the voting booths. For Ronald Reagan vaulted into the White House in 1980 largely on the strength of his biting attacks on the economy under President Carter and his telling question, "Are you better off today than you were four years ago?"

In the midterm Congressional elections two years ago, he suffered a stinging setback with the recession that eroded Republican ranks in the House of Representatives. Now this year, interviews showed, the President won a resounding vote of confidence for his handling of the economy and used it to power a coast-to-coast landslide for a second term in the White House.

His strategists were quick to contend that he had won a mandate for future policies. But the Times/CBS News poll showed that it was the electorate's feelings about the economy more than Mr. Reagan's appeals to traditional values or any specific vision for the future of what he likes to call his "second American revolution" that moved solid majorities in every region of the country into the President's column.

Broad Coalition for Reagan

Indeed, Walter F. Mondale gained more support than Mr. Reagan on his vision of the future, according to the poll. By nearly 2 to 1, however, the voters rejected Mr. Mondale's argument that a tax increase was necessary to reduce the Federal deficit, and Mr. Reagan won a big margin among those who opposed raising taxes.

Most significantly, the Election Day survey found that almost three-fifths of the voters felt the economy was better off today than four years ago, and that

Continued on Page A20, Column 2

PRESIDENT SWEEPS THE TRISTATE AREA

Connecticut Landslide Gives G.O.P. the Legislature

By FRANK LYNN

President Reagan swept New York, New Jersey and Connecticut yesterday. But except for Connecticut, he generally failed to translate his landslide margin into Republican victories in the House of Representatives and local offices.

In Connecticut, the Reagan tide enabled Republicans to gain control of both houses of the General Assembly for the first time in a decade, and to win the post held by Representative William R. Ratchford, a Democrat who was seeking his fourth term.

The President's victory over Walter F. Mondale, his Democratic opponent, in both New Jersey and Connecticut was approaching record proportions of at least 300,000 and 600,000 votes respectively.

He won New York State by at least 500,000 votes, triple his 1980 plurality in the state. He lost traditionally Democratic New York City by 300,000 votes but almost made up the entire deficit on Long Island, with victories of more than 100,000 votes each in Nassau and Suffolk Counties. The President lost only one upstate county, Albany, also a traditional Democratic stronghold.

In a hotly contested House campaign that was the most expensive in the country, Andrew J. Stein, the Democratic Manhattan Borough President,

Continued on Page B4, Column 1

State of Siege Is Imposed in Chile

By LYDIA CHAVEZ

Special to The New York Times

SANTIAGO, Chile, Nov. 6 — President Augusto Pinochet imposed a state of siege in Chile today for the first time in six years.

He acted after months of political unrest and a day after his Cabinet resigned to give him a freer hand to deal with the situation.

"It is precisely to save democracy and liberty that now more than ever it is necessary to be inflexible with respect to the institutional order that rules us," the President said at a ceremony at which he announced a new Cabinet.

Greater Powers for President

Minutes after the ceremony, a nightly curfew from midnight to 5 A.M. was imposed.

The President already had considerable powers to combat terrorism under the previous state of emergency. The press could be censored and political leaders exiled.

The main difference seems to be that under the state of siege the Goverment can hold terrorist suspects without charges for an indefinite period and trials can be delayed indefinately.

The new Cabinet brought only two minor changes. General Pinochet reappointed Interior Minister Sergio Onofre Jarpa, the chief minister, whose decision to step down Monday was followed immediately by the resignation of 15 other ministers.

Mr. Jarpa's resignation had been thought to be in protest against the Government's hard line against the opposition. But his decision to remain in the Cabinet indicated that he agrees with the Government's position.

The Government has taken an in-

Continued on Page A12, Column 1

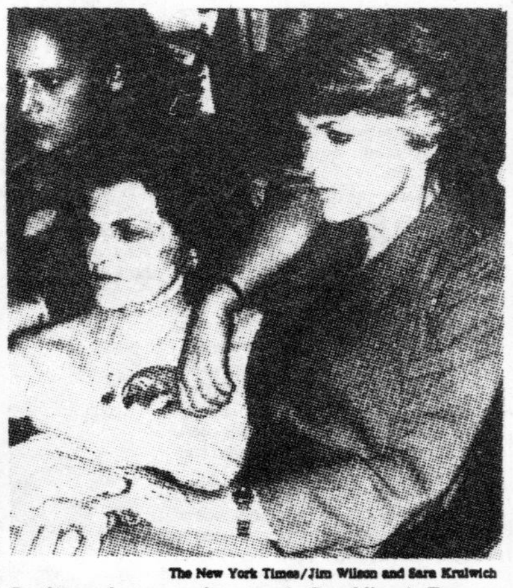

The New York Times/Jim Wilson and Sara Krulwich

Eleanor Mondale hugging her father as he appeared in St. Paul to make concession speech. Geraldine A. Ferraro was joined by her mother, Antonetta, and a daughter, Laura, in watching results at a Manhattan hotel.

Other News

Trade Talks With Russians

The United States and the Soviet Union plan talks in Moscow in January to explore ways to expand trade between the two nations. Page D1.

Catholics on Capitalism

A commission of conservative Roman Catholic business and professional leaders voiced strong support for American capitalism. Page A16.

Nicaragua Said to Get Soviet Attack Copters

By PHILIP TAUBMAN

Special to The New York Times

WASHINGTON, Wednesday, Nov. 7 — Nicaragua has received a number of Soviet-built attack helicopters in recent days, a senior Administration official said Tuesday night. He said the White House viewed their delivery as a "very serious development."

In addition, Administration officials said they were concerned about a Soviet freighter apparently headed for Nicaragua that intelligence reports indicated was carrying crates that could contain MIG fighter aircraft.

A spokesman for the Nicaragua Embassy denied that helicopters had been delivered or that MIG's were on the way.

A senior Defense Department official said the Administration was considering a variety of responses to the delivery of the helicopters because they could have an important impact on the military balance in Central America.

Although they do not represent as serious an increase in Nicaraguan fire power as would the delivery of advanced fighter planes, he said, they presented a more serious "practical problem."

Specifically, he said, the helicopters, which Soviet forces have used extensively in Afghanistan to combat insur-

Continued on Page A12, Column 1

Bradley Wins Handily in Jersey Despite Strong Vote for Reagan

By JOSEPH F. SULLIVAN

Senator Bill Bradley, Democrat of New Jersey, easily won re-election to a second term yesterday.

With more than two-thirds of the votes counted, the 41-year-old Senator led Mary V. Mochary, a 42-year-old lawyer and former Mayor of Montclair, 63 to 37 percent.

Mr. Bradley gained his victory as hundreds of thousands of voters moved between the Democratic and Republican lines on the ballot to give President Reagan an overwhelming margin in the state as well.

Mr. Reagan held a 64-to-36 percent lead over Walter F. Mondale with more than two-thirds of the votes counted. Mr. Reagan was leading in all 21 counties on his way to capturing the state's 16 electoral votes. The sweep would include Essex, Hudson and Mercer, three counties that he lost in 1980, when he won the state by 400,000 votes over President Jimmy Carter.

Mrs. Mochary telephoned Mr. Bradley at 8:45 P.M., 45 minutes after the polls closed, to congratulate him.

The Republican challenger was outspent by the incumbent, 3 to 1, and had to interrupt her campaign during the final three weeks to accompany her 44-year-old husband, Stephen, to the Stanford University Medical Center in California, where he is awaiting a heart transplant.

Mrs. Mochary said that she planned to leave for California this afternoon.

Mrs. Mochary, who talked to her supporters at the Somerset Hilton Hotel after telephoning Mr. Bradley, said she planned to run for office again, "and I'm not going to lower my sights."

Her comment prompted speculation she was thinking of running against New Jersey's other Democratic Sena-

Continued on Page B4, Column 5

"All the News That's Fit to Print"

The New York Times

Late Edition

Weather: Rain early today, tapering off to showers and ending in the afternoon; clearing tonight. Sunny tomorrow. Temperatures: today 41-49, tonight 33-37; yesterday 39-62. Details on page B2.

VOL.CXXXIV.. No. 46,346 · NEW YORK, TUESDAY, MARCH 12, 1985 · 30 CENTS

60 cents beyond 75 miles from New York City, except on Long Island.

CHERNENKO IS DEAD IN MOSCOW AT 73; GORBACHEV SUCCEEDS HIM AND URGES ARMS CONTROL AND ECONOMIC VIGOR

ISRAELI ARMY KILLS 24 IN RAID ON TOWN IN SOUTH LEBANON

Attack Across New Defense Line Follows Car-Bombing of a Military Convoy

By JOHN KIFNER

Special to The New York Times

ZRARIYAH, Lebanon, March 11 — Israeli troops stormed across their new defense line today and killed at least 24 people in a raid against this southern Lebanese village.

The raid, the fiercest of the current Israeli crackdown, came about 12 hours after a suicide car bomber crashed into an Israeli Army convoy, killing 12 Israeli soldiers.

The main street of this village was a scene of hysteria and chaos after the Israeli force withdrew just before dusk, with women shrieking and waving their hands in the air or sitting on the ground weeping.

The casualty figures were still in doubt tonight. An Israeli military announcement said 24 people it described as "terrorists" had been killed, but the Israeli radio later put the death toll at 30. The Lebanese police and local radio stations said 25 people had died.

Bodies in Burned-Out Cars

Western journalists saw six bodies in burned-out cars on the outskirts of the village and there were a number of others in the village itself.

The raid appeared to signal a determination by Israel that its "iron fist" policy would not be altered in the face of continued guerrilla resistance.

Today's raid, guerrillas and villagers said, actually began at about 11 P.M. Sunday when Israeli troops tried to infiltrate the village, which is a few miles north of their new second-stage defense line on the Litani River.

Members of the Amal Shiite militia, supported by a 30-man garrison that the Lebanese Army recently established here, fought back against the attack, militiamen and residents of the village said.

Israeli Force Put at 1,000

But at 6 A.M. today, after a heavy artillery barrage, the Israelis came from three directions in overwhelming force and pushed into the village of about 8,000 people, according to witnesses.

Militiamen and members of the local police force, who said they had been cuffed about by the Israelis, put the attacking force at as many as 1,000 soldiers and perhaps 200 to 300 vehicles.

Continued on Page A8, Column 4

Sygma/Regis Bossu; United Press International

Succession in Moscow

The announcement of the death of Konstantin U. Chernenko, above, the Soviet leader, was quickly followed by the naming of his successor, Mikhail S. Gorbachev. The move represents a shift to a new generation of Soviet leadership.

A Leader With Style — and Impatience

Special to The New York Times

MOSCOW, March 11 — Coming to power at the age of 54, Mikhail Sergeyevich Gorbachev, the peasant's son from southern Russia, is expected to bring a new style of leadership to the Kremlin. If the expectations prove correct, this leadership will be more open, perhaps, less obsessively suspicious, less burdened with memories of Stalin's terror and the war.

Man in the News

For the moment, Mr. Gorbachev seemed anxious to give fire to the program of economic change he had inherited from his mentor, Yuri V. Andropov.

He revealed his impatience in a major speech last December when he said, "We will have to carry out profound transformations in the economy and in the entire system of social relations."

'Intensive Development'

There was an echo of that today when he said, "We are to achieve a decisive turn in transferring the national economy to the tracks of intensive development."

He added, "A good deal is to be done."

What remained to be seen, however, was how Mr. Gorbachev (pronounced gore-bah-CHAWFF) would translate his impatience into action by the enormous bureaucracy that manages the Soviet Union's ponderous, creaky, centralized economy.

For all the fervor, style and obvious achievement he has displayed in reaching the highest position in the Soviet power structure, Mr. Gorbachev and the generation he represents remain an untested and largely unknown political force.

These are people who were reared after the war and after the Stalinist terrors, who grew up in a state more secure in its power and potential, men who got better educations than their predecessors and had more contact with the outside world.

Konstantin U. Chernenko was a dedicated Bolshevik but also a pragmatist. An obituary, page A14.

Yet these are also men who have made their careers in a Communist Party that has changed from an idealistic elite into an entrenched, privileged and self-perpetuating bureaucracy intolerant of too much independence or nonconformism among its members.

Under Mr. Andropov, Mr. Gorbachev worked under a seasoned politician who knew the power structure intimately from within as a consequence of his 15 years at the head of the K.G.B., the internal security and intelligence agency. And though he himself rose to the peak of Soviet power, Mr. Gorbachev's political biography did not conclusively prove his ability to wage the sort of brutal political struggle that is required to get change through the bureaucracy.

After a steady and apparently uneventful climb through the provincial party apparatus in the Stavropol region of southern Russia, north of the Caucasus, Mr. Gorbachev was brought to Moscow to take over as

Continued on Page A16, Column 1

BUSH SENT TO RITES

Reagan Decides Against Trip, but Says He Is Ready for Meeting

By BERNARD WEINRAUB

Special to The New York Times

WASHINGTON, March 11 — President Reagan decided today against attending the funeral of Konstantin U. Chernenko, but he said he was "more than ready" to meet the new Soviet leadership.

White House officials said Vice President Bush, who is in Geneva after a visit to drought-stricken African nations, would lead the American delegation to Mr. Chernenko's funeral in Moscow on Wednesday.

President's statement, page A17.

Mr. Bush also represented the United States at the funerals of Leonid I. Brezhnev in 1982 and Yuri V. Andropov in 1984. He is to be joined by Secretary of State George P. Shultz and the United States Ambassador to Moscow, Arthur A. Hartman.

'Looking Forward' to Meeting

Mr. Reagan, in his first public comments after Mr. Chernenko's death, said he was "looking forward" to meeting the new Soviet leader, Mikhail S. Gorbachev. But the President voiced doubt that Soviet policies would change in any substantive way as a result of the selection of Mr. Gorbachev.

White House officials indicated that Mr. Reagan had seriously considered flying to Moscow for the funeral to underscore American resolve to improve relations. But after a morning meeting with leading aides, Mr. Reagan decided against the trip, largely because he felt little would be accomplished by a brief visit.

"As of 4 A.M. this morning I started

Continued on Page A17, Column 1

Arms Talks Still On

The United States and the Soviet Union agreed that a new round of arms talks would go ahead as scheduled on Tuesday. Page A20.

TRANSFER IS SWIFT

New Leader, 54, Loses No Time in Offering His Own Program

By SERGE SCHMEMANN

Special to The New York Times

MOSCOW, March 11 — The Kremlin today announced the death of Konstantin U. Chernenko and, within hours, named Mikhail S. Gorbachev to succeed him as Soviet leader.

The announcement said Mr. Chernenko died Sunday evening after a grave illness at the age of 73. He had been in office 13 months, and had been ill much of the time, leaving a minor imprint on Soviet affairs.

The succession was the quickest in Soviet history, suggesting that it had been decided well in advance. Whereas the Central Committee had taken several days to name a successor to Leonid I. Brezhnev and Yuri V. Andropov, Mr. Gorbachev was confirmed in his new job 4 hours and 15 minutes after Mr. Chernenko's death was announced.

Youngest Leader Since Stalin

Mr. Gorbachev became, at 54, the youngest man to take charge of the Soviet Union since Stalin and the seventh to head the Soviet state.

"I am well aware of the great trust put in me and of the great responsibility connected with this," he said. "I promise you, comrades, to do my utmost to faithfully serve our party, our people and the great Leninist cause."

Kremlin statement and speech by Gorbachev, pages A15-A16. Autopsy report, page A19.

In his acceptance speech on being named General Secretary, he showed his impatience to start working.

"We are to achieve a decisive turn in transferring the national economy to the tracks of intensive development," he said. "We should, we are bound to attain within the briefest period the most advanced scientific and technical positions, the highest world level in the productivity of social labor."

Real Arms Cut Urged

In world affairs, he said he valued the "successes of détente, achieved in the 1970's." Referring to the Soviet-American arms talks starting Tuesday in Geneva, Mr. Gorbachev said the Soviet Union sought a "real and major reduction in arms stockpiles, and not the development of ever-new weapon systems, be it in space or on earth."

The speech was one sign that the leadership intended to pursue business as usual despite Mr. Chernenko's

Continued on Page A15, Column 1

Tass via Associated Press

Politburo members at the House of Unions in Moscow, where the body of Konstantin U. Chernenko lay in state. From the left were Vitaly I. Vorotnikov, Mikhail S. Gorbachev, the new Soviet leader, Prime Minister Nikolai A. Tikhonov, Foreign Minister Andrei A. Gromyko, Viktor V. Grishin and Grigory V. Romanov.

Reagan's Doctors Find a Growth, But Stress His Health Is Excellent

By PHILIP M. BOFFEY

Special to The New York Times

WASHINGTON, March 11 — Doctors discovered a second small growth in President Reagan's intestinal tract in his annual physical examination Friday, but the growth was not a precursor of cancer, the White House announced today.

The doctors also detected signs of blood in the President's stool, Larry Speakes, the White House spokesman, told reporters at a briefing where the doctors were not present. He said they had not determined the cause but believed it to be from the polyp or a false reading caused by the President's diet.

Over all, the results of the physical, perfomed at the Naval Medical Center in Betheeda, Md., were excellent, according to Mr. Reagan's doctors.

Capt. Walter Karney, chief of internal medicine at the naval hospital, who led the examining doctors, was quoted by the White House as saying:

"President Reagan continues to enjoy good health. His overall physical and mental condition is excellent. I am especially impressed with the fact that his blood pressure is lower than a year ago — this is quite remarkable."

The President's blood pressure while lying down was measured at 130 over 74. His pulse while resting was reported as 57 beats a minute, which Mr. Speakes described as "probably lower than most of us."

Mr. Reagan, who is 74 years old, is the oldest person ever to be President. His health and ability to perform in office became an issue in last year's campaign after he appeared to stumble verbally in a debate with the Demo-

Continued on Page A25, Column 1

INSIDE

Jets Strike Cities in Gulf

Iranian planes attacked the outskirts of Baghdad and Iraqi planes hit Iranian cities as stepped-up fighting continued for an eighth day. Page A3.

Bid-Rigging Charged

Key contractors acted to bar competition for concrete work on all major projects in New York City since 1978, a Federal lawsuit charged. Page B1.

In U.S., Cautious Hopes for Better Relations

By HEDRICK SMITH

Special to The New York Times

WASHINGTON, March 11 — The shift to a new generation of Soviet leadership has raised cautious hopes in the Reagan Administration that in the long run it will bring new vigor and decisiveness in the Kremlin and could lead to improvements in Soviet-American relations.

News Analysis

But President Reagan and his top advisers expect no significant changes in Soviet foreign policy to emerge over the next several months from the new leadership of Mikhail S. Gorbachev, a 54-year-old party official with a reputation for interest in modest internal economic changes.

The Soviet decision to pursue arms talks in Geneva, with only a token ceremonial interruption, is seen by Government specialists as a deliberate Kremlin move to project both strength of leadership and continuity of policy despite the death of the third Soviet leader in 28 months.

"Preserving the image of continuity at this point is at least as important as the fact of continuity," a State Department official said. "They are embarrassed at the succession of infirm leaders they've had," another Government specialist said, "and they don't want Chernenko's death to look as though it's hampering them."

The speed with which Mr. Gorbachev was named the General Secretary of the Communist Party was taken as evidence by officials here that the ruling Politburo made the key decision to select him as the new leader in late February, if not before.

Moreover, they see evidence that Mr. Gorbachev had been performing as the effective leader of both the party and the Soviet Defense Council in the final months of Konstantin U. Chernenko's life. Each of those developments adds

Continued on Page A17, Column 4

Young Team Takes Reins

Kremlin Starts Shift To a New Generation

By SETH MYDANS

Special to The New York Times

MOSCOW, March 11 — With the naming of Mikhail S. Gorbachev as its new leader, the Soviet Union has finally begun its long-awaited shift to a new generation of leadership.

News Analysis

The speed with which the announcement of his appointment was made and the fast pace of scheduled funeral rites suggested that plans for the succession had been firmly in place before the death of Konstantin U. Chernenko on Sunday.

The signposts of change contained in an address by the new leader, which was read immediately to the nation, showed that Mr. Gorbachev planned to take the Soviet Union forward toward changes in policy that have been on hold for the last year.

But Western and Soviet analysts here cautioned that although Mr. Gorbachev and his economic planners have been laying their plans for months, change in the Soviet Union comes slowly and with difficulty.

They said that although the new leader seemed to have stepped into his new role with vigor, it might take months or years for him to consolidate

Continued on Page A20, Column 1

"All the News That's Fit to Print"

The New York Times

Late Edition

Weather: Chance of morning showers today, sunny and cool this afternoon; clear tonight. Mostly sunny tomorrow. Temperatures: today 63-67, tonight 45-49; yesterday 60-78. Details, page C31

VOL.CXXXV. No. 46,559 | NEW YORK, FRIDAY, OCTOBER 11, 1985 | 60 cents beyond 75 miles from New York City, except on Long Island. | 30 CENTS

U.S. INTERCEPTS JET CARRYING HIJACKERS; FIGHTERS DIVERT IT TO NATO BASE IN ITALY; GUNMEN FACE TRIAL IN SLAYING OF HOSTAGE

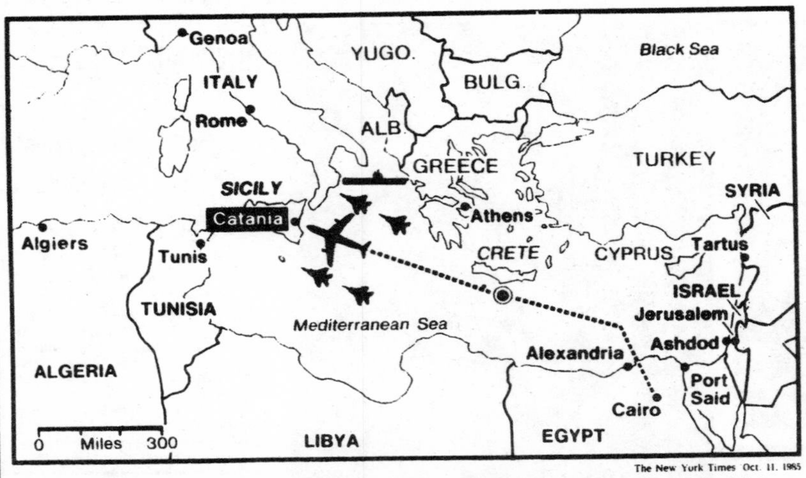

The New York Times Oct. 11, 1985

Planes from the carrier Saratoga near Albania intercepted jet south of Crete and escorted it to Sicily.

OFFICIALS SAY C.I.A. DID NOT TELL F.B.I. OF SPY CASE MOVES

Court Papers Assert Suspect Told Colleagues He Might Give Secrets to Soviet

The following article is based on reporting by Stephen Engelberg and Joel Brinkley and was written by Mr. Brinkley.

Special to The New York Times

WASHINGTON, Oct. 10 — The Central Intelligence Agency failed to notify the Federal Bureau of Investigation after it learned more than a year ago that Edward L. Howard was considering becoming a Soviet spy, Government officials said today.

According to court records, Mr. Howard told two agency employees in September 1984 that he was thinking of disclosing classified information to the Soviet Union.

Law Calls For Reporting

The bureau has sole responsibility for domestic espionage investigations and, under Federal law, the intelligence agency and all other Government agencies are supposed to report suspected espionage to the F.B.I. It is illegal for the C.I.A. or any other Federal agency to carry out surveillance or other actions within the United States to stop potential spies.

Mr. Howard, 33 years old, a former intelligence agency officer who is now a fugitive, has been charged with espionage, accused of giving Soviet officials details of American intelligence operations in Moscow. Federal officials have called the disclosures serious and damaging.

Soviet Defector Was the Key

Federal officials said the C.I.A. told the F.B.I. nothing about Mr. Howard until after the bureau began an investigation this fall based on information from a Soviet defector, Vitaly Yurchenko, who had been a senior official of the K.G.B., the Soviet intelligence agency.

The bureau began surveillance of Mr. Howard last month, but he slipped out of his home at night and is believed to have fled the country.

Senator Patrick J. Leahy, the Vermont Democrat who is vice chairman of the Select Committee on Intelligence, said today: "If the C.I.A. did not give the F.B.I. adequate information

Continued on Page B8, Column 4

PRAISE FOR PILOTS

Weinberger Will Not Say if Navy Planes Would Have Used Force

By BILL KELLER

Special to The New York Times

WASHINGTON, Friday, Oct. 11 — Secretary of Defense Caspar W. Weinberger praised Navy fighter pilots early this morning for "high military skill" in intercepting an Egyptian plane carrying four hijackers of an Italian cruise ship.

Mr. Weinberger, briefing reporters on the operation, refused to say whether the four F-14's from the aircraft carrier U.S.S. Saratoga had been prepared to use force if necessary to divert the Egyptian aircraft.

Mr. Weinberger also disclosed, in an apparent reference to American military special operations units reportedly deployed to the region, that before the hijackers of the Italian ship, the Achille Lauro, surrendered, the United States was "prepared to take action against the ship." He added, "We were prepared to do that, I think, effectively and successfully."

Details of Interception

Mr. Weinberger provided the first details of the interception.

He said the Saratoga was steaming west in the Eastern Mediterranean on a routine exercise near Albania when she received orders at about 9 P.M. local time Thursday to prepare for an interception.

At about 11 P.M., four swept-wing F-14 fighter planes took off, shortly before the Egyptian aircraft did so. Pentagon officials said two E-2C surveillance planes, smaller versions of the Awacs eavesdropping aircraft, had left the Saratoga earlier to track the Egyptian airliner. In addition, two KA-6 tankers accompanied the fighter planes in case they needed refueling.

'Very Good Intelligence'

Mr. Weinberger would not provide details of how the officers aboard the Saratoga knew the Egyptian plane was leaving the Cairo airport, or how they were certain they had the right plane. "I would say that we had very good intelligence," he said.

The fighters circled in the darkness near the island of Crete south of Greece and intercepted the Egyptian plane, a commercial Boeing 737 chartered by the Egyptian Government, at about 12:30 A.M., Mr. Weinberger said, and made radio contact.

"They were waiting in international

Continued on Page A10, Column 1

FLOWN FROM CAIRO

4 in Custody in Sicily — Washington Says It Wants Extradition

By BERNARD GWERTZMAN

Special to The New York Times

WASHINGTON, Friday, Oct. 11 — An Egyptian plane carrying the hijackers of an Italian cruise ship was intercepted by American Navy jets as it flew toward Tunisia Thursday night and was forced to land in Italy, the White House announced. A spokesman said the four terrorists had been taken into custody by Italian authorities.

In a late evening news conference, Larry Speakes, the White House spokesman, said President Reagan had ordered the dramatic military action after learning that Egypt had turned down repeated American pleas to prosecute the four gunmen and was flying them to freedom. The hijackers are believed to have killed an elderly American tourist aboard the cruise ship.

No Shots Fired

The United States intends to seek "the prompt extradition" of the hijackers from Italy, Mr. Speakes said. Later, Defense Secretary Caspar W. Weinberger said the United States hoped the Italians would waive their right to try the hijackers and would allow them to be prosecuted in the United States.

Mr. Speakes said that the Egyptian plane, a commercial 737 airliner with armed Egyptian security men aboard, was intercepted by the F-14's from the aircraft carrier Saratoga north of

News session excerpts, page A12.

Egypt in international waters. The F-14's "diverted" the plane to a joint Italian-NATO base at Sigonella in Sicily. Mr. Weinberger said four F-14's were involved.

The incident occurred without the American planes having to fire a shot, Mr. Speakes said.

Troops Surround Plane

He said the Egyptian aircraft had been headed for Tunisia but that the Tunisian Government had refused to grant it landing rights. For that, he said, the United States was grateful. Mr. Weinberger said the Egyptian plane had also been refused permission to land by authorities in Athens.

After the Egyptian plane landed, it was surrounded by American and Italian troops, Mr. Speakes said. Mr. Wein-

Continued on Page A10, Column 4

BUOYANT CAPITAL HAILS THE ACTION

Moynihan Sums Up the Mood: 'Thank God We Won One'

By BERNARD WEINRAUB

Special to The New York Times

WASHINGTON, Oct. 10 — Reagan Administration officials and legislators reacted exuberantly tonight to the news that American warplanes had seized the four hijackers who apparently killed an elderly American aboard an Italian cruise ship.

"Thank God we won one," said Senator Daniel Patrick Moynihan, Democrat of New York.

The comment summed up the mood in this startled capital after years of witnessing the Carter and Reagan administrations struggling in vain to cope with Middle East terrorism and attacks against the United States.

Iran Crisis Recalled

Officials pointed out that it was nearly six years ago that Iranian revolutionaries seized the United States Embassy in Teheran and virtually made a hostage of the Carter Administration. Mr. Carter found himself unable to fulfill his threats against terrorists and, in the case of a military raid to rescue the Americans held hostage in Iran, failed in a humiliating manner.

Mr. Reagan took office after criticiz-

Continued on Page A11, Column 4

Port in Israel Described as Target Of Terrorists Who Seized Vessel

By THOMAS L. FRIEDMAN

Special to The New York Times

JERUSALEM, Oct. 10 — The four Palestinians aboard the Achille Lauro intended to stay aboard as passengers until the cruise liner reached Ashdod, Israel, and then planned either to shoot up the harbor or take Israelis hostage, according to Israeli, Palestinian and other Arab informants. The Israelis were to be held to bargain for the release of 50 Palestinians held in Israeli jails.

The leader of the faction that ordered the operation, Mohammed Abbas, also known as Abul Abbas, is a close associate of Yasir Arafat, the chairman of the Palestine Liberation Organization, and was reportedly sent by Mr. Arafat to deal with the hijackers after their original plan to infiltrate Israel at Ashdod had gone awry.

Crew Discovered Arms Cache

According to the informants, the four members of the group aborted their plans and seized the ship when their weapons were discovered by the crew after the Achille Lauro had left Alexandria on Monday. The informants say the original plan and the hijacking were part of a bungled attempt to exact revenge for Israel's raid last week on the P.L.O. headquarters near Tunis.

When relations between the P.L.O. and Italy seemed jeopardized by the seizure of the ship and an American passenger was killed by the apparently panicked hijackers, Mr. Arafat and Abul Abbas ordered the hijackers to return to Port Said and surrender.

This picture was pieced together from information provided by Israeli Foreign Ministry and military officials, Arab analysts in Beirut and a statement issued today in Nicosia, Cyprus, by a spokesman of Abul Abbas's faction in the Palestine Liberation Front, one of the guerrilla groups in the Palestine Liberation Organization.

A copy of the statement was delivered to Reuters in Nicosia and virtually all its main points have been confirmed by Israeli or Arab sources.

The statement, which apologized to the cruise passengers for the hijacking, was believed to be the first time that a Palestinian guerrilla group has expressed regret for an attack. It was apparently occasioned by widespread condemnation of the incident in Italy and in the Arab world.

Retaliation Was Aim

According to Arab and Palestinian sources in Beirut and Nicosia, the gunmen had planned the assault on Ashdod in retaliation for the Israeli attack on the P.L.O. headquarters in Tunisia, in which about 60 people were killed. The message to Israel was to have been: "If you can reach out 1,500 miles and strike at us, we can reach out 1,500 miles and strike back at you."

Israeli merchant marine and Government sources say Israel has been on the lookout for seaborne attempts at infiltration. The sources noted that Israeli naval vessels had been observed and photographed by unidentified men when they docked at Western European ports. Now that overland routes into Israel — from Lebanon, Jordan

Continued on Page A14, Column 1

Orson Welles Is Dead at 70; Innovator of Film and Stage

United Press International

Orson Welles

Orson Welles, the Hollywood "boy wonder" who created the film classic "Citizen Kane," scared tens of thousands of Americans with a realistic radio report of a Martian invasion of New Jersey and changed the face of film and theater with his daring new ideas, died yesterday in Los Angeles, apparently of a heart attack. He was 70 years old and lived in Las Vegas, Nev.

An assistant coroner in Los Angeles, Donald Messerle, said Welles's death "appears to be natural in origin." He had been under treatment for diabetes as well as a heart ailment, his physician reported. Welles's body was found by his chauffeur.

An Unorthodox Style

Despite the feeling of many that his career — which evoked almost constant controversy over its 50 years — was one of largely unfulfilled promise, Welles eventually won the respect of his colleagues. He received the Life-time Achievement Award of the American Film Institute in 1975, and last year the Directors Guild of America gave him its highest honor, the D. W. Griffith Award.

His unorthodox casting and staging for the theater gave new meaning to the classics and to contemporary works. As the "Wonder Boy" of Broadway in the 1930's, he set the stage on its ear with a "Julius Caesar" set in Fascist Italy, an all-black "Macbeth" and his presentation of Marc Blitzstein's "Cradle Will Rock." His Mercury Theater of the Air set new standards for radio drama, and in one performance panicked thousands across the nation.

In film, his innovations in deep-focus technology and his use of theater esthetics — long takes without close-ups, making the viewer's eye search the screen as if it were a stage — created a new vocabulary for the cinema.

By age 24, he was already being described by the press as a has-been — a cliché that would dog him all his life. But at that very moment Welles was creating "Citizen Kane," generally considered one of the best motion pictures ever made. This scenario was re-

Continued on Page B6, Column 1

INSIDE

40 Salvador Soldiers Killed

A leftist rebel unit killed at least 40 Salvadoran soldiers and wounded 68 in a raid on the main army training base near La Unión. Page A3.

Yul Brynner Is Dead

The actor and director, the quintessential Siamese monarch in "The King and I," died in New York at the age of 65. Page B7.

Dodgers Go 2 Games Up

The Dodgers beat the Cardinals, 8-2, in Los Angeles and lead by 2-0, in the National League playoff, which shifts to St. Louis tomorrow. Page A29.

Hostage's Death: 'A Shot to Forehead'

By E. J. DIONNE Jr.

Special to The New York Times

PORT SAID, Egypt, Oct. 10 — Passengers from the hijacked Italian cruise liner were quoted today as describing how the terrorists had dragged an elderly American tourist in his wheelchair to the ship's side and shot him in cold blood.

The most vivid account, based on interviews with some of the more than 400 people held hostage aboard the Achille Lauro, came from the Italian Ambassador to Egypt, Giovanni Migliudo. The Ambassador told reporters that he had put together his account of the killing after six hours of interviews.

He said the killing of the tourist, Leon Klinghoffer, had taken place on Tuesday when the ship was near Tartus, Syria.

Answer 'Slow in Coming'

"The hijackers had asked to be put in contact with the Italian and U.S. Ambassadors in Damascus to demand the liberation of 50 Palestinians held in Israel," the Italian news agency, ANSA, quoted the Ambassador as saying. "But the answer was slow in coming and to exercise further pressure, the hijackers decided to kill a first hostage."

Mr. Migliudo said that all the American and British passengers on the ship were forced to lie on the deck.

"The hijackers pushed him in his chair and dragged him to the side of the boat where — in cold blood — they fired a shot to the forehead. Then the body was dumped into the sea, together with the wheelchair," the Ambassador said.

The Ambassador's story was one of many that emerged today as the ship, the Achille Lauro, lay under a searing sun in the Suez Canal harbor here.

The Austrian Ambassador to Egypt,

Continued on Page A13, Column 1

Agence France-Presse

Marilyn Klinghoffer, whose husband, Leon, was slain, being escorted off ship in Port Said. A family friend, Neil Kantor of Metuchen, N.J., is at left.

The New York Times

Late Edition

Weather: Mostly sunny and cold today, westerly winds; clear and cold tonight. Partly sunny and milder tomorrow. Temperatures: today 30-35, tonight 20-25; yesterday 20-41. Details on page 46.

VOL.CXXXV..No. 46,637 Copyright © 1986 The New York Times NEW YORK, SATURDAY, DECEMBER 28, 1985 60 cents beyond 75 miles from New York City, except on Long Island. **30 CENTS**

AIRPORT TERRORISTS KILL 13 AND WOUND 113 AT ISRAELI COUNTERS IN ROME AND VIENNA

REAGAN TO TRADE TELEVISION TALKS WITH GORBACHEV

New Year's Day Greetings Are to Be Broadcast at Same Time in Both Nations

By GERALD M. BOYD
Special to The New York Times

LOS ANGELES, Dec. 27 — President Reagan and Mikhail S. Gorbachev have agreed to exchange videotaped New Year's Day greetings that are intended for broadcast in the United States and the Soviet Union, the White House announced today.

The announcement said the exchanges would give Mr. Reagan his first chance to talk to the Soviet people directly on television and would give the Soviet leader the same chance to speak to the American people.

The announcement came as Mr. Gorbachev, in Moscow, offered a cautiously upbeat assessment of relations between the Soviet Union and the United States, saying points of "potential convergence" had emerged in arms control talks. [Page 3.]

'Barbaric Methods' Assailed

Shortly before the announcement, Mr. Reagan, who flew here today to begin a weeklong vacation, issued his latest statement condemning the Soviet intervention in Afghanistan.

The statement, noting the sixth anniversary of the intervention, accused the Russians and their surrogates of resorting "to barbaric methods of waging war" to try to crush a liberation effort in Afghanistan. Mr. Reagan said the United States stood "squarely on the side of the people of Afghanistan."

The videotape exchange will achieve a longtime Administration goal of having Mr. Reagan talk on Soviet television.

Three to Five Minutes Long

Late today, the news divisions of the American networks indicated that they all planned to broadcast both addresses.

The speeches, both of which are to be broadcast on Wednesday, are to be three to five minutes long and will contain New Year's greetings, the officials said. One White House aide said Mr.

Continued on Page 3, Column 5

Further Growth In the Economy Forecast for '86

But Inflation and Jobless Rate Worry Analysts

By ROBERT D. HERSHEY Jr.
Special to The New York Times

WASHINGTON, Dec. 27 — The United States economy seems headed for a fourth consecutive year of expansion in 1986, but its course will be marred by gradually rising inflation and stubbornly high unemployment, according to a consensus of business and academic forecasters.

The possibility of a recession, which at various times in the last year has seemed just over the horizon, has receded and is no longer regarded as an apparent threat.

One important reason is the roaring bull market in stocks and bonds. By making investors richer, it has raised both confidence and the outlook for consumer spending, which accounts for two-thirds of the economy.

'Rather Sluggish Fashion'

"The prospects for the economy in 1986 are quite good," said A. Gilbert Heebner, chief economist for the Philadelphia National Bank, in a prediction that typifies current professional thinking. "It's going to seem like more of the same, with the economy growing but in a rather sluggish fashion."

The Reagan Administration, for its part, is believed to have tentatively adopted a 4 percent growth forecast for next year, somewhat higher than that of most private analysts.

To be sure, few economists or politicians are satisfied with the current rate of American growth, less than 2.5 percent for 1985 after 6.6 percent in 1984. This year's rate has been barely enough to keep unemployment from rising and it has left industry with large amounts of idle productive capacity.

Moreover, agriculture and parts of the oil, real estate and banking industries are in disarray despite an expansion that this month reached its third anniversary. Weak farm and crude oil prices, as well as a glut of unrented office space in some cities, could cause more problems for banks in 1986.

Yet most economists predict solid growth for 1986. They cite several factors for this tempered optimism. Both

Continued on Page 31, Column 4

VICTIMS: Bodies bearing tags affixed by police on the floor at Leonardo da Vinci Airport near Rome. *Reuters*

SUSPECT: A man suspected as a terrorist being taken into custody after the attack on the Rome airport. *Agence France Presse*

4 ATTACKERS KILLED

Gunmen Fire Into Crowds and Throw Grenades Near Lines at El Al

By JOHN TAGLIABUE
Special to The New York Times

ROME, Dec. 27 — Terrorists hurled grenades and fired submachine guns at crowds of holiday travelers at airports in Rome and Vienna today in attacks on check-in counters of El Al Israel Airlines.

Authorities quoted by news services said the gunmen had killed at least 13 people, including 4 Americans, and wounded 113 in the two attacks. Four terrorists were killed, and three others were wounded and captured.

While El Al appeared to be a target in both attacks, the authorities said the terrorists in Rome had also thrown grenades and fired indiscriminately with Soviet-made assault rifles into crowds of New York-bound passengers checking in at Pan American World Airways and Trans World Airlines.

Terrorists Not Identified

The assailants, who were not immediately identified, left the two airline terminals strewn with bloodied and torn bodies, luggage, overturned furniture and broken glass.

Israeli Government officials asserted that the Palestine Liberation Organization might be responsible, but P.L.O. officials here and in Tunis denied any role in the apparently coordinated attacks.

Witnesses at the airport in Vienna said panic broke out as the explosions and firing began, with passengers and airport staff throwing themselves to the ground and crawling desperately for cover. [Page 4.]

Gunmen Jumped and Shrieked

Similar accounts were given in Rome, where survivors described chaos amid thundering explosions and raking bursts of gunfire unleashed by young masked men in blue jeans who jumped up and down and shrieked as their victims fell. Bystanders screamed and dived for cover.

"It was an inferno — they started throwing hand grenades and firing with submachine guns," said one witness who was wounded in Rome, Dora Silvestri. "We all threw ourselves to the ground. Blood spread over the floor. I

Washington said the attackers were "beyond the pale of civilization." Page 5. These comments were echoed worldwide. Page 6.

fell on the body of a girl, and a grenade splinter hit me in the face."

As the weary and shaken travelers caught in the airport attacks returned to New York, some of them told of their minutes of terror in a series of interviews. [Page 6.]

The authorities said seven terrorists were apparently involved — four in the attack in Rome, which began shortly after at 9 A.M. (3 A.M. New York time), and three in the attack in Vienna, which started a few minutes later.

At Leonardo da Vinci Airport at Rome, three terrorists were slain and one was seized after being wounded in a gun battle with the police and plainclothes Israeli security men in the terminal. Security had been increased there after recent hijackings and official warnings that airports might be attacked during the Christmas holidays.

A total of 13 people were killed in the Rome attack, including the three terrorists, and 70 wounded.

[A wounded American man died later at a Rome hospital, The Associated Press reported from Rome.]

At Schwechat Airport in Vienna, 3 were killed, including a gunman, and 47 wounded, one of them critically.

Two of the terrorists in Vienna were seized after a wild car chase and a run-

Continued on Page 4, Column 3

Road Repairs to Snarl Traffic On Both Sides of East River

By DEIRDRE CARMODY

A section of the Brooklyn-Queens Expressway near the Williamsburg Bridge will be closed in January for reconstruction, and the work is expected to cause heavy traffic on the Brooklyn and Manhattan ends of the bridge for more than a year.

The project, beginning in mid- to late January, is part of a five-year, $2.6 billion state program to rebuild many of the city's highways. The starting date depends on the availability of construction crews, according to the City Bureau of Traffic Operations.

70,000 Vehicles a Day

Westbound traffic on the expressway, which the Traffic Bureau says is used by about 70,000 vehicles a day, will be rerouted at the Wythe Avenue exit in Brooklyn onto Williamsburg Street West for two and a half blocks. Cars will be able to get back on the expressway at the Flushing Avenue entrance.

Williamsburg Street West has been widened by a lane and a shoulder has been added. The Flushing Avenue entrance has also been widened by a lane.

"It is not an easy detour, not one we look forward to," said Traffic Commissioner Samuel I. Schwartz.

The detour is not expected to be able to carry all the traffic, but according to Abel Silver, a spokesman for the City Transportation Department, some of the vehicles that normally take the Brooklyn and Manhattan Bridges into

Continued on Page 26, Column 1

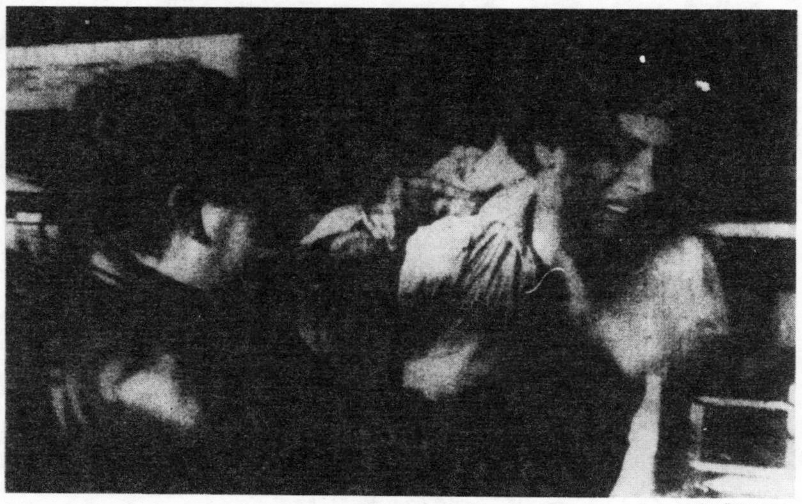

The New York Times/Dec. 28, 1985

Williamsburg Bridge will carry more Manhattan-bound traffic.

Israel, Blaming P.L.O., Issues a Warning

By THOMAS L. FRIEDMAN
Special to The New York Times

JERUSALEM, Dec. 27 — Although the Palestine Liberation Organization denied involvement in the attacks in Rome and Vienna, Israeli officials blamed the guerrilla group today and made it clear that Israel would respond at the appropriate time and place.

"Israel is shocked and outraged by these two new acts of senseless terror against innocent civilians," a Foreign Ministry statement said.

"The terrorist attacks come against a background of declarations by the head of the P.L.O., and those Arab states that support this organization, that these terrorists will cease terrorist operations outside of Israel. Israel will continue its struggle against terrorism in every place and at any time it sees fit."

Syrian Missiles in Lebanon

Meanwhile, Israeli analysts said Israel's ability to retaliate for the attacks had been limited by Syria's decision to move mobile surface-to-air missiles into Lebanon.

In the past, Israel has often retaliated for terrorist attacks abroad by bombing Palestinian guerrilla bases in Lebanon, regarding these as convenient "return addresses."

To do so now, however, Israeli jets would have to penetrate the new curtain of surface-to-air missiles Syria has drawn over the Bekaa region in Lebanon, which could lead to an all-out war with Syria, the analysts said.

Since Israel already destroyed the main P.L.O. compound in Tunisia last October, that too is no longer an option for retaliation. The analysts said new P.L.O. offices in Baghdad would not be easy to reach and were widely dispersed. This would seem to leave as the only option for retaliation a more surgical strike against specific individuals, the analysts said.

A Political Statement

To appreciate the full Israeli quandary, officials said, it must be understood that the Syrian decision to deploy the SAM-6 and SAM-8 mobile batteries a few miles inside Lebanon, for the second time in a month, was as much a political statement as a strategic military maneuver.

It was apparently designed, Israeli officials say, to send Israel and the United States clear signals about Damascus's intentions to change some of the rules in the Middle East.

To begin with, said Itamar Rabinovich, an authority on Syria at Tel Aviv University, the Syrians are apparently trying to establish a new relationship with Israel in Lebanon after the Israeli withdrawal.

While Israel wants to hold onto all of its old perquisites in Lebanon, particularly its freedom to fly reconnaissance missions over the Syrian-controlled Bekaa, the Syrians want to reverse once and for all this free Israeli access to their neighboring client state.

"By sending the missiles back, the

Continued on Page 5, Column 1

For Families of 2 Americans, Sudden Sorrow

By SARA RIMER

Natasha Simpson, the 11-year-old daughter of a foreign correspondent in Rome, was on her way to New York with her family for a three-week vacation with friends and relatives. John Buonocore 3d, a 20-year-old student, was on his way home to Wilmington, Del., after a semester in Rome, just in time for his father's 50th birthday.

Both died at Leonardo da Vinci Airport in Rome yesterday. They were among the 14 people killed there when terrorists hurled hand grenades and opened fire with submachine guns into crowds of holiday travelers. The Associated Press said two other Americans, Frederick Gage, of Madison,

Wis., and Don Maland, of New Port Richey, Fla., were also killed.

Natasha Simpson was killed apparently as her father, Victor L. Simpson, a New Yorker who is the news editor for The Associated Press in Rome, tried to shield her from the bullets. Mr. Simpson, 43, was wounded in the right wrist and hand.

'Put His Arm Around Her'

"I think he put his arm around her to try and push her down and that's how he injured his finger," said his wife, Daniela Petroff Simpson, who was reached by telephone at her parents' home in Rome.

Mrs. Simpson, 40, had been outside the terminal walking the family terrier

while her husband and two children — Natasha and 9-year-old Michael — checked in for their flight to Kennedy International Airport. Then she heard the exploding grenades.

"Suddenly there was a shattering noise as if something were collapsing," Mrs. Simpson, who is also a journalist, told The Associated Press in Rome. "And then there were machine-gun bursts. Two distinct machine-gun bursts. And then silence. I rushed into screams and cries and saw my husband dripping blood from his hand and my son on the floor shot in the stomach."

Mr. Simpson and his son were hospi-

Continued on Page 6, Column 3

INSIDE

3 on Miami Force Arrested
Three members of the Miami police force were charged with murder in the drownings of three men thought to have been dealing in drugs. Page 8.

West Side Rail Proposal
New York State and New York City are studying the possibility of a light rail line — perhaps a monorail — on Manhattan's West Side. Page 25.

ENTIRE STOCK REDUCED TO COST, TWO DAYS remaining. Sat. 12-28 & Sun. 12-29 9AM-9PM. Jenny Bailey Antiques. Call (212) 410-6210 or 831-6432. 1326 Mad. Ave. SW cor of 94th St.—ADVT

"All the News That's Fit to Print"

The New York Times

Late Edition

Weather: Partly cloudy and cold today, chance of snow; chance of snow tonight. Partly cloudy, cold tomorrow. Temperatures: today 27-30, tonight 13-19; yesterday 14-23. Details, page C19.

VOL.CXXXV . . . No. 46,669 NEW YORK, WEDNESDAY, JANUARY 29, 1986

50 cents beyond 75 miles from New York City, except on Long Island. 30 CENTS

THE SHUTTLE EXPLODES

6 IN CREW AND HIGH-SCHOOL TEACHER ARE KILLED 74 SECONDS AFTER LIFTOFF

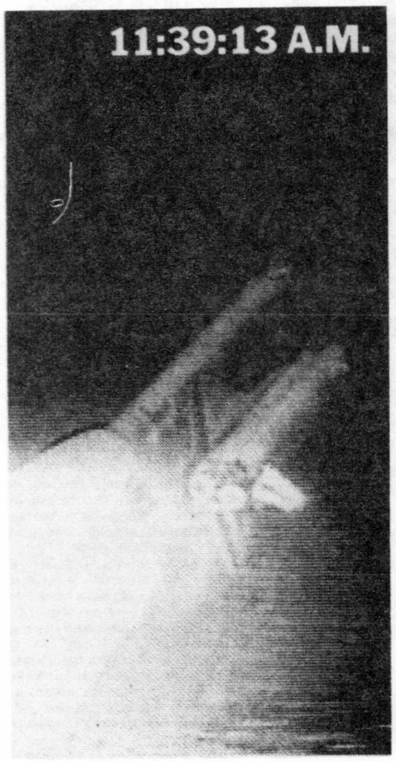

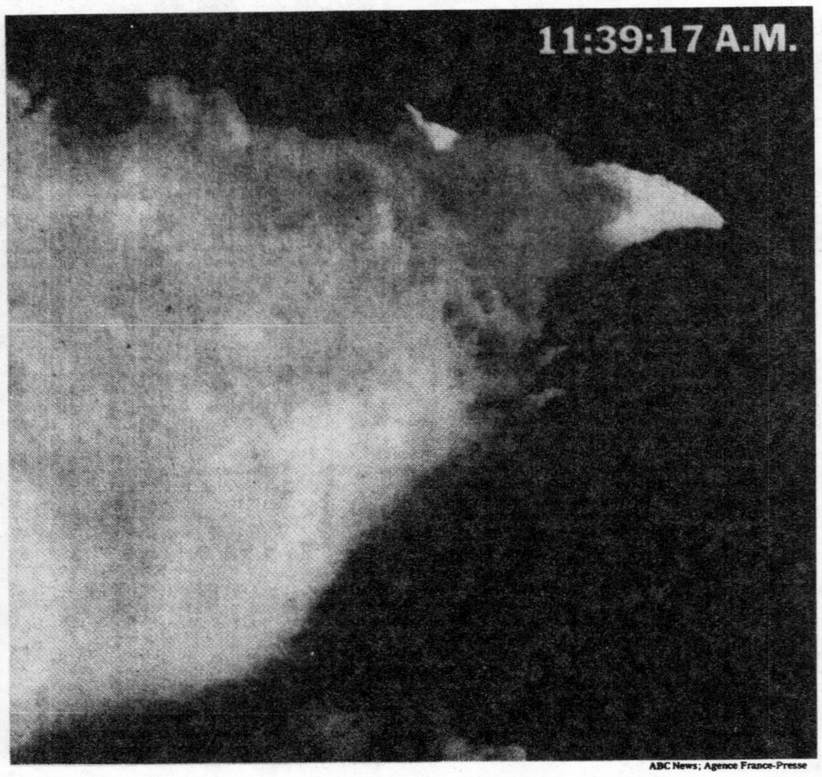

ABC News; Agence France-Presse

From the Beginning to the End

The last flight of the shuttle Challenger lasted about 74 seconds. Here is the transcript, as recorded by The New York Times, of its final moments, before and after liftoff.

PUBLIC AFFAIRS OFFICER: Coming up on the 90-second point in our countdown. Ninety seconds and counting. The 51-L Mission ready to go. . . .

T minus 10, 9, 8, 7, 6, we have main engine start, 4, 3, 2, 1. And liftoff. Liftoff of the 25th space shuttle mission and it has cleared the tower. . . .

MISSION CONTROL CENTER: Watch your roll, Challenger.

PUBLIC AFFAIRS OFFICER: Roll program confirmed. Challenger now heading down range. [Pause.] Engines beginning throttling down now at 94 percent. Normal throttle for most of flight 104 percent. Will throttle down to 65 percent shortly. Engines at 65 percent. Three engines running normally. Three good cells, three good ABU's. [Pause.] Velocity 2,257 feet per second, altitude 4.3 nautical miles, down range distance 3 nautical miles. [Pause.]

Engines throttling up, three engines now at 104 percent.

MISSION CONTROL: Challenger, go with throttle up.

FRANCIS R. SCOBEE, CHALLENGER COMMANDER: Roger, go with throttle up.

PUBLIC AFFAIRS OFFICER: One minute 15 seconds, velocity 2,900 feet per second, altitude 9 nautical miles, down range distance 7 nautical miles. [Long pause.]

Flight controllers here looking very carefully at the situation. [Pause.]

Obviously a major malfunction. We have no downlink [communications from Challenger]. [Long pause.]

We have a report from the flight dynamics officer that the vehicle has exploded.

After the Shock, a Need to Share Grief and Loss

By SARA RIMER

The nation came together yesterday in a moment of disaster and loss. Wherever Americans were when they heard the news — at work, at school or at home — they shared their grief over the death of the seven astronauts, among them one who had captured their imaginations, Christa McAuliffe, the teacher from Concord, N.H., who was to have been the first ordinary citizen to go into space.

Shortly before noon, when the first word of the explosion came, daily events seemed to stop as people awaited the details and asked the same questions: "What happened? Are there any survivors?"

In offices, restaurants and stores, people gathered in front of television sets, mesmerized by the terrible scene of the shuttle exploding, a scene that would be replayed throughout the day and night. Children who had learned about Mrs. McAuliffe were watching in classrooms across the country.

It seemed to be one of those moments, enlarged and frozen, that people would remember and recount for the rest of their lives — what they were doing and where they were when they heard that the space shuttle Challenger had exploded. The need to reach out, to speak of disbelief and pain, was everywhere. Family members telephoned one another, friends telephoned friends.

"It was like the Kennedy thing," said John Hannan, who heard the news when his sister called him at his office, a personnel recruiting concern in Philadelphia. "Everyone was numb."

'I Felt Very Close to Her'

Florine Israel, a legal secretary at the New York Civil Liberties Union, echoed the sentiments of many who spoke of Mrs. McAuliffe not as an astronaut but as a friend. "I felt very close to her," she said. "She was ordinary people. She was a mother, a working woman. I felt like I was a part of it."

The image of the shuttle exploding flashed across 100 television sets in the electronics department of Macy's, in midtown Manhattan, where a crowd of workers from nearby offices and facto-

Continued on Page A3, Column 1

How Could It Happen? Fuel Tank Leak Feared

By MALCOLM W. BROWNE

Debris from the explosion of the shuttle Challenger was scattered so widely over the Atlantic Ocean that investigators may never recover enough of it to pin down the cause of the disaster. But suspicions quickly focused on the craft's huge external fuel tank, a potential bomb that carried more than 385,000 gallons of liquid hydrogen and more than 140,000 gallons of liquid oxygen at liftoff.

The most logical explanation is that a large leak must have occurred either in the tank itself or in the pipeline and pumping system that carried liquid hydrogen to the orbiter's three main engines.

Barbara Schwartz, a spokesman for the Johnson Space Center, acknowledged that pure liquid or gaseous hydrogen cannot burn; only if the pure hydrogen carried in the rear section of the shuttle's tank were allowed to come into contact with air, or with the liquid oxygen in the tank's nose section, could it have burned or exploded.

Potential Dangers of Hydrogen Gas

But what might have started the leak, and what could have ignited the explosion that followed?

Parallel questions, never fully answered, were raised after the fire that destroyed the German airship Hindenburg as it was landing at Lakehurst, N.J., on May 6, 1937. The shuttle Challenger, like the Hindenburg, had been releasing hydrogen gas into the air shortly before the disaster, and some of the gas might have remained aboard the craft, mixed with air and ready to detonate if exposed to the smallest spark.

Neither NASA nor Martin Marietta Aerospace, the manufacturer of the external fuel tank, would comment yesterday on possible causes of the disaster.

But the geometry of the shuttle's external fuel tank, as described by official manuals from NASA and the Rockwell International Corporation, a major shuttle contractor, suggest one potential danger point in particular: the "intertank," or midsection of the structure, which separates the liquid oxygen tank from the liquid hydrogen tank. The bulk of the hydrogen fuel is closest to the liquid oxygen at this point, and a rupture or leak in the plumbing or walls of the intertank could have flooded the two fluids together to create a gigantic bomb.

Suggestions that the unseasonably cold weather at

Continued on Page A4, Column 1

Thousands Watch A Rain of Debris

By WILLIAM J. BROAD

Special to The New York Times

CAPE CANAVERAL, Fla., Jan. 28 — The space shuttle Challenger exploded in a ball of fire shortly after it left the launching pad today, and all seven astronauts on board were lost.

The worst accident in the history of the American space program, it was witnessed by thousands of spectators who watched in wonder, then horror, as the ship blew apart high in the air.

Flaming debris rained down on the Atlantic Ocean for an hour after the explosion, which occurred just after 11:39 A.M. It kept rescue teams from reaching the area where the craft would have fallen into the sea, about 18 miles offshore.

It seemed impossible that anyone could have lived through the terrific explosion 10 miles in the sky, and officials said this afternoon that there was no evidence to indicate that the five men and two women aboard had survived.

No Ideas Yet as to Cause

There were no clues to the cause of the accident. The space agency offered no immediate explanations, and said it was suspending all shuttle flights indefinitely while it conducted an inquiry. Officials discounted speculation that cold weather at Cape Canaveral or an accident several days ago that slightly damaged insulation on the external fuel tank might have been a factor.

Americans who had grown used to the idea of men and women soaring into space reacted with shock to the disaster, the first time United States astronauts had died in flight. President Reagan canceled the State of the Union Message that had been scheduled for tonight, expressing sympathy for the families of the crew but vowing that the nation's exploration of space would continue.

Killed in the explosion were the mission commander, Francis R. (Dick) Scobee; the pilot, Comdr. Michael J. Smith of the Navy; Dr. Judith A. Resnik; Dr. Ronald E. McNair; Lieut. Col. Ellison S. Onizuka of the Air Force; Gregory B. Jarvis, and Christa McAuliffe.

Mrs. McAuliffe, a high-school teacher from Concord, N.H., was to have been the first ordinary citizen in space.

After a Minute, Fire and Smoke

The Challenger lifted off flawlessly this morning, after three days of delays, for what was to have been the 25th mission of the reusable shuttle fleet that was intended to make space travel commonplace. The ship rose for about a minute on a column of smoke and fire from its five engines.

Suddenly, without warning, it erupted in a ball of flame.

The shuttle was about 10 miles above the earth, in the critical seconds when the two solid-fuel rocket boosters are firing as well as the shuttle's main engines. There was some discrepancy about the exact time of the blast: The National Aeronautics and Space Administration said they lost radio contact with the craft 74 seconds into the flight, plus or minus five seconds.

Two large white streamers raced away from the blast, followed by a rain of debris that etched white contrails in the cloudless sky and then slowly

Continued on Page A5, Column 4

Reagan Lauds 'Heroes'

President Reagan, shaken by the explosion of the space shuttle, postponed his State of the Union Message. "We mourn seven heroes," he said in a talk broadcast from the White House after the disaster. "There will be more shuttle flights and more shuttle crews and, yes, more volunteers, more civilians, more teachers in space."

He also sought to console the nation's pupils, many of whom saw telecasts of the loss of the teacher who was to have been sent into space. Article and transcript, page A9.

Francis R. Scobee
Commander

Michael J. Smith
Pilot

Judith A. Resnik
Electrical Engineer

Ellison S. Onizuka
Engineer

Ronald E. McNair
Physicist

Gregory B. Jarvis
Electrical Engineer

Christa McAuliffe
Teacher

"All the News That's Fit to Print"

The New York Times

Late Edition

Weather: Mostly cloudy, windy today, chance of snow; cloudy tonight. Partly cloudy and continued cold tomorrow. Temperatures: today 33-37, tonight 20-25; yesterday 19-25. Details on page 48.

VOL. CXXXV . . . No. 46,679 | Copyright © 1986 The New York Times | NEW YORK, SATURDAY, FEBRUARY 8, 1986 | 30 cents beyond 75 miles from New York City, except on Long Island. | 30 CENTS

DUVALIER FLEES HAITI TO END FAMILY'S 28 YEARS IN POWER; GENERAL LEADS NEW REGIME

Associated Press

President Jean-Claude Duvalier of Haiti, right, and his wife, Michèle, arriving at the airport in Port-au-Prince.

20 REPORTED DEAD

Cheers Turn to Violence —Ruler and Wife Fly to France in U.S. Jet

By JOSEPH B. TREASTER

Special to The New York Times

PORT-AU-PRINCE, Haiti, Feb. 7 — President Jean-Claude Duvalier boarded a United States Air Force jet and fled to France before dawn today, ending the 28-year grip of his family on this impoverished Caribbean nation.

In a videotaped message broadcast after he had been in the air several hours, Mr. Duvalier said he had stepped down after two months of tumultuous anti-Government protests to spare the nation of six million people a "nightmare of blood."

Moments later, Lieut. Gen. Henri Namphy, the commander of the armed forces, went on the air to announce that the army had taken over. He said he had acted with Haiti nearly paralyzed and the "specter of civil war" rising.

Interim Council to Rule

He said the armed forces would govern the country with an interim six-member ruling council that includes two civilians.

Mr. Duvalier's flight came after months of unrest over economic conditions and political repression in this country, the poorest in the Western hemisphere. It also came a week after the White House issued an erroneous announcement that Mr. Duvalier had fled.

General Namphy, 53 years old, gave assurances that the military did not "entertain any political ambition," indicating that it expected to perform its traditional mission of providing a transition power until elections could be held.

Cheers and Blaring Horns

Mr. Duvalier's departure, along with his wife, Michèle, their children, his mother and about 20 other relatives, was greeted in the capital with a riot of cheers and blaring horns. But the celebration soon turned violent.

A supervising doctor at the national university hospital said 20 people had been killed by early afternoon, half of them members of Mr. Duvalier's special police force, known as the Tontons Macoute. Seventy-five others were reported hurt.

At one point, mobs broke into the stone mausoleum of François Duvalier, Jean-Claude's father and predecessor as President, next to the presi-

Continued on Page 4, Column 3

Jamaica Said to Play a Key Role In Persuading Duvalier to Leave

By BERNARD GWERTZMAN

Special to The New York Times

WASHINGTON, Feb. 7 — The Jamaican Government secretly played a central role in persuading President Jean-Claude Duvalier to flee Haiti, United States and Jamaican officials said today.

The officials said Jamaica had convinced Mr. Duvalier, who called himself President for Life, that he had to leave for the sake of the people of Haiti and the Caribbean.

Jamaica Tells the U.S.

Mr. Duvalier and his family and associates were flown to France from Haiti early this morning aboard a United States Air Force C-141. But the primary impetus for his decision to leave was attributed by senior State Department officials to a member of the Jamaican Government whom the Duvalier family knew.

After the Jamaicans held discussions with the Duvaliers and persuaded them to leave, Jamaica told the United States, and American officials added pressure on Mr. Duvalier to leave, senior State Department officials said.

According to a Jamaican official, who confirmed the initial account by American officials, Prime Minister Edward P. G. Seaga of Jamaica sent a special representative to Haiti last Sunday.

The representative was Dr. Neville Gallimore, Minister of Social Security in the Jamaican Government. He met with Mr. Duvalier for three hours last Sunday in Port-au-Prince and discussed the options "facing the regime, and encouraged the President to leave office for the good of his people and the Caribbean in general," the Jamaican official said.

2d Meeting Is Held

A second meeting was held for one hour Monday, with Michèle Duvalier joining her husband in the talks. In that session, Dr. Gallimore requested a decision by Tuesday on whether he would leave.

On Tuesday, according to American and Jamaican officials, Mr. Duvalier told Dr. Gallimore that he would leave Wednesday. But on Wednesday he had no place to go to, and he began to waver, American officials said.

The Governments of Greece, Spain and Switzerland said Wednesday that they had turned down requests for asylum from Mr. Duvalier. But a senior American official said, "Those requests actually came from associates of Michèle, we think, and not from Duvalier himself."

The American Ambassador, Clayton E. McManaway Jr., and his staff in Haiti began telling all of President Duvalier's associates that Washington firmly believed that the only way he could survive as President would be to

Continued on Page 5, Column 1

Agence France-Presse

Haitians celebrating the departure of President Jean-Claude Duvalier as they rode through Port-au-Prince. News of his leaving was heralded by the ringing of a single church bell early yesterday morning. Page 4.

BOTH SIDES CLAIM THEY ARE LEADING IN PHILIPPINE VOTE

VIOLENCE REPORTED

Early Official Tally Gives Aquino Slight Edge — Marcos Confident

By SETH MYDANS

Special to The New York Times

MANILA, Saturday, Feb. 8 — Corazon C. Aquino claimed victory today in the Presidential election while President Ferdinand E. Marcos said only, "I probably have won."

The official Government vote count, after coming to a near halt on the afternoon and night of Election Day Friday, began moving slowly ahead and put Mrs. Aquino in a slight lead in sketchy early returns.

A respected poll-watching group that is relied on here to offer an independent assessment put Mrs. Aquino in the lead by a larger margin with more than a quarter of the vote recorded.

Aquino Statement

In a statement issued by her office, Mrs. Aquino said: "The trend is clear and irreversible. The people and I have won and we know it. Nothing can take our victory from us."

"Mrs. Aquino plans to call on Marcos to arrange for an orderly transition of power," an Aquino spokesman said today. He said the call would be made "when the trend is irreversible, probably within the next 48 hours."

A spokesman for the President called an urgent press conference at 3:30 A.M. to condemn Mrs. Aquino's statement and urged that no claims of victory be made until all returns are in.

'Systematic Harassment'

At least 30 people were reported killed in Election Day violence amid widespread reports of vote fraud and intimidation at the polls.

Senator Richard Lugar, the co-chairman of an official delegation of American observers, accused the Government today of trying to "shape the return" by reporting votes from areas where the President is strong while holding back on the results from Manila, where Mrs. Aquino has her heaviest support.

"The Manila vote has been held down by systematic harassment," said the Indiana Republican. "My own political judgment is that the Government concluded the results from Manila would not be good."

National Assembly's Role

Meanwhile, the speaker of the National Assembly, Nicanor Yniguez, appeared on Government television to remind voters that no matter what the various counts showed, it is his Government body that will assess them and declare the winner.

Mr. Yniguez, a close ally of Mr. Marcos, said the legislature would begin its

Continued on Page 6, Column 1

Reuters

A monitor for a citizens' group protecting a ballot box as it was removed from a voting station.

Gunmen Seize Votes At Polling Stations In Philippine Town

By FRANCIS X. CLINES

Special to The New York Times

MUNTINLUPA, the Philippines, Feb. 7 — The voting ended at 3 P.M., and 30 minutes later, just as the ballot boxes were unlocked for the counting, the gunmen arrived at the Bayanan elementary school.

They fired rifles into the air in the courtyard and burst into classroom after classroom, shouting and pointing their weapons at voters and poll watchers, seizing ballot boxes to be carried off or to be spilled and restuffed with false ballots.

Screaming in fright, the people fell to the floor and ducked under desks. "Mother of God!" someone shouted as the thugs darted past, wearing T-shirts with the message, "Vote Intelligently."

The gunmen moved quickly, kicking the long day's labor of marked ballots aside like chaff and moving into the room of Precinct 135 where they found Pedro San Juan, the poll inspector, defiantly hugging the voting box to his chest.

The intruders struck him with a gun butt. They cut his arm and finally tore the box loose.

In an adjoining room, Christina

Continued on Page 6, Column 4

Kremlin Shifts On 'Star Wars,' Diplomats Say

By PHILIP TAUBMAN

Special to The New York Times

MOSCOW, Feb. 7 — The Soviet Union will not insist that the United States abandon development of a space-based missile defense as a condition for an agreement to reduce medium-range nuclear weapons, Western diplomats said today.

They said that after some weeks of uncertainty about the Soviet position, American officials were recently told privately that Moscow would not link an accord on medium-range nuclear weapons to President Reagan's program to develop a space-based missile shield. The program, the Strategic Defense Initiative, is popularly known as the "Star Wars" plan.

Position Is 'Crystal Clear'

The diplomats said Mikhail S. Gorbachev, the Soviet leader, made a definitive statement about the issue in a meeting Thursday in the Kremlin with Senator Edward M. Kennedy, Democrat of Massachusetts.

"The Soviet position is now crystal clear, and it increases the odds that an interim agreement on medium-range weapons can be reached before the next summit meeting between Reagan and Gorbachev," one diplomat said.

[A new Joint Chiefs of Staff assessment disputes President Reagan's assertion that Moscow has violated a commitment on deployment of missile launchers and intercontinental bombers. Page 6.]

A Clear Separation

The diplomats said Moscow remained adamant in its insistence that progress on limiting long-range nuclear weapons is impossible unless Washington renounces development of the space defense program.

Mr. Kennedy is to return to Washington on Saturday. American diplomats said that he did not brief the United States Embassy about his conversations with Soviet officials but that

Continued on Page 6, Column 5

U.S. JUDGES HOLD NEW BUDGET LAW UNCONSTITUTIONAL

Supreme Court Is to Consider Ruling, Which Is Based on Separation of Powers

By ROBERT PEAR

Special to The New York Times

WASHINGTON, Feb. 7 — A panel of three Federal judges ruled unanimously today that a key provision of a new budget-balancing law was unconstitutional because it violated the principle requiring separation of powers among the branches of Government.

The Court ruled that Congress could delegate authority over the budget to the President or people answerable to him but could not shift it to the Comptroller General of the United States or other people removable by Congress itself through legislation. The ruling now goes to the Supreme Court for a final determination of new law's constitutionality.

Significance in Many Areas

The decision by the Federal District Court here has broad legal, political and economic significance. The statute in question was widely regarded as the most important step taken by Congress in many years to reduce the budget deficit.

The provision the panel struck down was intended to give teeth to the budget-balancing law, and some legislative leaders said today that its loss could undermine any effort to reach a compromise on shrinking the deficit to zero by 1991. [Page 9.]

More immediately, if upheld on appeal the decision would invalidate $11.7 billion of budget cuts for the current fiscal year that President Reagan ordered Saturday under the new law.

The judges stayed the effect of their ruling to permit supporters of the law to appeal. The law explicitly authorizes a direct appeal to the Supreme Court,

Continued on Page 9, Column 3

A Victory for Reagan

The ruling striking down provisions of the budget-balancing law is a significant but bittersweet victory for the President. News analysis, page 9.

Immunity Granted General Dynamics As Navy Lifts Ban

By RICHARD HALLORAN

Special to The New York Times

WASHINGTON, Feb. 7 — The Navy announced today that it had restored the General Dynamics Corporation's eligibility to bid for Government contracts because the company had made progress in correcting its shortcomings.

In addition, the Navy granted the leading military equipment contractor immunity from further suspensions that might be the consequence of new indictments arising from three grand jury investigations or 10 to 15 other investigations of the company that are under way.

The Navy had banned the company from receiving such orders Dec. 3, a day after it and four former or current executives were indicted on Federal fraud charges.

Government regulations require that a company be suspended from receiving all Government contracts if an indictment against it is handed up by a grand jury.

Everett Pyatt, the Assistant Secretary of the Navy who negotiated the agreement, told reporters late this afternoon that it would not make sense to suspend General Dynamics, already suspended twice in the last year, for wrongdoings that it was correcting.

"We believe they are in a major reformation in the way the company operates," Mr. Pyatt said. Left unsaid

Continued on Page 35, Column 1

After 9 Babies Die in 14 Years, Mother Is Held

By AMY WALLACE

Special to The New York Times

SCHENECTADY, N.Y., Feb. 7 — Year after year, one after the other, the babies of Mary Beth Tinning died, nine of them over the past 14 years. The causes were listed variously as natural or undetermined or sudden infant death syndrome.

There were six autopsies, but never any signs of abuse. There were whispers and suspicions. But somehow no one — not the police, the coroner, doctors, social workers or neighbors, not even Mrs. Tinning's husband — detected something evil in the strange pattern of deaths.

"There were so many of us in on it, I guess," said Dr. Robert L. Sullivan, Schenectady County's Chief Medical Examiner. "If anyone is negligent, I suppose I am. I probably should have said, 'There must be more to it than this.' But we all think, and don't do."

It was not until Wednesday, when the police charged Mrs. Tinning, who is 43 years old, with suffocating her 3-month-old daughter, Tami Lynne, with a pillow last Dec. 20, that investigators said they believed that all nine of her children, including one who was being adopted, may have been murdered by their mother since 1972.

Dr. Sullivan, 57, who has been the part-time medical examiner since 1968, said there might have been incomplete examinations of the deaths and lapses of communication among doctors and public officials.

The medical examiner, who is responsible for investigating all unexplained deaths, said he did not know why four of the deaths were not reported to his office.

He also said he regretted that he and other doctors who serve as his assistants had not been more diligent in noting the pattern of the deaths.

Investigators began looking into the case when an employee of St. Clare's Hospital called the police after Tami Lynne was brought to the hospital dead. They said Mrs. Tinning had made "statements and admissions" — which they declined to make public —

Continued on Page 30, Column 5

INSIDE

Conviction in Spy Case

A retired analyst for the Central Intelligence Agency was convicted by a Federal jury of spying for the Chinese for more than 30 years. Page 8.

Jobless Rate Drops to 6.6%

A sharp increase in job growth helped push the nation's jobless rate in January down to 6.6 percent, the lowest level in nearly six years. Page 50.

A Taste of Winter

Two storm systems with high winds brought four to eight inches of snow — the first real taste of winter — to New York City and its suburbs. Page 30.

2 California Banks to Merge

Two San Francisco banks will merge in a $1.08 billion transaction that will create the nation's 10th largest banking company. Page 33.

"All the News That's Fit to Print"

The New York Times

Late Edition

Weather: Mostly sunny and cold today; cloudy, chance of snow tonight. Continued cold, chance of snow tomorrow. Temperatures: today 28-32, tonight 20-23; yesterday 21-38. Details, page D11.

VOL.CXXXV.. No. 46,697 Copyright 1986 The New York Times NEW YORK, WEDNESDAY, FEBRUARY 26, 1986 50 cents beyond 75 miles from New York City, except on Long Island 30 CENTS

MARCOS FLEES AND IS TAKEN TO GUAM; U.S. RECOGNIZES AQUINO AS PRESIDENT

ROCKET ENGINEERS TELL OF PRESSURE FOR A LAUNCHING

Testify NASA Forced Them to Reverse Decision-Making Role on Shuttle Safety

By PHILIP M. BOFFEY
Special to The New York Times

WASHINGTON, Feb. 25 — Rocket engineers testified today that pressure from the space agency to launch the space shuttle Challenger forced them to reverse their normal role — that instead of having to prove that the shuttle was ready to go, it was up to them to show that a launching would be unsafe.

The engineers from Morton Thiokol Inc., which manufactured the shuttle's booster rockets, described a series of tense meetings and telephone conferences on Jan. 27, the day before the launching that resulted in an explosion that killed seven astronauts. They said that in those discussions they felt pressure from NASA officials to allow the launching to proceed unless they could prove beyond doubt that disaster would result.

Key hearing testimony, page B6.

Meanwhile today, James M. Beggs resigned as Administrator of the National Aeronautics and Space Administration. He had been on leave while facing fraud charges resulting from his tenure as an executive of the General Dynamics Corporation. [Page B7.]

The Thiokol engineers' testimony came at a hearing of the Presidential commission that is investigating the Challenger accident. "I felt pressure," said one of them, Brian Russell. "I felt we were in the position of having to

Continued on Page B7, Column 1

The New York Times/ Marilyn K. Yee
Allan J. McDonald, engineer for Morton Thiokol, as he testified.

Gorbachev Says U.S. Arms Note Is Not Adequate

Also Tells Party Change In Economy Is Urgent

By SERGE SCHMEMANN
Special to The New York Times

MOSCOW, Feb. 25 — Addressing a landmark meeting of the Soviet Communist Party, Mikhail S. Gorbachev today criticized President Reagan's recent response on arms reduction and said the timing of the next summit meeting could hinge on progress in arms control.

The Soviet leader's comments were included in a speech of five and a half hours on the state of the Soviet Union in

Excerpts from speech, page A11.

the opening session of the 27th congress of the ruling party.

Addressing 5,000 delegates and 152 foreign delegations, Mr. Gorbachev presented a sweeping overview of the problems facing the nation, most of which he blamed on stagnation under the 18-year rule of Leonid I. Brezhnev ending in 1982. Mr. Gorbachev said the key to the future was a qualitatively new approach to Soviet economic development.

Focus on Medium-Range Missiles

Two days ago, Mr. Reagan responded in a letter to a proposal made Jan. 15 by Mr. Gorbachev to eliminate nuclear arms by the year 2000 in a sequence of three stages. Mr. Reagan focused on the first of these stages, involving the elimination of medium-range nuclear missiles.

Mr. Gorbachev said in his speech that he presumed the timing of the response was intended to solicit his reaction at the congress.

He said that Mr. Reagan's proposal "seems to contain some reassuring opinions and theses," but that these "are swamped in various reservations, 'linkages' and 'conditions'".

"To put it in a nutshell," Mr. Gorbachev said, "it is hard to detect in the letter we have just received any serious readiness of the United States Administration to get down to solving the cardinal problems involved in eliminating the nuclear threat."

'No Sense in Empty Talks'

On the question of a summit meeting, Mr. Gorbachev essentially made any further planning contingent on progress in arms control.

"There is no sense in holding empty talks," he said.

Mr. Gorbachev and Mr. Reagan had agreed last November in Geneva that the Soviet leader would visit the United States this year, but officials in Washington have been saying that Moscow has evaded setting a date.

Mr. Gorbachev made clear that this

Continued on Page A10, Column 3

Associated Press
A looter slashing a painting of Ferdinand E. Marcos at presidential palace, which was stormed last night.

Shultz Praises 'Peaceful Transition' in Philippines

By GERALD M. BOYD
Special to The New York Times

WASHINGTON, Wednesday, Feb. 26 — The Reagan Administration moved quickly Tuesday to recognize the new Government of Corazon C. Aquino.

At the same time, the Administration praised what it called the peaceful manner in which Ferdinand E. Marcos had relinquished his 20-year rule as President of the Philippines.

The Administration had issued a statement Monday urging Mr. Marcos to resign. Tuesday, Secretary of State George P. Shultz welcomed the new Government only hours after Mr. Marcos, his family and other associates fled the presidential palace in Manila aboard United States helicopters.

Administration's Involvement

Mr. Marcos's abrupt departure capped days of close involvement by the Administration in the Philippines situation. That involvement was deepened when Senator Paul Laxalt, after conferring with President Reagan, told Mr. Marcos "the time has come" for him to surrender power. Senator Laxalt, a Republican of Nevada and a close friend of Mr. Reagan, had served as his special emissary to Manila last October.

"With the peaceful transition to a new Government of the Philippines, the United States extends recognition to this new Government headed by President Aquino," Mr. Shultz said in a statement pledging United States cooperation.

U.S. Encourages Reconciliation

Larry Speakes, the White House spokesman, said the Administration welcomed Mrs. Aquino's call for "reconciliation and nonviolence" and looked forward to working with the new Government on changes in political, military and economic areas. He said Philip C. Habib, the special Reagan envoy, was en route to Manila to discuss how the United States could help.

A senior Administration official said Mr. Reagan would telephone both Mrs. Aquino and Mr. Marcos, possibly as early as today. He said Mr. Reagan wanted to wait before contacting the new President because things were "unsettled" in the Philippines.

Mr. Shultz said the shift in power should have no effect on relations be-

Continued on Page A14, Column 1

From a Symbol to a Leader: The Rise of Corazon Aquino

Special to The New York Times

MANILA, Wednesday, Feb. 26 — Corazon C. Aquino began to exercise presidential power even before Ferdinand E. Marcos left the country today, telling some of the country's most powerful men what they would be doing in her Cabinet, and making a key decision about the nation's top financial institution.

She did so in the same quiet-spoken manner in which, as a self-described housewife, she had hovered in the background during the political career of her husband, Benigno S. Aquino Jr.

Her manner today, however, obscured a personal transformation that has been noted both by political analysts and by members of her own family, who say they have watched her grow in strength and confidence.

In the four months since she decided to run for office, Mrs. Aquino, a genuinely reluctant candidate, has moved from being a symbol around which the nation could unite to being a leader.

"It's astonishing," says a member of her husband's family. "She was just a housewife. Her strength has astonished all of us. The transformation is amazing. It has even affected her children, who have grown as well."

Mrs. Aquino's cool and even tone, her advisers say, overshadows the stubbornness and growing self-assurance that have put her in increasing command of their inner councils. Her self-assurance, they say, has been reinforced by the broad popular support that has continued to grow for the woman who has styled herself "almost the complete opposite" of Mr. Marcos.

One Aquino adviser, Teodoro Locsin, said, "By the end of the election, she realized that now she was speaking for the entire nation."

Mrs. Aquino had also come to demonstrate a greater familiarity with the issues than she had in an interview published

Continued on Page A13, Column 1

20-YEAR ERA ENDS

'New Life' for Philippines Seen by Successor — Nation Celebrates

By SETH MYDANS
Special to The New York Times

MANILA, Wednesday, Feb. 26 — Ferdinand E. Marcos fled the Philippines Tuesday, ending 20 years as President. Corazon C. Aquino succeeded him, saying "a new life" had begun for her country.

Mr. Marcos, facing pressure from all sides to step down, left the presidential palace shortly after 9 P.M. (8 A.M. Eastern standard time) and traveled by helicopter to Clark Air Base.

There, accompanied by his wife, Imelda, and Gen. Fabian C. Ver, a close associate and former chief of the Philippines military forces, he boarded an American Air Force plane for Guam, a United States territory in the Pacific.

[A Defense Deaparment statement said 55 people were in Mr. Marcos's party aboard two aircraft, The Associated Press reported from Agana, Guam.]

Greeted by Acting Governor

Mr. Marcos arrived at Andersen Air Force Base in Guam this morning, where he was greeted by Acting Gov. Edward D. Reyes.

In Washington, officials said the 68-year-old leader, who reportedly suffers from a kidney ailment, would receive treatment at the Naval Medical Center on Guam. One official described his hospitalization as precautionary.

According to a Defense Department spokesman in Washington, Mr. Marcos was to leave Guam this evening (between 5 A.M. and 8 A.M. E.S.T.) for an unspecified air base near Honolulu.

The departure of Mr. Marcos from Manila ended a day in which he pleaded with Washington for help in clinging to office, then went through an inaugural ceremony that was held apparently after he had decided to leave.

Aquino Too Is Inaugurated

Mrs. Aquino was also inaugurated in the morning to head what was dubbed a provisional government, and although Mr. Marcos made no public resignation when he departed, the United States immediately recognized her administration.

The news of Mr. Marcos's departure set off celebrations in the capital as hundreds of thousands of Filipinos surged into the streets, honking horns, setting off firecrackers and burning tires.

As crowds converged on the presidential palace, fighting broke out between supporters and opponents of Mr. Marcos. Stones and knives were used in the clashes, and a number of injuries were reported. Eventually, a noisy crowd surged into the palace, tearing down portraits of Mr. Marcos and his wife and helping themselves to souvenirs.

Earlier, three civilians were reported killed in Manila during a pitched battle between loyalist and rebel troops for control of a television transmitting tower.

In Washington, the Reagan Administration hailed Mrs. Aquino for "her commitment to nonviolence" while praising Mr. Marcos for a decision "characterized by the dignity and strength that have marked his many years of leadership."

Request to Stay Rejected

The official said that even after Mr. Marcos arrived at Clark Air Base, he asked if he could remain in his home province in northern Luzon, but that the Aquino side refused.

Legal questions remained to be resolved about Mrs. Aquino's mandate following the Feb. 7 election in which Mr. Marcos was proclaimed the winner

Continued on Page A12, Column 3

High Court Backs Use of Zoning To Regulate Showing of Sex Films

By STUART TAYLOR Jr.
Special to The New York Times

WASHINGTON, Feb. 25 — The Supreme Court held today that local zoning officials have broad powers to restrict the location of movie theaters showing sexually explicit material.

Extending a 1976 decision that allowed Detroit to prevent "skid row" concentrations of adult theaters by dispersing them around the city, the Court ruled that a town may limit such theaters to a small area away from homes, schools, churches and parks.

The Justices announced several other decisions today, including their ruling that states cannot require utility companies to include in their billing envelopes the messages of groups with which they disagree. [Page A20.]

Limit on Protection Reaffirmed

In the sex movie case, the seven-Justice majority rejected arguments by a theater owner that the zoning ordinance in Renton, Wash., might effectively ban adult theaters altogether by restricting them to an industrial area where no "commercially viable" sites were available.

While the First Amendment guarantees sexually explicit entertainment facilities "a reasonable opportunity to open and operate," Associate Justice William H. Rehnquist wrote for him-

self and five others, it does not require zoning under which they "will be able to obtain sites at bargain prices."

On Monday, in striking down an Indianapolis law that outlawed pornographic materials that "subordinate women" as a form of sex discrimina-

Continued on Page A20, Column 1

INSIDE

Cable TV and 3 Boroughs

Groups set up by three borough presidents have spent more than $700,000 on local programs for cable television systems still being readied. Page B1.

Consumer Prices Up 0.3%

The Consumer Price Index increased last month by the smallest amount since September. Food and energy costs were restrained. Page D1.

About New York ... B3	Man in the News ... B7	
Around Nation ... A18	Movies ... C17,C22	
Books ... C17,C21	Music ... C17,C20,C22	
Bridge ... C20	Obituaries ... B9	
Business Day ... D1-26	Op-Ed ... A23	
Crossword ... C21	Real Estate ... D26	
Dance ... C19,C21-22	Sports Pages ... B10-14	
Day by Day ... B4	Theaters ... C20	
Editorials ... A22	TV / Radio ... C22-23	
Going Out Guide ... C20	Washington Talk ... B8	
Living Section ... C1-15	Weather ... D11	

News Summary and Index, Page B1.

Classified Ads ... B15-N Auto Exchange ... B111

THE FIRST OFFICIAL SPECTATOR'S GUIDE TO One Lap of America by Brock Yate in The Sunday New York Times on April 7. Advertising details by calling 212-556-1564 ADVT

WAS THIS CITY'S THE TIMES delivered to you? Home and office delivery is available in many U.S. cities. Get details by calling toll free 1-800-631-2500 ADVT

The New York Times/ Larry C. Morris
NETS' STAR BANNED: Micheal Ray Richardson, who was barred from playing in the N.B.A. after a positive cocaine test. Page B11.

For Marcos, a Restless Night of Calls to U.S.

By BERNARD GWERTZMAN
Special to The New York Times

WASHINGTON, Feb. 25 — It was about 3 A.M. today in Manila and President Ferdinand E. Marcos was telephoning to find out whether the message he had received from Washington calling for "a peaceful transition" to a new government actually meant he should quit.

Senator Paul Laxalt, who received the call in Washington — where it was 2 P.M. Monday — told Mr. Marcos that Mr. Marcos was "a desperate man,

clutching at straws," even though he would be formally sworn in for another term as President in about nine hours.

Mr. Marcos told the Nevada Republican, whom he seemed to trust as a confidant of President Reagan, that he did not want to resign. Nor did he want to come to the United States, where he might be harassed by congressional committees.

The telephone call touched off the events that led to Mr. Marcos's reluctant decision to give up his fight to remain as President only hours after his inaugural ceremony. But, according to

senior Administration officials, Mr. Marcos has resisted accepting Mr. Reagan's offer of a safe haven in the United States.

Even after being taken to Clark Air Base by a United States Air Force helicopter, Mr. Marcos asked the United States Embassy to intercede with those close to Corazon C. Aquino and ask if he could be allowed to live in his home province of Ilocos Norte in northern Luzon.

According to a senior American official, the Aquino side refused on the grounds that passions were running too

Continued on Page A14, Column 4

CONCORDE/1ST CLASS DEEP DISCOUNT
NET FARE CORP (212) 645-1050 ADVT

MOOMSDAY HITS METROPOLITAN AREA.
HEAD FOR EINSTEIN MOOMJY ADVT

"All the News That's Fit to Print"

The New York Times

Late Edition

Weather: Partly cloudy and cool today, southwesterly winds; fair tonight. Mostly sunny and milder tomorrow. Temperatures: today 53-57, tonight 40-43; yesterday 41-52. Details, page C18.

VOL.CXXXV. No. 46,724 | NEW YORK, TUESDAY, MARCH 25, 1986 | 30 CENTS

80 cents beyond 75 miles from New York City, except on Long Island.

U.S., CITING LIBYAN FIRE, REPORTS ATTACKING A MISSILE SITE AND SETTING 2 SHIPS ABLAZE

Aquino May Disband Legislature While a New Charter Is Drafted

By FRANCIS X. CLINES
Special to The New York Times

MANILA, March 24 — President Corazon C. Aquino is expected to abolish the National Assembly and begin exercising "nearly absolute power," the national television station reported tonight.

The plan was described as a temporary step to having voters approve a new constitution and legislature.

After considerable internal dispute, Mrs. Aquino's plan is likely to provide for the drafting of a proposed constitution by committee rather than by an elected convention and for national elections this fall, according to Government officials familiar with the plan.

The President's spokesman, Rene Saguisag, cautioned tonight against speculation about Mrs. Aquino's decision, which is scheduled to be announced Tuesday. The President, who has kept her own Cabinet guessing and, in fact, furiously debating the shape of a reformed government, could alter existing plans at the last minute, he said.

November Elections Possible

While Mr. Saguisag was cautionary, Vice President Salvador Laurel has indicated that elections may be proposed for November to renew both local executive offices and national legislative offices under a plan submitted to Mrs. Aquino by a committee of advisers.

Mr. Laurel indicated that her current thinking is to abolish the parliamentary-style National Assembly, formally known as the Batasang Pambansa, and seek a constitution providing for a system with an elected bicameral legislature.

Such a step presumably would obviate the question of whether the National Assembly should rescind its certification of Ferdinand E. Marcos as President and proclaim her instead. The assembly acted following the disputed Feb. 7 election amid a national outcry that Mr. Marcos's majority in the assembly was stealing the election from Mrs. Aquino.

Interim Council Proposed

Some advisers have recommended keeping the assembly at least temporarily as a token indication of her wish to share power and not be absolutist in this provisional stage. Others have said the National Assembly remains too much a symbol of the Marcos era since its majority had routinely backed his authoritarian rule.

One recommendation she was reported considering was to try and ease this "absolutist" charge by designating some of her Cabinet members and other appointees as a "legislative council" designed to provide an additional governmental presence. This would, however, be merely advisory.

One point of considerable debate has been whether to define Mrs. Aquino's interim rule as "revolutionary," as

Continued on Page A3, Column 1

World Bank Plans $1.5 Billion In New Aid to Latin Debtors

By CLYDE H. FARNSWORTH
Special to The New York Times

WASHINGTON, March 24 — The World Bank, beginning Tuesday, is expected to approve $1.5 billion in loans to Latin America as part of its effort to help resolve the debt crisis.

The loans, all expected to be approved before the end of April, represent the bank's largest commitment ever to Latin America in such a brief period. The aid includes $1 billion for Mexico, which has been crippled by the collapse of world oil prices.

The loan agenda, described by World Bank officials, is a sign that the bank is responding to a call for increased lending by Treasury Secretary James A. Baker 3d. "These loans are a product of what Baker advocated in Seoul," said a bank spokesman, Peter Riddleberger, referring to a speech Mr. Baker made in South Korea last October at the annual meeting of the World Bank and its sister institution, the International Monetary Fund.

The bank's board of directors, representing its 149 member governments, is scheduled Tuesday to approve $465 million in loans to Mexico, including $400 million for reconstruction needed as a result of an earthquake last Sept. 19 that severely damaged Mexico City.

Other large loans in the final stages of negotiation include $500 million to Mexico to assist in trade liberalization and $350 million to Argentina to speed agricultural reforms. Colombia and Ecuador are among the other countries expected to receive World Bank aid.

Focus Is on Economies

The external debt of Latin American countries is about $380 billion, two-thirds of which is owed to commercial banks, so the World Bank loans are just a small step in solving the crisis. They are not intended to repay other loans, but to make the economies of the borrowing nations grow faster.

The loan negotiations, which have been going on for more than a year in some cases, have been influenced by Secretary Baker's agenda and the nations' increasing willingness to do their part under the Baker proposal to deregulate and free up their economies.

Mr. Riddleberger said the loan agreements were converging at this time because "this happens to be when the countries' internal policies now

Continued on Page D8, Column 5

Rocket Bombs Fired At the U.S. Embassy And Palace in Tokyo

By SUSAN CHIRA
Special to The New York Times

TOKYO, Tuesday, March 25 — Small homemade bombs were fired this afternoon at the United States Embassy and the Imperial Palace, the police said.

There were no injuries, and no damage was reported.

The bombs appeared to have been launched from parked cars outside the United States Embassy and the western gate of the Imperial Palace, known as the Hanzomon Gate, according to the Tokyo Metropolitan Police.

The bombs appeared to have been constructed from small aluminum cans that were filled with gasoline. The police found what appeared to be timing and launching devices inside the trunks of the cars.

The attacks occurred despite police measures to tighten security in preparation for the summit of industrialized nations to be held in Tokyo in May. The television news station NHK reported that Prime Minister Yasuhiro Nakasone called today for tighter security measures.

Police and United States Embassy officials said they did not know who had launched the bombs. But the police speculated that the attackers were left-

Continued on Page A3, Column 1

Reuters

An A-7 warplane taking off from the U.S. carrier Saratoga yesterday in the Gulf of Sidra.

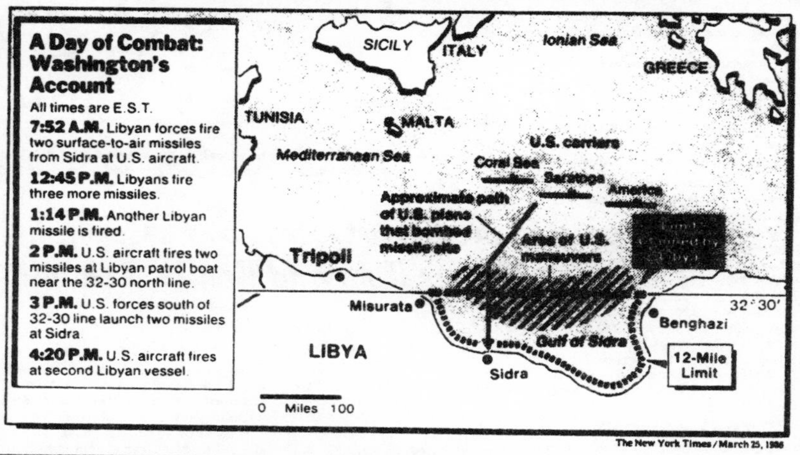
A Day of Combat: Washington's Account
All times are E.S.T.
7:52 A.M. Libyan forces fire two surface-to-air missiles from Sidra at U.S. aircraft.
12:45 P.M. Libyans fire three more missiles.
1:14 P.M. Another Libyan missile is fired.
2 P.M. U.S. aircraft fires two missiles at Libyan patrol boat near the 32-30 north line.
3 P.M. U.S. forces south of 32-30 line launch two missiles at Sidra.
4:20 P.M. U.S. aircraft fires at second Libyan vessel.
SICILY
ITALY
Ionian Sea
GREECE
TUNISIA
MALTA
Mediterranean Sea
U.S. carriers
Coral Sea
Saratoga
America
Approximate path of U.S. plane that bombed missile site
Area of U.S. maneuvers
Tripoli
Misurata
32°30'
Benghazi
Gulf of Sidra
LIBYA
Sidra
12-Mile Limit
0 Miles 100

The New York Times / March 25, 1986

Haiti's Exiles, Returning Steadily, Carry Home Formulas for Change

By MARLISE SIMONS
Special to The New York Times

PORT-AU-PRINCE, Haiti, March 24 — Jean Dominique was in from New York and walked into what used to be Haiti's most outspoken radio station, now a place covered with dust, unraveled tapes and smashed cabinets. The transmitters were carted off five years ago by the political police.

Today, as Haiti is testing life without the Duvalier family, Mr. Dominique is back from exile, ready to start over, joining many Haitians eager to come home.

In recent days, the cautious trickle of exiles returning has become a steady flow, with men and women arriving from Africa, Europe, the United States. They are here, celebrating, asking questions, offering recipes for change. Undaunted by the shake-up in the ruling council last week, some have already declared themselves political candidates.

Old-timers, away for 20 years, do not recognize the capital, which has tripled in size to about a million people and, by most indicators, also in misery and in the number of millionaires. Returnees say they see more villas on the cool hillsides, but also a town center and slums that look sadder and filthier, and more people hawking minutiae such as five cigarettes or a handful of lemons.

There are no exact accounts of the hundreds of thousands who left in the past few decades, people who were expelled, threatened or just felt trapped by a corrupt and harsh system.

Writers, Politicians, Guerrillas

It was poverty that forced many people to flee on rickety boats to Florida. But Haiti also lost much of its skilled and professional class, the teachers, doctors and economists who were caught in the perennial purges and power shifts dictated by the palace, or the people who looked for some intellectual and creative space elsewhere. Their role, in many cases, has been taken over by foreigners, whose freedom and salaries come from churches and development agencies abroad.

Today, nearly 1.5 million Haitians live outside Haiti, at least half of them

Continued on Page A14, Column 4

Associated Press

OSCAR WINNERS: William Hurt, left, after being named best actor for "Kiss of the Spider Woman." With him were Anjelica Huston, best supporting actress for "Prizzi's Honor;" Geraldine Page, best actress for "Trip to Bountiful" and Sydney Pollack, best director for "Out of Africa," also named best picture. Page C15.

IN DISPUTED AREA

Libya Says It Downed 3 Jets, but Washington Reports No Losses

By BERNARD WEINRAUB
Special to The New York Times

WASHINGTON, March 24 — American and Libyan forces clashed today in and around the disputed waters off the Libyan coast.

The Reagan Administration announced that the encounter began in the Gulf of Sidra when Libyan ground batteries fired six missiles at American planes. It said United States Navy aircraft had retaliated by attacking

News session excerpts, page A10.

two Libyan patrol boats and a missile site on Libyan soil.

It said one Libyan vessel was set afire and was "dead in the water" and the other was "severely damaged."

Missile Site 'Out of Action'

The damage to the missile site, according to Defense Secretary Caspar W. Weinberger, was still being assessed, but he said the installation was "out of action." Mr. Weinberger said that Navy warplanes had used long-range air-to-surface missiles to strike the Libyan missile site and the two Libyan vessels. [Page A10.]

Earlier, the Libyan state television and the official Libyan press agency reported that three American jets had been shot down.

The White House spokesman, Larry Speakes, said, "We have no reports of any U.S. casualties, and no loss of U.S. aircraft or ships has been reported."

A 30-Ship Task Force

The incident occurred as a 30-ship Navy task force, led by three aircraft carriers, was conducting maneuvers in the Mediterranean off Libya. The maneuvers began over the weekend.

Asked directly today why the United States had chosen this particular time to enter waters claimed by Libya, White House officials would say only that the United States wished to assert its right to navigate in international waters.

"The President approved the rules of engagement on March 14 as part of a pattern of asserting U.S. rights to navigate in international waters," said one senior official. The official said the United States had gone into the Gulf of Sidra eight times since 1981.

"We just couldn't allow Qaddafi to assert a right of sovereignty over international waters," the official said, referring to the Libyan leader, Col. Muammar el-Qaddafi.

Libya claims the entire Gulf of Sidra as its territorial waters, extending as far as 100 miles from the gulf's southern shore. But the United States and

Continued on Page A10, Column 5

LAWMAKERS BACK ACTIONS ON LIBYA

But Head of Committee Says Reagan Exceeded Powers

By ROBERT PEAR
Special to The New York Times

WASHINGTON, March 24 — Members of Congress today generally expressed support for the action taken by American warplanes against Libyan land and sea targets, but the chairman of the House Foreign Affairs Commitee charged that President Reagan had not fully complied with the War Powers Resolution of 1973.

The chairman, Representative Dante B. Fascell, said the deployment of American naval forces off the coast of Libya "constituted from the outset a situation where imminent involvement in hostilities was a distinct possibility clearly indicated by the circumstances even prior to today's development."

'The Right Course,' O'Neill Says

While some lawmakers said they needed more information to say for sure whether military action was justified, leading Democrats and Republicans in the House said they agreed with Mr. Reagan's actions against Libya and its leader, Col. Muammar el-Qaddafi.

"The Administration's handling of this matter is on the right course. Its actions in protecting America's armed forces in international waters are justified," said Thomas P. O'Neill, Jr., the Speaker of the House. "Based upon the briefing given me at the White House," Mr. O'Neill continued, "the American

Continued on Page A11, Column 1

INSIDE

Davis Bid for CBS Reported

Marvin Davis, the Denver millionaire, has apparently made an offer to buy CBS Inc., Wall Street sources disclosed last night. Page D1.

Genetic Test Draws Fine

A company accused of falsifying data has lost its permit to test a genetically engineered farm chemical and has been fined $20,000. Page A20.

Hondurans Meeting Amid U.S. Reports Of Nicaraguan Raid

By STEPHEN KINZER
Special to The New York Times

MANAGUA, Nicaragua, March 24 — President José Azcona Hoyo of Honduras tonight called an urgent meeting of his National Security Council to discuss reports of a Nicaraguan military incursion into Honduran territory.

A Government spokesman, Lisandro Quesada, said the Government could not verify the reports, which had been circulated earlier in the day by Reagan Administration officials in Washington.

"At this time, we know nothing about these reports," Mr. Quesada told reporters in Tegucigalpa. "The situation is being investigated by the armed forces."

The Honduran Foreign Minister, Carlos López Contreras, said before the National Security Council meeting that he could give no details of the alleged incursion. "We know nothing official at this time," he said.

In Managua, Western diplomats said they knew nothing of the supposed raid.

Administration officials in Washington told reporters today that 1,500 Nicaraguan troops had crossed into Honduras in what was described as their boldest cross-border strike ever. The officials said the troops had penetrated 10 miles or more into Honduras.

The Senate is scheduled to vote this

Continued on Page A18 Column 1

"All the News That's Fit to Print"

The New York Times

Late Edition

Weather: Partly cloudy and cool today, chance of showers; rain likely tonight. Cloudy, with continued rain tomorrow. Temperatures: today 54-58, tonight 43-47; yesterday 41-67. Details, page C14.

VOL.CXXXV. No. 46,745 NEW YORK, TUESDAY, APRIL 15, 1986 — 50 cents beyond 75 miles from New York City, except on Long Island — 30 CENTS

U.S. JETS HIT 'TERRORIST CENTERS' IN LIBYA; REAGAN WARNS OF NEW ATTACKS IF NEEDED; ONE PLANE MISSING IN RAIDS ON 5 TARGETS

The New York Times / Paul Hosefros

FORECAST ON TRADE GAP: Prime Minister Yasuhiro Nakasone in Washington. He predicted a decline in Japanese trade surplus with U.S. by fall. Page D1.

Crucial Portion Of Shuttle Joint Found in Ocean

By DAVID E. SANGER

Salvage crews off the Florida coast have recovered a burned-out section of the booster rocket joint whose rupture is thought to have led to the destruction of the space shuttle Challenger, the Navy said yesterday.

The discovery provides the first tangible evidence that a failure of the joint, whose questionable design had worried rocket engineers for nearly a year before the Jan. 28 explosion, caused the disaster, which took the lives of seven astronauts.

Key 4,000-Pound Segment

After discovery of the crew cabin, which was hauled ashore last month, the search for the booster joint was the top priority for the flotilla of surface ships and submarines still combing the ocean floor off Cape Canaveral.

The wreckage, a 4,000-pound section of the aft-center segment of the rocket, was recovered early Sunday morning by the salvage vessel Stena Workhorse and an unmanned submersible working in 560 feet of water. Along one edge, where a tang fits into a groove on an adjacent rocket segment, a 2-foot-wide hole is evident, burned through the hardened steel of the rocket casing.

"It looks like someone took a giant

Continued on Page C3, Column 3

PARIS BARRED JETS

Weinberger Says Rebuff Added 1,200 Miles to Flight From Britain

By NEIL A. LEWIS

Special to The New York Times

WASHINGTON, April 14 — President Reagan said today that the Western European allies had assisted the United States in its military attack against Libya, but according to other high officials the action was hampered by a lack of cooperation, notably from France.

According to Secretary of State George P. Shultz and Defense Secretary Caspar W. Weinberger, the degree of cooperation ranged from Britain's allowing American air bases there to be used to France's refusal to let the American planes fly through its airspace.

"With respect to our allies, we have a variety of opinions," Mr. Shultz said in the White House briefing room. Mr. Weinberger said Prime Minister Margaret Thatcher of Britain had allowed the use of the air bases.

Route Was 1,200 Miles Longer

But Mr. Weinberger said the pilots had to use a more dangerous route to avoid flying over countries that had barred the use of their airspace. He suggested that several countries had not cooperated, but in response to a question, he singled out France.

Mr. Weinberger, in showing the flight path on a map, said that the circuitous route was 2,800 nautical miles, 1,200 miles more than a direct route.

"Obviously, if we had permission to fly a direct route, we would not have subjected the pilots to such a long flight," he said.

'That Is a Fair Description'

In response to a question whether the United States sought and was refused permission to fly over France, he responded, "I think that is a fair description."

When asked whether countries other than France had refused permission to fly over their territory, Mr. Weinberger said, "No, that would have been the direct route," an allusion to French airspace.

Mr. Weinberger said that in addition to having to fly a longer route, pilots had to take evasive actions to avoid detection.

Mr. Reagan, in his speech, praised

Continued on Page A11, Column 1

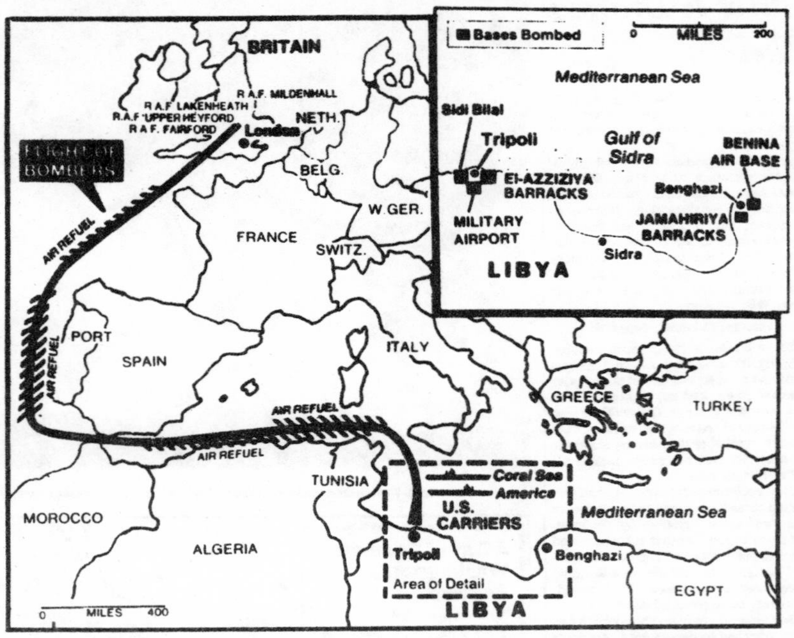

The New York Times April 15, 1986

United States conducted air strikes against five Libyan targets near Tripoli and Benghazi. The American jets were said to have taken off from a British base and from ships in the Mediterranean.

STRIKES IN 2 AREAS

White House Lays 'Direct Responsibility' in Blast in Berlin to Qaddafi

By BERNARD WEINRAUB

Special to The New York Times

WASHINGTON, Tuesday, April 15 — The United States conducted a series of air strikes on Monday night against what the White House called "terrorist centers" and military bases in Libya.

President Reagan, in a nationally broadcast speech, said the American forces had "succeeded" in their mission of retaliating against Libya for what he termed the "reign of terror" waged by Col. Muammar el-Qaddafi, the Libyan leader, against the United States.

Statements, pages A10 and A13.

Defense Secretary Caspar W. Weinberger said later that one United States plane, an F-111 with a crew of two, "is not accounted for at this time." But he declined to say if the plane had been shot down.

Libya Says 3 Jets Downed

The Libyan radio, monitored in London, said that three United States aircraft had been shot down and that Libyans had killed their pilots and crew.

Mr. Reagan said: "Today we have done what we had to do. If necessary we shall do it again."

Congressional leaders generally expressed support for the attack on Libya, but a leading Democrat warned that the raid could lead to more violence. [Page A10.]

The French Foreign Ministry said the French Embassy in Tripoli was hit in the bombing raid, but a spokesman said no one was injured.

Foreign reporters in Tripoli, after a Government-conducted tour of a residential district today, said that the rear of the French Embassy was heavily damaged, with windows blown out, and that five or six houses in the district were also damaged. A Libyan Government spokesman said an unknown number of civilians had been killed.

5 Targets Near Cities

In his address on Monday night, Mr. Reagan said the American attack was a retaliation for what he asserted was the "direct" Libyan role in the bombing on April 5 of a West Berlin discotheque frequented by American servicemen. One American soldier and a Turkish woman died, and more than 200 people were wounded, including 50 other servicemen.

"We believe that this pre-emptive action against his terrorist installations will not only diminish Colonel Qaddafi's capacity to export terror, it will provide him with incentives and reasons to alter his criminal behavior," said a grim-faced Mr. Reagan.

An Administration official said five military targets near Libya's two major cities, Tripoli and Benghazi, were attacked.

Mr. Weinberger said American planes were forced to fly a long route to

Continued on Page A10, Column 3

In the Skies Over Libya's Capital, Planes Roar and Bombs Resound

By EDWARD SCHUMACHER

Special to The New York Times

TRIPOLI, Libya, Tuesday, April 15 — For nearly 10 minutes, the night sky was ablaze with explosions from missiles and tracers as the American planes soared out of the distance.

Hours later, doctors said 60 to 100 wounded civilians had come to a hospital. It was not known how many people might have been killed, and the doctors did not offer an estimate.

Bombs fell on an upper-middle-class neighborhood that included the French Embassy. When reporters toured the area after daybreak, it was littered with broken glass, collapsed walls and destroyed cars.

The reporters saw one body.

The target appeared to be a communications building with a large antenna on top and several antennas behind it. The building's function was not clear, and officials would not say.

The bombs fell short of the building, and although its windows were blown out, the antennas stood intact on the roof.

The attacks began shortly before 2 A.M. (7 P.M. Monday, New York time), when the rumble of bombs could first be heard. For nearly 10 minutes afterward, the sky turned into a fireworks display of missiles and bombs.

Missiles could be seen rising into the air, but no American planes appeared to be hit.

Volleys of Antiaircraft Fire

The air strikes were met by volleys of antiaircraft fire. Smoke could be seen rising in the capital.

The reaction here was slow. The city's lights were not blacked out until 20 minutes after the attack began.

Even during the bombing, there was a strange calm on the city streets. Cars moved beneath the street lights around the harbor.

The state-run Libyan radio asserted that bombs had fallen on the barracks where Col. Muammar el-Qaddafi, the Libyan leader, maintains his headquarters, and that some members of his family were wounded in the raids. The reports could not be confirmed.

Officials said a downed American

Continued on Page A12, Column 1

PENTAGON DETAILS 2-PRONGED ATTACK

British-Based Jets Hit Tripoli, Navy Planes to Benghazi

By MICHAEL R. GORDON

Special to The New York Times

WASHINGTON, April 14 — Officials said tonight that the United States attack on five Libyan targets was a complex operation that involved separate attacks by Air Force and Navy planes and the use of aircraft for refueling, intelligence and electronic jamming.

The operation involved two strikes on separate regions of Libya, the officials said.

In one attack, Pentagon officials said, 18 United States Air Force F-111 bombers left England and attacked three targets near Tripoli. The targets were the military side of the Tripoli airport; a port section called Sidi Bilal, where Libyan commandos are trained, and the military barracks called el-Azziziya.

Planes From Carriers

In a separate attack, 15 A-6 and A-7 aircraft from the Coral Sea and the America, the two United States Navy aircraft carriers in the central Mediterranean, attacked two Libyan bases near Benghazi, Defense Secretary Caspar W. Weinberger said. They included an air base called Benina and a barracks called Jamahiriya.

Mr. Weinberger said that all the F-111's were accounted for except for

Continued on Page A11, Column 1

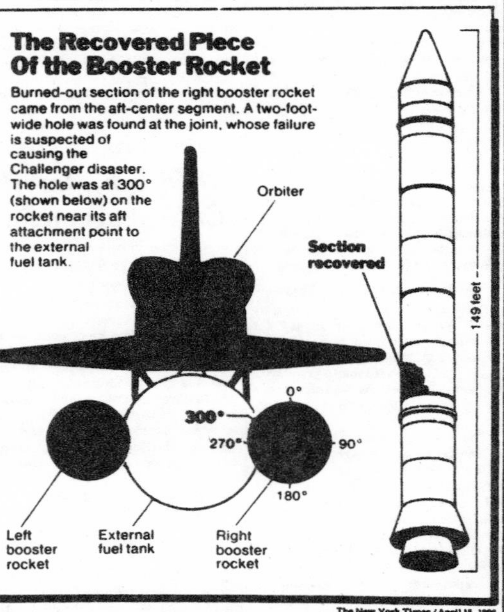

The New York Times / April 15, 1986

Plots on Global Scale Charged

By BERNARD GWERTZMAN

Special to The New York Times

WASHINGTON, April 14 — Secretary of State George P. Shultz said tonight that Libyan agents had been deployed around the world for attacks against United States embassies in as many as 30 countries.

At a news conference after the announcement of the American bombing attacks on Libya, Mr. Shultz said the raids had been necessary to deter Libya from future terrorist attacks and to retaliate for the bombing on April 5 of a West Berlin discothèque frequented by American soldiers.

He said that "we have reports and indications, quite substantial evidence, of Libyan efforts to attack — varying degrees of certainty on the evidence — up to 30 of our embassies."

Mr. Shultz said all United States embassies had been placed on special alert. Secretary of Defense Caspar W. Weinberger said United States military installations around the world were also on alert.

Administration officials said a plan by the Joint Chiefs of Staff for surgical bombing strikes against Libya was approved by President Reagan eight days ago. [Page A11.]

Larry Speakes, the White House spokesman, said tonight that Libyans were known to have been conducting surveillance and planning attacks against American diplomatic and commercial installations in Africa, Europe, the Middle East and Latin America.

He said that 10 attacks were planned in Africa alone and that in one African country, which he did not name, three Libyan agents arrived last week with the objective of bombing the United States Embassy and chancery and kidnapping the American Ambassador.

'The Primary Objective'

Discussing the American action tonight, Mr. Shultz said, "It's not a question of settling scores; it's a question of acting against terrorism, of saying to terrorists that the acts they perpetrate will cost them.

"If you raise the costs, you do something that should eventually act as a deterrent," he said. "And that is the primary objective, to defend ourselves both in the immediate sense and prospectively."

In his broadcast address tonight, Mr. Reagan said that "our evidence is direct, it is precise, it is irrefutable" that

Continued on Page A11, Column 4

The New York Times / Paul Hosefros

President Reagan speaking to journalists last night after broadcast.

INSIDE

Soviet Missile Said to Fail

United States experts said the Soviet Union had tested its largest new land-based missile, but that the test had apparently failed. Page A8.

Mets Lose Home Opener

An error by the Met third baseman, Howard Johnson, triggered a four-run burst that enabled the Cardinals to win, 6-2, in 13 innings. Page A25.

Simone de Beauvoir Dies

Simone de Beauvoir, the author and intellectual whose work helped inspire the women's movement, died in Paris at the age of 78. Page B9.

Horowitz Returns to Russia

Vladimir Horowitz, who left the Soviet Union 61 years ago, vowing never to return, arrived in Moscow to perform two piano recitals. Page C13.

"All the News That's Fit to Print"

The New York Times

Late Edition

Weather: Mostly sunny, warm today; increasing cloudiness tonight. Mostly cloudy, chance of showers tomorrow. Temperatures: today 78-82, tonight 50-59; yesterday 52-71. Details, page A18.

VOL.CXXXV . . . No. 46,760 NEW YORK, WEDNESDAY, APRIL 30, 1986 — 50 cents beyond 75 miles from New York City, except on Long Island. 30 CENTS

SOVIET, REPORTING ATOM PLANT 'DISASTER,' SEEKS HELP ABROAD TO FIGHT REACTOR FIRE

VIRTUAL CERTAINTY OF FAILURE SHOWN FOR SHUTTLE SEAL

New Tests Indicate That Cold and Design Flaws Doomed Challenger From Start

By DAVID E. SANGER

Special to The New York Times

WASHINGTON, April 29 — New and unpublished test results show that a failure of a safety seal on the space shuttle Challenger was virtually inevitable because of a combination of cold weather on the morning of the launching and serious design flaws.

The test results, conducted for the Presidential panel studying the accident and summarized for The New York Times, also determined that the joint would sometimes begin to fail at temperatures as high as 50 degrees Fahrenheit.

In the past, officials of the National Aeronautics and Space Administration have testified that they felt confident the shuttle could be launched at far lower temperatures without undue risk to the crew.

Failure Was Probable

The Challenger was launched Jan. 28 in 36-degree weather, but investigators estimate that the temperature of the joint that contained the failed seal was about 28 degrees, a temperature at which failure is more likely than not, the tests show.

The analysis of the accident, in which the seven crew members died, is expected to serve as the centerpiece of the Presidential commission's report, due in early June. On Monday panel members received a summary of the results, based on tests conducted in recent weeks primarily by NASA engineers and outside aerospace experts working for the commission's working group analyzing data and design.

'I Wouldn't Fly That Rocket'

"The bottom line is that temperature is the key variable, but temperature alone didn't cause it," Maj. Gen. Donald J. Kutyna, who led the working group, said in response to questions about the results. General Kutyna, a former fighter pilot, warned against a "quick fix" of the joint, saying that under the current design "even on a warm day I wouldn't fly that rocket."

The findings, when taken with testimony before the commission, strongly suggest that the middle-level NASA officials from the Marshall Space Flight Center who decided to go ahead with the launching, despite warnings about the low temperature from engineers working for the manufacturer of the booster rocket, acted with virtually no knowledge of the true performance limitations of the crucial joints and the synthetic rubber rings that were relied on to seal them.

Investigators say they are at a loss to

Continued on Page B7, Column 1

Agence France-Presse

AN IMPERIAL ANNIVERSARY: Emperor Hirohito reading a message at ceremony in Tokyo marking his 60th anniversary on the throne as well as his 85th birthday.

Indonesia Bars Two Journalists In Reagan Party

By GERALD M. BOYD

Special to The New York Times

DENPASAR, Bali, April 29 — President Reagan arrived today on this Indonesian island on the first major stop of his trip to the Far East, but the occasion was marred, White House officials said, when the Indonesian Government detained two Australian journalists in the President's party and barred them from the country.

In a separate incident, Indonesian authorities detained and expelled Barbara Crossette, a correspondent for The New York Times who was seeking to report on the Reagan visit. [Page A6].

Moments before Mr. Reagan was greeted at the island's airport by President Suharto, the Indonesian leader, and colorfully clad Balinese dancers, Indonesian authorities removed the two Australians from the White House press plane.

Ordered to Leave Country

The journalists, from the Australian Broadcasting Corporation, were ordered to leave the country in a move that White House officials said highlighted sharp differences between the United States and Indonesia over press and political freedoms.

The two correspondents, Jim Middleton and Richard D. Palfreyman, are based in Washington and had been told that they would not be allowed to enter, despite the protests of American officials, following unfavorable reports in

Continued on Page A6, Column 1

ASSESSMENT OF U.S.

Intelligence Sources Say Accident Began Days Ago and Continues

By PHILIP M. BOFFEY

Special to The New York Times

WASHINGTON, April 29 — United States intelligence sources said today that the nuclear disaster in the Soviet Union started as long as four or five days ago and was continuing to spread radioactive material into the atmosphere.

Most experts agreed that the graphite core of the Chernobyl reactor, at Pripyat in the Ukraine, had caught fire and was burning fiercely.

Details of the accident remained scarce today, the day after the Russians announced that an accident had taken place at the reactor. Without such details, experts found it difficult to speculate about the short- and long-term dangers the disaster posed to health and the environment.

Soviet Technology Faulted

But they faulted Soviet technology, which uses graphite, a form of carbon, to moderate nuclear reactions. In the United States, water is used as a moderator.

They also said the stricken reactor was not encased in a protective concrete containment dome, as is customary in the United States. The external shell could cut down on the radioactive material spewed into the atmosphere.

The experts warned that such graphite fires can be very difficult to extinguish, and that an unextinguished fire continues to release more radioactivity over the Soviet Union and other countries downwind of the reactor.

"The graphite is burning and will continue to burn for a good number of days," said Kenneth L. Adelman, the United States arms control administrator. He told Congress that, because the reactor is on a river, "there is concern over water contamination."

Europeans Are Critical

European officials and nuclear experts criticized the Soviet Union for not disclosing the accident as soon as it occurred. Some United States intelligence officials say they believe it happened Friday or possibly even Thursday. Moscow did not reveal the accident until Monday.

The Associated Press quoted a ranking information official, who was not identified, as saying that today "smoke was still billowing from the site" at the reactor.

"The roof had been blown off and large portions of the walls had caved in, and it seemed at the time that the nuclear unit just above it might still be in some danger," The A.P. said, adding that it was understood — but not officially confirmed — that much of the American intelligence information had been gathered by a KH-11 spy satellite.

Zhores Medvedev, the exiled Russian

Continued on Page A11, Column 2

Reuters

Photograph published in the February issue of Soviet Life magazine shows cooling system of a reactor at the Chernobyl nuclear power plant near Kiev.

The Nuclear Disaster

What Happened

In an unusual public admission, the Soviet state radio said a "disaster" had occurred at a nuclear power plant in the Ukraine. West German and Swedish officials said Soviet officials had asked for help in controlling a burning nuclear reactor. The nuclear accident, described by Swedish experts as potentially the worst ever at a power plant, sent a radioactive cloud across parts of the Soviet Union, Eastern Europe and Scandinavia. Moscow provided few details, but intelligence sources believe that the accident occurred last Thursday or Friday and that radiation was continuing to spew yesterday. Western experts say they believe graphite used to moderate the nuclear reaction in the plant caught fire. They disagree on whether the fire was associated with a meltdown, in which nuclear fuel rods burn out of control.

The Health Damage

The Russians reported that four nearby localities had been evacuated, two people had died and others had been treated. Western experts say they fear that a great many more, perhaps thousands, who lived near the plant may become ill or die from radiation poisoning in coming years or suffer cancers and genetic mutations later. So far, radiation levels reaching Scandinavia are not considered dangerous.

Could It Happen Here?

American commercial reactors use water rather than graphite, a flammable material, to moderate nuclear reactions. They also, unlike the Soviet reactor in the accident, have steel and concrete containment structures designed to prevent the escape of radiation. But experts say they do not have enough information to tell whether the accident holds any lessons for nuclear power safety here.

Unanswered Questions

These are among the unanswered questions: When did the accident begin? What caused the accident? How much radiation of what types has been released? How many people have been killed, injured or exposed to dangerous radiation? Have soils, crops, water and livestock in the Ukraine been dangerously contaminated?

2 DEATHS ADMITTED

Moscow, in Terse Report, Asserts the 'Radiation Situation' Is Stable

By SERGE SCHMEMANN

Special to The New York Times

MOSCOW, April 29 — The Soviet Government was reported today to have asked West Germany and Sweden for assistance in handling a fire in a nuclear reactor core.

The reports, from officials in those countries, came amid indications that a reactor accident reported Monday in the Ukraine, 70 miles north of Kiev, was a major disaster, perhaps the worst in the history of nuclear power.

[The United States formally offered humanitarian and technical assistance to the Soviet Union to help it deal with the accident. Page 6.]

'Radiation Situation' Stable

The developments came as the Soviet Government issued its second official statement on the accident in the Chernobyl nuclear power station at Pripyat, saying that the "radiation situation has now been stabilized."

The four-paragraph statement disclosed for the first time that the accident at the four-reactor plant had occurred in the No. 4 reactor, which went into service in 1983, and that the three others were in operating order, but had been shut down. Each of the four reactors had an electrical generating capacity of 1,000 megawatts.

[At one point, according to Reuters, the Moscow radio referred to the accident as "a disaster," but later dropped the word. United Press International quoted the radio as having said, "The disaster was the first one at a Soviet nuclear power plant in more than 30 years." There was a nuclear accident in the Urals in 1957 that the Soviet Government has never acknowledged.]

Four Localities Evacuated

The Soviet Government statement, which was read on the evening television news, said that two people had been killed in the accident and that the power-station settlement, an allusion to Pripyat, and three other nearby localities had been evacuated.

[Some Western officials questioned whether the death toll could be as low as two. In Washington, Kenneth L. Adelman, director of the Arms Control and Disarmament Agency, called the Soviet assertion "frankly preposterous."]

The reported Soviet request for assistance from West Germany and Sweden indicated to experts that the reactor's graphite core was burning uncontrollably, and therefore that the fuel rods in it might have melted down partly or completely. Some foreign scientists agreed that if this was the case, the accident was the worst nuclear-power disaster in history.

But the Soviet authorities provided

Continued on Page A10, Column 5

Casualties in Soviet Could Keep Rising, U.S. Experts Assert

By HAROLD M. SCHMECK Jr.

American experts said yesterday that deaths and injuries from the reactor accident in the Soviet Union may continue to mount for several weeks in the vicinity of the disaster if severe radiation has been released.

These experts on health and radiation said there appeared to be no danger for the Western Hemisphere and probably little in the Scandinavian countries, on the basis of what has been reported thus far.

When the Soviet Union announced that two people had been killed in the accident at the Chernobyl power plant in the Ukraine, there was no indication if the cause of death was radiation, fire or other nonnuclear effects.

There was an unconfirmed report from the area that many more may have died. If that report is confirmed, said Dr. Kenneth Mossman of Georgetown University Medical School, it would suggest extremely high levels of gamma radiation.

Two types of radiation exposure are likely to be involved in the damage at and near the reactor site.

The first and most immediately dangerous is external gamma radiation, which is similar to X-rays and equally penetrating. Gamma radiation can damage cells, genes and vital tissues,

Continued on Page A12, Column 1

The New York Times/Paul Hosefros

BODIES OF CHALLENGER'S CREW LEAVE FLORIDA: Coffin of Francis R. Scobee being carried from plane at Dover Air Force Base, Del. Remains of astronauts will be turned over to their families for burial. Page B7.

INSIDE

Dismissal in Secrets Case

Officials said a Pentagon aide was dismissed on the ground that he gave information about covert U.S. operations for a news article. Page A17.

Methodists' Nuclear Stand

The United Methodist Church's Council of Bishops voted to issue a pastoral letter declaring opposition to any use of nuclear weapons. Page A15.

Red Sox Pitcher Fans 20

Roger Clemens of Boston set a major league record by striking out 20 Seattle batters in the Red Sox 3-1 victory. He issued no walks. Page A27.

"All the News That's Fit to Print"

The New York Times

Late Edition

Weather: Mostly sunny, humid today; hazy, warm and humid tonight. Mostly sunny, humid and very hot tomorrow. Temperatures: today 90-92, tonight 73-77; yesterday 55-77. Details, page 17.

VOL.CXXXV. No. 46,826 · NEW YORK, SATURDAY, JULY 5, 1986 · 60 cents beyond 75 miles from New York City, except on Long Island. · 30 CENTS

A VERY SPECIAL DAY

Millions Watch Festive Harbor Salute to Liberty

The New York Times/Jim Wilson

SAILING TALL: Ships proceeding through the harbor, part of a stately six-hour parade that delighted an audience of millions on land and on water.

FIREWORKS FILL SKY

21-Gun Salutes Thunder as Warships and Tall Ships Ply the Bay

By ROBERT D. McFADDEN

A procession of tall ships joined an armada of mighty warships in New York Harbor yesterday, and an enormous fireworks show turned the night sky to blazing color in a salute to the Fourth of July and the centennial of a rekindled Statue of Liberty.

As darkness fell on a day of stately nautical maneuvers, the biggest fireworks display in American history — a booming, 28-minute barrage of skyrockets — burst like supernovas over the harbor and bathed millions of awed spectators and much of the metropolitan region in eerie light.

It was, to many, the highlight of a Fourth of July filled with delights, especially the spectacle of tall ships joining warships in the harbor, with President Reagan reviewing the fleet aboard the battleship Iowa and a parade of sail from Governors Island.

"We expected the best fireworks since Nero set Rome on fire, and we got them," Mayor Koch said after the fireworks.

40,000 Shells

From a necklace of 30 barges around the tip of Manhattan, stretching from the Brooklyn Bridge to the World Trade Center, more than 40,000 pyrotechnic shells shrieked skyward in a computer-controlled, nonstop cannonading, with smoke and blasts reminiscent of a battlefield.

Against the night sky, cascades of red, orange, yellow, blue, green and white exploded into gigantic flowerlike shapes of chrysanthemums, peonies, silvertails and morning glories. Others bloomed into palettes of swizzling color, forming dragonflies, swaying leaves, meteors.

The sound and light echoed and flashed off the towers of downtown Manhattan, washed over the floodlit Statue of Liberty, illuminated tens of thousands of boats dotting the harbor and overwhelmed the sparkling lights of the city in the distance.

Musical Score

The fireworks, choreographed by Grucci, Pyro Spectaculars and Zambelli Internationale, were accompanied by a musical score played on radio and television by the 140-member United States Marine Band aboard the aircraft carrier John F. Kennedy, anchored at midharbor. President Reagan and his wife, Nancy, had an admirable view from the deck of the carrier.

Millions of spectators, meanwhile, gasped, ooooed and aaaahed as they watched from the rim of the harbor and

Continued on Page 30, Column 1

STRIKE BY MINERS HITS SOUTH AFRICA

Workers at Diamond Company Seek Release of Unionists

By ALAN COWELL

Special to The New York Times

JOHANNESBURG, July 4 — Nearly 2,000 black mineworkers have gone on strike at four diamond mines to demand the release of detained labor leaders, their employer said today.

The stoppage at the De Beers mines, which started Thursday, was the first known protest in the economically crucial mining industry since the newest state of emergency was imposed June 12. South Africa's gold, diamond and other mines account for more than half the country's export earnings.

The police, meanwhile, said a bomb explosion, the 13th since the declaration of the emergency, wounded 20 people in a white suburb of Pretoria, the capital.

11 Blacks and 9 Whites Hurt

The Bureau for Information, the sole source of authorized news under the emergency decree, said the explosion was caused by a device left between two parked cars.

The bureau said 11 of the wounded were black — presumably blacks working for white employers in the area — and nine were white.

Three people have died and about 100, many of them white, have been wounded in bomb explosions since the emergency was declared. The overall death toll since June 12 is more than 100; most of the dead were blacks. Since September 1984, when the current period of protest and violence

Continued on Page 4, Column 4

The New York Times/Fred R. Conrad

BURSTING IN AIR: Fireworks providing brief but brilliant rivalry for statue's torch.

Family Sails Amid History For a Moment

By WILLIAM E. GEIST

Seven-year-old Josh Curtis wondered aloud yesterday what in the world the Statue of Liberty would say if she could speak. His question was lost in the roar of thousands of boat engines and the blare of their horns.

The boy had just entered New York Harbor, uttering a "Wow!" as the family motorboat emerged from a tributary. He beheld more boats than he had ever imagined existed — indeed, perhaps more than have ever been assembled — as they swirled about the statue's feet and swarms of

About New York

blimps, skywriters, helicopters and fighter planes buzzed around her head.

Josh's family had slept aboard their well-traveled, 26-foot boat at the New Elco Marina in Bayonne, N.J., for an early getaway. With American flags unfurled, they sailed across Newark Bay and down the Kill Van Kull, lined with salvage yards and oil tankers, a dreary approach that made the harbor view all the more dramatic.

•

His father, Skip Curtis, dressed in a red-white-and-blue "Liberty Park, New Jersey" T-shirt, enthusiastically loaded the family — Josh; his mother, Ellen, and Matthew, his 10-year-old brother — aboard, along with two coolers so full of beer, soda, cold cuts and nacho cheese chips that their sides were splitting. Also on board was a sack of fireworks and a radio playing rock-and-roll oldies.

Mr. Curtis, 42, said he wanted them to be "preeent and part of an unforgettable moment in American history." All they could do was hope this turned out better than Halley's comet, which he was also excited for them to see.

Mrs. Curtis went along reluctantly on the pilgrimage to the refurbished Statue of Liberty. Matthew had suggested to his father a little fluke fishing instead.

"They told us at school we had to contribute $5 to the statue," Matthew said, "or we were in trouble."

But now they were all excited — if occasionally afraid for their lives — as Mr. Curtis deftly wove them through this assemblage of virtually every type of vessel conceived by man to pay homage to the statue.

There were sloops, hydrofoils, junks, carriers, brigantines, the Queen Elizabeth 2, Jet-Skis, an oil barge with bleachers, schooners, water taxis, a submarine, a battleship and a thousand and one would-be Don Johnsons in sleek Cigarette boats.

The parade of breathtaking tall ships, the ostensible reason for the gathering of the masses, seemed but a sideshow at times.

The Curtis family, of North Bergen, N.J., beheld two seemingly crazed people out in a kayak in this hull-to-hull traffic. There was even a car, one of those small convertible automobiles that run on land or water, with waves breaking over the windshield wipers.

They next came upon what appeared

Continued on Page 27, Column 1

For Ronald Reagan, The Ceremonies Stir Pride and Patriotism

By BERNARD WEINRAUB

President Reagan blended politics and patriotism yesterday in what aides described as one of the most exuberant days of his Presidency.

Celebrating Independence Day and the rededication of the Statue of Liberty, Mr. Reagan flew by helicopter in the morning to the battleship Iowa and steamed south on the sun-drenched Hudson River to pass an international flotilla of warships. Many of the vessels fired guns in salute as the Iowa, a recommissioned World War II vessel, cruised down the Hudson at 8 knots.

As Mr. Reagan left the viewing booth, moments after F-16 Thunderbirds flew over and left a red, white and blue trail in the cloudless sky, he said to Capt. Larry Seaquist, the ship's commanding officer: "Absolutely brilliant. No word to describe my pride."

Larry Speakes, the White House spokesman, said the President was "exuberant for sure" during his visit to New York, which ends this morning. "There have been other days like these — inaugural days, the release of the Iranian hostages," Mr. Speakes said. "This ranks with them."

By nightfall Mr. Reagan and his

Continued on Page 31, Column 1

New York Relaxes as It Savors a Celebration

By JOSEPH BERGER

People moved about more lazily. Faces were less taut and many wore radiant smiles. Even the sky was flawless — blue, then a starry black. .

In short, New Yorkers and out-of town visitors yesterday were in a mood appropriate not only to the Fourth of July, but to a singular Fourth, one that celebrated their roots and their unabashed pride in their country.

"It's a custom-made day," said Gabriel De Los Rios, a 64-year-old Chilean-American pianist standing amid a light-hearted and relaxed throng on the Riverside Park promenade watching the tall ships glide up the Hudson.

"There's a brotherhood and everybody's friendly to everybody else," he added. "It happens on happy occasions."

"The last time I saw this was when the hostages came home from Iran and they had that rally," Police Officer Thomas Gulotta said as he took a lunch break on a shaded bench behind the promenade. "That's when everybody was pulling in the same direction. It's a pleasure. You don't mind working."

New Yorkers, who on most days seem to be heading in thousands of different directions, were indeed pulling in the same few directions yesterday and gently sharing an unspoken camaraderie.

Last night, as the fireworks began, the joyful screams of thousands matched the screams of thousands of rockets, and the whole of lower Manhattan seemed as if it had broken into a smile.

Couples embraced, children grasped their parents and those who could speak uttered superlatives and exclamations.

"Indescribable," said Jim Tully, a

Continued on Page 28, Column 2

INSIDE

Becker and Lendl in Final

Boris Becker, the champion last year, and Ivan Lendl, never the champion, advanced to tomorrow's singles final at Wimbledon. Page 19.

Neo-Nazi Dream Lives On

Members of a violent neo-Nazi group are dead or in prison, but their dream of a racist state in the Pacific Northwest refuses to die. Page 10.

Rudy Vallee Dies

Rudy Vallee, saxophonist, bandleader and singing idol of the 1930's and 40's, died at the age of 84 in his home in California. Page 8.

"All the News That's Fit to Print"

The New York Times

Late Edition
New York Today: Becoming cloudy, mild. High 66-72. Tonight, a few showers, mild. Low 53-58. Tomorrow, periods of rain. High 62-67. Yesterday: High 63, low 48. Details on page C18.

VOL.CXXXVI . . No. 46,926

NEW YORK, MONDAY, OCTOBER 13, 1986

50 cents beyond 75 miles from New York City, except on Long Island. 30 CENTS

REAGAN-GORBACHEV TALKS END IN STALEMATE AS U.S. REJECTS DEMAND TO CURB 'STAR WARS'

Agence France-Presse

A volunteer helping victims of the earthquake at a makeshift hospital set up on a San Salvador street.

Lack of Help Angers Poor In El Salvador

By JAMES LeMOYNE
Special to The New York Times

COMUNIDAD MODELO, El Salvador, Oct. 12 — The people of this miserable warren of mud shacks have been promised by the Government that it will help them rebuild from the earthquake that swept away their homes and buried their loved ones on Friday morning.

But tonight, as the rains of a violent thunderstorm added to their misery, they found it hard to believe that the promise would be kept any time soon.

"We have nobody, nobody," said Ana Lilia Vásquez Sibrian, 50 years old, as she watched friends dig out their crushed adobe home. "We are forgotten."

[The Salvadoran President, José Napoleón Duarte, said in a televised news conference late Sunday night that the death toll had risen to 890 and that some stricken areas had still not been reached to search for victims, the Associated Press reported. Mr. Duarte said 10,000 were injured and 150,000 left homeless.]

In his Sunday homily today, the Roman Catholic Archbishop of San Salvador, Arturo Rivera y Damas, harshly criticized the failure to provide greater relief services to the poor neighborhoods that appear to be those that sustained the most damage.

"What is most apparent, without of-

Continued on Page A11, Column 1

CLOSE AIDE TO BUSH LINKED TO FIGURE HELPING CONTRAS

National Security Adviser Had Served in C.I.A. With Man Directing Aid Flights

By PHILIP SHENON
Special to The New York Times

WASHINGTON, Oct. 12 — Vice President Bush acknowledged today that his national security adviser had ties to a Central Intelligence Agency veteran identified as a leader of a secret effort to supply Nicaraguan rebels.

But the Vice President continued to deny any involvement in overseeing the supply operations to the rebels, known as contras, who are fighting the Sandinista Government of Nicaragua.

Through a spokesman, the Vice President said he had met twice in his office with the former C.I.A. agent, known as Max or Felix Gomez and as Felix Rodriguez, but only to discuss El Salvador.

Worked for El Salvador

According to Mr. Bush's staff, Mr. Gomez had worked for the Salvadoran Air Force as a counterinsurgency specialist.

Mr. Bush's spokesman, Marlin Fitzwater, said in an interview that Mr. Gomez had been recommended for the job by Donald P. Gregg, a former intelligence agency official who is Mr. Bush's national security adviser.

Eugene Hasenfus, an American captured after his cargo plane was downed in Nicaragua last week, said Mr. Gomez was a C.I.A. employee and was running the supply operations to the rebels from a Salvadoran air base.

Denial by Agency

The Central Intelligence Agency has denied that Mr. Gomez works directly or indirectly for the agency.

Mr. Fitzwater said Mr. Bush had met twice with Mr. Gomez, most recently in May. On Saturday the Vice President called Mr. Gomez "a patriot."

Mr. Fitzwater said that the conversations in the Vice President's office in the Old Executive Office Building here were brief, 10 to 15 minutes, and did not involve the Nicaraguan rebels.

The conversations, the spokesman said, "had been entirely related to El Salvador." He said Mr. Bush "has never had any conversation of any kind about the contras or contra aid or Nicaragua with Mr. Gomez."

The Vice President, Mr. Fitzwater said, did not know then or now that Mr. Gomez might be involved in aiding the rebels. Congress has barred direct American Government support of the guerrillas.

President Reagan and the C.I.A.

Continued on Page A7, Column 4

The New York Times/Jose R. Lopez

President Reagan listening yesterday as an interpreter translated the farewell remarks of Mikhail S. Gorbachev.

Sticking Points in Iceland

'Historic' Gains on Arms Cuts Were Near, But Talks Foundered on 'Star Wars' Issue

By LESLIE H. GELB
Special to The New York Times

News Analysis

REYKJAVIK, Iceland, Oct. 12 — President Reagan and his aides came here with the expectation that Moscow was prepared to reach tentative agreements on medium-range missiles and other arms issues without first solving the problem of space-based defenses.

And they had reason to believe this, based on the two leaders' pledge last November in Geneva to seek an "interim" accord on medium-range weapons, and based on more recent public statements by Soviet leaders.

But today in the dramatic finale to their two-day get-together, Mikhail S. Gorbachev told them they were wrong.

To the Soviet leader, every agreement to reduce arms depended on American willingness essentially to scrap Mr. Reagan's dream for space-based defenses against missile attacks.

And he had a basis for this belief as well. That same joint statement in Geneva pledged the two sides to "accelerate" efforts to "prevent an arms race in space."

While each side accused the other of responsibility for a failure to reach agreement, both sides were at the same time careful not to charge one another with bad faith.

Progress on Arms Reduction

Mr. Reagan and Secretary of State George P. Shultz spoke hopefully about the potential progress made here on reducing offensive arms and about trying to pick up the pieces in the continuing arms talks in Geneva.

But Mr. Shultz appeared grim in his news conference, a seriousness matched by Mr. Gorbachev in his news conference, although he too referred to "positive" elements.

From all indications, neither side

Continued on Page A9, Column 3

NO U.S. SUMMIT DATE

Effect on Ties Unclear — Understandings Cited on Certain Issues

By BERNARD GWERTZMAN
Special to The New York Times

REYKJAVIK, Iceland, Oct. 12 — President Reagan and Mikhail S. Gorbachev ended two days of talks here today with no agreement on arms control and no date for a full-fledged summit meeting in the United States.

While officials said that the two leaders had succeeded in developing tentative understandings on most arms con-

Remarks by Reagan and Gorbachev, page A10, and Shultz, page A9.

trol issues, a possible accord foundered over Soviet insistence that the United States scrap its space-based missile-defense plans.

Secretary of State George P. Shultz said at a news conference, "We are deeply disappointed by this outcome."

Future Outlook Is in Doubt

It was not immediately clear whether Soviet-American relations would worsen because of the failure to achieve an agreement, or whether the tentative understandings on medium-range and long-range forces and on nuclear testing could be revived even in the absence of an understanding on the missile-defense issue.

The two leaders, after 11 hours of talks and all-night discussions by their experts, displayed frustration and disappointment. Each held the other responsible for the lack of results.

Mr. Reagan, speaking to American forces at the Keflavik Air Base near here, before returning home, said, "We came to Iceland to advance the cause of peace and, though we put on the table the most far-reaching arms control proposal in history, the General Secretary rejected it."

Mr. Gorbachev, at a news conference, attributed the failure to American intransigence on the plan for a space-based missile defense, known officially as the Strategic Defense Initiative, and popularly as "Star Wars."

Gorbachev Sees Chance Missed

The Soviet leader said he had told the President at the end of their meeting: "We missed a historic chance. Never have our positions been so close."

When the Iceland meeting was first arranged, it was expected to set a date for a regular summit meeting in the United States in the coming months, as called for by the two leaders at their first meeting in Geneva last year.

But Secretary of State Shultz said at his news conference after an unscheduled final three-and-a-half-hour session that no date was set.

He said the United States would not pay the price for having Mr. Gorbachev go to the United States if it meant accepting constraints on the missile defense program.

He said that the tentative package of "extremely important potential agreements," extending into areas other than arms control, failed when Mr. Gorbachev insisted that the 1972 treaty limiting defensive missiles, known as the antiballistic missile treaty, be changed to prevent research, testing

Continued on Page A8, Column 1

VIEW IN CONGRESS ON TALKS IS MIXED

Reagan Criticized and Praised for Stand on 'Star Wars'

By JOHN HERBERS
Special to The New York Times

WASHINGTON, Oct. 12 — Initial Congressional reaction tonight to the failure of President Reagan and Mikhail S. Gorbachev to reach agreement on nuclear arms control was mixed.

Some Democrats blamed the President for refusal to compromise on his missile defense program and some Republicans praised him for avoiding what they called a Soviet trap.

Senator Richard G. Lugar, Republican of Indiana and chairman of the Senate Foreign Relations committee, spoke out in Mr. Reagan's defense, saying the meeting was a "Soviet trap to put the United States in perpetual jeopardy of the remaining intercontinental ballistic missiles."

'Did Not Blink'

"The President did not blink," Mr. Lugar said, adding that he acted in an imaginative and proper way to "preserve the defense of our country."

Some leading Democrats, however, expressed disappointment that Mr. Reagan did not use his strategic defense initiative, popularly known as "Star Wars," as a bargaining chip.

"This is a sad day for mankind," said Senator Claiborne Pell of Rhode Island, ranking Democrat on the Foreign Relations Committee. "I deeply regret the failure to achieve an agreement

Continued on Page A8, Column 4

Reagan to Address Nation

President Reagan is to address the nation from the White House tonight at 8 P.M. All the television networks will carry the address live.

Associated Press

VISIT TO CHINA: Queen Elizabeth II being saluted by a youngster on her arrival in Peking for a six-day visit, the first to China by a British sovereign. At center is Lady Evans, wife of the British Ambassador to China. Page A5.

BankAmerica Recalling Clausen, Gone 5 Years, as Chief Executive

By ANDREW POLLACK
Special to The New York Times

SAN FRANCISCO, Oct. 12 — The board of directors of the troubled BankAmerica Corporation, in a special meeting today, named A. W. Clausen, former president of the World Bank, to resume the helm of the banking company he once led.

Mr. Clausen, who is 63 years old, was chief executive officer of BankAmerica from 1970 until 1981, when he left to join the World Bank. He returns as chairman and chief executive officer of both the bank holding company and its subsidiary, the Bank of America.

He will face the task of restoring the giant California bank to health after a long period of huge losses from bad loans, management turmoil and high costs.

The action of the board follows the resignation Friday of Samuel H. Armacost, 47, as president and chief executive officer of the BankAmerica Corporation and chairman and chief executive of its bank. He had presided over the bank since 1981, as its fortunes steadily diminished.

The board today also announced that Leland S. Prussia, the chairman of the board of the BankAmerica Corporation, would take early retirement and that Thomas A. Cooper, the No. 2 man at the Bank of America behind Mr. Armacost, would be given additional responsibilities.

The choice of Mr. Clausen, which had been suspected since Friday, has already become controversial.

Mr. Clausen, who is also known as Tom, led the bank during a decade of uninterrupted growth, as the bank rose to international prominence. Nevertheless, many analysts and bank officials say that the policies he put in place then were responsible for many of the problems that affected the bank after he left.

Still, the appointment is expected to end at least some uncertainty that had long permeated the bank because of rumors that Mr. Armacost was on the way out.

John R. Beckett, the chairman of the executive committee of the board of directors, said the board reached its decision reluctantly and took ac-

Continued on Page D3, Column 4

Apartment Builders Return to Prewar Design

By JOSEPH GIOVANNINI

A new generation of apartment buildings resembling the traditional, prewar structures of New York is being built in Manhattan, challenging the tall, thin apartment towers standing in plazas that have been typical of the last 25 years.

Behind the growing popularity of these buildings in the last year is a rare convergence of opinion among architects, preservationists, neighborhood activists and planners in the Department of City Planning.

After years of dismissing old neighborhoods, architects with a post-modernist interest in historical styles are now taking traditional buildings on old city blocks as architectural models.

Preservationists see the new buildings — which typically have storefronts on the street and whose upper stories step back in a "wedding cake" design — as compatible with older structures and with the social fabric of established neighborhoods.

"But the new buildings are not just happening because architects think it's nice," said the director of the Manhattan office of the Department of City Planning, Con Howe.

The new generation of buildings is largely a result of zoning changes made by the department, which has encouraged the buildings where appropriate. A sweeping neighborhood-by-neighborhood zoning review, called the Quality Housing program, that is under way will make these buildings an alternative that will no longer require spe-

Continued on Page B4, Column 1

INSIDE

The Pill: A New Kind

A drug may soon be available in France that both blocks and terminates pregnancy, a World Health Organization official said. Page A15.

Brazilians Mourn Priestess

Mourning has continued for weeks in Salvador, Brazil, over the death of a 92-year-old cult priestess who was revered across the country. Page A4.

U.S. Plans to Aid Patients

In a reversal after efforts to cut regulation of nursing homes, the Reagan Administration plans new rules to protect patients' rights. Page A13.

The New York Times/Barton Silverman

METS LOSE TO ASTROS, 3-1: Alan Ashby, right, after hitting a two-run homer. Denis Menke, third base coach, is at left. League championship series is tied at two each. SportsMonday, page C1.

"All the News That's Fit to Print"

The New York Times

Late Edition

New York Today: Rain, heavy in afternoon. High 51-56. Tonight, rain changing to showers. Low 42-47. Tomorrow, gradual clearing. High 48-53. Yesterday: High 52, low 39. Details on page B9.

VOL.CXXXVI .. No. 46,970 Copyright © 1986 The New York Times NEW YORK, WEDNESDAY, NOVEMBER 26, 1986 30 cents beyond 75 miles from New York City, except on Long Island 30 CENTS

IRAN PAYMENT FOUND DIVERTED TO CONTRAS; REAGAN SECURITY ADVISER AND AIDE ARE OUT

Friedman Is Guilty With 3 in Scandal

ALL PLAN TO APPEAL

Charges of Corruption in New York Case Carry Long Prison Terms

By RICHARD J. MEISLIN
Special to The New York Times

NEW HAVEN, Nov. 25 — A jury today returned guilty verdicts against Stanley M. Friedman, the Bronx Democratic leader and long one of New York City's most powerful political figures, on all charges against him in the first Federal trial stemming from New York City's corruption scandal.

Three other defendants were also found guilty of charges including racketeering, conspiracy and mail fraud for their participation in a "racketeering enterprise" that transformed the city's Parking Violations Bureau into a tool for their corrupt personal profit.

The 12 jurors, their expressions grim, delivered the verdict at 11:11 A.M. after deliberating for three days on the eight weeks of testimony and argument in the case. The jury found Mr. Friedman and each of his co-defendants guilty of racketeering, conspiracy and mail fraud charges carrying lengthy prison sentences and heavy financial penalties.

Sentencing Set for March 1

In addition to Mr. Friedman, those found guilty were Lester N. Shafran, the former director of the Parking Violations Bureau; Michael J. Lazar, a real-estate developer and former city transportation administrator, and Marvin B. Kaplan, the chairman of Citisource Inc., a company chosen to manufacture hand-held computers to issue summonses for the parking bureau. Mr. Kaplan was also found guilty of having perjured himself while testifying before the Securities and Exchange Commission last February.

Judge Whitman Knapp, who presided over the trial, scheduled sentencing for March 1 at 10 A.M. Lawyers for all four defendants said they would file appeals at that time.

The trial of the four defendants was the first to stem from Federal investigations into corruption in the New York City government, and the United States Attorney in Manhattan, Rudolph

Continued on Page B3, Column 1

More Inquiries to Come

The verdicts in New Haven cleared the way for other inquiries into New York City corruption, perhaps lasting for several years. Page B3.

Stanley M. Friedman and his daughter, Betty, leaving courthouse in New Haven after guilty verdict. Rudolph W. Giuliani, below, prosecuted case.
The New York Times/Jim Wilson

Manila and Rebels Say Cease-Fire Could Be Signed in a Day or Two

By BARBARA CROSSETTE
Special to The New York Times

MANILA, Nov. 25 — The Government of President Corazon C. Aquino said tonight that it might be within two days of signing a cease-fire agreement with Communist rebels.

Peace talks, broken off after the killing of a left-wing labor leader nearly two weeks ago, resumed this afternoon

less than 48 hours after the President said the talks would be called off if no accord was reached by Sunday.

Tonight, after eight hours of talks, the leader of the Government team, Agriculture Minister Ramon V. Mitra, told reporters, "I like to think we have just one more meeting, and then make an announcement."

He implied that the final meeting would take place Wednesday and that an agreement would be announced Thursday. "We are so close," he said.

'Technical Hitches' Cited

Declining to disclose the length of the cease-fire agreed on, Mr. Mitra said it was less than 100 days, the time sought by the Communists, but more than 30 days, the Government's proposal.

At the outset of the talks aimed at establishing a cease-fire, both sides said they hoped it would be a opportunity for more comprehensive negotiations to bring the insurgency to a formal end and bring guerrillas back into society.

It was not made clear today whether the Government had agreed to the rebels' preconditions, which included the scaling back of military deployment, the disbanding of certain paramilitary units and the restriction of the police to civilian law-enforcement duties.

The proposed truce, if begun early next month as planned, would extend through the Christmas season and pos-

Continued on Page A16, Column 1

INSIDE

Takeover Action Swings Up
A lull in merger activity abruptly ended, with billion-dollar offers for Cheseborough-Pond's, Borg-Warner and Carter Hawley Hale. Page D1.

Bumpers Case Revived
New York State's top court reinstated charges against a policeman who killed a knife-wielding, emotionally disturbed woman in 1984. Page B1.

President Reagan deferring reporters' questions to Attorney General Edwin Meese 3d at news conference yesterday in Washington. With them were Donald T. Regan, left, White House chief of staff, and Larry Speakes, the White House spokesman, next to the President. Mr. Reagan had just announced the resignation of Vice Adm. John M. Poindexter, far right, as national security adviser and the dismissal of Lieut. Col. Oliver L. North, right, for his role in the Iranian arms affair.
The New York Times: Paul Hosefros

The Iran Affair: A Presidency Damaged

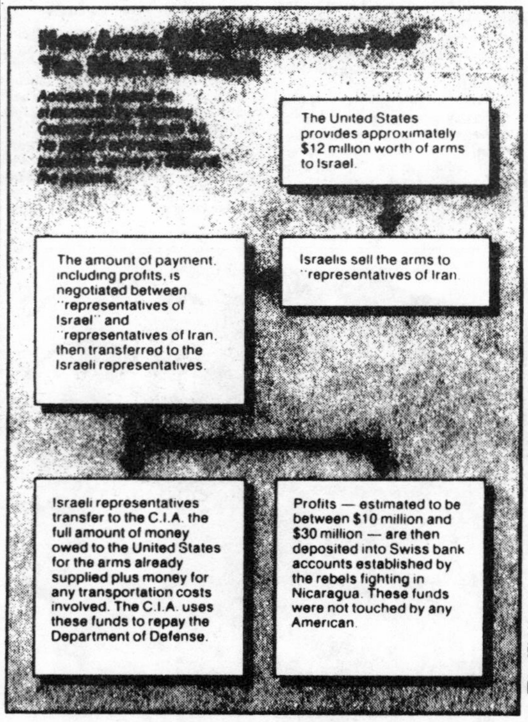

Both Friends and Foes See Reagan as Isolated

By R. W. APPLE Jr.
Special to The New York Times

WASHINGTON, Nov. 25 — After six years of seeming invulnerability, President Reagan has been grievously damaged by the crisis over secret arms shipments to Iran.

News Analysis With a unanimity rare in Washington, leading Republican and Democratic politicians agreed today that the disclosure of payments to the Nicaraguan rebels and the departure of two White House aides had probably hurt the Administration more than it helped. Some think the damage may be irreparable.

A week of unrelieved criticism of Mr. Reagan's secret decision to send arms to Iran, and of startling public bickering among senior Administration officials, has created the image of a President isolated, stuck with an unpopular policy and uncharacteristically defensive. The disclosures today produced a sensation in Washington unmatched, perhaps, since the days of the Watergate crisis.

'Probably No Smoking Gun'

"There is probably no smoking gun here," said a man who served in the White House during the Watergate years. "But there is a new mess in Washington, if not a new Watergate. There will be a whole string of fresh disclosures in the months to come, and that will throw the Administration off stride.

"It will hurt the effort in Nicaragua, it will hurt the campaign against terrorism and it will hurt Reagan — unless, of course, he gets lucky and something happens in Iran that shows he was right after all."

In the weeks to come, Mr. Reagan seems certain to find his credibility, his competence and his control under stern challenge.

On a personal level, Mr. Reagan remains the most popular President of modern times, and he has shown enormous resilience in the past. But he approaches the last two years of his Administration — a time when the strongest Presidents have seen their power slip slowly away — with the Senate and the House of Representatives under Democratic control, with severe budgetary problems demanding attention and now with months or perhaps even

Continued on Page A12, Column 5

The United States provides approximately $12 million worth of arms to Israel.

The amount of payment, including profits, is negotiated between "representatives of Israel" and "representatives of Iran," then transferred to the Israeli representatives.

Israelis sell the arms to "representatives of Iran."

Israeli representatives transfer to the C.I.A. the full amount of money owed to the United States for the arms already supplied plus money for any transportation costs involved. The C.I.A. uses these funds to repay the Department of Defense.

Profits — estimated to be between $10 million and $30 million — are then deposited into Swiss bank accounts established by the rebels fighting in Nicaragua. These funds were not touched by any American.

More on the Policy Crisis

Legal questions were raised by the operation involving the Nicaraguan rebels, including whether criminal laws had been broken. Page A11.

The contra-aid mystery may be explained by the disclosure, Congressional investigators and Administration officials said. Page A13.

Israel said it sent arms to Iran at the "request" of Washington and did not know some payments to the contras. Page A12.

A Saudi arms dealer played a central role in financing the Iranian purchase of arms, Israeli and American sources said. Page A13.

Doubts were raised by intelligence experts, officials and lawmakers con-

cerning the Administration's explanation of the arms shipments and assertions that only two American Government officials knew money was going to the contras. Page A11.

A sister of an American hostage held in Lebanon wrote to President Reagan in support of his Iran initiative and expressed "a deep sense of shame" that she had not spoken out sooner. Page A16.

Alton G. Keel Jr., the acting national security adviser, is described as an intelligent and hard-working man who has seldom taken a visible leadership role. Page A12.

Nancy Reagan dismissed the idea that the President had been badly damaged by the growing turmoil in his Administration. Page A16.

DISARRAY DEEPENS

Was Not 'Fully Informed' About Secret Moves, President Asserts

By BERNARD WEINRAUB
Special to The New York Times

WASHINGTON, Nov. 25 — President Reagan said today that he had not been in full control of his Administration's Iran policy, and the White House said that as a consequence up to $30 million intended to pay for American arms had been secretly diverted to rebel forces in Nicaragua.

At the same time, the President announced that two men he held responsible — Vice Adm. John M. Poindexter,

Statement by President Reagan and Meese's comments, page A10.

the national security adviser, and Lieut. Col. Oliver L. North, a member of the admiral's staff — had left their posts.

With the Administration already in turmoil over the earlier disclosure of clandestine arms shipments to Iran, and with speculation rampant about a major overhaul of the White House staff, the President's statement seemed to deepen a sense of disarray. By all accounts, Mr. Reagan now faces the most serious crisis in his six-year Presidency.

Shultz to Control Policy

The State Department, meanwhile, said Secretary of State George P. Shultz had been given control over future Iran policy, authority that apparently met his condition for remaining in office. State Department officials, including Mr. Shultz, have said they were left in the dark on much of the Iran operation. [Page A12.]

Mr. Reagan stunned legislators and ranking Administration officials by announcing in a televised session with reporters that he had not been "fully informed" of some details of the Iran operation and that Admiral Poindexter and Colonel North were leaving after "serious questions of propriety had been raised."

Inquiry Still Under Way

Mr. Reagan said that, "although not directly involved," Admiral Poindexter had "asked to be relieved of his assignment" and would return to Navy duties. Colonel North, the President said, "has been relieved of his duties on the National Security Council staff." Colonel North was widely reported to be the central figure in the Iran arms deal.

After Mr. Reagan's announcement, Attorney General Edwin Meese 3d said the Justice Department was still investigating how Nicaraguan rebel forces, known as contras, received "somewhere between $10 and $30 million."

Continued on Page A11, Column 1

TOP LEGISLATORS PROMISE INQUIRY

Likely Violations of Law Cited — Contra Aid May Suffer

By STEVEN V. ROBERTS
Special to The New York Times

WASHINGTON, Nov. 25 — Congressional leaders expressed astonishment today at the latest disclosures about United States dealings with Iran and vowed to investigate the Administration's actions.

The leaders asserted that several laws had probably been violated when funds paid by Iran for weapons were transferred to the Nicaraguan rebels.

The leaders also said Congress would probably approve legislation next year cutting off aid to the Nicaraguan rebels and would see to it that the head of the National Security Council would have to be confirmed by the Senate.

But the biggest question on Capitol Hill today was whether President Reagan and his chief aides had known about the operation.

Representative Jim Wright, the Texas Democrat who will become Speaker of the House in January, voiced skepticism about White House explanations that Vice Adm. John M. Poindexter, the national security adviser, had the highest ranking official to know about the operation.

It "defies logic," Mr. Wright told reporters, to believe that such a critical

Continued on Page A11, Column 1

"All the News That's Fit to Print"

The New York Times

Late Edition
New York: Today, increasing clouds. High 62-67. Tonight, cloudy, breezy, showers likely. Low 51-57. Tomorrow, showers ending. High 58-63. Yesterday: High 68, low 48. Details on page B6.

VOL.CXXXVII . . . No. 47,298 | Copyright © 1987 The New York Times | NEW YORK, TUESDAY, OCTOBER 20, 1987 | 50 cents beyond 75 miles from New York City, except on Long Island. | 30 CENTS

STOCKS PLUNGE 508 POINTS, A DROP OF 22.6%; 604 MILLION VOLUME NEARLY DOUBLES RECORD

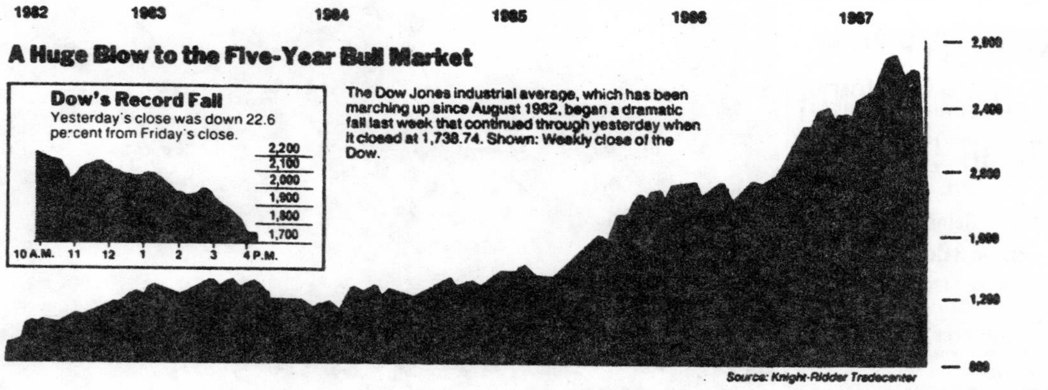
1982
1983
1984
1985
1986
1987
A Huge Blow to the Five-Year Bull Market
Dow's Record Fall
Yesterday's close was down 22.6 percent from Friday's close.
2,200
2,100
2,000
1,900
1,800
1,700
10 A.M.
11
12
1
2
3
4 P.M.
The Dow Jones industrial average, which has been marching up since August 1982, began a dramatic fall last week that continued through yesterday when it closed at 1,738.74. Shown: Weekly close of the Dow.
2,800
2,400
2,000
1,600
1,200
800
Source: Knight-Ridder Tradecenter

The New York Times/Oct. 20, 1987

U.S. Ships Shell Iran Installation In Gulf Reprisal

Offshore Target Termed a Base for Gunboats

By STEVEN V. ROBERTS

Special to The New York Times

WASHINGTON, Oct. 19 — United States naval forces struck back at Iran today for attacks on American-registered vessels and other Persian Gulf shipping by shelling two connected offshore platforms that American officials said were a base for Iranian gunboats.

A few hours later, a naval commando detachment boarded a third platform five miles away and destroyed radar and communications equipment, Pentagon officials said.

No American casualties were reported in the actions, which occurred 120 miles east of Bahrain at about 2 P.M. (7 A.M., Eastern daylight time).

A 20-Minute Warning

American officials said the attacking force took pains to avoid killing Iranians, giving the crew on the first two platforms a 20-minute warning before four destroyers, stationed about three miles away, began the shelling.

At the United Nations, an Iranian delegate said "several innocent people" had been killed in the attack, but the assertion could not be confirmed.

With the bombardment, the Administration intended to send a message to Iran: The United States had shown restraint in the level of its attack this time, but might respond with greater force if Iran continued "unprovoked attacks" on gulf shipping. [Military analysis, page A10.]

'Prudent Yet Restrained'

President Reagan issued a statement describing the actions as a "prudent yet restrained response." Defense Secretary Caspar W. Weinberger warned that "stronger countermeasures" would be taken if Iranian attacks continued.

Administration officials acknowledged that today's action was unlikely to halt the cycle of violence that has ensnared American forces in the gulf since 11 Kuwaiti tankers were placed under their protection this summer. "Nobody thinks that this will end it," Vice President Bush said today.

But the actions were necessary, Mr. Bush added, because American credibility was at stake in the region after a

Continued on Page A10, Column 1

ABC News

Two connected Iranian offshore platforms on fire after being shelled by American destroyers. A U.S. warship can be seen in the background.

Does 1987 Equal 1929?

By ERIC GELMAN

News Analysis

As stock prices soared this year, a chorus of pessimists warned that 1987 was looking more like 1929, when a stock market crash helped to usher in the Great Depression. Yesterday, after a plunge reminiscent of the worst days of 1929, one pressing question was whether the aftershocks would be as devastating to individuals and the nation.

The quick answer, many economists say, is no. The huge losses on Wall Street constitute a substantial blow to the economy at large. But there are many safeguards in place today — some instituted directly in response to the Depression — that would tend to prevent the cascading financial collapse that characterized the crash, impoverishing millions of Americans.

"A stock market crash doesn't ripple out into the economy with the same force" as it did in 1929, said Geoffrey H. Moore, director of the Center for International Business Cycle Research at Columbia University.

To be sure, there are some unsettling similarities between the current era and the pre-Depression years. Like the Roaring Twenties, the 1980's have seen an astonishing boom Wall Street. Now as then, individual and corporate debt are high, and some sectors of the economy are extremely weak. Trade relations are strained, with protectionist sentiment growing.

But today's economy is better equipped to handle financial shocks. "I don't see this decline in the stock market leading to a great breakdown in the economy," said Robert A. Kavesh, a professor of finance and economics at the New York University School of Business. "There are still many elements of strength in the economy —

Continued on Page D34, Column 5

Who Gets Hurt?

By ROBERT A. BENNETT

Unless the stock market bounces back quickly and substantially, most Americans are likely to be hurt by the dramatic decline in stock values — even those who own no stock at all.

Although it is a long jump from a record stock market plunge to a second Great Depression, it is much more likely that the plunging market may shake the economy and lead to a distinct downturn.

The biggest threat may be the spread of worry and fear. If investors feel poorer and employees begin to worry about the fortunes of their employers, consumers may draw back from spending of all kinds. They will postpone trading in the family car, do without a winter vacation and put off buying the home they wanted.

Reluctant to Build Plants

Similarly, businesses, stunned by the decline in their shares' value and facing the prospect of curtailed consumer spending, will shy away from building new plants or buying new equipment. Universities, churches, hospitals and other nonprofit institutions will likewise see their endowments shrink in value and are likely to brake their own spending.

And for all these diverse investors, the lower level of stock-market wealth will make it tougher to raise money by selling stock or borrowing against it.

"This affects even those who don't have direct investments in stocks," said Henry Kaufman, the chief economist of Salomon Brothers, a major

Continued on Page D34, Column 1

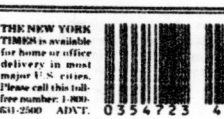

The New York Times/Marilynn K. Yee

Terrence J. McManus, a specialist with Spear, Leeds & Kellogg, on the floor of the New York Stock Exchange yesterday. Articles on Wall Street's day to remember and the sinking of investor hopes, page D1.

WORLDWIDE IMPACT

Frenzied Trading Raises Fears of Recession — Tape 2 Hours Late

By LAWRENCE J. De MARIA

Stock market prices plunged in a tumultuous wave of selling yesterday, giving Wall Street its worst day in history and raising fears of a recession.

The Dow Jones industrial average, considered a benchmark of the market's health, plummeted a record 508 points, to 1,738.74, based on preliminary calculations. That 22.6 percent decline was the worst since World War I and far greater than the 12.82 percent drop on Oct. 28, 1929, that along with the next day's 11.7 percent decline preceded the Great Depression.

Since hitting a record 2,722.42 on Aug. 25, the Dow has fallen almost 1,000 points, or 36 percent, putting the blue-chip indicator 157.5 points below the level at which it started the year. With Friday's plunge of 108.35 points, the Dow has fallen more than 26 percent in the last two sessions.

Unprecedented Trading

Yesterday's frenzied trading on the nation's stock exchanges lifted volume to unheard of levels. On the New York Stock Exchange, an estimated 604.3 million shares changed hands, almost double the previous record of 338.5 million shares set just last Friday.

With the tremendous volume, reports of brokers' trades on the New York Stock Exchange were delayed by more than two hours at one point. The New York Stock Exchange said that, as a result, it would not have definitive figures for the Dow's point decline and the exchange's volume until today.

Yesterday's big losers included International Business Machines, the bluest of the blue chips, which dropped $31, to $104. In August the stock was at $176. The other big losers among the blue chips were General Motors, which lost $13.875, to $52.125, and Exxon, which dropped $10.25, to $33.50.

More Than $1 Trillion Lost

According to Wilshire Associates, which tracks more than 5,000 stocks, the rout obliterated more than $500 billion in equity value from the nation's stock portfolios. That equity value now stands at $2.311 trillion. Since late summer, more than $1 trillion in stock values has been lost.

The losses were so great they sent shock waves to markets around the world, and many foreign exchanges posted record losses. In a sign of the continuing effect, the Tokyo Stock Exchange fell sharply today. The Nikkei Dow Jones average plummeted a record 3,395.95 yen, to 22,350.61, a drop of 13.2 percent, by late afternoon. Also, The Hong Kong exchange decided to close for the week.

In Washington yesterday, the White House spokesman, Marlin Fitzwater, issued a statement saying that President Reagan had "watched with concern" the stock market's collapse. But Mr. Reagan remained convinced that the economy was sound.

Economy Called Sound

Mr. Fitzwater said the President had directed Administration officials to contact leading financial experts. "Those consultations confirm our view that the underlying economy remains sound," he added.

Stock market analysts scrambled for explanations, which ranged from rising interest rates to the falling dollar to the possibility of war between the United States and Iran.

Indeed, the panic selling may have been bolstered by the news that the United States Navy destroyed an Iranian offshore oil platform in the central Persian Gulf yesterday, and Iran vowed retaliation.

But many experts seemed to think

Continued on Page D34, Column 1

Goetz Given 6-Month Term on Gun Charge

Bernhard H. Goetz, who ignited a nationwide debate about self-defense when he shot four teen-agers on a Manhattan subway train, was sentenced yesterday to six months in jail for carrying an unlicensed concealed pistol.

Mr. Goetz, who was acquitted of charges of attempted murder and assault at his trial last June, was also sentenced to five years' probation and ordered to undergo psychiatric counseling. He could have received as much as seven years' imprisonment.

The judge, Acting Justice Stephen G. Crane, stayed the sentence pending an appeal by Mr. Goetz, who left the courtroom without making any comment to reporters.

Outside the courthouse, however, Mr. Goetz's lead lawyer, Barry I. Slotnick, said, "We think that he's being treated harsher as a result of the fact that he's Bernhard Goetz."

The case began Dec. 22, 1984, when Mr. Goetz shot the youths on a downtown IRT train with a .38-caliber revolver. From his surrender that month through his indictments, the long legal maneuvering and the trial, Mr. Goetz steadfastly insisted that he had shot the youths because they were about to rob him.

Article, page B1.

More About the Markets

Bonn and the United States agreed that the dollar should be stabilized near current levels. Disagreement on currency levels and interest rates had contributed to unrest in the markets. Page D1.

Small investors searched for news much of the day. Many held on to their stocks, as they tried to determine what really was happening in the stock market. Page D1.

Washington officials hesitated to offer investors immediate advice. The shouts of panic on Wall Street echoed only faintly in the corridors of the Reagan Administration. The White House maintained that the underlying economy remained sound. News analysis, page D32.

Investors bought U.S. securities in a search for a safe place to put their money. Some interest rates hovered just below 10 percent. Page D1.

Tokyo's stock market plummeted to record losses today and the Hong Kong market suspended trading for the week as Asian investors reacted in fright to the collapse on Wall Street. Page D1.

Business leaders were shaken by the collapse, which wiped out huge amounts of the market value of their companies. And they seemed to have been caught by surprise. But many leaders were confident the panic would pass. Page D32.

Overseas investors sold actively on Wall Street after years of having poured money into the bull market. Accounts of the volume of foreign selling varied widely. Page D14.

Wall Street firms are uncertain about the effect the historic drop could have on them, but some analysts fear that smaller and poorly capitalized firms may find rough going in the days ahead. Page D33.

Mutual funds sold stock shares in huge numbers, feeding the historic drop. Several mutual fund management companies said the number of phone calls from investors was about double the normal volume. Page D33.

New York City could be affected significantly because of its large number of securities industry employees. Some experts maintain that the city's economy has grown too reliant on Wall Street. Page D32.

Trading tested computers' ability to handle a volume of trading that had not been expected until the early 1990's. Page D34.

The dollar closed lower against leading currencies except the Canadian dollar. Analysts said trading was quiet as traders were preoccupied by the jarring news from the stock market. Gold was $486.50 an ounce, up $15.50 from Friday to reach its highest level in over four years. Page D26.

Democratic leaders called for talks with President Reagan on a deficit-reduction package that would include tax increases. Page D32.

In politics, two questions loomed: How badly were the Republicans' 1988 chances hurt? How were the Democrats' prospects helped? Political Memo. Page A30.

INSIDE

Turnaround on Schools

A week after adopting a year-round term, the Los Angeles Board of Education reversed itself. A new vote was set for March 1. Page A17.

Senator Stennis to Retire

John C. Stennis, Democrat of Mississippi, will leave the Senate at the end of this term, when he will have served more than 41 years. Page A16.

Martin Back With Yankees

The Yankees promoted Lou Piniella to the post of general manager and brought Billy Martin back for his fifth stint as manager. Page B7.

"All the News That's Fit to Print"

The New York Times

Late Edition

New York: Today, partly sunny, breezy. High 45-50. Tonight, increasing clouds, colder. Low 26-36. Tomorrow, sunny periods, cold. High 35-40. Yesterday: High 70, low 48. Details on page C26.

VOL.CXXXVII . . No. 47,328 | NEW YORK, THURSDAY, NOVEMBER 19, 1987 | 50 cents beyond 75 miles from New York City, except on Long Island. | 30 CENTS

IRAN-CONTRA REPORT SAYS PRESIDENT BEARS 'ULTIMATE RESPONSIBILITY' FOR WRONGDOING

Mortgage Rates And Housing Construction

New private housing started, in millions.* Mortgage rates, at key points, are in parentheses.[1]

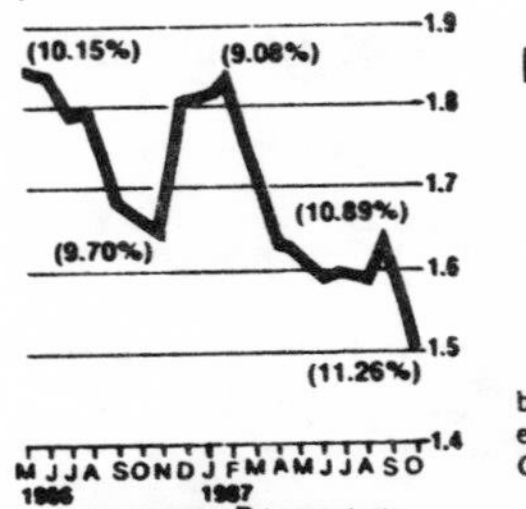

*Seasonally adjusted, annual rate
[1]30-year fixed rate mortgage, monthly average.
Source: Commerce Department; Federal Home Loan Mortgage Corp

The New York Times Nov. 19, 1987

Let Banks Enter Securities Field, Greenspan Says

By NATHANIEL C. NASH
Special to The New York Times

WASHINGTON, Nov. 18 — The Federal Reserve Board called today for repeal of legislation enacted during the Depression that places a barrier between the banking and securities industries.

Advocates of such change, including most banking regulators, say consumers would find a wider range of products at their banks and at lower cost.

Supporters of the barrier say enough competition already exists to provide consumers with a variety of investments at fair prices. There is not enough public benefit, they argue, to allow the industries to combine.

Testifying before a House banking subcommittee, Alan Greenspan, chairman of the Federal Reserve Board, said the central bank wanted commercial banks to be able to engage in the broadest range of securities underwriting. As a safeguard, Mr. Greenspan recommended that securities operations be confined to a separate unit of a bank holding company.

The legislation under assault is the Glass-Steagall Act of 1933, one of the nation's landmark banking laws. It was intended to increase the stability of the banking industry by preventing it from speculating in stocks and other securities. Now a concerted effort to repeal some of its key provisions is being

Continued on Page D10, Column 4

32 Are Killed in Fire At London Subway; 80 Reported Injured

By HOWELL RAINES
Special to The New York Times

LONDON, Thursday, Nov. 19 — At least 32 people were killed and about 80 injured Wednesday night when a fire broke out in a subway station in central London.

Witnesses described a scene of panic and confusion in the King's Cross station as commuters were trapped in the ticketing areas and on platforms of the Piccadilly Line. They reported seeing people with their clothes and hair aflame, clawing desperately to make their way to the exits.

"People were running everywhere, panicking and treading on each other," said Paul Medland, a survivor.

Another commuter, Doug McAdam, told of arriving in the station in a train just as smoke billowed down toward the tracks. "It was like coming into a pub full of smoke," he said. "The escalator had been shut down and the station guards sent us toward the Victoria Line escalator, which was working. As we went up, the smoke was worse."

The blaze started at the foot of a wooden escalator at about 7:50 P.M., catching the last of Wednesday's evening rush hour crowd at the city's busiest underground station, where five subway lines converge.

Early reports were that the fire started in the equipment room under the escalator that links the Piccadilly Line platforms with the main ticketing concourse of the station. Officials did not rule out the possibility that an incendiary device was involved, but they

Continued on Page A3, Column 4

STARTS IN HOUSING FALL 8% IN MONTH TO HIT 4-YEAR LOW

Most of October Drop Tied to Rise in Rates That Ended When Stocks Plunged

By PETER T. KILBORN
Special to The New York Times

WASHINGTON, Nov. 18 — Home building plunged in October to its lowest level in more than four years, the Government reported today.

Economists attributed most of the decline to the rise in interest rates that ended with the plunge of the stock market. Since then, rates have receded, but they are expected to stay high enough in the next year or so to prevent any burst of new construction.

Construction of houses and apartments dropped in October to an annual rate of 1.51 million, 8.2 percent below the September rate, the sharpest one-month drop in three years.

Between Boom and Recession

Despite the severity of the drop, that annual rate is midway between boom levels and recession levels, and economists predict it would remain there well into next year if mortgage rates continued in double digits, as they expect.

"We're busy as ever, just a little more nervous," said Richard A. Lewis, president of Lewis Homes in Upland, Calif., which builds 3,000 houses and apartments a year in one of the nation's strongest areas for new housing.

Economists predict little recovery from the October pace because they expect interest rates to remain above 10 percent; rates below that level lead to booms in construction. Rates for home mortgages, which were at a low of 9 percent on average last March, steadily rose to 10.5 percent in June, and then abated a bit in July.

At that point, investors and the Fed-

Continued on Page D11, Column 4

The New York Times/Paul Hosefros

Senator Warren B. Rudman, Republican of New Hampshire, commenting yesterday on the majority report of the Congressional committees that investigated the Iran-contra affair. With him were, from the right, Representative Lee H. Hamilton, Democrat of Indiana, and Senators Daniel K. Inouye, Democrat of Hawaii; Paul S. Trible Jr., Republican of Virginia; Paul S. Sarbanes, Democrat of Maryland; George J. Mitchell, Democrat of Maine, and William S. Cohen, Republican of Maine.

U.S. Aides Say Panama General Proposed Sabotage in Nicaragua

By STEPHEN ENGELBERG
Special to The New York Times

WASHINGTON, Nov. 18 — Panama's military leader offered to undertake sabotage and possibly assassinations in Nicaragua for the Reagan Administration, Government officials said today, explaining a veiled allusion to the matter in the Iran-contra report.

The officials said Lieut. Col. Oliver L. North, then a White House aide, had accepted the sabotage offer on the instructions of Rear Adm. John M. Poindexter, then the President's national security adviser. But they said the plan put forward by the Panamanian, Gen. Manuel Antonio Noriega, never got off the ground.

They said computer messages reviewed by the Congressional committees but not disclosed in the report suggested that General Noriega was also offering to undertake assassinations, but that Admiral Poindexter told Colonel North not to become involved. American Government officials are prohibited by executive order from conducting or taking part in assassinations.

The Enterprise's Activities

The Congressional report provides the fullest account yet of the activities kept secret from Congress by the Administration. It says White House officials were planning many more operations when their secret network was exposed last year.

Although it does not describe in detail the other covert operations planned by "the Enterprise," the private companies run by Richard V. Secord, a retired Air Force major general, and Albert Hakim, an Iranian-born middleman, the report says they included gathering intelligence on terrorists, freeing hostages and underwriting secret propaganda efforts.

The report also details completed operations, including Colonel North's use of a Danish ship to ferry arms around the world and his payments to Drug Enforcement Administration agents hoping to free American hostages in Lebanon.

In discussing the activities attributed by officials to Panama, the Congressional report says only that "a third party" offered to carry out the operations, and it does not indicate that a foreign government was involved.

According to the report, Admiral

Continued on Page A11, Column 1

Worst Is Past For President

Damage to Reputation Was Done Long Ago

By JOEL BRINKLEY
Special to The New York Times

WASHINGTON, Nov. 18 — Even with its arresting descriptions of "pervasive dishonesty" and "disarray at the highest levels of Government," the Congressional report on the Iran-contra affair is not likely to do significant new harm to the Reagan Presidency because the damage is already done.

News Analysis

The affair knocked President Reagan off his feet a year ago. As politicians of both parties say — and the failures, embarrassments and strident calls for stronger leadership of the last several months demonstrate — Mr. Reagan has never fully regained his stride.

'There Isn't Much New Here'

White House officials may be correct when they say, as one put it today, that "the public is tired" of the Iran-contra affair. In fact they were banking on that as they brushed off the report with a dismissive wave.

"There isn't much new here," said Marlin Fitzwater, the White House spokesman.

But while the White House may be correct that the report is not likely to set off new waves of criticism and angst, it is because the public view calcified many months ago that the affair had already diminished Mr. Reagan as a leader.

"The damage to Reagan's reputation came in the first two weeks," said an independent political consultant, Wil-

Continued on Page A11, Column 1

'CABAL OF ZEALOTS'

No Bush Role Is Found — Reagan Says It Is Time to Move On

By DAVID E. ROSENBAUM
Special to The New York Times

WASHINGTON, Nov. 18 — The Congressional committees on the Iran-contra affair blamed President Reagan in their final report today for failing to live up to his constitutional mandate to "take care that the laws be faithfully executed" and said he bore "the ultimate responsibility" for wrongdoing by his aides.

"Fundamental processes of governance were disregarded and the rule of law was subverted," the majority report of the committees asserted. "If the President did not know what his national security advisers were doing, he should have."

The White House reacted with a statement by Mr. Reagan's spokesman, Marlin Fitzwater, saying the President understood that mistakes had been made, accepted responsibility and believed that the time had come to move on to other, more pressing issues.

An Authoritative Narrative

The Congressional report provided the most accurate accounting to date on how nearly $48 million raised from the arms sales to Iran had been distributed and added some new details about other matters.

Although it included little important evidence that was not covered during the three months of public hearings last spring and summer, it marshaled the details of the complicated affair into an authoritative narrative that sought to underpin its severe judgments on the Reagan Administration.

The 11-month investigation, the most thorough and highly publicized Congressional inquiry since the Watergate scandal, grew out of the disclosures a year ago this month that the Reagan Administration had secretly sold arms to Iran and had run a clandestine operation to support the Nicaraguan rebels.

The focus now shifts to the special prosecutor, Lawrence E. Walsh, who is expected to seek indictments soon, perhaps in January.

Sweeping Criticism of Officials

"The Iran-contra affair was characterized by pervasive dishonesty and inordinate secrecy," the report said in a sweeping criticism of officials involved in the clandestine deals to ship arms to Iran and use the proceeds to finance the contras.

The report, which was accompanied

Continued on Page A10, Column 3

More on the Report

Key sections of the Congressional Iran-contra report and a transcript of the White House response are on pages A12-15. Also inside, a chronology, page A12; a cast of characters, page A13, and the special prosecutor's reaction, page A10.

Biological Mother Is Granted Custody of Boy in Abuse Case

The New York Times/William E. Sauro

Nicole Bridget Smigiel, right, biological mother of Mitchell Steinberg, and her mother, Graceann, arriving at Family Court.

By KIRK JOHNSON

The biological mother of a 17-month-old boy raised by a Manhattan couple who have been charged in the death of another child won temporary custody of the boy yesterday.

The woman, Nicole Bridget Smigiel, argued in an emotional hearing that the boy, Mitchell, had never been legally adopted. Miss Smigiel, who is 18 and lives in Massapequa Park, L.I., is seeking permanent custody.

The couple who had been raising the boy, Joel B. Steinberg and Hedda Nussbaum, are charged with murdering the other child, Lisa, and with neglect in the care of Mitchell, who was taken from the Steinberg home in Greenwich Village by the police on Nov. 2.

Mitchell, who began living with Mr. Steinberg and Ms. Nussbaum immediately after birth, was found tied to a chair and drinking spoiled milk. He has been in city foster care since Nov. 2. Yesterday, attorneys for Mr. Steinberg and Ms. Nussbaum strongly opposed Miss Smigiel's request for custody.

The court decision, at Family Court Building in lower Manhattan, was ordered held in abeyance by the judge, Jeffry H. Gallet, until 5 P.M. today to allow attorneys for Mr. Steinberg and Ms. Nussbaum to file appeals.

The attorneys for the city's Department of Social Services and the court-appointed lawyers speaking for Mitchell's interests supported the judge.

"I am not predeciding this case," Judge Gallet said in explaining the custody ruling, which will likely remain in effect pending a Family Court trial, to begin in January. "I just don't want this child bounced around," the judge said, referring to the foster-care program.

Under state law, blood relatives are given priority in temporary custody

Continued on Page B6, Column 4

INSIDE

Turmoil in Mexico

The peso fell by 59 percent against the dollar after the central bank stopped propping it up. And inflation reached 141 percent. Page D1.

Moscow Gives Arms Data

The Soviet Union gave the United States data on missiles as negotiators pressed to complete a missile treaty. Page A8.

New Post for Russian

Boris N. Yeltsin, removed as head of the Moscow Communist Party, was given a high post in the construction industry, Tass reported. Page A9.

Korean Fights His Past

For Roh Tae Woo, Government candidate for President of South Korea, unshackling himself from his military background is a key goal. Page A3.

Budget Plan Under Attack

Congressional negotiators criticized the emerging plan to reduce the budget deficit, raising doubts about its prospects for approval. Page A26.

CBS Returns to its Roots

CBS agreed to sell its records division to Sony for about $2 billion in cash, completing its sale of non-broadcast operations. Page D1.

Parents of Premature Infants Thrust Into a Life-Saving Role

Personal Health

New on Thursdays: The Health Page

A new life-saving role for parents of premature babies. And the Personal Health column reports on keeping the memory sharp. Page B12.

Also today: Parent & Child, a column starting this week in The Home Section, discusses neatness. Page C8.

Outlook for AIDS Victims

About 15 percent of the AIDS patients in New York City have survived at least five years, hinting at a less dire outlook for some victims. Page B1.

"All the News That's Fit to Print"

The New York Times

Late Edition
New York: Today, partly sunny skies. High 48-58. Tonight, partly cloudy. Low 40-45. Tomorrow, variable clouds and sun, showers. High 50-55. Yesterday: High 48, low 32. Details, page C32.

VOL.CXXXVII . . . No. 47,348 NEW YORK, WEDNESDAY, DECEMBER 9, 1987 — 50 cents beyond 75 miles from New York City, except on Long Island — 30 CENTS

REAGAN AND GORBACHEV SIGN MISSILE TREATY AND VOW TO WORK FOR GREATER REDUCTIONS

Associated Press

A.B.A. Rates Kennedy

Judge Anthony M. Kennedy, the Supreme Court nominee, has received the American Bar Association's highest rating. Page A29.

ECONOMY REPORTED HOLDING UP WELL SINCE STOCK SLIDE

A Recession Is Unlikely Soon, Analysts Say, Despite Slip in Consumer Spending

By ROBERT D. HERSHEY Jr.
Special to The New York Times

WASHINGTON, Dec. 8 — Defying widespread predictions, the economy has held up well since the stock market collapsed in mid-October and an imminent recession appears quite unlikely, private and Government analysts maintain.

Many forecasters who had initially slashed estimates for growth next year have been nudging them upward of late, prompted by successive sets of data indicating that the stock market tremors have yet to shake the economy's foundations.

These improved forecasts come despite consumer spending that slowed before the market plunge and seems to have lost further impetus since.

Spending Tied to Incomes

But while consumer spending has slowed, it has not dropped as sharply as many economists had feared. As best as economists can determine, people have apparently decided to base their spending on their incomes, not on their assets. And so their losses in the stock market have not dramatically affected their buying habits.

While the housing sector has been slumping, the decline in construction of new homes and sales of homes stems from the rising interest rates that preceded the stock market's collapse, and much of those increases have been reversed.

"I have zero evidence of an '88 early recession," said Joseph W. Duncan, chief economist for Dun & Bradstreet, who has just completed surveys of business expectations and production and investment plans. "Corporate America so far is saying, 'We're just going to move ahead because we have strong orders.' "

G.N.P. Loss 'Added Back'

An economist for a large New York bank said that, of a dozen economists with whom he lunched today, more than half had "added back" much or all of the loss of 1988 gross national product they had subtracted from their late-October G.N.P. estimates.

And in a survey last week, 51 economists polled by Blue Chip Economic Indicators, an Arizona-based newsletter,

Continued on Page D2, Column 5

Mikhail S. Gorbachev being welcomed yesterday by President Reagan at the White House. Associated Press

A MOOD OF WARMTH

As Summit Talks Begin, the Attention Shifts to Strategic Arms

By DAVID K. SHIPLER
Special to The New York Times

WASHINGTON, Dec. 8 — With fervent calls for a new era of peaceful understanding, President Reagan and Mikhail S. Gorbachev today signed the first treaty reducing the size of their nations' nuclear arsenals.

The President and the Soviet leader, beginning three days of talks aimed at even broader reductions, pledged to build on the accord by striving toward what Mr. Gorbachev called "the more important goal," reducing long-range nuclear weapons.

In their White House conversations, the leaders were said to have reviewed their previous proposals aimed at furthering those negotiations, and they established an arms-control working group of ranking officials to hold parallel sessions.

'Mine is Mikhail'

An immediate mood of warmth was established as the two leaders agreed this morning to call each other by their first names, a White House official said. He quoted the President as telling Mr. Gorbachev, "My first name is Ron."

Mr. Gorbachev answered, "Mine is Mikhail."

"When we're working in private session," Mr. Reagan reportedly said, "we can call each other that."

The new treaty, which provides for the dismantling of all Soviet and American medium- and shorter-range missiles, establishes the most extensive system of weapons inspection ever negotiated by the two countries, including placing technicians at sensitive sites on each other's territory.

The Mood for Talking

The signing, the fruition of years of negotiation, set the mood for two and a half hours of talks between the leaders. The talks were "very serious, substantive discussions," Secretary of State George P. Shultz said tonight before a formal dinner in the White House.

The visit to Washington by Mr. Gorbachev was the first by a Soviet leader since Leonid I. Brezhnev was here 14 years ago, and it took on immediate drama as Mr. Reagan, who entered office with deep suspicions of the Soviet Union, welcomed Mr. Gorbachev on the South Lawn of the White House.

"I have often felt that our people should have been better friends long ago," he told his guest as they stood

Continued on Page A20, Column 1

Estimate of Risk Of Dioxin Is Cut In Cancer Study

By PHILIP SHABECOFF
Special to The New York Times

WASHINGTON, Dec. 8 — The Environmental Protection Agency, in a new draft study with the potential for far-reaching policy implications, has sharply reduced its estimate of the cancer-causing potential of dioxin, a widespread chemical pollutant.

Dioxin has been described as among the most potent toxic substances known to man. But in a new risk assessment, the E.P.A. concludes that dioxin's potency as a cancer-inducing substance is one-sixteenth that of the agency's original estimate two years ago.

Agency officials said, however, that even considering the revised risk levels, dioxin is still the most toxic of the cancer-linked substances regulated by the agency.

Under the new risk assumptions, dioxin is 10,000 times more likely to cause cancer than PCB's, or polychlorinated biphenyls, at the same level of exposure, one agency official said. But the new assessment lowers the risk of dioxin by a significant amount and "brings it in out of left field," the official said.

Since dioxin appears in such minute quantities, the effect of the reassessment might be that previously troubling levels will be considered far less dangerous or even safe. The new report appears to strike a compromise between those scientists who see the alarm over dioxin as exaggerated and

Continued on Page D27, Column 1

HOW TO DESTROY THE 2,611 MISSILES

Treaty Details Ways but U.S. Withholds Data on Sites

By MICHAEL R. GORDON
Special to The New York Times

WASHINGTON, Dec. 8 — The text of the treaty signed today by President Reagan and Mikhail S. Gorbachev spells out how hundreds of American and Soviet inspectors will insure that 2,611 American and Soviet missiles are smashed, exploded, crushed, burned or launched to be destroyed.

But at American insistence, the text released today to the press and television does not include a 73-page annex that describes exactly where the weapons are kept.

American officials said that because of the danger from terrorists, the information was too sensitive to publish. Soviet officials, who have it, said that there was no reason why the information should be withheld and that it would be published in Moscow.

Rights of Inspectors

Under the treaty provisions, inspectors will have the right to visit installations on each side to confirm information provided by the other side. And when bases and support installations are eliminated, officials from each side will conduct special "close out" inspections. Inspectors will also observe the destruction of missiles.

Each side will have an annual quota of short-notice inspections for 13 years after the treaty goes into force.

Inspectors can make use of a camera that instantly produces two photographs, one for each side. The photos will be be taken not by the inspectors but by escorts from the nation being inspected. But the escorts are to photograph what the inspectors want.

To carry out inspections in the Soviet Union, American officials will fly to Moscow or Irkutsk. Once there, they

Continued on Page A21, Column 1

A Tempered Optimism

At the End of an Unlikely Journey, Reagan And Gorbachev Are Mindful of Differences

By R. W. APPLE Jr.
Special to The New York Times

News Analysis

WASHINGTON, Dec. 8 — Even for this city, which long ago mislaid its sense of wonder, this was a thrilling day, bathed in a glow of satisfaction at what has been achieved and of optimism about what may be just ahead.

Often Washington looks on the dark side, especially where the Soviet Union is concerned, but there were few in the capital who failed to feel a frisson of excitement as Mikhail S. Gorbachev stepped from his limousine and grasped Ronald Reagan's hand, few in the country who were immune to the drama of television pictures of the two leaders in profile with the red Soviet flag whipping in the wind behind them.

If, as Henry A. Kissinger once said, Americans oscillate between despair and euphoria in their attitudes toward the Soviet Union, today's emotions may be relatively short-lived. Certainly the hopes raised in June 1973, when Leonid I. Brezhnev was welcomed to the White House by Richard M. Nixon under steel-gray skies much like this morning's, proved ephemeral.

Both Mr. Reagan, with his call for "a heavy dose of realism," and Mr. Gorbachev, with his reminder of the "profound historical, ideological, socio-economic and cultural differences" that divide the superpowers, seemed to be warning of the limits of the process of accommodation they have begun.

But it is nonetheless remarkable that it has begun at all, and that these two men are those sponsoring it. For each, the moment at which they swapped pens after signing the treaty banning medium- and shorter-range nuclear arms represented the end of a long, im-

Continued on Page A20, Column 1

The Arms Treaty

The arms treaty and excerpts from the protocols to it are on pages A24-26. Additional coverage of yesterday's events, including remarks by President Reagan and Mikhail S. Gorbachev, appears on pages A20-23.

Air Crash Inquiry Is Said to Focus On Disgruntled Ex-Worker on Jet

By ROBERT REINHOLD
Special to The New York Times

TEMPLETON, Calif., Dec. 8 — The Federal Bureau of Investigation said today that criminal activity was strongly suspected in the crash of a jetliner that smashed into a cattle ranch here Monday after the pilot reported gunfire in the passenger cabin.

The crash killed all 43 people aboard the plane operated by Pacific Southwest Airlines, which last May was acquired by USAir.

Suspicion focused on a disgruntled former employee of USAir, dismissed last month on charges of stealing money from the company, who boarded the plane along with his former supervisor. The two men, together with all 36 other passengers and 5 crew members, died when the four-engine British Aerospace 146 Series 200 jet plunged into a green, oak-studded hillside near here in central California.

A Government official said he had been told that the employee, David A. Burke, had left a message on a friend's recording machine telling her that he was going to take care of the person who had dismissed him. But by the time she heard the message, the plane had crashed.

ABC News quoted unidentified officials as saying Mr. Burke left a suicide message indicating he intended to kill his former supervisor. The network said the authorities believed the former employee boarded the flight with a .44 magnum pistol.

Richard T. Bretzing, special agent in charge of the F.B.I.'s Los Angeles of-

Continued on Page D27, Column 3

The Emerging Candidate: Who Is Senator Simon?

By ROBIN TONER
Special to The New York Times

WASHINGTON, Dec. 8 — Senator Paul Simon of Illinois promises an administration of good deeds. He spins the vision of a nurturing Government.

If elected President, he says, he would give the unemployed an $8 billion-a-year job program. He would protect the elderly from the towering costs of nursing home care. The 11 books he has written bristle with Federal solutions to the nation's problems: a new program to rebuild the country's bridges and highways, a new Reconstruction Finance Corporation, a new drive to combat illiteracy.

"I want a Government that cares," he says. "I want a Government that helps people."

In a campaign dominated by tests of character, Mr. Simon's test has arisen not in his personal life but around his public policy. The issue is the cost of his unquestioned good intentions, the practicality of a politician who often affects a disdain for politics, the credibility of a man whose slogan is, "Isn't it time to believe again?"

In the simplest terms, his rivals for the Democratic nomination now demand that he explain how he would pay for it all and balance the budget in three years, as he promises.

"Paul, you're not a pay-as-you-go Democrat, you're a promise-as-you-go Democrat," Representative Richard A. Gephardt declared last week in a nationally

Continued on Page A28, Column 1

The New York Times/Paul Hosefros

Mr. Gorbachev applauding after he and Mr. Reagan signed copies of the treaty. At rear, staff members exchanged the copies so that each could be signed by the other leader.

News Summary, Page A2

INSIDE

Sandinistas Down American
An American pilot has been shot down over Nicaragua while "engaged in enemy activity," the Nicaraguan Defense Minister said. Page A3.

Reds Trade Dave Parker
The Cincinnati Reds traded Dave Parker, their aging but productive power hitter, to the Oakland Athletics for two young pitchers. Page A31.

Cardinal Krol to Retire
John Cardinal Krol, the Archbishop of Philadelphia, announced that he would retire on Feb. 11. Page A28.

$10 Million for Met Wing
Henry R. Kravis, a New York investor, has pledged $10 million to the Metropolitan Museum of Art to complete a new wing. Page C25.

Anti-Corruption Fund Asked
Top New York law-enforcement officials asked the Legislature for a $10 million fund to uncover corruption by officials and businesses. Page B1.

"All the News That's Fit to Print"

The New York Times

Late Edition
New York: Today, partly sunny and warmer. High 43-48. Tonight, clear and calm. Low 26-32. Tomorrow, sun then increasing clouds. High 45-50. Yesterday: High 43, low 29. Details, page C22.

VOL.CXXXVII . . No. 47,447 NEW YORK, THURSDAY, MARCH 17, 1988 — 50 cents beyond 75 miles from New York City, except on Long Island. — 30 CENTS

NORTH, POINDEXTER AND 2 OTHERS INDICTED ON IRAN-CONTRA FRAUD AND THEFT CHARGES

23 COUNTS DETAILED

Arms Middlemen Named — Walsh Acts After 14-Month Inquiry

By PHILIP SHENON
Special to The New York Times

WASHINGTON, March 16 — Lieut. Col. Oliver L. North, Rear Adm. John M. Poindexter and two other key participants in the Iran-contra affair were indicted today on charges of conspiracy to defraud the United States by illegally providing the Nicaraguan rebels with profits from the sale of American weapons to Iran.

The indictment was the most sweeping criminal action against former White House officials since the Watergate scandals, and presented to President Reagan the politically delicate issue of whether he should pardon his former aides before his term ends next January.

The long-awaited indictment, following a 14-month grand jury investigation, named Colonel North, who was a member of the National Security Council staff, and Admiral Poindexter, President Reagan's former national security adviser. It also med two middlemen in the arms nsfer — Richard V. Secord, a retired Air Force major general, and Albert A. Hakim, an Iranian-American businessman.

'Exploiting for Own Purposes'

All four were accused in the 23-count indictment of stealing money belonging to the Government — proceeds from the arms sales to Iran in 1985 and 1986 — and transfering a portion of the money to rebel groups, known as the contras, battling the Sandinista Government of Nicaragua.

They also were accused of wire fraud — using telephones or other wire communications to further their scheme.

The four have repeatedly denied wrongdoing, arguing their actions in the Iran-contra affair were motivated strictly by patriotism.

Money Involved Not Specified

According to the indictment the defendants, as part of what prosecutors described as the central conspiracy, defrauded the Government by "deceitfully exploiting for their own purposes" the Iran-contra initiative, "rather than pursuing solely the specified governmental objectives of the initiative, including the release of Americans being held hostage in Lebanon." [Excerpts from indictment, page D26.]

Today's indictment did not specify how much money may have been stolen. It said the arms sales to Iran generated about $30 million, of which the United States Government was paid $12 million.

Each of the defendants faces a different set of charges, and they could all go to prison for decades under the indictment. Law-enforcement officials said it

Continued on Page D27, Column 1

Indicted

The New York Times/Paul A. Souders
Lieut. Col. Oliver L. North

The New York Times
Rear Adm. John M. Poindexter

The Prosecutor

Agence France-Presse
Lawrence E. Walsh

3 Killed by Grenades at I.R.A. Funeral

Associated Press
Mourners ducking for cover as grenades exploded at a burial service in Belfast, Northern Ireland.

U.S. TO SEND FORCE TO AID HONDURAS, CITING 'INCURSION'

White House Charges a Raid by the Nicaraguan Army — 3,200 Troops to Go

By STEVEN V. ROBERTS
Special to The New York Times

WASHINGTON, March 16 — President Reagan tonight ordered the deployment of four battalions of American troops, about 3,200 men, to Honduras as a sign of support for the Government there.

In announcing the move, Marlin Fitzwater, the President's spokesman, said Honduras had suffered a "significant cross-border incursion" by 1,500 to 2,000 Sandinista troops.

That contention is disputed by President Daniel Ortega of Nicaragua, who has invited international observers to view the border region. [Page A12.]

Troops Will Be Restricted

Mr. Fitzwater called the troop movement an "emergency deployment readiness exercise," and said the soldiers would not be sent "to any area of ongoing hostilities." The troops, from Fort Bragg, N.C., and Fort Ord, Calif., are to leave Thursday morning. They are to be confined to the area surrounding the Palmerola Air Base in Honduras, about 125 miles from the Nicaraguan border.

The spokesman said the troops represented "an important signal and a deterrence, just by being in the region." The President, he added, sees the American forces as "an important show of solidarity" with Honduras.

Mr. Fitzwater insisted that President José Azcona Hoyo of Honduras had requested the military assistance tonight after consultation with Everett Briggs, the American ambassador to Honduras. "We are responding to his request," the spokesman asserted.

Military officials said, however, that

Continued on Page A12, Column 1

CONSUMER OUTLAYS SPURRING ECONOMY

Rebound From October Crash Surprises Many Analysts

By PETER T. KILBORN
Special to The New York Times

WASHINGTON, March 16 — The latest reports on jobs, consumer debt, production and the like are convincing many economists that the economy is a lot stronger these days than they were predicting just a few weeks ago. Today's announcement of an 8.9 percent jump in home construction last month is further evidence of the economy's surprising resilience.

The reason seems to be a consumer livelier than economists expected, particularly after the October rout of the stock market. Even without the rout, however, this was to have been a period when consumer spending, which had been pulling the economy through most of the last five years, would run out of steam.

The Earlier Assumption

The assumption had been that consumers would pass the baton to industry, which would sell more of its goods abroad, thanks to the cheaper dollar, and build more factories at home. During this first-quarter transition, the economy would slow down considerably and perhaps even slip into a recession.

But after pinching pennies for a month or two after the market's plunge, consumers are stepping up their spending again. They are still a lot more restrained than they were in recent years, but with industry pulling the weight expected of it, firmer consumer spending augurs a more robust economy than most forecasts showed. There is more talk now of inflation, the price the economy sometimes pays for strong growth, than of recession.

Right after the market collapsed, about half the members of the economics community revised their forecasts for the first quarter of this year from

Continued on Page D24, Column 1

Gunman Terrorizes Belfast Crowd Gathered at Rites for 3 Guerrillas

By FRANCIS X. CLINES
Special to The New York Times

BELFAST, Northern Ireland, March 16 — Three people were killed and dozens wounded today as an assailant threw grenades into a screaming crowd at a funeral and then fled across the graveyard from enraged mourners.

Panic broke out and grieving families dived for cover by the mud of the open grave as four grenades exploded amid thousands of mourners gathered for the burial of three Irish Republican Army guerrillas. The guerrillas, unarmed but on a bombing mission, were slain March 6 by British undercover agents in Gibraltar.

"Kill the bastard!" came cries from the crowd as dozens of mourners ignored the gunshots fired by the retreating assailant and chased him a quarter mile to an adjacent expressway.

Crowd Is Stunned

Families, clergy members, pallbearers and grave diggers watched stunned on the cemetery hill as the wounded mourners, who had been saying the rosary moments before, staggered bleeding among the headstones.

The collective screams of shock and panic soon changed to cheers when the crowd of more than 5,000 saw the blue-coated invader finally collared and pummelled after he coolly turned and threw the last of his grenades and fired bullets at furious pursuers.

"We beat him unmercifully," said George McMurray after racing down the hill toward the gunman, who was widely suspected of being on a terrorist mission for one of the paramilitary Protestant gangs. The gunman was rescued and arrested by officers of the Royal Ulster Constabulary.

Beyond the three dead men, four mourners were listed as seriously wounded among the dozen who were hospitalized. More than 30 others were treated and released, according to the hospital.

The attack on the eve of St. Patrick's Day in Milltown Cemetery pushed this city toward a fresh cycle of the sectarian vendetta and street violence that has marked the last two decades of Northern Irish life. Cars were hijacked and set afire by youths as anger built at nightfall in the heavily policed ghettos

Continued on Page A6, Column 3

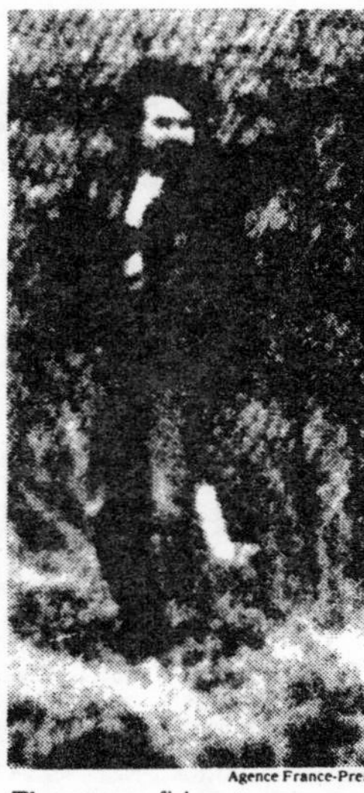

Agence France-Presse
The gunman firing at pursuers.

Noriega Foils Coup Attempt; Civilians Take to the Streets

By LARRY ROHTER
Special to The New York Times

PANAMA, March 16 — An attempt to overthrow Gen. Manuel Antonio Noriega failed here today, but it was followed by widespread civil disorders across Panama.

The uprising, which was marked by sharp exchanges of gunfire at military headquarters, was led by Col. Leónidas Macias, the chief of police, the Government said later.

General Noriega, the country's military leader, was apparently unhurt in the incident and later appeared on the doorstep of military headquarters to speak briefly to reporters.

No figure on the number of officers and men arrested in the coup attempt was given, and no mention was made of any casualties. But residents of the area around military headquarters said they had seen wounded soldiers being removed from the command building, which houses General Noriega's main office.

Senior United States officials in Washington said that the coup attempt demonstrated a deepening division within Panama's armed forces and police, but that they were uncertain whether it would weaken General Noriega's hold on power. [Page A6.]

The disturbances at military headquarters followed two days of demonstrations by doctors, teachers, dock workers and other Government employees protesting the Government's inability to pay them. The cash shortage stems from moves to block the Noriega Government from access to some $50 million in deposits in American banks.

A Display of Force

The United States has applied other economic sanctions as well in an effort to force the ouster of General Noriega, who is under indictment by two Federal grand juries in Florida on drug-trafficking and racketeering charges.

Rumors that the coup attempt had succeeded sent thousands of Panamanians into the streets of the capital this morning. They erected barricades, set cars, garbage dumpsters and tires on fire, brought traffic and commerce to a standstill and burned some buildings, including a military checkpoint.

But by midafternoon the military forces were back in action, firing shotguns and tear and pepper gas in a huge show of force as they sped down the palm-lined boulevards of the capital. Paramilitary squads in civilian clothes also took to the streets, firing shotguns and pistols at knots of confused civilians who had gathered on street corners to await the outcome of events.

"This morning, an attempt by some officers to seize and control the general headquarters of our institution was

Continued on Page A6, Column 4

Reagan Vetoes Bill That Would Widen Federal Rights Law

By JULIE JOHNSON
Special to The New York Times

WASHINGTON, March 16 — President Reagan disregarded warnings of a political backlash from Republican Congressional leaders today and vetoed a major civil rights bill.

The measure, which would expand the reach of Federal anti-discrimination laws that the Supreme Court had limited in 1984, was passed by both houses of Congress with more than enough votes to override a veto, and Senate leaders planned to call the bill up Thursday.

But Mr. Reagan offered an alternative that he said would "protect civil rights and at the same time preserve the independence of state and local governments, the freedom of religion and the right of America's citizens to order their lives and businesses without extensive Federal intrusion."

The President said Congress "has sent me a bill that would vastly and unjustifiably expand the power of the Federal Government over the decisions and affairs of private organizations, such as churches and synagogues, farms, businesses, and state and local governments," adding, "In the process, it would place at risk such cherished values as religious liberty."

The bill the President vetoed was intended to overturn the effects of a Supreme Court decision involving Grove City College in Pennsylvania. The

Continued on Page A14, Column 1

Bush vs. Dole: Behind the Turnaround

This article was reported by Gerald M. Boyd, E. J. Dionne Jr. and Bernard Weinraub and was written by Mr. Dionne.

History is written by the victors, and that is true even of political campaigns not yet concluded. In retrospect, the winning side's decisions invariably appear brilliant, and losers almost always look foolish.

And so it is now with the battle between Vice President Bush and Senator Bob Dole for the Republican Presidential nomination. A Bush victory is now spoken of as the inevitable product of a long-term battle plan that worked out exactly as it was supposed to. All the organizing the Bush campaign did in 1986 and 1987, discounted at the time by some, is now seen as critical to his victory.

'Firewall' in the South

And after Mr. Bush's sweep of Southern primaries on March 8, nothing looks more brilliant than having set up the South as a "firewall" against possible early defeats.

Mr. Dole, once the hero of the political circuit and even at times described as the inevitable nominee, is spoken of now in almost contemptuous terms, especially as he vows to continue his quest against impossible odds. His campaign, it is now said, was marked by blunders, internal rivalries, and the unpredictable personality of a candidate who switched signals and traveling plans with abandon. Mr. Dole, the argument goes, failed to appoint a single, dominant campaign manager and allowed his organization to go on a 1987 spending binge that left the cupboard bare when it came time for television commercials on Super Tuesday.

George Bush's success in transforming himself from a loser to an almost certain winner in just 29 days is one of the remarkable stories of recent American political history. It is also the lucky consequence of facing off against a foe, Mr. Dole, who at crucial moments seemed to do everything wrong.

What follows is an account of the rise of Mr. Bush and the fall of Mr. Dole, based on interviews with top officials and former officials of both campaigns and other Republican political professionals.

Staff, Organization, Planning

Mr. Bush won in large part because he had a better staff, a keener sense of organization and a more prescient long-term plan.

But in politics, one brilliant last-minute decision can make up for months of bad ones and a key strategic miss can leave even the best organization in chaos.

Thus amid the praise that Mr. Bush's campaign manager, Lee Atwater, receives now, what is not mentioned is that Mr. Bush, according to several aides, was prepared to dismiss or demote him if Mr. Dole won the New Hampshire primary.

And Mr. Dole, in the meantime, had many opportunities in the last month to turn the race around.

In New Hampshire, many of his allies believe he could have won if he

Continued on Page B7, Column 1

INSIDE

College Credits for Police
Two or more years of college will be required for members of the New York City force seeking promotion to sergeant, lieutenant or captain, Commissioner Benjamin Ward said. Supervisors now holding such posts will keep them, however. Page B1.

Reagan Firm on Mideast
After meeting with Prime Minister Yitzhak Shamir of Israel, President Reagan pledged to pursue his Middle East negotiating plan. Page A3.

Rogue Software Is Loose
A program that can secretly spread from computer to computer and destroy data has been found in commercial software. Page D1.

Prado Gains Collection
The Prado Museum in Madrid has been chosen to house several hundred pieces of the Thyssen-Bornemisza art collection. Page C23.

News Summary, Page A2

"All the News
That's Fit to Print"

The New York Times

Late Edition
New York: Today, partly sunny, breezy. High 63-69 inland, 50-55 coast. Tonight, showers late. Low 44-51. Tomorrow, showers likely. High 60-65. Yesterday: High 76, low 46. Details on page B16.

VOL.CXXXVII . . . No. 47,455 NEW YORK, FRIDAY, MARCH 25, 1988 — 50 cents beyond 75 miles from New York City, except on Long Island. — 30 CENTS

Associated Press

An unidentified New York City restaurant inspector in F.B.I. custody yesterday after his arrest.

Wedtech Figure Testifies He Hid Aid to D'Amato

By LYDIA CHAVEZ

A former Wedtech Corporation executive testified yesterday that he gave Senator Alfonse M. D'Amato more than $30,000 in illegal campaign contributions while the Senator was helping Wedtech win Government contracts.

But the witness, Mario Moreno, said that although he had hidden the contributions under different names, he did not feel he had bribed the Senator or been extorted by him. Mr. Moreno also testified that he saw nothing wrong in what Mr. D'Amato did for Wedtech.

Mr. D'Amato, a New York Republican, said through a spokesman that the allegations were "ridiculous."

Cooperating With Government

"We have absolutely no knowledge of any secret contributions," the spokesman, Edward Martin, said.

Mr. Moreno, Wedtech's former vice chairman, is cooperating with the Government in exchange for leniency. He testified yesterday under cross-examination by Maurice Nessen, the lawyer for the former Bronx Borough President, Stanley Simon.

Seven defendants, including Mr. Simon and Representative Mario Biaggi, Democrat of the Bronx, are on trial on charges of turning Wedtech, a Bronx military contractor, into a racketeering enterprise that paid millions of dollars in bribes to get Government contracts set aside for minority-owned companies.

Mr. D'Amato intervened repeatedly with the Army, the Navy and the Small Business Administration in behalf of Wedtech in its efforts to win Government contracts, but there is no evidence that he received any personal

Continued on Page B4, Column 4

Democrats Close In On Bush Nationally, Latest Survey Shows

By E. J. DIONNE Jr.

After months of having their Presidential candidates regarded as inferior to Republican counterparts, the Democrats have emerged as highly competitive with the Republicans in the 1988 Presidential election, the latest New York Times/CBS News Poll shows.

The survey shows that about a fifth of the voters who said they had voted for President Reagan in 1984 now expect to vote for a Democrat. The Democrats also keep almost all their 1984 voters, and the result is that the two parties are just about even nationally.

Gov. Michael S. Dukakis of Massachusetts now leads the Democratic field, and the Rev. Jesse Jackson is his only close competitor. Mr. Jackson has improved his image among Democrats in general and whites in particular.

Bush Achieves Dominance

Vice President Bush, in the meantime, has translated his string of primary victories into overwhelming dominance in the Republican Party. Among likely Republican primary voters, he now leads Senator Bob Dole of Kansas by 63 percent to 20 percent.

The poll of 1,654 adults, 1,271 of whom said they were registered voters, found that when Mr. Bush and Mr. Dukakis were matched in a hypothetical election, the result was a virtual tie among the registered voters: Mr. Bush had 46 percent, Mr. Dukakis 45. The poll had a margin of sampling error of plus or minus three percentage points.

Mr. Bush enjoys a clear lead when he is matched against Mr. Jackson or Senator Albert Gore Jr. of Tennessee. But when the registered voters were asked — without any candidate's name being mentioned — which party's Presidential candidate they would

Continued on Page B8, Column 1

INSPECTORS SEIZED IN WIDE EXTORTION FROM RESTAURANTS

28 CHARGED IN NEW YORK

Health Code Threats Against 300 Establishments Cited — Visits Suspended

By SELWYN RAAB

Twenty-eight current and former New York City health inspectors and supervisors were charged yesterday with extorting hundreds of thousands of dollars from restaurants by threatening to close them or cite them for sanitation violations.

More than 300 restaurants were forced to make payoffs ranging from $50 to $1,400 in a systematic corruption scheme by Health Department employees that authorities said dated back at least to the early 1980's.

The head of the Federal Bureau of Investigation in the city, James M. Fox, said the payoffs had doubled the incomes of most of the inspectors and allowed several of them to lead "lavish life styles."

Cadillacs and Rolexes

"Some restaurant owners dreaded to see them coming, driving up in Cadillacs and wearin_ Rolex watches," Mr. Fox said in announcing the filing of the Federal charges. In a single day, a team of two inspectors obtained $3,000 of payoffs from six restaurants, Mr. Fox asserted.

Andrew J. Maloney, the United States Attorney in Brooklyn, said the evidence suggested that usually the inspectors, rather than overlook unsanitary conditions, had threatened to cite restaurants falsely for nonexistent violations unless payments were made. Mr. Maloney said restaurateurs "dreaded" financial losses if cited for health code irregularities in a weekly list that was issued by the Health Department and published in newspapers.

The department said routine inspections of restaurants would be suspended, except for emergencies, until at least next week.

The New York Times, The Daily News and New York Newsday said yesterday that they would not print the current list of health code violations. [Page B6.]

Law-enforcement officials declined

Continued on Page B6, Column 1

SANDINISTA-CONTRA CEASE-FIRE OPENS WAY TO A DURABLE PEACE, RIVAL NICARAGUAN FACTIONS SAY

The New York Times/Samuel Barreto

Adolfo Calero, a contra leader, signing peace accord. Others included Defense Minister Humberto Ortega Saavedra, left, President Daniel Ortega Saavedra, third from left, and Miguel Cardinal Obando y Bravo.

TWO-MONTH TRUCE

Government to Release Prisoners in Steps — Exiles Can Return

By STEPHEN KINZER

Special to The New York Times

MANAGUA, Nicaragua, March 24 — Having recognized each other as authentic political forces for the first time, Government officials and contra leaders said today that the cease-fire agreement they signed Wednesday night held out the promise of a durable political settlement.

Under the agreement, the truce that was declared at the start of the talks on Monday will extend through May. During that time, contra leaders will meet with officials of the Sandinista Government here to discuss steps necessary to permanently end the six-year-old war.

The Government agreed that anti-Sandinista prisoners — those accused of contra activities and former members of the National Guard under the deposed Somoza family dictatorship — would be released in groups as t[illegible] peace process advances, with the f[illegible] 100 to be freed Sunday. The Sandinistas say there are 3,300 such prisoners.

Free Expression Guaranteed

The cases of former guardsmen are to be reviewed by the Inter-American Human Rights Court, which is part of the Organization of American States.

The Sandinistas also pledged to permit "unrestricted freedom of expression," and guaranteed that all exiles could return without fear of punishment for their "political-military activities." [Text of accord, page A8.]

In return, the contras agreed to recognize Sandinista rule and the legitimacy of President Daniel Ortega Saavedra. The contras embarked on a process aimed ultimately at disarming themselves and allowing them to return to a different and freer Nicaragua, although they will not be required to lay down their weapons until a final peace agreement is reached.

No Aid From the U.S.

The contras promised not to accept military aid from anyone, and to receive "humanitarian" aid — a term used in the agreement — only through "neutral organizations." This provision forbids them from receiving any form of direct aid from the United States.

If the plan succeeds, it would mark

Continued on Page A8, Column 1

Reversal on 'Star Wars'

U.S. Adopts Moscow's View That the Issue Cannot Be Ignored in Strategic Arms Talks

By MICHAEL R. GORDON

Special to The New York Times

News Analysis

WASHINGTON, March 24 — The United States is taking a new approach to strategic arms talks that stems from a worry that a new treaty could otherwise be a disturbing source of misunderstanding.

The new policy, disclosed by Secretary of State George P. Shultz on Wednesday night, is that the United States will try to negotiate a strategic arms pact and resolve the issue of space-based missile testing at the same time.

For years, the United States stressed the need to complete a strategic arms treaty even if the two sides couldn't resolve their differences over the development of the space-based missile defenses popularly known as "Star Wars." Moscow, in contrast, insisted the two issues had to be linked.

Under the latest American position, which has evolved over several years, the two sides finally agree on a basic negotiating approach, even though they remain far apart on what kind of testing and development of new anti-missile systems should be allowed.

'Predictability About Defenses'

Mr. Shultz, disclosing the new American position Wednesday after three days of meetings with Eduard A. Shevardnadze, the Soviet Foreign Minister, said: "I think that if we are going to have the kind of massive reductions in offensive arms that would be brought about by the strategic arms agreement, then we are as interested as they are in having predictability about defenses."

Asked if the two sides could conclude a strategic arms treaty while postponing a resolution of their differences over space defenses, Mr. Shultz said, "No, I don't think so." Last December, during the summit meeting in Washington, the American position was that the two sides had agreed to disagree over the issue while the negotiations on strategic arms moved ahead.

On Wednesday night, Mr. Shultz said that the two agreements in the two areas should be "completed more or less at the same time so the two things move in parallel."

The latest American approach

Continued on Page A11, Column 1

AT WHITE HOUSE, SOME 'DISCOMFORT'

Concern That the Rebels May Have Given Up Too Much

By JULIE JOHNSON

Special to The New York Times

WASHINGTON, March 24 — The Reagan Administration, caught by surprise by the terms of the cease-fire accord reached by the contras and Sandinistas, reacted ambivalently today.

Although Secretary of State George P. Shultz called the accord an important step forward, the White House pointedly declined to describe it as a positive development. In part this reflected concern in the Administration that the contras may have given up too much by agreeing to receive no more arms aid, thereby making moot the Administration's crusade for a renewal of such support for them.

U.S. Upset Over Terms

Lieut. Gen. Colin L. Powell, the President's national security adviser, told officials at a White House meeting today that he had been unaware that the contras were about to sign such an accord.

"There is discomfort over what the contras are apparently agreeing to," said a senior Administration official who was at the meeting.

He noted that the contra leadership had also indicated feelings of being "sold out" in the United States and added, "That is why they are making these kinds of agreements."

The Administration is concerned about the accord's provision that all

Continued on Page A8, Column 5

The New York Times/Jose R. Lopez

Iran-Contra Principals Plead Not Guilty

Rear Adm. John M. Poindexter, right, leaving court yesterday with his wife, Linda, and lawyer, Richard Beckler, after he was arraigned along with Lieut. Col. Oliver L. North and two arms dealers. Page A12.

U.S. Demand on Afghan Arms Aid Seen as Last Big Obstacle to Pact

By DAVID K. SHIPLER

Special to The New York Times

WASHINGTON, March 24 — The disagreement between the United States and the Soviet Union over the Reagan Administration's demand for a halt in Soviet weapon supplies to the Afghan Government has emerged as the only important obstacle to an accord on a Soviet troop withdrawal, American officials and Asian diplomats said today.

The other major problem was resolved because Pakistan has dropped its insistence that a transitional coalition government be established in Kabul before the withdrawal agreement is signed.

Instead, Pakistan is apparently ready to sign if the pro-Soviet Afghan Government commits itself to promoting the formation of an interim government, the officials said.

The American demand for a cutoff in Soviet military aid was recently added to conditions that Washington wants met before ending its military supplies to the Afghan guerrillas.

[In Geneva, officials said there was little chance the current talks on Afghanistan would produce a peace accord due to the aid dispute.]

In talks this week with the Soviet Foreign Minister, Eduard A. Shevardnadze, Secretary of State George P. Shultz proposed a moratorium in aid from both sides for three months longer than the time it takes the Soviet troops to leave, American officials said. Under the current plan for a nine-month withdrawal, the aid moratorium

Continued on Page A10, Column 1

Du Pont to Halt Chemicals That Peril Ozone

By PHILIP SHABECOFF

Special to The New York Times

WASHINGTON, March 24 — E.I. du Pont de Nemours & Company, the world's largest producer of chlorofluorocarbons, announced plans today to phase out all production of the chemicals that scientists say are contributing to the destruction of the earth's ozone shield.

While the company refused to set a target date for ending production of the chemicals, Joseph M. Steed, environmental manager of Du Pont's Freon products division, said that reducing output by at least 95 percent by the beginning of the next century was a "reasonable goal."

The company said it was taking the action, which would go well beyond its previous commitment only to reduce output of the chemicals, because of new scientific evidence that the threat to the atmospheric ozone layer was worse than had been thought.

An International Agreement

Du Pont's action indicated a readiness to surpass the goals of an international agreement reached in Montreal last fall calling for an initial freeze on production levels and then a 50 percent reduction in their use by the end of the century.

The company's decision is bound to have wide influence because Du Pont accounts for about 25 percent of the world's production of chlorofluorcarbons, or CFC's. The chemicals, which are widely used in refrigerants, foam insulation and cleaning solvents, among other products, are believed to combine with and destroy ozone molecules in the upper atmosphere.

The ozone shield blocks harmful ultraviolet rays from the sun that can cause skin cancer in humans, damage plants and harm animals.

Du Pont urged today that more countries quickly ratify the Montreal protocol. It also called for immediate reassessment of the problem and consider-

Continued on Page A20, Column 1

INSIDE

New York Landmarks Preservation Foundation

New Life for Ancient Turtle

After hundreds of years perched above the Bronx River, an Indian petroglyph of a turtle is rediscovered. A drawing of it has been outlined to make it more visible. Page B1.

A New Terror in Punjab

Sikh militants are attacking entire Sikh families who will not cooperate with the separatist campaign. Page A10.

A Troubled Savings Industry

A third of the nation's savings and loan associations lost money last year, giving the industry a record $6.8 billion net loss. Page D1.

News Summary, Page A2

"All the News That's Fit to Print"

The New York Times

Late Edition
New York: Today, rain and fog. High 44-48. Tonight, rain ending, fog. Low 37-40. Tomorrow, clouds, fog, afternoon clearing. High 47-52. Yesterday: High 45, low 41. Details are on page A19.

VOL.CXXXVII . . No. 47,469 NEW YORK, FRIDAY, APRIL 8, 1988 — 50 cents beyond 75 miles from New York City, except on Long Island. — 30 CENTS

GORBACHEV AND AFGHAN LEADER SAY WAY SEEMS CLEAR TO START SOVIET TROOP PULLOUT BY MAY 15

The New York Times/David Jennings
Governor Cuomo yesterday.

Hondurans Riot At U.S. Offices; Four Said to Die

By Reuters

TEGUCIGALPA, Honduras, Friday, April 8 — The United States Consulate was set afire Thursday night and at least four people were killed during a riot sparked by the expulsion of a suspected drug dealer to the United States, radio stations reported.

Witnesses said shots were fired from inside the consulate building and protesters responded with pistol fire. At least 4 students died and at least 2 were wounded as the crowd of 1,500 protesters scattered in panic, radio stations said. It was not clear who fired from inside the building.

The third floor of the consulate was reported burning fiercely and part of the outside of the main United States Embassy building across the street was also ablaze as firefighters arrived. Power was cut off, blacking out street lights and adding to the confusion as the shooting started, reports said.

20 Cars on Fire

The shots came after the protesters had set fire to part of the embassy, hurling rocks and flaming sticks, and had broken into the consulate building. At least 20 cars belonging to embassy personnel were burning in the street.

About 200 anti-riot officers and firefighters moved in to quell the violence, which was being called the worst anti-American riot ever in Honduras, traditionally a close American ally.

[The Associated Press quoted an embassy spokesman, Michael O'Brien, as saying that there was extensive damage to embassy buildings but that no American citizens had been injured. He said the Hondu-

Continued on Page A9, Column 1

Authorities Debate Increased Firepower For Narcotics Agents

By PETER KERR

A rise in the use of machine pistols by drug dealers in New York — and a decision to issue submachine guns this month to 300 Federal drug agents in the region — has officials arguing about the safest way to arm agents and the police in the densely populated city.

The growth of violent crack-dealing organizations in New York in the last two years has brought a new class of powerful handguns into general use in the underworld in the city, Federal officials said. The weapons hold 20 or more rounds and can be easily converted into machine guns that fire bursts of bullets with each pull of the trigger.

Crack organizations in Brooklyn and Queens are sending couriers, often by bus, to buy the guns in Texas, Georgia and Alabama, where firearms laws are more lax, according to the New York office of the Federal Bureau of Alcohol, Tobacco and Firearms.

Automatic weapons have been used by drug organizations in Florida and elsewhere in the country since the early 1980's. Drug dealers in New York have generally used cheaper less-powerful weapons, until recently.

The latest example of the danger posed by criminals armed with such weapons occurred Tuesday night, the police said, when four men sprayed a crowded Brooklyn intersection with

Continued on Page B5, Column 4

One Week of Killings

New York City police recorded 17 deaths by violence last week. Behind each police report is the story of a life. Page B1.

MAJOR DEMOCRATS IN NEW YORK STATE BACKING DUKAKIS

AN INITIATIVE BY CUOMO

Urging Leaders to Choose, He Remains Neutral to Avoid Anger in Jackson Camp

By FRANK LYNN

Governor Cuomo yesterday urged top New York Democrats to choose a Presidential candidate to support, and, as he expected, most of them started lining up behind Gov. Michael S. Dukakis of Massachusetts.

The move, orchestrated through the Democratic state chairman, Laurence J. Kirwan, allowed the Governor to bow to the preference of most of the state's Democratic leaders. At the same time, it permitted him to maintain his own public neutrality and thus not offend New York supporters of the Rev. Jesse Jackson, with whom Mr. Cuomo will have to deal long after 255 delegates to the Democratic National Convention are picked in the state's Presidential primary April 19.

"The Dukakis campaign people have been complaining that they can't get anywhere in the state with the Governor hanging back," said a leading Democrat.

Dukakis a Clear Choice

He added, "They asked the Governor that if he did not endorse Dukakis, to at least release the Democratic leaders on the ground that Dukakis had played the Cuomo game, showing him respect and deference."

Mr. Cuomo gave no personal signal of his own preference, party officials said. But he was aware that Governor Dukakis was the clear favorite among county leaders, legislators and other public officials who make up the state's Democratic leadership, particularly after the sweeping Dukakis victory in the Wisconsin primary last Tuesday.

So he knew what to expect when Mr. Kirwan, saying that he was speaking for the Governor, urged the leaders yesterday to choose one of the party's three remaining active Presidential candidates: Mr. Dukakis, Mr. Jackson or Senator Albert Gore Jr. of Tennessee.

'I Want You to Pick'

Addressing about half of the 300-member Democratic State Committee at the New York Hilton in Manhattan yesterday afternoon, Mr. Kirwan said, "The Governor now feels that there are three candidates in this race, and 'I want you to pick one of the three.' "

The first party leader to take the advice was Joseph F. Crangle, the Erie

Continued on Page A18, Column 4

Tass via Agence France-Presse
Najibullah, left, the Afghan leader, and Mikhail S. Gorbachev at meeting in Tashkent, U.S.S.R.

GENEVA PACT SEEN

Acceptance of U.S. Plan on Arms Aid Indicated in Joint Statement

By PHILIP TAUBMAN
Special to The New York Times

MOSCOW, April 7 — The Soviet Union and Afghanistan said today that they believed the last barriers to a negotiated settlement of the war in Afghanistan had been eliminated.

The two Governments indicated, but did not explicitly confirm, that they had accepted an American formula breaking the last remaining deadlock at the Geneva talks aimed at ending the eight-year-old war.

The compromise would permit Washington to continue providing military aid to the Afghan guerrillas during a withdrawal of Soviet forces at a level commensurate with the aid Moscow gives to the Afghan Government.

Signing Likely Next Week

Western diplomats here said the announcement appeared to clear the way for quick completion of the Geneva talks, with the signing of an agreement likely before the end of next week.

In Washington, Reagan Administration officials voiced cautious optimism that a settlement would soon be formally concluded and lead to a Soviet withdrawal. But they also said they were reserving final judgment until the United States received a formal response from the Soviet Union and reviewed the detailed Geneva accords. [Page A10.]

In a joint statement issued after a meeting today, Mikhail S. Gorbachev and the Afghan leader, Najibullah, said the Soviet Union would begin withdrawing its troops on May 15 if the Geneva accords were completed within the next few days. [Text of statement, page A10.]

Reagan Visit Seen as Factor

The departure date, originally set by Moscow for early February but postponed as the negotiations bogged down, suggested that Mr. Gorbachev wanted to start bringing Soviet soldiers home before President Reagan's visit to Moscow in late May.

Mr. Gorbachev and Mr. Najibullah met in the Soviet Central Asian city of Tashkent, 190 miles north of the Afghan border.

Mr. Gorbachev later told workers at two collective farms near Tashkent: "There is a certainty that an agreement will be signed on a political settlement. I think that Pakistan and Afghanistan will come to an agreement. And we with the Americans will agree to be guarantors, I think."

Resolution of the Afghan conflict, which Soviet forces entered in Decem-

Continued on Page A10, Column 3

Tokyo's Surging Stock Prices Top Record Set Before October Crash

By SUSAN CHIRA
Special to The New York Times

TOKYO, Friday, April 8 — Prices on the Tokyo stock market continued today to rise above the peak reached before last fall's global market collapse. No other major stock market has returned to its pre-crash levels.

Yesterday, the Nikkei average of 225 stocks closed at 26,769.22 yen, well above the previous record of 26,646.43 yen reached on Oct. 14, five days before share prices around the world collapsed. That increase was 258.05 yen, or 97-hundredths of 1 percent. In trading today the Nikkei has risen another 141.68 yen, to 26,910.90, by the close of the morning session.

The surge in prices demonstrates the underlying strength in the Tokyo Stock Exchange, the world's largest in terms of money invested. While the Tokyo market has now exceeded pre-crash levels, the New York and London markets have posted comparatively modest advances and are well below their record levels.

[In a move to bolster investor confidence in the market, the New York Stock Exchange proposed a sharp increase in the level of capital required for specialist brokers to buy or sell stocks. Page D1.]

High corporate profits, low interest rates, continuing economic growth, and Government actions to prevent any drastic fall in stock prices have driven the Tokyo market's rebound, analysts here said.

Fears of Overheating

Some Japanese officials, notably Satoshi Sumita, governor of the Bank of Japan, have expressed fears that the Tokyo market could be overheating. Mr. Sumita told reporters yesterday that share prices were rising too fast in relation to the rate of economic growth.

Other analysts point out that any panic in other stock markets might spread to Tokyo, given the degree to

Continued on Page D6, Column 1

ACCORD INDICATED ON STABLE DOLLAR

Officials Expect Action When 7 Nations Meet Next Week

By PETER T. KILBORN
Special to The New York Times

WASHINGTON, April 7 — American and foreign officials indicated today that they expect the United States and six other leading industrial nations to agree next week to try to keep the dollar's value roughly at its current level for the foreseeable future.

The officials thus confirmed speculation in the financial markets that after a couple of weeks of currency turbulence the countries want a steady dollar and will do what they can to keep it steady. Some economists had suggested that the dollar, which closed today at 125.72 Japanese yen, should decline some more.

The officials also said the countries, known as the Group of Seven, could report some progress on a proposal by Treasury Secretary James A. Baker 3d to use prices of gold and other commodities in guiding their economic policies. But they said that while Mr. Baker favors the immediate adoption of such a price index in making Group of Seven policy, other nations could urge delay.

The anticipation by market traders of a renewed commitment to a stable

Continued on Page D2, Column 1

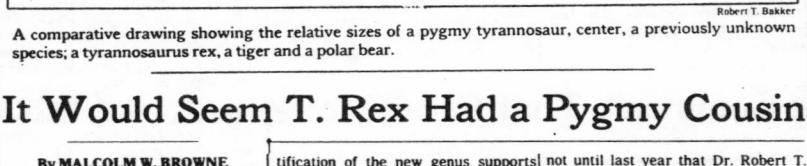

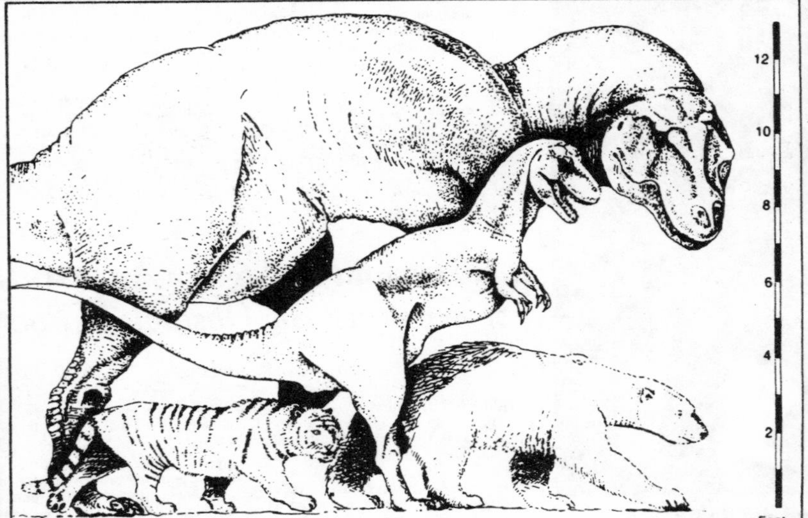

Robert T. Bakker
A comparative drawing showing the relative sizes of a pygmy tyrannosaur, center, a previously unknown species; a tyrannosaurus rex, a tiger and a polar bear.

It Would Seem T. Rex Had a Pygmy Cousin

By MALCOLM W. BROWNE

Paleontologists reported yesterday that a peculiar dinosaur skull, unearthed 46 years ago but erroneously identified at the time, is actually that of a previously unknown genus, a pygmy tyrannosaur possibly related to modern birds.

The announcement yesterday at the Cleveland Museum of Natural History culminated a yearlong study of the skull by three scientists who recognized it as a fossil of extraordinary importance.

Many paleontologists believe that the dinosaurs never entirely died out but merely evolved into birds, and the identification of the new genus supports that theory. Differences of opinion persist, however, as to which dinosaurs might have been the ancestors of birds.

The skull was found in Montana in 1942 but had never stirred particular scientific interest because it was assumed to have come from a gorgosaur, a large flesh-eating dinosaur of the late Cretaceous period, of which many specimens have been collected and studied.

Over the years several scientists questioned this assumption, but it was not until last year that Dr. Robert T. Bakker of the University of Colorado, on a visit to the museum, challenged the label on the skull and began an investigation.

He enlisted as collaborators Dr. Michael E. Williams of the Cleveland museum and Dr. Philip Currie of the Tyrrell Museum of Paleontology in Drumheller, Alberta, Canada. Dr. Currie is an expert in theropod, or "beast-footed," dinosaurs, a category to which the two-foot skull belonged.

"We found that this animal was much more like a tyrannosaur than a

Continued on Page A16, Column 1

Guard's Bullet Reportedly Struck Israeli Girl Killed on West Bank

By JOHN KIFNER
Special to The New York Times

ELON MOREH, Israeli-Occupied West Bank, April 7 — As angry, armed Jewish settlers turned the funeral here for a teen-age girl into a passionate rally, an army investigation was reported today to have found a bullet from an Israeli guard's rifle in the victim's body.

The report raised questions about the emotionally charged reports on Wednesday that the 15-year-old girl, Tirza Porat, had been stoned to death by Palestinian villagers. Army spokesmen said late tonight that it was not clear what had caused the girl's death and that an investigation was under way.

Israeli soldiers shot and killed a Palestinian youth outside the village of Beita today as they searched the hills surrounding the site where Wednesday's confrontation took place. The army said the unidentified youth was a suspect who was trying to flee. There was no independent confirmation of this report, and the death raised the number of Palestinians known to have been killed in four months of protest here to 123.

The army also blew up five houses in the sealed-off village, saying they were the homes of people known to have taken part in the clash on Wednesday.

Palestinian accounts of the events in Beita were not immediately available because the village and the surrounding area were sealed off by the army. The military order to shut the Palestine Press Service, which maintained a

Continued on Page A3, Column 1

INSIDE

Eggs Linked to Illness
Clean, inspected Grade A eggs may be responsible for an increase in food poisoning in the Northeast, Federal researchers say. Page A16.

Speakes Rolls the Capital
Larry Speakes, President Reagan's ex-spokesman, depicts him in a new book as inspiring but uninformed. Washington Talk, page A20.

News Summary, Page A2

"All the News That's Fit to Print"

The New York Times

New York: Today, mostly sunny and warm. High 81-87. Tonight, clear and mild. Low 59-66. Tomorrow, mostly sunny, very warm. High 84-90. Yesterday: High 88, low 61. Details, page 18.

VOL.CXXXVII . . . . No. 47,556 NEW YORK, MONDAY, JULY 4, 1988 — 50 cents beyond 75 miles from New York City, except on Long Island. 30 CENTS

U.S. DOWNS IRAN AIRLINER MISTAKEN FOR F-14; 290 REPORTED DEAD; A TRAGEDY, REAGAN SAYS

Two Churches in Paris Battle Across the Lefebvre Schism

Agence France-Presse

Jean-Marie Cardinal Lustiger calling for Church unity at Notre Dame in Paris yesterday.

By STEVEN GREENHOUSE

Special to The New York Times

PARIS, July 3 — It was a battle for the hearts, minds and souls of thousands of traditionalist followers of Marcel Lefebvre, the dissident Archbishop who was excommunicated Thursday.

It involved two churches less than a quarter mile apart. One was the rebel Left Bank church that Archbishop Lefebvre's ultraconservative followers took control of in 1977 in defiance of church superiors and the law, and the other was Notre Dame Cathedral, which was eager to win back the flocks that had strayed.

At St.-Nicolas-du-Chardonnet, the citadel of the Lefebvre movement in Paris, more than 2,000 worshipers flocked to morning Mass Sunday in defiance of Pope John Paul's threat that Catholics who continue to follow the rebel prelate might be excommunicated too.

Cardinal Gives Latin Mass

At the same time, Jean-Marie Cardinal Lustiger, the Archbishop of Paris, took a highly unusual step to woo back Lefebvre loyalists by holding the first traditional Latin Mass in Notre Dame in two decades. Five thousand worshipers, twice the usual number, crowded into Sunday's 10 A.M. Mass at the 12th-century landmark to hear the Cardinal implore traditionalists not to follow those who have broken with the Holy See.

As in most religious battles, the language was electric, and the stakes were high. Priests at St.-Nicolas sought to fight defections in the city where the Lefebvre movement is strongest, while Cardinal Lustiger struggled to bring unity back to Paris's Catholic Church. In ways it is a battle between those who want to bring the church into the 20th century and those who believe that the church is immutable and eternal and should not be tinkered with.

Archbishop Defied Pope

"A few of our people are anxious, but I can't say there is real fear about what the Vatican has done," said the Rev. François Pivert, a priest at St.-Nicolas. "We think the excommunications are null. Rome is excommunicating the real Catholics."

On Thursday, the Vatican said Archbishop Lefebvre was excommunicated because on that day he defied the orders of the Pope and consecrated four traditionalist bishops at his seminary

Continued on Page 28, Column 3

Because of holiday production requirements, The Times is printed today in two sections. SportsMonday begins on page 34, Business Day on page 29.

Israeli Decision On Emigré Curb Splits U.S. Aides

By MICHAEL R. GORDON

Special to The New York Times

WASHINGTON, July 3 — A debate has erupted in the State Department over whether the United States should counter a recent decision by the Israeli Cabinet that would require most Jews who leave the Soviet Union to settle in Israel.

Officials in the State Department's Office of Human Rights and Humanitarian Affairs say American refugee procedures should be changed so that Soviet Jews who travel to Israel would have the right to resettle in the United States quickly if they want to.

Broad Ramifications Seen

But this approach is opposed by the State Department officials in the Bureau of Near Eastern and South Asian Affairs, who say such a move would disrupt American-Israeli relations.

The issue, which has potential ramifications for refugees from other countries, has not yet been put to Secretary of State George P. Shultz for a decision.

At the heart of the dispute is a multifaceted legal, political and ethical debate about how best to aid Jewish emigration from the Soviet Union.

Under current arrangements, the overwhelming majority of Soviet Jews who are permitted to leave the Soviet Union do so by receiving Soviet exit permits and Israeli visas in Moscow. The Israeli visas are distributed by the Dutch Embassy in Moscow, which has represented Israel's interests there since the Soviet Union broke off rela-

Continued on Page 2, Column 3

Traffic Perils Economic Boom Of Suburbs Around New York

By RICHARD L. MADDEN

Jammed rush-hour traffic, once the bane of the big city, has become a pervasive part of daily life in the suburbs around New York City.

Fifty miles and more from Manhattan, highway traffic crawls bumper-to-bumper. Commuters, trying to avoid bottlenecks, leave home earlier, search out back roads, stay later at the office. Businesses that moved to the suburbs to escape the crowded city move again, even farther out.

What has happened, planners say, is that fundamental changes in where people work, where they live, and even

First of two articles.

how they live, have combined to overwhelm the metropolitan region's roads. The changes include these:

¶The spread of corporate headquarters and offices across Westchester County, Long Island, New Jersey and Connecticut has created hundreds of thousands of jobs in former bedroom communities. Since 1980 alone, the suburbs have gained 763,000 jobs, for a total of 4.9 million, compared with New York City's 3.6 million, a gain of 306,000.

¶The dispersal of those jobs has created new commuting patterns between far-flung suburbs, leaving most people no choice but to drive; nearly all mass transit runs in and out of New York City, not across the region.

¶Soaring housing costs have pushed more and more people farther out to find affordable homes, leaving them long commutes over crowded country roads never designed for heavy traffic.

¶The increase in families with two income-earners has sent more husbands and wives out of the house in separate cars and, often, in opposite directions. One consequence: the number of cars in the suburbs has far outstripped population growth.

Choking Suburbs

The result, according to planners, transportation officials, business people and commuters, is worsening traffic that threatens to choke the suburbs on their own success in becoming places to live and work. And they see no immediate solutions.

"No one really has realized it until it's on us," said Dr. Robert W. Burchell, acting director of the Center for Urban

Continued on Page 26, Column 1

Downing of Flight 655: The U.S. Account

Events occurred Sunday. Information is based on a briefing by Adm. William J. Crowe Jr., chairman of the Joint Chiefs of Staff.

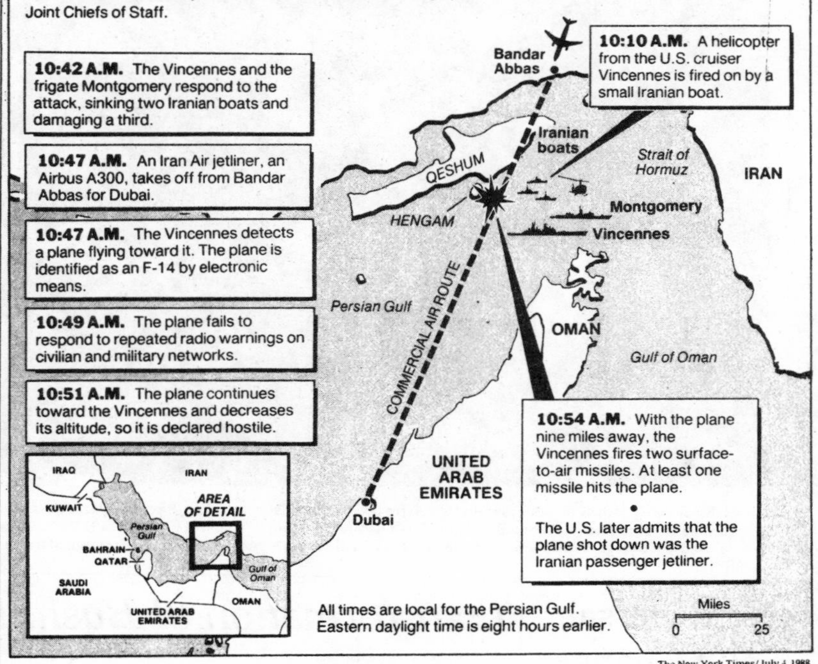
10:10 A.M. A helicopter from the U.S. cruiser Vincennes is fired on by a small Iranian boat.
10:42 A.M. The Vincennes and the frigate Montgomery respond to the attack, sinking two Iranian boats and damaging a third.
10:47 A.M. An Iran Air jetliner, an Airbus A300, takes off from Bandar Abbas for Dubai.
10:47 A.M. The Vincennes detects a plane flying toward it. The plane is identified as an F-14 by electronic means.
10:49 A.M. The plane fails to respond to repeated radio warnings on civilian and military networks.
10:51 A.M. The plane continues toward the Vincennes and decreases its altitude, so it is declared hostile.
10:54 A.M. With the plane nine miles away, the Vincennes fires two surface-to-air missiles. At least one missile hits the plane.
The U.S. later admits that the plane shot down was the Iranian passenger jetliner.
Bandar Abbas
Iranian boats
QESHUM
HENGAM
Strait of Hormuz
IRAN
Montgomery
Vincennes
Persian Gulf
COMMERCIAL AIR ROUTE
OMAN
Gulf of Oman
UNITED ARAB EMIRATES
Dubai
IRAQ
IRAN
KUWAIT
AREA OF DETAIL
Persian Gulf
BAHRAIN
QATAR
SAUDI ARABIA
UNITED ARAB EMIRATES
OMAN
Gulf of Oman
All times are local for the Persian Gulf. Eastern daylight time is eight hours earlier.
Miles
0
25

The New York Times/July 4, 1988

Failures Seen in Safeguards on Erroneous Attacks

By STEPHEN ENGELBERG

Special to The New York Times

WASHINGTON, July 3 — The downing of an Iranian jetliner is striking evidence of how split-second decisions in modern warfare may be based on incomplete electronic information.

Navy officers said today that based on the Government's account of the incident, it appeared that several precautions relied upon to prevent such an incident had inexplicably failed.

Iranian jetliners routinely monitor emergency frequencies used to send warnings and had always responded to such transmissions, these officers said, but the plane downed today did not answer three separate warnings on the civilian network. Four warnings were also sent on a military network, officials said.

Path Suited to Attack

Nor was radar able to identify the aircraft as a passenger plane. Civilian planes are supposed to be equipped with devices that emit signals identifying them on radar screens as civilian, but the Navy said no such signal had been received.

Finally, the Navy said the jetliner was following a path that was outside the normal civilian air corridors and would have been well suited to an attack on the American cruiser Vincennes in the Strait of Hormuz.

There are several unanswered questions about the incident, particularly how the jetliner and the control tower at Bandar Abbas in Iran failed to hear or heed the warnings said to have been sent by the Vincennes before it fired. It is not known whether the Reagan Administration will play tapes to establish that those warnings took place.

Navy officers asserted today that based on available information, the threat to the ship was sufficient to justify firing on the plane, and that, if anything, the captain of the Vincennes waited unusually long to fire his missiles. The Administration said the plane was nine miles away when the order was given, a distance well within the range of the air-to-surface missiles used by the Iranian military.

"If anything, the captain could be criticized for holding his fire as long as he did," said Joseph Metcalf 3d, the Navy's former deputy chief of naval operations for surface warfare. "From what they're saying, he waited a long

Continued on Page 6, Column 1

Reuters

The cruiser Vincennes, which shot down an Iranian jetliner yesterday.

Similarities With KAL Flight Are Rejected by U.S. Admiral

By STEVEN ERLANGER

The downing of an Iran Air passenger plane by American missiles yesterday prompted comparisons to the destruction of a South Korean airliner shot down by a Soviet fighter pilot nearly five years ago.

At a Washington news conference yesterday, the chairman of the Joint Chiefs of Staff, Adm. William J. Crowe Jr., rejected the comparison, citing "very fundamental differences" between the two events.

Unlike the Korean airliner, Admiral Crowe said, the Iran Air aircraft was flying in a war zone at low altitude during combat and had failed to change course or respond to three warnings on a civilian radio network and four warnings on a military network. Commercial pilots in the gulf have also been warned by the United States in recent months to identify themselves when challenged.

Admiral Crowe said there were reasons, including classified "electronic indications" he would not reveal, that led American crew members aboard the American cruiser Vincennes to believe that they were confronting an American-built F-14 of the Iranian Air Force.

But although the Navy said the Iranian plane was not emitting the signals that would have identified it as a commercial flight, the admiral did not explain in detail how a sophisticated American air defense system could confuse the radar signature of a small fighter jet and a wide-bodied passenger plane. This question of identification was raised both by the United States in the aftermath of the Korean airline disaster and by Iranian officials yesterday.

In the early hours of Sept 1, 1983, Korean Air Lines Flight 007, flying 365 miles off its normal course from An-

Continued on Page 6, Column 1

INSIDE

Inquiry Into Blimp Contract

The F.B.I. and the S.E.C. are investigating the competition between two military contractors for a $5 billion contract to build blimps. Page 10.

Rain at Wimbledon

The men's singles final between Boris Becker and Stefan Edberg was suspended by rain in the first set. It will resume today. Page 37.

Perestroika in China

China has largely undergone the type of economic restructuring sought by Moscow. But openness in public debate lags behind. Page 3.

Proudly Flies the Flag. . .

. . .and just about everywhere, too. Companies that make American flags say more and more people are showing their colors in a resurgence of patriotism. Page 7.

News Summary, Page 2

SKIPPER DEFENDED

Admiral Plans a Review of Rules for Firing — Embassies Alerted

By RICHARD HALLORAN

Special to The New York Times

WASHINGTON, July 3 — A United States Navy warship in the Persian Gulf shot down an Iranian passenger plane today that the Navy said it mistook for a jet fighter, and Iran said 290 lives were lost.

The Chairman of the Joint Chiefs of Staff, Admiral William J. Crowe Jr., said the missile cruiser Vincennes, while seeking to protect itself from what was thought to be a hostile aircraft, shot down the airliner with a surface-to-air missile. The downing of the jetliner, Iran Air flight 655, took place over the Strait of Hormuz, at the southern end of the gulf. [Transcript of news conference, pages 4 and 5.]

President Reagan, in a statement issued from the Presidential retreat in Camp David, Md., and Admiral Crowe, in a briefing at the Pentagon, both said the United States regretted the loss of life on the plane but defended the judgment of the warship's captain, Will C. Rogers 3d, saying the commander's first responsibility was to protect his ship and crew.

KAL Comparison Rejected

Admiral Crowe rejected a comparison with the episode on Sept. 1, 1983, in which a Soviet fighter plane shot down a Korean Air Lines passenger jet over international waters in the Sea of Japan, killing all 269 on board. The said the main difference was that the Korean plan "was not in a war zone" and that "there was no combat in progress" when it was shot down. The admiral said such was the case in the attack today.

The admiral said the actions aboard the Vincennes would be reviewed by Rear Adm. William N. Fogarty of the Central Command, which has its headquarters in Tampa, Fla. The Central Command is responsible for United States military operations in the gulf region.

'Obligation' to Crew

Admiral Crowe also said the rules of engagement, which govern the circumstances under which a commander may fire his weapons, would be reviewed. But he emphasized that "the commanding officer had a very heavy obligation to protect his ship, his people."

At the State Department, officials said the downing should not force the United States to revise its policy of seeking to keep the Persian Gulf open

Continued on Page 4, Column 1

'Saddened' Reagan Decides to Remain At Maryland Retreat

By JULIE JOHNSON

Special to The New York Times

WASHINGTON, July 3 — After a series of telephone calls that began before dawn, President Reagan decided today to remain at his Camp David retreat rather than return to the White House to deal with the shooting down of an Iranian airliner by an American warship.

The President's decision, Administration officials said, indicated the degree to which aides sought to keep the events from being characterized as a crisis.

The White House issued a written statement from Mr. Reagan, who was notified of the military action shortly before 5 A.M. but did not learn with certainty for five more hours that it was a commercial jetliner that had been shot down. The statement said the President was "saddened" by the incident and offered his condolences to the passengers, crew and their families. [Text of statement, page 6.]

Telephone Conference Call

The capital, emptied of officials over the Fourth of July holiday, was slow to react to today's events. With the President in Maryland, Vice President Bush in Maine, Secretary of State George P. Shultz in Massachusetts and the national security adviser, Lieut. Gen. Colin L. Powell, in Tennessee, the consultations that led to the Administration's response were worked out by telephone conference call.

At the heart of the effort to keep the crisis level at a minimum, Administration officials said, was a sensitivity to

Continued on Page 6, Column 4

"All the News That's Fit to Print"

The New York Times

Late Edition
New York: Today, sunny, windy, very cold. High 20-25. Tonight, clear, quite cold. Low 16-22. Tomorrow, partly sunny, windy, warmer. High 35-40. Yesterday: High 53, low 33. Details, page 49.

VOL.CXXXVIII . . No. 47,757 NEW YORK, SATURDAY, JANUARY 21, 1989 — 50 cents beyond 75 miles from New York City, except on Long Island. 35 CENTS

BUSH TAKES OFFICE ASKING BIPARTISAN HELP IN FIGHTING SOCIAL ILLS DESPITE THE DEFICIT

The New York Times/Angel Franco

George Bush being sworn in yesterday by Chief Justice William H. Rehnquist as Barbara Bush held two Bibles, the Bush family Bible and the one used by George Washington 200 years ago. Mr. Bush's 87-year-old mother, Dorothy, standing with Marilyn Quayle and surrounded by other family members, watched along with Vice President Dan Quayle, Congressional leaders and others.

'WILL' OVER 'WALLET'

41st President Also Says of Drug Abuse, 'This Scourge Will Stop'

By BERNARD WEINRAUB

Special to The New York Times

WASHINGTON, Jan. 20 — George Herbert Walker Bush of Texas, promising new efforts to heal social wounds and to end two decades of divisiveness between the White House and Congress, was inaugurated today as the 41st President of the United States.

In an Inaugural Address delivered from the flag-draped West Front of the Capitol, Mr. Bush, his voice strong and his manner self-assured, emphasized the urgency of dealing with the Federal budget deficit.

That deficit, the new President said, means that the Government alone cannot solve all pressing social problems. But he asserted that the problems could nonetheless be solved. "We have more will than wallet; but will is what we need," he said.

'This Scourge Will Stop'

Indeed, Mr. Bush offered an unqualified promise to put an end to one of those ills, the epidemic of drug abuse. "Take my word," he said. "This scourge will stop."

The 20-minute speech, delivered before tens of thousands of people at the Capitol and on the grounds beyond, was also marked by a theme of harmony and conciliation, as when the 64-year-old Republican called on the Democrats who control Congress to join him in dealing with homelessness, poverty and "the rough crime of the streets."

"A new breeze is blowing," he said, "and the old bipartisanship must be made new again. To my friends, and yes, I do mean friends, in the loyal opposition, and yes, I mean loyal: I put out my hand."

Three Minutes Late

The inauguration took place on a clear, cold day, the azure sky flecked with white.

Barbara Bush, the nation's new First Lady, smiled faintly as Chief Justice William H. Rehnquist administered the Presidential oath at 12:03 P.M., three minutes after Ronald Reagan's term had officially come to an end under the provisions of the 20th Amendment to the Constitution. Mr. Bush had his left hand on two Bibles held by his wife. One was a family Bible; the other was used by George Washington at his swearing-in 200 years ago.

Immediately after Mr. Bush had taken the oath, the United States Army Band broke into "Hail to the Chief." A 21-gun salute followed, the sound of the cannons echoing across the Mall.

Shortly before Mr. Bush took the

Continued on Page 6, Column 1

F.B.I. INTENSIFYING COMMODITY INQUIRY ON CHICAGO TRADES

Suspects Said to Be Pressed to Name Others Involved in Fraudulent Dealings

By KURT EICHENWALD

Special to The New York Times

CHICAGO, Jan. 20 — Capitalizing on fears in the commodity markets after subpoenas were served on 50 to 100 floor traders, Federal investigators are pressing those implicated in possible fraud to name others, lawyers and other sources said today.

A number of commodity traders with the Chicago Mercantile Exchange and the Chicago Board of Trade, the nation's two largest commodity exchanges, have begun to cooperate with the Government, these sources said. Some traders have agreed to testify before the grand jury conducting the inquiry, they added.

The investigation involves potential fraud charges based on, among other things, agreements among traders in the futures pits to cheat customers by illegally manipulating trades, law enforcement sources said. They added that clients might have been defrauded of millions of dollars.

Key Element of Strategy

The growing concern that many people might go to prison, fueled by the extensive publicity the case is receiving, appears to have become a key element of a strategy to convince traders to cooperate with the Government and testify, the sources said.

"This thing is being done to create the maximum effect, to create this big aura of inevitability," said John Troelstrup, a commodity lawyer involved in the case. "It's trying to tell people, 'You had better cooperate now before it's too late.'" By cooperating with the Government in the early stages of investigations, defendants typically stand a better chance of receiving lenient treatment in the courts.

The Mercantile Exchange said it had begun an inquiry into trading activities on its floor. The Board of Trade, the world's largest futures market, has also begun an investigation, said some officials who asked not to be identified. A Board of Trade spokesman declined to comment. [Page 39.]

Case Remains Sketchy

Lawyers involved in the case said today that they were telling their clients not to cooperate, simply because the case is very sketchy.

But the Government's strategy of surprise has won some cooperation, people directly involved in the investigation said.

Some people who have cooperated with the investigators were stunned when agents of the Federal Bureau of Investigation visited their homes beginning late Tuesday, armed with subpoenas and details of incriminating evidence against them.

Much of that evidence involved secret tape recordings, made on the trading floor, of conversations between the undercover agents and the people working at the exchanges.

In a scene more akin to a large drug

Continued on Page 39, Column 1

No Reversal, But Changes

'New Breeze' Signals A Shift From Reagan

By R. W. APPLE Jr.

Special to The New York Times

News Analysis

WASHINGTON, Jan. 20 — President Bush swore his oath with the same 35 words that George Washington uttered two centuries ago, resting his left hand on the same Bible that George Washington used, and he spoke of the orderly transfer of power that the inaugural ceremony so compellingly symbolizes.

But the thoughts that George Bush laid before the nation today as he stood on "the front porch of democracy," as he called it, were all about change. There was, of course, no hint of repudiation of the works of Ronald Reagan, whom the new President served for eight years and whom he thanked for "the wonderful things" Mr. Reagan had done. There was, all the same, a clear call from Mr. Bush for subtle yet significant corrections in the nation's course.

"A new breeze is blowing," the President said again and again, and he called upon the winds of change to carry away greed, both public and private, and sterile bickering between the White House and Congress, and seeming indifference, both public and private, to the plight of the poor and the sick, and the painful cleavages that still remain from the Vietnam War.

Though he briefly re-identified himself with the foes of abortion, and though he warned that the national finances could not stand much new spending, his was moderate, nonideological and modest. Where Mr.

Continued on Page 7, Column 4

Transformation of Bush: His Own Man

From Faithful Follower to Confident Leader in About 2 Months

By MAUREEN DOWD

Special to The New York Times

WASHINGTON, Jan. 20 — "I ——" the new President blurted out, a beat ahead of the moment he was supposed to begin repeating the Presidential oath after Chief Justice William H. Rehnquist. George Bush smiled nervously and began again.

The slip could not have surprised anyone who had been watching Mr. Bush bounding about the White House and the country since his election.

"He's loaded for bear," said his old friend Senator Alan K. Simpson of Wyoming. "It's what he's planned on for a long, long time."

For Mr. Bush, as for most Americans, the idea of George Bush as President took some getting used to. The morning after his election, alone with friends and family, his eyes had a lost look, the vulnerability that can come with getting exactly what you have always wanted. At a private buffet in Houston after his first news conference as President-elect, an aide recalled that Mr. Bush seemed nervous and subdued, his voice uncommonly low.

But by the next day, when he arrived in Florida for a vacation, his tentativeness had evaporated in a spray of water sports, and he met the press on the beach with an easy and joyful air of confidence. He had shed the "deferential Episcopalian tilt," as one friend called the self-effacing manner he assumed as Ronald Reagan's Vice President.

'The Man at the Desk'

After recalling all the Presidents he had known and worked for, after remembering all the contests he had endured and the jobs he had held to prepare himself, Mr. Bush was able to banish contemplation with the certainty that he was ready to be "the man at the desk."

"He was able to look at this whole thing and say, 'I can do this,'" said his friend and adviser Peter Teeley.

Or as his brother Jonathan put it in ebullient Bush fashion: "He's not cowed because he knows he has the combination of knowledge, experience and energy to form one great big assault on the management of the country."

Over the last 10 weeks, the 64-year-old Mr. Bush has made his passage from faithful and sometimes fumbling lieutenant to self-assured leader with an ease that has amazed all but those closest to him. Everyone has struggled for a metaphor to capture the striking change.

"It's as though a great shadow has lifted," said one of the men chosen for the Bush Cabinet. "It's like watching a balloon inflate," said another acquaintance.

But perhaps Jonathan Bush offered the best description of his older brother's giddy rush to self-expression: "It is as though you took a bottle of soda water and shook it up and down and then took the cork out, and boom goes

Continued on Page 9, Column 1

The New York Times/Jose R. Lopez

Ronald Reagan pausing to take a last look at his desk as he left the office of the President.

Tears, Handcuffs for Boy, 10, Facing Judge in Crack Sale

By MICHAEL WINERIP

Special to The New York Times

HAUPPAUGE, L.I., Jan. 20 — The 14-year-old boy drove the BMX bike, a Suffolk County police officer testified today. The 10-year-old sold crack from the back of the bike.

"I saw six such exchanges," the officer, John McGinley, testified in Family Court, describing how the boys, selling crack from a brown bag, rode up and down Straight Path in Wyandanch, a poor community plagued with drug dealing.

"God!" a relative of the 10-year-old said with a gasp.

In a highly unusual move this week, Suffolk County Judge Donald L. Auperin opened Family Court hearings concerning the 10-year-old boy, who the police said was carrying three small plastic bags of crack and $226 when he and his friend were arrested last Sunday night. He requested that the boy not be identified because of his age.

At the end of today's hearing, the judge found a reasonable likelihood that a crime had been committed and ordered that the boy continue to be held in a juvenile jail until a fact-finding hearing, the Family Court equivalent of a trial, on Jan. 31. Brought to court in handcuffs and carrying a Marvel comic book, he was led away in handcuffs and tears.

Family Court in New York is almost always closed, but can be opened at a judge's discretion. Judge Auperin, who acted today despite objections from both the prosecutor and the boy's legal guardian — the Family Court equivalent of a defense lawyer — indicated that his concern with society's drug

Continued on Page 33, Column 1

Reagan Packs Up a Presidency and Its Memories

By MAUREEN DOWD

Special to The New York Times

WASHINGTON, Jan. 20 — Ronald Reagan was wistful. Nancy Reagan was worried.

Mrs. Reagan, teary all morning, kept searching through drawers in the family quarters, making sure she had packed up all her things. Finally, her press secretary, Elaine Crispin, told her to stop. "If you leave something behind," she said to Mrs. Reagan, "they'll send it to you. They have your address."

Before she left, she tucked a note for Mrs. Bush in an empty drawer in the bedroom, and left a small white orchid. Mr. Reagan also put a humorous note for Mr. Bush in his dressing room, where the new President would change into formal clothes tonight for the inaugural balls.

Mr. Reagan left a more serious handwritten note with his prayers and his affection for Mr. Bush in the top desk drawer in the Oval Office. He went to the office in the morning to take one last look around and seemed quite sad to see it emptied of his belongings, including his sunny sign — "It CAN be done."

"He wanted to freeze a few vignettes in his memory," said Marlin Fitzwater, Mr. Reagan's spokesman, who was staying on with Mr. Bush.

Standing behind his desk, his head lowered, Mr. Reagan put out both hands to touch the desk as though to hold it in his memory. He received his last daily schedule from his personal secretary, Kathleen Osborne. He took a deep breath, lifted his head and walked out the door to the Rose Garden, stopping to look back.

Rex, the Reagans' energetic King Charles spaniel, dashed across the lawn and the President remarked, "There he goes — that's his last walk." This week the Presidential pet received a gift, a new doghouse built by Navy Seabees to resemble the White House and complete with a patch of carpet from Rex's favorite floor at Camp David.

Then Ronald Reagan carried on, in

Continued on Page 6, Column 1

Gorbachev Asks Stable Relations

Mikhail S. Gorbachev congratulated President Bush and expressed hope for stable relations.

Other countries also sent congratulations, while bidding farewell to Ronald Reagan.

Article, page 9.

INSIDE

Managua's Gesture to Bush

In a step to promote good relations with the new Bush Administration, Nicaragua lifted a freeze on visas for American diplomats. Page 5.

Zhukov on Stalin's War Role

Pravda published previously secret memoirs of Marshal Georgi K. Zhukov that shatter the Soviet image of Stalin as a war hero. Page 3.

Two Officers Wounded

Two New York City police officers were shot in Brooklyn when they tried to arrest a murder suspect. The man apparently escaped. Page 29.

Bea Lillie Dies at 94

The comedienne amused millions with her barbed wit and skillfully wielded cigarette holder. Page 34.

"All the News
That's Fit to Print"

The New York Times

Late Edition

New York: Today, morning showers, thunderstorms, then clearing skies and windy. High 82. Tonight, clear. Tomorrow, chance of late showers. Yesterday: High 86, low 65. Details are on page 41.

VOL.CXXXVIII — No. 47,891 NEW YORK, SUNDAY, JUNE 4, 1989 — $1.50 beyond 75 miles from New York City, except on Long Island. — $1.25

TROOPS ATTACK AND CRUSH BEIJING PROTEST; THOUSANDS FIGHT BACK, SCORES ARE KILLED

Khomeini, Imam of Iran And Foe of U.S., Is Dead

By The Associated Press

NICOSIA, Cyprus, Sunday June 4, — Ayatollah Ruhollah Khomeini, Iran's spiritual and political leader, died today, 12 days after he underwent surgery for bleeding in his digestive system, the official Iranian news agency reported. He was believed to be 89 years old.

"The leader of the Islamic revolution and founder of the Islamic Republic, Imam Khomeini, passed away at a Teheran Hospital," the Islamic Republic News Agency reported in an urgent dispatch.

[Reuters reported that a statement from his son, Hojatlislam Ahmad Khomeini, his chief aide, accompanied the announcement.

Associated Press, 1988

Ayatollah Ruhollah Khomeini

["The lofty spirit of the leader of Moslems and free men everywhere, His Excellency Imam Khomeini, has gone to Heaven and his heart, which was brimming with love for God and the oppressed of mankind, stopped beating," it said.]

The Ayatollah was referred to by Iranians as the imam, or spiritual leader. He led the 1979 revolution that toppled 2,500 years of monarchy and set up the Islamic Republic of Iran, turning the relatively Western-style country ruled by Shah Mohammed Riza Pahlevi into the most hard-line Islamic nation in the world.

He emerged as an implacable foe of the United States, which had supported the Shah, and it was under his direction that Iranian students overran the United States Embassy in Teheran and held many of the diplomats inside hostage for over a year, a development that was one of the chief causes of the electoral defeat of the Jimmy Carter Administration.

Reaction From Ex-Hostage

He was equally an enemy of the Soviet Union, referring to both the superpowers as "The Great Satans," and he led his country in an eight-year-war against neighboring Iraq.

A former American hostage in Iran said the Ayatollah's death ends a chapter for the former captives.

"I'm not the type to say I'm happy he's dead," said Barry Rosen, of Brooklyn, one of the 52 hostages held 444 days by radical Iranian students from 1979 to 1981. "But I do feel, to a certain degree, that that part of the

Continued on Page 39, Column 1

Associated Press

A student placing debris in front of a moving armored personnel carrier early today in Tiananmen Square.

SQUARE IS CLEARED

General Strike Is Urged as Officials Announce End of 'Rebellion'

By NICHOLAS D. KRISTOF

Special to The New York Times

BEIJING, Sunday, June 4 — Tens of thousands of Chinese troops retook the center of the capital from pro-democracy protesters early this morning, killing scores of students and workers and wounding hundreds more as they fired submachine guns at crowds of people who tried to resist.

Troops marched along the main roads surrounding central Tiananmen Square, sometimes firing in the air and sometimes firing directly at crowds who refused to move.

Early this morning, the troops finally cleared the square after first sweeping the area around it. Several thousand students who had remained on the square throughout the shooting left peacefully, still waving the banners of their universities. Several armored personnel carriers ran over their tents and destroyed the encampment.

Casualty Reports Sketchy

Reports on the number of dead were sketchy. Three Beijing hospitals reported receiving at least 68 corpses of civilians and said many others had not been picked up from the scene. Four other hospitals said they had received bodies of civilians but declined to disclose how many. Students said, however, that at least 500 people may have been killed in the crackdown.

[A report on the state-run radio put the death toll in the thousands and denounced the Government for the violence, The Associated Press reported. But the station later changed announcers and broadcast another report supporting the governing Communist Party, the A.P. said.]

Most of the dead had been shot, but some had been run over by personnel carriers that forced their way through the protesters' barricades.

Official Version

The official news programs this morning reported that the People's Liberation Army had crushed a "counter-revolutionary rebellion." They said that more than 1,000 police officers and troops had been injured and some killed, and that civilians had been killed, but did not give details.

[President Bush called for an end to the violence. "I deeply deplore the decision to use force against peaceful demonstrators," he said. Page 20.]

Changan Avenue, or the Avenue of Eternal Peace, Beijing's main east-

Continued on Page 20, Column 4

In the Streets, Anguish, Fury and Tears

Reuters

A protester injured in a clash with troops yesterday at the Great Hall of the People in Beijing.

By SHERYL WuDUNN

Special to The New York Times

BEIJING, Sunday, June 4 — As the crackle of automatic weapons filled the air today on the Avenue of Eternal Peace, tens of thousands of Beijing residents, even elderly men and women, rushed out to see what they could do to turn back the troops.

"The citizens have gone crazy," said a driver watching as a tank plowed its way down the main thoroughfare. "They throw themselves in front of the tank, and only when they see it won't stop, they scatter."

The driver himself was shaken by what he had seen: A tank had rammed into an army truck used as a barricade. As the truck turned over, it crushed a man to death. Elsewhere, he had seen three bloodied bodies lying in the street. Several soldiers still standing in their trucks were crying.

Students and workers threw beer bottles, gasoline bombs, lead pipes, whatever they could find, at the tanks and armed personnel trucks, which nevertheless continued rumbling down the avenue. One truck drove back and forth along the east side of the Changan Avenue, as the Avenue of Eternal Peace is known in Chinese, and did not stop when people stood in its path.

Amazement had already turned to fear and defiance earlier in the evening as citizens saw the military convoys entering the city. Some troops from other provinces practically paraded their AK-47 rifles as they stood in their trucks, stranded by the human blockades that had formed around the trucks.

By dark, tensions had soared throughout the city. Hundreds of thousands of people were impelled outdoors by their disbelief and anger, yet brought back to their homes by fear of the violence. The sound of tanks whizzing by and reports of open firing fanned their fears.

"You beasts! You beasts!" shouted the people at the troops.

'We Have to Obey Orders'

Around a convoy of about 45 military trucks in the eastern part of the city, people pushed and shoved their way to the troops, shouting and urging them to consider their role as fellow citizens. But the sympathy that had characterized the troops last week was gone; the soldiers seemed to have a certain resolve.

"Will you shoot at us if they order you to?" was a question asked by many of the people surrounding the truck. The soldiers gave weak assurances to the people that they would not fire, but they also admitted that

Continued on Page 20, Column 1

Soviet Emigré Mob Outgrows Brooklyn, and Fear Spreads

By RALPH BLUMENTHAL
with CELESTINE BOHLEN

A criminal underworld of Soviet émigrés, some of them skilled in white-collar crime and hardened by Soviet prison and labor camps, is reaching beyond its base in Brooklyn, using extortion and violence in its own neighborhoods and engaging in multimillion-dollar racketeering schemes on an international scale.

The network of Russian-speaking criminals is small and loosely grouped compared with the hierarchies of traditional American organized crime. But camouflaged within the country's growing Soviet immigrant communities, the network is fast outstripping the ability of local and Federal agencies to curb its illegal schemes, some of which are linked to Mafia crime families, officials of the Federal Bureau of Investigation and other agencies say.

Intelligence reports trace the network to black marketeers and other professional gangsters, many of whom plied their criminal trade in the Soviet Union before winning exit visas — or being planted — in the wave of Jewish emigration.

One mob boss who was said to have spent 10 years in Soviet prisons before turning up in Brooklyn was known to enforce his threats with an electric cattle prod he kept in his car. Investigators say he once extorted $15,000 from another immigrant by threatening to kill the man's daughter on her wedding day. Another crime kingpin, convicted of credit card fraud and now facing extradition from West Germany, is reputed to have amassed a fortune of more than $600 million from bootlegged gasoline in less than a decade after he arrived from Odessa.

Greater Numbers Coming

As Soviet emigration policies loosen up, greater numbers of Jews, Armenians and ethnic Germans have been given permission to leave. Since 1975, some 150,000 have come to the United States. About 50,000 have settled in the New York area; another 15,000 are expected to settle here this year.

Law-enforcement officials say that, while the network comprises no more than a few hundred active criminals out of all those who arrived, some of these are highly skilled mob enforcers, forgers and confidence men.

Their criminal activities range from old-fashioned jewelry swindles on 47th

Continued on Page 38, Column 1

Gingrich, Pursuer of Democrats, Now Finds Himself the Pursued

By E. J. DIONNE Jr.

Special to The New York Times

WASHINGTON, June 2 — Representative Newt Gingrich's role in bringing down House Speaker Jim Wright seems to have set him up for a Wright-style roasting that could determine his future as the leader of the young and aggressive backbenchers bidding for control of their party in the House.

Obviously a target for Democratic revenge, the 45-year-old Georgia Republican is also facing some criticism as a divisive figure within his own party.

One sign of Mr. Gingrich's political difficulties, party strategists say, is that his main competitor for leadership of the young conservatives, Representative Vin Weber of Minnesota, has already begun to distance himself from Mr. Gingrich, his longtime friend.

The strategists interpret recent comments by Mr. Weber as suggesting that while the party needs Mr. Gingrich's inspirational example right now, House members might want a cooler leader for the long haul.

Some Republicans scoff at Democratic suspicions that there is an organized "stink-tank" campaign under way, saying the majority party is merely suffering trouble that it brought on itself. [Page 34]

If Mr. Gingrich has his Republican

Continued on Page 34, Column 1

The Polish Vote

The Solidarity labor union takes a step toward becoming a broad political movement today as Poles vote in the first openly contested elections in the Soviet bloc.

Some say that, four years hence, the opposition will be in control. Others predict a splintering of Solidarity's factions.

Article, page 18.

The New York Times/Dith Pran

$12.1 Million Desk

An 18th-century American desk, which sold at a price usually paid for famous paintings. Page 36.

INSIDE

TODAY'S SECTIONS

Associated Press

Students in Beijing beating the driver of an armored personnel carrier after he rammed a crowd of protesters early today. The driver had been forced from the vehicle after demonstrators set fire to it.

"All the News That's Fit to Print"

The New York Times

Late Edition
New York: Today, increasing clouds, windy, cool. High 54. Tonight, clearing, breezy. Low near 40. Tomorrow, mostly sunny conditions. High 57. Yesterday: High 55, low 44. Details are on page 32.

VOL.CXXXIX . . No. 48,051 — NEW YORK, SATURDAY, NOVEMBER 11, 1989 — 40 CENTS
50 cents beyond 75 miles from New York City, except on Long Island.

JOYOUS EAST GERMANS POUR THROUGH WALL; PARTY PLEDGES FREEDOMS, AND CITY EXULTS

Agence France-Presse

East Germans pouring through a gate leading to the newly opened Berlin wall and, beyond it, West Berlin.

BERLIN A FESTIVAL

Communist Leadership Announces a Program of Radical Change

By SERGE SCHMEMANN
Special to The New York Times

WEST BERLIN, Nov. 10 — As hundreds of thousands of East Berliners romped through the newly porous wall in an unending celebration, West German leaders today proclaimed this the moment Germans had yearned for through 40 years of division.

At the same time, change continued unabated in East Berlin, where the Communist Party's Central Committee concluded a three-day session with the announcement of a program of radical changes. They included "free, democratic and secret elections," a "socialist planned economy oriented to market conditions," separation of party and state, parliamentary supervision of state security, freedom of assembly and a new law on the press and broadcasting.

'In the Midst of an Awakening'

"The German Democratic Republic is in the midst of an awakening," the Central Committee declared in the prologue to the newly adopted program. "A revolutionary people's movement has brought into motion a process of great change. The renewal of society is on the agenda."

Though the West Berlin police could give no estimate of the numbers of East Berliners who crossed over in the last 24 hours, the authorities said that only 1,500 so far had announced their intention to stay.

Beyond Berlin, only one of many points along the border between the two Germanys where people could cross, 55,500 East Germans crossed over the border between the two Germanys since the wall was opened on Thursday, and 3,250 remained in West Germany, the West German Interior Ministry said.

Chancellor Helmut Kohl, who interrupted a state visit to Poland to come to West Berlin, told an emotional crowd of East and West Berliners gathered outside the West Berlin city hall: "I want to call out to all in the German Democratic Republic: We're on your side, we are and remain one nation. We belong together."

Speaking on the steps of the city hall, from which President John F. Kennedy had made his "Ich bin ein Berliner" speech shortly after the wall was raised, Mr. Kohl declared: "Long live a free German fatherland! Long live a united Europe!"

Kurfürstendamm Is Packed

All through the night and through the day, East Berliners continued to flood into West Berlin in vast numbers, filling the glittering Kurfürstendamm until traffic came to a halt, forming long lines to pick up the 100-mark "welcome money" — about $55 — that West Germany has traditionally given East Germans on their first time in the West, gaping at shop windows and drinking in the heady new feeling of freedom.

A festival air seized the entire city. West Berliners lined entry points to greet East Berliners with champagne, cheers and hugs. Many restaurants offered the visitors free food. A television

Continued on Page 6, Column 1

D'AMATO BACKED SUPPORTERS' BID FOR H.U.D. MONEY

Senator's '84 Letter Appears to Contradict Assertions He Never Urged Grants

By MICHAEL WINERIP

Senator Alfonse M. D'Amato urged the Federal Housing Secretary to approve a grant worth several million dollars for a Buffalo housing-renovation project run in part by two of the Senator's supporters, according to a newly obtained document.

In a March 15, 1984, letter written on Mr. D'Amato's Washington office stationery, the Senator asked Secretary Samuel Pierce of the Department of Housing and Urban Development to use "deliberate speed" in approving the moderate-rehabilitation grant for the 65-unit Buffalo project. Within two months the grant was approved.

The letter, marked as having been hand delivered, appears to contradict repeated assertions by the Senator that he never asked department officials to approve specific moderate-rehabilitation projects. A statement issued to The New York Times last month by the Senator's office said, "The Senator has made no contact with any officials of H.U.D. on behalf of any development or developer as it relates to mod rehab."

Links to Projects

In May 1984, when the department's Buffalo office informed local officials of the moderate-rehabilitaton grants that had won approval that year, that letter was marked "cc: Sen. Alfonse M. D'Amato." He was the only elected official designated by the department to receive a copy of its letter about the Buffalo projects.

The Buffalo matter is the most recent in a series of disclosures that have linked the Senator with department projects that benefited his family members, friends and campaign contributors and that have stretched from his hometown, Island Park, L.I., throughout New York State and to Puerto Rico. Federal prosecutors and Congressional investigators are conducting inquiries into several of these programs although Mr. D'Amato has not been identified as a subject of any inquiry.

Allegations in '85

A spokeswoman for the Senator, Zenia Mucha, said last night that the Senator "can't be expected to remember every single letter over a nine-year period." She said that when Mr. D'Amato called on behalf of projects it was "based on merit and need, and no other factors were ever considered."

The moderate-rehabilitation program, which was intended to rebuild housing for low-income people, has been a central focus of inquiries into political favoritism by the department

Continued on Page 32, Column 1

Reuters

An East German border guard handing a flower back to West Berliners who sat atop the Berlin wall. (Detail from a scene that appears on page 7.)

Redefining Europe

As the Revelry Goes On, Politicians Ponder The Ramifications of Changes in Germany

By CRAIG R. WHITNEY
Special to The New York Times

News Analysis

WEST BERLIN, Nov. 10 — By the simple act of forcing their Communist rulers to open the Berlin wall and allow them to go wherever they wish, the people of East Germany have irrevocably changed the way Berlin, Germany and all of Europe have defined themselves for more than 40 years.

Thousands and thousands of East Berliners celebrated their triumph today by promenading up and down the elegant, tree-lined shopping boulevards of the western part of the city, which most of them had never before been allowed to see. They made the Kurfürstendamm into a street festival this evening as church bells pealed joyously into the night.

'A Different Relationship'

Willy Brandt, who was Mayor of West Berlin when the wall was built in 1961, said at a rally this evening, "The moving together of the German states is taking shape in reality in a different way than many of us expected." said . No one should act as if he knows in which concrete form the people in these two states will find a new relationship. But that they will find a relationship, that they will come together in freedom, that is the important point."

But the entire postwar European order has been based on the assumption that Germany, and Europe, would remain divided, and the countries of Eastern and Western Europe firmly anchored in their respective alliances.

In that assumption the United States, in the NATO alliance, guaranteed the security of Western Europe. And in that same assumption France, West Germany and the other major industrial countries of Western Europe began the economic and political unification of the European Community.

West German politicians, including Mr. Brandt and Chancellor Helmut Kohl, who interrupted an official visit to Poland today to fly to Berlin, all insist that West Germany's commitment to West European integration and the alliance remains.

But politicians, diplomats and business leaders all over Europe are considering new implications for both institutions now that the end of German partition is at last imaginable.

"Europe, though Europeans did not always appreciate it, has been a haven of order these past 44 years," The Economist wrote today. "For East Europeans the price of that stability has been high: a lifetime wasted under a government you loathed. For West Europeans the stability has been marvelous. They could get rich, and start to build a new unity, within a clearly defined zone which ended at the river Elbe and the Bohemian forest."

Now, a NATO diplomat in Brussels said, "The end of the wall raises questions of what's going to happen in Europe. The whole concept of the European Community now may have to change."

So would the concept of the NATO alliance, this diplomat conceded: "Our role will be to design a new role for the alliance — maintaining a balance of stability with the East while all this change is going on.

"There's a reassessment of the War-

Continued on Page 9, Column 4

U.S. ENTHUSIASTIC, BUT HAS CONCERNS

New Order in Eastern Europe Astonishes Washington

By THOMAS L. FRIEDMAN
Special to The New York Times

WASHINGTON, Nov. 10 — Like the rest of the world, Washington is scrambling to keep pace with the changes unfolding by the hour in Eastern Europe. But in contrast with the pivotal role the United States played 40 years ago in shaping the postwar European order that now seems to be coming apart, Washington finds itself more of a bystander — astonished, enthusiastic and concerned.

Twice in the last 24 hours, Secretary of State James A. Baker 3d found himself being slipped notes from aides informing him of major changes in Eastern Europe that only a week earlier no one had imagined, let alone predicted. Officials said a policy review that Mr. Baker ordered three weeks ago on how the United States should relate to changes in East Germany will have to be tossed out and begun anew.

The political changes reverberating across Europe, and the diminished threat of military conflict, also promised to stir new debate in Washington about the need for maintaining a large, expensive American military presence in Western Europe. Moving quickly to deflate such speculation, Defense Sec-

Continued on Page 8, Column 1

Bush Offers Housing Plan to Aid Poor, Homeless and New Buyers

By ANDREW ROSENTHAL
Special to The New York Times

DALLAS, Nov. 10 — President Bush today proposed a $7 billion, three-year package of housing programs and tax breaks to aid low-income families, first-time home buyers and the homeless "who live a nightmare in the midst of the American dream."

"This initiative will address the full range of housing concerns," Mr. Bush said in a speech to the National Association of Realtors here. He termed the program "a comprehensive agenda to help bring basic shelter and affordable housing within reach of millions of Americans."

The three-year program would provide mortgage assistance for low-income families and tax breaks for first-time buyers, but it does not include money for building new public and low-income housing units, which some advocates for the homeless regard as essential. Instead, it seeks to generate additional housing units through a variety of means that Republicans have been urging.

For example, a major element of the proposal involves matching grants to local authorities and nonprofit organizations for the acquisition of property and the rehabilitation of housing units.

Democratic legislators, advocates of low-income housing and spokesmen for the housing industry praised it as signaling a new interest in housing problems after years of relative inattention during the Reagan Administration. But several said the level of financing was insignificant compared to the needs of the homeless or people in substandard housing.

Jack F. Kemp, the Secretary of Housing and Urban Development, said the program was directed more toward stimulating the low-income housing industry than directly subsidizing individual purchases.

In announcing the plan, Mr. Bush

Continued on Page 13, Column 1

Bulgarian Chief Quits After 35 Years of Rigid Rule

By CLYDE HABERMAN
Special to The New York Times

SOFIA, Bulgaria, Nov. 10 — Todor I. Zhivkov, Eastern Europe's longest-serving leader, resigned today as Bulgaria's President and Communist Party leader, after 35 years of guiding the country with old-line orthodoxy.

Mr. Zhivkov, 78 years old, was immediately replaced as the party's General Secretary by his longtime Foreign Minister, Petar T. Mladenov, who is viewed here as likely to take a somewhat more flexible approach toward economic and political restructuring. It will be up to the politically weak National Assembly to choose his successor as President.

Since Mr. Zhivkov and other top officials recently began to talk about the need to separate state and party roles, it seemed possible that someone other than Mr. Mladenov could be selected.

Mr. Zhivkov's resignation came as a surprise but not as a total shock to Western diplomats, who said that the Bulgarian leader had apparently fallen victim to the fast-paced changes elsewhere in Eastern Europe.

Bulgarian officials reportedly said in confidence that Mr. Zhivkov did not want to stay too long and risk being forced from power in disgrace, as were Janos Kadar of Hungary or Erich Honecker of East Germany.

There were strong rumors of more shifts to come in top party echelons, but the state press agency and television network made no announcements. The prospects for genuine change here, several diplomats said, are likely to be determined by the extent of any future shake-up.

Doubts on Rapid Change

Mr. Mladenov, who is 53 and was Foreign Minister for 18 years, wasted no time as the new leader in warning that "there is no alternative to restructuring" Bulgaria's struggling economy and tightly controlled political apparatus. The present system has "handicapped progress in our society in all spheres," he told the party Central Committee, adding: "We have to turn Bulgaria into a modern, democratic and lawful country."

Despite his words, however, many

Continued on Page 9, Column 4

Agence France-Presse

Todor I. Zhivkov

INSIDE

The Debate on Child Care
Deep divisions have emerged in Congress over how much money should be spent on child care and who should benefit. Page 12.

Over 30 and Unmarried
Researchers whose study saw poor marriage prospects for well-educated women over 30 omit those findings in a revised paper. Page 10.

Warnings From Koch
He didn't exactly criticize David N. Dinkins, but the Mayor made it clear that he and his successor differ on many important issues. Page 29.

Chairman to Leave Ford
Donald E. Petersen, who led the company from a financial crisis to record profits, plans to retire. Page 35.

The New York Times

PAGE ONE

1990-1996

"All the News That's Fit to Print"

The New York Times

Late Edition
New York: Today, mostly cloudy, afternoon showers, mild. High 52. Tonight, showers ending. Low 37. Tomorrow, partly cloudy, cooler. High 44. Yesterday: High 52, low 35. Details, page C22.

VOL.CXXXIX . . No. 48,105 | Copyright © 1990 The New York Times | NEW YORK, THURSDAY, JANUARY 4, 1990 | 50 cents beyond 75 miles from New York City, except on Long Island. | 40 CENTS

NORIEGA GIVES HIMSELF UP TO U.S. MILITARY; IS FLOWN TO FLORIDA TO FACE DRUG CHARGES

DINKINS WILL DELAY HIRING OF RECRUITS FOR POLICE FORCE

Says That 'Real World' Move Will Help New York City Face Its Budget Gap

By TODD S. PURDUM

In his first major act as Mayor of New York, David N. Dinkins said yesterday that he would indefinitely delay hiring 1,848 police officers who were to have gone on the payroll on Jan. 16 as recruits at the Police Academy. He said he might also have to delay another class that was scheduled to start in June.

Mr. Dinkins's decision means that the city's Police Department will almost certainly fall below its current strength of 25,971 officers during the year. It will also make it harder for the Mayor to keep his campaign promise to double the number of community patrol officers, who walk neighborhood beats, in his first term.

Mr. Dinkins said the move would save $4 million a month and help keep the city's budget balanced in the face of deep fiscal uncertainty.

'Represents a Hardship'

"I realize that this represents a hardship both for the recruits awaiting induction and for the people of the city, who expect and deserve the protection that these new officers would afford," Mr. Dinkins said yesterday. His announcement came unexpectedly in the middle of a news conference called to discuss Gov. Mario M. Cuomo's State of the State Message.

State officials have predicted a budget gap for the city of as much as $185 million in the rest of the fiscal year that ends June 30 and a gap of at least several hundred million dollars in the following year.

"As I have said consistently, I will be bound by the requirements of fiscal prudence in making the difficult decisions that affect our city and our people," said Mr. Dinkins, whose liberal policies created concern in some quarters during the mayoral campaign that he might overspend. He was also faulted by his opponents as indecisive or unwilling to make unpopular decisions.

Discussion With Brown

"I would wish that every announcement I would make would speak of enhancements," he said. "But that's just not the real world."

Mr. Dinkins had vowed repeatedly during the mayoral campaign and in his inaugural address on Monday to be "the toughest mayor on crime this city has ever seen."

The January class was to have had 1,476 recruits for the Police Department, 230 for the transit police and 142 for the housing police. The transit police has about 3,600 officers, while the housing police has about 1,700. During his campaign, Mr. Dinkins had prom-

Continued on Page B2, Column 1

The New York Times/Sara Krulwich

Gov. Mario M. Cuomo delivering his State of the State address.

Savings Agency Ordered to Sell Real Estate Fast

By NATHANIEL C. NASH
Special to The New York Times

WASHINGTON, Jan. 3 — The new agency created to manage the huge savings and loan bailout was instructed today to sell the real estate it inherited from hundreds of insolvent institutions as quickly as possible. The directive from the Bush Administration raised concerns among bankers that the properties could be "dumped" in an already weakened real estate market.

While the mandate to the newly formed Resolution Trust Corporation could mean that billions of dollars in homes, apartment buildings, shopping centers and raw land would be available to investors at bargain prices in 1990, bankers warned that an overzealous sales program could do more harm than good.

"Dumping is an acute political hot button, and if that is mishandled, then the political problems will end up right on George Bush's door," said Kenneth A. Guenther, executive vice president of the Independent Bankers Association.

Largest in Nation's History

On Tuesday, the savings agency listed more than 30,000 parcels of commercial and residential property as the first group it will put on the market, making the real estate sale the nation's largest ever. The vast majority of parcels, 26,813, are residential, of which 11,918 are single-family homes.

The nonresidential properties range from a golf course in South Padre Island, Tex., to a Dairy Queen in Woodland Park, Colo. Also on the list are nursing homes, theaters, marinas and churches.

The heaviest concentration of properties is in the troubled Southwest. Although the trust agency has not disclosed the total value of the real estate,

Continued on Page D5, Column 1

HEALTH INSURANCE FOR ALL CHILDREN IS URGED BY CUOMO

State of State Message Calls for Score of New Programs in an Election Year

By ELIZABETH KOLBERT
Special to The New York Times

ALBANY, Jan. 3 — Presenting an election-year array of new programs, Gov. Mario M. Cuomo today proposed a universal health insurance program for children and an overhaul of the method that the state uses to distribute education aid.

Starting with a detailed recitation of his accomplishments and ending with a score of proposals aimed at almost as many constituencies, the Governor, who delivered his eighth State of the State address, sounded very much like a man preparing for the 1990 gubernatorial campaign.

"Wherever the need was, we were there — rebuilding New York," Mr. Cuomo said, listing the achievements of state government during his time in office. [Excerpts from the address, page B4.]

At a time when the state is facing enormous budget problems, the Governor proposed several major spending initiatives. Besides the new health insurance program for children, they included substantial expansion of the state's drug-treatment program and a $1.9 billion environmental bond issue.

A 'More Beautiful' Future

"It's time now for another solid down-payment on a better and more beautiful future for the generations to follow us," Mr. Cuomo said.

For the first time, the Governor also called for legislation eliminating so-called building tenure for principals in New York City schools. This prevents the principals from being transferred between schools without hearings.

Some of Mr. Cuomo's proposals, like the environmental bond issue, would not require a significant state investment for several years. But the Governor left open the question of how he would finance other new programs, saying this would be dealt with in the

Continued on Page B4, Column 1

Agence France-Presse

After the surrender of Gen. Manuel Antonio Noriega, an American soldier and a Panamanian woman celebrated in Panama City.

As Word Spreads in Panama, Thousands Turn Out to Cheer

By LARRY ROHTER
Special to The New York Times

PANAMA, Jan. 3 — Jubilant street celebrations broke out tonight as the news spread in the capital that the country's deposed military ruler, Gen. Manuel Antonio Noriega, had voluntarily handed himself over to the United States authorities and would be tried in a United States court.

Thousands of Panamanians took to their cars, honking their horns and snarling traffic across the city. Thousands came out of their homes onto the lawns or verandas of their homes to bang pots and pans as soon as General Noriega's surrender to the United States was announced over national radio and television.

On street corners, youths waved Panamanian flags and sang and danced. Some lighted firecrackers and hoisted pineapple effigies of General Noriega pierced with knives.

"Our full liberation from the dictatorship of Noriega is now complete," Vice President Ricardo Arias Calderón told the nation in a televised address. "All Panamanians feel great jubilation because we know now that a new day has begun, a new day of democracy and being brothers again, so as to reconstruct our country."

On the streets, the sentiment was identical and even more fervently expressed. "Now we are finally free," read one banner waved by a middle-aged woman. "Justice has been served," said another.

"The dictator is gone, once and for all," shouted a young Panamanian

Continued on Page A12, Column 5

U.S. GOAL ACHIEVED

Bush Speaks of Vatican 'Assistance' in Ending Panama Standoff

By ANDREW ROSENTHAL
Special to The New York Times

WASHINGTON, Jan. 3 — President Bush announced tonight that Gen. Manuel Antonio Noriega had surrendered to the United States military authorities in Panama, giving the President the final victory he had been seeking in the invasion of Panama.

General Noriega, who had defied American efforts to drive him from power for more than four years, was removed under cover of night from the Vatican Embassy in Panama, where he had taken refuge 10 days ago. He was then flown by United States military helicopter to Howard Air Base in Panama City, where he was arrested by agents of the United States Drug Enforcement Administration.

The general is under indictment in two Federal courts in Florida on drug trafficking charges and Mr. Bush has made bringing him to trial in the United States a major justification for invading Panama on Dec. 20 and an important aspect of his Latin American policy in general.

Bush Thanks the Vatican

Mr. Bush appeared in the White House briefing room at about 9:40 P.M., less than an hour after General Noriega surrendered, to announce that the deposed Panamanian strongman was aboard an Air Force C-131 transport plane bound for Homestead Air Force Base in southern Florida.

Thanking the Vatican for its "even-handed, statesmanlike assistance" in getting General Noriega into American hands, Mr. Bush told reporters at a hurriedly called White House briefing that the general would be arraigned in Federal District Court in Miami on the drug charges filed in Miami in 1988. He was also indicted in Tampa.

An Administration official who asked not to be identified said that the White House had been expecting a breakthrough in the negotiations for several days, but that General Noriega's final surrender came without warning.

General Sets 3 Conditions

The general had sought assurances earlier in the week that he would not face the death penalty if he surrendered and had been told that the charges against him did not carry the death penalty, the official said.

Tonight, General Noriega informed the United States through Vatican intermediaries that he was ready to surrender. The official said the general had set three conditions: he wanted the press to be kept away from the Vatican mission when he left, he wanted to be able to contact family and friends by telephone before being flown out of the country and he wanted to be able to wear his uniform when he surrendered.

The United States, acting through the Vatican diplomats, agreed to those conditions, the official said.

General Noriega left the mission at 8:48 P.M. and was aboard the C-131 transport plane by 9:08 P.M. His sur-

Continued on Page A12, Column 4

Reuters

Contras Deny Part in Attack on Nuns in Nicaragua

Roman Catholic nuns sitting beside the coffin of Sister Maureen Courtney yesterday in Managua. A leader of the American-backed Nicaraguan rebels denied that the contras played any part in the attack that killed Sister Maureen, an American, and Sister Teresa Rosales, a Nicaraguan. Page A10.

Teen-Agers Who Won't Join When Drug Dealers Recruit

By DIRK JOHNSON
Special to The New York Times

CHICAGO, Jan. 3 — One recent Saturday afternoon on the South Side here, a 14-year-old boy received a telephone call from a gang leader. He was calling, he said, to recruit drug dealers. The boy, who did not know the gang leader, politely declined.

"Well then," the caller asked, "who's going to fight for you?"

Street gangs here, which thrive on the commerce of illegal drugs, have become far more aggressive and insistent in trying to broaden their operations, schools and police officials say.

"The gangs used to be much more selective," said Mary Cannon, a counselor at Harper High School on the South Side, where a 16-year-old gang member was recently stabbed to death in a classroom by rival gang members. "Now they want anybody and everybody. It's big dollars, big business."

Teen-agers everywhere contend with peer pressure to use drugs just to fit in. But in the inner city, where poverty and frustration can make a drug high seem all the more appealing, there is also the pressure of street gangs, and their threats can be more ominous than any anti-drug message.

Despite these daunting forces, many young people in inner-city neighborhoods manage to resist drugs. They choose to work behind the counters of fast-food restaurants at the minimum wage even though they have heard they could earn a lot more money by selling cocaine.

They endure taunts, insults, even beatings, because they will not sell or use drugs.

Lacrista Ewing, an energetic 18-year-old, was warned about her strait-laced ways by the girls of a street gang

Continued on Page A20, Column 4

Soviets Reinforcing Troops Along Iranian Border

By FRANCIS X. CLINES
Special to The New York Times

MOSCOW, Jan. 3 — The Soviet Government reinforced its troops along the Iranian border today in the face of continuing reports of destructive protests by Azerbaijani crowds demanding an open frontier.

Soviet officials said angry throngs of thousands of people had destroyed guard towers, crossing alarms and wire fencing along miles of the border, demanding that ancient cultural and political ties between Azerbaijanis on both sides of the Soviet-Iranian border be restored.

Most of the Government reports of violence and protest, in which no deaths and no exchange of gunfire have been reported, centered on the autonomous republic of Nakhichevan, an Azerbaijani region that shares with Iran 102 miles of a common border area that is closed to Western reporters.

The Soviet Union shares a vast frontier with Iran, and Izvestia, the Soviet Government newspaper, reported that "a complex situation has emerged" with crowd protests reported at times along much of that length.

According to accounts in Izvestia, a group identified as the Nakhichevan Popular Front began staging protest rallies at the Nakhichevan segment of the border a month ago, demanding union with neighboring "southern Azerbaijan," which is now a part of

Continued on Page A15, Column 3

INSIDE

Federal AIDS Estimate Is Being Revised
Scientists say that while AIDS continues to rise sharply, there will be at least 10 percent fewer cases over the next three years than previously predicted. Experts are debating why the rate seems to be changing. Page D20.

Treatment for First Lady
Barbara Bush began the first of 10 daily radiation treatments to relieve the double vision, eye discomfort and tears caused by Graves' disease, a thyroid affliction. Page D20.

Oil Leak Threatens Birds
An Exxon pipeline has leaked more than 200,000 gallons of heating oil into the Arthur Kill between Staten Island and New Jersey, posing a threat to birds along the waterway. Page B1.

Tyrannosaurus Deflatus?
A leading paleontologist says a type of dinosaur as large and fierce as Tyrannosaurus rex flourished 30 million years earlier. Page A21.

"All the News That's Fit to Print"

The New York Times

Late Edition

New York: Today, light snow, becoming partly sunny. High 38. Tonight, clear, breezy late. Low 30. Tomorrow, partly cloudy, windy. High 49. Yesterday: High 48, low 32. Details, page C8.

VOL.CXXXIX . . . No. 48,144 | Copyright © 1990 The New York Times | NEW YORK, MONDAY, FEBRUARY 12, 1990 | 50 cents beyond 75 miles from New York City, except on Long Island | 40 CENTS

MANDELA, FREED, URGES STEP-UP IN PRESSURE TO END WHITE RULE

Nelson Mandela leaving Victor Verster prison yesterday after spending 27 years in South African jails. Reuters

SPEECH IS RESOLUTE

He Asks Other Nations Not to Lift Sanctions Against Pretoria

By CHRISTOPHER S. WREN

Special to The New York Times

CAPE TOWN, Feb. 11 — After 27 and a half years in prison, Nelson Mandela finally won his freedom today and promptly urged his supporters at home and abroad to increase their pressure against the white minority Goverment that had just released him.

"We have waited too long for our freedom," Mr. Mandela told a cheering crowd from a balcony of Cape Town's old City Hall. "We can wait no longer."

"Now is the time to intensify the struggle on all fronts," he said. "To relax our efforts now would be a mistake which generations to come will not able to forgive." [Transcript of the address, page A15.]

First Speech Since '64

Mr. Mandela's 20-minute speech, which he prepared before leaving prison today, constituted his first remarks in public since before he was sentenced in June 1964 to life imprisonment for conspiracy to overthrow the Government and engage in sabotage.

He asked the international community not to lift its sanctions against South Africa, despite the recent changes introduced by President F. W. de Klerk, which culminated in Mr. Mandela's release.

"To lift sanctions now would be to run the risk of aborting the process toward ending apartheid," he said.

An Eloquent Militancy

Mr. Mandela's voice sounded firm and his words as eloquently militant as when he defended violence as the ultimate recourse at his political trial in 1964. Though he looked all of his 71 years and was grayer than artists' renditions over the years had depicted, he walked out of Victor Verster prison erect and vigorous.

In Washington, President Bush rejoiced over the release of Mr. Mandela, spoke to him by telephone and invited the anti-apartheid leader to visit the White House. [Page A17.]

Mr. Mandela gave no evidence that his militant opposition to apartheid had been tempered by the more than 10,000 days he spent in confinement. But he also said nothing that would have surprised the Government had he said it during his years of incarceration. Indeed, there appeared to be nothing in Mr. Mandela's initial remarks after his release to give the Government much consolation or encouragement.

Although he has been viewed as a potential leader for all South Africans, he stressed time and again that his loyalty lay with the African National Congress, for which he was working under-

Continued on Page A14, Column 1

On Mandela's Walk, Hope and Violence

By JOHN F. BURNS

Special to The New York Times

PAARL, South Africa, Feb. 11 — When Nelson Mandela made his walk to freedom today, he did it with the same simplicity and command of occasion that made him a leader among millions of South African blacks when his imprisonment began more than 10,000 days ago.

At 4:14 P.M. on a sun-warmed day — 27 years, six months and one week after his arrest on Aug. 5, 1962 — Mr. Mandela stepped from the car that drove him to the last guard post at the Victor Verster prison.

From there, smiling gently, he passed under a raised barrier and flicked his right hand quickly out from his body in greeting. He then raised his right arm several times in the bolder, black nationalist salute, his left hand holding the hand of his wife, Winnie, and walked to the point where the prison entrance road abuts the highway running through the undulating wine country of the Western Cape.

It was a walk of perhaps 70 yards, through a corridor of policemen, and as he made it, Mr. Mandela said not a word, at least none that could be heard by any in the crowd of 5,000 blacks and whites chanting his name. But to those who have come to know Mr. Mandela in the only way that was possible under the total ban that the South African Government threw around the black leader in prison — through his speeches and writings of a generation ago — there was no mistaking the symbolism involved in beginning his life outside jail on foot.

About the time in 1961 when President John F. Kennedy was spending his first summer in the White House, Mr. Mandela, then about the same age as Mr. Kennedy, used a phrase that became the title of a book of Mr. Mandela's speeches and writings. The book has been passed hand to hand in dog-eared copies among South Africans, who were forbidden until today under censorship laws and statutes governing political prisoners to own any book by or about the black leader. There was, Mr. Mandela said, "no easy walk to freedom" for South African blacks after three centuries of white domination and repression.

Dignified and Resolute

The Nelson Mandela who made his own walk to freedom today, after more than 22 years in the fortress prison on Robben Island, in the gale-swept mouth of Cape Town harbor, and five more years in a series of other prisons, had hair that had turned to gray. He looked at least 30 pounds lighter than he had at his last public appearance, in June 1964 when, with the physique of the heavyweight boxer he had been in his youth, he stood in the dock at the Rivonia Trial in Johannesburg and acknowledged that he was guilty as charged of sabotage and attempting to overthrow the Government.

But in other respects, the 71-year-old

Continued on Page A14, Column 1

Agence France-Presse

A South African youth celebrating Nelson Mandela's release yesterday at an African National Congress rally in Soweto. Mr. Mandela urged supporters to increase their pressure against the white Government.

U.S. INVITES IDEAS FROM THE SOVIETS ON STRATEGIC CUTS

AN ADMINISTRATION SHIFT

Moscow's Earlier Suggestions on Reducing Nuclear Arms Have Been Spurned

By MICHAEL R. GORDON

Special to The New York Times

WASHINGTON, Feb. 11 — In a shift of position, the Bush Administration has told Moscow that it is now prepared to receive Soviet proposals about reductions in long-range nuclear arms that go beyond the emerging strategic arms treaty, Administration officials disclosed today.

Until recently, the Bush Administration has rebuffed Moscow's suggestions that the two sides open discussions on a possible second arms treaty that would make deeper reductions in long-range nuclear weapons, like ocean-spanning ballistic missiles, cruise missiles and bombers, than does the arms treaty now under negotiation.

But Secretary of State James A. Baker 3d told Soviet leaders in Moscow last week that the Administration is now ready to entertain new Soviet ideas on what sort of subsequent reductions in long-range nuclear arms should be carried out after the current Strategic Arms Reduction Talks are concluded.

Thinking of 'Next Phase'

"Up to now we have not been willing to discuss the Soviet ideas on Start-2 on the ground that we still have work to do on Start-1," said a senior Administration official. "Now we are saying you can raise your ideas if you want to. We are getting to the point where we need to think a little bit about the next phase."

The question of whether to seek further reductions in long-range nuclear weapons after an agreement is reached has been a contentious one for the Bush Administration. Some Administration officials, like the White House national security adviser, Brent Scowcroft, have argued that reductions in nuclear weapons should not be pursued for their own sake, and the Administration has yet to formulate a basic position of what additional cuts in long-range nuclear arms, if any, might be sought.

The treaty currently under negotia-

Continued on Page A11, Column 1

The Price of Peace

Movements that fought in the trenches of the cold war are flushed out as peace breaks out in Central and Eastern Europe. Page A10.

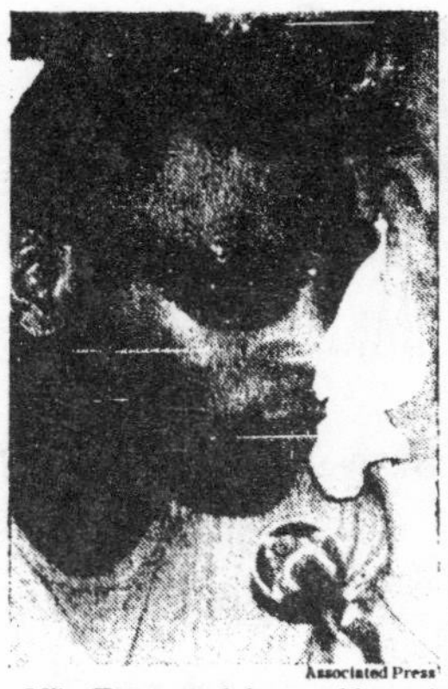

Associated Press

Mike Tyson applying a cold towel to his swollen eye during a news conference after the fight.

Boxing Officials Could Overturn Defeat of Tyson

By PHIL BERGER

James (Buster) Douglas knocked out Mike Tyson this weekend and won the world heavyweight championship in one of the greatest upsets in boxing history. But Douglas's victory in Tokyo may be undone by a rancorous dispute over a long count on Tyson's knockdown of Douglas in the eighth round.

Two of boxing's major governing bodies, the World Boxing Association and the World Boxing Council, suspended the result of the fight yesterday pending hearings into the controversy. The third major group that recognized Tyson as the champion, the International Boxing Federation, said it now considers Douglas to be the champion.

Tyson's corner had protested that Douglas received a long count, and, according to the W.B.C., a formal protest was later lodged by Japanese boxing authorities.

The result of the bout, fought Sunday in Tokyo (Saturday night in the United States), could ultimately be determined by the political and legal wrangling of the governing bodies as well as the considerable influence of Tyson's promoter, Don King.

Tunney-Dempsey Recalled

But this much is clear: By dominating the fight and knocking out the undefeated and seemingly invincible Tyson in the 10th round, Douglas, a relative unknown, shocked the sports world. And he also apparently upset the carefully laid plans for Tyson's boxing future, including a projected $22 million payday for a title defense against Evander Holyfield in June.

The knockdown in dispute, recalling the famous long count in the 1927 Gene Tunney-Jack Dempsey title fight, occurred after Tyson, battered by Douglas for most of eight rounds, connected on a right uppercut to Douglas's jaw that sent the challenger backward to the canvas.

Referee Octavio Meyran Sánchez leaped to Douglas's side and, after a pause, began counting with his fingers

Continued on Page C4, Column 5

Bush Homeless Plan: 'Godsend' or False Hope?

By JASON DePARLE

Federal Aid, New York Homeless

A special report.

On the night of Sept. 25, 1988, a previously obscure piece of Federal legislation was ushered onto political center stage before a television audience of millions.

During the season's first Presidential debate, a panelist asked George Bush what he would do for the homeless, "this voiceless segment of our society."

Mr. Bush answered without hesitation. "I want to see the McKinney Act fully funded," the Republican candidate said.

The McKinney Act?

The reference hardly resonated in the living rooms of America. Most viewers had never heard of the McKinney Act, and Mr. Bush's terse answer offered virtually no basis on which to judge it.

But Mr. Bush has kept his word. Last year, at his urging, Congress came close to fully financing most McKinney programs for the first time since the act was passed in 1987.

And the legislation remains a central provision of the Administration's plan for helping the homeless. As recently as last month, Mr. Bush pointed toward funds from the McKinney Act in telling a convention of home builders in Atlanta that "my Administration is going to do its part" in working to "solve the problems of the helpless and the homeless."

$67 Million for New York

The act itself is a quiver of 16 programs, each taking a different aim at homelessness. Some of the programs support shelters, with food or funds. Others provide services like job training, health care or treatment for alcohol or drug abuse.

The funds approved last year are likely to raise New York State's share to about $67 million, from $45 million. Because the money filters through a variety of governments and private organizations, it is impossible to determine how much of it is spent in New York City.

But despite the McKinney Act's broad aims and the recent increase in financing, many of those who provide shelter and services to the homeless say the McKinney Act falls short in at least these three respects:

¶It provides relatively little money.

¶It creates daunting bureaucratic obstacles.

¶And it provides almost no funds for low-income housing, which advocates argue must be part of a solution to homelessness.

"It's much ado about nothing," said Douglas H. Lasdon of the Legal Assistance Center for the Homeless in Manhattan. "It gives people the impression that something's being done, but it's not."

Measured in paint or plaster, protein or pajamas, the law has made a difference in the lives of dozens of New York organizations. Some money from the act, named for Representative Stewart B. McKinney, a Connecticut Republican

Continued on Page B8, Column 1

Rural Doctor's Struggle to Care for the Poorest

By PETER APPLEBOME

Special to The New York Times

TCHULA, Miss. — There aren't many doctors like Ronald Myers, a jazz-playing, Baptist-preaching family practitioner whose dream has always been to practice medicine in the kind of place most other doctors wouldn't even stop for a tank of gas.

But there are plenty of places like Tchula, a forlorn patch of Mississippi Delta poverty where it is hard to find a street that's not rutted, a sign that's not crooked, a paint job that's not peeling or a life that's not perched on the brink of economic ruin.

Dr. Myers's story — how hard it has been for him to get here and how hard it may be for him to stay — provides a dispiriting look at health care in rural America. The situation is worsening because the Government's program to provide doctors for the nation's neediest areas is being dismantled as health care needs continue to grow.

"Working in Tchula, Miss., is like working in a third world country," said Dr. Myers, who became Tchula's only doctor when he opened a clinic this month in an abandoned restaurant next to an empty liquor store. "The needs are that great. So how is it that here's a well-trained physician who wants to come to an area that's desperately poor, and I can't get any assistance? I can't get a loan. I'll take a tongue depressor if someone will give me one. There's a problem somewhere."

In poor rural areas, particularly in the South, regular medical care is seldom more than a distant dream. In areas like Tchula and nearby Belzoni, where Dr Myers previously worked, infant mortality rates are three times the national average, most women receive little if any prenatal care and people usually see a doctor only when they have no choice.

"The health problems in this area

Continued on Page B11, Column 1

INSIDE

Not Quite Watchdogs Yet

Across Eastern Europe, the once mighty official press is in even bigger trouble than the Communist parties it has praised for so long. Some papers have fallen into oblivion. Others are hoping for independence. Page A12.

A Turn in the Drug War?

In what experts hope is a turning point, the crime rate in and around Washington, D.C., is growing more slowly, and the number of suspects testing positive for cocaine use has dropped in recent months. Page B9.

Crisis Among Counselors

As the problems they confront grow more serious than those of 20 or even 10 years ago, guidance counselors in New York schools remain heavily overloaded. Page B1.

Checking-Account Bonus

Some banks are giving customers insurance that automatically protects goods bought by check against damage or loss and extends manufacturers' warranties. Page D1.

"All the News That's Fit to Print"

The New York Times

Late Edition
New York: **Today,** sunny. High 89. **Tonight,** clear, not as cool. Low 70. **Tomorrow,** mostly sunny, very warm, more humid. High 91. **Yesterday,** high 89, low 65. Details are on page C22.

VOL.CXXXIX . No. 48,316 — NEW YORK, FRIDAY, AUGUST 3, 1990 — 40 CENTS
50 cents beyond 75 miles from New York City, except on Long Island.

INVADING IRAQIS SEIZE KUWAIT AND ITS OIL; U.S. CONDEMNS ATTACK, URGES UNITED ACTION

The New York Times
Representative Floyd H. Flake

INDICTMENT NAMES QUEENS LAWMAKER IN MISUSE OF FUNDS

Rep. Flake Faces 17 Federal Counts Involving Church and Housing Complex

By ARNOLD H. LUBASCH

Representative Floyd H. Flake, a powerful Queens minister who rode his popularity into Congress four years ago, has been indicted on charges of diverting tens of thousands of dollars in church funds to his own use.

The 17-count Federal indictment, which was unsealed yesterday, charges that Mr. Flake and his wife, Margarett, engaged in a two-pronged conspiracy involving his church and the housing complex for the elderly that it built in Jamaica under his stewardship. They are accused of fraudulently obtaining $66,700 from the church, embezzling $75,000 from the housing complex and evading income taxes on both amounts.

Pastor Since '76

The Representative, a Democrat whose Sixth Congressional District covers southern Queens, issued a detailed statement denying the charges. His lawyer said he still intended to run for re-election in November, and Mrs. Flake's lawyer added that the charges would fuel "a perception that minority politicians are being unfairly targeted for prosecution."

Since 1976, the 45-year-old Congressman has been pastor of the Allen A.M.E. Church in Jamaica, one of the largest and oldest black churches in New York City, with 6,000 members and a history reaching back into the 1830's. During his tenure, Mr. Flake has built up the church, and his own influence, with a network of social-services for the largely poor and largely black Jamaica neighborhood.

3d Congressman to Be Indicted

And yesterday, under the warm afternoon sun, there was a wary feeling of racism at work and an insistence that the charges against the pastor had to be false. [Page B4.]

Mr. Flake is the third New York City Congressman indicted in the last three years. The others, Mario Biaggi and Robert Garcia, both Bronx Democrats, were convicted in the Wedtech racketeering case. Mr. Garcia's conviction was overturned in June.

In announcing the unsealing of the indictment, the United States Attorney

Continued on Page B4, Column 5

Covenant Report Is Said to Find Sex Misconduct

By M. A. FARBER

An investigation ordered by the Covenant House board of directors concludes that the Rev. Bruce Ritter, the charity's founder and longtime president, engaged in sexual misconduct with young men living at Covenant House shelters for runaway youths, according to people who have read the investigator's report.

They say the four-month investigation, headed by Robert J. McGuire, a former New York City Police Commissioner, finds that had Father Ritter not resigned last February, the board would have had to dismiss him.

A Secretive Personal Fund

The report, which is to be issued today, also says the Covenant House board, controlled by Father Ritter until this year, failed to exercise proper oversight. The report notes, for example, that the board did not know that Father Ritter was receiving a salary of $98,000, the bulk of which was going into a secretive personal fund.

The fund, called the Franciscan Charitable Trust, had accumulated close to $1 million. Plans now call for it to be liquidated, with the assets going to Covenant House, as Father Ritter says he intended all along.

Father Ritter, who has vehemently denied the allegations, calling them "garbage," has declined to be interviewed for months and is said to have refused to cooperate with Mr. McGuire's investigation. The 63-year-old

Continued on Page B4, Column 2

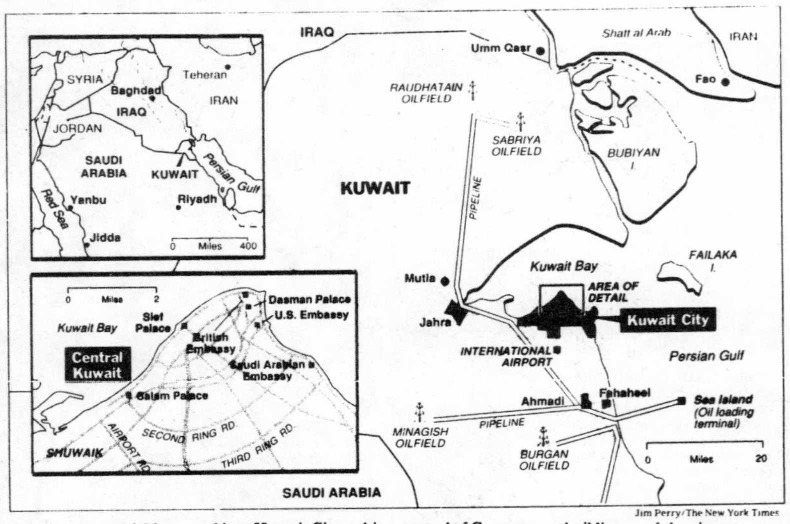

Jim Perry/The New York Times
Iraqi invaders quickly moved into Kuwait City, taking control of Government buildings and the airport.

IRAQ'S ADVANTAGE LIMITS U.S. OPTIONS

Lack of Warning or Proximity Hinders American Action

By MICHAEL R. GORDON
Special to The New York Times

WASHINGTON, Aug. 2 — The Bush Administration faced the sobering reality today that despite a longstanding commitment to defend America's vital interests in the Persian Gulf, there was no easy military means to compel Iraq to withdraw its forces from Kuwait.

With the forces of pro-Western Arab powers like Saudi Arabia no match militarily for Iraq's powerful army, and with only a token American military presence in the area, the Administration's immediate responses included condemning the invasion, freezing Iraqi assets in the United States and calling for international sanctions.

Pentagon officials said that the United States had undertaken some military preparations as a result of the Iraqi attack. One aircraft carrier, the Independence, was under way at high speed from the Indian Ocean toward the Arabian Sea, adjacent to the Persian Gulf. It is expected to reach the area in several days.

A 2d Carrier Is Shifted

Another aircraft carrier, the Eisenhower, was being shifted to the Eastern Mediterranean Sea to put its attack planes within range of Iraq. The modest fleet of American ships in the Persian Gulf was expanded from six to eight. And some Air Force aerial refueling tankers were said to have been dispatched to the Indian Ocean region.

Defense Secretary Dick Cheney canceled plans to go with President Bush to Aspen, Colo., for Mr. Bush's speech on military issues and instead monitored the Gulf crisis from the Penta-

Continued on Page A8, Column 4

A New Gulf Alignment

Iraqis, Bargaining on Anti-U.S. Sentiment, May Profit by Intimidating the Monarchies

By YOUSSEF M. IBRAHIM
Special to The New York Times

News Analysis

PARIS, Aug. 2 — Iraq's invasion of Kuwait ushers in a new alignment in which Iraqis, Iranians and Palestinian hard-liners appear to share an interest in subduing the oil-rich monarchies of the region and challenging United States influence in the Arab world.

In ordering his forces to attack Kuwait, President Saddam Hussein of Iraq calculated that the odds were largely in his favor.

Arab diplomats and military experts said the only serious risk for Iraq was swift retaliation from the United States military forces. But that is a move that Washington may not be ready to take, given that the Iraqi armed forces are widely considered the most tested and best equipped in the Gulf region.

The Iraqis have much to gain from their invasion of Kuwait. A successful offensive could establish Baghdad as the dominant power in the Middle East, giving it a much greater say in decisions on oil production and prices.

Beyond that, the attack could become a rallying point for those in the Arab world who resent United States influence in world affairs and who feel that some Middle Eastern nations like Egypt have gone too far in accommodating Washington. Lastly, it could finally settle Iraq's longstanding border disputes with Kuwait.

The prospects for an effective counter to the attack appear slimmer in view of evidence that the Iraqis coordinated their move with Iran, which helped exert diplomatic pressure on Kuwait and the United Arab Emirates to raise prices last month at a meeting of the Organization of Petroleum Exporting Countries.

Iran officially condemned the Iraqi move late today, but the suspicion remained that it had at the very least not discouraged Baghdad's action.

Sense of Powerlessness

In the wake of the invasion, the Arab world is discovering how powerless it is in countering an Iraqi attempt to assert its dominance.

Saudi Arabia is Kuwait's closest ally in the region and the founder of the Gulf Cooperation Council, the alliance to which both Kuwait and the United Arab Emirates belong. But it has hardly lifted a finger to halt the Iraqi invasion, giving the impression that it is powerless and ever more dependent on American assistance. Although the Saudis have spent billions of dollars on

Continued on Page A10, Column 3

'NAKED AGGRESSION'

Bush Suggests Action by U.N. — Emir Flees to Saudi Arabia Exile

By R. W. APPLE Jr.
Special to The New York Times

WASHINGTON, Aug. 2 — Iraqi troops stormed into the desert sheikdom of Kuwait today, seizing control of its capital city and its rich oilfields, driving its ruler into exile, plunging the strategic Persian Gulf region into crisis and sending tremors of anxiety around the world.

President Bush condemned the invasion as "naked aggression" and sought to enlist world leaders in collective action against Iraq.

Faced with a dire threat from the truculent Iraqi leader, Saddam Hussein, to a region containing much of the world's oil reserves and with world financial markets in turmoil, Mr. Bush banned nearly all imports from Iraq and froze the nation's assets in the United States. At a news conference in Woody Creek, Colo., the President and Prime Minister Margaret Thatcher of Britain raised the possibility of economic or even military action by the United Nations.

Iraq Suspends Payments

In response, Iraq, which had been accusing Kuwait for weeks of stealing its oil and violating production limits set by the Organization of Petroleum Exporting Countries, suspended debt payments to the United States. Western experts asserted that Iraq had been motivated by a financial squeeze that only more oil dollars could ease and by ambitions for regional dominance.

Although oil prices rose sharply today, analysts noted that world inventories are unusually high, and they saw no immediate threat to supplies.

Witnesses in Kuwait said that hundreds of people were killed or wounded today as Iraqi ground forces, led by columns of tanks, surged into the desert emirate at the head of the gulf. Other troops came by air.

For Mr. Bush, the invasion posed manifold problems: the difficulty of direct military action despite the huge commitment of money and resources to the gulf in recent years; fear of another surge in oil prices, which could hurt economic growth and rekindle inflation; the potential disruption of the fragile budget negotiations between the White House and the Congress, in which a gasoline tax has been considered, and possible damage to the Re-

Continued on Page A8, Column 1

Soviet Smokers Vow Strikes As Cigarettes, Too, Disappear

By CELESTINE BOHLEN
Special to The New York Times

MOSCOW, Aug. 2 — It happens like clockwork, all over the city. A truck pulls up to a boarded-up kiosk, unloads its wares, the sale window opens and within minutes smokers appear out of nowhere to take places in line, hopeful that for this day, anyway, their addiction can be fed.

Along with other ills, the Soviet Union is now in the throes of a nicotine fit, brought on by a painful and puzzling withdrawal of cigarettes from a nation of heavy smokers.

In many parts of the country, the cigarette shortage — caused by a series of typical economic lapses — has galvanized the patient, line-suffering Soviet consumer into action.

In the city of Perm last week, a demonstration that began in front of an empty tobacco shop spilled into downtown streets, ending in a rally outside City Hall, where 2,000 people chanted and waved banners, badgering the Communist Party for cigarettes. "Hey, you up there, your people have nothing to smoke as well as nothing to eat," one banner read. "Party, have you got a smoke?" asked another.

Aircraft Workers Threaten Strike

In Kuibyshev, smokers at an aircraft plant threatened a strike over the cigarette shortage and protesters mounted a daily vigil at a local tobacco plant that had been shut for repairs.

Warning strikes have also been reported in Ulyanovsk and Ufa, while in Voronezh and Orel, angry smokers have smashed the windows of tobacco kiosks. This month, at the height of the harvest in the Krasnador region, combine operators brought their machines to a stop with a nonnegotiable demand: "No tobacco, no work."

Such public vehemence has been absent during other shortages: when cheese, onions, lemons or sausages disappear from the stores, Soviet shoppers simply shift their queues from one

Continued on Page A4, Column 5

Reuters
Iraqi gunners yesterday on the coast near Kuwait City, where they fired on Kuwaiti naval vessels offshore.

2 Teen-Agers Shot As Violence Persists On New York Streets

The tide of violence in New York City in the last two weeks — four children killed by stray gunfire, an advertising executive shot dead in the West Village, two cab drivers murdered, a young couple bludgeoned in Central Park — continued yesterday as officials struggled to respond to growing fears.

A 14-year-old Queens boy was shot and killed after he told another teenager to stop riding a friend's moped. In the Bronx, a 15-year-old girl standing with friends in a park was critically wounded when a youth fired a gunshot into her group. A homeless drifter was charged with Monday's fatal shooting of the ad executive at a phone booth.

And pressure grew on city officials to cope with the latest wave of violence. Mayor David N. Dinkins today will announce a crackdown on gun users. Police Commissioner Lee P. Brown, in an interview, contended that the police alone could not solve the problems of crime and violence.

Articles, pages B1 and B3.

INSIDE

Why a Bishop Quit

The recent resignation of the Roman Catholic Archbishop of Atlanta came about after evidence of his "intimate relationship" with a woman, church officials said. Page A12.

A Troubled Savings Rescue

Almost a year after the Federal bailout of the savings and loan industry, economists see problems, including a danger to banks. Page D1.

Barry Case Goes to Jury

The drug case against Washington's Mayor is now in the hands of 12 of the city's residents. Page A12.

The Iraqi Invasion: Global Reverberations

OIL PRICES Spot market prices surged, with the American benchmark crude rising to $23.11 a barrel, up $1.57. The invasion stirred fears of slower economic growth, higher inflation and OPEC domination of the world oil market. But price increases should be limited by a near-record stockpile worldwide. Page A9.

FINANCIAL MARKETS The dollar rose, gold prices jumped and most stock markets fell. Japan, dependent on imported oil, was hard hit. As of today's close in Tokyo, its stock market had fallen 4.3 percent since the invasion took place. Page D1.

THE SOVIET UNION Moscow announced a suspension in the delivery of arms and military hardware to Iraq. The move interrupted Moscow's longtime role as Baghdad's chief arms supplier. Page A10.

UNITED NATIONS With Moscow and Washington in agreement, the Security Council voted 14 to 0 to condemn the invasion and demand an Iraqi withdrawal. Page A10.

DIPLOMACY Secretary of State James A. Baker 3d cut short a visit to Mongolia and plans to issue a joint statement about the crisis in Moscow today with the Soviet Foreign Minister, Eduard A. Shevardnadze. Syria condemned the invasion and called for an emergency Arab summit conference.

ISRAEL Israeli leaders condemned the invasion, but they also appeared relieved by the move. For months, President Saddam Hussein has been sharply threatening Israel. Officials in Jerusalem were openly frustrated that the rest of the world did not seem adequately concerned. Page A10.

THE EUROPEAN ALLIES Western European countries unanimously condemned the invasion, with Britain and France joining the United States in freezing billions of dollars worth of Kuwaiti assets. Page A10.

"All the News That's Fit to Print"

The New York Times

Late Edition

New York: Today, sunny, becoming windy. High 73. Tonight, breezy, mild. Low 62. Tomorrow, quite windy, sunny, warmer. High 77. Yesterday, high 69, low 56. Details are on page C7.

VOL. CXL .. No. 48,377

Copyright © 1990 The New York Times

NEW YORK, WEDNESDAY, OCTOBER 3, 1990

50 cents beyond 75 miles from New York City, except on Long Island.

40 CENTS

TWO GERMANYS UNITE AFTER 45 YEARS WITH JUBILATION AND A VOW OF PEACE

DINKINS PROPOSES RECORD EXPANSION OF POLICE FORCES

Mayor Offers New Programs for Corrections and Youth to Help Combat Crime

By RALPH BLUMENTHAL

Seeking to take command of an issue that has shaken his leadership, Mayor David N. Dinkins announced a barrage of proposals yesterday to fight crime, including a record expansion of New York City's police forces and ambitious new corrections, youth and education programs. The total cost would be $1.8 billion over the next four years.

With New York City already in financial straits, the Mayor proposed paying for the initiatives through a rise in the real-property tax, a new city payroll tax to be shared by workers and employers and a 25-cent surcharge on state lottery tickets.

The taxes, which would rise from $138 million in what remains of the first fiscal year to $644 million in the fourth year, would require approval by the City Council and the State Legislature.

'Assault on All Fronts'

"We will not wage war by degree," Mr. Dinkins said, releasing a 535-page police manpower study and a 57-page mayoral report that began a day of briefings and culminated in a news conference timed for live television coverage on the evening news. "Our strategy calls for an assault on all fronts." [Excerpts, page B2.]

The anti-crime program was hailed by many community leaders, but reaction to the tax plan was mixed. The State Senate majority leader, Ralph J. Marino, voiced strong reservations about the potentially negative effect on commuters and businesses. Gov. Mario M. Cuomo said that if it were necessary for public safety, he "could" support the payroll tax, but that he had yet to review the plan in detail.

Assembly Speaker Mel Miller also urged caution. "We're going to have to go slowly in weighing the tax package," most of which, he noted, would not take effect until the fiscal year beginning next July. The City Council Speaker, Peter F. Vallone, voiced general support for the plan but seemed taken aback that it went so far beyond the Council's own proposal to hire more officers through a lottery surcharge.

Thomas Reppetto, president of the

Continued on Page B2, Column 1

In Appeal for Support for Budget, President Calls Plan Best for Now

By DAVID E. ROSENBAUM
Special to The New York Times

WASHINGTON, Oct. 2 — Faced with a revolt in his party's Congressional ranks and wariness around the country, President Bush appealed on television tonight for public support of the budget compromise he and Congressional leaders struck last weekend. He predicted "economic chaos if we fail to reduce the deficit."

In a show of bipartisanship that verged on coalition Government, the President was followed with a broadcast by Senator George J. Mitchell of Maine, the Democratic leader. He urged support for the President "because the nation is more important than partisan differences." [Transcripts of the Bush and Mitchell speeches appear on page D28.]

Tough Task for Bush

Mr. Mitchell was preaching to the converted for the most part. Despite considerable opposition among liberals, a majority of Congressional Democrats appear to support the agreement.

But Mr. Bush has the more difficult task of swaying enough dissident Republicans to win enactment of the plan.

The President said that neither he

nor anyone else was completely satisfied with the compromise, but he said it was "the best agreement that can be legislated now."

In the strongest statement he has made about economic perils that might lie ahead, Mr. Bush emphasized: "If we fail to enact this agreement, our economy will falter, markets may tumble and recession will follow."

He called on the public to "tell your Congressmen and Senators you support this deficit-reduction agreement."

A Bipartisan Appeal

The President continued: "If they are Republicans, urge them to stand with the President. If they are Democrats, urge them to stand with their Congressional leaders."

"Those who dislike one part or another may pick our agreement apart," Mr. Bush said, "but if they do, believe me, the political reality is no one can put a better one back together again."

Senator Mitchell made almost identical points. He would have preferred "a budget that asks more from the wealthy and less from the elderly," he said. But as for the compromise, he

Continued on Page D27, Column 1

Pivotal Moment for Bush

By ANDREW ROSENTHAL
Special to The New York Times

WASHINGTON, Oct. 2 — With his speech tonight from the Oval Office, George Bush completed a fundamental transition: The President who succeeded for so long at giving Americans only good news is now telling them to prepare for economic pain at home and the possibility of war abroad.

News Analysis

With remarkable speed, Mr. Bush has moved from the most protracted honeymoon in recent White House his-

tory to twin crises that could determine the success of his Presidency.

The decision to confront the Republican rebellion on Capitol Hill over the budget agreement quickly and directly in a nationally televised speech represented a judgment that any delay could allow events to spin out of control. If the emerging prospects for passage of the budget package turn into defeat, Mr. Bush would immediately lose his calculated gamble that such an agreement would be good for the economy and thus bolster his re-election campaign in 1992.

For more than a year and a half, everything seemed to be going Mr. Bush's way, especially in Europe. Then on Aug. 8, six days after the Iraqi invasion of Kuwait, Mr. Bush went on national television to announce that he was sending troops to the Persian Gulf and to prepare the country for the possibility that American soldiers and civilians could die in a far-off war.

Tonight, less than two months later, Mr. Bush again spoke from the Oval

Continued on Page D27, Column 4

More on the Budget

A SECOND LOOK Some experts say the deficit will be cut less than predicted. Page D27.

TAX BREAKS Big companies may benefit from provisions aimed at small ones. Page D29.

PLANNING AHEAD How changes in deductions will affect some taxpayers. Page D29.

The German flag was unfurled in front of the Reichstag building in Berlin at midnight as the two Germanys were reunited.

Associated Press

Senate Confirms Souter, 90 to 9, As Supreme Court's 105th Justice

By RICHARD L. BERKE
Special to The New York Times

WASHINGTON, Oct. 2 — Ten weeks after President Bush nominated David H. Souter, a little-known New Hampshire judge, for the Supreme Court, the Senate voted overwhelmingly today to confirm him as the Court's 105th Justice.

The vote was 90 to 9, with only Democrats voting against confirmation. The balloting came after nearly four hours of speeches on the Senate floor in which supporters said they were confident Judge Souter would preserve fundamental constitutional values, while opponents said too much was not known about his positions on critical issues like abortion.

Case on Sensitive Issue

Chief Justice William H. Rehnquist will swear in Judge Souter at a relatively short ceremony at the Court on Tuesday morning, in time to sit for oral arguments later that day in the second week of the Court term.

On Wednesday, Judge Souter will be among the Justices hearing a major case on the lawfulness of corporate policies that exclude women from jobs that might endanger a developing fetus. Today the Court took up the major issue left unresolved from the era of official school segregation: what a school system that was segregated by law decades ago must do to free itself from Federal court supervision. [Education, page B8.]

With the Souter nomination behind him, Senator Joseph R. Biden Jr., the

Delaware Democrat who is chairman of the Judiciary Committee, was looking to future vacancies on the Court. He said he hoped that the Administration "will not learn the wrong lesson" from the strong bipartisan support the nominee received.

"Our overwhelming approval is not a sign that the Senate intends to be lax about exercising its advise-and-consent power, or intends to use that power only to screen out extremist nominees," Mr. Biden said. "Rather, it is a sign that we take this power seriously, and that we intend to exercise it responsibly. And in doing so, Judge Souter falls within the sphere of candidates acceptable to the Senate."

Mr. Biden emphasized, however, that he and several other Democrats who supported the nomination had serious misgivings because Judge Souter

Continued on Page A24, Column 1

INSIDE

Air Crash Mystery in China

Did a cockpit struggle cause a hijacked Chinese plane to crash into a parked jet at Canton's airport, killing 127 people? Chinese officials would not confirm the report. Page A3.

South African Rift Persists

The leader of the Inkatha movement spurned a meeting with the African National Congress, dampening prospects for a reconciliation between the two warring groups. Page A3.

Melee in Pakistan

A mob stormed the courtroom where former Prime Minister Benazir Bhutto is to stand trial on corruption charges. Page A6.

Women in Locker Rooms

Three recent incidents in football have reopened the issue of access to locker rooms by women covering men's sports. Page D31.

A MILLION IN BERLIN

Flag at Reichstag Marks Start of a New Era at Center of Europe

By SERGE SCHMEMANN
Special to The New York Times

BERLIN, Wednesday, Oct. 3 — Forty-five years after it was carved up in defeat and disgrace, Germany was reunited today in a midnight celebration of pealing bells, national hymns and the jubilant blare of good old German oom-pah-pah.

At the stroke of midnight Tuesday, a copy of the American Liberty Bell, a gift from the United States at the height of the cold war, tolled from the Town Hall, and the black, red and gold banner of the Federal Republic of Germany rose slowly before the Reichstag, the scarred seat of past German Parliaments.

Then the President, Richard von Weizsäcker, drawing on the words of the West German Constitution, proclaimed from the steps of the Reichstag: "In free self-determination, we want to achieve the unity in freedom of Germany. We are aware of our responsibility for these tasks before God and the people. We want to serve peace in the world in a united Europe."

Singing of Anthem

With that, a throng estimated at one million joined in the West German national anthem, now the anthem for united Germany: "Unity and justice and freedom for the German fatherland . . ." The words are from the third stanza of the prewar anthem, whose opening verses, now banned began, "Deutschland, Deutschland über Alles."

The moment marked the return of a nation severed along the front line between East and West to the center stage of Europe, this time as an economic powerhouse vowing never again to bring grief to a continent it had so terribly ravaged in the past century.

It is the smallest unified German state to rise in the 119 years since Otto von Bismarck first gathered the Germans under the Prussian crown.

Beer and Revelry

Hundreds of German flags waved and firecrackers snapped in the chilly autumn night. Beer and sparkling wine flowed freely and the strains of divergent bands mingled in a rowdy cacophony. Soon bottles began smashing on the pavement and celebration turned to intoxication, and by early morning the center of the new capital was deep in smashed bottles and weaving revelers.

A force of about 5,000 police officers had been massed in case radicals tried

Continued on Page A17, Column 1

Germany by the Numbers

In some respects, the united Germany is less than the sum of its parts. The statistical tale is told in charts and a map on page A16.

Bitter Dispute Is Threatening Program for Marrow Donors

By GINA KOLATA

A program that has the lofty goal of finding altruistic people to donate bone marrow to save the lives of dying patients has become enmeshed in a dispute that threatens its ability to function.

The conflict involves charges that a former subcontractor in the federally financed program provided misleading information to dying patients and volunteers who wanted to help them; withheld the names of thousands of potential marrow donors, and failed to account to families for large sums of money raised in their names.

The subcontractor, the Life-Savers Foundation of America, has denied the allegations and accused the National Marrow Donor Program of overcharging patients and being inefficient in matching patients and donors.

Registry of Potential Donors

The national program has amassed a file of 200,000 people who are willing to donate marrow if their tissue is compatible with that of a patient with leukemia or another disease. Without transplants, the patients will die, and the demand for donors far exceeds the supply.

But Federal officials, transplant surgeons and ethicists are worried that allegations of questionable conduct in the treatment of dying patients and their families could cause the network of

volunteer donors to fall apart. They say altruism is fragile at best, and any hint of misconduct is more than enough to make people shy away from donating.

The national program has asserted in court and in a letter to Senator Al Gore, Democrat of Tennessee, that Life-Savers caused patients unnecessary anguish by raising false hopes that there was a donor.

Officials of the national program, who say they have severed all ties with the subcontractor, say some families

Continued on Page A26, Column 1

Top Soviet General Tells U.S. Not to Attack in Gulf

Gen. Mikhail A. Moiseyev, left, chief of the Soviet General Staff, discussing options in the Persian Gulf crisis yesterday in New York City. With him was Gen. Colin L. Powell, the Chairman of the Joint Chiefs of Staff.

Jack Manning/The New York Times

By MICHAEL R. GORDON

The head of the Soviet military said yesterday that the economic sanctions against Iraq were working and that no force should be used in the Persian Gulf unless it was approved by the United Nations.

The remarks by the Soviet general, Mikhail A. Moiseyev, Chief of the Soviet General Staff, were the most explicit comments made so far by a Soviet official on the need to have United Nations approval for the use of force by the United States and other nations that have opposed the Iraqi invasion of Kuwait.

The Soviet general's comments — in

an unusual joint interview with Gen. Colin L. Powell, Chairman of the Joint Chiefs of Staff — signaled a basic disagreement with Washington about the circumstances under which military force could be used in the Persian Gulf.

"We cannot view the resolution of any crisis like this by means of using arms," said General Moiseyev, who is on a tour of the United States as a guest of General Powell. But General Powell pointedly said President Bush had not ruled out any options.

The two generals were interviewed by writers and editors of The New York Times.

Suggesting that military force was

not needed to force Iraqi troops out of Kuwait, General Moiseyev said the economic embargo was beginning to hurt Iraq.

"Saddam Hussein has really understood now finally how far he has gone," General Moiseyev said. "He is finding himself in economic and political isolation, and he can't survive very long that way."

General Moiseyev asserted that protests, uprisings and desertions in Iraqi were sapping the strength of the Iraqi military and impelling President Hussein to seek a diplomatic solution.

"You can't keep an army together

Continued on Page A12, Column 1

"All the News That's Fit to Print"

The New York Times

Late Edition

New York: Today, partly cloudy, windy. High 49. Tonight, clear, cold winds. Low 32. Tomorrow, variable clouds. High 40. Yesterday, high 55, low 38. Details are on page D22.

VOL.CXL — No. 48,483 Copyright © 1991 The New York Times NEW YORK, THURSDAY, JANUARY 17, 1991 50 cents beyond 75 miles from New York City, except on Long Island. 40 CENTS

U.S. AND ALLIES OPEN AIR WAR ON IRAQ; BOMB BAGHDAD AND KUWAITI TARGETS; 'NO CHOICE' BUT FORCE, BUSH DECLARES

A TENSE WAIT ENDS

News of Attack Sweeps the Country, Stirring Profound Feelings

By JAMES BARRON

In one long moment yesterday, word that the United States had attacked Baghdad swept the country.

In split-level suburban homes on the East Coast where dinner was in the oven, in big-city restaurants in the Midwest where bars were jammed with the happy-hour crowd and in skyscraper offices on the West Coast where people were still at work, there was an odd mixture of apprehension, sadness and relief.

In malls, shoppers emptied out of stores and cried. In supermarkets, cashiers rushed to call relatives and share the news that after five months of waiting and wondering America was at war. In department stores, people crowded in front of television sets, with some saying they were stunned that President Bush had decided to act so soon after the United States deadline for Iraq to withdraw from Kuwait.

A Scene Out of World War II

Suddenly, in public places where cacophony is the norm, there was an unusual silence, eerie rather than giddy. Grand Central Terminal in Manhattan — where even whispers can take on an echoing, high-decibel intensity — was quiet. On trains to Connecticut, passengers gathered around people who had radios with headsets. "The people with the radios would listen to the news and then relay it to the other passengers," said Dan Brucker, a spokesman for the Metro-North Commuter Railroad, "kind of like World War II radio dispatchers delivering the news."

The word that waves of air attacks were striking Iraq silenced black-tie galas in Manhattan. And in a Houston hotel, the chatter around the bar stopped when the President began his speech from the Oval Office. Only the machine making frozen margaritas kept whirring.

Some people applauded Mr. Bush's decision to order the attack. "It was direct and to the point," Lester Alexander, a New Orleans real-estate investor, said of Mr. Bush's speech. "He did not try to sell me on his reasons, but he

Continued on Page A19, Column 4

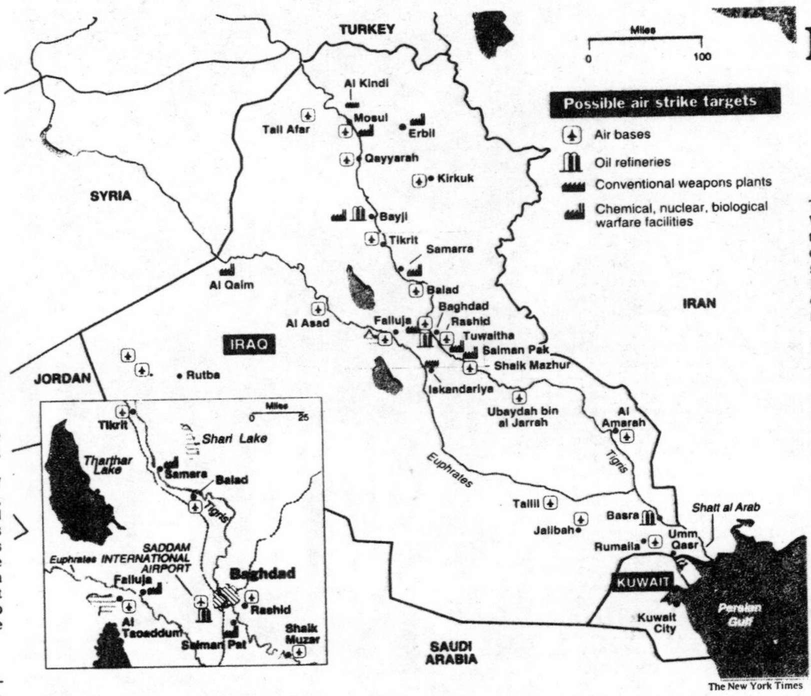

OTHER NEWS

Gorbachev Is Moving To Muzzle the Press

Faced with mounting condemnation of the assault by Soviet forces on demonstrators in Lithuania, President Mikhail S. Gorbachev moved to undermine a law guaranteeing freedom of the press — a hallmark of the era of openness that he himself ushered in. Page A8.

In a show of defiance in the Lithuanian capital, hundreds of thousands of mourners streamed through the streets to bury the dead. Page A8.

Dinkins Offers Budget With Layoffs and Cuts

Mayor David N. Dinkins presented a preliminary New York City budget of $29.3 billion for the next fiscal year. The announcement was met with a mix of pain and uncertainty. The plan includes thousands of layoffs and service cuts. Page B1.

Daily News Threatens To Close or Sell

The management of The Daily News threatened to close or sell the paper unless it stems heavy losses. Both sides in the 12-week-old strike agreed the move was an ultimatum to the unions to make major concessions or lose their jobs for good. Page B1.

News Summary	A2
Editorials/Op-Ed	A22-23
Obituaries	B10
Sports	B11-16
Weather	D22

Arts	C13-24	Health	B9
Bridge	C22	Media	D10
Chronicle	B22	TV Listings	C23
Crossword	C21	Word and Image	C21
Classified Index	B16	Auto Exchange	B12

Possible air strike targets
- Air bases
- Oil refineries
- Conventional weapons plants
- Chemical, nuclear, biological warfare facilities

The New York Times

Raids, on a Huge Scale, Seek to Destroy Iraqi Missiles

By MICHAEL R. GORDON
Special to The New York Times

WASHINGTON, Thursday, Jan. 17 — The military campaign to evict Iraq from Kuwait began, as expected, with night air strikes on a huge scale at targets deep in Iraq and Kuwait.

According to early reports of the night operation from the Pentagon, no American aircraft were lost and grave damage appeared to have been done to Iraqi military forces. Cable News Network reported that another series of sorties began at midmorning Baghdad time.

American officials said the first onslaught against Iraqi air defenses, communications and weapons sites included the firing of Tomahawk sea-launched cruise missiles, as well as F-117 Stealth fighter-bombers, F-15E fighter-bombers and a wide variety of other Air Force and Navy planes.

British and Saudis Join In

The American aircraft were accompanied by British and Saudi Tornado fighter-bombers, Saudi F-15's and Kuwaiti combat planes.

The aims of the nighttime attack were to damage the Iraqi military establishment by destroying command and control centers, including those in Baghdad, and to establish air superiority by knocking out Iraqi air defenses and airfields.

Pentagon officials said that all Navy planes in the night operation were reported to have returned safely. There were no reported Air Force losses, though the return of some of the planes to an air base near Taif, Saudi Arabia, was being delayed by bad weather there. Britain reported that all of its planes had returned safely.

Pentagon officials said that its bomb-damage assessments were still being conducted, and they disputed reports that the attacks had decimated the Republican Guards, the elite of the Iraqi Army.

Satellite Reports Awaited

Pentagon officials said the attack on Iraq appeared to be very successful because the Iraqi Air Force had not challenged the attacking planes and because the United States has no confirmed reports of launchings of Iraqi Scuds, long-range surface-to-surface missiles that are considered a threat to the allies' bases and to Israel. But they added that they were still awaiting definitive satellite and other reconnaissance reports.

Gen. Colin L. Powell, the chairman of the Joint Chiefs of Staff, said at a Pentagon news conference that "there has been no air resistance" from the Iraqis. Pentagon officials said that they hoped to destroy the Iraqi planes in their hardened shelters.

The allied air forces also attacked Scud batteries, and, as President Bush emphasized, American planes struck at Iraqi nuclear and chemical-weapons production sites. No ground forces were used in the operation, the Pentagon said.

In mounting the air attack, the United States is also trying to make good on assurances to the Israelis that Washington would blast the Scud missiles that threaten Israel to make it unnecessary for Israel to enter the war, the American officials said. Defense Secretary Dick Cheney said that the Pentagon had no information to confirm that Iraqi Scud missiles had struck Saudi Arabia.

The timing of the attack was de-

Continued on Page A15, Column 1

No Ground Fighting Yet; Call to Arms by Hussein

By ANDREW ROSENTHAL
Special to The New York Times

WASHINGTON, Thursday, Jan. 17 — The United States and allied forces Wednesday night opened the long-threatened war to drive President Saddam Hussein's army from Kuwait, striking Baghdad and other targets in Iraq and Kuwait with waves of bombers and cruise missiles launched from naval vessels.

"The liberation of Kuwait has begun," President Bush said in a three-sentence statement confirming the start of the attack that was read by his spokesman, Marlin Fitzwater, shortly after the raids began.

Later, in a televised address to the nation from the Oval Office, a somber Mr. Bush said that after months of continuous diplomatic overtures had failed to produce movement by Iraq, the United States and its allies "have no choice but to force Saddam from Kuwait by force. We will not fail." [Transcript, page A6.]

No Planes Reported Missing

United States officials said shortly after midnight Wednesday that none of the planes that took part in the night-time raids were reported missing.

In Baghdad, Mr. Hussein said in a speech broadcast by the Iraqi radio that "the mother of all battles has begun," according to news service reports. He called Mr. Bush a "hypocritical criminal" and vowed to crush "the satanic intentions of the White House." It was unclear when Mr. Hussein had read his remarks, whether they had been pre-recorded. or where he was at the time. [Page A18.]

Mr. Bush said his goal "is not the conquest of Iraq, it is the liberation of Kuwait." But he also said, "We are determined to knock out Saddam Hussein's nuclear bomb potential. We will also destroy his chemical-weapons facilities."

3 Other Nations Take Part

Defense Secretary Dick Cheney and Gen. Colin L. Powell, Chairman of the Joint Chiefs of Staff, told reporters at the Pentagon Wednesday night that those targets had been among those assigned to the first wave of American F-117 Stealth fighter-bombers, F-15 fighter-bombers, British Tornado attack planes and Saudi and Kuwaiti F-15's that raided Iraqi military targets about 3 A.M. local time Thursday (7 P.M. Wednesday Eastern standard time.)

Administration officials also said United States Navy ships in the waters off the Arabian Peninsula had fired ground-hugging cruise missiles at targets that had been programmed into their guidance systems for months. The officials said the ships fired a total of 50 Tomahawk missiles in an assault on Iraqi command and communications centers.

Seeking to Avoid Civilians

Mr. Cheney said the initial targets were spread throughout Iraq and Kuwait and were chosen to "do everything possible to avoid injury to civilians." Both officials declined to say if there had been any American or allied losses, or to describe in any detail how badly they thought they had damaged Baghdad or the other Iraqi targets.

"The response of the Iraqi forces at this point has been limited," Mr. Cheney said, leading analysts to conclude that the allies may have succeeded in their goal of largely incapacitating Iraq's Air Force at the outset.

But Mr. Cheney said that the war was just beginning and that "it is likely to run for a long period of time."

Reports of New Attack

Cable News Network reported that antiaircraft fire resumed in Baghdad about 9:30 A.M. Iraqi time and that its correspondents heard explosions that sounded like bombs in the far distance from their central Baghdad hotel.

The network also reported the first sighting of President Hussein since the start of the attacks, by a Western television technician at a Baghdad television center this afternoon.

Mr. Cheney said the United States could not confirm reports that Iraq had fired Soviet-made Scud missiles at allied positions after the attack began. Reuters reported from Bahrain that the civil defense authorities there had detected missile launches but that the weapons fell short of their targets.

Assuring Americans that ground forces were not yet engaged in the battle, the President added: "Five months ago, Saddam Hussein started this cruel war against Kuwait. Tonight, the battle has been joined."

He said initial reports indicated that "our operations are proceeding according to plan."

"Our objectives are clear," he said. "Saddam Hussein's forces will leave Kuwait, the legitimate Government of Kuwait will be restored to its rightful

Continued on Page A14, Column 1

President Bush as he announced in a televised address last night that an air attack had been launched against Iraq.

ABC News

Rumble in the Sky Ends a 5-Month Wait

By PHILIP SHENON
Special to The New York Times

IN SAUDI ARABIA, Thursday, Jan. 17 — "It's absolutely awesome, I mean the ground shook and you felt it," said Col. Ray Davies, describing the takeoff of the first planes to attack Iraq from a big Saudi air base where he is chief maintenance officer.

The 44-year-old colonel said the first group of jets left at 12:50 A.M., about an hour before the first word of attack was broadcast by television reporters in Baghdad.

"We've been waiting here for five months; now we finally got to do what

we were sent here to do," Colonel Davies told a group of American reporters who were brought to the base. "This is history in the making."

The F-15 fighter bombers, heavily loaded with bombs and supplemental underwing fuel tanks, thundered off in pairs into what had been a still desert night. The aircraft, which quickly became faint red dots, were also armed with cannon and air-to-air missiles to be used in their own defense.

The activity at the airfield, whose exact location cannot be identified under military reporting rules, was the first indication here that the assault

was under way. All commercial traffic at the airport had been suspended a short time earlier.

Just before 4 A.M. Saudi time, hundreds of journalists and other guests at the Dhahran International Hotel, including many Filipino and Pakistani workers, were herded into the bomb shelter in the hotel basement and instructed to put on gas masks. Sirens started to wail throughout the city.

Waiting for the Signal

As the guests, primarily journalists, waited for the signal "gas clear," a hotel employee serving as warden directed guests to spread out in the area, which serves as a kitchen. The air conditioning had been turned off to prevent the spread of chemical agents in case the hotel was hit by Iraqi missiles. The room was quiet except for the sound of a radio on which a news announcer was saying that the attack had begun.

A British defense consultant who is working for the hotel, Philip Congdon,

Continued on Page A17, Column 6

MORE ON THE GULF

Bush Evokes Glory Of Past, Not Vietnam

To tell Americans that war with Iraq had started, President Bush harked back to one of the great days in American military history — D-Day, June 6, 1944. News analysis, page A16.

In Cairo, Jubilation Among Kuwaiti Exiles

Hundreds of Kuwaitis drove their cars through the Egyptian capital, honking and waving flags after hearing news of the American-led attack. "Thank God! Thank God!" was a cry heard over and over again. Page A18.

Israel on Alert

Israel declared a state of emergency minutes after word of the attack. There was no indication of an Iraqi attack on Israel. Page A18.

The War Begins

"The liberation of Kuwait has begun. In conjunction with the forces of our coalition partners, the United States has moved under the code name Operation Desert Storm to enforce the mandates of the United Nations Security Council.

"As of 7 o'clock P.M. Operation Desert Storm forces were engaging targets in Iraq and Kuwait."

STATEMENT, PRESIDENT BUSH, 7:06 P.M.

"All the News That's Fit to Print"

The New York Times

Late Edition
New York: Today, partly cloudy, not as cold. High 43. Tonight, some clouds. Low near 40. Tomorrow, some sun, windy, warmer. High 58. Yesterday, high 36, low 26. Details, page B14.

VOL. CXL . . No. 48,525 NEW YORK, THURSDAY, FEBRUARY 28, 1991 50 cents beyond 75 miles from New York City, except on Long Island. 40 CENTS

BUSH HALTS OFFENSIVE COMBAT; KUWAIT FREED, IRAQIS CRUSHED

Associated Press

Under skies darkened by smoke from burning oil wells, Kuwaitis celebrated the recapture of Kuwait City from Iraq. The Kuwaiti flag, which had vanished from public display during Iraq's occupation, suddenly appeared everywhere. Page A6.

Associated Press

Gen. H. Norman Schwarzkopf as he discussed allied successes at a news briefing yesterday in Saudi Arabia.

MILITARY AIMS MET

Firing Ending After 100 Hours of Ground War, President Declares

By ANDREW ROSENTHAL

Special to The New York Times

WASHINGTON, Thursday, Feb. 28 — Declaring that "Kuwait is liberated" and Iraq's army defeated, President Bush ordered allied forces on Wednesday night to suspend offensive military operations against President Saddam Hussein's isolated and battered army.

Mr. Bush said the suspension, which began at midnight Eastern time, would continue as long as Iraq did not attack allied forces or launch missile attacks on any other country. In an address from the Oval Office that was televised around the world at 9 P.M. Eastern time, he called on Mr. Hussein to send his commanders to meet with allied officers in the war zone within 48 hours to settle the military terms of a permanent cease-fire.

For such a cease-fire to be approved, he said, Iraq must comply with all 12 United Nations resolutions concerning Kuwait, including measures calling for Iraq to void its annexation of the territory and agree in principle to pay reparations to Kuwait and other countries. Iraq must also free all prisoners of war and detained Kuwaiti citizens, and give the allies the location of all land and sea mines that Iraq had laid in the region, Mr. Bush said.

No Official Word From Iraq

Administration officials said they had received no authoritative response from the Iraqi Government. At the United Nations, Soviet diplomats said Iraq had submitted a letter signaling its willingness to comply with all 12 resolutions adopted by the Security Council. But the letter did not say whether Baghdad was willing to comply with the rest of Mr. Bush's demands, including the freeing of Kuwaiti civilians seized in recent days. [Text of the letter, page A10.]

Pentagon officials said this morning there were no reports of renewed Iraqi attacks on allied positions.

Speaking in a solemn voice, President Bush said: "This war is now behind us. Ahead of us is the difficult task of securing a potentially historic peace." [Transcript of his remarks, page A12.]

He seemed to invite the citizens of Iraq to overthrow the man who had defied the assembled military and political power of the international alliance. "Coalition forces fought this war only as a last resort," Mr. Bush said, "and look foward to the day when Iraq is led by people prepared to live in peace with their neighbors."

Unusually Low Casualties

Mr. Bush, who had staked his Presidency on being able to resolve a crisis that had shattered the post-cold war calm and led to the largest single American military offensive since World War II, declared an end to the war in his third nationally televised speech from the Oval Office since Iraq invaded Kuwait on Aug. 2.

To arrive at the point where he was able to declare victory last night, Mr. Bush had to command what military experts said was one of the largest combat operations ever conducted with such low casualties, counter political opposition at home and navigate the shoals of diplomacy complicated by last-minute Soviet peace ventures that plainly irritated the President and his war council.

"At midnight tonight, Eastern standard time, exactly 100 hours since ground operations commenced and six weeks since the start of Operation Desert Storm, all United States and

Continued on Page A12, Column 1

Freed Kuwaitis Tell of Iraqi Abuse Including Some Cases of Torture

By CHRIS HEDGES

Special to The New York Times

KUWAIT CITY, Feb. 27 — On the third floor of a gutted mansion, a Kuwaiti Army major slowly pushed open a door with his foot to what was once a laundry room. It had been converted by the Iraqis, he said, into a torture chamber.

In one corner were metal box springs, raised off the floor by chairs. Next to the springs was a crude brown box with bare electrical wires protruding from black cords.

"They put the prisoners on the springs, poured water over them and then applied the current," said the Kuwaiti Army officer, Maj. Jamal al-Hassan, who was a leader in the underground during the occupation. "If they were not happy with the answers, they turned up the voltage."

Accounts of Torture

Kuwaitis who were picked up by the Iraqi secret police had their own stories to tell.

"They beat me, did not let me sleep and made me sit naked on a bottle of hot sauce," said 21-year-old Faisal al-Anizi. "This went on for three days in what used to be the reform school."

Others tell of being rubbed down with sandpaper, having their heads thrust into cold water and being hung by their hands from a hook.

When an American correspondent arrived in Kuwait City on Tuesday, ahead of entering allied troops, he found Kuwaitis who were eager to tell the world that Saddam Hussein brought more to Kuwait than Iraqi license plates and innumerable portraits of himself. He had also brought the techniques of control that have kept his authoritarian Government in power.

Members of the Kuwaiti underground, acting on information provided by people who said they were tortured by the Iraqi secret police, have identified places where Kuwaitis were questioned, beaten and tortured.

A visitor is overwhelmed by reports that hundreds, perhaps thousands of young men were taken by the Iraqis, many in the final hours before the Iraqi forces left the city on Monday. Their parents and friends fear that they may not reappear.

"A lot of people have disappeared in Iraq and never been seen since," said

Continued on Page A6, Column 4

IRAQ ELITE ROUTED, U.S. SOLDIERS SAY

Officers Brace for Prisoners as Hussein's Force Retreats

By PHILIP SHENON

Special to The New York Times

WITH U.S. VII CORPS, in Iraq, Feb. 27 — American troops described a ferocious armored battle between the United States and troops of Iraq's Republican Guards that resulted, they said in interviews tonight, in devastating losses for the Iraqis and a torrent of thousands of battle-weary Iraqi prisoners of war.

In battlefield interviews with troops from three of the four Army divisions involved in the assault on the guards, American soldiers said that the tank clash raged across dozens of miles of the southern Iraqi desert. Speaking before President Bush ordered military operations suspended, the soldiers said that the Iraqi guards were offering fierce resistance despite overwhelming odds.

Tanks Are Charred Bits of Steel

During a helicopter tour today close to the front lines, the devastation wrought by allied forces on the Iraqi military in recent days and weeks was made plain.

The burned-out shells of scores of Iraqi tanks, some smoldering, some still on fire, sat in what had been extensive dug-in fortifications of sand and dirt. All that remained of several Iraqi tanks and artillery installations were charred bits of steel spread across hundreds of square yards of scrub-covered desert floor.

From the air, large bands of captured Iraqi soldiers could be seen in the custody of American soldiers.

The Americans described prisoners captured today from other, regular Iraqi units as desperate for food, water and medical attention, after a month-long allied bombing campaign cut them off from supply lines.

Some of the Iraqis said they had not been fed for days. As many as one-third

Continued on Page A7, Column 1

Allies Destroy Iraqis' Main Force; Kuwait Is Retaken After 7 Months

By R. W. APPLE Jr.

Special to The New York Times

DHAHRAN, Saudi Arabia, Thursday, Feb. 28 — Hours before President Bush announced the conditional suspension of offensive military operations in the Persian Gulf, allied armored units, which had trapped Iraq's vaunted Republican Guard, cut it to pieces in a furious tank battle that began Wednesday and raged until early this morning, American officials said.

At midday Wednesday, United States Marines captured the Kuwait International Airport after a smaller but nonetheless intense two-day fight, and later, marines and Kuwaiti and other Arab troops rode in triumph down the broad boulevards of Kuwait City, past scenes of devastation and desolation. That essentially completed the expulsion of President Saddam Hussein's forces from Kuwait, which they had overrun in a surprise assault last Aug. 2.

Casualties among coalition forces were light and Iraqi losses heavy, the allied command said.

But the honking horns, waving flags and scenes of jubilation as the capital was retaken scarcely concealed the agony generated by tales of torture, kidnapping, rape and pillage over the final days of occupation. As many as 40,000 Kuwaitis were said to have been taken hostage by the Iraqis as they fled north on Tuesday.

Gen. H. Norman Schwarzkopf, commander of the American-led coalition that has trounced Iraq in a lightning-fast ground war reminiscent of the World War II blitzkrieg, said the Iraqi leader had been stripped of the offensive weapons that made his army one of the most fearsome in the Middle East.

'Not Enough Left'

"There's not enough left for him to be a regional threat," the general said in a detailed briefing on the campaign Wednesday night, adding pointedly, "unless someone chooses to rearm them in the future." [Excerpts, page A8.]

"We've accomplished our mission," General Schwarzkopf said, hours before Mr. Bush spoke, "and when the decision-makers come to the decision that there should be a cease-fire, nobody will be happier than me."

With his army shattered and reeling after 100 hours of ground combat, Mr.

Continued on Page A9, Column 1

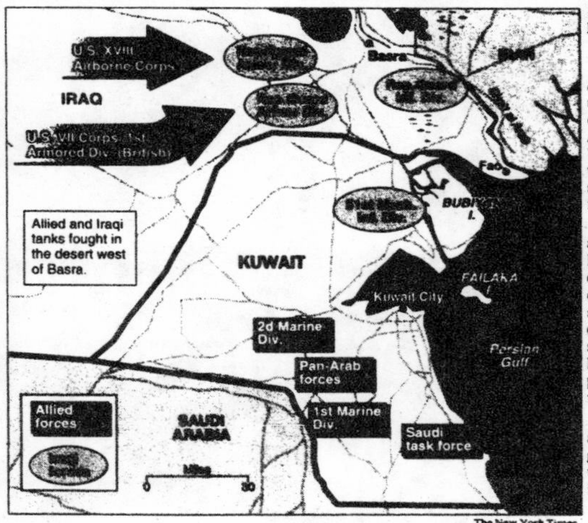

The New York Times

Ethics Unit Singles Out Cranston, Chides 4 Others in S.& L. Inquiry

By RICHARD L. BERKE

Special to The New York Times

WASHINGTON, Feb. 27 — Seeking to set standards for the way lawmakers raise money and do favors, the Senate Ethics Committee concluded today that Senator Alan Cranston engaged in "an impermissible pattern of conduct" that might warrant disciplinary action by the full Senate.

In written rebukes to four other Senators who were also investigated for their ties to Charles H. Keating Jr., a savings and loan executive and contributor to the Senators' campaigns or causes they supported, the committee asserted that their behavior reflected poor judgment at the very least.

The committee's finding on Mr. Cranston essentially clears the way for it to recommend that the full Senate reprimand him as the panel is expected to do. But the committee said the other lawmakers' actions were not significant enough to require such further action.

Aside from Mr. Cranston, a California Democrat, the findings against two other Democrats, Senators Dennis DeConcini of Arizona and Donald W. Riegle Jr. of Michigan, were the most stern. The committee said their conduct "gave the appearance of being improper and was certainly attended with insensitivity and poor judgment." The lightest rebukes went to Senators John Glenn, an Ohio Democrat, and John McCain, an Arizona Republican, who were found to have "exercised poor judgment." [Excerpts from the committee's statement, page B10.]

Today's announcement came after the committee voted unanimously on each Senator, ending a 14-month inves-

Continued on Page B10, Column 1

Women Among War Dead

At least three women were reported to be among the 28 American soldiers who were killed in an Iraqi missile attack on Tuesday. Page A13.

INSIDE

Condom Plan Approved

The New York City Board of Education narrowly approved a plan to make condoms available to the city's 250,000 high school students. Page B1.

New Rival to Phone Industry

Three cable television companies plan to build experimental networks that would allow people to use very small wireless telephones. Page D1.

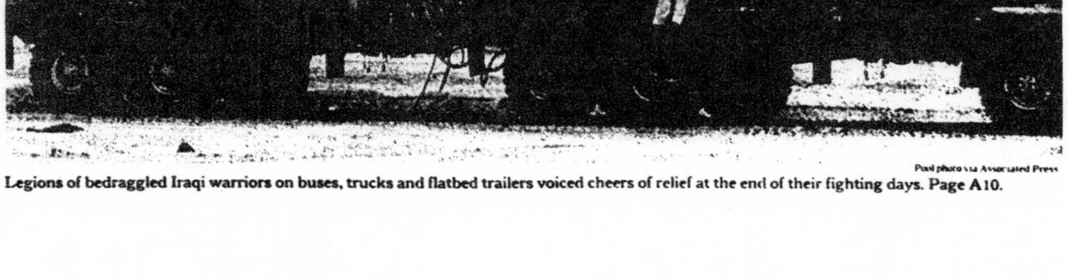

Paul photo via Associated Press

Legions of bedraggled Iraqi warriors on buses, trucks and flatbed trailers voiced cheers of relief at the end of their fighting days. Page A10.

"All the News That's Fit to Print"

The New York Times

Late Edition

New York: Today, cloudy, cool, early sprinkles. High near 60. Tonight, partial clearing. Low 46. Tomorrow, cloudy, late clearing. High 56. Yesterday, high 61, low 50. Details, page 17.

VOL.CXLI . . No. 48,751 — NEW YORK, SATURDAY, OCTOBER 12, 1991 — 50 CENTS

THOMAS ACCUSER TELLS HEARING OF OBSCENE TALK AND ADVANCES; JUDGE COMPLAINS OF 'LYNCHING'

Reuters

Kiichi Miyazawa at a meeting of his party faction yesterday.

Miyazawa Gets Party Approval To Lead Japan

By DAVID E. SANGER

Special to The New York Times

TOKYO, Oct. 11 — Kiichi Miyazawa, a stalwart of Japan's governing party and one of the architects of the country's postwar economic ascent, was virtually assured election as the next Japanese prime minister tonight, ending a bruising weeklong scramble for the leadership.

Mr. Miyazawa, an urbane 72-year-old politician who has held virtually every key political post in Japan except prime minister, was endorsed this evening by the largest and wealthiest faction in the Liberal Democratic Party, controlled by former Prime Minister Noboru Takeshita.

At a news conference earlier in the day, Mr. Miyazawa said he expected no significant changes in Japan's relations with Washington, where he has been a well-known and influential player in Japanese-American relations for more than two decades.

'The Same Values'

"We have the same values," he said of Japan and the United States. "If we have something to complain about to each other, we should do so frankly."

It was the Takeshita faction that withdrew its support from Prime Minister Toshiki Kaifu a week ago, forcing him to abandon his hopes of seeking a second term. Political analysts said they expected Mr. Miyazawa, a far more senior member of the party and a leader of a major faction, to hold somewhat more independent sway over the conduct of the Government than did Mr. Kaifu, who was widely viewed as a weak leader entirely dependent on the good graces of Mr. Takeshita and his aging ally in the governing party, Shin Kanemaru.

For Mr. Miyazawa, known as one of the party's keenest minds and one of its most fluent English speakers, the endorsement today completes a stunning political turnaround. Less than three years ago, he was forced to step down

Continued on Page 5, Column 5

SOVIET REPUBLICS AGREE TO CREATE AN ECONOMIC UNION

10 OF 12 PLEDGE SUPPORT

Yeltsin Leads Way in Pressing for an Accord — Gorbachev Calls Plan 'Last Hope'

By FRANCIS X. CLINES

Special to The New York Times

MOSCOW, Oct. 11 — Russia and a majority of the other republics announced their commitment today to soon forming a new economic community devoted to free-market resuscitation of the fallen Soviet nation.

President Boris N. Yeltsin of the Russian federation, the centerpiece republic in the complex plan, led the way in pressing nine other republics for a formal signing of the economic compact as early as next Tuesday.

The Soviet President, Mikhail S. Gorbachev, leading a meeting of 10 republic leaders at the Kremlin, warned that the economic plan represented the people's "last hope" for decisive action toward national reconstruction after the harrowing failed coup and collapse of the central Government in August.

Yeltsin's Return

"People's patience is at a breaking point," Mr. Gorbachev cautioned, according to the press agency Tass.

The news that Mr. Yeltsin was back from vacation and recommitting Russia to the economic plan immediately bolstered proponents of the free-market community.

In his absence for the last two weeks, critics of the plan came forward in his own cabinet to warn that Russia, the nation's dominant republic, would be slighted in creating such an economic community from the dregs of the Communist Soviet Union.

'Common Economic Space'

But Mr. Yeltsin reaffirmed his view that the plan for a "common economic space" of trade, currency, banking and customs procedures was the only hope for the crippled Soviet nation to turn itself toward reform and a chance of joining the global free market.

The most Mr. Yeltsin offered to critics, according to initial reports, was the possibility of a common banking system less central in nature. That was in concession to an apparent sensitive point among the now sovereign republics still fearful of echoes of the central monolith that marked Communism's handling of the economy.

The republics, meeting together as members of the new State Council emergency Government, also followed through on earlier agreements to reshape the K.G.B. state police into sepa-

Continued on Page 4, Column 6

Photographs by Jose R. Lopez/The New York Times

Professor Anita F. Hill and Judge Clarence Thomas as they were sworn in yesterday before testifying.

DRAMA IN SENATE

Court Nominee Rejects Charges Laid Out in Frank, Vivid Detail

By RICHARD L. BERKE

Special to The New York Times

WASHINGTON, Oct. 11 — Confronting a disputed nomination to the Supreme Court and a boiling political furor, the Senate Judiciary Committee heard gripping but contradictory testimony today from Judge Clarence Thomas and the woman accusing him of sexual harassment.

The proceedings in a jammed hearing room at the Russell Senate Office Building here amounted to a political drama centered on two extraordinarily composed figures, Judge Thomas and his accuser, Anita F. Hill, an Oklahoma law professor.

Judge Thomas and Professor Hill, who worked for him in two Federal agencies, both testified under oath and offered accounts of their social and professional relationships that differed so starkly that Senator Howell Heflin, an Alabama Democrat, said, "One of them is not telling the truth."

'I Had a Duty to Report'

Professor Hill complained of sexual approaches in vivid detail and said she had not volunteered to bring this issue to the Senate but was there because Senate aides had asked her if she was aware of any harassment. "I felt I had a duty to report — I have no personal vendetta against Clarence Thomas," she said.

Judge Thomas angrily denied the charge and compared his ordeal to a "lynching." [Excerpts from the hearing appear on pages 10-15.]

Testifying first in a hearing that lasted 12 hours and 35 minutes, Judge Thomas sounded by turns defiant and sorrowful in insisting to committee members that he never sexually harassed Professor Hill, depicting himself and his family as victims who were betrayed by the professor and a Senate confirmation process that had run amok.

The Process on Trial

In his opening statement in the morning, and even more strongly when he returned to the Congress tonight to testify, Judge Thomas tried to rebut the charges against him by putting the process on trial — a political process that has been widely disdained as cutthroat and out of control.

He called it "a travesty" that such "sleaze," "dirt," "gossip" and "lies," which he said were improperly disclosed by the committee, should be "displayed in prime time to an entire nation." In answer to a question, he said that he did not watch Professor Hill's testimony.

Professor Hill said that she, too, had been tormented by the issue and the intense scrutiny. Facing sometimes sharp questions from Republicans and more gentle questioning from Democrats, Professor Hill testified for near-

Continued on Page 9, Column 1

On Thomas: More Questions, Not Fewer

A Political Process Becomes the Focus

By R. W. APPLE Jr.

Special to The New York Times

News Analysis

WASHINGTON, Oct. 11 — The choices presented to the United States Senate by today's lurid, gut-wrenching proceedings on Capitol Hill could hardly have been much starker.

By the time Anita F. Hill had finished her testimony, filled with vivid and often excruciating sexual detail that few had anticipated, but delivered with a prim earnestness that seemed to bespeak reserve and reluctance to discuss such subjects, the Senators who must vote on Tuesday were left with only two options: Either she was telling the truth or she is a sociopath; either these horrifying events took place or she, for some reason, invented them.

By the time Judge Clarence Thomas had made his response, the Senators had been rocked even further back on their heels by a blast that have had few precedents as a statement by a senior Federal official in an official forum. Dropping his usual accommodating manner, he let the fury pour out of him, calling the current inquiry "a national disgrace" and "a high-tech lynching for uppity blacks."

He stopped only a hair short of explicity accusing the committee, composed entirely of white males, of racism.

He Said Them, Or He Didn't

What Professor Hill asserted, and what Judge Thomas said in his implacably resolute testimony, made it crystal clear that this was no case of tragic misunderstandings nor of ambiguous conversations that could be interpreted as sexual harassment or not, depending on one's frame of reference or state of mind. Either he said these wretched things to her — things that one associates with the seamiest of criminal cases or the raunchiest of locker rooms, not with the Senate or Supreme Court — or he did not. Yes or no. Up or down.

If Judge Thomas did say them, few, if any, Senators would vote to confirm, whatever the pull of partisan solidarity. So a vote to confirm the judge, in the rawest political terms, will mean the voter thinks Professor Hill fabricated (or was fed) these "ugly" incidents and phrases, to use her own word.

Such a vote will not be easy for the jury of 100 Senators, a group of professional politicians, a third of whom face re-election next year, who have already been burned by the wrath of women when they seemed willing to brush off Professor Hill's allegations earlier this week.

It will be harder because the judge's defenders struggled all day, with limited success, to suggest what kind of twisted motive she might have had for telling monstrous lies about him.

It will be hardest of all for the Democrats, and the arithmetic gives them the upper hand. If 51 of the 57 Democrats vote no on the nomination — vote, in effect, to back Professor Hill — then Judge Thomas will not make it to the Supreme Court, even if all 43 Republicans reject what she told them.

To bring about that result, only about five or six of the Democrats who had intended to support Judge Thomas before Professor Hill's allegations became public would have to change their minds. At least that many have indicated they had serious doubts by pressing to hold new hearings.

But what of Judge Thomas's testimony? Like Professor Hill a child of the civil rights movement, a success story that would have made the Rev. Dr. Martin Luther King Jr. beam with

Continued on Page 9, Column 1

Keith Meyers/The New York Times

Haitians in New York Rally for Ousted Leader

Tens of thousands of Haitian demonstrators spilled across the Brooklyn Bridge into lower Manhattan yesterday in a spirited display of support for Haiti's ousted President, Jean-Bertrand Aristide. Page 31.

In an Ugly Atmosphere, the Accusations Fly

By MAUREEN DOWD

Special to The New York Times

WASHINGTON, Oct. 11 — With a powerful invocation of racial imagery that he had not used in his public remarks before this day of testing, Clarence Thomas tried to put the Senate on trial tonight, accusing Congress of tactics that went "far beyond McCarthyism."

As his wife, Virginia, sat behind him with a trembling chin, wiping away tears, Judge Thomas delivered a forceful rebuttal to Anita F. Hill's accusations of sexual harassment with a stony face and a voice bristling with anger.

When his testimony, filled with racially charged images, collided with the counterpoint of the Oklahoma University law professor's cool, dispassionate testimony, nearly devoid of references to race, the hearing reached an emotional high point.

Furious Denunciations

Confounding those who thought he would give up after the testimony by Professor Hill, testimony that many Senators found impressive and credible, President Bush's nominee put the process on trial and offered a furious denunciation of the Judiciary Committee's handling of the case.

"You are ruining the country," he told the senators, accusing them of going "far beyond McCarthyism." At another point, he said that black men who did not "kowtow to an old order" would "be lynched, destroyed, caricatured by a committee of the U.S. Senate rather than hung from a tree."

In comparing his ordeal to a "high-tech lynching, for uppity blacks," Judge Thomas evoked one of the most powerful images of the civil rights movement, a movement with which he has long had an uneasy relationship.

It was during his tenure as chairman of the Equal Employment Opportunity Commission that he became an increasingly fervent spokesman against the approaches of the traditional civil rights groups. As his relations with those groups worsened, he complained in an interview with The Washington Post in 1984 that all the nation's traditional civil rights leaders do is, "bitch, bitch, bitch, moan and whine."

Offended by Justice Marshall

He said he was offended by Justice Thurgood Marshall who once complained that he did not want to celebrate the Constitution because it condoned slavery. But when he opened his testimony on Sept. 10, he was careful to give great credit to the civil rights movement for his own journey.

"So many others gave their lives, their talents. But for them, I would not be here today. Justice Marshall, whose seat I have been nominated to fill is one of those who had the courage and the intellect," he said.

Initially today, Mr. Thomas refused to rebut the individual charges, relying instead on monolithic outrage and a categorical denial. He said he had been "drawn and dragged" into a national forum to discuss allegations that "should have been discussed in a confidential way."

At first, Senator Howell Heflin,

Continued on Page 8, Column 1

America Listens In On a Private Subject

In cities and towns across the country, Americans took time out from their workaday lives to tune into the riveting collision between Judge Clarence Thomas and Anita F. Hill.

The hearing capped a week in which Professor Hill's charges became the leading topic in offices and on university campuses, in restaurants and on street corners, with many women applauding public discussion of a frequently private subject and many men wondering about their own conduct.

Article, page 8.

INSIDE

Bush Vetoes Benefits Bill

Citing a need for budget discipline, the President rejected legislation that would have given additional unemployment benefits to people out of work more than six months. Page 6.

One Step Closer

The President formed a Bush-Quayle '92 Primary Committee, a move that allows him to go ahead with already scheduled fund-raising events for his re-election campaign. Page 6.

Yes, He Is. No. Maybe.

Political contributors say Gov. Mario M. Cuomo told them he was considering running for President. But later he said he had no plans. Page 31.

Twins Win and Lead Playoff

A home run by Mike Pagliarulo in the 10th inning gave Minnesota a 3-2 victory over Toronto and a 2-1 lead in the American League playoff. Page 35.

"All the News That's Fit to Print"

The New York Times

Late Edition

New York: Today, limited sun, perhaps a shower late. High 62. Tonight, cooler Low 40. Tomorrow, cloudy, a light shower. High 41. Yesterday, high 59, low 45. Details are on page D10.

VOL.CXLI...No. 48,809

NEW YORK, MONDAY, DECEMBER 9, 1991

50 CENTS

DECLARING DEATH OF SOVIET UNION, RUSSIA AND 2 REPUBLICS FORM NEW COMMONWEALTH

Frantic Moves Came to Light In Days Before Maxwell Died

As the Empire Was Crumbling

A special report.

Robert Maxwell

By STEVEN PROKESCH
Special to The New York Times

LONDON, Dec. 8 — At the time of his mysterious death on Nov. 5, Robert Maxwell almost certainly knew he was about to be caught.

He had drained hundreds of millions of dollars from his two flagship public companies and from employee pension funds in a frantic attempt to keep his heavily indebted publishing empire afloat.

The auditors of the Maxwell empire, Coopers & Lybrand Deloitte, were to conduct their next regular audit of the pension funds in a couple of months. And Coopers would have quickly discovered the transactions, said a person very familiar with the details of a special financial examination of the empire conducted for the banks after Mr. Maxwell's death. He agreed to discuss the report only if his identity was not disclosed.

'Basically Grabbing Cash'

The Coopers team also found evidence that some of the diverted money went to The Daily News in New York to cover its losses. That raises more doubts about the future of the newspaper, which Mr. Maxwell acquired in March.

The maneuvering by Mr. Maxwell to prop up the private companies that controlled his empire "was doomed to failure," the person familiar with the Coopers report said.

"It wasn't a sophisticated fraud like B.C.C.I.," he said, referring to the scandal surrounding the Bank of Credit and Commerce International. "The guy was basically grabbing cash, and Coopers found it out within days of going in." The Coopers team was led by Richard Stone, the partner in charge of the accounting firm's corporate finance division.

That discovery led the main holding companies of the Maxwell empire to file Thursday for the British equivalent of bankruptcy protection.

It is now apparent that the pressure on Mr. Maxwell to find money for the private companies was increasing sharply in the weeks before his death, according to the Coopers report, bankers, and directors and executives of the Maxwell empire.

"It would appear that there was a desperate need for cash from June

Continued on Page D3 Column 1

The New and the Old

LATVIA — ESTONIA
LITHUANIA
BYELORUSSIA
UKRAINE • Brest • Minsk
Kiev Moscow RUSSIA
MOLDAVIA
GEORGIA
ARMENIA KAZAKHSTAN
AZERBAIJAN KIRGHIZIA
TURKMENIA TADZHIKISTAN
UZBEKISTAN

Miles
0 1,000

Source: The Statesman's Yearbook, 1991-92; U.S.S.R. Facts and Figures Annual, 1991

POPULATION
January 1990

Others 70.6 million
Baltics 8 million
Russia 148 million
Ukraine 51.8 million
Byelorussia 10.3 million

CONSUMER GOODS
Share of production 1988

Other 28.2%
Baltics 6.8%
Russia 47.0%
Ukraine 16.4%
Byelorussia 1.5%

AGRICULTURE
Share of total output, 1988

Other 21.4%
Baltics 4.4%
Russia 46.7%
Ukraine 22.1%
Byelorussia 5.4%

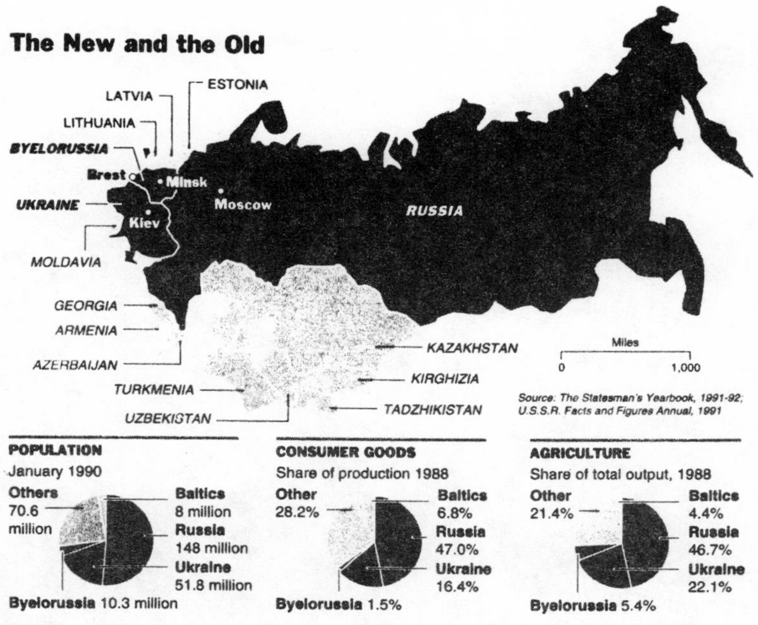

The New York Times

"We, the republic of Byelorussia, the Russian Federation and Ukraine . . . state that the U.S.S.R., as a subject of international law and geopolitical reality, is ceasing its existence."
— Brest declaration, Dec. 8, 1991

The Union Is Buried: What's Being Born?

By CELESTINE BOHLEN
Special to The New York Times

MOSCOW, Dec. 8 — Ever since the August coup d'état, the Soviet Union has been dying a lingering death, its final agony stretched over months of crisis and negotiations while it was kept alive largely by the frantic faith of one man, Mikhail S. Gorbachev, the Soviet President.

Today, the union died — if future historians will accept a death warrant signed by the patient itself as proof, which is how the leaders of Russia, Ukraine and Byelorussia intended their statement, signed in the Byelorus-

News Analysis

Gorbachev's Vain Pleas Make His Eclipse Clear

sian border town of Brest, to be read.

The Brest statement does not reckon with Mr. Gorbachev; it simply ignores him, which only made his appearance tonight on Soviet television all the more poignant as he once again pleaded, cajoled and banged his fists, making the case that without a union the country will fall apart.

But for some time now, Mr. Gorbachev's warnings have had a hollow ring, since for most people, the collapse

he keeps warning about has already happened. This is a fact they can confirm with their daily lives, as they go to factories that have run out of materials, to office jobs where they have stopped getting salaries or to shops where there are no goods.

A Fresh Start?

By sweeping the old structures out of the way, President Boris N. Yeltsin of Russia, President Leonid M. Kravchuk of Ukraine and the Byelorussian leader, Stanislav Shushkevich, have cleared the way for something new — assuming, of course, that the military or other conservative forces mount no effort to restore the center.

What exactly the new shape of things will be was not totally clear from today's statement, nor could it be, given the absence of some major players, most notably representatives of Kazakhstan and the Central Asian republics.

But the absence of Mr. Gorbachev seemed to make no difference one way or the other. Once the Houdini of Soviet politics, the man who could turn setbacks to his advantage, the master of the surprise move, the Soviet President had become a Johnny-one-note whose insistence on renovating old structures — the word perestroika means reconstruction — in the end got in the way of more radical but in the view of others more constructive approaches.

By bypassing him publicly, the lead-

Continued on Page A9, Column 1

West Europeans Gather to Seek A Tighter Union

By ALAN RIDING
Special to The New York Times

MAASTRICHT, the Netherlands, Dec. 8 — In an atmosphere of great expectation tinged with no small apprehension, European Community leaders gathered here tonight for a crucial two-day summit meeting that should determine the region's place in the world well into the 21st century.

Their aim is to prepare the 12-nation community to compete with regional economic groups led by the United States and Japan and to exercise greater political influence in international affairs. To achieve this, they hope to speed up Europe's 34-year-old march toward political and economic integration.

They will therefore be taking up proposals to establish a single currency and a regional central bank, to move toward common foreign and security policies, to give more power to the European Parliament and to harmonize their approaches to social and environmental questions.

Nowhere Near Full Union

The measures fall far short of creating anything resembling a United States of Europe. While some politicians like to evoke the centuries-old dream of full union, it is at least decades away.

Yet if approved, the changes will significantly bolster the community's existing plan to form a single regional market of 340 million consumers on Jan. 1, 1993, eventually turning what is already the world's largest trading bloc into the world's dominant financial power.

Adoption of the Maastricht agenda is far from assured. Britain, the long

Continued on Page A10, Column 1

U.S. Seeks to Trim 'Friendly Fire' Toll

Alarmed by the number of American soldiers killed and wounded by "friendly fire" in the Persian Gulf war, the military has begun top-to-bottom changes to decrease the frequency of such incidents in future conflicts.

The changes in training, equipment and procedures will affect tens of thousands of soldiers, the Army said, and are the most significant shifts so far in American military practices resulting from lessons learned in the gulf war.

"We're committed to addressing this problem in an institutional and effective way," Gen. Gordon R. Sullivan, the Army Chief of Staff, said.

The changes are to be announced later this week, at which time senior Army generals are also expected to discuss new policies on notifying relatives of American soldiers who were accidentally killed by their own forces.

Article, page A12.

TAKE OVER A-ARMS

Newborn Bureaucracy Is Inheriting Functions of Old Authority

By SERGE SCHMEMANN
Special to The New York Times

MOSCOW, Dec. 8 — The leaders of Russia, Ukraine and Byelorussia declared today that the Soviet Union had ceased to exist and proclaimed a new "Commonwealth of Independent States" open to all members of the former union.

In a series of statements issued after a two-day meeting at a Byelorussian government retreat, the leaders of the three Slavic republics declared void all efforts to create a new union on the ruins of the old one. But they called for the creation of new "coordinating bodies" for defense, foreign affairs and the economy that would have their seat in Minsk, the capital of Byelorussia, and decided to maintain the ruble as the common currency.

They declared that the "norms" and activities of the former union ceased as of the moment of signing, and that the new commonwealth assumed all international obligations of the Soviet Union, as well as control over its nuclear arsenal.

Gorbachev's Move

"The U.S.S.R., as a subject of international law and geopolitical reality, is ceasing its existence," the leaders declared. [Text, page A8.]

The action essentially stripped President Mikhail S. Gorbachev of his office and authority, and the immediate question was whether the tough and tenacious Soviet leader would resist — and if he did, whether the military or other levers of power would support him.

The three cofounders of the new commonwealth — President Boris N. Yeltsin of Russia, President Leonid M. Kravchuk of Ukraine and Stanislav Shushkevich, Chairman of the Byelorussian Parliament — were scheduled to meet on Monday with Mr. Gorbachev and with Nursultan A. Nazarbayev, the President of Kazakhstan and the unofficial spokesman for the Muslim republics of Central Asia.

Portents of Disaster

Mr. Gorbachev had no immediate reaction. But in a taped interview with French television broadcast today, he argued fervently that the consequences of dismantling the union would make the war in Yugoslavia "a simple joke by comparison."

The Central Asian republics had all indicated an interest in retaining some form of union, and it was not immediately clear why Mr. Nazarbayev was excluded from the Byelorussian declaration, or how he would respond. Arriving in Moscow today, he declared that he was still in favor of preserving an association, and at least in maintaining joint control over the nuclear arsenal.

The predominantly Slavic republics declared that they drew their authority to dissolve the union from the fact that they were its original cofounders. They and the Trans-Caucasus republic, later

Continued on Page A8, Column 3

INSIDE

Oiling the Machinery

The challenge for the President's new chief of staff will be to revitalize a domestic policy apparatus that rusted while John Sununu and Richard Darman held sway. Page A12.

Another View in Japan

Japan's Socialists said the nation had "turned its back on the historical truth" by refusing to "sincerely apologize" for wartime conduct. Page A7.

Who Knows Who Nanny Is?

Parents often know little about the people caring for their children, a fact highlighted by an au pair's arrest in a girl's arson death. Page B1.

Dallas Times Herald Shuts

The city's oldest daily newspaper ceases publication today, after selling its presses and subscription lists to its rival, The Morning News. Page D1.

Focus of AIDS Debate Dies

Kimberly Bergalis, who stirred a national debate over AIDS testing of doctors and other health workers, died of AIDS at the age of 23. Page D9.

0 35471 3 50

Short on funds, long on tolerance, Ira Levine and his team at Lafayette High School try to stay positive.
Jim Estrin for The New York Times

A Team Plays On in a Search for Normalcy

By HARVEY ARATON

Dexter Wooten's eyes grew wide and bright as he watched Antonio Carrasquillo score a layup against Midwood High School's undersized and helpless defenders under the basket.

"I could get me a lot of assists playing with Antonio," Wooten said at the game early last week, a smile breaking out from under the brim of his black-and-red Chicago Bulls cap.

That's what Ira Levine, the basketball coach at Lafayette High School, was thinking last June when Carrasquillo's improved class attendance enabled him to pass his academic subjects. Finally, as a senior, Carras-

Long Shots

A periodic visit with the Lafayette High School basketball team.

A Bruising Season in Brooklyn

quillo, an agile, 6-foot-9-inch basketball star-in-waiting, would make his debut in the New York City Public Schools Athletic League. He would arrive, unannounced, to make Levine's team a force in Brooklyn, a threat to the defending city champion and perennial divisional power, Lincoln.

But even the tallest and most gifted centers, as Patrick Ewing, the Knicks' $33 million man, knows, must be sur-

rounded by complementary players, and one by one Carrasquillo's began to disappear.

In many ways, the losses were just events in the life of public high school sports. They might have happened in Chicago, Los Angeles or Detroit. The situation was trying, but not debilitating. Short on funds, long on tolerance, the high school coach and his team play on.

Lafayette's team turned into an urban soap opera early this fall when

Continued on Page C8, Column 3

"All the News That's Fit to Print"

The New York Times

Late Edition
New York: Today, clear, mild for the season. High 44. Tonight, cloudy late, breezy. Low 34. Tomorrow, cloudy, then colder, windy. High 45. Yesterday, high 40, low 28. Details, page D12.

VOL. CXLI . . . No. 48,826 — NEW YORK, THURSDAY, DECEMBER 26, 1991 — 50 CENTS

GORBACHEV, LAST SOVIET LEADER, RESIGNS; U.S. RECOGNIZES REPUBLICS' INDEPENDENCE

RETAILERS REPORT SALES FELL SHORT OF DIM FORECASTS

Last-Minute Buying Spree Fails to Carry Merchants Ahead of Last Year's Receipts

By EBEN SHAPIRO

Retailers would probably like to forget Christmas 1991. While most merchants had been prepared for a sluggish season, many said sales turned out to be even worse than expected. Even the last-minute shopping frenzy was not enough to give merchants anything to cheer about.

As recently as a month ago, many retailers had hoped to exceed last year's sales by 5 percent. But results through the close of business on Monday indicate that spending will be flat or up slightly in December. The major retail chains are scheduled to release their final monthly sales results next week.

"We are disappointed with the season," Stephen E. Watson, president of the Dayton Hudson Corporation in Minneapolis, said in a telephone interview on Tuesday.

'Too Little Too Late'

Business surged in the final days, and a number of retailers said that Monday was the busiest day of the year. But Mr. Watson said, "In our view, it's really been too little too late." Dayton Hudson, which relies on California for one-third of its business, was hit hard by the slowdown in that state's economy.

This is the third consecutive sluggish Christmas shopping season — the make or break season for retailers — and many analysts say this year's dismal results are likely to force thousands of companies into bankruptcy.

The economy received most of the

Continued on Page D8, Column 3

Associated Press

Mikhail S. Gorbachev after announcing his resignation last night as President of the Soviet Union.

Communist Flag Is Removed; Yeltsin Gets Nuclear Controls

By FRANCIS X. CLINES
Special to The New York Times

MOSCOW, Dec. 25 — Mikhail S. Gorbachev, the trailblazer of the Soviet Union's retreat from the cold war and the spark for the democratic reforms that ended 70 years of Communist tyranny, told a weary, anxious nation tonight that he was resigning as President and closing out the union.

"I hereby discontinue my activities at the post of President of the Union of Soviet Socialist Republics," declared the 60-year-old politician, the last leader of a totalitarian empire that was undone across the six years and nine months of his stewardship.

Mr. Gorbachev made no attempt in his brief, leanly worded television address to mask his bitter regret and concern at being forced from office by the creation of the new Commonwealth of Independent States, composed of 11 former republics of the collapsed Soviet empire under the informal lead of President Boris N. Yeltsin of Russia.

'A New World'

Within hours of Mr. Gorbachev's resignation, Western and other nations began recognition of Russia and the other former republics.

"We're now living in a new world," Mr. Gorbachev declared in recognizing the rich history of his tenure. "An end has been put to the cold war and to the arms race, as well as to the mad militarization of the country, which has crippled our economy, public attitudes and morals. The threat of nuclear war has been removed." [A transcript of Mr. Gorbachev's speech and excerpts from interviews with Mr. Gorbachev and Mr. Yeltsin are on pages A12 and A13.]

Mr. Gorbachev's moment of farewell was stark. Kremlin guards were preparing to lower the red union flag for the last time. In minutes, Mr. Gorbachev would sign over the nuclear missile launching codes for safeguarding to Mr. Yeltsin, his rival and successor as the dominant politician of this agonized land.

Yeltsin's Assurance on Weapons

Earlier today, Mr. Yeltsin told his Russian Parliament that "there will be only a single nuclear button, and other presidents will not possess it."

But he said that to "push it" requires the approval of himself and the leaders of Ukraine, Byelorussia and Kazakhstan, the four former republics that have strategic nuclear weapons on their soil.

"Of course, we think this button must never be used," Mr. Yeltsin said.

Out in the night beyond the walled fortress as Mr. Gorbachev spoke, a disjointed people, freed from their decades of dictated misery, faced a frightening new course of shedding collectivism for the promises of individual enterprise. It is a course that remains a mystery for most of the commonwealth's 280 million people.

"I am very much concerned as I am leaving this post," the union President told the people. "However, I also have feelings of hope and faith in you, your wisdom and force of spirit. We are the heirs of a great civilization and it now depends on all and everyone whether or not this civilization will make a comeback to a new and decent living."

Still Against Commonwealth

In departing, the Soviet leader took comfort in the world's supporting his singular achievements in nuclear disarmament. But even more, he firmly warned his people that they had not yet learned to use their newly won freedom and that it could be put at risk by the

Continued on Page A12, Column 1

The Soviet State, Born of a Dream, Dies

By SERGE SCHMEMANN
Special to The New York Times

End of an Empire

A special report.

MOSCOW, Dec. 25 — The Soviet state, marked throughout its brief but tumultuous history by great achievement and terrible suffering, died today after a long and painful decline. It was 74 years old.

Conceived in utopian promise and born in the violent upheavals of the "Great October Revolution of 1917," the union heaved its last in the dreary darkness of late December 1991, stripped of ideology, dismembered, bankrupt and hungry — but awe-inspiring even in its fall.

The end of the Soviet Union came with the resignation of Mikhail S. Gorbachev to make way for a new "Commonwealth of Independent States." At 7:32 P.M., shortly after the conclusion of his televised address, the red flag with hammer-and-sickle was lowered over the Kremlin and the white-blue-red Russian flag rose in its stead.

No Ceremony, Only Chimes

There was no ceremony, only the tolling of chimes from the Spassky Gate, cheers from a handful of surprised foreigners and an angry tirade from a lone war veteran.

Reactions to the death varied widely, according to Pravda, the former mouthpiece of the empire: "Some joyfully exclaim, 'Finita la comedia!' Others, heaping ash on their heads, raise their hands to the sky in horror and ask, what will be?"

The reaction depended somewhat on whether one listened to the ominous gunfire from Georgia, or watched spellbound the bitter if dignified surrender of power by the last leader of the Union of Soviet Socialist Republics, Mr. Gorbachev.

Most people vacillated. The taboos and chains were gone, but so was the food. The Soviet Union had given them pitifully little, but there was no guarantee that the strange-sounding "Commonwealth of Independent States" would do any better.

As for Mr. Gorbachev, public opinion polls indicated a virtually universal agreement that it was time for him to move on — not because he had failed, but because there was nothing more he could do.

It was perhaps a paradox that the ruler who presided over the collapse of the Soviet Union was the only one of its ill-starred leaders to leave office with a measure of dignity intact. It was possible that history would reach a different verdict, but among many thoughtful Russians, it was to his undying credit that he lifted the chains of totalitarian dictatorship. Whether he could also have saved the economy was another question.

"Gorbachev was unable to change the living standards of the people, but he changed the people," Komsomolskaya Pravda wrote in a sympathetic farewell that seemed to capture the dominant mood. He didn't know how to make sausage, but he did know how to give freedom. And if someone believes that the former is more impor-

Continued on Page A14, Column 1

BUSH LAUDS VISION OF SOVIET LEADER

In Farewell, President Cites Gorbachev's Historic Role

By MICHAEL WINES
Special to The New York Times

WASHINGTON, Dec. 25 — President Bush moved quickly tonight to recognize Russia and other former republics of the now-extinct Soviet Union.

After praising the former Soviet leader, Mikhail S. Gorbachev, Mr. Bush went out of his way to express support for President Boris N. Yeltsin of Russia, who has emerged as the first among equals in the new Commonwealth of Independent States and as the custodian of the old Soviet Union's nuclear arsenal.

In his brief televised speech, Mr. Bush said that the United States now recognized the independence of the 11 former Soviet republics that have banded together, as well as a 12th, Georgia, which has shunned the alliance. [Text of Mr. Bush's remarks, page A16.]

But he indicated that the equally important step of establishing diplomatic ties between Washington and all 12 parts of the old Soviet empire would be more complicated.

The President said he was satisifed with the assurances on nuclear controls that he has received from Mr. Yeltsin and from leaders of other former republics with nuclear arms on their soil. Mr. Bush said that the United States would move rapidly to establish diplomatic relations with Russia, Armenia, Ukraine, Byelorussia, Kazakhstan and Kirghizia.

Diplomatic relations with the re-

Continued on Page A16, Column 3

On Tom Harkin

Mixing pugilism and politics, the Iowa Senator is running for President with an appeal built on his combative personality.

Strategies: The Democrats and '92. Page D11.

Pineapple, After Long Affair, Jilts Hawaii for Asian Suitors

By ROBERT REINHOLD
Special to The New York Times

LANAI CITY, Hawaii — For the last 13 years Kathleen Ruaburo dressed for work in thick rubberized pants and goggles and spent her days, just as her immigrant Filipino father did, in the heat and the dust picking pineapples on the Dole plantation. Now she dons a crisp white jacket with gold buttons and sets tables for wealthy tourists at the new Manele Bay Hotel here.

Mrs. Ruaburo's transition tells the story of pineapples in Hawaii. The crop that symbolizes this state and for decades has been a mainstay of the islands' economy is almost gone. Hawaiian pineapples can no longer compete in the world market.

Over the next 18 months, crews will harvest the last planting on this island, once the largest pineapple plantation in the world. Then the fields will go to alfalfa and oats, and the pineapple crews will either have to accept jobs in two new luxury hotels or leave the island for work. It is a future that some welcome and some fear on this tiny island, where 2,144 residents still live an isolated plantation life that has scarcely changed since James Drummond Dole started growing pineapples here 69 years ago.

A big worry is that the island's economy will be just as dependent as ever on one industry. When the hotels were first proposed, pineapple cultivation was expected to continue and tourism was intended as a way to diversify the types of jobs here. But gradually, Dole managers said, it became clear that pineapples were no longer profitable enough.

Seventy-two miles away in Honolulu the Dole Packaged Foods Company on Dec. 1 began laying off about 500 workers at the big cannery near downtown that has processed the Lanai fruits for more than half a century. Its largest competitor, Del Monte, ended canning almost a decade ago. Only one canner remains in Hawaii, the Maui Land and Pineapple Company, which produces private labels for supermarkets. The Dole brand will stay on the shelves, but the pineapples will come from its plantations in Asia, as some do now.

Some Hawaiian pineapples will be grown for local consumption and to provide fresh fruit to markets on the

Continued on Page A18, Column 2

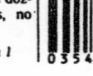

Lee Romero/The New York Times

Having a Home Is Not a Prerequisite for Having the Spirit of Christmas

Leroy Lewis built a Christmas tree at his sometime home under the Queensboro Bridge on First Avenue in Manhattan. Lenore Elners stopped yesterday to wish Mr. Lewis a merry Christmas.

From L.I. to Angry Illinois: A 5-Day Trash Odyssey

By SARAH LYALL
Special to The New York Times

TAYLORVILLE, Ill., Dec. 20 — The story of Ocke Ketelsen's garbage began Dec. 15, when he put it out on his curb in Westbury, L.I. It was nothing special, just things like an old milk carton and some scraps of aluminum foil, and Mr. Ketelsen didn't give it a second thought. "Garbage is garbage," he said.

Not really, not anymore.

Garbage has become a multimillion-dollar industry, a touchy environmental issue and a major headache for crowded states like New York and New Jersey. And the next day, while Mr. Ketelsen stayed home, his trash began an odyssey that took it north, south, and finally 900 miles west to the flat, open community of Taylorville, where the major industries are farming, paper and New York State refuse.

The system that got Mr. Ketelsen's garbage here is as messy as trash itself. Mr. Ketelsen now pays five times as much in waste-disposal taxes as he did 15 years ago. And as they deal with closing landfills, wildly varying environmental regulations, and a crazy-quilt pricing system that can draw garbage halfway across the country in search of a good deal, many municipalities are finding that garbage is their biggest worry and their biggest expense.

"Garbage is the most serious problem that we face," said Ernest J. Strada, who, as Mayor of Westbury, is responsible for removing Mr. Ketelsen's trash. "The general public talks about it in a general sense — we make garbage and it goes away. But it doesn't."

In the uneven picture of garbage in America, few places are as complicated as Long Island. The Island has dozens of overlapping jurisdictions, no

Continued on Page B4, Column 1

INSIDE

Health Care on Wheels

Home health care has emerged as a $15 billion industry with more than 12,500 companies and not-for-profit services, from simple nursing to mobile emergency rooms. Page D1.

11 Turks Die in Firebombing

Kurdish separatists threw firebombs at a department store in Istanbul, setting the seven-story building ablaze and killing 11. Page A5.

Television and radio news and listings appear today on pages D18-19.

"All the News
That's Fit to Print"

The New York Times

Late Edition

New York: Today, becoming mostly sunny. High 57-62. Tonight, showers late. Low 47. Tomorrow, clouds breaking, breezy. High 72. Yesterday, high 62, low 42. Details are on page B16.

VOL.CXLI . . No. 48,953 NEW YORK, FRIDAY, MAY 1, 1992 50 CENTS

23 DEAD AFTER 2D DAY OF LOS ANGELES RIOTS; FIRES AND LOOTING PERSIST DESPITE CURFEW

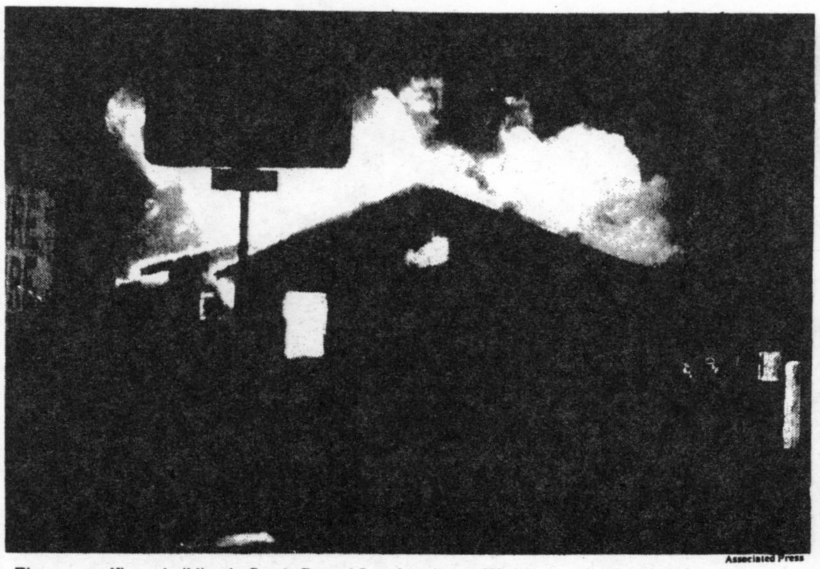

Flames engulfing a building in South-Central Los Angeles on Wednesday night as rioting spread. Associated Press

900 REPORTED HURT

National Guard on Patrol — Violence Spreads to San Francisco

By SETH MYDANS
Special to The New York Times

LOS ANGELES, April 30 — Social order broke down today across a broad area of the nation's second-largest city as vandals and looters roamed the streets, carloads of young men attacked pedestrians and uncounted fires burned out of control.

Mayor Tom Bradley and the Police Chief, Daryl F. Gates, appealed for order and imposed a dusk-to-dawn curfew, saying they had been overwhelmed by the violence and rioting that broke out after Wednesday's acquittal of four white police officers on trial for beating a black motorist, Rodney G. King.

The authorities said at least 23 people had been killed, more than 900 injured and nearly 500 people arrested. Hundreds of buildings burned as the violence spread from South-Central Los Angeles into wealthier white areas, and entire inner-city blocks lay in ruins.

National Guard Arrives

As the night wore on, officials said, the violence and lawlessness increased even as National Guard troops summoned by Gov. Pete Wilson were put on the streets.

"The situation is getting worse, despite the dusk-to-dawn curfew," said Deputy Larry Mead of the Los Angeles County Sherrif's Department. "There's been an increase in looting and fires in the southern sections of the city of L.A. and L.A. County."

Near midnight there were signs that the number of new fires was decreasing, but the police were still trying to control roving bands of looters. A police spokesman, Lieut. John Dunkin, said officers had killed three people in separate incidents since nightfall.

In Washington, the Justice Department announced that it was reopening an investigation into the March 3, 1991, videotaped beating of Mr. King to prepare the ground for a possible civil rights case against the four officers who were acquitted.

Violence in Other Cities

But it was clear from the words of the rioters, as well as black elected officials and others, that their anger ran far deeper than reaction to the acquittal. There were demonstrations around the nation, gangs on the loose in Atlanta and San Francisco and fears that the violence, shown vividly on television, might spread further. [Page A20.]

Just before 7 P.M., two white men on a motorcycle were attacked by a group of about 15 black men in Long Beach, south of Los Angeles. The two motorcyclists were beaten and shot, and one was killed, according to Comdr. Anthony Batts of the Long Beach Police Department.

The violence in Los Angeles spread today as smoke from burning buildings mingled with the city's smog. The first 1,200 of 4,000 National Guard members to be deployed took up positions this afternoon alongside hundreds of police and highway patrol officers in South-Central Los Angeles, the mostly black and Hispanic section where the violence began Wednesday afternoon.

Governor Wilson this afternoon doubled the original summons of 2,000 troops as the violence spread through-

Continued on Page A20, Column 1

Surprised, Police React Slowly as Violence Spreads

By ROBERT REINHOLD
Special to The New York Times

LOS ANGELES, April 30 — The Los Angeles Police, apparently caught off guard by the violent reaction to the acquittal of four white officers in the beating of a black motorist, were slow to react, even after the scope of the anarchy sweeping the city had become apparent.

As unruly demonstrators threatened to invade police headquarters downtown early Wednesday evening, Chief of Police Daryl F. Gates was attending an event in the affluent Brentwood area, about 11 miles away, to raise money to fight a proposal on the June ballot to limit the term of the police chief. Matthew Hunt, the deputy chief in charge of the affected area, was attending a community meeting about 6 miles from the police command center.

It was hours before the police entered many of the areas in South-Central Los Angeles where stores were being looted and motorists were being dragged from their cars and beaten.

Chief Resisted National Guard

As late as 11 P.M., with at least two dozen fires blazing out of control, Chief Gates resisted Mayor Tom Bradley's call for National Guard troops, telling Gov. Pete Wilson in a conference call with the Mayor that he was not sure the police needed help handling the situation, according to someone who is close to Mayor Bradley and who spoke on the condition of anonymity.

The Mayor prevailed with the Governor, and by this morning Mr. Gates agreed that the Guard was needed. But the first contingent, about 2,400 guardsmen, including 100 military police, was not deployed on the streets until mid-afternoon today. The Governor traced the delay in part to a shortage of ammunition.

Fires Burned Unattended

Similarly, the Los Angeles Fire Department, had no special contingency plan apart from declaring a tactical alert, meaning engine companies moved in special teams. The department was forced to let many fires burn unattended, not because it lacked sufficient engines at first but because the police did not have enough officers to protect firefighters. There were barely enough officers on hand to prevent Parker Center, the police headquarters downtown, from being overrun.

The slow response was due in part to the fact that almost nobody, including the Mayor, anticipated such a sweeping acquittal of all four officers and

Continued on Page A22, Column 1

Suspected looters, handcuffed and forced to lie down, in police custody. Reuters

Smell of Fear in Los Angeles

By JANE GROSS
Special to The New York Times

LOS ANGELES, April 30 — The City of Angels endured another siege of violence today with an acrid smell of smoke in its nostrils and a cold stone of fear heavy on its heart.

Hopes were dashed early that daylight would quiet the beating, looting and burning that followed Wednesday's verdict in the Rodney G. King case, and residents took to the streets warily, knowing that terrible things had happened here overnight, with more terrible things likely to come.

Throughout the sprawling metropolis, even in neighborhoods far from the epicenter of the violence, Angelenos sensed that the next car that passed might carry hooligans waving crowbars and axes, that the next store to burn or be looted could be the one on their corner. This was not a disturbance with a clear perimeter, they came to understand, and while some street corners were safer than others, there was really no place to hide.

The roadways were emptier than usual, but chaotic as a bumper-car ride as nervous motorists navigated a shifting maze of barricades and craned their heads skyward to track the newest plume of smoke rising in the heavy haze. The drivers' eyes darted from side to side, taking the measure of the stranger in the car beside them, plotting new routes as streets and highways closed and reopened, and gazing in horror at the ravaged and smoldering stores that dotted the city.

Evacuation in Koreatown

In some neighborhoods more than others, one could almost smell the fear. Four miles north from the genesis of the violence, Koreatown, for instance, was an edgy place this morning, braced for trouble because of longstanding tensions between the black and Asian communities here.

By midafternoon, the bands of looters were moving in waves toward the small strip shopping centers near Olympic Boulevard and Vermont Street, the heart of the Koreatown, but hours earlier some Korean merchants decided they were taking no

Continued on Page A21, Column 3

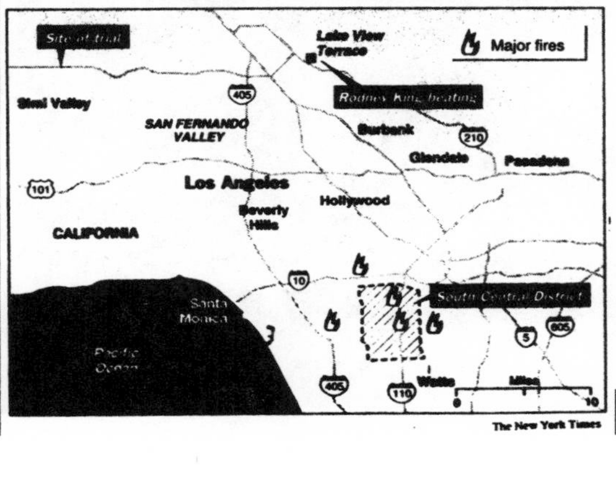

The New York Times

SENATORS APPROVE A BILL TO CURTAIL CAMPAIGN SPENDING

Curbs on Unrestricted Money Pass in Vote With Margin Too Thin for Override

By ADAM CLYMER
Special to The New York Times

WASHINGTON, April 30 — On a near party-line vote, the Senate today passed a campaign finance bill that would set voluntary spending limits in Congressional races and sharply reduce the role of money raised outside of existing Federal rules on contributions.

The 58-to-42 vote sent the most sweeping campaign finance legislation in 18 years to the White House, where it faces a certain veto. President Bush has said he would reject any legislation providing public money for candidates and setting spending limits, a move that he says would favor incumbents.

Neither today's margin nor the 259-to-165 tally by which the House approved the Democratic bill on April 9 is close to the two-thirds' vote required to override a veto.

A Milestone Vote

Despite that hard reality and the bill's failure to say how the Government would pay for the benefits it offers, supporters called today's vote and the agreement between House and Senate Democrats a milestone on the way to changing the current system.

The spending limits were the subject of the most heated argument as the Senate ended a three-day debate today. Senator Bob Dole of Kansas, the Republican leader, said: "Often the only way a challenger can compete with the built-in advantages of incumbency is to spend money. The bottom line is that spending limits are designed to prevent change at a time when the American people are demanding change."

Senator George J. Mitchell of Maine, the majority leader, called such arguments "nonsense." He said incumbents almost always raised more than their challengers, often three or four times as much, and therefore limits would help even the odds in those contests.

That partisan division was reflected

Continued on Page A16, Column 3

Leadership And Its Limits

Political Needs Prevail In Check-Scandal Vote

By ADAM CLYMER
Special to The New York Times

News Analysis

WASHINGTON, April 30 — The leaders wanted to resist. The followers didn't.

The leaders tried to look after the House as an institution. The ordinary members preferred to look after their own careers.

That is the quickest explanation of what happened when the House voted Wednesday night to comply with a subpoena from the Justice Department, asking for records of every check written on the now closed House bank between July 1988 and October 1991.

Indeed, dozens of members who voted to comply with the subpoena regarded it as an improper "fishing expedition" but one they could not effectively resist, and only 131 Democrats stood up and voted to challenge it in court. Perhaps 30 or 40 more had promised to do so if their votes mattered. They waited, saw it was hopeless and cast the vote that was easier to explain back home.

Spotlight on Foley

For months, some Democrats have faulted Speaker Thomas S. Foley for not anticipating the perils that the bank's tolerance of dubious checks posed for all of them. They also faulted him for being thoughtful and judicious but not political enough.

A Texan, John Bryant, took the floor four weeks ago to complain that the Speaker was not defending the House adequately. Mr. Foley is certainly not succeeding in defending the House against what he and most Democrats see as irresponsible intrusions by a zealous Justice Department. But on Tuesday night Mr. Bryant voted to surrender the records.

Yes, there are complaints about the leadership, but basically the followers have the leadership they want, leaders who plead with them but do not or cannot order them about. The demand that Mr. Foley become a stronger, firmer leader is not easily squared with the independent search for survival that marks the House today.

His circumstances were made al-

Continued on Page A24, Column 4

Afghans' Battle Lines Are Drawn As One Rebel Denounces Another

By EDWARD A. GARGAN
Special to The New York Times

KABUL, Afghanistan, April 30 — Afghanistan's strongest guerrilla leader, Ahmad Shah Masood, took charge of the security of Kabul today after entering the capital overnight with a three-mile-long convoy of military vehicles and an estimated 10,000 troops.

Shortly after arriving, Mr. Masood denounced the lone guerrilla leader who has refused to take part in the coalition that proclaimed an Islamic republic in Afghanistan on Tuesday.

The holdout, Gulbuddin Hekmatyar, who heads the hard-line Islamic group Hezb-i-Islami, has marshaled his guerrillas just south of Kabul in Logar Province, from where he is continuing to mount attacks on the capital.

A barrage of rockets, presumably fired by Mr. Hekmatyar's forces, hit the airport this evening. Mr. Masood's forces did not counterattack, but the guerrilla leader's criticism of Mr. Hekmatyar left little doubt that a new round of fighting could be in store.

"Every group which is fighting the Government, which is acceptable to the majority of the people, is baghi," Mr. Masood said. The word refers to un-Islamic behavior akin to criminality.

As late as Wednesday the new Government, headed by Sibgatullah Mojadedi, was considering some way to placate Mr. Hekmatyar by giving him a role in the new administration. But today, with the continuing attacks, Mr. Hekmatyar was branded an enemy.

Full Attack Weighed

"He's out," said Assam Akram, a spokesman for Mr. Mojadedi, who is to hand over leadership of the ruling coalition in two months to the head of Mr. Masood's guerrilla group, Jamiat-i-Islami or Islamic Society. Mr. Akram accused Mr. Hekmatyar of sabotaging Kabul's electrical grid; the capital has been without power for two days.

Nurul Haq Ullumi, a general in the

Continued on Page A10, Column 4

INSIDE

Familiar End in Mideast Talks

Israelis and Arabs ended their fifth round of talks without signs of progress on major issues or a commitment on meeting again. Page A6.

Navy Report on Sex Assaults

The Navy said many women, not just a few, were abused at an aviators' convention and said many officers would not aid the inquiry. Page A14.

An Everglades Cleanup Idea

A system of trading pollution credits could help to rid the Everglades waters of phosphorous from fertilizers, economists believe. Law, page B18.

Exxon Official Still Missing

The disappearance of the president of Exxon International remained a mystery and officials refused to discuss the investigation. Page B1.

Nets Walk the Plank

New Jersey's season of near-mutiny ended in a 98-89 loss to the Cleveland Cavaliers in the fourth game of their N.B.A. playoff series. Page B9.

MORE ON THE RIOTS

'I Know It's Not Right'

In some areas, looters said they were expressing their bitterness at the status of blacks in America. Page A21.

Clinton and Bush Spar

Gov. Bill Clinton and aides to President Bush criticized each other's response to the events. Page A22.

Public Topic No. 1

On call-in programs, at rallies and on the job, Americans voiced apprehension about race relations. Page A23.

How Lawyers See the Case

Los Angeles lawyers who have followed the case dissected the tactics of prosecution and defense. Page A20.

"All the News That's Fit to Print"

The New York Times

Late Edition

New York: **Today,** sun, then increasing clouds. High 44. **Tonight,** rain. Low 40. **Tomorrow,** morning rain, brighter by afternoon. High 46. **Yesterday,** high 43, low 27. Details are on page C20.

VOL.CXLII . . . No. 49,218 NEW YORK, THURSDAY, JANUARY 21, 1993 50 CENTS

CLINTON TAKES OATH AS 42D PRESIDENT, URGING SACRIFICE TO 'RENEW AMERICA'

Jose R. Lopez/The New York Times

Bill Clinton being sworn in yesterday by Chief Justice William H. Rehnquist as the 42d President of the United States. With him outside the Capitol were his wife, Hillary, their daughter, Chelsea, and Vice President Al Gore, who had taken his oath of office moments earlier.

Amid Pageant of Diversity, Homage to Election Themes

By THOMAS L. FRIEDMAN

Special to The New York Times

WASHINGTON, Jan. 20 — William Jefferson Clinton became the 42d President of the United States today, and in an Inaugural Address striking in its appeal for sacrifice, he told Americans that if they assume greater responsibility for their country's future, "there is nothing wrong with America that cannot be cured by what is right with America."

The 46-year-old Governor of Arkansas, virtually unknown to most Americans 18 months ago and a long shot for the White House, took the oath of office under a stunningly blue sky from Chief Justice William H. Rehnquist. President George Herbert Walker Bush, who once seemed sure to win a second term, watched stoically from his seat on the Capitol steps.

Under Mr. Clinton's left hand, his wife, Hillary, held a King James Bible given to Mr. Clinton by his grandmother. His 12-year-old daughter, Chelsea, stood at his right as he uttered the traditional oath at 11:58 A.M. Eastern time. He then spoke for 14 minutes to a sea of people, flowing down from the flag-draped Western facade of the Capitol to the Washington Monument.

'What America Does Best'

"We must do what America does best: offer more opportunity to all and demand more responsibility from all," Mr. Clinton declared in an echo of John F. Kennedy's Inaugural Address. "It is time to break the bad habit of expecting something for nothing, from our Government or from each other. Let us all take more responsibility, not only for ourselves and our families but for our communities and our country."

In a speech with the recurring theme of renewal, Mr. Clinton implored at one point: "To renew America we must be bold. We must do what no generation has had to do before." [Transcript, page A15.]

Washington never looked better, or felt better. Cheerful chaos reigned on the streets, in a subway system that is usually weirdly sedate and on the Mall, in front of the Capitol, where something like a quarter of a million people endured mobs and metal detectors and midwinter chill. Schools and Federal offices had a quadrennial holiday, so natives joined tourists beneath a Capitol that was dressed for the day in gowns of red, white and blue, and glittered in the January sun.

Walk Through the Crowd

In a day of ceremonies intended to be casual and intimate — with lots of Presidential bear hugs for friends and a conscious assertion of the passing of power to the post-World War II generation — the Clintons walked the last few blocks down Pennsylvania Avenue from the Capitol to the White House. Before the Clintons decided to get out of their new armor-plated Cadillac, the crowds along the route were chanting: "Walk! Walk!"

From the viewing stand in front of the White House's iron gates, the Clintons watched a politically inclusive parade, encompassing everyone from Arkansas bands to gay groups to Elvis impersonators — like the rest of the inaugural as meticulously scripted as any Hollywood production. Throughout, Mr. Clinton wore the amazed grin of a man whose lifelong dream had just come true.

The flag-waving crowds along the parade route were striking both for their enthusiasm and their racial diversity. The upbeat mood of the well-wishers seemed on track with that of recent national polls — one of guarded optimism about Mr. Clinton's prospects, coupled with a strong desire to give the new President a chance.

Short, Informal Speech

Mr. Clinton's Inaugural Address, far more compact than the lengthy oratory of his long 1988 Democratic National Convention speech, was informal and almost conversational.

It was typical of the New Age political style that helped him win the highest office in the land. While Mr. Clinton paid homage to many of the themes that won him the election — the need for renewal, health-care reform, economic revival and political reform — his address was not an agenda for action, but rather a call to service.

"You, my fellow Americans, have forced the spring," he said. "Now we must do the work the season demands."

The address was at times brutally frank in its assessment of the decline of the country under Mr. Bush and in its chastising of an aloof and self-absorbed

Continued on Page A14, Column 1

The Inauguration: Serious and Not So

DOWN TO BUSINESS As President Clinton's new team set about governing, the swirl of ceremony was almost an intrusion. Page A11.

CONFIRMING A CABINET The Senate confirmed new Secretaries of State, Defense and the Treasury, and agreed to move quickly on 11 other Cabinet posts. Page A12.

PRIVATE CITIZEN AGAIN Proclaiming his career "a hell of a ride," George Bush returned with little fanfare to Houston, where it began. Page A13.

STYLES AND PARTIES A new youthful feeling pervaded the fashions and forms of the Democrats' celebration. Page A16.

CLINTON SET TO END BAN ON GAY TROOPS

Military to Have Say on How Change Is Carried Out

By ERIC SCHMITT

Special to The New York Times

WASHINGTON, Jan. 20 — Refining a compromise on a volatile issue, President Clinton plans to issue an executive order that would lift the ban on homosexuals in the armed forces, but he will delay the directive for several months to give the Pentagon a chance to draft it, Clinton transition aides said today.

In the meantime, the military will be directed less formally to stop asking recruits about their sexual orientation and discharging people from the armed services when they are found to be homosexuals. These are the two points that would be the main practical effect once an executive order is in effect.

Tug of War on Issue

Mr. Clinton is expected to announce his new policy in the next few days, officials said.

The two-step process buys the Clinton Administration time to consult with senior military leaders on details of the policy, while at the same time fulfilling a campaign pledge Mr. Clinton made to repeal the ban with an executive order.

Under intense pressure from the military to back off that commitment, Mr. Clinton's aides had been considering a plan to lift the ban without a Presidential order. Homosexual-rights advocates vigorously protested, contending

Continued on Page A17, Column 5

January High Noon: Hail Meets Farewell

By DAVID E. ROSENBAUM

Special to The New York Times

WASHINGTON, Jan. 20 — At 11:30 sharp this morning, the Marine Band played "Hail to the Chief" for George Bush for the last time.

He walked through the archway on the West Front of the Capitol and, unsmiling, walked down to his chair on the inauguration stage, hardly acknowledging the lawmakers, Supreme Court Justices and others already seated.

Moments later, Bill Clinton — William Jefferson Clinton, as the doorkeeper of the House of Representatives, James T. Molloy, announced him — walked through the same arch. With a wide grin, he waved and shook hands all the way to his seat. Hillary and Chelsea Clinton were already there. So were Al and Tipper Gore and their four children.

The contrast in the families' moods was palpable throughout the ceremony. From below, the Bushes seemed to be maintaining their composure, but close up, on television, their eyes, while dry, showed the strain. Mr. Bush's were drawn and gray. During the Rev. Billy Graham's invocation, Barbara Bush's eyes were shut unusually tight.

Most of the Clintons and Gores could hardly contain their excitement, and after Mr. Gore took the oath of office from Justice Byron R. White, the new Vice President and Mr. Clinton threw their arms around each other in the bear hug they favor at festive occasions.

Chelsea Clinton, on the other hand, seemed wiped out. She had gone to the entertainment gala on Tuesday night and did not get back to Blair House, where the family was staying, until nearly 1:30 A.M. — quite a night

Smiles and Grim Eyes as Winners Exult and the Losers Depart

for a 12-year-old. She appeared to fall asleep at this morning's service at the Metropolitan African Methodist Episcopal church, and she yawned several times during Mr. Graham's invocation. But later she seemed to get a second wind and listened wide-eyed to her father's address.

Hats Off to Clinton

The mid-January weather has often played havoc with inaugurations. Eight years ago, with the temperature in single digits, Ronald Reagan took the oath inside the Capitol and the parade was canceled.

But today, the temperature climbed into the 40's, the sky was clear and wind was still. Mr. Clinton and Mr. Gore even took off their overcoats when they took their oaths.

But it was nippy enough that many wore hats. Chief Justice William H. Rehnquist, a stickler for precedent and tradition, wore the same black, wool skull cap he wore four years ago at Mr. Bush's inauguration ceremony.

The cap, it seems, is part of the official garb for Chief Justices at outdoor, cold-weather events. Chief Justice Charles Evans Hughes wore it to three of Franklin D. Roosevelt's inaugurations. But it fell into disuse thereafter, until Justice Rehnquist,

Continued on Page A13, Column 2

A Change of Power, but Barely a Break in Stride

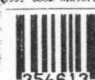

Agence France-Presse

President Bush welcoming the new tenant to 1600 Pennsylvania Avenue yesterday before they left for the inauguration.

In a Ritual of Continuity Bowing to History, Enter Clinton, With His Unwritten Chapter

By R. W. APPLE Jr.

Special to The New York Times

WASHINGTON, Jan. 20 — Today was the day of Bill Clinton's dreams, the day he and his party finished the arduous climb to a "joyful mountain-top of celebration," but like all Inauguration Days, it was more than that.

News Analysis

It was a day when the nation committed itself once more, with the recital of a simple 18th-century oath, to what the new President felicitously termed "the mystery of American renewal." The solemn magic of the moment, in this most telling of national rituals, lies in what it symbolizes: the unquestioned acceptance by victor, vanquished and public alike of the continuity and legitimacy of governance.

The United States crowns no kings. But as he stood before the Capitol and spoke the words George Washington first uttered in lower Manhattan on April 30, 1789, Mr. Clinton embodied this nation's unity, in something of the way a monarch embodies Britain's at the hour of coronation in Westminster Abbey.

Jack Valenti, who worked in the White House three decades ago, calls the man in the Oval Office "the keeper of the national integrity and the steward of our civic virtue."

As such, Mr. Clinton starts with the good wishes of most Americans. But he is the leader of a Government as well as an icon of nationhood, and in that capacity he begins with less than universal acceptance. He won the votes, after all, of only 43 percent of those who cast ballots last November, and since then, he has excited wariness as well as enthusiasm in the country.

Bitter Democratic Memories

Few will take exception to his message of hope and rebirth, but it is far less certain that he will carry the country with him in his appeal to "face hard truths and take strong steps" in a spirit of shared sacrifice. That will depend not only upon who is asked to give up what, and how fair the apportionment seems, but also upon Mr. Clinton's ability to stir a citizenry that has been more preoccupied with "me" than with "us" for much of the last two decades.

The Old Guard in his party remembers all too well the self-immolation of the last two Democratic Administrations, those headed by Lyndon B. Johnson and Jimmy Carter, and prays that

Continued on Page A12, Column 1

INSIDE

"All the News That's Fit to Print"

The New York Times

Late Edition

New York: **Today,** cold winds, mostly sunny. Clouds south of the city. High 33. **Tonight,** clear. Low 22. **Tomorrow,** mostly sunny, cold. High 35. Yesterday, high 27, low 21. Details, page 34.

VOL.CXLII .. No. 49,255 Copyright © 1993 The New York Times NEW YORK, SATURDAY, FEBRUARY 27, 1993 50 CENTS

BLAST HITS TRADE CENTER, BOMB SUSPECTED; 5 KILLED, THOUSANDS FLEE SMOKE IN TOWERS

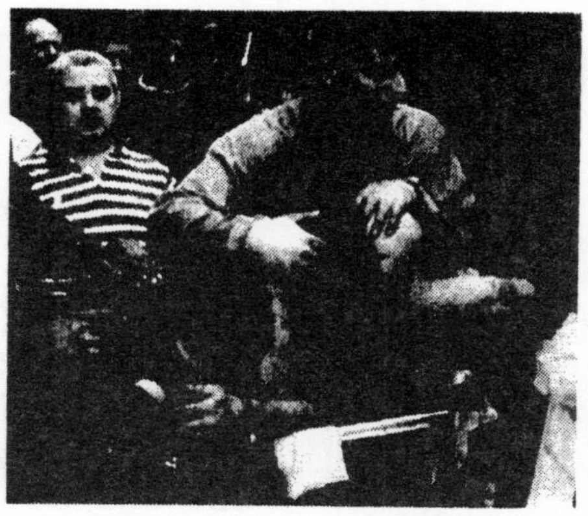

Associated Press; Carrie Borets for The New York Times; Marilynn K. Yee/The New York Times

ELEVATORS, STAIRS

SHOPPING ARCADE

VESEY STREET

LIBERTY STREET

VISTA HOTEL

WEST STREET

LOADING DOCK AND GENERATOR

PUBLIC PARKING

EMPLOYEE PARKING

EMPLOYEE PARKING

AIR-CONDITIONING, BACKUP GENERATOR

PATH TRACKS

❶ The blast occurred in a parking garage on the second level of the multi-level basement of the north World Trade Center tower.

❷ It carved a 200- by 100-foot crater on the public parking level, blew through a ceiling and knocked a hole in a wall.

❸ Cinder blocks and rubble from the collapsing wall fell to the tracks of the PATH station, and damaged lower levels.

This drawing is schematic and is based on information from reporters and officials at the scene.

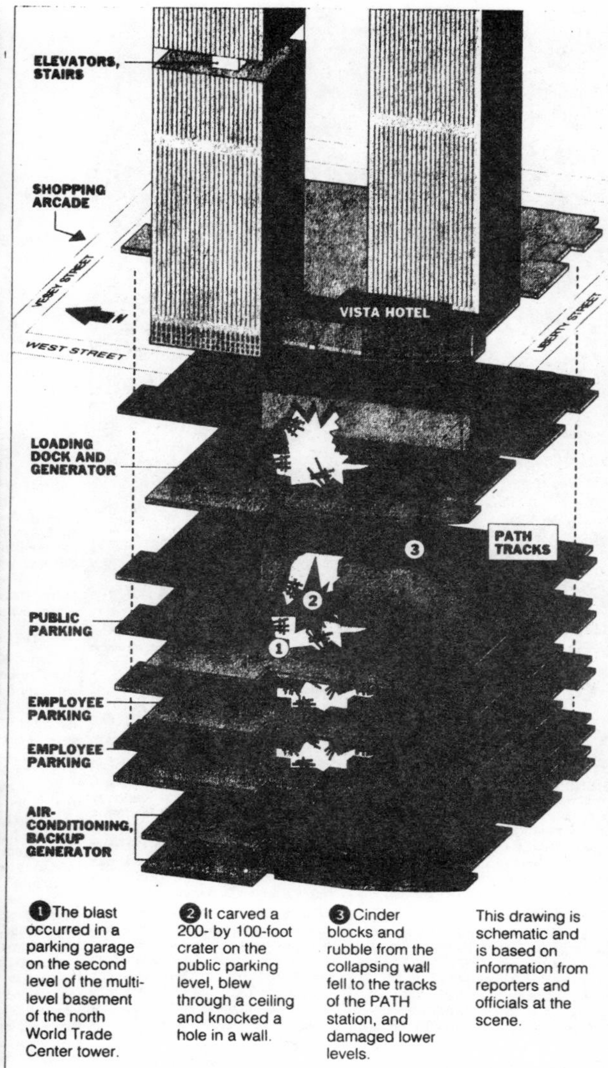

Jean Rutter/The New York Times; illustration by David Montesino and Julie Shaver

Many Are Trapped for Hours In Darkness and Confusion

By ROBERT D. McFADDEN

An explosion apparently caused by a car bomb in an underground garage shook the World Trade Center in lower Manhattan with the force of a small earthquake shortly after noon yesterday, collapsing walls and floors, igniting fires and plunging the city's largest building complex into a maelstrom of smoke, darkness and fearful chaos.

The police said the blast killed at least five people and left more than 650 others injured, mostly with smoke inhalation or minor burns, but dozens with cuts, bruises, broken bones or serious burns. The police said 476 were treated at hospitals and the rest by rescue and medical crews at the scene.

The explosion also trapped hundreds of people in debris or in smoke-filled stairwells and elevators of the towers overhead and forced the evacuation of more than 50,000 workers from a trade center bereft of power for lights and elevators for seven hours.

No Bomb Fragments Found

The blast, which was felt throughout the Wall Street area and a mile away on Ellis and Liberty Islands in New York Harbor, also knocked out the police command and operations centers for the towers, which officials said rendered the office complex's evacuation plans useless. [Page 23.]

James Fox, an assistant director of the Federal Bureau of Investigation in charge of the agency's New York office, said that no bomb fragments were found but that a joint terrorist task force of Federal agents and city detectives had examined the wreckage and believed that a car bomb had caused the explosion.

There was no warning of an impending explosion, Police Commissioner Raymond W. Kelly said. Jack Killorin, a spokesman in Washington for the Treasury Department's Bureau of Alcohol, Tobacco and Firearms, said that after the blast, authorities received at least nine telephone calls claiming responsibility.

Mr. Killorin said the first call was made 15 minutes after the blast to a non-emergency number of a New York Police Department precinct by an individual who mentioned the conflict in Bosnia. He said other claims were made between an hour and several hours after the event by callers who cited that and a variety of other reasons for the attack. He declined to elaborate.

Some law-enforcement officials said an explosion of such size, without a claim of responsibility in advance, might suggest that it went off accidentally.

Mr. Kelly was more oblique about the cause of the blast, saying only that a car bomb or other type of explosive device was not being ruled out.

Four hours after the explosion, a bomb threat forced the evacuation of the Empire State Building in midtown Manhattan, and there were numerous other bomb threats in the city, the police said. But it was unclear if any were related to the World Trade Center explosion or only the macabre work of pranksters.

As the day ended, a series of investigations began — into the cause of the explosion and its possible perpetrators, and into what went wrong in what many called a botched evacuation, with no alarms and no instructions for thousands caught in dark, smoky stairwells, in stark contrast to carefully laid plans.

Mayor David N. Dinkins, visiting in Osaka, Japan, was notified by City Hall and, in a telephone news conference, called the Fire Department response the largest for any non-natural disaster in the city's history. He said he had spoken with President Clinton and had thanked him for the cooperation of Federal investigators.

The effects of the blast radiated outward, disrupting most non-cable television transmissions throughout the metropolitan area, halting traffic in most of lower Manhattan and PATH train

Continued on Page 22, Column 1

Agence France-Presse

A man calling for help.

Manhattan Is Held in the Grip Of Traffic Snarls and Anxiety

By DEBORAH SONTAG

Traffic snarled to a standstill in lower Manhattan. Major arteries downtown closed, and a half-dozen subway lines were rerouted. Nervous relatives jammed the 911 emergency lines. And an anxiety that began in lower Manhattan at lunchtime yesterday grew infectious as the day grew long, generating a restless buzz throughout New York City.

As news spread that the explosion at the World Trade Center — which the F.B.I. said may have been caused by a car bomb — had been followed by a bomb scare at and evacuation of the Empire State Building, nerves began to fray. Drivers sitting bumper to bumper on Canal Street leaned on their horns, waiting over an hour to enter the Holland Tunnel. Subway riders jostled their way onto overcrowded trains, pondering their commuters' headaches as well as what seemed to be a different kind of urban terrorism.

An Eerie Quiet on Closed Streets

"It's frightening," said Charles Sampey, 34 years old, a building superintendent riding the IRT No. 3 downtown at 6 P.M. "You'd expect more to get robbed in New York than to get hit by a terrorist bomb."

After an underground explosion rocked the World Trade Center at noontime, the Franklin D. Roosevelt Drive, the West Side Highway, the Brooklyn Battery Tunnel and most side streets in lower Manhattan were closed to all but emergency vehicles. It grew eerily quiet — "like Sunday at dawn,"

said a Triborough Bridge and Tunnel Authority spokesman, Frank Pascual.

As trading on five commodities exchanges was disrupted and thousands of employees were evacuated from the smoke-filled office complex, transportation officials immediately began making emergency plans for an imminent rush hour. They added buses, trains and ferries to New Jersey to

Continued on Page 22, Column 1

INSIDE

Economy Ended 1992 With Robust Growth

The gross domestic product grew at the robust rate of 4.8 percent in the final three months of 1992, the best quarterly performance in five years and a full percentage point higher than initial estimates. Page 35.

Judge Rebuffs Gay Group On St. Patrick's Parade

A Federal judge ruled that New York City cannot order the Ancient Order of Hibernians to include a gay contingent in the annual St. Patrick's Day Parade up Fifth Avenue. The city will not appeal. Page 21.

Bosnia Sees a Turning Point

After hearing of American plans to airdrop relief supplies, many Bosnians said they sensed a major change in their plight. Page 6.

PRESIDENT URGES MORE RUSSIAN AID

In a Speech on World Trade, He Seeks a 2-Way Street

By R. W. APPLE Jr.

WASHINGTON, Feb. 26 — President Clinton declared today that having spent trillions of dollars to win the cold war, the United States must summon the will to spend much more than planned in Russia and the other former Soviet republics "to support democracy's success where Communism failed."

Documents sent to Capitol Hill with the President's economic message last week, but little noticed at the time, indicated the President will ask for $700 million in aid next year for the former Soviet republics, nearly doubling the $417 million allotted for this year. Mr. Clinton, who plans to meet with President Boris N. Yeltsin of Russia on April 4, said "the world will suffer" if Russia's tottering economic reforms collapse. [Excerpts, page 6.]

Wants America to Compete

In a speech at American University consciously evocative of one delivered there 30 years ago by John F. Kennedy, the President endorsed the broad thrust of former President George Bush's trade policies. But at the same time, he sent two signals of change with his call for greater support for Russia and a suggestion that he would demand progress on human rights as the price for continued growth in trade with China.

The speech was devoted to international economics and trade and was not

Continued on Page 6, Column 1

First, Darkness, Then Came the Smoke

By N. R. KLEINFIELD

It depended on where you were in the towers when it came. For some the warning was a trembling underfoot or just a blank computer screen and flickering lights. For others, it was a shocking noise. One woman was blown out of her high heels. Another, desk chair and all, sank into the floor. And then, instantly it seemed, came the billowing smoke and the chilling realization that you had to get out of there.

The Face of Death

There were those who panicked, those who coolly absorbed it, those who got sick to their stomach and those who saw the face of death. No one was sure what had happened; did a plane hit the building, was it an earthquake, had lightning struck? Many wondered why there seemed to be no evacuation plan and no guidance — not realizing that the blast had knocked out the center's operations center.

But thousands of people in the

For Workers in Offices, the First Imperative Was to Get Outside

World Trade Center yesterday afternoon knew they were in the grip of one of the most dreaded urban nightmares: they were in the city's tallest building and something was very wrong.

Joann Hilton was low. And, in this disaster, that was the worst place to be. A secretary working for the Port Authority of New York and New Jersey, she was at her desk in the command office on the B1 level of the building, musing about the weekend.

"All of a sudden, we heard this big boom," she said. "It sounded like an earthquake. And then the floor just collapsed and me and my chair sank into the floor. The ceiling started to come down, too, and I'm in my chair in the floor. Some of the lights went

out. And then it was all dark. Like a cave. Somebody pulled me out of that floor and we beat it out of there."

Denise Bosco was high. She was on the 82d floor, where she too works as a secretary for the Port Authority. "The whole building shook," she said. "The lights flashed on and off. The computers went down. Then, instantly, there was smoke. I was terrified. People panicked. They started pushing and shouting to get out. Some of them were throwing up. I said, 'Oh dear God, what is it? What is it? Is it my time? Is this the way?'"

Wrapped in a Bath Towel

Her coat was still in her office and she was wrapped in a white bath towel as she stood outside. She broke down into tears. "It was horrible," she said. "There was this awful feeling that we might not be able to get out. We were in the mighty, tall tower and we weren't getting out."

They didn't know whether to stay put or flee, but instinct said to run.

Continued on Page 22, Column 4

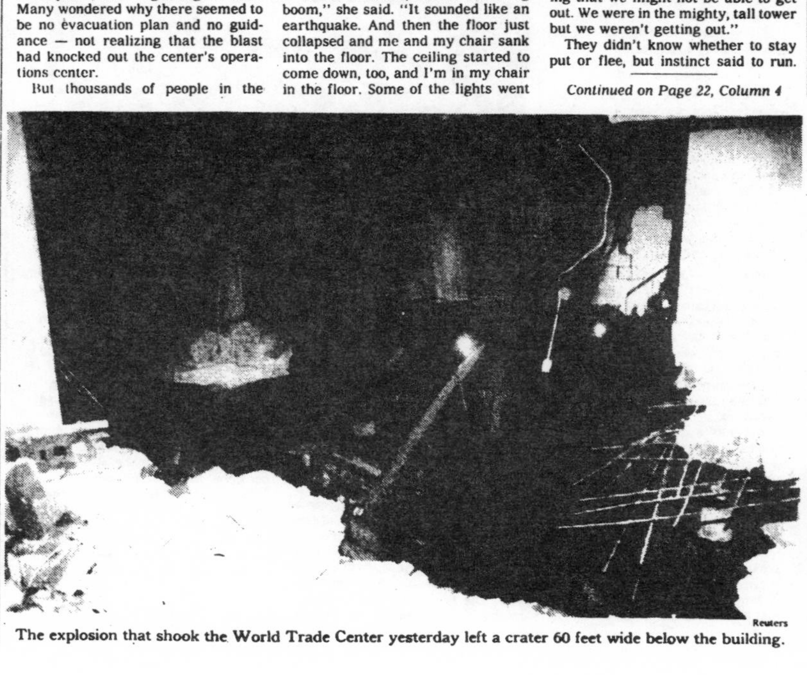

THE NEW YORK TIMES is available for home or office delivery in most major U.S. cities. Please call this toll-free number: 1-800-631-2500 ADVT

The explosion that shook the World Trade Center yesterday left a crater 60 feet wide below the building.

Reuters

354613

"All the News That's Fit to Print"

The New York Times

Late Edition

New York: **Today,** partly sunny warm winds. High 75, but cooler along south shores. **Tonight,** cloudy. Low 58. **Tomorrow,** showers. High 71. **Yesterday,** high 79, low 49. Details, page B16.

VOL.CXLII . . . No. 49,307 — NEW YORK, TUESDAY, APRIL 20, 1993 — 75 cents beyond 75 miles from New York City, except on Long Island — 50 CENTS

SCORES DIE AS CULT COMPOUND IS SET AFIRE AFTER F.B.I. SENDS IN TANKS WITH TEAR GAS

Agence France-Presse

The wood-frame compound of David Koresh and his cult followers turned into an inferno of death yesterday as a standoff of 51 days was ended.

Apparent Mass Suicide Ends A 51-Day Standoff in Texas

By SAM HOWE VERHOVEK

Special to The New York Times

WACO, Tex., April 19 — Hours after Federal agents began battering holes in the walls of the Branch Davidian compound and spraying tear gas inside, David Koresh and more than 80 followers — including at least 17 children — apparently perished today when flames engulfed the sprawling wooden complex on the Texas prairie.

Officials of the Federal Bureau of Investigation said they believed that Mr. Koresh, a self-described messiah who prophesied to his followers that they would meet their end in an apocalyptic confrontation with the law, gave the order to burn the compound down in the 51st day of a standoff with Federal agents.

F.B.I. officials said smashing the walls and filling the building with tear gas was intended to increase pressure on the cult members, who had resisted all previous demands for surrender. But the officials insisted that the tear gas was not flammable and that the fire was set by cult members who poured fuel around the perimeter of the compound and lit matches.

'They All Willingly Followed'

"David Koresh, we believe, gave the order to commit suicide and they all willingly followed," said Bob A. Ricks, a senior F.B.I. agent who has been here for most of the standoff, which began seven weeks ago with a deadly shootout between cult members and agents from the Federal Bureau of Alcohol, Tobacco and Firearms who wanted to search the compound.

Mr. Ricks said only nine people were rescued from the compound today, including one woman who had sought to return to the burning building and tried to fight off a Federal agent who came to her aid. Ammunition in the cult's storehouse of weapons sporadically exploded during the afternoon, hindering rescue workers.

Mr. Ricks said that so far "several bodies" had been found in a bus buried on the compound, and only "two or three" other bodies. The authorities believed that some of these were cult members who had been killed in the original confrontation on Feb. 28, he said.

"We had hoped the women would grab their children and flee," Mr. Ricks said. "That did not occur and they bunkered down the children and allowed them to go up in flames with them." Mr. Ricks said that it was only speculation at this point but that the authorities had received reports, apparently from some of the survivors, that the children had been injected with some kind of poison to ease their pain.

F.B.I. officials said they believed that 95 people were inside the compound when the fire began, including 17 children under the age of 10, and that it only knew of the 9 survivors, 4 of whom were at hospitals this evening and 5 of

Continued on Page A20, Column 3

RENO SEES ERROR IN MOVE ON CULT

Fatigue of Agents and Failure of Talks Brought Assault

By STEPHEN LABATON

Special to The New York Times

WASHINGTON, April 19 — Attorney General Janet Reno conceded tonight that in hindsight the Government's plan to assault the heavily armed cult near Waco, Tex., had been a mistake.

"It was based on what we knew then," she said this evening on the "Larry King Live" program on CNN. "Based on what we know now, it was obviously wrong."

Earlier in the day, a shaken and somber Ms. Reno said she had worried over the weekend that the plan could bring mass suicide, but she decided that it was "highly unlikely" and approved the operation.

Taking responsibility for the assault, she acknowledged that it had in fact led to a mass suicide, as members of the Branch Davidian cult burned down their wooden compound.

She added that Federal agents had decided to move in this morning in the 51st day of the standoff because negotiations had proved fruitless, because the cult members were prepared to hold out for many months and because there was no backup team to replace weary agents. She also said that the authorities had received reports that children in the compound were being beaten.

Ms. Reno said that the gassing of the

Continued on Page A21, Column 1

Italians Support Political Reform By a Big Margin

By ALAN COWELL

Special to The New York Times

ROME, April 19 — After months of scandal, recession and Government paralysis, Italians voted overwhelmingly for political change in a referendum on Sunday and today that repudiated the country's leadership of the last 48 years, but that left the future uncertain.

Final computer projections late tonight, 10 hours after polls closed, showed 82 percent of voters endorsing a proposal to scrap the current system of pure proportional representation for most of the Senate and replace it with the majority voting used in other parts of Europe and the United States.

The magnitude of the vote is expected to put heavy pressure on legislators to enact similar changes in the lower house, or Chamber of Deputies.

The ballot had assumed the proportions of a popular judgment on Italy's postwar political system, and the result was widely interpreted as a mandate for a new government to press through broader electoral reform.

That, in turn, would set a political calendar for new elections — and thus a fresh start — after a debilitating corruption scandal that has tainted much of the political and business elite and exposed ties between some government leaders and the Mafia.

While some of Italy's traditional parties, notably the Christian Democrats and the former Communists, would probably survive the process of re-

Continued on Page A8, Column 1

Vietnam Report on Prisoners A Fake, Reputed Author Says

By PHILIP SHENON

Special to The New York Times

HANOI, Vietnam, April 19 — A Vietnamese general denied today that he had written in 1972 that Hanoi held more than twice as many American prisoners as it ultimately released. Any such report attributed to Hanoi is a forgery, he declared.

And a special envoy, sent by President Clinton to tell the Vietnamese that relations could not improve until the matter was cleared up, said he saw no reason to disbelieve the Vietnamese denial.

Nearly two weeks ago, Russian archivists turned over to the United States a Russian translation of what was said to be a secret report to Hanoi's Politburo given by Gen. Tran Van Quang, described in the document as Deputy Chief of Staff of the Vietnamese armed forces at the time. The document said Hanoi held 1,205 American prisoners of war in September 1972.

591 Released in 1973

Because Vietnam released only 591 prisoners in 1973 and has maintained repeatedly that there were no other prisoners, the Russian translation raised the recurring question of whether Hanoi had kept some prisoners back, and if so, what happened to them. An alternative explanation offered by some experts was that Hanoi might have killed hundreds of prisoners.

Hanoi immediately denied the accuracy of the Russian document, saying it was a "fabrication."

In a meeting today, General Quang told President Clinton's special envoy, Gen. John W. Vessey Jr., that he did not write the 1972 report on which the Russian translation was supposedly based. If the Vietnamese report exists, General Quang said, it is a forgery that may have been prepared by someone interested "in undermining advances in relations between Vietnam and the United States."

At a news conference today after meeting with General Vessey, General Quang said of the 1972 report: "I did not write it. I tell you, never in my life have I made such a report, because it was not in my area of responsibility."

He stressed that although he was

Continued on Page A6, Column 4

Law Firm for S.& L. Is Fined $51 Million

Jones, Day, Reavis & Pogue, one of the nation's biggest law firms, agreed to pay the Government $51 million to settle charges that it aided the financier Charles H. Keating Jr. in the fraud that brought on the costliest bankruptcy in the savings and loan debacle. The agreement came as a trial was about to begin.

The settlement, which is the largest against a law firm in the savings and loan rescue, also ends litigation against the Jones, Day partner in charge of work for Mr. Keating's Lincoln Savings and Loan Association, which collapsed in 1989 at a cost to taxpayers of $2.5 billion.

Business Day, page D1.

John Kluge Gives Columbia $60 Million to Aid Minorities

By MARIA NEWMAN

John W. Kluge, the chairman of the Metromedia Company and a 1937 graduate of Columbia University, presented his alma mater last night with $60 million for minority scholarships. It is the largest gift the university has ever received.

In making his gift, Mr. Kluge recalled what a hardship it was for him to afford his tuition — only $500 a year at the time — when he was earning $7 a week working in the school dining hall. Fortunately for him, he said, Columbia helped by giving him a scholarship.

"Columbia made a difference really in my life and I really want to assure that it will continue to make a difference for others," Mr. Kluge said in an interview from his office in Manhattan. At 78, Mr. Kluge, who made his fortune building up a string of radio and television stations, is one of the wealthiest people in America.

By itself, the $60 million donation is believed to be the fifth largest to any university or college. When added to the $50 million Mr. Kluge already donated to Columbia in two previous gifts, it would be second only to the $125 million pledged to Louisiana State University in 1981 by Claude B. Pennington.

One of Mr. Kluge's two previous gifts of $25 million, presented in 1987, was also for minority scholarships and the other, in 1990, went to aid young scholars and junior faculty members.

The new gift comes at a critical time as Columbia battles serious fiscal problems. With its $1 billion operating budget, the university has a $15 million deficit this year and is working to cut costs to balance its budget for next year.

Luring Minority Candidates

But officials of the university said it was unclear whether the gift, because it was specifically for scholarships for undergraduates, would have any impact on the deficit.

The gift would, they said, help the university attract minority candidates who might otherwise go to other universities better able to help them with steep college costs.

Fred Knubel, a spokesman for Columbia, said last night that the gift would provide at least 300 students a year with grants of $10,000. Mr. Knubel said that the money would be used in

Continued on Page B7, Column 1

New Country Is Like Prison to Asenhat, 18

By DAVID GONZALEZ

Asenhat Gomez used to peer out the windows of her childhood home in the Dominican countryside and relish a landscape of willowy palm trees and verdant fields where her extended family would gather for daylong reunions.

In her new home in Brooklyn — a cramped apartment on Williamsburg's South Side — the windows frame a claustrophobic vista of brick walls, and the few relatives she has in this country are so preoccupied with making ends meet that family get-togethers seem as long gone as the father who died a dozen years ago.

It has been nearly a year since Asenhat was reunited with her mother, who six years before had left her children with their aunt and illegally entered the United States in search of the opportunities that had eluded the family in the Dominican Republic.

Longing for Home

But the immigrant journey of Asenhat Gomez is only beginning. For 18-year-old Asenhat, the joys of reunion are constantly tempered by the struggles of life in a hard new land. Hundreds of miles from all that was familiar, unable to shake her longing for home, she tentatively ventures into a future that beckons with equal measures of promise and fear.

In many ways, hers is the oldest of immigrant stories, played out time and again by wave after wave of newcomers to America's shores. But for today's immigrant children, in places like Williamsburg, that process of adjustment is made all the more difficult by the modern plagues of drugs, guns and recession.

Asenhat, a shy girl, has become even shyer since arriving last May, the strangeness and the frustrations coalescing in a sometimes overwhelming feeling that she is trapped.

'Sense of Confinement'

"Everybody talked about the sense of confinement," she said recently, recalling her first weeks in New York. "I expected that, but just not so much.

Monica Almeida/The New York Times

Children of the Shadows

The eighth of ten lives of the cities.

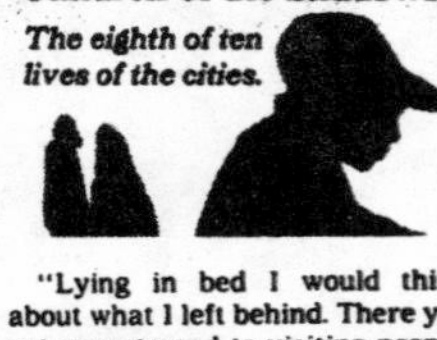

"Lying in bed I would think about what I left behind. There you got accustomed to visiting people, my friends from school, since we were infants. The whole place was different; you could go out to play. I miss my school."

Williamsburg — its bumpy narrow streets lined with age-worn two-family homes and apartment buildings closed in by the shadows of hulking waterfront factories and the Williamsburg Bridge — can seem forbidding to someone used to the easy freedom of the countryside. The family's two small bedrooms are shared by six people who subsist on meager earnings.

Still, even as she bridles at her confinement, it has become her defense mechanism in a city whose ways and language are not her own. She seldom ventures beyond her neighborhood, partly from fear of getting lost on unexplored streets and subway lines and partly from fear of drug dealing and violent crime on nearby blocks.

"It makes you feel insecure," said Asenhat, a short girl whose floppy ponytail and baggy jeans give her the look of someone just entering her teen-age years. "You can be going down the street and not know what can happen."

She has few friends, feeling that she has little in common with American-born teen-agers, who she says are too "liberal" — so preoccupied with boyfriends, clothes and the latest fads that

Continued on Page B6, Column 1

INSIDE

Arrest in Capital Shootings

The police arrested a suspect in a series of shootings that had left three people dead and terrorized Washington since Feb. 23. Page A12.

Slain South African Buried

South Africa turned the burial of a slain black Communist into the biggest political rite since Nelson Mandela's release from prison. Page A8.

New Abortion-Rights Politics

Now that abortion-rights supporters finally have an ally in the White House, they face a new set of priorities and challenges. Page A18.

Rustling Scholarly Feathers

Flightless bird or feathered dinosaur, a turkey-sized fossil from Mongolia has scientists debating the history of flying. Science Times, page C1.

Today's TV Listings

Television and radio listings and advertising appear today on pages B16-17.

"All the News That's Fit to Print"

The New York Times

Late Edition

New York: **Today,** partly sunny, windy, shower possible. High 84. **Tonight,** clearing, breezy. Low 57. **Tomorrow,** cool, windy. High 72. **Yesterday,** high 78, low 66. Details, page D17.

VOL.CXLII . . . No. 49,450 | NEW YORK, FRIDAY, SEPTEMBER 10, 1993 | 75 cents beyond the greater New York metropolitan area | 50 CENTS

P.L.O. AND ISRAEL ACCEPT EACH OTHER AFTER 3 DECADES OF RELENTLESS STRIFE

Mr. Prime Minister . . .
The P.L.O. recognizes the right of the State of Israel to exist in peace and security . . . renounces the use of terrorism and other acts of violence. . . .

Sincerely,
YASIR ARAFAT
CHAIRMAN
THE PALESTINE LIBERATION ORGANIZATION

Mr. Chairman . . .
The Government of Israel has decided to recognize the P.L.O. as the representative of the Palestinian people. . . .

YITZHAK RABIN
PRIME MINISTER OF ISRAEL

VIOLENCE REJECTED

An Exchange of Letters Clears the Way for a Pact on Self-Rule

By CLYDE HABERMAN
Special to The New York Times

JERUSALEM, Sept. 9 — Enemies to the death for three decades, Israel and the Palestine Liberation Organization opened a new era in their blood-soaked history today by recognizing each other's legitimacy and the rights of both to represent their people's dreams.

Yasir Arafat, the P.L.O. chairman, said in a letter to Prime Minister Yitzhak Rabin that his group recognized Israel's right "to exist in peace and security," renounced "the use of terrorism and other acts of violence," and was ready to discipline any of its loyalists who break this pledge.

And in a separate letter to Norway's Foreign Minister, who had served for months as an intermediary in secret talks between the two sides, Mr. Arafat called on Palestinians in the Israeli-occupied West Bank and Gaza Strip to begin "the normalization of life." Israeli officials took that as an Arafat appeal to end the Palestinian uprising known in Arabic as the intifada, although that was not spelled out.

Rabin Stood Firm

The Israelis said Mr. Rabin was adamant that the intifada be curtailed. It was a measure of Mr. Arafat's determination to reach an agreement that he yielded on this point even though most Palestinians in the territories consider the uprising an indispensable tool to resist the Israeli occupation.

For his part, Mr. Rabin wrote a terse letter to Mr. Arafat saying that in light of these Palestinian commitments, his Government "has decided to recognize the P.L.O. as the representative of the Palestinian people and to commence negotiations with the P.L.O. within the Middle East peace process." Unlike Mr. Arafat, who closed his letter with the word "sincerely," Mr. Rabin dispensed with such pleasantries and simply put his name. [Texts of the three letters, page A12.]

Mr. Arafat signed his letter to Mr. Rabin behind closed doors late tonight in Tunis, where the P.L.O. is based. When Mr. Rabin follows suit at a signing ceremony in Jerusalem on Friday morning, it will clear the way for yet another agreement on a plan to transfer authority in the territories from Israeli to Palestinian hands, starting with a form of self-rule in Gaza and the West Bank city of Jericho.

Breathtaking Change

That accord, the product of months of secret negotiations conducted mainly in Norway, is to be signed at the White House on Monday by high-ranking officials on each side. No names have been announced, but the Israelis said they would probably be represented by Foreign Minister Shimon Peres, and the Palestinians are expected to send Mahmoud Abbas, the P.L.O. official who supervised the negotiations. Farouk Kaddoumi, the P.L.O. foreign minister, opposed the agreements.

Washington has been the locale of the most recent Middle East peace talks, and both sides seem to want United States involvement in the peace process.

No amount of protocol or formal language, however, could obscure the breathtaking change that has now swept across this land for which Jews and Arabs have fought and died across the last century.

For Israel, recognition of the P.L.O., formally endorsed by the Rabin Cabinet this evening, means that it is pre-

Continued on Page A12, Column 1

U.S. Troops Fire on Somalis; Death Toll May Reach 100

By MICHAEL R. GORDON
Special to The New York Times

WASHINGTON, Sept. 9 — In a battle that is expected to heighten the debate over the United States role in Somalia, American and Pakistani forces opened fire today on a crowd of Somali soldiers, women and children after United Nations peacekeeping troops came under attack.

Two American Cobra attack helicopters and Pakistani tanks and armored personnel carriers fired cannons and rockets at the Somalis in Mogadishu, the Somali capital. United Nations officials said as many as 100 Somalis may have been killed in the fighting, and that some appeared to be women and children.

A Pakistani soldier was also killed, bringing the toll of United Nations peacekeepers killed in Somalia to 48. Four peacekeepers were wounded today, including two Americans.

Justified by U.N. Aide

Maj. David Stockwell, the chief United Nations spokesman in Mogadishu, justified the shooting of women and children as a "last-ditch, last resort effort to protect the United Nations troops."

"We saw all the people swarming on the vehicles as combatants," he was quoted as saying in news agency reports. "We've seen this before. If they reach our soldiers they tear them limb from limb."

Among the unresolved questions left by the fight was whether some of the women hit were armed collaborators of Gen. Mohammed Farah Aidid, the fugitive leader of a powerful Somali faction, as U.N. officials suggested, or rather civilians caught in the cross-fire.

United Nations and American officials gave this account of what appeared to be one of the deadliest battles since American forces were deployed in Somalia in December.

The officials said the fighting began when a contingent of American combat engineers protected by Pakistani troops was ambushed while trying to clear a roadblock. The officials said the attack was carried out by a well-armed force of more than 100 militiamen commanded by General Aidid.,

The engineers and Pakistani troops withdrew, the officials said, while American attack helicopters and Pakistani tanks went to the scene.

During the three-hour battle, United Nations officials said, the Somali militiamen mingled with women and children, in what the officials called a common tactic intended to deter United Nations forces from firing back.

"We have some evidence that he is proud of this tactic," Jonathan Howe, the retired admiral who serves as the United Nations envoy in Mogadishu, said in a reference to General Aidid.

Small Arms and Rockets

During the intense fighting along 21 October Road in Mogadishu, the American helicopters, designed to kill troops and destroy vehicles in combat, responded with 20-millimeter cannon and rocket fire, blowing up a bulldozer that had been seized by the Somalis.

The United Nations said its troops came under fire from small arms, machine guns, rocket-propelled grenades and a 106-millimeter recoilless gun that destroyed one of the Pakistanis' M-48 tanks.

"I think this is part of a continuing military effort to attack the United Nations," Admiral Howe added in a telephone interview.

A United Nations spokesman said

Continued on Page A9, Column 1

The Brave New Middle East

By THOMAS L. FRIEDMAN
Special to The New York Times

News Analysis

WASHINGTON, Sept. 9 — The Middle East will never be the same.

The mutual recognition agreement between Israel and the Palestine Liberation Organization today fundamentally alters both the political and psychological maps of the region. It may not bring peace tomorrow or the day after, but it will reshape the Middle East more than any other single event since the establishment of Israel in 1948.

This agreement creates the potential for dramatically new alliances that could knit together both Israel and Arab countries; it unearths a mother lode of diplomatic opportunities for the United States, which will no longer have to choose between friendships with Israel or the Arab world; it will make it much easier for the pro-American Arab countries to be identified with Washington; it will deprive the Arab and Muslim fundamentalists of their most potent issue for mobilizing the Arab street — the war with Israel — and, most important, it will lay a real foundation for Arab-Israeli coexistence.

Some Prefer the Status Quo

But precisely because this event is so transforming it will not go down peacefully between the Nile and the Euphrates. Many Israelis and Palestinians were devoted to the status quo — Israelis who do not want to give up land because they believe it is their biblical patrimony, or because they do not trust P.L.O. promises, and Palestinians who will never resign themselves to the notion that the Jews have a legitimate claim to the land of Israel, or because do not trust Israeli promises.

All of them have quietly been counting on the notion that the day would never come when Israel made

New Vistas Revealed On Every Side of Fray

peace with the P.L.O. They will be as deeply threatened by it as the advocates of peace will be uplifted.

To appreciate just how unexpected, how mind-bending, this change is, consider the fact that several years ago Life magazine ran a demonstration of trick photography in which it seamlessly grafted the heads of different people onto the bodies of others. To prove how wild such photography could be, Life created a picture of President Ronald Reagan bringing Yitzhak Shamir, who was then the Israeli Prime Minister, and the P.L.O. leader, Yasir Arafat, into a handshake on the White House lawn.

On Monday no trick photography will be needed. President Clinton is expected to be the host to just such a handshake between senior Israeli and P.L.O. officials in his backyard.

It is the psychological impact of that ceremony — two neighbors who for years never recognized the other's legal title to Palestine/Israel finally acknowledging that they each have an equally valid claim — that will be the most enduring.

For the Israelis, that moment will not only signify the beginning of the healing of the Arab-Israeli conflict, but, in some ways, it could also signify the first signs of recovery of the Israeli people from the trauma of the Holocaust.

For years, said the Israeli political theorist Yaron Ezrahi, Israeli leaders from Golda Meir to Yitzhak Shamir drew from the Holocaust the pessimistic lesson that the only way Jews could survive in the post-Holocaust

Continued on Page A14, Column 1

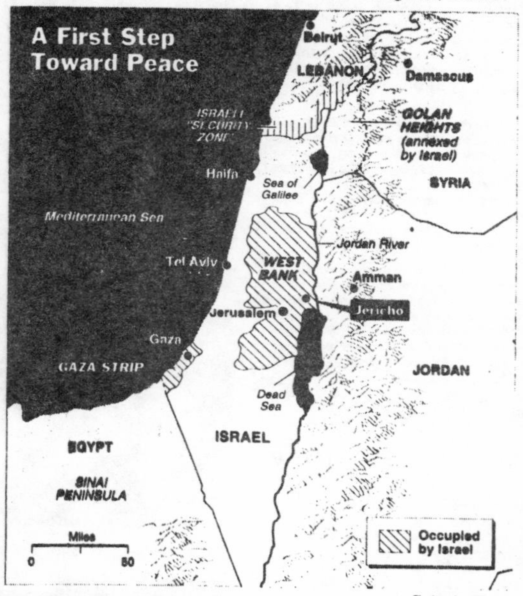

The New York Times

Accord clears the way for the granting of limited self-rule for Palestinians in the Gaza Strip and the West Bank town of Jericho.

Three pages on the Middle East accord: A12-14.

OTHER MAJOR NEWS

Proposed Settlement On Breast Implants

The Dow Corning Corporation announced a proposed $4.75 billion fund to compensate women with silicone breast implants. Lawyers on both sides of the bitter dispute said they expected it to be ratified.

Women who have suffered any one of eight diseases would be eligible for compensation ranging from $200,000 to $2 million, while others, even those claiming no physical effects, could receive lesser amounts. Page A16.

Baseball's New Lineup

If the players' union goes along, major league baseball will have a new look next season: three divisions in each league, instead of the current two, and a new round of playoffs in October. Page B11.

Masson v. Malcolm, Again

A Federal district judge ordered a new trial in the libel case between Jeffrey Masson and the writer Janet Malcolm but severed The New Yorker from the case. Page A20

Laura Pedrick for The New York Times

Wachtler Ordered to Prison

Sol Wachtler, above, New York State's former Chief Judge and one-time gubernatorial hopeful, was sentenced to 15 months in prison for threatening his ex-lover. Page B1

Penalties Proposed For High Drug Prices

The Clinton Administration has told Congress that it wants the Government to review prices of new prescription drugs so that Medicare coverage can be denied for drugs whose prices are deemed excessive.

Such a penalty, proposed as part the new health care plan, would be a powerful means of restraining prescription drug prices, which have risen twice as quickly as other consumer prices. Page A17.

No Early Holtzman Report

The New York City Comptroller, Elizabeth Holtzman, said in a candidates' debate that she would not allow the early release of the findings of a city investigation into a campaign loan that she received last year. Page B5.

P.L.O. Lining Up Palestinian Support for Accord

By YOUSSEF M. IBRAHIM
Special to The New York Times

TUNIS, Sept. 9 — In a mood of resignation and quiet satisfaction, top leaders of the Palestine Liberation Organization continued their final deliberations tonight on texts of agreements with Israel. And senior P.L.O. officials appeared to have made breakthroughs in taming opposition to the accords by Muslim militants and the organization's leftist flank.

A senior official asserted that the P.L.O. leadership in Tunis had succeeded in persuading Sheik Ahmad Yassin, the spiritual leader of the Palestinian Muslim militant Hamas movement in the Gaza Strip, who is held by the Israelis, to issue a statement calling on his followers not to use violence to demonstrate their opposition to the deal.

Yasir Arafat, the P.L.O. leader, signed the letter recognizing Israel and renouncing violence in a simple ceremony in his office tonight in the presence of Norway's Foreign Minister, Johan Jorgen Holst, who had acted as broker in the secret negotiations that led to the agreement.

In Paris, Mahmoud Darwish, a Palestinian poet who resigned from the P.L.O.'s Executive Committee last week to underline his opposition to any deals with Israel, is also expected to issue a statement now softening his stand against them, a P.L.O. official said.

Mr. Darwish, the P.L.O. official said, is expected to say that while he still opposes these accords, he now stands with the Palestinian leadership in its attempt to make them work and calls upon "all Palestinians" to do so.

Sheik Yassin has a great deal of influence among the rank and file of the Hamas movement, which has emerged as the most serious threat to the P.L.O.'s influence in Gaza and the West Bank.

It is too early to say whether his appeal will make a difference and it is not clear yet whether the P.L.O., with the cooperation of the Israeli authorities, has succeeded in proposing such a deal to him.

"We basically told him if you co-

Continued on Page A13, Column 1

"All the News That's Fit to Print"

The New York Times

Late Edition
New York: Today, patchy fog, then mostly sunny. High 86. Tonight, clear. Low 72. Tomorrow, sunshine mixed with clouds, humid. High 88. Yesterday, high 84, low 65. Details, page C16.

VOL.CXLII . . No. 49,454

NEW YORK, TUESDAY, SEPTEMBER 14, 1993

75 cents beyond the greater New York metropolitan area. 50 CENTS

RABIN AND ARAFAT SEAL THEIR ACCORD AS CLINTON APPLAUDS 'BRAVE GAMBLE'

Associated Press

"The children of Abraham . . . have embarked together on a bold journey." — President Clinton.

Old Warriors Now Face Task Of Building Upon Foundation

By THOMAS L. FRIEDMAN
Special to The New York Times

WASHINGTON, Sept. 13 — In a triumph of hope over history, Yitzhak Rabin, the Prime Minister of Israel, and Yasir Arafat, the chairman of the P.L.O., shook hands today on the White House lawn, sealing the first agreement between Jews and Palestinians to end their conflict and share the holy land along the River Jordan that they both call home.

At 11:43 A.M. on the sun-splashed South Lawn of the White House, Foreign Minister Shimon Peres of Israel and Mahmoud Abbas, the foreign policy aide for the Palestine Liberation Organization, signed a Declaration of Principles on Palestinian self-government in Israeli-occupied Gaza and the West Bank. Three thousand witnesses watched in amazement, including former Presidents Jimmy Carter and George Bush.

Mr. Rabin, whose face is etched with the memories of every Arab-Israeli war, captured in his remarks the exhaustion of all parties with the centuries-old conflict. "We the soldiers who have returned from the battle stained with blood," he said, "we who have fought against you, the Palestinians, we say to you today in a loud and clear voice: 'Enough of blood and tears! Enough!' "

Mr. Arafat, relishing his moment of acceptance on the White House lawn, strove to give Mr. Rabin the appropriate response, declaring in Arabic: "Our two peoples are awaiting today this historic hope, and they want to give peace a real chance."

An Awkward Moment

And President Clinton, who gracefully shepherded Mr. Arafat and Mr. Rabin through their awkward moment of public reconciliation, hailed them both for their "brave gamble that the future can be better than the past." [Transcripts of the leaders' remarks are on page A12.]

The agreement, which will eventually allow Palestinians to run their own affairs as Israeli troops pull back within months from the Gaza Strip and Jericho in a first step, was reached during secret negotiations over the past few months between Israelis and Palestinians, under the direction of Mr. Peres and Mr. Abbas, through the mediation of Norway.

The documents were signed on the same wooden table on which the Peace Treaty between Egypt and Israel was signed in 1979. That table stood today as a silent memorial to the assassinated Egyptian President, Anwar el-Sadat, whose path-breaking visit to Israel in 1977 and subsequent agreements at Camp David brought him denunciations as a traitor by Mr. Arafat.

But the audience in attendance, and perhaps the millions more watching back in the Middle East, seemed less interested in the formal signing than in the visual moment that would somehow make this tentative peace real: the handshake between the two old warriors who personified the conflict between their peoples.

A Nudge, a Hand, a Smile

Moments after the documents were signed, Mr. Clinton took Mr. Arafat in his left arm and Mr. Rabin in his right arm and gently coaxed them together, needing to give Mr. Rabin just a little extra nudge in the back. Mr. Arafat reached out his hand first, and then Mr. Rabin, after a split second of hesitation and with a wan smile on his face, received Mr. Arafat's hand. The audience let out a simultaneous sigh of relief and peal of joy, as a misty-eyed Mr. Clinton beamed away.

Two hands that had written the battle orders for so many young men, two fists that had been raised in anger at one another so many times in the past, locked together for a fleeting moment of reconciliation.

But much difficult work, many more compromises, will now have to be performed by these same two men to make it a lasting moment.

That reality was underscored by the fact that both Mr. Rabin and Mr. Arafat invoked their peoples' undying attachment to Jerusalem in their respective speeches.

[Later in Jerusalem, Israeli Radio reported that Mr. Rabin, accompanied by Foreign Minister Shimon Peres, was traveling to Morocco on Tuesday for a surprise meeting with King Hassan to discuss establishing diplomatic relations. The report said said Tunisia was among several Muslim and Arab countries now ready to establish ties with Israel.]

In an opening speech that was both eloquent and moving, Mr. Clinton described the history of the effort to make peace in the Middle East and paid tribute to Mr. Rabin and Mr. Arafat. He also pledged United States support for their effort.

"The United States is committed to insuring that the people who are affected by this agreement will be made more secure by it and to leading the world in marshaling the resources necessary to implement the difficult details that will make real the principles

Continued on Page A13, Column 1

MORE ON THE ACCORD

Arafat's Strategy: '2 Olive Branches'

Transforming one's image from guerrilla leader to statesman is not easy, but Yasir Arafat was trying hard to make it happen. Efforts in the past have had mixed results for all the countries involved. "This time," he said just an hour after making peace with Israel, "I am coming with two olive branches." Page A15.

Arabs and Jews Reflect

As many speak out about the events of recent days, there are new hopes, on both sides, but fears from years past remain. Page A16.

Divisions in Syria

Thousands marched in Syria, waving black flags in protest against Mr. Arafat, but elsewhere in the nation the response was more stunned, disbelieving, silence. Page A17.

Security Surprises

Security for the dignitaries was about what you would expect in the capital, but despite the hardware and planning, there were surprises. Page A14.

A 45-Year Struggle

Over the years since the birth of Israel in 1948, the Palestinian movement has drawn support from Palestinians inside Israel, in Israeli-occupied territories and in neighboring Arab countries while pressing for nationhood or self-rule. Page A15.

The Next Challenge for the U.S.

Peace Momentum Up to Washington

By R. W. APPLE Jr.
Special to The New York Times

WASHINGTON, Sept. 13 — As he himself said, this was not Bill Clinton's day. It was not he who brought together the sober old soldier and the grinning guerrilla fighter in the leafy calm of the South Lawn of the White House, far from the battlefields of the Middle East, for a paean to peace.

News Analysis

However deft, however sagacious, he was but the master of ceremonies. He thanked those who had labored to bring about the latest in a series of once-inconceivable changes that have remade the world in five short years. He bestowed the congratulations of the world's only superpower. And he gave Yitzhak Rabin a timely little nudge when he seemed reluctant to grasp the outstretched hand of Yasir Arafat.

Now, though, President Clinton will have to assume the central role if the momentum toward a comprehensive peace settlement is not to be lost. That is likely to be a long, messy job of diplomatic donkey work in the dark corners of history — a much less gratifying chapter than today's carefully scripted pageant of good intentions.

Israel and Jordan are poised to move forward tomorrow. But the other Arab nations whose representatives watched today's ceremony from the front rows know that only the United States can provide the impetus needed for the next round of negotiations. Mr. Arafat spoke for them, too, when he said his people "are relying on your role, Mr. President" to "usher in an age of peace."

So this President, who so longs to concentrate on problems at home, is thrust like so many of his predecessors into an international arena not of his choosing. Along with the rest of the world, the United States has a new ward, the inchoate entity called Palestine, and it has the main responsibility for fostering Israeli settlements with its other neighbors while deepening the one with the Palestinians.

It will be up to Mr. Clinton, who does not much like doing so, to butt heads between the Israelis and the Syrians, and perhaps take considerable heat from American Jews in the process, which he did not have to endure this time.

Neither Mr. Clinton nor any other American President has ever wanted to do business with Mr. Arafat and the Palestine Liberation Organization. As Mr. Rabin, the Israeli Prime Minister, said in one of his many moments of eloquence this morning, "It's not so

Continued on Page A13, Column 6

Jim Estrin/The New York Times

Palestinian women dancing with joy in Jericho, on the West Bank.

Reuters

Israelis watching the signing on television on a Jerusalem street.

Palestinians: Glee And Flag-Waving

Special to The New York Times

JERICHO, Israeli-Occupied West Bank, Sept. 13 — Palestinians took to the streets of the West Bank and Gaza Strip today in rapturous and noisy celebrations of the Palestine Liberation Organization accord with Israel and what they said was the cornerstone of their future state.

In the sleepy city of Jericho, the seat of the future Palestinian self-governing authority, it looked as though every one of the 15,000 residents was in the streets.

Savoring a new reality few had dared to imagine just a few weeks ago, they danced all day and into the night. In the Gaza Strip they handed flowers to Israeli soldiers. In East Jerusalem they shouted "Shalom!" to Israeli well-wishers.

The accord also changed the face of the occupied territories and East Jerusalem, where Palestinian flags, which had technically been banned, flew with impunity.

Israelis: Searching For New Bearings

Special to The New York Times

BEIT ZAYIT, Israel, Sept. 13 — When Yitzhak Rabin shook hands with Yasir Arafat, six Israelis watching it on television together on the western outskirts of Jerusalem might as well have been struck by lightning. They could only sigh deeply in disbelief before their thoughts and emotions unscrambled themselves.

The dominant feeling, in the room and across the country, is that there is no alternative to having Israelis and Palestinians come to terms with each other, as they are now trying to do.

Like many Israelis, Eliezer Shenhav, a surgeon who had friends into watch the ceremony, wrestled with religious convictions that taught him that God intended all of the biblical Land of Israel to be in Jewish hands.

Articles, page A17.

President's Tie Tells It All: Trumpets for a Day of Glory

By MAUREEN DOWD
Special to The New York Times

WASHINGTON, Sept. 13 — The President who loves to stay up late told his aides that he went to bed at 10 P.M. on Sunday, so he could be rested for the historic day.

They did not believe him, of course.

"No way," said Dee Dee Myers, the White House press secretary. "He got the big hand and the little hand mixed up."

"It was Jerusalem time," suggested Mark Gearan, the White House communications director.

But what happened next is not in contention: The President said he woke up at 3 A.M. and could not go back to sleep. He was worrying about the speech he would make to mark what was sure to be one of the most remarkable events of his Presidency: the moment when the two men who had been bitter enemies for so long, the Israeli Prime Minister, Yitzhak Rabin, and the Chairman of the Palestine Liberation Organization, Yasir Arafat, would recognize each other's existence on the South Lawn of the White House.

With his wife and daughter still asleep, Mr. Clinton put on a blue jogging suit and went into the study in the White House residence. He picked up a Bible. He read the entire Book of Joshua, wanting to review the part about the trumpets in Jericho that toppled walls and making sure he put a reference in his speech contrasting the victory of war and the victory of peace.

In another part of the White House, a team led by Jeremy Rosner, a National Security Council speechwriter, was scrambling to fulfill the President's last request: Mr. Clinton wanted a passage from the Koran to balance his Biblical allusions. The desperate White House staff members finally called Prince Bandar bin Sultan, the Saudi ambassador, who helped them pick out an appropriately soothing passage: "If the enemy inclines toward peace, do thou also incline toward peace."

Watching for the Dawn

At some point, Mr. Clinton moved from the study to the kitchen to read and drink coffee. He wanted to sit near the window, where he could keep track of when the dawn arrived and what the sky looked like.

The White House staff had worked over three days to compile a 26-page step-by-step log choreographing every movement that the leaders would make, and yet Mr. Clinton knew as well as anyone that, with this most delicate of all diplomatic meetings, a million things could go wrong — a look, a word, a handshake, the weather.

At dawn, as he later told aides, who

Continued on Page A14, Column 5

INSIDE

Primary Candidates Work on Voter Turnout

Appearing at subway stops and centers for the elderly and monopolizing the talk shows, candidates in the Democratic primaries for New York City offices played to their surest supporters in the closing hours of the campaign. The races could hinge on voter turnout. Page B1.

POLLING PLACES will be open from 6 A.M. to 9 P.M. today in New York City, Westchester and Nassau, and from 6 A.M. to 8 P.M. in Connecticut.

Fall Air Fares Cut by 45%

The nation's airlines cut fares by up to 45 percent on domestic flights through Dec. 16, but tickets must be bought by Saturday. Page D1.

"All the News
That's Fit to Print"

The New York Times

Late Edition
New York: **Today, some clouds,** windy, becoming very cold. **High 30. Tonight,** frigid. Low 4. **Tomorrow,** partly sunny, windy. **High 11. Yesterday,** high 47, low 12. **Details, page B8.**

VOL.CXLIII . . . No. 49,580 NEW YORK, TUESDAY, JANUARY 18, 1994 — 75 cents beyond the greater New York metropolitan area — 50 CENTS

SEVERE EARTHQUAKE HITS LOS ANGELES; AT LEAST 30 KILLED; FREEWAYS COLLAPSE

Reuters

The body of a motorcycle police officer lying near the wreckage of his vehicle in the center of an overpass that collapsed onto Interstate 5. He drove off the edge and fell 25 feet.

HUNDREDS INJURED

Predawn Tremor Levels Buildings and Ignites Dozens of Fires

By SETH MYDANS
Special to The New York Times

LOS ANGELES, Jan. 17 — A violent earthquake jolted millions of people out of bed before dawn today, crumpling freeway overpasses, leveling buildings and igniting scores of fires. Hundreds of people were injured and at least 30 were reported killed, including 15 at a three-level apartment complex that was reduced to two stories.

The quake, centered in the Northridge area in the San Fernando Valley, 20 miles northwest of downtown Los Angeles, measured 6.6 on the Richter scale of ground motion and was felt for hundreds of miles, knocking out power and water service for hundreds of thousands of residents.

In a region held together by its network of freeways, three overpasses collapsed, crippling major highways for weeks and possibly months. Roads cracked and buckled across the San Fernando Valley.

State of Emergency

People lingered on the streets throughout the day as the thuds of aftershocks sent dust rising above the mountains. Others formed long lines outside hardware stores and tried to buy batteries, water, propane or plywood to repair damaged homes. And when evening came, hundreds of people whose homes were destroyed or too dangerous to re-enter camped in city parks and on tennis courts in a nervously festive atmosphere, some of them with campfires and cases of beer.

A state of emergency was declared at the local, state and Federal levels in this latest disaster to strike the city. Aerial pictures of blocks of burning buildings evoked traumatic memories of the 1992 riots and last autumn's wildfires.

"I couldn't stop screaming as I ran out of the house," said Erik Wyler, 19, still shaking an hour after the quake. "I looked up and all I could see was darkness coming toward us, and it got real windy. I thought it was the sun exploding."

Hundreds of buildings were damaged, including Anaheim Stadium, which was expected to need $3.4 million in repairs. The quake, which struck at 4:31 A.M., was not the strongest to hit the region in recent years but was by far the most destructive because it struck in a heavily populated area.

Curfew Is Imposed

The Chief of Police, Willie L. Williams addressed the city on television this evening, telling people to remain calm and to stay home from work on Tuesday if possible. He said that city offices would be open on Tuesday but that schools in the Los Angeles Unified School District would be closed.

He also announced a dusk-to-dawn curfew and issued a warning against any potential looters, with reference to the rampage that overtook the city during the 1992 riots.

"We're not going to tolerate what

Continued on Page A17, Column 1

Associated Press

An injured man being treated at an emergency unit set up outside Olive View Medical Center in Sylmar.

Airborne in Bed: A Building Collapses, Leaving 15 Dead

By ELIZABETH KOLBERT
Special to The New York Times

LOS ANGELES, Jan. 17 — Erik Pearson heard a loud explosion and felt a jolt like a bomb. Still on their bed, he and his wife then fell 12 feet through the ceiling of the apartment below.

"We were airborne," said Mr. Pearson, a 27-year-old nursing student. "I heard the glass break from the glass sliding doors. Our apartment came down and pitched diagonally." The door was jammed shut, the couple said, but they climbed down to safety off their once third-floor, now second-floor, balcony.

But at least 15 other residents of the tan stucco apartment complex, the Northridge Meadows, did not. They died as building suffered some of the worst damage of the earthquake today and its residents bore the brunt of the casualties.

The building, half a block from California State University at Northridge, housed many college students. An identical building next to it, the Northridge, buckled but did not collapse.

The Meadows, a three-story, 164-unit apartment complex near the epicenter of the quake in the San Fernando Valley, looked like a cardboard box that someone had stepped on. In several sections of the building, the first floor no longer existed; it lay crushed beneath the two other floors. Windows had popped out of their frames, balconies dangled at odd angles and entire walls buckled.

Famous From Now On

Until 4:31 A.M. today this sleepy middle-class section of Los Angeles, about 20 miles northwest of downtown, was known only for its tree-lined branch of the California State University. From now, it will be known as the epicenter of a devastating 6.6 earthquake.

Simply put, city officials said the 15 deaths made this building the site of the largest number of earthquake fatalities in the city's history.

John William, 36, a survivor who lived on the first floor, managed to slither to safety by following a small path of light to a crack in the building's foundation.

"I pushed open the crack in the wall; my fiancée and I were pressed together, and we squeezed ourselves free," said Mr. William, who had cuts on both hands and arms. "I felt like we were going to lose circulation at any minute.

"I was hearing moans and whining and banging from people pinned in the other apartments. I'm not exaggerating: the second floor is now in the dirt. There is not two inches of room in my apartment."

Residents described a scene of panic in the hours before dawn as people tried to climb from their balconies or pick their way down dark staircases that had been torn apart by the quake.

Search for Bodies

This afternoon, many residents of the complex were still milling around in front of the ruined building, at 9565 Reseda Boulevard, as firefighters, sweaty and exhausted, continued to search the debris. Eight hours after the quake, firefighters held out little hope that anyone still trapped would be found alive, but they said they were inserting electronic listening devices into the rubble that could pick up sounds as soft as human breathing. Earlier, they brought in dogs trained to find survivors in building rubble.

There was no power in the area, most of the shops were closed and, in an incongruously festive gesture, people up and down the street had taken to eating half-melted ice cream cakes from a nearby Baskin-Robbins.

The force of the tremor ripped apart homes, businesses, roads and utilities, leaving thousands of people without water, power or shelter.

Reseda Boulevard, a main thoroughfare, resembled a war zone: broken water mains flooded streets; gas permeated the air, fuel for numerous fires that were controlled by the late afternoon. Traffic lights were knocked out, and accidents occurred throughout the area.

Many of the community's 20,000

Continued on Page A19, Column 1

OTHER MAJOR NEWS

U.S.-China Pact Averts Trade Fight

China and the United States reached an 11th-hour textile agreement, averting a major clash about the $7.3 billion in Chinese textiles sold annually in the American market.

The Clinton Administration had threatened to reduce Chinese textile imports by more than $1 billion unless a new agreement could be signed to end persistent instances of cheating by Chinese companies. Page D1.

Israelis Are Hopeful But Cautious on Syria

Israel said it saw a promise of peace, but expressed caution about remarks by Syria's President that he was ready for normal relations. "Normalization was also mentioned by the Syrians in the past," Prime Minister Yitzhak Rabin said. Page A8.

Facing Down Boos, Giuliani Praises King

After days of criticism over two confrontations between blacks and the police, Mayor Giuliani faced hecklers at a tribute to Martin Luther King Jr. He told his audience, "For you to succeed, I have to succeed." Page B1.

Collapsed Freeways Cripple City Where People Live Behind Wheel

By BERNARD WEINRAUB
Special to The New York Times

LOS ANGELES, Jan. 17 — The earthquake that struck Los Angeles before dawn today crippled crucial freeways, raising the prospect that the American city most defined by its cars and interlocking highways would be gripped by traffic chaos for months.

The city's freeways and highways, mostly built since World War II, soar and wind like roller coasters, often resting atop columns as they crisscross one another. The buckling and collapse today of three heavily traveled elevated portions raised the prospect of at least partial paralysis for a city where the automobile is seen as intrinsic to the region's life.

As a result, city officials said, almost every facet of life for the nine million people in the Los Angeles area is likely to be disrupted for up to a year or more.

With nearly 3 million vehicles using 616.3 miles of freeway in Los Angeles during the evening rush hour, the city's residents are extraordinarily dependent on main highway arteries. The city has never confronted, until today, the possibility that many of these freeways would be partially unusable for long periods.

The city's new subway line, the Metro Red Line, which opened in January 1993, is expected to offer little help. It runs through just 4.4 miles of downtown Los Angeles, from Union Station to MacArthur Park.

'Not Going to Be Easy'

The area's Metrolink commuter trains will operate on Tuesday, though some stations and stretches of track that were damaged will be closed. The service will add passenger cars to trains on the line from Santa Clarita and Antelope Valley, the Associated Press reported. Freeways linking those areas to Los Angeles were severed by the quake.

"It's not going to be easy," a grim Mayor Richard J. Riordan said this afternoon as Gov. Pete Wilson stood beside him.

Patricia Reid, a spokesman at Cal

Continued on Page A18, Column 1

Lives and Nerves Shattered, but Not Civility

By JANE GROSS
Special to The New York Times

LOS ANGELES, Jan. 17 — Ventura Boulevard, the main thoroughfare through the devastated San Fernando Valley, was ghostly this morning, its shops a shambles, its sidewalks littered with broken glass, its traffic signals out and its automatic teller machines useless.

But the stillness was misleading.

Behind a shuttered Thrifty drugstore in the Studio City section, where the aisles were clogged with fallen ceiling tiles, a tangle of toys and broken cosmetic bottles, employees peddled batteries and flashlights to a stunned throng of men and women still shaking from the jolt of a lifetime, which occurred before dawn.

"I need a good flashlight! And eight D batteries! And a couple of Triple A's! And one of those heavy-duty things!" sputtered one man in line, as harried clerks dispensed these limited goods from a shopping cart and apologized that nothing else was for sale because the store was knee-deep in ruined merchandise.

Across the region — from the eastern edge of the San Fernando Valley, where buildings shuddered and fell, to the graffiti-scarred streets of downtown, to the manicured confines of Beverly Hills and Pasadena — residents were stunned and shaken, but largely composed.

Some homes were ruined. Most were without power. Some lacked telephone service. And all of their inhabitants were shaken to the core. But residents of the City of Angels, where disasters have lately been heaped one upon the other, kept their heads.

The closest thing to bedlam, as of nightfall, was the scene at Hughes Market, the only open grocery store for

Continued on Page A19, Column 6

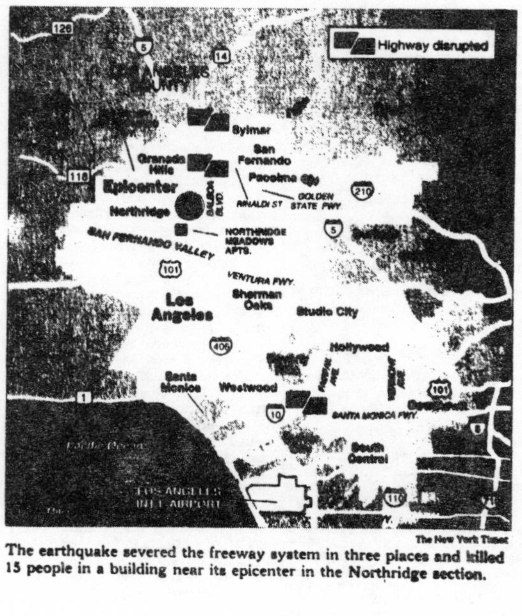

The New York Times

The earthquake severed the freeway system in three places and killed 15 people in a building near its epicenter in the Northridge section.

"All the News That's Fit to Print"

The New York Times

Late Edition

New York: **Today,** showers then clouds. High 61. **Tonight,** clearing. Low 51. **Tomorrow,** sun, scattered showers, thunder. High 66. **Yesterday,** high 66, low 51. Details, page C14.

VOL.CXLIII . . . No. 49,686 | NEW YORK, THURSDAY, MAY 5, 1994 | 50 CENTS

75 cents beyond the greater New York metropolitan area.

RABIN AND ARAFAT SIGN ACCORD ENDING ISRAEL'S 27-YEAR HOLD ON JERICHO AND THE GAZA STRIP

CEREMONY IN CAIRO

Pact Approved Despite Last-Minute Dispute Over Boundaries

By CHRIS HEDGES

Special to The New York Times

CAIRO, May 4 — Israel and the P.L.O. signed an agreement today that formally begins Israel's withdrawal from the Gaza Strip and the Jericho area of the West Bank — lands occupied for 27 years — and grants Palestinians a measure of self-government for the first time, though not sovereignty.

The accord, which follows up the agreement in principle signed in September in Washington, opens a new chapter in the Middle East. It provides for the possibility of Palestinian control of an area whose occupation by Israel has been a focus of Arab anger for decades, and holds out the chance for reconciliation between Israeli and Palestinian.

But for any of that to happen, there will have to be further agreements between Israel and the Palestine Liberation Organization during the next five years. During that time the Palestinians will be tested to show that they can govern the limited areas now being given to them.

The World Bank and many countries, including the United States, are committed to helping the Palestinian authority, as it is called, to survive.

The ceremonies here were led by President Hosni Mubarak of Egypt, whose country has been the only Arab land to make peace with Israel, and were attended by many dignitaries. The agreement was signed by Prime Minister Yitzhak Rabin of Israel and Yasir Arafat, chairman of the P.L.O.

Until last summer's negotiations leading up to the White House signing in September, the Israelis and the P.L.O. had been bitter enemies; now they are united in defending their accord.

Mr. Arafat, whose name was once anathema to Israelis, described the accord as a "true beginning — to complete the march of peace, guarantee the legitimate rights of the Palestinian people, and realize justice and equality." [Excerpts from speeches and from the agreement are on pages A16 and A18.]

But the ceremony faltered in a last-minute dispute over the boundaries of Jericho, and the Palestinian leader signed only after 35 awkward minutes of on- and off-stage negotiations with Mr. Mubarak and Secretary of State Warren Christopher.

After the heated consultations, Mr. Arafat added a handwritten note that

Continued on Page A16, Column 1

Agence France-Presse

Yasir Arafat caused an uproar in Cairo yesterday when he refused to sign part of the accord. Discussing the issue, which was resolved after 35 minutes of heated talks, were, from left, Foreign Minister Shimon Peres of Israel, Foreign Minister Andrei V. Kozyrev of Russia, Prime Minister Yitzhak Rabin of Israel, Foreign Minister Amr Moussa and President Hosni Mubarak of Egypt, and Mr. Arafat.

Arafat Signs and the Gaza Strip Shrugs

Some Palestinians Feel Only Abiding Distrust After a Long Wait

By CLYDE HABERMAN

Special to The New York Times

SHATI, Gaza Strip, May 4 — The picture was fuzzy on the balky old television set, but it was clear enough for Salameh al-Arouqi. What he saw did not please him one bit.

There was Yasir Arafat, master of political pyrotechnics and chairman of the Palestine Liberation Organization, taking out his pen to sign the agreement that he had finally reached with Prime Minister Yitzhak Rabin of Israel.

"Don't sign, you donkey, stop!" Mr. Arouqi shouted at the screen, which he watched with several friends in the bare three-room house in this coastal refugee camp that his family of 11 fills to the brim.

When Mr. Arafat paid him no mind and put pen to paper, Mr. Arouqi, who supports a P.L.O. faction opposed to the chairman, pressed his lips together and said quietly, "He's signing his own execution."

"For years we have been fighting and suffering, and this is the result — this silly document?" he said. "What is Gaza and Jericho?"

Not much, agreed the half-dozen friends who sat or knelt on cushions in the Arouqi home, watching the signing ceremony from Cairo.

Theirs was a widely shared view today across the Gaza Strip, where the dominant sound in ramshackle refugee camps and along garbage-lined city streets was that of one hand clapping even though this was one of those rare days that qualified immediately as historic.

With the signing, Israeli control formally ended over little Jericho in the West Bank and over teeming Gaza, except for buffer zones around the 19 Jewish settlements in the strip. It meant that for the first time Israel had ceded authority in Palestinian areas that it captured in the 1967 Arab-Israeli war. It meant that Palestinian police officers could start pouring in and Israeli soldiers start heading home. It meant a chance, effectively the first, to show that Palestinians can rule themselves without terrifying their neighbors.

In short, it was a big deal.

Yet while so much seemed to change, nothing actually did, and most of the 800,000 or so Gazans went about their daily business, ignoring the Cairo events or shrugging them

Continued on Page A17, Column 1

Agence France-Presse

In Jericho, Children Celebrate

The self-rule accord got a mixed reaction among Palestinians. While many went about their business with hardly a shrug, these children decorated a fence around the Israeli police station with flowers. Page A17.

Defense Dept. May Postpone Base Closings

Economic and Political Factors Are at Work

By ERIC SCHMITT

Special to The New York Times

WASHINGTON, May 4 — Fearful of damaging the economies of scores of communities nationwide, the Defense Department is preparing to seek authority to delay some decisions on base closings until after the 1996 elections, a senior Pentagon official said today.

Congress would have to approve such a plan. But Defense Secretary William J. Perry and Deputy Defense Secretary John M. Deutch favor dividing a final round of decisions scheduled for next year into two parts: choosing next year to close some bases and then waiting until 1997 or 1998 to decide the fate of many others, the official said.

By doing so, Mr. Perry and Mr. Deutch would place political and economic considerations above the strong objections of the Joint Chiefs of Staff, who are counting on saving billions of dollars by closing installations as quickly as possible to pay for future weapons, training and troop salaries.

Moreover, it would inject a political element into a process Congress invented four years ago specifically to be as free as possible from political influence. Critics say there is clearly a political incentive for President Clinton and some members of Congress to delay or diminish the economic pain of base closings until after the 1996 elections, or at least to limit closings in states like California, Texas and Florida, pivotal battlegrounds in 1996.

Three independent commissions, meeting in 1988, 1991 and 1993, have decided to close 70 major installations. It takes five to six years to shut a base. Lawmakers and Pentagon officials have predicted that the 1995 round of decisions, scheduled to be the last one, could close more installations than the previous three combined.

"As the defense budget goes down and we close bases, the issue now is the pace of closures so people and communities can adjust," the senior

Continued on Page B14, Column 1

11 MORE OFFICERS TAKEN OFF DUTIES IN 30TH PRECINCT

NEW YORK INQUIRY GROWS

25 of 191 Assigned Have Now Been Removed and Bratton Expects More to Follow

By CLIFFORD KRAUSS

Eleven more police officers were taken off the job in the 30th Precinct in Harlem yesterday, as a corruption investigation into the precinct continued to grow. A Federal investigator said the 11 were suspected of either knowing of or participating in crimes like stealing, selling drugs and shaking down drug dealers.

The officers' guns and badges were confiscated and they were placed on desk duty with pay. Police Commissioner William J. Bratton would not detail the accusations against them, except to say they were "very significant and disturbing."

But a Federal investigator said the allegations were linked to the previous corruption uncovered in the precinct in northwest Harlem, in which 14 officers have been arrested on charges including narcotics conspiracy, robbery, assault and civil-rights violations. The investigator, who spoke on the condition that he not be named, said the 11 officers now under investigation knew of, witnessed or participated in those crimes.

Police officials said several of the 11 officers would probably be suspended in the next few weeks, while others would be arrested on criminal charges. The Federal investigator said the department decided to move against the officers first because the charges were imminent.

The reassignment of the 11 officers — known as "modified assignment" in department jargon — brings to 25 the number of officers taken out of the 191-member precinct. Commissioner Bratton has said that more officers would be arrested in the 30th Precinct, and last month he estimated that 25 percent of the precinct might be implicated.

Yesterday, the Commissioner repeated his assessment that corrup-

Continued on Page B4, Column 4

Nations Help to Back Dollar As U.S. Acts to Show Resolve

By THOMAS L. FRIEDMAN

Special to The New York Times

WASHINGTON, May 4 — The United States teamed up with the central banks of 16 other nations today to buy dollars in a global campaign intended to show investors that the Clinton Administration is serious about maintaining the value of the ailing American currency.

It was the first such coordinated intervention since August 1992, and involved the Treasury Department and the Federal Reserve, joining with the central banks of Germany, France, Japan and 13 other countries. The move was planned in a series of secret phone calls overnight.

The dollar was sharply higher against the German mark and the Japanese yen in late trading in New York today, although it started to slip again near the end of the day. It ended at 1.6531 marks, up from 1.6370 on Tuesday, and at 101.88 yen, up from 101 on Tuesday.

Senior American Treasury officials said the main objective of Friday's effort and today's much larger intervention to support the dollar was to counter what they saw as a widening perception in global currency markets that the Administration was ready to allow the dollar to drift lower, either as matter of deliberate policy or of benign neglect.

But the real question is whether this kind of market intervention alone can change the mood in trading

Continued on Page D20, Column 1

Federal Judge Says Ban on Suicide Aid Is Unconstitutional

By TIMOTHY EGAN

Special to The New York Times

SEATTLE, May 4 — Abortion and suicide, two ends of the spectrum of life, have been linked for the first time by a Federal judge, who ruled on Tuesday that the Constitution guarantees people not only the right to terminate pregnancies without Government interference, but also the right to end their own lives.

In striking down a 140-year-old Washington State ban on assisted suicide, Judge Barbara Rothstein of United States District Court in Seattle said the law violated the 14th Amendment clause against state infringement of individual liberty.

"The suffering of a terminally ill person cannot be deemed any less intimate or personal, or any less deserving of protection from unwarranted governmental interference than that of a pregnant woman," Judge Rothstein wrote in her ruling on Tuesday.

The decision, the first by a Federal court on assisted suicide, came one day after a Michigan jury acquitted Dr. Jack Kevorkian of charges that he had violated that state's law against helping people kill themselves.

After Judge Rothstein's ruling, a group in Seattle that has been helping terminally ill people end their lives

Continued on Page A24, Column 1

INSIDE

Tokyo Official Speaks Out

A senior minister in Japan declared that the massacre of Chinese at Nanjing was a "fabrication." Page A9.

A Season for Goodbyes

In northern New England, the burying of those who died in winter is an unfailing sign of spring. Page A22.

Pact Breaks Grip of New York School Custodians

By CHARISSE JONES

Union negotiators for New York City's school custodians have agreed to concessions that would reduce the custodians' control over school buildings, a breakthrough that School Chancellor Ramon C. Cortines said would make schools cleaner for children and more accessible to community groups.

The tentative agreement between the union and the Board of Education, which is subject to the approval of union members and the Mayor's office, would effectively create a system of controls tying the promotion of the school system's 853 custodians to their job performance rather than seniority, and holding them accountable to the principals at their schools.

No longer would some custodians be able to set their own cleaning standards, opting for example to mop the bathrooms or sweep the floors of a school once a week if they chose. Instead, their cleaning responsibilities would be established by the custodian, the principal and a plant manager. The principal would have the primary responsibility to evaluate the custodians' performance every six months and decide whether or not those standards are being met.

"This tentative contract is not a small change from the previous one, as most labor settlements are," Chancellor Cortines said in a written statement. "It's revolutionary."

But while school officials applauded the tentative agreement, officials with the Mayor's office complained about how they learned of the agreement and what it included. They said they were informed of the preliminary settlement by press release and

Continued on Page B8, Column 3

Outcome of Voting In Zulu Heartland Remains in Doubt

By KENNETH B. NOBLE

Special to The New York Times

DURBAN, South Africa, May 4 — The outcome of elections in the volatile Zulu heartland of Natal remained uncertain today, with new vote totals showing a tight race between the African National Congress and its longtime adversary, the Inkatha Freedom Party.

Even though the polls closed five days ago, the battle for control of South Africa's most fiercely contested province intensified as officials of the Congress and Inkatha accused each other of widespread cheating. The latest tally showed the congress behind by 5 percentage points, with about half the vote still uncounted.

"We believe Inkatha had its own pirate polling stations, 54 of them," Ronnie Mamoepa, an African National Congress spokesman said. Other irregularities alleged by the African National Congress included tampering with the plastic seals used to close ballot boxes, chasing electoral monitors from polling stations and intimidating voters.

The Inkatha leader, Chief Mangosuthu G. Buthelezi, described the ac-

Continued on Page A13, Column 1

"All the News That's Fit to Print"

The New York Times

Late Edition

New York: Today, sunny with a few high clouds. High 75. Tonight, breezy, mild. Low 60. Tomorrow, showers, windy, cooler. High 68. Yesterday, high 72, low 54. Details, page B14.

VOL.CXLIII . . . No. 49,693 | NEW YORK, WEDNESDAY, MAY 11, 1994 | 75 cents beyond the greater New York metropolitan area. | 50 CENTS

SOUTH AFRICANS HAIL PRESIDENT MANDELA; FIRST BLACK LEADER PLEDGES RACIAL UNITY

Reuters

Nelson Mandela takes the oath of office as President from Chief Justice Michael Corbett in Pretoria.

DE KLERK PRAISED

An Inauguration Tumult for 'the Old Man' and His Diverse Guests

By BILL KELLER

Special to The New York Times

PRETORIA, South Africa, May 10 — With the commanding dignity that has carried him through more than half a century of defiance, captivity and conciliation, Nelson Rolihlahla Mandela became the first black President of South Africa today.

He stood before a crowd of world leaders who shunned this capital during its decades of infamy, and in a husky, resolute voice swore the oath to become the 10th leader of South Africa since its union in 1910, but the first elected with the participation of the black majority.

Then the 75-year-old leader opened his presidency with an intimate speech of shared patriotism, speaking of South Africans' common exhilaration in the seasons and the soil, their common pain for their country's humiliation before the world and their shared relief at being readmitted to the company of civilized nations.

"Never, never, and never again shall it be that this beautiful land will again experience the oppression of one by another and suffer the indignity of being the skunk of the world," he said. [Transcript, page A8.]

As a token of renewal, Mr. Mandela promised that an amnesty would soon be announced for "various categories" of prisoners.

He lavished praise on F. W. de Klerk, the President who collaborated with him in negotiating the end of white rule and who today took the oath as one of Mr. Mandela's two Vice Presidents in a unity Government.

In a post-inaugural visit to the 50,000 ordinary citizens celebrating on the lawn far below the Government buildings, Mr. Mandela held Mr. de Klerk's hand aloft and hailed his predecessor as "one of the greatest reformers, one of the greatest sons of our soil."

For the day, at least, blacks and whites were united by the mutual strain of taking in the recently unimaginable:

There was Fidel Castro on his first visit to the country that tried to pulverize his army in Angola, the only one among the scores of dignitaries singled out by the crowd for lusty shouts of "Viva!"

And Muslim and Hindu prayers broadcast into the air of what has been the most rigidly, officially Christian of capitals.

And the Navy band in dress whites entertaining the inaugural dignitaries with a Zulu migrant labor song.

And finally President Nelson Mandela, now Commander in Chief, reviewing the defense force that was built, in large part, to prevent some-

Continued on Page A8, Column 1

Dance for Joy! Come Dance a Toyi-Toyi!

By FRANCIS X. CLINES

Special to The New York Times

PRETORIA, South Africa, May 10 — Hours before Nelson Mandela took possession of the Government, and had his air force delight an outdoor throng with a fly-over wafting rainbow-hued vapors, Elsie Njokweni was dancing her shoes off in the most fitting of places.

She was a bobbing, crooning blur aboard one of the packed commuter trains from the Soweto ghetto, traditionally a sardine-can affair for the ostracized black underclass of apartheid, but today a vessel of historic exultation.

Numerous trains clacked and boomed along the rails with the special chanted resistance songs and the foot-stomping dances known as toyi-toyi that South African blacks turned into a swarming political art form in defeating racist oppression.

"I was arrested six years ago for behaving this way," Mrs. Njokweni said, sliding into a toyi-toyi with hip-swaying grace to join her neighbors from Soweto Extension No. 1, southwest of Johannesburg.

It was soon after dawn when they all crammed and capered onto one of the ceremonial excursion trains that carried scores of thousands of ordinary people to the grand Government Lawn to witness President Mandela's inaugural triumph.

Whatever the exuberance level of the formally choreographed proceedings, most of the watching world missed the full truth of South Africans' joy, not being aboard the toyi-toyi train nor trying to keep up with Mrs. Njokweni and three generations of her neighbors.

They were leaping, scuttling and back-sliding into a pounding version of "Hold On, Boys," a work-song for barracks laborers near the breaking point, a song intended to snatch courage from intimidation.

"Your gun, Mr. Policeman, only reminds me of our hero, Oliver Tambo," the Sowetans sang and danced, in praise of a founder of the African National Congress who died a year ago.

Their noise graced the passing countryside, stirring white suburbanites to wave V-signs and fists of triumph along the three-hour ride. More often, it was blacks looking out suddenly from their track-side shanties

Continued on Page A8, Column 1

Ozier Muhammad/The New York Times

Elsie Njokweni singing on her way to inauguration ceremonies.

Giuliani's Budget Proposes Cuts For Spending and Work Force

By JAMES C. McKINLEY Jr.

Mayor Rudolph W. Giuliani proposed a $31.6 billion budget for New York City yesterday that would reduce spending slightly for the first time in 16 years and sharply cut the municipal work force in almost every major agency except the Police and Fire Departments.

Submitting his first executive budget to the City Council, Mr. Giuliani said the city "has been spending itself beyond its economy" for more than a decade, creating perennial gaps between what it spends and what its tax base can support. The Mayor said the city's overspending had drained the local economy, driving private industry from the city.

"The purpose of this budget is to redirect the economy of New York," Mr. Giuliani said. Saying the city was "hemorrhaging jobs" while the rest of the nation was recovering, Mr. Giuliani added, "We can't employ people through government alone."

In drafting his plan, Mr. Giuliani needed to close a $2.3 billion gap between projected spending and revenues for the fiscal year that begins on July 1. To do that, he has suggested about $1.2 billion in spending cuts from city agencies, mostly through cutting 15,000 workers, or 7 percent of the city-financed work force. Mr. Giuliani said those cuts could be made without serious damage to services if managers learned to run agencies more efficiently. Over all, spending would fall by $102 million.

He also proposed some modest tax cuts totaling about $35 million.

The extent of the service cuts is likely to figure in the debate over Mr. Giuliani's budget as it moves to the City Council, particularly since the budget makes no cuts in the Police or Fire Departments. Already some lawmakers are asking whether protecting those agencies is worth the pain for schools, youth programs and hospitals. [News analysis, page B5.]

Besides cutting jobs, the Mayor relied in his efforts to close the budget gap on some actions that will still require the cooperation of the State Legislature, the Federal Government

Continued on Page B4, Column 4

Closing the Gap

Principal measures the Mayor proposes in his budget for fiscal year 1995 and the **PROJECTED SAVINGS (OR COST)** in millions.

Cuts to spending in city agencies	$1,269
Increased state aid	275
Increased Federal aid	125
Union co-payments for retirees' benefits	200
Refinancing of city debt	225
Asset sales (WNYC-FM, U.N. Plaza Hotel)	110
Changes in payments on pension debt	51
Fiscal year 1994 surplus	98
Cuts in hotel tax and commercial rent tax	(35)
TOTAL SAVINGS	$2,318

Trail of Despair by a Father Leaves 4 Dead and Son Hurt

By CLIFFORD J. LEVY

After being dismissed last week from his $7.50-an-hour job at a paper factory in Brooklyn, Jose Luis Berroa grew despondent about how he would care for his 2-year-old son. He had lived on the grim streets of New York City with little Carlos before, his friends said, and he could not bear to return. So he decided to give Carlos back to the boy's mother, Awilda Enriquez.

But something snapped in Mr. Berroa when he arrived at the home of Ms. Enriquez's family in Newark, something that caused him to go on a rampage that left a trail of death yesterday, ending when he wounded the child and then killed himself after a confrontation with police officers on a stairwell in Washington Heights.

The night before in Newark, Mr. Berroa killed two of Ms. Enriquez's brothers, the police said, and shot to death a woman who had earned a reputation for kindness in the neighborhood by adopting 12 children. [Page B6.] He then fled with the boy in her car and sought refuge in Washington Heights with a woman who had helped him build a new life after he immigrated from Cuba a decade ago.

It was there that his life ended. The police said they caught up with him and, instead of surrendering, Mr. Berroa fired a bullet into his son's face before shooting himself.

He left only two small plastic bags that he lugged from place to place in recent months, his friends said. They contained Carlos's baby clothes and tiny sneakers, a broken toy motorcycle and a box that once held shells for a 9-millimeter gun, the weapon the police said Mr. Berroa had used on his victims and himself.

"He told us he was going crazy about maybe losing the baby," said Georgina Gonzalez, 26, the daughter of Emma Maria, 50, in whose Washington Heights building Mr. Berroa died. She recalled how her mother had persuaded Mr. Berroa to stay with her recently after he had spent much of the winter sleeping on park benches, huddling with the child against the cold.

The police said Mr. Berroa, 33, showed up unexpectedly about 6:30 P.M. on Monday at the home of Ms. Enriquez's family at 231 Sixth Ave-

Continued on Page B6, Column 4

President Is Said to Pick Babbitt For Court Despite Senate Concern

By GWEN IFILL

Special to The New York Times

WASHINGTON, May 10 — In spite of last-minute concerns expressed by members of the Senate over the weekend, President Clinton has settled on Interior Secretary Bruce Babbitt as his nominee to the Supreme Court, officials said today.

A senior White House official said there was a "95 percent chance" that Mr. Babbitt, a former Arizona Governor and Attorney General, would be Mr. Clinton's choice to replace Justice Harry A. Blackmun, who is retiring at the end of the current term. Other advisers said Mr. Clinton was satisfied that Mr. Babbitt could face down any objections.

The President has been leaning toward Mr. Babbitt for several days, but he only disclosed his list of finalists for the Court to senators last weekend in a series of telephone conversations.

Mr. Clinton held a final one-hour meeting with his Supreme Court search team today, and aides said afterward that he was still "going through the calculus" to weigh the selection. One aide acknowledged that Mr. Babbitt could be a "political lightning rod," but said that the White House had determined it could overcome opposition led by Senator Orrin G. Hatch of Utah, the senior Republican on the Senate Judiciary Committee.

In an interview, Senator Hatch described Mr. Babbitt "as a nominee who would be pushed by the far left" and as the kind of judge "who would legislate from the bench laws that the liberal community doesn't have a tinker's chance of getting through the people's elected representatives."

Mr. Hatch suggested that Democratic and Republican senators would join his campaign to block a Babbitt nomination, but two other Western Senators who have tangled with Mr. Babbitt over environmental issues, Harry Reid of Nevada and Ben Nighthorse Campbell of Colorado, said today that they would welcome his

Continued on Page A17, Column 1

Fetal Harm Is Cited As Primary Hazard In Dioxin Exposure

By KEITH SCHNEIDER

In a report on dioxin, scientists at the Environmental Protection Agency have concluded that cancer is not the most serious health hazard at common exposure levels. Of greater concern, their report said, are subtle effects on fetal development and the immune system that may be the result of very low levels of exposure.

The scientists said that most people already have levels of dioxin in their bodies at or near the concentrations that cause such fetal and immune system problems in laboratory animals.

This new assessment of the risk of dioxin, one of a class of toxic chlorine-based compounds present everywhere in the environment, comes in a draft summary of a 2,000-page report scheduled to be made public this summer. The conclusion, that current levels of exposure may already pose human health problems, is based on new mathematical assumptions that have not been published in scientific journals.

And it has already caused a storm of dissent in Federal agencies, principally in the Food and Drug Administration and the Department of Agri-

Continued on Page A20, Column 1

Associated Press

Agence France-Presse

A Rare Sight

A solar eclipse darkened skies yesterday at midday in a 150-mile-deep swath across the United States. Sunlight filtered through tree branches in Chicago, above, projected the rare annular eclipse. Page B7.

INSIDE

Italian Government Formed

Italy's right-wing Prime Minister-designate formed a Government after weeks of wrangling, including five seats for neo-Fascists. Page A5.

Identifying a Real Lobbyist

The Government's new 30-page description of lobbying imposes micrometer precision on an activity that seemed kind of obvious. Page A16.

Collapse at Christie's

At an auction of Impressionist and modern art, only 38 of 76 works were sold; proceeds fell nearly $40 million below estimates. Page C18.

"All the News
That's Fit to Print"

The New York Times

Late Edition

New York: **Today,** clouds then sun, not as cool. High 65. **Tonight,** some clouds. Low 55. **Tomorrow,** partly sunny, pleasant. High 75. **Yesterday,** high 54, low 48. Details, page B10.

VOL.CXLIII . . . . No. 49,702 NEW YORK, FRIDAY, MAY 20, 1994 — 75 cents beyond the greater New York metropolitan area. 50 CENTS

Jacqueline Kennedy Onassis Dies of Cancer at 64

Widow of President, Ailing, Spent Final Day at Her Home

By ROBERT D. McFADDEN

Jacqueline Kennedy Onassis, the widow of President John F. Kennedy and of the Greek shipping magnate Aristotle Onassis, died of a form of cancer of the lymphatic system yesterday at her apartment in New York City. She was 64 years old.

Mrs. Onassis, who had enjoyed robust good health nearly all her life, began being treated for non-Hodgkin's lymphoma in early January and had been undergoing chemotherapy and other treatments in recent months while continuing her work as a book editor and her social, family and other personal routines.

But the disease, which attacks lymph nodes, an important component of the body's immune system, grew progressively worse. Mrs. Onassis entered the New York Hospital-Cornell Medical Center for the last time on Monday but returned to her Fifth Avenue apartment on Wednesday after her doctors said there was no more they could do.

In recent years Mrs. Onassis had lived quietly but not in seclusion, working at Doubleday; joining efforts to preserve historic New York buildings; spending time with her son, daughter and grandchildren; jogging in Central Park; getting away to her estates in New Jersey, at Hyannis, Mass., and on Martha's Vineyard, and going about town with Maurice Tempelsman, a financier who had become her closest companion.

She almost never granted interviews on her past — the last was nearly 30 years ago — and for decades she had not spoken publicly about Mr. Kennedy, his Presidency or their marriage.

Although she was one of the world's most famous women — an object of fascination to generations of Americans and the subject of countless articles and books that re-explored the myths and realities of the Kennedy years, the terrible images of the President's 1963 assassination in Dallas, and her made-for-tabloids marriage to the wealthy Mr. Onassis — she was a quintessentially private person, poised and glamorous, but shy and aloof.

They were qualities that spoke of her upbringing in the wealthy and fiercely independent Bouvier and Auchincloss families, of mansion life in East Hampton and Newport, commodious apartments in New York and Paris, of Miss Porter's finishing school and Vasser College and circles that valued a woman's skill with a verse-pen or a watercolor brush, at the reins of a chestnut mare or the center of a whirling charity cotillion.

She was only 23, working as an inquiring photographer for a Washington newspaper and taking in the capital nightlife of restaurants and parties, when she met John F. Kennedy, the young bachelor Congressman from Massachusetts, at a dinner party in 1952. She thought him quixot-

Continued on Page B8, Column 1

Susan Ragan/Associated Press, 1992

Jacqueline Kennedy Onassis

18 NAMED IN GRAFT TIED TO PROJECTS FOR SCHOOL BOARD

NEW YORK OFFICIALS HELD

Lease and Maintenance Unit, Shorn of Power to Build, Is Still Under Fire by U.S.

By SAM DILLON

Federal prosecutors charged yesterday that the division of the Board of Education that maintains schools and leases space remained rife with corruption, five years after it was stripped of the power to build new schools because of earlier scandals.

The prosecutors charged a senior lawyer for the Board of Education who resigned last week and 17 other people with paying or accepting bribes for awarding contracts, approving fake invoices and expediting board payments to contractors.

The sweeping charges against former board officials as well as lawyers and contractors underline how the Board of Education's management of its 1,100 buildings continues to be a target for bribery, fraud and racketeering, even though the State Legislature stripped the board of its power to build schools in 1989.

Before 1989, the racketeering detailed in the indictments focused largely on the construction of school buildings, particularly the badly botched construction of Fiorello H. La Guardia High School in the early 1980's. In 1989, after the La Guardia debacle and other troubles, the Legislature turned construction over to a new agency, the School Construction Authority, to stanch corruption in building schools. That agency was not involved in yesterday's allegations.

According to the indictments, since the change in 1989, corruption has largely focused on activities that have remained the responsibility of the board's Facilities Division, including leasing and renovating commercial buildings for use as schools, and removing asbestos and lead.

Because enrollments have surged amid the city's financial difficulties, the board has leased increasing numbers of buildings in recent years for use as schools and offices.

Responding to the indictments, the seven-member Board of Education voted in a closed session yesterday to suspend all new leasing, except the leasing of classroom space for the fall

Continued on Page B2, Column 4

Wide Immunity For Presidents Gains Support

Justice Dept. to Make Argument for Clinton

By NEIL A. LEWIS
Special to The New York Times

WASHINGTON, May 19 — The Justice Department is preparing to tell a Federal judge that the sexual harassment suit brought against President Clinton should be dismissed or delayed indefinitely because Presidents are entitled to broad immunity from lawsuits while in office, Administration officials said today.

The Justice Department argument is being readied to support a motion that Mr. Clinton's private lawyer, Robert S. Bennett, plans to file soon in Federal court in Little Rock. Mr. Bennett will ask that the suit brought by Paula Corbin Jones, a former Arkansas state employee, be dismissed or postponed until after the President leaves office. Mr. Bennett has indicated that he will argue that the President should be given immunity from all lawsuits because the need to defend himself would distract him from his official duties and throw the Government into disarray.

The Administration officials said that the Justice Department's Office of Legal Counsel is preparing a brief for the court that would back Mr. Bennett's claim of broad immunity for Presidents from civil lawsuits, even those resulting from actions before they take office.

Mr. Bennett's overall strategy is to crush Ms. Jones's suit at the earliest possible stage or to delay it until Mr. Clinton leaves office, according to a senior White House adviser who spoke on condition of anonymity.

The goal of Mr. Bennett and the President's other advisers is to avoid the spectacle of Mr. Clinton's testifying under oath about his behavior three years ago. Ms. Jones says in her legal complaint, which was filed on May 5, that she was invited to meet Mr. Clinton, then governor of Arkansas, in a Little Rock hotel room, where she alleges he made an explicit sexual overture.

White House officials acknowledged that Mr. Bennett's tactics were driven largely by political considerations, arising from the sexual nature of Ms. Jones's charges. "If this goes all the way to trial and the President wins, he will have really lost politically," said the senior White House adviser.

The official also said that any actions associated with the lawsuit, like

Continued on Page B20, Column 4

EXPERTS SAY U.S. FAILS TO ACCOUNT FOR ITS PLUTONIUM

DANGER OF THEFT IS CITED

Officials Say New Estimates Have Erased Large Gap in Bomb Fuel Inventory

By WILLIAM J. BROAD

Energy Secretary Hazel R. O'Leary's campaign to open the nation's atomic complex to public scrutiny has stumbled on the seeming inability of her department to assemble reliable figures on its production of plutonium, the main ingredient of nuclear warheads.

Experts say crude tallies and shifting numbers raise new doubts about the Government's attention to detail in guarding one of the deadliest substances on earth. In the past, private experts have charged that Federal plants were sloppy and prime targets for atomic theft and diversion.

The current trouble arose when private experts at the Natural Resources Defense Council, which specializes in nuclear issues, found a discrepancy between their calculations of plutonium production and what Mrs. O'Leary had announced last Dec. 7. The gap was 1.5 metric tons, enough to make 300 nuclear weapons.

Federal officials play down the discrepancy and say they have raised their production estimate to erase virtually all of the calculated gap. But the private experts accuse the Government of a laxity that raises questions about the plutonium's whereabouts.

Inconsistent numbers might also have diplomatic repercussions, since the declassified figures on plutonium production that Mrs. O'Leary delivered to her counterpart in Russia have turned out to be wrong.

"The accounting is not what it should have been," Michael Gauldin, the Energy Department's chief spokesman, said in an interview. "We've been trying to reconstruct the stuff from the early days and having a hard time."

Dr. Thomas B. Cochran, a senior scientist at the Natural Resources Defense Council in Washington, said: "The Government has never been through this accounting exercise before. That's troubling. Banks do this kind of thing once a day."

If Russia reported such discrepancies, some experts say, the West would be shocked.

Dr. Everet H. Beckner, a senior Federal official involved in tracking the nuclear materials and their production history, said the problem was nothing more than harmless errors of accounting and production. But Dr. Beckner added that the Energy Department, which runs the nation's nuclear complex, was committed to clearing up all apparent discrepancies.

"There are technical differences that need to be resolved," Dr. Beckner said in an interview. "And we think it's important to resolve them."

In atomic bombs, plutonium is often the sole ingredient fueling the nuclear blast; in hydrogen bombs, it is used as an atomic trigger to ignite

Continued on Page A19, Column 1

Clinton Spells Out Reasons He Might Use Force in Haiti

By DOUGLAS JEHL
Special to The New York Times

WASHINGTON, May 19 — President Clinton today offered the clearest explanation yet of why his Administration is considering the use of military force in Haiti while resisting it elsewhere in the world.

"It's in our backyard," the President said at a White House news conference as he ticked off the first in a list of six reasons why he is weighing military action to oust Haiti's leaders if economic sanctions do not force them to step down.

He said Haiti's proximity to the United States and the danger that more of its citizens could seek refuge in southern Florida meant that his Administration had an obligation to promote an end to the military dictatorship there.

Mr. Clinton's comments, in response to a question at a joint appearance with India's Prime Minister, also represented a response to Republican critics who say it would be wrong to risk American lives to restore the exiled President, the Rev. Jean-Bertrand Aristide.

With a tighter United Nations embargo on Haiti to take effect at midnight on Saturday, aides to Mr. Clinton emphasized that no American military action there was imminent. After facing criticism on past occasions in which the Administration has appeared to back away from tough talk on Bosnia, the aides said no decision on whether to use military force in Haiti would be made until the sanctions have been given time to work.

But with opinion polls showing mounting public dissatisfaction with his conduct of foreign policy, the aides say that Mr. Clinton has grown concerned that he has failed to cast the challenges he faces in proper context and that, in particular, he has not adequately explained why his Administration is suddenly devoting so much attention to Haiti after 32 months of military tyranny there.

A senior White House official, who said Mr. Clinton had planned his an-

Continued on Page A2, Column 3

Looser Rules on Water

Eight years after it voted for drastic tightening of the purity standards for tap water, the Senate decided to loosen them again. But whether the changes would increase the tiny risks of drinking tap water was in dispute, as environmentalists argued that the strict standards were warranted.

Article, page A12.

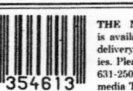

Angel Franco/The New York Times

Cause for Celebration, Twice

Barnard College graduates were showered with confetti and the fizz from a celebratory bottle yesterday as they joined their counterparts from Columbia University at commencement. The Barnard students, who celebrated at their own ceremony on Wednesday, received degrees yesterday. Page B6.

Vietnamese Also Extending A Search for Their M.I.A.'s

By MALCOLM W. BROWNE
Special to The New York Times

Vietnam Revisited
A periodic report.

HANOI, Vietnam — "For 2,000 years, wars have seeded our land with the bones of the missing in action," the general told a visitor, "and the American war produced a particularly rich crop. We'll never find most of our own dead soldiers, but they remain in our hearts."

The speaker, Maj. Gen. Nguyen Trong Vinh, spent most of his 68 years fighting the French and the Americans, and he now publishes a monthly magazine for North Vietnamese and Vietcong veterans listing grave sites and missing soldiers and guerrillas.

Sometimes families who see the photographs, eyewitness reports and maps that the magazine publishes have been able to identify the resting places of missing husbands, fathers and sons.

The quest by the United States for its war dead and missing in Vietnam seems to have brought increased efforts by Hanoi to account for Communist troops who remain missing.

Besides offering information that might help identify Communist dead, ordinary Vietnamese also sometimes respond to an American advertisement in the yellow pages of Hanoi's telephone book that asks for information that could lead to the recovery of American bones. The Veterans of Foreign Wars, which has given Hanoi a few tips on where to look for Vietcong remains, has thanked the Vietnamese who have helped in the search for American servicemen.

Most Vietnamese families gave up hope many years ago of learning the fates of their missing, most of whom were buried where they fell. During the war, this correspondent saw the unidentified corpses of hundreds of Communist soldiers shoveled into unmarked mass graves all over South

Continued on Page A8, Column 1

One of Africa's Last Dictators Bows to Democracy

By BILL KELLER
Special to The New York Times

JOHANNESBURG, May 19 — The last prominent ruler in the generation of African strongmen who displaced the European colonialists, Hastings Kamuzu Banda of Malawi, conceded today that voters had decisively ended his autocratic 30-year personality cult.

The self-proclaimed Life President, an eccentric leader in three-piece suit and homburg, accepted defeat in an extraordinary show of mutual graciousness. After a vote widely acclaimed as peaceful and fair, Dr. Banda, who is in his 90's, offered his cooperation to the new Government and was offered in turn generous praise and a comfortable pension.

"I consider him to be a father of the nation," said Bakili Muluzi, the victor, in a telephone interview tonight from his home in Blantyre. "Therefore we definitely want to look after him as much as possible. We are not looking for vengeance or retribution at all."

The President-elect is a 51-year-old businessman whose style is more Chamber of Commerce than inquisitional Star Chamber. He served in Dr. Banda's Cabinet and rose to the second-highest position in the governing party before resigning in 1982 because, he said tonight, he suspected Dr. Banda might have him killed.

Malawi is a land-locked sliver of mountain and lake whose 9.7 million people are among the poorest in the world.

Dr. Banda (he earned a medical degree from Meharry Medical College in Tennessee) outlasted all but one of the original African nationalists who took power from colonialists in the 1950's and 1960's and stamped

Continued on Page A10, Column 1

INSIDE

Insurer to Offer Clinic Care

Anticipating sweeping health care changes, New Jersey's largest health insurer plans to establish a statewide system of private clinics. Page B1.

A Long Night for the Icemen

Stephane Matteau's goal at 6 minutes 13 seconds of double overtime gave the Rangers a 3-2 victory over the New Jersey Devils. Page B11.

Tennis Star Seeks Treatment

Jennifer Capriati, arrested Monday on a drug charge, has entered a Miami rehabilitation facility. Page B11.

"All the News That's Fit to Print"

The New York Times

Late Edition

New York: **Today,** hot and humid, a few thunderstorms. High 95. **Tonight,** partly cloudy. Low 71. **Tomorrow,** sunny, cooler. High 84. **Yesterday,** high 92, low 72. Details are on page 33.

VOL.CXLIII . . No. 49,732

NEW YORK, SUNDAY, JUNE 19, 1994

$2.50 beyond the greater New York metropolitan area.

TWO DOLLARS

Simpson, Under Suicide Watch, Is Jailed on 2 Murder Charges

Former Football Star Is Described as Crying And Despondent

Associated Press

The police photo of O. J. Simpson being booked late Friday.

By SETH MYDANS

Special to The New York Times

LOS ANGELES, June 18 — O. J. Simpson, whose thrilling play on the football field seemed to symbolize freedom, today sat locked in a 9-foot-by-7-foot jail cell on a double-murder charge with only a toilet, a sink and a bunk for furnishings.

The authorities said they had taken sharp objects, shoelaces and his belt away from Mr. Simpson, who was described by his lawyer as being in tears today. Every few minutes, officials said, a deputy peered through a window into his cell to make sure he did not kill himself.

Mr. Simpson was admitted to Men's Central Jail at 10:20 on Friday night, said Sheriff's Deputy Angie McLaughlin, and was held without bail. His entry into jail ended an extraordinary day in which he was charged with murder in the slayings of his former wife and her friend, disappeared, and then led the police on a bizarre 90-minute tour of the freeways, broadcast live on television nationwide, before surrendering meekly at his house.

Al Cowlings, Mr. Simpson's driver in the chase, was freed early today on $250,000 bail after being arrested and booked for aiding and abetting a fugitive, the police said.

The police said Mr. Simpson could be arraigned as early as Monday, beginning what could be a long legal journey that will explore the brutal double killings of Nicole Brown Simpson, 35, and her friend Ronald Goldman, 25. On Friday, in a desperate open letter his lawyer described as a suicide note, Mr. Simpson denied involvement in the slayings.

Today, the lawyer, Robert Shapiro, talked to Mr. Simpson by telephone, and said his jailed client was deeply depressed and crying. "As bad as he has been in the past four days, it's the worst I've ever heard him," Mr. Shapiro, told The Associated Press.

The police's handling of the case was being scrutinized today, with politicians and former police officials criticizing what they saw as lax treatment that allowed Mr. Simpson to escape and elude capture for nearly nine hours. [Page 21.]

There was a sense of awe in the city today at the bizarreness of the spectacle as Mr. Simpson, holding a gun to his head, led the police on a low-speed

Continued on Page 20, Column 1

POLL FINDS A LACK OF FAITH IN POLICE

New Yorkers Concerned Over Protection and Integrity

By CLIFFORD KRAUSS

New Yorkers express anxiety about the Police Department's ability to protect them, and many say there is widespread corruption in the force, according to a New York Times/WCBS-TV News Poll.

The survey and follow-up interviews suggest a serious lack of confidence in the department because of a fear of crime and concern over revelations of corruption in several precincts.

Despite police reports of a slight though steady decrease in crime over the last four years, the poll found a general perception that crime has increased or remained at the same levels as last year. More than a third of those polled said that because of their fear of crime they had moved to new neighborhoods or were planning to. Many, especially in Hispanic and black neighborhoods, say they have taken measures like riding the subway less, staying home at night or avoiding places that they used to go to.

The telephone poll of 1,189 adult residents conducted from June 12 to June 15 is just a snapshot, and the extent to which opinions might have changed recently is uncertain, because many questions were asked for the first time. But the findings suggest that the image of the department is badly bruised just when it is introducing new crime-fighting strategies that rely on community cooperation, like having beat officers seek intelligence on drug dealers and gun traffickers from residents.

The worries about crime and police performance span racial, economic and ethnic lines. But skepticism about the Police Department is expressed most strongly by minority-

Continued on Page 30, Column 1

Liz Gilbert/Sygma, for The New York Times

Africa is falling further behind the rest of the world in health, education and general living standards. In Nairobi, Kenya, a health clinic sits next to an open sewer in a suburban shantytown.

'Lost Decade' Drains Africa's Vitality

Survival Test

Can Africa Rebound?

First of three articles.

By JOHN DARNTON

Special to The New York Times

OUAGADOUGOU, Burkina Faso — You don't have to be a detective to spot the decline in living standards in Africa. It hits you right away.

It can be seen in the shantytowns that surround every capital city, sprawls of humanity living in hovels with no windows, open sewers and garbage heaped in mounds chest-high.

It can be heard in the lessons sung out in ancient schoolrooms, where enrollments are dropping and yet class sizes swell to 120 pupils.

And it can be smelled in the fly-infested corridors of hospitals where diseases flourish, medication is scarce and people are increasingly turned away or left to suffer because they cannot afford treatment.

The countries south of the Sahara, the traditional division between black Africa and the Arab world, have turned in a decade and more of devastatingly bad economic performance. The economic failure is undercutting a drive for political liberalization, raising ethnic rivalries to a dangerous level and forcing countries to impose politically inflammatory austerity programs, often under the dictates of Western financial institutions.

But most of all it is spreading misery. In living standards, Africa is falling further behind the rest of the world. It is now the only continent where most poor people are getting still poorer and where health and education are deteriorating.

As political changes similar to those that shook Eastern Europe and the Soviet Union four and five years ago now reverberate in Africa, Africans seem more concerned about the social and welfare problems caused by the economic decline. Their views emerged during scores of interviews in the course of a six-week trip through nine countries in East, West and Southern Africa.

The statistics roll by in a blur: More than four million children born this year will die before the age of five. Nearly one-third of children are severely malnourished. One in three goes without primary school education.

But it is the individuals who remain fixed in memo-

Continued on Page 10, Column 1

ACCORD REACHED TO END WALKOUT AGAINST L.I.R.R.

PARTIAL SERVICE TODAY

Railroad Yields on Work Rules After Learning Congress Is Reluctant to Intervene

By MATTHEW L. WALD

Special to The New York Times

MELVILLE, L.I., June 18 — The Long Island Rail Road reached a contract agreement with its largest union late tonight, capitulating on work rule issues, after officials concluded that Congress would not step in soon to stop the strike.

The chairman of the Metropolitan Transportation Authority, Peter E. Stangl, appearing before reporters shortly before 11 P.M., said he had decided to settle the strike by giving up. "I made a decision that I'd pay the ransom before it got too bad out there," he said.

Mr. Stangl said he had been advised by Gov. Mario M. Cuomo and members of the state's Congressional delegation that Congress might not act soon. Senator Daniel Patrick Moynihan said the chance of Congressional action was "about 50-50."

Appearing after Mr. Stangl, Edward J. Yule Jr., the chairman of the United Transportation Union, said there was no ransom. "Ransom? I should have his money," Mr. Yule said of Mr. Stangl.

"That's called collective bargaining," he added. "We worked at this. I don't think we're winners."

Mr. Stangl said that between the pay package that had been agreed to and the failure to change the work rules, the accord would cost about $14 million more than the authority's last offer before the strike.

The deal ends a strike that began early Friday and promises limited service on Sunday and a normal Monday rush hour for 107,000 commuters.

The agreement was reached after a marathon day that began about 7:30 A.M., with the two sides meeting in separate rooms at the Huntington Hilton Hotel here, sending emissaries from room to room and conferring in hallways, elevators and the parking lot. The last contract expired nearly two and a half years ago.

But the deciding factor appears to have been Mr. Stangl's conclusion that he could not count on action by the Congress.

Presuming that the agreement is ratified by the union membership and the board of the M.T.A., it will be retroactive to Jan. 1, 1992, and will expire on New Year's Eve this year. Under the terms of the Railway Labor Act, the M.T.A. will send a notice to the union to begin renegotiation six months in advance of the expiration, which is less than two weeks from now. The schedule for the ratification vote was not certain tonight.

Governor Cuomo issued a statement saying, "We are grateful to the M.T.A. and the unions for saving the entire region from an enormous amount of inconvenience and damage. Reasonableness prevailed."

But the M.T.A.'s chief negotiator, Gary Dellaverson, said that the concession on work rules was "exceptionally damaging" to his agency's effort to win productivity improve-

Continued on Page 28, Column 3

Two Koreas Plan Summit Talks on Nuclear Issue

By DAVID E. SANGER

Special to The New York Times

SEOUL, South Korea, June 18 — For the first time since the Korean peninsula was divided five decades ago, the Presidents of North and South Korea agreed today to hold a summit meeting, which is likely to focus on defusing tensions over the North's suspected effort to build a nuclear weapon.

The agreement was brokered by former President Jimmy Carter, who delivered the offer from North Korea's 82-year-old leader, Kim Il Sung, after returning to Seoul this morning from a three-day visit to Pyongyang.

South Korea's President, Kim Young Sam, immediately met Mr. Carter at Blue House, the presidential mansion in the mountains ringing Seoul, and told him that "the sooner the better," aides said.

But South Korean officials acknowledged that there was reason to question whether a summit meeting between the two countries, still technically at war, would ever take place. They noted that many agreements between North and South have been thrown onto the scrap heap.

The state-run Korean Broadcasting System suggested in a television analysis tonight that "this could be another attempt by the North to buy time and escape from a tense situation."

Mr. Carter also used his visit to deliver a stinging critique of the Clinton Administration's strategy of seeking United Nations sanctions against the North as part of an effort to force Mr. Kim to give up his nuclear weapons program.

At a news conference outside the American Ambassador's house here, Mr. Carter said he believed that economic sanctions were doomed to failure and would do nothing but further poison relations between the North and the rest of the world.

"The declaration of sanctions by the U.N. would be regarded as an insult by them, branding it as an outlaw country," he said. It would also constitute "a personal insult to their so-called Great Leader," Kim Il Sung, Mr. Carter said, "by branding him as a liar and a criminal.

"This is something in my opinion

Continued on Page 12, Column 3

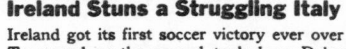

Life, Meet TV

The broadcasts of the fugitive's stately procession along California highways seemed so real because the scene differed so much from television's professionally crafted reality.

The Week in Review, Section 4.

David Cannon/Allsport

Ireland Stuns a Struggling Italy

Ireland got its first soccer victory ever over Italy, 1-0, in the World Cup opening round. Ireland's Andy Townsend, on the ground, took down Roberto Baggio at the Meadowlands. SportsSunday, section 8.

A Bitter Harvest for Ukraine From an American Seed Deal

By RAYMOND BONNER with JAMES BENNET

Special to The New York Times

KIEV, Ukraine — When an American company ventured into Ukraine last year with a deal to sell $70 million of corn seeds, herbicides and expensive farm equipment, it was hailed here and in Washington as a historic vote of confidence in this struggling nation and a model for cooperation between American businesses and former Communist countries.

Now, a year later, the deal looks like a model of a different sort, an embarrassing instance in which American companies took advantage of a country in turmoil to dispose of poor quality seeds it could not sell in the United States and reap large profits.

"It's a very black page," said David Sweere, chairman of the agriculture committee of the American Chamber of Commerce in Ukraine. "There was a time when the Ukrainian farmer held the American farmer in very high regard. Now, they have lost respect for us, because of deals like this. Yes, we in the West believe in commercial gain. But if that is your only goal, then this is what happens."

Some farms planted the seed and grew nothing. Most of the combines never moved from their sheds. And while the American seed company and brokers have been paid, Ukraine is struggling to repay the $70 million to Citibank, which financed the deal. If the country fails to repay the money, the United States Export-Import Bank, which guaranteed the loan, will have to repay it, a cost ultimately borne by American taxpayers.

The Ex-Im Bank, which promotes business abroad, is refusing to do business in Ukraine, partly because of the economic conditions here and delinquencies on the loan. This has dealt a blow to the Clinton Adminis-

Continued on Page 14, Column 1

INSIDE

Fear of No Health Care Bill

As the fight to overhaul health care enters a crucial phase, a powerful pressure on Congress is a possibility that was unthinkable until recently: that there might not be a major health care bill this year. Page 18.

6 Slain in Northern Ireland

Gunmen killed six people watching Ireland's World Cup soccer victory over Italy in a Northern Ireland pub, the police said. The militant Protestant Ulster Volunteer Force claimed responsibility. Page 5.

TODAY'S SECTIONS

** In New York City and the metropolitan region. († Elsewhere, auto pages are in section 3.)*

§ In most parts of New York City.

¶ In Long Island, Westchester, Connecticut and central and northern New Jersey.

"All the News That's Fit to Print"

The New York Times

Late Edition

New York: **Today,** mostly cloudy, mild, a drizzle. High 68. **Tonight,** cloudy, cooler late. Low 47. **Tomorrow,** some sun. High 58. **Yesterday,** high 70, low 48. Details, page D26.

VOL.CXLIV . No. 49,875

NEW YORK, WEDNESDAY, NOVEMBER 9, 1994

75 cents beyond the greater New York metropolitan area

60 CENTS

G.O.P. WINS CONTROL OF SENATE AND MAKES BIG GAINS IN HOUSE; PATAKI DENIES CUOMO 4TH TERM

OTHER HIGHLIGHTS

VIRGINIA

In Brutal Battle, Robb Defeats North

Robb

North

Chuck Robb, a one-term Democrat, narrowly defeated Oliver North. Mr. North, the former national security aide to President Ronald Reagan, rallied an intensely loyal following among the religious right, opponents of gun control laws and bitter voters wanting to shake up Washington. But his involvement in the Iran-contra affair proved more damaging than the allegations of marital misconduct against Mr. Robb. Page B3.

In what may have been the bitterest fight of a bitter year, Senator

GOVERNORSHIPS

Wilson and Weld Win; Bushes Split

Republicans swept all but one of the major governors' races. Gov. Pete Wilson, given up for politically dead two years ago as California staggered through a fierce recession, completed a stunning comeback by trouncing State Treasurer Kathleen Brown. Page B4.

In Masschusetts, Gov. William F. Weld easily turned back State Representative Mark Roosevelt, establishing himself as a possible player in the 1996 Republican Presidential sweepstakes. Page B3.

For two sons of President George Bush, it was a split decision, but not in the way experts had predicted. George W. Bush was elected in Texas, upsetting the incumbent, Ann Richards. But his younger brother, Jeb Bush, lost to Gov. Lawton Chiles in a close race in Florida.

G.W. Bush

Wilson

The Texas triumph was sweet revenge against one of President Bush's antagonists. The battle was close to the end, with Ms. Richards buoyed by the last-minute support of Ross Perot. Jeb Bush, a newcomer considered more conservative than his father, had been favored against the veteran Mr. Chiles. Page B4.

MASSACHUSETTS

Kennedy Beats Back Romney

Kennedy

Senator Edward M. Kennedy proved that after more than three decades on Capitol Hill, he is not ripe for replacing. In the toughest race of his career, the 62-year-old Senator beat a political newcomer with a large personal fortune and another famous name, Mitt Romney.

Mr. Romney, the 47-year-old son of George W. Romney, the former Governor of Michigan, had tried to tap this year's anti-incumbent fervor, arguing that it was time for a change, but on the stump and in political debates, Senator Kennedy underscored his long experience, his command of the issues and his intimacy with the legislative process.

ILLINOIS

Chicago Earthquake: Rostenkowski Is Out

If any seat in the House seemed safe at the outset of the year, it was that of Dan Rostenkowski of Chicago, longtime chairman of the House Ways and Means Committee. But reeling under an indictment and an anti-Democratic wave in Illinois, the 66-year-old Mr. Rostenkowski lost to a 31-year-old political neophyte, Michael Patrick Flanagan. Page B2.

NEW YORK

Moynihan Wins A Fourth Term

Moynihan

In a year when liberal incumbents faced stiff challenges from the right, Senator Daniel Patrick Moynihan, a Democrat who is the chairman of the Senate Finance Committee, easily defeated the Republican candidate, Bernadette Castro. Page B12.

TENNESSEE

A Senate Sweep For the G.O.P.

Tennessee had two Democratic Senators. Now it will have two Republicans. Jim Sasser, a three-term Democratic incumbent who is chairman of the Senate Budget Committee and a close ally of President Clinton, lost to William Frist, a wealthy heart and lung surgeon who has never held public office.

And Fred Dalton Thompson, a lawyer for the Republicans on the Senate Watergate committee in 1973, defeated Representative Jim Cooper for the seat left vacant when Al Gore was elected Vice President. Page B3.

WASHINGTON, D.C.

The Redemption Of Marion Barry

Barry

Marion Barry came back from the ignominy of a drug conviction to return as Mayor of Washington, despite a strong challenge from Carol Schwartz. In 1990, after 11 years as Mayor, Mr. Barry was videotaped smoking crack in a hotel room. In this campaign, he stressed his strength of character in overcoming his weaknesses. Page B4.

PENNSYLVANIA

Upset Winner in '90 Is the Loser in '94

A pitched battle of ideological opposites ended with Representative Rick Santorum, a conservative Republican, narrowly defeating Senator Harris Wofford, a liberal Democrat. Mr. Santorum had aggressively promoted less government, lower taxes, more military spending and his opposition to a ban on assault weapons. Mr. Wofford, whose own upset victory four years ago put health care at the top of the national agenda, made Social Security the pivotal issue in this election.

OHIO Metzenbaum's seat goes to the G.O.P.

NEW YORK Maloney defeats Millard on the Upper East Side.

TERM LIMITS Approved in Maine, Nebraska and Washington, D.C..

THE ELECTIONS: SECTION B

G. Paul Burnett/The New York Times

George E. Pataki celebrating at his Manhattan headquarters last night with his wife, Libby, after defeating Gov. Mario M. Cuomo. At right was Elizabeth McCaughey, who won election as Lieutenant Governor.

New York Voters End a Democratic Era

By KEVIN SACK

George Elmer Pataki, a lanky lawyer-legislator from the Hudson Valley who has promised to slash income taxes and restore the death penalty, was elected the 53d Governor of New York yesterday, ending 20 years of Democratic rule in Albany and toppling Mario M. Cuomo, a legendary figure in state and national politics.

In other New York races, H. Carl McCall became the first black New Yorker to win statewide elected office, defeating Herbert London in the race for state comptroller. Mr. McCall, a former State Senator, investment banker and president of the New York City Board of Education, was appointed Comptroller by the Legislature last year to fill a vacancy left by the midterm retirement of Edward V. Regan.

In the race for attorney general, the Republican, Dennis C. Vacco, a former United States Attorney from Buffalo, won a narrow victory over Karen S. Burstein, a former Family Court judge in Brooklyn.

Senator Daniel Patrick Moynihan, the New York Democrat, easily dispatched his Republican opponent, Bernadette Castro, to win a fourth term. But he lost the chairmanship of the Finance Committee to Senator Bob Packwood of Oregon when the Senate went Republican.

A HOMESPUN IMAGE

State Senator George E. Pataki, who will be New York's 55th Governor, is almost a millionaire, yet he comes off as homespun and unpretentious. Man in the News, page B1.

Mr. Pataki, a 49-year-old State Senator, won by drawing a strong turnout in upstate New York counties where Republicans traditionally fare well, by taking narrow majorities in the suburbs surrounding New York City, by winning Staten Island and by faring well in Erie County.

B. Thomas Golisano, a millionaire businessman from Rochester who was the gubernatorial candidate of the Independence Fusion Party, proved less of a factor than some had anticipated in siphoning anti-Cuomo votes from Mr. Pataki.

With 97 percent of the precincts reporting, the results were:

Pataki	2,405,631 (49%)
Cuomo	2,223,567 (45%)
Golisano	196,327 (4%)

Mr. Pataki's election represents a political triumph for his patron, Senator Alfonse M. D'Amato, and a potentially devastating defeat for Mayor Rudolph W. Giuliani, who alienat-

Continued on Page B11, Column 1

Rowland Wins Connecticut; Lautenberg Edges Haytaian

For the first time in a generation, Connecticut elected a Republican Governor yesterday, John G. Rowland.

His principal campaign promise was to repeal the 3-year-old state income tax, the legacy of Gov. Lowell P. Weicker Jr.

But because Mr. Rowland won only slightly more than a third of the vote in a five-way race, it will not be easy to deliver.

Mr. Rowland, 37, defeated William E. Curry, a Democrat, and Eunice S. Groark, the candidate of Mr. Weicker's A Connecticut Party, which stands to lose its major-party status.

With 98 percent of 820 precincts reporting, the vote was:

Rowland	36%
Curry	33%
Groark	19%
Scott	12%
Zdonczyk	1%

In New Jersey, Senator Frank R. Lautenberg, a Democrat, won a third term, defeating Assembly Speaker Chuck Haytaian, a Trenton insider who had strong support from Gov. Christine Todd Whitman. Mr. Haytaian, tried to portray himself as an outsider during the campaign.

With 99 percent of 6,010 districts reporting, the vote was:

Lautenberg	50%
Haytaian	47%

Mr. Haytaian had been a legislative champion of Mrs. Whitman's plan to reduce state income taxes by 30 percent. But last night she said it had been "difficult to communicate Haytaian's ability to do in Washington what we were able to accomplish here."

Articles, pages B13 and B14.

CONGRESS AT A GLANCE As of 2:00 A.M. Eastern time.

	CURRENT BALANCE	AT STAKE	WINNERS
SENATE			
Democrat	56	22 (6 OPEN)	13
Republican	44	13 (3 OPEN)	21
HOUSE			
Democrat	256	All 435	182
Republican	178	seats	216
Independent	1		1

NEW BALANCE

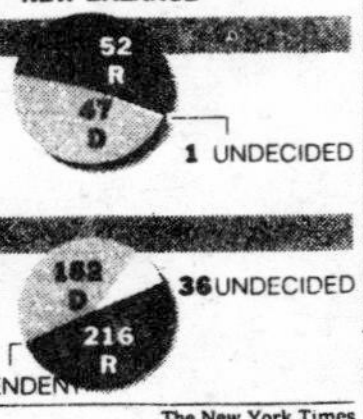

The New York Times

INSIDE

A Boost for Israel Talks

Israel agreed to pick up the pace of talks on Palestinian self-rule in an effort to blunt pressure from Islamic militants on Yasir Arafat. Page A10.

Black Ownership at Denny's

The Denny's chain, which has been accused of bias, said a black-owned company would run up to 47 outletsin the New York area. Page B15.

Bosnian Capital Bombarded

In its worst attack since February, Sarajevo was hit yesterday afternoon by artillery fire, probably from Bosnian Serb positions. Page A8.

BLOW FOR CLINTON

Democratic Mainstays Ousted in Big Upsets Around the Nation

By RICHARD L. BERKE

The Republican Party seized control of the Senate and moved within a few seats of capturing the House yesterday, winning eight Democratic seats in the Senate and at least 38 in the House. The gains were the Republicans' strongest in decades and put them in position to thwart President Clinton and his legislative proposals for the next two years.

The Republican tide also extended to the races for governor in several important states that will be critical to Mr. Clinton's hopes for reelection in 1996, including New York, Pennsylvania, Texas and California.

One after another, once unassailable Democrats like Gov. Mario M. Cuomo, Gov. Ann W. Richards of Texas, Representative Dan Rostenkowski of Chicago and Senators James Sasser of Tennessee and Harris Wofford of Pennsylvania fell to little-known Republican challengers.

But Republicans, who have held the Senate in only 6 of the last 40 years, were particularly overjoyed that they had picked up Democratic Senate seats in Pennsylvania, Michigan, Tennessee, Oklahoma, Minnesota, Michigan and Maine. Mr. Clinton had criss-crossed most of those states in a frenetic eight-day campaign swing, but it did no good. The Republicans ended the night with at least a 52-to-48 majority in the Senate.

"I've never known a better night in electoral politics for the Republican Party, and the best is yet to come," a beaming Bob Dole declared to an overflow crowd at the Republican National Committee headquarters in Washington. Mr. Dole, who will become the majority leader, studiously avoided saying whether he would focus on that job or on running for President in 1996, but the crowd was excited about the party's prospects, chanting, " '96! '96!, '96!"

The Democrats were not completely shut out. Senator Charles S. Robb, a Democrat, defeated Oliver L. North in one of the most closely watched races in a particularly volatile election season, and Senator Edward M. Kennedy of Massachusetts hung on to his seat after the biggest scare of his political life.

In metropolitan area races, two

Continued on Page B5, Column 1

A Vote Against Clinton

By R. W. APPLE Jr.

News Analysis

It was an immoderate campaign, coarse in its tone and unedifying in its substance, and the nation's politics are likely to stay that way for the next two years and beyond.

Dissatisfaction with President Clinton, with liberalism, with the Democratic Party and with Washington in general combined to create a surge by Republicans, especially conservative Republicans. If not quite a tidal wave, yesterday's results swept dozens of incumbents from office and set up two years of intense political confrontation between the White House and Congress.

Republicans will soon control the statehouses in seven of the eight largest states, giving them immensely useful building blocks for the next Presidential election. They will control the Senate for the first time since 1987, and perhaps Congress as a whole for the first time since the Eisenhower era.

Their leader in the House of Representatives, Representative Newt Gingrich, is at heart a revolutionary bent on fundamental change.

This was a realigning election that put the final nails in the coffin of the Solid South, the regional bastion upon which Democratic power was once built. Democratic seats in the House fell all across the region: three in Georgia, four in North Carolina, three in Tennessee.

If the victory of Senator Edward M. Kennedy of Massachusetts provided some balm, the defeats of major party luminaries — Representative Dan Rostenkowski of Illinois and Jack Brooks of Texas, Gov. Ann W. Richards of Texas and Gov. Mario M. Cuomo of New York — sent many Democrats into gloom bordering on despondency.

Stated most simply, the message from the electorate was disgust with big government and impatience with government activism, two of the things with which the Democrats are most closely identified.

The returns constituted a sharp rebuke to Mr. Clinton. Many of those

Continued on Page B5, Column 6

NEWS SUMMARY A2

"All the News That's Fit to Print"

The New York Times

Late Edition

New York: **Today,** cloudy, not as warm. Light rain, mainly east. High 54. **Tonight,** fog. Low 44. **Tomorrow** cloudy, cooler. High 48. **Yesterday** high 58, low 53. Details, page B8

VOL.CXLIV . . No. 49,943

NEW YORK, TUESDAY, JANUARY 17, 1995

75 cents beyond the greater New York metropolitan area. 60 CENTS

AT LEAST 597 ARE KILLED IN JAPANESE QUAKE; KOBE DEVASTATED AS 2,000 BUILDINGS BUCKLE

MANY FIRES IGNITED

Heaviest Urban Losses From Quake Since Tokyo in 1923

By NICHOLAS D. KRISTOF

Special to The New York Times

TOKYO, Tuesday, Jan. 17 — A powerful earthquake shook major cities in western Japan today, killing at least 597 people, starting dozens of fires and trapping hundreds of residents in the wreckage of collapsed buildings.

The national police and other authorities said 2,198 people were injured and 531 missing, and the casualty figures were expected to rise as the authorities combed the rubble. In the initial confusion, the official toll of injured was given as 13,000 but that number was later retracted.

The earthquake occurred at 5:46 A.M. (3:46 P.M. on Monday, Eastern time), when most people were still in their beds.

Today's temblor, which measured 7.2 on the Richter scale, apparently was the biggest to hit urban areas of Japan since a catastrophic quake struck Tokyo in 1923. Building collapses and widespread fires killed an estimated 140,000 in that quake.

While this morning's quake was not nearly so lethal, it caused enormous amounts of structural damage in one of Japan's most important economic zones. But there was no damage reported in Tokyo, where the quake could scarcely be felt.

Kobe, a major port city of 1.4 million people 280 miles west of Tokyo, bore the brunt. A modern industrial hub that was rebuilt after World War II, Kobe was covered by black smoke caused by more than 70 fires. Fires were still raging out of control eight hours after the quake.

An elevated freeway toppled on its side like a long ribbon, smashing cars beside it. Rescuers frantically searched through 2,000 collapsed buildings in Kobe.

The Government held an emergency cabinet meeting and dispatched troops to search the rubble with specially trained dogs.

"Mother! Mother!" a man in his 20's called out, as a television crew filmed him wandering over the debris of what had been his house. He stared blankly at the shattered

Continued on Page A6, Column 1

The New York Times

Center of quake was near Kobe.

Associated Press

Part of the Hanshin Expressway, which runs from Kobe to Osaka, collapsed in Nishinomiya, near Kobe.

Flu Casts Fevered Misery Across New York Region

By ELISABETH ROSENTHAL

Although her cubicle at the emergency room at St. Luke's-Roosevelt Hospital Center was uncomfortably warm, Martha Rivera of Manhattan wrapped herself in a sweater, scarf and thick winter coat, huddling fruitlessly against a chill that came from deep within.

"Oh, my God," she said. "I have never felt so terrible."

Her eyes were sunken, her nose red. "My joints hurt," she went on. "I have a splitting headache. Chills. A sore throat. A cough. My fever is 104. I feel like an old lady." (She is only 54.)

Two rooms down, Dan Auerbach, a 21-year-old violin student at Juilliard, slumped in his chair, coughing weakly; his shoes were untied, his hair on end. He had canceled all appointments for the day in deference to a cough, a high fever and a headache that would not go away.

The flu and cold season has singled out New York with particular fury this year. While much of the country has remained unusually healthy this winter, many New Yorkers have coughed, sneezed and wheezed their way into the new year.

Based on the surveillance system used by the Centers for Disease Control and Prevention and the World Health Organization, as of Jan. 6 more than 60 percent of the nation's flu cases were in New York, with Connecticut, Kentucky, Maryland and Virginia also reporting significant numbers of flu cases.

Most of the cases have been caused by the Shangdong strain of the influenza A virus. The strain is new to this country, so people have had no time to develop resistance to it, which may in part explain the large number of cases and their severity, experts say.

In addition to the flu, doctors say they have been deluged by patients with unusually severe coughs and intestinal problems.

"There seems to be a lot out there right now," said Steven J. Matthews a spokesman for the New York City Department of Health. "Probably a lot of what people are suffering from is not really the flu. But you know what? If you got it, it don't make no difference."

Hospital emergency depart-

Continued on Page B2, Column 1

New York City's Undying Deficit: Slash It, and It Just Grows Back

By ALISON MITCHELL

Although he has already slashed $2 billion from city programs, Mayor Rudolph W. Giuliani still faces another budget gap in the next 18 months that will be as large, if not larger.

And those grim figures do not take into account the real possibility of large cuts in aid from Washington and from Albany, where Gov. George E. Pataki is looking for ways to solve the state's own budget gaps and make good on his campaign promise of major cuts in taxes and spending.

"It's very, very bad," said City Comptroller Alan G. Hevesi. "The decisions are increasingly painful."

With business, sales and personal income tax collections all running lower than expected in December, the administration's first task is to close a gap now estimated at $600 million to $700 million in the $31.6 billion budget before the fiscal year ends in June.

At the same time, the Mayor must prepare a budget for next year to close a gap ranging from $2 billion, as his budget director predicts, to well above $2.5 billion, as several outside monitors expect.

To get through the year, administration officials are scrutinizing everything from a one-shot debt refinancing to cuts in contracts with nonprofit social-service providers. Next year, they are looking at vast reductions in welfare and Medicaid, as well as the elimination and consolidation of scores of city programs.

The municipal unions, which all open new rounds of contract talks with the city this year, have been told that there will be no raises that are not paid for through increased productivity.

The recurrence of annual $2 billion deficits testifies to the depth of the city's fiscal problems. When he came into office a year ago, inheriting a $2.3 billion deficit, Mr. Giuliani, the first Republican Mayor in more than two decades, promised to end New York City's long tradition of expansive government. And he has worked single-mindedly to carry out that pledge, despite demonstrations by constituent groups, a court battle with the City Council and growing criticisms from parents troubled by reductions in school aid and closing youth programs.

He won City Council approval for a budget that reduced city spending for the first time in 16 years, and removed 15,000 workers from the

Continued on Page B3, Column 1

Russian Guns Pound Deeper in Chechen Capital

By ALESSANDRA STANLEY

Special to The New York Times

GROZNY, Russia, Jan. 16 — Russian bombers and helicopters swung low over the capital of the secessionist region of Chechnya today, and artillery pounded deeper south toward Chechen-held territory. The besieged Chechen rebels, who say they have forced the Russians to retreat from some buildings in the city, appeared tired and dangerously edgy.

As artillery and rocket fire continued to hit the capital, Grozny, the Russian Prime Minister, Viktor S. Chernomyrdin, appeared on television in Moscow. He called for immediate peace talks and a cease-fire in Chechnya, where the Russian military campaign to seize control from the secessionist government entered its sixth week today.

Mr. Chernomyrdin, who has proposed such talks before, said that any negotiations would mean the end to the attacks in and around Grozny.

"Our main goal today," he said, "is to stop the bloodshed." As before, however, he blamed "illegal armed bands" in Chechnya for the war.

The children of Grozny, the capital are becoming hardened to the violence around them.

Ramon Gabayev, 10, had no words to describe the rain of fire that has turned his neighborhood into a burned-out ruin, and little to say even about the sniper fire that wounded his mother in front of his eyes. He stood silent and embar-

Continued on Page A8, Column 3

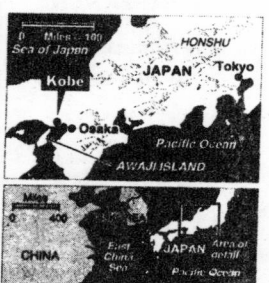

Reuters

In the besieged Chechen capital, a handicapped woman and a dog competed for a piece of meat.

Women's Five at Connecticut Make a Perfect Season Better

By MALCOLM MORAN

Special to The New York Times

STORRS, Conn., Jan. 16 — The players' joyful faces and the noise from all around transformed a basketball game into a milepost. And nobody wanted to leave.

The women from the University of Connecticut reached uncharted territory today by defeating the top-ranked Lady Vols of Tennessee. Their victory came before a roaring full house of 8,241 fans in Gampel Pavilion, before a national television audience and at the expense of the team whose three national championships make it the standard for challengers in women's college basketball.

The 77-66 victory was the 13th for the unbeaten and second-ranked Huskies this season, left them in position to become the top-ranked team in the nation for the first time, and preserved the only perfect record for men's and women's teams at the same major college.

This was the 25th time the top two women's teams had met in the 19 years that The Associated Press has conducted a women's poll. And it became the frantic start of a day that would turn the disease identified as Husky Mania into an epidemic.

The women received a standing ovation at the Hartford Civic Center tonight, where they held red roses

Continued on Page B11, Column 3

INSIDE

Budget Measure Unknowns

It is a good bet that an amendment calling for a balanced budget will pass the House of Representatives, but few can say what form the measure will take. Page A16.

Spotlight on Greenspan

Alan Greenspan, chairman of the Federal Reserve, is taking a more visible role in issues normally be beyond his purview. Page D1.

Red Sprites and Blue Jets

Researchers have spotted bizarre lightning bolts, some red and others blue, that shoot upward from thunderheads. Science Times, page C1.

Bishop Is Found Dead

Bishop David E. Johnson, who was retiring as leader of the largest Episcopal diocese in the nation, apparently committed suicide. Page B7.

"All the News That's Fit to Print"

The New York Times

Late Edition

New York: **Today,** sunny, mild, light winds. High 71. **Tonight,** increasing clouds. Low 50. **Tomorrow,** cloudy, cool, occasional rain. High 59. **Yesterday,** high 76, low 51. Details, page C13.

VOL.CXLIV . . . No. 50,037

NEW YORK, THURSDAY, APRIL 20, 1995

$1 beyond the greater New York metropolitan area. 60 CENTS

AT LEAST 31 ARE DEAD, SCORES ARE MISSING AFTER CAR BOMB ATTACK IN OKLAHOMA CITY WRECKS 9-STORY FEDERAL OFFICE BUILDING

CLUES ARE LACKING

U.S. Officials Scurry for Answers — Reno to Ask Death Penalty

By DAVID JOHNSTON

WASHINGTON, April 19 — The Federal authorities opened an intensive hunt today for whoever bombed a Federal office building in Oklahoma City, and proceeded on the theory that the bombing was a terrorist attack against the Government, law-enforcement officials said.

President Clinton appeared this afternoon in the White House press room and somberly promised that the Government would hunt down the "evil cowards" responsible. "These people are killers," he said, "and must be treated like killers."

Attorney General Janet Reno, speaking to reporters at the White House in early evening, said that casualty figures from the scene were climbing and that of the 550 people who worked in the building, 300 were unaccounted for.

Ms. Reno said Federal prosecutors would seek the death penalty against the bombers. "The death penalty is available," she said, "and we will seek it."

But questions about the identity of the bombers swirled around the case. The only solid fact was the explosion itself.

Some law-enforcement officials said the bombing might be linked to the second anniversary today of the F.B.I.'s ill-fated assault on the Branch Davidian compound near Waco, Tex., an operation that ended in a fire that killed about 80 people, including many children. Among the offices housed by the Federal building in Oklahoma City was one quartering local agents of the Bureau of Alcohol, Tobacco and Firearms, the agency that Branch Davidians and their sympathizers blamed for the confrontation.

But other officials said that neither the Branch Davidians nor right-wing "militia" groups that have protested the Government's handling of the Davidians were believed to have the technical exper-

Continued on Page B8, Column 1

David Longstreath/Associated Press

12 Victims Were Children in 2d-Floor Day-Care Center

By JOHN KIFNER

OKLAHOMA CITY, April 19 — A car bomb went off with a thunderous explosion here this morning, ripping through a Federal office building, collapsing walls and floors, and killing at least 31 people. Many others were buried in the wreckage, and the death toll seemed certain to rise.

At least 12 children whose parents had just dropped them off at a second-floor day-care center were among those immediately known dead in the deadliest bombing in the United States in 75 years.

As dusk fell, scores of the more than 500 people who normally work in the building were still missing. John Hansen, an Assistant Oklahoma City Fire Chief, said it appeared that dead and wounded victims were underneath the piles of concrete, plaster and glass. Late tonight, rain fell from the gray clouds that had threatened for much of the day, adding hardship to horror and raising the possibility the wreckage would shift, imperiling the trapped injured and their rescuers.

The National Guard has been called in, and late tonight limited martial law was declared to keep the streets clear.

Reflecting on the early report of the death toll, Fire Chief Gary Marrs said, "We're sure that it will go up, because we've seen fatalities in the building."

At the White House, President Clinton convened an inter-agency task force to coordinate Federal assistance and called on Americans to pray for the dead and stricken. He also dispatched a small army of Federal investigators to Oklahoma and pledged a relentless hunt for the killers.

Attorney General Janet Reno, noting that the dead children ranged from 1 to 7 years old, and that some had been burned beyond recognition in the day-care center just above the curb where the bomb detonated, said the crime was a capital one and that the Government would seek the death penalty if those responsible were caught. She also said that there were 550 people working in the building and that about 300 were still unaccounted for.

By late tonight, no one had claimed responsibility for the bombing, which occurred on the second anniversary of the Federal raid on

Associated Press

The Alfred P. Murrah building in Oklahoma City before its north side, facing left, was bombed.

the Branch Davidian compound near Waco, Tex., in which David Koresh and scores of his followers perished. There was no evidence that today's bombing, which was similar in intensity to the World Trade Center bombing in New York two years ago, but far more deadly, was linked to the Davidians.

Rescue teams, bringing in backhoes, bulldozers and other heavy equipment, dug in the rubble tonight in darkness, rain and a cutting wind, searching for victims in the flattened center of the nine-story Alfred P. Murrah Building.

Three survivors were pulled out of the wreckage by firefighters shortly after 9:30 P.M. There were cries from a woman in the basement, firefighters said, but they were having difficulty getting to her because there appeared to be bodies in the way. That vignette of horror was just one of hundreds played out all day long, from morning to dark.

Federal buildings in seven other cities were evacuated because of bomb threats, and security was tightened at Government buildings from coast to coast.

Shards of glass littered the street around the Federal building here, and much of the masonry was literally peeled away from the building, leaving a gaping nine-story hole. Federal Bureau of Investigation agents in bright yellow rain slickers,

Continued on Page B9, Column 1

OTHER NEWS

Gas Fumes Create Panic in Yokohama

In a chilling reminder of the gas attack last month in Tokyo, caustic fumes spread through Yokohama's railroad station and through a train, sending about 300 people to hospitals. No one took responsibility for release of the gas. Page A10.

Court Upholds Anonymity

In a decision threatening state election laws, the Supreme Court ruled the Constitution guarantees the right to distribute anonymous campaign literature. Page A20. Add two more lines of type in all.

Lugar Declares Candidacy

Saying he has an unblemished character, Senator Richard Lugar of Indiana announced that he would seek the Republican nomination for President in 1996. Page A16.

Mayor Wants to End Relief

A day after touting the success of new rules for a welfare program, Mayor Giuliani said he really favors abolishing the program. Page B1.

Charles H. Porter IV/Associated Press

Emergency workers remove a child injured in the explosion in downtown Oklahoma City, which occurred as employees began reporting for work yesterday. At least 31 were killed, including numerous children at a day-care center, and scores were injured or missing, some still buried in the rubble.

In Shock, Loathing, Denial: 'This Doesn't Happen Here'

By RICK BRAGG

OKLAHOMA CITY, April 19 — Before the dust and the rage had a chance to settle, a chilly rain started to fall on the blasted-out wreck of what had once been an office building, and on the shoulders of the small army of police, firefighters and medical technicians that surrounded it.

They were not used to this, if anyone is. On any other day, they would have answered calls to kitchen fires, domestic disputes, or even a cat up a tree. Oklahoma City is still, in some ways, a small town, said the people who live here.

This morning, as the blast trembled the morning coffee in cups miles away, the outside world came crashing hard onto Oklahoma City.

"I just took part in a surgery where a little boy had part of his brain hanging out of his head," said Terry Jones, a medical technician, as he searched in his pocket for a cigarette. Behind him, firefighters picked carefully through the skeleton of the building, still searching for the living and the dead.

"You tell me," he said, "how can anyone have so little respect for human life."

The shock of what the rescuers found in the rubble had long since worn off, replaced with a loathing for the people who had planted the bomb that killed their friends, neighbors and children.

One by one they said the same thing: this does not happen here. It happens in countries so far away, so different, they might as well be on the dark side of the moon. It happens in New York. It happens in Europe.

It does not happen in a place where, debarking at the airport, passengers see a woman holding a sign that welcomes them to the Lieutenant Governor's annual turkey shoot.

It does not happen in a city that has a sign just outside the city limits, "Oklahoma City, Home of Vince Gill," the country singer.

"We're just a little old cowtown," said Bill Finn, a grime-covered firefighter who propped himself wearily up against a brick wall as the rain turned the dust to mud on his face. "You can't get no more Middle America than Oklahoma City. You

Continued on Page B11, Column 1

More on the Blast

THE RESCUE When rescuers found the hundreds of cut, burned and terrified victims, it became a matter of grasping for the living while trying to ignore the dead. Page B10.

AROUND THE NATION Shocked and fearful, government officials at Federal, state and some local levels shut down offices in at least eight cities, including New York. Page B10.

THE BOMB The powerful bomb was very likely made of ingredients that are widely available from gardening centers, chemical suppliers and gasoline stations. Page B8.

"All the News That's Fit to Print"

The New York Times

Late Edition

New York: **Today,** becoming mostly sunny, mild. High 79. **Tonight,** mainly clear. Low 61. **Tomorrow,** sunshine and high clouds. High 77. **Yesterday,** high 75, low 50. Details, page B10.

VOL.CXLV . . . No. 50,202 | *NEW YORK, MONDAY, OCTOBER 2, 1995* | $1 beyond the greater New York metropolitan area. | *60 CENTS*

Reuters

Play On

The Yankees will play in their first post-season since 1981, facing Seattle or California tomorrow night. SportsMonday, page C1.

CLINTON TO EASE COMPUTER SALES

Advanced Models Would Be More Eligible for Export

By STEPHEN ENGELBERG

WASHINGTON, Oct. 1 — President Clinton is preparing to relax restrictions on the export of high-performance computers, handing a long-sought victory to the technology companies whose executives were among the most ardent supporters of his 1992 campaign.

Opponents of the move, including some on Capitol Hill and within the Administration, fear that the powerful American computers will be diverted to military uses, like the design of missiles or nuclear weapons.

Administration officials who support the proposal that is before Mr. Clinton say it recognizes a technological reality: computer manufacturers are making vastly more powerful machines every year. What the Administration defined two years ago as a supercomputer requiring Government approval for sale abroad is today a widely available desktop computer used by businesses from banks to movie animators.

The proposal, Administration officials said, would help American manufacturers sell billions of dollars of powerful computers to civilian customers in China, Russia, Israel, Pakistan and India.

They said exports to military customers in those countries would remain under tighter controls.

"If you try to control the uncontrollable, it's not tough and pious," one senior official said. "It's feckless

Continued on Page A2, Column 3

INSIDE

Jury to Center Stage

The jury in the O. J. Simpson case now has a decision to make, and among the endless supply of jury watchers, there is no agreement on what that decision will be or how long it will take. Page B9.

China Accepts Clinton Offer

China says that if the White House lacks the "political will" to honor its President with a formal visit in Washington, "a summit meeting in New York will do." Page A6.

Race to Reopen Subway Line

After a construction mishap shut one of the city's busiest subway lines, transit officials scrambled to avert chaos in the morning rush. Page B1.

Meaning Behind the Music

The Metropolitan Opera's $2.7 million titling system is to be unveiled tonight, as the season opens with "Otello." Page C11.

DOLE HINTS SWITCH ON TAX CUT PLAN BY SENATE G.O.P.

GINGRICH DISPUTES VIEW

Speaker Cites Party 'Contract' — the Senate Leader Sees Other Budget Needs

By JERRY GRAY

WASHINGTON, Oct. 1 — Senator Bob Dole, the majority leader, raised the prospect today that Senate Republicans might not go along with the entire $245 billion in tax cuts that they had agreed to with their House counterparts. But Speaker Newt Gingrich immediately took issue with the idea, vowing that he and the House were inexorably committed to the full reduction.

"There will be tax cuts," Mr. Dole said on the CBS News program "Face The Nation." But he went on: "There will be credits, child credits for families with children. Will it be $245 billion? I'm not certain at this point."

Mr. Dole's pronouncement was the first time he had spoken so pessimistically in public about the tax cut, and it came at a time when opinion polls showed that the Democratic strategy of linking budget cuts and planned reductions in Medicare and Medicaid with "a tax cut for the wealthy" was starting to take hold with the public.

Mr. Gingrich, appearing on the ABC program "This Week," said it would be "virtually impossible" to win approval in the House for a smaller tax cut.

"I don't think that the House Republicans who were elected on the Contract With America," Mr. Gingrich said, "are going to walk away from family tax credits for children, or walk off from an economic growth — tax cut — in the capital gains, and just say, 'Gee, we now give up.' I think that the Senate voted for $245 billion in tax cuts, and I think the Senate, frankly, is honor-bound to deliver on that."

By publicly wiggling on the tax issue, Mr. Dole raises the prospect of a rift between Senate and House Republicans at a time when the two chambers are already at odds over budget issues.

On Friday, House Republicans revolted against their leadership and joined with Democrats to defeat compromise legislation on spending bills for the Defense Department and the Interior Department because they were angry about Senate-

Continued on Page A14, Column 1

SHEIK AND 9 FOLLOWERS GUILTY OF A CONSPIRACY OF TERRORISM

SHEIK OMAR ABDEL RAHMAN

GUILTY OF

- Seditious conspiracy for leading a bombing and assassination campaign in the New York area.
- Solicitation and conspiracy to kill President Hosni Mubarak of Egypt.
- Solicitation to attack a United States military installation and bombing conspiracy for providing advice on targets.

BACKGROUND

Blind Muslim cleric, 57, from Jersey City. An Egyptian who arrived in the United States in 1990 after brief stays in the Sudan and Pakistan. Spiritual leader of fundamentalist group that has long sought to overthrow Egyptian Government.

Acquitted in Egypt of involvement in 1981 assassination of President Anwar el-Sadat and in two seditious rioting cases there, but convicted in absentia in 1994 retrial of one of the riot cases and sentenced to seven years in prison.

Profiles of the other defendants, page B5.

Fred R. Conrad/The New York Times

SECURITY IS TIGHT

Jury Finds Men Planned Four-Year Campaign of Urban Violence

By JOSEPH P. FRIED

Sheik Omar Abdel Rahman and nine other militant Muslims were convicted yesterday of conspiring to carry out a terrorist campaign of bombings and assassinations intended to destroy the United Nations and New York landmarks, kill hundreds of people and force America to abandon its support for Israel and Egypt.

Climaxing the biggest terrorism trial in the nation's history, a Federal jury that had deliberated over seven of the last nine days returned to a heavily guarded courtroom in Manhattan and pronounced the 10 defendants guilty on 48 of 50 charges.

It was a sweeping second victory for prosecutors in a trilogy of trials stemming from the 1993 bombing of the World Trade Center, which left six dead and terrorism at the fore of American consciousness. The defendants were not accused of that bombing, but prosecutors said four men convicted last year, and two to be tried next year, were co-conspirators of those convicted yesterday.

The centerpiece of the conspiracy, according to prosecutors who had no actual explosion to support their case and who relied heavily on secretly made tapes and a shady informer, was to be a cataclysmic "day of terror": five bombs that were to blow up the United Nations headquarters, the Lincoln and Holland tunnels, the George Washington Bridge and 26 Federal Plaza, the Government's main office building in New York.

"Guilty. Guilty. Guilty." The word rang out again and again as a jury of six women and six men, who had heard eight months of testimony, confronted the sober-faced defendants in Judge Michael B. Mukasey's courtroom at Foley Square.

Mr. Abdel Rahman, 57, a blind Egyptian cleric who came to this country in 1990 and attracted a devoted following of Islamic fundamentalists with his fiery denunciations of United States policies in the Middle East, was found guilty of directing a conspiracy to wage "a war of urban terrorism" against America and of plotting to kill Egyptian President Hosni Mubarak.

Mr. Abdel Rahman, his red clerical cap offering a bright dash of color at the cluster of defense tables, showed no emotion as Judge Mukasey read from the jurors' verdict sheet.

Another defendant, El Sayyid A. Nosair, was convicted of murdering Rabbi Meir Kahane in 1990, an assassination once regarded as a crazed gunman's isolated attack but later portrayed by prosecutors as the first blow in a four-year terrorist agenda. Mr. Nosair was acquitted of the murder in a state trial in 1991,

Continued on Page B4, Column 1

Giuliani Now Pressing Board To Name Interim Chancellor

By STEVEN LEE MYERS

Mayor Rudolph W. Giuliani and the Board of Education battled anew yesterday over how to proceed with the search for a chancellor of New York City's public schools, after a staggering 36 hours that saw one candidate withdraw under a cloud and then another get the job, only to have it snatched away.

Having orchestrated the dramatic reversal on Saturday night of the board's selection of Daniel A. Domenech, Mr. Giuliani called on the board yesterday to appoint an interim chancellor. He said the board should now take time to learn from its "mistakes" and then pointedly attacked its president, Carol A. Gresser, accusing her of dishonesty.

But Mrs. Gresser and other board members — echoed by some elected officials and education experts — said that to preserve some sense of stability in the nation's largest school system, they wanted to have a chancellor in place before Ramon C. Cortines stepped down on Oct. 13.

"The Mayor is insisting the game go on for a while," Mrs. Gresser said yesterday. "The question for us is how long. As far as I'm concerned, I would like to see this end."

The sharp divisions yesterday mirrored the tensions that have consumed the board's search for Mr. Cortines's replacement from the beginning. Those tensions reached new intensity on Friday, when the Mayor's choice, Leon M. Goldstein, abruptly withdrew from consideration and the board quickly decided, 4 to 3, to choose Dr. Domenech, the District Superintendent of western Suffolk County on Long Island.

Under intense pressure from the Mayor, Jerry F. Cammarata, the board member from Staten Island, switched his vote for Dr. Domenech only 24 hours later and joined three other members in voting to reopen the search, prompting Mrs. Gresser to accuse the Mayor of a tyrannical obsession with power and control.

The weekend's events left the leadership of the schools reeling less than two weeks before Mr. Cortines leaves town. Sandra E. Lerner, the board member from the Bronx, said the system faced numerous problems — particularly a projected gap of $150 million in its $8 billion budget — that needed immediate attention.

The tumult also led many elected officials and others to question

Continued on Page B3, Column 1

In Jail or Out, Sheik Preaches Views of Islam

By NEIL MacFARQUHAR

Around 8 P.M. on the night before his conviction, Sheik Omar Abdel Rahman placed a collect call from the Metropolitan Correctional Center in Manhattan to the Abu Bakr mosque in Brooklyn. There, his followers sat in a semicircle on the green carpet each Saturday, putting the telephone next to a microphone to listen to him preach for about an hour.

Over the years, the central defendant in the terrorism conspiracy trial combined veiled political lessons drawn from the Koran with diatribes against the Egyptian Government, along with occasional personal advice. Saturday night was no different. Anticipating a jail term for their leader, his followers said the 57-year-old blind cleric told them that all great religious believers had been tortured or imprisoned for their views and that it only increased interest in their teachings.

He also took the opportunity to lash out at the Cairo Government when a member of the congregation asked what they should do about recent reports that Israel shot Egyptian prisoners en masse during the 1967 Arab-Israeli war. "We have to make people aware that the Egyptian regime always lies to the public," he responded.

For the last 25 years, Mr. Abdel Rahman exhorted his small but relentlessly militant followers to rise up and smite secular rule in Arab lands, always keeping his incendiary encouragements rooted in Islam and balanced on the razor's edge of the law. Despite repeated detentions, house arrests and trials intended to

Continued on Page B4, Column 3

Lenore Victoria Davis for The New York Times

A Cathedral Ready to Resound Again With Joy

When Pope John Paul II visits Newark, he will see a troubled city that would be worse off if not for the church's presence. One stop is the grand but often empty Sacred Heart Cathedral, where Kimberly Tyler and her son Ronald attended a recent Mass. Articles and the Pope's itinerary, pages B1, B6 and B7.

A Free-for-All in Swapping Medicaid for Managed Care

By MARTIN GOTTLIEB

The Cutting Edge

Tennessee's Health Revolution

Second of two articles.

MEMPHIS — Funny things happened around this city last year when a half dozen health care plans battled to enroll a quarter of a million poor people.

The plans that signed up the most people could get tens of millions of dollars under TennCare, a new state health system. So, some promised new members free life insurance and secured credit cards. One offered holiday turkeys to members who enrolled friends. Homeless people recall being besieged by sales representatives and signing up with any number of them.

But no plan outdid OmniCare. One of its sales people, a recreation counselor at the state prison farm, was arrested for enrolling felons. Felons did not qualify for TennCare because they get medical services from the Department of Correction. The salesman was sentenced in September to 14 months behind bars.

For a time, the plan's sales representatives were coached by Coby Smith, a veteran political campaign worker in town. Mr. Smith said he had instructed them to go door to door through public housing projects, explaining the health plan as they would a political candidate, but not spending more than 15 minutes with a prospect.

"Knock on their doors," Mr. Smith said he told the representatives at about a dozen training sessions. "Be observant. If you see a physical problem, you don't need to sign those people. If you see someone who's very pregnant, you don't need to sign those people. If you see someone with eyes dilating, you don't need to sign those people.

"Do not create a risk situation for the company if you can."

Tennessee's health care overhaul

Continued on Page A14, Column 1

New Word of Advice for the Graduate: Software

By TRIP GABRIEL

A few years ago, Orion Letizi, an English major who graduated from the University of California at Berkeley, would probably have become a teacher, journalist or graduate student. But just three months after leaving behind Milton and the metaphysical poets, Mr. Letizi is up to his ears in computer software.

He has a job offering technical advice to customers of a company that sells access to the Internet. On his own time, he is learning computer programming. And with six other people, he is starting a service to distribute music on the Internet.

"Previous to my current experience I really was at sea when it comes to computers," said Mr. Letizi, who is 23 and lives in San Francisco. "I just walked into it."

Across the country, a generation of college graduates with no technical training is streaming into the software business, drawn by the industry's image as a generator of personal fortunes and cultural excitement.

"There's no doubt that being a computer software company — people see that as *the* place to work right now," said Lisa Mars, the vice president of human resources at Computer Associates in Islandia, L.I., the nation's second largest software company. Last spring, recruiters from Computer Associates, who visited more than 75 campuses nationwide, were besieged by applicants with majors ranging from economics to music composition to philosophy.

Call it the Netscape effect, after the company that this summer came

Continued on Page A11, Column 1

"All the News That's Fit to Print"

The New York Times

Late Edition
Today, cloudy, showers, more humid. High 75. **Tonight,** diminishing showers, patchy fog. Low 65. **Tomorrow,** showers. High 75. **Yesterday,** high 81, Low 60. Details are on page C10.

VOL.CXLV . No. 50,204 NEW YORK, WEDNESDAY, OCTOBER 4, 1995 — $1 beyond the greater New York metropolitan area. — 60 CENTS

Welcoming the Pope

TODAY

3 P.M. Arrival at Newark International Airport at restricted terminal. Welcoming ceremony, address and meeting with President Clinton.

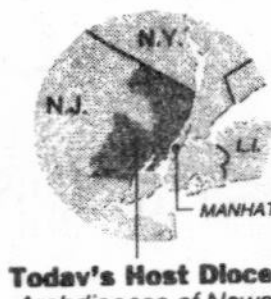

Today's Host Diocese
Archdiocese of Newark

5 P.M. Evening prayer at Sacred Heart Cathedral, Newark. Afterward, the Pope spends the night at the residence of the Vatican's representative to the United Nations on East 72d Street in Manhattan.

TRAFFIC Interstate 280 and New Jersey Turnpike closed as Pope and President pass; traffic barred from area around Sacred Heart Cathedral for much of the day. East 72d Street between Fifth and Madison Avenues closed to vehicles and pedestrians.

VIEWING ABC, NBC, WWOR, New York 1, FOX and CNN will provide live coverage of the arrival.

TOMORROW Addresses the United Nations and celebrates Mass and delivers homily at Giants Stadium.

FRIDAY Celebrates Mass and delivers homily at Aqueduct Racetrack in Queens. Leads evening prayer and delivers an address at St. Joseph's Seminary in Yonkers.

SATURDAY Celebrates Mass and delivers homily in Central Park. Recites rosary and delivers a brief address at St. Patrick's Cathedral.

Jury Clears Simpson in Double Murder; Spellbound Nation Divides on Verdict

Pool photo by Reuters

At the words "not guilty," a tense O. J. Simpson uncoiled and breathed a sigh of relief.

After 474 Days as a Prisoner, He Is Free

By DAVID MARGOLICK

LOS ANGELES, Oct. 3 — Orenthal James Simpson, a man who overcame the spindly legs left by a childhood case of rickets to run to fame and fortune, surmounted a very different sort of obstacle today, when a jury of 10 women and 2 men cleared him of charges that he murdered his former wife and one of her friends.

The verdict, coming 16 months after Nicole Brown Simpson and Ronald L. Goldman were slashed to death in the front yard of Mrs. Simpson's condominium and after 9 months of what often seemed like interminable testimony, sidebars and high-priced legal bickering, was reached in the end with breathtaking speed. When it was read, much of the nation, President Clinton included, stopped work to listen to it.

And with the Simpson verdict, as with the Simpson case, the nation once more divided — largely along racial lines. So, too, did defense lawyers, with the onetime chief of Mr. Simpson's legal team, Robert L. Shapiro, criticizing his successor.

"Not only did we play the race card, we dealt it from the bottom of the deck," Mr. Shapiro told Barbara Walters tonight in an interview on an ABC News special.

In a scene that lent a certain symmetry to the entire Simpson saga, Mr. Simpson immediately returned to the freeways of Los Angeles in a white van, and as fans waved from the streets he headed back to his home at 360 North Rockingham Avenue. While a dozen helicopters flew overhead, and fans festooned the fence with roses and balloons, he was met by A. C. Cowlings, who had been in the driver's seat of the white Ford Bronco on June 17, 1994, five days after the killings.

Mr. Simpson pursed his lips, gulped a few times and wore a forced, pained grin as Deirdre Robertson, the law clerk to Judge Lance A. Ito, read the verdict. Mrs. Robertson tripped over "Orenthal," but not over what came next: "not guilty." When she uttered those words, Mr. Simpson's body instantly uncoiled. He then breathed a sigh of relief, and a faint smile appeared.

As Mrs. Robertson's recitation continued — ". . . in violation of Penal Code Section 187A, a felony, upon Nicole Brown Simpson, a human being," Mr. Simpson waved at the panelists and mouthed the words "Thank you." The reading then unfolded again, with the name "Ronald L. Goldman" substituted for Mrs. Simpson. Mr. Simpson embraced his chief lawyer, Johnnie L. Cochran Jr., and silently thanked and rethanked the jury again.

"Ladies and gentlemen of the jury, is this your verdict, so say you one, so say you all?" Mrs. Robertson then asked. "Yes," the panel members — nine black, two whites and a Hispanic man — replied matter-of-factly. Critics of what the jurors did today maintained that they had been manipulated by a cynical defense team that talked more about the racism of the Los Angeles police than about the guilt or innocence of their client. Mr. Simpson's lawyers countered that prosecutors simply had not proven their case.

As he left court, one juror, a for-

Continued on Page A10, Column 1

Racial Split at the End, as at the Start

By MARTIN GOTTLIEB

The seven workers at the Pasqua Coffee Bar in lower Manhattan like to joke around with one another, to trade stories about family and regular customers, and to help one another out in jams.

But until the astonishingly abrupt culmination of the O. J. Simpson murder trial yesterday, they never seemed to get around to discussing what, for much of America, has been a prickly and divisive topic.

Then, as the voice of the court clerk intoning "not guilty" came over the restaurant's radio, Charmon Savage, a black man who works in the kitchen, jumped up, punched the air with both fists and exclaimed, "Yes! Yes! Yes!"

Geraldine Foney, the restaurant manager, who is white, lowered her head with disgust in her eyes. "I thought he should have rotted in hell," she said.

And several other women on the staff, including Debi Diaz, a counterwoman, grumbled in disbelief after hearing the verdict of the jurors, nine of whom are black. "They have to retry him," she said. "It's ridiculous, you know."

The scene at the Pasqua Bar was repeated in thousands of different settings across the country yesterday, with reactions that seemed often to be shaped by race — especially by race — sometimes by the person's sex and frequently by a jaded belief that personal wealth can triumph over just about anything.

At the Texas Bar-B-Q in downtown Dallas, a black-owned restaurant, a couple of black men greeted the verdict with eruptions of elation. Several white customers quietly left shortly afterward.

At Jocks n Jills Sports Bar at the CNN Center in Atlanta, the reaction was much the same as the verdict came over a bank of wall-to-wall television sets — black customers often embraced and cheered; whites sat in stony silence.

Over the Internet, the comments were often starkly racial.

Since it first began to transfix the country in June 1994, the Simpson murder case has been a combination soap opera, passion play and national Rorschach test laden with sex, celebrity, wealth, violence and, perhaps most sensitively, race.

The reactions to the verdict parallel the racial divide in every opinion poll taken since the trial began. Separated by a constant gap of about 40 percentage points, many whites seemed to hold fast to the belief that Mr. Simpson was guilty, while blacks believed as adamantly in his innocence. Several polls indicate that behind the response of many blacks is a deep suspicion of the police and the criminal justice system.

A poll taken by CBS News immedi-

Continued on Page A12, Column 1

Carrie Boretz for The New York Times

Ozier Muhammad/The New York Times

Passers-by watched the verdict with shock through the windows of the "Today" show studios at Rockefeller Center, left; at her restaurant in Harlem, Sylvia Woods cheered as she hugged her daughter and a waitress.

A Day (10 Minutes of It) the Country Stood Still

By N. R. KLEINFIELD

The country stopped.

Between 1 and 1:10 P.M. yesterday, people didn't work. They didn't go to math class. They didn't make phone calls. They didn't use the bathroom. They didn't walk the dog.

They listened to the O. J. Simpson verdicts.

Airplane flights had to wait. At Hartsfield International Airport in Atlanta, passengers and airport workers alike were so fixedly watching the television sets at the departure gates that several Delta Air Lines flights due to leave between 1:24 and 1:32 boarded late. When a Delta agent with poor timing tried to start her boarding instructions for a Louisville flight just as the verdicts were being read, a hundred passengers shouted her down.

Finance ceased. At the Barnett Bank branch on Biscayne Boulevard in Miami, tellers stopped counting bills and the lines of impatient customers evaporated as everyone turned, tantalized, to the television on the wall. Seeing the envelope containing the verdicts, a sales manager implored: "Open it. Open it."

It was an eerie moment of national communion, in which the routines and rituals of the country were subsumed by an unquenchable curiosity. Millions of people in millions of places seemed to spend 10 spellbinding minutes doing exactly the same thing.

The curiosity infected everyone, no matter what larger matters might be under consideration. President Clinton left the Oval Office at two minutes before 1 to catch the verdicts in his secretary's office with several of his aides.

The Supreme Court was hearing arguments at the big moment. Immediately after the verdicts were announced, two messengers appeared. One went to the side where Justice Ruth Bader Ginsburg sat, and the other to the side where Justice Stephen G. Breyer sat, and they

Continued on Page A12, Column 3

MORE ON THE TRIAL

A Free Man

O. J. Simpson left court free of criminal charges but not of the side effects of the case, from possible television deals to huge legal bills. Page A10.

The Cryptic Jury

Jurors who made an art form out of being unreadable finally showed a few small signs of emotion, but only for a moment. Page A11.

The Los Angeles Factor

The trial was a national event, but the dynamics of Los Angeles, particularly the Police Department's images, were crucial. Page A13.

Opinions Everywhere

There was rejoicing at a black college in Atlanta, cynicism at a health club in Massachusetts, disbelief at a bar in Michigan. Page A13.

The Reidys, All 11, Reflect On a Faith Proudly Lived

One Catholic Family Awaiting the Pope

By FELICIA R. LEE

To William J. Reidy, an Irish-Catholic father of nine, Pope John Paul II operates in the world in much the manner Mr. Reidy operates his large household in the affluent Riverdale section of the Bronx: offering guidelines and hoping his flock will believe.

"It's like a father," said Mr. Reidy, who was educated in Catholic schools from kindergarten through college and attends Mass every Sunday. "He talks first, makes a lot of noise, and you have guidelines." As a father, Mr. Reidy knows well that it's not at all certain how the message will be received.

"There is the presumption that the central voice is the universal voice," said the 54-year-old Mr. Reidy, adding, "but I am not sure what Catholic means."

Still, every last Reidy child — from Tim, 20, to Gavin, 3 — is a proud Catholic, and all are looking forward to the Pope's arrival today, each in his or her own way.

Ask Marcia Reidy, their mother, who spends much of her time taking care of her 10-year-old handicapped son, what Catholicism means to her, and she says: "It's an impossible question. It means to be a Christian. It means taking care of the children."

To 12-year-old Michael Reidy, an altar boy at St. Gabriel's in the Bronx, the Pope represents "the closest thing we have to God on earth." But already, his 14-year-old brother, Owen, also an altar boy, isn't so sure. "He's the Pope," he said. "I sort of find that just a name. How closer to God can he be than lay people? It's not like God is going to walk into his living room."

And then there is the Reidy's oldest, Tim. From the church, he learned that homosexual acts are sinful, but at Princeton, where he is a junior, he met openly gay people for the first time and has tried to fit them in with his idea of Catholicism.

Like so many area Catholics, the Reidys will be personally touched by the Pope's visit this week. Owen and his sisters Marcia, 16, and Anne, 17, will attend his Mass on the Great

Continued on Page B6, Column 1

A.M.A. Says Plan Would Drive Many Doctors Out of Medicare

By ROBERT PEAR

WASHINGTON, Oct. 3 — After months of public silence, the American Medical Association expressed deep concern today about Republican proposals to redesign Medicare, saying that new limits on payments would make the program unattractive to many doctors.

James H. Stacey, a spokesman for the medical association, said that under the Republican plan doctors in the standard Medicare program were facing not only a cut in the growth of Medicare payments, but also an absolute reduction in payment for many services.

"This causes real problems for the A.M.A.," Mr. Stacey said in response to a question. "It would be a major blow to the traditional fee-for-service Medicare program."

The doctors' concerns echo comments from the Clinton Administration and Democrats in Congress, who say the Republicans would cut payments to doctors so severely that many doctors would decide not to treat Medicare patients. As a result, they say, patients would be forced to obtain care through health maintenance organizations and other private health plans, even though the Republicans insist that beneficiaries will always be free to keep traditional Medicare coverage.

Until today, the American Medical Association had generally refrained from criticizing the Republican proposals on Medicare. Indeed, it has praised some of those proposals, including one that would relax antitrust laws for doctors and another that would limit payments to victims of medical malpractice.

By contrast, in the battle over President Clinton's health care plan in 1993 and 1994, the medical association regularly made itself heard. It supported Mr. Clinton's goal of guaranteeing health insurance coverage for all Americans, and it initially supported his proposal that all employers be required to buy such insurance for their employees. But the association later urged Congress to consider alternatives to the "employer mandate," and many doctors said Mr. Clinton's health plan envisioned too big a role for Government.

The specific points raised today concerned the fee schedule Medicare has used since 1992 to pay doctors. Each physician service is assigned a numerical value, and this number is multiplied by a fixed amount of money, called a dollar

Continued on Page A22, Column 1

INSIDE

Giuliani's Plan for Schools

Mayor Giuliani outlined a specific proposal for City Hall to gain control over the school system. Page B1.

Veto With a Message

President Clinton vetoed a bill to pay Congress's administrative expenses, scolding lawmakers. Page A22.

NEWS SUMMARY A2

BASEBALL '95 PLAYOFFS

Mariners	**6**
Yankees	**9**
Red Sox	**4**
Indians	**5**
Braves	**5**
Rockies	**4**
Reds	**7**
Dodgers	**2**

SportsWednesday, pages B10-B15.

"All the News
That's Fit to Print"

The New York Times

Late Edition

New York: Today, showers, heavy at times this morning, breezy. High 76. Tonight, showers. Low 70. Tomorrow, partly cloudy. High 83. Yesterday, high 73, low 69. Details, page B25.

VOL.CXLV . . . No. 50,205 NEW YORK, THURSDAY, OCTOBER 5, 1995 $1 beyond the greater New York metropolitan area. 60 CENTS

Pope Arrives, Urging America to Live Its Ideals

Keith Meyers/The New York Times

'Thank God for the extraordinary human epic that is the United States of America.'

Calls on U.S. to Preserve Openness

By ROBERT D. McFADDEN

Pope John Paul II returned to the New York City area after 16 years yesterday on a mission to strengthen his discordant church in America and press his crusades to undermine materialism and fortify peace in the post-cold-war world.

He was quickly engulfed in a swirl of secular pageantry, police security and religious solemnity, and responded with many of the themes he is expected to reiterate on a five-day visit: urging peace, support for the United Nations, openness to immigrants and a continuation of American social programs for the poor.

"It is my prayerful hope that America will persevere in its own best traditions of openness and opportunity," the Pope declared. [Transcript, page B2.]

On an extraordinary day that began at the papal apartments at St. Peter's Square, the Pope crossed the Atlantic, touched down on his fifth continent of the year, met this country's senior political and Catholic leaders, led vespers at a cathedral in the rundown drug-infested heart of Newark and retired, still ruggedly smiling, to the Vatican mission to the United Nations in Manhattan.

Ebullient despite an eight-hour flight from Rome and resplendent in robes as white as a swan's wing, the Pope arrived at midafternoon in a gray drizzle at Newark International Airport and was greeted by President Clinton and Hillary Rodham Clinton, the Governors of New York and New Jersey and 800 dignitaries, political leaders and almost the entire hierarchy of the Roman Catholic Church in this country.

A roar went up from 2,000 parochial-school children behind barricades as the Pope emerged from the door of a green-and-white Alitalia jetliner at 3:20 P.M., waved his blessing to the crowds and to the nation and carefully, but without help, descended steep steps to a red carpet on the tarmac, where he shook hands with Mr. and Mrs. Clinton and a receiving line of officials and church leaders.

It was a big day for New Jersey, which has often been in the shadow of major events in neighboring New York City. While he is the most-traveled Pope in history — 68 trips to 112 countries in a 17-year reign — John Paul had never been to New Jersey, and its millions of Catholics, its political and religious leaders and many other residents had been fairly bursting with anticipation.

Beaming, waving, blessing the crowds with the Sign of the Cross, but moving with the slow step that has become familiar in recent years as age and illness have overtaken him, the 75-year-old Pope did not bend down and kiss the tarmac, a formality reserved for his first visits to a country.

But he appeared hearty and was clearly delighted with his reception, which included renditions of the Vat-

Continued on Page B3, Column 1

Yeltsin's Heir Bows Out of Race, Raising Doubts About Reforms

By MICHAEL SPECTER

MOSCOW, Oct. 4 — In a surprise decision that throws the future leadership of Russia in doubt at a time when stability seemed likely, Prime Minister Viktor S. Chernomyrdin announced today that "I have never planned and I am not planning" to run for president next year.

The statement leaves an ailing and profoundly unpopular President Boris N. Yeltsin with no obvious political heir, and it raises questions about the course of the market-oriented economic changes that Mr. Chernomyrdin has shepherded over the last two years.

To many supporters of democracy and economic change in Russia, Mr. Chernomyrdin was the leader most likely to keep the country headed in the same direction despite a climate of disillusionment in the country's current political course.

Just this week, the Communist Party won 22 of the 24 seats in the Volgograd regional legislature. Independent polls repeatedly indicate that while no parties are popular in Russia, the Communists may do better than any other group in parliamentary elections in December.

Mr. Chernomyrdin seemed to have become an exception in the Yeltsin administration. He has grown steadily in his job, rarely shirked the tough choices needed to move Russia toward a market economy, and shown unusual maturity in dealing with a Parliament that he rarely agrees with. With a presidential field full of candidates nobody seems to like, politicians like the Communist Party chief Gennadi A. Zyuganov and the independent and outspoken Gen. Aleksandr I. Lebed are now considered leading possible successors to Mr. Yeltsin.

"It is the President we need to replace," Mr. Zyuganov said after hearing the news about Mr. Chernomyrdin today. "We need a president who can lead the government."

The decision by Mr. Chernomyr-

Continued on Page A7, Column 1

More on the Visit

A PAPAL CHAT Somewhere over the Atlantic Ocean en route to Newark, the Pope walked to the back of his plane to talk to reporters. He even showed his mastery of the news conference's finest art: ducking a question. Page B1.

OPPOSING VIEWS Some faithful Roman Catholics have no interest in seeing the best-known figure in all of Christendom. They believe that the Pope sees the world through a distorted prism of stained glass. Page B1.

THE SCENE The Pope did not kiss the ground when he arrived in New Jersey, but that was according to protocol. In Newark, the pageantry included a celebrity sighting. Notebook, page B1.

In Fleeting Moments, Pope Vitalizes Streets of Newark

By FRANK BRUNI

NEWARK, Oct. 4 — He passed by them first as a vague, white-robed blur behind the darkly tinted rear window of an indistinct black limousine, and later as a cloudy figure beneath the thick, bulletproof shroud over his special Popemobile. Each time, he came and went in a matter of seconds.

But to many of the people who waited long hours here on the sidewalks outside Sacred Heart Cathedral, that fleeting moment of communion with Pope John Paul II was enough. With just a wave and a smile, he gave them the heady, exalted feeling of being at the center of something holy and historic.

"I'm totally satisfied," said Lydia Masi, 69, of Newark, who spent more than 10 hours in the intermittent drizzle for her short-lived glimpse of the man she believes speaks for God on earth.

"Bravo Il Papa!" Mrs. Masi had shouted, as loudly as her lungs would let her, when the Pope neared her patch of sidewalk. Afterward, she said, "I got the chills."

In Mrs. Masi and the several thousand other people who gathered here today for the beginning of the Pope's brief American tour, the currents of emotion ran strong and deep. Their revelry and ardor transformed an inner-city neighborhood that is usually somewhat desolate into a crowded open-air arena of song and celebration as pride and jubilation swept through a city more accustomed to insult and injury.

Lisa Mendez, 35, said that usually when she tells people that she is from Newark, "they look at me funny." On this special day, their reaction was kinder. "They say, 'Oh, you're so lucky,'" Ms. Mendez said.

These were people whose paths do not typically cross. Spanning the economic extremes of the Archdiocese of Newark, in which the many pockets of urban poverty meant that roughly 40 percent of the 238 Catholic parishes operate at a deficit, they converged on the cathedral, both from tranquil suburbs an hour's drive away and city blocks within walking distance.

But on this day, in the presence of the Pope, they cut often identical figures: eager, jostling witnesses to a charmed occasion.

The Pope came to the cathedral from Newark International Airport for a 5 P.M. prayer service. The streets outside the majestic French Gothic structure, which crowns Newark's highest hill, were billed as the only place in the New York metropolitan region where people without tickets to specific events could hope to see the Pontiff up close.

Although the overall turnout fell far short of the crowd of 100,000 people for which the authorities had braced, there were still enough people — 15,000, by one police estimate that seemed generous — to fill nearly a half-mile stretch of the sidewalk along Clifton Avenue, the main street beside the cathedral.

They laughed, cheered and even

Continued on Page B4, Column 5

With Spotlight Shifted to Them, Some Simpson Jurors Talk Freely

By TIMOTHY EGAN

LOS ANGELES, Oct. 4 — Shadowed by news helicopters, limousines bearing network celebrities and tabloid-television producers offering up to $100,000 for exclusives, a few of the jurors in the O. J. Simpson murder trial emerged today to give insight into their celebrated verdicts.

"It wasn't a matter of sympathy, and it wasn't a matter of favoritism," said Brenda Moran, a 45-year-old computer technician. "It was a matter of evidence."

Ms. Moran, the first Simpson juror to go public, was offered a hair makeover, a limousine ride to an interview with the "Today" host Bryant Gumbel and numerous other enticements to talk, proffered by television producers at her doorstep in Gardena, south of Los Angeles.

She shunned those offers. Instead, she held a midday news conference on the roof of a Beverly Hills parking garage where she detailed how the verdicts were reached. At the same time, she held out for what her lawyer, Robert Ball, called "a later, person-to-person interview" with a personality whom Mr. Ball did not identify.

Another juror, Gina Rosborough, emerged on Oprah Winfrey's television show with her husband, Jerome. Mrs. Rosborough said she, like Ms. Moran, beyond simply believing that the prosecution had not made a good enough case to establish Mr. Simpson's guilt, thought that he had actually not killed his former wife.

Most of the other jurors, however, were nowhere to be found today. Some of them have asked for police protection from battalions of reporters and producers. Many of those producers are carrying cash for interviews with television outlets all over the world, and some said they had hired private investigators to help them track down the jurors.

By the accounts of Ms. Moran, Mrs. Rosborough and at least two other jurors, the panel thought there were so many flaws in the prosecution's case that even evidence as to motive did not seem to fit.

The prosecutors said Mr. Simpson had killed his former wife, Nicole Brown Simpson, in a jealous rage spawned by his obsession to control her, and in support of that contention they introduced an abundance of evidence concerning spousal abuse. But today Ms. Moran said: "This was a murder trial, not domestic abuse. If

Continued on Page B18, Column 4

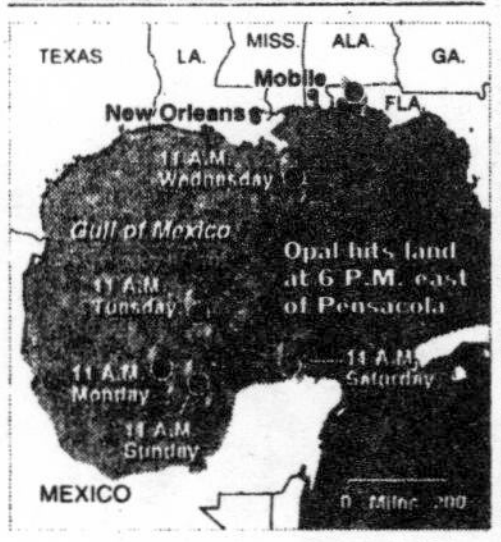

The New York Times

Storm Hits Florida

Hurricane Opal roared into Florida 25 miles east of Pensacola early last night with winds gusting to 145 miles an hour. Page B16.

NEWS SUMMARY A2

INSIDE

Yanks Win in 15 Innings On Leyritz's Home Run

Jim Leyritz ended a five-hour marathon with a home run that beat Seattle, 7-5. Then he survived the celebration as the Yankees took a 2-0 lead in the playoff series. Page B19.

Black Men and the Law

About one-third of black men in their 20's are in jail or under law enforcement supervision on any given day, a new study says. Page A18.

Term-Limit Bill Is Delayed

Freshman Republicans in the Senate conceded that they lacked the votes for a bill on term limits and asked that it be postponed. Page A23.

Bad Bet on a Star Property

For the real estate investment trust that holds the mortgage on Rockefeller Center, blue-chip names and a prestigious address proved to be no guarantees of success. Page D1.

A Top Apple Executive Quits

The chief financial officer of Apple Computer resigned, the apparent loser in a skirmish with the chief executive over whether Apple should remain independent. Page D1.

Interim Chancellor at Issue

Mayor Giuliani and the school board headed down divergent paths, as the Mayor sought an interim chancellor against board wishes. Page B14.

Associated Press

From the window of his Popemobile, the Pope greeted the waiting crowd as he arrived last night at Sacred Heart Cathedral in Newark.

"All the News That's Fit to Print"

The New York Times

Late Edition
New York: **Today,** sunny, not as windy, very cool. High 50. **Tonight,** clouds. Low 39. **Tomorrow,** becoming sunny, milder. High 59. **Yesterday,** high 55, low 38. Details, page 51.

VOL.CXLV . No. 50,236 | NEW YORK, SUNDAY, NOVEMBER 5, 1995 | $2.50

RABIN SLAIN AFTER PEACE RALLY IN TEL AVIV; ISRAELI GUNMAN HELD; SAYS HE ACTED ALONE

Associated Press

THE SPEECH Prime Minister Yitzhak Rabin addressing a peace rally yesterday in Tel Aviv before he was shot to death.

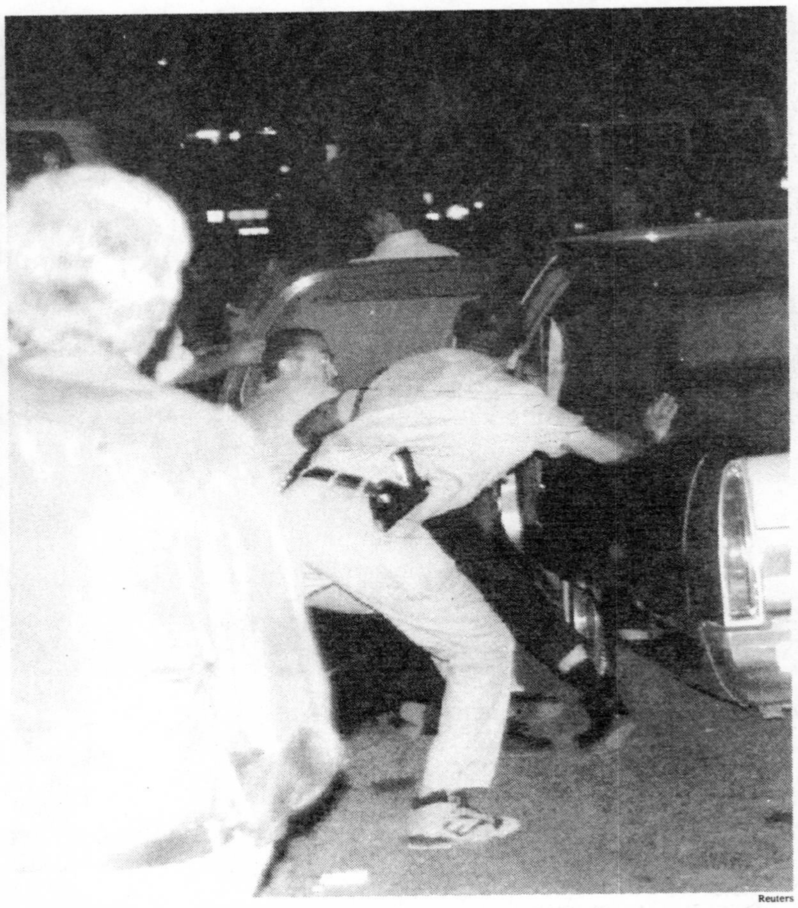

Reuters

THE ATTACK Mr. Rabin lying at the feet of security officers after he was shot before entering his car.

PERES TAKES OVER

Stunned Nation Asks if Talks With the P.L.O Are in Jeopardy

By SERGE SCHMEMANN

JERUSALEM, Nov. 4 — Prime Minister Yitzhak Rabin, who led Israel to victory in 1967 and began the march toward peace a generation later, was shot dead by a lone assassin this evening as he was leaving a vast rally in Tel Aviv.

Mr. Rabin, 73, was struck down by one or two bullets as he was entering his car. Police immediately seized a 27-year-old Israeli law student, Yigal Amir, who had been active in support of Israeli settlers but who told the police tonight that he had acted alone.

The police said Mr. Amir had also told them that he had tried twice before to attack the Prime Minister.

It was the first assassination of a prime minister in the 47-year history of the state of Israel, and it was certain to have extensive repercussions on Israeli politics and the future of the Arab-Israeli peace.

Mr. Rabin was to lead his Labor party in elections scheduled for November next year, and without him the prospects for a Labor victory, and of a continuation of his policies, were thrown into question.

In the immediate aftermath, Foreign Minister Shimon Peres, Mr. Rabin's partner in the peace negotiations, automatically became Acting Prime Minister. It was widely expected that he would be formally confirmed as Mr. Rabin's successor.

Mr. Rabin, who rose to national prominence as commander of the victorious Israeli army in the 1967 Six-Day War, became the second Middle Eastern leader, after President Anwar el-Sadat of Egypt, to be killed by extremists from his own side for seeking an Arab-Israeli peace. Mr. Sadat, the first Arab to make peace with Israel, was assassinated in 1984.

Mr. Rabin and his Labor Government have come under fierce attack from right-wing groups over the peace with the Palestinians, especially since the agreement transferring authority in the West Bank to the Palestine Liberation Organization was reached in September. Mr. Rabin has been heckled at many of his appearances in recent weeks and his security has been tight.

A gruff, chain-smoking career military man, Mr. Rabin led Israel both in its greatest military triumph and in one of its most dramatic bids for peace.

Shortly before his death, Mr. Rabin, obviously buoyed by the huge turnout of more than 100,000 supporters of the peace process, told the rally, "I have always believed that the majority of the people want peace and are ready to take a chance for peace." [Excerpts, page 16A.]

He then joined other participants in singing the "Song of Peace," a popular paean. Unfamiliar with the words, the prime minister followed from a text he tucked into his pocket.

Hours after the shooting, Mr. Peres said the blood-soaked sheet of music was found in his pocket and

Continued on Page 16A, Column 1

A Shaken Clinton Mourns Rabin, 'Martyr for His Nation's Peace'

By DAVID E. ROSENBAUM

WASHINGTON, Nov. 4 — President Clinton, who plans to leave on Sunday for the funeral of Prime Minister Yitzhak Rabin of Israel, went to the Rose Garden of the White House tonight and, his voice cracking, called Mr. Rabin "a martyr for his nation's peace."

"Peace must be and peace will be Prime Minister Rabin's lasting legacy," Mr. Clinton said.

The President and other officials here, though shocked and saddened by Mr. Rabin's assassination, said tonight that they expected the peace effort in the Middle East to continue uninterrupted.

Secretary of State Warren Christopher issued a statement in which he said, "History will record Prime Minister Rabin as one of the towering figures of this century."

As a political matter, Mr. Rabin was a crucial ally of Mr. Clinton's. The President's success in 1993 in bringing together Mr. Rabin and Yasir Arafat, the leader of the Palestine Liberation Organization, is the most important foreign policy success of the Clinton Presidency.

"Yitzhak Rabin was my partner and my friend," the President said. "I admired him, and I loved him very much."

To Israel's people, he said, "Just as America has stood by you in moments of crisis and triumph, so now we all stand by you in this moment."

The President was in his residence watching a college football game on television when Anthony Lake, his national security adviser, called about 3:20 P.M. to tell of the shooting, the White House said.

Other top officials rushed to the White House situation room to receive information from the United States Ambassador to Israel, Martin Indyk, who had gone to the hospital in Tel Aviv where Mr. Rabin died.

Around 4 P.M., Mr. Lake went to the President's office to tell him that Mr. Rabin had died.

Mr. Clinton then called Mr. Rabin's widow, Leah, and the new Acting Prime Minister, Shimon Peres, to express his sympathy.

Michael D. McCurry, the President's press secretary, said Mrs. Rabin and Mr. Peres had said they had never seen Mr. Rabin happier than he was tonight, right after his speech at the peace rally in Tel Aviv and just before he was shot.

Mr. McCurry said Mr. Clinton had invited leaders of Congress of both parties to join him at the funeral.

The President issued a proclama-

Continued on Page 16B, Column 1

Suspect Says He Tried to Kill Rabin Before

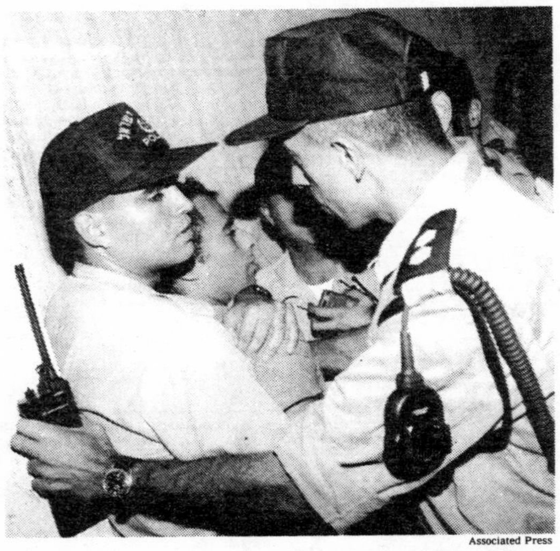

Associated Press

THE SUSPECT An Israeli police officer grabbed Yigal Amir, the suspected assassin, around the neck after the shooting.

Arrested Law Student Often Joined Protests Against Government

By JOEL GREENBERG

JERUSALEM, Nov. 4 — Yigal Amir, the 27-year-old law student who was arrested for the assassination of Prime Minister Yitzhak Rabin tonight, was described by acquaintances as a militant critic of the Government who regularly joined protests against Mr. Rabin's policies.

He told interrogators that he had carried out the killing on his own.

Under questioning by the police, Mr. Amir said he had been planning the assassination for a long time and had intended to kill Mr. Rabin on two previous occasions but was thwarted by tight security measures.

After his self-appointed mission tonight, Mr. Amir, a short, dark-haired man dressed in a blue shirt and light-colored pants, was pinned to a wall by police officers and rushed to a waiting police car.

"I have no regrets," he was quoted as telling investigators. "I acted alone and on orders from God."

According to some accounts, Mr. Amir had links to a small militant anti-Arab group known as Eyal that is virulently opposed to the Government's accords with the Palestine Liberation Organization.

A leader of the group, Avishai Raviv, acknowledged tonight that he knew Mr. Amir. But he denied that the assassin belonged to Eyal or that the group had anything to do with the shooting.

After the shooting, Israeli reporters received beeper messages signed Ain, a Hebrew acronym for the Israeli Avenging Organization, a previously unknown group. The group claimed responsibility for the killing, though it was not immediately known if it had any connection with Mr. Amir.

The assassination was the second incident of extreme violence by right-wing Jewish militants since the 1993 signing of the Israeli-Palestinian accord.

In February 1994, Baruch Goldstein, an American follower of the anti-Arab group Kach, massacred 29 Muslims at prayer at the Shrine of

Continued on Page 16A, Column 4

Teachers' Union Reaches Accord That Protects Jobs

By STEVEN LEE MYERS

Mayor Rudolph W. Giuliani and the leaders of New York City's teachers union announced a tentative agreement yesterday on a contract that would increase wages and benefits by 13 percent over five years and offer an unusual written commitment protecting union members from layoffs through 1998.

But the agreement included no significant concessions from the union's rank and file, even though the Mayor and his aides had vowed to achieve them to pay for raises. And by that measure, it fell short of the goal Mr. Giuliani set for himself: to scale back generous benefits and force employees to work harder for what they already earn.

The contract, subject to ratification by the union's 90,000 members and the Board of Education, provides no wage increases in the first two years, giving the city time, the Mayor said, to find ways to pay for raises of 3 to 4 percent in each succeeding year.

By the end of the pact in September of the year 2000, the top salary for teachers with 25 years experience would rise to $70,000, from $60,000 now. In the final year, the city would also contribute $75 per worker to the union's welfare fund. In all, the salary of a starting teacher would increase to $31,900, from $28,700.

"This contract is a historic breakthrough for the school system and for labor relations in the City of New York," the Mayor said. "It provides for much more educational value and at the same time is fiscally sound."

For Mr. Giuliani, the Republican Mayor nearing the midpoint of his term, the contract with the United Federation of Teachers was the first in the first round of bargaining conducted entirely by his administration. And it sets, he said, the general parameters for contracts with all of the city's 83 municipal unions.

Although the Mayor entered office

Continued on Page 46, Column 4

NEWS SUMMARY 2

TODAY'S SECTIONS

The New York Times
Education Life
Under the Glare of the Presidency

* *In New York City and the metropolitan region.*
  († Elsewhere, auto pages are in section 3.)
§ *In most parts of New York City.*
¶ *In Long Island, Westchester, Connecticut and central and northern New Jersey.*

THE DEATH OF RABIN

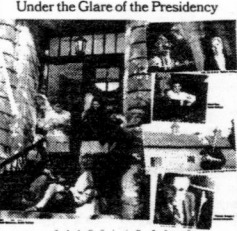

Associated Press

A Soldier-Statesman

Yitzhak Rabin was a soldier turned peacemaker, a man who tried to end the bloodshed that had plagued his country. Obituary, page 16.

Israeli Politics Clouded

The assassination threw a question mark over Israeli politics just a year before elections that could decide the future of the Arab-Israeli peace. News analysis, page 16A.

Horror and Condolences

Leaders of American Jewish groups were horrified by the killing. The head of the Palestine Liberation Organization offered condolences, while some other Arabs celebrated the assassination. Page 16B.

"All the News That's Fit to Print"

The New York Times

Late Edition

New York: **Today,** some sun, windy, a flurry. High 43. Tonight, part cloudy, chilly. Low 33. **Tomorrow,** mainly cloudy. High 46. **Yesterday,** high 54, low 43. Details are on page B16.

VOL.CXLV . . . No. 50,253

NEW YORK, WEDNESDAY, NOVEMBER 22, 1995

$1 beyond the greater New York metropolitan area.

60 CENTS

ACCORD REACHED TO END THE WAR IN BOSNIA; CLINTON PLEDGES U.S. TROOPS TO KEEP PEACE

Reuters

SERBIA Slobodan Milosevic, President — **BOSNIA-HERZEGOVINA** Alija Izetbegovic, President — **CROATIA** Franjo Tudjman, President — **UNITED STATES** Warren Christopher, Secretary of State

All Sides Make Concessions To End 4 Years of Conflict

By ELAINE SCIOLINO

DAYTON, Ohio, Nov. 21 — The presidents of three rival Balkan states agreed today to make peace in Bosnia, ending nearly four years of terror and ethnic bloodletting that have left a quarter of a million people dead in the worst war in Europe since World War II.

The leaders — Alija Izetbegovic of Bosnia, Franjo Tudjman of Croatia and Slobodan Milosevic of Serbia — initialed the peace agreement and 11 annexes in a hastily-arranged ceremony in the same conference room at Wright-Patterson Air Force Base where they opened their talks 21 days ago.

The agreement is to take effect when it is formally signed by the parties in Paris in mid-December.

Unlike previous peace accords that have collapsed, this one was reinforced by widespread fatigue of a war that has uprooted two million people from their homes and appalled the world with scenes of harrowing atrocities, and by the promise of enforcement by 60,000 NATO troops. President Clinton, hailing the agreement in a White House Rose Garden ceremony, reiterated his pledge that the NATO force would include 20,000 Americans.

"The agreement is a victory for all those who believe in a multi-ethnic democracy in Bosnia," said Secretary of State Warren Christopher, who spent several exhausting days brokering the final details of the accord. "It offers tangible hope that there will be no more days of dodging bullets, no more winters of freshly dug graves, no more years of isolation from the outside world."

But underneath the self-congratulation of today's ceremony was a grim awareness that the basic questions the parties failed to settle before the war remain: Can Bosnia, with its mutually suspicious populations of Muslims, Serbs and Croats, survive as a single state? What degree of self-government should be given to the Serb minority within its borders? And does Mr. Milosevic have the power to force the Serbs of Bosnia to do what he says?

Today the Bosnian Serb representatives who served in a delegation headed by Mr. Milosevic did not show up for the ceremony to initial the various annexes that affect the Serbian part of Bosnia.

The Bosnian Serbs were particularly upset by the military annexes in the agreement, which they charged essentially made NATO an occupying force, American and European negotiators said.

Under the agreement, NATO will have the right to remove or relocate specific forces and weapons from any location in the country whenever it determines that they constitute a threat to its troops.

The Bosnian Serbs were even

Continued on Page A10, Column 1

HIGHLIGHTS

TERRITORY Bosnia would maintain its current borders, but be divided into two entities — a Bosnian-Croat federation and a Bosnian Serb republic.

A central government, with a parliament and presidency, would remain in a united Sarajevo.

WAR CRIMINALS Would not be allowed to hold office, but no requirement to arrest them was specified.

TROOPS Forces would be withdrawn to agreed positions and an international force sent in to keep the peace. NATO has outlined a plan for a 60,000 member force — one-third of it American — to act as peacekeeper.

REFUGEES Would have the legal right to return home; human rights would be monitored by an independent commission.

ONE NATION, DIVIDED

Bosnian-Croat federation

Serb republic

The New York Times

An Imperfect Peace

By ROGER COHEN

News Analysis

DAYTON, Ohio, Nov. 21 — A cold Balkan peace was concluded today, one built over the graves of numberless victims by the very leaders who unleashed the Yugoslav wars, but still a peace that almost certainly offers the last hope for the stubborn vestiges of civilized life in Bosnia.

The American-brokered peace is necessarily imperfect and so could contain the seeds of future conflict. It divides Bosnia along ethnic lines, thus offering some endorsement to the racist politics of the Serbs who fought for secession. It offers no cast-iron guarantees that war criminals will be brought to justice. It will provide scant solace to the myriad bereaved and homeless of a long and savage conflict.

The possibility is real that the de facto division of Bosnia agreed upon today could prove permanent despite the establishment of central government institutions and the vows of the Bosnian, Croatian and Serbian presidents to work for the contrary.

For this peace remains to be defined. On paper, it is a bewildering, apparently unworkable jigsaw setting up two distinct self-governing units — a Muslim-Croat federation and a Serb republic — overseen by a rotating collective Bosnian presidency, a federal parliament, a constitutional court and other central institutions.

The Bosnian state laid out today has two armies — that of the Serbs and that of the federation. It has three administrations — that of the Serb republic, that of the federation, and that of the central Government. And it has an independent history made up entirely of a war whose legacy is one of deep mistrust and lingering anger.

Out of such confusion, it seems, a civil society could now grow; equally, a new and perhaps yet more savage conflict could erupt.

Even today, in an ominous sign, the Bosnian Serbs showed deep unhappiness with parts of the agreement, especially the establishment of a unified Sarajevo, and refused to initial all the documents.

For the Muslim-led Bosnian Government, it was another agonizing day. President Alija Izetbegovic showed no joy at the accord, shaking the hand of American officials and the Serbian and Croatian presidents in a distinctly perfunctory way. But

Continued on Page A11, Column 1

Study Finds Doctors Refuse Patients' Requests on Death

By SUSAN GILBERT

After 25 years of public outcry over the right to die with dignity, doctors are still ignoring patients' last wishes, according to a new study of terminally ill patients.

The study, reported in today's issue of The Journal of the American Medical Association, has found that doctors often misunderstand or ignore the patients' requests, with the result that large numbers of people still die alone, in pain and tethered to mechanical ventilators in intensive care units. Twenty-five years since the living will movement began, the study's authors say they have discovered that the wills, which are supposed to give terminally ill patients legal safeguards against unwanted medical treatment, offer virtually no protection.

The study also found that increasing communication between doctors and patients did not help.

"People think advance directives are solving the problem," said Dr. William Knaus, one of the researchers who directed the study. "We have very good information that they aren't, that nothing has changed — the amount of pain at the end of life, the number of people dying alone attached to machines."

The $28 million study, financed by the Robert Wood Johnson Foundation, took place at six medical centers around the country. It was divided into two parts, each one lasting two years and involving similar groups of terminally ill patients.

In the first phase, the researchers gathered base-line information, including the percentage of patients who did not want aggressive medical treatment like cardiopulmonary resuscitation and mechanical ventilation, the percentage of doctors who knew their patients' wishes, how often aggressive treatment was used and how much pain patients were in before they died.

The researchers found large gaps between what the patients wanted and what they got. Thirty-one percent of patients said they did not want cardiopulmonary resuscitation, but 80 percent of the doctors misunderstood or ignored their patients' wishes.

Forty-nine percent of the patients who wanted to avoid cardiopulmonary resuscitation by having their doctors write do-not-resuscitate orders did not get their wish.

The patients who did had to wait a long time for the doctors' orders. Depending on their medical specialty, doctors took an average of 22 to 73 days to write the orders after the patients requested them, and 46 percent of the orders were written within two days of the patient's death. Half the patients spent eight or more days in what the researchers de-

Continued on Page C7, Column 1

China Charges Leading Dissident With Trying to Overthrow Regime

By PATRICK E. TYLER

BEIJING, Nov. 21 — China formally charged the country's best-known dissident, Wei Jingsheng, today with trying to "overthrow the Chinese Government," a step that almost certainly will lead to conviction and a second, lengthy prison sentence for the 44-year-old democracy advocate.

Mr. Wei had been held incommunicado at an undisclosed police "guest house" without charge since April 1994, when he was seized by seven carloads of plainclothes policemen while driving into the Chinese capital from the nearby city of Tianjin.

At the time he was on parole after serving 14½ years of a 15-year prison sentence on charges of counter-revolutionary incitement and passing state secrets to foreigners for his activities during the 1978-79 Democracy Wall movement in Beijing.

Mr. Wei, an electrician turned political essayist, gained wide attention for his biting criticisms of the Communist Party leadership, particularly the Government's failure to pursue democratic reforms promised by Deng Xiaoping and other senior leaders during the years after the death of Mao in 1976.

Today's decision by the party leadership to bring criminal charges against Mr. Wei caught many of his supporters and family members by surprise and indicates a determined effort by the Government to prevent him from returning to Chinese society, where he has been a magnet for pro-democracy forces.

In one sense, the Government acted to ease the contradiction between its often-stated position that China seeks to become a nation ruled by law, and Mr. Wei's continued secret detention without charges in blatant violation of the country's own published criminal procedures.

The action against Mr. Wei went forward despite recent appeals by President Clinton and Chancellor Helmut Kohl of Germany. Mr. Kohl visited here this month seeking the release of China's political prisoners, especially Mr. Wei, who has now spent more than 16 years in detention, nearly half that time in solitary confinement.

Earlier this year, Mr. Wei's younger sister, Wei Shanshan, wrote a letter to Mr. Deng pointing out the illegality of his detention.

"No formal charges have been brought against him, nor is he being

Continued on Page A7, Column 1

Clinton's Next Task Will Be to Sell Plan To the U.S. Public

By ALISON MITCHELL

WASHINGTON, Nov. 21 — Even as he triumphantly announced the Balkan accord, President Clinton today began the difficult task of convincing a skeptical public and a hostile Congress to support sending 20,000 American troops to enforce the peace in Bosnia.

"We are at a decisive moment," the President said in a mid-morning appearance in the White House Rose Garden. "The parties have chosen peace. America must choose peace as well."

Clearly aiming his remarks at the American public, Mr. Clinton spoke of the "senseless slaughter of so many innocent people that our fellow citizens had to watch night after night after night for four long years on their television screens."

White House advisers were keenly aware that Mr. Clinton will have to make a major personal investment in the effort to convince Americans that their country's leadership responsibilities require that their soldiers be sent to a chaotic region to patrol a peace that could yet revert to war.

With a NATO plan to enforce a Balkans peace expected to be submitted to the President within a week — and large-scale deployment of troops possibly only weeks away — Mr. Clinton and his foreign policy team were preparing to mount a quick and extensive campaign, including a televised presidential ad-

Continued on Page A11, Column 1

Education Chief in Trenton Asks Legislature to Set School Budgets

By NEIL MacFARQUHAR

TRENTON, Nov. 21 — New Jersey officials, under court order to equalize spending between rich and poor school districts, today proposed that the State Legislature, rather than local voters, set the basic school budget for all districts.

The New Jersey Commissioner of Education, Leo F. Klagholz, presented the plan — the latest development in a 25-year legal battle — without actual dollar figures. The Commissioner said it would take weeks to determine whether following the recommendation would mean an increase in the state budget for education and what effect it might have on local property taxes.

The 77-page report released unexpectedly today was developed from suggestions put forward in 70 public hearings and meetings over the last year, Dr. Klagholz said. It now goes to the State Legislature for consideration.

Once combined with curriculum standards, which the department said it would submit by January, the government will determine what the state will pay for in every classroom, defining for the first time the minimum level of education that the state guarantees.

New Jersey is one of a dozen states that are under court orders to close the disparity in spending among school districts. Spending for students in New Jersey ranges from a low of $5,900 per pupil to a high of $11,500 per pupil in districts with kindergarten through 12th grade students. In districts with just kindergarten through eighth grade, spending runs from $4,800 to $15,900.

New Jersey joins a small group of states seeking to address such court orders to establish equity between wealthy and poor districts through the quality of the education delivered rather than the dollars spent.

Presently, each district determines its own curriculum, applying to the state for relief if it needs more money. New Jersey spends $12 billion a year on education — more per pupil than any other state — but Dr. Klagholz said the spending was not reflected in overall student achievement.

Under the new plan, the state would both establish the curriculum and outline school spending levels. It would determine everything from the number of teachers needed by an

Continued on Page B5, Column 1

Back to Square One At Columbus Circle

After more than a decade of neighborhood battles, environmental studies and court fights over the fate of the New York Coliseum, New York State and New York City have decided to turn the clock back to 1984 and look for a new buyer for the valuable Columbus Circle site.

Requests for new development proposals are to be issued before the end of the year.

Article, page B1.

354613

INSIDE

The Dow Surges Past 5,000

The extraordinary bull market in stocks shows no sign of letting up, with the Dow Jones industrial average surging past 5,000 for the first time. Market Place, page D1.

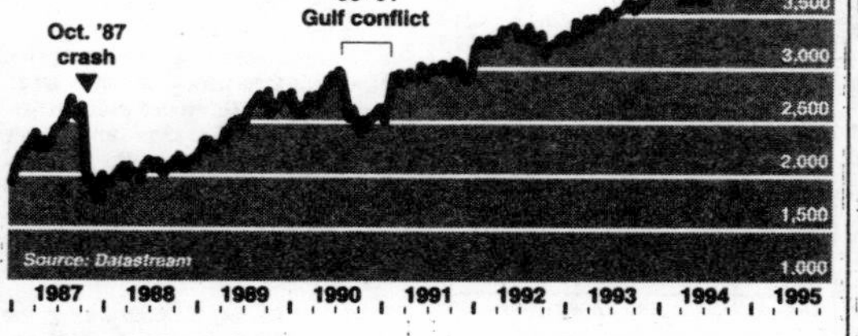

New Cabinet for Israel

Acting Prime Minister Shimon Peres of Israel announced his Cabinet, in which he will direct the Defense Ministry as troops leave parts of the West Bank. Page A3.

Crowded Day in the Skies

Airports across the nation will be busy today, but it will not be the busiest day of the year, a distinction that goes to the Sunday after Thanksgiving. Page A12.

NEWS SUMMARY A2

"All the News That's Fit to Print"

The New York Times

Late Edition
New York: Today, Cloudy, late showers. High 53. Tonight, showers. Low 42. Tomorrow, early showers, a brighter afternoon. High 48. Yesterday, high 60, low 38. Details, C18.

VOL.CXLV . . . No. 50,387 | NEW YORK, THURSDAY, APRIL 4, 1996 | 60 CENTS
$1 beyond the greater New York metropolitan area.

COMMERCE SECRETARY AMONG 33 LOST IN A CROATIA PLANE CRASH

ALL FEARED DEAD

Ronald Brown Headed a Business Mission to Rebuild Balkans

Reuters

Tragic End to Mission in Balkans

A plane carrying Commerce Secretary Ronald H. Brown, shown above arriving in Tuzla yesterday, crashed near the Croatian city of Dubrovnik. Secretary Brown was visiting the region with executives from U.S. companies.

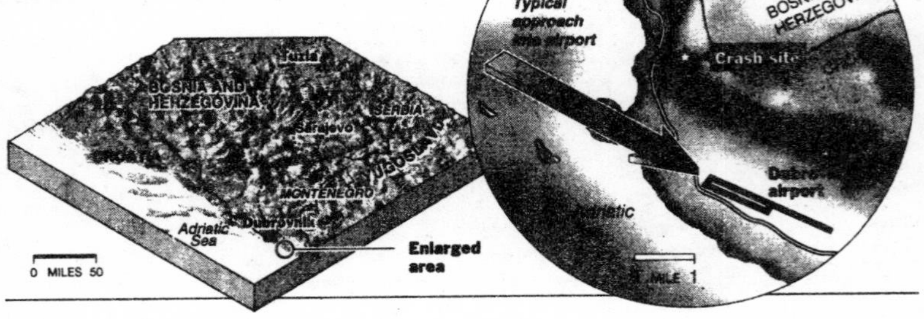

By R. W. APPLE Jr.

WASHINGTON, April 3 — A military plane carrying Commerce Secretary Ronald H. Brown and a delegation of American corporate executives slammed into a mountainside today as it approached the airport at Dubrovnik, on the Adriatic coast of Croatia. Chances that Mr. Brown had survived were "next to zero," a White House official said after more than 12 hours of rescue efforts.

Clambering over rocky, rugged terrain, working by flashlight in pelting rain, Croatian search parties found nine bodies and one survivor, described by a Dubrovnik doctor at the scene as "a woman who was bleeding profusely." She died later, Croatian officials said.

But there was no definitive word on the fate of Mr. Brown, a 54-year-old political insider who helped spark President Clinton's 1992 campaign. Glyn Davies, a State Department spokesman, said tonight that all 33 people aboard the plane were presumed dead, but later retracted his comment, saying they were considered missing. The Croatian television said all had perished.

Searchers at the scene and officials in Washington said they held out almost no hope that survivors would be found.

A United States military official in Germany said there was no indication the plane had been downed by hostile action.

One of those missing was Nathaniel C. Nash, 44, the Frankfurt bureau chief of The New York Times, who was accompanying Mr. Brown on a trip to Balkan nations for an article on reconstruction efforts. Commerce Department staff members were on board as well, including Charles Meissner, Assistant Secretary for International Economic Policy.

Names of the corporate executives aboard were not made public by the Government, but some companies issued statements confirming that their executives had been on board. Among them were Robert A. Whittaker chairman of Foster Wheeler Energy International of Clifton, N. J., and Robert E. Donovan, president of Asea Brown Boveri of Norwalk, Conn.

Several prominent businessmen who had planned to make the trip did not do so. One was Alfred A. Checchi, co-chairman of Northwest Airlines, who elected instead to attend a White House state dinner on Tuesday night.

A senior American official, speaking on the condition of anonymity, said the pilot of Mr. Brown's plane had flown up a valley parallel to the one he should have followed before turning for his final approach. When he turned, he hit the mountain, the official said on the basis of reports from the scene.

President Clinton went to Mr. Brown's Washington home to comfort the Commerce Secretary's wife, Alma, and then to the Commerce Department, where he spoke feelingly of the missing Cabinet member as "a magnificent life force." Mr. Clinton said Mr. Brown,

Continued on Page A8, Column 1

A Storm-Swept Mountain's Grim Story

In Rain and Darkness the Searchers Locate a Disaster's Debris

By CHRIS HEDGES

VELJI DO, Croatia, April 3 — Croatian special police officers wrapped in green army ponchos, their faces averted from withering sheets of rain, labored up the steep slope of St. John Mountain tonight in a huge search for the far-flung wreckage that had been the plane carrying Secretary of Commerce Ronald H. Brown and 32 others.

Debris and bodies were scattered down a dark, wooded hillside lit by the bobbing flashlights of the search teams and occasional, startling flashes of lightning.

Blasts of thunder rolled out over the rocky, razorbacked precipices that rise and fall in profusion along the Adriatic coast. The heavy rain, which had turned the dirt roads to mud, reduced visibility to a few feet. And soldiers said even walking to the remote site was difficult.

Two Croatian commanders of the operation, standing next to a stone hut, their hair matted down by the rain and their boots covered with mud, said they had found nine bodies and, to their astonishment, a surviving but unconscious woman. But the woman died as rescuers tried to get her to a hospital in Dubrovnik.

None of the passengers found had been identified by late tonight, and except for the woman, all were left to be recovered in the morning.

The heavy rain, fog and poor visibility made the use of helicopters impossible, the commanders said.

"We have sent as many men, as fast as we could, into the area," one said. "We will do the best we can, but the terrain is very, very difficult. The rain makes it hard for us to maneuver. We have 100 men now, another 100 are on the way. Our men will look all night. We all pray to God that some survived."

As he spoke, in the valley below, a convoy of six military trucks led by an army jeep with a flashing yellow light made its way up the steep road.

The officers in charge said the wreckage of the 737 military jet was strewn over a wide area near this tiny collection of stone huts about 20 miles by road east of the ancient walled city of Dubrovnik. They said that the bodies they had recovered, along with the woman, came from the fuselage of the plane, which had broken into two sections.

"This is a terrible, terrible tragedy," said one soldier as he came down from the mountain.

The gray stone houses near the steeply wooded tract where the plane went down look out over Cilipi

Continued on Page A8, Column 1

Jet Crash Casts a Sudden Shadow Over Official Washington

By TODD S. PURDUM

WASHINGTON, April 3 — At 10:30 this morning, President Clinton's national security adviser, Anthony Lake, walked into the Oval Office with the news: Commerce Secretary Ronald H. Brown's plane was missing in the Balkans and wreckage had been spotted. The rest was a welter of unconfirmed reports.

In that moment, a brilliant spring day turned to ashes. Minutes later, the deputy White House press secretaries, Ginny Terzano and Mary Ellen Glynn, crept into the office of their boss, Michael D. McCurry, with news service bulletins and spirited him off to the top-secret Situation Room in the basement of the West Wing.

By 11 A.M., Mr. Clinton was on the phone to Mr. Brown's wife, Alma, to tell her all he knew. She was home sick with the flu, not listening to radio or television, friends said, and the President's call came out of the blue.

"I want you to hear it from me first," aides said the President told her. Minutes later the President was making the rounds of the West Wing, consoling aides who were Mr. Brown's friends, and by midafternoon, he and his wife, Hillary Rodham Clinton, had arrived grim-faced at Mrs. Brown's house in Northwest Washington for a vigil.

From there, the Clintons went to the Commerce Department auditorium where the President brought hundreds of workers to their feet by repeating what he said Mrs. Brown had told him: that her husband had fought for the department and its workers, and that she hoped the President would too. Then Mr. Clinton brought a hush over the crowded room by recalling Mr. Brown's favorite passage from Scripture, Isaiah's words about how the faithful "shall mount up with wings as eagles."

"Ron Brown walked and ran and flew through life," Mr. Clinton said. "And he was a magnificent life force. And those of us who loved him will always be grateful for his friendship and his warmth."

So it went throughout the top echelons of the White House and Government, where almost everyone knew the affable Mr. Brown, one of the principal architects of the Democrats' 1992 victory.

Many had worked for him in his four-year tenure as chairman of the Democratic National Committee. Mr. McCurry was his press secretary for a time; later, so was Ms. Terzano.

The deputy White House chief of staff, Harold M. Ickes, worked with Mr. Brown on the Rev. Jesse Jackson's presidential campaign in 1988, and on Mr. Clinton's in 1992. Together with Paul Tully, the political director of the Democratic National Committee who died of a heart attack at the height of the 1992 campaign, Mr. Brown was the main institutional author of Mr. Clinton's victory, and he remained the odds-on

Continued on Page A9, Column 1

Ex-Professor Is Seized In Montana as Suspect In the Unabom Attacks

By DAVID JOHNSTON

WASHINGTON, April 3 — Federal agents today raided a remote Montana cabin where they seized a one-time university professor suspected of being the Unabomber, the elusive terrorist who has left a 17-year nationwide trail of mail bombs that have killed 3 people and maimed 23 others.

Law-enforcement officials said tonight that the agents had found explosive chemicals and other bomb-making material at the wilderness cabin belonging to the suspect, Theodore J. Kaczynski. They said they planned to charge Mr. Kaczynski on Thursday with the series of deadly attacks, which had long baffled the authorities.

The suspect is a 53-year-old former assistant professor of mathematics at the University of California at Berkeley, where he taught for two years in the late 1960's. He graduated from Harvard College in 1962 and then earned a doctorate in mathematics at the University of Michigan. His is just the sort of academic-oriented background that the authorities had attributed to the bomber, whose communications with the press had reflected an obsession with science and technology issues.

Since the early 1970's, Mr. Kaczynski has lived in his tiny cabin 50 miles northwest of Helena, Mont., near the Continental Divide on the edge of Lolo National Forest. The area is so remote that one of the F.B.I. agents who had kept him under surveillance there for the last several weeks is said to have watched a cougar attack and kill a deer.

Derek Pruitt for The New York Times

Theodore J. Kaczynski, the suspect in the Unabom attacks, was brought in for questioning in Helena, Mont., last night.

The agents confronted Mr. Kaczynski at the cabin today and, after a brief scuffle, searched it for evidence of bomb-related material. Federal investigators, who had said before the search that they did not have sufficient evidence to charge Mr. Kaczynski with the bombings, said afterward that the agents had found what they believe is enough to bring a complaint against him on Thursday in a Federal court in Helena.

The filing of formal charges against Mr. Kaczynski will mean that investigators can begin taking fingerprint and blood samples to determine whether they match the evidence collected over the years like the DNA, drawn from dried saliva, that the bomber left on stamps used to mail letters to his victims and to news organizations.

The Federal Bureau of Investigation put Mr. Kaczynski under scrutiny about two months ago, when — after years of false leads, fruitless searching across the country and the publication of a 35,000-word manifesto from the bomber — the long-awaited breakthrough came from the suspect's own family. According to law-enforcement officials, members of the Kaczynski family in the Chicago area, apparently while cleaning their house and preparing it for sale, discovered writings that seemed strikingly similar to the Unabomber's anarchist tracts.

The family members, who the officials said included Mr. Kaczynski's brother, turned the papers over to the F.B.I., apparently through a Washington lawyer acting as intermediary. They also permitted the F.B.I. to search their house, where, officials said, further evidence against Mr. Kaczynski was found.

Mr. Kaczynski was reared in Evergreen Park, Ill., a working-class suburb of Chicago that offers a tableau of Middle American images, from the Cape Cod house where the Kaczynski family once lived to the nearby park where children played soccer and touch football today. The family later moved to Lombard, another Chicago suburb, and it was at the house in that city that Mr. Kaczynski's papers were found.

The Unabom case, which came to be so called because some of the early targets were university employees and airlines, began in May 1978 with the first of 16 bombings or attempted bombings. The Unabomber mailed his last package bomb in April 1995, when a blast in Sacramento, Calif., killed the president of the California Forestry Association. During the 17 years in between, the bomber's meticulously built devices grew ever more powerful and lethal, and his communications to the authorities more menacing.

In an effort to showcase his anti-

Continued on Page B12, Column 1

Recalling Dodgers' Flight, Mayor Makes His Pitch for New Stadium

By STEVEN LEE MYERS

Recalling how New York City lost the Dodgers after a previous mayor refused to help the team build a new baseball stadium in Brooklyn, Mayor Rudolph W. Giuliani has begun to offer the economic justification — and with it the political one — for building the Yankees a new home on the West Side of Manhattan.

In news conferences on Tuesday and again yesterday, Mr. Giuliani said that while he felt an emotional bond with Yankee Stadium dating to his boyhood memories of Yankee heroes, the city had to do all it could to insure that the team's owner, George M. Steinbrenner 3d, does not move the team to New Jersey or anywhere else.

To do that, the Mayor is touting a proposal to build a new stadium above the rail yards beside the Hudson River, just south of the Jacob K. Javits Convention Center. On Tuesday, Mr. Giuliani said that revenue from a West Side stadium would be so high it "would be off the charts." Yesterday he said the city could not afford to repeat the mistakes of the past, ignoring the desires of one of the city's most valuable assets.

"It's also my responsibility to do the best that I can to make certain the Yankees stay in New York City." Mr. Giuliani said yesterday. "And that if, in fact, they are determined to leave the Bronx, that we not lose them to New Jersey, Tampa or someplace else."

No one has come right out and said Mr. Steinbrenner's Yankees plan to abandon their nostalgia-soaked 73-year-old stadium. But in his carefully measured remarks, the Mayor has made it clearer than ever that such a move is a distinct possibility and that the city had to have what he called "a fall-back strategy," name-

Continued on Page B10, Column 1

INSIDE

Move to Stamp Out Pushers

Using several new weapons, the Police Department will begin its biggest assault ever against drug dealers next week in several New York City neighborhoods. Page B1.

Carl Stokes Dies

Carl B. Stokes, a slave's great-grandson who became the first black Mayor of a major American city when he was elected to lead Cleveland in 1967, died at 68. Page D22.

"All the News That's Fit to Print"

The New York Times

Late Edition
New York: Today, sunny and warmer, cool sea breezes at the coast. High 77. Tonight, clear, calm. Low 58. Tomorrow, sunny. High 84. Yesterday, high 66, low 50. Details, page B7.

VOL. CXLV . . No. 50,444 — NEW YORK, FRIDAY, MAY 31, 1996 — 60 CENTS

$1 beyond the greater New York metropolitan area.

NETANYAHU, SET TO LEAD ISRAEL, TO SEEK 'PEACE WITH SECURITY'

Reuters

Likud supporters celebrated yesterday in Tel Aviv outside the hotel where Benjamin Netanyahu was staying.

FINAL TALLY TODAY

Likud Leader Launches Effort to Negotiate Coalition Cabinet

By SERGE SCHMEMANN

JERUSALEM, May 30 — Benjamin Netanyahu, the conservative opposition leader who campaigned on charges that Israel's Labor Government neglected the country's security in its search for peace with the Palestinians, stood on the brink of victory today, waiting only for the military vote to be counted before he could formally lay claim to the Prime Minister's job, now held by Shimon Peres.

With all the regular ballots counted, Mr. Netanyahu led by a scant 21,399 votes of the 2,811,161 cast, an edge of 0.7 percent. But 150,000 absentee ballots remained to be counted, most of them from military bases, and past experience indicated that a majority were likely to fall to Mr. Netanyahu. The final tally of the first direct election of an Israeli Prime Minister is expected Friday afternoon.

Though Mr. Netanyahu declined to claim victory openly, he held meetings throughout the day at a hotel in Tel Aviv with potential Cabinet ministers and coalition partners.

If the final tally confirms Mr. Netanyahu's victory, his first task will be to form a coalition in the Parliament and a Cabinet. The law gives him 45 days to present a government; if he fails, new elections for a Prime Minister would be called within 60 days.

Mr. Netanyahu was not expected to encounter any difficulty forging a majority coalition in the 120-seat Parliament. In addition to the 31 seats that Likud stood to win, he could count on support from three religious parties for 25 more seats, a party of Russian immigrants for 7, and two smaller parties for another 6. That would give him a total of 69.

Should he at some later time lose a vote of confidence in Parliament, new elections would be held for both Prime Minister and Parliament.

Mr. Netanyahu began immediate efforts to allay fears, in Israel as in Washington, that a conservative government would reverse the drive toward a settlement with the Palestinians that Mr. Peres pursued.

A statement issued by Dore Gold, a foreign affairs adviser, said: "Benjamin Netanyahu affirms that he is deeply committed to the continuation of the peace process, peace with security, between the state of Israel and all its neighbors, including the Palestinians. And he has committed himself as well to the strengthening of the peace between Israel and those Arab states with whom Israel

Continued on Page A10, Column 1

Terror Defendant Presents His Case

Ignoring a judge's advice that he not act as his own lawyer, the man accused of mounting an international campaign of terror that included the World Trade Center bombing began personally presenting his defense against charges that he plotted to blow up a dozen American jetliners.

After Judge Kevin Thomas Duffy reluctantly let him waive his right to a lawyer, Ramzi Ahmed Yousef contended that he was framed by two nations trying to curry favor with the United States.

Article, page B1.

Air Force Ousts 3 From Duties In Brown Case

By PHILIP SHENON

WASHINGTON, May 30 — The Air Force announced today that a general and two other senior commanders had been relieved of their duties in Germany as a result of an investigation into last month's crash of a jetliner in Croatia that killed Commerce Secretary Ronald H. Brown and 34 others.

With the investigation nearly completed, the Air Force said that Brig. Gen. William E. Stevens of the 86th Airlift Wing at Ramstein Air Base in Germany and two of his deputies had been removed from their posts because their commander had "lost his confidence in the ability" of the officers to "effectively discharge their responsibilities."

A senior Air Force official, speaking on condition that he not be identified, said the three officers had been removed because they had failed to follow rules that should have resulted months ago in a safety inspection of the airport at Dubrovnik, Croatia, where the plane was trying to land when it crashed into a mountainside during a violent rainstorm.

The airport had only rudimentary navigational equipment. Had the inspection occurred before April, it might have led to flying restrictions that would probably have prevented the crash, Pentagon officials said.

In fact, the Air Force command overseeing flights of United States-based planes had done such an inspection, and in February forbade planes under its control from landing at Dubrovnik, except in clear weather and in daylight. But officials said General Stevens did not order a similar inspection for transport aircraft based in Germany that might land at Dubrovnik, even though he was apparently under pressure to do so.

General Stevens and his deputies "chose not to do that," a senior officer said. "There's a very, very high operation tempo at Ramstein and insufficient resources to try to do everything, and the commander had to make some priorities," he said,

Continued on Page A16, Column 4

GIULIANI PLEDGES THOROUGH INQUIRY IN RACIAL BEATING

VICTIM REMAINS IN COMA

Detective Charged — Mayor Vows to Find Out if Other Officers Were Involved

By STEVEN LEE MYERS

A day after saying the arrest of a New York City detective in a racially charged assault outside a Long Island bar did not reflect badly on the police force, Mayor Rudolph W. Giuliani pledged a thorough investigation yesterday and spoke strongly about officers' responsibility to behave properly, even when off duty.

Faced with questions raised by the beating, the arrest and the possible complicity of other police officers, the Mayor insisted that the Police Department had cooperated fully with the authorities in Suffolk County within hours of the assault in the early morning hours of Sunday. He promised to "do everything possible" to make sure that if any other officers were involved in the assault, or the drunken brawling leading up to it, they would be punished.

Yesterday, investigators hunted for more suspects in the case, in which Detective Constantine Chronis is accused of beating Shane L. Daniels, 21, into a coma outside a nightclub in Westhampton Beach. Witnesses said one of Detective Chronis's companions had a gun, and investigators sought to determine whether any other officers were involved. [Page B6.]

At least two dozen detectives from the Police Department's internal affairs unit are helping in the investigation, and they have interviewed more than 100 of Detective Chronis's colleagues to determine whether any were with him.

Under the department's rules, an officer convicted of a misdemeanor or a felony is automatically dismissed from the force.

While the Police Department has strict rules against "behavior detrimental to the force," the Mayor said that officers should never drink to excess and certainly not while carrying their weapons. He also said they should never ignore violations of the law, such as a bartender's selling alcohol to minors.

"Police officers have a right off

Continued on Page B6, Column 1

Prosecutors v. Mayor

District attorneys from around the state condemned Mayor Rudolph W. Giuliani for continuing to challenge the Bronx District Attorney over his handling of the prosecution of a man charged in the death of a police officer last week.

Article, page B1.

Orthodox Welcome New Powers, And See Big Effects on Daily Life

By JOSEPH BERGER

BNEI BRAK, Israel, May 30 — Although it was not a Jewish holiday, the streets of this ardently Orthodox suburb of Tel Aviv had an uncommonly festive air today, with the talk at the bustling shops and restaurants all about the new power the Orthodox have snatched in Israel.

In Steisel's Restaurant, Hasidic men, seated in front of plates heaped with stuffed green peppers and potato pudding, took deep puffs of filtered cigarettes and chuckled as they passed their time with predictions of an Israel led by Benjamin Netanyahu and a Parliament with a record 25 deputies from religious parties.

"Hopefully, this will influence the country to go in the religious way," said Menachem Steisel, a 78-year-old Hasid with a wispy beard as he wandered among the tables in the homespun restaurant he owns. "They will close streets on Shabbos, there will be more education in Yiddishkeit," or Jewish tradition, in the public schools, he said.

"There's a great satisfaction that we are redeemed from the anti-religion government," said Mordechai Pollack, a 33-year-old Hasid with a broad, reddish beard.

While the race for Prime Minister focused almost entirely on the question of security and relations with the Arabs, some of the biggest effects of this week's election may be on daily life within Israel as the resurgent religious parties exert their new muscle in Parliament to deepen the hold of Jewish tradition.

Leaders of secular groups are apprehensive. The new power of the Orthodox, they said, will bring to the surface demands that have been kept relatively muffled under the Labor Government. The rising power of the Orthodox as lawmakers is sure to constitute a setback for the small Reform and Conservative movements here. They have been trying to

Continued on Page A11, Column 1

CLINTON IS SHAKEN, BUT REAFFIRMS TIE

As Ally Faces Electoral Defeat, He Vows Support for Israel

By ALISON MITCHELL

WASHINGTON, May 30 — Shaken by what might well be the defeat of one of its closest allies, the Clinton Administration struggled today to put the best face on Israel's election results and to reach out to Benjamin Netanyahu, the challenger whom President Clinton had all but campaigned against.

Mr. Clinton pledged his continued support to the Israeli people and said he hoped the search for Middle East peace could be maintained no matter what the final shape of the government that emerges in Israel.

"Whatever the results, the United States will continue its policy of support for the people of Israel, for the democratic process there, and for the process of peace," the President said, speaking at the White House before departing for a day of campaign-style events in Louisiana. "And our policy will be the same. If Israel is prepared to take risks for peace, we are determined to do our best to reduce the risks and increase the security of those who do that."

While the final tally was not yet in, the White House clearly believed that Mr. Netanyahu was likely to be declared the victor over Shimon Peres, the man Mr. Clinton had publicly embraced as the best hope for peace. Aides described the President as disappointed and said the mood in the White House was "crestfallen" over an expected outcome that they saw as setting back both the Clinton Administration's Middle East policy and the President's own election-year self-portrait as a peacemaker.

The results, officials said, would make it harder for Mr. Clinton to use

Continued on Page A10, Column 6

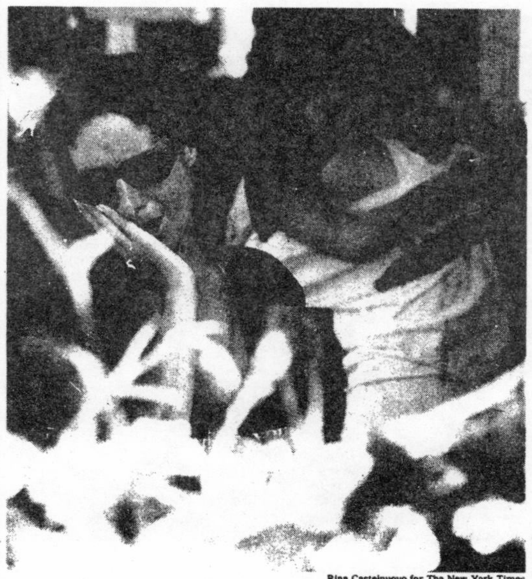

Rina Castelnuovo for The New York Times

At the flower-covered memorial to Yitzhak Rabin in Tel Aviv, some Israelis mourned what they saw as the death of the peace process.

Israel's Losingest Hero

Shimon Peres should rank as a great figure in Israeli history. But, if the current vote unwinds as many expect today, in his fourth defeat for Prime Minister, he may be remembered as the man who could not win.

Article, page A10.

The Verdict on Whitewater: It's in the Eye of the Beholder

By MICHAEL WINERIP

AN AMERICAN PLACE
Buzzing About Whitewater

CANTON, Ohio, May 30 — Jason Burnette, 25, a local television producer who votes Republican, was at home channel surfing the other day when he hit a CNN news bulletin on the Whitewater verdict.

"I kept it right there," he said, "and listened intently."

He put down his turkey and cheese sandwich. He was all alone, but when he heard that President Clinton's former business partners were guilty, he said, "Yes!"

Charles Brown, the Stark County Republican chairman, was driving home from his law office, listening to National Public Radio, when he heard. "Thank God!" he said.

He went right into the house and made 20 telephone calls to friends to spread the "good news."

At the North Canton Barber Shop on Main Street in that Republican suburb, it was not just the clippers that were buzzing these last two days. "We get mainly Republicans in here," said Don Schrader, the barber. "I'm a Republican myself. The Republicans have been looking for an in, so there's been lots of talk."

The first Whitewater trial did not directly involve President Clinton but there is no doubt that the outcome has energized Senator Bob Dole's supporters and caught the public's attention here in Stark County, a bellwether for national politics.

Which is not to say that it has changed many voters' minds yet or cut into the President's apparent lead here. At Democratic barber shops, like Downtowner Barber on Market Street in the Democratic city of Canton, customers mainly dismiss Whitewater as "politics."

"We're mostly working-class people," Fran DeMarco, a Democratic barber, said of his customers. "Their way of thinking is toward Mr. Clinton."

And at the taverns alongside the Timken Company's mills, where steelworkers gather at the end of their shift, the common reaction seems to be: All politicians are crooks and Clinton may be, too, but he is our crook.

"They all have skeletons in their closet," said Ray Cole, who voted for Mr. Clinton in 1992 and plans to again.

George Seich, another union man

Continued on Page A21, Column 1

Tokyo Journal

Japan vs. Korea, Again, and Both Cry 'Foul!'

By NICHOLAS D. KRISTOF

TOKYO, May 30 — Ask Chie Suzuki what she thinks of soccer, and the one thing she doesn't say is, "It's just a game."

Instead, this week, it is everything — at least to Japan and South Korea. The two countries are battling for the right to be host to the 2002 World Cup, the international championships held every four years. On Saturday one is expected to get it, and the other will be heartbroken.

Miss Suzuki, a computer company employee in Tokyo, is one of those whose heart is on the line. She scoffs that South Korea was mean-spirited even to compete with Japan for the World Cup, and she repeats the common complaints that South Korea is throwing money around to win votes.

"I don't like the way they are campaigning," Miss Suzuki said. "And they're only in this because Japan wanted it."

"Because Japan started campaigning for the World Cup, Korea followed," Miss Suzuki added. "Why else did Korea start its bid? It's because Korea didn't want to give the first World Cup in Asia to Japan."

Now, that is polite compared to what the Koreans say about the Japanese. And since the two countries — traditional enemies and contemporary allies — are the only bidders for the world's biggest single-sport event, all this is provoking a minor foreign policy crisis.

For South Korea, the problem is simple: if it loses, as 70,000 people gather in a sports stadium to watch the announcement live on television from the Zurich offices of FIFA, the sport's governing body, the result is national humiliation, crushing de-

Continued on Page A4, Column 3

INSIDE

Sales of New Homes Surge

Sales of new homes jumped in April, especially in the Northeast, providing further evidence of an increasingly strong economy. Page D1.

Candidates on Social Ills

President Clinton urged localities to impose curfews on youths, while Bob Dole said the welfare system magnified domestic violence. Page A20.

U.S. Won't Back China Dam

The U.S. Export-Import Bank refused to help finance the Three Gorges Dam in China, citing environmental concerns. Page D1.

Protection for Babies

Federal officials recommended strategies to cut the incidence bacterial infection in newborns. Page A12.

Pitino Turns Down Nets

Rick Pitino rejected an offer worth nearly $30 million to stay as coach at the University of Kentucky. Page B9.

"All the News That's Fit to Print"

The New York Times

Late Edition
New York: **Today,** fog, then partly sunny, humid. High 87. **Tonight,** showers. Low 70. **Tomorrow,** less humid, late thunderstorms. High 88. **Yesterday,** high 83, low 68. Details, page C9.

VOL.CXLV . . . . No. 50,456 | NEW YORK, WEDNESDAY, JUNE 12, 1996 | 60 CENTS
$1 beyond the greater New York metropolitan area.

Associated Press

Lightning Starts Fuel Tank Fire in New Jersey

Lightning struck a fuel tank holding three million gallons of gasoline in Woodbridge, N.J., yesterday, starting a blaze that shot 150 feet into the sky. Some 200 people were evacuated; there were no injuries. Page B1.

U.S. BLAMES ALLIES FOR UNDERCUTTING ITS CHINA POLICY

TRADE ACCORDS AT ISSUE

Asia Expert Says Europe and Japan 'Hold Our Coats and Gobble Up Contracts'

By DAVID E. SANGER

WASHINGTON, June 11 — The State Department's top official for Asian affairs said today that the Administration's efforts to force China to respect trade accords and halt the spread of weapons were being exploited by Europe and Japan, which he said were happy to "hold our coats" while they "gobble up our contracts."

The unusually blunt assessment by the official, Winston Lord, in testimony before the House Ways and Means Committee, came a day after Prime Minister Li Peng explicitly warned that he would use China's growing economic power to send more business to non-American companies unless Washington dropped its efforts to force China to change its ways.

Mr. Li, in an interview with The Financial Times, praised European leaders because "they do not attach political strings to cooperation with China, unlike the Americans who arbitrarily resort to the threat of sanctions or the use of sanctions."

Mr. Lord, a former Ambassador to China who is now Assistant Secretary of State for East Asia and the Pacific, and other Clinton Administration officials have privately expressed their frustration in recent months that Japan and the European Union have criticized America's tactics with China — while turning the tensions to their own benefit.

They have noted, for example, that among the biggest beneficiaries of America's crackdown on the piracy of music and video recordings in China are the Sony Corporation of Japan and Bertelsmann A. G. of Germany.

Through industry associations in Washington, the companies have lobbied the Administration heavily to take a tough line against China on behalf of their American subsidiaries.

But in Japan and Germany, the same companies and their Govern-

Continued on Page A7, Column 1

Citizen Dole Bids Farewell to the Senate

Associated Press

Bob Dole, with his wife, Elizabeth, left the Capitol yesterday after his official retirement from the Senate.

Mayor and Council Hold Strings For $276 Million Schools Pledge

By STEVEN LEE MYERS

Mayor Rudolph W. Giuliani and the City Council's leaders agreed yesterday to provide an immediate infusion of $276 million to repair New York City's public schools but only after making an unusual demand that they, not the Board of Education, dictate where the money is spent and on what.

The $276 million in new spending is the first installment of a larger proposal to borrow an additional $1.4 billion over the next four years to repair the city's aging, overcrowded schools.

The plan, a central component of an agreement on a $32.8 billion budget reached in the wee hours of the morning, would allow repair work to begin almost with the start of the new fiscal year on July 1, officials said yesterday. That would allow at least some projects to be completed before the new school year begins in September.

Although City Hall has no direct control over how the city's Board of Education spends its budget, Mr. Giuliani and the Council's leaders insisted on wresting away the power to approve repair projects as a condition of providing the $1.4 billion, which is to be raised by selling bonds to be repaid over the next 20 to 30 years. The board's seven members have not yet agreed to the demand, but both City Hall and school officials acknowledge that the board has little choice but to acquiesce.

The Mayor and the Council continued yesterday to negotiate with Schools Chancellor Rudy Crew's office over the exact wording of a written compact that is to establish the scope of City Hall's control. Officials on both sides of City Hall said they would decide to approve projects by category — choosing to repair, say, all the schools with leaky roofs — from project lists assembled by the board's engineers.

Mr. Giuliani, the Republican who

Continued on Page B4, Column 5

Dole, Ignoring His Advisers, Lashes Out at Abortion Foe

By RICHARD L. BERKE

WASHINGTON, June 11 — Bob Dole today brushed off the advice of some of his closest aides, who had urged him to pacify abortion opponents, and instead took the offensive against one of his most vociferous critics on the Republican right.

By insisting on a more inclusive position on abortion, Mr. Dole sent a clear signal that he was determined to win the support of abortion rights advocates in his own party, even at the expense of damaging relations with influential conservatives.

Several Dole advisers said some of his senior aides, including his campaign manager, Scott Reed, suggested to the all-but-certain Republican nominee today that the campaign put out a statement to soften his earlier comments that a plank in the Republican Party platform should contain a "declaration of tolerance" on abortion. The comments, in a television interview on Monday, had drawn an outcry from conservatives who insisted that any tempering language be included only in the preamble to the platform, and apply to a range of issues, not just abortion.

But aides to Mr. Dole said he was adamant that his remarks on Monday not be diluted. To further drive home the point, Mr. Dole went out of his way to express irritation with his critics among Republican conservatives, singling out Gary Bauer, president of the Family Research Council, an anti-abortion group.

"I don't know where these people come from, you know," Mr. Dole said in an interview with KMBC-TV, the ABC affiliate in Kansas City, Mo. "What's the difference if it's in the preamble or the platform? I mean this is a moral issue. I don't know where Gary Bauer's been all his life, but I've always known that we have had pro-choice Republicans and pro-life Republicans."

Mr. Dole went on: "I think Gary Bauer's tolerant. If he's not tolerant,

Continued on Page B7, Column 1

Full-Time Race for President Is Opened

By FRANCIS X. CLINES

WASHINGTON, June 11 — Bob Dole said goodbye to his Senate colleagues today, leaving the trappings and tribulations of the majority leader's post behind as he ventured off into America to campaign as "just a man" in pursuit of the ultimate political prize of the Presidency.

"My season in the Senate is about to come to an end," Mr. Dole declared in a farewell speech capped by a bipartisan wave of affectionate applause. "But the new season before me makes this moment far less the closing of one chapter than the opening of another."

The Senator resigned as of 2 P.M., walking down the East Capitol steps to close his cherished 35-year career as a Kansas Congressman and dominant Senate presence. His departure to cheers of "Dole '96!" instantly launched him into full-time campaigning as the Republican challenger to President Clinton, intent on reversing his underdog role in the early opinion polls.

In a rare moment of truce, Mr. Clinton, already campaigning in California, noted the Senator's service and urged a Los Angeles audience to wish Mr. Dole well. "I think we ought to give him a hand."

Mr. Dole was hardly looking back. "Our best tomorrows are yet to be lived," he told the senators at parting. His summary of his Capitol years was classically terse: "It's been a great ride, some bumps along the way."

His 37-minute speech, while rich in personal tributes to past and present Senate leaders of both parties, also touched on lingering Washington issues that Mr. Dole obviously intends to press as the Presidential campaign gathers heat.

"The one thing I would hope," he said, alluding to the failure of the proposed balanced-budget amendment in a clash with Mr. Clinton, "when they catalogue all the amendments and all the bills and do all the commentary, is that whenever it's all over for us here, that we've left our children something other than a legacy of debt."

Mr. Dole's last act after signing the resignation, aides said, was to pen a personal note to his daughter, Robin, just as he had done on the day he began his long incumbency, after arriving from Kansas at the dawning of the Kennedy Administration.

"We all take pride in the past," Mr. Dole told the Senate, fighting at several points to control his emotions as

Continued on Page B8, Column 1

James Hill for The New York Times

In Russia's Vote, a Clash Between Old and New

Workers erected a campaign billboard for President Boris N. Yeltsin in Penza, a town where voters are being pulled two ways — by the old Soviet values and the new drive for a more competitive society. Page A14.

Boards and Minds Are Little Changed By School Election

By JACQUES STEINBERG

It took 35 days, but the New York City Board of Elections finished counting the 172,000 ballots cast in the May 7 school board elections yesterday. Those who want to abolish the system of local school boards found no shortage of ammunition in this year's process.

Only 5 of every 100 eligible voters participated, according to the final tally, the lowest turnout in the 27 years since the local boards were given control of the city's elementary and junior high schools. The counting of the paper ballots, aided for the first time by computers that were supposed to speed the process, took nearly two weeks longer than it ever had when the counting was done by hand, officials said.

The 32 boards look much as they did before, with 82 percent of the incumbents who sought re-election winning new terms. Those incumbents included the presidents of three boards under suspension for wrongdoing or mismanagement.

"The system as it exists now is dysfunctional," said Assemblyman Steven Sanders of Manhattan, the chairman of the Assembly Education Committee, who has proposed abolishing the boards. "The 95 percent of the people who didn't vote were essentially voting no confidence in the current system. It has to

Continued on Page B5, Column 1

Drug Scandal Taints Panama's Reform Chief

By LARRY ROHTER

PANAMA, June 8 — Less than seven years ago, American troops invaded Panama and ousted Gen. Manuel Antonio Noriega and the drug-dealing army that he commanded. Now, with a friendly Government in power and the hand-over of the Panama Canal looming, the United States finds itself again facing a familiar quandary here.

Since taking office in 1994, President Ernesto Pérez Balladares has repeatedly pledged to crack down on drug trafficking here, and even followed through with some actions against Colombian cocaine cartels.

But he has been reluctant to respond to a trail of evidence that ties powerful figures in his own ruling party and Government to local companies that, American officials say, are deeply involved in money laundering and cocaine smuggling.

Those connections have come to light after the collapse here early this year of the Agro-Industrial and Commercial Bank, or Banaico, leaving more than $50 million unaccounted for and thousands of ordinary depositors broke and angry.

Named in several drug investigations in the United States, including a conspiracy to buy a fleet of planes for use by Colombian smugglers, Banaico is said by American law enforcement officials to have been a focal point of money laundering in Panama's flourishing off-shore banking center.

The bank's vice president and secretary was Mayor Alfredo Alemán

Continued on Page A10, Column 1

INSIDE

Beheading a Mob Empire

Federal prosecutors say they have broken the leadership of the most powerful mob clan in the nation by indicting 19 members of the Genovese crime family. Page B3.

Murder on Park Avenue

A woman known on the Upper East Side as "the lollipop lady" for giving sweets to children was fatally beaten at her dry cleaning shop. Page B1.

Signs of Neighbors 'Nearby'

An astronomer from the University of Pittsburgh has discovered evidence of planets at one of the stars closest to the sun. Page A24.

AN AMERICAN PLACE

Hard Choices in Ohio

Defiant workers at a Hoover vacuum factory in Ohio made a painful choice, rejecting a wage proposal even though jobs may now shift to a nonunion plant in Texas. Page A16.

Lessons in Leadership

In his long Senate career, Bob Dole came to know intimately the burdens of being a leader, a role that often found him balancing conflicting goals to achieve consensus and keep the Senate moving forward. His ability to listen and to ease tension with humor served him well.

News analysis, page B8.

"All the News That's Fit to Print"

The New York Times

Late Edition
New York: **Today,** sunny, some PM clouds. High 83. **Tonight,** variable clouds, possible shower. Low 67. **Tomorrow,** some sun. High 82. **Yesterday,** high 80, low 62. Details, page C18.

VOL.CXLV... No. 50,471

Copyright © 1996 The New York Times

NEW YORK, THURSDAY, JUNE 27, 1996

$1 beyond the greater New York metropolitan area.

60 CENTS

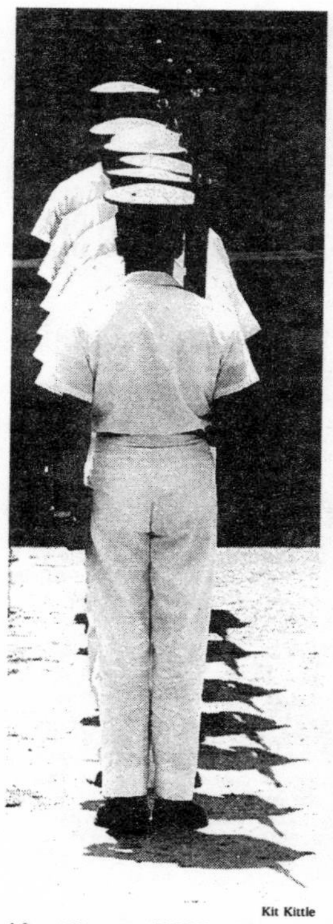

Kit Kittle

After 157 years, V.M.I. must do an about-face on admissions.

MILITARY COLLEGE CAN'T BAR WOMEN, HIGH COURT RULES

JUSTICES IN 7-1 DECISION

Separate Program Offered by Virginia Military Institute Is Deemed Inadequate

By LINDA GREENHOUSE

WASHINGTON, June 26 — The Supreme Court ruled today that under the "skeptical scrutiny" that applies to government action that treats men and women differently, the State of Virginia cannot justify keeping women out of its state-supported military college, the Virginia Military Institute.

"Women seeking and fit for a V.M.I.-quality education cannot be offered anything less under the state's obligation to afford them genuinely equal protection," Justice Ruth Bader Ginsburg said in a majority opinion for six Justices.

A seventh member of the Court, Chief Justice William H. Rehnquist, agreed in a separate opinion that the all-male admissions policy at the 157-year-old military college violated the Constitution and that the remedy accepted by the lower courts, a women's "leadership" program supported with state money at a nearby women's college, was inadequate.

The vote was therefore 7 to 1 on the basic constitutional holding in one of the Court's most important sex discrimination cases in years.

The lone dissenter was Justice Antonin Scalia, who objected that "change is forced upon Virginia, and reversion to single-sex education is prohibited nationwide, not by democratic processes but by order of this Court." Justice Clarence Thomas, whose son attends V.M.I., did not take part in the case.

The opinion leaves the state with the theoretical option of turning the college into a private institution, which would be free to exclude women. But officials at the school in Lexington, Va., indicated today that this option was probably not realistic.

"Whether or not it is feasible is very problematical," Maj. Gen. Josi-

Continued on Page B8, Column 1

Saudis, Aided by the F.B.I., Seek Blast Clues

Associated Press

Secretary of State Warren Christopher broke off a Middle East peacemaking trip to fly to the site of the blast, the second bombing in Saudi Arabia in seven months. He surveyed the damage yesterday with Saudi officials.

19 Killed in the 2d Explosion in 7 Months

By DOUGLAS JEHL

DHAHRAN, Saudi Arabia, June 26 — Surveying the ruins left by a blast that tore the face from an eight-story apartment building in a military complex here on Tuesday night and killed 19 American servicemen, American and Saudi officials insisted today that the attack would not diminish their close military cooperation.

The enormous explosion, which officials said was significantly more powerful than the bomb that demolished the Oklahoma City Federal Building in April 1995, left bathtubs and mattresses dangling from a structure rent open as if it were a doll house. It blew out windows a half-mile away, and wounded hundreds.

Secretary of State Warren Christopher, who interrupted a Middle East peacemaking trip to fly here and survey the damage, declared the blast "a direct and deliberate attack on the citizens of the United States and our friends and allies."

Twenty-four hours after the explosion, neither the motive nor the identity of those responsible was known, and American and Saudi officials said it was too soon to speculate about who would have carried out the attack, at the largest air base in Saudi Arabia.

American officials said a team sent by the Federal Bureau of Investigation was already moving in to assist Saudi investigators search for the clues that might identify who was behind the blast.

But they emphasized that the Saudi authorities would take the lead in the inquiry.

The bombing, the second aimed at American military personnel in Saudi Arabia in seven months, compounded an atmosphere of uncertainty in the country at a time when King Fahd has been weakened by a stroke and the leadership is contending with mounting internal dissent. [Page A11.]

Both Mr. Christopher and Prince Saud al-Faisal, the Saudi Foreign Minister, vowed that the attack would not deter their two countries from their extensive military cooperation, which has brought thousands of American service personnel to bases here as part of an effort to contain the threats posed by Iran and Iraq.

Visibly moved as he walked through broken glass and concrete rubble as dusk fell this evening, Mr. Christopher said, "It's a very bleak day for all of us."

Continued on Page A10, Column 4

New York City Acts to Tighten Begging Laws

By VIVIAN S. TOY

Mayor Rudolph W. Giuliani and the City Council reached agreement yesterday on an anti-begging law intended to crack down on insistent or menacing panhandlers and anyone who begs within 10 feet of automatic teller machines.

The bill, approved unanimously by the Council's Public Safety Committee yesterday, is expected to be approved by the full Council and signed by the Mayor next month. It would go into effect later this summer, giving police officers another weapon in what Council members and the Mayor call "quality of life" annoyances on the city's streets.

The proposed law would explicitly ban "aggressive" panhandling, which is defined as any begging that is threatening, involves physical contact or blocks a prospective donor's path. Administration officials said the bill's language was patterned after similar laws in other cities that had been upheld in court challenges.

The bill is also intended to put an end to the once seemingly ubiquitous "squeegee men" who sometimes still accost drivers at stoplights, demanding payment for an unwanted window washing. Officers now give squeegee men traffic tickets, but they add that some of the squeegee men ignore the summonses while

Continued on Page B4, Column 1

Victory for Parties

The Supreme Court said the Government may not limit how much political parties spend on their candidates unless it proves that party and candidate are working together.

Article, page B9.

Military Unprepared For Force of Attack

The United States had received a wave of threats against Americans and American installations in Saudi Arabia in recent weeks but failed to prepare adequately for a bomb of the size that killed 19 American military personnel on Tuesday, Clinton Administration officials said.

The Defense Department said it did all it reasonably could to protect service personnel, including the installation of concrete barriers around military installations. But one official said, "The surprise is not that there was an attack; the surprise is the severity of the attack."

Article, page A11.

Dole Campaign Plans an Attack On Clinton's Economic Record

By RICHARD W. STEVENSON

WASHINGTON, June 26 — Bob Dole's campaign advisers say they are planning a stepped-up attack on President Clinton's economic record, having concluded that despite low unemployment and inflation there is enough anxiety among voters about job security and stagnant incomes to leave the Administration vulnerable.

Their strategy, the advisers said, would be to argue that Mr. Clinton does not deserve credit for the ways in which the nation's economy is performing well, and should be blamed for tax increases and spending policies that they contend have undermined economic growth, creating a climate of insecurity and forcing workers to run harder just to stay in place.

The advisers said the economic campaign would begin in earnest this fall, after Mr. Dole announced his own economic policy package, probably about the time the Republican National Convention is held in San Diego this August.

Mr. Dole, the party's likely Presidential nominee, is expected to embrace a tax-cutting package as the centerpiece of a "pro-growth" economic platform, although he has yet to decide on details.

If the Dole campaign follows through on the plan to attack Mr. Clinton's economic record, it would be seeking to turn to its advantage — or at least to neutralize — an issue that the Administration has long considered one of its strengths.

The President often boasts of the economy's performance in creating more than eight million jobs since he took office, most of them paying good wages. He says the current combination of low inflation and unemployment with steady growth is one that no other Administration has sustained since the 1960's.

Democrats said they viewed the Dole camp as shifting away from a strategy of hoping that the economy would weaken this year, which has not happened, to one of asking wheth-

Continued on Page A18, Column 1

Survivors of Saudi Explosion Knew at Once It Was a Bomb

By STEVEN ERLANGER

DHAHRAN, Saudi Arabia, June 26 — Staff Sgt. Alfredo Guerrero saw it coming, unfolding before him like the nightmare his training courses had etched.

The Saudi base, where American, British and French troops are housed in a complex called Khobar Towers, was already on a heightened state of alert after warnings of possible attacks on Americans.

On Tuesday night, Sergeant Guerrero and two other Air Force security policemen were patrolling the roof of an eight-story barracks in the northernmost corner of Khobar Towers when a large gasoline truck and a passenger car pulled up to the perimeter fence.

The driver ran from his truck and threw himself into the car, which sped away, and Sergeant Guerrero knew immediately that it was a bomb. He and his fellow officers rushed down through the building urging those inside to evacuate.

They had perhaps three minutes for their task.

Sergeant Guerrero had only made it down two floors when the explosion struck, ripping the face off the building and killing 19 American servicemen. More than 400 other people were wounded, 250 of them American.

"Many are alive today because of his heroism," said Secretary of State Warren Christopher, who canceled a trip intended to help restart the Middle East peace effort to come here and see the victims of the kind of terrorism that has so often disrupted such efforts.

Prince Saud al-Faisal, the Saudi Foreign Minister, broke in. "This gentleman's name is Staff Sergeant Guerrero, and we're very grateful to him."

Maj. Gen. Kurt Anderson, commander of the joint task force, and

Continued on Page A10, Column 1

A Desperate Alarm Before The Blast

Here is a look at events that preceded the bombing of a U.S. military barracks near Dhahran, Saudi Arabia, killing 19 and injuring more than 400 others.

KHOBAR TOWERS COMPOUND (below) houses American, British and French military personnel assigned to the nearby air base.

① Three security guards patrolling the roof spot a truck pull up.

② The driver of the truck runs to a waiting car that speeds away.

③ Suspicious, the guards begin running downstairs yelling for residents to evacuate.

④ Minutes later, before most residents can leave the building, the truck explodes.

Security guards

BUILDING DAMAGED BY BLAST

N

Explosion occurred about 35 yards from building.

Concrete security barrier

ENLARGED AREA

Source: Department of Defense

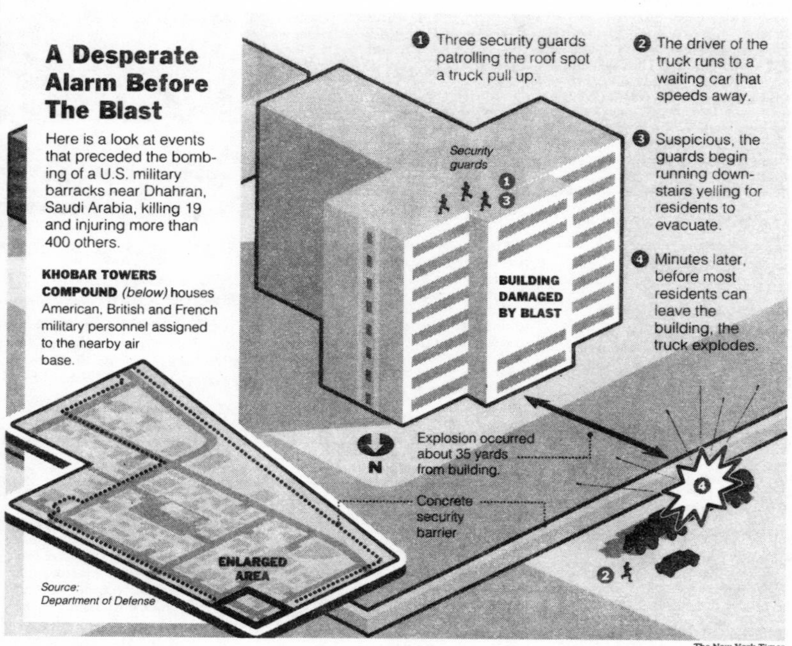

The New York Times

Honoring Ochs and the Newspaper He Built

By JANNY SCOTT

Early in a skit by Wendy Wasserstein and Frank Rich that opened and closed at the Metropolitan Museum of Art last night, a young newspaperman in Chattanooga, Tenn., named Adolph S. Ochs, and his wife, Effie, are describing a telegram just arrived from New York in summer 1896.

The telegram, Effie recalls, "said The New York Times was for sale."

"And I said, 'Adolph, so is the Brooklyn Bridge.' "

No one bought the bridge.

A century later, nearly 500 people gathered in black tie at the museum to toast the man who bought the newspaper. The museum's Temple of Dendur, the only complete Egyptian temple in the Western Hemi-

sphere, was rented for the occasion, while 100 musicians with 100 violins were hired to serenade the guests.

Thus The New York Times set out to honor Adolph S. Ochs, the immigrants' son who bought an almost bankrupt newspaper 100 years ago and turned it into one of the most influential in the world.

Politicians, publishers, artists, television anchors, business people and journalists filled the museum's

Great Hall as projectors hidden in towering boxwood topiaries flashed headlines on the museum's walls.

Dozens of tables draped in cloths imprinted with front pages were set up around the museum's reconstructed temple, and an enamel box bearing Mr. Ochs's likeness was left as a party favor at each place.

In a speech last night, Arthur Ochs Sulzberger, chairman of The New York Times Company, invoked Mr. Ochs's credo, "To give the news impartially, without fear or favor, regardless of any party, sect or interest involved."

"The principles it encompasses are now generally accepted as the underpinnings of a free and independent press," Mr. Sulzberger said. "And that, in turn, is an essential element in the imperfect yet won-

Continued on Page B4, Column 1

INSIDE

Power-Hungry Connecticut

With three nuclear plants shut for inspection, Connecticut is so short of power that the Navy, for one, is bringing its own. Page B1.

A New Health-Care Network

Catholic hospitals and nursing homes around New York are forming a network to compete better in the managed-care era. Page B2.

Stock Funds Low in Cash

Many mutual funds found themselves with little cash on hand this month, after fund managers rushed to buy stocks with the unprecedented inflows of money from eager investors so far this year. Page D1.

Underclassmen Dominate

The first seven players selected in the National Basketball Association draft decided to leave college early and join the pros. Allen Iverson went to the head of this class. Page B13.

"All the News That's Fit to Print"

The New York Times

Late Edition
New York: **Today,** increasing clouds, afternoon thunder. High 86. **Tonight,** scattered thunderstorms. Low 73. **Tomorrow,** showers. High 82. **Yesterday,** high 87, low 74. Details, page C18.

VOL. CXLV . No. 50,492 NEW YORK, THURSDAY, JULY 18, 1996 — $1 beyond the greater New York metropolitan area. — 60 CENTS

T.W.A. JETLINER LEAVING NEW YORK FOR PARIS CRASHES IN ATLANTIC; MORE THAN 220 ABOARD

U.S. Force in Saudi Arabia: Isolation as a Key to Safety

By PHILIP SHENON

WASHINGTON, July 17 — Defense Secretary William J. Perry announced "drastic changes" today in measures to protect American troops in Saudi Arabia from chemical and biological weapons, and from terrorist bombs four or five times as large as the one that killed 19 American airmen last month.

As many as 4,000 American troops, or about two-thirds of the American garrison there, will be moved to more remote areas of the kingdom where they would be better protected, he said.

Officials had suggested that only about 1,500 troops might be moved.

"We have to make some fundamental and drastic changes in the way we configure and deploy our forces," said Mr. Perry, who has been criticized in Congress over the inadequate security in Saudi Arabia before the bombing last month.

"We can't deal with those attacks adequately just by moving fences."

The Defense Department said last week that it had received intelligence reports suggesting that terrorists in Saudi Arabia might be planning to strike again, and that they might be able to build a far larger, far deadlier bomb than the one detonated last month at the Khobar Towers apartment complex outside the eastern Saudi city of Dhahran. The size of that bomb was estimated at 3,000 to 5,000 pounds.

After that attack, the Air Force was criticized for its assumption that Saudi terrorists were unable to build a bomb larger than 200 pounds.

Mr. Perry did not discuss the intelligence reports today, but he said, "We have to be prepared for a chemical-weapon attack, a biological-weapon attack, bombs even larger than 3,000 pounds, bombs in the 10,000 to 20,000-pound category, mortar attacks."

His blunt public comments were the first from a senior Pentagon official to quantify the new bomb threat, or to make mention of the possibility that terrorists operating in Saudi Arabia might have access to chemical or biological weapons.

Mr. Perry told Congress last week that he assumed the bombers who struck last month had support from a well-organized, well-financed international network and possibly from a foreign government.

Both Iraq and Iran have called for the overthrow of the Saudi Government, and both have sought to develop chemical and biological weapons.

"This is an initiative to provide adequate protection for our forces in the face of what I consider to be a threat of weapons of mass destruction in the hands of terrorists," Mr. Perry said in a brief news conference.

While the Defense Department has warned that terrorists in Saudi Arabia may be able to build far larger bombs, Pentagon officials do not appear to have any specific information to support the 10,000 to 20,000-pound range Mr. Perry suggested today.

He appeared to acknowledge that when he said the new security precautions were "worst-case planning," but said, "I believe we have to be prepared."

Another senior Pentagon official, speaking on condition of anonymity, said that the Defense Department also had no specific information that terrorists might be contemplating using chemical or biological weap-

Continued on Page A6, Column 1

Time Warner Near Approval In Turner Deal

By GERALDINE FABRIKANT

The Federal Trade Commission effectively cleared the way for the merger of Time Warner Inc. and Turner Broadcasting System Inc. yesterday but will require the new company's cable-television system to carry a second news channel as a rival to its own Cable News Network.

The requirement for the second channel is intended to increase competition in cable programming. According to communications lawyers, it is the first time that the Government has mandated that a cable company carry a particular type of programming on a broad national scale. Previously, cable companies have only been required to carry broadcast channels, to assure that customers continue to receive television programming that has historically been free.

The requirement is one of a series of concessions the agency seeks before it will approve the $6.3 billion merger, which would create the world's largest media company. Its holdings would include the nation's largest cable programmer, with Cable News Network, Home Box Office and Turner Network Television, to be distributed over Time Warner's extensive cable system, the second largest in the nation. Time Warner's businesses also include the Warner Brothers studios, Warner Music and magazines including Time, People, Sports Illustrated, Fortune and Entertainment Weekly.

F.T.C. staff members approved

Continued on Page D7, Column 1

Miles
0
20
NEW JERSEY
NEW YORK
Long Island Sound
BRONX
MANHATTAN
QUEENS
BROOKLYN
NASSAU
SUFFOLK
Kennedy International Airport
Lindenhurst
East Islip
Patchogue
East Moriches
Moriches Inlet
FIRE ISLAND NATIONAL SEASHORE
Atlantic Ocean
Departure
T.W.A. Flight 800 departs at 8:17 P.M. with at least 229 people aboard.
The plane
The 747-100 was the world's first jumbo jet. First flown in 1969, it can carry up to 366 passengers. The plane that crashed was first flown in 1971.
Approximate site of crash
Witnesses report seeing an explosion, and the plane disappears from radar around 8:40 P.M.
747
TRANS WORLD

A T.W.A. 747-100 as it appeared in 1991.

The New York Times

Accidental Witnesses to Airborne Tragedy

Tranquillity of Summer Is Shattered by Fire Falling From Sky

By JAMES BARRON

"Is that pyrotechnics in the sky?" someone on the radio asked Master Sgt. D. M. Richardson.

He was in the cockpit of an Air National Guard helicopter on a practice search-and-rescue mission off Long Island when the practice ended and the grim reality began. For the orange flash was not a fireworks display but a Trans World Airlines 747 crashing in flames in the Atlantic Ocean a few miles from Sergeant Richardson's home base in Westhampton Beach, L.I.

A long moment later, Sergeant Richardson's chopper was circling over the debris, the smoke and the ocean on fire.

"We saw this ball of fire coming down out of the sky," said Sergeant Richardson, the helicopter's flight engineer. "It was a ball of fire with black smoke and it was descending."

The chopper had been practicing search patterns and rescue maneuvers with a C-130 Hercules, a military cargo plane. The C-130's pilot, Col. Bill Stratemeier, banked and turned to where the passenger plane had gone down. "We're in the rescue business," he said. He and his crew were "looking for signs of life."

What they saw, he said, was flaming wreckage "about the size of a football field" and 15 to 20 bodies in the water. He also said he saw aircraft rescue slides in the water.

The explosions rocked the quiet summer evening on eastern Long Island and the orange fireball was confusing — it was as if the sunset was happening all over again, in fast-forward. On backyard decks with binoculars, in boats with fishing poles, in crowded bars with cool drinks in their hands, people watched and wondered and worried.

Like Victor S. Fehner, rocking on the water in his 17-foot runabout, some thought it was a small plane ditching into the water. But the explosions were too loud, the plumes of smoke too big, to have come from a single-engine plane.

And then all there was was a cloud over the ocean, and flaming wreckage.

"It looked like the wing came off," said Mr. Fehner, a 47-year-old cable splicer. "You could see two balls of flame, then everything disappeared."

Mr. Fehner figured it was a small plane with engine trouble, a two-seater, that had landed close to the beach after a frightening 8-to-10-second descent. Not until he had tied up his boat and called his son-in-law, a mechanic with the Coast Guard, did he learn the scope of the disaster he had seen: the plane was a jumbo jet bound for Paris and carrying more than 200 passengers.

"It was round, like a tropical sunset," said John Coyne, an area manager for the Peace Corps who saw the explosion through the sliding glass door of a condominium he had rented for the week in Westhampton,

Continued on Page B8, Column 5

NO SURVIVORS SEEN

L.I. Witnesses Describe Two Explosions, Then Fireball Into Ocean

By N. R. KLEINFIELD

A Trans World Airlines 747 airliner bound for Paris from New York City plunged in a fireball into the waters off Long Island last night with more than 220 people aboard.

The Coast Guard said there were no survivors, and officials said there was no immediate indication of what caused the crash. But Federal law enforcement authorities said early today that the F.B.I. would take jurisdiction over the case because witnesses reported an explosion, raising the possibility that a bomb went off on the jetliner.

But officials emphasized that they were not aware of any threats made to the airline or the airport and that if indeed an explosion did occur aboard the jet, there were other possible causes.

The plane, Flight 800, went down at around 8:40 P.M., on a partly cloudy night, minutes after taking off from Kennedy International Airport. Shedding pieces of its body as it fell, it crashed and sank into the choppy waters about 20 miles southeast of East Moriches in Suffolk County on the eastern end of Long Island, the Port Authority said.

Mike Kelly, an airline vice president, said there were 229 aboard — 212 passengers and 17 crew members, some of them travelers from an earlier canceled flight to Rome. Three hours before takeoff, the plane had arrived in New York from Athens as Flight 881.

The crash came as airline security has been elevated beyond customary levels because of the Olympic Games, the various trials of domestic and international terrorists and the bombings in Saudi Arabia, security experts said.

The crash broke the calm of a sultry summer evening for witnesses along the Long Island shore. "I looked to the ocean and I saw a ball in the sky that looked like a red glow," said Susan Kinscherf, who lives in Hampton Bays. "Then it went up and there was an explosion. It was a huge amount of fire. It was a fan of fire. Then it just fell from the sky."

Others spoke of a light dropping swiftly from the sky and then either one or two bursts of flame and an enormous black cloud. As the plane spiraled toward the water, they said they saw pieces peel off.

"There were two explosions, bright red up in the air," said John Keshal, who lives along the shore in Center Moriches. "There was a lot of flames and redness in the air. And a

Continued on Page B8, Column 1

PRIMARY COLORS
found out about later
rescient:
Chicago and

By Joe Anonymous

Joe Klein, a columnist for Newsweek, admitted yesterday that he was Anonymous, author of the campaign novel "Primary Colors." He spoke after The Washington Post compared notes on a manuscript of the book, left, with his handwriting. Article, page D23.

Photograph by Brian K. Diggs/The New York Times; Illustration by The Washington Post

Wall Street Is Calmer As Stocks Rise Again

Shoulders dropped a little on Wall Street yesterday, as a reassuring day ended with all the major market benchmarks higher in extremely heavy trading. The Dow Jones industrial average closed up 18.12 points, and the badly battered Nasdaq composite index, rose 33.18 points, or 3.15 percent — the index's largest single-day jump ever.

The tension-easing session suggested that investors had not fled the market in disgust after a two-week downturn. Corporate earnings that were better than expected helped spur the market.

Business Day, page D1.

Chang W. Lee/The New York Times

Accompanied by a Red Cross representative, people with relatives or friends on Flight 800 arrive in a bus outside the T.W.A. terminal.

Hondurans in 'Sweatshops' See Opportunity

By LARRY ROHTER

SAN PEDRO SULA, Honduras, July 13 — Each morning, the workers spill off the buses and past the guards at the front gates of the industrial parks here, rushing to punch the clock before the 7:30 start of their workday.

Outside, anxious onlookers are always waiting, hoping for a chance at least to fill out a job application that will allow them to become part of that throng.

With wages that start at less than 40 cents an hour, the apparel plants here offer little by American standards. But many of the people who work in them, having come from jobs that pay even less and offer no benefits or security, see employment here as the surest road to a better life.

"In the countryside, a peon is a peon for all of his life," said Yensy Meléndez, 29, a father of two and former farm worker who migrated seven years ago to this bustling city of 350,000 near Honduras's Caribbean coast and now has a factory job. "Here, it's not perfect, but at least you have a chance to improve your situation."

What residents of a rich country like the United States see as exploitation can seem a rare opportunity to residents of a poor country like Honduras, where the per capita income is $600 a year and unemployment is 40 percent. Such conflicts of standards and perceptions have become increasingly common as the global economy grows more intertwined, and have set off a heated debate about international norms of conduct and responsibility.

The recent controversy involving the television personality Kathie Lee Gifford and a line of clothing made here that bears her name provides a widely publicized case in point.

To critics in the United States, the apparel assembly plants here, known in Spanish as maquiladoras, are merely "monstrous sweatshops of the New World Order," to use the phrase of the National Labor Committee, the New York-based group that originally accused Mrs. Gifford of turning a blind eye to Hondurans working for "slave wages."

The National Labor Committee, a nonprofit group, is largely financed by foundations but also receives money from labor unions in the United States.

After the attacks on her, Mrs. Gifford has now endorsed efforts to

Continued on Page A14, Column 1

INSIDE

A Change on Pesticides

Long-divided factions on the House Commerce Committee voted unanimously for a compromise measure that would basically alter the regulation of pesticides in food. Page A20.

600 Suspected of Tax Fraud

At least 600 New York City employees, some of whom claim they are not subjects of the United States, are suspected of evading Federal and state income taxes. Page B4.

A Planet Within a Planet

Scientists have reported strong evidence that Earth's inner core is spinning freely and slightly faster than the rest of the planet. Page A20.

Kremlin Intrigue by Design

President Yeltsin appears to be building a new Government with an eye toward insuring maximum rivalry. News analysis, page A3.

MORE ON THE CRASH

Before Devastating News, T.W.A. Saw a Revival Ahead

Trans World Airlines, which has had to resuscitate itself after twice declaring bankruptcy, thought it had finally turned the corner financially. Then came bad news. Page B8.

A Gruesome Rescue Effort

The bodies floated, some in clusters, in dark, choppy waters that swelled two or three feet, eerily lit by rescue lamps and oily flames. Page B8.

Airline Security Tight

Airline security has been tighter than usual in recent months for several reasons, including the Olympics and Mideast bombings. Page B8.

"All the News That's Fit to Print"

The New York Times

Late Edition
New York: **Today**, mostly sunny, windy, less humid. High 80. **Tonight**, clear, not as windy, cool. Low 63. **Tomorrow**, sunny. High 81. Yesterday, high 85, low 72. Details, page 52.

VOL.CXLV.. No. 50,494 Copyright © 1996 The New York Times NEW YORK, SATURDAY, JULY 20, 1996 $1 beyond the greater New York metropolitan area. **60 CENTS**

Panel Advises F.D.A. To Allow Abortion Pill

Agency Foresees Final Action in September

By GINA KOLATA

GAITHERSBURG, Md., July 19 — Meeting in a windowless building here amid unusual security precautions, a committee of advisers to the Food and Drug Administration recommended today that the agency approve for marketing the abortion-inducing drug RU-486, or mifepristone.

The recommendation follows more than a decade in which American abortion protest has kept the drug, easily available in France, Britain and Sweden, out of the United States.

In deciding that mifepristone (pronounced mih-feh-PRISS-tone) should be considered safe and effective, the advisory committee may well have ordained a dramatic change in abortion procedure, and abortion politics, throughout the country.

Although the F.D.A. is not bound by its advisory committees' recommendations, in practice it almost always adopts them. Dr. David A. Kessler, the Commissioner of Food and Drugs, said today that the agency's goal in this case was to make a final decision by mid-September.

The reaction of abortion combatants who attended the hearing where the committee voted was predictable.

Eleanor Smeal, president of the Feminist Majority Foundation, said: "I'm thrilled. It's a medical breakthrough."

Olivia Gans, director of American Victims of Abortion, a national group of women who have had abortions and now regret them, said: "The Government has this very much on a fast track, and that's what we were most afraid of. It's not a good signal to American women."

Ms. Gans said that "many members of Congress are very concerned about this" but that "it was the will of this Administration to get this drug approved before the election," in the event that President Clinton, an abortion rights supporter, should be defeated this November by Bob Dole, an abortion opponent. The Commissioner of Food and Drugs is a Presidential appointee.

The committee that acted today had eight members, most of them physicians specializing in obstetrics and gynecology. Its chairman was Dr. Ezra C. Davidson Jr., a professor of obstetrics and gynecology at the Charles R. Drew University of Medicine and Science in Los Angeles.

Some members of the committee expressed concern at the cost and inconvenience entailed in the several visits to doctors' offices that would be required of women who partook in the drug regimen.

Some noted too that mifepristone had failed to induce abortion among a small percentage of women, leaving them with the choice of proceeding with surgical abortions or facing the prospect that the drug had caused a defect in the fetuses.

The panel nonetheless recommended approval, in a series of three votes: By 6 to 0, with 2 abstentions, it decided that the drug's benefits outweighed its risks; by 7 to 0, with 1 abstention, it decided that the drug was safe, and by 6 to 2 it decided that data from a French study were sufficient to support American use of the drug. The committee reserved the right to look at the research again if

Continued on Page 9, Column 1

TOP BOSNIAN SERB AGREES TO RESIGN

Karadzic Yields Political Role but He Will Not Be Exiled

By JANE PERLEZ

BELGRADE, Serbia, July 19 — Radovan Karadzic, the Bosnian Serb political chief who led his people in a brutal war of ethnic separation, has agreed to give up political power immediately, the special United States envoy, Richard C. Holbrooke, said here today.

The agreement removes an obstacle to September's national elections in Bosnia and Herzegovina and could aid the flagging peace effort by removing from visible public life a man indicted for genocide and other war crimes.

But Mr. Holbrooke acknowledged that it fell short of the goal of removing Dr. Karadzic from Bosnia and putting him on trial at the war crimes tribunal in The Hague, something Western nations have long demanded.

"This is a minimal acceptable package," Mr. Holbrooke said. Only a few days ago Mr. Holbrooke told Western and Bosnian officials that if Dr. Karadzic did not agree to leave Bosnia, the West would reimpose economic sanctions on Serbia. For now, Dr. Karadzic remains in his mountain hideaway of Pale, near Sarajevo, and the threat of sanctions has withered.

The signed agreement was negotiated with President Slobodan Milosevic of Serbia, who in turned exerted pressure on the Bosnian Serb leader.

The Bosnian Government and Western officials had considered Dr. Karadzic's presence as head of the major political party in the Serb part of Bosnia, and his control over the police, news media and politics

Continued on Page 4, Column 4

INSIDE

Growing Divisions in Mexico

An economic crisis is exaggerating an already wide income gap between rich and poor and giving rise to startling contrasts and clashes. Page 3.

Teachers for Newark

New Jersey plans to hire additional teachers for the embattled Newark schools by trimming more than 600 other employees. Page 21.

A New Look for Colorado

In Colorado, land where cattle once roamed is giving way to bulldozers clearing sites for shopping malls, offices and golf courses. Page 6.

Rough Seas Hamper Search for Clues in Plane Crash

Associated Press

Debris from the downed T.W.A. jetliner was collected in a hangar at a naval installation at Calverton, L.I.

Investors Pull Money Out of Stock Funds

Investors were clearly rattled by wild swings in the stock market, withdrawing $4 billion from stock mutual funds — the largest weekly withdrawal in four years.

While the data, released yesterday, do not reflect investor activity on Thursday and yesterday, when the stock market was calmer, they continue a trend.

Yesterday provided more fodder for skittish investors. After disappointing earnings reports from several technology companies. The Dow Jones industrial average declined 37.36 points, while the Nasdaq Composite index fell 12.14 points.

Business Day, page 39.

For Families, Few Answers Except the Ones They Fear

By JAMES BARRON

Their days now are bracketed by briefings.

In the morning and again in the evening, they listen to Government officials, who stand grimly in the front of a hotel ballroom near Kennedy International Airport and describe what, if anything, has been learned since the last such session.

In the long hours in between, the relatives and friends of passengers from T.W.A. Flight 800 keep their appointments with coroners and homicide detectives, who press for details: how can dental records be obtained?

And they try to adjust, to absorb the things they do not want to know. On Thursday, they did not want to know that there were no survivors among the 230 people who had barely settled in for the flight to Paris when the airliner went down. Yesterday, they did not want to know that rescuers might never find all of the bodies.

"I just wanted to see her," said Kyle Tennant of Sunset Park, Brooklyn, whose neighbor, Donna Griffith, was aboard the plane. "You don't know if she's in the water, if she blew up, if she burned, if she drowned."

And so the unanswerable questions remain, despite briefing after briefing that made the Ramada, near the Van Wyck Expressway in Queens, a center of attention. On the way into the hotel — a place more accustomed to being a backdrop for wedding receptions, medical society dinner dances and other quiet rituals of everyday life — the relatives had to run a gantlet of more than 100 reporters and camera people.

Some relatives are staying at the hotel, mostly people who, like their loved ones on the doomed flight, had made the journey to Kennedy from out of town. Some New York-area relatives have also checked in; others stop by, go home and come back again later. Some drift out to the parking lot and chat with reporters in the long hours when there seems to be no news. Some order room-service meal after room-service meal. Some spend time at trauma desks that have been set up: T.W.A., the Red Cross, the Mayor's office

Continued on Page 25, Column 1

The Olympics Open Amid Pageantry, and Anxiety

Associated Press

Muhammad Ali lighting the Olympic flame early today at the climax of opening ceremonies in Atlanta.

By JERE LONGMAN

ATLANTA, July 19 — After six years of preparation, Atlanta welcomed the world tonight for the opening of the centennial Summer Olympics, which began with idealistic hopes for peace among nations moderated by anxiety about terrorism in the wake of the explosion aboard Trans World Airlines Flight 800.

An estimated 7,000 athletes from 197 nations marched into the Olympic Stadium, filled with 83,100 spectators who paid up to $636 for a ticket, and witnessed a captivating and vibrant, if ear-splitting, celebration meant to honor 100 years of the modern Games and evoke the hospitable spirit of the modern American South. Competition will begin Saturday and continue through Aug. 4.

After speaking to the American contingent of 654 athletes in the Olympic Village, President Clinton attended tonight's four-hour ceremony to declare the Games open at midnight, and to watch the lighting of the Olympic flame. It was lighted by the great former heavyweight champion Muhammad Ali, a gold medalist at the 1960 Rome Olympics, and hoisted on a pulley to the Olympic cauldron.

But while the President came to celebrate the brotherhood of nations, united in the name of sport, the deaths of those aboard T.W.A. Flight 800 on Wednesday made the occasion "somewhat sadder by the tragedy that's now been suffered," the White House press secretary, Mike McCurry, said.

Security has been tight at the Olympics since the deaths of 11 Israeli athletes and coaches at the hands of Palestinian gunmen at the 1972 Summer Games in Munich, Germany. Tonight was no exception.

The Olympic Stadium, which will be downsized for baseball after the Games, is surrounded by a maze of eight-foot-high fences for at least a block on either side, and traffic is

Continued on Page 31, Column 4

Scores of Agents Seek Answers Worldwide

By JOHN KIFNER

Rough seas frustrated the search for the wreckage of Trans World Airlines Flight 800 yesterday, as Federal agents mounted an investigation in search of the method and motives behind what they think was a criminal act that blew up the plane in midair.

Federal officers set up a toll-free number and asked Suffolk County residents who saw the explosion and crash to call. They invited anyone with information to communicate with the Federal Bureau of Investigation through its Internet site.

Scores of agents also questioned not only witnesses, but also airport employees about baggage-handling routines and what happened while the plane sat on the tarmac at Kennedy International Airport for three hours before the departure for Paris.

They checked through the flight manifests both in New York and Athens for possible suspects, and pored over court records of previous terrorist cases.

But, one investigator said, "the most important piece of evidence is still on the ocean floor": the part of the fuselage from the midsection back to the cargo hold that could hold the evidence that shows how the plane blew up.

The bodies of at least 130 of the plane's passengers also presumably remain with the wreckage. Only about 100 have been recovered so far. [A list of the victims is on page 24.]

The search that was postponed yesterday was critical, another investigator said, because the searchers have recovered less than 1 percent of the wreckage, including parts of a wing and a tail, but nothing thus far that indicated where an explosion might have begun.

"If there was an explosion, the pieces that count are the ones that were near the explosion," this official said.

Investigators said they hope they can resume recovery operations today, adding that chemical residues and related evidence from an explosion would probably be lost if the wreckage stayed in the water as long as a week.

The possibility that an equipment failure was to blame seemed to ebb yesterday. Even the normally understated vice chairman of the National Transportation Safety Board, Robert Francis, said, "The possibility of a criminal act is a distinct one."

At a news briefing later, James Kallstrom, the head of the F.B.I. office in New York City, said, "we're looking at this as a criminal investigation."

Mr. Kallstrom, wearing an F.B.I. windbreaker field jacket, seemed determined to appear restrained as he opened his part of the news conference by saying: "We're not here to take over the investigation yet. We're not here to declare that this is a terrorist event, as has been speculated in the news media."

But, he added: "If it was a terrorist event, then we have the challenge to find out who these perpetrators were, who the cowards were who did this.

"Look," he said later, "something

Continued on Page 22, Column 2

Multiracial Americans Ready To Claim Their Own Identity

By MICHEL MARRIOTT

For Alison Perry, being multiracial has meant moving through life as if she had a giant question mark drawn on her forehead. Strangers frequently approach and begin a vexing guessing game: "Are you Israeli?" "Are you a Latina?" "Where are you from?"

Yet for this slender, almond-colored woman with delicate features drawn from both her black-American father and her Italian-American mother, race is not what defines her.

"I definitely say that I'm interracial," Ms. Perry said. "I do not identify myself as a black woman. I definitely don't identify myself as a white woman, either."

The very existence of multiracial people like Ms. Perry challenges this nation's traditionally rigid notions of race.

Their struggles of pride, loyalty and, occasionally, shame raise profound questions about the meaning of race and the promise and pitfalls of racial identity. Multiracial Americans often find themselves claimed by many groups and belonging wholly to none, in a society that often forces them to choose one identity — or imposes that identity on them.

Today, thousands of mixed-race Americans are expected to gather on the Mall in Washington in a display of pride, power and unity. Organized under the banner of the Multiracial Solidarity March, the afternoon demonstration is intended to celebrate multiracial identity and to pressure the Federal Government to add a multiracial category to the next census.

No one knows exactly how many Americans consider themselves multiracial, though the 1990 census counted two million children younger than 18 whose parents are of different races.

"People of mixed race in this country haven't belonged anywhere," said Charles Byrd, editor and publisher of Interracial Voice, an Internet news journal based in Queens

Continued on Page 7, Column 1

"All the News
That's Fit to Print"

The New York Times

Late Edition
New York: **Today,** plenty of sun, pleasant. High 82. **Tonight,** increasing clouds. Low 68. **Tomorrow,** some showers. High 78. **Yesterday,** high 78, low 66. Details are on page 39.

VOL.CXLV . No. 50,502

NEW YORK, SUNDAY, JULY 28, 1996

$3 beyond the greater New York metropolitan area. **$2.50**

OLYMPICS PARK BLAST KILLS ONE, HURTS 111; ATLANTA GAMES GO ON

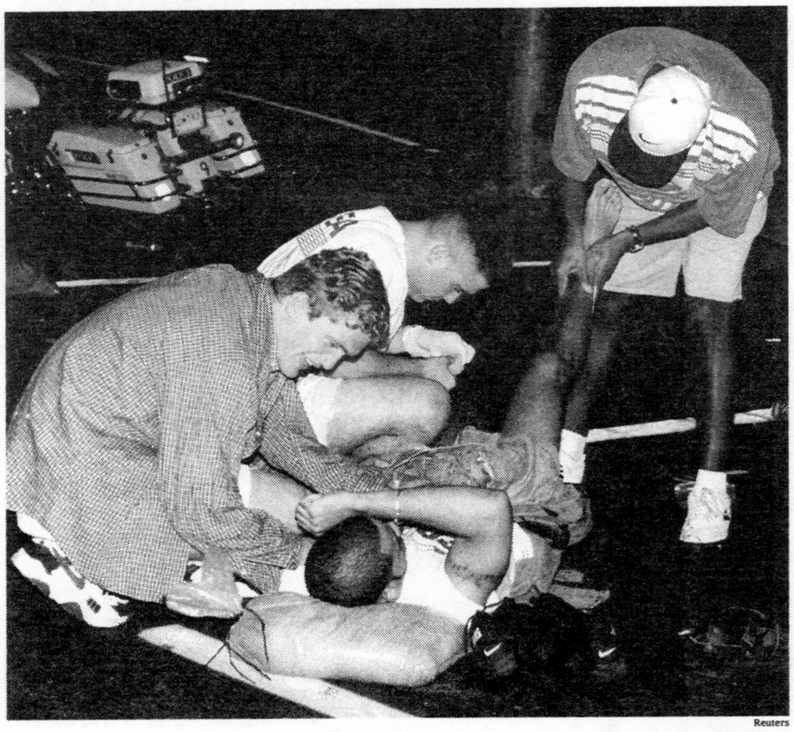

Reuters

A man wounded in a bombing at Centennial Olympic Park in Atlanta was aided as he awaited an ambulance.

WARNING TOO LATE

President Calls Attack 'Evil Act of Terror' — Flags at Half-Staff

By KEVIN SACK

ATLANTA, July 27 — A pipe bomb spiked with nails and screws shattered the Summer Olympic Games today, transforming an international celebration of sport and fellowship into a symbol of the dark side of modern life.

The homemade pipe bomb or bombs exploded at 1:25 A.M. in a crowded corner of Centennial Olympic Park, killing Alice S. Hawthorne, 44, of Albany, Ga., and wounding at least 111 people. A Turkish television cameraman died of a heart attack while running to cover the blast.

Most of the injured suffered shock or minor wounds from flying metal or other debris, officials said. Eleven people were hospitalized, and at least two underwent surgery.

President Clinton, who attended the Games twice in the first week, denounced the bombing as "an evil act of terror" and vowed that those responsible would be punished.

As of early evening, no arrests had been made. But Federal law-enforcement officials said they were beginning to theorize that the bombing was a case of domestic terrorism, based on recordings of a 911 telephone warning about 30 minutes before the bomb exploded and other unspecified evidence.

At a news conference this morning, Woody Johnson, the special agent in charge of the Atlanta office of the Federal Bureau of Investigation, said, "We will consider it an act of terrorism until information should arrive to the contrary."

Olympic officials said at 5:15 A.M. that the 17-day competition would continue, just as the Games did in 1972, when Palestinian terrorists killed 11 Israelis at the Munich Games. Olympic flags flew at half-staff at all Games sites as jittery athletes and subdued fans observed a moment of silence. [Page 21.]

During the concert in the park, at about the same time as the 911 call was made, a Georgia Bureau of Investigation agent noticed an unattended green knapsack that contained the bomb and called a team of explosives experts to the scene.

Officers began to clear the area, but the bomb detonated before they could move thousands of concert-goers out of the park, a new, 21-acre plaza that had become the physical and spiritual center of the Games.

The G.B.I. agent, Tom Davis, said

Continued on Page 21, Column 1

From Fun Under the Summer Stars to Terror

By RICK BRAGG

ATLANTA, July 27 — The city's downtown was alive in a way it had never been before the Olympics. The streets were still busy and vibrant even as 1 A.M. came and went, and at the heart of it all was the Centennial Olympic Park. Thousands of people sat on the grass under the spotlights and the stars, danced barefoot to the throb of live electric guitars, or rambled the brick walkways with plastic cups of beer, pleasantly numb.

Then, in an instant, the celebration was lost in a chorus of screams and the smell of gunpowder, and the character of Atlanta's Olympics was forever changed.

At 1:25 on a Saturday morning, the ground in front of the park's main music stage was strewn with wounded people. The bomb's blast drilled bits of metal into the crowd, missing some people, nicking others, boring deep into some. One man tried to reach around to the small of his back, where blood was leaking. A woman sat still as a statue, in shock, staring blankly at a neat round hole in her shoulder.

"We were listening to the band and trying to dance in the grass," said Meg Deckert, 31, an assistant to an Atlanta real estate lawyer. Then, she was surrounded by chaos.

"There was a guy who was grabbing his stomach," she said. "He was bleeding from the lower abdomen. He was in a lot of pain. We had him on a bench."

She and her husband, Ed, used the bench as a stretcher to carry the man to the ambulances, whose orange, flickering lights set a city block aglow. Mr. Deckert said, "We just talked to him and held his hand and told him it was O.K."

The blast, believed to have come from a bomb left beside a sound-and-light tower near the stage, came just as the band, Jack Mack and the Heart Attack, finished a set. The police had received a 911 call warning them of the bomb and where it was, but the call came too late to evacuate the tightly packed crowd. The authorities only had time to move people back, but that act prob-

Continued on Page 20, Column 1

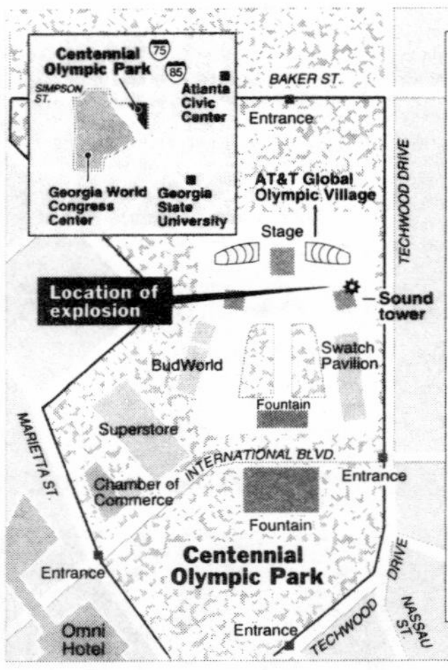

The Details

A WARNING
A 911 call is received warning that a bomb will go off in Centennial Olympic Park in 30 minutes. At about the same time, an unattended bag is spotted and bomb experts are alerted.

AN EVACUATION
Officers begin to clear the area that contains thousands of concert-goers.

AN EXPLOSION
Shortly after evacuation efforts begin, a bomb explodes killing one and injuring 111.

The New York Times

OFFICIAL DECISION The International Olympic Committee chose to continue the Games, just as it did in the 1972 Olympics when 11 Israeli athletes and officials were killed in Munich..

CHANGED FOREVER Competition has resumed, but the games will never be the same. Dave Anderson, Sports of The Times.

WORLD'S FASTEST After the disqualification of Linford Christie, the defending gold medalist, Donovan Bailey of Canada set a world record in the 100 meters. In other track events, Gail Devers of the United States won the women's 100 meters for the second straight Olympics, while Jackie Joyner-Kersee, twice a gold medalist in the heptathlon, withdrew with an injured hamstring.

TV COVERAGE Minutes after the bomb went off, television networks scrambled to provide coverage.

SportsSunday, section 8.

Associated Press

A pipe bomb that killed a woman during a rock concert at the Olympics in Centennial Olympic Park in Atlanta early yesterday left visitors to the Games in shock.

Despite His Reversals, Clinton Stays Centered

By ALISON MITCHELL

THE CLINTON RECORD
The Overview
First of seven articles.

WASHINGTON — His hands in restless motion, Bill Clinton sat in the Oval Office earlier this month assessing the Presidency he calls "this great adventure."

At times pensive, other times fiery, his finger stabbing the air as he disputed a point, he confidently made his case for a second term. "As Americans, what we have done in the last four years is put our economic house in order, restore growth and create opportunity," Mr. Clinton said. "We have succeeded in reducing the deficit, expanding trade, targeting investment in critical areas, and we have over 10 million new jobs."

"Now, what's missing in this picture?" he asked during an interview earlier this month, adding, "What's missing in this picture is that not every American has the capacity to take advantage of the opportunities."

Mr. Clinton ticked off a raft of ideas to help. Tax credits for community college tuition. Guarantees that pensions can be taken from job to job. Vouchers for job training. Ways to give more people access to health insurance.

What was striking about the proposals was their modesty. They sounded so humble from a President who had once fought for a $30 billion jobs program and who had made such a bold stand to give all Americans "health care that can never be taken away, health care that is always there."

What a contrast from the grand visions of 1993, when Mr. Clinton swept into Washington for his inauguration from Thomas Jefferson's Monticello, repeating the third President's maxim that "to preserve the very foundations of our nation we would need dramatic change from time to time."

"Well, my fellow Americans," the 46-year-old President had said then, "this is our time. Let's embrace it."

But America, as it watched the early Clinton Presidency, did not embrace it. The very people whom Mr. Clinton had said he would serve — "the hard-working Americans who make up our forgotten middle class" — deserted his Democrats in droves or stayed home in the 1994 midterm elections, giving the Republicans control of Congress for the first time in half a century.

That election sent shudders through the White House and virtually split Mr. Clinton's Presidency into two periods so distinct that his own advisers acknowledge that they could almost be viewed as two separate terms.

The first two years were marked by Government activism, culminating in Mr. Clin-

Continued on Page 28, Column 1

Stephen Crowley/The New York Times

'Every day I think about what was the vision I had for this country when I came here: Is it still valid? Is our strategy working? What do we still need to do? Where have we failed?'

PRESIDENT CLINTON,
Excerpts from interview at the White House, page 28.

While Cause of Crash Is Sought, Parallel Criminal Inquiry Goes On

By JOE SEXTON

While Federal officials have yet to conclude that an act of sabotage destroyed Trans World Airlines Flight 800, an elaborate criminal investigation has been under way from the first moments after the 747 smashed into the sea on July 17.

Agents from the Federal Bureau of Investigation have interviewed close to 1,500 people, from witnesses who saw the plane's explosion to officials at the Baltimore eye bank that shipped a box of corneas aboard the aircraft for transplant, according to investigators.

Known supporters of terrorist groups in the New York area are under surveillance. Prosecutors have begun subpoenaing basic records, and agents have interviewed all of the baggage handlers, maintenance workers and other personnel who had direct contact with the jetliner. But, reluctant to intrude on their grief, agents have moved slowly to interview relatives of the 230 people aboard the jet who died.

The quest for forensic evidence that might yield a lead to the cause entered its 10th full day yesterday, as investigators hauled a large section of the airliner's right wing from the ocean floor nine miles out in the Atlantic. The wing was taken for testing. Officials also said an examination by divers of two of the plane's four engines did not produce any evidence of mechanical malfunction. [Page 19A.]

Investigators and prosecutors have already assembled a long list of theories about who might have attacked the plane. According to senior investigators, they range from an attack by Middle Eastern terrorists to an act of arbitrary violence by a domestic militia organization. Officials are also considering

Continued on Page 19A, Column 4

Associated Press

Alice S. Hawthorne, 44, of Albany, Ga., the bombing victim. Page 20.

TODAY'S SECTIONS